PROFILES OF AMERICAN COLLEGES 2015

31st Edition

Compiled and Edited by
the College Division of
Barron's Educational Series

BARRON'S

All inquiries should be addressed to:
Barron's Educational Series, Inc.
250 Wireless Boulevard
Hauppauge, New York 11788
www.barronseduc.com

ISBN-13: 978-1-4380-0429-7

International Standard Serial No. 1065-5026

PRINTED IN THE UNITED STATES OF AMERICA
9 8 7 6 5 4 3 2 1

10%
POST-CONSUMER WASTE
Paper contains a minimum of 10% post-consumer waste (PCW). Paper used in this book was derived from certified, sustainable forestlands.

CONTENTS

PREFACE

Barron's *Profiles of American Colleges* is the most all-encompassing, easy-to-use guide available. All four-year institutions that offer bachelor's degrees are described if they are fully accredited or are recognized candidates for accreditation. The comprehensive, concise capsule and detailed essay on each school give an easy-to-absorb, complete picture of the colleges that interest the reader. The attractive graphic design provides added readability.

The capsule of each profile lists important information for quick reference: address and phone and fax numbers; enrollment; calendar; fall application deadline; size and salary level of the faculty; percentage of faculty members who hold doctorates; student/faculty ratio; tuition and fees; room-and-board costs; the number of students who applied to the freshman class, were accepted, and enrolled; the median SAT* and/or ACT scores; and finally, the College Admissions Selector Rating for the school. The information in the essay portion of each profile ranges from available housing and the financial aid climate to admissions requirements and the success of graduates. There are twenty-one categories of information under eight main headings: Student Life, Programs of Study, Admissions, Financial Aid, International Students, Computers, Graduates, and Admissions Contact. The Admissions Contact section also gives Internet addresses and video availability.

As a purchaser of the 31st edition of *Profiles of American Colleges*, you are eligible for a free six-month subscription to our *Profiles of American Colleges* on-line edition. The web site will simplify your college search and ease your college application process. To access, go to BarronsPAC.com and register today!

A Word of Thanks

To all the admissions officers, institutional research staff at the colleges, to participating high school advisers, to the students, parents, and other supporters of Barron's *Profiles of American Colleges*, over the last thirty editions, we offer our sincere thanks and appreciation.

Our appreciation to the editorial staff, including Bruce Morris, Lena Perfetto, and David Rodman; production department, including Frank Pasquale, Chris Ciaschini, and graphic artist Lou Vasquez. Thanks and appreciation to Greg Hammond of Reliable Internet Solutions for database management and technical support.

CONTRIBUTORS

Steven R. Antonoff, Ph.D.
Educational Consultant
Antonoff Associates, Inc.
Denver, Colorado

Barbara J. Aronson
Career Center Coordinator
Miramonte High School
Orinda, California

Marguerite J. Dennis
Former Vice President for
Enrollment and
International Programs
Suffolk University
Boston, Massachusetts

Benjamin W. Griffith
Former Dean
University of West Georgia
Carrolton, Georgia

Sheldon Halpern
Former Dean
Enrollment Management
Caldwell College
Caldwell, New Jersey

Anthony F. Capraro, III, Ph.D.
President, Teach Inc.
College Counseling
Ocoee, Florida

*SAT is a registered trademark owned by the College Entrance Examination Board. No endorsement of this product is implied or given.

AN EXPLANATION OF THE BOOK

You have been thinking about going to college within the coming years, and have decided that it's time to get serious and take the necessary steps that will lead to your ultimate college decisions, right?

But how do you take these steps? How much will your college education cost? How can you and your parents afford it? What about the entrance exams? What kinds of scores are you going to need to be considered? How do you decide what to major in? Which colleges offer the skills and career preparation that you're going to need? Even if you get past these hurdles, what if you decide which colleges you want to attend, apply to them, and then get turned down? Is there anything you can do to prevent *that* from happening?

So where do you begin? In addition to hundreds of two-year schools, there are more than 1,650 accredited four-year colleges in the United States, and your options are almost unlimited. Barron's *Profiles of American Colleges* can help by pointing you in the right direction, and guiding you through the coming months of preparation and decision making.

Within the pages of this directory, you will find articles that will assist you in evaluating your own needs and interests, selecting the colleges you want to apply to, filling out the application, writing the essay, going through the interview process, finding the money, and surviving your freshman year.

The Index of College Majors lists which colleges offer the field that you're interested in. The section also offers advice on deciding your major, career opportunities and the skills you are going to need for the occupation you choose. More than 700 majors are listed, along with the in-state costs and the Admissions Selector Rating in easy-to-read columns.

Advice for international students is included, as well as a list of schools' in-state costs from least to most expensive. The Colleges at a Glance geographic chart provides students quick information about the schools on a state-by-state basis.

The College Admissions Selector Ratings give applicants an idea of the competition they will encounter when applying to a particular school. For your convenience, a key to abbreviations is also included, as well as an explanation of the actual college entries.

The heart of the book, of course, is the detailed descriptions of the colleges, including a special section of religious schools, for those students wishing to pursue a career in the clergy and related fields. The college Profiles are arranged in alphabetical order by state. Each chapter opens with a map that pinpoints the geographic location of the colleges mentioned. Barron's *Profiles of American Colleges* covers the United States; and describes colleges in Puerto Rico, universities in Canada and abroad (along with advice for international students) as well as state and private systems of higher education, for a total of approximately 1700 Profile entries.

This updated and revised edition of *Profiles of American Colleges* will prove to be a valuable resource as you embark on a tremendous learning and growth time of your life – your college education.

KEY TO ABBREVIATIONS

DEGREES

A.A.—Associate of Arts
A.A.S.—Associate of Applied Science
A.B. or B.A.—Bachelor of Arts
A.B.J.—Bachelor of Arts in Journalism
A.S.—Associate of Science

B.A.—Bachelor of Arts
B.A.A.—Bachelor of Applied Arts
B.A.A.S. or **B.Applied A.S.**—Bachelor of Applied Arts and Sciences
B.Ac. or **B.Acc.**—Bachelor of Accountancy
B.A.C.—Bachelor of Science in Air Commerce
B.A.C.V.I.—Bachelor of Arts in Computer and Video Imaging
B.A.E. or **B.A.Ed.**—Bachelor of Arts in Education
B.A.G.E.—Bachelor of Arts in General Education
B.Agri.—Bachelor of Agriculture
B.A.G.S.—Bachelor of Arts in General Studies
B.A.J.S.—Bachelor of Arts in Judaic Studies
B.A.M.—Bachelor of Arts in Music
B.Applied Sc.—Bachelor of Applied Science
B.A.R.—Bachelor of Religion
B.Arch.—Bachelor of Architecture
B.Arch.Hist.—Bachelor of Architectural History
B.Arch.Tech.—Bachelor of Architectural Technology
B.Ar.Sc.—Baccalaurium Artium et Scientiae (honors college degree) (Bachelor of Arts & Sciences)
B.Art.Ed.—Bachelor of Art Education
B.A.S.—Bachelor of Applied Science
B.A.S.—Bachelor of Arts and Sciences
B.A.Sec.Ed.—Bachelor of Arts in Secondary Ed.
B.A.S.W.—Bachelor of Arts in Social Work
B.A.T.—Bachelor of Arts in Teaching
B.B. or B.Bus.—Bachelor of Business
B.B.A.—Bachelor of Business Administration
B.B.E.—Bachelor of Business Education
B.C. or **B.Com.** or **B.Comm.**—Bachelor of Commerce
B.C.A.—Bachelor of Creative Arts
B.C.E.—Bachelor of Civil Engineering
B.C.E.—Bachelor of Computer Engineering
B.Ch. or **B.Chem.**—Bachelor of Chemistry
B.Ch.E.—Bachelor of Chemical Engineering
B.C.J.—Bachelor of Criminal Justice
B.C.M.—Bachelor of Christian Ministries
B.Church Mus.—Bachelor of Church Music
B.C.S.—Bachelor of College Studies
B.E.—Bachelor of English
B.E. or **B.Ed.**—Bachelor of Education
B.E.—Bachelor of Engineering
B.E.D.—Bachelor of Environmental Design
B.E.E.—Bachelor of Electrical Engineering
B.En. or **B.Eng.**—Bachelor of Engineering
B.E.S. or **B.Eng.Sc.**—Bachelor of Engineering Science
B.E.T.—Bachelor of Engineering Technology
B.F.A.—Bachelor of Fine Arts
B.G.S.—Bachelor of General Studies
B.G.S.—Bachelor of Geological Sciences
B.H.E.—Bachelor of Health Education
B.H.P.E.—Bachelor of Health and Physical Education
B.H.S.—Bachelor of Health Science
B.I.D.—Bachelor of Industrial Design
B.I.M.—Bachelor of Industrial Management
B.Ind.Tech.—Bachelor of Industrial Technology
B.Int.Arch.—Bachelor of Interior Architecture
B.Int.Design—Bachelor of Interior Design
B.I.S.—Bachelor of Industrial Safety
B.I.S.—Bachelor of Interdisciplinary Studies
B.J.—Bachelor of Journalism
B.J.S.—Bachelor of Judaic Studies
B.L.A. or **B.Lib.Arts**—Bachelor of Liberal Arts
B.L.A. or **B.Land.Arch.**—Bachelor in Landscape Architecture
B.L.I.—Bachelor of Literary Interpretation
B.L.S.—Bachelor of Liberal Studies
B.M. or B.Mus. or **Mus.Bac.**—Bachelor of Music
B.M.E.—Bachelor of Mechanical Engineering
B.M.E. or **B.M.Ed.** or **B.Mus.Ed.**—Bachelor of Music Education
B.Med.Lab.Sc.—Bachelor of Medical Laboratory Science
B.Min—Bachelor of Ministry
B.M.P. or **B.Mu.**—Bachelor of Music in Performance
B.Mus.A.—Bachelor of Applied Music
B.M.T.—Bachelor of Music Therapy
B.O.T.—Bachelor of Occupational Therapy
B.P.A.—Bachelor of Public Administration
B.P.E.—Bachelor of Physical Education
B.Perf.Arts—Bachelor of Performing Arts
B.Ph.—Bachelor of Philosophy
B.Pharm.—Bachelor of Pharmacy
B.Phys.Hlth.Ed.—Bachelor of Physical Health Education
B.P.S.—Bachelor of Professional Studies
B.P.T.—Bachelor of Physical Therapy
B.R.E.—Bachelor of Religious Education
B.R.T.—Bachelor of Respiratory Therapy
B.S. or **B.Sc.** or **S.B.**—Bachelor of Science
B.S.A. or **B.S.Ag.** or B.S.Agr.—Bachelor of Science in Agriculture
B.Sacred Mus.—Bachelor of Sacred Music
B.Sacred Theol.—Bachelor of Sacred Theology
B.S.A.E.—Bachelor of Science in Agricultural Engineering
B.S.A.E. or **B.S.Art Ed.**—Bachelor of Science in Art Education
B.S.Ag.E.—Bachelor of Science in Agricultural Engineering
B.S.A.S.—Bachelor of Science in Administrative Sciences
B.S.A.T.—Bachelor of Science in Athletic Training
B.S.B.—Bachelor of Science (Business)
B.S.B.A. or **B.S.Bus. Adm.**—Bachelor of Science in Business Administration
B.S.Bus.—Bachelor of Science in Business
B.S.Bus.Ed.—Bachelor of Science in Business Education
B.S.C.—Bachelor of Science in Commerce
B.S.C.E. or **B.S.C.I.E.**—Bachelor of Science in Civil Engineering
B.S.C.E.T—B.S. in Computer Engineering Technology
B.S.Ch. or **B.S.Chem.** or **B.S. in Ch.**—Bachelor of Science in Chemistry
B.S.C.H.—Bachelor of Science in Community Health
B.S.Ch.E.—Bachelor of Science in Chemical Engineering
B.S.C.I.S.—Bachelor of Science in Computer Information Sciences
B.S.C.J.—Bachelor of Science in Criminal Justice
B.S.C.L.S.—Bachelor of Science in Clinical Laboratory Science
B.S.Comp.Eng.—Bachelor of Science in Computer Engineering
B.S.Comp.Sci. or **B.S.C.S.**—Bachelor of Science in Computer Science
B.S.Comp.Soft—Bachelor of Science in Computer Software
B.S.Comp.Tech.—Bachelor of Science in Computer Technology
B.Sc.(P.T.)—Bachelor of Science in Physical Therapy
B.S.C.S.T.—Bachelor of Science in Computer Science Technology
B.S.D.H.—Bachelor of Science in Dental Hygiene
B.S.Die—Bachelor of Science in Dietetics
B.S.E. or **B.S.Ed.** or **B.S.Educ.**—Bachelor of Science in Education
B.S.E. or **B.S in E.** or **B.S. in Eng.**—Bachelor of Science in Engineering
B.S.E.E.—Bachelor of Science in Electrical Engineering
B.S.E.E.T.—Bachelor of Science in Electrical Engineering Technology
B.S.E.H.—Bachelor of Science in Environmental Health
B.S.Elect.T.—Bachelor of Science in Electronics Technology
B.S.El.Ed. or **B.S. in Elem. Ed.**—Bachelor of Science in Elementary Education
B.S.E.P.H.—Bachelor of Science in Environmental and Public Health
B.S.E.S.—Bachelor of Science in Engineering Science
B.S.E.S.—Bachelor of Science in Environmental Studies
B.S.E.T.—Bachelor of Science in Engineering Technology
B.S.F.—Bachelor of Science in Forestry
B.S.F.R.—Bachelor of Science in Forestry Resources
B.S.F.W.—Bachelor of Science in Fisheries and Wildlife
B.S.G.—Bachelor of Science in Geology
B.S.G.—Bachelor of Science in Gerontology
B.S.G.E.—Bachelor of Science in Geological Engineering

B.S.G.S.—Bachelor of Science in General Studies
B.S.H.C.A.—Bachelor of Science in Health Care Administration
B.S.H.E.—Bachelor of Science in Home Economics
B.S.H.F.—Bachelor of Science in Health Fitness
B.S.H.M.S.—Bachelor of Science in Health Management Systems
B.S.H.S.—Bachelor of Science in Health Sciences
B.S.H.S.—Bachelor of Science in Human Services
B.S.I.A.—Bachelor of Science in Industrial Arts
B.S.I.E.—Bachelor of Science in Industrial Engineering
B.S.I.M.—Bachelor of Science in Industrial Management
B.S. in Biomed.Eng.—Bachelor of Science in Biomedical Engineering
B.S. in C.D.—Bachelor of Science in Communication Disorders
B.S.Ind.Ed.—Bachelor of Science in Industrial Education
B.S.Ind.Tech.—Bachelor of Science in Industrial Technology
B.S. in Sec.Ed.—Bachelor of Science in Secondary Education
B.S.I.S.—Bachelor of Science in Interdisciplinary Studies
B.S.I.T.—Bachelor of Science in Industrial Technology
B.S.J.—Bachelor of Science in Journalism
B.S.L.E.—Bachelor of Science in Law Enforcement
B.S.M.—Bachelor of Science in Management
B.S.M.—Bachelor of Science in Music
B.S.M.E.—Bachelor of Science in Mechanical Engineering
B.S.Med.Tech. or **B.S.M.T.**—Bachelor of Science in Medical Technology
B.S.Met.E.—Bachelor of Science in Metallurgical Engineering
B.S.M.R.A.—Bachelor of Science in Medical Records Administration
B.S.M.T.—Bachelor of Science in Medical Technology
B.S.M.T.—Bachelor of Science in Music Therapy
B.S.Mt.E.—Bachelor of Science in Materials Engineering
B.S.Mus.Ed.—Bachelor of Science in Music Education
B.S.N.—Bachelor of Science in Nursing
B.S.Nuc.T.—Bachelor of Science in Nuclear Technology
B.S.O.A.—Bachelor of Science in Office Administration
B.S.O.E.—Bachelor of Science in Occupational Education
B.S.O.T.—Bachelor of Science in Occupational Therapy
B.S.P. or **B.S.Pharm**—Bachelor of Science in Pharmacy
B.S.P.A.—Bachelor of Science in Public Administration
B.S.Pcs.—Bachelor of Science in Physics
B.S.P.E.—Bachelor of Science in Physical Education
B.S.P.T.—Bachelor of Science in Physical Therapy
B.S.Rad.Tech.—Bachelor of Science in Radiation Technology
B.S.R.C.—Bachelor of Science in Respiratory Care
B.S.R.S.—Bachelor of Science in Radiological Science
B.S.R.T.T.—Bachelor of Science in Radiation Therapy Technology
B.S.S.—Bachelor of Science in Surveying
B.S.S.—Bachelor of Special Studies
B.S.S.A.—Bachelor of Science in Systems Analysis
B.S.Soc. Work or **B.S.S.W.**—Bachelor of Science in Social Work
B.S.Sp.—Bachelor of Science in Speech
B.S.S.T.—Bachelor of Science in Surveying and Topography
B.S.T. or **B.S.Tech.**—Bachelor of Science in Technology
B.S.S.W.E.—Bachelor of Science in Software Engineering
B.S.V.T.E.—Bachelor of Science in Vocational Technical Education
B.S.W.—Bachelor of Social Work
B.T. or **B.Tech.**—Bachelor of Technology
B.Th.—Bachelor of Theology
B.T.S.—Bachelor of Technical Studies
B.U.S.—Bachelor of Urban Studies
B.V.M.—Bachelor of Veterinarian Medicine
B.Voc.Arts or **B.V.A.**—Bachelor of Vocational Arts
B.V.E.D. or **B.Voc.Ed.**—Bachelor of Vocational Education

D.D.S.—Doctor of Dental Surgery

Ed.D. —Doctor of Education
Ed.S.—Education Specialist

J.D.—Doctor of Jurisprudence

LL.B.—Bachelor of Laws

M.A.—Master of Arts
M.A.Ed.—Master of Arts in Education
M.A.T.—Master of Arts in Teaching
M.B.A.—Master of Business Administration
M.D.—Doctor of Medicine
M.F.A.—Master of Fine Arts
M.P.A.—Master of Public Administration
M.S.—Master of Science
Mus.B. or **Mus.Bac.**—Bachelor of Music

Ph.D.—Doctor of Philosophy

R.N.—Registered Nurse

S.B. or **B.S.** or **B.Sc.**—Bachelor of Science

OTHER ABBREVIATIONS

AAAHC—Accreditation Association for Ambulatory Health Care
AABC—Accrediting Association of Bible Colleges
AABI—Aviation Accreditation Board International
AACN—American Association of Colleges of Nursing
AACSB—American Assembly of Collegiate Schools of Business
AACT—American Association of Community Theatre
AACT—Advanced Application Certification Testing
AACTE—American Association of Colleges for Teacher Education
AAFCS—American Association of Family and Consumer Sciences
AAHE—American Association for Health Education
AAHE—American Association for Higher Education
AAHEP—Accreditation of Allied Health Programs
AAHPERD—American Alliance for Health, Physical Education, Recreation, and Dance
AAHPERD—American Association of Health, Physical Education, Recreation, and Dance
AALE—American Academy for Liberal Education
AALS—Association of American Law Schools
AAM—American Academy of Microbiology
AAMA—American Association for Medical Assistants
AAMA—American Alternative Medical Association
AAMC—Association of American Medical Colleges
AAMFT—American Association for Marriage and Family Therapy
AANA—American Association of Nurse Anesthetists
AAPAR—American Association for Physical Activity and Recreation
AATA—American Art Therapy Association, Inc.
AAVLD—American Association of Veterinary Laboratory Diagnosticians
ABA—American Bar Association
ABAI—American Board of Allergy & Immunology
ABE—Association of Building Engineers Association of Building Engineers
ABET—Accreditation Board for Engineering and Technology
ABFSE—American Board of Funeral Service Education
ABHE—Association for Biblical Higher Education
ABHES—Accrediting Bureau of Health Education Schools
ACA—American Chiropractic Association
ACAE—Accreditation Commission for Audiology Education
ACBSP—Accreditation Council for Business Schools and Programs
ACCE—American Council for Construction Education
ACCGC—Accrediting Council for Collegiate Graphic Communications
ACCME—Accreditation Council for Continuing Medical Education
ACCNE—American Catholic Church of New England
ACE HSA—Accrediting Commission on Education for Health Services Administration
ACEI—Association for Cultural Economics International
ACEJ—American Council on Education for Journalism

ACE JMC—American Council on Education in Journalism and Mass Communication
ACF—American Culinary Federation
ACFEF— American Culinary Federation's Education Foundation, Inc. Accrediting Commission
ACGME—Accreditation Council for Graduate Medical Education
ACICS—Accrediting Council for Independent Colleges and Schools
ACNM—American College of Nuclear Medicine
ACNM—American College of Nurse-Midwives
ACOT—American College of Technology
ACOT—Advanced Communications-Computer Officer Training
ACOTE—Accreditation Council for Occupational Therapy Education
ACPE—Association for Clinical Pastoral Education, Inc.
ACPE—Accreditation Council on Pharmaceutical Education
ACPHA—Accreditation Commission for Programs in Hospitality Administration
ACS—American Chemical Society
ACSCU—Accrediting Commission for Senior Colleges and Universities
ACSI—Association of Christian Schools International
ACT—American College Testing Program
ACTFL—American Council on the Teaching of Foreign Languages
ACU—Association of Commonwealth Universities
ADA—American Dietetic Association
ADA—American Dental Association
ADDA—American Design Drafting Association
AEE—Association for Experiential Education
AFIT—Accelerated Flight & Instrument Training
AFSA—Application for Federal Student Aid
AHEA—American Home Economics Association
AHIMA—American Health Information Management Association
AICE—Advanced International Certificate of Education
AIChe—American Institute of Chemical Engineers
ALA—American Library Association
ALIGU—American Language Institute of Georgetown University
AMA—American Medical Association
AMA- CAHEA—American Medical Association Committee on Allied Health Education and Accreditation
AMTA – American Music Therapy Association
AMTA—American Massage Therapy Association
AOA—American Osteopathic Association
AOA—American Optometric Association
AOBFP—American Osteopathic Board of Family Physicians
AOSA—American Optometric Student Association
AOSA—American Overseas Schools Archive
AOTA—American Occupational Therapy Association
AP—Advanced Placement
APA—American Podiatry Association
APA—American Psychological Association
APET—Asset Placement Evaluation Test
APIEL—Advance Placement International English Language Exam
APMA—American Podiatric Medical Association
APTA—American Physical Therapy Association
ARC-PA—Accreditation Review Commission on Education for the Physician Assistant, Inc.
ARC-PA—Accreditation Review Commission on Education for the Physician Assistant, Inc.
ASABE—American Society of Agricultural and Biological Engineers
ASC—Accredited Standards Committee
ASCP—Association of Collegiate Schools of Planning
ASCP—American Society of Concierge Physicians
ASCP—American Society of Cardiovascular Professionals
ASCP—American Society of Clinical Psychopharmacology
ASCP—American Society of Clinical Pathologists
ASHA—American Social Health Association
ASHA—American School Health Association
ASHA—American Speech-Language-Hearing Association
ASLH—American Society for Legal History
ASHA—American School Health Association
ASLA—American Society of Landscape Architects
ASLHA (ASHA)—American Speech-Language-Hearing Association
ASPT—American Society of Plant Taxonomists
ATEP—Athletic Training Education Program
ATMAE—Association of Technology, Management, and Applied Engineering
ATME—Association of Theatre Movement Educators
ATMNE—Association of Teachers of Mathematics in New England
ATS—Association of Theological Schools in the U.S. and Canada
ATSUSC—Association of Theological Schools in the United States and Canada
AUCC—Association of Universities and Colleges of Canada
AUPHA—Association of University Programs of Health Administration
AVMA—American Veterinary Medical Association
AWI—Agency for Workforce Innovation

BENHA—Board of Examiners of Nursing Home Administrators
BEOG—Basic Educational Opportunity Grant (now Pell Grant)

CAA—Council on Aviation Accreditation
CAADE—California Association for Alcohol/Drug Educators
CAAHEP—Commission on Accreditation of Allied Health Education Programs
CAAP—College Achievement Admission Program
CAAT—Center for Alternatives to Animal Testing
CAATE—Commission on Accreditation of Athletic Training Education
CACREP—Council for Accreditation of Counseling and Related Educational Programs
CADE—Commission on Accreditation for Dietetics Education
CAHEA—*See AMA-CAHEA*
CAHIIM—Commission on Accreditation for Health Informatics and Information Management Education
CAHME—Commission on Accreditation of Healthcare Management Education
CANAEP—Council on Accreditation of Nurse Anesthesia Educational Programs
CAPTE—Commission on Accreditation in Physical Therapy Education
CARC—Canadian Agri-Food Research Council
CARF—Commission on Accreditation of Rehabilitation Facilities
CAS—Certificate of Advanced Study
CCE—Council on Chiropractic Education
CCIE—California Colleges for International Education
CCNE—Commission on Collegiate Nursing Education
CCTC—California Commission on Teacher Credentialing
CDN—Canadian/Canada
CEA—Canadian Education Association
CEA—Colorado Education Association
CEC—Commission on Education and Communication
CEC—Community Education Council
CED—Council for Education of the Deaf
CEEB—College Entrance Examination Board
CELT—Comprehensive English Language Test
CEPH—Council on Education for Public Health
CHEA—Council for Higher Education Accreditation
CIDA—Council for Interior Design Accreditation
CLAST—College Level Academic Skills Test
CLEP—College-Level Examination Program
CNNE—Commission on Collegiate Nursing Education
CoA—Committee on Accreditation
CoA-NA—Council on Accreditation of Nurse Anesthesia Educational Programs
COA—Commission on Opticianry Accreditation

COAMFTE—Commission on Accreditation for Marriage and Family Therapy Education
CoARC—Committee on Accreditation for Respiratory Care
COAPRT—Council on Accreditation of Parks, Recreation, Tourism, and Related Professions
COC—Certificate of Completion
COCA—Comprehensive Outcomes of Cognitive Assessment
CODA—Commission on Dental Accreditation
COE—Council on Occupational Education
COLA—Commission on Office Laboratory Accreditation
COPRA—Commission on Peer Review and Accreditation
CORE—Central Operation of Resources for Educators
CORE—Council On Rehabilitation Education
CORE—Consortium for Oceanographic Research and Education
CORE—Center for Organ Recovery and Education
CPME—Council on Podiatric Medical Education
CRDA—Candidates Reply Date Agreement
CRE—Council on Rehabilitation Education
CSAB—Computing Science Accreditation Board
CSAC—Consensus Standards Advisory Committee (of NQF)
CSHSE—Council for Standards in Human Service Education
CSLE—Center for the Study of Law and Economics
CSS—College Scholarship Service
CSS/Profile—College Scholarship Service Financial Aid Profile
CSWE—Council on Social Work Education Office of Social Work Accreditation
CVTEA—Committee on Veterinary Technician Education and Activities
CWS—College Work-Study

DECA—Discovering the Educational Consequences of Advanced Technical Education (DECA), a National Science Foundation funded research grant
DECM—Department of Education of the Commonwealth of MA

EAC—Engineering Accreditation Commission
EESL—Examination of English as a Second Language
EHAC—National Environmental Health Science and Protection Accreditation Council
ELPT—English Language Proficiency Test (SAT subject)
ELS/ALA—English Language Services/American Language Academy
EMH—Educable Mentally Handicapped
EOP—Equal Opportunity Program
EPH—Epidemiology and Public Health
EPSB—Education Professional Standards Board
ESL—English as a Second Language
ETS—Educational Testing Service

FAFSA—Free Application for Federal Student Aid
FEF—Foundry Educational Foundation
FET—Full-time equivalent
FFS—Family Financial Statement
FIDER—Foundation for Interior Design Education Research
FISL—Federally Insured Student Loan
FTE—Full-Time Equivalent

GED—General Educational Development (high school equivalency examination)
GPA—Grade Point Average
GPSC—Georgia Professional Student Commission
GPSC—Graduate and Professional Student Council
GRE—Graduate Record Examination
GSLP—Guaranteed Student Loan Program
G-STEP—Georgia State Test for English Proficiency

HEPAC—Higher Education Program Alumni Council
HEOP—Higher Equal Opportunity Program
HLC—Higher Learning Commission
HPER—Health, Physical Education, and Recreation

IACBE—International Assembly for Collegiate Business Education
IAME—International Association for Management Education
IB—International Baccalaureate
IELTS—International English Language Testing System

JRC-AT—Joint Review Committee on Educational Programs in Athletic Training
JRCE—Joint Review Committee on Education
JRCDMS —Joint Review Committee on Education in Diagnostic Medical Sonography
JRCERT—Joint Review Committee on Education in Radiologic Technology
JRCNMT—Joint Review Committee on Educational Programs in Nuclear Medicine Technology

LAAB—Landscape Architectural Accreditation Board
LCME—Liaison Committee on Medical Education

MACTE—Montessori Accreditation Council for Teacher Education
MAPS—Multiple Assessment Program/Services
MBHE—Massachusetts Board of Higher Education
MDOE—Michigan Department of Education
MELAB—Michigan English Language Assessment Battery
MSACS—Middle States Association of Colleges and Schools
MSCHE (MSACHE)—Middle States Commission on Higher Education
MUSIC—Multi User System for Interactive Computing

NAAB—National Architectural Accrediting Board
NAACLS—National Accrediting Agency for Clinical Laboratory Sciences
NAALS—National Assessment of Adult Literacy Survey
NACEP—Nurse Aide Competency Evaluation Program
NAEYC—National Association for the Education of Young Children
NAIT—National Association of Industrial Technology
NAMT—National Association for Music Therapy
NAPNES—National Association for Practical Nurse Education and Service
NASAD—National Association of Schools of Art and Design
NASD—National Association of Schools of Dance
NASDTEC—National Association of State Development Teacher Education
NASSM—North American Society for Sport Management
NASM—National Association of Schools of Music
NASO—National Adult School Organization
NASP—National Association of School Psychologists
NASPAA—National Association of Schools of Public Affairs and Administration
NASPE—National Association of Sport and Physical Education
NAST—National Association of Schools of Theatre
NATA—National Athletic Trainers' Association
NCA—North Central Association of Colleges and Schools, Higher Learning Commission
NCAA—National Collegiate Athletic Association
NCACE—National Council for Accreditation of Coaching Education
NCACS—North Central Association of Colleges and Schools
NCA-HLC— North Central Association of Colleges and Schools, The Higher Learning Commission
NCATE—National Council for Accreditation of Teacher Education
NCCAA—National Christian College Athletic Association
NCDPI—North Carolina Department of Public Instruction
NCIDQ—National Council for Interior Design Qualification
NCOPE—National Commission on Orthotic and Prosthetic Education
NCTE—National Council of Teachers of English
NCTM—National Council of Teachers of Mathematics
NDEA—National Defense Education Act
NEASC-CIHE—New England Association of Schools and Colleges, Commission on Institutions of Higher Education

NEASC-CTCI—New England Association of Schools and Colleges, Commission on Technical and Career Institutions
NEHA—National Environmental Health Association
NEHSPAC—National Environmental Health Science and Protection Council
NLN—National League for Nursing
NLNAC—National League for Nursing Accrediting Commission, Inc.
NMPED—New Mexico Public Education Department
NMSA—National Middle School Association
NRPA—National Recreation and Park Association
NSTA—National Science Teachers Association
NWCCU—Northwest Commission on Colleges and Universities
NYSED—New York State Education Department

OAKE—Organization of American Kodály Educators
OBN—Ohio Board of Nursing
ODE—Ohio Department of Education
ODPS—Ohio Department of Public Safety

PAB—Planning Accreditation Board
PAIR—PHEAA Aid Information Request
PCS—Parents' Confidential Statement
PDE—Pennsylvania Department of Education
PEP—Proficiency Examination Program
PHEAA—Pennsylvania Higher Education Assistance Agency
PSAT/NMSQT—Preliminary Scholastic Aptitude Test/National Merit Scholarship Qualifying Test

ROTC—Reserve Officers Training Corps
RSE—Regents Scholarship Examination (New York State)

SAAC—Student Aid Application for California
SACU—Service for Admission to College and University (Canada)
SACS—Southern Association of Colleges and Schools, Commission on Colleges
SAF—Society of American Foresters
SAM—Single Application Method
SAR—Student Aid Report
SAT—Scholastic Assessment Testing *(formerly ATP–Admissions Testing Program)*
SATE—Security Awareness Training & Education
SBEC—State Board for Educator Certification (Texas)
SCAT—Scholastic College Aptitude Test
SCS—Students' Confidential Statement
SDBN—South Dakota Board of Nursing
SEOG—Supplementary Educational Opportunity Grant
SOA—Society of Actuaries

TAC—Technology Accreditation Commission
TAP—Tuition Assistance Program (New York State)
TDD/TTY—Telecommunications Device for the Deaf/TeleTYpewriter
TEA—Texas Education Agency
TEAC—Teacher Education Accreditation Council
TOEFL—Test of English as a Foreign Language
TRACS—Transnational Association of Christian Colleges and Schools, Accreditation Commission

UAP—Undergraduate Assessment Program
UMC—United Methodist Church
UP—Undergraduate Program (area tests)

VFAF—Virginia Financial Assistance Form

WASC-ACCJC—Western Association of Schools and Colleges, Accrediting Commission for Community and Junior Colleges
WASC-ACSCU—Western Association of Schools and Colleges, Accrediting Commission for Senior Colleges and Universities
WPCT—Washington Pre-College Test

PART I

AN INTRODUCTION TO COLLEGE

You'll soon be on your way to college—but how much thought have you given it so far? Have you started thinking about the career that's in your future?

- Which college will help you make the most of your natural abilities and interests, and get you ready for life?
- Which courses should you take?

This section will help you find answers to these questions. It will also give you advice on:

- how to apply to schools
- how to increase your chances of acceptance
- how to finance your education

And just as important, this introductory section will give you valuable tips on how to get through that critical freshman year.

KNOWING YOURSELF

It's not just about statistics like median SAT scores, the endowment, the number of majors or student-professor ratios; a college should feel right to you, from the structure of the classrooms to the food that's served in the dining halls.

Arielle Shipper, Connecticut College, Class of 2010

You have in your hands a book that will give you answers to your questions about the qualities and features of more than 1650 colleges. But before you start reading the descriptions and getting the answers, you need to know what questions to ask about finding the college that is right for you. Although you need to ask questions about "getting in" i.e., exploring colleges in terms of ease of admission for you, most of your questions should focus on the more significant issue of "fitting in." Fitting in means finding a college where you will be comfortable; where you are compatible with your peers, and where the overall atmosphere encourages your growth as a student and as a person.

This article is designed to help you assess some values and attitudes that will help you determine where you will fit in. It will enable you to ask the right questions. Not all colleges are for everyone; careful thinking about your interests, ideals, and values will lead you to find the college that is right *for you*. Colleges are not "good" or "bad" in a generic sense; they are either good or bad matches for you.

The two assessments that follow will be helpful in thinking about yourself as a future college student; they should help you make the right college choice.

THE COLLEGE PLANNING VALUES ASSESSMENT

Students have different reasons for going to college. Eleven reasons or values are found to be most important to students as they think about college. Knowing about your values is the important first step in identifying the colleges where you will fit in and be happy.

To complete the assessment, read through the list of ten values—A through K. Think about the outcomes you hope college will produce for you. Each student will rank them differently; hence, there are no "right" answers. Whereas several, or even most, of these values may be significant for you in one way or another, the goal is to decide which three are the most important. After you read each of the values, go back and circle the THREE most important ones on the basis of the following question:

What do you want college to do for you?

—— A. To provide me with a place to learn and study.
—— B. To provide me with opportunities to interact with teachers inside and outside the classroom.
—— C. To provide me with lots of fun experiences.
—— D. To prepare me to make a lot of money.
—— E. To provide me with recognition for accomplishments.
—— F. To get politically involved and/or to use much of my college years to help those who are disadvantaged.
—— G. To help me prepare for a career.
—— H. To enable me to be more independent.
—— I. To provide opportunities for me to grow religiously or spiritually.
—— J. To provide me with a variety of new experiences.
—— K. To enable me to receive a degree from a prestigious school.

What do your college planning values say about you?

If ***A*** was among the top three priorities on your list, you will want to explore the academic character of the colleges you are considering. Although all colleges are, by definition, intellectual centers, some put more priority on challenging students and pushing them to their limits. Reading about the academic features of the colleges you are considering will be important. (In the college Profiles, pay attention to the *special* section to learn about these features.) Your high ranking of this value says that you will be able to take advantage of intellectual opportunities at college. You may want to select a college where your SAT scores are similar to or slightly above the ranges of other admitted students—at those colleges you will be able to shine academically. You may desire to take an active part in classroom discussions and will want a college where the student faculty ratio is low.

If ***B*** was among your top three priorities, you feel challenged and stimulated by academics and classroom learning. You will want to find a college where your mind will be stretched. You will want to choose a college where you can explore a range of new academic subjects. A liberal arts and sciences college may give you an enriching breadth of academic offerings. You will want to look for a college where academic clubs are popular and where you have a good chance of knowing professors and sharing ideas with them. Access to faculty is important to you and you will want to look at the student faculty ratio in colleges you consider. Also note the ratio of undergraduate students to graduate students. Primarily undergraduate institutions will be the colleges that may best be able to meet your needs, because you will be the focus of teachers' attention. Teachers at such colleges place their priority on teaching and are not distracted by the needs of graduate students or by pressure to balance teaching and student time with research and writing.

If ***C*** was circled, you derive satisfaction from social opportunities. You will want a college where the academic demands will not diminish your ability to socialize. You likely will want a good balance between the social and academic sides of campus life. You will want to explore the percentage of students who get involved in intramural sports, clubs, or fraternities and sororities. (This information is listed in each college profile.) Look at your college choices on the basis of school spirit and sporting events offered. The profiles list popular campus events—see if they sound exciting to you. Also look at the percentage of students who stay on campus over the weekend. You will also want a college where it is easy to make friends. Both small and larger colleges would be appropriate for you. Although a larger college would expose you to more students and a larger quantity of potential friends, studies show that students at smaller colleges become more involved in activities and build deep friendships more quickly. Look for supportiveness and camaraderie in the student body.

If ***D*** is circled, you will want to consider earning potential, advancement opportunities, and the future market for the careers you consider. You will want to consider this value in your career planning. Remember, however, that there is no sure road to riches! You not only must pick a career direction carefully, but must choose a college where the potential for academic success—good grades—is high. The name of a particular college is less important than good grades or contributions to campus life when securing a good job or being admitted to graduate school. Even if you find that a particular career has tremendous earning potential, those earnings may come to only those who are most successful in the profession. Look at average salaries, but also consider your interests, values, and personality before making your final career choice. Be sure to take advantage of hands-on learning opportunities. Perhaps, for example, there are internships that meet your needs. Also, finding good, career-focused summer jobs can be helpful.

If ***E*** is high on your list, you take pleasure in being known for your success in an area of interest. For instance, you might feel good about being recognized or known in school as a good student, a top athlete, or a leader in a club. No doubt this type of recognition contributes to your confidence. You might look for colleges where you will be able to acquire or continue to receive this recognition. Often, recognition is easier to achieve at smaller colleges where you would not be competing against large numbers of students hoping to achieve the same recognition. You will also want to choose colleges where it is easy to get involved and where the activities offered are appealing to you. You may want to consider the benefits of being a "big fish in a small pond."

If ***F*** is important, that value will no doubt guide your vocational or avocational pursuits. You may find yourself choosing a career in which this value can be fulfilled, or you may seek opportunities on a college campus where you can be of service to others. You will want to choose a college where community service is valued. Look at the *activities* section and note whether community service-related involvements are available. Colleges vary a great deal in terms of political awareness. At some colleges, students are attuned to national and international events, often express feelings about current issues and policies, and in general, show interest in political affairs. Students at other colleges show little or no interest in these matters and find other ways to interact with peers.

If ***G*** was circled, you may know what career you want to pursue or you may be concerned but uncertain about your career decision. If you have tentatively selected a career, you will want to choose a college where you can take courses leading to the attainment of a degree in your chosen field. Explore the *programs of study* section in the profiles to determine whether a college you are considering offers the course work you desire. You will want to make a note of the most popular majors and the strongest majors as they are listed. If you don't yet know what career would suit you, remember, that for most careers, a broad, solid liberal arts foundation is considered good preparation. You will want to look at opportunities for internships and take advantage of the career planning and placement office at your chosen college. Finding a career that will be fulfilling is one of the most important choices you will make in your life. Your selection of a college will be your first step toward achieving your career goal.

If ***H*** is circled, it suggests that personal autonomy is important to you. College is, in general, a time for independence, and students are often anxious to make their own decisions without parental involvement. If you feel you can handle lots of independence, you will want to look for colleges where there is some freedom in choosing courses and where students are given responsibility for their own lives. Colleges vary in terms of these factors. Note particularly the *required* section under *programs of study,* which tells you the courses that must be fulfilled by all students. Be certain that you will not be stifled by too many rules and regulations. You may also want to look for colleges where the personal development of students receives high priority. A priority on independence also suggests that you will be comfortable being away from home and on your own.

If ***I*** is one of your top three choices, you will want to look first at the religious affiliation of each of your college options. There are two ways to consider religious life on college campuses. First is the question of how religion affects the day-to-day life of the college. For example, are biblical references made in class? Are religious convocations mandatory? Second is the question of whether there is a religious heritage at the college. Many hundreds of colleges have historical relationships with a religious denomination, but this tie does not affect the rules or the general life of the students. (For example, the college may have a certain number of religion classes required to graduate, but these classes are typically broad-based and not doctrinal.) You may want a college that has a relationship with your particular religious group. Or you may desire a large number of students who belong to the same denomination as you do. The profiles will also give you the percentage of students who are members of the major religious denominations. As you explore colleges, you will also want to see if the college has a commitment to the values and ideals held by you or your family.

If ***J*** is appealing, you like newness and will likely be stimulated by new experiences and new activities. You are in for a treat at most colleges. New experiences are the "stuff" of which college life is made. You may see college-going as an adventure and will want to pick colleges where you can meet your need for stimulation and excitement. Because you value newness, you should not hesitate to attend college in a different part of the country or to experience an environment or a climate that is quite different from your high school. You will also want to look for evidence of diversity in the student body. As you read the descriptions, look for colleges with lots of new opportunities for growth and for personal expansion.

If ***K*** is appealing, be cautious. Students who are overly concerned about this value might find college planning traumatic, and even painful, because of the admission selectivity of "name brand" colleges. Even though it is perfectly acceptable for students to be attuned to the overall excellence of a college, academic quality and prestige are not the same thing. Some colleges are well-known because of, say, a fine football team or because of academic excellence in a subject like psychology or physics. Although it is appropriate to look for a strong faculty and a highly regarded college, you want a college that will give you the greatest chance of academic success. It is success in college, not just academic reputation or prestige, that will lead to admission into graduate school or a broad selection of jobs.

Now that you've read about your top three values, answer the following question on a separate sheet of paper: In your own words, what do your top three values say about what you are looking for in a college? Then, share that information with your college adviser as he or she assists you in finding colleges that are right for you.

SELF-KNOWLEDGE QUESTIONNAIRE

The following seven items—A–G—will help you in thinking about yourself as a college student and the ease with which you will likely proceed through the college selection process. Read each statement and determine whether it is true or not true of you. After each question, you will see numbers ranging from 1 to 5. Circle 1 if the statement is very true of you. Circle 5 if the statement is not true of you. Use 2, 3, or 4 to reflect varying levels of preference. Be realistic and honest.

A. My academic abilities for college (such as reading, writing, and note taking) are good.

Very true of me 1 2 3 4 5 Not true of me

Academic abilities such as reading speed and comprehension, writing, note taking, calculating, speaking, and listening are important for college students. You will be called upon to use such skills in your college classes. If you are confident about your academic skills, you can approach picking a college with the ease of knowing that you will be able to master the academic rigors of college life. If you circled 3, 4, or 5 you will want to work on these skills in your remaining days in high school. You will want to choose colleges where you can work to strengthen these skills. Some colleges provide a learning skills center in which you are able to get help if you are having difficulty writing a paper or understanding the content of a class. If you are less than confident, you might look to colleges where you will not be intimidated by the skills of the other students.

B. My study skills and time management are good.

Very true of me 1 2 3 4 5 Not true of me

Study skills and time management are two of the most important qualities for an efficient and productive college student. Successful college students are average or above in organizing themselves for studying, scheduling, and using study time productively, and differentiating important content of a lecture or a book from supplementary information. In addition, they complete assignments on time and don't get flustered if they have several papers or a couple of tests due on the same day. If you circled 3, 4, or 5, it is important to work on improving these skills during your remaining high school days. You might consider the following:

- Seek help from your parents, a teacher, a counselor, or a learning specialist in becoming more organized.
- Try keeping a calendar. Anticipate each step necessary in preparing for every test and every paper.
- Be responsible for your own appointments.
- Check to see if a study skills course is offered at a local community college or university. Or consider reading a book on study skills.

C. I am motivated to succeed in college.

Very true of me 1 2 3 4 5 Not true of me

Motivation is definitely the most important skill you bring to college. Those students who want to succeed do succeed! Studies show that it is motivation, not your SAT scores, that determines academic success in college. And motivation means knowing not only that you want to go to college, but that you also want to be a student. Some students want to go to college for the fun aspects, but forget that college is primarily an academic experience. So if you circled 1 or 2, great, you're off to a good start. If you circled 3, 4, or 5, it may be an appropriate time to consider your wants and needs in a college. What sort of college would help motivate you? Would a college with a balance between academics and social life be appealing? Would you be more motivated if you were near a large and interesting city? Would nice weather be a distraction rather than an energizer? Is a trade or technical school best for you? Have you considered taking some time off between high school and college? Considering such questions is important, and the time to do that exploration is now.

D. I am a good decision maker.

Very true of me 1 2 3 4 5 Not true of me

Decisions, decisions, decisions. The college selection process is full of decisions! What colleges will I initially consider? To which colleges will I apply for admission? What college will I eventually attend? You will be facing those decisions in the upcoming months. If you circled 1 or 2, you are on your way. If you circled 3, 4, or 5, think about an important decision you made recently. Why didn't it go well? If you can analyze your decision-making weakness in that situation, it may help to avoid any potential pitfalls in your college decision-making. The following suggestions will help you improve your ability to make the right college choice:

- Clearly articulate what you're looking for in a college. Write down those features that will make a college right for you.
- Involve lots of people and resources in your search for a college. Your parents, counselors, and friends can help you.
- List and compare pros and cons of alternative colleges. Every college has both.
- Evaluate each college on the basis of the criteria you set for yourself.

Remember, you're looking for a college where you will get in *and* fit in.

E. I'm a good information gatherer; for example, I am usually able to find books, articles, and so on to help me do a research paper for, say, a history class.

Very true of me 1 2 3 4 5 Not true of me

Finding a college requires you to be a good researcher. There is so much information about colleges to sort through and analyze. If you feel you can do good research, fine, you're on your way. If you circled 3, 4, or 5, the following ideas may be helpful:

- Start with this book and look for colleges that are consistent with what you want. Remember that your primary concern is where you will fit in. Use your college-going values and your responses in this questionnaire to guide your thinking about colleges that will match you.
- Work closely with your college counselor, and seek impressions from students and others with reliable and up-to-date information about colleges of interest. You will make a better decision with credible and extensive input.
- Look for differences in features that are important to you. Is ease of making friends important to you? What about balance between academics and social life? Do you want teachers to know you?

F. I feel I adapt to new situations easily.

Very true of me 1 2 3 4 5 Not true of me

Everyone goes through changes in life. Some move through transition periods with great ease, others find them more difficult. You may have experienced the changes that come after a change of schools (even from middle school to high school), the illness or death of a relative, or the divorce of your parents. If you circled 1 or 2, you are not likely to be intimidated by a college in another part of the country or a college very different from your high school. If you circled 3, 4, or 5, you may want to carefully look at colleges that are a bit closer to home or colleges where the same values, perceptions, and attitudes exist as were true in your high school. Almost everyone has fear and apprehension about leaving for college. But if that fear is significant, you will want to choose a college where you will feel comfortable. Visits to college campuses may be particularly significant in feeling good about potential choices.

G. It is easy for me to meet people and establish friendships.

Very true of me 1 2 3 4 5 Not true of me

Identifying and nurturing friendships is an important skill for college adjustment. If you circled 3, 4, or 5, you will want to look carefully at colleges where there are few cliques, where there is an atmosphere of sharing, and where students report that it is relatively easy to integrate into the campus environment. Your choice of a college is a quest for a good social fit. Your thorough review of the profiles and even visits to college campuses will be helpful in assuring your ability to fit in and be comfortable.

FINAL THOUGHTS

If you took time to carefully consider the issues raised in both the Values Assessment and the Self-Knowledge Questionnaire, you should have gained new insights and perspectives about yourself. You will want to share these results with your parents and with your guidance counselor. Elicit their help in getting more insight as to how they see you as a prospective college student. Finally, two suggestions:

- As you research colleges, consider what you have learned about yourself. You want a college that is a good match with your values and interests.
- Spend time on your college search. It will take many hours of organized planning and investigation. But the time spent will result in a better choice and a greater likelihood that you will spend four productive and exciting years in college.

Good luck. There are lots of colleges out there that want you. Let your knowledge of yourself and your objective analysis of potential college options guide you to college environments where you will be able to shine. Success in college is in your hands. Make the most of the opportunity.

Steven R. Antonoff, Ph.D., Certified Educational Planner
Educational Consultant
Antonoff Associates, Inc.
Denver, Colorado

FINDING THE RIGHT COLLEGE

Location is a key factor in looking at colleges. Those seeking adventures should look toward city schools where there are endless possibilities, and those looking for a quiet atmosphere should look for schools in rural locations.

Bryan Cosca, Boston University College of Engineering, Class of 2014

Start your college search positively. Start with the knowledge that there are many schools out there that want you. Start with the idea that there are many good college choices for every student. Too often these days, articles on college admission make students and their parents apprehensive. You can have choices. You can get financial aid. You can have a happy, successful college career.

When you begin to think about college, you are embarking on a major research project. You have many choices available to you in order to get the best possible education for which you are qualified. This article is intended to help you think of some of the important variables in your college search.

Let us help make the book work for you!

THE CURRENT ADMISSION SCENE

Today there are approximately 1,650 four-year colleges and universities accredited. Most existing institutions have grown larger, and many have expanded their programs, offering master's and doctoral degrees as well as bachelor's.

Total graduate and undergraduate students has also grown, from under 4 million in 1960 to more than 16 million today. Almost 40 percent are part-time students, including many working adults. Part-time enrollments are mostly concentrated in the two-year colleges, which enroll about a third of all students.

What does this all mean to you? There is good news and bad news. The good news is that most of the colleges you will read about in this book are colleges you can get into! In other words, the vast majority of colleges in the U.S. admit more than 70 percent of those who apply. Many hundreds admit all of those who apply. So, on one level, you shouldn't worry that you won't be able to get a college education. The bad news is for the student with extremely high grades who seeks admission to the 50 or so most competitive colleges in the country. These "brand name" colleges have many times more candidates than they admit. Even incredibly qualified students are sometimes denied admission.

The key to good college planning is, as mentioned above, research. Find out about what makes one college different from another. Find out what students say about their experiences. Rely on many sources of information—many people, many books, many web sites, and so on. There are lots of people and materials available to help you. This book is one of them. Let the information be your guide. But also let your instincts and your sense of what's best for you play a part. The higher education opportunities in the U.S. are unlimited. The opportunity to let education help pave the way to achieving your dreams is a worthy goal of your college search.

MAKING A SHORT LIST

You have probably already started a list of colleges you know about from friends or relatives who have attended them, from recommendations by counselors or teachers, or by their academic or social reputations. This list will grow as you read the Profiles, receive college mailings, and attend college fairs. If you are interested in preparing for a very specific career, such as engineering, agriculture, nursing, or architecture, you should add only institutions that offer that program. If you want to study business, teacher education, or the arts and sciences, almost every college can provide a suitable major. Either way, your list will soon include dozens of institutions. Most students apply to between four and seven colleges. To narrow your list, you should keep the following process in mind:

- As you explore, be attuned to the admission requirements. You will want to have colleges on your list that span the admission selectivity continuum—from "reach" colleges (those where your grades, test scores, etc., suggest less chance of admission) to "safety" schools (those where your credentials are a bit better than the average student admitted), eliminating colleges at which you clearly would not qualify for admission.
- You also will want to keep an eye on cost. You want to consider colleges that are generally in line with your family's ability to finance your education. Be very cautious as you do this. Literally millions of dollars are available each year for students. There is both "need-based" aid (aid based on your family's ability to pay) and "merit-based" aid (aid based on such things as grades, test scores, and leadership ability).
- Screen the list according to your preferences, such as size, academic competitiveness, religious focus, and location.
- Make quality judgments, using published information and campus visits, to decide which colleges can give you the best quality and value.

The following sections are organized around the factors most important in researching a college. Discussion of admission competitiveness and cost comes first. After that, a wide range of factors important to consider as you evaluate colleges is examined. These include size, housing, the faculty, academic programs, internships, accreditation, libraries and computer technology, and religious/racial considerations. The final two sections are a discussion of campus visits and, finally, a checklist of 25 important questions to ask about each of the colleges you are exploring.

In the end, you must allow yourself to be a good decision maker. You will have to make some quality judgments. It is not as difficult as you may think. You have to be willing to read the information in this book and the literature that the schools make available, to visit a few campuses, and to ask plenty of questions. Usually you can ask questions of the admissions office by regular mail, e-mail, or in person during a campus visit. Because colleges sincerely are interested in helping you make the right choice, they generally will welcome your questions and answer them politely and honestly. In addition, your high school counselor is a key person who can offer advice and guidance. Finally, there are many resources available, in printed form and on the web, to help you.

SELECTION FACTORS

Admissions Competitiveness

The first question most students ask about a college is, "How hard is it to get in?" It should certainly not be the last question. Admissions competitiveness is not the only, or even the most important, measurement of institutional quality. It makes sense to avoid wasting time, money, and useless disappointment applying to institutions for which you clearly are not qualified. Nevertheless, there are many colleges for which you are qualified, and you can make a good choice from among them. The most prestigious institutions are rarely affected by market conditions. Most of the better known private and public colleges and universities have raised their admission standards in recent years. But there remain hundreds of fine public and private colleges, with good local reputations, that will welcome your application.

Use the College Admissions Selector to compare your qualifications to the admissions competitiveness of the institutions of your list. Make sure you read the descriptions of standards very carefully. Even if you meet the stated qualifications for *Most Competitive* or *Highly Competitive* institutions, you cannot assume that you will be offered admission. These colleges receive applications from many more students than they can enroll and reject far more than they accept. When considering colleges rated *Very Competitive* or *Competitive*, remember that the median test scores identify the middle of the most recent freshman class; half of the admitted students had scores lower than the median, and half were above. Students of average ability are admissible to most of the colleges and universities rated as *Competitive* and to virtually all of those rated as *Less Competitive*.

Cost

The basic cost of the most expensive colleges and universities can exceed $40,000 a year. This is widely publicized and very frightening, especially to your parents. But you don't have to spend that much for a good education. Private colleges charge an average of nearly $30,000 a year for tuition and room and board. Public institutions generally cost an average of $14,000 a year for in-state residents. Because many states have been cutting budgets in recent years, tuition at public institutions is now rising faster than at private ones. If you can commute to school from home, you can save about $6000 to $7000 in room and board, but should add the cost of transportation. The least expensive option is to attend a local community college for two years, at about $1500 a year, and then transfer to a four-year institution to complete your bachelor's degree. Depending on what you may qualify for in financial aid, and what your family is willing to sacrifice, you may have more choices than you think.

Size

Only one-fifth of American colleges and universities have enrollments of 5000 or more, but they account for more than half the ten million plus students who are pursuing bachelor's degrees. The rest are spread out among more than 1000 smaller schools. There are advantages and disadvantages that go with size.

At a college of 5000 or fewer students, you will get to know the campus quickly. You will not have to compete with many other students when registering for courses or for use of the library or other facilities. You can get to know your professors personally and become familiar with most of your fellow students. On the other hand, the school may not have as many majors and it may have less emphasis on spectator sports. Students at small schools are not able to be as "anonymous" as those at larger schools.

As colleges and universities enroll more students, they offer more courses and activities. Within a large campus community, you can probably find others who share your special interests and form a circle of good friends. But you may also find the facilities more crowded, classes closed out, and competition very stiff for athletic teams or musical groups.

Many of the largest institutions are universities offering medical, law, or other doctoral programs as well as bachelor's and master's degrees. Many colleges that do not offer these programs call themselves universities; and a few universities, Dartmouth among them, continue to call themselves colleges. Don't go by the name, but by the academic program. Universities emphasize research. University faculty need specialized laboratory equipment, computers, library material, and technical assistance for their research. Colleges tend to emphasize teaching.

Because research is very expensive, universities usually charge higher tuition than colleges, even to their undergraduate students. In effect, undergraduates at universities subsidize the high cost of graduate programs. Freshmen and sophomores usually receive some instruction from graduate student assistants and fellows, who are paid to be apprentice faculty members.

Of course, many larger private universities, and many public ones, have fine reputations. They have larger and more up-to-date libraries, laboratories, computers, and other special resources than colleges. They attract students from many states and countries and provide a rich social and cultural environment.

Housing

Deciding whether you will stay in a residence hall or at home is more than a matter of finances or how close to the college you live. You should be aware that students who live on campus, especially during the freshman year, are more likely to pass their courses and graduate than students who commute from home. Campus residents spend more time with faculty members, have more opportunity to use the library and laboratories, and are linked to other students who help one another with their studies. Residence hall life usually helps students mature faster as they participate in social and organizational activities.

If you commute to school, you can get maximum benefits from your college experience by spending time on campus between and after classes. If you need a part-time job, get employment in the college library, offices, or dining halls. Use the library to do homework in an environment that may be less distracting than home. If possible, have some dinners on campus, to make friends with other students and participate in evening social and cultural events. Get involved in campus activities, participating in athletics, working on the newspaper, attending a meeting, or rehearsing a play.

You will have a choice of food plans. Most meal plans include a certain number of meals per week. Other plans allow you to prepay a fixed dollar amount and purchase food by the item rather than by the meal. Choose a meal plan that fits your own eating habits. Most colleges today offer a tremendous variety of food and are accommodating to most diets and preferences.

Many students live off campus after their freshman or sophomore year, either by choice or because the school does not have room for them on campus. Schools try to provide listings of available off-campus rooms and apartments that meet good standards for safety and cleanliness. Many colleges also offer health care and food services to students who live off campus.

It is usually more expensive to live in an apartment than in a residence hall, especially if you plan to prepare your own meals. But that option is appealing to some students, particularly those in their junior or senior years.

The Faculty

The most important resources of any college or university are its professors. Admissions brochures usually point out the strengths of the faculty, but provide little detail. You should direct your questions about the faculty and other academic matters to the specific department or to the office that coordinates academic advising. Recruiting brochures also emphasize faculty research, because the prestige of professors depends largely on the books and articles they have published. Good researchers may or may not make good teachers. Ask how often the best researchers teach undergraduate courses, and whether they instruct small as well as large classes. For example, a Nobel prize chemist may lecture to 500 students at a time but never show up in the laboratories where graduate assistants actually teach individual students.

Also ask about class size, because this determines the amount of individual attention students get from professors. Student/faculty ratios, which usually range from 10 to 20 students per professor, don't really tell you much. Every school offers a mixture of large and small classes. Ask admission officers for the average size of a freshman class. You will want to look for such factors as those that follow:

- Science and technology courses should enroll only 25 to 30 students in each laboratory session, but may combine a number of laboratory classes for large weekly lectures.
- Skill development courses such as speech, foreign language, English composition, and fine and performing arts should have classes of 25 or fewer. Mathematics and computer science require considerable graded homework, and classes should be no larger than 35.

- Most other courses in humanities, social sciences, and professional areas are taught by classroom lectures and discussion. Classes should average 35 to 45 in introductory courses such as general psychology or American government. They should be smaller in advanced or specialized courses, such as Shakespeare or tax accounting.
- Many introductory courses, especially at universities, are taught in lecture classes of 100 or more. This is acceptable, if those courses also include small weekly discussion groups for individual instruction. Sometimes these discussion groups are taught by graduate student assistants rather than regular professors. Although graduate assistants lack teaching experience, they are very often highly capable. You should ask whether the teaching done by graduate assistants is closely supervised by regular faculty members.

Academic Programs

Even colleges and universities that boast fine and well qualified faculties can be short of professors in certain programs. Somo schools depend on instruction by part-time faculty members or fill in with available teachers from other specializations. Many international students are enrolled in technical doctoral programs, so you may find yourself being taught mathematics or engineering by a teaching assistant who is not a native English speaker. If you are interested in these subjects, check to see whether full-time faculty members teach the majority of the courses.

Other programs may have sufficient faculty but too few student majors. Majors such as physics and philosophy, for example, often have many students in required introductory courses, but few taking the major. Because of small enrollments, these departments may not be able to offer their advanced and specialized courses on a regular basis.

Academic departments give strength to the program by bringing together faculty members who share a common area of study and make sure their students get the classes they need. Some programs, usually called interdisciplinary, are taught by groups of faculty members from several departments. These programs generally have the word *studies* in their titles; for example, Middle-Eastern Studies, Communication Studies, Women's Studies, or Ethnic Studies. If you are enrolled in one of these programs, be sure to ask about the student advising. (Sometimes, advising suffers if faculty members are primarily loyal to their own department.)

Internships

Internships are available at many colleges. They provide an opportunity to experience work in your major and learn from experienced people in your field. Many students have received job offers after participating in an internship program during the school year or during summer vacation. These internships can make a big difference as you enter the job market.

Accreditation

General standards of academic quality are established by associations of colleges and universities through a process called voluntary accreditation. The criteria include: standards for admission of students; faculty qualifications; content of courses; grading standards; professional success of alumni; adequacy of libraries, laboratories, computers, and other support facilities; administrative systems and policy decision making; and financial support.

Six regional associations (New England, Middle States, Southern, North Central, Northwest, and Western) evaluate and accredit colleges as total institutions. Bible colleges have their own accrediting association. Other organizations evaluate and accredit specific programs, primarily in technical fields, like engineering and architecture; or those that require licensing, such as teaching and health care.

Libraries and Computer Technology

Most people judge libraries by the size of the collection, the bigger the better. Collection size is important, but only in relation to the variety and level of programs offered. A small liberal arts college can support its baccalaureate programs with a collection of 200,000 to 400,000 volumes. A university with many professional schools and doctoral programs may require over 2 million. Many books and journals are available through various methods of information technology, computer storage, and the Internet.

The main stacks should be open to students, with the possible exception of rare books, bound journals, and other special items. Open stacks encourage browsing and save students from waiting on line while a library assistant fetches a few books at a time. Instead, assistants constantly should be picking up unused materials from reading desks or carts and putting them back on the shelves.

Good circulation policies encourage students to check materials out for short periods and to return them promptly. One week or less loans are appropriate for books regularly used in courses, and four week loans should be the maximum for other materials. A recall system should be available to get back borrowed material when it is needed. Journals, reference material, or books placed on reserve for assigned reading should be used within the library while it is open, and circulated overnight only at closing time.

Using a computer is integral to university study. Some institutions require students to have personal computers. Colleges often offer the best price for new computers. You may want to check out the options on campus before you purchase a computer elsewhere. Many residence hall rooms are wired for computers and direct connections are linked to the main campus system. More and more campuses have wireless capability.

Religious/Ethnic Considerations

For some students, the religious life of the campus is important as college choices are reviewed. Religious life can vary from being pervasive to being absent. Most colleges are independent of religious influence. Some are historically affiliated with a religious group, yet religious matters are not part of student life. Other schools exist, in part, to educate students in the doctrine and the practices of their own religious perspective. Information you find on these pages will give you answers to some of your initial questions about religious life at particular schools.

If connecting with and learning from members of your racial/ethnic heritage is important, you will find many colleges and universities from which to choose. Again, this guide provides information about the diversity of the campus and the composition of students who are white, African-American, Hispanic, Asian-American, Latino, and so forth.

GETTING THE MOST FROM YOUR CAMPUS VISIT

It is best not to eliminate any options without at least visiting a few campuses of different types to judge their feeling and style first hand.

To learn everything important about a college, you need more than the standard presentation and tour given to visiting students and parents. Plan your visit for a weekday during the school term. This will let you see how classes are taught and how students live. It also is the best time to meet faculty and staff members. If the college does not schedule group presentations or tours at the time you want, call the office of admissions to arrange for an individual tour and interview. (This is more likely at a small college.) At the same time, ask the admissions office to make appointments with people you want to meet.

To find out about a specific academic program, ask to meet the department chairperson or a professor. If you are interested in athletics, religion, or music, arrange to meet with the coach, the chaplain, or the conductor of the orchestra. Your parents will also want to talk to a financial aid counselor about scholarships, grants, and loans. The office of academic affairs can help with your questions about courses or the faculty. The office of student affairs is in charge of residence halls, health services, and extracurricular activities. Each of these areas has a dean or vice president and a number of assistants, so you should be able to get your questions answered even if you go in without an appointment.

Take advantage of a group presentation and tour if one is scheduled on the day of your visit. Much of what you learn may be familiar, but other students and parents will ask about some of the same things you want to know. Student tour guides are also good sources of information. They love to talk about their own courses, professors, and campus experiences.

Finally, explore the campus on your own. Check the condition of the buildings and the grounds. If they appear well maintained, the college probably has good overall management. If they look run down, the college may have financial problems that also make it scrimp on the book budget or laboratory supplies. Visit a service office, such as the registrar, career planning, or academic advising. Observe whether they treat students courteously and seem genuinely interested in helping them. Look at bulletin boards for signs of campus activities.

And, perhaps most importantly, talk to some of the students who are already enrolled at the college. They will usually speak frankly about weekend activities, whether they find it easy to talk to professors out of class, and how much drinking or drug abuse there is on campus. Most importantly, meeting other students will help you discover how friendly the campus is and whether the college will suit you socially and intellectually.

More than buildings and courses of study, a college is a community of people. Only during a campus visit can you experience the human environment in which you will live and work during four critical years.

25 CRITICAL QUESTIONS

The following questions form a checklist to evaluate each college or university you are considering. Use the profiles, material from the colleges, and your own inquiries and observations to get the answers.

1. Do I have a reasonable chance of being admitted?
2. Can my family manage the costs?
3. Is the overall size of the school right for my personality?
4. Is the location right? (Consider such specifics as region, distance from a major city, distance from home, and weather.)
5. Are class sizes right for my learning style and my need for involvement in class?
6. Will I be comfortable with the setting of the campus?
7. Are the housing and food services suitable?
8. Does the college offer the program I want to study? (Or, often more importantly, does the college offer people and classes that will help me decide what I want to study?)
9. Will the college push me academically, but not shove me?
10. Do the best professors teach undergraduate courses?
11. Can I change majors easily, if I need to?
12. Do students say the majority of classes are taught by fun, stimulating, interesting professors?
13. Is the library collection adequate and accessible?
14. Are computer facilities readily available and are campus networking opportunities up-to-date?
15. Is the connection to the Internet adequate?
16. Are there resources for career development?
17. Do the people in the financial aid, housing, and other service offices seem attentive and genuinely interested in helping students?
18. Will I find activities that meet my interests?
19. Does the campus seem well maintained and managed?
20. Will the college meet my religious and/or ethnic needs?

And, finally, the five most critical questions:

21. Is there a good chance I will be academically successful there?
22. Will I be happy as a student there?
23. Do I seem compatible with the student population? Do they seem to enjoy what I enjoy?
24. Does the student life seem in sync with my personality and my goals? Is the student life what I'm looking for in a college?
25. Does the college "feel" right for me?

Steven R. Antonoff
Sheldon Halpern
Barbara Aronson

SCORING HIGH ON ENTRANCE EXAMINATIONS

Take your entrance exams seriously. When the opportunity of a lifetime presents itself, you'd better be ready for everything life has to offer, or live with regrets forever.

2Lt Jocelyn Booker, United States Air Force Academy, Class of 2010

COLLEGE ENTRANCE EXAMINATIONS

By providing you with exactly the same information about each of the colleges in which you are interested, the book you are now reading, *Profiles of American Colleges*, will help you narrow down the list of colleges to which you will apply. Of course, your final decision will be influenced by many other factors, many of which are far more important: actual visits to the colleges; virtual visits on the Internet; viewings of videotapes; advice from guidance counselors, parents, teachers, and friends.

In much the same way, by providing college admissions officers with the same information about thousands of applicants, the results of college entrance exams can help them narrow down the list of students they are considering accepting. The results of these exams help admissions officers compare students with widely differing backgrounds. Students from different high schools in different states who earn the same grade in their biology classes, B+ say, have used different textbooks, have performed different labs, have taken different tests, and in general often exhibit great disparity in their level of mastery of the subject; indeed, even within the same school, a grade of B+ from one teacher might not represent the same level of accomplishment as a B+ from another teacher. However, a grade of 650 on the Biology SAT Subject Test, or a 4 on the Biology AP test means the same thing whether it was earned by a student from a rural community in Idaho, an inner-city school in New York, or a private prep school in Massachusetts. Because students all across the country take the same standardized test on the same day, colleges can give greater credence to the results of those tests than they can to the results of final exams from different schools.

KINDS OF COLLEGE ENTRANCE EXAMINATIONS

Although some students who go from high school to two-year community colleges do not take any college entrance tests, most do, and virtually all students who are applying to four-year colleges will take some of the following exams:

- PSAT/NMSQT or the Preliminary SAT/National Merit Scholarship Qualifying Test.
- SAT Reasoning Test.
- SAT Subject Tests.
- Advanced Placement (AP) Examinations.
- The ACT Assessment.

The PSAT/NMSQT

The PSAT/NMSQT measures verbal and mathematical reasoning necessary for success in college. It is a standardized test taken by students in high schools throughout the country in October of their junior year. The test consists of five sections: two 25-minute critical reading sections, two 25-minute math sections, and one 30-minute writing section.

This Preliminary SAT is also the qualifying test for the scholarship competition conducted by the National Merit Scholarship Corporation, an independent, nonprofit organization supported by grants from over 600 corporations, private foundations, colleges, and universities. All students whose scores are in the top 5% of students taking the exam that year receive National Merit Letters of Commendation. In addition, students whose scores are in the top 1% of those taking the exam that year become National Merit Semifinalists. Those who advance to finalist standing by meeting additional requirements compete for one-time National Merit $2000 Scholarships and renewable four-year Merit Scholarships, which may be worth as much as $2000 a year or more for four years.

In addition, this test is used by the National Achievement Scholarship Program for outstanding African-American students. Top-scoring African-American students in each of the regional selection units established for the competition continue in the competition for nonrenewable National Achievement $2000 Scholarships and for four-year Achievement Scholarships sponsored by more than 175 organizations.

Test-Taking Strategies for the PSAT/NMSQT

1. Know what to expect. Each critical reading section has sentence completion questions and reading comprehension questions. A few of the reading questions are based on short passages (often a single paragraph), whereas most are based on longer passages (typically four to seven paragraphs). The first math section has 20 multiple-choice questions; the second math section has 8 quantitative comparison questions and 10 questions for which no choices are provided and whose answers must be entered in a special grid. Calculators may be used on any question in the math sections. The writing skills section, which does *not* have an essay, has three types of multiple-choice questions that test your knowledge of standard written English (grammar and usage).

2. On average, wild guessing has no effect on your score. Educated guessing, on the other hand, can improve your score dramatically. On all multiple-choice questions, try to eliminate as many obviously incorrect answer choices as possible, and then guess from among the choices still remaining.

3. Expect easy questions at the beginning of each set of the same question type. Within each set (except for the reading comprehension questions), the questions progress from easy to difficult. In other words, the first sentence completion questions in a set will be easier than the last sentence completion questions in that set; the first grid-in questions will be easier than the last ones.

4. Take advantage of the easy questions to boost your score. Remember: each question is worth the same number of points. Whether it is easy or difficult, whether it takes you ten seconds or two minutes to answer, you get the same number of points for each question you answer correctly. Your job is to answer as many questions as you can without rushing so fast that you make careless errors. Take enough time to get those easy questions right!

The SAT

The SAT is a reasoning test consisting of three parts—critical reading, mathematical reasoning, and writing. It is designed to measure your ability to do college work. Part of the test deals with verbal skills with an emphasis on critical reading, including a double passage with different points of view. The critical reading sections measure the extent of your vocabulary, your ability to interpret and create ideas, and your ability to reason logically and draw conclusions correctly. The mathematics part measures your ability to reason with numbers and mathematical concepts. It tests your ability to handle general number concepts rather than specific achievement in mathematics. Calculators are permitted on each math section.

The writing part consists of a short essay and multiple-choice questions that test your knowledge of standard written English (grammar and usage).

The SAT is given on seven Saturdays during the year—once each in January, March, May, June, October, November, and December. Applicants may request, for religious reasons, to take the test on the Sunday following the regularly scheduled date.

You can register online at *www.collegeboard.org* or by mail by using the registration form available at your school.

On each part of the SAT—critical reading, math, and writing—you will receive a scaled score between 200 and 800. On each part the national mean is approximately 500.

Test-Taking Strategies for the SAT

1. Pace yourself properly. It is much better to slow down and avoid careless errors than it is to speed up in an effort to answer all the questions. You can earn an above-average score (over 1000) by correctly answering fewer than half of the questions on the test and omitting the rest. Even scores of 1300 can be achieved by omitting more than 20% of the questions.
2. Read carefully. Make sure you are answering the question asked, not a similar one you once encountered. Underline key words (e.g., NOT and EXCEPT) to make sure you do not answer the opposite of the question asked.
3. Learn the directions for each type of question before taking the test. During the test, do not waste even one second reading the directions or looking at the sample questions.
4. Always answer the easy questions first (the ones at the beginning of each section). Do not panic if you can't answer a question. Do not spend too much time on any one question. If you are truly stuck, make an educated guess if possible (see below), and move on. Remember that each question is worth the same one point, and the next few questions may be much easier for you.
5. On average, wild guessing does not affect your score—it is unlikely to help, but it is equally unlikely to hurt you. The choice is yours. However, educated guessing—when you can eliminate one or more of the answer choices—can significantly increase your score! In particular, don't omit critical reading questions if you have read the passage; you can always eliminate some of the choices. Most math questions contain at least one or two choices that are absurd (for example, negative choices when you know that the answer must be positive); eliminate them and guess.

SAT Subject Tests

These tests are one-hour multiple-choice question tests. You may take one, two, or three tests on any one test date. Some colleges do not require SAT Subject Tests. Of those that do, some colleges require specific subject tests, whereas others allow applicants to choose the ones they wish to present with the admission application. Those colleges that do require these tests may use them to determine acceptance or placement in college courses. The tests in foreign language are used not only for placement but also for possible exemption from a foreign language requirement. If the college of your choice does not require these tests but you would like to demonstrate proficiency in a particular field, take the test anyway and have your scores sent. Tests are given in literature, history, mathematics, sciences, and several foreign languages.

Advanced Placement (AP) Examinations

The College Board also conducts Advanced Placement tests, given to high school students who have completed advanced or honors courses and wish to get college credit. Many secondary schools offer college-level courses in calculus, statistics, art, psychology, European history, American history, Latin, Spanish, French, German, biology, chemistry, and physics. As a result of scores obtained on these tests, colleges grant credit or use the results for placement in advanced college courses.

The ACT Assessment

The registration form for the ACT includes a detailed questionnaire that takes about one hour to complete. As a result of the answers to those questions about your high school courses, personal interests, and career plans, plus the scores on your ACT, an ACT Assessment Student Report is produced. This is made available to you, your high school, and to any college or scholarship source that you request. Decisions regarding college acceptance and award of scholarships are the result. This information is kept confidential and is released only according to your written instructions. To obtain an ACT application form, logon to www.actstudent.org, and click on online registration. When you visit the website you will find answers to other questions you may have as well.

The ACT measures knowledge, understanding, and skills acquired in the educational process. The test is made up of four distinct sections: English, mathematics, reading, and science reasoning.

In addition, you may register to take an optional fifth section: a 30-minute writing test. Some colleges require their applicants to take the writing test, but most do not. Check with the colleges to which you will be applying to know whether you need to take the writing part of the ACT.

On the ACT, you should answer all questions, because your score is based on the number of questions you answer correctly. There is no penalty for wrong answers. For each of the four tests the total number of correct responses yields a raw score. A table is used to convert the raw scores to *scaled scores*. The highest possible scaled score for each test is 36. The average of the four scaled scores yields the *composite score*.

The ACT English Test is a 75-question, 45-minute test that measures punctuation, grammar, usage, and sentence structure. The test consists of five passages, each accompanied by multiple-choice test items.

Test-Taking Strategies for the ACT English Test

1. Pace yourself. You have 45 minutes to complete 75 questions.
2. Read the sentences immediately before and after the one containing an underlined portion.

The ACT Mathematics Test has 60 questions to answer in 60 minutes. The test emphasizes quantitative reasoning rather than memorized formulas. Five content areas are included in the mathematics test. About 14 questions deal with pre-algebra topics, such as operations with whole numbers, decimals, fractions, and integers and about 10 questions deal with elementary algebra. Usually 18 questions are based on intermediate algebra and coordinate geometry. About 14 questions are based on plane geometry and usually four items are based on right triangle trigonometry and basic trigonometric identities.

Test-Taking Strategies for the ACT Mathematics Test

1. Spend an average of one minute on each question, less on the easy questions, more on the difficult ones.
2. Be sure to answer each question even if you have to guess.
3. Make sure your answers are reasonable.

The ACT Reading Test is a 40-question, 35-minute test that measures reading comprehension. Three scores are reported for this test: a total score, a subscore based on the 20 items in the social studies and natural sciences sections, and a subscore on the 20 items in the prose fiction and humanities sections.

Test-Taking Strategies for the ACT Reading Test

1. Read each passage carefully. Underline important ideas in the passage.
2. Pace yourself. You have 40 questions to answer in 35 minutes.
3. Refer to the passage and in particular to your underlined sections when answering the questions.

The ACT Science Reasoning Test presents seven sets of scientific information in three different formats: data representations (graphs, tables, and other schematic forms); research summaries (description of experiments); and conflicting viewpoints. The 40 questions are to be answered in 35 minutes. The content of the test is drawn from biology, chemistry, physics, geology, astronomy, and meteorology. Background knowledge at the level of a high school general science course is all that is needed to answer these questions. The test emphasizes scientific reasoning skills rather than recall of scientific content, skill in mathematics, or reading ability.

Test-Taking Strategies for the ACT Science Reasoning Test

1. Read the scientific material before you begin answering a question. Read tables and text carefully, underlining important ideas.
2. Look for flaws in the experiments and devise ways of improving the experiments.
3. When you are asked to compare viewpoints, make notes in the margin of the printed material summarizing each viewpoint.

A FINAL WORD

Don't take any examination without preparation, even though you will find descriptions of these tests that say they test skills developed over years of study both in and out of school. Don't walk in cold, even though you believe that you meet all the qualities colleges are looking for.

Although the College Board suggests no special preparation, it does distribute to applicants the booklet, "Taking the SAT Reasoning Test." It also makes available other publications containing former test questions along with advice on how to cope with the questions. Evidently, all candidates need some form of preparation.

The American College Testing Program furnishes the booklet, "Preparing for the ACT Assessment." This gives specific information about the test, test questions, and strategies for taking each of the four parts. It also describes what to expect on the test day and gives practice with typical questions.

Barron's Educational Series publishes books to help you prepare for these tests. They are available at all bookstores and in many libraries. You should be sure to use them before taking any of these tests.

Although no high school student takes all of the college-entrance exams described above, virtually all students planning to attend a four-year college take at least one of them—the SAT or ACT. Prepare conscientiously for each exam that you take and you will provide the colleges to which you are applying with valuable information about your abilities. Good luck!

Ira K. Wolf
President
PowerPrep, Inc.

GETTING IN

Don't be afraid to be yourself in every aspect of the applications process. No admissions officer wants to see the proverbial "perfect" application; rather, they're looking for individuals with unique stories, interests and voices that will contribute to the college community.

Arielle Shipper, Connecticut College, Class of 2010

The college admission process—getting in—begins the minute you start making your first choices in course selection and in cocurricular activities in junior high school, middle school, and high school. These initial and ongoing decisions are crucial to your future well-being. They lay the groundwork for the curriculum you will follow throughout your high school career: they are not easily reversed. These are the decisions that will allow you to market yourself to the colleges of your choice.

STUDENTS TAKE NOTE!

There is a myth prevalent among college-bound students throughout the country that the best way to gain entrance to the selective colleges is to be well rounded. This term usually refers to students who have earned good grades in high school (B+ or better) and participated in a wide range of cocurricular activities.

However, most admission officers at the selective colleges prefer applications from candidates they term angular—students who have demonstrated solid academic achievement in and out of school *and* who have developed one or two particularly strong cocurricular skills, interests, and activities. These angular students are very different in character from the well-rounded students who are very good at everything, yet excel at little, if anything.

William Fitzsimmons, Dean of Admission at Harvard, says that Harvard is looking for a well-rounded class, which means Harvard is most interested in admitting angular students—students who have excelled at something. He cautions, though, that "...It is a mistake to denigrate or underestimate that persuasive power of high grades, rank, triple 800s on the SAT, 36 on the ACT, and equally impressive SAT Subject Test scores. The selective colleges take many of these academically high profile applicants. But the numbers game alone often won't get you in! It would be fairly simple for Harvard to enroll an entire freshman class with a superior academic profile and little depth of quality in areas that make up the personality of the class. We just would not do that!"

Dean Fitzsimmons is saying that the majority of the successful applicants to selective colleges must have some major commitment(s) combined with excellent academic qualities. A strong impact results from quality involvements rather than a proliferation of joinings and transient interests. Essentially, the angular applicant is a committed individual, while the well-rounded candidate is merely involved.

STUDENTS AND PARENTS TAKE AN EARLY, ACTIVE ROLE

Students and parents must make time to ensure an early, active role in the college admissions process. Each year, starting in the seventh grade, students and parents should take the time to sit down with the student's guidance counselor and talk meaningfully about the following:

- selection and level of courses, projecting through the senior year of high school;
- cocurricular activities available, such as drama, music, athletics, academic clubs, community activities, student government, and other special interest groups; and
- summer study, work, or recreation.

Why is this important to getting in? As sure as taxes and death, there is going to come a time in your senior year when you, the college-bound student, will be asked to choose colleges, complete the college application, write your college essay(s), and have an interview—either on the college campus, or in your hometown.

You must create the personal marketing, which will take place during the application process in your senior year, long before your senior year starts. By the time you reach that long-awaited dream of being a senior, you and you alone have created the person you must market to the colleges of your choice. You must understand that the person you have created is the only person you have to market. There is no Madison Avenue glitz involved in this marketing process! You don't create a pseudo marketing campaign that shows you jumping off a bridge with a bungee cord tied to your sneakers. Admission counselors can tell the difference between a real marketing effort and a pseudo marketing campaign.

THE APPLICATION FORM

Today colleges are offering their application on hard copy, computer disk, E-mail, or through on-line services of the Internet. Each application form differs from college to college, with the exception of those colleges that use the common application. When you start to work, be sure to note all deadlines, follow all directions, be complete, be neat, fill out the geographical data with accurate facts, and type it all (unless you print exceptionally well). Always review the entire application before you start to fill it out, and complete the entire application before you start the next one. Remember the application is *you* to the admissions committee member reading it. Even though "a book should not be judged by its cover," appearances do influence opinions.

It is best to work through a rough draft of the application before you actually work on the application copy to be submitted. Remember to make a copy of all parts of the finished application in the event that yours gets lost and a replacement must be sent.

You are responsible for giving the Secondary School Report, found in each application, directly to your high school guidance counselor. Your counselor is responsible for sending official copies of grades, rank in class (if any), the school's profile, and a written recommendation regarding you. It also is your responsibility to call or fill out the appropriate forms for either the SAT and/or SAT Subject Tests or the ACT, to send the appropriate test information directly to each college to which you have applied, even if your scores are on your high school transcript. Your college file will not be considered complete, and will not be sent to the admission committee for a decision, without these official scores. Additionally, many colleges want recommendations from one or two teachers. Choose wisely and allow each teacher plenty of time. Request letters from teachers who know you best. If English is your interest, be sure to choose an English teacher. If you are fluent in Spanish and have future interest in Spanish at college, ask the Spanish teacher. Remember, though you have many interests and have participated in many activities—you are developing an admissions package as part of your marketing of yourself. Emphasize your strengths and show how they are integrated into your activities and achievements.

Cocurricular activities usually are athletic or nonathletic. If you have won athletic awards, note them. If you have had the starring role in the spring musical for the last two years, say so. If you are an editor on the school newspaper, specify this. Admissions people view your activities with special interest. They realize how very time consuming these activities can be and how they sometimes bring very few accolades. List these activities in the order of importance to you. If you do not believe that the application allows you the opportunity to show your depth of commitment to one or two cocurricular areas, you may add an addendum. Use the KISS (Keep It Short and Simple) method. This is an addendum, not an essay, letter, or dissertation. Be honest!

Some applications have mini essays. When space is provided, be sure you are concise, clear, and grammatically correct. Here, less is more. Your ability to organize your thoughts and present them concisely is being tested. You will receive your chance to impress each college with your prose in the long essay segment of the application. Some colleges have as many as four long essays, whereas some require none. In addition to the short and long essay questions, some colleges ask the student for a graded paper signed by the teacher.

Some colleges encourage you to support your application with additional materials. If you are given this option, consider what will strengthen your application: musical tapes, art and/or photography portfolios, published writings, an exceptional graded term paper, all the additional opportunities for the college to get to know you better and for you to increase your image as an angular candidate. Such additions help the admissions committee to get a better handle on who you are in relation to other applicants. Be sure your presentation is clear and as professional as possible. These additions are not going to be evaluated by the admissions committee. Your material will be directed to the appropriate department for evaluation and an evaluative note will be sent back to the admissions committee. It is this note that will become part of your admissions package, the same way an athletic coach evaluates potential student/athletes.

Proofread all parts of the application. Be sure you, the student, place your signature where it is required. If you are not sending your application on-line, then place everything, including the registration fee check, in a large manila envelope and give it to your college guidance counselor. After adding the completed Secondary School Report to the application, your guidance counselor will mail it. Your job is now finished and the waiting begins!

E-Mail, On-line Services through the College or the Internet

Applying online directly to the college(s) of your choice and communicating by e-mail has made the college application process less time consuming and easier than ever before. Certainly ecologically correct, by producing as close to a paperless process as possible, this method is still in cyberspace. Be sure you know what you are doing when you use any of these methods. It is seriously suggested that you take the time to call the college shortly after sending this type of application, to ensure that your application is on file. If you have an addendum or two, you may want to speak to an admission clerk to make sure each addendum has reached the office of admission in the format you desired. If it were my application and I chose any of these methods, I'd still send my musical tape, the slides for my art portfolio, and such, by certified or registered mail. Clarity is so important to the professionals who will be evaluating these addenda for your college admission process!

PC- and Mac-Based Computer Disk Applications

Since the emergence of on-line applications, fewer colleges have a computer disk application. If you wish to apply this way, make sure that your target college has authorized the disk: there are a number of organizations selling computer disk applications without the consent of the college. Make sure the service to which you have subscribed allows you to print a hard copy of the application, even if they want you to send the disk back to the service or to the college. Do yourself a favor and print an extra copy of the application for your personal college file—it is very easy for the post office or college to lose your information. It is also wise, if you have to send the disk with the application, to write, "DO NOT SCAN" on the envelope. It is highly probable that the information on the disk will be lost if it is passed through a scanning machine.

The Common Application

More than 450 colleges in the United States have agreed that students may apply to their colleges by completing one common application. Some of the colleges using the common application also have their own application. Students applying to a college that allows an applicant a choice of using either the college's own application or the common application, obviously face a choice. The use of the common application substantially reduces the time spent composing different essay answers and neatly typing separate application forms. If you are one of those who must make a choice between the common application and the application of the college, you should understand that each college using the common application (either as its only application or as an alternative application) has the right to ask for a supplement. If you choose the common application, be very sure to read the pages surrounding the common application carefully. Each college has a paragraph in which they discuss their deadlines, requirements for admission, and specify if they require supplemental information. The supplemental information can range from an additional essay or two, to additional information about your cocurricular activities.

All the colleges participating in the common application have each member of their admission staff sign a statement that they will NOT discriminate in the admissions process among students who submit the common application versus students who submit the college's application. However, there are counselors who believe that when there is a choice, the applicant has a better chance of conveying information by using the college's application; there is a vast difference in format between the two applications, even if the college requires a supplement. Check with your guidance counselor if you are unsure regarding your choice of format. To access the common application online, go to:

www.commonapp.org

College Web Sites

Most colleges today have their own web site. Here you will find a wealth of information. Some colleges have even put their viewbook, course curriculum guide, a campus tour, as well as their application, on their site. Visit each college's web page—the addresses are in the Admissions Contact section of the college Profiles in this book. You'll be a much better informed consumer.

THE INTERVIEW

The interview is a contrived situation that few people enjoy, of which many people misunderstand the value, and about which everyone is apprehensive. However, no information from a college catalog, no friend's friend, no high school guidance counselor's comments, and no parental remembrances from bygone days can surpass the value of your college campus visit and interview. This first hand opportunity to assess your future alma mater will confirm or contradict other impressions and help you make a sound college acceptance.

Many colleges will recommend or request a personal interview. It is best to travel to the campus to meet with a member of the admissions staff if you can; however, if you can't, many colleges will arrange to have one of their representatives, usually an alumnus, interview you in your hometown.

Even though the thought of an interview might give you enough butterflies to lift you to the top of your high school's flagpole, here are some tips that might make it a little easier.

1. **Go prepared.** Read the college's catalog and this book's Profile ahead of time so you won't ask "How many books are in your library?" or "How many students do you have?" Ask intelligent questions that introduce a topic of conversation that you want the interviewer to know about you. The key is to distin-

guish yourself in a positive way from thousands of other applicants. Forge the final steps in the marketing process you have been building since your first choices in the college admission process back in junior high school. The interview is your chance to enhance those decisions.

2. **Nervousness** is absolutely and entirely normal. The best way to handle it is to admit it, out loud, to the interviewer. Richard Shaw, Dean of Undergraduate Admissions and Financial Aid at Stanford University, sometimes relates this true story to his apprehensive applicants. One extremely agitated young applicant sat opposite him for her interview with her legs crossed, wearing loafers on her feet. She swung her top leg back and forth to some inaudible rhythm. The loafer on her top foot flew off her foot, hit him in the head, ricocheted to the desk lamp and broke it. She looked at him in terror, but when their glances met, they both dissolved in laughter. The moral of the story—the person on the other side of the desk is also a human being and wants to put you at ease. So admit to your anxiety, and don't swing your foot if you're wearing loafers! (And by the way, she was admitted.)
3. **Be yourself.** Nobody's perfect, and everyone knows nobody's perfect, so admit to a flaw or two before the interviewer goes hunting for them. The truly impressive candidate will convey a thorough knowledge of self.
4. **Interview the interviewer.** Don't passively sit there and allow the interviewer to ask all the questions and direct the conversation. Participate in this responsibility by assuming an active role. A thoughtful questioner will accomplish three important tasks in a successful interview:

   demonstrate interest, initiative, and maturity for taking partial responsibility for the content of the conversation;
   guide the conversation to areas where he/she feels most secure and accomplished; and
   obtain answers. Use your genuine feelings to react to the answers you hear. If you are delighted to learn of a certain program or activity, show it. If you are curious, ask more questions. If you are disappointed by something you learn, try to find a path to a positive answer. Then consider yourself lucky that you discovered this particular inadequacy in time.
5. **Parents** do belong in your college decision process as your advisers! Often it is they who spend the megabucks for your next four years. They can provide psychological support and a stabilizing influence for sensible, rational decisions. However, they do NOT belong in your interview session. In essence, the sage senior will find constructive ways to include parents in the decision-making process as catalysts, without letting them take over (as many are apt to do) the interview process. You may want your parents to meet and speak briefly to your interviewer prior to your interview and that is fine, but parents may not accompany you into the interview session! Arrange with your parents to meet somewhere out of the interview building after your interview is over. You do not want the interviewer inviting your parents back to the interview room. As intelligent as parents may be, they do not perceive the answers to questions the same way you do. The worst scenario I can imagine is the interviewer asking your parents some of the same questions that were asked you, and that is highly likely. Parents just answer questions differently than teenagers. At best, the scenario creates a long, long ride home, and when you get home you can't punish your parents by taking the car keys away from them, or grounding them for a week. At worst, the scenario has caused a blight in your admissions file. This is your time! Keep it that way!
6. **Practice makes perfect.** Begin your interviews at colleges that are low on your list of preferred choices, and leave your first-choice colleges until last. If you are shy, you will have a chance to practice vocalizing what your usually silent inner voice tells you. Others will have the opportunity to commit their inevitable first blunders where they won't count as much.
7. **Departing impressions.** There is a remarkable tendency for the student to base final college preferences on the quality of the interview only, or on the personal reaction to the interviewer as the personification of the entire institution. Do not do yourself the disservice of letting it influence an otherwise rational selection, one based on institutional programs, students, services, and environment. After the last good-bye and thank you has been smiled, and you exhale deeply on your way out the door, go ahead and congratulate yourself. If you used the interview properly, you will know whether or not you wish to attend that college and why.
8. **Send a thank-you note** to your interviewer. A short and simple handwritten or typed note will do—and if you forgot to mention something important about yourself at the interview, here's your chance.

WRITING THE COLLEGE ESSAY

Do the colleges read the essays you write on their applications? You bet your diploma they do. Here is your chance to strut your stuff, stand up, be counted, and stylize your way into the hearts of the decision makers.

Write it, edit it, review it. Rewrite it. Try to show why you are unique and how the college will benefit having you in its student body. This is not a routine homework assignment, but a college level essay that will be carefully examined for spelling, grammar, content, and style of a high school senior. As strenuous an effort as it may be, completing the essay gives the admissions committee a chance to know the real you, a three-dimensional human being with passions, preferences, strengths, weaknesses, imagination, energy, and ambition. Your ability to market yourself will help the deans and directors of admission remember your application from among the sea of thousands that flood their offices each year.

First, maximize your strengths—use your essays to say what you want to say. The answer to a specific question on the college's part still provides an opening for you to furnish background information about yourself, your interests, ambitions, and insights. For example, the essay that asks you to name your favorite book and the reason for your selection could be answered with the title of a Dr. Seuss book because you are considering a career as an elementary school teacher. If you are interested in business, read about a famous businessman you admire and then discuss your interest in business.

Whatever the essay questions are, autobiographical or otherwise, select the person or issue that puts you in the position to discuss the subject in which you are the most well versed. In essence, all of your essay responses are autobiographical in the sense that they will illustrate something important about yourself, your values, and the kind of person you are (or hope to become). If personal values are important to you, and they should be, then here is your opportunity to stress their importance.

Because many colleges will ask for more than one essay, make sure that the *sum* of the essays in any one college application covers your best points. Do not repeat your answers, even if the questions sound alike. Cover the most important academic and cocurricular activities (most important meaning the one in which you excelled and/or in which you spent the most quality time).

If you are fortunate to have a cooperative English teacher, you might request a critique of your first draft, but be sure to allow enough time for a careful evaluation and your revision.

Write the essays yourself—no substitutes or stand-ins. College admission professionals can discern mature adult prose from student prose.

PARTING WORDS

You may wish to ask yourself the following questions to help you decide which is your Paradise College. Most of this information is in the individual college Profiles in this book.

1. **Caliber of School Programs** Is the college known for its English department or chemistry department? What are its strengths?
2. **Selectivity of Admissions** Is the college Most Competitive, Highly Competitive, Very Competitive, Competitive, Less Competitive or Noncompetitive? Check the Selector Ratings.
3. **Chances of Admission** Be realistic. What are your chances of getting in? How far can you reach? Listen when you are given advice!
4. **Location of the School** Is the school near home, one hour away, 300 miles away, or across the United States?
5. **Rural, Suburban, Urban Campus** Is the school in the city or in a rural area?
6. **Size of the School** Can you spend four years at a small liberal arts college of 800 undergraduates? Do you need the larger atmosphere of a university? Do not equate size with social life!
7. **State College vs. Private College** Is the college a large state university with most of the student population from the state where it's located? Is it one of the public "Ivies"? Will you be a minority in the state school?
8. **Geographical Diversity** Is the college a regional one attracting students from the same state or region? Or is it a college, regardless of its size, which attracts students from all over the United States, or the world at large?
9. **Cost of College** What is the tuition? What are the living costs? What travel costs are there from home to campus? Are there hidden costs?
10. **Financial Aid** With a great percentage of undergraduates at many private colleges on financial aid of some type, where do you fit? What monies are available for the students at the schools of your choice? Is the college need blind in its admission program?
11. **Living Conditions** Is housing on campus guaranteed for all four years? Are the dorms coed? Are there single-sex dorms? Are alternatives in housing available?
12. **Socialization** Is it a grind school—all work, work, work? Is it fraternity- and sorority-oriented? What are the on-campus facilities for socialization?
13. **Safety on Campus** Are the dorms secure and locked? What's the safety system on the campus?
14. **Core Curriculum—Distribution Credits** Does the college require (for graduation) a specific number of credits in different academic disciplines? For example, does the student have to take six credits in philosophy before graduating? Is a self-designed curriculum possible?
15. **Sophomore Standing** Does the college accept AP credits? Does it offer advanced standing for an AP course, or just a credit toward graduation?
16. **Junior Year Abroad** Are there opportunities to study in Italy, Japan, or Australia, for example, while you are an undergraduate?
17. **Internships** Are there opportunities for hands-on experience while in college? Which departments have formal internship opportunities?
18. **Graduate School After College** What percentage of its graduates go on to graduate school immediately upon graduation, or within five years? What is the record of those who successfully get into the law, medical, or business school of their choice?
19. **Placement After Graduation** Is there an office for job placement after college? Is there an alumni network that helps in job placement?
20. **Weekend College** Do the students remain on campus on weekends, or is it a suitcase college?
21. **Minorities** What percentage of the students are minorities? Reflect on the racial, ethnic, and religious minority roles in the college you are considering. How would you feel being Jewish at a Roman Catholic college for example—or Catholic at a Jewish college?
22. **Sports Facilities** Is there a swimming pool? Are there horse stables? Is there an ice hockey rink on campus?
23. **Library Facilities** How many books are in the library? Is it computerized? Is the campus library tied into a larger network?
24. **Athletic Programs** Is the ice hockey team a varsity sport? Does the lacrosse team play Division I or III? Is basketball strong? Do they have a women's squash team?
25. **Honors Programs** Are honors programs available? What are they? Who is eligible?
26. **Student Body** Are the students politically active? Are they professional in orientation?
27. **Faculty** Are all classes taught by full professors? Or are TAs (teaching assistants) the norm?
28. **Computer Labs** Are computers required of incoming freshmen? What are the facilities on campus? Can you have your own PC in your room?
29. **Campus Visits** If possible, make a visit to the campus. Spend some time talking to students for a feel of the campus.
30. **Special Talents** Recognize your special talents and discover where they fit best. Often, a special talent becomes a scale-tipper in the admissions process.
31. **Special Family Circumstances** Talk with your parents about their expectations. Discuss your needs as well as their thoughts.
32. **Legacy** Does your family have a history at a specific school? Are you interested in continuing the tradition?
33. **Note Well—Final List** Be sure the final list is a realistic one. It should include "reaches," "targets," and "safeties." No matter which one admits you—it must fit!

Finding and applying to the best colleges for you is not supposed to be easy, but it can be fun. Parents, guidance counselors, and teachers are there to help you, so don't struggle alone. Keep your sense of humor and a smile on your face as you go about researching, exploring, and discovering your ideal college.

Last but not least is The Parent Credo: The right college is the one where your child will fit in scholastically and socially. Be realistic in your aspirations and support the child's choice!

Anthony F. Capraro, III, Ph.D.
President, Teach Inc.
College Counseling
Ocoee, Florida

FINDING THE MONEY

Sometimes getting more aid is a matter of simply applying for it.

Raymond A. Lutzky, Rensselaer Polytechnic Institute, Class of 2002

Postsecondary education is a major American industry. A greater proportion of students pursue postsecondary education in the United States than in any other industrialized country. Annually, more than 13 million students study at over 8000 institutions of higher learning. The diversity of our system of higher education is admired by educators and students throughout the world. There is no reason to believe that this system will change in the future. However, college costs and the resources available to parents and students to meet those costs have changed.

Unfortunately, many high school students and their parents believe either that there is no financial aid available or that they will not qualify for any type of financial assistance from any source. Neither assumption is correct. College costs have increased and will continue to increase. Federal allocations, for some financial aid programs, have decreased. But this decline has been met with generous increases in financial aid from state and school sources.

American students and their parents should realize that they must assume the primary role in planning to meet their future college costs and that the family financial planning process must begin much earlier than has been the case.

COLLEGE COSTS

- Nearly all parents believe college costs are too expensive.
- Currently, the average cost of education, including tuition and fees for one year at a public college would have been about $23,000 and for a private college and university, the cost could have exceeded $45,000.
- While college costs will increase each year, it is important to remember that currently a majority of all college students attend schools with tuition costs below $5,000.

STUDENT FINANCIAL AID

- In 2013, the total amount of financial aid available from federal, state, and institutional sources to postsecondary students is approximately $170 billion.
- A majority of all students enrolled in higher education receive some type of financial assistance.
- Federal student aid remains the largest source of funding.
- Not long ago the majority of federal financial assistance was grants. Today, a greater amount of financial aid is from loan money.

TIMETABLE FOR APPLYING FOR FINANCIAL AID

Sophomore Year of High School

Most families wait until a child has been accepted into a college or university to begin planning on how the family will meet those college costs. However, a family's college financial planning should begin much earlier.

Students, as early as the sophomore year of high school, should begin a systematic search for colleges that offer courses of study that are of interest. There are many computer programs that can be helpful in this process. These programs can match a student's interest with colleges fitting the profile. Considering that half of all students who enter college either drop out or transfer to another school, this type of early selection analysis can be invaluable.

After selecting certain schools for further consideration, you should write to the school and request a viewbook, catalog, and financial aid brochure. After receiving this information, you and your family should compare the schools. Your comparison should include academic considerations as well as financial. Don't rule out a school because you think you can't afford it. Remember the financial aid programs at that school may be more generous than at a lower-priced school. If possible, visit the college and speak with both an admission and financial aid counselor. If it is not possible to visit all the schools, call the schools and obtain answers to your questions about admission, financial aid, and placement after graduation.

Junior Year of High School

The comparative analysis of colleges and universities that you began in your sophomore year should continue in your junior year. By the completion of your junior year, you and your parents should have some idea of what it will cost to attend and the financial aid policies of each of the schools you are considering.

Some colleges and universities offer prospective applicants an early estimate of their financial aid award. This estimate is based upon information supplied by the family and can provide assistance in planning a family's budget. Remember that for most families, financial aid from federal, state, and school sources will probably not meet the total cost of attendance.

Families should remember that college costs can be met over the course of the academic year. It is not necessary to have all of the money needed to attend school available at the beginning of the academic year. Student and family savings, as well as student employment throughout the year, can be used to meet college costs.

Senior Year of High School

January

By January of your senior year of high school you should know which colleges and universities you want to receive your financial aid application forms. Be certain that you have completed not only the federal financial aid application form, but also any necessary state or school forms. Read carefully all of the instructions. Application methods and deadline dates may differ from one college to another. Submit an application clean of erasures or notations in the margins, and sign all of the application forms.

February

You will receive a report from the service agency you selected containing information on your family's expected contribution and your eligibility for financial aid. You and your parents should discuss the results of the financial aid application with regard to family contribution, educational costs, and how those costs can be met.

March

Beginning in March, most colleges begin to make financial aid decisions. If your application is complete, your chances of receiving an award letter early are greater than if additional information is required.

The financial aid award letter you receive from your school serves as your official document indicating the amount of financial aid you will receive for the year. You must sign and return a copy of the award letter to your school if you agree to accept their offer of financial aid.

If your family's financial circumstances change and you need additional funding, you should make an appointment to speak with your school's financial aid director or counselor. College financial aid personnel are permitted to exercise professional judgment and make adjustments to a student's financial need. Your letter of appeal should state explicitly how much money you need and why you need it.

TIPS ON APPLYING FOR FINANCIAL AID

1. Families can no longer wait until a child is accepted into college before deciding how they will finance that education. Earlier college financial planning is necessary.
2. Families should assume a much more active role in locating the resources necessary to fund future college costs.
3. Families should assume that college costs will continue to increase.
4. Families should assume that in the future the federal government will not substantially increase financial aid allocations.
5. Families should obtain information on a wide range of colleges including the many excellent low-cost schools.
6. Families should seek information about all of the funding sources available at each school they are considering.
7. Families should seek the advice and expertise of financial experts for college financing strategies. College financial planning should specify the amount of money a family should invest or save each month in order to meet future college bills.
8. Families should investigate all of the legitimate ways of reducing their income and assets before filing for financial aid.
9. Families should know how financial aid is awarded and the financial aid policies and programs of each school they are considering.
10. Families should realize that although the job of financing a college education rests primarily with them, they probably will not be able to save the entire cost of their child's college education. They probably will be eligible to receive some type of financial aid from some source and they will have to borrow a portion of their child's college education costs.
11. Families should be advised that the federal government frequently changes the rules and regulations governing financial aid eligibility. Check with your high school guidance counselor or college financial aid administrator for the latest program qualifications.
12. Part-time employment during the school year and full-time employment during the summer should be a part of every family's financing plan.
13. Families should investigate all colleges and universities that offer three-year graduation options.
14. Not every student can afford to live on campus. Commuting to college is one way to reduce college costs
15. It is important to find out a school's policy on awarding financial aid on the basis of need and merit.
16. Check with the financial aid office on the availability of loan forgiveness programs.
17. Find out if the aid awarded in the first year will be awarded in subsequent years if the family income does not change.
18. Find out the statistics on graduating seniors: how many were employed or accepted to graduate schools at the time of graduation.
19. Plan for the future. What was the average debt of graduating students in each of the schools you applied to?
20. Going to college should be a family decision. All family members should be aware of the financial implications of attendance, not just for the first year, but for all four years.

Marguerite J. Dennis
Former Vice President for Enrollment
and International Programs
Suffolk University
Boston, Massachusetts

SURVIVING THE FRESHMAN YEAR

Explore the campus and make yourself aware of all it has to offer. Most colleges have what seems like an endless supply of resources for its students. By taking advantage of these resources sooner, rather than later, they will prepare you for the years to come.

Shannon Scott, James Madison University, Class of 2013

COLLEGE: IT'S DIFFERENT

In college you are likely to hear fellow students say, "I don't know what that prof *wants*, and she won't *tell* me." "I wrote about three papers in high school, and now they want one every week." Though these students may be exaggerating a bit, college *is* different, both in the quality and the amount of work expected. Sometimes in high school the basic concepts of a course are reduced to a set of facts on a study sheet, handed to students to be reviewed and learned for a test.

In college, it is the concepts and ideas that are most important. These can only be grasped through a real understanding of the facts as they interrelate and form larger patterns. Writing papers and answering essay questions on tests can demonstrate a genuine understanding of the concepts, and this is why they are so important to college instructors. Learning to deal with ideas in this way can be a long-term asset, developing your independence, intellectual interests, and self-awareness.

Don't be discouraged; you are not alone. Most of your fellow students are having equally difficult times adjusting to a new learning method. Persist, and you will improve, leading to a lifetime habit of critical thinking and problem solving that can benefit you in many important ways.

College is also different outside of classes. Now that you have the freedom to choose how to spend time and what types of relationships to make, you have a bewildering number of possibilities.

MAKING A GOOD IMPRESSION

Here you are, plopped down in a strange place, feeling a bit like Dorothy transported to Oz. Your first goal is to make a good impression, showing your best self to those who will be important in your life for the next four years and even longer.

Impressing Faculty Members Favorably

Faculty members come in all ranks, from the graduate assistant, who teaches part-time while pursuing a degree, to a lofty full professor, who teaches primarily graduate students. Though different in rank and seniority, they respond to their students in roughly the same ways. They are, after all, people, with families and relationships much like your own. To have a good working relationship with them, try the following suggestions:

- **Make up your own mind about your instructors.** Listening to other students talk about teachers can be confusing. If you listen long enough, you will hear arguments for and against each of them. Don't allow hearsay to affect your own personal opinion.
- **Get to know your instructors firsthand.** Set up a meeting, during regular office hours. Don't try to settle important issues in the few moments before and after class.
- **Approach a discussion of grades carefully.** If you honestly believe that you have been graded too low, schedule a conference. Do not attack your instructor's integrity or judgment. Instead, say that you had expected your work to result in a better grade and would like to know ways to improve. Be serious about overcoming faults.
- **Don't make excuses.** Instructors have heard them all and can rarely be fooled. Accept responsibility for your mistakes, and learn from them.
- **Pay attention in class.** Conversing and daydreaming can insult your instructor and inhibit the learning process.
- **Arrive ahead of time for class.** You will be more relaxed, and you can use these moments to review notes or talk with classmates. You also demonstrate to your instructor a commitment to the class.
- **Participate in class discussions.** Ask questions and give answers to the instructor's questions. Nothing pleases an instructor more than an intelligent question that proves you are interested and prepared.
- **Learn from criticism.** It is an instructor's job to correct your errors in thinking. Don't take in-class criticism personally.

Impressing Fellow Students Favorably

Relationships with other students can be complex, but there are some basic suggestions that may make life easier in the residence halls and classrooms:

- **Don't get into the habit of bragging.** Frequent references to your wealth, your outstanding friends, your social status, or your family's successes are offensive to others.
- **Don't pry.** When your fellow students share their feelings and problems, listen carefully and avoid any tendency to intrude or ask embarrassing questions.
- **Don't borrow.** Borrowing a book, a basketball, or a few bucks may seem like a small thing to you, but some people who have trouble saying no may resent your request.
- **Divide chores.** Do your part; agree on a fair division of work in a lab project or a household task.
- **Support others.** Respect your friends' study time and the "Do not disturb" signs on their doors. Helping them to reach their goals will help you as well.
- **Allow others to be upset.** Sometimes, turning someone's anger into a joke, minimizing their difficulties, or belittling their frustration is your worst response. Support them by letting them release their emotions.
- **Don't preach.** Share your opinions when asked for, but don't try to reform the world around you.
- **Tell the truth.** Your reputation is your most important asset. When you make an agreement, keep it.

MANAGING YOUR TIME

Everyone, no matter how prominent or how insignificant, has 168 hours a week to spend. In this one asset we are all equal. There are students on every college campus, however, who seem to accomplish all their goals and still find time for play and socializing. There are others who seem to be alternating between frantic dashes and dull idleness, accomplishing very little. To the first group, college is a happy, fulfilling experience; to the latter, it is maddeningly frustrating. The first group has gained control of time, the second is controlled by that elusive and precious commodity.

- **Know where your time goes.** Unfortunately, we cannot store up time as we do money, to be used when the need is greatest. We use it as it comes, and it is amazing how it sometimes comes slowly (as in the last five minutes of a Friday afternoon class) or quickly (as in the last hour before a final exam). The first step in controlling time is to determine exactly how you use it. For a while, at least, you should carefully record how much time you spend in class, going to and from class, studying, sleeping, eating, listening to music, watching television, and running errands. You need to know what happens to your 168 hours. Only then can you make sensible decisions about managing them.

- **Make a weekly schedule.** You can schedule your routine for the week, using the time plan forms available at most college bookstores or by making your own forms.
- **First schedule the inflexible blocks of time.** Your class periods, transportation time, sleeping, and eating will form relatively routine patterns throughout the week. Trying to shave minutes off these important activities is often a mistake.
- **Plan your study time.** It is preferable, though not always possible, to set your study hours at the same time every weekday. Try to make your study time *prime time,* when your body and mind are ready for a peak performance.
- **Plan time for fun.** No one should plan to spend four years of college as a working robot. Fun and recreation are important, but they can be enjoyed in short periods just as well as long. For example, jogging with friends for 30 minutes can clear the mind, tone up the muscles, and give you those all-important social contacts. Parties and group activities can be scheduled for weekends.
- **Be reasonable in your time allotments.** As you progress through your freshman year, you will learn more precisely how much time is required to write a paper or complete a book report. Until then, schedule some extra minutes for these tasks. You are being unfair to yourself by planning one hour for a job that requires two.
- **Allow flexibility.** The unexpected is to be expected. There will be interruptions to your routine and errands that must be run at certain times. Allow for these unforeseen circumstances.

STUDYING EFFECTIVELY

Your most important activity in college is studying. Efficient study skills separate the inept student (who may spend just as many hours studying as an "A" student) from the excellent student, who thinks while studying and who uses common sense strategies to discover the important core of courses. The following suggested game plan for good study has worked in the past; it can work for you.

- **Make a commitment.** It is universally recommended that you spend two hours studying for every hour in class. At the beginning of your college career, be determined to do just that. It doesn't get easy until you make up your mind to do it.
- **Do the tough jobs first.** If certain courses are boring or particularly difficult, study them first. Don't read the interesting, enjoyable materials first, saving the toughies for the last sleepy twinges of your weary brain.
- **Study in short sessions.** Three two-hour sessions, separated from each other by a different activity, are much better than a long six-hour session.
- **Use your bits of time.** Use those minutes when you're waiting for a bus, a return call, laundry to wash, or a friend to arrive. Some of the best students I know carry 3 × 5 cards filled with definitions, formulas, or equations and learn during brief waiting periods. Most chief executives form the habit early of using bits of time wisely.

Digesting a Textbook

1. **Preview chapters.** Before you read a chapter in your textbook, preview it. Quickly examine the introductory paragraphs, headings, tables, illustrations, and other features of the chapter. The purpose is to discover the major topics. Then you can read with increased comprehension because you know where the author is leading.
2. **Underline the important points as you read.** Underlining should never be overdone; it can leave your textbook almost completely marked and less legible to read. Only the major ideas and concepts should be highlighted.
3. **Seven categories of information are commonly found in textbooks.** Be particularly alert when you see the following; get your marking pen ready.
   Definitions of terms.
   Types or *categories* of items.
   Methods of accomplishing certain tasks.
   Sequences of events or stages in a process.
   Reasons or *causes.*
   Results or *effects.*
   Contrasts or *comparisons* between items.
4. **Repeat information you need to learn.** When the object is to learn information, nothing is so effective as reciting the material, either silently or aloud.
5. **Don't read all material the same way.** Decide what you need to learn from the material and read accordingly. You read a work of fiction to learn the characters and the narrative; a poem, to learn an idea, an emotion, or a theme; a work of history, to learn the interrelationships of events. Do not read every sentence with the same speed and concentration; learn when to skim rapidly along. Remember, your study time is limited and the trick is to discriminate between the most important and the least important. No one can learn *everything* equally well.
6. **The five-minute golden secret.** As soon as possible after class is over—preferably at your desk in the classroom—skim through the chapter that has just been covered, marking the points primarily discussed. Copy what was written on the board. Now you know what the professor thinks is important!

TAKING TESTS SKILLFULLY

Try to predict the test questions. At some college libraries, copies of old examinations are made available to students. If you can legally find out your professor's previous test methods do so.

Ask your professor to describe the format of the upcoming test: multiple-choice? true-false? essay questions? problems? Adjust your study to the format described.

Listen for clues in the professor's lecture. Sometimes the questions posed in class have a way of reappearing on tests. If a statement is repeated several times or recurs in a subsequent lecture, note it as important.

As you review for the test, devise questions based on the material, and answer them. If you are part of a study group, have members ask questions of the others.

Common Sense Tactics

Arrive on the scene early; relax by breathing deeply. If the instructor gives instructions while distributing the test, listen very carefully.

- **Scan the whole test first.** Notice the point value for each section and budget your time accordingly.
- **Read the directions carefully** and then reread them. Don't lose points because you misread the directions.
- **Answer the short, easy questions first.** A bit of early success stimulates the mind and builds your confidence.
- **Leave space between answers.** You may think of a brilliant comment to add later.
- **Your first instinct is often the best** in answering true-false and multiple-choice questions. Look for qualifiers such as *never, all, often,* or *seldom* in true-false statements. Usually a qualifier that is absolute (*never, all,* or *none*) will indicate a false statement. Work fast on short-answer questions: they seldom count many points.

- **Open-book tests are no picnic.** Don't think that less study is required for an open-book test. They are often the most difficult of all examinations. If the material is unfamiliar, you won't have time to locate it and learn it during the test period.

Important Essay Strategies

- **Read the question carefully** and find out exactly what is asked for. If you are asked to contrast the French Revolution with the American Revolution and you spend your time describing each, without any contrasting references, your grade will be lowered.
- **Know the definitions of key words** used in essay questions:
  - **analyze:** discuss the component parts.
  - **compare:** examine for similarities.
  - **criticize:** give a judgment or evaluation.
  - **define:** state precise meaning of terms.
  - **describe:** give a detailed picture of qualities and characteristics.
  - **discuss:** give the pros and cons: debate them, and come to a conclusion.
  - **enumerate:** briefly mention a number of ideas, things, or events.
  - **evaluate:** give an opinion, with supporting evidence.
  - **illustrate:** give examples (illustrations) relating to a general statement.
  - **interpret:** usually means to state in other words, to explain, make clear.
  - **outline:** another way of asking for brief listings of principal ideas or characteristics. Normally the sentence or topic outline format is not required.
  - **prove:** give evidence and facts to support the premise stated in the test.
  - **summarize:** give an abbreviated account, with your conclusions.
- **Write a short outline** before you begin your essay. This organizes your thinking, making you less likely to leave out major topics.
- **Get to the point immediately.** Don't get bogged down in a lengthy introduction.
- **Read your essay over** before you hand it in. Words can be left out or misspelled. Remember that essay answers are graded somewhat subjectively, and papers that are correctly and neatly written make a better impression.
- **Learn from your test paper** when it is returned. Students who look at a test grade and discard the paper are throwing away a valuable tool. Analyze your mistakes honestly; look for clues for improvement in the professor's comments.

WRITING A TERM PAPER

Doing convincing library research and writing a term paper with correct footnotes and bibliography is a complicated procedure. Most first-year English composition courses include this process. Good students will work hard to master this skill because they know that research papers are integral parts of undergraduate and graduate courses.

Many students make the mistake of waiting until near the deadline to begin a term paper. At the busy end of the term, with final exams approaching, they embark on the uncertain time span of research and writing. Begin your term paper early, when the library staff is unhurried and ready to help and when you are under less pressure. It will pay dividends.

REGULATING YOUR RELATIONSHIPS

Find your special friends who believe in your definition of success. In a fast-paced environment like college, it is important to spend most of your time with people who share your ideas toward learning, where you can be yourself, without defensiveness. To find your kind of friends, first ask yourself: What is success? Is it a secure position and a comfortable home? A life of serving others? A position of power with a commodious executive suite? A challenging job that allows you to be creative? When you have answered honestly, you will have a set of long-range personal goals, and you can begin looking for kindred souls to walk with you on the road to success.

There will be, of course, some persons around you who are determined not to succeed, who for some reason program their lives for failure. Many college freshmen never receive a college degree; some may start college with no intention of passing courses. Their goal is to spend one hectic term as a party animal. If you intend to succeed at college, spending time among this type will be a considerable handicap. Consider making friends who will be around longer than the first year.

If possible, steer clear of highly emotional relationships during your first year of college. You don't have time for a broken heart, and relationships that begin with a rush often end that way.

MAINTAINING YOUR HEALTH

Poor health can threaten your success in the first year of college as nothing else can. No matter how busy you are, you must not forget your body and its needs: proper food, sufficient sleep, and healthy exercise. Many students, faced with the stress of college life, find themselves overmunching junk foods and gaining weight. Guard against this. Drugs and alcohol threaten the health and the success of many college students.

A FINAL WORD

So there it is. If you have read this far, you probably have a serious interest in succeeding in your first year of college. You probably have also realized that these suggestions, even if they sound a bit preachy, are practical and workable. They are based on many years of observing college students.

Benjamin W. Griffith
Former Dean,
University of West Georgia
Carrollton, Georgia

PART II

COLLEGE FACTS AND FINANCES

Now that you've read through Part I, you'll need specific information on the colleges that best match your needs and aptitudes. Here's where you'll find essential information in a nutshell.

Facts and figures on all schools are listed in chart form to help you make quick and easy comparisons. Thumbnail data include:

- campus environment
- degrees offered
- composition of the student body
- enrollment figures
- test scores of entering freshmen
- fall application deadlines

You'll also see at a glance how much it's going to cost you for tuition, room-and-board, and related expenses. In-state costs are broken down on a state-by-state basis, each range starting with colleges that don't charge tuition and going up the scale to the most expensive schools.

COLLEGES AT A GLANCE

The charts on these pages present some of the basic data that initially concerns many students. All of the four-year accredited schools in the United States are listed here alphabetically by state. The type of college environment (from urban to rural) is given, followed by degrees offered and whether the institution is public or private. Information about whether the student body is coed or primarily men or women, and whether fraternities or sororities are on campus follows. The undergraduate enrollment for the fall of 2013 is given as well as the median test scores for freshmen who took the ACT or the SAT. Finally, the fall admissions deadline is shown. "Open" usually indicates that admission applications will be accepted until a few weeks before classes begin.

NAME OF SCHOOL	TOWN	ENVIRONMENT U-Urban R-Rural SU-Suburban SM-Small Town	DEGREES AWARDED A-Associate B-Bachelor M-Master D-Doctorate	CONTROL Pri-Private, Pub-Public	FRATERNITIES AND SORORITIES F-Fraternities S-Sororities F, S-Both No-Neither	STUDENTS: C-Coed M-Men W-Women PM-Primarily Men PW-Primarily Women	UNDERGRADUATE ENROLLMENT FALL 2013	TEST SCORES: ACT						SAT CRITICAL READING					SAT MATHEMATICS					SAT WRITING					APPLICATION DEADLINE Month / Day
								Median	Below 21	21-23	24-26	27-28	Above 28	Median	Below 500	500-599	600-700	Above 700	Median	Below 500	500-599	600-700	Above 700	Median	Below 500	500-599	600-700	Above 700	
Alabama																													
Alabama Agricultural and Mechanical University	Normal	SU	A,M,D	Pub	F,S	C	4,415																						7/15
Alabama State University	Montgomery	SM	B,M,D	Pub	F,S	C	5,355	17	60	34	5			434	79	16	4	1	430	79	14	6							7/30
Amridge University	Montgomery	U	A,B,M,D	Pri	No	C	322																						Open
Auburn University	Auburn	SM	B,M,D		F,S	C	19,799	27	3	16	30	16	35	560	13	52	27	8	590	10	41	37	12	570	19	45	30	6	2/1
Auburn University at Montgomery	Montgomery	SU	B,M,D		F,S	C	4,225	22	34	42	16	5	3																8/1
Birmingham-Southern College	Birmingham	U	B	Pri	F,S	C	1,188	26	4	23	27	19	25	570	18	44	32	6	580	12	44	32	11	570	16	45	28	12	2/1
Concordia College - Alabama	Selma	SM	A,B	Pri	No	C	600																					12	2/1
Faulkner University	Montgomery	U	A,B,M,D	Pri	F,S	C	2,763	19	57	22	7	3	2	460	65	28	4	4	460	61	32	4	4	430	79	16	5		Open
Huntingdon College	Montgomery	SU	B	Pri	F,S	C	1,110	21	45	28	17	7	3	455	72	26	2		455	67	26	7							Open
Jacksonville State University	Jacksonville	SM	B,M	Pub	F,S	C	7,895																						Open
Judson College	Marion	SM	A,B	Pri	No	PW	347		60	18	6	8	8		17	16	50	17			50	50			17	33	50		Open
Miles College	Birmingham	U	B	Pri	F,S	C																							Open
Oakwood University	Huntsville	SU	A,B		No	C	1,825																						Open
Samford University	Birmingham	SU	B,M,D	Pri	F,S	C	3,013	25	7	26	27	17	23	565	18	43	32	7	565	18	47	29	6	560	23	48	26	3	Open
Spring Hill College	Mobile	SU	B,M	Pri	F,S	C	1,319	24	15	33	25	15	12	530	39	33	20	8	550	27	43	26	4	540	29	40	23	8	7/15
Stillman College	Tuscaloosa	SM	B		F,S	C	1,580																					8	7/15
Talladega College	Talladega	SM	B		F,S	C	740																						Open
Troy University	Troy	R	A,B,M	Pub	F,S	C	21,900																						Open
Tuskegee University	Tuskegee	R	B,M,D	Pri	F,S	C	2,598	21	17	61	15	6	1	500	67	27	4		480	64	26	8							Open
University of Alabama at Birmingham	Birmingham	U	B,M,D	Pub	F,S	C		25	15	25	25	14	21																6/1
University of Alabama at Huntsville	Huntsville	SU	B,M,D	Pub	F,S	C	5,696	26	16	13	25	17	29	570	19	42	21	18	570	17	40	31	12						6/1
University of Alabama at Tuscaloosa	Tuscaloosa	SU	B,M,D	Pub	F,S	C	26,234																						3/1
University of Mobile	Mobile	SU	B,M	Pri	No	C	1,481	23							37	38	25			38	40	19	3						8/1
University of Montevallo	Montevallo	SM	B,M	Pub	F,S	C	2,620	23																					8/1
University of North Alabama	Florence	U	B,M	Pub	F,S	C	6,161																						Open
University of South Alabama	Mobile	SU	B,M,D	Pub	F,S	C	11,315	23	33	26	23	9	9	514					513					501					Open
University of West Alabama	Livingston	SM	A,B,M	Pub	F,S	C	1,695																						Open
Alaska																													
Alaska Pacific University	Anchorage	SU	A,B,M	Pri	No	C	545																						Open
University of Alaska Anchorage	Anchorage	SM	A,B,M	Pub	No	C	10,825																						Open
University of Alaska Fairbanks	Fairbanks	SM	A,B,M,D	Pub	F,S	C	8,078	24	24	23	25	13	15	560	26	43	27	4	560	23	41	30	6	520	37	43	18	2	6/15
University of Alaska Southeast	Juneau	SU	A,B,M	Pub	No	C	2,095																						Open
Arizona																													
American Indian College	Phoenix	SM	A,B		No	C	130																						Open
Arizona State University	Tempe	U	B,M,D	Pub	F,S	C	59,382	24	18	26	27	13	16	540	28	42	24	6	560	23	39	30	8						2/1
Embry-Riddle Aeronautical University - Prescott Campus	Prescott	R	B,M	Pri	F,S	C	1,813	26	6	19	27	16	32	570	19	42	31	8	600	13	35	43	9	530	29	44	25	2	7/1
Grand Canyon University	Phoenix	SU	B,M,D	Pri	No	C	27,680																						Open
Northern Arizona University	Flagstaff	R	B,M,D	Pub	F,S	C	22,670	23	29	30	23	10	7	520	37	44	17	2	520	36	44	18	2	200	46	40	13	1	Open
Prescott College	Prescott	SM	B,M,D	Pri	No	C	545	23	8	42		33	17	565	29	41	18	12	520	44	26	24	6	534	33	50	11	6	8/15
University of Arizona	Tucson	U	B,M,D		F,S	C	31,670																					6	8/15
Arkansas																													
Arkansas Baptist College	Little Rock	SM	A,B		F,S	C	400																					6	8/15
Arkansas State University	State University	SM	A,B,M,D	Pub	F,S	C	10,098	23	24	31	24	12	8	470	67	25	8		509	47	33	7	13	445	75	25			8/18
Arkansas Tech University	Russellville	SM	A,B,M	Pub	F,S	C	10,482	21	42	22	22	10	5	420	79	11	11		470	71	29								Open
Harding University	Searcy	SM	B,M,D	Pri	F,S	C	4,390	25	16	23	23	15	23	560	25	40	26	9	550	24	38	30	8						6/1
Henderson State University	Arkadelphia	SM	B,M	Pub	F,S	C	3,199	21	45	26	19	6	4	500	58	42			536	37	42	21							Open

Hendrix College	Conway	SU	B,M	Pri	No	C	1,416	29	1	12	15	19	53	606	14	31	34	21	598	9	44	32	15						Open
John Brown University	Siloam Springs	SM	A,B,M	Pri	No	C	1,801	27	1	28	25	25	18	586	20	33	35	12	581	15	41	34	10	562	29	34	29	8	5/1
Lyon College	Batesville	SM	B	Pri	F,S	C	600	25	9	27	24	13	17	518	41	41	18		555	29	53	18		498	59	24	17		8/1
Ouachita Baptist University	Arkadelphia	SM	B	Pri	F,S	C	1,543	24	10	33	22	18	17	517	45	38	11	6	535	34	42	21	3						Open
Philander Smith College	Little Rock	U	B	Pri	F,S	C	732	18	81	9	8	1	1	450	67	29	5		439	62	38			437	76	24			7/15
Southern Arkansas University	Magnolia	SM	A,B,M	Pub	F,S	C	3,130																						Open
University of Arkansas at Fayetteville	Fayetteville	U	B,M,D	Pub	F,S	C	21,009	25	5	21	33	16	25	540	21	48	25	6	560	15	45	34	6						8/1
University of Arkansas at Little Rock	Little Rock	U	A,B,M,D	Pub	F,S	C		21	10	55			35	395	95	5			485	5	58	11							Open
University of Arkansas at Monticello	Monticello	SM	A,B,M	Pub	F,S	C	3,363		63	19	13	3	2																Open
University of Arkansas at Pine Bluff	Pine Bluff	SM	A,B,M	Pub	F,S	C	3,115																						Open
University of Central Arkansas	Conway	SM	A,B,M,D	Pub	F,S	C	9,604																						Open
University of the Ozarks	Clarksville	SM	B	Pri	No	C	660																						4/1
Williams Baptist College	Walnut Ridge	F	A,B	Pri	No	C	574	22																					Open

California

Academy of Art University	San Francisco	U	A,B,M	Pri	No	C																							Open
American Jewish University	Los Angeles	SU	B,M	Pri	No	C	110																						5/31
Art Center College of Design	Pasadena	SU	B,M	Pri	No	C	1,565																						Open
Azusa Pacific University	Azusa	SM	B,M,D	Pri	No	C	6,543	24						540	25	50	23	2	550	25	47	24	4	540	25	51	21	3	5/1
Biola University	La Mirada	SU	B,M,D	Pri	No	C	4,337	24	7	35	28	19	11	556	24	42	27	7	559	26	42	29	3	550	25	44	25	6	3/1
California Baptist University	Riverside	SU	B,M	Pri	No	C	4,954	21	44	31	16	5	4	480	56	34	9	1	490	54	33	12	1	480	58	32	9	1	3/1
California College of the Arts	San Francisco	SM	B,M	Pri	F,S	C	1,464	24	24	24	39	3	9	520	40	37	21	2	570	31	35	28	6	520	41	39	20		Open
California Institute of Technology	Pasadena	SU	B,M,D	Pri	No	C	997						100			1	20	79				1	99				22	78	1/3
California Institute of the Arts	Valencia	SU	B,M	Pri	No	C	895																						1/5
California Lutheran University	Thousand Oaks	SU	B,M,D	Pri	No	C	2,888	24	8	32	37	12	11	540	24	53	21	2	560	17	51	29	3	540	25	53	19	3	1/15
California Maritime Academy	Vallejo	SU	B	Pub	No	C	868																					3	1/15
California Polytechnic State University	San Luis Obispo	SU	B,M	Pub	F,S	C		28		14	59		27	595	8	43	39	10	630	2	29	48	21						11/30
California State Polytechnic University, Pomona	Pomona	SU	B,M,D	Pub	F,S	C	20,952	23	28	28	24	10	9	500	44	40	15	2	540	30	37	27	6						11/1
California State University, Bakersfield	Bakersfield	SM	B,M	Pub	F,S	C	5,370																						Open
California State University, Chico	Chico	SM	B,M	Pub	F,S	C	15,292	21						501	39	42	10	1	512	33	45	14	1						11/30
California State University, Dominguez Hills	Carson	SU	B,M	Pub	F,S	C	12,423		86	11	3				85	13	2			82	16	2			85	14	1		11/30
California State University, East Bay	Hayward	SM	B,M,D	Pub	F,S	C	11,853																						11/30
California State University, Fresno	Fresno	U	B,M,D	Pub	F,S	C	19,704								68	24	6	1		61	24	6	1		69	25	5	1	11/30
California State University, Fullerton	Fullerton	SU	B,M,D	Pub	F,S	C	33,086	21	43	32	19	4	3	490	51	39	9	1	520	38	45	15	2						11/30
California State University, Long Beach	Long Beach	SU	B,M	Pub	F,S	C	29,287	21	42	25	20	7	6	500	47	38	14	1	530	39	37	21	3						11/30
California State University, Los Angeles	Los Angeles	SM	B,M,D	Pub	F,S	C	18,074	17	79	12	6	2	1	430	77	19	3	1	440	72	22	5	1	430	77	19	3	1	6/15
California State University, Monterey Bay	Seaside	SU	B,M	Pub	F,S	C	5,308	21	21	54		24	1	485	53	36	10	1	495	52	36	11	1	485	56	35	8		3/15
California State University, Northridge	Northridge	U	B,M	Pub	F,S	C		19						455	69	26			465	63	28	8							3/15
California State University, Sacramento	Sacramento	SU	B,M,D	Pub	F,S	C	24,701																						11/30
California State University, San Bernardino	San Bernardino	SU	B,M	Pub	F,S	C	14,732																						Open
California State University, San Marcos	San Marcos	SU	B,M,D	Pub	F,S	C	9,482							470	60	32	7	1	490	52	37	10	1						11/30
California State University, Stanislaus	Turlock	SU	B,M	Pub	F,S	C	6,620																						11/30
Chapman University	Orange	SU	B,M,D	Pri	F,S	C	6,005	26	2	11	31	25	30	590	7	43	41	9	610	4	36	50	10	610	4	39	46	11	1/15
Claremont McKenna College	Claremont	SU	B,M	Pri	No	C	1,264	31						700		7	43	51	720		3	38	60	710		7	36	57	1/2
Cogswell Polytechnical College	Sunnyvale	SU	B,M	Pri	No	C	288		40	20	20	20			29	65	6			29	35	36			59	29	12		Open
Concordia University - Irvine	Irvine	SU	A,B,M	Pri	No	C	1,738																						Open
Dominican University of California	San Rafael	SU	B,M	Pri	No	C	1,625																						Open
Fresno Pacific University	Fresno	SU	A,B,M	Pri	No	C	2,439																						Open
Golden Gate University	San Francisco	U	B,M,D		No	C	645																						Open
Harvey Mudd College	Claremont	SU	B	Pri	No	C	803	34				2	98	730		3	32	65	770			9	91	720		5	31	64	1/1
Holy Names University	Oakland	U	B,M	Pri	No	C	640																					64	1/1
Hope International University	Fullerton	U	A,B,M	Pri	No	C	924																					64	1/1
Humboldt State University	Arcata	SM	B,M	Pub	F,S	C	6,830																					64	1/1
Humphreys College	Stockton	SU	A,B,D	Pri	No	C	620																						Open
La Sierra University	Riverside	SU	B,M,D		No	C	1,680																						Open
Laguna College of Art and Design	Laguna Beach	SM	B,M		No	C	514																						Open
Loyola Marymount University	Los Angeles	SU	B,M,D	Pri	F,S	C	6,205	27	4	12	31	24	29	593	9	42	42	7	603	7	38	47	8	597	7	43	43	7	1/15
Menlo College	Atherton	SU	B	Pri	No	C	713	20	50	12	25	10	3	470	63	33	3	1	500	46	43	9	2	480	64	30	6	7	1/15
Mills College	Oakland	U	B,M,D	Pri	No	W	985	26	7	33	16	26	18	600	13	36	40	11	560	22	45	30	3	570	20	38	37	5	1/15
Mount St. Mary's College/Chalon Campus	Los Angeles	U	A,B,M,D	Pri	S	PW	2,288		67	21	10	2	1		70	26	4			72	25	3			65	30	5		2/15
National University	La Jolla	U	A,B,M	Pri	No	C	5,920																						Open
Notre Dame de Namur University	Belmont	SU	B,M	Pri	No	C	1,147	20	54	29	12	2	3	470	60	31	8	1	470	63	28	9		480	59	37	4		Open
Occidental College	Los Angeles	U	B,M	Pri	F,S	C	2,128	30					34	650	1	20	53	26	650	1	19	54	27	660	1	18	53	28	1/10
Otis College of Art and Design	Los Angeles	U	B,M	Pri	No	C	1,158	19	46	31	8	8	7	510	46	34	17	3	500	36	38	20	6	480	48	35	15	2	Open

NAME OF SCHOOL	TOWN	ENVIRONMENT U-Urban R-Rural SU-Suburban SM-Small Town	DEGREES AWARDED A-Associate B-Bachelor M-Master D-Doctorate	CONTROL Pri-Private, Pub-Public	FRATERNITIES AND SORORITIES F-Fraternities S-Sororities F, S-Both No-Neither	STUDENTS: C-Coed M-Men W-Women PM-Primarily Men PW-Primarily Women	UNDERGRADUATE ENROLLMENT FALL 2013	TEST SCORES: ACT						SAT CRITICAL READING					SAT MATHEMATICS					SAT WRITING					APPLICATION DEADLINE Month / Day
								Median	Below 21	21-23	24-26	27-28	Above 28	Median	Below 500	500-599	600-700	Above 700	Median	Below 500	500-599	600-700	Above 700	Median	Below 500	500-599	600-700	Above 700	
Pacific Union College	Angwin	R	A,B,M	Pri	No	C	1,375																						Open
Pepperdine University	Malibu	SU	B,M,D	Pri	F,S	C	3,488	29	6	8	19	21	46	604	6	39	42	13	623	5	28	46	21	610	5	34	43	18	1/5
Pitzer College	Claremont	SU	B	Pri	No	C	1,099	30						652		15	60	25	641		24	60	16						1/1
Point Loma Nazarene University	San Diego	SU	B,M	Pri	F,S	C	2,415								14	44	35	7		14	42	37	7		16	47	31	6	3/1
Pomona College	Claremont	SU	B	Pri	F	C	1,612	33						730					730					730					1/1
Saint Mary's College of California	Moraga	SU	B,M,D	Pri	No	C	3,035	24	13	33	27	14	11	552	23	49	23	5	558	23	46	29	4						2/1
San Diego Christian College	El Cajon	SU	A,B	Pri	No	C	752																						Open
San Diego State University	San Diego	U	B,M,D	Pub	F,S	C	27,809	24	15	27	34	15	9	540	27	51	20	2	563	19	46	31	4						11/30
San Francisco Art Institute	San Francisco	U	B,M	Pri	No	C	478	24	13	38	13	25	13	560	32	39	26	3	500	48	39	13		540	35	32	32		2/1
San Francisco Conservatory of Music	San Francisco	U	B,M	Pri	No	C	175																						12/1
San Francisco State University	San Francisco	U	B,M,D	Pub	F,S	C								490	54	35	10	1	505	46	40	13							11/30
San Jose State University	San Jose	U	B,M,D	Pub	F,S	C	25,862																						11/30
Santa Clara University	Santa Clara	SU	B,M,D	Pri	No	C	5,435	29		5	16	22	57	630	4	30	48	18	660	3	18	50	29						1/7
Scripps College	Claremont	SU	B	Pri	No	W	945									10	47	44			12	6	29			5	45	50	1/2
Simpson University	Redding	SU	A,B,M	Pri	No	C	1,019	21	44	26	13	11	4	500	35	41	22	2	500	36	50	14		490	42	43	15		Open
Sonoma State University	Rohnert Park	SU	B,M	Pub	F,S	C	8,351	23	44	33	15	5	2	440	51	39	10	1	540	51	39	10	1						11/30
Stanford University	Stanford	SU	B,M,D	Pri	F,S	C	7,061				1	13	86			4	27	70			2	21	77			3	25	72	1/15
The Masters College	Santa Clarita	SU	B,M	Pri	No	C	1,098	24	23	32	24	6	15	552	24	50	17	7	536	31	37	20	7	538	27	38	22	5	3/2
Thomas Aquinas College	Santa Paula	R	B	Pri	No	C	366	28		30	4	15	52	650	2	26	44	28	610	2	39	46	12	630	9	23	51	18	Open
University of California at Berkeley	Berkeley	U	B,M,D	Pub	F,S	C	35,646	30						660	8	20	43	29	700	4	14	32	51	670	6	18	42	34	11/30
University of California at Davis	Davis	SU	B,M,D		F,S	C	25,096	27						600	14	34	40	11	640	8	23	46	22	600	12	34	40	13	11/30
University of California at Irvine	Irvine	SU	B,M,D	Pub	F,S	C	22,216							540	34	37	24	5	610	15	30	40	15	550	27	40	28	5	11/30
University of California at Los Angeles	Los Angeles	U	B,M,D	Pub	F,S	C	26,162	29	8	13	16	14	53	640	8	24	45	23	680	6	16	36	42	660	6	21	40	33	11/30
University of California at Riverside	Riverside	SU	B,M,D	Pub	F,S	C	18,612	23	27	29	25	10	9	540	26	45	22	6	540	17	39	34	9	580	26	48	23	2	11/30
University of California at San Diego	La Jolla	SU	B,M,D	Pub	F,S	C	20,475																						11/30
University of California at Santa Barbara	Santa Barbara	SU	B,M,D	Pub	F,S	C	19,362	27	7	14	21	17	41	610	10	32	42	16	640	6	23	45	27	630	6	29	45	19	11/30
University of California at Santa Cruz	Santa Cruz	SM	B,M,D	Pub	F,S	C	15,695	24	23	21	24	12	18	550	27	36	29	8	560	21	34	33	11	550	26	38	30	6	11/30
University of La Verne	La Verne	SU	A,B,M,D	Pri	F,S	C	2,682	22	35	35	21	7	3	510	42	44	14	1	520	34	51	14	1	510	45	44	10	1	2/1
University of Redlands	Redlands	SU	B,M	Pri	F,S	C	2,375																					1	2/1
University of San Diego	San Diego	U	B,M,D	Pri	F,S	C	5,665	28	3	11	19	26	41	600	9	39	42	10	620	7	30	49	14	610	8	34	46	12	12/15
University of San Francisco	San Francisco	U	B,M,D	Pri	F,S	C	6,344		8	24	36	16	16		14	47	34	5		12	49	34	4		10	47	38	5	12/15
University of Southern California	Los Angeles	U	B,M,D	Pri	F,S	C	18,316								3	14	47	36		1	8	34	57		1	9	39	50	1/10
University of the Pacific	Stockton	SU	B,M,D	Pri	F,S	C		25	4		30		66	570	21	38	31	10	605	15	29	34	22	570	23	37	29	11	2/15
Vanguard University of Southern California	Costa Mesa	SU	A,B,M	Pri	No	C	2,041																						3/2
Westmont College	Santa Barbara	SU	B	Pri	No	C	1,340																						3/2
Whittier College	Whittier	SU	B,M,D	Pri	F,S	C	1,368	22	36	27	23	8	6	526	38	42	17	3	532	36	41	21	2		40	42	16	2	2/1
Woodbury University	Burbank	SU	B,M	Pri	F,S	C	1,310																						Open
Colorado																													
Adams State College	Alamosa	SM	A,B,M	Pub	No	C	2,742	20	62	21	10	5	2	480	53	37	10		500	49	42	9		460	64	30	6		8/1
Colorado Christian University	Lakewood	SU	A,B,M	Pri	No	C	1,475																						8/1
Colorado College	Colorado Springs	U	B,M	Pri	F,S	C	2,040	30	1	2	16	17	64	660	2	20	48	31	660	2	15	50	33	660	2	16	55	28	1/15
Colorado Mesa University	Grand Junction	SM	A,B,M,D	Pub	No	C	9,414	20	52	25	15	5	3	480	60	29	9	2	490	53	34	11	2						Open
Colorado School of Mines	Golden	SM	B,M,D	Pub	F,S	C	3,320																						Open
Colorado State University-Fort Collins	Fort Collins	SU	B,M,D	Pub	F,S	C	22,565	25	11	28	30	14	16	560	20	46	30	5	580	17	43	35	5						2/1
Colorado State University-Pueblo	Pueblo	U	B,M	Pub	F,S	C	5,500																						2/1
Colorado Technical University	Colorado Springs	SU	A,B,M,D	Pri	No	C	1,200																						Open
Fort Lewis College	Durango	SM	B,M	Pub	No	C	4,028	22	37	30	21	8	5		38	44	14	3		33	48	17	1		43	39	16		8/1
Johnson and Wales University/Denver Campus	Denver	SU	A,B	Pri	S	C	1,672																						Open
Metropolitan State University of Denver	Denver	U	B	Pub	No	C	21,975																						Open
Naropa University	Boulder	U	B,M	Pri	No	C	383																						1/15
Regis University	Denver	SU	B,M,D	Pri	No	C	1,520	23	23	27	26	12	12		32	42	22	4		31	40	25	4						Open
Rocky Mountain College of Art and Design	Denver	SU	B,M	Pri	No	C	670																						Open
United States Air Force Academy	Colorado Springs	SU	B	Pub	No	C	4,470																						Open

University of Colorado at Colorado Springs	Colorado Springs	SM	B,M,D	Pub	F,S	C	6,750																						Open
University of Colorado Boulder	Boulder	SU	B,M,D	Pub	F,S	C	25,461	27	4	16	29	19	32	570	16	44	32	9	600	11	38	39	12						1/15
University of Colorado Denver	Denver	U	B,M,D	Pub	No	C	13,103	23						540	26	47	21	6	540	30	40	23	7						7/22
University of Denver	Denver	U	B,M,D	Pri	F,S	C	5,517	28	2	10	26	20	42	610	12	34	42	12	610	5	36	48	11	580	15	44	35	6	1/15
University of Northern Colorado	Greeley	SU	B,M,D	Pub	F,S	C	10,231	23	47	57	18	15	3	531	33	46	18	3	533	34	43	20	3	516	43	36	21		8/1
Western State Colorado University	Gunnison	R	B,M	Pub	No	C	2,185	22	43	28	17	8	4	509	47	42	11		516	52	39	9							6/1

Connecticut

Albertus Magnus College	New Haven	SU	A,B,M	Pri	No	C	1,605							456	43	41	14	2	448	53	30	15	1	472	48	36	15	1	Open
Central Connecticut State University	New Britain	SU	B,M,D	Pub	F,S	C	9,771							500	50	41	9	1	508	46	43	11	1	504	47	42	11	1	Open
Charter Oak State College	New Britain	SU	A,B	Pub	No	C	1,581																						Open
Connecticut College	New London	SM	B,M	Pri	No	C	1,926	29						670	1	14	49	36	650	1	14	59	26	690	1	6	49	44	1/1
Eastern Connecticut State University	Willimantic	SM	A,B,M	Pub	No	C	5,179	22	32	41	20	6	1	510	44	45	9	2	510	42	45	12	1	520	39	46	13	1	5/1
Fairfield University	Fairfield	SU	B,M,D	Pri	No	C	3,873	26	2	15	39	21	24	570	9	53	34	4	590	6	48	41	5	590	6	45	43	7	1/15
Goodwin College	East Hartford	SU	A,B	Pri	No	C	3,388																						Open
Mitchell College	New London	SU	A,B	Pri	No	C	858																						Open
Post University	Waterbury	U	A,B		No	C	1,275																						Open
Quinnipiac University	Hamden	SU	B,M,D	Pri	F,S	C	6,542	25	10	18	34	28	10	540	22	58	18	2	560	19	51	27	3	550	20	57	20	3	2/1
Sacred Heart University	Fairfield	SU	A,B,M,D	Pri	F,S	C	4,489		6	44	34	12	4	536	21	64	14	1	559	13	60	25	2					3	2/1
Saint Joseph College	West Hartford	SU	B,M,D	Pri	No	PW	1,060							500	46	44	10		500	49	39	12							Open
Southern Connecticut State University	New Haven	U	B,M	Pub	F,S	C	8,525	20	56	24	16	3	1	470	62	30	7	1	470	64	30	6		480	58	34	8		4/1
Trinity College	Hartford	U	B,M		F	C	2,308	28	1	11	24	34	30	610	2	22	49	27	650	3	32	48	17	630	4	25	54	16	1/1
United States Coast Guard Academy	New London	SU	B	Pub	No	C																						16	1/1
University of Bridgeport	Bridgeport	SM	A,B,M,D	Pri	F,S	C	2,503	20						468	67	27	6		472	70	23	6	1	457	74	23	3		4/1
University of Connecticut	Storrs	R	A,B,M,D	Pub	F,S	C	18,032	27						602	7	41	41	11	631	4	26	51	19		7	37	45	11	4/1
University of Hartford	West Hartford	SU	A,B,M,D	Pri	F,S	C	5,284	22	38	28	20	6	8	521	46	39	14	1	530	44	37	17	2						Open
University of New Haven	West Haven	SU	A,B,M,D	Pri	F,S	C	4,864	22	31	31	24	10	4	510	40	47	12	1	520	37	43	19	1	510	43	45	11	1	Open
Wesleyan University	Middletown	SU	B,M,D	Pri	F,S	C	2,906	32		1	3	7	88	710		7	33	60	700		6	39	55	720		6	33	61	1/1
Western Connecticut State University	Danbury	SU	A,B,M,D	Pub	F,S	C	5,583							490	52	38	9	1	480	54	36	9	1	490	52	38	9	1	5/1
Yale University	New Haven	U	B,M,D	Pri	F,S	C	5,405	33						750		2	22	76	750		2	7	81	760		2	16	81	12/31

Delaware

Delaware State University	Dover	SU	B,M	Pub	F,S	C	3,050																					81	12/31
Goldey-Beacom College	Wilmington	SU	A,B,M	Pri	No	C	625																						Open
University of Delaware	Newark	SM	A,B,M,D		F,S	C	17,427		1	21	62	16		599	8	42	38	12	610	7	34	46	13	595	9	41	41	9	1/15
Wesley College	Dover	SM	A,B,M		F,S	C	1,603							410	83	13	3	1	420	81	18	1		410	87	11	2		Open
Wilmington University	New Castle	U	A,B,M,D	Pri	No	C	8,115																						Open

District of Columbia

American University	Washington	SU	A,B,M,D	Pri	F,S	C	7,341	28	1	7	22	24	46	640	3	23	50	24	620	4	33	51	12	630	3	27	52	18	1/15
Corcoran College of Art and Design	Washington	U	A,B,M	Pri	No	C	420																						Open
Gallaudet University	Washington	U	B,M,D	Pri	F,S	C	1,077	17	76	19	8	4	3	395	88	8	4		410	75	25								Open
George Washington University	Washington	U	A,B,M,D	Pri	F,S	C	10,443																						Open
Georgetown University	Washington	U	B,M,D	Pri	No	C	7,552								1	9	33	57		1	8	36	56						1/10
Howard University	Washington	U	B,M,D	Pri	F,S	C	6,688	23	21	33	25	12	10	540	26	51	21	2	530	30	47	21	2	530	34	48	16	2	2/1
The Catholic University of America	Washington	U	B,M,D	Pri	F,S	C	3,799																						2/15
Trinity Washington University	Washington	U	A,B,M	Pri	No	W	1,391																						Open
University of the District of Columbia	Washington	SU	A,B,M	Pub	F,S	C	5,110																						Open

Florida

Adventist Universtiy cf Health Sciences	Orlando	U	A,B,M	Pri	No	C	2,576	19	71	21	4	2	2	455	72	23	5		440	73	24	3							7/1
Barry University	Miami Shores	SU	B,M,D	Pri	F,S	C	5,150																						Open
Beacon College	Leesburg	SM	A,B	Pri	F,S	C	140																						Open
Bethune-Cookman University	Daytona Beach	SM	B,M	Pri	F,S	C	3,527		93	5	1	1			91	8	1			91	8	1			91	8	1		7/30
Carlos Albizu University	Miami	SM	B,M,D	Pri	No	C	431																						Open
Clearwater Christian College	Clearwater	R	A,B,M	Pri	F,S	C	590																						Open
Eckerd College	St. Petersburg	SU	B	Pri	No	C	1,893	25	14	24	29	16	18	565	20	45	27	8	550	25	41	30	4						4/1
Edward Waters College	Jacksonville	U	B	Pri	F,S	C	1,400																						4/1
Embry-Riddle Aeronautical University - Daytona Beach	Daytona Beach	U	A,B,M,D	Pri	F,S	C	4,679	24	19	24	24	14	19	530	33	43	21	3	580	19	40	31	10	510	41	40	17	13	7/1
Embry-Riddle Aeronautical University - Worldwide	Daytona Beach	SU	A,B,M,D	Pri	No	C	10,412																						Open
Flagler College	St. Augustine	SM	B	Pri	No	C	2,878							562	10	69	18	1	554	11	76	11	1	549	14	71	11	1	3/1

NAME OF SCHOOL	TOWN	ENVIRONMENT (U-Urban R-Rural SU-Suburban SM-Small Town)	DEGREES AWARDED (A-Associate B-Bachelor M-Master D-Doctorate)	CONTROL (Pri-Private, Pub-Public)	FRATERNITIES AND SORORITIES (F-Fraternities S-Sororities F, S-Both No-Neither)	STUDENTS: C-Coed M-Men W-Women PM-Primarily Men PW-Primarily Women	UNDERGRADUATE ENROLLMENT FALL 2013	TEST SCORES: ACT Median	ACT Below 21	ACT 21-23	ACT 24-26	ACT 27-28	ACT Above 28	SAT CRITICAL READING Median	SAT CR Below 500	SAT CR 500-599	SAT CR 600-700	SAT CR Above 700	SAT MATHEMATICS Median	SAT M Below 500	SAT M 500-599	SAT M 600-700	SAT M Above 700	SAT WRITING Median	SAT W Below 500	SAT W 500-599	SAT W 600-700	SAT W Above 700	APPLICATION DEADLINE Month / Day
Florida Agricultural and Mechanical University	Tallahassee	U	A,B,M,D	Pub	F,S	C	10,053	20	55	29	10	4	2	470	64	27	7	1	470	66	27	6	1	460	72	24	3		5/15
Florida Atlantic University	Boca Raton	SU	A,B,M,D	Pub	F,S	C	24,823	23	13	47	25	8	6	534	30	53	15	2	539	26	53	19	2	527	32	54	13	1	5/1
Florida Gulf Coast University	Fort Myers	SU	A,B,M,D	Pub	F,S	C	12,861		5	70		23	2		43	46	10	1		41	46	12	1		52	40	7	1	5/1
Florida Institute of Technology	Melbourne	SU	B,M,D	Pri	F,S	C	2,978	25	12	23	25	17	23	550	24	44	25	7	590	12	40	36	12						Open
Florida International University	Miami	U	B,M,D	Pub	F,S	C	37,468	25	1	24	46	16	13	571	6	63	28	3	569	9	58	31	2	563	10	64	24	2	Open
Florida Memorial University	Miami	U	B		No	C																							Open
Florida Southern College	Lakeland	SU	B,M	Pri	F,S	C	2,192	25	5	30	35	14	16	540	23	54	19	4	540	18	57	23	2	530	33	47	19	3	5/1
Florida State University	Tallahassee	SU	A,B,M,D	Pub	F,S	C		27		6			94	600	2	48	42	8	595	3	46	43	6	600	3	49	43	5	1/25
Hodges University	Naples	SU	A,B,M	Pri	No	C	1,515																						Open
Jacksonville University	Jacksonville	SU	B,M	Pri	F,S	C	3,040																						Open
Johnson and Wales University/North Miami Campus	North Miami	SM	A,B	Pri	F,S	C	2,153																						Open
Lynn University	Boca Raton	SU	B,M,D	Pri	F,S	C	1,657	20	65	18	9	6	2	450	74	20	5	1	460	66	27	7		450	75	18	6	1	Open
New College of Florida	Sarasota	SU	B	Pub	No	C	801	29		4	14	24	58	680	1	8	48	43	620	2	28	54	17	640	1	21	57	21	Open
Northwood University	West Palm Beach	SU	A,B,M	Pri	No	C	497								67	28	4	1		42	42	12	4		80	15	4	1	Open
Nova Southeastern University	Fort Lauderdale	SU	A,B,M,D	Pri	F,S	C	5,156	23	23	27	18	18	13	520	37	39	20	4	530	31	43	22	5						Open
Palm Beach Atlantic University	West Palm Beach	U	A,B,M,D	Pri	No	C	2,887	24	12	30	26	16	16	550	20	52	21	7	550	21	46	32	1	550	25	48	24	3	Open
Ringling College of Art and Design	Sarasota	U	B	Pri	No	C	1,263																					3	Open
Rollins College	Winter Park	SU	B,M	Pri	F,S	C	1,884								5	46	41	9		7	39	43	9		9	46	35	9	2/15
Saint Leo University	Saint Leo	R	A,B,M	Pri	F,S	C	2,167	21	34	42	15	5	4	510	39	49	11	1	510	37	52	10	1	480	61	31	7	1	8/15
Southeastern University	Lakeland	SU	A,B,M,D	Pri	No	C	2,448	21	50	22	18	6	4	509	45	39	15	2	487	53	35	12	1	494	52	35	12	2	8/15
St. Thomas University	Miami	SU	B,M	Pri	No	C	1,145	17	83	13	4			440	78	20	2		440	80	18	2		430	79	19	2		Open
Stetson University	DeLand	SM	B,M	Pri	F,S	C	2,729	26	17	24	27	17	19	584	13	45	36	7	577	12	46	38	4	562	19	48	31	2	Open
University of Central Florida	Orlando	SU	A,B,M,D	Pub	F,S	C	51,269	26	2	26	36	18	18	585	9	50	33	8	595	7	45	40	8	560	18	52	26	4	5/1
University of Florida	Gainesville	SU	A,B,M,D	Pub	F,S	C	33,168	28	3	6	16	23	51	625	4	29	48	18	638	3	22	52	22	624	6	27	49	18	11/1
University of Miami	Coral Gables	SU	B,M,D	Pri	F,S	C	11,380	30					74	640	4	21	49	26	680	2	12	48	38	640	3	23	50	24	1/1
University of North Florida	Jacksonville	U	A,B,M,D	Pub	F,S	C	14,263	26		10	56	16	18	611	1	40	52	7	604	1	43	52	4		11	53	33	3	5/10
University of South Florida	Tampa	U	A,B,M,D	Pub	F,S	C	34,985																					3	5/10
University of South Florida/St. Petersburg	St. Petersburg	U	B,M	Pub	No	C	4,006	23						530					530					510					3/15
University of Tampa	Tampa	U	A,B,M	Pri	F,S	C	6,499	24	15	36	30	13	6	525	32	54	13	1	540	24	55	19	1	520	37	49	13	2	Open
University of West Florida	Pensacola	SU	A,B,M,D	Pub	F,S	C	10,332		8	56	32	2	2		44	44	10	1		49	41	9	1		60	34	5	1	6/30
Warner University	Lake Wales	R	A,B,M	Pri	No	C	1,090																						Open
Webber International University	Babson Park	SM	A,B,M	Pri	No	C	655		70	20		1			68	29	3			63	32	4	1						8/1
Georgia																													
Agnes Scott College	Decatur	U	B	Pri	No	W	913	26	16	19	26	16	23	590	17	38	33	12	570	19	40	27	14	570	16	40	36	8	3/1
Albany State University	Albany	U	A,B,M	Pub	F,S	C	3,025																						6/1
American InterContinental University	Atlanta	U	A,B		No	C	1,010																						Open
Armstrong Atlantic State University	Savannah	SU	A,B,M,D	Pub	F,S	C	6,377	21	49	32	13	5	2	500	45	44	9	1	490	53	39	9		480	57	36	7		7/15
Art Institute of Atlanta	Atlanta	SU	A,B	Pri	No	C	2,720																						Open
Berry College	Mount Berry	SU	B,M	Pri	No	C	2,141	26	1	22	30	18	28	590	8	46	38	8	580	7	52	36	4	550	18	51	27	4	2/1
Brenau University Women's College	Gainesville	SU	B,M	Pri	S	W	867		42	32	16	7	2		39	46	14	1		59	31	10							Open
Brewton-Parker College	Mt. Vernon	R	A,B	Pri	No	C	629			87		11	2		65	29	5	1		65	29	6			65	29	6		Open
Clark Atlanta University	Atlanta	U	B,M,D		F,S	C	2,629	18	74	16	8	2		430	83	17			420	82	17	1							Open
Clayton State University	Morrow	SU	A,B	Pub	F,S	C	5,230																						Open
Columbus State University	Columbus	SU	A,B,M,D	Pub	F,S	C	7,069	21	59	25	12	3	1	508	48	38	13	1	496	54	36	9	1	490	57	34	8	1	6/30
Covenant College	Lookout Mountain	SU	A,B,M	Pri	No	C		26	2	29			69	595	10	40	37	13	575	12	50	29	9	590	14	41	34	11	5/1
Emory University	Atlanta	SU	A,B,M,D		F,S	C	5,675																					11	5/1
Fort Valley State University	Fort Valley	R	A,B,M		F,S	C	3,421																					11	5/1
Georgia College and State University	Milledgeville	SM	B,M,D	Pub	F,S	C	5,729	24	9	29	42	14	6	573	11	55	30	4	570	13	51	33	3	557	18	53	26	2	4/1
Georgia Institute of Technology	Atlanta	U	B,M,D	Pub	F,S	C	14,558	31	1	1	7	11	80	660	1	12	52	34	710		3	36	61	670	1	11	54	34	1/10
Georgia Regents University	Augusta	U	A,B,M,D	Pub	F,S	C																						34	1/10
Georgia Southern University	Statesboro	SM	B,M,D	Pub	F,S	C	17,904	23	6	55	25	8	6	550	14	63	21	2	550	12	64	22	1	520	33	53	13	1	5/1
Georgia Southwestern State University	Americus	SM	A,B,M	Pub	F,S	C	2,105																					1	5/1
Georgia State University	Atlanta	U	B,M,D	Pub	F,S	C	18,975																					1	5/1

Kennesaw State University	Kennesaw	SU	B,M,D	Pub	F,S	C	22,621	22	22	52	21	4	1	540	18	60	20	2	530	26	56	17	1	510	39	47	13	1	5/8
LaGrange College	LaGrange	SM	B,M	Pri	F,S	C	856	21	44	34	15	5	3	490	50	39	11		500	52	40	7	1						Open
Mercer University	Macon	SU	B,M,D	Pri	F,S	C	2,538	26						580	9	47	35	9	590	7	48	37	8	560	19	46	29	6	4/1
Morehouse College	Atlanta	U	B	Pri	F		2,183	21	46	29	15	6	4	500	45	42	11	2	505	49	36	14	1	490	57	33	9	1	2/15
North Georgia College & State University	Dahlonega	SM	A,B,M	Pub	F,S	C	4,005																					1	2/15
Oglethorpe University	Atlanta	SU	B,M	Pri	F,S	C	1,073	24	11	30	29	14	16	570	12	50	28	10	550	19	48	30	3	550	26	44	24	6	2/15
Paine College	Augusta	U	B	Pri	F,S	C	837		91	8					90	8	2			93	5				93	5	2		7/1
Piedmont College	Demorest	SM	B,M,D	Pri	No	C	1,281	21	43	30	18	6	3	504	53	34	11	2	497	50	40	9	1						Open
Reinhardt College	Waleska	SM	A,B		No	C	1,120																						Open
Savannah College of Art and Design	Savannah	U	B,M	Pri	No	C	9,332	24	22	26	25	13	14	540	29	44	21	6	520	38	42	18	2	530	37	42	18	3	Open
Savannah State University	Savannah	SU	A,B,M	Pub	F,S	C	4,413																						7/15
Shorter University	Rome	SM	A,B,M	Pri	F,S	C	1,642	20	51	23	15	8	4	475	56	32	11	1	490	52	34	13	1	460	65	26	9		Open
South University	Savannah	U	A,B,M,D	Pri	No	C																							Open
Southern Polytechnic State University	Marietta	SU	A,B,M	Pub	F,S	C	5,402	24	17	29	29	12	13	550	20	52	24	4	590	9	45	39	7	520	39	46	14	1	7/1
Spelman College	Atlanta	U	B		S	W	2,318	23																					2/1
Thomas University	Thomasville	R	A,B,M		No	C	700																						Open
Toccoa Falls College	Toccoa Falls	SM	A,B	Pri	No	C	874	19	69	18	9	3	1	505	44	36	20		500	49	41	9	1						8/1
University of Georgia	Athens	SM	B,M,D		F,S	C	26,278																						1/15
University of West Georgia	Carrollton	R	B,M,D	Pub	F,S	C	9,959	20	62	25	9	3	1	485	71	25	4		476	75	21	4		470	75	22	3		6/1
Valdosta State University	Valdosta	SU	A,B	Pub	F,S	C	10,368	21						503	51	40	8		492	58	35	7		482	59	35	6		7/1
Wesleyan College	Macon	SU	B,M	Pri	No	W	592	22	36	27	25	7	7																2/1

Hawaii

Brigham Young University/Hawaii	Laie	R	B	Pri	No	C	2,397	23	26	22	24	16	12																2/15
Chaminade University of Honolulu	Honolulu	U	A,B,M	Pri	No	C	1,326	21	48	34	16	3		470	61	35	4	1	490	54	40	6	1						Open
Hawaii Pacific University	Honolulu	U	A,B,M	Pri	No	C	6,168	21	47	30	14	5	5	480	57	35	8	1	490	52	38	9	1	470	63	32	5		Open
University of Hawaii at Hilo	Hilo	SM	B,M	Pub	No	C	2,850																						Open
University of Hawaii at Manoa	Honolulu	SM	B,M,D	Pub	F,S	C	14,402	23	25	32	26	10	7	530	34	46	18	2	560	24	47	25	4	520	36	49	14	1	5/1

Idaho

Boise State University	Boise	U	A,B,M,D	Pub	F,S	C	19,653	19	24	28	24	12	12		36	44	17	3		33	42	23	2		44	36	13	2	5/15
Idaho State University	Pocatello	U	A,B,M,D	Pub	F,S	C	12,143	22	44	25	18	7	7	528	42	32	21	6	530	36	40	21	3	515	40	43	14	3	8/1
Lewis-Clark State College	Lewiston	U	A,B	Pub	No	C	3,495																						Open
Northwest Nazarene University	Nampa	SM	B,M	Pri	No	C	1,477	22	36	26	22	9	7	510	36	38	21	5	540	32	46	20	2	510	45	35	18	2	8/15
The College of Idaho	Caldwell	SM	B,M	Pri	F,S	C	1,042	24	20	23	27	14	16	545	33	30	23	13	540	33	38	27	3	525	39	35	24	2	7/15
University of Idaho	Moscow	SM	B,M,D	Pub	F,S	C	9,456	22	31	27	20	11	12	520	40	39	17	4	520	39	36	21	4	500	46	39	13	2	8/1

Illinois

Augustana College	Rock Island	SU	B	Pri	F,S	C	2,541	26	8	23	28	18	23																Open
Aurora University	Aurora	SU	B,M,D	Pri	F,S	C	2,391	22	32	37	20	7	4	470	69	22	9		470	69	22	9							6/20
Benedictine University	Lisle	SU	A,B,M,D	Pri	No	C	2,960	23	26	27	25	11	10																Open
Blackburn College	Carlinville	R	B	Pri	No	C	549	21	48	30	12	7	3																7/31
Bradley University	Peoria	U	B,M,D	Pri	F,S	C	5,061	25	12	23	30	17	17	540	27	44	23	6	570	20	38	34	8						Open
Chicago State University	Chicago	U	B,M,D	Pub	F,S	C	4,618		81	13	6	1																	7/15
Columbia College Chicago	Chicago	U	B,M		No	C	11,858																						7/15
Concordia University, River Forest	River Forest	SU	B,M,D	Pri	No	C	1,032		36	23	20	9	12																Open
DePaul University	Chicago	U	B,M,D	Pri	F,S	C	16,420	25	8	23	32	17	21	581	12	48	33	7	569	14	49	33	5						2/1
Dominican University	River Forest	SU	B,M,D	Pri	No	C	2,069	22	37	34	20	4	5	520	38	56	6		548	38	31	25	6	527	31	50	19		Open
Eastern Illinois University	Charleston	SM	B,M	Pub	F,S	C	8,347	22	40	34	16	6	4																Open
East-West University	Chicago	U	A,B		No	C	1,020																						Open
Elmhurst College	Elmhurst	SU	B,M	Pri	F,S	C	2,900	24	21	29	25	12	13	490	59	27	15		510	44	39	15	2	490	51	37	12		Open
Eureka College	Eureka	SM	B	Pri	F,S	C	550	23																					8/1
Greenville College	Greenville	SM	B,M	Pri	No	C	1,382	23	32	20	21	13	14	480	56	26	17	1	490	51	36	13		470	60	21	19		8/1
Illinois College	Jacksonville	SM	B	Pri	No	C	970																						Open
Illinois Institute of Technology	Chicago	U	B,M,D	Pri	F,S	C	2,801	28	2	10	24	24	40	600	14	31	44	11	660	1	17	54	28	590	15	40	37	8	Open
Illinois State University	Normal	U	B,M,D	Pub	F,S	C	17,749	24	11	35	36	11	8																3/1
Illinois Wesleyan University	Bloomington	SU	B	Pri	F,S	C	2,009	27						571	4	35	36	25	648	5	25	44	25						3/1
Judson University	Elgin	SU	B,M	Pri	No	C	1,195																						Open
Kendall College	Chicago	U	A,B	Pri	No	C	2,545																						Open
Knox College	Galesburg	SM	B	Pri	F,S	C	1,424		4	13	20	22	41		13	21	42	24		11	32	41	16		15	30	47	8	2/1
Lake Forest College	Lake Forest	SU	B,M	Pri	F,S	C	1,552																						2/15
Lewis University	Romeoville	SU	A,B,M	Pri	F,S	C	3,230																						Open

NAME OF SCHOOL	TOWN	ENVIRONMENT U-Urban R-Rural SU-Suburban SM-Small Town	DEGREES AWARDED A-Associate B-Bachelor M-Master D-Doctorate	CONTROL Pri-Private, Pub-Public	FRATERNITIES AND SORORITIES F-Fraternities S-Sororities F, S-Both No-Neither	STUDENTS: C-Coed M-Men W-Women PM-Primarily Men PW-Primarily Women	UNDERGRADUATE ENROLLMENT FALL 2013	TEST SCORES: ACT Median	ACT Below 21	ACT 21-23	ACT 24-26	ACT 27-28	ACT Above 28	SAT CRITICAL READING Median	SAT CR Below 500	SAT CR 500-599	SAT CR 600-700	SAT CR Above 700	SAT MATHEMATICS Median	SAT Math Below 500	SAT Math 500-599	SAT Math 600-700	SAT Math Above 700	SAT WRITING Median	SAT Writing Below 500	SAT Writing 500-599	SAT Writing 600-700	SAT Writing Above 700	APPLICATION DEADLINE Month / Day
Loyola University Chicago	Chicago	U	B,M,D	Pri	F,S	C	10,168	27	2	15	31	22	31	590	10	43	39	8	580	9	47	37	7	580	9	46	36	9	4/1
MacMurray College	Jacksonville	SM	A,B		F,S	C	701	21	50	28	15	4	3																Open
McKendree University	Lebanon	SU	B,M	Pri	F,S	C	2,194	24	27	34	27	4	7																Open
Millikin University	Decatur	SU	B,M,D	Pri	F,S	C	2,154	23	22	29	26	12	10	542	29	52	15	4	513	48	33	19		510	43	38	19		Open
Monmouth College	Monmouth	SM	B	Pri	F,S	C	1,248	23	30	35	21	8	6																Open
National Louis University	Chicago	SU	B,M,D	Pri	No	PW	2,084																						Open
North Central College	Naperville	SU	B,M	Pri	No	C	2,755	24	11	30	31	15	13																Open
North Park University	Chicago	U	B,M,D	Pri	No	C	2,224	22	41	25	16	9	9	530	33	49	17	1	500	40	43	14	3						4/1
Northeastern Illinois University	Chicago	U	B,M	Pub	F,S	C	9,140	19	69	20	9	2	1																7/1
Northern Illinois University	DeKalb	SM	B,M,D	Pub	F,S	C	18,277	22	37	30	21	7	5																8/1
Northwestern University	Evanston	SU	B,M,D	Pri	F,S	C	8,010																						8/1
Olivet Nazarene University	Bourbonnais	SU	A,B,M,D	Pri	No	C	3,187	23	27	25	22	12	15																5/1
Principia College	Elsah	R	B	Pri	No	C	491	24	12	45	15	16	12	549	31	37	21	11	525	40	35	18	7	537	39	36	15	10	5/1
Quincy University	Quincy	SM	A,B,M	Pri	F,S	C	1,241	21	44	30	15	8	3	450	79	21			460	53	32	10	5						Open
Rockford College	Rockford	SU	B,M	Pri	No	C	869	22	43	26	24	3																	Open
Roosevelt University	Chicago	U	B,M,D		F,S	C	4,300																						Open
Saint Xavier University	Chicago	U	B,M		No	C	3,070																						Open
School of the Art Institute of Chicago	Chicago	U	B,M		No	C	2,010																						Open
Shimer College	Chicago	U	B	Pri	No	C	127				50	50					66	33		33	66					33	66		Open
Southern Illinois University Carbondale	Carbondale	R	A,B,M,D	Pub	F,S	C	13,351	22	14	50	30		6	520	39	35	21	4	545	33	35	26	5						5/1
Southern Illinois University Edwardsville	Edwardsville	SU	B,M	Pub	F,S	C	11,341	23	31	30	22	9	8																5/1
Trinity Christian College	Palos Heights	SU	B	Pri	No	C	1,450	23	35	22	14	13	16	543	32	52	11	5	552	37	47	16							8/15
Trinity College of Nursing & Health Sciences	Rock Island	U	A,B	Pri	No	C																							8/15
Trinity International University	Deerfield	SU	B,M,D	Pri	No	C	1,265																						Open
University of Chicago	Chicago	U	B,M,D	Pri	F,S	C	5,590	33						744			16	84	742		1	18	81			1	21	78	1/2
University of Illinois at Chicago	Chicago	U	B,M,D	Pub	F,S	C	16,660	24	14	30	30	13	14	545	40	34	20	6	584	14	45	28	13	556				78	1/2
University of Illinois at Urbana-Champaign	Urbana	SM	B,M,D		F,S	C	30,900																					78	1/2
University of St. Francis	Joliet	SU	B,M,D	Pri	No	C	1,422	23	23	33	30	9	5		22	56	22			45	33	22			45	33	22		8/1
VanderCook College of Music	Chicago	U	B,M		F,S	C	90																						8/1
Western Illinois University	Macomb	R	B,M,D	Pub	F,S	C	9,873	23	50	27	12	5	5																5/15
Wheaton College	Wheaton	SU	B,M,D	Pri	No	C	2,444	30						660	2	22	44	32	650	2	24	47	27	660	2	18	53	27	1/10

Indiana

NAME OF SCHOOL	TOWN	ENVIRONMENT	DEGREES AWARDED	CONTROL	FRATERNITIES AND SORORITIES	STUDENTS	UNDERGRADUATE ENROLLMENT FALL 2013	ACT Median	ACT Below 21	ACT 21-23	ACT 24-26	ACT 27-28	ACT Above 28	SAT CR Median	SAT CR Below 500	SAT CR 500-599	SAT CR 600-700	SAT CR Above 700	SAT Math Median	SAT Math Below 500	SAT Math 500-599	SAT Math 600-700	SAT Math Above 700	SAT Writing Median	SAT Writing Below 500	SAT Writing 500-599	SAT Writing 600-700	SAT Writing Above 700	APPLICATION DEADLINE
Anderson University	Anderson	SU	A,B,M,D	Pri	No	C	2,016	23	23	32	27	9	9	515	43	43	13	1	527	34	46	17	3						Open
Ball State University	Muncie	SU	A,B,M,D	Pub	F,S	C	16,652	22						530	34	47	17	2	530	33	47	19	1	510	41	46	12	1	5/1
Bethel College	Mishawaka	SU	A,B,M	Pri	No	C	1,801	23	31	20	25	10	14	510	41	39	18	2	510	40	36	22	2	490	52	35	12	1	Open
Butler University	Indianapolis	SU	A,B,M	Pri	F,S	C	4,126	27	2	11	28	21	38	580	14	44	37	5	590	12	40	42	7	570	16	45	33	6	Open
Calumet College of St. Joseph	Whiting	SM	A,B,M		No	C	1,200																						Open
DePauw University	Greencastle	SM	B	Pri	F,S	C	2,336	27						580	14	40	35	10	600	8	36	41	14	580	13	42	37	7	3/1
Earlham College	Richmond	SM	B,M	Pri	No	C	1,064	28						640	17	33	32	18	600	15	29	42	14		16	37	36	11	2/15
Franklin College	Franklin	SM	B	Pri	F,S	C	1,014	22	12	33	16			500	46	42	11		510	41	43	15		480	55	36			Open
Goshen College	Goshen	SM	B,M	Pri	No	C	879																						Open
Grace College and Theological Seminary	Winona Lake	SM	A,B,M	Pri	No	C	870																						Open
Hanover College	Hanover	R	B	Pri	F,S	C	1,163	25	7	27	29	13	24	540	26	49	22	3	550	21	50	27	2	520	31	53	13	3	Open
Huntington University	Huntington	SM	A,B,M,D	Pri	No	C	1,053	24	7	42	44	30	8	509	43	42	12	3	503	49	36	12	3	486	56	33	10	1	Open
Indiana Institute of Technology	Fort Wayne	U	A,B,M,D	Pri	F,S	C	5,697	20	53	27	16	2	2	447	69	27	4		468	59	32	8	1	430	81	18	1		Open
Indiana State University	Terre Haute	U	A,B,M,D	Pub	F,S	C	8,565																						Open
Indiana University Bloomington	Bloomington	SM	B,M,D	Pub	F,S	C	36,862	27						575	18	44	30	8	600	10	39	37	15	565	19	45	29	7	2/1
Indiana University East	Richmond	SM	A,B,M	Pub	F,S	C	4,326	21						465	67	28	5		460	68	24	7		445	78	19	4		Open
Indiana University Kokomo	Kokomo	SM	A,B,M	Pub	F,S	C	3,981	20						475	64	30	6	1	470	59	32	8	1	460	69	26	5		Open
Indiana University Northwest	Gary	U	A,B,M	Pub	F,S	C	5,904	20						450	70	25	4	1	450	70	223	6		445	74	20	4		7/1
Indiana University South Bend	South Bend	SU	A,B,M	Pub	F,S	C	7,512	21						480	61	32	6	1	480	62	31	7	1	450	72	24	4		Open
Indiana University Southeast	New Albany	SU	A,B,M	Pub	F,S	C	6,148	20						475	61	31	8	1	475	61	33	6		460	67	28	4		8/17
Indiana University-Purdue University Fort Wayne	Fort Wayne	SU	A,B,M	Pub	F	C	12,928	22	41	28	14	7	9	495	54	36	9	1	505	50	35	13	2	478	64	28	7	1	8/1

Indiana University-Purdue University Indianapolis	Indianapolis	U	A,B,M,D	Pub	F,S	C	22,409	22						495	51	36	12	1	510	45	38	15	2	485	57	33	9	1	Open
Indiana Wesleyan University	Marion	SM	A,B,M,D	Pri	No	C		24	5	38	47		10	525	33	45	19	3	535	32	44	22	2	515	43	40	15	2	Open
Manchester College	North Manchester	SM	A,B	Pri	No	C	1,217																						Open
Marian University/Indianapolis	Indianapolis	SU	A,B,M,D	Pri	No	C	2,260	22	36	28	21	8	7	490	50	38	10	2	490	53	32	13	2	470	64	28	7		8/1
Martin University	Indianapolis	U	B,M	Pri	No	C	615																						Open
Oakland City University	Oakland City	SM	A,B,M	Pri	No	C	2,100																						Open
Purdue University/Calumet	Hammond	U	A,B,M	Pub	F,S	C	8,405																						Open
Purdue University/West Lafayette	West Lafayette	SU	A,B,M,D	Pub	F,S	C	29,440	27	4	14	24	19	39	574	17	46	29	8	626	8	30	38	24	573	18	43	32	7	3/1
Rose-Hulman Institute of Technology	Terre Haute	SU	B,M	Pri	F,S	C	2,205	30		6	16	15	62	630	4	34	46	17	680		10	58	32	600	12	38	42	8	3/1
Saint Joseph's College	Rensselaer	SM	A,B,M	Pri	No	C	1,148	22	40	32	19	4	5	492	55	32	11	2	501	48	42	10							Open
Saint Mary-of-the-Woods College	St Mary of the Woods	R	A,B,M	Pri	No	PW	748	20	60	20	5		15	460	66	30	2	2	440	68	32			450	75	16	7		Open
Saint Mary's College	Notre Dame	SU	B	Pri	No	W	1,479	25	12	21	29	18	20	560	23	46	26	6	540	28	46	22	5	550	23	49	21	6	2/15
Taylor University	Upland	R	A,B,M	Pri	No	C	2,246	26	11	15	22	15	38	590	20	33	32	15	580	20	37	37	8	560	25	36	32	7	12/1
Trine University	Angola	SM	A,B,M	Pri	F,S	C	1,943	24						510	42	43	15	2	570	22	43	32	4						8/1
University of Evansville	Evansville	U	A,B,M,D	Pri	F,S	C	2,477	26	12	18	26	17	27	550	25	47	23	5	570	24	39	33	4	540	31	41	24	4	2/3
University of Indianapolis	Indianapolis	SM	A,B,M,D	Pri	No	C	4,205								48	37	13	2		41	41	16	1						Open
University of Notre Dame	Notre Dame	SU	B,M,D	Pri	No	C	8,477	33				10	90	710	1	8	33	58	720		4	27	69	700	2	9	37	52	1/1
University of Saint Francis	Fort Wayne	SU	A,B,M	Pri	No	C	1,850																						Open
University of Southern Indiana	Evansville	SU	A,B,M,D	Pub	F,S	C	8,913	22	39	32	18	7	4	499	49	39	11	1	508	44	42	13	1	478	58	33	8	1	8/15
Valparaiso University	Valparaiso	SM	A,B,M,D	Pri	F,S	C	3,251	26	8	19	29	16	28	544	24	53	20	3	566	19	45	30	6	537	31	47	20	2	Open
Wabash College	Crawfordsville	SM	B	Pri	F		902	25	13	24	28	15	20	550	25	44	25	6	570	11	52	30	7	520	39	40	18	3	12/1

Iowa

Allen College	Waterloo	SU	A,B,M,D	Pri	No	PW	397																						2/1
Ashford University	Clinton	SM	A,B,M	Pri	No	C	9,866																						8/15
Briar Cliff University	Sioux City	SU	A,B,M	Pri	No	C	1,079	21	40	28	20	9	3																Open
Buena Vista University	Storm Lake	SM	B,M	Pri	No	C	920	23	35	29	21	7	8																Open
Central College	Pella	SM	B	Pri	F,S	C	1,604	24	18	34	25	11	12																3/1
Clarke University	Dubuque	SM	A,B,M,D	Pri	No	C	967	23	24	23	23	10	8	473	75	25			506	37	63								Open
Coe College	Cedar Rapids	U	B	Pri	F,S	C	1,420	25	17	18	29	16	20	597	21	30	27	24	583	27	27	33	12	560	42	16	26	16	Open
Cornell College	Mount Vernon	SM	B	Pri	F,S	C	1,122	26	5	17	29	17	32	610	13	33	35	19	570	19	37	34	10	580	18	42	33	7	3/1
Dordt College	Sioux Center	R	A,B,M		No	C	1,430	25	15	25	36	20	15		47	29	21	3		22	45	30	3		43	40	17		8/1
Drake University	Des Moines	U	B,M,D	Pri	F,S	C	3,581	27			16	57	26		14	42	31	13		10	36	36	19						8/1
Graceland University	Lamoni	SM	B,M	Pri	No	C	2,045																						8/1
Grand View University	Des Moines	U	B,M	Pri	No	C	2,094	21	48	27	18	3	5		96	4				80	20				96	4			Open
Grinnell College	Grinnell	SM	B	Pri	No	C	1,721								1	17	46	36		1	13	37	49						4/1
Iowa State University	Ames	U	B,M,D	Pub	F,S	C	21,985																						4/1
Iowa Wesleyan College	Mount Pleasant	SM	B		F,S	C	875																						Open
Kaplan University	Davenport	U	A,B	Pri	No	C	557																						Open
Loras College	Dubuque	SM	A,B,M		S	C	1,535																						Open
Luther College	Decorah	SM	B	Pri	F,S	C	2,466	26	8	21	28	17	26	525	37	31	26	6	550	22	40	26	12	530	34	45	16	5	Open
Maharishi University of Management	Fairfield	SM	B,M,D	Pri	No	C	220																						Open
Mercy College of Health Sciences	Des Moines	U	A,B	Pri	No	C	846																						6/15
Morningside College	Sioux City	SU	B,M	Pri	F,S	C	1,242	23	33	31	18	11	8																Open
Mount Mercy University	Cedar Rapids	U	B,M	Pri	No	C	1,476	21	36	45	14	2	3																Open
Northwestern College of Iowa	Orange City	SM	B	Pri	No	C	1,233	25	16	29	23	20	12	550	39	36	13	13	540	34	49	15	2	500	52	32	8	8	Open
Simpson College	Indianola	SM	B,M	Pri	F,S	C	1,817	24	20	33	22	14	11																Open
St. Ambrose University	Davenport	U	B,M,D	Pri	No	C	2,887	23	28	35	19	9	9																Open
University of Dubuque	Dubuque	SU	A,B,M,D	Pri	F,S	C	1,185																						Open
University of Iowa	Iowa City	SM	B,M,D	Pub	F,S	C	21,974	25	9	25	29	17	20	550	36	29	24	11	610	14	28	37	21						4/1
University of Northern Iowa	Cedar Falls	SM	B,M,D	Pub	F,S	C	10,380	23	28	33	24	7	8																8/15
Upper Iowa University	Fayette	R	A,B,M		F,S	C	720																						Open
Wartburg College	Waverly	SM	B	Pri	No	C	1,747																						Open
William Penn University	Oskaloosa	R	A,B,M	Pub	F,S	C	1,835																						Open

Kansas

Baker University	Baldwin City	R	B	Pri	F,S	C	942	24	24	26	31	9	11																Open
Benedictine College	Atchison	SM	A,B,M	Pri	No	C	1,993		22	29	19	15	15																Open
Bethany College	Lindsborg	SM	B	Pri	F,S	C	665		36	29	24	6	5		74	26				57	38	5							Open
Bethel College	North Newton	SU	B	Pri	No	C	946	23	4	56	30		10	455	73	14	10	3	500	48	38	7	7	445	72	21	7		Open
Emporia State University	Emporia	SM	B,M,D	Pub	F,S	C	3,873	22	35	31	19	9	8																Open
Fort Hays State University	Hays	SM	A,B,M	Pub	F,S	C	7,870																						Open
Friends University	Wichita	U	A,B,M	Pri	No	C	1,769								67	21	12			63	25	12							Open

NAME OF SCHOOL	TOWN	ENVIRONMENT (U-Urban R-Rural SU-Suburban SM-Small Town)	DEGREES AWARDED (A-Associate B-Bachelor M-Master D-Doctorate)	CONTROL (Pri-Private, Pub-Public)	FRATERNITIES AND SORORITIES (F-Fraternities S-Sororities F, S-Both No-Neither)	STUDENTS (C-Coed M-Men W-Women PM-Primarily Men PW-Primarily Women)	UNDERGRADUATE ENROLLMENT FALL 2013	TEST SCORES: ACT Median	ACT Below 21	ACT 21-23	ACT 24-26	ACT 27-28	ACT Above 28	SAT CRITICAL READING Median	SAT CR Below 500	SAT CR 500-599	SAT CR 600-700	SAT CR Above 700	SAT MATHEMATICS Median	SAT M Below 500	SAT M 500-599	SAT M 600-700	SAT M Above 700	SAT WRITING Median	SAT W Below 500	SAT W 500-599	SAT W 600-700	SAT W Above 700	APPLICATION DEADLINE Month / Day
Kansas State University	Manhattan	SU	A,B,M,D	Pub	F,S	C	20,169	24	17	27	26	12	18																Open
Kansas Wesleyan University	Salina	U	A,B,M	Pri	No	C	800																						Open
McPherson College	McPherson	SM	B,M	Pri	No	C	632																						Open
MidAmerica Nazarene University	Olathe	SU	A,B,M		No	C	1,320																						Open
Newman University	Wichita	U	A,B,M	Pri	No	C	2,795	24	15	32	24	13	16	509	38	46		8	548	31	38	31		487	46	46		8	Open
Ottawa University	Ottawa	SM	B		No	C	585																						Open
Pittsburg State University	Pittsburg	SM	A,B,M	Pub	F,S	C	6,166	22	40	32	16	6	6																Open
Southwestern College	Winfield	SM	B,M,D	Pri	F	C	522	22	31	29	27	9	4	455	69	25	3	3	486	61	29	7	3	433	75	22	3		8/1
Sterling College	Sterling	R	B	Pri	No	C	736	21	37	31	20	5	7	460	73	23	4		470	65	31	4		460	77	15	8		Open
Tabor College	Hillsboro	R	A,B	Pri	No	C	740																						Open
University of Kansas	Lawrence	SU	B,M,D	Pub	F,S	C	19,217	25	12	22	28	15	23																4/1
University of Saint Mary	Leavenworth	SM	A,B,M	Pri	No	C	825																						Open
Washburn University	Topeka	U	A,B,M,D	Pub	F,S	C	6,179	22	35	30	20	8	7																8/1
Wichita State University	Wichita	U	A,B,M,D	Pub	F,S	C	12,243	23	28	32	23	10	7	460	45	30	18	7	530	44	26	16	6						Open

Kentucky

NAME OF SCHOOL	TOWN	ENVIRONMENT	DEGREES AWARDED	CONTROL	FRATERNITIES AND SORORITIES	STUDENTS	UNDERGRADUATE ENROLLMENT FALL 2013	ACT Median	ACT Below 21	ACT 21-23	ACT 24-26	ACT 27-28	ACT Above 28	SAT CR Median	SAT CR Below 500	SAT CR 500-599	SAT CR 600-700	SAT CR Above 700	SAT M Median	SAT M Below 500	SAT M 500-599	SAT M 600-700	SAT M Above 700	SAT W Median	SAT W Below 500	SAT W 500-599	SAT W 600-700	SAT W Above 700	APPLICATION DEADLINE
Alice Lloyd College	Pippa Passes	R	B	Pri	No	C	612	20	48	35	13	3	1																Open
Asbury University	Wilmore	SM	A,B,M	Pri	No	C	1,532	24	17	27	26	11	19	568	21	41	33	5	558	24	40	32	4						Open
Bellarmine University	Louisville	SU	B,M,D	Pri	F,S	C	2,730	24	12	33	30	12	11	546	28	46	25	1	551	24	48	24	4						2/1
Berea College	Berea	SU	B	Pri	No	C	1,658	24	13	26	36	13	11	550	21	43	33	3	550	16	48	31	5	550	29	43	26	2	Open
Brescia University	Owensboro	U	A,B,M	Pri	No	C	801		20	45	17	15	3							53	47								Open
Campbellsville University	Campbellsville	SM	A,B,M	Pri	No	C	2,978	21	46	27	15	6	6																Open
Centre College	Danville	SM	B	Pri	F,S	C	1,189	28	2	6	25	22	45	625	6	31	38	25	615	6	28	56	10						2/1
Eastern Kentucky University	Richmond	SM	A,B,M	Pub	F,S	C	13,659																						8/1
Georgetown College	Georgetown	SU	B,M	Pri	F,S	C	1,116	23	23	32	24	6	8	515	39	27	28	6	521	44	27	6	6						8/1
Kentucky Christian University	Grayson	SM	B,M	Pri	No	C	570	19	62	22	10	3	2	450	73	20	7		460	53	40	7							Open
Kentucky State University	Frankfort	SM	A,B,M		F,S	C	2,300	17																					Open
Kentucky Wesleyan College	Owensboro	SU	B	Pri	F,S	C	678	22	38	29	16	7	10	470	58	36	6		490	55	36	9		460	61	36	3		Open
Lindsey Wilson College	Columbia	SM	A,B,M	Pri	No	C	2,200		42	8	26	14	9																Open
Midway College	Midway	R	A,B,M		No	PW	1,169	20	62	21	10	3	4																Open
Morehead State University	Morehead	SM	A,B,M,D	Pub	F,S	C		22	10	55			35																Open
Murray State University	Murray	SM	A,B,M,D	Pub	F,S	C	9,172	23	33	28	23	8	8																8/1
Northern Kentucky University	Highland Heights	SU	A,B,M,D	Pub	F,S	C	12,794		37	29	20	7	7		46	38	13	2		55	31	12	2						8/1
Spalding University	Louisville	U	A,B,M,D	Pri	No	C	1,371	20	58	25	20	7	3	480	42	58			500	57	40	3							Open
Thomas More College	Crestview Hills	SU	A,B,M	Pri	F,S	C	1,502	22	28	35	24	5	8	480	55	36	9		490	51	31	13	5						8/1
Transylvania University	Lexington	U	B	Pri	F,S	C	1,081	27	5	13	26	19	37	590	14	36	41	9	560	14	52	24	10						2/1
Union College	Barbourville	SM	B,M	Pri	No	C	818	22	41	25	26	5	3	469	58	38	4		506	54	38	8							Open
University of Kentucky	Lexington	SU	B,M,D	Pub	F,S	C	20,767								23	46	22	9		20	41	28	10		24	47	23	6	Open
University of Louisville	Louisville	U	A,B,M,D	Pub	F,S	C	15,957	24	85	5	5	3	2	540	24	41	24	11	570	20	40	32	8						8/19
University of Pikeville	Pikeville	SM	A,B,M,D	Pri	No	C	1,737	19	62	22	11	3	2							67	19	14			71	24	5		8/16
University of the Cumberlands	Williamsburg	SM	B,M	Pri	No	C	2,096	22	44	24	15	8	9	488	63	24	10	3	494	55	32	13							Open
Western Kentucky University	Bowling Green	SU	A,B,M	Pub	F,S	C	16,000	20	52	24	14	6	4																8/1

Louisiana

NAME OF SCHOOL	TOWN	ENVIRONMENT	DEGREES AWARDED	CONTROL	FRATERNITIES AND SORORITIES	STUDENTS	UNDERGRADUATE ENROLLMENT FALL 2013	ACT Median	ACT Below 21	ACT 21-23	ACT 24-26	ACT 27-28	ACT Above 28	SAT CR Median	SAT CR Below 500	SAT CR 500-599	SAT CR 600-700	SAT CR Above 700	SAT M Median	SAT M Below 500	SAT M 500-599	SAT M 600-700	SAT M Above 700	SAT W Median	SAT W Below 500	SAT W 500-599	SAT W 600-700	SAT W Above 700	APPLICATION DEADLINE
Centenary College of Louisiana	Shreveport	U	B,M	Pri	F,S	C	698	25	13	23	31	14	1																8/1
Dillard University	New Orleans	U	B	Pri	F,S	C	1,249																						8/1
Grambling State University	Grambling	SM	A,B,M,D	Pub	F,S	C	4,435	17	85	12	3	1		430	82	16	2		430	80	18	1							6/1
Louisiana College	Pineville	SM	A,B	Pri	F,S	C	1,056	22	38	29	16	9	8																Open
Louisiana State University	Baton Rouge	U	B,M,D	Pub	F,S	C	24,923	26	5	27	31	17	21	559	22	51	24	4	577	15	44	35	6						4/15
Louisiana State University in Shreveport	Shreveport	U	B,M	Pub	F,S	C	3,655	22	30	32	24	6	5	500	40	60			530	17	83								4/15
Louisiana Tech University	Ruston	SM	A,B,M,D	Pub	F,S	C	10,800																						4/15
Loyola University New Orleans	New Orleans	SU	B,M,D	Pri	F,S	C	3,200								4	42	43	10		7	50	39	4		7	44	42	7	Open
McNeese State University	Lake Charles	SU	A,B,M	Pub	F,S	C	7,501	20	36	37	17	5	5						490										Open

Nicholls State University	Thibodaux	SM	A,B,M	Pub	F,S	C	6,201	21	47	33	15	3	2																Open
Northwestern State University of Louisiana	Natchitoches	SM	A,B,M,D	Pub	F,S	C	7,836	21	42	30	17	7	4	480	68	28	3	1	500	51	40	7	1						7/6
Our Lady of Holy Cross College	New Orleans	U	A,B,M	Pri	No	C	1,314																						7/20
Southeastern Louisiana University	Hammond	SM	A,B,M,D	Pub	F,S	C	13,744	21	35	37	18	6	4																7/15
Southern University and A&M College	Baton Rouge	U	B,M,D	Pub	F,S	C	6,491	19	76	17	2	1	1		81	16	2			77	19	3	1						7/1
Southern University at New Orleans	New Orleans	SU	A,B,M	Pub	No	C	450																						7/1
Tulane University	New Orleans	U	A,B,M,D	Pri	F,S	C	8,352	30						656	2	15	54	29	660	1	14	59	27	669	2	10	54	34	1/15
University of Louisiana at Lafayette	Lafayette	U	B,M,D	Pub	F,S	C	14,560																						Open
University of Louisiana at Monroe	Monroe	U	A,B,M,D	Pub	F,S	C	7,276	22	34	30	22	6	7	500	45	32	22	1	540	37	37	22	4						Open
University of New Orleans	New Orleans	U	B,M,D	Pub	F,S	C	8,653	21	37	35	18	6	4	550	35	31	30	4	550	32	34	29	5	540	35	40	22	3	Open
Xavier University of Louisiana	New Orleans	U	B,M,D	Pri	F,S	C	2,750	22	14	56	29	29	1	480	55	35	9	1	480	57	32	11		470	63	31	6		7/1

Maine

Bates College	Lewiston	SM	B	Pri	No	C	1,791	31			5	11	84	680	1	8	49	42	680		9	59	32	680	1	8	52	39	1/1
Bowdoin College	Brunswick	SM	B	Pri	No	C	1,795	32			1	5	94	720		3	30	67	720		3	31	66	730		3	29	68	1/1
Colby College	Waterville	SM	B	Pri	No	C	1,820	30		1	8	16	74	660	2	15	51	31	680		12	49	39	670	1	14	48	36	1/1
College of the Atlantic	Bar Harbor	SM	B,M	Pri	No	C	356	28		50	30	20	50	640	2	23	54	21	610	5	42	53		610	7	33	58	2	2/15
Husson University	Bangor	SU	A,B,M,D	Pri	F,S	C	2,353	20	70	16	9	4	1	475	62	34	2	1	471	55	37	7	1	485	63	32	5		8/15
Maine College of Art	Portland	U	B,M	Pri	No	C	370																						Open
Maine Maritime Academy	Castine	SM	A,B,M	Pub	F	C	935																						5/1
Saint Joseph's College of Maine	Standish	R	A,B		No	C	930	21																					Open
Thomas College	Waterville	R	A,B,M	Pri	F	C	1,339	18	50	40	10			445	70	26	3	1	453	66	27	7		435	77	19	4		Open
Unity College	Unity	SM	A,B	Pri	No	C	554																						2/15
University of Maine	Orono	SM	B,M,D		F,S	C	9,182	24	21	27	25	16	12	530	34	45	17	4	540	31	43	22	4	510	40	43	16	1	Open
University of Maine at Augusta	Augusta	SM	A,B	Pub	No	C	4,990																						6/15
University of Maine at Farmington	Farmington	SM	B,M	Pub	No	C	1,901							520	44	34	19	3	500	50	37	12	1	500	50	34	15	1	Open
University of Maine at Fort Kent	Fort Kent	SM	A,B	Pub	F,S	C	1,167	18	64	27	9			450	73	25	2		450	75	23	2		440	78	19	3		Open
University of Maine at Machias	Machias	R	B	Pub	F,S	C	1,187	22	43	14	29	7	7																Open
University of Maine at Presque Isle	Presque Isle	R	A,B	Pub	F,S	C	1,536																						Open
University of New England	Biddeford	SM	B,M,D	Pri	No	C	2,179	24	17	35	31	13	7	522	37	49	13	1	536	30	51	17	1						2/15
University of Southern Maine	Gorham	U	A,B,M,D	Pub	F,S	C	7,618	21	45	32	15	3	5	500	47	39	12	2	500	50	40	9	1	490	51	37	11	1	2/15

Maryland

Bowie State University	Bowie	SU	B,M,D	Pub	F,S	C	4,311							410	77	21	2		400	82	16	2		390					4/1
Capitol College	Laurel	R	A,B,M		No	C	300																						Open
Coppin State University	Baltimore	U	B,M	Pub	F,S	C	3,242																						6/15
Frostburg State University	Frostburg	SM	B,M,D	Pub	F,S	C	4,704	20						488	59	33	6	1	492	58	34	8	1	469	66	27	6	1	Open
Goucher College	Baltimore	SU	B,M	Pri	No	C	1,449	26	14	17	21	24	24	590	18	33	33	14	570	22	42	29	6	560	22	34	32	10	2/1
Hood College	Frederick	SU	B,M	Pri	No	C	1,387	21	48	19	22	7	4	520	39	40	19	2	530	38	40	21	2	510	43	43	13	1	6/15
Johns Hopkins University	Baltimore	SU	B,M,D	Pri	F,S	C	4,591	31		2	13	11	74	680	1	11	51	37	710		7	39	53	680		13	51	35	1/1
Loyola University Maryland	Baltimore	U	B,M,D	Pri	No	C	3,917	26	4	12	39	19	26	586	10	47	38	5	591	12	37	46	5						1/15
Maryland Institute College of Art	Baltimore	SM	B,M	Pri	No	C	1,680																						1/15
McDaniel College	Westminster	SU	B,M	Pri	F,S	C	1,692	24	3	38		46	13	550	25	48	22	5	555	25	44	28	3						2/15
Morgan State University	Baltimore	SU	B,M,D	Pub	F,S	C	6,591																						2/15
Mount Saint Mary's University	Emmitsburg	R	B,M	Pri	No	C	1,741	21	49	26	20	3	2	550	23	52	22	3	530	28	50	21	1	530	31	46	21	2	Open
Notre Dame of Maryland University	Baltimore	SU	B,M		No	PW	1,620																						Open
Salisbury University	Salisbury	R	B,M,D	Pub	F,S	C	8,004	24	3	43		53	1	575	6	62	29	3	580	4	54	39	3	570	7	60	31	2	1/15
Sojourner-Douglass College	Baltimore	U	B		No	C	250																						Open
St. John's College-Annapolis	Annapolis	SM	B,M	Pri	No	C	463	27			12	46	42	640	2	10	40	48	570	4	29	44	23						Open
St. Mary's College of Maryland	St. Marys City	R	B,M	Pub	No	C	1,816	27	6	14	25	23	32	600	11	35	38	16	590	12	39	40	7	590	11	40	40	9	1/1
Stevenson University	Stevenson	SU	B,M	Pri	S	C	3,826								48	44	8			48	41	11			51	40	9		Open
Towson University	Towson	SU	B,M,D	Pub	F,S	C	16,230																						Open
United States Naval Academy	Annapolis	SM	B	Pub	No	C	4,526							656	6	30	46	18	676	1	19	51	29						1/31
University of Maryland	College Park	SU	B,M,D	Pub	F,S	C	26,487								6	26	47	21		4	16	43	37						1/20
University of Maryland/Baltimore County	Baltimore	SU	B,M,D	Pub	F,S	C	9,470																						1/20
University of Maryland/Eastern Shore	Princess Anne	R	B,M,D	Pub	F,S	C	3,335																						1/20
University of Maryland/University College	Adelphi	U	B,M,D	Pub	No	C	28,119																						Open
Washington Adventist University	Takoma Park	SU	A,B,M	Pri	No	C	995	18	56	24	20			451	74	21	4	1	429	76	22	2							8/1
Washington College	Chestertown	SM	B,M	Pri	F,S	C	1,512							585	9	48	38	5	570	12	47	37	4						2/15

Massachusetts

American International College	Springfield	U	A,B,M,D	Pri	F,S	C	1,729	19	60	30	4	4	2	467	67	28	4	1	471	64	26	10	1	461	66	29	5		Open

NAME OF SCHOOL	TOWN	ENVIRONMENT U-Urban R-Rural SU-Suburban SM-Small Town	DEGREES AWARDED A-Associate B-Bachelor M-Master D-Doctorate	CONTROL Pri-Private, Pub-Public	FRATERNITIES AND SORORITIES F-Fraternities S-Sororities F, S-Both No-Neither	STUDENTS: C-Coed M-Men W-Women PM-Primarily Men PW-Primarily Women	UNDERGRADUATE ENROLLMENT FALL 2013	TEST SCORES ACT Median	ACT Below 21	ACT 21-23	ACT 24-26	ACT 27-28	ACT Above 28	SAT CRITICAL READING Median	Below 500	500-599	600-700	Above 700	SAT MATHEMATICS Median	Below 500	500-599	600-700	Above 700	SAT WRITING Median	Below 500	500-599	600-700	Above 700	APPLICATION DEADLINE Month / Day
Amherst College	Amherst	SM	B	Pri	No	C	1,785									4	30	66			4	31	65			4	32	63	1/1
Anna Maria College	Paxton	R	A,B,M	Pri	No	C	930																						Open
Assumption College	Worcester	SU	B,M	Pri	No	C	2,002	25	11	20	42	16	11	550	18	57	22	5	570	15	50	32	2						2/15
Atlantic Union College	South Lancaster	SM	A,B,M	Pri	No	C	450																						2/15
Babson College	Babson Park	SU	B,M	Pri	F,S	C	1,800																						2/15
Bard College at Simon's Rock	Great Barrington	SM	A,B	Pri	No	C	350	27	10	10	30	30	20	690	9	9	27	55	650	9	18	46	27	640		9	45	46	5/1
Bay Path College	Longmeadow	SU	A,B,M		No	W	1,360																						Open
Becker College	Worcester	U	A,B	Pri	No	C	1,826	21						490	54	30	14	2	490	51	32	14	3	470	63	27	9	1	Open
Benjamin Franklin Institute of Technology	Boston	U	A,B	Pri	No	C	564																					1	Open
Bentley University	Waltham	SU	B,M,D	Pri	F,S	C	4,247	28	1	8	27	27	38	590	10	45	40	6	650	2	21	55	22	600	9	38	46	7	1/7
Berklee College of Music	Boston	U	B,M	Pri	No	C	4,090																					7	1/7
Boston Architectural College	Boston	U	B,M	Pri	No	C	407																						Open
Boston College	Chestnut Hill	SU	B,M,D	Pri	No	C	9,049	30					72	665	2	14	51	33	695	2	9	43	46	685	2	9	46	43	1/1
Boston Conservatory	Boston	U	B,M	Pri	F,S	C	512	25						549					577									43	1/1
Boston University	Boston	SM	B,M,D	Pri	F,S	C	18,714	28	1	5	26	25	44	630	1	27	59	13	650	1	22	59	19	640	1	22	60	17	1/1
Brandeis University	Waltham	SU	B,M,D	Pri	No	C	3,614	30		1	8	18	72	670	1	14	49	35	670	2	13	48	37	680	2	13	45	40	1/1
Bridgewater State University	Bridgewater	SU	B,M	Pub	F,S	C	9,684	21	46	43	7	2	2	499	48	41	10	1	511	40	47	12	1						2/15
Cambridge College	Cambridge	U	B,M,D	Pri	No	C	1,048																						Open
Clark University	Worcester	U	B,M,D	Pri	No	C	2,380	28		7	25	24	44	620	6	28	47	19	600	7	42	43	8	620	6	31	46	17	1/15
College of Art and Design at Lesley University	Boston	U	B,M	Pri	No	C	1,267		9	50	13	24	4		27	47	24	2		41	46	12	1		27	50	20	3	2/15
College of the Holy Cross	Worcester	SU	B	Pri	No	C	2,912	29						649	1	20	56	23	657	1	14	58	27	653	2	16	56	26	1/15
Curry College	Milton	SU	B,M	Pri	No	C	2,769	19						460	73	24	3		460	70	27	3		455	71	25	4		4/1
Eastern Nazarene College	Quincy	SU	A,B,M		No	C	640																						4/1
Elms College	Chicopee	SU	A,B,M		No	C	640																						Open
Emerson College	Boston	U	B,M,D	Pri	F,S	C	3,731	27	2	8	27	24	38	640	2	24	55	19	590	6	44	42	8	630	2	27	54	16	1/5
Emmanuel College	Boston	U	B,M	Pri	No	C	2,176	23	10	43	26	12	9	550	20	57	21	2	540	24	54	20	2	550	19	55	24	2	2/15
Endicott College	Beverly	SU	A,B,M,D	Pri	No	C	2,820	23						528	32	52	15	1	541	25	53	21	1	531	30	52	17	1	2/15
Fitchburg State University	Fitchburg	SU	B,M	Pub	F,S	C	4,239	21	41	37	11	7	4	500	48	40	11	1	510	40	46	14	1	490	51	39	9	1	3/1
Framingham State University	Framingham	SU	B,M	Pub	No	C	4,490	22						518	40	47	12	1	526	33	52	14	1	510	41	48	11		2/15
Franklin W. Olin College of Engineering	Needham	SU	B	Pri	No	C	355	34				8	92	730		5	24	71	770			9	91	710		1	41	58	1/1
Gordon College	Wenham	SU	B,M	Pri	No	C	1,707	26					15	582	14	43	34	9	570	20	43	29	8	575	18	41	32	9	8/1
Hampshire College	Amherst	R	B	Pri	No	C	1,491								5	20	47	27		14	35	41	10		8	27	46	19	8/1
Harvard University/Harvard College	Cambridge	U	B,M,D		No	C	6,670																					19	8/1
Hellenic College/Holy Cross Greek Orthodox School of Theology	Brookline	U	B,M	Pri	No	C	91	22	20	60	20			550	30	35	30	5	450	55	35	5	5	460	45	35	20		5/1
Lasell College	Newton	SU	B,M	Pri	No	C	1,687	20	60	24	5	7		480	58	35	6		480	58	35	6		480	60	35	5		Open
Lesley University	Cambridge	U	A,B,M,D	Pri	No	C	1,598		3	59	16	20	2		23	48	24	5		40	40	19	1		28	50	21	1	Open
Massachusetts College of Art and Design	Boston	U	B,M	Pub	No	C	1,772							560	18	47	30	5	540	26	49	22	3	540	23	49	24	3	2/1
Massachusetts College of Liberal Arts	North Adams	R	B,M	Pub	F,S	C	1,600	22	23	36	23	5	13	530	33	46	16	5	500	44	44	11	1						Open
Massachusetts College of Pharmacy and Health Sciences	Boston	U	B,M,D	Pri	F	C	2,883	24	20	28	34	14	4	525	31	55	13	1	570	16	47	34	4	540	26	51	22	1	2/1
Massachusetts Institute of Technology	Cambridge	U	B,M,D	Pri	F,S	C	4,503	34				2	98	730		4	32	65	780			10	90	740		3	28	69	1/1
Massachusetts Maritime Academy	Buzzards Bay	SM	B,M	Pub	No	C	975																						Open
Merrimack College	North Andover	SU	A,B,M	Pri	F,S	C	2,319																						2/15
Montserrat College of Art	Beverly	SU	B	Pri	No	C	305																						Open
Mount Holyoke College	South Hadley	SM	B,M	Pri	No	W	2,183	29		3	16	25	56	660		16	52	3	650	1	24	43	33	670		13	48	40	1/15
Mount Ida College	Newton	SU	A,B	Pri	No	C	1,130																						Open
New England Conservatory of Music	Boston	U	B,M,D	Pri	No	C	436																						12/1
Newbury College	Brookline	SU	A,B	Pri	No	C	962	20						430	88	9	3		430	83	14	3		430	89	8	3		Open
Nichols College	Dudley	SU	A,B,M	Pri	No	C	1,332	20	70	13	8	7	2	450	73	24	3		470	64	27	9		450	72	26	2		Open
Northeastern University	Boston	U	B,M,D	Pri	F,S	C	17,107	31						690	2	9	46	44	700	1	5	36	57	680	1	9	50	40	1/1
Pine Manor College	Chestnut Hill	SU	A,B,M	Pri	No	W	458																						Open
Regis College	Weston	SU	A,B,M,D	Pri	No	C	1,149	21	34	36	26	2	2	466	61	34	5		466	67	29	4		467	64	28	7		6/1
Salem State College	Salem	U	B,M	Pub	No	C	7,298																						Open
Simmons College	Boston	U	B,M,D	Pri	No	PW	1,792	26	21	30	28	16	6	575	18	47	29	6	570	13	53	29	5	580	12	46	35	7	2/1
Smith College	Northampton	SM	B,M,D	Pri	No	W	2,606	30			6	45	49	665	2	15	45	38	670	1	19	44	36	680	2	12	45	42	1/15

Springfield College	Springfield	SU	B,M,D		No	C	2,200																					42	1/15
Stonehill College	Easton	SU	B	Pri	No	C	2,582	26	1	10	32	33	24	590	4	43	47	6	600	4	37	52	7						1/15
Suffolk University	Boston	U	A,B,M,D	Pri	F,S	C	5,785	22	28	36	19	10	7	500	48	37	12	3	510	46	40	13	1	500	45	41	13	1	3/1
Tufts University	Medford	SU	B,M,D	Pri	F,S	C	5,232	32						715		6	30	64	720		3	28	69	720		4	32	64	1/1
University of Massachusetts Amherst	Amherst	SM	A,B,M,D	Pub	F,S	C		27	4	14	32	22	28	590	8	46	36	9	610	4	36	47	13						1/15
University of Massachusetts Boston	Boston	U	B,M,D	Pub	No	C	12,366							510	43	42	14	2	540	27	47	22	3						4/1
University of Massachusetts Dartmouth	North Dartmouth	SU	B,M,D	Pub	F,S	C	7,437	23	25	30	25	6	14	510	41	41	16	2	530	30	47	21	2	510	45	41	13	2	Open
University of Massachusetts Lowell	Lowell	U	A,B,M,D	Pub	No	C	10,548								34	48	16	2	555	23	47	27	3	528					Open
Wellesley College	Wellesley	SU	B	Pri	No	W	2,268	30					69	689		10	38	52	683		11	45	43	693		8	41	51	1/15
Wentworth Institute of Technology	Boston	U	A,B	Pri	No	C	3,728	23																				51	1/15
Western New England University	Springfield	SU	A,B,M,D	Pri	No	C	2,667	24	17	24	38	9	12	510	38	45	16	1	550	26	42	29	3						Open
Westfield State University	Westfield	SU	B,M	Pub	No	C	5,716	20	54	33	13			500	45	45	10		520	38	47	14	1	500	48	43	8		3/1
Wheaton College	Norton	SU	B	Pri	No	C	1,622	29			27	19	54	625	6	26	50	17	620	6	26	52	16						1/15
Wheelock College	Boston	U	A,B,M	Pri	No	C	680		56	11	33																		3/1
Williams College	Williamstown	SM	B,M	Pri	No	C	2,077	33						730	1	5	27	67	720	1	6	29	64			5	24	71	1/1
Worcester Polytechnic Institute	Worcester	SU	B,M,D	Pri	F,S	C	3,841	28	2	9	20	25	44	610	8	35	43	14	670		12	54	34	600	6	28	45	11	2/1
Worcester State University	Worcester	U	B,M	Pub	No	C	5,556	22	31	46	17	5	1	504	48	43	9	1	520	36	51	12	1						5/1
Michigan																													
Adrian College	Adrian	SM	A,B	Pri	F,S	C			32	31	24	7	6	490	57	37	3	3	490	52	35	13							3/30
Albion College	Albion	SM	B	Pri	F,S	C	1,382	24	16	23	25	13	16	540	39	29	26	6	550	29	32	23	16	540					Open
Alma College	Alma	SM	B	Pri	F,S	C	1,419	24	21	20	25	24	9	561	36	28	20	16	571	24	40	24	12	552	32	40	12	16	Open
Andrews University	Berrien Springs	R	A,B,M,D	Pri	F,S	C	1,964	23	34	26	21	11	8																Open
Aquinas College	Grand Rapids	SU	A,B,M	Pri	No	C	1,922	23	28	25	28	14	5																Open
Baker College of Flint	Flint	U	A,B		No	C	4,400																						Open
Calvin College	Grand Rapids	SU	B,M	Pri	No	C	3,960	26	9	18	25	18	29	575	17	40	31	11	595	16	34	37	13						8/15
Central Michigan University	Mount Pleasant	SM	B,M,D	Pub	F,S	C	20,580	22	34	34	20	7	5																Open
Cleary University	Ann Arbor	SU	A,B		No	C	700																						Open
College for Creative Studies	Detroit	U	B	Pri	No	C		22																					8/1
Concordia University, Ann Arbor	Ann Arbor	SU	A,B,M	Pri	No	C	521	22	36	20	27	11	6	575	36	21	21	22	550	28	43	29		560	43	7	29	21	Open
Cornerstone University and Grand Rapids Theological Seminary	Grand Rapids	SU	A,B,M	Pri	No	C	2,178	23	29	23	20	17	7																Open
Davenport University	Grand Rapids	SU	A,B,M	Pri	No	C	8,882																						Open
Eastern Michigan University	Ypsilanti	SU	B,M,D	Pub	F,S	C	18,561	22	36	29	22	7	5	512	48	33	17	2	521	42	38	17	3	493	50	39	9	2	8/30
Ferris State University	Big Rapids	SM	A,B,M,D	Pub	F,S	C	18,469	22	40	28	79	6	7																8/1
Grace Bible College	Grand Rapids	SU	A,B	Pri	No	C	194	21	45	26	19	7	3	560	35	66			540	34	66			500	34	33	33		Open
Grand Valley State University	Allendale	SM	B,M,D	Pub	F,S	C	21,231	24	19	31	28	12	10																7/23
Hillsdale College	Hillsdale	SM	B,M,D	Pri	F,S	C	1,486	29		3	22	21	54	690		10	47	43	620	2	25	48	25	670		16	44	40	2/15
Hope College	Holland	U	B	Pri	F,S	C	3,343	26						600	15	37	31	17	610	16	28	42	14						Open
Kalamazoo College	Kalamazoo	SU	B	Pri	No	C	1,458	28	3	11	26	24	35	615	12	34	37	17	640	7	31	39	22	605	12	35	43	11	2/1
Kendall College of Art and Design of Ferris State University	Grand Rapids	U	B,M	Pub	No	C	1,180	22																					Open
Kettering University	Flint	SU	B,M	Pri	F,S	C	2,178	26	3	12	40	17	28		17	47	27	9	630	6	25	51	18						Open
Lake Superior State University	Sault Sainte Marie	SM	A,B,M	Pub	F,S	C	2,521	21	35	29	21	9	6																Open
Lawrence Technological University	Southfield	SU	A,B,M,D	Pri	F,S	C	3,033	25	19	16	25	12	27	510	41	20	26	13	620	21	23	38	18	550	37	42	18	3	Open
Madonna University	Livonia	SU	A,B,M,D	Pri	No	C	3,368	23	27	29	25	11	8	630	20		60	20	580	20	40	20	20	560	20	60		20	Open
Marygrove College	Detroit	U	A,B,M	Pri	F,S	C	788	17																					8/15
Michigan State University	East Lansing	SU	B,M,D		F,S	C	35,678	24	14	26	32	14	14																7/25
Michigan Technological University	Houghton	SM	A,B,M,D	Pub	F,S	C	5,731	25	6	19	28	24	23	590					630	9	30	49	12	570					Open
Northern Michigan University	Marquette	U	A,B,M	Pub	F,S	C	8,578	23	33	30	22	8	7																Open
Northwood University	Midland	SU	A,B,M	Pri	F,S	C	1,819		48	27	16	6	3		76	17	3	3		55	34	10			64	29	7		8/1
Oakland University	Rochester	SU	B,M,D	Pub	F,S	C	16,190	22																					8/1
Olivet College	Olivet	SM	B,M	Pri	F,S	C	1,052	19	25	40	15	15	5																Open
Rochester College	Rochester Hills	SU	A,B,M	Pri	F,S	C	908	20	50	20	21	7	2																8/30
Saginaw Valley State University	University Center	SU	B,M	Pub	F,S	C	8,975	22	42	26	19	7	6																Open
Siena Heights University	Adrian	SM	A,B,M		F,S	C	1,100																						Open
Spring Arbor University	Spring Arbor	SM	A,B,M	Pri	No	C	1,555																						Open
University of Detroit Mercy	Detroit	U	B,M,D	Pri	F,S	C	3,400																						Open
University of Michigan/Ann Arbor	Ann Arbor	SU	B,M,D	Pub	F,S	C	27,366	30	2	4	13	31	50	640	3	23	51	23	690	2	10	39	49	660	3	17	46	31	2/1
University of Michigan/Dearborn	Dearborn	SU	B,M	Pub	F,S	C	7,328			29	28	13	12			1	1	1			1	2					1	1	2/1
University of Michigan-Flint	Flint	U	B,M,D	Pub	F,S	C	7,143	21	45	25	16	7	7	610	30	10	40	20	595	20	30	30	20	580	20	50		30	8/20
Wayne State University	Detroit	U	B,M,D	Pub	F,S	C	19,342	21	39	22	18	11	11																8/28
Western Michigan University	Kalamazoo	U	B,M,D	Pub	F,S	C	19,198	22	35	29	21	9	6																Open

NAME OF SCHOOL	TOWN	ENVIRONMENT U-Urban R-Rural SU-Suburban SM-Small Town	DEGREES AWARDED A-Associate B-Bachelor M-Master D-Doctorate	CONTROL Pri-Private, Pub-Public	FRATERNITIES AND SORORITIES F-Fraternities S-Sororities F, S-Both No-Neither	STUDENTS: C-Coed M-Men W-Women PM-Primarily Men PW-Primarily Women	UNDERGRADUATE ENROLLMENT FALL 2013	ACT Median	ACT Below 21	ACT 21-23	ACT 24-26	ACT 27-28	ACT Above 28	SAT CRITICAL READING Median	SAT CR Below 500	SAT CR 500-599	SAT CR 600-700	SAT CR Above 700	SAT MATHEMATICS Median	SAT Math Below 500	SAT Math 500-599	SAT Math 600-700	SAT Math Above 700	SAT WRITING Median	SAT Writing Below 500	SAT Writing 500-599	SAT Writing 600-700	SAT Writing Above 700	APPLICATION DEADLINE Month / Day
Minnesota																													
Augsburg College	Minneapolis	U	B,M	Pri	No	C	3,124	22	38	27	23	8	4	505	50	25	21	4	565	21	33	38	8						5/1
Bemidji State University	Bemidji	SM	A,B,M	Pub	F,S	C	4,744																						Open
Bethel University	St. Paul	SU	A,B,M,D	Pri	No	C	3,421	25	17	23	26	14	21	590	20	31	30	19	580	20	39	28	14						Open
Carleton College	Northfield	SM	B	Pri	No	C	2,045			5	6	8	81			7	30	63		1	5	31	63			6	38	56	1/15
College of Saint Benedict	St. Joseph	SM	B	Pri	No	C	2,051		12	22	34	13	19		37	40	15	8		30	38	32			37	37	18	8	Open
College of Saint Scholastica	Duluth	SU	B,M,D	Pri	No	C	2,936	24	29	22	19	17	13	470	67	20	13		480	67	20	13		470	60	40			Open
College of Visual Arts - School is Closed	St. Paul	U	B	Pri	No	C	207																						Open
Concordia College, Moorhead	Moorhead	SU	B,M	Pri	No	C	2,531	25	13	22	29	16	20	570	23	33	35	10	550	33	29	23	15		31	37	23	10	Open
Concordia University Saint Paul	St. Paul	U	A,B,M	Pri	No	C	2,171	21	49	25	20	4	2																8/1
Gustavus Adolphus College	St. Peter	SM	B	Pri	F,S	C	2,455	27	2	13	31	20	34																11/1
Hamline University	St. Paul	U	B,M,D	Pri	F,S	C	2,211	24	18	25	27	13	17	545	33	31	26	10	560	22	45	31	2	540	29	38	29	3	Open
Macalester College	St. Paul	SM	B	Pri	No	C	2,070	31		1	12	15	75	700		7	40	53	680		9	49	42	680	1	10	50	39	1/15
Metropolitan State University	St. Paul	U	B,M,D	Pub	No	C	6,974																						6/15
Minneapolis College of Art and Design	Minneapolis	U	B,M	Pri	No	C	740																						6/15
Minnesota State University, Mankato	Mankato	R	A,B,M,D	Pub	F,S	C	13,285	21	9	62	16	12	1																6/15
Minnesota State University, Moorhead	Moorhead	SU	A,B,M,D	Pub	F,S	C	7,012																						6/15
North Central University	Minneapolis	U	A,B	Pri	No	C	1,219	21																					6/1
Northwestern College	St. Paul	SU	A,B	Pri	No	C	1,865																						8/1
Saint John's University	Collegeville	R	B,M	Pri	No	C	1,871		7	23	29	18	23		38	32	26	4		38	32	22	8		42	39	18	1	Open
Saint Mary's University of Minnesota	Winona	SM	B,M,D	Pri	F,S	C	1,932	23	30	26	27	10	7	505	50	38	6	6	515	44	39	25		470	56	13	31		5/1
Southwest Minnesota State University	Marshall	R	A,B,M	Pub	No	C	2,710																						5/1
St. Catherine University	St. Paul	U	A,B,M,D	Pri	No	W	3,559	24	1		48	44	7	560	27	39	17	17	525	27	56	17							Open
St. Cloud State University	St. Cloud	SU	A,B,M,D	Pub	F,S	C	14,525																						Open
St. Olaf College	Northfield	SM	B	Pri	No	C	3,125	29	1	5	17	18	59	660	1	14	51	34	650	4	20	443	29	650	5	20	46	29	1/15
University of Minnesota Crookston	Crookston	SM	B	Pub	F,S	C	2,764	22	41	29	19	9	2	480	53	27	13		520	20	53	7	7	490	57	43			Open
University of Minnesota/Duluth	Duluth	SU	B,M,D		F,S	C	10,680	24	15	33	33	11	8	510	40	34	23	3	540	28	46	21	5	530	36	41	21	2	2/1
University of Minnesota/Morris	Morris	SM	B	Pub	No	C	1,850																					2	2/1
University of Minnesota/Twin Cities	Minneapolis	U	B,M,D	Pub	F,S	C	33,894	28	3	7	23	23	44	630	9	29	37	25	680	2	16	38	44	620	8	30	44	18	Open
University of Saint Thomas	St. Paul	U	B,M,D	Pri	No	C	6,350	25						580					590										Open
Winona State University	Winona	U	A,B,M,D	Pub	F,S	C	8,284	23	28	41	22	6	3																Open
Mississippi																													
Alcorn State University	Alcorn State	R	A,B,M	Pub	F,S	C	3,010																						Open
Belhaven University	Jackson	U	A,B,M	Pri	No	C	2,576	22	42	28	16	7	7	530	39	31	27	3	500	45	44	11							Open
Blue Mountain College	Blue Mountain	R	B,M	Pri	No	C	520	20	53	17	17	4	9	540	33	33	34		470	100				450	66	34			Open
Delta State University	Cleveland	SM	B,M,D	Pub	F,S	C	2,756	20	59	21	13	3	4	473	59	36	5		507	32	59	9							8/1
Jackson State University	Jackson	U	B,M,D	Pub	F,S	C	6,902	19	72	19	7	2	1																Open
Millsaps College	Jackson	U	B,M	Pri	F,S	C	744	26	9	23	27	18	23	540	25	39	28	8	560	17	47	33	3						Open
Mississippi College	Clinton	SU	B,M,D	Pri	F,S	C		23	30	23	20	12	16	550	43	30	24	4	520	41	33	19	7						Open
Mississippi University for Women	Columbus	SM	A,B,M,D	Pub	F,S	C	3,200																						Open
Mississippi Valley State University	Itta Bena	SM	B,M	Pub	F,S	C	2,748	17	91	6	3																		8/10
Rust College	Holly Springs	SM	A,B		F,S	C	1,015																						8/10
Tougaloo College	Tougaloo	SU	A,B	Pri	F,S	C	940																						Open
University of Mississippi	University	SM	B,M,D	Pub	F,S	C	16,060	24	24	25	22	12	17	530	31	44	20	5	540	29	43	24	4						7/1
University of Southern Mississippi	Hattiesburg	SU	B,M,D	Pub	F,S	C	13,658	22	41	24	19	7	9		35	43	18	4		42	40	18							6/30
William Carey University	Hattiesburg	SM	B,M		F,S	C	1,850																						6/30
Missouri																													
Avila University	Kansas City	SU	B,M	Pri	No	C	1,135																						Open
Central Methodist University	Fayette	SM	A,B,M	Pri	F,S	C	1,173																						Open
Chamberlain College of Nursing	St. Louis	U	A,B		No	C	400																						Open

College of the Ozarks	Point Lookout	SM	B	Pri	No	C	1,360																						Open
Columbia College	Columbia	U	A,B,M	Pri	No	C	953	23	25	28	25	11	10	483	58	33	8		535	33	42	17	8						8/13
Cox College	Springfield	U	A,B,M		No	C	600																						8/13
Culver-Stockton College	Canton	SM	B,M	Pri	F,S	C	830	21	51	26	15	5	3		53	40	7			33	67								Open
Drury University	Springfield	U	B,M	Pri	F,S	C	1,570	25	10	21	35	12	22		17	39	22	22		13	52	30	5		43	26	22	9	8/1
Evangel University	Springfield	U	A,B,M	Pri	No	C	1,879																					9	8/1
Fontbonne University	St. Louis	SU	B,M	Pri	No	C	2,085																					9	8/1
Hannibal-LaGrange University	Hannibal	SM	A,B,M	Pri	No	C	1,213		20	43	27	4	6																8/29
Harris-Stowe State University	St. Louis	U	B	Pub	No	C	1,298		88	11	2	1																	Open
Kansas City Art Institute	Kansas City	U	B	Pri	No	C	725																						2/1
Lincoln University	Jefferson City	SM	A,B,M	Pub	F,S	C	3,013	18	79	14	5	2		423	70	10	20		399	80	20								7/15
Lindenwood University	St. Charles	SU	B,M,D	Pri	F,S	C	5,905																						Open
Maryville University of Saint Louis	St. Louis	SU	B,M,D	Pri	No	C	2,829	25	7	28	31	21	13																Open
Missouri Baptist University	St. Louis	SU	A,B,M,D	Pri	No	C	3,950	22																					Open
Missouri Southern State University	Joplin	SM	A,B,M	Pub	F,S	C		21	18	53			29																Open
Missouri State University	Springfield	SU	B,M,D	Pub	F,S	C	17,434	24																					7/20
Missouri University of Science and Technology	Rolla	SM	B,M,D		F,S	C	6,146	28	1	8	26	19	46	590	14	35	36	15	640	5	21	54	21						7/1
Missouri Valley College	Marshall	SM	A,B	Pri	F,S	C	1,430																						Open
Missouri Western State University	St. Joseph	SU	A,B	Pub	F,S	C	5,250																						Open
Northwest Missouri State University	Maryville	SM	B,M	Pub	F,S	C	5,542	22	33	30	23	9	5	420					460										Open
Park University	Parkville	SU	A,B,M		No	C	1,674	21	50	29	9	5	7																Open
Research College of Nursing	Kansas City	U	B,M	Pri	F,S	C	330	23		33	37	17	13																6/30
Rockhurst University	Kansas City	U	B,M,D		F,S	C	2,325																						6/30
Saint Louis University	St. Louis	U	B,M,D	Pri	F,S	C	8,687	28	2	10	27	20	41		13	40	36	11		8	4	41	31						12/1
Southeast Missouri State University	Cape Girardeau	SM	A,B,M	Pub	F,S	C	10,755	23	31	30	20	9	9																7/1
Southwest Baptist University	Bolivar	SM	A,B,M,D	Pri	No	C	3,009																						Open
Stephens College	Columbia	U	A,B,M	Pri	S	PW	760																						Open
Truman State University	Kirksville	SM	B,M	Pub	F,S	C	5,468	27	3	14	29	16	38	600	12	40	34	14	610	12	28	49	11						3/1
University of Central Missouri	Warrensburg	SM	A,B,M	Pub	F,S	C	9,739	22	40	29	16	6	4																Open
University of Missouri/Columbia	Columbia	SU	B,M,D	Pub	F,S	C	26,996		6	23	31	18	23																5/1
University of Missouri-Kansas City	Kansas City	U	B,M,D	Pub	F,S	C	10,247	24	22	25	24	11	18						570	24	34	25	17	540	19	43	19	17	Open
University of Missouri-St. Louis	St. Louis	U	B,M,D	Pub	F,S	C	13,574	24	15	31	25	12	12	550	50	28	11	11	580	22	56	22		510	44	44	6	6	Open
Washington University in St. Louis	St. Louis	SU	A,B,M,D	Pri	F,S	C	7,336					1	99			1	24	75				11	89			1	24	75	1/15
Webster University	St. Louis	SU	B,M,D	Pri	S	C	2,962	24	25	24	24	12	15																8/1
Westminster College	Fulton	SM	B	Pri	F,S	C	1,044	24	17	28	27	13	14																Open
William Jewell College	Liberty	SU	B	Pri	F,S	C	1,030	26	9	22	25	18	26		24	30	39	7		21	34	39	11						8/15
William Woods University	Fulton	SM	A,B,M	Pri	F,S	C	1,069	23	37	22	20	9	12	560	30	39	29	2	510	44	44	12							Open

Montana

Carroll College	Helena	SM	A,B		No	C	1,550																						6/1
Montana State University	Bozeman	SM	B,M,D		F,S	C	11,579	24	21	24	23	13	19	550	27	39	27	6	560	24	39	29	7	540	31	43	21	4	Open
Montana State University-Billings	Billings	U	A,B,M	Pub	No	C	4,465	21	51	27	13	8	1	470	64	34	2		480	59	31	10							Open
Montana State University-Northern	Havre	SM	A,B,M	Pub	No	C	1,440																						Open
Montana Tech of The University of Montana	Butte	SM	A,B,M	Pub	No	C	2,757	24	14	31	31	12	12	545	25	44	26	4	610	11	31	46	13	530	38	36	24	3	Open
Rocky Mountain College	Billings	SU	A,B,M	Pri	No	C	988	22	32	30	24	9	2	510	43	38	17	2	500	46	36	16	3	480	58	34	8		Open
University of Great Falls	Great Falls	U	A,B,M		No	C	840																						Open
University of Montana	Missoula	U	A,B,M,D	Pub	F,S	C	12,254																						3/1
University of Montana-Western	Dillon	SM	A,B	Pub	No	C	1,255	20	62	23	13	3		460	68	20	10	2	470	63	29	8							7/1

Nebraska

Bellevue University	Bellevue	SU	B,M		No	C	3,775																						Open
Chadron State College	Chadron	SM	B,M	Pub	No	C	2,375																						Open
Clarkson College	Omaha	U	A,B,M	Pri	No	PW	770																						Open
College of Saint Mary	Omaha	U	A,B,M,D	Pri	No	PW	735	22	33	30	18	13	6																Open
Concordia University Nebraska	Seward	SM	B,M	Pri	No	C	1,085																						Open
Creighton University	Omaha	U	A,B,M,D	Pri	F,S	C	4,076	27	4	16	29	17	34	580	14	45	32	9	600	8	38	40	14	560	21	42	31	6	2/15
Doane College	Crete	SM	B	Pri	F,S	C	1,113	23	23	27	27	11	12																Open
Hastings College	Hastings	R	B,M	Pri	F,S	C	1,104	24	37	23	20	10	10																8/1
Midland University	Fremont	U	B,M	Pri	F,S	C	1,200																						Open
Nebraska Methodist College of Nursing and Allied Health	Omaha	SU	A,B,M	Pri	S	C	722		21	45	28	3	3																3/1
Nebraska Wesleyan University	Lincoln	SU	B,M	Pri	F,S	C	1,903	25	10	27	28	18	17																5/1
Peru State College	Peru	R	B,M	Pub	No	C	1,485																						Open

Header key: ENVIRONMENT: U-Urban R-Rural SU-Suburban SM-Small Town; DEGREES AWARDED: A-Associate B-Bachelor M-Master D-Doctorate; CONTROL: Pri-Private, Pub-Public; FRATERNITIES AND SORORITIES: F-Fraternities S-Sororities F, S-Both No-Neither; STUDENTS: C-Coed M-Men W-Women PM-Primarily Men PW-Primarily Women; UNDERGRADUATE ENROLLMENT FALL 2013; TEST SCORES; APPLICATION DEADLINE Month / Day

NAME OF SCHOOL	TOWN	Environment	Degrees Awarded	Control	Fraternities and Sororities	Students	Undergraduate Enrollment Fall 2013	ACT Median	ACT Below 21	ACT 21-23	ACT 24-26	ACT 27-28	ACT Above 28	SAT Critical Reading Median	SAT Critical Reading Below 500	SAT Critical Reading 500-599	SAT Critical Reading 600-700	SAT Critical Reading Above 700	SAT Mathematics Median	SAT Mathematics Below 500	SAT Mathematics 500-599	SAT Mathematics 600-700	SAT Mathematics Above 700	SAT Writing Median	SAT Writing Below 500	SAT Writing 500-599	SAT Writing 600-700	SAT Writing Above 700	Application Deadline Month / Day
Union College	Lincoln	SU	A,B,M	Pri	No	C	813	22																					Open
University of Nebraska - Lincoln	Lincoln	U	B,M,D	Pub	F,S	C	19,376	25	13	23	26	13	25	580	26	30	28	17	600	16	33	36	15						5/1
University of Nebraska at Kearney	Kearney	R	B,M	Pub	F,S	C	5,502	23	30	29	22	9	10		37	42	16	5		11	42	42	5						Open
University of Nebraska at Omaha	Omaha	SU	B,M,D	Pub	F,S	C	11,525																						8/1
Wayne State College	Wayne	R	B,M	Pub	F,S	C	2,991	21	45	26	15	8	6																Open
York College	York	SM	A,B	Pri	F,S	C	415																						Open
Nevada																													
Sierra Nevada College	Incline Village	R	B		No	C	195																						2/15
University of Nevada, Las Vegas	Las Vegas	U	B,M,D	Pub	F,S	C	22,708		16	52	15	14	3		50	36	13	1		42	38	17	3						2/1
University of Nevada/Reno	Reno	U	B,M,D	Pub	F,S	C	13,120																						2/1
New Hampshire																													
Colby-Sawyer College	New London	SM	A,B	Pri	No	C	1,440																						2/1
Daniel Webster College	Nashua	SU	A,B,M	Pri	No	C	725																						Open
Dartmouth College	Hanover	R	B,M,D	Pri	F,S	C	4,147								1	8	26	65			7	26	67		1	8	23	68	1/1
Franklin Pierce University	Rindge	R	A,B,M,D	Pri	No	C	1,687	21	9	72			19	480	58	36	6		480	54	37	7		470	63	32	5		Open
Granite State College	Concord	SM	A,B	Pub	No	C	1,518																						Open
Keene State College	Keene	SM	B,M	Pub	F,S	C	4,648							430	56	35	8	1	440	55	38	7	1	430	56	36	8		4/1
Mount Washington College	Manchester	SU	A,B	Pri	No	C	735																						4/1
New England College	Henniker	SM	A,B,M,D	Pri	F,S	C	1,635		40	40	20				69	25	5	1		68	29	3			78	15	7		Open
Plymouth State University	Plymouth	SM	B,M	Pub	S	C	4,064	20	59	20	14	4	1	479	62	31	7		484	57	34	8	1		65	30	5		4/1
Rivier College	Nashua	SU	A,B,M		No	C	1,630																						Open
Saint Anselm College	Manchester	SU	B	Pri	No	C	1,923	25	6	23	37	22	12	574	10	57	29	4	572	11	51	36	2	574	11	51	34	4	2/1
Southern New Hampshire University	Manchester	SU	A,B,M,D	Pri	F,S	C	1,995																					4	2/1
Thomas More College of Liberal Arts	Merrimack	SM	B	Pri	No	C	96																						Open
University of New Hampshire	Durham	SM	A,B,M,D		F,S	C	12,609	24	13	30	30	14	13	540	26	50	21	3	560	20	47	30	3	540	24	52	22	2	2/1
New Jersey																													
Berkeley College/New Jersey	Woodland Park	SU	A,B	Pri	No	C	3,052																						Open
Bloomfield College	Bloomfield	SU	B	Pri	F,S	C	1,969							421	86	13	1		435	83	14	2							8/1
Caldwell College	Caldwell	SU	B,M,D	Pri	No	C	1,705	21	46	31	20	3		490	60	30	9	1	480	50	37	12	1	490	52	39	9	1	Open
Centenary College	Hackettstown	SU	A,B,M	Pri	F,S	C	1,993	21	29	43	7	7	14	465	67	25	7	1	463	65	30	5							Open
College of New Jersey	Ewing	SU	B,M	Pub	F,S	C	6,653							610	7	38	43	12	640	4	27	51	18	620	8	32	44	16	1/15
College of Saint Elizabeth	Morristown	SU	B,M,D	Pri	No	PW	987							431	78	17	4	1	437	77	16	6	1	440	74	19	5	2	3/1
Drew University/College of Liberal Arts	Madison	SU	B,M,D	Pri	No	C	1,493	25	21	19	29	15	16	560	24	40	30	6	560	25	44	26	5						2/15
Fairleigh Dickinson University/College at Florham	Madison	SU	B,M	Pri	F,S	C	2,480							520	36	51	13	1	530	31	49	18	1	520	36	50	13	1	2/15
Fairleigh Dickinson University/Metropolitan Campus	Teaneck	SU	A,B,M,D	Pri	F,S	C	6,044							510	42	46	11		530	30	52	16	2	500	43	49	8		3/15
Felician College	Lodi	SU	A,B,M,D	Pri	No	C	1,621	17	68	20	8	4		435	85	13	2		440	76	21	2		420	84	13	2		Open
Georgian Court University	Lakewood	SU	B,M	Pri	No	C	1,567							440	73	24	3		450	69	26	4	1	440	73	24	3		8/1
Kean University	Union	SU	B,M,D	Pub	F,S	C	12,078																						5/31
Monmouth University	West Long Branch	SU	A,B,M,D	Pri	F,S	C	4,607	23	11	40	34	11	3	520	37	49	13	1	540	28	50	21	1	520	35	48	16	1	3/1
Montclair State University	Montclair	SU	B,M,D	Pub	F,S	C	14,432							487	58	34	7	1	502	48	42	9	1	497	52	39	8	1	3/1
New Jersey City University	Jersey City	U	B,M,D	Pub	F,S	C	6,438							450	72	25	3		480	60	34	6							4/1
New Jersey Institute of Technology	Newark	U	B,M,D	Pub	F,S	C	7,111							549	34	40	21	5	614	4	43	40	13	540	37	41	18	4	6/1
Princeton University	Princeton	SM	B,M,D	Pri	No	C	5,244	33			1	6	93	740		3	21	76	760		1	19	80	750		3	18	79	1/1
Ramapo College of New Jersey	Mahwah	SU	B,M	Pub	F,S	C		23	12	42	40		6	540	29	51	18	3	555	21	49	25	5	530	32	47	18	3	3/1
Richard Stockton College of New Jersey	Pomona	SU	B,M,D	Pub	F,S	C	6,790																					3	3/1
Rider University	Lawrenceville	SU	A,B,M	Pri	F,S	C	4,549	22						510	44	42	12	2	520	35	44	18	2	520	43	40	14	2	Open
Rowan University	Glassboro	SU	B,M,D	Pub	F,S	C	10,951							586	5	55	33	7	614	2	39	46	13	562	15	56	26	3	3/1
Rutgers, The State University of New Jersey/Camden Campus	Camden	U	B,M,D	Pub	No	C	4,842							520	37	47	15	1	540	28	53	16	3	510	39	48	12	1	Open

Rutgers, The State University of New Jersey/New Brunswick	Piscataway	U	A,B,M,D	Pub	F,S	C	33,900							590	7	44	37	12	640	2	28	45	25	610	5	40	40	15	Open
Rutgers, The State University of New Jersey/Newark Campus	Newark	U	B,M,D	Pub	No	C	7,217							510	37	49	12	2	550	21	48	26	5	520	33	50	14	3	Open
Saint Peter's College	Jersey City	U	A,B,M,D	Pri	No	C	2,317																						Open
Seton Hall University	South Orange	SU	B,M,D	Pri	F,S	C	5,148	23	20	33	27	8	13	530	29	49	21	1	540	26	49	24	2	550	24	43	26	2	Open
Stevens Institute of Technology	Hoboken	U	B,M,D	Pri	F,S	C	2,234	27		18		58	24	600	9	41	41	9	670		14	58	28	600	11	39	41	9	2/1
Thomas Edison State College	Trenton	U	A,B,M	Pub	No	C	19,596																						Open
Westminster Choir College	Princeton	SU	B,M	Pri	No	C	355																						Open
William Paterson University of New Jersey	Wayne	SU	B,M,D	Pub	F,S	C	10,089							517	49	39	9	2	526	42	46	12							6/1

New Mexico

Eastern New Mexico University	Portales	SM	A,B,M	Pub	F,S	C	4,572	21	56	25	15	2	2	470	60	23	9		490	54	33	9	1						Open
New Mexico Highlands University	Las Vegas	SM	A,B,M	Pub	No	C	2,396	18						430	76	23	1		435	76	19	6		430	81	19			Open
New Mexico Institute of Mining and Technology	Socorro	SM	A,B,M,D	Pub	No	C	1,425	27	5	21	24	20	30	600	13	34	36	17	630	5	32	43	20						8/1
New Mexico State University	Las Cruces	SM	A,B,M,D		F,S	C	13,582	21	47	26	16	7	4	470	57	33	9	1	480	56	32	11	1	460	66	27	6	1	Open
Santa Fe University of Art and Design	Santa Fe	SU	B	Pri	No	C	544																						Open
St. John's College, Santa Fe	Santa Fe	SU	B,M	Pri	No	C	349	28						680	4	19	29	48	630	20	21	40	19						Open
University of New Mexico	Albuquerque	U	A,B,M,D	Pub	F,S	C	20,852						7																6/15
University of the Southwest	Hobbs	SM	B,M	Pri	No	C	425																						Open
Western New Mexico University	Silver City	SM	A,B,M	Pub	F,S	C	660																						7/21

New York

Adelphi University	Garden City	SU	A,B,M,D	Pri	F,S	C	5,040	25						553	25	50	20	5	564	18	48	29	5	575	19	47	29	5	Open
Albany College of Pharmacy and Health Sciences	Albany	SM	B,M,D	Pri	F,S	C	1,075	26	4	18	29	21	28	570	11	52	36	2	610	2	35	55	8	570	14	50	32	4	2/1
Albert A. List College of Jewish Studies	New York	U	B		No	C	210																					4	2/1
Alfred State / SUNY College of Technology	Alfred	R	A,B	Pub	F,S	C		23						520					540					490					Open
Alfred University	Alfred	R	B,M,D	Pri	No	C	1,960	24	16	28	30	15	11	530	27	51	19	3	550	20	49	27	4	510	43	40	15	2	2/1
Bard College	Annandale-on-Hudson	R	A,B,M,D	Pri	No	C	2,022							650					620										1/1
Berkeley College	New York	U	A,B	Pri	No	C	2,622																						Open
Berkeley College/Westchester Campus	White Plains	SU	A,B		No	C	640																						Open
Binghamton University / The State University of New York	Binghamton	SU	B,M,D	Pub	F,S	C	12,997	29	1	5	14	25	55	630	5	25	55	15	670	1	13	54	32	620	3	21	56	20	Open
Boricua College	New York	U	A,B	Pri	No	C	1,170																						Open
Buffalo State/State University of Buffalo	Buffalo	U	B,M	Pub	F,S	C	9,822							480	57	36	7	1	490	51	41	8							Open
Canisius College	Buffalo	U	B,M	Pri	F,S	C	3,084	24	21	28	23	14	14	520	40	40	17	3	500	35	38	23	4						3/1
Cazenovia College	Cazenovia	SM	A,B	Pri	No	C	1,105																						Open
City University of New York/Baruch College	New York	U	B,M	Pub	F,S	C	14,082								12	48	31	8		1	21	50	27						2/1
City University of New York/Brooklyn College	Brooklyn	U	B,M	Pub	F,S	C	13,099								30	50	15	5		12	54	26	8						2/1
Clarkson University	Potsdam	R	B,M,D	Pri	F,S	C	3,110	26	4	20	32	20	24	560	15	50	28	7	620	5	31	51	13	550	23	50	22	4	1/15
Colgate University	Hamilton	R	B,M		F,S	C	2,825	30	1	3	9	13	76	661	4	12	47	37	680	2	11	45	42						1/15
College of Staten Island / The City University of New York	Staten Island	U	A,B,M,D	Pub	No	C	13,398							490	54	38	7	1	525	84	14	2		479	61	31	7	1	Open
College of Mount Saint Vincent	Riverdale	U	A,B,M	Pri	No	C	1,595																						4/2
College of New Rochelle - School of New Resources	New Rochelle	U	B	Pri	No	C	4,360																						8/15
Columbia University in the City of New York	New York	U	B,M,D	Pri	F,S	C	6,084	33				10	90	740		3	21	76	750		2	20	78	750		2	24	74	1/1
Columbia University/Barnard College	New York	U	B	Pri	No	W	2,355																						1/1
Columbia University/School of General Studies	New York	U	B	Pri	F,S	C	1,499				11		89		2	17	27	54			15	40	45			1	35	54	6/1
Concordia College New York	Bronxville	SU	A,B	Pri	F,S	C	735																						3/15
Cooper Union for the Advancement of Science and Art	New York	U	B,M	Pri	F	C	868	31				25	75	650	3	19	47	31	730	9	17	18	57						1/1
Cornell University	Ithaca	R	B,M,D	Pri	F,S	C	14,393									10	40	50			5	29	66						1/2
CUNY-City College	New York	U	B,M,D	Pub	F,S	C								510	9	67	17	7	550	14	43	31	12						12/1
Daemen College	Amherst	SU	B,M,D	Pri	F,S	C	1,685																						Open
Dominican College	Orangeburg	SU	A,B,M,D	Pri	No	C	1,677	18	32	58	5	5		451	77	20	2	1	451	75	21	4		448	75	21	3	1	Open
Dowling College	Oakdale	SU	B,M,D	Pri	No	C	3,435																						Open
D'Youville College	Buffalo	U	B,M,D	Pri	No	C	1,866	23	20	37	27	10	7	520	44	48	8		530	33	53	14	1	510	49	46	6		Open
Eastman School of Music	Rochester	U	B,M,D	Pri	F,S	C	505																						12/1
Elmira College	Elmira	SU	A,B,M	Pri	No	C	1,408	24	2	5	16	20	7	540	37	42	16	5	530	35	46	16	3						12/1
Eugene Lang College - The New School for Liberal Arts	New York	U	B	Pri	No	C	1,437	24	11	18	26	20	25	560	11	32	43	14	555	20	51	27	2	570	11	37	44	8	1/6
Excelsior College	Albany	SU	A,B,M	Pri	No	C	33,422																						Open
Farmingdale State College	Farmingdale	SU	A,B	Pub	F,S	C	8,163	22	27	45	21	7	1	497	54	40	5	1	534	28	54	17	1	485					Open
Fashion Institute of Technology/State University of New York	New York	U	A,B,M	Pub	No	C	10,710																						Open
Five Towns College	Dix Hills	SU	A,B,M,D	Pri	No	C	749	21	40	45	15			450	67	26	5	2	430	68	24	7	1	430	75	21	3	1	Open

NAME OF SCHOOL	TOWN	ENVIRONMENT U-Urban R-Rural SU-Suburban SM-Small Town	DEGREES AWARDED A-Associate B-Bachelor M-Master D-Doctorate	CONTROL Pri-Private, Pub-Public	FRATERNITIES AND SORORITIES F-Fraternities S-Sororities F, S-Both No-Neither	STUDENTS: C-Coed M-Men W-Women PM-Primarily Men PW-Primarily Women	UNDERGRADUATE ENROLLMENT FALL 2013	TEST SCORES: ACT Median	ACT Below 21	ACT 21-23	ACT 24-26	ACT 27-28	ACT Above 28	SAT CRITICAL READING Median	SAT CR Below 500	SAT CR 500-599	SAT CR 600-700	SAT CR Above 700	SAT MATHEMATICS Median	SAT M Below 500	SAT M 500-599	SAT M 600-700	SAT M Above 700	SAT WRITING Median	SAT W Below 500	SAT W 500-599	SAT W 600-700	SAT W Above 700	APPLICATION DEADLINE Month / Day
Fordham University	Bronx	U	B,M,D	Pri	No	C	8,325							620	5	31	48	16	640	3	26	51	20	630	4	27	50	19	Open
Hamilton College	Clinton	R	B	Pri	F,S	C	1,884	31	1	1	9	8	82	700	1	10	38	51	700	1	7	42	51	700	1	11	36	52	1/1
Hartwick College	Oneonta	SM	B	Pri	F,S	C	1,615	25					9	560	24	44	29	3	560	21	49	28	2	540	28	45	21	5	Open
Hilbert College	Hamburg	SU	A,B,M	Pri	No	C	1,019	21	49	30	16	5		460	64	36			470	58	34	7	1	450	78	19	3		Open
Hobart and William Smith Colleges	Geneva	SM	B,M		F	C	1,885																						2/1
Hofstra University	Hempstead	SU	B,M,D	Pri	F,S	C	6,893	25	2	24	35	20	19	580	9	51	36	4	590	7	48	40	5						2/1
Houghton College	Houghton	R	A,B,M	Pri	No	C	1,081	25	17	20	26	19	19	569	22	41	29	8	548	27	44	25	4	547	32	36	28	4	Open
Hunter College / The City University of New York	New York	U	B,M	Pub	F,S	C	16,638							574	12	54	26	8	598	3	50	37	10						Open
Iona College	New Rochelle	SU	B,M	Pri	F,S	C	3,462	22	28	37	20	6	10	500	49	41	9	1	500	44	42	13	2						2/15
Ithaca College	Ithaca	SM	B,M,D	Pri	F,S	C	6,234							590	9	46	38	7	590	9	44	41	6	590	11	41	41	7	2/1
John Jay College of Criminal Justice / The City University of New York	New York	U	B,M	Pub	No	C	13,217							460	71	25	4		480	59	34	7							Open
Juilliard School	New York	U	B,M,D	Pri	No	C	495																						12/1
Keuka College	Keuka Park	R	B,M		No	C	1,829		79				2		59	36	5			61	31	8			73	26	1		12/1
Le Moyne College	Syracuse	SU	B,M	Pri	No	C	2,785	24	18	29	24	11	18	540	34	46	17	3	550	22	47	24	7						3/1
Lehman College / The City University of New York	Bronx	U	B,M	Pub	No	C	9,577							470	67	26	5	2	490	51	38	9	2	460	69	24	5	2	3/1
LIM College	New York	SM	A,B,M	Pri	No	C	1,357	20	58	29	13			483	61	34	5		474	67	28	5							Open
Long Island University/Brooklyn Campus	Brooklyn	U	A,B,M,D	Pri	F,S	C	5,370																						Open
Long Island University/C.W. Post Campus	Brookville	SU	A,B,M,D		F,S	C	6,600	21	44	27	10	4		520	62	30	7	1	500	55	33	11	1	510	63	30	7		Open
Manhattan College	Riverdale	U	B,M	Pri	F,S	C	3,351	24	16	27	30	12	15	526	38	44	16	2	535	29	40	27	4	528	35	45	19	2	3/1
Manhattan School of Music	New York	U	B,M,D		F,S	C	430																					2	3/1
Manhattanville College	Purchase	SU	B,M	Pri	No	C	1,842	24	25	33	26	8	8	530	5	74	20	1	540	5	67	26	2						Open
Mannes College New School for Music	New York	U	B,M	Pri	No	C	210																						12/1
Marist College	Poughkeepsie	SU	B,M	Pri	F,S	C	4,875																						2/15
Maritime College / State University of New York	Throgs Neck	SU	A,B,M	Pub	No	C	1,575	22	35	40	16	4	5	510	42	45	11	2	550	20	52	26	2						2/15
Marymount Manhattan College	New York	U	A,B	Pri	S	C	1,945																						Open
Medaille College	Buffalo	U	A,B,M	Pri	No	C	1,843	21						460	80	17	2	1	460	72	22	6							Open
Medgar Evers College / The City University of New York	Brooklyn	U	A,B	Pub	No	C	7,081							380	91	8	1		380	92	8			380	93	6	1		Open
Mercy College	Dobbs Ferry	SU	A,B,M,D	Pri	No	C	8,154																						Open
Metropolitan College of New York	New York	U	A,B,M	Pri	No	C	676																						Open
Molloy College	Rockville Centre	SU	A,B,M,D	Pri	No	C	3,375	23	27	33	27	8	5	520	34	53	13	1	540	25	55	20	1	520	39	45	15	1	Open
Monroe College	Bronx		A,B,M	Pri	No	C	5,480																						8/15
Mount Saint Mary College	Newburgh	SU	B,M	Pri	No	C	2,203	22	33	41	18	7	2	503	50	40	9	1	508	44	45	10	1	494	53	38	9		Open
Nazareth College of Rochester	Rochester	SU	B,M,D	Pri	No	C	2,034	25	15	26	31	14	14	540	29	49	20	2	540	24	49	23	4	520	33	45	19	3	2/1
New York City College of Technology / The City University of New York	Brooklyn	U	A,B	Pub	No	C	16,207																						2/1
New York Institute of Technology	Old Westbury	SU	A,B,M,D	Pri	F,S	C	4,796	25						533	29	48	17	4	593	8	45	36	11						2/1
New York University	New York	U	A,B,M,D	Pri	F,S	C	22,615	30		1	10	18	71	670	1	14	50	35	680	1	13	43	43	680	1	10	47	42	1/1
Niagara University	Niagara University	SU	A,B,M,D	Pri	F,S	C	3,227	23	25	34	30	7	4	510	44	43	12	1	510	41	45	13	1	490	54	36	9	1	1/1
Nyack College	Nyack	SU	A,B,M,D	Pri	No	C	1,831																						Open
Oswego / State University of New York	Oswego	SM	B,M	Pub	F,S	C	7,628	24	11	40	29	15	5	540	22	58	18	2	560	16	59	23	2						1/15
Pace University	New York	U	A,B,M,D	Pri	F,S	C	8,289		6	33	33	15	13	547	20	58	20	2	548	22	54	22	2						2/15
Parsons The New School for Design	New York	U	A,B,M	Pri	No	C	4,260		29	24	32	7	8		32	41	25	2		28	43	26	3		28	49	22	2	Open
Polytechnic Institute of New York University	Brooklyn	U	B,M,D	Pri	F,S	C	2,071	28			25	26	48	600	11	38	40	11	680	1	10	45	44	600	9	40	41	10	Open
Pratt Institute	Brooklyn	U	A,B,M	Pri	F,S	C	3,021	26	3	16	37	23	21	585	14	38	39	9	605	10	31	47	12	595	7	41	44	8	1/5
Purchase College / State University of New York	Purchase	SU	B,M	Pub	No	C	3,830																						8/15
Queens College / The City University of New York	Flushing	U	B,M	Pub	F,S	C	15,351							540	35	47	13	5	574	6	60	28	6		39	45	13	4	8/15
Rensselaer Polytechnic Institute	Troy	SU	B,M,D	Pri	F,S	C	5,452	29		5	18	21	56	660	1	17	48	34	720		3	33	64						1/15
Roberts Wesleyan College	Rochester	SU	A,B,M		No	C	1,323	24	23	18	18	23	18	542	35	39	21	5	533	40	39	17	4		51	31	14	4	2/1
Rochester Institute of Technology	Rochester	SU	A,B,M,D	Pri	F,S	C	14,224		2	12	23	34	29		12	42	37	9		6	33	45	16		20	45	30	5	3/1
Russell Sage College	Troy	U	B,M	Pri	No	W	823	22						500					500									5	3/1
Sarah Lawrence College	Bronxville	SU	B,M	Pri	No	C	1,330																					5	3/1
School of Visual Arts	New York	U	B,M		No	C	3,335																						2/1
Siena College	Loudonville	SU	B,M	Pri	No	C	3,161	25	16	24	27	13	20	540	31	44	20	5	550	29	38	27	6	530	30	45	22	3	2/15
Skidmore College	Saratoga Springs	SM	B,M	Pri	No	C	2,684	28	2	8	19	28	43	620	7	31	43	9	620	4	34	45	17	630	5	29	46	20	1/15
St. Bonaventure University	St. Bonaventure	SM	B,M	Pri	No	C	1,959	23	27	25	26	9	13	520	38	42	18	2	530	32	45	20	3	510	41	41	14	4	7/1

St. Francis College	Brooklyn	U	A,B,M	Pri	F,S	C	2,764							474	67	28	5		472	66	29	5							4/1
St. John Fisher College	Rochester	SU	B,M,D	Pri	No	C	2,959	24	7	33	34	21	6	520	34	52	14	1	550	45	42	12	1	510	45	42	12	1	Open
St. John's University	Queens	SU	A,B,M,D	Pri	F,S	C	15,773	24	20	30	25	10	15	540	29	48	20	3	550	24	43	24	9						Open
St. Joseph's College, New York / Brooklyn Campus	Brooklyn	U	B,M	Pri	F,S	C	1,231	23	29	21	43	4	4	490	53	40	8		480	53	38	8	1	470	59	30	10	1	8/15
St. Joseph's College, New York / Suffolk Campus	Patchogue	SU	B,M	Pri	F,S	C	3,298	23	20	34	29	13	4	520	34	50	15	1	540	23	52	21	3	510	40	46	14	1	8/15
St. Lawrence University	Canton	SM	B,M	Pri	F,S	C	2,361							618	3	35	50	12	602		3	60	9	620	6	32	49	12	2/1
St. Thomas Aquinas College	Sparkill	SU	A,B,M		No	C	2,120																					12	2/1
State University of New York / College of Environmental Science and Forestry	Syracuse	U	A,B,M,D	Pub	F,S	C	2,177	25	6	29	35	21	9	584	7	50	37	6	600	5	44	46	5					12	2/1
State University of New York Institute of Technology at Utica / Rome	Utica	SU	B,M	Pub	No	C	1,688	22	2	29	29		3	510	42	40	14	1	550	19	50	25	3						8/1
State University of New York/Empire State College	Saratoga Springs		A,B,M	Pub	No	C	10,851																						6/1
Stony Brook University / State University of New York	Stony Brook	SU	B,M,D	Pub	F,S	C	16,159	28	1	5	28	24	42	600	7	37	45	11	660	1	16	57	26	610	7	37	46	10	1/15
SUNY College at Geneseo	Geneseo	SM	B,M	Pub	F,S	C	5,388	28	4			81	15	630	6	24	49	21	639	6	19	57	18						1/1
SUNY College at Old Westbury	Old Westbury	SU	B,M	Pub	F,S	C	4,158							490	55	39	5	1		40	50	10			64	32	4		Open
SUNY Cortland / The State University of New York	Cortland	SM	B,M	Pub	F,S	C																							Open
SUNY Fredonia / The State University of New York at Fredonia	Fredonia	SM	B,M	Pub	F,S	C	5,129	24	8	39	31	12	10	540	28	54	16	2	545	23	58	17	3						Open
SUNY New Paltz	New Paltz	SM	B,M	Pub	F,S	C	6,130																						4/1
SUNY Oneonta / State University of New York	Oneonta	R	B,M	Pub	F,S	C	5,863	24						538	23	62	14	1	563	14	59	25	2						Open
SUNY Plattsburgh / State University of New York	Plattsburgh	SU	B,M	Pub	F,S	C	5,639		19	42	25	10	4	525	33	51	14	2	535	25	53	21	1						8/1
Syracuse University	Syracuse	U	A,B,M,D	Pri	F,S	C	15,097								21	45	29	5		12	37	40	11		18	43	33	6	1/1
The College at Brockport / State University of New York	Brockport	SM	B,M	Pub	F,S	C	7,138	23	12	36	32	13	6	530	6	57	15	2	550	17	57	24	2	510	40	48	12		Open
The College of New Rochelle	New Rochelle	SU	B,M	Pri	No	PW	1,025																						8/15
The College of Saint Rose	Albany	U	B,M	Pri	No	C	2,891	23	28	23	28	11	11	520	37	44	17	2	520	35	47	16	3						2/1
The State University of New York at Potsdam	Potsdam	R	B,M	Pub	F,S	C	3,707	23	34	19	27	7	13	520	38	41	16	5	520	37	44	18	1						Open
The State University of New York College of Agriculture and Tech at Cobleskill	Cobleskill	R	A,B	Pub	No	C	2,470	20	52	32	9	6	1	440	73	22	4	1	440	73	23	4							Open
Touro College	New York	U	A,B,M,D	Pri	No	C	9,740	24	3	45	31	13	8	580	8	46	34	12	550	17	48	27	8	560	15	44	32	9	Open
Union College	Schenectady	SM	B	Pri	F,S	C	2,246								3	25	54	18			12	49	38			25	54	21	1/15
United States Merchant Marine Academy	Kings Point	SU	B,M	Pub	No	C	987			2	35	35	28	614	4	40	45	11	643		15	66	19						3/1
United States Military Academy	West Point	SM	B	Pub	No	C	4,175																						3/1
University at Albany / SUNY	Albany	SU	B,M,D	Pub	F,S	C	12,542	24	8	33	35	14	10	540	25	59	15	2	560	16	54	26	4						8/1
University at Buffalo / The State University of New York	Buffalo	SU	B,M,D	Pub	F,S	C	19,505	26						550	23	50	23	4	601	8	40	40	12						8/1
University of Rochester	Rochester	SU	B,M,D	Pri	F,S	C	6,177																						1/1
Utica College	Utica	SU	B,M,D	Pri	F,S	C	2,881						22		69	26	4	1		60	32	6	1		72	24	3	1	Open
Vassar College	Poughkeepsie	SU	B,M	Pri	No	C	2,406	31			2	11	87	704		7	35	58	690		5	48	47	700		7	38	54	1/1
Vaughn College of Aeronautics and Technology	Flushing	U	A,B,M	Pri	No	C	1,799	22	16	67			17	498	54	37	8	1	547	25	48	24	3						Open
Wagner College	Staten Island	SU	B,M	Pri	F,S	C	1,818	25	5	28	42	17	8	560	9	42	42	7	540	10	40	42	7	530	11	39	42	7	2/15
Webb Institute	Glen Cove	SU	B		No	C	85																					7	2/15
Wells College	Aurora	SM	B	Pri	No	C	560																					7	2/15
Yeshiva University	New York	U	A,B		No	C	2,869	26						619	6	35	39	20	622	5	35	40	20	610	6	37	40	17	2/15
York College / City University of New York	Jamaica	U	B,M	Pub	No	C	8,350													71	25	3							Open

North Carolina

Appalachian State University	Boone	SM	B,M,D	Pub	F,S	C	15,712	26	3	14	47	19	17	572	11	55	30	4	581	6	52	38	4	548	22	55	21	2	3/15
Barton College	Wilson	SU	B	Pri	F,S	C	1,150	19	85	17	4	2		460	74	21	4	1	470	67	24	7	2						Open
Belmont Abbey College	Belmont	SU	B	Pri	F,S	C	1,706	23	27	33	28	4	7	510	54	29	13	3	510	42	39	17	2						Open
Bennett College	Greensboro	U	B	Pri	S	W	766								90	10	1			92		8							Open
Cabarrus College of Health Sciences	Concord	SU	A,B	Pri	No	C	355																						Open
Campbell University	Buies Creek	R	A,B,M,D	Pri	No	C	2,945																						Open
Catawba College	Salisbury	SM	B,M	Pri	No	C	1,298	21	45	28	16	6	4	490	60	31	6	3	500	55	32	12	1						Open
Davidson College	Davidson	SM	B	Pri	F,S	C	1,788	31		1	6	10	83	675	1	13	47	39	660	3	20	46	31	660	2	18	47	33	1/2
Duke University	Durham	SU	B,M,D	Pri	F,S	C	6,270																					33	1/2
East Carolina University	Greenville	U	B,M,D	Pub	F,S	C	21,298	22	18	55	19	6	3	510	49	43	7	1	540	32	55	12	1	490	57	37	6		3/15
Elizabeth City State University	Elizabeth City	SM	B,M	Pub	F,S	C	3,395								89	10	1			83	16	1			92	8			Open
Elon University	Elon	SU	B,M,D	Pri	F,S	C	5,599	27	4	11	29	24	32	610	8	43	40	9	612	8	36	48	8	610	8	38	43	11	1/10
Fayetteville State University	Fayetteville	U	B,M,D	Pub	F,S	C	5,287																					11	1/10
Gardner-Webb University	Boiling Springs	SM	A,B,M,D	Pri	No	C	2,572		36	31	19	8	6		47	39	13	1		45	38	16	1						Open
Greensboro College	Greensboro	U	B,M	Pri	F,S	C	1,066								70	24	5	1		63	26	11							Open
Guilford College	Greensboro	SU	B	Pri	No	C	2,462	23	24	28	24	10	14	550	29	41	25	5	540	29	47	21	3	520	36	37	23	4	2/15
High Point University	High Point	SU	B,M,D	Pri	F,S	C	3,964	22	28	37	24	7	5	530	30	52	16	2	545	32	49	18	1	530	31	52	16	1	3/15
Johnson and Wales University/Charlotte Campus	Charlotte	U	A,B	Pri	No	C	2,537																						Open
Johnson C. Smith University	Charlotte	U	B	Pri	F,S	C	1,387	17	87	9	4			420	83	14	2		420	90	9	1							Open
Lees-McRae College	Banner Elk	R	B	Pri	No	C	890								59	34	6	1		53	35	12							Open

NAME OF SCHOOL	TOWN	ENVIRONMENT U-Urban R-Rural SU-Suburban SM-Small Town	DEGREES AWARDED A-Associate B-Bachelor M-Master D-Doctorate	CONTROL Pri-Private, Pub-Public	FRATERNITIES AND SORORITIES F-Fraternities S-Sororities F, S-Both No-Neither	STUDENTS: C-Coed M-Men W-Women PM-Primarily Men PW-Primarily Women	UNDERGRADUATE ENROLLMENT FALL 2013	ACT Median	ACT Below 21	ACT 21-23	ACT 24-26	ACT 27-28	ACT Above 28	SAT CRITICAL READING Median	SAT CRITICAL READING Below 500	SAT CRITICAL READING 500-599	SAT CRITICAL READING 600-700	SAT CRITICAL READING Above 700	SAT MATHEMATICS Median	SAT MATHEMATICS Below 500	SAT MATHEMATICS 500-599	SAT MATHEMATICS 600-700	SAT MATHEMATICS Above 700	SAT WRITING Median	SAT WRITING Below 500	SAT WRITING 500-599	SAT WRITING 600-700	SAT WRITING Above 700	APPLICATION DEADLINE Month / Day
Lenoir-Rhyne College	Hickory	SU	B,M		F,S	C	1,564	21	74	6	17	2	1	480	57	33	10		500	46	39	14	1						Open
Livingstone College	Salisbury	SM	B		F,S	C	895	15																					6
Mars Hill College	Mars Hill	R	B		F,S	C	1,250																						Open
Meredith College	Raleigh	U	B,M	Pri	No	W	1,967	21	47	24	21	5	6	519	41	42	16	1	520	39	43	17	1						2/15
Methodist University	Fayetteville	SU	A,B,M	Pri	F,S	C	2,280	21	50	30	10	6	4	484	59	34	6	1	510	45	40	14	1	466	60	33	6	1	Open
Montreat College	Montreat	R	A,B,M	Pri	No	C								475	20	73	7	1	466	16	76	7	1	445					Open
Mount Olive College	Mount Olive	SM	A,B		No	C	3,116																						Open
North Carolina Agricultural and Technical State University	Greensboro	U	B,M,D	Pub	F,S	C	8,872	18	44	49	6			450	78	20	2		460	72	24	4		16	88	11		1	Open
North Carolina Central University	Durham	U	B,M	Pub	F,S	C	5,300																					1	Open
North Carolina State University	Raleigh	U	A,B,M,D		F,S	C	24,833	26						590	7	47	28	8	630	3	27	54	16	570	13	52	30	5	11/1
North Carolina Wesleyan College	Rocky Mount	SU	B	Pri	F,S	C	1,756																						Open
Pfeiffer University	Misenheimer	R	B,M	Pri	No	C	955	20	55	32	7	5		460	63	31	6		500	49	40	11		450	71	26	2	1	8/25
Queens University of Charlotte	Charlotte	SU	B,M	Pri	F,S	C	1,703	24	22	26	29	13	10	520	41	44	11	3	520	39	43	17	1	510	45	37	15	3	Open
Saint Augustine's University	Raleigh	U	B		F,S	C	1,360																					3	Open
Salem College	Winston-Salem	U	B,M	Pri	No	PW	871	28																					Open
Shaw University	Raleigh	U	A,B,M	Pri	F,S	C	2,572																						7/30
St. Andrews University	Laurinburg	SM	B,M	Pri	No	C	460	19					2	460	67	27	4		480	66	29	5							Open
University of North Carolina at Asheville	Asheville	U	B,M	Pub	F,S	C	3,693	25	5	22	39	17	18	600	7	41	42	11	590	5	46	42	7	570	15	47	31	6	2/15
University of North Carolina at Chapel Hill	Chapel Hill	SU	B,M,D	Pub	F,S	C	18,370	29	1	7	19	19	53	640	3	24	47	27	660	2	19	49	30	640	4	24	47	24	1/7
University of North Carolina at Charlotte	Charlotte	SU	B,M,D	Pub	F,S	C	21,503	22	28	35	24	7	6	520	36	50	13	1	540	21	53	23	3	500	44	46	9	1	7/1
University of North Carolina at Greensboro	Greensboro	U	B,M,D	Pub	F,S	C	14,674							510	44	42	12	2	520	40	46	12	2	500	54	36	9	1	3/1
University of North Carolina at Wilmington	Wilmington	SU	B,M,D	Pub	F,S	C	11,770	26	10	30	39	14	8	592	6	56	35	3	605	4	50	42	4	561	16	56	26	2	2/1
University of North Carolina School of the Arts	Winston-Salem	U	B,M	Pub	No	C	781																						3/1
Wake Forest University	Winston-Salem	SU	B,M,D	Pri	F,S	C	4,815			5	31	31	64		3	13	55	27		1	11	52	35						1/15
Warren Wilson College	Asheville	SM	B,M	Pri	No	C	906							599	12	38	38	12	540	27	50	22	1	571	19	41	35	5	1/15
Western Carolina University	Cullowhee	R	B,M,D	Pub	F,S	C	7,979	22	34	38	16	6	6	515	43	43	13	1	526	36	47	16	1	486	60	32	7	1	3/1
William Peace University	Raleigh	U	B	Pri	S	C	791	18	64	10	15	3	8	440	72	23	5		440	73	24	3							Open
Wingate University	Wingate	SM	B,M,D	Pri	F,S	C	1,773	22	34	35	19	6	6	500	49	39	11	1	520	37	42	21	1	490	53	37	9	1	Open
Winston-Salem State University	Winston-Salem	SU	B,M	Pub	F,S	C	5,458												440	78	12	1		420	79	7	1		Open
North Dakota																													
Dickinson State University	Dickinson	R	A,B	Pub	No	C	2,669	22	51	25	15	3	3																Open
Mayville State University	Mayville	R	A,B	Pub	No	C	1,036	19	68	20	7	3	2																Open
Minot State University	Minot	SM	A,B,M	Pub	No	C	3,298																						Open
North Dakota State University	Fargo	U	B,M,D	Pub	F,S	C	11,948	23						557	26	39	27	8	569	25	37	29	9	523	42	36	17	5	Open
University of Jamestown	Jamestown	SM	B,M,D	Pri	No	C	938	22	32	32	24	8	4	498	55	28	13	2	495	57	28	11	2						Open
University of Mary	Bismarck	SU	B,M	Pri	No	C	2,060	23	27	33	27	8	5																8/15
University of North Dakota	Grand Forks	U	B,M,D	Pub	F,S	C	11,724	23	18	31	26	8	11																7/1
Valley City State University	Valley City	SM	B,M	Pub	F,S	C	1,211	20	58	24	12	4	2	444	90		10		460	56	27	17							Open
Ohio																													
Art Academy of Cincinnati	Cincinnati	U	A,B,M	Pri	No	C	138	21	43	36	14		7	550	33	50	6	1	460	68	26	6		500	47	47		6	6/30
Ashland University	Ashland	SM	A,B,M,D		F,S	C	2,785																						Open
Baldwin Wallace University	Berea	SU	B,M	Pri	F,S	C	3,425	24	20	24	28	15	13	540	33	39	20	8	540	31	46	20	3						Open
Bluffton University	Bluffton	SM	B,M	Pri	No	C	1,077	22	45	26	19	5	6	495	48	33	11	8	510	51	23	20	3						5/31
Bowling Green State University	Bowling Green	SM	B,M,D	Pub	F,S	C	14,477	23	28	32	25	9	7	510	42	42	14	1	510	40	46	13	1	490	52	40	8	1	7/15
Capital University	Columbus	SU	B,M,D	Pri	F,S	C	2,720	24	17	29	25	15	14	545	33	39	21	7	542	30	40	24	6	545	44	36	16	4	7/15
Case Western Reserve University	Cleveland	U	B,M,D	Pri	F,S	C	4,661	31			9	12	79	660	1	22	44	33	720		5	32	63	670		16	50	34	1/15
Cedarville University	Cedarville	SM	B,M,D	Pri	No	C	3,220	26	7	19	29	19	26	590	10	41	35	14	600	13	37	40	10	580	16	42	32	11	Open
Central State University	Wilberforce	R	B,M	Pub	F,S	C	1,335																					11	Open
Chancellor University	Cleveland	U	A,B,M		No	C	1,105																						Open
Cincinnati College of Mortuary Science	Cincinnati	U	A,B		No	C	137																						Open

Cleveland Institute of Art	Cleveland	U	B	Pri	F,S	C	568	22	33	28	17	10	12	550	27	40	28	5	520	41	32	22	5	500	44	32	22	2	3/1
Cleveland Institute of Music	Cleveland	U	B,M,D	Pri	No	C	240																					2	3/1
Cleveland State University	Cleveland	U	B,M,D	Pub	F,S	C	12,376	22						510	43	40	16	2	520	39	39	20	2					2	3/1
College of Mount Saint Joseph	Cincinnati	SU	A,B,M,D	Pri	No	C	1,795	22	40	29	22	6	3	475	62	30	7	1	468	61	30	9						2	3/1
College of Wooster	Wooster	SU	B	Pri	F,S	C	1,820																					2	3/1
Columbus College of Art and Design	Columbus	U	B,M	Pri	No	C	1,333	22	40	23	22	9	6	540	33	37	27	3	570	39	42	18	1	570	49	37	14		8/15
Defiance College	Defiance	SM	A,B,M	Pri	F,S	C	957	22	42	25	22	6	3	470	60	32	8		490	48	48	4		430	72	28			Open
Denison University	Granville	SM	B	Pri	F,S	C	2,336	29	1	1	13	36	49	647	3	22	44	31	639		37	42	21						1/15
Franciscan University of Steubenville	Steubenville	SM	A,B,M	Pri	S	C	2,040																						1/15
Franklin University	Columbus	U	A,B,M		No	C	7,055																						Open
Heidelberg University	Tiffin	SM	B,M	Pri	F,S	C	1,110	22	48	24	16	7	5	420	51	35	12	2	490	52	35	13		400	60	30	9	2	8/1
Hiram College	Hiram	R	B,M	Pri	No	C	1,380																						Open
John Carroll University	University Heights	SU	B,M	Pri	F,S	C		24	14	25	32	14	15	540	28	48	21	3	550	21	51	26	2	540	29	45	24	2	2/1
Kent State University	Kent	SU	A,B,M,D	Pub	F,S	C	22,968	22	26	35	23	9	7	520	35	44	18	3	520	35	45	18	2	500	44	41	14	2	Open
Kenyon College	Gambier	R	B	Pri	F,S	C	1,705	30					61	680	1	15	43	42	650	1	22	56	22	670	1	13	49	37	1/15
Lake Erie College	Painesville	SM	B,M	Pri	F,S	C	1,034	21	49	13	10	5	7	485	52	33	9	5	510	41	50	6	2	460	62	26	9	1	8/1
Lourdes University	Sylvania	SU	A,B,M	Pri	No	C	2,118	20	63	25	10	3		422	79	21			438	80	13	7							Open
Malone University	Canton	SU	B,M	Pri	No	C	1,656	22	36	26	19	7	13	520	36	44	16	5	510	38	47	16							Open
Marietta College	Marietta	SM	A,B,M	Pri	F,S	C	1,487	24	23	27	23	13	15	539	33	40	25	2	555	27	36	34	3	517	40	42	17	1	4/15
Miami University	Oxford	SM	A,B,M,D	Pub	F,S	C	15,071	27	3	13	33	21	29	580	11	46	34	9	610	7	35	45	13						2/1
Mount Vernon Nazarene University	Mount Vernon	SM	A,B,M	Pri	No	C	1,756	23	26	28	20	15	12	493	34	39	20	6	524	39	37	24							5/1
Muskingum University	New Concord	SM	B,M	Pri	F,S	C	1,741	22	40	28	19	6	6	491	50	43	5	2	513	45	36	14	5						5/1
Notre Dame College	South Euclid	SU	A,B,M	Pri	No	C	1,363																						Open
Oberlin College	Oberlin	SM	B,M	Pri	No	C	2,930	30		4		38	58	700	1	9	41	49	670	1	13	48	38	700	1	11	47	41	1/15
Ohio Dominican University	Columbus	U	A,B,M	Pri	No	C	2,005		33	33	22	7	4		53	23	14	5		35	42	23							Open
Ohio Northern University	Ada	SM	B,D		F,S	C	2,305																						Open
Ohio State University at Lima	Lima	SU	A,B,M	Pub	No	C	1,059	22						480	39	39	18	4	520	48	26	26		450	48	39	13		Open
Ohio State University at Mansfield	Mansfield	U	A,B,M	Pub	No	C	1,155	22	38	28	16	16	2	530	41	49	10		520	34	38	23	5	490	62	28	10		Open
Ohio State University at Marion	Marion	R	A,B,M	Pub	No	C		29		6			94	600	13	32	41	14	665	2	18	46	34	605	9	35	44	12	Open
Ohio State University at Newark	Newark	SU	A,B,M	Pub	No	C	2,263	22						500	45	42	10	3	510	46	35	17	2	480	59	30	10	1	Open
Ohio University	Athens	SM	A,B,M,D	Pub	F,S	C	23,519	24	14	34	30	11	11	540	30	44	20	6	540	28	46	22	4	520	35	44	19	2	2/1
Ohio University at Lancaster	Lancaster		B		No																							2	2/1
Ohio Wesleyan University	Delaware	SM	B	Pri	F,S	C	1,821	26	11	23	26	19	25	569	20	44	26	10	581	13	41	36	10						3/1
Otterbein College	Westerville	SU	B,M	Pri	F,S	C	2,715	23	31	29	24	9	7	530	35	41	22	2	531	33	43	22	2	527					3/1
Shawnee State University	Portsmouth	SM	A,B,M	Pub	F,S	C	4,255	20	54	23	15	5	3	510	44	33	21	2	515	44	31	25		460	65	33	2		Open
The Ohio State University	Columbus	U	A,B,M,D	Pub	F,S	C	44,201	29					38	600	13	32	41	14	660	2	18	46	34	600	9	35	44	12	5/1
Tiffin University	Tiffin	SM	A,B,M	Pri	F,S	C	3,764	20	50	25	15	6	4	480	54	39	5	2	480	54	39	7							Open
Union Institute & University	Cincinnati	SM	B,M,D	Pri	No	C	1,129																						10/1
University of Akron	Akron	U	A,B,M,D	Pub	F,S	C	20,581	21	41	24	17	8	10	520	38	39	20	3	540	34	36	25	5						8/11
University of Cincinnati	Cincinnati	U	A,B,M,D	Pub	F,S	C	22,893	24	8	29	32	15	16	560	24	44	25	7	580	18	40	34	9	535	32	44	19	5	7/31
University of Dayton	Dayton	SU	B,M,D	Pri	F,S	C	8,069	26	4	18	30	20	28	560	20	48	26	6	590	15	39	38	8	580	19	40	31	10	7/31
University of Findlay	Findlay	SM	A,B,M,D	Pri	F,S	C	4,004	23	16	31	27	15	11	510	37	45	16	2	530	31	46	21	2	515	36	41	19	4	8/1
University of Mount Union	Alliance	SU	B,M	Pri	F,S	C	2,175	22	30	34	18	11	7																Open
University of Rio Grande	Rio Grande	R	A,B,M		F,S	C	1,855																						Open
University of Toledo	Toledo	U	A,B,M,D	Pub	F,S	C	16,877	22	41	25	19	8	6																Open
Urbana University	Urbana	SM	A,B,M	Pri	No	C	1,457																						Open
Ursuline College	Pepper Pike	SU	B,M,D	Pri	No	PW	953	20	56	26	15	2	2	456	68	21	11		459	74	21	5		441	74	21	5		Open
Walsh University	North Canton	SM	A,B,M,D	Pri	No	C	2,385	22	30	31	23	10	6	500	50	36	13	1	530	34	47	19							Open
Wilberforce University	Wilberforce	R	B,M		F,S	C	800																						Open
Wilmington College	Wilmington	SM	B,M	Pri	F,S	C	1,395	21	20	59	10	10	1	510	61	28	9	1	550	49	35	16							Open
Wittenberg University	Springfield	SU	B,M	Pri	F,S	C	1,959	26	6	21	34	19	20	560	15	51	24	10	580	16	41	39	4						3/15
Wright State University	Dayton	SU	A,B,M,D	Pub	F,S	C	13,143	21	46	25	17	7	5	499	49	35	12	4	503	47	32	18	3	481	56	34	9	1	Open
Xavier University	Cincinnati	SM	A,B,M,D	Pri	No	C	4,652	25	13	29	30	14	14	550	23	50	21	6	560	19	47	29	5		29	47	21	3	2/1
Youngstown State University	Youngstown	SM	A,B,M,D	Pub	F,S	C	12,172	20	52	24	13	5	6	460	64	28	6	2	470	61	26	12	1	440	72	21	6	1	8/1

Oklahoma

Cameron University	Lawton	SU	A,B,M	Pub	F,S	C	5,362	19	59	22	13	3	3																Open
East Central University	Ada	SM	B,M	Pub	F,S	C	3,757	20	52	23	16	5	3																Open
Langston University	Langston	R	A,B,M	Pub	F,S	C	4,020																						Open
Northeastern State University	Tahlequah	SM	B,M,D	Pub	F,S	C	8,659	24																					Open
Northwestern Oklahoma State University	Alva	SM	B,M	Pub	F,S	C	1,809	19	68	22	8	1	1																Open
Oklahoma Baptist University	Shawnee	SM	A,B,M	Pri	F,S	C	2,019	24	21	27	25	12	15	536	32	40	23	5	536	25	47	25	3						8/1
Oklahoma Christian University	Oklahoma City	SU	B,M	Pri	No	C	1,966	25	17	26	22	20	15	520	37	32	24	7	535	36	35	20	9	510					Open
Oklahoma City University	Oklahoma City	U	B,M,D	Pri	F,S	C	1,768	25	11	20	31	12	26																Open

NAME OF SCHOOL	TOWN	ENVIRONMENT U-Urban R-Rural SU-Suburban SM-Small Town	DEGREES AWARDED A-Associate B-Bachelor M-Master D-Doctorate	CONTROL Pri-Private, Pub-Public	FRATERNITIES AND SORORITIES F-Fraternities S-Sororities F, S-Both No-Neither	STUDENTS: C-Coed M-Men W-Women PM-Primarily Men PW-Primarily Women	UNDERGRADUATE ENROLLMENT FALL 2013	TEST SCORES: ACT Median	ACT Below 21	ACT 21-23	ACT 24-26	ACT 27-28	ACT Above 28	SAT CRITICAL READING Median	SAT CR Below 500	SAT CR 500-599	SAT CR 600-700	SAT CR Above 700	SAT MATHEMATICS Median	SAT M Below 500	SAT M 500-599	SAT M 600-700	SAT M Above 700	SAT WRITING Median	SAT W Below 500	SAT W 500-599	SAT W 600-700	SAT W Above 700	APPLICATION DEADLINE Month / Day
Oklahoma Panhandle State University	Goodwell	R	A,B	Pub	F	C	1,387	22	25	35	28	11	1	525	16	67	17		520	33	50	17							Open
Oklahoma State University	Stillwater	SM	B,M,D		F,S	C	20,130	25	13	23	31	14	19	540	27	48	21	4	560	19	42	33	6						Open
Oklahoma Wesleyan University	Bartlesville	SU	A,B,M	Pri	No	C	1,059																						Open
Oral Roberts University	Tulsa	U	B,M,D	Pri	No	C	2,782	22	35	28	21	9	8	530	32	43	19	7	510	44	33	18	5						Open
Southeastern Oklahoma State University	Durant	R	B,M	Pub	F,S	C	3,615	18	60	23	12	4	1																Open
Southern Nazarene University	Bethany	SU	A,B,M	Pri	No	C	1,653	23	36	26	18	8	12																Open
Southwestern Oklahoma State University	Weatherford	SM	A,B,M,D	Pub	F,S	C	4,517	21																					Open
St. Gregory's University	Shawnee	SU	A,B,M	Pri	F,S	C	770																						Open
University of Central Oklahoma	Edmond	SU	B,M	Pub	F,S	C	15,367	21	35	33	19	7	6																Open
University of Oklahoma	Norman	SU	B,M,D	Pub	F,S	C	20,985	25	7	23	29	15	26	560	21	43	24	12	580	13	41	33	13						4/1
University of Science and Arts of Oklahoma	Chickasha	SM	B	Pub	F,S	C	983	24	18	29	28	16	9																5/8
University of Tulsa	Tulsa	U	B,M,D	Pri	F,S	C	3,428	28	2	10	18	19	51	620	9	29	35	27	630	7	27	43	23						Open
Oregon																													
Art Institute of Portland	Portland	U	A,B		No	C	1,327																						Open
Concordia University	Portland	U	A,B,M,D	Pri	No	C	998	21	40	35	16	9	2																Open
Corban University	Salem	SU	A,B,M,D	Pri	No	C	949	22	26	30	24	14	6	517	31	41	17	1	520	24	41	18	1	506	36	36	13	1	8/1
Eastern Oregon University	La Grande	R	B,M	Pub	No	C	3,050																						Open
George Fox University	Newberg	SM	B,M,D	Pri	No	C	2,443	23	35	21	22	8	13	540	27	37	21	5	530	33	40	23	4	520	40	37	20	3	2/1
Lewis & Clark College	Portland	SU	B,M,D	Pri	No	C	2,126			6	24	18	52		3	21	49	27		1	32	52	15		3	25	52	20	1/15
Linfield College-McMinnville Campus	McMinnville	SM	B	Pri	F,S	C	1,671	23	32	20	26	11	11	530	29	43	21	6	550	24	47	26	3	520	35	48	15	2	2/15
Marylhurst University	Marylhurst	SU	B,M	Pri	No	C	817																						Open
Northwest Christian University	Eugene	U	A,B,M	Pri	No	C	400	20	57	21	7	14																	Open
Oregon Institute of Technology	Klamath Falls	SM	A,B,M	Pub	F,S	C	3,070																						6/1
Oregon State University	Corvallis	SM	B,M,D		F,S	C	23,161	24	20	25	24	14	17	540	30	43	23	4	550	25	40	28	7	530	38	41	19	3	9/1
Pacific Northwest College of Art	Portland	U	B,M	Pri	No	C	446																						8/15
Pacific University	Forest Grove	SM	B,M,D	Pub	F,S	C	1,640								29	49	17	5		23	49	24	4						2/15
Portland State University	Portland	U	B,M,D	Pub	F,S	C	23,170	22	38	26	20	10	6	520	39	39	19	3	510	42	4	16	1		50	36	13	1	Open
Reed College	Portland	U	B,M	Pri	No	C	1,395			2	7	18	73	710		5	36	59	670		16	49	35	680	1	8	52	39	1/15
Southern Oregon University	Ashland	SM	B,M	Pub	No	C	5,414	22	46	26	16	9	3	510	45	36	16	3	500	49	38	11	2	480	56	32	10	2	Open
University of Oregon	Eugene	SU	B,M,D	Pub	F,S	C	20,797							550	26	43	26	5	560	23	42	29	6						1/15
University of Portland	Portland	U	B,M,D		No	C	3,468							590	12	42	32	13	600	9	39	42	10						2/1
Warner Pacific College	Portland	U	A,B	Pri	No	C	1,550								54	36	8	2		57	31	11	1						Open
Western Oregon University	Monmouth	R	A,B,M	Pub	No	C	4,875	20	56	32	7	4	1	480	57	33	9	1	490	55	36	8	1	450	72	23	4	1	Open
Willamette University	Salem	U	B,M,D	Pri	F,S	C	3,058	27	2	9	35	19	35	610	11	38	39	13	600	9	46	34	12	600	12	42	39	7	2/1
Pennsylvania																													
Albright College	Reading	SU	B,M	Pri	F,S	C	1,751							510	42	43	14	1	520	36	48	14	2						Open
Allegheny College	Meadville	SU	B	Pri	F,S	C	2,161	26	7	21	25	21	26	590	11	41	39	9	600	12	36	45	7	575	6	42	36	6	2/15
Alvernia University	Reading	SU	A,B,M,D	Pri	No	C	2,371	20	53	33	11	6		490	52	41	6	1	500	49	43	7	1	480	58	36	5	1	Open
Arcadia University	Glenside	SU	B,M,D	Pri	No	C	1,957	25																					Open
Bloomsburg University of Pennsylvania	Bloomsburg	SM	A,B,M,D	Pub	F,S	C	8,605							500	49	42	8	1	510	40	46	13	1						Open
Bryn Athyn College	Bryn Athyn	SU	A,B,M	Pri	No	C	267	22	11	56	11		22	510	44	27	25	4	510	44	35	18	3	470	56	26	12	6	Open
Bryn Mawr College	Bryn Mawr	SU	B,M,D	Pri	No	W	1,328	28		7	22	24	47	650	3	19	45	33	670	3	24	39	34	670	1	18	45	37	1/15
Bucknell University	Lewisburg	SM	B,M	Pri	F,S	C	3,532	30		2	13	23	62	640	1	24	54	21	670	1	14	51	35	650	2	21	54	24	1/15
Cabrini College	Radnor	SU	B,M	Pri	No	C	1,312	20	55	23	16	6		450	70	26	4		440	73	23	4		440	74	24	2		Open
Cairn University	Langhorne	SU	B,M	Pri	No	C	846	23	33	19	22	7	19	520	39	33	24	4	510	43	40	16	1						Open
California University of Pennsylvania	California	SM	A,B,M	Pub	F,S	C	5,970	20	68	21	7	3	1																Open
Carlow University	Pittsburgh	U	B,M,D	Pri	No	PW	1,818	21	46	32	15	3	4	480	58	32	8	2	470	65	32	3		475	60	30	9	1	7/1
Carnegie Mellon University	Pittsburgh	SU	B,M,D	Pri	F,S	C	5,951	31	2	3	6	11	78	670	1	14	16	69	730	1	5	28	66	680	1	13	47	39	7/1
Cedar Crest College	Allentown	SU	B,M	Pri	No	W	1,286	22						460	64	30	6		470	57	38	5		460	70	23	7		Open
Chatham University	Pittsburgh	U	B,M,D	Pri	No	PW	977	22	26	37	26		11	545	26	41	29	4	540	27	53	17	3	545	25	40	30	5	Open
Chestnut Hill College	Philadelphia	SU	A,B,M,D	Pri	No	C	1,507	21	76	12	4	4	4	480	59	34	6	1	470	62	30	7	1	460	65	30	5		Open

Cheyney University of Pennsylvania	Cheyney	SU	A,B,M	Pub	F,S	C	1,224								94	5	1			94	6				96	3	1		5/30
Clarion University of Pennsylvania	Clarion	SM	A,B,M	Pub	F,S	C	5,199							471	66	27	7		477	68	30	8		458					Open
Curtis Institute of Music	Philadelphia	U	B		No	C	130																						Open
De Sales University	Center Valley	SU	B,M,D	Pri	No	C	2,482	25	12	28	37	13	10	530	31	46	18	5	550	31	40	25	4						Open
Delaware Valley College	Doylestown	SU	A,B,M	Pri	F,S	C	2,000	22	38	25	25	13																	Open
Dickinson College	Carlisle	SU	B	Pri	F,S	C	2,352	29	2	2	11	31	55	640	3	25	53	18	640	3	20	55	22	635	4	22	57	17	2/1
Drexel University	Philadelphia	U	A,B,M,D	Pri	F,S	C	16,616	27	3	18	23	19	37	570	18	43	31	8	630	6	30	44	20	570	19	43	31	7	1/15
Duquesne University	Pittsburgh	U	B,M,D	Pri	F,S	C	5,970	25	9	30	31	17	13	561	17	59	22	2	578	13	52	32	3	558	20	53	25	2	7/1
East Stroudsburg University of Pennsylvania	East Stroudsburg	SM	B,M	Pub	F,S	C	6,186							480	61	34	5		490	52	38	9		480	62	34	4	1	4/1
Eastern University	St. Davids	SU	A,B,M,D	Pri	No	C	2,701	22	34	23	27	12	4	527	33	48	17	2	520	35	44	17	4	527	39	41	15	2	Open
Edinboro University of Pennsylvania	Edinboro	SM	A,B,M	Pub	F,S	C	6,090	20					1	482	63	29	7	1	478	62	30	7	1	462					Open
Elizabethtown College	Elizabethtown	SM	B,M	Pri	No	C	1,844	23	20	32	21	11	16	550	24	48	25	3	560	22	40	33	5						Open
Elizabethtown College School of Continuing and Professional Studies	Elizabethtown	SM	A,B,M	Pri	No	C	372																						Open
Franklin and Marshall College	Lancaster	SU	B	Pri	F,S	C	2,297	29						640	2	22	53	23	662	1	11	58	30						1/15
Gannon University	Erie	U	A,B,M,D	Pri	F,S	C	3,111	24	26	24	30	10	10	520	41	46	12	1	540	34	42	22	2	500	50	35	13	1	Open
Geneva College	Beaver Falls	SM	A,B,M	Pri	No	C	1,395																						Open
Gettysburg College	Gettysburg	SU	B	Pri	F,S	C	2,533									18	64	18			16	69	15						2/1
Grove City College	Grove City	SM	B	Pri	F,S	C	2,491	27	7	12	16	23	42	605	8	39	40	13	601	9	37	43	11						2/1
Gwynedd-Mercy College	Gwynedd Valley	SU	A,B,M	Pri	No	C	2,196							490	48	41	10	1	490	56	36	7	1						2/1
Haverford College	Haverford	SU	B	Pri	No	C	1,187	32				20	80	710		6	43	51	700		6	39	55	710		6	38	56	1/15
Holy Family University	Philadelphia	SU	A,B,M,D	Pri	No	C	2,139							471	71	25	4		476	64	32	4		472					Open
Immaculata University	Immaculata	SU	A,B,M,D	Pri	No	C	2,883																						3/1
Indiana University of Pennsylvania	Indiana	SM	A,B,M,D	Pub	F,S	C	12,471							480	58	34	8	1	490	53	38	9	1	470	63	30	6		Open
Juniata College	Huntingdon	SM	B,M	Pri	No	C	1,625							570	17	42	31	10	580	9	51	33	7						3/15
Keystone College	La Plume	R	A,B	Pri	No	C	1,641	17	86	6			8	445	80	19	1	1	440	79	18	4		445	82	16	1	1	3/15
King's College	Wilkes Barre	U	A,B,M	Pri	No	C	2,144							519	38	48	13	1	528	38	48	12	2	511	45	42	11	2	Open
Kutztown University of Pennsylvania	Kutztown	SM	B,M	Pub	F,S	C	8,815	20	58	28	10	2	2	483	60	35	5		486	58	34	7	1	470	67	29	4		Open
La Roche College	Pittsburgh	SU	A,B,M	Pri	No	C	1,363	20	55	17	18	5	5	460	68	26	5	1	480	63	31	6		430	79	17	4		Open
La Salle University	Philadelphia	U	A,B,M,D	Pri	F,S	C	4,409	21	42	31	13	7	7	510	41	44	13	2	510	42	40	14	3						4/1
Lafayette College	Easton	SU	B	Pri	F,S	C	2,537	28	3				37	617	6	31	48	15	658	2	18	50	30	631	4	25	53	18	1/15
Lebanon Valley College	Annville	SM	A,B,M,D	Pri	F,S	C	1,747	22	35	23	28	8	6	540	31	48	19	3	560	24	41	32	4	530	36	43	20	1	Open
Lehigh University	Bethlehem	SU	B,M,D	Pri	F,S	C	4,931	30						630	5	28	50	17	690		9	46	45						1/1
Lock Haven University of Pennsylvania	Lock Haven	R	A,B,M	Pub	F,S	C	4,783	20	54	22	12	4	8	472	66	29	4	1	480	60	33	7		456	74	22	4		Open
Lycoming College	Williamsport	SM	B	Pri	F,S	C	1,307	22	26	36	17	15	6	520	42	41	15	2	520	38	46	15	2	490	51	38	10	1	3/1
Mansfield University	Mansfield	R	A,B,M	Pub	F,S	C	2,717							476	60	32	7	1	484	57	33	9	1	451	77	21	5	1	3/1
Marywood University	Scranton	SU	B,M,D	Pri	S	C	2,255	22	33	32	21	10	4	510	42	46	11		520	34	51	15		510	44	41	15		Open
Mercyhurst University	Erie	SU	A,B,M,D	Pri	No	C	3,840	23	21	46	33			550					530					510					Open
Messiah College	Mechanicsburg	SM	B,M	Pri	No	C	2,772	25	13	19	26	16	26	570	19	44	27	10	580	19	38	35	8	560	23	43	27	7	Open
Millersville University of Pennsylvania	Millersville	SM	A,B,M	Pub	F,S	C	7,388	22	39	26	24	4	7	500	47	41	10	2	510	42	45	12	1	490	54	37	8	1	Open
Misericordia University	Dallas	SU	B,M,D	Pri	No	C	2,417	23	26	33	23	11	7	520	33	52	13	2	540	23	61	15	1						Open
Moore College of Art and Design	Philadelphia	U	B	Pri	No	W	635																						Open
Moravian College	Bethlehem	SU	B,M	Pri	F,S	C	1,770	19						553	21	52	23	4	561	20	49	26	5	545	29	47	20	4	3/1
Mount Aloysius College	Cresson	SM	A,B,M	Pri	No	C	1,611								49	49	2			45	52	2						4	3/1
Muhlenberg College	Allentown	SU	A,B	Pri	F,S	C	2,448	27					23	617	3	35	45	17	614	4	33	52	11	617	3	36	45	16	2/15
Neumann University	Aston	SU	A,B,M,D	Pri	No	C	2,501								76	22	2			80	18	2			75	23	1		Open
Peirce College	Philadelphia	U	A,B	Pri	No	C	1,962																						Open
Penn State Erie/The Behrend College	Erie	SU	A,B,M	Pub	F,S	C	4,015																						Open
Penn State University/Altoona	Altoona	SU	A,B,M		F,S	C	4,032																						Open
Penn State University/University Park	University Park	SU	A,B,M,D	Pub	F,S	C	37,830							570	15	47	33	5	620	9	30	46	15	590	13	42	38	7	11/30
Pennsylvania College of Technology	Williamsport	SU	A,B	Pub	F	C	5,678																						7/1
Philadelphia University	Philadelphia	SU	A,B,M,D	Pri	F,S	C	2,888																						Open
Point Park University	Pittsburgh	U	A,B,M	Pri	No	C	3,226		34	22	25	20	6		45	39	14	2		57	34	8	1		52	35	12	2	Open
Robert Morris University	Moon Township	SU	B,M,D	Pri	F,S	C	4,459	23						513	42	44	12	1	535	32	44	20	3	500	43	40	9	1	5/1
Rosemont College	Rosemont	SU	B,M	Pri	No	C	524	23	8	10	57	18	7	504	52	33	13	2	493	50	41	5	4	500	53	32	6	4	Open
Saint Francis University	Loretto	R	B,M	Pri	F,S	C	1,772																					4	Open
Saint Joseph's University	Philadelphia	SU	A,B,M,D	Pri	F,S	C	5,374	24	13	30	34	10	13	550	18	58	21	3	560	16	52	28	3	550	13	53	25	3	2/1
Saint Vincent College	Latrobe	SU	B,M,D	Pri	No	C	1,660	22	29	30	22	11	6	510	36	45	16	2	520	28	49	21	2	520	42	42	15	1	4/1
Seton Hill University	Greensburg	SM	B,M	Pri	No	C	1,572																						Open
Shippensburg University of Pennsylvania	Shippensburg	R	B,M	Pub	F,S	C	6,712	20	53	30	12	4	1	490	53	38	8	1	500	48	40	11	1	470	62	32	6		Open
Slippery Rock University of Pennsylvania	Slippery Rock	SM	B,M,D	Pub	F,S	C	7,065																						Open
Susquehanna University	Selinsgrove	SM	B	Pri	F,S	C	2,177								19	48	26	6		17	49	29	5		28	45	24	4	3/1
Swarthmore College	Swarthmore	SU	B	Pri	F,S	C	1,534	32			5	9	86	730		3	31	66	720		3	31	66	730		4	26	70	1/1
Temple University	Philadelphia	U	A,B,M,D	Pub	F,S	C	28,243	24	16	27	28	12	17	558	22	43	25	5	571	17	46	30	7	553	24	46	25	5	3/1
The Lincoln University	Lincoln University	R	B,M	Pub	F,S	C	1,624	16	67	33				410	88	11	1		490	88	11	1			86	11	1		Open
Thiel College	Greenville	R	A,B	Pri	F,S	C	999	20						450					470										Open

NAME OF SCHOOL	TOWN	ENVIRONMENT U-Urban R-Rural SU-Suburban SM-Small Town	DEGREES AWARDED A-Associate B-Bachelor M-Master D-Doctorate	CONTROL Pri-Private, Pub-Public	FRATERNITIES AND SORORITIES F-Fraternities S-Sororities F, S-Both No-Neither	STUDENTS: C-Coed M-Men W-Women PM-Primarily Men PW-Primarily Women	UNDERGRADUATE ENROLLMENT FALL 2013	TEST SCORES ACT Median	ACT Below 21	ACT 21-23	ACT 24-26	ACT 27-28	ACT Above 28	SAT CRITICAL READING Median	SAT CR Below 500	SAT CR 500-599	SAT CR 600-700	SAT CR Above 700	SAT MATHEMATICS Median	SAT Math Below 500	SAT Math 500-599	SAT Math 600-700	SAT Math Above 700	SAT WRITING Median	SAT Writing Below 500	SAT Writing 500-599	SAT Writing 600-700	SAT Writing Above 700	APPLICATION DEADLINE Month / Day
University of Pennsylvania	Philadelphia	U	A,B,M,D	Pri	F,S	C	9,682			1	10	10	80			6	33	62			3	24	73			4	28	68	1/1
University of Pittsburgh at Bradford	Bradford	SM	A,B	Pub	F,S	C	1,481	20	58	20	15	5	2	470	62	28	10		500	49	36	13	2	450	70	25	5		Open
University of Pittsburgh at Greensburg	Greensburg	SU	B	Pub	No	C	1,795																						Open
University of Pittsburgh at Johnstown	Johnstown	SU	A,B	Pub	F,S	C	2,932	20	52	36	10	1	1	505	50	41	8	1	520	41	43	15	1	500	55	38	6	1	Open
University of Pittsburgh at Pittsburgh	Pittsburgh	SM	B,M,D	Pub	F,S	C	18,615	29	1	4	24	20	51	625	3	33	48	16	649	1	20	55	24	623	3	32	49	16	Open
University of Scranton	Scranton	U	A,B,M,D	Pri	No	C	4,041								15	56	25	4		12	51	31	5						3/1
University of the Arts	Philadelphia	U	B,M	Pri	No	C	2,079	22	48	11	27	7	7																Open
University of the Sciences	Philadelphia	U	B,M,D	Pri	F,S	C	2,438	25	3	34	31	16	16	557	15	61	21	3	603	6	43	40	11	567	16	52	26	6	Open
Ursinus College	Collegeville	SU	B	Pri	F,S	C	1,596	26		20	27	27	26	580	13	45	34	8	590	7	42	40	11	590	14	43	34	9	2/15
Villanova University	Villanova	SU	A,B,M,D	Pri	F,S	C	7,042	30			2	36	62	640	2	23	54	21	670	2	13	50	35	640	3	20	53	24	1/15
Washington and Jefferson College	Washington	SM	B,M	Pri	F,S	C	1,328	25	6	16	27	15	9	560	15	55	27	3	581	11	50	33	6						3/1
Waynesburg University	Waynesburg	SM	B,M,D	Pri	No	C	1,598																						Open
West Chester University of Pennsylvania	West Chester	SU	B,M,D	Pub	F,S	C	13,711							530	28	55	16	1	550	20	56	22	2	530	32	51	17	1	Open
Westminster College	New Wilmington	R	B,M		F,S	C	1,469	24	73	13	8	2	3															1	Open
Widener University	Chester	SU	A,B,M,D	Pri	F,S	C	3,534							490	49	43	7	1	510	36	42	17	2						2/15
Wilkes University	Wilkes Barre	U	B,M,D	Pri	No	C	2,388							500	45	39	15	1	530	34	42	21	3	490	51	37	11	1	Open
Wilson College	Chambersburg	SM	A,B	Pri	No	W	729	22	50	10	30		10																Open
York College of Pennsylvania	York	SU	A,B,M,D	Pri	F,S	C	5,008	22	31	32	21	12	4	510	41	46	12	1	520	32	50	16	2	500	47	45	8		Open
Puerto Rico																													
American University of Puerto Rico	Bayamon	U	A,B	Pri	No	C	1,211																						Open
Caribbean University	Bayamon	U	A,B,M	Pri	No		3,931																						Open
Central University of Bayamon	Bayamon	U	A,B,M		No	C	2,910																						Open
Conservatory of Music of Puerto Rico	San Juan	U	B	Pub	No	C	255																						Open
Escuela de Artes Plasticas de Puerto Rico	San Juan	U	B	Pub	No	C	515																						Open
Inter-American University of Puerto Rico/Aguadilla Campus	Aguadilla	SU	A,B,M	Pri	No	C	4,357																						5/1
Inter-American University of Puerto Rico/Arecibo Campus	Arecibo	SU	A,B,M		F,S	C	4,135																						5/1
Inter-American University of Puerto Rico/Barranquitas	Barranquitas	SM	A,B		No	C	1,720																						5/1
Inter-American University of Puerto Rico/Bayamon University College	Bayamon	U	A,B,M	Pri	No	C	4,942																						5/1
Inter-American University of Puerto Rico/Fajardo Campus	Fajardo	U	A,B,M,D	Pri	No	C	2,171																						8/15
Inter-American University of Puerto Rico/Metropolitan Campus	San Juan	U	A,B,M,D	Pri	No	C	7,100																						8/15
Inter-American University of Puerto Rico/Ponce	Ponce	U	B		No	C																							8/15
Inter-American University of Puerto Rico/San Germán	San Germán	R	A,B,M,D		No	C	5,090																						8/15
Pontifical Catholic University of Puerto Rico	Ponce	U	A,B,M,D	Pri	F,S	C	8,020																						8/15
Universidad Adventista de las Antillas	Mayaguez	SM	A,B,M	Pri	F,S	C	760																						Open
Universidad del Turabo	Gurabo	SU	A,B,M		No																								Open
Universidad Metropolitana	Rio Piedras	U	A,B,M		No	C																							Open
Universidad Politecnica de Puerto Rico	Hato Rey	U	A,B,M	Pri	F	C	3,861																						Open
University of Puerto Rico Recinto de Rio Piedras	San Juan	U	B,M,D	Pub	F,S	C	17,860																						Open
University of Puerto Rico/Arecibo	Arecibo	U	A,B	Pub	No	C	4,146																						11/30
University of Puerto Rico/Bayamon	Bayamon	SU	A,B	Pub	No	C	5,327																						11/30
University of Puerto Rico/Cayey	Cayey	U	A,B	Pub	No	C	3,659																						11/30
University of Puerto Rico/Humacao	Humacao	SU	A,B	Pub	S	C	4,542																						11/14
University of Puerto Rico/Mayaguez	Mayaguez	U	A,B,M,D	Pub	F,S	C	11,095																						11/14
University of the Sacred Heart	Santurce	U	A,B,M		No	C	4,565																						11/14
Rhode Island																													
Brown University	Providence	SM	B,M,D	Pri	F,S	C	12,428	31					79	720		8	30	62	730		6	27	67	720		6	27	67	1/1

Bryant University	Smithfield	SU	B,M	Pri	F,S	C	3,287	25	3	23	45	16	13	550	18	59	20	3	585	8	48	37	7	545	22	53	23	2	1/1
Johnson and Wales University/Providence Campus	Providence	SM	A,B,M,D	Pri	F,S	C	9,839																						Open
Providence College	Providence	SU	A,B,M	Pri	No	C	3,866	25	9	25	31	17	19	570	15	50	31	5	580	13	44	37	7	585	12	43	36	9	1/15
Rhode Island College	Providence	SU	B,M,D	Pub	F,S	C	7,261	20	61	23	12	1	3	470	63	31	5	1	460	66	28	6		470	65	30	5		3/15
Rhode Island School of Design	Providence	U	B,M	Pri	No	C	2,005																						2/1
Roger Williams University	Bristol	SM	A,B,M	Pri	No	C	4,411							535	35	50	14	1	524	29	50	20	1	523	36	49	14	1	2/1
Salve Regina University	Newport	SU	A,B,M,D	Pri	No	C	2,026	24	10	37	39	10	4	550	17	59	22	2	550	16	57	24	2	560	21	52	25	1	2/1
University of Rhode Island	Kingston	SM	B,M,D		F,S	C	13,427	24					7	530	26	52	19	3	540	22	51	24	4	430	26	51	20	2	2/1
South Carolina																													
Allen University	Columbia	SM	A,B	Pri	F,S	C	350																						Open
Benedict College	Columbia	U	B	Pri	F,S	C	2,641																						Open
Charleston Southern University	Charleston	SU	A,B,M		No	C	2,490																						Open
Citadel, The	Charleston	SU	B,M	Pub	No	C	2,735	23	22	35	27	7	9	538	36	46	15	3	549	23	51	23	3						Open
Claflin University	Orangeburg	SU	B,M	Pri	F,S	C	1,883	18	77	17	8			436	78	18	4		440	72	19	8	2						Open
Clemson University	Clemson	SM	B,M,D	Pub	F,S	C	15,836	27	8	15	31	15	31	600	8	41	42	9	630	4	25	54	17	540	24	49	23	2	5/1
Coastal Carolina University	Conway	SU	B,M	Pub	F,S	C	8,867	21	42	31	13	6	3	490	54	38	7	1	500	46	44	9	1						6/1
Coker College	Hartsville	SM	B,M	Pri	No	C	1,178	19	60	23	16			460	66	24	10		480	58	31	10	1						Open
College of Charleston	Charleston	U	B,M	Pub	F,S	C	10,488		2	22	37	19	19	589	12	49	31	7	579	13	53	29	4						4/1
Columbia College	Columbia	U	B,M	Pri	No	PW	1,239							500	49	32	16	3	500	50	36	13	1						8/1
Converse College	Spartanburg	U	B,M	Pri	No	W	690	23	32	25	25	13	6	530	29	43	25	3	520	35	50	14	1						8/1
Erskine College	Due West	R	B,M,D	Pri	No	C	553							531	40	36	19	5	543	37	35	23	5						Open
Francis Marion University	Florence	R	B,M	Pub	F,S	C	3,714	20	69	15	12	3	1	476	65	26	8	1	476	64	28	7	1	446	74	24	2		8/15
Furman University	Greenville	SU	B,M	Pri	F,S	C	2,798	28	3	11	22	26	38	610	7	35	42	16	620	5	28	50	17	610	10	33	42	15	1/15
Lander University	Greenwood	SM	B,M	Pub	F,S	C	2,363	21	47	32	15	4	2	470	59	32	8		500	47	38	14	1						Open
Limestone College	Gaffney	SU	A,B,M	Pri	F	C	1,059	21	41	43	11	2	3	480	55	37	7	1	520	33	57	10							Open
Morris College	Sumter	SM	B	Pri	F,S	C	824																						4/30
Newberry College	Newberry	SM	B	Pri	F,S	C	795																						Open
Presbyterian College	Clinton	SM	B,D	Pri	F,S	C	1,123	24	16	26	24	15	19	550	27	46	24	3	550	18	50	28	4						2/1
South Carolina State University	Orangeburg	SM	B,M,D		F,S	C	4,030																						7/31
Southern Wesleyan University	Central	SM	A,B,M	Pri	No	C	1,677	20						490	54	39	7		490	54	33	13		480	56	36	8		Open
University of South Carolina at Aiken	Aiken	SU	B,M	Pub	F,S	C	3,169	22	55	23	16	4	3	510	56	35	9		500	60	32	8		460	67	28	5		Open
University of South Carolina at Columbia	Columbia	U	A,B,M,D	Pub	F,S	C	23,363	27	3	17	29	22	29	590	10	45	36	10	610	5	37	48	11						12/1
University of South Carolina Upstate	Spartanburg	U	B,M	Pub	F,S	C	5,224	20	64	21	10	3	2	430	63	28	5	1	520	61	33	6		410	74	23	3		Open
Voorhees College	Denmark	SM	B		F,S	C	533																						Open
Winthrop University	Rock Hill	SM	B,M	Pub	F,S	C		23	36	28	17	13	9	525	37	39	18	3	525	37	43	17	1						5/1
Wofford College	Spartanburg	U	B	Pri	F,S	C	1,584	26	3	15	27	23	32	585	12	40	42	6	597	11	35	42	11		21	38	37	4	2/1
South Dakota																													
Augustana College	Sioux Falls	U	B,M	Pri	No	C	1,697	26	3	24	30	28	15																Open
Black Hills State University	Spearfish	SM	A,B,M	Pub	F,S	C	4,002																						Open
Dakota State University	Madison	R	A,B,M,D	Pub	No	C																							Open
Dakota Wesleyan University	Mitchell	SM	A,B,M	Pri	No	C	756	21	12	62			26																8/25
Mount Marty College	Yankton	SM	A,B,M	Pri	No	C	1,092		10	50	30	5	5																Open
National American University	Rapid City	SM	A,B,M	Pri	No	C	477																						Open
Northern State University	Aberdeen	U	A,B,M	Pub	No	C	2,829	22	24	47	19	5	5		58	30	11	1		51	37	12	1						Open
Oglala Lakota College	Kyle	R	B		No	C																							Open
Presentation College	Aberdeen	SM	A,B		No	C	630	21																					Open
Sinte Gleska University	Rosebud	R	A,B,M		No	C	341																						Open
South Dakota School of Mines and Technology	Rapid City	SU	A,B,M,D	Pub	F,S	C	2,101	26	4	17	35	20	24	560	31	40	22	7	600	12	40	29	19	500	42	40	16	2	Open
South Dakota State University	Brookings	SM	A,B,M,D		F,S	C																							Open
University of Sioux Falls	Sioux Falls	SU	A,B,M	Pri	No	C	1,261	22	36	24	27	5	8	525	44	33		23	525	55	34		11						Open
University of South Dakota	Vermillion	SM	A,B,M,D	Pub	F,S	C	7,633	23	24	31	26	11	8	509	46	34	18	2	527	39	32	25	4						Open
Tennessee																													
Aquinas College	Nashville	U	A,B,M	Pri	No	C	508	24	15	30	27	18	6	480	50	25	25		415	100									Open
Austin Peay State University	Clarksville	U	A,B,M	Pub	F,S	C	9,550	22	43	30	16	5	6																8/5
Belmont University	Nashville	U	B,M,D	Pri	F,S	C	5,506	27	3	24	34	19	20	590	8	48	36	8	580	14	45	34	7						8/1
Bethel University	McKenzie	SM	B,M	Pri	F,S	C	2,232		62	24	15	3	2																8/30
Bryan College	Dayton	SM	A,B,M	Pri	No	C	1,011																						Open
Carson-Newman University	Jefferson City	SM	A,B,M	Pri	F,S	C	1,646	23	35	30	20	7	8	455					520										8/15
Christian Brothers University	Memphis	SM	B,M	Pri	F,S	C	1,351	25	4	42	28	11	15																8/1

NAME OF SCHOOL	TOWN	ENVIRONMENT U-Urban R-Rural SU-Suburban SM-Small Town	DEGREES AWARDED A-Associate B-Bachelor M-Master D-Doctorate	CONTROL Pri-Private, Pub-Public	FRATERNITIES AND SORORITIES F-Fraternities S-Sororities F, S-Both No-Neither	STUDENTS: C-Coed M-Men W-Women PM-Primarily Men PW-Primarily Women	UNDERGRADUATE ENROLLMENT FALL 2013	TEST SCORES: ACT Median	ACT Below 21	ACT 21-23	ACT 24-26	ACT 27-28	ACT Above 28	SAT CRITICAL READING Median	SAT CR Below 500	SAT CR 500-599	SAT CR 600-700	SAT CR Above 700	SAT MATHEMATICS Median	SAT Math Below 500	SAT Math 500-599	SAT Math 600-700	SAT Math Above 700	SAT WRITING Median	SAT Writing Below 500	SAT Writing 500-599	SAT Writing 600-700	SAT Writing Above 700	APPLICATION DEADLINE Month / Day
Cumberland University	Lebanon	SM	A,B,M	Pri	F,S	C	623	21	44	33	10	11	2		65	30		5		50	50					88	12		Open
East Tennessee State University	Johnson City	SM	A,B,M,D	Pub	F,S	C	9,580																						Open
Fisk University	Nashville	U	B,M	Pri	F,S	C	868	20	60	21	14	3	1																Open
Freed-Hardeman University	Henderson	SM	A,B,M		No	C	1,479	23	30	27	21	10	12																Open
King University	Bristol	SM	B,M	Pri	No	C	1,963	23	6	47	43		4	485	47	47	6		509	36	51	12	1						Open
Lane College	Jackson	SM	B	Pri	F,S	C	965																						Open
Lee University	Cleveland	SU	B,M	Pri	F,S	C	4,016	24	25	18	23	18	16	550	34	37	23	6	530	37	34	26	3						9/1
LeMoyne-Owen College	Memphis	U	B	Pri	F,S	C	785																						9/1
Lincoln Memorial University	Harrogate	R	A,B,M	Pri	F,S	C	1,654																						Open
Lipscomb University	Nashville	SU	A,B,M,D	Pri	F,S	C	2,890	25	12	23	26	15	24	570	17	42	28	13	590	15	38	35	12						Open
Maryville College	Maryville	SU	B	Pri	No	C	1,176	24	20	26	23	16	15	537	35	34	27	4	535	34	42	23	1	528	35	37	25	3	3/1
Memphis College of Art	Memphis	U	B,M	Pri	No	C	377	22	23	39	23	13	3																Open
Middle Tennessee State University	Murfreesboro	U	B,M,D	Pub	F,S	C	22,299	22	32	35	20	7	5																7/1
Milligan College	Milligan College	SU	B,M	Pri	No	C	903	23	26	30	26	7	11	530	34	45	18	3	520	38	43	15	3	510	39	44	10	7	8/15
Rhodes College	Memphis	U	B,M	Pri	F,S	C	1,905	28		4	22	24	50	630	3	30	44	23	630	2	26	53	19	620					1/15
Sewanee: The University of the South	Sewanee	SM	B,M,D	Pri	F,S	C	1,620	28	2	8	27	26	37	630	4	29	49	18	610	5	38	47	10	610	5	36	44	15	2/1
Southern Adventist University	Collegedale	SM	A,B,M	Pri	No	C	2,477	22	34	27	21	10	8																Open
Tennessee State University	Nashville	U	A,B,M,D	Pub	F,S	C	6,919	18	77	17	5	1	1																8/1
Tennessee Technological University	Cookeville	SM	B,M,D	Pub	F,S	C	8,060	23							38	30	28	4		26	38	6	30		42	35	21	2	8/1
Tennessee Wesleyan College	Athens	SM	B	Pri	F,S	C	1,070		31	35	22	5	6		61	25	11	3		72	22	3	3						8
Trevecca Nazarene University	Nashville	U	A,B,M,D	Pri	No	C	1,492	23	23	28	25	11	13	540	26	49	23	2	520	37	37	21	5						8
Tusculum College	Greeneville	SM	B,M	Pri	No	C	2,446	22																					Open
Union University	Jackson	SU	A,B,M,D	Pri	F,S	C	2,829	25	16	21	22	12	29	590	13	23	30	23	590	13	35	36	10						Open
University of Memphis	Memphis	U	B,M,D	Pub	F,S	C	17,647	23																					7/1
University of Tennessee at Chattanooga	Chattanooga	U	B,M,D	Pub	F,S	C	10,297	23	21	37	26	10	6	530	36	40	17	7	530	38	40	20	2						5/1
University of Tennessee at Knoxville	Knoxville	U	B,M,D	Pub	F,S	C	21,033	27		12	22	9	22	580	12	46	32	10	590	12	39	38	10						12/1
University of Tennessee at Martin	Martin	R	B,M	Pub	F,S	C	7,025	22	34	28	19	6	12																Open
Vanderbilt University	Nashville	U	B,M,D	Pri	F,S	C	6,835		1	1	2	34	62		2	3	19	76		1	4	15	80		1	5	27	67	1/3
Victory University	Memphis	U	B	Pri	No	C	1,007																						Open

Texas

NAME OF SCHOOL	TOWN	ENVIRONMENT	DEGREES AWARDED	CONTROL	FRATERNITIES AND SORORITIES	STUDENTS	UNDERGRADUATE ENROLLMENT FALL 2013	ACT Median	ACT Below 21	ACT 21-23	ACT 24-26	ACT 27-28	ACT Above 28	SAT CR Median	SAT CR Below 500	SAT CR 500-599	SAT CR 600-700	SAT CR Above 700	SAT Math Median	SAT Math Below 500	SAT Math 500-599	SAT Math 600-700	SAT Math Above 700	SAT Writing Median	SAT Writing Below 500	SAT Writing 500-599	SAT Writing 600-700	SAT Writing Above 700	APPLICATION DEADLINE Month / Day
Abilene Christian University	Abilene	SM	A,B,M,D	Pri	F,S	C	3,727	24	18	27	26	12	17	532	36	43	15	6	547	27	45	24	4	511	46	39	13	2	2/15
Angelo State University	San Angelo	U	B,M,D	Pub	F,S	C	5,546	20	51	27	15	5	3	460	66	26	6	1	480	55	34	10	1	460					8/25
Austin College	Sherman	SU	B,M	Pri	F,S	C	1,335	26	13	20	35	12	20	615	10	31	48	12	625	6	27	50	17	595	16	36	36	12	3/1
Baylor University	Waco	SM	B,M,D	Pri	F,S	C	13,292	27	1	14	30	24	32	600	5	43	39	13	620	2	32	54	13	590	11	42	37	10	2/1
Concordia University Texas	Austin	U	A,B,M	Pri	No	C	1,030																						8/15
Dallas Baptist University	Dallas	SU	A,B,M,D	Pri	F,S	C	3,435	22	36	32	22	5	5	563	18	48	31	4	560	14	59	25	2						Open
East Texas Baptist University	Marshall	SM	B,M	Pri	F,S	C	1,196	20	55	30	9	4	2	470	64	30	6		490	54	37	8	1						8/15
Hardin-Simmons University	Abilene	U	B,M,D	Pri	F,S	C	2,030	22	39	25	24	6	6	510	43	35	20	2	520	38	44	17	1	510	43	45	11	1	Open
Houston Baptist University	Houston	U	A,B,M		F,S	C	1,992	22	40	30	16	8	6	530	37	38	22	3	540	35	41	22	2	520	39	40	17	4	Open
Howard Payne University	Brownwood	SM	A,B		F,S	C	1,371	21	47	29	14	7	3																8/1
Huston-Tillotson University	Austin	U	B	Pri	F,S	C	844		94	7	1	1			87	12	1	2		88	10	2							7/1
Jarvis Christian College	Hawkins	R	B	Pri	F,S	C	632	15	90	9	1			388	95	5			380	92	8			365	97	3			8/1
Lamar University	Beaumont	U	A,B,M,D	Pub	F,S	C	8,430																						8/1
LeTourneau University	Longview	SM	A,B,M	Pri	No	C	2,450																						8/1
Lubbock Christian University	Lubbock	SU	A,B,M	Pri	F,S	C	1,468	22	29	29	29	8	5	500	46	40	11	3	520	39	44	16	1	490	51	40	9		Open
McMurry University	Abilene	U	B	Pri	F,S	C	1,509	20	53	19	16	5	7	460	61	28	10	1	500	49	38	13							8/13
Midwestern State University	Wichita Falls	U	A,B,M	Pub	F,S	C	5,348	21	52	28	14	5	2	490	53	34	12	1	500	48	38	13	1	490	55	38	7		8/7
Northwood University	Cedar Hill	SU	A,B,M	Pri	F,S	C	514		66	21	11	1	2		68	25	6	1		54	32	14			73	23	5		8/1
Our Lady of the Lake University of San Antonio	San Antonio	U	B,M,D		No	C	1,792	19	68	23	6	2																	Open
Paul Quinn College	Dallas	U	B	Pri	F,S	C	193																						Open
Prairie View A&M University	Prairie View	SM	B,M,D	Pub	F,S	C	6,757	17	57	36	4	4		410	85	13	1		420	82	16	2		417					6/1
Rice University	Houston	U	B,M,D	Pri	No	C	3,102	30	3		18		79	650	2	9	37	53	670		9	26	65	640	3	9	37	51	6/1
Saint Mary's University	San Antonio	SU	B,M,D	Pri	F,S	C	2,391	22	25	42	21	6	6	510	43	42	12	2	530	31	51	17	1	490	52	38	9	1	Open

Sam Houston State University	Huntsville	SM	B,M,D	Pub	F,S	C	14,995		25	12	5	2	1		46	30	6	1		40	33	9	1						Open
Schreiner University	Kerrville	R	A,B,M	Pri	F,S	C	1,065								55	34	8	3		41	48	10	1		68	26	5	1	8/1
Southern Methodist University	Dallas	SU	B,M,D	Pri	F,S	C	6,357	29						640	3	20	53	24	660	2	14	55	29	640	5	22	54	19	1/15
Southwestern Adventist University	Keene	R	A,B,M	Pri	No	C	875																					19	1/15
Southwestern University	Georgetown	SU	B	Pri	F,S	C	1,535	26	9	20	28	16	26	590	16	39	35	10	580	7	44	37	9						2/1
St. Edward's University	Austin	U	B,M	Pri	No	C	4,089	24	14	33	30	12	12	560	20	49	26	5	560	19	48	29	4	550	25	46	27	2	5/1
Stephen F. Austin State University	Nacogdoches	SM	B,M,D	Pub	F,S	C	11,269	20	52	26	16	4	2	470	62	29	8	1	490	55	35	10	1	460	67	28	5	1	Open
Sul Ross State University	Alpine	R	A,B,M	Pub	No	C	1,310								91	8	1			87	12	1			94	6			Open
Tarleton State University	Stephenville	SM	A,B,M,D	Pub	F,S	C	9,585	20	47	32	16	3	1	470	60	31	8	1	500	48	41	10	1	460	63	27	4		8/1
Texas A&M University	College Station	U	B,M,D		F,S	C	44,072	26	5	15	26	18	36	570	18	41	33	8	610	8	33	45	14	550	25	44	26	5	2/15
Texas A&M University at Commerce	Commerce	SM	B,M,D	Pub	F,S	C	5,185																						8/6
Texas A&M University at Galveston	Galveston	SU	B,M	Pub	No	C	1,565	23	20	30	40	7	3	520	30	55	14	1	540	30	55	14	1						Open
Texas A&M University at Kingsville	Kingsville	SM	B,M,D	Pub	F,S	C	5,580																						Open
Texas Christian University	Fort Worth	SU	B,M,D	Pri	F,S	C	8,640																						2/15
Texas Lutheran University	Seguin	SM	B,M	Pri	F,S	C	1,329	22	35	31	23	7	4	500	48	38	13	1	530	33	50	16	1	490	54	37	8	1	6/1
Texas Southern University	Houston	U	B,M,D	Pub	F,S	C	7,021	17	93	5	2			400	90	9	1		420	86	13	1		400	92	8			8/15
Texas State University	San Marcos	SU	B,M,D	Pub	F,S	C	31,032	24	8	41	31	11	9	540	27	53	17	3	551	17	59	22	2	509	44	45	10	1	5/1
Texas Tech University	Lubbock	U	B,M,D	Pub	F,S	C	23,021	23	17	33	29	11	10	530	31	43	19	2	560	22	49	27	2	510					5/1
Texas Wesleyan University	Fort Worth	U	B,M,D	Pri	F,S	C	1,941	21	67	20	10	1		512	52	37	10	1	521	40	57	7	1	471	64	29	8		Open
Texas Woman's University	Denton	U	B,M,D	Pub	F,S	PW	9,441																						7/15
Trinity University	San Antonio	U	B,M	Pri	F,S	C	2,353	29		7	21	23	49	620	3	34	44	18	620	2	27	54	17	600	9	35	41	14	2/1
University of Dallas	Irving	U	B,M,D	Pri	No	C	1,353	26	4	22	29	14	31	610	7	36	39	18	580	12	44	29	15	580	13	40	30	17	3/1
University of Houston	Houston	U	B,M,D	Pub	F,S	C	31,587	24	17	28	27	12	16	551	25	45	24	6	588	11	43	38	8						4/1
University of Houston-Downtown	Houston	U	B,M	Pub	F,S	C		16						380	51	17	2		420	51	29	4			47	16	1		4/1
University of Mary Hardin-Baylor	Belton	SM	B,M,D	Pri	No	C	3,056	24	28	30	22	11	9	516	42	44	12	2	530	34	49	16	1	485	60	32	7	1	Open
University of North Texas	Denton	SU	B,M,D	Pub	F,S	C	28,283	23	21	31	25	13	11	540	29	44	23	4	550	23	45	25	6	520	39	42	17	2	8/1
University of St. Thomas - Houston	Houston	U	B,M,D	Pri	No	C	1,610	25	8	21	40	8	23	540	28	48	19	5	560	21	45	32	2	530	32	46	20	1	5/1
University of Texas at Arlington	Arlington	U	B,M,D	Pub	F,S	C	19,604																						6/1
University of Texas at Austin	Austin	U	B,M,D	Pub	F,S	C	39,955	26	10	16	26	18	30																2/1
University of Texas at Dallas	Richardson	SU	B,M,D	Pub	F,S	C	13,049	27	3	10	20	20	47	600	9	35	38	18	640	3	21	48	28	590	13	40	34	13	7/1
University of Texas at El Paso	El Paso	U	B,M,D	Pub	F,S	C	15,806																						7/31
University of Texas at San Antonio	San Antonio	SU	B,M,D	Pub	F,S	C	24,342	22	38	29	21	7	5	500	49	36	13	2	530	35	45	18	2						7/1
University of Texas-Pan American	Edinburg	SM	B,M,D	Pub	F,S	C	17,602	19	66	23	8	2	1	460	67	26	6	1	490	52	39	8	2	450	72	23	4		8/8
University of the Incarnate Word	San Antonio	U	A,B,M,D	Pri	F,S	C	6,491	20	53	27	14	4	2	470	61	30	8	1	490	53	36	10	1	460	69	25	5	1	Open
Wayland Baptist University	Plainview	SM	A,B,M	Pri	F,S	C	1,385	19	59	19	14	6	2	455	63	25	10	2	470	59	26	15		425	76	17	6	1	Open
West Texas A&M University	Canyon	SM	B,M,D	Pub	F,S	C	6,908	21	49	28	15	5	2																Open
Wiley College	Marshall	SM	B		No		741																						Open

Utah

Brigham Young University	Provo	SU	B,M,D	Pri	No	C	27,767		2	6	20	25	47		6	28	43	23		4	24	50	22		10	37	41	12	2/15
Southern Utah University	Cedar City	SM	A,B,M	Pub	F,S	C	7,017								38	45	14	3		41	40	17	2		47	40	12	1	5/1
University of Utah	Salt Lake City	U	B,M,D	Pub	F,S	C	24,840	24	20	23	26	12	19	580	18	42	30	10	580	19	36	34	11	550	25	42	28	5	4/1
Utah State University	Logan	SM	A,B,M,D	Pub	F,S	C	24,385	23	23	27	23	11	16																4/1
Westminster College	Salt Lake City	U	B,M	Pri	No	C	2,295	25	15	23	28	17	17	550	24	48	23	5	550	21	50	26	3						Open

Vermont

Bennington College	Bennington	SM	B,M	Pri	No	C	688	29	5		23	23	50	690		13	46	41	610	2	38	48	13	660	2	21	51	27	1/3
Burlington College	Burlington	U	A,B,M	Pri	No	C	219																						8
Castleton State College	Castleton	R	A,B,M	Pub	No	C	2,059	20						490	54	38	6	2	500	56	35	9		470	69	27	4		Open
Champlain College	Burlington	U	A,B,M	Pri	No	C	2,252	25	17	19	29	15	20	568	22	42	27	9	556	25	41	29	5	544	28	47	22	3	2/1
College of St Joseph	Rutland	SM	A,B,M	Pri	No	C	176	17	100					417	25	75			427	100				435	25	75			Open
Goddard College	Plainfield	R	B,M	Pri	No	C	244																						Open
Green Mountain College	Poultney	SM	B,M	Pri	No	C	765	20	41	39	11	8	1																Open
Johnson State College	Johnson	SM	A,B,M	Pub	No	C	1,540	20						500					500										Open
Lyndon State College	Lyndonville	SM	A,B,M	Pub	No	C	1,430																						Open
Marlboro College	Marlboro	R	B,M	Pri	No	C	336	25		35	29	29	7																2/15
Middlebury College	Middlebury	SM	B,M,D	Pri	No	C	2,495	31		2	25		73	688	1	13	34	52	692	1	9	38	52	697	1	10	34	56	2/15
Norwich University	Northfield	R	A,B	Pri	No	C	1,903	22	40	28	20	7	5																Open
Saint Michael's College	Colchester	SU	B,M	Pri	No	C	1,971	25	14	14	32	17	23	580	13	43	39	5	570	15	46	34	5	570	15	47	33	5	2/1
Southern Vermont College	Bennington	SM	A,B	Pri	No	C	532	19	5	2	1	1		450	78	19	2	1	450	76	24	1			78	19	1		Open
Sterling College	Craftsbury Common	R	B	Pri	No	C	105																						2/15
University of Vermont	Burlington	SU	B,M,D	Pub	F,S	C	10,912	26	3	15	32	23	27	590	10	41	39	10	595	10	41	41	8	595	10	42	39	9	1/15
Vermont Technical College	Randolph Center	R	A,B	Pub	No	C	1,356																						Open

NAME OF SCHOOL	TOWN	ENVIRONMENT (U-Urban R-Rural SU-Suburban SM-Small Town)	DEGREES AWARDED (A-Associate B-Bachelor M-Master D-Doctorate)	CONTROL (Pri-Private, Pub-Public)	FRATERNITIES AND SORORITIES (F-Fraternities S-Sororities F, S-Both No-Neither)	STUDENTS: C-Coed M-Men W-Women PM-Primarily Men PW-Primarily Women	UNDERGRADUATE ENROLLMENT FALL 2013	TEST SCORES: ACT Median	ACT Below 21	ACT 21-23	ACT 24-26	ACT 27-28	ACT Above 28	SAT CRITICAL READING Median	SAT CR Below 500	SAT CR 500-599	SAT CR 600-700	SAT CR Above 700	SAT MATHEMATICS Median	SAT M Below 500	SAT M 500-599	SAT M 600-700	SAT M Above 700	SAT WRITING Median	SAT W Below 500	SAT W 500-599	SAT W 600-700	SAT W Above 700	APPLICATION DEADLINE Month / Day
Woodbury Institute of Champlain College in Burlington	Montpelier	SM	A,B		No	C	131																						Open
Virginia																													
Averett University	Danville	SM	A,B,M	Pri	S	C	886	19	71	14	13	1	1	470	66	29	4	1	480	60	35	4							7/15
Bluefield College	Bluefield	SM	B	Pri	F,S	C	776	21	57	20	13	3	7																Open
Bridgewater College	Bridgewater	SM	B	Pri	No	C	1,848	23	27	24	36	5	8	520	41	44	13	2	510	42	42	15	1	490	54	35	11		Open
Christendom College	Front Royal	R	A,B,M		No	C	411	25	3	28	50	12	7	632	5	33	33	29	570	20	46	24	10	616	11	24	43	22	3/1
Christopher Newport University	Newport News	SU	B,M	Pub	F,S	C	5,094	25	7	24	31	19	19	580	7	53	34	6	580	7	57	33	3						2/1
College of William & Mary	Williamsburg	SM	B,M,D	Pub	F,S	C	6,271	30	2	4	10	15	70	690	1	12	42	46	680	1	14	45	40	670	2	13	47	38	1/1
Eastern Mennonite University	Harrisonburg	SM	A,B,M	Pri	No	C	897	25	17	21	30	9	23																Open
Emory and Henry College	Emory	R	B,M	Pri	F,S	C	1,211								53	34	11	2		43	42	14	1		55	35	9	1	4/15
Ferrum College	Ferrum	R	B	Pri	F,S	C	1,240																						Open
George Mason University	Fairfax	SU	B,M,D	Pub	F,S	C	19,702	25	4	30	37	15	14	560	15	52	28	6	570	12	49	34	5						1/15
Hampden-Sydney College	Hampden-Sydney	R	B	Pri	F		1,070	23						555	25	48	22	5	562	21	46	28	5	524					3/1
Hampton University	Hampton	U	A,B,M,D	Pri	F,S	C	3,851	20	40	34	15	1	1	514	45	43	10	2	517	44	44	12	1						3/1
Hollins University	Roanoke	SU	B,M	Pri	No	PW	610	24	20	26	16	23	15	586	19	33	34	14	526	33	45	20	2	559	32	33	25	10	5/1
James Madison University	Harrisonburg	SM	B,M,D	Pub	F,S	C	18,107							570	13	52	31	4	580	10	47	39	4	565	14	51	31	4	1/15
Liberty University	Lynchburg	SU	A,B,M,D		No	C	6,330																						Open
Longwood University	Farmville	SM	B,M	Pub	F,S	C	4,497	21						500	43	44	10	1	500	44	45	9							3/1
Lynchburg College	Lynchburg	SU	B,M,D	Pri	F,S	C	2,178	21	41	28	17	8	6	500	50	38	10	2	500	49	36	14	1	490	54	36	10		3/1
Mary Baldwin College	Staunton	SM	B,M,D	Pri	No	PW	1,431	21	31	31	27	4		500	58	28	12	2	480	70	22	8		480	63	26	9	2	4/15
Marymount University	Arlington	SU	B,M,D	Pri	No	C	2,470	21	43	32	19	3	3	500	46	43	9	2	490	52	38	10		490	51	40	8	1	Open
Norfolk State University	Norfolk	U	A,B,M,D	Pub	F,S	C	5,337	18	81	13	6																		5/31
Old Dominion University	Norfolk	U	B,M,D	Pub	F,S	C	19,819	21	49	26	16	5	4	510	42	44	13	1	510	41	43	15	1						2/1
Radford University	Radford	SM	B,M,D	Pub	F,S	C	8,913	20	57	25	14	2	2	490	54	37	9	1	490	54	38	8		480	62	34	4		2/1
Randolph College	Lynchburg	SU	B,M	Pri	No	C	665	25						550	26	44	23	3	535	34	41	22	3	535	34	41	20	5	3/15
Randolph-Macon College	Ashland	SU	B	Pri	F,S	C	1,315	24						547	26	51	19	4	545	28	48	22	3	530	36	44	19	1	3/1
Roanoke College	Salem	SU	B	Pri	F,S	C	2,029	24	22	27	28	13	10	540	26	46	24	4	540	28	50	21	2	530	30	49	18	3	3/15
Saint Paul's College	Lawrenceville	SM	B		F,S	C	690																						Open
Shenandoah University	Winchester	SM	B,M,D	Pri	No	C	2,150	21	46	28	13	6	7	480	57	34	7	2	490	55	33	11	1	470	63	27	8	2	Open
Sweet Briar College	Sweet Briar	R	B,M	Pri	No	W	723	25	15	23	32	17	12	560	28	42	24	6	510	42	42	13	3	530	39	37	23	1	2/1
University of Mary Washington	Fredericksburg	SU	B,M	Pub	No	C	4,515	25	7	24	34	18	17	570	10	42	37	10	560	14	47	34	4	560	12	45	37	6	2/1
University of Virginia	Charlottesville	SU	B,M,D	Pub	F,S	C	16,087	30	1	3	7	12	77	670	2	14	47	37	680	2	12	40	46	670	2	12	47	39	1/1
University of Virginia's College at Wise	Wise	SM	B	Pub	F,S	C	1,892	20	58	24	11	4	3																8/1
Virginia Commonwealth University	Richmond	U	B,M,D	Pub	F,S	C	23,951	23	18	34	26	11	12	550	22	49	24	5	550	21	49	24	4	540	29	47	20	4	1/15
Virginia Intermont College	Bristol	U	A,B	Pri	No	C	496	20	60	21	16	2	1																Open
Virginia Military Institute	Lexington	SM	B	Pub	No	C	1,378	23	21	36	32	6	5	550	18	52	27	3	560	11	56	30	3	530	30	49	20	1	2/1
Virginia Polytechnic Institute and State University	Blacksburg	R	B,M,D	Pub	F,S	C	30,855							590					621					586					1/15
Virginia State University	Petersburg	SU	B,M		F,S	C	3,600																						1/15
Virginia Union University	Richmond	U	B,M,D		F,S	C	1,260																						1/15
Virginia Wesleyan College	Norfolk	SU	B	Pri	F,S	C	1,671	20	55	23	19	2	2																Open
Washington and Lee University	Lexington	SM	B,M,D	Pri	F,S	C	1,838	30				27	73	691		4	47	49	693		3	50	47	683		10	44	46	1/1
Washington																													
Central Washington University	Ellensburg	R	B,M	Pub	No	C	8,587	20	51	23	12	12	2																4/1
City University of Seattle	Seattle	U	A,B,M,D	Pri	No	C	1,190																						Open
Cornish College of the Arts	Seattle	U	B	Pri	No	C	710																						8/15
Eastern Washington University	Cheney	SM	B,M	Pub	F,S	C		21	20	55			25	485	57	33	9	1	495	51	38	11		470	64	30	6		5/15
Evergreen State College	Olympia	SM	B,M	Pub	No	C	4,282	24	17	30	28	13	12	580	17	41	33	9	530	36	40	22	2						3/1
Gonzaga University	Spokane	U	B,M,D	Pri	No	C	4,896	27		12	33	20	35	596	6	44	40	10	605	3	40	46	11						2/1
Heritage University	Toppenish	R	A,B,M	Pri	No	C	876																						Open
Northwest University	Kirkland	SU	A,B,M	Pri	No	C	1,057																						8/1
Pacific Lutheran University	Tacoma	SU	B,M	Pri	No	C	3,166	25	4	24	27	15	18	548	28	41	26	5	550	29	41	24	6		33	43	21	3	Open

Saint Martin's University	Lacey	SU	B,M	Pri	No	C	1,479	22	63	17	12	2	6	519	39	41	16	4	630	35	42	21	2	503	45	44	11		3/1
Seattle Pacific University	Seattle	U	B,M,D	Pri	No	C	3,395	25	9	22	30	18	21	570	16	47	28	9	570	19	46	32	3	550	23	45	27	5	3/1
Seattle University	Seattle	U	B,M,D	Pri	No	C	4,666	27						580	11	46	34	9	580	11	50	32	7	580	12	45	36	7	2/1
University of Puget Sound	Tacoma	SM	B,M,D	Pri	F,S	C		27		11		59	29	620	5	32	44	18	590	7	37	45	11	610	5	38	43	14	1/15
University of Washington	Seattle	U	B,M,D	Pub	F,S	C	28,570		9	16	27	20	28		16	36	36	12		9	32	44	16		17	42	34	8	1/15
Walla Walla University	College Place	SM	A,B,M	Pri	No	C	1,563																						Open
Washington State University	Pullman	SM	B,M,D		F,S	C	22,763		26	26	24	11	10		38	42	18	2		33	43	22	3		44	42	13	1	1/31
Western Washington University	Bellingham	SM	B,M	Pub	No	C	13,925	25	13	26	28	15	18	550	25	43	27	5	550	25	47	26	3	530	32	45	21	2	3/1
Whitman College	Walla Walla	SM	B	Pri	F,S	C	1,541	30		6	12	15	67	670	4	15	42	39	660	2	20	53	25	660	5	16	53	26	1/15
Whitworth University	Spokane	SU	B,M	Pri	No	C	2,358	26						600	11	36	44	9	600	11	38	43	8	590	11	42	39	8	3/1

West Virginia

Alderson Broaddus University	Philippi	SM	A,B,M	Pri	F,S	C	1,052	21	47	29	19	3	2	470	57	38	5		470	61	32	7		470	69	29	2		8/1
Bethany College	Bethany	R	B,M	Pri	F,S	C	694	21	45	27	22	4	1	450	64	26	9	1	430	65	30	5		460	74	19	6	1	Open
Bluefield State College	Bluefield	SM	A,B	Pub	F,S	C	2,063	18	73	17	8	1	1		55	43	2			57	33	10							Open
Concord University	Athens	SM	A,B,M	Pub	F,S	C	2,652	21						486	58	32	10		482	58	34	7	1		68	23	8	1	Open
Davis and Elkins College	Elkins	SM	A,B		No	C	874																						Open
Fairmont State University	Fairmont	SM	A,B,M	Pub	F,S	C	4,362	21						468	69	29	2		484	65	33	2							Open
Glenville State College	Glenville	R	A,B	Pub	F,S	C	1,719	20	61	24	12	2	1	428	75	20	4	1	438	77	19	4							Open
Marshall University	Huntington	U	A,B,M,D	Pub	F,S	C	9,762																						Open
Mountain State University	Beckley	SM	A,B,M,D	Pri	F,S	C	4,890	18	73	15	9	3							525	50	50								Open
Ohio Valley University	Vienna	SU	A,B	Pri	No	C	659	23	75	25	9	3	2																Open
Salem International University	Salem	R	A,B,M	Pri	F,S	C	340	21	51	29	18	2																	Open
Shepherd University	Shepherdstown	SM	B,M	Pub	F,S	C	3,990	21	43	27	19	7	4	490	49	37	11	3	480	55	35	10							Open
University of Charleston	Charleston	SM	A,B,M,D	Pri	F,S	C	1,386	22	38	29	21	6	7	470	69	24	4	4	480	58	29	11	1						Open
West Liberty University	West Liberty	R	A,B	Pub	F,S	C	2,266																						Open
West Virginia State University	Institute	SU	A,B	Pub	F,S	C	3,449	19																					Open
West Virginia University	Morgantown	SM	B,M,D	Pub	F,S	C	22,757	24	54	20	18	7	2	516	41	44	13	2	536	33	45	19	3						8/1
West Virginia University Institute of Technology	Montgomery	SM	B	Pub	F,S	C	2,400																						8/1
West Virginia Wesleyan College	Buckhannon	SM	B,M	Pri	F,S	C	1,327	23	18	19	16	6	4																8/1
Wheeling Jesuit University	Wheeling	SU	B,M,D	Pri	No	C	1,173	22	31	31	23	9	6	500	41	46	13		510	35	52	10	2	480	57	33	5		Open

Wisconsin

Alverno College	Milwaukee	SM	A,B,M	Pri	S	W	1,862	19	66	23	7	3	1																Open
Beloit College	Beloit	SM	B	Pri	F,S	C		27	2	22		47	30	630	14	30	28	29	600	14	36	36	15						1/15
Cardinal Stritch University	Milwaukee	SU	A,B,M,D		No	C	3,130																						1/15
Carroll University	Waukesha	SU	B,M	Pri	F,S	C	3,066	23	31	34	22	9	4																Open
Carthage College	Kenosha	SU	B,M	Pri	F,S	C	2,265																						Open
Concordia University Wisconsin	Mequon	SU	A,B,M,D	Pri	No	C	4,419	22																					8/1
Edgewood College	Madison	SU	B,M		No	C	2,206	22	38	31	22	7	3																8/25
Lakeland College	Sheboygan	R	B,M	Pri	F,S	C	840																						8/25
Lawrence University	Appleton	U	B	Pri	F,S	C	1,496		1	6	15	20	58		1	21	48	30		2	26	48	24		6	31	38	25	1/15
Marian University	Fond du Lac	SM	B,M,D	Pri	F,S	C	1,688	20	58	24	13	4	1																Open
Marquette University	Milwaukee	U	B,M,D	Pri	F,S	C	8,293	27	3	13	27	23	35	580	13	44	36	7	600	10	36	45	10	580	14	44	37	5	12/1
Milwaukee Institute of Art and Design	Milwaukee	U	B	Pri	No	C	628																					5	12/1
Milwaukee School of Engineering	Milwaukee	U	B,M	Pri	F,S	C	2,378	27	3	13	29	35	20	570	17	53	19	11	630	8	19	58	15						Open
Mount Mary University	Milwaukee	U	B,M,D	Pri	No	PW	926	20	61	12	19	3	5																Open
Northland College	Ashland	SM	B		F,S	C	739	23	27	20	28	10	15																Open
Ripon College	Ripon	SM	B	Pri	F,S	C	1,065	24	19	29	28	14	10	500	53	35	9	3	528	36	38	23	3						8/1
Silver Lake College	Manitowoc	R	A,B,M	Pri	No	C	1,540																						Open
St. Norbert College	De Pere	SU	B,M	Pri	F,S	C	2,160	25	9	29	32	17	13																Open
University of Wisconsin Whitewater	Whitewater	SM	A,B,M	Pub	F,S	C	10,687	1050						530					520					525					Open
University of Wisconsin/Eau Claire	Eau Claire	U	A,B,M,D	Pub	F,S	C	10,383	24	11	9	36	34	10		29	31	34	6		9	40	31	20						Open
University of Wisconsin/Green Bay	Green Bay	SU	A,B,M	Pub	F,S	C	6,444	23	24	35	28	9	4																1/1
University of Wisconsin/La Crosse	La Crosse	SM	A,B,M	Pub	F,S	C	9,441	25	5	28	41	17	9																Open
University of Wisconsin/Madison	Madison	U	B,M,D	Pub	F,S	C	31,126								7	39	40	14		1	14	40	45		5	24	52	19	2/1
University of Wisconsin/Oshkosh	Oshkosh	U	A,B,M	Pub	F,S	C	9,800																					19	2/1
University of Wisconsin/Parkside	Kenosha	SU	B,M	Pub	No	C	6,640																						8/1
University of Wisconsin/Platteville	Platteville	SM	A,B,M	Pub	F,S	C	7,682	23	21	32	26	11	10																Open
University of Wisconsin/River Falls	River Falls	SU	B,M	Pub	F,S	C	6,390																						Open
University of Wisconsin/Stevens Point	Stevens Point	SM	A,B,M,D	Pub	F,S	C	9,118	23	27	37	23	8	5	546	23	55	14	9	536	32	41	23	5	528	46	32	23		Open
University of Wisconsin/Stout	Menomonie	R	B,M	Pub	F,S	C	8,270	21	42	35	17	5	2																Open
University of Wisconsin/Superior	Superior	U	A,B,M	Pub	No	C	2,522	22	38	31	22	5	5																8/1

NAME OF SCHOOL	TOWN	ENVIRONMENT U-Urban R-Rural SU-Suburban SM-Small Town	DEGREES AWARDED A-Associate B-Bachelor M-Master D-Doctorate	CONTROL Pri-Private, Pub-Public	FRATERNITIES AND SORORITIES F-Fraternities S-Sororities F, S-Both No-Neither	STUDENTS: C-Coed M-Men W-Women PM-Primarily Men PW-Primarily Women	UNDERGRADUATE ENROLLMENT FALL 2013	TEST SCORES: ACT Median	ACT Below 21	ACT 21-23	ACT 24-26	ACT 27-28	ACT Above 28	SAT CRITICAL READING Median	SAT CR Below 500	SAT CR 500-599	SAT CR 600-700	SAT CR Above 700	SAT MATHEMATICS Median	SAT M Below 500	SAT M 500-599	SAT M 600-700	SAT M Above 700	SAT WRITING Median	SAT W Below 500	SAT W 500-599	SAT W 600-700	SAT W Above 700	APPLICATION DEADLINE Month / Day
University of Wisconsin-Milwaukee	Milwaukee	U	B,M,D	Pub	F,S	C	23,004	22	38	30	21	7	5																7/1
Viterbo University	La Crosse	SU	A,B,M	Pri	No	C	2,105	23	24	34	29	8	5																Open
Wisconsin Lutheran College	Milwaukee	SU	B	Pri	No	C	740																						Open
Wyoming																													
University of Wyoming	Laramie	SM	B,M,D		F,S	C	10,194	24	16	28	28	12	15	543	33	38	25	4	557	25	39	30	6						8/10

IN-STATE COST RANGES DIRECTORY

The breakdown of in-state tuition, room, and board costs for the 2013-2014 academic year is arranged from least expensive to most expensive. Within each range are lists of schools that don't charge for tuition or room and board, and those that do. Listings that say (no R & B) means complete information was not provided by the school at press time. For any late additions, please refer to the school profile on our website, *barronspac.com.*

Colleges Where There Are No Fees For Tuition, Room/Board

United States Coast Guard Academy, CT
United States Merchant Marine Academy, NY (no R & B)
United States Air Force Academy, CO
United States Military Academy, NY
United States Naval Academy, MD

Less Than $2000

Colleges with Tuition, Room, and Board

Conservatory of Music of Puerto Rico, PR (no R & B)
Excelsior College, NY (no R & B)
Southern University at New Orleans, LA
University of Puerto Rico/Bayamon , PR (no R & B)
University of Puerto Rico/Cayey, PR (no R & B)
University of Puerto Rico/Humacao, PR (no R & B)
University of Puerto Rico/Mayaguez, PR (no R & B)

$2000-$3999

Colleges with Tuition, Room, and Board

Bluefield State College, WV (no R & B)
Central University of Bayamon, PR (no R & B)
Escuela de Artes Plasticas de Puerto Rico, PR (no R & B)
Inter-American University of Puerto Rico/Arecibo Campus, PR (no R & B)
Inter-American University of Puerto Rico/Barranquitas , PR (no R & B)
Inter-American University of Puerto Rico/Ponce , PR (no R & B)
Langston University, OK
Oglala Lakota College, SD (no R & B)
Sinte Gleska University, SD (no R & B)
Universidad Metropolitana, PR

$4000-$5999

Colleges with Tuition, Room, and Board

Alice Lloyd College, KY
American University of Puerto Rico, PR (no R & B)
Bellevue University, NE (no R & B)
Chicago State University, IL (no R & B)
City University of New York/Brooklyn College, NY (no R & B)
Inter-American University of Puerto Rico/Aguadilla Campus, PR (no R & B)
Inter-American University of Puerto Rico/Bayamon University College, PR (no R & B)
Inter-American University of Puerto Rico/Fajardo Campus, PR (no R & B)
Inter-American University of Puerto Rico/Metropolitan Campus, PR (no R & B)
Lehman College / The City University of New York, NY
Louisiana State University in Shreveport, LA (no R & B)
Medgar Evers College / The City University of New York, NY (no R & B)
Metropolitan State University, MN (no R & B)
Metropolitan State University of Denver, CO (no R & B)
New York City College of Technology / The City University of New York, NY (no R & B)
Thomas Edison State College, NJ (no R & B)
Universidad del Turabo, PR (no R & B)
University of Puerto Rico Recinto de Rio Piedras, PR
University of the Sacred Heart, PR
York College / City University of New York, NY (no R & B)

$6000-$7999

Colleges with Tuition, Room, and Board

Amridge University, AL (no R & B)
Baker College of Flint, MI
Berea College, KY
Chadron State College, NE
Franklin University, OH (no R & B)
Granite State College, NH (no R & B)
Indiana University East, IN (no R & B)
Indiana University Kokomo, IN
Indiana University Northwest, IN
Inter-American University of Puerto Rico/San Germán, PR
John Jay College of Criminal Justice / The City University of New York, NY (no R & B)
Lamar University, TX
Lewis-Clark State College, ID
Mississippi University for Women, MS
Nicholls State University, LA
Northwestern Oklahoma State University, OK
Ohio State University at Lima, OH (no R & B)
Pontifical Catholic University of Puerto Rico, PR
South Carolina State University, SC
Southeastern Oklahoma State University, OK
State University of New York/Empire State College, NY (no R & B)
Texas A&M University at Kingsville, TX
Universidad Adventista de las Antillas, PR
University of Hawaii at Hilo, HI
University of Houston-Downtown, TX (no R & B)
University of Louisiana at Lafayette, LA
University of Maine at Augusta, ME (no R & B)
University of Maryland/University College, MD (no R & B)
University of North Carolina School of the Arts, NC
University of Puerto Rico/Arecibo, PR (no R & B)
University of the District of Columbia, DC (no R & B)
Webb Institute, NY (no R & B)
Wilmington University, DE (no R & B)

$8000-$9999

Colleges with Tuition, Room, and Board

Albany State University, GA
Alcorn State University, MS
Arkansas Baptist College, AR
Boricua College, NY (no R & B)
Brigham Young University/Hawaii, HI
California State University, Bakersfield, CA
Cameron University, OK
Central State University, OH
Charter Oak State College, CT (no R & B)
Dickinson State University, ND
East Tennessee State University, TN
Louisiana Tech University, LA
Middle Tennessee State University, TN
Midwestern State University, TX
Mississippi Valley State University, MS
New Mexico Highlands University, NM
North Carolina Central University, NC
North Georgia College & State University, GA
Northeastern State University, OK
Ohio State University at Marion, OH (no R & B)
Oklahoma Panhandle State University, OK
Oregon Institute of Technology, OR
Our Lady of Holy Cross College, LA (no R & B)
Peru State College, NE
Sojourner-Douglass College, MD (no R & B)
Southern University and A&M College, LA
Southwestern Oklahoma State University, OK
Tennessee State University, TN
Union Institute & University, OH (no R & B)
University of Arkansas at Monticello, AR
University of Michigan/Dearborn, MI (no R & B)
University of Montana-Western, MT
University of New Orleans, LA
University of North Alabama, AL
University of Rio Grande, OH
University of Texas at El Paso, TX
University of West Alabama, AL
University of Wisconsin/River Falls, WI
West Liberty University, WV
West Virginia State University, WV
Western New Mexico University, NM
Wiley College, TX
Winston-Salem State University, NC

$10,000-$11,999

Colleges with Tuition, Room, and Board

Cabarrus College of Health Sciences, NC (no R & B)
Caribbean University, PR
Central Washington University, WA
Chancellor University, OH (no R & B)
Cleary University, MI (no R & B)
East Central University, OK
Eastern Kentucky University, KY
Eastern New Mexico University, NM
Eastern Oregon University, OR
Elizabeth City State University, NC
Fayetteville State University, NC
Fort Hays State University, KS
Fort Valley State University, GA
Glenville State College, WV
Idaho State University, ID
Kentucky State University, KY
Lane College, TN
Lincoln University, MO
Martin University, IN (no R & B)
Mayville State University, ND
Minot State University, ND
Missouri Southern State University, MO
Morehead State University, KY
Norfolk State University, VA
Penn State University/Altoona, PA
Rust College, MS
Slippery Rock University of Pennsylvania, PA
Southern Utah University, UT
St. Cloud State University, MN
Tennessee Technological University, TN
Texas A&M University at Commerce, TX
Texas A&M University at Corpus Christi, TX
Texas A&M University at Galveston, TX
Thomas University, GA
Troy University, AL
University of Alaska Southeast, AK
University of Arkansas at Pine Bluff, AR
University of Central Arkansas, AR
University of Maine at Machias, ME
University of Massachusetts Boston, MA (no R & B)
University of Science and Arts of Oklahoma, OK
University of Texas at Arlington, TX
University of Virginia's College at Wise, VA
University of Wisconsin/Oshkosh, WI
University of Wisconsin/Parkside, WI
Utah State University, UT
Valdosta State University, GA
Virginia State University, VA
Wayne State College, NE
Weber State University, UT
Western Kentucky University, KY

$12,000-$13,999

Colleges with Tuition, Room, and Board

Adams State College, CO
American InterContinental University, GA (no R & B)
Appalachian State University, NC
Arkansas Tech University, AR
Auburn University at Montgomery, AL
Bemidji State University, MN
Black Hills State University, SD
Bloomsburg University of Pennsylvania, PA
Blue Mountain College, MS
Boise State University, ID
Brigham Young University, UT
California State University, San Bernardino, CA
Cambridge College, MA (no R & B)
Carlos Albizu University, FL (no R & B)
Cincinnati College of Mortuary Science, OH (no R & B)
Clayton State University, GA
Colorado State University-Pueblo, CO
Columbus State University, GA
Concord University, WV
Concordia College - Alabama, AL
Dakota State University, SD
Delta State University, MS
Emporia State University, KS
Evergreen State College, WA
Fairmont State University, WV
Fashion Institute of Technology/State University of New York, NY
Georgia Southwestern State University, GA (no R & B)
Georgia State University, GA
Grambling State University, LA
Henderson State University, AR
Hodges University, FL (no R & B)
Jackson State University, MS
Jacksonville State University, AL
Kennesaw State University, GA
LeMoyne-Owen College, TN
Michigan State University, MI

Minnesota State University, Moorhead, MN
Missouri State University, MO
Missouri Western State University, MO
Montana State University-Billings, MT
Montana State University-Northern, MT
New Mexico Institute of Mining and Technology, NM
New Mexico State University, NM
North Carolina Agricultural and Technical State University, NC
Ohio State University at Mansfield, OH
Peirce College, PA (no R & B)
Pittsburg State University, KS
Salem State College, MA
Savannah State University, GA
Southeastern Louisiana University, LA
Southern Polytechnic State University, GA
Sul Ross State University, TX
Talladega College, AL
Tarleton State University, TX
Texas Woman's University, TX
Truman State University, MO
University of Alaska Fairbanks, AK
University of Central Oklahoma, OK
University of Louisiana at Monroe, LA
University of Montana, MT
University of Nebraska at Omaha, NE
University of North Carolina at Asheville, NC
University of North Carolina at Greensboro, NC
University of North Carolina at Wilmington, NC
University of South Alabama, AL
University of South Florida, FL
University of South Florida/St. Petersburg, FL
University of Southern Mississippi, MS
University of Tennessee at Martin, TN
University of Texas-Pan American, TX
University of Utah, UT
University of Wisconsin Whitewater, WI
University of Wyoming, WY
Valley City State University, ND
Washburn University, KS
West Texas A&M University, TX
Western Carolina University, NC
Wichita State University, KS
William Carey University, MS

$14,000-$15,999

Colleges with Tuition, Room, and Board

Alabama State University, AL
Angelo State University, TX
Arkansas State University, AR
Austin Peay State University, TN
Buffalo State/State University of Buffalo, NY
California Maritime Academy, CA
California State University, Los Angeles, CA
California State University, San Marcos, CA
California University of Pennsylvania, PA
Calumet College of St. Joseph, IN (no R & B)
City University of New York/Baruch College, NY (no R & B)
City University of Seattle, WA (no R & B)
Coppin State University, MD
Cox College, MO
Delaware State University, DE
East Carolina University, NC
Edinboro University of Pennsylvania, PA
Embry-Riddle Aeronautical University - Worldwide, FL
Florida Agricultural and Mechanical University, FL
Florida State University, FL
Fort Lewis College, CO
Frostburg State University, MD
George Mason University, VA
Harris-Stowe State University, MO
Hunter College / The City University of New York, NY
Indiana University South Bend, IN
Indiana University Southeast, IN
Indiana University-Purdue University Fort Wayne, IN
Kansas State University, KS
Kaplan University, IA
Louisiana College, LA
Lyndon State College, VT
Marshall University, WV
Massachusetts Maritime Academy, MA
Mercy College of Health Sciences, IA (no R & B)
Minnesota State University, Mankato, MN
Mississippi State University, MS
Montana State University, MT
Montana Tech of The University of Montana, MT
Morgan State University, MD
Mountain State University, WV
Murray State University, KY
National University, CA (no R & B)
New College of Florida, FL
North Dakota State University, ND
Northern Kentucky University, KY
Northern Michigan University, MI
Northern State University, SD
Northwest Missouri State University, MO
Northwestern State University of Louisiana, LA
Oklahoma State University, OK
Ottawa University, KS (no R & B)
Prairie View A&M University, TX
Presentation College, SD
Purdue University/Calumet, IN
Saint Augustine's University, NC
Shaw University, NC
Shepherd University, WV
South Dakota School of Mines and Technology, SD
South Dakota State University, SD
Southeast Missouri State University, MO
Southern Arkansas University, AR
Southwest Minnesota State University, MN
Stephen F. Austin State University, TX
SUNY New Paltz, NY
Texas Tech University, TX
The Lincoln University, PA
Tougaloo College, MS
University of Alaska Anchorage, AK
University of Central Florida, FL
University of Central Missouri, MO
University of Colorado at Colorado Springs, CO
University of Florida, FL
University of Idaho, ID
University of Maine at Fort Kent, ME
University of Maine at Presque Isle, ME
University of Maryland/Eastern Shore, MD
University of Memphis, TN
University of Mississippi, MS
University of Nebraska at Kearney, NE
University of Nevada/Reno, NV
University of New Mexico, NM
University of North Carolina at Charlotte, NC
University of North Dakota, ND
University of North Florida, FL
University of North Texas, TX
University of Northern Colorado, CO
University of Northern Iowa, IA
University of South Dakota, SD
University of Southern Indiana, IN
University of the Southwest, NM
University of Washington, WA
University of West Florida, FL
University of West Georgia, GA
University of Wisconsin/Eau Claire, WI
University of Wisconsin/Green Bay, WI
University of Wisconsin/La Crosse, WI
University of Wisconsin/Platteville, WI
University of Wisconsin/Stevens Point, WI
University of Wisconsin/Superior, WI
Vermont Technical College, VT
Virginia Polytechnic Institute and State University, VA
West Virginia University, WV
West Virginia University Institute of Technology, WV
Western Oregon University, OR
Wilberforce University, OH
Woodbury Institute of Champlain College in Burlington, VT

$16,000-$17,999

Colleges with Tuition, Room, and Board

Adventist Universtiy of Health Sciences, FL
Allen University, SC (no R & B)
American Indian College , AZ
Armstrong Atlantic State University, GA
Ball State University, IN
Bluefield College, VA
California State University, Dominguez Hills, CA
California State University, East Bay, CA
California State University, Fresno, CA
California State University, Long Beach, CA
California State University, Sacramento, CA
Clarion University of Pennsylvania, PA
Clarkson College, NE
Coastal Carolina University, SC
College of Staten Island / The City University of New York, NY
Colorado Mesa University, CO
East Stroudsburg University of Pennsylvania, PA
Eastern Michigan University, MI
Eastern Washington University, WA
East-West University, IL (no R & B)
Edward Waters College, FL
Fitchburg State University, MA
Florida Atlantic University, FL
Florida International University, FL
Framingham State University, MA
Francis Marion University, SC
Georgia Southern University, GA
Goddard College, VT
Golden Gate University, CA (no R & B)
Grand Valley State University, MI
Heritage University, WA (no R & B)
Howard Payne University, TX
Humphreys College, CA
Indiana State University, IN
Indiana University-Purdue University Indianapolis, IN
Iowa State University, IA
Johnson State College, VT
Kentucky Christian University, KY
Kutztown University of Pennsylvania, PA
Livingstone College, NC
Lock Haven University of Pennsylvania, PA
Maritime College / State University of New York, NY
Massachusetts College of Liberal Arts, MA
Metropolitan College of New York, NY (no R & B)
Miles College, AL
Monroe College, NY
Morris College, SC
National American University, SD (no R & B)
National Louis University, IL (no R & B)
North Carolina State University, NC
Ohio State University at Newark, OH
Ohio Valley University, WV
Park University, MO
Penn State Erie/The Behrend College, PA
Purchase College / State University of New York , NY
Queens College / The City University of New York, NY
Radford University, VA
Rhode Island College, RI
Saginaw Valley State University, MI
Saint Paul's College, VA
Sam Houston State University, TX
Shawnee State University, OH
Shippensburg University of Pennsylvania, PA
Siena Heights University, MI
Southern Illinois University Edwardsville, IL
Southern Oregon University, OR
St. Gregory's University, OK
SUNY College at Old Westbury, NY
SUNY Oneonta / State University of New York, NY
Texas A&M University, TX
Texas State University, TX
The State University of New York at Potsdam, NY
Towson University, MD
University of Alabama at Huntsville, AL
University of Alabama at Tuscaloosa, AL
University of Arkansas at Fayetteville, AR
University of Arkansas at Little Rock, AR
University of Colorado Denver , CO
University of Iowa, IA
University of Kansas, KS
University of Louisville, KY
University of Maine at Farmington, ME
University of Mary, ND
University of Michigan-Flint, MI
University of Minnesota Crookston, MN
University of Minnesota/Morris, MN
University of Montevallo, AL
University of Nebraska - Lincoln, NE
University of Nevada, Las Vegas, NV
University of North Carolina at Pembroke, NC
University of Oklahoma, OK
University of Pittsburgh at Greensburg, PA
University of South Carolina at Aiken, SC
University of South Carolina Upstate, SC
University of Southern Maine, ME
University of Tennessee at Chattanooga, TN
Virginia Military Institute, VA
Wayland Baptist University, TX
West Chester University of Pennsylvania, PA
Western State Colorado University, CO
Winona State University, MN
Wright State University, OH
Youngstown State University, OH

$18,000-$19,999

Colleges with Tuition, Room, and Board

Alfred State / SUNY College of Technology , NY
Arizona State University, AZ
Berkeley College, NY (no R & B)
Bethel University, TN
Boston Architectural College, MA (no R & B)
Bowling Green State University, OH
Bridgewater State University, MA
California Polytechnic State University, CA
California State Polytechnic University, Pomona, CA
California State University, Chico, CA
California State University, Stanislaus, CA
Castleton State College, VT
Central Connecticut State University, CT
Central Michigan University, MI
Christian Brothers University, TN
Citadel, The, SC
Clemson University, SC
Colorado School of Mines, CO
CUNY-City College, NY
Eureka College, IL
Farmingdale State College, NY
Ferris State University, MI
Fisk University, TN
Freed-Hardeman University, TN
Georgia College and State University, GA
Goodwin College, CT (no R & B)
Humboldt State University, CA
Huston-Tillotson University, TX
Indiana University Bloomington, IN
James Madison University, VA

Jarvis Christian College, TX
Kent State University, OH
Lake Superior State University, MI
Lee University, TN
Liberty University, VA
Lincoln Memorial University, TN
Louisiana State University, LA
Mansfield University, PA
Marylhurst University, OR (no R & B)
Millersville University of Pennsylvania, PA
Missouri University of Science and Technology, MO
Mount Olive College, NC
Northern Arizona University, AZ
Northern Illinois University, IL
Northwest University, WA
Oakland University, MI
Old Dominion University, VA
Olivet College, MI
Oregon State University, OR
Paine College, GA
Philander Smith College, AR
Portland State University, OR
Rochester College, MI
Salem International University, WV
Salisbury University, MD
San Francisco State University, CA
San Jose State University, CA
Southern Connecticut State University, CT
State University of New York / College of Environmental Science and Forestry, NY
Stillman College, AL
Stony Brook University / State University of New York, NY
SUNY College at Geneseo , NY
SUNY Cortland / The State University of New York, NY
SUNY Fredonia / The State University of New York at Fredonia, NY
SUNY Plattsburgh / State University of New York, NY
Texas Southern University, TX
The College at Brockport / State University of New York, NY
The Ohio State University, OH
The State University of New York College of Agriculture and Tech at Cobleskill, NY
Universidad Politecnica de Puerto Rico, PR
University at Albany / SUNY, NY
University of Alabama at Birmingham, AL
University of Georgia, GA
University of Hawaii at Manoa, HI
University of Houston, TX
University of Kentucky, KY
University of Maine, ME
University of Mary Washington, VA
University of Maryland, MD
University of Maryland/Baltimore County, MD
University of Massachusetts Lowell, MA
University of Minnesota/Duluth, MN
University of Missouri/Columbia, MO
University of Missouri-Kansas City, MO
University of Missouri-St. Louis, MO
University of North Carolina at Chapel Hill, NC
University of South Carolina at Columbia, SC
University of Texas at San Antonio, TX
University of Toledo, OH
University of Wisconsin/Madison, WI
University of Wisconsin-Milwaukee, WI
Victory University, TN
Virginia Commonwealth University, VA
Virginia Union University, VA
Voorhees College, SC
Warner University, FL
Wayne State University, MI
Western Connecticut State University, CT
Western Michigan University, MI
Western Washington University, WA
Westfield State University, MA
Worcester State University, MA
York College, NE

$20,000-$21,999

Colleges with Tuition, Room, and Board

Albert A. List College of Jewish Studies, NY
Ashford University, IA
Auburn University, AL
Benedict College, SC
Bennett College, NC
Binghamton University / The State University of New York, NY
Blackburn College, IL
Capitol College, MD
Cheyney University of Pennsylvania, PA
Christopher Newport University, VA
Cleveland State University, OH
College of Charleston, SC
Colorado State University-Fort Collins, CO
Cornish College of the Arts, WA (no R & B)
Cumberland University, TN
Davenport University, MI
Dillard University, LA
Eastern Connecticut State University, CT
Eastern Illinois University, IL
Florida Memorial University, FL
Georgia Institute of Technology, GA
Grace Bible College, MI
Harding University, AR
Indiana University of Pennsylvania, PA
Keene State College, NH
Kendall College of Art and Design of Ferris State University, MI
Lindenwood University, MO
Longwood University, VA
MacMurray College, IL
Maine Maritime Academy, ME
Marygrove College, MI
Midway College, KY
Mississippi College, MS
Mount Washington College, NH
New Jersey City University, NJ
North Central University, MN
Ohio University, OH
Oklahoma Wesleyan University, OK
Oswego / State University of New York, NY
Purdue University/West Lafayette, IN
Richard Stockton College of New Jersey, NJ
Rockhurst University, MO
San Diego State University, CA
Sonoma State University, CA
Southern Illinois University Carbondale, IL
St. Joseph's College, New York / Brooklyn Campus, NY (no R & B)
St. Joseph's College, New York / Suffolk Campus, NY (no R & B)
Tennessee Wesleyan College, TN
University at Buffalo / The State University of New York, NY
University of Akron, OH
University of Arizona, AZ
University of California at San Diego, CA
University of Cincinnati, OH
University of Oregon, OR
University of Pittsburgh at Bradford, PA
University of Pittsburgh at Johnstown, PA
University of Tennessee at Knoxville, TN
University of Texas at Dallas, TX
Urbana University, OH
Washington State University, WA
Western Illinois University, IL
William Paterson University of New Jersey, NJ
Williams Baptist College, AR
Winthrop University, SC

$22,000-$23,999

Colleges with Tuition, Room, and Board

Art Institute of Portland, OR (no R & B)
Bethune-Cookman University, FL
Bowie State University, MD
Charleston Southern University, SC
Claflin University, SC
Clearwater Christian College, FL
Concordia University Texas, TX
Dakota Wesleyan University, SD
Elms College, MA
Evangel University, MO
Faulkner University, AL
Grove City College, PA
Hardin-Simmons University, TX
Houston Baptist University, TX
Husson University, ME
Illinois State University, IL
Kean University, NJ
Lakeland College, WI
Lander University, SC
Lewis University, IL
Mars Hill College, NC
Massachusetts College of Art and Design, MA
Michigan Technological University, MI
Missouri Valley College, MO
Montclair State University, NJ
Nebraska Methodist College of Nursing and Allied Health, NE
Oakwood University, AL
Our Lady of the Lake University of San Antonio, TX
Plymouth State University, NH
Rocky Mountain College of Art and Design, CO (no R & B)
Roosevelt University, IL
Rowan University, NJ
Silver Lake College, WI
Southwestern Adventist University, TX
State University of New York Institute of Technology at Utica / Rome, NY
Toccoa Falls College, GA
Touro College, NY
Union College, NE
University of California at Berkeley, CA
University of Colorado Boulder, CO
University of Connecticut, CT
University of Delaware, DE
University of Massachusetts Amherst, MA
University of Massachusetts Dartmouth, MA
University of Michigan/Ann Arbor, MI
University of Rhode Island, RI
University of Sioux Falls, SD
University of the Ozarks, AR
University of Virginia, VA
University of Wisconsin/Stout, WI
Wisconsin Lutheran College, WI

$24,000-$25,999

Colleges with Tuition, Room, and Board

Art Academy of Cincinnati, OH
Art Institute of Atlanta, GA
Ashland University, OH
Atlantic Union College, MA
Bryan College, TN
California State University, Fullerton, CA
Campbell University, NC
Cardinal Stritch University, WI
Carroll University, WI
College of New Jersey, NJ
College of William & Mary, VA
Columbia College, MO
Daniel Webster College, NH
Dowling College, NY
Flagler College, FL
Gallaudet University, DC
Grand Canyon University, AZ
Hannibal-LaGrange University, MO
Illinois College, IL
Johnson C. Smith University, NC
Judson College, AL
Judson University, IL
Lubbock Christian University, TX
Madonna University, MI
McMurry University, TX
Miami University, OH
Northwest Nazarene University, ID
Northwestern College, MN
Northwood University, TX
Oakland City University, IN
Oklahoma Christian University, OK
Paul Quinn College, TX
Penn State University/University Park , PA
Pennsylvania College of Technology, PA
Ramapo College of New Jersey, NJ
Reinhardt College, GA
Rutgers, The State University of New Jersey/Camden Campus, NJ
Rutgers, The State University of New Jersey/New Brunswick, NJ
Rutgers, The State University of New Jersey/Newark Campus, NJ
Southern Nazarene University, OK
Southern Wesleyan University, SC
Southwest Baptist University, MO
Spelman College, GA
Springfield College, MA
Temple University, PA
Tusculum College, TN
University of California at Davis, CA
University of California at Irvine, CA
University of California at Los Angeles, CA
University of Illinois at Chicago, IL
University of Illinois at Urbana-Champaign, IL
University of Jamestown, ND
University of New Hampshire, NH
University of Pikeville, KY
Warner Pacific College, OR
Washington Adventist University, MD
Webber International University, FL
Wesleyan College, GA
William Woods University, MO
Xavier University of Louisiana, LA

$26,000-$29,999

Colleges with Tuition, Room, and Board

Alderson Broaddus University, WV
Allen College, IA
Andrews University, MI
Aquinas College, TN
Aurora University, IL
Avila University, MO
Barton College, NC
Belhaven University, MS
Benedictine College, KS
Benjamin Franklin Institute of Technology, MA
Berkeley College/New Jersey, NJ
Berkeley College/Westchester Campus, NY
Bethel College, KS
Brenau University Women's College, GA
Brescia University, KY
Briar Cliff University, IA
Bryn Athyn College , PA
California State University, Monterey Bay, CA
California State University, Northridge, CA
Campbellsville University, KY
Carroll College, MT
Carson-Newman University, TN
Central Methodist University, MO
Christendom College, VA
Colorado Christian University, CO
Columbia College, SC
Concordia University Nebraska, NE
Concordia University Saint Paul, MN
Concordia University Wisconsin, WI
Concordia University, Ann Arbor, MI
Concordia University, River Forest, IL
Dallas Baptist University, TX
Delaware Valley College, PA
D'Youville College, NY
East Texas Baptist University, TX
Ferrum College, VA
Franciscan University of Steubenville, OH
Friends University, KS
Geneva College, PA
Goldey-Beacom College, DE
Grace College and Theological Seminary, IN
Graceland University, IA
Greensboro College, NC
Greenville College, IL
Hampton University, VA
Hastings College, NE
Hilbert College, NY
Kentucky Wesleyan College, KY
Keystone College, PA
Laguna College of Art and Design, CA (no R & B)
LeTourneau University, TX
Limestone College, SC

Long Island University/Brooklyn Campus, NY
Lourdes University, OH
Maine College of Art, ME
McKendree University, IL
McPherson College, KS
Mercy College, NY
MidAmerica Nazarene University, KS
Milligan College, TN
Mount Aloysius College, PA
Mount Marty College, SD
Mount Vernon Nazarene University, OH
Nebraska Wesleyan University, NE
New Jersey Institute of Technology, NJ
Newberry College, SC
North Carolina Wesleyan College, NC
Northland College, WI
Northwest Christian University, OR
Northwood University, MI
Norwich University, VT
Notre Dame of Maryland University, MD
Oklahoma Baptist University, OK
Olivet Nazarene University, IL
Ouachita Baptist University, AR
Pacific Union College, CA
Piedmont College, GA
Saint Leo University, FL
Salem College, NC
Shorter University, GA
Simpson University, CA
Southeastern University, FL
Southern Adventist University, TN
Southwestern College, KS
Spring Arbor University, MI
St. Mary's College of Maryland, MD
Sterling College, KS
Sterling College, VT
Tabor College, KS
Texas Wesleyan University, TX
The College of Saint Rose, NY
Thomas College, ME
Thomas More College of Liberal Arts, NH
Trinity Christian College, IL
Tuskegee University, AL
Union College, KY
Union University, TN
University of California at Riverside, CA
University of California at Santa Barbara, CA
University of California at Santa Cruz, CA
University of Charleston, WV
University of Great Falls, MT
University of Mobile, AL
University of Pittsburgh at Pittsburgh, PA
University of Saint Francis, IN
University of Saint Mary, KS
University of the Cumberlands, KY
University of Vermont, VT
VanderCook College of Music, IL
Virginia Wesleyan College, VA
Walla Walla University, WA
Waynesburg University, PA
Wentworth Institute of Technology, MA
West Virginia Wesleyan College, WV
William Penn University, IA
Wilmington College, OH
Wilson College, PA
York College of Pennsylvania, PA

$30,000 and over

Colleges with Tuition, Room, and Board

Abilene Christian University, TX
Adelphi University, NY
Adrian College, MI
Agnes Scott College, GA
Alabama Agricultural and Mechanical University, AL
Alaska Pacific University, AK
Albany College of Pharmacy and Health Sciences, NY
Albertus Magnus College, CT
Albion College, MI
Albright College, PA
Alfred University, NY
Allegheny College, PA
Alma College, MI
Alvernia University, PA
Alverno College, WI
American International College, MA
American Jewish University , CA
American University, DC
Amherst College, MA
Anderson University, IN
Anna Maria College, MA
Aquinas College, MI
Arcadia University, PA
Art Center College of Design, CA (no R & B)
Asbury University, KY
Assumption College, MA
Augsburg College, MN
Augustana College, IL
Augustana College, SD
Austin College, TX
Averett University, VA
Azusa Pacific University, CA
Babson College, MA
Baker University, KS
Baldwin Wallace University, OH
Bard College, NY
Bard College at Simon's Rock, MA
Barry University, FL
Bates College, ME
Bay Path College, MA
Baylor University, TX
Beacon College, FL
Becker College, MA
Bellarmine University, KY
Belmont Abbey College, NC
Belmont University, TN
Beloit College, WI
Benedictine University, IL
Bennington College, VT
Bentley University, MA
Berklee College of Music, MA
Berry College, GA
Bethany College, KS
Bethany College, WV
Bethel College, IN
Bethel University, MN
Biola University, CA
Birmingham-Southern College, AL
Bloomfield College, NJ
Bluffton University, OH
Boston College, MA
Boston Conservatory, MA
Boston University, MA
Bowdoin College, ME
Bradley University, IL
Brandeis University, MA
Brewton-Parker College, GA
Bridgewater College, VA
Brown University, RI
Bryant University, RI
Bryn Mawr College, PA
Bucknell University, PA
Buena Vista University, IA
Burlington College, VT
Butler University, IN
Cabrini College, PA
Cairn University, PA
Caldwell College, NJ
California Baptist University, CA
California College of the Arts, CA
California Institute of Technology, CA
California Institute of the Arts, CA
California Lutheran University, CA
Calvin College, MI
Canisius College, NY
Capital University, OH
Carleton College, MN
Carlow University, PA
Carnegie Mellon University, PA
Carthage College, WI
Case Western Reserve University, OH
Catawba College, NC
Cazenovia College, NY
Cedar Crest College, PA
Cedarville University, OH
Centenary College, NJ
Centenary College of Louisiana, LA
Central College, IA
Centre College, KY
Chaminade University of Honolulu, HI
Champlain College, VT
Chapman University, CA
Chatham University, PA
Chestnut Hill College, PA
Claremont McKenna College, CA
Clark Atlanta University, GA
Clark University, MA
Clarke University, IA
Clarkson University, NY
Cleveland Institute of Art, OH
Cleveland Institute of Music, OH
Coe College, IA
Cogswell Polytechnical College, CA
Coker College, SC
Colby College, ME
Colby-Sawyer College, NH
Colgate University, NY
College for Creative Studies, MI
College of Art and Design at Lesley University, MA
College of Mount Saint Joseph, OH
College of Mount Saint Vincent, NY
College of Saint Benedict , MN
College of Saint Elizabeth, NJ
College of Saint Mary, NE
College of Saint Scholastica, MN
College of St Joseph, VT
College of the Atlantic, ME
College of the Holy Cross, MA
College of Wooster, OH
Colorado College, CO
Columbia College Chicago, IL
Columbia University in the City of New York, NY
Columbia University/Barnard College, NY
Columbia University/School of General Studies, NY
Columbus College of Art and Design, OH
Concordia College New York, NY
Concordia College, Moorhead, MN
Concordia University, OR
Concordia University - Irvine, CA
Connecticut College, CT
Converse College, SC
Cooper Union for the Advancement of Science and Art, NY
Corban University, OR
Corcoran College of Art and Design, DC
Cornell College, IA
Cornell University, NY
Cornerstone University and Grand Rapids Theological Seminary, MI
Covenant College, GA
Creighton University, NE
Culver-Stockton College, MO
Curry College, MA
Daemen College, NY
Dartmouth College, NH
Davidson College, NC
Davis and Elkins College, WV
De Sales University, PA
Defiance College, OH
Denison University, OH
DePaul University, IL
DePauw University, IN
Dickinson College, PA
Doane College, NE
Dominican College, NY
Dominican University, IL
Dominican University of California, CA
Dordt College, IA
Drake University, IA
Drew University/College of Liberal Arts, NJ
Drexel University, PA
Drury University, MO
Duke University, NC
Duquesne University, PA
Earlham College, IN
Eastern Mennonite University, VA
Eastern Nazarene College, MA
Eastern University, PA
Eastman School of Music, NY
Eckerd College, FL
Edgewood College, WI
Elizabethtown College, PA
Elmhurst College, IL
Elmira College, NY
Elon University, NC
Embry-Riddle Aeronautical University - Daytona Beach, FL
Embry-Riddle Aeronautical University - Prescott Campus, AZ
Emerson College, MA
Emmanuel College, MA
Emory and Henry College, VA
Emory University, GA
Endicott College, MA
Erskine College, SC
Eugene Lang College - The New School for Liberal Arts, NY
Fairfield University, CT
Fairleigh Dickinson University/College at Florham, NJ
Fairleigh Dickinson University/ Metropolitan Campus, NJ
Felician College, NJ
Five Towns College, NY
Florida Institute of Technology, FL
Florida Southern College, FL
Fontbonne University, MO
Fordham University, NY
Franklin and Marshall College, PA
Franklin College, IN
Franklin Pierce University, NH
Franklin W. Olin College of Engineering, MA
Fresno Pacific University, CA
Furman University, SC
Gannon University, PA
Gardner-Webb University, NC
George Fox University, OR
George Washington University, DC
Georgetown College, KY
Georgetown University, DC
Georgian Court University, NJ
Gettysburg College, PA
Gonzaga University, WA
Gordon College, MA
Goshen College, IN
Goucher College, MD
Grand View University, IA
Green Mountain College, VT
Grinnell College, IA
Guilford College, NC
Gustavus Adolphus College, MN
Gwynedd-Mercy College, PA
Hamilton College, NY
Hamline University, MN
Hampden-Sydney College, VA
Hampshire College, MA
Hanover College, IN
Hartwick College, NY
Harvard University/Harvard College, MA
Harvey Mudd College, CA
Haverford College, PA
Hawaii Pacific University, HI
Heidelberg University, OH
Hellenic College/Holy Cross Greek Orthodox School of Theology, MA
Hendrix College, AR
High Point University, NC (no R & B)
Hillsdale College, MI
Hiram College, OH
Hobart and William Smith Colleges, NY
Hofstra University, NY
Hollins University, VA
Holy Family University, PA
Holy Names University, CA
Hood College, MD
Hope College, MI
Hope International University, CA
Houghton College, NY
Howard University, DC
Huntingdon College, AL
Huntington University, IN
Illinois Institute of Technology, IL
Illinois Wesleyan University, IL
Immaculata University, PA
Indiana Institute of Technology, IN
Indiana Wesleyan University, IN
Iona College, NY
Iowa Wesleyan College, IA
Ithaca College, NY
Jacksonville University, FL
John Brown University, AR
John Carroll University, OH
Johns Hopkins University, MD
Johnson and Wales University/ Charlotte Campus, NC
Johnson and Wales University/ Denver Campus, CO
Johnson and Wales University/North Miami Campus, FL
Johnson and Wales University/ Providence Campus, RI
Juilliard School, NY
Juniata College, PA
Kalamazoo College, MI
Kansas City Art Institute, MO
Kansas Wesleyan University, KS
Kendall College, IL
Kenyon College, OH
Kettering University, MI
Keuka College, NY
King University, TN
King's College, PA
La Roche College, PA
La Salle University, PA
La Sierra University, CA
Lafayette College, PA
LaGrange College, GA
Lake Erie College, OH
Lake Forest College, IL
Lasell College, MA

Lawrence Technological University, MI
Lawrence University, WI
Le Moyne College, NY
Lebanon Valley College, PA
Lees-McRae College, NC
Lehigh University, PA
Lenoir-Rhyne College, NC
Lesley University, MA
Lewis & Clark College, OR
LIM College, NY
Lindsey Wilson College, KY
Linfield College-McMinnville Campus, OR
Lipscomb University, TN
Long Island University/C.W. Post Campus, NY
Loras College, IA
Loyola Marymount University, CA
Loyola University Chicago, IL
Loyola University New Orleans, LA
Luther College, IA
Lycoming College, PA
Lynchburg College, VA
Lynn University, FL
Lyon College, AR
Macalester College, MN
Maharishi University of Management, IA
Malone University, OH
Manchester College, IN
Manhattan College, NY
Manhattan School of Music, NY
Manhattanville College, NY
Mannes College New School for Music, NY
Marian University, WI
Marian University/Indianapolis, IN
Marietta College, OH
Marist College, NY
Marlboro College, VT
Marquette University, WI
Mary Baldwin College, VA
Maryland Institute College of Art, MD
Marymount Manhattan College, NY
Marymount University, VA
Maryville College, TN
Maryville University of Saint Louis, MO
Marywood University, PA
Massachusetts College of Pharmacy and Health Sciences, MA
Massachusetts Institute of Technology, MA
McDaniel College, MD
Medaille College, NY
Memphis College of Art, TN
Menlo College, CA
Mercer University, GA
Mercyhurst University, PA
Meredith College, NC
Merrimack College, MA
Messiah College, PA
Methodist University, NC
Middlebury College, VT
Midland University, NE
Millikin University, IL
Mills College, CA
Millsaps College, MS
Milwaukee Institute of Art and Design, WI
Milwaukee School of Engineering, WI
Minneapolis College of Art and Design, MN
Misericordia University, PA
Missouri Baptist University, MO
Mitchell College, CT
Molloy College, NY
Monmouth College, IL
Monmouth University, NJ
Montreat College, NC
Montserrat College of Art, MA
Moore College of Art and Design, PA
Moravian College, PA
Morehouse College, GA
Morningside College, IA
Mount Holyoke College, MA
Mount Ida College, MA
Mount Mary University, WI
Mount Mercy University, IA
Mount Saint Mary College, NY
Mount Saint Mary's University, MD
Mount St. Mary's College/Chalon Campus, CA
Muhlenberg College, PA
Muskingum University, OH
Naropa University, CO
Nazareth College of Rochester, NY
Neumann University, PA
New England College, NH
New England Conservatory of Music, MA
New York Institute of Technology, NY
New York University, NY
Newbury College, MA
Newman University, KS
Niagara University, NY
Nichols College, MA
North Central College, IL
North Park University, IL
Northeastern University, MA
Northwestern College of Iowa, IA
Northwestern University, IL
Northwood University, FL
Notre Dame College, OH
Notre Dame de Namur University, CA
Nova Southeastern University, FL
Nyack College, NY
Oberlin College, OH
Occidental College, CA
Oglethorpe University, GA
Ohio Dominican University, OH
Ohio Northern University, OH
Ohio Wesleyan University, OH
Oklahoma City University, OK
Oral Roberts University, OK
Otis College of Art and Design, CA (no R & B)
Otterbein College, OH
Pace University, NY
Pacific Lutheran University, WA
Pacific Northwest College of Art, OR
Pacific University, OR
Palm Beach Atlantic University, FL
Parsons The New School for Design, NY
Pepperdine University, CA
Pfeiffer University, NC
Philadelphia University, PA
Pine Manor College, MA
Pitzer College, CA
Point Loma Nazarene University, CA
Point Park University, PA
Polytechnic Institute of New York University, NY
Pomona College, CA
Post University, CT
Pratt Institute, NY
Presbyterian College, SC
Prescott College, AZ
Princeton University, NJ
Principia College, IL
Providence College, RI
Queens University of Charlotte, NC
Quincy University, IL
Quinnipiac University, CT
Randolph College, VA
Randolph-Macon College, VA
Reed College, OR
Regis College, MA
Regis University, CO
Rensselaer Polytechnic Institute, NY
Research College of Nursing, MO
Rhode Island School of Design, RI
Rhodes College, TN
Rice University, TX
Rider University, NJ
Ringling College of Art and Design, FL
Ripon College, WI
Rivier College, NH
Roanoke College, VA
Robert Morris University, PA
Roberts Wesleyan College, NY
Rochester Institute of Technology, NY
Rockford College, IL
Rocky Mountain College, MT
Roger Williams University, RI
Rollins College, FL
Rose-Hulman Institute of Technology, IN
Rosemont College, PA
Russell Sage College, NY
Sacred Heart University, CT
Saint Anselm College, NH
Saint Francis University, PA
Saint John's University, MN
Saint Joseph College, CT
Saint Joseph's College, IN
Saint Joseph's College of Maine, ME
Saint Joseph's University, PA
Saint Louis University, MO
Saint Martin's University, WA
Saint Mary-of-the-Woods College, IN
Saint Mary's College, IN
Saint Mary's College of California, CA
Saint Mary's University , TX
Saint Mary's University of Minnesota, MN
Saint Michael's College, VT
Saint Peter's College, NJ
Saint Vincent College, PA
Saint Xavier University, IL
Salve Regina University, RI
Samford University, AL
San Diego Christian College, CA
San Francisco Art Institute, CA
San Francisco Conservatory of Music, CA
Santa Clara University, CA
Santa Fe University of Art and Design, NM
Sarah Lawrence College, NY
Savannah College of Art and Design, GA
School of the Art Institute of Chicago, IL
School of Visual Arts, NY
Schreiner University, TX
Scripps College, CA
Seattle Pacific University, WA
Seattle University, WA
Seton Hall University, NJ
Seton Hill University, PA
Sewanee: The University of the South, TN
Shenandoah University, VA
Shimer College, IL
Siena College, NY
Sierra Nevada College, NV
Simmons College, MA
Simpson College, IA
Skidmore College, NY
Smith College, MA
Southern Methodist University, TX
Southern New Hampshire University, NH
Southern Vermont College, VT
Southwestern University, TX
Spalding University, KY
Spring Hill College, AL
St. Ambrose University, IA
St. Andrews University, NC
St. Bonaventure University, NY
St. Catherine University, MN
St. Edward's University, TX
St. Francis College, NY
St. John Fisher College, NY
St. John's College, Santa Fe, NM
St. John's College-Annapolis, MD
St. John's University, NY
St. Lawrence University, NY
St. Norbert College, WI
St. Olaf College, MN
St. Thomas Aquinas College, NY
St. Thomas University, FL
Stanford University, CA
Stephens College, MO
Stetson University, FL
Stevens Institute of Technology, NJ
Stevenson University, MD
Stonehill College, MA
Suffolk University, MA
Susquehanna University, PA
Swarthmore College, PA
Sweet Briar College, VA
Syracuse University, NY
Taylor University, IN
Texas Christian University, TX
Texas Lutheran University, TX
The Catholic University of America, DC
The College of Idaho, ID
The College of New Rochelle, NY
The Masters College, CA
Thiel College, PA
Thomas Aquinas College, CA
Thomas More College, KY
Tiffin University, OH
Transylvania University, KY
Trevecca Nazarene University, TN
Trine University, IN
Trinity College of Nursing & Health Sciences, IL
Trinity International University, IL
Trinity University, TX
Trinity Washington University, DC
Tufts University, MA
Tulane University, LA
Union College, NY
Unity College, ME
University of Bridgeport, CT
University of Chicago, IL
University of Dallas, TX
University of Dayton, OH
University of Denver, CO
University of Detroit Mercy, MI
University of Dubuque, IA
University of Evansville, IN
University of Findlay, OH
University of Hartford, CT
University of Indianapolis, IN
University of La Verne, CA
University of Mary Hardin-Baylor, TX
University of Miami, FL
University of Mount Union , OH
University of New England, ME
University of New Haven, CT
University of Notre Dame, IN
University of Pennsylvania, PA
University of Portland, OR
University of Puget Sound, WA
University of Redlands, CA
University of Richmond, VA
University of Rochester, NY
University of Saint Thomas, MN
University of San Diego, CA
University of San Francisco, CA
University of Scranton, PA
University of Southern California, CA
University of St. Francis, IL
University of St. Thomas - Houston, TX
University of Tampa, FL
University of Texas at Austin, TX
University of the Arts, PA
University of the Incarnate Word, TX
University of the Pacific, CA
University of the Sciences , PA
University of Tulsa, OK
Upper Iowa University, IA
Ursinus College, PA
Ursuline College, OH
Utica College, NY
Valparaiso University, IN
Vanderbilt University, TN
Vanguard University of Southern California, CA
Vassar College, NY
Vaughn College of Aeronautics and Technology, NY
Villanova University, PA
Virginia Intermont College, VA
Viterbo University, WI
Wabash College, IN
Wagner College, NY
Wake Forest University, NC
Walsh University, OH
Warren Wilson College, NC
Wartburg College, IA
Washington and Jefferson College, PA
Washington and Lee University, VA
Washington College, MD
Washington University in St. Louis, MO
Webster University, MO
Wellesley College, MA
Wells College, NY
Wesley College, DE
Wesleyan University, CT
Western New England University, MA
Westminster Choir College, NJ
Westminster College, MO
Westminster College, PA
Westminster College, UT
Westmont College, CA
Wheaton College, IL
Wheaton College, MA
Wheeling Jesuit University, WV
Wheelock College, MA
Whitman College, WA
Whittier College, CA
Whitworth University, WA
Widener University, PA
Wilkes University, PA
Willamette University, OR
William Jewell College, MO
William Peace University, NC
Williams College, MA
Wingate University, NC
Wittenberg University, OH
Wofford College, SC
Woodbury University, CA
Worcester Polytechnic Institute, MA
Xavier University, OH
Yale University, CT
Yeshiva University, NY

PART III

INDEX OF COLLEGE MAJORS

By now, you either have a clear idea about what your college major will be, or you are worrying about it. This section presents an overview of academic majors as well as information about some of the careers for which each major prepares you.

Majors are listed alphabetically in chart form. This lets you compare the various schools that offer the majors that interest you. You'll also be able to compare each school's Selector Rating and in-state costs.

After you've found a representative sampling of the schools that offer majors in the fields you may want to pursue, go on to the college Profiles that make up this book's main section.

DECIDING ON A COLLEGE MAJOR AND CAREER

What Is a College Major? A major is a field of study in which a student chooses an academic specialty to receive a college degree. A major consists of a concentration of specialized subject matter in a field of study. Most majors occupy about one-quarter to two-thirds of courses in that subject. Most college and university students must complete a required number of courses in their major to earn a Bachelor of Arts (B.A.) or a Bachelor of Science (B.S.) degree. The other twenty-five to fifty percent of courses are occupied by "general education" requirements for graduation, or electives that enhance and broaden a student's academic knowledge. Students' choice of major should be made carefully considering their interests and special talents.

What Is a College Minor? A minor in a field of study usually consists of a number of courses in a field of study other than the major. However, the required units of study are fewer than those required of the major. Many colleges today do not require a formal minor for graduation. The practical reason for a minor is to supplement and strengthen a major. For example, a computer science major may require specified courses in mathematics that, when totaled up, meet the definition of a minor, or perhaps a dual major.

Majors and Careers. Choosing a field of study is one of the most important decisions a student will make in the process of choosing a college major leading to an associate or bachelor's degree. A major with a structured course of study not only provides for intellectual growth, self-improvement, general knowledge, and a search for truth and understanding, but often provides the required technical training to enter and become successful in the world of work. Personal enlightenment is a noble goal, but most students no longer can afford the monetary expenses and the time to pursue courses that do not lead to a major that ties into career goals. Information on majors and careers is presented here to help students to make wise educational and career decisions. Informed educational and career decisions should include interests, academic abilities, and work values.

WHAT ARE SOME DIFFERENT APPROACHES TO CHOOSING A COLLEGE MAJOR?

JOB TRAINING: A student may want to go to college for one main reason: to acquire specific job skills to qualify for direct job entry. Job training course work is usually work-related and technical and it is evident that the skills learned in class can be directly applied to an occupation. For example, students who want to work as engineers in one of the many engineering specialties should pursue a two-year program course work as engineering technicians, or a four- to five-year engineering curriculum to become professional engineers.

Technical preparation: Technical preparation students generally enroll in associate degree programs that provide them with advanced skills through studies and experiences in applied academics, skills, and advanced technology. These students join the workforce after grade 14 or continue their formal preparation by working toward a baccalaureate degree in applied technology. Technical majors can be planned in agriculture, arts and communications, business, engineering and mechanics, health, human service, and natural science.

A general approach: Students may want to pursue a more general major that may not directly tie in to job entry, but will improve their general knowledge and prepare them as generalists with intellectual and problem-solving skills rather than technical training. This kind of major is often referred to as liberal arts, humanities, or general studies. Liberal arts majors can be planned in Social and Behavioral Sciences, The Arts, Communications, Humanities, and Ethnic Studies. A liberal arts major, leading to a baccalaureate degree, may not guarantee direct entry into an occupation associated with the major.

Special talent approach: Students may want to select a major because of a special talent and a strong interest in a certain field of study. Students with a strong interest in writing, drama, music, art, or an academic subject should select a major that helps to further the talent. College life will be more enjoyable if students select majors that will provide personal satisfaction. Designing a career plan that will allow a lifestyle compatible with the special talent will also provide personal satisfaction.

Double major approach: Students often decide to choose two majors in preparation for a career. A double major may be necessary in preparing for occupations in the science field where it is essential to be well-grounded in both the physical and biological sciences.

Independent approach: Students may have highly divergent interests that cut across two or more fields of study. Many colleges allow students to design a major to satisfy their goals. For example, students may have artistic talents and scientific interests. They might combine the two interests and design a scientific illustration major that meets faculty approval.

CONNECTING COLLEGE MAJOR PLANNING AND CAREER PLANNING

All students from the ninth grade through postsecondary school should be following a program of study that will prepare them for specific careers—studies that blend appropriate academics with appropriate skills and knowledge in a particular career area. All students in postsecondary studies should be preparing for life and work after completing their studies. This assertion eliminates a justification for a "general plan" of studies that in theory "leads anywhere," but in fact "leads nowhere." Students should either be in a postsecondary associate, technical, or baccalaureate educational plan that leads to a satisfying career.

The next section presents relevant educational and career information on 14 fields of study from which students may choose a major based on career plans. Each of the 14 fields of study has specific information on majors and careers that students should consider carefully when choosing a college major. Information about employment, growth, and earnings is taken from the Department of Labor figures for 2012, with growth projected to 2022.

1. AGRICULTURAL SCIENCES

Agriculture is a broad and diverse field of study that trains scientists for many rewarding and satisfying careers. These play an important part in maintaining the nation's food supply through ensuring agricultural productivity and the safety of the food supply. Agricultural scientists engage in research, development, and production of farm crops and animals, food sciences, plant sciences, and soil sciences. Others manage marketing or production operations in companies that produce food products or agricultural chemicals, supplies, and machinery. Other agricultural scientists are consultants to business firms, private clients, or governmental agencies.

Interests: Agricultural research, development, and production of farm crops and animals, and development of ways to improve their quantity and quality

Popular majors in this field of study: Agribusiness, Agricultural Education, Agronomy, Animal Science, Entomology, Farm and Ranch Management, Fisheries and Wildlife, Food Sciences, Forestry, Horticultural Science, and Soil Sciences

Employment information/outlook: More than 2,024,179 people worked in related occupations in this field of study in 2012. The 2012-2022 employment growth is expected to be 9%.

In May 2012, median annual wages of food scientists and technologists were $58,070; soil and plant scientists, $58,740; and animal scientists, $61,680. Incomes of farmers and ranchers vary greatly from year to year, because prices of farm products fluctuate with weather conditions and other factors that influence the quantity and quality of farm output and the demand for those products. In addition to farm business income, farmers often receive government subsidies or other payments that supplement their incomes and reduce some of the risk of farming. Many farmers—primarily operators of small farms—have recently been relying more and more on off-farm sources of income. Full-time, salaried agricultural managers had median weekly earnings of $1,332.80 in 2012. Farm income can vary substantially depending on a number of factors, including the type of crop or livestock being raised, price fluctuations for various agricultural products, and weather conditions that affect yield. In some cases, government subsidies may supplement a farmer's income. For a growing number of farmers and ranchers, particularly those working on farms for residential and lifestyle reasons, crop or livestock production is not their major occupation or source of income.

Agribusiness

Agribusiness majors will learn the business aspect of farms, firms, and industries that supply and service the farmer and other farm-related businesses. They will study merchandising, advertising, finance, marketing, and international trade.

Interests: Taking initiative, leadership, decision making, problem solving, analyzing data, global interdependence, working with people

Skills and abilities: Planning, organizing, making business decisions, leadership, teamwork, creative and critical thinking, working with people, written and verbal skills, adapting to change

Occupations related to this major: Agricultural Crop Farm Managers, Farm Products Purchasing Agents and Buyers, Farm and Ranch Managers, Fish Hatchery Managers, Farmers and Ranchers, Agricultural Statisticians, and Farm and Home Management advisers.

Agricultural Education

Agricultural Education majors will study those basic courses in agriculture that will prepare them to teach agricultural science in high schools, community colleges, or universities. They will also complete general preparation for a service-type career in agriculture, such as extension services. They will learn to supervise youth and adult groups and to direct programs in both agricultural and human resources.

Interests: Working with people, working with plants, working with animals

Skills and abilities: Communication, science (especially natural sciences and chemistry)

Occupations related to this major: Farm and Home Management Advisers, Park Naturalists, Farmers and Ranchers, Agricultural Science Teachers, and 4-H and Agricultural Extension Agents

Agronomy

Agronomy majors will learn about three basic natural elements—crops, soils, and climates—and their interdependence in producing food, feed, fiber, and fuel. Agronomists study theory and practices for improving crop production while conserving natural resources and maintaining environmental quality.

Interests: Nature and the outdoors, environmental quality (soil, water, and air), conservation of natural resources, biological and physical sciences, problem solving, plant growth and experimentation, weather, climate, geologic formations

Skills and qualities: Oral and written communication skills, group dynamics, leadership, organizational (interpersonal) skills, analytic reasoning, creative thinking

Occupations related to this major: Agricultural Climatologists, Agrochemical Technologists, Environmental Technicians, Food and Drug Inspectors, Farm or Ranch Managers, Plant Breeders, Agricultural Technicians, Soil and Water Conservationists, and Greenhouse Managers

Animal Science

Animal Science majors will learn how to manage livestock and poultry. They will study the role of animals in the economy, how animal products influence eating habits and are part of the global food supply, and how animals help serve people's recreation needs. They will carry out investigations and experiments in the areas of breeding, feeding, management, and disease control in farm and domestic animals.

Interests: Working with plants, working with animals, working with people

Skills and abilities: Speaking and writing effectively

Occupations related to this major: Animal Scientists, Soil and Plant Scientists, Park Naturalists, Biologists, Farm and Ranch Managers, and Soil Conservationists

Entomology

Entomology majors will study the biology, ecology, classification, distribution, physiology, economic importance, and management of insects and their relation to plant and animal life. They will learn to identify species of insects and allied forms, such as mites and spiders. They will study methods of controlling and eliminating agricultural, structural, and forest pests by developing new and improved pesticides and cultural and biological methods, including using natural enemies of pests. They will also study insect distribution and habitat, and methods to prevent importation and spread of injurious species.

Interests: Science, techniques of scientific research, the environment, the health and well-being of people

Skills and abilities: Curiosity, rational thinking, objective thinking, performing laboratory tasks carefully

Occupations related to this major: Entomologists, Environmental Scientists, Soil and Plant Scientists, Biologists, Clinical Laboratory Technologists, and Pest Control Workers

Farm and Ranch Management

Farm and Ranch Management majors will learn to guide and assist farmers and ranchers in maximizing the financial returns to their land by managing the day-to-day activities. Duties and responsibilities may vary widely. For example, the owner of a very large livestock farm may employ a farm manager to oversee a single activity, such as feeding livestock. When managing a small crop farm, on the other hand, a farm manager may assume responsibility for all functions, from selecting the crop to participating in planting and harvesting.

Interests: Directing and coordinating worker activities, decision making, problem solving, nature and the outdoors, conservation of natural resources, biological and physical science

Skills and abilities: Speaking, motivating people, creative and critical thinking, oral and written expression and comprehension, organizational skills, leadership

Occupations related to this major: Agricultural Crop Farm Managers, Farm and Ranch Managers, Foresters, Dairy Farm Managers, Poultry Farm Managers, and Farm and Home Management Advisers

Fisheries and Wildlife

Fisheries and Wildlife majors will learn about fish eggs, larvae, fish parasites, and diseases. They will learn to operate fish culture facilities, tag and mark fish, detect problems of water pollution, analyze, identify, collect, control, and preserve populations of fur and game animals.

Interests: Nature and the outdoors, science, research

Skills and abilities: Solving problems, communicating effectively, working with others

Occupations related to this major: Fish Culturists, Fish Hatchery Managers, Environmental Scientists, Zoo Workers, Fisheries and Wildlife Biologists, and Park Naturalists

Food Sciences

Food Science majors will learn to use biological, physical, and social sciences to transform raw materials into safe, nutritious, and economical foods. They will learn to apply scientific and engineering principles in research, development, and food production technology. They will also work to improve methods of processing, preserving, packaging, distributing, and preparing food.

Interests: Biological and physical science, public well-being, teamwork, observing details, solving complex problems

Skills and abilities: Good laboratory technique, oral and written expression and comprehension, mathematical reasoning

Occupations related to this major: Food Scientists, Food Science Technicians, Food Chemists, Food Plant Managers, Food Microbiologists, and Biological and Agricultural Technologists

Forestry

Forestry majors will learn to manage, protect, and develop forest lands and other resources for economic and recreational purposes; plan and supervise the cutting and harvesting of timber; carry out forestation and reforestation activities and manage parks and camps.

Interests: Nature and the outdoors, working with people, planning activities, investigative research, solving problems

Skills and abilities: Communicating effectively, working with quantitative and qualitative problems, presenting ideas to others

Occupations related to this major: Foresters, Soil Conservationists, Environmental Scientists, Biologists, Range Managers, Nursery and Greenhouse Managers, Agricultural Engineers, and Forest and Conservation Technicians

Horticultural Science

Horticultural Science majors will study problems of plant production, processing, and disease resistance. They will also study soil and climate to learn the conditions in which different types of plants thrive. They will be concerned with orchards, garden plants, flowers, ornamental plants, and nursery stock.

Interests: Science, working with plants, business, working with people, solving problems, improving the environment

Skills and abilities: Biological and physical sciences, written and oral communication, organization, creativity, quantitative thinking, computer competency, working with people

Occupations related to this major: Horticulturists, Foresters, Conservation Scientists, Landscape Architects, Plant Scientists, Farmers, and Farm Managers

Soil Sciences

Soil Science majors will study the physical, chemical, and geological characteristics and behaviors of soils. They will learn how to investigate soil both in the field and in the lab, and to classify soils in terms of their capability in producing crops, grasses, and trees. They also will learn how to make land appraisals.

Interests: Nature and the outdoors, conservation of natural resources, the environment, science

Skills and abilities: Quantitative reasoning, keen observation of natural phenomena, oral and written communication, applying scientific knowledge to complex systems

Occupations related to this major: Plant Scientists, Conservation Scientists, Botanists, Biochemists, Park Naturalists, and Farm and Range Managers

2. ARCHITECTURE AND DESIGN

Architects learn to plan, design, and supervise the construction of buildings, houses, factories, skyscrapers, schools, and other structures. They learn to make them attractive, usable, energy efficient, and economical. Architects must qualify for a state license after graduation. Most architects work for architectural firms. Others work directly for builders, real estate developers, or large construction projects, as well as governmental agencies responsible for housing and community planning, such as the Department of Defense, Interior, and Housing and Urban Development. Students interested in the field of architecture will do well in such courses as architectural theory design, computer graphics, computer science, general engineering urban planning, mathematics, physics, and economics.

Interests: Architects have an interest in planning, designing, and supervising the construction of buildings, houses, factories, skyscrapers, schools, and other structures.

Popular majors in this field of study: Architectural Engineering, Architecture, City and Regional Planning, Construction Science, Interior Design, Landscape Architecture, Marine Architecture, and Surveying

Employment information/outlook: More than 2,474,500 people worked in related occupations in this field of study in 2012. The 2012-2022 employment growth is expected to be 7.3%.

Median annual wages of wage-and-salary architects were $73,900 in May 2012. Those just starting their internships can expect to earn considerably less. Earnings of partners in established architectural firms may fluctuate because of changing business conditions. Some architects may have difficulty establishing their own practices and may go through a period when their expenses are greater than their incomes, requiring substantial financial resources. Many firms pay tuition and fees toward continuing education requirements for their employees. Median annual wages of urban and regional planners were $65,230 in May 2012. Earnings also vary by the worker's education and experience, type of work, complexity of the construction project, and geographic location. Wages of construction workers often are affected when poor weather prevents them from working. Traditionally, winter is the slack period for construction activity, especially in colder parts of the country, but there is a trend toward more year-round construction, even in colder areas. Construction trades are dependent on one another to complete specific parts of a project—especially on large projects—so work delays affecting one trade can delay or stop the work of another trade.

Architectural Engineering

Architectural Engineering majors will learn how different materials interact. They also will learn to calculate loads and stress and study the strength, durability, and safety-factor of materials. They will use artistic, applied physics, and material science skills in the design of buildings.

Interests: Mathematics, physical science, building things, applying mathematics and science to practical use, design, computers

Skills and abilities: Oral and written expression and comprehension, speech clarity, logical thinking, interpersonal skills, teamwork

Occupations related to this major: Architects, Civil Engineers, Marine Architects, Materials Engineers, and Architectural Drafters

Architecture

Architecture majors learn to plan, design, and supervise the construction of buildings, houses, factories, skyscrapers, schools, and other structures. They learn to make them attractive, usable, energy efficient, and economical. They must qualify for a license after graduation. They work in design studios that develop skills and foster creative expression. Architecture students also study the history of the building environment (rooms, buildings, landscapes, cities), the technology required to create it, and related graphic communication.

Interests: The formation of the physical environment; the history of buildings, cities, and landscapes; applied creative expression

Skills and abilities: Communicating by sketching and drafting; solving spatial problems; sensitivity to visual forms, proportions, and colors

Occupations related to this major: Architects, Naval Architects, Landscape Architects, Civil Engineers, Industrial Designers, Interior Designers, and Drafters

City and Regional Planning

City and Regional Planning majors learn to deal with land use and environmental issues created by population movements. They learn how to draw plans for new city environments including streets, sewers, water, and electricity. They also learn to zone areas for residential, commercial, or industrial use. Students commit themselves, through planning, to the future, and to social and environmental improvement.

Interests: Solving problems, working with people, helping groups, communities, and organizations improve people's lives

Skills and abilities: Working with numbers, listening, interpreting and communicating what was observed or heard

Occupations related to this major: Urban and Regional Planners, Architects, Landscape Architects, City Managers, Civil Engineers, and Environmental Engineers

Construction Science

Construction Science majors learn about all areas of construction technology. These areas include contracting, remodeling, cabinet making, building inspection, carpentry, and estimating the costs of building projects.

Interests: Starting and completing projects; leading people and making decisions; risk taking; activities that include practical, hands-on problems and solutions

Skills and abilities: Listening to and understanding information; reading and understanding information; managing one's own time and the time of others; communicating information and ideas in writing

Occupations related to this major: Architects, Property and Real Estate Managers, Real Estate Appraisers, Construction and Building Inspectors, and Industrial Engineers

Interior Design

Interior Design majors learn to arrange the interiors of buildings to fit the functional and aesthetic needs of their owners. They will design everything from lighting and furniture to home decorating accessories. Interior design majors study all aspects of the building environment: scale, proportion, arrangement, light, acoustics, temperature, textures, colors, and materials. They learn how to develop surroundings that are satisfying, creative, and appropriate to human needs.

Interests: Architecture, design (interior, industrial, graphic), building construction, interaction of colors, nature of materials, and textures

Skills and abilities: Design, organization, working with people, drawing, communicating ideas

Occupations related to this major: Interior Designers, Fashion, Furniture, Textile, and Floral Designers, Exhibition Designers, Architects, and Landscape Architects

Landscape Architecture

Landscape Architecture majors learn skills and techniques for planning, designing, and managing the land. They learn about weather, drainage, botany, and construction. They are frequently involved in mapping and consultation. They creatively apply information and principles drawn from both the arts and the sciences to reshape and conserve landscapes.

Interests: Visual arts, ecology, nature, environmental issues

Skills and abilities: Drawing and graphic expression, problem solving, written communication

Occupations related to this major: Landscape Architects, Architects, Surveyors, Civil Engineers, Urban and Regional Planners, Botanists, and Park Naturalists

Marine Architecture

Marine Architecture majors learn to design and oversee construction and repair of marine craft and floating structures, such as ships, barges, tugs, dredges, submarines, torpedoes, floats, and buoys. May confer with marine engineers.

Interests: Design techniques, engineering science and technology, building materials, construction and repair of structures

Skills and abilities: Problem solving, listening and understanding information and ideas, creativity, communicating information and ideas in writing, fluency of ideas

Occupations related to this major: Marine Architects, Aerospace Engineers, Civil Engineers, Materials Engineers, Engineering Technicians, and Drafters

Surveying

Surveying majors learn to make exact measurements and determine property boundaries. They learn to provide data relevant to the shape, contour, gravitation, location, elevation, or dimension of land, or land features on or near the earth's surface, for engineering, mapping, mining, land evaluation, construction, and other purposes.

Interests: Shapes and elevations of geomorphic and topographic features, geography, and methods for describing the features of land, sea, and air masses

Skills and abilities: Communicating effectively in writing; using mathematics to solve problems; understanding written information; using scientific methods to solve problems; motivating, developing, and directing people as they work

Occupations related to this major: Surveyors, Cartographers, Urban Planners, Civil Drafters, Agricultural Engineers, and Landscape Architects

3. THE ARTS

The Arts is a field of study that includes a wider range of subjects than found in other areas of concentration. If students major in one of the arts, they will learn to design products, articles, and materials; they will develop talents as actors; they will study the theory and practice of film production; they will develop talents to draw, paint, or design interpretations of objects, people, and nature, or they will develop talents dealing with the art of sound that express ideas and emotions either by song, dance, or by instrumental musical instruments. This field, in contrast to a liberal arts education, is often thought of as professional training. A major in this field gives information, methods, procedures, and techniques needed in a career. A professional program in this field will offer students good training to make a contribution in the world of art.

Interests: Developing talents to draw, paint, or design interpretations of objects, people, and nature; or developing the art of sound that expresses ideas and emotions either by speech, song, dance, or musical instruments.

Popular majors in this field of study: Art Education, Art History, Arts Management, Dance, Dramatic Arts, Film Arts, Fine Arts, Graphic Design, Music Business Management, Music Education, Music Performance, Music Therapy, Photography, Religious Music, and Studio Art

Employment information/outlook: More than 2,570,900 people worked in related occupations in this field of study in 2012. The 2012-2022 employment growth is expected to be 7.0%.

In May 2012, median annual wages of salaried art directors were $80,880; advertising, public relations and related services, $115,750; salaried craft artists, $44,380; multimedia artists and animators were $61,370; motion picture and video industries, $71,350; advertising and related services, $46,290. The hourly wages of actors were $20.26; hourly wages for performing arts companies were $15.87; and motion picture and video industry occupations came in at $34.31. The median annual wages in May 2012 for producers and directors were $71,350; radio and television broadcasting, $37,090; graphic designers, $44,150. Hourly wages of wage-and-salary musicians and singers were $23.50; performing arts companies, $18.33; and religious organizations, $14.69. The median annual wages for salaried music directors and composers were $47,350 in May 2012. Self-employed artist wages vary considerably. Most artists, including actors, musicians, and singers, were not available because of the variation in the number of hours they work, and the lack of guaranteed employment. The more successful performers may belong to one of the talent unions, such as SAG/AFTRA, American Guild of Musical Artists, or The American Federation of Musicians, which negotiates minimum contracts.

Art Education

Art Education majors learn to develop their artistic talents and gain the knowledge and skills needed to teach art at various education levels. They will explore the value of art both to the individual and to various cultures throughout history.

Interests: Visual arts, creating art, teaching

Skills and abilities: Working with others, solving problems creatively, manipulating materials creatively, responding to other people's art with sensitivity

Occupations related to this major: Art Teachers, Curriculum Specialists, Art Administrators, Manual Arts Therapists, Craft Demonstrators, Curators, Archivists, and Museum Research Workers

Art History

Art History majors study works of art—how they came about and what they mean. They will examine works of art as they appear now and also consider appearance and function in their original contexts. Through their visual analysis and extensive reading and writing, students explore the traditions of appearance and technique that guided the creation of art in different cultures.

Interests: Visual arts, past civilizations, the connections between different aspects of a civilization, artists, art technique

Skills and abilities: Observing carefully, information gathering, reading critically, written expression and comprehension

Occupations related to this major: High School Teachers, College Teachers, Curators, Archivists, Conservators, Museum Directors, and Museum Technicians

Arts Management

Arts Management majors learn to organize and manage art organizations and facilities. They receive instruction in business and financial management and labor relations, event promotion and management, public relations and arts advocacy, and arts law. They will learn to analyze and address the issues concerning the health of theaters, dance companies, museums, and other arts organizations.

Interests: Visual and performance arts, leadership, working with people

Skills and abilities: Oral and written communication, organizational ability, creative thinking, critical thinking

Occupations related to this major: Theater Managers, Symphony Orchestra Managers, Dance Company Managers, Curators, and Museum Technicians and Conservators

Dance

Dance majors learn to interpret an idea or a story through physical expression or rhythm and/or sound. Dance forms vary from ballet and modern interpretative dance to tap and chorus lines. Dance is a demanding discipline. Students learn to develop their bodies as articulate instruments for dance expression: to understand contributions that dance has made to the arts, and to create their own dances.

Interests: Dance, other arts, the physicality of movement

Skills and abilities: Sense of rhythm and musicality, physical stamina, dynamic strength, speed of limb movement, gross body coordination

Occupations related to this major: Dance Teachers, Actors and Performers, Choreographers, Dance Researchers, and Dance Therapists

Dramatic Arts

Dramatic Arts majors learn how to play a part to entertain, inform, or instruct an audience. They learn to be involved in interpreting plays or scripts, selecting plays or scripts, or planning and supervising performances. They gain breadth of knowledge about past and present culture, art, literature, politics, psychology, and philosophy.

Interests: Self-expression, communication of ideas and feelings, literature and language, art and music, human personality and motivation

Skills and abilities: Speech clarity, memorization, originality, oral and written expression and comprehension, emotional openness

Occupations related to this major: Actors, Directors, Designers, Playwrights, Stage Managers, Talent Directors, and Teachers

Film Arts

Film Arts majors study the theory and practice of film production and the techniques used in this medium of communication. They learn to do creative work, as well as learn the rapidly changing technology. They study cinema history, screenwriting, and the aesthetic and technical aspects of cinema production, including directing, cinematography, and editing. They also examine the economic, technical, social, cultural, and ideological aspects of film as a medium for communication and personal expression.

Interests: Film literature, psychology, theater, music, art history, biography, current events

Skills and abilities: Creativity, ability to express oneself verbally and visually, self-discipline, understanding of human psychology, organization, attention to detail, flexibility, working with people

Occupations related to this major: Directors—Stage, Motion Pictures, Television and Radio, Cinematographers, Technical Directors, Programming and Script Editors, Production Assistants

Fine Arts

Fine Arts majors learn to draw or design their interpretations of objects, people, and nature, using a wide variety of materials from watercolors and oils to stone and metal. They learn to create art to satisfy their own need for self-expression. They learn about the creation of art historically, in contemporary society, and through their own efforts in studio classes. They may display their work in museums, art galleries, corporate collections, and private homes.

Interests: Making things with the hands, other cultures, history, paintings, sculpture, film, self-expression

Skills and abilities: Oral and written expression and comprehension, fluency of ideas, originality, visual color discrimination, manual and finger dexterity

Occupations related to this major: Fine Artists, Graphic Artists, Sculptors, Painters, Illustrators, and Cartoonists and Animators

Graphic Design

Graphic Design majors study the principles of design to learn how to create attractive and effective advertisements, flyers, brochures, logos, magazines, or books. They learn how to create images through the use of silkscreen, computers, and printing presses. Students learn to communicate information visually using words and images. They also study how people perceive and interpret information.

Interests: Visual arts, creativity, critical thinking, working with people

Skills and abilities: Drawing, photography, originality, fluency of ideas, oral expression, visual color discrimination

Occupations related to this major: Graphic Designers, Painters, Illustrators, Cartoonists, Animators, Fashion Designers, and Interior Designers

Music Business Management

Music Business Management majors learn to organize and manage music operations, facilities, and personnel. They receive instruction in business and financial management, personnel management and labor relations, event promotion, and music products merchandising. They study the functional area of business as well as music performance, history, and theory.

Interests: Music, leadership, organizing people, business, solving problems, negotiating

Skills and abilities: Oral expression and comprehension, written expression and comprehension, leadership, organization, creative thinking

Occupations related to this major: Music Facilities Managers, Recording Studio Managers, Artists' Representatives, Orchestra Managers, Music Directors, and Concert Booking Agents

Music Education

Music Education majors learn to become music teachers in public and private schools. They learn the basics of music and the fundamentals of teaching to share music with people of all ages and abilities.

Interests: Listening to music, performing, working with young people, leadership

Skills and abilities: Musical ability, a sense of rhythm and pitch, oral and written expression and comprehension, speech clarity, discriminating listening

Occupations related to this major: Music Teachers, Music Therapists, Choir Directors, Conductors, Composers, Arrangers, and Music Librarians

Music Performance

Music Performance majors learn to develop a high level of performance skill and musical understanding. They reach a high level of technical proficiency and musical sensitivity as music performance majors. They become well-rounded musicians through the study of core music theory and history courses.

Interests: Communicating through music performance, the theoretical and historical aspects of musical structure and style, the relation of music to society

Skills and abilities: Natural aptitude for music, technical skill, strong background in piano

Occupations related to this major: Musicians, Singers, Music Directors, Music Composers, Music Teachers, and Positions with Orchestras and Ensembles

Music Therapy

Music Therapy majors learn to design music experiences and activities to the treatment of individuals and groups in all age categories who have psychological, emotional, physical, social, intellectual, or medical disorders.

Interests: Music, the arts, behavioral and life sciences, helping others

Skills and abilities: Competency in music performance and theory, oral and written expression and comprehension, working with people

Occupations related to this major: Music Therapists, Occupational Therapists, Physical Therapists, Musicians, Singers, and Music Directors

Photography

Photography majors learn the use of camera and film to portray people, places, and events. They become involved in everything from creating motion pictures and video/television to still, portrait, aerial, and commercial photography. They learn both the artistic and technical aspects of photography and a broad understanding of the social, political, and interpersonal aspects of society.

Interests: Expressing oneself in a visual medium, creating images from ideas, helping people see and understand subjects to which they might not otherwise have access

Skills and abilities: Visualization, far vision, fluency of ideas, arm-hand steadiness, control precision, color discrimination

Occupations related to this major: Commercial Photographers, Portrait Photographers, Graphic Designers, Photojournalists, Photo Editors, and Technical and Science Photographers

Religious Music

Religious Music majors develop their skills and interests as musicians and learn to use music in religious celebrations while focusing on the role and history of music in worship. They study the history, theory, composition, and performance of music for religious or sacred purposes.

Interests: Music, music history, the fine arts, the place of music in religious celebrations, matters of faith, working with people

Skills and abilities: Ability to listen carefully, hearing sensitivity, auditory attention, oral expression and comprehension, working with people

Occupations related to this major: Music Directors, Music Teachers, Music Conductors, Organists, Cantors, Musicians, and Singers

Studio Art

Studio Art majors learn to create works of art by exploring a variety of techniques and materials. They learn to focus on learning to master new media, discovering unique solutions to visual problems, exploring fresh ways to create satisfying images, and evaluating what is worth doing.

Interests: Visual arts, manipulating materials, observing visual phenomena in nature and works of art, communicating and experimenting with forms, colors, images, and symbols

Skills and abilities: Working independently, creativity, problem solving, oral and written expression and comprehension

Occupations related to this major: Fine Artists, Commercial Artists, Graphic Designers, Art Teachers, Exhibit Designers, and Set Designers

4. BIOLOGICAL AND LIFE SCIENCES

Biological and Life Sciences majors are concerned with the world of living things—people and microbes, wild and domestic animals, plants and insects, birds and fish. Some biological scientists conduct research. Still others apply biological knowledge to the solution of practical problems, such as the development of new drugs and vaccines or new strains of plants. Biological scientists, who may also be called life scientists, study the structure of living organisms, their life processes, and evolutionary development. They may be classified into groups characterized by the type of organism with which they work or the specific activity they perform. Examples of these groups are botanists who study plants, microbiologists who work with microorganisms, and zoologists who work with animals.

Interests: The world of living things—people and microbes, wild and domestic animals, plants and insects, birds and fish—or the evolutionary development of living organisms.

Popular majors in this field of study: Biochemistry, Biology, Biophysics, Biotechnology, Botany, Marine/Aquatic Biology, Microbiology, Molecular and Cell Biology, Science Education, Wildlife Management, and Zoology

Employment information/outlook: More than 103,100 people worked in related occupations in this field of study in 2012. The 2012-2022 employment growth is expected to be 13%.

In May 2012, median annual wages of biochemists and biophysicists were $81,480; microbiologists, $66,260. Median annual wages of zoologists and wildlife biologists were $57,710 in May 2012.

Biochemistry

Biochemistry majors learn how chemical substances enter into or are created in living things; how drugs, foods, hormones, serums, and other substances can influence organisms. They perform tests to identify, classify, and analyze various chemical reactions. They learn to use the physical and biological sciences to explore the nature of living organisms. They study the structure and behavior of complex molecules and how they interact to form cells, tissues, and entire organisms. They also gain a fundamental grasp of metabolism, energy flow, and the regulation of various life processes.

Interests: Nature, problem solving, investigative research

Skills and abilities: Using information from many areas of science, inductive and deductive reasoning, handling and interpreting data, written expression and comprehension

Occupations related to this major: Microbiologists, Biologists, Toxicologists, Plant Pathologists, Physiologists, Cytologists, and Food Scientists

Biology

Biology majors learn about the structure of living organisms, their life processes and evolutionary development, and the relation between these organisms and their environment. They may specialize in research centering on plants, animals, or human organisms. They study animals, plants, and microorganisms that constitute the living world at the levels of molecule, cell, organism, and population.

Interests: Quality of life, investigative laboratory work, fieldwork

Skills and abilities: Problem solving, deductive and inductive reasoning, information gathering, written expression and comprehension

Occupations related to this major: Biologists, Biochemists, Botanists, Microbiologists, Geneticists, and Zoologists

Biophysics

Biophysics majors learn to apply the laws of physics to biological systems. They study vision, hearing, nerve action, blood flow, and even the behavior of DNA. They also study the effects of radiation and radioactivity on biological systems, and the use of ultrasound scanners to construct images of body interiors. They use biology, physics, chemistry, and mathematics to explore the properties of biological molecules and groups of molecules. They study the inner workings of biological systems with precision to learn how proteins fold, how genes are switched on and off, how organisms respond to light, how cells move, and how the nervous system works.

Interests: Natural history, investigative problem solving

Skills and abilities: Curiosity, deductive and inductive reasoning, written expression and comprehension, information ordering, manual dexterity

Occupations related to this major: Biophysicists, Biologists, Botanists, Geneticists, Microbiologists, and Soil Scientists

Biotechnology

Biotechnology is an interdisciplinary field of study involving the molecular life sciences and engineering fields of study. Students learn techniques for using living matter to develop new products and services in agriculture (plant growth hormones, food additives), health care (vaccines, improved drugs and vitamins), the environment (detoxification of chemicals), and other areas.

Interests: Science, treating and preventing disease, investigative research, and problem solving

Skills and abilities: Creative thinking, oral and written expression and comprehension, deductive and inductive reasoning, problem sensitivity

Occupations related to this major: Biological Technologists, Agricultural Technologists, Environmental Scientists, Food Scientists, Animal Scientists, Botanists, and Microbiologists

Botany

Botany majors focus on all aspects of plant life including taxonomy, genetics, physiology, and plant anatomy. They learn about the economic value of plants in their application to agronomy, forestry, horticulture, and pharmacology. Students study all aspects of plant biology to become familiar with the cellular and molecular functioning of life.

Interests: Nature, investigative problem solving, analytic reasoning

Skills and abilities: Deductive and inductive reasoning, information ordering, written expression and comprehension

Occupations related to this major: Botanists, Agricultural Scientists, Soil Scientists, Ecologists, Microbiologists, Physiologists

Marine/Aquatic Biology

Marine/Aquatic Biology majors learn to research and study marine organisms and their environments. They receive instruction in freshwater and saltwater organisms, physiological and anatomical marine adaptations, ocean and freshwater ecologies, marine microbiology, marine mammalogy, ichthyology, marine botany, and biochemical products of marine life used by humans. They learn about the diversity of life in the ocean, how ocean species relate to each other as food and prey, and how different species depend on and use the physical and chemical structures of the ocean.

Interests: Life in the ocean, how organisms use the sea as a habitat

Skills and abilities: Quantitative thinking, deductive and inductive reasoning, information ordering, written expression and comprehension

Occupations related to this major: Marine Biologists, Aquatic Biologists, Biochemists, Botanists, Agricultural Scientists, and Zoologists

Microbiology

Microbiology majors concentrate on microorganisms, bacteria, yeasts, fungi, protozoa, and one-celled algae. They learn about the application of these organisms in the production of food products, antibiotics, and industrial chemicals. They learn to use the basic knowledge acquired from other biological sciences, chemistry/biochemistry, and physics to study microscopic organisms such as bacteria, yeasts, molds, viruses, rickettsia, and protozoa.

Interests: Biological sciences, health and medicine, ecology, food production, investigative research

Skills and abilities: Working with detail, analytic thinking, deductive and inductive reasoning, information ordering

Occupations related to this major: Microbiologists, Botanists, Medical Scientists, Zoologists, Physiologists, and Geneticists

Molecular and Cell Biology

Molecular and Cell Biology majors study the nature of biological phenomena at the molecular level through the study of DNA proteins and other macromolecules relating to genetic information and cell function. They study what cells are, how they are put together, what makes them work, what makes them differ from each other, how they associate and interact, what goes wrong in disease states, and how they can intervene beneficially in these processes. They study how molecular biology underlies many aspects of genetic engineering, protein engineering, and other new approaches to improving upon nature.

Interests: Organisms and their development, how things work, the molecular basis of plant, animal, and human disease, disease prevention

Skills and abilities: Investigative research, laboratory skills, information gathering, deductive and inductive reasoning, oral and written expression and comprehension

Occupations related to this major: Molecular Biologists, Medical Doctors, Toxicologists, Botanists, Plant Pathologists, and Biologists

Science Education

Science Education majors prepare to teach science in grades 7 through 12. Students typically major in one science and take additional course work in two other sciences. They learn techniques for teaching science.

Interests: Working with young people, helping others, the learning process, solving practical problems, understanding complex processes, learning how things work

Skills and abilities: Oral and written expression and comprehension, speech clarity, fluency of ideas, deductive reasoning, working with numbers

Occupations related to this major: Biological Technicians, Health Specialties Teachers, Elementary School Teachers, Dietitians, Nutritionists, Pharmacists, Psychiatrists, Veterinarians, and Medical and Clinical Laboratory Technologists

Wildlife Management

Wildlife Management majors receive a solid background in basic biology. They study natural resources and wildlife management. They study conservation of animal populations and their habitats, paying special attention to species that are hunted regularly and species that are threatened or endangered. They learn to analyze characteristics of animals to identify and classify them; to conduct experimental studies with live animals in controlled or natural surroundings; to study animals in their natural habitats; and to study characteristics of animals such as origin, interrelationships, classification, life histories and diseases, development, genetics, and distribution.

Interests: Nature, conservation of natural resources, hunting, bird-watching

Skills and abilities: Using scientific rules and methods to solve problems, mathematics, deductive and inductive reasoning, problem sensitivity

Occupations related to this major: Wildlife Biologists, Environmental Scientists, Park Naturalists, and Research Wildlife Biologists

Zoology

Zoology majors study the identification, description, and classification of animals. They study life histories, habits, diseases, life processes, and distribution of animal species within the environment. They study living organisms in the animal kingdom, exploring their form and function, chemistry and structure, growth, reproduction, maintenance, and interactions with each other and their world. They study the transmission of characteristics from one generation to the next (genetics and evolution).

Interests: Natural history, wildlife, the outdoors, bird-watching, how things work, living things, fossils, working with animals

Skills and abilities: Deductive and inductive reasoning, synthesizing information, gathering and analyzing information, working with numbers

Occupations related to this major: Zoologists, Ecologists, Agricultural Scientists, Physiologists, Cytologists, Microbiologists, and Botanists

5. BUSINESS AND MANAGEMENT

Business and Management majors are found in every industry. Business executives, administrators, managers, and support staff are found in every organization. They direct and coordinate operations and activities of an organization. Business majors must be comfortable with numbers and the manipulation of data, enjoy working with a computer, and have good communication skills, both written and oral. Business majors deal with large amounts of information to make production, personnel, financial, and marketing decisions.

Interests: Business managers and support workers have an interest in directing and coordinating operations and activities of a business or organization; an interest in making production, personnel, financial, and market decisions of a business.

Popular majors in this field of study: Accounting, Business Administration, Business Education, Finance, Human Resource Management, Insurance and Risk Management, International Business Management, Labor Relations Management, Management, Management Information Systems, Management Science, Marketing, and Real Estate

Employment information/outlook: More than 10,228,200 people worked in related occupations in this field of study in 2012. The 2012-2022 employment growth is expected to be 13.8%.

In May 2012, median annual wages of wage and salary accountants and auditors were $63,550. Median annual wages, excluding annual bonuses and stock options, of wage and salary financial managers were $109,740. Annual salary rates for human resources workers vary according to occupation, level of experience, training, location, and firm size. Median annual wages in May 2012 were $80,220 for advertising and promotions managers, $134,250 for marketing managers, $129,870 for sales managers, and $108,260 for public relations managers. Median annual wages of salaried property, real estate, and community association managers were $52,610 in May 2012.

Accounting

Accounting majors learn to keep track of expenditures, income, profit and loss, prepare financial reports, and calculate taxes. They may specialize in auditing, taxes, or consulting. Many accountants seek Certified Public Accountant (CPA) certification after graduation. Students will learn to apply this knowledge in all areas of business, government, and nonprofit enterprises.

Interests: Working with numbers, competition, economics, computers, mathematics, entrepreneurship, social and political activism, moral and ethical responsibility

Skills and abilities: Mathematical reasoning, written and oral expression and comprehension, working with people, leadership

Occupations related to this major: Accountants, Auditors, Loan Officers, Loan Counselors, Credit Analysts, Tax Preparers, Budget Analysts, and Marketing Managers

Business Administration

Business Administration majors learn about a variety of managerial opportunities in finance, accounting, marketing, information management, operations and production, general management, retailing, and consulting. They learn the fundamental principles, concepts, and applications of accounting, finance, and management.

Interests: Leadership, organizing people, taking initiative, starting and running a business, working with numbers, solving problems, competing, taking risks, working with people

Skills and abilities: Oral and written expression and comprehension, speech clarity, inductive reasoning, creative and critical thinking

Occupations related to this major: Private Sector Executives, Administrative Services Managers, Human Resources Specialists, Production Managers, Labor Relations Specialists, and Financial Analysts

Business Education

Business Education majors learn to teach vocational business programs at various education levels. They develop instructional methods and training techniques including curriculum design principles, learning theory, group and individual teaching techniques, design of individual development plans, and test design principles.

Interests: Teaching young people, helping people develop their academic interests in business, and helping people develop career plans

Skills and abilities: Working with young people, speech clarity, oral and written expression and comprehension, teaching, learning, understanding human behavior

Occupations related to this major: Business Education Teacher, Education Administrators, Training and Development Managers, and Educational Program Directors

Finance

Finance majors study financial and accounting information, economic models, and analytic techniques that can be applied to financing problems. They learn to determine prices of assets such as stocks, bonds, and businesses, and to manage assets to maximize their economic value.

Interests: Business, the stock market, the economy, budgets

Skills and abilities: Logical thinking, organizational skills, oral and written expression and comprehension, problem sensitivity, mathematical reasoning, working with people, solving problems with computers

Occupations related to this major: Financial Managers, Financial Planners, Treasurers, Controllers, Chief Financial Officers, and Loan Officers and Counselors

Human Resource Management

Human Resource Management majors learn to deal with many personnel activities, including hiring competent workers and dismissing workers when necessary, keeping records, classifying jobs, evaluating and properly placing workers, analyzing and assisting in morale and discipline problems, and promoting and rewarding employees. They learn to deal with issues that affect men and women at work.

Interests: Solving problems, working with numbers, working with people of different ages and backgrounds, leadership

Skills and abilities: Logical and critical thinking, speech clarity, oral and written expression and comprehension, analyzing numerical data, teamwork

Occupations related to this major: Human Resource Specialists, Training and Development Managers, Labor Relations Managers, Employee Assistance Specialists, Employee Benefits Managers, and Career Planning and Placement Counselors

Insurance and Risk Management

Insurance and Risk Management majors learn to analyze and solve problems involving loss of personal and corporate assets. They study programs, integrate knowledge from finance, quantitative analysis, and management, and include study of the legal, social, and institutional environment in which losses may occur.

Interests: Working with numbers, solving problems, competing, leadership, taking initiative

Skills and abilities: Oral and written expression and comprehension, fluency of ideas, problem sensitivity, deductive and inductive reasoning, creative and critical thinking

Occupations related to this major: Insurance Adjusters, Insurance Appraisers, Risk Managers, Insurance Brokers, Insurance Sales Representatives, and Insurance Underwriters

International Business Management

International Business Management majors learn to determine and formulate policies, and provide the overall direction of international companies or private and public sector organizations with international business activities. They learn to conduct management guidelines set up by a board of directors or similar governing body. They learn basic business management techniques and practices and how business is conducted in other countries and between different countries.

Interests: Business operations, other cultures, different people and environments

Skills and abilities: Learning languages, organizing and managing people, oral and written expression and comprehension, deductive and inductive reasoning, fluency of ideas

Occupations related to this major: International Business Managers, International Purchasing Agents and Buyers, International Marketing Managers, International Advertising and Promotions Managers, Compliance Officers and Inspectors, and Investment Bankers

Labor Relations Management

Labor Relations Management majors learn to deal with various aspects of employer-employee relations. They learn to deal with wage and salary negotiations, benefits and welfare, affirmative action, grievances, abuses and demands, labor laws, union organization, and collective bargaining. Particular attention is given to government policies, labor unions, and human resources management.

Interests: The employment relationship, human behavior, problem solving

Skills and abilities: Working with people, oral and written expression and comprehension, problem sensitivity, inductive reasoning

Occupations related to this major: Labor Relations Managers, Human Resource Managers, Training and Development Managers, Employee Assistance Specialists, Employee Benefits Managers, and Union Organizers

Management

Management majors study courses designed for the generalist who wants a broad business background. They take courses in business areas, such as accounting, marketing, finance, and business law, and courses that prepare them to function as managers in any organization.

Interests: Working with people, listening, persuading, leading, starting new systems

Skills and abilities: Thinking analytically, problem sensitivity, oral and written expression and comprehension, speech clarity

Occupations related to this major: General and Operations Managers, Marketing Managers, Public Relations Managers, Corporate Communications Specialists, Human Resource Specialists, and Human Resources Recruiters

Management Information Systems

Management Information Systems majors unite studies in computer science and business knowledge. They learn to act as intermediaries between persons with information needs and the computer programmers who provide the solutions to the problems.

Interests: Computer languages, computer programming, problem solving, logic, taking initiative, organizing groups

Skills and abilities: Oral and written expression and comprehension, deductive and inductive reasoning, information ordering, fluency of ideas, creativity

Occupations related to this major: Management Information Systems Managers, Systems Analysts, Computer Support Specialists, Database Administrators, and Computer Programmers

Management Science

Management Science majors learn to plan, organize, direct, and control the functions and processes of a business firm or organization. They learn about management theory, human resources, management and behavior, accounting and other quantitative methods, purchasing and logistics organization and production, marketing and business decision making. They learn to use mathematics, computers, and statistical and economic analysis to solve managerial and business problems.

Interests: Mathematics, solving business and management problems, computer languages, computer programming

Skills and abilities: Quantitative thinking, computer programming, creativity, oral and written expression and comprehension, speech clarity

Occupations related to this major: Employee Training Specialists, Administrative Service Managers, Purchasing Managers, Association Managers, and Property Managers

Marketing

Marketing majors learn to increase sales of products or services by analyzing and compiling data, and researching and influencing the purchasing power of the public through inventory procedures. They study trend forecasting, product development, management, wholesale selling, and operations. They learn how to display and to buy and sell items through showrooms, department stores, and specialty shops. They learn to make decisions about product design and quality, pricing, advertising, selling, and distribution.

Interests: Running a business, economic issues, social issues, working on new products, problem solving, analyzing data, understanding how people buy, use, and sell products and services

Skills and abilities: Oral and written expression and comprehension, speech clarity, originality, fluency of ideas, mathematical reasoning, persuasion

Occupations related to this major: Marketing Managers, Sales Managers, Public Relations Representatives, Advertising and Promotions Managers, Market Research Analysts, and Advertising Account Executives

Real Estate

Real Estate majors learn to show real estate properties to clients, evaluate and list properties for sale, and advise and arrange financing. They study property management and insurance. They act as independent agents, brokers, or appraisers. They gain an understanding of and proficiency in the business and social principles that affect how real property—buildings and land—is developed, operated, and traded.

Interests: Business, people and social conditions, the economy, public affairs

Skills and abilities: Oral and written expression and comprehension, mathematical reasoning, working independently, critical and analytic thinking

Occupations related to this major: Property Managers, Real Estate Sales Agents, Real Estate Financial Analysts, Real Estate Brokers, Loan Processors, and Real Estate Appraisers

6. COMMUNICATIONS

Communications is the giving or exchanging of information. It is a way to share facts, experiences, or emotions with others. A message can be conveyed through a wide variety of means. These can include writing, speaking, drawing, or using face, hand, and body movements. People receive messages through each of the five senses: taste, touch, sight, smell, and hearing. Communications studies involve the understanding of the role of mass communication in society; broadcast satellites, cable television transmitters, computer networks, and other mass media technology provide a global communication system. The field of communications includes training for those occupations necessary for the system to work efficiently.

Interests: The ways and means of exchanging information; an interest in broadcast satellites, television transmitters, computer networks, and other mass media technology.

Popular majors in this field of study: Advertising, Communications, Creative Writing, Journalism, Public Relations, Radio/Television Broadcasting, and Speech

Employment information/outlook: More than 1,531,000 people worked in related occupations in this field of study in 2012. The 2012-2022 employment growth is expected to be 10.8%.

In 2012, nonsupervisory workers in advertising and public relations services earned an average of $747 a week—significantly higher than the $608 a week for all nonsupervisory workers in private industry.

Median annual wages for salaried writers and authors were $51,510 in May 2012. Median annual wages were $76,790 for those working in advertising, public relations, and related services and $51,510 for those working for newspaper, periodical, book and directory publishers. In May 2012, median annual wages for salaried editors were $53,880; those working for newspaper, periodical, book, and directory publishers were $52,000. Freelance writers earn income from their articles, books, and less commonly, television and movie scripts. While most work on an individual project basis for multiple publishers, many support themselves with income derived from other sources. Unless gotten from another job, freelancers generally have to provide for their own health insurance and pension. Weekly earnings of nonsupervisory workers in broadcasting averaged $852 in 2012, higher than the average of $608 for all private industry. Earnings of broadcast personnel typically are highest in large metropolitan areas.

Advertising

Advertising majors learn to plan and prepare advertisements for newspapers, magazines, radio, television, billboards, and brochures. They may specialize in writing copy, layout, or research. They use creative talents to market a product to prospective clients. They learn how advertising campaigns are produced, how advertising is coordinated with marketing, and how advertising strategies develop from research. They learn to write advertising copy for broadcasting and print, and to select media for advertising campaigns.

Interests: Writing, art and design, analysis, knowing something about lots of things, investigative research

Skills and abilities: Oral and written expression and comprehension, originality, fluency of ideas, analytic reasoning, public speaking, art and design

Occupations related to this major: Advertising and Promotions Managers, Advertising Agency Account Executives, Marketing Managers, Sales Managers, Fund-raising Directors, and Advertising Research Specialists

Communications

Communications majors study the role of mass communication in society. They study the nature, function, content, values, and effects of communication on public policy and opinion. They study the nature of language and how it is communicated. They study the history of political and religious oratory; explore the sociology of interpersonal relations, group dynamics, and messages; examine ways of thinking about human symbol systems (semiotics); and examine the ethics of communication.

Interests: Politics, presentations, advertising, television, film, analyzing oral and electronic messages

Skills and abilities: Oral and written expression and comprehension, critical listening, logical analysis, leadership

Occupations related to this major: Communications Managers, Public Relations Specialists, Television Producers and Directors, Press Secretaries, Reporters, and Speech Writers

Creative Writing

Creative Writing majors study the processes and techniques of original composition in various literary forms, such as short stories, novels, biographies, articles, plays, and scripts. They receive instruction in technical and editorial skills, criticism, and the marketing of finished manuscripts.

Interests: Reading, fiction and nonfiction prose, writing, factual information, English language, critical thinking, computers

Skills and abilities: Written and oral expression and comprehension, information ordering, deductive and inductive reasoning, fluency of ideas

Occupations related to this major: Radio and Television Announcers, Broadcast News Analysts, Reporters and Correspondents, Editors, Technical Writers, and Poets and Lyricists

Journalism

Journalism majors learn to write, edit, manage, and produce newspapers and magazines. They learn to interview people, review records, observe events, and conduct journalistic research. They study the liberal arts and sciences to acquire the depth and breadth of knowledge they need to understand the world better and communicate information about it to others. They learn special skills needed by reporters, editors, broadcasters, and photojournalists.

Interests: Human psychology and behavior, reading widely, photography, world events

Skills and abilities: Writing, oral and written expression and comprehension, speech clarity, learning quickly about a wide range of topics

Occupations related to this major: Reporters and Correspondents, Magazine Writers and Editors, Columnists, Critics, Commentators, Creative Writers, Radio and Television Reporters, and Photojournalists

Public Relations

Public Relations majors learn how to manage an organization's or an individual's communication and relationship with others. They develop skills to build trust between an organization and the public. They learn how to write news articles and press releases, give speeches, and create audiovisual presentations designed to build trust. They learn technical and managerial skills, such as writing and producing printed and visual materials, and study strategic planning and problem solving.

Interests: Solving problems, mediating between opposing groups, writing, public speaking, giving advice

Skills and abilities: Communicating clearly, oral and written expression and comprehension, speech clarity, fluency of ideas, creative and critical thinking

Occupations related to this major: Public Relations Specialists, Publicity Writers, Advertising and Promotions Managers, Corporate Video Producers, Staff Writers and Editors, Special Events Planners, and Reporters and Correspondents

Radio/Television Broadcasting

Radio/Television Broadcasting majors learn about the planning, preparation, and production of radio and television programs. They may specialize in announcing, programming, engineering, or sales. They study the relationship between the mass media and society and develop skills in such specialties as reporting, performance, production, sales, and management

Interests: Writing, speaking, editing words, pictures, or sound; operating a camera; sound recording

Skills and abilities: Interviewing people, oral and written expression and comprehension, speech clarity, persuasion, operating technical equipment

Occupations related to this major: Broadcast News Analysts, Reporters and Correspondents, Radio/Television Announcers, Radio/Television Producers, Station Managers, Radio/Television Writers

Speech

Speech majors learn about the human communication process. They learn the principles and practical application of speech communication, and the skills and techniques essential for effective interpersonal communication. They learn to develop listening skills.

Interests. Public speaking, human behavior

Skills and abilities: Working with people, oral and written expression and comprehension, speech clarity

Occupations related to this major: Speech Teachers, Speech Writers, Public Relations Specialists, Journalists, Writers, Editors, and Radio and Television Reporters

7. COMPUTER AND INFORMATION SCIENCES

Computer and Information Sciences field of study prepares students for a wide variety of occupations in most sectors of the economy. This field of study prepares a wide range of professionals who design computers and the software that runs them. Information technology occupations are comprised of computer-related occupations engaged in either managing, storing, transmitting, or generating the information organizations use to make decisions, as well as installing and repairing computer hardware and software used to perform such tasks. Computer science is distinguished by a high level of theoretical expertise and innovation applied to complex problems, as well as the creation or application of new technology. Computer scientists and technicians can be theorists, researchers, or inventors. They may work at an academic institution on theory, hardware, or language design. Others work in industry to apply theory, develop specialized languages, or design programming tools and knowledge-based systems.

Interests: Designing computers and the software that runs them; managing, storing, transmitting, or generating and repairing computer hardware and software used to perform such tasks

Popular majors in this field of study: Computer Software Engineering, Computer Science, Information Sciences and Systems, Computer Programming, Mathematics, Mathematics Education, and Statistics

Employment information/outlook: More than 1,549,700 people worked in related occupations in this field of study in 2012. The 2012-2022 employment growth is expected to be 16.8%.

In May 2012, median annual wages of wage-and-salary computer applications software engineers were $85,430; computer systems software engineers, $92,430; mathematicians, $95,150; and statisticians, $72,610.

Computer Software Engineering

Computer Software Engineering majors study applied mathematical and scientific principles to the design, development, and operational evaluation of computer hardware and software systems and related equipment and facilities. They learn to develop, create, and test applications software and/or operating systems level software. They learn to analyze specific problems in computer applications.

Interests: Computers and electronics, computer programming, problem solving, engineering technology, design

Skills and abilities: Using mathematics to solve problems, computer programming, critical thinking, oral and written expression and comprehension, speech clarity, problem sensitivity

Occupations related to this major: Computer Support Specialists, Mathematical Technicians, Computer Science Teachers, and Numerical Tool and Process Control Programmers

Computer Science

Computer Science majors learn to design new computers, computer languages, and related devices, and research new ways to use computers effectively. They become involved in aspects of artificial intelligence, from pattern recognition to problem solving. They learn how computers work and how to program computers to perform tasks and provide services. They study the physical hardware components of computer systems and software procedures for making computers work.

Interests: Mathematics, electronics, investigative research

Skills and abilities: Oral and written expression and comprehension, mathematical reasoning, problem solving, abstract reasoning, working with people

Occupations related to this major: Computer Scientists, Computer Engineers, Computer Science Teachers, Computer Programmers, Software and Hardware Developers

Information Sciences and Systems

Information Sciences and Systems majors receive broad exposure to computer and programming concepts. They learn to bring people and computers together to solve problems in businesses and other organizations. They learn to plan, direct, and coordinate activities in such fields as electronic data processing, information systems, systems analysis, and computer programming.

Interests: Solving problems, working with details, taking initiative, working with numbers, organizing information, working with people

Skills and abilities: Oral and written expression and comprehension, mathematical reasoning, deductive reasoning, critical and logical thinking, working with changing technology

Occupations related to this major: Computer Programmers, Information Systems Designers, Information Systems Analysts, Computer Security Specialists, Database Administrators

Computer Programming

Computer Programming majors learn to write step-by-step instructions in several computer languages and create video games and software packages. They learn how to write software to handle specific jobs. They learn to convert project specifications and statements of problems and procedures to detailed logical flowcharts for coding into computer language. They learn to develop and write computer programs to store, locate, and retrieve specific documents, data, and information. They learn how to maintain software that controls the operations of entire computer systems.

Interests: Mathematics, electronics, using computers, investigative research, problem solving

Skills and abilities: Programming, critical thinking, active listening, oral and written expression and comprehension, mathematical reasoning, fluency of ideas, problem sensitivity

Occupations related to this major: Computer Programmers, Computer and Information Systems Managers, Computer Support Specialists, Computer Systems Analysts, Numerical Tool and Process Control Programmers, and Computer Science Teachers

Mathematics

Mathematics majors learn to solve both theoretical and practical problems that can be explained in mathematical terms. They study all aspects of algebra, geometry, advanced mathematics, and computer languages. They develop the abilities to explore, conjecture, and reason logically as well as the ability to use various mathematical methods effectively to solve problems.

Interests: Problem solving, working with numbers, games requiring analytic reasoning, investigative research

Skills and abilities: Oral and written comprehension, number facility, mathematical reasoning, deductive reasoning, analytic skills

Occupations related to this major: Mathematicians, Statisticians, Mathematics Teachers, and Financial Analysts

Mathematics Education

Mathematics Education majors learn to teach mathematics at the high school or middle school level. They learn techniques to help students develop skills and knowledge in the field of mathematics; they also take professional education courses.

Interests: Problem solving, analytic reasoning, working with young students, working with computers, leadership, organizing people

Skills and abilities: Oral and written expression and comprehension, speech clarity, organizational skills, creativity, using computers

Occupations related to this major: Middle School Teachers, High School Teachers, Insurance Underwriters, Business Training Specialists, and Education Administrators

Statistics

Statistics majors learn the science of dealing with data. They learn to design efficient data collection systems and to analyze and interpret information derived from the data. They learn to use mathematical theory or apply statistical theory and methods to collect, organize, interpret, and summarize numerical data to provide usable information. They may specialize in fields such as biostatistics, agricultural statistics, business statistics, economic statistics, or other fields.

Interests: Mathematics, working with numbers, problem solving, quantitative problems

Skills and abilities: Mathematical reasoning, computer operations, critical thinking, deductive and inductive reasoning, written expression

Occupations related to this major: Statisticians, Actuaries, Mathematicians, Operations Research Analysts, and Cost Estimators

8. EDUCATION

Education is a people-oriented field of study providing teachers, librarians, and school counselors involved in helping others to learn, acquire information, or gain insight into it. There are many levels on which one can teach. These include preschool and day care facilities, elementary schools, secondary schools, colleges and universities, as well as public and private vocational education institutions, dance, music, and art studios, and many other places. Librarianship and counseling are smaller fields than teaching. Archivists and curators are more involved with things than people. They may also help people learn and gain information, but they do not usually work as closely with people as do teachers, librarians, and counselors. All of these professions usually require a bachelor's degree, although some require a master's or doctoral degree.

Interest: Helping others learn, acquire information; teaching, counseling, or librarianship

Popular majors in this field of study: Early Childhood Education, Elementary School Education, Library Science, Middle School Education, Parks and Recreation Management, Physical Education, Secondary School Education, Special Education, Technology Education, and Vocational and Educational Counseling

Employment information/outlook: More than 6,758,700 people worked in related occupations in this field of study in 2012. The 2012-2022 employment growth is expected to be 15%.

In May 2012, median annual wages of preschool teachers was $27,130; kindergarten, elementary, middle, and secondary school teachers ranged from $53,090 to $57,810 in that same period. In 2012, the majority of all elementary, middle, and secondary school teachers belonged to unions—mainly the American Federation of Teachers and the National Education Association—that bargain with school systems over salaries, hours, and other terms and conditions of employment. Median annual wages in May 2012 of special education teachers who worked primarily in preschools, kindergartens, and elementary schools was $55,060; middle school special education teachers, $87,760; and special education teachers who worked primarily in secondary schools, $51,260. Median annual wages of vocational education teachers in elementary and secondary schools in May 2012 were $56,270.

Early Childhood Education

Early Childhood Education majors learn to teach preschool students through art, music, play, poetry, and stories to prepare for learning language, science, numbers, and social studies. They learn to design programs to develop students' mental capacities, learning abilities, and emotional health. They learn a variety of appropriate teaching methods and strategies.

Interests: Childhood development, working with children, communicating with children and their parents

Skills and abilities: Oral expression and comprehension, speech clarity, problem sensitivity, time sharing, creativity, music or artistic ability

Occupations related to this major: Preschool Teachers, Kindergarten Teachers, Elementary School Teachers, Early Childhood Education Program Directors, Child Care Administrators, and Family Service Coordinators

Elementary School Education

Elementary School Education majors learn to teach young students (kindergarten through grade 6) basic academic, social, and manipulative skills. They learn to instill good study and work habits and an appreciation for learning. They learn to prepare lesson plans, tests, records, and reports, and to conduct conferences with parents. They learn a variety of methods for understanding how and why children develop socially and intellectually, and get professional experience that includes research in teaching and learning.

Interests: Communication, creativity, problem solving, flexibility, ability to organize, energy, enthusiasm

Skills and abilities: Oral and written expression and comprehension, speech clarity, problem sensitivity

Occupations related to this major: Elementary School Teachers, Kindergarten Teachers, Middle School Teachers, Secondary School Teachers, Special Education Teachers, and School Counselors

Library Science

Library Science majors learn the science of acquiring and organizing collections of books, pamphlets, manuscripts, clippings, and reports, and assisting readers in their use. They learn how to analyze reader needs, prepare bibliographies, and organize films, tapes, and maps.

Interests: Reading, multimedia communication, working with people, computers

Skills and abilities: Reading comprehension, active listening, oral and written expression and comprehension, speech clarity, fluency of ideas, information ordering

Occupations related to this major: Librarians, Computer and Information Systems Managers, Elementary School Teachers, Secondary School Teachers, and School Administrators

Middle School Education

Middle School Education majors learn to develop a wide array of instructional skills, which include multimedia approaches, classroom management, advisory ability, effective communication, and alternatives to teacher-centered instruction. They learn to build on and extend basic academic skills developed in elementary school students, and introduce them to the world of more abstract thinking and knowledge that they will encounter in high school.

Interests: Helping or providing service to others, communicating with young people, teaching young people, working with ideas

Skills and abilities: Instructing others, active listening, social perceptiveness, oral and written expression and comprehension, speech clarity, problem sensitivity

Occupations related to this major: Middle School Teachers, High School Teachers, Vocational Education Teachers, School Counselors, and Librarians

Parks and Recreation Management

Parks and Recreation Management majors study how individuals and communities pursue leisure and recreation. They explore what recreation is, investigate what motivates people's recreational choices, and develop skills to manage a variety of leisure and recreation enterprises and organizations.

Interests: Working with people; scientific, historic, and natural features of parks, forests, and other attractions

Skills and abilities: Helping others, leadership, solving problems, oral and written expression, speech clarity, problem sensitivity

Occupations related to this major: Community Recreation Planners/Directors, Social Directors, Park Naturalists, Forest Rangers, Amusement and Recreation Establishment Managers, and Camp Directors

Physical Education

Physical Education majors learn to teach and supervise individual and team sports. They learn to demonstrate sports techniques, analyze physical capabilities and needs of students, and administer corrective exercises and physical conditioning. They learn to provide students with activities to maximize physical fitness.

Interests: Physical activity, sports, working with people, health-related issues, biological science

Skills and abilities: Physical stamina, leadership, oral expression, speech clarity, multilimb coordination

Occupations related to this major: Physical Education Teachers, Sports Coaches, Physical Training Instructors, Aerobic Dance Instructors, Athletic Trainers, Fitness Directors, and Athletic Administrators

Secondary School Education

Secondary School Education majors learn to teach one or more high school subjects using various teaching methods. They learn to develop and plan teaching materials and assignments. They learn to construct tests to evaluate learning. They gain depth of knowledge in the subject they intend to teach and develop teaching skills in subject matters such as science, mathematics, social studies, English, music, art, business, physical education, or other subjects.

Interests: Serving others, teaching young people and helping them develop their academic interests and career choices

Skills and abilities: Working with people, teaching, learning, understanding human behavior, oral and written expression and comprehension, speech clarity

Occupations related to this major: Secondary School Teachers, Middle School Teachers, Special Education Teachers, Vocational Education Teachers, and Vocational and Educational School Counselors

Special Education

Special Education majors prepare for a career working with disabled children and adults in a variety of settings. They learn to coordinate the services available to people with disabilities, and provide appropriate educational experiences for people with varying disabilities, including deafness, blindness, aphasia, and mobility impairments.

Interests: Helping others, working with people

Skills and abilities: Accepting differences in people, communicating effectively, teaching, oral and written expression and comprehension, speech clarity, problem sensitivity

Occupations related to this major: Special Education Teachers; Teachers of the Emotionally and Mentally Impaired; Teachers of the Physically, Visually, and Hearing Impaired; Rehabilitation Counselors

Technology Education

Technology Education majors are trained to teach the design, operation, and impact of technological systems to students. They learn technical skills to be used in advanced communication, applied higher mathematics, and science. This major prepares students to teach technical pathway programs found in middle schools, high schools, and colleges. Technical majors can be planned in agriculture, arts, communication, business, engineering, information science, mechanics, and other fields.

Interests: Helping people, design, technological systems, network technology, graphics and multimedia, system designs, programming, teaching

Skills and abilities: Working with people, oral and written expression and comprehension, analyzing and describing technological systems

Occupations related to this major: Agriculture Teachers, Art Teachers, Computer Science Teachers, Business Teachers, Engineering Technology Teachers, and Science Teachers

Vocational and Educational Counseling

Vocational and Educational Counseling majors learn to counsel individuals and provide group educational and vocational guidance services. They learn to promote and enhance student learning through three broad and interrelated areas of student development: academic development, career development, and personal/social development.

Interests: Working with, communicating with, and teaching people; providing service to others

Skills and abilities: Speaking, active listening, oral and written expression and comprehension, problem sensitivity, speech clarity, fluency of ideas

Occupations related to this major: Educational and Vocational School Counselors, Child, Family, and School Social Workers, Health Educators, and Probation Officers

9. ENGINEERING

Engineering field of study involves planning and designing various things. Engineers design machines, processes, systems, and structures. They apply physical laws and mathematical theories and principles to solve practical technical problems. Engineers work in research, development, design, manufacturing and construction, operations, management, technical sales, teaching, and consulting services.

Interests: Designing machines, processes, systems and structures; research, development, design, manufacturing and construction, operations, management, and technical consulting services

Popular majors in this field of study: Aerospace/Aeronautical Engineering, Agricultural Engineering, Chemical Engineering, Civil Engineering, Computer Engineering, Electrical Engineering, Industrial Engineering, Materials Engineering, Mechanical Engineering, and Petroleum Engineering

Employment information/outlook: More than 1,166,700 people worked in related occupations in this field of study in 2012. The 2012-2022 employment growth is expected to be 9.7%.

Earnings for engineers vary significantly by specialty, industry, and education. Variation in median earnings and in the earnings distributions for engineers in a number of specialties is especially significant. Median annual wages of aerospace engineers in May 2012 was $103,720; agricultural engineers, $74,000; chemical engineers, $94,350; civil engineers, $79,340; computer engineers, $100,920; electrical engineers, $89,630; industrial engineers, $78,860; materials engineers, $85,150; mechanical engineers, $80,580; and petroleum engineers, $130,280.

Aerospace/Aeronautical Engineering

Aerospace/Aeronautical Engineering majors learn to perform a variety of engineering work in designing, constructing, and testing aircraft, missiles, and spacecraft. They learn to conduct basic and applied research to evaluate adaptability of materials and equipment to aircraft design and manufacture. They learn to make improvements in testing equipment and techniques.

Interests: Model aircraft and rocketry, astronomy, piloting, space exploration, computers, problem solving, working with people

Skills and abilities: Leadership, computer technology, physical science, oral and written expression and comprehension, mathematical reasoning, deductive and inductive reasoning

Occupations related to this major: Aerospace/Aeronautical Engineers, Electronics Engineers, Nuclear Engineers, Ceramic Engineers, Chemical Engineers, and Civil Engineers

Agricultural Engineering

Agricultural Engineering majors learn to apply knowledge of engineering technology and biological science to agricultural problems concerned with power and machinery, electrification, structures, soil and water conservation, and processing of agricultural products.

Interests: Solving problems, improving the quality of life, computers, leadership

Skills and abilities: Problem solving, oral and written expression and comprehension, computer operation, deductive and inductive reasoning, number facility

Occupations related to this major: Soil Conservationists, Landscape Architects, Geoscientists, Foresters, Chemical Engineers, Industrial Engineers, and Mechanical Engineers

Chemical Engineering

Chemical Engineering majors learn to turn chemicals into products through research and development. They learn to devise economical and efficient production processes. They learn to work in a number of fields, such as cosmetics, fertilizers, paints, dyes, pesticides, oil refining, and pollution prevention.

Interests: Science, chemistry, mathematics

Skills and abilities: Applying knowledge of science and mathematics to real-world problems, written expression and comprehension, mathematical reasoning, originality, deductive reasoning

Occupations related to this major: Chemical Engineers, Nuclear Engineers, Civil Engineers, Petroleum Engineers, Agricultural Engineers, and Electrical Engineers

Civil Engineering

Civil Engineering majors learn to solve technical problems involved in providing buildings, bridges, airports, transportation systems, foundations, coastal facilities, environmental control systems, and water supply and purification systems. They become involved in the conception, planning, design, construction, operation, and maintenance of these important public facilities. Studies will include soil mechanics, hydraulics, and structural engineering.

Interests: Mathematics, physical sciences, computers, building things, public service, applying mathematics and science to practical uses

Skills and abilities: Mathematics, physical sciences, logical thinking, interpersonal skills, oral and written expression and comprehension, inductive and deductive reasoning

Occupations related to this major: Civil Engineers, Civil Engineering Technicians, Architectural Engineers, Nuclear Engineers, Electrical Engineers, and Industrial Engineers

Computer Engineering

Computer Engineering majors learn to design and develop computer and computer-related systems. These systems include software systems, hardware systems, and combined hardware/software systems. Students take courses in basic sciences, mathematics, and engineering science and design.

Interests: Mathematics, science, computing, investigative research

Skills and abilities: Mathematics, computer operations, oral and written expression and comprehension, inductive and deductive reasoning

Occupations related to this major: Computer Hardware Engineers, Computer Software Engineers, Electronics Engineers, and Computer Service Technicians

Electrical Engineering

Electrical Engineering majors learn to design, develop, test, or supervise the manufacturing and installation of electrical equipment components or systems for commercial, industrial, military, or scientific use. They learn to design and manufacture a broad array of electrical and electronic devices and systems to meet society's needs.

Interests: Computer languages, computer programming, electronic equipment

Skills and abilities: Mathematics, physical science, oral and written expression and comprehension, deductive reasoning

Occupations related to this major: Electrical Engineers, Electronics Engineers, Mechanical Engineers, Electricians, Nuclear Engineers, and Production Engineers

Industrial Engineering

Industrial Engineering majors learn to plan, design, and implement complex systems for industry that take into account the availability, capabilities, and needs of people, machines, and materials. They learn to plan the layout of factories for efficiency, and engage in time, motion, and incentive studies. They learn about safety studies, cost, and quality control measures, and long-range planning goals.

Interests: Problem solving, leadership

Skills and abilities: Working with people, critical thinking, written and oral expression and comprehension, fluency of ideas, mathematical reasoning

Occupations related to this major: Aerospace Engineers, Materials Engineers, Petroleum Engineers, Industrial Engineers, Mechanical Engineers, and Engineering Technicians

Materials Engineering

Materials Engineering majors learn to evaluate properties of materials used to manufacture products that must meet specialized design and performance criteria. They learn to develop machinery and processes to manufacture materials, such as polymers, plastics, and alloys.

Interests: Nature and the physical sciences, problem solving, computer operations, working with ideas

Skills and abilities: Creative and critical thinking, problem sensitivity, oral and written expression and comprehension, deductive and inductive reasoning

Occupations related to this major: Materials Engineers, Marine Architects, Mechanical Engineers, Electrical Drafters, and Electrical Engineering Technicians

Mechanical Engineering

Mechanical Engineering majors learn to plan and design tools, engines, machines, and other mechanically functioning equipment. They learn to oversee installation, operation, maintenance, and repair of such equipment as centralized heat, gas, water, and steam systems. They learn to create and build machines, devices, and systems that perform useful services.

Interests: Mechanical devices, computers, cars, solving problems, mathematics, physical science

Skills and abilities: Mathematics, critical thinking, complex problem solving, mathematical reasoning, deductive and inductive reasoning, oral and written comprehension

Occupations related to this major: Mechanical Engineers, Marine Architects, Materials Engineers, Petroleum Engineers, Engineering Technicians, and Mechanical Drafters

Petroleum Engineering

Petroleum Engineering majors learn about exploring and drilling for fossil fuel, both on land and under the sea, and how to maximize the recovery of oil and gas through engineering processes. They learn methods of searching for new sources of energy, for example, geothermal energy. They learn to devise methods to improve oil and gas well production and determine the need for new or modified tool designs.

Interests: Solving problems, working with others, using computers, outdoor activities

Skills and abilities: Mathematics, physics, oral and written expression and comprehension, inductive and deductive reasoning, problem sensitivity, fluency of ideas

Occupations related to this major: Petroleum Engineers, Aerospace Engineers, Marine Engineers, Materials Engineers, Mining and Geological Engineers, and Geologists

10. FAMILY AND CONSUMER SCIENCES

Family and Consumer Sciences majors concentrate on issues concerning feeding, clothing, and caring for children, managing resources, and providing housing for individuals and families. Family and Consumer Science majors provide information, gained through research, about families and individuals as consumers and decision makers. These majors provide information about child care, elder care, food, clothing, housing, finance, and other issues of resource management.

Interests: Issues concerning feeding, clothing, and caring for children, managing resources, and providing housing for individuals and families; an interest in families as consumers and decision makers.

Popular majors in this field of study: Day Care Administration, Family and Consumer Education, Fashion Merchandising, Food Science and Nutrition, Hotel and Motel Management, Housing and Human Development, Individual and Family Development, Leisure Studies, Textile Sciences, and Tourism

Employment information/outlook: More than 1,011,500 people worked in related occupations in this field of study in 2012. The 2012-2022 employment growth is expected to be 7.8%.

Pay depends on the educational attainment of the worker and the type of establishment. Although the pay generally is very low, more education usually means higher earnings. Median hourly wages of child care workers were $9.38 in May 2012. Hourly earnings of nonsupervisory workers in clothing, accessory, and general merchandise stores in 2012 were well below the average for all workers in private industry. This reality reflects both the high proportion of part-time and less experienced workers in these stores and the fact that even experienced workers receive relatively low pay compared with the pay of experienced workers in many other industries. Median annual wages of dietitians and nutritionists were $55,240 in May 2012. For that same period, lodging managers were $46,810; lodging managers in traveler accommodations, $53,780. Salaries of lodging managers vary greatly according to their responsibilities, location, and the segment of the hotel industry in which they work.

Day Care Administration

Day Care Administration majors learn to manage programs that provide education or social services to young children and their families. They gain knowledge of child development and develop skills in teaching young children, in supervising staff, and in business management.

Interests: Leadership, management, supervising people, administering programs, working with children

Skills and abilities: Organizational and managerial skills, program development, oral and written expression and comprehension, speech clarity

Occupations related to this major: Day Care Director, Preschool Director, Head Start Directors, Early Childhood Education Program Directors, and Child Care Workers

Family and Consumer Education

Family and Consumer Education majors learn to use community resources to meet the needs of the individual and the family in the management of time, energy, and money. They learn about parenting skills, communication skills, relationship skills, wellness, foods and nutrition, consumerism, clothing selection, and job skills. They prepare to become family and consumer teachers for preschool through adult education in subjects related to the family. They study various aspects of family life including human development, nutrition, and decision making, in addition to teaching strategies.

Interests: Family life, using current technology, working with people

Skills and abilities: Critical and analytical thinking, oral and written expression and comprehension, speech clarity

Occupations related to this major: Family and Consumer Science Teachers, Consumer Advocates, Education Consultants, Extension Agents, Financial Planners, Housing Administrators

Fashion Merchandising

Fashion Merchandising majors study how to manufacture fashions for consumers and effectively sell those fashions.

Interests: Current trends in apparel, arts, furnishings, travel and leisure, food business trends, fabrics, fashion and fashion designers

Skills and abilities: Motivating people, leadership, organizational ability, originality, fluency of ideas, color discrimination, oral comprehension

Occupations related to this major: Retail Buyers, Manufacturers' Representatives, Product Designer-Pattern Makers, and Fashion Designers

Food Science and Nutrition

Food Science and Nutrition majors study the nature of foods, the causes of their deterioration, and the principles of food processing. They will learn about the selection, preservation, processing, packaging, distribution, and use of safe, nutritious, and wholesome food.

Interests: Social, health, economic, and political issues involved in food production and availability; chemical reactions and what happens to food when it enters the human body; solving problems

Skills and abilities: Organizational abilities, critical thinking, oral and written expression and comprehension, speech clarity, mathematical reasoning

Occupations related to this major: Dietitians, Nutritionists, Nutrition Educators, and Food Scientists and Technicians

Hotel and Motel Management

Hotel Management majors learn the operation of a hotel. They learn the principles of managing lodging facilities efficiently and profitably. They learn about personnel management, services, supplies, business aspects, decision making, accounting, and public relations. They are introduced to the principles of managing these key components of the hospitality industry.

Interests: Working with people, problem solving, attention to detail, leadership

Skills and abilities: Organization ability, creativity, oral and written expression and comprehension, speech clarity, speech recognition

Occupations related to this major: Lodging Managers, Food Service Managers, Retail Store Managers, and Office Managers

Housing and Human Development

Housing and Human Development majors learn to analyze the use of investment in housing and its impact on families, the community, and the larger economy and society.

Interests: Working with people, serving others, real estate, home automation, the family, marketing, management, interior design, environmental design, finance

Skills and abilities: Computer skills, analytical skills, oral and written expression and comprehension, problem sensitivity

Occupations related to this major: Real Estate Managers, Property Managers, Consumer Affairs Specialists, Extension Agents, and Financial/Mortgage Specialists

Individual and Family Development

Individual and Family Development majors study interpersonal relationships and human development from infancy to old age. They study theories of development with an emphasis on techniques to improve quality of life for individuals and families.

Interests: Helping others, family and individual well-being, prevention and elimination of problems facing people in their daily lives

Skills and abilities: Working with people, critical thinking, oral and written expression and comprehension, curiosity about interpersonal and family dynamics, speech clarity

Occupations related to this major: Child Life Specialists, Day Care Teachers, Recreation Activities Directors, Drug and Alcohol Rehabilitation Counselors, and Crisis Center Directors

Leisure Studies

Leisure Studies majors learn to design, manage, and deliver leisure services to a variety of people in diverse settings. They learn about the impact of leisure services upon individual satisfaction and the quality of life.

Interests: Helping people, leadership, organizing individual and group activities

Skills and abilities: Working with people, oral and written expression and comprehension, speech clarity, problem sensitivity, fluency of ideas, memorization

Occupations related to this major: Amusement and Recreation Establishment Managers, Recreation Workers, Tour Guides and Escorts, Social and Community Service Managers, and Meeting and Convention Planners

Textile Sciences

Textile Sciences majors learn how to design fabrics for garments, upholstery, rugs, and other products. They study print, woven, and embroidery styles, and learn how to buy and sell certain fabrics and trims. They learn how to analyze fabric performance in the marketplace.

Interests: Fashion design, garment fashion, art, history of textiles, textile technology, design principles

Skills and abilities: Originality, visualization, visual color discrimination, fluency of ideas, oral expression and comprehension

Occupations related to this major: Textile Designers, Fashion Designers, Quality Control Analysts, Sales Representatives, and Wardrobe Planners

Tourism

Tourism majors study how to manage travel-related enterprises and conventions and tour services. They learn about travel agency management, travel industry operations and procedures, tourism marketing and promotion strategies, and travel industry law.

Interests: Travel, tourism planning, human resource management, travel industry operations, marketing

Skills and abilities: Oral and written expression and comprehension, mathematical reasoning, speech clarity, fluency of ideas

Occupations related to this major: Travel Agents, Travel Guides, Tour Guides and Escorts, Reservation and Transportation Ticket Agents, and Amusement and Recreation Establishment Managers

11. HEALTH SCIENCE

The **Health Science** field of study trains workers in a vast array of occupations. Occupational titles vary, and the training necessary to fill these occupations requires lengthy postgraduate education. Health practitioners diagnose, treat, and prevent illness and disease. While all health practitioners practice the art of healing, they differ in methods of treatment and areas of specialization. Training for this profession is more rigorous than training for most other professional occupations, but practice also offers unusual rewards. Incomes of health practitioners generally are higher than those of other professional workers with similar years of education. Furthermore, most health practitioners derive considerable satisfaction from knowing that their work contributes directly to the well-being of others. Workers in the industry must have the ability and perseverance to complete the years of study required. They should be emotionally stable, able to make decisions in emergencies, and have a strong desire to help the sick and injured. Sincerity and an ability to gain the confidence of patients are important qualities.

Interests: Diagnosing, treating, and preventing illness and disease; an interest in the well-being of others and a desire to help the sick and injured

Popular majors in this field of study: Athletic Training, Clinical Laboratory Science, Dental Hygiene, Health Services Management, Medical Record Administration, Nuclear Medical Technology, Nursing, Occupational Therapy, Pharmacy, and Physical Therapy

Employment information/outlook: More than 2,775,600 people worked in related occupations in this field of study in 2012. The 2012-2022 employment growth is expected to be 27%.

Most athletic trainers work in full-time positions, and typically receive benefits. The salary of an athletic trainer depends on experience and job responsibilities, and varies by job setting. In May 2012, median annual wages for athletic trainers were $42,690; medical and clinical laboratory technologists, $47,820; and dental hygienists, $70,210; Earnings vary by geographic location, employment setting, and years of experience. Dental hygienists may be paid on an hourly, daily, salary, or commission basis. Median annual wages of wage and salary medical and health services managers were $88,580; medical records and health information technicians, $34,160. The median annual wage in May 2012 of nuclear medicine technologists was $70,180; registered nurses, $65,470; occupational therapists, $75,400; salary pharmacists, $116,670; physical therapists, $79,860; and speech-language pathologists, $69,870.

Athletic Training

Athletic Training majors learn to prevent, recognize, refer, and treat injuries and illnesses sustained by athletes. They learn about the administration of athletic training programs in public and private schools, colleges, universities, and with professional teams. They study exercise sciences and the medical aspects of sport. Together with clinical experience, this prepares students for national certification in the field.

Interests: Sports, helping others, health and medicine, physical fitness and exercise, anatomy, nutrition, first aid

Skills and abilities: Manual skills, science, problem solving, interpersonal communication, integrity, oral expression, speech clarity, physical strength

Occupations related to this major: Athletic Trainers, Sports Medicine Clinic Administrators, Exercise Physiologists, Physical and Corrective Therapists, and Occupational Therapists

Clinical Laboratory Science

Clinical Laboratory Science majors learn to perform medical tests to determine the presence and cause of disease. They study sophisticated instrumentation used to perform a variety of laboratory procedures. They study blood and other body fluids that aid in the diagnosis of disease and the maintenance of health.

Interests: Solving problems, working with complex machinery, computer science, laboratory work, helping others, medicine, biological science

Skills and abilities: Computer skills, analytic skills, oral and written expression and comprehension, arm-hand steadiness, visual color discrimination

Occupations related to this major: Laboratory Technologists and Technicians, Research Analysts, Coroners, Clinical Scientists, Environmental Health Officers, and Toxicologists

Dental Hygiene

Dental Hygiene majors learn to work under the supervision of a dentist to clean and polish teeth, massage gums, apply fluoride to prevent decay, and provide dental health education. They obtain the knowledge and clinical skills needed to provide preventive oral health care. They learn skills as an assistant to a dentist performing a number of duties.

Interests: Working with people, helping individuals maintain their health, science

Skills and abilities: Critical thinking, oral expression, arm-hand steadiness, manual dexterity, near vision

Occupations related to this major: Dental Hygienists, Dental Assistants, Dentists, and Medical Assistants

Health Services Management

Health Services Management majors prepare for entry-level positions managing a wide variety of health care organizations such as hospitals, nursing homes, insurance companies, and public agencies. They learn to direct the many activities of health care organizations and coordinate administrative duties with medical services. They learn about space needs, staffing, and supplies. They learn to supervise personnel, prepare budgets, and direct the policies of the organization.

Interests: Working with people, taking initiative, solving problems, working with data

Skills and abilities: Oral and written expression and comprehension, speech clarity, organizational skills, interpersonal skills, critical thinking

Occupations related to this major: Medical and Health Services Managers, Public Health Directors, Educational Program Directors, Nursing Directors, Social Welfare Administrators, and Health Insurance Underwriters

Medical Record Administration

Medical Record Administration majors learn to supervise and manage the preparation, storage, and use of medical records and related information systems. They study the legal and technical aspects of medical records, and the design and management of secure data systems. They learn to merge the study of business and medicine. Students prepare to direct medical record departments in varied health care settings by exploring the health care environment, health care organizations, clinical information systems, medical record department operations, and health care reimbursement systems.

Interests: Leadership, working with people, designing and implementing systems, problem solving, working with detail

Skills and abilities: Writing and speaking effectively, working in a changing environment, oral and written expression and comprehension, near vision, mathematical reasoning

Occupations related to this major: Medical Records Administrators and Directors, Quality Assurance Coordinators, Health Care Administrators, Medical Records Educators, and Research Coordinators

Nuclear Medicine Technology

Nuclear Medicine Technology majors learn how to administer radionuclides to patients and to monitor the characteristics and functions of tissues or organs in which they localize. They learn to operate the cameras that detect the radionuclides and maintain patient records. They learn to prepare and administer radioactive drugs to patients, operate radiation detection equipment, and perform the calculations or computer analysis needed to complete the patient's examination.

Interests: Biological sciences, new technologies, helping others, working in a medical setting, working with people

Skills and abilities: Biological and physical science, working with others, oral and written expression and comprehension, problem sensitivity

Occupations related to this major: Nuclear Medicine Technologists, Radiation Therapists, Radiologic Technologists, Electroneurodiagnostic Technologists, and Medical and Clinical Laboratory Technologists

Nursing

Nursing majors learn to administer nursing care to ill or injured persons. They learn to administer medication and treatments prescribed by medical doctors, observe and record symptoms and behaviors of patients, and promote good health. They learn how to rehabilitate, counsel, and educate patients, and how to work as part of a health care team in many settings. They study humanities, natural sciences, and nursing theory to serve individuals, families, groups, and communities.

Interests: Provide intimate helping services to people, ethical care, chemistry, physics, anatomy, biology

Skills and abilities: Clear thinking, oral and written expression and comprehension, problem sensitivity, speech clarity

Occupations related to this major: Registered Nurses, Doctors of Medicine, Nursing Instructors, Physical Therapists, Medical Assistants, Chiropractors, and Podiatrists

Occupational Therapy

Occupational Therapy majors learn to determine the educational, recreational, and vocational activities needed to hasten a patient's recovery from physical, psychological, social, or developmental problems. They learn to instruct patients in the use of artificial limbs or to regain the use of muscles. They learn to help patients function independently so that they may work, play, take care of themselves, and relate to others in a productive and satisfying manner.

Interests: Solving problems, anatomy, working with people, medicine, health, rehabilitation

Skills and abilities: Logical thinking, working with others, oral and written expression and comprehension, deductive reasoning

Occupations related to this major: Occupational Therapists, Respiratory Therapists, Physical Therapists, Speech-Language Pathologists and Audiologists, Recreational Therapists, and Exercise Physiologists

Pharmacy

Pharmacy majors study the science of drugs, including their chemical and physical properties and composition. They learn to understand the effects of drugs, to test those drugs for purity and strength. They learn to provide drug products and drug information in all areas of patient care. They learn to monitor drug therapy to ensure that the treatment is appropriate, safe, therapeutically effective, and cost-effective.

Interests: Chemistry, biology, mathematics, solving problems, helping others

Skills and abilities: Patience, tact, adapting to change, working carefully, oral and written expression and comprehension, information ordering, mathematical reasoning

Occupations related to this major: Pharmacists, Pharmacy Technicians, Physician Assistants, Opticians, Licensed Practical Nurses, and Dietitians and Nutritionists

Physical Therapy

Physical Therapy majors learn to assist and help persons with injuries, muscle, nerve, and joint problems, burns, and bone diseases. They learn to use exercise, massage, and heat and light to assist in healing. They prepare to take state licensure examinations in this field and qualify for service in the prevention of disabilities and the rehabilitation of the disabled. They learn to test, evaluate, and plan a treatment program for patients who are physically incapacitated as the result of accidents or disease, and for healthy individuals who wish to prevent injuries in work or recreational settings.

Interests: Biological and physical sciences, exercise and fitness, people, analytic reasoning

Skills and abilities: Interpersonal communication, problem solving, visual spatial perception, emotional sensitivity, oral and written expression, speech clarity, problem sensitivity, manual dexterity

Occupations related to this major: Physical Therapists, Occupational Therapists, Respiratory Therapists, Manual Arts Therapists, Corrective Therapists, and Speech-Language Pathologists and Audiologists

Speech Pathology/Audiology

Speech Pathology majors learn to treat people with speech, language, voice, hearing, and communication disorders. These disorders may be the result of hearing loss, brain injury or deterioration, cerebral palsy, stroke, cleft palate, mental retardation, or emotional problems. They receive training in the identification and treatment of human communication disorders. They learn about the normal processes of speech and language development, why problems may occur, and what can be done to minimize their impact.

Interests: Working with children, working with adults, identifying and solving behavioral problems, applying technology to human needs

Skills and abilities: Oral and written expression and comprehension, speech clarity, creativity, working cooperatively in groups

Occupations related to this major: Speech-Language Pathologists and Audiologists, Recreation Therapists, Corrective Therapists, Exercise Physiologists, Occupational Therapists, and Respiratory Therapists

12. HUMANITIES

Humanities students explore thought and expression through aesthetic, historical, philosophical, social, political, psychological, and symbolic contexts. Humanities studies serve as a liberal and broad training for professional careers. Students will enjoy courses in English, literature, history, classics, culture studies, history of art and music, philosophy, foreign language, social and natural sciences. Graduates with a bachelor's degree may qualify for management trainee positions in corporations, banks, and federal and state governmental agencies. Many students use humanities as an undergraduate degree for the teaching or law professions. Other students may become writers or communications specialists in humanistic endeavors.

Interests: Exploring thoughts and expressions through aesthetic, historical, philosophical, social, political, psychological and symbolic contests; literature, history, foreign language, social and natural sciences

Popular majors in this field of study: American Literature, Anthropology, Classics, Comparative Literature, English, English Education, Foreign Language, History, Linguistics, Philosophy, Religion, and Sociology

Employment information/outlook: More than 972,100 people worked in related occupations in this field of study in 2012. The 2012-2022 employment growth is expected to be 11%.

In May 2012, median annual wages for anthropologists and archaeologists were $57,420; historians, $52,480; sociologists, $74,960. Wages of anthropologists and archaeologists, geographers, and historians vary. The same applies to English and Foreign Language specialists and people in the clergy.

American Literature

American Literature majors study the historical development of the culture in which they live. They study the literature and literary development of the United States from the Colonial Era to the present. They learn about the forces—intellectual, economic, geographic, and social—that have shaped their own character. They study periods and genres, authors, literary criticism, and regional and oral traditions.

Interests: Sensitivity to language, the power of ideas, exploring the development of different regional and ethnic traditions that make up American culture

Skills and abilities: Assessing conflicting points of view, oral and written expression and comprehension, speech clarity

Occupations related to this major: English Teachers, Creative Writers, Art, Drama, and Music Teachers, Reporters and Correspondents, and Publicity Writers

Anthropology

Anthropology majors learn to make comparative studies of the distribution, origin, and evolution of man, cultures that man has created, and their social and physical characteristics. Studies include ancient as well as modern man.

Interests: Writing, archeology, sociology, social sciences, investigative research

Skills and abilities: Writing, science, critical thinking, oral and written expression and comprehension, inductive reasoning, fluency of ideas

Occupations related to this major: Anthropologists, Archeologists, Historians, Sociologists, Linguistic Scientists, and Genealogists

Classics

Classics majors immerse themselves in two cultures fundamental to the West—the cultures of ancient Greece and ancient Rome. Students explore the literature, history, art, philosophy, and architecture of those civilizations. Connecting with the past creates a sense of belonging to humanity and participating in human achievement and evokes reflections on the present. Students will explore their poetry, prose, and drama, and consider the relation of literature to other arts and to other fields of study.

Interests: Language, literature, exploring the past, acquiring a broad liberal education

Skills and abilities: Oral and written expression and comprehension, information ordering, skills of analysis and criticism

Occupations related to this major: Classicists, Anthropologists, Art History Teachers, English Teachers, Foreign Language Teachers, and Literature Teachers

Comparative Literature

Comparative Literature majors study the literature of different countries, cultures, and languages. They explore their poetry, prose, and drama, and consider the relation of literature to other arts and to other fields of study.

Interests: Literature, foreign languages, differences between cultures as expressed in their languages and works of art

Skills and abilities: Reading critically, speaking, active listening, oral and written expression and comprehension, speech recognition, information ordering

Occupations related to this major: English Teachers, Foreign Language Teachers, Postsecondary Teachers, Journalists, Lawyers, Reporters and Correspondents, and Writers

English

English majors study the linguistic and literary richness of the English language as well as some of the cultural history of the English-speaking world. They concentrate on specific areas such as creative writing, comparative or American literature, or semantics. They study important works of literature—drama, prose, and poetry—focusing on the point of view, organization, and language of the works. They develop critical and analytical reading skills, and practice language use and composition.

Interests: Reading, talking, writing about literature; music, theater, and film

Skills and abilities: Speaking, writing, oral and written expression and comprehension, speech clarity

Occupations related to this major: English Teachers, Teachers, Journalists, Publishers, Radio and Television Broadcasters, and Social Workers

English Education

English Education majors learn to teach students about English grammar and linguistics. They learn to instruct students in different types of literature such as poetry, short stories, plays, and novels. They learn how to teach students to research and prepare research papers. They learn how to teach public speaking, drama, and English as a second language

Interests: Nature and history of languages, reading, literature, journalism, creative writing, linguistic development of children and teenagers

Skills and abilities: Speaking, working with students, art, guiding discussions

Occupations related to this major: Elementary School Teachers, Secondary School Teachers, Postsecondary School Teachers, Linguistic Scientists, and Speech-Language Pathologists and Audiologists

Foreign Language

Foreign Language majors study foreign languages (French, German, Italian, Japanese, Russian, Spanish, etc.). They study the language, literature, and culture of the country where the language is spoken.

Interests: Literature, history, culture of a language

Skills and abilities: Fluency in speaking and writing, learning languages, oral and written expression and comprehension, speech clarity

Occupations related to this major: Foreign Language Teachers, Translators, Journalists, Foreign Travel Consultants, Diplomats, and Linguists

History

History majors study the social, economic, and political developments of societies. They learn to analyze historical happenings and, as reporters, writers, or teachers, report on their significance. Students expand their knowledge and understanding of the past. Working with written, oral, visual, and art factual evidence they examine the causes, contexts, and chronologies of historical events, thus cultivating a sense of continuity and change in human experiences.

Interests: Curiosity about when, where, and why historical happenings occurred; what it was like to have lived in different times and places

Skills and abilities: Reading carefully, writing clearly, speaking articulately, thinking analytically, oral and written expression and comprehension, expressing ideas with clarity and precision

Occupations related to this major: Historians, Archeologists, Anthropologists, Genealogists, Curators, Archivists, and Teachers

Linguistics

Linguistics majors study the common properties of the world's languages. They study the structure and development of a specific language or language group. They trace the origin and evolution of words through comparative analysis of ancient parent languages and modern language groups. They study word and structural characteristics, such as phonetics and phonology, morphology, syntax, and semantics.

Interests: Language, foreign languages, how people talk and express themselves

Skills and abilities: Learning foreign languages, problem solving, oral and written expression and comprehension, speech recognition

Occupations related to this major: Linguistic Scientists, English as a Second Language Teachers, English Teachers, Foreign Language Teachers, Interpreters, Translators, Public Relations Specialists, and Speech Pathologists

Philosophy

Philosophy majors learn the process of developing a philosophy. They gain insight into how the great minds of the past and present have attempted to answer the most serious questions of the universe. They participate in a tradition of thought as old as civilized life and as new as artificial intelligence and medical ethics. They examine issues of morality, reality, and knowledge. Philosophy is a foundation for teaching, religion, wisdom, and logical thinking.

Interests: Solitary meditation, argument with family and friends, reading, asking the "why" question, seeing the connections between different things

Skills and abilities: Writing, debating, thinking logically, mathematics, oral and written expression and comprehension, speech recognition, information ordering

Occupations related to this major: Philologists, Political Scientists, Anthropologists, Psychologists, Sociologists, and Historians

Religion

Religion majors study and compare the major world religions, as well as many of the lesser-known religions. They study the various branches, sects, and denominations of particular religions. They learn how religion plays an integral part in all societies. They learn to use a range of approaches when examining religion—historical, textual, psychological, philosophical, sociological, and anthropological.

Interests: Different cultures and societies, world religions, human problems and mysteries, such as birth, growth, love, death, grief

Skills and abilities: Reading carefully and critically, foreign languages, oral and written expression and comprehension, problem sensitivity, speech clarity

Occupations related to this major: Clergy, Directors of Religious Activities and Education, Therapists and Counselors, Psychologists, Social Workers, and Teachers

Sociology

Sociology majors study the origin, development, organization, and functions of human society. They trace the origin and growth of human organizations and the behavior and interaction within social groups. They analyze the influence of group activities on individual and group behavior.

Interests: Anthropology, geography, criminology, psychology, investigative research, politics

Skills and abilities: Reading critically, critical thinking, solving problems, oral and written expression and comprehension, deductive reasoning

Occupations related to this major: Sociologists, Anthropologists, Political Scientists, Counseling Psychologists, Historians, and Linguistic Scientists

13. PHYSICAL SCIENCES

Physical Sciences majors in this field of study investigate the structure and composition of the Earth and the universe. Everything in our physical environment, whether naturally occurring or of human design, is composed of chemicals. Chemists search for, and put to practical use, new knowledge about chemicals. Geological scientists play an important role in preserving and cleaning up the environment. Meteorologists forecast the weather. Physicists design and perform experiments with lasers, cyclotrons, telescopes, mass spectrometers, and other equipment. Physical science technicians use the principles and theories of science and mathematics to solve problems in research and development and to help invent and improve products and processes.

Interests: The structure and composition of the Earth and the universe; an interest in our physical environment, whether naturally occurring or of human design

Popular majors in this field of study: Astronomy, Atmospheric Sciences, Chemistry, Environmental Sciences, Geology, Geophysics, and Physics

Employment information/outlook: More than 978,300 people worked in related occupations in this field of study in 2012. The 2012-2022 employment growth is expected to be 10%.

In May 2012, median wages for physicists and astronomers were $106,360; chemists were $73,060; and environmental scientists, $63,570.

Astronomy

Astronomy majors study the sizes, shapes, motions, and all other physical properties of the sun, moon, stars, and planets. They may use knowledge of astronomy in space exploration and the development of space technology. Students seek to understand the entire universe—its constituent parts, such as the stars and planets, and the physical and mathematical laws that govern them.

Interests: Nature, the night sky, the expanding universe, physical science, astronomical science

Skills and abilities: Mathematics, science, computers, inductive and deductive reasoning, written comprehension

Occupations related to this major: Astronomers, Geophysicists, Physicists, Geologists, Chemists, and Atmospheric and Space Scientists

Atmospheric Sciences

Atmospheric Sciences majors learn to investigate atmospheric phenomena and interpret meteorological data gathered by surface and air stations, satellites, and radar to prepare reports and weather forecasts for public and other uses. They study the basic principles of atmospheric physics and dynamics and are concerned with understanding and forecasting weather.

Interests: Weather, environment, climate, science, mathematics, computer science, geography, serving the public

Skills and abilities: Analytic reasoning, mechanical reasoning, problem solving, oral and written expression and comprehension, speech clarity, inductive reasoning

Occupations related to this major: Atmospheric Scientists, Space Scientists, Climatologists, Geophysicists, Astronomers, and Meteorologists

Chemistry

Chemistry majors study the sciences of physical substances, atoms, molecules, elements, and compounds. They learn to perform chemical tests, develop new chemical products, and monitor the purity of air, food, and drugs. Because it is an experimental science, students learn to design and perform the experiments that allow a better understanding of the physical world.

Interests: Investigative research, problem solving, curiosity about how things work

Skills and abilities: Analytic and mathematical skills, oral and written expression and comprehension, deductive reasoning, mathematical reasoning

Occupations related to this major: Chemists, Chemical Engineers, Chemical Engineering Technicians, Agricultural Scientists, Biological Scientists, and Physicists

Environmental Sciences

Environmental Sciences majors study the biological and physical aspects of the environment. They learn about the conservation and/or improvement of natural resources, such as air, soil, water, land, fish, and wildlife, as well as methods of controlling environmental pollution. They conduct research or perform investigation for the purpose of identifying, abating, or eliminating sources of pollutants or hazards that affect either the environment or the health of the population.

Interests: Investigative research, solving problems, working with ideas

Skills and abilities: Working with others, oral and written expression and comprehension, problem sensitivity, mathematical reasoning, inductive reasoning

Occupations related to this major: Environmental Scientists, Materials Scientists, Geographers, Geologists, Atmospheric Scientists, and Space Scientists

Geology

Geology majors study the Earth's structure, composition, and history. They examine rocks, minerals, and fossils. They record data, prepare maps, conduct surveys, and advise suitability of sites. They develop skills that are useful for basic research and applied problem solving.

Interests: The outdoors, remote places, problem solving, collecting minerals or fossils

Skills and abilities: Reasoning ability, critical thinking, mathematics, oral and written expression and comprehension, number facility, inductive reasoning

Occupations related to this major: Geologists, Physicists, Geophysicists, Materials Scientists, Geological Data Technicians, and Geographers

Geophysics

Geophysics majors study aspects of the earth, including the atmosphere and hydrosphere. They investigate and measure seismic, gravitational, electrical, thermal, and magnetic forces affecting the Earth, and utilize principles of physics, mathematics, and chemistry. They study the Earth and its atmosphere by physical measurements. Students learn to use mathematics and physics, along with electrical engineering, computer science, geology, and other earth sciences to analyze measurements taken at the surface to infor properties and processes deep within the Earth's complex interior.

Interests: The outdoors, travel, taking measurements, computer languages, graphics, computer programming

Skills and abilities: Natural curiosity, mathematics, physical science, computers, oral and written comprehension, mathematical reasoning, deductive reasoning

Occupations related to this major: Geophysicists, Geologists, Astronomers, Physicists, Atmospheric Scientists, Space Scientists, and Chemists

Physics

Physics majors learn to explore and identify the basic principles of the structure and behavior of matter, the generation and transfer of energy, and the interaction of matter and energy. They learn to use these principles in theoretical areas such as the origin of the universe, or in practical areas to develop advanced materials, electronic devices, or medical equipment.

Interests: Investigative research, mathematics, problem solving, improving the quality of life

Skills and abilities: Computational skills, reasoning logically, solving problems, oral and written expression and comprehension, mathematical reasoning

Occupations related to this major: Physicists, Astronomers, Geologists, Atmospheric Scientists, Space Scientists, Geophysicists, and Environmental Scientists

14. SOCIAL AND BEHAVIORAL SCIENCES

Social and Behavioral Sciences majors learn about the social needs of people. Clinical psychologists help the mentally or emotionally disturbed adjust to life through behavior modification programs and other techniques. Social workers address the needs of individuals, families, groups, and communities. Their work may involve everything from helping an elderly person adjust to life in a nursing home, to organizing fund-raising for community social welfare activities. Other social scientists conduct basic and applied research in the social sciences. They use established methods to assemble a body of fact and theory that contributes to human knowledge. Social scientists investigate all aspects of human society—from anthropologists studying the origins of the human race, or historians studying an ancient civilization—to political scientists analyzing the results of presidential elections.

Interests: Social and emotional needs of people; an interest in all aspects of society—from the origins of the human race, or an ancient civilization, to political results of presidential elections

Popular majors in this field of study: Criminal Justice Studies, Economics, Geography, Gerontology, Political Sciences, Psychology, Public Administration, Social Studies Education, and Social Work

Employment information/outlook: More than 4,153,700 people worked in related occupations in this field of study in 2012. The 2012-2022 employment growth is expected to be 19%.

In May 2012, median annual wages of probation officers and correctional treatment specialists were $38,970; economists, $91,860; salary clinical, counseling, and school psychologists, $69,280; social and human service assistants, $28,850; political scientists, $102,000; sociologists, $74,960; child, family, and school social workers, $44,200. Public administration positions vary by occupation, size of the state or locality, and region of the country.

Criminal Justice Studies

Criminal Justice Studies majors learn about the dimensions and causes of crime and delinquency; the structure of the American criminal justice system; the operation of criminal courts; and the techniques and theories of law enforcement.

Interests: Serving others, court procedures, criminal law, private security, criminal justice

Skills and abilities: Working with others, making decisions, oral and written expression and comprehension, inductive reasoning, speech clarity, problem sensitivity

Occupations related to this major: Criminal Investigators, United States Marshals, Police Detectives, Sheriffs and Deputy Sheriffs, Correction Officers and Jailers, and Child Support and Missing Persons Investigators

Economics

Economics majors learn to plan, design, and conduct research into activities devoted to satisfying human wants. They learn to analyze the relationship between supply and demand. They study the problems of inflation, unemployment, tariffs, taxation, and foreign trade. They learn to analyze such issues as inflation, unemployment, monopoly, and economic growth. They study theory, policy, and trends and explore ways to deal with the economic problems of society and the individual.

Interests: Current issues such as taxes, poverty, health, inflation, the environment, human behavior

Skills and abilities: Solving problems, oral and written expression and comprehension, mathematical reasoning, logical reasoning

Occupations related to this major: Economists, Market Research Analysts, Urban and Regional Planners, Financial Managers, Financial Analysts, and Underwriters

Geography

Geography majors study the activities of people. Students study where people live, why they are located there, and how they earn a living. Students study the physical characteristics of the Earth, such as landforms, vegetation, climate, locale, and mineral and water resources. They study how people relate to and are shaped by their environment. They gain a broad perspective on the world's environments and its peoples while gaining a strong background in the physical and social sciences.

Interests: Analyzing and solving social and environmental problems, doing social and physical scientific research, the relationship between people and their environment

Skills and abilities: Oral and written expression and comprehension, spatial orientation, working individually and in groups, information gathering, working with computers

Occupations related to this major: Geographers, Geophysicists, Geologists, Atmospheric and Space Scientists, Environmental Scientists, and Materials Scientists

Gerontology

Gerontology majors learn about aging and older persons. They study physical, emotional, and intellectual changes in the elderly, cultural aspects of aging, and governmental policies and programs for the aging.

Interests: Helping people, human development, older people, family relations, improving the quality of life

Skills and abilities: Oral and written expression and comprehension, listening, objectivity, deductive reasoning, determining needs and interests, organizing and managing projects

Occupations related to this major: Gerontologists, Geriatric Nurses, Nursing Home Administrators, Social Welfare Administrators, and Occupational and Physical Therapists

Political Sciences

Political Sciences majors study government and the nature of politics. They analyze the operations of different forms of government, and attempt to find theoretical and practical solutions to political problems. Students learn about the origins, historical development, and social functions of government. They study how electoral, legislative, judicial, and administrative structures and processes vary from one country and one age to another; how and why governments change, fall, and engage in wars. They study the behavior of public officials and other citizens involved in politics.

Interests: Public policy issues such as health care and environmental protection; politicians and public figures, justice, good and bad government, law, criminal justice, the legal system

Skills and abilities: Reading critically, thinking analytically, oral and written expression and comprehension, understanding graphic material

Occupations related to this major: Political Scientists, Legislators, Sociologists, Historians, Anthropologists, and Political Science Teachers

Psychology

Psychology majors learn to collect and interpret scientific data relating to human behavior to understand people and explain their actions. They learn to interview patients, give diagnostic tests, and offer therapy to help people make behavioral adjustments. Students study human and animal behavior and explore the processes involved in normal and abnormal thoughts, feelings, and actions. They increase their understanding of behavior while learning psychological facts, methods, principles, and generalizations about individuals and groups.

Interests: Working with people, scientific method, human and animal behavior

Skills and abilities: Critical thinking, oral and written expression and comprehension, inductive reasoning

Occupations related to this major: Developmental Psychologists, Experimental Psychologists, Educational Psychologists, Social Psychologists, Clinical Psychologists, and Counseling Psychologists

Public Administration

Public Administration majors may study in five areas of specialization: personnel, management, public relations, finance, and planning. They learn to establish government policy, and develop laws, rules and regulations. These studies will prepare students to find positions managing public agencies. Students deal with the operations of all forms and levels of government. Students learn about the many skills and challenges associated with implementing public policy in government and in nonprofit organizations.

Interests: Public and community service, organizing people, leadership, working with people from different backgrounds

Skills and abilities: Leadership, organizational ability, problem solving, oral and written expression and comprehension, inductive reasoning

Occupations related to this major: Government Service Executives, City Managers, Management Analysts, Government Affairs Specialists, and Legislators

Social Studies Education

Social Studies Education majors learn to teach courses pertaining to human society and its characteristic elements. They learn to teach subjects such as psychology, economics, history, political science, and sociology. They learn to teach students in middle school and high school courses in history, citizenship, and other social sciences.

Interests: Serving people, working with people, history, social sciences

Skills and abilities: Speaking, organizing working with people, oral and written expression and comprehension, speech clarity

Occupations related to this major: Middle School Teachers, High School Teachers, Postsecondary School Teachers, Historians, Sociologists, and Psychologists

Social Work

Social Work majors study many types of social issues and needs. They learn to aid families with physical, mental, or social problems, such as poverty, unemployment, illness, broken homes, various disabilities, antisocial behavior, and inadequate housing. Students acquire the knowledge and skills to assist individuals, families, groups, and communities in preventing and alleviating the problems of a modern, rapidly changing society. They learn to help others and to modify harmful social conditions, promote social and economic well being, and increase opportunities for all people to live with dignity and freedom.

Interests: Helping those in need, particularly children, the poor, minorities, the aged, the disabled, and women, enabling others to develop unique, positive responses and solutions to their problems

Skills and abilities: Objectivity, ability to listen, analytic ability, oral and written expression and comprehension, problem sensitivity

Occupations related to this major: Social Workers, Medical and Psychiatric Social Workers, Community Organization Social Workers, Residential Counselors, Probation and Correctional Treatment Specialists, and Human Services Workers

LOCATING OCCUPATIONAL INFORMATION RELATED TO YOUR MAJOR

Students may find occupations in a Field of Study in which they have a work interest. They may wish to conduct research to find specific information about an occupation. Good sources for occupational information are public libraries, high school and college career resource centers, One-Stop Career Centers, America's InfoNet (*www.acinet.org*) and O*Net (*www.online.onetcenter.org*), the occupational information Network.

Recommended books for occupations and college entry research:

Occupational Outlook Handbook, 2012–2022 Edition,
U.S. Bureau of Labor Statistics, Postal Square Building
2 Massachusetts Avenue, NE, Washington, DC 20212-0001
www.bls.gov

A Guide to the College Admission Process,
National Association for College Admissions Counseling,
1050 North Highland Street, Suite 400, Arlington, VA 22201
www.nacacnet.org

College Major Handbook, 3rd Edition, CFKR Career Materials, Inc.
11860 Kemper Road, # 7, Auburn, CA 95603
www.cfkr.com

Federal Student Aid Information Center,
An Office of the U.S. Department of Education, P.O. Box 84
Washington, DC 20044-0084
www.fafsa.ed.gov

CHOOSING A COLLEGE

A student's choice of institution may depend on individual needs and talents. A person's career goals, career plans, and choice of college major are very important criteria in choosing a college. A student's choice may be limited by financial or other considerations. However, if at all possible, students should give high priority to their career plans and choice of a college major when choosing a college that best matches their career plans. Students' choice of their college major may influence their final college choice.

Some majors are rare and specialized. Special attention must be given to those majors that are fairly rare and specialized. Students will be limited in the number of colleges from which to choose. There are more than 1800 four-year colleges in the United States; only 78 offer aerospace engineering; 42 offer landscape architecture; 81 offer astronomy; 24 offer petroleum engineering; 8 offer statistics; 8 offer business statistics; 26 offer oceanography; 59 offer pharmacy; and 115 offer occupational therapy majors. This is a partial listing. A student who chooses a specialized major may find it necessary to travel a distance to find a college offering that major. School career centers and public libraries may carry listings of colleges that offer the major of the student's choice.

The most widely offered baccalaureate-level majors are found in four-year colleges. No college, not even the largest university, offers every major; some offer relatively few. Students will want to attend a college that offers several of the majors they are considering. Students can keep their choice of major open by selecting a university or college that offers a wide range of majors. The most common majors are found in the Art, Business, Computer and Information Science, Education, Engineering, Health, Humanities, and the Social and Behavioral Science fields of study.

MAKING THE FINAL DECISION

Making important decisions and setting long-range goals is never an easy task. Making a decision on what to study in college for four or more years, and how this will fit into students' lifestyles and career goals is very important and very personal. With the soaring costs of education and the increasing complexity of the job market, students cannot afford the luxury of trial and error in preparing for a career that requires college training; entering college without a career or major in mind can add time and expense to the entire journey. Good decision-making calls for awareness of one's needs and the matching of those needs with a wide variety of alternate choices. It is to this end that sufficient information has been explored for making a final decision.

In making a final decision, students must take a broad view of the fourteen Fields of Study. They should look carefully at all career and major options within the fourteen fields. Students should not limit themselves to a career or major that has been recommended to them by family or friends. The final decision should be the student's, along with the responsibility to reach their goals. In the final analysis, students will have to look at themselves. As Plato once said, "Know thyself, and to thine own self be true."

- **Assess work interests.** Identify work-related interests. Discover the type of work activities and occupations that match work interests. Identify and learn about the most relevant broad interest areas. Use interest results to explore the world of work.
- **Assess work values.** Pinpoint what is important in a job. Identify occupations that provide satisfaction based on the similarity among work values, conditions of work, and the characteristics of an occupation.
- **Assess work abilities.** Identify user ability strength, parts of work that the user likes to do, parts of work that the user finds important, and training needs of the user.

The more students know about their interests, work values, abilities, and career goals, the better their decisions will be. In the final analysis, good decision-making by students is based on knowing oneself and being flexible enough to sense whether they are on the right track, and to alter decisions when they are not in their best interest. No matter what major is chosen, students must keep in ming that intellectual flexibility is the skill that enables them to work productively when the knowledge they have mastered is challenged or replaced by new ideas.

We wish all students well in their college studies and in the career path that they have chosen.

Robert Kauk and Francis Ferry

Occupational information was gathered from *O*Net,* U.S. Department of Labor.

INDEX OF COLLEGE MAJORS

This section of *Profiles of American Colleges* will help you quickly determine which schools offer the major in which you are interested, the in-state tuition, room and board costs, and the Selector Rating. The colleges are listed alphabetically and the first column indicates the state where each is located. These data reflect the 2013-2014 academic year. You will be able to compare schools offering those majors that interest you the most and see what their in-state costs and Selector Ratings are, before reading the Profiles in the main section of the book (see page 249 for Selector Rating details). You may also discover some new schools or majors that interset you.

(BIOLOGICAL) PRE-HEALTH STUDIES

School	ST	$IS	SR
Bethel College	IN	31,560	C
Elmhurst College	IL	42,032	₵
John Carroll Univ	OH	44,520	₵
Oswego / SUNY	NY	20,009	VC
Shippensburg Univ of Pennsylvania	PA	17,064	LC
Univ of Arkansas at Little Rock	AR		C

(EDUCATION) CHILDHOOD EDUCATION

School	ST	$IS	SR
Aquinas College	MI	33,060	C
Bethel College	IN	31,560	C
Canisius College	NY	45,602	VC
CUNY/Brooklyn College	NY	5,884	₵
Dordt College	IA	34,160	VC
Hofstra Univ	NY	48,020	V₵
Houghton College	NY	35,740	VC
Iona College	NY	44,028	C
Kennesaw State Univ	GA	13,017	VC
Marshall Univ	WV	14,820	C
Mass College of Liberal Arts	MA	16,733	C
Mount Aloysius College	PA	27,970	C
New York Univ	NY	61,470	MC
Nyack College	NY	32,000	C
Oswego / SUNY	NY	20,009	VC
Point Park Univ	PA	36,390	C
St. Mary's Univ of Minn	MN	37,015	C
Taylor Univ	IN	36,742	V₵
Univ of Arkansas at Fayetteville	AR	16,860	VC
Univ of Nebr - Lincoln	NE	17,507	VC
Univ of Texas at San Antonio	TX	18,372	C
Wright State Univ	OH	16,983	C
Youngstown State Univ	OH	16,374	LC

(SOCIAL SCIENCE) GLOBAL STUDIES

School	ST	$IS	SR
Aquinas College	MI	33,060	C
Bryant Univ	RI	49,179	VC
Colby College	ME	57,510	MC
Hofstra Univ	NY	48,020	V₵
Lehigh Univ	PA	55,080	MC
Missouri State Univ	MO	13,996	VC
New York Univ	NY	61,470	MC
St. Mary's Univ of Minn	MN	37,015	C
Southeast Missouri State Univ	MO	14,983	LC
Univ of Calif at Irvine	CA	25,961	VC
Univ of Central Florida	FL	15,711	V₵
Univ of Nebr - Lincoln	NE	17,507	VC
Univ of New Haven	CT	47,740	C
Warren Wilson College	NC	34,888	VC
Wheeling Jesuit Univ	WV	34,668	C
Winona State Univ	MN	16,530	C

ACCOUNTING

School	ST	$IS	SR
Abilene Christian Univ	TX	38,400	VC
Adams State College	CO	13,358	LC
Adelphi Univ	NY	43,130	VC
Adrian College	MI	33,800	C
Alabama A&M Univ	AL	96,100	C
Alabama State Univ	AL	14,142	NC
Albany State Univ	GA	8,500	C
Albertus Magnus College	CT	37,382	LC
Albright College	PA	46,660	C
Alcorn State Univ	MS	9,500	C
Alderson Broaddus Univ	WV	28,656	C
Alfred Univ	NY	40,392	VC
Alvernia Univ	PA	39,250	C
Alverno College	WI	30,483	LC
American International College	MA	36,100	LC
Anderson Univ	IN	35,390	C
Andrews Univ	MI	28,030	₵
Angelo State Univ	TX	15,049	NC
Appalachian State Univ	NC	12,919	VC
Aquinas College	MI	33,060	C
Arcadia Univ	PA	33,570	₵
Arizona State Univ	AZ	18,818	₵
Arkansas Baptist College	AR	9,000	NC
Arkansas State Univ	AR	14,980	C
Arkansas Tech Univ	AR	13,164	LC
Asbury Univ	KY	32,038	VC
Ashford Univ	IA	21,780	C
Ashland Univ	OH	25,000	C
Assumption College	MA	45,721	VC
Atlantic Union College	MA	24,600	LC
Auburn Univ	AL	20,052	V₵
Auburn Univ at Montgomery	AL	12,120	C
Augsburg College	MN	35,142	C
Augustana College	IL	43,398	HC
Augustana College	SD	35,500	VC
Aurora Univ	IL	26,870	C
Avila Univ	MO	26,900	C
Azusa Pacific Univ	CA	39,946	C
Baker College of Flint	MI	7,800	NC
Baker Univ	KS	33,350	₵
Baldwin Wallace Univ	OH	36,980	VC
Ball State Univ	IN	17,850	C
Barry Univ	FL	38,190	C
Barton College	NC	27,660	C
Baylor Univ	TX	46,720	HC
Belhaven Univ	MS	27,170	C
Bellarmine Univ	KY	42,950	VC
Bellevue Univ	NE	4,600	NC
Belmont Abbey College	NC	37,716	C
Belmont Univ	TN	37,380	V₵
Bemidji State Univ	MN	13,500	C
Benedict College	SC	20,454	NC
Benedictine College	KS	29,180	VC
Benedictine Univ	IL	35,220	C
Bennett College	NC		LC
Bentley Univ	MA	54,555	H₵
Berkeley College	NY	18,300	LC
Berkeley College/New Jersey	NJ	27,300	LC
Berkeley College/ Westchester Campus	NY	28,500	LC
Berry College	GA	39,254	HC
Bethany College	KS	30,605	NC
Bethany College	WV	35,282	C
Bethel College	IN	31,560	C
Bethel Univ	MN	34,940	VC
Bethune-Cookman Univ	FL	22,290	LC
Binghamton Univ / The SUNY	NY	20,832	H₵
Biola Univ	CA	40,320	VC
Birmingham-Southern College	AL	42,370	V₵
Black Hills State Univ	SD	13,562	LC
Blackburn College	IL	21,350	C
Bloomfield College	NJ	36,960	C
Bloomsburg Univ of Pennsylvania	PA	13,598	C
Bluefield State College	WV	3,140	LC
Bluffton Univ	OH	37,864	C
Boise State Univ	ID	12,802	C
Boston College	MA	58,506	MC
Boston Univ	MA	54,130	H₵
Bowling Green State Univ	OH	18,970	C
Bradley Univ	IL	31,874	VC
Brenau Univ Women's College	GA	26,650	₵
Brescia Univ	KY	26,140	V₵
Brewton-Parker College	GA	33,388	LC
Briar Cliff Univ	IA	29,514	C
Bridgewater State Univ	MA	18,752	C
Brigham Young Univ	UT	12,100	HC
Brigham Young Univ/ Hawaii	HI	8,614	VC
Bryant Univ	RI	49,179	VC
Bucknell Univ	PA	58,160	MC
Buena Vista Univ	IA	37,954	C
Butler Univ	IN	45,898	V₵
Cabrini College	PA	40,859	LC
Cairn Univ	PA	31,255	C
Caldwell College	NJ	35,602	LC
Calif Baptist Univ	CA	35,890	C
Calif Lutheran Univ	CA	47,640	C
Cal State, Chico	CA	18,952	C
Cal State, East Bay	CA	16,549	C
Cal State, Fresno	CA	17,405	C
Cal State, Long Beach	CA	17,534	₵
Cal State, Northridge	CA	28,313	C
Cal State, Sacramento	CA	16,200	C
Cal State, San Bernardino	CA	12,000	C
Calif Univ of Pennsylvania	PA	14,217	C
Calumet College of St. Joseph	IN	15,000	LC
Calvin College	MI	37,585	V₵
Cameron Univ	OK	9,267	LC
Campbell Univ	NC	25,500	C
Campbellsville Univ	KY	27,720	C
Canisius College	NY	45,602	VC
Capital Univ	OH	39,824	VC
Cardinal Stritch Univ	WI	24,054	C
Caribbean Univ	PR	10,375	
Carlow Univ	PA	30,272	C
Carroll College	MT	28,000	C
Carroll Univ	WI	24,000	C
Carson-Newman Univ	TN	29,058	₵
Carthage College	WI	33,000	C
Case Western Reserve Univ	OH	55,178	MC
Catawba College	NC	37,105	C
Cedar Crest College	PA	43,240	C
Cedarville Univ	OH	31,036	V₵
Centenary College	NJ	38,618	LC
Centenary College of Louisiana	LA	39,070	₵
Central College	IA	36,980	VC
Central Conn State Univ	CT	19,212	C
Central Methodist Univ	MO	28,240	VC
Central Mich Univ	MI	18,066	C
Central State Univ	OH	9,010	C
Central Univ of Bayamon	PR	3,350	
Central Washington Univ	WA	11,730	C
Chaminade Univ of Honolulu	HI	31,664	C
Champlain College	VT	44,850	VC
Chancellor Univ	OH	11,000	C
Chapman Univ	CA	56,019	V₵
Chatham Univ	PA	42,440	VC
Chestnut Hill College	PA	39,785	LC
Cheyney Univ of Pennsylvania	PA	20,372	LC
Chicago State Univ	IL	5,482	C
Christian Brothers Univ	TN	19,140	HC
Christopher Newport Univ	VA	21,050	VC
CUNY/Baruch College	NY	15,831	VC
CUNY/Brooklyn College	NY	5,884	₵
City Univ of Seattle	WA	14,880	NC
Claremont McKenna College	CA	58,065	MC
Clarion Univ of Pennsylvania	PA	17,370	C
Clark Atlanta Univ	GA	30,006	C
Clarke Univ	IA	36,400	C
Clarkson Univ	NY	53,538	HC
Clayton State Univ	GA	12,000	LC
Clearwater Christian College	FL	23,720	C
Cleary Univ	MI	11,000	C
Clemson Univ	SC	19,136	HC
Cleveland State Univ	OH	21,357	C
Coastal Carolina Univ	SC	17,620	C
Coe College	IA	43,590	VC
College of Staten Island / The CUNY	NY	16,778	NC
College of Charleston	SC	21,273	VC
College of Mount St. Joseph	OH	33,880	C
College of New Jersey	NJ	25,376	HC
College of St. Benedict	MN	47,570	VC
College of St. Scholastica	MN	39,960	C
College of St Joseph	VT	30,600	LC
College of the Holy Cross	MA	56,232	MC
College of the Ozarks	MO	5,605	VC
College of William & Mary	VA	25,085	MC
Colo Christian Univ	CO	27,500	VC
Colo Mesa Univ	CO	16,669	LC
Colo State Univ-Pueblo	CO	13,532	LC
Columbia College	MO	24,578	C
Columbia College	SC	27,882	C
Columbus State Univ	GA	13,176	C
Concord Univ	WV	13,102	C
Concordia College, Moorhead	MN	39,974	₵
Concordia Univ Nebr	NE	26,000	VC
Concordia Univ St. Paul	MN	27,200	C
Concordia Univ Texas	TX	23,640	C
Concordia Univ Wisc	WI	28,980	C
Concordia Univ, River Forest	IL	26,300	C
Converse College	SC	37,130	C
Coppin State Univ	MD	14,905	VC
Corban Univ	OR	34,764	C
Cornerstone Univ and Grand Rapids Theological Seminary	MI	30,866	C
Creighton Univ	NE	44,058	V₵
Culver-Stockton College	MO	30,900	C
Cumberland Univ	TN	21,220	C
Daemen College	NY	31,510	C
Dakota Wesleyan Univ	SD	23,000	C
Dallas Baptist Univ	TX	29,118	C
Davenport Univ	MI	21,002	LC
Davis and Elkins College	WV	33,742	C
De Sales Univ	PA	42,670	C
Defiance College	OH	30,645	C
Delaware State Univ	DE	14,700	LC
Delaware Valley College	PA	29,944	C
Delta State Univ	MS	12,292	LC
DePaul Univ	IL	46,120	VC
Dickinson State Univ	ND	8,550	NC
Dillard Univ	LA	20,940	VC
Doane College	NE	33,730	VC
Dominican College	NY	31,270	C
Dominican Univ	IL	37,628	C
Dordt College	IA	34,160	VC
Dowling College	NY	25,000	LC
Drake Univ	IA	30,980	V₵
Drexel Univ	PA	51,920	HC
Drury Univ	MO	30,319	VC
Duquesne Univ	PA	42,017	VC
D'Youville College	NY	29,850	C
East Carolina Univ	NC	14,169	C
East Central Univ	OK	10,223	LC
East Tenn State Univ	TN	9,000	C
Eastern Conn State Univ	CT	20,584	C
Eastern Illinois Univ	IL	20,502	C
Eastern Kentucky Univ	KY	11,161	C
Eastern Mennonite Univ	VA	38,850	VC
Eastern Mich Univ	MI	17,961	C
Eastern Nazarene College	MA	30,000	C
Eastern New Mexico Univ	NM	10,682	C
Eastern Oregon Univ	OR	10,400	C
Eastern Univ	PA	37,704	C
Eastern Washington Univ	WA	16,388	C
Edgewood College	WI	33,294	C
Edward Waters College	FL	17,856	LC
Elizabeth City State Univ	NC	11,638	C
Elizabethtown College	PA	47,600	VC
Elizabethtown College School of Continuing and Professional Studies	PA		VC
Elmhurst College	IL	42,032	₵
Elmira College	NY	49,950	₵
Elms College	MA	23,900	VC
Elon Univ	NC	40,046	HC
Emmanuel College	MA	47,985	VC
Emory Univ	GA	45,000	MC
Emporia State Univ	KS	12,897	C
Endicott College	MA	42,390	C
Eureka College	IL	19,280	C
Evangel Univ	MO	23,090	C
Excelsior College	NY	895	SP
Fairfield Univ	CT	55,850	VC
Fairleigh Dickinson Univ/ College at Florham	NJ	42,142	C
Fairleigh Dickinson Univ/ Metropolitan Campus	NJ	40,254	C
Fairmont State Univ	WV	12,098	LC
Faulkner Univ	AL	22,530	LC
Fayetteville State Univ	NC	10,816	C
Felician College	NJ	41,640	C
Ferris State Univ	MI	19,698	C
Ferrum College	VA	27,740	LC
Fitchburg State Univ	MA	17,241	C
Flagler College	FL	24,960	VC
Florida A&M Univ	FL	14,935	LC
Florida Atlantic Univ	FL	17,339	C
Florida Gulf Coast Univ	FL		C
Florida Inst of Technology	FL	48,290	VC
Florida International Univ	FL	17,747	VC
Florida Memorial Univ	FL	20,716	LC
Florida Southern College	FL	38,240	VC
Florida State Univ	FL	15,238	HC
Fontbonne Univ	MO	31,384	C
Fordham Univ	NY	58,927	HC
Fort Hays State Univ	KS	11,354	C
Fort Lewis College	CO	15,513	C
Fort Valley State Univ	GA	11,200	VC
Francis Marion Univ	SC	16,464	LC
Franciscan Univ of Steubenville	OH	27,320	VC
Franklin College	IN	35,885	C
Franklin Pierce Univ	NH	41,598	C
Franklin Univ	OH	7,000	SP
Freed-Hardeman Univ	TN	19,697	VC
Fresno Pacific Univ	CA	32,136	C
Friends Univ	KS	29,100	C
Frostburg State Univ	MD	15,264	LC
Furman Univ	SC	54,006	HC
Gallaudet Univ	DC	25,380	SP
Gannon Univ	PA	37,940	C
Gardner-Webb Univ	NC	34,375	₵
Geneva College	PA	27,280	C
George Fox Univ	OR	40,750	₵
George Mason Univ	VA	15,724	VC
George Washington Univ	DC	57,108	MC
Georgetown College	KY	38,690	C
Georgetown Univ	DC	52,910	MC
Georgia College and State Univ	GA	18,216	VC

ST = STATE **$IS** = IN-STATE COSTS **SR** = SELECTOR RATING

INDEX OF COLLEGE MAJORS

School	ST	$IS	SR
Georgia Regents Univ	GA		C
Georgia Southern Univ	GA	16,414	C
Georgia Southwestern State Univ	GA	12,218	C
Georgia State Univ	GA	12,000	VC
Georgian Court Univ	NJ	39,726	LC
Glenville State College	WV	11,348	NC
Golden Gate Univ	CA	17,000	C
Goldey-Beacom College	DE	27,493	C
Gonzaga Univ	WA	44,247	HC
Gordon College	MA	42,660	VG
Goshen College	IN	35,900	VC
Grace College and Theological Seminary	IN	28,800	C
Graceland Univ	IA	28,020	C
Grambling State Univ	LA	13,384	LC
Grand Canyon Univ	AZ	24,540	VC
Grand Valley State Univ	MI	17,998	VC
Grand View Univ	IA	31,050	C
Greensboro College	NC	28,740	LC
Greenville College	IL	27,012	C
Grove City College	PA	22,988	HC
Guilford College	NC	35,340	C
Gustavus Adolphus College	MN	48,170	HC
Gwynedd-Mercy College	PA	33,560	C
Hamline Univ	MN	44,198	VC
Hampton Univ	VA	28,528	C
Hannibal-LaGrange Univ	MO	24,490	C
Harding Univ	AR	21,432	G
Hardin-Simmons Univ	TX	23,560	G
Harris-Stowe State Univ	MO	14,000	NC
Hartwick College	NY	49,815	G
Hastings College	NE	27,782	G
Hawaii Pacific Univ	HI	36,690	C
Heidelberg Univ	OH	34,100	C
Henderson State Univ	AR	13,634	C
Hendrix College	AR	48,436	HG
Heritage Univ	WA	17,664	NC
High Point Univ	NC	39,800	C
Hilbert College	NY	28,550	C
Hillsdale College	MI	31,890	HG
Hiram College	OH	37,300	VC
Hodges Univ	FL	12,000	LC
Hofstra Univ	NY	48,020	VG
Holy Family Univ	PA	40,030	LC
Hope College	MI	36,320	VG
Hope International Univ	CA	34,650	C
Houghton College	NY	35,740	VC
Houston Baptist Univ	TX	23,815	G
Howard Payne Univ	TX	17,115	C
Howard Univ	DC	35,957	C
Humphreys College	CA	17,000	NC
Hunter College / The CUNY	NY	14,429	VC
Huntingdon College	AL	31,850	C
Huntington Univ	IN	32,220	C
Husson Univ	ME	23,386	LC
Idaho State Univ	ID	11,908	C
Illinois College	IL	25,770	VC
Illinois State Univ	IL	22,634	VC
Illinois Wesleyan Univ	IL	48,452	VG
Immaculata Univ	PA	43,000	C
Indiana Inst of Technology	IN	34,240	LC
Indiana State Univ	IN	16,000	C
Indiana Univ Bloomington	IN	19,358	HC
Indiana Univ Kokomo	IN	6,674	LC
Indiana Univ of Pennsylvania	PA	20,180	LC
Indiana Univ South Bend	IN	15,293	C
Indiana Univ Southeast	IN	15,807	LC
Indiana Univ-Purdue Univ Fort Wayne	IN	15,425	C
Indiana Univ-Purdue Univ Indianapolis	IN	17,290	C
Indiana Wesleyan Univ	IN	31,815	VC
Inter-American Univ of PR/ Aguadilla Campus	PR	5,578	
Inter-American Univ of PR/ Arecibo Campus	PR	3,350	
Inter-American Univ of PR/ Barranquitas	PR	3,350	
Inter-American Univ of PR/ Bayamon Univ College	PR	4,428	
Inter-American Univ of PR/ Fajardo Campus	PR	4,200	
Inter-American Univ of PR/ Metropolitan Campus	PR	4,320	
Inter-American Univ of PR/ Ponce	PR	3,700	
Inter-American Univ of PR/ San Germán	PR	6,720	
Iona College	NY	44,028	C
Iowa State Univ	IA	16,403	C
Iowa Wesleyan College	IA	30,850	LC
Ithaca College	NY	52,300	HC
Jackson State Univ	MS	13,512	LC
Jacksonville State Univ	AL	12,280	LC
Jacksonville Univ	FL	37,780	C
James Madison Univ	VA	18,049	VC
John Brown Univ	AR	30,996	VG
John Carroll Univ	OH	44,520	G
Johnson and Wales Univ/ Charlotte Campus	NC	35,421	C
Johnson and Wales Univ/ Denver Campus	CO	34,368	C
Johnson and Wales Univ/ North Miami Campus	FL	34,368	C
Johnson and Wales Univ/ Providence Campus	RI	34,668	C
Judson Univ	IL	25,130	C
Juniata College	PA	49,340	VC
Kansas State Univ	KS	15,497	VC
Kansas Wesleyan Univ	KS	32,000	C
Kean Univ	NJ	22,060	LC
Kennesaw State Univ	GA	13,017	VC
Kent State Univ	OH	19,352	C
Kentucky Wesleyan College	KY	27,440	VG
Keuka College	NY	30,300	C
Keystone College	PA	28,680	LC
King Univ	TN	33,140	C
King's College	PA	41,678	C
Kutztown Univ of Pennsylvania	PA	16,909	LC
La Roche College	PA	34,802	LC
La Salle Univ	PA	50,270	C
La Sierra Univ	CA	35,694	VC
LaGrange College	GA	34,480	C
Lake Erie College	OH	35,704	C
Lake Superior State Univ	MI	18,121	C
Lakeland College	WI	22,990	C
Lamar Univ	TX	6,820	LC
Langston Univ	OK	3,000	LC
Lasell College	MA	42,500	LC
Le Moyne College	NY	42,200	VC
Lebanon Valley College	PA	38,570	C
Lee Univ	TN	18,690	G
Lehigh Univ	PA	55,080	MC
Lehman College / The CUNY	NY	5,778	LC
LeMoyne-Owen College	TN	13,100	C
Lenoir-Rhyne College	NC	35,984	C
LeTourneau Univ	TX	26,230	C
Lewis Univ	IL	23,050	C
Liberty Univ	VA	19,101	C
Limestone College	SC	29,880	C
Lincoln Memorial Univ	TN	18,144	C
Lincoln Univ	MO	11,996	NC
Lindenwood Univ	MO	20,750	C
Lindsey Wilson College	KY	30,470	VC
Linfield College-McMinnville Campus	OR	46,166	C
Lipscomb Univ	TN	35,722	VC
Livingstone College	NC	17,815	LC
LIU/Brooklyn Campus	NY	26,500	C
LIU/C.W. Post Campus	NY	38,888	C
Louisiana State Univ	LA	18,677	VG
Louisiana State Univ in Shreveport	LA	5,606	C
Louisiana Tech Univ	LA	8,000	C
Lourdes Univ	OH	26,055	LC
Loyola Marymount Univ	CA	53,240	VG
Loyola Univ Chicago	IL	49,560	VG
Loyola Univ Maryland	MD		VC
Loyola Univ New Orleans	LA	46,581	VC
Lubbock Christian Univ	TX	25,518	C
Luther College	IA	44,380	VG
Lycoming College	PA	43,636	C
Lynchburg College	VA	42,645	C
Lyndon State College	VT	14,233	C
Lyon College	AR	30,246	VC
MacMurray College	IL	20,755	C
Madonna Univ	MI	24,540	VC
Malone Univ	OH	34,334	C
Manchester College	IN	35,070	C
Manhattan College	NY	44,955	VC
Marian Univ	WI	30,980	LC
Marian Univ/Indianapolis	IN	37,058	C
Marietta College	OH	42,135	VC
Marist College	NY	35,500	C
Marquette Univ	WI	43,664	VG
Mars Hill College	NC	22,950	LC
Marshall Univ	WV	14,820	C
Martin Univ	IN	11,000	SP
Marymount Manhattan College	NY	40,118	VC
Maryville Univ of St. Louis	MO	34,920	VC
Marywood Univ	PA	40,695	C
Mass College of Liberal Arts	MA	16,733	C
McKendree Univ	IL	29,920	G
McMurry Univ	TX	25,962	LC
McNeese State Univ	LA		C
Medgar Evers College / The CUNY	NY	4,920	NC
Menlo College	CA	49,002	C
Mercer Univ	GA	44,201	VG
Mercy College	NY	29,996	C
Mercyhurst Univ	PA	40,700	C
Meredith College	NC	31,420	C
Merrimack College	MA	44,215	C
Messiah College	PA	39,540	VC
Methodist Univ	NC	37,185	C
Metropolitan State Univ	MN	5,923	SP
Metropolitan State Univ of Denver	CO	4,835	LC
Miami Univ	OH	24,191	HC
Mich State Univ	MI	13,689	VC
Mich Tech Univ	MI	22,105	VC
MidAmerica Nazarene Univ	KS	28,000	C
Middle Tenn State Univ	TN	8,650	C
Midland Univ	NE	34,000	C
Midwestern State Univ	TX	9,722	C
Miles College	AL	16,530	NC
Milligan College	TN	27,510	C
Millikin Univ	IL	37,462	C
Millsaps College	MS	43,888	VG
Minn State Univ, Mankato	MN	14,900	C
Minn State Univ, Moorhead	MN	13,392	C
Minot State Univ	ND	10,915	C
Misericordia Univ	PA	39,840	C
Miss College	MS	21,998	VC
Miss Univ for Women	MS	7,400	LC
Miss Valley State Univ	MS	9,706	LC
Missouri Baptist Univ	MO	30,310	C
Missouri Southern State Univ	MO	11,910	C
Missouri State Univ	MO	13,996	VC
Missouri Valley College	MO	22,200	C
Missouri Western State Univ	MO	12,260	NC
Molloy College	NY	38,950	C
Monmouth College	IL	39,290	C
Monmouth Univ	NJ	42,252	C
Monroe College	NY	17,700	C
Montclair State Univ	NJ	22,614	C
Moravian College	PA	36,381	VC
Morehead State Univ	KY	10,900	C
Morgan State Univ	MD	14,500	VC
Mount Aloysius College	PA	27,970	C
Mount Marty College	SD	29,638	C
Mount Mary Univ	WI	32,836	LC
Mount Mercy Univ	IA	34,385	C
Mount Olive College	NC	18,426	C
Mount St. Mary College	NY	39,540	C
Mount St. Mary's Univ	MD	46,158	C
Mount Vernon Nazarene Univ	OH	29,590	C
Mount Washington College	NH	21,500	NC
Mountain State Univ	WV	14,330	NC
Muhlenberg College	PA	52,837	HC
Murray State Univ	KY	14,944	C
Muskingum Univ	OH	30,502	C
National American Univ	SD	16,712	NC
National Univ	CA	14,730	SP
Nazareth College of Rochester	NY	41,590	VC
Nebr Wesleyan Univ	NE	29,774	G
Neumann Univ	PA	31,078	LC
New Jersey City Univ	NJ	21,060	G
New Mexico Highlands Univ	NM	9,720	NC
New Mexico State Univ	NM	13,955	LC
New York Inst of Technology	NY	40,590	VC
New York Univ	NY	61,470	MC
Newbury College	MA	41,850	C
Newman Univ	KS	30,380	G
Niagara Univ	NY	39,800	C
Nicholls State Univ	LA	7,095	C
Nichols College	MA	37,240	LC
Norfolk State Univ	VA	10,531	LC
N Car Agricultural and Technical State Univ	NC	13,175	LC
N Car Central Univ	NC	9,000	LC
N Car State Univ	NC	16,202	HC
N Car Wesleyan College	NC	29,440	C
North Central College	IL	38,343	VC
N Dak State Univ	ND	14,642	C
North Georgia College & State Univ	GA	8,500	C
North Park Univ	IL	30,130	C
Northeastern Illinois Univ	IL		C
Northeastern State Univ	OK	8,615	VC
Northeastern Univ	MA	55,296	MC
Northern Arizona Univ	AZ	18,592	C
Northern Illinois Univ	IL	19,768	C
Northern Kentucky Univ	KY	15,302	LC
Northern Mich Univ	MI	15,300	VC
Northern State Univ	SD	14,021	C
Northwest Christian Univ	OR	27,399	C
Northwest Missouri State Univ	MO	14,229	C
Northwest Nazarene Univ	ID	24,275	NC
Northwestern College	MN	24,000	C
Northwestern College of Iowa	IA	34,848	G
Northwestern Okla State Univ	OK	7,275	NC
Northwestern State Univ of Louisiana	LA	14,368	C
Northwood Univ	FL	30,746	LC
Northwood Univ	MI	26,331	LC
Northwood Univ	TX	25,296	LC
Norwich Univ	VT	28,212	C
Notre Dame College	OH	34,942	VC
Notre Dame de Namur Univ	CA	41,610	LC
Notre Dame of Maryland Univ	MD	27,700	C
Nova Southeastern Univ	FL	34,016	VC
Nyack College	NY	32,000	C
Oakland City Univ	IN	24,500	NC
Oakland Univ	MI	19,391	VC
Oakwood Univ	AL	23,035	C
Oglethorpe Univ	GA	42,580	VC
Ohio Dominican Univ	OH	38,380	G
Ohio Northern Univ	OH	42,075	VC
Ohio Univ	OH	20,676	VC
Ohio Valley Univ	WV	17,752	C
Ohio Wesleyan Univ	OH	49,460	G
Okla Baptist Univ	OK	28,202	VC
Okla Christian Univ	OK	24,975	VC
Okla City Univ	OK	33,546	VC
Okla Panhandle State Univ	OK	8,996	NC
Okla State Univ	OK	14,310	VC
Okla Wesleyan Univ	OK	21,300	C
Old Dominion Univ	VA	18,662	C
Olivet College	MI	19,984	C
Olivet Nazarene Univ	IL	29,990	C
Oral Roberts Univ	OK	31,734	C
Oregon State Univ	OR	19,017	G
Oswego / SUNY	NY	20,009	VC
Ottawa Univ	KS	15,000	VC
Otterbein College	OH	32,214	C
Ouachita Baptist Univ	AR	29,010	VC
Our Lady of Holy Cross College	LA	8,090	LC
Our Lady of the Lake Univ of San Antonio	TX	22,430	LC
Pace Univ	NY	48,094	VC
Park Univ	MO	17,525	C
Paul Quinn College	TX	25,350	LC
Peirce College	PA	12,760	NC
Penn State Erie/The Behrend College	PA	16,256	C
Penn State Univ/Univ Park	PA	25,404	VC
Pennsylvania College of Technology	PA	25,653	NC
Pepperdine Univ	CA	55,372	HG
Peru State College	NE	8,600	NC
Pfeiffer Univ	NC	33,700	C
Philadelphia Univ	PA	44,160	C
Pittsburg State Univ	KS	12,032	C
Plymouth State Univ	NH	23,148	LC
Point Loma Nazarene Univ	CA	38,610	VC
Point Park Univ	PA	36,390	C
Pontifical Catholic Univ of PR	PR	7,310	
Portland State Univ	OR	18,672	C
Post Univ	CT	35,750	C
Prairie View A&M Univ	TX	15,205	LC
Providence College	RI	55,995	HC
Purdue Univ/Calumet	IN	14,336	C
Purdue Univ/West Lafayette	IN	20,278	HC
Queens College / The CUNY	NY	17,107	VC
Queens Univ of Charlotte	NC	39,543	VC
Quincy Univ	IL	34,980	LC
Quinnipiac Univ	CT	53,580	VC
Radford Univ	VA	17,132	LC
Ramapo College of New Jersey	NJ	24,938	G
Randolph-Macon College	VA	45,086	C
Regis Univ	CO	41,318	C
Rhode Island College	RI	17,132	LC
Richard Stockton College of New Jersey	NJ	20,000	VC
Rider Univ	NJ	45,720	C
Robert Morris Univ	PA	36,699	C
Roberts Wesleyan College	NY	37,384	G
Rochester College	MI	18,320	C
Rochester Inst of Technology	NY	42,450	VG
Rockford College	IL	31,000	C
Rocky Mountain College	MT	32,242	C
Roger Williams Univ	RI	45,788	C
Roosevelt Univ	IL	22,605	VC
Rosemont College	PA	42,350	C
Rowan Univ	NJ	23,570	VC
Rutgers, The State Univ of New Jersey/Camden Campus	NJ	24,254	C
Rutgers, The State Univ of New Jersey/New Brunswick	NJ	25,077	VC
Rutgers, The State Univ of New Jersey/Newark Campus	NJ	25,376	C
Sacred Heart Univ	CT	48,564	VC
Saginaw Valley State Univ	MI	16,869	C
St. Anselm College	NH	48,324	VC
St. Augustine's Univ	NC	14,000	C
St. Francis Univ	PA	30,029	LC
St. John's Univ	MN	46,146	C
St. Joseph College	CT	45,630	LC
St. Joseph's College	IN	35,790	C
St. Joseph's Univ	PA	52,272	VC
St. Leo Univ	FL	27,990	C
St. Louis Univ	MO	46,594	VG
St. Martin's Univ	WA	38,082	C
St. Mary-of-the-Woods College	IN	37,722	LC
St. Mary's College	IN	45,160	VC
St. Mary's College of Calif	CA	53,550	C
St. Mary's Univ	TX	33,854	C
St. Mary's Univ of Minn	MN	37,015	C
St. Michael's College	VT	48,740	VC
St. Peter's College	NJ	44,240	C
St. Vincent College	PA	40,244	C
St. Xavier Univ	IL	32,840	C
Salem College	NC	29,326	VC
Salem State College	MA	13,161	LC
Salisbury Univ	MD	18,368	VC
Salve Regina Univ	RI	47,250	VC
Sam Houston State Univ	TX	17,082	C
Samford Univ	AL	35,700	VG
San Diego State Univ	CA	20,578	VC
San Francisco State Univ	CA	18,514	C

School	ST	$IS	SR
San Jose State Univ	CA	19,707	C
Santa Clara Univ	CA	54,702	MC
Savannah State Univ	GA	13,156	C
Schreiner Univ	TX	32,734	LC
Seattle Pacific Univ	WA	41,559	VC+
Seattle Univ	WA	47,010	VC+
Seton Hall Univ	NJ	45,902	C
Seton Hill Univ	PA	35,172	C
Shaw Univ	NC	15,488	LC
Shepherd Univ	WV	14,996	C
Shippensburg Univ of Pennsylvania	PA	17,064	LC
Shorter Univ	GA	26,470	C
Siena College	NY	43,863	VC
Siena Heights Univ	MI	17,000	LC
Silver Lake College	WI	22,600	LC
Simpson College	IA	36,086	VC
Simpson Univ	CA	28,900	C
Slippery Rock Univ of Pennsylvania	PA	10,360	LC
S Car State Univ	SC	6,700	LC
Southeast Missouri State Univ	MO	14,983	LC
Southeastern Louisiana Univ	LA	13,325	C
Southeastern Okla State Univ	OK	7,966	C
Southeastern Univ	FL	27,201	C+
Southern Adventist Univ	TN	26,190	C
Southern Arkansas Univ	AR	14,316	C
Southern Conn State Univ	CT	18,033	C
Southern Illinois Univ Carbondale	IL	21,620	C
Southern Illinois Univ Edwardsville	IL	17,532	C
Southern Methodist Univ	TX	57,755	MC
Southern Nazarene Univ	OK	24,354	NC
Southern New Hampshire Univ	NH	38,100	C
Southern Oregon Univ	OR	17,874	C
Southern Polytechnic State Univ	GA	13,958	VC
Southern Univ and A&M College	LA	9,761	C+
Southern Univ at New Orleans	LA	1,000	NC
Southwest Baptist Univ	MO	24,710	C
Southwest Minn State Univ	MN	14,000	C
Southwestern College	KS	29,270	C
Southwestern Okla State Univ	OK	9,160	C
Southwestern Univ	TX	45,660	VC
Spalding Univ	KY	31,850	LC
Spring Arbor Univ	MI	26,740	C
Spring Hill College	AL	42,130	VC
St. Ambrose Univ	IA		C
St. Bonaventure Univ	NY	38,831	C
St. Catherine Univ	MN	37,782	C+
St. Cloud State Univ	MN	10,600	C
St. Edward's Univ	TX	44,674	VC
St. Francis College	NY	34,200	LC
St. John Fisher College	NY	39,370	C+
St. John's Univ	NY	52,840	C+
St. Joseph's College, New York / Brooklyn Campus	NY	21,878	C
St. Joseph's College, New York / Suffolk Campus	NY	21,878	VC
St. Norbert College	WI	39,992	VC
St. Thomas Aquinas College	NY	30,000	C
St. Thomas Univ	FL	32,310	C+
SUNY Inst of Technology at Utica / Rome	NY	23,818	C
SUNY/Empire State College	NY	6,315	SP
Stephen F. Austin State Univ	TX	14,668	C
Stephens College	MO	34,500	VC
Stetson Univ	FL	49,512	VC+
Stevenson Univ	MD	39,572	C
Stonehill College	MA	46,780	VC+
Suffolk Univ	MA	46,548	C
Sul Ross State Univ	TX	13,410	LC
SUNY College at Geneseo	NY	18,055	HC+
SUNY College at Old Westbury	NY	16,324	C
SUNY Fredonia / The SUNY at Fredonia	NY	18,702	VC
SUNY New Paltz	NY	15,010	C
SUNY Oneonta / SUNY	NY	16,919	VC
SUNY Plattsburgh / SUNY	NY	18,083	VC
Susquehanna Univ	PA	49,170	C
Syracuse Univ	NY	54,512	HC
Tabor College	KS	29,010	LC
Talladega College	AL	13,000	C
Tarleton State Univ	TX	13,489	LC
Taylor Univ	IN	36,742	VC+
Temple Univ	PA	24,392	VC
Tenn State Univ	TN	9,048	C
Tenn Tech Univ	TN	11,310	C
Tenn Wesleyan College	TN	21,250	C
Texas A&M Univ	TX	16,956	VC+
Texas A&M Univ at Commerce	TX	10,496	C
Texas A&M Univ at Corpus Christi	TX	11,544	LC
Texas A&M Univ at Kingsville	TX	7,500	LC

School	ST	$IS	SR
Texas Christian Univ	TX	47,570	HC
Texas Lutheran Univ	TX	34,070	C
Texas Southern Univ	TX	18,212	LC
Texas State Univ	TX	16,495	VC
Texas Wesleyan Univ	TX	29,886	C
Texas Woman's Univ	TX	13,633	LC
The Catholic Univ of America	DC	52,852	VC
The College at Brockport / SUNY	NY	18,362	VC
The College of Idaho	ID	31,277	VC
The College of St. Rose	NY	26,750	C
The Lincoln Univ	PA	15,154	LC
Ohio State Univ	OH	19,887	MC
Thiel College	PA	31,378	LC
Thomas College	ME	26,270	LC
Thomas Edison State College	NJ	5,700	SP
Thomas More College	KY	34,760	C
Tiffin Univ	OH	30,273	LC
Touro College	NY	23,150	VC
Towson Univ	MD	16,000	VC
Transylvania Univ	KY	40,310	VC+
Trevecca Nazarene Univ	TN	30,118	C
Trine Univ	IN	39,400	VC
Trinity Christian College	IL	28,869	C
Trinity International Univ	IL	31,070	C
Troy Univ	AL	10,650	C
Truman State Univ	MO	13,546	HC
Tulane Univ	LA	58,942	MC
Tuskegee Univ	AL	26,750	C
Union College	KY	28,775	C
Union College	NE	23,270	VC
Union Univ	TN	28,260	VC
Universidad del Turabo	PR	4,110	
Universidad Metropolitana	PR		
Univ at Albany / SUNY	NY	18,674	VC
Univ of Akron	OH	20,436	C
Univ of Alabama at Birmingham	AL	18,484	C+
Univ of Alabama at Huntsville	AL	17,625	VC
Univ of Alabama at Tuscaloosa	AL	17,164	C+
Univ of Alaska Anchorage	AK	15,290	NC
Univ of Alaska Fairbanks	AK	13,955	C
Univ of Alaska Southeast	AK	11,493	C
Univ of Arizona	AZ	20,105	C
Univ of Arkansas at Fayetteville	AR	16,860	VC
Univ of Arkansas at Little Rock	AR		C
Univ of Arkansas at Monticello	AR	8,470	NC
Univ of Arkansas at Pine Bluff	AR	10,600	C
Univ of Bridgeport	CT	39,030	LC
Univ of Calif at Santa Barbara	CA	27,551	HC
Univ of Central Arkansas	AR	10,840	VC
Univ of Central Florida	FL	15,711	VC+
Univ of Central Missouri	MO	14,605	C
Univ of Central Okla	OK	12,293	C
Univ of Charleston	WV	28,650	C
Univ of Cincinnati	OH	20,199	VC
Univ of Colo Boulder	CO	22,605	VC+
Univ of Conn	CT	23,744	HC
Univ of Dayton	OH	43,750	VC
Univ of Delaware	DE	22,728	VC
Univ of Denver	CO	51,787	VC+
Univ of Detroit Mercy	MI	30,450	C
Univ of Dubuque	IA	30,200	C
Univ of Evansville	IN	41,056	VC+
Univ of Findlay	OH	31,916	C
Univ of Florida	FL	15,783	HC+
Univ of Georgia	GA	19,508	VC
Univ of Great Falls	MT	27,970	C
Univ of Hartford	CT	42,674	C
Univ of Hawaii at Manoa	HI	19,379	VC
Univ of Houston	TX	19,184	VC
Univ of Houston-Downtown	TX	6,267	LC
Univ of Idaho	ID	14,558	C
Univ of Illinois at Chicago	IL	24,293	VC
Univ of Illinois at Urbana-Champaign	IL	24,300	HC
Univ of Indianapolis	IN	31,740	LC
Univ of Iowa	IA	17,481	VC
Univ of Jamestown	ND	24,738	C
Univ of Kansas	KS	16,980	C+
Univ of Kentucky	KY	19,868	C
Univ of La Verne	CA	47,010	VC
Univ of Louisiana at Lafayette	LA	6,130	C
Univ of Louisiana at Monroe	LA	12,998	C
Univ of Louisville	KY	17,460	VC
Univ of Maine	ME	19,712	C+
Univ of Maine at Augusta	ME	6,855	C
Univ of Maine at Machias	ME	10,523	C
Univ of Maine at Presque Isle	ME	15,011	LC
Univ of Mary	ND	16,714	C
Univ of Mary Hardin-Baylor	TX	31,950	C+
Univ of Maryland	MD	18,801	HC
Univ of Maryland/Eastern Shore	MD	14,000	C
Univ of Maryland/Univ College	MD	6,168	SP

School	ST	$IS	SR
Univ of Mass Amherst	MA	23,697	VC+
Univ of Mass Dartmouth	MA	22,223	C
Univ of Memphis	TN	15,094	C
Univ of Miami	FL	55,166	MC
Univ of Mich/Dearborn	MI	9,885	VC
Univ of Mich-Flint	MI	17,547	C+
Univ of Minn Crookston	MN	17,834	C
Univ of Minn/Duluth	MN	18,964	C+
Univ of Minn/Twin Cities	MN		HC
Univ of Miss	MS	15,482	VC
Univ of Missouri/Columbia	MO	18,201	MC
Univ of Missouri-Kansas City	MO	19,603	C
Univ of Missouri-St. Louis	MO	18,304	VC
Univ of Mobile	AL	27,070	VC
Univ of Montana	MT	13,670	C
Univ of Montevallo	AL	17,320	C
Univ of Mount Union	OH	35,130	C
Univ of Nebr - Lincoln	NE	17,507	VC
Univ of Nebr at Kearney	NE	14,855	LC
Univ of Nebr at Omaha	NE	12,700	C
Univ of Nevada, Las Vegas	NV	17,303	C
Univ of Nevada/Reno	NV	14,500	NC
Univ of New Haven	CT	47,740	C
Univ of New Orleans	LA	9,224	VC
Univ of North Alabama	AL	9,960	C
Univ of N Car at Asheville	NC	13,500	VC+
Univ of N Car at Charlotte	NC	15,847	C
Univ of N Car at Greensboro	NC	12,848	C
Univ of N Car at Wilmington	NC	13,572	VC+
Univ of N Dak	ND	14,094	C
Univ of North Florida	FL	15,578	VC
Univ of North Texas	TX	15,628	C
Univ of Northern Iowa	IA	14,776	C
Univ of Notre Dame	IN		MC
Univ of Okla	OK	17,634	VC+
Univ of Oregon	OR	20,872	VC
Univ of Pennsylvania	PA	56,106	MC
Univ of Pittsburgh at Bradford	PA	21,316	LC
Univ of Pittsburgh at Greensburg	PA	17,640	C
Univ of Pittsburgh at Johnstown	PA	20,862	LC
Univ of Pittsburgh at Pittsburgh	PA	27,800	HC+
Univ of Portland	OR	47,874	VC
Univ of PR Recinto de Rio Piedras	PR	5,750	
Univ of PR/Arecibo	PR	7,227	
Univ of PR/Bayamon	PR	1,600	
Univ of PR/Cayey	PR	1,504	
Univ of PR/Humacao	PR	1,877	
Univ of PR/Mayaguez	PR	1,250	
Univ of Redlands	CA	40,500	VC
Univ of Rio Grande	OH	8,750	NC
Univ of St. Francis	IN	29,810	C
Univ of St. Mary	KS	28,400	C+
Univ of San Diego	CA	53,302	HC+
Univ of San Francisco	CA	49,674	VC
Univ of Scranton	PA	51,940	VC
Univ of Sioux Falls	SD	22,990	C
Univ of South Alabama	AL	13,510	C
Univ of S Car at Columbia	SC	19,725	VC+
Univ of S Car Upstate	SC	17,673	LC
Univ of S Dak	SD	15,111	C
Univ of South Florida	FL	13,000	C
Univ of South Florida/St. Petersburg	FL	12,769	VC
Univ of Southern Calif	CA	56,903	MC
Univ of Southern Indiana	IN	14,657	C
Univ of Southern Maine	ME	16,576	C
Univ of Southern Miss	MS	13,170	C
Univ of St. Francis	IL	36,490	C
Univ of St. Thomas - Houston	TX	36,490	VC
Univ of Tampa	FL	35,160	VC
Univ of Tenn at Knoxville	TN	20,364	VC+
Univ of Tenn at Martin	TN	13,217	C
Univ of Texas at Arlington	TX	10,908	LC
Univ of Texas at Austin	TX	44,074	HC
Univ of Texas at Dallas	TX	21,046	HC
Univ of Texas at El Paso	TX	8,764	NC
Univ of Texas at San Antonio	TX	18,372	C
Univ of Texas-Pan American	TX	12,432	LC
Univ of the Cumberlands	KY	27,500	LC
Univ of the District of Columbia	DC	7,244	LC
Univ of the Ozarks	AR	22,100	C
Univ of the Sacred Heart	PR	5,590	
Univ of the Southwest	NM	15,000	C
Univ of Toledo	OH	18,464	C
Univ of Tulsa	OK	45,311	HC+
Univ of Utah	UT	13,462	VC
Univ of Virginia's College at Wise	VA	11,076	C
Univ of Washington	WA	14,722	VC
Univ of West Alabama	AL	9,415	C
Univ of West Florida	FL	14,656	C
Univ of West Georgia	GA	14,852	LC
Univ of Wisc Whitewater	WI	13,314	C
Univ of Wisc/Eau Claire	WI	15,430	VC
Univ of Wisc/Green Bay	WI	14,900	C
Univ of Wisc/La Crosse	WI	14,755	VC

School	ST	$IS	SR
Univ of Wisc/Madison	WI	18,757	HC
Univ of Wisc/Oshkosh	WI	10,426	LC
Univ of Wisc/Platteville	WI	14,274	C
Univ of Wisc/River Falls	WI	9,722	LC
Univ of Wisc/Stevens Point	WI	14,043	C
Univ of Wisc/Superior	WI	14,106	C
Univ of Wisc-Milwaukee	WI	18,436	C
Univ of Wyoming	WY	13,855	C+
Upper Iowa Univ	IA	30,426	NC
Ursuline College	OH	33,198	LC
Utah State Univ	UT	11,803	C
Utica College	NY	44,734	C
Valparaiso Univ	IN	43,040	VC+
Vanguard Univ of Southern Calif	CA	35,833	VC
Villanova Univ	PA	56,436	MC
Virginia Commonwealth Univ	VA	18,633	C
Virginia Polytechnic Inst and State Univ	VA	14,629	HC
Virginia State Univ	VA	11,318	C+
Virginia Union Univ	VA	18,432	C
Viterbo Univ	WI	30,070	C
Voorhees College	SC	18,126	C
Wagner College	NY	48,600	VC
Wake Forest Univ	NC	51,000	MC
Walsh Univ	OH	35,100	C
Warner Univ	FL	18,000	C
Wartburg College	IA	41,055	VC
Washburn Univ	KS	12,165	NC
Washington Adventist Univ	MD	25,859	C+
Washington and Jefferson College	PA	49,990	VC
Washington and Lee Univ	VA	52,812	MC
Washington State Univ	WA	20,461	C
Washington Univ in St. Louis	MO	58,818	MC
Wayland Baptist Univ	TX	16,058	LC
Wayne State Univ	MI	19,493	C
Waynesburg Univ	PA	29,100	C
Webber International Univ	FL	25,664	C
Webster Univ	MO	33,990	C+
Wesley College	DE	31,115	LC
West Chester Univ of Pennsylvania	PA	16,836	C
West Liberty Univ	WV	9,142	LC
West Texas A&M Univ	TX	13,478	C
West Virginia State Univ	WV	8,378	NC
West Virginia Univ	WV	15,794	C+
West Virginia Univ Inst of Technology	WV	14,094	NC
West Virginia Wesleyan College	WV	26,880	C
Western Carolina Univ	NC	13,965	C+
Western Conn State Univ	CT	18,327	C
Western Illinois Univ	IL	20,130	C
Western Kentucky Univ	KY	11,000	LC
Western Mich Univ	MI	19,042	C
Western New England Univ	MA	45,590	C
Western New Mexico Univ	NM	8,500	LC
Western State Colo Univ	CO	16,135	C
Western Washington Univ	WA	18,519	VC
Westminster College	MO	30,490	VC
Westminster College	PA	31,290	C+
Westminster College	UT	37,708	VC
Wheeling Jesuit Univ	WV	34,668	C
Whitworth Univ	WA	45,826	VC+
Wichita State Univ	KS	12,539	C
Widener Univ	PA	50,368	C
Wilberforce Univ	OH	15,100	LC
Wilkes Univ	PA	42,786	C
William Jewell College	MO	31,000	VC+
William Paterson Univ of New Jersey	NJ	21,694	C
William Penn Univ	IA	26,000	C
William Woods Univ	MO		C
Wilmington College	OH	29,784	C
Wilmington Univ	DE	7,778	NC
Wilson College	PA	27,660	C
Wingate Univ	NC	34,990	C
Winona State Univ	MN	16,530	C
Winston-Salem State Univ	NC	9,418	LC
Wofford College	SC	45,795	VC
Woodbury Univ	CA	34,500	LC
Wright State Univ	OH	16,983	C
Xavier Univ	OH	43,740	VC
Xavier Univ of Louisiana	LA	25,300	C
Yeshiva Univ	NY	47,250	VC+
York College	NE	19,475	C
York College / CUNY	NY	5,496	NC
York College of Pennsylvania	PA	26,590	C
Youngstown State Univ	OH	16,374	LC

ACCOUNTING/CPA

Thomas Edison State College	NJ	5,700	SP
Univ of Georgia	GA	19,508	VC

ACTING

Chapman Univ	CA	56,019	VC+
Elon Univ	NC	40,046	HC
Millikin Univ	IL	37,462	C
Shenandoah Univ	VA	39,268	C
St. Edward's Univ	TX	44,674	VC

School	ST	$IS	SR
Webster Univ	MO	33,990	C+

ACTUARIAL MATHEMATICS

School	ST	$IS	SR
Asbury Univ	KY	32,038	VC
Binghamton Univ / The SUNY	NY	20,832	HC+
Bryant Univ	RI	49,179	VC
Ferris State Univ	MI	19,698	C
Lycoming College	PA	43,636	C
Univ of Pittsburgh at Pittsburgh	PA	27,800	HC+
Univ of Texas at San Antonio	TX	18,372	C
Youngstown State Univ	OH	16,374	LC

ACTUARIAL SCIENCE

School	ST	$IS	SR
Appalachian State Univ	NC	12,919	VC
Auburn Univ	AL	20,052	VC+
Aurora Univ	IL	26,870	C
Ball State Univ	IN	17,850	C
Bellarmine Univ	KY	42,950	VC
Bentley Univ	MA	54,555	HC+
Bradley Univ	IL	31,874	VC
Brigham Young Univ	UT	12,100	HC
Bryant Univ	RI	49,179	VC
Butler Univ	IN	45,898	VC+
Carroll Univ	WI	24,860	C
Central College	IA	36,980	VC
Central Mich Univ	MI	18,066	C
Central Washington Univ	WA	11,730	C
CUNY/Baruch College	NY	15,831	VC
Dordt College	IA	34,160	VC
Drake Univ	IA	30,980	VC+
Eastern Mich Univ	MI	17,961	C
Elizabethtown College	PA	47,600	VC
Florida A&M Univ	FL	14,935	LC
Florida State Univ	FL	15,238	HC
Georgia State Univ	GA	12,000	VC
High Point Univ	NC	39,800	C
Indiana Univ Northwest	IN	6,738	LC
Indiana Univ South Bend	IN	15,293	C
Indiana Univ-Purdue Univ Fort Wayne	IN	15,425	C
Indiana Univ-Purdue Univ Indianapolis	IN	17,290	C
Le Moyne College	NY	42,200	VC
Lebanon Valley College	PA	38,570	C
Maryville Univ of St. Louis	MO	34,920	VC
Millikin Univ	IL	37,462	C
Milwaukee School of Engineering	WI	39,948	VC+
New York Univ	NY	61,470	MC
North Central College	IL	38,343	VC
N Dak State Univ	ND	14,642	C
Northwestern College of Iowa	IA	34,848	C+
Ohio Univ	OH	20,676	VC
Olivet Nazarene Univ	IL	29,990	C
Penn State Univ/Univ Park	PA	25,404	VC
Pittsburg State Univ	KS	12,032	C
Purdue Univ/West Lafayette	IN	20,278	HC
Queens College / The CUNY	NY	17,107	VC
Rider Univ	NJ	45,720	C
Robert Morris Univ	PA	36,699	C
Roosevelt Univ	IL	22,605	VC
St. Joseph's Univ	PA	52,272	VC
St. Mary's Univ of Minn	MN	37,015	C
Seton Hill Univ	PA	35,172	C
Siena College	NY	43,863	VC
Simpson College	IA	36,086	VC
Southern Illinois Univ Edwardsville	IL	17,532	C
St. John's Univ	NY	52,840	C+
Temple Univ	PA	24,392	VC
Ohio State Univ	OH	19,887	MC
Thiel College	PA	31,378	LC
Univ at Albany / SUNY	NY	18,674	VC
Univ of Calif at Santa Barbara	CA	27,551	HC
Univ of Central Missouri	MO	14,605	C
Univ of Central Okla	OK	12,293	C
Univ of Illinois at Urbana-Champaign	IL	24,300	HC
Univ of Iowa	IA	17,481	VC
Univ of Maine at Farmington	ME	17,841	C
Univ of Minn/Duluth	MN	18,964	C+
Univ of Minn/Twin Cities	MN		HC
Univ of Nebr - Lincoln	NE	17,507	VC
Univ of Pennsylvania	PA	56,106	MC
Univ of Texas at Dallas	TX	21,046	HC
Univ of Texas at San Antonio	TX	18,372	C
Univ of Wisc/Madison	WI	18,757	HC
Univ of Wisc-Milwaukee	WI	18,436	C
Valparaiso Univ	IN	43,040	VC+
West Chester Univ of Pennsylvania	PA	16,836	C
Worcester Polytechnic Inst	MA	53,440	HC+
Xavier Univ	OH	43,740	VC

ADDICTION STUDIES

School	ST	$IS	SR
Bethany College	KS	30,605	NC
Brescia Univ	KY	26,140	VC+
Elizabethtown College School of Continuing and Professional Studies	PA		VC
Goddard College	VT	16,418	VC
Graceland Univ	IA	28,020	C
Grand Canyon Univ	AZ	24,540	VC
Indiana Wesleyan Univ	IN	31,815	VC
Kansas Wesleyan Univ	KS	32,000	C
Keene State College	NH	21,538	C
Metropolitan State Univ	MN	5,923	SP
Minot State Univ	ND	10,915	C
Missouri Valley College	MO	22,200	C
Northwestern State Univ of Louisiana	LA	14,368	C
Okla City Univ	OK	33,546	VC
Prescott College	AZ	33,284	C+
Rhode Island College	RI	17,132	LC
Southern Univ at New Orleans	LA	1,000	NC
Texas Tech Univ	TX	14,243	C
Univ of Central Okla	OK	12,293	C
Univ of Detroit Mercy	MI	30,450	C
Univ of Mary	ND	16,714	C
Univ of S Dak	SD	15,111	C
Viterbo Univ	WI	30,070	C

ADMINISTRATION OF JUSTICE

School	ST	$IS	SR
Catawba College	NC	37,105	C
Howard Univ	DC	35,957	C
Texas Southern Univ	TX	18,212	LC
Univ of Louisville	KY	17,460	VC
Univ of Pittsburgh at Pittsburgh	PA	27,800	HC+

ADVERTISING

School	ST	$IS	SR
Abilene Christian Univ	TX	38,400	VC
Academy of Art Univ	CA		
Adams State College	CO	13,358	LC
American International College	MA	36,100	LC
Appalachian State Univ	NC	12,919	VC
Art Center College of Design	CA	34,044	SP
Art Inst of Atlanta	GA	24,000	SP
Art Inst of Portland	OR	23,040	SP
Barry Univ	FL	38,190	C
Biola Univ	CA	40,320	VC
Brigham Young Univ	UT	12,100	HC
Butler Univ	IN	45,898	VC+
Cal State, East Bay	CA	16,549	C
Cal State, Fullerton	CA	25,188	C+
Campbell Univ	NC	25,500	C
Central State Univ	OH	9,010	C
Champlain College	VT	44,850	VC
CUNY/Baruch College	NY	15,831	VC
Clarke Univ	IA	36,400	C
College for Creative Studies	MI		SP
College of St. Scholastica	MN	39,960	C
Columbia College Chicago	IL	30,940	LC
Columbus College of Art and Design	OH	37,732	SP
Cornerstone Univ and Grand Rapids Theological Seminary	MI	30,866	C
Davenport Univ	MI	21,002	LC
Dordt College	IA	34,160	VC
Drake Univ	IA	30,980	VC+
Drury Univ	MO	30,319	VC
Duquesne Univ	PA	42,017	VC
East Central Univ	OK	10,223	LC
Eastern Mich Univ	MI	17,961	C
Eastern Nazarene College	MA	30,000	C
Emerson College	MA	50,246	HC
Fashion Inst of Technology/SUNY	NY	12,468	SP
Ferris State Univ	MI	19,698	C
Florida Southern College	FL	38,240	VC
Florida State Univ	FL	15,238	HC
Fontbonne Univ	MO	31,384	C
Gannon Univ	PA	37,940	C
Grand Valley State Univ	MI	17,998	VC
Harding Univ	AR	21,432	C+
Hawaii Pacific Univ	HI	36,690	C
Howard Univ	DC	35,957	C
Indiana Univ South Bend	IN	15,293	C
Iowa State Univ	IA	16,403	C
Johnson and Wales Univ/ Providence Campus	RI	34,668	C
Kent State Univ	OH	19,352	C
Lamar Univ	TX	6,820	LC
Lasell College	MA	42,500	LC
Le Moyne College	NY	42,200	VC
Loyola Univ Chicago	IL	49,560	VC+
Lynn Univ	FL	43,500	C
Marietta College	OH	42,135	VC
Marquette Univ	WI	43,664	VC+
Marshall Univ	WV	14,820	C
Marywood Univ	PA	40,695	C
Mercyhurst Univ	PA	40,700	C
Metropolitan State Univ	MN	5,923	SP
Mich State Univ	MI	18,689	VC
Midland Univ	NE	34,000	C
Minneapolis College of Art and Design	MN	36,700	SP
Morningside College	IA	32,620	C
Murray State Univ	KY	14,944	C
New York Inst of Technology	NY	40,590	VC
North Park Univ	IL	30,130	C
Northeastern State Univ	OK	8,615	VC
Northwest Missouri State Univ	MO	14,229	C
Northwood Univ	FL	30,746	LC
Northwood Univ	MI	26,331	LC
Ohio Univ	OH	20,676	VC
Okla Christian Univ	OK	24,975	VC
Okla City Univ	OK	33,546	VC
Otis College of Art and Design	CA	35,404	SP
Pace Univ	NY	48,094	VC
Parsons The New School for Design	NY	56,610	SP
Penn State Univ/Univ Park	PA	25,404	VC
Pepperdine Univ	CA	55,372	HC+
Pittsburg State Univ	KS	12,032	C
Point Park Univ	PA	36,390	C
Portland State Univ	OR	18,672	C
Purdue Univ/West Lafayette	IN	20,278	HC
Quinnipiac Univ	CT	53,580	VC
Rider Univ	NJ	45,720	C
Ringling College of Art and Design	FL	46,130	SP
Roosevelt Univ	IL	22,605	VC
Rowan Univ	NJ	23,570	VC
Salem State College	MA	13,161	LC
San Diego State Univ	CA	20,578	VC
San Jose State Univ	CA	19,707	C
Savannah College of Art and Design	GA	46,824	SP
School of Visual Arts	NY	36,500	SP
Southeast Missouri State Univ	MO	14,983	LC
Southern Methodist Univ	TX	57,755	MC
Southern New Hampshire Univ	NH	38,100	C
Spring Arbor Univ	MI	26,740	C
St. Cloud State Univ	MN	10,600	C
St. John's Univ	NY	52,840	C+
Suffolk Univ	MA	46,548	C
Syracuse Univ	NY	54,512	HC
Temple Univ	PA	24,392	VC
Texas A&M Univ at Commerce	TX	10,496	C
Texas State Univ	TX	16,495	VC
Texas Tech Univ	TX	14,243	C
Texas Wesleyan Univ	TX	29,886	C
Union Univ	TN	28,260	VC
Univ of Alabama at Tuscaloosa	AL	17,164	C+
Univ of Arkansas at Fayetteville	AR	16,860	VC
Univ of Arkansas at Little Rock	AR		C
Univ of Central Florida	FL	15,711	VC+
Univ of Central Okla	OK	12,293	C
Univ of Colo Boulder	CO	22,605	VC+
Univ of Florida	FL	15,783	HC+
Univ of Georgia	GA	19,508	VC
Univ of Idaho	ID	14,558	C
Univ of Illinois at Urbana-Champaign	IL	24,300	HC
Univ of Kentucky	KY	19,868	C
Univ of Louisiana at Lafayette	LA	6,130	C
Univ of Miami	FL	55,166	MC
Univ of Missouri/Columbia	MO	18,201	MC
Univ of Nebr - Lincoln	NE	17,507	VC
Univ of Nebr at Kearney	NE	14,855	LC
Univ of New Haven	CT	47,740	C
Univ of Okla	OK	17,634	VC+
Univ of Oregon	OR	20,872	VC
Univ of S Car at Columbia	SC	19,725	VC+
Univ of Southern Indiana	IN	14,657	C
Univ of Southern Miss	MS	13,170	C
Univ of Tampa	FL	35,160	VC
Univ of Tenn at Knoxville	TN	20,364	VC+
Univ of Texas at Austin	TX	44,074	HC
Univ of the Sacred Heart	PR	5,590	
Washington State Univ	WA	20,461	C
Washington Univ in St. Louis	MO	58,818	MC
Waynesburg Univ	PA	29,100	C
Webster Univ	MO	33,990	C+
Wesleyan College	GA	24,000	C+
West Virginia Univ	WV	15,794	C+
Western Kentucky Univ	KY	11,000	LC
Western Mich Univ	MI	19,042	C
Western New England Univ	MA	45,590	C
Wilmington College	OH	29,784	C
Xavier Univ	OH	43,740	VC
Youngstown State Univ	OH	16,374	LC

AERONAUTICAL ENGINEERING

School	ST	$IS	SR
Arizona State Univ	AZ	18,818	C+
Auburn Univ	AL	20,052	VC+
Boston Univ	MA	54,130	HC+
Calif Polytechnic State Univ	CA	19,847	HC
Case Western Reserve Univ	OH	55,178	MC
Clarkson Univ	NY	53,538	HC
Daniel Webster College	NH	25,380	C
Embry-Riddle Aeronautical Univ - Daytona Beach	FL	40,884	C+
Florida Inst of Technology	FL	48,290	VC
Georgia Inst of Technology	GA	20,464	MC
Illinois Inst of Technology	IL	38,512	HC+
Iowa State Univ	IA	16,403	C
Mass Inst of Technology	MA	54,238	MC
Missouri Univ of Science and Technology	MO	18,655	VC+
New York Inst of Technology	NY	40,590	VC
N Car State Univ	NC	16,202	HC
Princeton Univ	NJ	53,795	MC
Purdue Univ/West Lafayette	IN	20,278	HC
Rensselaer Polytechnic Inst	NY	59,229	MC
St. Louis Univ	MO	46,594	VC+
San Diego State Univ	CA	20,578	VC
San Jose State Univ	CA	19,707	C
Stanford Univ	CA	56,411	MC
Syracuse Univ	NY	54,512	HC
Texas A&M Univ	TX	16,956	VC+
Ohio State Univ	OH	19,887	MC
Tuskegee Univ	AL	26,750	C
United States Air Force Academy	CO		MC
United States Naval Academy	MD		MC
Univ of Arizona	AZ	20,105	C
Univ of Calif at Davis	CA	24,482	HC
Univ of Calif at Irvine	CA	25,961	VC
Univ of Calif at Los Angeles	CA	25,686	MC
Univ of Central Florida	FL	15,711	VC+
Univ of Cincinnati	OH	20,199	VC
Univ of Colo Boulder	CO	22,605	VC+
Univ of Florida	FL	15,783	HC+
Univ of Illinois at Urbana-Champaign	IL	24,300	HC
Univ of Kansas	KS	16,980	C+
Univ of Maryland	MD	18,801	HC
Univ of Mich/Ann Arbor	MI	22,102	HC+
Univ of Notre Dame	IN		MC
Univ of Okla	OK	17,634	VC+
Univ of Southern Calif	CA	56,903	MC
Univ of Washington	WA	14,722	VC
West Virginia Univ	WV	15,794	C+
Western Mich Univ	MI	19,042	C
Wichita State Univ	KS	12,539	C
Worcester Polytechnic Inst	MA	53,440	HC+

AERONAUTICAL SCIENCE

School	ST	$IS	SR
Bridgewater State Univ	MA	18,752	C
Dowling College	NY	25,000	LC
Embry-Riddle Aeronautical Univ - Daytona Beach	FL	40,884	C+
Embry-Riddle Aeronautical Univ - Prescott Campus	AZ	40,584	VC
Embry-Riddle Aeronautical Univ - Worldwide	FL	15,512	C
Farmingdale State College	NY	18,985	C
Florida Inst of Technology	FL	48,290	VC
Inter-American Univ of PR/ Bayamon Univ College	PR	4,428	
Kent State Univ	OH	19,352	C
LeTourneau Univ	TX	26,230	C
Rocky Mountain College	MT	32,242	C
Univ of Maryland/Eastern Shore	MD	14,000	C
Wilmington Univ	DE	7,778	NC

AERONAUTICAL TECHNOLOGY

School	ST	$IS	SR
Andrews Univ	MI	28,030	C+
Arizona State Univ	AZ	18,818	C+
Central Washington Univ	WA	11,730	C
Dowling College	NY	25,000	LC
Indiana State Univ	IN	16,000	C
Inter-American Univ of PR/ Bayamon Univ College	PR	4,428	
Kansas State Univ	KS	15,497	VC
Kent State Univ	OH	19,352	C
LeTourneau Univ	TX	26,230	C
Ohio Univ	OH	20,676	VC
Purdue Univ/West Lafayette	IN	20,278	HC
St. Louis Univ	MO	46,594	VC+
Tenn State Univ	TN	9,048	C
Univ of Alaska Anchorage	AK	15,290	NC

AEROSPACE STUDIES

School	ST	$IS	SR
Cal State, Long Beach	CA	17,534	C+
Embry-Riddle Aeronautical Univ - Daytona Beach	FL	40,884	C+
Embry-Riddle Aeronautical Univ - Prescott Campus	AZ	40,584	VC
Mass Inst of Technology	MA	54,238	MC
New Mexico State Univ	NM	13,955	LC
Okla State Univ	OK	14,310	VC
Penn State Univ/Univ Park	PA	25,404	VC

ST = STATE **$IS** = IN-STATE COSTS **SR** = SELECTOR RATING

School	ST	$IS	SR
Rochester Inst of Technology	NY	42,450	VC+
St. Louis Univ	MO	46,594	VC+
United States Air Force Academy	CO		MC
Univ at Buffalo / The SUNY	NY	20,283	VC
Univ of Alabama at Tuscaloosa	AL	17,164	C+
Univ of Alaska Anchorage	AK	15,290	NC
Univ of Calif at Los Angeles	CA	25,686	MC
Univ of Calif at San Diego	CA	21,000	VC
Univ of Central Florida	FL	15,711	VC+
Univ of Miami	FL	55,166	MC
Univ of Mich/Ann Arbor	MI	22,102	HC+
Univ of Minn/Twin Cities	MN		HC
Univ of Southern Calif	CA	56,903	MC
Univ of Tenn at Knoxville	TN	20,364	VC+
Univ of Texas at Austin	TX	44,074	HC
Univ of Virginia	VA	22,175	MC
Virginia Polytechnic Inst and State Univ	VA	14,629	HC
West Virginia Univ	WV	15,794	C+

AFRICAN AMERICAN STUDIES

School	ST	$IS	SR
Amherst College	MA	58,744	MC
Arizona State Univ	AZ	18,818	C+
Bard College at Simon's Rock	MA	58,963	HC+
Bates College	ME	58,950	MC
Berea College	KY	7,220	HC
Brandeis Univ	MA	58,820	HC
Brown Univ	RI	56,150	MC
Cabrini College	PA	40,859	LC
Cal State, Fresno	CA	17,405	C
Cal State, Fullerton	CA	25,188	C+
Cal State, Long Beach	CA	17,534	C+
Cal State, Los Angeles	CA	15,829	C
Cal State, Northridge	CA	28,313	C
Carleton College	MN	58,149	MC
Chicago State Univ	IL	5,482	C
Claflin Univ	SC	22,368	C+
Coe College	IA	43,590	VC
Colby College	ME	57,510	MC
College of Staten Island / The CUNY	NY	16,778	NC
College of Wooster	OH	52,600	VC
Columbia Univ in the City of New York	NY	61,116	MC
Columbia Univ/School of General Studies	NY	54,083	MC
Dartmouth College	NH	57,996	MC
Denison Univ	OH	54,670	HC+
DePauw Univ	IN	48,950	VC+
Duke Univ	NC	50,250	MC
Earlham College	IN	49,710	VC+
East Carolina Univ	NC	14,169	C
Eastern Mich Univ	MI	17,961	C
Emory Univ	GA	45,000	MC
Fordham Univ	NY	58,927	HC
Georgia State Univ	GA	12,000	VC
Guilford College	NC	35,340	C
Hampshire College	MA	58,320	MC
Harvard Univ/Harvard College	MA	49,000	MC
Howard Univ	DC	35,957	C
Hunter College / The CUNY	NY	14,429	VC
Indiana State Univ	IN	16,000	C
Indiana Univ Bloomington	IN	19,358	HC
Indiana Univ Northwest	IN	6,738	LC
Knox College	IL		VC
Lehman College / The CUNY	NY	5,778	LC
Loyola Marymount Univ	CA	53,240	VC+
Luther College	IA	44,380	VC+
Martin Univ	IN	11,000	SP
Metropolitan State Univ of Denver	CO	4,835	LC
Miami Univ	OH	24,191	HC
Middlebury College	VT	57,470	MC
Morehouse College	GA	38,640	C
Morgan State Univ	MD	14,500	VC
Mount Holyoke College	MA	53,596	HC+
New York Univ	NY	61,470	MC
Northeastern Illinois Univ	IL		C
Northeastern Univ	MA	55,296	MC
Northwestern Univ	IL	37,595	MC
Oakland Univ	MI	19,391	VC
Oberlin College	OH	57,025	MC
Ohio Univ	OH	20,676	VC
Ohio Wesleyan Univ	OH	49,460	C+
Old Dominion Univ	VA	18,662	C
Penn State Univ/Univ Park	PA	25,404	VC
Pitzer College	CA	54,988	MC
Purdue Univ/West Lafayette	IN	20,278	HC
Rhode Island College	RI	17,132	LC
Roosevelt Univ	IL	22,605	VC
Rutgers, The State Univ of New Jersey/Camden Campus	NJ	24,254	C
Rutgers, The State Univ of New Jersey/New Brunswick	NJ	25,077	VC
Rutgers, The State Univ of New Jersey/Newark Campus	NJ	25,376	C
St. Augustine's Univ	NC	14,000	C
St. Louis Univ	MO	46,594	VC+
St. Peter's College	NJ	44,240	C
San Diego State Univ	CA	20,578	VC
Scripps College	CA	54,900	MC
Seton Hall Univ	NJ	45,902	C
Simmons College	MA	48,770	VC
Smith College	MA	57,524	MC
Sonoma State Univ	CA	20,541	C
Southern Methodist Univ	TX	57,755	MC
Stanford Univ	CA	56,411	MC
Suffolk Univ	MA	46,548	C
SUNY College at Geneseo	NY	18,055	HC+
SUNY Cortland / The SUNY	NY	19,117	C
SUNY New Paltz	NY	15,010	C
Syracuse Univ	NY	54,512	HC
Temple Univ	PA	24,392	VC
The College at Brockport / SUNY	NY	18,362	VC
Ohio State Univ	OH	19,887	MC
Univ at Albany / SUNY	NY	18,674	VC
Univ at Buffalo / The SUNY	NY	20,283	VC
Univ of Alabama at Birmingham	AL	18,484	C+
Univ of Arkansas at Fayetteville	AR	16,860	VC
Univ of Calif at Berkeley	CA	23,322	MC
Univ of Calif at Irvine	CA	25,961	VC
Univ of Calif at Los Angeles	CA	25,686	MC
Univ of Calif at Riverside	CA	27,204	C
Univ of Calif at Santa Barbara	CA	27,551	HC
Univ of Central Arkansas	AR	10,840	VC
Univ of Chicago	IL	55,416	MC
Univ of Cincinnati	OH	20,199	VC
Univ of Georgia	GA	19,508	VC
Univ of Illinois at Chicago	IL	24,293	VC
Univ of Iowa	IA	17,481	VC
Univ of Kansas	KS	16,980	C+
Univ of Maryland	MD	18,801	HC
Univ of Maryland/Baltimore County	MD	18,000	VC
Univ of Mass Amherst	MA	23,697	VC+
Univ of Mass Boston	MA	11,966	C
Univ of Memphis	TN	15,094	C
Univ of Mich/Ann Arbor	MI	22,102	HC+
Univ of Minn/Twin Cities	MN		HC
Univ of Miss	MS	15,482	VC
Univ of Nebr at Omaha	NE	12,700	C
Univ of N Car at Chapel Hill	NC	18,348	MC
Univ of N Car at Charlotte	NC	15,847	C
Univ of N Car at Greensboro	NC	12,848	C
Univ of Northern Colo	CO	15,973	C
Univ of Okla	OK	17,634	VC+
Univ of Pennsylvania	PA	56,106	MC
Univ of Rochester	NY	58,500	MC
Univ of S Car at Columbia	SC	19,725	VC+
Univ of South Florida	FL	13,000	C
Univ of Southern Calif	CA	56,903	MC
Univ of Virginia	VA	22,175	MC
Univ of Washington	WA	14,722	VC
Univ of Wisc/Madison	WI	18,757	HC
Univ of Wisc-Milwaukee	WI	18,436	C
Vanderbilt Univ	TN	57,072	MC
Virginia Commonwealth Univ	VA	18,633	C
Washington Univ in St. Louis	MO	58,818	MC
Wellesley College	MA	49,848	MC
Wesleyan Univ	CT	59,844	MC
Western Illinois Univ	IL	20,130	C
Wheaton College	MA	54,934	HC+
William Paterson Univ of New Jersey	NJ	21,694	C
Wofford College	SC	45,795	VC
Wright State Univ	OH	16,983	C
Yale Univ	CT	55,300	MC
York College / CUNY	NY	5,496	NC

AFRICAN LANGUAGES

School	ST	$IS	SR
Cal State, Northridge	CA	28,313	C
Duke Univ	NC	50,250	MC
Univ of Wisc/Madison	WI	18,757	HC

AFRICAN STUDIES

School	ST	$IS	SR
Agnes Scott College	GA	45,323	VC+
Bard College	NY	59,872	HC
Berea College	KY	7,220	HC
Bowling Green State Univ	OH	18,970	C
Brown Univ	RI	56,150	MC
Cal State, Dominguez Hills	CA	17,056	LC
Carleton College	MN	58,149	MC
CUNY/Brooklyn College	NY	5,884	C+
Claflin Univ	SC	22,368	C+
Colgate Univ	NY	50,930	MC
College of William & Mary	VA	25,085	MC
Conn College	CT	54,970	MC
Creighton Univ	NE	44,058	VC+
DePaul Univ	IL	46,120	VC
Dickinson College	PA	57,662	HC+
Drew Univ/College of Liberal Arts	NJ	55,862	VC
Duke Univ	NC	50,250	MC
Eastern Illinois Univ	IL	20,502	C
Eastern Mich Univ	MI	17,961	C
Emory Univ	GA	45,000	MC
Fordham Univ	NY	58,927	HC
Franklin and Marshall College	PA	58,295	MC
Hamilton College	NY	55,620	MC
Hampshire College	MA	58,320	MC
Hobart and William Smith Colleges	NY	43,000	VC
Hofstra Univ	NY	48,020	VC+
Howard Univ	DC	35,957	C
Indiana Univ Bloomington	IN	19,358	HC
Johns Hopkins Univ	MD	47,492	MC
Kennesaw State Univ	GA	13,017	VC
Kent State Univ	OH	19,352	C
Lafayette College	PA	57,050	HC+
Lehigh Univ	PA	55,080	MC
Loyola Univ Chicago	IL	49,560	VC+
Mercer Univ	GA	44,201	VC+
New York Univ	NY	61,470	MC
North Park Univ	IL	30,130	C
Ohio Univ	OH	20,676	VC
Old Dominion Univ	VA	18,662	C
Queens College / The CUNY	NY	17,107	VC
Ramapo College of New Jersey	NJ	24,938	C+
Rowan Univ	NJ	23,570	VC
San Francisco State Univ	CA	18,514	C
Savannah State Univ	GA	13,156	C
Shaw Univ	NC	15,488	LC
Smith College	MA	57,524	MC
St. Lawrence Univ	NY	53,740	HC
Stony Brook Univ / SUNY	NY	19,359	HC
SUNY Oneonta / SUNY	NY	16,919	VC
Tenn State Univ	TN	9,048	C
The College at Brockport / SUNY	NY	18,362	VC
Tufts Univ	MA	58,780	MC
Tulane Univ	LA	58,942	MC
Univ of Arizona	AZ	20,105	C
Univ of Arkansas at Fayetteville	AR	16,860	VC
Univ of Calif at Davis	CA	24,482	HC
Univ of Calif at Los Angeles	CA	25,686	MC
Univ of Kansas	KS	16,980	C+
Univ of Mich/Ann Arbor	MI	22,102	HC+
Univ of Minn/Twin Cities	MN		HC
Univ of Notre Dame	IN		MC
Univ of Pennsylvania	PA	56,106	MC
Vassar College	NY	59,070	MC
Washington Univ in St. Louis	MO	58,818	MC
Wayne State Univ	MI	19,493	C
Western Mich Univ	MI	19,042	C
Wheaton College	MA	54,934	HC+
Yale Univ	CT	55,300	MC
Youngstown State Univ	OH	16,374	LC

AFRICANA STUDIES

School	ST	$IS	SR
Binghamton Univ / The SUNY	NY	20,832	HC+
Bowdoin College	ME	57,834	MC
Cornell Univ	NY	59,037	MC
Davidson College	NC	54,683	MC
Indiana Univ-Purdue Univ Indianapolis	IN	17,290	C
New York Univ	NY	61,470	MC
Pomona College	CA	57,680	MC
Univ of Miami	FL	55,166	MC
Univ of New Mexico	NM	15,300	C
Univ of Pittsburgh at Pittsburgh	PA	27,800	HC+

AGRICULTURAL BUSINESS MANAGEMENT

School	ST	$IS	SR
Abilene Christian Univ	TX	38,400	VC
Adams State College	CO	13,358	LC
Alabama A&M Univ	AL	96,100	C
Alcorn State Univ	MS	9,500	C
Angelo State Univ	TX	15,049	NC
Appalachian State Univ	NC	12,919	VC
Arizona State Univ	AZ	18,818	C+
Arkansas State Univ	AR	14,980	C
Arkansas Tech Univ	AR	13,164	LC
Auburn Univ	AL	20,052	VC+
Brigham Young Univ	UT	12,100	HC
Calif Polytechnic State Univ	CA	19,847	HC
Calif State Polytechnic Univ, Pomona	CA	18,932	C
Cal State, Chico	CA	18,952	C
Cal State, Fresno	CA	17,405	C
College of the Ozarks	MO	5,605	VC
Colo State Univ-Fort Collins	CO	20,090	VC
Delaware State Univ	DE	14,700	LC
Dickinson State Univ	ND	8,550	NC
Dordt College	IA	34,160	VC
Eastern New Mexico Univ	NM	10,682	C
Eastern Oregon Univ	OR	10,400	C
Florida Southern College	FL	38,240	VC
Fort Hays State Univ	KS	11,354	C
Hardin-Simmons Univ	TX	23,560	C+
Illinois State Univ	IL	22,634	VC
Iowa State Univ	IA	16,403	C
Kansas State Univ	KS	15,497	VC
Lincoln Univ	MO	11,996	NC
Louisiana State Univ	LA	18,677	VC+
Louisiana Tech Univ	LA	8,000	C
Lubbock Christian Univ	TX	25,518	C
Middle Tenn State Univ	TN	8,650	C
Montana State Univ	MT	14,068	VC
New Mexico State Univ	NM	13,955	LC
Nicholls State Univ	LA	7,095	C
N Car Agricultural and Technical State Univ	NC	13,175	LC
N Car State Univ	NC	16,202	HC
N Dak State Univ	ND	14,642	C
Northwest Missouri State Univ	MO	14,229	C
Northwestern College of Iowa	IA	34,848	C+
Northwestern Okla State Univ	OK	7,275	NC
Okla Panhandle State Univ	OK	8,996	NC
Okla State Univ	OK	14,310	VC
Oregon State Univ	OR	19,017	C+
Penn State Univ/Univ Park	PA	25,404	VC
Prairie View A&M Univ	TX	15,205	LC
Purdue Univ/West Lafayette	IN	20,278	HC
San Diego State Univ	CA	20,578	VC
S Car State Univ	SC	6,700	LC
S Dak State Univ	SD	14,296	C
Southeast Missouri State Univ	MO	14,983	LC
Southern Arkansas Univ	AR	14,316	C
Southwest Minn State Univ	MN	14,000	C
Stephen F. Austin State Univ	TX	14,668	C
Sul Ross State Univ	TX	13,410	LC
Tarleton State Univ	TX	13,489	LC
Texas A&M Univ	TX	16,956	VC+
Texas A&M Univ at Kingsville	TX	7,500	LC
Texas State Univ	TX	16,495	VC
Texas Tech Univ	TX	14,243	C
Ohio State Univ	OH	19,887	MC
The SUNY College of Agriculture and Tech at Cobleskill	NY	18,869	VC
Truman State Univ	MO	13,546	HC
Univ of Arizona	AZ	20,105	C
Univ of Arkansas at Fayetteville	AR	16,860	VC
Univ of Calif at Davis	CA	24,482	HC
Univ of Central Missouri	MO	14,605	C
Univ of Delaware	DE	22,728	VC
Univ of Florida	FL	15,783	HC+
Univ of Idaho	ID	14,558	C
Univ of Illinois at Urbana-Champaign	IL	24,300	HC
Univ of Louisiana at Monroe	LA	12,998	C
Univ of Maryland	MD	18,801	HC
Univ of Minn Crookston	MN	17,834	C
Univ of Minn/Twin Cities	MN		HC
Univ of Missouri/Columbia	MO	18,201	MC
Univ of Nebr - Lincoln	NE	17,507	VC
Univ of Tenn at Martin	TN	13,217	C
Univ of Wisc/Madison	WI	18,757	HC
Univ of Wisc/Platteville	WI	14,274	C
Univ of Wisc/River Falls	WI	9,722	LC
Univ of Wyoming	WY	13,855	C+
Utah State Univ	UT	11,803	C
Washington State Univ	WA	20,461	C
West Texas A&M Univ	TX	13,478	C
Wilmington College	OH	29,784	C

AGRICULTURAL COMMUNICATIONS

School	ST	$IS	SR
Auburn Univ	AL	20,052	VC+
Calif Polytechnic State Univ	CA	19,847	HC
Cal State, Fresno	CA	17,405	C
Kansas State Univ	KS	15,497	VC
N Dak State Univ	ND	14,642	C
Okla State Univ	OK	14,310	VC
Purdue Univ/West Lafayette	IN	20,278	HC
S Dak State Univ	SD	14,296	C
Texas A&M Univ	TX	16,956	VC+
Texas Tech Univ	TX	14,243	C
Univ of Arkansas at Fayetteville	AR	16,860	VC
Univ of Georgia	GA	19,508	VC
Univ of Idaho	ID	14,558	C
Univ of Illinois at Urbana-Champaign	IL	24,300	HC
Univ of Nebr - Lincoln	NE	17,507	VC
Univ of Wisc/Madison	WI	18,757	HC
Univ of Wyoming	WY	13,855	C+
Washington State Univ	WA	20,461	C

ST = STATE **$IS** = IN-STATE COSTS **SR** = SELECTOR RATING

AGRICULTURAL ECONOMICS

School	ST	$IS	SR
Alabama A&M Univ	AL	96,100	C
Alcorn State Univ	MS	9,500	C
Auburn Univ	AL	20,052	VC+
Colo State Univ-Fort Collins	CO	20,090	VC
Eastern Oregon Univ	OR	10,400	C
Fort Valley State Univ	GA	11,200	VC
Kansas State Univ	KS	15,497	VC
Langston Univ	OK	3,000	LC
New Mexico State Univ	NM	13,955	LC
N Car Agricultural and Technical State Univ	NC	13,175	LC
N Car State Univ	NC	16,202	HC
N Dak State Univ	ND	14,642	C
Okla State Univ	OK	14,310	VC
Oregon State Univ	OR	19,017	C+
Prairie View A&M Univ	TX	15,205	LC
Purdue Univ/West Lafayette	IN	20,278	HC
S Dak State Univ	SD	14,296	C
Southern Illinois Univ Carbondale	IL	21,620	C
Southern Univ and A&M College	LA	9,761	C+
Tarleton State Univ	TX	13,489	LC
Tenn Tech Univ	TN	11,310	C
Texas A&M Univ	TX	16,956	VC+
Texas A&M Univ at Commerce	TX	10,496	C
Texas Tech Univ	TX	14,243	C
Ohio State Univ	OH	19,887	MC
Tuskegee Univ	AL	26,750	C
Univ of Arizona	AZ	20,105	C
Univ of Arkansas at Fayetteville	AR	16,860	VC
Univ of Calif at Davis	CA	24,482	HC
Univ of Conn	CT	23,744	HC
Univ of Delaware	DE	22,728	VC
Univ of Georgia	GA	19,508	VC
Univ of Idaho	ID	14,558	C
Univ of Illinois at Urbana-Champaign	IL	24,300	HC
Univ of Kentucky	KY	19,868	C
Univ of Maryland	MD	18,801	HC
Univ of Mass Amherst	MA	23,697	VC+
Univ of Minn/Twin Cities	MN		HC
Univ of Missouri/Columbia	MO	18,201	MC
Univ of Nebr - Lincoln	NE	17,507	VC
Univ of Nevada/Reno	NV	14,500	NC
Univ of Tenn at Knoxville	TN	20,364	VC+
Univ of Wisc/Madison	WI	18,757	HC
Univ of Wyoming	WY	13,855	C+
Utah State Univ	UT	11,803	C
Virginia Polytechnic Inst and State Univ	VA	14,629	HC
Washington State Univ	WA	20,461	C
West Texas A&M Univ	TX	13,478	C

AGRICULTURAL EDUCATION

School	ST	$IS	SR
Alabama A&M Univ	AL	96,100	C
Arkansas Tech Univ	AR	13,164	LC
Calif Polytechnic State Univ	CA	19,847	HC
Cal State, Chico	CA	18,952	C
Cal State, Fresno	CA	17,405	C
Clemson Univ	SC	19,136	HC
College of the Ozarks	MO	5,605	VC
Colo State Univ-Fort Collins	CO	20,090	VC
Delaware State Univ	DE	14,700	LC
Dordt College	IA	34,160	VC
Eastern New Mexico Univ	NM	10,682	C
Fort Valley State Univ	GA	11,200	VC
Iowa State Univ	IA	16,403	C
Kansas State Univ	KS	15,497	VC
Louisiana State Univ	LA	18,677	VC+
Mich State Univ	MI	13,689	VC
Missouri State Univ	MO	13,996	VC
Montana State Univ	MT	14,068	VC
Morehead State Univ	KY	10,900	C
Murray State Univ	KY	14,944	C
New Mexico State Univ	NM	13,955	LC
N Car Agricultural and Technical State Univ	NC	13,175	LC
N Car State Univ	NC	16,202	HC
N Dak State Univ	ND	14,642	C
Northwest Missouri State Univ	MO	14,229	C
Okla Panhandle State Univ	OK	8,996	NC
Okla State Univ	OK	14,310	VC
Oswego / SUNY	NY	20,009	VC
Prescott College	AZ	33,284	C+
Purdue Univ/West Lafayette	IN	20,278	HC
S Dak State Univ	SD	14,296	C
Southeast Missouri State Univ	MO	14,983	LC
Southern Arkansas Univ	AR	14,316	C
Southern Univ and A&M College	LA	9,761	C+
Stephen F. Austin State Univ	TX	14,668	C
Tarleton State Univ	TX	13,489	LC
Tenn Tech Univ	TN	11,310	C
Texas A&M Univ	TX	16,956	VC+
Texas A&M Univ at Commerce	TX	10,496	C
Texas A&M Univ at Kingsville	TX	7,500	LC
Ohio State Univ	OH	19,887	MC
Univ of Arizona	AZ	20,105	C
Univ of Arkansas at Fayetteville	AR	16,860	VC
Univ of Arkansas at Pine Bluff	AR	10,600	C
Univ of Central Missouri	MO	14,605	C
Univ of Conn	CT	23,744	HC
Univ of Florida	FL	15,783	HC+
Univ of Georgia	GA	19,508	VC
Univ of Idaho	ID	14,558	C
Univ of Illinois at Urbana-Champaign	IL	24,300	HC
Univ of Kentucky	KY	19,868	C
Univ of Louisiana at Lafayette	LA	6,130	C
Univ of Maryland/Eastern Shore	MD	14,000	C
Univ of Minn/Twin Cities	MN		HC
Univ of Nebr - Lincoln	NE	17,507	VC
Univ of Wisc/Platteville	WI	14,274	C
Univ of Wisc/River Falls	WI	9,722	LC
Univ of Wyoming	WY	13,855	C+
Utah State Univ	UT	11,803	C
Virginia Polytechnic Inst and State Univ	VA	14,629	HC
Washington State Univ	WA	20,461	C
Wilmington College	OH	29,784	C

AGRICULTURAL ENGINEERING

School	ST	$IS	SR
Auburn Univ	AL	20,052	VC+
Clemson Univ	SC	19,136	HC
Iowa State Univ	IA	16,403	C
Kansas State Univ	KS	15,497	VC
New Mexico State Univ	NM	13,955	LC
N Car State Univ	NC	16,202	HC
N Dak State Univ	ND	14,642	C
Oregon State Univ	OR	19,017	C+
Penn State Univ/Univ Park	PA	25,404	VC
Purdue Univ/West Lafayette	IN	20,278	HC
S Dak State Univ	SD	14,296	C
Texas A&M Univ	TX	16,956	VC+
Univ of Arizona	AZ	20,105	C
Univ of Calif at Davis	CA	24,482	HC
Univ of Florida	FL	15,783	HC+
Univ of Georgia	GA	19,508	VC
Univ of Idaho	ID	14,558	C
Univ of Illinois at Urbana-Champaign	IL	24,300	HC
Univ of Nebr - Lincoln	NE	17,507	VC
Univ of Wisc/River Falls	WI	9,722	LC
Utah State Univ	UT	11,803	C
Virginia Polytechnic Inst and State Univ	VA	14,629	HC
Washington State Univ	WA	20,461	C

AGRICULTURAL ENGINEERING TECHNOLOGY

School	ST	$IS	SR
Fort Valley State Univ	GA	11,200	VC
Kansas State Univ	KS	15,497	VC
Montana State Univ	MT	14,068	VC
N Dak State Univ	ND	14,642	C
S Dak State Univ	SD	14,296	C
Univ of Central Missouri	MO	14,605	C
Univ of Minn Crookston	MN	17,834	C

AGRICULTURAL MECHANICS

School	ST	$IS	SR
Calif Polytechnic State Univ	CA	19,847	HC
Montana State Univ-Northern	MT	12,500	NC
N Dak State Univ	ND	14,642	C
Northwest Missouri State Univ	MO	14,229	C
Penn State Univ/Univ Park	PA	25,404	VC
Stephen F. Austin State Univ	TX	14,668	C
Tarleton State Univ	TX	13,489	LC
The SUNY College of Agriculture and Tech at Cobleskill	NY	18,869	VC
Univ of Idaho	ID	14,558	C
Univ of Illinois at Urbana-Champaign	IL	24,300	HC
Univ of Nebr - Lincoln	NE	17,507	VC
Washington State Univ	WA	20,461	C

AGRICULTURAL SCIENCES

School	ST	$IS	SR
Calif Polytechnic State Univ	CA	19,847	HC
Cornell Univ	NY	59,037	MC
Univ of Idaho	ID	14,558	C

AGRICULTURE

School	ST	$IS	SR
Andrews Univ	MI	28,030	C+
Arkansas State Univ	AR	14,980	C
Auburn Univ	AL	20,052	VC+
Austin Peay State Univ	TN	14,650	C
Beloit College	WI	49,970	HC
Berea College	KY	7,220	HC
Calif State Polytechnic Univ, Pomona	CA	18,932	C
Cal State, Chico	CA	18,952	C
Cal State, Stanislaus	CA	18,582	C
Cameron Univ	OK	9,267	LC
Clemson Univ	SC	19,136	HC
College of the Ozarks	MO	5,605	VC
Dordt College	IA	34,160	VC
Eastern Kentucky Univ	KY	11,161	C
Eastern New Mexico Univ	NM	10,682	C
Ferrum College	VA	27,740	LC
Florida Southern College	FL	38,240	VC
Fort Hays State Univ	KS	11,354	C
Hampshire College	MA	58,320	MC
Hardin-Simmons Univ	TX	23,560	C+
Illinois State Univ	IL	22,634	VC
Iowa State Univ	IA	16,403	C
Lincoln Univ	MO	11,996	NC
Lubbock Christian Univ	TX	25,518	C
McNeese State Univ	LA		C
Mich State Univ	MI	13,689	VC
Missouri State Univ	MO	13,996	VC
Morehead State Univ	KY	10,900	C
Murray State Univ	KY	14,944	C
New Mexico State Univ	NM	13,955	LC
N Car State Univ	NC	16,202	HC
N Dak State Univ	ND	14,642	C
Northwest Missouri State Univ	MO	14,229	C
Northwestern Okla State Univ	OK	7,275	NC
Oregon State Univ	OR	19,017	C+
Penn State Univ/Univ Park	PA	25,404	VC
Prescott College	AZ	33,284	C+
Purdue Univ/West Lafayette	IN	20,278	HC
Rutgers, The State Univ of New Jersey/New Brunswick	NJ	25,077	VC
Sam Houston State Univ	TX	17,082	C
S Dak State Univ	SD	14,296	C
Southern Arkansas Univ	AR	14,316	C
Southern Illinois Univ Carbondale	IL	21,620	C
Southern Univ and A&M College	LA	9,761	C+
Stephen F. Austin State Univ	TX	14,668	C
Sterling College	VT	26,160	C
Tarleton State Univ	TX	13,489	LC
Tenn State Univ	TN	9,048	C
Tenn Tech Univ	TN	11,310	C
Texas A&M Univ at Commerce	TX	10,496	C
Texas State Univ	TX	16,495	VC
Truman State Univ	MO	13,546	HC
Unity College	ME	34,054	C
Univ of Arkansas at Monticello	AR	8,470	NC
Univ of Arkansas at Pine Bluff	AR	10,600	C
Univ of Conn	CT	23,744	HC
Univ of Delaware	DE	22,728	VC
Univ of Hawaii at Hilo	HI	6,500	C
Univ of Idaho	ID	14,558	C
Univ of Kentucky	KY	19,868	C
Univ of Maine	ME	19,712	C+
Univ of Maryland	MD	18,801	HC
Univ of Maryland/Eastern Shore	MD	14,000	C
Univ of Missouri/Columbia	MO	18,201	MC
Univ of Nebr - Lincoln	NE	17,507	VC
Univ of Tenn at Knoxville	TN	20,364	VC+
Univ of Tenn at Martin	TN	13,217	C
Univ of Vermont	VT	26,120	VC+
Univ of Wyoming	WY	13,855	C+
Virginia State Univ	VA	11,318	C+
Warren Wilson College	NC	34,888	VC
Washington State Univ	WA	20,461	C
West Texas A&M Univ	TX	13,478	C
West Virginia Univ	WV	15,794	C+
Western Illinois Univ	IL	20,130	C
Western Kentucky Univ	KY	11,000	LC
Xavier Univ	OH	43,740	VC

AGRONOMY

School	ST	$IS	SR
Alabama A&M Univ	AL	96,100	C
Auburn Univ	AL	20,052	VC+
Calif Polytechnic State Univ	CA	19,847	HC
College of the Ozarks	MO	5,605	VC
Delaware Valley College	PA	29,944	C
Iowa State Univ	IA	16,403	C
Kansas State Univ	KS	15,497	VC
New Mexico State Univ	NM	13,955	LC
N Car State Univ	NC	16,202	HC
Northwest Missouri State Univ	MO	14,229	C
Okla Panhandle State Univ	OK	8,996	NC
Oregon State Univ	OR	19,017	C+
Prairie View A&M Univ	TX	15,205	LC
Purdue Univ/West Lafayette	IN	20,278	HC
S Dak State Univ	SD	14,296	C
Tarleton State Univ	TX	13,489	LC
Texas A&M Univ	TX	16,956	VC+
Texas Tech Univ	TX	14,243	C
Truman State Univ	MO	13,546	HC
Univ of Conn	CT	23,744	HC
Univ of Florida	FL	15,783	HC+
Univ of Illinois at Urbana-Champaign	IL	24,300	HC
Univ of Minn Crookston	MN	17,834	C
Univ of Nebr - Lincoln	NE	17,507	VC
Univ of Wisc/Madison	WI	18,757	HC
Univ of Wisc/River Falls	WI	9,722	LC
Washington State Univ	WA	20,461	C
West Virginia Univ	WV	15,794	C+
Wilmington College	OH	29,784	C

AIR TRAFFIC CONTROL

School	ST	$IS	SR
Arizona State Univ	AZ	18,818	C+
Daniel Webster College	NH	25,380	C
Embry-Riddle Aeronautical Univ - Daytona Beach	FL	40,884	C+
Florida Memorial Univ	FL	20,716	LC
Kent State Univ	OH	19,352	C
Purdue Univ/West Lafayette	IN	20,278	HC
Thomas Edison State College	NJ	5,700	SP
Univ of Alaska Anchorage	AK	15,290	NC
Univ of N Dak	ND	14,094	C
Vaughn College of Aeronautics and Technology	NY	31,360	SP

AIRCRAFT MECHANICS

School	ST	$IS	SR
Andrews Univ	MI	28,030	C+
Embry-Riddle Aeronautical Univ - Worldwide	FL	15,512	C
Idaho State Univ	ID	11,908	C
Lewis Univ	IL	23,050	C
Pennsylvania College of Technology	PA	25,653	NC
Vaughn College of Aeronautics and Technology	NY	31,360	SP
Western Mich Univ	MI	19,042	C

AIRLINE PILOTING AND NAVIGATION

School	ST	$IS	SR
Averett Univ	VA	36,000	LC
Baylor Univ	TX	46,720	HC
Daniel Webster College	NH	25,380	C
Eastern Kentucky Univ	KY	11,161	C
Eastern Mich Univ	MI	17,961	C
Embry-Riddle Aeronautical Univ - Daytona Beach	FL	40,884	C+
Indiana State Univ	IN	16,000	C
Kansas State Univ	KS	15,497	VC
Lewis Univ	IL	23,050	C
Louisiana Tech Univ	LA	8,000	C
Metropolitan State Univ of Denver	CO	4,835	LC
Ohio Univ	OH	20,676	VC
Pacific Union College	CA	28,150	VC
Purdue Univ/West Lafayette	IN	20,278	HC
St. Louis Univ	MO	46,594	VC+
Univ of Alaska Anchorage	AK	15,290	NC
Univ of Illinois at Urbana-Champaign	IL	24,300	HC
Univ of Minn Crookston	MN	17,834	C
Vaughn College of Aeronautics and Technology	NY	31,360	SP
Western Mich Univ	MI	19,042	C

ALLIED HEALTH

School	ST	$IS	SR
Adams State College	CO	13,358	LC
Albany State Univ	GA	8,500	C
Andrews Univ	MI	28,030	C+
Black Hills State Univ	SD	13,562	LC
Bloomfield College	NJ	36,960	C
Cedarville Univ	OH	31,036	VC+
Clayton State Univ	GA	12,000	LC
College of Mount St. Vincent	NY	41,040	MC
East Tenn State Univ	TN	9,000	C
Eastern Mich Univ	MI	17,961	C
Fairleigh Dickinson Univ/College at Florham	NJ	42,142	C
Fairleigh Dickinson Univ/Metropolitan Campus	NJ	40,254	C
Felician College	NJ	41,640	C
Ferris State Univ	MI	19,698	C
George Fox Univ	OR	40,750	C+
Georgian Court Univ	NJ	39,726	LC
Hendrix College	AR	48,436	HC+
Hofstra Univ	NY	48,020	VC+
Howard Univ	DC	35,957	C

School	ST	$IS	SR
Ithaca College	NY	52,300	HC
Johnson State College	VT	16,721	C
Madonna Univ	MI	24,540	VC
Mars Hill College	NC	22,950	LC
Marshall Univ	WV	14,820	C
Mass College of Liberal Arts	MA	16,733	C
Merrimack College	MA	44,215	C
Millersville Univ of Pennsylvania	PA	18,498	C
Millikin Univ	IL	37,462	C
Montclair State Univ	NJ	22,614	C
Mount Aloysius College	PA	27,970	C
National Univ	CA	14,730	SP
Nebr Methodist College of Nursing and Allied Health	NE	22,872	SP
Northwestern State Univ of Louisiana	LA	14,368	C
Oakland Univ	MI	19,391	VC
Ramapo College of New Jersey	NJ	24,938	₵
Rochester Inst of Technology	NY	42,450	V₵
Roosevelt Univ	IL	22,605	VC
Rutgers, The State Univ of New Jersey/New Brunswick	NJ	25,077	VC
Rutgers, The State Univ of New Jersey/Newark Campus	NJ	25,376	C
Tuskegee Univ	AL	26,750	C
Univ of Central Okla	OK	12,293	C
Univ of Florida	FL	15,783	H₵
Univ of Illinois at Chicago	IL	24,293	VC
Univ of St. Francis	IL	36,490	C
Univ of Texas at El Paso	TX	8,764	NC
Washington Univ in St. Louis	MO	58,818	MC
West Texas A&M Univ	TX	13,478	C
Youngstown State Univ	OH	16,374	LC

AMERICAN INDIAN STUDIES

School	ST	$IS	SR
Arizona State Univ	AZ	18,818	₵
Black Hills State Univ	SD	13,562	LC
Fort Lewis College	CO	15,513	C
San Diego State Univ	CA	20,578	VC
Sonoma State Univ	CA	20,541	C
Southern Oregon Univ	OR	17,874	C
Univ of Arizona	AZ	20,105	C
Univ of Calif at Los Angeles	CA	25,686	MC
Univ of Minn/Twin Cities	MN		HC
Univ of Science and Arts of Okla	OK	10,560	VC
Univ of S Dak	SD	15,111	C
Univ of Wisc/Eau Claire	WI	15,430	VC
Univ of Wisc/Green Bay	WI	14,900	C
Univ of Wyoming	WY	13,855	₵

AMERICAN LITERATURE

School	ST	$IS	SR
American Univ	DC	54,829	H₵
Bennington College	VT	56,990	H₵
Biola Univ	CA	40,320	VC
Brown Univ	RI	56,150	MC
Eastern Mich Univ	MI	17,961	C
Florida State Univ	FL	15,238	HC
Hofstra Univ	NY	48,020	V₵
Lubbock Christian Univ	TX	25,518	C
New York Univ	NY	61,470	MC
Southern Illinois Univ Edwardsville	IL	17,532	C
Univ of Calif at Los Angeles	CA	25,686	MC
Washington Univ in St. Louis	MO	58,818	MC
Wheeling Jesuit Univ	WV	34,668	C

AMERICAN SIGN LANGUAGE

School	ST	$IS	SR
Augustana College	SD	35,500	VC
Bethel College	IN	31,560	C
Biola Univ	CA	40,320	VC
Bloomsburg Univ of Pennsylvania	PA	13,598	C
Gallaudet Univ	DC	25,380	SP
Gardner-Webb Univ	NC	34,375	₵
Goshen College	IN	35,900	VC
Indiana Univ-Purdue Univ Indianapolis	IN	17,290	C
Kent State Univ	OH	19,352	C
Keuka College	NY	30,300	C
Maryville College	TN	33,150	VC
Mount Aloysius College	PA	27,970	C
Northeastern Univ	MA	55,296	MC
St. Catherine Univ	MN	37,782	₵
Univ of Arkansas at Little Rock	AR		C
Univ of Houston	TX	19,184	VC
Univ of Louisville	KY	17,460	VC
Univ of New Mexico	NM	15,300	C
Univ of North Florida	FL	15,578	VC
Univ of Northern Colo	CO	15,973	C
Univ of Rochester	NY	58,500	MC
Western Oregon Univ	OR	15,021	C
Wright State Univ	OH	16,983	C

AMERICAN STUDIES

School	ST	$IS	SR
Albion College	MI	43,884	VC
Albright College	PA	46,660	C
American Univ	DC	54,829	H₵
Amherst College	MA	58,744	MC
Arizona State Univ	AZ	18,818	₵
Ashland Univ	OH	25,000	C
Austin College	TX	36,940	HC
Bard College	NY	59,872	HC
Bard College at Simon's Rock	MA	58,963	H₵
Bates College	ME	58,950	MC
Baylor Univ	TX	40,720	HC
Bennington College	VT	56,990	H₵
Boston Univ	MA	54,130	H₵
Bowling Green State Univ	OH	18,970	C
Brandeis Univ	MA	58,820	HC
Brigham Young Univ	UT	12,100	HC
Brown Univ	RI	56,150	MC
Bryant Univ	RI	49,179	VC
Cabrini College	PA	40,859	LC
Cal State, Fullerton	CA	25,188	₵
Cal State, San Bernardino	CA	12,000	C
Carleton College	MN	58,149	MC
Case Western Reserve Univ	OH	55,178	MC
Cedarville Univ	OH	31,036	V₵
Christopher Newport Univ	VA	21,050	VC
CUNY/Brooklyn College	NY	5,884	₵
Claflin Univ	SC	22,368	₵
Claremont McKenna College	CA	58,065	MC
Clarkson Univ	NY	53,538	HC
Coe College	IA	43,590	VC
Colby College	ME	57,510	MC
College of Staten Island / The CUNY	NY	16,778	NC
College of St. Elizabeth	NJ	43,839	LC
College of William & Mary	VA	25,085	MC
Columbia College	MO	24,578	C
Columbia Univ in the City of New York	NY	61,116	MC
Columbia Univ/Barnard College	NY	39,000	MC
Conn College	CT	54,970	MC
Cornell Univ	NY	59,037	MC
Creighton Univ	NE	44,058	V₵
Cumberland Univ	TN	21,220	C
CUNY-City College	NY	19,576	H₵
DePaul Univ	IL	46,120	VC
Dickinson College	PA	57,662	H₵
Dominican Univ	IL	37,628	C
Drury Univ	MO	30,319	VC
Eckerd College	FL	43,902	VC
Elmhurst College	IL	42,032	₵
Elmira College	NY	49,950	₵
Elms College	MA	23,900	VC
Emmanuel College	MA	47,985	VC
Emory Univ	GA	45,000	MC
Erskine College	SC	37,360	C
Fairfield Univ	CT	55,850	VC
Florida State Univ	FL	15,238	HC
Fordham Univ	NY	58,927	HC
Franklin and Marshall College	PA	58,295	MC
Franklin College	IN	35,885	C
Franklin Pierce Univ	NH	41,598	C
George Washington Univ	DC	57,108	MC
Georgetown College	KY	38,690	C
Georgetown Univ	DC	52,910	MC
Goucher College	MD	50,252	V₵
Hamilton College	NY	55,620	MC
Hampshire College	MA	58,320	MC
Harding Univ	AR	21,432	₵
Harvard Univ/Harvard College	MA	49,000	MC
Hendrix College	AR	48,436	H₵
Hillsdale College	MI	31,890	H₵
Hobart and William Smith Colleges	NY	43,000	VC
Hofstra Univ	NY	48,020	V₵
Illinois College	IL	25,770	VC
Illinois Wesleyan Univ	IL	48,452	V₵
Indiana Univ Bloomington	IN	19,358	HC
Keene State College	NH	21,538	C
Kent State Univ	OH	19,352	C
Kenyon College	OH	56,810	MC
Knox College	IL		VC
Lafayette College	PA	57,050	H₵
Lake Forest College	IL	45,580	VC
Lebanon Valley College	PA	38,570	C
Lehman College / The CUNY	NY	5,778	LC
Lenoir-Rhyne College	NC	35,984	C
Lindsey Wilson College	KY	30,470	VC
Lipscomb Univ	TN	35,722	VC
Lycoming College	PA	43,636	C
Macalester College	MN	53,419	MC
Manhattanville College	NY	46,260	VC
Marist College	NY	35,500	C
Mary Baldwin College	VA	37,110	C
Meredith College	NC	31,420	C
Miami Univ	OH	24,191	HC
Mich State Univ	MI	13,689	VC
Middlebury College	VT	57,470	MC
Mills College	CA	54,119	HC
Miss College	MS	21,998	VC
Montreat College	NC	31,298	VC
Mount St. Mary's College/ Chalon Campus	CA	43,897	V₵
Muhlenberg College	PA	52,837	HC
Muskingum Univ	OH	30,502	C
Nazareth College of Rochester	NY	41,590	VC
New York Univ	NY	61,470	MC
Northwestern Univ	IL	37,595	MC
Oberlin College	OH	57,025	MC
Occidental College	CA	59,592	M₵
Oglethorpe Univ	GA	42,580	VC
Okla State Univ	OK	14,310	VC
Oregon State Univ	OR	19,017	₵
Oswego / SUNY	NY	20,009	VC
Pace Univ	NY	48,094	VC
Pitzer College	CA	54,988	MC
Pomona College	CA	57,680	MC
Providence College	RI	55,995	HC
Queens College / The CUNY	NY	17,107	VC
Ramapo College of New Jersey	NJ	24,938	₵
Reed College	OR	57,780	MC
Rider Univ	NJ	45,720	C
Roger Williams Univ	RI	45,788	C
Roosevelt Univ	IL	22,605	VC
Rowan Univ	NJ	23,570	VC
Rutgers, The State Univ of New Jersey/New Brunswick	NJ	25,077	VC
Rutgers, The State Univ of New Jersey/Newark Campus	NJ	25,376	C
St. Louis Univ	MO	46,594	V₵
St. Michael's College	VT	48,740	VC
St. Peter's College	NJ	44,240	C
Salem College	NC	29,326	VC
Salve Regina Univ	RI	47,250	VC
San Diego State Univ	CA	20,578	VC
San Francisco State Univ	CA	18,514	C
Scripps College	CA	54,900	MC
Sewanee: The Univ of the South	TN	47,700	H₵
Siena College	NY	43,863	VC
Siena Heights Univ	MI	17,000	LC
Skidmore College	NY	57,926	HC
Smith College	MA	57,524	MC
Southern Nazarene Univ	OK	24,354	NC
St. John Fisher College	NY	39,370	₵
St. Olaf College	MN	49,960	H₵
Stanford Univ	CA	56,411	MC
Stetson Univ	FL	49,512	V₵
Stonehill College	MA	46,780	V₵
Stony Brook Univ / SUNY	NY	19,359	HC
Suffolk Univ	MA	46,548	C
SUNY College at Geneseo	NY	18,055	H₵
SUNY College at Old Westbury	NY	16,324	C
Temple Univ	PA	24,392	VC
Texas State Univ	TX	16,495	VC
The College of St. Rose	NY	26,750	C
Trinity College	CT		H₵
Tufts Univ	MA	58,780	MC
Tulane Univ	LA	58,942	MC
Union College	NY		MC
Univ at Buffalo / The SUNY	NY	20,283	VC
Univ of Alabama at Tuscaloosa	AL	17,164	₵
Univ of Arkansas at Fayetteville	AR	16,860	VC
Univ of Calif at Berkeley	CA	23,322	MC
Univ of Calif at Davis	CA	24,482	HC
Univ of Calif at Santa Cruz	CA	27,807	VC
Univ of Dayton	OH	43,750	VC
Univ of Florida	FL	15,783	H₵
Univ of Hawaii at Manoa	HI	19,379	VC
Univ of Idaho	ID	14,558	C
Univ of Iowa	IA	17,481	VC
Univ of Kansas	KS	16,980	₵
Univ of Mary Washington	VA	19,484	VC
Univ of Maryland	MD	18,801	HC
Univ of Maryland/Baltimore County	MD	18,000	VC
Univ of Mass Boston	MA	11,966	C
Univ of Mass Lowell	MA	19,316	C
Univ of Miami	FL	55,166	MC
Univ of Mich/Ann Arbor	MI	22,102	H₵
Univ of Mich/Dearborn	MI	9,885	VC
Univ of Minn/Twin Cities	MN		HC
Univ of Mount Union	OH	35,130	C
Univ of New Mexico	NM	15,300	C
Univ of N Car at Chapel Hill	NC	18,348	MC
Univ of Notre Dame	IN		MC
Univ of Pennsylvania	PA	56,106	MC
Univ of Pittsburgh at Greensburg	PA	17,640	C
Univ of Pittsburgh at Johnstown	PA	20,862	LC
Univ of Rio Grande	OH	8,750	NC
Univ of Rochester	NY	58,500	MC
Univ of St. Francis	IN	29,810	C
Univ of South Florida	FL	13,300	C
Univ of Southern Calif	CA	56,903	MC
Univ of Texas at Austin	TX	44,074	HC
Univ of Texas at Dallas	TX	21,046	HC
Univ of Texas at San Antonio	TX	18,372	C
Univ of Wisc/Stevens Point	WI	14,043	C
Univ of Wyoming	WY	13,855	₵
Upper Iowa Univ	IA	30,426	NC
Ursinus College	PA	55,630	V₵
Utah State Univ	UT	11,803	C
Valparaiso Univ	IN	43,040	V₵
Vanderbilt Univ	TN	57,072	MC
Vassar College	NY	59,070	MC
Virginia Wesleyan College	VA	28,433	LC
Warner Pacific College	OR	25,550	C
Washington College	MD	48,768	VC
Washington Univ in St. Louis	MO	58,818	MC
Webster Univ	MO	33,990	₵
Wellesley College	MA	49,848	MC
Wells College	NY	38,680	VC
Wesley College	DE	31,115	LC
Wesleyan College	GA	24,000	₵
Wesleyan Univ	CT	59,844	MC
West Chester Univ of Pennsylvania	PA	16,836	C
Western Conn State Univ	CT	18,327	C
Western Washington Univ	WA	18,519	VC
Wheaton College	MA	54,934	H₵
Whitworth Univ	WA	55,826	V₵
Willamette Univ	OR	56,450	V₵
Williams College	MA	58,900	MC
Wittenberg Univ	OH	47,766	VC
Yale Univ	CT	55,300	MC
Youngstown State Univ	OH	16,374	LC

ANATOMY

School	ST	$IS	SR
Andrews Univ	MI	28,030	₵
Duke Univ	NC	50,250	MC
Howard Univ	DC	35,957	C
Marshall Univ	WV	14,820	C
Univ of Illinois at Chicago	IL	24,293	VC

ANIMAL FEED SCIENCE

School	ST	$IS	SR
Kansas State Univ	KS	15,497	VC

ANIMAL SCIENCE

School	ST	$IS	SR
Abilene Christian Univ	TX	38,400	VC
Alabama A&M Univ	AL	96,100	C
Andrews Univ	MI	28,030	₵
Angelo State Univ	TX	15,049	NC
Arkansas State Univ	AR	14,980	C
Auburn Univ	AL	20,052	V₵
Becker College	MA	41,420	LC
Berry College	GA	39,254	HC
Bucknell Univ	PA	58,160	MC
Calif Polytechnic State Univ	CA	19,847	HC
Calif State Polytechnic Univ, Pomona	CA	18,932	C
Cal State, Chico	CA	18,952	C
Cal State, Fresno	CA	17,405	C
Clemson Univ	SC	19,136	HC
College of the Ozarks	MO	5,605	VC
Colo State Univ-Fort Collins	CO	20,090	VC
Cornell Univ	NY	59,037	MC
Delaware Valley College	PA	29,944	C
Dordt College	IA	34,160	VC
Eastern New Mexico Univ	NM	10,682	C
Florida A&M Univ	FL	14,935	LC
Fort Valley State Univ	GA	11,200	VC
Hampshire College	MA	58,320	MC
Hardin-Simmons Univ	TX	23,560	₵
Iowa State Univ	IA	16,403	C
Kansas State Univ	KS	15,497	VC
Langston Univ	OK	3,000	LC
Louisiana State Univ	LA	18,677	V₵
Louisiana Tech Univ	LA	8,000	C
Lubbock Christian Univ	TX	25,518	C
Mich State Univ	MI	13,689	VC
Middle Tenn State Univ	TN	8,650	C
Missouri State Univ	MO	13,996	VC
Montana State Univ	MT	14,068	VC
New Mexico State Univ	NM	13,955	LC
N Car Agricultural and Technical State Univ	NC	13,175	LC
N Car State Univ	NC	16,202	HC
N Dak State Univ	ND	14,642	C
Northwest Missouri State Univ	MO	14,229	C
Okla Panhandle State Univ	OK	8,996	NC
Okla State Univ	OK	14,310	VC
Oregon State Univ	OR	19,017	₵
Penn State Univ/Univ Park	PA	25,404	VC
Prairie View A&M Univ	TX	15,205	LC
Purdue Univ/West Lafayette	IN	20,278	HC
Rutgers, The State Univ of New Jersey/New Brunswick	NJ	25,077	VC
Sam Houston State Univ	TX	17,082	C
S Dak State Univ	SD	14,296	C
Southeast Missouri State Univ	MO	14,983	LC
Southern Illinois Univ Carbondale	IL	21,620	C
Southwestern Univ	TX	45,660	VC

INDEX OF COLLEGE MAJORS

School	ST	$IS	SR
SUNY / College of Environmental Science and Forestry	NY	18,351	HC
Stephen F. Austin State Univ	TX	14,668	C
Sul Ross State Univ	TX	13,410	LC
Tarleton State Univ	TX	13,489	LC
Tenn Tech Univ	TN	11,310	C
Texas A&M Univ	TX	16,956	VC+
Texas A&M Univ at Commerce	TX	10,496	C
Texas A&M Univ at Kingsville	TX	7,500	LC
Texas State Univ	TX	16,495	VC
Texas Tech Univ	TX	14,243	C
Ohio State Univ	OH	19,887	MC
The SUNY College of Agriculture and Tech at Cobleskill	NY	18,869	VC
Truman State Univ	MO	13,546	HC
Tuskegee Univ	AL	26,750	C
Unity College	ME	34,054	C
Univ of Arizona	AZ	20,105	C
Univ of Arkansas at Fayetteville	AR	16,860	VC
Univ of Calif at Davis	CA	24,482	HC
Univ of Calif at San Diego	CA	21,000	VC
Univ of Conn	CT	23,744	HC
Univ of Delaware	DE	22,728	VC
Univ of Florida	FL	15,783	HC+
Univ of Georgia	GA	19,508	VC
Univ of Hawaii at Manoa	HI	19,379	VC
Univ of Idaho	ID	14,558	C
Univ of Illinois at Urbana-Champaign	IL	24,300	HC
Univ of Kentucky	KY	19,868	C
Univ of Maine	ME	19,712	C+
Univ of Maryland	MD	18,801	HC
Univ of Mass Amherst	MA	23,697	VC+
Univ of Minn Crookston	MN	17,834	C
Univ of Minn/Twin Cities	MN		HC
Univ of Missouri/Columbia	MO	18,201	MC
Univ of Montana-Western	MT	9,753	LC
Univ of Nebr - Lincoln	NE	17,507	VC
Univ of Nevada/Reno	NV	14,500	NC
Univ of New England	ME	46,145	C+
Univ of New Hampshire	NH	24,702	VC
Univ of PR/Mayaguez	PR	1,250	
Univ of Tenn at Knoxville	TN	20,364	VC+
Univ of Tenn at Martin	TN	13,217	C
Univ of Vermont	VT	26,120	VC+
Univ of Wisc/Madison	WI	18,757	HC
Univ of Wisc/Platteville	WI	14,274	C
Univ of Wisc/River Falls	WI	9,722	LC
Univ of Wyoming	WY	13,855	C+
Utah State Univ	UT	11,803	C
Virginia Polytechnic Inst and State Univ	VA	14,629	HC
Washington State Univ	WA	20,461	C
West Texas A&M Univ	TX	13,478	C
West Virginia Univ	WV	15,794	C+
Wilmington College	OH	29,784	C

ANIMATION

School	ST	$IS	SR
Academy of Art Univ	CA		
Art Inst of Atlanta	GA	24,000	SP
Art Inst of Portland	OR	23,040	SP
Bennington College	VT	56,990	HC+
Brigham Young Univ	UT	12,100	HC
Calif College of the Arts	CA	48,334	SP
Calif Inst of the Arts	CA	46,368	SP
Cleveland Inst of Art	OH	48,641	SP
Cogswell Polytechnical College	CA	30,531	C
College for Creative Studies	MI		SP
Columbus College of Art and Design	OH	37,732	SP
Daemen College	NY	31,510	C
DePaul Univ	IL	46,120	VC
Eastern Mich Univ	MI	17,961	C
Fairleigh Dickinson Univ/College at Florham	NJ	42,142	C
Huntington Univ	IN	32,220	C
Kansas City Art Inst	MO	38,000	SP
Laguna College of Art and Design	CA	26,500	SP
Lawrence Tech Univ	MI	37,630	VC
Loyola Marymount Univ	CA	53,240	VC+
Maryland Inst College of Art	MD	39,500	SP
Mass College of Art and Design	MA	23,600	SP
Memphis College of Art	TN	33,550	SP
Minneapolis College of Art and Design	MN	36,700	SP
New Mexico State Univ	NM	13,955	LC
New York Univ	NY	61,470	MC
Northwestern College	MN	24,000	C
Rochester Inst of Technology	NY	42,450	VC+
Rocky Mountain College of Art and Design	CO	22,470	NC
Santa Fe Univ of Art and Design	NM	39,666	SP
Savannah College of Art and Design	GA	46,824	SP
School of Visual Arts	NY	36,500	SP
Southern Adventist Univ	TN	26,190	C
SUNY Fredonia / The SUNY at Fredonia	NY	18,702	VC
Univ of Denver	CO	51,787	VC+
Univ of Idaho	ID	14,558	C
Webster Univ	MO	33,990	C+
Woodbury Univ	CA	34,500	LC

ANTHROPOLOGY

School	ST	$IS	SR
Adelphi Univ	NY	43,130	VC
Agnes Scott College	GA	45,323	VC+
Albion College	MI	43,884	VC
Alma College	MI	42,400	VC
American Univ	DC	54,829	HC+
Amherst College	MA	58,744	MC
Andrews Univ	MI	28,030	C+
Appalachian State Univ	NC	12,919	VC
Arizona State Univ	AZ	18,818	C+
Auburn Univ	AL	20,052	VC+
Augustana College	IL	43,398	HC
Augustana College	SD	35,500	VC
Ball State Univ	IN	17,850	C
Bard College	NY	59,872	HC
Bates College	ME	58,950	MC
Baylor Univ	TX	46,720	HC
Beloit College	WI	49,970	HC
Bennington College	VT	56,990	HC+
Berry College	GA	39,254	HC
Binghamton Univ / The SUNY	NY	20,832	HC+
Biola Univ	CA	40,320	VC
Bloomsburg Univ of Pennsylvania	PA	13,598	C
Boise State Univ	ID	12,802	C
Boston Univ	MA	54,130	HC+
Bowdoin College	ME	57,834	MC
Brandeis Univ	MA	58,820	HC
Bridgewater State Univ	MA	18,752	C
Brigham Young Univ	UT	12,100	HC
Brown Univ	RI	56,150	MC
Bryn Mawr College	PA	57,760	MC
Bucknell Univ	PA	58,160	MC
Buffalo State/State Univ of Buffalo	NY	15,733	C+
Butler Univ	IN	45,898	VC+
Calif Baptist Univ	CA	35,890	C
Calif Polytechnic State Univ	CA	19,847	HC
Calif State Polytechnic Univ, Pomona	CA	18,932	C
Cal State, Bakersfield	CA	8,000	LC
Cal State, Chico	CA	18,952	C
Cal State, Dominguez Hills	CA	17,056	LC
Cal State, East Bay	CA	16,549	C
Cal State, Fresno	CA	17,405	C
Cal State, Fullerton	CA	25,188	C+
Cal State, Long Beach	CA	17,534	C+
Cal State, Los Angeles	CA	15,829	C
Cal State, Northridge	CA	28,313	C
Cal State, Sacramento	CA	16,200	C
Cal State, San Bernardino	CA	12,000	C
Cal State, Stanislaus	CA	18,582	C
Canisius College	NY	45,602	VC
Carleton College	MN	58,149	MC
Case Western Reserve Univ	OH	55,178	MC
Central College	IA	36,980	VC
Central Conn State Univ	CT	19,212	C
Central Mich Univ	MI	18,066	C
Central Washington Univ	WA	11,730	C
Centre College	KY	35,000	HC+
CUNY/Brooklyn College	NY	5,884	C+
Clarion Univ of Pennsylvania	PA	17,370	C
Cleveland State Univ	OH	21,357	C
Colby College	ME	57,510	MC
College of Charleston	SC	21,273	VC
College of the Holy Cross	MA	56,232	MC
College of William & Mary	VA	25,085	MC
College of Wooster	OH	52,600	VC
Colo College	CO	54,534	MC
Colo State Univ-Fort Collins	CO	20,090	VC
Columbia Univ in the City of New York	NY	61,116	MC
Columbia Univ/Barnard College	NY	39,000	MC
Columbia Univ/School of General Studies	NY	54,083	MC
Conn College	CT	54,970	MC
Cornell Univ	NY	59,037	MC
Creighton Univ	NE	44,058	VC+
CUNY-City College	NY	19,576	HC+
Dartmouth College	NH	57,996	MC
Davidson College	NC	54,683	MC
Denison Univ	OH	54,670	HC+
DePaul Univ	IL	46,120	VC
DePauw Univ	IN	48,950	VC+
Dickinson College	PA	57,662	HC+
Drew Univ/College of Liberal Arts	NJ	55,862	VC
Duke Univ	NC	50,250	MC
Earlham College	IN	49,710	VC+
East Carolina Univ	NC	14,169	C
Eastern Kentucky Univ	KY	11,161	C
Eastern Mich Univ	MI	17,961	C
Eastern New Mexico Univ	NM	10,682	C
Eastern Oregon Univ	OR	10,400	C
Eastern Washington Univ	WA	16,388	C
Eckerd College	FL	43,902	VC
Edinboro Univ of Pennsylvania	PA	15,940	LC
Elmira College	NY	49,950	C+
Elon Univ	NC	40,046	HC
Emory Univ	GA	45,000	MC
Eugene Lang College - The New School for Liberal Arts	NY	55,650	VC
Florida Atlantic Univ	FL	17,339	C
Florida Gulf Coast Univ	FL		C
Florida State Univ	FL	15,238	HC
Fordham Univ	NY	58,927	HC
Fort Lewis College	CO	15,513	C
Franciscan Univ of Steubenville	OH	27,320	VC
Franklin and Marshall College	PA	58,295	MC
Franklin Pierce Univ	NH	41,598	C
George Mason Univ	VA	15,724	VC
George Washington Univ	DC	57,108	MC
Georgetown Univ	DC	52,910	MC
Georgia Southern Univ	GA	16,414	C
Georgia State Univ	GA	12,000	VC
Gettysburg College	PA	56,820	HC
Goucher College	MD	50,252	VC+
Grand Valley State Univ	MI	17,998	VC
Grinnell College	IA	53,654	HC
Guilford College	NC	35,310	C
Gustavus Adolphus College	MN	48,170	HC
Hamilton College	NY	55,620	MC
Hamline Univ	MN	44,198	VC
Hampshire College	MA	58,320	MC
Hanover College	IN	41,450	VC
Hartwick College	NY	49,815	C+
Harvard Univ/Harvard College	MA	49,000	MC
Haverford College	PA	59,236	MC
Hawaii Pacific Univ	HI	36,690	C
Heidelberg Univ	OH	34,100	C
Hendrix College	AR	48,436	HC+
Hobart and William Smith Colleges	NY	43,000	VC
Hofstra Univ	NY	48,020	VC+
Howard Univ	DC	35,957	C
Humboldt State Univ	CA	18,400	C
Hunter College / The CUNY	NY	14,429	VC
Idaho State Univ	ID	11,908	C
Illinois State Univ	IL	22,634	VC
Illinois Wesleyan Univ	IL	48,452	VC+
Indiana State Univ	IN	16,000	C
Indiana Univ Bloomington	IN	19,358	HC
Indiana Univ Northwest	IN	6,738	LC
Indiana Univ of Pennsylvania	PA	20,180	LC
Indiana Univ South Bend	IN	15,293	C
Indiana Univ-Purdue Univ Fort Wayne	IN	15,425	C
Indiana Univ-Purdue Univ Indianapolis	IN	17,290	C
Iowa State Univ	IA	16,403	C
Ithaca College	NY	52,300	HC
James Madison Univ	VA	18,049	VC
Johns Hopkins Univ	MD	47,492	MC
Johnson State College	VT	16,721	C
Judson Univ	IL	25,130	C
Juniata College	PA	49,340	VC
Kalamazoo College	MI	47,825	HC+
Kansas State Univ	KS	15,497	VC
Keene State College	NH	21,538	C
Kennesaw State Univ	GA	13,017	VC
Kent State Univ	OH	19,352	C
Kenyon College	OH	56,810	MC
Knox College	IL		VC
Kutztown Univ of Pennsylvania	PA	16,909	LC
Lafayette College	PA	57,050	HC+
Lake Forest College	IL	45,580	VC
Lawrence Univ	WI	46,371	HC
Le Moyne College	NY	42,200	VC
Lee Univ	TN	18,690	C+
Lehigh Univ	PA	55,080	MC
Lehman College / The CUNY	NY	5,778	LC
Lewis & Clark College	OR	52,656	VC
Linfield College-McMinnville Campus	OR	46,166	C
LIU/Brooklyn Campus	NY	26,500	C
Longwood Univ	VA	20,924	C
Louisiana State Univ	LA	18,677	VC+
Loyola Univ Chicago	IL	49,560	VC+
Loyola Univ New Orleans	LA	46,581	VC
Luther College	IA	44,380	VC+
Lycoming College	PA	43,636	C
Macalester College	MN	53,419	MC
Mansfield Univ	PA	19,468	LC
Marlboro College	VT	35,980	VC
Marquette Univ	WI	43,664	VC+
Mary Baldwin College	VA	37,110	C
Mass Inst of Technology	MA	54,238	MC
Mercer Univ	GA	44,201	VC+
Mercyhurst Univ	PA	40,700	C
Metropolitan State Univ of Denver	CO	4,835	LC
Miami Univ	OH	24,191	HC
Mich State Univ	MI	13,689	VC
Mich Tech Univ	MI	22,105	VC
Middle Tenn State Univ	TN	8,650	C
Middlebury College	VT	57,470	MC
Millersville Univ of Pennsylvania	PA	18,498	C
Mills College	CA	54,119	HC
Millsaps College	MS	43,888	VC+
Minn State Univ, Mankato	MN	14,900	C
Minn State Univ, Moorhead	MN	13,392	C
Missouri State Univ	MO	13,996	VC
Missouri Valley College	MO	22,200	C
Monmouth College	IL	39,290	C
Monmouth Univ	NJ	42,252	C
Montana State Univ	MT	14,068	VC
Montclair State Univ	NJ	22,614	C
Mount Holyoke College	MA	53,596	HC+
Muhlenberg College	PA	52,837	HC
National Louis Univ	IL	16,915	LC
Nazareth College of Rochester	NY	41,590	VC
New College of Florida	FL	14,504	HC+
New Mexico Highlands Univ	NM	9,720	NC
New Mexico State Univ	NM	13,955	LC
New York Univ	NY	61,470	MC
North Central College	IL	38,343	VC
N Dak State Univ	ND	14,642	C
North Park Univ	IL	30,130	C
Northeastern Illinois Univ	IL		C
Northeastern Univ	MA	55,296	MC
Northern Arizona Univ	AZ	18,592	C
Northern Illinois Univ	IL	19,768	C
Northern Kentucky Univ	KY	15,302	LC
Northwestern Univ	IL	37,595	MC
Nova Southeastern Univ	FL	34,016	VC
Oakland Univ	MI	19,391	VC
Oberlin College	OH	57,025	MC
Ohio Univ	OH	20,676	VC
Ohio Wesleyan Univ	OH	49,460	C+
Olivet College	MI	19,984	C
Oregon State Univ	OR	19,017	C+
Oswego / SUNY	NY	20,009	VC
Pacific Lutheran Univ	WA	44,840	VC
Penn State Univ/Univ Park	PA	25,404	VC
Pitzer College	CA	54,988	MC
Plymouth State Univ	NH	23,148	LC
Pomona College	CA	57,680	MC
Portland State Univ	OR	18,672	C
Prescott College	AZ	33,284	C+
Princeton Univ	NJ	53,795	MC
Purchase College / SUNY	NY	16,951	C
Purdue Univ/West Lafayette	IN	20,278	HC
Queens College / The CUNY	NY	17,107	VC
Radford Univ	VA	17,132	LC
Reed College	OR	57,780	MC
Rhode Island College	RI	17,132	LC
Rhodes College	TN	47,596	HC+
Rice Univ	TX	43,288	MC
Richard Stockton College of New Jersey	NJ	20,000	VC
Ripon College	WI	36,959	C+
Rockford College	IL	31,000	C
Rocky Mountain College	MT	32,242	C
Roger Williams Univ	RI	45,788	C
Rollins College	FL	52,370	HC
Rutgers, The State Univ of New Jersey/New Brunswick	NJ	25,077	VC
Rutgers, The State Univ of New Jersey/Newark Campus	NJ	25,376	C
St. Louis Univ	MO	46,594	VC+
St. Mary's College of Calif	CA	53,550	C
St. Michael's College	VT	48,740	VC
St. Vincent College	PA	40,244	C
San Diego State Univ	CA	20,578	VC
San Francisco State Univ	CA	18,514	C
San Jose State Univ	CA	19,707	C
Santa Clara Univ	CA	54,702	MC
Sarah Lawrence College	NY	48,000	HC
Scripps College	CA	54,900	MC
Seattle Univ	WA	47,010	VC+
Seton Hall Univ	NJ	45,902	C
Sewanee: The Univ of the South	TN	47,700	HC+
Skidmore College	NY	57,926	HC
Slippery Rock Univ of Pennsylvania	PA	10,360	LC
Smith College	MA	57,524	MC
Sonoma State Univ	CA	20,541	C
Southern Illinois Univ Carbondale	IL	21,620	C
Southern Illinois Univ Edwardsville	IL	17,532	C
Southern Methodist Univ	TX	57,755	MC
Southern Oregon Univ	OR	17,874	C
Southwestern Univ	TX	45,660	VC
Spelman College	GA	24,650	VC
St. Cloud State Univ	MN	10,600	C
St. John Fisher College	NY	39,370	C+
St. John's Univ	NY	52,840	C+
St. Lawrence Univ	NY	53,740	HC

School	ST	$IS	SR
St. Mary's College of Maryland	MD	26,699	HC
Stanford Univ	CA	56,411	MC
Stony Brook Univ / SUNY	NY	19,359	HC
SUNY College at Geneseo	NY	18,055	HC+
SUNY Cortland / The SUNY	NY	19,117	C
SUNY New Paltz	NY	15,010	C
SUNY Oneonta / SUNY	NY	16,919	VC
SUNY Plattsburgh / SUNY	NY	18,083	VC
Susquehanna Univ	PA	49,170	C
Swarthmore College	PA	57,870	MC
Sweet Briar College	VA	43,765	C+
Syracuse Univ	NY	54,512	HC
Temple Univ	PA	24,392	VC
Texas A&M Univ	TX	16,956	VC+
Texas A&M Univ at Commerce	TX	10,496	C
Texas A&M Univ at Kingsville	TX	7,500	LC
Texas Christian Univ	TX	47,570	HC
Texas State Univ	TX	16,495	VC
Texas Tech Univ	TX	14,243	C
The Catholic Univ of America	DC	52,852	VC
The College at Brockport / SUNY	NY	18,362	VC
The College of Idaho	ID	31,277	VC
The Lincoln Univ	PA	15,154	LC
Ohio State Univ	OH	19,887	MC
The SUNY at Potsdam	NY	17,754	C
Thomas Edison State College	NJ	5,700	SP
Towson Univ	MD	16,000	VC
Transylvania Univ	KY	40,310	VC+
Trinity College	CT		HC+
Trinity Univ	TX	44,174	HC+
Truman State Univ	MO	13,546	HC
Tufts Univ	MA	58,780	MC
Tulane Univ	LA	58,942	MC
Union College	NY		MC
Univ at Albany / SUNY	NY	18,674	VC
Univ at Buffalo / The SUNY	NY	20,283	VC
Univ of Akron	OH	20,436	C
Univ of Alabama at Birmingham	AL	18,484	C+
Univ of Alabama at Tuscaloosa	AL	17,164	C+
Univ of Alaska Anchorage	AK	15,290	NC
Univ of Alaska Fairbanks	AK	13,955	C
Univ of Arizona	AZ	20,105	C
Univ of Arkansas at Fayetteville	AR	16,860	VC
Univ of Calif at Berkeley	CA	23,322	MC
Univ of Calif at Davis	CA	24,482	HC
Univ of Calif at Irvine	CA	25,961	VC
Univ of Calif at Los Angeles	CA	25,686	MC
Univ of Calif at Riverside	CA	27,204	C
Univ of Calif at San Diego	CA	21,000	VC
Univ of Calif at Santa Barbara	CA	27,551	HC
Univ of Calif at Santa Cruz	CA	27,807	VC
Univ of Central Florida	FL	15,711	VC+
Univ of Chicago	IL	55,416	MC
Univ of Cincinnati	OH	20,199	VC
Univ of Colo at Colo Springs	CO	15,000	VC
Univ of Colo Boulder	CO	22,605	VC+
Univ of Colo Denver	CO	17,904	C
Univ of Conn	CT	23,744	HC
Univ of Delaware	DE	22,728	VC
Univ of Denver	CO	51,787	VC+
Univ of Florida	FL	15,783	HC+
Univ of Georgia	GA	19,508	VC
Univ of Hawaii at Hilo	HI	6,500	C
Univ of Hawaii at Manoa	HI	19,379	VC
Univ of Houston	TX	19,184	VC
Univ of Idaho	ID	14,558	C
Univ of Illinois at Chicago	IL	24,293	VC
Univ of Illinois at Urbana-Champaign	IL	24,300	HC
Univ of Indianapolis	IN	31,740	LC
Univ of Iowa	IA	17,481	VC
Univ of Kansas	KS	16,980	C+
Univ of Kentucky	KY	19,868	C
Univ of La Verne	CA	47,010	VC
Univ of Louisiana at Lafayette	LA	6,130	C
Univ of Louisville	KY	17,460	VC
Univ of Maine	ME	19,712	C+
Univ of Mary Washington	VA	19,484	VC
Univ of Maryland	MD	18,801	HC
Univ of Maryland/Baltimore County	MD	18,000	VC
Univ of Mass Amherst	MA	23,697	VC+
Univ of Mass Boston	MA	11,966	C
Univ of Mass Dartmouth	MA	22,223	C
Univ of Memphis	TN	15,094	C
Univ of Miami	FL	55,166	MC
Univ of Mich/Ann Arbor	MI	22,102	HC+
Univ of Mich/Dearborn	MI	9,885	VC
Univ of Mich-Flint	MI	17,547	C+
Univ of Minn/Duluth	MN	18,964	C+
Univ of Minn/Morris	MN	17,150	VC
Univ of Minn/Twin Cities	MN		HC
Univ of Miss	MS	15,482	VC
Univ of Missouri/Columbia	MO	18,201	MC
Univ of Missouri-St. Louis	MO	18,304	VC
Univ of Montana	MT	13,670	C
Univ of Montana-Western	MT	9,753	LC
Univ of Nebr - Lincoln	NE	17,507	VC
Univ of Nevada, Las Vegas	NV	17,303	C
Univ of Nevada/Reno	NV	14,500	NC
Univ of New Hampshire	NH	24,702	VC
Univ of New Mexico	NM	15,300	C
Univ of New Orleans	LA	9,224	VC
Univ of N Car at Asheville	NC	13,500	VC+
Univ of N Car at Chapel Hill	NC	18,348	MC
Univ of N Car at Charlotte	NC	15,847	C
Univ of N Car at Greensboro	NC	12,848	C
Univ of N Car at Wilmington	NC	13,572	VC+
Univ of N Dak	ND	14,094	C
Univ of North Florida	FL	15,578	VC
Univ of North Texas	TX	15,628	C
Univ of Northern Colo	CO	15,973	C
Univ of Northern Iowa	IA	14,776	C
Univ of Notre Dame	IN		MC
Univ of Okla	OK	17,634	VC+
Univ of Oregon	OR	20,872	VC
Univ of Pennsylvania	PA	56,106	MC
Univ of Pittsburgh at Greensburg	PA	17,640	C
Univ of Pittsburgh at Pittsburgh	PA	27,800	HC+
Univ of PR Recinto de Rio Piedras	PR	5,750	
Univ of Redlands	CA	40,500	VC
Univ of Rochester	NY	58,500	MC
Univ of San Diego	CA	53,302	HC+
Univ of South Alabama	AL	13,510	C
Univ of S Car at Columbia	SC	19,725	VC+
Univ of S Dak	SD	15,111	C
Univ of South Florida	FL	13,000	C
Univ of South Florida/St. Petersburg	FL	12,769	VC
Univ of Southern Calif	CA	56,903	MC
Univ of Southern Indiana	IN	14,657	C
Univ of Southern Maine	ME	16,576	C
Univ of Southern Miss	MS	13,170	C
Univ of Tenn at Knoxville	TN	20,364	VC+
Univ of Texas at Arlington	TX	10,908	LC
Univ of Texas at Austin	TX	44,074	HC
Univ of Texas at El Paso	TX	8,764	NC
Univ of Texas at San Antonio	TX	18,372	C
Univ of Texas-Pan American	TX	12,432	LC
Univ of Toledo	OH	18,464	C
Univ of Tulsa	OK	45,311	HC+
Univ of Utah	UT	13,462	VC
Univ of Vermont	VT	26,120	VC+
Univ of Virginia	VA	22,175	MC
Univ of Washington	WA	14,722	VC
Univ of West Georgia	GA	14,852	LC
Univ of Wisc/Madison	WI	18,757	HC
Univ of Wisc/Oshkosh	WI	10,426	LC
Univ of Wisc-Milwaukee	WI	18,436	C
Univ of Wyoming	WY	13,855	C+
Ursinus College	PA	55,630	VC+
Vanderbilt Univ	TN	57,072	MC
Vanguard Univ of Southern Calif	CA	35,833	VC
Vassar College	NY	59,070	MC
Virginia Commonwealth Univ	VA	18,633	C
Wagner College	NY	48,600	VC
Wake Forest Univ	NC	51,000	MC
Warren Wilson College	NC	34,888	VC
Washburn Univ	KS	12,165	NC
Washington and Lee Univ	VA	52,812	MC
Washington College	MD	48,768	VC
Washington State Univ	WA	20,461	C
Washington Univ in St. Louis	MO	58,818	MC
Wayne State Univ	MI	19,493	C
Wellesley College	MA	49,848	MC
Wells College	NY	38,680	VC
Wesleyan Univ	CT	59,844	MC
West Chester Univ of Pennsylvania	PA	16,836	C
West Virginia Univ	WV	15,794	C+
Western Carolina Univ	NC	13,965	C+
Western Conn State Univ	CT	18,327	C
Western Illinois Univ	IL	20,130	C
Western Kentucky Univ	KY	11,000	LC
Western Mich Univ	MI	19,042	C
Western Oregon Univ	OR	15,021	C
Western State Colo Univ	CO	16,135	C
Western Washington Univ	WA	18,519	VC
Westminster College	MO	30,490	VC
Wheaton College	IL	39,650	HC+
Wheaton College	MA	54,934	HC+
Whitman College	WA	54,400	MC
Wichita State Univ	KS	12,539	C
Widener Univ	PA	50,368	C
Willamette Univ	OR	56,450	VC+
William Paterson Univ of New Jersey	NJ	21,694	C
Williams College	MA	58,900	MC
Wright State Univ	OH	16,983	C
Yale Univ	CT	55,300	MC
York College / CUNY	NY	5,496	NC
Youngstown State Univ	OH	16,374	LC

APPAREL AND ACCESSORIES MARKETING

School	ST	$IS	SR
Auburn Univ	AL	20,052	VC+
Calif State Polytechnic Univ, Pomona	CA	18,932	C
Cheyney Univ of Pennsylvania	PA	20,372	LC
Colo State Univ-Fort Collins	CO	20,090	VC
Dominican Univ	IL	37,628	C
Eastern Mich Univ	MI	17,961	C
Fashion Inst of Technology/SUNY	NY	12,468	SP
Fontbonne Univ	MO	31,384	C
Indiana Univ Bloomington	IN	19,358	HC
Kansas State Univ	KS	15,497	VC
Kentucky State Univ	KY	11,000	LC
S Dak State Univ	SD	14,296	C
Univ of Arkansas at Fayetteville	AR	16,860	VC
Univ of Nebr - Lincoln	NE	17,507	VC
Univ of N Car at Greensboro	NC	12,848	C
Virginia Polytechnic Inst and State Univ	VA	14,629	HC
Youngstown State Univ	OH	16,374	LC

APPAREL AND TEXTILES

School	ST	$IS	SR
Missouri State Univ	MO	13,996	VC
Southern Polytechnic State Univ	GA	13,958	VC
Univ of Nebr - Lincoln	NE	17,507	VC

APPAREL DESIGN

School	ST	$IS	SR
Appalachian State Univ	NC	12,919	VC
Art Inst of Portland	OR	23,040	SP
Auburn Univ	AL	20,052	VC+
Boston Univ	MA	54,130	HC+
Bowling Green State Univ	OH	18,970	C
Central Mich Univ	MI	18,066	C
Colo State Univ-Fort Collins	CO	20,090	VC
Dominican Univ	IL	37,628	C
Florida State Univ	FL	15,238	HC
Kansas State Univ	KS	15,497	VC
Kent State Univ	OH	19,352	C
N Dak State Univ	ND	14,642	C
Oregon State Univ	OR	19,017	C+
Purdue Univ/West Lafayette	IN	20,278	HC
Rhode Island School of Design	RI	55,204	SP
San Francisco State Univ	CA	18,514	C
Texas Tech Univ	TX	14,243	C
Univ of Delaware	DE	22,728	VC
Univ of Hawaii at Manoa	HI	19,379	VC
Univ of Idaho	ID	14,558	C
Univ of Minn/Twin Cities	MN		HC
Univ of Nebr - Lincoln	NE	17,507	VC
Univ of Wisc/Stout	WI	23,942	C
Western Washington Univ	WA	18,519	VC

APPLIED ART

School	ST	$IS	SR
Centenary College	NJ	38,618	LC
Daemen College	NY	31,510	C
Edinboro Univ of Pennsylvania	PA	15,940	LC
Georgian Court Univ	NJ	39,726	LC
Goddard College	VT	16,418	VC
Marshall Univ	WV	14,820	C
Memphis College of Art	TN	33,550	SP
Oral Roberts Univ	OK	31,734	C
Oregon State Univ	OR	19,017	C+
Point Park Univ	PA	36,390	C
Roberts Wesleyan College	NY	37,384	C+
Rochester Inst of Technology	NY	42,450	VC+
Santa Fe Univ of Art and Design	NM	39,666	SP
Tabor College	KS	29,010	LC
Texas State Univ	TX	16,495	VC
Univ of Idaho	ID	14,558	C
Univ of Maine at Presque Isle	ME	15,011	LC
Univ of North Texas	TX	15,628	C
West Texas A&M Univ	TX	13,478	C

APPLIED AVIATION

School	ST	$IS	SR
Calif Baptist Univ	CA	35,890	C
Eastern Mich Univ	MI	17,961	C
Univ of Minn Crookston	MN	17,834	C

APPLIED ECONOMICS / MANAGEMENT

School	ST	$IS	SR
Bryant Univ	RI	49,179	VC
Cornell Univ	NY	59,037	MC
Farmingdale State College	NY	18,985	C
Ithaca College	NY	52,300	HC

APPLIED MATHEMATICS

School	ST	$IS	SR
American Univ	DC	54,829	HC+
Andrews Univ	MI	28,030	C+
Arizona State Univ	AZ	18,818	C+
Asbury Univ	KY	32,038	VC
Auburn Univ	AL	20,052	VC+
Baylor Univ	TX	46,720	HC
Belmont Univ	TN	37,380	VC+
Berea College	KY	7,220	HC
Bethany College	WV	35,282	C
Biola Univ	CA	40,320	VC
Bloomfield College	NJ	36,960	C
Brown Univ	RI	56,150	MC
Bryant Univ	RI	49,179	VC
Calif Inst of Technology	CA	54,045	MC
Cal State, Chico	CA	18,952	C
Cal State, Fullerton	CA	25,188	C+
Cal State, Long Beach	CA	17,534	C+
Case Western Reserve Univ	OH	55,178	MC
Christopher Newport Univ	VA	21,050	VC
Clarkson Univ	NY	53,538	HC
Colby College	ME	57,510	MC
Colo State Univ-Fort Collins	CO	20,090	VC
Columbia Univ in the City of New York	NY	61,116	MC
Columbia Univ/School of General Studies	NY	54,083	MC
DePaul Univ	IL	46,120	VC
Dowling College	NY	25,000	LC
East Central Univ	OK	10,223	LC
Eastern Mich Univ	MI	17,961	C
Elizabethtown College	PA	47,600	VC
Elon Univ	NC	40,046	HC
Endicott College	MA	42,390	C
Farmingdale State College	NY	18,985	C
Ferris State Univ	MI	19,698	C
Fitchburg State Univ	MA	17,241	C
Florida Inst of Technology	FL	48,290	VC
Florida State Univ	FL	15,238	HC
Geneva College	PA	27,280	C
George Washington Univ	DC	57,108	MC
Georgia Inst of Technology	GA	20,464	MC
Hampden-Sydney College	VA	48,848	C
Harvard Univ/Harvard College	MA	49,000	MC
Hawaii Pacific Univ	HI	36,690	C
Hofstra Univ	NY	48,020	VC+
Illinois Inst of Technology	IL	38,512	HC+
Indiana Univ South Bend	IN	15,293	C
Iona College	NY	44,028	C
Johns Hopkins Univ	MD	47,492	MC
Johnson C. Smith Univ	NC	25,336	LC
Kent State Univ	OH	19,352	C
Kentucky State Univ	KY	11,000	LC
Kettering Univ	MI	31,456	HC
Lasell College	MA	42,500	LC
Le Moyne College	NY	42,200	VC
Lipscomb Univ	TN	35,722	VC
Marshall Univ	WV	14,820	C
Mary Baldwin College	VA	37,110	C
Metropolitan State Univ	MN	5,923	SP
Millsaps College	MS	43,888	VC+
Missouri Univ of Science and Technology	MO	18,655	VC+
Montclair State Univ	NJ	22,614	C
New College of Florida	FL	14,504	HC+
New Jersey Inst of Technology	NJ	26,490	VC
New York City College of Technology / The CUNY	NY	5,769	NC
North Central College	IL	38,343	VC
Northwestern Univ	IL	37,595	MC
Oberlin College	OH	57,025	MC
Ohio Univ	OH	20,676	VC
Old Dominion Univ	VA	18,662	C
Oswego / SUNY	NY	20,009	VC
Pacific Union College	CA	28,150	VC
Piedmont College	GA	29,260	C
Purdue Univ/West Lafayette	IN	20,278	HC
Rice Univ	TX	43,288	MC
Robert Morris Univ	PA	36,699	C
Rochester Inst of Technology	NY	42,450	VC+
Rutgers, The State Univ of New Jersey/Newark Campus	NJ	25,376	C
Saginaw Valley State Univ	MI	16,869	C
St. Augustine's Univ	NC	14,000	C
San Diego State Univ	CA	20,578	VC
San Francisco State Univ	CA	18,514	C
San Jose State Univ	CA	19,707	C
Seattle Univ	WA	47,010	VC+
Southern Illinois Univ Edwardsville	IL	17,532	C
SUNY Inst of Technology at Utica / Rome	NY	23,818	C
Stevenson Univ	MD	39,572	C
Stony Brook Univ / SUNY	NY	19,359	HC
Temple Univ	PA	24,392	VC
Tufts Univ	MA	58,780	MC
Univ at Albany / SUNY	NY	18,674	VC
Univ of Akron	OH	20,436	C
Univ of Arizona	AZ	20,105	C

School	ST	$IS	SR
Univ of Arkansas at Little Rock	AR		C
Univ of Arkansas at Pine Bluff	AR	10,600	C
Univ of Calif at Berkeley	CA	23,322	MC
Univ of Calif at Los Angeles	CA	25,686	MC
Univ of Calif at San Diego	CA	21,000	VC
Univ of Central Arkansas	AR	10,840	VC
Univ of Central Okla	OK	12,293	C
Univ of Chicago	IL	55,416	MC
Univ of Colo Boulder	CO	22,605	VC+
Univ of Houston-Downtown	TX	6,267	LC
Univ of Idaho	ID	14,558	C
Univ of Mass Lowell	MA	19,316	C
Univ of Miami	FL	55,166	MC
Univ of Montana-Western	MT	9,753	LC
Univ of New Haven	CT	47,740	C
Univ of N Car at Chapel Hill	NC	18,348	MC
Univ of North Florida	FL	15,578	VC
Univ of Pittsburgh at Bradford	PA	21,316	LC
Univ of Pittsburgh at Greensburg	PA	17,640	C
Univ of Pittsburgh at Pittsburgh	PA	27,800	HC+
Univ of PR Recinto de Rio Piedras	PR	5,750	
Univ of Rochester	NY	58,500	MC
Univ of S Car at Aiken	SC	16,278	C
Univ of Southern Calif	CA	56,903	MC
Univ of St. Thomas - Houston	TX	30,490	VC
Univ of Tenn at Chattanooga	TN	16,883	C
Univ of Texas at El Paso	TX	8,764	NC
Univ of the Pacific	CA	52,146	VC
Univ of Tulsa	OK	45,311	HC+
Univ of Utah	UT	13,462	VC
Univ of Wisc/Madison	WI	18,757	HC
Univ of Wisc/Stout	WI	23,942	C
Univ of Wisc-Milwaukee	WI	18,436	C
Washington State Univ	WA	20,461	C
Washington Univ in St. Louis	MO	58,818	MC
West Virginia State Univ	WV	8,378	NC
Western Mich Univ	MI	19,042	C
Western Washington Univ	WA	18,519	VC
Wofford College	SC	45,795	VC
Wright State Univ	OH	16,983	C
Yale Univ	CT	55,300	MC
Youngstown State Univ	OH	16,374	LC

APPLIED MUSIC

School	ST	$IS	SR
Baldwin Wallace Univ	OH	36,980	VC
Baylor Univ	TX	46,720	HC
Concordia College New York	NY	31,500	VC
Cornerstone Univ and Grand Rapids Theological Seminary	MI	30,866	C
Dallas Baptist Univ	TX	29,118	C
Eastern Mich Univ	MI	17,961	C
Geneva College	PA	27,280	C
Indiana Wesleyan Univ	IN	31,815	VC
Inter-American Univ of PR/ Fajardo Campus	PR	4,200	
Inter-American Univ of PR/ Ponce	PR	3,700	
Judson College	AL	24,690	C
Kansas State Univ	KS	15,497	VC
Lenoir-Rhyne College	NC	35,984	C
Mannes College New School for Music	NY	44,500	C
Meredith College	NC	31,420	C
Miss College	MS	21,998	VC
Nebr Wesleyan Univ	NE	29,774	C+
New England Conservatory of Music	MA	52,550	SP
Newberry College	SC	26,850	LC
Ouachita Baptist Univ	AR	29,010	VC
Roberts Wesleyan College	NY	37,384	C+
Seton Hall Univ	NJ	45,902	C
Trinity Christian College	IL	28,869	C
Univ of Delaware	DE	22,728	VC
Univ of Houston	TX	19,184	VC
Univ of Idaho	ID	14,558	C
Univ of Illinois at Chicago	IL	24,293	VC
Univ of Nevada/Reno	NV	14,500	NC
Univ of Texas at Austin	TX	44,074	HC
Wartburg College	IA	41,055	VC
Youngstown State Univ	OH	16,374	LC

APPLIED PHYSICS

School	ST	$IS	SR
Angelo State Univ	TX	15,049	NC
Armstrong Atlantic State Univ	GA	16,276	C
Beloit College	WI	49,970	HC
Bethel Univ	MN	34,940	VC
Bridgewater College	VA	39,880	C
Cal State, San Bernardino	CA	12,000	C
Cal State, Stanislaus	CA	18,582	C
Christopher Newport Univ	VA	21,050	VC
Columbia Univ in the City of New York	NY	61,116	MC
Creighton Univ	NE	44,058	VC+
East Carolina Univ	NC	14,169	C
Georgia Inst of Technology	GA	20,464	MC
Hofstra Univ	NY	48,020	VC+
Houghton College	NY	35,740	VC
Kettering Univ	MI	31,456	HC
Linfield College-McMinnville Campus	OR	46,166	C
Marietta College	OH	42,135	VC
Mich Tech Univ	MI	22,105	VC
New Jersey Inst of Technology	NJ	26,490	VC
Northeastern Univ	MA	55,296	MC
Ohio Univ	OH	20,676	VC
Pacific Lutheran Univ	WA	44,840	VC
Piedmont College	GA	29,260	C
Providence College	RI	55,995	HC
Purdue Univ/West Lafayette	IN	20,278	HC
Rensselaer Polytechnic Inst	NY	59,229	MC
Rutgers, The State Univ of New Jersey/Newark Campus	NJ	25,376	C
Shippensburg Univ of Pennsylvania	PA	17,064	LC
SUNY College at Geneseo	NY	18,055	HC+
Tufts Univ	MA	58,780	MC
Univ of Alaska Fairbanks	AK	13,955	C
Univ of Calif at San Diego	CA	21,000	VC
Univ of Iowa	IA	17,481	VC
Univ of Minn/Duluth	MN	18,964	C+
Univ of Nevada, Las Vegas	NV	17,303	C
Univ of Notre Dame	IN		MC
Western Washington Univ	WA	18,519	VC
Wheeling Jesuit Univ	WV	34,668	C
Whitworth Univ	WA	45,826	VC+
Xavier Univ	OH	43,740	VC
Yale Univ	CT	55,300	MC

APPLIED PSYCHOLOGY

School	ST	$IS	SR
Arizona State Univ	AZ	18,818	C+
Belmont Abbey College	NC	37,716	C
Biola Univ	CA	40,320	VC
Boston College	MA	58,506	MC
Bryant Univ	RI	49,179	VC
Cal State, Chico	CA	18,952	C
Cedarville Univ	OH	31,036	VC+
Christian Brothers Univ	TN	19,140	HC
College of St. Mary	NE	34,334	C
Coppin State Univ	MD	14,905	VC
Farmingdale State College	NY	18,985	C
Franklin Univ	OH	7,000	SP
Ithaca College	NY	52,300	HC
Loyola Univ Chicago	IL	49,560	VC+
Mayville State Univ	ND	11,401	NC
New York Univ	NY	61,470	MC
Pace Univ	NY	48,094	VC
Russell Sage College	NY	39,370	C
The SUNY College of Agriculture and Tech at Cobleskill	NY	18,869	VC
Univ of Illinois at Chicago	IL	24,293	VC
Univ of Mich-Flint	MI	17,547	C+
Univ of North Texas	TX	15,628	C+
Univ of Pittsburgh at Pittsburgh	PA	27,800	HC+
Univ of St. Mary	KS	28,400	C+
Wright State Univ	OH	16,983	C

APPLIED SCIENCE

School	ST	$IS	SR
Alcorn State Univ	MS	9,500	C
Arizona State Univ	AZ	18,818	C+
Concordia College, Moorhead	MN	39,974	C+
Florida Gulf Coast Univ	FL		C
Granite State College	NH	6,195	SP
Indiana Univ Bloomington	IN	19,358	HC
Lehigh Univ	PA	55,080	MC
Madonna Univ	MI	24,540	VC
Northern Arizona Univ	AZ	18,592	C
Saginaw Valley State Univ	MI	16,869	C
Southern Polytechnic State Univ	GA	13,958	VC
Southwest Minn State Univ	MN	14,000	C
Southwestern Univ	TX	45,660	VC
Texas Lutheran Univ	TX	34,070	C
Univ of Arizona	AZ	20,105	C
Univ of Arkansas at Monticello	AR	8,470	NC
Univ of Central Florida	FL	15,711	VC+
Univ of Maine at Augusta	ME	6,855	C
Univ of Mich-Flint	MI	17,547	C+
Univ of Nebr - Lincoln	NE	17,507	VC
Univ of N Car at Chapel Hill	NC	18,348	MC
Univ of Pennsylvania	PA	56,106	MC
Univ of Wisc/Stout	WI	23,942	C
Winona State Univ	MN	16,530	C

APPLIED SOCIAL SCIENCE

School	ST	$IS	SR
Bryant Univ	RI	49,179	VC
East Carolina Univ	NC	14,169	C
Univ of Wisc/Stout	WI	23,942	C

ARABIC

School	ST	$IS	SR
American Univ	DC	54,829	HC+
Bard College	NY	59,872	HC
Binghamton Univ / The SUNY	NY	20,832	HC+
Dartmouth College	NH	57,996	MC
DePaul Univ	IL	46,120	VC
Georgetown Univ	DC	52,910	MC
Howard Univ	DC	35,957	C
Middlebury College	VT	57,470	MC
New York Univ	NY	61,470	MC
Ohio State Univ	OH	19,887	MC
Thomas Edison State College	NJ	5,700	SP
Tufts Univ	MA	58,780	MC
United States Naval Academy	MD		MC
Univ of Calif at Los Angeles	CA	25,686	MC
Univ of Georgia	GA	19,508	VC
Univ of Iowa	IA	17,481	VC
Univ of Maryland	MD	18,801	HC
Univ of Mich/Ann Arbor	MI	22,102	HC+
Univ of Notre Dame	IN		MC
Univ of Okla	OK	17,634	VC+
Univ of Texas at Austin	TX	44,074	HC
Univ of Utah	UT	13,462	VC
Washington Univ in St. Louis	MO	58,818	MC
Williams College	MA	58,900	MC

ARCHEOLOGY

School	ST	$IS	SR
Baylor Univ	TX	46,720	HC
Biola Univ	CA	40,320	VC
Boston Univ	MA	54,130	HC+
Brigham Young Univ	UT	12,100	HC
Brown Univ	RI	56,150	MC
Bryn Mawr College	PA	57,760	MC
College of Wooster	OH	52,600	VC
Columbia Univ in the City of New York	NY	61,116	MC
Columbia Univ/School of General Studies	NY	54,083	MC
Cornell College	IA	44,930	HC
Cornell Univ	NY	59,037	MC
Dickinson College	PA	57,662	HC+
George Washington Univ	DC	57,108	MC
Hamilton College	NY	55,620	MC
Haverford College	PA	59,236	MC
Hood College	MD	44,630	C
Hunter College / The CUNY	NY	14,429	VC
Lycoming College	PA	43,636	C
Mass Inst of Technology	MA	54,238	MC
Mercyhurst Univ	PA	40,700	C
Oberlin College	OH	57,025	MC
Penn State Univ/Univ Park	PA	25,404	VC
Prescott College	AZ	33,284	C+
Princeton Univ	NJ	53,795	MC
Randolph-Macon College	VA	45,086	C
Stanford Univ	CA	56,411	MC
Sweet Briar College	VA	43,765	C+
Texas A&M Univ at Galveston	TX	11,258	C
The SUNY at Potsdam	NY	17,754	C
Tufts Univ	MA	58,780	MC
Univ of Evansville	IN	41,056	VC+
Univ of Indianapolis	IN	31,740	LC
Univ of Kansas	KS	16,980	C+
Univ of Mich/Ann Arbor	MI	22,102	HC+
Univ of Missouri/Columbia	MO	18,201	MC
Univ of N Car at Chapel Hill	NC	18,348	MC
Univ of Rochester	NY	58,500	MC
Univ of Texas at Austin	TX	44,074	HC
Univ of Wisc/La Crosse	WI	14,755	VC
Washington and Lee Univ	VA	52,812	MC
Washington Univ in St. Louis	MO	58,818	MC
Wellesley College	MA	49,848	MC
Wesleyan Univ	CT	59,844	MC
Wheaton College	IL	39,650	HC+
Yale Univ	CT	55,300	MC

ARCHITECTURAL ENGINEERING

School	ST	$IS	SR
Calif Polytechnic State Univ	CA	19,847	HC
Dordt College	IA	34,160	VC
Drexel Univ	PA	51,920	HC
Illinois Inst of Technology	IL	38,512	HC+
Kansas State Univ	KS	15,497	VC
Lawrence Tech Univ	MI	37,630	VC
Milwaukee School of Engineering	WI	39,948	VC+
Missouri Univ of Science and Technology	MO	18,655	VC+
N Car Agricultural and Technical State Univ	NC	13,175	LC
Northern Kentucky Univ	KY	15,302	LC
Okla State Univ	OK	14,310	VC
Parsons The New School for Design	NY	56,610	SP
Penn State Univ/Univ Park	PA	25,404	VC
Princeton Univ	NJ	53,795	MC
Rice Univ	TX	43,288	MC
Stanford Univ	CA	56,411	MC
Tenn State Univ	TN	9,048	C
Univ of Cincinnati	OH	20,199	VC
Univ of Colo Boulder	CO	22,605	VC+
Univ of Hartford	CT	42,674	C
Univ of Illinois at Urbana-Champaign	IL	24,300	HC
Univ of Kansas	KS	16,980	C+
Univ of Miami	FL	55,166	MC
Univ of Nebr - Lincoln	NE	17,507	VC
Univ of Nevada, Las Vegas	NV	17,303	C
Univ of Okla	OK	17,634	VC+
Univ of Texas at Austin	TX	44,074	HC
Univ of Wyoming	WY	13,855	C+
Vermont Technical College	VT	15,751	C
Worcester Polytechnic Inst	MA	53,440	HC+

ARCHITECTURAL HISTORY

School	ST	$IS	SR
Brown Univ	RI	56,150	MC
DePaul Univ	IL	46,120	VC
Miami Univ	OH	24,191	HC
Middlebury College	VT	57,470	MC
Savannah College of Art and Design	GA	46,824	SP
Syracuse Univ	NY	54,512	HC
Univ of Kansas	KS	16,980	C+
Univ of Virginia	VA	22,175	MC

ARCHITECTURAL STUDIES

School	ST	$IS	SR
Amherst College	MA	58,744	MC
Arizona State Univ	AZ	18,818	C+
Bowling Green State Univ	OH	18,970	C
Indiana Univ of Pennsylvania	PA	20,180	LC
Ithaca College	NY	52,300	HC
Lawrence Tech Univ	MI	37,630	VC
New York Univ	NY	61,470	MC
Univ of Arkansas at Fayetteville	AR	16,860	VC
Univ of Illinois at Chicago	IL	24,293	VC
Univ of Nebr - Lincoln	NE	17,507	VC
Univ of Pittsburgh at Pittsburgh	PA	27,800	HC+
Univ of San Diego	CA	53,302	HC+
Univ of Utah	UT	13,462	VC

ARCHITECTURAL TECHNOLOGY

School	ST	$IS	SR
Alfred State / SUNY College of Technology	NY	18,034	C
Brown Univ	RI	56,150	MC
Fairmont State Univ	WV	12,098	LC
Farmingdale State College	NY	18,985	C
Fitchburg State Univ	MA	17,241	C
New York City College of Technology / The CUNY	NY	5,769	NC
Pennsylvania College of Technology	PA	25,653	NC
Univ of Cincinnati	OH	20,199	VC
Univ of Southern Miss	MS	13,170	C
Washington Univ in St. Louis	MO	58,818	MC

ARCHITECTURE

School	ST	$IS	SR
Academy of Art Univ	CA		
Andrews Univ	MI	28,030	C+
Appalachian State Univ	NC	12,919	VC
Arizona State Univ	AZ	18,818	C+
Auburn Univ	AL	20,052	VC+
Ball State Univ	IN	17,850	C
Baylor Univ	TX	46,720	HC
Bennington College	VT	56,990	HC+
Boston Architectural College	MA	18,622	SP
Brown Univ	RI	56,150	MC
Calif College of the Arts	CA	48,334	SP
Calif Polytechnic State Univ	CA	19,847	HC
Calif State Polytechnic Univ, Pomona	CA	18,932	C
Case Western Reserve Univ	OH	55,178	MC
Cleveland Inst of Art	OH	48,641	SP
College of the Holy Cross	MA	56,232	MC
Columbia Univ in the City of New York	NY	61,116	MC
Columbia Univ/Barnard College	NY	39,000	MC
Columbia Univ/School of General Studies	NY	54,083	MC
Conn College	CT	54,970	MC
Cooper Union for the Advancement of Science and Art	NY	55,600	MC
Cornell Univ	NY	59,037	MC
CUNY-City College	NY	19,576	HC+
Drexel Univ	PA	51,920	HC
Drury Univ	MO	30,319	VC
Florida Atlantic Univ	FL	17,339	C
Florida International Univ	FL	17,747	VC
Georgia Inst of Technology	GA	20,464	MC
Hampshire College	MA	58,320	MC

ST = STATE **$IS** = IN-STATE COSTS **SR** = SELECTOR RATING

School	ST	$IS	SR
Hampton Univ	VA	28,528	C
Hobart and William Smith Colleges	NY	43,000	VC
Howard Univ	DC	35,957	C
Illinois Inst of Technology	IL	38,512	HC+
Iowa State Univ	IA	16,403	C
Kansas State Univ	KS	15,497	VC
Keene State College	NH	21,538	C
Kent State Univ	OH	19,352	C
Lawrence Tech Univ	MI	37,630	VC
Lehigh Univ	PA	55,080	MC
Louisiana State Univ	LA	18,677	VC+
Louisiana Tech Univ	LA	8,000	C
Marywood Univ	PA	40,695	C
Mass College of Art and Design	MA	23,600	SP
Mass Inst of Technology	MA	54,238	MC
Miami Univ	OH	24,191	HC
Mount Holyoke College	MA	53,596	HC+
New Jersey Inst of Technology	NJ	26,490	VC
New York Inst of Technology	NY	40,590	VC
N Car State Univ	NC	16,202	HC
N Dak State Univ	ND	14,642	C
Northeastern Univ	MA	55,296	MC
Northern Mich Univ	MI	15,300	VC
Norwich Univ	VT	28,212	C
Okla State Univ	OK	14,310	VC
Otis College of Art and Design	CA	35,404	SP
Penn State Univ/Univ Park	PA	25,404	VC
Philadelphia Univ	PA	44,160	C
Portland State Univ	OR	18,672	C
Prairie View A&M Univ	TX	15,205	LC
Pratt Inst	NY	49,520	SP
Princeton Univ	NJ	53,795	MC
Rensselaer Polytechnic Inst	NY	59,229	MC
Rhode Island School of Design	RI	55,204	SP
Rice Univ	TX	43,288	MC
Roger Williams Univ	RI	45,788	C
Savannah College of Art and Design	GA	46,824	SP
Smith College	MA	57,524	MC
S Dak State Univ	SD	14,296	C
Southern Illinois Univ Carbondale	IL	21,620	C
Southern Polytechnic State Univ	GA	13,958	VC
Southern Univ and A&M College	LA	9,761	C+
Syracuse Univ	NY	54,512	HC
Temple Univ	PA	24,392	VC
Texas Tech Univ	TX	14,243	C
The Catholic Univ of America	DC	52,852	VC
Ohio State Univ	OH	19,887	MC
Tufts Univ	MA	58,780	MC
Tulane Univ	LA	58,942	MC
Tuskegee Univ	AL	26,750	C
Univ at Buffalo / The SUNY	NY	20,283	VC
Univ of Arizona	AZ	20,105	C
Univ of Arkansas at Fayetteville	AR	16,860	VC
Univ of Calif at Berkeley	CA	23,322	MC
Univ of Calif at Los Angeles	CA	25,686	MC
Univ of Central Florida	FL	15,711	VC+
Univ of Colo Denver	CO	17,904	C
Univ of Detroit Mercy	MI	30,450	C
Univ of Florida	FL	15,783	HC+
Univ of Houston	TX	19,184	VC
Univ of Idaho	ID	14,558	C
Univ of Illinois at Chicago	IL	24,293	VC
Univ of Illinois at Urbana-Champaign	IL	24,300	HC
Univ of Kansas	KS	16,980	C+
Univ of Maine at Augusta	ME	6,855	C
Univ of Maryland	MD	18,801	HC
Univ of Mass Amherst	MA	23,697	VC+
Univ of Memphis	TN	15,094	C
Univ of Miami	FL	55,166	MC
Univ of Mich/Ann Arbor	MI	22,102	HC+
Univ of Minn/Twin Cities	MN		HC
Univ of Nebr - Lincoln	NE	17,507	VC
Univ of New Mexico	NM	15,300	C
Univ of N Car at Charlotte	NC	15,847	C
Univ of Notre Dame	IN		MC
Univ of Okla	OK	17,634	VC+
Univ of Oregon	OR	20,872	VC
Univ of Pennsylvania	PA	56,106	MC
Univ of San Francisco	CA	49,674	VC
Univ of Southern Calif	CA	56,903	MC
Univ of Tenn at Knoxville	TN	20,364	VC+
Univ of Texas at Arlington	TX	10,908	LC
Univ of Texas at Austin	TX	44,074	HC
Univ of Texas at San Antonio	TX	18,372	C
Univ of the District of Columbia	DC	7,244	LC
Univ of Utah	UT	13,462	VC
Univ of Virginia	VA	22,175	MC
Univ of Wisc-Milwaukee	WI	18,436	C
Virginia Polytechnic Inst and State Univ	VA	14,629	HC
Washington State Univ	WA	20,461	C
Washington Univ in St. Louis	MO	58,818	MC
Wellesley College	MA	49,848	MC
Wentworth Inst of Technology	MA	29,800	SP
Woodbury Univ	CA	34,500	LC
Yale Univ	CT	55,300	MC

AREA STUDIES

School	ST	$IS	SR
American Univ	DC	54,829	HC+
Appalachian State Univ	NC	12,919	VC
Bard College	NY	59,872	HC
Beloit College	WI	49,970	HC
Calvin College	MI	37,585	VC+
Castleton State College	VT	19,424	C
College of Wooster	OH	52,600	VC
Columbia Univ in the City of New York	NY	61,116	MC
CUNY-City College	NY	19,576	HC+
Duke Univ	NC	50,250	MC
Eastern Mich Univ	MI	17,961	C
Huntington Univ	IN	32,220	C
Ithaca College	NY	52,300	HC
Lake Forest College	IL	45,580	VC
Mercer Univ	GA	44,201	VC+
New York Univ	NY	61,470	MC
Prescott College	AZ	33,284	C+
Rutgers, The State Univ of New Jersey/Newark Campus	NJ	25,376	C
Stanford Univ	CA	56,411	MC
Univ of Alaska Fairbanks	AK	13,955	C
Univ of Miss	MS	15,482	VC
Univ of Okla	OK	17,634	VC+
Univ of Vermont	VT	26,120	VC+
Univ of Virginia	VA	22,175	MC
Washington Univ in St. Louis	MO	58,818	MC
Webster Univ	MO	33,990	C+

ART

School	ST	$IS	SR
Abilene Christian Univ	TX	38,400	VC
Adams State College	CO	13,358	LC
Alabama A&M Univ	AL	96,100	C
Alabama State Univ	AL	14,142	NC
Albany State Univ	GA	8,500	C
Albion College	MI	43,884	VC
Albright College	PA	46,660	C
Allegheny College	PA	49,020	HC
Alma College	MI	42,400	VC
Alverno College	WI	30,483	LC
Andrews Univ	MI	28,030	C+
Angelo State Univ	TX	15,049	NC
Anna Maria College	MA	34,600	LC
Appalachian State Univ	NC	12,919	VC
Aquinas College	MI	33,060	C
Arizona State Univ	AZ	18,818	C+
Arkansas State Univ	AR	14,980	C
Arkansas Tech Univ	AR	13,164	LC
Armstrong Atlantic State Univ	GA	16,276	C
Asbury Univ	KY	32,038	VC
Ashland Univ	OH	25,000	C
Atlantic Union College	MA	24,600	LC
Auburn Univ	AL	20,052	VC+
Augustana College	IL	43,398	HC
Augustana College	SD	35,500	VC
Aurora Univ	IL	26,870	C
Austin College	TX	36,940	HC
Austin Peay State Univ	TN	14,650	C
Averett Univ	VA	36,000	LC
Avila Univ	MO	26,900	C
Ball State Univ	IN	17,850	C
Barry Univ	FL	38,190	C
Baylor Univ	TX	46,720	HC
Belhaven Univ	MS	27,170	C
Benedictine College	KS	29,180	VC
Bennington College	VT	56,990	HC+
Berea College	KY	7,220	HC
Berry College	GA	39,254	HC
Bethany College	KS	30,605	NC
Bethel College	IN	31,560	C
Bethel College	KS	29,100	C
Bethel Univ	MN	34,940	VC
Binghamton Univ / The SUNY	NY	20,832	HC+
Biola Univ	CA	40,320	VC
Black Hills State Univ	SD	13,562	LC
Blackburn College	IL	21,350	C
Bluffton Univ	OH	37,864	C
Boise State Univ	ID	12,802	C
Bowling Green State Univ	OH	18,970	C
Brescia Univ	KY	26,140	VC+
Briar Cliff Univ	IA	29,514	C
Bridgewater College	VA	39,880	C
Bridgewater State Univ	MA	18,752	C
Brigham Young Univ	UT	12,100	HC
Brigham Young Univ/ Hawaii	HI	8,614	VC
Brown Univ	RI	56,150	MC
Bucknell Univ	PA	58,160	MC
Buena Vista Univ	IA	37,954	C
Buffalo State/State Univ of Buffalo	NY	15,733	C+
Butler Univ	IN	45,898	VC+
Caldwell College	NJ	35,602	LC
Calif College of the Arts	CA	48,334	SP
Calif Lutheran Univ	CA	47,640	C
Calif State Polytechnic Univ, Pomona	CA	18,932	C
Cal State, Bakersfield	CA	8,000	LC
Cal State, Chico	CA	18,952	C
Cal State, Dominguez Hills	CA	17,056	LC
Cal State, East Bay	CA	16,549	C
Cal State, Fresno	CA	17,405	C
Cal State, Fullerton	CA	25,188	C+
Cal State, Long Beach	CA	17,534	C+
Cal State, Northridge	CA	28,313	C
Cal State, San Bernardino	CA	12,000	C
Cal State, Stanislaus	CA	18,582	C
Calif Univ of Pennsylvania	PA	14,217	C
Calvin College	MI	37,585	VC+
Cameron Univ	OK	9,267	LC
Campbell Univ	NC	25,500	C
Campbellsville Univ	KY	27,720	C
Capital Univ	OH	39,824	VC
Cardinal Stritch Univ	WI	24,054	C
Carlow Univ	PA	30,272	C
Carroll Univ	WI	24,860	C
Carthage College	WI	33,000	C
Castleton State College	VT	19,424	C
Cedar Crest College	PA	43,240	C
Centenary College of Louisiana	LA	39,070	C+
Central College	IA	36,980	VC
Central Conn State Univ	CT	19,212	C
Central Mich Univ	MI	18,066	C
Central Washington Univ	WA	11,730	C
Chadron State College	NE	7,400	NC
Chapman Univ	CA	56,019	VC+
Chestnut Hill College	PA	39,785	LC
Chicago State Univ	IL	5,482	C
CUNY/Brooklyn College	NY	5,884	C+
Claflin Univ	SC	22,368	C+
Clarion Univ of Pennsylvania	PA	17,370	C
Clark Atlanta Univ	GA	30,006	C
Clarke Univ	IA	36,400	C
Cleveland State Univ	OH	21,357	C
Coe College	IA	43,590	VC
Coker College	SC	32,256	LC
Colby-Sawyer College	NH	47,870	C
College of Staten Island / The CUNY	NY	16,778	NC
College of Mount St. Joseph	OH	33,880	C
College of New Jersey	NJ	25,376	HC
College of St. Benedict	MN	47,570	VC
College of St. Elizabeth	NJ	43,839	LC
College of St. Mary	NE	34,334	C
College of the Ozarks	MO	5,605	VC
College of William & Mary	VA	25,085	MC
Colo Christian Univ	CO	27,500	VC
Colo Mesa Univ	CO	16,669	LC
Colo State Univ-Fort Collins	CO	20,090	VC
Colo State Univ-Pueblo	CO	13,532	LC
Columbia College	MO	24,578	C
Columbia College Chicago	IL	30,940	LC
Columbus State Univ	GA	13,176	C
Concordia College, Moorhead	MN	39,974	C+
Concordia Univ - Irvine	CA	35,390	VC
Concordia Univ St. Paul	MN	27,200	C
Concordia Univ Wisc	WI	28,980	C
Concordia Univ, Ann Arbor	MI	27,220	VC
Concordia Univ, River Forest	IL	26,300	C
Conn College	CT	54,970	MC
Covenant College	GA		VC+
Creighton Univ	NE	44,058	VC+
Culver-Stockton College	MO	30,900	C
CUNY-City College	NY	19,576	HC+
Daemen College	NY	31,510	C
Dakota Wesleyan Univ	SD	23,000	C
Dallas Baptist Univ	TX	29,118	C
Davidson College	NC	54,683	MC
Davis and Elkins College	WV	33,742	C
Defiance College	OH	30,645	C
Delta State Univ	MS	12,292	LC
DePaul Univ	IL	46,120	VC
Dillard Univ	LA	20,940	VC
Doane College	NE	33,730	VC
Dominican Univ of Calif	CA	51,250	C
Dordt College	IA	34,160	VC
Drew Univ/College of Liberal Arts	NJ	55,862	VC
Earlham College	IN	49,710	VC+
East Carolina Univ	NC	14,169	C
East Central Univ	OK	10,223	LC
East Stroudsburg Univ of Pennsylvania	PA	16,636	C
East Tenn State Univ	TN	9,000	C
Eastern Illinois Univ	IL	20,502	C
Eastern Kentucky Univ	KY	11,161	C
Eastern Mennonite Univ	VA	38,850	VC
Eastern Mich Univ	MI	17,961	C
Eastern New Mexico Univ	NM	10,682	C
Eastern Oregon Univ	OR	10,400	C
Eastern Washington Univ	WA	16,388	C
Edgewood College	WI	33,294	C
Edinboro Univ of Pennsylvania	PA	15,940	LC
Elizabeth City State Univ	NC	11,638	C
Elmhurst College	IL	42,032	C+
Elmira College	NY	49,950	C+
Elon Univ	NC	40,046	HC
Emory and Henry College	VA	387,460	C
Emory Univ	GA	45,000	MC
Emporia State Univ	KS	12,897	C
Erskine College	SC	37,360	C
Evangel Univ	MO	23,090	C
Felician College	NJ	41,640	C
Ferrum College	VA	27,740	LC
Florida Atlantic Univ	FL	17,339	C
Florida Gulf Coast Univ	FL		C
Florida International Univ	FL	17,747	VC
Fontbonne Univ	MO	31,384	C
Fort Hays State Univ	KS	11,354	C
Fort Lewis College	CO	15,513	C
Franklin College	IN	35,885	C
Freed-Hardeman Univ	TN	19,697	VC
Friends Univ	KS	29,100	C
Furman Univ	SC	54,006	HC
Gardner-Webb Univ	NC	34,375	C+
George Fox Univ	OR	40,750	C+
Georgetown College	KY	38,690	C
Georgetown Univ	DC	52,910	MC
Georgia College and State Univ	GA	18,216	VC
Georgia Regents Univ	GA		C
Georgia Southern Univ	GA	16,414	C
Georgia State Univ	GA	12,000	VC
Georgian Court Univ	NJ	39,726	LC
Goddard College	VT	16,418	VC
Gonzaga Univ	WA	44,247	HC
Gordon College	MA	42,660	VC+
Goshen College	IN	35,900	VC
Goucher College	MD	50,252	VC+
Grace College and Theological Seminary	IN	28,800	C
Grand Valley State Univ	MI	17,998	VC
Green Mountain College	VT	33,547	LC
Greensboro College	NC	28,740	LC
Greenville College	IL	27,012	C
Grinnell College	IA	53,654	HC
Guilford College	NC	35,340	C
Hamilton College	NY	55,620	MC
Hamline Univ	MN	44,198	VC
Hampton Univ	VA	28,528	C
Hannibal-LaGrange Univ	MO	24,490	C
Hanover College	IN	41,450	VC
Harding Univ	AR	21,432	C+
Hardin-Simmons Univ	TX	23,560	C+
Hartwick College	NY	49,815	C+
Hendrix College	AR	48,436	HC+
Heritage Univ	WA	17,664	NC
High Point Univ	NC	39,800	C
Hiram College	OH	37,300	VC
Holy Family Univ	PA	40,030	LC
Hood College	MD	44,630	C
Houghton College	NY	35,740	VC
Houston Baptist Univ	TX	23,815	C+
Howard Payne Univ	TX	17,115	C
Humboldt State Univ	CA	18,400	C
Huntingdon College	AL	31,850	C
Huntington Univ	IN	32,220	C
Idaho State Univ	ID	11,908	C
Illinois State Univ	IL	22,634	VC
Illinois Wesleyan Univ	IL	48,452	VC+
Indiana Univ of Pennsylvania	PA	20,180	LC
Indiana Wesleyan Univ	IN	31,815	VC
Ithaca College	NY	52,300	HC
Jackson State Univ	MS	13,512	LC
James Madison Univ	VA	18,049	VC
Johnson State College	VT	16,721	C
Judson College	AL	24,690	C
Kalamazoo College	MI	47,825	HC+
Kansas State Univ	KS	15,497	VC
Keene State College	NH	21,538	C
Kennesaw State Univ	GA	13,017	VC
Kentucky State Univ	KY	11,000	LC
Kentucky Wesleyan College	KY	27,440	VC+
Kenyon College	OH	56,810	MC
La Sierra Univ	CA	35,694	VC
Lafayette College	PA	57,050	HC+
LaGrange College	GA	34,480	C
Lake Forest College	IL	45,580	VC
Lakeland College	WI	22,990	C
Lebanon Valley College	PA	38,570	C
Lees-McRae College	NC	33,624	C
Lehigh Univ	PA	55,080	MC
LeMoyne-Owen College	TN	13,100	C
Lindsey Wilson College	KY	30,470	VC
Linfield College-McMinnville Campus	OR	46,166	C
Lipscomb Univ	TN	35,722	VC
Longwood Univ	VA	20,924	C
Lourdes Univ	OH	26,055	LC
Luther College	IA	44,380	VC+
Lycoming College	PA	43,636	C
Lynchburg College	VA	42,645	C
Lyon College	AR	30,246	VC
Macalester College	MN	53,419	MC
MacMurray College	IL	20,755	C
Madonna Univ	MI	24,540	VC

School	ST	$IS	SR
Malone Univ	OH	34,334	C
Manchester College	IN	35,070	C
Manhattanville College	NY	46,260	VC
Marian Univ	WI	30,980	LC
Marshall Univ	WV	14,820	C
Mary Baldwin College	VA	37,110	C
Marygrove College	MI	21,290	C
Marylhurst Univ	OR	18,945	NC
Marymount Univ	VA	36,178	C
Maryville College	TN	33,150	VC
Mass College of Liberal Arts	MA	16,733	C
McKendree Univ	IL	29,920	₵
McMurry Univ	TX	25,962	LC
McNeese State Univ	LA		C
McPherson College	KS	28,138	C
Mercer Univ	GA	44,201	V₵
Meredith College	NC	31,420	C
Methodist Univ	NC	37,185	C
Metropolitan State Univ of Denver	CO	4,835	LC
Miami Univ	OH	24,191	HC
Millersville Univ of Pennsylvania	PA	18,498	C
Millikin Univ	IL	37,462	C
Minn State Univ, Mankato	MN	14,900	C
Minot State Univ	ND	10,915	C
Miss College	MS	21,998	VC
Miss Valley State Univ	MS	9,706	LC
Missouri Southern State Univ	MO	11,910	C
Missouri State Univ	MO	13,996	VC
Missouri Valley College	MO	22,200	C
Molloy College	NY	38,950	C
Monmouth College	IL	39,290	C
Monmouth Univ	NJ	42,252	C
Montana State Univ	MT	14,068	VC
Montana State Univ-Billings	MT	12,425	LC
Montclair State Univ	NJ	22,614	C
Morehouse College	GA	38,640	C
Morningside College	IA	32,620	C
Mount Mercy Univ	IA	34,385	C
Mount Olive College	NC	18,426	C
Mount St. Mary's College/Chalon Campus	CA	43,897	V₵
Mount Vernon Nazarene Univ	OH	29,590	C
Muhlenberg College	PA	52,837	HC
Muskingum Univ	OH	30,502	C
Nazareth College of Rochester	NY	41,590	VC
Nebr Wesleyan Univ	NE	29,774	₵
New College of Florida	FL	14,504	H₵
New Mexico Highlands Univ	NM	9,720	NC
New Mexico State Univ	NM	13,955	LC
Newberry College	SC	26,850	LC
Newman Univ	KS	30,380	₵
Nicholls State Univ	LA	7,095	C
N Car Central Univ	NC	9,000	LC
North Central College	IL	38,343	VC
N Dak State Univ	ND	14,642	C
North Georgia College & State Univ	GA	8,500	C
Northeastern Illinois Univ	IL		C
Northeastern Univ	MA	55,296	MC
Northern Illinois Univ	IL	19,768	C
Northern Kentucky Univ	KY	15,302	LC
Northwest Missouri State Univ	MO	14,229	C
Northwest Nazarene Univ	ID	24,275	NC
Northwestern Univ	IL	37,595	MC
Notre Dame College	OH	34,942	VC
Notre Dame de Namur Univ	CA	41,610	LC
Oberlin College	OH	57,025	MC
Oglethorpe Univ	GA	42,580	VC
Ohio Dominican Univ	OH	38,380	₵
Ohio Univ	OH	20,676	VC
Okla Christian Univ	OK	24,975	VC
Okla City Univ	OK	33,546	VC
Okla State Univ	OK	14,310	VC
Olivet Nazarene Univ	IL	29,990	C
Oregon State Univ	OR	19,017	₵
Oswego / SUNY	NY	20,009	VC
Ottawa Univ	KS	15,000	VC
Otterbein College	OH	32,214	C
Ouachita Baptist Univ	AR	29,010	VC
Our Lady of the Lake Univ of San Antonio	TX	22,430	LC
Pace Univ	NY	48,094	VC
Pacific Lutheran Univ	WA	44,840	VC
Palm Beach Atlantic Univ	FL	33,882	LC
Penn State Univ/Univ Park	PA	25,404	VC
Pepperdine Univ	CA	55,372	H₵
Pfeiffer Univ	NC	33,700	C
Piedmont College	GA	29,260	C
Pine Manor College	MA	32,659	LC
Pittsburg State Univ	KS	12,032	C
Pitzer College	CA	54,988	MC
Plymouth State Univ	NH	23,148	LC
Prairie View A&M Univ	TX	15,205	LC
Presbyterian College	SC	42,678	VC
Prescott College	AZ	33,284	₵
Queens College / The CUNY	NY	17,107	VC
Queens Univ of Charlotte	NC	39,543	VC
Radford Univ	VA	17,132	LC
Ramapo College of New Jersey	NJ	24,938	₵
Randolph College	VA	43,960	VC
Reed College	OR	57,780	MC
Rhodes College	TN	47,596	H₵
Ringling College of Art and Design	FL	46,130	SP
Ripon College	WI	36,959	₵
Roanoke College	VA	47,996	₵
Roberts Wesleyan College	NY	37,384	₵
Rockford College	IL	31,000	C
Rocky Mountain College	MT	32,242	C
Rowan Univ	NJ	23,570	VC
Rutgers, The State Univ of New Jersey/Camden Campus	NJ	24,254	C
Rutgers, The State Univ of New Jersey/New Brunswick	NJ	25,077	VC
Rutgers, The State Univ of New Jersey/Newark Campus	NJ	25,376	C
Saginaw Valley State Univ	MI	16,869	C
St. John's Univ	MN	46,146	C
St. Joseph's College	IN	35,790	C
St. Joseph's Univ	PA	52,272	VC
St. Mary-of-the-Woods College	IN	37,722	LC
St. Mary's College	IN	45,160	VC
St. Mary's College of Calif	CA	53,550	C
St. Mary's Univ of Minn	MN	37,015	C
St. Vincent College	PA	40,244	C
Salisbury Univ	MD	10,000	VC
Sam Houston State Univ	TX	17,082	C
Samford Univ	AL	35,700	V₵
San Diego State Univ	CA	20,578	VC
San Francisco State Univ	CA	18,514	C
Savannah College of Art and Design	GA	46,824	SP
Schreiner Univ	TX	32,734	LC
Seattle Pacific Univ	WA	41,559	V₵
Shepherd Univ	WV	14,996	C
Shippensburg Univ of Pennsylvania	PA	17,064	LC
Shorter Univ	GA	26,470	C
Simmons College	MA	48,770	VC
Simpson College	IA	36,086	VC
Sinte Gleska Univ	SD	2,300	NC
Skidmore College	NY	57,926	HC
Sonoma State Univ	CA	20,541	C
S Dak State Univ	SD	14,296	C
Southeast Missouri State Univ	MO	14,983	LC
Southeastern Louisiana Univ	LA	13,325	C
Southeastern Okla State Univ	OK	7,966	C
Southern Adventist Univ	TN	26,190	C
Southern Arkansas Univ	AR	14,316	C
Southern Illinois Univ Carbondale	IL	21,620	C
Southern Illinois Univ Edwardsville	IL	17,532	C
Southern Oregon Univ	OR	17,874	C
Southwest Baptist Univ	MO	24,710	C
Southwest Minn State Univ	MN	14,000	C
Southwestern Univ	TX	45,660	VC
Spelman College	GA	24,650	VC
Spring Arbor Univ	MI	26,740	C
St. Catherine Univ	MN	37,782	₵
St. Edward's Univ	TX	44,674	VC
St. Lawrence Univ	NY	53,740	HC
St. Mary's College of Maryland	MD	26,699	HC
St. Norbert College	WI	39,992	VC
Stanford Univ	CA	56,411	MC
Stephen F. Austin State Univ	TX	14,668	C
Sterling College	KS	27,216	C
Stetson Univ	FL	49,512	V₵
Stevenson Univ	MD	39,572	C
Stillman College	AL	18,460	C
SUNY Cortland / The SUNY	NY	19,117	C
SUNY Oneonta / SUNY	NY	16,919	VC
SUNY Plattsburgh / SUNY	NY	18,083	VC
Swarthmore College	PA	57,870	MC
Syracuse Univ	NY	54,512	HC
Tarleton State Univ	TX	13,489	LC
Taylor Univ	IN	36,742	V₵
Temple Univ	PA	24,392	VC
Tenn State Univ	TN	9,048	C
Texas A&M Univ at Corpus Christi	TX	11,544	LC
Texas Lutheran Univ	TX	34,070	C
Texas Southern Univ	TX	18,212	LC
Texas State Univ	TX	16,495	VC
Texas Wesleyan Univ	TX	29,886	C
Texas Woman's Univ	TX	13,633	LC
The Catholic Univ of America	DC	52,852	VC
The College of Idaho	ID	31,277	VC
Ohio State Univ	OH	19,887	MC
The SUNY at Potsdam	NY	17,754	C
Thiel College	PA	31,378	LC
Thomas Edison State College	NJ	5,700	SP
Thomas More College	KY	34,760	C
Tougaloo College	MS	15,275	NC
Towson Univ	MD	16,000	VC
Transylvania Univ	KY	40,310	V₵
Trinity Christian College	IL	28,869	C
Trinity Univ	TX	44,174	H₵
Troy Univ	AL	10,650	C
Truman State Univ	MO	13,546	HC
Union Univ	TN	28,260	VC
Unity College	ME	34,054	C
Univ at Buffalo / The SUNY	NY	20,283	VC
Univ of Akron	OH	20,436	C
Univ of Alabama at Birmingham	AL	18,484	₵
Univ of Alabama at Huntsville	AL	17,625	VC
Univ of Alaska Anchorage	AK	15,290	NC
Univ of Alaska Fairbanks	AK	13,955	C
Univ of Alaska Southeast	AK	11,493	C
Univ of Arizona	AZ	20,105	C
Univ of Arkansas at Fayetteville	AR	16,860	VC
Univ of Arkansas at Little Rock	AR		C
Univ of Arkansas at Monticello	AR	8,470	NC
Univ of Arkansas at Pine Bluff	AR	10,600	C
Univ of Calif at Berkeley	CA	23,322	MC
Univ of Calif at Los Angeles	CA	25,686	MC
Univ of Calif at Riverside	CA	27,204	C
Univ of Calif at Santa Barbara	CA	27,551	HC
Univ of Calif at Santa Cruz	CA	27,807	VC
Univ of Central Florida	FL	15,711	V₵
Univ of Central Okla	OK	12,293	C
Univ of Charleston	WV	28,650	C
Univ of Conn	CT	23,744	HC
Univ of Dayton	OH	43,750	VC
Univ of Delaware	DE	22,728	VC
Univ of Denver	CO	51,787	V₵
Univ of Evansville	IN	41,056	V₵
Univ of Florida	FL	15,783	H₵
Univ of Georgia	GA	19,508	VC
Univ of Great Falls	MT	27,970	C
Univ of Hawaii at Hilo	HI	6,500	C
Univ of Hawaii at Manoa	HI	19,379	VC
Univ of Houston	TX	19,184	VC
Univ of Idaho	ID	14,558	C
Univ of Indianapolis	IN	31,740	LC
Univ of Iowa	IA	17,481	VC
Univ of Kansas	KS	16,980	₵
Univ of La Verne	CA	47,010	VC
Univ of Louisiana at Monroe	LA	12,998	C
Univ of Louisville	KY	17,460	VC
Univ of Maine	ME	19,712	₵
Univ of Maine at Augusta	ME	6,855	C
Univ of Maine at Farmington	ME	17,841	C
Univ of Maine at Presque Isle	ME	15,011	LC
Univ of Mary Hardin-Baylor	TX	31,950	₵
Univ of Mass Boston	MA	11,966	C
Univ of Memphis	TN	15,094	C
Univ of Miami	FL	55,166	MC
Univ of Mich/Ann Arbor	MI	22,102	H₵
Univ of Mich-Flint	MI	17,547	₵
Univ of Minn/Duluth	MN	18,964	₵
Univ of Minn/Twin Cities	MN		HC
Univ of Miss	MS	15,482	VC
Univ of Missouri/Columbia	MO	18,201	MC
Univ of Mobile	AL	27,870	VC
Univ of Montana-Western	MT	9,753	LC
Univ of Montevallo	AL	17,320	C
Univ of Mount Union	OH	35,130	C
Univ of Nebr - Lincoln	NE	17,507	VC
Univ of Nebr at Omaha	NE	12,700	C
Univ of Nevada/Reno	NV	14,500	NC
Univ of New Haven	CT	47,740	C
Univ of New Mexico	NM	15,300	C
Univ of New Orleans	LA	9,224	VC
Univ of North Alabama	AL	9,960	C
Univ of N Car at Asheville	NC	13,500	V₵
Univ of N Car at Charlotte	NC	15,847	C
Univ of N Car at Greensboro	NC	12,848	C
Univ of N Car at Wilmington	NC	13,572	V₵
Univ of North Florida	FL	15,578	VC
Univ of North Texas	TX	15,628	C
Univ of Northern Colo	CO	15,973	C
Univ of Okla	OK	17,634	V₵
Univ of Oregon	OR	20,872	VC
Univ of Pikeville	KY	24,750	NC
Univ of Puget Sound	WA	52,648	H₵
Univ of Redlands	CA	40,500	VC
Univ of Rio Grande	OH	8,750	NC
Univ of St. Mary	KS	28,400	₵
Univ of Science and Arts of Okla	OK	10,560	VC
Univ of S Dak	SD	15,111	C
Univ of Southern Indiana	IN	14,657	C
Univ of Tampa	FL	35,160	VC
Univ of Tenn at Chattanooga	TN	16,883	C
Univ of Tenn at Knoxville	TN	20,364	V₵
Univ of Texas at El Paso	TX	8,764	NC
Univ of Texas at San Antonio	TX	18,372	C
Univ of Texas-Pan American	TX	12,432	LC
Univ of the Cumberlands	KY	27,500	LC
Univ of the Incarnate Word	TX	35,200	LC
Univ of the Ozarks	AR	22,100	C
Univ of the Pacific	CA	52,146	VC
Univ of Tulsa	OK	45,311	H₵
Univ of Utah	UT	13,462	VC
Univ of Vermont	VT	26,120	V₵
Univ of Virginia	VA	22,175	MC
Univ of Virginia's College at Wise	VA	11,076	C
Univ of West Georgia	GA	14,852	LC
Univ of Wisc/Eau Claire	WI	15,430	VC
Univ of Wisc/Green Bay	WI	14,900	C
Univ of Wisc/La Crosse	WI	14,755	VC
Univ of Wisc/Madison	WI	18,757	HC
Univ of Wisc/Oshkosh	WI	10,426	LC
Univ of Wisc/Platteville	WI	14,274	C
Univ of Wisc/River Falls	WI	9,722	LC
Univ of Wisc/Stevens Point	WI	14,043	C
Univ of Wisc/Stout	WI	23,942	C
Univ of Wisc/Superior	WI	14,106	C
Univ of Wisc-Milwaukee	WI	18,436	C
Univ of Wyoming	WY	13,855	₵
Upper Iowa Univ	IA	30,426	NC
Ursinus College	PA	55,630	V₵
Ursuline College	OH	33,198	LC
Valley City State Univ	ND	12,286	LC
Valparaiso Univ	IN	43,040	V₵
Vassar College	NY	59,070	MC
Virginia Intermont College	VA	32,411	LC
Virginia Polytechnic Inst and State Univ	VA	14,629	HC
Virginia Wesleyan College	VA	28,433	LC
Viterbo Univ	WI	30,070	C
Wabash College	IN	44,160	VC
Wake Forest Univ	NC	51,000	MC
Walla Walla Univ	WA	26,256	NC
Warren Wilson College	NC	34,888	VC
Wartburg College	IA	41,055	VC
Washburn Univ	KS	12,165	NC
Washington and Jefferson College	PA	49,990	VC
Washington College	MD	48,768	VC
Wayland Baptist Univ	TX	16,058	LC
Wayne State College	NE	11,764	NC
Wayne State Univ	MI	19,493	C
Waynesburg Univ	PA	29,100	C
Webster Univ	MO	33,990	₵
West Chester Univ of Pennsylvania	PA	16,836	C
West Texas A&M Univ	TX	13,478	C
West Virginia Univ	WV	15,794	₵
Western Carolina Univ	NC	13,965	₵
Western Conn State Univ	CT	18,327	C
Western Illinois Univ	IL	20,130	C
Western Mich Univ	MI	19,042	C
Western Oregon Univ	OR	15,021	C
Western State Colo Univ	CO	16,135	C
Western Washington Univ	WA	18,519	VC
Westfield State Univ	MA	18,489	C
Westminster College	PA	31,290	₵
Westminster College	UT	37,708	VC
Westmont College	CA	41,500	HC
Wheaton College	IL	39,650	H₵
Whittier College	CA	43,416	C
Whitworth Univ	WA	45,826	V₵
Wichita State Univ	KS	12,539	C
Widener Univ	PA	50,368	C
William Carey Univ	MS	13,500	LC
William Jewell College	MO	31,000	V₵
William Woods Univ	MO		
Williams Baptist College	AR	20,070	C
Williams College	MA	58,900	MC
Wilmington College	OH	29,784	C
Winston-Salem State Univ	NC	9,418	LC
Winthrop Univ	SC	21,120	VC
Wisc Lutheran College	WI	23,510	VC
Wright State Univ	OH	16,983	C
Xavier Univ	OH	43,740	VC
Yale Univ	CT	55,300	MC
Youngstown State Univ	OH	16,374	LC

ART AND DESIGN

School	ST	$IS	SR
Bryant Univ	RI	49,179	VC
Calif Polytechnic State Univ	CA	19,847	HC
Univ of San Diego	CA	53,302	H₵

ART EDUCATION

School	ST	$IS	SR
Abilene Christian Univ	TX	38,400	VC
Academy of Art Univ	CA		
Adams State College	CO	13,358	LC
Adelphi Univ	NY	43,130	VC
Alabama A&M Univ	AL	96,100	C
Alabama State Univ	AL	14,142	NC
Alfred Univ	NY	40,392	VC
Alverno College	WI	30,483	LC
Anderson Univ	IN	35,390	C
Andrews Univ	MI	28,030	₵
Appalachian State Univ	NC	12,919	VC
Aquinas College	MI	33,060	C

School	ST	$IS	SR
Arcadia Univ	PA	33,570	C+
Arkansas Tech Univ	AR	13,164	LC
Armstrong Atlantic State Univ	GA	16,276	C
Asbury Univ	KY	32,038	VC
Ashland Univ	OH	25,000	C
Augustana College	IL	43,398	HC
Averett Univ	VA	36,000	LC
Azusa Pacific Univ	CA	39,946	C
Baker Univ	KS	33,350	C+
Baldwin Wallace Univ	OH	36,980	VC
Barton College	NC	27,660	C
Baylor Univ	TX	46,720	HC
Beloit College	WI	40,070	HC
Bemidji State Univ	MN	13,500	C
Berry College	GA	39,254	HC
Bethany College	KS	30,605	NC
Bethany College	WV	35,282	C
Bethel College	IN	31,560	C
Birmingham-Southern College	AL	42,370	VC+
Black Hills State Univ	SD	13,562	LC
Blackburn College	IL	21,350	C
Boise State Univ	ID	12,802	C
Boston Univ	MA	54,130	HC+
Bowling Green State Univ	OH	18,970	C
Bradley Univ	IL	31,874	VC
Brenau Univ Women's College	GA	26,650	C+
Brescia Univ	KY	26,140	VC+
Bridgewater State Univ	MA	18,752	C
Brigham Young Univ	UT	12,100	HC
Brigham Young Univ/Hawaii	HI	8,614	VC
Buena Vista Univ	IA	37,954	C
Buffalo State/State Univ of Buffalo	NY	15,733	C+
Cal State, Chico	CA	18,952	C
Calvin College	MI	37,585	VC+
Capital Univ	OH	39,824	VC
Carlow Univ	PA	30,272	C
Carroll Univ	WI	24,860	C
Carson-Newman Univ	TN	29,058	C+
Case Western Reserve Univ	OH	55,178	MC
Central Conn State Univ	CT	19,212	C
Central State Univ	OH	9,010	C
Central Washington Univ	WA	11,730	C
Chicago State Univ	IL	5,482	C
CUNY/Brooklyn College	NY	5,884	C+
Claflin Univ	SC	22,368	C+
Clarke Univ	IA	36,400	C
Coker College	SC	32,256	LC
Colby-Sawyer College	NH	47,870	C
College for Creative Studies	MI		SP
College of Mount St. Joseph	OH	33,880	C
College of New Jersey	NJ	25,376	HC
College of the Ozarks	MO	5,605	VC
Colo State Univ-Fort Collins	CO	20,090	VC
Columbus State Univ	GA	13,176	C
Concord Univ	WV	13,102	C
Concordia College, Moorhead	MN	39,974	C+
Concordia Univ St. Paul	MN	27,200	C
Converse College	SC	37,130	C
Corcoran College of Art and Design	DC	36,500	SP
Cornell College	IA	44,930	HC
Culver-Stockton College	MO	30,900	C
CUNY-City College	NY	19,576	HC+
Daemen College	NY	31,510	C
Defiance College	OH	30,645	C
Delaware State Univ	DE	14,700	LC
DePaul Univ	IL	46,120	VC
Dickinson State Univ	ND	8,550	NC
Dordt College	IA	34,160	VC
Dowling College	NY	25,000	LC
East Carolina Univ	NC	14,169	C
East Central Univ	OK	10,223	LC
Eastern Kentucky Univ	KY	11,161	C
Eastern Mich Univ	MI	17,961	C
Eastern Washington Univ	WA	16,388	C
Edinboro Univ of Pennsylvania	PA	15,940	LC
Elizabethtown College	PA	47,600	VC
Elmhurst College	IL	42,032	C+
Elmira College	NY	49,950	C+
Emporia State Univ	KS	12,897	C
Escuela de Artes Plasticas de PR	PR	2,660	
Fairmont State Univ	WV	12,098	LC
Ferris State Univ	MI	19,698	C
Fisk Univ	TN	19,830	C
Flagler College	FL	24,960	VC
Florida A&M Univ	FL	14,935	LC
Florida International Univ	FL	17,747	VC
Florida Southern College	FL	38,240	VC
Florida State Univ	FL	15,238	HC
Fort Hays State Univ	KS	11,354	C
Francis Marion Univ	SC	16,464	LC
Freed-Hardeman Univ	TN	19,697	VC
Friends Univ	KS	29,100	C
Georgia Southwestern State Univ	GA	12,218	C
Georgia State Univ	GA	12,000	VC
Goddard College	VT	16,418	VC
Goshen College	IN	35,900	VC
Grace College and Theological Seminary	IN	28,800	C
Grand Valley State Univ	MI	17,998	VC
Grand View Univ	IA	31,050	C
Green Mountain College	VT	33,547	LC
Greensboro College	NC	28,740	LC
Gustavus Adolphus College	MN	48,170	HC
Hardin-Simmons Univ	TX	23,560	C+
Hastings College	NE	27,782	C+
Henderson State Univ	AR	13,634	C
Heritage Univ	WA	17,664	NC
Hillsdale College	MI	31,890	HC+
Hofstra Univ	NY	48,020	VC+
Hope College	MI	36,320	VC+
Houghton College	NY	35,740	VC
Houston Baptist Univ	TX	23,815	C+
Howard Univ	DC	35,957	C
Hunter College / The CUNY	NY	14,429	VC
Huntington Univ	IN	32,220	C
Indiana State Univ	IN	16,000	C
Indiana Univ Bloomington	IN	19,358	HC
Indiana Univ of Pennsylvania	PA	20,180	LC
Indiana Univ-Purdue Univ Fort Wayne	IN	15,425	C
Indiana Univ-Purdue Univ Indianapolis	IN	17,290	C
Indiana Wesleyan Univ	IN	31,815	VC
Inter-American Univ of PR/San Germán	PR	6,720	
Iowa Wesleyan College	IA	30,850	LC
Ithaca College	NY	52,300	HC
Jacksonville Univ	FL	37,780	C
Johnson State College	VT	16,721	C
Kansas State Univ	KS	15,497	VC
Kansas Wesleyan Univ	KS	32,000	C
Kendall College of Art and Design of Ferris State Univ	MI	21,048	SP
Kennesaw State Univ	GA	13,017	VC
Kent State Univ	OH	19,352	C
Kentucky State Univ	KY	11,000	LC
Kentucky Wesleyan College	KY	27,440	VC+
Keystone College	PA	28,680	LC
Kutztown Univ of Pennsylvania	PA	16,909	LC
Lamar Univ	TX	6,820	LC
Lehman College / The CUNY	NY	5,778	LC
Lincoln Univ	MO	11,996	NC
Lindsey Wilson College	KY	30,470	VC
Lipscomb Univ	TN	35,722	VC
LIU/Brooklyn Campus	NY	26,500	C
LIU/C.W. Post Campus	NY	38,888	C
Longwood Univ	VA	20,924	C
Louisiana College	LA	15,746	C
Louisiana Tech Univ	LA	8,000	C
Lubbock Christian Univ	TX	25,518	C
Madonna Univ	MI	24,540	VC
Malone Univ	OH	34,334	C
Manchester College	IN	35,070	C
Mansfield Univ	PA	19,468	LC
Marian Univ	WI	30,980	LC
Mars Hill College	NC	22,950	LC
Marymount Univ	VA	36,178	C
Maryville Univ of St. Louis	MO	34,920	VC
Marywood Univ	PA	40,695	C
Mass College of Art and Design	MA	23,600	SP
McKendree Univ	IL	29,920	C+
McMurry Univ	TX	25,962	LC
Mercyhurst Univ	PA	40,700	C
Messiah College	PA	39,540	VC
Methodist Univ	NC	37,185	C
Miami Univ	OH	24,191	HC
Mich State Univ	MI	13,689	VC
Middle Tenn State Univ	TN	8,650	C
Midland Univ	NE	34,000	C
Millersville Univ of Pennsylvania	PA	18,498	C
Millikin Univ	IL	37,462	C
Minn State Univ, Mankato	MN	14,900	C
Minn State Univ, Moorhead	MN	13,392	C
Miss College	MS	21,998	VC
Miss Univ for Women	MS	7,400	LC
Missouri Southern State Univ	MO	11,910	C
Missouri Western State Univ	MO	12,260	NC
Monmouth Univ	NJ	42,252	C
Montana State Univ-Billings	MT	12,425	LC
Montclair State Univ	NJ	22,614	C
Montserrat College of Art	MA	31,000	SP
Moore College of Art and Design	PA	38,124	SP
Moravian College	PA	36,381	VC
Morningside College	IA	32,620	C
Mount Mary Univ	WI	32,836	LC
Mount Vernon Nazarene Univ	OH	29,590	C
Murray State Univ	KY	14,944	C
Nazareth College of Rochester	NY	41,590	VC
New Jersey City Univ	NJ	21,060	C+
New York Inst of Technology	NY	40,590	VC
New York Univ	NY	61,470	MC
N Car Agricultural and Technical State Univ	NC	13,175	LC
North Central College	IL	38,343	VC
North Georgia College & State Univ	GA	8,500	C
Northeastern State Univ	OK	8,615	VC
Northern Illinois Univ	IL	19,768	C
Northern Kentucky Univ	KY	15,302	LC
Northern Mich Univ	MI	15,300	VC
Northern State Univ	SD	14,021	C
Northwest Missouri State Univ	MO	14,229	C
Northwest Nazarene Univ	ID	24,275	NC
Northwestern College	MN	24,000	C
Northwestern College of Iowa	IA	34,848	C+
Notre Dame of Maryland Univ	MD	27,700	C
Nova Southeastern Univ	FL	34,016	VC
Oakland City Univ	IN	24,500	NC
Ohio Wesleyan Univ	OH	49,460	C+
Okla Baptist Univ	OK	28,202	VC
Old Dominion Univ	VA	18,662	C
Olivet Nazarene Univ	IL	29,990	C
Oral Roberts Univ	OK	31,734	C
Ouachita Baptist Univ	AR	29,010	VC
Our Lady of the Lake Univ of San Antonio	TX	22,430	LC
Palm Beach Atlantic Univ	FL	33,882	LC
Peru State College	NE	8,600	NC
Piedmont College	GA	29,260	C
Pittsburg State Univ	KS	12,032	C
Plymouth State Univ	NH	23,148	LC
Point Loma Nazarene Univ	CA	38,610	VC
Pontifical Catholic Univ of PR	PR	7,310	
Pratt Inst	NY	49,520	SP
Prescott College	AZ	33,284	C+
Purdue Univ/West Lafayette	IN	20,278	HC
Queens College / The CUNY	NY	17,107	VC
Rhode Island College	RI	17,132	LC
Rivier College	NH	35,000	VC
Roberts Wesleyan College	NY	37,384	C+
Rocky Mountain College	MT	32,242	C
Rocky Mountain College of Art and Design	CO	22,470	NC
Rosemont College	PA	42,350	C
Rowan Univ	NJ	23,570	VC
Saginaw Valley State Univ	MI	16,869	C
St. Joseph's Univ	PA	52,272	VC
St. Mary-of-the-Woods College	IN	37,722	LC
St. Michael's College	VT	48,740	VC
St. Vincent College	PA	40,244	C
St. Xavier Univ	IL	32,840	C
Salem State College	MA	13,161	LC
School of the Art Inst of Chicago	IL	44,000	SP
Seton Hill Univ	PA	35,172	C
Shepherd Univ	WV	14,996	C
Shippensburg Univ of Pennsylvania	PA	17,064	LC
Silver Lake College	WI	22,600	LC
S Car State Univ	SC	6,700	LC
S Dak State Univ	SD	14,296	C
Southeast Missouri State Univ	MO	14,983	LC
Southeastern Okla State Univ	OK	7,966	C
Southern Arkansas Univ	AR	14,316	C
Southern Conn State Univ	CT	18,033	C
Southern Illinois Univ Edwardsville	IL	17,532	C
Southern Methodist Univ	TX	57,755	MC
Southern Univ and A&M College	LA	9,761	C+
Southern Univ at New Orleans	LA	1,000	NC
Southwest Baptist Univ	MO	24,710	C
Southwest Minn State Univ	MN	14,000	C
Southwestern Okla State Univ	OK	9,160	C
Spelman College	GA	24,650	VC
St. Ambrose Univ	IA		C
St. Catherine Univ	MN	37,782	C+
St. Cloud State Univ	MN	10,600	C
St. Edward's Univ	TX	44,674	VC
St. Thomas Aquinas College	NY	30,000	C
Sul Ross State Univ	TX	13,410	LC
SUNY New Paltz	NY	15,010	C
Syracuse Univ	NY	54,512	HC
Tarleton State Univ	TX	13,489	LC
Taylor Univ	IN	36,742	VC+
Temple Univ	PA	24,392	VC
Tenn Tech Univ	TN	11,310	C
Texas Christian Univ	TX	47,570	HC
The Catholic Univ of America	DC	52,852	VC
The College of New Rochelle	NY	33,600	VC
The College of St. Rose	NY	26,750	C
Ohio State Univ	OH	19,887	MC
Thomas More College	KY	34,760	C
Towson Univ	MD	16,000	VC
Trinity Christian College	IL	28,869	C
Troy Univ	AL	10,650	C
Union College	NE	23,270	VC
Univ of Akron	OH	20,436	C
Univ of Arizona	AZ	20,105	C
Univ of Arkansas at Pine Bluff	AR	10,600	C
Univ of Central Arkansas	AR	10,840	VC
Univ of Central Florida	FL	15,711	VC+
Univ of Central Missouri	MO	14,605	C
Univ of Central Okla	OK	12,293	C
Univ of Cincinnati	OH	20,199	VC
Univ of Dallas	TX	43,510	VC+
Univ of Dayton	OH	43,750	VC
Univ of Evansville	IN	41,056	VC+
Univ of Findlay	OH	31,916	C
Univ of Florida	FL	15,783	HC+
Univ of Georgia	GA	19,508	VC
Univ of Idaho	ID	14,558	C
Univ of Illinois at Chicago	IL	24,293	VC
Univ of Illinois at Urbana-Champaign	IL	24,300	HC
Univ of Indianapolis	IN	31,740	LC
Univ of Iowa	IA	17,481	VC
Univ of Kansas	KS	16,980	C+
Univ of Kentucky	KY	19,868	C
Univ of Louisiana at Lafayette	LA	6,130	C
Univ of Louisville	KY	17,460	VC
Univ of Maine	ME	19,712	C+
Univ of Maine at Presque Isle	ME	15,011	LC
Univ of Mary Hardin-Baylor	TX	31,950	C+
Univ of Maryland	MD	18,801	HC
Univ of Maryland/Eastern Shore	MD	14,000	C
Univ of Mass Dartmouth	MA	22,223	C
Univ of Minn/Duluth	MN	18,964	C+
Univ of Minn/Twin Cities	MN		HC
Univ of Missouri/Columbia	MO	18,201	MC
Univ of Montana-Western	MT	9,753	LC
Univ of Montevallo	AL	17,320	C
Univ of Nebr at Kearney	NE	14,855	LC
Univ of New England	ME	46,145	C+
Univ of New Mexico	NM	15,300	C
Univ of North Alabama	AL	9,960	C
Univ of N Car at Charlotte	NC	15,847	C
Univ of N Car at Greensboro	NC	12,848	C
Univ of North Florida	FL	15,578	VC
Univ of Northern Iowa	IA	14,776	C
Univ of Rio Grande	OH	8,750	NC
Univ of St. Francis	IN	29,810	C
Univ of Sioux Falls	SD	22,990	C
Univ of S Car at Columbia	SC	19,725	VC+
Univ of S Car Upstate	SC	17,673	LC
Univ of S Dak	SD	15,111	C
Univ of South Florida	FL	13,000	C
Univ of Southern Indiana	IN	14,657	C
Univ of Southern Miss	MS	13,170	C
Univ of St. Francis	IL	36,490	C
Univ of Tenn at Chattanooga	TN	16,883	C
Univ of the Cumberlands	KY	27,500	LC
Univ of the Incarnate Word	TX	35,200	LC
Univ of Toledo	OH	18,464	C
Univ of Utah	UT	13,462	VC
Univ of Vermont	VT	26,120	VC+
Univ of West Florida	FL	14,656	C
Univ of Wisc Whitewater	WI	13,314	C
Univ of Wisc/Green Bay	WI	14,900	C
Univ of Wisc/Madison	WI	18,757	HC
Univ of Wisc/Oshkosh	WI	10,426	LC
Univ of Wisc/Platteville	WI	14,274	C
Univ of Wisc/River Falls	WI	9,722	LC
Univ of Wisc/Stout	WI	23,942	C
Univ of Wisc/Superior	WI	14,106	C
Univ of Wisc-Milwaukee	WI	18,436	C
Utah State Univ	UT	11,803	C
Valparaiso Univ	IN	43,040	VC+
Virginia Commonwealth Univ	VA	18,633	C
Virginia Union Univ	VA	18,432	C
Virginia Wesleyan College	VA	28,433	LC
Viterbo Univ	WI	30,070	C
Wartburg College	IA	41,055	VC
Washburn Univ	KS	12,165	NC
Washington and Jefferson College	PA	49,990	VC
Washington Univ in St. Louis	MO	58,818	MC
Wayne State Univ	MI	19,493	C
Webster Univ	MO	33,990	C+
West Liberty Univ	WV	9,142	LC
West Texas A&M Univ	TX	13,478	C
West Virginia State Univ	WV	8,378	NC
West Virginia Wesleyan College	WV	26,880	C
Western Carolina Univ	NC	13,965	C+
Western Kentucky Univ	KY	11,000	LC
Western Mich Univ	MI	19,042	C
Western New Mexico Univ	NM	8,500	LC
Western State Colo Univ	CO	16,135	C
Western Washington Univ	WA	18,519	VC

School	ST	$IS	SR
Westmont College	CA	41,500	HC
Wichita State Univ	KS	12,539	C
Winona State Univ	MN	16,530	C
Wright State Univ	OH	16,983	C
Xavier Univ of Louisiana	LA	25,300	C
Youngstown State Univ	OH	16,374	LC

ART HISTORY

School	ST	$IS	SR
Academy of Art Univ	CA		
Amherst College	MA	58,744	MC
Aquinas College	MI	33,060	C
Arizona State Univ	AZ	18,818	C+
Assumption College	MA	45,721	VC
Baldwin Wallace Univ	OH	36,980	VC
Belmont Univ	TN	37,380	VC+
Binghamton Univ / The SUNY	NY	20,832	HC+
Bowdoin College	ME	57,834	MC
Bowling Green State Univ	OH	18,970	C
Cal State, Chico	CA	18,952	C
Cal State, Fullerton	CA	25,188	C+
Calvin College	MI	37,585	VC+
Canisius College	NY	45,602	VC
Colby College	ME	57,510	MC
College of Charleston	SC	21,273	VC
College of Mount St. Joseph	OH	33,880	C
Cornell Univ	NY	59,037	MC
Creighton Univ	NE	44,058	VC+
DePaul Univ	IL	46,120	VC
Dickinson College	PA	57,002	HC+
Dominican Univ	IL	37,628	C
Dordt College	IA	34,160	VC
Elon Univ	NC	40,046	HC
Flagler College	FL	24,960	VC
Fordham Univ	NY	58,927	HC
Franklin College	IN	35,885	C
Georgetown Univ	DC	52,910	MC
Goucher College	MD	50,252	VC+
Hamline Univ	MN	44,198	VC
Indiana Univ Bloomington	IN	19,358	HC
Indiana Univ-Purdue Univ Indianapolis	IN	17,290	C
Ithaca College	NY	52,300	HC
John Carroll Univ	OH	44,520	C+
Keene State College	NH	21,538	C
Kennesaw State Univ	GA	13,017	VC
Kenyon College	OH	56,810	MC
Loyola Univ Chicago	IL	49,560	VC+
Mills College	CA	54,119	HC
Missouri State Univ	MO	13,996	VC
Nazareth College of Rochester	NY	41,590	VC
New York Univ	NY	61,470	MC
North Central College	IL	38,343	VC
Northeastern Illinois Univ	IL		C
Oberlin College	OH	57,025	MC
Occidental College	CA	59,592	MC+
Ohio Univ	OH	20,676	VC
Pace Univ	NY	48,094	VC
Plymouth State Univ	NH	23,148	LC
Providence College	RI	55,995	HC
St. Louis Univ	MO	46,594	VC+
San Diego State Univ	CA	20,578	VC+
San Jose State Univ	CA	19,707	C
Seattle Univ	WA	47,010	VC+
Seton Hall Univ	NJ	45,902	C
Sewanee: The Univ of the South	TN	47,700	HC+
Southern Oregon Univ	OR	17,874	C
Southwestern Univ	TX	45,660	VC
St. Bonaventure Univ	NY	38,831	C
Syracuse Univ	NY	54,512	HC
Texas Christian Univ	TX	47,570	HC
The Catholic Univ of America	DC	52,852	VC
The SUNY at Potsdam	NY	17,754	C
Transylvania Univ	KY	40,310	VC+
Univ of Arizona	AZ	20,105	C
Univ of Calif at Irvine	CA	25,961	VC
Univ of Calif at Riverside	CA	27,204	C
Univ of Central Okla	OK	12,293	C
Univ of Colo Boulder	CO	22,605	VC+
Univ of Denver	CO	51,787	VC+
Univ of Evansville	IN	41,056	VC+
Univ of Georgia	GA	19,508	VC
Univ of Illinois at Chicago	IL	24,293	VC
Univ of Louisville	KY	17,460	VC
Univ of Maine	ME	19,712	C+
Univ of Miami	FL	55,166	MC
Univ of Nebr - Lincoln	NE	17,507	VC
Univ of New Mexico	NM	15,300	C
Univ of San Diego	CA	53,302	HC+
Univ of Tenn at Knoxville	TN	20,364	VC+
Univ of Tulsa	OK	45,311	HC+
Univ of Utah	UT	13,462	VC
Univ of Wisc/Superior	WI	14,106	C
Wake Forest Univ	NC	51,000	MC
Webster Univ	MO	33,990	C+
Western Mich Univ	MI	19,042	C
Whitman College	WA	54,400	MC
Wofford College	SC	45,795	VC
Wright State Univ	OH	16,983	C
Yale Univ	CT	55,300	MC
Youngstown State Univ	OH	16,374	LC

ART HISTORY AND APPRECIATION

School	ST	$IS	SR
Adams State College	CO	13,358	LC
Adelphi Univ	NY	43,130	VC
Agnes Scott College	GA	45,323	VC+
Albion College	MI	43,884	VC
Alfred Univ	NY	40,392	VC
Allegheny College	PA	49,020	HC
American Univ	DC	54,829	HC+
Aquinas College	MI	33,060	C
Arcadia Univ	PA	33,570	C+
Art Academy of Cincinnati	OH	25,940	SP
Augsburg College	MN	35,142	C
Augustana College	IL	43,398	HC
Baker Univ	KS	33,350	C+
Bard College	NY	59,872	HC
Bard College at Simon's Rock	MA	58,963	HC+
Baylor Univ	TX	46,720	HC
Beloit College	WI	49,970	HC
Berry College	GA	39,254	HC
Birmingham-Southern College	AL	42,370	VC+
Bloomsburg Univ of Pennsylvania	PA	13,598	C
Boston College	MA	58,506	MC
Bradley Univ	IL	31,874	VC
Brandeis Univ	MA	58,820	HC
Bridgewater State Univ	MA	18,752	C
Brigham Young Univ	UT	12,100	HC
Brown Univ	RI	56,150	MC
Bryn Mawr College	PA	57,760	MC
Bucknell Univ	PA	58,160	MC
Buffalo State/State Univ of Buffalo	NY	15,733	C+
Cal State, San Bernardino	CA	12,000	C
Cal State, Stanislaus	CA	18,582	C
Calvin College	MI	37,585	VC+
Carleton College	MN	58,149	MC
Carlow Univ	PA	30,272	C
Case Western Reserve Univ	OH	55,178	MC
Centre College	KY	35,000	HC+
Chapman Univ	CA	56,019	VC+
Chatham Univ	PA	42,440	VC
CUNY/Brooklyn College	NY	5,884	C+
Clark Univ	MA	47,020	HC+
Clarke Univ	IA	36,400	C
Coe College	IA	43,590	VC
Colgate Univ	NY	50,930	MC
College of New Jersey	NJ	25,376	HC
College of the Holy Cross	MA	56,232	MC
College of William & Mary	VA	25,085	MC
Colo College	CO	54,534	MC
Colo State Univ-Fort Collins	CO	20,090	VC
Columbia Univ in the City of New York	NY	61,116	MC
Columbia Univ/Barnard College	NY	39,000	MC
Columbia Univ/School of General Studies	NY	54,083	MC
Conn College	CT	54,970	MC
Cornell College	IA	44,930	HC
Dartmouth College	NH	57,996	MC
Denison Univ	OH	54,670	HC+
DePauw Univ	IN	48,950	VC+
Dominican Univ of Calif	CA	51,250	C
Drake Univ	IA	30,980	VC+
Drew Univ/College of Liberal Arts	NJ	55,862	VC
Drury Univ	MO	30,319	VC
Duke Univ	NC	50,250	MC
Duquesne Univ	PA	42,017	VC
East Carolina Univ	NC	14,169	C
Eastern Mich Univ	MI	17,961	C
Eastern Washington Univ	WA	16,388	C
Edinboro Univ of Pennsylvania	PA	15,940	LC
Elizabethtown College	PA	47,600	VC
Emory Univ	GA	45,000	MC
Ferris State Univ	MI	19,698	C
Florida International Univ	FL	17,747	VC
Florida Southern College	FL	38,240	VC
Florida State Univ	FL	15,238	HC
Framingham State Univ	MA	16,750	C
Franklin and Marshall College	PA	58,295	MC
Gallaudet Univ	DC	25,380	SP
George Mason Univ	VA	15,724	VC
George Washington Univ	DC	57,108	MC
Georgia State Univ	GA	12,000	VC
Gettysburg College	PA	56,820	HC
Grand Valley State Univ	MI	17,998	VC
Hamilton College	NY	55,620	MC
Hampshire College	MA	58,320	MC
Hanover College	IN	41,450	VC
Hartwick College	NY	49,815	C+
Harvard Univ/Harvard College	MA	49,000	MC
Haverford College	PA	59,236	MC
Hobart and William Smith Colleges	NY	43,000	VC
Hofstra Univ	NY	48,020	VC+
Hollins Univ	VA	43,295	VC
Howard Univ	DC	35,957	C
Indiana State Univ	IN	16,000	C
Ithaca College	NY	52,300	HC
Jacksonville Univ	FL	37,780	C
James Madison Univ	VA	18,049	VC
John Carroll Univ	OH	44,520	C+
Johns Hopkins Univ	MD	47,492	MC
Juniata College	PA	49,340	VC
Kalamazoo College	MI	47,825	HC+
Kansas City Art Inst	MO	38,000	SP
Kean Univ	NJ	22,060	LC
Kendall College of Art and Design of Ferris State Univ	MI	21,048	SP
Kent State Univ	OH	19,352	C
Knox College	IL		VC
Lawrence Univ	WI	46,371	HC
Lehigh Univ	PA	55,080	MC
Lewis & Clark College	OR	52,656	VC
Lindenwood Univ	MO	20,750	C
Lourdes Univ	OH	26,055	LC
Loyola Marymount Univ	CA	53,240	VC+
Lycoming College	PA	43,636	C
Manhattanville College	NY	46,260	VC
Mansfield Univ	PA	19,468	LC
Marian Univ/Indianapolis	IN	37,058	C
Mars Hill College	NC	22,950	LC
Mary Baldwin College	VA	37,110	C
Maryland Inst College of Art	MD	39,500	SP
Maryville College	TN	33,150	VC
Mass College of Art and Design	MA	23,600	SP
McDaniel College	MD	45,600	VC
Messiah College	PA	39,540	VC
Miami Univ	OH	24,191	HC
Mich State Univ	MI	13,689	VC
Millsaps College	MS	43,888	VC+
Monmouth Univ	NJ	42,252	C
Montclair State Univ	NJ	22,614	C
Moravian College	PA	36,381	VC
Mount Holyoke College	MA	53,596	HC+
New College of Florida	FL	14,504	HC+
New England College	NH	45,930	LC
New York Univ	NY	61,470	MC
Northern Illinois Univ	IL	19,768	C
Northern Kentucky Univ	KY	15,302	LC
Northwestern Univ	IL	37,595	MC
Notre Dame of Maryland Univ	MD	27,700	C
Oakland Univ	MI	19,391	VC
Oglethorpe Univ	GA	42,580	VC
Ohio Univ	OH	20,676	VC
Old Dominion Univ	VA	18,662	C
Pace Univ	NY	48,094	VC
Penn State Univ/Univ Park	PA	25,404	VC
Pepperdine Univ	CA	55,372	HC+
Pomona College	CA	57,680	MC
Portland State Univ	OR	18,672	C
Pratt Inst	NY	49,520	SP
Presbyterian College	SC	42,678	VC
Purchase College / SUNY	NY	16,951	C
Purdue Univ/West Lafayette	IN	20,278	HC
Queens College / The CUNY	NY	17,107	VC
Randolph-Macon College	VA	45,086	C
Rhode Island College	RI	17,132	LC
Rice Univ	TX	43,288	MC
Ripon College	WI	36,959	C+
Roanoke College	VA	47,996	C+
Rockford College	IL	31,000	C
Roger Williams Univ	RI	45,788	C
Rollins College	FL	52,370	HC
Roosevelt Univ	IL	22,605	VC
Rutgers, The State Univ of New Jersey/Camden Campus	NJ	24,254	C
Rutgers, The State Univ of New Jersey/New Brunswick	NJ	25,077	VC
St. Joseph College	CT	45,630	LC
St. Peter's College	NJ	44,240	C
St. Vincent College	PA	40,244	C
Salem College	NC	29,326	VC
Salve Regina Univ	RI	47,250	VC
San Francisco Art Inst	CA	52,492	SP
Santa Clara Univ	CA	54,702	MC
Sarah Lawrence College	NY	48,000	HC
Savannah College of Art and Design	GA	46,824	SP
School of the Art Inst of Chicago	IL	44,000	SP
Scripps College	CA	54,900	MC
Seton Hill Univ	PA	35,172	C
Siena Heights Univ	MI	17,000	LC
Skidmore College	NY	57,926	HC
Smith College	MA	57,524	MC
Southern Conn State Univ	CT	18,033	C
Southern Illinois Univ Edwardsville	IL	17,532	C
Southern Methodist Univ	TX	57,755	MC
St. Lawrence Univ	NY	53,740	HC
St. Mary's College of Maryland	MD	26,699	HC
St. Olaf College	MN	49,960	HC+
Stanford Univ	CA	56,411	MC
Stonehill College	MA	46,780	VC+
Stony Brook Univ / SUNY	NY	19,359	HC
Suffolk Univ	MA	46,548	C
SUNY College at Geneseo	NY	18,055	HC+
SUNY New Paltz	NY	15,010	C
Susquehanna Univ	PA	49,170	C
Swarthmore College	PA	57,870	MC
Sweet Briar College	VA	43,765	C+
Temple Univ	PA	24,392	VC
Texas Tech Univ	TX	14,243	C
The Catholic Univ of America	DC	52,852	VC
The College of New Rochelle	NY	33,600	VC
Trinity College	CT		HC+
Trinity Univ	TX	44,174	HC+
Troy Univ	AL	10,650	C
Truman State Univ	MO	13,546	HC
Tufts Univ	MA	58,780	MC
Tulane Univ	LA	58,942	MC
Univ at Albany / SUNY	NY	18,674	VC
Univ at Buffalo / The SUNY	NY	20,283	VC
Univ of Alabama at Tuscaloosa	AL	17,164	C+
Univ of Arkansas at Little Rock	AR		C
Univ of Calif at Berkeley	CA	23,322	MC
Univ of Calif at Davis	CA	24,482	HC
Univ of Calif at Los Angeles	CA	25,686	MC
Univ of Calif at Riverside	CA	27,204	C
Univ of Calif at San Diego	CA	21,000	VC
Univ of Calif at Santa Barbara	CA	27,551	HC
Univ of Calif at Santa Cruz	CA	27,807	VC
Univ of Chicago	IL	55,416	MC
Univ of Colo Boulder	CO	22,605	VC+
Univ of Conn	CT	23,744	HC
Univ of Dallas	TX	43,510	VC+
Univ of Dayton	OH	43,750	VC
Univ of Delaware	DE	22,728	VC
Univ of Denver	CO	51,787	VC+
Univ of Florida	FL	15,783	HC+
Univ of Georgia	GA	19,508	VC
Univ of Hartford	CT	42,674	C
Univ of Illinois at Chicago	IL	24,293	VC
Univ of Illinois at Urbana-Champaign	IL	24,300	HC
Univ of Iowa	IA	17,481	VC
Univ of Kansas	KS	16,980	C+
Univ of Kentucky	KY	19,868	C
Univ of La Verne	CA	47,010	VC
Univ of Louisville	KY	17,460	VC
Univ of Mary Washington	VA	19,484	VC
Univ of Maryland	MD	18,801	HC
Univ of Mass Amherst	MA	23,697	VC+
Univ of Mass Dartmouth	MA	22,223	C
Univ of Memphis	TN	15,094	C
Univ of Mich/Ann Arbor	MI	22,102	HC+
Univ of Mich/Dearborn	MI	9,885	VC
Univ of Minn/Duluth	MN	18,964	C+
Univ of Minn/Morris	MN	17,150	VC
Univ of Minn/Twin Cities	MN		HC
Univ of Miss	MS	15,482	VC
Univ of Missouri/Columbia	MO	18,201	MC
Univ of Missouri-Kansas City	MO	19,603	C
Univ of Missouri-St. Louis	MO	18,304	VC
Univ of Nebr - Lincoln	NE	17,507	VC
Univ of Nebr at Omaha	NE	12,700	C
Univ of Nevada, Las Vegas	NV	17,303	C
Univ of New Orleans	LA	9,224	VC
Univ of N Car at Chapel Hill	NC	18,348	MC
Univ of N Car at Charlotte	NC	15,847	C
Univ of N Car at Wilmington	NC	13,572	VC+
Univ of North Texas	TX	15,628	C
Univ of Northern Iowa	IA	14,776	C
Univ of Notre Dame	IN		MC
Univ of Okla	OK	17,634	VC+
Univ of Oregon	OR	20,872	VC
Univ of Pennsylvania	PA	56,106	MC
Univ of Rochester	NY	58,500	MC
Univ of San Francisco	CA	49,674	VC
Univ of S Car at Columbia	SC	19,725	VC+
Univ of Southern Calif	CA	56,903	MC
Univ of Texas at Arlington	TX	10,908	LC
Univ of Texas at Austin	TX	44,074	HC
Univ of Texas at San Antonio	TX	18,372	C
Univ of Toledo	OH	18,464	C
Univ of Utah	UT	13,462	VC
Univ of Vermont	VT	26,120	VC+
Univ of Washington	WA	14,722	VC
Univ of Wisc Whitewater	WI	13,314	C
Univ of Wisc/Madison	WI	18,757	HC
Univ of Wisc-Milwaukee	WI	18,436	C
Villanova Univ	PA	56,436	MC
Virginia Commonwealth Univ	VA	18,633	C
Washburn Univ	KS	12,165	NC
Washington and Lee Univ	VA	52,812	MC
Washington Univ in St. Louis	MO	58,818	MC
Wayne State Univ	MI	19,493	C
Webster Univ	MO	33,990	C+
Wellesley College	MA	49,848	MC
Wesleyan College	GA	24,000	C+
Wesleyan Univ	CT	59,844	MC

School	ST	$IS	SR
Wheaton College	MA	54,934	H₲
Wichita State Univ	KS	12,539	C
Willamette Univ	OR	56,450	V₲
William Paterson Univ of New Jersey	NJ	21,694	C
Williams College	MA	58,900	MC
Winthrop Univ	SC	21,120	VC
Wright State Univ	OH	16,983	C
York College / CUNY	NY	5,496	NC
Youngstown State Univ	OH	16,374	LC

ART THERAPY

School	ST	$IS	SR
Albertus Magnus College	CT	37,382	LC
Alverno College	WI	30,483	LC
Andrews Univ	MI	20,030	₲
Anna Maria College	MA	34,600	LC
Arcadia Univ	PA	33,570	₲
Bethany College	KS	30,605	NC
Bethel College	IN	31,560	C
Capital Univ	OH	39,824	VC
Carlow Univ	PA	30,272	C
Converse College	SC	37,130	C
DePaul Univ	IL	46,120	VC
Edgewood College	WI	33,294	C
Emmanuel College	MA	47,985	VC
Endicott College	MA	42,390	C
Lipscomb Univ	TN	35,722	VC
LIU/C.W. Post Campus	NY	38,888	C
Marygrove College	MI	21,290	C
Marywood Univ	PA	40,695	C
Mercyhurst Univ	PA	40,700	C
Millikin Univ	IL	37,462	C
Mount Mary Univ	WI	32,836	LC
New York Univ	NY	61,470	MC
Prescott College	AZ	33,284	₲
Russell Sage College	NY	39,370	C
Seton Hill Univ	PA	35,172	C
Springfield College	MA	25,000	C
The College of New Rochelle	NY	33,600	VC
Univ of Central Okla	OK	12,293	C
Univ of Indianapolis	IN	31,740	LC
Univ of Montana-Western	MT	9,753	LC
Univ of Wisc/Superior	WI	14,106	C

ART/ART STUDIES

School	ST	$IS	SR
Bard College at Simon's Rock	MA	58,963	H₲
St. Joseph's Univ	PA	52,272	VC
Univ of Denver	CO	51,787	V₲
Univ of Illinois at Chicago	IL	24,293	VC

ART/VISUAL CULTURE

School	ST	$IS	SR
Bates College	ME	58,950	MC
Bryant Univ	RI	49,179	VC

ARTS ADMINISTRATION/ MANAGEMENT

School	ST	$IS	SR
Adrian College	MI	33,800	C
Appalachian State Univ	NC	12,919	VC
Aquinas College	MI	33,060	C
Belhaven Univ	MS	27,170	C
Bellarmine Univ	KY	42,950	VC
Benedictine Univ	IL	35,220	C
Bennett College	NC		LC
Bethany College	KS	30,605	NC
Blackburn College	IL	21,350	C
Brenau Univ Women's College	GA	26,650	₲
Buena Vista Univ	IA	37,954	C
Butler Univ	IN	45,898	V₲
Chatham Univ	PA	42,440	VC
College of Charleston	SC	21,273	VC
Concordia College New York	NY	31,500	VC
Culver-Stockton College	MO	30,900	C
Daemen College	NY	31,510	C
Drury Univ	MO	30,319	VC
Eastern Mich Univ	MI	17,961	C
Elmhurst College	IL	42,032	₲
Elon Univ	NC	40,046	HC
Franklin Pierce Univ	NH	41,598	C
Green Mountain College	VT	33,547	LC
Indiana Univ Bloomington	IN	19,358	HC
Lake Erie College	OH	35,704	C
LIU/C.W. Post Campus	NY	38,888	C
Mary Baldwin College	VA	37,110	C
Marywood Univ	PA	40,695	C
Mass College of Liberal Arts	MA	16,733	C
Messiah College	PA	39,540	VC
New York Univ	NY	61,470	MC
Nichols College	MA	37,240	LC
North Georgia College & State Univ	GA	8,500	C
Piedmont College	GA	29,260	C
Point Park Univ	PA	36,390	C
Prescott College	AZ	33,284	₲
Randolph-Macon College	VA	45,086	C
St. Vincent College	PA	40,244	C
Salem College	NC	29,326	VC
Seton Hill Univ	PA	35,172	C
Simmons College	MA	48,770	VC
Spring Hill College	AL	42,130	VC
SUNY Fredonia / The SUNY at Fredonia	NY	18,702	VC
Tiffin Univ	OH	30,273	LC
Univ of Findlay	OH	31,916	C
Univ of Kentucky	KY	19,868	C
Univ of Mich/Dearborn	MI	9,885	VC
Univ of Montana-Western	MT	9,753	LC
Univ of San Francisco	CA	49,674	VC
Univ of Tulsa	OK	45,311	H₲
Univ of Wisc/Green Bay	WI	14,900	C
Univ of Wisc/Stevens Point	WI	14,043	C
Upper Iowa Univ	IA	30,426	NC
Viterbo Univ	WI	30,070	C
Wagner College	NY	48,600	VC
Wartburg College	IA	41,055	VC
Waynesburg Univ	PA	29,100	C
Westminster College	UT	37,708	VC
Wright State Univ	OH	16,983	C

ASIAN STUDIES

School	ST	$IS	SR
Amherst College	MA	58,744	MC
Bates College	ME	58,950	MC
Bowdoin College	ME	57,834	MC
Cal State, Chico	CA	18,952	C
Cornell Univ	NY	59,037	MC
Indiana Univ Bloomington	IN	19,358	HC
Kenyon College	OH	56,810	MC
McDaniel College	MD	45,600	VC
Nazareth College of Rochester	NY	41,590	VC
New York Univ	NY	61,470	MC
Occidental College	CA	59,592	M₲
St. Joseph's Univ	PA	52,272	VC
Seattle Univ	WA	47,010	V₲
Univ of Arkansas at Fayetteville	AR	16,860	VC
Univ of Colo Boulder	CO	22,605	V₲
Univ of Mass Boston	MA	11,966	C

ASIAN/AMERICAN STUDIES

School	ST	$IS	SR
Arizona State Univ	AZ	18,818	₲
Binghamton Univ / The SUNY	NY	20,832	H₲
Brigham Young Univ	UT	12,100	HC
Cal State, Fullerton	CA	25,188	₲
Cal State, Northridge	CA	28,313	C
Columbia Univ in the City of New York	NY	61,116	MC
Emory Univ	GA	45,000	MC
New York Univ	NY	61,470	MC
Ohio Univ	OH	20,676	VC
Pitzer College	CA	54,988	MC
Pomona College	CA	57,680	MC
Providence College	RI	55,995	HC
Purdue Univ/West Lafayette	IN	20,278	HC
San Francisco State Univ	CA	18,514	C
Scripps College	CA	54,900	MC
St. Olaf College	MN	49,960	H₲
Stanford Univ	CA	56,411	MC
Stony Brook Univ / SUNY	NY	19,359	HC
Univ of Calif at Berkeley	CA	23,322	MC
Univ of Calif at Irvine	CA	25,961	VC
Univ of Calif at Los Angeles	CA	25,686	MC
Univ of Calif at Riverside	CA	27,204	C
Univ of Calif at Santa Barbara	CA	27,551	HC
Univ of Denver	CO	51,787	V₲
Univ of Northern Colo	CO	15,973	C
Univ of Southern Calif	CA	56,903	MC
Univ of Washington	WA	14,722	VC
Univ of Wisc-Milwaukee	WI	18,436	C

ASIAN/ORIENTAL STUDIES

School	ST	$IS	SR
Arizona State Univ	AZ	18,818	₲
Augustana College	IL	43,398	HC
Bard College	NY	59,872	HC
Bard College at Simon's Rock	MA	58,963	H₲
Baylor Univ	TX	46,720	HC
Belmont Univ	TN	37,380	V₲
Berea College	KY	7,220	HC
Birmingham-Southern College	AL	42,370	V₲
Boston Univ	MA	54,130	H₲
Bowling Green State Univ	OH	18,970	C
Brigham Young Univ	UT	12,100	HC
Cal State, Long Beach	CA	17,534	₲
Calvin College	MI	37,585	V₲
Carleton College	MN	58,149	MC
Case Western Reserve Univ	OH	55,178	MC
Central Washington Univ	WA	11,730	C
Claremont McKenna College	CA	58,065	MC
Clark Univ	MA	47,020	H₲
Coe College	IA	43,590	VC
Colgate Univ	NY	50,930	MC
College of St. Benedict	MN	47,570	VC
College of the Holy Cross	MA	56,232	MC
Colo College	CO	54,534	MC
CUNY-City College	NY	19,576	H₲
Dartmouth College	NH	57,996	MC
Duke Univ	NC	50,250	MC
Eastern Mich Univ	MI	17,961	C
Emory Univ	GA	45,000	MC
Florida International Univ	FL	17,747	VC
Florida State Univ	FL	15,238	HC
Furman Univ	SC	54,006	HC
Hamilton College	NY	55,620	MC
Hampshire College	MA	58,320	MC
Harvard Univ/Harvard College	MA	49,000	MC
Hobart and William Smith Colleges	NY	43,000	VC
Indiana Univ of Pennsylvania	PA	20,180	LC
John Carroll Univ	OH	44,520	₲
Kean Univ	NJ	22,060	LC
Knox College	IL		VC
Lafayette College	PA	57,050	H₲
Lake Forest College	IL	45,580	VC
Lehigh Univ	PA	55,080	MC
Loyola Marymount Univ	CA	53,240	V₲
Macalester College	MN	53,419	MC
Manhattanville College	NY	46,260	VC
Marietta College	OH	42,135	VC
Mary Baldwin College	VA	37,110	C
Mount Holyoke College	MA	53,596	H₲
New York Univ	NY	61,470	MC
Northeastern Univ	MA	55,296	MC
Ohio Univ	OH	20,676	VC
Old Dominion Univ	VA	18,662	C
Pacific Lutheran Univ	WA	44,840	VC
Penn State Univ/Univ Park	PA	25,404	VC
Pitzer College	CA	54,988	MC
Pomona College	CA	57,680	MC
Purdue Univ/West Lafayette	IN	20,278	HC
Randolph-Macon College	VA	45,086	C
Rice Univ	TX	43,288	MC
Rollins College	FL	52,370	HC
Rutgers, The State Univ of New Jersey/New Brunswick	NJ	25,077	VC
St. John's Univ	MN	46,146	C
San Diego State Univ	CA	20,578	VC
Sarah Lawrence College	NY	48,000	HC
Scripps College	CA	54,900	MC
Seton Hall Univ	NJ	45,902	C
Sewanee: The Univ of the South	TN	47,700	H₲
Simmons College	MA	48,770	VC
Skidmore College	NY	57,926	HC
St. John's Univ	NY	52,840	₲
St. Lawrence Univ	NY	53,740	HC
St. Mary's College of Maryland	MD	26,699	HC
SUNY New Paltz	NY	15,010	C
Swarthmore College	PA	57,870	MC
Temple Univ	PA	24,392	VC
Texas State Univ	TX	16,495	VC
Tufts Univ	MA	58,780	MC
Tulane Univ	LA	58,942	MC
Union College	NY		MC
Univ at Albany / SUNY	NY	18,674	VC
Univ at Buffalo / The SUNY	NY	20,283	VC
Univ of Calif at Berkeley	CA	23,322	MC
Univ of Calif at Los Angeles	CA	25,686	MC
Univ of Calif at Riverside	CA	27,204	C
Univ of Calif at Santa Barbara	CA	27,551	HC
Univ of Cincinnati	OH	20,199	VC
Univ of Colo Boulder	CO	22,605	V₲
Univ of Florida	FL	15,783	H₲
Univ of Hawaii at Manoa	HI	19,379	VC
Univ of Iowa	IA	17,481	VC
Univ of Maryland/Univ College	MD	6,168	SP
Univ of Mich/Ann Arbor	MI	22,102	H₲
Univ of Minn/Twin Cities	MN		HC
Univ of New Mexico	NM	15,300	C
Univ of N Car at Chapel Hill	NC	18,348	MC
Univ of Okla	OK	17,634	V₲
Univ of Oregon	OR	20,872	VC
Univ of Pennsylvania	PA	56,106	MC
Univ of Puget Sound	WA	52,648	H₲
Univ of Redlands	CA	40,500	VC
Univ of Texas at Austin	TX	44,074	HC
Univ of Utah	UT	13,462	VC
Univ of Vermont	VT	26,120	V₲
Univ of Washington	WA	14,722	VC
Univ of Wisc/Madison	WI	18,757	HC
Vassar College	NY	59,070	MC
Washington State Univ	WA	20,461	C
Washington Univ in St. Louis	MO	58,818	MC
Wayne State Univ	MI	19,493	C
Wellesley College	MA	49,848	MC
Wheaton College	MA	54,934	H₲
Whitman College	WA	54,400	MC
Willamette Univ	OR	56,450	V₲
Williams College	MA	58,900	MC

ASTRONOMY

School	ST	$IS	SR
Amherst College	MA	58,744	MC
Benedictine College	KS	29,180	VC
Bennington College	VT	56,990	H₲
Boston Univ	MA	54,130	H₲
Brigham Young Univ	UT	12,100	HC
Bryn Mawr College	PA	57,760	MC
Case Western Reserve Univ	OH	55,178	MC
Colgate Univ	NY	50,930	MC
College of Charleston	SC	21,273	VC
Columbia Univ in the City of New York	NY	61,116	MC
Columbia Univ/Barnard College	NY	39,000	MC
Columbia Univ/School of General Studies	NY	54,083	MC
Cornell Univ	NY	59,037	MC
Eastern Mich Univ	MI	17,961	C
Embry-Riddle Aeronautical Univ - Prescott Campus	AZ	40,584	VC
Florida Inst of Technology	FL	48,290	VC
Franklin and Marshall College	PA	58,295	MC
George Mason Univ	VA	15,724	VC
Harvard Univ/Harvard College	MA	49,000	MC
Haverford College	PA	59,236	MC
Indiana Univ Bloomington	IN	19,358	HC
Lehigh Univ	PA	55,080	MC
Lycoming College	PA	43,636	C
Minn State Univ, Mankato	MN	14,900	C
Montclair State Univ	NJ	22,614	C
Mount Holyoke College	MA	53,596	H₲
Northern Arizona Univ	AZ	18,592	C
Northwestern Univ	IL	37,595	MC
Oberlin College	OH	57,025	MC
Penn State Univ/Univ Park	PA	25,404	VC
San Diego State Univ	CA	20,578	VC
San Francisco State Univ	CA	18,514	C
Smith College	MA	57,524	MC
Stony Brook Univ / SUNY	NY	19,359	HC
Swarthmore College	PA	57,870	MC
Ohio State Univ	OH	19,887	MC
Union College	NY		MC
Univ of Arizona	AZ	20,105	C
Univ of Colo Boulder	CO	22,605	V₲
Univ of Delaware	DE	22,728	VC
Univ of Florida	FL	15,783	H₲
Univ of Hawaii at Hilo	HI	6,500	C
Univ of Illinois at Urbana-Champaign	IL	24,300	HC
Univ of Iowa	IA	17,481	VC
Univ of Kansas	KS	16,980	₲
Univ of Maryland	MD	18,801	HC
Univ of Mass Amherst	MA	23,697	V₲
Univ of Mich/Ann Arbor	MI	22,102	H₲
Univ of Mount Union	OH	35,130	C
Univ of Nebr - Lincoln	NE	17,507	VC
Univ of Okla	OK	17,634	V₲
Univ of Pittsburgh at Pittsburgh	PA	27,800	H₲
Univ of Rochester	NY	58,500	MC
Univ of Southern Calif	CA	56,903	MC
Univ of Texas at Austin	TX	44,074	HC
Univ of Virginia	VA	22,175	MC
Univ of Washington	WA	14,722	VC
Univ of Wisc/Madison	WI	18,757	HC
Valparaiso Univ	IN	43,040	V₲
Vassar College	NY	59,070	MC
Villanova Univ	PA	56,436	MC
Wayne State Univ	MI	19,493	C
Wellesley College	MA	49,848	MC
Wesleyan Univ	CT	59,844	MC
Whitman College	WA	54,400	MC
Williams College	MA	58,900	MC
Wilmington College	OH	29,784	C
Yale Univ	CT	55,300	MC

ASTRONOMY AND PHYSICS

School	ST	$IS	SR
Texas Christian Univ	TX	47,570	HC
Univ of Georgia	GA	19,508	VC
Univ of Mass Dartmouth	MA	22,223	C
Univ of Wyoming	WY	13,855	₲
Youngstown State Univ	OH	16,374	LC

ASTROPHYSICS

School	ST	$IS	SR
Agnes Scott College	GA	45,323	V₲
Boston Univ	MA	54,130	H₲
Calif Inst of Technology	CA	54,045	MC
Cal State, Northridge	CA	28,313	C
Colgate Univ	NY	50,930	MC
College of Charleston	SC	21,273	VC
Columbia Univ in the City of New York	NY	61,116	MC
Dartmouth College	NH	57,996	MC
Florida Inst of Technology	FL	48,290	VC
Franklin and Marshall College	PA	58,295	MC
Haverford College	PA	59,236	MC
Indiana Univ Bloomington	IN	19,358	HC
Lehigh Univ	PA	55,080	MC
Lycoming College	PA	43,636	C
Mich State Univ	MI	13,689	VC
Ohio Univ	OH	20,676	VC
Princeton Univ	NJ	53,795	MC
Rutgers, The State Univ of New Jersey/New Brunswick	NJ	25,077	VC

ST = STATE **$IS** = IN-STATE COSTS **SR** = SELECTOR RATING

School	ST	$IS	SR
San Francisco State Univ	CA	18,514	C
Swarthmore College	PA	57,870	MC
Ohio State Univ	OH	19,887	MC
Tufts Univ	MA	58,780	MC
Univ of Calif at Berkeley	CA	23,322	MC
Univ of Calif at Los Angeles	CA	25,686	MC
Univ of Mich/Ann Arbor	MI	22,102	H₲
Univ of Minn/Twin Cities	MN		HC
Univ of New Mexico	NM	15,300	C
Univ of Okla	OK	17,634	V₲
Villanova Univ	PA	56,436	MC
Wellesley College	MA	49,848	MC
Williams College	MA	58,900	MC

ATHLETIC TRAINING

School	ST	$IS	SR
Adams State College	CO	13,358	LC
Albion College	MI	43,884	VC
Alderson Broaddus Univ	WV	28,656	C
Alfred Univ	NY	40,392	VC
Alma College	MI	42,400	VC
Alvernia Univ	PA	39,250	C
Angelo State Univ	TX	15,049	NC
Appalachian State Univ	NC	12,919	VC
Aquinas College	MI	33,060	C
Arkansas State Univ	AR	14,980	C
Ashland Univ	OH	25,000	C
Augustana College	SD	35,500	VC
Aurora Univ	IL	26,870	C
Averett Univ	VA	36,000	LC
Baldwin Wallace Univ	OH	36,980	VC
Barton College	NC	27,660	C
Baylor Univ	TX	46,720	HC
Belhaven Univ	MS	27,170	C
Benedictine College	KS	29,180	VC
Bethany College	KS	30,605	NC
Bethel College	KS	29,100	C
Bethel Univ	MN	34,940	VC
Boston Univ	MA	54,130	H₲
Bowling Green State Univ	OH	18,970	C
Bridgewater College	VA	39,880	C
Bridgewater State Univ	MA	18,752	C
Cal State, Fullerton	CA	25,188	₲
Calif Univ of Pennsylvania	PA	14,217	C
Campbell Univ	NC	25,500	C
Campbellsville Univ	KY	27,720	C
Canisius College	NY	45,602	VC
Capital Univ	OH	39,824	VC
Carroll Univ	WI	24,860	C
Castleton State College	VT	19,424	C
Catawba College	NC	37,105	C
Cedarville Univ	OH	31,036	V₲
Central College	IA	36,980	V₲
Central Conn State Univ	CT	19,212	C
Central Methodist Univ	MO	28,240	VC
Central Mich Univ	MI	18,066	C
Chapman Univ	CA	56,019	V₲
Clarion Univ of Pennsylvania	PA	17,370	C
Clarke Univ	IA	36,400	C
Coe College	IA	43,590	VC
Colby-Sawyer College	NH	47,870	C
College of Charleston	SC	21,273	VC
College of Mount St. Joseph	OH	33,880	C
College of William & Mary	VA	25,085	MC
Concordia Univ Wisc	WI	28,980	C
Culver-Stockton College	MO	30,900	C
Dakota Wesleyan Univ	SD	23,000	C
Defiance College	OH	30,645	C
Delta State Univ	MS	12,292	LC
Dominican College	NY	31,270	C
Dordt College	IA	34,160	VC
Duquesne Univ	PA	42,017	VC
East Carolina Univ	NC	14,169	C
East Central Univ	OK	10,223	LC
East Texas Baptist Univ	TX	29,135	C
Eastern Illinois Univ	IL	20,502	C
Eastern Mich Univ	MI	17,961	C
Eastern Nazarene College	MA	30,000	C
Eastern Univ	PA	37,704	C
Emporia State Univ	KS	12,897	C
Endicott College	MA	42,390	C
Erskine College	SC	37,360	C
Eureka College	IL	19,280	C
Florida Gulf Coast Univ	FL		C
Florida Southern College	FL	38,240	VC
Florida State Univ	FL	15,238	HC
Fort Lewis College	CO	15,513	C
Franklin College	IN	35,885	C
Gardner-Webb Univ	NC	34,375	₲
George Fox Univ	OR	40,750	₲
George Mason Univ	VA	15,724	VC
Georgetown College	KY	38,690	C
Georgia College and State Univ	GA	18,216	VC
Georgia Southern Univ	GA	16,414	C
Graceland Univ	IA	28,020	C
Grand Canyon Univ	AZ	24,540	VC
Grand Valley State Univ	MI	17,998	VC
Greensboro College	NC	28,740	LC
Hamline Univ	MN	44,198	VC
Harding Univ	AR	21,432	₲
Hardin-Simmons Univ	TX	23,560	₲
Heidelberg Univ	OH	34,100	C
Henderson State Univ	AR	13,634	C
High Point Univ	NC	39,800	C
Hofstra Univ	NY	48,020	V₲
Howard Payne Univ	TX	17,115	C
Huntingdon College	AL	31,850	C
Illinois State Univ	IL	22,634	VC
Indiana Univ Bloomington	IN	19,358	HC
Indiana Univ of Pennsylvania	PA	20,180	LC
Indiana Wesleyan Univ	IN	31,815	VC
Ithaca College	NY	52,300	HC
James Madison Univ	VA	18,049	VC
Johnson State College	VT	16,721	C
Kansas State Univ	KS	15,497	VC
Kean Univ	NJ	22,060	LC
Keene State College	NH	21,538	C
Kent State Univ	OH	19,352	C
King Univ	TN	33,140	C
Lake Superior State Univ	MI	18,121	C
Lasell College	MA	42,500	LC
Lee Univ	TN	18,690	₲
Lees-McRae College	NC	33,624	C
Lenoir-Rhyne College	NC	35,984	C
Lewis Univ	IL	23,050	C
Liberty Univ	VA	19,101	C
Limestone College	SC	29,880	C
Lincoln Memorial Univ	TN	18,144	C
Lindenwood Univ	MO	20,750	C
Linfield College-McMinnville Campus	OR	46,166	C
Longwood Univ	VA	20,924	C
Loras College	IA	37,432	VC
Louisiana College	LA	15,740	C
Louisiana State Univ	LA	18,677	V₲
Loyola Marymount Univ	CA	53,240	V₲
Luther College	IA	44,380	V₲
Lynchburg College	VA	42,645	C
Marietta College	OH	42,135	VC
Marist College	NY	35,500	C
Marquette Univ	WI	43,664	V₲
Mars Hill College	NC	22,950	LC
Marshall Univ	WV	14,820	C
Marywood Univ	PA	40,695	C
Mass College of Liberal Arts	MA	16,733	C
McKendree Univ	IL	29,920	₲
McMurry Univ	TX	25,962	LC
McNeese State Univ	LA		C
Mercyhurst Univ	PA	40,700	C
Messiah College	PA	39,540	VC
Methodist Univ	NC	37,185	C
Miami Univ	OH	24,191	HC
MidAmerica Nazarene Univ	KS	28,000	C
Middle Tenn State Univ	TN	8,650	C
Millikin Univ	IL	37,462	C
Minn State Univ, Mankato	MN	14,900	C
Minn State Univ, Moorhead	MN	13,392	C
Missouri State Univ	MO	13,996	VC
Montclair State Univ	NJ	22,614	C
Mount Marty College	SD	29,638	C
Murray State Univ	KY	19,944	C
National American Univ	SD	16,712	NC
Nebr Wesleyan Univ	NE	29,774	₲
Neumann Univ	PA	31,078	LC
New Mexico State Univ	NM	13,955	LC
North Central College	IL	38,343	VC
N Dak State Univ	ND	14,642	C
North Park Univ	IL	30,130	C
Northern Kentucky Univ	KY	15,302	LC
Northwestern College of Iowa	IA	34,848	₲
Ohio Northern Univ	OH	42,075	VC
Ohio Univ	OH	20,676	VC
Okla State Univ	OK	14,310	VC
Olivet College	MI	19,984	C
Olivet Nazarene Univ	IL	29,990	C
Otterbein College	OH	32,214	C
Palm Beach Atlantic Univ	FL	33,882	LC
Park Univ	MO	17,525	C
Piedmont College	GA	29,260	C
Plymouth State Univ	NH	23,148	LC
Point Loma Nazarene Univ	CA	38,610	VC
Purdue Univ/West Lafayette	IN	20,278	HC
Quinnipiac Univ	CT	53,580	VC
Radford Univ	VA	17,132	LC
Roanoke College	VA	47,996	₲
Rowan Univ	NJ	23,570	VC
Sacred Heart Univ	CT	48,564	VC
Saginaw Valley State Univ	MI	16,869	C
St. Joseph's College	IN	35,790	C
St. Louis Univ	MO	46,594	V₲
Salem International Univ	WV	18,020	C
Salisbury Univ	MD	18,368	VC
Samford Univ	AL	35,700	V₲
San Diego State Univ	CA	20,578	VC
Shaw Univ	NC	15,488	LC
Shawnee State Univ	OH	16,545	NC
Simpson College	IA	36,086	VC
S Dak State Univ	SD	14,296	C
Southeast Missouri State Univ	MO	14,983	LC
Southeastern Louisiana Univ	LA	13,325	C
Southern Nazarene Univ	OK	24,354	NC
Southwest Baptist Univ	MO	24,710	C
Southwestern College	KS	29,270	C
Southwestern Okla State Univ	OK	9,160	C
St. Edward's Univ	TX	44,674	VC
Sterling College	KS	27,216	C
Stony Brook Univ / SUNY	NY	19,359	HC
SUNY Cortland / The SUNY	NY	19,117	C
Tabor College	KS	29,010	LC
Temple Univ	PA	24,392	VC
Texas Christian Univ	TX	47,570	HC
Texas Lutheran Univ	TX	34,070	C
Texas State Univ	TX	16,495	VC
Texas Wesleyan Univ	TX	29,886	C
Ohio State Univ	OH	19,887	MC
Towson Univ	MD	16,000	VC
Trinity International Univ	IL	31,070	C
Troy Univ	AL	10,650	C
Truman State Univ	MO	13,546	HC
Tusculum College	TN	24,295	C
Union College	KY	28,775	C
Univ of Akron	OH	20,436	C
Univ of Alabama at Tuscaloosa	AL	17,164	₲
Univ of Central Arkansas	AR	10,840	VC
Univ of Central Florida	FL	15,711	V₲
Univ of Central Okla	OK	12,293	C
Univ of Charleston	WV	28,650	C
Univ of Conn	CT	23,744	HC
Univ of Delaware	DE	22,728	VC
Univ of Evansville	IN	41,056	V₲
Univ of Georgia	GA	19,508	VC
Univ of Idaho	ID	14,558	C
Univ of Illinois at Urbana-Champaign	IL	24,300	HC
Univ of Indianapolis	IN	31,740	LC
Univ of Iowa	IA	17,481	VC
Univ of Kansas	KS	16,980	₲
Univ of La Verne	CA	47,010	VC
Univ of Maine	ME	19,712	₲
Univ of Maine at Presque Isle	ME	15,011	LC
Univ of Mary	ND	16,714	C
Univ of Miami	FL	55,166	MC
Univ of Mich/Ann Arbor	MI	22,102	H₲
Univ of Minn/Duluth	MN	18,964	₲
Univ of Mobile	AL	27,870	VC
Univ of Montana-Western	MT	9,753	LC
Univ of Mount Union	OH	35,130	C
Univ of Nebr - Lincoln	NE	17,507	VC
Univ of New England	ME	46,145	₲
Univ of New Hampshire	NH	24,702	VC
Univ of New Mexico	NM	15,300	C
Univ of N Car at Charlotte	NC	15,847	C
Univ of N Car at Wilmington	NC	13,572	V₲
Univ of N Dak	ND	14,094	C
Univ of North Florida	FL	15,578	VC
Univ of Northern Colo	CO	15,973	C
Univ of Northern Iowa	IA	14,776	C
Univ of Pittsburgh at Bradford	PA	21,316	LC
Univ of Pittsburgh at Pittsburgh	PA	27,800	H₲
Univ of San Francisco	CA	49,674	VC
Univ of Tampa	FL	35,160	VC
Univ of the Incarnate Word	TX	35,200	LC
Univ of Tulsa	OK	45,311	H₲
Univ of Vermont	VT	26,120	V₲
Univ of West Alabama	AL	9,415	C
Univ of Wisc/Eau Claire	WI	15,430	VC
Univ of Wisc/La Crosse	WI	14,755	VC
Univ of Wisc/Madison	WI	18,757	HC
Univ of Wisc/Stevens Point	WI	14,043	C
Univ of Wisc-Milwaukee	WI	18,436	C
Upper Iowa Univ	IA	30,426	NC
Vanguard Univ of Southern Calif	CA	35,833	VC
Virginia State Univ	VA	11,318	₲
Washburn Univ	KS	12,165	NC
Washington State Univ	WA	20,461	C
Waynesburg Univ	PA	29,100	C
West Chester Univ of Pennsylvania	PA	16,836	C
West Texas A&M Univ	TX	13,478	C
West Virginia Univ	WV	15,794	₲
Western Illinois Univ	IL	20,130	C
Western Mich Univ	MI	19,042	C
Westfield State Univ	MA	18,489	C
Wheeling Jesuit Univ	WV	34,668	C
Whitworth Univ	WA	45,826	V₲
William Woods Univ	MO		C
Wilmington College	OH	29,784	C
Wingate Univ	NC	34,990	C
Winona State Univ	MN	16,530	C
Winthrop Univ	SC	21,120	VC
Wright State Univ	OH	16,983	C
Xavier Univ	OH	43,740	VC

ATMOSPHERIC SCIENCES AND METEOROLOGY

School	ST	$IS	SR
Cal State, Chico	CA	18,952	C
Cornell Univ	NY	59,037	MC
CUNY-City College	NY	19,576	H₲
East Carolina Univ	NC	14,169	C
Embry-Riddle Aeronautical Univ - Daytona Beach	FL	40,884	₲
Embry-Riddle Aeronautical Univ - Prescott Campus	AZ	40,584	VC
Florida Inst of Technology	FL	48,290	VC
Florida State Univ	FL	15,238	HC
Howard Univ	DC	35,957	C
Iowa State Univ	IA	16,403	C
Jackson State Univ	MS	13,512	LC
Lewis Univ	IL	23,050	C
Lyndon State College	VT	14,233	C
Maritime College / SUNY	NY	16,020	C
Metropolitan State Univ of Denver	CO	4,835	LC
Millersville Univ of Pennsylvania	PA	18,498	C
N Car State Univ	NC	16,202	HC
Northern Illinois Univ	IL	19,768	C
Northland College	WI	26,680	C
Ohio Univ	OH	20,676	VC
Oswego / SUNY	NY	20,009	VC
Penn State Univ/Univ Park	PA	25,404	VC
Plymouth State Univ	NH	23,148	LC
Purdue Univ/West Lafayette	IN	20,278	HC
Rutgers, The State Univ of New Jersey/New Brunswick	NJ	25,077	VC
St. Louis Univ	MO	46,594	V₲
San Francisco State Univ	CA	18,514	C
St. Cloud State Univ	MN	10,600	C
Stony Brook Univ / SUNY	NY	19,359	HC
SUNY Oneonta / SUNY	NY	16,919	VC
Texas A&M Univ	TX	16,956	V₲
The College at Brockport / SUNY	NY	18,362	VC
Ohio State Univ	OH	19,887	MC
United States Air Force Academy	CO		MC
Univ at Albany / SUNY	NY	18,674	VC
Univ of Arizona	AZ	20,105	C
Univ of Calif at Davis	CA	24,482	HC
Univ of Calif at Los Angeles	CA	25,686	MC
Univ of Hawaii at Manoa	HI	19,379	VC
Univ of Kansas	KS	16,980	₲
Univ of Louisiana at Monroe	LA	12,998	C
Univ of Louisville	KY	17,460	VC
Univ of Maryland	MD	18,801	HC
Univ of Miami	FL	55,166	MC
Univ of Mich/Ann Arbor	MI	22,102	H₲
Univ of Missouri/Columbia	MO	18,201	MC
Univ of Nebr - Lincoln	NE	17,507	VC
Univ of N Car at Asheville	NC	13,500	V₲
Univ of N Car at Charlotte	NC	15,847	C
Univ of N Dak	ND	14,094	C
Univ of Okla	OK	17,634	V₲
Univ of South Alabama	AL	13,510	C
Univ of Utah	UT	13,462	VC
Univ of Washington	WA	14,722	VC
Univ of Wisc/Madison	WI	18,757	HC
Univ of Wisc-Milwaukee	WI	18,436	C
Valparaiso Univ	IN	43,040	V₲
Western Conn State Univ	CT	18,327	C

AUDIO TECHNOLOGY

School	ST	$IS	SR
American Univ	DC	54,829	H₲
Belmont Univ	TN	37,380	V₲
Brigham Young Univ	UT	12,100	HC
Cogswell Polytechnical College	CA	30,531	C
Columbia College Chicago	IL	30,940	LC
Cornerstone Univ and Grand Rapids Theological Seminary	MI	30,866	C
Five Towns College	NY	34,550	SP
Hofstra Univ	NY	48,020	V₲
Ithaca College	NY	52,300	HC
Lawrence Tech Univ	MI	37,630	VC
Lebanon Valley College	PA	38,570	C
Mich Tech Univ	MI	22,105	VC
Ohio Univ	OH	20,676	VC
Purdue Univ/West Lafayette	IN	20,278	HC
Savannah College of Art and Design	GA	46,824	SP
School of the Art Inst of Chicago	IL	44,000	SP
SUNY Fredonia / The SUNY at Fredonia	NY	18,702	VC
Texas State Univ	TX	16,495	VC
Univ of Hartford	CT	42,674	C
Univ of Mich/Ann Arbor	MI	22,102	H₲
Univ of New Haven	CT	47,740	C
Univ of Rochester	NY	58,500	MC
Webster Univ	MO	33,990	₲

AUTOMOTIVE TECHNOLOGY

School	ST	$IS	SR
Benjamin Franklin Inst of Technology	MA	27,190	SP
Colo State Univ-Pueblo	CO	13,532	LC
Ferris State Univ	MI	19,698	C
Idaho State Univ	ID	11,908	C
Minn State Univ, Mankato	MN	14,900	C
Montana State Univ-Northern	MT	12,500	NC

School	ST	$IS	SR
Pennsylvania College of Technology	PA	25,653	NC
Pittsburg State Univ	KS	12,032	C
Southern Illinois Univ Carbondale	IL	21,620	C
Thomas Edison State College	NJ	5,700	SP
Univ of Akron	OH	20,436	C
Univ of Central Missouri	MO	14,605	C
Walla Walla Univ	WA	26,256	NC

AVIAN SCIENCES

School	ST	$IS	SR
Bowling Green State Univ	OH	18,970	C
Eastern New Mexico Univ	NM	10,682	C
Southern Illinois Univ Carbondale	IL	21,620	C
Ohio State Univ	OH	19,887	MC
Univ of Calif at Davis	CA	24,482	HC

AVIATION ADMINISTRATION/ MANAGEMENT

School	ST	$IS	SR
Andrews Univ	MI	28,030	₵
Auburn Univ	AL	20,052	V₵
Averett Univ	VA	36,000	LC
Baker College of Flint	MI	7,800	NC
Calif Baptist Univ	CA	35,890	C
Central Washington Univ	WA	11,730	C
Daniel Webster College	NH	25,380	C
Delta State Univ	MS	12,292	LC
Dowling College	NY	25,000	LC
Eastern Mich Univ	MI	17,961	C
Embry-Riddle Aeronautical Univ - Prescott Campus	AZ	40,584	VC
Farmingdale State College	NY	18,985	C
Florida Inst of Technology	FL	48,290	VC
Florida Memorial Univ	FL	20,716	LC
Geneva College	PA	27,280	C
Henderson State Univ	AR	13,634	C
Inter-American Univ of PR/ Bayamon Univ College	PR	4,428	
Jacksonville Univ	FL	37,780	C
Lewis Univ	IL	23,050	C
Louisiana Tech Univ	LA	8,000	C
Lynn Univ	FL	43,500	C
Marywood Univ	PA	40,695	C
Metropolitan State Univ of Denver	CO	4,835	LC
Minn State Univ, Mankato	MN	14,900	C
Mountain State Univ	WV	14,330	NC
Ohio Univ	OH	20,676	VC
Park Univ	MO	17,525	C
Purdue Univ/West Lafayette	IN	20,278	HC
Quincy Univ	IL	34,980	LC
Rocky Mountain College	MT	32,242	C
St. Louis Univ	MO	46,594	V₵
Salem International Univ	WV	18,020	C
San Diego Christian College	CA	31,012	C
S Dak State Univ	SD	14,296	C
Southeastern Okla State Univ	OK	7,966	C
Southern Illinois Univ Carbondale	IL	21,620	C
Southern Nazarene Univ	OK	24,354	NC
St. Cloud State Univ	MN	10,600	C
Texas Southern Univ	TX	18,212	LC
Univ of Dubuque	IA	30,200	C
Univ of Illinois at Urbana-Champaign	IL	24,300	HC
Univ of Louisiana at Monroe	LA	12,998	C
Univ of Nebr at Kearney	NE	14,855	LC
Univ of Nebr at Omaha	NE	12,700	C
Univ of North Texas	TX	15,628	C
Univ of Okla	OK	17,634	V₵
Univ of the District of Columbia	DC	7,244	LC
Vaughn College of Aeronautics and Technology	NY	31,360	SP
Western Mich Univ	MI	19,042	C
Westminster College	UT	37,708	VC
Wilmington Univ	DE	7,778	NC

AVIATION COMPUTER TECHNOLOGY

School	ST	$IS	SR
Andrews Univ	MI	28,030	₵
Florida Inst of Technology	FL	48,290	VC
Florida Memorial Univ	FL	20,716	LC
Inter-American Univ of PR/ Bayamon Univ College	PR	4,428	
Metropolitan State Univ of Denver	CO	4,835	LC
Purdue Univ/West Lafayette	IN	20,278	HC
Southern Illinois Univ Carbondale	IL	21,620	C
Univ of Central Missouri	MO	14,605	C
Walla Walla Univ	WA	26,256	NC
Westminster College	UT	37,708	VC

AVIATION FLIGHT TECHNOLOGY

School	ST	$IS	SR
Thomas Edison State College	NJ	5,700	SP

AVIATION MAINTENANCE MANAGEMENT

School	ST	$IS	SR
Central Washington Univ	WA	11,730	C
Embry-Riddle Aeronautical Univ - Daytona Beach	FL	40,884	₵
Embry-Riddle Aeronautical Univ - Prescott Campus	AZ	40,584	VC
S Dak State Univ	SD	14,296	C
Univ of N Dak	ND	14,094	C

AVIATION MAINTENANCE TECHNOLOGY

School	ST	$IS	SR
Thomas Edison State College	NJ	5,700	SP

BACTERIOLOGY

School	ST	$IS	SR
Univ of Calif at Davis	CA	24,482	HC
Wilmington College	OH	29,784	C

BAKERY SCIENCE

School	ST	$IS	SR
Kansas State Univ	KS	15,497	VC

BALLET

School	ST	$IS	SR
Belhaven Univ	MS	27,170	C
Friends Univ	KS	29,100	C
Indiana Univ Bloomington	IN	19,358	HC
Texas Christian Univ	TX	47,570	HC
Univ of N Car School of the Arts	NC	7,401	SP
Univ of Utah	UT	13,462	VC
Webster Univ	MO	33,990	₵

BALLET MODERN DANCE

School	ST	$IS	SR
Texas Christian Univ	TX	47,570	HC

BANKING AND FINANCE

School	ST	$IS	SR
Adams State College	CO	13,358	LC
Adelphi Univ	NY	43,130	VC
Alabama A&M Univ	AL	96,100	C
Alabama State Univ	AL	14,142	NC
Alfred State / SUNY College of Technology	NY	18,034	C
Anderson Univ	IN	35,390	C
Andrews Univ	MI	28,030	₵
Angelo State Univ	TX	15,049	NC
Appalachian State Univ	NC	12,919	VC
Arcadia Univ	PA	33,570	₵
Arizona State Univ	AZ	18,818	₵
Arkansas State Univ	AR	14,980	C
Ashland Univ	OH	25,000	C
Auburn Univ	AL	20,052	V₵
Auburn Univ at Montgomery	AL	12,120	C
Avila Univ	MO	26,900	C
Ball State Univ	IN	17,850	C
Baylor Univ	TX	46,720	HC
Bellarmine Univ	KY	42,950	VC
Benedictine Univ	IL	35,220	C
Bethel Univ	MN	34,940	VC
Boston College	MA	58,506	MC
Boston Univ	MA	54,130	H₵
Bradley Univ	IL	31,874	VC
Brescia Univ	KY	26,140	V₵
Bryant Univ	RI	49,179	VC
Buena Vista Univ	IA	37,954	C
Butler Univ	IN	45,898	V₵
Cal State, Long Beach	CA	17,534	₵
Cal State, Northridge	CA	28,313	C
Cal State, Sacramento	CA	16,200	C
Cal State, San Bernardino	CA	12,000	C
Canisius College	NY	45,602	VC
Caribbean Univ	PR	10,375	
Centenary College of Louisiana	LA	39,070	₵
Central Mich Univ	MI	18,066	C
Central State Univ	OH	9,010	C
Central Washington Univ	WA	11,730	C
Chicago State Univ	IL	5,482	C
CUNY/Brooklyn College	NY	5,884	₵
Clarion Univ of Pennsylvania	PA	17,370	C
Cleary Univ	MI	11,000	C
Clemson Univ	SC	19,136	HC
Coastal Carolina Univ	SC	17,620	C
College of William & Mary	VA	25,085	MC
Colo State Univ-Fort Collins	CO	20,090	VC
Columbia College	MO	24,578	C
Columbus State Univ	GA	13,176	C
Concord Univ	WV	13,102	C
Concordia Univ St. Paul	MN	27,200	C
Concordia Univ Wisc	WI	28,980	C
Creighton Univ	NE	44,058	V₵
Dallas Baptist Univ	TX	29,118	C
Davenport Univ	MI	21,002	LC
De Sales Univ	PA	42,670	C
Defiance College	OH	30,645	C
DePaul Univ	IL	46,120	VC
Dominican College	NY	31,270	C
Dordt College	IA	34,160	VC
Dowling College	NY	25,000	LC
Drake Univ	IA	30,980	V₵
Drury Univ	MO	30,319	VC
Duquesne Univ	PA	42,017	VC
East Carolina Univ	NC	14,169	C
East Central Univ	OK	10,223	LC
Eastern Illinois Univ	IL	20,502	C
Eastern Kentucky Univ	KY	11,161	C
Eastern Mich Univ	MI	17,961	C
Eastern Washington Univ	WA	16,388	C
Emory Univ	GA	45,000	MC
Excelsior College	NY	895	SP
Fairleigh Dickinson Univ/ College at Florham	NJ	42,142	C
Fairmont State Univ	WV	12,098	LC
Fayetteville State Univ	NC	10,816	C
Ferris State Univ	MI	19,698	C
Florida A&M Univ	FL	14,935	LC
Florida Atlantic Univ	FL	17,339	C
Florida Gulf Coast Univ	FL		C
Florida International Univ	FL	17,747	VC
Florida State Univ	FL	15,238	HC
Fort Hays State Univ	KS	11,354	C
Francis Marion Univ	SC	16,464	LC
Franklin Pierce Univ	NH	41,598	C
Franklin Univ	OH	7,000	SP
Freed-Hardeman Univ	TN	19,697	VC
Friends Univ	KS	29,100	C
Gannon Univ	PA	37,940	C
George Mason Univ	VA	15,724	VC
George Washington Univ	DC	57,108	MC
Georgetown College	KY	38,690	C
Georgetown Univ	DC	52,910	MC
Georgia Regents Univ	GA		C
Georgia State Univ	GA	12,000	VC
Golden Gate Univ	CA	17,000	C
Goldey-Beacom College	DE	27,493	C
Gordon College	MA	42,660	V₵
Grand Valley State Univ	MI	17,998	VC
Gwynedd-Mercy College	PA	33,560	C
Hampton Univ	VA	28,528	C
Harding Univ	AR	21,432	₵
Hardin-Simmons Univ	TX	23,560	₵
Hawaii Pacific Univ	HI	36,690	C
Hillsdale College	MI	31,890	H₵
Hofstra Univ	NY	48,020	V₵
Houston Baptist Univ	TX	23,815	₵
Howard Univ	DC	35,957	C
Husson Univ	ME	23,386	LC
Idaho State Univ	ID	11,908	C
Illinois State Univ	IL	22,634	VC
Immaculata Univ	PA	43,000	C
Indiana State Univ	IN	16,000	C
Indiana Univ South Bend	IN	15,293	C
Indiana Univ-Purdue Univ Fort Wayne	IN	15,425	C
Indiana Wesleyan Univ	IN	31,815	VC
Inter-American Univ of PR/ Bayamon Univ College	PR	4,428	
Inter-American Univ of PR/ Fajardo Campus	PR	4,200	
Inter-American Univ of PR/ Metropolitan Campus	PR	4,320	
Inter-American Univ of PR/ Ponce	PR	3,700	
Inter-American Univ of PR/ San Germán	PR	6,720	
Iowa State Univ	IA	16,403	C
Jacksonville State Univ	AL	12,280	LC
Jacksonville Univ	FL	37,780	C
James Madison Univ	VA	18,049	VC
John Carroll Univ	OH	44,520	₵
Johnson and Wales Univ/ Denver Campus	CO	34,368	C
Juniata College	PA	49,340	VC
Kansas State Univ	KS	15,497	VC
Kent State Univ	OH	19,352	C
King's College	PA	41,678	C
Kutztown Univ of Pennsylvania	PA	16,909	LC
La Roche College	PA	34,802	LC
La Salle Univ	PA	50,270	C
La Sierra Univ	CA	35,694	VC
Lake Superior State Univ	MI	18,121	C
Lasell College	MA	42,500	LC
Le Moyne College	NY	42,200	VC
Lewis Univ	IL	23,050	C
Lindenwood Univ	MO	20,750	C
Linfield College-McMinnville Campus	OR	46,166	C
LIU/Brooklyn Campus	NY	26,500	C
LIU/C.W. Post Campus	NY	38,888	C
Loras College	IA	37,432	VC
Louisiana State Univ	LA	18,677	V₵
Louisiana State Univ in Shreveport	LA	5,606	C
Louisiana Tech Univ	LA	8,000	C
Loyola Univ New Orleans	LA	46,581	VC
Lubbock Christian Univ	TX	25,518	C
Manchester College	IN	35,070	C
Manhattan College	NY	44,955	VC
Manhattanville College	NY	46,260	VC
Marian Univ/Indianapolis	IN	37,058	C
Marietta College	OH	42,135	VC
Marshall Univ	WV	14,820	C
Marywood Univ	PA	40,695	C
McKendree Univ	IL	29,920	₵
McMurry Univ	TX	25,962	LC
Mercy College	NY	29,996	C
Mercyhurst Univ	PA	40,700	C
Metropolitan State Univ	MN	5,923	SP
Metropolitan State Univ of Denver	CO	4,835	LC
Miami Univ	OH	24,191	HC
Mich State Univ	MI	13,680	VC
Middle Tenn State Univ	TN	8,650	C
Midwestern State Univ	TX	9,722	C
Minn State Univ, Mankato	MN	14,900	C
Minn State Univ, Moorhead	MN	13,392	C
Minot State Univ	ND	10,915	C
Missouri Southern State Univ	MO	11,910	C
Monmouth Univ	NJ	42,252	C
Montclair State Univ	NJ	22,614	C
Morehead State Univ	KY	10,900	C
Muhlenberg College	PA	52,837	HC
Murray State Univ	KY	14,944	C
National Univ	CA	14,730	SP
New Mexico Highlands Univ	NM	9,720	NC
New York Inst of Technology	NY	40,590	VC
New York Univ	NY	61,470	MC
Nicholls State Univ	LA	7,095	C
Norfolk State Univ	VA	10,531	LC
North Georgia College & State Univ	GA	8,500	C
North Park Univ	IL	30,130	C
Northeastern Illinois Univ	IL		C
Northeastern State Univ	OK	8,615	VC
Northern Illinois Univ	IL	19,768	C
Northern Mich Univ	MI	15,300	VC
Northern State Univ	SD	14,021	C
Northwest Missouri State Univ	MO	14,229	C
Northwestern College	MN	24,000	C
Northwood Univ	MI	26,331	LC
Notre Dame of Maryland Univ	MD	27,700	C
Oakland Univ	MI	19,391	VC
Ohio Dominican Univ	OH	38,380	₵
Ohio Univ	OH	20,676	VC
Okla Baptist Univ	OK	28,202	VC
Okla City Univ	OK	33,546	VC
Okla State Univ	OK	14,310	VC
Old Dominion Univ	VA	18,662	C
Oral Roberts Univ	OK	31,734	C
Pace Univ	NY	48,094	VC
Palm Beach Atlantic Univ	FL	33,882	LC
Penn State Erie/The Behrend College	PA	16,256	C
Philadelphia Univ	PA	44,160	C
Pittsburg State Univ	KS	12,032	C
Pontifical Catholic Univ of PR	PR	7,310	
Post Univ	CT	35,750	C
Prairie View A&M Univ	TX	15,205	LC
Providence College	RI	55,995	HC
Purdue Univ/Calumet	IN	14,336	C
Purdue Univ/West Lafayette	IN	20,278	HC
Queens College / The CUNY	NY	17,107	VC
Quincy Univ	IL	34,980	LC
Quinnipiac Univ	CT	53,580	VC
Radford Univ	VA	17,132	LC
Rhode Island College	RI	17,132	LC
Richard Stockton College of New Jersey	NJ	20,000	VC
Rider Univ	NJ	45,720	C
Robert Morris Univ	PA	36,699	C
Rochester Inst of Technology	NY	42,450	V₵
Roger Williams Univ	RI	45,788	C
Roosevelt Univ	IL	22,605	VC
Rutgers, The State Univ of New Jersey/Camden Campus	NJ	24,254	C
Rutgers, The State Univ of New Jersey/New Brunswick	NJ	25,077	VC
Rutgers, The State Univ of New Jersey/Newark Campus	NJ	25,376	C
Sacred Heart Univ	CT	48,564	VC
Saginaw Valley State Univ	MI	16,869	C
St. Anselm College	NH	48,324	VC
St. Mary's Univ	TX	33,854	C
St. Vincent College	PA	40,244	C
St. Xavier Univ	IL	32,840	C
Salem State College	MA	13,161	LC
Salisbury Univ	MD	18,368	VC
Sam Houston State Univ	TX	17,082	C
San Francisco State Univ	CA	18,514	C
San Jose State Univ	CA	19,707	C
Shippensburg Univ of Pennsylvania	PA	17,064	LC
Siena College	NY	43,863	VC

School	ST	$IS	SR
Southeastern Univ	FL	27,201	₲
Southern Adventist Univ	TN	26,190	C
Southern Conn State Univ	CT	18,033	C
Southern Illinois Univ Carbondale	IL	21,620	C
Southern Methodist Univ	TX	57,755	MC
Southern Nazarene Univ	OK	24,354	NC
Southern Univ and A&M College	LA	9,761	₲
Southwestern Okla State Univ	OK	9,160	C
St. Bonaventure Univ	NY	38,831	C
St. Cloud State Univ	MN	10,600	C
St. Edward's Univ	TX	44,674	VC
St. Thomas Aquinas College	NY	30,000	C
St. Thomas Univ	FL	32,310	₲
SUNY Inst of Technology at Utica / Rome	NY	23,818	C
Stephen F. Austin State Univ	TX	14,668	C
Stetson Univ	FL	49,512	V₲
Stonehill College	MA	46,780	V₲
Suffolk Univ	MA	46,548	C
SUNY College at Old Westbury	NY	16,324	C
SUNY New Paltz	NY	15,010	C
Talladega College	AL	13,000	C
Tarleton State Univ	TX	13,489	LC
Taylor Univ	IN	36,742	V₲
Temple Univ	PA	24,392	VC
Tenn Tech Univ	TN	11,310	C
Tenn Wesleyan College	TN	21,250	C
Texas A&M Univ	TX	16,956	V₲
Texas A&M Univ at Commerce	TX	10,496	C
Texas A&M Univ at Corpus Christi	TX	11,544	LC
Texas A&M Univ at Kingsville	TX	7,500	LC
Texas Southern Univ	TX	18,212	LC
Texas State Univ	TX	16,495	VC
Texas Tech Univ	TX	14,243	C
The Catholic Univ of America	DC	52,852	VC
Ohio State Univ	OH	19,887	MC
Tiffin Univ	OH	30,273	LC
Touro College	NY	23,150	VC
Trine Univ	IN	39,400	VC
Troy Univ	AL	10,650	C
Tulane Univ	LA	58,942	MC
Tuskegee Univ	AL	26,750	C
Union College	NE	23,270	VC
Union Univ	TN	28,260	VC
Univ of Akron	OH	20,436	C
Univ of Alabama at Birmingham	AL	18,484	₲
Univ of Alabama at Huntsville	AL	17,625	VC
Univ of Alaska Anchorage	AK	15,290	NC
Univ of Arkansas at Fayetteville	AR	16,860	VC
Univ of Arkansas at Little Rock	AR		C
Univ of Bridgeport	CT	39,030	LC
Univ of Central Arkansas	AR	10,840	VC
Univ of Central Florida	FL	15,711	V₲
Univ of Central Okla	OK	12,293	C
Univ of Cincinnati	OH	20,199	VC
Univ of Conn	CT	23,744	HC
Univ of Dayton	OH	43,750	VC
Univ of Delaware	DE	22,728	VC
Univ of Denver	CO	51,787	V₲
Univ of Findlay	OH	31,916	C
Univ of Florida	FL	15,783	H₲
Univ of Hartford	CT	42,674	C
Univ of Hawaii at Manoa	HI	19,379	VC
Univ of Houston-Downtown	TX	6,267	LC
Univ of Illinois at Chicago	IL	24,293	VC
Univ of Illinois at Urbana-Champaign	IL	24,300	HC
Univ of Indianapolis	IN	31,740	LC
Univ of Iowa	IA	17,481	VC
Univ of Kentucky	KY	19,868	C
Univ of Louisiana at Lafayette	LA	6,130	C
Univ of Louisville	KY	17,460	VC
Univ of Maryland	MD	18,801	HC
Univ of Mass Amherst	MA	23,697	V₲
Univ of Memphis	TN	15,094	C
Univ of Mich-Flint	MI	17,547	₲
Univ of Miss	MS	15,482	VC
Univ of Missouri/Columbia	MO	18,201	MC
Univ of Montana	MT	13,670	C
Univ of Montevallo	AL	17,320	C
Univ of Nebr - Lincoln	NE	17,507	VC
Univ of Nebr at Kearney	NE	14,855	LC
Univ of Nebr at Omaha	NE	12,700	C
Univ of Nevada, Las Vegas	NV	17,303	C
Univ of Nevada/Reno	NV	14,500	NC
Univ of New Haven	CT	47,740	C
Univ of New Orleans	LA	9,224	VC
Univ of North Alabama	AL	9,960	C
Univ of N Car at Charlotte	NC	15,847	C
Univ of N Car at Greensboro	NC	12,848	C
Univ of N Car at Wilmington	NC	13,572	V₲
Univ of N Dak	ND	14,094	C
Univ of North Florida	FL	15,578	VC
Univ of North Texas	TX	15,628	C
Univ of Northern Iowa	IA	14,776	C
Univ of Notre Dame	IN		MC
Univ of Okla	OK	17,634	V₲
Univ of Pittsburgh at Johnstown	PA	20,862	LC
Univ of Pittsburgh at Pittsburgh	PA	27,800	H₲
Univ of Portland	OR	47,874	VC
Univ of PR Recinto de Rio Piedras	PR	5,750	
Univ of PR/Arecibo	PR	7,227	
Univ of PR/Bayamon	PR	1,600	
Univ of PR/Mayaguez	PR	1,250	
Univ of San Francisco	CA	49,674	VC
Univ of Scranton	PA	51,940	VC
Univ of South Alabama	AL	13,510	C
Univ of S Car at Columbia	SC	19,725	V₲
Univ of S Dak	SD	15,111	C
Univ of South Florida	FL	13,000	C
Univ of Southern Miss	MS	13,170	C
Univ of St. Francis	IL	36,490	C
Univ of St. Thomas - Houston	TX	36,490	VC
Univ of Tampa	FL	35,160	VC
Univ of Texas at Arlington	TX	10,908	LC
Univ of Texas at Austin	TX	44,074	HC
Univ of Texas at Dallas	TX	21,046	HC
Univ of Texas at El Paso	TX	8,764	NC
Univ of Texas-Pan American	TX	12,432	LC
Univ of the District of Columbia	DC	7,244	LC
Univ of Toledo	OH	18,464	C
Univ of Tulsa	OK	45,311	H₲
Univ of Washington	WA	14,722	VC
Univ of West Florida	FL	14,656	C
Univ of Wisc Whitewater	WI	13,314	C
Univ of Wisc/Eau Claire	WI	15,430	VC
Univ of Wisc/La Crosse	WI	14,755	VC
Univ of Wisc/Madison	WI	18,757	HC
Univ of Wisc/Oshkosh	WI	10,426	LC
Upper Iowa Univ	IA	30,426	NC
Utah State Univ	UT	11,803	C
Valparaiso Univ	IN	43,040	V₲
Villanova Univ	PA	56,436	MC
Virginia Polytechnic Inst and State Univ	VA	14,629	HC
Virginia Union Univ	VA	18,432	C
Wake Forest Univ	NC	51,000	MC
Warner Univ	FL	18,000	C
Wartburg College	IA	41,055	VC
Washburn Univ	KS	12,165	NC
Washington Univ in St. Louis	MO	58,818	MC
Wayne State Univ	MI	19,493	C
Webber International Univ	FL	25,664	C
West Chester Univ of Pennsylvania	PA	16,836	C
West Liberty Univ	WV	9,142	LC
West Texas A&M Univ	TX	13,478	C
West Virginia State Univ	WV	8,378	NC
West Virginia Univ	WV	15,794	₲
Western Carolina Univ	NC	13,965	₲
Western Conn State Univ	CT	18,327	C
Western Illinois Univ	IL	20,130	C
Western Kentucky Univ	KY	11,000	LC
Western Mich Univ	MI	19,042	C
Westminster College	PA	31,290	₲
Westminster College	UT	37,708	VC
Wichita State Univ	KS	12,539	C
Wilberforce Univ	OH	15,100	LC
William Paterson Univ of New Jersey	NJ	21,694	C
Wilmington Univ	DE	7,778	NC
Winona State Univ	MN	16,530	C
Wofford College	SC	45,795	VC
Wright State Univ	OH	16,983	C
Xavier Univ	OH	43,740	VC
York College of Pennsylvania	PA	26,590	C
Youngstown State Univ	OH	16,374	LC

BEHAVIORAL SCIENCE

School	ST	$IS	SR
Alvernia Univ	PA	39,250	C
Andrews Univ	MI	28,030	₲
Calif Baptist Univ	CA	35,890	C
Cal State, Dominguez Hills	CA	17,056	LC
Cal State, Monterey Bay	CA	26,871	LC
Capital Univ	OH	39,824	VC
Chaminade Univ of Honolulu	HI	31,664	C
College of St. Scholastica	MN	39,960	C
Concordia College New York	NY	31,500	VC
Concordia Univ - Irvine	CA	35,390	VC
Concordia Univ Nebr	NE	26,000	VC
Concordia Univ Texas	TX	23,640	C
Dakota Wesleyan Univ	SD	23,000	C
Duquesne Univ	PA	42,017	VC
East-West Univ	IL	16,076	C
Elizabethtown College School of Continuing and Professional Studies	PA		VC
Erskine College	SC	37,360	C
Fontbonne Univ	MO	31,384	C
George Fox Univ	OR	40,750	₲
Grand Valley State Univ	MI	17,998	VC
Granite State College	NH	6,195	SP
Green Mountain College	VT	33,547	LC
Johnson State College	VT	16,721	C
Lakeland College	WI	22,990	C
Lehigh Univ	PA	55,080	MC
Mercy College	NY	29,996	C
Metropolitan State Univ of Denver	CO	4,835	LC
Missouri Baptist Univ	MO	30,310	C
Mount Aloysius College	PA	27,970	C
Mount Marty College	SD	29,638	C
Mount Mary Univ	WI	32,836	LC
National Univ	CA	14,730	SP
New York Inst of Technology	NY	40,590	VC
North Central Univ	MN	20,946	C
Northwest Univ	WA	18,854	C
Nova Southeastern Univ	FL	34,016	VC
Oglethorpe Univ	GA	42,580	VC
Okla City Univ	OK	33,546	VC
Okla Wesleyan Univ	OK	21,300	C
Our Lady of Holy Cross College	LA	8,090	LC
Our Lady of the Lake Univ of San Antonio	TX	22,430	LC
Point Park Univ	PA	36,390	C
Purdue Univ/West Lafayette	IN	20,278	HC
Rochester College	MI	18,320	C
Savannah State Univ	GA	13,156	C
Southern Adventist Univ	TN	26,190	C
Sterling College	KS	27,216	C
Tenn Wesleyan College	TN	21,250	C
Trevecca Nazarene Univ	TN	30,118	C
United States Air Force Academy	CO		MC
United States Military Academy	NY		MC
Univ of Calif at Davis	CA	24,482	HC
Univ of Kansas	KS	16,980	₲
Univ of La Verne	CA	47,010	VC
Univ of Maine at Fort Kent	ME	14,975	LC
Univ of Maine at Machias	ME	10,523	C
Univ of Mary	ND	16,714	C
Univ of Mich/Ann Arbor	MI	22,102	H₲
Univ of Mich/Dearborn	MI	9,885	VC
Univ of New Haven	CT	47,740	C
Univ of Rio Grande	OH	8,750	NC
Univ of San Diego	CA	53,302	H₲
Univ of Utah	UT	13,462	VC
Univ of Wisc-Milwaukee	WI	18,436	C
Western Mich Univ	MI	19,042	C
Western Washington Univ	WA	18,519	VC
Widener Univ	PA	50,368	C
Wilmington Univ	DE	7,778	NC
York College of Pennsylvania	PA	26,590	C

BIBLICAL LANGUAGES

School	ST	$IS	SR
Asbury Univ	KY	32,038	VC
Baylor Univ	TX	46,720	HC
Belmont Univ	TN	37,380	V₲
Concordia Univ - Irvine	CA	35,390	VC
Concordia Univ Wisc	WI	28,980	C
Concordia Univ, Ann Arbor	MI	27,220	VC
Harding Univ	AR	21,432	₲
Houston Baptist Univ	TX	23,815	₲
Lipscomb Univ	TN	35,722	VC
Luther College	IA	44,380	V₲
North Central Univ	MN	20,946	C
Northwest Nazarene Univ	ID	24,275	NC
Ouachita Baptist Univ	AR	29,010	VC
Union Univ	TN	28,260	VC
Walla Walla Univ	WA	26,256	NC

BIBLICAL STUDIES

School	ST	$IS	SR
Abilene Christian Univ	TX	38,400	VC
Albert A. List College of Jewish Studies	NY	21,600	
Amridge Univ	AL	6,870	LC
Asbury Univ	KY	32,038	VC
Azusa Pacific Univ	CA	39,946	C
Belhaven Univ	MS	27,170	C
Belmont Univ	TN	37,380	V₲
Bethel College	IN	31,560	C
Bethel Univ	MN	34,940	VC
Biola Univ	CA	40,320	VC
Blue Mountain College	MS	13,550	LC
Bluffton Univ	OH	37,864	C
Cairn Univ	PA	31,255	C
Campbellsville Univ	KY	27,720	C
Canisius College	NY	45,602	VC
Cedarville Univ	OH	31,036	V₲
Clearwater Christian College	FL	23,720	C
Colo Christian Univ	CO	27,500	VC
Corban Univ	OR	34,764	C
Cornerstone Univ and Grand Rapids Theological Seminary	MI	30,866	C
Covenant College	GA		V₲
Dallas Baptist Univ	TX	29,118	C
East Texas Baptist Univ	TX	29,135	C
Eastern Mennonite Univ	VA	38,850	VC
Eastern Univ	PA	37,704	C
Elizabethtown College	PA	47,600	VC
Evangel Univ	MO	23,090	C
Faulkner Univ	AL	22,530	LC
Freed-Hardeman Univ	TN	19,697	VC
Geneva College	PA	27,280	C
George Fox Univ	OR	40,750	₲
Gordon College	MA	42,660	V₲
Goshen College	IN	35,900	VC
Grace Bible College	MI	20,770	C
Grace College and Theological Seminary	IN	28,800	C
Grove City College	PA	22,988	HC
Hannibal-LaGrange Univ	MO	24,490	C
Harding Univ	AR	21,432	₲
Hardin-Simmons Univ	TX	23,560	₲
Hope International Univ	CA	34,650	C
Houghton College	NY	35,740	VC
Huntington Univ	IN	32,220	C
Indiana Wesleyan Univ	IN	31,815	VC
John Brown Univ	AR	30,996	V₲
Kentucky Christian Univ	KY	17,622	LC
King Univ	TN	33,140	C
Lee Univ	TN	18,690	₲
LeTourneau Univ	TX	26,230	C
Lipscomb Univ	TN	35,722	VC
Lubbock Christian Univ	TX	25,518	C
Malone Univ	OH	34,334	C
Milligan College	TN	27,510	C
Montreat College	NC	31,208	VC
Mount Vernon Nazarene Univ	OH	29,590	C
North Park Univ	IL	30,130	C
Northwest Univ	WA	18,854	C
Northwestern College	MN	24,000	C
Nyack College	NY	32,000	C
Ohio Valley Univ	WV	17,752	C
Okla Christian Univ	OK	24,975	VC
Olivet Nazarene Univ	IL	29,990	C
Oral Roberts Univ	OK	31,734	C
Ouachita Baptist Univ	AR	29,010	VC
Palm Beach Atlantic Univ	FL	33,882	LC
Point Loma Nazarene Univ	CA	38,610	VC
Roberts Wesleyan College	NY	37,384	₲
Rochester College	MI	18,320	C
San Diego Christian College	CA	31,012	C
Simpson Univ	CA	28,900	C
Southeastern Univ	FL	27,201	₲
Southwest Baptist Univ	MO	24,710	C
Spring Arbor Univ	MI	26,740	C
Tabor College	KS	29,010	LC
Taylor Univ	IN	36,742	V₲
The Masters College	CA	38,160	₲
Toccoa Falls College	GA	23,210	C
Trinity Bible College	ND		
Trinity Christian College	IL	28,869	C
Trinity International Univ	IL	31,070	C
Union Univ	TN	28,260	VC
Univ of Evansville	IN	41,056	V₲
Univ of Mary Hardin-Baylor	TX	31,950	₲
Univ of Mich/Ann Arbor	MI	22,102	H₲
Vanguard Univ of Southern Calif	CA	35,833	VC
Victory Univ	TN	19,118	C
Warner Univ	FL	18,000	C
Waynesburg Univ	PA	29,100	C
Wheaton College	IL	39,650	H₲
York College	NE	19,475	C

BILINGUAL EARLY CHILDHOOD EDUCATION

School	ST	$IS	SR
Texas Christian Univ	TX	47,570	HC

BILINGUAL/BICULTURAL EDUCATION

School	ST	$IS	SR
Boston Univ	MA	54,130	H₲
Cal State, San Bernardino	CA	12,000	C
Chicago State Univ	IL	5,482	C
CUNY/Brooklyn College	NY	5,884	₲
CUNY-City College	NY	19,576	H₲
Eastern Mich Univ	MI	17,961	C
Elms College	MA	23,900	VC
Loyola Univ Chicago	IL	49,560	V₲
Mount Mary Univ	WI	32,836	LC
New York Univ	NY	61,470	MC
Northeastern Illinois Univ	IL		C
St. Thomas Aquinas College	NY	30,000	C
SUNY College at Old Westbury	NY	16,324	C
Univ of Central Okla	OK	12,293	C
Univ of Findlay	OH	31,916	C
Univ of Minn/Twin Cities	MN		HC
Washington State Univ	WA	20,461	C
Western Illinois Univ	IL	20,130	C

BIOCHEMISTRY

School	ST	$IS	SR
Abilene Christian Univ	TX	38,400	VC
Adams State College	CO	13,358	LC
Adelphi Univ	NY	43,130	VC
Agnes Scott College	GA	45,323	V₲

School	ST	$IS	SR
Albright College	PA	46,660	C
Allegheny College	PA	49,020	HC
Alma College	MI	42,400	VC
Alvernia Univ	PA	39,250	C
American International College	MA	36,100	LC
American Univ	DC	54,829	H¢
Amherst College	MA	58,744	MC
Andrews Univ	MI	28,030	¢
Angelo State Univ	TX	15,049	NC
Arizona State Univ	AZ	18,818	¢
Asbury Univ	KY	32,038	VC
Auburn Univ	AL	20,052	V¢
Augustana College	IL	43,308	HC
Augustana College	SD	35,500	VC
Austin College	TX	36,940	HC
Azusa Pacific Univ	CA	39,946	C
Bates College	ME	58,950	MC
Baylor Univ	TX	46,720	HC
Bellarmine Univ	KY	42,950	VC
Belmont Univ	TN	37,380	V¢
Beloit College	WI	49,970	HC
Benedictine College	KS	29,180	VC
Benedictine Univ	IL	35,220	C
Berry College	GA	39,254	HC
Bethany College	WV	35,282	C
Bethel Univ	MN	34,940	VC
Binghamton Univ / The SUNY	NY	20,832	H¢
Biola Univ	CA	40,320	VC
Blackburn College	IL	21,350	C
Boston College	MA	58,506	MC
Boston Univ	MA	54,130	H¢
Bowdoin College	ME	57,834	MC
Bradley Univ	IL	31,874	VC
Brandeis Univ	MA	58,820	HC
Brescia Univ	KY	26,140	V¢
Brigham Young Univ	UT	12,100	HC
Brown Univ	RI	56,150	MC
Bucknell Univ	PA	58,160	MC
Calif Baptist Univ	CA	35,890	C
Calif Lutheran Univ	CA	47,640	C
Calif Polytechnic State Univ	CA	19,847	HC
Cal State, Chico	CA	18,952	C
Cal State, Dominguez Hills	CA	17,056	LC
Cal State, Fullerton	CA	25,188	¢
Cal State, Long Beach	CA	17,534	¢
Cal State, Los Angeles	CA	15,829	C
Cal State, Northridge	CA	28,313	C
Cal State, San Bernardino	CA	12,000	C
Cal State, San Marcos	CA	14,576	C
Calvin College	MI	37,585	V¢
Campbell Univ	NC	25,500	C
Canisius College	NY	45,602	VC
Capital Univ	OH	39,824	VC
Carroll Univ	WI	24,860	C
Case Western Reserve Univ	OH	55,178	MC
Cedar Crest College	PA	43,240	C
Centenary College of Louisiana	LA	39,070	¢
Central College	IA	36,980	VC
Central Conn State Univ	CT	19,212	C
Central Mich Univ	MI	18,066	C
Centre College	KY	35,000	H¢
Chaminade Univ of Honolulu	HI	31,664	C
Chapman Univ	CA	56,019	V¢
Charleston Southern Univ	SC	22,420	C
Chatham Univ	PA	42,440	VC
Chestnut Hill College	PA	39,785	LC
Chicago State Univ	IL	5,482	C
Christian Brothers Univ	TN	19,140	HC
Christopher Newport Univ	VA	21,050	VC
Claflin Univ	SC	22,368	¢
Claremont McKenna College	CA	58,065	MC
Clark Univ	MA	47,020	H¢
Clarke Univ	IA	36,400	C
Clemson Univ	SC	19,136	HC
Coastal Carolina Univ	SC	17,620	C
Coe College	IA	43,590	VC
Colby College	ME	57,510	MC
Colgate Univ	NY	50,930	MC
College of Staten Island / The CUNY	NY	16,778	NC
College of Charleston	SC	21,273	VC
College of Mount St. Joseph	OH	33,880	C
College of Mount St. Vincent	NY	41,040	MC
College of St. Benedict	MN	47,570	VC
College of St. Elizabeth	NJ	43,839	LC
College of St. Scholastica	MN	39,960	C
College of Wooster	OH	52,600	VC
Colo College	CO	54,534	MC
Colo State Univ-Fort Collins	CO	20,090	VC
Colo State Univ-Pueblo	CO	13,532	LC
Columbia Univ in the City of New York	NY	61,116	MC
Columbia Univ/Barnard College	NY	39,000	MC
Conn College	CT	54,970	MC
Cornell College	IA	44,930	HC
Creighton Univ	NE	44,058	V¢
Culver-Stockton College	MO	30,900	C
Daemen College	NY	31,510	C
Dartmouth College	NH	57,996	MC
De Sales Univ	PA	42,670	C
Denison Univ	OH	54,670	H¢
DePauw Univ	IN	48,950	V¢
Dickinson College	PA	57,662	H¢
Doane College	NE	33,730	VC
Dominican Univ	IL	37,628	C
Drew Univ/College of Liberal Arts	NJ	55,862	VC
Duquesne Univ	PA	42,017	VC
Earlham College	IN	49,710	V¢
East Carolina Univ	NC	14,169	C
East Stroudsburg Univ of Pennsylvania	PA	16,636	C
Eastern Conn State Univ	CT	20,584	C
Eastern Mennonite Univ	VA	38,850	VC
Eastern Mich Univ	MI	17,961	C
Eastern New Mexico Univ	NM	10,682	C
Eastern Univ	PA	37,704	C
Eastern Washington Univ	WA	16,388	C
Eckerd College	FL	43,902	VC
Elizabethtown College	PA	47,600	VC
Elmira College	NY	49,950	¢
Elon Univ	NC	40,046	HC
Emmanuel College	MA	47,985	VC
Emporia State Univ	KS	12,897	C
Fairfield Univ	CT	55,850	VC
Fairleigh Dickinson Univ/ College at Florham	NJ	42,142	C
Fairleigh Dickinson Univ/ Metropolitan Campus	NJ	40,254	C
Ferris State Univ	MI	19,698	C
Florida Inst of Technology	FL	48,290	VC
Florida Southern College	FL	38,240	VC
Florida State Univ	FL	15,238	HC
Fort Lewis College	CO	15,513	C
Franklin and Marshall College	PA	58,295	MC
Freed-Hardeman Univ	TN	19,697	VC
Georgetown Univ	DC	52,910	MC
Georgia Inst of Technology	GA	20,464	MC
Georgian Court Univ	NJ	39,726	LC
Gettysburg College	PA	56,820	HC
Gonzaga Univ	WA	44,247	HC
Goshen College	IN	35,900	VC
Goucher College	MD	50,252	V¢
Grand View Univ	IA	31,050	C
Grinnell College	IA	53,654	HC
Grove City College	PA	22,988	HC
Gustavus Adolphus College	MN	48,170	HC
Hamilton College	NY	55,620	MC
Hamline Univ	MN	44,198	VC
Hanover College	IN	41,150	VC
Harding Univ	AR	21,432	¢
Hardin-Simmons Univ	TX	23,560	¢
Hartwick College	NY	49,815	¢
Harvard Univ/Harvard College	MA	49,000	MC
Hawaii Pacific Univ	HI	36,690	C
Heidelberg Univ	OH	34,100	C
Hendrix College	AR	48,436	H¢
High Point Univ	NC	39,800	C
Hiram College	OH	37,300	VC
Hofstra Univ	NY	48,020	V¢
Holy Family Univ	PA	40,030	LC
Hood College	MD	44,630	C
Houghton College	NY	35,740	VC
Howard Univ	DC	35,957	C
Huntingdon College	AL	31,850	C
Idaho State Univ	ID	11,908	C
Illinois College	IL	25,770	VC
Illinois Inst of Technology	IL	38,512	H¢
Illinois State Univ	IL	22,634	VC
Immaculata Univ	PA	43,000	C
Indiana Univ Bloomington	IN	19,358	HC
Indiana Univ East	IN	6,639	LC
Indiana Univ Kokomo	IN	6,674	LC
Indiana Univ of Pennsylvania	PA	20,180	LC
Indiana Univ South Bend	IN	15,293	C
Indiana Univ Southeast	IN	15,807	LC
Indiana Univ-Purdue Univ Fort Wayne	IN	15,425	C
Iona College	NY	44,028	C
Iowa State Univ	IA	16,403	C
Ithaca College	NY	52,300	HC
John Brown Univ	AR	30,996	V¢
John Carroll Univ	OH	44,520	¢
Juniata College	PA	49,340	VC
Kansas State Univ	KS	15,497	VC
Kennesaw State Univ	GA	13,017	VC
Kenyon College	OH	56,810	MC
Kettering Univ	MI	31,456	HC
Keuka College	NY	30,300	C
King Univ	TN	33,140	C
Knox College	IL		VC
Kutztown Univ of Pennsylvania	PA	16,909	LC
La Salle Univ	PA	50,270	C
La Sierra Univ	CA	35,694	VC
Lafayette College	PA	57,050	H¢
LaGrange College	GA	34,480	C
Lawrence Tech Univ	MI	37,630	VC
Lawrence Univ	WI	46,371	HC
Le Moyne College	NY	42,200	VC
Lebanon Valley College	PA	38,570	C
Lee Univ	TN	18,690	¢
Lehigh Univ	PA	55,080	MC
Lewis & Clark College	OR	52,656	VC
Lewis Univ	IL	23,050	C
Linfield College-McMinnville Campus	OR	46,166	C
Lipscomb Univ	TN	35,722	VC
Loras College	IA	37,432	VC
Louisiana State Univ	LA	18,677	V¢
Louisiana State Univ in Shreveport	LA	5,606	C
Loyola Marymount Univ	CA	53,240	V¢
Loyola Univ Chicago	IL	49,560	V¢
Madonna Univ	MI	24,540	VC
Manchester College	IN	35,070	C
Manhattan College	NY	44,955	VC
Manhattanville College	NY	46,260	VC
Mansfield Univ	PA	19,468	LC
Marietta College	OH	42,135	VC
Marlboro College	VT	35,980	VC
Marquette Univ	WI	43,664	V¢
Marshall Univ	WV	14,820	C
Maryville College	TN	33,150	VC
Maryville Univ of St. Louis	MO	34,920	VC
McMurry Univ	TX	25,962	LC
Mercer Univ	GA	44,201	V¢
Mercyhurst Univ	PA	40,700	C
Merrimack College	MA	44,215	C
Messiah College	PA	39,540	VC
Miami Univ	OH	24,191	HC
Mich State Univ	MI	13,689	VC
Mich Tech Univ	MI	22,105	VC
Middlebury College	VT	57,470	MC
Millikin Univ	IL	37,462	C
Mills College	CA	54,119	HC
Millsaps College	MS	43,888	V¢
Minn State Univ, Mankato	MN	14,900	C
Misericordia Univ	PA	39,840	C
Miss College	MS	21,998	VC
Missouri Baptist Univ	MO	30,310	C
Monmouth College	IL	39,290	C
Montclair State Univ	NJ	22,614	C
Moravian College	PA	36,381	VC
Mount Holyoke College	MA	53,596	H¢
Mount St. Mary's Univ	MD	46,158	C
Mount St. Mary's College/ Chalon Campus	CA	43,897	V¢
Muhlenberg College	PA	52,837	HC
Nazareth College of Rochester	NY	41,590	VC
Nebr Wesleyan Univ	NE	29,774	¢
New College of Florida	FL	14,504	H¢
New Mexico State Univ	NM	13,955	LC
New York Univ	NY	61,470	MC
Newman Univ	KS	30,380	¢
Niagara Univ	NY	39,800	C
N Car State Univ	NC	16,202	HC
North Central College	IL	38,343	VC
Northeastern Univ	MA	55,296	MC
Northern Mich Univ	MI	15,300	VC
Northwest Nazarene Univ	ID	24,275	NC
Northwestern College	MN	24,000	C
Norwich Univ	VT	28,212	C
Notre Dame de Namur Univ	CA	41,610	LC
Oakland Univ	MI	19,391	VC
Oakwood Univ	AL	23,035	C
Oberlin College	OH	57,025	MC
Occidental College	CA	59,592	M¢
Ohio Northern Univ	OH	42,075	VC
Ohio Univ	OH	20,676	VC
Ohio Valley Univ	WV	17,752	C
Ohio Wesleyan Univ	OH	49,460	¢
Okla Christian Univ	OK	24,975	VC
Okla City Univ	OK	33,546	VC
Okla State Univ	OK	14,310	VC
Old Dominion Univ	VA	18,662	C
Olivet College	MI	19,984	C
Oregon State Univ	OR	19,017	¢
Oswego / SUNY	NY	20,009	VC
Otterbein College	OH	32,214	C
Penn State Univ/Univ Park	PA	25,404	VC
Philadelphia Univ	PA	44,160	C
Pittsburg State Univ	KS	12,032	C
Pitzer College	CA	54,988	MC
Portland State Univ	OR	18,672	C
Presbyterian College	SC	42,678	VC
Providence College	RI	55,995	HC
Purdue Univ/West Lafayette	IN	20,278	HC
Queens Univ of Charlotte	NC	39,543	VC
Quinnipiac Univ	CT	53,580	VC
Ramapo College of New Jersey	NJ	24,938	¢
Reed College	OR	57,780	MC
Regis College	MA	47,565	LC
Regis Univ	CO	41,318	C
Rensselaer Polytechnic Inst	NY	59,229	MC
Rhodes College	TN	47,596	H¢
Richard Stockton College of New Jersey	NJ	20,000	VC
Rider Univ	NJ	45,720	C
Ripon College	WI	36,959	¢
Roanoke College	VA	47,996	¢
Roberts Wesleyan College	NY	37,384	¢
Rochester Inst of Technology	NY	42,450	V¢
Rockford College	IL	31,000	C
Rockhurst Univ	MO	20,625	C
Rocky Mountain College	MT	32,242	C
Roger Williams Univ	RI	45,788	C
Rollins College	FL	52,370	HC
Rose-Hulman Inst of Technology	IN	51,738	MC
Rosemont College	PA	42,350	C
Rowan Univ	NJ	23,570	VC
Russell Sage College	NY	39,370	C
Rutgers, The State Univ of New Jersey/Camden Campus	NJ	24,254	C
Rutgers, The State Univ of New Jersey/New Brunswick	NJ	25,077	VC
Saginaw Valley State Univ	MI	16,869	C
St. Anselm College	NH	48,324	VC
St. John's Univ	MN	46,146	C
St. Joseph College	CT	45,630	LC
St. Joseph's Univ	PA	52,272	VC
St. Louis Univ	MO	46,594	V¢
St. Mary's Univ	TX	33,854	C
St. Mary's Univ of Minn	MN	37,015	C
St. Michael's College	VT	48,740	VC
St. Peter's College	NJ	44,240	C
St. Vincent College	PA	40,244	C
Samford Univ	AL	35,700	V¢
San Francisco State Univ	CA	18,514	C
San Jose State Univ	CA	19,707	C
Santa Clara Univ	CA	54,702	MC
Schreiner Univ	TX	32,734	LC
Seattle Pacific Univ	WA	41,559	V¢
Seattle Univ	WA	47,010	V¢
Seton Hall Univ	NJ	45,902	C
Seton Hill Univ	PA	35,172	C
Sewanee: The Univ of the South	TN	47,700	H¢
Siena College	NY	43,863	VC
Simmons College	MA	48,770	VC
Simpson College	IA	36,086	VC
Skidmore College	NY	57,926	HC
Smith College	MA	57,524	MC
Sonoma State Univ	CA	20,541	C
S Dak State Univ	SD	14,296	C
Southern Conn State Univ	CT	18,033	C
Southern Illinois Univ Edwardsville	IL	17,532	C
Southern Methodist Univ	TX	57,755	MC
Southern Nazarene Univ	OK	24,354	NC
Southwestern College	KS	29,270	C
Southwestern Univ	TX	45,660	VC
Spelman College	GA	24,650	VC
Spring Arbor Univ	MI	26,740	C
Spring Hill College	AL	42,130	VC
Springfield College	MA	25,000	C
St. Bonaventure Univ	NY	38,831	C
St. Catherine Univ	MN	37,782	¢
St. Edward's Univ	TX	44,674	VC
St. Lawrence Univ	NY	53,740	HC
St. Mary's College of Maryland	MD	26,699	HC
Stetson Univ	FL	49,512	V¢
Stevens Inst of Technology	NJ	50,130	HC
Stonehill College	MA	46,780	V¢
Stony Brook Univ / SUNY	NY	19,359	HC
Suffolk Univ	MA	46,548	C
SUNY College at Geneseo	NY	18,055	H¢
SUNY College at Old Westbury	NY	16,324	C
SUNY Fredonia / The SUNY at Fredonia	NY	18,702	VC
SUNY Plattsburgh / SUNY	NY	18,083	VC
Susquehanna Univ	PA	49,170	C
Swarthmore College	PA	57,870	MC
Sweet Briar College	VA	43,765	¢
Syracuse Univ	NY	54,512	HC
Temple Univ	PA	24,392	VC
Tenn Tech Univ	TN	11,310	C
Texas A&M Univ	TX	16,956	V¢
Texas Christian Univ	TX	47,570	HC
Texas State Univ	TX	16,495	VC
Texas Tech Univ	TX	14,243	C
Texas Wesleyan Univ	TX	29,886	C
The Catholic Univ of America	DC	52,852	VC
The College of St. Rose	NY	26,750	C
Ohio State Univ	OH	19,887	MC
The SUNY at Potsdam	NY	17,754	C
Transylvania Univ	KY	40,310	V¢
Trinity College	CT		H¢
Trinity Univ	TX	44,174	H¢
Trinity Washington Univ	DC	30,250	¢
Tufts Univ	MA	58,780	MC
Tulane Univ	LA	58,942	MC
Union College	NY		MC
Univ at Albany / SUNY	NY	18,674	VC
Univ at Buffalo / The SUNY	NY	20,283	VC
Univ of Arizona	AZ	20,105	C
Univ of Calif at Davis	CA	24,482	HC
Univ of Calif at Irvine	CA	25,961	VC
Univ of Calif at Los Angeles	CA	25,686	MC
Univ of Calif at Riverside	CA	27,204	C
Univ of Calif at San Diego	CA	21,000	VC

School	ST	$IS	SR
Univ of Calif at Santa Barbara	CA	27,551	HC
Univ of Calif at Santa Cruz	CA	27,807	VC
Univ of Chicago	IL	55,416	MC
Univ of Cincinnati	OH	20,199	VC
Univ of Colo Boulder	CO	22,605	VC+
Univ of Dallas	TX	43,510	VC+
Univ of Dayton	OH	43,750	VC
Univ of Delaware	DE	22,728	VC
Univ of Denver	CO	51,787	VC+
Univ of Detroit Mercy	MI	30,450	C
Univ of Evansville	IN	41,056	VC+
Univ of Georgia	GA	19,508	VC
Univ of Idaho	ID	14,558	C
Univ of Illinois at Chicago	IL	24,293	VC
Univ of Iowa	IA	17,481	VC
Univ of Jamestown	ND	24,738	C
Univ of Kansas	KS	16,980	C+
Univ of Maine	ME	19,712	C+
Univ of Maryland	MD	18,801	HC
Univ of Maryland/Baltimore County	MD	18,000	VC
Univ of Mass Amherst	MA	23,697	VC+
Univ of Mass Boston	MA	11,966	C
Univ of Mass Dartmouth	MA	22,223	C
Univ of Miami	FL	55,166	MC
Univ of Mich/Ann Arbor	MI	22,102	HC+
Univ of Mich/Dearborn	MI	9,885	VC
Univ of Minn/Duluth	MN	18,964	C+
Univ of Minn/Twin Cities	MN		HC
Univ of Miss	MS	15,482	VC
Univ of Missouri/Columbia	MO	18,201	MC
Univ of Missouri-St. Louis	MO	18,304	VC
Univ of Mount Union	OH	35,130	C
Univ of Nebr - Lincoln	NE	17,507	VC
Univ of Nevada/Reno	NV	14,500	NC
Univ of New England	ME	46,145	C+
Univ of New Hampshire	NH	24,702	VC
Univ of New Haven	CT	47,740	C
Univ of New Mexico	NM	15,300	C
Univ of N Car at Greensboro	NC	12,848	C
Univ of N Car at Wilmington	NC	13,572	VC+
Univ of North Texas	TX	15,628	C
Univ of Northern Iowa	IA	14,776	C
Univ of Notre Dame	IN		MC
Univ of Okla	OK	17,634	VC+
Univ of Oregon	OR	20,872	VC
Univ of Pennsylvania	PA	56,106	MC
Univ of PR/Mayaguez	PR	1,250	
Univ of Puget Sound	WA	52,648	HC+
Univ of Redlands	CA	40,500	VC
Univ of Rochester	NY	58,500	MC
Univ of San Diego	CA	53,302	HC+
Univ of Scranton	PA	51,940	VC
Univ of St. Thomas - Houston	TX	36,490	VC
Univ of Tampa	FL	35,160	VC
Univ of Texas at Arlington	TX	10,908	LC
Univ of Texas at Austin	TX	44,074	HC
Univ of Texas at Dallas	TX	21,046	HC
Univ of Texas at San Antonio	TX	18,372	C
Univ of the Pacific	CA	52,146	VC
Univ of the Sciences	PA	48,320	VC+
Univ of Tulsa	OK	45,311	HC+
Univ of Vermont	VT	26,120	VC+
Univ of Washington	WA	14,722	VC
Univ of Wisc/Eau Claire	WI	15,430	VC
Univ of Wisc/Madison	WI	18,757	HC
Univ of Wisc/Stevens Point	WI	14,043	C
Univ of Wisc-Milwaukee	WI	18,436	C
Ursinus College	PA	55,630	VC+
Utah State Univ	UT	11,803	C
Utica College	NY	44,734	C
Valparaiso Univ	IN	43,040	VC+
Vanguard Univ of Southern Calif	CA	35,833	VC
Vassar College	NY	59,070	MC
Villanova Univ	PA	56,436	MC
Virginia Polytechnic Inst and State Univ	VA	14,629	HC
Viterbo Univ	WI	30,070	C
Wabash College	IN	44,160	VC
Walla Walla Univ	WA	26,256	NC
Walsh Univ	OH	35,100	C
Wartburg College	IA	41,055	VC
Washburn Univ	KS	12,165	NC
Washington Adventist Univ	MD	25,859	C+
Washington and Jefferson College	PA	49,990	VC
Washington and Lee Univ	VA	52,812	MC
Washington State Univ	WA	20,461	C
Washington Univ in St. Louis	MO	58,818	MC
Wayne State Univ	MI	19,493	C
Wellesley College	MA	49,848	MC
Wells College	NY	38,680	VC
West Chester Univ of Pennsylvania	PA	16,836	C
Western Kentucky Univ	KY	11,000	LC
Western Mich Univ	MI	19,042	C
Western Washington Univ	WA	18,519	VC
Westminster College	MO	30,490	VC
Wheaton College	MA	54,934	HC+
Whitman College	WA	54,400	MC
Whittier College	CA	43,416	C
Widener Univ	PA	50,368	C
Wilkes Univ	PA	42,786	C
William Jewell College	MO	31,000	VC+
Wilmington College	OH	29,784	C
Worcester Polytechnic Inst	MA	53,440	HC+
Xavier Univ of Louisiana	LA	25,300	C
Yale Univ	CT	55,300	MC

BIOENGINEERING

School	ST	$IS	SR
Binghamton Univ / The SUNY	NY	20,832	HC+
Colo State Univ-Fort Collins	CO	20,090	VC
Cornell Univ	NY	59,037	MC
Dordt College	IA	34,160	VC
Endicott College	MA	42,390	C
Florida State Univ	FL	15,238	HC
Indiana Univ-Purdue Univ Indianapolis	IN	17,290	C
Lehigh Univ	PA	55,080	MC
Louisiana State Univ	LA	18,677	VC+
Marquette Univ	WI	43,664	VC+
Mass Inst of Technology	MA	54,238	MC
Miami Univ	OH	24,191	HC
Ohio Univ	OH	20,676	VC
Okla State Univ	OK	14,310	VC
Oral Roberts Univ	OK	31,734	C
Oregon State Univ	OR	19,017	C+
Purdue Univ/West Lafayette	IN	20,278	HC
Rice Univ	TX	43,288	MC
St. Louis Univ	MO	46,594	VC+
Santa Clara Univ	CA	54,702	MC
Stanford Univ	CA	56,411	MC
Syracuse Univ	NY	54,512	HC
Texas A&M Univ	TX	16,956	VC+
Union College	NY		MC
Univ of Arkansas at Fayetteville	AR	16,860	VC
Univ of Calif at Berkeley	CA	23,322	MC
Univ of Calif at Davis	CA	24,482	HC
Univ of Calif at Los Angeles	CA	25,686	MC
Univ of Calif at Riverside	CA	27,204	C
Univ of Calif at San Diego	CA	21,000	VC
Univ of Colo Boulder	CO	22,605	VC+
Univ of Colo Denver	CO	17,904	C
Univ of Delaware	DE	22,728	VC
Univ of Denver	CO	51,787	VC+
Univ of Hawaii at Manoa	HI	19,379	VC
Univ of Idaho	ID	14,558	C
Univ of Illinois at Chicago	IL	24,293	VC
Univ of Illinois at Urbana-Champaign	IL	24,300	HC
Univ of Louisville	KY	17,460	VC
Univ of Maine	ME	19,712	C+
Univ of Mass Dartmouth	MA	22,223	C
Univ of Minn/Twin Cities	MN		HC
Univ of Nebr - Lincoln	NE	17,507	VC
Univ of Pennsylvania	PA	56,106	MC
Univ of Pittsburgh at Pittsburgh	PA	27,800	HC+
Univ of Toledo	OH	18,464	C
Univ of Utah	UT	13,462	VC
Univ of Wisc/Madison	WI	18,757	HC
Vanderbilt Univ	TN	57,072	MC
Virginia Commonwealth Univ	VA	18,633	C
Walla Walla Univ	WA	26,256	NC
Washington State Univ	WA	20,461	C
Washington Univ in St. Louis	MO	58,818	MC
Western New England Univ	MA	45,590	C

BIOINFORMATICS

School	ST	$IS	SR
Baylor Univ	TX	46,720	HC
Brigham Young Univ	UT	12,100	HC
Canisius College	NY	45,602	VC
Claflin Univ	SC	22,368	C+
Clarke Univ	IA	36,400	C
Gannon Univ	PA	37,940	C
Inter-American Univ of PR/Bayamon Univ College	PR	4,428	
Loyola Univ Chicago	IL	49,560	VC+
Mich State Univ	MI	13,689	VC
Mich Tech Univ	MI	22,105	VC
New York City College of Technology / The CUNY	NY	5,769	NC
Ramapo College of New Jersey	NJ	24,938	C+
Rochester Inst of Technology	NY	42,450	VC+
Rockhurst Univ	MO	20,625	C
Rowan Univ	NJ	23,570	VC
St. Vincent College	PA	40,244	C
St. Bonaventure Univ	NY	38,831	C
St. Edward's Univ	TX	44,674	VC
Stevens Inst of Technology	NJ	50,130	HC
The College of St. Rose	NY	26,750	C
Univ at Buffalo / The SUNY	NY	20,283	VC
Univ of Arkansas at Little Rock	AR		C
Univ of Calif at Irvine	CA	25,961	VC
Univ of Calif at San Diego	CA	21,000	VC
Univ of Calif at Santa Cruz	CA	27,807	VC
Univ of Denver	CO	51,787	VC+
Univ of Georgia	GA	19,508	VC
Univ of Maryland/Baltimore County	MD	18,000	VC
Univ of Missouri-Kansas City	MO	19,603	C
Univ of Nebr at Omaha	NE	12,700	C
Univ of Northern Iowa	IA	14,776	C
Univ of Pittsburgh at Pittsburgh	PA	27,800	HC+
Univ of St. Thomas - Houston	TX	36,490	VC
Univ of the Sciences	PA	48,320	VC+
Virginia Commonwealth Univ	VA	18,633	C
Walsh Univ	OH	35,100	C
Washington Univ in St. Louis	MO	58,818	MC
Wheaton College	MA	54,934	HC+

BIOLOGY

School	ST	$IS	SR
Bowling Green State Univ	OH	18,970	C
Bryant Univ	RI	49,179	VC
Cabrini College	PA	40,859	LC
Drexel Univ	PA	51,920	HC
Elon Univ	NC	40,046	HC
Indiana Univ Bloomington	IN	19,358	HC
Indiana Univ East	IN	6,639	LC
Indiana Univ Kokomo	IN	6,674	LC
Indiana Univ Northwest	IN	6,738	LC
Indiana Univ South Bend	IN	15,293	C
Indiana Univ Southeast	IN	15,807	LC
Indiana Univ-Purdue Univ Indianapolis	IN	17,290	C
Northwestern State Univ of Louisiana	LA	14,368	C
Nova Southeastern Univ	FL	34,016	VC
Ohio Valley Univ	WV	17,752	C
Okla City Univ	OK	33,546	VC
St. Louis Univ	MO	46,594	VC+
Southern Oregon Univ	OR	17,874	C
Thomas Edison State College	NJ	5,700	SP
Univ of Denver	CO	51,787	VC+
Univ of Georgia	GA	19,508	VC
Univ of Louisiana at Monroe	LA	12,998	C
Univ of Miami	FL	55,166	MC
Univ of Wisc/Superior	WI	14,106	C
Univ of Wyoming	WY	13,855	C+
Whitman College	WA	54,400	MC

BIOLOGY AND SOCIETY

School	ST	$IS	SR
Cornell Univ	NY	59,037	MC

BIOLOGY/ADOLESCENCE EDUCATION

School	ST	$IS	SR
Bethany College	WV	35,282	C
Biola Univ	CA	40,320	VC
Duquesne Univ	PA	42,017	VC
Elizabethtown College	PA	47,600	VC
Gannon Univ	PA	37,940	C
Houghton College	NY	35,740	VC
Indiana Univ Northwest	IN	6,738	LC
Indiana Univ of Pennsylvania	PA	20,180	LC
Indiana Univ Southeast	IN	15,807	LC
Indiana Univ-Purdue Univ Indianapolis	IN	17,290	C
Lipscomb Univ	TN	35,722	VC
Messiah College	PA	39,540	VC
Millikin Univ	IL	37,462	C
Nazareth College of Rochester	NY	41,590	VC
Oswego / SUNY	NY	20,009	VC
Pace Univ	NY	48,094	VC
Seattle Univ	WA	47,010	VC+
St. John's Univ	NY	52,840	C+
SUNY Plattsburgh / SUNY	NY	18,083	VC
Taylor Univ	IN	36,742	VC+
Temple Univ	PA	24,392	VC
The College of St. Rose	NY	26,750	C
Univ of Mary Hardin-Baylor	TX	31,950	C+

BIOLOGY/BIOLOGICAL SCIENCE

School	ST	$IS	SR
Abilene Christian Univ	TX	38,400	VC
Adams State College	CO	13,358	LC
Adelphi Univ	NY	43,130	VC
Adrian College	MI	33,800	C
Agnes Scott College	GA	45,323	VC+
Alabama A&M Univ	AL	16,400	C
Alabama State Univ	AL	14,142	NC
Albany State Univ	GA	8,500	C
Albertus Magnus College	CT	37,382	LC
Albion College	MI	43,884	VC
Albright College	PA	46,660	C
Alcorn State Univ	MS	9,500	C
Alderson Broaddus Univ	WV	28,656	C
Alfred Univ	NY	40,392	VC
Alice Lloyd College	KY	4,900	C
Allegheny College	PA	49,020	HC
Allen Univ	SC	16,124	NC
Alma College	MI	42,400	VC
Alvernia Univ	PA	39,250	C
Alverno College	WI	30,483	LC
American International College	MA	36,100	LC
American Univ	DC	54,829	HC+
Amherst College	MA	58,744	MC
Anderson Univ	IN	35,390	C
Andrews Univ	MI	28,030	C+
Angelo State Univ	TX	15,049	NC
Appalachian State Univ	NC	12,919	VC
Aquinas College	MI	33,060	C
Arcadia Univ	PA	33,570	C+
Arizona State Univ	AZ	18,818	C+
Arkansas State Univ	AR	14,980	C
Arkansas Tech Univ	AR	13,164	LC
Armstrong Atlantic State Univ	GA	16,276	C
Asbury Univ	KY	32,038	VC
Ashford Univ	IA	21,780	C
Ashland Univ	OH	25,000	C
Assumption College	MA	45,721	VC
Atlantic Union College	MA	24,600	LC
Auburn Univ	AL	20,052	VC+
Auburn Univ at Montgomery	AL	12,120	C
Augsburg College	MN	35,142	C
Augustana College	IL	43,398	HC
Augustana College	SD	35,500	VC
Aurora Univ	IL	26,870	C
Austin College	TX	36,940	HC
Austin Peay State Univ	TN	14,650	C
Averett Univ	VA	36,000	LC
Avila Univ	MO	26,900	C
Azusa Pacific Univ	CA	39,946	C
Baker Univ	KS	33,350	C+
Baldwin Wallace Univ	OH	36,980	VC
Ball State Univ	IN	17,850	C
Bard College	NY	59,872	HC
Bard College at Simon's Rock	MA	58,963	HC+
Barry Univ	FL	38,190	C
Barton College	NC	27,660	C
Bates College	ME	58,950	MC
Bay Path College	MA	34,565	C
Baylor Univ	TX	46,720	HC
Becker College	MA	41,420	LC
Belhaven Univ	MS	27,170	C
Bellarmine Univ	KY	42,950	VC
Belmont Abbey College	NC	37,716	C
Belmont Univ	TN	37,380	VC+
Beloit College	WI	49,970	HC
Bemidji State Univ	MN	13,500	C
Benedict College	SC	20,454	NC
Benedictine College	KS	29,180	VC
Benedictine Univ	IL	35,220	C
Bennett College	NC		LC
Bennington College	VT	56,990	HC+
Berea College	KY	7,220	HC
Berry College	GA	39,254	HC
Bethany College	KS	30,605	NC
Bethany College	WV	35,282	C
Bethel College	IN	31,560	C
Bethel College	KS	29,100	C
Bethel Univ	MN	34,940	VC
Bethel Univ	TN	19,186	C
Bethune-Cookman Univ	FL	22,290	LC
Binghamton Univ / The SUNY	NY	20,832	HC+
Biola Univ	CA	40,320	VC
Birmingham-Southern College	AL	42,370	VC+
Black Hills State Univ	SD	13,562	LC
Blackburn College	IL	21,350	C
Bloomfield College	NJ	36,960	C
Bloomsburg Univ of Pennsylvania	PA	13,598	C
Blue Mountain College	MS	13,550	LC
Bluefield College	VA	17,230	C+
Bluefield State College	WV	3,140	LC
Bluffton Univ	OH	37,864	C
Boise State Univ	ID	12,802	C
Boston College	MA	58,506	MC
Boston Univ	MA	54,130	HC+
Bowdoin College	ME	57,834	MC
Bowie State Univ	MD	23,990	LC
Bradley Univ	IL	31,874	VC
Brandeis Univ	MA	58,820	HC
Brenau Univ Women's College	GA	26,650	C+
Brescia Univ	KY	26,140	VC+
Brewton-Parker College	GA	33,388	LC
Briar Cliff Univ	IA	29,514	C
Bridgewater College	VA	39,880	C
Bridgewater State Univ	MA	18,752	C
Brigham Young Univ	UT	12,100	HC
Brigham Young Univ/Hawaii	HI	8,614	VC
Brown Univ	RI	56,150	MC
Bryan College	TN	24,194	C
Bryant Univ	RI	49,179	VC
Bryn Athyn College	PA	27,984	C
Bryn Mawr College	PA	57,760	MC
Bucknell Univ	PA	58,160	MC
Buena Vista Univ	IA	37,954	C
Buffalo State/State Univ of Buffalo	NY	15,733	C+

School	ST	$IS	SR
Butler Univ	IN	45,898	VC+
Caldwell College	NJ	35,602	LC
Calif Baptist Univ	CA	35,890	C
Calif Inst of Technology	CA	54,045	MC
Calif Lutheran Univ	CA	47,640	C
Calif Polytechnic State Univ	CA	19,847	HC
Calif State Polytechnic Univ, Pomona	CA	18,932	C
Cal State, Bakersfield	CA	8,000	LC
Cal State, Chico	CA	18,952	C
Cal State, Dominguez Hills	CA	17,056	LC
Cal State, East Bay	CA	16,549	C
Cal State, Fresno	CA	17,405	C
Cal State, Fullerton	CA	25,188	C+
Cal State, Long Beach	CA	17,534	C+
Cal State, Los Angeles	CA	15,829	C
Cal State, Monterey Bay	CA	26,871	LC
Cal State, Northridge	CA	28,313	C
Cal State, Sacramento	CA	16,200	C
Cal State, San Bernardino	CA	12,000	C
Cal State, San Marcos	CA	14,576	C
Cal State, Stanislaus	CA	18,582	C
Calif Univ of Pennsylvania	PA	14,217	C
Calvin College	MI	37,585	VC+
Cameron Univ	OK	9,267	LC
Campbell Univ	NC	25,500	C
Campbellsville Univ	KY	27,720	C
Canisius College	NY	45,602	VC
Capital Univ	OH	39,824	VC
Cardinal Stritch Univ	WI	24,054	C
Caribbean Univ	PR	10,375	
Carleton College	MN	58,149	MC
Carlow Univ	PA	30,272	C
Carnegie Mellon Univ	PA	51,260	MC
Carroll College	MT	28,000	C
Carroll Univ	WI	24,860	C
Carson-Newman Univ	TN	29,058	C+
Carthage College	WI	33,000	C
Case Western Reserve Univ	OH	55,178	MC
Castleton State College	VT	19,424	C
Catawba College	NC	37,105	C
Cedar Crest College	PA	43,240	C
Cedarville Univ	OH	31,036	VC+
Centenary College	NJ	38,618	LC
Centenary College of Louisiana	LA	39,070	C+
Central College	IA	36,980	VC
Central Conn State Univ	CT	19,212	C
Central Methodist Univ	MO	28,240	VC
Central Mich Univ	MI	18,066	C
Central State Univ	OH	9,010	C
Central Univ of Bayamon	PR	3,350	
Central Washington Univ	WA	11,730	C
Centre College	KY	35,000	HC+
Chadron State College	NE	7,400	NC
Chaminade Univ of Honolulu	HI	31,664	C
Chapman Univ	CA	56,019	VC+
Charleston Southern Univ	SC	22,420	C
Chatham Univ	PA	42,440	VC
Chestnut Hill College	PA	39,785	LC
Cheyney Univ of Pennsylvania	PA	20,372	LC
Chicago State Univ	IL	5,482	C
Christian Brothers Univ	TN	19,140	HC
Christopher Newport Univ	VA	21,050	VC
Citadel, The	SC		C
CUNY/Brooklyn College	NY	5,884	C+
Claflin Univ	SC	22,368	C+
Claremont McKenna College	CA	58,065	MC
Clarion Univ of Pennsylvania	PA	17,370	C
Clark Atlanta Univ	GA	30,006	C
Clark Univ	MA	47,020	HC+
Clarke Univ	IA	36,400	C
Clarkson Univ	NY	53,538	HC
Clearwater Christian College	FL	23,720	C
Clemson Univ	SC	19,136	HC
Cleveland State Univ	OH	21,357	C
Coastal Carolina Univ	SC	17,620	C
Coe College	IA	43,590	VC
Coker College	SC	32,256	LC
Colby College	ME	57,510	MC
Colby-Sawyer College	NH	47,870	C
Colgate Univ	NY	50,930	MC
College of Staten Island / The CUNY	NY	16,778	NC
College of Charleston	SC	21,273	VC
College of Mount St. Joseph	OH	33,880	C
College of Mount St. Vincent	NY	41,040	MC
College of New Jersey	NJ	25,376	HC
College of St. Benedict	MN	47,570	VC
College of St. Elizabeth	NJ	43,839	LC
College of St. Mary	NE	34,334	C
College of St. Scholastica	MN	39,960	C
College of the Holy Cross	MA	56,232	MC
College of the Ozarks	MO	5,605	VC
College of William & Mary	VA	25,085	MC
College of Wooster	OH	52,600	VC
Colo Christian Univ	CO	27,500	VC
Colo College	CO	54,534	MC
Colo Mesa Univ	CO	16,669	LC

School	ST	$IS	SR
Colo State Univ-Fort Collins	CO	20,090	VC
Colo State Univ-Pueblo	CO	13,532	LC
Columbia College	MO	24,578	C
Columbia College	SC	27,882	C
Columbia Univ in the City of New York	NY	61,116	MC
Columbia Univ/Barnard College	NY	39,000	MC
Columbia Univ/School of General Studies	NY	54,083	MC
Columbus State Univ	GA	13,176	C
Concord Univ	WV	13,102	C
Concordia College New York	NY	31,500	VC
Concordia College, Moorhead	MN	39,974	C+
Concordia Univ	OR	34,930	C
Concordia Univ - Irvine	CA	35,390	VC
Concordia Univ Nebr	NE	26,000	VC
Concordia Univ St. Paul	MN	27,200	C
Concordia Univ Wisc	WI	28,980	C
Concordia Univ, Ann Arbor	MI	27,220	VC
Concordia Univ, River Forest	IL	26,300	C
Conn College	CT	54,970	MC
Converse College	SC	37,130	C
Coppin State Univ	MD	14,905	VC
Cornell College	IA	44,930	HC
Cornell Univ	NY	59,037	MC
Cornerstone Univ and Grand Rapids Theological Seminary	MI	30,866	C
Covenant College	GA		VC+
Creighton Univ	NE	44,058	VC+
Culver-Stockton College	MO	30,900	C
Cumberland Univ	TN	21,220	C
CUNY-City College	NY	19,576	HC+
Curry College	MA	47,545	LC
Daemen College	NY	31,510	C
Dakota State Univ	SD	13,811	C
Dakota Wesleyan Univ	SD	23,000	C
Dallas Baptist Univ	TX	29,118	C
Dartmouth College	NH	57,996	MC
Davidson College	NC	54,683	MC
Davis and Elkins College	WV	33,742	C
De Sales Univ	PA	42,670	C
Defiance College	OH	30,645	C
Delaware State Univ	DE	14,700	LC
Delaware Valley College	PA	29,944	C
Delta State Univ	MS	12,292	LC
Denison Univ	OH	54,670	HC+
DePaul Univ	IL	46,120	VC
DePauw Univ	IN	48,950	VC+
Dickinson College	PA	57,662	HC+
Dickinson State Univ	ND	8,550	NC
Dillard Univ	LA	20,940	VC
Doane College	NE	33,730	VC
Dominican College	NY	31,270	C
Dominican Univ	IL	37,628	C
Dominican Univ of Calif	CA	51,250	C
Dordt College	IA	34,160	VC
Dowling College	NY	25,000	LC
Drake Univ	IA	30,980	VC+
Drew Univ/College of Liberal Arts	NJ	55,862	VC
Drexel Univ	PA	51,920	HC
Drury Univ	MO	30,319	VC
Duke Univ	NC	50,250	MC
Duquesne Univ	PA	42,017	VC
D'Youville College	NY	29,850	C
Earlham College	IN	49,710	VC+
East Carolina Univ	NC	14,169	C
East Central Univ	OK	10,223	LC
East Stroudsburg Univ of Pennsylvania	PA	16,636	C
East Tenn State Univ	TN	9,000	C
East Texas Baptist Univ	TX	29,135	C
Eastern Conn State Univ	CT	20,584	C
Eastern Illinois Univ	IL	20,502	C
Eastern Kentucky Univ	KY	11,161	C
Eastern Mennonite Univ	VA	38,850	VC
Eastern Mich Univ	MI	17,961	C
Eastern Nazarene College	MA	30,000	C
Eastern New Mexico Univ	NM	10,682	C
Eastern Oregon Univ	OR	10,400	C
Eastern Univ	PA	37,704	C
Eastern Washington Univ	WA	16,388	C
Eckerd College	FL	43,902	VC
Edgewood College	WI	33,294	C
Edinboro Univ of Pennsylvania	PA	15,940	LC
Edward Waters College	FL	17,856	LC
Elizabeth City State Univ	NC	11,638	C
Elizabethtown College	PA	47,600	VC
Elmhurst College	IL	42,032	C+
Elmira College	NY	49,950	C+
Elms College	MA	23,900	VC
Emmanuel College	MA	47,985	VC
Emory and Henry College	VA	387,460	C
Emory Univ	GA	45,000	MC
Emporia State Univ	KS	12,897	C
Erskine College	SC	37,360	C
Eureka College	IL	19,280	C
Evangel Univ	MO	23,090	C
Excelsior College	NY	895	SP
Fairfield Univ	CT	55,850	VC

School	ST	$IS	SR
Fairleigh Dickinson Univ/College at Florham	NJ	42,142	C
Fairleigh Dickinson Univ/Metropolitan Campus	NJ	40,254	C
Fairmont State Univ	WV	12,098	LC
Farmingdale State College	NY	18,985	C
Faulkner Univ	AL	22,530	LC
Fayetteville State Univ	NC	10,816	C
Felician College	NJ	41,640	C
Ferris State Univ	MI	19,698	C
Ferrum College	VA	27,740	LC
Fisk Univ	TN	19,830	C
Fitchburg State Univ	MA	17,241	C
Florida A&M Univ	FL	14,935	LC
Florida Atlantic Univ	FL	17,009	C
Florida Gulf Coast Univ	FL		C
Florida Inst of Technology	FL	48,290	VC
Florida International Univ	FL	17,747	VC
Florida Memorial Univ	FL	20,716	LC
Florida Southern College	FL	38,240	VC
Florida State Univ	FL	15,238	HC
Fontbonne Univ	MO	31,384	C
Fordham Univ	NY	58,927	HC
Fort Hays State Univ	KS	11,354	C
Fort Lewis College	CO	15,513	C
Fort Valley State Univ	GA	11,200	VC
Framingham State Univ	MA	16,750	C
Francis Marion Univ	SC	16,464	LC
Franciscan Univ of Steubenville	OH	27,320	VC
Franklin and Marshall College	PA	58,295	MC
Franklin College	IN	35,885	C
Franklin Pierce Univ	NH	41,598	C
Freed-Hardeman Univ	TN	19,697	VC
Fresno Pacific Univ	CA	32,136	C
Friends Univ	KS	29,100	C
Frostburg State Univ	MD	15,264	LC
Furman Univ	SC	54,006	HC
Gallaudet Univ	DC	25,380	SP
Gannon Univ	PA	37,940	C
Gardner-Webb Univ	NC	34,375	C+
Geneva College	PA	27,280	C
George Fox Univ	OR	40,750	C+
George Mason Univ	VA	15,724	VC
George Washington Univ	DC	57,108	MC
Georgetown College	KY	38,690	C
Georgetown Univ	DC	52,910	MC
Georgia College and State Univ	GA	18,216	VC
Georgia Inst of Technology	GA	20,464	MC
Georgia Regents Univ	GA		C
Georgia Southern Univ	GA	16,414	C
Georgia Southwestern State Univ	GA	12,218	C
Georgia State Univ	GA	12,000	VC
Georgian Court Univ	NJ	39,726	LC
Gettysburg College	PA	56,820	HC
Glenville State College	WV	11,348	NC
Gonzaga Univ	WA	44,247	HC
Gordon College	MA	42,660	VC+
Goshen College	IN	35,900	VC
Goucher College	MD	50,252	VC+
Grace College and Theological Seminary	IN	28,800	C
Graceland Univ	IA	28,020	C
Grambling State Univ	LA	13,384	LC
Grand Canyon Univ	AZ	24,540	VC
Grand Valley State Univ	MI	17,998	VC
Grand View Univ	IA	31,050	C
Green Mountain College	VT	33,547	LC
Greensboro College	NC	28,740	LC
Greenville College	IL	27,012	C
Grinnell College	IA	53,654	HC
Grove City College	PA	22,988	HC
Guilford College	NC	35,340	C
Gustavus Adolphus College	MN	48,170	HC
Gwynedd-Mercy College	PA	33,560	C
Hamilton College	NY	55,620	MC
Hamline Univ	MN	44,198	VC
Hampden-Sydney College	VA	48,848	C
Hampshire College	MA	58,320	MC
Hampton Univ	VA	28,528	C
Hannibal-LaGrange Univ	MO	24,490	C
Hanover College	IN	41,450	VC
Harding Univ	AR	21,432	C+
Hardin-Simmons Univ	TX	23,560	C+
Harris-Stowe State Univ	MO	14,360	NC
Hartwick College	NY	49,815	C+
Harvard Univ/Harvard College	MA	49,000	MC
Harvey Mudd College	CA	61,660	MC
Hastings College	NE	27,782	C+
Haverford College	PA	59,236	MC
Hawaii Pacific Univ	HI	36,690	C
Heidelberg Univ	OH	34,100	C
Henderson State Univ	AR	13,634	C
Hendrix College	AR	48,436	HC+
High Point Univ	NC	39,800	C
Hillsdale College	MI	31,890	HC+
Hiram College	OH	37,300	VC
Hobart and William Smith Colleges	NY	43,000	VC
Hofstra Univ	NY	48,020	VC+
Hollins Univ	VA	43,295	VC
Holy Family Univ	PA	40,030	LC

School	ST	$IS	SR
Holy Names Univ	CA	40,310	NC
Hood College	MD	44,630	C
Hope College	MI	36,320	VC+
Houghton College	NY	35,740	VC
Houston Baptist Univ	TX	23,815	C+
Howard Payne Univ	TX	17,115	C
Howard Univ	DC	35,957	C
Humboldt State Univ	CA	18,400	C
Hunter College / The CUNY	NY	14,429	VC
Huntingdon College	AL	31,850	C
Huntington Univ	IN	32,220	C
Husson Univ	ME	23,386	LC
Huston-Tillotson Univ	TX	18,124	C+
Idaho State Univ	ID	11,908	C
Illinois College	IL	25,770	VC
Illinois Inst of Technology	IL	38,512	HC+
Illinois State Univ	IL	22,634	VC
Illinois Wesleyan Univ	IL	48,452	VC+
Immaculata Univ	PA	43,000	C
Indiana State Univ	IN	16,000	C
Indiana Univ Kokomo	IN	6,674	LC
Indiana Univ of Pennsylvania	PA	20,180	LC
Indiana Univ South Bend	IN	15,293	C
Indiana Univ-Purdue Univ Fort Wayne	IN	15,425	C
Indiana Wesleyan Univ	IN	31,815	VC
Inter-American Univ of PR/ Aguadilla Campus	PR	5,578	
Inter-American Univ of PR/ Arecibo Campus	PR	3,350	
Inter-American Univ of PR/ Bayamon Univ College	PR	4,428	
Inter-American Univ of PR/ Fajardo Campus	PR	4,200	
Inter-American Univ of PR/ Metropolitan Campus	PR	4,320	
Inter-American Univ of PR/ Ponce	PR	3,700	
Inter-American Univ of PR/ San Germán	PR	6,720	
Iona College	NY	44,028	C
Iowa State Univ	IA	16,403	C
Iowa Wesleyan College	IA	30,850	LC
Ithaca College	NY	52,300	HC
Jackson State Univ	MS	13,512	LC
Jacksonville State Univ	AL	12,280	LC
Jacksonville Univ	FL	37,780	C
James Madison Univ	VA	18,049	VC
Jarvis Christian College	TX	19,552	NC
John Brown Univ	AR	30,996	VC+
John Carroll Univ	OH	44,520	C+
Johns Hopkins Univ	MD	47,492	MC
Johnson C. Smith Univ	NC	25,336	LC
Johnson State College	VT	16,721	C
Judson College	AL	24,690	C
Judson Univ	IL	25,130	C
Juniata College	PA	49,340	VC
Kalamazoo College	MI	47,825	HC+
Kansas State Univ	KS	15,497	VC
Kansas Wesleyan Univ	KS	32,000	C
Kean Univ	NJ	22,060	LC
Keene State College	NH	21,538	C
Kennesaw State Univ	GA	13,017	VC
Kent State Univ	OH	19,352	C
Kentucky State Univ	KY	11,000	LC
Kentucky Wesleyan College	KY	27,440	VC+
Kenyon College	OH	56,810	MC
Keuka College	NY	30,300	C
Keystone College	PA	28,680	LC
King Univ	TN	33,140	C
King's College	PA	41,678	C
Knox College	IL		VC
Kutztown Univ of Pennsylvania	PA	16,909	LC
La Roche College	PA	34,802	LC
La Salle Univ	PA	50,270	C
La Sierra Univ	CA	35,694	VC
Lafayette College	PA	57,050	HC+
LaGrange College	GA	34,480	C
Lake Erie College	OH	35,704	C
Lake Forest College	IL	45,580	VC
Lake Superior State Univ	MI	18,121	C
Lakeland College	WI	22,990	C
Lamar Univ	TX	6,820	LC
Lander Univ	SC	22,514	C+
Lane College	TN	11,212	C
Langston Univ	OK	3,000	LC
Lawrence Univ	WI	46,371	HC
Le Moyne College	NY	42,200	VC
Lebanon Valley College	PA	38,570	C
Lee Univ	TN	18,690	C+
Lees-McRae College	NC	33,624	C
Lehigh Univ	PA	55,080	MC
Lehman College / The CUNY	NY	5,778	LC
LeMoyne-Owen College	TN	13,100	C
Lenoir-Rhyne College	NC	35,984	C
LeTourneau Univ	TX	26,230	C
Lewis & Clark College	OR	52,656	VC
Lewis Univ	IL	23,050	C
Lewis-Clark State College	ID	6,990	C
Liberty Univ	VA	19,101	C
Limestone College	SC	29,880	C
Lincoln Memorial Univ	TN	18,144	C
Lincoln Univ	MO	11,996	NC

ST = STATE **$IS** = IN-STATE COSTS **SR** = SELECTOR RATING

School	ST	$IS	SR
Lindenwood Univ	MO	20,750	C
Lindsey Wilson College	KY	30,470	VC
Linfield College-McMinnville Campus	OR	46,166	C
Lipscomb Univ	TN	35,722	VC
Livingstone College	NC	17,815	LC
Lock Haven Univ of Pennsylvania	PA	17,587	LC
LIU/Brooklyn Campus	NY	26,500	C
LIU/C.W. Post Campus	NY	38,888	C
Longwood Univ	VA	20,924	C
Loras College	IA	37,432	VC
Louisiana College	LA	15,746	C
Louisiana State Univ	LA	18,677	V₲
Louisiana State Univ in Shreveport	LA	5,606	C
Louisiana Tech Univ	LA	8,000	C
Lourdes Univ	OH	26,055	LC
Loyola Marymount Univ	CA	53,240	V₲
Loyola Univ Chicago	IL	49,560	V₲
Loyola Univ Maryland	MD		VC
Loyola Univ New Orleans	LA	46,581	VC
Lubbock Christian Univ	TX	25,518	C
Luther College	IA	44,380	V₲
Lycoming College	PA	43,636	C
Lynchburg College	VA	42,645	C
Lynn Univ	FL	43,500	C
Lyon College	AR	30,246	VC
Macalester College	MN	53,419	MC
MacMurray College	IL	20,755	C
Madonna Univ	MI	24,540	VC
Malone Univ	OH	34,334	C
Manchester College	IN	35,070	C
Manhattan College	NY	44,955	VC
Manhattanville College	NY	46,260	VC
Mansfield Univ	PA	19,468	LC
Marian Univ	WI	30,980	LC
Marian Univ/Indianapolis	IN	37,058	C
Marietta College	OH	42,135	VC
Marist College	NY	35,500	C
Marlboro College	VT	35,980	VC
Marquette Univ	WI	43,664	V₲
Mars Hill College	NC	22,950	LC
Marshall Univ	WV	14,820	C
Martin Univ	IN	11,000	SP
Mary Baldwin College	VA	37,110	C
Marygrove College	MI	21,290	C
Marymount Manhattan College	NY	40,118	VC
Marymount Univ	VA	36,178	C
Maryville College	TN	33,150	VC
Maryville Univ of St. Louis	MO	34,920	VC
Marywood Univ	PA	40,695	C
Mass College of Liberal Arts	MA	16,733	C
Mass Inst of Technology	MA	54,238	MC
Mayville State Univ	ND	11,401	NC
McDaniel College	MD	45,600	VC
McKendree Univ	IL	29,920	₲
McMurry Univ	TX	25,962	LC
McNeese State Univ	LA		C
McPherson College	KS	28,138	C
Medaille College	NY	35,112	VC
Medgar Evers College / The CUNY	NY	4,920	NC
Mercer Univ	GA	44,201	V₲
Mercy College	NY	29,996	C
Mercyhurst Univ	PA	40,700	C
Meredith College	NC	31,420	C
Merrimack College	MA	44,215	C
Messiah College	PA	39,540	VC
Methodist Univ	NC	37,185	C
Metropolitan State Univ	MN	5,923	SP
Metropolitan State Univ of Denver	CO	4,835	LC
Mich State Univ	MI	13,689	VC
Mich Tech Univ	MI	22,105	VC
MidAmerica Nazarene Univ	KS	28,000	C
Middle Tenn State Univ	TN	8,650	C
Middlebury College	VT	57,470	MC
Midland Univ	NE	34,000	C
Midway College	KY	20,150	C
Midwestern State Univ	TX	9,722	C
Miles College	AL	16,530	NC
Millersville Univ of Pennsylvania	PA	18,498	C
Milligan College	TN	27,510	C
Millikin Univ	IL	37,462	C
Mills College	CA	54,119	HC
Millsaps College	MS	43,888	V₲
Minn State Univ, Mankato	MN	14,900	C
Minn State Univ, Moorhead	MN	13,392	C
Minot State Univ	ND	10,915	C
Misericordia Univ	PA	39,840	C
Miss College	MS	21,998	VC
Miss Univ for Women	MS	7,400	LC
Miss Valley State Univ	MS	9,706	LC
Missouri Baptist Univ	MO	30,310	C
Missouri Southern State Univ	MO	11,910	C
Missouri State Univ	MO	13,996	VC
Missouri Univ of Science and Technology	MO	18,655	V₲
Missouri Valley College	MO	22,200	C
Missouri Western State Univ	MO	12,260	NC
Molloy College	NY	38,950	C
Monmouth College	IL	39,290	C
Monmouth Univ	NJ	42,252	C
Montana State Univ	MT	14,068	VC
Montana State Univ-Billings	MT	12,425	LC
Montana State Univ-Northern	MT	12,500	NC
Montana Tech of The Univ of Montana	MT	14,650	VC
Montclair State Univ	NJ	22,614	C
Moravian College	PA	36,381	VC
Morehead State Univ	KY	10,900	C
Morehouse College	GA	38,640	C
Morgan State Univ	MD	14,500	VC
Morningside College	IA	32,620	C
Morris College	SC	16,006	LC
Mount Aloysius College	PA	27,970	C
Mount Holyoke College	MA	53,596	H₲
Mount Marty College	SD	29,638	C
Mount Mary Univ	WI	32,836	LC
Mount Mercy Univ	IA	34,385	C
Mount Olive College	NC	18,426	C
Mount St. Mary College	NY	39,540	C
Mount St. Mary's Univ	MD	46,158	C
Mount St. Mary's College/Chalon Campus	CA	43,897	V₲
Mount Vernon Nazarene Univ	OH	29,590	C
Mountain State Univ	WV	14,330	NC
Muhlenberg College	PA	52,837	HC
Murray State Univ	KY	14,944	C
Muskingum Univ	OH	30,502	C
National Louis Univ	IL	16,915	LC
Nazareth College of Rochester	NY	41,590	VC
Nebr Wesleyan Univ	NE	29,774	₲
Neumann Univ	PA	31,078	LC
New College of Florida	FL	14,504	H₲
New England College	NH	45,930	LC
New Jersey City Univ	NJ	21,060	₲
New Jersey Inst of Technology	NJ	26,490	VC
New Mexico Highlands Univ	NM	9,720	NC
New Mexico Inst of Mining and Technology	NM	12,892	HC
New Mexico State Univ	NM	13,955	LC
New York Inst of Technology	NY	40,590	VC
New York Univ	NY	61,470	MC
Newberry College	SC	26,850	LC
Newman Univ	KS	30,380	₲
Niagara Univ	NY	39,800	C
Nicholls State Univ	LA	7,095	C
Norfolk State Univ	VA	10,531	LC
N Car Agricultural and Technical State Univ	NC	13,175	LC
N Car Central Univ	NC	9,000	LC
N Car State Univ	NC	16,202	HC
N Car Wesleyan College	NC	29,440	C
North Central College	IL	38,343	VC
N Dak State Univ	ND	14,642	C
North Georgia College & State Univ	GA	8,500	C
North Park Univ	IL	30,130	C
Northeastern Illinois Univ	IL		C
Northeastern State Univ	OK	8,615	VC
Northeastern Univ	MA	55,296	MC
Northern Arizona Univ	AZ	18,592	C
Northern Illinois Univ	IL	19,768	C
Northern Kentucky Univ	KY	15,302	LC
Northern Mich Univ	MI	15,300	VC
Northern State Univ	SD	14,021	C
Northland College	WI	26,680	C
Northwest Missouri State Univ	MO	14,229	C
Northwest Nazarene Univ	ID	24,275	NC
Northwestern College	MN	24,000	C
Northwestern College of Iowa	IA	34,848	₲
Northwestern Okla State Univ	OK	7,275	NC
Northwestern State Univ of Louisiana	LA	14,368	C
Northwestern Univ	IL	37,595	MC
Norwich Univ	VT	28,212	C
Notre Dame College	OH	34,942	VC
Notre Dame de Namur Univ	CA	41,610	LC
Notre Dame of Maryland Univ	MD	27,700	C
Nyack College	NY	32,000	C
Oakland City Univ	IN	24,500	NC
Oakland Univ	MI	19,391	VC
Oakwood Univ	AL	23,035	C
Oberlin College	OH	57,025	MC
Occidental College	CA	59,592	M₲
Oglethorpe Univ	GA	42,580	VC
Ohio Dominican Univ	OH	38,380	₲
Ohio Northern Univ	OH	42,075	VC
Ohio State Univ at Lima	OH	7,140	C
Ohio Univ	OH	20,676	VC
Ohio Wesleyan Univ	OH	49,460	₲
Okla Baptist Univ	OK	28,202	VC
Okla Christian Univ	OK	24,975	VC
Okla Panhandle State Univ	OK	8,996	NC
Okla State Univ	OK	14,310	VC
Okla Wesleyan Univ	OK	21,300	C
Old Dominion Univ	VA	18,662	C
Olivet College	MI	19,984	C
Olivet Nazarene Univ	IL	29,990	C
Oral Roberts Univ	OK	31,734	C
Oregon State Univ	OR	19,017	₲
Oswego / SUNY	NY	20,009	VC
Ottawa Univ	KS	15,000	VC
Ouachita Baptist Univ	AR	29,010	VC
Our Lady of Holy Cross College	LA	8,090	LC
Our Lady of the Lake Univ of San Antonio	TX	22,430	LC
Pace Univ	NY	48,094	VC
Pacific Lutheran Univ	WA	44,840	VC
Pacific Union College	CA	28,150	VC
Pacific Univ	OR	42,815	C
Paine College	GA	18,594	LC
Palm Beach Atlantic Univ	FL	33,882	LC
Park Univ	MO	17,525	C
Penn State Erie/The Behrend College	PA	16,256	C
Penn State Univ/Altoona	PA	11,464	C
Penn State Univ/Univ Park	PA	25,404	VC
Pepperdine Univ	CA	55,372	H₲
Peru State College	NE	8,600	NC
Pfeiffer Univ	NC	33,700	C
Philadelphia Univ	PA	44,160	C
Philander Smith College	AR	19,760	LC
Piedmont College	GA	29,260	C
Pine Manor College	MA	32,659	LC
Pittsburg State Univ	KS	12,032	C
Pitzer College	CA	54,988	MC
Plymouth State Univ	NH	23,148	LC
Point Loma Nazarene Univ	CA	38,610	VC
Point Park Univ	PA	36,390	C
Pomona College	CA	57,680	MC
Pontifical Catholic Univ of PR	PR	7,310	
Portland State Univ	OR	18,672	C
Prairie View A&M Univ	TX	15,205	LC
Presbyterian College	SC	42,678	VC
Prescott College	AZ	33,284	₲
Presentation College	SD	14,800	LC
Principia College	IL	35,140	₲
Providence College	RI	55,995	HC
Purchase College / SUNY	NY	16,951	C
Purdue Univ/Calumet	IN	14,336	C
Purdue Univ/West Lafayette	IN	20,278	HC
Queens College / The CUNY	NY	17,107	VC
Queens Univ of Charlotte	NC	39,543	VC
Quincy Univ	IL	34,980	LC
Quinnipiac Univ	CT	53,580	VC
Radford Univ	VA	17,132	LC
Ramapo College of New Jersey	NJ	24,938	₲
Randolph College	VA	43,960	VC
Randolph-Macon College	VA	45,086	C
Reed College	OR	57,780	MC
Regis College	MA	47,565	LC
Regis Univ	CO	41,318	C
Reinhardt College	GA	25,000	C
Rensselaer Polytechnic Inst	NY	59,229	MC
Rhode Island College	RI	17,132	LC
Rhodes College	TN	47,596	H₲
Rice Univ	TX	43,288	MC
Richard Stockton College of New Jersey	NJ	20,000	VC
Rider Univ	NJ	45,720	C
Ripon College	WI	36,959	₲
Rivier College	NH	35,000	VC
Roanoke College	VA	47,996	₲
Robert Morris Univ	PA	36,699	C
Roberts Wesleyan College	NY	37,384	₲
Rochester Inst of Technology	NY	42,450	V₲
Rockford College	IL	31,000	C
Rockhurst Univ	MO	20,625	C
Rocky Mountain College	MT	32,242	C
Roger Williams Univ	RI	45,788	C
Rollins College	FL	52,370	HC
Roosevelt Univ	IL	22,605	VC
Rose-Hulman Inst of Technology	IN	51,738	MC
Rosemont College	PA	42,350	C
Rowan Univ	NJ	23,570	VC
Russell Sage College	NY	39,370	C
Rust College	MS	10,600	C
Rutgers, The State Univ of New Jersey/Camden Campus	NJ	24,254	C
Rutgers, The State Univ of New Jersey/New Brunswick	NJ	25,077	VC
Rutgers, The State Univ of New Jersey/Newark Campus	NJ	25,376	C
Sacred Heart Univ	CT	48,564	VC
Saginaw Valley State Univ	MI	16,869	C
St. Anselm College	NH	48,324	VC
St. Augustine's Univ	NC	14,000	C
St. Francis Univ	PA	30,029	LC
St. John's Univ	MN	46,146	C
St. Joseph College	CT	45,630	LC
St. Joseph's College	IN	35,790	C
St. Joseph's College of Maine	ME	31,580	C
St. Joseph's Univ	PA	52,272	VC
St. Leo Univ	FL	27,990	C
St. Louis Univ	MO	46,594	V₲
St. Martin's Univ	WA	38,082	C
St. Mary-of-the-Woods College	IN	37,722	LC
St. Mary's College	IN	45,160	VC
St. Mary's College of Calif	CA	53,550	C
St. Mary's Univ	TX	33,854	C
St. Mary's Univ of Minn	MN	37,015	C
St. Michael's College	VT	48,740	VC
St. Paul's College	VA	16,030	NC
St. Peter's College	NJ	44,240	C
St. Vincent College	PA	40,244	C
St. Xavier Univ	IL	32,840	C
Salem College	NC	29,326	VC
Salem International Univ	WV	18,020	C
Salem State College	MA	13,161	LC
Salisbury Univ	MD	18,368	VC
Salve Regina Univ	RI	47,250	VC
Sam Houston State Univ	TX	17,082	C
Samford Univ	AL	35,700	V₲
San Diego Christian College	CA	31,012	C
San Diego State Univ	CA	20,578	VC
San Francisco State Univ	CA	18,514	C
San Jose State Univ	CA	19,707	C
Santa Clara Univ	CA	54,702	MC
Sarah Lawrence College	NY	48,000	HC
Savannah State Univ	GA	13,156	C
Schreiner Univ	TX	32,734	LC
Scripps College	CA	54,900	MC
Seattle Pacific Univ	WA	41,559	V₲
Seattle Univ	WA	47,010	V₲
Seton Hall Univ	NJ	45,902	C
Seton Hill Univ	PA	35,172	C
Sewanee: The Univ of the South	TN	47,700	H₲
Shaw Univ	NC	15,488	LC
Shawnee State Univ	OH	16,545	NC
Shenandoah Univ	VA	39,268	C
Shepherd Univ	WV	14,996	C
Shippensburg Univ of Pennsylvania	PA	17,064	LC
Shorter Univ	GA	26,470	C
Siena College	NY	43,863	VC
Siena Heights Univ	MI	17,000	LC
Silver Lake College	WI	22,600	LC
Simmons College	MA	48,770	VC
Simpson College	IA	36,086	VC
Simpson Univ	CA	28,900	C
Skidmore College	NY	57,926	HC
Slippery Rock Univ of Pennsylvania	PA	10,360	LC
Smith College	MA	57,524	MC
Sonoma State Univ	CA	20,541	C
S Car State Univ	SC	6,700	LC
S Dak State Univ	SD	14,296	C
Southeast Missouri State Univ	MO	14,983	LC
Southeastern Louisiana Univ	LA	13,325	C
Southeastern Okla State Univ	OK	7,966	C
Southeastern Univ	FL	27,201	₲
Southern Adventist Univ	TN	26,190	C
Southern Arkansas Univ	AR	14,316	C
Southern Conn State Univ	CT	18,033	C
Southern Illinois Univ Carbondale	IL	21,620	C
Southern Illinois Univ Edwardsville	IL	17,532	C
Southern Methodist Univ	TX	57,755	MC
Southern Nazarene Univ	OK	24,354	NC
Southern Oregon Univ	OR	17,874	C
Southern Polytechnic State Univ	GA	13,958	VC
Southern Univ and A&M College	LA	9,761	₲
Southern Univ at New Orleans	LA	1,000	NC
Southern Wesleyan Univ	SC	25,600	C
Southwest Baptist Univ	MO	24,710	C
Southwest Minn State Univ	MN	14,000	C
Southwestern Adventist Univ	TX	23,026	LC
Southwestern College	KS	29,270	C
Southwestern Okla State Univ	OK	9,160	C
Southwestern Univ	TX	45,660	VC
Spalding Univ	KY	31,850	LC
Spelman College	GA	24,650	VC
Spring Arbor Univ	MI	26,740	C
Spring Hill College	AL	42,130	VC
Springfield College	MA	25,000	C
St. Ambrose Univ	IA		C
St. Andrews Univ	NC	32,050	LC
St. Bonaventure Univ	NY	38,831	C
St. Catherine Univ	MN	37,782	₲
St. Cloud State Univ	MN	10,600	C
St. Edward's Univ	TX	44,674	VC
St. Francis College	NY	34,200	LC
St. John Fisher College	NY	39,370	₲
St. John's Univ	NY	52,840	₲
St. Joseph's College, New York / Brooklyn Campus	NY	21,878	C
St. Joseph's College, New York / Suffolk Campus	NY	21,878	VC

ST = STATE **$IS** = IN-STATE COSTS **SR** = SELECTOR RATING

School	ST	$IS	SR
St. Lawrence Univ	NY	53,740	HC
St. Mary's College of Maryland	MD	26,699	HC
St. Norbert College	WI	39,992	VC
St. Olaf College	MN	49,960	HC+
St. Thomas Univ	FL	32,310	C+
Stanford Univ	CA	56,411	MC
SUNY / College of Environmental Science and Forestry	NY	18,351	HC
Stephen F. Austin State Univ	TX	14,668	C
Stephens College	MO	34,500	VC
Sterling College	KS	27,216	C
Stetson Univ	FL	49,512	VC+
Stevenson Univ	MD	39,572	C
Stillman College	AL	18,460	C
Stonehill College	MA	46,780	VC+
Stony Brook Univ / SUNY	NY	19,359	HC
Suffolk Univ	MA	46,548	C
Sul Ross State Univ	TX	13,410	LC
SUNY College at Geneseo	NY	18,055	HC+
SUNY College at Old Westbury	NY	16,324	C
SUNY Cortland / The SUNY	NY	19,117	C
SUNY Fredonia / The SUNY at Fredonia	NY	18,702	VC
SUNY New Paltz	NY	15,010	C
SUNY Oneonta / SUNY	NY	16,919	VC
SUNY Plattsburgh / SUNY	NY	18,083	VC
Susquehanna Univ	PA	49,170	C
Swarthmore College	PA	57,870	MC
Sweet Briar College	VA	43,765	C+
Syracuse Univ	NY	54,512	HC
Tabor College	KS	29,010	LC
Talladega College	AL	13,000	C
Tarleton State Univ	TX	13,489	LC
Taylor Univ	IN	36,742	VC+
Temple Univ	PA	24,392	VC
Tenn State Univ	TN	9,048	C
Tenn Tech Univ	TN	11,310	C
Tenn Wesleyan College	TN	21,250	C
Texas A&M Univ	TX	16,956	VC+
Texas A&M Univ at Commerce	TX	10,496	C
Texas A&M Univ at Corpus Christi	TX	11,544	LC
Texas A&M Univ at Galveston	TX	11,258	C
Texas A&M Univ at Kingsville	TX	7,500	LC
Texas Christian Univ	TX	47,570	HC
Texas Lutheran Univ	TX	34,070	C
Texas Southern Univ	TX	18,212	LC
Texas State Univ	TX	16,495	VC
Texas Tech Univ	TX	14,243	C
Texas Wesleyan Univ	TX	29,886	C
Texas Woman's Univ	TX	13,633	LC
The Catholic Univ of America	DC	52,852	VC
The College at Brockport / SUNY	NY	18,362	VC
The College of Idaho	ID	31,277	VC
The College of New Rochelle	NY	33,600	VC
The College of St. Rose	NY	26,750	C
The Lincoln Univ	PA	15,154	LC
The Masters College	CA	38,160	C+
Ohio State Univ	OH	19,887	MC
The SUNY at Potsdam	NY	17,754	C
Thiel College	PA	31,378	LC
Thomas More College	KY	34,760	C
Thomas Univ	GA	11,520	NC
Toccoa Falls College	GA	23,210	C
Tougaloo College	MS	15,275	NC
Touro College	NY	23,150	VC
Towson Univ	MD	16,000	VC
Transylvania Univ	KY	40,310	VC+
Trevecca Nazarene Univ	TN	30,118	C
Trine Univ	IN	39,400	VC
Trinity Christian College	IL	28,869	C
Trinity College	CT		HC+
Trinity International Univ	IL	31,070	C
Trinity Univ	TX	44,174	HC+
Trinity Washington Univ	DC	30,250	C+
Troy Univ	AL	10,650	C
Truman State Univ	MO	13,546	HC
Tufts Univ	MA	58,780	MC
Tusculum College	TN	24,295	C
Tuskegee Univ	AL	26,750	C
Union College	KY	28,775	C
Union College	NE	23,270	VC
Union College	NY		MC
Union Univ	TN	28,260	VC
United States Air Force Academy	CO		MC
Unity College	ME	34,054	C
Universidad Adventista de las Antillas	PR	7,360	
Universidad del Turabo	PR	4,110	
Univ at Albany / SUNY	NY	18,674	VC
Univ at Buffalo / The SUNY	NY	20,283	VC
Univ of Akron	OH	20,436	C
Univ of Alabama at Birmingham	AL	18,484	C+
Univ of Alabama at Huntsville	AL	17,625	VC
Univ of Alabama at Tuscaloosa	AL	17,164	C+
Univ of Alaska Anchorage	AK	15,290	NC
Univ of Alaska Fairbanks	AK	13,955	C
Univ of Alaska Southeast	AK	11,493	C
Univ of Arizona	AZ	20,105	C
Univ of Arkansas at Fayetteville	AR	16,860	VC
Univ of Arkansas at Little Rock	AR		C
Univ of Arkansas at Monticello	AR	8,470	NC
Univ of Arkansas at Pine Bluff	AR	10,600	C
Univ of Bridgeport	CT	30,030	LC
Univ of Calif at Berkeley	CA	23,322	MC
Univ of Calif at Davis	CA	24,482	HC
Univ of Calif at Irvine	CA	25,961	VC
Univ of Calif at Los Angeles	CA	25,686	MC
Univ of Calif at Riverside	CA	27,204	C
Univ of Calif at San Diego	CA	21,000	VC
Univ of Calif at Santa Barbara	CA	27,551	HC
Univ of Calif at Santa Cruz	CA	27,807	VC
Univ of Central Arkansas	AR	10,840	VC
Univ of Central Florida	FL	15,711	VC+
Univ of Central Missouri	MO	14,605	C
Univ of Central Okla	OK	12,293	C
Univ of Charleston	WV	28,650	C
Univ of Chicago	IL	55,416	MC
Univ of Cincinnati	OH	20,199	VC
Univ of Colo at Colo Springs	CO	15,000	VC
Univ of Colo Denver	CO	17,904	C
Univ of Conn	CT	23,744	HC
Univ of Dallas	TX	43,510	VC+
Univ of Dayton	OH	43,750	VC
Univ of Delaware	DE	22,728	VC
Univ of Denver	CO	51,787	VC+
Univ of Detroit Mercy	MI	30,450	C
Univ of Dubuque	IA	30,200	C
Univ of Evansville	IN	41,056	VC+
Univ of Findlay	OH	31,916	C
Univ of Georgia	GA	19,508	VC
Univ of Great Falls	MT	27,970	C
Univ of Hartford	CT	42,674	C
Univ of Hawaii at Hilo	HI	6,500	C
Univ of Hawaii at Manoa	HI	19,379	VC
Univ of Houston	TX	19,184	VC
Univ of Houston-Downtown	TX	6,267	LC
Univ of Idaho	ID	14,558	C
Univ of Illinois at Chicago	IL	24,293	VC
Univ of Illinois at Urbana-Champaign	IL	24,300	HC
Univ of Indianapolis	IN	31,740	LC
Univ of Iowa	IA	17,481	VC
Univ of Jamestown	ND	24,738	C
Univ of Kansas	KS	16,980	C+
Univ of Kentucky	KY	19,868	C
Univ of La Verne	CA	47,010	VC
Univ of Louisiana at Monroe	LA	12,998	C
Univ of Louisville	KY	17,460	VC
Univ of Maine	ME	19,712	C+
Univ of Maine at Augusta	ME	6,855	C
Univ of Maine at Farmington	ME	17,841	C
Univ of Maine at Fort Kent	ME	14,975	LC
Univ of Maine at Machias	ME	10,523	C
Univ of Maine at Presque Isle	ME	15,011	LC
Univ of Mary	ND	16,714	C
Univ of Mary Hardin-Baylor	TX	31,950	C+
Univ of Mary Washington	VA	19,484	VC
Univ of Maryland	MD	18,801	HC
Univ of Maryland/Baltimore County	MD	18,000	VC
Univ of Maryland/Eastern Shore	MD	14,000	C
Univ of Mass Amherst	MA	23,697	VC+
Univ of Mass Boston	MA	11,966	C
Univ of Mass Dartmouth	MA	22,223	C
Univ of Mass Lowell	MA	19,316	C
Univ of Memphis	TN	15,094	C
Univ of Mich/Ann Arbor	MI	22,102	HC+
Univ of Mich/Dearborn	MI	9,885	VC
Univ of Mich-Flint	MI	17,547	C+
Univ of Minn Crookston	MN	17,834	C
Univ of Minn/Duluth	MN	18,964	C+
Univ of Minn/Morris	MN	17,150	VC
Univ of Minn/Twin Cities	MN		HC
Univ of Miss	MS	15,482	VC
Univ of Missouri/Columbia	MO	18,201	MC
Univ of Missouri-Kansas City	MO	19,603	C
Univ of Missouri-St. Louis	MO	18,304	VC
Univ of Mobile	AL	27,870	VC
Univ of Montana	MT	13,670	C
Univ of Montevallo	AL	17,320	C
Univ of Mount Union	OH	35,130	C
Univ of Nebr - Lincoln	NE	17,507	VC
Univ of Nebr at Kearney	NE	14,855	LC
Univ of Nebr at Omaha	NE	12,700	C
Univ of Nevada, Las Vegas	NV	17,303	C
Univ of Nevada/Reno	NV	14,500	NC
Univ of New England	ME	46,145	C+
Univ of New Hampshire	NH	24,702	VC
Univ of New Haven	CT	47,740	C
Univ of New Mexico	NM	15,300	C
Univ of New Orleans	LA	9,224	VC
Univ of North Alabama	AL	9,960	C
Univ of N Car at Asheville	NC	13,500	VC+
Univ of N Car at Chapel Hill	NC	18,348	MC
Univ of N Car at Charlotte	NC	15,847	C
Univ of N Car at Greensboro	NC	12,848	C
Univ of N Car at Wilmington	NC	13,572	VC+
Univ of N Dak	ND	14,094	C
Univ of North Florida	FL	15,578	VC
Univ of North Texas	TX	15,020	C
Univ of Northern Colo	CO	15,973	C
Univ of Northern Iowa	IA	14,776	C
Univ of Notre Dame	IN		MC
Univ of Oregon	OR	20,872	VC
Univ of Pennsylvania	PA	56,106	MC
Univ of Pikeville	KY	24,750	NC
Univ of Pittsburgh at Bradford	PA	21,316	LC
Univ of Pittsburgh at Greensburg	PA	17,640	C
Univ of Pittsburgh at Johnstown	PA	20,862	LC
Univ of Pittsburgh at Pittsburgh	PA	27,800	HC+
Univ of Portland	OR	47,874	VC
Univ of PR Recinto de Rio Piedras	PR	5,750	
Univ of PR/Cayey	PR	1,504	
Univ of PR/Humacao	PR	1,877	
Univ of PR/Mayaguez	PR	1,250	
Univ of Puget Sound	WA	52,648	HC+
Univ of Redlands	CA	40,500	VC
Univ of Rio Grande	OH	8,750	NC
Univ of Rochester	NY	58,500	MC
Univ of St. Francis	IN	29,810	C
Univ of St. Mary	KS	28,400	C+
Univ of San Diego	CA	53,302	HC+
Univ of San Francisco	CA	49,674	VC
Univ of Science and Arts of Okla	OK	10,560	VC
Univ of Scranton	PA	51,940	VC
Univ of Sioux Falls	SD	22,990	C
Univ of South Alabama	AL	13,510	C
Univ of S Car at Aiken	SC	16,278	C
Univ of S Car at Columbia	SC	19,725	VC+
Univ of S Car Upstate	SC	17,673	LC
Univ of S Dak	SD	15,111	C
Univ of South Florida	FL	13,000	C
Univ of South Florida/St. Petersburg	FL	12,769	VC
Univ of Southern Calif	CA	56,903	MC
Univ of Southern Indiana	IN	14,657	C
Univ of Southern Maine	ME	16,576	C
Univ of Southern Miss	MS	13,170	C
Univ of St. Francis	IL	36,490	C
Univ of St. Thomas - Houston	TX	36,490	VC
Univ of Tampa	FL	35,160	VC
Univ of Tenn at Chattanooga	TN	16,883	C
Univ of Tenn at Knoxville	TN	20,364	VC+
Univ of Tenn at Martin	TN	13,217	C
Univ of Texas at Arlington	TX	10,908	LC
Univ of Texas at Austin	TX	44,074	HC
Univ of Texas at Dallas	TX	21,046	HC
Univ of Texas at El Paso	TX	8,764	NC
Univ of Texas at San Antonio	TX	18,372	C
Univ of Texas-Pan American	TX	12,432	LC
Univ of the Cumberlands	KY	27,500	LC
Univ of the District of Columbia	DC	7,244	LC
Univ of the Incarnate Word	TX	35,200	LC
Univ of the Ozarks	AR	22,100	C
Univ of the Pacific	CA	52,146	VC
Univ of the Sacred Heart	PR	5,590	
Univ of the Sciences	PA	48,320	VC+
Univ of the Southwest	NM	15,000	C
Univ of Toledo	OH	18,464	C
Univ of Tulsa	OK	45,311	HC+
Univ of Utah	UT	13,462	VC
Univ of Vermont	VT	26,120	VC+
Univ of Virginia	VA	22,175	MC
Univ of Virginia's College at Wise	VA	11,076	C
Univ of Washington	WA	14,722	VC
Univ of West Alabama	AL	9,415	C
Univ of West Florida	FL	14,656	C
Univ of West Georgia	GA	14,852	LC
Univ of Wisc Whitewater	WI	13,314	C
Univ of Wisc/Eau Claire	WI	15,430	VC
Univ of Wisc/Green Bay	WI	14,900	C
Univ of Wisc/La Crosse	WI	14,755	VC
Univ of Wisc/Madison	WI	18,757	HC
Univ of Wisc/Oshkosh	WI	10,426	LC
Univ of Wisc/Parkside	WI	10,181	LC
Univ of Wisc/Platteville	WI	14,274	C
Univ of Wisc/River Falls	WI	9,722	LC
Univ of Wisc/Stevens Point	WI	14,043	C
Univ of Wisc/Superior	WI	14,106	C
Univ of Wisc-Milwaukee	WI	18,436	C
Upper Iowa Univ	IA	30,426	NC
Ursinus College	PA	55,630	VC+
Ursuline College	OH	33,198	LC
Utah State Univ	UT	11,803	C
Utica College	NY	44,734	C
Valley City State Univ	ND	12,286	LC
Valparaiso Univ	IN	43,040	VC+
Vanderbilt Univ	TN	57,072	MC
Vanguard Univ of Southern Calif	CA	35,833	VC
Vassar College	NY	59,070	MC
Victory Univ	TN	19,118	C
Villanova Univ	PA	56,436	MC
Virginia Commonwealth Univ	VA	18,633	C
Virginia Intermont College	VA	32,411	LC
Virginia Military Inst	VA	16,156	C
Virginia Polytechnic Inst and State Univ	VA	14,629	HC
Virginia State Univ	VA	11,318	C+
Virginia Union Univ	VA	18,432	C
Virginia Wesleyan College	VA	28,433	LC
Viterbo Univ	WI	30,070	C
Voorhees College	SC	18,126	C
Wabash College	IN	44,160	VC
Wagner College	NY	48,600	VC
Wake Forest Univ	NC	51,000	MC
Walla Walla Univ	WA	26,256	NC
Walsh Univ	OH	35,100	C
Warner Pacific College	OR	25,550	C
Warner Univ	FL	18,000	C
Warren Wilson College	NC	34,888	VC
Wartburg College	IA	41,055	VC
Washburn Univ	KS	12,165	NC
Washington Adventist Univ	MD	25,859	C+
Washington and Jefferson College	PA	49,990	VC
Washington and Lee Univ	VA	52,812	MC
Washington College	MD	48,768	VC
Washington State Univ	WA	20,461	C
Washington Univ in St. Louis	MO	58,818	MC
Wayland Baptist Univ	TX	16,058	LC
Wayne State College	NE	11,764	NC
Wayne State Univ	MI	19,493	C
Waynesburg Univ	PA	29,100	C
Webster Univ	MO	33,990	C+
Wellesley College	MA	49,848	MC
Wells College	NY	38,680	VC
Wesley College	DE	31,115	LC
Wesleyan College	GA	24,000	C+
Wesleyan Univ	CT	59,844	MC
West Chester Univ of Pennsylvania	PA	16,836	C
West Liberty Univ	WV	9,142	LC
West Texas A&M Univ	TX	13,478	C
West Virginia State Univ	WV	8,378	NC
West Virginia Univ	WV	15,794	C+
West Virginia Univ Inst of Technology	WV	14,094	NC
West Virginia Wesleyan College	WV	26,880	C
Western Carolina Univ	NC	13,965	C+
Western Conn State Univ	CT	18,327	C
Western Illinois Univ	IL	20,130	C
Western Kentucky Univ	KY	11,000	LC
Western Mich Univ	MI	19,042	C
Western New England Univ	MA	45,590	C
Western New Mexico Univ	NM	8,500	LC
Western Oregon Univ	OR	15,021	C
Western State Colo Univ	CO	16,135	C
Western Washington Univ	WA	18,519	VC
Westfield State Univ	MA	18,489	C
Westminster College	MO	30,490	VC
Westminster College	PA	31,290	C+
Westminster College	UT	37,708	VC
Westmont College	CA	41,500	HC
Wheaton College	IL	39,650	HC+
Wheaton College	MA	54,934	HC+
Wheeling Jesuit Univ	WV	34,668	C
Whittier College	CA	43,416	C
Whitworth Univ	WA	45,826	VC+
Wichita State Univ	KS	12,539	C
Widener Univ	PA	50,368	C
Wilberforce Univ	OH	15,100	LC
Wiley College	TX		LC
Wilkes Univ	PA	42,786	C
Willamette Univ	OR	56,450	VC+
William Carey Univ	MS	13,500	LC
William Jewell College	MO	31,000	VC+
William Paterson Univ of New Jersey	NJ	21,694	C
William Peace Univ	NC	32,900	LC
William Penn Univ	IA	26,000	C
William Woods Univ	MO		C
Williams Baptist College	AR	20,070	C
Williams College	MA	58,900	MC
Wilmington College	OH	29,784	C
Wilson College	PA	27,660	C
Wingate Univ	NC	34,990	C
Winona State Univ	MN	16,530	C
Winston-Salem State Univ	NC	9,418	LC
Winthrop Univ	SC	21,120	VC
Wisc Lutheran College	WI	23,510	VC
Wittenberg Univ	OH	47,766	VC
Wofford College	SC	45,795	VC
Worcester State Univ	MA	18,657	C
Wright State Univ	OH	16,983	C

ST = STATE **$IS** = IN-STATE COSTS **SR** = SELECTOR RATING

School	ST	$IS	SR
Xavier Univ	OH	43,740	VC
Xavier Univ of Louisiana	LA	25,300	C
Yale Univ	CT	55,300	MC
Yeshiva Univ	NY	47,250	V₲
York College	NE	19,475	C
York College / CUNY	NY	5,496	NC
York College of Pennsylvania	PA	26,590	C
Youngstown State Univ	OH	16,374	LC

BIOMATHEMATICS

School	ST	$IS	SR
Emmanuel College	MA	47,985	VC
Florida Inst of Technology	FL	48,290	VC
Rutgers, The State Univ of New Jersey/New Brunswick	NJ	25,077	VC
Univ of Montana-Western	MT	9,753	LC
Univ of Scranton	PA	51,940	VC
Washington Univ in St. Louis	MO	58,818	MC

BIOMEDICAL ART

School	ST	$IS	SR
Cleveland Inst of Art	OH	48,641	SP

BIOMEDICAL ELECTRONICS

School	ST	$IS	SR
Thomas Edison State College	NJ	5,700	SP

BIOMEDICAL ENGINEERING

School	ST	$IS	SR
Arizona State Univ	AZ	18,818	₲
Boston Univ	MA	54,130	H₲
Bucknell Univ	PA	58,160	MC
Butler Univ	IN	45,898	V₲
Calif Polytechnic State Univ	CA	19,847	HC
Case Western Reserve Univ	OH	55,178	MC
College of New Jersey	NJ	25,376	HC
Colo State Univ-Fort Collins	CO	20,090	VC
Columbia Univ in the City of New York	NY	61,116	MC
CUNY-City College	NY	19,576	H₲
Drexel Univ	PA	51,920	HC
Duke Univ	NC	50,250	MC
Elon Univ	NC	40,046	HC
Florida Inst of Technology	FL	48,290	VC
Florida International Univ	FL	17,747	VC
Florida State Univ	FL	15,238	HC
Gannon Univ	PA	37,940	C
Georgia Inst of Technology	GA	20,464	MC
Harding Univ	AR	21,432	₲
Hofstra Univ	NY	48,020	V₲
Indiana Inst of Technology	IN	34,240	LC
Indiana Univ-Purdue Univ Indianapolis	IN	17,290	C
Johns Hopkins Univ	MD	47,492	MC
Lawrence Tech Univ	MI	37,630	VC
Louisiana Tech Univ	LA	8,000	C
Marquette Univ	WI	43,664	V₲
Mass Inst of Technology	MA	54,238	MC
Mich Tech Univ	MI	22,105	VC
Milwaukee School of Engineering	WI	39,948	V₲
New Jersey Inst of Technology	NJ	26,490	VC
New York Inst of Technology	NY	40,590	VC
New York Univ	NY	61,470	MC
N Dak State Univ	ND	14,642	C
Northwestern Univ	IL	37,595	MC
Penn State Univ/Univ Park	PA	25,404	VC
Purdue Univ/West Lafayette	IN	20,278	HC
Rensselaer Polytechnic Inst	NY	59,229	MC
Rochester Inst of Technology	NY	42,450	V₲
Rose-Hulman Inst of Technology	IN	51,738	MC
Rowan Univ	NJ	23,570	VC
Rutgers, The State Univ of New Jersey/New Brunswick	NJ	25,077	VC
St. Louis Univ	MO	46,594	V₲
San Jose State Univ	CA	19,707	C
Stevens Inst of Technology	NJ	50,130	HC
Stony Brook Univ / SUNY	NY	19,359	HC
Texas A&M Univ	TX	16,956	V₲
The Catholic Univ of America	DC	52,852	VC
Ohio State Univ	OH	19,887	MC
Tufts Univ	MA	58,780	MC
Tulane Univ	LA	58,942	MC
Tuskegee Univ	AL	26,750	C
Univ at Buffalo / The SUNY	NY	20,283	VC
Univ of Akron	OH	20,436	C
Univ of Alabama at Birmingham	AL	18,484	₲
Univ of Arizona	AZ	20,105	C
Univ of Calif at Irvine	CA	25,961	VC
Univ of Calif at Los Angeles	CA	25,686	MC
Univ of Central Okla	OK	12,293	C
Univ of Conn	CT	23,744	HC
Univ of Hartford	CT	42,674	C
Univ of Houston	TX	19,184	VC
Univ of Idaho	ID	14,558	C
Univ of Iowa	IA	17,481	VC
Univ of Memphis	TN	15,094	C
Univ of Miami	FL	55,166	MC
Univ of Mich/Ann Arbor	MI	22,102	H₲
Univ of Missouri/Columbia	MO	18,201	MC
Univ of Rochester	NY	58,500	MC
Univ of S Car at Columbia	SC	19,725	V₲
Univ of Southern Calif	CA	56,903	MC
Univ of Tenn at Knoxville	TN	20,364	V₲
Univ of Texas at Austin	TX	44,074	HC
Univ of Texas at Dallas	TX	21,046	HC
Univ of Texas at San Antonio	TX	18,372	C
Univ of Utah	UT	13,462	VC
Univ of Virginia	VA	22,175	MC
Univ of Wisc/Madison	WI	18,757	HC
Virginia Commonwealth Univ	VA	18,633	C
Washington State Univ	WA	20,461	C
Washington Univ in St. Louis	MO	58,818	MC
Wayne State Univ	MI	19,493	C
Wentworth Inst of Technology	MA	29,800	SP
Western New England Univ	MA	45,590	C
Widener Univ	PA	50,368	C
Worcester Polytechnic Inst	MA	53,440	H₲
Wright State Univ	OH	16,983	C
Yale Univ	CT	55,300	MC

BIOMEDICAL EQUIPMENT TECHNOLOGY

School	ST	$IS	SR
Andrews Univ	MI	28,030	₲

BIOMEDICAL SCIENCE

School	ST	$IS	SR
Adventist Universtiy of Health Sciences	FL	16,344	NC
Albany College of Pharmacy and Health Sciences	NY	38,900	SP
Andrews Univ	MI	28,030	₲
Auburn Univ	AL	20,052	V₲
Averett Univ	VA	36,000	LC
Brown Univ	RI	56,150	MC
Cal State, Northridge	CA	28,313	C
Central Mich Univ	MI	18,066	C
Christian Brothers Univ	TN	19,140	HC
Colo State Univ-Fort Collins	CO	20,090	VC
CUNY-City College	NY	19,576	H₲
Grand Valley State Univ	MI	17,998	VC
Heritage Univ	WA	17,664	NC
Hiram College	OH	37,300	VC
LIU/C.W. Post Campus	NY	38,888	C
Lynchburg College	VA	42,645	C
Marquette Univ	WI	43,664	V₲
McMurry Univ	TX	25,962	LC
Northern Arizona Univ	AZ	18,592	C
Okla City Univ	OK	33,546	VC
Oral Roberts Univ	OK	31,734	C
Quinnipiac Univ	CT	53,580	VC
Rutgers, The State Univ of New Jersey/New Brunswick	NJ	25,077	VC
St. Peter's College	NJ	44,240	C
Southern Oregon Univ	OR	17,874	C
Texas A&M Univ	TX	16,956	V₲
Ohio State Univ	OH	19,887	MC
Univ at Buffalo / The SUNY	NY	20,283	VC
Univ of Calif at Riverside	CA	27,204	C
Univ of Central Florida	FL	15,711	V₲
Univ of Georgia	GA	19,508	VC
Univ of Illinois at Urbana-Champaign	IL	24,300	HC
Univ of New England	ME	46,145	₲
Univ of New Hampshire	NH	24,702	VC
Univ of St. Mary	KS	28,400	₲
Univ of South Alabama	AL	13,510	C
Univ of Vermont	VT	26,120	V₲
Victory Univ	TN	19,118	C
Washington State Univ	WA	20,461	C
Western Mich Univ	MI	19,042	C

BIOMETRICS AND BIOSTATISTICS

School	ST	$IS	SR
Cornell Univ	NY	59,037	MC
La Sierra Univ	CA	35,694	VC
Simmons College	MA	48,770	VC
Univ of Arizona	AZ	20,105	C
Univ of N Car at Chapel Hill	NC	18,348	MC

BIOPHYSICS

School	ST	$IS	SR
Amherst College	MA	58,744	MC
Andrews Univ	MI	28,030	₲
Bellarmine Univ	KY	42,950	VC
Brandeis Univ	MA	58,820	HC
Brigham Young Univ	UT	12,100	HC
Brown Univ	RI	56,150	MC
Cal State, Fresno	CA	17,405	C
Centenary College of Louisiana	LA	39,070	₲
Claremont McKenna College	CA	58,065	MC
Columbia Univ in the City of New York	NY	61,116	MC
Elon Univ	NC	40,046	HC
Harvard Univ/Harvard College	MA	49,000	MC
Illinois Inst of Technology	IL	38,512	H₲
Iowa State Univ	IA	16,403	C
Johns Hopkins Univ	MD	47,492	MC
La Sierra Univ	CA	35,694	VC
Lipscomb Univ	TN	35,722	VC
Loyola Univ Chicago	IL	49,560	V₲
Pacific Union College	CA	28,150	VC
Rensselaer Polytechnic Inst	NY	59,229	MC
St. Mary's Univ of Minn	MN	37,015	C
Southern Nazarene Univ	OK	24,354	NC
Southwestern Okla State Univ	OK	9,160	C
St. Bonaventure Univ	NY	38,831	C
St. Lawrence Univ	NY	53,740	HC
SUNY College at Geneseo	NY	18,055	H₲
Syracuse Univ	NY	54,512	HC
Temple Univ	PA	24,392	VC
Tufts Univ	MA	58,780	MC
Univ of Calif at Los Angeles	CA	25,686	MC
Univ of Calif at San Diego	CA	21,000	VC
Univ of Conn	CT	23,744	HC
Univ of Illinois at Chicago	IL	24,293	VC
Univ of Illinois at Urbana-Champaign	IL	24,300	HC
Univ of Mich/Ann Arbor	MI	22,102	H₲
Univ of Pennsylvania	PA	56,106	MC
Univ of San Diego	CA	53,302	H₲
Univ of Scranton	PA	51,940	VC
Univ of Southern Calif	CA	56,903	MC
Univ of Southern Indiana	IN	14,657	C
Walla Walla Univ	WA	26,256	NC
Washington and Jefferson College	PA	49,990	VC
Washington Univ in St. Louis	MO	58,818	MC
Wayne State Univ	MI	19,493	C
Whitworth Univ	WA	45,826	V₲
Xavier Univ	OH	43,740	VC
Yale Univ	CT	55,300	MC

BIOPSYCHOLOGY

School	ST	$IS	SR
Birmingham-Southern College	AL	42,370	V₲
Columbia Univ/Barnard College	NY	39,000	MC
Grand Valley State Univ	MI	17,998	VC
Messiah College	PA	39,540	VC
Mills College	CA	54,119	HC
Monmouth College	IL	39,290	C
Nebr Wesleyan Univ	NE	29,774	₲
Oglethorpe Univ	GA	42,580	VC
Pace Univ	NY	48,094	VC
Philadelphia Univ	PA	44,160	C
Rider Univ	NJ	45,720	C
Simmons College	MA	48,770	VC
Spring Hill College	AL	42,130	VC
The Lincoln Univ	PA	15,154	LC
Tufts Univ	MA	58,780	MC
Univ of Calif at Santa Barbara	CA	27,551	HC
Vassar College	NY	59,070	MC
Viterbo Univ	WI	30,070	C
Washington Univ in St. Louis	MO	58,818	MC
York College	NE	19,475	C

BIORESOURCE ENGINEERING

School	ST	$IS	SR
Calif Polytechnic State Univ	CA	19,847	HC
Rutgers, The State Univ of New Jersey/New Brunswick	NJ	25,077	VC
Univ of Maryland	MD	18,801	HC

BIOTECHNOLOGY

School	ST	$IS	SR
Alma College	MI	42,400	VC
Arkansas State Univ	AR	14,980	C
Assumption College	MA	45,721	VC
Brigham Young Univ	UT	12,100	HC
Calif State Polytechnic Univ, Pomona	CA	18,932	C
Cal State, San Marcos	CA	14,576	C
Calvin College	MI	37,585	V₲
Claflin Univ	SC	22,368	₲
Colo State Univ-Pueblo	CO	13,532	LC
Elizabethtown College	PA	47,600	VC
Endicott College	MA	42,390	C
Ferris State Univ	MI	19,698	C
Fitchburg State Univ	MA	17,241	C
Florida Gulf Coast Univ	FL		
Grand View Univ	IA	31,050	C
Indiana Univ Bloomington	IN	19,358	HC
Indiana Univ East	IN	6,639	LC
Indiana Univ-Purdue Univ Indianapolis	IN	17,290	C
Inter-American Univ of PR/ Bayamon Univ College	PR	4,428	
James Madison Univ	VA	18,049	VC
Kennesaw State Univ	GA	13,017	VC
Kent State Univ	OH	19,352	C
Lawrence Tech Univ	MI	37,630	VC
Marshall Univ	WV	14,820	C
Marywood Univ	PA	40,695	C
Mich State Univ	MI	13,689	VC
Minn State Univ, Mankato	MN	14,900	C
Missouri Baptist Univ	MO	30,310	C
Missouri Southern State Univ	MO	11,910	C
Montana State Univ	MT	14,068	VC
Mount Aloysius College	PA	27,970	C
N Dak State Univ	ND	14,642	C
Ohio Univ	OH	20,676	VC
Oregon State Univ	OR	19,017	₲
Plymouth State Univ	NH	23,148	LC
Point Park Univ	PA	36,390	C
Purdue Univ/Calumet	IN	14,336	C
Quinnipiac Univ	CT	53,580	VC
Rochester Inst of Technology	NY	42,450	V₲
Rutgers, The State Univ of New Jersey/New Brunswick	NJ	25,077	VC
S Dak State Univ	SD	14,296	C
Southeastern Okla State Univ	OK	7,966	C
Springfield College	MA	25,000	C
SUNY / College of Environmental Science and Forestry	NY	18,351	HC
Stevenson Univ	MD	39,572	C
Suffolk Univ	MA	46,548	C
Syracuse Univ	NY	54,512	HC
The Catholic Univ of America	DC	52,852	VC
The SUNY College of Agriculture and Tech at Cobleskill	NY	18,869	VC
Tufts Univ	MA	58,780	MC
Univ at Buffalo / The SUNY	NY	20,283	VC
Univ of Calif at San Diego	CA	21,000	VC
Univ of Central Florida	FL	15,711	V₲
Univ of Delaware	DE	22,728	VC
Univ of Georgia	GA	19,508	VC
Univ of Houston-Downtown	TX	6,267	LC
Univ of Illinois at Urbana-Champaign	IL	24,300	HC
Univ of Maine	ME	19,712	₲
Univ of Maryland/Univ College	MD	6,168	SP
Univ of Mass Dartmouth	MA	22,223	C
Univ of Missouri-Kansas City	MO	19,603	C
Univ of Missouri-St. Louis	MO	18,304	VC
Univ of Nebr at Omaha	NE	12,700	C
Univ of New Haven	CT	47,740	C
Univ of Northern Iowa	IA	14,776	C
Univ of PR/Mayaguez	PR	1,250	
Univ of Wisc/River Falls	WI	9,722	LC
Ursuline College	OH	33,198	LC
West Texas A&M Univ	TX	13,478	C
William Paterson Univ of New Jersey	NJ	21,694	C
William Penn Univ	IA	26,000	C
Worcester Polytechnic Inst	MA	53,440	H₲
Worcester State Univ	MA	18,657	C
York College / CUNY	NY	5,496	NC

BOTANY

School	ST	$IS	SR
Andrews Univ	MI	28,030	₲
Auburn Univ	AL	20,052	V₲
Bennington College	VT	56,990	H₲
Brigham Young Univ	UT	12,100	HC
Cal State, Chico	CA	18,952	C
Cal State, Long Beach	CA	17,534	₲
Colo State Univ-Fort Collins	CO	20,090	VC
Conn College	CT	54,970	MC
Delaware State Univ	DE	14,700	LC
Eastern Washington Univ	WA	16,388	C
Hampshire College	MA	58,320	MC
Humboldt State Univ	CA	18,400	C
Idaho State Univ	ID	11,908	C
Kent State Univ	OH	19,352	C
Marlboro College	VT	35,980	VC
Mars Hill College	NC	22,950	LC
Miami Univ	OH	24,191	HC
Mich State Univ	MI	13,689	VC
N Car State Univ	NC	16,202	HC
N Dak State Univ	ND	14,642	C
Northern Mich Univ	MI	15,300	VC
Northwest Missouri State Univ	MO	14,229	C
Ohio Univ	OH	20,676	VC
Ohio Wesleyan Univ	OH	49,460	₲
Okla State Univ	OK	14,310	VC
Oregon State Univ	OR	19,017	₲
Rutgers, The State Univ of New Jersey/New Brunswick	NJ	25,077	VC

School	ST	$IS	SR
Rutgers, The State Univ of New Jersey/Newark Campus	NJ	25,376	C
San Diego State Univ	CA	20,578	VC
San Francisco State Univ	CA	18,514	C
San Jose State Univ	CA	19,707	C
Southern Illinois Univ Carbondale	IL	21,620	C
SUNY / College of Environmental Science and Forestry	NY	18,351	HC
Texas A&M Univ	TX	16,956	V₲
Texas A&M Univ at Commerce	TX	10,496	C
Univ of Calif at Davis	CA	24,482	HC
Univ of Calif at Irvine	CA	25,961	VC
Univ of Florida	FL	15,783	H₲
Univ of Great Falls	MT	27,970	C
Univ of Hawaii at Manoa	HI	19,379	VC
Univ of Idaho	ID	14,558	C
Univ of Illinois at Urbana-Champaign	IL	24,300	HC
Univ of Kentucky	KY	19,868	C
Univ of Maine	ME	19,712	₲
Univ of Mich/Ann Arbor	MI	22,102	H₲
Univ of Minn/Twin Cities	MN		HC
Univ of Montana	MT	13,670	C
Univ of Okla	OK	17,634	V₲
Univ of Vermont	VT	26,120	V₲
Univ of Washington	WA	14,722	VC
Univ of Wisc/Madison	WI	18,757	HC
Univ of Wyoming	WY	13,855	₲
Western New Mexico Univ	NM	8,500	LC

BROADCASTING

School	ST	$IS	SR
Alabama State Univ	AL	14,142	NC
Ashland Univ	OH	25,000	C
Baldwin Wallace Univ	OH	36,980	VC
Barry Univ	FL	38,190	C
Baylor Univ	TX	46,720	HC
Belhaven Univ	MS	27,170	C
Bemidji State Univ	MN	13,500	C
Biola Univ	CA	40,320	VC
Black Hills State Univ	SD	13,562	LC
Bluffton Univ	OH	37,864	C
Buffalo State/State Univ of Buffalo	NY	15,733	₲
Cedarville Univ	OH	31,036	V₲
Central Methodist Univ	MO	28,240	VC
Central Mich Univ	MI	18,066	C
Central State Univ	OH	9,010	C
Central Washington Univ	WA	11,730	C
Champlain College	VT	44,850	VC
Chapman Univ	CA	56,019	V₲
Chicago State Univ	IL	5,482	C
CUNY/Brooklyn College	NY	5,884	₲
College of the Ozarks	MO	5,605	VC
Colo State Univ-Pueblo	CO	13,532	LC
Concord Univ	WV	13,102	C
Dordt College	IA	34,160	VC
Drake Univ	IA	30,980	V₲
Eastern Kentucky Univ	KY	11,161	C
Eastern Nazarene College	MA	30,000	C
Eastern Washington Univ	WA	16,388	C
Elon Univ	NC	40,046	HC
Emerson College	MA	50,246	HC
Evangel Univ	MO	23,090	C
Florida Southern College	FL	38,240	VC
Florida State Univ	FL	15,238	HC
Freed-Hardeman Univ	TN	19,697	VC
Geneva College	PA	27,280	C
George Washington Univ	DC	57,108	MC
Gonzaga Univ	WA	44,247	HC
Goshen College	IN	35,900	VC
Grand Valley State Univ	MI	17,998	VC
Grand View Univ	IA	31,050	C
Harding Univ	AR	21,432	₲
Hardin-Simmons Univ	TX	23,560	₲
Hastings College	NE	27,782	₲
Howard Univ	DC	35,957	C
Huntington Univ	IN	32,220	C
Ithaca College	NY	52,300	HC
John Brown Univ	AR	30,996	V₲
Kean Univ	NJ	22,060	LC
Lewis Univ	IL	23,050	C
Lincoln Memorial Univ	TN	18,144	C
LIU/Brooklyn Campus	NY	26,500	C
LIU/C.W. Post Campus	NY	38,888	C
Loras College	IA	37,432	VC
Madonna Univ	MI	24,540	VC
Malone Univ	OH	34,334	C
Manhattan College	NY	44,955	VC
Mansfield Univ	PA	19,468	LC
Marietta College	OH	42,135	VC
Marquette Univ	WI	43,664	V₲
Marshall Univ	WV	14,820	C
Marywood Univ	PA	40,695	C
Mercy College	NY	29,996	C
Mercyhurst Univ	PA	40,700	C
Messiah College	PA	39,540	VC
Minn State Univ, Moorhead	MN	13,392	C
Minot State Univ	ND	10,915	C
Montclair State Univ	NJ	22,614	C
Mount Vernon Nazarene Univ	OH	29,590	C
Murray State Univ	KY	14,944	C
North Central College	IL	38,343	VC
Northern Mich Univ	MI	15,300	VC
Northwest Missouri State Univ	MO	14,229	C
Northwestern College	MN	24,000	C
Northwestern Okla State Univ	OK	7,275	NC
Ohio Northern Univ	OH	42,075	VC
Ohio Univ	OH	20,676	VC
Okla Baptist Univ	OK	28,202	VC
Okla Christian Univ	OK	24,975	VC
Okla City Univ	OK	33,546	VC
Okla State Univ	OK	14,310	VC
Oral Roberts Univ	OK	31,734	C
Oswego / SUNY	NY	20,009	VC
Otterbein College	OH	32,214	C
Pittsburg State Univ	KS	12,032	C
Point Loma Nazarene Univ	CA	38,610	VC
Point Park Univ	PA	36,390	C
Prairie View A&M Univ	TX	15,205	LC
Purdue Univ/Calumet	IN	14,336	C
Purdue Univ/West Lafayette	IN	20,278	HC
Roosevelt Univ	IL	22,605	VC
Rowan Univ	NJ	23,570	VC
San Francisco State Univ	CA	18,514	C
San Jose State Univ	CA	19,707	C
Savannah College of Art and Design	GA	46,824	SP
Seton Hall Univ	NJ	45,902	C
Shaw Univ	NC	15,488	LC
Sojourner-Douglass College	MD	9,160	LC
Southeastern Univ	FL	27,201	₲
Southern Adventist Univ	TN	26,190	C
Southern Arkansas Univ	AR	14,316	C
Southern Illinois Univ Carbondale	IL	21,620	C
Southern Methodist Univ	TX	57,755	MC
Southwestern Adventist Univ	TX	23,026	LC
Spring Arbor Univ	MI	26,740	C
St. Cloud State Univ	MN	10,600	C
Stephen F. Austin State Univ	TX	14,668	C
Suffolk Univ	MA	46,548	C
Syracuse Univ	NY	54,512	HC
Temple Univ	PA	24,392	VC
Texas A&M Univ at Commerce	TX	10,496	C
Texas State Univ	TX	16,495	VC
Texas Tech Univ	TX	14,243	C
Texas Wesleyan Univ	TX	29,886	C
The Lincoln Univ	PA	15,154	LC
Troy Univ	AL	10,650	C
Union Univ	TN	28,260	VC
Univ of Central Florida	FL	15,711	V₲
Univ of Central Missouri	MO	14,605	C
Univ of Central Okla	OK	12,293	C
Univ of Cincinnati	OH	20,199	VC
Univ of Colo Boulder	CO	22,605	V₲
Univ of Findlay	OH	31,916	C
Univ of Georgia	GA	19,508	VC
Univ of Idaho	ID	14,558	C
Univ of Illinois at Urbana-Champaign	IL	24,300	HC
Univ of Indianapolis	IN	31,740	LC
Univ of La Verne	CA	47,010	VC
Univ of Louisiana at Lafayette	LA	6,130	C
Univ of Missouri/Columbia	MO	18,201	MC
Univ of Nebr - Lincoln	NE	17,507	VC
Univ of Nebr at Kearney	NE	14,855	LC
Univ of Nebr at Omaha	NE	12,700	C
Univ of North Texas	TX	15,628	C
Univ of Northern Iowa	IA	14,776	C
Univ of Okla	OK	17,634	V₲
Univ of S Car at Columbia	SC	19,725	V₲
Univ of Southern Calif	CA	56,903	MC
Univ of Southern Indiana	IN	14,657	C
Univ of Texas at Arlington	TX	10,908	LC
Vanguard Univ of Southern Calif	CA	35,833	VC
Wartburg College	IA	41,055	VC
Washington State Univ	WA	20,461	C
Waynesburg Univ	PA	29,100	C
West Texas A&M Univ	TX	13,478	C
West Virginia Univ	WV	15,794	₲
Western Illinois Univ	IL	20,130	C
Western Kentucky Univ	KY	11,000	LC
Western Mich Univ	MI	19,042	C
Westminster College	PA	31,290	₲
Winona State Univ	MN	16,530	C
York College of Pennsylvania	PA	26,590	C
Youngstown State Univ	OH	16,374	LC

BUSINESS (DUAL MAJOR PROGRAM)

School	ST	$IS	SR
Bentley Univ	MA	54,555	H₲
CUNY/Brooklyn College	NY	5,884	₲
Franklin College	IN	35,885	C
John Carroll Univ	OH	44,520	₲
Mercy College	NY	29,996	C
Southern Oregon Univ	OR	17,874	C
Univ of Pittsburgh at Pittsburgh	PA	27,800	H₲
Univ of Tulsa	OK	45,311	H₲

BUSINESS ADMINISTRATION AND MANAGEMENT

School	ST	$IS	SR
Adams State College	CO	13,358	LC
Adelphi Univ	NY	43,130	VC
Adrian College	MI	33,800	C
Agnes Scott College	GA	45,323	V₲
Alabama A&M Univ	AL	96,100	C
Alabama State Univ	AL	14,142	NC
Alaska Pacific Univ	AK	33,360	VC
Albertus Magnus College	CT	37,382	LC
Albright College	PA	46,660	C
Alcorn State Univ	MS	9,500	C
Alderson Broaddus Univ	WV	28,656	C
Alfred Univ	NY	40,392	VC
Alice Lloyd College	KY	4,900	C
Allen Univ	SC	16,124	NC
Alma College	MI	42,400	VC
Alvernia Univ	PA	39,250	C
Alverno College	WI	30,483	LC
American InterContinental Univ	GA	13,500	NC
American International College	MA	36,100	LC
American Jewish Univ	CA	32,600	C
American Univ	DC	54,829	H₲
Amridge Univ	AL	6,870	LC
Anderson Univ	IN	35,390	C
Andrews Univ	MI	28,030	₲
Angelo State Univ	TX	15,049	NC
Anna Maria College	MA	34,600	LC
Aquinas College	MI	33,060	C
Aquinas College	TN	29,250	₲
Arcadia Univ	PA	33,570	₲
Arizona State Univ	AZ	18,818	₲
Arkansas Baptist College	AR	9,000	NC
Arkansas State Univ	AR	14,980	C
Asbury Univ	KY	32,038	VC
Ashford Univ	IA	21,780	C
Ashland Univ	OH	25,000	C
Assumption College	MA	45,721	VC
Atlantic Union College	MA	24,600	LC
Auburn Univ	AL	20,052	V₲
Auburn Univ at Montgomery	AL	12,120	C
Augsburg College	MN	35,142	C
Augustana College	IL	43,398	HC
Augustana College	SD	35,500	VC
Aurora Univ	IL	26,870	C
Austin College	TX	36,940	HC
Austin Peay State Univ	TN	14,650	C
Averett Univ	VA	36,000	LC
Avila Univ	MO	26,900	C
Azusa Pacific Univ	CA	39,946	C
Babson College	MA	51,940	HC
Baker College of Flint	MI	7,800	NC
Baker Univ	KS	33,350	₲
Baldwin Wallace Univ	OH	36,980	VC
Ball State Univ	IN	17,850	C
Barton College	NC	27,660	C
Bay Path College	MA	34,565	C
Baylor Univ	TX	46,720	HC
Becker College	MA	41,420	LC
Belhaven Univ	MS	27,170	C
Bellarmine Univ	KY	42,950	VC
Bellevue Univ	NE	4,600	NC
Belmont Abbey College	NC	37,716	C
Belmont Univ	TN	37,380	V₲
Beloit College	WI	49,970	HC
Bemidji State Univ	MN	13,500	C
Benedict College	SC	20,454	NC
Benedictine College	KS	29,180	VC
Benedictine Univ	IL	35,220	C
Bennett College	NC		LC
Bentley Univ	MA	54,555	H₲
Berea College	KY	7,220	HC
Berkeley College	NY	18,300	LC
Berkeley College/New Jersey	NJ	27,300	LC
Berkeley College/Westchester Campus	NY	28,500	LC
Berry College	GA	39,254	HC
Bethany College	KS	30,605	NC
Bethany College	WV	35,282	C
Bethel College	IN	31,560	C
Bethel College	KS	29,100	C
Bethel Univ	MN	34,940	VC
Bethel Univ	TN	19,186	C
Bethune-Cookman Univ	FL	22,290	LC
Binghamton Univ / The SUNY	NY	20,832	H₲
Biola Univ	CA	40,320	VC
Birmingham-Southern College	AL	42,370	V₲
Black Hills State Univ	SD	13,562	LC
Blackburn College	IL	21,350	C
Bloomfield College	NJ	36,960	C
Bloomsburg Univ of Pennsylvania	PA	13,598	C
Blue Mountain College	MS	13,550	LC
Bluefield College	VA	17,230	₲
Bluefield State College	WV	3,140	LC
Bluffton Univ	OH	37,864	C
Boise State Univ	ID	12,802	C
Boricua College	NY	8,600	C
Boston College	MA	58,506	MC
Boston Univ	MA	54,130	H₲
Bowie State Univ	MD	23,990	LC
Bowling Green State Univ	OH	18,970	C
Bradley Univ	IL	31,874	VC
Brandeis Univ	MA	58,820	HC
Brenau Univ Women's College	GA	26,650	₲
Brescia Univ	KY	26,140	V₲
Brewton-Parker College	GA	33,388	LC
Briar Cliff Univ	IA	29,514	C
Bridgewater College	VA	39,880	C
Brigham Young Univ	UT	12,100	HC
Bryan College	TN	24,194	C
Bryant Univ	RI	49,179	VC
Bucknell Univ	PA	58,160	MC
Buena Vista Univ	IA	37,954	C
Buffalo State/State Univ of Buffalo	NY	15,733	₲
Cabrini College	PA	40,859	LC
Cairn Univ	PA	31,255	C
Caldwell College	NJ	35,602	LC
Calif Baptist Univ	CA	35,890	C
Calif Inst of Technology	CA	54,045	MC
Calif Lutheran Univ	CA	47,640	C
Calif Maritime Academy	CA	15,496	C
Calif Polytechnic State Univ	CA	19,847	HC
Calif State Polytechnic Univ, Pomona	CA	18,932	C
Cal State, Bakersfield	CA	8,000	LC
Cal State, Chico	CA	18,952	C
Cal State, Dominguez Hills	CA	17,056	LC
Cal State, East Bay	CA	16,540	C
Cal State, Fresno	CA	17,405	C
Cal State, Fullerton	CA	25,188	₲
Cal State, Long Beach	CA	17,534	₲
Cal State, Los Angeles	CA	15,829	C
Cal State, Monterey Bay	CA	26,871	LC
Cal State, Northridge	CA	28,313	C
Cal State, Sacramento	CA	16,200	C
Cal State, San Bernardino	CA	12,000	C
Cal State, San Marcos	CA	14,576	C
Cal State, Stanislaus	CA	18,582	C
Calif Univ of Pennsylvania	PA	14,217	C
Calumet College of St. Joseph	IN	15,000	LC
Calvin College	MI	37,585	V₲
Cameron Univ	OK	9,267	LC
Campbell Univ	NC	25,500	C
Campbellsville Univ	KY	27,720	C
Canisius College	NY	45,602	VC
Capital Univ	OH	39,824	VC
Cardinal Stritch Univ	WI	24,054	C
Caribbean Univ	PR	10,375	
Carlos Albizu Univ	FL	12,053	LC
Carlow Univ	PA	30,272	C
Carnegie Mellon Univ	PA	51,260	MC
Carroll College	MT	28,000	C
Carroll Univ	WI	24,860	C
Carson-Newman Univ	TN	29,058	₲
Carthage College	WI	33,000	C
Case Western Reserve Univ	OH	55,178	MC
Castleton State College	VT	19,424	C
Catawba College	NC	37,105	C
Cazenovia College	NY	30,800	C
Cedar Crest College	PA	43,240	C
Cedarville Univ	OH	31,036	V₲
Centenary College	NJ	38,618	LC
Centenary College of Louisiana	LA	39,070	₲
Central College	IA	36,980	VC
Central Conn State Univ	CT	19,212	C
Central Methodist Univ	MO	28,240	VC
Central Mich Univ	MI	18,066	C
Central State Univ	OH	9,010	C
Central Univ of Bayamon	PR	3,350	
Central Washington Univ	WA	11,730	C
Chadron State College	NE	7,400	NC
Chaminade Univ of Honolulu	HI	31,664	C
Champlain College	VT	44,850	VC
Chancellor Univ	OH	11,000	C
Chapman Univ	CA	56,019	V₲
Charleston Southern Univ	SC	22,420	C
Chatham Univ	PA	42,440	VC
Chestnut Hill College	PA	39,785	LC
Cheyney Univ of Pennsylvania	PA	20,372	LC
Chicago State Univ	IL	5,482	C
Christian Brothers Univ	TN	19,140	HC
Christopher Newport Univ	VA	21,050	VC
Citadel, The	SC		C
CUNY/Brooklyn College	NY	5,884	₲
City Univ of Seattle	WA	14,880	NC
Claflin Univ	SC	22,368	₲
Clarion Univ of Pennsylvania	PA	17,370	C
Clark Atlanta Univ	GA	30,006	C
Clark Univ	MA	47,020	H₲
Clarke Univ	IA	36,400	C
Clarkson College	NE	16,300	VC
Clarkson Univ	NY	53,538	HC
Clayton State Univ	GA	12,000	LC

ST = STATE $IS = IN-STATE COSTS   SR = SELECTOR RATING

School	ST	$IS	SR
Clearwater Christian College	FL	23,720	C
Cleary Univ	MI	11,000	C
Clemson Univ	SC	19,136	HC
Coastal Carolina Univ	SC	17,620	C
Coe College	IA	43,590	VC
Coker College	SC	32,256	LC
Colby-Sawyer College	NH	47,870	C
College of Staten Island / The CUNY	NY	16,778	NC
College of Charleston	SC	21,273	VC
College of Mount St. Joseph	OH	33,880	C
College of Mount St. Vincent	NY	41,040	MC
College of New Jersey	NJ	25,376	HC
College of St. Elizabeth	NJ	43,839	LC
College of St. Mary	NE	34,334	C
College of St. Scholastica	MN	39,960	C
College of St Joseph	VT	30,600	LC
College of the Ozarks	MO	5,605	VC
College of William & Mary	VA	25,085	MC
Colo Christian Univ	CO	27,500	VC
Colo Mesa Univ	CO	16,669	LC
Colo State Univ-Fort Collins	CO	20,090	VC
Colo State Univ-Pueblo	CO	13,532	LC
Colo Technical Univ	CO	10,500	LC
Columbia College	MO	24,578	C
Columbia College	SC	27,882	C
Columbus State Univ	GA	13,176	C
Concord Univ	WV	13,102	C
Concordia College - Alabama	AL	12,200	NC
Concordia College New York	NY	31,500	VC
Concordia College, Moorhead	MN	39,974	¢
Concordia Univ	OR	34,930	C
Concordia Univ - Irvine	CA	35,390	VC
Concordia Univ Nebr	NE	26,000	VC
Concordia Univ St. Paul	MN	27,200	C
Concordia Univ Texas	TX	23,640	C
Concordia Univ Wisc	WI	28,980	C
Concordia Univ, Ann Arbor	MI	27,220	VC
Concordia Univ, River Forest	IL	26,300	C
Converse College	SC	37,130	C
Coppin State Univ	MD	14,905	VC
Corban Univ	OR	34,764	C
Cornerstone Univ and Grand Rapids Theological Seminary	MI	30,866	C
Covenant College	GA		V¢
Creighton Univ	NE	44,058	V¢
Culver-Stockton College	MO	30,900	C
Cumberland Univ	TN	21,220	C
CUNY-City College	NY	19,576	H¢
Curry College	MA	47,545	LC
Daemen College	NY	31,510	C
Dakota State Univ	SD	13,811	C
Dakota Wesleyan Univ	SD	23,000	C
Dallas Baptist Univ	TX	29,118	C
Daniel Webster College	NH	25,380	C
Davenport Univ	MI	21,002	LC
Davis and Elkins College	WV	33,742	C
De Sales Univ	PA	42,670	C
Defiance College	OH	30,645	C
Delaware State Univ	DE	14,700	LC
Delaware Valley College	PA	29,944	C
Delta State Univ	MS	12,292	LC
DePaul Univ	IL	46,120	VC
Dickinson State Univ	ND	8,550	NC
Dillard Univ	LA	20,940	VC
Doane College	NE	33,730	VC
Dominican College	NY	31,270	C
Dominican Univ	IL	37,628	C
Dominican Univ of Calif	CA	51,250	C
Dordt College	IA	34,160	VC
Dowling College	NY	25,000	LC
Drake Univ	IA	30,980	V¢
Drexel Univ	PA	51,920	HC
Drury Univ	MO	30,319	VC
Duquesne Univ	PA	42,017	VC
D'Youville College	NY	29,850	C
Earlham College	IN	49,710	V¢
East Carolina Univ	NC	14,169	C
East Central Univ	OK	10,223	LC
East Stroudsburg Univ of Pennsylvania	PA	16,636	C
East Texas Baptist Univ	TX	29,135	C
Eastern Conn State Univ	CT	20,584	C
Eastern Illinois Univ	IL	20,502	C
Eastern Kentucky Univ	KY	11,161	C
Eastern Mennonite Univ	VA	38,850	VC
Eastern Mich Univ	MI	17,961	C
Eastern Nazarene College	MA	30,000	C
Eastern New Mexico Univ	NM	10,682	C
Eastern Oregon Univ	OR	10,400	C
Eastern Univ	PA	37,704	C
Eastern Washington Univ	WA	16,388	C
East-West Univ	IL	16,076	C
Eckerd College	FL	43,902	VC
Edgewood College	WI	33,294	C
Edinboro Univ of Pennsylvania	PA	15,940	LC
Edward Waters College	FL	17,856	LC
Elizabeth City State Univ	NC	11,638	C

School	ST	$IS	SR
Elizabethtown College	PA	47,600	VC
Elizabethtown College School of Continuing and Professional Studies	PA		VC
Elmhurst College	IL	42,032	¢
Elmira College	NY	49,950	¢
Elms College	MA	23,900	VC
Elon Univ	NC	40,046	HC
Embry-Riddle Aeronautical Univ - Daytona Beach	FL	40,884	¢
Embry-Riddle Aeronautical Univ - Worldwide	FL	15,512	C
Emmanuel College	MA	47,985	VC
Emory and Henry College	VA	387,460	C
Emory Univ	GA	45,000	MC
Emporia State Univ	KS	12,897	C
Endicott College	MA	42,390	C
Erskine College	SC	37,360	C
Eureka College	IL	19,280	C
Excelsior College	NY	895	SP
Fairfield Univ	CT	55,850	VC
Fairleigh Dickinson Univ/ College at Florham	NJ	42,142	C
Fairleigh Dickinson Univ/ Metropolitan Campus	NJ	40,254	C
Fairmont State Univ	WV	12,098	LC
Farmingdale State College	NY	18,985	C
Faulkner Univ	AL	22,530	LC
Fayetteville State Univ	NC	10,816	C
Felician College	NJ	41,640	C
Ferris State Univ	MI	19,698	C
Ferrum College	VA	27,740	LC
Fisk Univ	TN	19,830	C
Fitchburg State Univ	MA	17,241	C
Flagler College	FL	24,960	VC
Florida A&M Univ	FL	14,935	LC
Florida Atlantic Univ	FL	17,339	C
Florida Inst of Technology	FL	48,290	VC
Florida International Univ	FL	17,747	VC
Florida Memorial Univ	FL	20,716	LC
Florida Southern College	FL	38,240	VC
Florida State Univ	FL	15,238	HC
Fontbonne Univ	MO	31,384	C
Fordham Univ	NY	58,927	HC
Fort Hays State Univ	KS	11,354	C
Fort Lewis College	CO	15,513	C
Fort Valley State Univ	GA	11,200	VC
Framingham State Univ	MA	16,750	C
Francis Marion Univ	SC	16,464	LC
Franciscan Univ of Steubenville	OH	27,320	VC
Franklin and Marshall College	PA	58,295	MC
Franklin Pierce Univ	NH	41,598	C
Franklin Univ	OH	7,000	SP
Freed-Hardeman Univ	TN	19,697	VC
Fresno Pacific Univ	CA	32,136	C
Friends Univ	KS	29,100	C
Frostburg State Univ	MD	15,264	LC
Furman Univ	SC	54,006	HC
Gallaudet Univ	DC	25,380	SP
Gannon Univ	PA	37,940	C
Gardner-Webb Univ	NC	34,375	¢
Geneva College	PA	27,280	C
George Fox Univ	OR	40,750	¢
George Mason Univ	VA	15,724	VC
George Washington Univ	DC	57,108	MC
Georgetown College	KY	38,690	C
Georgetown Univ	DC	52,910	MC
Georgia College and State Univ	GA	18,216	VC
Georgia Inst of Technology	GA	20,464	MC
Georgia Regents Univ	GA		C
Georgia Southwestern State Univ	GA	12,218	C
Georgia State Univ	GA	12,000	VC
Georgian Court Univ	NJ	39,726	LC
Gettysburg College	PA	56,820	HC
Glenville State College	WV	11,348	NC
Goldey-Beacom College	DE	27,493	C
Gonzaga Univ	WA	44,247	HC
Goodwin College	CT	19,400	LC
Gordon College	MA	42,660	V¢
Goshen College	IN	35,900	VC
Goucher College	MD	50,252	V¢
Grace Bible College	MI	20,770	C
Grace College and Theological Seminary	IN	28,800	C
Graceland Univ	IA	28,020	C
Grambling State Univ	LA	13,384	LC
Grand Canyon Univ	AZ	24,540	VC
Grand Valley State Univ	MI	17,998	VC
Grand View Univ	IA	31,050	C
Green Mountain College	VT	33,547	LC
Greensboro College	NC	28,740	LC
Greenville College	IL	27,012	C
Grove City College	PA	22,988	HC
Guilford College	NC	35,340	C
Gustavus Adolphus College	MN	48,170	HC
Gwynedd-Mercy College	PA	33,560	C
Hamline Univ	MN	44,198	VC
Hampton Univ	VA	28,528	C
Hannibal-LaGrange Univ	MO	24,490	C
Harding Univ	AR	21,432	¢
Hardin-Simmons Univ	TX	23,560	¢
Harris-Stowe State Univ	MO	14,360	NC
Hartwick College	NY	49,815	¢

School	ST	$IS	SR
Hastings College	NE	27,782	¢
Hawaii Pacific Univ	HI	36,690	C
Heidelberg Univ	OH	34,100	C
Hellenic College/Holy Cross Greek Orthodox School of Theology	MA	33,190	VC
Henderson State Univ	AR	13,634	C
Heritage Univ	WA	17,664	NC
High Point Univ	NC	39,800	C
Hilbert College	NY	28,550	C
Hillsdale College	MI	31,890	H¢
Hodges Univ	FL	12,000	LC
Hofstra Univ	NY	48,020	V¢
Hollins Univ	VA	43,295	VC
Holy Family Univ	PA	40,030	LC
Holy Names Univ	CA	40,310	NC
Hood College	MD	44,630	C
Hope College	MI	36,320	V¢
Hope International Univ	CA	34,650	C
Houghton College	NY	35,740	VC
Houston Baptist Univ	TX	23,815	¢
Howard Payne Univ	TX	17,115	C
Howard Univ	DC	35,957	C
Humboldt State Univ	CA	18,400	C
Humphreys College	CA	17,000	NC
Huntingdon College	AL	31,850	C
Huntington Univ	IN	32,220	C
Husson Univ	ME	23,386	LC
Huston-Tillotson Univ	TX	18,124	¢
Idaho State Univ	ID	11,908	C
Illinois College	IL	25,770	VC
Illinois State Univ	IL	22,634	VC
Illinois Wesleyan Univ	IL	48,452	V¢
Immaculata Univ	PA	43,000	C
Indiana Inst of Technology	IN	34,240	LC
Indiana State Univ	IN	16,000	C
Indiana Univ Bloomington	IN	19,358	HC
Indiana Univ East	IN	6,639	LC
Indiana Univ Kokomo	IN	6,674	LC
Indiana Univ Northwest	IN	6,738	LC
Indiana Univ of Pennsylvania	PA	20,180	LC
Indiana Univ South Bend	IN	15,293	C
Indiana Univ Southeast	IN	15,807	LC
Indiana Univ-Purdue Univ Fort Wayne	IN	15,425	C
Indiana Univ-Purdue Univ Indianapolis	IN	17,290	C
Indiana Wesleyan Univ	IN	31,815	VC
Inter-American Univ of PR/ Aguadilla Campus	PR	5,578	
Inter-American Univ of PR/ Arecibo Campus	PR	3,350	
Inter-American Univ of PR/ Barranquitas	PR	3,350	
Inter-American Univ of PR/ Bayamon Univ College	PR	4,428	
Inter-American Univ of PR/ Fajardo Campus	PR	4,200	
Inter-American Univ of PR/ Metropolitan Campus	PR	4,320	
Inter-American Univ of PR/ Ponce	PR	3,700	
Inter-American Univ of PR/ San Germán	PR	6,720	
Iona College	NY	44,028	C
Iowa State Univ	IA	16,403	C
Iowa Wesleyan College	IA	30,850	LC
Ithaca College	NY	52,300	HC
Jackson State Univ	MS	13,512	LC
Jacksonville Univ	FL	37,780	C
James Madison Univ	VA	18,049	VC
Jarvis Christian College	TX	19,552	NC
John Brown Univ	AR	30,996	V¢
John Carroll Univ	OH	44,520	¢
Johnson and Wales Univ/ Charlotte Campus	NC	35,421	C
Johnson and Wales Univ/ North Miami Campus	FL	34,368	C
Johnson and Wales Univ/ Providence Campus	RI	34,668	C
Johnson C. Smith Univ	NC	25,336	LC
Johnson State College	VT	16,721	C
Judson College	AL	24,690	C
Judson Univ	IL	25,130	C
Juniata College	PA	49,340	VC
Kansas State Univ	KS	15,497	VC
Kaplan Univ	IA	14,025	NC
Keene State College	NH	21,538	C
Kendall College	IL	32,610	NC
Kennesaw State Univ	GA	13,017	VC
Kent State Univ	OH	19,352	C
Kentucky Christian Univ	KY	17,622	LC
Kentucky State Univ	KY	11,000	LC
Kentucky Wesleyan College	KY	27,440	V¢
Keuka College	NY	30,300	C
Keystone College	PA	28,680	LC
King Univ	TN	33,140	C
King's College	PA	41,678	C
Kutztown Univ of Pennsylvania	PA	16,909	LC
La Roche College	PA	34,802	LC
La Salle Univ	PA	50,270	C
La Sierra Univ	CA	35,694	VC
LaGrange College	GA	34,480	C
Lake Erie College	OH	35,704	C
Lake Superior State Univ	MI	18,121	C

School	ST	$IS	SR
Lakeland College	WI	22,990	C
Lamar Univ	TX	6,820	LC
Lander Univ	SC	22,514	¢
Lane College	TN	11,212	C
Langston Univ	OK	3,000	LC
Lasell College	MA	42,500	LC
Lawrence Tech Univ	MI	37,630	VC
Le Moyne College	NY	42,200	VC
Lebanon Valley College	PA	38,570	C
Lee Univ	TN	18,690	¢
Lees-McRae College	NC	33,624	C
Lehman College / The CUNY	NY	5,778	LC
LeMoyne-Owen College	TN	13,100	C
Lenoir-Rhyne College	NC	35,984	C
LeTourneau Univ	TX	26,230	C
Lewis Univ	IL	23,050	C
Lewis-Clark State College	ID	6,990	C
Liberty Univ	VA	19,101	C
LIM College	NY	41,575	LC
Limestone College	SC	29,880	C
Lincoln Memorial Univ	TN	18,144	C
Lincoln Univ	MO	11,996	NC
Lindenwood Univ	MO	20,750	C
Lindsey Wilson College	KY	30,470	VC
Linfield College-McMinnville Campus	OR	46,166	C
Lipscomb Univ	TN	35,722	VC
Livingstone College	NC	17,815	LC
Lock Haven Univ of Pennsylvania	PA	17,587	LC
LIU/Brooklyn Campus	NY	26,500	C
LIU/C.W. Post Campus	NY	38,888	C
Longwood Univ	VA	20,924	C
Loras College	IA	37,432	VC
Louisiana College	LA	15,746	C
Louisiana State Univ	LA	18,677	V¢
Louisiana State Univ in Shreveport	LA	5,606	C
Louisiana Tech Univ	LA	8,000	C
Lourdes Univ	OH	26,055	LC
Loyola Marymount Univ	CA	53,240	V¢
Loyola Univ Chicago	IL	49,560	V¢
Loyola Univ Maryland	MD		VC
Loyola Univ New Orleans	LA	46,581	VC
Lubbock Christian Univ	TX	25,518	C
Lycoming College	PA	43,636	C
Lynchburg College	VA	42,645	C
Lyndon State College	VT	14,233	C
Lyon College	AR	30,246	VC
MacMurray College	IL	20,755	C
Madonna Univ	MI	24,540	VC
Malone Univ	OH	34,334	C
Manchester College	IN	35,070	C
Mansfield Univ	PA	19,468	LC
Marian Univ	WI	30,980	LC
Marian Univ/Indianapolis	IN	37,058	C
Marietta College	OH	42,135	VC
Marist College	NY	35,500	C
Maritime College / SUNY	NY	16,020	C
Marquette Univ	WI	43,664	V¢
Mars Hill College	NC	22,950	LC
Martin Univ	IN	11,000	SP
Mary Baldwin College	VA	37,110	C
Marygrove College	MI	21,290	C
Marylhurst Univ	OR	18,945	NC
Marymount Manhattan College	NY	40,118	VC
Marymount Univ	VA	36,178	C
Maryville College	TN	33,150	VC
Maryville Univ of St. Louis	MO	34,920	VC
Marywood Univ	PA	40,695	C
Mass College of Liberal Arts	MA	16,733	C
Mayville State Univ	ND	11,401	NC
McDaniel College	MD	45,600	VC
McKendree Univ	IL	29,920	¢
McMurry Univ	TX	25,962	LC
McNeese State Univ	LA		C
McPherson College	KS	28,138	C
Medaille College	NY	35,112	VC
Medgar Evers College / The CUNY	NY	4,920	NC
Mercer Univ	GA	44,201	V¢
Mercy College	NY	29,996	C
Mercyhurst Univ	PA	40,700	C
Meredith College	NC	31,420	C
Merrimack College	MA	44,215	C
Messiah College	PA	39,540	VC
Methodist Univ	NC	37,185	C
Metropolitan College of New York	NY	16,720	VC
Metropolitan State Univ	MN	5,923	SP
Mich State Univ	MI	13,689	VC
Mich Tech Univ	MI	22,105	VC
MidAmerica Nazarene Univ	KS	28,000	C
Middle Tenn State Univ	TN	8,650	C
Midland Univ	NE	34,000	C
Midway College	KY	20,150	C
Midwestern State Univ	TX	9,722	C
Miles College	AL	16,530	NC
Millersville Univ of Pennsylvania	PA	18,498	C
Milligan College	TN	27,510	C
Millikin Univ	IL	37,462	C
Millsaps College	MS	43,888	V¢

School	ST	$IS	SR
Milwaukee School of Engineering	WI	39,948	VC+
Minn State Univ, Mankato	MN	14,900	C
Minn State Univ, Moorhead	MN	13,392	C
Misericordia Univ	PA	39,840	C
Miss College	MS	21,998	VC
Miss Univ for Women	MS	7,400	LC
Miss Valley State Univ	MS	9,706	LC
Missouri Baptist Univ	MO	30,310	C
Missouri Southern State Univ	MO	11,910	C
Missouri State Univ	MO	13,996	VC
Missouri Univ of Science and Technology	MO	18,655	VC+
Missouri Valley College	MO	22,200	C
Missouri Western State Univ	MO	12,260	NC
Mitchell College	CT	40,983	C
Molloy College	NY	38,950	C
Monmouth College	IL	39,290	C
Monmouth Univ	NJ	42,252	C
Monroe College	NY	17,700	C
Montana State Univ	MT	14,068	VC
Montana State Univ-Billings	MT	12,425	LC
Montclair State Univ	NJ	22,614	C
Montreat College	NC	31,298	VC
Moravian College	PA	36,381	VC
Morehouse College	GA	38,640	C
Morgan State Univ	MD	14,500	VC
Morningside College	IA	32,620	C
Morris College	SC	16,006	LC
Mount Aloysius College	PA	27,970	C
Mount Ida College	MA	30,115	LC
Mount Marty College	SD	29,638	C
Mount Mary Univ	WI	32,836	LC
Mount Mercy Univ	IA	34,385	C
Mount Olive College	NC	18,426	C
Mount St. Mary College	NY	39,540	C
Mount St. Mary's Univ	MD	46,158	C
Mount St. Mary's College/Chalon Campus	CA	43,897	VC+
Mount Vernon Nazarene Univ	OH	29,590	C
Mount Washington College	NH	21,500	NC
Mountain State Univ	WV	14,330	NC
Muhlenberg College	PA	52,837	HC
Murray State Univ	KY	14,944	C
Muskingum Univ	OH	30,502	C
National American Univ	SD	16,712	NC
National Louis Univ	IL	16,915	LC
Nazareth College of Rochester	NY	41,590	VC
Nebr Wesleyan Univ	NE	29,774	C+
Neumann Univ	PA	31,078	LC
New England College	NH	45,930	LC
New Jersey City Univ	NJ	21,060	C+
New Mexico Highlands Univ	NM	9,720	NC
New Mexico Inst of Mining and Technology	NM	12,892	HC
New Mexico State Univ	NM	13,955	LC
New York Inst of Technology	NY	40,590	VC
New York Univ	NY	61,470	MC
Newberry College	SC	26,850	LC
Newbury College	MA	41,850	LC
Newman Univ	KS	30,380	C+
Niagara Univ	NY	39,800	C
Nicholls State Univ	LA	7,095	C
Nichols College	MA	37,240	LC
N Car Agricultural and Technical State Univ	NC	13,175	LC
N Car Central Univ	NC	9,000	LC
N Car State Univ	NC	16,202	HC
N Car Wesleyan College	NC	29,440	C
North Central College	IL	38,343	VC
N Dak State Univ	ND	14,642	C
North Georgia College & State Univ	GA	8,500	C
North Park Univ	IL	30,130	C
Northeastern Illinois Univ	IL		C
Northeastern State Univ	OK	8,615	VC
Northeastern Univ	MA	55,296	MC
Northern Arizona Univ	AZ	18,592	C
Northern Illinois Univ	IL	19,768	C
Northern Kentucky Univ	KY	15,302	LC
Northern Mich Univ	MI	15,300	VC
Northern State Univ	SD	14,021	C
Northland College	WI	26,680	C
Northwest Christian Univ	OR	27,399	C
Northwest Missouri State Univ	MO	14,229	C
Northwest Nazarene Univ	ID	24,275	NC
Northwest Univ	WA	18,854	C
Northwestern College	MN	24,000	C
Northwestern College of Iowa	IA	34,848	C+
Northwestern Okla State Univ	OK	7,275	NC
Northwestern State Univ of Louisiana	LA	14,368	C
Northwood Univ	FL	30,746	LC
Northwood Univ	MI	26,331	LC
Norwich Univ	VT	28,212	C
Notre Dame de Namur Univ	CA	41,610	LC
Notre Dame of Maryland Univ	MD	27,700	C
Nova Southeastern Univ	FL	34,016	VC
Nyack College	NY	32,000	C
Oakland City Univ	IN	24,500	NC
Oakland Univ	MI	19,391	VC
Oakwood Univ	AL	23,035	C
Oglala Lakota College	SD	2,000	NC
Oglethorpe Univ	GA	42,580	VC
Ohio Dominican Univ	OH	38,380	C+
Ohio Northern Univ	OH	42,075	VC
Ohio State Univ at Lima	OH	7,140	C
Ohio State Univ at Mansfield	OH	13,160	C
Ohio State Univ at Marion	OH	9,850	MC
Ohio State Univ at Newark	OH	17,510	C
Ohio Univ	OH	20,676	VC
Ohio Valley Univ	WV	17,752	C
Okla Baptist Univ	OK	28,202	VC
Okla Christian Univ	OK	24,975	VC
Okla City Univ	OK	33,546	VC
Okla Panhandle State Univ	OK	8,996	NC
Okla State Univ	OK	14,310	VC
Okla Wesleyan Univ	OK	21,300	C
Old Dominion Univ	VA	18,662	C
Olivet College	MI	19,984	C
Olivet Nazarene Univ	IL	29,990	C
Oral Roberts Univ	OK	31,734	C
Oregon State Univ	OR	19,017	C+
Oswego / SUNY	NY	20,009	VC
Ottawa Univ	KS	15,000	VC
Otterbein College	OH	32,214	C
Ouachita Baptist Univ	AR	29,010	VC
Our Lady of Holy Cross College	LA	8,090	LC
Our Lady of the Lake Univ of San Antonio	TX	22,430	LC
Pace Univ	NY	48,094	VC
Pacific Lutheran Univ	WA	44,840	VC
Pacific Union College	CA	28,150	VC
Pacific Univ	OR	42,815	C
Paine College	GA	18,594	LC
Palm Beach Atlantic Univ	FL	33,882	LC
Park Univ	MO	17,525	C
Paul Quinn College	TX	25,350	LC
Peirce College	PA	12,760	NC
Penn State Erie/The Behrend College	PA	16,256	C
Penn State Univ/Altoona	PA	11,464	C
Pennsylvania College of Technology	PA	25,653	NC
Pepperdine Univ	CA	55,372	HC+
Peru State College	NE	8,600	NC
Pfeiffer Univ	NC	33,700	C
Philander Smith College	AR	19,760	LC
Piedmont College	GA	29,260	C
Pine Manor College	MA	32,659	LC
Pittsburg State Univ	KS	12,032	C
Plymouth State Univ	NH	23,148	LC
Point Loma Nazarene Univ	CA	38,610	VC
Point Park Univ	PA	36,390	C
Polytechnic Inst of New York Univ	NY	53,064	HC+
Pontifical Catholic Univ of PR	PR	7,310	
Portland State Univ	OR	18,672	C
Post Univ	CT	35,750	C
Prairie View A&M Univ	TX	15,205	LC
Presbyterian College	SC	42,678	VC
Presentation College	SD	14,800	LC
Principia College	IL	35,140	C+
Providence College	RI	55,995	HC
Queens College / The CUNY	NY	17,107	VC
Queens Univ of Charlotte	NC	39,543	VC
Quincy Univ	IL	34,980	LC
Quinnipiac Univ	CT	53,580	VC
Radford Univ	VA	17,132	LC
Ramapo College of New Jersey	NJ	24,938	C+
Randolph College	VA	43,960	VC
Regis Univ	CO	41,318	C
Reinhardt College	GA	25,000	C
Rhode Island College	RI	17,132	LC
Rhodes College	TN	47,596	HC+
Richard Stockton College of New Jersey	NJ	20,000	VC
Rider Univ	NJ	45,720	C
Ripon College	WI	36,959	C+
Rivier College	NH	35,000	VC
Roanoke College	VA	47,996	C+
Robert Morris Univ	PA	36,699	C
Roberts Wesleyan College	NY	37,384	C+
Rochester Inst of Technology	NY	42,450	VC+
Rockford College	IL	31,000	C
Rockhurst Univ	MO	20,625	C
Rocky Mountain College	MT	32,242	C
Roger Williams Univ	RI	45,788	C
Roosevelt Univ	IL	22,605	VC
Rosemont College	PA	42,350	C
Rowan Univ	NJ	23,570	VC
Rust College	MS	10,600	C
Rutgers, The State Univ of New Jersey/New Brunswick	NJ	25,077	VC
Rutgers, The State Univ of New Jersey/Newark Campus	NJ	25,376	C
Sacred Heart Univ	CT	48,564	VC
Saginaw Valley State Univ	MI	16,869	C
St. Anselm College	NH	48,324	VC
St. Augustine's Univ	NC	14,000	C
St. Joseph's College	IN	35,790	C
St. Joseph's College of Maine	ME	31,580	C
St. Joseph's Univ	PA	52,272	VC
St. Leo Univ	FL	27,990	C
St. Louis Univ	MO	46,594	VC+
St. Martin's Univ	WA	38,082	C
St. Mary-of-the-Woods College	IN	37,722	LC
St. Mary's College	IN	45,160	VC
St. Mary's College of Calif	CA	53,550	C
St. Mary's Univ	TX	33,854	C
St. Mary's Univ of Minn	MN	37,015	C
St. Michael's College	VT	48,740	VC
St. Paul's College	VA	16,030	NC
St. Peter's College	NJ	44,240	C
St. Vincent College	PA	40,244	C
St. Xavier Univ	IL	32,840	C
Salem College	NC	29,326	VC
Salem International Univ	WV	18,020	C
Salem State College	MA	13,161	LC
Salisbury Univ	MD	18,368	VC
Salve Regina Univ	RI	47,250	VC
Sam Houston State Univ	TX	17,082	C
San Diego Christian College	CA	31,012	C
San Diego State Univ	CA	20,578	VC
San Francisco State Univ	CA	18,514	C
San Jose State Univ	CA	19,707	C
Savannah State Univ	GA	13,156	C
Schreiner Univ	TX	32,734	LC
Seattle Pacific Univ	WA	41,559	VC+
Seattle Univ	WA	47,010	VC+
Seton Hall Univ	NJ	45,902	C
Seton Hill Univ	PA	35,172	C
Shaw Univ	NC	15,488	LC
Shawnee State Univ	OH	16,545	NC
Shenandoah Univ	VA	39,268	C
Shepherd Univ	WV	14,996	C
Shippensburg Univ of Pennsylvania	PA	17,064	LC
Shorter Univ	GA	26,470	C
Siena College	NY	43,863	VC
Siena Heights Univ	MI	17,000	LC
Sierra Nevada College	NV	32,700	VC
Silver Lake College	WI	22,600	LC
Simmons College	MA	48,770	VC
Simpson College	IA	36,086	VC
Simpson Univ	CA	28,900	C
Skidmore College	NY	57,926	HC
Slippery Rock Univ of Pennsylvania	PA	10,360	LC
Sojourner-Douglass College	MD	9,160	LC
Sonoma State Univ	CA	20,541	C
S Car State Univ	SC	6,700	LC
South Univ	GA		LC
Southeast Missouri State Univ	MO	14,983	LC
Southeastern Louisiana Univ	LA	13,325	C
Southeastern Okla State Univ	OK	7,966	C
Southeastern Univ	FL	27,201	C+
Southern Adventist Univ	TN	26,190	C
Southern Arkansas Univ	AR	14,316	C
Southern Conn State Univ	CT	18,033	C
Southern Illinois Univ Carbondale	IL	21,620	C
Southern Illinois Univ Edwardsville	IL	17,532	C
Southern Methodist Univ	TX	57,755	MC
Southern Nazarene Univ	OK	24,354	NC
Southern New Hampshire Univ	NH	38,100	C
Southern Oregon Univ	OR	17,874	C
Southern Polytechnic State Univ	GA	13,958	VC
Southern Univ and A&M College	LA	9,761	C+
Southern Univ at New Orleans	LA	1,000	NC
Southern Vermont College	VT	30,740	LC
Southern Wesleyan Univ	SC	25,600	C
Southwest Baptist Univ	MO	24,710	C
Southwest Minn State Univ	MN	14,000	C
Southwestern Adventist Univ	TX	23,026	LC
Southwestern College	KS	29,270	C
Southwestern Okla State Univ	OK	9,160	C
Southwestern Univ	TX	45,660	VC
Spalding Univ	KY	31,850	LC
Spring Arbor Univ	MI	26,740	C
Spring Hill College	AL	42,130	VC
Springfield College	MA	25,000	C
St. Ambrose Univ	IA		C
St. Andrews Univ	NC	32,050	LC
St. Catherine Univ	MN	37,782	C+
St. Cloud State Univ	MN	10,600	C
St. Edward's Univ	TX	44,674	VC
St. Francis College	NY	34,200	LC
St. John Fisher College	NY	39,370	C+
St. John's Univ	NY	52,840	C+
St. Joseph's College, New York / Brooklyn Campus	NY	21,878	C
St. Joseph's College, New York / Suffolk Campus	NY	21,878	VC
St. Norbert College	WI	39,992	VC
St. Thomas Aquinas College	NY	30,000	C
St. Thomas Univ	FL	32,310	C+
SUNY Inst of Technology at Utica / Rome	NY	23,818	C
SUNY/Empire State College	NY	6,315	SP
Stephen F. Austin State Univ	TX	14,668	C
Stephens College	MO	34,500	VC
Sterling College	KS	27,216	C
Stetson Univ	FL	40,512	VC+
Stevens Inst of Technology	NJ	50,130	HC
Stevenson Univ	MD	39,572	C
Stillman College	AL	18,460	C
Stonehill College	MA	46,780	VC+
Stony Brook Univ / SUNY	NY	19,359	HC
Sul Ross State Univ	TX	13,410	LC
SUNY College at Geneseo	NY	18,055	HC+
SUNY College at Old Westbury	NY	16,324	C
SUNY Fredonia / The SUNY at Fredonia	NY	18,702	VC
SUNY New Paltz	NY	15,010	C
SUNY Plattsburgh / SUNY	NY	18,083	VC
Susquehanna Univ	PA	49,170	C
Sweet Briar College	VA	43,765	C+
Tabor College	KS	29,010	LC
Talladega College	AL	13,000	C
Tarleton State Univ	TX	13,489	LC
Taylor Univ	IN	36,742	VC+
Temple Univ	PA	24,392	VC
Tenn State Univ	TN	9,048	C
Tenn Tech Univ	TN	11,310	C
Tenn Wesleyan College	TN	21,250	C
Texas A&M Univ at Commerce	TX	10,496	C
Texas A&M Univ at Corpus Christi	TX	11,544	LC
Texas A&M Univ at Kingsville	TX	7,500	LC
Texas Lutheran Univ	TX	34,070	C
Texas Southern Univ	TX	18,212	LC
Texas State Univ	TX	16,495	VC
Texas Tech Univ	TX	14,243	C
Texas Wesleyan Univ	TX	29,886	C
Texas Woman's Univ	TX	13,633	LC
The Catholic Univ of America	DC	52,852	VC
The College at Brockport / SUNY	NY	18,362	VC
The College of Idaho	ID	31,277	VC
The College of New Rochelle	NY	33,600	VC
The College of St. Rose	NY	26,750	C
The Masters College	CA	38,160	C+
Ohio State Univ	OH	19,887	MC
The SUNY at Potsdam	NY	17,754	C
The SUNY College of Agriculture and Tech at Cobleskill	NY	18,869	VC
Thiel College	PA	31,378	LC
Thomas College	ME	26,270	LC
Thomas More College	KY	34,760	C
Thomas Univ	GA	11,520	NC
Tiffin Univ	OH	30,273	LC
Toccoa Falls College	GA	23,210	C
Touro College	NY	23,150	VC
Towson Univ	MD	16,000	VC
Transylvania Univ	KY	40,310	VC+
Trevecca Nazarene Univ	TN	30,118	C
Trine Univ	IN	39,400	VC
Trinity Christian College	IL	28,869	C
Trinity International Univ	IL	31,070	C
Trinity Univ	TX	44,174	HC+
Trinity Washington Univ	DC	30,250	C+
Troy Univ	AL	10,650	C
Truman State Univ	MO	13,546	HC
Tulane Univ	LA	58,942	MC
Tuskegee Univ	AL	26,750	C
Union College	KY	28,775	C
Union College	NE	23,270	VC
Union Inst & Univ	OH	8,912	SP
Union Univ	TN	28,260	VC
Universidad Adventista de las Antillas	PR	7,360	
Universidad del Turabo	PR	4,110	
Universidad Metropolitana	PR		
Universidad Politecnica de PR	PR	19,252	
Univ at Albany / SUNY	NY	18,674	VC
Univ at Buffalo / The SUNY	NY	20,283	VC
Univ of Akron	OH	20,436	C
Univ of Alabama at Huntsville	AL	17,625	VC
Univ of Alaska Anchorage	AK	15,290	NC
Univ of Alaska Fairbanks	AK	13,955	C
Univ of Alaska Southeast	AK	11,493	C
Univ of Arizona	AZ	20,105	C
Univ of Arkansas at Fayetteville	AR	16,860	VC
Univ of Arkansas at Little Rock	AR		C

ST = STATE   **$IS** = IN-STATE COSTS   **SR** = SELECTOR RATING

School	ST	$IS	SR
Univ of Arkansas at Monticello	AR	8,470	NC
Univ of Arkansas at Pine Bluff	AR	10,600	C
Univ of Bridgeport	CT	39,030	LC
Univ of Calif at Berkeley	CA	23,322	MC
Univ of Calif at Irvine	CA	25,961	VC
Univ of Calif at Riverside	CA	27,204	C
Univ of Central Arkansas	AR	10,840	VC
Univ of Central Florida	FL	15,711	VC+
Univ of Central Missouri	MO	14,605	C
Univ of Central Okla	OK	12,293	C
Univ of Charleston	WV	28,650	C
Univ of Cincinnati	OH	20,199	VC
Univ of Colo at Colo Springs	CO	15,000	VC
Univ of Colo Boulder	CO	22,605	VC+
Univ of Colo Denver	CO	17,904	C
Univ of Conn	CT	23,744	HC
Univ of Dallas	TX	43,510	VC+
Univ of Dayton	OH	43,750	VC
Univ of Delaware	DE	22,728	VC
Univ of Denver	CO	51,787	VC+
Univ of Detroit Mercy	MI	30,450	C
Univ of Dubuque	IA	30,200	C
Univ of Evansville	IN	41,056	VC+
Univ of Findlay	OH	31,916	C
Univ of Florida	FL	15,783	HC+
Univ of Georgia	GA	19,508	VC
Univ of Great Falls	MT	27,970	C
Univ of Hartford	CT	42,674	C
Univ of Hawaii at Hilo	HI	6,500	C
Univ of Hawaii at Manoa	HI	19,379	VC
Univ of Houston-Downtown	TX	6,267	LC
Univ of Idaho	ID	14,558	C
Univ of Illinois at Chicago	IL	24,293	VC
Univ of Indianapolis	IN	31,740	LC
Univ of Iowa	IA	17,481	VC
Univ of Jamestown	ND	24,738	C
Univ of Kansas	KS	16,980	C+
Univ of La Verne	CA	47,010	VC
Univ of Louisiana at Lafayette	LA	6,130	C
Univ of Louisiana at Monroe	LA	12,998	C
Univ of Louisville	KY	17,460	VC
Univ of Maine	ME	19,712	C+
Univ of Maine at Augusta	ME	6,855	C
Univ of Maine at Farmington	ME	17,841	C
Univ of Maine at Fort Kent	ME	14,975	LC
Univ of Maine at Machias	ME	10,523	C
Univ of Maine at Presque Isle	ME	15,011	LC
Univ of Mary	ND	16,714	C
Univ of Mary Hardin-Baylor	TX	31,950	C+
Univ of Mary Washington	VA	19,484	VC
Univ of Maryland	MD	18,801	HC
Univ of Maryland/Eastern Shore	MD	14,000	C
Univ of Maryland/Univ College	MD	6,168	SP
Univ of Mass Amherst	MA	23,697	VC+
Univ of Mass Dartmouth	MA	22,223	C
Univ of Mass Lowell	MA	19,316	C
Univ of Mich/Ann Arbor	MI	22,102	HC+
Univ of Mich/Dearborn	MI	9,885	VC
Univ of Mich-Flint	MI	17,547	C+
Univ of Minn Crookston	MN	17,834	C
Univ of Minn/Duluth	MN	18,964	C+
Univ of Minn/Twin Cities	MN		HC
Univ of Miss	MS	15,482	VC
Univ of Missouri/Columbia	MO	18,201	MC
Univ of Missouri-Kansas City	MO	19,603	C
Univ of Missouri-St. Louis	MO	18,304	VC
Univ of Mobile	AL	27,870	VC
Univ of Montana	MT	13,670	C
Univ of Montevallo	AL	17,320	C
Univ of Mount Union	OH	35,130	C
Univ of Nebr - Lincoln	NE	17,507	VC
Univ of Nebr at Kearney	NE	14,855	LC
Univ of New England	ME	46,145	C+
Univ of New Hampshire	NH	24,702	VC
Univ of New Haven	CT	47,740	C
Univ of New Mexico	NM	15,300	C
Univ of New Orleans	LA	9,224	VC
Univ of N Car at Asheville	NC	13,500	VC+
Univ of N Car at Chapel Hill	NC	18,348	MC
Univ of N Car at Charlotte	NC	15,847	C
Univ of N Car at Greensboro	NC	12,848	C
Univ of N Car at Wilmington	NC	13,572	VC+
Univ of North Florida	FL	15,578	VC
Univ of North Texas	TX	15,628	C
Univ of Northern Colo	CO	15,973	C
Univ of Okla	OK	17,634	VC+
Univ of Oregon	OR	20,872	VC
Univ of Pennsylvania	PA	56,106	MC
Univ of Pikeville	KY	24,750	NC
Univ of Pittsburgh at Bradford	PA	21,316	LC
Univ of Pittsburgh at Johnstown	PA	20,862	LC
Univ of Pittsburgh at Pittsburgh	PA	27,800	HC+
Univ of PR Recinto de Rio Piedras	PR	5,750	
Univ of PR/Arecibo	PR	7,227	
Univ of PR/Bayamon	PR	1,600	
Univ of PR/Cayey	PR	1,504	
Univ of PR/Humacao	PR	1,877	
Univ of PR/Mayaguez	PR	1,250	
Univ of Puget Sound	WA	52,648	HC+
Univ of Redlands	CA	40,500	VC
Univ of Rio Grande	OH	8,750	NC
Univ of Rochester	NY	58,500	MC
Univ of St. Francis	IN	29,810	C
Univ of St. Mary	KS	28,400	C+
Univ of San Diego	CA	53,302	HC+
Univ of San Francisco	CA	49,674	VC
Univ of Science and Arts of Okla	OK	10,560	VC
Univ of Scranton	PA	51,940	VC
Univ of Sioux Falls	SD	22,990	C
Univ of South Alabama	AL	13,510	C
Univ of S Car at Aiken	SC	16,278	C
Univ of S Car at Columbia	SC	19,725	VC+
Univ of S Car Upstate	SC	17,673	LC
Univ of South Florida	FL	13,000	C
Univ of South Florida/St. Petersburg	FL	12,769	VC
Univ of Southern Calif	CA	56,903	MC
Univ of Southern Indiana	IN	14,657	C
Univ of Southern Maine	ME	16,576	C
Univ of Southern Miss	MS	13,170	C
Univ of St. Francis	IL	36,490	C
Univ of St. Thomas - Houston	TX	36,490	VC
Univ of Tampa	FL	35,160	VC
Univ of Tenn at Chattanooga	TN	16,883	C
Univ of Tenn at Martin	TN	13,217	C
Univ of Texas at Arlington	TX	10,908	LC
Univ of Texas at Austin	TX	44,074	HC
Univ of Texas at Dallas	TX	21,046	HC
Univ of Texas at San Antonio	TX	18,372	C
Univ of the Cumberlands	KY	27,500	LC
Univ of the District of Columbia	DC	7,244	LC
Univ of the Incarnate Word	TX	35,200	LC
Univ of the Ozarks	AR	22,100	C
Univ of the Pacific	CA	52,146	VC
Univ of the Sacred Heart	PR	5,590	
Univ of the Southwest	NM	15,000	C
Univ of Toledo	OH	18,464	C
Univ of Tulsa	OK	45,311	HC+
Univ of Utah	UT	13,462	VC
Univ of Vermont	VT	26,120	VC+
Univ of Virginia	VA	22,175	MC
Univ of Virginia's College at Wise	VA	11,076	C
Univ of Washington	WA	14,722	VC
Univ of West Alabama	AL	9,415	C
Univ of West Florida	FL	14,656	C
Univ of West Georgia	GA	14,852	LC
Univ of Wisc Whitewater	WI	13,314	C
Univ of Wisc/Eau Claire	WI	15,430	VC
Univ of Wisc/Green Bay	WI	14,900	C
Univ of Wisc/La Crosse	WI	14,755	VC
Univ of Wisc/Oshkosh	WI	10,426	LC
Univ of Wisc/Parkside	WI	10,181	LC
Univ of Wisc/Platteville	WI	14,274	C
Univ of Wisc/River Falls	WI	9,722	LC
Univ of Wisc/Stevens Point	WI	14,043	C
Univ of Wisc/Stout	WI	23,942	C
Univ of Wisc/Superior	WI	14,106	C
Univ of Wisc-Milwaukee	WI	18,436	C
Univ of Wyoming	WY	13,855	C+
Upper Iowa Univ	IA	30,426	NC
Urbana Univ	OH	21,190	C
Ursuline College	OH	33,198	LC
Utah State Univ	UT	11,803	C
Utica College	NY	44,734	C
Valley City State Univ	ND	12,286	LC
Valparaiso Univ	IN	43,040	VC+
Vanguard Univ of Southern Calif	CA	35,833	VC
Vaughn College of Aeronautics and Technology	NY	31,360	SP
Victory Univ	TN	19,118	C
Villanova Univ	PA	56,436	MC
Virginia Commonwealth Univ	VA	18,633	C
Virginia Intermont College	VA	32,411	LC
Virginia State Univ	VA	11,318	C+
Virginia Union Univ	VA	18,432	C
Virginia Wesleyan College	VA	28,433	LC
Voorhees College	SC	18,126	C
Wagner College	NY	48,600	VC
Wake Forest Univ	NC	51,000	MC
Walla Walla Univ	WA	26,256	NC
Walsh Univ	OH	35,100	C
Warner Pacific College	OR	25,550	C
Warner Univ	FL	18,000	C
Wartburg College	IA	41,055	VC
Washburn Univ	KS	12,165	NC
Washington Adventist Univ	MD	25,859	C+
Washington and Jefferson College	PA	49,990	VC
Washington and Lee Univ	VA	52,812	MC
Washington College	MD	48,768	VC
Washington State Univ	WA	20,461	C
Washington Univ in St. Louis	MO	58,818	MC
Wayland Baptist Univ	TX	16,058	LC
Wayne State College	NE	11,764	NC
Wayne State Univ	MI	19,493	C
Webber International Univ	FL	25,664	C
Webster Univ	MO	33,990	C+
Wells College	NY	38,680	VC
Wesley College	DE	31,115	LC
Wesleyan College	GA	24,000	C+
West Chester Univ of Pennsylvania	PA	16,836	C
West Liberty Univ	WV	9,142	LC
West Texas A&M Univ	TX	13,478	C
West Virginia State Univ	WV	8,378	NC
West Virginia Univ	WV	15,794	C+
West Virginia Univ Inst of Technology	WV	14,094	NC
West Virginia Wesleyan College	WV	26,880	C
Western Conn State Univ	CT	18,327	C
Western Illinois Univ	IL	20,130	C
Western Mich Univ	MI	19,042	C
Western New England Univ	MA	45,590	C
Western New Mexico Univ	NM	8,500	LC
Western Oregon Univ	OR	15,021	C
Western State Colo Univ	CO	16,135	C
Western Washington Univ	WA	18,519	VC
Westfield State Univ	MA	18,489	C
Westminster College	MO	30,490	VC
Westminster College	PA	31,290	C+
Westminster College	UT	37,708	VC
Wheeling Jesuit Univ	WV	34,668	C
Whittier College	CA	43,416	C
Whitworth Univ	WA	45,826	VC+
Wichita State Univ	KS	12,539	C
Widener Univ	PA	50,368	C
Wilberforce Univ	OH	15,100	LC
Wiley College	TX		LC
Wilkes Univ	PA	42,786	C
William Carey Univ	MS	13,500	LC
William Jewell College	MO	31,000	VC+
William Paterson Univ of New Jersey	NJ	21,694	C
William Peace Univ	NC	32,900	LC
William Penn Univ	IA	26,000	C
William Woods Univ	MO		C
Williams Baptist College	AR	20,070	C
Wilmington College	OH	29,784	C
Wilmington Univ	DE	7,778	NC
Wingate Univ	NC	34,990	C
Winona State Univ	MN	16,530	C
Winston-Salem State Univ	NC	9,418	LC
Winthrop Univ	SC	21,120	VC
Wittenberg Univ	OH	47,766	VC
Woodbury Univ	CA	34,500	LC
Worcester Polytechnic Inst	MA	53,440	HC+
Worcester State Univ	MA	18,657	C
Xavier Univ	OH	43,740	VC
Xavier Univ of Louisiana	LA	25,300	C
Yeshiva Univ	NY	47,250	VC+
York College	NE	19,475	C
York College / CUNY	NY	5,496	NC
York College of Pennsylvania	PA	26,590	C
Youngstown State Univ	OH	16,374	LC

BUSINESS ADMINISTRATION, MGMT, OPERATIONS

Univ of Georgia	GA	19,508	VC

BUSINESS COMMUNICATIONS

Aquinas College	MI	33,060	C
Arizona State Univ	AZ	18,818	C+
Augustana College	SD	35,500	VC
Bentley Univ	MA	54,555	HC+
Biola Univ	CA	40,320	VC
Bryant Univ	RI	49,179	VC
Calvin College	MI	37,585	VC+
Canisius College	NY	45,602	VC
Carlow Univ	PA	30,272	C
Chestnut Hill College	PA	39,785	LC
Duquesne Univ	PA	42,017	VC
George Fox Univ	OR	40,750	C+
Ithaca College	NY	52,300	HC
Nichols College	MA	37,240	LC
Olivet Nazarene Univ	IL	29,990	C
Point Loma Nazarene Univ	CA	38,610	VC
Rockhurst Univ	MO	20,625	C
St. Leo Univ	FL	27,990	C
Southwestern College	KS	29,270	C
Stevenson Univ	MD	39,572	C
Univ of Akron	OH	20,436	C
Univ of Indianapolis	IN	31,740	LC
Univ of Mary	ND	16,714	C
Univ of Nebr at Omaha	NE	12,700	C
Univ of Southern Indiana	IN	14,657	C
Walsh Univ	OH	35,100	C
Webber International Univ	FL	25,664	C
Westminster College	MO	30,490	VC

BUSINESS DATA PROCESSING

School	ST	$IS	SR
Bryant Univ	RI	49,179	VC
Cal State, Fresno	CA	17,405	C
Eastern Mich Univ	MI	17,961	C
Idaho State Univ	ID	11,908	C
John Carroll Univ	OH	44,520	C+
Mount Vernon Nazarene Univ	OH	29,590	C

BUSINESS ECONOMICS

Adams State College	CO	13,358	LC
Alabama State Univ	AL	14,142	NC
American International College	MA	36,100	LC
Andrews Univ	MI	28,030	C+
Aquinas College	MI	33,060	C
Arkansas State Univ	AR	14,980	C
Ashland Univ	OH	25,000	C
Auburn Univ	AL	20,052	VC+
Auburn Univ at Montgomery	AL	12,120	C
Ball State Univ	IN	17,850	C
Baylor Univ	TX	46,720	HC
Benedictine Univ	IL	35,220	C
Bentley Univ	MA	54,555	HC+
Bethany College	KS	30,605	NC
Bethel College	IN	31,560	C
Biola Univ	CA	40,320	VC
Bloomsburg Univ of Pennsylvania	PA	13,598	C
Boston College	MA	58,506	MC
Brescia Univ	KY	26,140	VC+
Bryant Univ	RI	49,179	VC
Buena Vista Univ	IA	37,954	C
Cal State, Fullerton	CA	25,188	C+
Cal State, San Bernardino	CA	12,000	C
Campbellsville Univ	KY	27,720	C
Canisius College	NY	45,602	VC
Carnegie Mellon Univ	PA	51,260	MC
Carson-Newman Univ	TN	29,058	C+
Centenary College of Louisiana	LA	39,070	C+
Central Washington Univ	WA	11,730	C
Clarion Univ of Pennsylvania	PA	17,370	C
Cleveland State Univ	OH	21,357	C
College of the Ozarks	MO	5,605	VC
College of Wooster	OH	52,600	VC
Cornell College	IA	44,930	HC
DePaul Univ	IL	46,120	VC
Dominican College	NY	31,270	C
Dordt College	IA	34,160	VC
Drexel Univ	PA	51,920	HC
Duquesne Univ	PA	42,017	VC
Eastern Mich Univ	MI	17,961	C
Elizabethtown College	PA	47,600	VC
Elmira College	NY	49,950	C+
Emory Univ	GA	45,000	MC
Eureka College	IL	19,280	C
Fairleigh Dickinson Univ/Metropolitan Campus	NJ	40,254	C
Fairmont State Univ	WV	12,098	LC
Fayetteville State Univ	NC	10,816	C
Florida A&M Univ	FL	14,935	LC
Florida Atlantic Univ	FL	17,339	C
Fordham Univ	NY	58,927	HC
Fort Lewis College	CO	15,513	C
Francis Marion Univ	SC	16,464	LC
Friends Univ	KS	29,100	C
George Washington Univ	DC	57,108	MC
Georgetown College	KY	38,690	C
Georgia State Univ	GA	12,000	VC
Gonzaga Univ	WA	44,247	HC
Grambling State Univ	LA	13,384	LC
Grand Valley State Univ	MI	17,998	VC
Grove City College	PA	22,988	HC
Gustavus Adolphus College	MN	48,170	HC
Hampden-Sydney College	VA	48,848	C
Hawaii Pacific Univ	HI	36,690	C
Heidelberg Univ	OH	34,100	C
Hendrix College	AR	48,436	HC+
Hofstra Univ	NY	48,020	VC+
Humboldt State Univ	CA	18,400	C
Indiana Univ-Purdue Univ Fort Wayne	IN	15,425	C
Inter-American Univ of PR/Bayamon Univ College	PR	4,428	
James Madison Univ	VA	18,049	VC
Johnson C. Smith Univ	NC	25,336	LC
Kalamazoo College	MI	47,825	HC+
Kansas Wesleyan Univ	KS	32,000	C
Kentucky Wesleyan College	KY	27,440	VC+
King Univ	TN	33,140	C
Kutztown Univ of Pennsylvania	PA	16,909	LC
Lafayette College	PA	57,050	HC+
Lake Forest College	IL	45,580	VC
Lakeland College	WI	22,990	C
Lamar Univ	TX	6,820	LC
Lehigh Univ	PA	55,080	MC
Limestone College	SC	29,880	C
Louisiana Tech Univ	LA	8,000	C
Loyola Univ Chicago	IL	49,560	VC+
Manhattan College	NY	44,955	VC
Mansfield Univ	PA	19,468	LC
Marquette Univ	WI	43,664	VC+

ST = STATE **$IS** = IN-STATE COSTS **SR** = SELECTOR RATING

School	ST	$IS	SR
Marshall Univ	WV	14,820	C
Merrimack College	MA	44,215	C
Miami Univ	OH	24,191	HC
Midland Univ	NE	34,000	C
Midwestern State Univ	TX	9,722	C
Mills College	CA	54,119	HC
Missouri Southern State Univ	MO	11,910	C
Monmouth Univ	NJ	42,252	C
Montclair State Univ	NJ	22,614	C
Moravian College	PA	36,381	VC
Morehead State Univ	KY	10,900	C
Mount Aloysius College	PA	27,970	C
Murray State Univ	KY	14,944	C
New Mexico State Univ	NM	13,955	LC
New York Univ	NY	61,470	MC
Niagara Univ	NY	39,800	C
N Car State Univ	NC	16,202	HC
North Georgia College & State Univ	GA	8,500	C
Northern Arizona Univ	AZ	18,592	C
Northern Kentucky Univ	KY	15,302	LC
Northern State Univ	SD	14,021	C
Northland College	WI	26,680	C
Northwest Missouri State Univ	MO	14,229	C
Northwestern College of Iowa	IA	34,848	C+
Northwood Univ	MI	26,331	LC
Norwich Univ	VT	28,212	C
Notre Dame College	OH	34,942	VC
Oakland Univ	MI	19,391	VC
Ohio Northern Univ	OH	42,075	VC
Ohio Univ	OH	20,676	VC
Ohio Wesleyan Univ	OH	49,460	C+
Pace Univ	NY	48,094	VC
Park Univ	MO	17,525	C
Penn State Erie/The Behrend College	PA	16,256	C
Pittsburg State Univ	KS	12,032	C
Pontifical Catholic Univ of PR	PR	7,310	
Presbyterian College	SC	42,678	VC
Providence College	RI	55,995	HC
Purdue Univ/Calumet	IN	14,336	C
Quinnipiac Univ	CT	53,580	VC
Randolph-Macon College	VA	45,086	C
Regis Univ	CO	41,318	C
Rider Univ	NJ	45,720	C
Rockhurst Univ	MO	20,625	C
Rocky Mountain College	MT	32,242	C
Sacred Heart Univ	CT	48,564	VC
Saginaw Valley State Univ	MI	16,869	C
St. Louis Univ	MO	46,594	VC+
Seattle Univ	WA	47,010	VC+
Seton Hall Univ	NJ	45,902	C
Seton Hill Univ	PA	35,172	C
Skidmore College	NY	57,926	HC
S Car State Univ	SC	6,700	LC
Southern Conn State Univ	CT	18,033	C
Southern Illinois Univ Carbondale	IL	21,620	C
Southern Illinois Univ Edwardsville	IL	17,532	C
Southern Univ and A&M College	LA	9,761	C+
St. Ambrose Univ	IA		C
St. Cloud State Univ	MN	10,600	C
St. John's Univ	NY	52,840	C+
Stetson Univ	FL	49,512	VC+
SUNY Fredonia / The SUNY at Fredonia	NY	18,702	VC
SUNY Oneonta / SUNY	NY	16,919	VC
Tenn State Univ	TN	9,048	C
Texas A&M Univ at Kingsville	TX	7,500	LC
Texas State Univ	TX	16,495	VC
Texas Tech Univ	TX	14,243	C
Texas Wesleyan Univ	TX	29,886	C
The SUNY at Potsdam	NY	17,754	C
Thomas College	ME	26,270	LC
Trinity Washington Univ	DC	30,250	C+
Troy Univ	AL	10,650	C
Tuskegee Univ	AL	26,750	C
Univ of Arizona	AZ	20,105	C
Univ of Arkansas at Fayetteville	AR	16,860	VC
Univ of Calif at Irvine	CA	25,961	VC
Univ of Calif at Los Angeles	CA	25,686	MC
Univ of Calif at Riverside	CA	27,204	C
Univ of Calif at Santa Cruz	CA	27,807	VC
Univ of Central Arkansas	AR	10,840	VC
Univ of Central Florida	FL	15,711	VC+
Univ of Dayton	OH	43,750	VC
Univ of Denver	CO	51,787	VC+
Univ of Findlay	OH	31,916	C
Univ of Idaho	ID	14,558	C
Univ of Illinois at Chicago	IL	24,293	VC
Univ of Indianapolis	IN	31,740	LC
Univ of Iowa	IA	17,481	VC
Univ of Kentucky	KY	19,868	C
Univ of La Verne	CA	47,010	VC
Univ of Louisville	KY	17,460	VC
Univ of Maine	ME	19,712	C+
Univ of Maine at Farmington	ME	17,841	C
Univ of Memphis	TN	15,094	C
Univ of Miss	MS	15,482	VC
Univ of Missouri/Columbia	MO	18,201	MC
Univ of Nebr - Lincoln	NE	17,507	VC
Univ of Nebr at Kearney	NE	14,855	LC
Univ of Nevada/Reno	NV	14,500	NC
Univ of North Alabama	AL	9,960	C
Univ of N Car at Charlotte	NC	15,847	C
Univ of N Car at Greensboro	NC	12,848	C
Univ of N Car at Wilmington	NC	13,572	VC+
Univ of N Dak	ND	14,094	C
Univ of North Florida	FL	15,578	VC
Univ of Okla	OK	17,004	VC+
Univ of Pittsburgh at Johnstown	PA	20,862	LC
Univ of PR Recinto de Rio Piedras	PR	5,750	
Univ of PR/Mayaguez	PR	1,250	
Univ of Rio Grande	OH	8,750	NC
Univ of San Diego	CA	53,302	HC+
Univ of Scranton	PA	51,940	VC
Univ of Sioux Falls	SD	22,990	C
Univ of South Alabama	AL	13,510	C
Univ of S Car at Columbia	SC	19,725	VC+
Univ of South Florida	FL	13,000	C
Univ of Southern Miss	MS	13,170	C
Univ of Tampa	FL	35,160	VC
Univ of Tenn at Martin	TN	13,217	C
Univ of Texas at Arlington	TX	10,908	LC
Univ of Texas at El Paso	TX	8,764	NC
Univ of Washington	WA	14,722	VC
Univ of West Florida	FL	14,656	C
Univ of West Georgia	GA	14,852	LC
Univ of Wisc Whitewater	WI	13,314	C
Univ of Wyoming	WY	13,855	C+
Ursinus College	PA	55,630	VC+
Utah State Univ	UT	11,803	C
Utica College	NY	44,734	C
Villanova Univ	PA	56,436	MC
Virginia Military Inst	VA	16,156	C
Virginia Polytechnic Inst and State Univ	VA	14,629	HC
Warren Wilson College	NC	34,888	VC
Washburn Univ	KS	12,165	NC
Washington State Univ	WA	20,461	C
Washington Univ in St. Louis	MO	58,818	MC
West Liberty Univ	WV	9,142	LC
West Texas A&M Univ	TX	13,478	C
Western Kentucky Univ	KY	11,000	LC
Western Mich Univ	MI	19,042	C
Westmont College	CA	41,500	HC
Wheaton College	IL	39,650	HC+
Widener Univ	PA	50,368	C
Wilberforce Univ	OH	15,100	LC
William Jewell College	MO	31,000	VC+
Wilson College	PA	27,660	C
Winona State Univ	MN	16,530	C
Wisc Lutheran College	WI	23,510	VC
Wofford College	SC	45,795	VC
Wright State Univ	OH	16,983	C
Xavier Univ	OH	43,740	VC
Xavier Univ of Louisiana	LA	25,300	C
Youngstown State Univ	OH	16,374	LC

BUSINESS EDUCATION

School	ST	$IS	SR
Adams State College	CO	13,358	LC
Alabama State Univ	AL	14,142	NC
Alfred Univ	NY	40,392	VC
Appalachian State Univ	NC	12,919	VC
Arkansas State Univ	AR	14,980	C
Arkansas Tech Univ	AR	13,164	LC
Ashford Univ	IA	21,780	C
Auburn Univ	AL	20,052	VC+
Avila Univ	MO	26,900	C
Ball State Univ	IN	17,850	C
Baylor Univ	TX	46,720	HC
Bethany College	KS	30,605	NC
Bethel Univ	MN	34,940	VC
Bethune-Cookman Univ	FL	22,290	LC
Black Hills State Univ	SD	13,562	LC
Bloomsburg Univ of Pennsylvania	PA	13,598	C
Bowling Green State Univ	OH	18,970	C
Brigham Young Univ/ Hawaii	HI	8,614	VC
Bryant Univ	RI	49,179	VC
Buena Vista Univ	IA	37,954	C
Buffalo State/State Univ of Buffalo	NY	15,733	C+
Cal State, Northridge	CA	28,313	C
Cal State, Sacramento	CA	16,200	C
Canisius College	NY	45,602	VC
Caribbean Univ	PR	10,375	
Central Mich Univ	MI	18,066	C
Central Washington Univ	WA	11,730	C
Chicago State Univ	IL	5,482	C
Clark Atlanta Univ	GA	30,006	C
College of the Ozarks	MO	5,605	VC
Concord Univ	WV	13,102	C
Concordia College, Moorhead	MN	39,974	C+
Concordia Univ Nebr	NE	26,000	VC
Corban Univ	OR	34,764	C
Dakota State Univ	SD	13,811	C
Delaware State Univ	DE	14,700	LC
Dickinson State Univ	ND	8,550	NC
Doane College	NE	33,730	VC
Dordt College	IA	34,160	VC
East Carolina Univ	NC	14,169	C
East Central Univ	OK	10,223	LC
Eastern Kentucky Univ	KY	11,161	C
Eastern Mich Univ	MI	17,961	C
Eastern New Mexico Univ	NM	10,682	C
Elizabeth City State Univ	NC	11,638	C
Emporia State Univ	KS	12,897	C
Evangel Univ	MO	23,090	C
Fairmont State Univ	WV	12,098	LC
Fayetteville State Univ	NC	10,816	C
Ferris State Univ	MI	19,698	C
Florida A&M Univ	FL	14,935	LC
Framingham State Univ	MA	16,750	C
Friends Univ	KS	29,100	C
Georgia Southwestern State Univ	GA	12,218	C
Glenville State College	WV	11,348	NC
Goshen College	IN	35,900	VC
Grace College and Theological Seminary	IN	28,800	C
Gustavus Adolphus College	MN	48,170	HC
Gwynedd-Mercy College	PA	33,560	C
Hardin-Simmons Univ	TX	23,560	C+
Hastings College	NE	27,782	C+
Henderson State Univ	AR	13,634	C
Hofstra Univ	NY	48,020	VC+
Humboldt State Univ	CA	18,400	C
Illinois State Univ	IL	22,634	VC
Indiana State Univ	IN	16,000	C
Jackson State Univ	MS	13,512	LC
Lakeland College	WI	22,990	C
Langston Univ	OK	3,000	LC
Lee Univ	TN	18,690	C+
Lehman College / The CUNY	NY	5,778	LC
LeTourneau Univ	TX	26,230	C
Lincoln Memorial Univ	TN	18,144	C
Lincoln Univ	MO	11,996	NC
Lindenwood Univ	MO	20,750	C
LIU/Brooklyn Campus	NY	26,500	C
Louisiana College	LA	15,746	C
Lubbock Christian Univ	TX	25,518	C
McKendree Univ	IL	29,920	C+
McMurry Univ	TX	25,962	LC
Mercyhurst Univ	PA	40,700	C
MidAmerica Nazarene Univ	KS	28,000	C
Middle Tenn State Univ	TN	8,650	C
Midland Univ	NE	34,000	C
Minot State Univ	ND	10,915	C
Miss College	MS	21,998	VC
Missouri Baptist Univ	MO	30,310	C
Missouri Southern State Univ	MO	11,910	C
Missouri State Univ	MO	13,996	VC
Montana State Univ-Northern	MT	12,500	NC
Montclair State Univ	NJ	22,614	C
Morehead State Univ	KY	10,900	C
Mount Mary Univ	WI	32,836	LC
Mount Vernon Nazarene Univ	OH	29,590	C
Nazareth College of Rochester	NY	41,590	VC
New York Inst of Technology	NY	40,590	VC
Niagara Univ	NY	39,800	C
Nicholls State Univ	LA	7,095	C
Norfolk State Univ	VA	10,531	LC
N Car Agricultural and Technical State Univ	NC	13,175	LC
Northern Kentucky Univ	KY	15,302	LC
Northern Mich Univ	MI	15,300	VC
Northern State Univ	SD	14,021	C
Northwest Missouri State Univ	MO	14,229	C
Northwestern College of Iowa	IA	34,848	C+
Northwestern Okla State Univ	OK	7,275	NC
Oakland City Univ	IN	24,500	NC
Oakwood Univ	AL	23,035	C
Oglala Lakota College	SD	2,000	NC
Ohio Univ	OH	20,676	VC
Okla Panhandle State Univ	OK	8,996	NC
Okla Wesleyan Univ	OK	21,300	C
Oral Roberts Univ	OK	31,734	C
Oswego / SUNY	NY	20,009	VC
Ouachita Baptist Univ	AR	29,010	VC
Philander Smith College	AR	19,760	LC
Pontifical Catholic Univ of PR	PR	7,310	
Rider Univ	NJ	45,720	C
Robert Morris Univ	PA	36,699	C
Rust College	MS	10,600	C
Sacred Heart Univ	CT	48,564	VC
St. Augustine's Univ	NC	14,000	C
St. Mary's Univ	TX	33,854	C
St. Paul's College	VA	16,030	NC
St. Vincent College	PA	40,244	C
Salem State College	MA	13,161	LC
Shippensburg Univ of Pennsylvania	PA	17,064	LC
Siena Heights Univ	MI	17,000	LC
S Car State Univ	SC	6,700	LC
Southeast Missouri State Univ	MO	14,983	LC
Southeastern Okla State Univ	OK	7,966	C
Southern Arkansas Univ	AR	14,316	C
Southern New Hampshire Univ	NH	38,100	C
Southern Univ at New Orleans	LA	1,000	NC
Southwestern Adventist Univ	TX	23,026	LC
Suffolk Univ	MA	46,548	C
SUNY Oneonta / SUNY	NY	16,919	VC
Tabor College	KS	29,010	LC
Tarleton State Univ	TX	13,489	LC
Texas A&M Univ at Commerce	TX	10,496	C
Thomas College	ME	26,270	LC
Thomas More College	KY	34,760	C
Trevecca Nazarene Univ	TN	30,118	C
Union College	NE	23,270	VC
Univ of Arkansas at Fayetteville	AR	16,860	VC
Univ of Arkansas at Pine Bluff	AR	10,600	C
Univ of Central Florida	FL	15,711	VC+
Univ of Central Missouri	MO	14,605	C
Univ of Cincinnati	OH	20,199	VC
Univ of Idaho	ID	14,558	C
Univ of Indianapolis	IN	31,740	LC
Univ of Kentucky	KY	19,868	C
Univ of Louisville	KY	17,460	VC
Univ of Maine at Machias	ME	10,523	C
Univ of Maryland/Eastern Shore	MD	14,000	C
Univ of Minn/Twin Cities	MN		HC
Univ of Montana-Western	MT	9,753	LC
Univ of Nebr - Lincoln	NE	17,507	VC
Univ of Nebr at Kearney	NE	14,855	LC
Univ of North Alabama	AL	9,960	C
Univ of N Dak	ND	14,094	C
Univ of Northern Iowa	IA	14,776	C
Univ of Pittsburgh at Bradford	PA	21,316	LC
Univ of Rio Grande	OH	8,750	NC
Univ of St. Francis	IN	29,810	C
Univ of South Florida	FL	13,000	C
Univ of Southern Indiana	IN	14,657	C
Univ of Southern Miss	MS	13,170	C
Univ of St. Thomas - Houston	TX	36,490	VC
Univ of the Cumberlands	KY	27,500	LC
Univ of the Ozarks	AR	22,100	C
Univ of Toledo	OH	18,464	C
Univ of West Georgia	GA	14,852	LC
Univ of Wisc Whitewater	WI	13,314	C
Utah State Univ	UT	11,803	C
Valley City State Univ	ND	12,286	LC
Vermont Technical College	VT	15,751	C
Virginia Polytechnic Inst and State Univ	VA	14,629	HC
Virginia State Univ	VA	11,318	C+
Virginia Union Univ	VA	18,432	C
Viterbo Univ	WI	30,070	C
Walla Walla Univ	WA	26,256	NC
Warner Univ	FL	18,000	C
Wayland Baptist Univ	TX	16,058	LC
West Texas A&M Univ	TX	13,478	C
Western Kentucky Univ	KY	11,000	LC
Western Mich Univ	MI	19,042	C
Western New Mexico Univ	NM	8,500	LC
Wiley College	TX		LC
Winona State Univ	MN	16,530	C
Wright State Univ	OH	16,983	C

BUSINESS INFORMATION SYSTEMS

School	ST	$IS	SR
Biola Univ	CA	40,320	VC
Bryant Univ	RI	49,179	VC
CUNY/Brooklyn College	NY	5,884	C+
Lehigh Univ	PA	55,080	MC
Texas Christian Univ	TX	47,570	HC
Univ of Arkansas at Fayetteville	AR	16,860	VC
Univ of Illinois at Chicago	IL	24,293	VC
Univ of Pittsburgh at Pittsburgh	PA	27,800	HC+

BUSINESS INTELLIGENCE AND ANALYTICS

School	ST	$IS	SR
Bryant Univ	RI	49,179	VC
College of St. Mary	NE	34,334	C
Creighton Univ	NE	44,058	VC+
Old Dominion Univ	VA	18,662	C
St. Mary's Univ of Minn	MN	37,015	C

BUSINESS LAW

School	ST	$IS	SR
Adams State College	CO	13,358	LC
Arizona State Univ	AZ	18,818	C+
Bryant Univ	RI	49,179	VC
Cal State, Fresno	CA	17,405	C
Hofstra Univ	NY	48,020	VC+
Lamar Univ	TX	6,820	LC

INDEX OF COLLEGE MAJORS

School	ST	$IS	SR
Mountain State Univ	WV	14,330	NC
New York Univ	NY	61,470	MC
Ohio Univ	OH	20,676	VC
Peirce College	PA	12,760	NC
Roger Williams Univ	RI	45,788	C
Warner Univ	FL	18,000	C
Washington State Univ	WA	20,461	C
Western Carolina Univ	NC	13,965	₲

BUSINESS STATISTICS

School	ST	$IS	SR
Arizona State Univ	AZ	18,818	₲
Baylor Univ	TX	46,720	HC
Bryant Univ	RI	49,179	VC
Univ of Denver	CO	51,787	V₲
Univ of PR Recinto de Rio Piedras	PR	5,750	
Univ of Texas at San Antonio	TX	18,372	C
Washington State Univ	WA	20,461	C

BUSINESS SYSTEMS ANALYSIS

School	ST	$IS	SR
Baylor Univ	TX	46,720	HC
Bryant Univ	RI	49,179	VC
CUNY/Brooklyn College	NY	5,884	₲
Clarkson Univ	NY	53,538	HC
Eastern Mich Univ	MI	17,961	C
Elizabethtown College	PA	47,600	VC
Husson Univ	ME	23,386	LC
Johnson State College	VT	16,721	C
Louisiana Tech Univ	LA	8,000	C
Montana Tech of The Univ of Montana	MT	14,650	VC
Oregon State Univ	OR	19,017	₲
Rochester Inst of Technology	NY	42,450	V₲
Stevenson Univ	MD	39,572	C
Texas A&M Univ	TX	16,956	V₲
Univ of Findlay	OH	31,916	C
Univ of N Car at Wilmington	NC	13,572	V₲
Univ of Tenn at Knoxville	TN	20,364	V₲

CANADIAN STUDIES

School	ST	$IS	SR
Duke Univ	NC	50,250	MC
Franklin College	IN	35,885	C
St. Lawrence Univ	NY	53,740	HC
SUNY Plattsburgh / SUNY	NY	18,083	VC
Univ of Washington	WA	14,722	VC
Western Washington Univ	WA	18,519	VC

CARDIAC SONOGRAPHY

School	ST	$IS	SR
St. Mary's Univ of Minn	MN	37,015	C
Thomas Edison State College	NJ	5,700	SP

CAREER, TECHNICAL EDUCATION & TRAINING

School	ST	$IS	SR
Temple Univ	PA	24,392	VC
Univ of Arkansas at Fayetteville	AR	16,860	VC
Univ of Wisc/Stout	WI	23,942	C
Wright State Univ	OH	16,983	C

CARIBBEAN STUDIES

School	ST	$IS	SR
Binghamton Univ / The SUNY	NY	20,832	H₲
Burlington College	VT	32,510	SP
CUNY/Brooklyn College	NY	5,884	₲
Emory Univ	GA	45,000	MC
Florida State Univ	FL	15,238	HC
Hofstra Univ	NY	48,020	V₲
Pitzer College	CA	54,988	MC
Union College	NY		MC
Univ at Albany / SUNY	NY	18,674	VC
Univ of Mich/Ann Arbor	MI	22,102	H₲

CARTOGRAPHY

School	ST	$IS	SR
East Central Univ	OK	10,223	LC
Salem State College	MA	13,161	LC
Texas State Univ	TX	16,495	VC
Univ of Wisc/Madison	WI	18,757	HC

CELL BIOLOGY

School	ST	$IS	SR
Adams State College	CO	13,358	LC
Auburn Univ	AL	20,052	V₲
Beloit College	WI	49,970	HC
Bethel College	IN	31,560	C
Binghamton Univ / The SUNY	NY	20,832	H₲
Bucknell Univ	PA	58,160	MC
Cal State, Long Beach	CA	17,534	₲
Canisius College	NY	45,602	VC
Dallas Baptist Univ	TX	29,118	C
Florida State Univ	FL	15,238	HC
Grand Valley State Univ	MI	17,998	VC
Huntingdon College	AL	31,850	C
John Carroll Univ	OH	44,520	₲
Johns Hopkins Univ	MD	47,492	MC
Johnson State College	VT	16,721	C
Marshall Univ	WV	14,820	C
Missouri State Univ	MO	13,996	VC
Montana State Univ	MT	14,068	VC
New York Univ	NY	61,470	MC
Northwest Nazarene Univ	ID	24,275	NC
Ohio Univ	OH	20,676	VC
Okla City Univ	OK	33,546	VC
Okla State Univ	OK	14,310	VC
Pittsburg State Univ	KS	12,032	C
Purdue Univ/West Lafayette	IN	20,278	HC
Rutgers, The State Univ of New Jersey/New Brunswick	NJ	25,077	VC
San Francisco State Univ	CA	18,514	C
Seattle Univ	WA	47,010	V₲
Texas Tech Univ	TX	14,243	C
Tulane Univ	LA	58,942	MC
Univ of Arizona	AZ	20,105	C
Univ of Calif at Irvine	CA	25,961	VC
Univ of Calif at Los Angeles	CA	25,686	MC
Univ of Calif at Riverside	CA	27,204	C
Univ of Calif at Santa Barbara	CA	27,551	HC
Univ of Calif at Santa Cruz	CA	27,807	VC
Univ of Illinois at Urbana-Champaign	IL	24,300	HC
Univ of Maine	ME	19,712	₲
Univ of Mich/Ann Arbor	MI	22,102	H₲
Univ of Minn/Duluth	MN	18,964	₲
Univ of Minn/Twin Cities	MN		HC
Univ of Montana-Western	MT	9,753	LC
Univ of Puget Sound	WA	52,648	H₲
Univ of Rochester	NY	58,500	MC
Washington and Jefferson College	PA	49,990	VC
Washington State Univ	WA	20,461	C
West Chester Univ of Pennsylvania	PA	16,836	C
Western Washington Univ	WA	18,519	VC

CELTIC STUDIES

School	ST	$IS	SR
Bard College	NY	59,872	HC
Univ of Calif at Berkeley	CA	23,322	MC

CERAMIC ART AND DESIGN

School	ST	$IS	SR
Adams State College	CO	13,358	LC
Alfred Univ	NY	40,392	VC
Andrews Univ	MI	28,030	₲
Aquinas College	MI	33,060	C
Arizona State Univ	AZ	18,818	₲
Bard College at Simon's Rock	MA	58,963	H₲
Bennington College	VT	56,990	H₲
Calif College of the Arts	CA	48,334	SP
Cal State, San Bernardino	CA	12,000	C
Cleveland Inst of Art	OH	48,641	SP
College for Creative Studies	MI		SP
Columbia College	MO	24,578	C
Hofstra Univ	NY	48,020	V₲
Howard Univ	DC	35,957	C
Indiana Univ Southeast	IN	15,807	LC
Indiana Univ-Purdue Univ Indianapolis	IN	17,290	C
Indiana Wesleyan Univ	IN	31,815	VC
Kansas City Art Inst	MO	38,000	SP
Kent State Univ	OH	19,352	C
Kutztown Univ of Pennsylvania	PA	16,909	LC
Marshall Univ	WV	14,820	C
Maryland Inst College of Art	MD	39,500	SP
Marywood Univ	PA	40,695	C
Mass College of Art and Design	MA	23,600	SP
Northwest Nazarene Univ	ID	24,275	NC
Ohio Northern Univ	OH	42,075	VC
Ohio Univ	OH	20,676	VC
Pittsburg State Univ	KS	12,032	C
Rhode Island School of Design	RI	55,204	SP
Rochester Inst of Technology	NY	42,450	V₲
School of the Art Inst of Chicago	IL	44,000	SP
Syracuse Univ	NY	54,512	HC
Temple Univ	PA	24,392	VC
Texas Christian Univ	TX	47,570	HC
The Catholic Univ of America	DC	52,852	VC
Univ of Dallas	TX	43,510	V₲
Univ of Hartford	CT	42,674	C
Univ of Iowa	IA	17,481	VC
Univ of Kansas	KS	16,980	₲
Univ of Mass Dartmouth	MA	22,223	C
Univ of Miami	FL	55,166	MC
Univ of Mich/Ann Arbor	MI	22,102	H₲
Univ of Oregon	OR	20,872	VC
Washington Univ in St. Louis	MO	58,818	MC
Webster Univ	MO	33,990	₲
Western Washington Univ	WA	18,519	VC

CERAMIC ENGINEERING

School	ST	$IS	SR
Alfred Univ	NY	40,392	VC
Clemson Univ	SC	19,136	HC
Missouri Univ of Science and Technology	MO	18,655	V₲
Rutgers, The State Univ of New Jersey/New Brunswick	NJ	25,077	VC
Univ of Illinois at Urbana-Champaign	IL	24,300	HC
Univ of Washington	WA	14,722	VC

CERAMIC SCIENCE

School	ST	$IS	SR
Maine College of Art	ME	28,812	SP

CHEMICAL ENGINEERING

School	ST	$IS	SR
Arizona State Univ	AZ	18,818	₲
Auburn Univ	AL	20,052	V₲
Bethel College	IN	31,560	C
Brigham Young Univ	UT	12,100	HC
Bucknell Univ	PA	58,160	MC
Calif Inst of Technology	CA	54,045	MC
Calif State Polytechnic Univ, Pomona	CA	18,932	C
Cal State, Long Beach	CA	17,534	₲
Calvin College	MI	37,585	V₲
Carnegie Mellon Univ	PA	51,260	MC
Case Western Reserve Univ	OH	55,178	MC
Christian Brothers Univ	TN	19,140	HC
Clarkson Univ	NY	53,538	HC
Clemson Univ	SC	19,136	HC
Cleveland State Univ	OH	21,357	C
Colo School of Mines	CO	18,000	HC
Colo State Univ-Fort Collins	CO	20,090	VC
Columbia Univ in the City of New York	NY	61,116	MC
Cooper Union for the Advancement of Science and Art	NY	55,600	MC
Cornell Univ	NY	59,037	MC
CUNY-City College	NY	19,576	H₲
Delaware State Univ	DE	14,700	LC
Dordt College	IA	34,160	VC
Drexel Univ	PA	51,920	HC
Elon Univ	NC	40,046	HC
Florida A&M Univ	FL	14,935	LC
Florida Inst of Technology	FL	48,290	VC
Florida State Univ	FL	15,238	HC
Geneva College	PA	27,280	C
Georgia Inst of Technology	GA	20,464	MC
Hampton Univ	VA	28,528	C
Howard Univ	DC	35,957	C
Illinois Inst of Technology	IL	38,512	H₲
Iowa State Univ	IA	16,403	C
Johns Hopkins Univ	MD	47,492	MC
Kansas State Univ	KS	15,497	VC
Lafayette College	PA	57,050	H₲
Lamar Univ	TX	6,820	LC
Lehigh Univ	PA	55,080	MC
Louisiana State Univ	LA	18,677	V₲
Louisiana Tech Univ	LA	8,000	C
Manhattan College	NY	44,955	VC
Mass Inst of Technology	MA	54,238	MC
Miami Univ	OH	24,191	HC
Mich State Univ	MI	13,689	VC
Mich Tech Univ	MI	22,105	VC
Missouri Univ of Science and Technology	MO	18,655	V₲
Montana State Univ	MT	14,068	VC
New Jersey Inst of Technology	NJ	26,490	VC
New Mexico Inst of Mining and Technology	NM	12,892	HC
New Mexico State Univ	NM	13,955	LC
New York Univ	NY	61,470	MC
N Car Agricultural and Technical State Univ	NC	13,175	LC
N Car State Univ	NC	16,202	HC
Northeastern Univ	MA	55,296	MC
Northwestern Univ	IL	37,595	MC
Ohio Univ	OH	20,676	VC
Okla State Univ	OK	14,310	VC
Oregon State Univ	OR	19,017	₲
Penn State Univ/Univ Park	PA	25,404	VC
Polytechnic Inst of New York Univ	NY	53,064	H₲
Prairie View A&M Univ	TX	15,205	LC
Princeton Univ	NJ	53,795	MC
Purdue Univ/West Lafayette	IN	20,278	HC
Rensselaer Polytechnic Inst	NY	59,229	MC
Rice Univ	TX	43,288	MC
Rochester Inst of Technology	NY	42,450	V₲
Rose-Hulman Inst of Technology	IN	51,738	MC
Rowan Univ	NJ	23,570	VC
Rutgers, The State Univ of New Jersey/New Brunswick	NJ	25,077	VC
San Jose State Univ	CA	19,707	C
S Dak School of Mines and Technology	SD	15,260	VC
Stanford Univ	CA	56,411	MC
SUNY / College of Environmental Science and Forestry	NY	18,351	HC
Stevens Inst of Technology	NJ	50,130	HC
Stony Brook Univ / SUNY	NY	19,359	HC
Syracuse Univ	NY	54,512	HC
Tenn Tech Univ	TN	11,310	C
Texas A&M Univ	TX	16,956	V₲
Texas A&M Univ at Kingsville	TX	7,500	LC
Texas Tech Univ	TX	14,243	C
Ohio State Univ	OH	19,887	MC
Trine Univ	IN	39,400	VC
Tufts Univ	MA	58,780	MC
Tulane Univ	LA	58,942	MC
Tuskegee Univ	AL	26,750	C
Universidad Politecnica de PR	PR	19,252	
Univ at Buffalo / The SUNY	NY	20,283	VC
Univ of Akron	OH	20,436	C
Univ of Alabama at Huntsville	AL	17,625	VC
Univ of Alabama at Tuscaloosa	AL	17,164	₲
Univ of Arizona	AZ	20,105	C
Univ of Arkansas at Fayetteville	AR	16,860	VC
Univ of Calif at Berkeley	CA	23,322	MC
Univ of Calif at Davis	CA	24,482	HC
Univ of Calif at Irvine	CA	25,961	VC
Univ of Calif at Los Angeles	CA	25,686	MC
Univ of Calif at Riverside	CA	27,204	C
Univ of Calif at San Diego	CA	21,000	VC
Univ of Calif at Santa Barbara	CA	27,551	HC
Univ of Cincinnati	OH	20,199	VC
Univ of Colo Boulder	CO	22,605	V₲
Univ of Conn	CT	23,744	HC
Univ of Dayton	OH	43,750	VC
Univ of Delaware	DE	22,728	VC
Univ of Florida	FL	15,783	H₲
Univ of Houston	TX	19,184	VC
Univ of Idaho	ID	14,558	C
Univ of Illinois at Chicago	IL	24,293	VC
Univ of Illinois at Urbana-Champaign	IL	24,300	HC
Univ of Iowa	IA	17,481	VC
Univ of Kansas	KS	16,980	₲
Univ of Kentucky	KY	19,868	C
Univ of Louisiana at Lafayette	LA	6,130	C
Univ of Louisville	KY	17,460	VC
Univ of Maine	ME	19,712	₲
Univ of Maryland	MD	18,801	HC
Univ of Maryland/Baltimore County	MD	18,000	VC
Univ of Mass Amherst	MA	23,697	V₲
Univ of Mass Lowell	MA	19,316	C
Univ of Mich/Ann Arbor	MI	22,102	H₲
Univ of Minn/Duluth	MN	18,964	₲
Univ of Minn/Twin Cities	MN		HC
Univ of Miss	MS	15,482	VC
Univ of Missouri/Columbia	MO	18,201	MC
Univ of Nebr - Lincoln	NE	17,507	VC
Univ of Nevada/Reno	NV	14,500	NC
Univ of New Hampshire	NH	24,702	VC
Univ of New Haven	CT	47,740	C
Univ of New Mexico	NM	15,300	C
Univ of N Dak	ND	14,094	C
Univ of Notre Dame	IN		MC
Univ of Okla	OK	17,634	V₲
Univ of Pennsylvania	PA	56,106	MC
Univ of Pittsburgh at Pittsburgh	PA	27,800	H₲
Univ of PR/Mayaguez	PR	1,250	
Univ of Rochester	NY	58,500	MC
Univ of South Alabama	AL	13,510	C
Univ of S Car at Columbia	SC	19,725	V₲
Univ of South Florida	FL	13,000	C
Univ of Southern Calif	CA	56,903	MC
Univ of Tenn at Chattanooga	TN	16,883	C
Univ of Tenn at Knoxville	TN	20,364	V₲
Univ of Texas at Austin	TX	44,074	HC
Univ of Toledo	OH	18,464	C
Univ of Tulsa	OK	45,311	H₲
Univ of Utah	UT	13,462	VC
Univ of Virginia	VA	22,175	MC
Univ of Washington	WA	14,722	VC
Univ of Wisc/Madison	WI	18,757	HC
Univ of Wyoming	WY	13,855	₲
Vanderbilt Univ	TN	57,072	MC
Villanova Univ	PA	56,436	MC
Virginia Commonwealth Univ	VA	18,633	C
Virginia Polytechnic Inst and State Univ	VA	14,629	HC
Washington and Lee Univ	VA	52,812	MC
Washington State Univ	WA	20,461	C
Washington Univ in St. Louis	MO	58,818	MC
Wayne State Univ	MI	19,493	C
West Virginia Univ	WV	15,794	₲

School	ST	$IS	SR
West Virginia Univ Inst of Technology	WV	14,094	NC
Western Mich Univ	MI	19,042	C
Widener Univ	PA	50,368	C
Worcester Polytechnic Inst	MA	53,440	HC+
Yale Univ	CT	55,300	MC
Youngstown State Univ	OH	16,374	LC

CHEMICAL ENGINEERING TECHNOLOGY

School	ST	$IS	SR
Purdue Univ/West Lafayette	IN	20,278	HC
Univ of Hartford	CT	42,674	C
Univ of PR/Arecibo	PR	7,227	

CHEMICAL PHYSICS

School	ST	$IS	SR
Adams State College	CO	13,358	LC
Augustana College	SD	35,500	VC
Bowdoin College	ME	57,834	MC
Brown Univ	RI	56,150	MC
Centre College	KY	35,000	HC+
Hamilton College	NY	55,620	MC
Hendrix College	AR	48,436	HC+
Maryville College	TN	33,150	VC
Mich State Univ	MI	13,689	VC
Reed College	OR	57,780	MC
Saginaw Valley State Univ	MI	16,869	C
San Diego State Univ	CA	20,578	VC
Swarthmore College	PA	57,870	MC
The Catholic Univ of America	DC	52,852	VC
Tufts Univ	MA	58,780	MC

CHEMICAL TECHNOLOGY

School	ST	$IS	SR
Florida State Univ	FL	15,238	HC
Inter-American Univ of PR/ Arecibo Campus	PR	3,350	
Inter-American Univ of PR/ Bayamon Univ College	PR	4,428	
Inter-American Univ of PR/ Fajardo Campus	PR	4,200	
Inter-American Univ of PR/ Ponce	PR	3,700	
Midwestern State Univ	TX	9,722	C
Univ of Cincinnati	OH	20,199	VC

CHEMISTRY

School	ST	$IS	SR
Abilene Christian Univ	TX	38,400	VC
Adams State College	CO	13,358	LC
Adelphi Univ	NY	43,130	VC
Adrian College	MI	33,800	C
Agnes Scott College	GA	45,323	VC+
Alabama A&M Univ	AL	96,100	C
Alabama State Univ	AL	14,142	NC
Albany College of Pharmacy and Health Sciences	NY	38,900	SP
Albany State Univ	GA	8,500	C
Albion College	MI	43,884	VC
Albright College	PA	46,660	C
Alcorn State Univ	MS	9,500	C
Alderson Broaddus Univ	WV	28,656	C
Alfred Univ	NY	40,392	VC
Allegheny College	PA	49,020	HC
Alma College	MI	42,400	VC
Alvernia Univ	PA	39,250	C
Alverno College	WI	30,483	LC
American International College	MA	36,100	LC
American Univ	DC	54,829	HC+
Amherst College	MA	58,744	MC
Anderson Univ	IN	35,390	C
Andrews Univ	MI	28,030	C+
Angelo State Univ	TX	15,049	NC
Appalachian State Univ	NC	12,919	VC
Aquinas College	MI	33,060	C
Arcadia Univ	PA	33,570	C+
Arizona State Univ	AZ	18,818	C+
Arkansas State Univ	AR	14,980	C
Arkansas Tech Univ	AR	13,164	LC
Armstrong Atlantic State Univ	GA	16,276	C
Asbury Univ	KY	32,038	VC
Ashland Univ	OH	25,000	C
Assumption College	MA	45,721	VC
Auburn Univ	AL	20,052	VC+
Augsburg College	MN	35,142	C
Augustana College	IL	43,398	HC
Augustana College	SD	35,500	VC
Austin College	TX	36,940	HC
Austin Peay State Univ	TN	14,650	C
Avila Univ	MO	26,900	C
Azusa Pacific Univ	CA	39,946	C
Baker Univ	KS	33,350	C+
Baldwin Wallace Univ	OH	36,980	VC
Ball State Univ	IN	17,850	C
Bard College	NY	59,872	HC
Bard College at Simon's Rock	MA	58,963	HC+
Barry Univ	FL	38,190	C
Barton College	NC	27,660	C
Bates College	ME	58,950	MC
Baylor Univ	TX	46,720	HC
Belhaven Univ	MS	27,170	C
Bellarmine Univ	KY	42,950	VC
Belmont Univ	TN	37,380	VC+
Beloit College	WI	49,970	HC
Bemidji State Univ	MN	13,500	C
Benedict College	SC	20,454	NC
Benedictine College	KS	29,180	VC
Benedictine Univ	IL	35,220	C
Bennett College	NC		LC
Bennington College	VT	56,990	HC+
Berea College	KY	7,220	HC
Berry College	GA	39,254	HC
Bethany College	KS	30,605	NC
Bethany College	WV	35,282	C
Bethel College	IN	31,500	C
Bethel College	KS	29,100	C
Bethel Univ	MN	34,940	VC
Bethel Univ	TN	19,186	C
Bethune-Cookman Univ	FL	22,290	LC
Binghamton Univ / The SUNY	NY	20,832	HC+
Biola Univ	CA	40,320	VC
Birmingham-Southern College	AL	42,370	VC+
Black Hills State Univ	SD	13,562	LC
Blackburn College	IL	21,350	C
Bloomfield College	NJ	36,960	C
Bloomsburg Univ of Pennsylvania	PA	13,598	C
Bluefield College	VA	17,230	C+
Bluffton Univ	OH	37,864	C
Boise State Univ	ID	12,802	C
Boston College	MA	58,506	MC
Boston Univ	MA	54,130	HC+
Bowdoin College	ME	57,834	MC
Bowling Green State Univ	OH	18,970	C
Bradley Univ	IL	31,874	VC
Brandeis Univ	MA	58,820	HC
Brescia Univ	KY	26,140	VC+
Briar Cliff Univ	IA	29,514	C
Bridgewater College	VA	39,880	C
Bridgewater State Univ	MA	18,752	C
Brigham Young Univ	UT	12,100	HC
Brown Univ	RI	56,150	MC
Bryn Mawr College	PA	57,760	MC
Bucknell Univ	PA	58,160	MC
Buena Vista Univ	IA	37,954	C
Buffalo State/State Univ of Buffalo	NY	15,733	C+
Butler Univ	IN	45,898	VC+
Cabrini College	PA	40,859	LC
Caldwell College	NJ	35,602	LC
Calif Baptist Univ	CA	35,890	C
Calif Inst of Technology	CA	54,045	MC
Calif Lutheran Univ	CA	47,640	C
Calif Polytechnic State Univ	CA	19,847	HC
Calif State Polytechnic Univ, Pomona	CA	18,932	C
Cal State, Bakersfield	CA	8,000	LC
Cal State, Chico	CA	18,952	C
Cal State, Dominguez Hills	CA	17,056	LC
Cal State, East Bay	CA	16,549	C
Cal State, Fresno	CA	17,405	C
Cal State, Fullerton	CA	25,188	C+
Cal State, Long Beach	CA	17,534	C+
Cal State, Los Angeles	CA	15,829	C
Cal State, Northridge	CA	28,313	C
Cal State, Sacramento	CA	16,200	C
Cal State, San Bernardino	CA	12,000	C
Cal State, San Marcos	CA	14,576	C
Cal State, Stanislaus	CA	18,582	C
Calif Univ of Pennsylvania	PA	14,217	C
Calvin College	MI	37,585	VC+
Cameron Univ	OK	9,267	LC
Campbell Univ	NC	25,500	C
Campbellsville Univ	KY	27,720	C
Canisius College	NY	45,602	VC
Capital Univ	OH	39,824	VC
Cardinal Stritch Univ	WI	24,054	C
Carleton College	MN	58,149	MC
Carlow Univ	PA	30,272	C
Carnegie Mellon Univ	PA	51,260	MC
Carroll College	MT	28,000	C
Carroll Univ	WI	24,860	C
Carthage College	WI	33,000	C
Case Western Reserve Univ	OH	55,178	MC
Catawba College	NC	37,105	C
Cedar Crest College	PA	43,240	C
Cedarville Univ	OH	31,036	VC+
Centenary College of Louisiana	LA	39,070	C+
Central College	IA	36,980	VC
Central Conn State Univ	CT	19,212	C
Central Methodist Univ	MO	28,240	VC
Central Mich Univ	MI	18,066	C
Central State Univ	OH	9,010	C
Central Univ of Bayamon	PR	3,350	
Central Washington Univ	WA	11,730	C
Centre College	KY	35,000	HC+
Chadron State College	NE	7,400	NC
Chapman Univ	CA	56,019	VC+
Charleston Southern Univ	SC	22,420	C
Chatham Univ	PA	42,440	VC
Chestnut Hill College	PA	39,785	LC
Cheyney Univ of Pennsylvania	PA	20,372	LC
Chicago State Univ	IL	5,482	C
Christian Brothers Univ	TN	19,140	HC
Christopher Newport Univ	VA	21,050	VC
Citadel, The	SC		C
CUNY/Brooklyn College	NY	5,884	C+
Claflin Univ	SC	22,368	C+
Claremont McKenna College	CA	58,065	MC
Clarion Univ of Pennsylvania	PA	17,370	C
Clark Atlanta Univ	GA	30,006	C
Clark Univ	MA	47,020	HC+
Clarke Univ	IA	36,400	C
Clarkson Univ	NY	53,538	HC
Clemson Univ	SC	19,136	HC
Cleveland State Univ	OH	21,357	C
Coastal Carolina Univ	SC	17,620	C
Coe College	IA	43,590	VC
Coker College	SC	32,256	LC
Colby College	ME	57,510	MC
Colgate Univ	NY	50,930	MC
College of Staten Island / The CUNY	NY	16,778	NC
College of Charleston	SC	21,273	VC
College of Mount St. Joseph	OH	33,880	C
College of Mount St. Vincent	NY	41,040	MC
College of New Jersey	NJ	25,376	HC
College of St. Benedict	MN	47,570	VC
College of St. Elizabeth	NJ	43,839	LC
College of St. Mary	NE	34,334	C
College of St. Scholastica	MN	39,960	C
College of the Holy Cross	MA	56,232	MC
College of the Ozarks	MO	5,605	VC
College of William & Mary	VA	25,085	MC
College of Wooster	OH	52,600	VC
Colo College	CO	54,534	MC
Colo School of Mines	CO	18,000	HC
Colo State Univ-Fort Collins	CO	20,090	VC
Colo State Univ-Pueblo	CO	13,532	LC
Columbia College	MO	24,578	C
Columbia College	SC	27,882	C
Columbia Univ in the City of New York	NY	61,116	MC
Columbia Univ/Barnard College	NY	39,000	MC
Columbia Univ/School of General Studies	NY	54,083	MC
Columbus State Univ	GA	13,176	C
Concord Univ	WV	13,102	C
Concordia College, Moorhead	MN	39,974	C+
Concordia Univ	OR	34,930	C
Concordia Univ - Irvine	CA	35,390	VC
Concordia Univ Nebr	NE	26,000	VC
Concordia Univ, Ann Arbor	MI	27,220	VC
Concordia Univ, River Forest	IL	26,300	C
Conn College	CT	54,970	MC
Converse College	SC	37,130	C
Coppin State Univ	MD	14,905	VC
Cornell College	IA	44,930	HC
Cornerstone Univ and Grand Rapids Theological Seminary	MI	30,866	C
Covenant College	GA		VC+
Creighton Univ	NE	44,058	VC+
CUNY-City College	NY	19,576	HC+
Curry College	MA	47,545	LC
Dartmouth College	NH	57,996	MC
Davidson College	NC	54,683	MC
Davis and Elkins College	WV	33,742	C
De Sales Univ	PA	42,670	C
Delaware State Univ	DE	14,700	LC
Delaware Valley College	PA	29,944	C
Delta State Univ	MS	12,292	LC
Denison Univ	OH	54,670	HC+
DePaul Univ	IL	46,120	VC
DePauw Univ	IN	48,950	VC+
Dickinson College	PA	57,662	HC+
Dickinson State Univ	ND	8,550	NC
Dillard Univ	LA	20,940	VC
Doane College	NE	33,730	VC
Dominican Univ	IL	37,628	C
Dordt College	IA	34,160	VC
Drake Univ	IA	30,980	VC+
Drew Univ/College of Liberal Arts	NJ	55,862	VC
Drexel Univ	PA	51,920	HC
Drury Univ	MO	30,319	VC
Duke Univ	NC	50,250	MC
Duquesne Univ	PA	42,017	VC
Earlham College	IN	49,710	VC+
East Carolina Univ	NC	14,169	C
East Central Univ	OK	10,223	LC
East Stroudsburg Univ of Pennsylvania	PA	16,636	C
East Tenn State Univ	TN	9,000	C
East Texas Baptist Univ	TX	29,135	C
Eastern Illinois Univ	IL	20,502	C
Eastern Kentucky Univ	KY	11,161	C
Eastern Mennonite Univ	VA	38,850	VC
Eastern Mich Univ	MI	17,961	C
Eastern Nazarene College	MA	30,000	C
Eastern New Mexico Univ	NM	10,682	C
Eastern Oregon Univ	OR	10,400	C
Eastern Univ	PA	37,704	C
Eastern Washington Univ	WA	16,388	C
Eckerd College	FL	43,902	VC
Edgewood College	WI	33,294	C
Edinboro Univ of Pennsylvania	PA	15,940	LC
Elizabeth City State Univ	NC	11,638	C
Elizabethtown College	PA	47,600	VC
Elmhurst College	IL	42,032	C+
Elmira College	NY	49,950	C+
Elms College	MA	23,900	VC
Elon Univ	NC	40,046	HC
Emmanuel College	MA	47,985	VC
Emory and Henry College	VA	387,460	C
Emory Univ	GA	45,000	MC
Emporia State Univ	KS	12,897	C
Erskine College	SC	37,360	C
Eureka College	IL	19,280	C
Evangel Univ	MO	23,090	C
Excelsior College	NY	895	SP
Fairfield Univ	CT	55,850	VC
Fairleigh Dickinson Univ/ College at Florham	NJ	42,142	C
Fairleigh Dickinson Univ/ Metropolitan Campus	NJ	40,254	C
Fairmont State Univ	WV	12,098	LC
Fayetteville State Univ	NC	10,816	C
Ferris State Univ	MI	19,698	C
Ferrum College	VA	27,740	LC
Fisk Univ	TN	19,830	C
Fitchburg State Univ	MA	17,241	C
Florida A&M Univ	FL	14,935	LC
Florida Atlantic Univ	FL	17,339	C
Florida Gulf Coast Univ	FL		C
Florida Inst of Technology	FL	48,290	VC
Florida International Univ	FL	17,747	VC
Florida Memorial Univ	FL	20,716	LC
Florida Southern College	FL	38,240	VC
Florida State Univ	FL	15,238	HC
Fordham Univ	NY	58,927	HC
Fort Hays State Univ	KS	11,354	C
Fort Lewis College	CO	15,513	C
Fort Valley State Univ	GA	11,200	VC
Framingham State Univ	MA	16,750	C
Francis Marion Univ	SC	16,464	LC
Franciscan Univ of Steubenville	OH	27,320	VC
Franklin and Marshall College	PA	58,295	MC
Franklin College	IN	35,885	C
Freed-Hardeman Univ	TN	19,697	VC
Fresno Pacific Univ	CA	32,136	C
Friends Univ	KS	29,100	C
Frostburg State Univ	MD	15,264	LC
Furman Univ	SC	54,006	HC
Gallaudet Univ	DC	25,380	SP
Gannon Univ	PA	37,940	C
Gardner-Webb Univ	NC	34,375	C+
Geneva College	PA	27,280	C
George Fox Univ	OR	40,750	C+
George Mason Univ	VA	15,724	VC
George Washington Univ	DC	57,108	MC
Georgetown College	KY	38,690	C
Georgetown Univ	DC	52,910	MC
Georgia College and State Univ	GA	18,216	VC
Georgia Inst of Technology	GA	20,464	MC
Georgia Regents Univ	GA		C
Georgia Southern Univ	GA	16,414	C
Georgia Southwestern State Univ	GA	12,218	C
Georgia State Univ	GA	12,000	VC
Georgian Court Univ	NJ	39,726	LC
Gettysburg College	PA	56,820	HC
Glenville State College	WV	11,348	NC
Gonzaga Univ	WA	44,247	HC
Gordon College	MA	42,660	VC+
Goshen College	IN	35,900	VC
Goucher College	MD	50,252	VC+
Graceland Univ	IA	28,020	C
Grambling State Univ	LA	13,384	LC
Grand Valley State Univ	MI	17,998	VC
Greensboro College	NC	28,740	LC
Greenville College	IL	27,012	C
Grinnell College	IA	53,654	HC
Grove City College	PA	22,988	HC
Guilford College	NC	35,340	C
Gustavus Adolphus College	MN	48,170	HC
Hamilton College	NY	55,620	MC
Hamline Univ	MN	44,198	VC
Hampden-Sydney College	VA	48,848	C
Hampshire College	MA	58,320	MC
Hampton Univ	VA	28,528	C
Hanover College	IN	41,450	VC
Harding Univ	AR	21,432	C+
Hardin-Simmons Univ	TX	23,560	C+
Hartwick College	NY	49,815	C+
Harvard Univ/Harvard College	MA	49,000	MC
Harvey Mudd College	CA	61,660	MC
Hastings College	NE	27,782	C+
Haverford College	PA	59,236	MC
Hawaii Pacific Univ	HI	36,690	C
Heidelberg Univ	OH	34,100	C

ST = STATE $IS = IN-STATE COSTS SR = SELECTOR RATING

School	ST	$IS	SR
Henderson State Univ	AR	13,634	C
Hendrix College	AR	48,436	H¢
High Point Univ	NC	39,800	C
Hillsdale College	MI	31,890	H¢
Hiram College	OH	37,300	VC
Hobart and William Smith Colleges	NY	43,000	VC
Hofstra Univ	NY	48,020	V¢
Hollins Univ	VA	43,295	VC
Hood College	MD	44,630	C
Hope College	MI	36,320	V¢
Houghton College	NY	35,740	VC
Houston Baptist Univ	TX	23,815	¢
Howard Payne Univ	TX	17,115	C
Howard Univ	DC	35,957	C
Humboldt State Univ	CA	18,400	C
Hunter College / The CUNY	NY	14,429	VC
Huntingdon College	AL	31,850	C
Huntington Univ	IN	32,220	C
Husson Univ	ME	23,386	LC
Huston-Tillotson Univ	TX	18,124	¢
Idaho State Univ	ID	11,908	C
Illinois College	IL	25,770	VC
Illinois Inst of Technology	IL	38,512	H¢
Illinois State Univ	IL	22,634	VC
Illinois Wesleyan Univ	IL	48,452	V¢
Indiana State Univ	IN	16,000	C
Indiana Univ Bloomington	IN	19,358	HC
Indiana Univ Kokomo	IN	6,674	LC
Indiana Univ Northwest	IN	6,738	LC
Indiana Univ of Pennsylvania	PA	20,180	LC
Indiana Univ South Bend	IN	15,293	C
Indiana Univ Southeast	IN	15,807	LC
Indiana Univ-Purdue Univ Fort Wayne	IN	15,425	C
Indiana Univ-Purdue Univ Indianapolis	IN	17,290	C
Indiana Wesleyan Univ	IN	31,815	VC
Inter-American Univ of PR/ Arecibo Campus	PR	3,350	
Inter-American Univ of PR/ Bayamon Univ College	PR	4,428	
Inter-American Univ of PR/ Fajardo Campus	PR	4,200	
Inter-American Univ of PR/ Metropolitan Campus	PR	4,320	
Inter-American Univ of PR/ Ponce	PR	3,700	
Inter-American Univ of PR/ San Germán	PR	6,720	
Iona College	NY	44,028	C
Iowa State Univ	IA	16,403	C
Iowa Wesleyan College	IA	30,850	LC
Ithaca College	NY	52,300	HC
Jackson State Univ	MS	13,512	LC
Jacksonville State Univ	AL	12,280	LC
Jacksonville Univ	FL	37,780	C
James Madison Univ	VA	18,049	VC
Jarvis Christian College	TX	19,552	NC
John Brown Univ	AR	30,996	V¢
John Carroll Univ	OH	44,520	¢
Johns Hopkins Univ	MD	47,492	MC
Johnson C. Smith Univ	NC	25,336	LC
Judson College	AL	24,690	C
Judson Univ	IL	25,130	C
Juniata College	PA	49,340	VC
Kalamazoo College	MI	47,825	H¢
Kansas State Univ	KS	15,497	VC
Kansas Wesleyan Univ	KS	32,000	C
Kean Univ	NJ	22,060	LC
Keene State College	NH	21,538	C
Kennesaw State Univ	GA	13,017	VC
Kent State Univ	OH	19,352	C
Kentucky State Univ	KY	11,000	LC
Kentucky Wesleyan College	KY	27,440	V¢
Kenyon College	OH	56,810	MC
Kettering Univ	MI	31,456	HC
King Univ	TN	33,140	C
King's College	PA	41,678	C
Knox College	IL		VC
Kutztown Univ of Pennsylvania	PA	16,909	LC
La Roche College	PA	34,802	LC
La Salle Univ	PA	50,270	C
La Sierra Univ	CA	35,694	VC
Lafayette College	PA	57,050	H¢
LaGrange College	GA	34,480	C
Lake Erie College	OH	35,704	C
Lake Forest College	IL	45,580	VC
Lake Superior State Univ	MI	18,121	C
Lakeland College	WI	22,990	C
Lamar Univ	TX	6,820	LC
Lander Univ	SC	22,514	¢
Lane College	TN	11,212	C
Langston Univ	OK	3,000	LC
Lawrence Tech Univ	MI	37,630	VC
Lawrence Univ	WI	46,371	HC
Le Moyne College	NY	42,200	VC
Lebanon Valley College	PA	38,570	C
Lee Univ	TN	18,690	¢
Lehigh Univ	PA	55,080	MC
Lehman College / The CUNY	NY	5,778	LC
LeMoyne-Owen College	TN	13,100	C
Lenoir-Rhyne College	NC	35,984	C
LeTourneau Univ	TX	26,230	C
Lewis & Clark College	OR	52,656	VC
Lewis Univ	IL	23,050	C
Lewis-Clark State College	ID	6,990	C
Limestone College	SC	29,880	C
Lincoln Memorial Univ	TN	18,144	C
Lincoln Univ	MO	11,996	NC
Lindenwood Univ	MO	20,750	C
Linfield College-McMinnville Campus	OR	46,166	C
Lipscomb Univ	TN	35,722	VC
Livingstone College	NC	17,815	LC
Lock Haven Univ of Pennsylvania	PA	17,587	LC
LIU/Brooklyn Campus	NY	26,500	C
LIU/C.W. Post Campus	NY	38,888	C
Longwood Univ	VA	20,924	C
Loras College	IA	37,432	VC
Louisiana College	LA	15,746	C
Louisiana State Univ	LA	18,677	V¢
Louisiana State Univ in Shreveport	LA	5,606	C
Louisiana Tech Univ	LA	8,000	C
Loyola Marymount Univ	CA	53,240	V¢
Loyola Univ Chicago	IL	49,560	V¢
Loyola Univ Maryland	MD		VC
Loyola Univ New Orleans	LA	46,581	VC
Lubbock Christian Univ	TX	25,518	C
Luther College	IA	44,380	V¢
Lycoming College	PA	43,636	C
Lynchburg College	VA	42,645	C
Lyon College	AR	30,246	VC
Macalester College	MN	53,419	MC
MacMurray College	IL	20,755	C
Madonna Univ	MI	24,540	VC
Malone Univ	OH	34,334	C
Manchester College	IN	35,070	C
Manhattan College	NY	44,955	VC
Manhattanville College	NY	46,260	VC
Mansfield Univ	PA	19,468	LC
Marian Univ	WI	30,980	LC
Marian Univ/Indianapolis	IN	37,058	C
Marietta College	OH	42,135	VC
Marist College	NY	35,500	C
Marlboro College	VT	35,980	VC
Marquette Univ	WI	43,664	V¢
Mars Hill College	NC	22,950	LC
Marshall Univ	WV	14,820	C
Martin Univ	IN	11,000	SP
Mary Baldwin College	VA	37,110	C
Marygrove College	MI	21,290	C
Maryville College	TN	33,150	VC
Maryville Univ of St. Louis	MO	34,920	VC
Mass College of Liberal Arts	MA	16,733	C
Mass College of Pharmacy and Health Sciences	MA	36,450	SP
Mass Inst of Technology	MA	54,238	MC
Mayville State Univ	ND	11,401	NC
McDaniel College	MD	45,600	VC
McKendree Univ	IL	29,920	¢
McMurry Univ	TX	25,962	LC
McNeese State Univ	LA		C
McPherson College	KS	28,138	C
Mercer Univ	GA	44,201	V¢
Mercyhurst Univ	PA	40,700	C
Meredith College	NC	31,420	C
Merrimack College	MA	44,215	C
Messiah College	PA	39,540	VC
Methodist Univ	NC	37,185	C
Metropolitan State Univ of Denver	CO	4,835	LC
Miami Univ	OH	24,191	HC
Mich State Univ	MI	13,689	VC
Mich Tech Univ	MI	22,105	VC
MidAmerica Nazarene Univ	KS	28,000	C
Middle Tenn State Univ	TN	8,650	C
Middlebury College	VT	57,470	MC
Midland Univ	NE	34,000	C
Midway College	KY	20,150	C
Midwestern State Univ	TX	9,722	C
Miles College	AL	16,530	NC
Millersville Univ of Pennsylvania	PA	18,498	C
Milligan College	TN	27,510	C
Millikin Univ	IL	37,462	C
Mills College	CA	54,119	HC
Millsaps College	MS	43,888	V¢
Minn State Univ, Mankato	MN	14,900	C
Minn State Univ, Moorhead	MN	13,392	C
Minot State Univ	ND	10,915	C
Misericordia Univ	PA	39,840	C
Miss College	MS	21,998	VC
Miss Univ for Women	MS	7,400	LC
Miss Valley State Univ	MS	9,706	LC
Missouri Baptist Univ	MO	30,310	C
Missouri Southern State Univ	MO	11,910	C
Missouri State Univ	MO	13,996	VC
Missouri Univ of Science and Technology	MO	18,655	V¢
Missouri Western State Univ	MO	12,260	NC
Monmouth College	IL	39,290	C
Monmouth Univ	NJ	42,252	C
Montana State Univ	MT	14,068	VC
Montana State Univ-Billings	MT	12,425	LC
Montana State Univ-Northern	MT	12,500	NC
Montana Tech of The Univ of Montana	MT	14,650	VC
Montclair State Univ	NJ	22,614	C
Moravian College	PA	36,381	VC
Morehead State Univ	KY	10,900	C
Morehouse College	GA	38,640	C
Morgan State Univ	MD	14,500	VC
Morningside College	IA	32,620	C
Mount Holyoke College	MA	53,596	H¢
Mount Marty College	SD	29,638	C
Mount Mary Univ	WI	32,836	LC
Mount St. Mary College	NY	39,540	C
Mount St. Mary's Univ	MD	46,158	C
Mount St. Mary's College/ Chalon Campus	CA	43,897	V¢
Mount Vernon Nazarene Univ	OH	29,590	C
Muhlenberg College	PA	52,837	HC
Murray State Univ	KY	14,944	C
Muskingum Univ	OH	30,502	C
Nazareth College of Rochester	NY	41,590	VC
Nebr Wesleyan Univ	NE	29,774	¢
New College of Florida	FL	14,504	H¢
New Jersey City Univ	NJ	21,060	¢
New Jersey Inst of Technology	NJ	26,490	VC
New Mexico Highlands Univ	NM	9,720	NC
New Mexico Inst of Mining and Technology	NM	12,892	HC
New Mexico State Univ	NM	13,955	LC
New York Inst of Technology	NY	40,590	VC
New York Univ	NY	61,470	MC
Newberry College	SC	26,850	LC
Newman Univ	KS	30,380	¢
Niagara Univ	NY	39,800	C
Nicholls State Univ	LA	7,095	C
Norfolk State Univ	VA	10,531	LC
N Car Agricultural and Technical State Univ	NC	13,175	LC
N Car Central Univ	NC	9,000	LC
N Car State Univ	NC	16,202	HC
N Car Wesleyan College	NC	29,440	C
North Central College	IL	38,343	VC
N Dak State Univ	ND	14,642	C
North Georgia College & State Univ	GA	8,500	C
North Park Univ	IL	30,130	C
Northeastern Illinois Univ	IL		C
Northeastern State Univ	OK	8,615	VC
Northeastern Univ	MA	55,296	MC
Northern Arizona Univ	AZ	18,592	C
Northern Illinois Univ	IL	19,768	C
Northern Kentucky Univ	KY	15,302	LC
Northern Mich Univ	MI	15,300	VC
Northern State Univ	SD	14,021	C
Northland College	WI	26,680	C
Northwest Missouri State Univ	MO	14,229	C
Northwest Nazarene Univ	ID	24,275	NC
Northwestern College of Iowa	IA	34,848	¢
Northwestern Okla State Univ	OK	7,275	NC
Northwestern Univ	IL	37,595	MC
Norwich Univ	VT	28,212	C
Notre Dame College	OH	34,942	VC
Notre Dame of Maryland Univ	MD	27,700	C
Nova Southeastern Univ	FL	34,016	VC
Oakland Univ	MI	19,391	VC
Oakwood Univ	AL	23,035	C
Oberlin College	OH	57,025	MC
Occidental College	CA	59,592	M¢
Oglethorpe Univ	GA	42,580	VC
Ohio Dominican Univ	OH	38,380	¢
Ohio Northern Univ	OH	42,075	VC
Ohio Univ	OH	20,676	VC
Ohio Wesleyan Univ	OH	49,460	¢
Okla Baptist Univ	OK	28,202	VC
Okla Christian Univ	OK	24,975	VC
Okla City Univ	OK	33,546	VC
Okla Panhandle State Univ	OK	8,996	NC
Okla State Univ	OK	14,310	VC
Okla Wesleyan Univ	OK	21,300	C
Old Dominion Univ	VA	18,662	C
Olivet College	MI	19,984	C
Olivet Nazarene Univ	IL	29,990	C
Oral Roberts Univ	OK	31,734	C
Oregon State Univ	OR	19,017	¢
Oswego / SUNY	NY	20,009	VC
Ottawa Univ	KS	15,000	VC
Otterbein College	OH	32,214	C
Ouachita Baptist Univ	AR	29,010	VC
Our Lady of the Lake Univ of San Antonio	TX	22,430	LC
Pace Univ	NY	48,094	VC
Pacific Lutheran Univ	WA	44,840	VC
Pacific Union College	CA	28,150	VC
Pacific Univ	OR	42,815	C
Paine College	GA	18,594	LC
Palm Beach Atlantic Univ	FL	33,882	LC
Park Univ	MO	17,525	C
Penn State Erie/The Behrend College	PA	16,256	C
Penn State Univ/Univ Park	PA	25,404	VC
Pepperdine Univ	CA	55,372	H¢
Pfeiffer Univ	NC	33,700	C
Philadelphia Univ	PA	44,160	C
Philander Smith College	AR	19,760	LC
Piedmont College	GA	29,260	C
Pittsburg State Univ	KS	12,032	C
Pitzer College	CA	54,988	MC
Plymouth State Univ	NH	23,148	LC
Point Loma Nazarene Univ	CA	38,610	VC
Polytechnic Inst of New York Univ	NY	53,064	H¢
Pomona College	CA	57,680	MC
Pontifical Catholic Univ of PR	PR	7,310	
Portland State Univ	OR	18,672	C
Prairie View A&M Univ	TX	15,205	LC
Presbyterian College	SC	42,678	VC
Princeton Univ	NJ	53,795	MC
Principia College	IL	35,140	¢
Providence College	RI	55,995	HC
Purchase College / SUNY	NY	16,951	C
Purdue Univ/Calumet	IN	14,336	C
Purdue Univ/West Lafayette	IN	20,278	HC
Queens College / The CUNY	NY	17,107	VC
Queens Univ of Charlotte	NC	39,543	VC
Quincy Univ	IL	34,980	LC
Quinnipiac Univ	CT	53,580	VC
Radford Univ	VA	17,132	LC
Ramapo College of New Jersey	NJ	24,938	¢
Randolph College	VA	43,960	VC
Randolph-Macon College	VA	45,086	C
Reed College	OR	57,780	MC
Regis College	MA	47,565	LC
Regis Univ	CO	41,318	C
Rensselaer Polytechnic Inst	NY	59,229	MC
Rhode Island College	RI	17,132	LC
Rhodes College	TN	47,596	H¢
Rice Univ	TX	43,288	MC
Richard Stockton College of New Jersey	NJ	20,000	VC
Rider Univ	NJ	45,720	C
Ripon College	WI	36,959	¢
Roanoke College	VA	47,996	¢
Roberts Wesleyan College	NY	37,384	¢
Rochester Inst of Technology	NY	42,450	V¢
Rockford College	IL	31,000	C
Rockhurst Univ	MO	20,625	C
Rocky Mountain College	MT	32,242	C
Roger Williams Univ	RI	45,788	C
Rollins College	FL	52,370	HC
Roosevelt Univ	IL	22,605	VC
Rose-Hulman Inst of Technology	IN	51,738	MC
Rosemont College	PA	42,350	C
Rowan Univ	NJ	23,570	VC
Russell Sage College	NY	39,370	C
Rust College	MS	10,600	C
Rutgers, The State Univ of New Jersey/Camden Campus	NJ	24,254	C
Rutgers, The State Univ of New Jersey/New Brunswick	NJ	25,077	VC
Rutgers, The State Univ of New Jersey/Newark Campus	NJ	25,376	C
Sacred Heart Univ	CT	48,564	VC
Saginaw Valley State Univ	MI	16,869	C
St. Anselm College	NH	48,324	VC
St. Augustine's Univ	NC	14,000	C
St. Francis Univ	PA	30,029	LC
St. John's Univ	MN	46,146	C
St. Joseph College	CT	45,630	LC
St. Joseph's College	IN	35,790	C
St. Joseph's College of Maine	ME	31,580	C
St. Joseph's Univ	PA	52,272	VC
St. Louis Univ	MO	46,594	V¢
St. Martin's Univ	WA	38,082	C
St. Mary's College	IN	45,160	VC
St. Mary's College of Calif	CA	53,550	C
St. Mary's Univ	TX	33,854	C
St. Mary's Univ of Minn	MN	37,015	C
St. Michael's College	VT	48,740	VC
St. Peter's College	NJ	44,240	C
St. Vincent College	PA	40,244	C
St. Xavier Univ	IL	32,840	C
Salem College	NC	29,326	VC
Salem State College	MA	13,161	LC
Salisbury Univ	MD	18,368	VC
Salve Regina Univ	RI	47,250	VC
Sam Houston State Univ	TX	17,082	C
Samford Univ	AL	35,700	V¢
San Diego State Univ	CA	20,578	VC
San Francisco State Univ	CA	18,514	C
San Jose State Univ	CA	19,707	C
Santa Clara Univ	CA	54,702	MC
Sarah Lawrence College	NY	48,000	HC
Savannah State Univ	GA	13,156	C
Schreiner Univ	TX	32,734	LC

ST = STATE **$IS** = IN-STATE COSTS **SR** = SELECTOR RATING

School	ST	$IS	SR
Scripps College	CA	54,900	MC
Seattle Pacific Univ	WA	41,559	VC+
Seattle Univ	WA	47,010	VC+
Seton Hall Univ	NJ	45,902	C
Seton Hill Univ	PA	35,172	C
Sewanee: The Univ of the South	TN	47,700	HC+
Shaw Univ	NC	15,488	LC
Shawnee State Univ	OH	16,545	NC
Shenandoah Univ	VA	39,268	C
Shepherd Univ	WV	14,996	C
Shippensburg Univ of Pennsylvania	PA	17,064	LC
Shorter Univ	GA	26,470	C
Siena College	NY	43,863	VC
Siena Heights Univ	MI	17,000	LC
Simmons College	MA	48,770	VC
Simpson College	IA	36,086	VC
Skidmore College	NY	57,926	HC
Slippery Rock Univ of Pennsylvania	PA	10,360	LC
Smith College	MA	57,524	MC
Sonoma State Univ	CA	20,541	C
S Car State Univ	SC	6,700	LC
S Dak School of Mines and Technology	SD	15,260	VC
S Dak State Univ	SD	14,296	C
Southeast Missouri State Univ	MO	14,983	LC
Southeastern Louisiana Univ	LA	13,325	C
Southeastern Okla State Univ	OK	7,966	C
Southern Adventist Univ	TN	26,190	C
Southern Arkansas Univ	AR	14,316	C
Southern Conn State Univ	CT	18,033	C
Southern Illinois Univ Carbondale	IL	21,620	C
Southern Illinois Univ Edwardsville	IL	17,532	C
Southern Methodist Univ	TX	57,755	MC
Southern Nazarene Univ	OK	24,354	NC
Southern Oregon Univ	OR	17,874	C
Southern Polytechnic State Univ	GA	13,958	VC
Southern Univ and A&M College	LA	9,761	C+
Southern Univ at New Orleans	LA	1,000	NC
Southern Wesleyan Univ	SC	25,600	C
Southwest Baptist Univ	MO	24,710	C
Southwest Minn State Univ	MN	14,000	C
Southwestern Adventist Univ	TX	23,026	LC
Southwestern College	KS	29,270	C
Southwestern Okla State Univ	OK	9,160	C
Southwestern Univ	TX	45,660	VC
Spelman College	GA	24,650	VC
Spring Arbor Univ	MI	26,740	C
Spring Hill College	AL	42,130	VC
Springfield College	MA	25,000	C
St. Ambrose Univ	IA		C
St. Bonaventure Univ	NY	38,831	C
St. Catherine Univ	MN	37,782	C+
St. Cloud State Univ	MN	10,600	C
St. Edward's Univ	TX	44,674	VC
St. Francis College	NY	34,200	LC
St. John Fisher College	NY	39,370	C+
St. John's Univ	NY	52,840	C+
St. Joseph's College, New York / Brooklyn Campus	NY	21,878	C
St. Joseph's College, New York / Suffolk Campus	NY	21,878	VC
St. Lawrence Univ	NY	53,740	HC
St. Mary's College of Maryland	MD	26,699	HC
St. Norbert College	WI	39,992	VC
St. Olaf College	MN	49,960	HC+
Stanford Univ	CA	56,411	MC
SUNY / College of Environmental Science and Forestry	NY	18,351	HC
Stephen F. Austin State Univ	TX	14,668	C
Sterling College	KS	27,216	C
Stetson Univ	FL	49,512	VC+
Stevens Inst of Technology	NJ	50,130	HC
Stevenson Univ	MD	39,572	C
Stonehill College	MA	46,780	VC+
Stony Brook Univ / SUNY	NY	19,359	HC
Suffolk Univ	MA	46,548	C
SUNY College at Geneseo	NY	18,055	HC+
SUNY College at Old Westbury	NY	16,324	C
SUNY Cortland / The SUNY	NY	19,117	C
SUNY Fredonia / The SUNY at Fredonia	NY	18,702	VC
SUNY New Paltz	NY	15,010	C
SUNY Oneonta / SUNY	NY	16,919	VC
SUNY Plattsburgh / SUNY	NY	18,083	VC
Susquehanna Univ	PA	49,170	C
Swarthmore College	PA	57,870	MC
Sweet Briar College	VA	43,765	C+
Syracuse Univ	NY	54,512	HC
Tabor College	KS	29,010	LC
Talladega College	AL	13,000	C
Tarleton State Univ	TX	13,489	LC
Taylor Univ	IN	36,742	VC+
Temple Univ	PA	24,392	VC
Tenn State Univ	TN	9,048	C
Tenn Tech Univ	TN	11,310	C
Tenn Wesleyan College	TN	21,250	C
Texas A&M Univ	TX	16,956	VC+
Texas A&M Univ at Commerce	TX	10,496	C
Texas A&M Univ at Corpus Christi	TX	11,544	LC
Texas A&M Univ at Kingsville	TX	7,500	LC
Texas Christian Univ	TX	47,570	HC
Texas Lutheran Univ	TX	31,070	C
Texas Southern Univ	TX	18,212	LC
Texas State Univ	TX	16,495	VC
Texas Tech Univ	TX	14,243	C
Texas Wesleyan Univ	TX	29,886	C
Texas Woman's Univ	TX	13,633	LC
The Catholic Univ of America	DC	52,852	VC
The College at Brockport / SUNY	NY	18,362	VC
The College of Idaho	ID	31,277	VC
The College of New Rochelle	NY	33,600	VC
The College of St. Rose	NY	26,750	C
The Lincoln Univ	PA	15,154	LC
Ohio State Univ	OH	19,887	MC
The SUNY at Potsdam	NY	17,754	C
Thiel College	PA	31,378	LC
Thomas More College	KY	34,760	C
Tougaloo College	MS	15,275	NC
Touro College	NY	23,150	VC
Towson Univ	MD	16,000	VC
Transylvania Univ	KY	40,310	VC+
Trevecca Nazarene Univ	TN	30,118	C
Trine Univ	IN	39,400	VC
Trinity Christian College	IL	28,869	C
Trinity College	CT		HC+
Trinity International Univ	IL	31,070	C
Trinity Univ	TX	44,174	HC+
Trinity Washington Univ	DC	30,250	C+
Troy Univ	AL	10,650	C
Truman State Univ	MO	13,546	HC
Tufts Univ	MA	58,780	MC
Tulane Univ	LA	58,942	MC
Tuskegee Univ	AL	26,750	C
Union College	KY	28,775	C
Union College	NE	23,270	VC
Union College	NY		MC
Union Univ	TN	28,260	VC
United States Air Force Academy	CO		MC
United States Military Academy	NY		MC
United States Naval Academy	MD		MC
Universidad del Turabo	PR	4,110	
Univ at Albany / SUNY	NY	18,674	VC
Univ at Buffalo / The SUNY	NY	20,283	VC
Univ of Akron	OH	20,436	C
Univ of Alabama at Birmingham	AL	18,484	C+
Univ of Alabama at Huntsville	AL	17,625	VC
Univ of Alabama at Tuscaloosa	AL	17,164	C+
Univ of Alaska Anchorage	AK	15,290	NC
Univ of Alaska Fairbanks	AK	13,955	C
Univ of Arizona	AZ	20,105	C
Univ of Arkansas at Fayetteville	AR	16,860	VC
Univ of Arkansas at Little Rock	AR		C
Univ of Arkansas at Monticello	AR	8,470	NC
Univ of Arkansas at Pine Bluff	AR	10,600	C
Univ of Calif at Berkeley	CA	23,322	MC
Univ of Calif at Davis	CA	24,482	HC
Univ of Calif at Irvine	CA	25,961	VC
Univ of Calif at Los Angeles	CA	25,686	MC
Univ of Calif at Riverside	CA	27,204	C
Univ of Calif at San Diego	CA	21,000	VC
Univ of Calif at Santa Barbara	CA	27,551	HC
Univ of Calif at Santa Cruz	CA	27,807	VC
Univ of Central Arkansas	AR	10,840	VC
Univ of Central Florida	FL	15,711	VC+
Univ of Central Missouri	MO	14,605	C
Univ of Central Okla	OK	12,293	C
Univ of Charleston	WV	28,650	C
Univ of Chicago	IL	55,416	MC
Univ of Cincinnati	OH	20,199	VC
Univ of Colo at Colo Springs	CO	15,000	VC
Univ of Colo Boulder	CO	22,605	VC+
Univ of Colo Denver	CO	17,904	C
Univ of Conn	CT	23,744	HC
Univ of Dallas	TX	43,510	VC+
Univ of Dayton	OH	43,750	VC
Univ of Delaware	DE	22,728	VC
Univ of Denver	CO	51,787	VC+
Univ of Detroit Mercy	MI	30,450	C
Univ of Evansville	IN	41,056	VC+
Univ of Findlay	OH	31,916	C
Univ of Florida	FL	15,783	HC+
Univ of Georgia	GA	19,508	VC
Univ of Hartford	CT	42,674	C
Univ of Hawaii at Hilo	HI	6,500	C
Univ of Hawaii at Manoa	HI	19,379	VC
Univ of Houston	TX	19,184	VC
Univ of Houston-Downtown	TX	6,267	LC
Univ of Idaho	ID	14,558	C
Univ of Illinois at Chicago	IL	24,293	VC
Univ of Illinois at Urbana-Champaign	IL	24,300	HC
Univ of Indianapolis	IN	31,740	LC
Univ of Iowa	IA	17,481	VC
Univ of Jamestown	ND	24,738	C
Univ of Kansas	KS	16,980	C+
Univ of Kentucky	KY	19,868	C
Univ of La Verne	CA	47,010	VC
Univ of Louisiana at Lafayette	LA	6,130	C
Univ of Louisville	KY	17,460	VC
Univ of Maine	ME	19,712	C+
Univ of Mary Hardin-Baylor	TX	31,950	C+
Univ of Mary Washington	VA	19,484	VC
Univ of Maryland	MD	18,801	HC
Univ of Maryland/Baltimore County	MD	18,000	VC
Univ of Maryland/Eastern Shore	MD	14,000	C
Univ of Mass Amherst	MA	23,697	VC+
Univ of Mass Boston	MA	11,966	C
Univ of Mass Dartmouth	MA	22,223	C
Univ of Mass Lowell	MA	19,316	C
Univ of Memphis	TN	15,094	C
Univ of Miami	FL	55,166	MC
Univ of Mich/Ann Arbor	MI	22,102	HC+
Univ of Mich/Dearborn	MI	9,885	VC
Univ of Mich-Flint	MI	17,547	C+
Univ of Minn/Duluth	MN	18,964	C+
Univ of Minn/Morris	MN	17,150	VC
Univ of Minn/Twin Cities	MN		HC
Univ of Miss	MS	15,482	VC
Univ of Missouri/Columbia	MO	18,201	MC
Univ of Missouri-Kansas City	MO	19,603	C
Univ of Missouri-St. Louis	MO	18,304	VC
Univ of Montana	MT	13,670	C
Univ of Montevallo	AL	17,320	C
Univ of Mount Union	OH	35,130	C
Univ of Nebr - Lincoln	NE	17,507	VC
Univ of Nebr at Kearney	NE	14,855	LC
Univ of Nebr at Omaha	NE	12,700	C
Univ of Nevada, Las Vegas	NV	17,303	C
Univ of Nevada/Reno	NV	14,500	NC
Univ of New England	ME	46,145	C+
Univ of New Hampshire	NH	24,702	VC
Univ of New Haven	CT	47,740	C
Univ of New Mexico	NM	15,300	C
Univ of New Orleans	LA	9,224	VC
Univ of North Alabama	AL	9,960	C
Univ of N Car at Asheville	NC	13,500	VC+
Univ of N Car at Chapel Hill	NC	18,348	MC
Univ of N Car at Charlotte	NC	15,847	C
Univ of N Car at Greensboro	NC	12,848	C
Univ of N Car at Wilmington	NC	13,572	VC+
Univ of N Dak	ND	14,094	C
Univ of North Florida	FL	15,578	VC
Univ of North Texas	TX	15,628	C
Univ of Northern Colo	CO	15,973	C
Univ of Northern Iowa	IA	14,776	C
Univ of Notre Dame	IN		MC
Univ of Okla	OK	17,634	VC+
Univ of Oregon	OR	20,872	VC
Univ of Pennsylvania	PA	56,106	MC
Univ of Pikeville	KY	24,750	NC
Univ of Pittsburgh at Bradford	PA	21,316	LC
Univ of Pittsburgh at Johnstown	PA	20,862	LC
Univ of Pittsburgh at Pittsburgh	PA	27,800	HC+
Univ of Portland	OR	47,874	VC
Univ of PR Recinto de Rio Piedras	PR	5,750	
Univ of PR/Cayey	PR	1,504	
Univ of PR/Humacao	PR	1,877	
Univ of PR/Mayaguez	PR	1,250	
Univ of Puget Sound	WA	52,648	HC+
Univ of Redlands	CA	40,500	VC
Univ of Rio Grande	OH	8,750	NC
Univ of Rochester	NY	58,500	MC
Univ of St. Francis	IN	29,810	C
Univ of St. Mary	KS	28,400	C+
Univ of San Diego	CA	53,302	HC+
Univ of San Francisco	CA	49,674	VC
Univ of Science and Arts of Okla	OK	10,560	VC
Univ of Scranton	PA	51,940	VC
Univ of Sioux Falls	SD	22,990	C
Univ of South Alabama	AL	13,510	C
Univ of S Car at Aiken	SC	16,278	C
Univ of S Car at Columbia	SC	19,725	VC+
Univ of S Car Upstate	SC	17,673	LC
Univ of S Dak	SD	15,111	C
Univ of South Florida	FL	13,000	C
Univ of Southern Calif	CA	56,903	MC
Univ of Southern Indiana	IN	14,657	C
Univ of Southern Maine	ME	16,576	C
Univ of Southern Miss	MS	13,170	C
Univ of St. Thomas - Houston	TX	36,490	VC
Univ of Tampa	FL	35,160	VC
Univ of Tenn at Chattanooga	TN	16,883	C
Univ of Tenn at Knoxville	TN	20,364	VC+
Univ of Tenn at Martin	TN	13,217	C
Univ of Texas at Arlington	TX	10,908	LC
Univ of Texas at Austin	TX	44,074	HC
Univ of Texas at Dallas	TX	21,046	HC
Univ of Texas at El Paso	TX	8,764	NC
Univ of Texas at San Antonio	TX	18,372	C
Univ of Texas-Pan American	TX	12,432	LC
Univ of the Cumberlands	KY	27,500	LC
Univ of the District of Columbia	DC	7,244	LC
Univ of the Incarnate Word	TX	35,200	LC
Univ of the Ozarks	AR	22,100	C
Univ of the Pacific	CA	52,146	VC
Univ of the Sacred Heart	PR	5,590	
Univ of the Sciences	PA	48,320	VC+
Univ of Toledo	OH	18,464	C
Univ of Tulsa	OK	45,311	HC+
Univ of Utah	UT	13,462	VC
Univ of Vermont	VT	26,120	VC+
Univ of Virginia	VA	22,175	MC
Univ of Virginia's College at Wise	VA	11,076	C
Univ of West Alabama	AL	9,415	C
Univ of West Florida	FL	14,656	C
Univ of West Georgia	GA	14,852	LC
Univ of Wisc Whitewater	WI	13,314	C
Univ of Wisc/Eau Claire	WI	15,430	VC
Univ of Wisc/Green Bay	WI	14,900	C
Univ of Wisc/La Crosse	WI	14,755	VC
Univ of Wisc/Madison	WI	18,757	HC
Univ of Wisc/Oshkosh	WI	10,426	LC
Univ of Wisc/Parkside	WI	10,181	LC
Univ of Wisc/Platteville	WI	14,274	C
Univ of Wisc/River Falls	WI	9,722	LC
Univ of Wisc/Stevens Point	WI	14,043	C
Univ of Wisc/Superior	WI	14,106	C
Univ of Wisc-Milwaukee	WI	18,436	C
Univ of Wyoming	WY	13,855	C+
Upper Iowa Univ	IA	30,426	NC
Ursinus College	PA	55,630	VC+
Utah State Univ	UT	11,803	C
Utica College	NY	44,734	C
Valley City State Univ	ND	12,286	LC
Valparaiso Univ	IN	43,040	VC+
Vanderbilt Univ	TN	57,072	MC
Vanguard Univ of Southern Calif	CA	35,833	VC
Vassar College	NY	59,070	MC
Victory Univ	TN	19,118	C
Villanova Univ	PA	56,436	MC
Virginia Commonwealth Univ	VA	18,633	C
Virginia Military Inst	VA	16,156	C
Virginia Polytechnic Inst and State Univ	VA	14,629	HC
Virginia State Univ	VA	11,318	C+
Virginia Union Univ	VA	18,432	C
Virginia Wesleyan College	VA	28,433	LC
Viterbo Univ	WI	30,070	C
Wabash College	IN	44,160	VC
Wagner College	NY	48,600	VC
Wake Forest Univ	NC	51,000	MC
Walla Walla Univ	WA	26,256	NC
Walsh Univ	OH	35,100	C
Warren Wilson College	NC	34,888	VC
Wartburg College	IA	41,055	VC
Washburn Univ	KS	12,165	NC
Washington Adventist Univ	MD	25,859	C+
Washington and Jefferson College	PA	49,990	VC
Washington and Lee Univ	VA	52,812	MC
Washington College	MD	48,768	VC
Washington State Univ	WA	20,461	C
Washington Univ in St. Louis	MO	58,818	MC
Wayland Baptist Univ	TX	16,058	LC
Wayne State College	NE	11,764	NC
Wayne State Univ	MI	19,493	C
Waynesburg Univ	PA	29,100	C
Wellesley College	MA	49,848	MC
Wells College	NY	38,680	VC
Wesleyan College	GA	24,000	C+
Wesleyan Univ	CT	59,844	MC
West Chester Univ of Pennsylvania	PA	16,836	C
West Liberty Univ	WV	9,142	LC
West Texas A&M Univ	TX	13,478	C
West Virginia State Univ	WV	8,378	NC
West Virginia Univ	WV	15,794	C+
West Virginia Univ Inst of Technology	WV	14,094	NC
West Virginia Wesleyan College	WV	26,880	C
Western Carolina Univ	NC	13,965	C+
Western Conn State Univ	CT	18,327	C
Western Illinois Univ	IL	20,130	C

School	ST	$IS	SR
Western Kentucky Univ	KY	11,000	LC
Western Mich Univ	MI	19,042	C
Western New England Univ	MA	45,590	C
Western New Mexico Univ	NM	8,500	LC
Western Oregon Univ	OR	15,021	C
Western State Colo Univ	CO	16,135	C
Western Washington Univ	WA	18,519	VC
Westfield State Univ	MA	18,489	C
Westminster College	MO	30,490	VC
Westminster College	PA	31,290	Ȼ
Westminster College	UT	37,708	VC
Westmont College	CA	41,500	HC
Wheaton College	IL	39,650	HȻ
Wheaton College	MA	54,934	HȻ
Wheeling Jesuit Univ	WV	34,668	C
Whitman College	WA	54,400	MC
Whittier College	CA	43,416	C
Whitworth Univ	WA	45,826	VȻ
Wichita State Univ	KS	12,539	C
Widener Univ	PA	50,368	C
Wilberforce Univ	OH	15,100	LC
Wiley College	TX		LC
Wilkes Univ	PA	42,786	C
Willamette Univ	OR	56,450	VȻ
William Carey Univ	MS	13,500	LC
William Jewell College	MO	31,000	VȻ
William Paterson Univ of New Jersey	NJ	21,694	C
Williams College	MA	58,900	MC
Wilmington College	OH	29,784	C
Wilson College	PA	27,660	C
Wingate Univ	NC	34,990	C
Winona State Univ	MN	16,530	C
Winston-Salem State Univ	NC	9,418	LC
Winthrop Univ	SC	21,120	VC
Wisc Lutheran College	WI	23,510	VC
Wittenberg Univ	OH	47,766	VC
Wofford College	SC	45,795	VC
Worcester Polytechnic Inst	MA	53,440	HȻ
Worcester State Univ	MA	18,657	C
Wright State Univ	OH	16,983	C
Xavier Univ	OH	43,740	VC
Xavier Univ of Louisiana	LA	25,300	C
Yale Univ	CT	55,300	MC
Yeshiva Univ	NY	47,250	VȻ
York College / CUNY	NY	5,496	NC
York College of Pennsylvania	PA	26,590	C
Youngstown State Univ	OH	16,374	LC

CHEMISTRY / CHEMICAL BIOLOGY

School	ST	$IS	SR
Case Western Reserve Univ	OH	55,178	MC
Cornell Univ	NY	59,037	MC
Georgia Southern Univ	GA	16,414	C

CHEMISTRY/ADOLESCENCE EDUCATION

School	ST	$IS	SR
Bethany College	WV	35,282	C
Duquesne Univ	PA	42,017	VC
Elizabethtown College	PA	47,600	VC
Houghton College	NY	35,740	VC
Indiana Univ Northwest	IN	6,738	LC
Indiana Univ-Purdue Univ Indianapolis	IN	17,290	C
Lipscomb Univ	TN	35,722	VC
Messiah College	PA	39,540	VC
Millikin Univ	IL	37,462	C
Nazareth College of Rochester	NY	41,590	VC
St. Mary's Univ of Minn	MN	37,015	C
Seattle Univ	WA	47,010	VȻ
SUNY Plattsburgh / SUNY	NY	18,083	VC
Temple Univ	PA	24,392	VC
The College of St. Rose	NY	26,750	C
Trevecca Nazarene Univ	TN	30,118	C
Univ of Mary Hardin-Baylor	TX	31,950	Ȼ
Univ of Nebr - Lincoln	NE	17,507	VC

CHILD CARE/CHILD AND FAMILY STUDIES

School	ST	$IS	SR
Albright College	PA	46,660	C
Ashland Univ	OH	25,000	C
Baylor Univ	TX	46,720	HC
Berea College	KY	7,220	HC
Cal State, Fresno	CA	17,405	C
Cal State, Fullerton	CA	25,188	Ȼ
Cameron Univ	OK	9,267	LC
Chestnut Hill College	PA	39,785	LC
CUNY/Brooklyn College	NY	5,884	Ȼ
Concordia Univ St. Paul	MN	27,200	C
East Carolina Univ	NC	14,169	C
Eastern Kentucky Univ	KY	11,161	C
Eastern Mich Univ	MI	17,961	C
Edgewood College	WI	33,294	C
Eureka College	IL	19,280	C
Florida State Univ	FL	15,238	HC
Fontbonne Univ	MO	31,384	C
Freed-Hardeman Univ	TN	19,697	VC
Gallaudet Univ	DC	25,380	SP
Goodwin College	CT	19,400	LC
Harding Univ	AR	21,432	Ȼ
Indiana State Univ	IN	16,000	C
Indiana Univ of Pennsylvania	PA	20,180	LC
Iowa State Univ	IA	16,403	C
Jackson State Univ	MS	13,512	LC
Kansas State Univ	KS	15,497	VC
Lasell College	MA	42,500	LC
Louisiana State Univ	LA	18,677	VȻ
Mayville State Univ	ND	11,401	NC
Messiah College	PA	39,540	VC
Metropolitan College of New York	NY	16,720	VC
Mount Aloysius College	PA	27,970	C
New York Univ	NY	61,470	MC
N Car Central Univ	NC	9,000	LC
N Dak State Univ	ND	14,642	C
Northern Illinois Univ	IL	19,768	C
Northwest Missouri State Univ	MO	14,229	C
Ohio Univ	OH	20,676	VC
Okla Christian Univ	OK	24,975	VC
Okla State Univ	OK	14,310	VC
Park Univ	MO	17,525	C
Plymouth State Univ	NH	23,148	LC
Portland State Univ	OR	18,672	C
Rutgers, The State Univ of New Jersey/Camden Campus	NJ	24,254	C
Seton Hill Univ	PA	35,172	C
St. Bonaventure Univ	NY	38,831	C
SUNY/Empire State College	NY	6,315	SP
SUNY Oneonta / SUNY	NY	16,919	VC
SUNY Plattsburgh / SUNY	NY	18,083	VC
Syracuse Univ	NY	54,512	HC
Tenn Tech Univ	TN	11,310	C
Texas A&M Univ at Kingsville	TX	7,500	LC
Texas State Univ	TX	16,495	VC
The SUNY College of Agriculture and Tech at Cobleskill	NY	18,869	VC
Univ of Idaho	ID	14,558	C
Univ of Maine	ME	19,712	Ȼ
Univ of Missouri/Columbia	MO	18,201	MC
Univ of Nebr - Lincoln	NE	17,507	VC
Univ of Nevada/Reno	NV	14,500	NC
Univ of New Mexico	NM	15,300	C
Univ of N Car at Chapel Hill	NC	18,348	MC
Univ of N Car at Charlotte	NC	15,847	C
Univ of N Car at Greensboro	NC	12,848	C
Univ of North Texas	TX	15,628	C
Univ of Tenn at Knoxville	TN	20,364	VȻ
Univ of Tenn at Martin	TN	13,217	C
Univ of Texas at Austin	TX	44,074	HC
Univ of Texas at San Antonio	TX	18,372	C
Univ of the Incarnate Word	TX	35,200	LC
Univ of Vermont	VT	26,120	VȻ
Univ of Wisc/Madison	WI	18,757	HC
Univ of Wisc/Stout	WI	23,942	C
Utah State Univ	UT	11,803	C
West Virginia Univ	WV	15,794	Ȼ
Western Mich Univ	MI	19,042	C
Wheelock College	MA	33,075	C
Youngstown State Univ	OH	16,374	LC

CHILD PSYCHOLOGY/ DEVELOPMENT

School	ST	$IS	SR
Alcorn State Univ	MS	9,500	C
Angelo State Univ	TX	15,049	NC
Appalachian State Univ	NC	12,919	VC
Bay Path College	MA	34,565	C
Bennington College	VT	56,990	HȻ
Bethel Univ	TN	19,186	C
Bluffton Univ	OH	37,864	C
Calif Polytechnic State Univ	CA	19,847	HC
Cal State, Bakersfield	CA	8,000	LC
Cal State, Chico	CA	18,952	C
Cal State, Dominguez Hills	CA	17,056	LC
Cal State, Fresno	CA	17,405	C
Cal State, Los Angeles	CA	15,829	C
Cal State, Northridge	CA	28,313	C
Cal State, San Bernardino	CA	12,000	C
Cal State, Stanislaus	CA	18,582	C
Central Mich Univ	MI	18,066	C
Colby-Sawyer College	NH	47,870	C
College of the Ozarks	MO	5,605	VC
East Tenn State Univ	TN	9,000	C
East Texas Baptist Univ	TX	29,135	C
Eastern Nazarene College	MA	30,000	C
Florida Gulf Coast Univ	FL		C
Fort Valley State Univ	GA	11,200	VC
Hope International Univ	CA	34,650	C
Howard Univ	DC	35,957	C
Humboldt State Univ	CA	18,400	C
Iowa State Univ	IA	16,403	C
Madonna Univ	MI	24,540	VC
Marygrove College	MI	21,290	C
Meredith College	NC	31,420	C
Metropolitan State Univ	MN	5,923	SP
Mich State Univ	MI	13,689	VC
Mills College	CA	54,119	HC
Missouri Baptist Univ	MO	30,310	C
Missouri State Univ	MO	13,996	VC
Mount Ida College	MA	30,115	LC
Mount St. Mary's College/ Chalon Campus	CA	43,897	VȻ
New Mexico State Univ	NM	13,955	LC
N Car Agricultural and Technical State Univ	NC	13,175	LC
N Car Central Univ	NC	9,000	LC
Olivet Nazarene Univ	IL	29,990	C
Point Loma Nazarene Univ	CA	38,610	VC
St. Joseph College	CT	45,630	LC
San Diego State Univ	CA	20,578	VC
Siena Heights Univ	MI	17,000	LC
Southern New Hampshire Univ	NH	38,100	C
Spelman College	GA	24,650	VC
St. Joseph's College, New York / Brooklyn Campus	NY	21,878	C
St. Joseph's College, New York / Suffolk Campus	NY	21,878	VC
Stephen F. Austin State Univ	TX	14,668	C
Texas Christian Univ	TX	47,570	HC
Texas Tech Univ	TX	14,243	C
Texas Woman's Univ	TX	13,633	LC
Tougaloo College	MS	15,275	NC
Tufts Univ	MA	58,780	MC
Univ of Central Okla	OK	12,293	C
Univ of Illinois at Urbana-Champaign	IL	24,300	HC
Univ of La Verne	CA	47,010	VC
Univ of Minn/Twin Cities	MN		HC
Univ of N Car at Charlotte	NC	15,847	C
Univ of St. Mary	KS	28,400	Ȼ
Univ of Texas at Dallas	TX	21,046	HC
Utica College	NY	44,734	C
Vanderbilt Univ	TN	57,072	MC
Western Washington Univ	WA	18,519	VC
Whittier College	CA	43,416	C

CHILDHOOD EDUCATION: 1-6

School	ST	$IS	SR
CUNY/Brooklyn College	NY	5,884	Ȼ
Concordia Univ St. Paul	MN	27,200	C
Fontbonne Univ	MO	31,384	C
Houghton College	NY	35,740	VC
New York Univ	NY	61,470	MC
St. John's Univ	NY	52,840	Ȼ
SUNY Plattsburgh / SUNY	NY	18,083	VC
The College of St. Rose	NY	26,750	C
Univ of Arkansas at Fayetteville	AR	16,860	VC
Univ of Illinois at Chicago	IL	24,293	VC
Univ of Louisiana at Monroe	LA	12,998	C

CHINA ASIA-PACIFIC STUDIES

School	ST	$IS	SR
Cornell Univ	NY	59,037	MC
Hofstra Univ	NY	48,020	VȻ

CHINESE

School	ST	$IS	SR
American Univ	DC	54,829	HȻ
Bard College	NY	59,872	HC
Bates College	ME	58,950	MC
Bennington College	VT	56,990	HȻ
Brigham Young Univ	UT	12,100	HC
Bryant Univ	RI	49,179	VC
Calvin College	MI	37,585	VȻ
Central Washington Univ	WA	11,730	C
Colgate Univ	NY	50,930	MC
College of the Holy Cross	MA	56,232	MC
College of William & Mary	VA	25,085	MC
Concordia College, Moorhead	MN	39,974	Ȼ
Conn College	CT	54,970	MC
Dartmouth College	NH	57,996	MC
DePaul Univ	IL	46,120	VC
Drew Univ/College of Liberal Arts	NJ	55,862	VC
Emory Univ	GA	45,000	MC
George Washington Univ	DC	57,108	MC
Georgetown Univ	DC	52,910	MC
Grand Valley State Univ	MI	17,998	VC
Grinnell College	IA	53,654	HC
Hamilton College	NY	55,620	MC
Harvard Univ/Harvard College	MA	49,000	MC
Hofstra Univ	NY	48,020	VȻ
Hunter College / The CUNY	NY	14,429	VC
Lawrence Univ	WI	46,371	HC
Lehigh Univ	PA	55,080	MC
Macalester College	MN	53,419	MC
Middlebury College	VT	57,470	MC
Nazareth College of Rochester	NY	41,590	VC
New College of Florida	FL	14,504	HȻ
North Central College	IL	38,343	VC
Oakland Univ	MI	19,391	VC
Occidental College	CA	59,592	MȻ
Penn State Univ/Univ Park	PA	25,404	VC
Pomona College	CA	57,680	MC
Portland State Univ	OR	18,672	C
Queens College / The CUNY	NY	17,107	VC
Reed College	OR	57,780	MC
Rutgers, The State Univ of New Jersey/New Brunswick	NJ	25,077	VC
San Francisco State Univ	CA	18,514	C
San Jose State Univ	CA	19,707	C
Scripps College	CA	54,900	MC
Stanford Univ	CA	56,411	MC
Swarthmore College	PA	57,870	MC
Ohio State Univ	OH	19,887	MC
Thomas Edison State College	NJ	5,700	SP
Trinity Univ	TX	44,174	HȻ
Tufts Univ	MA	58,780	MC
United States Naval Academy	MD		MC
Univ at Albany / SUNY	NY	18,674	VC
Univ of Calif at Berkeley	CA	23,322	MC
Univ of Calif at Davis	CA	24,482	HC
Univ of Calif at Los Angeles	CA	25,686	MC
Univ of Calif at Riverside	CA	27,204	C
Univ of Calif at San Diego	CA	21,000	VC
Univ of Calif at Santa Barbara	CA	27,551	HC
Univ of Colo Boulder	CO	22,605	VȻ
Univ of Georgia	GA	19,508	VC
Univ of Hawaii at Manoa	HI	19,379	VC
Univ of Houston	TX	19,184	VC
Univ of Iowa	IA	17,481	VC
Univ of Maryland	MD	18,801	HC
Univ of Mass Amherst	MA	23,697	VȻ
Univ of Minn/Twin Cities	MN		HC
Univ of Miss	MS	15,482	VC
Univ of N Dak	ND	14,094	C
Univ of Notre Dame	IN		MC
Univ of Okla	OK	17,634	VȻ
Univ of Oregon	OR	20,872	VC
Univ of Pittsburgh at Pittsburgh	PA	27,800	HȻ
Univ of Puget Sound	WA	52,648	HȻ
Univ of Utah	UT	13,462	VC
Univ of Vermont	VT	26,120	VȻ
Univ of Wisc/Madison	WI	18,757	HC
Vassar College	NY	59,070	MC
Wake Forest Univ	NC	51,000	MC
Washington State Univ	WA	20,461	C
Washington Univ in St. Louis	MO	58,818	MC
Wellesley College	MA	49,848	MC
Whittier College	CA	43,416	C
Wofford College	SC	45,795	VC
Yale Univ	CT	55,300	MC

CHINESE STUDIES

School	ST	$IS	SR
Binghamton Univ / The SUNY	NY	20,832	HȻ
Eugene Lang College - The New School for Liberal Arts	NY	55,650	VC
Hofstra Univ	NY	48,020	VȻ
Messiah College	PA	39,540	VC
Swarthmore College	PA	57,870	MC
Univ of Calif at Irvine	CA	25,961	VC

CHIROPRACTIC

School	ST	$IS	SR
Colo State Univ-Pueblo	CO	13,532	LC
Mount Aloysius College	PA	27,970	C
Northern Mich Univ	MI	15,300	VC

CHORAL MUSIC

School	ST	$IS	SR
Baylor Univ	TX	46,720	HC
Concordia Univ St. Paul	MN	27,200	C
Mannes College New School for Music	NY	44,500	C
Mount Aloysius College	PA	27,970	C
Ohio Univ	OH	20,676	VC
Toccoa Falls College	GA	23,210	C
Univ of Kansas	KS	16,980	Ȼ
Univ of North Texas	TX	15,628	C
Webster Univ	MO	33,990	Ȼ

CHRISTIAN EDUCATION

School	ST	$IS	SR
Anderson Univ	IN	35,390	C
Asbury Univ	KY	32,038	VC
Bethany College	KS	30,605	NC
Biola Univ	CA	40,320	VC
Cedarville Univ	OH	31,036	VȻ
Columbia College	SC	27,882	C
Concordia Univ - Irvine	CA	35,390	VC
Concordia Univ Nebr	NE	26,000	VC
Concordia Univ St. Paul	MN	27,200	C
Defiance College	OH	30,645	C
Erskine College	SC	37,360	C
Hannibal-LaGrange Univ	MO	24,490	C
Harding Univ	AR	21,432	Ȼ
Houghton College	NY	35,740	VC
Huntingdon College	AL	31,850	C
Lenoir-Rhyne College	NC	35,984	C
Malone Univ	OH	34,334	C
MidAmerica Nazarene Univ	KS	28,000	C
Muskingum Univ	OH	30,502	C
Northwest Nazarene Univ	ID	24,275	NC

School	ST	$IS	SR
Northwestern College of Iowa	IA	34,848	C+
Olivet Nazarene Univ	IL	29,990	C
Pfeiffer Univ	NC	33,700	C
Southern Nazarene Univ	OK	24,354	NC
Spring Arbor Univ	MI	26,740	C
Taylor Univ	IN	36,742	VC+
Westminster College	PA	31,290	C+
Wheaton College	IL	39,650	HC+

CHRISTIAN STUDIES

School	ST	$IS	SR
Alderson Broaddus Univ	WV	28,656	C
Aquinas College	MI	33,060	C
Belmont Univ	TN	37,380	VC+
Bethel College	IN	31,560	C
Bluefield College	VA	17,230	C+
Brewton-Parker College	GA	33,388	LC
Bryan College	TN	24,194	C
Calif Baptist Univ	CA	35,890	C
Campbellsville Univ	KY	27,720	C
Cornerstone Univ and Grand Rapids Theological Seminary	MI	30,866	C
Eastern Nazarene College	MA	30,000	C
Friends Univ	KS	29,100	C
Grand Canyon Univ	AZ	24,540	VC
Hillsdale College	MI	31,890	HC+
Houghton College	NY	35,740	VC
Houston Baptist Univ	TX	23,815	C+
Howard Payne Univ	TX	17,115	C
Lewis Univ	IL	23,050	C
Mercer Univ	GA	44,201	VC+
Miss College	MS	21,998	VC
Missouri Baptist Univ	MO	30,310	C
Ouachita Baptist Univ	AR	29,010	VC
Roanoke College	VA	47,996	C+
Roberts Wesleyan College	NY	37,384	C+
Seattle Pacific Univ	WA	41,559	VC+
Shorter Univ	GA	26,470	C
Stonehill College	MA	46,780	VC+
Toccoa Falls College	GA	23,210	C
Trinity International Univ	IL	31,070	C
Union Univ	TN	28,260	VC
Univ of Mary Hardin-Baylor	TX	31,950	C+
Vanguard Univ of Southern Calif	CA	35,833	VC
Wayland Baptist Univ	TX	16,058	LC

CHURCH MUSIC

School	ST	$IS	SR
Cedarville Univ	OH	31,036	VC+
Concordia Univ St. Paul	MN	27,200	C
Dordt College	IA	34,160	VC
Hope International Univ	CA	34,650	C
Okla City Univ	OK	33,546	VC
Ouachita Baptist Univ	AR	29,010	VC
Samford Univ	AL	35,700	VC+
Shenandoah Univ	VA	39,268	C
Texas Christian Univ	TX	47,570	HC
Univ of Mary Hardin-Baylor	TX	31,950	C+

CITY/COMMUNITY/REGIONAL PLANNING

School	ST	$IS	SR
Alabama A&M Univ	AL	96,100	C
Arizona State Univ	AZ	18,818	C+
Brigham Young Univ	UT	12,100	HC
Calif Polytechnic State Univ	CA	19,847	HC
East Carolina Univ	NC	14,169	C
Eastern Mich Univ	MI	17,961	C
Iowa State Univ	IA	16,403	C
Mansfield Univ	PA	19,468	LC
Mich State Univ	MI	13,689	VC
New Mexico State Univ	NM	13,955	LC
Plymouth State Univ	NH	23,148	LC
Temple Univ	PA	24,392	VC
Texas State Univ	TX	16,495	VC
Ohio State Univ	OH	19,887	MC
Univ of Cincinnati	OH	20,199	VC
Univ of Illinois at Urbana-Champaign	IL	24,300	HC
Univ of New Hampshire	NH	24,702	VC
Univ of Virginia	VA	22,175	MC
Univ of Wisc/Green Bay	WI	14,900	C
Western Mich Univ	MI	19,042	C
Westfield State Univ	MA	18,489	C

CIVIL ENGINEERING

School	ST	$IS	SR
Alabama A&M Univ	AL	96,100	C
Arizona State Univ	AZ	18,818	C+
Auburn Univ	AL	20,052	VC+
Bethel College	IN	31,560	C
Boise State Univ	ID	12,802	C
Bradley Univ	IL	31,874	VC
Brigham Young Univ	UT	12,100	HC
Bucknell Univ	PA	58,160	MC
Calif Baptist Univ	CA	35,890	C
Calif Polytechnic State Univ	CA	19,847	HC
Calif State Polytechnic Univ, Pomona	CA	18,932	C
Cal State, Chico	CA	18,952	C
Cal State, Fresno	CA	17,405	C
Cal State, Fullerton	CA	25,188	C+
Cal State, Long Beach	CA	17,534	C+
Cal State, Los Angeles	CA	15,829	C
Cal State, Sacramento	CA	16,200	C
Calvin College	MI	37,585	VC+
Caribbean Univ	PR	10,375	
Carnegie Mellon Univ	PA	51,260	MC
Carroll College	MT	28,000	C
Case Western Reserve Univ	OH	55,178	MC
Central Conn State Univ	CT	19,212	C
Christian Brothers Univ	TN	19,140	HC
Citadel, The	SC		C
Clarkson Univ	NY	53,538	HC
Clemson Univ	SC	19,136	HC
Cleveland State Univ	OH	21,357	C
College of New Jersey	NJ	25,376	HC
Colo State Univ-Fort Collins	CO	20,090	VC
Columbia Univ in the City of New York	NY	61,116	MC
Cooper Union for the Advancement of Science and Art	NY	55,600	MC
Cornell Univ	NY	59,037	MC
CUNY-City College	NY	19,576	HC+
Delaware State Univ	DE	14,700	LC
Dordt College	IA	34,160	VC
Drexel Univ	PA	51,920	HC
Duke Univ	NC	50,250	MC
Embry-Riddle Aeronautical Univ - Daytona Beach	FL	40,884	C+
Florida A&M Univ	FL	14,935	LC
Florida Atlantic Univ	FL	17,339	C
Florida Gulf Coast Univ	FL		C
Florida Inst of Technology	FL	48,290	VC
Florida International Univ	FL	17,747	VC
Florida State Univ	FL	15,238	HC
George Mason Univ	VA	15,724	VC
George Washington Univ	DC	57,108	MC
Georgia Inst of Technology	GA	20,464	MC
Georgia Southern Univ	GA	16,414	C
Gonzaga Univ	WA	44,247	HC
Hofstra Univ	NY	48,020	VC+
Howard Univ	DC	35,957	C
Idaho State Univ	ID	11,908	C
Illinois Inst of Technology	IL	38,512	HC+
Indiana Univ-Purdue Univ Fort Wayne	IN	15,425	C
Iowa State Univ	IA	16,403	C
Jackson State Univ	MS	13,512	LC
Johns Hopkins Univ	MD	47,492	MC
Kansas State Univ	KS	15,497	VC
Lafayette College	PA	57,050	HC+
Lamar Univ	TX	6,820	LC
Lawrence Tech Univ	MI	37,630	VC
Lehigh Univ	PA	55,080	MC
Lipscomb Univ	TN	35,722	VC
Louisiana State Univ	LA	18,677	VC+
Louisiana Tech Univ	LA	8,000	C
Loyola Marymount Univ	CA	53,240	VC+
Manhattan College	NY	44,955	VC
Marquette Univ	WI	43,664	VC+
Marshall Univ	WV	14,820	C
Mass Inst of Technology	MA	54,238	MC
Merrimack College	MA	44,215	C
Mich State Univ	MI	13,689	VC
Mich Tech Univ	MI	22,105	VC
Minn State Univ, Mankato	MN	14,900	C
Missouri Univ of Science and Technology	MO	18,655	VC+
Montana State Univ	MT	14,068	VC
Morgan State Univ	MD	14,500	VC
New Jersey Inst of Technology	NJ	26,490	VC
New Mexico Inst of Mining and Technology	NM	12,892	HC
New Mexico State Univ	NM	13,955	LC
New York Univ	NY	61,470	MC
N Car Agricultural and Technical State Univ	NC	13,175	LC
N Car State Univ	NC	16,202	HC
N Dak State Univ	ND	14,642	C
Northeastern Univ	MA	55,296	MC
Northern Arizona Univ	AZ	18,592	C
Northwestern Univ	IL	37,595	MC
Norwich Univ	VT	28,212	C
Ohio Northern Univ	OH	42,075	VC
Ohio Univ	OH	20,676	VC
Okla State Univ	OK	14,310	VC
Old Dominion Univ	VA	18,662	C
Oregon Inst of Technology	OR	8,910	C
Oregon State Univ	OR	19,017	C+
Penn State Univ/Univ Park	PA	25,404	VC
Point Park Univ	PA	36,390	C
Polytechnic Inst of New York Univ	NY	53,064	HC+
Portland State Univ	OR	18,672	C
Prairie View A&M Univ	TX	15,205	LC
Princeton Univ	NJ	53,795	MC
Purdue Univ/West Lafayette	IN	20,278	HC
Quinnipiac Univ	CT	53,580	VC
Rensselaer Polytechnic Inst	NY	59,229	MC
Rice Univ	TX	43,288	MC
Rose-Hulman Inst of Technology	IN	51,738	MC
Rowan Univ	NJ	23,570	VC
Rutgers, The State Univ of New Jersey/New Brunswick	NJ	25,077	VC
St. Louis Univ	MO	46,594	VC+
St. Martin's Univ	WA	38,082	C
San Diego State Univ	CA	20,578	VC
San Francisco State Univ	CA	18,514	C
San Jose State Univ	CA	19,707	C
Santa Clara Univ	CA	54,702	MC
Savannah State Univ	GA	13,156	C
Seattle Univ	WA	47,010	VC+
S Dak School of Mines and Technology	SD	15,260	VC
S Dak State Univ	SD	14,296	C
Southern Illinois Univ Carbondale	IL	21,020	C
Southern Illinois Univ Edwardsville	IL	17,532	C
Southern Methodist Univ	TX	57,755	MC
Southern Polytechnic State Univ	GA	13,958	VC
Southern Univ and A&M College	LA	9,761	C+
Stanford Univ	CA	56,411	MC
Stevens Inst of Technology	NJ	50,130	HC
Syracuse Univ	NY	54,512	HC
Temple Univ	PA	24,392	VC
Tenn State Univ	TN	9,048	C
Tenn Tech Univ	TN	11,310	C
Texas A&M Univ	TX	16,956	VC+
Texas A&M Univ at Galveston	TX	11,258	C
Texas A&M Univ at Kingsville	TX	7,500	LC
Texas Tech Univ	TX	14,243	C
The Catholic Univ of America	DC	52,852	VC
Ohio State Univ	OH	19,887	MC
Trine Univ	IN	39,400	VC
Tufts Univ	MA	58,780	MC
United States Air Force Academy	CO		MC
United States Coast Guard Academy	CT		HC
United States Military Academy	NY		MC
Universidad Politecnica de PR	PR	19,252	
Univ at Buffalo / The SUNY	NY	20,283	VC
Univ of Akron	OH	20,436	C
Univ of Alabama at Birmingham	AL	18,484	C+
Univ of Alabama at Huntsville	AL	17,625	VC
Univ of Alabama at Tuscaloosa	AL	17,164	C+
Univ of Alaska Anchorage	AK	15,290	NC
Univ of Alaska Fairbanks	AK	13,955	C
Univ of Arizona	AZ	20,105	C
Univ of Arkansas at Fayetteville	AR	16,860	VC
Univ of Calif at Berkeley	CA	23,322	MC
Univ of Calif at Davis	CA	24,482	HC
Univ of Calif at Irvine	CA	25,961	VC
Univ of Calif at Los Angeles	CA	25,686	MC
Univ of Central Florida	FL	15,711	VC+
Univ of Cincinnati	OH	20,199	VC
Univ of Colo Boulder	CO	22,605	VC+
Univ of Colo Denver	CO	17,904	C
Univ of Conn	CT	23,744	HC
Univ of Dayton	OH	43,750	VC
Univ of Delaware	DE	22,728	VC
Univ of Detroit Mercy	MI	30,450	C
Univ of Evansville	IN	41,056	VC+
Univ of Florida	FL	15,783	HC+
Univ of Georgia	GA	19,508	VC
Univ of Hartford	CT	42,674	C
Univ of Hawaii at Manoa	HI	19,379	VC
Univ of Houston	TX	19,184	VC
Univ of Idaho	ID	14,558	C
Univ of Illinois at Chicago	IL	24,293	VC
Univ of Illinois at Urbana-Champaign	IL	24,300	HC
Univ of Iowa	IA	17,481	VC
Univ of Kansas	KS	16,980	C+
Univ of Kentucky	KY	19,868	C
Univ of Louisiana at Lafayette	LA	6,130	C
Univ of Louisville	KY	17,460	VC
Univ of Maine	ME	19,712	C+
Univ of Maryland	MD	18,801	HC
Univ of Mass Amherst	MA	23,697	VC+
Univ of Mass Dartmouth	MA	22,223	C
Univ of Mass Lowell	MA	19,316	C
Univ of Memphis	TN	15,094	C
Univ of Miami	FL	55,166	MC
Univ of Mich/Ann Arbor	MI	22,102	HC+
Univ of Minn/Duluth	MN	18,964	C+
Univ of Minn/Twin Cities	MN		HC
Univ of Miss	MS	15,482	VC
Univ of Missouri/Columbia	MO	18,201	MC
Univ of Missouri-Kansas City	MO	19,603	C
Univ of Missouri-St. Louis	MO	18,304	VC
Univ of Mount Union	OH	35,130	C
Univ of Nebr - Lincoln	NE	17,507	VC
Univ of Nevada, Las Vegas	NV	17,303	C
Univ of Nevada/Reno	NV	14,500	NC
Univ of New Hampshire	NH	24,702	VC
Univ of New Haven	CT	47,740	C
Univ of New Mexico	NM	15,300	C
Univ of New Orleans	LA	9,224	VC
Univ of N Car at Charlotte	NC	15,847	C
Univ of N Dak	ND	14,094	C
Univ of North Florida	FL	15,578	VC
Univ of Notre Dame	IN		MC
Univ of Okla	OK	17,634	VC+
Univ of Pennsylvania	PA	56,106	MC
Univ of Pittsburgh at Pittsburgh	PA	27,800	HC+
Univ of Portland	OR	47,874	VC
Univ of PR/Mayaguez	PR	1,250	
Univ of South Alabama	AL	13,510	C
Univ of S Car at Columbia	SC	19,725	VC+
Univ of South Florida	FL	13,000	C
Univ of Southern Calif	CA	56,903	MC
Univ of Tenn at Chattanooga	TN	16,883	C
Univ of Tenn at Knoxville	TN	20,364	VC+
Univ of Texas at Arlington	TX	10,908	LC
Univ of Texas at Austin	TX	44,074	HC
Univ of Texas at El Paso	TX	8,764	NC
Univ of Texas at San Antonio	TX	18,372	C
Univ of Texas-Pan American	TX	12,432	LC
Univ of the District of Columbia	DC	7,244	LC
Univ of the Pacific	CA	52,146	VC
Univ of Toledo	OH	18,464	C
Univ of Utah	UT	13,462	VC
Univ of Vermont	VT	26,120	VC+
Univ of Virginia	VA	22,175	MC
Univ of Washington	WA	14,722	VC
Univ of Wisc/Madison	WI	18,757	HC
Univ of Wisc/Platteville	WI	14,274	C
Univ of Wisc-Milwaukee	WI	18,436	C
Univ of Wyoming	WY	13,855	C+
Utah State Univ	UT	11,803	C
Valparaiso Univ	IN	43,040	VC+
Vanderbilt Univ	TN	57,072	MC
Villanova Univ	PA	56,436	MC
Virginia Military Inst	VA	16,156	C
Virginia Polytechnic Inst and State Univ	VA	14,629	HC
Washington State Univ	WA	20,461	C
Washington Univ in St. Louis	MO	58,818	MC
Wayne State Univ	MI	19,493	C
West Virginia Univ	WV	15,794	C+
West Virginia Univ Inst of Technology	WV	14,094	NC
Western Kentucky Univ	KY	11,000	LC
Western Mich Univ	MI	19,042	C
Western New England Univ	MA	45,590	C
Widener Univ	PA	50,368	C
Worcester Polytechnic Inst	MA	53,440	HC+
Youngstown State Univ	OH	16,374	LC

CIVIL ENGINEERING TECHNOLOGY

School	ST	$IS	SR
Alabama A&M Univ	AL	96,100	C
Arkansas State Univ	AR	14,980	C
Cal State, Fresno	CA	17,405	C
Central Conn State Univ	CT	19,212	C
Colo State Univ-Pueblo	CO	13,532	LC
Fairleigh Dickinson Univ/Metropolitan Campus	NJ	40,254	C
Fairmont State Univ	WV	12,098	LC
Idaho State Univ	ID	11,908	C
Lincoln Univ	MO	11,996	NC
Metropolitan State Univ of Denver	CO	4,835	LC
Montana State Univ-Northern	MT	12,500	NC
Murray State Univ	KY	14,944	C
Old Dominion Univ	VA	18,662	C
Pennsylvania College of Technology	PA	25,653	NC
Point Park Univ	PA	36,390	C
Rochester Inst of Technology	NY	42,450	VC+
S Car State Univ	SC	6,700	LC
Southern Polytechnic State Univ	GA	13,958	VC
SUNY Inst of Technology at Utica / Rome	NY	23,818	C
Texas Southern Univ	TX	18,212	LC
Univ of N Car at Charlotte	NC	15,847	C
Univ of Pittsburgh at Johnstown	PA	20,862	LC
Wentworth Inst of Technology	MA	29,800	SP
Youngstown State Univ	OH	16,374	LC

CLASSICAL AND NEAR EASTERN CIVILIZATION

School	ST	$IS	SR
Creighton Univ	NE	44,058	VC+

CLASSICAL LANGUAGES

School	ST	$IS	SR
Agnes Scott College	GA	45,323	VC+

School	ST	$IS	SR
Asbury Univ	KY	32,038	VC
Ball State Univ	IN	17,850	C
Bard College	NY	59,872	HC
Beloit College	WI	49,970	HC
Brigham Young Univ	UT	12,100	HC
Bryn Mawr College	PA	57,760	MC
Calvin College	MI	37,585	VG
Canisius College	NY	45,602	VC
Carroll College	MT	28,000	C
Christopher Newport Univ	VA	21,050	VC
Concordia College, Moorhead	MN	39,974	G
Creighton Univ	NE	44,058	VG
Dartmouth College	NH	57,996	MC
DePauw Univ	IN	48,950	VG
Dickinson College	PA	57,662	HG
Duke Univ	NC	50,250	MC
Duquesne Univ	PA	42,017	VC
Eastern Mich Univ	MI	17,961	C
Fordham Univ	NY	58,927	HC
John Carroll Univ	OH	44,520	G
La Salle Univ	PA	50,270	C
Luther College	IA	44,380	VG
Marquette Univ	WI	43,664	VG
Miami Univ	OH	24,191	HC
New York Univ	NY	61,470	MC
St. Louis Univ	MO	46,594	VG
St. Mary's College of Calif	CA	53,550	C
St. Peter's College	NJ	44,240	C
Scripps College	CA	54,900	MC
Sewanee: The Univ of the South	TN	47,700	HG
St. Bonaventure Univ	NY	38,831	C
Univ of Calif at Berkeley	CA	23,322	MC
Univ of Calif at Riverside	CA	27,204	C
Univ of Calif at Santa Cruz	CA	27,807	VC
Univ of Georgia	GA	19,508	VC
Univ of Kansas	KS	16,980	G
Univ of Mass Boston	MA	11,966	C
Univ of Miami	FL	55,166	MC
Univ of Mich/Ann Arbor	MI	22,102	HG
Univ of Minn/Twin Cities	MN		HC
Univ of Nebr - Lincoln	NE	17,507	VC
Univ of N Car at Greensboro	NC	12,848	C
Univ of N Dak	ND	14,094	C
Vanderbilt Univ	TN	57,072	MC
Washington Univ in St. Louis	MO	58,818	MC
Wheaton College	IL	39,650	HG
Wright State Univ	OH	16,983	C
Yeshiva Univ	NY	47,250	VG

CLASSICAL/ANCIENT CIVILIZATION

School	ST	$IS	SR
Agnes Scott College	GA	45,323	VG
Bard College	NY	59,872	HC
Bates College	ME	58,950	HC
Beloit College	WI	49,970	HC
Binghamton Univ / The SUNY	NY	20,832	HG
Boston College	MA	58,506	MC
Boston Univ	MA	54,130	HG
Bowdoin College	ME	57,834	MC
Brigham Young Univ	UT	12,100	HC
Brown Univ	RI	56,150	MC
Carleton College	MN	58,149	MC
Centre College	KY	35,000	HG
Christendom College	VA	28,120	VC
Clark Univ	MA	47,020	HG
Cleveland State Univ	OH	21,357	C
Colby College	ME	57,510	MC
College of William & Mary	VA	25,085	MC
Columbia Univ in the City of New York	NY	61,116	MC
Columbia Univ/Barnard College	NY	39,000	MC
Columbia Univ/School of General Studies	NY	54,083	MC
Cornell College	IA	44,930	HC
Dartmouth College	NH	57,996	MC
Denison Univ	OH	54,670	HG
DePauw Univ	IN	48,950	VG
Dickinson College	PA	57,662	HG
Duke Univ	NC	50,250	MC
Duquesne Univ	PA	42,017	VC
Earlham College	IN	49,710	VG
Eckerd College	FL	43,902	VC
Emory Univ	GA	45,000	MC
Florida State Univ	FL	15,238	HC
Fordham Univ	NY	58,927	HC
Gonzaga Univ	WA	44,247	HC
Hawaii Pacific Univ	HI	36,690	C
Hollins Univ	VA	43,295	VC
Howard Univ	DC	35,957	C
Indiana Univ Bloomington	IN	19,358	HC
Kalamazoo College	MI	47,825	HG
Lehigh Univ	PA	55,080	MC
Loyola Marymount Univ	CA	53,240	VG
Loyola Univ Chicago	IL	49,560	VG
Loyola Univ Maryland	MD		VC
Loyola Univ New Orleans	LA	46,581	VC
Mich State Univ	MI	13,689	VC
Mount Holyoke College	MA	53,596	HG
New York Univ	NY	61,470	MC
North Central College	IL	38,343	VC
Ohio Univ	OH	20,676	VC
Queens College / The CUNY	NY	17,107	VC
Rhodes College	TN	47,596	HG
Rice Univ	TX	43,288	MC
Rollins College	FL	52,370	HC
Rutgers, The State Univ of New Jersey/Newark Campus	NJ	25,376	C
St. Peter's College	NJ	44,240	C
Santa Clara Univ	CA	54,702	MC
Scripps College	CA	54,900	MC
Smith College	MA	57,524	MC
St. Olaf College	MN	49,960	HG
Swarthmore College	PA	57,870	MC
Sweet Briar College	VA	43,765	G
Syracuse Univ	NY	54,512	HC
Trinity College	CT		HG
Univ of Arkansas at Fayetteville	AR	16,860	VC
Univ of Calif at Berkeley	CA	23,322	MC
Univ of Calif at Davis	CA	24,482	HC
Univ of Calif at Irvine	CA	25,961	VC
Univ of Calif at Los Angeles	CA	25,686	MC
Univ of Calif at Riverside	CA	27,204	C
Univ of Chicago	IL	55,416	MC
Univ of Cincinnati	OH	20,199	VC
Univ of Evansville	IN	41,056	VG
Univ of Florida	FL	15,783	HG
Univ of Illinois at Chicago	IL	24,293	VC
Univ of Iowa	IA	17,481	VC
Univ of Kansas	KS	16,980	G
Univ of Maryland/Baltimore County	MD	18,000	VC
Univ of Miami	FL	55,166	MC
Univ of Mich/Ann Arbor	MI	22,102	HG
Univ of Miss	MS	15,482	VC
Univ of Nebr - Lincoln	NE	17,507	VC
Univ of Notre Dame	IN		MC
Univ of Oregon	OR	20,872	VC
Univ of Southern Calif	CA	56,903	MC
Univ of Texas at Arlington	TX	10,908	LC
Univ of Texas at Austin	TX	44,074	HC
Vassar College	NY	59,070	MC
Wellesley College	MA	49,848	MC
Wesleyan Univ	CT	59,844	MC
Willamette Univ	OR	56,450	VG
Yale Univ	CT	55,300	MC

CLASSICS

School	ST	$IS	SR
Alabama A&M Univ	AL	96,100	C
Amherst College	MA	58,744	MC
Assumption College	MA	45,721	VC
Augustana College	IL	43,398	HC
Augustana College	SD	35,500	VC
Austin College	TX	36,940	HC
Ball State Univ	IN	17,850	C
Baylor Univ	TX	46,720	HC
Belmont Univ	TN	37,380	VG
Binghamton Univ / The SUNY	NY	20,832	HG
Boston College	MA	58,506	MC
Boston Univ	MA	54,130	HG
Bowdoin College	ME	57,834	MC
Bowling Green State Univ	OH	18,970	C
Brandeis Univ	MA	58,820	HC
Brigham Young Univ	UT	12,100	HC
Brown Univ	RI	56,150	MC
Bryn Mawr College	PA	57,760	MC
Bucknell Univ	PA	58,160	MC
Calvin College	MI	37,585	VG
Carleton College	MN	58,149	MC
Case Western Reserve Univ	OH	55,178	MC
CUNY/Brooklyn College	NY	5,884	G
Claremont McKenna College	CA	58,065	MC
Colby College	ME	57,510	MC
Colgate Univ	NY	50,930	MC
College of Charleston	SC	21,273	VC
College of St. Benedict	MN	47,570	VC
College of the Holy Cross	MA	56,232	MC
Colo College	CO	54,534	MC
Columbia Univ in the City of New York	NY	61,116	MC
Columbia Univ/Barnard College	NY	39,000	MC
Columbia Univ/School of General Studies	NY	54,083	MC
Concordia College, Moorhead	MN	39,974	G
Conn College	CT	54,970	MC
Cornell Univ	NY	59,037	MC
Dartmouth College	NH	57,996	MC
Davidson College	NC	54,683	MC
Drew Univ/College of Liberal Arts	NJ	55,862	VC
Elmira College	NY	49,950	G
Emory Univ	GA	45,000	MC
Florida State Univ	FL	15,238	HC
Fordham Univ	NY	58,927	HC
Franciscan Univ of Steubenville	OH	27,320	VC
Franklin and Marshall College	PA	58,295	MC
Furman Univ	SC	54,006	HC
George Washington Univ	DC	57,108	MC
Georgetown Univ	DC	52,910	MC
Georgia State Univ	GA	12,000	VC
Gettysburg College	PA	56,820	HC
Gonzaga Univ	WA	44,247	HC
Grand Valley State Univ	MI	17,998	VC
Grinnell College	IA	53,654	HC
Gustavus Adolphus College	MN	48,170	HC
Hamilton College	NY	55,620	MC
Hampden-Sydney College	VA	48,848	C
Hanover College	IN	41,450	VC
Harvard Univ/Harvard College	MA	49,000	MC
Haverford College	PA	59,236	MC
Hellenic College/Holy Cross Greek Orthodox School of Theology	MA	33,190	VC
Hendrix College	AR	48,436	HG
Hillsdale College	MI	31,890	HG
Hobart and William Smith Colleges	NY	43,000	VC
Hofstra Univ	NY	48,020	VG
Hunter College / The CUNY	NY	14,429	VC
Illinois Wesleyan Univ	IL	48,452	VG
John Carroll Univ	OH	44,520	G
Johns Hopkins Univ	MD	47,492	MC
Kent State Univ	OH	19,352	C
Kenyon College	OH	56,810	MC
Knox College	IL		VC
Lawrence Univ	WI	46,371	HC
Lehigh Univ	PA	55,080	MC
Lewis & Clark College	OR	52,656	VC
Loyola Marymount Univ	CA	53,240	VG
Macalester College	MN	53,419	MC
Marquette Univ	WI	43,664	VG
Marshall Univ	WV	14,820	C
Miami Univ	OH	24,191	HC
Middlebury College	VT	57,470	MC
Millsaps College	MS	43,888	VG
Monmouth College	IL	39,290	C
Montclair State Univ	NJ	22,614	C
Moravian College	PA	36,381	VC
Mount Holyoke College	MA	53,596	HG
New College of Florida	FL	14,504	HG
New York Univ	NY	61,470	MC
Northwestern Univ	IL	37,595	MC
Notre Dame of Maryland Univ	MD	27,700	C
Oberlin College	OH	57,025	MC
Ohio Univ	OH	20,676	VC
Pacific Lutheran Univ	WA	44,840	VC
Penn State Univ/Univ Park	PA	25,404	VC
Pitzer College	CA	54,988	MC
Pomona College	CA	57,680	MC
Princeton Univ	NJ	53,795	MC
Purdue Univ/West Lafayette	IN	20,278	HC
Randolph College	VA	43,960	VC
Randolph-Macon College	VA	45,086	C
Reed College	OR	57,780	MC
Rice Univ	TX	43,288	MC
Rockford College	IL	31,000	C
Rutgers, The State Univ of New Jersey/New Brunswick	NJ	25,077	VC
St. Anselm College	NH	48,324	VC
St. John's Univ	MN	46,146	C
St. Louis Univ	MO	46,594	VG
Samford Univ	AL	35,700	VG
San Diego State Univ	CA	20,578	VC
San Francisco State Univ	CA	18,514	C
Sarah Lawrence College	NY	48,000	HC
Seattle Pacific Univ	WA	41,559	VG
Seton Hall Univ	NJ	45,902	C
Siena College	NY	43,863	VC
Skidmore College	NY	57,926	HC
Smith College	MA	57,524	MC
Southern Illinois Univ Carbondale	IL	21,620	C
Southwestern Univ	TX	45,660	VC
St. Catherine Univ	MN	37,782	G
St. Olaf College	MN	49,960	HG
Stanford Univ	CA	56,411	MC
Swarthmore College	PA	57,870	MC
Syracuse Univ	NY	54,512	HC
Temple Univ	PA	24,392	VC
Texas Tech Univ	TX	14,243	C
The Catholic Univ of America	DC	52,852	VC
The College of New Rochelle	NY	33,600	VC
Ohio State Univ	OH	19,887	MC
Transylvania Univ	KY	40,310	VG
Trinity College	CT		HG
Trinity Univ	TX	44,174	HG
Truman State Univ	MO	13,546	HC
Tufts Univ	MA	58,780	MC
Tulane Univ	LA	58,942	MC
Union College	NY		MC
Univ at Buffalo / The SUNY	NY	20,283	VC
Univ of Akron	OH	20,436	C
Univ of Alabama at Tuscaloosa	AL	17,164	G
Univ of Arizona	AZ	20,105	C
Univ of Calif at Irvine	CA	25,961	VC
Univ of Calif at Los Angeles	CA	25,686	MC
Univ of Calif at San Diego	CA	21,000	VC
Univ of Calif at Santa Barbara	CA	27,551	HC
Univ of Chicago	IL	55,416	MC
Univ of Colo Boulder	CO	22,605	VG
Univ of Conn	CT	23,744	HC
Univ of Dallas	TX	43,510	VG
Univ of Hawaii at Manoa	HI	19,379	VC
Univ of Illinois at Urbana-Champaign	IL	24,300	HC
Univ of Iowa	IA	17,481	VC
Univ of Mary Washington	VA	19,484	VC
Univ of Maryland	MD	18,801	HC
Univ of Mass Amherst	MA	23,697	VG
Univ of Mass Boston	MA	11,966	C
Univ of Miami	FL	55,166	MC
Univ of Mich/Ann Arbor	MI	22,102	HG
Univ of Missouri/Columbia	MO	18,201	MC
Univ of Montana	MT	13,670	C
Univ of Nebr - Lincoln	NE	17,507	VC
Univ of New Hampshire	NH	24,702	VC
Univ of New Mexico	NM	15,300	C
Univ of N Car at Asheville	NC	13,500	VG
Univ of N Car at Chapel Hill	NC	18,348	MC
Univ of Okla	OK	17,634	VG
Univ of Oregon	OR	20,872	VC
Univ of Pennsylvania	PA	56,106	MC
Univ of Pittsburgh at Pittsburgh	PA	27,800	HG
Univ of Puget Sound	WA	52,648	HG
Univ of Rochester	NY	58,500	MC
Univ of S Car at Columbia	SC	19,725	VG
Univ of South Florida	FL	13,000	C
Univ of Southern Calif	CA	56,903	MC
Univ of Tenn at Knoxville	TN	20,364	VG
Univ of Texas at Austin	TX	44,074	HC
Univ of Texas at San Antonio	TX	18,372	C
Univ of Utah	UT	13,462	VC
Univ of Vermont	VT	26,120	VG
Univ of Virginia	VA	22,175	MC
Univ of Washington	WA	14,722	VC
Univ of Wisc/Madison	WI	18,757	HC
Univ of Wisc-Milwaukee	WI	18,436	C
Ursinus College	PA	55,630	VG
Valparaiso Univ	IN	43,040	VG
Vanderbilt Univ	TN	57,072	MC
Villanova Univ	PA	56,436	MC
Virginia Wesleyan College	VA	28,433	LC
Wabash College	IN	44,160	VC
Wake Forest Univ	NC	51,000	MC
Washington and Lee Univ	VA	52,812	MC
Washington Univ in St. Louis	MO	58,818	MC
Wayne State Univ	MI	19,493	C
Wesleyan Univ	CT	59,844	MC
Western Washington Univ	WA	18,519	VC
Wheaton College	MA	54,934	HG
Whitman College	WA	54,400	MC
Williams College	MA	58,900	MC
Xavier Univ	OH	43,740	VC
Yale Univ	CT	55,300	MC

CLINICAL LABORATORY SCIENCE

School	ST	$IS	SR
Arkansas State Univ	AR	14,980	C
Indiana Univ Southeast	IN	15,807	LC
Indiana Univ-Purdue Univ Indianapolis	IN	17,290	C
Monmouth Univ	NJ	42,252	C
St. Louis Univ	MO	46,594	VG
Thomas Edison State College	NJ	5,700	SP
Univ of Evansville	IN	41,056	VG
Univ of Mary Hardin-Baylor	TX	31,950	G

CLINICAL PSYCHOLOGY

School	ST	$IS	SR
American Univ	DC	54,829	HG
Eastern Nazarene College	MA	30,000	C
Goddard College	VT	16,418	VC
Kutztown Univ of Pennsylvania	PA	16,909	LC
Marywood Univ	PA	40,695	C
Seattle Pacific Univ	WA	41,559	VG
The Lincoln Univ	PA	15,154	LC
Univ of Louisiana at Monroe	LA	12,998	C
Univ of New Haven	CT	47,740	C

CLINICAL SCIENCE

School	ST	$IS	SR
Ashford Univ	IA	21,780	C
Bellarmine Univ	KY	42,950	VC
Benedictine Univ	IL	35,220	C
Bethune-Cookman Univ	FL	22,290	LC
Bloomfield College	NJ	36,960	C
Brigham Young Univ	UT	12,100	HC
Cal State, Bakersfield	CA	8,000	LC
Cal State, Dominguez Hills	CA	17,056	LC
Campbell Univ	NC	25,500	C
Canisius College	NY	45,602	VC
Carroll College	MT	28,000	C

School	ST	$IS	SR
Carroll Univ	WI	24,860	C
Concordia College, Moorhead	MN	39,974	₵
DePaul Univ	IL	46,120	VC
Fairleigh Dickinson Univ/ College at Florham	NJ	42,142	C
Fairleigh Dickinson Univ/ Metropolitan Campus	NJ	40,254	C
Florida Gulf Coast Univ	FL		C
George Washington Univ	DC	57,108	MC
Georgian Court Univ	NJ	39,726	LC
Grand Valley State Univ	MI	17,998	VC
Gwynedd-Mercy College	PA	33,560	C
Howard Univ	DC	35,957	C
Indiana Univ of Pennsylvania	PA	20,180	LC
Ithaca College	NY	52,300	HC
Lake Superior State Univ	MI	18,121	C
Loyola Univ Chicago	IL	49,560	V₵
Marquette Univ	WI	43,664	V₵
Mary Baldwin College	VA	37,110	C
Maryville Univ of St. Louis	MO	34,920	VC
McNeese State Univ	LA		C
Miami Univ	OH	24,191	HC
Mich State Univ	MI	13,689	VC
Mich Tech Univ	MI	22,105	VC
Minn State Univ, Mankato	MN	14,900	C
Missouri State Univ	MO	13,996	VC
New Mexico State Univ	NM	13,955	LC
New York Inst of Technology	NY	40,590	VC
N Dak State Univ	ND	14,642	C
Northern Illinois Univ	IL	19,768	C
Northern Mich Univ	MI	15,300	VC
Purdue Univ/West Lafayette	IN	20,278	HC
Quincy Univ	IL	34,980	LC
Ramapo College of New Jersey	NJ	24,938	₵
Rockhurst Univ	MO	20,625	C
Rutgers, The State Univ of New Jersey/Newark Campus	NJ	25,376	C
St. Louis Univ	MO	46,594	V₵
San Francisco State Univ	CA	18,514	C
S Dak State Univ	SD	14,296	C
St. John's Univ	NY	52,840	₵
Stony Brook Univ / SUNY	NY	19,359	HC
Texas A&M Univ at Corpus Christi	TX	11,544	LC
Texas State Univ	TX	16,495	VC
The College of Idaho	ID	31,277	VC
Truman State Univ	MO	13,546	HC
Univ of Idaho	ID	14,558	C
Univ of Jamestown	ND	24,738	C
Univ of Louisiana at Monroe	LA	12,998	C
Univ of Maine	ME	19,712	₵
Univ of Mass Dartmouth	MA	22,223	C
Univ of Mass Lowell	MA	19,316	C
Univ of Nevada, Las Vegas	NV	17,303	C
Univ of N Car at Chapel Hill	NC	18,348	MC
Univ of N Car at Wilmington	NC	13,572	V₵
Univ of N Dak	ND	14,094	C
Univ of St. Mary	KS	28,400	₵
Univ of Tenn at Knoxville	TN	20,364	V₵
Univ of Texas at El Paso	TX	8,764	NC
Univ of Texas-Pan American	TX	12,432	LC
Univ of Wisc/Stevens Point	WI	14,043	C
Virginia Commonwealth Univ	VA	18,633	C
Walsh Univ	OH	35,100	C
Washburn Univ	KS	12,165	NC
Wayne State Univ	MI	19,493	C
West Liberty Univ	WV	9,142	LC
Wright State Univ	OH	16,983	C
Youngstown State Univ	OH	16,374	LC

CLOTHING AND TEXTILES MANAGEMENT/ PRODUCTION/SERVICES

School	ST	$IS	SR
Cheyney Univ of Pennsylvania	PA	20,372	LC
College of the Ozarks	MO	5,605	VC
East Carolina Univ	NC	14,169	C
Eastern Mich Univ	MI	17,961	C
Florida State Univ	FL	15,238	HC
Johnson and Wales Univ/ Charlotte Campus	NC	35,421	C
Johnson and Wales Univ/ North Miami Campus	FL	34,368	C
Johnson and Wales Univ/ Providence Campus	RI	34,668	C
N Car Agricultural and Technical State Univ	NC	13,175	LC
N Car State Univ	NC	16,202	HC
San Francisco State Univ	CA	18,514	C
Southern Illinois Univ Carbondale	IL	21,620	C
Texas Tech Univ	TX	14,243	C
Univ of Alabama at Tuscaloosa	AL	17,164	₵
Univ of Northern Iowa	IA	14,776	C
Washington State Univ	WA	20,461	C

School	ST	$IS	SR
Western Mich Univ	MI	19,042	C

COGNITIVE SCIENCE

School	ST	$IS	SR
Bard College	NY	59,872	HC
Brown Univ	RI	56,150	MC
Cal State, Stanislaus	CA	18,582	C
Canisius College	NY	45,602	VC
Case Western Reserve Univ	OH	55,178	MC
Central Mich Univ	MI	18,066	C
Dartmouth College	NH	57,996	MC
Fitchburg State Univ	MA	17,241	C
George Fox Univ	OR	40,750	₵
Hampshire College	MA	58,320	MC
Indiana Univ Bloomington	IN	19,358	HC
Johns Hopkins Univ	MD	47,492	MC
Lawrence Univ	WI	46,371	HC
Lehigh Univ	PA	55,080	MC
Mass Inst of Technology	MA	54,238	MC
Northwestern Univ	IL	37,595	MC
Occidental College	CA	59,592	M₵
Oswego / SUNY	NY	20,009	VC
Pomona College	CA	57,680	MC
Rice Univ	TX	43,288	MC
Smith College	MA	57,524	MC
Tufts Univ	MA	58,780	MC
Tulane Univ	LA	58,942	MC
Univ at Buffalo / The SUNY	NY	20,283	VC
Univ of Calif at Berkeley	CA	23,322	MC
Univ of Calif at Los Angeles	CA	25,686	MC
Univ of Calif at San Diego	CA	21,000	VC
Univ of Denver	CO	51,787	V₵
Univ of Evansville	IN	41,056	V₵
Univ of Georgia	GA	19,508	VC
Univ of Mich/Ann Arbor	MI	22,102	H₵
Univ of Mount Union	OH	35,130	C
Univ of Pennsylvania	PA	56,106	MC
Univ of Rochester	NY	58,500	MC
Univ of Texas at Dallas	TX	21,046	HC
Univ of Wisc/Stout	WI	23,942	C
Vanderbilt Univ	TN	57,072	MC
Vassar College	NY	59,070	MC
Wellesley College	MA	49,848	MC
Wright State Univ	OH	16,983	C
Yale Univ	CT	55,300	MC

COLLABORATIVE EDUCATION

School	ST	$IS	SR
Birmingham-Southern College	AL	42,370	V₵
Goddard College	VT	16,418	VC
Rowan Univ	NJ	23,570	VC
Troy Univ	AL	10,650	C

COLLABORATIVE PIANO

School	ST	$IS	SR
Shenandoah Univ	VA	39,268	C

COMMERCIAL ART

School	ST	$IS	SR
American InterContinental Univ	GA	13,500	NC
Ashland Univ	OH	25,000	C
Brenau Univ Women's College	GA	26,650	₵
Calif Univ of Pennsylvania	PA	14,217	C
Cazenovia College	NY	30,800	C
Fort Valley State Univ	GA	11,200	VC
Graceland Univ	IA	28,020	C
Madonna Univ	MI	24,540	VC
Millikin Univ	IL	37,462	C
Northern Kentucky Univ	KY	15,302	LC
Oral Roberts Univ	OK	31,734	C
Pittsburg State Univ	KS	12,032	C
Southwest Baptist Univ	MO	24,710	C
St. Norbert College	WI	39,992	VC
St. Thomas Aquinas College	NY	30,000	C
Univ of Central Missouri	MO	14,605	C
Univ of Indianapolis	IN	31,740	LC
Univ of North Texas	TX	15,628	C
Univ of S Car Upstate	SC	17,673	LC
Washington Univ in St. Louis	MO	58,818	MC

COMMUNICATION

School	ST	$IS	SR
American Univ	DC	54,829	H₵
Bowling Green State Univ	OH	18,970	C
Bryant Univ	RI	49,179	VC
Cabrini College	PA	40,859	LC
Cal State, Chico	CA	18,952	C
Chestnut Hill College	PA	39,785	LC
Cornell Univ	NY	59,037	MC
Dordt College	IA	34,160	VC
Fairfield Univ	CT	55,850	VC
Ferris State Univ	MI	19,698	C
Fordham Univ	NY	58,927	HC
Houghton College	NY	35,740	VC
Indiana Univ Bloomington	IN	19,358	HC
Indiana Univ Northwest	IN	6,738	LC
Indiana Univ South Bend	IN	15,293	C
Indiana Univ Southeast	IN	15,807	LC
Ithaca College	NY	52,300	HC
Mansfield Univ	PA	19,468	LC
McNeese State Univ	LA		C
Millikin Univ	IL	37,462	C
Southern Oregon Univ	OR	17,874	C
Univ of Arkansas at Fayetteville	AR	16,860	VC
Univ of Louisiana at Monroe	LA	12,998	C
Univ of Maine	ME	19,712	₵
Univ of Miami	FL	55,166	MC
Univ of Wyoming	WY	13,855	₵
Viterbo Univ	WI	30,070	C

COMMUNICATION DESIGN

School	ST	$IS	SR
Bryant Univ	RI	49,179	VC
Cal State, Chico	CA	18,952	C
Dallas Baptist Univ	TX	29,118	C
Texas State Univ	TX	16,495	VC

COMMUNICATION RHETORIC/ COMMUNICATION

School	ST	$IS	SR
Bryant Univ	RI	49,179	VC
Cal State, Chico	CA	18,952	C
Florida Southern College	FL	38,240	VC
Marshall Univ	WV	14,820	C
Mercer Univ	GA	44,201	V₵
Nazareth College of Rochester	NY	41,590	VC
Nyack College	NY	32,000	C
Southeast Missouri State Univ	MO	14,983	LC
Univ of Nebr - Lincoln	NE	17,507	VC
Univ of Pittsburgh at Pittsburgh	PA	27,800	H₵
Washington and Jefferson College	PA	49,990	VC
Waynesburg Univ	PA	29,100	C
Wheeling Jesuit Univ	WV	34,668	C
Xavier Univ	OH	43,740	VC

COMMUNICATION SCIENCE

School	ST	$IS	SR
Abilene Christian Univ	TX	38,400	VC
Bryant Univ	RI	49,179	VC
Cal State, Chico	CA	18,952	C
Eastern Illinois Univ	IL	20,502	C
Elmhurst College	IL	42,032	₵
Howard Univ	DC	35,957	C
Idaho State Univ	ID	11,908	C
Missouri State Univ	MO	13,996	VC
Univ of Georgia	GA	19,508	VC
Univ of Miss	MS	15,482	VC
Univ of Oregon	OR	20,872	VC
Univ of Pittsburgh at Pittsburgh	PA	27,800	H₵
Univ of Wisc/Madison	WI	18,757	HC
Wayne State Univ	MI	19,493	C

COMMUNICATION SCIENCES & DISORDERS

School	ST	$IS	SR
Baldwin Wallace Univ	OH	36,980	VC
Cal State, Chico	CA	18,952	C
Fontbonne Univ	MO	31,384	C
Jackson State Univ	MS	13,512	LC
Mercy College	NY	29,996	C
Nazareth College of Rochester	NY	41,590	VC
SUNY Plattsburgh / SUNY	NY	18,083	VC
The College of St. Rose	NY	26,750	C
Univ of Georgia	GA	19,508	VC
Univ of Louisiana at Monroe	LA	12,998	C
Univ of Tulsa	OK	45,311	H₵
Univ of Wisc/Eau Claire	WI	15,430	VC

COMMUNICATION STUDIES

School	ST	$IS	SR
Baldwin Wallace Univ	OH	36,980	VC
Bryant Univ	RI	49,179	VC
Calif Polytechnic State Univ	CA	19,847	HC
Creighton Univ	NE	44,058	V₵
Indiana Univ Bloomington	IN	19,358	HC
Indiana Univ Bloomington	IN	19,358	HC
Indiana Univ East	IN	6,639	LC
Indiana Univ Kokomo	IN	6,674	LC
Indiana Univ-Purdue Univ Indianapolis	IN	17,290	C
Nova Southeastern Univ	FL	34,016	VC
San Diego State Univ	CA	20,578	VC
San Jose State Univ	CA	19,707	C
Tiffin Univ	OH	30,273	LC
Univ of Denver	CO	51,787	V₵
Univ of Georgia	GA	19,508	VC
Univ of Louisiana at Monroe	LA	12,998	C
Univ of Miami	FL	55,166	MC
Winona State Univ	MN	16,530	C

COMMUNICATIONS

School	ST	$IS	SR
Abilene Christian Univ	TX	38,400	VC
Adams State College	CO	13,358	LC
Adelphi Univ	NY	43,130	VC
Adrian College	MI	33,800	C
Alabama State Univ	AL	14,142	NC
Albertus Magnus College	CT	37,382	LC
Albright College	PA	46,660	C
Alcorn State Univ	MS	9,500	C
Alderson Broaddus Univ	WV	28,656	C
Alfred Univ	NY	40,392	VC
Allegheny College	PA	49,020	HC
Alma College	MI	42,400	VC
Alvernia Univ	PA	39,250	C
Alverno College	WI	30,483	LC
American International College	MA	36,100	LC
American Univ	DC	54,829	H₵
Anderson Univ	IN	35,390	C
Andrews Univ	MI	28,030	₵
Angelo State Univ	TX	15,049	NC
Appalachian State Univ	NC	12,919	VC
Aquinas College	MI	33,060	C
Arcadia Univ	PA	33,570	₵
Arizona State Univ	AZ	18,818	₵
Arkansas State Univ	AR	14,980	C
Arkansas Tech Univ	AR	13,164	LC
Asbury Univ	KY	32,038	VC
Ashland Univ	OH	25,000	C
Auburn Univ	AL	20,052	V₵
Auburn Univ at Montgomery	AL	12,120	C
Augsburg College	MN	35,142	C
Augustana College	IL	43,398	HC
Augustana College	SD	35,500	VC
Aurora Univ	IL	26,870	C
Austin College	TX	36,940	HC
Austin Peay State Univ	TN	14,650	C
Avila Univ	MO	26,900	C
Azusa Pacific Univ	CA	39,946	C
Baker Univ	KS	33,350	₵
Barry Univ	FL	38,190	C
Barton College	NC	27,660	C
Bay Path College	MA	34,565	C
Baylor Univ	TX	46,720	HC
Becker College	MA	41,420	LC
Belhaven Univ	MS	27,170	C
Bellarmine Univ	KY	42,950	VC
Bellevue Univ	NE	4,600	NC
Belmont Univ	TN	37,380	V₵
Bemidji State Univ	MN	13,500	C
Benedictine Univ	IL	35,220	C
Bennett College	NC		LC
Berea College	KY	7,220	HC
Berry College	GA	39,254	HC
Bethany College	KS	30,605	NC
Bethany College	WV	35,282	C
Bethel College	IN	31,560	C
Bethel College	KS	29,100	C
Bethel Univ	MN	34,940	VC
Bethune-Cookman Univ	FL	22,290	LC
Biola Univ	CA	40,320	VC
Black Hills State Univ	SD	13,562	LC
Blackburn College	IL	21,350	C
Bloomsburg Univ of Pennsylvania	PA	13,598	C
Bluefield College	VA	17,230	₵
Bluffton Univ	OH	37,864	C
Boise State Univ	ID	12,802	C
Boston College	MA	58,506	MC
Boston Univ	MA	54,130	H₵
Bradley Univ	IL	31,874	VC
Brenau Univ Women's College	GA	26,650	₵
Brewton-Parker College	GA	33,388	LC
Briar Cliff Univ	IA	29,514	C
Bridgewater College	VA	39,880	C
Brigham Young Univ	UT	12,100	HC
Bryan College	TN	24,194	C
Bryant Univ	RI	49,179	VC
Buena Vista Univ	IA	37,954	C
Buffalo State/State Univ of Buffalo	NY	15,733	₵
Butler Univ	IN	45,898	V₵
Caldwell College	NJ	35,602	LC
Calif Baptist Univ	CA	35,890	C
Calif Lutheran Univ	CA	47,640	C
Calif State Polytechnic Univ, Pomona	CA	18,932	C
Cal State, Bakersfield	CA	8,000	LC
Cal State, Chico	CA	18,952	C
Cal State, Dominguez Hills	CA	17,056	LC
Cal State, East Bay	CA	16,549	C
Cal State, Fresno	CA	17,405	C
Cal State, Fullerton	CA	25,188	₵
Cal State, Long Beach	CA	17,534	₵
Cal State, Sacramento	CA	16,200	C
Cal State, San Bernardino	CA	12,000	C
Cal State, San Marcos	CA	14,576	C
Cal State, Stanislaus	CA	18,582	C
Calvin College	MI	37,585	V₵
Cameron Univ	OK	9,267	LC
Campbell Univ	NC	25,500	C
Campbellsville Univ	KY	27,720	C
Canisius College	NY	45,602	VC
Capital Univ	OH	39,824	VC
Cardinal Stritch Univ	WI	24,054	C
Carlow Univ	PA	30,272	C
Carnegie Mellon Univ	PA	51,260	MC
Carroll College	MT	28,000	C
Carroll Univ	WI	24,860	C
Carson-Newman Univ	TN	29,058	₵

School	ST	$IS	SR
Castleton State College	VT	19,424	C
Catawba College	NC	37,105	C
Cazenovia College	NY	30,800	C
Cedar Crest College	PA	43,240	C
Cedarville Univ	OH	31,036	V₵
Centenary College	NJ	38,618	LC
Centenary College of Louisiana	LA	39,070	₵
Central College	IA	36,980	VC
Central Conn State Univ	CT	19,212	C
Central Methodist Univ	MO	28,240	VC
Central Mich Univ	MI	18,066	C
Central Washington Univ	WA	11,730	C
Chaminade Univ of Honolulu	HI	31,664	C
Champlain College	VT	44,850	VC
Chapman Univ	CA	56,019	V₵
Chatham Univ	PA	42,440	VC
Cheyney Univ of Pennsylvania	PA	20,372	LC
Christopher Newport Univ	VA	21,050	VC
CUNY/Baruch College	NY	15,831	VC
CUNY/Brooklyn College	NY	5,884	₵
Claflin Univ	SC	22,368	₵
Clarion Univ of Pennsylvania	PA	17,370	C
Clark Atlanta Univ	GA	30,006	C
Clark Univ	MA	47,020	H₵
Clarke Univ	IA	36,400	C
Clarkson Univ	NY	53,538	HC
Clearwater Christian College	FL	23,720	C
Clemson Univ	SC	10,100	HC
Cleveland State Univ	OH	21,357	C
Coastal Carolina Univ	SC	17,620	C
Coe College	IA	43,590	VC
Coker College	SC	32,256	LC
Colby-Sawyer College	NH	47,870	C
College of Staten Island / The CUNY	NY	16,778	NC
College of Charleston	SC	21,273	VC
College of Mount St. Joseph	OH	33,880	C
College of Mount St. Vincent	NY	41,040	MC
College of New Jersey	NJ	25,376	HC
College of St. Benedict	MN	47,570	VC
College of St. Elizabeth	NJ	43,839	LC
College of St. Scholastica	MN	39,960	C
College of the Ozarks	MO	5,605	VC
College of Wooster	OH	52,600	VC
Colo Christian Univ	CO	27,500	VC
Colo Mesa Univ	CO	16,669	LC
Colo State Univ-Fort Collins	CO	20,090	VC
Colo State Univ-Pueblo	CO	13,532	LC
Columbia College	MO	24,578	C
Columbia College	SC	27,882	C
Columbus State Univ	GA	13,176	C
Concord Univ	WV	13,102	C
Concordia College, Moorhead	MN	39,974	₵
Concordia Univ - Irvine	CA	35,390	VC
Concordia Univ Nebr	NE	26,000	VC
Concordia Univ St. Paul	MN	27,200	C
Concordia Univ Texas	TX	23,640	C
Concordia Univ Wisc	WI	28,980	C
Concordia Univ, Ann Arbor	MI	27,220	VC
Concordia Univ, River Forest	IL	26,300	C
Corban Univ	OR	34,764	C
Cornerstone Univ and Grand Rapids Theological Seminary	MI	30,866	C
Culver-Stockton College	MO	30,900	C
CUNY-City College	NY	19,576	H₵
Curry College	MA	47,545	LC
Dakota Wesleyan Univ	SD	23,000	C
Dallas Baptist Univ	TX	29,118	C
Davis and Elkins College	WV	33,742	C
De Sales Univ	PA	42,670	C
Defiance College	OH	30,645	C
Delta State Univ	MS	12,292	LC
Denison Univ	OH	54,670	H₵
DePaul Univ	IL	46,120	VC
DePauw Univ	IN	48,950	V₵
Dickinson State Univ	ND	8,550	NC
Dillard Univ	LA	20,940	VC
Dominican Univ	IL	37,628	C
Dominican Univ of Calif	CA	51,250	C
Dordt College	IA	34,160	VC
Dowling College	NY	25,000	LC
Drake Univ	IA	30,980	V₵
Drexel Univ	PA	51,920	HC
Drury Univ	MO	30,319	VC
Duquesne Univ	PA	42,017	VC
East Carolina Univ	NC	14,169	C
East Central Univ	OK	10,223	LC
East Stroudsburg Univ of Pennsylvania	PA	16,636	C
East Tenn State Univ	TN	9,000	C
East Texas Baptist Univ	TX	29,135	C
Eastern Conn State Univ	CT	20,584	C
Eastern Illinois Univ	IL	20,502	C
Eastern Mennonite Univ	VA	38,850	VC
Eastern Mich Univ	MI	17,961	C
Eastern Nazarene College	MA	30,000	C
Eastern New Mexico Univ	NM	10,682	C
Eastern Univ	PA	37,704	C
Eastern Washington Univ	WA	16,388	C
East-West Univ	IL	16,076	C
Eckerd College	FL	43,902	VC
Edinboro Univ of Pennsylvania	PA	15,940	LC
Edward Waters College	FL	17,856	LC
Elizabethtown College	PA	47,600	VC
Elizabethtown College School of Continuing and Professional Studies	PA		VC
Elmhurst College	IL	42,032	₵
Elon Univ	NC	40,046	HC
Embry-Riddle Aeronautical Univ - Daytona Beach	FL	40,884	₵
Embry-Riddle Aeronautical Univ - Prescott Campus	AZ	40,584	VC
Emerson College	MA	50,246	HC
Emmanuel College	MA	47,985	VC
Emory and Henry College	VA	387,460	C
Emporia State Univ	KS	12,897	C
Endicott College	MA	42,390	C
Eureka College	IL	19,280	C
Evangel Univ	MO	23,090	C
Excelsior College	NY	895	SP
Fairleigh Dickinson Univ/ College at Florham	NJ	42,142	C
Fairleigh Dickinson Univ/ Metropolitan Campus	NJ	40,254	C
Fairmont State Univ	WV	12,098	LC
Felician College	NJ	41,640	C
Ferris State Univ	MI	19,698	C
Fitchburg State Univ	MA	17,241	C
Five Towns College	NY	34,550	SP
Flagler College	FL	24,960	VC
Florida Atlantic Univ	FL	17,339	C
Florida Gulf Coast Univ	FL		C
Florida Inst of Technology	FL	48,290	VC
Florida Southern College	FL	38,240	VC
Florida State Univ	FL	15,238	HC
Fontbonne Univ	MO	31,384	C
Fordham Univ	NY	58,927	HC
Fort Hays State Univ	KS	11,354	C
Fort Valley State Univ	GA	11,200	VC
Framingham State Univ	MA	16,750	C
Francis Marion Univ	SC	16,464	LC
Franciscan Univ of Steubenville	OH	27,320	VC
Franklin Pierce Univ	NH	41,598	C
Freed-Hardeman Univ	TN	19,697	VC
Friends Univ	KS	29,100	C
Frostburg State Univ	MD	15,264	LC
Furman Univ	SC	54,006	HC
Gallaudet Univ	DC	25,380	SP
Gannon Univ	PA	37,940	C
Gardner-Webb Univ	NC	34,375	₵
Geneva College	PA	27,280	C
George Fox Univ	OR	40,750	₵
George Mason Univ	VA	15,724	VC
George Washington Univ	DC	57,108	MC
Georgetown College	KY	38,690	C
Georgia Regents Univ	GA		C
Georgian Court Univ	NJ	39,726	LC
Gonzaga Univ	WA	44,247	HC
Gordon College	MA	42,660	V₵
Goshen College	IN	35,900	VC
Goucher College	MD	50,252	V₵
Grace College and Theological Seminary	IN	28,800	C
Graceland Univ	IA	28,020	C
Grambling State Univ	LA	13,384	LC
Grand Canyon Univ	AZ	24,540	VC
Grand Valley State Univ	MI	17,998	VC
Grand View Univ	IA	31,050	C
Green Mountain College	VT	33,547	LC
Greenville College	IL	27,012	C
Grove City College	PA	22,988	HC
Gustavus Adolphus College	MN	48,170	HC
Gwynedd-Mercy College	PA	33,560	C
Hamilton College	NY	55,620	MC
Hamline Univ	MN	44,198	VC
Hampshire College	MA	58,320	MC
Hampton Univ	VA	28,528	C
Hannibal-LaGrange Univ	MO	24,490	C
Hanover College	IN	41,450	VC
Harding Univ	AR	21,432	₵
Hardin-Simmons Univ	TX	23,560	₵
Hastings College	NE	27,782	₵
Hawaii Pacific Univ	HI	36,690	C
Heidelberg Univ	OH	34,100	C
Henderson State Univ	AR	13,634	C
High Point Univ	NC	39,800	C
Hiram College	OH	37,300	VC
Hollins Univ	VA	43,295	VC
Holy Family Univ	PA	40,030	LC
Holy Names Univ	CA	40,310	NC
Hood College	MD	44,630	C
Hope College	MI	36,320	V₵
Hope International Univ	CA	34,650	C
Houston Baptist Univ	TX	23,815	₵
Howard Payne Univ	TX	17,115	C
Howard Univ	DC	35,957	C
Humboldt State Univ	CA	18,400	C
Huntingdon College	AL	31,850	C
Huntington Univ	IN	32,220	C
Idaho State Univ	ID	11,908	C
Illinois College	IL	25,770	VC
Illinois State Univ	IL	22,634	VC
Indiana Inst of Technology	IN	34,240	LC
Indiana State Univ	IN	16,000	C
Indiana Univ Kokomo	IN	6,674	LC
Indiana Univ of Pennsylvania	PA	20,180	LC
Indiana Univ-Purdue Univ Fort Wayne	IN	15,425	C
Indiana Wesleyan Univ	IN	31,815	VC
Iona College	NY	44,028	C
Iowa State Univ	IA	16,403	C
Iowa Wesleyan College	IA	30,850	LC
Ithaca College	NY	52,300	HC
Jackson State Univ	MS	13,512	LC
Jacksonville State Univ	AL	12,280	LC
Jacksonville Univ	FL	37,780	C
James Madison Univ	VA	18,049	VC
John Carroll Univ	OH	44,520	₵
Johnson C. Smith Univ	NC	25,336	LC
Judson Univ	IL	25,130	C
Juniata College	PA	49,340	VC
Kansas State Univ	KS	15,497	VC
Kansas Wesleyan Univ	KS	32,000	C
Kaplan Univ	IA	14,025	NC
Kean Univ	NJ	22,060	LC
Keene State College	NH	21,538	C
Kennesaw State Univ	GA	13,017	VC
Kent State Univ	OH	19,352	C
Kentucky Wesleyan College	KY	27,440	V₵
Keuka College	NY	30,300	C
Keystone College	PA	28,680	LC
King's College	PA	41,678	C
La Roche College	PA	34,802	LC
La Salle Univ	PA	50,270	C
La Sierra Univ	CA	35,694	VC
Lake Erie College	OH	35,704	C
Lake Forest College	IL	45,580	VC
Lake Superior State Univ	MI	18,121	C
Lamar Univ	TX	6,820	LC
Lander Univ	SC	22,514	₵
Lane College	TN	11,212	C
Lasell College	MA	42,500	LC
Lawrence Tech Univ	MI	37,630	VC
Le Moyne College	NY	42,200	VC
Lee Univ	TN	18,690	₵
Lees-McRae College	NC	33,624	C
Lehman College / The CUNY	NY	5,778	LC
Lenoir-Rhyne College	NC	35,984	C
Lewis & Clark College	OR	52,656	VC
Lewis Univ	IL	23,050	C
Lewis-Clark State College	ID	6,990	C
Liberty Univ	VA	19,101	C
Limestone College	SC	29,880	C
Lincoln Memorial Univ	TN	18,144	C
Lindenwood Univ	MO	20,750	C
Lindsey Wilson College	KY	30,470	VC
Linfield College-McMinnville Campus	OR	46,166	C
Lipscomb Univ	TN	35,722	VC
Lock Haven Univ of Pennsylvania	PA	17,587	LC
LIU/Brooklyn Campus	NY	26,500	C
LIU/C.W. Post Campus	NY	38,888	C
Longwood Univ	VA	20,924	C
Louisiana College	LA	15,746	C
Louisiana State Univ	LA	18,677	V₵
Louisiana State Univ in Shreveport	LA	5,606	C
Loyola Marymount Univ	CA	53,240	V₵
Loyola Univ Chicago	IL	49,560	V₵
Loyola Univ Maryland	MD		VC
Loyola Univ New Orleans	LA	46,581	VC
Lubbock Christian Univ	TX	25,518	C
Luther College	IA	44,380	V₵
Lycoming College	PA	43,636	C
Lynchburg College	VA	42,645	C
Lyndon State College	VT	14,233	C
Lynn Univ	FL	43,500	C
Madonna Univ	MI	24,540	VC
Malone Univ	OH	34,334	C
Manchester College	IN	35,070	C
Manhattan College	NY	44,955	VC
Manhattanville College	NY	46,260	VC
Marian Univ	WI	30,980	LC
Marian Univ/Indianapolis	IN	37,058	C
Marietta College	OH	42,135	VC
Marist College	NY	35,500	C
Marquette Univ	WI	43,664	V₵
Mars Hill College	NC	22,950	LC
Marshall Univ	WV	14,820	C
Martin Univ	IN	11,000	SP
Mary Baldwin College	VA	37,110	C
Marylhurst Univ	OR	18,945	NC
Marymount Manhattan College	NY	40,118	VC
Marymount Univ	VA	36,178	C
Maryville Univ of St. Louis	MO	34,920	VC
Marywood Univ	PA	40,695	C
Mass College of Liberal Arts	MA	16,733	C
Mayville State Univ	ND	11,401	NC
McDaniel College	MD	45,600	VC
McPherson College	KS	28,138	C
Medaille College	NY	35,112	VC
Mercer Univ	GA	44,201	V₵
Mercy College	NY	29,996	C
Mercyhurst Univ	PA	40,700	C
Meredith College	NC	31,420	C
Merrimack College	MA	44,215	C
Messiah College	PA	39,540	VC
Methodist Univ	NC	37,185	C
Metropolitan State Univ	MN	5,923	SP
Metropolitan State Univ of Denver	CO	4,835	LC
Miami Univ	OH	24,191	HC
Mich State Univ	MI	13,689	VC
Mich Tech Univ	MI	22,105	VC
MidAmerica Nazarene Univ	KS	28,000	C
Middle Tenn State Univ	TN	8,650	C
Midland Univ	NE	34,000	C
Midwestern State Univ	TX	9,722	C
Miles College	AL	16,530	NC
Millersville Univ of Pennsylvania	PA	18,498	C
Milligan College	TN	27,510	C
Millsaps College	MS	43,888	V₵
Minn State Univ, Mankato	MN	14,900	C
Minn State Univ, Moorhead	MN	13,392	C
Minot State Univ	ND	10,915	C
Misericordia Univ	PA	39,840	C
Miss College	MS	21,998	VC
Miss Univ for Women	MS	7,400	LC
Miss Valley State Univ	MS	9,706	LC
Missouri Baptist Univ	MO	30,310	C
Missouri Southern State Univ	MO	11,910	C
Missouri State Univ	MO	13,996	VC
Missouri Valley College	MO	22,200	C
Missouri Western State Univ	MO	12,260	NC
Mitchell College	CT	40,983	C
Molloy College	NY	38,950	C
Monmouth College	IL	39,290	C
Monmouth Univ	NJ	42,252	C
Montana State Univ-Billings	MT	12,425	LC
Montana State Univ-Northern	MT	12,500	NC
Montana Tech of The Univ of Montana	MT	14,650	VC
Montclair State Univ	NJ	22,614	C
Morehead State Univ	KY	10,900	C
Morningside College	IA	32,620	C
Morris College	SC	16,006	LC
Mount Ida College	MA	30,115	LC
Mount Mary Univ	WI	32,836	LC
Mount Mercy Univ	IA	34,385	C
Mount Olive College	NC	18,426	C
Mount St. Mary's Univ	MD	46,158	C
Mount Vernon Nazarene Univ	OH	29,590	C
Muhlenberg College	PA	52,837	HC
Murray State Univ	KY	14,944	C
Muskingum Univ	OH	30,502	C
Nebr Wesleyan Univ	NE	29,774	₵
Neumann Univ	PA	31,078	LC
New England College	NH	45,930	LC
New Jersey Inst of Technology	NJ	26,490	VC
New Mexico Highlands Univ	NM	9,720	NC
New Mexico State Univ	NM	13,955	LC
New York City College of Technology / The CUNY	NY	5,769	NC
New York Inst of Technology	NY	40,590	VC
New York Univ	NY	61,470	MC
Newberry College	SC	26,850	LC
Newbury College	MA	41,850	C
Newman Univ	KS	30,380	₵
Niagara Univ	NY	39,800	C
Nicholls State Univ	LA	7,095	C
Norfolk State Univ	VA	10,531	LC
N Car Agricultural and Technical State Univ	NC	13,175	LC
N Car State Univ	NC	16,202	HC
North Central College	IL	38,343	VC
North Central Univ	MN	20,946	C
N Dak State Univ	ND	14,642	C
North Park Univ	IL	30,130	C
Northeastern Illinois Univ	IL		C
Northeastern State Univ	OK	8,615	VC
Northeastern Univ	MA	55,296	MC
Northern Arizona Univ	AZ	18,592	C
Northern Illinois Univ	IL	19,768	C
Northern Kentucky Univ	KY	15,302	LC
Northern Mich Univ	MI	15,300	VC
Northwest Christian Univ	OR	27,399	C
Northwest Missouri State Univ	MO	14,229	C
Northwest Nazarene Univ	ID	24,275	NC
Northwest Univ	WA	18,854	C
Northwestern College	MN	24,000	C
Northwestern Okla State Univ	OK	7,275	NC
Northwestern State Univ of Louisiana	LA	14,368	C
Northwestern Univ	IL	37,595	MC
Norwich Univ	VT	28,212	C
Notre Dame College	OH	34,942	VC
Notre Dame de Namur Univ	CA	41,610	LC

ST = STATE **$IS** = IN-STATE COSTS **SR** = SELECTOR RATING

School	ST	$IS	SR
Notre Dame of Maryland Univ	MD	27,700	C
Nyack College	NY	32,000	C
Oakland Univ	MI	19,391	VC
Oakwood Univ	AL	23,035	C
Oglethorpe Univ	GA	42,580	VC
Ohio Dominican Univ	OH	38,380	C+
Ohio Northern Univ	OH	42,075	VC
Ohio Univ	OH	20,676	VC
Okla Baptist Univ	OK	28,202	VC
Okla Christian Univ	OK	24,975	VC
Okla City Univ	OK	33,546	VC
Okla Wesleyan Univ	OK	21,300	C
Old Dominion Univ	VA	18,662	C
Olivet College	MI	19,984	C
Olivet Nazarene Univ	IL	20,090	C
Oral Roberts Univ	OK	31,734	C
Oswego / SUNY	NY	20,009	VC
Ottawa Univ	KS	15,000	VC
Otterbein College	OH	32,214	C
Ouachita Baptist Univ	AR	29,010	VC
Our Lady of the Lake Univ of San Antonio	TX	22,430	LC
Pace Univ	NY	48,094	VC
Pacific Lutheran Univ	WA	44,840	VC
Pacific Union College	CA	28,150	VC
Paine College	GA	18,594	LC
Palm Beach Atlantic Univ	FL	33,882	LC
Park Univ	MO	17,525	C
Paul Quinn College	TX	25,350	LC
Penn State Erie/The Behrend College	PA	16,256	C
Penn State Univ/Altoona	PA	11,464	C
Penn State Univ/Univ Park	PA	25,404	VC
Pepperdine Univ	CA	55,372	HC+
Pfeiffer Univ	NC	33,700	C
Piedmont College	GA	29,260	C
Pine Manor College	MA	32,659	LC
Pittsburg State Univ	KS	12,032	C
Plymouth State Univ	NH	23,148	LC
Point Loma Nazarene Univ	CA	38,610	VC
Point Park Univ	PA	36,390	C
Pontifical Catholic Univ of PR	PR	7,310	
Prairie View A&M Univ	TX	15,205	LC
Pratt Inst	NY	49,520	SP
Prescott College	AZ	33,284	C+
Presentation College	SD	14,800	LC
Principia College	IL	35,140	C+
Purdue Univ/Calumet	IN	14,336	C
Purdue Univ/West Lafayette	IN	20,278	HC
Queens Univ of Charlotte	NC	39,543	VC
Quincy Univ	IL	34,980	LC
Quinnipiac Univ	CT	53,580	VC
Radford Univ	VA	17,132	LC
Ramapo College of New Jersey	NJ	24,938	C+
Randolph College	VA	43,960	VC
Randolph-Macon College	VA	45,086	C
Regis College	MA	47,565	LC
Regis Univ	CO	41,318	C
Reinhardt College	GA	25,000	C
Rensselaer Polytechnic Inst	NY	59,229	MC
Rhode Island College	RI	17,132	LC
Richard Stockton College of New Jersey	NJ	20,000	VC
Rider Univ	NJ	45,720	C
Ripon College	WI	36,959	C+
Rivier College	NH	35,000	VC
Roanoke College	VA	47,996	C+
Robert Morris Univ	PA	36,699	C
Roberts Wesleyan College	NY	37,384	C+
Rochester College	MI	18,320	C
Rochester Inst of Technology	NY	42,450	VC+
Rockhurst Univ	MO	20,625	C
Rocky Mountain College	MT	32,242	C
Roger Williams Univ	RI	45,788	C
Rollins College	FL	52,370	HC
Roosevelt Univ	IL	22,605	VC
Rosemont College	PA	42,350	C
Rowan Univ	NJ	23,570	VC
Rust College	MS	10,600	C
Rutgers, The State Univ of New Jersey/New Brunswick	NJ	25,077	VC
Sacred Heart Univ	CT	48,564	VC
Saginaw Valley State Univ	MI	16,869	C
St. Augustine's Univ	NC	14,000	C
St. Francis Univ	PA	30,029	LC
St. John's Univ	MN	46,146	C
St. Joseph's College	IN	35,790	C
St. Joseph's College of Maine	ME	31,580	C
St. Joseph's Univ	PA	52,272	VC
St. Mary's College	IN	45,160	VC
St. Mary's College of Calif	CA	53,550	C
St. Mary's Univ	TX	33,854	C
St. Peter's College	NJ	44,240	C
St. Vincent College	PA	40,244	C
St. Xavier Univ	IL	32,840	C
Salem College	NC	29,326	VC
Salem International Univ	WV	18,020	C
Salem State College	MA	13,161	LC
Salisbury Univ	MD	18,368	VC
Salve Regina Univ	RI	47,250	VC
Samford Univ	AL	35,700	VC+
San Diego Christian College	CA	31,012	C
San Diego State Univ	CA	20,578	VC
San Francisco State Univ	CA	18,514	C
Santa Clara Univ	CA	54,702	MC
Savannah College of Art and Design	GA	46,824	SP
Savannah State Univ	GA	13,156	C
Scripps College	CA	54,900	MC
Seattle Pacific Univ	WA	41,559	VC+
Seattle Univ	WA	47,010	VC+
Seton Hall Univ	NJ	45,902	C
Seton Hill Univ	PA	35,172	C
Shenandoah Univ	VA	39,268	C
Shepherd Univ	WV	14,996	C
Shippensburg Univ of Pennsylvania	PA	17,064	LC
Shorter Univ	GA	26,470	C
Siena Heights Univ	MI	17,000	LC
Simmons College	MA	48,770	VC
Simpson College	IA	36,086	VC
Simpson Univ	CA	28,900	C
Slippery Rock Univ of Pennsylvania	PA	10,360	LC
Sonoma State Univ	CA	20,541	C
S Dak State Univ	SD	14,296	C
Southeastern Louisiana Univ	LA	13,325	C
Southeastern Okla State Univ	OK	7,966	C
Southeastern Univ	FL	27,201	C+
Southern Adventist Univ	TN	26,190	C
Southern Arkansas Univ	AR	14,316	C
Southern Conn State Univ	CT	18,033	C
Southern Illinois Univ Edwardsville	IL	17,532	C
Southern Methodist Univ	TX	57,755	MC
Southern Nazarene Univ	OK	24,354	NC
Southern New Hampshire Univ	NH	38,100	C
Southern Univ and A&M College	LA	9,761	C+
Southern Vermont College	VT	30,740	LC
Southern Wesleyan Univ	SC	25,600	C
Southwest Baptist Univ	MO	24,710	C
Southwest Minn State Univ	MN	14,000	C
Southwestern Adventist Univ	TX	23,026	LC
Southwestern College	KS	29,270	C
Southwestern Okla State Univ	OK	9,160	C
Southwestern Univ	TX	45,660	VC
Spring Arbor Univ	MI	26,740	C
Spring Hill College	AL	42,130	VC
St. Ambrose Univ	IA		C
St. Bonaventure Univ	NY	38,831	C
St. Catherine Univ	MN	37,782	C+
St. Cloud State Univ	MN	10,600	C
St. Edward's Univ	TX	44,674	VC
St. Francis College	NY	34,200	LC
St. John Fisher College	NY	39,370	C+
St. John's Univ	NY	52,840	C+
St. Lawrence Univ	NY	53,740	HC
St. Norbert College	WI	39,992	VC
St. Thomas Aquinas College	NY	30,000	C
St. Thomas Univ	FL	32,310	C+
Stanford Univ	CA	56,411	MC
Stephen F. Austin State Univ	TX	14,668	C
Sterling College	KS	27,216	C
Stetson Univ	FL	49,512	VC+
Stonehill College	MA	46,780	VC+
Suffolk Univ	MA	46,548	C
Sul Ross State Univ	TX	13,410	LC
SUNY College at Geneseo	NY	18,055	HC+
SUNY College at Old Westbury	NY	16,324	C
SUNY Cortland / The SUNY	NY	19,117	C
SUNY Fredonia / The SUNY at Fredonia	NY	18,702	VC
SUNY New Paltz	NY	15,010	C
SUNY Oneonta / SUNY	NY	16,919	VC
SUNY Plattsburgh / SUNY	NY	18,083	VC
Susquehanna Univ	PA	49,170	C
Syracuse Univ	NY	54,512	HC
Tabor College	KS	29,010	LC
Taylor Univ	IN	36,742	VC+
Temple Univ	PA	24,392	VC
Texas A&M Univ at Corpus Christi	TX	11,544	LC
Texas A&M Univ at Kingsville	TX	7,500	LC
Texas Christian Univ	TX	47,570	HC
Texas Lutheran Univ	TX	34,070	C
Texas Southern Univ	TX	18,212	LC
Texas State Univ	TX	16,495	VC
Texas Tech Univ	TX	14,243	C
Texas Woman's Univ	TX	13,633	LC
The Catholic Univ of America	DC	52,852	VC
The College at Brockport / SUNY	NY	18,362	VC
The College of New Rochelle	NY	33,600	VC
The College of St. Rose	NY	26,750	C
The Masters College	CA	38,160	C+
Ohio State Univ	OH	19,887	MC
The SUNY College of Agriculture and Tech at Cobleskill	NY	18,869	VC
Thiel College	PA	31,378	LC
Thomas College	ME	26,270	LC
Thomas Edison State College	NJ	5,700	SP
Thomas More College	KY	34,760	C
Tiffin Univ	OH	30,273	LC
Toccoa Falls College	GA	23,210	C
Tougaloo College	MS	15,275	NC
Towson Univ	MD	16,000	VC
Trevecca Nazarene Univ	TN	30,118	C
Trine Univ	IN	39,400	VC
Trinity Christian College	IL	28,809	C
Trinity International Univ	IL	31,070	C
Trinity Univ	TX	44,174	HC+
Trinity Washington Univ	DC	30,250	C+
Troy Univ	AL	10,650	C
Truman State Univ	MO	13,546	HC
Tulane Univ	LA	58,942	MC
Union College	KY	28,775	C
Union College	NE	23,270	VC
Union Inst & Univ	OH	8,912	SP
Union Univ	TN	28,260	VC
Univ at Albany / SUNY	NY	18,674	VC
Univ at Buffalo / The SUNY	NY	20,283	VC
Univ of Alabama at Birmingham	AL	18,484	C+
Univ of Alabama at Huntsville	AL	17,625	VC
Univ of Alabama at Tuscaloosa	AL	17,164	C+
Univ of Alaska Anchorage	AK	15,290	NC
Univ of Alaska Fairbanks	AK	13,955	C
Univ of Alaska Southeast	AK	11,493	C
Univ of Arizona	AZ	20,105	C
Univ of Bridgeport	CT	39,030	LC
Univ of Calif at Berkeley	CA	23,322	MC
Univ of Calif at Davis	CA	24,482	HC
Univ of Calif at Los Angeles	CA	25,686	MC
Univ of Calif at San Diego	CA	21,000	VC
Univ of Calif at Santa Barbara	CA	27,551	HC
Univ of Central Arkansas	AR	10,840	VC
Univ of Central Florida	FL	15,711	VC+
Univ of Central Missouri	MO	14,605	C
Univ of Central Okla	OK	12,293	C
Univ of Charleston	WV	28,650	C
Univ of Cincinnati	OH	20,199	VC
Univ of Colo at Colo Springs	CO	15,000	VC
Univ of Colo Boulder	CO	22,605	VC+
Univ of Colo Denver	CO	17,904	C
Univ of Conn	CT	23,744	HC
Univ of Dayton	OH	43,750	VC
Univ of Delaware	DE	22,728	VC
Univ of Detroit Mercy	MI	30,450	C
Univ of Evansville	IN	41,056	VC+
Univ of Findlay	OH	31,916	C
Univ of Hartford	CT	42,674	C
Univ of Hawaii at Hilo	HI	6,500	C
Univ of Hawaii at Manoa	HI	19,379	VC
Univ of Houston	TX	19,184	VC
Univ of Houston-Downtown	TX	6,267	LC
Univ of Illinois at Chicago	IL	24,293	VC
Univ of Illinois at Urbana-Champaign	IL	24,300	HC
Univ of Indianapolis	IN	31,740	LC
Univ of Iowa	IA	17,481	VC
Univ of Jamestown	ND	24,738	C
Univ of Kentucky	KY	19,868	C
Univ of La Verne	CA	47,010	VC
Univ of Louisiana at Lafayette	LA	6,130	C
Univ of Louisiana at Monroe	LA	12,998	C
Univ of Louisville	KY	17,460	VC
Univ of Maine	ME	19,712	C+
Univ of Mary	ND	16,714	C
Univ of Mary Hardin-Baylor	TX	31,950	C+
Univ of Maryland	MD	18,801	HC
Univ of Maryland/Baltimore County	MD	18,000	VC
Univ of Maryland/Univ College	MD	6,168	SP
Univ of Mass Amherst	MA	23,697	VC+
Univ of Mass Boston	MA	11,966	C
Univ of Memphis	TN	15,094	C
Univ of Mich/Ann Arbor	MI	22,102	HC+
Univ of Mich/Dearborn	MI	9,885	VC
Univ of Mich-Flint	MI	17,547	C+
Univ of Minn Crookston	MN	17,834	C
Univ of Minn/Duluth	MN	18,964	C+
Univ of Missouri/Columbia	MO	18,201	MC
Univ of Missouri-Kansas City	MO	19,603	C
Univ of Missouri-St. Louis	MO	18,304	VC
Univ of Mobile	AL	27,870	VC
Univ of Montana	MT	13,670	C
Univ of Montana-Western	MT	9,753	LC
Univ of Montevallo	AL	17,320	C
Univ of Mount Union	OH	35,130	C
Univ of Nebr - Lincoln	NE	17,507	VC
Univ of Nebr at Kearney	NE	14,855	LC
Univ of Nebr at Omaha	NE	12,700	C
Univ of Nevada, Las Vegas	NV	17,303	C
Univ of New England	ME	46,145	C+
Univ of New Hampshire	NH	24,702	VC
Univ of New Haven	CT	47,740	C
Univ of New Mexico	NM	15,300	C
Univ of New Orleans	LA	9,224	VC
Univ of North Alabama	AL	9,960	C
Univ of N Car at Asheville	NC	13,500	VC+
Univ of N Car at Chapel Hill	NC	18,348	MC
Univ of N Car at Charlotte	NC	15,847	C
Univ of N Car at Greensboro	NC	12,848	C
Univ of N Car at Wilmington	NC	13,572	VC+
Univ of N Dak	ND	14,094	C
Univ of North Florida	FL	15,578	VC
Univ of North Texas	TX	15,628	C
Univ of Northern Colo	CO	15,973	C
Univ of Northern Iowa	IA	14,776	C
Univ of Okla	OK	17,634	VC+
Univ of Oregon	OR	20,872	VC
Univ of Pennsylvania	PA	56,106	MC
Univ of Pikeville	KY	24,750	NC
Univ of Pittsburgh at Bradford	PA	21,316	LC
Univ of Pittsburgh at Greensburg	PA	17,640	C
Univ of Pittsburgh at Johnstown	PA	20,862	LC
Univ of Pittsburgh at Pittsburgh	PA	27,800	HC+
Univ of Portland	OR	47,874	VC
Univ of Puget Sound	WA	52,648	HC+
Univ of Rio Grande	OH	8,750	NC
Univ of St. Francis	IN	29,810	C
Univ of San Diego	CA	53,302	HC+
Univ of San Francisco	CA	49,674	VC
Univ of Science and Arts of Okla	OK	10,560	VC
Univ of Scranton	PA	51,940	VC
Univ of Sioux Falls	SD	22,990	C
Univ of South Alabama	AL	13,510	C
Univ of S Car at Aiken	SC	16,278	C
Univ of S Car at Columbia	SC	19,725	VC+
Univ of S Car Upstate	SC	17,673	LC
Univ of South Florida	FL	13,000	C
Univ of South Florida/St. Petersburg	FL	12,769	VC
Univ of Southern Calif	CA	56,903	MC
Univ of Southern Indiana	IN	14,657	C
Univ of Southern Maine	ME	16,576	C
Univ of Southern Miss	MS	13,170	C
Univ of St. Francis	IL	36,490	C
Univ of St. Thomas - Houston	TX	36,490	VC
Univ of Tampa	FL	35,160	VC
Univ of Tenn at Chattanooga	TN	16,883	C
Univ of Tenn at Knoxville	TN	20,364	VC+
Univ of Tenn at Martin	TN	13,217	C
Univ of Texas at Arlington	TX	10,908	LC
Univ of Texas at El Paso	TX	8,764	NC
Univ of Texas at San Antonio	TX	18,372	C
Univ of Texas-Pan American	TX	12,432	LC
Univ of the Arts	PA	38,450	SP
Univ of the Cumberlands	KY	27,500	LC
Univ of the Incarnate Word	TX	35,200	LC
Univ of the Ozarks	AR	22,100	C
Univ of the Pacific	CA	52,146	VC
Univ of the Sacred Heart	PR	5,590	
Univ of Toledo	OH	18,464	C
Univ of Tulsa	OK	45,311	HC+
Univ of Utah	UT	13,462	VC
Univ of Vermont	VT	26,120	VC+
Univ of Virginia's College at Wise	VA	11,076	C
Univ of Washington	WA	14,722	VC
Univ of West Florida	FL	14,656	C
Univ of Wisc Whitewater	WI	13,314	C
Univ of Wisc/Eau Claire	WI	15,430	VC
Univ of Wisc/Green Bay	WI	14,900	C
Univ of Wisc/La Crosse	WI	14,755	VC
Univ of Wisc/Madison	WI	18,757	HC
Univ of Wisc/Parkside	WI	10,181	LC
Univ of Wisc/River Falls	WI	9,722	LC
Univ of Wisc/Stevens Point	WI	14,043	C
Univ of Wisc/Stout	WI	23,942	C
Univ of Wisc/Superior	WI	14,106	C
Univ of Wisc-Milwaukee	WI	18,436	C
Upper Iowa Univ	IA	30,426	NC
Urbana Univ	OH	21,190	C
Ursinus College	PA	55,630	VC+
Utica College	NY	44,734	C
Valparaiso Univ	IN	43,040	VC+
Vanderbilt Univ	TN	57,072	MC
Vanguard Univ of Southern Calif	CA	35,833	VC
Villanova Univ	PA	56,436	MC
Virginia Commonwealth Univ	VA	18,633	C
Virginia Polytechnic Inst and State Univ	VA	14,629	HC
Virginia Wesleyan College	VA	28,433	LC
Voorhees College	SC	18,126	C

ST = STATE **$IS** = IN-STATE COSTS **SR** = SELECTOR RATING

School	ST	$IS	SR
Wake Forest Univ	NC	51,000	MC
Walla Walla Univ	WA	26,256	NC
Walsh Univ	OH	35,100	C
Warner Univ	FL	18,000	C
Wartburg College	IA	41,055	VC
Washburn Univ	KS	12,165	NC
Washington Adventist Univ	MD	25,859	C+
Washington State Univ	WA	20,461	C
Washington Univ in St. Louis	MO	58,818	MC
Wayland Baptist Univ	TX	16,058	LC
Wayne State College	NE	11,764	NC
Wayne State Univ	MI	19,493	C
Webster Univ	MO	33,990	C+
Wesleyan College	GA	24,000	C+
West Chester Univ of Pennsylvania	PA	16,836	C
West Liberty Univ	WV	9,142	LC
West Virginia State Univ	WV	8,378	NC
West Virginia Univ	WV	15,794	C+
Western Carolina Univ	NC	13,965	C+
Western Conn State Univ	CT	18,327	C
Western Illinois Univ	IL	20,130	C
Western Kentucky Univ	KY	11,000	LC
Western Mich Univ	MI	19,042	C
Western New England Univ	MA	45,590	C
Western State Colo Univ	CO	16,135	C
Western Washington Univ	WA	18,519	VC
Westfield State Univ	MA	18,489	C
Westminster College	PA	31,290	C+
Westminster College	UT	37,708	VC
Westmont College	CA	41,500	HC
Wheaton College	IL	39,650	HC+
Wheeling Jesuit Univ	WV	34,668	C
Whitworth Univ	WA	45,826	VC+
Wichita State Univ	KS	12,539	C
Widener Univ	PA	50,368	C
Wilberforce Univ	OH	15,100	LC
Wiley College	TX		LC
Wilkes Univ	PA	42,786	C
William Carey Univ	MS	13,500	LC
William Jewell College	MO	31,000	VC+
William Paterson Univ of New Jersey	NJ	21,694	C
William Peace Univ	NC	32,900	LC
William Penn Univ	IA	26,000	C
William Woods Univ	MO		C
Wilmington College	OH	29,784	C
Wilson College	PA	27,660	C
Wingate Univ	NC	34,990	C
Winston-Salem State Univ	NC	9,418	LC
Winthrop Univ	SC	21,120	VC
Wisc Lutheran College	WI	23,510	VC
Wittenberg Univ	OH	47,766	VC
Woodbury Univ	CA	34,500	LC
Worcester State Univ	MA	18,657	C
Wright State Univ	OH	16,983	C
Xavier Univ of Louisiana	LA	25,300	C
Yeshiva Univ	NY	47,250	VC+
York College	NE	19,475	C
York College of Pennsylvania	PA	26,590	C
Youngstown State Univ	OH	16,374	LC

COMMUNICATIONS TECHNOLOGY

School	ST	$IS	SR
Alverno College	WI	30,483	LC
Calif College of the Arts	CA	48,334	SP
Cal State, Monterey Bay	CA	26,871	LC
Champlain College	VT	44,850	VC
Chestnut Hill College	PA	39,785	LC
Dakota State Univ	SD	13,811	C
Eastern Mich Univ	MI	17,961	C
George Mason Univ	VA	15,724	VC
Grand Canyon Univ	AZ	24,540	LC
Indiana Univ of Pennsylvania	PA	20,180	LC
Inter-American Univ of PR/ Bayamon Univ College	PR	4,428	
James Madison Univ	VA	18,049	VC
Lebanon Valley College	PA	38,570	C
Lewis Univ	IL	23,050	C
Montana Tech of The Univ of Montana	MT	14,650	VC
Montclair State Univ	NJ	22,614	C
New York Univ	NY	61,470	MC
Northwestern Univ	IL	37,595	MC
Ohio Univ	OH	20,676	VC
Penn State Univ/Univ Park	PA	25,404	VC
Rochester Inst of Technology	NY	42,450	VC+
Sacred Heart Univ	CT	48,564	VC
Salve Regina Univ	RI	47,250	VC
Southern Methodist Univ	TX	57,755	MC
SUNY Inst of Technology at Utica / Rome	NY	23,818	C
Taylor Univ	IN	36,742	VC+
Univ of New Haven	CT	47,740	C
Univ of S Dak	SD	15,111	C
Wilmington Univ	DE	7,778	NC

COMMUNITY HEALTH WORK

School	ST	$IS	SR
Baylor Univ	TX	46,720	HC
Bethel Univ	MN	34,940	VC
Brown Univ	RI	56,150	MC

School	ST	$IS	SR
Central Washington Univ	WA	11,730	C
Concordia Univ St. Paul	MN	27,200	C
Delaware State Univ	DE	14,700	LC
Florida Gulf Coast Univ	FL		C
Florida State Univ	FL	15,238	HC
George Mason Univ	VA	15,724	VC
Georgia College and State Univ	GA	18,216	VC
Hofstra Univ	NY	48,020	VC+
Howard Univ	DC	35,957	C
Ithaca College	NY	52,300	HC
John Brown Univ	AR	30,996	VC+
Johnson C. Smith Univ	NC	25,336	LC
Kent State Univ	OH	19,352	C
Lewis Univ	IL	23,050	C
Liberty Univ	VA	19,101	C
Longwood Univ	VA	20,924	C
Louisiana State Univ in Shreveport	LA	5,606	C
Malone Univ	OH	34,334	C
Minn State Univ, Moorhead	MN	13,392	C
Montclair State Univ	NJ	22,614	C
Morris College	SC	16,006	LC
New Mexico State Univ	NM	13,955	LC
Northern Illinois Univ	IL	19,768	C
Ohio Univ	OH	20,676	VC
Prescott College	AZ	33,284	C+
Slippery Rock Univ of Pennsylvania	PA	10,360	LC
Southern Illinois Univ Edwardsville	IL	17,532	C
SUNY College at Old Westbury	NY	16,324	C
The SUNY at Potsdam	NY	17,754	C
Tufts Univ	MA	58,780	MC
Univ of Calif at Davis	CA	24,482	HC
Univ of Central Okla	OK	12,293	C
Univ of Illinois at Urbana-Champaign	IL	24,300	HC
Univ of Kansas	KS	16,980	C+
Univ of Maine at Farmington	ME	17,841	C
Univ of Maryland	MD	18,801	HC
Univ of Mass Lowell	MA	19,316	C
Univ of Nebr at Omaha	NE	12,700	C
Univ of Scranton	PA	51,940	VC
Univ of Wisc/La Crosse	WI	14,755	VC
Univ of Wisc/Superior	WI	14,106	C
Western Mich Univ	MI	19,042	C
William Paterson Univ of New Jersey	NJ	21,694	C
Winona State Univ	MN	16,530	C
Wright State Univ	OH	16,983	C
York College / CUNY	NY	5,496	NC

COMMUNITY PSYCHOLOGY

School	ST	$IS	SR
Mount Aloysius College	PA	27,970	C
Southwestern Okla State Univ	OK	9,160	C
Univ of Mich-Flint	MI	17,547	C+
Univ of New Haven	CT	47,740	C

COMMUNITY SERVICES

School	ST	$IS	SR
Alverno College	WI	30,483	LC
Aquinas College	MI	33,060	C
Bemidji State Univ	MN	13,500	C
Bryant Univ	RI	49,179	VC
Cal State, Chico	CA	18,952	C
Central Mich Univ	MI	18,066	C
DePaul Univ	IL	46,120	VC
Emory and Henry College	VA	387,460	C
Guilford College	NC	35,340	C
Humphreys College	CA	17,000	NC
Martin Univ	IN	11,000	SP
Metropolitan College of New York	NY	16,720	VC
Midland Univ	NE	34,000	C
New Mexico State Univ	NM	13,955	LC
Northern State Univ	SD	14,021	C
Ohio Univ	OH	20,676	VC
Portland State Univ	OR	18,672	C
Prescott College	AZ	33,284	C+
Providence College	RI	55,995	HC
Queens Univ of Charlotte	NC	39,543	VC
Roger Williams Univ	RI	45,788	C
St. Martin's Univ	WA	38,082	C
Southern Arkansas Univ	AR	14,316	C
St. Joseph's College, New York / Brooklyn Campus	NY	21,878	C
St. Joseph's College, New York / Suffolk Campus	NY	21,878	VC
SUNY/Empire State College	NY	6,315	SP
Ohio State Univ	OH	19,887	MC
Univ of Calif at Santa Cruz	CA	27,807	VC
Univ of Mass Boston	MA	11,966	C
Univ of Toledo	OH	18,464	C
Woodbury Inst of Champlain College in Burlington	VT	15,150	LC

COMPARATIVE LITERATURE

School	ST	$IS	SR
Beloit College	WI	49,970	HC
Bennington College	VT	56,990	HC+
Binghamton Univ / The SUNY	NY	20,832	HC+
Brandeis Univ	MA	58,820	HC
Brigham Young Univ	UT	12,100	HC
Brown Univ	RI	56,150	MC
Bryant Univ	RI	49,179	VC
Bryn Mawr College	PA	57,760	MC
Cal State, Fullerton	CA	25,188	C+
Cal State, Long Beach	CA	17,534	C+
Case Western Reserve Univ	OH	55,178	MC
CUNY/Brooklyn College	NY	5,884	C+
Clark Univ	MA	47,020	HC+
College of Wooster	OH	52,600	VC
Colo College	CO	54,534	MC
Columbia Univ in the City of New York	NY	61,116	MC
Columbia Univ/Barnard College	NY	39,000	MC
Columbia Univ/School of General Studies	NY	54,083	MC
Cornell Univ	NY	59,037	MC
CUNY-City College	NY	19,576	HC+
Dartmouth College	NH	57,996	MC
Eckerd College	FL	43,902	VC
Emory Univ	GA	45,000	MC
Fordham Univ	NY	58,927	HC
Georgetown Univ	DC	52,910	MC
Goddard College	VT	16,418	VC
Hamilton College	NY	55,620	MC
Hampshire College	MA	58,320	MC
Haverford College	PA	59,236	MC
Hillsdale College	MI	31,890	HC+
Hobart and William Smith Colleges	NY	43,000	VC
Hofstra Univ	NY	48,020	VC+
Hunter College / The CUNY	NY	14,429	VC
Indiana Univ Bloomington	IN	19,358	HC
Lehman College / The CUNY	NY	5,778	LC
Middlebury College	VT	57,470	MC
Mills College	CA	54,119	HC
New England College	NH	45,930	LC
New York Univ	NY	61,470	MC
Northwestern Univ	IL	37,595	MC
Oberlin College	OH	57,025	MC
Penn State Univ/Univ Park	PA	25,404	VC
Princeton Univ	NJ	53,795	MC
Purdue Univ/West Lafayette	IN	20,278	HC
Queens College / The CUNY	NY	17,107	VC
Rutgers, The State Univ of New Jersey/New Brunswick	NJ	25,077	VC
San Diego State Univ	CA	20,578	VC
San Francisco State Univ	CA	18,514	C
Smith College	MA	57,524	MC
Stanford Univ	CA	56,411	MC
Stony Brook Univ / SUNY	NY	19,359	HC
SUNY College at Geneseo	NY	18,055	HC+
Swarthmore College	PA	57,870	MC
Syracuse Univ	NY	54,512	HC
Trinity College	CT		HC+
Univ of Calif at Berkeley	CA	23,322	MC
Univ of Calif at Davis	CA	24,482	HC
Univ of Calif at Irvine	CA	25,961	VC
Univ of Calif at Riverside	CA	27,204	C
Univ of Calif at Santa Barbara	CA	27,551	HC
Univ of Chicago	IL	55,416	MC
Univ of Cincinnati	OH	20,199	VC
Univ of Delaware	DE	22,728	VC
Univ of Georgia	GA	19,508	VC
Univ of Illinois at Urbana-Champaign	IL	24,300	HC
Univ of Iowa	IA	17,481	VC
Univ of La Verne	CA	47,010	VC
Univ of Mass Amherst	MA	23,697	VC+
Univ of Mich/Ann Arbor	MI	22,102	HC+
Univ of New Mexico	NM	15,300	C
Univ of N Car at Chapel Hill	NC	18,348	MC
Univ of Okla	OK	17,634	VC+
Univ of Oregon	OR	20,872	VC
Univ of Pennsylvania	PA	56,106	MC
Univ of PR Recinto de Rio Piedras	PR	5,750	
Univ of Rochester	NY	58,500	MC
Univ of S Car at Columbia	SC	19,725	VC+
Univ of Southern Calif	CA	56,903	MC
Univ of Utah	UT	13,462	VC
Univ of Virginia	VA	22,175	MC
Univ of Washington	WA	14,722	VC
Univ of Wisc/Madison	WI	18,757	HC
Univ of Wisc-Milwaukee	WI	18,436	C
Washington Univ in St. Louis	MO	58,818	MC
Wellesley College	MA	49,848	MC
Willamette Univ	OR	56,450	VC+

COMPOSITION

School	ST	$IS	SR
Indiana Univ Bloomington	IN	19,358	HC
Shenandoah Univ	VA	39,268	C

COMPUTATIONAL SCIENCES

School	ST	$IS	SR
Biola Univ	CA	40,320	VC
Brown Univ	RI	56,150	MC
Bryant Univ	RI	49,179	VC
Canisius College	NY	45,602	VC
Champlain College	VT	44,850	VC
Creighton Univ	NE	44,058	VC+
DePaul Univ	IL	46,120	VC
George Mason Univ	VA	15,724	VC
Hood College	MD	44,630	C
Marquette Univ	WI	43,664	VC+
Mercer Univ	GA	44,201	VC+
Mich State Univ	MI	13,689	VC
Mount Aloysius College	PA	27,970	C
New College of Florida	FL	14,504	HC+
New York Univ	NY	61,470	MC
Park Univ	MO	17,525	C
Purdue Univ/West Lafayette	IN	20,278	HC
Richard Stockton College of New Jersey	NJ	20,000	VC
Stevens Inst of Technology	NJ	50,130	HC
The College at Brockport / SUNY	NY	18,362	VC
Univ at Buffalo / The SUNY	NY	20,283	VC
Univ of Illinois at Urbana-Champaign	IL	24,300	HC

COMPUTER EDUCATION

School	ST	$IS	SR
Appalachian State Univ	NC	12,919	VC
Baylor Univ	TX	46,720	HC
Concordia Univ, River Forest	IL	26,300	C
Dakota State Univ	SD	13,811	C
Duquesne Univ	PA	42,017	VC
Eastern Mich Univ	MI	17,961	C
Eastern Washington Univ	WA	16,388	C
Hardin-Simmons Univ	TX	23,560	C+
Indiana Univ-Purdue Univ Fort Wayne	IN	15,425	C
Missouri State Univ	MO	13,996	VC
Northern Mich Univ	MI	15,300	VC
Union College	NE	23,270	VC
Univ of Illinois at Urbana-Champaign	IL	24,300	HC
Univ of Montana-Western	MT	9,753	LC
Univ of Nebr - Lincoln	NE	17,507	VC
Youngstown State Univ	OH	16,374	LC

COMPUTER ENGINEERING

School	ST	$IS	SR
Arizona State Univ	AZ	18,818	C+
Auburn Univ	AL	20,052	VC+
Baylor Univ	TX	46,720	HC
Bellarmine Univ	KY	42,950	VC
Benedict College	SC	20,454	NC
Bethune-Cookman Univ	FL	22,290	LC
Binghamton Univ / The SUNY	NY	20,832	HC+
Boston Univ	MA	54,130	HC+
Brigham Young Univ	UT	12,100	HC
Bucknell Univ	PA	58,160	MC
Calif Baptist Univ	CA	35,890	C
Calif Inst of Technology	CA	54,045	MC
Calif Polytechnic State Univ	CA	19,847	HC
Cal State, Chico	CA	18,952	C
Cal State, Fresno	CA	17,405	C
Cal State, Fullerton	CA	25,188	C+
Cal State, Long Beach	CA	17,534	C+
Cal State, Sacramento	CA	16,200	C
Calvin College	MI	37,585	VC+
Capitol College	MD	21,250	C
Carnegie Mellon Univ	PA	51,260	MC
Case Western Reserve Univ	OH	55,178	MC
Cedarville Univ	OH	31,036	VC+
Christopher Newport Univ	VA	21,050	VC
Claflin Univ	SC	22,368	C+
Clarkson Univ	NY	53,538	HC
Clemson Univ	SC	19,136	HC
Cogswell Polytechnical College	CA	30,531	C
College of New Jersey	NJ	25,376	HC
Colo State Univ-Fort Collins	CO	20,090	VC
Colo Technical Univ	CO	10,500	LC
Columbia Univ in the City of New York	NY	61,116	MC
CUNY-City College	NY	19,576	HC+
Dordt College	IA	34,160	VC
Drexel Univ	PA	51,920	HC
Eastern Mich Univ	MI	17,961	C
Eastern Nazarene College	MA	30,000	C
Elizabethtown College	PA	47,600	VC
Elon Univ	NC	40,046	HC
Embry-Riddle Aeronautical Univ - Daytona Beach	FL	40,884	C+
Embry-Riddle Aeronautical Univ - Prescott Campus	AZ	40,584	VC
Fairfield Univ	CT	55,850	VC
Florida Atlantic Univ	FL	17,339	C
Florida Inst of Technology	FL	48,290	VC
Florida International Univ	FL	17,747	VC
Florida State Univ	FL	15,238	HC

School	ST	$IS	SR
George Mason Univ	VA	15,724	VC
George Washington Univ	DC	57,108	MC
Georgia Inst of Technology	GA	20,464	MC
Gonzaga Univ	WA	44,247	HC
Harding Univ	AR	21,432	C+
Hofstra Univ	NY	48,020	VC+
Howard Univ	DC	35,957	C
Illinois Inst of Technology	IL	38,512	HC+
Indiana Inst of Technology	IN	34,240	LC
Indiana Univ-Purdue Univ Fort Wayne	IN	15,425	C
Indiana Univ-Purdue Univ Indianapolis	IN	17,290	C
Iowa State Univ	IA	16,403	C+
Jackson State Univ	MS	13,512	LC
Johns Hopkins Univ	MD	47,402	MC
Johnson C. Smith Univ	NC	25,336	LC
Kansas State Univ	KS	15,497	VC
Kettering Univ	MI	31,456	HC
Lake Superior State Univ	MI	18,121	C
Lawrence Tech Univ	MI	37,630	VC
Lehigh Univ	PA	55,080	MC
LeTourneau Univ	TX	26,230	C
Lipscomb Univ	TN	35,722	VC
Louisiana State Univ	LA	18,677	VC+
Marquette Univ	WI	43,664	VC+
Miami Univ	OH	24,191	HC
Mich State Univ	MI	13,689	VC
Mich Tech Univ	MI	22,105	VC
Milwaukee School of Engineering	WI	39,948	VC+
Minn State Univ, Mankato	MN	14,900	C
Missouri Univ of Science and Technology	MO	18,655	VC+
Montana State Univ	MT	14,068	VC
Montana Tech of The Univ of Montana	MT	14,650	VC
Murray State Univ	KY	14,944	C
New Jersey Inst of Technology	NJ	26,490	VC
New York City College of Technology / The CUNY	NY	5,769	NC
New York Inst of Technology	NY	40,590	VC
New York Univ	NY	61,470	MC
N Car State Univ	NC	16,202	HC
N Dak State Univ	ND	14,642	C
Northeastern Univ	MA	55,296	MC
Northwestern Univ	IL	37,595	MC
Norwich Univ	VT	28,212	C
Nova Southeastern Univ	FL	34,016	VC
Oakland Univ	MI	19,391	VC
Ohio Northern Univ	OH	42,075	VC
Ohio Univ	OH	20,676	VC
Okla Christian Univ	OK	24,975	VC
Okla State Univ	OK	14,310	VC
Old Dominion Univ	VA	18,662	C
Olivet Nazarene Univ	IL	29,990	C
Oral Roberts Univ	OK	31,734	C
Oregon State Univ	OR	19,017	C+
Pacific Lutheran Univ	WA	44,840	VC
Penn State Erie/The Behrend College	PA	16,256	C
Penn State Univ/Univ Park	PA	25,404	VC
Pennsylvania College of Technology	PA	25,653	NC
Polytechnic Inst of New York Univ	NY	53,064	HC+
Portland State Univ	OR	18,672	C
Prairie View A&M Univ	TX	15,205	LC
Purdue Univ/Calumet	IN	14,336	C
Purdue Univ/West Lafayette	IN	20,278	HC
Rensselaer Polytechnic Inst	NY	59,229	MC
Rochester Inst of Technology	NY	42,450	VC+
Rose-Hulman Inst of Technology	IN	51,738	MC
St. Louis Univ	MO	46,594	VC+
St. Mary's Univ	TX	33,854	C
San Diego State Univ	CA	20,578	VC
San Francisco State Univ	CA	18,514	C
San Jose State Univ	CA	19,707	C
Seattle Univ	WA	47,010	VC+
Shepherd Univ	WV	14,996	C
Shippensburg Univ of Pennsylvania	PA	17,064	LC
S Dak School of Mines and Technology	SD	15,260	VC
Southern Illinois Univ Carbondale	IL	21,620	C
Southern Illinois Univ Edwardsville	IL	17,532	C
Southern Methodist Univ	TX	57,755	MC
Southwestern Okla State Univ	OK	9,160	C
Stevens Inst of Technology	NJ	50,130	HC
Stony Brook Univ / SUNY	NY	19,359	HC
Suffolk Univ	MA	46,548	C
SUNY New Paltz	NY	15,010	C
Syracuse Univ	NY	54,512	HC
Taylor Univ	IN	36,742	VC+
Texas A&M Univ	TX	16,956	VC+
The Catholic Univ of America	DC	52,852	VC
Ohio State Univ	OH	19,887	MC
Trine Univ	IN	39,400	VC
Tufts Univ	MA	58,780	MC
Union College	NY		MC
United States Air Force Academy	CO		MC
United States Naval Academy	MD		MC
Universidad Politecnica de PR	PR	19,252	
Univ at Buffalo / The SUNY	NY	20,283	VC
Univ of Akron	OH	20,436	C
Univ of Alabama at Huntsville	AL	17,625	VC
Univ of Alaska Fairbanks	AK	13,955	C
Univ of Arkansas at Fayetteville	AR	16,860	VC
Univ of Bridgeport	CT	39,030	LC
Univ of Calif at Berkeley	CA	23,322	MC
Univ of Calif at Davis	CA	24,482	HC
Univ of Calif at Irvine	CA	25,961	VC
Univ of Calif at Los Angeles	CA	25,686	MC
Univ of Calif at San Diego	CA	21,000	VC
Univ of Calif at Santa Barbara	CA	27,551	HC
Univ of Calif at Santa Cruz	CA	27,807	VC
Univ of Central Florida	FL	15,711	VC+
Univ of Cincinnati	OH	20,199	VC
Univ of Colo Boulder	CO	22,605	VC+
Univ of Conn	CT	23,744	HC
Univ of Dayton	OH	43,750	VC
Univ of Delaware	DE	22,728	VC
Univ of Denver	CO	51,787	VC+
Univ of Evansville	IN	41,056	VC+
Univ of Florida	FL	15,783	HC+
Univ of Hartford	CT	42,674	C
Univ of Houston	TX	19,184	VC
Univ of Idaho	ID	14,558	C
Univ of Illinois at Chicago	IL	24,293	VC
Univ of Illinois at Urbana-Champaign	IL	24,300	HC
Univ of Kansas	KS	16,980	C+
Univ of La Verne	CA	47,010	VC
Univ of Louisiana at Lafayette	LA	6,130	C
Univ of Louisville	KY	17,460	VC
Univ of Maine	ME	19,712	C+
Univ of Maryland	MD	18,801	HC
Univ of Maryland/Baltimore County	MD	18,000	VC
Univ of Mass Amherst	MA	23,697	VC+
Univ of Mass Dartmouth	MA	22,223	C
Univ of Memphis	TN	15,094	C
Univ of Miami	FL	55,166	MC
Univ of Mich/Ann Arbor	MI	22,102	HC+
Univ of Mich/Dearborn	MI	9,885	VC
Univ of Minn/Duluth	MN	18,964	C+
Univ of Missouri/Columbia	MO	18,201	MC
Univ of Nebr - Lincoln	NE	17,507	VC
Univ of Nevada, Las Vegas	NV	17,303	C
Univ of New Hampshire	NH	24,702	VC
Univ of New Haven	CT	47,740	C
Univ of New Mexico	NM	15,300	C
Univ of N Car at Charlotte	NC	15,847	C
Univ of North Texas	TX	15,628	C
Univ of Notre Dame	IN		MC
Univ of Okla	OK	17,634	VC+
Univ of Pennsylvania	PA	56,106	MC
Univ of Pittsburgh at Johnstown	PA	20,862	LC
Univ of Pittsburgh at Pittsburgh	PA	27,800	HC+
Univ of PR/Mayaguez	PR	1,250	
Univ of Scranton	PA	51,940	VC
Univ of South Alabama	AL	13,510	C
Univ of S Car at Columbia	SC	19,725	VC+
Univ of South Florida	FL	13,000	C
Univ of Southern Calif	CA	56,903	MC
Univ of Tenn at Knoxville	TN	20,364	VC+
Univ of Texas at Arlington	TX	10,908	LC
Univ of Texas at Dallas	TX	21,046	HC
Univ of Texas at San Antonio	TX	18,372	C
Univ of Texas-Pan American	TX	12,432	LC
Univ of the Pacific	CA	52,146	VC
Univ of Toledo	OH	18,464	C
Univ of Utah	UT	13,462	VC
Univ of Virginia	VA	22,175	MC
Univ of Washington	WA	14,722	VC
Univ of West Florida	FL	14,656	C
Univ of Wisc/Madison	WI	18,757	HC
Univ of Wisc/Stout	WI	23,942	C
Univ of Wisc-Milwaukee	WI	18,436	C
Univ of Wyoming	WY	13,855	C+
Valparaiso Univ	IN	43,040	VC+
Vanderbilt Univ	TN	57,072	MC
Vermont Technical College	VT	15,751	C
Villanova Univ	PA	56,436	MC
Virginia Commonwealth Univ	VA	18,633	C
Virginia Polytechnic Inst and State Univ	VA	14,629	HC
Washington State Univ	WA	20,461	C
Washington Univ in St. Louis	MO	58,818	MC
West Virginia Univ	WV	15,794	C+
Western Mich Univ	MI	19,042	C
Western New England Univ	MA	45,590	C
Wichita State Univ	KS	12,539	C
Wright State Univ	OH	16,983	C
York College of Pennsylvania	PA	26,590	C

COMPUTER ENGINEERING TECHNOLOGY

School	ST	$IS	SR
Cal State, Fresno	CA	17,405	C
Central Conn State Univ	CT	19,212	C
Farmingdale State College	NY	18,985	C
Howard Univ	DC	35,957	C
Indiana Univ-Purdue Univ Indianapolis	IN	17,290	C
Mount Vernon Nazarene Univ	OH	29,590	C
Murray State Univ	KY	14,944	C
New York Univ	NY	61,470	MC
Northern Kentucky Univ	KY	15,302	LC
Nova Southeastern Univ	FL	34,016	VC
Santa Clara Univ	CA	54,702	MC
Shawnee State Univ	OH	16,545	NC
Southern Polytechnic State Univ	GA	13,958	VC
Syracuse Univ	NY	54,512	HC
Taylor Univ	IN	36,742	VC+
Univ of S Car Upstate	SC	17,673	LC

COMPUTER GAME DESIGN/ DEVELOPMENT

School	ST	$IS	SR
Abilene Christian Univ	TX	38,400	VC
Becker College	MA	41,420	LC
Champlain College	VT	44,850	VC
Dakota State Univ	SD	13,811	C
DePaul Univ	IL	46,120	VC
Elmhurst College	IL	42,032	C+
Indiana Inst of Technology	IN	34,240	LC
Marshall Univ	WV	14,820	C
Shawnee State Univ	OH	16,545	NC
Southern Polytechnic State Univ	GA	13,958	VC
Univ of Calif at Santa Cruz	CA	27,807	VC
Univ of Denver	CO	51,787	VC+
Univ of Miami	FL	55,166	MC

COMPUTER GRAPHICS

School	ST	$IS	SR
Andrews Univ	MI	28,030	C+
Arizona State Univ	AZ	18,818	C+
Art Inst of Atlanta	GA	24,000	SP
Ashford Univ	IA	21,780	C
Cal State, Chico	CA	18,952	C
Cogswell Polytechnical College	CA	30,531	C
Columbia College Chicago	IL	30,940	LC
Dakota State Univ	SD	13,811	C
DePaul Univ	IL	46,120	VC
Eastern Mich Univ	MI	17,961	C
Escuela de Artes Plasticas de PR	PR	2,660	
Fashion Inst of Technology/SUNY	NY	12,468	SP
Indiana Univ Northwest	IN	6,738	LC
Indiana Univ-Purdue Univ Fort Wayne	IN	15,425	C
Indiana Univ-Purdue Univ Indianapolis	IN	17,290	C
Indiana Wesleyan Univ	IN	31,815	VC
Jacksonville Univ	FL	37,780	C
La Salle Univ	PA	50,270	C
Lawrence Tech Univ	MI	37,630	VC
Lewis Univ	IL	23,050	C
Millikin Univ	IL	37,462	C
Monmouth Univ	NJ	42,252	C
Murray State Univ	KY	14,944	C
New York Inst of Technology	NY	40,590	VC
Pennsylvania College of Technology	PA	25,653	NC
Pratt Inst	NY	49,520	SP
Purdue Univ/Calumet	IN	14,336	C
Purdue Univ/West Lafayette	IN	20,278	HC
Ringling College of Art and Design	FL	46,130	SP
Rochester Inst of Technology	NY	42,450	VC+
Sacred Heart Univ	CT	48,564	VC
Savannah College of Art and Design	GA	46,824	SP
School of Visual Arts	NY	36,500	SP
Springfield College	MA	25,000	C
Syracuse Univ	NY	54,512	HC
Taylor Univ	IN	36,742	VC+
Univ of Dubuque	IA	30,200	C
Univ of Great Falls	MT	27,970	C
Univ of Mary Hardin-Baylor	TX	31,950	C+
Univ of Miami	FL	55,166	MC
Univ of Tampa	FL	35,160	VC
Worcester Polytechnic Inst	MA	53,440	HC+

COMPUTER INFORMATION SYSTEMS

School	ST	$IS	SR
Bryant Univ	RI	49,179	VC
Cabrini College	PA	40,859	LC
Ferris State Univ	MI	19,698	C
Indiana Univ Northwest	IN	6,738	LC
Nova Southeastern Univ	FL	34,016	VC
St. Louis Univ	MO	46,594	VC+
Southern Oregon Univ	OR	17,874	C
Texas State Univ	TX	16,495	VC
Thomas Edison State College	NJ	5,700	SP
Univ of Louisiana at Monroe	LA	12,998	C
Univ of Miami	FL	55,166	MC
Univ of Texas-Pan American	TX	12,432	LC

COMPUTER INFORMATION TECHNOLOGY

School	ST	$IS	SR
Biola Univ	CA	40,320	VC
Bryant Univ	RI	49,179	VC
Champlain College	VT	44,850	VC
City Univ of Seattle	WA	14,880	NC
Franklin College	IN	35,885	C
Grove City College	PA	22,988	HC
Indiana Univ-Purdue Univ Indianapolis	IN	17,290	C
John Jay College of Criminal Justice / The CUNY	NY	6,059	C
Limestone College	SC	29,880	C
Northern Arizona Univ	AZ	18,592	C
Ohio Valley Univ	WV	17,752	C
St. Edward's Univ	TX	44,674	VC
St. Joseph's College, New York / Brooklyn Campus	NY	21,878	C
St. Joseph's College, New York / Suffolk Campus	NY	21,878	VC
Texas Christian Univ	TX	47,570	HC
Thomas College	ME	26,270	LC
Washington and Jefferson College	PA	49,990	VC

COMPUTER MANAGEMENT

School	ST	$IS	SR
Bryant Univ	RI	49,179	VC
Caldwell College	NJ	35,602	LC
Chestnut Hill College	PA	39,785	LC
Colo Christian Univ	CO	27,500	VC
Eastern Mennonite Univ	VA	38,850	VC
Emory and Henry College	VA	387,460	C
Johnson and Wales Univ/ Providence Campus	RI	34,668	C
Lake Superior State Univ	MI	18,121	C
Mayville State Univ	ND	11,401	NC
Metropolitan State Univ of Denver	CO	4,835	LC
Mount Olive College	NC	18,426	C
Murray State Univ	KY	14,944	C
New Jersey Inst of Technology	NJ	26,490	VC
Northwest Missouri State Univ	MO	14,229	C
Northwest Univ	WA	18,854	C
Northwood Univ	MI	26,331	LC
Peirce College	PA	12,760	NC
Peru State College	NE	8,600	NC
Rochester College	MI	18,320	C
Southern Adventist Univ	TN	26,190	C
Southern Illinois Univ Edwardsville	IL	17,532	C
Univ of Great Falls	MT	27,970	C
Univ of Illinois at Urbana-Champaign	IL	24,300	HC
Univ of New Haven	CT	47,740	C
Univ of Northern Iowa	IA	14,776	C
Webster Univ	MO	33,990	C+

COMPUTER MATHEMATICS

School	ST	$IS	SR
Arizona State Univ	AZ	18,818	C+
Ashford Univ	IA	21,780	C
Bethany College	WV	35,282	C
Biola Univ	CA	40,320	VC
Bowdoin College	ME	57,834	MC
Calif Inst of Technology	CA	54,045	MC
Colo College	CO	54,534	MC
Florida Southern College	FL	38,240	VC
Ithaca College	NY	52,300	HC
Keene State College	NH	21,538	C
LeTourneau Univ	TX	26,230	C
Lewis & Clark College	OR	52,656	VC
Marist College	NY	35,500	C
Missouri Southern State Univ	MO	11,910	C
New York Univ	NY	61,470	MC
Oakwood Univ	AL	23,035	C
Piedmont College	GA	29,260	C
Rochester Inst of Technology	NY	42,450	VC+
Salem International Univ	WV	18,020	C
Southern Oregon Univ	OR	17,874	C
Univ of Illinois at Chicago	IL	24,293	VC
Univ of Illinois at Urbana-Champaign	IL	24,300	HC
Univ of New Haven	CT	47,740	C
Univ of S Car at Aiken	SC	16,278	C
Wheaton College	MA	54,934	HC+

COMPUTER PROGRAMMING

School	ST	$IS	SR
Arizona State Univ	AZ	18,818	C+
Baker College of Flint	MI	7,800	NC
Calvin College	MI	37,585	VC+
Caribbean Univ	PR	10,375	
Carnegie Mellon Univ	PA	51,260	MC
Central Washington Univ	WA	11,730	C
City Univ of Seattle	WA	14,880	NC
Cogswell Polytechnical College	CA	30,531	C
Concord Univ	WV	13,102	C
Concordia Univ, River Forest	IL	26,300	C
Dakota State Univ	SD	13,811	C
DePaul Univ	IL	46,120	VC
Dickinson State Univ	ND	8,550	NC
Dordt College	IA	34,160	VC
Eastern Kentucky Univ	KY	11,161	C
Eastern Mich Univ	MI	17,961	C
Farmingdale State College	NY	18,985	C
Ferris State Univ	MI	19,698	C
Freed-Hardeman Univ	TN	19,697	VC
Georgia Southwestern State Univ	GA	12,218	C
Goshen College	IN	35,900	VC
Hannibal-LaGrange Univ	MO	24,490	C
Hawaii Pacific Univ	HI	36,690	C
Husson Univ	ME	23,386	LC
Idaho State Univ	ID	11,908	C
Indiana Univ-Purdue Univ Fort Wayne	IN	15,425	C
Lamar Univ	TX	6,820	LC
Le Moyne College	NY	42,200	VC
Limestone College	SC	29,880	C
Mayville State Univ	ND	11,401	NC
Midland Univ	NE	34,000	C
Missouri Western State Univ	MO	12,260	NC
Monmouth College	IL	39,290	C
Montana Tech of The Univ of Montana	MT	14,650	VC
Murray State Univ	KY	14,944	C
Northeastern Univ	MA	55,296	MC
Northern Mich Univ	MI	15,300	VC
Pacific Lutheran Univ	WA	44,840	VC
Peirce College	PA	12,760	NC
Pennsylvania College of Technology	PA	25,653	NC
Peru State College	NE	8,600	NC
Pontifical Catholic Univ of PR	PR	7,310	
Purdue Univ/Calumet	IN	14,336	C
Salem State College	MA	13,161	LC
Southern Oregon Univ	OR	17,874	C
Southwestern Okla State Univ	OK	9,160	C
St. Thomas Univ	FL	32,310	C+
Stephen F. Austin State Univ	TX	14,668	C
Suffolk Univ	MA	46,548	C
Tarleton State Univ	TX	13,489	LC
Universidad del Turabo	PR	4,110	
Univ of Arkansas at Little Rock	AR		C
Univ of Great Falls	MT	27,970	C
Univ of Illinois at Urbana-Champaign	IL	24,300	HC
Univ of Nebr at Kearney	NE	14,855	LC
Univ of New Haven	CT	47,740	C
Univ of St. Francis	IL	36,490	C
Univ of Wisc Whitewater	WI	13,314	C
Univ of Wisc/River Falls	WI	9,722	LC
Washington Univ in St. Louis	MO	58,818	MC
West Virginia Univ Inst of Technology	WV	14,094	NC
Youngstown State Univ	OH	16,374	LC

COMPUTER SCIENCE

School	ST	$IS	SR
Abilene Christian Univ	TX	38,400	VC
Adams State College	CO	13,358	LC
Adelphi Univ	NY	43,130	VC
Agnes Scott College	GA	45,323	VC+
Alabama A&M Univ	AL	96,100	C
Albany State Univ	GA	8,500	C
Albion College	MI	43,884	VC
Albright College	PA	46,660	C
Alcorn State Univ	MS	9,500	C
Alderson Broaddus Univ	WV	28,656	C
Allegheny College	PA	49,020	HC
Alma College	MI	42,400	VC
American Univ	DC	54,829	HC+
Amherst College	MA	58,744	MC
Anderson Univ	IN	35,390	C
Andrews Univ	MI	28,030	C+
Angelo State Univ	TX	15,049	NC
Anna Maria College	MA	34,600	LC
Appalachian State Univ	NC	12,919	VC
Arcadia Univ	PA	33,570	C+
Arizona State Univ	AZ	18,818	C+
Arkansas Baptist College	AR	9,000	NC
Arkansas State Univ	AR	14,980	C
Arkansas Tech Univ	AR	13,164	LC
Armstrong Atlantic State Univ	GA	16,276	C
Ashford Univ	IA	21,780	C
Ashland Univ	OH	25,000	C
Assumption College	MA	45,721	VC
Atlantic Union College	MA	24,600	LC
Auburn Univ	AL	20,052	VC+
Augsburg College	MN	35,142	C
Augustana College	IL	43,398	HC
Augustana College	SD	35,500	VC
Aurora Univ	IL	26,870	C
Austin College	TX	36,940	HC
Austin Peay State Univ	TN	14,650	C
Averett Univ	VA	36,000	LC
Avila Univ	MO	26,900	C
Azusa Pacific Univ	CA	39,946	C
Baker Univ	KS	33,350	C+
Baldwin Wallace Univ	OH	36,980	VC
Ball State Univ	IN	17,850	C
Bard College	NY	59,872	HC
Bard College at Simon's Rock	MA	58,963	HC+
Barry Univ	FL	38,190	C
Baylor Univ	TX	46,720	HC
Belhaven Univ	MS	27,170	C
Bellarmine Univ	KY	42,950	VC
Belmont Univ	TN	37,380	VC+
Beloit College	WI	49,970	HC
Bemidji State Univ	MN	13,500	C
Benedict College	SC	20,454	NC
Benedictine College	KS	29,180	VC
Benedictine Univ	IL	35,220	C
Bennett College	NC		LC
Bennington College	VT	58,990	HC+
Berea College	KY	7,220	HC
Bethany College	WV	35,282	C
Bethel Univ	MN	34,940	VC
Bethune-Cookman Univ	FL	22,290	LC
Binghamton Univ / The SUNY	NY	20,832	HC+
Biola Univ	CA	40,320	VC
Birmingham-Southern College	AL	42,370	VC+
Blackburn College	IL	21,350	C
Bloomsburg Univ of Pennsylvania	PA	13,598	C
Bluefield State College	WV	3,140	LC
Bluffton Univ	OH	37,864	C
Boise State Univ	ID	12,802	C
Boston College	MA	58,506	MC
Boston Univ	MA	54,130	HC+
Bowdoin College	ME	57,834	MC
Bowie State Univ	MD	23,990	LC
Bowling Green State Univ	OH	18,970	C
Bradley Univ	IL	31,874	VC
Brandeis Univ	MA	58,820	HC
Brescia Univ	KY	26,140	VC+
Briar Cliff Univ	IA	29,514	C
Bridgewater College	VA	39,880	C
Bridgewater State Univ	MA	18,752	C
Brigham Young Univ	UT	12,100	HC
Brigham Young Univ/Hawaii	HI	8,614	VC
Brown Univ	RI	56,150	MC
Bryan College	TN	24,194	C
Bryn Mawr College	PA	57,760	MC
Bucknell Univ	PA	58,160	MC
Buena Vista Univ	IA	37,954	C
Butler Univ	IN	45,898	VC+
Caldwell College	NJ	35,602	LC
Calif Inst of Technology	CA	54,045	MC
Calif Lutheran Univ	CA	47,640	C
Calif Polytechnic State Univ	CA	19,847	HC
Calif State Polytechnic Univ, Pomona	CA	18,932	C
Cal State, Bakersfield	CA	8,000	LC
Cal State, Chico	CA	18,952	C
Cal State, Dominguez Hills	CA	17,056	LC
Cal State, East Bay	CA	16,549	C
Cal State, Fresno	CA	17,405	C
Cal State, Fullerton	CA	25,188	C+
Cal State, Long Beach	CA	17,534	C+
Cal State, Los Angeles	CA	15,829	C
Cal State, Monterey Bay	CA	26,871	LC
Cal State, Northridge	CA	28,313	C
Cal State, Sacramento	CA	16,200	C
Cal State, San Bernardino	CA	12,000	C
Cal State, San Marcos	CA	14,576	C
Cal State, Stanislaus	CA	18,582	C
Calvin College	MI	37,585	VC+
Cameron Univ	OK	9,267	LC
Campbell Univ	NC	25,500	C
Campbellsville Univ	KY	27,720	C
Canisius College	NY	45,602	VC
Capital Univ	OH	39,824	VC
Cardinal Stritch Univ	WI	24,054	C
Caribbean Univ	PR	10,375	
Carleton College	MN	58,149	MC
Carnegie Mellon Univ	PA	51,260	MC
Carroll College	MT	28,000	C
Carroll Univ	WI	24,860	C
Case Western Reserve Univ	OH	55,178	MC
Castleton State College	VT	19,424	C
Catawba College	NC	37,105	C
Cedar Crest College	PA	43,240	C
Cedarville Univ	OH	31,036	VC+
Central College	IA	36,980	VC
Central Conn State Univ	CT	19,212	C
Central Methodist Univ	MO	28,240	VC
Central Mich Univ	MI	18,066	C
Central State Univ	OH	9,010	C
Central Univ of Bayamon	PR	3,350	
Central Washington Univ	WA	11,730	C
Centre College	KY	35,000	HC+
Chaminade Univ of Honolulu	HI	31,664	C
Champlain College	VT	44,850	VC
Chapman Univ	CA	56,019	VC+
Charleston Southern Univ	SC	22,420	C
Chestnut Hill College	PA	39,785	LC
Cheyney Univ of Pennsylvania	PA	20,372	LC
Chicago State Univ	IL	5,482	C
Christian Brothers Univ	TN	19,140	HC
Christopher Newport Univ	VA	21,050	VC
Citadel, The	SC		C
CUNY/Brooklyn College	NY	5,884	C+
Claflin Univ	SC	22,368	C+
Clarion Univ of Pennsylvania	PA	17,370	C
Clark Atlanta Univ	GA	30,006	C
Clark Univ	MA	47,020	HC+
Clarke Univ	IA	36,400	C
Clarkson Univ	NY	53,538	HC
Clemson Univ	SC	19,136	HC
Cleveland State Univ	OH	21,357	C
Coastal Carolina Univ	SC	17,620	C
Coe College	IA	43,590	VC
Coker College	SC	32,266	LC
Colby College	ME	57,510	MC
Colgate Univ	NY	50,930	MC
College of Staten Island / The CUNY	NY	16,778	NC
College of Charleston	SC	21,273	VC
College of Mount St. Vincent	NY	41,040	MC
College of New Jersey	NJ	25,376	HC
College of St. Benedict	MN	47,570	VC
College of St. Elizabeth	NJ	43,839	LC
College of St. Scholastica	MN	39,960	C
College of the Holy Cross	MA	56,232	MC
College of the Ozarks	MO	5,605	VC
College of William & Mary	VA	25,085	MC
College of Wooster	OH	52,600	VC
Colo College	CO	54,534	MC
Colo Mesa Univ	CO	16,669	LC
Colo State Univ-Fort Collins	CO	20,090	VC
Colo Technical Univ	CO	10,500	LC
Columbia College	MO	24,578	C
Columbia Univ in the City of New York	NY	61,116	MC
Columbia Univ/Barnard College	NY	39,000	MC
Columbia Univ/School of General Studies	NY	54,083	MC
Columbus State Univ	GA	13,176	C
Concord Univ	WV	13,102	C
Concordia Univ Nebr	NE	26,000	VC
Concordia Univ Texas	TX	23,640	C
Concordia Univ, River Forest	IL	26,300	C
Converse College	SC	37,130	C
Coppin State Univ	MD	14,905	VC
Cornell College	IA	44,930	HC
Cornell Univ	NY	59,037	MC
Covenant College	GA		VC+
Creighton Univ	NE	44,058	VC+
CUNY-City College	NY	19,576	HC+
Dakota State Univ	SD	13,811	C
Dallas Baptist Univ	TX	29,118	C
Daniel Webster College	NH	25,380	C
Dartmouth College	NH	57,996	MC
Davis and Elkins College	WV	33,742	C
De Sales Univ	PA	42,670	C
Delaware State Univ	DE	14,700	LC
Delaware Valley College	PA	29,944	C
Denison Univ	OH	54,670	HC+
DePaul Univ	IL	46,120	VC
DePauw Univ	IN	48,950	VC+
Dickinson College	PA	57,662	HC+
Dickinson State Univ	ND	8,550	NC
Dillard Univ	LA	20,940	VC
Doane College	NE	33,730	VC
Dominican College	NY	31,270	C
Dominican Univ	IL	37,628	C
Dordt College	IA	34,160	VC
Dowling College	NY	25,000	LC
Drake Univ	IA	30,980	VC+
Drew Univ/College of Liberal Arts	NJ	55,862	VC
Drexel Univ	PA	51,920	HC
Drury Univ	MO	30,319	VC
Duke Univ	NC	50,250	MC
Duquesne Univ	PA	42,017	VC
Earlham College	IN	49,710	VC+
East Carolina Univ	NC	14,169	C
East Central Univ	OK	10,223	LC
East Stroudsburg Univ of Pennsylvania	PA	16,636	C
East Tenn State Univ	TN	9,000	C
Eastern Conn State Univ	CT	20,584	C
Eastern Illinois Univ	IL	20,502	C
Eastern Kentucky Univ	KY	11,161	C
Eastern Mennonite Univ	VA	38,850	VC
Eastern Mich Univ	MI	17,961	C
Eastern Nazarene College	MA	30,000	C
Eastern New Mexico Univ	NM	10,682	C
Eastern Oregon Univ	OR	10,400	C
Eastern Washington Univ	WA	16,388	C
East-West Univ	IL	16,076	C
Eckerd College	FL	43,902	VC
Edinboro Univ of Pennsylvania	PA	15,940	LC
Edward Waters College	FL	17,856	LC
Elizabeth City State Univ	NC	11,638	C
Elizabethtown College	PA	47,600	VC
Elmhurst College	IL	42,032	C+
Elms College	MA	23,900	VC
Elon Univ	NC	40,046	HC
Embry-Riddle Aeronautical Univ - Daytona Beach	FL	40,884	C+
Emory and Henry College	VA	387,460	C
Emory Univ	GA	45,000	MC
Emporia State Univ	KS	12,897	C
Endicott College	MA	42,390	C
Eureka College	IL	19,280	C
Evangel Univ	MO	23,090	C
Fairfield Univ	CT	55,850	VC
Fairleigh Dickinson Univ/College at Florham	NJ	42,142	C
Fairleigh Dickinson Univ/Metropolitan Campus	NJ	40,254	C
Fairmont State Univ	WV	12,098	LC
Faulkner Univ	AL	22,530	LC
Fayetteville State Univ	NC	10,816	C
Fisk Univ	TN	19,830	C
Fitchburg State Univ	MA	17,241	C
Florida A&M Univ	FL	14,935	LC
Florida Atlantic Univ	FL	17,339	C
Florida Gulf Coast Univ	FL		C
Florida Inst of Technology	FL	48,290	VC
Florida International Univ	FL	17,747	VC
Florida Memorial Univ	FL	20,716	LC
Florida Southern College	FL	38,240	VC
Florida State Univ	FL	15,238	HC
Fontbonne Univ	MO	31,384	C
Fordham Univ	NY	58,927	HC
Fort Hays State Univ	KS	11,354	C
Fort Valley State Univ	GA	11,200	VC
Framingham State Univ	MA	16,750	C
Francis Marion Univ	SC	16,464	LC
Franciscan Univ of Steubenville	OH	27,320	VC
Franklin College	IN	35,885	C
Franklin Univ	OH	7,000	SP
Freed-Hardeman Univ	TN	19,697	VC
Friends Univ	KS	29,100	C
Frostburg State Univ	MD	15,264	LC
Furman Univ	SC	54,006	HC
Gallaudet Univ	DC	25,380	SP
Gannon Univ	PA	37,940	C
Gardner-Webb Univ	NC	34,375	C+
Geneva College	PA	27,280	C
George Fox Univ	OR	40,750	C+
George Mason Univ	VA	15,724	VC
George Washington Univ	DC	57,108	MC
Georgetown College	KY	38,690	C
Georgetown Univ	DC	52,910	MC
Georgia College and State Univ	GA	18,216	VC
Georgia Inst of Technology	GA	20,464	MC
Georgia Regents Univ	GA		C
Georgia Southern Univ	GA	16,414	C
Georgia Southwestern State Univ	GA	12,218	C
Georgia State Univ	GA	12,000	VC
Gettysburg College	PA	56,820	HC
Gonzaga Univ	WA	44,247	HC
Gordon College	MA	42,660	VC+
Goucher College	MD	50,252	VC+
Graceland Univ	IA	28,020	C
Grambling State Univ	LA	13,384	LC
Grand Valley State Univ	MI	17,998	VC
Grand View Univ	IA	31,050	C
Greenville College	IL	27,012	C
Grinnell College	IA	53,654	HC
Grove City College	PA	22,988	HC
Gustavus Adolphus College	MN	48,170	HC
Gwynedd-Mercy College	PA	33,560	C
Hamilton College	NY	55,620	MC
Hampden-Sydney College	VA	48,848	C
Hampshire College	MA	58,320	MC
Hampton Univ	VA	28,528	C
Hanover College	IN	41,450	VC
Harding Univ	AR	21,432	C+
Hardin-Simmons Univ	TX	23,560	C+
Hartwick College	NY	49,815	C+
Harvard Univ/Harvard College	MA	49,000	MC
Harvey Mudd College	CA	61,660	MC
Hastings College	NE	27,782	C+
Haverford College	PA	59,236	MC
Hawaii Pacific Univ	HI	36,690	C
Heidelberg Univ	OH	34,100	C
Henderson State Univ	AR	13,634	C
Hendrix College	AR	48,436	HC+
Heritage Univ	WA	17,664	NC
High Point Univ	NC	39,800	C
Hiram College	OH	37,300	VC

ST = STATE **$IS** = IN-STATE COSTS **SR** = SELECTOR RATING

School	ST	$IS	SR
Hobart and William Smith Colleges	NY	43,000	VC
Hofstra Univ	NY	48,020	V₵
Holy Names Univ	CA	40,310	NC
Hood College	MD	44,630	C
Hope College	MI	36,320	V₵
Houghton College	NY	35,740	VC
Howard Payne Univ	TX	17,115	C
Howard Univ	DC	35,957	C
Hunter College / The CUNY	NY	14,429	VC
Huntington Univ	IN	32,220	C
Huston-Tillotson Univ	TX	18,124	₵
Idaho State Univ	ID	11,908	C
Illinois College	IL	25,770	VC
Illinois Inst of Technology	IL	38,512	H₵
Illinois State Univ	IL	22,634	VC
Illinois Wesleyan Univ	IL	48,452	V₵
Indiana Inst of Technology	IN	34,240	LC
Indiana State Univ	IN	16,000	C
Indiana Univ Bloomington	IN	19,358	HC
Indiana Univ of Pennsylvania	PA	20,180	LC
Indiana Univ South Bend	IN	15,293	C
Indiana Univ Southeast	IN	15,807	LC
Indiana Univ-Purdue Univ Fort Wayne	IN	15,425	C
Indiana Wesleyan Univ	IN	31,815	VC
Inter-American Univ of PR/ Aguadilla Campus	PR	5,578	
Inter-American Univ of PR/ Arecibo Campus	PR	3,350	
Inter-American Univ of PR/ Bayamon Univ College	PR	4,428	
Inter-American Univ of PR/ Fajardo Campus	PR	4,200	
Inter-American Univ of PR/ Metropolitan Campus	PR	4,320	
Inter-American Univ of PR/ Ponce	PR	3,700	
Inter-American Univ of PR/ San Germán	PR	6,720	
Iona College	NY	44,028	C
Iowa State Univ	IA	16,403	C
Iowa Wesleyan College	IA	30,850	LC
Ithaca College	NY	52,300	HC
Jackson State Univ	MS	13,512	LC
Jacksonville State Univ	AL	12,280	LC
Jacksonville Univ	FL	37,780	C
James Madison Univ	VA	18,049	VC
John Brown Univ	AR	30,996	V₵
John Carroll Univ	OH	44,520	₵
Johns Hopkins Univ	MD	47,492	MC
Johnson and Wales Univ/ Providence Campus	RI	34,668	C
Johnson C. Smith Univ	NC	25,336	LC
Judson Univ	IL	25,130	C
Juniata College	PA	49,340	VC
Kalamazoo College	MI	47,825	H₵
Kansas State Univ	KS	15,497	VC
Kansas Wesleyan Univ	KS	32,000	C
Kean Univ	NJ	22,060	LC
Keene State College	NH	21,538	C
Kennesaw State Univ	GA	13,017	VC
Kent State Univ	OH	19,352	C
Kentucky State Univ	KY	11,000	LC
Kentucky Wesleyan College	KY	27,440	V₵
Kettering Univ	MI	31,456	HC
King's College	PA	41,678	C
Knox College	IL		VC
Kutztown Univ of Pennsylvania	PA	16,909	LC
La Roche College	PA	34,802	LC
La Salle Univ	PA	50,270	C
La Sierra Univ	CA	35,694	VC
Lafayette College	PA	57,050	H₵
LaGrange College	GA	34,480	C
Lake Forest College	IL	45,580	VC
Lake Superior State Univ	MI	18,121	C
Lakeland College	WI	22,990	C
Lamar Univ	TX	6,820	LC
Lander Univ	SC	22,514	₵
Lane College	TN	11,212	C
Langston Univ	OK	3,000	LC
Lawrence Tech Univ	MI	37,630	VC
Lawrence Univ	WI	46,371	HC
Le Moyne College	NY	42,200	VC
Lebanon Valley College	PA	38,570	C
Lehigh Univ	PA	55,080	MC
Lehman College / The CUNY	NY	5,778	LC
LeMoyne-Owen College	TN	13,100	C
Lenoir-Rhyne Univ	NC	35,984	C
LeTourneau Univ	TX	26,230	C
Lewis & Clark College	OR	52,656	VC
Lewis Univ	IL	23,050	C
Lewis-Clark State College	ID	6,990	C
Liberty Univ	VA	19,101	C
Limestone College	SC	29,880	C
Lincoln Univ	MO	11,996	NC
Lindenwood Univ	MO	20,750	C
Linfield College-McMinnville Campus	OR	46,166	C
Lipscomb Univ	TN	35,722	VC
Livingstone College	NC	17,815	LC
Lock Haven Univ of Pennsylvania	PA	17,587	LC

School	ST	$IS	SR
LIU/Brooklyn Campus	NY	26,500	C
LIU/C.W. Post Campus	NY	38,888	C
Longwood Univ	VA	20,924	C
Loras College	IA	37,432	VC
Louisiana State Univ	LA	18,677	V₵
Louisiana State Univ in Shreveport	LA	5,606	C
Louisiana Tech Univ	LA	8,000	C
Loyola Marymount Univ	CA	53,240	V₵
Loyola Univ Chicago	IL	49,560	V₵
Loyola Univ Maryland	MD		VC
Luther College	IA	44,380	V₵
Lynchburg College	VA	42,645	C
Macalester College	MN	53,419	MC
MacMurray College	IL	20,755	C
Madonna Univ	MI	24,540	VC
Maharishi Univ of Management	IA	31,000	VC
Malone Univ	OH	34,334	C
Manchester College	IN	35,070	C
Manhattan College	NY	44,955	VC
Manhattanville College	NY	46,260	VC
Mansfield Univ	PA	19,468	LC
Marietta College	OH	42,135	VC
Marist College	NY	35,500	C
Marlboro College	VT	35,980	VC
Marquette Univ	WI	43,664	V₵
Mars Hill College	NC	22,950	LC
Marshall Univ	WV	14,820	C
Marygrove College	MI	21,290	C
Maryville College	TN	33,150	VC
Mass College of Liberal Arts	MA	16,733	C
Mass Inst of Technology	MA	54,238	MC
McDaniel College	MD	45,600	VC
McKendree Univ	IL	29,920	₵
McMurry Univ	TX	25,962	LC
McNeese State Univ	LA		C
Medgar Evers College / The CUNY	NY	4,920	NC
Mercer Univ	GA	44,201	V₵
Mercy College	NY	29,996	C
Meredith College	NC	31,420	C
Merrimack College	MA	44,215	C
Messiah College	PA	39,540	VC
Methodist Univ	NC	37,185	C
Metropolitan State Univ	MN	5,923	SP
Motropolitan State Univ of Denver	CO	4,835	LC
Miami Univ	OH	24,191	HC
Mich State Univ	MI	13,689	VC
Mich Tech Univ	MI	22,105	VC
MidAmerica Nazarene Univ	KS	28,000	C
Middle Tenn State Univ	TN	8,650	C
Middlebury College	VT	57,470	MC
Midland Univ	NE	34,000	C
Midwestern State Univ	TX	9,722	C
Miles College	AL	16,530	NC
Millersville Univ of Pennsylvania	PA	18,498	C
Mills College	CA	54,119	HC
Minn State Univ, Moorhead	MN	13,392	C
Minot State Univ	ND	10,915	C
Misericordia Univ	PA	39,840	C
Miss College	MS	21,998	VC
Miss Valley State Univ	MS	9,706	LC
Missouri Southern State Univ	MO	11,910	C
Missouri State Univ	MO	13,996	VC
Missouri Univ of Science and Technology	MO	18,655	V₵
Missouri Western State Univ	MO	12,260	NC
Molloy College	NY	38,950	C
Monmouth College	IL	39,290	C
Monmouth Univ	NJ	42,252	C
Montana State Univ	MT	14,068	VC
Montana Tech of The Univ of Montana	MT	14,650	VC
Montclair State Univ	NJ	22,614	C
Moravian College	PA	36,381	VC
Morehead State Univ	KY	10,900	C
Morehouse College	GA	38,640	C
Morgan State Univ	MD	14,500	VC
Morningside College	IA	32,620	C
Mount Holyoke College	MA	53,596	H₵
Mount Marty College	SD	29,638	C
Mount Mercy Univ	IA	34,385	C
Mount St. Mary's Univ	MD	46,158	C
Mount Vernon Nazarene Univ	OH	29,590	C
Mountain State Univ	WV	14,330	NC
Muhlenberg College	PA	52,837	HC
Murray State Univ	KY	14,944	C
Muskingum Univ	OH	30,502	C
National Univ	CA	14,730	SP
Nebr Wesleyan Univ	NE	29,774	₵
Neumann Univ	PA	31,078	LC
New England College	NH	45,930	LC
New Jersey City Univ	NJ	21,060	₵
New Jersey Inst of Technology	NJ	26,490	VC
New Mexico Highlands Univ	NM	9,720	NC
New Mexico Inst of Mining and Technology	NM	12,892	HC
New Mexico State Univ	NM	13,955	LC

School	ST	$IS	SR
New York Inst of Technology	NY	40,590	VC
New York Univ	NY	61,470	MC
Newberry College	SC	26,850	LC
Newbury College	MA	41,850	C
Niagara Univ	NY	39,800	C
Nicholls State Univ	LA	7,095	C
Norfolk State Univ	VA	10,531	LC
N Car Agricultural and Technical State Univ	NC	13,175	LC
N Car Central Univ	NC	9,000	LC
N Car State Univ	NC	16,202	HC
North Central College	IL	38,343	VC
N Dak State Univ	ND	14,642	C
North Georgia College & State Univ	GA	8,600	C
Northeastern Illinois Univ	IL		C
Northeastern State Univ	OK	8,615	VC
Northeastern Univ	MA	55,296	MC
Northern Arizona Univ	AZ	18,592	C
Northern Illinois Univ	IL	19,768	C
Northern Kentucky Univ	KY	15,302	LC
Northern Mich Univ	MI	15,300	VC
Northwest Christian Univ	OR	27,399	C
Northwest Missouri State Univ	MO	14,229	C
Northwest Nazarene Univ	ID	24,275	NC
Northwestern College of Iowa	IA	34,848	₵
Northwestern Okla State Univ	OK	7,275	NC
Northwestern Univ	IL	37,595	MC
Norwich Univ	VT	28,212	C
Notre Dame de Namur Univ	CA	41,610	LC
Notre Dame of Maryland Univ	MD	27,700	C
Nova Southeastern Univ	FL	34,016	VC
Nyack College	NY	32,000	C
Oakland Univ	MI	19,391	VC
Oakwood Univ	AL	23,035	C
Oberlin College	OH	57,025	MC
Ohio Dominican Univ	OH	38,380	₵
Ohio Northern Univ	OH	42,075	VC
Ohio Univ	OH	20,676	VC
Ohio Wesleyan Univ	OH	49,460	₵
Okla Baptist Univ	OK	28,202	VC
Okla Christian Univ	OK	24,975	VC
Okla State Univ	OK	14,310	VC
Old Dominion Univ	VA	18,662	C
Olivet College	MI	19,984	C
Olivet Nazarene Univ	IL	29,990	C
Oral Roberts Univ	OK	31,734	C
Oregon State Univ	OR	19,017	₵
Oswego / SUNY	NY	20,009	VC
Otterbein College	OH	32,214	C
Ouachita Baptist Univ	AR	29,010	VC
Pace Univ	NY	48,094	VC
Pacific Lutheran Univ	WA	44,840	VC
Pacific Union College	CA	28,150	VC
Pacific Univ	OR	42,815	C
Palm Beach Atlantic Univ	FL	33,882	LC
Park Univ	MO	17,525	C
Penn State Erie/The Behrend College	PA	16,256	C
Penn State Univ/Univ Park	PA	25,404	VC
Pepperdine Univ	CA	55,372	H₵
Peru State College	NE	8,000	NC
Philander Smith College	AR	19,760	LC
Plymouth State Univ	NH	23,148	LC
Point Loma Nazarene Univ	CA	38,610	VC
Point Park Univ	PA	36,390	C
Polytechnic Inst of New York Univ	NY	53,064	H₵
Pomona College	CA	57,680	MC
Portland State Univ	OR	18,672	C
Prairie View A&M Univ	TX	15,205	LC
Princeton Univ	NJ	53,795	MC
Principia College	IL	35,140	₵
Providence College	RI	55,995	HC
Purdue Univ/Calumet	IN	14,336	C
Purdue Univ/West Lafayette	IN	20,278	HC
Queens College / The CUNY	NY	17,107	VC
Quincy Univ	IL	34,980	LC
Quinnipiac Univ	CT	53,580	VC
Radford Univ	VA	17,132	LC
Ramapo College of New Jersey	NJ	24,938	₵
Randolph-Macon College	VA	45,086	C
Regis College	MA	47,565	LC
Regis Univ	CO	41,318	C
Rensselaer Polytechnic Inst	NY	59,229	MC
Rhode Island College	RI	17,132	LC
Rhodes College	TN	47,596	H₵
Rice Univ	TX	43,288	MC
Richard Stockton College of New Jersey	NJ	20,000	VC
Ripon College	WI	36,959	₵
Rivier College	NH	35,000	VC
Roanoke College	VA	47,996	₵
Roberts Wesleyan College	NY	37,384	₵
Rochester Inst of Technology	NY	42,450	V₵
Rockford College	IL	31,000	C
Rockhurst Univ	MO	20,625	C

School	ST	$IS	SR
Rocky Mountain College	MT	32,242	C
Roger Williams Univ	RI	45,788	C
Rollins College	FL	52,370	HC
Roosevelt Univ	IL	22,605	VC
Rose-Hulman Inst of Technology	IN	51,738	MC
Rowan Univ	NJ	23,570	VC
Rust College	MS	10,600	C
Rutgers, The State Univ of New Jersey/Camden Campus	NJ	24,254	C
Rutgers, The State Univ of New Jersey/New Brunswick	NJ	25,077	VC
Rutgers, The State Univ of New Jersey/Newark Campus	NJ	25,376	C
Sacred Heart Univ	CT	48,564	VC
Saginaw Valley State Univ	MI	16,869	C
St. Anselm College	NH	48,324	VC
St. Augustine's Univ	NC	14,000	C
St. Francis Univ	PA	30,029	LC
St. John's Univ	MN	46,146	C
St. Joseph's College	IN	35,790	C
St. Joseph's Univ	PA	52,272	VC
St. Martin's Univ	WA	38,082	C
St. Mary-of-the-Woods College	IN	37,722	LC
St. Mary's College of Calif	CA	53,550	C
St. Mary's Univ	TX	33,854	C
St. Mary's Univ of Minn	MN	37,015	C
St. Michael's College	VT	48,740	VC
St. Peter's College	NJ	44,240	C
St. Vincent College	PA	40,244	C
St. Xavier Univ	IL	32,840	C
Salisbury Univ	MD	18,368	VC
Sam Houston State Univ	TX	17,082	C
Samford Univ	AL	35,700	V₵
San Diego State Univ	CA	20,578	VC
San Francisco State Univ	CA	18,514	C
San Jose State Univ	CA	19,707	C
Santa Clara Univ	CA	54,702	MC
Savannah State Univ	GA	13,156	C
Scripps College	CA	54,900	MC
Seattle Pacific Univ	WA	41,559	V₵
Seattle Univ	WA	47,010	V₵
Seton Hall Univ	NJ	45,902	C
Seton Hill Univ	PA	35,172	C
Sewanee: The Univ of the South	TN	47,700	H₵
Shaw Univ	NC	15,488	LC
Shepherd Univ	WV	14,996	C
Shippensburg Univ of Pennsylvania	PA	17,064	LC
Siena College	NY	43,863	VC
Silver Lake College	WI	22,600	LC
Simmons College	MA	48,770	VC
Simpson College	IA	36,086	VC
Skidmore College	NY	57,926	HC
Slippery Rock Univ of Pennsylvania	PA	10,360	LC
Smith College	MA	57,524	MC
Sonoma State Univ	CA	20,541	C
S Car State Univ	SC	6,700	LC
S Dak School of Mines and Technology	SD	15,260	VC
S Dak State Univ	SD	14,296	C
Southeast Missouri State Univ	MO	14,903	LC
Southeastern Louisiana Univ	LA	13,325	C
Southeastern Okla State Univ	OK	7,966	C
Southern Adventist Univ	TN	26,190	C
Southern Arkansas Univ	AR	14,316	C
Southern Conn State Univ	CT	18,033	C
Southern Illinois Univ Carbondale	IL	21,620	C
Southern Illinois Univ Edwardsville	IL	17,532	C
Southern Methodist Univ	TX	57,755	MC
Southern Nazarene Univ	OK	24,354	NC
Southern New Hampshire Univ	NH	38,100	C
Southern Oregon Univ	OR	17,874	C
Southern Polytechnic State Univ	GA	13,958	VC
Southern Univ and A&M College	LA	9,761	₵
Southern Univ at New Orleans	LA	1,000	NC
Southern Wesleyan Univ	SC	25,600	C
Southwest Baptist Univ	MO	24,710	C
Southwest Minn State Univ	MN	14,000	C
Southwestern Adventist Univ	TX	23,026	LC
Southwestern College	KS	29,270	C
Southwestern Okla State Univ	OK	9,160	C
Spelman College	GA	24,650	VC
Spring Arbor Univ	MI	26,740	C
Spring Hill College	AL	42,130	VC
St. Ambrose Univ	IA		C
St. Bonaventure Univ	NY	38,831	C
St. Cloud State Univ	MN	10,600	C
St. Edward's Univ	TX	44,674	VC
St. John Fisher College	NY	39,370	₵
St. John's Univ	NY	52,840	₵

ST = STATE **$IS** = IN-STATE COSTS **SR** = SELECTOR RATING

School	ST	$IS	SR
St. Joseph's College, New York / Brooklyn Campus	NY	21,878	C
St. Joseph's College, New York / Suffolk Campus	NY	21,878	VC
St. Lawrence Univ	NY	53,740	HC
St. Mary's College of Maryland	MD	26,699	HC
St. Norbert College	WI	39,992	VC
St. Olaf College	MN	49,960	HC+
St. Thomas Univ	FL	32,310	C+
Stanford Univ	CA	56,411	MC
SUNY Inst of Technology at Utica / Rome	NY	23,818	C
SUNY/Empire State College	NY	6,315	SP
Stephen F. Austin State Univ	TX	14,668	C
Stetson Univ	FL	49,512	VC+
Stevens Inst of Technology	NJ	50,130	HC
Stillman College	AL	18,460	C
Stonehill College	MA	46,780	VC+
Stony Brook Univ / SUNY	NY	19,359	HC
Suffolk Univ	MA	46,548	C
Sul Ross State Univ	TX	13,410	LC
SUNY College at Old Westbury	NY	16,324	C
SUNY Fredonia / The SUNY at Fredonia	NY	18,702	VC
SUNY New Paltz	NY	15,010	C
SUNY Oneonta / SUNY	NY	16,919	VC
SUNY Plattsburgh / SUNY	NY	18,083	VC
Susquehanna Univ	PA	49,170	C
Swarthmore College	PA	57,870	MC
Syracuse Univ	NY	54,512	HC
Tabor College	KS	29,010	LC
Talladega College	AL	13,000	C
Tarleton State Univ	TX	13,489	LC
Taylor Univ	IN	36,742	VC+
Temple Univ	PA	24,392	VC
Tenn State Univ	TN	9,048	C
Tenn Tech Univ	TN	11,310	C
Texas A&M Univ	TX	16,956	VC+
Texas A&M Univ at Commerce	TX	10,496	C
Texas A&M Univ at Corpus Christi	TX	11,544	LC
Texas A&M Univ at Kingsville	TX	7,500	LC
Texas Christian Univ	TX	47,570	HC
Texas Lutheran Univ	TX	34,070	C
Texas Southern Univ	TX	18,212	LC
Texas State Univ	TX	16,495	VC
Texas Tech Univ	TX	14,243	C
Texas Wesleyan Univ	TX	29,886	C
Texas Woman's Univ	TX	13,633	LC
The Catholic Univ of America	DC	52,852	VC
The College at Brockport / SUNY	NY	18,362	VC
The College of St. Rose	NY	26,750	C
The Lincoln Univ	PA	15,154	LC
Ohio State Univ	OH	19,887	MC
The SUNY at Potsdam	NY	17,754	C
Thiel College	PA	31,378	LC
Thomas College	ME	26,270	LC
Thomas More College	KY	34,760	C
Tougaloo College	MS	15,275	NC
Touro College	NY	23,150	VC
Towson Univ	MD	16,000	VC
Transylvania Univ	KY	40,310	VC+
Trine Univ	IN	39,400	VC
Trinity Christian College	IL	28,869	C
Trinity College	CT		HC+
Trinity Univ	TX	44,174	HC+
Troy Univ	AL	10,650	C
Truman State Univ	MO	13,546	HC
Tufts Univ	MA	58,780	MC
Tusculum College	TN	24,295	C
Tuskegee Univ	AL	26,750	C
Union College	NE	23,270	VC
Union College	NY		MC
Union Inst & Univ	OH	8,912	SP
Union Univ	TN	28,260	VC
United States Air Force Academy	CO		MC
United States Military Academy	NY		MC
United States Naval Academy	MD		MC
Universidad Adventista de las Antillas	PR	7,360	
Universidad Politecnica de PR	PR	19,252	
Univ at Albany / SUNY	NY	18,674	VC
Univ at Buffalo / The SUNY	NY	20,283	VC
Univ of Akron	OH	20,436	C
Univ of Alabama at Birmingham	AL	18,484	C+
Univ of Alabama at Huntsville	AL	17,625	VC
Univ of Alabama at Tuscaloosa	AL	17,164	C+
Univ of Alaska Anchorage	AK	15,290	NC
Univ of Alaska Fairbanks	AK	13,955	C
Univ of Arizona	AZ	20,105	C
Univ of Arkansas at Fayetteville	AR	16,860	VC
Univ of Arkansas at Little Rock	AR		C
Univ of Arkansas at Pine Bluff	AR	10,600	C
Univ of Bridgeport	CT	39,030	LC
Univ of Calif at Berkeley	CA	23,322	MC
Univ of Calif at Davis	CA	24,482	HC
Univ of Calif at Irvine	CA	25,961	VC
Univ of Calif at Los Angeles	CA	25,686	MC
Univ of Calif at Riverside	CA	27,204	C
Univ of Calif at San Diego	CA	21,000	VC
Univ of Calif at Santa Barbara	CA	27,551	HC
Univ of Calif at Santa Cruz	CA	27,807	VC
Univ of Central Arkansas	AR	10,840	VC
Univ of Central Florida	FL	15,711	VC+
Univ of Central Missouri	MO	14,605	C
Univ of Central Okla	OK	12,293	C
Univ of Chicago	IL	55,416	MC
Univ of Cincinnati	OH	20,199	VC
Univ of Colo at Colo Springs	CO	15,000	VC
Univ of Colo Boulder	CO	22,605	VC+
Univ of Colo Denver	CO	17,904	C
Univ of Conn	CT	23,744	HC
Univ of Dallas	TX	43,510	VC+
Univ of Dayton	OH	43,750	VC
Univ of Delaware	DE	22,728	VC
Univ of Denver	CO	51,787	VC+
Univ of Detroit Mercy	MI	30,450	C
Univ of Dubuque	IA	30,200	C
Univ of Evansville	IN	41,056	VC+
Univ of Findlay	OH	31,916	C
Univ of Florida	FL	15,783	HC+
Univ of Georgia	GA	19,508	VC
Univ of Great Falls	MT	27,970	C
Univ of Hartford	CT	42,674	C
Univ of Hawaii at Hilo	HI	6,500	C
Univ of Hawaii at Manoa	HI	19,379	VC
Univ of Houston-Downtown	TX	6,267	LC
Univ of Idaho	ID	14,558	C
Univ of Illinois at Chicago	IL	24,293	VC
Univ of Indianapolis	IN	31,740	LC
Univ of Iowa	IA	17,481	VC
Univ of Jamestown	ND	24,738	C
Univ of Kansas	KS	16,980	C+
Univ of Kentucky	KY	19,868	C
Univ of La Verne	CA	47,010	VC
Univ of Louisiana at Lafayette	LA	6,130	C
Univ of Louisiana at Monroe	LA	12,998	C
Univ of Louisville	KY	17,460	VC
Univ of Maine	ME	19,712	C+
Univ of Maine at Farmington	ME	17,841	C
Univ of Maine at Fort Kent	ME	14,975	LC
Univ of Mary Hardin-Baylor	TX	31,950	C+
Univ of Mary Washington	VA	19,484	VC
Univ of Maryland	MD	18,801	HC
Univ of Maryland/Baltimore County	MD	18,000	VC
Univ of Maryland/Eastern Shore	MD	14,000	C
Univ of Maryland/Univ College	MD	6,168	SP
Univ of Mass Amherst	MA	23,697	VC+
Univ of Mass Boston	MA	11,966	C
Univ of Mass Dartmouth	MA	22,223	C
Univ of Mass Lowell	MA	19,316	C
Univ of Memphis	TN	15,094	C
Univ of Miami	FL	55,166	MC
Univ of Mich/Ann Arbor	MI	22,102	HC+
Univ of Mich/Dearborn	MI	9,885	VC
Univ of Mich-Flint	MI	17,547	C+
Univ of Minn/Duluth	MN	18,964	C+
Univ of Minn/Morris	MN	17,150	VC
Univ of Minn/Twin Cities	MN		HC
Univ of Miss	MS	15,482	VC
Univ of Missouri/Columbia	MO	18,201	MC
Univ of Missouri-Kansas City	MO	19,603	C
Univ of Missouri-St. Louis	MO	18,304	VC
Univ of Montana	MT	13,670	C
Univ of Mount Union	OH	35,130	C
Univ of Nebr - Lincoln	NE	17,507	VC
Univ of Nebr at Kearney	NE	14,855	LC
Univ of Nebr at Omaha	NE	12,700	C
Univ of Nevada, Las Vegas	NV	17,303	C
Univ of Nevada/Reno	NV	14,500	NC
Univ of New Hampshire	NH	24,702	VC
Univ of New Haven	CT	47,740	C
Univ of New Mexico	NM	15,300	C
Univ of New Orleans	LA	9,224	VC
Univ of North Alabama	AL	9,960	C
Univ of N Car at Asheville	NC	13,500	VC+
Univ of N Car at Chapel Hill	NC	18,348	MC
Univ of N Car at Charlotte	NC	15,847	C
Univ of N Car at Greensboro	NC	12,848	C
Univ of N Car at Wilmington	NC	13,572	VC+
Univ of N Dak	ND	14,094	C
Univ of North Florida	FL	15,578	VC
Univ of North Texas	TX	15,628	C
Univ of Northern Iowa	IA	14,776	C
Univ of Notre Dame	IN		MC
Univ of Okla	OK	17,634	VC+
Univ of Oregon	OR	20,872	VC
Univ of Pennsylvania	PA	56,106	MC
Univ of Pikeville	KY	24,750	NC
Univ of Pittsburgh at Johnstown	PA	20,862	LC
Univ of Pittsburgh at Pittsburgh	PA	27,800	HC+
Univ of Portland	OR	47,874	VC
Univ of PR Recinto de Rio Piedras	PR	5,750	
Univ of PR/Arecibo	PR	7,227	
Univ of PR/Bayamon	PR	1,600	
Univ of PR/Mayaguez	PR	1,250	
Univ of Puget Sound	WA	52,648	HC+
Univ of Redlands	CA	40,500	VC
Univ of Rio Grande	OH	8,750	NC
Univ of Rochester	NY	58,500	MC
Univ of San Diego	CA	53,302	HC+
Univ of San Francisco	CA	49,674	VC
Univ of Scranton	PA	51,940	VC
Univ of Sioux Falls	SD	22,990	C
Univ of South Alabama	AL	13,510	C
Univ of S Car at Columbia	SC	19,725	VC+
Univ of S Car Upstate	SC	17,673	LC
Univ of S Dak	SD	15,111	C
Univ of Southern Calif	CA	56,903	MC
Univ of Southern Indiana	IN	14,657	C
Univ of Southern Maine	ME	16,576	C
Univ of Southern Miss	MS	13,170	C
Univ of St. Francis	IL	36,100	C
Univ of St. Thomas - Houston	TX	36,490	VC
Univ of Tenn at Chattanooga	TN	16,883	C
Univ of Tenn at Knoxville	TN	20,364	VC+
Univ of Tenn at Martin	TN	13,217	C
Univ of Texas at Arlington	TX	10,908	LC
Univ of Texas at Austin	TX	44,074	HC
Univ of Texas at Dallas	TX	21,046	HC
Univ of Texas at El Paso	TX	8,764	NC
Univ of Texas at San Antonio	TX	18,372	C
Univ of Texas-Pan American	TX	12,432	LC
Univ of the District of Columbia	DC	7,244	LC
Univ of the Pacific	CA	52,146	VC
Univ of the Sacred Heart	PR	5,590	
Univ of the Sciences	PA	48,320	VC+
Univ of Toledo	OH	18,464	C
Univ of Tulsa	OK	45,311	HC+
Univ of Utah	UT	13,462	VC
Univ of Vermont	VT	26,120	VC+
Univ of Virginia	VA	22,175	MC
Univ of Washington	WA	14,722	VC
Univ of West Alabama	AL	9,415	C
Univ of West Florida	FL	14,656	C
Univ of West Georgia	GA	14,852	LC
Univ of Wisc/Eau Claire	WI	15,430	VC
Univ of Wisc/Green Bay	WI	14,900	C
Univ of Wisc/La Crosse	WI	14,755	VC
Univ of Wisc/Madison	WI	18,757	HC
Univ of Wisc/Oshkosh	WI	10,426	LC
Univ of Wisc/Parkside	WI	10,181	LC
Univ of Wisc/Platteville	WI	14,274	C
Univ of Wisc/Superior	WI	14,106	C
Univ of Wisc-Milwaukee	WI	18,436	C
Univ of Wyoming	WY	13,855	C+
Ursinus College	PA	55,630	VC+
Utah State Univ	UT	11,803	C
Utica College	NY	44,734	C
Valparaiso Univ	IN	43,040	VC+
Vassar College	NY	59,070	MC
Villanova Univ	PA	56,436	MC
Virginia Commonwealth Univ	VA	18,633	C
Virginia Military Inst	VA	16,156	C
Virginia Polytechnic Inst and State Univ	VA	14,629	HC
Virginia Wesleyan College	VA	28,433	LC
Voorhees College	SC	18,126	C
Wagner College	NY	48,600	VC
Wake Forest Univ	NC	51,000	MC
Walla Walla Univ	WA	26,256	NC
Walsh Univ	OH	35,100	C
Wartburg College	IA	41,055	VC
Washburn Univ	KS	12,165	NC
Washington Adventist Univ	MD	25,859	C+
Washington and Lee Univ	VA	52,812	MC
Washington College	MD	48,768	VC
Washington State Univ	WA	20,461	C
Washington Univ in St. Louis	MO	58,818	MC
Wayne State College	NE	11,764	NC
Wayne State Univ	MI	19,493	C
Waynesburg Univ	PA	29,100	C
Webster Univ	MO	33,990	C+
Wellesley College	MA	49,848	MC
Wells College	NY	38,680	VC
Wentworth Inst of Technology	MA	29,800	SP
Wesleyan Univ	CT	59,844	MC
West Chester Univ of Pennsylvania	PA	16,836	C
West Texas A&M Univ	TX	13,478	C
West Virginia Univ	WV	15,794	C+
West Virginia Univ Inst of Technology	WV	14,094	NC
West Virginia Wesleyan College	WV	26,880	C
Western Carolina Univ	NC	13,965	C+
Western Conn State Univ	CT	18,327	C
Western Illinois Univ	IL	20,130	C
Western Kentucky Univ	KY	11,000	LC
Western Mich Univ	MI	19,042	C
Western New England Univ	MA	45,590	C
Western New Mexico Univ	NM	8,500	LC
Western Oregon Univ	OR	15,021	C
Western State Colo Univ	CO	16,135	C
Western Washington Univ	WA	18,519	VC
Westfield State Univ	MA	18,489	C
Westminster College	MO	30,490	VC
Westminster College	PA	31,290	C+
Westminster College	UT	37,708	VC
Westmont College	CA	41,500	HC
Wheaton College	IL	39,650	HC+
Wheaton College	MA	54,934	HC+
Wheeling Jesuit Univ	WV	34,668	C
Whitworth Univ	WA	45,826	VC+
Wichita State Univ	KS	12,539	C
Widener Univ	PA	50,368	C
Wilberforce Univ	OH	15,100	LC
Wiley College	TX		LC
Wilkes Univ	PA	42,786	C
Willamette Univ	OR	56,450	VC+
William Paterson Univ of New Jersey	NJ	21,694	C
William Penn Univ	IA	26,000	C
William Woods Univ	MO		C
Williams Baptist College	AR	20,070	C
Williams College	MA	58,900	MC
Wilmington College	OH	29,784	C
Winona State Univ	MN	16,530	C
Winston-Salem State Univ	NC	9,418	LC
Winthrop Univ	SC	21,120	VC
Wittenberg Univ	OH	47,766	VC
Wofford College	SC	45,795	VC
Worcester Polytechnic Inst	MA	53,440	HC+
Worcester State Univ	MA	18,657	C
Wright State Univ	OH	16,983	C
Xavier Univ	OH	43,740	VC
Xavier Univ of Louisiana	LA	25,300	C
Yale Univ	CT	55,300	MC
Yeshiva Univ	NY	47,250	VC+
York College of Pennsylvania	PA	26,590	C
Youngstown State Univ	OH	16,374	LC

COMPUTER SECURITY AND INFORMATION ASSURANCE

School	ST	$IS	SR
Baldwin Wallace Univ	OH	36,980	VC
Champlain College	VT	44,850	VC
Charter Oak State College	CT	8,280	SP
Clarke Univ	IA	36,400	C
Dakota State Univ	SD	13,811	C
DePaul Univ	IL	46,120	VC
Eastern Mich Univ	MI	17,961	C
Felician College	NJ	41,640	C
Florida Atlantic Univ	FL	17,339	C
Fontbonne Univ	MO	31,384	C
Frostburg State Univ	MD	15,264	LC
Hilbert College	NY	28,550	C
Kennesaw State Univ	GA	13,017	VC
Limestone College	SC	29,880	C
Loyola Univ Chicago	IL	49,560	VC+
Marshall Univ	WV	14,820	C
Metropolitan State Univ	MN	5,923	SP
Minn State Univ, Mankato	MN	14,900	C
Minn State Univ, Moorhead	MN	13,392	C
Mount Aloysius College	PA	27,970	C
Norwich Univ	VT	28,212	C
Pace Univ	NY	48,094	VC
Pennsylvania College of Technology	PA	25,653	NC
Pittsburg State Univ	KS	12,032	C
Roger Williams Univ	RI	45,788	C
Sacred Heart Univ	CT	48,564	VC
St. John's Univ	NY	52,840	C+
Stevens Inst of Technology	NJ	50,130	HC
Stevenson Univ	MD	39,572	C
Thomas College	ME	26,270	LC
Univ of Akron	OH	20,436	C
Univ of Maryland/Univ College	MD	6,168	SP
Univ of Texas at San Antonio	TX	18,372	C
Utica College	NY	44,734	C
Webber International Univ	FL	25,664	C
Youngstown State Univ	OH	16,374	LC

COMPUTER TECHNOLOGY

School	ST	$IS	SR
Alcorn State Univ	MS	9,500	C
Alfred State / SUNY College of Technology	NY	18,034	C
Alverno College	WI	30,483	LC
Andrews Univ	MI	28,030	C+
Appalachian State Univ	NC	12,919	VC
Bellarmine Univ	KY	42,950	VC
Biola Univ	CA	40,320	VC
Bowie State Univ	MD	23,990	LC

ST = STATE **$IS** = IN-STATE COSTS **SR** = SELECTOR RATING

School	ST	$IS	SR
Calif State Polytechnic Univ, Pomona	CA	18,932	C
Cal State, Dominguez Hills	CA	17,056	LC
Calif Univ of Pennsylvania	PA	14,217	C
Central Mich Univ	MI	18,066	C
Chestnut Hill College	PA	39,785	LC
Colo State Univ-Fort Collins	CO	20,090	VC
Daniel Webster College	NH	25,380	C
DePaul Univ	IL	46,120	VC
Duquesne Univ	PA	42,017	VC
Eastern Mich Univ	MI	17,961	C
Eastern Washington Univ	WA	16,388	C
Excelsior College	NY	806	SP
Georgia Southwestern State Univ	GA	12,218	C
Guilford College	NC	35,340	C
Hodges Univ	FL	12,000	LC
Idaho State Univ	ID	11,908	C
Indiana State Univ	IN	16,000	C
Indiana Univ-Purdue Univ Indianapolis	IN	17,290	C
Inter-American Univ of PR/ Bayamon Univ College	PR	4,428	
Kent State Univ	OH	19,352	C
LeTourneau Univ	TX	26,230	C
Limestone College	SC	29,880	C
Martin Univ	IN	11,000	SP
Methodist Univ	NC	37,185	C
Minn State Univ, Mankato	MN	14,900	C
Missouri Southern State Univ	MO	11,910	C
Mountain State Univ	WV	14,330	NC
Murray State Univ	KY	14,944	C
New Jersey Inst of Technology	NJ	26,490	VC
New Mexico State Univ	NM	13,955	LC
Norfolk State Univ	VA	10,531	LC
Oregon Inst of Technology	OR	8,910	C
Peirce College	PA	12,760	NC
Purdue Univ/Calumet	IN	14,336	C
Purdue Univ/West Lafayette	IN	20,278	HC
Rochester Inst of Technology	NY	42,450	VC+
Rockhurst Univ	MO	20,625	C
Shepherd Univ	WV	14,996	C
Southern Wesleyan Univ	SC	25,600	C
SUNY Inst of Technology at Utica / Rome	NY	23,818	C
Union College	KY	28,775	C
Univ of Arkansas at Little Rock	AR		C
Univ of Dayton	OH	43,750	VC
Univ of Illinois at Urbana-Champaign	IL	24,300	HC
Univ of Maryland/Univ College	MD	6,168	SP
Univ of Memphis	TN	15,094	C
Univ of Minn Crookston	MN	17,834	C
Univ of Northern Iowa	IA	14,776	C
Univ of Rio Grande	OH	8,750	NC
Univ of Southern Miss	MS	13,170	C
Univ of St. Francis	IL	36,490	C
Univ of Wisc/Stevens Point	WI	14,043	C
Valparaiso Univ	IN	43,040	VC+
Wayne State Univ	MI	19,493	C
Wentworth Inst of Technology	MA	29,800	SP
Youngstown State Univ	OH	16,374	LC

CONSERVATION AND REGULATION

School	ST	$IS	SR
Arizona State Univ	AZ	18,818	C+
College of the Ozarks	MO	5,605	VC
Florida Inst of Technology	FL	48,290	VC
Kent State Univ	OH	19,352	C
Lipscomb Univ	TN	35,722	VC
LIU/C.W. Post Campus	NY	38,888	C
Mount Mercy Univ	IA	34,385	C
Muskingum Univ	OH	30,502	C
N Car State Univ	NC	16,202	HC
Northwest Missouri State Univ	MO	14,229	C
Northwestern Okla State Univ	OK	7,275	NC
Southeastern Okla State Univ	OK	7,966	C
St. Lawrence Univ	NY	53,740	HC
Texas Tech Univ	TX	14,243	C
Unity College	ME	34,054	C
Univ of Arkansas at Pine Bluff	AR	10,600	C
Univ of Calif at Berkeley	CA	23,322	MC
Univ of Central Missouri	MO	14,605	C
Univ of Idaho	ID	14,558	C
Univ of Wisc/River Falls	WI	9,722	LC
Upper Iowa Univ	IA	30,426	NC

CONSTRUCTION

School	ST	$IS	SR
Thomas Edison State College	NJ	5,700	SP
Univ of Louisiana at Monroe	LA	12,998	C

CONSTRUCTION ENGINEERING

School	ST	$IS	SR
Arizona State Univ	AZ	18,818	C+
Bradley Univ	IL	31,874	VC
Fairleigh Dickinson Univ/ Metropolitan Campus	NJ	40,254	C
Florida Inst of Technology	FL	48,290	VC
Florida International Univ	FL	17,747	VC
Iowa State Univ	IA	16,403	C
Louisiana Tech Univ	LA	8,000	C
Marquette Univ	WI	43,664	VC+
Montana State Univ	MT	14,068	VC
National Univ	CA	14,730	SP
N Dak State Univ	ND	14,642	C
Purdue Univ/West Lafayette	IN	20,278	HC
Rensselaer Polytechnic Inst	NY	59,229	MC
San Diego State Univ	CA	20,578	VC
Southern Polytechnic State Univ	GA	13,958	VC
Texas A&M Univ	TX	16,956	VC+
The Catholic Univ of America	DC	52,852	VC
Univ of Arkansas at Little Rock	AR		C
Univ of Central Florida	FL	15,711	VC+
Univ of Florida	FL	15,783	HC+
Univ of Nebr - Lincoln	NE	17,507	VC
Univ of New Mexico	NM	15,300	C
Univ of North Florida	FL	15,578	VC
Univ of North Texas	TX	15,628	C
Univ of Southern Calif	CA	56,903	MC
Univ of the District of Columbia	DC	7,244	LC
Univ of Washington	WA	14,722	VC
Virginia Polytechnic Inst and State Univ	VA	14,629	HC
Western Mich Univ	MI	19,042	C

CONSTRUCTION MANAGEMENT

School	ST	$IS	SR
Alfred State / SUNY College of Technology	NY	18,034	C
Appalachian State Univ	NC	12,919	VC
Arizona State Univ	AZ	18,818	C+
Auburn Univ	AL	20,052	VC+
Boise State Univ	ID	12,802	C
Bowling Green State Univ	OH	18,970	C
Brigham Young Univ	UT	12,100	HC
Calif Baptist Univ	CA	35,890	C
Calif Polytechnic State Univ	CA	19,847	HC
Cal State, Chico	CA	18,952	C
Cal State, Fresno	CA	17,405	C
Central Conn State Univ	CT	19,212	C
Central Washington Univ	WA	11,730	C
Clemson Univ	SC	19,136	HC
Colo State Univ-Fort Collins	CO	20,090	VC
Dordt College	IA	34,160	VC
Drexel Univ	PA	51,920	HC
East Carolina Univ	NC	14,169	C
Eastern Mich Univ	MI	17,961	C
Ferris State Univ	MI	19,698	C
Florida Inst of Technology	FL	48,290	VC
Georgia Inst of Technology	GA	20,464	MC
Georgia Southern Univ	GA	16,414	C
Illinois State Univ	IL	22,634	VC
John Brown Univ	AR	30,996	VC+
Kansas State Univ	KS	15,497	VC
Lawrence Tech Univ	MI	37,630	VC
Louisiana State Univ	LA	18,677	VC+
Mich State Univ	MI	13,689	VC
Mich Tech Univ	MI	22,105	VC
Milwaukee School of Engineering	WI	39,948	VC+
Minn State Univ, Mankato	MN	14,900	C
Minn State Univ, Moorhead	MN	13,392	C
Missouri State Univ	MO	13,996	VC
National Univ	CA	14,730	SP
New York Univ	NY	61,470	MC
N Car State Univ	NC	16,202	HC
N Dak State Univ	ND	14,642	C
Northern Arizona Univ	AZ	18,592	C
Northern Kentucky Univ	KY	15,302	LC
Northern Mich Univ	MI	15,300	VC
Okla State Univ	OK	14,310	VC
Oregon State Univ	OR	19,017	C+
Pennsylvania College of Technology	PA	25,653	NC
Pittsburg State Univ	KS	12,032	C
Polytechnic Inst of New York Univ	NY	53,064	HC+
Pratt Inst	NY	49,520	SP
Purdue Univ/West Lafayette	IN	20,278	HC
Roger Williams Univ	RI	45,788	C
S Dak State Univ	SD	14,296	C
Southern Illinois Univ Edwardsville	IL	17,532	C
Southern Polytechnic State Univ	GA	13,958	VC
SUNY / College of Environmental Science and Forestry	NY	18,351	HC
Temple Univ	PA	24,392	VC
Texas State Univ	TX	16,495	VC
Ohio State Univ	OH	19,887	MC
Tuskegee Univ	AL	26,750	C
Univ of Arkansas at Little Rock	AR		C
Univ of Central Missouri	MO	14,605	C
Univ of Cincinnati	OH	20,199	VC
Univ of Denver	CO	51,787	VC+
Univ of Houston	TX	19,184	VC
Univ of Louisiana at Monroe	LA	12,998	C
Univ of Nebr - Lincoln	NE	17,507	VC
Univ of Nebr at Kearney	NE	14,855	LC
Univ of Nevada, Las Vegas	NV	17,303	C
Univ of New Mexico	NM	15,300	C
Univ of N Car at Charlotte	NC	15,847	C
Univ of North Florida	FL	15,578	VC
Univ of Northern Iowa	IA	14,776	C
Univ of Okla	OK	17,634	VC+
Univ of Tenn at Chattanooga	TN	16,883	C
Univ of Texas at San Antonio	TX	18,372	C
Utica College	NY	44,734	C
Virginia Polytechnic Inst and State Univ	VA	14,629	HC
Washington State Univ	WA	20,461	C
Wayne State Univ	MI	19,493	C
Wentworth Inst of Technology	MA	29,800	SP
Western Carolina Univ	NC	13,965	C+
Western Illinois Univ	IL	20,130	C
Western Kentucky Univ	KY	11,000	LC

CONSTRUCTION TECHNOLOGY

School	ST	$IS	SR
Appalachian State Univ	NC	12,919	VC
Calif State Polytechnic Univ, Pomona	CA	18,932	C
Eastern Kentucky Univ	KY	11,161	C
Fitchburg State Univ	MA	17,241	C
Florida International Univ	FL	17,747	VC
Idaho State Univ	ID	11,908	C
Indiana State Univ	IN	16,000	C
Montana State Univ-Northern	MT	12,500	NC
Norfolk State Univ	VA	10,531	LC
Northern Kentucky Univ	KY	15,302	LC
Okla State Univ	OK	14,310	VC
Pennsylvania College of Technology	PA	25,653	NC
Pittsburg State Univ	KS	12,032	C
Purdue Univ/Calumet	IN	14,336	C
Purdue Univ/West Lafayette	IN	20,278	HC
Texas State Univ	TX	16,495	VC
Texas Tech Univ	TX	14,243	C
Univ of Akron	OH	20,436	C
Univ of Arkansas at Little Rock	AR		C
Univ of Maine	ME	19,712	C+
Univ of Maryland/Eastern Shore	MD	14,000	C
Univ of Mass Amherst	MA	23,697	VC+
Univ of Southern Miss	MS	13,170	C
Univ of Wisc/Stout	WI	23,942	C
Wentworth Inst of Technology	MA	29,800	SP

CONSUMER SERVICES

School	ST	$IS	SR
San Francisco State Univ	CA	18,514	C
S Dak State Univ	SD	14,296	C
Texas Woman's Univ	TX	13,633	LC
Univ of Utah	UT	13,462	VC

CONTEMPORARY CHRISTIAN MUSIC

School	ST	$IS	SR
Greenville College	IL	27,012	C

CORE STUDIES

School	ST	$IS	SR
Shenandoah Univ	VA	39,268	C

CORRECTIONS

School	ST	$IS	SR
Adams State College	CO	13,358	LC
College of the Ozarks	MO	5,605	VC
Eastern Kentucky Univ	KY	11,161	C
Hardin-Simmons Univ	TX	23,560	C+
Jackson State Univ	MS	13,512	LC
Minn State Univ, Mankato	MN	14,900	C
St. Louis Univ	MO	46,594	VC+
Southeast Missouri State Univ	MO	14,983	LC
Stephen F. Austin State Univ	TX	14,668	C
Texas State Univ	TX	16,495	VC
Tiffin Univ	OH	30,273	LC
Univ of Indianapolis	IN	31,740	LC
Univ of New Haven	CT	47,740	C
Washburn Univ	KS	12,165	NC
Western Oregon Univ	OR	15,021	C

COSTUME DESIGN

School	ST	$IS	SR
Shenandoah Univ	VA	39,268	C
Webster Univ	MO	33,990	C+

COUNSELING/PSYCHOLOGY

School	ST	$IS	SR
Adams State College	CO	13,358	LC
Arizona State Univ	AZ	18,818	C+
Biola Univ	CA	40,320	VC
Blackburn College	IL	21,350	C
Cal State, Fresno	CA	17,405	C
City Univ of Seattle	WA	14,880	NC
Corban Univ	OR	34,764	C
Dallas Baptist Univ	TX	29,118	C
East Central Univ	OK	10,223	LC
Eastern Mich Univ	MI	17,961	C
Eastern New Mexico Univ	NM	10,682	C
Edinboro Univ of Pennsylvania	PA	15,940	LC
Emmanuel College	MA	47,985	VC
Faulkner Univ	AL	22,530	LC
Florida Gulf Coast Univ	FL		C
Friends Univ	KS	29,100	C
Geneva College	PA	27,280	C
Goddard College	VT	16,418	VC
Grace College and Theological Seminary	IN	28,800	C
Houghton College	NY	35,740	VC
Howard Univ	DC	35,957	C
Huntington Univ	IN	32,220	C
Husson Univ	ME	23,386	LC
Kentucky Christian Univ	KY	17,622	LC
Kutztown Univ of Pennsylvania	PA	16,909	LC
Martin Univ	IN	11,000	SP
Missouri State Univ	MO	13,996	VC
Mount St. Mary's College/ Chalon Campus	CA	43,897	VC+
New York Univ	NY	61,470	MC
Newman Univ	KS	30,380	C+
Northwest Univ	WA	18,854	C
Pittsburg State Univ	KS	12,032	C
Prescott College	AZ	33,284	C+
Rochester College	MI	18,320	C
Samford Univ	AL	35,700	VC+
SUNY/Empire State College	NY	6,315	SP
Toccoa Falls College	GA	23,210	C
Univ of Arizona	AZ	20,105	C
Univ of Georgia	GA	19,508	VC
Univ of Great Falls	MT	27,970	C
Univ of Idaho	ID	14,558	C
Univ of Louisiana at Monroe	LA	12,998	C
Univ of Missouri/Columbia	MO	18,201	MC
Univ of New Haven	CT	47,740	C
Univ of North Florida	FL	15,578	VC
Univ of St. Francis	IL	36,490	C
Univ of Wyoming	WY	13,855	C+
Washington Adventist Univ	MD	25,859	C+
Wayne State College	NE	11,764	NC
Williams Baptist College	AR	20,070	C

COURT REPORTING

School	ST	$IS	SR
Humphreys College	CA	17,000	NC

CRAFTS

School	ST	$IS	SR
Indiana Univ-Purdue Univ Fort Wayne	IN	15,425	C
Kent State Univ	OH	19,352	C
Kutztown Univ of Pennsylvania	PA	16,909	LC
Rochester Inst of Technology	NY	42,450	VC+
Univ of Illinois at Urbana-Champaign	IL	24,300	HC
Virginia Commonwealth Univ	VA	18,633	C

CREATIVE WRITING

School	ST	$IS	SR
Adams State College	CO	13,358	LC
Agnes Scott College	GA	45,323	VC+
Alderson Broaddus Univ	WV	28,656	C
American Univ	DC	54,829	HC+
Andrews Univ	MI	28,030	C+
Arkansas Tech Univ	AR	13,164	LC
Asbury Univ	KY	32,038	VC
Ashland Univ	OH	25,000	C
Baldwin Wallace Univ	OH	36,980	VC
Bard College	NY	59,872	HC
Bard College at Simon's Rock	MA	58,963	HC+
Baylor Univ	TX	46,720	HC
Belhaven Univ	MS	27,170	C
Beloit College	WI	49,970	HC
Benedictine Univ	IL	35,220	C
Bennington College	VT	56,990	HC+
Bethany College	WV	35,282	C
Bethel College	IN	31,560	C

School	ST	$IS	SR
Binghamton Univ / The SUNY	NY	20,832	HȻ
Blackburn College	IL	21,350	C
Bluffton Univ	OH	37,864	C
Bowling Green State Univ	OH	18,970	C
Brandeis Univ	MA	58,820	HC
Burlington College	VT	32,510	SP
Calif College of the Arts	CA	48,334	SP
Calvin College	MI	37,585	VȻ
Canisius College	NY	45,602	VC
Capital Univ	OH	39,824	VC
Cardinal Stritch Univ	WI	24,054	C
Carlow Univ	PA	30,272	C
Carroll College	MT	28,000	C
Chapman Univ	CA	56,019	VȻ
Chatham Univ	PA	42,440	VC
CUNY/Brooklyn College	NY	5,884	Ȼ
Coe College	IA	43,590	VC
Colby College	ME	57,510	MC
Colby-Sawyer College	NH	47,870	C
Colo College	CO	54,534	MC
Colo State Univ-Fort Collins	CO	20,090	VC
Columbia College Chicago	IL	30,940	LC
Concordia Univ St. Paul	MN	27,200	C
Corban Univ	OR	34,764	C
DePaul Univ	IL	46,120	VC
Dominican Univ of Calif	CA	51,250	C
Eastern Mich Univ	MI	17,961	C
Eastern Washington Univ	WA	16,388	C
Eckerd College	FL	43,902	VC
Elon Univ	NC	40,046	HC
Emerson College	MA	50,246	HC
Emory and Henry College	VA	387,460	C
Emory Univ	GA	45,000	MC
Fairleigh Dickinson Univ/ College at Florham	NJ	42,142	C
Florida Southern College	FL	38,240	VC
Florida State Univ	FL	15,238	HC
Geneva College	PA	27,280	C
George Fox Univ	OR	40,750	Ȼ
Goddard College	VT	16,418	VC
Goshen College	IN	35,900	VC
Grand Valley State Univ	MI	17,998	VC
Green Mountain College	VT	33,547	LC
Hamilton College	NY	55,620	MC
Hamline Univ	MN	44,198	VC
Hampshire College	MA	58,320	MC
Harvard Univ/Harvard College	MA	49,000	MC
Hiram College	OH	37,300	VC
Hofstra Univ	NY	48,020	VȻ
Hunter College / The CUNY	NY	14,429	VC
Huntington Univ	IN	32,220	C
Indiana Wesleyan Univ	IN	31,815	VC
Ithaca College	NY	52,300	HC
Johns Hopkins Univ	MD	47,492	MC
Johnson State College	VT	16,721	C
Kansas City Art Inst	MO	38,000	SP
Knox College	IL		VC
La Roche College	PA	34,802	LC
Lakeland College	WI	22,990	C
Le Moyne College	NY	42,200	VC
Lindenwood Univ	MO	20,750	C
Linfield College-McMinnville Campus	OR	46,166	C
Loras College	IA	37,432	VC
Loyola Univ Maryland	MD		VC
Loyola Univ New Orleans	LA	46,581	VC
Lubbock Christian Univ	TX	25,518	C
Malone Univ	OH	34,334	C
Marlboro College	VT	35,980	VC
Marshall Univ	WV	14,820	C
Maryville College	TN	33,150	VC
Mass Inst of Technology	MA	54,238	MC
Mercer Univ	GA	44,201	VȻ
Methodist Univ	NC	37,185	C
Mills College	CA	54,119	HC
Millsaps College	MS	43,888	VȻ
Montclair State Univ	NJ	22,614	C
Murray State Univ	KY	14,944	C
New England College	NH	45,930	LC
New York Univ	NY	61,470	MC
Northland College	WI	26,680	C
Oberlin College	OH	57,025	MC
Ohio Northern Univ	OH	42,075	VC
Ohio Univ	OH	20,676	VC
Okla Christian Univ	OK	24,975	VC
Oswego / SUNY	NY	20,009	VC
Pacific Univ	OR	42,815	C
Pepperdine Univ	CA	55,372	HȻ
Pfeiffer Univ	NC	33,700	C
Pittsburg State Univ	KS	12,032	C
Pratt Inst	NY	49,520	SP
Prescott College	AZ	33,284	Ȼ
Purchase College / SUNY	NY	16,951	C
Purdue Univ/West Lafayette	IN	20,278	HC
Queens Univ of Charlotte	NC	39,543	VC
Roanoke College	VA	47,996	Ȼ
Roger Williams Univ	RI	45,788	C
Sacred Heart Univ	CT	48,564	VC
Saginaw Valley State Univ	MI	16,869	C
St. Joseph's College	IN	35,790	C
St. Mary-of-the-Woods College	IN	37,722	LC
St. Mary's College	IN	45,160	VC
San Francisco State Univ	CA	18,514	C
Santa Fe Univ of Art and Design	NM	39,666	SP
Sarah Lawrence College	NY	48,000	HC
School of the Art Inst of Chicago	IL	44,000	SP
Seattle Pacific Univ	WA	41,559	VȻ
Seattle Univ	WA	47,010	VȻ
Seton Hall Univ	NJ	45,902	C
Seton Hill Univ	PA	35,172	C
Smith College	MA	57,524	MC
Southern Methodist Univ	TX	57,755	MC
Southern New Hampshire Univ	NH	38,100	C
Southern Vermont College	VT	30,740	LC
Southwest Minn State Univ	MN	14,000	C
Spalding Univ	KY	31,850	LC
St. Andrews Univ	NC	32,050	LC
St. Lawrence Univ	NY	53,740	HC
Stephens College	MO	34,500	VC
Suffolk Univ	MA	46,548	C
Sweet Briar College	VA	43,765	Ȼ
The College of Idaho	ID	31,277	VC
The SUNY at Potsdam	NY	17,754	C
Univ of Arizona	AZ	20,105	C
Univ of Calif at Riverside	CA	27,204	C
Univ of Central Okla	OK	12,293	C
Univ of Evansville	IN	41,056	VȻ
Univ of Idaho	ID	14,558	C
Univ of Maine at Farmington	ME	17,841	C
Univ of Mich/Ann Arbor	MI	22,102	HȻ
Univ of Missouri/Columbia	MO	18,201	MC
Univ of Montana-Western	MT	9,753	LC
Univ of Mount Union	OH	35,130	C
Univ of Nebr at Omaha	NE	12,700	C
Univ of New Haven	CT	47,740	C
Univ of N Car at Wilmington	NC	13,572	VȻ
Univ of Pittsburgh at Greensburg	PA	17,640	C
Univ of Pittsburgh at Johnstown	PA	20,862	LC
Univ of Redlands	CA	40,500	VC
Univ of Southern Calif	CA	56,903	MC
Univ of Tampa	FL	35,160	VC
Univ of Wisc/Green Bay	WI	14,900	C
Valparaiso Univ	IN	43,040	VȻ
Warren Wilson College	NC	34,888	VC
Wartburg College	IA	41,055	VC
Washington Univ in St. Louis	MO	58,818	MC
Waynesburg Univ	PA	29,100	C
Webster Univ	MO	33,990	Ȼ
Western Mich Univ	MI	19,042	C
Western New England Univ	MA	45,590	C
Western Washington Univ	WA	18,519	VC
Wheaton College	MA	54,934	HȻ
Wheeling Jesuit Univ	WV	34,668	C
Widener Univ	PA	50,368	C
Wofford College	SC	45,795	VC
Wright State Univ	OH	16,983	C
York College of Pennsylvania	PA	26,590	C

CRIMINAL JUSTICE

School	ST	$IS	SR
Abilene Christian Univ	TX	38,400	VC
Adelphi Univ	NY	43,130	VC
Adrian College	MI	33,800	C
Alabama State Univ	AL	14,142	NC
Albany State Univ	GA	8,500	C
Albright College	PA	46,660	C
Alcorn State Univ	MS	9,500	C
Alfred Univ	NY	40,392	VC
Alvernia Univ	PA	39,250	C
American International College	MA	36,100	LC
American Univ	DC	54,829	HȻ
Anderson Univ	IN	35,390	C
Angelo State Univ	TX	15,049	NC
Anna Maria College	MA	34,600	LC
Appalachian State Univ	NC	12,919	VC
Arcadia Univ	PA	33,570	Ȼ
Arizona State Univ	AZ	18,818	Ȼ
Armstrong Atlantic State Univ	GA	16,276	C
Asbury Univ	KY	32,038	VC
Ashford Univ	IA	21,780	C
Ashland Univ	OH	25,000	C
Auburn Univ at Montgomery	AL	12,120	C
Aurora Univ	IL	26,870	C
Austin Peay State Univ	TN	14,650	C
Averett Univ	VA	36,000	LC
Baldwin Wallace Univ	OH	36,980	VC
Ball State Univ	IN	17,850	C
Barton College	NC	27,660	C
Bay Path College	MA	34,565	C
Becker College	MA	41,420	LC
Bellarmine Univ	KY	42,950	VC
Bellevue Univ	NE	4,600	NC
Belmont Abbey College	NC	37,716	C
Bemidji State Univ	MN	13,500	C
Benedict College	SC	20,454	NC
Bethany College	KS	30,605	NC
Bethel College	IN	31,560	C
Bethune-Cookman Univ	FL	22,290	LC
Blackburn College	IL	21,350	C
Bloomsburg Univ of Pennsylvania	PA	13,598	C
Bluefield College	VA	17,230	Ȼ
Bluefield State College	WV	3,140	LC
Bluffton Univ	OH	37,864	C
Boise State Univ	ID	12,802	C
Bowie State Univ	MD	23,990	LC
Bowling Green State Univ	OH	18,970	C
Bradley Univ	IL	31,874	VC
Briar Cliff Univ	IA	29,514	C
Bridgewater State Univ	MA	18,752	C
Buena Vista Univ	IA	37,954	C
Buffalo State/State Univ of Buffalo	NY	15,733	Ȼ
Butler Univ	IN	45,898	VȻ
Caldwell College	NJ	35,602	LC
Calif Baptist Univ	CA	35,890	C
Calif Lutheran Univ	CA	47,640	C
Cal State, Bakersfield	CA	8,000	LC
Cal State, Chico	CA	18,952	C
Cal State, Dominguez Hills	CA	17,056	LC
Cal State, East Bay	CA	16,549	C
Cal State, Fullerton	CA	25,188	Ȼ
Cal State, Los Angeles	CA	15,829	C
Cal State, Sacramento	CA	16,200	C
Cal State, San Bernardino	CA	12,000	C
Cal State, Stanislaus	CA	18,582	C
Calif Univ of Pennsylvania	PA	14,217	C
Calumet College of St. Joseph	IN	15,000	LC
Cameron Univ	OK	9,267	LC
Campbell Univ	NC	25,500	C
Campbellsville Univ	KY	27,720	C
Canisius College	NY	45,602	VC
Capital Univ	OH	39,824	VC
Caribbean Univ	PR	10,375	
Carroll Univ	WI	24,860	C
Carthage College	WI	33,000	C
Castleton State College	VT	19,424	C
Cedar Crest College	PA	43,240	C
Cedarville Univ	OH	31,036	VȻ
Centenary College	NJ	38,618	LC
Central Methodist Univ	MO	28,240	VC
Central Mich Univ	MI	18,066	C
Central Washington Univ	WA	11,730	C
Chadron State College	NE	7,400	NC
Chaminade Univ of Honolulu	HI	31,664	C
Champlain College	VT	44,850	VC
Charleston Southern Univ	SC	22,420	C
Chestnut Hill College	PA	39,785	LC
Cheyney Univ of Pennsylvania	PA	20,372	LC
Chicago State Univ	IL	5,482	C
Citadel, The	SC		C
City Univ of Seattle	WA	14,880	NC
Claflin Univ	SC	22,368	Ȼ
College of New Jersey	NJ	25,376	HC
College of St Joseph	VT	30,600	LC
College of the Ozarks	MO	5,605	VC
Colo Technical Univ	CO	10,500	LC
Columbia College	MO	24,578	C
Columbus State Univ	GA	13,176	C
Concordia Univ St. Paul	MN	27,200	C
Concordia Univ Wisc	WI	28,980	C
Concordia Univ, Ann Arbor	MI	27,220	VC
Coppin State Univ	MD	14,905	VC
Corban Univ	OR	34,764	C
Culver-Stockton College	MO	30,900	C
Cumberland Univ	TN	21,220	C
Curry College	MA	47,545	LC
Dakota Wesleyan Univ	SD	23,000	C
Dallas Baptist Univ	TX	29,118	C
De Sales Univ	PA	42,670	C
Defiance College	OH	30,645	C
Delaware Valley College	PA	29,944	C
Delta State Univ	MS	12,292	LC
Dominican College	NY	31,270	C
Dominican Univ	IL	37,628	C
Dordt College	IA	34,160	VC
Drury Univ	MO	30,319	VC
East Carolina Univ	NC	14,169	C
East Central Univ	OK	10,223	LC
East Stroudsburg Univ of Pennsylvania	PA	16,636	C
East Tenn State Univ	TN	9,000	C
East Texas Baptist Univ	TX	29,135	C
Eastern Mich Univ	MI	17,961	C
Eastern New Mexico Univ	NM	10,682	C
Eastern Washington Univ	WA	16,388	C
Edgewood College	WI	33,294	C
Edinboro Univ of Pennsylvania	PA	15,940	LC
Edward Waters College	FL	17,856	LC
Elizabeth City State Univ	NC	11,638	C
Elizabethtown College	PA	47,600	VC
Elizabethtown College School of Continuing and Professional Studies	PA		VC
Elmhurst College	IL	42,032	Ȼ
Elmira College	NY	49,950	Ȼ
Emporia State Univ	KS	12,897	C
Endicott College	MA	42,390	C
Evangel Univ	MO	23,090	C
Excelsior College	NY	895	SP
Fairleigh Dickinson Univ/ Metropolitan Campus	NJ	40,254	C
Fairmont State Univ	WV	12,098	LC
Farmingdale State College	NY	18,985	C
Faulkner Univ	AL	22,530	LC
Fayetteville State Univ	NC	10,816	C
Felician College	NJ	41,640	C
Ferris State Univ	MI	19,698	C
Ferrum College	VA	27,740	LC
Fitchburg State Univ	MA	17,241	C
Florida A&M Univ	FL	14,935	LC
Florida Atlantic Univ	FL	17,339	C
Florida Gulf Coast Univ	FL		C
Florida International Univ	FL	17,747	VC
Florida Memorial Univ	FL	20,716	LC
Fort Hays State Univ	KS	11,354	C
Fort Valley State Univ	GA	11,200	VC
Franklin Pierce Univ	NH	41,598	C
Freed-Hardeman Univ	TN	19,697	VC
Friends Univ	KS	29,100	C
Frostburg State Univ	MD	15,264	LC
Gannon Univ	PA	37,940	C
George Mason Univ	VA	15,724	VC
George Washington Univ	DC	57,108	MC
Georgia College and State Univ	GA	18,216	VC
Georgia Regents Univ	GA		C
Georgia State Univ	GA	12,000	VC
Georgian Court Univ	NJ	39,726	LC
Glenville State College	WV	11,348	NC
Gonzaga Univ	WA	44,247	HC
Grace College and Theological Seminary	IN	28,800	C
Graceland Univ	IA	28,020	C
Grambling State Univ	LA	13,384	LC
Grand Valley State Univ	MI	17,998	VC
Grand View Univ	IA	31,050	C
Granite State College	NH	6,195	SP
Greenville College	IL	27,012	C
Guilford College	NC	35,340	C
Gwynedd-Mercy College	PA	33,560	C
Hamline Univ	MN	44,198	VC
Hannibal-LaGrange Univ	MO	24,490	C
Harding Univ	AR	21,432	Ȼ
Hardin-Simmons Univ	TX	23,560	Ȼ
Harris-Stowe State Univ	MO	14,360	NC
Hawaii Pacific Univ	HI	36,690	C
Heidelberg Univ	OH	34,100	C
Henderson State Univ	AR	13,634	C
High Point Univ	NC	39,800	C
Hilbert College	NY	28,550	C
Hodges Univ	FL	12,000	LC
Holy Family Univ	PA	40,030	LC
Howard Univ	DC	35,957	C
Huntington Univ	IN	32,220	C
Husson Univ	ME	23,386	LC
Huston-Tillotson Univ	TX	18,124	Ȼ
Illinois State Univ	IL	22,634	VC
Indiana Inst of Technology	IN	34,240	LC
Indiana Univ Bloomington	IN	19,358	HC
Indiana Univ East	IN	6,639	LC
Indiana Univ Kokomo	IN	6,674	LC
Indiana Univ Northwest	IN	6,738	LC
Indiana Univ South Bend	IN	15,293	C
Indiana Univ Southeast	IN	15,807	LC
Indiana Univ-Purdue Univ Fort Wayne	IN	15,425	C
Indiana Univ-Purdue Univ Indianapolis	IN	17,290	C
Indiana Wesleyan Univ	IN	31,815	VC
Inter-American Univ of PR/ Aguadilla Campus	PR	5,578	
Inter-American Univ of PR/ Arecibo Campus	PR	3,350	
Inter-American Univ of PR/ Barranquitas	PR	3,350	
Inter-American Univ of PR/ Fajardo Campus	PR	4,200	
Inter-American Univ of PR/ Metropolitan Campus	PR	4,320	
Inter-American Univ of PR/ Ponce	PR	3,700	
Iona College	NY	44,028	C
Iowa Wesleyan College	IA	30,850	LC
Jackson State Univ	MS	13,512	LC
Jacksonville State Univ	AL	12,280	LC
James Madison Univ	VA	18,049	VC
Jarvis Christian College	TX	19,552	NC
John Carroll Univ	OH	44,520	Ȼ
John Jay College of Criminal Justice / The CUNY	NY	6,059	C
Johnson and Wales Univ/ Denver Campus	CO	34,368	C
Johnson and Wales Univ/ North Miami Campus	FL	34,368	C
Johnson and Wales Univ/ Providence Campus	RI	34,668	C
Johnson C. Smith Univ	NC	25,336	LC
Judson College	AL	24,690	C
Kansas Wesleyan Univ	KS	32,000	C
Kaplan Univ	IA	14,025	NC
Kean Univ	NJ	22,060	LC
Keene State College	NH	21,538	C
Kennesaw State Univ	GA	13,017	VC
Kentucky State Univ	KY	11,000	LC

ST = STATE **$IS** = IN-STATE COSTS **SR** = SELECTOR RATING

School	ST	$IS	SR
Kentucky Wesleyan College	KY	27,440	VC+
Keuka College	NY	30,300	C
Keystone College	PA	28,680	LC
King's College	PA	41,678	C
Kutztown Univ of Pennsylvania	PA	16,909	LC
La Roche College	PA	34,802	LC
La Salle Univ	PA	50,270	C
Lake Erie College	OH	35,704	C
Lake Superior State Univ	MI	18,121	C
Lakeland College	WI	22,990	C
Lamar Univ	TX	6,820	LC
Lane College	TN	11,212	C
Langston Univ	OK	3,000	LC
Lasell College	MA	42,500	LC
Le Moyne College	NY	42,200	VC
Lebanon Valley College	PA	38,570	C
Lees-McRae College	NC	33,624	C
LeMoyne-Owen College	TN	13,100	C
Lewis Univ	IL	23,050	C
Lewis-Clark State College	ID	6,990	C
Limestone College	SC	29,880	C
Lincoln Univ	MO	11,996	NC
Lindenwood Univ	MO	20,750	C
Lindsey Wilson College	KY	30,470	VC
Livingstone College	NC	17,815	LC
Lock Haven Univ of Pennsylvania	PA	17,587	LC
LIU/C.W. Post Campus	NY	38,888	C
Longwood Univ	VA	20,924	C
Loras College	IA	37,432	VC
Louisiana College	LA	15,746	C
Lourdes Univ	OH	26,055	LC
Loyola Univ Chicago	IL	49,560	VC+
Loyola Univ New Orleans	LA	46,581	VC
Lubbock Christian Univ	TX	25,518	C
Lycoming College	PA	43,636	C
Lynn Univ	FL	43,500	C
MacMurray College	IL	20,755	C
Madonna Univ	MI	24,540	VC
Mansfield Univ	PA	19,468	LC
Marian Univ	WI	30,980	LC
Marist College	NY	35,500	C
Marshall Univ	WV	14,820	C
Martin Univ	IN	11,000	SP
Mary Baldwin College	VA	37,110	C
Marygrove College	MI	21,290	C
Marymount Univ	VA	36,178	C
Marywood Univ	PA	40,695	C
McKendree Univ	IL	29,920	C+
McNeese State Univ	LA		C
Medaille College	NY	35,112	VC
Mercer Univ	GA	44,201	VC+
Mercy College	NY	29,996	C
Mercyhurst Univ	PA	40,700	C
Messiah College	PA	39,540	VC
Methodist Univ	NC	37,185	C
Metropolitan State Univ	MN	5,923	SP
Metropolitan State Univ of Denver	CO	4,835	LC
Miami Univ	OH	24,191	HC
Mich State Univ	MI	13,689	VC
MidAmerica Nazarene Univ	KS	28,000	C
Middle Tenn State Univ	TN	8,650	C
Midwestern State Univ	TX	9,722	C
Miles College	AL	16,530	NC
Minn State Univ, Moorhead	MN	13,392	C
Minot State Univ	ND	10,915	C
Miss College	MS	21,998	VC
Miss Valley State Univ	MS	9,706	LC
Missouri Baptist Univ	MO	30,310	C
Missouri Southern State Univ	MO	11,910	C
Missouri Valley College	MO	22,200	C
Missouri Western State Univ	MO	12,260	NC
Mitchell College	CT	40,983	C
Molloy College	NY	38,950	C
Monmouth Univ	NJ	42,252	C
Monroe College	NY	17,700	C
Montana State Univ-Billings	MT	12,425	LC
Montclair State Univ	NJ	22,614	C
Moravian College	PA	36,381	VC
Morris College	SC	16,006	LC
Mount Aloysius College	PA	27,970	C
Mount Ida College	MA	30,115	LC
Mount Marty College	SD	29,638	C
Mount Mary Univ	WI	32,836	LC
Mount Mercy Univ	IA	34,385	C
Mount Olive College	NC	18,426	C
Mount St. Mary's Univ	MD	46,158	C
Mount Vernon Nazarene Univ	OH	29,590	C
Mount Washington College	NH	21,500	NC
Mountain State Univ	WV	14,330	NC
Murray State Univ	KY	14,944	C
Muskingum Univ	OH	30,502	C
National Univ	CA	14,730	SP
Neumann Univ	PA	31,078	LC
New England College	NH	45,930	LC
New Jersey City Univ	NJ	21,060	C+
New Mexico State Univ	NM	13,955	LC
Newbury College	MA	41,850	C
Newman Univ	KS	30,380	C+
Niagara Univ	NY	39,800	C
Nichols College	MA	37,240	LC
N Car Central Univ	NC	9,000	LC
N Car State Univ	NC	16,202	HC
N Car Wesleyan College	NC	29,440	C
N Dak State Univ	ND	14,642	C
North Georgia College & State Univ	GA	8,500	C
North Park Univ	IL	30,130	C
Northeastern Illinois Univ	IL		C
Northeastern State Univ	OK	8,615	VC
Northeastern Univ	MA	55,296	MC
Northern Arizona Univ	AZ	18,592	C
Northern Kentucky Univ	KY	15,302	LC
Northern Mich Univ	MI	15,300	VC
Northern State Univ	SD	14,021	C
Northwestern College	MN	24,000	C
Northwestern Okla State Univ	OK	7,275	NC
Northwestern State Univ of Louisiana	LA	14,368	C
Norwich Univ	VT	28,212	C
Nova Southeastern Univ	FL	34,016	VC
Nyack College	NY	32,000	C
Ohio Dominican Univ	OH	38,380	C+
Ohio Northern Univ	OH	42,075	VC
Ohio Univ	OH	20,676	VC
Ohio Valley Univ	WV	17,752	C
Old Dominion Univ	VA	18,662	C
Olivet College	MI	19,984	C
Olivet Nazarene Univ	IL	29,990	C
Oswego / SUNY	NY	20,009	VC
Pace Univ	NY	48,094	VC
Park Univ	MO	17,525	C
Penn State Univ/Altoona	PA	11,464	C
Penn State Univ/Univ Park	PA	25,404	VC
Pfeiffer Univ	NC	33,700	C
Piedmont College	GA	29,260	C
Pittsburg State Univ	KS	12,032	C
Plymouth State Univ	NH	23,148	LC
Point Park Univ	PA	36,390	C
Post Univ	CT	35,750	C
Prairie View A&M Univ	TX	15,205	LC
Purdue Univ/Calumet	IN	14,336	C
Purdue Univ/West Lafayette	IN	20,278	HC
Quincy Univ	IL	34,980	LC
Quinnipiac Univ	CT	53,580	VC
Radford Univ	VA	17,132	LC
Rhode Island College	RI	17,132	LC
Richard Stockton College of New Jersey	NJ	20,000	VC
Roanoke College	VA	47,996	C+
Roberts Wesleyan College	NY	37,384	C+
Rochester Inst of Technology	NY	42,450	VC+
Roger Williams Univ	RI	45,788	C
Rowan Univ	NJ	23,570	VC
Russell Sage College	NY	39,370	C
Rutgers, The State Univ of New Jersey/Camden Campus	NJ	24,254	C
Rutgers, The State Univ of New Jersey/New Brunswick	NJ	25,077	VC
Rutgers, The State Univ of New Jersey/Newark Campus	NJ	25,376	C
Sacred Heart Univ	CT	48,564	VC
Saginaw Valley State Univ	MI	16,869	C
St. Anselm College	NH	48,324	VC
St. Augustine's Univ	NC	14,000	C
St. Francis Univ	PA	30,029	LC
St. Joseph's College	IN	35,790	C
St. Joseph's College of Maine	ME	31,580	C
St. Joseph's Univ	PA	52,272	VC
St. Leo Univ	FL	27,990	C
St. Louis Univ	MO	46,594	VC+
St. Martin's Univ	WA	38,082	C
St. Mary's Univ	TX	33,854	C
St. Mary's Univ of Minn	MN	37,015	C
St. Peter's College	NJ	44,240	C
St. Xavier Univ	IL	32,840	C
Salem International Univ	WV	18,020	C
Salem State College	MA	13,161	LC
Salve Regina Univ	RI	47,250	VC
Sam Houston State Univ	TX	17,082	C
San Diego State Univ	CA	20,578	VC
San Francisco State Univ	CA	18,514	C
San Jose State Univ	CA	19,707	C
Savannah State Univ	GA	13,156	C
Seattle Univ	WA	47,010	VC+
Seton Hall Univ	NJ	45,902	C
Seton Hill Univ	PA	35,172	C
Shaw Univ	NC	15,488	LC
Shenandoah Univ	VA	39,268	C
Shippensburg Univ of Pennsylvania	PA	17,064	LC
Siena Heights Univ	MI	17,000	LC
Simpson College	IA	36,086	VC
Sojourner-Douglass College	MD	9,160	LC
Sonoma State Univ	CA	20,541	C
S Car State Univ	SC	6,700	LC
South Univ	GA		LC
Southeast Missouri State Univ	MO	14,983	LC
Southeastern Louisiana Univ	LA	13,325	C
Southeastern Okla State Univ	OK	7,966	C
Southeastern Univ	FL	27,201	C+
Southern Illinois Univ Carbondale	IL	21,620	C
Southern Illinois Univ Edwardsville	IL	17,532	C
Southern Methodist Univ	TX	57,755	MC
Southern Oregon Univ	OR	17,874	C
Southern Univ and A&M College	LA	9,761	C+
Southern Univ at New Orleans	LA	1,000	NC
Southern Vermont College	VT	30,740	LC
Southern Wesleyan Univ	SC	25,600	C
Southwest Baptist Univ	MO	24,710	C
Southwestern Okla State Univ	OK	9,160	C
St. Ambrose Univ	IA		C
St. Cloud State Univ	MN	10,600	C
St. Edward's Univ	TX	44,674	VC
St. Francis College	NY	34,200	LC
St. John's Univ	NY	52,840	C+
St. Joseph's College, New York / Brooklyn Campus	NY	21,878	C
St. Joseph's College, New York / Suffolk Campus	NY	21,878	VC
St. Thomas Aquinas College	NY	30,000	C
St. Thomas Univ	FL	32,310	C+
SUNY Inst of Technology at Utica / Rome	NY	23,818	C
SUNY/Empire State College	NY	6,315	SP
Stephen F. Austin State Univ	TX	14,668	C
Suffolk Univ	MA	46,548	C
Sul Ross State Univ	TX	13,410	LC
SUNY Oneonta / SUNY	NY	16,919	VC
SUNY Plattsburgh / SUNY	NY	18,083	VC
Tarleton State Univ	TX	13,489	LC
Temple Univ	PA	24,392	VC
Tenn State Univ	TN	9,048	C
Texas A&M Univ at Commerce	TX	10,496	C
Texas A&M Univ at Corpus Christi	TX	11,544	LC
Texas Christian Univ	TX	47,570	HC
Texas Southern Univ	TX	18,212	LC
Texas State Univ	TX	16,495	VC
Texas Wesleyan Univ	TX	29,886	C
Texas Woman's Univ	TX	13,633	LC
The College at Brockport / SUNY	NY	18,362	VC
The College of St. Rose	NY	26,750	C
The Lincoln Univ	PA	15,154	LC
Ohio State Univ	OH	19,887	MC
The SUNY at Potsdam	NY	17,754	C
Thiel College	PA	31,378	LC
Thomas College	ME	26,270	LC
Thomas Edison State College	NJ	5,700	SP
Thomas More College	KY	34,760	C
Thomas Univ	GA	11,520	NC
Tiffin Univ	OH	30,273	LC
Trevecca Nazarene Univ	TN	30,118	C
Trine Univ	IN	39,400	VC
Trinity Christian College	IL	28,869	C
Trinity Washington Univ	DC	30,250	C+
Troy Univ	AL	10,650	C
Truman State Univ	MO	13,546	HC
Union College	KY	28,775	C
Union Inst & Univ	OH	8,912	SP
Univ at Albany / SUNY	NY	18,674	VC
Univ of Akron	OH	20,436	C
Univ of Alabama at Birmingham	AL	18,484	C+
Univ of Alabama at Tuscaloosa	AL	17,164	C+
Univ of Alaska Fairbanks	AK	13,955	C
Univ of Arkansas at Fayetteville	AR	16,860	VC
Univ of Arkansas at Little Rock	AR		C
Univ of Arkansas at Monticello	AR	8,470	NC
Univ of Arkansas at Pine Bluff	AR	10,600	C
Univ of Bridgeport	CT	39,030	LC
Univ of Central Florida	FL	15,711	VC+
Univ of Central Missouri	MO	14,605	C
Univ of Central Okla	OK	12,293	C
Univ of Charleston	WV	28,650	C
Univ of Cincinnati	OH	20,199	VC
Univ of Colo Denver	CO	17,904	C
Univ of Dayton	OH	43,750	VC
Univ of Delaware	DE	22,728	VC
Univ of Detroit Mercy	MI	30,450	C
Univ of Evansville	IN	41,056	VC+
Univ of Findlay	OH	31,916	C
Univ of Georgia	GA	19,508	VC
Univ of Great Falls	MT	27,970	C
Univ of Hartford	CT	42,674	C
Univ of Hawaii at Hilo	HI	6,500	C
Univ of Houston-Downtown	TX	6,267	LC
Univ of Idaho	ID	14,558	C
Univ of Illinois at Chicago	IL	24,293	VC
Univ of Jamestown	ND	24,738	C
Univ of Louisiana at Lafayette	LA	6,130	C
Univ of Louisiana at Monroe	LA	12,998	C
Univ of Louisville	KY	17,460	VC
Univ of Maine at Fort Kent	ME	14,975	LC
Univ of Maine at Presque Isle	ME	15,011	LC
Univ of Mary	ND	16,714	C
Univ of Mary Hardin-Baylor	TX	31,950	C+
Univ of Maryland	MD	18,801	HC
Univ of Maryland/Eastern Shore	MD	14,000	C
Univ of Maryland/Univ College	MD	6,168	SP
Univ of Mass Boston	MA	11,966	C
Univ of Mass Dartmouth	MA	22,220	C
Univ of Mass Lowell	MA	19,316	C
Univ of Memphis	TN	15,094	C
Univ of Mich/Dearborn	MI	9,885	VC
Univ of Mich-Flint	MI	17,547	C+
Univ of Minn Crookston	MN	17,834	C
Univ of Missouri-Kansas City	MO	19,603	C
Univ of Missouri-St. Louis	MO	18,304	VC
Univ of Montana-Western	MT	9,753	LC
Univ of Mount Union	OH	35,130	C
Univ of Nebr at Kearney	NE	14,855	LC
Univ of Nebr at Omaha	NE	12,700	C
Univ of Nevada, Las Vegas	NV	17,303	C
Univ of Nevada/Reno	NV	14,500	NC
Univ of New Haven	CT	47,740	C
Univ of North Alabama	AL	9,960	C
Univ of N Car at Charlotte	NC	15,847	C
Univ of N Car at Wilmington	NC	13,572	VC+
Univ of N Dak	ND	14,094	C
Univ of North Florida	FL	15,578	VC
Univ of North Texas	TX	15,628	C
Univ of Northern Colo	CO	15,973	C
Univ of Okla	OK	17,634	VC+
Univ of Pikeville	KY	24,750	NC
Univ of Pittsburgh at Bradford	PA	21,316	LC
Univ of Pittsburgh at Johnstown	PA	20,862	LC
Univ of Scranton	PA	51,940	VC
Univ of South Alabama	AL	13,510	C
Univ of S Car at Columbia	SC	19,725	VC+
Univ of S Car Upstate	SC	17,673	LC
Univ of S Dak	SD	15,111	C
Univ of Southern Indiana	IN	14,657	C
Univ of Southern Miss	MS	13,170	C
Univ of St. Francis	IL	36,490	C
Univ of Tenn at Chattanooga	TN	16,883	C
Univ of Tenn at Martin	TN	13,217	C
Univ of Texas at Arlington	TX	10,908	LC
Univ of Texas at El Paso	TX	8,764	NC
Univ of Texas at San Antonio	TX	18,372	C
Univ of Texas-Pan American	TX	12,432	LC
Univ of the District of Columbia	DC	7,244	LC
Univ of the Sacred Heart	PR	5,590	
Univ of the Southwest	NM	15,000	C
Univ of Toledo	OH	18,464	C
Univ of Virginia's College at Wise	VA	11,076	C
Univ of West Florida	FL	14,656	C
Univ of Wisc/Eau Claire	WI	15,430	VC
Univ of Wisc/Oshkosh	WI	10,426	LC
Univ of Wisc/Platteville	WI	14,274	C
Univ of Wisc/Superior	WI	14,106	C
Univ of Wisc-Milwaukee	WI	18,436	C
Univ of Wyoming	WY	13,855	C+
Urbana Univ	OH	21,190	C
Utica College	NY	44,734	C
Villanova Univ	PA	56,436	MC
Virginia Commonwealth Univ	VA	18,633	C
Virginia Intermont College	VA	32,411	LC
Virginia Wesleyan College	VA	28,433	LC
Viterbo Univ	WI	30,070	C
Voorhees College	SC	18,126	C
Walsh Univ	OH	35,100	C
Washburn Univ	KS	12,165	NC
Washington State Univ	WA	20,461	C
Wayland Baptist Univ	TX	16,058	LC
Wayne State College	NE	11,764	NC
Wayne State Univ	MI	19,493	C
Waynesburg Univ	PA	29,100	C
West Chester Univ of Pennsylvania	PA	16,836	C
West Liberty Univ	WV	9,142	LC
West Texas A&M Univ	TX	13,478	C
West Virginia State Univ	WV	8,378	NC
Western Carolina Univ	NC	13,965	C+
Western Conn State Univ	CT	18,327	C
Western Mich Univ	MI	19,042	C
Western New England Univ	MA	45,590	C
Westfield State Univ	MA	18,489	C
Westminster College	PA	31,290	C+
Westminster College	UT	37,708	VC
Wheeling Jesuit Univ	WV	34,668	C
Wichita State Univ	KS	12,539	C
Widener Univ	PA	50,368	C

School	ST	$IS	SR
Wilmington College	OH	29,784	C
Wilmington Univ	DE	7,778	NC
Wingate Univ	NC	34,990	C
Winona State Univ	MN	16,530	C
Worcester State Univ	MA	18,657	C
Wright State Univ	OH	16,983	C
Xavier Univ	OH	43,740	VC
York College of Pennsylvania	PA	26,590	C
Youngstown State Univ	OH	16,374	LC

CRIMINOLOGY

School	ST	$IS	SR
Adams State College	CO	13,358	LC
Alabama A&M Univ	AL	96,100	C
Albertus Magnus College	CT	37,382	LC
Alderson Broaddus Univ	WV	28,656	C
Arkansas State Univ	AR	14,980	C
Auburn Univ	AL	20,052	VC+
Barry Univ	FL	38,190	C
Cabrini College	PA	40,859	LC
Cal State, Fresno	CA	17,405	C
Cal State, Northridge	CA	28,313	C
Cal State, San Marcos	CA	14,576	C
Cazenovia College	NY	30,800	C
Central Conn State Univ	CT	19,212	C
Clarke Univ	IA	36,400	C
Cleveland State Univ	OH	21,357	C
Coker College	SC	32,256	LC
College of Mount St. Joseph	OH	33,880	C
College of the Ozarks	MO	5,605	VC
Colo State Univ-Pueblo	CO	13,532	LC
Drury Univ	MO	30,319	VC
Faulkner Univ	AL	22,530	LC
Florida Gulf Coast Univ	FL		C
Florida Southern College	FL	38,240	VC
Florida State Univ	FL	15,238	HC
Framingham State Univ	MA	16,750	C
Hilbert College	NY	28,550	C
Hofstra Univ	NY	48,020	VC+
Indiana Inst of Technology	IN	34,240	LC
Indiana State Univ	IN	16,000	C
Indiana Univ of Pennsylvania	PA	20,180	LC
Indiana Univ Southeast	IN	15,807	LC
John Carroll Univ	OH	44,520	C+
John Jay College of Criminal Justice / The CUNY	NY	6,059	C
Le Moyne College	NY	42,200	VC
Longwood Univ	VA	20,924	C
Lycoming College	PA	43,636	C
Lynchburg College	VA	42,645	C
Marquette Univ	WI	43,664	VC+
Maryville Univ of St. Louis	MO	34,920	VC
Missouri State Univ	MO	13,996	VC
Mount Aloysius College	PA	27,970	C
Northern Arizona Univ	AZ	18,592	C
Ohio Univ	OH	20,676	VC
Pontifical Catholic Univ of PR	PR	7,310	
St. Mary-of-the-Woods College	IN	37,722	LC
Southeast Missouri State Univ	MO	14,983	LC
Southern Oregon Univ	OR	17,874	C
St. Ambrose Univ	IA		C
St. Edward's Univ	TX	44,674	VC
St. John Fisher College	NY	39,370	C+
Stonehill College	MA	46,780	VC+
SUNY College at Old Westbury	NY	16,324	C
Ohio State Univ	OH	19,887	MC
Universidad del Turabo	PR	4,110	
Univ of Akron	OH	20,436	C
Univ of Calif at Irvine	CA	25,961	VC
Univ of Denver	CO	51,787	VC+
Univ of Florida	FL	15,783	HC+
Univ of Illinois at Chicago	IL	24,293	VC
Univ of La Verne	CA	47,010	VC
Univ of Maryland	MD	18,801	HC
Univ of Memphis	TN	15,094	C
Univ of Miami	FL	55,166	MC
Univ of Minn/Duluth	MN	18,964	C+
Univ of New Haven	CT	47,740	C
Univ of New Mexico	NM	15,300	C
Univ of Northern Iowa	IA	14,776	C
Univ of St. Mary	KS	28,400	C+
Univ of South Florida	FL	13,000	C
Univ of South Florida/St. Petersburg	FL	12,769	VC
Univ of Tampa	FL	35,160	VC
Univ of Texas at Dallas	TX	21,046	HC
Univ of West Georgia	GA	14,852	LC
Upper Iowa Univ	IA	30,426	NC
Valparaiso Univ	IN	43,040	VC+
Virginia Union Univ	VA	18,432	C
Wheeling Jesuit Univ	WV	34,668	C
Wilkes Univ	PA	42,786	C
William Penn Univ	IA	26,000	C

CROSSCULTURAL STUDIES

School	ST	$IS	SR
Alfred Univ	NY	40,392	VC
Andrews Univ	MI	28,030	C+
Bard College at Simon's Rock	MA	58,963	HC+
Biola Univ	CA	40,320	VC
Chatham Univ	PA	42,440	VC
Columbia College Chicago	IL	30,940	LC
Corban Univ	OR	34,764	C
Goddard College	VT	16,418	VC
Hampshire College	MA	58,320	MC
Hope International Univ	CA	34,650	C
Houghton College	NY	35,740	VC
John Brown Univ	AR	30,996	VC+
Kentucky Christian Univ	KY	17,622	LC
Lee Univ	TN	18,690	C+
Linfield College-McMinnville Campus	OR	46,166	C
National Louis Univ	IL	16,915	LC
Northern Arizona Univ	AZ	18,592	C
Northwestern College	MN	24,000	C
Nyack College	NY	32,000	C
Olivet Nazarene Univ	IL	29,990	C
Palm Beach Atlantic Univ	FL	33,882	LC
Rollins College	FL	52,370	HC
Simpson Univ	CA	28,900	C
Stanford Univ	CA	56,411	MC
Toccoa Falls College	GA	23,210	C
Towson Univ	MD	16,000	VC
Villanova Univ	PA	56,436	MC
Washington State Univ	WA	20,461	C
Whitworth Univ	WA	45,826	VC+
Wofford College	SC	45,795	VC

CULINARY ARTS

School	ST	$IS	SR
Art Inst of Atlanta	GA	24,000	SP
Atlantic Union College	MA	24,600	LC
Idaho State Univ	ID	11,908	C
Kendall College	IL	32,610	NC
Miss Univ for Women	MS	7,400	LC
Mountain State Univ	WV	14,330	NC
Pennsylvania College of Technology	PA	25,653	NC
Southern New Hampshire Univ	NH	38,100	C
The SUNY College of Agriculture and Tech at Cobleskill	NY	18,869	VC
Univ of Alaska Anchorage	AK	15,290	NC
Univ of Charleston	WV	28,650	C
Univ of Nebr - Lincoln	NE	17,507	VC
Virginia Intermont College	VA	32,411	LC

CULTURAL ANTHROPOLOGY

School	ST	$IS	SR
Creighton Univ	NE	44,058	VC+
Webster Univ	MO	33,990	C+

CULTURAL STUDIES/CRITICAL THEORY & ANALYSIS

School	ST	$IS	SR
Bard College at Simon's Rock	MA	58,963	HC+
Goddard College	VT	16,418	VC
Occidental College	CA	59,592	MC+

CYTOTECHNOLOGY

School	ST	$IS	SR
Ashford Univ	IA	21,780	C
Barry Univ	FL	38,190	C
Edgewood College	WI	33,294	C
Indiana Univ-Purdue Univ Indianapolis	IN	17,290	C
Marian Univ	WI	30,980	LC
Marshall Univ	WV	14,820	C
Mass College of Liberal Arts	MA	16,733	C
Northern Mich Univ	MI	15,300	VC
Old Dominion Univ	VA	18,662	C
St. Louis Univ	MO	46,594	VC+
St. Mary's Univ of Minn	MN	37,015	C
Stony Brook Univ / SUNY	NY	19,359	HC
SUNY Plattsburgh / SUNY	NY	18,083	VC
The College of St. Rose	NY	26,750	C
Thiel College	PA	31,378	LC
United States Naval Academy	MD		MC
Univ of Alabama at Birmingham	AL	18,484	C+
Univ of Conn	CT	23,744	HC
Univ of Kansas	KS	16,980	C+
Univ of Mass Dartmouth	MA	22,223	C
Univ of N Dak	ND	14,094	C
Univ of North Texas	TX	15,628	C
Winona State Univ	MN	16,530	C

DAIRY SCIENCE

School	ST	$IS	SR
Calif Polytechnic State Univ	CA	19,847	HC
Cal State, Fresno	CA	17,405	C
Delaware Valley College	PA	29,944	C
Iowa State Univ	IA	16,403	C
S Dak State Univ	SD	14,296	C
Texas A&M Univ	TX	16,956	VC+
Univ of Florida	FL	15,783	HC+
Univ of Georgia	GA	19,508	VC
Univ of Idaho	ID	14,558	C
Univ of New Hampshire	NH	24,702	VC
Univ of Wisc/Madison	WI	18,757	HC
Utah State Univ	UT	11,803	C
Virginia Polytechnic Inst and State Univ	VA	14,629	HC

DANCE

School	ST	$IS	SR
Adelphi Univ	NY	43,130	VC
Agnes Scott College	GA	45,323	VC+
Amherst College	MA	58,744	MC
Appalachian State Univ	NC	12,919	VC
Arizona State Univ	AZ	18,818	C+
Ball State Univ	IN	17,850	C
Bard College	NY	59,872	HC
Bard College at Simon's Rock	MA	58,963	HC+
Belhaven Univ	MS	27,170	C
Bennington College	VT	56,990	HC+
Binghamton Univ / The SUNY	NY	20,832	HC+
Birmingham-Southern College	AL	42,370	VC+
Boston Conservatory	MA	56,380	SP
Bowling Green State Univ	OH	18,970	C
Brenau Univ Women's College	GA	26,650	C+
Brigham Young Univ	UT	12,100	HC
Butler Univ	IN	45,898	VC+
Calif Inst of the Arts	CA	46,368	SP
Cal State, Fullerton	CA	25,188	C+
Cal State, Long Beach	CA	17,534	C+
Cal State, Northridge	CA	28,313	C
Cal State, San Bernardino	CA	12,000	C
Case Western Reserve Univ	OH	55,178	MC
Cedar Crest College	PA	43,240	C
Centenary College of Louisiana	LA	39,070	C+
Chapman Univ	CA	56,019	VC+
Coker College	SC	32,256	LC
College of Charleston	SC	21,273	VC
Colo College	CO	54,534	MC
Colo State Univ-Fort Collins	CO	20,090	VC
Columbia College	SC	27,882	C
Columbia College Chicago	IL	30,940	LC
Columbia Univ in the City of New York	NY	61,116	MC
Columbia Univ/Barnard College	NY	39,000	MC
Columbia Univ/School of General Studies	NY	54,083	MC
Conn College	CT	54,970	MC
Cornell Univ	NY	59,037	MC
Cornish College of the Arts	WA	21,200	SP
Creighton Univ	NE	44,058	VC+
De Sales Univ	PA	42,670	C
Denison Univ	OH	54,670	HC+
Dickinson College	PA	57,662	HC+
Dominican Univ of Calif	CA	51,250	C
East Carolina Univ	NC	14,169	C
Eastern Mich Univ	MI	17,961	C
Eastern Univ	PA	37,704	C
Eastern Washington Univ	WA	16,388	C
Elon Univ	NC	40,046	HC
Emory Univ	GA	45,000	MC
Eugene Lang College - The New School for Liberal Arts	NY	55,650	VC
Florida Southern College	FL	38,240	VC
Florida State Univ	FL	15,238	HC
Fordham Univ	NY	58,927	HC
Franklin Pierce Univ	NH	41,598	C
George Mason Univ	VA	15,724	VC
George Washington Univ	DC	57,108	MC
Georgian Court Univ	NJ	39,726	LC
Goucher College	MD	50,252	VC+
Grand Valley State Univ	MI	17,998	VC
Gustavus Adolphus College	MN	48,170	HC
Hamilton College	NY	55,620	MC
Hampshire College	MA	58,320	MC
Hobart and William Smith Colleges	NY	43,000	VC
Hofstra Univ	NY	48,020	VC+
Hollins Univ	VA	43,295	VC
Hope College	MI	36,320	VC+
Howard Univ	DC	35,957	C
Hunter College / The CUNY	NY	14,429	VC
Indiana Univ Bloomington	IN	19,358	HC
Jacksonville Univ	FL	37,780	C
James Madison Univ	VA	18,049	VC
Juilliard School	NY	44,460	SP
Keene State College	NH	21,538	C
Kennesaw State Univ	GA	13,017	VC
Kent State Univ	OH	19,352	C
Kenyon College	OH	56,810	MC
La Roche College	PA	34,802	LC
Lehman College / The CUNY	NY	5,778	LC
Lindenwood Univ	MO	20,750	C
LIU/C.W. Post Campus	NY	38,888	C
Loyola Marymount Univ	CA	53,240	VC+
Loyola Univ Chicago	IL	49,560	VC+
Luther College	IA	44,380	VC+
Manhattanville College	NY	46,260	VC
Marlboro College	VT	35,980	VC
Marygrove College	MI	21,290	C
Marymount Manhattan College	NY	40,118	VC
Mercyhurst Univ	PA	40,700	C
Meredith College	NC	31,420	C
Messiah College	PA	39,540	VC
Middlebury College	VT	57,470	MC
Mills College	CA	54,119	HC
Minn State Univ, Mankato	MN	14,900	C
Montclair State Univ	NJ	22,614	C
Mount Holyoke College	MA	53,596	HC+
Muhlenberg College	PA	52,837	HC
New Mexico State Univ	NM	13,955	LC
New York Univ	NY	61,470	MC
Northeastern Illinois Univ	IL		C
Northwestern Univ	IL	37,595	MC
Nova Southeastern Univ	FL	34,016	VC
Oakland Univ	MI	19,391	VC
Oberlin College	OH	57,025	MC
Ohio Univ	OH	20,676	VC
Okla City Univ	OK	33,546	VC
Old Dominion Univ	VA	18,662	C
Oral Roberts Univ	OK	31,734	C
Pace Univ	NY	48,094	VC
Palm Beach Atlantic Univ	FL	33,882	LC
Pitzer College	CA	54,988	MC
Point Park Univ	PA	36,390	C
Pomona College	CA	57,680	MC
Prescott College	AZ	33,284	C+
Purchase College / SUNY	NY	16,951	C
Queens College / The CUNY	NY	17,107	VC
Radford Univ	VA	17,132	LC
Randolph College	VA	43,960	VC
Rhode Island College	RI	17,132	LC
Richard Stockton College of New Jersey	NJ	20,000	VC
Rider Univ	NJ	45,720	C
Roger Williams Univ	RI	45,788	C
Rutgers, The State Univ of New Jersey/New Brunswick	NJ	25,077	VC
Sam Houston State Univ	TX	17,082	C
San Diego State Univ	CA	20,578	VC
San Francisco State Univ	CA	18,514	C
San Jose State Univ	CA	19,707	C
Santa Fe Univ of Art and Design	NM	39,666	SP
Sarah Lawrence College	NY	48,000	HC
Scripps College	CA	54,900	MC
Shenandoah Univ	VA	39,268	C
Skidmore College	NY	57,926	HC
Slippery Rock Univ of Pennsylvania	PA	10,360	LC
Smith College	MA	57,524	MC
Southern Illinois Univ Edwardsville	IL	17,532	C
Southern Methodist Univ	TX	57,755	MC
St. Olaf College	MN	49,960	HC+
Stephen F. Austin State Univ	TX	14,668	C
Stephens College	MO	34,500	VC
SUNY Fredonia / The SUNY at Fredonia	NY	18,702	VC
Swarthmore College	PA	57,870	MC
Sweet Briar College	VA	43,765	C+
Temple Univ	PA	24,392	VC
Texas State Univ	TX	16,495	VC
Texas Tech Univ	TX	14,243	C
Texas Woman's Univ	TX	13,633	LC
The College at Brockport / SUNY	NY	18,362	VC
Ohio State Univ	OH	19,887	MC
The SUNY at Potsdam	NY	17,754	C
Towson Univ	MD	16,000	VC
Trinity College	CT		HC+
Tulane Univ	LA	58,942	MC
Univ at Buffalo / The SUNY	NY	20,283	VC
Univ of Akron	OH	20,436	C
Univ of Alabama at Tuscaloosa	AL	17,164	C+
Univ of Arizona	AZ	20,105	C
Univ of Arkansas at Little Rock	AR		C
Univ of Calif at Berkeley	CA	23,322	MC
Univ of Calif at Irvine	CA	25,961	VC
Univ of Calif at Riverside	CA	27,204	C
Univ of Calif at San Diego	CA	21,000	VC
Univ of Calif at Santa Barbara	CA	27,551	HC
Univ of Central Okla	OK	12,293	C
Univ of Cincinnati	OH	20,199	VC
Univ of Colo Boulder	CO	22,605	VC+
Univ of Florida	FL	15,783	HC+
Univ of Georgia	GA	19,508	VC
Univ of Hartford	CT	42,674	C
Univ of Hawaii at Manoa	HI	19,379	VC
Univ of Houston	TX	19,184	VC
Univ of Idaho	ID	14,558	C
Univ of Illinois at Urbana-Champaign	IL	24,300	HC
Univ of Iowa	IA	17,481	VC
Univ of Kansas	KS	16,980	C+
Univ of Louisiana at Lafayette	LA	6,130	C
Univ of Maryland	MD	18,801	HC
Univ of Maryland/Baltimore County	MD	18,000	VC

School	ST	$IS	SR
Univ of Mass Amherst	MA	23,697	VC+
Univ of Mich/Ann Arbor	MI	22,102	HC+
Univ of Minn/Twin Cities	MN		HC
Univ of Missouri-Kansas City	MO	19,603	C
Univ of Missouri-St. Louis	MO	18,304	VC
Univ of Nebr - Lincoln	NE	17,507	VC
Univ of Nevada, Las Vegas	NV	17,303	C
Univ of New Mexico	NM	15,300	C
Univ of N Car at Charlotte	NC	15,847	C
Univ of N Car at Greensboro	NC	12,848	C
Univ of N Car School of the Arts	NC	7,401	SP
Univ of North Texas	TX	15,028	C
Univ of Okla	OK	17,634	VC+
Univ of Oregon	OR	20,872	VC
Univ of S Car at Columbia	SC	19,725	VC+
Univ of South Florida	FL	13,000	C
Univ of Southern Miss	MS	13,170	C
Univ of Texas at Austin	TX	44,074	HC
Univ of Texas-Pan American	TX	12,432	LC
Univ of the Arts	PA	38,450	SP
Univ of Utah	UT	13,462	VC
Univ of Washington	WA	14,722	VC
Univ of Wisc/Madison	WI	18,757	HC
Univ of Wisc/Stevens Point	WI	14,043	C
Univ of Wisc-Milwaukee	WI	18,436	C
Ursinus College	PA	55,630	VC+
Utah State Univ	UT	11,803	C
Virginia Commonwealth Univ	VA	18,633	C
Virginia Intermont College	VA	32,411	LC
Washington Univ in St. Louis	MO	58,818	MC
Wayne State Univ	MI	19,493	C
Webster Univ	MO	33,990	C+
Wells College	NY	38,680	VC
Wesleyan Univ	CT	59,844	MC
West Chester Univ of Pennsylvania	PA	16,836	C
West Texas A&M Univ	TX	13,478	C
Western Mich Univ	MI	19,042	C
Western Oregon Univ	OR	15,021	C
Western Washington Univ	WA	18,519	VC
Wheaton College	MA	54,934	HC+
Whitman College	WA	54,400	MC
Winthrop Univ	SC	21,120	VC
Wright State Univ	OH	16,983	C
Youngstown State Univ	OH	16,374	LC

DANCE EDUCATION

School	ST	$IS	SR
Birmingham-Southern College	AL	42,370	VC+
Brenau Univ Women's College	GA	26,650	C+
Bridgewater State Univ	MA	18,752	C
Brigham Young Univ	UT	12,100	HC
Columbia College	SC	27,882	C
East Carolina Univ	NC	14,169	C
Grand Canyon Univ	AZ	24,540	VC
Hofstra Univ	NY	48,020	VC+
Jacksonville Univ	FL	37,780	C
Keene State College	NH	21,538	C
Marywood Univ	PA	40,695	C
New York Univ	NY	61,470	MC
Old Dominion Univ	VA	18,662	C
Point Park Univ	PA	36,390	C
Shenandoah Univ	VA	39,268	C
Southern Methodist Univ	TX	57,755	MC
Ohio State Univ	OH	19,887	MC
Towson Univ	MD	16,000	VC
Univ of Central Okla	OK	12,293	C
Univ of N Car at Charlotte	NC	15,847	C
Univ of N Car at Greensboro	NC	12,848	C
Univ of the Arts	PA	38,450	SP

DENTAL EDUCATION

School	ST	$IS	SR
Indiana Univ South Bend	IN	15,293	C
Thomas Edison State College	NJ	5,700	SP

DENTAL HYGIENE

School	ST	$IS	SR
Clayton State Univ	GA	12,000	LC
Creighton Univ	NE	44,058	VC+
East Tenn State Univ	TN	9,000	C
Eastern Washington Univ	WA	16,388	C
Farmingdale State College	NY	18,985	C
Ferris State Univ	MI	19,698	C
Georgia Regents Univ	GA		C
Howard Univ	DC	35,957	C
Idaho State Univ	ID	11,908	C
Indiana Univ Northwest	IN	6,738	LC
Indiana Univ South Bend	IN	15,293	C
Indiana Univ-Purdue Univ Indianapolis	IN	17,290	C
Mass College of Pharmacy and Health Sciences	MA	36,450	SP
Metropolitan State Univ	MN	5,923	SP
Midwestern State Univ	TX	9,722	C
Minn State Univ, Mankato	MN	14,900	C
New York Univ	NY	61,470	MC
Northern Arizona Univ	AZ	18,592	C
Ohio State Univ at Lima	OH	7,140	C
Old Dominion Univ	VA	18,662	C
Oregon Inst of Technology	OR	8,910	C
Pennsylvania College of Technology	PA	25,653	NC
Southern Illinois Univ Carbondale	IL	21,620	C
Tenn State Univ	TN	9,048	C
Texas Woman's Univ	TX	13,633	LC
Ohio State Univ	OH	19,887	MC
Thomas Edison State College	NJ	5,700	SP
Univ of Bridgeport	CT	39,030	LC
Univ of Detroit Mercy	MI	30,450	C
Univ of Hawaii at Manoa	HI	19,379	VC
Univ of Illinois at Chicago	IL	24,293	VC
Univ of Louisiana at Monroe	LA	12,998	C
Univ of Louisville	KY	17,460	VC
Univ of Maine at Augusta	ME	6,855	C
Univ of Mich/Ann Arbor	MI	22,102	HC+
Univ of Minn/Twin Cities	MN		HC
Univ of Missouri-Kansas City	MO	19,603	C
Univ of New England	ME	46,145	C+
Univ of New Haven	CT	47,740	C
Univ of New Mexico	NM	15,300	C
Univ of N Car at Chapel Hill	NC	18,348	MC
Univ of Pittsburgh at Pittsburgh	PA	27,800	HC+
Univ of S Dak	SD	15,111	C
Univ of Southern Calif	CA	56,903	MC
Univ of Southern Indiana	IN	14,657	C
Univ of Tenn at Knoxville	TN	20,364	VC+
Univ of Washington	WA	14,722	VC
Univ of Wyoming	WY	13,855	C+
Virginia Commonwealth Univ	VA	18,633	C
West Liberty Univ	WV	9,142	LC
West Virginia Univ	WV	15,794	C+
Western Kentucky Univ	KY	11,000	LC
Youngstown State Univ	OH	16,374	LC

DENTAL LABORATORY TECHNOLOGY

School	ST	$IS	SR
Minot State Univ	ND	10,915	C
Southern Illinois Univ Carbondale	IL	21,620	C
Southwest Minn State Univ	MN	14,000	C
Univ of Louisiana at Monroe	LA	12,998	C

DESIGN

School	ST	$IS	SR
Adams State College	CO	13,358	LC
Adelphi Univ	NY	43,130	VC
Andrews Univ	MI	28,030	C+
Arizona State Univ	AZ	18,818	C+
Art Center College of Design	CA	34,044	SP
Auburn Univ	AL	20,052	VC+
Becker College	MA	41,420	LC
Belmont Univ	TN	37,380	VC+
Bennington College	VT	56,990	HC+
Boston Architectural College	MA	18,622	SP
Bowling Green State Univ	OH	18,970	C
Buffalo State/State Univ of Buffalo	NY	15,733	C+
Cal State, Long Beach	CA	17,534	C+
Carnegie Mellon Univ	PA	51,260	MC
Central Mich Univ	MI	18,066	C
Clemson Univ	SC	19,136	HC
College of Art and Design at Lesley Univ	MA	39,730	SP
Concordia Univ St. Paul	MN	27,200	C
Cornish College of the Arts	WA	21,200	SP
Drexel Univ	PA	51,920	HC
Drury Univ	MO	30,319	VC
East Carolina Univ	NC	14,169	C
Eastern Mich Univ	MI	17,961	C
Evangel Univ	MO	23,090	C
Fashion Inst of Technology/SUNY	NY	12,468	SP
Grand Valley State Univ	MI	17,998	VC
Harding Univ	AR	21,432	C+
Hofstra Univ	NY	48,020	VC+
Howard Univ	DC	35,957	C
Iowa State Univ	IA	16,403	C
John Brown Univ	AR	30,996	VC+
Kansas City Art Inst	MO	38,000	SP
Lamar Univ	TX	6,820	LC
Lees-McRae College	NC	33,624	C
Lehigh Univ	PA	55,080	MC
Memphis College of Art	TN	33,550	SP
Minneapolis College of Art and Design	MN	36,700	SP
Missouri State Univ	MO	13,996	VC
National Univ	CA	14,730	SP
New York Univ	NY	61,470	MC
N Car State Univ	NC	16,202	HC
Northern Mich Univ	MI	15,300	VC
Ohio Univ	OH	20,676	VC
Okla Christian Univ	OK	24,975	VC
Okla State Univ	OK	14,310	VC
Olivet College	MI	19,984	C
Otis College of Art and Design	CA	35,404	SP
Parsons The New School for Design	NY	56,610	SP
Penn State Univ/Univ Park	PA	25,404	VC
Radford Univ	VA	17,132	LC
Rochester Inst of Technology	NY	42,450	VC+
Saginaw Valley State Univ	MI	16,869	C
Salem State College	MA	13,161	LC
San Francisco State Univ	CA	18,514	C
San Jose State Univ	CA	19,707	C
Savannah College of Art and Design	GA	46,824	SP
School of the Art Inst of Chicago	IL	44,000	SP
Southern Illinois Univ Carbondale	IL	21,620	C
Texas Tech Univ	TX	14,243	C
Troy Univ	AL	10,650	C
Tusculum College	TN	24,295	C
Univ of Calif at Davis	CA	24,482	HC
Univ of Cincinnati	OH	20,199	VC
Univ of Hartford	CT	42,674	C
Univ of Idaho	ID	14,558	C
Univ of Kansas	KS	16,980	C+
Univ of Mich/Ann Arbor	MI	22,102	HC+
Univ of Missouri/Columbia	MO	18,201	MC
Univ of New Haven	CT	47,740	C
Univ of North Texas	TX	15,628	C
Univ of Notre Dame	IN		MC
Univ of Oregon	OR	20,872	VC
Univ of Pennsylvania	PA	56,106	MC
Univ of Southern Miss	MS	13,170	C
Univ of Texas at Austin	TX	44,074	HC
Univ of Wisc/Green Bay	WI	14,900	C
Washington Univ in St. Louis	MO	58,818	MC
Wayne State Univ	MI	19,493	C
Western Kentucky Univ	KY	11,000	LC
Western Washington Univ	WA	18,519	VC
Xavier Univ	OH	43,740	VC
Youngstown State Univ	OH	16,374	LC

DESIGN AND ENVIRONMENTAL ANALYSIS

School	ST	$IS	SR
Cornell Univ	NY	59,037	MC

DEVELOPMENT ECONOMICS

School	ST	$IS	SR
Calvin College	MI	37,585	VC+
Eastern Mennonite Univ	VA	38,850	VC
Taylor Univ	IN	36,742	VC+

DEVELOPMENTAL PSYCHOLOGY

School	ST	$IS	SR
Brown Univ	RI	56,150	MC
Cal State, Stanislaus	CA	18,582	C
Emmanuel College	MA	47,985	VC
Fitchburg State Univ	MA	17,241	C
Metropolitan State Univ	MN	5,923	SP
New York Univ	NY	61,470	MC
Univ of Kansas	KS	16,980	C+

DEVELOPMENTAL SOCIOLOGY

School	ST	$IS	SR
Cornell Univ	NY	59,037	MC

DIAGNOSTIC MEDICAL SONOGRAPHY

School	ST	$IS	SR
Nova Southeastern Univ	FL	34,016	VC
Thomas Edison State College	NJ	5,700	SP
Univ of Charleston	WV	28,650	C

DIETETICS

School	ST	$IS	SR
Andrews Univ	MI	28,030	C+
Arkansas State Univ	AR	14,980	C
Ball State Univ	IN	17,850	C
Baylor Univ	TX	46,720	HC
Bowling Green State Univ	OH	18,970	C
Bradley Univ	IL	31,874	VC
Brigham Young Univ	UT	12,100	HC
Buffalo State/State Univ of Buffalo	NY	15,733	C+
Cal State, Chico	CA	18,952	C
Cal State, Los Angeles	CA	15,829	C
Central Mich Univ	MI	18,066	C
College of the Ozarks	MO	5,605	VC
Dominican Univ	IL	37,628	C
D'Youville College	NY	29,850	C
East Carolina Univ	NC	14,169	C
Eastern Kentucky Univ	KY	11,161	C
Eastern Mich Univ	MI	17,961	C
Florida International Univ	FL	17,747	VC
Florida State Univ	FL	15,238	HC
Fontbonne Univ	MO	31,384	C
Harding Univ	AR	21,432	C+
Idaho State Univ	ID	11,908	C
Immaculata Univ	PA	43,000	C
Indiana State Univ	IN	16,000	C
Indiana Univ Bloomington	IN	19,358	HC
Iowa State Univ	IA	16,403	C
James Madison Univ	VA	18,049	VC
Kansas State Univ	KS	15,497	VC
Lehman College / The CUNY	NY	5,778	LC
Lipscomb Univ	TN	35,722	VC
Louisiana Tech Univ	LA	8,000	C
Madonna Univ	MI	24,540	VC
Mansfield Univ	PA	19,468	LC
Marshall Univ	WV	14,820	C
Marywood Univ	PA	40,695	C
Messiah College	PA	39,540	VC
Mich State Univ	MI	13,689	VC
Minn State Univ, Mankato	MN	14,900	C
Missouri State Univ	MO	13,996	VC
Montclair State Univ	NJ	22,614	C
Mount Mary Univ	WI	32,836	LC
Nicholls State Univ	LA	7,095	C
N Dak State Univ	ND	14,642	C
Northern Illinois Univ	IL	19,768	C
Oakwood Univ	AL	23,035	C
Ohio Univ	OH	20,676	VC
Olivet Nazarene Univ	IL	29,990	C
Ouachita Baptist Univ	AR	29,010	VC
Point Loma Nazarene Univ	CA	38,610	VC
Prairie View A&M Univ	TX	15,205	LC
Purdue Univ/West Lafayette	IN	20,278	HC
Radford Univ	VA	17,132	LC
Rochester Inst of Technology	NY	42,450	VC+
Samford Univ	AL	35,700	VC+
San Francisco State Univ	CA	18,514	C
Seton Hill Univ	PA	35,172	C
Simmons College	MA	48,770	VC
St. Catherine Univ	MN	37,782	C+
Stephen F. Austin State Univ	TX	14,668	C
SUNY Oneonta / SUNY	NY	16,919	VC
Tarleton State Univ	TX	13,489	LC
Texas Christian Univ	TX	47,570	HC
Texas Southern Univ	TX	18,212	LC
Texas Tech Univ	TX	14,243	C
Texas Woman's Univ	TX	13,633	LC
Thomas Edison State College	NJ	5,700	SP
Tuskegee Univ	AL	26,750	C
Univ of Akron	OH	20,436	C
Univ of Arkansas at Fayetteville	AR	16,860	VC
Univ of Calif at Davis	CA	24,482	HC
Univ of Central Arkansas	AR	10,840	VC
Univ of Central Missouri	MO	14,605	C
Univ of Conn	CT	23,744	HC
Univ of Dayton	OH	43,750	VC
Univ of Delaware	DE	22,728	VC
Univ of Georgia	GA	19,508	VC
Univ of Illinois at Chicago	IL	24,293	VC
Univ of Illinois at Urbana-Champaign	IL	24,300	HC
Univ of Louisiana at Lafayette	LA	6,130	C
Univ of Miss	MS	15,482	VC
Univ of Nebr - Lincoln	NE	17,507	VC
Univ of New Haven	CT	47,740	C
Univ of N Dak	ND	14,094	C
Univ of North Florida	FL	15,578	VC
Univ of Northern Colo	CO	15,973	C
Univ of Texas at Austin	TX	44,074	HC
Univ of Texas-Pan American	TX	12,432	LC
Univ of Vermont	VT	26,120	VC+
Univ of Wisc/Green Bay	WI	14,900	C
Univ of Wisc/Stevens Point	WI	14,043	C
Univ of Wisc/Stout	WI	23,942	C
Virginia Polytechnic Inst and State Univ	VA	14,629	HC
Viterbo Univ	WI	30,070	C
Wayne State Univ	MI	19,493	C
West Chester Univ of Pennsylvania	PA	16,836	C
Western Carolina Univ	NC	13,965	C+
Western Mich Univ	MI	19,042	C
Youngstown State Univ	OH	16,374	LC

DIGITAL ARTS/TECHNOLOGY

School	ST	$IS	SR
Arizona State Univ	AZ	18,818	C+
Arkansas State Univ	AR	14,980	C
Art Academy of Cincinnati	OH	25,940	SP
Baldwin Wallace Univ	OH	36,980	VC
Bennington College	VT	56,990	HC+
Bethel College	IN	31,560	C
Bowling Green State Univ	OH	18,970	C
Calif Baptist Univ	CA	35,890	C
Calif College of the Arts	CA	48,334	SP
Cal State, Dominguez Hills	CA	17,056	LC
Calvin College	MI	37,585	VC+
Chapman Univ	CA	56,019	VC+
Claflin Univ	SC	22,368	C+
Clarkson Univ	NY	53,538	HC
Cogswell Polytechnical College	CA	30,531	C
College for Creative Studies	MI		SP
College of New Jersey	NJ	25,376	HC
Dakota State Univ	SD	13,811	C

ST = STATE **$IS** = IN-STATE COSTS **SR** = SELECTOR RATING

School	ST	$IS	SR
DePaul Univ	IL	46,120	VC
Dominican Univ	IL	37,628	C
Drexel Univ	PA	51,920	HC
Elon Univ	NC	40,046	HC
Gallaudet Univ	DC	25,380	SP
Grace Bible College	MI	20,770	C
Grand Canyon Univ	AZ	24,540	VC
Greenville College	IL	27,012	C
Hamline Univ	MN	44,198	VC
Illinois State Univ	IL	22,634	VC
John Brown Univ	AR	30,996	VC+
Kansas City Art Inst	MO	38,000	SP
Kendall College of Art and Design of Ferris State Univ	MI	21,048	SP
Lake Erie College	OH	35,704	C
Marist College	NY	35,500	C
Memphis College of Art	TN	33,550	SP
Mercy College	NY	29,996	C
Messiah College	PA	39,540	VC
Minneapolis College of Art and Design	MN	36,700	SP
New York Univ	NY	61,470	MC
Northeastern Univ	MA	55,296	MC
Northwest Nazarene Univ	ID	24,275	NC
Ohio Univ	OH	20,676	VC
Olivet Nazarene Univ	IL	29,990	C
Otis College of Art and Design	CA	35,404	SP
Parsons The New School for Design	NY	56,610	SP
Philadelphia Univ	PA	44,160	C
Point Park Univ	PA	36,390	C
Quinnipiac Univ	CT	53,580	VC
Ringling College of Art and Design	FL	46,130	SP
San Francisco Art Inst	CA	52,492	SP
Santa Fe Univ of Art and Design	NM	39,666	SP
Savannah College of Art and Design	GA	46,824	SP
School of the Art Inst of Chicago	IL	44,000	SP
Seattle Univ	WA	47,010	VC+
Southern New Hampshire Univ	NH	38,100	C
Southern Oregon Univ	OR	17,874	C
Southwestern College	KS	29,270	C
Stetson Univ	FL	49,512	VC+
Stevens Inst of Technology	NJ	50,130	HC
Univ of Central Florida	FL	15,711	VC+
Univ of Denver	CO	51,787	VC+
Univ of Idaho	ID	14,558	C
Univ of Illinois at Chicago	IL	24,293	VC
Univ of Maryland/Univ College	MD	6,168	SP
Univ of Oregon	OR	20,872	VC
Univ of Pennsylvania	PA	56,106	MC
Univ of Tampa	FL	35,160	VC
Viterbo Univ	WI	30,070	C
Walla Walla Univ	WA	26,256	NC
Washington State Univ	WA	20,461	C
Worcester Polytechnic Inst	MA	53,440	HC+
Youngstown State Univ	OH	16,374	LC

DIGITAL COMMUNICATIONS

School	ST	$IS	SR
Albright College	PA	46,660	C
Arkansas State Univ	AR	14,980	C
Bennington College	VT	56,990	HC+
Bethany College	WV	35,282	C
Calvin College	MI	37,585	VC+
Canisius College	NY	45,602	VC
Endicott College	MA	42,390	C
Florida Southern College	FL	38,240	VC
Hilbert College	NY	28,550	C
Indiana Inst of Technology	IN	34,240	LC
Juniata College	PA	49,340	VC
Kansas City Art Inst	MO	38,000	SP
King Univ	TN	33,140	C
Lycoming College	PA	43,636	C
Marywood Univ	PA	40,695	C
Mass Inst of Technology	MA	54,238	MC
Muskingum Univ	OH	30,502	C
Neumann Univ	PA	31,078	LC
New York Univ	NY	61,470	MC
Ohio Univ	OH	20,676	VC
Olivet Nazarene Univ	IL	29,990	C
Queens Univ of Charlotte	NC	39,543	VC
Spring Hill College	AL	42,130	VC
St. Edward's Univ	TX	44,674	VC
St. John Fisher College	NY	39,370	C+
Syracuse Univ	NY	54,512	HC
Trevecca Nazarene Univ	TN	30,118	C
Univ of Cincinnati	OH	20,199	VC
Univ of Idaho	ID	14,558	C
Univ of Oregon	OR	20,872	VC
Valparaiso Univ	IN	43,040	VC+
Vanguard Univ of Southern Calif	CA	35,833	VC
Washington State Univ	WA	20,461	C
Webster Univ	MO	33,990	C+
Wheeling Jesuit Univ	WV	34,668	C
William Penn Univ	IA	26,000	C

DRAFTING AND DESIGN

School	ST	$IS	SR
Pennsylvania College of Technology	PA	25,653	NC

DRAFTING AND DESIGN TECHNOLOGY

School	ST	$IS	SR
Alabama A&M Univ	AL	96,100	C
Baker College of Flint	MI	7,800	NC
Montana State Univ-Northern	MT	12,500	NC
Norfolk State Univ	VA	10,531	LC
School of the Art Inst of Chicago	IL	44,000	SP
Texas Southern Univ	TX	18,212	LC
Trine Univ	IN	39,400	VC
Univ of Central Missouri	MO	14,605	C
Univ of Rio Grande	OH	8,750	NC
Western Mich Univ	MI	19,042	C

DRAMA EDUCATION

School	ST	$IS	SR
Appalachian State Univ	NC	12,919	VC
Augustana College	SD	35,500	VC
Averett Univ	VA	36,000	LC
Baylor Univ	TX	46,720	HC
Bennington College	VT	56,990	HC+
Boston Univ	MA	54,130	HC+
Bradley Univ	IL	31,874	VC
Bridgewater State Univ	MA	18,752	C
Brigham Young Univ	UT	12,100	HC
Columbus State Univ	GA	13,176	C
Culver-Stockton College	MO	30,900	C
East Carolina Univ	NC	14,169	C
East Texas Baptist Univ	TX	29,135	C
Eastern Mich Univ	MI	17,961	C
Fontbonne Univ	MO	31,384	C
Friends Univ	KS	29,100	C
Greensboro College	NC	28,740	LC
Hardin-Simmons Univ	TX	23,560	C+
Lees-McRae College	NC	33,624	C
Mars Hill College	NC	22,950	LC
Minot State Univ	ND	10,915	C
Missouri Southern State Univ	MO	11,910	C
Morehouse College	GA	38,640	C
Old Dominion Univ	VA	18,662	C
Oral Roberts Univ	OK	31,734	C
Point Park Univ	PA	36,390	C
Saginaw Valley State Univ	MI	16,869	C
Southwestern College	KS	29,270	C
St. Edward's Univ	TX	44,674	VC
The Catholic Univ of America	DC	52,852	VC
Trevecca Nazarene Univ	TN	30,118	C
Univ of Evansville	IN	41,056	VC+
Univ of Indianapolis	IN	31,740	LC
Univ of Maryland	MD	18,801	HC
Univ of Montana-Western	MT	9,753	LC
Univ of Nebr - Lincoln	NE	17,507	VC
Univ of New Mexico	NM	15,300	C
Univ of N Car at Charlotte	NC	15,847	C
Univ of N Car at Greensboro	NC	12,848	C
West Texas A&M Univ	TX	13,478	C
York College	NE	19,475	C

DRAMATIC ARTS

School	ST	$IS	SR
Abilene Christian Univ	TX	38,400	VC
Adams State College	CO	13,358	LC
Adelphi Univ	NY	43,130	VC
Adrian College	MI	33,800	C
Agnes Scott College	GA	45,323	VC+
Alabama A&M Univ	AL	96,100	C
Alabama State Univ	AL	14,142	NC
Albany State Univ	GA	8,500	C
Albertus Magnus College	CT	37,382	LC
Albright College	PA	46,660	C
Alfred Univ	NY	40,392	VC
Allegheny College	PA	49,020	HC
Alma College	MI	42,400	VC
American Univ	DC	54,829	HC+
Anderson Univ	IN	35,390	C
Appalachian State Univ	NC	12,919	VC
Arcadia Univ	PA	33,570	C+
Arizona State Univ	AZ	18,818	C+
Armstrong Atlantic State Univ	GA	16,276	C
Asbury Univ	KY	32,038	VC
Ashland Univ	OH	25,000	C
Auburn Univ	AL	20,052	VC+
Augsburg College	MN	35,142	C
Augustana College	IL	43,398	HC
Augustana College	SD	35,500	VC
Aurora Univ	IL	26,870	C
Averett Univ	VA	36,000	LC
Avila Univ	MO	26,900	C
Baker Univ	KS	33,350	C+
Ball State Univ	IN	17,850	C
Bard College	NY	59,872	HC
Bard College at Simon's Rock	MA	58,963	HC+
Barry Univ	FL	38,190	C
Barton College	NC	27,660	C
Baylor Univ	TX	46,720	HC
Belhaven Univ	MS	27,170	C
Beloit College	WI	49,970	HC
Benedictine College	KS	29,180	VC
Bennington College	VT	56,990	HC+
Berea College	KY	7,220	HC
Bethel College	IN	31,560	C
Bethel Univ	MN	34,940	VC
Bethune-Cookman Univ	FL	22,290	LC
Binghamton Univ / The SUNY	NY	20,832	HC+
Biola Univ	CA	40,320	VC
Birmingham-Southern College	AL	42,370	VC+
Bloomsburg Univ of Pennsylvania	PA	13,598	C
Boise State Univ	ID	12,802	C
Boston College	MA	58,506	MC
Boston Univ	MA	54,130	HC+
Bradley Univ	IL	31,874	VC
Brenau Univ Women's College	GA	26,650	C+
Brewton-Parker College	GA	33,388	LC
Briar Cliff Univ	IA	29,514	C
Brigham Young Univ	UT	12,100	HC
Bucknell Univ	PA	58,160	MC
Buffalo State/State Univ of Buffalo	NY	15,733	C+
Butler Univ	IN	45,898	VC+
Calif Baptist Univ	CA	35,890	C
Calif Inst of the Arts	CA	46,368	SP
Calif State Polytechnic Univ, Pomona	CA	18,932	C
Cal State, Bakersfield	CA	8,000	LC
Cal State, Dominguez Hills	CA	17,056	LC
Cal State, East Bay	CA	16,549	C
Cal State, Fresno	CA	17,405	C
Cal State, Fullerton	CA	25,188	C+
Cal State, Long Beach	CA	17,534	C+
Cal State, Los Angeles	CA	15,829	C
Cal State, Northridge	CA	28,313	C
Cal State, Sacramento	CA	16,200	C
Cal State, San Bernardino	CA	12,000	C
Cal State, Stanislaus	CA	18,582	C
Calif Univ of Pennsylvania	PA	14,217	C
Calvin College	MI	37,585	VC+
Campbell Univ	NC	25,500	C
Capital Univ	OH	39,824	VC
Cardinal Stritch Univ	WI	24,054	C
Carnegie Mellon Univ	PA	51,260	MC
Carroll College	MT	28,000	C
Carroll Univ	WI	24,860	C
Case Western Reserve Univ	OH	55,178	MC
Castleton State College	VT	19,424	C
Cedar Crest College	PA	43,240	C
Centenary College	NJ	38,618	LC
Centenary College of Louisiana	LA	39,070	C+
Central College	IA	36,980	VC
Central Conn State Univ	CT	19,212	C
Central Methodist Univ	MO	28,240	VC
Central Mich Univ	MI	18,066	C
Central Washington Univ	WA	11,730	C
Centre College	KY	35,000	HC+
Chadron State College	NE	7,400	NC
Chapman Univ	CA	56,019	VC+
Charleston Southern Univ	SC	22,420	C
Cheyney Univ of Pennsylvania	PA	20,372	LC
Clarion Univ of Pennsylvania	PA	17,370	C
Clark Univ	MA	47,020	HC+
Clarke Univ	IA	36,400	C
Cleveland State Univ	OH	21,357	C
Coastal Carolina Univ	SC	17,620	C
Coker College	SC	32,256	LC
Colgate Univ	NY	50,930	MC
College of Staten Island / The CUNY	NY	16,778	NC
College of the Holy Cross	MA	56,232	MC
College of the Ozarks	MO	5,605	VC
College of William & Mary	VA	25,085	MC
College of Wooster	OH	52,600	VC
Colo College	CO	54,534	MC
Colo State Univ-Fort Collins	CO	20,090	VC
Columbia College Chicago	IL	30,940	LC
Columbia Univ in the City of New York	NY	61,116	MC
Columbia Univ/Barnard College	NY	39,000	MC
Columbia Univ/School of General Studies	NY	54,083	MC
Columbus State Univ	GA	13,176	C
Concordia College, Moorhead	MN	39,974	C+
Concordia Univ - Irvine	CA	35,390	VC
Concordia Univ Nebr	NE	26,000	VC
Concordia Univ St. Paul	MN	27,200	C
Concordia Univ, Ann Arbor	MI	27,220	VC
Conn College	CT	54,970	MC
Cornell College	IA	44,930	HC
Cornish College of the Arts	WA	21,200	SP
Covenant College	GA		VC+
Creighton Univ	NE	44,058	VC+
Culver-Stockton College	MO	30,900	C
CUNY-City College	NY	19,576	HC+
Dakota Wesleyan Univ	SD	23,000	C
Dartmouth College	NH	57,996	MC
Davidson College	NC	54,683	MC
Davis and Elkins College	WV	33,742	C
De Sales Univ	PA	42,670	C
Denison Univ	OH	54,670	HC+
DePaul Univ	IL	46,120	VC
Doane College	NE	33,730	VC
Dominican Univ	IL	37,628	C
Dordt College	IA	34,160	VC
Drake Univ	IA	30,980	VC+
Drury Univ	MO	30,319	VC
Duke Univ	NC	50,250	MC
Duquesne Univ	PA	42,017	VC
Earlham College	IN	49,710	VC+
East Carolina Univ	NC	14,169	C
East Central Univ	OK	10,223	LC
East Stroudsburg Univ of Pennsylvania	PA	16,636	C
East Texas Baptist Univ	TX	29,135	C
Eastern Illinois Univ	IL	20,502	C
Eastern Kentucky Univ	KY	11,161	C
Eastern Mennonite Univ	VA	38,850	VC
Eastern Mich Univ	MI	17,961	C
Eastern Nazarene College	MA	30,000	C
Eastern New Mexico Univ	NM	10,682	C
Eastern Oregon Univ	OR	10,400	C
Eastern Washington Univ	WA	16,388	C
Eckerd College	FL	43,902	VC
Edinboro Univ of Pennsylvania	PA	15,940	LC
Elizabethtown College	PA	47,600	VC
Elmira College	NY	49,950	C+
Elon Univ	NC	40,046	HC
Emerson College	MA	50,246	HC
Emory and Henry College	VA	387,460	C
Emory Univ	GA	45,000	MC
Emporia State Univ	KS	12,897	C
Eugene Lang College - The New School for Liberal Arts	NY	55,650	VC
Eureka College	IL	19,280	C
Evangel Univ	MO	23,090	C
Fairleigh Dickinson Univ/College at Florham	NJ	42,142	C
Fayetteville State Univ	NC	10,816	C
Ferrum College	VA	27,740	LC
Fisk Univ	TN	19,830	C
Fitchburg State Univ	MA	17,241	C
Five Towns College	NY	34,550	SP
Flagler College	FL	24,960	VC
Florida A&M Univ	FL	14,935	LC
Florida Atlantic Univ	FL	17,339	C
Florida International Univ	FL	17,747	VC
Florida Southern College	FL	38,240	VC
Florida State Univ	FL	15,238	HC
Fontbonne Univ	MO	31,384	C
Fordham Univ	NY	58,927	HC
Fort Lewis College	CO	15,513	C
Francis Marion Univ	SC	16,464	LC
Franciscan Univ of Steubenville	OH	27,320	VC
Franklin and Marshall College	PA	58,295	MC
Franklin Pierce Univ	NH	41,598	C
Freed-Hardeman Univ	TN	19,697	VC
Frostburg State Univ	MD	15,264	LC
Furman Univ	SC	54,006	HC
Gannon Univ	PA	37,940	C
George Fox Univ	OR	40,750	C+
George Mason Univ	VA	15,724	VC
George Washington Univ	DC	57,108	MC
Georgetown College	KY	38,690	C
Georgia College and State Univ	GA	18,216	VC
Gettysburg College	PA	56,820	HC
Goddard College	VT	16,418	VC
Gonzaga Univ	WA	44,247	HC
Gordon College	MA	42,660	VC+
Goshen College	IN	35,900	VC
Graceland Univ	IA	28,020	C
Grand Valley State Univ	MI	17,998	VC
Greensboro College	NC	28,740	LC
Greenville College	IL	27,012	C
Grinnell College	IA	53,654	HC
Guilford College	NC	35,340	C
Gustavus Adolphus College	MN	48,170	HC
Hamilton College	NY	55,620	MC
Hamline Univ	MN	44,198	VC
Hampshire College	MA	58,320	MC
Hampton Univ	VA	28,528	C
Hannibal-LaGrange Univ	MO	24,490	C
Hanover College	IN	41,450	VC
Harding Univ	AR	21,432	C+
Hardin-Simmons Univ	TX	23,560	C+
Hartwick College	NY	49,815	C+
Hastings College	NE	27,782	C+
Heidelberg Univ	OH	34,100	C
Henderson State Univ	AR	13,634	C
Hendrix College	AR	48,436	HC+
Hillsdale College	MI	31,890	HC+
Hiram College	OH	37,300	VC
Hofstra Univ	NY	48,020	VC+
Hollins Univ	VA	43,295	VC
Hope College	MI	36,320	VC+
Howard Payne Univ	TX	17,115	C

School	ST	$IS	SR
Howard Univ	DC	35,957	C
Humboldt State Univ	CA	18,400	C
Hunter College / The CUNY	NY	14,429	VC
Huntington Univ	IN	32,220	C
Idaho State Univ	ID	11,908	C
Illinois College	IL	25,770	VC
Illinois State Univ	IL	22,634	VC
Indiana State Univ	IN	16,000	C
Indiana Univ-Purdue Univ Fort Wayne	IN	15,425	C
Ithaca College	NY	52,300	HC
Jacksonville State Univ	AL	12,280	LC
Jacksonville Univ	FL	37,780	C
James Madison Univ	VA	18,049	VC
Judson Univ	IL	25,130	C
Juilliard School	NY	44,460	SP
Juniata College	PA	49,340	VC
Kalamazoo College	MI	47,825	HC+
Kansas State Univ	KS	15,497	VC
Kansas Wesleyan Univ	KS	32,000	C
Kent State Univ	OH	19,352	C
Kenyon College	OH	56,810	MC
King's College	PA	41,678	C
Knox College	IL		VC
Kutztown Univ of Pennsylvania	PA	16,909	LC
Lakeland College	WI	22,990	C
Lamar Univ	TX	6,820	LC
Lander Univ	SC	22,514	C+
Langston Univ	OK	3,000	LC
Lawrence Univ	WI	46,371	HC
Le Moyne College	NY	42,200	VC
Lee Univ	TN	18,690	C+
Lees-McRae College	NC	33,624	C
Lenoir-Rhyne College	NC	35,984	C
Lewis & Clark College	OR	52,656	VC
Lewis Univ	IL	23,050	C
Lindenwood Univ	MO	20,750	C
Linfield College-McMinnville Campus	OR	46,166	C
Livingstone College	NC	17,815	LC
LIU/C.W. Post Campus	NY	38,888	C
Louisiana College	LA	15,746	C
Louisiana State Univ	LA	18,677	VC+
Loyola Marymount Univ	CA	53,240	VC+
Loyola Univ New Orleans	LA	46,581	VC
Luther College	IA	44,380	VC+
Lycoming College	PA	43,636	C
Lynn Univ	FL	43,500	C
Lyon College	AR	30,246	VC
Macalester College	MN	53,419	MC
MacMurray College	IL	20,755	C
Maharishi Univ of Management	IA	31,000	VC
Manhattanville College	NY	46,260	VC
Marietta College	OH	42,135	VC
Marlboro College	VT	35,980	VC
Marquette Univ	WI	43,664	VC+
Mars Hill College	NC	22,950	LC
Mary Baldwin College	VA	37,110	C
Marymount Manhattan College	NY	40,118	VC
Maryville College	TN	33,150	VC
Marywood Univ	PA	40,695	C
McDaniel College	MD	45,600	VC
McKendree Univ	IL	29,920	C+
McMurry Univ	TX	25,962	LC
McPherson College	KS	28,138	C
Mercer Univ	GA	44,201	VC+
Meredith College	NC	31,420	C
Messiah College	PA	39,540	VC
Methodist Univ	NC	37,185	C
Metropolitan State Univ	MN	5,923	SP
Miami Univ	OH	24,191	HC
Mich State Univ	MI	13,689	VC
MidAmerica Nazarene Univ	KS	28,000	C
Middlebury College	VT	57,470	MC
Midwestern State Univ	TX	9,722	C
Millikin Univ	IL	37,462	C
Minn State Univ, Mankato	MN	14,900	C
Minn State Univ, Moorhead	MN	13,392	C
Missouri Southern State Univ	MO	11,910	C
Missouri Valley College	MO	22,200	C
Monmouth College	IL	39,290	C
Montana State Univ-Billings	MT	12,425	LC
Montana State Univ-Northern	MT	12,500	NC
Montclair State Univ	NJ	22,614	C
Moravian College	PA	36,381	VC
Morehead State Univ	KY	10,900	C
Morgan State Univ	MD	14,500	VC
Morningside College	IA	32,620	C
Mount Holyoke College	MA	53,596	HC+
Mount Vernon Nazarene Univ	OH	29,590	C
Muhlenberg College	PA	52,837	HC
Murray State Univ	KY	14,944	C
Muskingum Univ	OH	30,502	C
Nebr Wesleyan Univ	NE	29,774	C+
New England College	NH	45,930	LC
New Mexico State Univ	NM	13,955	LC
New York Univ	NY	61,470	MC
Newberry College	SC	26,850	LC
Niagara Univ	NY	39,800	C
N Car Agricultural and Technical State Univ	NC	13,175	LC
N Car Central Univ	NC	9,000	LC
N Car Wesleyan College	NC	29,440	C
N Dak State Univ	ND	14,642	C
Northeastern Univ	MA	55,296	MC
Northern Illinois Univ	IL	19,768	C
Northern Kentucky Univ	KY	15,302	LC
Northern Mich Univ	MI	15,300	VC
Northwest Missouri State Univ	MO	14,229	C
Northwestern College	MN	24,000	C
Northwestern College of Iowa	IA	34,848	C+
Northwestern Okla State Univ	OK	7,276	NC
Northwestern State Univ of Louisiana	LA	14,308	C
Northwestern Univ	IL	37,595	MC
Notre Dame de Namur Univ	CA	41,610	LC
Nova Southeastern Univ	FL	34,016	VC
Oakland Univ	MI	19,391	VC
Oberlin College	OH	57,025	MC
Ohio Northern Univ	OH	42,075	VC
Ohio Univ	OH	20,676	VC
Ohio Wesleyan Univ	OH	49,460	C+
Okla Baptist Univ	OK	28,202	VC
Okla State Univ	OK	14,310	VC
Old Dominion Univ	VA	18,662	C
Olivet Nazarene Univ	IL	29,990	C
Oral Roberts Univ	OK	31,734	C
Oswego / SUNY	NY	20,009	VC
Ottawa Univ	KS	15,000	VC
Otterbein College	OH	32,214	C
Ouachita Baptist Univ	AR	29,010	VC
Our Lady of the Lake Univ of San Antonio	TX	22,430	LC
Pacific Univ	OR	42,815	C
Park Univ	MO	17,525	C
Pepperdine Univ	CA	55,372	HC+
Piedmont College	GA	29,260	C
Pittsburg State Univ	KS	12,032	C
Pitzer College	CA	54,988	MC
Point Loma Nazarene Univ	CA	38,610	VC
Point Park Univ	PA	36,390	C
Portland State Univ	OR	18,672	C
Prairie View A&M Univ	TX	15,205	LC
Presbyterian College	SC	42,070	VC
Prescott College	AZ	33,284	C+
Principia College	IL	35,140	C+
Providence College	RI	55,995	HC
Purchase College / SUNY	NY	16,951	C
Purdue Univ/West Lafayette	IN	20,278	HC
Queens College / The CUNY	NY	17,107	VC
Queens Univ of Charlotte	NC	39,543	VC
Quinnipiac Univ	CT	53,580	VC
Ramapo College of New Jersey	NJ	24,938	C+
Randolph College	VA	43,960	VC
Randolph-Macon College	VA	45,086	C
Reed College	OR	57,780	MC
Rhode Island College	RI	17,132	LC
Richard Stockton College of New Jersey	NJ	20,000	VC
Rider Univ	NJ	45,720	C
Ripon College	WI	36,959	C+
Rockford College	IL	31,000	C
Rocky Mountain College	MT	32,242	C
Roger Williams Univ	RI	45,788	C
Rollins College	FL	52,370	HC
Roosevelt Univ	IL	22,605	VC
Rowan Univ	NJ	23,570	VC
Rutgers, The State Univ of New Jersey/Camden Campus	NJ	24,254	C
Rutgers, The State Univ of New Jersey/New Brunswick	NJ	25,077	VC
Rutgers, The State Univ of New Jersey/Newark Campus	NJ	25,376	C
Saginaw Valley State Univ	MI	16,869	C
St. Joseph's College	IN	35,790	C
St. Louis Univ	MO	46,594	VC+
St. Michael's College	VT	48,740	VC
Salem State College	MA	13,161	LC
Salve Regina Univ	RI	47,250	VC
Sam Houston State Univ	TX	17,082	C
San Francisco State Univ	CA	18,514	C
San Jose State Univ	CA	19,707	C
Santa Fe Univ of Art and Design	NM	39,666	SP
Sarah Lawrence College	NY	48,000	HC
Schreiner Univ	TX	32,734	LC
Scripps College	CA	54,900	MC
Seton Hill Univ	PA	35,172	C
Shenandoah Univ	VA	39,268	C
Shorter Univ	GA	26,470	C
Simpson College	IA	36,086	VC
Skidmore College	NY	57,926	HC
Smith College	MA	57,524	MC
S Car State Univ	SC	6,700	LC
S Dak State Univ	SD	14,296	C
Southeastern Okla State Univ	OK	7,966	C
Southeastern Univ	FL	27,201	C+
Southern Conn State Univ	CT	18,033	C
Southern Illinois Univ Carbondale	IL	21,620	C
Southern Illinois Univ Edwardsville	IL	17,532	C
Southern Methodist Univ	TX	57,755	MC
Southern Oregon Univ	OR	17,874	C
Southern Univ and A&M College	LA	9,761	C+
Southwest Minn State Univ	MN	14,000	C
Southwestern College	KS	29,270	C
Southwestern Univ	TX	45,660	VC
Spelman College	GA	24,650	VC
St. Bonaventure Univ	NY	38,831	C
St. Catherine Univ	MN	37,782	C+
St. Cloud State Univ	MN	10,600	C
St. John's Univ	NY	52,840	C+
St. Lawrence Univ	NY	53,740	HC
St. Mary's College of Maryland	MD	26,699	HC
Stanford Univ	CA	56,411	MC
Stephen F. Austin State Univ	TX	14,668	C
Stephens College	MO	34,500	VC
Sterling College	KS	27,216	C
Stetson Univ	FL	49,512	VC+
Stevenson Univ	MD	39,572	C
Stony Brook Univ / SUNY	NY	19,359	HC
Suffolk Univ	MA	46,548	C
Sul Ross State Univ	TX	13,410	LC
SUNY Fredonia / The SUNY at Fredonia	NY	18,702	VC
SUNY New Paltz	NY	15,010	C
SUNY Oneonta / SUNY	NY	16,919	VC
Swarthmore College	PA	57,870	MC
Sweet Briar College	VA	43,765	C+
Syracuse Univ	NY	54,512	HC
Tarleton State Univ	TX	13,489	LC
Taylor Univ	IN	36,742	VC+
Tenn State Univ	TN	9,048	C
Texas A&M Univ at Commerce	TX	10,496	C
Texas A&M Univ at Corpus Christi	TX	11,544	LC
Texas A&M Univ at Kingsville	TX	7,500	LC
Texas Lutheran Univ	TX	34,070	C
Texas Southern Univ	TX	18,212	LC
Texas State Univ	TX	16,495	VC
Texas Tech Univ	TX	14,243	C
Texas Wesleyan Univ	TX	29,886	C
Texas Woman's Univ	TX	13,633	LC
The Catholic Univ of America	DC	52,852	VC
Thomas More College	KY	34,760	C
Transylvania Univ	KY	40,310	VC+
Trevecca Nazarene Univ	TN	30,118	C
Trinity College	CT		HC+
Trinity Univ	TX	44,174	HC+
Troy Univ	AL	10,650	C
Truman State Univ	MO	13,546	HC
Tufts Univ	MA	58,780	MC
Tulane Univ	LA	58,942	MC
Union College	KY	28,775	C
Union Univ	TN	28,260	VC
Univ of Alabama at Birmingham	AL	18,484	C+
Univ of Alaska Anchorage	AK	15,290	NC
Univ of Arkansas at Fayetteville	AR	16,860	VC
Univ of Arkansas at Little Rock	AR		C
Univ of Calif at Berkeley	CA	23,322	MC
Univ of Calif at Davis	CA	24,482	HC
Univ of Calif at Irvine	CA	25,961	VC
Univ of Calif at Los Angeles	CA	25,686	MC
Univ of Calif at Riverside	CA	27,204	C
Univ of Calif at San Diego	CA	21,000	VC
Univ of Calif at Santa Barbara	CA	27,551	HC
Univ of Calif at Santa Cruz	CA	27,807	VC
Univ of Central Florida	FL	15,711	VC+
Univ of Cincinnati	OH	20,199	VC
Univ of Conn	CT	23,744	HC
Univ of Dallas	TX	43,510	VC+
Univ of Dayton	OH	43,750	VC
Univ of Denver	CO	51,787	VC+
Univ of Detroit Mercy	MI	30,450	C
Univ of Evansville	IN	41,056	VC+
Univ of Findlay	OH	31,916	C
Univ of Hartford	CT	42,674	C
Univ of Hawaii at Manoa	HI	19,379	VC
Univ of Idaho	ID	14,558	C
Univ of Illinois at Chicago	IL	24,293	VC
Univ of Illinois at Urbana-Champaign	IL	24,300	HC
Univ of Indianapolis	IN	31,740	LC
Univ of Iowa	IA	17,481	VC
Univ of Kansas	KS	16,980	C+
Univ of Kentucky	KY	19,868	C
Univ of La Verne	CA	47,010	VC
Univ of Louisiana at Lafayette	LA	6,130	C
Univ of Louisville	KY	17,460	VC
Univ of Maine	ME	19,712	C+
Univ of Mary Washington	VA	19,484	VC
Univ of Maryland	MD	18,801	HC
Univ of Maryland/Baltimore County	MD	18,000	VC
Univ of Mass Amherst	MA	23,697	VC+
Univ of Mass Boston	MA	11,966	C
Univ of Memphis	TN	15,094	C
Univ of Mich/Ann Arbor	MI	22,102	HC+
Univ of Mich-Flint	MI	17,547	C+
Univ of Minn/Duluth	MN	18,964	C+
Univ of Minn/Morris	MN	17,150	VC
Univ of Missouri/Columbia	MO	18,201	MC
Univ of Missouri-Kansas City	MO	19,603	C
Univ of Missouri-St. Louis	MO	18,304	VC
Univ of Montana	MT	13,670	C
Univ of Montana-Western	MT	9,753	LC
Univ of Montevallo	AL	17,320	C
Univ of Mount Union	OH	35,130	C
Univ of Nebr - Lincoln	NE	17,507	VC
Univ of Nebr at Kearney	NE	14,855	LC
Univ of Nebr at Omaha	NE	12,700	C
Univ of Nevada, Las Vegas	NV	17,303	C
Univ of Nevada/Reno	NV	14,500	NC
Univ of New Orleans	LA	9,224	VC
Univ of North Alabama	AL	9,960	C
Univ of N Car at Asheville	NC	13,500	VC+
Univ of N Car at Chapel Hill	NC	18,348	MC
Univ of N Car at Charlotte	NC	15,847	C
Univ of N Car at Greensboro	NC	12,848	C
Univ of N Car at Wilmington	NC	13,572	VC+
Univ of N Car School of the Arts	NC	7,401	SP
Univ of North Texas	TX	15,628	C
Univ of Northern Iowa	IA	14,776	C
Univ of Okla	OK	17,634	VC+
Univ of Oregon	OR	20,872	VC
Univ of Pennsylvania	PA	56,106	MC
Univ of Pittsburgh at Johnstown	PA	20,862	LC
Univ of Portland	OR	47,874	VC
Univ of PR Recinto de Rio Piedras	PR	5,750	
Univ of Puget Sound	WA	52,648	HC+
Univ of Redlands	CA	40,500	VC
Univ of St. Mary	KS	28,400	C+
Univ of Science and Arts of Okla	OK	10,560	VC
Univ of South Alabama	AL	13,510	C
Univ of S Car at Columbia	SC	19,725	VC+
Univ of S Dak	SD	15,111	C
Univ of South Florida	FL	13,000	C
Univ of Southern Calif	CA	56,903	MC
Univ of Southern Maine	ME	16,576	C
Univ of Southern Miss	MS	13,170	C
Univ of St. Thomas - Houston	TX	36,490	VC
Univ of Tampa	FL	35,160	VC
Univ of Tenn at Chattanooga	TN	16,883	C
Univ of Texas at Arlington	TX	10,908	LC
Univ of Texas at Austin	TX	44,074	HC
Univ of Texas at El Paso	TX	8,764	NC
Univ of Texas-Pan American	TX	12,432	LC
Univ of the Cumberlands	KY	27,500	LC
Univ of the District of Columbia	DC	7,244	LC
Univ of the Incarnate Word	TX	35,200	LC
Univ of the Ozarks	AR	22,100	C
Univ of the Pacific	CA	52,146	VC
Univ of Toledo	OH	18,464	C
Univ of Utah	UT	13,462	VC
Univ of Vermont	VT	26,120	VC+
Univ of Virginia	VA	22,175	MC
Univ of Virginia's College at Wise	VA	11,076	C
Univ of Washington	WA	14,722	VC
Univ of Wisc Whitewater	WI	13,314	C
Univ of Wisc/Green Bay	WI	14,900	C
Univ of Wisc/La Crosse	WI	14,755	VC
Univ of Wisc/Madison	WI	18,757	HC
Univ of Wisc/Parkside	WI	10,181	LC
Univ of Wisc/Stevens Point	WI	14,043	C
Univ of Wisc/Superior	WI	14,106	C
Univ of Wisc-Milwaukee	WI	18,436	C
Ursinus College	PA	55,630	VC+
Utah State Univ	UT	11,803	C
Valparaiso Univ	IN	43,040	VC+
Vanguard Univ of Southern Calif	CA	35,833	VC
Vassar College	NY	59,070	MC
Virginia Commonwealth Univ	VA	18,633	C
Virginia Intermont College	VA	32,411	LC
Virginia Polytechnic Inst and State Univ	VA	14,629	HC
Virginia Wesleyan College	VA	28,433	LC
Viterbo Univ	WI	30,070	C
Wabash College	IN	44,160	VC
Wagner College	NY	48,600	VC
Wartburg College	IA	41,055	VC
Washburn Univ	KS	12,165	NC
Washington and Lee Univ	VA	52,812	MC
Washington College	MD	48,768	VC

ST = STATE $IS = IN-STATE COSTS SR = SELECTOR RATING

School	ST	$IS	SR
Washington Univ in St. Louis	MO	58,818	MC
Wayland Baptist Univ	TX	16,058	LC
Wayne State College	NE	11,764	NC
Wayne State Univ	MI	19,493	C
Webster Univ	MO	33,990	C+
Wellesley College	MA	49,848	MC
Wells College	NY	38,680	VC
Wesleyan College	GA	24,000	C+
Wesleyan Univ	CT	59,844	MC
West Chester Univ of Pennsylvania	PA	16,836	C
West Texas A&M Univ	TX	13,478	C
West Virginia Univ	WV	15,794	C+
West Virginia Wesleyan College	WV	26,880	C
Western Carolina Univ	NC	13,965	C+
Western Conn State Univ	CT	18,327	C
Western Illinois Univ	IL	20,130	C
Western Kentucky Univ	KY	11,000	LC
Western Mich Univ	MI	19,042	C
Western Oregon Univ	OR	15,021	C
Western State Colo Univ	CO	16,135	C
Western Washington Univ	WA	18,519	VC
Westfield State Univ	MA	18,489	C
Westminster College	PA	31,290	C+
Westminster College	UT	37,708	VC
Westmont College	CA	41,500	HC
Wheaton College	MA	54,934	HC+
Whittier College	CA	43,416	C
Whitworth Univ	WA	45,826	VC+
Wilkes Univ	PA	42,786	C
Willamette Univ	OR	56,450	VC+
William Carey Univ	MS	13,500	LC
William Jewell College	MO	31,000	VC+
William Paterson Univ of New Jersey	NJ	21,694	C
William Woods Univ	MO		C
Williams College	MA	58,900	MC
Wilmington College	OH	29,784	C
Winona State Univ	MN	16,530	C
Wisc Lutheran College	WI	23,510	VC
Wittenberg Univ	OH	47,766	VC
Wofford College	SC	45,795	VC
Wright State Univ	OH	16,983	C
Yale Univ	CT	55,300	MC
York College / CUNY	NY	5,496	NC
York College of Pennsylvania	PA	26,590	C
Youngstown State Univ	OH	16,374	LC

DRAWING

School	ST	$IS	SR
Adams State College	CO	13,358	LC
Aquinas College	MI	33,060	C
Art Academy of Cincinnati	OH	25,940	SP
Bard College at Simon's Rock	MA	58,963	HC+
Bennington College	VT	56,990	HC+
Biola Univ	CA	40,320	VC
Calif College of the Arts	CA	48,334	SP
Cleveland Inst of Art	OH	48,641	SP
College of Visual Arts - School is Closed	MN	24,310	SP
Ferris State Univ	MI	19,698	C
Indiana Univ South Bend	IN	15,293	C
Indiana Univ Southeast	IN	15,807	LC
Indiana Univ-Purdue Univ Fort Wayne	IN	15,425	C
Kendall College of Art and Design of Ferris State Univ	MI	21,048	SP
Kutztown Univ of Pennsylvania	PA	16,909	LC
Laguna College of Art and Design	CA	26,500	SP
Lewis Univ	IL	23,050	C
Maryland Inst College of Art	MD	39,500	SP
Memphis College of Art	TN	33,550	SP
Milwaukee Inst of Art and Design	WI	31,938	SP
Minneapolis College of Art and Design	MN	36,700	SP
Olivet Nazarene Univ	IL	29,990	C
Pacific Northwest College of Art	OR	38,494	SP
School of the Art Inst of Chicago	IL	44,000	SP
Univ of Hartford	CT	42,674	C
Univ of Iowa	IA	17,481	VC
Univ of Mich/Ann Arbor	MI	22,102	HC+
Univ of San Francisco	CA	49,674	VC
Washington Univ in St. Louis	MO	58,818	MC

DUTCH

School	ST	$IS	SR
Calvin College	MI	37,585	VC+
Dordt College	IA	34,160	VC
Univ of Calif at Berkeley	CA	23,322	MC

EARLY CHILDHOOD EDUCATION

School	ST	$IS	SR
Abilene Christian Univ	TX	38,400	VC
Alabama A&M Univ	AL	96,100	C
Alabama State Univ	AL	14,142	NC
Albany State Univ	GA	8,500	C
Alfred Univ	NY	40,392	VC
American International College	MA	36,100	LC
American Univ	DC	54,829	HC+
Anna Maria College	MA	34,600	LC
Aquinas College	MI	33,060	C
Arcadia Univ	PA	33,570	C+
Arizona State Univ	AZ	18,818	C+
Arkansas State Univ	AR	14,980	C
Arkansas Tech Univ	AR	13,164	LC
Ashland Univ	OH	25,000	C
Atlantic Union College	MA	24,600	LC
Auburn Univ	AL	20,052	VC+
Averett Univ	VA	36,000	LC
Baldwin Wallace Univ	OH	36,980	VC
Ball State Univ	IN	17,850	C
Barry Univ	FL	38,190	C
Bay Path College	MA	34,565	C
Becker College	MA	41,420	LC
Belmont Univ	TN	37,380	VC+
Bemidji State Univ	MN	13,500	C
Benedict College	SC	20,454	NC
Bennington College	VT	56,990	HC+
Berry College	GA	39,254	HC
Bethel College	IN	31,560	C
Bethel Univ	MN	34,940	VC
Biola Univ	CA	40,320	VC
Bloomsburg Univ of Pennsylvania	PA	13,598	C
Bluffton Univ	OH	37,864	C
Boston College	MA	58,506	MC
Boston Univ	MA	54,130	HC+
Bowie State Univ	MD	23,990	LC
Bowling Green State Univ	OH	18,970	C
Bradley Univ	IL	31,874	VC
Brenau Univ Women's College	GA	26,650	C+
Brescia Univ	KY	26,140	VC+
Brewton-Parker College	GA	33,388	LC
Bridgewater State Univ	MA	18,752	C
Brigham Young Univ	UT	12,100	HC
Bucknell Univ	PA	58,160	MC
Cal State, Sacramento	CA	16,200	C
Calif Univ of Pennsylvania	PA	14,217	C
Calvin College	MI	37,585	VC+
Cameron Univ	OK	9,267	LC
Campbellsville Univ	KY	27,720	C
Canisius College	NY	45,602	VC
Cardinal Stritch Univ	WI	24,054	C
Carlow Univ	PA	30,272	C
Carroll Univ	WI	24,860	C
Carson-Newman Univ	TN	29,058	C+
Cazenovia College	NY	30,800	C
Cedar Crest College	PA	43,240	C
Cedarville Univ	OH	31,036	VC+
Central Methodist Univ	MO	28,240	VC
Central Washington Univ	WA	11,730	C
Chadron State College	NE	7,400	NC
Chaminade Univ of Honolulu	HI	31,664	C
Champlain College	VT	44,850	VC
Charleston Southern Univ	SC	22,420	C
Chatham Univ	PA	42,440	VC
Chestnut Hill College	PA	39,785	LC
Cheyney Univ of Pennsylvania	PA	20,372	LC
Chicago State Univ	IL	5,482	C
Christian Brothers Univ	TN	19,140	HC
CUNY/Brooklyn College	NY	5,884	C+
Claflin Univ	SC	22,368	C+
Clarion Univ of Pennsylvania	PA	17,370	C
Clark Atlanta Univ	GA	30,006	C
Clemson Univ	SC	19,136	HC
Cleveland State Univ	OH	21,357	C
Coastal Carolina Univ	SC	17,620	C
Coker College	SC	32,256	LC
Colby-Sawyer College	NH	47,870	C
College of Charleston	SC	21,273	VC
College of Mount St. Joseph	OH	33,880	C
College of New Jersey	NJ	25,376	HC
College of St. Mary	NE	34,334	C
College of the Ozarks	MO	5,605	VC
Columbia College	SC	27,882	C
Columbia College Chicago	IL	30,940	LC
Columbus State Univ	GA	13,176	C
Concord Univ	WV	13,102	C
Concordia College - Alabama	AL	12,200	NC
Concordia College New York	NY	31,500	VC
Concordia Univ	OR	34,930	C
Concordia Univ - Irvine	CA	35,390	VC
Concordia Univ Nebr	NE	26,000	VC
Concordia Univ St. Paul	MN	27,200	C
Concordia Univ Wisc	WI	28,980	C
Concordia Univ, Ann Arbor	MI	27,220	VC
Concordia Univ, River Forest	IL	26,300	C
Converse College	SC	37,130	C
CUNY-City College	NY	19,576	HC+
Curry College	MA	47,545	LC
Daemen College	NY	31,510	C
Dallas Baptist Univ	TX	29,118	C
De Sales Univ	PA	42,670	C
Defiance College	OH	30,645	C
Delaware State Univ	DE	14,700	LC
DePaul Univ	IL	46,120	VC
Dickinson State Univ	ND	8,550	NC
Dominican Univ	IL	37,628	C
Dordt College	IA	34,160	VC
Duquesne Univ	PA	42,017	VC
East Carolina Univ	NC	14,169	C
East Central Univ	OK	10,223	LC
East Stroudsburg Univ of Pennsylvania	PA	16,636	C
East Texas Baptist Univ	TX	29,135	C
Eastern Conn State Univ	CT	20,584	C
Eastern Illinois Univ	IL	20,502	C
Eastern Mennonite Univ	VA	38,850	VC
Eastern Mich Univ	MI	17,961	C
Eastern New Mexico Univ	NM	10,682	C
Eastern Univ	PA	37,704	C
Edgewood College	WI	33,294	C
Edinboro Univ of Pennsylvania	PA	15,940	LC
Edward Waters College	FL	17,856	LC
Elizabethtown College	PA	47,600	VC
Elmhurst College	IL	42,032	C+
Elms College	MA	23,900	VC
Elon Univ	NC	40,046	HC
Erskine College	SC	37,360	C
Evangel Univ	MO	23,090	C
Fairmont State Univ	WV	12,098	LC
Fayetteville State Univ	NC	10,816	C
Felician College	NJ	41,640	C
Ferris State Univ	MI	19,698	C
Fitchburg State Univ	MA	17,241	C
Florida A&M Univ	FL	14,935	LC
Florida Gulf Coast Univ	FL		C
Florida International Univ	FL	17,747	VC
Florida State Univ	FL	15,238	HC
Fontbonne Univ	MO	31,384	C
Fort Valley State Univ	GA	11,200	VC
Framingham State Univ	MA	16,750	C
Francis Marion Univ	SC	16,464	LC
Freed-Hardeman Univ	TN	19,697	VC
Frostburg State Univ	MD	15,264	LC
Gallaudet Univ	DC	25,380	SP
Gannon Univ	PA	37,940	C
Georgia College and State Univ	GA	18,216	VC
Georgia Southern Univ	GA	16,414	C
Georgia Southwestern State Univ	GA	12,218	C
Georgia State Univ	GA	12,000	VC
Glenville State College	WV	11,348	NC
Goddard College	VT	16,418	VC
Gordon College	MA	42,660	VC+
Goshen College	IN	35,900	VC
Grambling State Univ	LA	13,384	LC
Granite State College	NH	6,195	SP
Greensboro College	NC	28,740	LC
Greenville College	IL	27,012	C
Grove City College	PA	22,988	HC
Hannibal-LaGrange Univ	MO	24,490	C
Harding Univ	AR	21,432	C+
Hardin-Simmons Univ	TX	23,560	C+
Harris-Stowe State Univ	MO	14,360	NC
Henderson State Univ	AR	13,634	C
Heritage Univ	WA	17,664	NC
Hillsdale College	MI	31,890	HC+
Holy Family Univ	PA	40,030	LC
Hood College	MD	44,630	C
Houston Baptist Univ	TX	23,815	C+
Howard Univ	DC	35,957	C
Humphreys College	CA	17,000	NC
Hunter College / The CUNY	NY	14,429	VC
Idaho State Univ	ID	11,908	C
Illinois State Univ	IL	22,634	VC
Immaculata Univ	PA	43,000	C
Indiana State Univ	IN	16,000	C
Indiana Univ Bloomington	IN	19,358	HC
Indiana Univ Kokomo	IN	6,674	LC
Indiana Univ of Pennsylvania	PA	20,180	LC
Indiana Univ-Purdue Univ Fort Wayne	IN	15,425	C
Inter-American Univ of PR/ Aguadilla Campus	PR	5,578	
Inter-American Univ of PR/ Barranquitas	PR	3,350	
Inter-American Univ of PR/ Fajardo Campus	PR	4,200	
Inter-American Univ of PR/ Metropolitan Campus	PR	4,320	
Inter-American Univ of PR/ Ponce	PR	3,700	
Inter-American Univ of PR/ San Germán	PR	6,720	
Iona College	NY	44,028	C
Iowa State Univ	IA	16,403	C
Iowa Wesleyan College	IA	30,850	LC
Jacksonville State Univ	AL	12,280	LC
John Brown Univ	AR	30,996	VC+
John Carroll Univ	OH	44,520	C+
Judson Univ	IL	25,130	C
Juniata College	PA	49,340	VC
Kansas State Univ	KS	15,497	VC
Kean Univ	NJ	22,060	LC
Keene State College	NH	21,538	C
Kendall College	IL	32,610	NC
Kennesaw State Univ	GA	13,017	VC
Kent State Univ	OH	19,352	C
Kentucky State Univ	KY	11,000	LC
Keystone College	PA	28,680	LC
King's College	PA	41,678	C
Kutztown Univ of Pennsylvania	PA	16,909	LC
LaGrange College	GA	34,480	C
Lake Erie College	OH	35,704	C
Lake Superior State Univ	MI	18,121	C
Lakeland College	WI	22,990	C
Lamar Univ	TX	6,820	LC
Lander Univ	SC	22,514	C+
Lasell College	MA	42,500	LC
Lebanon Valley College	PA	38,570	C
Lehman College / The CUNY	NY	5,778	LC
LeMoyne-Owen College	TN	13,100	C
Lenoir-Rhyne College	NC	35,984	C
Lesley Univ	MA	46,350	C
Limestone College	SC	29,880	C
Lincoln Memorial Univ	TN	18,144	C
Lindenwood Univ	MO	20,750	C
Lipscomb Univ	TN	35,722	VC
Livingstone College	NC	17,815	LC
Lock Haven Univ of Pennsylvania	PA	17,587	LC
LIU/Brooklyn Campus	NY	26,500	C
LIU/C.W. Post Campus	NY	38,888	C
Loras College	IA	37,432	VC
Louisiana State Univ	LA	18,677	VC+
Louisiana Tech Univ	LA	8,000	C
Loyola Univ Chicago	IL	49,560	VC+
Lubbock Christian Univ	TX	25,518	C
Lyndon State College	VT	14,233	C
Lyon College	AR	30,246	VC
Malone Univ	OH	34,334	C
Manhattan College	NY	44,955	VC
Mansfield Univ	PA	19,468	C
Marian Univ	WI	30,980	LC
Marietta College	OH	42,135	VC
Marshall Univ	WV	14,820	C
Martin Univ	IN	11,000	SP
Marygrove College	MI	21,290	C
Maryville Univ of St. Louis	MO	34,920	VC
Marywood Univ	PA	40,695	C
Mayville State Univ	ND	11,401	NC
McNeese State Univ	LA		C
Medaille College	NY	35,112	VC
Mercer Univ	GA	44,201	VC+
Mercyhurst Univ	PA	40,700	C
Messiah College	PA	39,540	VC
Metropolitan College of New York	NY	16,720	VC
Metropolitan State Univ	MN	5,923	SP
Miami Univ	OH	24,191	HC
Middle Tenn State Univ	TN	8,650	C
Midland Univ	NE	34,000	C
Miles College	AL	16,530	NC
Millersville Univ of Pennsylvania	PA	18,498	C
Milligan College	TN	27,510	C
Millikin Univ	IL	37,462	C
Minn State Univ, Mankato	MN	14,900	C
Minn State Univ, Moorhead	MN	13,392	C
Miss Valley State Univ	MS	9,706	LC
Missouri Baptist Univ	MO	30,310	C
Missouri Southern State Univ	MO	11,910	C
Missouri State Univ	MO	13,996	VC
Missouri Western State Univ	MO	12,260	NC
Mitchell College	CT	40,983	C
Montana State Univ-Billings	MT	12,425	LC
Montclair State Univ	NJ	22,614	C
Morris College	SC	16,006	LC
Mount Aloysius College	PA	27,970	C
Mount Ida College	MA	30,115	LC
Mount Mary Univ	WI	32,836	LC
Mount Mercy Univ	IA	34,385	C
Mount Vernon Nazarene Univ	OH	29,590	C
Mountain State Univ	WV	14,330	NC
Murray State Univ	KY	14,944	C
Muskingum Univ	OH	30,502	C
Naropa Univ	CO	37,875	SP
National Louis Univ	IL	16,915	LC
Neumann Univ	PA	31,078	LC
New Jersey City Univ	NJ	21,060	C+
New Mexico Highlands Univ	NM	9,720	NC
New Mexico State Univ	NM	13,955	LC
New York Univ	NY	61,470	MC
Newberry College	SC	26,850	LC
Newman Univ	KS	30,380	C+
Niagara Univ	NY	39,800	C
Norfolk State Univ	VA	10,531	LC
N Car Agricultural and Technical State Univ	NC	13,175	LC
North Georgia College & State Univ	GA	8,500	C
North Park Univ	IL	30,130	C
Northeastern Illinois Univ	IL		C
Northeastern State Univ	OK	8,615	VC
Northern Arizona Univ	AZ	18,592	C
Northern Illinois Univ	IL	19,768	C
Northern Kentucky Univ	KY	15,302	LC

School	ST	$IS	SR
Northern State Univ	SD	14,021	C
Northwest Missouri State Univ	MO	14,229	C
Northwestern College	MN	24,000	C
Northwestern College of Iowa	IA	34,848	₵
Northwestern Okla State Univ	OK	7,275	NC
Northwestern State Univ of Louisiana	LA	14,368	C
Notre Dame College	OH	34,942	VC
Notre Dame of Maryland Univ	MD	27,700	C
Nyack College	NY	32,000	C
Ohio Dominican Univ	OH	38,380	₵
Ohio Northern Univ	OH	42,075	VC
Ohio Univ	OH	20,676	VC
Ohio Wesleyan Univ	OH	49,460	₵
Okla Baptist Univ	OK	28,202	VC
Okla Christian Univ	OK	24,975	VC
Okla City Univ	OK	33,546	VC
Old Dominion Univ	VA	18,662	C
Olivet Nazarene Univ	IL	29,990	C
Oral Roberts Univ	OK	31,734	C
Ouachita Baptist Univ	AR	29,010	VC
Our Lady of the Lake Univ of San Antonio	TX	22,430	LC
Pacific Union College	CA	28,150	VC
Paine College	GA	18,594	LC
Park Univ	MO	17,525	C
Philander Smith College	AR	19,760	LC
Piedmont College	GA	29,260	C
Pittsburg State Univ	KS	12,032	C
Point Park Univ	PA	36,390	C
Presbyterian College	SC	42,678	VC
Prescott College	AZ	33,284	₵
Purdue Univ/Calumet	IN	14,336	C
Purdue Univ/West Lafayette	IN	20,278	HC
Queens College / The CUNY	NY	17,107	VC
Rhode Island College	RI	17,132	LC
Rider Univ	NJ	45,720	C
Ripon College	WI	36,959	₵
Rivier College	NH	35,000	VC
Roberts Wesleyan College	NY	37,384	₵
Roosevelt Univ	IL	22,605	VC
Rowan Univ	NJ	23,570	VC
St. Joseph's Univ	PA	52,272	VC
St. Mary-of-the-Woods College	IN	37,722	LC
St. Vincent College	PA	40,244	C
St. Xavier Univ	IL	32,840	C
Salisbury Univ	MD	18,368	VC
Salve Regina Univ	RI	47,250	VC
Samford Univ	AL	35,700	V₵
San Jose State Univ	CA	19,707	C
Schreiner Univ	TX	32,734	LC
Seton Hill Univ	PA	35,172	C
Shawnee State Univ	OH	16,545	NC
Shippensburg Univ of Pennsylvania	PA	17,064	LC
Shorter Univ	GA	26,470	C
Silver Lake College	WI	22,600	LC
Simmons College	MA	48,770	VC
Sinte Gleska Univ	SD	2,300	NC
Slippery Rock Univ of Pennsylvania	PA	10,360	LC
Smith College	MA	57,524	MC
Sojourner-Douglass College	MD	9,160	LC
S Car State Univ	SC	6,700	LC
S Dak State Univ	SD	14,296	C
Southeast Missouri State Univ	MO	14,983	LC
Southeastern Louisiana Univ	LA	13,325	C
Southeastern Okla State Univ	OK	7,966	C
Southern Conn State Univ	CT	18,033	C
Southern Illinois Univ Carbondale	IL	21,620	C
Southern Illinois Univ Edwardsville	IL	17,532	C
Southern Nazarene Univ	OK	24,354	NC
Southern New Hampshire Univ	NH	38,100	C
Southern Oregon Univ	OR	17,874	C
Southern Univ and A&M College	LA	9,761	₵
Southern Wesleyan Univ	SC	25,600	C
Southwest Baptist Univ	MO	24,710	C
Southwest Minn State Univ	MN	14,000	C
Southwestern College	KS	29,270	C
Spring Hill College	AL	42,130	VC
Springfield College	MA	25,000	C
St. Ambrose Univ	IA		C
St. Catherine Univ	MN	37,782	₵
St. Cloud State Univ	MN	10,600	C
St. John's Univ	NY	52,840	₵
Stephens College	MO	34,500	VC
Stevenson Univ	MD	39,572	C
SUNY College at Geneseo	NY	18,055	H₵
SUNY College at Old Westbury	NY	16,324	C
SUNY Fredonia / The SUNY at Fredonia	NY	18,702	VC
SUNY New Paltz	NY	15,010	C
Susquehanna Univ	PA	49,170	C
Syracuse Univ	NY	54,512	HC
Taylor Univ	IN	36,742	V₵
Temple Univ	PA	24,392	VC
Tenn State Univ	TN	9,048	C
Tenn Wesleyan College	TN	21,250	C
Texas A&M Univ at Commerce	TX	10,496	C
Texas Christian Univ	TX	47,570	HC
Texas State Univ	TX	16,495	VC
Texas Tech Univ	TX	14,243	C
The Catholic Univ of America	DC	52,852	VC
The College of St. Rose	NY	26,750	C
The Lincoln Univ	PA	15,154	LC
The SUNY at Potsdam	NY	17,754	C
Thomas College	ME	26,270	LC
Thomas Univ	GA	11,520	NC
Toccoa Falls College	GA	23,210	C
Towson Univ	MD	16,000	VC
Trevecca Nazarene Univ	TN	30,118	C
Trinity Washington Univ	DC	30,250	₵
Troy Univ	AL	10,650	C
Tulane Univ	LA	58,942	MC
Tusculum College	TN	24,295	C
Tuskegee Univ	AL	26,750	C
Univ of Akron	OH	20,436	C
Univ of Alabama at Birmingham	AL	18,484	₵
Univ of Alabama at Tuscaloosa	AL	17,164	₵
Univ of Alaska Fairbanks	AK	13,955	C
Univ of Arizona	AZ	20,105	C
Univ of Arkansas at Fayetteville	AR	16,860	VC
Univ of Arkansas at Little Rock	AR		C
Univ of Arkansas at Monticello	AR	8,470	NC
Univ of Arkansas at Pine Bluff	AR	10,600	C
Univ of Central Arkansas	AR	10,840	VC
Univ of Central Florida	FL	15,711	V₵
Univ of Central Missouri	MO	14,605	C
Univ of Central Okla	OK	12,293	C
Univ of Cincinnati	OH	20,199	VC
Univ of Dayton	OH	43,750	VC
Univ of Delaware	DE	22,728	VC
Univ of Detroit Mercy	MI	30,450	C
Univ of Georgia	GA	19,508	VC
Univ of Hartford	CT	42,674	C
Univ of Illinois at Chicago	IL	24,293	VC
Univ of Illinois at Urbana-Champaign	IL	24,300	HC
Univ of Kansas	KS	16,980	₵
Univ of Kentucky	KY	19,868	C
Univ of Louisville	KY	17,460	VC
Univ of Maine at Farmington	ME	17,841	C
Univ of Mary	ND	16,714	C
Univ of Mary Hardin-Baylor	TX	31,950	₵
Univ of Maryland	MD	18,801	HC
Univ of Mass Boston	MA	11,966	C
Univ of Mich/Dearborn	MI	9,885	VC
Univ of Mich-Flint	MI	17,547	₵
Univ of Minn Crookston	MN	17,834	C
Univ of Minn/Twin Cities	MN		HC
Univ of Missouri/Columbia	MO	18,201	MC
Univ of Missouri-Kansas City	MO	19,603	C
Univ of Missouri-St. Louis	MO	18,304	VC
Univ of Mobile	AL	27,870	VC
Univ of Montana-Western	MT	9,753	LC
Univ of Mount Union	OH	35,130	C
Univ of Nebr - Lincoln	NE	17,507	VC
Univ of Nebr at Kearney	NE	14,855	LC
Univ of New Mexico	NM	15,300	C
Univ of New Orleans	LA	9,224	VC
Univ of North Alabama	AL	9,960	C
Univ of N Car at Greensboro	NC	12,848	C
Univ of N Car at Wilmington	NC	13,572	V₵
Univ of N Dak	ND	14,094	C
Univ of Northern Iowa	IA	14,776	C
Univ of Okla	OK	17,634	V₵
Univ of PR/Bayamon	PR	1,600	
Univ of Rio Grande	OH	8,750	NC
Univ of Science and Arts of Okla	OK	10,560	VC
Univ of Scranton	PA	51,940	VC
Univ of Sioux Falls	SD	22,990	C
Univ of South Alabama	AL	13,510	C
Univ of S Car at Aiken	SC	16,278	C
Univ of S Car at Columbia	SC	19,725	V₵
Univ of S Car Upstate	SC	17,673	LC
Univ of Southern Indiana	IN	14,657	C
Univ of Southern Miss	MS	13,170	C
Univ of Tenn at Chattanooga	TN	16,883	C
Univ of Texas at San Antonio	TX	18,372	C
Univ of the District of Columbia	DC	7,244	LC
Univ of the Ozarks	AR	22,100	C
Univ of Toledo	OH	18,464	C
Univ of Vermont	VT	26,120	V₵
Univ of West Alabama	AL	9,415	C
Univ of West Florida	FL	14,656	C
Univ of West Georgia	GA	14,852	LC
Univ of Wisc Whitewater	WI	13,314	C
Univ of Wisc/Stevens Point	WI	14,043	C
Univ of Wisc/Stout	WI	23,942	C
Ursuline College	OH	33,198	LC
Utah State Univ	UT	11,803	C
Vanderbilt Univ	TN	57,072	MC
Virginia Union Univ	VA	18,432	C
Walsh Univ	OH	35,100	C
Washburn Univ	KS	12,165	NC
Washington State Univ	WA	20,461	C
Wayland Baptist Univ	TX	16,058	LC
Waynesburg Univ	PA	29,100	C
Webster Univ	MO	33,990	₵
Wesleyan College	GA	24,000	₵
West Chester Univ of Pennsylvania	PA	16,836	C
West Liberty Univ	WV	9,142	LC
West Virginia State Univ	WV	8,378	NC
Western Carolina Univ	NC	13,965	₵
Western Kentucky Univ	KY	11,000	LC
Western Mich Univ	MI	19,042	C
Western Washington Univ	WA	18,519	VC
Westfield State Univ	MA	18,489	C
Westminster College	UT	37,708	VC
Wheeling Jesuit Univ	WV	34,668	C
Wheelock College	MA	33,075	C
Widener Univ	PA	50,368	C
William Woods Univ	MO		C
Wilmington College	OH	29,784	C
Wilmington Univ	DE	7,778	NC
Winona State Univ	MN	16,530	C
Winthrop Univ	SC	21,120	VC
Worcester State Univ	MA	18,657	C
Wright State Univ	OH	16,983	C
Xavier Univ	OH	43,740	VC
Youngstown State Univ	OH	16,374	LC

EARLY CHILDHOOD STUDIES

School	ST	$IS	SR
Becker College	MA	41,420	LC
Biola Univ	CA	40,320	VC
Bluffton Univ	OH	37,864	C
Boise State Univ	ID	12,802	C
Calif Baptist Univ	CA	35,890	C
Central Mich Univ	MI	18,066	C
Grace Bible College	MI	20,770	C
Idaho State Univ	ID	11,908	C
Langston Univ	OK	3,000	LC
Mayville State Univ	ND	11,401	NC
Metropolitan State Univ	MN	5,923	SP
Mills College	CA	54,119	HC
National Univ	CA	14,730	SP
New York Univ	NY	61,470	MC
Northern Illinois Univ	IL	19,768	C
Pittsburg State Univ	KS	12,032	C
Plymouth State Univ	NH	23,148	LC
Point Park Univ	PA	36,390	C
Rochester College	MI	18,320	C
Shippensburg Univ of Pennsylvania	PA	17,064	LC
S Dak State Univ	SD	14,296	C
SUNY/Empire State College	NY	6,315	SP
SUNY Fredonia / The SUNY at Fredonia	NY	18,702	VC
Univ of Dayton	OH	43,750	VC
Univ of Maryland	MD	18,801	HC
Univ of Minn/Duluth	MN	18,964	₵
Univ of Missouri/Columbia	MO	18,201	MC
Univ of Nebr - Lincoln	NE	17,507	VC
Univ of N Dak	ND	14,094	C
Univ of Texas-Pan American	TX	12,432	LC
Wayne State College	NE	11,764	NC
Youngstown State Univ	OH	16,374	LC

EARTH SCIENCE

School	ST	$IS	SR
Adams State College	CO	13,358	LC
Adrian College	MI	33,800	C
Alaska Pacific Univ	AK	33,360	VC
Albion College	MI	43,884	VC
Arizona State Univ	AZ	18,818	₵
Augustana College	IL	43,398	HC
Baylor Univ	TX	46,720	HC
Bemidji State Univ	MN	13,500	C
Boston Univ	MA	54,130	H₵
Bowdoin College	ME	57,834	MC
Bowling Green State Univ	OH	18,970	C
Bridgewater State Univ	MA	18,752	C
Buffalo State/State Univ of Buffalo	NY	15,733	₵
Calif Polytechnic State Univ	CA	19,847	HC
Cal State, Long Beach	CA	17,534	₵
Cal State, Monterey Bay	CA	26,871	LC
Cal State, Northridge	CA	28,313	C
Calvin College	MI	37,585	V₵
Central Conn State Univ	CT	19,212	C
Central Mich Univ	MI	18,066	C
Central Washington Univ	WA	11,730	C
CUNY/Brooklyn College	NY	5,884	₵
Columbia Univ in the City of New York	NY	61,116	MC
Columbus State Univ	GA	13,176	C
CUNY-City College	NY	19,576	H₵
Dartmouth College	NH	57,996	MC
DePauw Univ	IN	48,950	V₵
Dickinson College	PA	57,662	H₵
Dickinson State Univ	ND	8,550	NC
East Stroudsburg Univ of Pennsylvania	PA	16,636	C
Eastern Mich Univ	MI	17,961	C
Edinboro Univ of Pennsylvania	PA	15,940	LC
Emporia State Univ	KS	12,897	C
Fitchburg State Univ	MA	17,241	C
George Mason Univ	VA	15,724	VC
Georgia Inst of Technology	GA	20,464	MC
Grand Valley State Univ	MI	17,998	VC
Indiana Univ Bloomington	IN	19,358	HC
Indiana Univ of Pennsylvania	PA	20,180	LC
Indiana Univ-Purdue Univ Fort Wayne	IN	15,425	C
Iowa State Univ	IA	16,403	C
Jackson State Univ	MS	13,512	LC
Johns Hopkins Univ	MD	47,492	MC
Kean Univ	NJ	22,060	LC
Keene State College	NH	21,538	C
Kent State Univ	OH	19,352	C
Lehigh Univ	PA	55,080	MC
Lock Haven Univ of Pennsylvania	PA	17,587	LC
Mass Inst of Technology	MA	54,238	MC
Mercer Univ	GA	44,201	V₵
Mercyhurst Univ	PA	40,700	C
Miami Univ	OH	24,191	HC
Mich State Univ	MI	13,689	VC
Millersville Univ of Pennsylvania	PA	18,498	C
Minn State Univ, Mankato	MN	14,900	C
Minn State Univ, Moorhead	MN	13,392	C
Minot State Univ	ND	10,915	C
Montana State Univ	MT	14,068	VC
Morehead State Univ	KY	10,900	C
Murray State Univ	KY	14,944	C
Muskingum Univ	OH	30,502	C
National Univ	CA	14,730	SP
New Mexico Inst of Mining and Technology	NM	12,892	HC
New York Univ	NY	61,470	MC
N Car State Univ	NC	16,202	HC
N Dak State Univ	ND	14,642	C
Northeastern Illinois Univ	IL		C
Northeastern Univ	MA	55,296	MC
Northern Mich Univ	MI	15,300	VC
Northland College	WI	26,680	C
Northwest Missouri State Univ	MO	14,229	C
Ohio Univ	OH	20,676	VC
Ohio Wesleyan Univ	OH	49,460	₵
Old Dominion Univ	VA	18,662	C
Oregon State Univ	OR	19,017	₵
Oswego / SUNY	NY	20,009	VC
Point Park Univ	PA	36,390	C
Prescott College	AZ	33,284	₵
Purdue Univ/West Lafayette	IN	20,278	HC
Rice Univ	TX	43,288	MC
St. Louis Univ	MO	46,594	V₵
St. Mary's Univ	TX	33,854	C
Salem State College	MA	13,161	LC
Salisbury Univ	MD	18,368	VC
San Francisco State Univ	CA	18,514	C
Shippensburg Univ of Pennsylvania	PA	17,064	LC
Slippery Rock Univ of Pennsylvania	PA	10,360	LC
Southern Conn State Univ	CT	18,033	C
Southern Illinois Univ Edwardsville	IL	17,532	C
St. Cloud State Univ	MN	10,600	C
Stanford Univ	CA	56,411	MC
Stony Brook Univ / SUNY	NY	19,359	HC
SUNY Fredonia / The SUNY at Fredonia	NY	18,702	VC
SUNY Oneonta / SUNY	NY	16,919	VC
Susquehanna Univ	PA	49,170	C
Syracuse Univ	NY	54,512	HC
Tarleton State Univ	TX	13,489	LC
Texas A&M Univ at Commerce	TX	10,496	C
Texas A&M Univ at Galveston	TX	11,258	C
The College at Brockport / SUNY	NY	18,362	VC
Ohio State Univ	OH	19,887	MC
Towson Univ	MD	16,000	VC
Tulane Univ	LA	58,942	MC
Univ at Albany / SUNY	NY	18,674	VC
Univ of Alabama at Huntsville	AL	17,625	VC
Univ of Alaska Fairbanks	AK	13,955	C
Univ of Arkansas at Fayetteville	AR	16,860	VC
Univ of Calif at Berkeley	CA	23,322	MC
Univ of Calif at Irvine	CA	25,961	VC
Univ of Calif at Los Angeles	CA	25,686	MC
Univ of Calif at San Diego	CA	21,000	VC
Univ of Calif at Santa Barbara	CA	27,551	HC

School	ST	$IS	SR
Univ of Calif at Santa Cruz	CA	27,807	VC
Univ of Central Missouri	MO	14,605	C
Univ of Florida	FL	15,783	HC+
Univ of Illinois at Chicago	IL	24,293	VC
Univ of Indianapolis	IN	31,740	LC
Univ of Maine	ME	19,712	C+
Univ of Mass Amherst	MA	23,697	VC+
Univ of Mass Boston	MA	11,966	C
Univ of Memphis	TN	15,094	C
Univ of Mich/Ann Arbor	MI	22,102	HC+
Univ of Nevada, Las Vegas	NV	17,303	C
Univ of New Hampshire	NH	24,702	VC
Univ of New Mexico	NM	15,300	C
Univ of New Orleans	LA	9,224	VC
Univ of N Car at Charlotte	NC	15,847	C
Univ of Northern Colo	CO	15,973	C
Univ of Northern Iowa	IA	14,776	C
Univ of S Dak	SD	15,111	C
Univ of Texas at El Paso	TX	8,764	NC
Univ of Utah	UT	13,462	VC
Univ of Wisc/Green Bay	WI	14,900	C
Univ of Wyoming	WY	13,855	C+
Utah State Univ	UT	11,803	C
Vassar College	NY	59,070	MC
Virginia Wesleyan College	VA	28,433	LC
Washington Univ in St. Louis	MO	58,818	MC
Wesleyan Univ	CT	59,844	MC
West Chester Univ of Pennsylvania	PA	16,836	C
Western Conn State Univ	CT	18,327	C
Western Mich Univ	MI	19,042	C
Western Oregon Univ	OR	15,021	C
Western Washington Univ	WA	18,519	VC
Wilkes Univ	PA	42,786	C
Winona State Univ	MN	16,530	C

EARTH SCIENCE / ADOLESCENCE EDUCATION

School	ST	$IS	SR
Elizabethtown College	PA	47,600	VC
Indiana Univ-Purdue Univ Indianapolis	IN	17,290	C
Oswego / SUNY	NY	20,009	VC
Temple Univ	PA	24,392	VC
The College of St. Rose	NY	26,750	C
Univ of Nebr - Lincoln	NE	17,507	VC
Univ of West Georgia	GA	14,852	LC
Winona State Univ	MN	16,530	C

EAST ASIAN LANGUAGES AND LITERATURE

School	ST	$IS	SR
Beloit College	WI	49,970	HC
Boston Univ	MA	54,130	HC+
Indiana Univ Bloomington	IN	19,358	HC
Miami Univ	OH	24,191	HC
Mich State Univ	MI	13,689	VC
Rutgers, The State Univ of New Jersey/New Brunswick	NJ	25,077	VC
Smith College	MA	57,524	MC
Univ of Chicago	IL	55,416	MC
Univ of Florida	FL	15,783	HC+
Univ of Illinois at Urbana-Champaign	IL	24,300	HC
Univ of Kansas	KS	16,980	C+
Univ of Puget Sound	WA	52,648	HC+
Univ of Southern Calif	CA	56,903	MC
Washington Univ in St. Louis	MO	58,818	MC
Yale Univ	CT	55,300	MC

EAST ASIAN STUDIES

School	ST	$IS	SR
Appalachian State Univ	NC	12,919	VC
Augsburg College	MN	35,142	C
Bates College	ME	58,950	MC
Binghamton Univ / The SUNY	NY	20,832	HC+
Boston Univ	MA	54,130	HC+
Brandeis Univ	MA	58,820	HC
Brown Univ	RI	56,150	MC
Bryn Mawr College	PA	57,760	MC
Bucknell Univ	PA	58,160	MC
Colby College	ME	57,510	MC
Columbia Univ in the City of New York	NY	61,116	MC
Columbia Univ/Barnard College	NY	39,000	MC
Columbia Univ/School of General Studies	NY	54,083	MC
Conn College	CT	54,970	MC
Denison Univ	OH	54,670	HC+
DePaul Univ	IL	46,120	VC
DePauw Univ	IN	48,950	VC+
Dickinson College	PA	57,662	HC+
Eckerd College	FL	43,902	VC
Emory and Henry College	VA	387,460	C
George Washington Univ	DC	57,108	MC
Hamline Univ	MN	44,198	VC
Haverford College	PA	59,236	MC
Indiana Univ Bloomington	IN	19,358	HC
John Carroll Univ	OH	44,520	C+
Johns Hopkins Univ	MD	47,492	MC
Lawrence Univ	WI	46,371	HC
Lewis & Clark College	OR	52,656	VC
Mary Baldwin College	VA	37,110	C
Middlebury College	VT	57,470	MC
Minn State Univ, Moorhead	MN	13,392	C
Mount Holyoke College	MA	53,596	HC+
New York Univ	NY	61,470	MC
North Central College	IL	38,343	VC
Oakland Univ	MI	19,391	VC
Oberlin College	OH	57,025	MC
Occidental College	CA	59,592	MC+
Princeton Univ	NJ	53,795	MC
Queens College / The CUNY	NY	17,107	VC
Stanford Univ	CA	56,411	MC
Univ at Albany / SUNY	NY	18,674	VC
Univ of Arizona	AZ	20,105	C
Univ of Calif at Davis	CA	24,482	HC
Univ of Calif at Irvine	CA	25,961	VC
Univ of Calif at Los Angeles	CA	25,686	MC
Univ of Delaware	DE	22,728	VC
Univ of Illinois at Urbana-Champaign	IL	24,300	HC
Univ of Minn/Twin Cities	MN		HC
Univ of Rochester	NY	58,500	MC
Univ of Southern Calif	CA	56,903	MC
Ursinus College	PA	55,630	VC+
Valparaiso Univ	IN	43,040	VC+
Vanderbilt Univ	TN	57,072	MC
Washington and Lee Univ	VA	52,812	MC
Washington Univ in St. Louis	MO	58,818	MC
Wesleyan Univ	CT	59,844	MC
Western Washington Univ	WA	18,519	VC
Wittenberg Univ	OH	47,766	VC
Yale Univ	CT	55,300	MC

EASTERN EUROPEAN STUDIES

School	ST	$IS	SR
Boston Univ	MA	54,130	HC+
Bowdoin College	ME	57,834	MC
Florida State Univ	FL	15,238	HC
Indiana Univ Bloomington	IN	19,358	HC
Kent State Univ	OH	19,352	C
Oberlin College	OH	57,025	MC
Ohio Univ	OH	20,676	VC
Rutgers, The State Univ of New Jersey/Newark Campus	NJ	25,376	C
Univ of Mich/Ann Arbor	MI	22,102	HC+
Univ of Okla	OK	17,634	VC+
Univ of Texas at Austin	TX	44,074	HC
Washington Univ in St. Louis	MO	58,818	MC
Yale Univ	CT	55,300	MC

ECOLOGY

School	ST	$IS	SR
Adams State College	CO	13,358	LC
Angelo State Univ	TX	15,049	NC
Appalachian State Univ	NC	12,919	VC
Bard College at Simon's Rock	MA	58,963	HC+
Beloit College	WI	49,970	HC
Bennington College	VT	56,990	HC+
Boston Univ	MA	54,130	HC+
Cal State, Chico	CA	18,952	C
Cal State, Long Beach	CA	17,534	C+
Colo State Univ-Fort Collins	CO	20,090	VC
Defiance College	OH	30,645	C
Florida Inst of Technology	FL	48,290	VC
Florida State Univ	FL	15,238	HC
Goshen College	IN	35,900	VC
Hampshire College	MA	58,320	MC
Idaho State Univ	ID	11,908	C
Kutztown Univ of Pennsylvania	PA	16,909	LC
Le Moyne College	NY	42,200	VC
Marshall Univ	WV	14,820	C
Mich Tech Univ	MI	22,105	VC
Missouri Southern State Univ	MO	11,910	C
Montana State Univ-Northern	MT	12,500	NC
Morehead State Univ	KY	10,900	C
New Mexico State Univ	NM	13,955	LC
Northern Mich Univ	MI	15,300	VC
Northwest Nazarene Univ	ID	24,275	NC
Northwestern Univ	IL	37,595	MC
Ohio Univ	OH	20,676	VC
Oregon State Univ	OR	19,017	C+
Prescott College	AZ	33,284	C+
Princeton Univ	NJ	53,795	MC
Purdue Univ/West Lafayette	IN	20,278	HC
Rutgers, The State Univ of New Jersey/New Brunswick	NJ	25,077	VC
Sacred Heart Univ	CT	48,564	VC
San Diego State Univ	CA	20,578	VC
San Francisco State Univ	CA	18,514	C
S Dak State Univ	SD	14,296	C
Southern Illinois Univ Edwardsville	IL	17,532	C
SUNY / College of Environmental Science and Forestry	NY	18,351	HC
Sterling College	VT	26,160	C
Stony Brook Univ / SUNY	NY	19,359	HC
SUNY Plattsburgh / SUNY	NY	18,083	VC
Susquehanna Univ	PA	49,170	C
Ohio State Univ	OH	19,887	MC
Tulane Univ	LA	58,942	MC
Unity College	ME	34,054	C
Univ of Arizona	AZ	20,105	C
Univ of Calif at Davis	CA	24,482	HC
Univ of Calif at Irvine	CA	25,961	VC
Univ of Calif at Los Angeles	CA	25,686	MC
Univ of Calif at San Diego	CA	21,000	VC
Univ of Calif at Santa Barbara	CA	27,551	HC
Univ of Calif at Santa Cruz	CA	27,807	VC
Univ of Colo Boulder	CO	22,605	VC+
Univ of Denver	CO	51,787	VC+
Univ of Georgia	GA	19,508	VC
Univ of Mich/Ann Arbor	MI	22,102	HC+
Univ of Mich-Flint	MI	17,547	C+
Univ of Minn/Twin Cities	MN		HC
Univ of Pittsburgh at Pittsburgh	PA	27,800	HC+
Univ of Rochester	NY	58,500	MC
Univ of Wyoming	WY	13,855	C+
Washington Univ in St. Louis	MO	58,818	MC
West Chester Univ of Pennsylvania	PA	16,836	C
Western Washington Univ	WA	18,519	VC

ECONOMICS

School	ST	$IS	SR
Adams State College	CO	13,358	LC
Adelphi Univ	NY	43,130	VC
Adrian College	MI	33,800	C
Agnes Scott College	GA	45,323	VC+
Alabama A&M Univ	AL	96,100	C
Albion College	MI	43,884	VC
Albright College	PA	46,660	C
Alcorn State Univ	MS	9,500	C
Allegheny College	PA	49,020	HC
Alma College	MI	42,400	VC
American International College	MA	36,100	LC
American Univ	DC	54,829	HC+
Amherst College	MA	58,744	MC
Anderson Univ	IN	35,390	C
Andrews Univ	MI	28,030	C+
Appalachian State Univ	NC	12,919	VC
Aquinas College	MI	33,060	C
Arizona State Univ	AZ	18,818	C+
Arkansas State Univ	AR	14,980	C
Arkansas Tech Univ	AR	13,164	LC
Armstrong Atlantic State Univ	GA	16,276	C
Ashland Univ	OH	25,000	C
Assumption College	MA	45,721	VC
Auburn Univ	AL	20,052	VC+
Augsburg College	MN	35,142	C
Augustana College	IL	43,398	HC
Augustana College	SD	35,500	VC
Austin College	TX	36,940	HC
Baker Univ	KS	33,350	C+
Baldwin Wallace Univ	OH	36,980	VC
Ball State Univ	IN	17,850	C
Bard College	NY	59,872	HC
Barry Univ	FL	38,190	C
Barton College	NC	27,660	C
Bates College	ME	58,950	MC
Baylor Univ	TX	46,720	HC
Bellarmine Univ	KY	42,950	VC
Belmont Univ	TN	37,380	VC+
Beloit College	WI	49,970	HC
Bemidji State Univ	MN	13,500	C
Benedict College	SC	20,454	NC
Benedictine College	KS	29,180	VC
Benedictine Univ	IL	35,220	C
Bentley Univ	MA	54,555	HC+
Berea College	KY	7,220	HC
Berry College	GA	39,254	HC
Bethany College	WV	35,282	C
Bethel College	IN	31,560	C
Bethel Univ	MN	34,940	VC
Binghamton Univ / The SUNY	NY	20,832	HC+
Biola Univ	CA	40,320	VC
Birmingham-Southern College	AL	42,370	VC+
Bloomsburg Univ of Pennsylvania	PA	13,598	C
Bluffton Univ	OH	37,864	C
Boise State Univ	ID	12,802	C
Boston College	MA	58,506	MC
Boston Univ	MA	54,130	HC+
Bowdoin College	ME	57,834	MC
Bowling Green State Univ	OH	18,970	C
Bradley Univ	IL	31,874	VC
Brandeis Univ	MA	58,820	HC
Bridgewater College	VA	39,880	C
Bridgewater State Univ	MA	18,752	C
Brigham Young Univ	UT	12,100	HC
Brown Univ	RI	56,150	MC
Bryant Univ	RI	49,179	VC
Bryn Mawr College	PA	57,760	MC
Bucknell Univ	PA	58,160	MC
Buena Vista Univ	IA	37,954	C
Buffalo State/State Univ of Buffalo	NY	15,733	C+
Butler Univ	IN	45,898	VC+
Cabrini College	PA	40,859	LC
Calif Inst of Technology	CA	54,045	MC
Calif Lutheran Univ	CA	47,640	C
Calif Polytechnic State Univ	CA	19,847	HC
Calif State Polytechnic Univ, Pomona	CA	18,932	C
Cal State, Bakersfield	CA	8,000	LC
Cal State, Chico	CA	18,952	C
Cal State, East Bay	CA	16,549	C
Cal State, Fresno	CA	17,405	C
Cal State, Fullerton	CA	25,188	C+
Cal State, Long Beach	CA	17,534	C+
Cal State, Los Angeles	CA	15,829	C
Cal State, Northridge	CA	28,313	C
Cal State, Sacramento	CA	16,200	C
Cal State, San Bernardino	CA	12,000	C
Cal State, San Marcos	CA	14,576	C
Cal State, Stanislaus	CA	18,582	C
Calvin College	MI	37,585	VC+
Campbell Univ	NC	25,500	C
Campbellsville Univ	KY	27,720	C
Capital Univ	OH	39,824	VC
Carleton College	MN	58,149	MC
Carnegie Mellon Univ	PA	51,260	MC
Carson-Newman Univ	TN	29,058	C+
Carthage College	WI	33,000	C
Case Western Reserve Univ	OH	55,170	MC
Catawba College	NC	37,105	C
Centenary College of Louisiana	LA	39,070	C+
Central College	IA	36,980	VC
Central Conn State Univ	CT	19,212	C
Central Mich Univ	MI	18,066	C
Central State Univ	OH	9,010	C
Central Washington Univ	WA	11,730	C
Centre College	KY	35,000	HC+
Chancellor Univ	OH	11,000	C
Chapman Univ	CA	56,019	VC+
Charleston Southern Univ	SC	22,420	C
Chatham Univ	PA	42,440	VC
Cheyney Univ of Pennsylvania	PA	20,372	LC
Chicago State Univ	IL	5,482	C
Christopher Newport Univ	VA	21,050	VC
CUNY/Baruch College	NY	15,831	VC
CUNY/Brooklyn College	NY	5,884	C+
Claremont McKenna College	CA	58,065	MC
Clarion Univ of Pennsylvania	PA	17,370	C
Clark Atlanta Univ	GA	30,006	C
Clark Univ	MA	47,020	HC+
Clemson Univ	SC	19,136	HC
Cleveland State Univ	OH	21,357	C
Coastal Carolina Univ	SC	17,620	C
Coe College	IA	43,590	VC
Colby College	ME	57,510	MC
Colgate Univ	NY	50,930	MC
College of Staten Island / The CUNY	NY	16,778	NC
College of Charleston	SC	21,273	VC
College of Mount St. Vincent	NY	41,040	MC
College of New Jersey	NJ	25,376	HC
College of St. Benedict	MN	47,570	VC
College of St. Elizabeth	NJ	43,839	LC
College of St. Scholastica	MN	39,960	C
College of the Holy Cross	MA	56,232	MC
College of William & Mary	VA	25,085	MC
College of Wooster	OH	52,600	VC
Colo College	CO	54,534	MC
Colo School of Mines	CO	18,000	HC
Colo State Univ-Fort Collins	CO	20,090	VC
Colo State Univ-Pueblo	CO	13,532	LC
Columbia Univ in the City of New York	NY	61,116	MC
Columbia Univ/Barnard College	NY	39,000	MC
Columbia Univ/School of General Studies	NY	54,083	MC
Conn College	CT	54,970	MC
Converse College	SC	37,130	C
Cornell College	IA	44,930	HC
Cornell Univ	NY	59,037	MC
Covenant College	GA		VC+
Creighton Univ	NE	44,058	VC+
CUNY-City College	NY	19,576	HC+
Dartmouth College	NH	57,996	MC
Davidson College	NC	54,683	MC
Davis and Elkins College	WV	33,742	C
Delaware State Univ	DE	14,700	LC
Denison Univ	OH	54,670	HC+
DePaul Univ	IL	46,120	VC
DePauw Univ	IN	48,950	VC+
Dickinson College	PA	57,662	HC+
Dillard Univ	LA	20,940	VC
Doane College	NE	33,730	VC
Dominican Univ	IL	37,628	C
Dordt College	IA	34,160	VC
Dowling College	NY	25,000	LC
Drake Univ	IA	30,980	VC+

ST = STATE **$IS** = IN-STATE COSTS **SR** = SELECTOR RATING

School	ST	$IS	SR
Drew Univ/College of Liberal Arts	NJ	55,862	VC
Drexel Univ	PA	51,920	HC
Drury Univ	MO	30,319	VC
Duke Univ	NC	50,250	MC
Duquesne Univ	PA	42,017	VC
Earlham College	IN	49,710	VC+
East Carolina Univ	NC	14,169	C
East Stroudsburg Univ of Pennsylvania	PA	16,636	C
East Tenn State Univ	TN	9,000	C
Eastern Conn State Univ	CT	20,584	C
Eastern Illinois Univ	IL	20,502	C
Eastern Kentucky Univ	KY	11,161	C
Eastern Mennonite Univ	VA	38,850	VC
Eastern Mich Univ	MI	17,961	C
Eastern Washington Univ	WA	16,388	C
Eckerd College	FL	43,902	VC
Edgewood College	WI	33,294	C
Edinboro Univ of Pennsylvania	PA	15,940	LC
Elizabethtown College	PA	47,600	VC
Elmhurst College	IL	42,032	C+
Elon Univ	NC	40,046	HC
Emory and Henry College	VA	387,460	C
Emory Univ	GA	45,000	MC
Emporia State Univ	KS	12,897	C
Eugene Lang College - The New School for Liberal Arts	NY	55,650	VC
Excelsior College	NY	895	SP
Fairfield Univ	CT	55,850	VC
Fairleigh Dickinson Univ/College at Florham	NJ	42,142	C
Fairleigh Dickinson Univ/Metropolitan Campus	NJ	40,254	C
Fayetteville State Univ	NC	10,816	C
Fisk Univ	TN	19,830	C
Fitchburg State Univ	MA	17,241	C
Flagler College	FL	24,960	VC
Florida A&M Univ	FL	14,935	LC
Florida Atlantic Univ	FL	17,339	C
Florida Gulf Coast Univ	FL		C
Florida International Univ	FL	17,747	VC
Florida Southern College	FL	38,240	VC
Florida State Univ	FL	15,238	HC
Fordham Univ	NY	58,927	HC
Fort Hays State Univ	KS	11,354	C
Fort Lewis College	CO	15,513	C
Fort Valley State Univ	GA	11,200	VC
Framingham State Univ	MA	16,750	C
Francis Marion Univ	SC	16,464	LC
Franciscan Univ of Steubenville	OH	27,320	VC
Franklin and Marshall College	PA	58,295	MC
Franklin College	IN	35,885	C
Frostburg State Univ	MD	15,264	LC
Furman Univ	SC	54,006	HC
Gallaudet Univ	DC	25,380	SP
George Fox Univ	OR	40,750	C+
George Mason Univ	VA	15,724	VC
George Washington Univ	DC	57,108	MC
Georgetown Univ	DC	52,910	MC
Georgia College and State Univ	GA	18,216	VC
Georgia Inst of Technology	GA	20,464	MC
Georgia Southern Univ	GA	16,414	C
Georgia State Univ	GA	12,000	VC
Gettysburg College	PA	56,820	HC
Goldey-Beacom College	DE	27,493	C
Gonzaga Univ	WA	44,247	HC
Gordon College	MA	42,660	VC+
Goshen College	IN	35,900	VC
Goucher College	MD	50,252	VC+
Graceland Univ	IA	28,020	C
Grambling State Univ	LA	13,384	LC
Grand Valley State Univ	MI	17,998	VC
Grinnell College	IA	53,654	HC
Grove City College	PA	22,988	HC
Guilford College	NC	35,340	C
Gustavus Adolphus College	MN	48,170	HC
Hamilton College	NY	55,620	MC
Hamline Univ	MN	44,198	VC
Hampden-Sydney College	VA	48,848	C
Hampshire College	MA	58,320	MC
Hampton Univ	VA	28,528	C
Hanover College	IN	41,450	VC
Harding Univ	AR	21,432	C+
Hardin-Simmons Univ	TX	23,560	C+
Hartwick College	NY	49,815	C+
Harvard Univ/Harvard College	MA	49,000	MC
Hastings College	NE	27,782	C+
Haverford College	PA	59,236	MC
Hawaii Pacific Univ	HI	36,690	C
Heidelberg Univ	OH	34,100	C
Hendrix College	AR	48,436	HC+
Hillsdale College	MI	31,890	HC+
Hiram College	OH	37,300	VC
Hobart and William Smith Colleges	NY	43,000	VC
Hofstra Univ	NY	48,020	VC+
Hollins Univ	VA	43,295	VC
Hood College	MD	44,630	C
Hope College	MI	36,320	VC+
Houston Baptist Univ	TX	23,815	C+
Howard Univ	DC	35,957	C
Hunter College / The CUNY	NY	14,429	VC
Huntington Univ	IN	32,220	C
Idaho State Univ	ID	11,908	C
Illinois College	IL	25,770	VC
Illinois State Univ	IL	22,634	VC
Illinois Wesleyan Univ	IL	48,452	VC+
Immaculata Univ	PA	43,000	C
Indiana State Univ	IN	16,000	C
Indiana Univ Bloomington	IN	19,358	HC
Indiana Univ Kokomo	IN	6,674	LC
Indiana Univ Northwest	IN	6,738	LC
Indiana Univ of Pennsylvania	PA	20,180	LC
Indiana Univ South Bend	IN	15,293	C
Indiana Univ Southeast	IN	15,807	LC
Indiana Univ-Purdue Univ Fort Wayne	IN	15,425	C
Indiana Univ-Purdue Univ Indianapolis	IN	17,290	C
Indiana Wesleyan Univ	IN	31,815	VC
Inter-American Univ of PR/San Germán	PR	6,720	
Iona College	NY	44,028	C
Iowa State Univ	IA	16,403	C
Ithaca College	NY	52,300	HC
Jackson State Univ	MS	13,512	LC
Jacksonville State Univ	AL	12,280	LC
Jacksonville Univ	FL	37,780	C
James Madison Univ	VA	18,049	VC
John Carroll Univ	OH	44,520	C+
John Jay College of Criminal Justice / The CUNY	NY	6,059	C
Johns Hopkins Univ	MD	47,492	MC
Johnson C. Smith Univ	NC	25,336	LC
Juniata College	PA	49,340	VC
Kalamazoo College	MI	47,825	HC+
Kansas State Univ	KS	15,497	VC
Kean Univ	NJ	22,060	LC
Keene State College	NH	21,538	C
Kennesaw State Univ	GA	13,017	VC
Kent State Univ	OH	19,352	C
Kenyon College	OH	56,810	MC
King Univ	TN	33,140	C
King's College	PA	41,678	C
Knox College	IL		VC
La Salle Univ	PA	50,270	C
Lafayette College	PA	57,050	HC+
Lake Forest College	IL	45,580	VC
Lake Superior State Univ	MI	18,121	C
Lakeland College	WI	22,990	C
Lamar Univ	TX	6,820	LC
Langston Univ	OK	3,000	LC
Lawrence Univ	WI	46,371	HC
Le Moyne College	NY	42,200	VC
Lebanon Valley College	PA	38,570	C
Lehigh Univ	PA	55,080	MC
Lehman College / The CUNY	NY	5,778	LC
Lenoir-Rhyne College	NC	35,984	C
Lewis & Clark College	OR	52,656	VC
Lewis Univ	IL	23,050	C
Limestone College	SC	29,880	C
Linfield College-McMinnville Campus	OR	46,166	C
Lipscomb Univ	TN	35,722	VC
Lock Haven Univ of Pennsylvania	PA	17,587	LC
LIU/Brooklyn Campus	NY	26,500	C
LIU/C.W. Post Campus	NY	38,888	C
Longwood Univ	VA	20,924	C
Loras College	IA	37,432	VC
Louisiana College	LA	15,746	C
Louisiana State Univ	LA	18,677	VC+
Loyola Marymount Univ	CA	53,240	VC+
Loyola Univ Chicago	IL	49,560	VC+
Loyola Univ Maryland	MD		VC
Loyola Univ New Orleans	LA	46,581	VC
Luther College	IA	44,380	VC+
Lycoming College	PA	43,636	C
Lynchburg College	VA	42,645	C
Lyon College	AR	30,246	VC
Macalester College	MN	53,419	MC
Manchester College	IN	35,070	C
Manhattan College	NY	44,955	VC
Manhattanville College	NY	46,260	VC
Mansfield Univ	PA	19,468	LC
Marian Univ	WI	30,980	LC
Marian Univ/Indianapolis	IN	37,058	C
Marietta College	OH	42,135	VC
Marist College	NY	35,500	C
Marlboro College	VT	35,980	VC
Marquette Univ	WI	43,664	VC+
Marshall Univ	WV	14,820	C
Mary Baldwin College	VA	37,110	C
Marymount Univ	VA	36,178	C
Maryville College	TN	33,150	VC
Mass Inst of Technology	MA	54,238	MC
McDaniel College	MD	45,600	VC
McKendree Univ	IL	29,920	C+
Mercer Univ	GA	44,201	VC+
Meredith College	NC	31,420	C
Merrimack College	MA	44,215	C
Messiah College	PA	39,540	VC
Methodist Univ	NC	37,185	C
Metropolitan State Univ	MN	5,923	SP
Metropolitan State Univ of Denver	CO	4,835	LC
Miami Univ	OH	24,191	HC
Mich State Univ	MI	13,689	VC
Mich Tech Univ	MI	22,105	VC
Middle Tenn State Univ	TN	8,650	C
Middlebury College	VT	57,470	MC
Midland Univ	NE	34,000	C
Midwestern State Univ	TX	9,722	C
Millersville Univ of Pennsylvania	PA	18,498	C
Mills College	CA	54,119	HC
Millsaps College	MS	43,888	VC+
Minn State Univ, Mankato	MN	14,900	C
Minn State Univ, Moorhead	MN	13,392	C
Minot State Univ	ND	10,915	C
Missouri Southern State Univ	MO	11,910	C
Missouri State Univ	MO	13,996	VC
Missouri Univ of Science and Technology	MO	18,655	VC+
Missouri Valley College	MO	22,200	C
Missouri Western State Univ	MO	12,260	NC
Monmouth College	IL	39,290	C
Montana State Univ	MT	14,068	VC
Montclair State Univ	NJ	22,614	C
Moravian College	PA	36,381	VC
Morehouse College	GA	38,640	C
Morgan State Univ	MD	14,500	VC
Mount Holyoke College	MA	53,596	HC+
Mount St. Mary's Univ	MD	46,158	C
Muhlenberg College	PA	52,837	HC
Murray State Univ	KY	14,944	C
Muskingum Univ	OH	30,502	C
Nazareth College of Rochester	NY	41,590	VC
Nebr Wesleyan Univ	NE	29,774	C+
New College of Florida	FL	14,504	HC+
New Jersey City Univ	NJ	21,060	C+
New Mexico State Univ	NM	13,955	LC
New York Univ	NY	61,470	MC
Nichols College	MA	37,240	LC
N Car Agricultural and Technical State Univ	NC	13,175	LC
N Car State Univ	NC	16,202	HC
North Central College	IL	38,343	VC
N Dak State Univ	ND	14,642	C
North Park Univ	IL	30,130	C
Northeastern Illinois Univ	IL		C
Northeastern Univ	MA	55,296	MC
Northern Illinois Univ	IL	19,768	C
Northern Kentucky Univ	KY	15,302	LC
Northern Mich Univ	MI	15,300	VC
Northern State Univ	SD	14,021	C
Northwest Missouri State Univ	MO	14,229	C
Northwestern College of Iowa	IA	34,848	C+
Northwestern Okla State Univ	OK	7,275	NC
Northwestern Univ	IL	37,595	MC
Notre Dame College	OH	34,942	VC
Notre Dame of Maryland Univ	MD	27,700	C
Oakland Univ	MI	19,391	VC
Oberlin College	OH	57,025	MC
Occidental College	CA	59,592	MC+
Oglethorpe Univ	GA	42,580	VC
Ohio Dominican Univ	OH	38,380	C+
Ohio Univ	OH	20,676	VC
Ohio Wesleyan Univ	OH	49,460	C+
Okla City Univ	OK	33,546	VC
Okla State Univ	OK	14,310	VC
Old Dominion Univ	VA	18,662	C
Olivet College	MI	19,984	C
Olivet Nazarene Univ	IL	29,990	C
Oregon State Univ	OR	19,017	C+
Oswego / SUNY	NY	20,009	VC
Otterbein College	OH	32,214	C
Pace Univ	NY	48,094	VC
Pacific Lutheran Univ	WA	44,840	VC
Pacific Univ	OR	42,815	C
Park Univ	MO	17,525	C
Penn State Erie/The Behrend College	PA	16,256	C
Penn State Univ/Univ Park	PA	25,404	VC
Pepperdine Univ	CA	55,372	HC+
Pitzer College	CA	54,988	MC
Plymouth State Univ	NH	23,148	LC
Pomona College	CA	57,680	MC
Portland State Univ	OR	18,672	C
Prescott College	AZ	33,284	C+
Princeton Univ	NJ	53,795	MC
Principia College	IL	35,140	C+
Providence College	RI	55,995	HC
Purchase College / SUNY	NY	16,951	C
Purdue Univ/West Lafayette	IN	20,278	HC
Queens College / The CUNY	NY	17,107	VC
Quinnipiac Univ	CT	53,580	VC
Radford Univ	VA	17,132	LC
Ramapo College of New Jersey	NJ	24,938	C+
Randolph College	VA	43,960	VC
Randolph-Macon College	VA	45,086	C
Reed College	OR	57,780	MC
Regis Univ	CO	41,318	C
Rensselaer Polytechnic Inst	NY	59,229	MC
Rhode Island College	RI	17,132	LC
Rhodes College	TN	47,596	HC+
Rice Univ	TX	43,288	MC
Richard Stockton College of New Jersey	NJ	20,000	VC
Rider Univ	NJ	45,720	C
Ripon College	WI	36,959	C+
Roanoke College	VA	47,996	C+
Robert Morris Univ	PA	36,699	C
Rochester Inst of Technology	NY	42,450	VC+
Rockford College	IL	31,000	C
Rockhurst Univ	MO	20,625	C
Roger Williams Univ	RI	45,788	C
Rollins College	FL	52,370	HC
Roosevelt Univ	IL	22,605	VC
Rose-Hulman Inst of Technology	IN	51,738	MC
Rosemont College	PA	42,350	C
Rowan Univ	NJ	23,570	VC
Rutgers, The State Univ of New Jersey/Camden Campus	NJ	24,254	C
Rutgers, The State Univ of New Jersey/New Brunswick	NJ	25,077	VC
Rutgers, The State Univ of New Jersey/Newark Campus	NJ	25,376	C
Saginaw Valley State Univ	MI	16,869	C
St. Anselm College	NH	48,324	VC
St. Francis Univ	PA	30,029	LC
St. John's Univ	MN	46,146	C
St. Joseph's College	IN	35,790	C
St. Joseph's Univ	PA	52,272	VC
St. Mary's College	IN	45,160	VC
St. Mary's College of Calif	CA	53,550	C
St. Mary's Univ	TX	33,854	C
St. Michael's College	VT	48,740	VC
St. Peter's College	NJ	44,240	C
St. Vincent College	PA	40,244	C
Salem College	NC	29,326	VC
Salem State College	MA	13,161	LC
Salisbury Univ	MD	18,368	VC
Salve Regina Univ	RI	47,250	VC
Sam Houston State Univ	TX	17,082	C
Samford Univ	AL	35,700	VC+
San Diego State Univ	CA	20,578	VC
San Francisco State Univ	CA	18,514	C
San Jose State Univ	CA	19,707	C
Santa Clara Univ	CA	54,702	MC
Sarah Lawrence College	NY	48,000	HC
Scripps College	CA	54,900	MC
Seattle Pacific Univ	WA	41,559	VC+
Seattle Univ	WA	47,010	VC+
Seton Hall Univ	NJ	45,902	C
Seton Hill Univ	PA	35,172	C
Sewanee: The Univ of the South	TN	47,700	HC+
Shepherd Univ	WV	14,996	C
Shippensburg Univ of Pennsylvania	PA	17,064	LC
Shorter Univ	GA	26,470	C
Siena College	NY	43,863	VC
Simmons College	MA	48,770	VC
Simpson College	IA	36,086	VC
Skidmore College	NY	57,926	HC
Slippery Rock Univ of Pennsylvania	PA	10,360	LC
Smith College	MA	57,524	MC
Sonoma State Univ	CA	20,541	C
S Dak State Univ	SD	14,296	C
Southeast Missouri State Univ	MO	14,983	LC
Southeastern Okla State Univ	OK	7,966	C
Southern Conn State Univ	CT	18,033	C
Southern Illinois Univ Carbondale	IL	21,620	C
Southern Illinois Univ Edwardsville	IL	17,532	C
Southern Methodist Univ	TX	57,755	MC
Southern Oregon Univ	OR	17,874	C
Southern Univ at New Orleans	LA	1,000	NC
Southwest Baptist Univ	MO	24,710	C
Southwestern Univ	TX	45,660	VC
Spelman College	GA	24,650	VC
Spring Hill College	AL	42,130	VC
St. Ambrose Univ	IA		C
St. Catherine Univ	MN	37,782	C+
St. Cloud State Univ	MN	10,600	C
St. Edward's Univ	TX	44,674	VC
St. Francis College	NY	34,200	LC
St. John Fisher College	NY	39,370	C+
St. John's Univ	NY	52,840	C+
St. Lawrence Univ	NY	53,740	HC
St. Mary's College of Maryland	MD	26,699	HC
St. Norbert College	WI	39,992	VC
St. Olaf College	MN	49,960	HC+
Stanford Univ	CA	56,411	MC
SUNY/Empire State College	NY	6,315	SP

School	ST	$IS	SR
Stephen F. Austin State Univ	TX	14,668	C
Stetson Univ	FL	49,512	V₵
Stonehill College	MA	46,780	V₵
Stony Brook Univ / SUNY	NY	19,359	HC
Suffolk Univ	MA	46,548	C
SUNY College at Geneseo	NY	18,055	H₵
SUNY Cortland / The SUNY	NY	19,117	C
SUNY Fredonia / The SUNY at Fredonia	NY	18,702	VC
SUNY New Paltz	NY	15,010	C
SUNY Oneonta / SUNY	NY	16,919	VC
SUNY Plattsburgh / SUNY	NY	18,083	VC
Susquehanna Univ	PA	49,170	C
Swarthmore College	PA	57,870	MC
Sweet Briar College	VA	43,765	₵
Syracuse Univ	NY	54,512	HC
Talladega College	AL	13,000	C
Tarleton State Univ	TX	13,489	LC
Taylor Univ	IN	36,742	V₵
Temple Univ	PA	24,392	VC
Tenn Tech Univ	TN	11,310	C
Texas A&M Univ	TX	16,956	V₵
Texas A&M Univ at Commerce	TX	10,496	C
Texas Christian Univ	TX	47,570	HC
Texas Lutheran Univ	TX	34,070	C
Texas Southern Univ	TX	18,212	LC
Texas State Univ	TX	16,495	VC
Texas Tech Univ	TX	14,243	C
Texas Wesleyan Univ	TX	29,886	C
The Catholic Univ of America	DC	52,852	VC
The College of New Rochelle	NY	33,600	VC
The College of St. Rose	NY	26,750	C
Ohio State Univ	OH	19,887	MC
The SUNY at Potsdam	NY	17,754	C
Thomas Edison State College	NJ	5,700	SP
Thomas More College	KY	34,760	C
Tougaloo College	MS	15,275	NC
Touro College	NY	23,150	VC
Towson Univ	MD	16,000	VC
Transylvania Univ	KY	40,310	V₵
Trinity College	CT		H₵
Trinity Univ	TX	44,174	H₵
Trinity Washington Univ	DC	30,250	₵
Truman State Univ	MO	13,546	HC
Tufts Univ	MA	58,780	MC
Tulane Univ	LA	58,942	MC
Tuskegee Univ	AL	26,750	C
Union College	NY		MC
Union Univ	TN	28,260	VC
United States Air Force Academy	CO		MC
United States Military Academy	NY		MC
United States Naval Academy	MD		MC
Universidad del Turabo	PR	4,110	
Univ at Albany / SUNY	NY	18,674	VC
Univ at Buffalo / The SUNY	NY	20,283	VC
Univ of Akron	OH	20,436	C
Univ of Alabama at Birmingham	AL	18,484	₵
Univ of Alabama at Tuscaloosa	AL	17,164	₵
Univ of Alaska Anchorage	AK	15,290	NC
Univ of Alaska Fairbanks	AK	13,955	C
Univ of Arizona	AZ	20,105	C
Univ of Arkansas at Fayetteville	AR	16,860	VC
Univ of Arkansas at Little Rock	AR		C
Univ of Calif at Berkeley	CA	23,322	MC
Univ of Calif at Davis	CA	24,482	HC
Univ of Calif at Irvine	CA	25,961	VC
Univ of Calif at Los Angeles	CA	25,686	MC
Univ of Calif at Riverside	CA	27,204	C
Univ of Calif at San Diego	CA	21,000	VC
Univ of Calif at Santa Barbara	CA	27,551	HC
Univ of Calif at Santa Cruz	CA	27,807	VC
Univ of Central Arkansas	AR	10,840	VC
Univ of Central Florida	FL	15,711	V₵
Univ of Central Missouri	MO	14,605	C
Univ of Central Okla	OK	12,293	C
Univ of Chicago	IL	55,416	MC
Univ of Cincinnati	OH	20,199	VC
Univ of Colo at Colo Springs	CO	15,000	VC
Univ of Colo Boulder	CO	22,605	V₵
Univ of Colo Denver	CO	17,904	C
Univ of Conn	CT	23,744	HC
Univ of Dallas	TX	43,510	V₵
Univ of Dayton	OH	43,750	VC
Univ of Delaware	DE	22,728	VC
Univ of Denver	CO	51,787	V₵
Univ of Detroit Mercy	MI	30,450	C
Univ of Evansville	IN	41,056	V₵
Univ of Findlay	OH	31,916	C
Univ of Florida	FL	15,783	H₵
Univ of Georgia	GA	19,508	VC
Univ of Hartford	CT	42,674	C
Univ of Hawaii at Hilo	HI	6,500	C
Univ of Hawaii at Manoa	HI	19,379	VC
Univ of Idaho	ID	14,558	C
Univ of Illinois at Chicago	IL	24,293	VC
Univ of Illinois at Urbana-Champaign	IL	24,300	HC
Univ of Indianapolis	IN	31,740	LC
Univ of Iowa	IA	17,481	VC
Univ of Kansas	KS	16,980	₵
Univ of Kentucky	KY	19,868	C
Univ of Louisiana at Lafayette	LA	6,130	C
Univ of Louisiana at Monroe	LA	12,998	C
Univ of Maine	ME	19,712	₵
Univ of Mary Hardin-Baylor	TX	31,950	₵
Univ of Mary Washington	VA	19,484	VC
Univ of Maryland	MD	18,801	HC
Univ of Maryland/Baltimore County	MD	18,000	VC
Univ of Mass Amherst	MA	23,697	V₵
Univ of Mass Boston	MA	11,966	C
Univ of Mass Dartmouth	MA	22,223	C
Univ of Mass Lowell	MA	19,316	C
Univ of Memphis	TN	15,094	C
Univ of Miami	FL	55,166	MC
Univ of Mich/Ann Arbor	MI	22,102	H₵
Univ of Mich/Dearborn	MI	9,885	VC
Univ of Mich-Flint	MI	17,547	₵
Univ of Minn/Duluth	MN	18,964	₵
Univ of Minn/Morris	MN	17,150	VC
Univ of Minn/Twin Cities	MN		HC
Univ of Miss	MS	15,182	VC
Univ of Missouri/Columbia	MO	18,201	MC
Univ of Missouri-Kansas City	MO	19,603	C
Univ of Missouri-St. Louis	MO	18,304	VC
Univ of Montana	MT	13,670	C
Univ of Mount Union	OH	35,130	C
Univ of Nebr - Lincoln	NE	17,507	VC
Univ of Nebr at Kearney	NE	14,855	LC
Univ of Nebr at Omaha	NE	12,700	C
Univ of Nevada, Las Vegas	NV	17,303	C
Univ of New Hampshire	NH	24,702	VC
Univ of New Haven	CT	47,740	C
Univ of New Mexico	NM	15,300	C
Univ of New Orleans	LA	9,224	VC
Univ of N Car at Asheville	NC	13,500	V₵
Univ of N Car at Chapel Hill	NC	18,348	MC
Univ of N Car at Charlotte	NC	15,847	C
Univ of N Car at Greensboro	NC	12,848	C
Univ of N Car at Wilmington	NC	13,572	V₵
Univ of N Dak	ND	14,094	C
Univ of North Florida	FL	15,578	VC
Univ of North Texas	TX	15,628	C
Univ of Northern Colo	CO	15,973	C
Univ of Northern Iowa	IA	14,776	C
Univ of Notre Dame	IN		MC
Univ of Okla	OK	17,634	V₵
Univ of Oregon	OR	20,872	VC
Univ of Pennsylvania	PA	56,106	MC
Univ of Pittsburgh at Bradford	PA	21,316	LC
Univ of Pittsburgh at Johnstown	PA	20,862	LC
Univ of Pittsburgh at Pittsburgh	PA	27,800	H₵
Univ of Portland	OR	47,874	VC
Univ of PR Recinto de Rio Piedras	PR	5,750	
Univ of PR/Cayey	PR	1,504	
Univ of PR/Mayaguez	PR	1,250	
Univ of Puget Sound	WA	52,648	H₵
Univ of Redlands	CA	40,500	VC
Univ of Rio Grande	OH	8,750	NC
Univ of Rochester	NY	58,500	MC
Univ of San Diego	CA	53,302	H₵
Univ of San Francisco	CA	49,674	VC
Univ of Science and Arts of Okla	OK	10,560	VC
Univ of Scranton	PA	51,940	VC
Univ of S Car at Columbia	SC	19,725	V₵
Univ of S Car Upstate	SC	17,673	LC
Univ of S Dak	SD	15,111	C
Univ of South Florida	FL	13,000	C
Univ of South Florida/St. Petersburg	FL	12,769	VC
Univ of Southern Calif	CA	56,903	MC
Univ of Southern Indiana	IN	14,657	C
Univ of Southern Maine	ME	16,576	C
Univ of Southern Miss	MS	13,170	C
Univ of St. Thomas - Houston	TX	36,490	VC
Univ of Tampa	FL	35,160	VC
Univ of Tenn at Chattanooga	TN	16,883	C
Univ of Tenn at Knoxville	TN	20,364	V₵
Univ of Tenn at Martin	TN	13,217	C
Univ of Texas at Arlington	TX	10,908	LC
Univ of Texas at Austin	TX	44,074	HC
Univ of Texas at Dallas	TX	21,046	HC
Univ of Texas at El Paso	TX	8,764	NC
Univ of Texas at San Antonio	TX	18,372	C
Univ of Texas-Pan American	TX	12,432	LC
Univ of the District of Columbia	DC	7,244	LC
Univ of the Ozarks	AR	22,100	C
Univ of the Pacific	CA	52,146	VC
Univ of Toledo	OH	18,464	C
Univ of Tulsa	OK	45,311	H₵
Univ of Utah	UT	13,462	VC
Univ of Vermont	VT	26,120	V₵
Univ of Virginia	VA	22,175	MC
Univ of Virginia's College at Wise	VA	11,076	C
Univ of Washington	WA	14,722	VC
Univ of West Georgia	GA	14,852	LC
Univ of Wisc Whitewater	WI	13,314	C
Univ of Wisc/Eau Claire	WI	15,430	VC
Univ of Wisc/Green Bay	WI	14,900	C
Univ of Wisc/La Crosse	WI	14,755	VC
Univ of Wisc/Madison	WI	18,757	HC
Univ of Wisc/Oshkosh	WI	10,426	LC
Univ of Wisc/Parkside	WI	10,181	LC
Univ of Wisc/River Falls	WI	9,722	LC
Univ of Wisc/Stevens Point	WI	14,043	C
Univ of Wisc/Superior	WI	14,106	C
Univ of Wisc-Milwaukee	WI	18,436	C
Univ of Wyoming	WY	13,855	₵
Utah State Univ	UT	11,803	C
Utica College	NY	44,734	C
Valparaiso Univ	IN	43,040	V₵
Vanderbilt Univ	TN	57,072	MC
Vassar College	NY	59,070	MC
Villanova Univ	PA	56,436	MC
Virginia Commonwealth Univ	VA	18,633	C
Virginia Polytechnic Inst and State Univ	VA	14,629	HC
Virginia State Univ	VA	11,318	₵
Wabash College	IN	44,160	VC
Wake Forest Univ	NC	51,000	MC
Wartburg College	IA	41,055	VC
Washburn Univ	KS	12,165	NC
Washington and Jefferson College	PA	49,990	VC
Washington and Lee Univ	VA	52,812	MC
Washington College	MD	48,768	VC
Washington State Univ	WA	20,461	C
Washington Univ in St. Louis	MO	58,818	MC
Wayland Baptist Univ	TX	16,058	LC
Wayne State Univ	MI	19,493	C
Webster Univ	MO	33,990	₵
Wellesley College	MA	49,848	MC
Wells College	NY	38,680	VC
Wesleyan College	GA	24,000	₵
Wesleyan Univ	CT	59,844	MC
West Chester Univ of Pennsylvania	PA	16,836	C
West Liberty Univ	WV	9,142	LC
West Texas A&M Univ	TX	13,478	C
West Virginia State Univ	WV	8,378	NC
West Virginia Univ	WV	15,794	₵
West Virginia Wesleyan College	WV	26,880	C
Western Conn State Univ	CT	18,327	C
Western Illinois Univ	IL	20,130	C
Western Kentucky Univ	KY	11,000	LC
Western Mich Univ	MI	19,042	C
Western New England Univ	MA	45,590	C
Western Oregon Univ	OR	15,021	C
Western State Colo Univ	CO	16,135	C
Western Washington Univ	WA	18,519	VC
Westfield State Univ	MA	18,489	C
Westminster College	MO	30,490	VC
Westminster College	PA	31,290	₵
Westminster College	UT	37,708	VC
Wheaton College	IL	39,650	H₵
Wheaton College	MA	54,934	H₵
Whitman College	WA	54,400	MC
Whittier College	CA	43,416	C
Whitworth Univ	WA	45,826	V₵
Wichita State Univ	KS	12,539	C
Widener Univ	PA	50,368	C
Wilberforce Univ	OH	15,100	LC
Willamette Univ	OR	56,450	V₵
William Paterson Univ of New Jersey	NJ	21,694	C
Williams College	MA	58,900	MC
Wilmington College	OH	29,784	C
Winona State Univ	MN	16,530	C
Winston-Salem State Univ	NC	9,418	LC
Winthrop Univ	SC	21,120	VC
Wittenberg Univ	OH	47,766	VC
Wofford College	SC	45,795	VC
Worcester Polytechnic Inst	MA	53,440	H₵
Worcester State Univ	MA	18,657	C
Wright State Univ	OH	16,983	C
Xavier Univ	OH	43,740	VC
Yale Univ	CT	55,300	MC
Yeshiva Univ	NY	47,250	V₵
York College / CUNY	NY	5,496	NC
York College of Pennsylvania	PA	26,590	C
Youngstown State Univ	OH	16,374	LC

ECONOMICS – STATISTICS

School	ST	$IS	SR
Biola Univ	CA	40,320	VC
Boise State Univ	ID	12,802	C
Bryant Univ	RI	49,179	VC
Univ of Alabama at Huntsville	AL	17,625	VC
Univ of Calif at Irvine	CA	25,961	VC
Univ of Pittsburgh at Pittsburgh	PA	27,800	H₵
Univ of West Georgia	GA	14,852	LC

EDUCATION

School	ST	$IS	SR
Adams State College	CO	13,358	LC
Albertus Magnus College	CT	37,382	LC
Appalachian State Univ	NC	12,919	VC
Aquinas College	MI	33,060	C
Arizona State Univ	AZ	18,818	₵
Arkansas Tech Univ	AR	13,164	LC
Auburn Univ	AL	20,052	V₵
Averett Univ	VA	36,000	LC
Belmont Abbey College	NC	37,716	C
Beloit College	WI	49,970	HC
Bennington College	VT	56,990	H₵
Berea College	KY	7,220	HC
Bethany College	WV	35,282	C
Bethel College	IN	31,560	C
Bethel Univ	MN	34,940	VC
Bethune-Cookman Univ	FL	22,290	LC
Bloomfield College	NJ	36,960	C
Boise State Univ	ID	12,802	C
Boston Univ	MA	54,130	H₵
Bowling Green State Univ	OH	18,970	C
Brown Univ	RI	56,150	MC
Bryant Univ	HI	49,179	VC
Bryn Athyn College	PA	27,984	C
Bucknell Univ	PA	58,160	MC
Cabrini College	PA	40,859	LC
Cairn Univ	PA	31,255	C
Calif Polytechnic State Univ	CA	19,847	HC
Cal State, Chico	CA	18,952	C
Cal State, Monterey Bay	CA	26,871	LC
Calif Univ of Pennsylvania	PA	14,217	C
Calvin College	MI	37,585	V₵
Canisius College	NY	45,602	VC
Case Western Reserve Univ	OH	55,178	MC
Catawba College	NC	37,105	C
Cedar Crest College	PA	43,240	C
Central Mich Univ	MI	18,066	C
Chapman Univ	CA	56,019	V₵
Chatham Univ	PA	42,440	VC
Coker College	SC	32,256	LC
Colgate Univ	NY	50,930	MC
College of St. Elizabeth	NJ	43,839	LC
College of St. Mary	NE	34,334	C
College of St. Scholastica	MN	39,960	C
Colo College	CO	54,534	MC
Colo State Univ-Fort Collins	CO	20,090	VC
Columbia College	MO	24,578	C
Columbia Univ in the City of New York	NY	61,116	MC
Concordia College New York	NY	31,500	VC
Corban Univ	OR	34,764	C
Cornerstone Univ and Grand Rapids Theological Seminary	MI	30,866	C
Culver-Stockton College	MO	30,900	C
Dallas Baptist Univ	TX	29,118	C
Denison Univ	OH	54,670	H₵
DePaul Univ	IL	46,120	VC
Dominican Univ	IL	37,628	C
Dordt College	IA	34,160	VC
Drexel Univ	PA	51,920	HC
Duquesne Univ	PA	42,017	VC
East Texas Baptist Univ	TX	29,135	C
Eastern Mich Univ	MI	17,961	C
Eastern Nazarene College	MA	30,000	C
Eastern Oregon Univ	OR	10,400	C
Elizabethtown College	PA	47,600	VC
Elon Univ	NC	40,046	HC
Endicott College	MA	42,390	C
Eugene Lang College - The New School for Liberal Arts	NY	55,650	VC
Eureka College	IL	19,280	C
Felician College	NJ	41,640	C
Fitchburg State Univ	MA	17,241	C
Florida International Univ	FL	17,747	VC
Fontbonne Univ	MO	31,384	C
Franklin Pierce Univ	NH	41,598	C
Friends Univ	KS	29,100	C
Furman Univ	SC	54,006	HC
Georgian Court Univ	NJ	39,726	LC
Goddard College	VT	16,418	VC
Goucher College	MD	50,252	V₵
Grand Canyon Univ	AZ	24,540	VC
Guilford College	NC	35,340	C
Hamline Univ	MN	44,198	VC
Hampshire College	MA	58,320	MC
Hardin-Simmons Univ	TX	23,560	₵
Harris-Stowe State Univ	MO	14,360	NC
Henderson State Univ	AR	13,634	C
Hiram College	OH	37,300	VC
Hope International Univ	CA	34,650	C
Howard Univ	DC	35,957	C
Huntington Univ	IN	32,220	C

School	ST	$IS	SR
Huston-Tillotson Univ	TX	18,124	C+
Illinois Wesleyan Univ	IL	48,452	VC+
Indiana Univ Bloomington	IN	19,358	HC
Ithaca College	NY	52,300	HC
John Carroll Univ	OH	44,520	C+
Johnson State College	VT	16,721	C
Keene State College	NH	21,538	C
LaGrange College	GA	34,480	C
Lake Forest College	IL	45,580	VC
Lees-McRae College	NC	33,624	C
Lipscomb Univ	TN	35,722	VC
Loras College	IA	37,432	VC
Lourdes Univ	OH	26,055	LC
Lynchburg College	VA	42,645	C
Macalester College	MN	53,119	MC
Maharishi Univ of Management	IA	31,000	VC
Manhattan College	NY	44,955	VC
Manhattanville College	NY	46,260	VC
Marquette Univ	WI	43,664	VC+
Marshall Univ	WV	14,820	C
Martin Univ	IN	11,000	SP
Mary Baldwin College	VA	37,110	C
Mass College of Liberal Arts	MA	16,733	C
Mayville State Univ	ND	11,401	NC
Mercer Univ	GA	44,201	VC+
Mich State Univ	MI	13,689	VC
Midway College	KY	20,150	C
Millikin Univ	IL	37,462	C
Millsaps College	MS	43,888	VC+
Montana State Univ-Billings	MT	12,425	LC
Morehouse College	GA	38,640	C
Morningside College	IA	32,620	C
Mount Aloysius College	PA	27,970	C
Mount St. Mary College	NY	39,540	C
New England College	NH	45,930	LC
New York Inst of Technology	NY	40,590	VC
New York Univ	NY	61,470	MC
N Car State Univ	NC	16,202	HC
Northwest Christian Univ	OR	27,399	C
Northwest Univ	WA	18,854	C
Northwestern Univ	IL	37,595	MC
Nova Southeastern Univ	FL	34,016	VC
Ohio State Univ at Lima	OH	7,140	C
Ohio State Univ at Marion	OH	9,850	MC
Okla City Univ	OK	33,546	VC
Okla State Univ	OK	14,310	VC
Oregon State Univ	OR	19,017	C+
Pacific Lutheran Univ	WA	44,840	VC
Piedmont College	GA	29,260	C
Pittsburg State Univ	KS	12,032	C
Point Park Univ	PA	36,390	C
Prescott College	AZ	33,284	C+
Purdue Univ/West Lafayette	IN	20,278	HC
Quincy Univ	IL	34,980	LC
Randolph College	VA	43,960	VC
Regis Univ	CO	41,318	C
Richard Stockton College of New Jersey	NJ	20,000	VC
Rocky Mountain College	MT	32,242	C
Roger Williams Univ	RI	45,788	C
Rosemont College	PA	42,350	C
Rowan Univ	NJ	23,570	VC
Sacred Heart Univ	CT	48,564	VC
St. Louis Univ	MO	46,594	VC+
Salem State College	MA	13,161	LC
Salisbury Univ	MD	18,368	VC
San Diego Christian College	CA	31,012	C
Schreiner Univ	TX	32,734	LC
Seattle Pacific Univ	WA	41,559	VC+
Shawnee State Univ	OH	16,545	NC
Simmons College	MA	48,770	VC
Smith College	MA	57,524	MC
S Dak State Univ	SD	14,296	C
Southern Nazarene Univ	OK	24,354	NC
Southern New Hampshire Univ	NH	38,100	C
Southern Oregon Univ	OR	17,874	C
Southern Polytechnic State Univ	GA	13,958	VC
Southwestern Univ	TX	45,660	VC
Spalding Univ	KY	31,850	LC
St. Bonaventure Univ	NY	38,831	C
St. Francis College	NY	34,200	LC
St. John's Univ	NY	52,840	C+
St. Joseph's College, New York / Brooklyn Campus	NY	21,878	C
St. Joseph's College, New York / Suffolk Campus	NY	21,878	VC
SUNY/Empire State College	NY	6,315	SP
Stonehill College	MA	46,780	VC+
SUNY Fredonia / The SUNY at Fredonia	NY	18,702	VC
Swarthmore College	PA	57,870	MC
Syracuse Univ	NY	54,512	HC
Taylor Univ	IN	36,742	VC+
Texas A&M Univ at Corpus Christi	TX	11,544	LC
Texas Lutheran Univ	TX	34,070	C
Texas Wesleyan Univ	TX	29,886	C
The Catholic Univ of America	DC	52,852	VC
The College of Idaho	ID	31,277	VC
Ohio State Univ	OH	19,887	MC
Towson Univ	MD	16,000	VC
Transylvania Univ	KY	40,310	VC+
Trevecca Nazarene Univ	TN	30,118	C
Trinity Christian College	IL	28,869	C
Trinity College	CT		HC+
Trinity Washington Univ	DC	30,250	C+
Tusculum College	TN	24,295	C
Union College	KY	28,775	C
Union Inst & Univ	OH	8,912	SP
Union Univ	TN	28,260	VC
Unity College	ME	34,054	C
Univ of Akron	OH	20,436	C
Univ of Arizona	AZ	20,105	C
Univ of Colo Denver	CO	17,904	C
Univ of Conn	CT	23,744	HC
Univ of Delaware	DE	22,728	VC
Univ of Dubuque	IA	30,200	C
Univ of Idaho	ID	14,558	C
Univ of Illinois at Urbana-Champaign	IL	24,300	HC
Univ of La Verne	CA	47,010	VC
Univ of Maryland	MD	18,801	HC
Univ of Mass Amherst	MA	23,697	VC+
Univ of Mich/Dearborn	MI	9,885	VC
Univ of Mich-Flint	MI	17,547	C+
Univ of Missouri/Columbia	MO	18,201	MC
Univ of Missouri-St. Louis	MO	18,304	VC
Univ of Montana-Western	MT	9,753	LC
Univ of Nebr - Lincoln	NE	17,507	VC
Univ of New England	ME	46,145	C+
Univ of Northern Colo	CO	15,973	C
Univ of Oregon	OR	20,872	VC
Univ of PR Recinto de Rio Piedras	PR	5,750	
Univ of South Alabama	AL	13,510	C
Univ of South Florida	FL	13,000	C
Univ of South Florida/St. Petersburg	FL	12,769	VC
Univ of St. Thomas - Houston	TX	36,490	VC
Univ of Tenn at Chattanooga	TN	16,883	C
Univ of Tenn at Knoxville	TN	20,364	VC+
Univ of Texas at San Antonio	TX	18,372	C
Univ of the Pacific	CA	52,146	VC
Univ of Tulsa	OK	45,311	HC+
Univ of Vermont	VT	26,120	VC+
Univ of Wisc/Green Bay	WI	14,900	C
Univ of Wisc/Parkside	WI	10,181	LC
Univ of Wisc/Platteville	WI	14,274	C
Univ of Wisc/Stevens Point	WI	14,043	C
Univ of Wisc-Milwaukee	WI	18,436	C
Utica College	NY	44,734	C
Vanderbilt Univ	TN	57,072	MC
Vanguard Univ of Southern Calif	CA	35,833	VC
Victory Univ	TN	19,118	C
Virginia Intermont College	VA	32,411	LC
Wake Forest Univ	NC	51,000	MC
Washburn Univ	KS	12,165	NC
Washington and Jefferson College	PA	49,990	VC
Washington State Univ	WA	20,461	C
Washington Univ in St. Louis	MO	58,818	MC
Webster Univ	MO	33,990	C+
Western Mich Univ	MI	19,042	C
Western Oregon Univ	OR	15,021	C
Wheeling Jesuit Univ	WV	34,668	C
William Peace Univ	NC	32,900	LC
Wilmington College	OH	29,784	C
Wright State Univ	OH	16,983	C
Xavier Univ	OH	43,740	VC
York College	NE	19,475	C
York College of Pennsylvania	PA	26,590	C
Youngstown State Univ	OH	16,374	LC

EDUCATION ADMINISTRATION

School	ST	$IS	SR
Ashland Univ	OH	25,000	C
Auburn Univ	AL	20,052	VC+
Bryant Univ	RI	49,179	VC
Cairn Univ	PA	31,255	C
Canisius College	NY	45,602	VC
DePaul Univ	IL	46,120	VC
Howard Univ	DC	35,957	C
Missouri State Univ	MO	13,996	VC
Salisbury Univ	MD	18,368	VC
San Jose State Univ	CA	19,707	C
Southwestern Okla State Univ	OK	9,160	C
Univ of Arkansas at Little Rock	AR		C
Univ of Georgia	GA	19,508	VC
Univ of Idaho	ID	14,558	C
Univ of Louisiana at Monroe	LA	12,998	C
Univ of Missouri/Columbia	MO	18,201	MC
Univ of Tenn at Martin	TN	13,217	C
Western Washington Univ	WA	18,519	VC

EDUCATION OF THE DEAF AND HEARING IMPAIRED

School	ST	$IS	SR
Barton College	NC	27,660	C
Boston Univ	MA	54,130	HC+
Bowling Green State Univ	OH	18,970	C
Cal State, Northridge	CA	28,313	C
Canisius College	NY	45,602	VC
College of New Jersey	NJ	25,376	HC
Eastern Kentucky Univ	KY	11,161	C
Eastern Mich Univ	MI	17,961	C
Flagler College	FL	24,960	VC
Fontbonne Univ	MO	31,384	C
Ithaca College	NY	52,300	HC
MacMurray College	IL	20,755	C
Marywood Univ	PA	40,695	C
Minot State Univ	ND	10,915	C
Rochester Inst of Technology	NY	42,450	VC+
San Jose State Univ	CA	19,707	C
Southern Univ at New Orleans	LA	1,000	NC
Stephen F. Austin State Univ	TX	14,668	C
Towson Univ	MD	16,000	VC
Univ of Arkansas at Little Rock	AR		C
Univ of Montevallo	AL	17,320	C
Univ of Nebr - Lincoln	NE	17,507	VC
Univ of N Car at Greensboro	NC	12,848	C
Univ of Science and Arts of Okla	OK	10,560	VC
Univ of Tulsa	OK	45,311	HC+

EDUCATION OF THE EMOTIONALLY HANDICAPPED

School	ST	$IS	SR
Concordia Univ St. Paul	MN	27,200	C
CUNY-City College	NY	19,576	HC+
East Carolina Univ	NC	14,169	C
Eastern Mich Univ	MI	17,961	C
Florida State Univ	FL	15,238	HC
Manhattan College	NY	44,955	VC
Prescott College	AZ	33,284	C+
Univ of South Florida	FL	13,000	C
Walsh Univ	OH	35,100	C
Western Mich Univ	MI	19,042	C

EDUCATION OF THE EXCEPTIONAL CHILD

School	ST	$IS	SR
Ashland Univ	OH	25,000	C
Bethel Univ	TN	19,186	C
Bethune-Cookman Univ	FL	22,290	LC
Canisius College	NY	45,602	VC
Edgewood College	WI	33,294	C
Flagler College	FL	24,960	VC
Florida Atlantic Univ	FL	17,339	C
Houghton College	NY	35,740	VC
Jacksonville Univ	FL	37,780	C
Mansfield Univ	PA	19,468	LC
Mayville State Univ	ND	11,401	NC
Minot State Univ	ND	10,915	C
Northwest Nazarene Univ	ID	24,275	NC
Nova Southeastern Univ	FL	34,016	VC
Prescott College	AZ	33,284	C+
St. Augustine's Univ	NC	14,000	C
Southeast Missouri State Univ	MO	14,983	LC
Southeastern Univ	FL	27,201	C+
Univ of Central Arkansas	AR	10,840	VC
Univ of Central Florida	FL	15,711	VC+
Univ of Great Falls	MT	27,970	C
Univ of Miami	FL	55,166	MC
Univ of Tenn at Chattanooga	TN	16,883	C
Univ of Wisc/Stevens Point	WI	14,043	C
Walsh Univ	OH	35,100	C
Warner Univ	FL	18,000	C
Western Kentucky Univ	KY	11,000	LC

EDUCATION OF THE MENTALLY HANDICAPPED

School	ST	$IS	SR
Brescia Univ	KY	26,140	VC+
CUNY-City College	NY	19,576	HC+
East Carolina Univ	NC	14,169	C
Eastern Mich Univ	MI	17,961	C
Florida State Univ	FL	15,238	HC
Kutztown Univ of Pennsylvania	PA	16,909	LC
Minot State Univ	ND	10,915	C
Northern Mich Univ	MI	15,300	VC
Northwest Missouri State Univ	MO	14,229	C
Prescott College	AZ	33,284	C+
Southeastern Okla State Univ	OK	7,966	C
Univ of N Car at Charlotte	NC	15,847	C
Univ of Rio Grande	OH	8,750	NC
Univ of South Florida	FL	13,000	C
Walsh Univ	OH	35,100	C
Western Mich Univ	MI	19,042	C

EDUCATION OF THE MULTIPLY HANDICAPPED

School	ST	$IS	SR
Aquinas College	MI	33,060	C
Ball State Univ	IN	17,850	C
Bowling Green State Univ	OH	18,970	C
Eastern Mich Univ	MI	17,961	C
Univ of Illinois at Urbana-Champaign	IL	24,300	HC

EDUCATION OF THE PHYSICALLY HANDICAPPED

School	ST	$IS	SR
Aquinas College	MI	33,060	C
Eastern Mich Univ	MI	17,961	C
Kutztown Univ of Pennsylvania	PA	16,000	LC
Walsh Univ	OH	35,100	C

EDUCATION OF THE VISUALLY HANDICAPPED

School	ST	$IS	SR
Eastern Mich Univ	MI	17,961	C
Florida State Univ	FL	15,238	HC
Kutztown Univ of Pennsylvania	PA	16,909	LC
Stephen F. Austin State Univ	TX	14,668	C

EDUCATION SERVICES

School	ST	$IS	SR
Birmingham-Southern College	AL	42,370	VC+
SUNY Cortland / The SUNY	NY	19,117	C

EDUCATIONAL MEDIA

School	ST	$IS	SR
Eastern Mich Univ	MI	17,961	C

EDUCATIONAL STATISTICS AND RESEARCH

School	ST	$IS	SR
Bryant Univ	RI	49,179	VC
Bucknell Univ	PA	58,160	MC
Emory Univ	GA	45,000	MC
Penn State Univ/Univ Park	PA	25,404	VC

ELECTRICAL AND COMPUTER ENGINEERING

School	ST	$IS	SR
Bowling Green State Univ	OH	18,970	C
Cornell Univ	NY	59,037	MC
Franklin W. Olin College of Engineering	MA	57,500	SP
Indiana Univ-Purdue Univ Indianapolis	IN	17,290	C
New York Univ	NY	61,470	MC
Northern Arizona Univ	AZ	18,592	C
Oswego / SUNY	NY	20,009	VC
Univ of Denver	CO	51,787	VC+
Univ of Idaho	ID	14,558	C
Univ of Mass Boston	MA	11,966	C

ELECTRICAL TECHNOLOGY

School	ST	$IS	SR
Thomas Edison State College	NJ	5,700	SP

ELECTRICAL/ELECTRONICS ENGINEERING

School	ST	$IS	SR
Alabama A&M Univ	AL	96,100	C
Andrews Univ	MI	28,030	C+
Arizona State Univ	AZ	18,818	C+
Arkansas State Univ	AR	14,980	C
Arkansas Tech Univ	AR	13,164	LC
Auburn Univ	AL	20,052	VC+
Baylor Univ	TX	46,720	HC
Benedict College	SC	20,454	NC
Bethel College	IN	31,560	C
Binghamton Univ / The SUNY	NY	20,832	HC+
Bloomsburg Univ of Pennsylvania	PA	13,598	C
Boise State Univ	ID	12,802	C
Boston Univ	MA	54,130	HC+
Bradley Univ	IL	31,874	VC
Brigham Young Univ	UT	12,100	HC
Bucknell Univ	PA	58,160	MC
Calif Baptist Univ	CA	35,890	C
Calif Inst of Technology	CA	54,045	MC
Calif Polytechnic State Univ	CA	19,847	HC
Calif State Polytechnic Univ, Pomona	CA	18,932	C
Cal State, Chico	CA	18,952	C
Cal State, Fresno	CA	17,405	C
Cal State, Fullerton	CA	25,188	C+
Cal State, Long Beach	CA	17,534	C+
Cal State, Los Angeles	CA	15,829	C
Cal State, Sacramento	CA	16,200	C
Calvin College	MI	37,585	VC+
Capitol College	MD	21,250	C
Carnegie Mellon Univ	PA	51,260	MC

School	ST	$IS	SR
Case Western Reserve Univ	OH	55,178	MC
Cedarville Univ	OH	31,036	V₵
Central Mich Univ	MI	18,066	C
Central Washington Univ	WA	11,730	C
Christian Brothers Univ	TN	19,140	HC
Citadel, The	SC		C
Clarkson Univ	NY	53,538	HC
Clemson Univ	SC	19,136	HC
Cleveland State Univ	OH	21,357	C
College of New Jersey	NJ	25,376	HC
Colo State Univ-Fort Collins	CO	20,090	VC
Colo Technical Univ	CO	10,500	LC
Columbia Univ in the City of New York	NY	61,116	MC
Cooper Union for the Advancement of Science and Art	NY	55,600	MC
CUNY-City College	NY	19,576	H₵
Delaware State Univ	DE	14,700	LC
Dordt College	IA	34,160	VC
Drexel Univ	PA	51,920	HC
Duke Univ	NC	50,250	MC
Elizabethtown College	PA	47,600	VC
Embry-Riddle Aeronautical Univ - Daytona Beach	FL	40,884	₵
Embry-Riddle Aeronautical Univ - Prescott Campus	AZ	40,584	VC
Fairfield Univ	CT	55,850	VC
Fairleigh Dickinson Univ/ Metropolitan Campus	NJ	40,254	C
Florida A&M Univ	FL	14,935	LC
Florida Atlantic Univ	FL	17,339	C
Florida Inst of Technology	FL	48,290	VC
Florida International Univ	FL	17,747	VC
Florida State Univ	FL	15,238	HC
Gannon Univ	PA	37,940	C
George Mason Univ	VA	15,724	VC
George Washington Univ	DC	57,108	MC
Georgia Inst of Technology	GA	20,464	MC
Georgia Southern Univ	GA	16,414	C
Gonzaga Univ	WA	44,247	HC
Grove City College	PA	22,988	HC
Hampton Univ	VA	28,528	C
Harding Univ	AR	21,432	₵
Hofstra Univ	NY	48,020	V₵
Howard Univ	DC	35,957	C
Idaho State Univ	ID	11,908	C
Illinois Inst of Technology	IL	38,512	H₵
Indiana Inst of Technology	IN	34,240	LC
Indiana Univ-Purdue Univ Fort Wayne	IN	15,425	C
Indiana Univ-Purdue Univ Indianapolis	IN	17,290	C
Inter-American Univ of PR/ Bayamon Univ College	PR	4,428	
Iowa State Univ	IA	16,403	C
Jackson State Univ	MS	13,512	LC
Jacksonville Univ	FL	37,780	C
John Brown Univ	AR	30,996	V₵
Johns Hopkins Univ	MD	47,492	MC
Johnson and Wales Univ/ North Miami Campus	FL	34,368	C
Johnson and Wales Univ/ Providence Campus	RI	34,668	C
Kansas State Univ	KS	15,497	VC
Kettering Univ	MI	31,456	HC
Lafayette College	PA	57,050	H₵
Lake Superior State Univ	MI	18,121	C
Lamar Univ	TX	6,820	LC
Lawrence Tech Univ	MI	37,630	VC
Lehigh Univ	PA	55,080	MC
LeTourneau Univ	TX	26,230	C
Lipscomb Univ	TN	35,722	VC
Loras College	IA	37,432	VC
Louisiana State Univ	LA	18,677	V₵
Loyola Marymount Univ	CA	53,240	V₵
Manhattan College	NY	44,955	VC
Maritime College / SUNY	NY	16,020	C
Marquette Univ	WI	43,664	V₵
Mass Inst of Technology	MA	54,238	MC
Merrimack College	MA	44,215	C
Miami Univ	OH	24,191	HC
Mich State Univ	MI	13,689	VC
Mich Tech Univ	MI	22,105	VC
Milwaukee School of Engineering	WI	39,948	V₵
Minn State Univ, Mankato	MN	14,900	C
Missouri Univ of Science and Technology	MO	18,655	V₵
Montana State Univ	MT	14,068	VC
Morgan State Univ	MD	14,500	VC
New Jersey Inst of Technology	NJ	26,490	VC
New Mexico Inst of Mining and Technology	NM	12,892	HC
New Mexico State Univ	NM	13,955	LC
New York Inst of Technology	NY	40,590	VC
New York Univ	NY	61,470	MC
N Car Agricultural and Technical State Univ	NC	13,175	LC
N Car State Univ	NC	16,202	HC
N Dak State Univ	ND	14,642	C
Northeastern Univ	MA	55,296	MC
Northern Illinois Univ	IL	19,768	C
Northwestern Univ	IL	37,595	MC
Norwich Univ	VT	28,212	C
Oakland Univ	MI	19,391	VC
Ohio Northern Univ	OH	42,075	VC
Ohio Univ	OH	20,676	VC
Okla Christian Univ	OK	24,975	VC
Okla State Univ	OK	14,310	VC
Old Dominion Univ	VA	18,662	C
Oral Roberts Univ	OK	31,734	C
Oregon State Univ	OR	19,017	₵
Penn State Univ/Univ Park	PA	25,404	VC
Point Park Univ	PA	36,390	C
Polytechnic Inst of New York Univ	NY	53,064	H₵
Portland State Univ	OR	18,672	C
Prairie View A&M Univ	TX	15,205	LC
Princeton Univ	NJ	53,795	MC
Purdue Univ/Calumet	IN	14,336	C
Purdue Univ/West Lafayette	IN	20,278	HC
Rensselaer Polytechnic Inst	NY	59,229	MC
Rice Univ	TX	43,288	MC
Rochester Inst of Technology	NY	42,450	V₵
Rose-Hulman Inst of Technology	IN	51,738	MC
Rutgers, The State Univ of New Jersey/New Brunswick	NJ	25,077	VC
Saginaw Valley State Univ	MI	16,869	C
St. Louis Univ	MO	46,594	V₵
St. Mary's Univ	TX	33,854	C
San Diego State Univ	CA	20,578	VC
San Francisco State Univ	CA	18,514	C
San Jose State Univ	CA	19,707	C
Santa Clara Univ	CA	54,702	MC
Seattle Pacific Univ	WA	41,559	V₵
Seattle Univ	WA	47,010	V₵
S Dak School of Mines and Technology	SD	15,260	VC
S Dak State Univ	SD	14,296	C
Southern Illinois Univ Carbondale	IL	21,620	C
Southern Illinois Univ Edwardsville	IL	17,532	C
Southern Methodist Univ	TX	57,755	MC
Southern Polytechnic State Univ	GA	13,958	VC
Southern Univ and A&M College	LA	9,761	₵
St. Cloud State Univ	MN	10,600	C
Stanford Univ	CA	56,411	MC
SUNY Inst of Technology at Utica / Rome	NY	23,818	C
Stevens Inst of Technology	NJ	50,130	HC
Stony Brook Univ / SUNY	NY	19,359	HC
Suffolk Univ	MA	46,548	C
SUNY New Paltz	NY	15,010	C
Syracuse Univ	NY	54,512	HC
Temple Univ	PA	24,392	VC
Tenn State Univ	TN	9,048	C
Tenn Tech Univ	TN	11,310	C
Texas A&M Univ	TX	16,956	V₵
Texas A&M Univ at Kingsville	TX	7,500	LC
Texas Christian Univ	TX	47,570	HC
Texas State Univ	TX	16,495	VC
Texas Tech Univ	TX	14,243	C
The Catholic Univ of America	DC	52,852	VC
Ohio State Univ	OH	19,887	MC
Trine Univ	IN	39,400	VC
Tufts Univ	MA	58,780	MC
Tuskegee Univ	AL	26,750	C
Union College	NY		MC
United States Air Force Academy	CO		MC
United States Coast Guard Academy	CT		HC
United States Military Academy	NY		MC
Universidad Politecnica de PR	PR	19,252	
Univ at Buffalo / The SUNY	NY	20,283	VC
Univ of Akron	OH	20,436	C
Univ of Alabama at Birmingham	AL	18,484	₵
Univ of Alabama at Huntsville	AL	17,625	VC
Univ of Alabama at Tuscaloosa	AL	17,164	₵
Univ of Alaska Anchorage	AK	15,290	NC
Univ of Alaska Fairbanks	AK	13,955	C
Univ of Arizona	AZ	20,105	C
Univ of Arkansas at Fayetteville	AR	16,860	VC
Univ of Calif at Berkeley	CA	23,322	MC
Univ of Calif at Davis	CA	24,482	HC
Univ of Calif at Irvine	CA	25,961	VC
Univ of Calif at Los Angeles	CA	25,686	MC
Univ of Calif at Riverside	CA	27,204	C
Univ of Calif at San Diego	CA	21,000	VC
Univ of Calif at Santa Barbara	CA	27,551	HC
Univ of Calif at Santa Cruz	CA	27,807	VC
Univ of Central Florida	FL	15,711	V₵
Univ of Central Missouri	MO	14,605	C
Univ of Central Okla	OK	12,293	C
Univ of Cincinnati	OH	20,199	VC
Univ of Colo at Colo Springs	CO	15,000	VC
Univ of Colo Boulder	CO	22,605	V₵
Univ of Colo Denver	CO	17,904	C
Univ of Conn	CT	23,744	HC
Univ of Dayton	OH	43,750	VC
Univ of Delaware	DE	22,728	VC
Univ of Denver	CO	51,787	V₵
Univ of Detroit Mercy	MI	30,450	C
Univ of Evansville	IN	41,056	V₵
Univ of Florida	FL	15,783	H₵
Univ of Georgia	GA	19,508	VC
Univ of Hartford	CT	42,674	C
Univ of Hawaii at Manoa	HI	19,379	VC
Univ of Houston	TX	19,184	VC
Univ of Idaho	ID	14,558	C
Univ of Illinois at Chicago	IL	24,293	VC
Univ of Illinois at Urbana-Champaign	IL	24,300	HC
Univ of Indianapolis	IN	31,740	LC
Univ of Iowa	IA	17,481	VC
Univ of Kansas	KS	16,980	₵
Univ of Kentucky	KY	19,868	C
Univ of Louisiana at Lafayette	LA	6,130	C
Univ of Louisville	KY	17,460	VC
Univ of Maine	ME	19,712	₵
Univ of Maryland	MD	18,801	HC
Univ of Mass Amherst	MA	23,697	V₵
Univ of Mass Dartmouth	MA	22,223	C
Univ of Mass Lowell	MA	19,316	C
Univ of Memphis	TN	15,094	C
Univ of Miami	FL	55,166	MC
Univ of Mich/Ann Arbor	MI	22,102	H₵
Univ of Minn/Duluth	MN	18,964	₵
Univ of Minn/Twin Cities	MN		HC
Univ of Miss	MS	15,482	VC
Univ of Missouri/Columbia	MO	18,201	MC
Univ of Missouri-Kansas City	MO	19,603	C
Univ of Missouri-St. Louis	MO	18,304	VC
Univ of Nebr - Lincoln	NE	17,507	VC
Univ of Nevada, Las Vegas	NV	17,303	C
Univ of Nevada/Reno	NV	14,500	NC
Univ of New Hampshire	NH	24,702	VC
Univ of New Haven	CT	47,740	C
Univ of New Mexico	NM	15,300	C
Univ of New Orleans	LA	9,224	VC
Univ of N Car at Charlotte	NC	15,847	C
Univ of N Dak	ND	14,094	C
Univ of North Florida	FL	15,578	VC
Univ of North Texas	TX	15,628	C
Univ of Notre Dame	IN		MC
Univ of Okla	OK	17,634	V₵
Univ of Pennsylvania	PA	56,106	MC
Univ of Pittsburgh at Pittsburgh	PA	27,800	H₵
Univ of Portland	OR	47,874	VC
Univ of PR/Mayaguez	PR	1,250	
Univ of Rochester	NY	58,500	MC
Univ of San Diego	CA	53,302	H₵
Univ of Scranton	PA	51,940	VC
Univ of South Alabama	AL	13,510	C
Univ of S Car at Columbia	SC	19,725	V₵
Univ of South Florida	FL	13,000	C
Univ of Southern Calif	CA	56,903	MC
Univ of Southern Maine	ME	16,576	C
Univ of Tenn at Chattanooga	TN	16,883	C
Univ of Tenn at Knoxville	TN	20,364	V₵
Univ of Texas at Arlington	TX	10,908	LC
Univ of Texas at Austin	TX	44,074	HC
Univ of Texas at Dallas	TX	21,046	HC
Univ of Texas at El Paso	TX	8,764	NC
Univ of Texas at San Antonio	TX	18,372	C
Univ of Texas-Pan American	TX	12,432	LC
Univ of the District of Columbia	DC	7,244	LC
Univ of the Pacific	CA	52,146	VC
Univ of Toledo	OH	18,464	C
Univ of Tulsa	OK	45,311	H₵
Univ of Utah	UT	13,462	VC
Univ of Vermont	VT	26,120	V₵
Univ of Virginia	VA	22,175	MC
Univ of Washington	WA	14,722	VC
Univ of West Florida	FL	14,656	C
Univ of Wisc/Madison	WI	18,757	HC
Univ of Wisc/Platteville	WI	14,274	C
Univ of Wisc-Milwaukee	WI	18,436	C
Univ of Wyoming	WY	13,855	₵
Utah State Univ	UT	11,803	C
Valparaiso Univ	IN	43,040	V₵
Vanderbilt Univ	TN	57,072	MC
Villanova Univ	PA	56,436	MC
Virginia Commonwealth Univ	VA	18,633	C
Virginia Military Inst	VA	16,156	C
Virginia Polytechnic Inst and State Univ	VA	14,629	HC
Washington State Univ	WA	20,461	C
Washington Univ in St. Louis	MO	58,818	MC
Wayne State Univ	MI	19,493	C
West Virginia Univ	WV	15,794	₵
West Virginia Univ Inst of Technology	WV	14,094	NC
Western Carolina Univ	NC	13,965	₵
Western Kentucky Univ	KY	11,000	LC
Western Mich Univ	MI	19,042	C
Western New England Univ	MA	45,590	C
Western Washington Univ	WA	18,519	VC
Wichita State Univ	KS	12,539	C
Widener Univ	PA	50,368	C
Wilkes Univ	PA	42,786	C
Worcester Polytechnic Inst	MA	53,440	H₵
Wright State Univ	OH	16,983	C
Yale Univ	CT	55,300	MC
York College of Pennsylvania	PA	26,590	C
Youngstown State Univ	OH	16,374	LC

ELECTRICAL/ELECTRONICS ENGINEERING TECHNOLOGY

School	ST	$IS	SR
Alabama A&M Univ	AL	96,100	C
Alfred State / SUNY College of Technology	NY	18,034	C
Appalachian State Univ	NC	12,919	VC
Arizona State Univ	AZ	18,818	₵
Baker College of Flint	MI	7,800	NC
Bowling Green State Univ	OH	18,970	C
Brigham Young Univ	UT	12,100	HC
Buffalo State/State Univ of Buffalo	NY	15,733	₵
Calif Univ of Pennsylvania	PA	14,217	C
Cameron Univ	OK	9,267	LC
Central Conn State Univ	CT	19,212	C
Cleveland State Univ	OH	21,357	C
Colo State Univ-Pueblo	CO	13,532	LC
Colo Technical Univ	CO	10,500	LC
East Carolina Univ	NC	14,169	C
Eastern Mich Univ	MI	17,961	C
Eastern New Mexico Univ	NM	10,682	C
East-West Univ	IL	16,076	C
Excelsior College	NY	895	SP
Fairleigh Dickinson Univ/ Metropolitan Campus	NJ	40,254	C
Fairmont State Univ	WV	12,098	LC
Farmingdale State College	NY	18,985	C
Ferris State Univ	MI	19,698	C
Fitchburg State Univ	MA	17,241	C
Fort Valley State Univ	GA	11,200	VC
Indiana State Univ	IN	16,000	C
Indiana Univ-Purdue Univ Fort Wayne	IN	15,425	C
Inter-American Univ of PR/ Aguadilla Campus	PR	5,578	
Inter-American Univ of PR/ Bayamon Univ College	PR	4,428	
Inter-American Univ of PR/ Fajardo Campus	PR	4,200	
Inter-American Univ of PR/ Ponce	PR	3,700	
Kansas State Univ	KS	15,497	VC
Louisiana Tech Univ	LA	8,000	C
Metropolitan State Univ of Denver	CO	4,835	LC
Mich Tech Univ	MI	22,105	VC
Minn State Univ, Mankato	MN	14,900	C
Montana State Univ-Northern	MT	12,500	NC
New York Inst of Technology	NY	40,590	VC
Norfolk State Univ	VA	10,531	LC
Northern Kentucky Univ	KY	15,302	LC
Northern Mich Univ	MI	15,300	VC
Northwestern State Univ of Louisiana	LA	14,368	C
Okla State Univ	OK	14,310	VC
Old Dominion Univ	VA	18,662	C
Oregon Inst of Technology	OR	8,910	C
Pennsylvania College of Technology	PA	25,653	NC
Pittsburg State Univ	KS	12,032	C
Point Park Univ	PA	36,390	C
Purdue Univ/Calumet	IN	14,336	C
Purdue Univ/West Lafayette	IN	20,278	HC
Rochester Inst of Technology	NY	42,450	V₵
Roosevelt Univ	IL	22,605	VC
Savannah State Univ	GA	13,156	C
S Car State Univ	SC	6,700	LC
S Dak State Univ	SD	14,296	C
Southern Illinois Univ Carbondale	IL	21,620	C
Southern Polytechnic State Univ	GA	13,958	VC
Southwestern Okla State Univ	OK	9,160	C
SUNY Inst of Technology at Utica / Rome	NY	23,818	C
Texas A&M Univ at Galveston	TX	11,258	C
Texas Southern Univ	TX	18,212	LC
Texas Tech Univ	TX	14,243	C
Thomas Edison State College	NJ	5,700	SP
Tuskegee Univ	AL	26,750	C
United States Naval Academy	MD		MC

School	ST	$IS	SR
Univ of Akron	OH	20,436	C
Univ of Arkansas at Little Rock	AR		C
Univ of Central Missouri	MO	14,605	C
Univ of Cincinnati	OH	20,199	VC
Univ of Dayton	OH	43,750	VC
Univ of Hartford	CT	42,674	C
Univ of Maine	ME	19,712	C+
Univ of Memphis	TN	15,094	C
Univ of Mich/Dearborn	MI	9,885	VC
Univ of N Car at Charlotte	NC	15,847	C
Univ of North Texas	TX	15,628	C
Univ of Pittsburgh at Johnstown	PA	20,862	LC
Univ of PR/Bayamon	PR	1,600	
Univ of Rio Grande	OH	8,750	NC
Univ of Southern Miss	MS	13,170	C
Vaughn College of Aeronautics and Technology	NY	31,360	SP
Virginia Commonwealth Univ	VA	18,633	C
Wayne State Univ	MI	19,493	C
Wentworth Inst of Technology	MA	29,800	SP
West Virginia Univ Inst of Technology	WV	14,094	NC
Western Carolina Univ	NC	13,965	C+
Western Washington Univ	WA	18,519	VC
Youngstown State Univ	OH	16,374	LC

ELECTROMECHANICAL TECHNOLOGY

School	ST	$IS	SR
Idaho State Univ	ID	11,908	C
Murray State Univ	KY	14,944	C
Penn State Univ/Altoona	PA	11,464	C
Texas A&M Univ at Galveston	TX	11,258	C
Univ of Northern Iowa	IA	14,776	C
Univ of the District of Columbia	DC	7,244	LC
Univ of Toledo	OH	18,464	C
Vermont Technical College	VT	15,751	C
Wayne State Univ	MI	19,493	C
Wentworth Inst of Technology	MA	29,800	SP
Western Kentucky Univ	KY	11,000	LC

ELECTRONIC BUSINESS

School	ST	$IS	SR
Champlain College	VT	44,850	VC
Davenport Univ	MI	21,002	LC
Florida Inst of Technology	FL	48,290	VC
Kent State Univ	OH	19,352	C
La Sierra Univ	CA	35,694	VC
Limestone College	SC	29,880	C
Mountain State Univ	WV	14,330	NC
Old Dominion Univ	VA	18,662	C
San Francisco State Univ	CA	18,514	C
Southern Univ and A&M College	LA	9,761	C+
Thiel College	PA	31,378	LC
Trevecca Nazarene Univ	TN	30,118	C
Univ of La Verne	CA	47,010	VC
Univ of North Texas	TX	15,628	C
Univ of Scranton	PA	51,940	VC
Univ of Southern Indiana	IN	14,657	C
Winthrop Univ	SC	21,120	VC

ELEMENTARY EDUCATION

School	ST	$IS	SR
Abilene Christian Univ	TX	38,400	VC
Adams State College	CO	13,358	LC
Adrian College	MI	33,800	C
Alabama A&M Univ	AL	96,100	C
Alabama State Univ	AL	14,142	NC
Alaska Pacific Univ	AK	33,360	VC
Albright College	PA	46,660	C
Alcorn State Univ	MS	9,500	C
Alderson Broaddus Univ	WV	28,656	C
Alice Lloyd College	KY	4,900	C
Alma College	MI	42,400	VC
Alvernia Univ	PA	39,250	C
Alverno College	WI	30,483	LC
American Indian College	AZ	16,702	C
American International College	MA	36,100	LC
American Univ	DC	54,829	HC+
Anderson Univ	IN	35,390	C
Andrews Univ	MI	28,030	C+
Anna Maria College	MA	34,600	LC
Appalachian State Univ	NC	12,919	VC
Aquinas College	MI	33,060	C
Aquinas College	TN	29,250	C+
Arcadia Univ	PA	33,570	C+
Arizona State Univ	AZ	18,818	C+
Arkansas Baptist College	AR	9,000	NC
Arkansas Tech Univ	AR	13,164	LC
Armstrong Atlantic State Univ	GA	16,276	C
Asbury Univ	KY	32,038	VC
Ashford Univ	IA	21,780	C
Ashland Univ	OH	25,000	C
Atlantic Union College	MA	24,600	LC
Auburn Univ	AL	20,052	VC+
Auburn Univ at Montgomery	AL	12,120	C
Augsburg College	MN	35,142	C
Augustana College	IL	43,398	HC
Augustana College	SD	35,500	VC
Aurora Univ	IL	26,870	C
Averett Univ	VA	36,000	LC
Avila Univ	MO	26,900	C
Baker Univ	KS	33,350	C+
Ball State Univ	IN	17,850	C
Barton College	NC	27,660	C
Bay Path College	MA	34,565	C
Baylor Univ	TX	46,720	HC
Becker College	MA	41,420	LC
Belhaven Univ	MS	27,170	C
Bellarmine Univ	KY	42,950	VC
Belmont Abbey College	NC	37,716	C
Belmont Univ	TN	37,380	VC+
Bemidji State Univ	MN	13,500	C
Benedict College	SC	20,454	NC
Benedictine College	KS	29,180	VC
Benedictine Univ	IL	35,220	C
Bennett College	NC		LC
Bennington College	VT	56,990	HC+
Berea College	KY	7,220	HC
Bethany College	KS	30,605	NC
Bethany College	WV	35,282	C
Bethel College	IN	31,560	C
Bethel College	KS	29,100	C
Bethel Univ	MN	34,940	VC
Bethune-Cookman Univ	FL	22,290	LC
Black Hills State Univ	SD	13,562	LC
Blackburn College	IL	21,350	C
Blue Mountain College	MS	13,550	LC
Bluefield State College	WV	3,140	LC
Boise State Univ	ID	12,802	C
Boricua College	NY	8,600	C
Boston College	MA	58,506	MC
Boston Univ	MA	54,130	HC+
Bowie State Univ	MD	23,990	LC
Bowling Green State Univ	OH	18,970	C
Bradley Univ	IL	31,874	VC
Brescia Univ	KY	26,140	VC+
Briar Cliff Univ	IA	29,514	C
Bridgewater State Univ	MA	18,752	C
Brigham Young Univ	UT	12,100	HC
Brigham Young Univ/ Hawaii	HI	8,614	VC
Bryan College	TN	24,194	C
Bucknell Univ	PA	58,160	MC
Buena Vista Univ	IA	37,954	C
Buffalo State/State Univ of Buffalo	NY	15,733	C+
Butler Univ	IN	45,898	VC+
Cabrini College	PA	40,859	LC
Caldwell College	NJ	35,602	LC
Cal State, Long Beach	CA	17,534	C+
Calif Univ of Pennsylvania	PA	14,217	C
Calumet College of St. Joseph	IN	15,000	LC
Calvin College	MI	37,585	VC+
Cameron Univ	OK	9,267	LC
Campbell Univ	NC	25,500	C
Campbellsville Univ	KY	27,720	C
Canisius College	NY	45,602	VC
Capital Univ	OH	39,824	VC
Cardinal Stritch Univ	WI	24,054	C
Caribbean Univ	PR	10,375	
Carlos Albizu Univ	FL	12,053	LC
Carlow Univ	PA	30,272	C
Carroll College	MT	28,000	C
Carroll Univ	WI	24,860	C
Carson-Newman Univ	TN	29,058	C+
Carthage College	WI	33,000	C
Catawba College	NC	37,105	C
Cazenovia College	NY	30,800	C
Cedar Crest College	PA	43,240	C
Cedarville Univ	OH	31,036	VC+
Centenary College	NJ	38,618	LC
Centenary College of Louisiana	LA	39,070	C+
Central College	IA	36,980	VC
Central Conn State Univ	CT	19,212	C
Central Methodist Univ	MO	28,240	VC
Central Mich Univ	MI	18,066	C
Central State Univ	OH	9,010	C
Central Univ of Bayamon	PR	3,350	
Central Washington Univ	WA	11,730	C
Centre College	KY	35,000	HC+
Chadron State College	NE	7,400	NC
Chaminade Univ of Honolulu	HI	31,664	C
Champlain College	VT	44,850	VC
Charleston Southern Univ	SC	22,420	C
Chatham Univ	PA	42,440	VC
Chestnut Hill College	PA	39,785	LC
Cheyney Univ of Pennsylvania	PA	20,372	LC
Chicago State Univ	IL	5,482	C
CUNY/Brooklyn College	NY	5,884	C+
City Univ of Seattle	WA	14,880	NC
Claflin Univ	SC	22,368	C+
Clarion Univ of Pennsylvania	PA	17,370	C
Clarke Univ	IA	36,400	C
Clearwater Christian College	FL	23,720	C
Clemson Univ	SC	19,136	HC
Cleveland State Univ	OH	21,357	C
Coastal Carolina Univ	SC	17,620	C
Coe College	IA	43,590	VC
Coker College	SC	32,256	LC
College of Charleston	SC	21,273	VC
College of Mount St. Joseph	OH	33,880	C
College of New Jersey	NJ	25,376	HC
College of St. Benedict	MN	47,570	VC
College of St. Elizabeth	NJ	43,839	LC
College of St. Mary	NE	34,334	C
College of St Joseph	VT	30,600	LC
College of the Ozarks	MO	5,605	VC
Colo Christian Univ	CO	27,500	VC
Columbia College	MO	24,578	C
Columbia College	SC	27,882	C
Concord Univ	WV	13,102	C
Concordia College - Alabama	AL	12,200	NC
Concordia College New York	NY	31,500	VC
Concordia College, Moorhead	MN	39,974	C+
Concordia Univ	OR	34,930	C
Concordia Univ Nebr	NE	26,000	VC
Concordia Univ St. Paul	MN	27,200	C
Concordia Univ Texas	TX	23,640	C
Concordia Univ Wisc	WI	28,980	C
Concordia Univ, Ann Arbor	MI	27,220	VC
Concordia Univ, River Forest	IL	26,300	C
Converse College	SC	37,130	C
Coppin State Univ	MD	14,905	VC
Corban Univ	OR	34,764	C
Cornell College	IA	44,930	HC
Cornerstone Univ and Grand Rapids Theological Seminary	MI	30,866	C
Covenant College	GA		VC+
Creighton Univ	NE	44,058	VC+
Culver-Stockton College	MO	30,900	C
Cumberland Univ	TN	21,220	C
CUNY-City College	NY	19,576	HC+
Curry College	MA	47,545	LC
Daemen College	NY	31,510	C
Dakota State Univ	SD	13,811	C
Dakota Wesleyan Univ	SD	23,000	C
Dallas Baptist Univ	TX	29,118	C
Davis and Elkins College	WV	33,742	C
De Sales Univ	PA	42,670	C
Defiance College	OH	30,645	C
Delaware State Univ	DE	14,700	LC
Delta State Univ	MS	12,292	LC
DePaul Univ	IL	46,120	VC
DePauw Univ	IN	48,950	VC+
Dickinson State Univ	ND	8,550	NC
Doane College	NE	33,730	VC
Dominican College	NY	31,270	C
Dominican Univ	IL	37,628	C
Dordt College	IA	34,160	VC
Dowling College	NY	25,000	LC
Drake Univ	IA	30,980	VC+
Drury Univ	MO	30,319	VC
East Carolina Univ	NC	14,169	C
East Central Univ	OK	10,223	LC
East Stroudsburg Univ of Pennsylvania	PA	16,636	C
East Texas Baptist Univ	TX	29,135	C
Eastern Conn State Univ	CT	20,584	C
Eastern Illinois Univ	IL	20,502	C
Eastern Kentucky Univ	KY	11,161	C
Eastern Mennonite Univ	VA	38,850	VC
Eastern Mich Univ	MI	17,961	C
Eastern Nazarene College	MA	30,000	C
Eastern New Mexico Univ	NM	10,682	C
Eastern Washington Univ	WA	16,388	C
Edgewood College	WI	33,294	C
Edinboro Univ of Pennsylvania	PA	15,940	LC
Edward Waters College	FL	17,856	LC
Elizabeth City State Univ	NC	11,638	C
Elizabethtown College	PA	47,600	VC
Elmhurst College	IL	42,032	C+
Elmira College	NY	49,950	C+
Elms College	MA	23,900	VC
Elon Univ	NC	40,046	HC
Emmanuel College	MA	47,985	VC
Emporia State Univ	KS	12,897	C
Erskine College	SC	37,360	C
Eureka College	IL	19,280	C
Evangel Univ	MO	23,090	C
Fairmont State Univ	WV	12,098	LC
Faulkner Univ	AL	22,530	LC
Fayetteville State Univ	NC	10,816	C
Felician College	NJ	41,640	C
Ferris State Univ	MI	19,698	C
Fitchburg State Univ	MA	17,241	C
Five Towns College	NY	34,550	SP
Flagler College	FL	24,960	VC
Florida A&M Univ	FL	14,935	LC
Florida Atlantic Univ	FL	17,339	C
Florida Gulf Coast Univ	FL		C
Florida International Univ	FL	17,747	VC
Florida Memorial Univ	FL	20,716	LC
Florida Southern College	FL	38,240	VC
Florida State Univ	FL	15,238	HC
Fontbonne Univ	MO	31,384	C
Fort Hays State Univ	KS	11,354	C
Framingham State Univ	MA	16,750	C
Francis Marion Univ	SC	16,464	LC
Franciscan Univ of Steubenville	OH	27,320	VC
Franklin College	IN	35,885	C
Franklin Pierce Univ	NH	41,598	C
Freed-Hardeman Univ	TN	19,697	VC
Friends Univ	KS	29,100	C
Frostburg State Univ	MD	15,264	LC
Furman Univ	SC	54,006	HC
Gallaudet Univ	DC	25,380	SP
Gannon Univ	PA	37,940	C
Gardner-Webb Univ	NC	34,375	C+
Geneva College	PA	27,280	C
George Fox Univ	OR	40,750	C+
Georgetown College	KY	38,690	C
Georgia Regents Univ	GA		C
Georgia Southwestern State Univ	GA	12,218	C
Gettysburg College	PA	56,820	HC
Glenville State College	WV	11,348	NC
Goddard College	VT	16,418	VC
Gordon College	MA	42,660	VC+
Goshen College	IN	35,900	VC
Grace Bible College	MI	20,770	C
Grace College and Theological Seminary	IN	28,800	C
Graceland Univ	IA	28,020	C
Grambling State Univ	LA	13,384	LC
Grand Canyon Univ	AZ	24,540	VC
Grand Valley State Univ	MI	17,998	VC
Grand View Univ	IA	31,050	C
Green Mountain College	VT	33,547	LC
Greensboro College	NC	28,740	LC
Greenville College	IL	27,012	C
Grove City College	PA	22,988	HC
Gustavus Adolphus College	MN	48,170	HC
Gwynedd-Mercy College	PA	33,560	C
Hamline Univ	MN	44,198	VC
Hannibal-LaGrange Univ	MO	24,490	C
Hanover College	IN	41,450	VC
Harding Univ	AR	21,432	C+
Hardin-Simmons Univ	TX	23,560	C+
Harris-Stowe State Univ	MO	14,360	NC
Hastings College	NE	27,782	C+
Hawaii Pacific Univ	HI	36,690	C
Heidelberg Univ	OH	34,100	C
Hellenic College/Holy Cross Greek Orthodox School of Theology	MA	33,190	VC
Heritage Univ	WA	17,664	NC
High Point Univ	NC	39,800	C
Hillsdale College	MI	31,890	HC+
Hofstra Univ	NY	48,020	VC+
Holy Family Univ	PA	40,030	LC
Hood College	MD	44,630	C
Hope College	MI	36,320	VC+
Houghton College	NY	35,740	VC
Houston Baptist Univ	TX	23,815	C+
Howard Payne Univ	TX	17,115	C
Howard Univ	DC	35,957	C
Humboldt State Univ	CA	18,400	C
Hunter College / The CUNY	NY	14,429	VC
Huntingdon College	AL	31,850	C
Huntington Univ	IN	32,220	C
Husson Univ	ME	23,386	LC
Huston-Tillotson Univ	TX	18,124	C+
Idaho State Univ	ID	11,908	C
Illinois College	IL	25,770	VC
Illinois State Univ	IL	22,634	VC
Immaculata Univ	PA	43,000	C
Indiana Inst of Technology	IN	34,240	LC
Indiana State Univ	IN	16,000	C
Indiana Univ Bloomington	IN	19,358	HC
Indiana Univ East	IN	6,639	LC
Indiana Univ Kokomo	IN	6,674	LC
Indiana Univ Northwest	IN	6,738	LC
Indiana Univ South Bend	IN	15,293	C
Indiana Univ Southeast	IN	15,807	LC
Indiana Univ-Purdue Univ Fort Wayne	IN	15,425	C
Indiana Univ-Purdue Univ Indianapolis	IN	17,290	C
Indiana Wesleyan Univ	IN	31,815	VC
Inter-American Univ of PR/ Aguadilla Campus	PR	5,578	
Inter-American Univ of PR/ Arecibo Campus	PR	3,350	
Inter-American Univ of PR/ Barranquitas	PR	3,350	
Inter-American Univ of PR/ Fajardo Campus	PR	4,200	
Inter-American Univ of PR/ Metropolitan Campus	PR	4,320	
Inter-American Univ of PR/ Ponce	PR	3,700	
Inter-American Univ of PR/ San Germán	PR	6,720	
Iowa State Univ	IA	16,403	C
Iowa Wesleyan College	IA	30,850	LC
Jackson State Univ	MS	13,512	LC
Jacksonville State Univ	AL	12,280	LC
Jacksonville Univ	FL	37,780	C
Jarvis Christian College	TX	19,552	NC

School	ST	$IS	SR
John Brown Univ	AR	30,996	V₵
Johnson State College	VT	16,721	C
Judson College	AL	24,690	C
Judson Univ	IL	25,130	C
Juniata College	PA	49,340	VC
Kansas State Univ	KS	15,497	VC
Kean Univ	NJ	22,060	LC
Keene State College	NH	21,538	C
Kentucky Christian Univ	KY	17,622	LC
Kentucky State Univ	KY	11,000	LC
Kentucky Wesleyan College	KY	27,440	V₵
Keuka College	NY	30,300	C
Keystone College	PA	28,680	LC
King Univ	TN	33,140	C
King's College	PA	41,678	C
Knox College	IL		VC
Kutztown Univ of Pennsylvania	PA	16,909	LC
La Roche College	PA	34,802	LC
La Salle Univ	PA	50,270	C
La Sierra Univ	CA	35,694	VC
Lake Superior State Univ	MI	18,121	C
Lakeland College	WI	22,990	C
Lamar Univ	TX	6,820	LC
Lander Univ	SC	22,514	₵
Langston Univ	OK	3,000	LC
Lasell College	MA	42,500	LC
Le Moyne College	NY	42,200	VC
Lebanon Valley College	PA	38,570	C
Lee Univ	TN	18,690	₵
Lees-McRae College	NC	33,624	C
Lehman College / The CUNY	NY	5,778	LC
Lenoir-Rhyne College	NC	35,984	C
Lesley Univ	MA	46,350	C
LeTourneau Univ	TX	26,230	C
Lewis Univ	IL	23,050	C
Lewis-Clark State College	ID	6,990	C
Liberty Univ	VA	19,101	C
Limestone College	SC	29,880	C
Lincoln Memorial Univ	TN	18,144	C
Lincoln Univ	MO	11,996	NC
Lindenwood Univ	MO	20,750	C
Lindsey Wilson College	KY	30,470	VC
Linfield College-McMinnville Campus	OR	46,166	C
Lipscomb Univ	TN	35,722	VC
Livingstone College	NC	17,815	LC
Lock Haven Univ of Pennsylvania	PA	17,587	LC
LIU/Brooklyn Campus	NY	26,500	C
LIU/C.W. Post Campus	NY	38,888	C
Longwood Univ	VA	20,924	C
Loras College	IA	37,432	VC
Louisiana College	LA	15,746	C
Louisiana State Univ	LA	18,677	V₵
Louisiana State Univ in Shreveport	LA	5,606	C
Louisiana Tech Univ	LA	8,000	C
Loyola Univ Chicago	IL	49,560	V₵
Loyola Univ Maryland	MD		VC
Lubbock Christian Univ	TX	25,518	C
Luther College	IA	44,380	V₵
Lynchburg College	VA	42,645	C
Lyndon State College	VT	14,233	C
Lynn Univ	FL	43,500	C
MacMurray College	IL	20,755	C
Manchester College	IN	35,070	C
Manhattan College	NY	44,955	VC
Mansfield Univ	PA	19,468	LC
Marian Univ	WI	30,980	LC
Marian Univ/Indianapolis	IN	37,058	C
Mars Hill College	NC	22,950	LC
Marshall Univ	WV	14,820	C
Marymount Manhattan College	NY	40,118	VC
Maryville College	TN	33,150	VC
Maryville Univ of St. Louis	MO	34,920	VC
Marywood Univ	PA	40,695	C
Mayville State Univ	ND	11,401	NC
McKendree Univ	IL	29,920	₵
McMurry Univ	TX	25,962	LC
McNeese State Univ	LA		C
McPherson College	KS	28,138	C
Medaille College	NY	35,112	VC
Medgar Evers College / The CUNY	NY	4,920	NC
Mercer Univ	GA	44,201	V₵
Mercy College	NY	29,996	C
Mercyhurst Univ	PA	40,700	C
Merrimack College	MA	44,215	C
Messiah College	PA	39,540	VC
Methodist Univ	NC	37,185	C
Miami Univ	OH	24,191	HC
MidAmerica Nazarene Univ	KS	28,000	C
Midland Univ	NE	34,000	C
Miles College	AL	16,530	NC
Millersville Univ of Pennsylvania	PA	18,498	C
Millikin Univ	IL	37,462	C
Minn State Univ, Mankato	MN	14,900	C
Minn State Univ, Moorhead	MN	13,392	C
Minot State Univ	ND	10,915	C
Misericordia Univ	PA	39,840	C
Miss College	MS	21,998	VC
Miss Univ for Women	MS	7,400	LC
Miss Valley State Univ	MS	9,706	LC
Missouri Baptist Univ	MO	30,310	C
Missouri Southern State Univ	MO	11,910	C
Missouri State Univ	MO	13,996	VC
Missouri Valley College	MO	22,200	C
Missouri Western State Univ	MO	12,260	NC
Molloy College	NY	38,950	C
Monmouth College	IL	39,290	C
Montana State Univ	MT	14,068	VC
Montana State Univ-Billings	MT	12,425	LC
Montana State Univ-Northern	MT	12,500	NC
Montreat College	NC	31,298	VC
Moravian College	PA	36,381	VC
Morehead State Univ	KY	10,900	C
Morgan State Univ	MD	14,500	VC
Morningside College	IA	32,620	C
Morris College	SC	16,006	LC
Mount Aloysius College	PA	27,970	C
Mount Marty College	SD	29,638	C
Mount Mary Univ	WI	32,836	LC
Mount Mercy Univ	IA	34,385	C
Mount St. Mary's Univ	MD	46,158	C
Mount St. Mary's College/ Chalon Campus	CA	43,897	V₵
Murray State Univ	KY	14,944	C
Muskingum Univ	OH	30,502	C
National Louis Univ	IL	16,915	LC
Nazareth College of Rochester	NY	41,590	VC
Nebr Wesleyan Univ	NE	29,774	₵
Neumann Univ	PA	31,078	LC
New England College	NH	45,930	LC
New Jersey City Univ	NJ	21,060	₵
New Mexico Highlands Univ	NM	9,720	NC
New Mexico State Univ	NM	13,955	LC
New York Inst of Technology	NY	40,590	VC
New York Univ	NY	61,470	MC
Newberry College	SC	26,850	LC
Newman Univ	KS	30,380	₵
Niagara Univ	NY	39,800	C
Nicholls State Univ	LA	7,095	C
N Car Central Univ	NC	9,000	LC
N Car Wesleyan College	NC	29,440	C
North Central College	IL	38,343	VC
North Central Univ	MN	20,946	C
N Dak State Univ	ND	14,642	C
North Georgia College & State Univ	GA	8,500	C
North Park Univ	IL	30,130	C
Northeastern Illinois Univ	IL		C
Northeastern State Univ	OK	8,615	VC
Northern Arizona Univ	AZ	18,592	C
Northern Illinois Univ	IL	19,768	C
Northern Kentucky Univ	KY	15,302	LC
Northern Mich Univ	MI	15,300	VC
Northern State Univ	SD	14,021	C
Northland College	WI	26,680	C
Northwest Christian Univ	OR	27,399	C
Northwest Missouri State Univ	MO	14,229	C
Northwest Nazarene Univ	ID	24,275	NC
Northwest Univ	WA	18,854	C
Northwestern College	MN	24,000	C
Northwestern College of Iowa	IA	34,848	₵
Northwestern Okla State Univ	OK	7,275	NC
Northwestern State Univ of Louisiana	LA	14,368	C
Notre Dame College	OH	34,942	VC
Notre Dame of Maryland Univ	MD	27,700	C
Nova Southeastern Univ	FL	34,016	VC
Nyack College	NY	32,000	C
Oakland City Univ	IN	24,500	NC
Oakland Univ	MI	19,391	VC
Oakwood Univ	AL	23,035	C
Oglala Lakota College	SD	2,000	NC
Ohio State Univ at Mansfield	OH	13,160	C
Ohio State Univ at Marion	OH	9,850	MC
Ohio State Univ at Newark	OH	17,510	C
Ohio Valley Univ	WV	17,752	C
Ohio Wesleyan Univ	OH	49,460	₵
Okla Baptist Univ	OK	28,202	VC
Okla Christian Univ	OK	24,975	VC
Okla City Univ	OK	33,546	VC
Okla State Univ	OK	14,310	VC
Okla Wesleyan Univ	OK	21,300	C
Old Dominion Univ	VA	18,662	C
Olivet College	MI	19,984	C
Olivet Nazarene Univ	IL	29,990	C
Oral Roberts Univ	OK	31,734	C
Oswego / SUNY	NY	20,009	VC
Ottawa Univ	KS	15,000	VC
Otterbein College	OH	32,214	C
Ouachita Baptist Univ	AR	29,010	VC
Our Lady of Holy Cross College	LA	8,090	LC
Pace Univ	NY	48,094	VC
Palm Beach Atlantic Univ	FL	33,882	LC
Park Univ	MO	17,525	C
Penn State Univ/Altoona	PA	11,464	C
Penn State Univ/Univ Park	PA	25,404	VC
Pepperdine Univ	CA	55,372	H₵
Peru State College	NE	8,600	NC
Pfeiffer Univ	NC	33,700	C
Pittsburg State Univ	KS	12,032	C
Point Park Univ	PA	36,390	C
Pontifical Catholic Univ of PR	PR	7,310	
Prescott College	AZ	33,284	₵
Principia College	IL	35,140	₵
Providence College	RI	55,995	HC
Purdue Univ/Calumet	IN	14,336	C
Purdue Univ/West Lafayette	IN	20,278	HC
Queens Univ of Charlotte	NC	39,543	VC
Quincy Univ	IL	34,980	LC
Quinnipiac Univ	CT	53,580	VC
Rhode Island College	RI	17,132	LC
Rider Univ	NJ	45,720	C
Ripon College	WI	36,959	₵
Rivier College	NH	35,000	VC
Robert Morris Univ	PA	36,699	C
Roberts Wesleyan College	NY	37,384	₵
Rockford College	IL	31,000	C
Rockhurst Univ	MO	20,625	C
Rocky Mountain College	MT	32,242	C
Roger Williams Univ	RI	45,788	C
Rollins College	FL	52,370	HC
Roosevelt Univ	IL	22,605	VC
Rowan Univ	NJ	23,570	VC
Russell Sage College	NY	39,370	C
Rust College	MS	10,600	C
Sacred Heart Univ	CT	48,564	VC
Saginaw Valley State Univ	MI	16,869	C
St. Augustine's Univ	NC	14,000	C
St. Francis Univ	PA	30,029	LC
St. John's Univ	MN	46,146	C
St. Joseph's College	IN	35,790	C
St. Joseph's College of Maine	ME	31,580	C
St. Joseph's Univ	PA	52,272	VC
St. Leo Univ	FL	27,990	C
St. Louis Univ	MO	46,594	V₵
St. Martin's Univ	WA	38,082	C
St. Mary-of-the-Woods College	IN	37,722	LC
St. Mary's College	IN	45,160	VC
St. Mary's Univ	TX	33,854	C
St. Mary's Univ of Minn	MN	37,015	C
St. Michael's College	VT	48,740	VC
St. Paul's College	VA	16,030	NC
St. Peter's College	NJ	44,240	C
St. Xavier Univ	IL	32,840	C
Salem International Univ	WV	18,020	C
Salisbury Univ	MD	18,368	VC
Salve Regina Univ	RI	47,250	VC
San Francisco State Univ	CA	18,514	C
Schreiner Univ	TX	32,734	LC
Seattle Pacific Univ	WA	41,559	V₵
Seton Hall Univ	NJ	45,902	C
Seton Hill Univ	PA	35,172	C
Shaw Univ	NC	15,488	LC
Shawnee State Univ	OH	16,545	NC
Shepherd Univ	WV	14,996	C
Shippensburg Univ of Pennsylvania	PA	17,064	LC
Siena Heights Univ	MI	17,000	LC
Silver Lake College	WI	22,600	LC
Simmons College	MA	48,770	VC
Simpson College	IA	36,086	VC
Simpson Univ	CA	28,900	C
Sinte Gleska Univ	SD	2,300	NC
Skidmore College	NY	57,926	HC
Slippery Rock Univ of Pennsylvania	PA	10,360	LC
Smith College	MA	57,524	MC
S Car State Univ	SC	6,700	LC
Southeast Missouri State Univ	MO	14,983	LC
Southeastern Louisiana Univ	LA	13,325	C
Southeastern Okla State Univ	OK	7,966	C
Southeastern Univ	FL	27,201	₵
Southern Adventist Univ	TN	26,190	C
Southern Arkansas Univ	AR	14,316	C
Southern Conn State Univ	CT	18,033	C
Southern Illinois Univ Carbondale	IL	21,620	C
Southern Illinois Univ Edwardsville	IL	17,532	C
Southern Methodist Univ	TX	57,755	MC
Southern Nazarene Univ	OK	24,354	NC
Southern New Hampshire Univ	NH	38,100	C
Southern Oregon Univ	OR	17,874	C
Southern Univ and A&M College	LA	9,761	₵
Southern Univ at New Orleans	LA	1,000	NC
Southern Wesleyan Univ	SC	25,600	C
Southwest Baptist Univ	MO	24,710	C
Southwest Minn State Univ	MN	14,000	C
Southwestern Adventist Univ	TX	23,026	LC
Southwestern College	KS	29,270	C
Southwestern Okla State Univ	OK	9,160	C
Spalding Univ	KY	31,850	LC
Spring Hill College	AL	42,130	VC
Springfield College	MA	25,000	C
St. Ambrose Univ	IA		C
St. Andrews Univ	NC	32,050	LC
St. Bonaventure Univ	NY	38,831	C
St. Catherine Univ	MN	37,782	₵
St. Cloud State Univ	MN	10,600	C
St. Francis College	NY	34,200	LC
St. John Fisher College	NY	39,370	₵
St. John's Univ	NY	52,840	₵
St. Joseph's College, New York / Brooklyn Campus	NY	21,878	C
St. Norbert College	WI	39,992	VC
St. Thomas Aquinas College	NY	30,000	C
St. Thomas Univ	FL	32,310	₵
Stephens College	MO	34,500	VC
Sterling College	KS	27,216	C
Stetson Univ	FL	49,512	V₵
Stevenson Univ	MD	39,572	C
Stillman College	AL	18,460	C
Sul Ross State Univ	TX	13,410	LC
SUNY College at Geneseo	NY	18,055	H₵
SUNY College at Old Westbury	NY	16,324	C
SUNY Fredonia / The SUNY at Fredonia	NY	18,702	VC
SUNY New Paltz	NY	15,010	C
SUNY Oneonta / SUNY	NY	16,919	VC
Syracuse Univ	NY	54,512	HC
Tabor College	KS	29,010	LC
Taylor Univ	IN	36,742	V₵
Temple Univ	PA	24,392	VC
Tenn Wesleyan College	TN	21,250	C
Texas A&M Univ	TX	16,956	V₵
Texas A&M Univ at Commerce	TX	10,496	C
Texas A&M Univ at Kingsville	TX	7,500	LC
Texas State Univ	TX	16,495	VC
Texas Wesleyan Univ	TX	29,886	C
The Catholic Univ of America	DC	52,852	VC
The College of Idaho	ID	31,277	VC
The Masters College	CA	38,160	₵
The SUNY at Potsdam	NY	17,754	C
Thiel College	PA	31,378	LC
Thomas College	ME	26,270	LC
Thomas More College	KY	34,760	C
Tougaloo College	MS	15,275	NC
Touro College	NY	23,150	VC
Towson Univ	MD	16,000	VC
Transylvania Univ	KY	40,310	V₵
Trine Univ	IN	39,400	VC
Trinity Bible College	ND		
Trinity Christian College	IL	28,869	C
Trinity International Univ	IL	31,070	C
Trinity Washington Univ	DC	30,250	₵
Troy Univ	AL	10,650	C
Tusculum College	TN	24,295	C
Tuskegee Univ	AL	26,750	C
Union College	KY	28,775	C
Union College	NE	23,270	VC
Union Univ	TN	28,260	VC
Universidad Adventista de las Antillas	PR	7,360	
Universidad del Turabo	PR	4,110	
Universidad Metropolitana	PR		
Univ of Alabama at Birmingham	AL	18,484	₵
Univ of Alabama at Huntsville	AL	17,625	VC
Univ of Alabama at Tuscaloosa	AL	17,164	₵
Univ of Alaska Anchorage	AK	15,290	NC
Univ of Alaska Fairbanks	AK	13,955	C
Univ of Alaska Southeast	AK	11,493	C
Univ of Arizona	AZ	20,105	C
Univ of Arkansas at Fayetteville	AR	16,860	VC
Univ of Arkansas at Little Rock	AR		C
Univ of Central Arkansas	AR	10,840	VC
Univ of Central Florida	FL	15,711	V₵
Univ of Central Missouri	MO	14,605	C
Univ of Central Okla	OK	12,293	C
Univ of Charleston	WV	28,650	C
Univ of Cincinnati	OH	20,199	VC
Univ of Conn	CT	23,744	HC
Univ of Dallas	TX	43,510	V₵
Univ of Dayton	OH	43,750	VC
Univ of Delaware	DE	22,728	VC
Univ of Detroit Mercy	MI	30,450	C
Univ of Evansville	IN	41,056	V₵
Univ of Findlay	OH	31,916	C
Univ of Florida	FL	15,783	H₵
Univ of Georgia	GA	19,508	VC
Univ of Great Falls	MT	27,970	C
Univ of Hartford	CT	42,674	C
Univ of Hawaii at Manoa	HI	19,379	VC
Univ of Idaho	ID	14,558	C
Univ of Illinois at Chicago	IL	24,293	VC
Univ of Illinois at Urbana-Champaign	IL	24,300	HC
Univ of Indianapolis	IN	31,740	LC
Univ of Iowa	IA	17,481	VC
Univ of Jamestown	ND	24,738	C

School	ST	$IS	SR
Univ of Kansas	KS	16,980	C+
Univ of Kentucky	KY	19,868	C
Univ of Louisiana at Lafayette	LA	6,130	C
Univ of Louisiana at Monroe	LA	12,998	C
Univ of Louisville	KY	17,460	VC
Univ of Maine	ME	19,712	C+
Univ of Maine at Farmington	ME	17,841	C
Univ of Maine at Fort Kent	ME	14,975	LC
Univ of Maine at Machias	ME	10,523	C
Univ of Maine at Presque Isle	ME	15,011	LC
Univ of Mary	ND	16,714	C
Univ of Mary Hardin-Baylor	TX	31,950	C+
Univ of Maryland	MD	18,801	HC
Univ of Maryland/Eastern Shore	MD	14,000	C
Univ of Miami	FL	55,166	MC
Univ of Mich/Ann Arbor	MI	22,102	HC+
Univ of Mich/Dearborn	MI	9,885	VC
Univ of Mich-Flint	MI	17,547	C+
Univ of Minn Crookston	MN	17,834	C+
Univ of Minn/Duluth	MN	18,964	C+
Univ of Minn/Morris	MN	17,150	VC
Univ of Minn/Twin Cities	MN		HC
Univ of Miss	MS	15,482	VC
Univ of Missouri/Columbia	MO	18,201	MC
Univ of Missouri-Kansas City	MO	19,603	C
Univ of Missouri-St. Louis	MO	18,304	VC
Univ of Mobile	AL	27,870	VC
Univ of Montana	MT	13,670	C
Univ of Montana-Western	MT	9,753	LC
Univ of Montevallo	AL	17,320	C
Univ of Mount Union	OH	35,130	C
Univ of Nebr - Lincoln	NE	17,507	VC
Univ of Nebr at Kearney	NE	14,855	LC
Univ of Nebr at Omaha	NE	12,700	C
Univ of Nevada, Las Vegas	NV	17,303	C
Univ of Nevada/Reno	NV	14,500	NC
Univ of New England	ME	46,145	C+
Univ of New Mexico	NM	15,300	C
Univ of New Orleans	LA	9,224	VC
Univ of North Alabama	AL	9,960	C
Univ of N Car at Chapel Hill	NC	18,348	MC
Univ of N Car at Charlotte	NC	15,847	C
Univ of N Car at Greensboro	NC	12,848	C
Univ of N Car at Wilmington	NC	13,572	VC+
Univ of N Dak	ND	14,094	C
Univ of North Florida	FL	15,578	VC
Univ of Northern Iowa	IA	14,776	C
Univ of Okla	OK	17,634	VC+
Univ of Pennsylvania	PA	56,106	MC
Univ of Pikeville	KY	24,750	NC
Univ of Pittsburgh at Bradford	PA	21,316	LC
Univ of Pittsburgh at Johnstown	PA	20,862	LC
Univ of Portland	OR	47,874	VC
Univ of PR Recinto de Rio Piedras	PR	5,750	
Univ of PR/Arecibo	PR	7,227	
Univ of PR/Bayamon	PR	1,600	
Univ of PR/Cayey	PR	1,504	
Univ of PR/Humacao	PR	1,877	
Univ of Rio Grande	OH	8,750	NC
Univ of St. Francis	IN	29,810	C
Univ of St. Mary	KS	28,400	C+
Univ of San Francisco	CA	49,674	VC
Univ of Science and Arts of Okla	OK	10,560	VC
Univ of Scranton	PA	51,940	VC
Univ of Sioux Falls	SD	22,990	C
Univ of South Alabama	AL	13,510	C
Univ of S Car at Aiken	SC	16,278	C
Univ of S Car at Columbia	SC	19,725	VC+
Univ of S Car Upstate	SC	17,673	LC
Univ of S Dak	SD	15,111	C
Univ of South Florida	FL	13,000	C
Univ of Southern Indiana	IN	14,657	C
Univ of Southern Miss	MS	13,170	C
Univ of St. Francis	IL	36,490	C
Univ of Tampa	FL	35,160	VC
Univ of Tenn at Martin	TN	13,217	C
Univ of the Cumberlands	KY	27,500	LC
Univ of the District of Columbia	DC	7,244	LC
Univ of the Incarnate Word	TX	35,200	LC
Univ of the Sacred Heart	PR	5,590	
Univ of the Southwest	NM	15,000	C
Univ of Toledo	OH	18,464	C
Univ of Tulsa	OK	45,311	HC+
Univ of Utah	UT	13,462	VC
Univ of Vermont	VT	26,120	VC+
Univ of West Alabama	AL	9,415	C
Univ of West Florida	FL	14,656	C
Univ of Wisc Whitewater	WI	13,314	C
Univ of Wisc/Eau Claire	WI	15,430	VC
Univ of Wisc/Green Bay	WI	14,900	C
Univ of Wisc/La Crosse	WI	14,755	VC
Univ of Wisc/Madison	WI	18,757	HC
Univ of Wisc/Oshkosh	WI	10,426	LC
Univ of Wisc/Platteville	WI	14,274	C
Univ of Wisc/River Falls	WI	9,722	LC
Univ of Wisc/Stevens Point	WI	14,043	C
Univ of Wisc/Superior	WI	14,106	C
Univ of Wyoming	WY	13,855	C+
Upper Iowa Univ	IA	30,426	NC
Urbana Univ	OH	21,190	C
Ursuline College	OH	33,198	LC
Utah State Univ	UT	11,803	C
Valley City State Univ	ND	12,286	LC
Valparaiso Univ	IN	43,040	VC+
Vanderbilt Univ	TN	57,072	MC
Vanguard Univ of Southern Calif	CA	35,833	VC
Victory Univ	TN	19,118	C
Virginia Union Univ	VA	18,432	C
Virginia Wesleyan College	VA	28,433	LC
Viterbo Univ	WI	30,070	C
Wagner College	NY	48,600	VC
Walla Walla Univ	WA	26,256	NC
Walsh Univ	OH	35,100	C
Warner Univ	FL	18,000	C
Wartburg College	IA	41,055	VC
Washburn Univ	KS	12,165	NC
Washington Adventist Univ	MD	25,859	C+
Washington Univ in St. Louis	MO	58,818	MC
Wayne State College	NE	11,764	NC
Wayne State Univ	MI	19,493	C
Waynesburg Univ	PA	29,100	C
Webster Univ	MO	33,990	C+
Wells College	NY	38,680	VC
Wesley College	DE	31,115	LC
West Chester Univ of Pennsylvania	PA	16,836	C
West Liberty Univ	WV	9,142	LC
West Virginia State Univ	WV	8,378	NC
West Virginia Wesleyan College	WV	26,880	C
Western Carolina Univ	NC	13,965	C+
Western Conn State Univ	CT	18,327	C
Western Illinois Univ	IL	20,130	C
Western Kentucky Univ	KY	11,000	LC
Western Mich Univ	MI	19,042	C
Western New England Univ	MA	45,590	C
Western New Mexico Univ	NM	8,500	LC
Western State Colo Univ	CO	16,135	C
Western Washington Univ	WA	18,519	VC
Westfield State Univ	MA	18,489	C
Westminster College	MO	30,490	VC
Westminster College	PA	31,290	C+
Westminster College	UT	37,708	VC
Wheaton College	IL	39,650	HC+
Wheeling Jesuit Univ	WV	34,668	C
Wheelock College	MA	33,075	C
Whitworth Univ	WA	45,826	VC+
Wichita State Univ	KS	12,539	C
Widener Univ	PA	50,368	C
Wiley College	TX		LC
Wilkes Univ	PA	42,786	C
William Carey Univ	MS	13,500	LC
William Jewell College	MO	31,000	VC+
William Penn Univ	IA	26,000	C
William Woods Univ	MO		C
Williams Baptist College	AR	20,070	C
Wilmington College	OH	29,784	C
Wilmington Univ	DE	7,778	NC
Wilson College	PA	27,660	C
Wingate Univ	NC	34,990	C
Winona State Univ	MN	16,530	C
Winston-Salem State Univ	NC	9,418	LC
Winthrop Univ	SC	21,120	VC
Wisc Lutheran College	WI	23,510	VC
Wittenberg Univ	OH	47,766	VC
Worcester State Univ	MA	18,657	C
Wright State Univ	OH	16,983	C
Xavier Univ of Louisiana	LA	25,300	C
York College	NE	19,475	C
York College of Pennsylvania	PA	26,590	C

ELEMENTARY PARTICLE PHYSICS

School	ST	$IS	SR
The Catholic Univ of America	DC	52,852	VC

EMERGENCY MEDICAL SERVICES

School	ST	$IS	SR
Creighton Univ	NE	44,058	VC+

EMERGENCY MEDICAL TECHNOLOGIES

School	ST	$IS	SR
Central Washington Univ	WA	11,730	C
George Washington Univ	DC	57,108	MC
Idaho State Univ	ID	11,908	C
Mountain State Univ	WV	14,330	NC
Pennsylvania College of Technology	PA	25,653	NC
Springfield College	MA	25,000	C
Univ of Maryland/Baltimore County	MD	18,000	VC
Univ of New Mexico	NM	15,300	C
Univ of Pittsburgh at Pittsburgh	PA	27,800	HC+
Univ of South Alabama	AL	13,510	C
Western Carolina Univ	NC	13,965	C+

EMERGENCY/DISASTER SCIENCE

School	ST	$IS	SR
Arkansas State Univ	AR	14,980	C
Arkansas Tech Univ	AR	13,164	LC
N Dak State Univ	ND	14,642	C
St. Louis Univ	MO	46,594	VC+
Univ of Akron	OH	20,436	C
Univ of Alaska Fairbanks	AK	13,955	C
Univ of Florida	FL	15,783	HC+
Univ of Maryland/Univ College	MD	6,168	SP
Univ of North Texas	TX	15,628	C
West Texas A&M Univ	TX	13,478	C
Western Carolina Univ	NC	13,965	C+

ENERGY MANAGEMENT TECHNOLOGY

School	ST	$IS	SR
Creighton Univ	NE	44,058	VC+
Fitchburg State Univ	MA	17,241	C
Hunter College / The CUNY	NY	14,429	VC
Idaho State Univ	ID	11,908	C
Illinois State Univ	IL	22,634	VC
Ohio Univ	OH	20,676	VC
Texas Tech Univ	TX	14,243	C
Univ of Northern Iowa	IA	14,776	C
Univ of Tulsa	OK	45,311	HC+
Univ of Wyoming	WY	13,855	C+

ENERGY SCIENCE

School	ST	$IS	SR
Creighton Univ	NE	44,058	VC+
Indiana Univ-Purdue Univ Indianapolis	IN	17,290	C
Syracuse Univ	NY	54,512	HC

ENERGY SYSTEMS TECHNOLOGY

School	ST	$IS	SR
Thomas Edison State College	NJ	5,700	SP
Univ of Illinois at Chicago	IL	24,293	VC
Univ of Wyoming	WY	13,855	C+

ENERGY UTILITY TECHNOLOGY

School	ST	$IS	SR
Thomas Edison State College	NJ	5,700	SP

ENGINEERING

School	ST	$IS	SR
Abilene Christian Univ	TX	38,400	VC
Agnes Scott College	GA	45,323	VC+
Alabama State Univ	AL	14,142	NC
Andrews Univ	MI	28,030	C+
Arcadia Univ	PA	33,570	C+
Arizona State Univ	AZ	18,818	C+
Arkansas State Univ	AR	14,980	C
Ball State Univ	IN	17,850	C
Baylor Univ	TX	46,720	HC
Benedictine College	KS	29,180	VC
Bethel College	IN	31,560	C
Binghamton Univ / The SUNY	NY	20,832	HC+
Biola Univ	CA	40,320	VC
Boston Univ	MA	54,130	HC+
Brown Univ	RI	56,150	MC
Bucknell Univ	PA	58,160	MC
Butler Univ	IN	45,898	VC+
Calif Baptist Univ	CA	35,890	C
Calif State Polytechnic Univ, Pomona	CA	18,932	C
Cal State, East Bay	CA	16,549	C
Cal State, Los Angeles	CA	15,829	C
Cal State, Northridge	CA	28,313	C
Calvin College	MI	37,585	VC+
Carnegie Mellon Univ	PA	51,260	MC
Case Western Reserve Univ	OH	55,178	MC
Cedarville Univ	OH	31,036	VC+
Colo School of Mines	CO	18,000	HC
Colo State Univ-Fort Collins	CO	20,090	VC
Cooper Union for the Advancement of Science and Art	NY	55,600	MC
Dominican Univ	IL	37,628	C
Dordt College	IA	34,160	VC
East Carolina Univ	NC	14,169	C
Eastern Illinois Univ	IL	20,502	C
Eastern Washington Univ	WA	16,388	C
Elizabethtown College	PA	47,600	VC
Elon Univ	NC	40,046	HC
Embry-Riddle Aeronautical Univ - Daytona Beach	FL	40,884	C+
Florida Atlantic Univ	FL	17,339	C
Franklin W. Olin College of Engineering	MA	57,500	SP
Geneva College	PA	27,280	C
George Washington Univ	DC	57,108	MC
Grand Valley State Univ	MI	17,998	VC
Harvard Univ/Harvard College	MA	49,000	MC
Harvey Mudd College	CA	61,660	MC
Hope College	MI	36,320	VC+
Indiana Inst of Technology	IN	34,240	LC
Indiana Univ-Purdue Univ Fort Wayne	IN	15,425	C
Iowa State Univ	IA	16,403	C
James Madison Univ	VA	18,049	VC
John Brown Univ	AR	30,996	VC+
Johns Hopkins Univ	MD	47,492	MC
Johnson C. Smith Univ	NC	25,336	LC
Lafayette College	PA	57,050	HC+
Lake Superior State Univ	MI	18,121	C
Lawrence Tech Univ	MI	37,000	VC
LeTourneau Univ	TX	26,230	C
Lindenwood Univ	MO	20,750	C
Loyola Univ Maryland	MD		VC
Lubbock Christian Univ	TX	25,518	C
Maine Maritime Academy	ME	21,073	C
Manchester College	IN	35,070	C
Maritime College / SUNY	NY	16,020	C
Marquette Univ	WI	43,664	VC+
Marshall Univ	WV	14,820	C
Maryville College	TN	33,150	VC
Maryville Univ of St. Louis	MO	34,920	VC
Mass Inst of Technology	MA	54,238	MC
McNeese State Univ	LA		C
Mercer Univ	GA	44,201	VC+
Messiah College	PA	39,540	VC
Miami Univ	OH	24,191	HC
Mich State Univ	MI	13,689	VC
Mich Tech Univ	MI	22,105	VC
Milwaukee School of Engineering	WI	39,948	VC+
Montana Tech of The Univ of Montana	MT	14,650	VC
Morehouse College	GA	38,640	C
Mountain State Univ	WV	14,330	NC
Muskingum Univ	OH	30,502	C
New Mexico Highlands Univ	NM	9,720	NC
New York Univ	NY	61,470	MC
N Car State Univ	NC	16,202	HC
Northwest Nazarene Univ	ID	24,275	NC
Northwestern Univ	IL	37,595	MC
Olivet Nazarene Univ	IL	29,990	C
Oral Roberts Univ	OK	31,734	C
Penn State Erie/The Behrend College	PA	16,256	C
Penn State Univ/Univ Park	PA	25,404	VC
Pepperdine Univ	CA	55,372	HC+
Philadelphia Univ	PA	44,160	C
Purdue Univ/Calumet	IN	14,336	C
Quinnipiac Univ	CT	53,580	VC
Rensselaer Polytechnic Inst	NY	59,229	MC
Robert Morris Univ	PA	36,699	C
Rochester Inst of Technology	NY	42,450	VC+
Roger Williams Univ	RI	45,788	C
Rowan Univ	NJ	23,570	VC
St. Anselm College	NH	48,324	VC
St. Louis Univ	MO	46,594	VC+
St. Mary's Univ	TX	33,854	C
St. Vincent College	PA	40,244	C
San Diego State Univ	CA	20,578	VC
San Jose State Univ	CA	19,707	C
Santa Clara Univ	CA	54,702	MC
Seattle Pacific Univ	WA	41,559	VC+
Seton Hill Univ	PA	35,172	C
Smith College	MA	57,524	MC
S Dak State Univ	SD	14,296	C
Spelman College	GA	24,650	VC
Spring Hill College	AL	42,130	VC
Stanford Univ	CA	56,411	MC
Swarthmore College	PA	57,870	MC
Temple Univ	PA	24,392	VC
Tenn Tech Univ	TN	11,310	C
Texas Christian Univ	TX	47,570	HC
Texas Tech Univ	TX	14,243	C
The Catholic Univ of America	DC	52,852	VC
Trinity College	CT		HC+
Tufts Univ	MA	58,780	MC
United States Air Force Academy	CO		MC
United States Naval Academy	MD		MC
Univ of Akron	OH	20,436	C
Univ of Arizona	AZ	20,105	C
Univ of Calif at Irvine	CA	25,961	VC
Univ of Calif at San Diego	CA	21,000	VC
Univ of Central Missouri	MO	14,605	C
Univ of Central Okla	OK	12,293	C
Univ of Cincinnati	OH	20,199	VC
Univ of Delaware	DE	22,728	VC
Univ of Detroit Mercy	MI	30,450	C
Univ of Georgia	GA	19,508	VC
Univ of Hartford	CT	42,674	C
Univ of Idaho	ID	14,558	C
Univ of Illinois at Chicago	IL	24,293	VC
Univ of Illinois at Urbana-Champaign	IL	24,300	HC
Univ of Iowa	IA	17,481	VC
Univ of Louisville	KY	17,460	VC
Univ of Maryland	MD	18,801	HC
Univ of Mass Boston	MA	11,966	C

School	ST	$IS	SR
Univ of Mich/Ann Arbor	MI	22,102	HC+
Univ of Mich/Dearborn	MI	9,885	VC
Univ of Mich-Flint	MI	17,547	C+
Univ of Missouri/Columbia	MO	18,201	MC
Univ of New Haven	CT	47,740	C
Univ of N Car at Asheville	NC	13,500	VC+
Univ of Okla	OK	17,634	VC+
Univ of Pittsburgh at Bradford	PA	21,316	LC
Univ of Portland	OR	47,874	VC
Univ of PR/Mayaguez	PR	1,250	
Univ of South Florida	FL	13,000	C
Univ of Southern Indiana	IN	14,657	C
Univ of Tenn at Chattanooga	TN	16,883	C
Univ of Tenn at Martin	TN	13,217	C
Univ of Texas at San Antonio	TX	18,372	C
Univ of Toledo	OH	18,464	C
Univ of Utah	UT	13,462	VC
Univ of Vermont	VT	26,120	VC+
Univ of Washington	WA	14,722	VC
Univ of Wisc/Platteville	WI	14,274	C
Univ of Wisc-Milwaukee	WI	18,436	C
Utah State Univ	UT	11,803	C
Walla Walla Univ	WA	26,256	NC
Washington Univ in St. Louis	MO	58,818	MC
Waynesburg Univ	PA	29,100	C
West Virginia Univ	WV	15,794	C+
Western Illinois Univ	IL	20,130	C
Wheaton College	IL	39,650	HC+
Wheeling Jesuit Univ	WV	34,668	C
Widener Univ	PA	50,368	C
Yale Univ	CT	55,300	MC
York College of Pennsylvania	PA	26,590	C
Youngstown State Univ	OH	16,374	LC

ENGINEERING AND APPLIED SCIENCE

School	ST	$IS	SR
Arizona State Univ	AZ	18,818	C+
Benedictine Univ	IL	35,220	C
Bethel Univ	MN	34,940	VC
Calif Inst of Technology	CA	54,045	MC
Cal State, Fullerton	CA	25,188	C+
College of Staten Island / The CUNY	NY	16,778	NC
College of New Jersey	NJ	25,376	HC
Colo State Univ-Fort Collins	CO	20,090	VC
Dartmouth College	NH	57,996	MC
George Fox Univ	OR	40,750	C+
Hofstra Univ	NY	48,020	VC+
New Jersey Inst of Technology	NJ	26,490	VC
Pacific Lutheran Univ	WA	44,840	VC
Penn State Univ/Univ Park	PA	25,404	VC
Rutgers, The State Univ of New Jersey/New Brunswick	NJ	25,077	VC
Seattle Pacific Univ	WA	41,559	VC+
Stony Brook Univ / SUNY	NY	19,359	HC
Sweet Briar College	VA	43,765	C+
Trinity Univ	TX	44,174	HC+
Tufts Univ	MA	58,780	MC
United States Air Force Academy	CO		MC
Univ of Calif at Berkeley	CA	23,322	MC
Univ of Calif at Riverside	CA	27,204	C
Univ of Florida	FL	15,783	HC+
Univ of Mary	ND	16,714	C
Univ of Rochester	NY	58,500	MC
Univ of Virginia	VA	22,175	MC
Vanderbilt Univ	TN	57,072	MC
Wartburg College	IA	41,055	VC
Wilkes Univ	PA	42,786	C
Yale Univ	CT	55,300	MC

ENGINEERING CHEMISTRY

School	ST	$IS	SR
Ithaca College	NY	52,300	HC
New York Univ	NY	61,470	MC
Oakland Univ	MI	19,391	VC
Stony Brook Univ / SUNY	NY	19,359	HC

ENGINEERING MANAGEMENT

School	ST	$IS	SR
Arizona State Univ	AZ	18,818	C+
Christian Brothers Univ	TN	19,140	HC
Clarkson Univ	NY	53,538	HC
Columbia Univ in the City of New York	NY	61,116	MC
Illinois Inst of Technology	IL	38,512	HC+
Kansas State Univ	KS	15,497	VC
Lake Superior State Univ	MI	18,121	C
Miami Univ	OH	24,191	HC
Missouri Univ of Science and Technology	MO	18,655	VC+
N Dak State Univ	ND	14,642	C
Oral Roberts Univ	OK	31,734	C
Park Univ	MO	17,525	C
Point Park Univ	PA	36,390	C
Purdue Univ/West Lafayette	IN	20,278	HC
Southern Methodist Univ	TX	57,755	MC
Stevens Inst of Technology	NJ	50,130	HC
Sweet Briar College	VA	43,765	C+
Texas A&M Univ at Kingsville	TX	7,500	LC
Trine Univ	IN	39,400	VC
United States Military Academy	NY		MC
Univ of Louisville	KY	17,460	VC
Univ of N Car at Asheville	NC	13,500	VC+
Univ of Tenn at Chattanooga	TN	16,883	C
Univ of the Incarnate Word	TX	35,200	LC
Univ of the Pacific	CA	52,146	VC
Univ of Vermont	VT	26,120	VC+
Western Mich Univ	MI	19,042	C
Wilkes Univ	PA	42,786	C
York College of Pennsylvania	PA	26,590	C

ENGINEERING MECHANICS

School	ST	$IS	SR
Columbia Univ in the City of New York	NY	61,116	MC
Johns Hopkins Univ	MD	47,492	MC
Lehigh Univ	PA	55,080	MC
Mich State Univ	MI	13,689	VC
Missouri Univ of Science and Technology	MO	18,655	VC+
New York Univ	NY	61,470	MC
United States Air Force Academy	CO		MC
Univ of Arkansas at Little Rock	AR		C
Univ of Calif at Riverside	CA	27,204	C
Univ of Cincinnati	OH	20,199	VC
Univ of Illinois at Urbana-Champaign	IL	24,300	HC
Univ of Wisc/Madison	WI	18,757	HC
Virginia Polytechnic Inst and State Univ	VA	14,629	HC
Washington Univ in St. Louis	MO	58,818	MC

ENGINEERING PHYSICS

School	ST	$IS	SR
Arkansas Tech Univ	AR	13,164	LC
Augustana College	IL	43,398	HC
Augustana College	SD	35,500	VC
Belmont Univ	TN	37,380	VC+
Bethel College	IN	31,560	C
Bradley Univ	IL	31,874	VC
Case Western Reserve Univ	OH	55,178	MC
Christian Brothers Univ	TN	19,140	HC
Colo State Univ-Fort Collins	CO	20,090	VC
Cornell Univ	NY	59,037	MC
Dartmouth College	NH	57,996	MC
Eastern Mich Univ	MI	17,961	C
Eastern Nazarene College	MA	30,000	C
Edinboro Univ of Pennsylvania	PA	15,940	LC
Elon Univ	NC	40,046	HC
Embry-Riddle Aeronautical Univ - Daytona Beach	FL	40,884	C+
Fordham Univ	NY	58,927	HC
Henderson State Univ	AR	13,634	C
Ithaca College	NY	52,300	HC
Jacksonville Univ	FL	37,780	C
John Carroll Univ	OH	44,520	C+
Juniata College	PA	49,340	VC
Kettering Univ	MI	31,456	HC
Lehigh Univ	PA	55,080	MC
Loyola Marymount Univ	CA	53,240	VC+
Miami Univ	OH	24,191	HC
Miss College	MS	21,998	VC
Morgan State Univ	MD	14,500	VC
Murray State Univ	KY	14,944	C
New Mexico State Univ	NM	13,955	LC
New York Univ	NY	61,470	MC
N Car Agricultural and Technical State Univ	NC	13,175	LC
Northwest Nazarene Univ	ID	24,275	NC
Oakland Univ	MI	19,391	VC
Ohio Univ	OH	20,676	VC
Okla Christian Univ	OK	24,975	VC
Oregon State Univ	OR	19,017	C+
Point Loma Nazarene Univ	CA	38,610	VC
Ramapo College of New Jersey	NJ	24,938	C+
Randolph College	VA	43,960	VC
Randolph-Macon College	VA	45,086	C
Rensselaer Polytechnic Inst	NY	59,229	MC
Rose-Hulman Inst of Technology	IN	51,738	MC
St. Louis Univ	MO	46,594	VC+
St. Mary's Univ of Minn	MN	37,015	C
Samford Univ	AL	35,700	VC+
Santa Clara Univ	CA	54,702	MC
S Dak State Univ	SD	14,296	C
Southeast Missouri State Univ	MO	14,983	LC
Southwestern Okla State Univ	OK	9,160	C
St. Ambrose Univ	IA		C
St. Bonaventure Univ	NY	38,831	C
Stanford Univ	CA	56,411	MC
Stevens Inst of Technology	NJ	50,130	HC
Taylor Univ	IN	36,742	VC+
Texas Tech Univ	TX	14,243	C
Ohio State Univ	OH	19,887	MC
Tufts Univ	MA	58,780	MC
Tulane Univ	LA	58,942	MC
United States Military Academy	NY		MC
Univ at Buffalo / The SUNY	NY	20,283	VC
Univ of Calif at Berkeley	CA	23,322	MC
Univ of Calif at San Diego	CA	21,000	VC
Univ of Central Okla	OK	12,293	C
Univ of Colo Boulder	CO	22,605	VC+
Univ of Illinois at Chicago	IL	24,293	VC
Univ of Illinois at Urbana-Champaign	IL	24,300	HC
Univ of Kansas	KS	16,980	C+
Univ of Maine	ME	19,712	C+
Univ of Mass Boston	MA	11,966	C
Univ of Mich/Ann Arbor	MI	22,102	HC+
Univ of Nebr at Omaha	NE	12,700	C
Univ of Nevada/Reno	NV	14,500	NC
Univ of North Texas	TX	15,628	C
Univ of Okla	OK	17,634	VC+
Univ of Pittsburgh at Pittsburgh	PA	27,800	HC+
Univ of the Pacific	CA	52,146	VC
Univ of Tulsa	OK	45,311	HC+
Univ of Wisc/Madison	WI	18,757	HC
Washington and Lee Univ	VA	52,812	MC
West Chester Univ of Pennsylvania	PA	16,836	C
West Virginia Wesleyan College	WV	26,880	C
Westmont College	CA	41,500	HC
Whitworth Univ	WA	45,826	VC+
Worcester Polytechnic Inst	MA	53,440	HC+
Wright State Univ	OH	16,983	C

ENGINEERING SCIENCE

School	ST	$IS	SR
Calif Polytechnic State Univ	CA	19,847	HC
Univ of Mary Hardin-Baylor	TX	31,950	C+
Univ of Miami	FL	55,166	MC

ENGINEERING TECHNOLOGY

School	ST	$IS	SR
Appalachian State Univ	NC	12,919	VC
Austin Peay State Univ	TN	14,650	C
Bluefield State College	WV	3,140	LC
Bowling Green State Univ	OH	18,970	C
Calif Maritime Academy	CA	15,496	C
Calif State Polytechnic Univ, Pomona	CA	18,932	C
Cal State, Long Beach	CA	17,534	C+
Cal State, Sacramento	CA	16,200	C
Calif Univ of Pennsylvania	PA	14,217	C
Capitol College	MD	21,250	C
Central Mich Univ	MI	18,066	C
Central Washington Univ	WA	11,730	C
Colo Mesa Univ	CO	16,669	LC
East Tenn State Univ	TN	9,000	C
Eastern Mich Univ	MI	17,961	C
Eastern Washington Univ	WA	16,388	C
Embry-Riddle Aeronautical Univ - Daytona Beach	FL	40,884	C+
Fairmont State Univ	WV	12,098	LC
Farmingdale State College	NY	18,985	C
Ferris State Univ	MI	19,698	C
Florida A&M Univ	FL	14,935	LC
Grambling State Univ	LA	13,384	LC
Indiana Univ-Purdue Univ Fort Wayne	IN	15,425	C
Iowa State Univ	IA	16,403	C
Kansas State Univ	KS	15,497	VC
Lake Superior State Univ	MI	18,121	C
Lawrence Tech Univ	MI	37,630	VC
LeTourneau Univ	TX	26,230	C
Maine Maritime Academy	ME	21,073	C
McNeese State Univ	LA		C
Miami Univ	OH	24,191	HC
Middle Tenn State Univ	TN	8,650	C
Midwestern State Univ	TX	9,722	C
Milwaukee School of Engineering	WI	39,948	VC+
Minn State Univ, Mankato	MN	14,900	C
Missouri Western State Univ	MO	12,260	NC
Montana State Univ-Northern	MT	12,500	NC
New Jersey Inst of Technology	NJ	26,490	VC
New Mexico State Univ	NM	13,955	LC
New York Inst of Technology	NY	40,590	VC
Ohio Univ	OH	20,676	VC
Old Dominion Univ	VA	18,662	C
Oregon Inst of Technology	OR	8,910	C
Penn State Erie/The Behrend College	PA	16,256	C
Pennsylvania College of Technology	PA	25,653	NC
Point Park Univ	PA	36,390	C
Prairie View A&M Univ	TX	15,205	LC
Purdue Univ/Calumet	IN	14,336	C
Rochester Inst of Technology	NY	42,450	VC+
Saginaw Valley State Univ	MI	16,869	C
Shawnee State Univ	OH	16,545	NC
S Car State Univ	SC	6,700	LC
S Dak State Univ	SD	14,296	C
Southeast Missouri State Univ	MO	14,983	LC
Southeastern Louisiana Univ	LA	13,325	C
Southern Illinois Univ Carbondale	IL	21,620	C
Southern Univ and A&M College	LA	9,761	C+
Southwestern Okla State Univ	OK	9,160	C
St. Cloud State Univ	MN	10,600	C
Temple Univ	PA	24,392	VC
Texas A&M Univ	TX	16,956	VC+
Texas A&M Univ at Commerce	TX	10,496	C
Texas A&M Univ at Corpus Christi	TX	11,544	LC
Texas Southern Univ	TX	18,212	LC
Texas State Univ	TX	16,495	VC
Texas Tech Univ	TX	14,243	C
Univ of Arkansas at Little Rock	AR		C
Univ of Central Missouri	MO	14,605	C
Univ of Cincinnati	OH	20,199	VC
Univ of Dayton	OH	43,750	VC
Univ of Delaware	DE	22,728	VC
Univ of Hartford	CT	42,674	C
Univ of Houston-Downtown	TX	6,267	LC
Univ of Maryland/Eastern Shore	MD	14,000	C
Univ of Mass Lowell	MA	19,316	C
Univ of Memphis	TN	15,094	C
Univ of N Car at Charlotte	NC	15,847	C
Univ of North Texas	TX	15,628	C
Univ of S Car Upstate	SC	17,673	LC
Univ of Southern Miss	MS	13,170	C
Univ of Toledo	OH	18,464	C
Univ of Wisc/Green Bay	WI	14,900	C
Univ of Wisc/Stout	WI	23,942	C
Virginia State Univ	VA	11,318	C+
West Texas A&M Univ	TX	13,478	C
West Virginia Univ Inst of Technology	WV	14,094	NC
Western Carolina Univ	NC	13,965	C+
Western Washington Univ	WA	18,519	VC

ENGLISH

School	ST	$IS	SR
Abilene Christian Univ	TX	38,400	VC
Adams State College	CO	13,358	LC
Adelphi Univ	NY	43,130	VC
Adrian College	MI	33,800	C
Alabama A&M Univ	AL	96,100	C
Alabama State Univ	AL	14,142	NC
Albany State Univ	GA	8,500	C
Albertus Magnus College	CT	37,382	LC
Albion College	MI	43,884	VC
Albright College	PA	46,660	C
Alcorn State Univ	MS	9,500	C
Alfred Univ	NY	40,392	VC
Alice Lloyd College	KY	4,900	C
Allegheny College	PA	49,020	HC
Allen Univ	SC	16,124	NC
Alma College	MI	42,400	VC
Alvernia Univ	PA	39,250	C
Alverno College	WI	30,483	LC
American International College	MA	36,100	LC
Amherst College	MA	58,744	MC
Anderson Univ	IN	35,390	C
Andrews Univ	MI	28,030	C+
Angelo State Univ	TX	15,049	NC
Anna Maria College	MA	34,600	LC
Appalachian State Univ	NC	12,919	VC
Aquinas College	MI	33,060	C
Aquinas College	TN	29,250	C+
Arcadia Univ	PA	33,570	C+
Arizona State Univ	AZ	18,818	C+
Arkansas State Univ	AR	14,980	C
Armstrong Atlantic State Univ	GA	16,276	C
Asbury Univ	KY	32,038	VC
Ashford Univ	IA	21,780	C
Ashland Univ	OH	25,000	C
Assumption College	MA	45,721	VC
Atlantic Union College	MA	24,600	LC
Auburn Univ	AL	20,052	VC+
Auburn Univ at Montgomery	AL	12,120	C
Augsburg College	MN	35,142	C
Augustana College	IL	43,398	HC
Augustana College	SD	35,500	VC
Aurora Univ	IL	26,870	C
Austin College	TX	36,940	HC
Austin Peay State Univ	TN	14,650	C
Averett Univ	VA	36,000	LC
Avila Univ	MO	26,900	C
Azusa Pacific Univ	CA	39,946	C
Baker Univ	KS	33,350	C+
Baldwin Wallace Univ	OH	36,980	VC
Ball State Univ	IN	17,850	C
Barry Univ	FL	38,190	C
Barton College	NC	27,660	C
Bates College	ME	58,950	MC

School	ST	$IS	SR
Baylor Univ	TX	46,720	HC
Belhaven Univ	MS	27,170	C
Bellarmine Univ	KY	42,950	VC
Bellevue Univ	NE	4,600	NC
Belmont Abbey College	NC	37,716	C
Belmont Univ	TN	37,380	VǤ
Beloit College	WI	49,970	HC
Bemidji State Univ	MN	13,500	C
Benedict College	SC	20,454	NC
Benedictine College	KS	29,180	VC
Bennett College	NC		LC
Bennington College	VT	56,990	HǤ
Berea College	KY	7,220	HC
Berry College	GA	39,254	HC
Bethany College	KS	30,605	NC
Bethany College	WV	35,282	C
Bethel College	IN	31,560	C
Bethel College	KS	29,100	C
Bethel Univ	MN	34,940	VC
Bethel Univ	TN	19,186	C
Bethune-Cookman Univ	FL	22,290	LC
Binghamton Univ / The SUNY	NY	20,832	HǤ
Biola Univ	CA	40,320	VC
Birmingham-Southern College	AL	42,370	VǤ
Black Hills State Univ	SD	13,562	LC
Bloomfield College	NJ	36,960	C
Bloomsburg Univ of Pennsylvania	PA	13,598	C
Blue Mountain College	MS	13,550	LC
Bluefield College	VA	17,230	Ǥ
Bluffton Univ	OH	37,864	C
Boise State Univ	ID	12,802	C
Boston College	MA	58,506	MC
Boston Univ	MA	54,130	HǤ
Bowdoin College	ME	57,834	MC
Bowie State Univ	MD	23,990	LC
Bowling Green State Univ	OH	18,970	C
Bradley Univ	IL	31,874	VC
Brandeis Univ	MA	58,820	HC
Brenau Univ Women's College	GA	26,650	Ǥ
Brescia Univ	KY	26,140	VǤ
Brewton-Parker College	GA	33,388	LC
Briar Cliff Univ	IA	29,514	C
Bridgewater College	VA	39,880	C
Bridgewater State Univ	MA	18,752	C
Brigham Young Univ	UT	12,100	HC
Brigham Young Univ/Hawaii	HI	8,614	VC
Brown Univ	RI	56,150	MC
Bryan College	TN	24,194	C
Bryant Univ	RI	49,179	VC
Bryn Athyn College	PA	27,984	C
Bryn Mawr College	PA	57,760	MC
Bucknell Univ	PA	58,160	MC
Buena Vista Univ	IA	37,954	C
Buffalo State/State Univ of Buffalo	NY	15,733	Ǥ
Butler Univ	IN	45,898	VǤ
Cabrini College	PA	40,859	LC
Cairn Univ	PA	31,255	C
Caldwell College	NJ	35,602	LC
Calif Baptist Univ	CA	35,890	C
Calif College of the Arts	CA	48,334	SP
Calif Lutheran Univ	CA	47,640	C
Calif Polytechnic State Univ	CA	19,847	HC
Calif State Polytechnic Univ, Pomona	CA	18,932	C
Cal State, Bakersfield	CA	8,000	LC
Cal State, Chico	CA	18,952	C
Cal State, Dominguez Hills	CA	17,056	LC
Cal State, East Bay	CA	16,549	C
Cal State, Fresno	CA	17,405	C
Cal State, Fullerton	CA	25,188	Ǥ
Cal State, Long Beach	CA	17,534	Ǥ
Cal State, Los Angeles	CA	15,829	C
Cal State, Northridge	CA	28,313	C
Cal State, Sacramento	CA	16,200	C
Cal State, San Bernardino	CA	12,000	C
Cal State, Stanislaus	CA	18,582	C
Calif Univ of Pennsylvania	PA	14,217	C
Calumet College of St. Joseph	IN	15,000	LC
Calvin College	MI	37,585	VǤ
Cameron Univ	OK	9,267	LC
Campbell Univ	NC	25,500	C
Campbellsville Univ	KY	27,720	C
Canisius College	NY	45,602	VC
Capital Univ	OH	39,824	VC
Cardinal Stritch Univ	WI	24,054	C
Carleton College	MN	58,149	MC
Carlow Univ	PA	30,272	C
Carnegie Mellon Univ	PA	51,260	MC
Carroll College	MT	28,000	C
Carroll Univ	WI	24,860	C
Carson-Newman Univ	TN	29,058	Ǥ
Carthage College	WI	33,000	C
Case Western Reserve Univ	OH	55,178	MC
Catawba College	NC	37,105	C
Cazenovia College	NY	30,800	C
Cedar Crest College	PA	43,240	C
Cedarville Univ	OH	31,036	VǤ
Centenary College	NJ	38,618	LC
Centenary College of Louisiana	LA	39,070	Ǥ
Central College	IA	36,980	VC
Central Conn State Univ	CT	19,212	C
Central Methodist Univ	MO	28,240	VC
Central Mich Univ	MI	18,066	C
Central State Univ	OH	9,010	C
Central Washington Univ	WA	11,730	C
Centre College	KY	35,000	HǤ
Chadron State College	NE	7,400	NC
Chaminade Univ of Honolulu	HI	31,664	C
Chapman Univ	CA	56,019	VǤ
Charleston Southern Univ	SC	22,420	C
Chatham Univ	PA	42,440	VC
Cheyney Univ of Pennsylvania	PA	20,372	LC
Chicago State Univ	IL	5,482	C
Christendom College	VA	28,120	VC
Christian Brothers Univ	TN	19,140	HC
Christopher Newport Univ	VA	21,050	VC
Citadel, The	SC		C
CUNY/Baruch College	NY	15,831	VC
CUNY/Brooklyn College	NY	5,884	Ǥ
Claflin Univ	SC	22,368	Ǥ
Clarion Univ of Pennsylvania	PA	17,370	C
Clark Atlanta Univ	GA	30,006	C
Clark Univ	MA	47,020	HǤ
Clarke Univ	IA	36,400	C
Clearwater Christian College	FL	23,720	C
Clemson Univ	SC	19,136	HC
Cleveland State Univ	OH	21,357	C
Coastal Carolina Univ	SC	17,620	C
Coe College	IA	43,590	VC
Coker College	SC	32,256	LC
Colby College	ME	57,510	MC
Colby-Sawyer College	NH	47,870	C
Colgate Univ	NY	50,930	MC
College of Staten Island / The CUNY	NY	16,778	NC
College of Charleston	SC	21,273	VC
College of Mount St. Joseph	OH	33,880	C
College of Mount St. Vincent	NY	41,040	MC
College of New Jersey	NJ	25,376	HC
College of St. Benedict	MN	47,570	VC
College of St. Elizabeth	NJ	43,839	LC
College of St. Mary	NE	34,334	C
College of St. Scholastica	MN	39,960	C
College of St Joseph	VT	30,600	LC
College of the Holy Cross	MA	56,232	MC
College of the Ozarks	MO	5,605	VC
College of William & Mary	VA	25,085	MC
College of Wooster	OH	52,600	VC
Colo Christian Univ	CO	27,500	VC
Colo College	CO	54,534	MC
Colo Mesa Univ	CO	16,669	LC
Colo State Univ-Fort Collins	CO	20,090	VC
Colo State Univ-Pueblo	CO	13,532	LC
Columbia College	MO	24,578	C
Columbia College	SC	27,882	C
Columbia Univ in the City of New York	NY	61,116	MC
Columbia Univ/Barnard College	NY	39,000	MC
Columbus State Univ	GA	13,176	C
Concord Univ	WV	13,102	C
Concordia College New York	NY	31,500	VC
Concordia College, Moorhead	MN	39,974	Ǥ
Concordia Univ	OR	34,930	C
Concordia Univ - Irvine	CA	35,390	VC
Concordia Univ Nebr	NE	26,000	VC
Concordia Univ St. Paul	MN	27,200	C
Concordia Univ Texas	TX	23,640	C
Concordia Univ Wisc	WI	28,980	C
Concordia Univ, Ann Arbor	MI	27,220	VC
Concordia Univ, River Forest	IL	26,300	C
Conn College	CT	54,970	MC
Converse College	SC	37,130	C
Coppin State Univ	MD	14,905	VC
Corban Univ	OR	34,764	C
Cornell College	IA	44,930	HC
Cornell Univ	NY	59,037	MC
Cornerstone Univ and Grand Rapids Theological Seminary	MI	30,866	C
Covenant College	GA		VǤ
Creighton Univ	NE	44,058	VǤ
Culver-Stockton College	MO	30,900	C
Cumberland Univ	TN	21,220	C
CUNY-City College	NY	19,576	HǤ
Curry College	MA	47,545	LC
Daemen College	NY	31,510	C
Dakota State Univ	SD	13,811	C
Dakota Wesleyan Univ	SD	23,000	C
Dallas Baptist Univ	TX	29,118	C
Dartmouth College	NH	57,996	MC
Davidson College	NC	54,683	MC
Davis and Elkins College	WV	33,742	C
De Sales Univ	PA	42,670	C
Delaware State Univ	DE	14,700	LC
Delaware Valley College	PA	29,944	C
Delta State Univ	MS	12,292	LC
Denison Univ	OH	54,670	HǤ
DePaul Univ	IL	46,120	VC
DePauw Univ	IN	48,950	VǤ
Dickinson College	PA	57,662	HǤ
Dickinson State Univ	ND	8,550	NC
Dillard Univ	LA	20,940	VC
Doane College	NE	33,730	VC
Dominican College	NY	31,270	C
Dominican Univ	IL	37,628	C
Dordt College	IA	34,160	VC
Dowling College	NY	25,000	LC
Drake Univ	IA	30,980	VǤ
Drew Univ/College of Liberal Arts	NJ	55,002	VC
Drury Univ	MO	30,319	VC
Duke Univ	NC	50,250	MC
Duquesne Univ	PA	42,017	VC
D'Youville College	NY	29,850	C
Earlham College	IN	49,710	VǤ
East Carolina Univ	NC	14,169	C
East Central Univ	OK	10,223	LC
East Stroudsburg Univ of Pennsylvania	PA	16,636	C
East Tenn State Univ	TN	9,000	C
East Texas Baptist Univ	TX	29,135	C
Eastern Conn State Univ	CT	20,584	C
Eastern Illinois Univ	IL	20,502	C
Eastern Kentucky Univ	KY	11,161	C
Eastern Mennonite Univ	VA	38,850	VC
Eastern Mich Univ	MI	17,961	C
Eastern Nazarene College	MA	30,000	C
Eastern New Mexico Univ	NM	10,682	C
Eastern Oregon Univ	OR	10,400	C
Eastern Univ	PA	37,704	C
Eastern Washington Univ	WA	16,388	C
East-West Univ	IL	16,076	C
Edgewood College	WI	33,294	C
Edinboro Univ of Pennsylvania	PA	15,940	LC
Edward Waters College	FL	17,856	LC
Elizabeth City State Univ	NC	11,638	C
Elizabethtown College	PA	47,600	VC
Elmhurst College	IL	42,032	Ǥ
Elms College	MA	23,900	VC
Elon Univ	NC	40,046	HC
Emmanuel College	MA	47,985	VC
Emory Univ	GA	45,000	MC
Emporia State Univ	KS	12,897	C
Endicott College	MA	42,390	C
Erskine College	SC	37,360	C
Eureka College	IL	19,280	C
Evangel Univ	MO	23,090	C
Fairfield Univ	CT	55,850	VC
Fairmont State Univ	WV	12,098	LC
Faulkner Univ	AL	22,530	LC
Fayetteville State Univ	NC	10,816	C
Felician College	NJ	41,640	C
Ferris State Univ	MI	19,698	C
Ferrum College	VA	27,740	LC
Fisk Univ	TN	19,830	C
Fitchburg State Univ	MA	17,241	C
Flagler College	FL	24,960	VC
Florida A&M Univ	FL	14,935	LC
Florida Atlantic Univ	FL	17,339	C
Florida Gulf Coast Univ	FL		C
Florida International Univ	FL	17,747	VC
Florida Memorial Univ	FL	20,716	LC
Florida Southern College	FL	38,240	VC
Florida State Univ	FL	15,238	HC
Fontbonne Univ	MO	31,384	C
Fordham Univ	NY	58,927	HC
Fort Hays State Univ	KS	11,354	C
Fort Lewis College	CO	15,513	C
Fort Valley State Univ	GA	11,200	VC
Framingham State Univ	MA	16,750	C
Francis Marion Univ	SC	16,464	LC
Franciscan Univ of Steubenville	OH	27,320	VC
Franklin and Marshall College	PA	58,295	MC
Franklin College	IN	35,885	C
Franklin Pierce Univ	NH	41,598	C
Freed-Hardeman Univ	TN	19,697	VC
Fresno Pacific Univ	CA	32,136	C
Friends Univ	KS	29,100	C
Frostburg State Univ	MD	15,264	LC
Furman Univ	SC	54,006	HC
Gallaudet Univ	DC	25,380	SP
Gannon Univ	PA	37,940	C
Gardner-Webb Univ	NC	34,375	Ǥ
Geneva College	PA	27,280	C
George Mason Univ	VA	15,724	VC
George Washington Univ	DC	57,108	MC
Georgetown College	KY	38,690	C
Georgetown Univ	DC	52,910	MC
Georgia College and State Univ	GA	18,216	VC
Georgia Regents Univ	GA		C
Georgia Southern Univ	GA	16,414	C
Georgia Southwestern State Univ	GA	12,218	C
Georgia State Univ	GA	12,000	VC
Georgian Court Univ	NJ	39,726	LC
Gettysburg College	PA	56,820	HC
Glenville State College	WV	11,348	NC
Goddard College	VT	16,418	VC
Gonzaga Univ	WA	44,247	HC
Gordon College	MA	42,660	VǤ
Goshen College	IN	35,900	VC
Goucher College	MD	50,252	VǤ
Grace College and Theological Seminary	IN	28,800	C
Graceland Univ	IA	28,020	C
Grambling State Univ	LA	13,384	LC
Grand Canyon Univ	AZ	24,540	VC
Grand Valley State Univ	MI	17,998	VC
Grand View Univ	IA	31,050	C
Green Mountain College	VT	33,547	LC
Greensboro College	NC	28,740	LC
Greenville College	IL	27,012	C
Grinnell College	IA	53,654	HC
Grove City College	PA	22,900	HC
Guilford College	NC	35,340	C
Gustavus Adolphus College	MN	48,170	HC
Gwynedd-Mercy College	PA	33,560	C
Hamilton College	NY	55,620	MC
Hamline Univ	MN	44,198	VC
Hampden-Sydney College	VA	48,848	C
Hampton Univ	VA	28,528	C
Hannibal-LaGrange Univ	MO	24,490	C
Hanover College	IN	41,450	VC
Harding Univ	AR	21,432	Ǥ
Hardin-Simmons Univ	TX	23,560	Ǥ
Hartwick College	NY	49,815	Ǥ
Harvard Univ/Harvard College	MA	49,000	MC
Hastings College	NE	27,782	Ǥ
Haverford College	PA	59,236	MC
Hawaii Pacific Univ	HI	36,690	C
Heidelberg Univ	OH	34,100	C
Henderson State Univ	AR	13,634	C
Hendrix College	AR	48,436	HǤ
Heritage Univ	WA	17,664	NC
Hilbert College	NY	28,550	C
Hillsdale College	MI	31,890	HǤ
Hiram College	OH	37,300	VC
Hobart and William Smith Colleges	NY	43,000	VC
Hollins Univ	VA	43,295	VC
Holy Family Univ	PA	40,030	LC
Holy Names Univ	CA	40,310	NC
Hood College	MD	44,630	C
Hope College	MI	36,320	VǤ
Houghton College	NY	35,740	VC
Houston Baptist Univ	TX	23,815	Ǥ
Howard Payne Univ	TX	17,115	C
Howard Univ	DC	35,957	C
Humboldt State Univ	CA	18,400	C
Hunter College / The CUNY	NY	14,429	VC
Huntingdon College	AL	31,850	C
Huntington Univ	IN	32,220	C
Husson Univ	ME	23,386	LC
Huston-Tillotson Univ	TX	18,124	Ǥ
Idaho State Univ	ID	11,908	C
Illinois College	IL	25,770	VC
Illinois State Univ	IL	22,634	VC
Illinois Wesleyan Univ	IL	48,452	VǤ
Immaculata Univ	PA	43,000	C
Indiana State Univ	IN	16,000	C
Indiana Univ Bloomington	IN	19,358	HC
Indiana Univ East	IN	6,639	LC
Indiana Univ Kokomo	IN	6,674	LC
Indiana Univ Northwest	IN	6,738	LC
Indiana Univ of Pennsylvania	PA	20,180	LC
Indiana Univ South Bend	IN	15,293	C
Indiana Univ Southeast	IN	15,807	LC
Indiana Univ-Purdue Univ Fort Wayne	IN	15,425	C
Indiana Univ-Purdue Univ Indianapolis	IN	17,290	C
Indiana Wesleyan Univ	IN	31,815	VC
Inter-American Univ of PR/ San Germán	PR	6,720	
Iona College	NY	44,028	C
Iowa State Univ	IA	16,403	C
Iowa Wesleyan College	IA	30,850	LC
Ithaca College	NY	52,300	HC
Jackson State Univ	MS	13,512	LC
Jacksonville State Univ	AL	12,280	LC
Jacksonville Univ	FL	37,780	C
James Madison Univ	VA	18,049	VC
Jarvis Christian College	TX	19,552	NC
John Brown Univ	AR	30,996	VǤ
John Carroll Univ	OH	44,520	Ǥ
John Jay College of Criminal Justice / The CUNY	NY	6,059	C
Johns Hopkins Univ	MD	47,492	MC
Johnson C. Smith Univ	NC	25,336	LC
Johnson State College	VT	16,721	C
Judson College	AL	24,690	C
Judson Univ	IL	25,130	C
Juniata College	PA	49,340	VC
Kalamazoo College	MI	47,825	HǤ
Kansas State Univ	KS	15,497	VC
Kansas Wesleyan Univ	KS	32,000	C
Kean Univ	NJ	22,060	LC
Keene State College	NH	21,538	C
Kennesaw State Univ	GA	13,017	VC

ST = STATE **$IS** = IN-STATE COSTS **SR** = SELECTOR RATING

School	ST	$IS	SR
Kent State Univ	OH	19,352	C
Kentucky State Univ	KY	11,000	LC
Kentucky Wesleyan College	KY	27,440	VC+
Kenyon College	OH	56,810	MC
Keuka College	NY	30,300	C
King Univ	TN	33,140	C
King's College	PA	41,678	C
Kutztown Univ of Pennsylvania	PA	16,909	LC
La Roche College	PA	34,802	LC
La Salle Univ	PA	50,270	C
La Sierra Univ	CA	35,694	VC
Lafayette College	PA	57,050	HC+
LaGrange College	GA	34,480	C
Lake Erie College	OH	35,704	C
Lake Forest College	IL	45,580	VC
Lake Superior State Univ	MI	18,121	C
Lakeland College	WI	22,990	C
Lamar Univ	TX	6,820	LC
Lander Univ	SC	22,514	C+
Lane College	TN	11,212	C
Langston Univ	OK	3,000	LC
Lasell College	MA	42,500	LC
Lawrence Tech Univ	MI	37,630	VC
Lawrence Univ	WI	46,371	HC
Le Moyne College	NY	42,200	VC
Lebanon Valley College	PA	38,570	C
Lee Univ	TN	18,690	C+
Lees-McRae College	NC	33,624	C
Lehigh Univ	PA	55,080	MC
Lehman College / The CUNY	NY	5,778	LC
LeMoyne-Owen College	TN	13,100	C
Lenoir-Rhyne Univ	NC	35,984	C
LeTourneau Univ	TX	26,230	C
Lewis & Clark College	OR	52,656	VC
Lewis Univ	IL	23,050	C
Lewis-Clark State College	ID	6,990	C
Liberty Univ	VA	19,101	C
Limestone College	SC	29,880	C
Lincoln Memorial Univ	TN	18,144	C
Lincoln Univ	MO	11,996	NC
Lindenwood Univ	MO	20,750	C
Lindsey Wilson College	KY	30,470	VC
Linfield College-McMinnville Campus	OR	46,166	C
Lipscomb Univ	TN	35,722	VC
Livingstone College	NC	17,815	LC
Lock Haven Univ of Pennsylvania	PA	17,587	LC
LIU/Brooklyn Campus	NY	26,500	C
LIU/C.W. Post Campus	NY	38,888	C
Longwood Univ	VA	20,924	C
Louisiana College	LA	15,746	C
Louisiana State Univ	LA	18,677	VC+
Louisiana State Univ in Shreveport	LA	5,606	C
Louisiana Tech Univ	LA	8,000	C
Lourdes Univ	OH	26,055	LC
Loyola Marymount Univ	CA	53,240	VC+
Loyola Univ Chicago	IL	49,560	VC+
Loyola Univ Maryland	MD		VC
Luther College	IA	44,380	VC+
Lycoming College	PA	43,636	C
Lynchburg College	VA	42,645	C
Lyndon State College	VT	14,233	C
Lyon College	AR	30,246	VC
Macalester College	MN	53,419	MC
MacMurray College	IL	20,755	C
Madonna Univ	MI	24,540	VC
Malone Univ	OH	34,334	C
Manchester College	IN	35,070	C
Manhattan College	NY	44,955	VC
Manhattanville College	NY	46,260	VC
Mansfield Univ	PA	19,468	LC
Marian Univ	WI	30,980	LC
Marian Univ/Indianapolis	IN	37,058	C
Marietta College	OH	42,135	VC
Marist College	NY	35,500	C
Marlboro College	VT	35,980	VC
Marquette Univ	WI	43,664	VC+
Mars Hill College	NC	22,950	LC
Marshall Univ	WV	14,820	C
Mary Baldwin College	VA	37,110	C
Marygrove College	MI	21,290	C
Marymount Manhattan College	NY	40,118	VC
Marymount Univ	VA	36,178	C
Maryville College	TN	33,150	VC
Maryville Univ of St. Louis	MO	34,920	VC
Marywood Univ	PA	40,695	C
Mass College of Liberal Arts	MA	16,733	C
Mayville State Univ	ND	11,401	NC
McDaniel College	MD	45,600	VC
McKendree Univ	IL	29,920	C+
McMurry Univ	TX	25,962	LC
McNeese State Univ	LA		C
McPherson College	KS	28,138	C
Medaille College	NY	35,112	VC
Medgar Evers College / The CUNY	NY	4,920	NC
Mercy College	NY	29,996	C
Mercyhurst Univ	PA	40,700	C
Meredith College	NC	31,420	C
Merrimack College	MA	44,215	C

School	ST	$IS	SR
Messiah College	PA	39,540	VC
Methodist Univ	NC	37,185	C
Metropolitan State Univ	MN	5,923	SP
Metropolitan State Univ of Denver	CO	4,835	LC
Miami Univ	OH	24,191	HC
Mich State Univ	MI	13,689	VC
Mich Tech Univ	MI	22,105	VC
MidAmerica Nazarene Univ	KS	28,000	C
Middle Tenn State Univ	TN	8,650	C
Middlebury College	VT	57,470	MC
Midland Univ	NE	34,000	C
Midway College	KY	20,150	C
Midwestern State Univ	TX	9,722	C
Miles College	AL	16,530	NC
Millersville Univ of Pennsylvania	PA	18,498	C
Milligan College	TN	27,510	C
Millikin Univ	IL	37,462	C
Mills College	CA	54,119	HC
Millsaps College	MS	43,888	VC+
Minn State Univ, Mankato	MN	14,900	C
Minn State Univ, Moorhead	MN	13,392	C
Minot State Univ	ND	10,915	C
Misericordia Univ	PA	39,840	C
Miss College	MS	21,998	VC
Miss Univ for Women	MS	7,400	LC
Miss Valley State Univ	MS	9,706	LC
Missouri Baptist Univ	MO	30,310	C
Missouri Southern State Univ	MO	11,910	C
Missouri State Univ	MO	13,996	VC
Missouri Univ of Science and Technology	MO	18,655	VC+
Missouri Valley College	MO	22,200	C
Missouri Western State Univ	MO	12,260	NC
Molloy College	NY	38,950	C
Monmouth College	IL	39,290	C
Monmouth Univ	NJ	42,252	C
Montana State Univ	MT	14,068	VC
Montana State Univ-Billings	MT	12,425	LC
Montana State Univ-Northern	MT	12,500	NC
Montclair State Univ	NJ	22,614	C
Montreat College	NC	31,298	VC
Moravian College	PA	36,381	VC
Morehead State Univ	KY	10,900	C
Morehouse College	GA	38,640	C
Morgan State Univ	MD	14,500	VC
Morningside College	IA	32,620	C
Morris College	SC	16,006	LC
Mount Aloysius College	PA	27,970	C
Mount Holyoke College	MA	53,596	HC+
Mount Marty College	SD	29,638	C
Mount Mary Univ	WI	32,836	LC
Mount Mercy Univ	IA	34,385	C
Mount Olive College	NC	18,426	C
Mount St. Mary College	NY	39,540	C
Mount St. Mary's Univ	MD	46,158	C
Mount St. Mary's College/ Chalon Campus	CA	43,897	VC+
Mount Vernon Nazarene Univ	OH	29,590	C
Muhlenberg College	PA	52,837	HC
Murray State Univ	KY	14,944	C
Muskingum Univ	OH	30,502	C
Naropa Univ	CO	37,875	SP
National Louis Univ	IL	16,915	LC
National Univ	CA	14,730	SP
Nazareth College of Rochester	NY	41,590	VC
Nebr Wesleyan Univ	NE	29,774	C+
Neumann Univ	PA	31,078	LC
New College of Florida	FL	14,504	HC+
New Jersey City Univ	NJ	21,060	C+
New Mexico Highlands Univ	NM	9,720	NC
New Mexico State Univ	NM	13,955	LC
New York Inst of Technology	NY	40,590	VC
New York Univ	NY	61,470	MC
Newberry College	SC	26,850	LC
Newman Univ	KS	30,380	C+
Niagara Univ	NY	39,800	C
Nicholls State Univ	LA	7,095	C
Nichols College	MA	37,240	LC
Norfolk State Univ	VA	10,531	LC
N Car Agricultural and Technical State Univ	NC	13,175	LC
N Car Central Univ	NC	9,000	LC
N Car State Univ	NC	16,202	HC
N Car Wesleyan College	NC	29,440	C
North Central College	IL	38,343	VC
N Dak State Univ	ND	14,642	C
North Georgia College & State Univ	GA	8,500	C
North Park Univ	IL	30,130	C
Northeastern Illinois Univ	IL		C
Northeastern State Univ	OK	8,615	VC
Northeastern Univ	MA	55,296	MC
Northern Arizona Univ	AZ	18,592	C
Northern Illinois Univ	IL	19,768	C
Northern Kentucky Univ	KY	15,302	LC
Northern Mich Univ	MI	15,300	VC
Northern State Univ	SD	14,021	C
Northland College	WI	26,680	C

School	ST	$IS	SR
Northwest Missouri State Univ	MO	14,229	C
Northwest Nazarene Univ	ID	24,275	NC
Northwest Univ	WA	18,854	C
Northwestern College	MN	24,000	C
Northwestern Okla State Univ	OK	7,275	NC
Northwestern State Univ of Louisiana	LA	14,368	C
Northwestern Univ	IL	37,595	MC
Norwich Univ	VT	28,212	C
Notre Dame College	OH	34,942	VC
Notre Dame de Namur Univ	CA	41,610	LC
Notre Dame of Maryland Univ	MD	27,700	C
Nyack College	NY	32,000	C
Oakland City Univ	IN	24,500	NC
Oakland Univ	MI	19,391	VC
Oakwood Univ	AL	23,035	C
Oberlin College	OH	57,025	MC
Occidental College	CA	59,592	MC+
Oglethorpe Univ	GA	42,580	VC
Ohio Dominican Univ	OH	38,380	C+
Ohio Northern Univ	OH	42,075	VC
Ohio State Univ at Lima	OH	7,140	C
Ohio State Univ at Mansfield	OH	13,160	C
Ohio State Univ at Marion	OH	9,850	MC
Ohio State Univ at Newark	OH	17,510	C
Ohio Univ	OH	20,676	VC
Ohio Valley Univ	WV	17,752	C
Ohio Wesleyan Univ	OH	49,460	C+
Okla Baptist Univ	OK	28,202	VC
Okla Christian Univ	OK	24,975	VC
Okla City Univ	OK	33,546	VC
Okla Panhandle State Univ	OK	8,996	NC
Okla State Univ	OK	14,310	VC
Okla Wesleyan Univ	OK	21,300	C
Old Dominion Univ	VA	18,662	C
Olivet College	MI	19,984	C
Olivet Nazarene Univ	IL	29,990	C
Oral Roberts Univ	OK	31,734	C
Oregon State Univ	OR	19,017	C+
Oswego / SUNY	NY	20,009	VC
Ottawa Univ	KS	15,000	VC
Otterbein College	OH	32,214	C
Ouachita Baptist Univ	AR	29,010	VC
Our Lady of Holy Cross College	LA	8,090	LC
Our Lady of the Lake Univ of San Antonio	TX	22,430	LC
Pace Univ	NY	48,094	VC
Pacific Lutheran Univ	WA	44,840	VC
Pacific Union College	CA	28,150	VC
Paine College	GA	18,594	LC
Palm Beach Atlantic Univ	FL	33,882	LC
Park Univ	MO	17,525	C
Paul Quinn College	TX	25,350	LC
Penn State Erie/The Behrend College	PA	16,256	C
Penn State Univ/Altoona	PA	11,464	C
Pepperdine Univ	CA	55,372	HC+
Peru State College	NE	8,600	NC
Philander Smith College	AR	19,760	LC
Piedmont College	GA	29,260	C
Pine Manor College	MA	32,659	LC
Pittsburg State Univ	KS	12,032	C
Pitzer College	CA	54,988	MC
Plymouth State Univ	NH	23,148	LC
Point Park Univ	PA	36,390	C
Pomona College	CA	57,680	MC
Pontifical Catholic Univ of PR	PR	7,310	
Portland State Univ	OR	18,672	C
Post Univ	CT	35,750	C
Prairie View A&M Univ	TX	15,205	LC
Presbyterian College	SC	42,678	VC
Prescott College	AZ	33,284	C+
Princeton Univ	NJ	53,795	MC
Principia College	IL	35,140	C+
Providence College	RI	55,995	HC
Purdue Univ/Calumet	IN	14,336	C
Purdue Univ/West Lafayette	IN	20,278	HC
Queens College / The CUNY	NY	17,107	VC
Quincy Univ	IL	34,980	LC
Quinnipiac Univ	CT	53,580	VC
Radford Univ	VA	17,132	LC
Randolph College	VA	43,960	VC
Randolph-Macon College	VA	45,086	C
Regis College	MA	47,565	LC
Regis Univ	CO	41,318	C
Rhode Island College	RI	17,132	LC
Rhodes College	TN	47,596	HC+
Rice Univ	TX	43,288	MC
Rider Univ	NJ	45,720	C
Ripon College	WI	36,959	C+
Rivier College	NH	35,000	VC
Robert Morris Univ	PA	36,699	C
Roberts Wesleyan College	NY	37,384	C+
Rochester College	MI	18,320	C
Rockford College	IL	31,000	C
Rockhurst Univ	MO	20,625	C
Roger Williams Univ	RI	45,788	C
Rollins College	FL	52,370	HC
Roosevelt Univ	IL	22,605	VC

School	ST	$IS	SR
Rosemont College	PA	42,350	C
Rowan Univ	NJ	23,570	VC
Russell Sage College	NY	39,370	C
Rust College	MS	10,600	C
Rutgers, The State Univ of New Jersey/Camden Campus	NJ	24,254	C
Rutgers, The State Univ of New Jersey/New Brunswick	NJ	25,077	VC
Rutgers, The State Univ of New Jersey/Newark Campus	NJ	25,376	C
Sacred Heart Univ	CT	48,564	VC
Saginaw Valley State Univ	MI	16,869	C
St. Anselm College	NH	48,324	VC
St. Augustine's Univ	NC	14,000	C
St. Francis Univ	PA	30,029	LC
St. John's Univ	MN	46,146	C
St. Joseph College	CT	45,630	LC
St. Joseph's College	IN	35,790	C
St. Joseph's College of Maine	ME	31,580	C
St. Joseph's Univ	PA	52,272	VC
St. Leo Univ	FL	27,990	C
St. Louis Univ	MO	46,594	VC+
St. Martin's Univ	WA	38,082	C
St. Mary-of-the-Woods College	IN	37,722	LC
St. Mary's College of Calif	CA	53,550	C
St. Mary's Univ	TX	33,854	C
St. Michael's College	VT	48,740	VC
St. Paul's College	VA	16,030	NC
St. Peter's College	NJ	44,240	C
St. Vincent College	PA	40,244	C
St. Xavier Univ	IL	32,840	C
Salem College	NC	29,326	VC
Salem State College	MA	13,161	LC
Salisbury Univ	MD	18,368	VC
Salve Regina Univ	RI	47,250	VC
Sam Houston State Univ	TX	17,082	C
Samford Univ	AL	35,700	VC+
San Diego Christian College	CA	31,012	C
San Diego State Univ	CA	20,578	VC
San Francisco State Univ	CA	18,514	C
San Jose State Univ	CA	19,707	C
Santa Clara Univ	CA	54,702	MC
Sarah Lawrence College	NY	48,000	HC
Savannah State Univ	GA	13,156	C
Schreiner Univ	TX	32,734	LC
Scripps College	CA	54,900	MC
Seattle Pacific Univ	WA	41,559	VC+
Seattle Univ	WA	47,010	VC+
Seton Hall Univ	NJ	45,902	C
Seton Hill Univ	PA	35,172	C
Sewanee: The Univ of the South	TN	47,700	HC+
Shaw Univ	NC	15,488	LC
Shawnee State Univ	OH	16,545	NC
Shenandoah Univ	VA	39,268	C
Shepherd Univ	WV	14,996	C
Shippensburg Univ of Pennsylvania	PA	17,064	LC
Shorter Univ	GA	26,470	C
Siena College	NY	43,863	VC
Siena Heights Univ	MI	17,000	LC
Silver Lake College	WI	22,600	LC
Simmons College	MA	48,770	VC
Simpson College	IA	36,086	VC
Simpson Univ	CA	28,900	C
Skidmore College	NY	57,926	HC
Slippery Rock Univ of Pennsylvania	PA	10,360	LC
Smith College	MA	57,524	MC
Sonoma State Univ	CA	20,541	C
S Car State Univ	SC	6,700	LC
S Dak State Univ	SD	14,296	C
Southeast Missouri State Univ	MO	14,983	LC
Southeastern Louisiana Univ	LA	13,325	C
Southeastern Okla State Univ	OK	7,966	C
Southeastern Univ	FL	27,201	C+
Southern Adventist Univ	TN	26,190	C
Southern Arkansas Univ	AR	14,316	C
Southern Conn State Univ	CT	18,033	C
Southern Illinois Univ Carbondale	IL	21,620	C
Southern Illinois Univ Edwardsville	IL	17,532	C
Southern Methodist Univ	TX	57,755	MC
Southern Nazarene Univ	OK	24,354	NC
Southern New Hampshire Univ	NH	38,100	C
Southern Oregon Univ	OR	17,874	C
Southern Univ and A&M College	LA	9,761	C+
Southern Univ at New Orleans	LA	1,000	NC
Southern Vermont College	VT	30,740	LC
Southern Wesleyan Univ	SC	25,600	C
Southwest Baptist Univ	MO	24,710	C
Southwestern Adventist Univ	TX	23,026	LC
Southwestern College	KS	29,270	C

ST = STATE **$IS** = IN-STATE COSTS **SR** = SELECTOR RATING

School	ST	$IS	SR
Southwestern Okla State Univ	OK	9,160	C
Southwestern Univ	TX	45,660	VC
Spelman College	GA	24,650	VC
Spring Arbor Univ	MI	26,740	C
Spring Hill College	AL	42,130	VC
Springfield College	MA	25,000	C
St. Ambrose Univ	IA		C
St. Bonaventure Univ	NY	38,831	C
St. Catherine Univ	MN	37,782	C+
St. Cloud State Univ	MN	10,600	C
St. Francis College	NY	34,200	LC
St. John Fisher College	NY	39,370	C+
St. John's Univ	NY	52,040	C+
St. Joseph's College, New York / Brooklyn Campus	NY	21,878	C
St. Joseph's College, New York / Suffolk Campus	NY	21,878	VC
St. Lawrence Univ	NY	53,740	HC
St. Mary's College of Maryland	MD	26,699	HC
St. Norbert College	WI	39,992	VC
St. Olaf College	MN	49,960	HC+
St. Thomas Aquinas College	NY	30,000	C
St. Thomas Univ	FL	32,310	C+
Stanford Univ	CA	56,411	MC
Stephen F. Austin State Univ	TX	14,668	C
Stephens College	MO	34,500	VC
Sterling College	KS	27,216	C
Stetson Univ	FL	49,512	VC+
Stillman College	AL	18,460	C
Stonehill College	MA	46,780	VC+
Stony Brook Univ / SUNY	NY	19,359	HC
Suffolk Univ	MA	46,548	C
Sul Ross State Univ	TX	13,410	LC
SUNY College at Geneseo	NY	18,055	HC+
SUNY Cortland / The SUNY	NY	19,117	C
SUNY Fredonia / The SUNY at Fredonia	NY	18,702	VC
SUNY New Paltz	NY	15,010	C
SUNY Oneonta / SUNY	NY	16,919	VC
SUNY Plattsburgh / SUNY	NY	18,083	VC
Susquehanna Univ	PA	49,170	C
Sweet Briar College	VA	43,765	C+
Syracuse Univ	NY	54,512	HC
Tabor College	KS	29,010	LC
Talladega College	AL	13,000	C
Tarleton State Univ	TX	13,489	LC
Taylor Univ	IN	36,742	VC+
Temple Univ	PA	24,392	VC
Tenn State Univ	TN	9,048	C
Tenn Tech Univ	TN	11,310	C
Tenn Wesleyan College	TN	21,250	C
Texas A&M Univ	TX	16,956	VC+
Texas A&M Univ at Commerce	TX	10,496	C
Texas A&M Univ at Corpus Christi	TX	11,544	LC
Texas A&M Univ at Kingsville	TX	7,500	LC
Texas Christian Univ	TX	47,570	HC
Texas Lutheran Univ	TX	34,070	C
Texas Southern Univ	TX	18,212	LC
Texas State Univ	TX	16,495	VC
Texas Tech Univ	TX	14,243	C
Texas Wesleyan Univ	TX	29,886	C
Texas Woman's Univ	TX	13,633	LC
The Catholic Univ of America	DC	52,852	VC
The College at Brockport / SUNY	NY	18,362	VC
The College of New Rochelle	NY	33,600	VC
The College of St. Rose	NY	26,750	C
The Masters College	CA	38,160	C+
Ohio State Univ	OH	19,887	MC
The SUNY at Potsdam	NY	17,754	C
Thiel College	PA	31,378	LC
Thomas College	ME	26,270	LC
Thomas Edison State College	NJ	5,700	SP
Thomas More College	KY	34,760	C
Thomas Univ	GA	11,520	NC
Tiffin Univ	OH	30,273	LC
Toccoa Falls College	GA	23,210	C
Tougaloo College	MS	15,275	NC
Touro College	NY	23,150	VC
Towson Univ	MD	16,000	VC
Transylvania Univ	KY	40,310	VC+
Trevecca Nazarene Univ	TN	30,118	C
Trinity Christian College	IL	28,869	C
Trinity College	CT		HC+
Trinity International Univ	IL	31,070	C
Trinity Univ	TX	44,174	HC+
Trinity Washington Univ	DC	30,250	C+
Troy Univ	AL	10,650	C
Truman State Univ	MO	13,546	HC
Tufts Univ	MA	58,780	MC
Tulane Univ	LA	58,942	MC
Tusculum College	TN	24,295	C
Tuskegee Univ	AL	26,750	C
Union College	KY	28,775	C
Union College	NE	23,270	VC
Union College	NY		MC
Union Univ	TN	28,260	VC
United States Air Force Academy	CO		MC
United States Naval Academy	MD		MC
Unity College	ME	34,054	C
Universidad del Turabo	PR	4,110	
Univ at Albany / SUNY	NY	18,674	VC
Univ at Buffalo / The SUNY	NY	20,283	VC
Univ of Akron	OH	20,436	C
Univ of Alabama at Birmingham	AL	18,484	C+
Univ of Alabama at Huntsville	AL	17,625	VC
Univ of Alabama at Tuscaloosa	AL	17,164	C+
Univ of Alaska Anchorage	AK	15,290	NC
Univ of Alaska Fairbanks	AK	13,955	C
Univ of Arizona	AZ	20,105	C
Univ of Arkansas at Fayetteville	AR	16,860	VC
Univ of Arkansas at Little Rock	AR		C
Univ of Arkansas at Monticello	AR	8,470	NC
Univ of Arkansas at Pine Bluff	AR	10,600	C
Univ of Bridgeport	CT	39,030	LC
Univ of Calif at Berkeley	CA	23,322	MC
Univ of Calif at Davis	CA	24,482	HC
Univ of Calif at Irvine	CA	25,961	VC
Univ of Calif at Los Angeles	CA	25,686	MC
Univ of Calif at Riverside	CA	27,204	C
Univ of Calif at Santa Barbara	CA	27,551	HC
Univ of Central Arkansas	AR	10,840	VC
Univ of Central Florida	FL	15,711	VC+
Univ of Central Missouri	MO	14,605	C
Univ of Central Okla	OK	12,293	C
Univ of Chicago	IL	55,416	MC
Univ of Cincinnati	OH	20,199	VC
Univ of Colo at Colo Springs	CO	15,000	VC
Univ of Colo Boulder	CO	22,605	VC+
Univ of Colo Denver	CO	17,904	C
Univ of Conn	CT	23,744	HC
Univ of Dallas	TX	43,510	VC+
Univ of Dayton	OH	43,750	VC
Univ of Delaware	DE	22,728	VC
Univ of Denver	CO	51,787	VC+
Univ of Detroit Mercy	MI	30,450	C
Univ of Dubuque	IA	30,200	C
Univ of Findlay	OH	31,916	C
Univ of Florida	FL	15,783	HC+
Univ of Georgia	GA	19,508	VC
Univ of Great Falls	MT	27,970	C
Univ of Hartford	CT	42,674	C
Univ of Hawaii at Hilo	HI	6,500	C
Univ of Hawaii at Manoa	HI	19,379	VC
Univ of Houston	TX	19,184	VC
Univ of Houston-Downtown	TX	6,267	LC
Univ of Idaho	ID	14,558	C
Univ of Illinois at Chicago	IL	24,293	VC
Univ of Illinois at Urbana-Champaign	IL	24,300	HC
Univ of Indianapolis	IN	31,740	LC
Univ of Iowa	IA	17,481	VC
Univ of Jamestown	ND	24,738	C
Univ of Kansas	KS	16,980	C+
Univ of Kentucky	KY	19,868	C
Univ of La Verne	CA	47,010	VC
Univ of Louisiana at Lafayette	LA	6,130	C
Univ of Louisiana at Monroe	LA	12,998	C
Univ of Louisville	KY	17,460	VC
Univ of Maine	ME	19,712	C+
Univ of Maine at Augusta	ME	6,855	C
Univ of Maine at Farmington	ME	17,841	C
Univ of Maine at Fort Kent	ME	14,975	LC
Univ of Maine at Machias	ME	10,523	C
Univ of Maine at Presque Isle	ME	15,011	LC
Univ of Mary	ND	16,714	C
Univ of Mary Hardin-Baylor	TX	31,950	C+
Univ of Mary Washington	VA	19,484	VC
Univ of Maryland	MD	18,801	HC
Univ of Maryland/Baltimore County	MD	18,000	VC
Univ of Maryland/Eastern Shore	MD	14,000	C
Univ of Maryland/Univ College	MD	6,168	SP
Univ of Mass Amherst	MA	23,697	VC+
Univ of Mass Boston	MA	11,966	C
Univ of Mass Dartmouth	MA	22,223	C
Univ of Mass Lowell	MA	19,316	C
Univ of Memphis	TN	15,094	C
Univ of Miami	FL	55,166	MC
Univ of Mich/Ann Arbor	MI	22,102	HC+
Univ of Mich/Dearborn	MI	9,885	VC
Univ of Mich-Flint	MI	17,547	C+
Univ of Minn/Duluth	MN	18,964	C+
Univ of Minn/Morris	MN	17,150	VC
Univ of Minn/Twin Cities	MN		HC
Univ of Miss	MS	15,482	VC
Univ of Missouri/Columbia	MO	18,201	MC
Univ of Missouri-Kansas City	MO	19,603	C
Univ of Missouri-St. Louis	MO	18,304	VC
Univ of Mobile	AL	27,870	VC
Univ of Montana	MT	13,670	C
Univ of Montana-Western	MT	9,753	LC
Univ of Montevallo	AL	17,320	C
Univ of Mount Union	OH	35,130	C
Univ of Nebr - Lincoln	NE	17,507	VC
Univ of Nebr at Kearney	NE	14,855	LC
Univ of Nebr at Omaha	NE	12,700	C
Univ of Nevada, Las Vegas	NV	17,303	C
Univ of Nevada/Reno	NV	14,500	NC
Univ of New England	ME	46,145	C+
Univ of New Hampshire	NH	24,702	VC
Univ of New Haven	CT	47,740	C
Univ of New Mexico	NM	15,300	C
Univ of New Orleans	LA	9,224	VC
Univ of North Alabama	AL	9,960	C
Univ of N Car at Chapel Hill	NC	18,348	MC
Univ of N Car at Charlotte	NC	15,847	C
Univ of N Car at Greensboro	NC	12,848	C
Univ of N Car at Wilmington	NC	13,572	VC+
Univ of N Dak	ND	14,094	C
Univ of North Florida	FL	15,578	VC
Univ of North Texas	TX	15,628	C
Univ of Northern Colo	CO	15,973	C
Univ of Northern Iowa	IA	14,776	C
Univ of Notre Dame	IN		MC
Univ of Okla	OK	17,634	VC+
Univ of Oregon	OR	20,872	VC
Univ of Pennsylvania	PA	56,106	MC
Univ of Pikeville	KY	24,750	NC
Univ of Pittsburgh at Bradford	PA	21,316	LC
Univ of Pittsburgh at Johnstown	PA	20,862	LC
Univ of Portland	OR	47,874	VC
Univ of PR Recinto de Rio Piedras	PR	5,750	
Univ of PR/Cayey	PR	1,504	
Univ of PR/Humacao	PR	1,877	
Univ of PR/Mayaguez	PR	1,250	
Univ of Puget Sound	WA	52,648	HC+
Univ of Redlands	CA	40,500	VC
Univ of Rio Grande	OH	8,750	NC
Univ of Rochester	NY	58,500	MC
Univ of St. Francis	IN	29,810	C
Univ of St. Mary	KS	28,400	C+
Univ of San Diego	CA	53,302	HC+
Univ of San Francisco	CA	49,674	VC
Univ of Science and Arts of Okla	OK	10,560	VC
Univ of Scranton	PA	51,940	VC
Univ of Sioux Falls	SD	22,990	C
Univ of South Alabama	AL	13,510	C
Univ of S Car at Aiken	SC	16,278	C
Univ of S Car at Columbia	SC	19,725	VC+
Univ of S Car Upstate	SC	17,673	LC
Univ of S Dak	SD	15,111	C
Univ of South Florida/St. Petersburg	FL	12,769	VC
Univ of Southern Calif	CA	56,903	MC
Univ of Southern Indiana	IN	14,657	C
Univ of Southern Maine	ME	16,576	C
Univ of Southern Miss	MS	13,170	C
Univ of St. Francis	IL	36,490	C
Univ of St. Thomas - Houston	TX	36,490	VC
Univ of Tampa	FL	35,160	VC
Univ of Tenn at Chattanooga	TN	16,883	C
Univ of Tenn at Knoxville	TN	20,364	VC+
Univ of Tenn at Martin	TN	13,217	C
Univ of Texas at Arlington	TX	10,908	LC
Univ of Texas at Austin	TX	44,074	HC
Univ of Texas at El Paso	TX	8,764	NC
Univ of Texas at San Antonio	TX	18,372	C
Univ of Texas-Pan American	TX	12,432	LC
Univ of the Cumberlands	KY	27,500	LC
Univ of the District of Columbia	DC	7,244	LC
Univ of the Incarnate Word	TX	35,200	LC
Univ of the Ozarks	AR	22,100	C
Univ of the Pacific	CA	52,146	VC
Univ of the Southwest	NM	15,000	C
Univ of Toledo	OH	18,464	C
Univ of Tulsa	OK	45,311	HC+
Univ of Utah	UT	13,462	VC
Univ of Vermont	VT	26,120	VC+
Univ of Virginia	VA	22,175	MC
Univ of Virginia's College at Wise	VA	11,076	C
Univ of Washington	WA	14,722	VC
Univ of West Alabama	AL	9,415	C
Univ of West Florida	FL	14,656	C
Univ of West Georgia	GA	14,852	LC
Univ of Wisc Whitewater	WI	13,314	C
Univ of Wisc/Eau Claire	WI	15,430	VC
Univ of Wisc/Green Bay	WI	14,900	C
Univ of Wisc/La Crosse	WI	14,755	VC
Univ of Wisc/Madison	WI	18,757	HC
Univ of Wisc/Oshkosh	WI	10,426	LC
Univ of Wisc/Parkside	WI	10,181	LC
Univ of Wisc/Platteville	WI	14,274	C
Univ of Wisc/River Falls	WI	9,722	LC
Univ of Wisc/Stevens Point	WI	14,043	C
Univ of Wisc/Superior	WI	14,106	C
Univ of Wisc-Milwaukee	WI	18,436	C
Univ of Wyoming	WY	13,855	C+
Upper Iowa Univ	IA	30,426	NC
Urbana Univ	OH	21,190	C
Ursinus College	PA	55,630	VC+
Ursuline College	OH	33,198	LC
Utah State Univ	UT	11,803	C
Utica College	NY	44,734	C
Valley City State Univ	ND	12,286	LC
Valparaiso Univ	IN	43,040	VC+
Vanderbilt Univ	TN	57,072	MC
Vanguard Univ of Southern Calif	CA	35,833	VC
Vassar College	NY	59,070	MC
Victory Univ	TN	19,118	C
Villanova Univ	PA	56,436	MC
Virginia Commonwealth Univ	VA	18,633	C
Virginia Intermont College	VA	32,411	LC
Virginia Military Inst	VA	16,156	C
Virginia Polytechnic Inst and State Univ	VA	14,629	HC
Virginia Union Univ	VA	18,432	C
Virginia Wesleyan College	VA	28,433	LC
Viterbo Univ	WI	30,070	C
Voorhees College	SC	18,126	C
Wabash College	IN	44,160	VC
Wagner College	NY	48,600	VC
Wake Forest Univ	NC	51,000	MC
Walla Walla Univ	WA	26,256	NC
Walsh Univ	OH	35,100	C
Warner Pacific College	OR	25,550	C
Warner Univ	FL	18,000	C
Warren Wilson College	NC	34,888	VC
Wartburg College	IA	41,055	VC
Washburn Univ	KS	12,165	NC
Washington Adventist Univ	MD	25,859	C+
Washington and Jefferson College	PA	49,990	VC
Washington and Lee Univ	VA	52,812	MC
Washington College	MD	48,768	VC
Washington State Univ	WA	20,461	C
Washington Univ in St. Louis	MO	58,818	MC
Wayland Baptist Univ	TX	16,058	LC
Wayne State College	NE	11,764	NC
Wayne State Univ	MI	19,493	C
Waynesburg Univ	PA	29,100	C
Webster Univ	MO	33,990	C+
Wellesley College	MA	49,848	MC
Wells College	NY	38,680	VC
Wesley College	DE	31,115	LC
Wesleyan College	GA	24,000	C+
Wesleyan Univ	CT	59,844	MC
West Chester Univ of Pennsylvania	PA	16,836	C
West Liberty Univ	WV	9,142	LC
West Texas A&M Univ	TX	13,478	C
West Virginia State Univ	WV	8,378	NC
West Virginia Univ	WV	15,794	C+
West Virginia Wesleyan College	WV	26,880	C
Western Carolina Univ	NC	13,965	C+
Western Conn State Univ	CT	18,327	C
Western Illinois Univ	IL	20,130	C
Western Kentucky Univ	KY	11,000	LC
Western Mich Univ	MI	19,042	C
Western New England Univ	MA	45,590	C
Western New Mexico Univ	NM	8,500	LC
Western Oregon Univ	OR	15,021	C
Western State Colo Univ	CO	16,135	C
Western Washington Univ	WA	18,519	VC
Westfield State Univ	MA	18,489	C
Westminster College	MO	30,490	VC
Westminster College	PA	31,290	C+
Westminster College	UT	37,708	VC
Westmont College	CA	41,500	HC
Wheaton College	IL	39,650	HC+
Wheaton College	MA	54,934	HC+
Wheeling Jesuit Univ	WV	34,668	C
Whitman College	WA	54,400	MC
Whittier College	CA	43,416	C
Whitworth Univ	WA	45,826	VC+
Wichita State Univ	KS	12,539	C
Widener Univ	PA	50,368	C
Wiley College	TX		LC
Wilkes Univ	PA	42,786	C
Willamette Univ	OR	56,450	VC+
William Carey Univ	MS	13,500	LC
William Jewell College	MO	31,000	VC+
William Paterson Univ of New Jersey	NJ	21,694	C
William Peace Univ	NC	32,900	LC
William Penn Univ	IA	26,000	C
William Woods Univ	MO		C
Williams Baptist College	AR	20,070	C
Williams College	MA	58,900	MC
Wilmington College	OH	29,784	C
Wilson College	PA	27,660	C
Wingate Univ	NC	34,990	C
Winona State Univ	MN	16,530	C
Winston-Salem State Univ	NC	9,418	LC

ST = STATE **$IS** = IN-STATE COSTS **SR** = SELECTOR RATING

School	ST	$IS	SR
Winthrop Univ	SC	21,120	VC
Wisc Lutheran College	WI	23,510	VC
Wittenberg Univ	OH	47,766	VC
Wofford College	SC	45,795	VC
Worcester State Univ	MA	18,657	C
Wright State Univ	OH	16,983	C
Xavier Univ	OH	43,740	VC
Xavier Univ of Louisiana	LA	25,300	C
Yale Univ	CT	55,300	MC
Yeshiva Univ	NY	47,250	V₲
York College	NE	19,475	C
York College / CUNY	NY	5,496	NC
York College of Pennsylvania	PA	26,590	C
Youngstown State Univ	OH	16,374	LC

ENGLISH AND PROFESSIONAL COMMUNICATION

School	ST	$IS	SR
Farmingdale State College	NY	18,985	C
Southeast Missouri State Univ	MO	14,983	LC
Southern Polytechnic State Univ	GA	13,958	VC
Taylor Univ	IN	36,742	V₲
Wheeling Jesuit Univ	WV	34,668	C

ENGLISH AS A SECOND/ FOREIGN LANGUAGE

School	ST	$IS	SR
Doane College	NE	33,730	VC
Dordt College	IA	34,160	VC
Holy Names Univ	CA	40,310	NC
Houghton College	NY	35,740	VC
Huntington Univ	IN	32,220	C
La Sierra Univ	CA	35,694	VC
Lenoir-Rhyne College	NC	35,984	C
Liberty Univ	VA	19,101	C
Maryville College	TN	33,150	VC
Northwestern College	MN	24,000	C
Oswego / SUNY	NY	20,009	VC
Penn State Univ/Univ Park	PA	25,404	VC
Salem International Univ	WV	18,020	C
Salisbury Univ	MD	18,368	VC
Southern New Hampshire Univ	NH	38,100	C
Union Univ	TN	28,260	VC
Univ of Arizona	AZ	20,105	C
Univ of Central Okla	OK	12,293	C
Univ of Findlay	OH	31,916	C
Univ of Hawaii at Manoa	HI	19,379	VC
Univ of Nebr - Lincoln	NE	17,507	VC
Univ of Wisc/Green Bay	WI	14,900	C

ENGLISH EDUCATION

School	ST	$IS	SR
Adams State College	CO	13,358	LC
Alabama State Univ	AL	14,142	NC
Andrews Univ	MI	28,030	₲
Appalachian State Univ	NC	12,919	VC
Aquinas College	MI	33,060	C
Arkansas State Univ	AR	14,980	C
Arkansas Tech Univ	AR	13,164	LC
Asbury Univ	KY	32,038	VC
Ashland Univ	OH	25,000	C
Auburn Univ	AL	20,052	V₲
Averett Univ	VA	36,000	LC
Baker Univ	KS	33,350	₲
Baylor Univ	TX	46,720	HC
Bennett College	NC		LC
Bethany College	KS	30,605	NC
Bethany College	WV	35,282	C
Bethel College	IN	31,560	C
Bethel Univ	MN	34,940	VC
Bethune-Cookman Univ	FL	22,290	LC
Blackburn College	IL	21,350	C
Blue Mountain College	MS	13,550	LC
Boise State Univ	ID	12,802	C
Boston Univ	MA	54,130	H₲
Brigham Young Univ	UT	12,100	HC
Brigham Young Univ/ Hawaii	HI	8,614	VC
Bryant Univ	RI	49,179	VC
Cal State, Chico	CA	18,952	C
Calvin College	MI	37,585	V₲
Cameron Univ	OK	9,267	LC
Canisius College	NY	45,602	VC
Carthage College	WI	33,000	C
Cedarville Univ	OH	31,036	V₲
Central Univ of Bayamon	PR	3,350	
Central Washington Univ	WA	11,730	C
CUNY/Brooklyn College	NY	5,884	₲
Claflin Univ	SC	22,368	₲
Coker College	SC	32,256	LC
Colby-Sawyer College	NH	47,870	C
College of New Jersey	NJ	25,376	HC
College of the Ozarks	MO	5,605	VC
Colo State Univ-Fort Collins	CO	20,090	VC
Concordia Univ St. Paul	MN	27,200	C
Cornerstone Univ and Grand Rapids Theological Seminary	MI	30,866	C
Covenant College	GA		V₲
CUNY-City College	NY	19,576	H₲
Daemen College	NY	31,510	C
Dakota State Univ	SD	13,811	C
Delta State Univ	MS	12,292	LC
Dordt College	IA	34,160	VC
Duquesne Univ	PA	42,017	VC
East Carolina Univ	NC	14,169	C
East Central Univ	OK	10,223	LC
East Texas Baptist Univ	TX	29,135	C
Eastern Mich Univ	MI	17,961	C
Elizabethtown College	PA	47,600	VC
Emory and Henry College	VA	387,460	C
Faulkner Univ	AL	22,530	LC
Ferris State Univ	MI	19,698	C
Florida Atlantic Univ	FL	17,339	C
Florida State Univ	FL	15,238	HC
Fontbonne Univ	MO	31,384	C
Franklin College	IN	35,885	C
Fresno Pacific Univ	CA	32,136	C
Friends Univ	KS	29,100	C
Gannon Univ	PA	37,940	C
Georgia Southwestern State Univ	GA	12,218	C
Glenville State College	WV	11,348	NC
Goddard College	VT	16,418	VC
Goshen College	IN	35,900	VC
Grace College and Theological Seminary	IN	28,800	C
Grambling State Univ	LA	13,384	LC
Green Mountain College	VT	33,547	LC
Greensboro College	NC	28,740	LC
Greenville College	IL	27,012	C
Hardin-Simmons Univ	TX	23,560	₲
Hofstra Univ	NY	48,020	V₲
Hood College	MD	11,600	C
Houghton College	NY	35,740	VC
Humboldt State Univ	CA	18,400	C
Huntingdon College	AL	31,850	C
Huntington Univ	IN	32,220	C
Husson Univ	ME	23,386	LC
Indiana Univ Northwest	IN	6,738	LC
Indiana Univ South Bend	IN	15,293	C
Indiana Univ Southeast	IN	15,807	LC
Indiana Univ-Purdue Univ Fort Wayne	IN	15,425	C
Indiana Univ-Purdue Univ Indianapolis	IN	17,290	C
Indiana Univ-Purdue Univ Indianapolis	IN	17,290	C
Indiana Wesleyan Univ	IN	31,815	VC
Ithaca College	NY	52,300	HC
Johnson State College	VT	16,721	C
Judson College	AL	24,690	C
Judson Univ	IL	25,130	C
Juniata College	PA	49,340	VC
Kennesaw State Univ	GA	13,017	VC
Kentucky Christian Univ	KY	17,622	LC
Kutztown Univ of Pennsylvania	PA	16,909	LC
La Roche College	PA	34,802	LC
Le Moyne College	NY	42,200	VC
Lenoir-Rhyne College	NC	35,984	C
Limestone College	SC	29,880	C
Lincoln Univ	MO	11,996	NC
Lipscomb Univ	TN	35,722	VC
LIU/C.W. Post Campus	NY	38,888	C
Louisiana College	LA	15,746	C
Lyndon State College	VT	14,233	C
Mansfield Univ	PA	19,468	LC
Marian Univ	WI	30,980	LC
Marshall Univ	WV	14,820	C
Marymount Univ	VA	36,178	C
Marywood Univ	PA	40,695	C
Mayville State Univ	ND	11,401	NC
McMurry Univ	TX	25,962	LC
Messiah College	PA	39,540	VC
MidAmerica Nazarene Univ	KS	28,000	C
Millikin Univ	IL	37,462	C
Minn State Univ, Moorhead	MN	13,392	C
Minot State Univ	ND	10,915	C
Miss Valley State Univ	MS	9,706	LC
Missouri Southern State Univ	MO	11,910	C
Monmouth Univ	NJ	42,252	C
Morningside College	IA	32,620	C
Morris College	SC	16,006	LC
Mount Aloysius College	PA	27,970	C
Mount Mary Univ	WI	32,836	LC
Mount Vernon Nazarene Univ	OH	29,590	C
Nazareth College of Rochester	NY	41,590	VC
Nebr Wesleyan Univ	NE	29,774	₲
New York Univ	NY	61,470	MC
Niagara Univ	NY	39,800	C
N Car Agricultural and Technical State Univ	NC	13,175	LC
Northeastern Illinois Univ	IL		C
Northwest Nazarene Univ	ID	24,275	NC
Northwestern College	MN	24,000	C
Northwestern Okla State Univ	OK	7,275	NC
Nova Southeastern Univ	FL	34,016	VC
Oakwood Univ	AL	23,035	C
Ohio Valley Univ	WV	17,752	C
Okla Christian Univ	OK	24,975	VC
Okla Wesleyan Univ	OK	21,300	C
Old Dominion Univ	VA	18,662	C
Olivet Nazarene Univ	IL	29,990	C
Oral Roberts Univ	OK	31,734	C
Oswego / SUNY	NY	20,009	VC
Palm Beach Atlantic Univ	FL	33,882	LC
Pfeiffer Univ	NC	33,700	C
Piedmont College	GA	29,260	C
Pittsburg State Univ	KS	12,032	C
Providence College	RI	55,995	HC
Purdue Univ/West Lafayette	IN	20,278	HC
Rider Univ	NJ	45,720	C
Rivier College	NH	35,000	VC
Roberts Wesleyan College	NY	37,384	₲
Rocky Mountain College	MT	32,242	C
Rust College	MS	10,600	C
Sacred Heart Univ	CT	48,564	VC
Saginaw Valley State Univ	MI	16,869	C
St. Augustine's Univ	NC	14,000	C
St. Mary's Univ of Minn	MN	37,015	C
Samford Univ	AL	35,700	V₲
Schreiner Univ	TX	32,734	LC
Seton Hill Univ	PA	35,172	C
Shaw Univ	NC	15,488	LC
Shepherd Univ	WV	14,996	C
Shippensburg Univ of Pennsylvania	PA	17,064	LC
Simpson Univ	CA	28,900	C
Southeast Missouri State Univ	MO	14,983	LC
Southeastern Louisiana Univ	LA	13,325	C
Southern Nazarene Univ	OK	24,354	NC
Southern New Hampshire Univ	NH	38,100	C
Southern Oregon Univ	OR	17,874	C
Southern Univ and A&M College	LA	9,761	₲
Southern Univ at New Orleans	LA	1,000	NC
Southern Wesleyan Univ	SC	25,600	C
Southwestern Okla State Univ	OK	9,160	C
St. Edward's Univ	TX	44,674	VC
St. John Fisher College	NY	39,370	₲
St. John's Univ	NY	52,840	₲
Suffolk Univ	MA	46,548	C
SUNY Fredonia / The SUNY at Fredonia	NY	18,702	VC
SUNY New Paltz	NY	15,010	C
SUNY Oneonta / SUNY	NY	16,919	VC
SUNY Plattsburgh / SUNY	NY	18,083	VC
Syracuse Univ	NY	54,512	HC
Taylor Univ	IN	36,742	V₲
Texas Christian Univ	TX	47,570	HC
Texas Southern Univ	TX	18,212	LC
The Catholic Univ of America	DC	52,852	VC
The College of St. Rose	NY	26,750	C
The Lincoln Univ	PA	15,154	LC
The SUNY at Potsdam	NY	17,754	C
Tiffin Univ	OH	30,273	LC
Tougaloo College	MS	15,275	NC
Trevecca Nazarene Univ	TN	30,118	C
Trine Univ	IN	39,400	VC
Troy Univ	AL	10,650	C
Union College	NE	23,270	VC
Universidad del Turabo	PR	4,110	
Univ of Arkansas at Pine Bluff	AR	10,600	C
Univ of Central Florida	FL	15,711	V₲
Univ of Central Missouri	MO	14,605	C
Univ of Central Okla	OK	12,293	C
Univ of Charleston	WV	28,650	C
Univ of Conn	CT	23,744	HC
Univ of Delaware	DE	22,728	VC
Univ of Evansville	IN	41,056	V₲
Univ of Georgia	GA	19,508	VC
Univ of Illinois at Chicago	IL	24,293	VC
Univ of Illinois at Urbana-Champaign	IL	24,300	HC
Univ of Indianapolis	IN	31,740	LC
Univ of Louisiana at Lafayette	LA	6,130	C
Univ of Louisiana at Monroe	LA	12,998	C
Univ of Mary	ND	16,714	C
Univ of Mary Hardin-Baylor	TX	31,950	₲
Univ of Minn/Twin Cities	MN		HC
Univ of Miss	MS	15,482	VC
Univ of Missouri/Columbia	MO	18,201	MC
Univ of Montana-Western	MT	9,753	LC
Univ of Nebr - Lincoln	NE	17,507	VC
Univ of New Hampshire	NH	24,702	VC
Univ of New Orleans	LA	9,224	VC
Univ of N Car at Charlotte	NC	15,847	C
Univ of N Car at Greensboro	NC	12,848	C
Univ of North Florida	FL	15,578	VC
Univ of Pittsburgh at Bradford	PA	21,316	C
Univ of Pittsburgh at Johnstown	PA	20,862	LC
Univ of Rio Grande	OH	8,750	NC
Univ of St. Francis	IN	29,810	C
Univ of S Car Upstate	SC	17,673	LC
Univ of South Florida	FL	13,000	C
Univ of Southern Indiana	IN	14,657	C
Univ of Tenn at Chattanooga	TN	16,883	C
Univ of the Cumberlands	KY	27,500	LC
Univ of Utah	UT	13,462	VC
Univ of Vermont	VT	26,120	V₲
Univ of Wisc/Green Bay	WI	14,900	C
Univ of Wisc/Superior	WI	14,106	C
Valparaiso Univ	IN	43,040	V₲
Viterbo Univ	WI	30,070	C
Warner Univ	FL	18,000	C
Wartburg College	IA	41,055	VC
Washington Adventist Univ	MD	25,859	₲
Washington State Univ	WA	20,461	C
Wayne State Univ	MI	19,493	C
West Chester Univ of Pennsylvania	PA	16,836	C
West Texas A&M Univ	TX	13,478	C
West Virginia Univ	WV	15,794	₲
Western Carolina Univ	NC	13,965	₲
Westmont College	CA	41,500	HC
Wheeling Jesuit Univ	WV	34,668	C
Whitworth Univ	WA	45,826	V₲
Wiley College	TX		LC
Wilmington College	OH	29,784	C
Wingate Univ	NC	34,990	C
Xavier Univ of Louisiana	LA	25,300	C
York College	NE	19,475	C
York College of Pennsylvania	PA	26,590	C

ENGLISH LITERATURE

School	ST	$IS	SR
Agnes Scott College	GA	45,323	V₲
Aquinas College	MI	33,060	C
Arkansas Tech Univ	AR	13,164	LC
Bard College	NY	59,872	HC
Bennington College	VT	56,990	H₲
Berry College	GA	39,254	HC
Bethany College	WV	35,282	C
Bethel Univ	MN	34,940	VC
Binghamton Univ / The SUNY	NY	20,832	H₲
Blackburn College	IL	21,350	C
Boise State Univ	ID	12,802	C
Bowling Green State Univ	OH	18,970	C
Cal State, Chico	CA	18,952	C
Calvin College	MI	37,585	V₲
Chatham Univ	PA	42,440	VC
Chestnut Hill College	PA	39,785	LC
Columbia Univ/School of General Studies	NY	54,083	MC
DePauw Univ	IN	48,950	V₲
Dominican Univ of Calif	CA	51,250	C
Eastern Mich Univ	MI	17,961	C
Edinboro Univ of Pennsylvania	PA	15,940	LC
Elizabethtown College	PA	47,600	VC
Elmira College	NY	49,950	₲
Emmanuel College	MA	47,985	VC
Emory and Henry College	VA	387,460	C
Excelsior College	NY	895	SP
Fairleigh Dickinson Univ/ Metropolitan Campus	NJ	40,254	C
Ferris State Univ	MI	19,698	C
Fontbonne Univ	MO	31,384	C
Fordham Univ	NY	58,927	HC
Hamilton College	NY	55,620	MC
High Point Univ	NC	39,800	C
Hope International Univ	CA	34,650	C
Houghton College	NY	35,740	VC
Hunter College / The CUNY	NY	14,429	VC
Huntington Univ	IN	32,220	C
Indiana Univ-Purdue Univ Fort Wayne	IN	15,425	C
Ithaca College	NY	52,300	HC
Keene State College	NH	21,538	C
Knox College	IL		VC
Loras College	IA	37,432	VC
Loyola Univ New Orleans	LA	46,581	VC
Marshall Univ	WV	14,820	C
Marylhurst Univ	OR	18,945	NC
Mass College of Liberal Arts	MA	16,733	C
Mercer Univ	GA	44,201	V₲
Mills College	CA	54,119	HC
New England College	NH	45,930	LC
New York Univ	NY	61,470	MC
North Central College	IL	38,343	VC
Northeastern Illinois Univ	IL		C
Oral Roberts Univ	OK	31,734	C
Pfeiffer Univ	NC	33,700	C
Purdue Univ/Calumet	IN	14,336	C
Queens Univ of Charlotte	NC	39,543	VC
Reed College	OR	57,780	MC
Rider Univ	NJ	45,720	C
St. Louis Univ	MO	46,594	V₲
St. Mary's College	IN	45,160	VC
Santa Fe Univ of Art and Design	NM	39,666	SP
Southern Illinois Univ Carbondale	IL	21,620	C
Southern New Hampshire Univ	NH	38,100	C
St. Edward's Univ	TX	44,674	VC
Stevenson Univ	MD	39,572	C
SUNY Plattsburgh / SUNY	NY	18,083	VC
Swarthmore College	PA	57,870	MC
Syracuse Univ	NY	54,512	HC
Taylor Univ	IN	36,742	V₲

ST = STATE **$IS** = IN-STATE COSTS **SR** = SELECTOR RATING

School	ST	$IS	SR
The Catholic Univ of America	DC	52,852	VC
The Lincoln Univ	PA	15,154	LC
The SUNY at Potsdam	NY	17,754	C
Union Univ	TN	28,260	VC
Univ of Calif at San Diego	CA	21,000	VC
Univ of Illinois at Chicago	IL	24,293	VC
Univ of Illinois at Urbana-Champaign	IL	24,300	HC
Univ of Maryland	MD	18,801	HC
Univ of Mass Dartmouth	MA	22,223	C
Univ of Mich/Ann Arbor	MI	22,102	H¢
Univ of Missouri/Columbia	MO	18,201	MC
Univ of Montana-Western	MT	9,753	LC
Univ of New Hampshire	NH	24,702	VC
Univ of North Florida	FL	15,578	VC
Univ of Pittsburgh at Greensburg	PA	17,640	C
Univ of Pittsburgh at Pittsburgh	PA	27,800	H¢
Univ of Redlands	CA	40,500	VC
Univ of Rochester	NY	58,500	MC
Univ of South Florida	FL	13,000	C
Univ of Southern Calif	CA	56,903	MC
Virginia State Univ	VA	11,318	¢
Warren Wilson College	NC	34,888	VC
Washington Univ in St. Louis	MO	58,818	MC
Wesleyan Univ	CT	59,844	MC
Wheeling Jesuit Univ	WV	34,668	C
Winthrop Univ	SC	21,120	VC
York College of Pennsylvania	PA	26,590	C
Youngstown State Univ	OH	16,374	LC

ENGLISH WRITING

School	ST	$IS	SR
Aquinas College	MI	33,060	C
Bethel College	IN	31,560	C
Boise State Univ	ID	12,802	C
Concordia Univ St. Paul	MN	27,200	C
Cornerstone Univ and Grand Rapids Theological Seminary	MI	30,866	C
Elizabethtown College	PA	47,600	VC
Fontbonne Univ	MO	31,384	C
Fordham Univ	NY	58,927	HC
Goddard College	VT	16,418	VC
Goshen College	IN	35,900	VC
High Point Univ	NC	39,800	C
Houghton College	NY	35,740	VC
Ithaca College	NY	52,300	HC
Keene State College	NH	21,538	C
Limestone College	SC	29,880	C
Marylhurst Univ	OR	18,945	NC
Mass College of Liberal Arts	MA	16,733	C
Mills College	CA	54,119	HC
North Central College	IL	38,343	VC
Oswego / SUNY	NY	20,009	VC
Southern Oregon Univ	OR	17,874	C
Spring Hill College	AL	42,130	VC
St. Edward's Univ	TX	44,674	VC
SUNY Plattsburgh / SUNY	NY	18,083	VC
Taylor Univ	IN	36,742	V¢
The SUNY at Potsdam	NY	17,754	C
Univ of Colo Denver	CO	17,904	C
Univ of Idaho	ID	14,558	C
Univ of Mass Dartmouth	MA	22,223	C
Univ of Pittsburgh at Pittsburgh	PA	27,800	H¢
Valparaiso Univ	IN	43,040	V¢
Warren Wilson College	NC	34,888	VC

ENTOMOLOGY

School	ST	$IS	SR
Cornell Univ	NY	59,037	MC
Iowa State Univ	IA	16,403	C
Mich State Univ	MI	13,689	VC
Okla State Univ	OK	14,310	VC
Purdue Univ/West Lafayette	IN	20,278	HC
SUNY / College of Environmental Science and Forestry	NY	18,351	HC
Texas A&M Univ	TX	16,956	V¢
Ohio State Univ	OH	19,887	MC
Univ of Arizona	AZ	20,105	C
Univ of Calif at Davis	CA	24,482	HC
Univ of Calif at Riverside	CA	27,204	C
Univ of Delaware	DE	22,728	VC
Univ of Florida	FL	15,783	H¢
Univ of Georgia	GA	19,508	VC
Univ of Illinois at Urbana-Champaign	IL	24,300	HC
Univ of Nebr - Lincoln	NE	17,507	VC
Univ of Wisc/Madison	WI	18,757	HC
Washington State Univ	WA	20,461	C

ENTREPRENEURIAL STUDIES

School	ST	$IS	SR
American International College	MA	36,100	LC
Baldwin Wallace Univ	OH	36,980	VC
Ball State Univ	IN	17,850	C
Baylor Univ	TX	46,720	HC
Belmont Univ	TN	37,380	V¢
Binghamton Univ / The SUNY	NY	20,832	H¢
Boston Univ	MA	54,130	H¢
Bradley Univ	IL	31,874	VC
Brown Univ	RI	56,150	MC
Bryant Univ	RI	49,179	VC
Cal State, Fullerton	CA	25,188	¢
Canisius College	NY	45,602	VC
Central Mich Univ	MI	18,066	C
Clarkson Univ	NY	53,538	HC
Cogswell Polytechnical College	CA	30,531	C
College of William & Mary	VA	25,085	MC
Creighton Univ	NE	44,058	V¢
Davenport Univ	MI	21,002	LC
Duquesne Univ	PA	42,017	VC
Eastern Mich Univ	MI	17,961	C
Eastern Univ	PA	37,704	C
Elon Univ	NC	40,046	HC
Fairleigh Dickinson Univ/ College at Florham	NJ	42,142	C
Fairleigh Dickinson Univ/ Metropolitan Campus	NJ	40,254	C
Florida State Univ	FL	15,238	HC
Gannon Univ	PA	37,940	C
Grand Canyon Univ	AZ	24,540	VC
Grove City College	PA	22,988	HC
Hawaii Pacific Univ	HI	36,690	C
Hofstra Univ	NY	48,020	V¢
Houston Baptist Univ	TX	23,815	¢
Huntington Univ	IN	32,220	C
Indiana Univ Bloomington	IN	19,358	HC
Jackson State Univ	MS	13,512	LC
John Carroll Univ	OH	44,520	¢
Johnson and Wales Univ/ Charlotte Campus	NC	35,421	C
Johnson and Wales Univ/ Denver Campus	CO	34,368	C
Johnson and Wales Univ/ North Miami Campus	FL	34,368	C
Johnson and Wales Univ/ Providence Campus	RI	34,668	C
Kansas State Univ	KS	15,497	VC
Lake Erie College	OH	35,704	C
Lasell College	MA	42,500	LC
Lipscomb Univ	TN	35,722	VC
Loyola Marymount Univ	CA	53,240	V¢
Loyola Univ Chicago	IL	49,560	V¢
Lynn Univ	FL	43,500	C
Marquette Univ	WI	43,664	V¢
Menlo College	CA	49,002	C
Mercy College	NY	29,996	C
Middle Tenn State Univ	TN	8,650	C
Millikin Univ	IL	37,462	C
Missouri State Univ	MO	13,996	VC
Mount Aloysius College	PA	27,970	C
Northern Mich Univ	MI	15,300	VC
Okla State Univ	OK	14,310	VC
Pace Univ	NY	48,094	VC
Paul Quinn College	TX	25,350	LC
Peirce College	PA	12,760	NC
Purdue Univ/West Lafayette	IN	20,278	HC
Quinnipiac Univ	CT	53,580	VC
Rowan Univ	NJ	23,570	VC
St. Joseph's Univ	PA	52,272	VC
St. Mary's Univ of Minn	MN	37,015	C
Samford Univ	AL	35,700	V¢
San Francisco State Univ	CA	18,514	C
Seton Hill Univ	PA	35,172	C
Shenandoah Univ	VA	39,268	C
S Dak State Univ	SD	14,296	C
Southern Adventist Univ	TN	26,190	C
Southern Illinois Univ Edwardsville	IL	17,532	C
Southern Vermont College	VT	30,740	LC
St. Edward's Univ	TX	44,674	VC
Suffolk Univ	MA	46,548	C
SUNY Plattsburgh / SUNY	NY	18,083	VC
Syracuse Univ	NY	54,512	HC
Temple Univ	PA	24,392	VC
Texas Christian Univ	TX	47,570	HC
Thomas Edison State College	NJ	5,700	SP
Tulane Univ	LA	58,942	MC
Univ of Alaska Anchorage	AK	15,290	NC
Univ of Arizona	AZ	20,105	C
Univ of Dayton	OH	43,750	VC
Univ of Hartford	CT	42,674	C
Univ of Illinois at Chicago	IL	24,293	VC
Univ of Illinois at Urbana-Champaign	IL	24,300	HC
Univ of Indianapolis	IN	31,740	LC
Univ of Miami	FL	55,166	MC
Univ of Nebr - Lincoln	NE	17,507	VC
Univ of N Car at Greensboro	NC	12,848	C
Univ of N Dak	ND	14,094	C
Univ of North Texas	TX	15,628	C
Univ of Pennsylvania	PA	56,106	MC
Univ of Portland	OR	47,874	VC
Univ of South Florida/St. Petersburg	FL	12,769	VC
Univ of St. Francis	IL	36,490	C
Univ of Tampa	FL	35,160	VC
Univ of Utah	UT	13,462	VC
Univ of Vermont	VT	26,120	V¢
Univ of Wisc-Milwaukee	WI	18,436	C
Virginia Polytechnic Inst and State Univ	VA	14,629	HC
Washington State Univ	WA	20,461	C
Washington Univ in St. Louis	MO	58,818	MC
Waynesburg Univ	PA	29,100	C
Western Carolina Univ	NC	13,965	¢
Wichita State Univ	KS	12,539	C
Wilkes Univ	PA	42,786	C
Xavier Univ	OH	43,740	VC
York College of Pennsylvania	PA	26,590	C

ENVIRONMENTAL BIOLOGY

School	ST	$IS	SR
Aquinas College	MI	33,060	C
Averett Univ	VA	36,000	LC
Belmont Univ	TN	37,380	V¢
Beloit College	WI	49,970	HC
Bennington College	VT	56,990	H¢
Bethel College	IN	31,560	C
Blackburn College	IL	21,350	C
Boston Univ	MA	54,130	H¢
Cal State, Northridge	CA	28,313	C
Cedar Crest College	PA	43,240	C
Christopher Newport Univ	VA	21,050	VC
Colby College	ME	57,510	MC
Columbia Univ in the City of New York	NY	61,116	MC
Fitchburg State Univ	MA	17,241	C
Georgetown Univ	DC	52,910	MC
Greenville College	IL	27,012	C
Hanover College	IN	41,450	VC
Heidelberg Univ	OH	34,100	C
Houghton College	NY	35,740	VC
Lock Haven Univ of Pennsylvania	PA	17,587	LC
Mercer Univ	GA	44,201	V¢
Mich State Univ	MI	13,689	VC
Missouri Univ of Science and Technology	MO	18,655	V¢
Montclair State Univ	NJ	22,614	C
Mount Aloysius College	PA	27,970	C
Norfolk State Univ	VA	10,531	LC
Ohio Univ	OH	20,676	VC
Pittsburg State Univ	KS	12,032	C
Plymouth State Univ	NH	23,148	LC
Prescott College	AZ	33,284	¢
Queens College / The CUNY	NY	17,107	VC
St. Mary's Univ of Minn	MN	37,015	C
Sewanee: The Univ of the South	TN	47,700	H¢
S Dak State Univ	SD	14,296	C
SUNY / College of Environmental Science and Forestry	NY	18,351	HC
Texas A&M Univ at Galveston	TX	11,258	C
Tulane Univ	LA	58,942	MC
Univ of Calif at Davis	CA	24,482	HC
Univ of Dayton	OH	43,750	VC
Univ of La Verne	CA	47,010	VC
Univ of Mount Union	OH	35,130	C
Univ of North Alabama	AL	9,960	C
West Chester Univ of Pennsylvania	PA	16,836	C
Wilmington College	OH	29,784	C
Wingate Univ	NC	34,990	C

ENVIRONMENTAL CHEMISTRY

School	ST	$IS	SR
Binghamton Univ / The SUNY	NY	20,832	H¢
Lawrence Tech Univ	MI	37,630	VC
Marshall Univ	WV	14,820	C
Pittsburg State Univ	KS	12,032	C
Sewanee: The Univ of the South	TN	47,700	H¢
St. Edward's Univ	TX	44,674	VC
Univ of Denver	CO	51,787	V¢
Univ of Georgia	GA	19,508	VC

ENVIRONMENTAL DESIGN

School	ST	$IS	SR
Art Center College of Design	CA	34,044	SP
Ball State Univ	IN	17,850	C
Bethel College	IN	31,560	C
Binghamton Univ / The SUNY	NY	20,832	H¢
Brigham Young Univ	UT	12,100	HC
Hampshire College	MA	58,320	MC
Harvard Univ/Harvard College	MA	49,000	MC
Maryland Inst College of Art	MD	39,500	SP
Marywood Univ	PA	40,695	C
Montana State Univ	MT	14,068	VC
New York Inst of Technology	NY	40,590	VC
N Car State Univ	NC	16,202	HC
N Dak State Univ	ND	14,642	C
Olivet Nazarene Univ	IL	29,990	C
Prescott College	AZ	33,284	¢
Rutgers, The State Univ of New Jersey/New Brunswick	NJ	25,077	VC
SUNY / College of Environmental Science and Forestry	NY	18,351	HC
Stony Brook Univ / SUNY	NY	19,359	HC
Syracuse Univ	NY	54,512	HC
Texas A&M Univ	TX	16,956	V¢
Univ at Buffalo / The SUNY	NY	20,283	VC
Univ of Calif at Davis	CA	24,482	HC
Univ of Colo Boulder	CO	22,605	V¢
Univ of Houston	TX	19,184	VC
Univ of Mass Amherst	MA	23,697	V¢
Univ of Minn/Twin Cities	MN		HC
Univ of New Mexico	NM	15,300	C
Univ of Okla	OK	17,634	V¢
Univ of PR Recinto de Rio Piedras	PR	5,750	

ENVIRONMENTAL EARTH RESOURCES

School	ST	$IS	SR
Binghamton Univ / The SUNY	NY	20,832	H¢
Texas Christian Univ	TX	47,570	HC

ENVIRONMENTAL EDUCATION

School	ST	$IS	SR
Catawba College	NC	37,105	C
Goshen College	IN	35,900	VC
Johnson State College	VT	16,721	C
Messiah College	PA	39,540	VC
Prescott College	AZ	33,284	¢
Seattle Univ	WA	47,010	V¢
Southern Oregon Univ	OR	17,874	C
SUNY / College of Environmental Science and Forestry	NY	18,351	HC
Ohio State Univ	OH	19,887	MC
Univ of Montana-Western	MT	9,753	LC
Univ of New Hampshire	NH	24,702	VC
Univ of Pittsburgh at Bradford	PA	21,316	LC
Virginia Polytechnic Inst and State Univ	VA	14,629	HC
West Virginia Univ	WV	15,794	¢

ENVIRONMENTAL ENGINEERING

School	ST	$IS	SR
Alabama A&M Univ	AL	96,100	C
Arizona State Univ	AZ	18,818	¢
Calif Polytechnic State Univ	CA	19,847	HC
Clarkson Univ	NY	53,538	HC
Colo State Univ-Fort Collins	CO	20,090	VC
Cornell Univ	NY	59,037	MC
CUNY-City College	NY	19,576	H¢
Drexel Univ	PA	51,920	HC
Elon Univ	NC	40,046	HC
Florida Gulf Coast Univ	FL		C
Florida International Univ	FL	17,747	VC
Florida State Univ	FL	15,238	HC
Gannon Univ	PA	37,940	C
Georgia Inst of Technology	GA	20,464	MC
Humboldt State Univ	CA	18,400	C
Johns Hopkins Univ	MD	47,492	MC
Lehigh Univ	PA	55,080	MC
Louisiana State Univ	LA	18,677	V¢
Manhattan College	NY	44,955	VC
Marquette Univ	WI	43,664	V¢
Mass Inst of Technology	MA	54,238	MC
Mass Maritime Academy	MA	15,340	C
Mich Tech Univ	MI	22,105	VC
Missouri Univ of Science and Technology	MO	18,655	V¢
Montana Tech of The Univ of Montana	MT	14,650	VC
New Jersey Inst of Technology	NJ	26,490	VC
New Mexico Inst of Mining and Technology	NM	12,892	HC
New Mexico State Univ	NM	13,955	LC
N Car State Univ	NC	16,202	HC
Northern Arizona Univ	AZ	18,592	C
Northwestern Univ	IL	37,595	MC
Ohio Univ	OH	20,676	VC
Oregon State Univ	OR	19,017	¢
Rensselaer Polytechnic Inst	NY	59,229	MC
Rice Univ	TX	43,288	MC
San Diego State Univ	CA	20,578	VC
Seattle Univ	WA	47,010	V¢
S Dak School of Mines and Technology	SD	15,260	VC
S Dak State Univ	SD	14,296	C
Southern Methodist Univ	TX	57,755	MC
Stanford Univ	CA	56,411	MC
SUNY / College of Environmental Science and Forestry	NY	18,351	HC
Stevens Inst of Technology	NJ	50,130	HC
Suffolk Univ	MA	46,548	C
Syracuse Univ	NY	54,512	HC
Taylor Univ	IN	36,742	V¢
Tenn Tech Univ	TN	11,310	C
Texas Tech Univ	TX	14,243	C
The Catholic Univ of America	DC	52,852	VC

School	ST	$IS	SR
Ohio State Univ	OH	19,887	MC
Tufts Univ	MA	58,780	MC
United States Air Force Academy	CO		MC
United States Military Academy	NY		MC
Universidad Politecnica de PR	PR	19,252	
Univ at Buffalo / The SUNY	NY	20,283	VC
Univ of Arizona	AZ	20,105	C
Univ of Calif at Berkeley	CA	23,322	MC
Univ of Calif at Irvine	CA	25,961	VC
Univ of Calif at Riverside	CA	27,204	C
Univ of Calif at San Diego	CA	21,000	VC
Univ of Central Florida	FL	15,711	VC+
Univ of Colo Boulder	CO	22,605	VC+
Univ of Conn	CT	23,744	HC
Univ of Delaware	DE	22,728	VC
Univ of Florida	FL	15,783	HC+
Univ of Georgia	GA	19,508	VC
Univ of Idaho	ID	14,558	C
Univ of Miami	FL	55,166	MC
Univ of Mich/Ann Arbor	MI	22,102	HC+
Univ of New Hampshire	NH	24,702	VC
Univ of Okla	OK	17,634	VC+
Univ of Southern Calif	CA	56,903	MC
Univ of Tenn at Chattanooga	TN	16,883	C
Univ of Vermont	VT	26,120	VC+
Univ of Wisc/Platteville	WI	14,274	C
Wilkes Univ	PA	42,786	C
Worcester Polytechnic Inst	MA	53,440	HC
Yale Univ	CT	55,300	MC

ENVIRONMENTAL ENGINEERING TECHNOLOGY

School	ST	$IS	SR
East Carolina Univ	NC	14,169	C
Indiana Inst of Technology	IN	34,240	LC
Inter-American Univ of PR/ Bayamon Univ College	PR	4,428	
Lake Superior State Univ	MI	18,121	C
New York Inst of Technology	NY	40,590	VC
Rochester Inst of Technology	NY	42,450	VC+
Shawnee State Univ	OH	16,545	NC
Southwestern Okla State Univ	OK	9,160	C
Texas Southern Univ	TX	18,212	LC

ENVIRONMENTAL GEOLOGY

School	ST	$IS	SR
Allegheny College	PA	49,020	HC
Beloit College	WI	49,970	HC
Binghamton Univ / The SUNY	NY	20,832	HC+
Calvin College	MI	37,585	VC+
Hanover College	IN	41,450	VC
Kutztown Univ of Pennsylvania	PA	16,909	LC
Ohio Univ	OH	20,676	VC
Oswego / SUNY	NY	20,009	VC
Prescott College	AZ	33,284	C+
Queens College / The CUNY	NY	17,107	VC
Samford Univ	AL	35,700	VC+
Southern Methodist Univ	TX	57,755	MC
SUNY New Paltz	NY	15,010	C
Univ of Akron	OH	20,436	C
Univ of Calif at Irvine	CA	25,961	VC
Univ of Dayton	OH	43,750	VC
Univ of Illinois at Chicago	IL	24,293	VC
Univ of Mich/Ann Arbor	MI	22,102	HC+
Univ of Okla	OK	17,634	VC+
Univ of Pittsburgh at Pittsburgh	PA	27,800	HC+
Univ of Utah	UT	13,462	VC
Univ of Wyoming	WY	13,855	C+

ENVIRONMENTAL HEALTH SCIENCE

School	ST	$IS	SR
Benedict College	SC	20,454	NC
Boise State Univ	ID	12,802	C
Calif Inst of Technology	CA	54,045	MC
Cal State, Chico	CA	18,952	C
Cal State, Sacramento	CA	16,200	C
Cal State, San Bernardino	CA	12,000	C
Clarkson Univ	NY	53,538	HC
Colo State Univ-Fort Collins	CO	20,090	VC
Colo State Univ-Pueblo	CO	13,532	LC
Delaware State Univ	DE	14,700	LC
Drury Univ	MO	30,319	VC
East Carolina Univ	NC	14,169	C
East Central Univ	OK	10,223	LC
East Tenn State Univ	TN	9,000	C
Eastern Kentucky Univ	KY	11,161	C
Illinois State Univ	IL	22,634	VC
Indiana State Univ	IN	16,000	C
Iowa Wesleyan College	IA	30,850	LC
Lake Superior State Univ	MI	18,121	C
Miss Valley State Univ	MS	9,706	LC
Missouri Southern State Univ	MO	11,910	C
New Mexico State Univ	NM	13,955	LC
New York Univ	NY	61,470	MC
Ohio Univ	OH	20,676	VC
Old Dominion Univ	VA	18,662	C
Point Park Univ	PA	36,390	C
Purdue Univ/West Lafayette	IN	20,278	HC
Salisbury Univ	MD	18,368	VC
San Diego State Univ	CA	20,578	VC
Springfield College	MA	25,000	C
Texas Southern Univ	TX	18,212	LC
Univ of Arizona	AZ	20,105	C
Univ of Arkansas at Little Rock	AR		C
Univ of Calif at Davis	CA	24,482	HC
Univ of Georgia	GA	19,508	VC
Univ of Mich-Flint	MI	17,547	C+
Univ of N Car at Chapel Hill	NC	18,348	MC
Univ of Southern Maine	ME	16,576	C
Univ of Washington	WA	14,722	VC
Western Carolina Univ	NC	13,965	C+
Western Kentucky Univ	KY	11,000	LC
Wright State Univ	OH	16,983	C
York College / CUNY	NY	5,496	NC

ENVIRONMENTAL SCIENCE

School	ST	$IS	SR
Abilene Christian Univ	TX	38,400	VC
Adrian College	MI	33,800	C
Alaska Pacific Univ	AK	33,360	VC
Albright College	PA	46,660	C
Alderson Broaddus Univ	WV	28,656	C
Allegheny College	PA	49,020	HC
Alverno College	WI	30,483	LC
American Univ	DC	54,829	HC+
Andrews Univ	MI	28,030	C+
Anna Maria College	MA	34,600	LC
Appalachian State Univ	NC	12,919	VC
Aquinas College	MI	33,060	C
Arcadia Univ	PA	33,570	C+
Ashland Univ	OH	25,000	C
Assumption College	MA	45,721	VC
Auburn Univ	AL	20,052	VC+
Averett Univ	VA	36,000	LC
Barton College	NC	27,660	C
Baylor Univ	TX	46,720	HC
Beloit College	WI	49,970	HC
Benedictine Univ	IL	35,220	C
Bennington College	VT	56,990	HC+
Bentley Univ	MA	54,555	HC+
Berry College	GA	39,254	HC
Bethany College	WV	35,282	C
Bethel College	IN	31,560	C
Bethel Univ	MN	34,940	VC
Binghamton Univ / The SUNY	NY	20,832	HC+
Biola Univ	CA	40,320	VC
Boston College	MA	58,506	MC
Boston Univ	MA	54,130	HC+
Bowling Green State Univ	OH	18,970	C
Bradley Univ	IL	31,874	VC
Briar Cliff Univ	IA	29,514	C
Bridgewater College	VA	39,880	C
Brown Univ	RI	56,150	MC
Bryant Univ	RI	49,179	VC
Bucknell Univ	PA	58,160	MC
Buena Vista Univ	IA	37,954	C
Cabrini College	PA	40,859	LC
Calif Baptist Univ	CA	35,890	C
Calif Polytechnic State Univ	CA	19,847	HC
Cal State, Chico	CA	18,952	C
Cal State, East Bay	CA	16,549	C
Calif Univ of Pennsylvania	PA	14,217	C
Calvin College	MI	37,585	VC+
Canisius College	NY	45,602	VC
Capital Univ	OH	39,824	VC
Carroll College	MT	28,000	C
Carroll Univ	WI	24,860	C
Case Western Reserve Univ	OH	55,178	MC
Castleton State College	VT	19,424	C
Catawba College	NC	37,105	C
Cedarville Univ	OH	31,036	VC+
Centenary College of Louisiana	LA	39,070	C+
Central College	IA	36,980	VC
Central Methodist Univ	MO	28,240	VC
Central Mich Univ	MI	18,066	C
Chapman Univ	CA	56,019	VC+
Charleston Southern Univ	SC	22,420	C
Chatham Univ	PA	42,440	VC
Chestnut Hill College	PA	39,785	LC
Christopher Newport Univ	VA	21,050	VC
Claflin Univ	SC	22,368	C+
Claremont McKenna College	CA	58,065	MC
Clarion Univ of Pennsylvania	PA	17,370	C
Clark Univ	MA	47,020	HC+
Clarkson Univ	NY	53,538	HC
Cleveland State Univ	OH	21,357	C
Coe College	IA	43,590	VC
Colby-Sawyer College	NH	47,870	C
Colgate Univ	NY	50,930	MC
Colo College	CO	54,534	MC
Colo Mesa Univ	CO	16,669	LC
Columbia Univ in the City of New York	NY	61,116	MC
Columbia Univ/Barnard College	NY	39,000	MC
Columbia Univ/School of General Studies	NY	54,083	MC
Concordia College New York	NY	31,500	VC
Concordia College, Moorhead	MN	39,974	C+
Concordia Univ	OR	34,930	C
Concordia Univ Texas	TX	23,640	C
Conn College	CT	54,970	MC
Cornell College	IA	44,930	HC
Creighton Univ	NE	44,058	VC+
CUNY-City College	NY	19,576	HC+
Curry College	MA	47,545	LC
Dallas Baptist Univ	TX	29,118	C
Dartmouth College	NH	57,996	MC
Davis and Elkins College	WV	33,742	C
Defiance College	OH	30,645	C
Delaware Valley College	PA	29,944	C
Delta State Univ	MS	12,292	LC
DePaul Univ	IL	46,120	VC
DePauw Univ	IN	48,950	VC+
Dickinson College	PA	57,662	HC+
Doane College	NE	33,730	VC
Dominican Univ	IL	37,628	C
Dordt College	IA	34,160	VC
Drake Univ	IA	30,980	VC+
Drexel Univ	PA	51,920	HC
Drury Univ	MO	30,319	VC
Duke Univ	NC	50,250	MC
Duquesne Univ	PA	42,017	VC
Earlham College	IN	49,710	VC+
East Stroudsburg Univ of Pennsylvania	PA	16,636	C
Eastern Conn State Univ	CT	20,584	C
Eastern Kentucky Univ	KY	11,161	C
Eastern Mennonite Univ	VA	38,850	VC
Eastern Nazarene College	MA	30,000	C
Eastern New Mexico Univ	NM	10,682	C
Edinboro Univ of Pennsylvania	PA	15,940	LC
Elizabethtown College	PA	47,600	VC
Elmhurst College	IL	42,032	C+
Elmira College	NY	49,950	C+
Elon Univ	NC	40,046	HC
Emory and Henry College	VA	387,460	C
Endicott College	MA	42,390	C
Ferrum College	VA	27,740	LC
Flagler College	FL	24,960	VC
Florida Inst of Technology	FL	48,290	VC
Florida International Univ	FL	17,747	VC
Florida State Univ	FL	15,238	HC
Fordham Univ	NY	58,927	HC
Framingham State Univ	MA	16,750	C
Franklin and Marshall College	PA	58,295	MC
Franklin Pierce Univ	NH	41,598	C
Fresno Pacific Univ	CA	32,136	C
Friends Univ	KS	29,100	C
Frostburg State Univ	MD	15,264	LC
Furman Univ	SC	54,006	HC
Gannon Univ	PA	37,940	C
George Washington Univ	DC	57,108	MC
Georgetown College	KY	38,690	C
Georgia College and State Univ	GA	18,216	VC
Gettysburg College	PA	56,820	HC
Glenville State College	WV	11,348	NC
Goshen College	IN	35,900	VC
Hampshire College	MA	58,320	MC
Hanover College	IN	41,450	VC
Hardin-Simmons Univ	TX	23,560	C+
Hartwick College	NY	49,815	C+
Harvard Univ/Harvard College	MA	49,000	MC
Hawaii Pacific Univ	HI	36,690	C
Heritage Univ	WA	17,664	NC
Hiram College	OH	37,300	VC
Hobart and William Smith Colleges	NY	43,000	VC
Hood College	MD	44,630	C
Houghton College	NY	35,740	VC
Howard Univ	DC	35,957	C
Humboldt State Univ	CA	18,400	C
Hunter College / The CUNY	NY	14,429	VC
Husson Univ	ME	23,386	LC
Idaho State Univ	ID	11,908	C
Illinois College	IL	25,770	VC
Indiana Univ Bloomington	IN	19,358	HC
Indiana Univ-Purdue Univ Indianapolis	IN	17,290	C
Iona College	NY	44,028	C
Iowa State Univ	IA	16,403	C
Ithaca College	NY	52,300	HC
Jacksonville Univ	FL	37,780	C
John Brown Univ	AR	30,996	VC+
John Carroll Univ	OH	44,520	C+
Johns Hopkins Univ	MD	47,492	MC
Johnson State College	VT	16,721	C
Juniata College	PA	49,340	VC
Keuka College	NY	30,300	C
Keystone College	PA	28,680	LC
Knox College	IL		VC
Kutztown Univ of Pennsylvania	PA	16,909	LC
La Salle Univ	PA	50,270	C
Lake Forest College	IL	45,580	VC
Lake Superior State Univ	MI	18,121	C
Lander Univ	SC	22,514	C+
Le Moyne College	NY	42,200	VC
Lehigh Univ	PA	55,080	MC
Lewis Univ	IL	23,050	C
Lincoln Memorial Univ	TN	18,144	C
Lincoln Univ	MO	11,996	NC
Lipscomb Univ	TN	35,722	VC
Louisiana State Univ	LA	18,677	VC+
Louisiana Tech Univ	LA	8,000	C
Lourdes Univ	OH	26,055	LC
Loyola Marymount Univ	CA	53,240	VC+
Loyola Univ Chicago	IL	49,560	VC+
Lynchburg College	VA	42,645	C
Madonna Univ	MI	24,540	VC
Mansfield Univ	PA	19,468	LC
Marian Univ/Indianapolis	IN	37,058	C
Marietta College	OH	42,135	VC
Marist College	NY	35,500	C
Maritime College / SUNY	NY	16,020	C
Marshall Univ	WV	14,820	C
Martin Univ	IN	11,000	SP
Marygrove College	MI	21,290	C
Maryville Univ of St. Louis	MO	34,920	VC
Marywood Univ	PA	40,695	C
McDaniel College	MD	45,600	VC
Medgar Evers College / The CUNY	NY	4,920	NC
Mercyhurst Univ	PA	40,700	C
Merrimack College	MA	44,215	C
Messiah College	PA	39,540	VC
Metropolitan State Univ of Denver	CO	4,835	LC
Miami Univ	OH	24,191	HC
Middle Tenn State Univ	TN	8,650	C
Midway College	KY	20,150	C
Midwestern State Univ	TX	9,722	C
Miles College	AL	16,530	NC
Mills College	CA	54,119	HC
Minn State Univ, Mankato	MN	14,900	C
Molloy College	NY	38,950	C
Monmouth College	IL	39,290	C
Montana State Univ	MT	14,068	VC
Montana State Univ-Billings	MT	12,425	LC
Montana State Univ-Northern	MT	12,500	NC
Montreat College	NC	31,298	VC
Mount Aloysius College	PA	27,970	C
Mount Marty College	SD	29,638	C
Mount Olive College	NC	18,426	C
Mount St. Mary's Univ	MD	46,158	C
Muhlenberg College	PA	52,837	HC
Muskingum Univ	OH	30,502	C
National Univ	CA	14,730	SP
Nazareth College of Rochester	NY	41,590	VC
New England College	NH	45,930	LC
New Jersey Inst of Technology	NJ	26,490	VC
New Mexico Highlands Univ	NM	9,720	NC
New Mexico Inst of Mining and Technology	NM	12,892	HC
New Mexico State Univ	NM	13,955	LC
N Car Central Univ	NC	9,000	LC
N Car State Univ	NC	16,202	HC
N Car Wesleyan College	NC	29,440	C
North Park Univ	IL	30,130	C
Northeastern Univ	MA	55,296	MC
Northern Arizona Univ	AZ	18,592	C
Northern Kentucky Univ	KY	15,302	LC
Northern State Univ	SD	14,021	C
Northland College	WI	26,680	C
Northwest Univ	WA	18,854	C
Northwestern Univ	IL	37,595	MC
Norwich Univ	VT	28,212	C
Notre Dame College	OH	34,942	VC
Nova Southeastern Univ	FL	34,016	VC
Oakland Univ	MI	19,391	VC
Ohio Wesleyan Univ	OH	49,460	C+
Okla State Univ	OK	14,310	VC
Olivet College	MI	19,984	C
Olivet Nazarene Univ	IL	29,990	C
Oregon Inst of Technology	OR	8,910	C
Oregon State Univ	OR	19,017	C+
Pace Univ	NY	48,094	VC
Pacific Lutheran Univ	WA	44,840	VC
Pfeiffer Univ	NC	33,700	C
Philadelphia Univ	PA	44,160	C
Piedmont College	GA	29,260	C
Pitzer College	CA	54,988	MC
Point Loma Nazarene Univ	CA	38,610	VC
Point Park Univ	PA	36,390	C
Portland State Univ	OR	18,672	C
Prescott College	AZ	33,284	C+
Principia College	IL	35,140	C+
Purchase College / SUNY	NY	16,951	C
Purdue Univ/West Lafayette	IN	20,278	HC
Queens College / The CUNY	NY	17,107	VC
Queens Univ of Charlotte	NC	39,543	VC

School	ST	$IS	SR
Ramapo College of New Jersey	NJ	24,938	C+
Randolph College	VA	43,960	VC
Rhodes College	TN	47,596	HC+
Richard Stockton College of New Jersey	NJ	20,000	VC
Rider Univ	NJ	45,720	C
Ripon College	WI	36,959	C+
Robert Morris Univ	PA	36,699	C
Rochester Inst of Technology	NY	42,450	VC+
Rocky Mountain College	MT	32,242	C
Roger Williams Univ	RI	45,788	C
Rollins College	FL	52,370	HC
Roosevelt Univ	IL	22,605	VC
Rosemont College	PA	42,350	C
Russell Sage College	NY	39,370	C
Rutgers, The State Univ of New Jersey/New Brunswick	NJ	25,077	VC
Rutgers, The State Univ of New Jersey/Newark Campus	NJ	25,376	C
St. Anselm College	NH	48,324	VC
St. Joseph's College of Maine	ME	31,580	C
St. Joseph's Univ	PA	52,272	VC
St. Leo Univ	FL	27,990	C
St. Louis Univ	MO	46,594	VC+
St. Mary's College of Calif	CA	53,550	C
St. Mary's Univ	TX	33,854	C
St. Paul's College	VA	16,030	NC
St. Vincent College	PA	40,244	C
Salem International Univ	WV	18,020	C
Sam Houston State Univ	TX	17,082	C
Samford Univ	AL	35,700	VC+
San Diego State Univ	CA	20,578	VC
Santa Clara Univ	CA	54,702	MC
Savannah State Univ	GA	13,156	C
Scripps College	CA	54,900	MC
Seattle Univ	WA	47,010	VC+
Shaw Univ	NC	15,488	LC
Shenandoah Univ	VA	39,268	C
Shippensburg Univ of Pennsylvania	PA	17,064	LC
Siena College	NY	43,863	VC
Sierra Nevada College	NV	32,700	VC
Simpson College	IA	36,086	VC
Smith College	MA	57,524	MC
Sonoma State Univ	CA	20,541	C
Southeast Missouri State Univ	MO	14,983	LC
Southern Methodist Univ	TX	57,755	MC
Southern Oregon Univ	OR	17,874	C
Southwest Minn State Univ	MN	14,000	C
St. Bonaventure Univ	NY	38,831	C
St. Edward's Univ	TX	44,674	VC
St. Lawrence Univ	NY	53,740	HC
St. Norbert College	WI	39,992	VC
SUNY / College of Environmental Science and Forestry	NY	18,351	HC
Stephen F. Austin State Univ	TX	14,668	C
Stetson Univ	FL	49,512	VC+
Stony Brook Univ / SUNY	NY	19,359	HC
Suffolk Univ	MA	46,548	C
SUNY Cortland / The SUNY	NY	19,117	C
SUNY Fredonia / The SUNY at Fredonia	NY	18,702	VC
SUNY Oneonta / SUNY	NY	16,919	VC
SUNY Plattsburgh / SUNY	NY	18,083	VC
Susquehanna Univ	PA	49,170	C
Sweet Briar College	VA	43,765	C+
Taylor Univ	IN	36,742	VC+
Temple Univ	PA	24,392	VC
Texas A&M Univ	TX	16,956	VC+
Texas A&M Univ at Corpus Christi	TX	11,544	LC
Texas A&M Univ at Galveston	TX	11,258	C
Texas Christian Univ	TX	47,570	HC
Texas State Univ	TX	16,495	VC
The Catholic Univ of America	DC	52,852	VC
The College at Brockport / SUNY	NY	18,362	VC
The Lincoln Univ	PA	15,154	LC
Ohio State Univ	OH	19,887	MC
Thiel College	PA	31,378	LC
Thomas Edison State College	NJ	5,700	SP
Thomas More College	KY	34,760	C
Towson Univ	MD	16,000	VC
Trine Univ	IN	39,400	VC
Trinity College	CT		HC+
Troy Univ	AL	10,650	C
Tufts Univ	MA	58,780	MC
Tulane Univ	LA	58,942	MC
Tusculum College	TN	24,295	C
Union College	NY		MC
Unity College	ME	34,054	C
Univ of Alabama at Tuscaloosa	AL	17,164	C+
Univ of Alaska Southeast	AK	11,493	C
Univ of Arizona	AZ	20,105	C
Univ of Arkansas at Fayetteville	AR	16,860	VC
Univ of Calif at Berkeley	CA	23,322	MC
Univ of Calif at Davis	CA	24,482	HC
Univ of Calif at Irvine	CA	25,961	VC
Univ of Calif at Los Angeles	CA	25,686	MC
Univ of Calif at Riverside	CA	27,204	C
Univ of Calif at San Diego	CA	21,000	VC
Univ of Calif at Santa Barbara	CA	27,551	HC
Univ of Central Arkansas	AR	10,840	VC
Univ of Chicago	IL	55,416	MC
Univ of Colo Boulder	CO	22,605	VC+
Univ of Conn	CT	20,744	HC
Univ of Delaware	DE	22,728	VC
Univ of Denver	CO	51,787	VC+
Univ of Dubuque	IA	30,200	C
Univ of Evansville	IN	41,056	VC+
Univ of Findlay	OH	31,916	C
Univ of Hawaii at Manoa	HI	19,379	VC
Univ of Houston	TX	19,184	VC
Univ of Idaho	ID	14,558	C
Univ of Indianapolis	IN	31,740	LC
Univ of Iowa	IA	17,481	VC
Univ of La Verne	CA	47,010	VC
Univ of Maine	ME	19,712	C+
Univ of Maine at Farmington	ME	17,841	C
Univ of Maine at Fort Kent	ME	14,975	LC
Univ of Maine at Machias	ME	10,523	C
Univ of Maine at Presque Isle	ME	15,011	LC
Univ of Mary Washington	VA	19,484	VC
Univ of Maryland	MD	18,801	HC
Univ of Maryland/Baltimore County	MD	18,000	VC
Univ of Maryland/Eastern Shore	MD	14,000	C
Univ of Maryland/Univ College	MD	6,168	SP
Univ of Mass Amherst	MA	23,697	VC+
Univ of Mass Lowell	MA	19,316	C
Univ of Miami	FL	55,166	MC
Univ of Mich/Dearborn	MI	9,885	VC
Univ of Minn Crookston	MN	17,834	C
Univ of Minn/Duluth	MN	18,964	C+
Univ of Missouri-Kansas City	MO	19,603	C
Univ of Montana-Western	MT	9,753	LC
Univ of Montevallo	AL	17,320	C
Univ of Mount Union	OH	35,130	C
Univ of Nebr - Lincoln	NE	17,507	VC
Univ of Nevada, Las Vegas	NV	17,303	C
Univ of Nevada/Reno	NV	14,500	NC
Univ of New England	ME	46,145	C+
Univ of New Hampshire	NH	24,702	VC
Univ of New Haven	CT	47,740	C
Univ of New Mexico	NM	15,300	C
Univ of New Orleans	LA	9,224	VC
Univ of N Car at Asheville	NC	13,500	VC+
Univ of N Car at Chapel Hill	NC	18,348	MC
Univ of N Car at Wilmington	NC	13,572	VC+
Univ of Northern Iowa	IA	14,776	C
Univ of Notre Dame	IN		MC
Univ of Okla	OK	17,634	VC+
Univ of Oregon	OR	20,872	VC
Univ of Portland	OR	47,874	VC
Univ of Redlands	CA	40,500	VC
Univ of Rio Grande	OH	8,750	NC
Univ of Rochester	NY	58,500	MC
Univ of St. Francis	IN	29,810	C
Univ of San Francisco	CA	49,674	VC
Univ of Scranton	PA	51,940	VC
Univ of S Car at Columbia	SC	19,725	VC+
Univ of South Florida	FL	13,000	C
Univ of South Florida/St. Petersburg	FL	12,769	VC
Univ of Southern Calif	CA	56,903	MC
Univ of Southern Indiana	IN	14,657	C
Univ of Southern Maine	ME	16,576	C
Univ of St. Francis	IL	36,490	C
Univ of St. Thomas - Houston	TX	36,490	VC
Univ of Tampa	FL	35,160	VC
Univ of Tenn at Chattanooga	TN	16,883	C
Univ of Tenn at Knoxville	TN	20,364	VC+
Univ of Texas at San Antonio	TX	18,372	C
Univ of Texas-Pan American	TX	12,432	LC
Univ of the District of Columbia	DC	7,244	LC
Univ of the Incarnate Word	TX	35,200	LC
Univ of the Ozarks	AR	22,100	C
Univ of the Pacific	CA	52,146	VC
Univ of the Sciences	PA	48,320	VC+
Univ of Toledo	OH	18,464	C
Univ of Vermont	VT	26,120	VC+
Univ of Virginia	VA	22,175	MC
Univ of Virginia's College at Wise	VA	11,076	C
Univ of West Alabama	AL	9,415	C
Univ of West Georgia	GA	14,852	LC
Univ of Wisc/Green Bay	WI	14,900	C
Univ of Wisc/Madison	WI	18,757	HC
Univ of Wisc-Milwaukee	WI	18,436	C
Ursinus College	PA	55,630	VC+
Utah State Univ	UT	11,803	C
Valparaiso Univ	IN	43,040	VC+
Villanova Univ	PA	56,436	MC
Virginia Polytechnic Inst and State Univ	VA	14,629	HC
Walla Walla Univ	WA	26,256	NC
Walsh Univ	OH	35,100	C
Warren Wilson College	NC	34,888	VC
Washington and Lee Univ	VA	52,812	MC
Washington State Univ	WA	20,461	C
Washington Univ in St. Louis	MO	58,818	MC
Wayland Baptist Univ	TX	16,058	LC
Wayne State Univ	MI	19,493	C
Waynesburg Univ	PA	29,100	C
Wentworth Inst of Technology	MA	29,800	SP
Wesley College	DE	31,115	LC
Wesleyan College	GA	24,000	C+
West Texas A&M Univ	TX	13,478	C
West Virginia Univ	WV	15,794	C+
Western Conn State Univ	CT	18,327	C
Western Washington Univ	WA	18,519	VC
Westfield State Univ	MA	18,489	C
Westminster College	MO	30,490	VC
Wheaton College	IL	39,650	HC+
Wheaton College	MA	54,934	HC+
Wheeling Jesuit Univ	WV	34,668	C
Whitman College	WA	54,400	MC
Whittier College	CA	43,416	C
Widener Univ	PA	50,368	C
Willamette Univ	OR	56,450	VC+
William Paterson Univ of New Jersey	NJ	21,694	C
William Penn Univ	IA	26,000	C
Wilson College	PA	27,660	C
Winthrop Univ	SC	21,120	VC
Wittenberg Univ	OH	47,766	VC
Wright State Univ	OH	16,983	C
Xavier Univ	OH	43,740	VC

ENVIRONMENTAL STUDIES

School	ST	$IS	SR
Adelphi Univ	NY	43,130	VC
Adrian College	MI	33,800	C
Alaska Pacific Univ	AK	33,360	VC
Alfred Univ	NY	40,392	VC
Allegheny College	PA	49,020	HC
Alma College	MI	42,400	VC
American Univ	DC	54,829	HC+
Amherst College	MA	58,744	MC
Appalachian State Univ	NC	12,919	VC
Aquinas College	MI	33,060	C
Bard College	NY	59,872	HC
Bard College at Simon's Rock	MA	58,963	HC+
Bates College	ME	58,950	MC
Bemidji State Univ	MN	13,500	C
Bennington College	VT	56,990	HC+
Bethel Univ	MN	34,940	VC
Binghamton Univ / The SUNY	NY	20,832	HC+
Birmingham-Southern College	AL	42,370	VC+
Boise State Univ	ID	12,802	C
Boston Univ	MA	54,130	HC+
Bowdoin College	ME	57,834	MC
Bowling Green State Univ	OH	18,970	C
Brandeis Univ	MA	58,820	HC
Brenau Univ Women's College	GA	26,650	C+
Brigham Young Univ	UT	12,100	HC
Calif Lutheran Univ	CA	47,640	C
Cal State, East Bay	CA	16,549	C
Cal State, San Bernardino	CA	12,000	C
Calvin College	MI	37,585	VC+
Canisius College	NY	45,602	VC
Carleton College	MN	58,149	MC
Catawba College	NC	37,105	C
Cazenovia College	NY	30,800	C
Central Mich Univ	MI	18,066	C
Chaminade Univ of Honolulu	HI	31,664	C
Chatham Univ	PA	42,440	VC
CUNY/Brooklyn College	NY	5,884	C+
Claremont McKenna College	CA	58,065	MC
Coe College	IA	43,590	VC
Colby College	ME	57,510	MC
Colby-Sawyer College	NH	47,870	C
College of St. Benedict	MN	47,570	VC
College of the Holy Cross	MA	56,232	MC
Columbia College	MO	24,578	C
Daemen College	NY	31,510	C
Dartmouth College	NH	57,996	MC
Davidson College	NC	54,683	MC
Denison Univ	OH	54,670	HC+
Dickinson College	PA	57,662	HC+
Dominican Univ of Calif	CA	51,250	C
Drew Univ/College of Liberal Arts	NJ	55,862	VC
Drury Univ	MO	30,319	VC
Earlham College	IN	49,710	VC+
Eastern Univ	PA	37,704	C
Eckerd College	FL	43,902	VC
Elon Univ	NC	40,046	HC
Emmanuel College	MA	47,985	VC
Emory Univ	GA	45,000	MC
Eugene Lang College - The New School for Liberal Arts	NY	55,650	VC
Florida Gulf Coast Univ	FL		C
Florida Inst of Technology	FL	48,290	VC
Florida Southern College	FL	38,240	VC
Florida State Univ	FL	15,238	HC
Fort Lewis College	CO	15,513	C
Franklin and Marshall College	PA	58,295	MC
George Mason Univ	VA	15,724	VC
Goddard College	VT	16,418	VC
Gonzaga Univ	WA	44,247	HC
Goodwin College	CT	19,400	LC
Goshen College	IN	35,900	VC
Goucher College	MD	50,252	VC+
Green Mountain College	VT	33,547	LC
Guilford College	NC	35,340	C
Gustavus Adolphus College	MN	48,170	HC
Hamilton College	NY	55,620	MC
Hamline Univ	MN	44,198	VC
Hawaii Pacific Univ	HI	36,690	C
Hendrix College	AR	48,436	HC+
Hofstra Univ	NY	48,020	VC+
Hollins Univ	VA	43,295	VC
Illinois Wesleyan Univ	IL	48,452	VC+
Indiana Univ Bloomington	IN	19,358	HC
Ithaca College	NY	52,300	HC
Juniata College	PA	49,340	VC
Keene State College	NH	21,538	C
King's College	PA	41,678	C
Lasell College	MA	42,500	LC
Lawrence Univ	WI	46,371	HC
Lehigh Univ	PA	55,080	MC
Lenoir-Rhyne College	NC	35,984	C
Lewis & Clark College	OR	52,656	VC
Linfield College-McMinnville Campus	OR	46,166	C
Lipscomb Univ	TN	35,722	VC
Louisiana State Univ	LA	18,677	VC+
Loyola Univ New Orleans	LA	46,581	VC
Luther College	IA	44,380	VC+
Lynchburg College	VA	42,645	C
Lynn Univ	FL	43,500	C
Lyon College	AR	30,246	VC
Macalester College	MN	53,419	MC
Manchester College	IN	35,070	C
Marietta College	OH	42,135	VC
Maryville College	TN	33,150	VC
Maryville Univ of St. Louis	MO	34,920	VC
Mass College of Liberal Arts	MA	16,733	C
Mercer Univ	GA	44,201	VC+
Meredith College	NC	31,420	C
Messiah College	PA	39,540	VC
Mich State Univ	MI	13,689	VC
Middlebury College	VT	57,470	MC
Mills College	CA	54,119	HC
Missouri State Univ	MO	13,996	VC
Mitchell College	CT	40,983	C
Mount Holyoke College	MA	53,596	HC+
Mountain State Univ	WV	14,330	NC
Naropa Univ	CO	37,875	SP
Neumann Univ	PA	31,078	LC
New College of Florida	FL	14,504	HC+
New York Univ	NY	61,470	MC
Northeastern Illinois Univ	IL		C
Northeastern Univ	MA	55,296	MC
Northern Arizona Univ	AZ	18,592	C
Oberlin College	OH	57,025	MC
Ohio Dominican Univ	OH	38,380	C+
Ohio Northern Univ	OH	42,075	VC
Okla City Univ	OK	33,546	VC
Pace Univ	NY	48,094	VC
Penn State Univ/Altoona	PA	11,464	C
Penn State Univ/Univ Park	PA	25,404	VC
Piedmont College	GA	29,260	C
Pittsburg State Univ	KS	12,032	C
Plymouth State Univ	NH	23,148	LC
Point Park Univ	PA	36,390	C
Pomona College	CA	57,680	MC
Prescott College	AZ	33,284	C+
Queens College / The CUNY	NY	17,107	VC
Queens Univ of Charlotte	NC	39,543	VC
Ramapo College of New Jersey	NJ	24,938	C+
Randolph College	VA	43,960	VC
Randolph-Macon College	VA	45,086	C
Reed College	OR	57,780	MC
Regis Univ	CO	41,318	C
Rhodes College	TN	47,596	HC+
Roanoke College	VA	47,996	C+
Rocky Mountain College	MT	32,242	C
Rowan Univ	NJ	23,570	VC
St. John's Univ	MN	46,146	C
St. Mary's College of Calif	CA	53,550	C
St. Michael's College	VT	48,740	VC
Salisbury Univ	MD	18,368	VC
San Diego State Univ	CA	20,578	VC
San Francisco State Univ	CA	18,514	C
San Jose State Univ	CA	19,707	C

School	ST	$IS	SR
Scripps College	CA	54,900	MC
Seattle Univ	WA	47,010	VC+
Seton Hall Univ	NJ	45,902	C
Sewanee: The Univ of the South	TN	47,700	HC+
Shepherd Univ	WV	14,996	C
Simmons College	MA	48,770	VC
Skidmore College	NY	57,926	HC
Southeastern Okla State Univ	OK	7,966	C
Southern Nazarene Univ	OK	24,354	NC
Southern New Hampshire Univ	NH	38,100	C
Southern Oregon Univ	OR	17,874	C
Southwestern Univ	TX	45,660	VC
St. John's Univ	NY	52,840	C+
St. Lawrence Univ	NY	53,740	HC
St. Olaf College	MN	49,960	HC+
SUNY / College of Environmental Science and Forestry	NY	18,351	HC
Stonehill College	MA	46,780	VC+
Stony Brook Univ / SUNY	NY	19,359	HC
Suffolk Univ	MA	46,548	C
Sweet Briar College	VA	43,765	C+
Taylor Univ	IN	36,742	VC+
Temple Univ	PA	24,392	VC
Tenn Wesleyan College	TN	21,250	C
Texas A&M Univ at Galveston	TX	11,258	C
The College of Idaho	ID	31,277	VC
The College of New Rochelle	NY	33,600	VC
The SUNY at Potsdam	NY	17,754	C
Thomas Edison State College	NJ	5,700	SP
Union College	NY		MC
Unity College	ME	34,054	C
Univ at Albany / SUNY	NY	18,674	VC
Univ at Buffalo / The SUNY	NY	20,283	VC
Univ of Arizona	AZ	20,105	C
Univ of Calif at Irvine	CA	25,961	VC
Univ of Calif at Los Angeles	CA	25,686	MC
Univ of Calif at San Diego	CA	21,000	VC
Univ of Calif at Santa Cruz	CA	27,807	VC
Univ of Evansville	IN	41,056	VC+
Univ of Illinois at Chicago	IL	24,293	VC
Univ of Kansas	KS	16,980	C+
Univ of Maine at Farmington	ME	17,841	C
Univ of Maryland/Baltimore County	MD	18,000	VC
Univ of Mich/Ann Arbor	MI	22,102	HC+
Univ of Mich/Dearborn	MI	9,885	VC
Univ of Minn/Duluth	MN	18,964	C+
Univ of Mobile	AL	27,870	VC
Univ of Montana	MT	13,670	C
Univ of Montana-Western	MT	9,753	LC
Univ of Nebr - Lincoln	NE	17,507	VC
Univ of Nebr at Omaha	NE	12,700	C
Univ of New England	ME	46,145	C+
Univ of New Hampshire	NH	24,702	VC
Univ of N Car at Chapel Hill	NC	18,348	MC
Univ of N Dak	ND	14,094	C
Univ of Oregon	OR	20,872	VC
Univ of Pennsylvania	PA	56,106	MC
Univ of Pittsburgh at Bradford	PA	21,316	LC
Univ of Pittsburgh at Johnstown	PA	20,862	LC
Univ of Pittsburgh at Pittsburgh	PA	27,800	HC+
Univ of Redlands	CA	40,500	VC
Univ of Rochester	NY	58,500	MC
Univ of San Diego	CA	53,302	HC+
Univ of Southern Calif	CA	56,903	MC
Univ of St. Thomas - Houston	TX	36,490	VC
Univ of Tulsa	OK	45,311	HC+
Univ of Utah	UT	13,462	VC
Univ of Vermont	VT	26,120	VC+
Univ of West Georgia	GA	14,852	LC
Univ of Wisc/Green Bay	WI	14,900	C
Univ of Wisc/Madison	WI	18,757	HC
Univ of Wyoming	WY	13,855	C+
Vassar College	NY	59,070	MC
Villanova Univ	PA	56,436	MC
Virginia Commonwealth Univ	VA	18,633	C
Virginia Wesleyan College	VA	28,433	LC
Viterbo Univ	WI	30,070	C
Warren Wilson College	NC	34,888	VC
Washington and Jefferson College	PA	49,990	VC
Washington College	MD	48,768	VC
Washington Univ in St. Louis	MO	58,818	MC
Wayland Baptist Univ	TX	16,058	LC
Webster Univ	MO	33,990	C+
Wellesley College	MA	49,848	MC
Wells College	NY	38,680	VC
Wesleyan Univ	CT	59,844	MC
West Chester Univ of Pennsylvania	PA	16,836	C
Western Mich Univ	MI	19,042	C
Western State Colo Univ	CO	16,135	C
Western Washington Univ	WA	18,519	VC
Westminster College	UT	37,708	VC
Wheeling Jesuit Univ	WV	34,668	C
Whitman College	WA	54,400	MC
Winthrop Univ	SC	21,120	VC
Wofford College	SC	45,795	VC
Worcester Polytechnic Inst	MA	53,440	HC+
Yale Univ	CT	55,300	MC
Youngstown State Univ	OH	16,374	LC

EQUINE SCIENCE

School	ST	$IS	SR
Asbury Univ	KY	32,038	VC
Auburn Univ	AL	20,052	VC+
Averett Univ	VA	36,000	LC
Bethany College	WV	35,282	C
Centenary College	NJ	38,618	LC
Colo State Univ-Fort Collins	CO	20,090	VC
Delaware Valley College	PA	29,944	C
Houghton College	NY	35,740	VC
Johnson and Wales Univ/ Providence Campus	RI	34,668	C
Judson College	AL	24,690	C
Lake Erie College	OH	35,704	C
Midway College	KY	20,150	C
Mount Ida College	MA	30,115	LC
National American Univ	SD	16,712	NC
N Dak State Univ	ND	14,642	C
Okla Panhandle State Univ	OK	8,996	NC
Otterbein College	OH	32,214	C
Rocky Mountain College	MT	32,242	C
St. Mary-of-the-Woods College	IN	37,722	LC
Salem International Univ	WV	18,020	C
Savannah College of Art and Design	GA	46,824	SP
Stephens College	MO	34,500	VC
Truman State Univ	MO	13,546	HC
Univ of Findlay	OH	31,916	C
Univ of Louisville	KY	17,460	VC
Univ of Minn Crookston	MN	17,834	C
Univ of Montana-Western	MT	9,753	LC
Virginia Intermont College	VA	32,411	LC
William Woods Univ	MO		C
Wilmington College	OH	29,784	C
Wilson College	PA	27,660	C

ESKIMO

School	ST	$IS	SR
Univ of Alaska Fairbanks	AK	13,955	C

ETHICS, POLITICS, AND SOCIAL POLICY

School	ST	$IS	SR
American Jewish Univ	CA	32,600	C
Drake Univ	IA	30,980	VC+
Goddard College	VT	16,418	VC
Millikin Univ	IL	37,462	C
Northwestern Univ	IL	37,595	MC
Pine Manor College	MA	32,659	LC
Prescott College	AZ	33,284	C+
Smith College	MA	57,524	MC
Syracuse Univ	NY	54,512	HC
Unity College	ME	34,054	C
Univ of Dayton	OH	43,750	VC
Univ of Mass Boston	MA	11,966	C
Univ of Northern Colo	CO	15,973	C
Univ of Southern Calif	CA	56,903	MC
Wells College	NY	38,680	VC
Wheeling Jesuit Univ	WV	34,668	C
Yale Univ	CT	55,300	MC

ETHNIC STUDIES

School	ST	$IS	SR
Albion College	MI	43,884	VC
Arizona State Univ	AZ	18,818	C+
Bowling Green State Univ	OH	18,970	C
Brown Univ	RI	56,150	MC
Calif Polytechnic State Univ	CA	19,847	HC
Cal State, East Bay	CA	16,549	C
Cal State, Fullerton	CA	25,188	C+
Cal State, San Bernardino	CA	12,000	C
Cal State, Stanislaus	CA	18,582	C
Colo State Univ-Fort Collins	CO	20,090	VC
Cornell College	IA	44,930	HC
CUNY-City College	NY	19,576	HC+
Kansas State Univ	KS	15,497	VC
Kent State Univ	OH	19,352	C
Messiah College	PA	39,540	VC
Metropolitan State Univ	MN	5,923	SP
Mills College	CA	54,119	HC
Minn State Univ, Mankato	MN	14,900	C
New York Univ	NY	61,470	MC
Oregon State Univ	OR	19,017	C+
Purchase College / SUNY	NY	16,951	C
Santa Clara Univ	CA	54,702	MC
Simmons College	MA	48,770	VC
Sonoma State Univ	CA	20,541	C
St. Catherine Univ	MN	37,782	C+
St. Olaf College	MN	49,960	HC+
Stony Brook Univ / SUNY	NY	19,359	HC
Univ of Alaska Fairbanks	AK	13,955	C
Univ of Calif at Berkeley	CA	23,322	MC
Univ of Calif at Riverside	CA	27,204	C
Univ of Calif at San Diego	CA	21,000	VC
Univ of Colo Boulder	CO	22,605	VC+
Univ of Colo Denver	CO	17,904	C
Univ of Hawaii at Manoa	HI	19,379	VC
Univ of Illinois at Chicago	IL	24,293	VC
Univ of Nebr - Lincoln	NE	17,507	VC
Univ of North Florida	FL	15,578	VC
Univ of Oregon	OR	20,872	VC
Univ of San Diego	CA	53,302	HC+
Univ of Texas at Austin	TX	44,074	HC
Univ of Utah	UT	13,462	VC
Univ of Vermont	VT	26,120	VC+
Univ of Washington	WA	14,722	VC
Univ of Wisc-Milwaukee	WI	18,436	C
Washington State Univ	WA	20,461	C
Washington Univ in St. Louis	MO	58,818	MC
Westfield State Univ	MA	18,489	C
Whitman College	WA	54,400	MC
Wichita State Univ	KS	12,539	C
Yale Univ	CT	55,300	MC

EUROPEAN STUDIES

School	ST	$IS	SR
Amherst College	MA	58,744	MC
Bates College	ME	58,950	MC
Belmont Univ	TN	37,380	VC+
Bennington College	VT	56,990	HC+
Brandeis Univ	MA	58,820	HC
Cal State, Fullerton	CA	25,188	C+
Canisius College	NY	45,602	VC
Central Mich Univ	MI	10,000	C
Columbia Univ/Barnard College	NY	39,000	MC
Emory and Henry College	VA	387,460	C
George Washington Univ	DC	57,108	MC
Georgetown College	KY	38,690	C
Harvard Univ/Harvard College	MA	49,000	MC
Hillsdale College	MI	31,890	HC+
Hobart and William Smith Colleges	NY	43,000	VC
John Carroll Univ	OH	44,520	C+
Lipscomb Univ	TN	35,722	VC
Loyola Marymount Univ	CA	53,240	VC+
Middlebury College	VT	57,470	MC
Millsaps College	MS	43,888	VC+
New York Univ	NY	61,470	MC
Northwestern Univ	IL	37,595	MC
Ohio Univ	OH	20,676	VC
Pitzer College	CA	54,988	MC
St. Joseph's Univ	PA	52,272	VC
San Diego State Univ	CA	20,578	VC
Scripps College	CA	54,900	MC
Seattle Pacific Univ	WA	41,559	VC+
Smith College	MA	57,524	MC
Stony Brook Univ / SUNY	NY	19,359	HC
Suffolk Univ	MA	46,548	C
Syracuse Univ	NY	54,512	HC
Texas State Univ	TX	16,495	VC
Univ of Arkansas at Fayetteville	AR	16,860	VC
Univ of Calif at Irvine	CA	25,961	VC
Univ of Calif at Los Angeles	CA	25,686	MC
Univ of Delaware	DE	22,728	VC
Univ of Kansas	KS	16,980	C+
Univ of Mich/Ann Arbor	MI	22,102	HC+
Univ of Minn/Morris	MN	17,150	VC
Univ of Nebr - Lincoln	NE	17,507	VC
Univ of New Hampshire	NH	24,702	VC
Univ of New Mexico	NM	15,300	C
Univ of N Car at Chapel Hill	NC	18,348	MC
Univ of Okla	OK	17,634	VC+
Univ of S Car at Columbia	SC	19,725	VC+
Univ of Vermont	VT	26,120	VC+
Vanderbilt Univ	TN	57,072	MC
Washington Univ in St. Louis	MO	58,818	MC
Webster Univ	MO	33,990	C+
Westmont College	CA	41,500	HC

EVOLUTIONARY BIOLOGY

School	ST	$IS	SR
Angelo State Univ	TX	15,049	NC
Bennington College	VT	56,990	HC+
Binghamton Univ / The SUNY	NY	20,832	HC+
Case Western Reserve Univ	OH	55,178	MC
Florida State Univ	FL	15,238	HC
Marshall Univ	WV	14,820	C
Princeton Univ	NJ	53,795	MC
Rutgers, The State Univ of New Jersey/New Brunswick	NJ	25,077	VC
Ohio State Univ	OH	19,887	MC
Tulane Univ	LA	58,942	MC
Univ of Calif at Santa Barbara	CA	27,551	HC
Univ of Calif at Santa Cruz	CA	27,807	VC
Univ of Colo Boulder	CO	22,605	VC+
Univ of Conn	CT	23,744	HC
Univ of Mich/Ann Arbor	MI	22,102	HC+
Univ of Minn/Twin Cities	MN		HC
Yale Univ	CT	55,300	MC

EXERCISE SCIENCE

School	ST	$IS	SR
Abilene Christian Univ	TX	38,400	VC
Adams State College	CO	13,358	LC
Adrian College	MI	33,800	C
Alma College	MI	42,400	VC
Angelo State Univ	TX	15,049	NC
Appalachian State Univ	NC	12,919	VC
Arizona State Univ	AZ	18,818	C+
Arkansas State Univ	AR	14,980	C
Asbury Univ	KY	32,038	VC
Augustana College	SD	35,500	VC
Baker Univ	KS	33,350	C+
Baldwin Wallace Univ	OH	36,980	VC
Barton College	NC	27,660	C
Becker College	MA	41,420	LC
Belhaven Univ	MS	27,170	C
Bellarmine Univ	KY	42,950	VC
Belmont Univ	TN	37,380	VC+
Berry College	GA	39,254	HC
Bethel College	IN	31,560	C
Bethel Univ	MN	34,940	VC
Bloomsburg Univ of Pennsylvania	PA	13,598	C
Blue Mountain College	MS	13,550	LC
Bluefield College	VA	17,230	C+
Boston Univ	MA	54,130	HC+
Bowling Green State Univ	OH	18,970	C
Bridgewater College	VA	39,880	C
Brigham Young Univ	UT	12,100	HC
Bryan College	TN	24,194	C
Cabrini College	PA	40,859	LC
Calif Baptist Univ	CA	35,890	C
Calif Lutheran Univ	CA	47,640	C
Cal State, Fullerton	CA	25,188	C+
Cal State, Northridge	CA	28,313	C
Cal State, San Bernardino	CA	12,000	C
Calvin College	MI	37,585	VC+
Campbellsville Univ	KY	27,720	C
Canisius College	NY	45,602	VC
Capital Univ	OH	29,824	VC
Carroll Univ	WI	24,860	C
Castleton State College	VT	19,424	C
Cedarville Univ	OH	31,036	VC+
Centenary College of Louisiana	LA	39,070	C+
Central College	IA	36,980	VC
Central Washington Univ	WA	11,730	C
Chatham Univ	PA	42,440	VC
Cleveland State Univ	OH	21,357	C
Coastal Carolina Univ	SC	17,620	C
Colby-Sawyer College	NH	47,870	C
College of Charleston	SC	21,273	VC
College of New Jersey	NJ	25,376	HC
College of St. Scholastica	MN	39,960	C
Colo State Univ-Fort Collins	CO	20,090	VC
Colo State Univ-Pueblo	CO	13,532	LC
Columbus State Univ	GA	13,176	C
Concordia College, Moorhead	MN	39,974	C+
Concordia Univ - Irvine	CA	35,390	VC
Concordia Univ Nebr	NE	26,000	VC
Corban Univ	OR	34,764	C
Cornerstone Univ and Grand Rapids Theological Seminary	MI	30,866	C
Creighton Univ	NE	44,058	VC+
De Sales Univ	PA	42,670	C
Dordt College	IA	34,160	VC
Drury Univ	MO	30,319	VC
D'Youville College	NY	29,850	C
East Carolina Univ	NC	14,169	C
East Central Univ	OK	10,223	LC
Eastern Mich Univ	MI	17,961	C
Eastern Univ	PA	37,704	C
Elmhurst College	IL	42,032	C+
Elon Univ	NC	40,046	HC
Fitchburg State Univ	MA	17,241	C
Florida Gulf Coast Univ	FL		C
Florida International Univ	FL	17,747	VC
Fort Lewis College	CO	15,513	C
Franklin College	IN	35,885	C
Frostburg State Univ	MD	15,264	LC
Furman Univ	SC	54,006	HC
Georgetown College	KY	38,690	C
Georgia College and State Univ	GA	18,216	VC
Georgia Southern Univ	GA	16,414	C
Georgia State Univ	GA	12,000	VC
Georgian Court Univ	NJ	39,726	LC
Gonzaga Univ	WA	44,247	HC
Grand Canyon Univ	AZ	24,540	VC
Grand Valley State Univ	MI	17,998	VC
Greensboro College	NC	28,740	LC
Grove City College	PA	22,988	HC
Guilford College	NC	35,340	C
Hamline Univ	MN	44,198	VC
Harding Univ	AR	21,432	C+
Hardin-Simmons Univ	TX	23,560	C+
Hendrix College	AR	48,436	HC+
High Point Univ	NC	39,800	C
Hofstra Univ	NY	48,020	VC+
Howard Payne Univ	TX	17,115	C
Huntingdon College	AL	31,850	C
Huntington Univ	IN	32,220	C
Illinois College	IL	25,770	VC

School	ST	$IS	SR
Illinois State Univ	IL	22,634	VC
Indiana Univ Bloomington	IN	19,358	HC
Indiana Univ-Purdue Univ Indianapolis	IN	17,290	C
Ithaca College	NY	52,300	HC
John Carroll Univ	OH	44,520	C+
Kansas State Univ	KS	15,497	VC
Keene State College	NH	21,538	C
Kennesaw State Univ	GA	13,017	VC
La Sierra Univ	CA	35,694	VC
LaGrange College	GA	34,480	C
Lake Superior State Univ	MI	18,121	C
Lander Univ	SC	22,514	C+
Lenoir-Rhyne College	NC	35,984	C
Liberty Univ	VA	19,101	C
Linfield College-McMinnville Campus	OR	46,166	C
Lipscomb Univ	TN	35,722	VC
Loras College	IA	37,432	VC
Louisiana College	LA	15,746	C
Loyola Univ Chicago	IL	49,560	VC+
Lubbock Christian Univ	TX	25,518	C
Lynchburg College	VA	42,645	C
Malone Univ	OH	34,334	C
Marquette Univ	WI	43,664	VC+
Marshall Univ	WV	14,820	C
McMurry Univ	TX	25,962	LC
Mercy College	NY	29,996	C
Meredith College	NC	31,420	C
Messiah College	PA	39,540	VC
Mich Tech Univ	MI	22,105	VC
Milligan College	TN	27,510	C
Minn State Univ, Moorhead	MN	13,392	C
Missouri Baptist Univ	MO	30,310	C
Missouri State Univ	MO	13,996	VC
Missouri Valley College	MO	22,200	C
Monmouth College	IL	39,290	C
Mount Vernon Nazarene Univ	OH	29,590	C
Murray State Univ	KY	14,944	C
Nebr Wesleyan Univ	NE	29,774	C+
Norfolk State Univ	VA	10,531	LC
N Car Wesleyan College	NC	29,440	C
North Central College	IL	38,343	VC
North Park Univ	IL	30,130	C
Northern Arizona Univ	AZ	18,592	C
Northwest Christian Univ	OR	27,399	C
Northwestern College	MN	24,000	C
Northwestern State Univ of Louisiana	LA	14,368	C
Nova Southeastern Univ	FL	34,016	VC
Ohio Dominican Univ	OH	38,380	C+
Ohio Univ	OH	20,676	VC
Okla City Univ	OK	33,546	VC
Old Dominion Univ	VA	18,662	C
Olivet Nazarene Univ	IL	29,990	C
Oregon State Univ	OR	19,017	C+
Palm Beach Atlantic Univ	FL	33,882	LC
Pennsylvania College of Technology	PA	25,653	NC
Pfeiffer Univ	NC	33,700	C
Point Loma Nazarene Univ	CA	38,610	VC
Purdue Univ/West Lafayette	IN	20,278	HC
Queens College / The CUNY	NY	17,107	VC
Queens Univ of Charlotte	NC	39,543	VC
Quincy Univ	IL	34,980	LC
Rice Univ	TX	43,288	MC
Ripon College	WI	36,959	C+
Roanoke College	VA	47,996	C+
Rutgers, The State Univ of New Jersey/New Brunswick	NJ	25,077	VC
Sacred Heart Univ	CT	48,564	VC
Saginaw Valley State Univ	MI	16,869	C
St. Louis Univ	MO	46,594	VC+
Salisbury Univ	MD	18,368	VC
Samford Univ	AL	35,700	VC+
San Diego State Univ	CA	20,578	VC
San Francisco State Univ	CA	18,514	C
Schreiner Univ	TX	32,734	LC
Seattle Pacific Univ	WA	41,559	VC+
Seattle Univ	WA	47,010	VC+
Shenandoah Univ	VA	39,268	C
Shippensburg Univ of Pennsylvania	PA	17,064	LC
Simmons College	MA	48,770	VC
Simpson College	IA	36,086	VC
Skidmore College	NY	57,926	HC
Smith College	MA	57,524	MC
S Dak State Univ	SD	14,296	C
Southern Illinois Univ Edwardsville	IL	17,532	C
Southern Nazarene Univ	OK	24,354	NC
Southwestern Adventist Univ	TX	23,026	LC
Southwestern Univ	TX	45,660	VC
Spring Arbor Univ	MI	26,740	C
St. Catherine Univ	MN	37,782	C+
St. Olaf College	MN	49,960	HC+
Sterling College	KS	27,216	C
Taylor Univ	IN	36,742	VC+
Tenn Wesleyan College	TN	21,250	C
Texas State Univ	TX	16,495	VC
Texas Tech Univ	TX	14,243	C
Texas Wesleyan Univ	TX	29,886	C
The College at Brockport / SUNY	NY	18,362	VC
The College of Idaho	ID	31,277	VC
Ohio State Univ	OH	19,887	MC
Towson Univ	MD	16,000	VC
Transylvania Univ	KY	40,310	VC+
Trevecca Nazarene Univ	TN	30,118	C
Trinity Washington Univ	DC	30,250	C+
Truman State Univ	MO	13,546	HC
Union College	KY	28,775	C
Univ at Buffalo / The SUNY	NY	20,283	VC
Univ of Akron	OH	20,436	C
Univ of Arkansas at Fayetteville	AR	16,860	VC
Univ of Arkansas at Monticello	AR	8,470	NC
Univ of Central Arkansas	AR	10,840	VC
Univ of Central Florida	FL	15,711	VC+
Univ of Central Okla	OK	12,293	C
Univ of Conn	CT	23,744	HC
Univ of Dayton	OH	43,750	VC
Univ of Evansville	IN	41,056	VC+
Univ of Florida	FL	15,783	HC+
Univ of Georgia	GA	19,508	VC
Univ of Hawaii at Manoa	HI	19,379	VC
Univ of Idaho	ID	14,558	C
Univ of Illinois at Chicago	IL	24,293	VC
Univ of Illinois at Urbana-Champaign	IL	24,300	HC
Univ of Indianapolis	IN	31,740	LC
Univ of Jamestown	ND	24,738	C
Univ of Louisiana at Monroe	LA	12,998	C
Univ of Mary	ND	16,714	C
Univ of Mary Hardin-Baylor	TX	31,950	C+
Univ of Mass Amherst	MA	23,697	VC+
Univ of Mass Boston	MA	11,966	C
Univ of Mass Lowell	MA	19,316	C
Univ of Miami	FL	55,166	MC
Univ of Mich/Ann Arbor	MI	22,102	HC+
Univ of Miss	MS	15,482	VC
Univ of Mount Union	OH	35,130	C
Univ of Nebr - Lincoln	NE	17,507	VC
Univ of Nevada, Las Vegas	NV	17,303	C
Univ of New England	ME	46,145	C+
Univ of New Mexico	NM	15,300	C
Univ of N Car at Chapel Hill	NC	18,348	MC
Univ of N Car at Charlotte	NC	15,847	C
Univ of N Car at Greensboro	NC	12,848	C
Univ of Northern Colo	CO	15,973	C
Univ of Puget Sound	WA	52,648	HC+
Univ of St. Francis	IN	29,810	C
Univ of San Francisco	CA	49,674	VC
Univ of Scranton	PA	51,940	VC
Univ of S Car at Aiken	SC	16,278	C
Univ of S Car at Columbia	SC	19,725	VC+
Univ of Southern Calif	CA	56,903	MC
Univ of Southern Indiana	IN	14,657	C
Univ of Tampa	FL	35,160	VC
Univ of Tulsa	OK	45,311	HC+
Univ of Utah	UT	13,462	VC
Univ of Vermont	VT	26,120	VC+
Univ of Wisc/Green Bay	WI	14,900	C
Univ of Wisc/La Crosse	WI	14,755	VC
Univ of Wisc/Superior	WI	14,106	C
Univ of Wisc-Milwaukee	WI	18,436	C
Ursinus College	PA	55,630	VC+
Valparaiso Univ	IN	43,040	VC+
Vanguard Univ of Southern Calif	CA	35,833	VC
Wake Forest Univ	NC	51,000	MC
Walsh Univ	OH	35,100	C
Warner Univ	FL	18,000	C
Washington Adventist Univ	MD	25,859	C+
Washington State Univ	WA	20,461	C
Wayne State College	NE	11,764	NC
Wayne State Univ	MI	19,493	C
Waynesburg Univ	PA	29,100	C
Wesley College	DE	31,115	LC
West Chester Univ of Pennsylvania	PA	16,836	C
West Texas A&M Univ	TX	13,478	C
Western Illinois Univ	IL	20,130	C
Western Mich Univ	MI	19,042	C
Westmont College	CA	41,500	HC
Willamette Univ	OR	56,450	VC+
Wilson College	PA	27,660	C
Winona State Univ	MN	16,530	C
Winthrop Univ	SC	21,120	VC
Wright State Univ	OH	16,983	C
York College / CUNY	NY	5,496	NC
Youngstown State Univ	OH	16,374	LC

EXPERIMENTAL PSYCHOLOGY

School	ST	$IS	SR
Blackburn College	IL	21,350	C
Immaculata Univ	PA	43,000	C
Prescott College	AZ	33,284	C+
Univ of Louisiana at Monroe	LA	12,998	C
Univ of S Car at Columbia	SC	19,725	VC+

FAMILY AND COMMUNITY SERVICES

School	ST	$IS	SR
Central Washington Univ	WA	11,730	C
East Carolina Univ	NC	14,169	C
John Brown Univ	AR	30,996	VC+
Kansas State Univ	KS	15,497	VC
Mich State Univ	MI	13,689	VC
Montclair State Univ	NJ	22,614	C
Ohio Univ	OH	20,676	VC
Point Loma Nazarene Univ	CA	38,610	VC
Prairie View A&M Univ	TX	15,205	LC
Purdue Univ/West Lafayette	IN	20,278	HC
Union Univ	TN	28,260	VC
Univ of Delaware	DE	22,728	VC
Univ of New Haven	CT	47,740	C
Univ of Northern Iowa	IA	14,776	C
Univ of Oregon	OR	20,872	VC

FAMILY/CONSUMER RESOURCE MANAGEMENT

School	ST	$IS	SR
Arizona State Univ	AZ	18,818	C+
Cal State, Northridge	CA	28,313	C
East Central Univ	OK	10,223	LC
Iowa State Univ	IA	16,403	C
Mich State Univ	MI	13,689	VC
Northwest Missouri State Univ	MO	14,229	C
Ohio State Univ at Lima	OH	7,140	C
Ohio Univ	OH	20,676	VC
Pittsburg State Univ	KS	12,032	C
Seattle Pacific Univ	WA	41,559	VC+
Seton Hill Univ	PA	35,172	C
S Dak State Univ	SD	14,296	C
Southern Illinois Univ Carbondale	IL	21,620	C
Texas Tech Univ	TX	14,243	C
Ohio State Univ	OH	19,887	MC
Univ of Hawaii at Manoa	HI	19,379	VC
Univ of Missouri/Columbia	MO	18,201	MC
West Virginia Univ	WV	15,794	C+

FAMILY/CONSUMER STUDIES

School	ST	$IS	SR
Abilene Christian Univ	TX	38,400	VC
Alabama A&M Univ	AL	96,100	C
Alderson Broaddus Univ	WV	28,656	C
Anderson Univ	IN	35,390	C
Andrews Univ	MI	28,030	C+
Appalachian State Univ	NC	12,919	VC
Ball State Univ	IN	17,850	C
Baylor Univ	TX	46,720	HC
Bluffton Univ	OH	37,864	C
Bowling Green State Univ	OH	18,970	C
Bradley Univ	IL	31,874	VC
Bridgewater College	VA	39,880	C
Brigham Young Univ	UT	12,100	HC
Cal State, Fresno	CA	17,405	C
Cal State, Northridge	CA	28,313	C
Campbell Univ	NC	25,500	C
Central Mich Univ	MI	18,066	C
Central Washington Univ	WA	11,730	C
College of the Ozarks	MO	5,605	VC
Colo State Univ-Fort Collins	CO	20,090	VC
Concordia Univ, Ann Arbor	MI	27,220	VC
Cornerstone Univ and Grand Rapids Theological Seminary	MI	30,866	C
Delta State Univ	MS	12,292	LC
East Central Univ	OK	10,223	LC
Eastern Illinois Univ	IL	20,502	C
Fairmont State Univ	WV	12,098	LC
Florida State Univ	FL	15,238	HC
Fontbonne Univ	MO	31,384	C
Framingham State Univ	MA	16,750	C
Freed-Hardeman Univ	TN	19,697	VC
Gallaudet Univ	DC	25,380	SP
George Fox Univ	OR	40,750	C+
Hampshire College	MA	58,320	MC
Henderson State Univ	AR	13,634	C
Idaho State Univ	ID	11,908	C
Illinois State Univ	IL	22,634	VC
Indiana Univ of Pennsylvania	PA	20,180	LC
Iowa State Univ	IA	16,403	C
Kansas State Univ	KS	15,497	VC
Lamar Univ	TX	6,820	LC
Liberty Univ	VA	19,101	C
Lipscomb Univ	TN	35,722	VC
Lubbock Christian Univ	TX	25,518	C
Madonna Univ	MI	24,540	VC
Marywood Univ	PA	40,695	C
Mercyhurst Univ	PA	40,700	C
Meredith College	NC	31,420	C
Messiah College	PA	39,540	VC
Miami Univ	OH	24,191	HC
Mich State Univ	MI	13,689	VC
Middle Tenn State Univ	TN	8,650	C
Minn State Univ, Mankato	MN	14,900	C
Miss College	MS	21,998	VC
Missouri State Univ	MO	13,996	VC
Mount Vernon Nazarene Univ	OH	29,590	C
New Mexico State Univ	NM	13,955	LC
Nicholls State Univ	LA	7,095	C
Northwestern State Univ of Louisiana	LA	14,368	C
Oakwood Univ	AL	23,035	C
Ohio Univ	OH	20,676	VC
Olivet Nazarene Univ	IL	29,990	C
Oregon State Univ	OR	19,017	C+
Oswego / SUNY	NY	20,009	VC
Pittsburg State Univ	KS	12,032	C
Purdue Univ/West Lafayette	IN	20,278	HC
Queens College / The CUNY	NY	17,107	VC
St. Joseph College	CT	45,630	LC
San Francisco State Univ	CA	18,514	C
Seattle Pacific Univ	WA	41,559	VC+
Seton Hill Univ	PA	35,172	C
Shepherd Univ	WV	14,996	C
S Dak State Univ	SD	14,296	C
Southeast Missouri State Univ	MO	14,983	LC
Southeastern Louisiana Univ	LA	13,325	C
Southern Univ and A&M College	LA	9,761	C+
St. Catherine Univ	MN	37,782	C+
Stephen F. Austin State Univ	TX	14,668	C
Tenn State Univ	TN	9,048	C
Texas State Univ	TX	16,495	VC
Texas Tech Univ	TX	14,243	C
Texas Woman's Univ	TX	13,633	LC
Ohio State Univ	OH	19,887	MC
Towson Univ	MD	16,000	VC
Univ of Akron	OH	20,436	C
Univ of Arizona	AZ	20,105	C
Univ of Arkansas at Pine Bluff	AR	10,600	C
Univ of Central Arkansas	AR	10,840	VC
Univ of Central Okla	OK	12,293	C
Univ of Idaho	ID	14,558	C
Univ of Illinois at Urbana-Champaign	IL	24,300	HC
Univ of Maryland	MD	18,801	HC
Univ of Miss	MS	15,482	VC
Univ of Montevallo	AL	17,320	C
Univ of Nebr - Lincoln	NE	17,507	VC
Univ of Nebr at Kearney	NE	14,855	LC
Univ of New Hampshire	NH	24,702	VC
Univ of New Mexico	NM	15,300	C
Univ of PR Recinto de Rio Piedras	PR	5,750	
Univ of Utah	UT	13,462	VC
Univ of Wisc/Madison	WI	18,757	HC
Univ of Wisc/Stevens Point	WI	14,043	C
Univ of Wisc/Stout	WI	23,942	C
Univ of Wyoming	WY	13,855	C+
Walsh Univ	OH	35,100	C
Washington State Univ	WA	20,461	C
Wayne State College	NE	11,764	NC
Western Illinois Univ	IL	20,130	C
Western Mich Univ	MI	19,042	C
Youngstown State Univ	OH	16,374	LC

FAMILY/JUVENILE JUSTICE

School	ST	$IS	SR
Univ of Akron	OH	20,436	C
Univ of New Haven	CT	47,740	C
William Woods Univ	MO		C

FASHION DESIGN AND TECHNOLOGY

School	ST	$IS	SR
Academy of Art Univ	CA		
American InterContinental Univ	GA	13,500	NC
Baylor Univ	TX	46,720	HC
Bennington College	VT	56,990	HC+
Bluffton Univ	OH	37,864	C
Calif College of the Arts	CA	48,334	SP
Cazenovia College	NY	30,800	C
Centenary College	NJ	38,618	LC
Columbus College of Art and Design	OH	37,732	SP
Dominican Univ	IL	37,628	C
Drexel Univ	PA	51,920	HC
Fashion Inst of Technology/SUNY	NY	12,468	SP
Florida State Univ	FL	15,238	HC
Framingham State Univ	MA	16,750	C
Howard Univ	DC	35,957	C
Illinois State Univ	IL	22,634	VC
Indiana Univ Bloomington	IN	19,358	HC
Iowa State Univ	IA	16,403	C
Kent State Univ	OH	19,352	C
Lasell College	MA	42,500	LC
Lindenwood Univ	MO	20,750	C
Marist College	NY	35,500	C
Marymount Univ	VA	36,178	C
Mass College of Art and Design	MA	23,600	SP
Missouri State Univ	MO	13,996	VC
Moore College of Art and Design	PA	38,124	SP
Mount Ida College	MA	30,115	LC
Mount Mary Univ	WI	32,836	LC

School	ST	$IS	SR
Otis College of Art and Design	CA	35,404	SP
Parsons The New School for Design	NY	56,610	SP
Philadelphia Univ	PA	44,160	C
Pratt Inst	NY	49,520	SP
Purdue Univ/West Lafayette	IN	20,278	HC
Savannah College of Art and Design	GA	46,824	SP
School of the Art Inst of Chicago	IL	44,000	SP
St. Catherine Univ	MN	37,782	C+
Stephens College	MO	34,500	VC
Stevenson Univ	MD	39,572	C
Syracuse Univ	NY	54,512	HC
Texas Woman's Univ	TX	13,633	LC
Univ of Delaware	DE	22,728	VC
Univ of North Texas	TX	15,628	C
Univ of the Incarnate Word	TX	35,200	LC
Ursuline College	OH	33,198	LC
Virginia Commonwealth Univ	VA	18,633	C
Washington Univ in St. Louis	MO	58,818	MC
Woodbury Univ	CA	34,500	LC

FASHION MERCHANDISING

School	ST	$IS	SR
Albright College	PA	46,660	C
American InterContinental Univ	GA	13,500	NC
Ashland Univ	OH	25,000	C
Auburn Univ	AL	20,052	VC+
Baylor Univ	TX	46,720	HC
Bluffton Univ	OH	37,864	C
Brenau Univ Women's College	GA	26,650	C+
Canisius College	NY	45,602	VC
Central Washington Univ	WA	11,730	C
Delaware State Univ	DE	14,700	LC
Dominican Univ	IL	37,628	C
Drexel Univ	PA	51,920	HC
Eastern Mich Univ	MI	17,961	C
Fashion Inst of Technology/SUNY	NY	12,468	SP
Florida State Univ	FL	15,238	HC
Fontbonne Univ	MO	31,384	C
Framingham State Univ	MA	16,750	C
Georgia Southern Univ	GA	16,414	C
Harding Univ	AR	21,432	C+
Howard Univ	DC	35,957	C
Immaculata Univ	PA	43,000	C
Indiana Inst of Technology	IN	34,240	LC
Indiana Univ of Pennsylvania	PA	20,180	LC
Iowa State Univ	IA	16,403	C
Johnson and Wales Univ/ Providence Campus	RI	34,668	C
Kent State Univ	OH	19,352	C
Lasell College	MA	42,500	LC
LIM College	NY	41,575	LC
Lipscomb Univ	TN	35,722	VC
Lynn Univ	FL	43,500	C
Marist College	NY	35,500	C
Mars Hill College	NC	22,950	LC
Marymount Univ	VA	36,178	C
Mercyhurst Univ	PA	40,700	C
Meredith College	NC	31,420	C
Missouri State Univ	MO	13,996	VC
Mount Ida College	MA	30,115	LC
Mount Mary Univ	WI	32,836	LC
New Mexico State Univ	NM	13,955	LC
Newbury College	MA	41,850	LC
Northwood Univ	MI	26,331	LC
Ohio Univ	OH	20,676	VC
Old Dominion Univ	VA	18,662	C
Olivet Nazarene Univ	IL	29,990	C
Philadelphia Univ	PA	44,160	C
Pittsburg State Univ	KS	12,032	C
Purdue Univ/West Lafayette	IN	20,278	HC
Sacred Heart Univ	CT	48,564	VC
Savannah College of Art and Design	GA	46,824	SP
Southern Illinois Univ Carbondale	IL	21,620	C
Southern New Hampshire Univ	NH	38,100	C
St. Catherine Univ	MN	37,782	C+
Stephen F. Austin State Univ	TX	14,668	C
Stephens College	MO	34,500	VC
Stevenson Univ	MD	39,572	C
SUNY Oneonta / SUNY	NY	16,919	VC
Tarleton State Univ	TX	13,489	LC
Texas A&M Univ at Kingsville	TX	7,500	LC
Texas Christian Univ	TX	47,570	HC
Texas State Univ	TX	16,495	VC
Texas Woman's Univ	TX	13,633	LC
Ohio State Univ	OH	19,887	MC
Univ of Akron	OH	20,436	C
Univ of Bridgeport	CT	39,030	LC
Univ of Central Okla	OK	12,293	C
Univ of Georgia	GA	19,508	VC
Univ of Louisiana at Lafayette	LA	6,130	C
Univ of Nebr - Lincoln	NE	17,507	VC
Univ of the Incarnate Word	TX	35,200	LC
Ursuline College	OH	33,198	LC
Utah State Univ	UT	11,803	C
West Virginia Univ	WV	15,794	C+
Western Mich Univ	MI	19,042	C
Western Washington Univ	WA	18,519	VC
Woodbury Univ	CA	34,500	LC
Youngstown State Univ	OH	16,374	LC

FEMINIST, GENDER, SEXUALITY STUDIES

School	ST	$IS	SR
Bryant Univ	RI	49,179	VC
Cornell Univ	NY	59,037	MC

FIBER SCIENCE AND APPAREL DESIGN

School	ST	$IS	SR
Cornell Univ	NY	59,037	MC

FIBER/TEXTILES/WEAVING

School	ST	$IS	SR
Adams State College	CO	13,358	LC
Fashion Inst of Technology/SUNY	NY	12,468	SP
Florida State Univ	FL	15,238	HC
Kansas City Art Inst	MO	38,000	SP
Kutztown Univ of Pennsylvania	PA	16,909	LC
Maryland Inst College of Art	MD	39,500	SP
Mass College of Art and Design	MA	23,600	SP
Savannah College of Art and Design	GA	46,824	SP
School of the Art Inst of Chicago	IL	44,000	SP
Temple Univ	PA	24,392	VC
Univ of Kansas	KS	16,980	C+
Univ of Mass Dartmouth	MA	22,223	C
Univ of Mich/Ann Arbor	MI	22,102	HC+
Univ of Oregon	OR	20,872	VC

FILM ARTS

School	ST	$IS	SR
American Univ	DC	54,829	HC+
Arizona State Univ	AZ	18,818	C+
Art Center College of Design	CA	34,044	SP
Bard College	NY	59,872	HC
Bennington College	VT	56,990	HC+
Berklee College of Music	MA	47,100	SP
Binghamton Univ / The SUNY	NY	20,832	HC+
Biola Univ	CA	40,320	VC
Boston College	MA	58,506	MC
Boston Univ	MA	54,130	HC+
Bowling Green State Univ	OH	18,970	C
Brandeis Univ	MA	58,820	HC
Burlington College	VT	32,510	SP
Calif Baptist Univ	CA	35,890	C
Calif College of the Arts	CA	48,334	SP
Cal State, Long Beach	CA	17,534	C+
Cal State, Northridge	CA	28,313	C
Calvin College	MI	37,585	VC+
Champlain College	VT	44,850	VC
Chapman Univ	CA	56,019	VC+
CUNY/Brooklyn College	NY	5,884	C+
Claremont McKenna College	CA	58,065	MC
Clark Univ	MA	47,020	HC+
Coe College	IA	43,590	VC
College of Staten Island / The CUNY	NY	16,778	NC
Colo College	CO	54,534	MC
Columbia College Chicago	IL	30,940	LC
Columbia Univ in the City of New York	NY	61,116	MC
Columbia Univ/Barnard College	NY	39,000	MC
Columbia Univ/School of General Studies	NY	54,083	MC
Columbus College of Art and Design	OH	37,732	SP
Concordia Univ - Irvine	CA	35,390	VC
Conn College	CT	54,970	MC
Cornell Univ	NY	59,037	MC
CUNY-City College	NY	19,576	HC+
Dartmouth College	NH	57,996	MC
De Sales Univ	PA	42,670	C
Denison Univ	OH	54,670	HC+
Dominican Univ	IL	37,628	C
Drexel Univ	PA	51,920	HC
Eastern Mich Univ	MI	17,961	C
Elon Univ	NC	40,046	HC
Emerson College	MA	50,246	HC
Emory Univ	GA	45,000	MC
Fairleigh Dickinson Univ/ College at Florham	NJ	42,142	C
Florida State Univ	FL	15,238	HC
George Fox Univ	OR	40,750	C+
George Mason Univ	VA	15,724	VC
Georgia State Univ	GA	12,000	VC
Grand Valley State Univ	MI	17,998	VC
Hampshire College	MA	58,320	MC
Hofstra Univ	NY	48,020	VC+
Hollins Univ	VA	43,295	VC
Howard Univ	DC	35,957	C
Hunter College / The CUNY	NY	14,429	VC
Huntington Univ	IN	32,220	C
Ithaca College	NY	52,300	HC
Kean Univ	NJ	22,060	LC
Keene State College	NH	21,538	C
Kenyon College	OH	56,810	MC
Le Moyne College	NY	42,200	VC
LIU/C.W. Post Campus	NY	38,888	C
Lynn Univ	FL	43,500	C
Mass College of Art and Design	MA	23,600	SP
Memphis College of Art	TN	33,550	SP
Middlebury College	VT	57,470	MC
Minneapolis College of Art and Design	MN	36,700	SP
Minn State Univ, Moorhead	MN	13,392	C
Montclair State Univ	NJ	22,614	C
Mount Holyoke College	MA	53,596	HC+
Mount St. Mary's College/ Chalon Campus	CA	43,897	VC+
Muhlenberg College	PA	52,837	HC
New Mexico State Univ	NM	13,955	LC
New York Univ	NY	61,470	MC
Northeastern Univ	MA	55,296	MC
Oakland Univ	MI	19,391	VC
Oberlin College	OH	57,025	MC
Ohio Univ	OH	20,676	VC
Okla City Univ	OK	33,546	VC
Old Dominion Univ	VA	18,662	C
Oral Roberts Univ	OK	31,734	C
Oswego / SUNY	NY	20,009	VC
Pace Univ	NY	48,094	VC
Palm Beach Atlantic Univ	FL	33,882	LC
Penn State Univ/Univ Park	PA	25,404	VC
Pepperdine Univ	CA	55,372	HC+
Pitzer College	CA	54,988	MC
Point Park Univ	PA	36,390	C
Pratt Inst	NY	49,520	SP
Purchase College / SUNY	NY	16,951	C
Purdue Univ/West Lafayette	IN	20,278	HC
Queens College / The CUNY	NY	17,107	VC
Rhode Island College	RI	17,132	LC
Rhode Island School of Design	RI	55,204	SP
Rochester Inst of Technology	NY	42,450	VC+
San Francisco Art Inst	CA	52,492	SP
San Francisco State Univ	CA	18,514	C
San Jose State Univ	CA	19,707	C
Santa Fe Univ of Art and Design	NM	39,666	SP
Sarah Lawrence College	NY	48,000	HC
Savannah College of Art and Design	GA	46,824	SP
School of the Art Inst of Chicago	IL	44,000	SP
School of Visual Arts	NY	36,500	SP
Seattle Univ	WA	47,010	VC+
Smith College	MA	57,524	MC
Southern Adventist Univ	TN	26,190	C
Southern Illinois Univ Carbondale	IL	21,620	C
Southern Methodist Univ	TX	57,755	MC
Spring Arbor Univ	MI	26,740	C
St. Mary's College of Maryland	MD	26,699	HC
Stanford Univ	CA	56,411	MC
Stephens College	MO	34,500	VC
Stevenson Univ	MD	39,572	C
Stony Brook Univ / SUNY	NY	19,359	HC
Suffolk Univ	MA	46,548	C
SUNY Cortland / The SUNY	NY	19,117	C
Swarthmore College	PA	57,870	MC
Syracuse Univ	NY	54,512	HC
Taylor Univ	IN	36,742	VC+
Temple Univ	PA	24,392	VC
Tulane Univ	LA	58,942	MC
Univ at Buffalo / The SUNY	NY	20,283	VC
Univ of Alaska Fairbanks	AK	13,955	C
Univ of Arizona	AZ	20,105	C
Univ of Calif at Berkeley	CA	23,322	MC
Univ of Calif at Irvine	CA	25,961	VC
Univ of Calif at Los Angeles	CA	25,686	MC
Univ of Calif at Riverside	CA	27,204	C
Univ of Calif at Santa Barbara	CA	27,551	HC
Univ of Calif at Santa Cruz	CA	27,807	VC
Univ of Central Florida	FL	15,711	VC+
Univ of Chicago	IL	55,416	MC
Univ of Colo Boulder	CO	22,605	VC+
Univ of Denver	CO	51,787	VC+
Univ of Hartford	CT	42,674	C
Univ of Illinois at Chicago	IL	24,293	VC
Univ of Illinois at Urbana-Champaign	IL	24,300	HC
Univ of Iowa	IA	17,481	VC
Univ of Kansas	KS	16,980	C+
Univ of Maryland	MD	18,801	HC
Univ of Miami	FL	55,166	MC
Univ of Mich/Ann Arbor	MI	22,102	HC+
Univ of Minn/Twin Cities	MN		HC
Univ of Nebr - Lincoln	NE	17,507	VC
Univ of Nevada, Las Vegas	NV	17,303	C
Univ of N Car at Wilmington	NC	13,572	VC+
Univ of N Car School of the Arts	NC	7,401	SP
Univ of Notre Dame	IN		MC
Univ of Okla	OK	17,634	VC+
Univ of Oregon	OR	20,872	VC
Univ of Pittsburgh at Pittsburgh	PA	27,800	HC+
Univ of Rochester	NY	58,500	MC
Univ of Southern Calif	CA	56,903	MC
Univ of Tampa	FL	35,160	VC
Univ of Texas at Austin	TX	44,074	HC
Univ of the Arts	PA	38,450	SP
Univ of Toledo	OH	18,464	C
Univ of Tulsa	OK	45,311	HC+
Univ of Utah	UT	13,462	VC
Univ of Vermont	VT	26,120	VC+
Univ of Wisc-Milwaukee	WI	18,436	C
Vassar College	NY	59,070	MC
Virginia Commonwealth Univ	VA	18,633	C
Washington Univ in St. Louis	MO	58,818	MC
Wayne State Univ	MI	19,493	C
Webster Univ	MO	33,990	C+
Wellesley College	MA	49,848	MC
Wesleyan Univ	CT	59,844	MC
Wheaton College	MA	54,934	HC+
Whitman College	WA	54,400	MC
Wright State Univ	OH	16,983	C
Yale Univ	CT	55,300	MC

FILM, TELEVISION AND DIGITAL MEDIA

School	ST	$IS	SR
Amherst College	MA	58,744	MC
Asbury Univ	KY	32,038	VC
Baldwin Wallace Univ	OH	36,980	VC
Chapman Univ	CA	56,019	VC+
Chatham Univ	PA	42,440	VC
Cleveland State Univ	OH	21,357	C
Dordt College	IA	34,160	VC
Mercy College	NY	29,996	C
Messiah College	PA	39,540	VC
Northern Arizona Univ	AZ	18,592	C
Southern Oregon Univ	OR	17,874	C
St. John's Univ	NY	52,840	C+
Taylor Univ	IN	36,742	VC+
Texas Christian Univ	TX	47,570	HC
Univ of Illinois at Chicago	IL	24,293	VC
Univ of Nebr - Lincoln	NE	17,507	VC
Univ of New Mexico	NM	15,300	C
Univ of Pikeville	KY	24,750	NC

FINANCE

School	ST	$IS	SR
Abilene Christian Univ	TX	38,400	VC
Baldwin Wallace Univ	OH	36,980	VC
Belmont Univ	TN	37,380	VC+
Bentley Univ	MA	54,555	HC+
Berry College	GA	39,254	HC
Bethany College	KS	30,605	NC
Bethany College	WV	35,282	C
Binghamton Univ / The SUNY	NY	20,832	HC+
Boise State Univ	ID	12,802	C
Bridgewater State Univ	MA	18,752	C
Bryant Univ	RI	49,179	VC
Cabrini College	PA	40,859	LC
Cal State, Chico	CA	18,952	C
Cal State, Fullerton	CA	25,188	C+
Canisius College	NY	45,602	VC
Case Western Reserve Univ	OH	55,178	MC
Cedarville Univ	OH	31,036	VC+
Centenary College of Louisiana	LA	39,070	C+
Central Conn State Univ	CT	19,212	C
Christopher Newport Univ	VA	21,050	VC
Clarkson Univ	NY	53,538	HC
Cleveland State Univ	OH	21,357	C
College of St. Scholastica	MN	39,960	C
Columbia College	MO	24,578	C
Culver-Stockton College	MO	30,900	C
Dallas Baptist Univ	TX	29,118	C
DePaul Univ	IL	46,120	VC
Dominican Univ	IL	37,628	C
Elmhurst College	IL	42,032	C+
Elon Univ	NC	40,046	HC
Endicott College	MA	42,390	C
Fairfield Univ	CT	55,850	VC
Ferris State Univ	MI	19,698	C
Fordham Univ	NY	58,927	HC
Georgetown Univ	DC	52,910	MC
Georgia Southern Univ	GA	16,414	C
Gordon College	MA	42,660	VC+
Grove City College	PA	22,988	HC
Holy Family Univ	PA	40,030	LC
Indiana Univ Bloomington	IN	19,358	HC
Indiana Univ East	IN	6,639	LC
Indiana Univ Kokomo	IN	6,674	LC
Indiana Univ of Pennsylvania	PA	20,180	LC
Indiana Univ South Bend	IN	15,293	C

ST = STATE **$IS** = IN-STATE COSTS **SR** = SELECTOR RATING

School	ST	$IS	SR
Indiana Univ Southeast	IN	15,807	LC
Indiana Univ-Purdue Univ Indianapolis	IN	17,290	C
Iona College	NY	44,028	C
Jackson State Univ	MS	13,512	LC
John Carroll Univ	OH	44,520	C+
Kean Univ	NJ	22,060	LC
Kennesaw State Univ	GA	13,017	VC
Lake Erie College	OH	35,704	C
Lake Forest College	IL	45,580	VC
Lehigh Univ	PA	55,080	MC
Limestone College	SC	29,880	C
Lipscomb Univ	TN	35,722	VC
Lourdes Univ	OH	26,055	LC
Loyola Univ Chicago	IL	49,560	VC+
Lubbock Christian Univ	TX	25,518	C
Marquette Univ	WI	43,664	VC+
Marshall Univ	WV	14,820	C
Menlo College	CA	49,002	C
Mercer Univ	GA	44,201	VC+
Millikin Univ	IL	37,462	C
Missouri State Univ	MO	13,996	VC
Molloy College	NY	38,950	C
Mount Mercy Univ	IA	34,385	C
Mount Vernon Nazarene Univ	OH	29,590	C
Nazareth College of Rochester	NY	41,590	VC
New York Univ	NY	61,470	MC
North Central College	IL	38,343	VC
N Dak State Univ	ND	14,642	C
Northern Arizona Univ	AZ	18,592	C
Northern Kentucky Univ	KY	15,302	LC
Northwood Univ	FL	30,746	LC
Nova Southeastern Univ	FL	34,016	VC
Ohio Univ	OH	20,676	VC
Oswego / SUNY	NY	20,009	VC
Pace Univ	NY	48,094	VC
Point Park Univ	PA	36,390	C
Queens Univ of Charlotte	NC	39,543	VC
Quinnipiac Univ	CT	53,580	VC
Rutgers, The State Univ of New Jersey/New Brunswick	NJ	25,077	VC
Rutgers, The State Univ of New Jersey/Newark Campus	NJ	25,376	C
Saginaw Valley State Univ	MI	16,869	C
St. Joseph's Univ	PA	52,272	VC
St. Louis Univ	MO	46,594	VC+
St. Mary's Univ of Minn	MN	37,015	C
Samford Univ	AL	35,700	VC+
San Diego State Univ	CA	20,578	VC
Santa Clara Univ	CA	54,702	MC
Seattle Univ	WA	47,010	VC+
Seton Hall Univ	NJ	45,902	C
Simmons College	MA	48,770	VC
Southeast Missouri State Univ	MO	14,983	LC
St. John's Univ	NY	52,840	C+
SUNY Fredonia / The SUNY at Fredonia	NY	18,702	VC
SUNY Plattsburgh / SUNY	NY	18,083	VC
Syracuse Univ	NY	54,512	HC
Taylor Univ	IN	36,742	VC+
Temple Univ	PA	24,392	VC
Texas Christian Univ	TX	47,570	HC
The Catholic Univ of America	DC	52,852	VC
The College at Brockport / SUNY	NY	18,362	VC
The Lincoln Univ	PA	15,154	LC
Thomas College	ME	26,270	LC
Thomas Edison State College	NJ	5,700	SP
Univ of Arizona	AZ	20,105	C
Univ of Arkansas at Fayetteville	AR	16,860	VC
Univ of Central Okla	OK	12,293	C
Univ of Charleston	WV	28,650	C
Univ of Colo Boulder	CO	22,605	VC+
Univ of Denver	CO	51,787	VC+
Univ of Evansville	IN	41,056	VC+
Univ of Georgia	GA	19,508	VC
Univ of Illinois at Chicago	IL	24,293	VC
Univ of Kansas	KS	16,980	C+
Univ of Louisiana at Monroe	LA	12,998	C
Univ of Mary Hardin-Baylor	TX	31,950	C+
Univ of Mass Dartmouth	MA	22,223	C
Univ of Miami	FL	55,166	MC
Univ of Miss	MS	15,482	VC
Univ of Missouri-St. Louis	MO	18,304	VC
Univ of Nebr - Lincoln	NE	17,507	VC
Univ of N Car at Charlotte	NC	15,847	C
Univ of N Car at Greensboro	NC	12,848	C
Univ of North Florida	FL	15,578	VC
Univ of Pittsburgh at Pittsburgh	PA	27,800	HC+
Univ of San Diego	CA	53,302	HC+
Univ of South Florida/St. Petersburg	FL	12,769	VC
Univ of Southern Indiana	IN	14,657	C
Univ of St. Thomas - Houston	TX	36,490	VC
Univ of Tenn at Knoxville	TN	20,364	VC+
Univ of Texas at San Antonio	TX	18,372	C
Univ of Texas-Pan American	TX	12,432	LC
Univ of Utah	UT	13,462	VC
Univ of West Georgia	GA	14,852	LC
Univ of Wisc/Green Bay	WI	14,900	C
Univ of Wisc/Superior	WI	14,106	C
Univ of Wisc-Milwaukee	WI	18,436	C
Univ of Wyoming	WY	13,855	C+
Valparaiso Univ	IN	43,040	VC+
Waynesburg Univ	PA	29,100	C
Webster Univ	MO	33,990	C+
Western Illinois Univ	IL	20,130	C
Western Mich Univ	MI	19,042	C
Western New England Univ	MA	45,590	C
Widener Univ	PA	50,368	C
Wingate Univ	NC	34,990	C
Wofford College	SC	45,795	VC

FINANCIAL INSTITUTIONS MANAGEMENT

School	ST	$IS	SR
Thomas Edison State College	NJ	5,700	SP

FINANCIAL SERVICES

School	ST	$IS	SR
Bryant Univ	RI	49,179	VC
San Diego State Univ	CA	20,578	VC

FINE ARTS

School	ST	$IS	SR
Abilene Christian Univ	TX	38,400	VC
Academy of Art Univ	CA		
Adelphi Univ	NY	43,130	VC
Alabama State Univ	AL	14,142	NC
Albany State Univ	GA	8,500	C
Albertus Magnus College	CT	37,382	LC
Alfred Univ	NY	40,392	VC
American Univ	DC	54,829	HC+
Amherst College	MA	58,744	MC
Anderson Univ	IN	35,390	C
Aquinas College	MI	33,060	C
Arcadia Univ	PA	33,570	C+
Arizona State Univ	AZ	18,818	C+
Arkansas State Univ	AR	14,980	C
Art Academy of Cincinnati	OH	25,940	SP
Art Center College of Design	CA	34,044	SP
Ashland Univ	OH	25,000	C
Auburn Univ	AL	20,052	VC+
Auburn Univ at Montgomery	AL	12,120	C
Bellarmine Univ	KY	42,950	VC
Bellevue Univ	NE	4,600	NC
Bemidji State Univ	MN	13,500	C
Benedictine Univ	IL	35,220	C
Bennington College	VT	56,990	HC+
Bethany College	WV	35,282	C
Biola Univ	CA	40,320	VC
Black Hills State Univ	SD	13,562	LC
Bloomfield College	NJ	36,960	C
Blue Mountain College	MS	13,550	LC
Bluefield College	VA	17,230	C+
Boise State Univ	ID	12,802	C
Bowie State Univ	MD	23,990	LC
Bowling Green State Univ	OH	18,970	C
Brenau Univ Women's College	GA	26,650	C+
Bridgewater State Univ	MA	18,752	C
Brigham Young Univ	UT	12,100	HC
Brigham Young Univ/Hawaii	HI	8,614	VC
Bryn Mawr College	PA	57,760	MC
Bucknell Univ	PA	58,160	MC
Buffalo State/State Univ of Buffalo	NY	15,733	C+
Burlington College	VT	32,510	SP
Caldwell College	NJ	35,602	LC
Calif Inst of the Arts	CA	46,368	SP
Cal State, Chico	CA	18,952	C
Cal State, Fullerton	CA	25,188	C+
Cal State, Stanislaus	CA	18,582	C
Calvin College	MI	37,585	VC+
Canisius College	NY	45,602	VC
Cardinal Stritch Univ	WI	24,054	C
Carnegie Mellon Univ	PA	51,260	MC
Carson-Newman Univ	TN	29,058	C+
Carthage College	WI	33,000	C
Cedar Crest College	PA	43,240	C
Central Washington Univ	WA	11,730	C
Centre College	KY	35,000	HC+
Champlain College	VT	44,850	VC
Charleston Southern Univ	SC	22,420	C
Christopher Newport Univ	VA	21,050	VC
Clark Univ	MA	47,020	HC+
Clemson Univ	SC	19,136	HC
Coastal Carolina Univ	SC	17,620	C
College for Creative Studies	MI		SP
College of Art and Design at Lesley Univ	MA	39,730	SP
College of Mount St. Joseph	OH	33,880	C
College of New Jersey	NJ	25,376	HC
College of St. Elizabeth	NJ	43,839	LC
College of Visual Arts - School is Closed	MN	24,310	SP
College of Wooster	OH	52,600	VC
Colo State Univ-Fort Collins	CO	20,090	VC
Columbia College	MO	24,578	C
Columbus College of Art and Design	OH	37,732	SP
Concordia Univ Nebr	NE	26,000	VC
Converse College	SC	37,130	C
Cooper Union for the Advancement of Science and Art	NY	55,600	MC
Corcoran College of Art and Design	DC	36,500	SP
Cornell College	IA	44,930	HC
Cornell Univ	NY	59,037	MC
Cornerstone Univ and Grand Rapids Theological Seminary	MI	30,866	C
Cornish College of the Arts	WA	21,200	SP
Creighton Univ	NE	44,058	VC+
Culver-Stockton College	MO	30,900	C
Cumberland Univ	TN	21,220	C
CUNY-City College	NY	19,576	HC+
Daemen College	NY	31,510	C
Dallas Baptist Univ	TX	29,118	C
Denison Univ	OH	54,670	HC+
DePaul Univ	IL	46,120	VC
Dickinson State Univ	ND	8,550	NC
Dominican Univ	IL	37,628	C
Dordt College	IA	34,160	VC
Dowling College	NY	25,000	LC
Drury Univ	MO	30,319	VC
East Stroudsburg Univ of Pennsylvania	PA	16,636	C
East Tenn State Univ	TN	9,000	C
Eastern Mich Univ	MI	17,961	C
Edinboro Univ of Pennsylvania	PA	15,940	LC
Elizabethtown College	PA	47,600	VC
Elmira College	NY	49,950	C+
Elms College	MA	23,900	VC
Emory Univ	GA	45,000	MC
Endicott College	MA	42,390	C
Eureka College	IL	19,280	C
Fairleigh Dickinson Univ/College at Florham	NJ	42,142	C
Fairleigh Dickinson Univ/Metropolitan Campus	NJ	40,254	C
Felician College	NJ	41,640	C
Ferris State Univ	MI	19,698	C
Fisk Univ	TN	19,830	C
Flagler College	FL	24,960	VC
Florida A&M Univ	FL	14,935	LC
Florida Atlantic Univ	FL	17,339	C
Florida International Univ	FL	17,747	VC
Florida Memorial Univ	FL	20,716	LC
Fontbonne Univ	MO	31,384	C
Fordham Univ	NY	58,927	HC
Fort Hays State Univ	KS	11,354	C
Franklin and Marshall College	PA	58,295	MC
Franklin Pierce Univ	NH	41,598	C
Freed-Hardeman Univ	TN	19,697	VC
Friends Univ	KS	29,100	C
George Washington Univ	DC	57,108	MC
Georgetown Univ	DC	52,910	MC
Georgia Southwestern State Univ	GA	12,218	C
Georgia State Univ	GA	12,000	VC
Goddard College	VT	16,418	VC
Grand Valley State Univ	MI	17,998	VC
Green Mountain College	VT	33,547	LC
Gustavus Adolphus College	MN	48,170	HC
Hamline Univ	MN	44,198	VC
Hampden-Sydney College	VA	48,848	C
Hampshire College	MA	58,320	MC
Harding Univ	AR	21,432	C+
Harvard Univ/Harvard College	MA	49,000	MC
Hastings College	NE	27,782	C+
Haverford College	PA	59,236	MC
High Point Univ	NC	39,800	C
Hillsdale College	MI	31,890	HC+
Hobart and William Smith Colleges	NY	43,000	VC
Hofstra Univ	NY	48,020	VC+
Hope College	MI	36,320	VC+
Humboldt State Univ	CA	18,400	C
Hunter College / The CUNY	NY	14,429	VC
Huntington Univ	IN	32,220	C
Illinois College	IL	25,770	VC
Indiana State Univ	IN	16,000	C
Indiana Univ Bloomington	IN	19,358	HC
Indiana Univ East	IN	6,639	LC
Indiana Univ Kokomo	IN	6,674	LC
Indiana Univ Northwest	IN	6,738	LC
Indiana Univ of Pennsylvania	PA	20,180	LC
Indiana Univ South Bend	IN	15,293	C
Indiana Univ Southeast	IN	15,807	LC
Indiana Univ-Purdue Univ Fort Wayne	IN	15,425	C
Indiana Univ-Purdue Univ Indianapolis	IN	17,290	C
Inter-American Univ of PR/San Germán	PR	6,720	
Iowa State Univ	IA	16,403	C
Iowa Wesleyan College	IA	30,850	LC
Ithaca College	NY	52,300	HC
James Madison Univ	VA	18,049	VC
Johnson State College	VT	16,721	C
Judson Univ	IL	25,130	C
Kean Univ	NJ	22,060	LC
Kendall College of Art and Design of Ferris State Univ	MI	21,048	SP
Kentucky State Univ	KY	11,000	LC
Kentucky Wesleyan College	KY	27,440	VC+
Kutztown Univ of Pennsylvania	PA	16,909	LC
La Salle Univ	PA	50,270	C
La Sierra Univ	CA	35,694	VC
Lake Erie College	OH	35,704	C
Lake Superior State Univ	MI	18,121	C
Lamar Univ	TX	6,820	LC
Lehman College / The CUNY	NY	5,778	LC
Lewis & Clark College	OR	52,656	VC
Lincoln Memorial Univ	TN	18,144	C
Lincoln Univ	MO	11,996	NC
Lock Haven Univ of Pennsylvania	PA	17,587	LC
LIU/Brooklyn Campus	NY	26,500	C
LIU/C.W. Post Campus	NY	38,888	C
Louisiana State Univ in Shreveport	LA	5,606	C
Louisiana Tech Univ	LA	8,000	C
Loyola Univ Chicago	IL	49,560	VC+
Loyola Univ Maryland	MD		VC
Loyola Univ New Orleans	LA	46,581	VC
Madonna Univ	MI	24,540	VC
Maharishi Univ of Management	IA	31,000	VC
Marist College	NY	35,500	C
Marlboro College	VT	35,980	VC
Martin Univ	IN	11,000	SP
Maryland Inst College of Art	MD	39,500	SP
Marylhurst Univ	OR	18,945	NC
Marymount Manhattan College	NY	40,118	VC
Mass College of Art and Design	MA	23,600	SP
Mass College of Liberal Arts	MA	16,733	C
McDaniel College	MD	45,600	VC
Memphis College of Art	TN	33,550	SP
Mercy College	NY	29,996	C
Meredith College	NC	31,420	C
Metropolitan State Univ of Denver	CO	4,835	LC
Midland Univ	NE	34,000	C
Midwestern State Univ	TX	9,722	C
Milligan College	TN	27,510	C
Milwaukee Inst of Art and Design	WI	31,938	SP
Minn State Univ, Moorhead	MN	13,392	C
Miss Univ for Women	MS	7,400	LC
Miss Valley State Univ	MS	9,706	LC
Missouri Southern State Univ	MO	11,910	C
Missouri Western State Univ	MO	12,260	NC
Montana State Univ	MT	14,068	VC
Montana State Univ-Northern	MT	12,500	NC
Montclair State Univ	NJ	22,614	C
Montserrat College of Art	MA	31,000	SP
Moore College of Art and Design	PA	38,124	SP
Morgan State Univ	MD	14,500	VC
Mount Mary Univ	WI	32,836	LC
Mount Olive College	NC	18,426	C
Mount St. Mary's Univ	MD	46,158	C
Murray State Univ	KY	14,944	C
National Louis Univ	IL	16,915	LC
Nazareth College of Rochester	NY	41,590	VC
New England College	NH	45,930	LC
New Jersey City Univ	NJ	21,060	C+
New Mexico State Univ	NM	13,955	LC
New York Inst of Technology	NY	40,590	VC
New York Univ	NY	61,470	MC
Norfolk State Univ	VA	10,531	LC
Northeastern State Univ	OK	8,615	VC
Northern Kentucky Univ	KY	15,302	LC
Northern Mich Univ	MI	15,300	VC
Northern State Univ	SD	14,021	C
Northland College	WI	26,680	C
Northwest Missouri State Univ	MO	14,229	C
Northwestern State Univ of Louisiana	LA	14,368	C
Northwestern Univ	IL	37,595	MC
Notre Dame de Namur Univ	CA	41,610	LC
Nova Southeastern Univ	FL	34,016	VC
Oakland City Univ	IN	24,500	NC
Oberlin College	OH	57,025	MC
Ohio Northern Univ	OH	42,075	VC

School	ST	$IS	SR
Ohio Wesleyan Univ	OH	49,460	C+
Okla Baptist Univ	OK	28,202	VC
Okla Panhandle State Univ	OK	8,996	NC
Old Dominion Univ	VA	18,662	C
Olivet College	MI	19,984	C
Our Lady of the Lake Univ of San Antonio	TX	22,430	LC
Pace Univ	NY	48,094	VC
Pacific Lutheran Univ	WA	44,840	VC
Pacific Northwest College of Art	OR	38,494	SP
Pacific Union College	CA	28,150	VC
Park Univ	MO	17,525	C
Parsons The New School for Design	NY	56,610	SP
Piedmont College	GA	29,260	C
Pomona College	CA	57,680	MC
Pontifical Catholic Univ of PR	PR	7,310	
Portland State Univ	OR	18,672	C
Pratt Inst	NY	49,520	SP
Prescott College	AZ	33,284	C+
Principia College	IL	35,140	C+
Purdue Univ/West Lafayette	IN	20,278	HC
Radford Univ	VA	17,132	LC
Richard Stockton College of New Jersey	NJ	20,000	VC
Rider Univ	NJ	45,720	C
Ringling College of Art and Design	FL	46,130	SP
Roberts Wesleyan College	NY	37,384	C+
Rochester Inst of Technology	NY	42,450	VC+
Rocky Mountain College of Art and Design	CO	22,470	NC
Rosemont College	PA	42,350	C
Rowan Univ	NJ	23,570	VC
Saginaw Valley State Univ	MI	16,869	C
St. Anselm College	NH	48,324	VC
St. Augustine's Univ	NC	14,000	C
St. Louis Univ	MO	46,594	VC+
St. Mary's College	IN	45,160	VC
St. Michael's College	VT	48,740	VC
St. Peter's College	NJ	44,240	C
St. Vincent College	PA	40,244	C
Salem State College	MA	13,161	LC
Salisbury Univ	MD	18,368	VC
San Jose State Univ	CA	19,707	C
Santa Fe Univ of Art and Design	NM	39,666	SP
Sarah Lawrence College	NY	48,000	HC
School of Visual Arts	NY	36,500	SP
Seattle Pacific Univ	WA	41,559	VC+
Seattle Univ	WA	47,010	VC+
Seton Hall Univ	NJ	45,902	C
Seton Hill Univ	PA	35,172	C
Sewanee: The Univ of the South	TN	47,700	HC+
Shawnee State Univ	OH	16,545	NC
Siena Heights Univ	MI	17,000	LC
Sierra Nevada College	NV	32,700	VC
Silver Lake College	WI	22,600	LC
Slippery Rock Univ of Pennsylvania	PA	10,360	LC
Sonoma State Univ	CA	20,541	C
S Car State Univ	SC	6,700	LC
Southeastern Okla State Univ	OK	7,966	C
Southern Adventist Univ	TN	26,190	C
Southern Conn State Univ	CT	18,033	C
Southern Illinois Univ Carbondale	IL	21,620	C
Southern Oregon Univ	OR	17,874	C
Southern Univ and A&M College	LA	9,761	C+
Southern Univ at New Orleans	LA	1,000	NC
Spelman College	GA	24,650	VC
Springfield College	MA	25,000	C
St. Ambrose Univ	IA		C
St. Catherine Univ	MN	37,782	C+
St. Cloud State Univ	MN	10,600	C
St. John's Univ	NY	52,840	C+
St. Lawrence Univ	NY	53,740	HC
St. Thomas Aquinas College	NY	30,000	C
Stanford Univ	CA	56,411	MC
Stonehill College	MA	46,780	VC+
Suffolk Univ	MA	46,548	C
Sul Ross State Univ	TX	13,410	LC
SUNY Fredonia / The SUNY at Fredonia	NY	18,702	VC
SUNY Oneonta / SUNY	NY	16,919	VC
Syracuse Univ	NY	54,512	HC
Tarleton State Univ	TX	13,489	LC
Taylor Univ	IN	36,742	VC+
Tenn Tech Univ	TN	11,310	C
Texas A&M Univ at Commerce	TX	10,496	C
Texas A&M Univ at Kingsville	TX	7,500	LC
Texas Woman's Univ	TX	13,633	LC
Ohio State Univ	OH	19,887	MC
The SUNY at Potsdam	NY	17,754	C
Trinity College	CT		HC+
Truman State Univ	MO	13,546	HC
Tusculum College	TN	24,295	C
Union College	KY	28,775	C
Union College	NY		MC
Univ at Albany / SUNY	NY	18,674	VC
Univ of Alaska Anchorage	AK	15,290	NC
Univ of Arizona	AZ	20,105	C
Univ of Calif at Davis	CA	24,482	HC
Univ of Central Florida	FL	15,711	VC+
Univ of Cincinnati	OH	20,199	VC
Univ of Colo at Colo Springs	CO	15,000	VC
Univ of Colo Boulder	CO	22,605	VC+
Univ of Colo Denver	CO	17,904	C
Univ of Dayton	OH	43,750	VC
Univ of Delaware	DE	22,728	VC
Univ of Great Falls	MT	27,970	C
Univ of Houston-Downtown	TX	6,267	LC
Univ of Idaho	ID	14,558	C
Univ of Illinois at Chicago	IL	24,293	VC
Univ of Illinois at Urbana-Champaign	IL	24,300	HC
Univ of Iowa	IA	17,481	VC
Univ of Jamestown	ND	24,738	C
Univ of Kansas	KS	16,980	C+
Univ of Louisiana at Lafayette	LA	6,130	C
Univ of Maine at Machias	ME	10,523	C
Univ of Maryland/Baltimore County	MD	18,000	VC
Univ of Mass Lowell	MA	19,316	C
Univ of Miami	FL	55,166	MC
Univ of Montana	MT	13,670	C
Univ of Nebr - Lincoln	NE	17,507	VC
Univ of Nebr at Kearney	NE	14,855	LC
Univ of Nebr at Omaha	NE	12,700	C
Univ of Nevada, Las Vegas	NV	17,303	C
Univ of New Hampshire	NH	24,702	VC
Univ of New Orleans	LA	9,224	VC
Univ of N Car at Asheville	NC	13,500	VC+
Univ of N Car at Charlotte	NC	15,847	C
Univ of N Car at Greensboro	NC	12,848	C
Univ of North Florida	FL	15,578	VC
Univ of Northern Colo	CO	15,973	C
Univ of Northern Iowa	IA	14,776	C
Univ of Oregon	OR	20,872	VC
Univ of Pennsylvania	PA	56,106	MC
Univ of PR Recinto de Rio Piedras	PR	5,750	
Univ of PR/Mayaguez	PR	1,250	
Univ of Rio Grande	OH	8,750	NC
Univ of St. Francis	IN	29,810	C
Univ of San Francisco	CA	49,674	VC
Univ of Science and Arts of Okla	OK	10,560	VC
Univ of South Alabama	AL	13,510	C
Univ of S Car at Aiken	SC	16,278	C
Univ of S Car at Columbia	SC	19,725	VC+
Univ of Southern Calif	CA	56,903	MC
Univ of Southern Maine	ME	16,576	C
Univ of Southern Miss	MS	13,170	C
Univ of Tenn at Chattanooga	TN	16,883	C
Univ of Tenn at Martin	TN	13,217	C
Univ of Texas at Dallas	TX	21,046	HC
Univ of the District of Columbia	DC	7,244	LC
Univ of the Southwest	NM	15,000	C
Univ of Toledo	OH	18,464	C
Univ of Utah	UT	13,462	VC
Univ of Wisc/Green Bay	WI	14,900	C
Univ of Wisc/La Crosse	WI	14,755	VC
Univ of Wisc/Oshkosh	WI	10,426	LC
Univ of Wisc/Parkside	WI	10,181	LC
Univ of Wisc/River Falls	WI	9,722	LC
Univ of Wisc/Stevens Point	WI	14,043	C
Univ of Wisc/Stout	WI	23,942	C
Univ of Wisc/Superior	WI	14,106	C
Upper Iowa Univ	IA	30,426	NC
Utah State Univ	UT	11,803	C
Vanderbilt Univ	TN	57,072	MC
Virginia Intermont College	VA	32,411	LC
Wagner College	NY	48,600	VC
Washington College	MD	48,768	VC
Washington State Univ	WA	20,461	C
Washington Univ in St. Louis	MO	58,818	MC
Wayne State Univ	MI	19,493	C
Wells College	NY	38,680	VC
West Liberty Univ	WV	9,142	LC
West Virginia State Univ	WV	8,378	NC
Western New Mexico Univ	NM	8,500	LC
Western State Colo Univ	CO	16,135	C
Western Washington Univ	WA	18,519	VC
Westminster College	PA	31,290	C+
Westminster College	UT	37,708	VC
Wheaton College	MA	54,934	HC+
Whitman College	WA	54,400	MC
Widener Univ	PA	50,368	C
Wilberforce Univ	OH	15,100	LC
William Paterson Univ of New Jersey	NJ	21,694	C
William Penn Univ	IA	26,000	C
Williams College	MA	58,900	MC
Wilson College	PA	27,660	C
Wingate Univ	NC	34,990	C
Winona State Univ	MN	16,530	C
Winthrop Univ	SC	21,120	VC
Wittenberg Univ	OH	47,766	VC
Wright State Univ	OH	16,983	C
Xavier Univ	OH	43,740	VC
Xavier Univ of Louisiana	LA	25,300	C
York College of Pennsylvania	PA	26,590	C

FIRE CONTROL AND SAFETY TECHNOLOGY

School	ST	$IS	SR
Cogswell Polytechnical College	CA	30,531	C
Okla State Univ	OK	14,310	VC
Univ of New Haven	CT	47,740	C
Univ of N Car at Charlotte	NC	15,847	C

FIRE PROTECTION

School	ST	$IS	SR
Cal State, Los Angeles	CA	15,829	C
Cogswell Polytechnical College	CA	30,531	C
Eastern Kentucky Univ	KY	11,161	C
Park Univ	MO	17,525	C
Southern Illinois Univ Carbondale	IL	21,620	C
Univ of New Haven	CT	47,740	C
Western Oregon Univ	OR	15,021	C
Worcester Polytechnic Inst	MA	53,440	HC+

FIRE PROTECTION ENGINEERING

School	ST	$IS	SR
Univ of Houston-Downtown	TX	6,267	LC
Univ of Maryland	MD	18,801	HC
Univ of New Haven	CT	47,740	C

FIRE PROTECTION SCIENCE

School	ST	$IS	SR
Thomas Edison State College	NJ	5,700	SP
Western Illinois Univ	IL	20,130	C

FIRE SCIENCE

School	ST	$IS	SR
Anna Maria College	MA	34,600	LC
Embry-Riddle Aeronautical Univ - Worldwide	FL	15,512	C
John Jay College of Criminal Justice / The CUNY	NY	6,059	C
Lake Superior State Univ	MI	18,121	C
Madonna Univ	MI	24,540	VC
Providence College	RI	55,995	HC
Univ of Maryland/Univ College	MD	6,168	SP
Univ of New Haven	CT	47,740	C
Univ of the District of Columbia	DC	7,244	LC

FIRE SERVICES ADMINISTRATION

School	ST	$IS	SR
Bowling Green State Univ	OH	18,970	C
Colo State Univ-Fort Collins	CO	20,090	VC
Columbia College	MO	24,578	C
Holy Family Univ	PA	40,030	LC
Idaho State Univ	ID	11,908	C
John Jay College of Criminal Justice / The CUNY	NY	6,059	C
Park Univ	MO	17,525	C
SUNY/Empire State College	NY	6,315	SP
Univ of New Haven	CT	47,740	C

FISH AND GAME MANAGEMENT

School	ST	$IS	SR
Delaware State Univ	DE	14,700	LC
Frostburg State Univ	MD	15,264	LC
Kansas State Univ	KS	15,497	VC
Lake Superior State Univ	MI	18,121	C
S Dak State Univ	SD	14,296	C
Stephen F. Austin State Univ	TX	14,668	C
Tenn Tech Univ	TN	11,310	C
Texas A&M Univ	TX	16,956	VC+
Texas Tech Univ	TX	14,243	C
Univ of Montana-Western	MT	9,753	LC
Univ of Nebr - Lincoln	NE	17,507	VC
Univ of Wyoming	WY	13,855	C+
West Virginia Univ	WV	15,794	C+

FISHING AND FISHERIES

School	ST	$IS	SR
Auburn Univ	AL	20,052	VC+
Colo State Univ-Fort Collins	CO	20,090	VC
Humboldt State Univ	CA	18,400	C
Mansfield Univ	PA	19,468	LC
Mich State Univ	MI	13,689	VC
Murray State Univ	KY	14,944	C
N Car State Univ	NC	16,202	HC
Oregon State Univ	OR	19,017	C+
Purdue Univ/West Lafayette	IN	20,278	HC
SUNY / College of Environmental Science and Forestry	NY	18,351	HC
Texas A&M Univ	TX	16,956	VC+
Texas A&M Univ at Galveston	TX	11,258	C
Ohio State Univ	OH	19,887	MC
The SUNY College of Agriculture and Tech at Cobleskill	NY	18,869	VC
Univ of Alaska Fairbanks	AK	13,955	C
Univ of Arkansas at Pine Bluff	AR	10,600	C
Univ of Georgia	GA	19,508	VC
Univ of Idaho	ID	14,558	C
Univ of Maine	ME	19,712	C+
Univ of Minn/Twin Cities	MN		HC
Univ of Missouri/Columbia	MO	18,201	MC
Univ of N Dak	ND	14,094	C
Univ of Vermont	VT	26,120	VC+
Univ of Washington	WA	14,722	VC
Univ of Wisc/Stevens Point	WI	14,043	C
West Virginia Univ	WV	15,794	C+

FLUID AND THERMAL SCIENCE

School	ST	$IS	SR
Case Western Reserve Univ	OH	55,178	MC

FOLKLORE AND MYTHOLOGY

School	ST	$IS	SR
Goddard College	VT	16,418	VC
Harvard Univ/Harvard College	MA	49,000	MC
Indiana Univ Bloomington	IN	19,358	HC
Univ of Oregon	OR	20,872	VC
Univ of Pennsylvania	PA	56,106	MC

FOOD PRODUCTION/ MANAGEMENT/SERVICES

School	ST	$IS	SR
Arizona State Univ	AZ	18,818	C+
Central Mich Univ	MI	18,066	C
Concordia Univ St. Paul	MN	27,200	C
Delaware Valley College	PA	29,944	C
Dominican Univ	IL	37,628	C
Drexel Univ	PA	51,920	HC
Johnson and Wales Univ/ Charlotte Campus	NC	35,421	C
Johnson and Wales Univ/ Denver Campus	CO	34,368	C
Johnson and Wales Univ/ North Miami Campus	FL	34,368	C
Johnson and Wales Univ/ Providence Campus	RI	34,668	C
Lipscomb Univ	TN	35,722	VC
Metropolitan State Univ	MN	5,923	SP
Mich State Univ	MI	13,689	VC
Miss Univ for Women	MS	7,400	LC
Montclair State Univ	NJ	22,614	C
Mount Marty College	SD	29,638	C
Newbury College	MA	41,850	C
Nicholls State Univ	LA	7,095	C
Purdue Univ/West Lafayette	IN	20,278	HC
Rochester Inst of Technology	NY	42,450	VC+
St. Louis Univ	MO	46,594	VC+
Seton Hill Univ	PA	35,172	C
Simmons College	MA	48,770	VC
S Dak State Univ	SD	14,296	C
Texas A&M Univ at Kingsville	TX	7,500	LC
Texas Christian Univ	TX	47,570	HC
Texas Tech Univ	TX	14,243	C
Univ of Central Florida	FL	15,711	VC+
Univ of Delaware	DE	22,728	VC
Univ of Georgia	GA	19,508	VC
Univ of Illinois at Urbana-Champaign	IL	24,300	HC
Univ of Nebr - Lincoln	NE	17,507	VC
Univ of Nevada, Las Vegas	NV	17,303	C
Univ of Wisc/Stout	WI	23,942	C
Western Mich Univ	MI	19,042	C

FOOD SCIENCE

School	ST	$IS	SR
Alabama A&M Univ	AL	96,100	C
Ashland Univ	OH	25,000	C
Auburn Univ	AL	20,052	VC+
Bluffton Univ	OH	37,864	C
Brigham Young Univ	UT	12,100	HC
Calif Polytechnic State Univ	CA	19,847	HC
Calif State Polytechnic Univ, Pomona	CA	18,932	C
Cal State, Fresno	CA	17,405	C
Cal State, San Bernardino	CA	12,000	C
Central Washington Univ	WA	11,730	C
Clemson Univ	SC	19,136	HC
College of the Ozarks	MO	5,605	VC
Colo State Univ-Fort Collins	CO	20,090	VC
Cornell Univ	NY	59,037	MC
Delaware Valley College	PA	29,944	C
Dominican Univ	IL	37,628	C
Florida State Univ	FL	15,238	HC

School	ST	$IS	SR
Framingham State Univ	MA	16,750	C
Immaculata Univ	PA	43,000	C
Indiana State Univ	IN	16,000	C
Iowa State Univ	IA	16,403	C
Kansas State Univ	KS	15,497	VC
Madonna Univ	MI	24,540	VC
Mich State Univ	MI	13,689	VC
Minn State Univ, Mankato	MN	14,900	C
N Car State Univ	NC	16,202	HC
N Dak State Univ	ND	14,642	C
Northwest Missouri State Univ	MO	14,229	C
Okla State Univ	OK	14,310	VC
Oregon State Univ	OR	19,017	₵
Penn State Univ/Univ Park	PA	25,404	VC
Purdue Univ/West Lafayette	IN	20,278	HC
Rutgers, The State Univ of New Jersey/New Brunswick	NJ	25,077	VC
St. Louis Univ	MO	46,594	V₵
San Jose State Univ	CA	19,707	C
Seattle Pacific Univ	WA	41,559	V₵
S Car State Univ	SC	6,700	LC
S Dak State Univ	SD	14,296	C
Southern Illinois Univ Carbondale	IL	21,620	C
Texas A&M Univ at Kingsville	TX	7,500	LC
Texas Tech Univ	TX	14,243	C
Tuskegee Univ	AL	26,750	C
Univ of Alabama at Tuscaloosa	AL	17,164	₵
Univ of Arkansas at Fayetteville	AR	16,860	VC
Univ of Calif at Davis	CA	24,482	HC
Univ of Delaware	DE	22,728	VC
Univ of Florida	FL	15,783	H₵
Univ of Georgia	GA	19,508	VC
Univ of Hawaii at Manoa	HI	19,379	VC
Univ of Idaho	ID	14,558	C
Univ of Illinois at Urbana-Champaign	IL	24,300	HC
Univ of Kentucky	KY	19,868	C
Univ of Maine	ME	19,712	₵
Univ of Mass Amherst	MA	23,697	V₵
Univ of Minn/Twin Cities	MN		HC
Univ of Missouri/Columbia	MO	18,201	MC
Univ of Nebr - Lincoln	NE	17,507	VC
Univ of Tenn at Knoxville	TN	20,364	V₵
Univ of the District of Columbia	DC	7,244	LC
Univ of Vermont	VT	26,120	V₵
Univ of Washington	WA	14,722	VC
Univ of Wisc/Madison	WI	18,757	HC
Univ of Wisc/River Falls	WI	9,722	LC
Utah State Univ	UT	11,803	C
Virginia Polytechnic Inst and State Univ	VA	14,629	HC
Washington State Univ	WA	20,461	C
Wayne State Univ	MI	19,493	C
Youngstown State Univ	OH	16,374	LC

FOOD SERVICES TECHNOLOGY

School	ST	$IS	SR
Brigham Young Univ	UT	12,100	HC
Delaware Valley College	PA	29,944	C
Inter-American Univ of PR/Bayamon Univ College	PR	4,428	
Johnson and Wales Univ/Charlotte Campus	NC	35,421	C
Johnson and Wales Univ/North Miami Campus	FL	34,368	C
Johnson and Wales Univ/Providence Campus	RI	34,668	C
Purdue Univ/West Lafayette	IN	20,278	HC
St. Louis Univ	MO	46,594	V₵
St. Catherine Univ	MN	37,782	₵
Univ of Central Florida	FL	15,711	V₵
Univ of Wisc/Stout	WI	23,942	C

FOOD TECHNOLOGY FOR COMPANION ANIMALS

School	ST	$IS	SR
Univ of Nebr - Lincoln	NE	17,507	VC

FOREIGN LANGUAGE

School	ST	$IS	SR
Bowling Green State Univ	OH	18,970	C
Bryant Univ	RI	49,179	VC
Northwestern State Univ of Louisiana	LA	14,368	C
Southern Oregon Univ	OR	17,874	C
Thomas Edison State College	NJ	5,700	SP
Univ of Louisiana at Monroe	LA	12,998	C

FOREIGN LANGUAGES EDUCATION

School	ST	$IS	SR
Abilene Christian Univ	TX	38,400	VC
Adams State College	CO	13,358	LC
Alabama State Univ	AL	14,142	NC
American International College	MA	36,100	LC
American Univ	DC	54,829	H₵
Anderson Univ	IN	35,390	C
Appalachian State Univ	NC	12,919	VC
Arizona State Univ	AZ	18,818	₵
Arkansas State Univ	AR	14,980	C
Arkansas Tech Univ	AR	13,164	LC
Asbury Univ	KY	32,038	VC
Ashland Univ	OH	25,000	C
Auburn Univ	AL	20,052	V₵
Baylor Univ	TX	46,720	HC
Bemidji State Univ	MN	13,500	C
Bennington College	VT	56,990	H₵
Bethel Univ	MN	34,940	VC
Blue Mountain College	MS	13,550	LC
Boston Univ	MA	54,130	H₵
Bowling Green State Univ	OH	18,970	C
Bryant Univ	RI	49,179	VC
Buffalo State/State Univ of Buffalo	NY	15,733	₵
Cameron Univ	OK	9,267	LC
Canisius College	NY	45,602	VC
Carroll College	MT	28,000	C
Carroll Univ	WI	24,860	C
Carson-Newman Univ	TN	29,058	₵
Carthage College	WI	33,000	C
Cedarville Univ	OH	31,036	V₵
Centenary College of Louisiana	LA	39,070	₵
Central Mich Univ	MI	18,066	C
Central Washington Univ	WA	11,730	C
CUNY/Brooklyn College	NY	5,884	₵
Clarion Univ of Pennsylvania	PA	17,370	C
College of the Ozarks	MO	5,605	VC
Colo State Univ-Fort Collins	CO	20,090	VC
Columbus State Univ	GA	13,176	C
Concordia College, Moorhead	MN	39,974	₵
Converse College	SC	37,130	C
Cornell College	IA	44,930	HC
CUNY-City College	NY	19,576	H₵
Daemen College	NY	31,510	C
Delta State Univ	MS	12,292	LC
DePaul Univ	IL	46,120	VC
DePauw Univ	IN	48,950	V₵
Dordt College	IA	34,160	VC
Duquesne Univ	PA	42,017	VC
East Carolina Univ	NC	14,169	C
East Stroudsburg Univ of Pennsylvania	PA	16,636	C
East Tenn State Univ	TN	9,000	C
East Texas Baptist Univ	TX	29,135	C
Eastern Kentucky Univ	KY	11,161	C
Eastern Mich Univ	MI	17,961	C
Eastern Washington Univ	WA	16,388	C
Edinboro Univ of Pennsylvania	PA	15,940	LC
Elmira College	NY	49,950	₵
Elms College	MA	23,900	VC
Elon Univ	NC	40,046	HC
Emporia State Univ	KS	12,897	C
Erskine College	SC	37,360	C
Eugene Lang College - The New School for Liberal Arts	NY	55,650	VC
Evangel Univ	MO	23,090	C
Fairmont State Univ	WV	12,098	LC
Florida Atlantic Univ	FL	17,339	C
Florida State Univ	FL	15,238	HC
Friends Univ	KS	29,100	C
Gannon Univ	PA	37,940	C
Gardner-Webb Univ	NC	34,375	₵
Georgetown College	KY	38,690	C
Georgia Regents Univ	GA		C
Georgia Southwestern State Univ	GA	12,218	C
Gettysburg College	PA	56,820	HC
Goshen College	IN	35,900	VC
Grace College and Theological Seminary	IN	28,800	C
Grand Valley State Univ	MI	17,998	VC
Greensboro College	NC	28,740	LC
Gustavus Adolphus College	MN	48,170	HC
Hamline Univ	MN	44,198	VC
Harding Univ	AR	21,432	₵
Hardin-Simmons Univ	TX	23,560	₵
Hastings College	NE	27,782	₵
Heidelberg Univ	OH	34,100	C
Hillsdale College	MI	31,890	H₵
Hofstra Univ	NY	48,020	V₵
Holy Family Univ	PA	40,030	LC
Hood College	MD	44,630	C
Hope College	MI	36,320	V₵
Houghton College	NY	35,740	VC
Hunter College / The CUNY	NY	14,429	VC
Illinois College	IL	25,770	VC
Immaculata Univ	PA	43,000	C
Indiana State Univ	IN	16,000	C
Indiana Univ-Purdue Univ Fort Wayne	IN	15,425	C
Ithaca College	NY	52,300	HC
Juniata College	PA	49,340	VC
King's College	PA	41,678	C
Kutztown Univ of Pennsylvania	PA	16,909	LC
La Salle Univ	PA	50,270	C
Lamar Univ	TX	6,820	LC
Le Moyne College	NY	42,200	VC
Lehman College / The CUNY	NY	5,778	LC
Lenoir-Rhyne College	NC	35,984	C
Lipscomb Univ	TN	35,722	VC
Lock Haven Univ of Pennsylvania	PA	17,587	LC
LIU/C.W. Post Campus	NY	38,888	C
Louisiana Tech Univ	LA	8,000	C
Malone Univ	OH	34,334	C
Manhattan College	NY	44,955	VC
Mansfield Univ	PA	19,468	LC
Marshall Univ	WV	14,820	C
Marywood Univ	PA	40,695	C
Messiah College	PA	39,540	VC
Miami Univ	OH	24,191	HC
Minn State Univ, Mankato	MN	14,900	C
Minn State Univ, Moorhead	MN	13,392	C
Minot State Univ	ND	10,915	C
Missouri Southern State Univ	MO	11,910	C
Missouri Western State Univ	MO	12,260	NC
Monmouth Univ	NJ	42,252	C
Mount Mary Univ	WI	32,836	LC
Murray State Univ	KY	14,944	C
Muskingum Univ	OH	30,502	C
Nazareth College of Rochester	NY	41,590	VC
New York Univ	NY	61,470	MC
Niagara Univ	NY	39,800	C
N Car State Univ	NC	16,202	HC
North Georgia College & State Univ	GA	8,500	C
Northern State Univ	SD	14,021	C
Northwestern College of Iowa	IA	34,848	₵
Notre Dame of Maryland Univ	MD	27,700	C
Ohio Wesleyan Univ	OH	49,460	₵
Okla Baptist Univ	OK	28,202	VC
Old Dominion Univ	VA	18,662	C
Oral Roberts Univ	OK	31,734	C
Oswego / SUNY	NY	20,009	VC
Ouachita Baptist Univ	AR	29,010	VC
Prescott College	AZ	33,284	₵
Providence College	RI	55,995	HC
Purdue Univ/Calumet	IN	14,336	C
Purdue Univ/West Lafayette	IN	20,278	HC
Radford Univ	VA	17,132	LC
Rhode Island College	RI	17,132	LC
Rider Univ	NJ	45,720	C
Rockhurst Univ	MO	20,625	C
Rosemont College	PA	42,350	C
Rowan Univ	NJ	23,570	VC
Sacred Heart Univ	CT	48,564	VC
Saginaw Valley State Univ	MI	16,869	C
St. Mary's Univ of Minn	MN	37,015	C
St. Michael's College	VT	48,740	VC
St. Xavier Univ	IL	32,840	C
Seton Hill Univ	PA	35,172	C
Shippensburg Univ of Pennsylvania	PA	17,064	LC
Slippery Rock Univ of Pennsylvania	PA	10,360	LC
Southeast Missouri State Univ	MO	14,983	LC
Southern Conn State Univ	CT	18,033	C
Southern Univ at New Orleans	LA	1,000	NC
Southwest Minn State Univ	MN	14,000	C
St. Cloud State Univ	MN	10,600	C
St. Edward's Univ	TX	44,674	VC
St. John Fisher College	NY	39,370	₵
St. John's Univ	NY	52,840	₵
St. Thomas Aquinas College	NY	30,000	C
SUNY College at Old Westbury	NY	16,324	C
SUNY Cortland / The SUNY	NY	19,117	C
SUNY Fredonia / The SUNY at Fredonia	NY	18,702	VC
SUNY New Paltz	NY	15,010	C
SUNY Oneonta / SUNY	NY	16,919	VC
Taylor Univ	IN	36,742	V₵
Texas Southern Univ	TX	18,212	LC
Texas Wesleyan Univ	TX	29,886	C
Universidad del Turabo	PR	4,110	
Univ of Central Arkansas	AR	10,840	VC
Univ of Central Florida	FL	15,711	V₵
Univ of Central Missouri	MO	14,605	C
Univ of Central Okla	OK	12,293	C
Univ of Cincinnati	OH	20,199	VC
Univ of Conn	CT	23,744	HC
Univ of Delaware	DE	22,728	VC
Univ of Evansville	IN	41,056	V₵
Univ of Findlay	OH	31,916	C
Univ of Idaho	ID	14,558	C
Univ of Illinois at Urbana-Champaign	IL	24,300	HC
Univ of Indianapolis	IN	31,740	LC
Univ of Iowa	IA	17,481	VC
Univ of Kentucky	KY	19,868	C
Univ of Louisiana at Lafayette	LA	6,130	C
Univ of Louisiana at Monroe	LA	12,998	C
Univ of Louisville	KY	17,460	VC
Univ of Mary Hardin-Baylor	TX	31,950	₵
Univ of Mich-Flint	MI	17,547	₵
Univ of Minn/Duluth	MN	18,964	₵
Univ of Nebr - Lincoln	NE	17,507	VC
Univ of Nebr at Kearney	NE	14,855	LC
Univ of New Orleans	LA	9,224	VC
Univ of North Alabama	AL	9,960	C
Univ of N Car at Charlotte	NC	15,847	C
Univ of N Car at Greensboro	NC	12,818	C
Univ of Northern Iowa	IA	14,770	C
Univ of Okla	OK	17,634	V₵
Univ of PR/Mayaguez	PR	1,250	
Univ of South Florida	FL	13,000	C
Univ of Southern Miss	MS	13,170	C
Univ of Toledo	OH	18,464	C
Univ of Vermont	VT	26,120	V₵
Univ of West Georgia	GA	14,852	LC
Univ of Wisc Whitewater	WI	13,314	C
Univ of Wisc/Green Bay	WI	14,900	C
Univ of Wisc/River Falls	WI	9,722	LC
Utah State Univ	UT	11,803	C
Utica College	NY	44,734	C
Valparaiso Univ	IN	43,040	V₵
Vassar College	NY	59,070	MC
Virginia Commonwealth Univ	VA	18,633	C
Virginia Polytechnic Inst and State Univ	VA	14,629	HC
Wartburg College	IA	41,055	VC
Washington State Univ	WA	20,461	C
Washington Univ in St. Louis	MO	58,818	MC
Webster Univ	MO	33,990	₵
West Texas A&M Univ	TX	13,478	C
West Virginia Univ	WV	15,794	₵
Western Carolina Univ	NC	13,965	₵
Western Mich Univ	MI	19,042	C
Western State Colo Univ	CO	16,135	C
Western Washington Univ	WA	18,519	VC
Wheeling Jesuit Univ	WV	34,668	C
Whitworth Univ	WA	45,826	V₵
Winona State Univ	MN	16,530	C
Wittenberg Univ	OH	47,766	VC
Wright State Univ	OH	16,983	C

FORENSIC PSYCHOLOGY

School	ST	$IS	SR
The College of St. Rose	NY	26,750	C
Univ of Central Okla	OK	12,293	C
Univ of Louisiana at Monroe	LA	12,998	C

FORENSIC SCIENCE

School	ST	$IS	SR
Alvernia Univ	PA	39,250	C
Bethany College	KS	30,605	NC
Bethany College	WV	35,282	C
Bryant Univ	RI	49,179	VC
Duquesne Univ	PA	42,017	VC
Embry-Riddle Aeronautical Univ - Prescott Campus	AZ	40,584	VC
Hilbert College	NY	28,550	C
Indiana Univ-Purdue Univ Indianapolis	IN	17,290	C
Pace Univ	NY	48,094	VC
Point Park Univ	PA	36,390	C
San Jose State Univ	CA	19,707	C
The College of St. Rose	NY	26,750	C
Univ of Central Okla	OK	12,293	C
Univ of Illinois at Chicago	IL	24,293	VC
Univ of Nebr - Lincoln	NE	17,507	VC
Waynesburg Univ	PA	29,100	C

FORENSIC STUDIES

School	ST	$IS	SR
Albany State Univ	GA	8,500	C
Arkansas State Univ	AR	14,980	C
Bay Path College	MA	34,565	C
Baylor Univ	TX	46,720	HC
Becker College	MA	41,420	LC
Bryant Univ	RI	49,179	VC
Cal State, Fresno	CA	17,405	C
Carlow Univ	PA	30,272	C
Cedarville Univ	OH	31,036	V₵
Chaminade Univ of Honolulu	HI	31,664	C
Champlain College	VT	44,850	VC
Chatham Univ	PA	42,440	VC
Chestnut Hill College	PA	39,785	LC
Columbia College	MO	24,578	C
Defiance College	OH	30,645	C
Eastern Kentucky Univ	KY	11,161	C
Eastern New Mexico Univ	NM	10,682	C
Edinboro Univ of Pennsylvania	PA	15,940	LC
Emmanuel College	MA	47,985	VC
Florida Gulf Coast Univ	FL		C
Florida Inst of Technology	FL	48,290	VC
Friends Univ	KS	29,100	C
Grand Canyon Univ	AZ	24,540	VC

School	ST	$IS	SR
Guilford College	NC	35,340	C
Hamline Univ	MN	44,198	VC
Heidelberg Univ	OH	34,100	C
Hilbert College	NY	28,550	C
Hofstra Univ	NY	48,020	VC+
Husson Univ	ME	23,386	LC
Inter-American Univ of PR/ Aguadilla Campus	PR	5,578	
Inter-American Univ of PR/ Bayamon Univ College	PR	4,428	
John Jay College of Criminal Justice / The CUNY	NY	6,059	C
Keystone College	PA	28,680	LC
King Univ	TN	33,140	C
Lake Superior State Univ	MI	18,121	C
LIU/C.W. Post Campus	NY	38,888	C
Loyola Univ Chicago	IL	49,560	VC+
Loyola Univ New Orleans	LA	46,581	VC
Lynn Univ	FL	43,500	C
Marshall Univ	WV	14,820	C
Marygrove College	MI	21,290	C
Marymount Univ	VA	36,178	C
Maryville Univ of St. Louis	MO	34,920	VC
Mercyhurst Univ	PA	40,700	C
Mountain State Univ	WV	14,330	NC
Newman Univ	KS	30,380	C+
Northern Kentucky Univ	KY	15,302	LC
Ohio Univ	OH	20,676	VC
Pace Univ	NY	48,094	VC
Penn State Univ/Univ Park	PA	25,404	VC
Russell Sage College	NY	39,370	C
Seattle Univ	WA	47,010	VC+
Seton Hill Univ	PA	35,172	C
Simpson College	IA	36,086	VC
Southern Illinois Univ Edwardsville	IL	17,532	C
Southern Wesleyan Univ	SC	25,600	C
St. Ambrose Univ	IA		C
St. Andrews Univ	NC	32,050	LC
St. Edward's Univ	TX	44,674	VC
Syracuse Univ	NY	54,512	HC
Thomas More College	KY	34,760	C
Tiffin Univ	OH	30,273	LC
Trine Univ	IN	39,400	VC
Univ of Central Florida	FL	15,711	VC+
Univ of Central Okla	OK	12,293	C
Univ of Findlay	OH	31,916	C
Univ of Illinois at Chicago	IL	24,293	VC
Univ of Miss	MS	15,482	VC
Univ of New Haven	CT	47,740	C
Univ of N Dak	ND	14,094	C
Univ of Scranton	PA	51,940	VC
Univ of Tampa	FL	35,160	VC
Univ of Wisc/Platteville	WI	14,274	C
Univ of Wisc-Milwaukee	WI	18,436	C
Virginia Commonwealth Univ	VA	18,633	C
Washburn Univ	KS	12,165	NC
West Chester Univ of Pennsylvania	PA	16,836	C
Western Carolina Univ	NC	13,965	C+
Western New England Univ	MA	45,590	C
Youngstown State Univ	OH	16,374	LC

FOREST ENGINEERING

School	ST	$IS	SR
Auburn Univ	AL	20,052	VC+
Oregon State Univ	OR	19,017	C+
SUNY / College of Environmental Science and Forestry	NY	18,351	HC
Univ of Maine	ME	19,712	C+
Univ of Washington	WA	14,722	VC

FORESTRY AND RELATED SCIENCES

School	ST	$IS	SR
Alabama A&M Univ	AL	96,100	C
Baylor Univ	TX	46,720	HC
Calif Polytechnic State Univ	CA	19,847	HC
Clemson Univ	SC	19,136	HC
Colo State Univ-Fort Collins	CO	20,090	VC
Eastern Oregon Univ	OR	10,400	C
Elizabethtown College	PA	47,600	VC
Glenville State College	WV	11,348	NC
Humboldt State Univ	CA	18,400	C
Iowa State Univ	IA	16,403	C
Louisiana State Univ	LA	18,677	VC+
Louisiana Tech Univ	LA	8,000	C
Mich State Univ	MI	13,689	VC
Mich Tech Univ	MI	22,105	VC
N Car State Univ	NC	16,202	HC
Northern Arizona Univ	AZ	18,592	C
Northwest Missouri State Univ	MO	14,229	C
Oregon State Univ	OR	19,017	C+
Penn State Univ/Univ Park	PA	25,404	VC
Prescott College	AZ	33,284	C+
Purdue Univ/West Lafayette	IN	20,278	HC
Sewanee: The Univ of the South	TN	47,700	HC+
S Dak State Univ	SD	14,296	C
Southern Illinois Univ Carbondale	IL	21,620	C
Southern Univ and A&M College	LA	9,761	C+
SUNY / College of Environmental Science and Forestry	NY	18,351	HC
Stephen F. Austin State Univ	TX	14,668	C
Texas A&M Univ	TX	16,956	VC+
Ohio State Univ	OH	19,887	MC
Univ of Arkansas at Monticello	AR	8,470	NC
Univ of Calif at Berkeley	CA	23,322	MC
Univ of Florida	FL	15,783	HC+
Univ of Georgia	GA	19,508	VC
Univ of Idaho	ID	14,558	C
Univ of Illinois at Urbana-Champaign	IL	24,300	HC
Univ of Kentucky	KY	19,868	C
Univ of Maine	ME	19,712	C+
Univ of Maine at Fort Kent	ME	14,975	LC
Univ of Minn/Twin Cities	MN		HC
Univ of Missouri/Columbia	MO	18,201	MC
Univ of Montana	MT	13,670	C
Univ of New Hampshire	NH	24,702	VC
Univ of Tenn at Knoxville	TN	20,364	VC+
Univ of Vermont	VT	26,120	VC+
Univ of Wisc/Madison	WI	18,757	HC
Univ of Wisc/Stevens Point	WI	14,043	C
Utah State Univ	UT	11,803	C
Virginia Polytechnic Inst and State Univ	VA	14,629	HC
Warren Wilson College	NC	34,888	VC
West Virginia Univ	WV	15,794	C+
Western New Mexico Univ	NM	8,500	LC

FORESTRY PRODUCTION AND PROCESSING

School	ST	$IS	SR
Auburn Univ	AL	20,052	VC+
Clemson Univ	SC	19,136	HC
Oregon State Univ	OR	19,017	C+
Penn State Univ/Univ Park	PA	25,404	VC
Stephen F. Austin State Univ	TX	14,668	C
Univ of Idaho	ID	14,558	C
Univ of Minn/Twin Cities	MN		HC
Univ of Washington	WA	14,722	VC

FRENCH

School	ST	$IS	SR
Adelphi Univ	NY	43,130	VC
Adrian College	MI	33,800	C
Agnes Scott College	GA	45,323	VC+
Alabama A&M Univ	AL	96,100	C
Alabama State Univ	AL	14,142	NC
Albany State Univ	GA	8,500	C
Albion College	MI	43,884	VC
Albright College	PA	46,660	C
Allegheny College	PA	49,020	HC
Alma College	MI	42,400	VC
American Univ	DC	54,829	HC+
Amherst College	MA	58,744	MC
Anderson Univ	IN	35,390	C
Andrews Univ	MI	28,030	C+
Angelo State Univ	TX	15,049	NC
Appalachian State Univ	NC	12,919	VC
Aquinas College	MI	33,060	C
Arizona State Univ	AZ	18,818	C+
Arkansas State Univ	AR	14,980	C
Asbury Univ	KY	32,038	VC
Ashland Univ	OH	25,000	C
Assumption College	MA	45,721	VC
Auburn Univ	AL	20,052	VC+
Augsburg College	MN	35,142	C
Augustana College	IL	43,398	HC
Augustana College	SD	35,500	VC
Austin College	TX	36,940	HC
Baker Univ	KS	33,350	C+
Baldwin Wallace Univ	OH	36,980	VC
Ball State Univ	IN	17,850	C
Bard College	NY	59,872	HC
Barry Univ	FL	38,190	C
Baylor Univ	TX	46,720	HC
Belmont Univ	TN	37,380	VC+
Beloit College	WI	49,970	HC
Benedictine College	KS	29,180	VC
Bennington College	VT	56,990	HC+
Berea College	KY	7,220	HC
Berry College	GA	39,254	HC
Bethel Univ	MN	34,940	VC
Binghamton Univ / The SUNY	NY	20,832	HC+
Birmingham-Southern College	AL	42,370	VC+
Bloomsburg Univ of Pennsylvania	PA	13,598	C
Boise State Univ	ID	12,802	C
Boston College	MA	58,506	MC
Boston Univ	MA	54,130	HC+
Bowdoin College	ME	57,834	MC
Bowling Green State Univ	OH	18,970	C
Bradley Univ	IL	31,874	VC
Brandeis Univ	MA	58,820	HC
Bridgewater College	VA	39,880	C
Brigham Young Univ	UT	12,100	HC
Bryant Univ	RI	49,179	VC
Bryn Mawr College	PA	57,760	MC
Bucknell Univ	PA	58,160	MC
Buffalo State/State Univ of Buffalo	NY	15,733	C+
Butler Univ	IN	45,898	VC+
Cabrini College	PA	40,859	LC
Caldwell College	NJ	35,602	LC
Calif Lutheran Univ	CA	47,640	C
Cal State, Fresno	CA	17,405	C
Cal State, Fullerton	CA	25,188	C+
Cal State, Long Beach	CA	17,534	C+
Cal State, Los Angeles	CA	15,829	C
Cal State, Northridge	CA	28,313	C
Cal State, Sacramento	CA	16,200	C
Cal State, San Bernardino	CA	12,000	C
Cal State, Stanislaus	CA	18,582	C
Calif Univ of Pennsylvania	PA	14,217	C
Calvin College	MI	37,585	VC+
Campbell Univ	NC	25,500	C
Canisius College	NY	45,602	VC
Capital Univ	OH	39,824	VC
Cardinal Stritch Univ	WI	24,054	C
Carleton College	MN	58,149	MC
Carnegie Mellon Univ	PA	51,260	MC
Carroll College	MT	28,000	C
Carson-Newman Univ	TN	29,058	C+
Carthage College	WI	33,000	C
Case Western Reserve Univ	OH	55,178	MC
Centenary College of Louisiana	LA	39,070	C+
Central College	IA	36,980	VC
Central Conn State Univ	CT	19,212	C
Central Mich Univ	MI	18,066	C
Central Washington Univ	WA	11,730	C
Centre College	KY	35,000	HC+
Chapman Univ	CA	56,019	VC+
Chestnut Hill College	PA	39,785	LC
Christopher Newport Univ	VA	21,050	VC
Citadel, The	SC		C
CUNY/Brooklyn College	NY	5,884	C+
Claremont McKenna College	CA	58,065	MC
Clarion Univ of Pennsylvania	PA	17,370	C
Clark Univ	MA	47,020	HC+
Clemson Univ	SC	19,136	HC
Cleveland State Univ	OH	21,357	C
Coe College	IA	43,590	VC
Colgate Univ	NY	50,930	MC
College of Mount St. Vincent	NY	41,040	MC
College of St. Benedict	MN	47,570	VC
College of the Holy Cross	MA	56,232	MC
College of William & Mary	VA	25,085	MC
College of Wooster	OH	52,600	VC
Colo State Univ-Fort Collins	CO	20,090	VC
Columbia College	SC	27,882	C
Columbia Univ in the City of New York	NY	61,116	MC
Columbia Univ/Barnard College	NY	39,000	MC
Columbia Univ/School of General Studies	NY	54,083	MC
Columbus State Univ	GA	13,176	C
Concordia College, Moorhead	MN	39,974	C+
Conn College	CT	54,970	MC
Converse College	SC	37,130	C
Cornell College	IA	44,930	HC
Cornell Univ	NY	59,037	MC
Covenant College	GA		VC+
CUNY-City College	NY	19,576	HC+
Daemen College	NY	31,510	C
Dartmouth College	NH	57,996	MC
Davidson College	NC	54,683	MC
Delaware State Univ	DE	14,700	LC
Denison Univ	OH	54,670	HC+
DePaul Univ	IL	46,120	VC
DePauw Univ	IN	48,950	VC+
Dickinson College	PA	57,662	HC+
Doane College	NE	33,730	VC
Dominican Univ	IL	37,628	C
Drew Univ/College of Liberal Arts	NJ	55,862	VC
Drury Univ	MO	30,319	VC
Earlham College	IN	49,710	VC+
East Carolina Univ	NC	14,169	C
East Stroudsburg Univ of Pennsylvania	PA	16,636	C
Eastern Kentucky Univ	KY	11,161	C
Eastern Mennonite Univ	VA	38,850	VC
Eastern Mich Univ	MI	17,961	C
Eastern Nazarene College	MA	30,000	C
Eastern Washington Univ	WA	16,388	C
Eckerd College	FL	43,902	VC
Edgewood College	WI	33,294	C
Elizabethtown College	PA	47,600	VC
Elmhurst College	IL	42,032	C+
Elmira College	NY	49,950	C+
Elon Univ	NC	40,046	HC
Emory Univ	GA	45,000	MC
Fairmont State Univ	WV	12,098	LC
Fisk Univ	TN	19,830	C
Florida Atlantic Univ	FL	17,339	C
Florida International Univ	FL	17,747	VC
Florida State Univ	FL	15,238	HC
Fordham Univ	NY	58,927	HC
Fort Hays State Univ	KS	11,354	C
Franciscan Univ of Steubenville	OH	27,320	VC
Franklin and Marshall College	PA	58,295	MC
Franklin College	IN	35,885	C
Furman Univ	SC	54,006	HC
Gardner-Webb Univ	NC	34,375	C+
George Mason Univ	VA	15,724	VC
George Washington Univ	DC	57,108	MC
Georgetown College	KY	38,690	C
Georgetown Univ	DC	52,910	MC
Georgia College and State Univ	GA	18,216	VC
Georgia Regents Univ	GA		C
Georgia State Univ	GA	12,000	VC
Gettysburg College	PA	56,820	HC
Gonzaga Univ	WA	44,247	HC
Gordon College	MA	42,660	VC+
Goucher College	MD	50,252	VC+
Grace College and Theological Seminary	IN	28,800	C
Grand Valley State Univ	MI	17,998	VC
Greensboro College	NC	28,740	LC
Grinnell College	IA	53,654	HC
Grove City College	PA	22,988	HC
Guilford College	NC	35,340	C
Gustavus Adolphus College	MN	48,170	HC
Hamilton College	NY	55,620	MC
Hamline Univ	MN	44,198	VC
Hampden-Sydney College	VA	48,848	C
Hanover College	IN	41,450	VC
Harding Univ	AR	21,432	C+
Hartwick College	NY	49,815	C+
Harvard Univ/Harvard College	MA	49,000	MC
Haverford College	PA	59,236	MC
Hendrix College	AR	48,436	HC+
High Point Univ	NC	39,800	C
Hillsdale College	MI	31,890	HC+
Hiram College	OH	37,300	VC
Hobart and William Smith Colleges	NY	43,000	VC
Hofstra Univ	NY	48,020	VC+
Hollins Univ	VA	43,295	VC
Hood College	MD	44,630	C
Hope College	MI	36,320	VC+
Houston Baptist Univ	TX	23,815	C+
Howard Univ	DC	35,957	C
Humboldt State Univ	CA	18,400	C
Hunter College / The CUNY	NY	14,429	VC
Idaho State Univ	ID	11,908	C
Illinois College	IL	25,770	VC
Illinois State Univ	IL	22,634	VC
Illinois Wesleyan Univ	IL	48,452	VC+
Immaculata Univ	PA	43,000	C
Indiana State Univ	IN	16,000	C
Indiana Univ Bloomington	IN	19,358	HC
Indiana Univ Northwest	IN	6,738	LC
Indiana Univ South Bend	IN	15,293	C
Indiana Univ Southeast	IN	15,807	LC
Indiana Univ-Purdue Univ Fort Wayne	IN	15,425	C
Indiana Univ-Purdue Univ Indianapolis	IN	17,290	C
Iona College	NY	44,028	C
Iowa State Univ	IA	16,403	C
Ithaca College	NY	52,300	HC
Jacksonville Univ	FL	37,780	C
John Carroll Univ	OH	44,520	C+
Johns Hopkins Univ	MD	47,492	MC
Juniata College	PA	49,340	VC
Kalamazoo College	MI	47,825	HC+
Keene State College	NH	21,538	C
Kent State Univ	OH	19,352	C
Kenyon College	OH	56,810	MC
King Univ	TN	33,140	C
King's College	PA	41,678	C
Knox College	IL		VC
Kutztown Univ of Pennsylvania	PA	16,909	LC
La Salle Univ	PA	50,270	C
Lafayette College	PA	57,050	HC+
Lake Forest College	IL	45,580	VC
Lamar Univ	TX	6,820	LC
Lane College	TN	11,212	C
Lawrence Univ	WI	46,371	HC
Le Moyne College	NY	42,200	VC
Lebanon Valley College	PA	38,570	C
Lee Univ	TN	18,690	C+
Lehigh Univ	PA	55,080	MC
Lehman College / The CUNY	NY	5,778	LC
Lenoir-Rhyne College	NC	35,984	C
Lindenwood Univ	MO	20,750	C
Linfield College-McMinnville Campus	OR	46,166	C
Lipscomb Univ	TN	35,722	VC
Lock Haven Univ of Pennsylvania	PA	17,587	LC
LIU/C.W. Post Campus	NY	38,888	C
Louisiana College	LA	15,746	C
Louisiana State Univ	LA	18,677	VC+
Louisiana Tech Univ	LA	8,000	C

School	ST	$IS	SR
Loyola Marymount Univ	CA	53,240	VC+
Loyola Univ Chicago	IL	49,560	VC+
Loyola Univ Maryland	MD		VC
Loyola Univ New Orleans	LA	46,581	VC
Luther College	IA	44,380	VC+
Lycoming College	PA	43,636	C
Lynchburg College	VA	42,645	C
Macalester College	MN	53,419	MC
Manchester College	IN	35,070	C
Manhattan College	NY	44,955	VC
Manhattanville College	NY	46,260	VC
Mansfield Univ	PA	19,468	LC
Marian Univ/Indianapolis	IN	37,058	C
Marist College	NY	35,500	C
Marlboro College	VT	35,980	VC
Marquette Univ	WI	43,664	VC+
Marshall Univ	WV	14,820	C
Marywood Univ	PA	40,695	C
McDaniel College	MD	45,600	VC
Mercer Univ	GA	44,201	VC+
Meredith College	NC	31,420	C
Messiah College	PA	39,540	VC
Methodist Univ	NC	37,185	C
Miami Univ	OH	24,191	HC
Mich State Univ	MI	13,689	VC
Middle Tenn State Univ	TN	8,650	C
Middlebury College	VT	57,470	MC
Millersville Univ of Pennsylvania	PA	18,498	C
Mills College	CA	54,119	HC
Minn State Univ, Mankato	MN	14,900	C
Minot State Univ	ND	10,915	C
Miss College	MS	21,998	VC
Missouri Southern State Univ	MO	11,910	C
Missouri State Univ	MO	13,996	VC
Missouri Western State Univ	MO	12,260	NC
Monmouth College	IL	39,290	C
Montana State Univ-Northern	MT	12,500	NC
Montclair State Univ	NJ	22,614	C
Moravian College	PA	36,381	VC
Morehouse College	GA	38,640	C
Mount Holyoke College	MA	53,596	HC+
Mount St. Mary's Univ	MD	46,158	C
Mount St. Mary's College/ Chalon Campus	CA	43,897	VC+
Muhlenberg College	PA	52,837	HC
Murray State Univ	KY	14,944	C
Muskingum Univ	OH	30,502	C
Nazareth College of Rochester	NY	41,590	VC
Nebr Wesleyan Univ	NE	29,774	C+
New College of Florida	FL	14,504	HC+
New York Univ	NY	61,470	MC
Newberry College	SC	26,850	LC
Niagara Univ	NY	39,800	C
Nicholls State Univ	LA	7,095	C
N Car Agricultural and Technical State Univ	NC	13,175	LC
N Car Central Univ	NC	9,000	LC
N Car State Univ	NC	16,202	HC
North Central College	IL	38,343	VC
N Dak State Univ	ND	14,642	C
North Georgia College & State Univ	GA	8,500	C
North Park Univ	IL	30,130	C
Northeastern Illinois Univ	IL		C
Northern Illinois Univ	IL	19,768	C
Northern Kentucky Univ	KY	15,302	LC
Northern Mich Univ	MI	15,300	VC
Northern State Univ	SD	14,021	C
Northwestern Univ	IL	37,595	MC
Oakland Univ	MI	19,391	VC
Oakwood Univ	AL	23,035	C
Oberlin College	OH	57,025	MC
Occidental College	CA	59,592	MC+
Oglethorpe Univ	GA	42,580	VC
Ohio Northern Univ	OH	42,075	VC
Ohio Univ	OH	20,676	VC
Ohio Wesleyan Univ	OH	49,460	C+
Okla Baptist Univ	OK	28,202	VC
Okla City Univ	OK	33,546	VC
Okla State Univ	OK	14,310	VC
Old Dominion Univ	VA	18,662	C
Oral Roberts Univ	OK	31,734	C
Oregon State Univ	OR	19,017	C+
Oswego / SUNY	NY	20,009	VC
Otterbein College	OH	32,214	C
Pacific Lutheran Univ	WA	44,840	VC
Pacific Union College	CA	28,150	VC
Penn State Univ/Univ Park	PA	25,404	VC
Pepperdine Univ	CA	55,372	HC+
Pittsburg State Univ	KS	12,032	C
Pitzer College	CA	54,988	MC
Plymouth State Univ	NH	23,148	LC
Pomona College	CA	57,680	MC
Portland State Univ	OR	18,672	C
Presbyterian College	SC	42,678	VC
Princeton Univ	NJ	53,795	MC
Principia College	IL	35,140	C+
Providence College	RI	55,995	HC
Purdue Univ/Calumet	IN	14,336	C
Purdue Univ/West Lafayette	IN	20,278	HC
Queens College / The CUNY	NY	17,107	VC
Queens Univ of Charlotte	NC	39,543	VC
Randolph College	VA	43,960	VC
Randolph-Macon College	VA	45,086	C
Regis Univ	CO	41,318	C
Rhode Island College	RI	17,132	LC
Rhodes College	TN	47,596	HC+
Rider Univ	NJ	45,720	C
Ripon College	WI	36,959	C+
Roanoke College	VA	47,996	C+
Rockford College	IL	31,000	C
Rockhurst Univ	MO	20,625	C
Rollins College	FL	52,370	HC
Roosevelt Univ	IL	22,605	VC
Rosemont College	PA	42,350	C
Rutgers, The State Univ of New Jersey/Camden Campus	NJ	24,254	C
Rutgers, The State Univ of New Jersey/New Brunswick	NJ	25,077	VC
Rutgers, The State Univ of New Jersey/Newark Campus	NJ	25,376	C
Saginaw Valley State Univ	MI	16,869	C
St. Anselm College	NH	48,324	VC
St. Augustine's Univ	NC	14,000	C
St. Francis Univ	PA	30,029	LC
St. John's Univ	MN	46,146	C
St. Joseph's Univ	PA	52,272	VC
St. Mary's College	IN	45,160	VC
St. Mary's College of Calif	CA	53,550	C
St. Mary's Univ	TX	33,854	C
St. Michael's College	VT	48,740	VC
St. Vincent College	PA	40,244	C
St. Xavier Univ	IL	32,840	C
Salem College	NC	29,326	VC
Salisbury Univ	MD	18,368	VC
Salve Regina Univ	RI	47,250	VC
Sam Houston State Univ	TX	17,082	C
Samford Univ	AL	35,700	VC+
San Diego State Univ	CA	20,578	VC
San Francisco State Univ	CA	18,514	C
San Jose State Univ	CA	19,707	C
Sarah Lawrence College	NY	48,000	HC
Seattle Pacific Univ	WA	41,559	VC+
Seattle Univ	WA	47,010	VC+
Seton Hall Univ	NJ	45,902	C
Sewanee: The Univ of the South	TN	47,700	HC+
Shippensburg Univ of Pennsylvania	PA	17,064	LC
Shorter Univ	GA	26,470	C
Siena College	NY	43,863	VC
Simmons College	MA	48,770	VC
Simpson College	IA	36,086	VC
Skidmore College	NY	57,926	HC
Slippery Rock Univ of Pennsylvania	PA	10,360	LC
Smith College	MA	57,524	MC
Sonoma State Univ	CA	20,541	C
S Car State Univ	SC	6,700	LC
Southern Conn State Univ	CT	18,033	C
Southern Illinois Univ Carbondale	IL	21,620	C
Southern Illinois Univ Edwardsville	IL	17,532	C
Southern Methodist Univ	TX	57,755	MC
Southern Univ and A&M College	LA	9,761	C+
Southwestern Univ	TX	45,660	VC
Spelman College	GA	24,650	VC
St. Ambrose Univ	IA		C
St. Bonaventure Univ	NY	38,831	C
St. Catherine Univ	MN	37,782	C+
St. Edward's Univ	TX	44,674	VC
St. John Fisher College	NY	39,370	C+
St. John's Univ	NY	52,840	C+
St. Lawrence Univ	NY	53,740	HC
St. Norbert College	WI	39,992	VC
St. Olaf College	MN	49,960	HC+
Stanford Univ	CA	56,411	MC
Stephen F. Austin State Univ	TX	14,668	C
Stetson Univ	FL	49,512	VC
Stonehill College	MA	46,780	VC+
Suffolk Univ	MA	46,548	C
SUNY College at Geneseo	NY	18,055	HC+
SUNY Fredonia / The SUNY at Fredonia	NY	18,702	VC
SUNY New Paltz	NY	15,010	C
SUNY Oneonta / SUNY	NY	16,919	VC
SUNY Plattsburgh / SUNY	NY	18,083	VC
Susquehanna Univ	PA	49,170	C
Swarthmore College	PA	57,870	MC
Sweet Briar College	VA	43,765	C+
Syracuse Univ	NY	54,512	HC
Temple Univ	PA	24,392	VC
Tenn Tech Univ	TN	11,310	C
Texas A&M Univ	TX	16,956	VC+
Texas A&M Univ at Commerce	TX	10,496	C
Texas Christian Univ	TX	47,570	HC
Texas State Univ	TX	16,495	VC
Texas Tech Univ	TX	14,243	C
The Catholic Univ of America	DC	52,852	VC
The College at Brockport / SUNY	NY	18,362	VC
The College of New Rochelle	NY	33,600	VC
The Lincoln Univ	PA	15,154	LC
Ohio State Univ	OH	19,887	MC
The SUNY at Potsdam	NY	17,754	C
Thomas Edison State College	NJ	5,700	SP
Towson Univ	MD	16,000	VC
Transylvania Univ	KY	40,310	VC+
Trinity College	CT		HC+
Trinity Univ	TX	44,174	HC+
Truman State Univ	MO	13,546	HC
Tufts Univ	MA	58,780	MC
Tulane Univ	LA	58,942	MC
Union College	NE	23,270	VC
Union Univ	TN	28,260	VC
Univ at Buffalo / The SUNY	NY	20,283	VC
Univ of Akron	OH	20,436	C
Univ of Alabama at Birmingham	AL	18,484	C+
Univ of Alabama at Tuscaloosa	AL	17,164	C+
Univ of Alaska Fairbanks	AK	13,955	C
Univ of Arizona	AZ	20,105	C
Univ of Arkansas at Fayetteville	AR	16,860	VC
Univ of Arkansas at Little Rock	AR		C
Univ of Calif at Berkeley	CA	23,322	MC
Univ of Calif at Davis	CA	24,482	HC
Univ of Calif at Irvine	CA	25,961	VC
Univ of Calif at Los Angeles	CA	25,686	MC
Univ of Calif at Riverside	CA	27,204	C
Univ of Calif at Santa Barbara	CA	27,551	HC
Univ of Central Arkansas	AR	10,840	VC
Univ of Central Florida	FL	15,711	VC+
Univ of Central Missouri	MO	14,605	C
Univ of Central Okla	OK	12,293	C
Univ of Cincinnati	OH	20,199	VC
Univ of Colo Boulder	CO	22,605	VC+
Univ of Colo Denver	CO	17,904	C
Univ of Conn	CT	23,744	HC
Univ of Dallas	TX	43,510	VC+
Univ of Dayton	OH	43,750	VC
Univ of Denver	CO	51,787	VC+
Univ of Evansville	IN	41,056	VC+
Univ of Florida	FL	15,783	HC+
Univ of Georgia	GA	19,508	VC
Univ of Hawaii at Manoa	HI	19,379	VC
Univ of Houston	TX	19,184	VC
Univ of Idaho	ID	14,558	C
Univ of Illinois at Chicago	IL	24,293	VC
Univ of Illinois at Urbana-Champaign	IL	24,300	HC
Univ of Indianapolis	IN	31,740	LC
Univ of Iowa	IA	17,481	VC
Univ of Jamestown	ND	24,738	C
Univ of Kansas	KS	16,980	C+
Univ of Kentucky	KY	19,868	C
Univ of La Verne	CA	47,010	VC
Univ of Louisiana at Lafayette	LA	6,130	C
Univ of Louisiana at Monroe	LA	12,998	C
Univ of Louisville	KY	17,460	VC
Univ of Maine	ME	19,712	C+
Univ of Maine at Fort Kent	ME	14,975	LC
Univ of Mary Washington	VA	19,484	VC
Univ of Maryland	MD	18,801	HC
Univ of Maryland/Baltimore County	MD	18,000	VC
Univ of Mass Boston	MA	11,966	C
Univ of Mass Dartmouth	MA	22,223	C
Univ of Miami	FL	55,166	MC
Univ of Mich/Ann Arbor	MI	22,102	HC+
Univ of Mich/Dearborn	MI	9,885	VC
Univ of Mich-Flint	MI	17,547	C+
Univ of Minn/Morris	MN	17,150	VC
Univ of Minn/Twin Cities	MN		HC
Univ of Miss	MS	15,482	VC
Univ of Missouri/Columbia	MO	18,201	MC
Univ of Missouri-Kansas City	MO	19,603	C
Univ of Missouri-St. Louis	MO	18,304	VC
Univ of Montana	MT	13,670	C
Univ of Montevallo	AL	17,320	C
Univ of Mount Union	OH	35,130	C
Univ of Nebr - Lincoln	NE	17,507	VC
Univ of Nebr at Kearney	NE	14,855	LC
Univ of Nebr at Omaha	NE	12,700	C
Univ of Nevada, Las Vegas	NV	17,303	C
Univ of Nevada/Reno	NV	14,500	NC
Univ of New Hampshire	NH	24,702	VC
Univ of New Mexico	NM	15,300	C
Univ of New Orleans	LA	9,224	VC
Univ of North Alabama	AL	9,960	C
Univ of N Car at Asheville	NC	13,500	VC+
Univ of N Car at Charlotte	NC	15,847	C
Univ of N Car at Greensboro	NC	12,848	C
Univ of N Car at Wilmington	NC	13,572	VC+
Univ of N Dak	ND	14,094	C
Univ of North Texas	TX	15,628	C
Univ of Northern Colo	CO	15,973	C
Univ of Notre Dame	IN		MC
Univ of Okla	OK	17,634	VC+
Univ of Oregon	OR	20,872	VC
Univ of Pennsylvania	PA	56,106	MC
Univ of Pittsburgh at Pittsburgh	PA	27,800	HC+
Univ of PR/Mayaguez	PR	1,250	
Univ of Puget Sound	WA	52,648	HC+
Univ of Redlands	CA	40,500	VC
Univ of Rochester	NY	58,500	MC
Univ of San Diego	CA	53,302	HC+
Univ of San Francisco	CA	49,674	VC
Univ of Scranton	PA	51,940	VC
Univ of S Car at Columbia	SC	19,725	VC+
Univ of South Florida	FL	13,000	C
Univ of Southern Calif	CA	56,903	MC
Univ of Southern Indiana	IN	14,657	C
Univ of Southern Maine	ME	16,576	C
Univ of St. Thomas - Houston	TX	36,490	VC
Univ of Tenn at Chattanooga	TN	16,883	C
Univ of Tenn at Knoxville	TN	20,364	VC+
Univ of Tenn at Martin	TN	13,217	C
Univ of Texas at Arlington	TX	10,908	LC
Univ of Texas at Austin	TX	44,074	HC
Univ of Texas at El Paso	TX	8,764	NC
Univ of the District of Columbia	DC	7,244	LC
Univ of the Pacific	CA	52,146	VC
Univ of Toledo	OH	18,464	C
Univ of Tulsa	OK	45,311	HC+
Univ of Utah	UT	13,462	VC
Univ of Vermont	VT	26,120	VC+
Univ of Virginia	VA	22,175	MC
Univ of Virginia's College at Wise	VA	11,076	C
Univ of Washington	WA	14,722	VC
Univ of Wisc Whitewater	WI	13,314	C
Univ of Wisc/Eau Claire	WI	15,430	VC
Univ of Wisc/Green Bay	WI	14,900	C
Univ of Wisc/La Crosse	WI	14,755	VC
Univ of Wisc/Madison	WI	18,757	HC
Univ of Wisc/Oshkosh	WI	10,426	LC
Univ of Wisc/Parkside	WI	10,181	LC
Univ of Wisc/Stevens Point	WI	14,043	C
Univ of Wisc-Milwaukee	WI	18,436	C
Univ of Wyoming	WY	13,855	C+
Ursinus College	PA	55,630	VC+
Utah State Univ	UT	11,803	C
Valparaiso Univ	IN	43,040	VC+
Vanderbilt Univ	TN	57,072	MC
Vassar College	NY	59,070	MC
Villanova Univ	PA	56,436	MC
Virginia Polytechnic Inst and State Univ	VA	14,629	HC
Virginia Wesleyan College	VA	28,433	LC
Wabash College	IN	44,160	VC
Wake Forest Univ	NC	51,000	MC
Walla Walla Univ	WA	26,256	NC
Walsh Univ	OH	35,100	C
Wartburg College	IA	41,055	VC
Washburn Univ	KS	12,165	NC
Washington and Jefferson College	PA	49,990	VC
Washington and Lee Univ	VA	52,812	MC
Washington College	MD	48,768	VC
Washington State Univ	WA	20,461	C
Washington Univ in St. Louis	MO	58,818	MC
Webster Univ	MO	33,990	C+
Wellesley College	MA	49,848	MC
Wells College	NY	38,680	VC
Wesleyan College	GA	24,000	C+
West Chester Univ of Pennsylvania	PA	16,836	C
Western Carolina Univ	NC	13,965	C+
Western Illinois Univ	IL	20,130	C
Western Kentucky Univ	KY	11,000	LC
Western Mich Univ	MI	19,042	C
Western Washington Univ	WA	18,519	VC
Westminster College	MO	30,490	VC
Westminster College	PA	31,290	C+
Westmont College	CA	41,500	HC
Wheaton College	IL	39,650	HC+
Wheeling Jesuit Univ	WV	34,668	C
Whitman College	WA	54,400	MC
Whittier College	CA	43,416	C
Whitworth Univ	WA	45,826	VC+
Wichita State Univ	KS	12,539	C
Widener Univ	PA	50,368	C
Willamette Univ	OR	56,450	VC+
William Jewell College	MO	31,000	VC+
Williams College	MA	58,900	MC
Wilson College	PA	27,660	C
Winthrop Univ	SC	21,120	VC
Wittenberg Univ	OH	47,766	VC
Wofford College	SC	45,795	VC
Wright State Univ	OH	16,983	C
Xavier Univ	OH	43,740	VC
Xavier Univ of Louisiana	LA	25,300	C
Yale Univ	CT	55,300	MC
Yeshiva Univ	NY	47,250	VC+
York College / CUNY	NY	5,496	NC
Youngstown State Univ	OH	16,374	LC

ST = STATE **$IS** = IN-STATE COSTS **SR** = SELECTOR RATING

FRENCH AND FRANCOPHONE STUDIES

School	ST	$IS	SR
Bates College	ME	58,950	MC
Creighton Univ	NE	44,058	V¢
Linfield College-McMinnville Campus	OR	46,166	C
St. Louis Univ	MO	46,594	V¢
Univ of Illinois at Chicago	IL	24,293	VC

FRENCH STUDIES

School	ST	$IS	SR
American Univ	DC	54,829	H¢
Appalachian State Univ	NC	12,919	VC
Aquinas College	MI	33,060	C
Bard College	NY	59,872	HC
Bard College at Simon's Rock	MA	58,963	H¢
Boston Univ	MA	54,130	H¢
Brown Univ	RI	56,150	MC
Cal State, Chico	CA	18,952	C
Cal State, Fresno	CA	17,405	C
Cal State, Northridge	CA	28,313	C
Case Western Reserve Univ	OH	55,178	MC
Coe College	IA	43,590	VC
Colby College	ME	57,510	MC
College of Charleston	SC	21,273	VC
Colo College	CO	54,534	MC
Columbia Univ/School of General Studies	NY	54,083	MC
Dartmouth College	NH	57,996	MC
Duke Univ	NC	50,250	MC
Emory Univ	GA	45,000	MC
Fairleigh Dickinson Univ/ College at Florham	NJ	42,142	C
Fordham Univ	NY	58,927	HC
Lake Erie College	OH	35,704	C
Lake Superior State Univ	MI	18,121	C
Lewis & Clark College	OR	52,656	VC
Mills College	CA	54,119	HC
New College of Florida	FL	14,504	H¢
New York Univ	NY	61,470	MC
North Park Univ	IL	30,130	C
Northeastern Illinois Univ	IL		C
Northern Kentucky Univ	KY	15,302	LC
Oswego / SUNY	NY	20,009	VC
Purdue Univ/West Lafayette	IN	20,278	HC
Reed College	OR	57,780	MC
Rice Univ	TX	43,288	MC
St. Joseph's Univ	PA	52,272	VC
Santa Clara Univ	CA	54,702	MC
Scripps College	CA	54,900	MC
Sewanee: The Univ of the South	TN	47,700	H¢
Skidmore College	NY	57,926	HC
Smith College	MA	57,524	MC
S Dak State Univ	SD	14,296	C
Southeast Missouri State Univ	MO	14,983	LC
Stony Brook Univ / SUNY	NY	19,359	HC
SUNY Plattsburgh / SUNY	NY	18,083	VC
The Catholic Univ of America	DC	52,852	VC
Ohio State Univ	OH	19,887	MC
The SUNY at Potsdam	NY	17,754	C
Union College	NY		MC
Univ of Calif at Los Angeles	CA	25,686	MC
Univ of Calif at San Diego	CA	21,000	VC
Univ of Illinois at Chicago	IL	24,293	VC
Univ of Mass Amherst	MA	23,697	V¢
Univ of New Hampshire	NH	24,702	VC
Univ of North Florida	FL	15,578	VC
Univ of Portland	OR	47,874	VC
Univ of S Dak	SD	15,111	C
Univ of Texas-Pan American	TX	12,432	LC
Univ of Wisc/Green Bay	WI	14,900	C
Wartburg College	IA	41,055	VC
Wellesley College	MA	49,848	MC
Wesleyan Univ	CT	59,844	MC
Wheaton College	MA	54,934	H¢
Youngstown State Univ	OH	16,374	LC

FUNERAL HOME SERVICES

School	ST	$IS	SR
Cincinnati College of Mortuary Science	OH	13,500	SP
Gannon Univ	PA	37,940	C
Mount Ida College	MA	30,115	LC
Point Park Univ	PA	36,390	C
Southern Illinois Univ Carbondale	IL	21,620	C
St. John's Univ	NY	52,840	¢
Univ of Central Okla	OK	12,293	C
Wayne State Univ	MI	19,493	C

FURNITURE DESIGN

School	ST	$IS	SR
Calif College of the Arts	CA	48,334	SP
Cal State, Fresno	CA	17,405	C
Ferris State Univ	MI	19,698	C
Indiana Univ-Purdue Univ Indianapolis	IN	17,290	C
Kendall College of Art and Design of Ferris State Univ	MI	21,048	SP
Minneapolis College of Art and Design	MN	36,700	SP
N Car State Univ	NC	16,202	HC
Rhode Island School of Design	RI	55,204	SP
Rochester Inst of Technology	NY	42,450	V¢
Savannah College of Art and Design	GA	46,824	SP

GAME DESIGN AND DEVELOPMENT

School	ST	$IS	SR
Abilene Christian Univ	TX	38,400	VC
Cleveland Inst of Art	OH	48,641	SP
Lawrence Tech Univ	MI	37,630	VC
Rocky Mountain College of Art and Design	CO	22,470	NC
St. Edward's Univ	TX	44,674	VC
Univ of Wisc/Stout	WI	23,942	C
William Peace Univ	NC	32,900	LC

GENDER STUDIES

School	ST	$IS	SR
Albion College	MI	43,884	VC
American Univ	DC	54,829	H¢
Bard College	NY	59,872	HC
Bard College at Simon's Rock	MA	58,963	H¢
Bowdoin College	ME	57,834	MC
Brown Univ	RI	56,150	MC
Bryant Univ	RI	49,179	VC
Butler Univ	IN	45,898	V¢
Calif State Polytechnic Univ, Pomona	CA	18,932	C
Coe College	IA	43,590	VC
College of St. Benedict	MN	47,570	VC
Colo College	CO	54,534	MC
Conn College	CT	54,970	MC
Davidson College	NC	54,683	MC
DePauw Univ	IN	48,950	V¢
Dominican Univ	IL	37,628	C
Eastern Mich Univ	MI	17,961	C
Eugene Lang College - The New School for Liberal Arts	NY	55,650	VC
Fort Lewis College	CO	15,513	C
Guilford College	NC	35,340	C
Hanover College	IN	41,450	VC
Hollins Univ	VA	43,295	VC
Indiana Univ Bloomington	IN	19,358	HC
John Carroll Univ	OH	44,520	¢
John Jay College of Criminal Justice / The CUNY	NY	6,059	C
Lawrence Univ	WI	46,371	HC
McNeese State Univ	LA		C
Mercer Univ	GA	44,201	V¢
Mount Holyoke College	MA	53,596	H¢
New College of Florida	FL	14,504	H¢
New York Univ	NY	61,470	MC
Northeastern Illinois Univ	IL		C
Northwestern Univ	IL	37,595	MC
Oberlin College	OH	57,025	MC
Ohio Univ	OH	20,676	VC
Prescott College	AZ	33,284	¢
St. John's Univ	MN	46,146	C
St. Michael's College	VT	48,740	VC
Simmons College	MA	48,770	VC
Skidmore College	NY	57,926	HC
Sonoma State Univ	CA	20,541	C
Southern Oregon Univ	OR	17,874	C
Stonehill College	MA	46,780	V¢
SUNY Plattsburgh / SUNY	NY	18,083	VC
Swarthmore College	PA	57,870	MC
Texas State Univ	TX	16,495	VC
Tulane Univ	LA	58,942	MC
Univ of Arizona	AZ	20,105	C
Univ of Calif at San Diego	CA	21,000	VC
Univ of Chicago	IL	55,416	MC
Univ of Illinois at Chicago	IL	24,293	VC
Univ of Iowa	IA	17,481	VC
Univ of Maryland/Baltimore County	MD	18,000	VC
Univ of Mass Amherst	MA	23,697	V¢
Univ of Miami	FL	55,166	MC
Univ of Pennsylvania	PA	56,106	MC
Univ of Utah	UT	13,462	VC
Univ of Vermont	VT	26,120	V¢
Univ of Wisc/Green Bay	WI	14,900	C
Univ of Wisc/Madison	WI	18,757	HC
Villanova Univ	PA	56,436	MC
Warren Wilson College	NC	34,888	VC
Wesleyan Univ	CT	59,844	MC
Western Mich Univ	MI	19,042	C
Westminster College	UT	37,708	VC
Widener Univ	PA	50,368	C
Wofford College	SC	45,795	VC
Xavier Univ	OH	43,740	VC

GENERAL STUDIES

School	ST	$IS	SR
College of Mount St. Joseph	OH	33,880	C
Fontbonne Univ	MO	31,384	C
Houghton College	NY	35,740	VC
Indiana Univ Bloomington	IN	19,358	HC
Indiana Univ East	IN	6,639	LC
Indiana Univ Kokomo	IN	6,674	LC
Indiana Univ Northwest	IN	6,738	LC
Indiana Univ Southeast	IN	15,807	LC
Indiana Univ-Purdue Univ Indianapolis	IN	17,290	C
Kent State Univ	OH	19,352	C
New York Univ	NY	61,470	MC
Nova Southeastern Univ	FL	34,016	VC
St. Louis Univ	MO	46,594	V¢
Texas Christian Univ	TX	47,570	HC
Univ of Central Okla	OK	12,293	C
Univ of Idaho	ID	14,558	C
Western Illinois Univ	IL	20,130	C
Youngstown State Univ	OH	16,374	LC

GENETICS

School	ST	$IS	SR
Cal State, Northridge	CA	28,313	C
Cedar Crest College	PA	43,240	C
Dartmouth College	NH	57,996	MC
Florida State Univ	FL	15,238	HC
Howard Univ	DC	35,957	C
Iowa State Univ	IA	16,403	C
Missouri Southern State Univ	MO	11,910	C
New Mexico State Univ	NM	13,955	LC
Ohio Wesleyan Univ	OH	49,460	¢
Purdue Univ/West Lafayette	IN	20,278	HC
Rutgers, The State Univ of New Jersey/New Brunswick	NJ	25,077	VC
Southern Illinois Univ Edwardsville	IL	17,532	C
SUNY Fredonia / The SUNY at Fredonia	NY	18,702	VC
Texas A&M Univ	TX	16,956	V¢
Univ of Arizona	AZ	20,105	C
Univ of Calif at Davis	CA	24,482	HC
Univ of Calif at Irvine	CA	25,961	VC
Univ of Calif at Riverside	CA	27,204	C
Univ of Conn	CT	23,744	HC
Univ of Georgia	GA	19,508	VC
Univ of Minn/Twin Cities	MN		HC
Univ of New Hampshire	NH	24,702	VC
Univ of Vermont	VT	26,120	V¢
Univ of Wisc/Madison	WI	18,757	HC
Washington State Univ	WA	20,461	C
Western Kentucky Univ	KY	11,000	LC

GEOCHEMISTRY

School	ST	$IS	SR
Bridgewater State Univ	MA	18,752	C
Calif Inst of Technology	CA	54,045	MC
Columbia Univ in the City of New York	NY	61,116	MC
Grand Valley State Univ	MI	17,998	VC
Oswego / SUNY	NY	20,009	VC
SUNY College at Geneseo	NY	18,055	H¢
SUNY Cortland / The SUNY	NY	19,117	C
Western Mich Univ	MI	19,042	C

GEODETIC SCIENCE

School	ST	$IS	SR
Univ of Arkansas at Monticello	AR	8,470	NC

GEOENVIRONMENTAL STUDIES

School	ST	$IS	SR
Northeastern Illinois Univ	IL		C
Shippensburg Univ of Pennsylvania	PA	17,064	LC
Univ of Illinois at Chicago	IL	24,293	VC
Univ of Notre Dame	IN		MC

GEOGRAPHY

School	ST	$IS	SR
Adams State College	CO	13,358	LC
Appalachian State Univ	NC	12,919	VC
Aquinas College	MI	33,060	C
Arizona State Univ	AZ	18,818	¢
Arkansas State Univ	AR	14,980	C
Auburn Univ	AL	20,052	V¢
Augustana College	IL	43,398	HC
Ball State Univ	IN	17,850	C
Bard College at Simon's Rock	MA	58,963	H¢
Baylor Univ	TX	46,720	HC
Bellevue Univ	NE	4,600	NC
Bemidji State Univ	MN	13,500	C
Binghamton Univ / The SUNY	NY	20,832	H¢
Bloomsburg Univ of Pennsylvania	PA	13,598	C
Boston Univ	MA	54,130	H¢
Bowling Green State Univ	OH	18,970	C
Bridgewater State Univ	MA	18,752	C
Brigham Young Univ	UT	12,100	HC
Bucknell Univ	PA	58,160	MC
Buffalo State/State Univ of Buffalo	NY	15,733	¢
Calif State Polytechnic Univ, Pomona	CA	18,932	C
Cal State, Chico	CA	18,952	C
Cal State, Dominguez Hills	CA	17,056	LC
Cal State, East Bay	CA	16,549	C
Cal State, Fresno	CA	17,405	C
Cal State, Fullerton	CA	25,188	¢
Cal State, Long Beach	CA	17,534	¢
Cal State, Los Angeles	CA	15,829	C
Cal State, Northridge	CA	28,313	C
Cal State, Sacramento	CA	16,200	C
Cal State, San Bernardino	CA	12,000	C
Cal State, Stanislaus	CA	18,582	C
Calif Univ of Pennsylvania	PA	14,217	C
Calvin College	MI	37,585	V¢
Carthage College	WI	33,000	C
Central Conn State Univ	CT	19,212	C
Central Mich Univ	MI	18,066	C
Central Washington Univ	WA	11,730	C
Charleston Southern Univ	SC	22,420	C
Cheyney Univ of Pennsylvania	PA	20,372	LC
Chicago State Univ	IL	5,482	C
Clark Univ	MA	47,020	H¢
Colgate Univ	NY	50,930	MC
Concord Univ	WV	13,102	C
Concordia Univ Nebr	NE	26,000	VC
Concordia Univ, River Forest	IL	26,300	C
Dartmouth College	NH	57,996	MC
DePaul Univ	IL	46,120	VC
DePauw Univ	IN	48,950	V¢
Dickinson State Univ	ND	8,550	NC
East Carolina Univ	NC	14,169	C
East Stroudsburg Univ of Pennsylvania	PA	16,636	C
East Tenn State Univ	TN	9,000	C
Eastern Illinois Univ	IL	20,502	C
Eastern Kentucky Univ	KY	11,161	C
Eastern Mich Univ	MI	17,961	C
Eastern Washington Univ	WA	16,388	C
Edinboro Univ of Pennsylvania	PA	15,940	LC
Elmhurst College	IL	42,032	¢
Emory and Henry College	VA	387,460	C
Excelsior College	NY	895	SP
Fayetteville State Univ	NC	10,816	C
Fitchburg State Univ	MA	17,241	C
Florida Atlantic Univ	FL	17,339	C
Florida International Univ	FL	17,747	VC
Florida State Univ	FL	15,238	HC
Framingham State Univ	MA	16,750	C
Frostburg State Univ	MD	15,264	LC
George Mason Univ	VA	15,724	VC
George Washington Univ	DC	57,108	MC
Georgia College and State Univ	GA	18,216	VC
Georgia Southern Univ	GA	16,414	C
Georgia State Univ	GA	12,000	VC
Grand Valley State Univ	MI	17,998	VC
Gustavus Adolphus College	MN	48,170	HC
Hampshire College	MA	58,320	MC
Hofstra Univ	NY	48,020	V¢
Howard Univ	DC	35,957	C
Humboldt State Univ	CA	18,400	C
Hunter College / The CUNY	NY	14,429	VC
Illinois State Univ	IL	22,634	VC
Indiana State Univ	IN	16,000	C
Indiana Univ Bloomington	IN	19,358	HC
Indiana Univ of Pennsylvania	PA	20,180	LC
Indiana Univ-Purdue Univ Indianapolis	IN	17,290	C
Jacksonville State Univ	AL	12,280	LC
Jacksonville Univ	FL	37,780	C
James Madison Univ	VA	18,049	VC
Kansas State Univ	KS	15,497	VC
Keene State College	NH	21,538	C
Kennesaw State Univ	GA	13,017	VC
Kent State Univ	OH	19,352	C
Kutztown Univ of Pennsylvania	PA	16,909	LC
Lehman College / The CUNY	NY	5,778	LC
Lock Haven Univ of Pennsylvania	PA	17,587	LC
LIU/C.W. Post Campus	NY	38,888	C
Louisiana State Univ	LA	18,677	V¢
Louisiana Tech Univ	LA	8,000	C
Macalester College	MN	53,419	MC
Mansfield Univ	PA	19,468	LC
Marshall Univ	WV	14,820	C
Miami Univ	OH	24,191	HC
Mich State Univ	MI	13,689	VC
Middle Tenn State Univ	TN	8,650	C
Middlebury College	VT	57,470	MC
Millersville Univ of Pennsylvania	PA	18,498	C
Minn State Univ, Mankato	MN	14,900	C
Missouri State Univ	MO	13,996	VC
Montclair State Univ	NJ	22,614	C
Morehead State Univ	KY	10,900	C
Mount Holyoke College	MA	53,596	H¢
New Jersey City Univ	NJ	21,060	¢
New Mexico State Univ	NM	13,955	LC
N Car Central Univ	NC	9,000	LC

School	ST	$IS	SR
Northeastern Illinois Univ	IL		C
Northeastern State Univ	OK	8,615	VC
Northern Arizona Univ	AZ	18,592	C
Northern Illinois Univ	IL	19,768	C
Northern Kentucky Univ	KY	15,302	LC
Northern Mich Univ	MI	15,300	VC
Northwest Missouri State Univ	MO	14,229	C
Northwestern State Univ of Louisiana	LA	14,368	C
Northwestern Univ	IL	37,595	MC
Ohio Univ	OH	20,676	VC
Ohio Wesleyan Univ	OH	49,460	C+
Okla State Univ	OK	14,310	VC
Old Dominion Univ	VA	10,002	C
Olivet Nazarene Univ	IL	29,990	C
Park Univ	MO	17,525	C
Penn State Univ/Univ Park	PA	25,404	VC
Pittsburg State Univ	KS	12,032	C
Plymouth State Univ	NH	23,148	LC
Portland State Univ	OR	18,672	C
Prairie View A&M Univ	TX	15,205	LC
Prescott College	AZ	33,284	C+
Radford Univ	VA	17,132	LC
Rhode Island College	RI	17,132	LC
Rowan Univ	NJ	23,570	VC
Rutgers, The State Univ of New Jersey/New Brunswick	NJ	25,077	VC
Salem State College	MA	13,161	LC
Salisbury Univ	MD	18,368	VC
Sam Houston State Univ	TX	17,082	C
Samford Univ	AL	35,700	VC+
San Diego State Univ	CA	20,578	VC
San Francisco State Univ	CA	18,514	C
San Jose State Univ	CA	19,707	C
Shippensburg Univ of Pennsylvania	PA	17,064	LC
Slippery Rock Univ of Pennsylvania	PA	10,360	LC
Sonoma State Univ	CA	20,541	C
S Dak State Univ	SD	14,296	C
Southern Conn State Univ	CT	18,033	C
Southern Illinois Univ Carbondale	IL	21,620	C
Southern Illinois Univ Edwardsville	IL	17,532	C
Southern Oregon Univ	OR	17,874	C
St. Cloud State Univ	MN	10,600	C
Stephen F. Austin State Univ	TX	14,668	C
Stetson Univ	FL	49,512	VC+
SUNY College at Geneseo	NY	18,055	HC+
SUNY Cortland / The SUNY	NY	19,117	C
SUNY New Paltz	NY	15,010	C
SUNY Oneonta / SUNY	NY	16,919	VC
SUNY Plattsburgh / SUNY	NY	18,083	VC
Syracuse Univ	NY	54,512	HC
Taylor Univ	IN	36,742	VC+
Temple Univ	PA	24,392	VC
Texas A&M Univ at Commerce	TX	10,496	C
Texas A&M Univ at Corpus Christi	TX	11,544	LC
Texas A&M Univ at Galveston	TX	11,258	C
Texas A&M Univ at Kingsville	TX	7,500	LC
Texas Christian Univ	TX	47,570	HC
Texas State Univ	TX	16,495	VC
Texas Tech Univ	TX	14,243	C
Ohio State Univ	OH	19,887	MC
Towson Univ	MD	16,000	VC
United States Air Force Academy	CO		MC
United States Military Academy	NY		MC
Univ at Albany / SUNY	NY	18,674	VC
Univ at Buffalo / The SUNY	NY	20,283	VC
Univ of Akron	OH	20,436	C
Univ of Alabama at Tuscaloosa	AL	17,164	C+
Univ of Alaska Fairbanks	AK	13,955	C
Univ of Arizona	AZ	20,105	C
Univ of Arkansas at Fayetteville	AR	16,860	VC
Univ of Calif at Berkeley	CA	23,322	MC
Univ of Calif at Davis	CA	24,482	HC
Univ of Calif at Los Angeles	CA	25,686	MC
Univ of Calif at Santa Barbara	CA	27,551	HC
Univ of Central Arkansas	AR	10,840	VC
Univ of Central Missouri	MO	14,605	C
Univ of Central Okla	OK	12,293	C
Univ of Chicago	IL	55,416	MC
Univ of Cincinnati	OH	20,199	VC
Univ of Colo at Colo Springs	CO	15,000	VC
Univ of Colo Boulder	CO	22,605	VC+
Univ of Colo Denver	CO	17,904	C
Univ of Conn	CT	23,744	HC
Univ of Delaware	DE	22,728	VC
Univ of Denver	CO	51,787	VC+
Univ of Florida	FL	15,783	HC+
Univ of Georgia	GA	19,508	VC
Univ of Hawaii at Hilo	HI	6,500	C
Univ of Hawaii at Manoa	HI	19,379	VC
Univ of Idaho	ID	14,558	C
Univ of Illinois at Urbana-Champaign	IL	24,300	HC
Univ of Iowa	IA	17,481	VC
Univ of Kansas	KS	16,980	C+
Univ of Kentucky	KY	19,868	C
Univ of Louisville	KY	17,460	VC
Univ of Maine at Farmington	ME	17,841	C
Univ of Mary Washington	VA	19,484	VC
Univ of Maryland	MD	18,801	HC
Univ of Maryland/Baltimore County	MD	18,000	VC
Univ of Mass Amherst	MA	23,697	VC+
Univ of Mass Boston	MA	11,966	C
Univ of Memphis	TN	15,094	C
Univ of Miami	FL	55,166	MC
Univ of Mich-Flint	MI	17,547	C+
Univ of Minn/Duluth	MN	18,964	C+
Univ of Minn/Twin Cities	MN		HC
Univ of Missouri/Columbia	MO	18,201	MC
Univ of Missouri-Kansas City	MO	19,603	C
Univ of Montana	MT	13,670	C
Univ of Nebr - Lincoln	NE	17,507	VC
Univ of Nebr at Kearney	NE	14,855	LC
Univ of Nebr at Omaha	NE	12,700	C
Univ of Nevada/Reno	NV	14,500	NC
Univ of New Mexico	NM	15,300	C
Univ of New Orleans	LA	9,224	VC
Univ of North Alabama	AL	9,960	C
Univ of N Car at Chapel Hill	NC	18,348	MC
Univ of N Car at Charlotte	NC	15,847	C
Univ of N Car at Greensboro	NC	12,848	C
Univ of N Car at Wilmington	NC	13,572	VC+
Univ of N Dak	ND	14,094	C
Univ of North Texas	TX	15,628	C
Univ of Northern Colo	CO	15,973	C
Univ of Northern Iowa	IA	14,776	C
Univ of Okla	OK	17,634	VC+
Univ of Oregon	OR	20,872	VC
Univ of Pittsburgh at Johnstown	PA	20,862	LC
Univ of PR Recinto de Rio Piedras	PR	5,750	
Univ of South Alabama	AL	13,510	C
Univ of S Car at Columbia	SC	19,725	VC+
Univ of South Florida	FL	13,000	C
Univ of Southern Calif	CA	56,903	MC
Univ of Southern Maine	ME	16,576	C
Univ of Southern Miss	MS	13,170	C
Univ of Tenn at Knoxville	TN	20,364	VC+
Univ of Tenn at Martin	TN	13,217	C
Univ of Texas at Austin	TX	44,074	HC
Univ of Texas at Dallas	TX	21,046	HC
Univ of Texas at San Antonio	TX	18,372	C
Univ of the District of Columbia	DC	7,244	LC
Univ of Toledo	OH	18,464	C
Univ of Utah	UT	13,462	VC
Univ of Vermont	VT	26,120	VC+
Univ of Washington	WA	14,722	VC
Univ of West Georgia	GA	14,852	LC
Univ of Wisc Whitewater	WI	13,314	C
Univ of Wisc/Eau Claire	WI	15,430	VC
Univ of Wisc/La Crosse	WI	14,755	VC
Univ of Wisc/Madison	WI	18,757	HC
Univ of Wisc/Oshkosh	WI	10,426	LC
Univ of Wisc/Parkside	WI	10,181	LC
Univ of Wisc/Platteville	WI	14,274	C
Univ of Wisc/River Falls	WI	9,722	LC
Univ of Wisc/Stevens Point	WI	14,043	C
Univ of Wisc-Milwaukee	WI	18,436	C
Univ of Wyoming	WY	13,855	C+
Utah State Univ	UT	11,803	C
Valparaiso Univ	IN	43,040	VC+
Vassar College	NY	59,070	MC
Villanova Univ	PA	56,436	MC
Virginia Polytechnic Inst and State Univ	VA	14,629	HC
Wayne State College	NE	11,764	NC
West Chester Univ of Pennsylvania	PA	16,836	C
West Texas A&M Univ	TX	13,478	C
West Virginia Univ	WV	15,794	C+
Western Carolina Univ	NC	13,965	C+
Western Illinois Univ	IL	20,130	C
Western Kentucky Univ	KY	11,000	LC
Western Mich Univ	MI	19,042	C
Western Oregon Univ	OR	15,021	C
Western Washington Univ	WA	18,519	VC
William Paterson Univ of New Jersey	NJ	21,694	C
Wittenberg Univ	OH	47,766	VC
Worcester State Univ	MA	18,657	C
Wright State Univ	OH	16,983	C
Youngstown State Univ	OH	16,374	LC

GEOLOGICAL ENGINEERING

School	ST	$IS	SR
Colo School of Mines	CO	18,000	HC
Mich Tech Univ	MI	22,105	VC
Missouri Univ of Science and Technology	MO	18,655	VC+
Montana Tech of The Univ of Montana	MT	14,650	VC
Olivet Nazarene Univ	IL	29,990	C
Oregon State Univ	OR	19,017	C+
Rutgers, The State Univ of New Jersey/Newark Campus	NJ	25,376	C
S Dak School of Mines and Technology	SD	15,260	VC
Univ of Akron	OH	20,436	C
Univ of Alaska Fairbanks	AK	13,955	C
Univ of Calif at Los Angeles	CA	25,686	MC
Univ of Idaho	ID	14,558	C
Univ of Illinois at Urbana-Champaign	IL	24,300	HC
Univ of Mich/Ann Arbor	MI	22,102	HC+
Univ of Minn/Twin Cities	MN		HC
Univ of Miss	MS	15,482	VC
Univ of Nevada/Reno	NV	14,500	NC
Univ of N Dak	ND	14,094	C
Univ of Rochester	NY	58,500	MC
Univ of Utah	UT	13,462	VC
Univ of Wisc/Madison	WI	18,757	HC

GEOLOGY

School	ST	$IS	SR
Adams State College	CO	13,358	LC
Alfred Univ	NY	40,392	VC
Allegheny College	PA	49,020	HC
Amherst College	MA	58,744	MC
Appalachian State Univ	NC	12,919	VC
Arizona State Univ	AZ	18,818	C+
Arkansas Tech Univ	AR	13,164	LC
Ashland Univ	OH	25,000	C
Auburn Univ	AL	20,052	VC+
Augustana College	IL	43,398	HC
Ball State Univ	IN	17,850	C
Bates College	ME	58,950	MC
Baylor Univ	TX	46,720	HC
Beloit College	WI	49,970	HC
Bemidji State Univ	MN	13,500	C
Binghamton Univ / The SUNY	NY	20,832	HC+
Boise State Univ	ID	12,802	C
Boston College	MA	58,506	MC
Bowling Green State Univ	OH	18,970	C
Brigham Young Univ	UT	12,100	HC
Brown Univ	RI	56,150	MC
Bryn Mawr College	PA	57,760	MC
Bucknell Univ	PA	58,160	MC
Buffalo State/State Univ of Buffalo	NY	15,733	C+
Calif Inst of Technology	CA	54,045	MC
Calif Lutheran Univ	CA	47,640	C
Calif State Polytechnic Univ, Pomona	CA	18,932	C
Cal State, Bakersfield	CA	8,000	LC
Cal State, Chico	CA	18,952	C
Cal State, Dominguez Hills	CA	17,056	LC
Cal State, East Bay	CA	16,549	C
Cal State, Fresno	CA	17,405	C
Cal State, Fullerton	CA	25,188	C+
Cal State, Long Beach	CA	17,534	C+
Cal State, Los Angeles	CA	15,829	C
Cal State, Northridge	CA	28,313	C
Cal State, Sacramento	CA	16,200	C
Cal State, San Bernardino	CA	12,000	C
Cal State, Stanislaus	CA	18,582	C
Calif Univ of Pennsylvania	PA	14,217	C
Calvin College	MI	37,585	VC+
Carleton College	MN	58,149	MC
Case Western Reserve Univ	OH	55,178	MC
Castleton State College	VT	19,424	C
Cedarville Univ	OH	31,036	VC+
Centenary College of Louisiana	LA	39,070	C+
Central Mich Univ	MI	18,066	C
Central Washington Univ	WA	11,730	C
Charleston Southern Univ	SC	22,420	C
CUNY/Brooklyn College	NY	5,884	C+
Clarion Univ of Pennsylvania	PA	17,370	C
Clemson Univ	SC	10,136	HC
Cleveland State Univ	OH	21,357	C
Colby College	ME	57,510	MC
Colgate Univ	NY	50,930	MC
College of Charleston	SC	21,273	VC
College of William & Mary	VA	25,085	MC
College of Wooster	OH	52,600	VC
Colo College	CO	54,534	MC
Colo State Univ-Fort Collins	CO	20,090	VC
Columbia Univ in the City of New York	NY	61,116	MC
Cornell College	IA	44,930	HC
CUNY-City College	NY	19,576	HC+
Denison Univ	OH	54,670	HC+
DePauw Univ	IN	48,950	VC+
Duke Univ	NC	50,250	MC
Earlham College	IN	49,710	VC+
East Carolina Univ	NC	14,169	C
Eastern Illinois Univ	IL	20,502	C
Eastern Kentucky Univ	KY	11,161	C
Eastern Mich Univ	MI	17,961	C
Eastern New Mexico Univ	NM	10,682	C
Eastern Washington Univ	WA	16,388	C
Edinboro Univ of Pennsylvania	PA	15,940	LC
Elizabeth City State Univ	NC	11,638	C
Excelsior College	NY	895	SP
Florida Atlantic Univ	FL	17,339	C
Florida International Univ	FL	17,747	VC
Florida State Univ	FL	15,238	HC
Fort Hays State Univ	KS	11,354	C
Fort Lewis College	CO	15,513	C
Franklin and Marshall College	PA	58,295	MC
George Mason Univ	VA	15,724	VC
George Washington Univ	DC	57,108	MC
Georgia Southern Univ	GA	16,414	C
Georgia Southwestern State Univ	GA	12,218	C
Georgia State Univ	GA	12,000	VC
Grand Valley State Univ	MI	17,998	VC
Guilford College	NC	35,340	C
Gustavus Adolphus College	MN	48,170	HC
Hampshire College	MA	58,320	MC
Hanover College	IN	41,450	VC
Hardin-Simmons Univ	TX	23,560	C+
Hartwick College	NY	49,815	C+
Harvard Univ/Harvard College	MA	49,000	MC
Haverford College	PA	59,236	MC
Hofstra Univ	NY	48,020	VC+
Hope College	MI	36,320	VC+
Humboldt State Univ	CA	18,400	C
Idaho State Univ	ID	11,908	C
Illinois State Univ	IL	22,634	VC
Indiana State Univ	IN	16,000	C
Indiana Univ Bloomington	IN	19,358	HC
Indiana Univ Northwest	IN	6,738	LC
Indiana Univ of Pennsylvania	PA	20,180	LC
Indiana Univ-Purdue Univ Fort Wayne	IN	15,425	C
Indiana Univ-Purdue Univ Indianapolis	IN	17,290	C
Iowa State Univ	IA	16,403	C
James Madison Univ	VA	18,049	VC
Juniata College	PA	49,340	VC
Kansas State Univ	KS	15,497	VC
Keene State College	NH	21,538	C
Kent State Univ	OH	19,352	C
Kutztown Univ of Pennsylvania	PA	16,909	LC
La Salle Univ	PA	50,270	C
Lafayette College	PA	57,050	HC+
Lake Superior State Univ	MI	18,121	C
Lamar Univ	TX	6,820	LC
Lawrence Univ	WI	46,371	HC
Lehman College / The CUNY	NY	5,778	LC
Lock Haven Univ of Pennsylvania	PA	17,587	LC
LIU/C.W. Post Campus	NY	38,888	C
Louisiana State Univ	LA	18,677	VC+
Louisiana Tech Univ	LA	8,000	C
Macalester College	MN	53,419	MC
Marietta College	OH	42,135	VC
Marshall Univ	WV	14,820	C
Mercyhurst Univ	PA	40,700	C
Miami Univ	OH	24,191	HC
Mich State Univ	MI	13,689	VC
Mich Tech Univ	MI	22,105	VC
Middlebury College	VT	57,470	MC
Midwestern State Univ	TX	9,722	C
Millersville Univ of Pennsylvania	PA	18,498	C
Millsaps College	MS	43,888	VC+
Minot State Univ	ND	10,915	C
Missouri State Univ	MO	13,996	VC
Missouri Univ of Science and Technology	MO	18,655	VC+
Morehead State Univ	KY	10,900	C
Mount Holyoke College	MA	53,596	HC+
Muskingum Univ	OH	30,502	C
New Jersey City Univ	NJ	21,060	C+
New Mexico State Univ	NM	13,955	LC
N Car State Univ	NC	16,202	HC
N Dak State Univ	ND	14,642	C
Northern Arizona Univ	AZ	18,592	C
Northern Illinois Univ	IL	19,768	C
Northern Kentucky Univ	KY	15,302	LC
Northwest Missouri State Univ	MO	14,229	C
Northwestern Univ	IL	37,595	MC
Norwich Univ	VT	28,212	C
Oberlin College	OH	57,025	MC
Occidental College	CA	59,592	MC+
Ohio Univ	OH	20,676	VC
Ohio Wesleyan Univ	OH	49,460	C+
Okla State Univ	OK	14,310	VC
Old Dominion Univ	VA	18,662	C
Oswego / SUNY	NY	20,009	VC
Penn State Univ/Univ Park	PA	25,404	VC
Pomona College	CA	57,680	MC
Portland State Univ	OR	18,672	C
Prescott College	AZ	33,284	C+
Purdue Univ/West Lafayette	IN	20,278	HC

School	ST	$IS	SR
Queens College / The CUNY	NY	17,107	VC
Radford Univ	VA	17,132	LC
Rensselaer Polytechnic Inst	NY	59,229	MC
Rice Univ	TX	43,288	MC
Richard Stockton College of New Jersey	NJ	20,000	VC
Rocky Mountain College	MT	32,242	C
Rutgers, The State Univ of New Jersey/New Brunswick	NJ	25,077	VC
Rutgers, The State Univ of New Jersey/Newark Campus	NJ	25,376	C
St. Louis Univ	MO	46,594	VC+
Salem State College	MA	13,161	LC
Sam Houston State Univ	TX	17,082	C
San Diego State Univ	CA	20,578	VC
San Francisco State Univ	CA	18,514	C
San Jose State Univ	CA	19,707	C
Scripps College	CA	54,900	MC
Sewanee: The Univ of the South	TN	47,700	HC+
Skidmore College	NY	57,926	HC
Slippery Rock Univ of Pennsylvania	PA	10,360	LC
Smith College	MA	57,524	MC
Sonoma State Univ	CA	20,541	C
S Dak School of Mines and Technology	SD	15,260	VC
Southern Illinois Univ Carbondale	IL	21,620	C
Southern Methodist Univ	TX	57,755	MC
St. Cloud State Univ	MN	10,600	C
St. Lawrence Univ	NY	53,740	HC
St. Norbert College	WI	39,992	VC
Stanford Univ	CA	56,411	MC
Stephen F. Austin State Univ	TX	14,668	C
Stony Brook Univ / SUNY	NY	19,359	HC
Sul Ross State Univ	TX	13,410	LC
SUNY College at Geneseo	NY	18,055	HC+
SUNY Cortland / The SUNY	NY	19,117	C
SUNY Fredonia / The SUNY at Fredonia	NY	18,702	VC
SUNY New Paltz	NY	15,010	C
SUNY Oneonta / SUNY	NY	16,919	VC
SUNY Plattsburgh / SUNY	NY	18,083	VC
Syracuse Univ	NY	54,512	HC
Tarleton State Univ	TX	13,489	LC
Temple Univ	PA	24,392	VC
Tenn Tech Univ	TN	11,310	C
Texas A&M Univ	TX	16,956	VC+
Texas A&M Univ at Commerce	TX	10,496	C
Texas A&M Univ at Corpus Christi	TX	11,544	LC
Texas A&M Univ at Kingsville	TX	7,500	LC
Texas Christian Univ	TX	47,570	HC
Texas Tech Univ	TX	14,243	C
The College at Brockport / SUNY	NY	18,362	VC
The College of St. Rose	NY	26,750	C
Ohio State Univ	OH	19,887	MC
The SUNY at Potsdam	NY	17,754	C
Towson Univ	MD	16,000	VC
Tufts Univ	MA	58,780	MC
Tulane Univ	LA	58,942	MC
Union College	NY		MC
Unity College	ME	34,054	C
Univ at Buffalo / The SUNY	NY	20,283	VC
Univ of Akron	OH	20,436	C
Univ of Alabama at Tuscaloosa	AL	17,164	C+
Univ of Alaska Fairbanks	AK	13,955	C
Univ of Arizona	AZ	20,105	C
Univ of Arkansas at Fayetteville	AR	16,860	VC
Univ of Arkansas at Little Rock	AR		C
Univ of Calif at Davis	CA	24,482	HC
Univ of Calif at Irvine	CA	25,961	VC
Univ of Calif at Los Angeles	CA	25,686	MC
Univ of Calif at Riverside	CA	27,204	C
Univ of Calif at Santa Barbara	CA	27,551	HC
Univ of Calif at Santa Cruz	CA	27,807	VC
Univ of Central Missouri	MO	14,605	C
Univ of Cincinnati	OH	20,199	VC
Univ of Colo Boulder	CO	22,605	VC+
Univ of Conn	CT	23,744	HC
Univ of Dayton	OH	43,750	VC
Univ of Delaware	DE	22,728	VC
Univ of Florida	FL	15,783	HC+
Univ of Georgia	GA	19,508	VC
Univ of Hawaii at Hilo	HI	6,500	C
Univ of Hawaii at Manoa	HI	19,379	VC
Univ of Houston	TX	19,184	VC
Univ of Idaho	ID	14,558	C
Univ of Illinois at Urbana-Champaign	IL	24,300	HC
Univ of Iowa	IA	17,481	VC
Univ of Kansas	KS	16,980	C+
Univ of Kentucky	KY	19,868	C
Univ of Louisiana at Lafayette	LA	6,130	C
Univ of Maine at Farmington	ME	17,841	C
Univ of Maryland	MD	18,801	HC
Univ of Mass Amherst	MA	23,697	VC+
Univ of Miami	FL	55,166	MC
Univ of Mich/Ann Arbor	MI	22,102	HC+
Univ of Mich/Dearborn	MI	9,885	VC
Univ of Minn/Duluth	MN	18,964	C+
Univ of Minn/Morris	MN	17,150	VC
Univ of Minn/Twin Cities	MN		HC
Univ of Miss	MS	15,482	VC
Univ of Missouri/Columbia	MO	18,201	MC
Univ of Missouri-Kansas City	MO	19,603	C
Univ of Montana	MT	13,670	C
Univ of Montana-Western	MT	9,753	LC
Univ of Mount Union	OH	35,130	C
Univ of Nebr - Lincoln	NE	17,507	VC
Univ of Nebr at Omaha	NE	12,700	C
Univ of Nevada, Las Vegas	NV	17,303	C
Univ of Nevada/Reno	NV	14,500	NC
Univ of New Hampshire	NH	24,702	VC
Univ of New Orleans	LA	9,224	VC
Univ of North Alabama	AL	9,960	C
Univ of N Car at Chapel Hill	NC	18,348	MC
Univ of N Car at Charlotte	NC	15,847	C
Univ of N Car at Wilmington	NC	13,572	VC+
Univ of N Dak	ND	14,094	C
Univ of Northern Colo	CO	15,970	C
Univ of Northern Iowa	IA	14,776	C
Univ of Okla	OK	17,634	VC+
Univ of Oregon	OR	20,872	VC
Univ of Pennsylvania	PA	56,106	MC
Univ of Pittsburgh at Johnstown	PA	20,862	LC
Univ of Pittsburgh at Pittsburgh	PA	27,800	HC+
Univ of PR/Mayaguez	PR	1,250	
Univ of Puget Sound	WA	52,648	HC+
Univ of Rochester	NY	58,500	MC
Univ of South Alabama	AL	13,510	C
Univ of S Car at Columbia	SC	19,725	VC+
Univ of South Florida	FL	13,000	C
Univ of Southern Calif	CA	56,903	MC
Univ of Southern Indiana	IN	14,657	C
Univ of Southern Maine	ME	16,576	C
Univ of Southern Miss	MS	13,170	C
Univ of Tenn at Chattanooga	TN	16,883	C
Univ of Tenn at Knoxville	TN	20,364	VC+
Univ of Tenn at Martin	TN	13,217	C
Univ of Texas at Arlington	TX	10,908	LC
Univ of Texas at Austin	TX	44,074	HC
Univ of Texas at El Paso	TX	8,764	NC
Univ of Texas at San Antonio	TX	18,372	C
Univ of the Pacific	CA	52,146	VC
Univ of Toledo	OH	18,464	C
Univ of Tulsa	OK	45,311	HC+
Univ of Utah	UT	13,462	VC
Univ of Vermont	VT	26,120	VC+
Univ of Washington	WA	14,722	VC
Univ of West Georgia	GA	14,852	LC
Univ of Wisc/Eau Claire	WI	15,430	VC
Univ of Wisc/Madison	WI	18,757	HC
Univ of Wisc/Oshkosh	WI	10,426	LC
Univ of Wisc/Parkside	WI	10,181	LC
Univ of Wisc/River Falls	WI	9,722	LC
Univ of Wisc-Milwaukee	WI	18,436	C
Univ of Wyoming	WY	13,855	C+
Utah State Univ	UT	11,803	C
Valparaiso Univ	IN	43,040	VC+
Vanderbilt Univ	TN	57,072	MC
Vassar College	NY	59,070	MC
Virginia Polytechnic Inst and State Univ	VA	14,629	HC
Washington and Lee Univ	VA	52,812	MC
Washington State Univ	WA	20,461	C
Washington Univ in St. Louis	MO	58,818	MC
Wayland Baptist Univ	TX	16,058	LC
Wayne State Univ	MI	19,493	C
Wellesley College	MA	49,848	MC
West Chester Univ of Pennsylvania	PA	16,836	C
West Texas A&M Univ	TX	13,478	C
West Virginia Univ	WV	15,794	C+
Western Carolina Univ	NC	13,965	C+
Western Illinois Univ	IL	20,130	C
Western Kentucky Univ	KY	11,000	LC
Western Mich Univ	MI	19,042	C
Western State Colo Univ	CO	16,135	C
Western Washington Univ	WA	18,519	VC
Wheaton College	IL	39,650	HC+
Whitman College	WA	54,400	MC
Wichita State Univ	KS	12,539	C
Williams College	MA	58,900	MC
Wilmington College	OH	29,784	C
Winona State Univ	MN	16,530	C
Wittenberg Univ	OH	47,766	VC
Wright State Univ	OH	16,983	C
Yale Univ	CT	55,300	MC
York College / CUNY	NY	5,496	NC
Youngstown State Univ	OH	16,374	LC

GEOPHYSICAL ENGINEERING

School	ST	$IS	SR
Colo School of Mines	CO	18,000	HC
Montana Tech of The Univ of Montana	MT	14,650	VC
New Jersey Inst of Technology	NJ	26,490	VC
Oregon State Univ	OR	19,017	C+
Univ of Mich/Ann Arbor	MI	22,102	HC+
Univ of Texas at Austin	TX	44,074	HC

GEOPHYSICS AND SEISMOLOGY

School	ST	$IS	SR
Baylor Univ	TX	46,720	HC
Boise State Univ	ID	12,802	C
Boston College	MA	58,506	MC
Boston Univ	MA	54,130	HC+
Calif Inst of Technology	CA	54,045	MC
Colgate Univ	NY	50,930	MC
Columbia Univ in the City of New York	NY	61,116	MC
Harvard Univ/Harvard College	MA	49,000	MC
Mich State Univ	MI	13,689	VC
Mich Tech Univ	MI	22,105	VC
Missouri Univ of Science and Technology	MO	18,655	VC+
Rice Univ	TX	43,288	MC
St. Louis Univ	MO	46,594	VC+
Southern Methodist Univ	TX	57,755	MC
Stanford Univ	CA	56,411	MC
SUNY College at Geneseo	NY	18,055	HC+
SUNY Cortland / The SUNY	NY	19,117	C
Texas A&M Univ	TX	16,956	VC+
Texas Tech Univ	TX	14,243	C
Univ of Akron	OH	20,436	C
Univ of Calif at Los Angeles	CA	25,686	MC
Univ of Calif at Riverside	CA	27,204	C
Univ of Calif at Santa Barbara	CA	27,551	HC
Univ of Hawaii at Manoa	HI	19,379	VC
Univ of Minn/Twin Cities	MN		HC
Univ of Nevada/Reno	NV	14,500	NC
Univ of New Orleans	LA	9,224	VC
Univ of Okla	OK	17,634	VC+
Univ of S Car at Columbia	SC	19,725	VC+
Univ of Texas at Austin	TX	44,074	HC
Univ of Texas at El Paso	TX	8,764	NC
Univ of the Pacific	CA	52,146	VC
Univ of Tulsa	OK	45,311	HC+
Univ of Utah	UT	13,462	VC
Univ of Wisc/Madison	WI	18,757	HC
Washington Univ in St. Louis	MO	58,818	MC
Western Mich Univ	MI	19,042	C
Wright State Univ	OH	16,983	C

GEOSCIENCE

School	ST	$IS	SR
Albion College	MI	43,884	VC
Angelo State Univ	TX	15,049	NC
Austin Peay State Univ	TN	14,650	C
Bloomsburg Univ of Pennsylvania	PA	13,598	C
Boise State Univ	ID	12,802	C
Cal State, Chico	CA	18,952	C
Cedarville Univ	OH	31,036	VC+
Colby College	ME	57,510	MC
Columbia Univ/School of General Studies	NY	54,083	MC
Eckerd College	FL	43,902	VC
Hamilton College	NY	55,620	MC
Hobart and William Smith Colleges	NY	43,000	VC
Idaho State Univ	ID	11,908	C
Indiana Univ Southeast	IN	15,807	LC
Lewis-Clark State College	ID	6,990	C
Mich State Univ	MI	13,689	VC
Minn State Univ, Moorhead	MN	13,392	C
Montclair State Univ	NJ	22,614	C
Murray State Univ	KY	14,944	C
Northern Illinois Univ	IL	19,768	C
Ohio Univ	OH	20,676	VC
Olivet Nazarene Univ	IL	29,990	C
Pacific Lutheran Univ	WA	44,840	VC
Princeton Univ	NJ	53,795	MC
Rider Univ	NJ	45,720	C
Rutgers, The State Univ of New Jersey/Newark Campus	NJ	25,376	C
S Dak State Univ	SD	14,296	C
Stanford Univ	CA	56,411	MC
Texas A&M Univ at Galveston	TX	11,258	C
Texas Christian Univ	TX	47,570	HC
Texas Tech Univ	TX	14,243	C
Towson Univ	MD	16,000	VC
Trinity Univ	TX	44,174	HC+
Univ of Alaska Fairbanks	AK	13,955	C
Univ of Arizona	AZ	20,105	C
Univ of Calif at Riverside	CA	27,204	C
Univ of Chicago	IL	55,416	MC
Univ of Miami	FL	55,166	MC
Univ of Mich/Ann Arbor	MI	22,102	HC+
Univ of Montana-Western	MT	9,753	LC
Univ of Okla	OK	17,634	VC+
Univ of Southern Maine	ME	16,576	C
Univ of Texas at Dallas	TX	21,046	HC
Univ of Tulsa	OK	45,311	HC+
Univ of Utah	UT	13,462	VC
Univ of Wisc/Green Bay	WI	14,900	C
Univ of Wisc/Stevens Point	WI	14,043	C
Utica College	NY	44,734	C
West Chester Univ of Pennsylvania	PA	16,836	C
West Virginia Univ	WV	15,794	C+

GERMAN

School	ST	$IS	SR
Adrian College	MI	33,800	C
Agnes Scott College	GA	45,323	VC+
Alabama A&M Univ	AL	96,100	C
Albion College	MI	43,884	VC
Allegheny College	PA	49,020	HC
Alma College	MI	42,400	VC
American Univ	DC	54,829	HC+
Amherst College	MA	58,744	MC
Aquinas College	MI	33,060	C
Arizona State Univ	AZ	18,818	C+
Auburn Univ	AL	20,052	VC+
Augsburg College	MN	35,142	C
Augustana College	IL	43,398	HC
Augustana College	SD	35,500	VC
Austin College	TX	36,940	HC
Baker Univ	KS	33,350	C+
Baldwin Wallace Univ	OH	30,900	VC
Ball State Univ	IN	17,850	C
Bates College	ME	58,950	MC
Baylor Univ	TX	46,720	HC
Belmont Univ	TN	37,380	VC+
Beloit College	WI	49,970	HC
Bemidji State Univ	MN	13,500	C
Berea College	KY	7,220	HC
Berry College	GA	39,254	HC
Binghamton Univ / The SUNY	NY	20,832	HC+
Birmingham-Southern College	AL	42,370	VC+
Bloomsburg Univ of Pennsylvania	PA	13,598	C
Boise State Univ	ID	12,802	C
Boston Univ	MA	54,130	HC+
Bowdoin College	ME	57,834	MC
Bowling Green State Univ	OH	18,970	C
Bradley Univ	IL	31,874	VC
Brandeis Univ	MA	58,820	HC
Brigham Young Univ	UT	12,100	HC
Bryn Mawr College	PA	57,760	MC
Bucknell Univ	PA	58,160	MC
Butler Univ	IN	45,898	VC+
Calif Lutheran Univ	CA	47,640	C
Cal State, Chico	CA	18,952	C
Cal State, Fresno	CA	17,405	C
Cal State, Long Beach	CA	17,534	C+
Cal State, Northridge	CA	28,313	C
Cal State, Sacramento	CA	16,200	C
Calvin College	MI	37,585	VC+
Canisius College	NY	45,602	VC
Carleton College	MN	58,149	MC
Carnegie Mellon Univ	PA	51,260	MC
Carthage College	WI	33,000	C
Case Western Reserve Univ	OH	55,178	MC
Centenary College of Louisiana	LA	39,070	C+
Central College	IA	36,980	VC
Central Conn State Univ	CT	19,212	C
Central Mich Univ	MI	18,066	C
Central Washington Univ	WA	11,730	C
Centre College	KY	35,000	HC+
Christopher Newport Univ	VA	21,050	VC
Citadel, The	SC		C
Clemson Univ	SC	19,136	HC
Coe College	IA	43,590	VC
Colgate Univ	NY	50,930	MC
College of Charleston	SC	21,273	VC
College of St. Benedict	MN	47,570	VC
College of the Holy Cross	MA	56,232	MC
College of William & Mary	VA	25,085	MC
College of Wooster	OH	52,600	VC
Colo State Univ-Fort Collins	CO	20,090	VC
Columbia Univ in the City of New York	NY	61,116	MC
Columbia Univ/Barnard College	NY	39,000	MC
Columbia Univ/School of General Studies	NY	54,083	MC
Concordia College, Moorhead	MN	39,974	C+
Conn College	CT	54,970	MC
Cornell College	IA	44,930	HC
Cornell Univ	NY	59,037	MC
Dartmouth College	NH	57,996	MC
Davidson College	NC	54,683	MC
Denison Univ	OH	54,670	HC+
DePaul Univ	IL	46,120	VC
DePauw Univ	IN	48,950	VC+
Dickinson College	PA	57,662	HC+
Doane College	NE	33,730	VC
Dordt College	IA	34,160	VC

School	ST	$IS	SR
Drew Univ/College of Liberal Arts	NJ	55,862	VC
Drury Univ	MO	30,319	VC
Earlham College	IN	49,710	VC+
East Carolina Univ	NC	14,169	C
Eastern Mennonite Univ	VA	38,850	VC
Eastern Mich Univ	MI	17,961	C
Eastern Washington Univ	WA	16,388	C
Elizabethtown College	PA	47,600	VC
Elmhurst College	IL	42,032	C+
Florida Atlantic Univ	FL	17,339	C
Florida State Univ	FL	15,238	HC
Fordham Univ	NY	58,927	HC
Fort Hays State Univ	KS	11,354	C
Franciscan Univ of Steubenville	OH	27,320	VC
Franklin and Marshall College	PA	58,295	MC
Furman Univ	SC	54,006	HC
George Washington Univ	DC	57,108	MC
Georgetown College	KY	38,690	C
Georgetown Univ	DC	52,910	MC
Georgia State Univ	GA	12,000	VC
Gettysburg College	PA	56,820	HC
Gordon College	MA	42,660	VC+
Grace College and Theological Seminary	IN	28,800	C
Graceland Univ	IA	28,020	C
Grand Valley State Univ	MI	17,998	VC
Grinnell College	IA	53,654	HC
Guilford College	NC	35,340	C
Hamline Univ	MN	44,198	VC
Hampden-Sydney College	VA	48,848	C
Hanover College	IN	41,450	VC
Hartwick College	NY	49,815	C+
Harvard Univ/Harvard College	MA	49,000	MC
Hastings College	NE	27,782	C+
Haverford College	PA	59,236	MC
Heidelberg Univ	OH	34,100	C
Hendrix College	AR	48,436	HC+
Hillsdale College	MI	31,890	HC+
Hofstra Univ	NY	48,020	VC+
Hood College	MD	44,630	C
Hope College	MI	36,320	VC+
Humboldt State Univ	CA	18,400	C
Hunter College / The CUNY	NY	14,429	VC
Idaho State Univ	ID	11,908	C
Illinois College	IL	25,770	VC
Illinois State Univ	IL	22,634	VC
Illinois Wesleyan Univ	IL	48,452	VC+
Indiana State Univ	IN	16,000	C
Indiana Univ Bloomington	IN	19,358	HC
Indiana Univ South Bend	IN	15,293	C
Indiana Univ Southeast	IN	15,807	LC
Indiana Univ-Purdue Univ Fort Wayne	IN	15,425	C
Indiana Univ-Purdue Univ Indianapolis	IN	17,290	C
Iowa State Univ	IA	16,403	C
Ithaca College	NY	52,300	HC
John Carroll Univ	OH	44,520	C+
Johns Hopkins Univ	MD	47,492	MC
Juniata College	PA	49,340	VC
Kalamazoo College	MI	47,825	HC+
Kent State Univ	OH	19,352	C
Kenyon College	OH	56,810	MC
Knox College	IL		VC
Kutztown Univ of Pennsylvania	PA	16,909	LC
La Salle Univ	PA	50,270	C
Lafayette College	PA	57,050	HC+
Lakeland College	WI	22,990	C
Lawrence Univ	WI	46,371	HC
Lebanon Valley College	PA	38,570	C
Lehigh Univ	PA	55,080	MC
Lehman College / The CUNY	NY	5,778	LC
Lenoir-Rhyne College	NC	35,984	C
Linfield College-McMinnville Campus	OR	46,166	C
Lipscomb Univ	TN	35,722	VC
Lock Haven Univ of Pennsylvania	PA	17,587	LC
LIU/C.W. Post Campus	NY	38,888	C
Loyola Univ Maryland	MD		VC
Luther College	IA	44,380	VC+
Lycoming College	PA	43,636	C
Manchester College	IN	35,070	C
Marlboro College	VT	35,980	VC
Marquette Univ	WI	43,664	VC+
Marshall Univ	WV	14,820	C
McDaniel College	MD	45,600	VC
Mercer Univ	GA	44,201	VC+
Messiah College	PA	39,540	VC
Miami Univ	OH	24,191	HC
Mich State Univ	MI	13,689	VC
Middle Tenn State Univ	TN	8,650	C
Middlebury College	VT	57,470	MC
Millersville Univ of Pennsylvania	PA	18,498	C
Minn State Univ, Mankato	MN	14,900	C
Minot State Univ	ND	10,915	C
Missouri Southern State Univ	MO	11,910	C
Missouri State Univ	MO	13,996	VC
Moravian College	PA	36,381	VC
Mount St. Mary's Univ	MD	46,158	C
Muhlenberg College	PA	52,837	HC
Murray State Univ	KY	14,944	C
Muskingum Univ	OH	30,502	C
Nazareth College of Rochester	NY	41,590	VC
Nebr Wesleyan Univ	NE	29,774	C+
New York Univ	NY	61,470	MC
Newberry College	SC	26,850	LC
North Central College	IL	38,343	VC
Northern Illinois Univ	IL	19,768	C
Northern Kentucky Univ	KY	15,302	LC
Northern State Univ	SD	14,021	C
Northwestern Univ	IL	37,595	MC
Oakland Univ	MI	19,391	VC
Oberlin College	OH	57,025	MC
Ohio Univ	OH	20,676	VC
Ohio Wesleyan Univ	OH	49,460	C+
Okla Baptist Univ	OK	28,202	VC
Okla State Univ	OK	14,310	VC
Old Dominion Univ	VA	18,662	C
Oral Roberts Univ	OK	31,734	C
Oregon State Univ	OR	19,017	C+
Oswego / SUNY	NY	20,009	VC
Pacific Lutheran Univ	WA	44,840	VC
Penn State Univ/Univ Park	PA	25,404	VC
Pepperdine Univ	CA	55,372	HC+
Portland State Univ	OR	18,672	C
Princeton Univ	NJ	53,795	MC
Purdue Univ/Calumet	IN	14,336	C
Purdue Univ/West Lafayette	IN	20,278	HC
Queens College / The CUNY	NY	17,107	VC
Randolph-Macon College	VA	45,086	C
Rhodes College	TN	47,596	HC+
Rider Univ	NJ	45,720	C
Ripon College	WI	36,959	C+
Rockford College	IL	31,000	C
Rosemont College	PA	42,350	C
Rutgers, The State Univ of New Jersey/Camden Campus	NJ	24,254	C
Rutgers, The State Univ of New Jersey/New Brunswick	NJ	25,077	VC
Rutgers, The State Univ of New Jersey/Newark Campus	NJ	25,376	C
St. John's Univ	MN	46,146	C
St. Joseph's Univ	PA	52,272	VC
St. Mary's Univ	TX	33,854	C
Salem College	NC	29,326	VC
Sam Houston State Univ	TX	17,082	C
Samford Univ	AL	35,700	VC+
San Diego State Univ	CA	20,578	VC
San Francisco State Univ	CA	18,514	C
San Jose State Univ	CA	19,707	C
Sarah Lawrence College	NY	48,000	HC
Seattle Pacific Univ	WA	41,559	VC+
Sewanee: The Univ of the South	TN	47,700	HC+
Simpson College	IA	36,086	VC
Skidmore College	NY	57,926	HC
Slippery Rock Univ of Pennsylvania	PA	10,360	LC
S Dak State Univ	SD	14,296	C
Southern Conn State Univ	CT	18,033	C
Southern Illinois Univ Carbondale	IL	21,620	C
Southern Illinois Univ Edwardsville	IL	17,532	C
Southern Methodist Univ	TX	57,755	MC
Southwestern Univ	TX	45,660	VC
St. Ambrose Univ	IA		C
St. Lawrence Univ	NY	53,740	HC
St. Norbert College	WI	39,992	VC
St. Olaf College	MN	49,960	HC+
Stetson Univ	FL	49,512	VC+
SUNY New Paltz	NY	15,010	VC
Susquehanna Univ	PA	49,170	C
Swarthmore College	PA	57,870	MC
Sweet Briar College	VA	43,765	C+
Temple Univ	PA	24,392	VC
Tenn Tech Univ	TN	11,310	C
Texas A&M Univ	TX	16,956	VC+
Texas A&M Univ at Commerce	TX	10,496	C
Texas Christian Univ	TX	47,570	HC
Texas State Univ	TX	16,495	VC
Texas Tech Univ	TX	14,243	C
The Catholic Univ of America	DC	52,852	VC
Ohio State Univ	OH	19,887	MC
Thomas Edison State College	NJ	5,700	SP
Towson Univ	MD	16,000	VC
Trinity College	CT		HC+
Trinity Univ	TX	44,174	HC+
Truman State Univ	MO	13,546	HC
Tufts Univ	MA	58,780	MC
Tulane Univ	LA	58,942	MC
Union College	NE	23,270	VC
Univ at Buffalo / The SUNY	NY	20,283	VC
Univ of Alabama at Tuscaloosa	AL	17,164	C+
Univ of Alaska Fairbanks	AK	13,955	C
Univ of Arkansas at Fayetteville	AR	16,860	VC
Univ of Calif at Berkeley	CA	23,322	MC
Univ of Calif at Davis	CA	24,482	HC
Univ of Calif at Los Angeles	CA	25,686	MC
Univ of Calif at Riverside	CA	27,204	C
Univ of Calif at Santa Barbara	CA	27,551	HC
Univ of Central Missouri	MO	14,605	C
Univ of Central Okla	OK	12,293	C
Univ of Chicago	IL	55,416	MC
Univ of Cincinnati	OH	20,199	VC
Univ of Conn	CT	23,744	HC
Univ of Dallas	TX	43,510	VC+
Univ of Dayton	OH	43,750	VC
Univ of Denver	CO	51,787	VC+
Univ of Evansville	IN	41,056	VC+
Univ of Florida	FL	15,783	HC+
Univ of Georgia	GA	19,508	VC
Univ of Hawaii at Manoa	HI	19,379	VC
Univ of Illinois at Chicago	IL	24,293	VC
Univ of Indianapolis	IN	31,740	LC
Univ of Iowa	IA	17,481	VC
Univ of Jamestown	ND	24,738	C
Univ of Kansas	KS	16,980	C+
Univ of Kentucky	KY	19,868	C
Univ of La Verne	CA	47,010	VC
Univ of Maine	ME	19,712	C+
Univ of Mary Washington	VA	19,484	VC
Univ of Maryland/Baltimore County	MD	18,000	VC
Univ of Miami	FL	55,166	MC
Univ of Mich/Ann Arbor	MI	22,102	HC+
Univ of Minn/Morris	MN	17,150	VC
Univ of Minn/Twin Cities	MN		HC
Univ of Miss	MS	15,482	VC
Univ of Missouri/Columbia	MO	18,201	MC
Univ of Missouri-Kansas City	MO	19,603	C
Univ of Missouri-St. Louis	MO	18,304	VC
Univ of Montana	MT	13,670	C
Univ of Montevallo	AL	17,320	C
Univ of Mount Union	OH	35,130	C
Univ of Nebr - Lincoln	NE	17,507	VC
Univ of Nebr at Kearney	NE	14,855	LC
Univ of Nebr at Omaha	NE	12,700	C
Univ of Nevada, Las Vegas	NV	17,303	C
Univ of Nevada/Reno	NV	14,500	NC
Univ of New Hampshire	NH	24,702	VC
Univ of New Mexico	NM	15,300	C
Univ of North Alabama	AL	9,960	C
Univ of N Car at Asheville	NC	13,500	VC+
Univ of N Car at Chapel Hill	NC	18,348	MC
Univ of N Car at Charlotte	NC	15,847	C
Univ of N Car at Greensboro	NC	12,848	C
Univ of N Car at Wilmington	NC	13,572	VC+
Univ of N Dak	ND	14,094	C
Univ of North Texas	TX	15,628	C
Univ of Northern Colo	CO	15,973	C
Univ of Notre Dame	IN		MC
Univ of Okla	OK	17,634	VC+
Univ of Oregon	OR	20,872	VC
Univ of Pennsylvania	PA	56,106	MC
Univ of Pittsburgh at Pittsburgh	PA	27,800	HC+
Univ of Puget Sound	WA	52,648	HC+
Univ of Redlands	CA	40,500	VC
Univ of Rochester	NY	58,500	MC
Univ of Scranton	PA	51,940	VC
Univ of S Car at Columbia	SC	19,725	VC+
Univ of S Dak	SD	15,111	C
Univ of South Florida	FL	13,000	C
Univ of Southern Indiana	IN	14,657	C
Univ of Tenn at Knoxville	TN	20,364	VC+
Univ of Texas at Arlington	TX	10,908	LC
Univ of Texas at Austin	TX	44,074	HC
Univ of Texas at El Paso	TX	8,764	NC
Univ of the Pacific	CA	52,146	VC
Univ of Toledo	OH	18,464	C
Univ of Tulsa	OK	45,311	HC+
Univ of Utah	UT	13,462	VC
Univ of Vermont	VT	26,120	VC+
Univ of Virginia	VA	22,175	MC
Univ of Wisc Whitewater	WI	13,314	C
Univ of Wisc/Eau Claire	WI	15,430	VC
Univ of Wisc/Green Bay	WI	14,900	C
Univ of Wisc/Madison	WI	18,757	HC
Univ of Wisc/Oshkosh	WI	10,426	LC
Univ of Wisc/Parkside	WI	10,181	LC
Univ of Wisc/Platteville	WI	14,274	C
Univ of Wisc/Stevens Point	WI	14,043	C
Univ of Wyoming	WY	13,855	C+
Ursinus College	PA	55,630	VC+
Utah State Univ	UT	11,803	C
Valparaiso Univ	IN	43,040	VC+
Vanderbilt Univ	TN	57,072	MC
Vassar College	NY	59,070	MC
Virginia Polytechnic Inst and State Univ	VA	14,629	HC
Virginia Wesleyan College	VA	28,433	LC
Wabash College	IN	44,160	VC
Wake Forest Univ	NC	51,000	MC
Walla Walla Univ	WA	26,256	NC
Wartburg College	IA	41,055	VC
Washburn Univ	KS	12,165	NC
Washington and Jefferson College	PA	49,990	VC
Washington and Lee Univ	VA	52,812	MC
Washington College	MD	48,768	VC
Washington Univ in St. Louis	MO	58,818	MC
Wayne State Univ	MI	19,493	C
Webster Univ	MO	33,990	C+
Wellesley College	MA	49,848	MC
Wells College	NY	38,680	VC
West Chester Univ of Pennsylvania	PA	16,836	C
Western Carolina Univ	NC	13,965	C+
Western Kentucky Univ	KY	11,000	LC
Western Mich Univ	MI	10,042	C
Western Washington Univ	WA	18,519	VC
Westminster College	PA	31,290	C+
Wheaton College	IL	39,650	HC+
Wheaton College	MA	54,934	HC+
Whitman College	WA	54,400	MC
Willamette Univ	OR	56,450	VC+
Williams College	MA	58,900	MC
Winthrop Univ	SC	21,120	VC
Wittenberg Univ	OH	47,766	VC
Wofford College	SC	45,795	VC
Wright State Univ	OH	16,983	C
Xavier Univ	OH	43,740	VC

GERMAN AREA STUDIES

School	ST	$IS	SR
American Univ	DC	54,829	HC+
Appalachian State Univ	NC	12,919	VC
Bard College	NY	59,872	HC
Bard College at Simon's Rock	MA	50,963	HC+
Boston College	MA	58,506	MC
Brown Univ	RI	56,150	MC
Cal State, Northridge	CA	28,313	C
Case Western Reserve Univ	OH	55,178	MC
Coe College	IA	43,590	VC
College of the Holy Cross	MA	56,232	MC
Columbia Univ/School of General Studies	NY	54,083	MC
Cornell Univ	NY	59,037	MC
Dartmouth College	NH	57,996	MC
Emory Univ	GA	45,000	MC
Fordham Univ	NY	58,927	HC
Hamilton College	NY	55,620	MC
Indiana Univ Southeast	IN	15,807	LC
Ithaca College	NY	52,300	HC
Lake Erie College	OH	35,704	C
Lewis & Clark College	OR	52,656	VC
Linfield College-McMinnville Campus	OR	46,166	C
Macalester College	MN	53,419	MC
Moravian College	PA	36,381	VC
Mount Holyoke College	MA	53,596	HC+
Muhlenberg College	PA	52,837	HC
New College of Florida	FL	14,504	HC+
Pomona College	CA	57,680	MC
Rice Univ	TX	43,288	MC
Santa Clara Univ	CA	54,702	MC
Scripps College	CA	54,900	MC
Southeast Missouri State Univ	MO	14,983	LC
Southern Illinois Univ Carbondale	IL	21,620	C
Southern Methodist Univ	TX	57,755	MC
Stanford Univ	CA	56,411	MC
Suffolk Univ	MA	46,548	C
Swarthmore College	PA	57,870	MC
Sweet Briar College	VA	43,765	C+
Tufts Univ	MA	58,780	MC
Union College	NY		MC
Univ of Arizona	AZ	20,105	C
Univ of Calif at Irvine	CA	25,961	VC
Univ of Calif at Santa Cruz	CA	27,807	VC
Univ of Colo Boulder	CO	22,605	VC+
Univ of Illinois at Chicago	IL	24,293	VC
Univ of Minn/Duluth	MN	18,964	C+
Univ of N Car at Wilmington	NC	13,572	VC+
Univ of Portland	OR	47,874	VC
Univ of Wisc/La Crosse	WI	14,755	VC
Wartburg College	IA	41,055	VC
Wellesley College	MA	49,848	MC
Wesleyan Univ	CT	59,844	MC
Yale Univ	CT	55,300	MC

GERMAN STUDIES

School	ST	$IS	SR
Creighton Univ	NE	44,058	VC+
Indiana Univ Bloomington	IN	19,358	HC

GERMANIC LANGUAGES AND LITERATURE

School	ST	$IS	SR
Bard College	NY	59,872	HC
Bennington College	VT	56,990	HC
Binghamton Univ / The SUNY	NY	20,832	HC+
Boston Univ	MA	54,130	HC+
Colby College	ME	57,510	MC
Colo College	CO	54,534	MC

School	ST	$IS	SR
Columbia Univ in the City of New York	NY	61,116	MC
Duke Univ	NC	50,250	MC
Indiana Univ Bloomington	IN	19,358	HC
New College of Florida	FL	14,504	HC+
New York Univ	NY	61,470	MC
Oberlin College	OH	57,025	MC
Reed College	OR	57,780	MC
St. Louis Univ	MO	46,594	VC+
Scripps College	CA	54,900	MC
Smith College	MA	57,524	MC
Stony Brook Univ / SUNY	NY	19,359	HC
Syracuse Univ	NY	54,512	HC
Ohio State Univ	OH	19,887	MC
Transylvania Univ	KY	40,310	VC+
Univ of Calif at Riverside	CA	27,204	C
Univ of Calif at San Diego	CA	21,000	VC
Univ of Calif at Santa Barbara	CA	27,551	HC
Univ of Georgia	GA	19,508	VC
Univ of Illinois at Chicago	IL	24,293	VC
Univ of Illinois at Urbana-Champaign	IL	24,300	HC
Univ of Kansas	KS	16,980	C+
Univ of Maryland	MD	18,801	HC
Univ of Mass Amherst	MA	23,697	VC+
Univ of Mich/Ann Arbor	MI	22,102	HC+
Univ of Missouri-St. Louis	MO	18,304	VC
Univ of Pittsburgh at Pittsburgh	PA	27,800	HC+
Univ of Washington	WA	14,722	VC
Univ of Wisc/Green Bay	WI	14,900	C
Univ of Wisc Milwaukee	WI	10,400	C
Vassar College	NY	59,070	MC
Washington and Lee Univ	VA	52,812	MC
Washington Univ in St. Louis	MO	58,818	MC
Yale Univ	CT	55,300	MC

GERONTOLOGY

School	ST	$IS	SR
Alfred Univ	NY	40,392	VC
Barton College	NC	27,660	C
Bethune-Cookman Univ	FL	22,290	LC
Bowling Green State Univ	OH	18,970	C
Cal State, Chico	CA	18,952	C
Cal State, Fresno	CA	17,405	C
Cal State, San Bernardino	CA	12,000	C
Calif Univ of Pennsylvania	PA	14,217	C
Canisius College	NY	45,602	VC
Case Western Reserve Univ	OH	55,178	MC
Central Washington Univ	WA	11,730	C
College of the Ozarks	MO	5,605	VC
Eastern Mich Univ	MI	17,961	C
Gwynedd-Mercy College	PA	33,560	C
Ithaca College	NY	52,300	HC
Langston Univ	OK	3,000	LC
Madonna Univ	MI	24,540	VC
Marywood Univ	PA	40,695	C
McKendree Univ	IL	29,920	C+
Metropolitan College of New York	NY	16,720	VC
Miami Univ	OH	24,191	HC
Minn State Univ, Moorhead	MN	13,392	C
Missouri State Univ	MO	13,996	VC
Montclair State Univ	NJ	22,614	C
Mount St. Mary's College/ Chalon Campus	CA	43,897	VC+
Northeastern Illinois Univ	IL		C
Pontifical Catholic Univ of PR	PR	7,310	
Quinnipiac Univ	CT	53,580	VC
San Diego State Univ	CA	20,578	VC
Shaw Univ	NC	15,488	LC
Sojourner-Douglass College	MD	9,160	LC
Southeastern Okla State Univ	OK	7,966	C
Southern Illinois Univ Edwardsville	IL	17,532	C
Springfield College	MA	25,000	C
St. Bonaventure Univ	NY	38,831	C
SUNY Oneonta / SUNY	NY	16,919	VC
Towson Univ	MD	16,000	VC
Univ of Arkansas at Pine Bluff	AR	10,600	C
Univ of Central Arkansas	AR	10,840	VC
Univ of Central Okla	OK	12,293	C
Univ of Louisiana at Monroe	LA	12,998	C
Univ of Maryland/Univ College	MD	6,168	SP
Univ of Mass Boston	MA	11,966	C
Univ of Northern Colo	CO	15,973	C
Univ of Northern Iowa	IA	14,776	C
Univ of South Florida	FL	13,000	C
Univ of Southern Calif	CA	56,903	MC
Utica College	NY	44,734	C
Wichita State Univ	KS	12,539	C
York College / CUNY	NY	5,496	NC
Youngstown State Univ	OH	16,374	LC

GLASS

School	ST	$IS	SR
Alfred Univ	NY	40,392	VC
Calif College of the Arts	CA	48,334	SP
Cleveland Inst of Art	OH	48,641	SP
College for Creative Studies	MI		SP
Mass College of Art and Design	MA	23,600	SP
Rhode Island School of Design	RI	55,204	SP
Rochester Inst of Technology	NY	42,450	VC+
Temple Univ	PA	24,392	VC

GLOBAL MANAGEMENT

School	ST	$IS	SR
Bryant Univ	RI	49,179	VC

GLOBAL/GENERAL MANAGEMENT

School	ST	$IS	SR
Bryant Univ	RI	49,179	VC
Hamline Univ	MN	44,198	VC
Thomas Edison State College	NJ	5,700	SP
Univ of North Florida	FL	15,578	VC
Univ of Pittsburgh at Pittsburgh	PA	27,800	HC+
Univ of South Florida/St. Petersburg	FL	12,769	VC

GOLF ENTERPRISE MANAGEMENT

School	ST	$IS	SR
Univ of Nebr - Lincoln	NE	17,507	VC
Univ of Wisc/Stout	WI	23,942	C

GOVERNMENT

School	ST	$IS	SR
American Univ	DC	54,829	HC+
Cornell Univ	NY	59,037	MC
Mills College	CA	54,119	HC

GRAPHIC AND PRINTING PRODUCTION

School	ST	$IS	SR
Brenau Univ Women's College	GA	26,650	C+
New York City College of Technology / The CUNY	NY	5,769	NC
Pittsburg State Univ	KS	12,032	C
Rochester Inst of Technology	NY	42,450	VC+
Univ of Wisc/Stout	WI	23,942	C
Western Mich Univ	MI	19,042	C
Youngstown State Univ	OH	16,374	LC

GRAPHIC ARTS TECHNOLOGY

School	ST	$IS	SR
Andrews Univ	MI	28,030	C+
Appalachian State Univ	NC	12,919	VC
Arizona State Univ	AZ	18,818	C+
Ball State Univ	IN	17,850	C
Bloomfield College	NJ	36,960	C
Carroll Univ	WI	24,860	C
Central State Univ	OH	9,010	C
Clemson Univ	SC	19,136	HC
College of the Ozarks	MO	5,605	VC
Colo Mesa Univ	CO	16,669	LC
Colo Technical Univ	CO	10,500	LC
Emmanuel College	MA	47,985	VC
Florida State Univ	FL	15,238	HC
Idaho State Univ	ID	11,908	C
Minn State Univ, Moorhead	MN	13,392	C
New York Univ	NY	61,470	MC
North Central College	IL	38,343	VC
Pacific Union College	CA	28,150	VC
Pennsylvania College of Technology	PA	25,653	NC
Pittsburg State Univ	KS	12,032	C
Rochester Inst of Technology	NY	42,450	VC+
Univ of Central Missouri	MO	14,605	C
Univ of Wisc/Stout	WI	23,942	C

GRAPHIC COMMUNICATIONS

School	ST	$IS	SR
Calif Polytechnic State Univ	CA	19,847	HC

GRAPHIC COMMUNICATIONS MANAGEMENT

School	ST	$IS	SR
Bethany College	WV	35,282	C
Georgia Southern Univ	GA	16,414	C
Murray State Univ	KY	14,944	C
Univ of Wisc/Stout	WI	23,942	C

GRAPHIC DESIGN

School	ST	$IS	SR
Abilene Christian Univ	TX	38,400	VC
Academy of Art Univ	CA		
Adams State College	CO	13,358	LC
Alabama A&M Univ	AL	96,100	C
American Univ	DC	54,829	HC+
Anderson Univ	IN	35,390	C
Andrews Univ	MI	28,030	C+
Anna Maria College	MA	34,600	LC
Appalachian State Univ	NC	12,919	VC
Arcadia Univ	PA	33,570	C+
Arizona State Univ	AZ	18,818	C+
Arkansas State Univ	AR	14,980	C
Art Academy of Cincinnati	OH	25,940	SP
Art Center College of Design	CA	34,044	SP
Art Inst of Atlanta	GA	24,000	SP
Art Inst of Portland	OR	23,040	SP
Assumption College	MA	45,721	VC
Auburn Univ	AL	20,052	VC+
Barton College	NC	27,660	C
Becker College	MA	41,420	LC
Bethel College	IN	31,560	C
Biola Univ	CA	40,320	VC
Blackburn College	IL	21,350	C
Boston Univ	MA	54,130	HC+
Bowling Green State Univ	OH	18,970	C
Bradley Univ	IL	31,874	VC
Brescia Univ	KY	26,140	VC+
Briar Cliff Univ	IA	29,514	C
Brigham Young Univ	UT	12,100	HC
Buena Vista Univ	IA	37,954	C
Burlington College	VT	32,510	SP
Cabrini College	PA	40,859	LC
Calif Baptist Univ	CA	35,890	C
Calif College of the Arts	CA	48,334	SP
Calif State Polytechnic Univ, Pomona	CA	18,932	C
Cal State, Chico	CA	18,952	C
Cal State, Fresno	CA	17,405	C
Cal State, Los Angeles	CA	15,829	C
Cal State, San Bernardino	CA	12,000	C
Calif Univ of Pennsylvania	PA	14,217	C
Calvin College	MI	37,585	VC+
Carthage College	WI	33,000	C
Cedarville Univ	OH	31,036	VC+
Central Conn State Univ	CT	19,212	C
Central Mich Univ	MI	18,066	C
Champlain College	VT	44,850	VC
Chapman Univ	CA	56,019	VC+
Cleveland Inst of Art	OH	48,641	SP
Coastal Carolina Univ	SC	17,620	C
Coker College	SC	32,256	LC
Colby-Sawyer College	NH	47,870	C
College for Creative Studies	MI		SP
College of Mount St. Joseph	OH	33,880	C
College of New Jersey	NJ	25,376	HC
College of Visual Arts - School is Closed	MN	24,310	SP
Columbia College	MO	24,578	C
Columbus College of Art and Design	OH	37,732	SP
Concordia Univ St. Paul	MN	27,200	C
Concordia Univ Wisc	WI	28,980	C
Cooper Union for the Advancement of Science and Art	NY	55,600	MC
Corcoran College of Art and Design	DC	36,500	SP
Cornerstone Univ and Grand Rapids Theological Seminary	MI	30,866	C
Culver-Stockton College	MO	30,900	C
Curry College	MA	47,545	LC
Daemen College	NY	31,510	C
Defiance College	OH	30,645	C
DePaul Univ	IL	46,120	VC
Dominican Univ	IL	37,628	C
Dominican Univ of Calif	CA	51,250	C
Dordt College	IA	34,160	VC
Drake Univ	IA	30,980	VC+
Drexel Univ	PA	51,920	HC
Eastern Mich Univ	MI	17,961	C
Eastern Washington Univ	WA	16,388	C
Edgewood College	WI	33,294	C
Edinboro Univ of Pennsylvania	PA	15,940	LC
Elmhurst College	IL	42,032	C+
Endicott College	MA	42,390	C
Fashion Inst of Technology/SUNY	NY	12,468	SP
Felician College	NJ	41,640	C
Ferris State Univ	MI	19,698	C
Fitchburg State Univ	MA	17,241	C
Flagler College	FL	24,960	VC
Florida Atlantic Univ	FL	17,339	C
Florida Southern College	FL	38,240	VC
Fordham Univ	NY	58,927	HC
Franklin Pierce Univ	NH	41,598	C
Gallaudet Univ	DC	25,380	SP
Georgia Southern Univ	GA	16,414	C
Goshen College	IN	35,900	VC
Grace College and Theological Seminary	IN	28,800	C
Graceland Univ	IA	28,020	C
Grand View Univ	IA	31,050	C
Harding Univ	AR	21,432	C+
Hardin-Simmons Univ	TX	23,560	C+
High Point Univ	NC	39,800	C
Howard Univ	DC	35,957	C
Huntington Univ	IN	32,220	C
Indiana Univ South Bend	IN	15,293	C
Indiana Univ Southeast	IN	15,807	LC
Indiana Univ-Purdue Univ Fort Wayne	IN	15,425	C
Iowa State Univ	IA	16,403	C
John Brown Univ	AR	30,996	VC+
Keene State College	NH	21,538	C
Kendall College of Art and Design of Ferris State Univ	MI	21,048	SP
Kutztown Univ of Pennsylvania	PA	16,909	LC
La Roche College	PA	34,802	LC
La Sierra Univ	CA	35,694	VC
Laguna College of Art and Design	CA	26,500	SP
Lasell College	MA	42,500	LC
Lenoir-Rhyne College	NC	35,984	C
Limestone College	SC	29,880	C
Lipscomb Univ	TN	35,722	VC
Louisiana College	LA	15,746	C
Loyola Univ New Orleans	LA	46,581	VC
Lyndon State College	VT	14,233	C
Madonna Univ	MI	24,540	VC
Maine College of Art	ME	28,812	SP
Mansfield Univ	PA	19,468	LC
Marian Univ/Indianapolis	IN	37,058	C
Marietta College	OH	42,135	VC
Marshall Univ	WV	14,820	C
Maryland Inst College of Art	MD	39,500	SP
Marymount Univ	VA	36,178	C
Maryville Univ of St. Louis	MO	34,920	VC
Marywood Univ	PA	40,695	C
Mass College of Art and Design	MA	23,600	SP
Memphis College of Art	TN	33,550	SP
Mercyhurst Univ	PA	40,700	C
Miami Univ	OH	24,191	HC
MidAmerica Nazarene Univ	KS	28,000	C
Middle Tenn State Univ	TN	8,650	C
Milwaukee Inst of Art and Design	WI	31,938	SP
Minneapolis College of Art and Design	MN	36,700	SP
Miss College	MS	21,998	VC
Missouri Southern State Univ	MO	11,910	C
Missouri Western State Univ	MO	12,260	NC
Monmouth Univ	NJ	42,252	C
Montclair State Univ	NJ	22,614	C
Montserrat College of Art	MA	31,000	SP
Moore College of Art and Design	PA	38,124	SP
Moravian College	PA	36,381	VC
Morningside College	IA	32,620	C
Mount Ida College	MA	30,115	LC
Mount Mary Univ	WI	32,836	LC
Mount Mercy Univ	IA	34,385	C
Mount Vernon Nazarene Univ	OH	29,590	C
Mountain State Univ	WV	14,330	NC
New Mexico Highlands Univ	NM	9,720	NC
New York Inst of Technology	NY	40,590	VC
New York Univ	NY	61,470	MC
Newbury College	MA	41,850	C
Norfolk State Univ	VA	10,531	LC
N Car State Univ	NC	16,202	HC
Northeastern Univ	MA	55,296	MC
Northern Kentucky Univ	KY	15,302	LC
Northwest Nazarene Univ	ID	24,275	NC
Northwestern College	MN	24,000	C
Northwestern College of Iowa	IA	34,848	C+
Notre Dame College	OH	34,942	VC
Notre Dame de Namur Univ	CA	41,610	LC
Notre Dame of Maryland Univ	MD	27,700	C
Ohio Dominican Univ	OH	38,380	C+
Ohio Northern Univ	OH	42,075	VC
Ohio Univ	OH	20,676	VC
Old Dominion Univ	VA	18,662	C
Oswego / SUNY	NY	20,009	VC
Otis College of Art and Design	CA	35,404	SP
Ouachita Baptist Univ	AR	29,010	VC
Pacific Northwest College of Art	OR	38,494	SP
Pacific Union College	CA	28,150	VC
Palm Beach Atlantic Univ	FL	33,882	LC
Park Univ	MO	17,525	C
Parsons The New School for Design	NY	56,610	SP
Penn State Univ/Univ Park	PA	25,404	VC
Pennsylvania College of Technology	PA	25,653	NC
Philadelphia Univ	PA	44,160	C
Plymouth State Univ	NH	23,148	LC
Point Loma Nazarene Univ	CA	38,610	VC
Purdue Univ/West Lafayette	IN	20,278	HC
Queens College / The CUNY	NY	17,107	VC
Queens Univ of Charlotte	NC	39,543	VC
Quincy Univ	IL	34,980	LC
Rhode Island School of Design	RI	55,204	SP
Ringling College of Art and Design	FL	46,130	SP
Rivier College	NH	35,000	VC
Roberts Wesleyan College	NY	37,384	C+

School	ST	$IS	SR
Rochester Inst of Technology	NY	42,450	VC+
Rocky Mountain College of Art and Design	CO	22,470	NC
Roger Williams Univ	RI	45,788	C
Sacred Heart Univ	CT	48,564	VC
St. Mary's Univ of Minn	MN	37,015	C
St. Peter's College	NJ	44,240	C
Sam Houston State Univ	TX	17,082	C
Samford Univ	AL	35,700	VC+
San Diego State Univ	CA	20,578	VC
Santa Fe Univ of Art and Design	NM	39,666	SP
Savannah College of Art and Design	GA	46,824	SP
School of Visual Arts	NY	36,500	SP
Schreiner Univ	TX	32,734	LC
Seton Hall Univ	NJ	45,902	C
Seton Hill Univ	PA	35,172	C
Simpson College	IA	36,086	VC
S Dak State Univ	SD	14,296	C
South Univ	GA		LC
Southern Adventist Univ	TN	26,190	C
Southern Nazarene Univ	OK	24,354	NC
Southern New Hampshire Univ	NH	38,100	C
Southern Oregon Univ	OR	17,874	C
Southwestern Okla State Univ	OK	9,160	C
Spring Hill College	AL	42,130	VC
St. Ambrose Univ	IA		C
St. Edward's Univ	TX	44,674	VC
St. John's Univ	NY	52,840	C+
St. Norbert College	WI	39,992	VC
Stephens College	MO	34,500	VC
Suffolk Univ	MA	46,548	C
SUNY Fredonia / The SUNY at Fredonia	NY	18,702	VC
SUNY New Paltz	NY	15,010	C
Susquehanna Univ	PA	49,170	C
Syracuse Univ	NY	54,512	HC
Tabor College	KS	29,010	LC
Temple Univ	PA	24,392	VC
Texas Christian Univ	TX	47,570	HC
The College of St. Rose	NY	26,750	C
The SUNY College of Agriculture and Tech at Cobleskill	NY	18,869	VC
Union College	NE	23,270	VC
Union Univ	TN	28,260	VC
Univ of Bridgeport	CT	39,030	LC
Univ of Central Okla	OK	12,293	C
Univ of Evansville	IN	41,056	VC+
Univ of Florida	FL	15,783	HC+
Univ of Illinois at Chicago	IL	24,293	VC
Univ of Illinois at Urbana-Champaign	IL	24,300	HC
Univ of Iowa	IA	17,481	VC
Univ of Kansas	KS	16,980	C+
Univ of Mass Dartmouth	MA	22,223	C
Univ of Miami	FL	55,166	MC
Univ of Mich/Ann Arbor	MI	22,102	HC+
Univ of Minn/Duluth	MN	18,964	C+
Univ of New Haven	CT	47,740	C
Univ of N Dak	ND	14,094	C
Univ of Northern Colo	CO	15,973	C
Univ of Northern Iowa	IA	14,776	C
Univ of San Francisco	CA	49,674	VC
Univ of S Car Upstate	SC	17,673	LC
Univ of South Florida/St. Petersburg	FL	12,769	VC
Univ of Tampa	FL	35,160	VC
Univ of Tenn at Knoxville	TN	20,364	VC+
Univ of the Arts	PA	38,450	SP
Univ of the Pacific	CA	52,146	VC
Univ of Washington	WA	14,722	VC
Upper Iowa Univ	IA	30,426	NC
Ursuline College	OH	33,198	LC
Virginia Commonwealth Univ	VA	18,633	C
Viterbo Univ	WI	30,070	C
Walla Walla Univ	WA	26,256	NC
Walsh Univ	OH	35,100	C
Wartburg College	IA	41,055	VC
Washington Univ in St. Louis	MO	58,818	MC
Wayland Baptist Univ	TX	16,058	LC
Wayne State College	NE	11,764	NC
Waynesburg Univ	PA	29,100	C
Webster Univ	MO	33,990	C+
West Liberty Univ	WV	9,142	LC
West Texas A&M Univ	TX	13,478	C
Western Mich Univ	MI	19,042	C
Wichita State Univ	KS	12,539	C
William Woods Univ	MO		C
Winona State Univ	MN	16,530	C
Woodbury Univ	CA	34,500	LC
York College of Pennsylvania	PA	26,590	C
Youngstown State Univ	OH	16,374	LC

GRAPHIC DESIGN & MEDIA

School	ST	$IS	SR
Creighton Univ	NE	44,058	VC+
Southern Oregon Univ	OR	17,874	C
Univ of Illinois at Chicago	IL	24,293	VC

GREAT PLAINS STUDIES

School	ST	$IS	SR
Univ of Nebr - Lincoln	NE	17,507	VC

GREEK

School	ST	$IS	SR
Brigham Young Univ	UT	12,100	HC
Bryn Mawr College	PA	57,760	MC
Calvin College	MI	37,585	VC+
Carleton College	MN	58,149	MC
Colgate Univ	NY	50,930	MC
Columbia Univ in the City of New York	NY	61,116	MC
Columbia Univ/Barnard College	NY	39,000	MC
Concordia Univ, Ann Arbor	MI	27,220	VC
Creighton Univ	NE	44,058	VC+
DePauw Univ	IN	48,950	VC+
Dickinson College	PA	57,662	HC+
Emory Univ	GA	45,000	MC
Florida State Univ	FL	15,238	HC
Franklin and Marshall College	PA	58,295	MC
Furman Univ	SC	54,006	HC
Gettysburg College	PA	56,820	HC
Hampden-Sydney College	VA	48,848	C
Harvard Univ/Harvard College	MA	49,000	MC
Haverford College	PA	59,236	MC
Hunter College / The CUNY	NY	14,429	VC
John Carroll Univ	OH	44,520	C+
Lehman College / The CUNY	NY	5,778	LC
Loyola Marymount Univ	CA	53,240	VC+
Loyola Univ Chicago	IL	49,560	VC+
Marlboro College	VT	35,980	VC
Monmouth College	IL	39,290	C
Mount Holyoke College	MA	53,596	HC+
New York Univ	NY	61,470	MC
Ohio Univ	OH	20,676	VC
Randolph-Macon College	VA	45,086	C
Samford Univ	AL	35,700	VC+
Santa Clara Univ	CA	54,702	MC
Sarah Lawrence College	NY	48,000	HC
Sewanee: The Univ of the South	TN	47,700	HC+
Smith College	MA	57,524	MC
Southwestern Univ	TX	45,660	VC
St. Olaf College	MN	49,960	HC+
Swarthmore College	PA	57,870	MC
Syracuse Univ	NY	54,512	HC
Ohio State Univ	OH	19,887	MC
Trinity Univ	TX	44,174	HC+
Tufts Univ	MA	58,780	MC
Union Univ	TN	28,260	VC
Univ of Calif at Berkeley	CA	23,322	MC
Univ of Calif at Davis	CA	24,482	HC
Univ of Calif at Los Angeles	CA	25,686	MC
Univ of Georgia	GA	19,508	VC
Univ of Iowa	IA	17,481	VC
Univ of Mich/Ann Arbor	MI	22,102	HC+
Univ of Minn/Twin Cities	MN		HC
Univ of New Hampshire	NH	24,702	VC
Univ of Notre Dame	IN		MC
Univ of Oregon	OR	20,872	VC
Univ of Scranton	PA	51,940	VC
Univ of Tenn at Chattanooga	TN	16,883	C
Univ of Texas at Austin	TX	44,074	HC
Univ of Vermont	VT	26,120	VC+
Wabash College	IN	44,160	VC
Wake Forest Univ	NC	51,000	MC
Wellesley College	MA	49,848	MC
Wheaton College	MA	54,934	HC+
Wright State Univ	OH	16,983	C

GREEK (CLASSICAL)

School	ST	$IS	SR
Baylor Univ	TX	46,720	HC
Boston Univ	MA	54,130	HC+
Butler Univ	IN	45,898	VC+
College of Wooster	OH	52,600	VC
Duquesne Univ	PA	42,017	VC
Indiana Univ Bloomington	IN	19,358	HC
Kenyon College	OH	56,810	MC
Knox College	IL		VC
New York Univ	NY	61,470	MC
Ohio Univ	OH	20,676	VC
The Catholic Univ of America	DC	52,852	VC
Univ of Miami	FL	55,166	MC
Washington Univ in St. Louis	MO	58,818	MC

GREEK (MODERN)

School	ST	$IS	SR
Boston Univ	MA	54,130	HC+
New York Univ	NY	61,470	MC
Queens College / The CUNY	NY	17,107	VC
Tulane Univ	LA	58,942	MC
Univ of Mich/Ann Arbor	MI	22,102	HC+

GUIDANCE EDUCATION

School	ST	$IS	SR
Calif Univ of Pennsylvania	PA	14,217	C
Eastern Washington Univ	WA	16,388	C
Prescott College	AZ	33,284	C+
S Car State Univ	SC	6,700	LC
St. Cloud State Univ	MN	10,600	C
Texas A&M Univ at Commerce	TX	10,496	C
Univ of Central Arkansas	AR	10,840	VC
Univ of Cincinnati	OH	20,199	VC
Univ of Southern Miss	MS	13,170	C
Westminster College	PA	31,290	C+

GUITAR

School	ST	$IS	SR
Boston Conservatory	MA	56,380	SP
Central Washington Univ	WA	11,730	C
Illinois Wesleyan Univ	IL	48,452	VC+
Indiana Univ Bloomington	IN	19,358	HC
Loyola Univ New Orleans	LA	46,581	VC
Mannes College New School for Music	NY	44,500	C
Okla City Univ	OK	33,546	VC
Roosevelt Univ	IL	22,605	VC
San Francisco Conservatory of Music	CA	53,923	SP
Stetson Univ	FL	49,512	VC+
Wright State Univ	OH	16,983	C

HABILITATION OF THE DEAF

School	ST	$IS	SR
Texas Christian Univ	TX	47,570	HC

HAWAIIAN

School	ST	$IS	SR
Univ of Hawaii at Manoa	HI	19,379	VC

HAWAIIAN STUDIES

School	ST	$IS	SR
Brigham Young Univ/ Hawaii	HI	8,614	VC
Univ of Hawaii at Hilo	HI	6,500	C
Univ of Hawaii at Manoa	HI	19,379	VC

HEALTH

School	ST	$IS	SR
Aquinas College	MI	30,060	C
Arizona State Univ	AZ	18,818	C+
Averett Univ	VA	36,000	LC
Boston Univ	MA	54,130	HC+
Buffalo State/State Univ of Buffalo	NY	15,733	C+
Cal State, Monterey Bay	CA	26,871	LC
Cal State, Northridge	CA	28,313	C
Central Mich Univ	MI	18,066	C
Chicago State Univ	IL	5,482	C
Coastal Carolina Univ	SC	17,620	C
College of the Ozarks	MO	5,605	VC
Concordia College, Moorhead	MN	39,974	C+
Concordia Univ Nebr	NE	26,000	VC
Coppin State Univ	MD	14,905	VC
DePauw Univ	IN	48,950	VC+
Eastern Illinois Univ	IL	20,502	C
Eastern Oregon Univ	OR	10,400	C
George Fox Univ	OR	40,750	C+
Georgetown Univ	DC	52,910	MC
Georgian Court Univ	NJ	39,726	LC
Goddard College	VT	16,418	VC
Graceland Univ	IA	28,020	C
Harding Univ	AR	21,432	C+
Hodges Univ	FL	12,000	LC
Husson Univ	ME	23,386	LC
Idaho State Univ	ID	11,908	C
Indiana Univ-Purdue Univ Indianapolis	IN	17,290	C
Indiana Wesleyan Univ	IN	31,815	VC
Ithaca College	NY	52,300	HC
Kentucky Wesleyan College	KY	27,440	VC+
Lebanon Valley College	PA	38,570	C
LeTourneau Univ	TX	26,230	C
Luther College	IA	44,380	VC+
McKendree Univ	IL	29,920	C+
Molloy College	NY	38,950	C+
Montana State Univ	MT	14,068	VC
Morehouse College	GA	38,640	C
Nebr Wesleyan Univ	NE	29,774	C+
New Mexico Highlands Univ	NM	9,720	NC
Northeastern Illinois Univ	IL		C
Ohio Northern Univ	OH	42,075	VC
Ohio Valley Univ	WV	17,752	C
Olivet College	MI	19,984	C
Oregon State Univ	OR	19,017	C+
Prairie View A&M Univ	TX	15,205	LC
Rowan Univ	NJ	23,570	VC
Rust College	MS	10,600	C
Sam Houston State Univ	TX	17,082	C
Southeastern Louisiana Univ	LA	13,325	C
Southern Oregon Univ	OR	17,874	C
Southwestern Adventist Univ	TX	23,026	LC
SUNY Inst of Technology at Utica / Rome	NY	23,818	C
SUNY College at Old Westbury	NY	16,324	C
Tenn Wesleyan College	TN	21,250	C
Texas Christian Univ	TX	47,570	HC
Texas Southern Univ	TX	18,212	LC
Texas Tech Univ	TX	14,243	C
The College of Idaho	ID	31,277	VC
Union College	KY	28,775	C
Union Inst & Univ	OH	8,912	SP
Univ of Delaware	DE	22,728	VC
Univ of Houston	TX	19,184	VC
Univ of Louisiana at Monroe	LA	12,998	C
Univ of Louisville	KY	17,460	VC
Univ of Mich/Dearborn	MI	9,005	VC
Univ of Minn Crookston	MN	17,834	C
Univ of Missouri-Kansas City	MO	19,603	C
Univ of Mount Union	OH	35,130	C
Univ of New Mexico	NM	15,300	C
Univ of New Orleans	LA	9,224	VC
Univ of N Car at Asheville	NC	13,500	VC+
Univ of North Texas	TX	15,628	C
Univ of Pennsylvania	PA	56,106	MC
Univ of Rochester	NY	58,500	MC
Univ of Texas at San Antonio	TX	18,372	C
Univ of Texas-Pan American	TX	12,432	LC
Univ of the Cumberlands	KY	27,500	LC
Univ of Wisc/Stout	WI	23,942	C
Univ of Wisc/Superior	WI	14,106	C
Upper Iowa Univ	IA	30,426	NC
Voorhees College	SC	18,126	C
Walla Walla Univ	WA	26,256	NC
West Chester Univ of Pennsylvania	PA	16,836	C

HEALTH ADMINISTRATION AND POLICY

School	ST	$IS	SR
Creighton Univ	NE	44,058	VC+
Indiana Univ Bloomington	IN	19,358	HC
Indiana Univ Kokomo	IN	6,674	LC
Indiana Univ Northwest	IN	6,738	LC
Indiana Univ-Purdue Univ Indianapolis	IN	17,290	C
Univ of Miami	FL	55,166	MC
Univ of St. Francis	IL	36,400	C

HEALTH AND PHYSICAL ACTIVITY

School	ST	$IS	SR
Hanover College	IN	41,450	VC
Millikin Univ	IL	37,462	C
Univ of Wisc/Superior	WI	14,106	C

HEALTH CARE ADMINISTRATION

School	ST	$IS	SR
Adams State College	CO	13,358	LC
Alaska Pacific Univ	AK	33,360	VC
Alma College	MI	42,400	VC
Appalachian State Univ	NC	12,919	VC
Arcadia Univ	PA	33,570	C+
Auburn Univ	AL	20,052	VC+
Baker College of Flint	MI	7,800	NC
Baldwin Wallace Univ	OH	36,980	VC
Benedictine Univ	IL	35,220	C
Berkeley College/New Jersey	NJ	27,300	LC
Black Hills State Univ	SD	13,562	LC
Cabarrus College of Health Sciences	NC	10,000	SP
Calif Baptist Univ	CA	35,890	C
Cal State, Chico	CA	18,952	C
Cal State, Long Beach	CA	17,534	C+
Cal State, Northridge	CA	28,313	C
Cal State, San Bernardino	CA	12,000	C
Calumet College of St. Joseph	IN	15,000	LC
Carlow Univ	PA	30,272	C
Carroll College	MT	28,000	C
Central Mich Univ	MI	18,066	C
Chancellor Univ	OH	11,000	C
Charter Oak State College	CT	8,280	SP
Chestnut Hill College	PA	39,785	LC
Chicago State Univ	IL	5,482	C
Clayton State Univ	GA	12,000	LC
Cleary Univ	MI	11,000	C
Coastal Carolina Univ	SC	17,620	C
College of St. Scholastica	MN	39,960	C
Columbia College	MO	24,578	C
Concordia Univ	OR	34,930	C
Corban Univ	OR	34,764	C
Dallas Baptist Univ	TX	29,118	C
Dominican College	NY	31,270	C
Duquesne Univ	PA	42,017	VC
D'Youville College	NY	29,850	C
East Carolina Univ	NC	14,169	C
Eastern Kentucky Univ	KY	11,161	C
Eastern Mich Univ	MI	17,961	C
Eastern Washington Univ	WA	16,388	C
Emporia State Univ	KS	12,897	C
Ferris State Univ	MI	19,698	C
Florida Atlantic Univ	FL	17,339	C
Florida International Univ	FL	17,747	VC

School	ST	$IS	SR
Franklin Pierce Univ	NH	41,598	C
Franklin Univ	OH	7,000	SP
Gardner-Webb Univ	NC	34,375	Ǥ
George Fox Univ	OR	40,750	Ǥ
Gwynedd-Mercy College	PA	33,560	C
Harding Univ	AR	21,432	Ǥ
Harris-Stowe State Univ	MO	14,360	NC
Hastings College	NE	27,782	Ǥ
Hodges Univ	FL	12,000	LC
Howard Univ	DC	35,957	C
Husson Univ	ME	23,386	LC
Idaho State Univ	ID	11,908	C
Illinois State Univ	IL	22,634	VC
Indiana Univ Bloomington	IN	19,358	HC
Indiana Univ Northwest	IN	6,738	LC
Indiana Univ South Bend	IN	15,293	C
Indiana Univ Southeast	IN	15,807	LC
Indiana Univ-Purdue Univ Fort Wayne	IN	15,425	C
Jackson State Univ	MS	13,512	LC
James Madison Univ	VA	18,049	VC
Langston Univ	OK	3,000	LC
Lebanon Valley College	PA	38,570	C
Lee Univ	TN	18,690	Ǥ
Lehman College / The CUNY	NY	5,778	LC
Lewis Univ	IL	23,050	C
Limestone College	SC	29,880	C
LIU/C.W. Post Campus	NY	38,888	C
Lourdes Univ	OH	26,055	LC
Mary Baldwin College	VA	37,110	C
Marywood Univ	PA	40,095	C
Mercy College of Health Sciences	IA	14,460	SP
Metropolitan State Univ of Denver	CO	4,835	LC
Midwestern State Univ	TX	9,722	C
Minn State Univ, Moorhead	MN	13,392	C
Missouri Baptist Univ	MO	30,310	C
Missouri State Univ	MO	13,996	VC
Monroe College	NY	17,700	C
Montana State Univ-Billings	MT	12,425	LC
Mount Aloysius College	PA	27,970	C
Mount Marty College	SD	29,638	C
Mount Mercy Univ	IA	34,385	C
Mount St. Mary's College/ Chalon Campus	CA	43,897	VǤ
Mountain State Univ	WV	14,330	NC
National American Univ	SD	16,712	NC
National Louis Univ	IL	16,915	LC
Nebr Methodist College of Nursing and Allied Health	NE	22,872	SP
New York City College of Technology / The CUNY	NY	5,769	NC
New York Univ	NY	61,470	MC
Newbury College	MA	41,850	C
Norfolk State Univ	VA	10,531	LC
Northwest Christian Univ	OR	27,399	C
Ohio Univ	OH	20,676	VC
Okla City Univ	OK	33,546	VC
Oregon State Univ	OR	19,017	Ǥ
Park Univ	MO	17,525	C
Penn State Univ/Univ Park	PA	25,404	VC
Pennsylvania College of Technology	PA	25,653	NC
Point Park Univ	PA	36,390	C
Presentation College	SD	14,800	LC
Providence College	RI	55,995	HC
Rhode Island College	RI	17,132	LC
Robert Morris Univ	PA	36,699	C
Roger Williams Univ	RI	45,788	C
St. Joseph's Univ	PA	52,272	VC
St. Leo Univ	FL	27,990	C
St. Louis Univ	MO	46,594	VǤ
St. Mary-of-the-Woods College	IN	37,722	LC
St. Peter's College	NJ	44,240	C
Salisbury Univ	MD	18,368	VC
Shenandoah Univ	VA	39,268	C
Shippensburg Univ of Pennsylvania	PA	17,064	LC
Simpson Univ	CA	28,900	C
Sojourner-Douglass College	MD	9,160	LC
South Univ	GA		LC
Southern Adventist Univ	TN	26,190	C
Southern Illinois Univ Carbondale	IL	21,620	C
Southern Univ at New Orleans	LA	1,000	NC
Southern Vermont College	VT	30,740	LC
Southwestern Okla State Univ	OK	9,160	C
Springfield College	MA	25,000	C
St. Catherine Univ	MN	37,782	Ǥ
St. Francis College	NY	34,200	LC
St. John's Univ	NY	52,840	Ǥ
St. Joseph's College, New York / Brooklyn Campus	NY	21,878	C
St. Joseph's College, New York / Suffolk Campus	NY	21,878	VC
SUNY Inst of Technology at Utica / Rome	NY	23,818	C
SUNY/Empire State College	NY	6,315	SP
Stonehill College	MA	46,780	VǤ
SUNY Fredonia / The SUNY at Fredonia	NY	18,702	VC
Tenn State Univ	TN	9,048	C
Texas Southern Univ	TX	18,212	LC
Texas State Univ	TX	16,495	VC
Thomas More College	KY	34,760	C
Towson Univ	MD	16,000	VC
Univ of Central Arkansas	AR	10,840	VC
Univ of Central Florida	FL	15,711	VǤ
Univ of Colo at Colo Springs	CO	15,000	VC
Univ of Conn	CT	23,744	HC
Univ of Detroit Mercy	MI	30,450	C
Univ of Evansville	IN	41,056	VǤ
Univ of Great Falls	MT	27,970	C
Univ of Illinois at Urbana-Champaign	IL	24,300	HC
Univ of La Verne	CA	47,010	VC
Univ of Miami	FL	55,166	MC
Univ of Mich-Flint	MI	17,547	Ǥ
Univ of Minn Crookston	MN	17,834	C
Univ of Nebr at Omaha	NE	12,700	C
Univ of Nevada, Las Vegas	NV	17,303	C
Univ of New England	ME	46,145	Ǥ
Univ of New Hampshire	NH	24,702	VC
Univ of N Car at Chapel Hill	NC	18,348	MC
Univ of North Florida	FL	15,578	VC
Univ of Pennsylvania	PA	56,106	MC
Univ of Scranton	PA	51,940	VC
Univ of S Dak	SD	15,111	C
Univ of Southern Indiana	IN	14,057	C
Univ of St. Francis	IL	36,490	C
Univ of Washington	WA	14,722	VC
Univ of Wisc/Eau Claire	WI	15,430	VC
Upper Iowa Univ	IA	30,426	NC
Ursuline College	OH	33,198	LC
Valparaiso Univ	IN	43,040	VǤ
Viterbo Univ	WI	30,070	C
Washburn Univ	KS	12,165	NC
Washington Adventist Univ	MD	25,859	Ǥ
Washington Univ in St. Louis	MO	58,818	MC
Wayland Baptist Univ	TX	16,058	LC
West Virginia Univ Inst of Technology	WV	14,094	NC
Western Carolina Univ	NC	13,965	Ǥ
Western Conn State Univ	CT	18,327	C
Western Kentucky Univ	KY	11,000	LC
Wichita State Univ	KS	12,539	C
Wilberforce Univ	OH	15,100	LC
Winona State Univ	MN	16,530	C

HEALTH COMMUNICATION

School	ST	$IS	SR
San Diego State Univ	CA	20,578	VC

HEALTH EDUCATION

School	ST	$IS	SR
Albany State Univ	GA	8,500	C
Anderson Univ	IN	35,390	C
Appalachian State Univ	NC	12,919	VC
Aquinas College	MI	33,060	C
Arkansas Tech Univ	AR	13,164	LC
Ashland Univ	OH	25,000	C
Auburn Univ	AL	20,052	VǤ
Augsburg College	MN	35,142	C
Austin Peay State Univ	TN	14,650	C
Averett Univ	VA	36,000	LC
Ball State Univ	IN	17,850	C
Baylor Univ	TX	46,720	HC
Bemidji State Univ	MN	13,500	C
Bethany College	KS	30,605	NC
Bethel College	KS	29,100	C
Bethel Univ	MN	34,940	VC
Black Hills State Univ	SD	13,562	LC
Briar Cliff Univ	IA	29,514	C
Bridgewater State Univ	MA	18,752	C
Calif Baptist Univ	CA	35,890	C
Cal State, Chico	CA	18,952	C
Cal State, Sacramento	CA	16,200	C
Cal State, San Bernardino	CA	12,000	C
Cal State, Stanislaus	CA	18,582	C
Campbellsville Univ	KY	27,720	C
Carson-Newman Univ	TN	29,058	Ǥ
Castleton State College	VT	19,424	C
Central State Univ	OH	9,010	C
Central Washington Univ	WA	11,730	C
Chadron State College	NE	7,400	NC
Citadel, The	SC		C
Cleveland State Univ	OH	21,357	C
College of Mount St. Vincent	NY	41,040	MC
College of New Jersey	NJ	25,376	HC
Columbus State Univ	GA	13,176	C
Concordia College, Moorhead	MN	39,974	Ǥ
Concordia Univ, Ann Arbor	MI	27,220	VC
Curry College	MA	47,545	LC
Dakota State Univ	SD	13,811	C
Defiance College	OH	30,645	C
Delaware State Univ	DE	14,700	LC
Delta State Univ	MS	12,292	LC
DePaul Univ	IL	46,120	VC
East Carolina Univ	NC	14,169	C
East Stroudsburg Univ of Pennsylvania	PA	16,636	C
Eastern Kentucky Univ	KY	11,161	C
Eastern Mich Univ	MI	17,961	C
Eastern Washington Univ	WA	16,388	C
Edinboro Univ of Pennsylvania	PA	15,940	LC
Elon Univ	NC	40,046	HC
Emporia State Univ	KS	12,897	C
Fairmont State Univ	WV	12,098	LC
Fayetteville State Univ	NC	10,816	C
Florida State Univ	FL	15,238	HC
Freed-Hardeman Univ	TN	19,697	VC
Friends Univ	KS	29,100	C
Gardner-Webb Univ	NC	34,375	Ǥ
Georgia Regents Univ	GA		C
Georgia Southern Univ	GA	16,414	C
Glenville State College	WV	11,348	NC
Goddard College	VT	16,418	VC
Goshen College	IN	35,900	VC
Gustavus Adolphus College	MN	48,170	HC
Hofstra Univ	NY	48,020	VǤ
Houghton College	NY	35,740	VC
Howard Univ	DC	35,957	C
Hunter College / The CUNY	NY	14,429	VC
Idaho State Univ	ID	11,908	C
Illinois State Univ	IL	22,634	VC
Indiana State Univ	IN	16,000	C
Indiana Univ Bloomington	IN	19,358	HC
Indiana Univ of Pennsylvania	PA	20,180	LC
Indiana Univ-Purdue Univ Indianapolis	IN	17,290	C
Inter-American Univ of PR/ San Germán	PR	6,720	
Iowa State Univ	IA	16,403	C
Ithaca College	NY	52,300	HC
Jackson State Univ	MS	13,512	LC
Jacksonville State Univ	AL	12,280	LC
Johnson C. Smith Univ	NC	25,336	LC
Kennesaw State Univ	GA	13,017	VC
Lamar Univ	TX	6,820	LC
Lee Univ	TN	18,690	Ǥ
Lehman College / The CUNY	NY	5,778	LC
Lenoir-Rhyne College	NC	35,984	C
Lincoln Memorial Univ	TN	18,144	C
Linfield College-McMinnville Campus	OR	46,166	C
Lipscomb Univ	TN	35,722	VC
LIU/C.W. Post Campus	NY	38,888	C
Louisiana College	LA	15,746	C
Malone Univ	OH	34,334	C
Manchester College	IN	35,070	C
Manhattan College	NY	44,955	VC
Mayville State Univ	ND	11,401	NC
McNeese State Univ	LA		C
MidAmerica Nazarene Univ	KS	28,000	C
Middle Tenn State Univ	TN	8,650	C
Minn State Univ, Mankato	MN	14,900	C
Minn State Univ, Moorhead	MN	13,392	C
Missouri Baptist Univ	MO	30,310	C
Missouri Southern State Univ	MO	11,910	C
Monmouth Univ	NJ	42,252	C
Montana State Univ-Billings	MT	12,425	LC
Montclair State Univ	NJ	22,614	C
Morehead State Univ	KY	10,900	C
Morgan State Univ	MD	14,500	VC
Mountain State Univ	WV	14,330	NC
Murray State Univ	KY	14,944	C
New Jersey City Univ	NJ	21,060	Ǥ
New York Inst of Technology	NY	40,590	VC
N Car Central Univ	NC	9,000	LC
N Dak State Univ	ND	14,642	C
Northeastern Illinois Univ	IL		C
Northeastern State Univ	OK	8,615	VC
Northern Illinois Univ	IL	19,768	C
Northern Mich Univ	MI	15,300	VC
Northern State Univ	SD	14,021	C
Northwest Nazarene Univ	ID	24,275	NC
Northwestern State Univ of Louisiana	LA	14,368	C
Ohio Northern Univ	OH	42,075	VC
Ohio Valley Univ	WV	17,752	C
Okla State Univ	OK	14,310	VC
Old Dominion Univ	VA	18,662	C
Oral Roberts Univ	OK	31,734	C
Otterbein College	OH	32,214	C
Pfeiffer Univ	NC	33,700	C
Plymouth State Univ	NH	23,148	LC
Portland State Univ	OR	18,672	C
Purdue Univ/West Lafayette	IN	20,278	HC
Rhode Island College	RI	17,132	LC
St. Mary's College of Calif	CA	53,550	C
Salisbury Univ	MD	18,368	VC
Shepherd Univ	WV	14,996	C
Slippery Rock Univ of Pennsylvania	PA	10,360	LC
S Car State Univ	SC	6,700	LC
S Dak State Univ	SD	14,296	C
Southeastern Louisiana Univ	LA	13,325	C
Southern Arkansas Univ	AR	14,316	C
Southern Conn State Univ	CT	18,033	C
Southern Illinois Univ Carbondale	IL	21,620	C
Southern Illinois Univ Edwardsville	IL	17,532	C
Southern Methodist Univ	TX	57,755	MC
Southwest Baptist Univ	MO	24,710	C
Southwest Minn State Univ	MN	14,000	C
Southwestern Okla State Univ	OK	9,160	C
Springfield College	MA	25,000	C
St. Cloud State Univ	MN	10,600	C
SUNY Cortland / The SUNY	NY	19,117	C
Syracuse Univ	NY	54,512	HC
Tabor College	KS	29,010	LC
Taylor Univ	IN	36,742	VǤ
Tenn State Univ	TN	9,048	C
Texas A&M Univ	TX	16,956	VǤ
Texas A&M Univ at Commerce	TX	10,496	C
Texas A&M Univ at Kingsville	TX	7,500	LC
Texas State Univ	TX	16,495	VC
The Lincoln Univ	PA	15,154	LC
Troy Univ	AL	10,650	C
Univ of Alabama at Birmingham	AL	18,484	Ǥ
Univ of Arkansas at Little Rock	AR		C
Univ of Arkansas at Monticello	AR	8,470	NC
Univ of Cincinnati	OH	20,100	VC
Univ of Florida	FL	15,783	HǤ
Univ of Georgia	GA	19,508	VC
Univ of Great Falls	MT	27,970	C
Univ of Illinois at Chicago	IL	24,293	VC
Univ of Iowa	IA	17,481	VC
Univ of Kansas	KS	16,980	Ǥ
Univ of Kentucky	KY	19,868	C
Univ of Louisiana at Lafayette	LA	6,130	C
Univ of Louisiana at Monroe	LA	12,998	C
Univ of Maine	ME	19,712	Ǥ
Univ of Maine at Farmington	ME	17,841	C
Univ of Maine at Presque Isle	ME	15,011	LC
Univ of Maryland/Eastern Shore	MD	14,000	C
Univ of Minn/Duluth	MN	18,964	Ǥ
Univ of Montana-Western	MT	9,753	LC
Univ of Nebr at Kearney	NE	14,855	LC
Univ of Nevada, Las Vegas	NV	17,303	C
Univ of New Mexico	NM	15,300	C
Univ of Northern Iowa	IA	14,776	C
Univ of Pittsburgh at Bradford	PA	21,316	LC
Univ of Rio Grande	OH	8,750	NC
Univ of St. Francis	IN	29,810	C
Univ of South Alabama	AL	13,510	C
Univ of Southern Miss	MS	13,170	C
Univ of the Cumberlands	KY	27,500	LC
Univ of the District of Columbia	DC	7,244	LC
Univ of Toledo	OH	18,464	C
Univ of Utah	UT	13,462	VC
Univ of West Florida	FL	14,656	C
Univ of Wisc/La Crosse	WI	14,755	VC
Univ of Wisc/Stevens Point	WI	14,043	C
Univ of Wisc/Superior	WI	14,106	C
Univ of Wyoming	WY	13,855	Ǥ
Utah State Univ	UT	11,803	C
Valley City State Univ	ND	12,286	LC
Virginia Commonwealth Univ	VA	18,633	C
Wayne State College	NE	11,764	NC
Wayne State Univ	MI	19,493	C
West Chester Univ of Pennsylvania	PA	16,836	C
West Liberty Univ	WV	9,142	LC
Western Mich Univ	MI	19,042	C
Western Oregon Univ	OR	15,021	C
Western Washington Univ	WA	18,519	VC
William Paterson Univ of New Jersey	NJ	21,694	C
William Penn Univ	IA	26,000	C
Wilmington College	OH	29,784	C
Winona State Univ	MN	16,530	C
Worcester State Univ	MA	18,657	C
Youngstown State Univ	OH	16,374	LC

HEALTH INFORMATION MANAGEMENT

School	ST	$IS	SR
Arkansas Tech Univ	AR	13,164	LC
Champlain College	VT	44,850	VC
Charter Oak State College	CT	8,280	SP
College of Mount St. Joseph	OH	33,880	C
Coppin State Univ	MD	14,905	VC
Dakota State Univ	SD	13,811	C
Duquesne Univ	PA	42,017	VC
Georgia Regents Univ	GA		C
Idaho State Univ	ID	11,908	C
Indiana Inst of Technology	IN	34,240	LC
Indiana Univ Northwest	IN	6,738	LC
Indiana Univ Southeast	IN	15,807	LC

School	ST	$IS	SR
Indiana Univ-Purdue Univ Indianapolis	IN	17,290	C
John Carroll Univ	OH	44,520	G
Kean Univ	NJ	22,060	LC
Loyola Univ Chicago	IL	49,560	VG
Marymount Univ	VA	36,178	C
Miami Univ	OH	24,191	HC
Montana Tech of The Univ of Montana	MT	14,650	VC
Northern Kentucky Univ	KY	15,302	LC
Ohio State Univ at Lima	OH	7,140	C
Rutgers, The State Univ of New Jersey/New Brunswick	NJ	25,077	VC
St. Louis Univ	MO	46,604	VG
Southeast Missouri State Univ	MO	14,983	LC
Southern Illinois Univ Edwardsville	IL	17,532	C
Temple Univ	PA	24,392	VC
Ohio State Univ	OH	19,887	MC
Thomas Edison State College	NJ	5,700	SP
Univ of Central Florida	FL	15,711	VG
Univ of Illinois at Chicago	IL	24,293	VC
Univ of Kansas	KS	16,980	G
Univ of Maine at Farmington	ME	17,841	C
Univ of Pittsburgh at Pittsburgh	PA	27,800	HG
Univ of S Car Upstate	SC	17,673	LC
Univ of Tenn at Knoxville	TN	20,364	VG
Univ of Wisc/Green Bay	WI	14,900	C

HEALTH PROMOTION

School	ST	$IS	SR
Arkansas State Univ	AR	14,980	C
Baldwin Wallace Univ	OH	36,980	VC
Georgia Southern Univ	GA	16,414	C
Goddard College	VT	16,418	VC
Keene State College	NH	21,538	C
Lynchburg College	VA	42,645	C
Miami Univ	OH	24,191	HC
Missouri State Univ	MO	13,996	VC
Nova Southeastern Univ	FL	34,016	VC
Samford Univ	AL	35,700	VG
Univ of Georgia	GA	19,508	VC
Univ of N Car at Asheville	NC	13,500	VG
Univ of Wisc/Superior	WI	14,106	C
Western Conn State Univ	CT	18,327	C

HEALTH SCIENCE

School	ST	$IS	SR
Adventist University of Health Sciences	FL	16,344	NC
Albany College of Pharmacy and Health Sciences	NY	38,900	SP
Alcorn State Univ	MS	9,500	C
Alderson Broaddus Univ	WV	28,656	C
Alma College	MI	42,400	VC
Alvernia Univ	PA	39,250	C
American Univ	DC	54,829	HG
Appalachian State Univ	NC	12,919	VC
Arizona State Univ	AZ	18,818	G
Armstrong Atlantic State Univ	GA	16,276	C
Asbury Univ	KY	32,038	VC
Aurora Univ	IL	26,870	C
Baylor Univ	TX	46,720	HC
Benedictine Univ	IL	35,220	C
Bloomsburg Univ of Pennsylvania	PA	13,598	C
Boise State Univ	ID	12,802	C
Boston Univ	MA	54,130	HG
Bowling Green State Univ	OH	18,970	C
Bradley Univ	IL	31,874	VC
Brandeis Univ	MA	58,820	HC
Brigham Young Univ	UT	12,100	HC
Butler Univ	IN	45,898	VG
Calif Baptist Univ	CA	35,890	C
Cal State, Chico	CA	18,952	C
Cal State, Dominguez Hills	CA	17,056	LC
Cal State, East Bay	CA	16,549	C
Cal State, Fresno	CA	17,405	C
Cal State, Fullerton	CA	25,188	G
Cal State, Long Beach	CA	17,534	G
Cal State, Los Angeles	CA	15,829	C
Cal State, San Bernardino	CA	12,000	C
Castleton State College	VT	19,424	C
Chapman Univ	CA	56,019	VG
Chicago State Univ	IL	5,482	C
CUNY/Brooklyn College	NY	5,884	G
Cleveland State Univ	OH	21,357	C
College of St. Scholastica	MN	39,960	C
College of St Joseph	VT	30,600	LC
College of William & Mary	VA	25,085	MC
Colo State Univ-Fort Collins	CO	20,090	VC
Columbus State Univ	GA	13,176	C
Corban Univ	OR	34,764	C
Creighton Univ	NE	44,058	VG
Daemen College	NY	31,510	C
DePaul Univ	IL	46,120	VC
Dordt College	IA	34,160	VC
Drury Univ	MO	30,319	VC
East Tenn State Univ	TN	9,000	C
Elms College	MA	23,900	VC
Emporia State Univ	KS	12,897	C
Excelsior College	NY	895	SP
Ferrum College	VA	27,740	LC
Fitchburg State Univ	MA	17,241	C
Florida Atlantic Univ	FL	17,339	C
Florida Gulf Coast Univ	FL		C
Franklin Pierce Univ	NH	41,598	C
Friends Univ	KS	29,100	C
Furman Univ	SC	54,006	HC
Gannon Univ	PA	37,940	C
George Mason Univ	VA	15,724	VC
Gettysburg College	PA	56,820	HC
Goddard College	VT	16,418	VC
Goodwin College	CT	19,400	LC
Grand Canyon Univ	AZ	24,540	VC
Grand Valley State Univ	MI	17,998	VC
Guilford College	NC	35,340	C
Hampshire College	MA	58,320	MC
Harding Univ	AR	21,432	G
Hardin-Simmons Univ	TX	23,560	G
Hofstra Univ	NY	48,020	VG
Hope International Univ	CA	34,650	C
Howard Univ	DC	35,957	C
Idaho State Univ	ID	11,908	C
Indiana Univ Bloomington	IN	19,358	HC
Indiana Univ Kokomo	IN	6,674	LC
Indiana Univ-Purdue Univ Indianapolis	IN	17,290	C
Ithaca College	NY	52,300	HC
James Madison Univ	VA	18,049	VC
Johnson State College	VT	16,721	C
Kalamazoo College	MI	47,825	HG
King Univ	TN	33,140	C
La Sierra Univ	CA	35,694	VC
Lee Univ	TN	18,690	G
Lock Haven Univ of Pennsylvania	PA	17,587	LC
Loyola Marymount Univ	CA	53,240	VG
Marietta College	OH	42,135	VC
Marshall Univ	WV	14,820	C
Marymount Univ	VA	36,178	C
Maryville Univ of St. Louis	MO	34,920	VC
Marywood Univ	PA	40,695	C
Mass College of Pharmacy and Health Sciences	MA	36,450	SP
Mercy College	NY	29,996	C
Mercy College of Health Sciences	IA	14,460	SP
Middle Tenn State Univ	TN	8,650	C
Midwestern State Univ	TX	9,722	C
Minn State Univ, Mankato	MN	14,900	C
Missouri Baptist Univ	MO	30,310	C
Nazareth College of Rochester	NY	41,590	VC
New England College	NH	45,930	LC
Newman Univ	KS	30,380	G
Nicholls State Univ	LA	7,095	C
Norfolk State Univ	VA	10,531	LC
Northeastern Univ	MA	55,296	MC
Northern Arizona Univ	AZ	18,592	C
Northern Illinois Univ	IL	19,768	C
Oakland Univ	MI	19,391	VC
Old Dominion Univ	VA	18,662	C
Oral Roberts Univ	OK	31,734	C
Oregon Inst of Technology	OR	8,910	C
Our Lady of Holy Cross College	LA	8,090	LC
Pennsylvania College of Technology	PA	25,653	NC
Purdue Univ/West Lafayette	IN	20,278	HC
Quinnipiac Univ	CT	53,580	VC
Randolph College	VA	43,960	VC
Sacred Heart Univ	CT	48,564	VC
Saginaw Valley State Univ	MI	16,869	C
St. Joseph's Univ	PA	52,272	VC
St. Mary's College of Calif	CA	53,550	C
San Diego State Univ	CA	20,578	VC
San Francisco State Univ	CA	18,514	C
San Jose State Univ	CA	19,707	C
South Univ	GA		LC
Southern Adventist Univ	TN	26,190	C
Southwestern Okla State Univ	OK	9,160	C
St. Ambrose Univ	IA		C
St. Francis College	NY	34,200	LC
Stephen F. Austin State Univ	TX	14,668	C
Stetson Univ	FL	49,512	VG
Stony Brook Univ / SUNY	NY	19,359	HC
SUNY Cortland / The SUNY	NY	19,117	C
Syracuse Univ	NY	54,512	HC
Taylor Univ	IN	36,742	VG
Texas A&M Univ at Corpus Christi	TX	11,544	LC
Texas Woman's Univ	TX	13,633	LC
The College at Brockport / SUNY	NY	18,362	VC
The Lincoln Univ	PA	15,154	LC
Ohio State Univ	OH	19,887	MC
Towson Univ	MD	16,000	VC
Truman State Univ	MO	13,546	HC
Universidad Adventista de las Antillas	PR	7,360	
Univ of Alabama at Birmingham	AL	18,484	G
Univ of Arkansas at Fayetteville	AR	16,860	VC
Univ of Arkansas at Little Rock	AR		C
Univ of Calif at Santa Cruz	CA	27,807	VC
Univ of Central Arkansas	AR	10,840	VC
Univ of Central Florida	FL	15,711	VG
Univ of Delaware	DE	22,728	VC
Univ of Findlay	OH	31,916	C
Univ of Florida	FL	15,783	HG
Univ of Hartford	CT	42,674	C
Univ of Maryland/Baltimore County	MD	18,000	VC
Univ of Mass Dartmouth	MA	22,223	C
Univ of Memphis	TN	15,094	C
Univ of Miami	FL	55,166	MC
Univ of Mich-Flint	MI	17,547	G
Univ of Minn Crookston	MN	17,834	C
Univ of Missouri-Kansas City	MO	19,603	C
Univ of Nebr - Lincoln	NE	17,507	VC
Univ of New England	ME	46,145	G
Univ of New Hampshire	NH	24,702	VC
Univ of North Florida	FL	15,578	VC
Univ of Okla	OK	17,634	VG
Univ of South Florida/St. Petersburg	FL	12,769	VC
Univ of Southern Maine	ME	16,576	C
Univ of Tenn at Martin	TN	13,217	C
Univ of Texas at El Paso	TX	8,764	NC
Univ of the Sciences	PA	48,320	VG
Univ of Wisc/Stevens Point	WI	14,043	C
Univ of Wyoming	WY	13,855	G
Washington Univ in St. Louis	MO	58,818	MC
Wayne State Univ	MI	19,493	C
West Chester Univ of Pennsylvania	PA	16,836	C
Western Conn State Univ	CT	18,327	C
Western Illinois Univ	IL	20,130	C
Western New England Univ	MA	45,590	C
Wheaton College	IL	39,650	HG
Wheeling Jesuit Univ	WV	34,668	C
Whitworth Univ	WA	45,826	VG
William Paterson Univ of New Jersey	NJ	21,694	C
Yeshiva Univ	NY	47,250	VG

HEALTH SERVICES TECHNOLOGY

School	ST	$IS	SR
Indiana Univ Northwest	IN	6,738	LC
Thomas Edison State College	NJ	5,700	SP
Univ of Pittsburgh at Pittsburgh	PA	27,800	HG

HEBREW

School	ST	$IS	SR
American Univ	DC	54,829	HG
Bard College	NY	59,872	HC
Binghamton Univ / The SUNY	NY	20,832	HG
Harvard Univ/Harvard College	MA	49,000	MC
Hofstra Univ	NY	48,020	VG
Hunter College / The CUNY	NY	14,429	VC
Lehman College / The CUNY	NY	5,778	LC
New York Univ	NY	61,470	MC
Queens College / The CUNY	NY	17,107	VC
Ohio State Univ	OH	19,887	MC
Thomas Edison State College	NJ	5,700	SP
Touro College	NY	23,150	VC
Univ of Calif at Los Angeles	CA	25,686	MC
Univ of Illinois at Urbana-Champaign	IL	24,300	HC
Univ of Mich/Ann Arbor	MI	22,102	HG
Univ of Minn/Twin Cities	MN		HC
Univ of Texas at Austin	TX	44,074	HC
Univ of Utah	UT	13,462	VC
Univ of Wisc/Madison	WI	18,757	HC
Washington Univ in St. Louis	MO	58,818	MC
Yeshiva Univ	NY	47,250	VG

HISPANIC AMERICAN STUDIES

School	ST	$IS	SR
Arizona State Univ	AZ	18,818	G
Boston College	MA	58,506	MC
Boston Univ	MA	54,130	HG
Brown Univ	RI	56,150	MC
Cal State, Long Beach	CA	17,534	G
CUNY/Brooklyn College	NY	5,884	G
Claremont McKenna College	CA	58,065	MC
College of St. Benedict	MN	47,570	VC
Colo College	CO	54,534	MC
Columbia Univ in the City of New York	NY	61,116	MC
Columbia Univ/School of General Studies	NY	54,083	MC
Conn College	CT	54,970	MC
East Carolina Univ	NC	14,169	C
Hamilton College	NY	55,620	MC
Hofstra Univ	NY	48,020	VG
Hunter College / The CUNY	NY	14,429	VC
Lewis & Clark College	OR	52,656	VC
Loyola Marymount Univ	CA	53,240	VG
Mills College	CA	54,119	HC
Mount St. Mary College	NY	39,540	C
Northeastern Illinois Univ	IL		C
Pepperdine Univ	CA	55,372	HG
Pomona College	CA	57,680	MC
Rice Univ	TX	43,288	MC
Rutgers, The State Univ of New Jersey/New Brunswick	NJ	25,077	VC
St. John's Univ	MN	46,146	C
Scripps College	CA	54,900	MC
St. Olaf College	MN	49,960	HG
Stanford Univ	CA	56,411	MC
SUNY Oneonta / SUNY	NY	16,919	VC
Univ at Albany / SUNY	NY	18,674	VC
Univ of Calif at Berkeley	CA	23,322	MC
Univ of Calif at Irvine	CA	25,961	VC
Univ of Mass Boston	MA	11,966	C
Univ of Mich/Ann Arbor	MI	22,102	HG
Univ of Mich/Dearborn	MI	9,885	VC
Univ of Pennsylvania	PA	56,106	MC
Univ of PR/Cayey	PR	1,504	
Univ of Tenn at Knoxville	TN	20,364	VG
Vassar College	NY	59,070	MC
Wesleyan Univ	CT	59,844	MC
Western New Mexico Univ	NM	8,500	LC
Wheaton College	MA	54,934	HG

HISTORIC PRESERVATION

School	ST	$IS	SR
College of Charleston	SC	21,273	VC
Eastern Mich Univ	MI	17,961	C
Roger Williams Univ	RI	45,788	C
Salve Regina Univ	RI	47,250	VC
Savannah College of Art and Design	GA	46,824	SP
Southeast Missouri State Univ	MO	14,983	LC
Univ of Delaware	DE	22,728	VC
Univ of Georgia	GA	19,508	VC
Univ of Mary Washington	VA	19,484	VC
Univ of Mich/Ann Arbor	MI	22,102	HG
Ursuline College	OH	33,198	LC

HISTORY

School	ST	$IS	SR
Abilene Christian Univ	TX	38,400	VC
Adams State College	CO	13,358	LC
Adelphi Univ	NY	43,130	VC
Adrian College	MI	33,800	C
Agnes Scott College	GA	45,323	VG
Alabama A&M Univ	AL	96,100	C
Alabama State Univ	AL	14,142	NC
Albany State Univ	GA	8,500	C
Albertus Magnus College	CT	37,382	LC
Albion College	MI	43,884	VC
Albright College	PA	46,660	C
Alcorn State Univ	MS	9,500	C
Alderson Broaddus Univ	WV	28,656	C
Alfred Univ	NY	40,392	VC
Alice Lloyd College	KY	4,900	C
Allegheny College	PA	49,020	HC
Allen Univ	SC	16,124	NC
Alma College	MI	42,400	VC
Alvernia Univ	PA	39,250	C
Alverno College	WI	30,483	LC
American International College	MA	36,100	LC
American Univ	DC	54,829	HG
Amherst College	MA	58,744	MC
Anderson Univ	IN	35,390	C
Andrews Univ	MI	28,030	G
Angelo State Univ	TX	15,049	NC
Anna Maria College	MA	34,600	LC
Appalachian State Univ	NC	12,919	VC
Aquinas College	MI	33,060	C
Aquinas College	TN	29,250	G
Arcadia Univ	PA	33,570	G
Arizona State Univ	AZ	18,818	G
Arkansas State Univ	AR	14,980	C
Arkansas Tech Univ	AR	13,164	LC
Armstrong Atlantic State Univ	GA	16,276	C
Asbury Univ	KY	32,038	VC
Ashland Univ	OH	25,000	C
Assumption College	MA	45,721	VC
Atlantic Union College	MA	24,600	LC
Auburn Univ	AL	20,052	VG
Auburn Univ at Montgomery	AL	12,120	C
Augsburg College	MN	35,142	C
Augustana College	IL	43,398	HC
Augustana College	SD	35,500	VC
Aurora Univ	IL	26,870	C
Austin College	TX	36,940	HC
Austin Peay State Univ	TN	14,650	C
Averett Univ	VA	36,000	LC
Avila Univ	MO	26,900	C
Azusa Pacific Univ	CA	39,946	C
Baker Univ	KS	33,350	G
Baldwin Wallace Univ	OH	36,980	VC

INDEX OF COLLEGE MAJORS

School	ST	$IS	SR
Ball State Univ	IN	17,850	C
Bard College	NY	59,872	HC
Bard College at Simon's Rock	MA	58,963	HC+
Barry Univ	FL	38,190	C
Barton College	NC	27,660	C
Bates College	ME	58,950	MC
Baylor Univ	TX	46,720	HC
Belhaven Univ	MS	27,170	C
Bellarmine Univ	KY	42,950	VC
Bellevue Univ	NE	4,600	NC
Belmont Abbey College	NC	37,716	C
Belmont Univ	TN	37,380	VC+
Beloit College	WI	49,970	HC
Bemidji State Univ	MN	13,500	C
Benedict College	SC	20,454	NC
Benedictine College	KS	29,180	VC
Benedictine Univ	IL	35,220	C
Bennington College	VT	56,990	HC+
Bentley Univ	MA	54,555	HC+
Berea College	KY	7,220	HC
Berry College	GA	39,254	HC
Bethany College	KS	30,605	NC
Bethany College	WV	35,282	C
Bethel College	IN	31,560	C
Bethel College	KS	29,100	C
Bethel Univ	MN	34,940	VC
Bethel Univ	TN	19,186	C
Bethune-Cookman Univ	FL	22,290	LC
Binghamton Univ / The SUNY	NY	20,832	HC+
Biola Univ	CA	40,320	VC
Birmingham-Southern College	AL	42,370	VC+
Black Hills State Univ	SD	13,562	LC
Blackburn College	IL	21,350	C
Bloomfield College	NJ	36,960	C
Bloomsburg Univ of Pennsylvania	PA	13,598	C
Blue Mountain College	MS	13,550	LC
Bluefield College	VA	17,230	C+
Bluffton Univ	OH	37,864	C
Boise State Univ	ID	12,802	C
Boston College	MA	58,506	MC
Boston Univ	MA	54,130	HC+
Bowdoin College	ME	57,834	MC
Bowie State Univ	MD	23,990	LC
Bowling Green State Univ	OH	18,970	C
Bradley Univ	IL	31,874	VC
Brandeis Univ	MA	58,820	HC
Brenau Univ Women's College	GA	26,650	C+
Brescia Univ	KY	26,140	VC+
Brewton-Parker College	GA	33,388	LC
Briar Cliff Univ	IA	29,514	C
Bridgewater College	VA	39,880	C
Brigham Young Univ	UT	12,100	HC
Brigham Young Univ/ Hawaii	HI	8,614	VC
Brown Univ	RI	56,150	MC
Bryan College	TN	24,194	C
Bryant Univ	RI	49,179	VC
Bryn Athyn College	PA	27,984	C
Bryn Mawr College	PA	57,760	MC
Bucknell Univ	PA	58,160	MC
Buena Vista Univ	IA	37,954	C
Buffalo State/State Univ of Buffalo	NY	15,733	C+
Butler Univ	IN	45,898	VC+
Cairn Univ	PA	31,255	C
Caldwell College	NJ	35,602	LC
Calif Baptist Univ	CA	35,890	C
Calif Inst of Technology	CA	54,045	MC
Calif Lutheran Univ	CA	47,640	C
Calif Polytechnic State Univ	CA	19,847	HC
Calif State Polytechnic Univ, Pomona	CA	18,932	C
Cal State, Bakersfield	CA	8,000	LC
Cal State, Chico	CA	18,952	C
Cal State, Dominguez Hills	CA	17,056	LC
Cal State, East Bay	CA	16,549	C
Cal State, Fresno	CA	17,405	C
Cal State, Fullerton	CA	25,188	C+
Cal State, Long Beach	CA	17,534	C+
Cal State, Los Angeles	CA	15,829	C
Cal State, Northridge	CA	28,313	C
Cal State, Sacramento	CA	16,200	C
Cal State, San Bernardino	CA	12,000	C
Cal State, San Marcos	CA	14,576	C
Cal State, Stanislaus	CA	18,582	C
Calif Univ of Pennsylvania	PA	14,217	C
Calvin College	MI	37,585	VC+
Cameron Univ	OK	9,267	LC
Campbell Univ	NC	25,500	C
Campbellsville Univ	KY	27,720	C
Canisius College	NY	45,602	VC
Capital Univ	OH	39,824	VC
Cardinal Stritch Univ	WI	24,054	C
Carleton College	MN	58,149	MC
Carlow Univ	PA	30,272	C
Carnegie Mellon Univ	PA	51,260	MC
Carroll College	MT	28,000	C
Carroll Univ	WI	24,860	C
Carson-Newman Univ	TN	29,058	C+
Carthage College	WI	33,000	C
Case Western Reserve Univ	OH	55,178	MC
Castleton State College	VT	19,424	C
Catawba College	NC	37,105	C
Cedar Crest College	PA	43,240	C
Cedarville Univ	OH	31,036	VC+
Centenary College	NJ	38,618	LC
Centenary College of Louisiana	LA	39,070	C+
Central College	IA	36,980	VC
Central Conn State Univ	CT	19,212	C
Central Methodist Univ	MO	28,240	VC
Central Mich Univ	MI	18,066	C
Central State Univ	OH	9,010	C
Central Washington Univ	WA	11,730	C
Centre College	KY	35,000	HC+
Chadron State College	NE	7,400	NC
Chaminade Univ of Honolulu	HI	31,664	C
Chapman Univ	CA	56,019	VC+
Charleston Southern Univ	SC	22,420	C
Chatham Univ	PA	42,440	VC
Chestnut Hill College	PA	39,785	LC
Chicago State Univ	IL	5,482	C
Christendom College	VA	28,120	VC
Christian Brothers Univ	TN	19,140	HC
Christopher Newport Univ	VA	21,050	VC
Citadel, The	SC		C
CUNY/Baruch College	NY	15,831	VC
CUNY/Brooklyn College	NY	5,884	C+
Claflin Univ	SC	22,368	C+
Claremont McKenna College	CA	58,065	MC
Clarion Univ of Pennsylvania	PA	17,370	C
Clark Atlanta Univ	GA	30,006	C
Clark Univ	MA	47,020	HC+
Clarke Univ	IA	36,400	C
Clarkson Univ	NY	53,538	HC
Clayton State Univ	GA	12,000	LC
Clearwater Christian College	FL	23,720	C
Clemson Univ	SC	19,136	HC
Cleveland State Univ	OH	21,357	C
Coastal Carolina Univ	SC	17,620	C
Coe College	IA	43,590	VC
Coker College	SC	32,256	LC
Colby College	ME	57,510	MC
Colby-Sawyer College	NH	47,870	C
Colgate Univ	NY	50,930	MC
College of Staten Island / The CUNY	NY	16,778	NC
College of Charleston	SC	21,273	VC
College of Mount St. Joseph	OH	33,880	C
College of Mount St. Vincent	NY	41,040	MC
College of New Jersey	NJ	25,376	HC
College of St. Benedict	MN	47,570	VC
College of St. Elizabeth	NJ	43,839	LC
College of St. Scholastica	MN	39,960	C
College of St Joseph	VT	30,600	LC
College of the Holy Cross	MA	56,232	MC
College of the Ozarks	MO	5,605	VC
College of William & Mary	VA	25,085	MC
College of Wooster	OH	52,600	VC
Colo Christian Univ	CO	27,500	VC
Colo College	CO	54,534	MC
Colo Mesa Univ	CO	16,669	LC
Colo State Univ-Fort Collins	CO	20,090	VC
Colo State Univ-Pueblo	CO	13,532	LC
Columbia College	MO	24,578	C
Columbia College	SC	27,882	C
Columbia Univ in the City of New York	NY	61,116	MC
Columbia Univ/Barnard College	NY	39,000	MC
Columbia Univ/School of General Studies	NY	54,083	MC
Columbus State Univ	GA	13,176	C
Concord Univ	WV	13,102	C
Concordia College New York	NY	31,500	VC
Concordia College, Moorhead	MN	39,974	C+
Concordia Univ - Irvine	CA	35,390	VC
Concordia Univ Nebr	NE	26,000	VC
Concordia Univ St. Paul	MN	27,200	C
Concordia Univ Texas	TX	23,640	C
Concordia Univ Wisc	WI	28,980	C
Concordia Univ, Ann Arbor	MI	27,220	VC
Concordia Univ, River Forest	IL	26,300	C
Conn College	CT	54,970	MC
Converse College	SC	37,130	C
Coppin State Univ	MD	14,905	VC
Corban Univ	OR	34,764	C
Cornell College	IA	44,930	HC
Cornell Univ	NY	59,037	MC
Cornerstone Univ and Grand Rapids Theological Seminary	MI	30,866	C
Covenant College	GA		VC+
Creighton Univ	NE	44,058	VC+
Culver-Stockton College	MO	30,900	C
Cumberland Univ	TN	21,220	C
CUNY-City College	NY	19,576	HC+
Curry College	MA	47,545	LC
Daemen College	NY	31,510	C
Dakota Wesleyan Univ	SD	23,000	C
Dallas Baptist Univ	TX	29,118	C
Dartmouth College	NH	57,996	MC
Davidson College	NC	54,683	MC
Davis and Elkins College	WV	33,742	C
De Sales Univ	PA	42,670	C
Defiance College	OH	30,645	C
Delaware State Univ	DE	14,700	LC
Delta State Univ	MS	12,292	LC
Denison Univ	OH	54,670	HC+
DePaul Univ	IL	46,120	VC
DePauw Univ	IN	48,950	VC+
Dickinson College	PA	57,662	HC+
Dickinson State Univ	ND	8,550	NC
Dillard Univ	LA	20,940	VC
Doane College	NE	33,730	VC
Dominican College	NY	31,270	C
Dominican Univ	IL	37,628	C
Dominican Univ of Calif	CA	51,250	C
Dordt College	IA	34,160	VC
Dowling College	NY	25,000	LC
Drake Univ	IA	30,980	VC+
Drew Univ/College of Liberal Arts	NJ	55,862	VC
Drexel Univ	PA	51,920	HC
Drury Univ	MO	30,319	VC
Duke Univ	NC	50,250	MC
Duquesne Univ	PA	42,017	VC
D'Youville College	NY	29,850	C
Earlham College	IN	40,710	VC+
East Carolina Univ	NC	14,169	C
East Central Univ	OK	10,223	LC
East Stroudsburg Univ of Pennsylvania	PA	16,636	C
East Tenn State Univ	TN	9,000	C
East Texas Baptist Univ	TX	29,135	C
Eastern Conn State Univ	CT	20,584	C
Eastern Illinois Univ	IL	20,502	C
Eastern Kentucky Univ	KY	11,161	C
Eastern Mennonite Univ	VA	38,850	VC
Eastern Mich Univ	MI	17,961	C
Eastern Nazarene College	MA	30,000	C
Eastern New Mexico Univ	NM	10,682	C
Eastern Oregon Univ	OR	10,400	C
Eastern Univ	PA	37,704	C
Eastern Washington Univ	WA	16,388	C
Eckerd College	FL	43,902	VC
Edgewood College	WI	33,294	C
Edinboro Univ of Pennsylvania	PA	15,940	LC
Edward Waters College	FL	17,856	LC
Elizabeth City State Univ	NC	11,638	C
Elizabethtown College	PA	47,600	VC
Elmhurst College	IL	42,032	C+
Elmira College	NY	49,950	C+
Elon Univ	NC	40,046	HC
Emmanuel College	MA	47,985	VC
Emory and Henry College	VA	387,460	C
Emory Univ	GA	45,000	MC
Emporia State Univ	KS	12,897	C
Endicott College	MA	42,390	C
Erskine College	SC	37,360	C
Eugene Lang College - The New School for Liberal Arts	NY	55,650	VC
Eureka College	IL	19,280	C
Evangel Univ	MO	23,090	C
Excelsior College	NY	895	SP
Fairfield Univ	CT	55,850	VC
Fairleigh Dickinson Univ/ College at Florham	NJ	42,142	C
Fairleigh Dickinson Univ/ Metropolitan Campus	NJ	40,254	C
Fairmont State Univ	WV	12,098	LC
Faulkner Univ	AL	22,530	LC
Fayetteville State Univ	NC	10,816	C
Felician College	NJ	41,640	C
Ferris State Univ	MI	19,698	C
Ferrum College	VA	27,740	LC
Fisk Univ	TN	19,830	C
Fitchburg State Univ	MA	17,241	C
Flagler College	FL	24,960	VC
Florida A&M Univ	FL	14,935	LC
Florida Atlantic Univ	FL	17,339	C
Florida Gulf Coast Univ	FL		C
Florida International Univ	FL	17,747	VC
Florida Southern College	FL	38,240	VC
Florida State Univ	FL	15,238	HC
Fontbonne Univ	MO	31,384	C
Fordham Univ	NY	58,927	HC
Fort Hays State Univ	KS	11,354	C
Fort Lewis College	CO	15,513	C
Framingham State Univ	MA	16,750	C
Francis Marion Univ	SC	16,464	LC
Franciscan Univ of Steubenville	OH	27,320	VC
Franklin and Marshall College	PA	58,295	MC
Franklin College	IN	35,885	C
Franklin Pierce Univ	NH	41,598	C
Freed-Hardeman Univ	TN	19,697	VC
Fresno Pacific Univ	CA	32,136	C
Friends Univ	KS	29,100	C
Frostburg State Univ	MD	15,264	LC
Furman Univ	SC	54,006	HC
Gallaudet Univ	DC	25,380	SP
Gannon Univ	PA	37,940	C
Gardner-Webb Univ	NC	34,375	C+
Geneva College	PA	27,280	C
George Fox Univ	OR	40,750	C+
George Mason Univ	VA	15,724	VC
George Washington Univ	DC	57,108	MC
Georgetown College	KY	38,690	C
Georgetown Univ	DC	52,910	MC
Georgia College and State Univ	GA	18,216	VC
Georgia Regents Univ	GA		C
Georgia Southern Univ	GA	16,414	C
Georgia Southwestern State Univ	GA	12,218	C
Georgia State Univ	GA	12,000	VC
Georgian Court Univ	NJ	39,726	LC
Gettysburg College	PA	56,820	HC
Glenville State College	WV	11,348	NC
Goddard College	VT	16,418	VC
Gonzaga Univ	WA	44,247	HC
Gordon College	MA	42,660	VC+
Goshen College	IN	35,900	VC
Goucher College	MD	50,252	VC+
Graceland Univ	IA	28,020	C
Grambling State Univ	LA	13,384	LC
Grand Canyon Univ	AZ	24,540	VC
Grand Valley State Univ	MI	17,998	VC
Green Mountain College	VT	33,547	LC
Greensboro College	NC	28,740	LC
Greenville College	IL	27,012	C
Grinnell College	IA	53,651	HC
Grove City College	PA	22,988	HC
Guilford College	NC	35,340	C
Gustavus Adolphus College	MN	48,170	HC
Gwynedd-Mercy College	PA	33,560	C
Hamilton College	NY	55,620	MC
Hamline Univ	MN	44,198	VC
Hampden-Sydney College	VA	48,848	C
Hampshire College	MA	58,320	MC
Hampton Univ	VA	28,528	C
Hannibal-LaGrange Univ	MO	24,490	C
Hanover College	IN	41,450	VC
Harding Univ	AR	21,432	C+
Hardin-Simmons Univ	TX	23,560	C+
Hartwick College	NY	49,815	C+
Harvard Univ/Harvard College	MA	49,000	MC
Hastings College	NE	27,782	C+
Haverford College	PA	59,236	MC
Hawaii Pacific Univ	HI	36,690	C
Heidelberg Univ	OH	34,100	C
Hellenic College/Holy Cross Greek Orthodox School of Theology	MA	33,190	VC
Henderson State Univ	AR	13,634	C
Hendrix College	AR	48,436	HC+
High Point Univ	NC	39,800	C
Hillsdale College	MI	31,890	HC+
Hiram College	OH	37,300	VC
Hobart and William Smith Colleges	NY	43,000	VC
Hofstra Univ	NY	48,020	VC+
Hollins Univ	VA	43,295	VC
Holy Family Univ	PA	40,030	LC
Holy Names Univ	CA	40,310	NC
Hood College	MD	44,630	C
Hope College	MI	36,320	VC+
Houghton College	NY	35,740	VC
Houston Baptist Univ	TX	23,815	C+
Howard Payne Univ	TX	17,115	C
Howard Univ	DC	35,957	C
Humboldt State Univ	CA	18,400	C
Hunter College / The CUNY	NY	14,429	VC
Huntingdon College	AL	31,850	C
Huntington Univ	IN	32,220	C
Huston-Tillotson Univ	TX	18,124	C+
Idaho State Univ	ID	11,908	C
Illinois College	IL	25,770	VC
Illinois State Univ	IL	22,634	VC
Illinois Wesleyan Univ	IL	48,452	VC+
Immaculata Univ	PA	43,000	C
Indiana State Univ	IN	16,000	C
Indiana Univ Bloomington	IN	19,358	HC
Indiana Univ East	IN	6,639	LC
Indiana Univ Kokomo	IN	6,674	LC
Indiana Univ Northwest	IN	6,738	LC
Indiana Univ of Pennsylvania	PA	20,180	LC
Indiana Univ South Bend	IN	15,293	C
Indiana Univ South Bend	IN	15,293	C
Indiana Univ Southeast	IN	15,807	LC
Indiana Univ-Purdue Univ Fort Wayne	IN	15,425	C
Indiana Univ-Purdue Univ Indianapolis	IN	17,290	C
Indiana Wesleyan Univ	IN	31,815	VC
Inter-American Univ of PR/ Fajardo Campus	PR	4,200	
Inter-American Univ of PR/ Metropolitan Campus	PR	4,320	
Inter-American Univ of PR/ Ponce	PR	3,700	
Inter-American Univ of PR/ San Germán	PR	6,720	
Iona College	NY	44,028	C

ST = STATE **$IS** = IN-STATE COSTS **SR** = SELECTOR RATING

School	ST	$IS	SR
Iowa State Univ	IA	16,403	C
Iowa Wesleyan College	IA	30,850	LC
Ithaca College	NY	52,300	HC
Jackson State Univ	MS	13,512	LC
Jacksonville State Univ	AL	12,280	LC
Jacksonville Univ	FL	37,780	C
James Madison Univ	VA	18,049	VC
Jarvis Christian College	TX	19,552	NC
John Brown Univ	AR	30,996	VȻ
John Carroll Univ	OH	44,520	Ȼ
Johns Hopkins Univ	MD	47,492	MC
Johnson C. Smith Univ	NC	25,336	LC
Johnson State College	VT	16,721	C
Judson College	AL	24,690	C
Judson Univ	IL	25,130	C
Juniata College	PA	49,340	VC
Kalamazoo College	MI	47,825	HȻ
Kansas State Univ	KS	15,497	VC
Kansas Wesleyan Univ	KS	32,000	C
Kean Univ	NJ	22,060	LC
Keene State College	NH	21,538	C
Kennesaw State Univ	GA	13,017	VC
Kent State Univ	OH	19,352	C
Kentucky Christian Univ	KY	17,622	LC
Kentucky State Univ	KY	11,000	LC
Kentucky Wesleyan College	KY	27,440	VȻ
Kenyon College	OH	56,810	MC
King Univ	TN	33,140	C
King's College	PA	41,678	C
Knox College	IL		VC
Kutztown Univ of Pennsylvania	PA	16,909	LC
La Roche College	PA	34,802	LC
La Salle Univ	PA	50,270	C
La Sierra Univ	CA	35,694	VC
Lafayette College	PA	57,050	HȻ
LaGrange College	GA	34,480	C
Lake Erie College	OH	35,704	C
Lake Forest College	IL	45,580	VC
Lake Superior State Univ	MI	18,121	C
Lakeland College	WI	22,990	C
Lamar Univ	TX	6,820	LC
Lander Univ	SC	22,514	Ȼ
Lane College	TN	11,212	C
Langston Univ	OK	3,000	LC
Lasell College	MA	42,500	LC
Lawrence Univ	WI	46,371	HC
Le Moyne College	NY	42,200	VC
Lebanon Valley College	PA	38,570	C
Lee Univ	TN	18,690	Ȼ
Lehigh Univ	PA	55,080	MC
Lehman College / The CUNY	NY	5,778	LC
LeMoyne-Owen College	TN	13,100	C
Lenoir-Rhyne College	NC	35,984	C
LeTourneau Univ	TX	26,230	C
Lewis & Clark College	OR	52,656	VC
Lewis Univ	IL	23,050	C
Lewis-Clark State College	ID	6,990	C
Liberty Univ	VA	19,101	C
Limestone College	SC	29,880	C
Lincoln Memorial Univ	TN	18,144	C
Lincoln Univ	MO	11,996	NC
Lindenwood Univ	MO	20,750	C
Lindsey Wilson College	KY	30,470	VC
Linfield College-McMinnville Campus	OR	46,166	C
Lipscomb Univ	TN	35,722	VC
Livingstone College	NC	17,815	LC
Lock Haven Univ of Pennsylvania	PA	17,587	LC
LIU/Brooklyn Campus	NY	26,500	C
LIU/C.W. Post Campus	NY	38,888	C
Longwood Univ	VA	20,924	C
Loras College	IA	37,432	VC
Louisiana College	LA	15,746	C
Louisiana State Univ	LA	18,677	VȻ
Louisiana State Univ in Shreveport	LA	5,606	C
Louisiana Tech Univ	LA	8,000	C
Lourdes Univ	OH	26,055	LC
Loyola Marymount Univ	CA	53,240	VȻ
Loyola Univ Chicago	IL	49,560	VȻ
Loyola Univ Maryland	MD		VC
Loyola Univ New Orleans	LA	46,581	VC
Luther College	IA	44,380	VȻ
Lycoming College	PA	43,636	C
Lynchburg College	VA	42,645	C
Lyon College	AR	30,246	VC
Macalester College	MN	53,419	MC
MacMurray College	IL	20,755	C
Madonna Univ	MI	24,540	VC
Malone Univ	OH	34,334	C
Manchester College	IN	35,070	C
Manhattan College	NY	44,955	VC
Manhattanville College	NY	46,260	VC
Mansfield Univ	PA	19,468	LC
Marian Univ	WI	30,980	LC
Marian Univ/Indianapolis	IN	37,058	C
Marietta College	OH	42,135	VC
Marist College	NY	35,500	C
Marlboro College	VT	35,980	VC
Marquette Univ	WI	43,664	VȻ
Mars Hill College	NC	22,950	LC
Marshall Univ	WV	14,820	C
Martin Univ	IN	11,000	SP
Mary Baldwin College	VA	37,110	C
Marygrove College	MI	21,290	C
Marymount Manhattan College	NY	40,118	VC
Marymount Univ	VA	36,178	C
Maryville College	TN	33,150	VC
Maryville Univ of St. Louis	MO	34,920	VC
Marywood Univ	PA	40,695	C
Mass College of Liberal Arts	MA	16,733	C
Mass Inst of Technology	MA	54,238	MC
McDaniel College	MD	45,600	VC
McKendree Univ	IL	29,920	Ȼ
McMurry Univ	TX	25,962	LC
McNeese State Univ	LA		C
McPherson College	KS	28,138	C
Mercer Univ	GA	44,201	VȻ
Mercy College	NY	29,996	C
Mercyhurst Univ	PA	40,700	C
Meredith College	NC	31,420	C
Merrimack College	MA	44,215	C
Messiah College	PA	39,540	VC
Methodist Univ	NC	37,185	C
Metropolitan State Univ	MN	5,923	SP
Metropolitan State Univ of Denver	CO	4,835	LC
Miami Univ	OH	24,191	HC
Mich State Univ	MI	13,689	VC
Mich Tech Univ	MI	22,105	VC
MidAmerica Nazarene Univ	KS	28,000	C
Middle Tenn State Univ	TN	8,650	C
Middlebury College	VT	57,470	MC
Midland Univ	NE	34,000	C
Midwestern State Univ	TX	9,722	C
Miles College	AL	16,530	NC
Millersville Univ of Pennsylvania	PA	18,498	C
Milligan College	TN	27,510	C
Millikin Univ	IL	37,462	C
Mills College	CA	54,119	HC
Millsaps College	MS	43,888	VȻ
Minn State Univ, Mankato	MN	14,900	C
Minn State Univ, Moorhead	MN	13,392	C
Minot State Univ	ND	10,915	C
Misericordia Univ	PA	39,840	C
Miss College	MS	21,998	VC
Miss Univ for Women	MS	7,400	LC
Miss Valley State Univ	MS	9,706	LC
Missouri Baptist Univ	MO	30,310	C
Missouri Southern State Univ	MO	11,910	C
Missouri State Univ	MO	13,996	VC
Missouri Univ of Science and Technology	MO	18,655	VȻ
Missouri Valley College	MO	22,200	C
Missouri Western State Univ	MO	12,260	NC
Molloy College	NY	38,950	C
Monmouth College	IL	39,290	C
Monmouth Univ	NJ	42,252	C
Montana State Univ	MT	14,068	VC
Montana State Univ-Billings	MT	12,425	LC
Montana State Univ-Northern	MT	12,500	NC
Montclair State Univ	NJ	22,614	C
Montreat College	NC	31,298	VC
Moravian College	PA	36,381	VC
Morehead State Univ	KY	10,900	C
Morehouse College	GA	38,640	C
Morgan State Univ	MD	14,500	VC
Morningside College	IA	32,620	C
Morris College	SC	16,006	LC
Mount Aloysius College	PA	27,970	C
Mount Holyoke College	MA	53,596	HȻ
Mount Marty College	SD	29,638	C
Mount Mary Univ	WI	32,836	LC
Mount Mercy Univ	IA	34,385	C
Mount Olive College	NC	18,426	C
Mount St. Mary College	NY	39,540	C
Mount St. Mary's Univ	MD	46,158	C
Mount St. Mary's College/Chalon Campus	CA	43,897	VȻ
Mount Vernon Nazarene Univ	OH	29,590	C
Muhlenberg College	PA	52,837	HC
Murray State Univ	KY	14,944	C
Muskingum Univ	OH	30,502	C
National Univ	CA	14,730	SP
Nazareth College of Rochester	NY	41,590	VC
Nebr Wesleyan Univ	NE	29,774	Ȼ
New College of Florida	FL	14,504	HȻ
New Jersey City Univ	NJ	21,060	Ȼ
New Jersey Inst of Technology	NJ	26,490	VC
New Mexico Highlands Univ	NM	9,720	NC
New Mexico State Univ	NM	13,955	LC
New York Univ	NY	61,470	MC
Newberry College	SC	26,850	LC
Newman Univ	KS	30,380	Ȼ
Niagara Univ	NY	39,800	C
Nicholls State Univ	LA	7,095	C
Nichols College	MA	37,240	LC
Norfolk State Univ	VA	10,531	LC
N Car Agricultural and Technical State Univ	NC	13,175	LC
N Car Central Univ	NC	9,000	LC
N Car State Univ	NC	16,202	HC
N Car Wesleyan College	NC	29,440	C
North Central College	IL	38,343	VC
N Dak State Univ	ND	14,642	C
North Georgia College & State Univ	GA	8,500	C
North Park Univ	IL	30,130	C
Northeastern Illinois Univ	IL		C
Northeastern State Univ	OK	8,615	VC
Northeastern Univ	MA	55,296	MC
Northern Arizona Univ	AZ	18,592	C
Northern Illinois Univ	IL	19,768	C
Northern Kentucky Univ	KY	15,302	LC
Northern Mich Univ	MI	15,300	VC
Northern State Univ	SD	14,021	C
Northland College	WI	26,680	C
Northwest Missouri State Univ	MO	14,229	C
Northwest Nazarene Univ	ID	24,275	NC
Northwest Univ	WA	18,854	C
Northwestern College	MN	24,000	C
Northwestern College of Iowa	IA	34,848	Ȼ
Northwestern Okla State Univ	OK	7,275	NC
Northwestern State Univ of Louisiana	LA	14,368	C
Northwestern Univ	IL	37,595	MC
Norwich Univ	VT	28,212	C
Notre Dame College	OH	34,942	VC
Notre Dame de Namur Univ	CA	41,610	LC
Notre Dame of Maryland Univ	MD	27,700	C
Nyack College	NY	32,000	C
Oakland Univ	MI	19,391	VC
Oakwood Univ	AL	23,035	C
Oberlin College	OH	57,025	MC
Occidental College	CA	59,592	MȻ
Oglala Lakota College	SD	2,000	NC
Oglethorpe Univ	GA	42,580	VC
Ohio Dominican Univ	OH	38,380	Ȼ
Ohio Northern Univ	OH	42,075	VC
Ohio State Univ at Lima	OH	7,140	C
Ohio State Univ at Mansfield	OH	13,160	C
Ohio State Univ at Marion	OH	9,850	MC
Ohio State Univ at Newark	OH	17,510	C
Ohio Univ	OH	20,676	VC
Ohio Valley Univ	WV	17,752	C
Ohio Wesleyan Univ	OH	49,460	Ȼ
Okla Baptist Univ	OK	28,202	VC
Okla Christian Univ	OK	24,975	VC
Okla City Univ	OK	33,546	VC
Okla Panhandle State Univ	OK	8,996	NC
Okla State Univ	OK	14,310	VC
Okla Wesleyan Univ	OK	21,300	C
Old Dominion Univ	VA	18,662	C
Olivet College	MI	19,984	C
Olivet Nazarene Univ	IL	29,990	C
Oral Roberts Univ	OK	31,734	C
Oregon State Univ	OR	19,017	Ȼ
Oswego / SUNY	NY	20,009	VC
Ottawa Univ	KS	15,000	VC
Otterbein College	OH	32,214	C
Ouachita Baptist Univ	AR	29,010	VC
Our Lady of Holy Cross College	LA	8,090	LC
Our Lady of the Lake Univ of San Antonio	TX	22,430	LC
Pace Univ	NY	48,094	VC
Pacific Lutheran Univ	WA	44,840	VC
Pacific Union College	CA	28,150	VC
Pacific Univ	OR	42,815	C
Paine College	GA	18,594	LC
Palm Beach Atlantic Univ	FL	33,882	LC
Park Univ	MO	17,525	C
Penn State Erie/The Behrend College	PA	16,256	C
Penn State Univ/Altoona	PA	11,464	C
Penn State Univ/Univ Park	PA	25,404	VC
Pepperdine Univ	CA	55,372	HȻ
Peru State College	NE	8,600	NC
Pfeiffer Univ	NC	33,700	C
Piedmont College	GA	29,260	C
Pine Manor College	MA	32,659	LC
Pittsburg State Univ	KS	12,032	C
Pitzer College	CA	54,988	MC
Plymouth State Univ	NH	23,148	LC
Point Loma Nazarene Univ	CA	38,610	VC
Point Park Univ	PA	36,390	C
Pomona College	CA	57,680	MC
Pontifical Catholic Univ of PR	PR	7,310	
Portland State Univ	OR	18,672	C
Post Univ	CT	35,750	C
Prairie View A&M Univ	TX	15,205	LC
Presbyterian College	SC	42,678	VC
Prescott College	AZ	33,284	Ȼ
Princeton Univ	NJ	53,795	MC
Principia College	IL	35,140	Ȼ
Providence College	RI	55,995	HC
Purchase College / SUNY	NY	16,951	C
Purdue Univ/Calumet	IN	14,336	C
Purdue Univ/West Lafayette	IN	20,278	HC
Queens College / The CUNY	NY	17,107	VC
Queens Univ of Charlotte	NC	39,543	VC
Quincy Univ	IL	34,980	LC
Quinnipiac Univ	CT	53,580	VC
Radford Univ	VA	17,132	LC
Ramapo College of New Jersey	NJ	24,938	Ȼ
Randolph College	VA	43,960	VC
Randolph-Macon College	VA	45,086	C
Reed College	OR	57,780	MC
Regis College	MA	47,565	LC
Regis Univ	CO	41,318	C
Rhode Island College	RI	17,132	LC
Rhodes College	TN	47,596	HȻ
Rice Univ	TX	43,288	MC
Richard Stockton College of New Jersey	NJ	20,000	VC
Rider Univ	NJ	45,720	C
Ripon College	WI	36,959	Ȼ
Rivier College	NH	35,000	VC
Roanoke College	VA	47,996	Ȼ
Roberts Wesleyan College	NY	37,384	Ȼ
Rochester College	MI	18,320	C
Rockford College	IL	31,000	C
Rockhurst Univ	MO	20,625	C
Rocky Mountain College	MT	32,242	C
Roger Williams Univ	RI	45,788	C
Rollins College	FL	52,370	HC
Roosevelt Univ	IL	22,605	VC
Rosemont College	PA	42,350	C
Rowan Univ	NJ	23,570	VC
Russell Sage College	NY	39,370	C
Rutgers, The State Univ of New Jersey/Camden Campus	NJ	24,254	C
Rutgers, The State Univ of New Jersey/New Brunswick	NJ	25,077	VC
Rutgers, The State Univ of New Jersey/Newark Campus	NJ	25,376	C
Sacred Heart Univ	CT	48,564	VC
Saginaw Valley State Univ	MI	16,869	C
St. Anselm College	NH	48,324	VC
St. Augustine's Univ	NC	14,000	C
St. Francis Univ	PA	30,029	LC
St. John's Univ	MN	46,146	C
St. Joseph College	CT	45,630	LC
St. Joseph's College	IN	35,790	C
St. Joseph's College of Maine	ME	31,580	C
St. Joseph's Univ	PA	52,272	VC
St. Leo Univ	FL	27,990	C
St. Louis Univ	MO	46,594	VȻ
St. Martin's Univ	WA	38,082	C
St. Mary's College	IN	45,160	VC
St. Mary's College of Calif	CA	53,550	C
St. Mary's Univ	TX	33,854	C
St. Mary's Univ of Minn	MN	37,015	C
St. Michael's College	VT	48,740	VC
St. Peter's College	NJ	44,240	C
St. Vincent College	PA	40,244	C
St. Xavier Univ	IL	32,840	C
Salem College	NC	29,326	VC
Salem State College	MA	13,161	LC
Salisbury Univ	MD	18,368	VC
Salve Regina Univ	RI	47,250	VC
Sam Houston State Univ	TX	17,082	C
Samford Univ	AL	35,700	VȻ
San Diego Christian College	CA	31,012	C
San Diego State Univ	CA	20,578	VC
San Francisco State Univ	CA	18,514	C
San Jose State Univ	CA	19,707	C
Santa Clara Univ	CA	54,702	MC
Sarah Lawrence College	NY	48,000	HC
Savannah State Univ	GA	13,156	C
Schreiner Univ	TX	32,734	LC
Scripps College	CA	54,900	MC
Seattle Pacific Univ	WA	41,559	VȻ
Seattle Univ	WA	47,010	VȻ
Seton Hall Univ	NJ	45,902	C
Seton Hill Univ	PA	35,172	C
Sewanee: The Univ of the South	TN	47,700	HȻ
Shawnee State Univ	OH	16,545	NC
Shenandoah Univ	VA	39,268	C
Shepherd Univ	WV	14,996	C
Shippensburg Univ of Pennsylvania	PA	17,064	LC
Shorter Univ	GA	26,470	C
Siena College	NY	43,863	VC
Siena Heights Univ	MI	17,000	LC
Silver Lake College	WI	22,600	LC
Simmons College	MA	48,770	VC
Simpson College	IA	36,086	VC
Simpson Univ	CA	28,900	C
Skidmore College	NY	57,926	HC
Slippery Rock Univ of Pennsylvania	PA	10,360	LC
Smith College	MA	57,524	MC
Sonoma State Univ	CA	20,541	C
S Car State Univ	SC	6,700	LC
S Dak State Univ	SD	14,296	C
Southeast Missouri State Univ	MO	14,983	LC
Southeastern Louisiana Univ	LA	13,325	C

ST = STATE **$IS** = IN-STATE COSTS **SR** = SELECTOR RATING

INDEX OF COLLEGE MAJORS

School	ST	$IS	SR
Southeastern Okla State Univ	OK	7,966	C
Southeastern Univ	FL	27,201	C+
Southern Adventist Univ	TN	26,190	C
Southern Arkansas Univ	AR	14,316	C
Southern Conn State Univ	CT	18,033	C
Southern Illinois Univ Carbondale	IL	21,620	C
Southern Illinois Univ Edwardsville	IL	17,532	C
Southern Methodist Univ	TX	57,755	MC
Southern Nazarene Univ	OK	24,354	NC
Southern New Hampshire Univ	NH	38,100	C
Southern Oregon Univ	OR	17,874	C
Southern Univ and A&M College	LA	9,761	C+
Southern Univ at New Orleans	LA	1,000	NC
Southern Vermont College	VT	30,740	LC
Southern Wesleyan Univ	SC	25,600	C
Southwest Baptist Univ	MO	24,710	C
Southwest Minn State Univ	MN	14,000	C
Southwestern Adventist Univ	TX	23,026	LC
Southwestern College	KS	29,270	C
Southwestern Okla State Univ	OK	9,160	C
Southwestern Univ	TX	45,660	VC
Spelman College	GA	24,650	VC
Spring Arbor Univ	MI	26,740	C
Spring Hill College	AL	42,130	VC
Springfield College	MA	25,000	C
St. Ambrose Univ	IA		C
St. Bonaventure Univ	NY	38,831	C
St. Catherine Univ	MN	37,782	C+
St. Cloud State Univ	MN	10,600	C
St. Edward's Univ	TX	44,674	VC
St. Francis College	NY	34,200	LC
St. John Fisher College	NY	39,370	C+
St. John's Univ	NY	52,840	C+
St. Joseph's College, New York / Brooklyn Campus	NY	21,878	C
St. Joseph's College, New York / Suffolk Campus	NY	21,878	VC
St. Lawrence Univ	NY	53,740	HC
St. Mary's College of Maryland	MD	26,699	HC
St. Norbert College	WI	39,992	VC
St. Olaf College	MN	49,960	HC+
St. Thomas Aquinas College	NY	30,000	C
St. Thomas Univ	FL	32,310	C+
Stanford Univ	CA	56,411	MC
SUNY/Empire State College	NY	6,315	SP
Stephen F. Austin State Univ	TX	14,668	C
Sterling College	KS	27,216	C
Stetson Univ	FL	49,512	VC+
Stevens Inst of Technology	NJ	50,130	HC
Stevenson Univ	MD	39,572	C
Stillman College	AL	18,460	C
Stonehill College	MA	46,780	VC+
Stony Brook Univ / SUNY	NY	19,359	HC
Suffolk Univ	MA	46,548	C
Sul Ross State Univ	TX	13,410	LC
SUNY College at Geneseo	NY	18,055	HC+
SUNY College at Old Westbury	NY	16,324	C
SUNY Cortland / The SUNY	NY	19,117	C
SUNY Fredonia / The SUNY at Fredonia	NY	18,702	VC
SUNY New Paltz	NY	15,010	C
SUNY Oneonta / SUNY	NY	16,919	VC
SUNY Plattsburgh / SUNY	NY	18,083	VC
Susquehanna Univ	PA	49,170	C
Swarthmore College	PA	57,870	MC
Sweet Briar College	VA	43,765	C+
Syracuse Univ	NY	54,512	HC
Tabor College	KS	29,010	LC
Talladega College	AL	13,000	C
Tarleton State Univ	TX	13,489	LC
Taylor Univ	IN	36,742	VC+
Temple Univ	PA	24,392	VC
Tenn State Univ	TN	9,048	C
Tenn Tech Univ	TN	11,310	C
Tenn Wesleyan College	TN	21,250	C
Texas A&M Univ	TX	16,956	VC+
Texas A&M Univ at Commerce	TX	10,496	C
Texas A&M Univ at Corpus Christi	TX	11,544	LC
Texas A&M Univ at Kingsville	TX	7,500	LC
Texas Christian Univ	TX	47,570	HC
Texas Lutheran Univ	TX	34,070	C
Texas Southern Univ	TX	18,212	LC
Texas State Univ	TX	16,495	VC
Texas Tech Univ	TX	14,243	C
Texas Wesleyan Univ	TX	29,886	C
Texas Woman's Univ	TX	13,633	LC
The Catholic Univ of America	DC	52,852	VC
The College at Brockport / SUNY	NY	18,362	VC
The College of Idaho	ID	31,277	VC
The College of New Rochelle	NY	33,600	VC
The College of St. Rose	NY	26,750	C
The Lincoln Univ	PA	15,154	LC
The Masters College	CA	38,160	C+
Ohio State Univ	OH	19,887	MC
The SUNY at Potsdam	NY	17,754	C
Thiel College	PA	31,378	LC
Thomas Edison State College	NJ	5,700	SP
Thomas More College	KY	34,760	C
Tiffin Univ	OH	30,273	LC
Toccoa Falls College	GA	23,210	C
Tougaloo College	MS	15,275	NC
Touro College	NY	23,150	VC
Towson Univ	MD	16,000	VC
Transylvania Univ	KY	40,310	VC+
Trevecca Nazarene Univ	TN	30,118	C
Trinity Christian College	IL	28,869	C
Trinity College	CT		HC+
Trinity International Univ	IL	31,070	C
Trinity Univ	TX	44,174	HC+
Trinity Washington Univ	DC	30,250	C+
Troy Univ	AL	10,650	C
Truman State Univ	MO	13,546	HC
Tufts Univ	MA	58,780	MC
Tulane Univ	LA	58,942	MC
Tusculum College	TN	24,295	C
Tuskegee Univ	AL	26,750	C
Union College	KY	28,775	C
Union College	NE	23,270	VC
Union College	NY		MC
Union Univ	TN	28,260	VC
United States Air Force Academy	CO		MC
United States Military Academy	NY		MC
United States Naval Academy	MD		MC
Universidad Adventista de las Antillas	PR	7,360	
Universidad del Turabo	PR	4,110	
Univ at Albany / SUNY	NY	18,674	VC
Univ at Buffalo / The SUNY	NY	20,283	VC
Univ of Akron	OH	20,436	C
Univ of Alabama at Birmingham	AL	18,484	C+
Univ of Alabama at Huntsville	AL	17,625	VC
Univ of Alabama at Tuscaloosa	AL	17,164	C+
Univ of Alaska Anchorage	AK	15,290	NC
Univ of Alaska Fairbanks	AK	13,955	C
Univ of Arizona	AZ	20,105	C
Univ of Arkansas at Fayetteville	AR	16,860	VC
Univ of Arkansas at Little Rock	AR		C
Univ of Arkansas at Monticello	AR	8,470	NC
Univ of Arkansas at Pine Bluff	AR	10,600	C
Univ of Calif at Berkeley	CA	23,322	MC
Univ of Calif at Davis	CA	24,482	HC
Univ of Calif at Irvine	CA	25,961	VC
Univ of Calif at Los Angeles	CA	25,686	MC
Univ of Calif at Riverside	CA	27,204	C
Univ of Calif at San Diego	CA	21,000	VC
Univ of Calif at Santa Barbara	CA	27,551	HC
Univ of Calif at Santa Cruz	CA	27,807	VC
Univ of Central Arkansas	AR	10,840	VC
Univ of Central Florida	FL	15,711	VC+
Univ of Central Missouri	MO	14,605	C
Univ of Central Okla	OK	12,293	C
Univ of Charleston	WV	28,650	C
Univ of Chicago	IL	55,416	MC
Univ of Cincinnati	OH	20,199	VC
Univ of Colo at Colo Springs	CO	15,000	VC
Univ of Colo Boulder	CO	22,605	VC+
Univ of Colo Denver	CO	17,904	C
Univ of Conn	CT	23,744	HC
Univ of Dallas	TX	43,510	VC+
Univ of Dayton	OH	43,750	VC+
Univ of Delaware	DE	22,728	VC
Univ of Denver	CO	51,787	VC+
Univ of Detroit Mercy	MI	30,450	C
Univ of Evansville	IN	41,056	VC+
Univ of Findlay	OH	31,916	C
Univ of Florida	FL	15,783	HC+
Univ of Georgia	GA	19,508	VC
Univ of Great Falls	MT	27,970	C
Univ of Hartford	CT	42,674	C
Univ of Hawaii at Hilo	HI	6,500	C
Univ of Hawaii at Manoa	HI	19,379	VC
Univ of Houston-Downtown	TX	6,267	LC
Univ of Idaho	ID	14,558	C
Univ of Illinois at Chicago	IL	24,293	VC
Univ of Illinois at Urbana-Champaign	IL	24,300	HC
Univ of Indianapolis	IN	31,740	LC
Univ of Iowa	IA	17,481	VC
Univ of Jamestown	ND	24,738	C
Univ of Kansas	KS	16,980	C+
Univ of Kentucky	KY	19,868	C
Univ of La Verne	CA	47,010	VC
Univ of Louisiana at Lafayette	LA	6,130	C
Univ of Louisiana at Monroe	LA	12,998	C
Univ of Louisville	KY	17,460	VC
Univ of Maine	ME	19,712	C+
Univ of Maine at Farmington	ME	17,841	C
Univ of Maine at Machias	ME	10,523	C
Univ of Mary Hardin-Baylor	TX	31,950	C+
Univ of Mary Washington	VA	19,484	VC
Univ of Maryland	MD	18,801	HC
Univ of Maryland/Baltimore County	MD	18,000	VC
Univ of Maryland/Eastern Shore	MD	14,000	C
Univ of Maryland/Univ College	MD	6,168	SP
Univ of Mass Amherst	MA	23,697	VC+
Univ of Mass Boston	MA	11,966	C
Univ of Mass Dartmouth	MA	22,223	C
Univ of Mass Lowell	MA	19,316	C
Univ of Memphis	TN	15,094	C
Univ of Miami	FL	55,166	MC
Univ of Mich/Ann Arbor	MI	22,102	HC+
Univ of Mich/Dearborn	MI	9,885	VC
Univ of Mich-Flint	MI	17,547	C+
Univ of Minn/Duluth	MN	18,964	C+
Univ of Minn/Morris	MN	17,150	VC
Univ of Minn/Twin Cities	MN		HC
Univ of Miss	MS	15,482	VC
Univ of Missouri/Columbia	MO	18,201	MC
Univ of Missouri-Kansas City	MO	19,003	C
Univ of Missouri-St. Louis	MO	18,304	VC
Univ of Mobile	AL	27,870	VC
Univ of Montana	MT	13,670	C
Univ of Montana-Western	MT	9,753	LC
Univ of Montevallo	AL	17,320	C
Univ of Mount Union	OH	35,130	C
Univ of Nebr - Lincoln	NE	17,507	VC
Univ of Nebr at Kearney	NE	14,855	LC
Univ of Nebr at Omaha	NE	12,700	C
Univ of Nevada, Las Vegas	NV	17,303	C
Univ of Nevada/Reno	NV	14,500	NC
Univ of New England	ME	46,145	C+
Univ of New Hampshire	NH	24,702	VC
Univ of New Haven	CT	47,740	C
Univ of New Mexico	NM	15,300	C
Univ of New Orleans	LA	9,224	VC
Univ of North Alabama	AL	9,960	C
Univ of N Car at Asheville	NC	13,500	VC+
Univ of N Car at Chapel Hill	NC	18,348	MC
Univ of N Car at Charlotte	NC	15,847	C
Univ of N Car at Greensboro	NC	12,848	C
Univ of N Car at Wilmington	NC	13,572	VC+
Univ of N Dak	ND	14,094	C
Univ of North Florida	FL	15,578	VC
Univ of North Texas	TX	15,628	C
Univ of Northern Colo	CO	15,973	C
Univ of Northern Iowa	IA	14,776	C
Univ of Notre Dame	IN		MC
Univ of Okla	OK	17,634	VC+
Univ of Oregon	OR	20,872	VC
Univ of Pennsylvania	PA	56,106	MC
Univ of Pikeville	KY	24,750	NC
Univ of Pittsburgh at Bradford	PA	21,316	LC
Univ of Pittsburgh at Johnstown	PA	20,862	LC
Univ of Pittsburgh at Pittsburgh	PA	27,800	HC+
Univ of Portland	OR	47,874	VC
Univ of PR Recinto de Rio Piedras	PR	5,750	
Univ of PR/Cayey	PR	1,504	
Univ of PR/Mayaguez	PR	1,250	
Univ of Puget Sound	WA	52,648	HC+
Univ of Redlands	CA	40,500	VC
Univ of Rio Grande	OH	8,750	NC
Univ of Rochester	NY	58,500	MC
Univ of St. Francis	IN	29,810	C
Univ of St. Mary	KS	28,400	C+
Univ of San Diego	CA	53,302	HC+
Univ of San Francisco	CA	49,674	VC
Univ of Science and Arts of Okla	OK	10,560	VC
Univ of Scranton	PA	51,940	VC
Univ of Sioux Falls	SD	22,990	C
Univ of South Alabama	AL	13,510	C
Univ of S Car at Aiken	SC	16,278	C
Univ of S Car at Columbia	SC	19,725	VC+
Univ of S Car Upstate	SC	17,673	LC
Univ of S Dak	SD	15,111	C
Univ of South Florida	FL	13,000	C
Univ of South Florida/St. Petersburg	FL	12,769	VC
Univ of Southern Calif	CA	56,903	MC
Univ of Southern Indiana	IN	14,657	C
Univ of Southern Maine	ME	16,576	C
Univ of Southern Miss	MS	13,170	C
Univ of St. Francis	IL	36,490	C
Univ of St. Thomas - Houston	TX	36,490	VC
Univ of Tampa	FL	35,160	VC
Univ of Tenn at Chattanooga	TN	16,883	C
Univ of Tenn at Knoxville	TN	20,364	VC+
Univ of Tenn at Martin	TN	13,217	C
Univ of Texas at Arlington	TX	10,908	LC
Univ of Texas at Austin	TX	44,074	HC
Univ of Texas at Dallas	TX	21,046	HC
Univ of Texas at El Paso	TX	8,764	NC
Univ of Texas at San Antonio	TX	18,372	C
Univ of Texas-Pan American	TX	12,432	LC
Univ of the Cumberlands	KY	27,500	LC
Univ of the District of Columbia	DC	7,244	LC
Univ of the Incarnate Word	TX	35,200	LC
Univ of the Ozarks	AR	22,100	C
Univ of the Pacific	CA	52,146	VC
Univ of the Southwest	NM	15,000	C
Univ of Toledo	OH	18,464	C
Univ of Tulsa	OK	45,311	HC+
Univ of Utah	UT	13,462	VC
Univ of Vermont	VT	26,120	VC+
Univ of Virginia	VA	22,175	MC
Univ of Virginia's College at Wise	VA	11,076	C
Univ of Washington	WA	14,722	VC
Univ of West Alabama	AL	9,415	C
Univ of West Florida	FL	14,656	C
Univ of West Georgia	GA	14,852	LC
Univ of Wisc Whitewater	WI	13,314	C
Univ of Wisc/Eau Claire	WI	15,430	VC
Univ of Wisc/Green Bay	WI	14,000	C
Univ of Wisc/La Crosse	WI	14,755	VC
Univ of Wisc/Madison	WI	18,757	HC
Univ of Wisc/Oshkosh	WI	10,426	LC
Univ of Wisc/Parkside	WI	10,181	LC
Univ of Wisc/Platteville	WI	14,274	C
Univ of Wisc/River Falls	WI	9,722	LC
Univ of Wisc/Stevens Point	WI	14,043	C
Univ of Wisc/Superior	WI	14,106	C
Univ of Wisc-Milwaukee	WI	18,436	C
Univ of Wyoming	WY	13,855	C+
Ursinus College	PA	55,630	VC+
Ursuline College	OH	33,198	LC
Utah State Univ	UT	11,803	C
Utica College	NY	44,734	C
Valley City State Univ	ND	12,286	LC
Valparaiso Univ	IN	43,040	VC+
Vanderbilt Univ	TN	57,072	MC
Vanguard Univ of Southern Calif	CA	35,833	VC
Vassar College	NY	59,070	MC
Victory Univ	TN	19,118	C
Villanova Univ	PA	56,436	MC
Virginia Commonwealth Univ	VA	18,633	C
Virginia Intermont College	VA	32,411	LC
Virginia Military Inst	VA	16,156	C
Virginia Polytechnic Inst and State Univ	VA	14,629	HC
Virginia State Univ	VA	11,318	C+
Virginia Union Univ	VA	18,432	C
Virginia Wesleyan College	VA	28,433	LC
Viterbo Univ	WI	30,070	C
Wabash College	IN	44,160	VC
Wagner College	NY	48,600	VC
Wake Forest Univ	NC	51,000	MC
Walla Walla Univ	WA	26,256	NC
Walsh Univ	OH	35,100	C
Warner Pacific College	OR	25,550	C
Warner Univ	FL	18,000	C
Warren Wilson College	NC	34,888	VC
Wartburg College	IA	41,055	VC
Washburn Univ	KS	12,165	NC
Washington Adventist Univ	MD	25,859	C+
Washington and Jefferson College	PA	49,990	VC
Washington and Lee Univ	VA	52,812	MC
Washington College	MD	48,768	VC
Washington State Univ	WA	20,461	C
Washington Univ in St. Louis	MO	58,818	MC
Wayland Baptist Univ	TX	16,058	LC
Wayne State College	NE	11,764	NC
Wayne State Univ	MI	19,493	C
Waynesburg Univ	PA	29,100	C
Webster Univ	MO	33,990	C+
Wellesley College	MA	49,848	MC
Wells College	NY	38,680	VC
Wesley College	DE	31,115	LC
Wesleyan College	GA	24,000	C+
Wesleyan Univ	CT	59,844	MC
West Chester Univ of Pennsylvania	PA	16,836	C
West Liberty Univ	WV	9,142	LC
West Texas A&M Univ	TX	13,478	C
West Virginia State Univ	WV	8,378	NC
West Virginia Univ	WV	15,794	C+
West Virginia Univ Inst of Technology	WV	14,094	NC
West Virginia Wesleyan College	WV	26,880	C
Western Carolina Univ	NC	13,965	C+
Western Conn State Univ	CT	18,327	C
Western Illinois Univ	IL	20,130	C
Western Kentucky Univ	KY	11,000	LC
Western Mich Univ	MI	19,042	C

ST = STATE **$IS** = IN-STATE COSTS **SR** = SELECTOR RATING

School	ST	$IS	SR
Western New England Univ	MA	45,590	C
Western New Mexico Univ	NM	8,500	LC
Western Oregon Univ	OR	15,021	C
Western State Colo Univ	CO	16,135	C
Western Washington Univ	WA	18,519	VC
Westfield State Univ	MA	18,489	C
Westminster College	MO	30,490	VC
Westminster College	PA	31,290	C+
Westminster College	UT	37,708	VC
Westmont College	CA	41,500	HC
Wheaton College	IL	39,650	HC+
Wheaton College	MA	54,934	HC+
Wheeling Jesuit Univ	WV	34,668	C
Whitman College	WA	54,400	MC
Whittier College	CA	43,416	C
Whitworth Univ	WA	45,826	VC+
Wichita State Univ	KS	12,539	C
Widener Univ	PA	50,368	C
Wiley College	TX		LC
Wilkes Univ	PA	42,786	C
Willamette Univ	OR	56,450	VC+
William Carey Univ	MS	13,500	LC
William Jewell College	MO	31,000	VC+
William Paterson Univ of New Jersey	NJ	21,694	C
William Penn Univ	IA	26,000	C
William Woods Univ	MO		C
Williams Baptist College	AR	20,070	C
Williams College	MA	58,900	MC
Wilmington College	OH	29,784	C
Wilson College	PA	27,660	C
Wingate Univ	NC	34,990	C
Winona State Univ	MN	16,530	C
Winston-Salem State Univ	NC	9,418	LC
Winthrop Univ	SC	21,120	VC
Wisc Lutheran College	WI	23,510	VC
Wittenberg Univ	OH	47,766	VC
Wofford College	SC	45,795	VC
Woodbury Univ	CA	34,500	LC
Worcester State Univ	MA	18,657	C
Wright State Univ	OH	16,983	C
Xavier Univ	OH	43,740	VC
Xavier Univ of Louisiana	LA	25,300	C
Yale Univ	CT	55,300	MC
Yeshiva Univ	NY	47,250	VC+
York College	NE	19,475	C
York College / CUNY	NY	5,496	NC
York College of Pennsylvania	PA	26,590	C
Youngstown State Univ	OH	16,374	LC

HISTORY OF ARCHITECTURE / URBAN DEVELOPMENT

School	ST	$IS	SR
Cornell Univ	NY	59,037	MC
Univ of Illinois at Chicago	IL	24,293	VC

HISTORY OF PHILOSOPHY

School	ST	$IS	SR
Colo College	CO	54,534	MC
Univ of Pittsburgh at Pittsburgh	PA	27,800	HC+

HISTORY OF SCIENCE

School	ST	$IS	SR
Calif Inst of Technology	CA	54,045	MC
Case Western Reserve Univ	OH	55,178	MC
Georgia Inst of Technology	GA	20,464	MC
Johns Hopkins Univ	MD	47,492	MC
Univ of Jamestown	ND	24,738	C
Univ of Pennsylvania	PA	56,106	MC
Univ of Wisc/Madison	WI	18,757	HC
Yale Univ	CT	55,300	MC

HOME ECONOMICS

School	ST	$IS	SR
Cal State, Fresno	CA	17,405	C
College of the Ozarks	MO	5,605	VC
Florida State Univ	FL	15,238	HC
Harding Univ	AR	21,432	C+
Illinois State Univ	IL	22,634	VC
Indiana State Univ	IN	16,000	C
Langston Univ	OK	3,000	LC
Montclair State Univ	NJ	22,614	C
Morgan State Univ	MD	14,500	VC
Oakwood Univ	AL	23,035	C
Queens College / The CUNY	NY	17,107	VC
San Diego State Univ	CA	20,578	VC
SUNY Oneonta / SUNY	NY	16,919	VC
SUNY Plattsburgh / SUNY	NY	18,083	VC
Tarleton State Univ	TX	13,489	LC
Texas A&M Univ at Kingsville	TX	7,500	LC
Texas Tech Univ	TX	14,243	C
The Masters College	CA	38,160	C+
Univ of Florida	FL	15,783	HC+
Univ of Georgia	GA	19,508	VC
Univ of Maryland/Eastern Shore	MD	14,000	C
Univ of PR Recinto de Rio Piedras	PR	5,750	
Utah State Univ	UT	11,803	C
Virginia State Univ	VA	11,318	C+

HOME ECONOMICS EDUCATION

School	ST	$IS	SR
Alabama A&M Univ	AL	96,100	C
Ashland Univ	OH	25,000	C
Auburn Univ	AL	20,052	VC+
Baylor Univ	TX	46,720	HC
Bluffton Univ	OH	37,864	C
Brigham Young Univ	UT	12,100	HC
Cal State, Northridge	CA	28,313	C
Carson-Newman Univ	TN	29,058	C+
Central Washington Univ	WA	11,730	C
Cheyney Univ of Pennsylvania	PA	20,372	LC
Concordia Univ Nebr	NE	26,000	VC
Delaware State Univ	DE	14,700	LC
East Carolina Univ	NC	14,169	C
Eastern Kentucky Univ	KY	11,161	C
Eastern New Mexico Univ	NM	10,682	C
Florida State Univ	FL	15,238	HC
Fort Valley State Univ	GA	11,200	VC
Immaculata Univ	PA	43,000	C
Indiana State Univ	IN	16,000	C
Jacksonville State Univ	AL	12,280	LC
Langston Univ	OK	3,000	LC
Mercyhurst Univ	PA	40,700	C
Montclair State Univ	NJ	22,614	C
New Mexico State Univ	NM	13,955	LC
N Car Agricultural and Technical State Univ	NC	13,175	LC
N Dak State Univ	ND	14,642	C
Oakwood Univ	AL	23,035	C
Pittsburg State Univ	KS	12,032	C
Pontifical Catholic Univ of PR	PR	7,310	
Queens College / The CUNY	NY	17,107	VC
San Francisco State Univ	CA	18,514	C
Seattle Pacific Univ	WA	41,559	VC+
Seton Hill Univ	PA	35,172	C
Shepherd Univ	WV	14,996	C
S Car State Univ	SC	6,700	LC
S Dak State Univ	SD	14,296	C
St. Catherine Univ	MN	37,702	C+
SUNY Oneonta / SUNY	NY	16,919	VC
Tarleton State Univ	TX	13,489	LC
Tenn Tech Univ	TN	11,310	C
Univ of Akron	OH	20,436	C
Univ of Arkansas at Pine Bluff	AR	10,600	C
Univ of Louisiana at Lafayette	LA	6,130	C
Univ of Maryland/Eastern Shore	MD	14,000	C
Univ of Minn/Twin Cities	MN		HC
Univ of Montevallo	AL	17,320	C
Univ of Nebr - Lincoln	NE	17,507	VC
Univ of North Alabama	AL	9,960	C
Univ of Southern Miss	MS	13,170	C
Univ of Wisc/Stout	WI	23,942	C
Univ of Wyoming	WY	13,855	C+
Utah State Univ	UT	11,803	C
Wayne State College	NE	11,764	NC
Western Kentucky Univ	KY	11,000	LC

HOME FURNISHINGS AND EQUIPMENT MANAGEMENT/ PRODUCTION/SERVICES

School	ST	$IS	SR
Auburn Univ	AL	20,052	VC+
Fashion Inst of Technology/SUNY	NY	12,468	SP
High Point Univ	NC	39,800	C
Univ of North Texas	TX	15,628	C

HOMELAND SECURITY

School	ST	$IS	SR
Angelo State Univ	TX	15,049	NC
Cal State, Sacramento	CA	16,200	C
Marian Univ	WI	30,980	LC
Mitchell College	CT	40,983	C
Monmouth Univ	NJ	42,252	C
Savannah State Univ	GA	13,156	C
St. John's Univ	NY	52,840	C+
Univ of Alaska Fairbanks	AK	13,955	C
Virginia Commonwealth Univ	VA	18,633	C
Westminster College	UT	37,708	VC

HOMELAND SECURITY/ EMERGENCY PREPAREDNESS

School	ST	$IS	SR
Thomas Edison State College	NJ	5,700	SP

HORTICULTURE

School	ST	$IS	SR
Alabama A&M Univ	AL	96,100	C
Andrews Univ	MI	28,030	C+
Auburn Univ	AL	20,052	VC+
Cal State, Chico	CA	18,952	C
Clemson Univ	SC	19,136	HC
College of the Ozarks	MO	5,605	VC
Colo State Univ-Fort Collins	CO	20,090	VC
Delaware Valley College	PA	29,944	C
Eastern Kentucky Univ	KY	11,161	C
Farmingdale State College	NY	18,985	C
Ferrum College	VA	27,740	LC
Florida A&M Univ	FL	14,935	LC
Florida Southern College	FL	38,240	VC
Fort Valley State Univ	GA	11,200	VC
Iowa State Univ	IA	16,403	C
Kansas State Univ	KS	15,497	VC
Mich State Univ	MI	13,689	VC
Montana State Univ	MT	14,068	VC
Murray State Univ	KY	14,944	C
New Mexico State Univ	NM	13,955	LC
N Car State Univ	NC	16,202	HC
N Dak State Univ	ND	14,642	C
Northwest Missouri State Univ	MO	14,229	C
Okla State Univ	OK	14,310	VC
Oregon State Univ	OR	19,017	C+
Penn State Univ/Univ Park	PA	25,404	VC
Purdue Univ/West Lafayette	IN	20,278	HC
Sam Houston State Univ	TX	17,082	C
S Dak State Univ	SD	14,296	C
Southeast Missouri State Univ	MO	14,983	LC
Stephen F. Austin State Univ	TX	14,668	C
Tarleton State Univ	TX	13,489	LC
Temple Univ	PA	24,392	VC
Texas A&M Univ	TX	16,956	VC+
Texas Tech Univ	TX	14,243	C
Truman State Univ	MO	13,546	HC
Tuskegee Univ	AL	26,750	C
Univ of Arkansas at Fayetteville	AR	16,860	VC
Univ of Conn	CT	23,744	HC
Univ of Florida	FL	15,783	HC+
Univ of Georgia	GA	19,508	VC
Univ of Idaho	ID	14,558	C
Univ of Illinois at Urbana-Champaign	IL	24,300	HC
Univ of Maine	ME	19,712	C+
Univ of Minn Crookston	MN	17,834	C
Univ of Nebr - Lincoln	NE	17,507	VC
Univ of New Hampshire	NH	24,702	VC
Univ of PR/Mayaguez	PR	1,250	
Univ of Vermont	VT	26,120	VC+
Univ of Wisc/Madison	WI	18,757	HC
Univ of Wisc/Platteville	WI	14,274	C
Univ of Wisc/River Falls	WI	9,722	LC
Virginia Polytechnic Inst and State Univ	VA	14,629	HC
Washington State Univ	WA	20,461	C
West Virginia Univ	WV	15,794	C+

HOSPICE CARE

School	ST	$IS	SR
Madonna Univ	MI	24,540	VC

HOSPITAL ADMINISTRATION

School	ST	$IS	SR
Missouri State Univ	MO	13,996	VC
Thomas Edison State College	NJ	5,700	SP
Univ of Minn/Duluth	MN	18,964	C+
Univ of Wisc-Milwaukee	WI	18,436	C

HOSPITALITY MANAGEMENT SERVICES

School	ST	$IS	SR
Appalachian State Univ	NC	12,919	VC
Arkansas Tech Univ	AR	13,164	LC
Brigham Young Univ/ Hawaii	HI	8,614	VC
Buffalo State/State Univ of Buffalo	NY	15,733	C+
Burlington College	VT	32,510	SP
Central Conn State Univ	CT	19,212	C
Central Mich Univ	MI	18,066	C
College of Charleston	SC	21,273	VC
Colo State Univ-Fort Collins	CO	20,090	VC
Concordia Univ, Ann Arbor	MI	27,220	VC
Dallas Baptist Univ	TX	29,118	C
Davis and Elkins College	WV	33,742	C
Delta State Univ	MS	12,292	LC
DePaul Univ	IL	46,120	VC
East Carolina Univ	NC	14,169	C
Eastern Mich Univ	MI	17,961	C
Endicott College	MA	42,390	C
Ferris State Univ	MI	19,698	C
Florida Atlantic Univ	FL	17,339	C
Florida International Univ	FL	17,747	VC
Georgia State Univ	GA	12,000	VC
Green Mountain College	VT	33,547	LC
Harris-Stowe State Univ	MO	14,360	NC
Husson Univ	ME	23,386	LC
Indiana Univ Kokomo	IN	6,674	LC
Indiana Univ-Purdue Univ Fort Wayne	IN	15,425	C
James Madison Univ	VA	18,049	VC
Johnson and Wales Univ/ Charlotte Campus	NC	35,421	C
Johnson and Wales Univ/ North Miami Campus	FL	34,368	C
Johnson and Wales Univ/ Providence Campus	RI	34,668	C
Johnson State College	VT	16,721	C
Kendall College	IL	32,610	NC
Kent State Univ	OH	19,352	C
Lakeland College	WI	22,990	C
Lasell College	MA	42,500	LC
Madonna Univ	MI	24,540	VC
Marywood Univ	PA	40,695	C
Metropolitan State Univ	MN	5,923	SP
Metropolitan State Univ of Denver	CO	4,835	LC
Mich State Univ	MI	13,689	VC
Mitchell College	CT	40,983	C
Monroe College	NY	17,700	C
Montclair State Univ	NJ	22,614	C
Morgan State Univ	MD	14,500	VC
Mount Ida College	MA	30,115	LC
New York City College of Technology / The CUNY	NY	5,769	NC
New York Inst of Technology	NY	40,590	VC
Norfolk State Univ	VA	10,531	LC
N Dak State Univ	ND	14,642	C
Northwestern State Univ of Louisiana	LA	14,368	C
Pace Univ	NY	48,094	VC
Penn State Univ/Univ Park	PA	25,404	VC
Purdue Univ/West Lafayette	IN	20,278	HC
Robert Morris Univ	PA	36,699	C
Rutgers, The State Univ of New Jersey/Camden Campus	NJ	24,254	C
St. Leo Univ	FL	27,990	C
St. Louis Univ	MO	46,594	VC+
San Diego State Univ	CA	20,578	VC
San Francisco State Univ	CA	18,514	C
Southeast Missouri State Univ	MO	14,983	LC
Southern New Hampshire Univ	NH	38,100	C
Southern Oregon Univ	OR	17,874	C
St. John's Univ	NY	52,840	C+
St. Joseph's College, New York / Suffolk Campus	NY	21,878	VC
St. Thomas Univ	FL	32,310	C+
Stephen F. Austin State Univ	TX	14,668	C
Ohio State Univ	OH	19,887	MC
Thomas Edison State College	NJ	5,700	SP
Tougaloo College	MS	15,275	NC
Tuskegee Univ	AL	26,750	C
Univ of Arkansas at Fayetteville	AR	16,860	VC
Univ of Central Florida	FL	15,711	VC+
Univ of Denver	CO	51,787	VC+
Univ of Findlay	OH	31,916	C
Univ of Illinois at Urbana-Champaign	IL	24,300	HC
Univ of Mass Amherst	MA	23,697	VC+
Univ of Memphis	TN	15,094	C
Univ of Miss	MS	15,482	VC
Univ of Nebr - Lincoln	NE	17,507	VC
Univ of New Hampshire	NH	24,702	VC
Univ of New Haven	CT	47,740	C
Univ of N Car at Greensboro	NC	12,848	C
Univ of North Texas	TX	15,628	C
Univ of Pittsburgh at Bradford	PA	21,316	LC
Univ of San Francisco	CA	49,674	VC
Univ of Wisc/Stout	WI	23,942	C
Webber International Univ	FL	25,664	C
Western Carolina Univ	NC	13,965	C+
Western Kentucky Univ	KY	11,000	LC
Widener Univ	PA	50,368	C
Youngstown State Univ	OH	16,374	LC

HOTEL AND RESTAURANT ADMINISTRATION

School	ST	$IS	SR
Cornell Univ	NY	59,037	MC
N Dak State Univ	ND	14,642	C
Southern Oregon Univ	OR	17,874	C

HOTEL/MOTEL AND RESTAURANT MANAGEMENT

School	ST	$IS	SR
Ashland Univ	OH	25,000	C
Auburn Univ	AL	20,052	VC+
Bethune-Cookman Univ	FL	22,290	LC
Black Hills State Univ	SD	13,562	LC
Boston Univ	MA	54,130	HC+
Calif State Polytechnic Univ, Pomona	CA	18,932	C
Cheyney Univ of Pennsylvania	PA	20,372	LC
College of the Ozarks	MO	5,605	VC
Colo State Univ-Fort Collins	CO	20,090	VC
Concord Univ	WV	13,102	C
Delaware State Univ	DE	14,700	LC
Drexel Univ	PA	51,920	HC
East Stroudsburg Univ of Pennsylvania	PA	16,636	C

School	ST	$IS	SR
Eastern Mich Univ	MI	17,961	C
Endicott College	MA	42,390	C
Fairleigh Dickinson Univ/ College at Florham	NJ	42,142	C
Fairleigh Dickinson Univ/ Metropolitan Campus	NJ	40,254	C
Florida State Univ	FL	15,238	HC
Grambling State Univ	LA	13,384	LC
Grand Valley State Univ	MI	17,998	VC
Green Mountain College	VT	33,547	LC
Indiana Univ of Pennsylvania	PA	20,180	LC
Inter-American Univ of PR/ Aguadilla Campus	PR	5,578	
Iowa State Univ	IA	16,403	C
Johnson and Wales Univ/ Charlotte Campus	NC	35,421	C
Johnson and Wales Univ/ Denver Campus	CO	34,368	C
Johnson and Wales Univ/ North Miami Campus	FL	34,368	C
Johnson and Wales Univ/ Providence Campus	RI	34,668	C
Kansas State Univ	KS	15,497	VC
Kendall College	IL	32,610	NC
Keuka College	NY	30,300	C
Lynn Univ	FL	43,500	C
Mercyhurst Univ	PA	40,700	C
New Mexico State Univ	NM	13,955	LC
New York Univ	NY	61,470	MC
Newbury College	MA	41,850	C
Niagara Univ	NY	39,800	C
N Car Wesleyan College	NC	29,440	C
N Dak State Univ	ND	14,642	C
Northern Arizona Univ	AZ	18,592	C
Northwood Univ	FL	30,746	LC
Northwood Univ	MI	26,331	LC
Ohio Univ	OH	20,676	VC
Okla State Univ	OK	14,310	VC
Purdue Univ/Calumet	IN	14,336	C
Rochester Inst of Technology	NY	42,450	VC+
Roosevelt Univ	IL	22,605	VC
San Francisco State Univ	CA	18,514	C
Siena Heights Univ	MI	17,000	LC
S Dak State Univ	SD	14,296	C
Southwest Minn State Univ	MN	14,000	C
St. Joseph's College, New York / Brooklyn Campus	NY	21,878	C
SUNY Plattsburgh / SUNY	NY	18,083	VC
Tenn State Univ	TN	9,048	C
Texas Tech Univ	TX	14,243	C
Univ of Alaska Anchorage	AK	15,290	NC
Univ of Central Missouri	MO	14,605	C
Univ of Delaware	DE	22,728	VC
Univ of Houston	TX	19,184	VC
Univ of Kentucky	KY	19,868	C
Univ of Louisiana at Lafayette	LA	6,130	C
Univ of Maryland/Eastern Shore	MD	14,000	C
Univ of Missouri/Columbia	MO	18,201	MC
Univ of Nevada, Las Vegas	NV	17,303	C
Univ of New Hampshire	NH	24,702	VC
Univ of New Haven	CT	47,740	C
Univ of New Orleans	LA	9,224	VC
Univ of San Francisco	CA	49,674	VC
Univ of S Car at Columbia	SC	19,725	VC+
Univ of Southern Miss	MS	13,170	C
Univ of Tenn at Knoxville	TN	20,364	VC+
Univ of Wisc/Stout	WI	23,942	C
Virginia Polytechnic Inst and State Univ	VA	14,629	HC
Virginia State Univ	VA	11,318	C+
Washington State Univ	WA	20,461	C
Wiley College	TX		LC
Youngstown State Univ	OH	16,374	LC

HUMAN BIOLOGY, HEALTH, AND SOCIETY

School	ST	$IS	SR
Cornell Univ	NY	59,037	MC
Indiana Univ Bloomington	IN	19,358	HC

HUMAN DEVELOPMENT

School	ST	$IS	SR
Alabama A&M Univ	AL	96,100	C
Amridge Univ	AL	6,870	LC
Andrews Univ	MI	28,030	C+
Anna Maria College	MA	34,600	LC
Arizona State Univ	AZ	18,818	C+
Auburn Univ	AL	20,052	VC+
Binghamton Univ / The SUNY	NY	20,832	HC+
Boston College	MA	58,506	MC
Bowling Green State Univ	OH	18,970	C
Brigham Young Univ	UT	12,100	HC
Brown Univ	RI	56,150	MC
Cal State, East Bay	CA	16,549	C
Cal State, Long Beach	CA	17,534	C+
Cal State, San Bernardino	CA	12,000	C
Cal State, San Marcos	CA	14,576	C
Colo State Univ-Fort Collins	CO	20,090	VC
Conn College	CT	54,970	MC
Cornell Univ	NY	59,037	MC
Earlham College	IN	49,710	VC+
East Tenn State Univ	TN	9,000	C
Eckerd College	FL	43,902	VC
Goddard College	VT	16,418	VC
Hellenic College/Holy Cross Greek Orthodox School of Theology	MA	33,190	VC
Hope International Univ	CA	34,650	C
Howard Univ	DC	35,957	C
Kalamazoo College	MI	47,825	HC+
Kent State Univ	OH	19,352	C
Lee Univ	TN	18,690	C+
Marylhurst Univ	OR	18,945	NC
Messiah College	PA	39,540	VC
Minn State Univ, Mankato	MN	14,900	C
Mitchell College	CT	40,983	C
Montana State Univ	MT	14,068	VC
National Louis Univ	IL	16,915	LC
N Dak State Univ	ND	14,642	C
Northwestern Univ	IL	37,595	MC
Nova Southeastern Univ	FL	34,016	VC
Oakwood Univ	AL	23,035	C
Ohio Univ	OH	20,676	VC
Okla State Univ	OK	14,310	VC
Oregon State Univ	OR	19,017	C+
Oswego / SUNY	NY	20,009	VC
Penn State Univ/Altoona	PA	11,464	C
Penn State Univ/Univ Park	PA	25,404	VC
Prescott College	AZ	33,284	C+
Rivier College	NH	35,000	VC
Samford Univ	AL	35,700	VC+
San Diego Christian College	CA	31,012	C
Sonoma State Univ	CA	20,541	C
S Dak State Univ	SD	14,296	C
Southern Nazarene Univ	OK	24,354	NC
St. Joseph's College, New York / Suffolk Campus	NY	21,878	VC
SUNY/Empire State College	NY	6,315	SP
Suffolk Univ	MA	46,548	C
SUNY Plattsburgh / SUNY	NY	18,083	VC
Tarleton State Univ	TX	13,489	LC
Tenn Wesleyan College	TN	21,250	C
Texas Tech Univ	TX	14,243	C
Ohio State Univ	OH	19,887	MC
Univ of Alabama at Tuscaloosa	AL	17,164	C+
Univ of Arizona	AZ	20,105	C
Univ of Arkansas at Fayetteville	AR	16,860	VC
Univ of Bridgeport	CT	39,030	LC
Univ of Calif at Davis	CA	24,482	HC
Univ of Calif at San Diego	CA	21,000	VC
Univ of Chicago	IL	55,416	MC
Univ of Conn	CT	23,744	HC
Univ of Delaware	DE	22,728	VC
Univ of Georgia	GA	19,508	VC
Univ of Idaho	ID	14,558	C
Univ of Illinois at Urbana-Champaign	IL	24,300	HC
Univ of Memphis	TN	15,094	C
Univ of Miami	FL	55,166	MC
Univ of Missouri/Columbia	MO	18,201	MC
Univ of Nebr at Kearney	NE	14,855	LC
Univ of New Mexico	NM	15,300	C
Univ of N Car at Greensboro	NC	12,848	C
Univ of Okla	OK	17,634	VC+
Univ of Pittsburgh at Bradford	PA	21,316	LC
Univ of Utah	UT	13,462	VC
Univ of Vermont	VT	26,120	VC+
Univ of Wisc/Green Bay	WI	14,900	C
Univ of Wisc/Madison	WI	18,757	HC
Univ of Wisc/Stout	WI	23,942	C
Utah State Univ	UT	11,803	C
Vanderbilt Univ	TN	57,072	MC
Virginia Polytechnic Inst and State Univ	VA	14,629	HC
Warner Pacific College	OR	25,550	C
Washington State Univ	WA	20,461	C
Wheelock College	MA	33,075	C

HUMAN ECOLOGY

School	ST	$IS	SR
College of the Atlantic	ME	48,204	HC+
Goddard College	VT	16,418	VC
Kansas State Univ	KS	15,497	VC
Montclair State Univ	NJ	22,614	C
Prescott College	AZ	33,284	C+
Tenn Tech Univ	TN	11,310	C
Ohio State Univ	OH	19,887	MC
Univ of Calif at Davis	CA	24,482	HC
Univ of Nevada/Reno	NV	14,500	NC
Univ of Texas at Austin	TX	44,074	HC
Virginia Wesleyan College	VA	28,433	LC

HUMAN RESOURCES

School	ST	$IS	SR
Adelphi Univ	NY	43,130	VC
Alderson Broaddus Univ	WV	28,656	C
Alvernia Univ	PA	39,250	C
American International College	MA	36,100	LC
Amridge Univ	AL	6,870	LC
Aquinas College	MI	33,060	C
Baldwin Wallace Univ	OH	36,980	VC
Ball State Univ	IN	17,850	C
Barton College	NC	27,660	C
Baylor Univ	TX	46,720	HC
Black Hills State Univ	SD	13,562	LC
Bluffton Univ	OH	37,864	C
Boston College	MA	58,506	MC
Brescia Univ	KY	26,140	VC+
Briar Cliff Univ	IA	29,514	C
Bryant Univ	RI	49,179	VC
Calif State Polytechnic Univ, Pomona	CA	18,932	C
Cal State, San Bernardino	CA	12,000	C
Carlow Univ	PA	30,272	C
Central Mich Univ	MI	18,066	C
Chestnut Hill College	PA	39,785	LC
Cleary Univ	MI	11,000	C
Colo Christian Univ	CO	27,500	VC
Columbia College	MO	24,578	C
Davenport Univ	MI	21,002	LC
De Sales Univ	PA	42,670	C
Defiance College	OH	30,645	C
DePaul Univ	IL	46,120	VC
Dominican College	NY	31,270	C
Elizabethtown College School of Continuing and Professional Studies	PA		VC
Excelsior College	NY	895	SP
Faulkner Univ	AL	22,530	LC
Ferris State Univ	MI	19,698	C
Florida Atlantic Univ	FL	17,339	C
Franklin Univ	OH	7,000	SP
Friends Univ	KS	29,100	C
George Washington Univ	DC	57,108	MC
Golden Gate Univ	CA	17,000	C
Goldey-Beacom College	DE	27,493	C
Gwynedd-Mercy College	PA	33,560	C
Hawaii Pacific Univ	HI	36,690	C
Holy Names Univ	CA	40,310	NC
Idaho State Univ	ID	11,908	C
Indiana Univ of Pennsylvania	PA	20,180	LC
Inter-American Univ of PR/ Aguadilla Campus	PR	5,578	
Inter-American Univ of PR/ Bayamon Univ College	PR	4,428	
John Carroll Univ	OH	44,520	C+
Juniata College	PA	49,340	VC
Kentucky Wesleyan College	KY	27,440	VC+
Lake Erie College	OH	35,704	C
Le Moyne College	NY	42,200	VC
Lewis Univ	IL	23,050	C
Limestone College	SC	29,880	C
Lindenwood Univ	MO	20,750	C
Louisiana State Univ	LA	18,677	VC+
Lourdes Univ	OH	26,055	LC
Loyola Univ Chicago	IL	49,560	VC+
Lynchburg College	VA	42,645	C
Marietta College	OH	42,135	VC
Marquette Univ	WI	43,664	VC+
Menlo College	CA	49,002	C
Metropolitan State Univ	MN	5,923	SP
Mich State Univ	MI	13,689	VC
Midway College	KY	20,150	C
Mount Aloysius College	PA	27,970	C
Mount Mercy Univ	IA	34,385	C
Mount Olive College	NC	18,426	C
New York Univ	NY	61,470	MC
Niagara Univ	NY	39,800	C
Nichols College	MA	37,240	LC
North Central College	IL	38,343	VC
Northeastern Illinois Univ	IL		C
Northern Kentucky Univ	KY	15,302	LC
Notre Dame College	OH	34,942	VC
Oakland Univ	MI	19,391	VC
Okla Wesleyan Univ	OK	21,300	C
Oswego / SUNY	NY	20,009	VC
Our Lady of the Lake Univ of San Antonio	TX	22,430	LC
Park Univ	MO	17,525	C
Peirce College	PA	12,760	NC
Pennsylvania College of Technology	PA	25,653	NC
Point Park Univ	PA	36,390	C
Purdue Univ/West Lafayette	IN	20,278	HC
Rider Univ	NJ	45,720	C
Rowan Univ	NJ	23,570	VC
Rutgers, The State Univ of New Jersey/New Brunswick	NJ	25,077	VC
St. Joseph's Univ	PA	52,272	VC
St. Leo Univ	FL	27,990	C
St. Mary-of-the-Woods College	IN	37,722	LC
St. Mary's Univ	TX	33,854	C
Seton Hill Univ	PA	35,172	C
Silver Lake College	WI	22,600	LC
Simpson Univ	CA	28,900	C
Southern Illinois Univ Edwardsville	IL	17,532	C
St. Joseph's College, New York / Brooklyn Campus	NY	21,878	C
St. Joseph's College, New York / Suffolk Campus	NY	21,878	VC
SUNY/Empire State College	NY	6,315	SP
Tarleton State Univ	TX	13,489	LC
Tenn Wesleyan College	TN	21,250	C
Ohio State Univ	OH	19,887	MC
Thomas College	ME	26,270	LC
Trinity International Univ	IL	31,070	C
Univ of Arkansas at Fayetteville	AR	16,860	VC
Univ of Central Missouri	MO	14,605	C
Univ of Central Okla	OK	12,293	C
Univ of Findlay	OH	31,916	C
Univ of Florida	FL	15,783	HC+
Univ of Georgia	GA	19,508	VC
Univ of Hawaii at Manoa	HI	19,379	VC
Univ of Idaho	ID	14,558	C
Univ of Illinois at Urbana-Champaign	IL	24,300	HC
Univ of Maryland/Univ College	MD	6,168	SP
Univ of Mich-Flint	MI	17,547	C+
Univ of Mount Union	OH	35,130	C
Univ of Nebr - Lincoln	NE	17,507	VC
Univ of Nevada, Las Vegas	NV	17,303	C
Univ of N Dak	ND	14,094	C
Univ of North Texas	TX	15,628	C
Univ of Okla	OK	17,634	VC+
Univ of Pennsylvania	PA	56,106	MC
Univ of Pittsburgh at Pittsburgh	PA	27,800	HC+
Univ of PR/Humacao	PR	1,877	
Univ of Scranton	PA	51,940	VC
Univ of Tenn at Knoxville	TN	20,364	VC+
Univ of Texas at San Antonio	TX	18,372	C
Univ of the Incarnate Word	TX	35,200	LC
Univ of Wisc/Green Bay	WI	14,900	C
Univ of Wisc/Madison	WI	18,757	HC
Univ of Wisc/Oshkosh	WI	10,426	LC
Univ of Wisc-Milwaukee	WI	18,436	C
Ursuline College	OH	33,198	LC
Valley City State Univ	ND	12,286	LC
Washington Univ in St. Louis	MO	58,818	MC
Western Mich Univ	MI	19,042	C
Western Washington Univ	WA	18,519	VC
Wichita State Univ	KS	12,539	C
Xavier Univ	OH	43,740	VC
York College	NE	19,475	C
Youngstown State Univ	OH	16,374	LC

HUMAN RESOURCES/ ORGANIZATIONAL MGMT

School	ST	$IS	SR
Indiana Univ South Bend	IN	15,293	C
Indiana Univ Southeast	IN	15,807	LC
Lipscomb Univ	TN	35,722	VC
Thomas Edison State College	NJ	5,700	SP
Univ of Miami	FL	55,166	MC
Winona State Univ	MN	16,530	C

HUMAN SERVICES

School	ST	$IS	SR
Alaska Pacific Univ	AK	33,360	VC
Albertus Magnus College	CT	37,382	LC
Aquinas College	MI	33,060	C
Arkansas Baptist College	AR	9,000	NC
Assumption College	MA	45,721	VC
Beacon College	FL	38,000	C
Bethel College	IN	31,560	C
Bethel Univ	TN	19,186	C
Black Hills State Univ	SD	13,562	LC
Boricua College	NY	8,600	C
Brewton-Parker College	GA	33,388	LC
Burlington College	VT	32,510	SP
Cal State, Dominguez Hills	CA	17,056	LC
Cal State, Fullerton	CA	25,188	C+
Cal State, Monterey Bay	CA	26,871	LC
Cal State, San Bernardino	CA	12,000	C
Calumet College of St. Joseph	IN	15,000	LC
Cambridge College	MA	13,392	NC
Cazenovia College	NY	30,800	C
Chestnut Hill College	PA	39,785	LC
Coe College	IA	43,590	VC
College of St Joseph	VT	30,600	LC
Columbia College	MO	24,578	C
Dakota Wesleyan Univ	SD	23,000	C
Drury Univ	MO	30,319	VC
East Central Univ	OK	10,223	LC
Eastern New Mexico Univ	NM	10,682	C
Elizabethtown College School of Continuing and Professional Studies	PA		VC
Elmira College	NY	49,950	C+
Elon Univ	NC	40,046	HC
Fitchburg State Univ	MA	17,241	C
Fontbonne Univ	MO	31,384	C
Friends Univ	KS	29,100	C
Geneva College	PA	27,280	C
George Washington Univ	DC	57,108	MC
Goodwin College	CT	19,400	LC
Grace Bible College	MI	20,770	C
Graceland Univ	IA	28,020	C
Grand View Univ	IA	31,050	C
Gwynedd-Mercy College	PA	33,560	C
Hannibal-LaGrange Univ	MO	24,490	C
Hastings College	NE	27,782	C+
Hawaii Pacific Univ	HI	36,690	C

School	ST	$IS	SR
Henderson State Univ	AR	13,634	C
High Point Univ	NC	39,800	C
Hilbert College	NY	28,550	C
Holy Names Univ	CA	40,310	NC
Hope International Univ	CA	34,650	C
Indiana Inst of Technology	IN	34,240	LC
Indiana Univ Kokomo	IN	6,674	LC
Indiana Univ-Purdue Univ Fort Wayne	IN	15,425	C
Indiana Univ-Purdue Univ Indianapolis	IN	17,290	C
Kennesaw State Univ	GA	13,017	VC
La Roche College	PA	34,802	LC
Lake Superior State Univ	MI	18,121	C
Lasell College	MA	42,500	LC
Le Moyne College	NY	42,200	VC
Lenoir-Rhyne College	NC	35,984	C
Lesley Univ	MA	46,350	C
Lindenwood Univ	MO	20,750	C
Lindsey Wilson College	KY	30,470	VC
Loyola Univ Chicago	IL	49,560	VC+
Lyndon State College	VT	14,233	C
Metropolitan College of New York	NY	16,720	VC
Metropolitan State Univ	MN	5,923	SP
Metropolitan State Univ of Denver	CO	4,835	LC
Millikin Univ	IL	37,462	C
Missouri Baptist Univ	MO	30,310	C
Missouri Valley College	MO	22,200	C
Montana State Univ-Billings	MT	12,425	LC
Montreat College	NC	31,298	VC
Mount Olive College	NC	18,426	C
Mount St. Mary College	NY	39,540	C
National Louis Univ	IL	16,915	LC
New York City College of Technology / The CUNY	NY	5,769	NC
N Car Central Univ	NC	9,000	LC
Northern State Univ	SD	14,021	C
Northwest Christian Univ	OR	27,399	C
Notre Dame de Namur Univ	CA	41,610	LC
Nova Southeastern Univ	FL	34,016	VC
Oglala Lakota College	SD	2,000	NC
Old Dominion Univ	VA	18,662	C
Ottawa Univ	KS	15,000	VC
Park Univ	MO	17,525	C
Pfeiffer Univ	NC	33,700	C
Prescott College	AZ	33,284	C+
Queens Univ of Charlotte	NC	39,543	VC
Quincy Univ	IL	34,980	LC
St. Leo Univ	FL	27,990	C
St. Mary-of-the-Woods College	IN	37,722	LC
St. Mary's Univ of Minn	MN	37,015	C
Salem International Univ	WV	18,020	C
Seton Hill Univ	PA	35,172	C
Siena Heights Univ	MI	17,000	LC
Sinte Gleska Univ	SD	2,300	NC
S Car State Univ	SC	6,700	LC
Southern Oregon Univ	OR	17,874	C
Southern Wesleyan Univ	SC	25,600	C
Southwest Baptist Univ	MO	24,710	C
Springfield College	MA	25,000	C
St. John's Univ	NY	52,840	C+
St. Joseph's College, New York / Brooklyn Campus	NY	21,878	C
St. Joseph's College, New York / Suffolk Campus	NY	21,878	VC
St. Thomas Univ	FL	32,310	C+
Stevenson Univ	MD	39,572	C
Suffolk Univ	MA	46,548	C
SUNY Cortland / The SUNY	NY	19,117	C
Tenn Wesleyan College	TN	21,250	C
Texas Southern Univ	TX	18,212	LC
The Lincoln Univ	PA	15,154	LC
Thomas Edison State College	NJ	5,700	SP
Touro College	NY	23,150	VC
Trinity Washington Univ	DC	30,250	C+
Troy Univ	AL	10,650	C
Univ of Alaska Anchorage	AK	15,290	NC
Univ of Bridgeport	CT	39,030	LC
Univ of Delaware	DE	22,728	VC
Univ of Detroit Mercy	MI	30,450	C
Univ of Great Falls	MT	27,970	C
Univ of Hartford	CT	42,674	C
Univ of Maine at Machias	ME	10,523	C
Univ of Mass Boston	MA	11,966	C
Univ of New Mexico	NM	15,300	C
Univ of North Texas	TX	15,628	C
Univ of Northern Colo	CO	15,973	C
Univ of Scranton	PA	51,940	VC
Univ of Wisc/Oshkosh	WI	10,426	LC
Upper Iowa Univ	IA	30,426	NC
Washburn Univ	KS	12,165	NC
Wayland Baptist Univ	TX	16,058	LC
Waynesburg Univ	PA	29,100	C
Western New Mexico Univ	NM	8,500	LC
Western Washington Univ	WA	18,519	VC
William Penn Univ	IA	26,000	C
Wingate Univ	NC	34,990	C
Woodbury Inst of Champlain College in Burlington	VT	15,150	LC
York College	NE	19,475	C

HUMANITIES

School	ST	$IS	SR
Albertus Magnus College	CT	37,382	LC
Anna Maria College	MA	34,600	LC
Belhaven Univ	MS	27,170	C
Bennington College	VT	56,990	HC+
Biola Univ	CA	40,320	VC
Bluefield State College	WV	3,140	LC
Brigham Young Univ	UT	12,100	HC
Bucknell Univ	PA	58,160	MC
Buffalo State/State Univ of Buffalo	NY	15,733	C+
Cal State, Chico	CA	18,952	C
Cal State, Fresno	CA	17,405	C
Cal State, Monterey Bay	CA	26,871	LC
Cal State, Northridge	CA	28,313	C
Cal State, San Bernardino	CA	12,000	C
Chaminade Univ of Honolulu	HI	31,664	C
Charleston Southern Univ	SC	22,420	C
Clarkson Univ	NY	53,538	HC
Clearwater Christian College	FL	23,720	C
Colby-Sawyer College	NH	47,870	C
Colgate Univ	NY	50,930	MC
College of St. Benedict	MN	47,570	VC
College of St. Mary	NE	34,334	C
College of St. Scholastica	MN	39,960	C
Concordia College, Moorhead	MN	39,974	C+
Concordia Univ	OR	34,930	C
Concordia Univ - Irvine	CA	35,390	VC
Concordia Univ Wisc	WI	28,980	C
Corban Univ	OR	34,764	C
Cornerstone Univ and Grand Rapids Theological Seminary	MI	30,866	C
Defiance College	OH	30,645	C
DePaul Univ	IL	46,120	VC
Dominican College	NY	31,270	C
Dominican Univ of Calif	CA	51,250	C
Dowling College	NY	25,000	LC
Duquesne Univ	PA	42,017	VC
Eastern Washington Univ	WA	16,388	C
Eckerd College	FL	43,902	VC
Edinboro Univ of Pennsylvania	PA	15,940	LC
Fairleigh Dickinson Univ/ College at Florham	NJ	42,142	C
Fairleigh Dickinson Univ/ Metropolitan Campus	NJ	40,254	C
Felician College	NJ	41,640	C
Florida Inst of Technology	FL	48,290	VC
Florida Southern College	FL	38,240	VC
Florida State Univ	FL	15,238	HC
Fort Lewis College	CO	15,513	C
George Washington Univ	DC	57,108	MC
Georgian Court Univ	NJ	39,726	LC
Hampden-Sydney College	VA	48,848	C
Hampshire College	MA	58,320	MC
Harding Univ	AR	21,432	C+
Harvard Univ/Harvard College	MA	49,000	MC
Hawaii Pacific Univ	HI	36,690	C
Holy Family Univ	PA	40,030	LC
Holy Names Univ	CA	40,310	NC
Houghton College	NY	35,740	VC
Illinois Inst of Technology	IL	38,512	HC+
Indiana Univ East	IN	6,639	LC
Indiana Univ Kokomo	IN	6,674	LC
Jacksonville Univ	FL	37,780	C
John Carroll Univ	OH	44,520	C+
Johns Hopkins Univ	MD	47,492	MC
Johnson State College	VT	16,721	C
Kansas State Univ	KS	15,497	VC
Kentucky Christian Univ	KY	17,622	LC
Lasell College	MA	42,500	LC
Lawrence Tech Univ	MI	37,630	VC
Lee Univ	TN	18,690	C+
Lees-McRae College	NC	33,624	C
LeMoyne-Owen College	TN	13,100	C
Lesley Univ	MA	46,350	C
Loyola Marymount Univ	CA	53,240	VC+
Lubbock Christian Univ	TX	25,518	C
Macalester College	MN	53,419	MC
Maritime College / SUNY	NY	16,020	C
Marshall Univ	WV	14,820	C
Martin Univ	IN	11,000	SP
Mass Inst of Technology	MA	54,238	MC
Messiah College	PA	39,540	VC
Mich State Univ	MI	13,689	VC
Mich Tech Univ	MI	22,105	VC
Midwestern State Univ	TX	9,722	C
Milligan College	TN	27,510	C
Minn State Univ, Mankato	MN	14,900	C
Montana State Univ-Northern	MT	12,500	NC
Montclair State Univ	NJ	22,614	C
Mount Aloysius College	PA	27,970	C
Mount Mercy Univ	IA	34,385	C
Mountain State Univ	WV	14,330	NC
New College of Florida	FL	14,504	HC+
New York Univ	NY	61,470	MC
N Dak State Univ	ND	14,642	C
Northwest Christian Univ	OR	27,399	C
Northwest Missouri State Univ	MO	14,229	C
Northwestern State Univ of Louisiana	LA	14,368	C
Notre Dame de Namur Univ	CA	41,610	LC
Oberlin College	OH	57,025	MC
Ohio Valley Univ	WV	17,752	C
Okla City Univ	OK	33,546	VC
Pacific Univ	OR	42,815	C
Paul Quinn College	TX	25,350	LC
Pepperdine Univ	CA	55,372	HC+
Plymouth State Univ	NH	23,148	LC
Polytechnic Inst of New York Univ	NY	53,064	HC+
Prescott College	AZ	33,284	C+
Providence College	RI	55,995	HC
Quincy Univ	IL	34,980	LC
Roberts Wesleyan College	NY	37,384	C+
Rockford College	IL	31,000	C
Roger Williams Univ	RI	45,788	C
Rollins College	FL	52,370	HC
Rosemont College	PA	42,350	C
Rutgers, The State Univ of New Jersey/New Brunswick	NJ	25,077	VC
St. John's Univ	MN	46,146	C
St. Louis Univ	MO	46,594	VC+
St. Mary-of-the-Woods College	IN	37,722	LC
St. Mary's College	IN	45,160	VC
St. Peter's College	NJ	44,240	C
San Diego State Univ	CA	20,578	VC
San Francisco State Univ	CA	18,514	C
Schreiner Univ	TX	32,734	LC
Scripps College	CA	54,900	MC
Seattle Univ	WA	47,010	VC+
Shawnee State Univ	OH	16,545	NC
Shimer College	IL	32,875	VC
Siena Heights Univ	MI	17,000	LC
Sierra Nevada College	NV	32,700	VC
Southern Methodist Univ	TX	57,755	MC
Spring Hill College	AL	42,130	VC
St. Andrews Univ	NC	32,050	LC
St. Norbert College	WI	39,992	VC
Stetson Univ	FL	49,512	VC+
Stony Brook Univ / SUNY	NY	19,359	HC
Suffolk Univ	MA	46,548	C
SUNY College at Old Westbury	NY	16,324	C
Tabor College	KS	29,010	LC
Taylor Univ	IN	36,742	VC+
Thomas Edison State College	NJ	5,700	SP
Thomas More College	KY	34,760	C
Thomas Univ	GA	11,520	NC
Tougaloo College	MS	15,275	NC
Trinity International Univ	IL	31,070	C
Tulane Univ	LA	58,942	MC
Union College	NY		MC
United States Air Force Academy	CO		MC
Universidad del Turabo	PR	4,110	
Universidad Metropolitana	PR		
Univ of Calif at Irvine	CA	25,961	VC
Univ of Central Florida	FL	15,711	VC+
Univ of Central Okla	OK	12,293	C
Univ of Chicago	IL	55,416	MC
Univ of Colo Boulder	CO	22,605	VC+
Univ of Houston-Downtown	TX	6,267	LC
Univ of Illinois at Chicago	IL	24,293	VC
Univ of Illinois at Urbana-Champaign	IL	24,300	HC
Univ of Kansas	KS	16,980	C+
Univ of Louisville	KY	17,460	VC
Univ of Maryland/Univ College	MD	6,168	SP
Univ of Mich/Ann Arbor	MI	22,102	HC+
Univ of Mich/Dearborn	MI	9,885	VC
Univ of Minn/Twin Cities	MN		HC
Univ of Mobile	AL	27,870	VC
Univ of New Hampshire	NH	24,702	VC
Univ of Northern Iowa	IA	14,776	C
Univ of Oregon	OR	20,872	VC
Univ of Pittsburgh at Greensburg	PA	17,640	C
Univ of Pittsburgh at Johnstown	PA	20,862	LC
Univ of Pittsburgh at Pittsburgh	PA	27,800	HC+
Univ of PR/Cayey	PR	1,504	
Univ of Rio Grande	OH	8,750	NC
Univ of San Diego	CA	53,302	HC+
Univ of South Florida	FL	13,000	C
Univ of Tenn at Chattanooga	TN	16,883	C
Univ of Texas at Austin	TX	44,074	HC
Univ of Texas at Dallas	TX	21,046	HC
Univ of Texas at San Antonio	TX	18,372	C
Univ of the Southwest	NM	15,000	C
Univ of Toledo	OH	18,464	C
Univ of Utah	UT	13,462	VC
Univ of Wisc/Green Bay	WI	14,900	C
Univ of Wisc/Parkside	WI	10,181	LC
Univ of Wyoming	WY	13,855	C+
Ursuline College	OH	33,198	LC
Valparaiso Univ	IN	43,040	VC+
Villanova Univ	PA	56,436	MC
Virginia Wesleyan College	VA	28,433	LC
Walla Walla Univ	WA	26,256	NC
Washington College	MD	48,768	VC
Washington State Univ	WA	20,461	C
Washington Univ in St. Louis	MO	58,818	MC
Wesleyan College	GA	24,000	C+
Western New Mexico Univ	NM	8,500	LC
Western Oregon Univ	OR	15,021	C
Widener Univ	PA	50,368	C
Willamette Univ	OR	56,450	VC+
Wofford College	SC	45,795	VC
Worcester Polytechnic Inst	MA	53,440	HC+
Wright State Univ	OH	16,983	C
Xavier Univ	OH	43,740	VC
Yale Univ	CT	55,300	MC
York College of Pennsylvania	PA	26,590	C

HUMANITIES AND SOCIAL SCIENCE

School	ST	$IS	SR
Alabama A&M Univ	AL	96,100	C
Bennington College	VT	56,990	HC+
Canisius College	NY	45,602	VC
Franciscan Univ of Steubenville	OH	27,320	VC
Goddard College	VT	16,418	VC
John Jay College of Criminal Justice / The CUNY	NY	6,059	C
Lock Haven Univ of Pennsylvania	PA	17,587	LC
Mount Aloysius College	PA	27,970	C
New York Univ	NY	61,470	MC
Northwestern State Univ of Louisiana	LA	14,368	C
Prescott College	AZ	33,284	C+
San Francisco State Univ	CA	18,514	C
Spalding Univ	KY	31,850	LC
SUNY/Empire State College	NY	6,315	SP
Texas A&M Univ at Galveston	TX	11,258	C
Univ of Calif at Riverside	CA	27,204	C
Univ of the Sciences	PA	40,020	VC+

HYDROGEOLOGY

School	ST	$IS	SR
Eastern Mich Univ	MI	17,961	C
Rensselaer Polytechnic Inst	NY	59,229	MC
Western Mich Univ	MI	19,042	C

HYDROLOGY

School	ST	$IS	SR
Texas A&M Univ at Galveston	TX	11,258	C
Univ of Arizona	AZ	20,105	C
Univ of Calif at Davis	CA	24,482	HC
Univ of Calif at Santa Barbara	CA	27,551	HC
Univ of Nevada/Reno	NV	14,500	NC

IBERIAN STUDIES

School	ST	$IS	SR
New York Univ	NY	61,470	MC
Stanford Univ	CA	56,411	MC
Univ of PR/Arecibo	PR	7,227	

ILLUSTRATION

School	ST	$IS	SR
Academy of Art Univ	CA		
Arcadia Univ	PA	33,570	C+
Art Academy of Cincinnati	OH	25,940	SP
Art Center College of Design	CA	34,044	SP
Bennington College	VT	56,990	HC+
Brigham Young Univ	UT	12,100	HC
Calif College of the Arts	CA	48,334	SP
Cleveland Inst of Art	OH	48,641	SP
College for Creative Studies	MI		SP
College of Art and Design at Lesley Univ	MA	39,730	SP
College of Visual Arts - School is Closed	MN	24,310	SP
Columbus College of Art and Design	OH	37,732	SP
Fashion Inst of Technology/SUNY	NY	12,468	SP
Indiana Wesleyan Univ	IN	31,815	VC
John Brown Univ	AR	30,996	VC+
Kansas City Art Inst	MO	38,000	SP
Kendall College of Art and Design of Ferris State Univ	MI	21,048	SP
Kutztown Univ of Pennsylvania	PA	16,909	LC
Laguna College of Art and Design	CA	26,500	SP
Lawrence Tech Univ	MI	37,630	VC
Lewis Univ	IL	23,050	C
Maryland Inst College of Art	MD	39,500	SP
Marywood Univ	PA	40,695	C
Mass College of Art and Design	MA	23,600	SP
Memphis College of Art	TN	33,550	SP

School	ST	$IS	SR
Milwaukee Inst of Art and Design	WI	31,938	SP
Minneapolis College of Art and Design	MN	36,700	SP
Montserrat College of Art	MA	31,000	SP
Moore College of Art and Design	PA	38,124	SP
Ohio Univ	OH	20,676	VC
Olivet College	MI	19,984	C
Otis College of Art and Design	CA	35,404	SP
Pacific Northwest College of Art	OR	38,494	SP
Parsons The New School for Design	NY	56,610	SP
Rhode Island School of Design	RI	55,204	SP
Ringling College of Art and Design	FL	46,130	SP
Rivier College	NH	35,000	VC
Rochester Inst of Technology	NY	42,450	VG
Rocky Mountain College of Art and Design	CO	22,470	NC
Savannah College of Art and Design	GA	46,824	SP
School of Visual Arts	NY	36,500	SP
St. John's Univ	NY	52,840	G
Syracuse Univ	NY	54,512	HC
Univ of Bridgeport	CT	39,030	LC
Univ of Findlay	OH	31,916	C
Univ of Hartford	CT	42,674	C
Univ of Kansas	KS	16,980	G
Univ of Mass Dartmouth	MA	22,223	C
Univ of Mich/Ann Arbor	MI	22,102	HG
Univ of Montana-Western	MT	9,753	LC
Univ of San Francisco	CA	49,674	VC
Univ of the Arts	PA	38,450	SP
Washington Univ in St. Louis	MO	58,818	MC
Western Conn State Univ	CT	18,327	C

IMAGING SCIENCES

School	ST	$IS	SR
Thomas Edison State College	NJ	5,700	SP

INDUSTRIAL ADMINISTRATION/ MANAGEMENT

School	ST	$IS	SR
Central Mich Univ	MI	18,066	C
Chancellor Univ	OH	11,000	C
Clarion Univ of Pennsylvania	PA	17,370	C
Clemson Univ	SC	19,136	HC
Colo State Univ-Pueblo	CO	13,532	LC
Gardner-Webb Univ	NC	34,375	G
Grove City College	PA	22,988	HC
Illinois Inst of Technology	IL	38,512	HG
Inter-American Univ of PR/ Bayamon Univ College	PR	4,428	
Lawrence Tech Univ	MI	37,630	VC
LeTourneau Univ	TX	26,230	C
Mercer Univ	GA	44,201	VG
Metropolitan State Univ of Denver	CO	4,835	LC
Okla State Univ	OK	14,310	VC
Oregon Inst of Technology	OR	8,910	C
Purdue Univ/West Lafayette	IN	20,278	HC
Saginaw Valley State Univ	MI	16,869	C
St. Augustine's Univ	NC	14,000	C
San Francisco State Univ	CA	18,514	C
S Dak State Univ	SD	14,296	C
Southwestern Okla State Univ	OK	9,160	C
Trine Univ	IN	39,400	VC
Universidad Politecnica de PR	PR	19,252	
Univ of Alabama at Birmingham	AL	18,484	G
Univ of Alabama at Tuscaloosa	AL	17,164	G
Univ of Arkansas at Little Rock	AR		C
Univ of Cincinnati	OH	20,199	VC
Univ of Illinois at Urbana-Champaign	IL	24,300	HC
Univ of Iowa	IA	17,481	VC
Univ of Mass Lowell	MA	19,316	C
Univ of Minn Crookston	MN	17,834	C
Univ of Nebr at Kearney	NE	14,855	LC
Univ of N Car at Asheville	NC	13,500	VG
Univ of N Car at Charlotte	NC	15,847	C
Univ of Southern Indiana	IN	14,657	C
Univ of Wisc/Parkside	WI	10,181	LC
Univ of Wisc/Stout	WI	23,942	C
Wentworth Inst of Technology	MA	29,800	SP
West Virginia Univ Inst of Technology	WV	14,094	NC
William Penn Univ	IA	26,000	C

INDUSTRIAL AND LABOR RELATIONS

School	ST	$IS	SR
Cornell Univ	NY	59,037	MC
Eastern Conn State Univ	CT	20,584	C
New York Univ	NY	61,470	MC

INDUSTRIAL AND ORGANIZATIONAL PSYCHOLOGY

School	ST	$IS	SR
Albertus Magnus College	CT	37,382	LC
Baldwin Wallace Univ	OH	36,980	VC
Cedar Crest College	PA	43,240	C
CUNY/Baruch College	NY	15,831	VC
Coe College	IA	43,590	VC
Fitchburg State Univ	MA	17,241	C
Goddard College	VT	16,418	VC
High Point Univ	NC	39,800	C
Holy Family Univ	PA	40,030	LC
Ithaca College	NY	52,300	HC
Kutztown Univ of Pennsylvania	PA	16,909	LC
Marywood Univ	PA	40,695	C
Northwest Missouri State Univ	MO	14,229	C
Oregon Inst of Technology	OR	8,910	C
Point Loma Nazarene Univ	CA	38,610	VC
Texas Wesleyan Univ	TX	29,886	C
Ohio State Univ	OH	19,887	MC
Univ of Georgia	GA	19,508	VC
Univ of PR/Arecibo	PR	7,227	
Washington Univ in St. Louis	MO	58,818	MC

INDUSTRIAL ARTS EDUCATION

School	ST	$IS	SR
Alabama A&M Univ	AL	96,100	C
Auburn Univ	AL	20,052	VG
Ball State Univ	IN	17,850	C
Bemidji State Univ	MN	13,500	C
Buffalo State/State Univ of Buffalo	NY	15,733	G
Cal State, Los Angeles	CA	15,829	C
Central Washington Univ	WA	11,730	C
Chicago State Univ	IL	5,482	C
Clemson Univ	SC	19,136	HC
Concordia Univ Nebr	NE	26,000	VC
Eastern Kentucky Univ	KY	11,161	C
Eastern Mich Univ	MI	17,961	C
Elizabeth City State Univ	NC	11,638	C
Fitchburg State Univ	MA	17,241	C
Florida A&M Univ	FL	14,935	LC
Humboldt State Univ	CA	18,400	C
Indiana State Univ	IN	16,000	C
Iowa State Univ	IA	16,403	C
Langston Univ	OK	3,000	LC
Montana State Univ-Northern	MT	12,500	NC
Morehead State Univ	KY	10,900	C
Murray State Univ	KY	14,944	C
N Car Agricultural and Technical State Univ	NC	13,175	LC
N Car State Univ	NC	16,202	HC
Northeastern State Univ	OK	8,615	VC
Northern Kentucky Univ	KY	15,302	LC
Northern Mich Univ	MI	15,300	VC
San Diego State Univ	CA	20,578	VC
San Francisco State Univ	CA	18,514	C
S Car State Univ	SC	6,700	LC
Southeast Missouri State Univ	MO	14,983	LC
Southwestern Okla State Univ	OK	9,160	C
St. Cloud State Univ	MN	10,600	C
Tarleton State Univ	TX	13,489	LC
Texas A&M Univ at Commerce	TX	10,496	C
Univ of Arkansas at Pine Bluff	AR	10,600	C
Univ of Central Missouri	MO	14,605	C
Univ of Cincinnati	OH	20,199	VC
Univ of Idaho	ID	14,558	C
Univ of Louisiana at Lafayette	LA	6,130	C
Univ of Maryland/Eastern Shore	MD	14,000	C
Univ of Minn/Twin Cities	MN		HC
Univ of Montana-Western	MT	9,753	LC
Univ of Southern Miss	MS	13,170	C
Utah State Univ	UT	11,803	C
Wayne State College	NE	11,764	NC
Western Illinois Univ	IL	20,130	C

INDUSTRIAL DESIGN

School	ST	$IS	SR
Academy of Art Univ	CA		
Appalachian State Univ	NC	12,919	VC
Arizona State Univ	AZ	18,818	G
Art Center College of Design	CA	34,044	SP
Auburn Univ	AL	20,052	VG
Brigham Young Univ	UT	12,100	HC
Calif College of the Arts	CA	48,334	SP
Cedarville Univ	OH	31,036	VG
Cleveland Inst of Art	OH	48,641	SP
College for Creative Studies	MI		SP
Columbus College of Art and Design	OH	37,732	SP
Escuela de Artes Plasticas de PR	PR	2,660	
Georgia Inst of Technology	GA	20,464	MC
Kean Univ	NJ	22,060	LC
Kendall College of Art and Design of Ferris State Univ	MI	21,048	SP
Lawrence Tech Univ	MI	37,630	VC
Mass College of Art and Design	MA	23,600	SP
Metropolitan State Univ of Denver	CO	4,835	LC
Milwaukee Inst of Art and Design	WI	31,938	SP
N Car State Univ	NC	16,202	HC
Otis College of Art and Design	CA	35,404	SP
Parsons The New School for Design	NY	56,610	SP
Philadelphia Univ	PA	44,160	C
Pratt Inst	NY	49,520	SP
Purdue Univ/West Lafayette	IN	20,278	HC
Rhode Island School of Design	RI	55,204	SP
Rochester Inst of Technology	NY	42,450	VG
Savannah College of Art and Design	GA	46,824	SP
Syracuse Univ	NY	54,512	HC
Ohio State Univ	OH	19,887	MC
Univ of Bridgeport	CT	39,030	LC
Univ of Houston	TX	19,184	VC
Univ of Illinois at Chicago	IL	24,293	VC
Univ of Illinois at Urbana-Champaign	IL	24,300	HC
Univ of Kansas	KS	16,980	G
Univ of Mich/Ann Arbor	MI	22,102	HG
Univ of the Arts	PA	38,450	SP
Virginia Polytechnic Inst and State Univ	VA	14,629	HC
Wentworth Inst of Technology	MA	29,800	SP

INDUSTRIAL ENGINEERING

School	ST	$IS	SR
Alabama A&M Univ	AL	96,100	C
Arizona State Univ	AZ	18,818	G
Auburn Univ	AL	20,052	VG
Binghamton Univ / The SUNY	NY	20,832	HG
Bradley Univ	IL	31,874	VC
Calif Polytechnic State Univ	CA	19,847	HC
Calif State Polytechnic Univ, Pomona	CA	18,932	C
Cal State, East Bay	CA	16,549	C
Cal State, Fresno	CA	17,405	C
Clemson Univ	SC	19,136	HC
Colo State Univ-Pueblo	CO	13,532	LC
Elizabethtown College	PA	47,600	VC
Florida A&M Univ	FL	14,935	LC
Florida State Univ	FL	15,238	HC
Francis Marion Univ	SC	16,464	LC
George Mason Univ	VA	15,724	VC
Georgia Inst of Technology	GA	20,464	MC
Hofstra Univ	NY	48,020	VG
Indiana Inst of Technology	IN	34,240	LC
Inter-American Univ of PR/ Bayamon Univ College	PR	4,428	
Kansas State Univ	KS	15,497	VC
Kettering Univ	MI	31,456	HC
Lamar Univ	TX	6,820	LC
Lawrence Tech Univ	MI	37,630	VC
Lehigh Univ	PA	55,080	MC
Louisiana State Univ	LA	18,677	VG
Louisiana Tech Univ	LA	8,000	C
Mass Maritime Academy	MA	15,340	C
Milwaukee School of Engineering	WI	39,948	VG
Montana State Univ	MT	14,068	VC
New Jersey Inst of Technology	NJ	26,490	VC
New Mexico State Univ	NM	13,955	LC
New York Inst of Technology	NY	40,590	VC
N Car Agricultural and Technical State Univ	NC	13,175	LC
N Car State Univ	NC	16,202	HC
N Dak State Univ	ND	14,642	C
Northeastern Univ	MA	55,296	MC
Northern Illinois Univ	IL	19,768	C
Northwestern State Univ of Louisiana	LA	14,368	C
Northwestern Univ	IL	37,595	MC
Oakland Univ	MI	19,391	VC
Okla State Univ	OK	14,310	VC
Oregon State Univ	OR	19,017	G
Penn State Univ/Univ Park	PA	25,404	VC
Philadelphia Univ	PA	44,160	C
Purdue Univ/West Lafayette	IN	20,278	HC
Quinnipiac Univ	CT	53,580	VC
Rensselaer Polytechnic Inst	NY	59,229	MC
Rochester Inst of Technology	NY	42,450	VG
Rutgers, The State Univ of New Jersey/New Brunswick	NJ	25,077	VC
St. Augustine's Univ	NC	14,000	C
St. Mary's Univ	TX	33,854	C
San Jose State Univ	CA	19,707	C
S Dak School of Mines and Technology	SD	15,260	VC
Southern Illinois Univ Edwardsville	IL	17,532	C
St. Ambrose Univ	IA		C
Stanford Univ	CA	56,411	MC
SUNY Inst of Technology at Utica / Rome	NY	23,818	C
Tenn Tech Univ	TN	11,310	C
Texas State Univ	TX	16,495	VC
Texas Tech Univ	TX	14,243	C
Ohio State Univ	OH	19,887	MC
Universidad Politecnica de PR	PR	19,252	
Univ at Buffalo / The SUNY	NY	20,283	VC
Univ of Alabama at Huntsville	AL	17,625	VC
Univ of Alabama at Tuscaloosa	AL	17,164	G
Univ of Arizona	AZ	20,105	C
Univ of Arkansas at Fayetteville	AR	16,860	VC
Univ of Calif at Berkeley	CA	23,322	MC
Univ of Central Florida	FL	15,711	VG
Univ of Houston	TX	19,184	VC
Univ of Illinois at Urbana-Champaign	IL	24,300	HC
Univ of Iowa	IA	17,481	VC
Univ of Louisiana at Lafayette	LA	6,130	C
Univ of Louisville	KY	17,460	VC
Univ of Mass Amherst	MA	23,697	VG
Univ of Miami	FL	55,166	MC
Univ of Mich/Ann Arbor	MI	22,102	HG
Univ of Minn/Duluth	MN	18,964	G
Univ of Minn/Twin Cities	MN		HC
Univ of Missouri/Columbia	MO	18,201	MC
Univ of Okla	OK	17,634	VG
Univ of Pittsburgh at Pittsburgh	PA	27,800	HG
Univ of PR/Mayaguez	PR	1,250	
Univ of San Diego	CA	53,302	HG
Univ of South Florida	FL	13,000	C
Univ of Southern Calif	CA	56,903	MC
Univ of Tenn at Chattanooga	TN	16,883	C
Univ of Tenn at Knoxville	TN	20,364	VG
Univ of Toledo	OH	18,464	C
Univ of Wisc/Madison	WI	18,757	HC
Univ of Wisc/Platteville	WI	14,274	C
Univ of Wisc-Milwaukee	WI	18,436	C
Utah State Univ	UT	11,803	C
Virginia Polytechnic Inst and State Univ	VA	14,629	HC
Wayne State Univ	MI	19,493	C
Western Mich Univ	MI	19,042	C
Western New England Univ	MA	45,590	C
Wichita State Univ	KS	12,539	C
Worcester Polytechnic Inst	MA	53,440	HG
Wright State Univ	OH	16,983	C
Youngstown State Univ	OH	16,374	LC

INDUSTRIAL ENGINEERING TECHNOLOGY

School	ST	$IS	SR
Alabama A&M Univ	AL	96,100	C
Appalachian State Univ	NC	12,919	VC
Arizona State Univ	AZ	18,818	G
Ball State Univ	IN	17,850	C
Bemidji State Univ	MN	13,500	C
Berea College	KY	7,220	HC
Buffalo State/State Univ of Buffalo	NY	15,733	G
Cal State, Fresno	CA	17,405	C
Cal State, Los Angeles	CA	15,829	C
Calif Univ of Pennsylvania	PA	14,217	C
Caribbean Univ	PR	10,375	
Central Conn State Univ	CT	19,212	C
Central Washington Univ	WA	11,730	C
Chadron State College	NE	7,400	NC
Columbia Univ in the City of New York	NY	61,116	MC
East Carolina Univ	NC	14,169	C
Eastern Illinois Univ	IL	20,502	C
Elizabeth City State Univ	NC	11,638	C
Farmingdale State College	NY	18,985	C
Fitchburg State Univ	MA	17,241	C
Grand Valley State Univ	MI	17,998	VC
Humboldt State Univ	CA	18,400	C
Illinois State Univ	IL	22,634	VC
Indiana State Univ	IN	16,000	C
Indiana Univ-Purdue Univ Fort Wayne	IN	15,425	C
Iowa State Univ	IA	16,403	C
Jackson State Univ	MS	13,512	LC
Kent State Univ	OH	19,352	C
Lamar Univ	TX	6,820	LC
Langston Univ	OK	3,000	LC
Metropolitan State Univ of Denver	CO	4,835	LC
Middle Tenn State Univ	TN	8,650	C

School	ST	$IS	SR
Millersville Univ of Pennsylvania	PA	18,498	C
Minn State Univ, Moorhead	MN	13,392	C
Miss Valley State Univ	MS	9,706	LC
Morehead State Univ	KY	10,900	C
Morgan State Univ	MD	14,500	VC
Northern Kentucky Univ	KY	15,302	LC
Northern Mich Univ	MI	15,300	VC
Northwestern State Univ of Louisiana	LA	14,368	C
Ohio Univ	OH	20,676	VC
Okla Panhandle State Univ	OK	8,996	NC
Prairie View A&M Univ	TX	15,205	LC
Purdue Univ/Calumet	IN	14,336	C
Purdue Univ/West Lafayette	IN	20,278	HC
Roger Williams Univ	RI	45,788	C
San Francisco State Univ	CA	18,514	C
Southeastern Louisiana Univ	LA	13,325	C
Southern Illinois Univ Carbondale	IL	21,620	C
Southern Polytechnic State Univ	GA	13,958	VC
Southwestern Okla State Univ	OK	9,160	C
Tarleton State Univ	TX	13,489	LC
Tenn Tech Univ	TN	11,310	C
Texas A&M Univ	TX	16,956	VC+
Texas A&M Univ at Kingsville	TX	7,500	LC
Texas Southern Univ	TX	18,212	LC
Texas State Univ	TX	16,495	VC
Univ of Arkansas at Pine Bluff	AR	10,600	C
Univ of Central Missouri	MO	14,605	C
Univ of Cincinnati	OH	20,199	VC
Univ of Dayton	OH	43,750	VC
Univ of Florida	FL	15,783	HC+
Univ of Illinois at Chicago	IL	24,293	VC
Univ of Mass Lowell	MA	19,316	C
Univ of Mich/Dearborn	MI	9,885	VC
Univ of N Dak	ND	14,094	C
Univ of Northern Iowa	IA	14,776	C
Univ of Rio Grande	OH	8,750	NC
Univ of Southern Maine	ME	16,576	C
Univ of Texas at Arlington	TX	10,908	LC
Univ of Texas at El Paso	TX	8,764	NC
Univ of West Alabama	AL	9,415	C
Univ of Wisc/Platteville	WI	14,274	C
Univ of Wisc/Stout	WI	23,942	C
Utah State Univ	UT	11,803	C
Wayne State Univ	MI	19,493	C
West Virginia Univ Inst of Technology	WV	14,094	NC
Western Illinois Univ	IL	20,130	C
Western Kentucky Univ	KY	11,000	LC
Western Mich Univ	MI	19,042	C
Western Washington Univ	WA	18,519	VC
William Penn Univ	IA	26,000	C

INDUSTRIAL HYGIENE

School	ST	$IS	SR
Ohio Univ	OH	20,676	VC
St. Augustine's Univ	NC	14,000	C
South Univ	GA		LC
Univ of Central Okla	OK	12,293	C
Univ of North Alabama	AL	9,960	C

INDUSTRIAL TECHNOLOGY

School	ST	$IS	SR
Calif Polytechnic State Univ	CA	19,847	HC
San Diego State Univ	CA	20,578	VC

INFORMATICS AND COMPUTER SCIENCE

School	ST	$IS	SR
Arkansas State Univ	AR	14,980	C
Bryant Univ	RI	49,179	VC
Creighton Univ	NE	44,058	VC+
Indiana Univ Bloomington	IN	19,358	HC

INFORMATION & COMMUNICATION TECHNOLOGY

School	ST	$IS	SR
Abilene Christian Univ	TX	38,400	VC
Aquinas College	MI	33,060	C
Guilford College	NC	35,340	C
Northern Kentucky Univ	KY	15,302	LC
St. John's Univ	NY	52,840	C+
Univ of Scranton	PA	51,940	VC
Univ of Wisc/Stout	WI	23,942	C

INFORMATION SCIENCE

School	ST	$IS	SR
Bryant Univ	RI	49,179	VC
Cornell Univ	NY	59,037	MC

INFORMATION SCIENCES AND SYSTEMS

School	ST	$IS	SR
Abilene Christian Univ	TX	38,400	VC
Alabama State Univ	AL	14,142	NC
Albany State Univ	GA	8,500	C
Albright College	PA	46,660	C
Alfred State / SUNY College of Technology	NY	18,034	C
American InterContinental Univ	GA	13,500	NC
Andrews Univ	MI	28,030	C+
Aquinas College	MI	33,060	C+
Arizona State Univ	AZ	18,818	C+
Arkansas State Univ	AR	14,980	C
Arkansas Tech Univ	AR	13,164	LC
Armstrong Atlantic State Univ	GA	16,276	C
Atlantic Union College	MA	24,600	LC
Auburn Univ at Montgomery	AL	12,120	C
Augustana College	SD	35,500	VC
Averett Univ	VA	36,000	LC
Avila Univ	MO	26,900	C
Azusa Pacific Univ	CA	39,946	C
Barton College	NC	27,660	C
Baylor Univ	TX	46,720	HC
Beacon College	FL	38,000	C
Belhaven Univ	MS	27,170	C
Bellevue Univ	NE	4,600	NC
Bentley Univ	MA	54,555	HC+
Bethune-Cookman Univ	FL	22,290	LC
Binghamton Univ / The SUNY	NY	20,832	HC+
Biola Univ	CA	40,320	VC
Bloomfield College	NJ	36,960	C
Bluffton Univ	OH	37,864	C
Boise State Univ	ID	12,802	C
Boston College	MA	58,506	MC
Bradley Univ	IL	31,874	VC
Brewton-Parker College	GA	33,388	LC
Briar Cliff Univ	IA	29,514	C
Brigham Young Univ	UT	12,100	HC
Brigham Young Univ/Hawaii	HI	8,614	VC
Bryant Univ	RI	49,179	VC
Buffalo State/State Univ of Buffalo	NY	15,733	C+
Cabrini College	PA	40,859	LC
Caldwell College	NJ	35,602	LC
Calif Lutheran Univ	CA	47,640	C
Calif State Polytechnic Univ, Pomona	CA	18,932	C
Cal State, Fullerton	CA	25,188	C+
Cal State, Los Angeles	CA	15,829	C
Cal State, Stanislaus	CA	18,582	C
Calif Univ of Pennsylvania	PA	14,217	C
Calumet College of St. Joseph	IN	15,000	LC
Calvin College	MI	37,585	VC+
Campbell Univ	NC	25,500	C
Campbellsville Univ	KY	27,720	C
Canisius College	NY	45,602	VC
Carlow Univ	PA	30,272	C
Carnegie Mellon Univ	PA	51,260	MC
Carroll Univ	WI	24,860	C
Catawba College	NC	37,105	C
Cedar Crest College	PA	43,240	C
Cedarville Univ	OH	31,036	VC+
Central Mich Univ	MI	18,066	C
Central Washington Univ	WA	11,730	C
Chaminade Univ of Honolulu	HI	31,664	C
Champlain College	VT	44,850	VC
Chancellor Univ	OH	11,000	C
Chapman Univ	CA	56,019	VC+
Chestnut Hill College	PA	39,785	LC
Chicago State Univ	IL	5,482	C
Christopher Newport Univ	VA	21,050	VC
CUNY/Baruch College	NY	15,831	VC
CUNY/Brooklyn College	NY	5,884	C+
Clarion Univ of Pennsylvania	PA	17,370	C
Clarke Univ	IA	36,400	C
Clarkson Univ	NY	53,538	HC
Clayton State Univ	GA	12,000	LC
Cleary Univ	MI	11,000	C
Clemson Univ	SC	19,136	HC
Cleveland State Univ	OH	21,357	C
Coastal Carolina Univ	SC	17,620	C
College of the Ozarks	MO	5,605	VC
Colo State Univ-Fort Collins	CO	20,090	VC
Colo State Univ-Pueblo	CO	13,532	LC
Colo Technical Univ	CO	10,500	LC
Columbia College	MO	24,578	C
Columbia College	SC	27,882	C
Concord Univ	WV	13,102	C
Concordia Univ St. Paul	MN	27,200	C
Corban Univ	OR	34,764	C
Cornell Univ	NY	59,037	MC
Curry College	MA	47,545	LC
Dakota State Univ	SD	13,811	C
Daniel Webster College	NH	25,380	C
Davenport Univ	MI	21,002	LC
Defiance College	OH	30,645	C
Delta State Univ	MS	12,292	LC
DePaul Univ	IL	46,120	VC
Doane College	NE	33,730	VC
Dominican College	NY	31,270	C
Dordt College	IA	34,160	VC
Dowling College	NY	25,000	LC
Drake Univ	IA	30,980	VC+
Drexel Univ	PA	51,920	HC
D'Youville College	NY	29,850	C
East Carolina Univ	NC	14,169	C
East Tenn State Univ	TN	9,000	C
Eastern Conn State Univ	CT	20,584	C
Eastern Mich Univ	MI	17,961	C
Eastern New Mexico Univ	NM	10,682	C
Eastern Washington Univ	WA	16,388	C
Edgewood College	WI	33,294	C
Edinboro Univ of Pennsylvania	PA	15,940	LC
Elizabethtown College	PA	47,600	VC
Elmhurst College	IL	42,032	C+
Elon Univ	NC	40,046	HC
Emporia State Univ	KS	12,897	C
Excelsior College	NY	895	SP
Fairfield Univ	CT	55,850	VC
Fairleigh Dickinson Univ/Metropolitan Campus	NJ	40,254	C
Farmingdale State College	NY	18,985	C
Faulkner Univ	AL	22,530	LC
Felician College	NJ	41,640	C
Ferrum College	VA	27,740	LC
Florida Atlantic Univ	FL	17,339	C
Florida Inst of Technology	FL	48,290	VC
Florida State Univ	FL	15,238	HC
Fontbonne Univ	MO	31,384	C
Fordham Univ	NY	58,927	HC
Fort Hays State Univ	KS	11,354	C
Fort Valley State Univ	GA	11,200	VC
Francis Marion Univ	SC	16,464	LC
Franciscan Univ of Steubenville	OH	27,320	VC
Franklin College	IN	35,885	C
Freed-Hardeman Univ	TN	19,697	VC
Friends Univ	KS	29,100	C
Frostburg State Univ	MD	15,264	LC
Furman Univ	SC	54,006	HC
Gallaudet Univ	DC	25,380	SP
Gannon Univ	PA	37,940	C
Gardner-Webb Univ	NC	34,375	C+
George Fox Univ	OR	40,750	C+
George Mason Univ	VA	15,724	VC
George Washington Univ	DC	57,108	MC
Georgia College and State Univ	GA	18,216	VC
Glenville State College	WV	11,348	NC
Goldey-Beacom College	DE	27,493	C
Goshen College	IN	35,900	VC
Graceland Univ	IA	28,020	C
Grambling State Univ	LA	13,384	LC
Grand Valley State Univ	MI	17,998	VC
Guilford College	NC	35,340	C
Gwynedd-Mercy College	PA	33,560	C
Hampton Univ	VA	28,528	C
Hannibal-LaGrange Univ	MO	24,490	C
Harding Univ	AR	21,432	C+
Hartwick College	NY	49,815	C+
Haverford College	PA	59,236	MC
Heidelberg Univ	OH	34,100	C
Henderson State Univ	AR	13,634	C
Hodges Univ	FL	12,000	LC
Hofstra Univ	NY	48,020	VC+
Holy Family Univ	PA	40,030	LC
Houston Baptist Univ	TX	23,815	C+
Humboldt State Univ	CA	18,400	C
Huntington Univ	IN	32,220	C
Idaho State Univ	ID	11,908	C
Illinois College	IL	25,770	VC
Illinois Inst of Technology	IL	38,512	HC+
Illinois State Univ	IL	22,634	VC
Immaculata Univ	PA	43,000	C
Indiana Inst of Technology	IN	34,240	LC
Indiana Univ-Purdue Univ Fort Wayne	IN	15,425	C
Indiana Wesleyan Univ	IN	31,815	VC
Inter-American Univ of PR/Aguadilla Campus	PR	5,578	
Iona College	NY	44,028	C
Ithaca College	NY	52,300	HC
Jacksonville Univ	FL	37,780	C
James Madison Univ	VA	18,049	VC
Johnson and Wales Univ/Providence Campus	RI	34,668	C
Juniata College	PA	49,340	VC
Kansas State Univ	KS	15,497	VC
Kaplan Univ	IA	14,025	NC
Kean Univ	NJ	22,060	LC
Kennesaw State Univ	GA	13,017	VC
Keystone College	PA	28,680	LC
King's College	PA	41,678	C
Kutztown Univ of Pennsylvania	PA	16,909	LC
La Roche College	PA	34,802	LC
La Salle Univ	PA	50,270	C
La Sierra Univ	CA	35,694	VC
Lake Superior State Univ	MI	18,121	C
Lamar Univ	TX	6,820	LC
Lawrence Tech Univ	MI	37,630	VC
Le Moyne College	NY	42,200	VC
Lee Univ	TN	18,690	C+
Limestone College	SC	29,880	C
Lincoln Memorial Univ	TN	18,144	C
Lincoln Univ	MO	11,996	NC
Lock Haven Univ of Pennsylvania	PA	17,587	LC
LIU/Brooklyn Campus	NY	26,500	C
LIU/C.W. Post Campus	NY	38,888	C
Louisiana State Univ	LA	18,677	VC+
Loyola Univ Chicago	IL	49,560	VC+
Lubbock Christian Univ	TX	25,518	C
Madonna Univ	MI	24,540	VC
Manhattan College	NY	44,955	VC
Mansfield Univ	PA	19,468	LC
Marian Univ	WI	30,980	LC
Marietta College	OH	42,135	VC
Marist College	NY	35,500	C
Marshall Univ	WV	14,820	C
Marymount Manhattan College	NY	40,118	VC
Maryville Univ of St. Louis	MO	34,920	VC
Marywood Univ	PA	40,695	C
McKendree Univ	IL	29,920	C+
Mercer Univ	GA	44,201	VC+
Mercy College	NY	29,996	C
Meredith College	NC	31,420	C
Metropolitan State Univ	MN	5,923	SP
Metropolitan State Univ of Denver	CO	4,835	LC
Mich State Univ	MI	13,689	VC
Middle Tenn State Univ	TN	8,650	C
Midwestern State Univ	TX	9,722	C
Milligan College	TN	27,510	C
Millikin Univ	IL	37,462	C
Minn State Univ, Mankato	MN	14,900	C
Misericordia Univ	PA	39,840	C
Missouri Baptist Univ	MO	30,310	C
Missouri Southern State Univ	MO	11,910	C
Missouri Univ of Science and Technology	MO	18,655	VC+
Missouri Valley College	MO	22,200	C
Missouri Western State Univ	MO	12,260	NC
Molloy College	NY	38,950	C
Monroe College	NY	17,700	C
Montana State Univ-Billings	MT	12,425	LC
Montclair State Univ	NJ	22,614	C
Morgan State Univ	MD	14,500	VC
Mount Aloysius College	PA	27,970	C
Mount Olive College	NC	18,426	C
Mount St. Mary's Univ	MD	46,158	C
Mountain State Univ	WV	14,330	NC
Murray State Univ	KY	14,944	C
National American Univ	SD	16,712	NC
National Louis Univ	IL	16,915	LC
National Univ	CA	14,730	SP
Nebr Wesleyan Univ	NE	29,774	C+
New Jersey Inst of Technology	NJ	26,490	VC
New Mexico Inst of Mining and Technology	NM	12,892	HC
New Mexico State Univ	NM	13,955	LC
New York City College of Technology / The CUNY	NY	5,769	NC
New York Univ	NY	61,470	MC
Newman Univ	KS	30,380	C+
Niagara Univ	NY	39,800	C
Nicholls State Univ	LA	7,095	C
N Car Wesleyan College	NC	29,440	C
Northeastern State Univ	OK	8,615	VC
Northeastern Univ	MA	55,296	MC
Northern Illinois Univ	IL	19,768	C
Northern Kentucky Univ	KY	15,302	LC
Northern Mich Univ	MI	15,300	VC
Northland College	WI	26,680	C
Northwest Missouri State Univ	MO	14,229	C
Northwestern College of Iowa	IA	34,848	C+
Northwestern State Univ of Louisiana	LA	14,368	C
Northwestern Univ	IL	37,595	MC
Norwich Univ	VT	28,212	C
Notre Dame College	OH	34,942	VC
Notre Dame de Namur Univ	CA	41,610	LC
Notre Dame of Maryland Univ	MD	27,700	C
Oakland Univ	MI	19,391	VC
Oakwood Univ	AL	23,035	C
Okla Baptist Univ	OK	28,202	VC
Okla Christian Univ	OK	24,975	VC
Okla Panhandle State Univ	OK	8,996	NC
Old Dominion Univ	VA	18,662	C
Olivet Nazarene Univ	IL	29,990	C
Oswego / SUNY	NY	20,009	VC
Ottawa Univ	KS	15,000	VC
Our Lady of the Lake Univ of San Antonio	TX	22,430	LC
Pace Univ	NY	48,094	VC
Park Univ	MO	17,525	C
Peirce College	PA	12,760	NC
Penn State Univ/Univ Park	PA	25,404	VC
Pennsylvania College of Technology	PA	25,653	NC
Pfeiffer Univ	NC	33,700	C
Pittsburg State Univ	KS	12,032	C
Plymouth State Univ	NH	23,148	LC
Point Loma Nazarene Univ	CA	38,610	VC
Point Park Univ	PA	36,390	C
Polytechnic Inst of New York Univ	NY	53,064	HC+
Portland State Univ	OR	18,672	C
Purdue Univ/Calumet	IN	14,336	C

ST = STATE **$IS** = IN-STATE COSTS **SR** = SELECTOR RATING

INFORMATION TECHNOLOGY

INSTITUTIONAL MANAGEMENT

INSTRUMENTAL MUSIC EDUCATION

INSTRUMENTAL PERFORMANCE

INSURANCE

INSURANCE AND RISK MANAGEMENT

INTEGRATED LEADERSHIP STUDIES

INTERDISCIPLINARY STUDIES

School	ST	$IS	SR
Cal State, Dominguez Hills	CA	17,056	LC
Cal State, Long Beach	CA	17,534	G
Cal State, Los Angeles	CA	15,829	C
Cal State, Stanislaus	CA	18,582	C
Calvin College	MI	37,585	VG
Cambridge College	MA	13,392	NC
Cameron Univ	OK	9,267	LC
Centenary College	NJ	38,618	LC
Centenary College of Louisiana	LA	39,070	G
Central Methodist Univ	MO	28,240	VC
Central Mich Univ	MI	18,066	C
Chatham Univ	PA	42,440	VC
Christopher Newport Univ	VA	21,050	VC
CUNY/Brooklyn College	NY	5,884	G
Claremont McKenna College	CA	58,065	MC
Clarkson Univ	NY	53,538	HC
Clayton State Univ	GA	12,000	LC
Coastal Carolina Univ	SC	17,620	C
Coe College	IA	43,590	VC
College of the Ozarks	MO	5,605	VC
College of William & Mary	VA	25,085	MC
College of Wooster	OH	52,600	VC
Colo College	CO	54,534	MC
Colo State Univ-Fort Collins	CO	20,090	VC
Columbia College	MO	24,578	C
Concordia College New York	NY	31,500	VC
Coppin State Univ	MD	14,905	VC
Corban Univ	OR	34,764	C
Cornerstone Univ and Grand Rapids Theological Seminary	MI	30,866	C
Covenant College	GA		VG
Dallas Baptist Univ	TX	29,118	C
Davidson College	NC	54,683	MC
Delta State Univ	MS	12,292	LC
DePauw Univ	IN	48,950	VG
D'Youville College	NY	29,850	C
East Tenn State Univ	TN	9,000	C
East Texas Baptist Univ	TX	29,135	C
Eastern Mich Univ	MI	17,961	C
Embry-Riddle Aeronautical Univ - Prescott Campus	AZ	40,584	VC
Emerson College	MA	50,246	HC
Emmanuel College	MA	47,985	VC
Emory and Henry College	VA	387,460	C
Emory Univ	GA	45,000	MC
Eugene Lang College - The New School for Liberal Arts	NY	55,650	VC
Fairleigh Dickinson Univ/ Metropolitan Campus	NJ	40,254	C
Fitchburg State Univ	MA	17,241	C
Florida Atlantic Univ	FL	17,339	C
Florida Inst of Technology	FL	48,290	VC
Fort Lewis College	CO	15,513	C
Framingham State Univ	MA	16,750	C
Franklin and Marshall College	PA	58,295	MC
Franklin Pierce Univ	NH	41,598	C
Geneva College	PA	27,280	C
George Mason Univ	VA	15,724	VC
George Washington Univ	DC	57,108	MC
Georgetown College	KY	38,690	C
Georgetown Univ	DC	52,910	MC
Georgia State Univ	GA	12,000	VC
Goddard College	VT	16,418	VC
Gonzaga Univ	WA	44,247	HC
Goshen College	IN	35,900	VC
Goucher College	MD	50,252	VG
Grace Bible College	MI	20,770	C
Grand Canyon Univ	AZ	24,540	VC
Guilford College	NC	35,340	C
Hamilton College	NY	55,620	MC
Haverford College	PA	59,236	MC
Hendrix College	AR	48,436	HG
Heritage Univ	WA	17,664	NC
Hodges Univ	FL	12,000	LC
Hollins Univ	VA	43,295	VC
Houghton College	NY	35,740	VC
Howard Univ	DC	35,957	C
Huston-Tillotson Univ	TX	18,124	G
Illinois State Univ	IL	22,634	VC
Illinois Wesleyan Univ	IL	48,452	VG
Indiana State Univ	IN	16,000	C
Indiana Univ Bloomington	IN	19,358	HC
Indiana Univ-Purdue Univ Indianapolis	IN	17,290	C
Ithaca College	NY	52,300	HC
John Brown Univ	AR	30,996	VG
Johns Hopkins Univ	MD	47,492	MC
Judson College	AL	24,690	C
Kalamazoo College	MI	47,825	HG
Kennesaw State Univ	GA	13,017	VC
King Univ	TN	33,140	C
Lafayette College	PA	57,050	HG
LaGrange College	GA	34,480	C
Lake Erie College	OH	35,704	C
Lander Univ	SC	22,514	G
Lane College	TN	11,212	C
Lasell College	MA	42,500	LC
Lee Univ	TN	18,690	G
Lees-McRae College	NC	33,624	C
LeTourneau Univ	TX	26,230	C
Lewis & Clark College	OR	52,656	VC

School	ST	$IS	SR
Liberty Univ	VA	19,101	C
Lipscomb Univ	TN	35,722	VC
Louisiana State Univ	LA	18,677	VG
Lourdes Univ	OH	26,055	LC
Lyndon State College	VT	14,233	C
Manchester College	IN	35,070	C
Marian Univ	WI	30,980	LC
Marietta College	OH	42,135	VC
Marist College	NY	35,500	C
Marlboro College	VT	35,980	VC
Marquette Univ	WI	43,664	VG
Marylhurst Univ	OR	18,945	NC
Mass College of Liberal Arts	MA	16,733	C
Mass Inst of Technology	MA	54,238	MC
McMurry Univ	TX	25,962	LC
Mercy College	NY	29,996	C
Messiah College	PA	39,540	VC
Miami Univ	OH	24,191	HC
Mich State Univ	MI	13,689	VC
Middle Tenn State Univ	TN	8,650	C
Midwestern State Univ	TX	9,722	C
Millikin Univ	IL	37,462	C
Misericordia Univ	PA	39,840	C
Molloy College	NY	38,950	C
Montana State Univ-Northern	MT	12,500	NC
Mount St. Mary College	NY	39,540	C
Mount St. Mary's Univ	MD	46,158	C
Mountain State Univ	WV	14,330	NC
Naropa Univ	CO	37,875	SP
National Univ	CA	14,730	SP
New York Inst of Technology	NY	40,590	VC
Newman Univ	KS	30,380	G
Norfolk State Univ	VA	10,531	LC
N Car State Univ	NC	16,202	HC
Northeastern Illinois Univ	IL		C
Northeastern Univ	MA	55,296	MC
Northern Arizona Univ	AZ	18,592	C
Northwest Christian Univ	OR	27,399	C
Northwest Nazarene Univ	ID	24,275	NC
Northwest Univ	WA	18,854	C
Northwestern College	MN	24,000	C
Notre Dame of Maryland Univ	MD	27,700	C
Nyack College	NY	32,000	C
Ohio Dominican Univ	OH	38,380	G
Ohio Valley Univ	WV	17,752	C
Old Dominion Univ	VA	18,662	C
Palm Beach Atlantic Univ	FL	33,882	LC
Piedmont College	GA	29,260	C
Plymouth State Univ	NH	23,148	LC
Prairie View A&M Univ	TX	15,205	LC
Queens College / The CUNY	NY	17,107	VC
Radford Univ	VA	17,132	LC
Rensselaer Polytechnic Inst	NY	59,229	MC
Rhodes College	TN	47,596	HG
Roberts Wesleyan College	NY	37,384	G
Rochester College	MI	18,320	C
Russell Sage College	NY	39,370	C
Rutgers, The State Univ of New Jersey/Camden Campus	NJ	24,254	C
Rutgers, The State Univ of New Jersey/Newark Campus	NJ	25,376	C
Saginaw Valley State Univ	MI	16,869	C
St. Martin's Univ	WA	38,082	C
St. Peter's College	NJ	44,240	C
Salisbury Univ	MD	18,368	VC
San Diego Christian College	CA	31,012	C
San Diego State Univ	CA	20,578	VC
San Francisco State Univ	CA	18,514	C
Shawnee State Univ	OH	16,545	NC
Shippensburg Univ of Pennsylvania	PA	17,064	LC
Simmons College	MA	48,770	VC
Simpson College	IA	36,086	VC
Sonoma State Univ	CA	20,541	C
S Dak School of Mines and Technology	SD	15,260	VC
Southeast Missouri State Univ	MO	14,983	LC
Southeastern Univ	FL	27,201	G
Southern Oregon Univ	OR	17,874	C
Southwest Baptist Univ	MO	24,710	C
Southwest Minn State Univ	MN	14,000	C
Southwestern College	KS	29,270	C
St. Andrews Univ	NC	32,050	LC
St. Edward's Univ	TX	44,674	VC
St. John Fisher College	NY	39,370	G
St. Lawrence Univ	NY	53,740	HC
St. Olaf College	MN	49,960	HG
SUNY/Empire State College	NY	6,315	SP
Stephen F. Austin State Univ	TX	14,668	C
Stevenson Univ	MD	39,572	C
Stonehill College	MA	46,780	VG
Stony Brook Univ / SUNY	NY	19,359	HC
SUNY Fredonia / The SUNY at Fredonia	NY	18,702	VC
SUNY Plattsburgh / SUNY	NY	18,083	VC
Sweet Briar College	VA	43,765	G

School	ST	$IS	SR
Tarleton State Univ	TX	13,489	LC
Taylor Univ	IN	36,742	VG
Tenn State Univ	TN	9,048	C
Tenn Wesleyan College	TN	21,250	C
Texas Southern Univ	TX	18,212	LC
Texas State Univ	TX	16,495	VC
Texas Wesleyan Univ	TX	29,886	C
Texas Woman's Univ	TX	13,633	LC
The College at Brockport / SUNY	NY	18,362	VC
The College of St. Rose	NY	26,750	C
Touro College	NY	23,150	VC
Towson Univ	MD	16,000	VC
Trinity College	CT		HG
Truman State Univ	MO	13,546	HC
Union College	NY		MC
Univ at Albany / SUNY	NY	18,674	VC
Univ of Akron	OH	20,436	C
Univ of Alabama at Tuscaloosa	AL	17,164	G
Univ of Alaska Anchorage	AK	15,290	NC
Univ of Alaska Fairbanks	AK	13,955	C
Univ of Arizona	AZ	20,105	C
Univ of Bridgeport	CT	39,030	LC
Univ of Calif at Berkeley	CA	23,322	MC
Univ of Calif at Irvine	CA	25,961	VC
Univ of Calif at Riverside	CA	27,204	C
Univ of Calif at Santa Barbara	CA	27,551	HC
Univ of Central Florida	FL	15,711	VG
Univ of Chicago	IL	55,416	MC
Univ of Colo Denver	CO	17,904	C
Univ of Delaware	DE	22,728	VC
Univ of Denver	CO	51,787	VG
Univ of Evansville	IN	41,056	VG
Univ of Florida	FL	15,783	HG
Univ of Georgia	GA	19,508	VC
Univ of Hartford	CT	42,674	C
Univ of Hawaii at Manoa	HI	19,379	VC
Univ of Houston	TX	19,184	VC
Univ of Houston-Downtown	TX	6,267	LC
Univ of Idaho	ID	14,558	C
Univ of Maine	ME	19,712	G
Univ of Maine at Augusta	ME	6,855	C
Univ of Maine at Farmington	ME	17,841	C
Univ of Maryland	MD	18,801	HC
Univ of Maryland/Baltimore County	MD	18,000	VC
Univ of Mass Amherst	MA	23,697	VG
Univ of Mass Dartmouth	MA	22,223	C
Univ of Memphis	TN	15,094	C
Univ of Miami	FL	55,166	MC
Univ of Mich/Ann Arbor	MI	22,102	HG
Univ of Minn/Duluth	MN	18,964	G
Univ of Missouri-St. Louis	MO	18,304	VC
Univ of Nebr - Lincoln	NE	17,507	VC
Univ of Nebr at Omaha	NE	12,700	C
Univ of Nevada, Las Vegas	NV	17,303	C
Univ of New Mexico	NM	15,300	C
Univ of N Car at Chapel Hill	NC	18,348	MC
Univ of N Dak	ND	14,094	C
Univ of North Florida	FL	15,578	VC
Univ of North Texas	TX	15,628	C
Univ of Northern Colo	CO	15,973	C
Univ of Okla	OK	17,634	VG
Univ of Pikeville	KY	24,750	NC
Univ of Pittsburgh at Bradford	PA	21,316	LC
Univ of Pittsburgh at Pittsburgh	PA	27,800	HG
Univ of Portland	OR	47,874	VC
Univ of PR Recinto de Rio Piedras	PR	5,750	
Univ of Redlands	CA	40,500	VC
Univ of Rochester	NY	58,500	MC
Univ of St. Mary	KS	28,400	G
Univ of S Car at Aiken	SC	16,278	C
Univ of S Car at Columbia	SC	19,725	VG
Univ of S Car Upstate	SC	17,673	LC
Univ of Tenn at Knoxville	TN	20,364	VG
Univ of Texas at Arlington	TX	10,908	LC
Univ of Texas at Dallas	TX	21,046	HC
Univ of Texas at El Paso	TX	8,764	NC
Univ of Texas at San Antonio	TX	18,372	C
Univ of Texas-Pan American	TX	12,432	LC
Univ of the Sciences	PA	48,320	VG
Univ of Virginia	VA	22,175	MC
Univ of Wisc/Green Bay	WI	14,900	C
Univ of Wisc/Superior	WI	14,106	C
Univ of Wisc-Milwaukee	WI	18,436	C
Univ of Wyoming	WY	13,855	G
Valparaiso Univ	IN	43,040	VG
Vanderbilt Univ	TN	57,072	MC
Victory Univ	TN	19,118	C
Villanova Univ	PA	56,436	MC
Virginia Commonwealth Univ	VA	18,633	C
Virginia Intermont College	VA	32,411	LC
Virginia Polytechnic Inst and State Univ	VA	14,629	HC
Virginia State Univ	VA	11,318	G
Virginia Wesleyan College	VA	28,433	LC
Warren Wilson College	NC	34,888	VC
Washburn Univ	KS	12,165	NC

School	ST	$IS	SR
Washington and Jefferson College	PA	49,990	VC
Washington and Lee Univ	VA	52,812	MC
Washington College	MD	48,768	VC
Washington State Univ	WA	20,461	C
Washington Univ in St. Louis	MO	58,818	MC
Wayland Baptist Univ	TX	16,058	LC
Wayne State College	NE	11,764	NC
Webster Univ	MO	33,990	G
Wesleyan College	GA	24,000	G
West Liberty Univ	WV	9,142	LC
West Texas A&M Univ	TX	13,478	C
West Virginia Univ	WV	15,794	G
Western Illinois Univ	IL	20,130	C
Western Mich Univ	MI	19,042	C
Western Oregon Univ	OR	15,021	C
Western Washington Univ	WA	18,519	VC
Wheaton College	IL	39,650	HG
William Woods Univ	MO		C
Wisc Lutheran College	WI	23,510	VC
Woodbury Inst of Champlain College in Burlington	VT	15,150	LC
Woodbury Univ	CA	34,500	LC
Worcester Polytechnic Inst	MA	53,440	HG

INTERIOR ARCHITECTURE

School	ST	$IS	SR
Cleveland Inst of Art	OH	48,641	SP
Lawrence Tech Univ	MI	37,630	VC

INTERIOR DESIGN

School	ST	$IS	SR
Abilene Christian Univ	TX	38,400	VC
Academy of Art Univ	CA		
Adrian College	MI	33,800	C
American InterContinental Univ	GA	13,500	NC
Appalachian State Univ	NC	12,919	VC
Arcadia Univ	PA	33,570	G
Arizona State Univ	AZ	18,818	G
Art Inst of Atlanta	GA	24,000	SP
Art Inst of Portland	OR	23,040	SP
Auburn Univ	AL	20,052	VG
Baker College of Flint	MI	7,800	NC
Bay Path College	MA	34,565	C
Baylor Univ	TX	46,720	HC
Boston Architectural College	MA	18,622	SP
Bowling Green State Univ	OH	18,970	C
Brenau Univ Women's College	GA	26,650	G
Calif College of the Arts	CA	48,334	SP
Cal State, Chico	CA	18,952	C
Cal State, Fresno	CA	17,405	C
Cazenovia College	NY	30,800	C
Central Mich Univ	MI	18,066	C
Chaminade Univ of Honolulu	HI	31,664	C
Chatham Univ	PA	42,440	VC
College for Creative Studies	MI		SP
Colo State Univ-Fort Collins	CO	20,090	VC
Columbus College of Art and Design	OH	37,732	SP
Concordia Univ Wisc	WI	28,980	C
Converse College	SC	37,130	C
Drexel Univ	PA	51,920	HC
East Carolina Univ	NC	14,169	C
Eastern Kentucky Univ	KY	11,161	C
Eastern Mich Univ	MI	17,961	C
Endicott College	MA	42,390	C
Fashion Inst of Technology/SUNY	NY	12,468	SP
Ferris State Univ	MI	19,698	C
Florida International Univ	FL	17,747	VC
Florida State Univ	FL	15,238	HC
Georgia Southern Univ	GA	16,414	C
Harding Univ	AR	21,432	G
High Point Univ	NC	39,800	C
Howard Univ	DC	35,957	C
Indiana State Univ	IN	16,000	C
Indiana Univ Bloomington	IN	19,358	HC
Indiana Univ of Pennsylvania	PA	20,180	LC
Indiana Univ-Purdue Univ Fort Wayne	IN	15,425	C
Indiana Univ-Purdue Univ Indianapolis	IN	17,290	C
Indiana Wesleyan Univ	IN	31,815	VC
Iowa State Univ	IA	16,403	C
Kansas State Univ	KS	15,497	VC
Kean Univ	NJ	22,060	LC
Kendall College of Art and Design of Ferris State Univ	MI	21,048	SP
Kent State Univ	OH	19,352	C
La Roche College	PA	34,802	LC
Lawrence Tech Univ	MI	37,630	VC
Louisiana State Univ	LA	18,677	VG
Marymount Univ	VA	36,178	C
Maryville Univ of St. Louis	MO	34,920	VC
Marywood Univ	PA	40,695	C
Mercyhurst Univ	PA	40,700	C
Meredith College	NC	31,420	C
Miami Univ	OH	24,191	HC

School	ST	$IS	SR
Mich State Univ	MI	13,689	VC
Middle Tenn State Univ	TN	8,650	C
Milwaukee Inst of Art and Design	WI	31,938	SP
Minn State Univ, Mankato	MN	14,900	C
Miss College	MS	21,998	VC
Missouri State Univ	MO	13,996	VC
Moore College of Art and Design	PA	38,124	SP
Mount Ida College	MA	30,115	LC
Mount Mary Univ	WI	32,836	LC
New York Inst of Technology	NY	40,590	VC
Newbury College	MA	41,850	C
N Dak State Univ	ND	14,642	C
Northern Arizona Univ	AZ	18,592	C
Ohio Univ	OH	20,676	VC
Okla Christian Univ	OK	24,975	VC
Oregon State Univ	OR	19,017	₲
Park Univ	MO	17,525	C
Parsons The New School for Design	NY	56,610	SP
Philadelphia Univ	PA	44,160	C
Pittsburg State Univ	KS	12,032	C
Pratt Inst	NY	49,520	SP
Purdue Univ/West Lafayette	IN	20,278	HC
Queens Univ of Charlotte	NC	39,543	VC
Rhode Island School of Design	RI	55,204	SP
Ringling College of Art and Design	FL	46,130	SP
Rochester Inst of Technology	NY	42,450	V₲
Rocky Mountain College of Art and Design	CO	22,470	NC
Salem College	NC	29,326	VC
Samford Univ	AL	35,700	V₲
San Diego State Univ	CA	20,578	VC
San Francisco State Univ	CA	18,514	C
San Jose State Univ	CA	19,707	C
Savannah College of Art and Design	GA	46,824	SP
School of the Art Inst of Chicago	IL	44,000	SP
School of Visual Arts	NY	36,500	SP
Seattle Pacific Univ	WA	41,559	V₲
S Dak State Univ	SD	14,296	C
Southern Illinois Univ Carbondale	IL	21,620	C
Stephen F. Austin State Univ	TX	14,668	C
Stephens College	MO	34,500	VC
Suffolk Univ	MA	46,548	C
Texas A&M Univ at Kingsville	TX	7,500	LC
Texas Christian Univ	TX	47,570	HC
Texas State Univ	TX	16,495	VC
Texas Tech Univ	TX	14,243	C
Ohio State Univ	OH	19,887	MC
Univ of Akron	OH	20,436	C
Univ of Alabama at Tuscaloosa	AL	17,164	₲
Univ of Arkansas at Fayetteville	AR	16,860	VC
Univ of Bridgeport	CT	39,030	LC
Univ of Central Arkansas	AR	10,840	VC
Univ of Central Missouri	MO	14,605	C
Univ of Central Okla	OK	12,293	C
Univ of Charleston	WV	28,650	C
Univ of Florida	FL	15,783	H₲
Univ of Idaho	ID	14,558	C
Univ of Kansas	KS	16,980	₲
Univ of Louisiana at Lafayette	LA	6,130	C
Univ of Minn/Twin Cities	MN		HC
Univ of Nebr - Lincoln	NE	17,507	VC
Univ of Nebr at Kearney	NE	14,855	LC
Univ of Nevada, Las Vegas	NV	17,303	C
Univ of Nevada/Reno	NV	14,500	NC
Univ of New Haven	CT	47,740	C
Univ of North Alabama	AL	9,960	C
Univ of N Car at Greensboro	NC	12,848	C
Univ of North Texas	TX	15,628	C
Univ of Okla	OK	17,634	V₲
Univ of Tenn at Chattanooga	TN	16,883	C
Univ of Tenn at Knoxville	TN	20,364	V₲
Univ of Texas at Arlington	TX	10,908	LC
Univ of Texas at Austin	TX	44,074	HC
Univ of Texas at San Antonio	TX	18,372	C
Univ of the Incarnate Word	TX	35,200	LC
Univ of Wisc/Madison	WI	18,757	HC
Univ of Wisc/Stevens Point	WI	14,043	C
Utah State Univ	UT	11,803	C
Virginia Commonwealth Univ	VA	18,633	C
Virginia Polytechnic Inst and State Univ	VA	14,629	HC
Washington State Univ	WA	20,461	C
Wentworth Inst of Technology	MA	29,800	SP
West Virginia Univ	WV	15,794	₲
Western Carolina Univ	NC	13,965	₲
Western Mich Univ	MI	19,042	C
Winthrop Univ	SC	21,120	VC
Woodbury Univ	CA	34,500	LC

INTERMEDIA/MULTIMEDIA

School	ST	$IS	SR
Bard College at Simon's Rock	MA	58,963	H₲
Goddard College	VT	16,418	VC

INTERNATIONAL ACCOUNTING

School	ST	$IS	SR
Bryant Univ	RI	49,179	VC
Texas Christian Univ	TX	47,570	HC

INTERNATIONAL AGRICULTURE

School	ST	$IS	SR
Eastern Mennonite Univ	VA	38,850	VC
Iowa State Univ	IA	16,403	C
MidAmerica Nazarene Univ	KS	28,000	C
Tarleton State Univ	TX	13,489	LC
Univ of Calif at Davis	CA	24,482	HC
Utah State Univ	UT	11,803	C

INTERNATIONAL AGRICULTURE / RURAL DEVELOPMENT

School	ST	$IS	SR
Cornell Univ	NY	59,037	MC

INTERNATIONAL BUSINESS

School	ST	$IS	SR
Arkansas State Univ	AR	14,980	C
Baldwin Wallace Univ	OH	36,980	VC
Bryant Univ	RI	49,179	VC
Indiana Univ Bloomington	IN	19,358	HC
Indiana Univ Kokomo	IN	6,674	LC
Indiana Univ South Bend	IN	15,293	C
Indiana Univ Southeast	IN	15,807	LC
Indiana Univ Southeast	IN	15,807	LC
St. Louis Univ	MO	46,594	V₲
St. Mary's Univ of Minn	MN	37,015	C
Thomas Edison State College	NJ	5,700	SP
Univ of Evansville	IN	41,056	V₲
Univ of Georgia	GA	19,508	VC
Univ of Mary Hardin-Baylor	TX	31,950	₲
Univ of Wisc/Eau Claire	WI	15,430	VC
Univ of Wisc-Milwaukee	WI	18,436	C

INTERNATIONAL BUSINESS INFORMATION SYSTEMS

School	ST	$IS	SR
Bryant Univ	RI	49,179	VC
Holy Family Univ	PA	40,030	LC
Texas Christian Univ	TX	47,570	HC

INTERNATIONAL BUSINESS MANAGEMENT

School	ST	$IS	SR
Adams State College	CO	13,358	LC
Adrian College	MI	33,800	C
Alma College	MI	42,400	VC
Alverno College	WI	30,483	LC
American International College	MA	36,100	LC
American Univ	DC	54,829	H₲
Angelo State Univ	TX	15,049	NC
Appalachian State Univ	NC	12,919	VC
Aquinas College	MI	33,060	C
Arcadia Univ	PA	33,570	₲
Assumption College	MA	45,721	VC
Auburn Univ	AL	20,052	V₲
Augsburg College	MN	35,142	C
Augustana College	IL	43,398	HC
Avila Univ	MO	26,900	C
Baker Univ	KS	33,350	₲
Barry Univ	FL	38,190	C
Bay Path College	MA	34,565	C
Baylor Univ	TX	46,720	HC
Belmont Univ	TN	37,380	V₲
Benedictine Univ	IL	35,220	C
Berkeley College	NY	18,300	LC
Berkeley College/New Jersey	NJ	27,300	LC
Berkeley College/ Westchester Campus	NY	28,500	LC
Bethel College	IN	31,560	C
Bethune-Cookman Univ	FL	22,290	LC
Biola Univ	CA	40,320	VC
Birmingham-Southern College	AL	42,370	V₲
Boise State Univ	ID	12,802	C
Boston Univ	MA	54,130	H₲
Bradley Univ	IL	31,874	VC
Brigham Young Univ/ Hawaii	HI	8,614	VC
Bryant Univ	RI	49,179	VC
Buena Vista Univ	IA	37,954	C
Butler Univ	IN	45,898	V₲
Caldwell College	NJ	35,602	LC
Calif State Polytechnic Univ, Pomona	CA	18,932	C
Cal State, Fullerton	CA	25,188	₲
Cal State, Long Beach	CA	17,534	₲
Cal State, Sacramento	CA	16,200	C
Cal State, San Bernardino	CA	12,000	C
Campbell Univ	NC	25,500	C
Canisius College	NY	45,602	VC
Cardinal Stritch Univ	WI	24,054	C
Catawba College	NC	37,105	C
Central College	IA	36,980	VC
Central Conn State Univ	CT	19,212	C
Central Mich Univ	MI	18,066	C
Central Washington Univ	WA	11,730	C
Champlain College	VT	44,850	VC
Chatham Univ	PA	42,440	VC
Clarion Univ of Pennsylvania	PA	17,370	C
College of Charleston	SC	21,273	VC
College of the Ozarks	MO	5,605	VC
Columbia College	MO	24,578	C
Concordia College, Moorhead	MN	39,974	₲
Cornerstone Univ and Grand Rapids Theological Seminary	MI	30,866	C
Creighton Univ	NE	44,058	V₲
Davenport Univ	MI	21,002	LC
Dickinson College	PA	57,662	H₲
Dominican College	NY	31,270	C
Dominican Univ	IL	37,628	C
Dominican Univ of Calif	CA	51,250	C
Dowling College	NY	25,000	LC
Drake Univ	IA	30,980	V₲
Duquesne Univ	PA	42,017	VC
Eastern Mennonite Univ	VA	38,850	VC
Eastern Mich Univ	MI	17,001	C
Eckerd College	FL	43,902	VC
Elizabethtown College	PA	47,600	VC
Elmhurst College	IL	42,032	₲
Elmira College	NY	49,950	₲
Elms College	MA	23,900	VC
Elon Univ	NC	40,046	HC
Endicott College	MA	42,390	C
Excelsior College	NY	895	SP
Felician College	NJ	41,640	C
Ferris State Univ	MI	19,698	C
Fitchburg State Univ	MA	17,241	C
Florida Atlantic Univ	FL	17,339	C
Florida Inst of Technology	FL	48,290	VC
Florida International Univ	FL	17,747	VC
Florida State Univ	FL	15,238	HC
Fordham Univ	NY	58,927	HC
Friends Univ	KS	29,100	C
Gannon Univ	PA	37,940	C
Gardner-Webb Univ	NC	34,375	₲
George Washington Univ	DC	57,108	MC
Georgetown College	KY	38,690	C
Georgetown Univ	DC	52,910	MC
Golden Gate Univ	CA	17,000	C
Goldey-Beacom College	DE	27,493	C
Graceland Univ	IA	28,020	C
Grand Valley State Univ	MI	17,998	VC
Grove City College	PA	22,988	HC
Guilford College	NC	35,340	C
Gustavus Adolphus College	MN	48,170	HC
Gwynedd-Mercy College	PA	33,560	C
Hamline Univ	MN	44,198	VC
Harding Univ	AR	21,432	₲
Hawaii Pacific Univ	HI	36,690	C
High Point Univ	NC	39,800	C
Hilbert College	NY	28,550	C
Hillsdale College	MI	31,890	H₲
Hofstra Univ	NY	48,020	V₲
Howard Univ	DC	35,957	C
Illinois State Univ	IL	22,634	VC
Illinois Wesleyan Univ	IL	48,452	V₲
Indiana Univ of Pennsylvania	PA	20,180	LC
Iona College	NY	44,028	C
Iowa State Univ	IA	16,403	C
Jacksonville Univ	FL	37,780	C
James Madison Univ	VA	18,049	VC
John Carroll Univ	OH	44,520	₲
Johnson and Wales Univ/ Denver Campus	CO	34,368	C
Johnson and Wales Univ/ Providence Campus	RI	34,668	C
Judson Univ	IL	25,130	C
Juniata College	PA	49,340	VC
Kennesaw State Univ	GA	13,017	VC
King Univ	TN	33,140	C
King's College	PA	41,678	C
Kutztown Univ of Pennsylvania	PA	16,909	LC
La Roche College	PA	34,802	LC
La Sierra Univ	CA	35,694	VC
Lake Erie College	OH	35,704	C
Lake Superior State Univ	MI	18,121	C
Lakeland College	WI	22,990	C
Lasell College	MA	42,500	LC
Lawrence Tech Univ	MI	37,630	VC
Lenoir-Rhyne College	NC	35,984	C
Linfield College- McMinnville Campus	OR	46,166	C
Lipscomb Univ	TN	35,722	VC
Loyola Univ Chicago	IL	49,560	V₲
Loyola Univ New Orleans	LA	46,581	VC
Lynn Univ	FL	43,500	C
Madonna Univ	MI	24,540	VC
Maine Maritime Academy	ME	21,073	C
Manhattan College	NY	44,955	VC
Mansfield Univ	PA	19,468	LC
Marietta College	OH	42,135	VC
Marquette Univ	WI	43,664	V₲
Marshall Univ	WV	14,820	C
Maryville Univ of St. Louis	MO	34,920	VC
Marywood Univ	PA	40,695	C
Mass Maritime Academy	MA	15,340	C
Menlo College	CA	49,002	C
Mercer Univ	GA	44,201	V₲
Meredith College	NC	31,420	C
Merrimack College	MA	44,215	C
Messiah College	PA	39,540	VC
Metropolitan State Univ	MN	5,923	SP
MidAmerica Nazarene Univ	KS	28,000	C
Millikin Univ	IL	37,462	C
Milwaukee School of Engineering	WI	39,948	V₲
Minn State Univ, Mankato	MN	14,900	C
Minn State Univ, Moorhead	MN	13,392	C
Minot State Univ	ND	10,915	C
Missouri Southern State Univ	MO	11,910	C
Monmouth College	IL	39,290	C
Monmouth Univ	NJ	42,252	C
Montclair State Univ	NJ	22,614	C
Moravian College	PA	36,381	VC
Mount Vernon Nazarene Univ	OH	29,590	C
Murray State Univ	KY	14,944	C
Muskingum Univ	OH	30,502	C
Nazareth College of Rochester	NY	41,590	VC
Nebr Wesleyan Univ	NE	29,774	₲
Neumann Univ	PA	31,078	LC
New Mexico State Univ	NM	13,955	LC
New York Univ	NY	61,470	MC
Newbury College	MA	41,850	C
Nichols College	MA	37,240	LC
North Central College	IL	38,343	VC
North Park Univ	IL	30,130	C
Northeastern Univ	MA	55,296	MC
Northern State Univ	SD	14,021	C
Northwest Missouri State Univ	MO	14,229	C
Northwestern College	MN	24,000	C
Northwood Univ	FL	30,746	LC
Northwood Univ	MI	26,331	LC
Notre Dame de Namur Univ	CA	41,610	LC
Notre Dame of Maryland Univ	MD	27,700	C
Ohio Dominican Univ	OH	38,380	₲
Ohio Northern Univ	OH	42,075	VC
Ohio Univ	OH	20,676	VC
Ohio Wesleyan Univ	OH	49,460	₲
Okla State Univ	OK	14,310	VC
Old Dominion Univ	VA	18,662	C
Olivet College	MI	19,984	C
Olivet Nazarene Univ	IL	29,990	C
Oral Roberts Univ	OK	31,734	C
Pace Univ	NY	48,094	VC
Palm Beach Atlantic Univ	FL	33,882	LC
Pepperdine Univ	CA	55,372	H₲
Pfeiffer Univ	NC	33,700	C
Philadelphia Univ	PA	44,160	C
Pittsburg State Univ	KS	12,032	C
Queens College / The CUNY	NY	17,107	VC
Quinnipiac Univ	CT	53,580	VC
Ramapo College of New Jersey	NJ	24,938	₲
Regis Univ	CO	41,318	C
Rider Univ	NJ	45,720	C
Roberts Wesleyan College	NY	37,384	₲
Rochester Inst of Technology	NY	42,450	V₲
Roger Williams Univ	RI	45,788	C
Rollins College	FL	52,370	HC
Saginaw Valley State Univ	MI	16,869	C
St. Augustine's Univ	NC	14,000	C
St. Joseph's Univ	PA	52,272	VC
St. Mary's Univ	TX	33,854	C
St. Peter's College	NJ	44,240	C
St. Vincent College	PA	40,244	C
St. Xavier Univ	IL	32,840	C
Salem College	NC	29,326	VC
Salve Regina Univ	RI	47,250	VC
San Diego State Univ	CA	20,578	VC
San Francisco State Univ	CA	18,514	C
San Jose State Univ	CA	19,707	C
Seattle Univ	WA	47,010	V₲
Seton Hill Univ	PA	35,172	C
Simpson College	IA	36,086	VC
Slippery Rock Univ of Pennsylvania	PA	10,360	LC
Southeast Missouri State Univ	MO	14,983	LC
Southern Adventist Univ	TN	26,190	C
Southern Illinois Univ Edwardsville	IL	17,532	C
Southern New Hampshire Univ	NH	38,100	C
Southwest Baptist Univ	MO	24,710	C
Spring Hill College	AL	42,130	VC
St. Ambrose Univ	IA		C
St. Catherine Univ	MN	37,782	₲
St. Cloud State Univ	MN	10,600	C

School	ST	$IS	SR
St. Edward's Univ	TX	44,674	VC
St. Norbert College	WI	39,992	VC
St. Thomas Univ	FL	32,310	C+
Stephen F. Austin State Univ	TX	14,668	C
Stetson Univ	FL	49,512	VC+
Stonehill College	MA	46,780	VC+
Suffolk Univ	MA	46,548	C
SUNY New Paltz	NY	15,010	C
SUNY Plattsburgh / SUNY	NY	18,083	VC
Taylor Univ	IN	36,742	VC+
Temple Univ	PA	24,392	VC
Texas A&M Univ at Galveston	TX	11,258	C
Texas Tech Univ	TX	14,243	C
The College at Brockport / SUNY	NY	18,362	VC
Ohio State Univ	OH	19,887	MC
Thiel College	PA	31,378	LC
Trinity International Univ	IL	31,070	C
Truman State Univ	MO	13,546	HC
Union College	KY	28,775	C
Univ of Akron	OH	20,436	C
Univ of Arkansas at Fayetteville	AR	16,860	VC
Univ of Bridgeport	CT	39,030	LC
Univ of Dayton	OH	43,750	VC
Univ of Denver	CO	51,787	VC+
Univ of Findlay	OH	31,916	C
Univ of Hawaii at Manoa	HI	19,379	VC
Univ of Houston-Downtown	TX	6,267	LC
Univ of Indianapolis	IN	31,740	LC
Univ of La Verne	CA	47,010	VC
Univ of Maryland	MD	18,801	HC
Univ of Memphis	TN	15,094	C
Univ of Missouri-St. Louis	MO	18,304	VC
Univ of Mount Union	OH	35,130	C
Univ of Nebr - Lincoln	NE	17,507	VC
Univ of Nevada, Las Vegas	NV	17,303	C
Univ of N Car at Charlotte	NC	15,847	C
Univ of N Car at Greensboro	NC	12,848	C
Univ of North Florida	FL	15,578	VC
Univ of Okla	OK	17,634	VC+
Univ of Pittsburgh at Pittsburgh	PA	27,800	HC+
Univ of Portland	OR	47,874	VC
Univ of PR/Humacao	PR	1,877	
Univ of Rio Grande	OH	8,750	NC
Univ of San Diego	CA	53,302	HC+
Univ of San Francisco	CA	49,674	VC
Univ of Scranton	PA	51,940	VC
Univ of Southern Calif	CA	56,903	MC
Univ of Southern Miss	MS	13,170	C
Univ of St. Francis	IL	36,490	C
Univ of Tampa	FL	35,160	VC
Univ of Texas at Dallas	TX	21,046	HC
Univ of Texas-Pan American	TX	12,432	LC
Univ of Tulsa	OK	45,311	HC+
Univ of Washington	WA	14,722	VC
Univ of Wisc/La Crosse	WI	14,755	VC
Univ of Wisc/Madison	WI	18,757	HC
Univ of Wisc/Superior	WI	14,106	C
Utah State Univ	UT	11,803	C
Vanguard Univ of Southern Calif	CA	35,833	VC
Villanova Univ	PA	56,436	MC
Walsh Univ	OH	35,100	C
Wartburg College	IA	41,055	VC
Washington and Jefferson College	PA	49,990	VC
Washington State Univ	WA	20,461	C
Washington Univ in St. Louis	MO	58,818	MC
Waynesburg Univ	PA	29,100	C
Wesleyan College	GA	24,000	C+
Western Carolina Univ	NC	13,965	C
Western New Mexico Univ	NM	8,500	LC
Western Washington Univ	WA	18,519	VC
Westminster College	MO	30,490	VC
Westminster College	PA	31,290	C+
Westminster College	UT	37,708	VC
Whitworth Univ	WA	45,826	VC+
Wichita State Univ	KS	12,539	C
Widener Univ	PA	50,368	C
William Jewell College	MO	31,000	VC+
Xavier Univ	OH	43,740	VC

INTERNATIONAL ECONOMICS

School	ST	$IS	SR
Austin College	TX	36,940	HC
Belmont Univ	TN	37,380	VC+
Bethany College	WV	35,282	C
Bryant Univ	RI	49,179	VC
Cal State, Chico	CA	18,952	C
Carthage College	WI	33,000	C
Colo College	CO	54,534	MC
Cornerstone Univ and Grand Rapids Theological Seminary	MI	30,866	C
Elon Univ	NC	40,046	HC
Fitchburg State Univ	MA	17,241	C
Georgia Inst of Technology	GA	20,464	MC
La Salle Univ	PA	50,270	C
Lafayette College	PA	57,050	HC+
Louisiana State Univ	LA	18,677	VC+
Mary Baldwin College	VA	37,110	C
Middlebury College	VT	57,470	MC
Midwestern State Univ	TX	9,722	C
Pontifical Catholic Univ of PR	PR	7,310	
San Diego State Univ	CA	20,578	VC
Seattle Univ	WA	47,010	VC+
Southwestern Adventist Univ	TX	23,026	LC
St. Catherine Univ	MN	37,782	C+
St. Lawrence Univ	NY	53,740	HC
Suffolk Univ	MA	46,548	C
Texas Christian Univ	TX	47,570	HC
Texas Tech Univ	TX	14,243	C
The Catholic Univ of America	DC	52,852	VC
The College of Idaho	ID	31,277	VC
Univ of Bridgeport	CT	39,030	LC
Univ of Calif at Santa Cruz	CA	27,807	VC
Univ of Puget Sound	WA	52,648	HC+
Univ of Vermont	VT	26,120	VC+
Univ of West Georgia	GA	14,852	LC
Valparaiso Univ	IN	43,040	VC+
Washington Univ in St. Louis	MO	58,818	MC
Western Washington Univ	WA	18,519	VC

INTERNATIONAL ENTREPRENEURIAL MANAGEMENT

School	ST	$IS	SR
Bryant Univ	RI	49,179	VC
Texas Christian Univ	TX	47,570	HC

INTERNATIONAL FINANCE

School	ST	$IS	SR
Bryant Univ	RI	49,179	VC
Texas Christian Univ	TX	47,570	HC
Univ of Miami	FL	55,166	MC

INTERNATIONAL MARKETING

School	ST	$IS	SR
Bryant Univ	RI	49,179	VC
Texas Christian Univ	TX	47,570	HC
Univ of Miami	FL	55,166	MC

INTERNATIONAL POLITICAL SCIENCE

School	ST	$IS	SR
Reed College	OR	57,780	MC
Simmons College	MA	48,770	VC
Texas Christian Univ	TX	47,570	HC

INTERNATIONAL PUBLIC SERVICE

School	ST	$IS	SR
Baylor Univ	TX	46,720	HC
Union College	NE	23,270	VC
Univ of New Haven	CT	47,740	C
Univ of Texas at Dallas	TX	21,046	HC
Valparaiso Univ	IN	43,040	VC+

INTERNATIONAL REAL ESTATE FINANCE

School	ST	$IS	SR
Texas Christian Univ	TX	47,570	HC

INTERNATIONAL RELATIONS

School	ST	$IS	SR
Abilene Christian Univ	TX	38,400	VC
Agnes Scott College	GA	45,323	VC+
Alverno College	WI	30,483	LC
American International College	MA	36,100	LC
Aquinas College	MI	33,060	C
Augsburg College	MN	35,142	C
Beloit College	WI	49,970	HC
Bennington College	VT	56,990	HC+
Bethany College	WV	35,282	C
Bethel Univ	MN	34,940	VC
Boston Univ	MA	54,130	HC+
Bridgewater College	VA	39,880	C
Brigham Young Univ	UT	12,100	HC
Brown Univ	RI	56,150	MC
Bucknell Univ	PA	58,160	MC
Cal State, Chico	CA	18,952	C
Cal State, Sacramento	CA	16,200	C
Calvin College	MI	37,585	VC+
Canisius College	NY	45,602	VC
Capital Univ	OH	39,824	VC
Carleton College	MN	58,149	MC
Carroll College	MT	28,000	C
Carroll Univ	WI	24,860	C
Centre College	KY	35,000	HC+
Chaminade Univ of Honolulu	HI	31,664	C
Chatham Univ	PA	42,440	VC
Claremont McKenna College	CA	58,065	MC
Clark Univ	MA	47,020	HC+
Cleveland State Univ	OH	21,357	C
Colgate Univ	NY	50,930	MC
College of William & Mary	VA	25,085	MC
College of Wooster	OH	52,600	VC
Conn College	CT	54,970	MC
Cornell College	IA	44,930	HC
Creighton Univ	NE	44,058	VC+
Dominican Univ	IL	37,628	C
Drake Univ	IA	30,980	VC+
Duquesne Univ	PA	42,017	VC
Eastern Mich Univ	MI	17,961	C
Eastern Washington Univ	WA	16,388	C
Eckerd College	FL	43,902	VC
Edgewood College	WI	33,294	C
Florida International Univ	FL	17,747	VC
Florida State Univ	FL	15,238	HC
George Mason Univ	VA	15,724	VC
George Washington Univ	DC	57,108	MC
Georgetown Univ	DC	52,910	MC
Georgia Inst of Technology	GA	20,464	MC
Gettysburg College	PA	56,820	HC
Goucher College	MD	50,252	VC+
Grand Valley State Univ	MI	17,998	VC
Hamilton College	NY	55,620	MC
Hampshire College	MA	58,320	MC
Hawaii Pacific Univ	HI	36,690	C
Hendrix College	AR	48,436	HC+
High Point Univ	NC	39,800	C
Hobart and William Smith Colleges	NY	43,000	VC
Hunter College / The CUNY	NY	14,429	VC
Illinois College	IL	25,770	VC
Immaculata Univ	PA	43,000	C
Iowa State Univ	IA	16,403	C
Kent State Univ	OH	19,352	C
Knox College	IL		VC
La Roche College	PA	34,802	LC
Lafayette College	PA	57,050	HC+
Lake Forest College	IL	45,580	VC
Le Moyne College	NY	42,200	VC
Lehigh Univ	PA	55,080	MC
Lehman College / The CUNY	NY	5,778	LC
Lewis & Clark College	OR	52,656	VC
Linfield College-McMinnville Campus	OR	46,166	C
Lynchburg College	VA	42,645	C
Marquette Univ	WI	43,664	VC+
Marshall Univ	WV	14,820	C
Mary Baldwin College	VA	37,110	C
Maryville College	TN	33,150	VC
McKendree Univ	IL	29,920	C+
Miami Univ	OH	24,191	HC
Middle Tenn State Univ	TN	8,650	C
Mills College	CA	54,119	HC
Morningside College	IA	32,620	C
Mount Holyoke College	MA	53,596	HC+
Muskingum Univ	OH	30,502	C
New York Univ	NY	61,470	MC
North Park Univ	IL	30,130	C
Northern Arizona Univ	AZ	18,592	C
Northern Kentucky Univ	KY	15,302	LC
Northwestern State Univ of Louisiana	LA	14,368	C
Notre Dame of Maryland Univ	MD	27,700	C
Nova Southeastern Univ	FL	34,016	VC
Oakland Univ	MI	19,391	VC
Occidental College	CA	59,592	MC+
Ohio Wesleyan Univ	OH	49,460	C+
Oral Roberts Univ	OK	31,734	C
Penn State Univ/Univ Park	PA	25,404	VC
Pitzer College	CA	54,988	MC
Pomona College	CA	57,680	MC
Prescott College	AZ	33,284	C+
Princeton Univ	NJ	53,795	MC
Principia College	IL	35,140	C+
Regis College	MA	47,565	LC
Roanoke College	VA	47,996	C+
Rockhurst Univ	MO	20,625	C
Roger Williams Univ	RI	45,788	C
Rollins College	FL	52,370	HC
St. Joseph's Univ	PA	52,272	VC
St. Louis Univ	MO	46,594	VC+
St. Mary's Univ	TX	33,854	C
Salem College	NC	29,326	VC
Samford Univ	AL	35,700	VC+
San Francisco State Univ	CA	18,514	C
Seton Hall Univ	NJ	45,902	C
Shaw Univ	NC	15,488	LC
Shawnee State Univ	OH	16,545	NC
Simpson College	IA	36,086	VC
Skidmore College	NY	57,926	HC
Smith College	MA	57,524	MC
Southwestern Adventist Univ	TX	23,026	LC
St. Catherine Univ	MN	37,782	C+
St. Cloud State Univ	MN	10,600	C
St. Edward's Univ	TX	44,674	VC
St. Norbert College	WI	39,992	VC
St. Thomas Univ	FL	32,310	C+
Stanford Univ	CA	56,411	MC
Suffolk Univ	MA	46,548	C
SUNY College at Geneseo	NY	18,055	HC+
SUNY New Paltz	NY	15,010	C+
Sweet Briar College	VA	43,765	C+
Syracuse Univ	NY	54,512	HC
Taylor Univ	IN	36,742	VC+
Texas State Univ	TX	16,495	VC
Texas Wesleyan Univ	TX	29,886	C
Trinity Univ	TX	44,174	HC+
Tufts Univ	MA	58,780	MC
Univ of Arkansas at Fayetteville	AR	16,860	VC
Univ of Calif at Davis	CA	24,482	HC
Univ of Colo Boulder	CO	22,605	VC+
Univ of Delaware	DE	22,728	VC
Univ of Idaho	ID	14,558	C
Univ of Indianapolis	IN	31,740	LC
Univ of Mary Washington	VA	19,484	VC
Univ of Minn/Twin Cities	MN		HC
Univ of Nevada/Reno	NV	14,500	NC
Univ of New Haven	CT	47,740	C
Univ of Northern Colo	CO	15,973	C
Univ of Pennsylvania	PA	56,106	MC
Univ of Redlands	CA	40,500	VC
Univ of Rochester	NY	58,500	MC
Univ of San Diego	CA	53,302	HC+
Univ of South Florida	FL	13,000	C
Univ of Southern Calif	CA	56,903	MC
Univ of the Pacific	CA	52,146	VC
Univ of Toledo	OH	18,464	C
Univ of Virginia	VA	22,175	MC
Univ of Washington	WA	14,722	VC
Univ of Wisc/Madison	WI	18,757	HC
Ursinus College	PA	55,630	VC+
Utah State Univ	UT	11,803	C
Valparaiso Univ	IN	43,040	VC+
Virginia Wesleyan College	VA	28,433	LC
Walsh Univ	OH	35,100	C
Wartburg College	IA	41,055	VC
Washington Univ in St. Louis	MO	58,818	MC
Webster Univ	MO	33,990	C+
Wellesley College	MA	49,848	MC
Wesleyan College	GA	24,000	C+
West Chester Univ of Pennsylvania	PA	16,836	C
Westminster College	PA	31,290	C+
Wheaton College	IL	39,650	HC+
Wheaton College	MA	54,934	HC+
Widener Univ	PA	50,368	C
William Jewell College	MO	31,000	VC+
Wittenberg Univ	OH	47,766	VC
Wright State Univ	OH	16,983	C

INTERNATIONAL SECURITY/ CONFLICT RESOLUTION MGMT

School	ST	$IS	SR
San Diego State Univ	CA	20,578	VC

INTERNATIONAL STUDIES

School	ST	$IS	SR
Adrian College	MI	33,800	C
Albion College	MI	43,884	VC
Allegheny College	PA	49,020	HC
American Univ	DC	54,829	HC+
Aquinas College	MI	33,060	C
Arcadia Univ	PA	33,570	C+
Arizona State Univ	AZ	18,818	C+
Arkansas Tech Univ	AR	13,164	LC
Ashland Univ	OH	25,000	C
Assumption College	MA	45,721	VC
Auburn Univ at Montgomery	AL	12,120	C
Augustana College	SD	35,500	VC
Austin College	TX	36,940	HC
Azusa Pacific Univ	CA	39,946	C
Baker Univ	KS	33,350	C+
Baldwin Wallace Univ	OH	36,980	VC
Bard College	NY	59,872	HC
Barry Univ	FL	38,190	C
Belhaven Univ	MS	27,170	C
Bellarmine Univ	KY	42,950	VC
Benedictine Univ	IL	35,220	C
Bennington College	VT	56,990	HC+
Bentley Univ	MA	54,555	HC+
Berry College	GA	39,254	HC
Bethel College	IN	31,560	C
Bethune-Cookman Univ	FL	22,290	LC
Binghamton Univ / The SUNY	NY	20,832	HC+
Birmingham-Southern College	AL	42,370	VC+
Bowling Green State Univ	OH	18,970	C
Bradley Univ	IL	31,874	VC
Brandeis Univ	MA	58,820	HC
Brenau Univ Women's College	GA	26,650	C+
Brigham Young Univ/ Hawaii	HI	8,614	VC
Bryant Univ	RI	49,179	VC
Bryn Mawr College	PA	57,760	MC
Butler Univ	IN	45,898	VC+
Calif Baptist Univ	CA	35,890	C
Calif Lutheran Univ	CA	47,640	C
Cal State, East Bay	CA	16,549	C
Cal State, Long Beach	CA	17,534	C+
Cal State, Monterey Bay	CA	26,871	LC
Calvin College	MI	37,585	VC+
Case Western Reserve Univ	OH	55,178	MC
Cedarville Univ	OH	31,036	VC+
Centenary College	NJ	38,618	LC
Central College	IA	36,980	VC
Central Conn State Univ	CT	19,212	C
Chestnut Hill College	PA	39,785	LC
Clark Univ	MA	47,020	HC+

INTERNATIONAL SUPPLY AND VALUE CHAIN MANAGEMENT

INTERPRETER FOR THE DEAF

INVESTMENTS AND SECURITIES

ISLAMIC STUDIES

ITALIAN

School	ST	$IS	SR
New York Univ	NY	61,470	MC
Northeastern Illinois Univ	IL		C
Northwestern Univ	IL	37,595	MC
Penn State Univ/Univ Park	PA	25,404	VC
Pepperdine Univ	CA	55,372	HC+
Princeton Univ	NJ	53,795	MC
Providence College	RI	55,995	HC
Queens College / The CUNY	NY	17,107	VC
Rutgers, The State Univ of New Jersey/New Brunswick	NJ	25,077	VC
Rutgers, The State Univ of New Jersey/Newark Campus	NJ	25,376	C
St. Joseph's Univ	PA	52,272	VC
St. Louis Univ	MO	46,594	VC+
St. Mary's College	IN	45,160	VC
San Francisco State Univ	CA	18,514	C
Sarah Lawrence College	NY	48,000	HC
Scripps College	CA	54,900	MC
Seton Hall Univ	NJ	45,902	C
Smith College	MA	57,524	MC
Southern Conn State Univ	CT	18,033	C
St. John's Univ	NY	52,840	C+
Stanford Univ	CA	56,411	MC
Susquehanna Univ	PA	49,170	C
Temple Univ	PA	24,392	VC
The Catholic Univ of America	DC	52,852	VC
Ohio State Univ	OH	19,887	MC
Thomas Edison State College	NJ	5,700	SP
Trinity College	CT		HC+
Tufts Univ	MA	58,780	MC
Tulane Univ	LA	58,942	MC
Univ at Buffalo / The SUNY	NY	20,283	VC
Univ of Arizona	AZ	20,105	C
Univ of Calif at Berkeley	CA	23,322	MC
Univ of Calif at Davis	CA	24,482	HC
Univ of Calif at Los Angeles	CA	25,686	MC
Univ of Colo Boulder	CO	22,605	VC+
Univ of Delaware	DE	22,728	VC
Univ of Denver	CO	51,787	VC+
Univ of Georgia	GA	19,508	VC
Univ of Illinois at Chicago	IL	24,293	VC
Univ of Illinois at Urbana-Champaign	IL	24,300	HC
Univ of Iowa	IA	17,481	VC
Univ of Kentucky	KY	19,868	C
Univ of Mass Boston	MA	11,966	C
Univ of Mich/Ann Arbor	MI	22,102	HC+
Univ of Minn/Twin Cities	MN		HC
Univ of Notre Dame	IN		MC
Univ of Okla	OK	17,634	VC+
Univ of Oregon	OR	20,872	VC
Univ of Pittsburgh at Pittsburgh	PA	27,800	HC+
Univ of South Florida	FL	13,000	C
Univ of Southern Calif	CA	56,903	MC
Univ of Tenn at Knoxville	TN	20,364	VC+
Univ of Texas at Austin	TX	44,074	HC
Univ of Virginia	VA	22,175	MC
Univ of Washington	WA	14,722	VC
Univ of Wisc/Madison	WI	18,757	HC
Villanova Univ	PA	56,436	MC
Washington Univ in St. Louis	MO	58,818	MC
Yale Univ	CT	55,300	MC
Youngstown State Univ	OH	16,374	LC

ITALIAN STUDIES

School	ST	$IS	SR
Assumption College	MA	45,721	VC
Bard College	NY	59,872	HC
Boston Univ	MA	54,130	HC+
Brown Univ	RI	56,150	MC
College of Staten Island / The CUNY	NY	16,778	NC
College of the Holy Cross	MA	56,232	MC
Colo College	CO	54,534	MC
Columbia Univ in the City of New York	NY	61,116	MC
Columbia Univ/School of General Studies	NY	54,083	MC
Conn College	CT	54,970	MC
Dickinson College	PA	57,662	HC+
Duke Univ	NC	50,250	MC
Emory Univ	GA	45,000	MC
Fordham Univ	NY	58,927	HC
Gonzaga Univ	WA	44,247	HC
Ithaca College	NY	52,300	HC
Lake Erie College	OH	35,704	C
Miami Univ	OH	24,191	HC
New York Univ	NY	61,470	MC
Purdue Univ/West Lafayette	IN	20,278	HC
Rosemont College	PA	42,350	C
Santa Clara Univ	CA	54,702	MC
Scripps College	CA	54,900	MC
Southern Methodist Univ	TX	57,755	MC
Stony Brook Univ / SUNY	NY	19,359	HC
Syracuse Univ	NY	54,512	HC
Univ of Calif at Los Angeles	CA	25,686	MC
Univ of Calif at San Diego	CA	21,000	VC
Univ of Calif at Santa Barbara	CA	27,551	HC
Univ of Calif at Santa Cruz	CA	27,807	VC
Univ of Conn	CT	23,744	HC
Univ of Houston	TX	19,184	VC
Univ of Illinois at Chicago	IL	24,293	VC
Univ of Maryland	MD	18,801	HC
Univ of Mass Amherst	MA	23,697	VC+
Univ of Pennsylvania	PA	56,106	MC
Univ of San Diego	CA	53,302	HC+
Univ of Vermont	VT	26,120	VC+
Univ of Wisc-Milwaukee	WI	18,436	C
Wellesley College	MA	49,848	MC
Wesleyan Univ	CT	59,844	MC
Wheaton College	MA	54,934	HC+
Youngstown State Univ	OH	16,374	LC

JAPANESE

School	ST	$IS	SR
American Univ	DC	54,829	HC+
Ball State Univ	IN	17,850	C
Bates College	ME	58,950	MC
Bennington College	VT	56,990	HC+
Brigham Young Univ	UT	12,100	HC
Cal State, Fullerton	CA	25,188	C+
Cal State, Long Beach	CA	17,534	C+
Cal State, Los Angeles	CA	15,829	C
Calvin College	MI	37,585	VC+
Central Washington Univ	WA	11,730	C
Colgate Univ	NY	50,930	MC
Conn College	CT	54,970	MC
Eastern Mich Univ	MI	17,961	C
Elizabethtown College	PA	47,600	VC
Emory Univ	GA	45,000	MC
George Washington Univ	DC	57,108	MC
Georgetown Univ	DC	52,910	MC
Harvard Univ/Harvard College	MA	49,000	MC
Lawrence Univ	WI	46,371	HC
Linfield College-McMinnville Campus	OR	46,166	C
Macalester College	MN	53,419	MC
Marshall Univ	WV	14,820	C
Middlebury College	VT	57,470	MC
Murray State Univ	KY	14,944	C
North Central College	IL	38,343	VC
Oakland Univ	MI	19,391	VC
Occidental College	CA	59,592	MC+
Pacific Univ	OR	42,815	C
Penn State Univ/Univ Park	PA	25,404	VC
Pomona College	CA	57,680	MC
Portland State Univ	OR	18,672	C
Purdue Univ/West Lafayette	IN	20,278	HC
San Diego State Univ	CA	20,578	VC
San Francisco State Univ	CA	18,514	C
San Jose State Univ	CA	19,707	C
Scripps College	CA	54,900	MC
Stanford Univ	CA	56,411	MC
Ohio State Univ	OH	19,887	MC
Thomas Edison State College	NJ	5,700	SP
Tufts Univ	MA	58,780	MC
Univ of Calif at Berkeley	CA	23,322	MC
Univ of Calif at Davis	CA	24,482	HC
Univ of Calif at Irvine	CA	25,961	VC
Univ of Calif at Los Angeles	CA	25,686	MC
Univ of Calif at Riverside	CA	27,204	C
Univ of Calif at Santa Barbara	CA	27,551	HC
Univ of Colo Boulder	CO	22,605	VC+
Univ of Findlay	OH	31,916	C
Univ of Georgia	GA	19,508	VC
Univ of Hawaii at Manoa	HI	19,379	VC
Univ of Iowa	IA	17,481	VC
Univ of Maryland	MD	18,801	HC
Univ of Mass Amherst	MA	23,697	VC+
Univ of Minn/Twin Cities	MN		HC
Univ of Missouri-St. Louis	MO	18,304	VC
Univ of Montana	MT	13,670	C
Univ of Mount Union	OH	35,130	C
Univ of Notre Dame	IN		MC
Univ of Oregon	OR	20,872	VC
Univ of Pittsburgh at Pittsburgh	PA	27,800	HC+
Univ of Puget Sound	WA	52,648	HC+
Univ of Rochester	NY	58,500	MC
Univ of the Pacific	CA	52,146	VC
Univ of Utah	UT	13,462	VC
Univ of Vermont	VT	26,120	VC+
Univ of Washington	WA	14,722	VC
Univ of Wisc/Madison	WI	18,757	HC
Vassar College	NY	59,070	MC
Wake Forest Univ	NC	51,000	MC
Washington Univ in St. Louis	MO	58,818	MC
Wellesley College	MA	49,848	MC
Western Washington Univ	WA	18,519	VC
Yale Univ	CT	55,300	MC

JAPANESE STUDIES

School	ST	$IS	SR
Adrian College	MI	33,800	C
Binghamton Univ / The SUNY	NY	20,832	HC+
Boston Univ	MA	54,130	HC+
Case Western Reserve Univ	OH	55,178	MC
Earlham College	IN	49,710	VC+
Gettysburg College	PA	56,820	HC
Linfield College-McMinnville Campus	OR	46,166	C
Madonna Univ	MI	24,540	VC
New York Univ	NY	61,470	MC
Purdue Univ/West Lafayette	IN	20,278	HC
Salem International Univ	WV	18,020	C
Smith College	MA	57,524	MC
Swarthmore College	PA	57,870	MC
Univ of Alaska Fairbanks	AK	13,955	C
Univ of Calif at San Diego	CA	21,000	VC
Univ of Hawaii at Hilo	HI	6,500	C
Univ of N Car at Charlotte	NC	15,847	C
Wellesley College	MA	49,848	MC
Willamette Univ	OR	56,450	VC+
William Jewell College	MO	31,000	VC+

JAZZ

School	ST	$IS	SR
Alabama A&M Univ	AL	96,100	C
Aquinas College	MI	33,060	C
Bennington College	VT	56,990	HC+
Berklee College of Music	MA	47,100	SP
Bowling Green State Univ	OH	18,970	C
Brigham Young Univ	UT	12,100	HC
Cal State, Fresno	CA	17,405	C
DePaul Univ	IL	46,120	VC
Eastman School of Music	NY	58,802	SP
Elmhurst College	IL	42,032	C+
Five Towns College	NY	34,550	SP
Florida Atlantic Univ	FL	17,339	C
Florida State Univ	FL	15,238	HC
Hofstra Univ	NY	48,020	VC+
Howard Univ	DC	35,957	C
Indiana Univ Bloomington	IN	19,358	HC
Ithaca College	NY	52,300	HC
Johnson State College	VT	16,721	C
Limestone College	SC	29,880	C
Loyola Univ New Orleans	LA	46,581	VC
Manhattan School of Music	NY	55,850	SP
Marshall Univ	WV	14,820	C
Mich State Univ	MI	13,689	VC
New England Conservatory of Music	MA	52,550	SP
N Car Central Univ	NC	9,000	LC
North Central College	IL	38,343	VC
Northwestern Univ	IL	37,595	MC
Roosevelt Univ	IL	22,605	VC
Rowan Univ	NJ	23,570	VC
San Jose State Univ	CA	19,707	C
Shenandoah Univ	VA	39,268	C
Temple Univ	PA	24,392	VC
Texas State Univ	TX	16,495	VC
Ohio State Univ	OH	19,887	MC
Tulane Univ	LA	58,942	MC
Univ of Cincinnati	OH	20,199	VC
Univ of Denver	CO	51,787	VC+
Univ of Hartford	CT	42,674	C
Univ of Iowa	IA	17,481	VC
Univ of Maine at Augusta	ME	6,855	C
Univ of Miami	FL	55,166	MC
Univ of Mich/Ann Arbor	MI	22,102	HC+
Univ of Minn/Duluth	MN	18,964	C+
Univ of N Car at Greensboro	NC	12,848	C
Univ of North Florida	FL	15,578	VC
Univ of North Texas	TX	15,628	C
Univ of Oregon	OR	20,872	VC
Univ of Rochester	NY	58,500	MC
Univ of Southern Calif	CA	56,903	MC
Univ of Washington	WA	14,722	VC
Webster Univ	MO	33,990	C+
Western Mich Univ	MI	19,042	C
Youngstown State Univ	OH	16,374	LC

JOURNALISM

School	ST	$IS	SR
Abilene Christian Univ	TX	38,400	VC
Adrian College	MI	33,800	C
Alabama A&M Univ	AL	96,100	C
American Jewish Univ	CA	32,600	C
American Univ	DC	54,829	HC+
Andrews Univ	MI	28,030	C+
Angelo State Univ	TX	15,049	NC
Appalachian State Univ	NC	12,919	VC
Aquinas College	MI	33,060	C
Arizona State Univ	AZ	18,818	C+
Arkansas State Univ	AR	14,980	C
Arkansas Tech Univ	AR	13,164	LC
Asbury Univ	KY	32,038	VC
Ashland Univ	OH	25,000	C
Auburn Univ	AL	20,052	VC+
Augustana College	SD	35,500	VC
Averett Univ	VA	36,000	LC
Ball State Univ	IN	17,850	C
Baylor Univ	TX	46,720	HC
Belmont Univ	TN	37,380	VC+
Bemidji State Univ	MN	13,500	C
Benedict College	SC	20,454	NC
Benedictine College	KS	29,180	VC
Bennington College	VT	56,990	HC+
Bethel College	IN	31,560	C
Bethel Univ	MN	34,940	VC
Biola Univ	CA	40,320	VC
Boston Univ	MA	54,130	HC+
Bowling Green State Univ	OH	18,970	C
Briar Cliff Univ	IA	29,514	C
Buffalo State/State Univ of Buffalo	NY	15,733	C+
Butler Univ	IN	45,898	VC+
Calif Baptist Univ	CA	35,890	C
Calif Polytechnic State Univ	CA	19,847	HC
Cal State, Chico	CA	18,952	C
Cal State, Fresno	CA	17,405	C
Cal State, Fullerton	CA	25,188	C+
Cal State, Long Beach	CA	17,534	C+
Cal State, Northridge	CA	28,313	C
Cal State, Sacramento	CA	16,200	C
Campbell Univ	NC	25,500	C
Canisius College	NY	45,602	VC
Carnegie Mellon Univ	PA	51,260	MC
Cedarville Univ	OH	31,036	VC+
Central Conn State Univ	CT	19,212	C
Central Mich Univ	MI	18,066	C
Central State Univ	OH	9,010	C
Central Univ of Bayamon	PR	3,350	
Central Washington Univ	WA	11,730	C
Champlain College	VT	44,850	VC
CUNY/Baruch College	NY	15,831	VC
CUNY/Brooklyn College	NY	5,884	C+
College of St. Scholastica	MN	39,960	C
College of the Ozarks	MO	5,605	VC
Colo State Univ-Fort Collins	CO	20,090	VC
Colo State Univ-Pueblo	CO	13,532	LC
Columbia College Chicago	IL	30,940	LC
Concordia College, Moorhead	MN	39,974	C+
Concordia Univ, Ann Arbor	MI	27,220	VC
Corban Univ	OR	34,764	C
Creighton Univ	NE	44,058	VC+
Delaware State Univ	DE	14,700	LC
Delta State Univ	MS	12,292	LC
DePaul Univ	IL	46,120	VC
Dickinson State Univ	ND	8,550	NC
Doane College	NE	33,730	VC
Dominican Univ	IL	37,628	C
Dordt College	IA	34,160	VC
Drake Univ	IA	30,980	VC+
Duquesne Univ	PA	42,017	VC
Eastern Illinois Univ	IL	20,502	C
Eastern Kentucky Univ	KY	11,161	C
Eastern Mich Univ	MI	17,961	C
Eastern Nazarene College	MA	30,000	C
Eastern Washington Univ	WA	16,388	C
Edinboro Univ of Pennsylvania	PA	15,940	LC
Elon Univ	NC	40,046	HC
Emerson College	MA	50,246	HC
Emory and Henry College	VA	387,460	C
Emory Univ	GA	45,000	MC
Evangel Univ	MO	23,090	C
Felician College	NJ	41,640	C
Florida A&M Univ	FL	14,935	LC
Florida Atlantic Univ	FL	17,339	C
Florida Southern College	FL	38,240	VC
Fordham Univ	NY	58,927	HC
Franklin College	IN	35,885	C
Freed-Hardeman Univ	TN	19,697	VC
Gannon Univ	PA	37,940	C
George Washington Univ	DC	57,108	MC
Georgia College and State Univ	GA	18,216	VC
Georgia State Univ	GA	12,000	VC
Gonzaga Univ	WA	44,247	HC
Goshen College	IN	35,900	VC
Grace College and Theological Seminary	IN	28,800	C
Grand Valley State Univ	MI	17,998	VC
Grand View Univ	IA	31,050	C
Hampshire College	MA	58,320	MC
Harding Univ	AR	21,432	C+
Hawaii Pacific Univ	HI	36,690	C
Hofstra Univ	NY	48,020	VC+
Howard Univ	DC	35,957	C
Humboldt State Univ	CA	18,400	C
Huntington Univ	IN	32,220	C
Illinois State Univ	IL	22,634	VC
Indiana State Univ	IN	16,000	C
Indiana Univ Bloomington	IN	19,358	HC
Indiana Univ of Pennsylvania	PA	20,180	LC
Indiana Univ South Bend	IN	15,293	C
Indiana Univ Southeast	IN	15,807	LC
Indiana Univ-Purdue Univ Indianapolis	IN	17,290	C
Iowa State Univ	IA	16,403	C
Ithaca College	NY	52,300	HC
John Brown Univ	AR	30,996	VC+
Johnson State College	VT	16,721	C
Kansas State Univ	KS	15,497	VC
Keene State College	NH	21,538	C
Lasell College	MA	42,500	LC
Le Moyne College	NY	42,200	VC
Lehigh Univ	PA	55,080	MC
Lenoir-Rhyne College	NC	35,984	C
Lewis Univ	IL	23,050	C
Lincoln Univ	MO	11,996	NC

School	ST	$IS	SR
Linfield College-McMinnville Campus	OR	46,166	C
Lipscomb Univ	TN	35,722	VC
Lock Haven Univ of Pennsylvania	PA	17,587	LC
LIU/Brooklyn Campus	NY	26,500	C
LIU/C.W. Post Campus	NY	38,888	C
Loras College	IA	37,432	VC
Louisiana College	LA	15,746	C
Louisiana State Univ	LA	18,677	V₲
Louisiana Tech Univ	LA	8,000	C
Loyola Univ Chicago	IL	49,560	V₲
Lyndon State College	VT	14,233	C
Madonna Univ	MI	24,540	VC
Malone Univ	OH	34,334	C
Manhattan College	NY	44,955	VC
Mansfield Univ	PA	19,468	LC
Marietta College	OH	42,135	VC
Marquette Univ	WI	43,664	V₲
Marshall Univ	WV	14,820	C
Mercer Univ	GA	44,201	V₲
Mercy College	NY	29,996	C
Mercyhurst Univ	PA	40,700	C
Messiah College	PA	39,540	VC
Metropolitan State Univ of Denver	CO	4,835	LC
Miami Univ	OH	24,191	HC
Mich State Univ	MI	13,689	VC
Midland Univ	NE	34,000	C
Millikin Univ	IL	37,462	C
Minn State Univ, Mankato	MN	14,900	C
Minn State Univ, Moorhead	MN	13,000	C
Missouri Baptist Univ	MO	30,310	C
Missouri State Univ	MO	13,996	VC
Mount Ida College	MA	30,115	LC
Mount Marty College	SD	29,638	C
Mount Mercy Univ	IA	34,385	C
Mount Vernon Nazarene Univ	OH	29,590	C
Murray State Univ	KY	14,944	C
Muskingum Univ	OH	30,502	C
New Mexico State Univ	NM	13,955	LC
New York Univ	NY	61,470	MC
Nicholls State Univ	LA	7,095	C
Norfolk State Univ	VA	10,531	LC
North Central College	IL	38,343	VC
Northeastern State Univ	OK	8,615	VC
Northeastern Univ	MA	55,296	MC
Northern Arizona Univ	AZ	18,592	C
Northern Illinois Univ	IL	19,768	C
Northern Kentucky Univ	KY	15,302	LC
Northwest Missouri State Univ	MO	14,229	C
Northwest Nazarene Univ	ID	24,275	NC
Northwest Univ	WA	18,854	C
Northwestern College	MN	24,000	C
Northwestern College of Iowa	IA	34,848	₲
Northwestern Univ	IL	37,595	MC
Oakland Univ	MI	19,391	VC
Ohio Northern Univ	OH	42,075	VC
Ohio Univ	OH	20,676	VC
Ohio Wesleyan Univ	OH	49,460	₲
Okla Baptist Univ	OK	28,202	VC
Okla Christian Univ	OK	24,975	VC
Okla State Univ	OK	14,310	VC
Old Dominion Univ	VA	18,662	C
Olivet College	MI	19,984	C
Olivet Nazarene Univ	IL	29,990	C
Oswego / SUNY	NY	20,009	VC
Otterbein College	OH	32,214	C
Pacific Union College	CA	28,150	VC
Palm Beach Atlantic Univ	FL	33,882	LC
Penn State Univ/Univ Park	PA	25,404	VC
Pepperdine Univ	CA	55,372	H₲
Pittsburg State Univ	KS	12,032	C
Point Loma Nazarene Univ	CA	38,610	VC
Point Park Univ	PA	36,390	C
Prairie View A&M Univ	TX	15,205	LC
Prescott College	AZ	33,284	₲
Purchase College / SUNY	NY	16,951	C
Purdue Univ/West Lafayette	IN	20,278	HC
Quinnipiac Univ	CT	53,580	VC
Rider Univ	NJ	45,720	C
Roger Williams Univ	RI	45,788	C
Roosevelt Univ	IL	22,605	VC
Rowan Univ	NJ	23,570	VC
Rust College	MS	10,600	C
Rutgers, The State Univ of New Jersey/New Brunswick	NJ	25,077	VC
Rutgers, The State Univ of New Jersey/Newark Campus	NJ	25,376	C
St. Mary-of-the-Woods College	IN	37,722	LC
St. Mary's Univ of Minn	MN	37,015	C
St. Michael's College	VT	48,740	VC
Sam Houston State Univ	TX	17,082	C
Samford Univ	AL	35,700	V₲
San Diego State Univ	CA	20,578	VC
San Francisco State Univ	CA	18,514	C
San Jose State Univ	CA	19,707	C
Seattle Univ	WA	47,010	V₲
Seton Hall Univ	NJ	45,902	C
Seton Hill Univ	PA	35,172	C
Shippensburg Univ of Pennsylvania	PA	17,064	LC
Simpson College	IA	36,086	VC
S Dak State Univ	SD	14,296	C
Southeast Missouri State Univ	MO	14,983	LC
Southeastern Univ	FL	27,201	₲
Southern Adventist Univ	TN	26,190	C
Southern Arkansas Univ	AR	14,316	C
Southern Conn State Univ	CT	18,033	C
Southern Illinois Univ Carbondale	IL	21,620	C
Southern Illinois Univ Edwardsville	IL	17,532	C
Southern Methodist Univ	TX	57,755	MC
Southern Nazarene Univ	OK	24,354	NC
Southern Univ at New Orleans	LA	1,000	NC
Southwest Baptist Univ	MO	24,710	C
Southwestern Adventist Univ	TX	23,026	LC
Spring Hill College	AL	42,130	VC
St. Bonaventure Univ	NY	38,831	C
St. Cloud State Univ	MN	10,600	C
St. John's Univ	NY	52,840	₲
St. Joseph's College, New York / Brooklyn Campus	NY	21,878	C
St. Joseph's College, New York / Suffolk Campus	NY	21,878	VC
Stephen F. Austin State Univ	TX	14,668	C
Suffolk Univ	MA	46,548	C
SUNY Fredonia / The SUNY at Fredonia	NY	18,702	VC
SUNY New Paltz	NY	15,010	C
SUNY Plattsburgh / SUNY	NY	18,083	VC
Syracuse Univ	NY	54,512	HC
Taylor Univ	IN	36,742	V₲
Temple Univ	PA	24,392	VC
Tenn Tech Univ	TN	11,310	C
Texas A&M Univ	TX	16,956	V₲
Texas A&M Univ at Commerce	TX	10,496	C
Texas Christian Univ	TX	47,570	HC
Texas State Univ	TX	16,495	VC
Texas Tech Univ	TX	14,243	C
Texas Wesleyan Univ	TX	29,886	C
The College at Brockport / SUNY	NY	18,362	VC
The Lincoln Univ	PA	15,154	LC
Ohio State Univ	OH	19,887	MC
Thomas Edison State College	NJ	5,700	SP
Tougaloo College	MS	15,275	NC
Trevecca Nazarene Univ	TN	30,118	C
Troy Univ	AL	10,650	C
Truman State Univ	MO	13,546	HC
Tulane Univ	LA	58,942	MC
Union College	NE	23,270	VC
Union Univ	TN	28,260	VC
Univ of Alabama at Tuscaloosa	AL	17,164	₲
Univ of Alaska Anchorage	AK	15,290	NC
Univ of Alaska Fairbanks	AK	13,955	C
Univ of Arizona	AZ	20,105	C
Univ of Arkansas at Fayetteville	AR	16,860	VC
Univ of Arkansas at Little Rock	AR		C
Univ of Arkansas at Pine Bluff	AR	10,600	C
Univ of Bridgeport	CT	39,030	LC
Univ of Calif at Irvine	CA	25,961	VC
Univ of Central Arkansas	AR	10,840	VC
Univ of Central Florida	FL	15,711	V₲
Univ of Central Missouri	MO	14,605	C
Univ of Central Okla	OK	12,293	C
Univ of Colo Boulder	CO	22,605	V₲
Univ of Conn	CT	23,744	HC
Univ of Delaware	DE	22,728	VC
Univ of Denver	CO	51,787	V₲
Univ of Florida	FL	15,783	H₲
Univ of Georgia	GA	19,508	VC
Univ of Hawaii at Manoa	HI	19,379	VC
Univ of Idaho	ID	14,558	C
Univ of Illinois at Urbana-Champaign	IL	24,300	HC
Univ of Indianapolis	IN	31,740	LC
Univ of Iowa	IA	17,481	VC
Univ of Kansas	KS	16,980	₲
Univ of Kentucky	KY	19,868	C
Univ of La Verne	CA	47,010	VC
Univ of Maine	ME	19,712	₲
Univ of Mary Hardin-Baylor	TX	31,950	₲
Univ of Maryland	MD	18,801	HC
Univ of Mass Amherst	MA	23,697	V₲
Univ of Memphis	TN	15,094	C
Univ of Miami	FL	55,166	MC
Univ of Miss	MS	15,482	VC
Univ of Missouri/Columbia	MO	18,201	MC
Univ of Montana	MT	13,670	C
Univ of Montevallo	AL	17,320	C
Univ of Nebr - Lincoln	NE	17,507	VC
Univ of Nebr at Kearney	NE	14,855	LC
Univ of Nebr at Omaha	NE	12,700	C
Univ of Nevada/Reno	NV	14,500	NC
Univ of New Haven	CT	47,740	C
Univ of New Mexico	NM	15,300	C
Univ of North Alabama	AL	9,960	C
Univ of N Car at Chapel Hill	NC	18,348	MC
Univ of North Texas	TX	15,628	C
Univ of Northern Colo	CO	15,973	C
Univ of Okla	OK	17,634	V₲
Univ of Oregon	OR	20,872	VC
Univ of Pittsburgh at Johnstown	PA	20,862	LC
Univ of PR Recinto de Rio Piedras	PR	5,750	
Univ of S Car at Columbia	SC	19,725	V₲
Univ of S Dak	SD	15,111	C
Univ of Southern Calif	CA	56,903	MC
Univ of Southern Indiana	IN	14,657	C
Univ of Southern Miss	MS	13,170	C
Univ of St. Francis	IL	36,490	C
Univ of Tenn at Knoxville	TN	20,364	V₲
Univ of Texas at Arlington	TX	10,908	LC
Univ of Texas at Austin	TX	44,074	HC
Univ of Texas at El Paso	TX	8,764	NC
Univ of Texas-Pan American	TX	12,432	LC
Univ of West Georgia	GA	14,852	LC
Univ of Wisc Whitewater	WI	13,314	C
Univ of Wisc/Eau Claire	WI	15,430	VC
Univ of Wisc/Madison	WI	18,757	HC
Univ of Wisc/Oshkosh	WI	10,426	LC
Univ of Wisc/River Falls	WI	9,722	LC
Univ of Wyoming	WY	13,855	₲
Utah State Univ	UT	11,803	C
Utica College	NY	44,704	C
Virginia Union Univ	VA	18,432	C
Virginia Wesleyan College	VA	28,433	LC
Wartburg College	IA	41,055	VC
Washington Adventist Univ	MD	25,859	₲
Washington and Lee Univ	VA	52,812	MC
Washington State Univ	WA	20,461	C
Washington Univ in St. Louis	MO	58,818	MC
Wayne State Univ	MI	19,493	C
Webster Univ	MO	33,990	₲
West Virginia Univ	WV	15,794	₲
Western Illinois Univ	IL	20,130	C
Western Kentucky Univ	KY	11,000	LC
Western Mich Univ	MI	19,042	C
Western Washington Univ	WA	18,519	VC
Whitworth Univ	WA	45,826	V₲
William Penn Univ	IA	26,000	C
William Woods Univ	MO		C
Wilmington College	OH	29,784	C
Wingate Univ	NC	34,990	C
Winona State Univ	MN	16,530	C
Youngstown State Univ	OH	16,374	LC

JOURNALISM EDUCATION

School	ST	$IS	SR
Baylor Univ	TX	46,720	HC
Cal State, Northridge	CA	28,313	C
Carlow Univ	PA	30,272	C
Georgia Southern Univ	GA	16,414	C
Grace College and Theological Seminary	IN	28,800	C
Univ of Nebr - Lincoln	NE	17,507	VC
Wartburg College	IA	41,055	VC
Webster Univ	MO	33,990	₲

JUDAIC STUDIES

School	ST	$IS	SR
Albert A. List College of Jewish Studies	NY	21,600	
American Jewish Univ	CA	32,600	C
American Univ	DC	54,829	H₲
Arizona State Univ	AZ	18,818	₲
Bard College	NY	59,872	HC
Bennington College	VT	56,990	H₲
Binghamton Univ / The SUNY	NY	20,832	H₲
Brandeis Univ	MA	58,820	HC
Brown Univ	RI	56,150	MC
CUNY/Brooklyn College	NY	5,884	₲
DePaul Univ	IL	46,120	VC
Dickinson College	PA	57,662	H₲
Emory Univ	GA	45,000	MC
Florida Atlantic Univ	FL	17,339	C
George Washington Univ	DC	57,108	MC
Gettysburg College	PA	56,820	HC
Hampshire College	MA	58,320	MC
Hofstra Univ	NY	48,020	V₲
Hunter College / The CUNY	NY	14,429	VC
Indiana Univ Bloomington	IN	19,358	HC
New York Univ	NY	61,470	MC
Northeastern Univ	MA	55,296	MC
Oberlin College	OH	57,025	MC
Purdue Univ/West Lafayette	IN	20,278	HC
Queens College / The CUNY	NY	17,107	VC
Rutgers, The State Univ of New Jersey/New Brunswick	NJ	25,077	VC
San Francisco State Univ	CA	18,514	C
Scripps College	CA	54,900	MC
Smith College	MA	57,524	MC
Syracuse Univ	NY	54,512	HC
Ohio State Univ	OH	19,887	MC
Touro College	NY	23,150	VC
Trinity College	CT		H₲
Tufts Univ	MA	58,780	MC
Tulane Univ	LA	58,942	MC
Univ of Arizona	AZ	20,105	C
Univ of Calif at Los Angeles	CA	25,686	MC
Univ of Calif at San Diego	CA	21,000	VC
Univ of Chicago	IL	55,416	MC
Univ of Cincinnati	OH	20,199	VC
Univ of Colo Boulder	CO	22,605	V₲
Univ of Denver	CO	51,787	V₲
Univ of Florida	FL	15,783	H₲
Univ of Hartford	CT	42,674	C
Univ of Illinois at Chicago	IL	24,293	VC
Univ of Maryland	MD	18,801	HC
Univ of Mass Amherst	MA	23,697	V₲
Univ of Miami	FL	55,166	MC
Univ of Mich/Ann Arbor	MI	22,102	H₲
Univ of Missouri-Kansas City	MO	19,603	C
Univ of Okla	OK	17,634	V₲
Univ of Oregon	OR	20,872	VC
Univ of Pennsylvania	PA	56,106	MC
Univ of Southern Calif	CA	56,903	MC
Univ of Texas at Austin	TX	44,074	HC
Univ of Washington	WA	14,722	VC
Univ of Wisc/Madison	WI	18,757	HC
Univ of Wisc-Milwaukee	WI	18,436	C
Vassar College	NY	59,070	MC
Washington Univ in St. Louis	MO	58,818	MC
Wellesley College	MA	49,848	MC
Yale Univ	CT	55,300	MC

JUSTICE AND SOCIETY

School	ST	$IS	SR
Creighton Univ	NE	44,058	V₲
Goddard College	VT	16,418	VC

KEYBOARD - PIANO CONCENTRATION

School	ST	$IS	SR
Baldwin Wallace Univ	OH	36,980	VC
Cedarville Univ	OH	31,036	V₲
Chapman Univ	CA	56,019	V₲
Ouachita Baptist Univ	AR	29,010	VC
Texas Christian Univ	TX	47,570	HC
Youngstown State Univ	OH	16,374	LC

KINESIOLOGY

School	ST	$IS	SR
Calif Polytechnic State Univ	CA	19,847	HC
Cal State, Fullerton	CA	25,188	₲
Chapman Univ	CA	56,019	V₲
Hanover College	IN	41,450	VC
Indiana Univ Bloomington	IN	19,358	HC
Indiana Univ Bloomington	IN	19,358	HC
Indiana Univ-Purdue Univ Indianapolis	IN	17,290	C
Nova Southeastern Univ	FL	34,016	VC
St. Louis Univ	MO	46,594	V₲
Shenandoah Univ	VA	39,268	C
Univ of Georgia	GA	19,508	VC
Univ of Louisiana at Monroe	LA	12,998	C
Univ of Maine	ME	19,712	₲
Univ of Wisc/Madison	WI	18,757	HC
Univ of Wyoming	WY	13,855	₲
Western Illinois Univ	IL	20,130	C

KITCHEN AND BATH DESIGN

School	ST	$IS	SR
Thomas Edison State College	NJ	5,700	SP

KNOWLEDGE MANAGEMENT

School	ST	$IS	SR
St. Louis Univ	MO	46,594	V₲

KOREAN

School	ST	$IS	SR
American Univ	DC	54,829	H₲
Binghamton Univ / The SUNY	NY	20,832	H₲
Brigham Young Univ	UT	12,100	HC
Northeastern Illinois Univ	IL		C
Ohio State Univ	OH	19,887	MC
Thomas Edison State College	NJ	5,700	SP
Univ of Calif at Irvine	CA	25,961	VC
Univ of Calif at Los Angeles	CA	25,686	MC
Univ of Hawaii at Manoa	HI	19,379	VC

LABOR STUDIES

School	ST	$IS	SR
Cal State, Dominguez Hills	CA	17,056	LC
Cleveland State Univ	OH	21,357	C
Eastern Mich Univ	MI	17,961	C
Hofstra Univ	NY	48,020	V₲
Howard Univ	DC	35,957	C
Indiana Univ Bloomington	IN	19,358	HC
Indiana Univ Kokomo	IN	6,674	LC
Indiana Univ Northwest	IN	6,738	LC
Indiana Univ South Bend	IN	15,293	C

School	ST	$IS	SR
Indiana Univ-Purdue Univ Fort Wayne	IN	15,425	C
Indiana Univ-Purdue Univ Indianapolis	IN	17,290	C
Manhattan College	NY	44,955	VC
Northern Kentucky Univ	KY	15,302	LC
Penn State Univ/Univ Park	PA	25,404	VC
Queens College / The CUNY	NY	17,107	VC
Rutgers, The State Univ of New Jersey/New Brunswick	NJ	25,077	VC
San Francisco State Univ	CA	18,514	C
SUNY/Empire State College	NY	6,315	SP
SUNY College at Old Westbury	NY	16,324	C
Thomas Edison State College	NJ	5,700	SP
Univ of Akron	OH	20,436	C
Univ of Illinois at Urbana-Champaign	IL	24,300	HC
Univ of Mass Boston	MA	11,966	C
Univ of PR Recinto de Rio Piedras	PR	5,750	
Wayne State Univ	MI	19,493	C

LABORATORY ANIMAL SCIENCE

School	ST	$IS	SR
Thomas Edison State College	NJ	5,700	SP

LAND USE MANAGEMENT AND RECLAMATION

School	ST	$IS	SR
Cal State, Bakersfield	CA	8,000	LC
Eastern Mich Univ	MI	17,961	C
Humboldt State Univ	CA	18,400	C
Metropolitan State Univ of Denver	CO	4,835	LC
Montana State Univ	MT	14,068	VC
Prescott College	AZ	33,284	C+
Texas A&M Univ at Galveston	TX	11,258	C
Texas State Univ	TX	16,495	VC
Unity College	ME	34,054	C
Univ of Louisiana at Lafayette	LA	6,130	C
Univ of Okla	OK	17,634	VC+
Univ of Wisc/Platteville	WI	14,274	C
Univ of Wisc/River Falls	WI	9,722	LC

LANDSCAPE ARCHITECTURE

School	ST	$IS	SR
Calif Polytechnic State Univ	CA	19,847	HC
Cornell Univ	NY	59,037	MC
Univ of Arkansas at Fayetteville	AR	16,860	VC
Univ of Georgia	GA	19,508	VC
Univ of Maine	ME	19,712	C+
Univ of Nebr - Lincoln	NE	17,507	VC

LANDSCAPE ARCHITECTURE/DESIGN

School	ST	$IS	SR
Academy of Art Univ	CA		
Andrews Univ	MI	28,030	C+
Arizona State Univ	AZ	18,818	C+
Auburn Univ	AL	20,052	VC+
Augustana College	IL	43,398	HC
Ball State Univ	IN	17,850	C
Boston Architectural College	MA	18,622	SP
Brigham Young Univ	UT	12,100	HC
Calif State Polytechnic Univ, Pomona	CA	18,932	C
Clemson Univ	SC	19,136	HC
Colo State Univ-Fort Collins	CO	20,090	VC
CUNY-City College	NY	19,576	HC+
Florida International Univ	FL	17,747	VC
Florida Southern College	FL	38,240	VC
Iowa State Univ	IA	16,403	C
Kansas State Univ	KS	15,497	VC
Louisiana State Univ	LA	18,677	VC+
Mich State Univ	MI	13,689	VC
N Car Agricultural and Technical State Univ	NC	13,175	LC
N Car State Univ	NC	16,202	HC
N Dak State Univ	ND	14,642	C
Northeastern Univ	MA	55,296	MC
Okla State Univ	OK	14,310	VC
Penn State Univ/Univ Park	PA	25,404	VC
Philadelphia Univ	PA	44,160	C
Purdue Univ/West Lafayette	IN	20,278	HC
S Dak State Univ	SD	14,296	C
SUNY / College of Environmental Science and Forestry	NY	18,351	HC
Temple Univ	PA	24,392	VC
Texas A&M Univ	TX	16,956	VC+
Texas Tech Univ	TX	14,243	C
Ohio State Univ	OH	19,887	MC
The SUNY College of Agriculture and Tech at Cobleskill	NY	18,869	VC
Univ of Arizona	AZ	20,105	C
Univ of Arkansas at Fayetteville	AR	16,860	VC
Univ of Calif at Berkeley	CA	23,322	MC
Univ of Calif at Davis	CA	24,482	HC
Univ of Conn	CT	23,744	HC
Univ of Delaware	DE	22,728	VC
Univ of Florida	FL	15,783	HC+
Univ of Idaho	ID	14,558	C
Univ of Illinois at Urbana-Champaign	IL	24,300	HC
Univ of Kentucky	KY	19,868	C
Univ of Maine	ME	19,712	C+
Univ of Maryland	MD	18,801	HC
Univ of Mass Amherst	MA	23,697	VC+
Univ of Minn/Twin Cities	MN		HC
Univ of Nebr - Lincoln	NE	17,507	VC
Univ of Nevada, Las Vegas	NV	17,303	C
Univ of Oregon	OR	20,872	VC
Univ of Texas at Arlington	TX	10,908	LC
Univ of Texas at Austin	TX	44,074	HC
Univ of Vermont	VT	26,120	VC+
Univ of Washington	WA	14,722	VC
Univ of Wisc/Madison	WI	18,757	HC
Utah State Univ	UT	11,803	C
Virginia Polytechnic Inst and State Univ	VA	14,629	HC
Washington State Univ	WA	20,461	C
West Virginia Univ	WV	15,794	C+

LANGUAGE ARTS

School	ST	$IS	SR
Aquinas College	MI	33,060	C
Calvin College	MI	37,585	VC+
Catawba College	NC	37,105	C
Central Mich Univ	MI	18,066	C
Central Washington Univ	WA	11,730	C
College of St. Mary	NE	34,334	C
Concordia Univ, Ann Arbor	MI	27,220	VC
Eastern Mich Univ	MI	17,961	C
Lake Erie College	OH	35,704	C
LeMoyne-Owen College	TN	13,100	C
Madonna Univ	MI	24,540	VC
Malone Univ	OH	34,334	C
Marygrove College	MI	21,290	C
Miles College	AL	16,530	NC
Nebr Wesleyan Univ	NE	29,774	C+
Northern Mich Univ	MI	15,300	VC
Ohio Northern Univ	OH	42,075	VC
Ohio Univ	OH	20,676	VC
Samford Univ	AL	35,700	VC+
Seattle Pacific Univ	WA	41,559	VC+
Spring Arbor Univ	MI	26,740	C
Univ of Calif at Santa Cruz	CA	27,807	VC
Univ of Mich/Dearborn	MI	9,885	VC
Univ of Nebr - Lincoln	NE	17,507	VC
Univ of Okla	OK	17,634	VC+
Wayne State Univ	MI	19,493	C
Wells College	NY	38,680	VC
Western Kentucky Univ	KY	11,000	LC
Wright State Univ	OH	16,983	C

LANGUAGES

School	ST	$IS	SR
Adelphi Univ	NY	43,130	VC
Arkansas Tech Univ	AR	13,164	LC
Assumption College	MA	45,721	VC
Auburn Univ	AL	20,052	VC+
Austin Peay State Univ	TN	14,650	C
Baylor Univ	TX	46,720	HC
Bellarmine Univ	KY	42,950	VC
Bemidji State Univ	MN	13,500	C
Bennington College	VT	56,990	HC+
Bethany College	WV	35,282	C
Cal State, Northridge	CA	28,313	C
Cameron Univ	OK	9,267	LC
Carnegie Mellon Univ	PA	51,260	MC
Carson-Newman Univ	TN	29,058	C+
Carthage College	WI	33,000	C
Clark Atlanta Univ	GA	30,006	C
Clark Univ	MA	47,020	HC+
College of St. Scholastica	MN	39,960	C
Colo State Univ-Fort Collins	CO	20,090	VC
Columbia College	SC	27,882	C
Converse College	SC	37,130	C
Cornell College	IA	44,930	HC
Davis and Elkins College	WV	33,742	C
Denison Univ	OH	54,670	HC+
Dordt College	IA	34,160	VC
Dowling College	NY	25,000	LC
Earlham College	IN	49,710	VC+
Eastern Illinois Univ	IL	20,502	C
Elmira College	NY	49,950	C+
Excelsior College	NY	895	SP
Frostburg State Univ	MD	15,264	LC
Gordon College	MA	42,660	VC+
Grand Valley State Univ	MI	17,998	VC
Hamilton College	NY	55,620	MC
Hartwick College	NY	49,815	C+
Hunter College / The CUNY	NY	14,429	VC
Indiana Univ Bloomington	IN	19,358	HC
Ithaca College	NY	52,300	HC
Jackson State Univ	MS	13,512	LC
Lehman College / The CUNY	NY	5,778	LC
Lewis & Clark College	OR	52,656	VC
LIU/Brooklyn Campus	NY	26,500	C
Louisiana College	LA	15,746	C
McNeese State Univ	LA		C
Mercyhurst Univ	PA	40,700	C
Miss College	MS	21,998	VC
New Mexico State Univ	NM	13,955	LC
New York Univ	NY	61,470	MC
Newberry College	SC	26,850	LC
Northeastern Univ	MA	55,296	MC
Occidental College	CA	59,592	MC+
Pomona College	CA	57,680	MC
Portland State Univ	OR	18,672	C
Principia College	IL	35,140	C+
Richard Stockton College of New Jersey	NJ	20,000	VC
Roger Williams Univ	RI	45,788	C
Roosevelt Univ	IL	22,605	VC
Samford Univ	AL	35,700	VC+
San Francisco State Univ	CA	18,514	C
Scripps College	CA	54,900	MC
Southern Illinois Univ Edwardsville	IL	17,532	C
Southern Methodist Univ	TX	57,755	MC
Southern Oregon Univ	OR	17,874	C
St. Cloud State Univ	MN	10,600	C
St. John's Univ	NY	52,840	C+
St. Lawrence Univ	NY	53,740	HC
St. Mary's College of Maryland	MD	26,699	HC
Tenn State Univ	TN	9,048	C
Texas A&M Univ at Commerce	TX	10,496	C
United States Military Academy	NY		MC
Univ of Alabama at Huntsville	AL	17,625	VC
Univ of Alaska Anchorage	AK	15,290	NC
Univ of Calif at Riverside	CA	27,204	C
Univ of Central Florida	FL	15,711	VC+
Univ of Delaware	DE	22,728	VC
Univ of Denver	CO	51,787	VC+
Univ of Hartford	CT	42,674	C
Univ of Memphis	TN	15,094	C
Univ of Minn/Twin Cities	MN		HC
Univ of New Mexico	NM	15,300	C
Univ of Okla	OK	17,634	VC+
Univ of PR Recinto de Rio Piedras	PR	5,750	
Univ of South Alabama	AL	13,510	C
Univ of Southern Miss	MS	13,170	C
Univ of Texas at El Paso	TX	8,764	NC
Vassar College	NY	59,070	MC
Virginia Commonwealth Univ	VA	18,633	C
Virginia Wesleyan College	VA	28,433	LC
Washington Univ in St. Louis	MO	58,818	MC
Wilson College	PA	27,660	C
Xavier Univ of Louisiana	LA	25,300	C

LASER ELECTRO-OPTICS TECHNOLOGY

School	ST	$IS	SR
Idaho State Univ	ID	11,908	C
Oregon Inst of Technology	OR	8,910	C

LATIN

School	ST	$IS	SR
Austin College	TX	36,940	HC
Baylor Univ	TX	46,720	HC
Binghamton Univ / The SUNY	NY	20,832	HC+
Boston Univ	MA	54,130	HC+
Bowling Green State Univ	OH	18,970	C
Brigham Young Univ	UT	12,100	HC
Bryn Mawr College	PA	57,760	MC
Butler Univ	IN	45,898	VC+
Calvin College	MI	37,585	VC+
Carleton College	MN	58,149	MC
Centenary College of Louisiana	LA	39,070	C+
Colgate Univ	NY	50,930	MC
College of Wooster	OH	52,600	VC
Columbia Univ in the City of New York	NY	61,116	MC
Columbia Univ/Barnard College	NY	39,000	MC
Concordia College, Moorhead	MN	39,974	C+
Creighton Univ	NE	44,058	VC+
Denison Univ	OH	54,670	HC+
DePauw Univ	IN	48,950	HC+
Dickinson College	PA	57,662	HC+
Duquesne Univ	PA	42,017	VC
Emory Univ	GA	45,000	MC
Florida State Univ	FL	15,238	HC
Fordham Univ	NY	58,927	HC
Franklin and Marshall College	PA	58,295	MC
Furman Univ	SC	54,006	HC
Gettysburg College	PA	56,820	HC
Hampden-Sydney College	VA	48,848	C
Harvard Univ/Harvard College	MA	49,000	MC
Haverford College	PA	59,236	MC
Hofstra Univ	NY	48,020	VC+
Hope College	MI	36,320	VC+
Hunter College / The CUNY	NY	14,429	VC
Indiana Univ Bloomington	IN	19,358	HC
John Carroll Univ	OH	44,520	C+
Kent State Univ	OH	19,352	C
Kenyon College	OH	56,810	MC
Knox College	IL		VC
Lehman College / The CUNY	NY	5,778	LC
Loyola Marymount Univ	CA	53,240	VC+
Loyola Univ Chicago	IL	49,560	VC+
Loyola Univ Maryland	MD		VC
Marlboro College	VT	35,980	VC
Mercer Univ	GA	44,201	VC+
Mich State Univ	MI	13,689	VC
Missouri State Univ	MO	13,996	VC
Monmouth College	IL	39,290	C
Montclair State Univ	NJ	22,614	C
Mount Holyoke College	MA	53,596	HC+
New York Univ	NY	61,470	MC
Ohio Univ	OH	20,676	VC
Purdue Univ/West Lafayette	IN	20,278	HC
Purdue Univ/West Lafayette	IN	20,278	HC
Randolph-Macon College	VA	45,086	C
Rockford College	IL	31,000	C
Rutgers, The State Univ of New Jersey/New Brunswick	NJ	25,077	VC
St. Joseph's Univ	PA	52,272	VC
Samford Univ	AL	35,700	VC+
Santa Clara Univ	CA	54,702	MC
Sarah Lawrence College	NY	48,000	HC
Seattle Pacific Univ	WA	41,559	VC+
Sewanee: The Univ of the South	TN	47,700	HC+
Smith College	MA	57,524	MC
Southwestern Univ	TX	45,660	VC
St. Catherine Univ	MN	37,782	C+
St. Olaf College	MN	49,960	HC+
Swarthmore College	PA	57,870	MC
The Catholic Univ of America	DC	52,852	VC
Trinity Univ	TX	44,174	HC+
Tufts Univ	MA	58,780	MC
Univ of Calif at Berkeley	CA	23,322	MC
Univ of Calif at Davis	CA	24,482	HC
Univ of Calif at Los Angeles	CA	25,686	MC
Univ of Georgia	GA	19,508	VC
Univ of Iowa	IA	17,481	VC
Univ of Maine	ME	19,712	C+
Univ of Mich/Ann Arbor	MI	22,102	HC+
Univ of Minn/Twin Cities	MN		HC
Univ of Nebr - Lincoln	NE	17,507	VC
Univ of New Hampshire	NH	24,702	VC
Univ of Oregon	OR	20,872	VC
Univ of Scranton	PA	51,940	VC
Univ of Tenn at Chattanooga	TN	16,883	C
Univ of Texas at Austin	TX	44,074	HC
Univ of Vermont	VT	26,120	VC+
Univ of Wisc/Madison	WI	18,757	HC
Wabash College	IN	44,160	VC
Wake Forest Univ	NC	51,000	MC
Washington Univ in St. Louis	MO	58,818	MC
Wellesley College	MA	49,848	MC
West Chester Univ of Pennsylvania	PA	16,836	C
Western Mich Univ	MI	19,042	C
Westminster College	PA	31,290	C+
Wheaton College	MA	54,934	HC+
Wichita State Univ	KS	12,539	C
Wright State Univ	OH	16,983	C

LATIN AMERICAN STUDIES

School	ST	$IS	SR
Adelphi Univ	NY	43,130	VC
Albright College	PA	46,660	C
American Univ	DC	54,829	HC+
Appalachian State Univ	NC	12,919	VC
Arizona State Univ	AZ	18,818	C+
Assumption College	MA	45,721	VC
Austin College	TX	36,940	HC
Ball State Univ	IN	17,850	C
Bard College	NY	59,872	HC
Bates College	ME	58,950	MC
Baylor Univ	TX	46,720	HC
Bennington College	VT	56,990	HC+
Binghamton Univ / The SUNY	NY	20,832	HC+
Birmingham-Southern College	AL	42,370	VC+
Boston Univ	MA	54,130	HC+
Bowdoin College	ME	57,834	MC
Brandeis Univ	MA	58,820	HC
Brigham Young Univ	UT	12,100	HC
Brown Univ	RI	56,150	MC
Bucknell Univ	PA	58,160	MC
Cal State, Chico	CA	18,952	C
Cal State, East Bay	CA	16,549	C
Cal State, Fresno	CA	17,405	C
Cal State, Fullerton	CA	25,188	C+

School	ST	$IS	SR
Cal State, Los Angeles	CA	15,829	C
Canisius College	NY	45,602	VC
Carleton College	MN	58,149	MC
CUNY/Brooklyn College	NY	5,884	C+
Colby College	ME	57,510	MC
Colgate Univ	NY	50,930	MC
College of Charleston	SC	21,273	VC
College of William & Mary	VA	25,085	MC
Columbia Univ in the City of New York	NY	61,116	MC
Columbia Univ/School of General Studies	NY	54,083	MC
Conn College	CT	54,970	MC
Cornell College	IA	44,930	HC
CUNY-City College	NY	19,576	HC+
Dartmouth College	NH	57,996	MC
Davidson College	NC	54,683	MC
Denison Univ	OH	54,670	HC+
DePaul Univ	IL	46,120	VC
Dickinson College	PA	57,662	HC+
Earlham College	IN	49,710	VC+
Eastern Mich Univ	MI	17,961	C
Emory Univ	GA	45,000	MC
Flagler College	FL	24,960	VC
Florida State Univ	FL	15,238	HC
Fordham Univ	NY	58,927	HC
George Mason Univ	VA	15,724	VC
George Washington Univ	DC	57,108	MC
Gettysburg College	PA	56,820	HC
Hamline Univ	MN	44,198	VC
Hampshire College	MA	58,320	MC
Hobart and William Smith Colleges	NY	43,000	VC
Hofstra Univ	NY	48,020	VC+
Hood College	MD	44,630	C
Hunter College / The CUNY	NY	14,429	VC
Johns Hopkins Univ	MD	47,492	MC
Kent State Univ	OH	19,352	C
Lake Forest College	IL	45,580	VC
Lock Haven Univ of Pennsylvania	PA	17,587	LC
Loyola Univ New Orleans	LA	46,581	VC
Macalester College	MN	53,419	MC
Miami Univ	OH	24,191	HC
Middlebury College	VT	57,470	MC
Millsaps College	MS	43,888	VC+
Mount Holyoke College	MA	53,596	HC+
New College of Florida	FL	14,504	HC+
New York Univ	NY	61,470	MC
Oakland Univ	MI	19,391	VC
Oberlin College	OH	57,025	MC
Occidental College	CA	59,592	MC+
Ohio Univ	OH	20,676	VC
Pace Univ	NY	48,094	VC
Penn State Univ/Univ Park	PA	25,404	VC
Pitzer College	CA	54,988	MC
Pomona College	CA	57,680	MC
Prescott College	AZ	33,284	C+
Queens College / The CUNY	NY	17,107	VC
Rhode Island College	RI	17,132	LC
Rhodes College	TN	47,596	HC+
Ripon College	WI	36,959	C+
Rollins College	FL	52,370	HC
Rutgers, The State Univ of New Jersey/New Brunswick	NJ	25,077	VC
Sacred Heart Univ	CT	48,564	VC
St. Louis Univ	MO	46,594	VC+
St. Mary's Univ	TX	33,854	C
St. Peter's College	NJ	44,240	C
Samford Univ	AL	35,700	VC+
San Diego State Univ	CA	20,578	VC
Santa Clara Univ	CA	54,702	MC
Scripps College	CA	54,900	MC
Seattle Pacific Univ	WA	41,559	VC+
Seton Hall Univ	NJ	45,902	C
Smith College	MA	57,524	MC
Sonoma State Univ	CA	20,541	C
Southern Methodist Univ	TX	57,755	MC
Southern Nazarene Univ	OK	24,354	NC
Southwestern Univ	TX	45,660	VC
St. Edward's Univ	TX	44,674	VC
Stanford Univ	CA	56,411	MC
SUNY New Paltz	NY	15,010	C
SUNY Plattsburgh / SUNY	NY	18,083	VC
Syracuse Univ	NY	54,512	HC
Temple Univ	PA	24,392	VC
Texas Tech Univ	TX	14,243	C
Tufts Univ	MA	58,780	MC
Tulane Univ	LA	58,942	MC
Union College	KY	28,775	C
Univ at Albany / SUNY	NY	18,674	VC
Univ of Arizona	AZ	20,105	C
Univ of Arkansas at Fayetteville	AR	16,860	VC
Univ of Calif at Berkeley	CA	23,322	MC
Univ of Calif at Los Angeles	CA	25,686	MC
Univ of Calif at Riverside	CA	27,204	C
Univ of Calif at San Diego	CA	21,000	VC
Univ of Calif at Santa Barbara	CA	27,551	HC
Univ of Calif at Santa Cruz	CA	27,807	VC
Univ of Central Florida	FL	15,711	VC+
Univ of Chicago	IL	55,416	MC
Univ of Cincinnati	OH	20,199	VC
Univ of Conn	CT	23,744	HC
Univ of Delaware	DE	22,728	VC
Univ of Georgia	GA	19,508	VC
Univ of Idaho	ID	14,558	C
Univ of Illinois at Chicago	IL	24,293	VC
Univ of Illinois at Urbana-Champaign	IL	24,300	HC
Univ of Kansas	KS	16,980	C+
Univ of Kentucky	KY	19,868	C
Univ of Miami	FL	55,166	MC
Univ of Mich/Ann Arbor	MI	22,102	HC+
Univ of Minn/Morris	MN	17,150	VC
Univ of Nebr - Lincoln	NE	17,507	VC
Univ of Nebr at Omaha	NE	12,700	C
Univ of New Mexico	NM	15,300	C
Univ of N Car at Chapel Hill	NC	18,348	MC
Univ of N Car at Charlotte	NC	15,847	C
Univ of Okla	OK	17,634	VC+
Univ of Oregon	OR	20,872	VC
Univ of Pennsylvania	PA	56,106	MC
Univ of San Francisco	CA	49,674	VC
Univ of S Car at Columbia	SC	19,725	VC+
Univ of Southern Calif	CA	56,903	MC
Univ of Texas at Austin	TX	44,074	HC
Univ of Texas at El Paso	TX	8,764	NC
Univ of Texas-Pan American	TX	12,432	LC
Univ of Utah	UT	13,462	VC
Univ of Vermont	VT	26,120	VC+
Univ of Wisc/Eau Claire	WI	15,130	VC
Univ of Wisc/Madison	WI	18,757	HC
Univ of Wisc-Milwaukee	WI	18,436	C
Vanderbilt Univ	TN	57,072	MC
Vassar College	NY	59,070	MC
Villanova Univ	PA	56,436	MC
Washington Univ in St. Louis	MO	58,818	MC
Wellesley College	MA	49,848	MC
Wesleyan Univ	CT	59,844	MC
Willamette Univ	OR	56,450	VC+
Wofford College	SC	45,795	VC
Yale Univ	CT	55,300	MC

LAW

School	ST	$IS	SR
American Univ	DC	54,829	HC+
Amherst College	MA	58,744	MC
Bay Path College	MA	34,565	C
Bryant Univ	RI	49,179	VC
Central Mich Univ	MI	18,066	C
Dickinson College	PA	57,662	HC+
Florida Gulf Coast Univ	FL		C
Franciscan Univ of Steubenville	OH	27,320	VC
Grand Valley State Univ	MI	17,998	VC
Hampshire College	MA	58,320	MC
Hood College	MD	44,630	C
Howard Univ	DC	35,957	C
Indiana Inst of Technology	IN	34,240	LC
John Jay College of Criminal Justice / The CUNY	NY	6,059	C
Kaplan Univ	IA	14,025	NC
Lasell College	MA	42,500	LC
Minn State Univ, Moorhead	MN	13,392	C
Montclair State Univ	NJ	22,614	C
Mount Aloysius College	PA	27,970	C
Mount Ida College	MA	30,115	LC
Mountain State Univ	WV	14,330	NC
New England College	NH	45,930	LC
New York Univ	NY	61,470	MC
Nichols College	MA	37,240	LC
Oberlin College	OH	57,025	MC
Park Univ	MO	17,525	C
Ramapo College of New Jersey	NJ	24,938	C+
Regis College	MA	47,565	LC
Scripps College	CA	54,900	MC
South Univ	GA		LC
Southern Illinois Univ Carbondale	IL	21,620	C
The College of St. Rose	NY	26,750	LC
Towson Univ	MD	16,000	VC
United States Air Force Academy	CO		MC
United States Military Academy	NY		MC
Univ of Arizona	AZ	20,105	C
Univ of Arkansas at Little Rock	AR		C
Univ of Calif at Berkeley	CA	23,322	MC
Univ of Calif at Santa Cruz	CA	27,807	VC
Univ of Chicago	IL	55,416	MC
Univ of Georgia	GA	19,508	VC
Univ of Hartford	CT	42,674	C
Univ of Mass Amherst	MA	23,697	VC+
Univ of Pennsylvania	PA	56,106	MC
Univ of Wisc/Madison	WI	18,757	HC
Univ of Wisc/Superior	WI	14,106	C
Ursuline College	OH	33,198	LC
Western New England Univ	MA	45,590	C
Wilson College	PA	27,660	C
Woodbury Inst of Champlain College in Burlington	VT	15,150	LC

LAW ENFORCEMENT AND CORRECTIONS

School	ST	$IS	SR
Adams State College	CO	13,358	LC
Amridge Univ	AL	6,870	LC
Calumet College of St. Joseph	IN	15,000	LC
College of the Ozarks	MO	5,605	VC
Frostburg State Univ	MD	15,264	LC
Idaho State Univ	ID	11,908	C
Indiana Inst of Technology	IN	34,240	LC
Indiana Wesleyan Univ	IN	31,815	VC
Le Moyne College	NY	42,200	VC
Metropolitan State Univ	MN	5,923	SP
Minn State Univ, Mankato	MN	14,900	C
Mount Aloysius College	PA	27,970	C
Point Park Univ	PA	36,390	C
Portland State Univ	OR	18,672	C
St. Paul's College	VA	16,030	NC
Sam Houston State Univ	TX	17,082	C
Shenandoah Univ	VA	39,268	C
Southeast Missouri State Univ	MO	14,983	LC
Southwest Minn State Univ	MN	14,000	C
Stephen F. Austin State Univ	TX	14,668	C
Tarleton State Univ	TX	13,489	LC
Texas State Univ	TX	16,495	VC
Tiffin Univ	OH	30,273	LC
Unity College	ME	34,054	C
Univ of Great Falls	MT	27,970	C
Univ of Illinois at Chicago	IL	24,293	VC
Univ of Indianapolis	IN	31,740	LC
Univ of Maine at Augusta	ME	6,855	C
Univ of New Haven	CT	47,740	C
Univ of San Francisco	CA	49,674	VC
Univ of Virginia's College at Wise	VA	11,076	C
Washburn Univ	KS	12,165	NC
Western Conn State Univ	CT	18,327	C
Western Illinois Univ	IL	20,130	C
Western New Mexico Univ	NM	8,500	LC
Western Oregon Univ	OR	15,021	C
Youngstown State Univ	OH	16,374	LC

LEARNER DESIGNED AREA OF STUDY

School	ST	$IS	SR
Bowling Green State Univ	OH	18,970	C
Goddard College	VT	16,418	VC
Thomas Edison State College	NJ	5,700	SP
Univ of Illinois at Chicago	IL	24,293	VC

LEGAL STUDIES

School	ST	$IS	SR
Bryant Univ	RI	49,179	VC
Burlington College	VT	32,510	SP
Cal State, Chico	CA	18,952	C
Champlain College	VT	44,850	VC
Claremont McKenna College	CA	58,065	MC
Culver-Stockton College	MO	30,900	C
Dominican Univ	IL	37,628	C
Elizabethtown College	PA	47,600	VC
Faulkner Univ	AL	22,530	LC
Gannon Univ	PA	37,940	C
Harding Univ	AR	21,432	C+
Howard Univ	DC	35,957	C
Indiana Univ Bloomington	IN	19,358	HC
Ithaca College	NY	52,300	HC
Lipscomb Univ	TN	35,722	VC
Mercy College	NY	29,996	C
Nazareth College of Rochester	NY	41,590	VC
New England College	NH	45,930	LC
Nova Southeastern Univ	FL	34,016	VC
Paul Quinn College	TX	25,350	LC
Point Park Univ	PA	36,390	C
Roger Williams Univ	RI	45,788	C
St. Louis Univ	MO	46,594	VC+
St. John Fisher College	NY	39,370	C+
St. John's Univ	NY	52,840	C+
Temple Univ	PA	24,392	VC
Univ at Buffalo / The SUNY	NY	20,283	VC
Univ of Central Florida	FL	15,711	VC+
Univ of Central Okla	OK	12,293	C
Univ of Miami	FL	55,166	MC
Univ of New Haven	CT	47,740	C
Univ of Pittsburgh at Pittsburgh	PA	27,800	HC+
Webster Univ	MO	33,990	C+
Wesley College	DE	31,115	LC

LIBERAL ARTS/ENGINEERING STUDIES

School	ST	$IS	SR
Calif Polytechnic State Univ	CA	19,847	HC

LIBERAL ARTS/GENERAL STUDIES

School	ST	$IS	SR
Abilene Christian Univ	TX	38,400	VC
Adams State College	CO	13,358	LC
Alaska Pacific Univ	AK	33,360	VC
Albertus Magnus College	CT	37,382	LC
Alvernia Univ	PA	39,250	C
American International College	MA	36,100	LC
American Jewish Univ	CA	32,600	C
Amridge Univ	AL	6,870	LC
Angelo State Univ	TX	15,049	NC
Anna Maria College	MA	34,600	LC
Aquinas College	MI	33,060	C
Aquinas College	TN	29,250	C+
Arcadia Univ	PA	33,570	C+
Arizona State Univ	AZ	18,818	C+
Armstrong Atlantic State Univ	GA	16,276	C
Atlantic Union College	MA	24,600	LC
Auburn Univ at Montgomery	AL	12,120	C
Austin Peay State Univ	TN	14,650	C
Averett Univ	VA	36,000	LC
Azusa Pacific Univ	CA	39,946	C
Ball State Univ	IN	17,850	C
Barry Univ	FL	38,190	C
Bay Path College	MA	34,565	C
Beacon College	FL	38,000	C
Becker College	MA	41,420	LC
Bellarmine Univ	KY	42,950	VC
Belmont Abbey College	NC	37,716	C
Belmont Univ	TN	37,380	VC+
Benedictine College	KS	29,180	VC
Bennington College	VT	56,990	HC+
Bentley Univ	MA	54,555	HC+
Bethel College	IN	31,560	C
Bethune-Cookman Univ	FL	22,290	LC
Biola Univ	CA	40,320	VC
Boricua College	NY	8,600	C
Bowling Green State Univ	OH	18,970	C
Bradley Univ	IL	31,874	VC
Brenau Univ Women's College	GA	26,650	C+
Brescia Univ	KY	26,140	VC+
Brewton-Parker College	GA	33,388	LC
Bridgewater College	VA	39,880	C
Bryan College	TN	24,194	C
Burlington College	VT	32,510	SP
Cabrini College	PA	40,859	LC
Cairn Univ	PA	31,255	C
Calif Baptist Univ	CA	35,890	C
Calif Lutheran Univ	CA	47,640	C
Calif Polytechnic State Univ	CA	19,847	HC
Calif State Polytechnic Univ, Pomona	CA	18,932	C
Cal State, Bakersfield	CA	8,000	LC
Cal State, Chico	CA	18,952	C
Cal State, Dominguez Hills	CA	17,056	LC
Cal State, East Bay	CA	16,549	C
Cal State, Fresno	CA	17,405	C
Cal State, Fullerton	CA	25,188	C+
Cal State, Los Angeles	CA	15,829	C
Cal State, Monterey Bay	CA	26,871	LC
Cal State, Northridge	CA	28,313	C
Cal State, San Bernardino	CA	12,000	C
Cal State, San Marcos	CA	14,576	C
Cal State, Stanislaus	CA	18,582	C
Calif Univ of Pennsylvania	PA	14,217	C
Calumet College of St. Joseph	IN	15,000	LC
Canisius College	NY	45,602	VC
Carlow Univ	PA	30,272	C
Castleton State College	VT	19,424	C
Cazenovia College	NY	30,800	C
Cedarville Univ	OH	31,036	VC+
Centenary College of Louisiana	LA	39,070	C+
Central Washington Univ	WA	11,730	C
Chaminade Univ of Honolulu	HI	31,664	C
Champlain College	VT	44,850	VC
Charter Oak State College	CT	8,280	SP
Chestnut Hill College	PA	39,785	LC
Cheyney Univ of Pennsylvania	PA	20,372	LC
Christian Brothers Univ	TN	19,140	HC
City Univ of Seattle	WA	14,880	NC
Clarion Univ of Pennsylvania	PA	17,370	C
Clarke Univ	IA	36,400	C
Cleveland State Univ	OH	21,357	C
College of Mount St. Joseph	OH	33,880	C
College of Mount St. Vincent	NY	41,040	MC
College of New Rochelle - School of New Resources	NY		VC
College of St. Benedict	MN	47,570	VC
College of St. Mary	NE	34,334	C
College of St Joseph	VT	30,600	LC
College of Visual Arts - School is Closed	MN	24,310	SP
Colo Christian Univ	CO	27,500	VC
Colo College	CO	54,534	MC
Colo Mesa Univ	CO	16,669	LC
Colo State Univ-Fort Collins	CO	20,090	VC
Columbia College	MO	24,578	C
Concordia Univ - Irvine	CA	35,390	VC
Concordia Univ Texas	TX	23,640	C

School	ST	$IS	SR
Coppin State Univ	MD	14,905	VC
Cornerstone Univ and Grand Rapids Theological Seminary	MI	30,866	C
Dallas Baptist Univ	TX	29,118	C
De Sales Univ	PA	42,670	C
Dominican Univ of Calif	CA	51,250	C
Dowling College	NY	25,000	LC
Duquesne Univ	PA	42,017	VC
East Carolina Univ	NC	14,169	C
East Central Univ	OK	10,223	LC
East Tenn State Univ	TN	9,000	C
Eastern Conn State Univ	CT	20,584	C
Eastern Illinois Univ	IL	20,502	C
Eastern Mennonite Univ	VA	38,850	VC
Eastern Oregon Univ	OR	10,400	C
Edinboro Univ of Pennsylvania	PA	15,940	LC
Elmhurst College	IL	42,032	C+
Emmanuel College	MA	47,985	VC
Emporia State Univ	KS	12,897	C
Endicott College	MA	42,390	C
Eureka College	IL	19,280	C
Evergreen State College	WA	12,969	C+
Excelsior College	NY	895	SP
Fairleigh Dickinson Univ/ College at Florham	NJ	42,142	C
Fairleigh Dickinson Univ/ Metropolitan Campus	NJ	40,254	C
Faulkner Univ	AL	22,530	LC
Felician College	NJ	41,640	C
Ferrum College	VA	27,740	LC
Flagler College	FL	24,960	VC
Florida Atlantic Univ	FL	17,339	C
Florida Gulf Coast Univ	FL		C
Florida International Univ	FL	17,747	VC
Fontbonne Univ	MO	31,384	C
Fort Hays State Univ	KS	11,354	C
Francis Marion Univ	SC	16,464	LC
Friends Univ	KS	29,100	C
Frostburg State Univ	MD	15,264	LC
Gallaudet Univ	DC	25,380	SP
Gannon Univ	PA	37,940	C
George Washington Univ	DC	57,108	MC
Georgetown College	KY	38,690	C
Georgia College and State Univ	GA	18,216	VC
Glenville State College	WV	11,348	NC
Goddard College	VT	16,418	VC
Gonzaga Univ	WA	44,247	HC
Graceland Univ	IA	28,020	C
Grand Valley State Univ	MI	17,998	VC
Granite State College	NH	6,195	SP
Green Mountain College	VT	33,547	LC
Greenville College	IL	27,012	C
Hannibal-LaGrange Univ	MO	24,490	C
Harding Univ	AR	21,432	C+
Harris-Stowe State Univ	MO	14,360	NC
Haverford College	PA	59,236	MC
Hilbert College	NY	28,550	C
Hofstra Univ	NY	48,020	VC+
Holy Names Univ	CA	40,310	NC
Hope International Univ	CA	34,650	C
Houghton College	NY	35,740	VC
Houston Baptist Univ	TX	23,815	C+
Howard Payne Univ	TX	17,115	C
Humboldt State Univ	CA	18,400	C
Idaho State Univ	ID	11,908	C
Indiana State Univ	IN	16,000	C
Indiana Univ-Purdue Univ Fort Wayne	IN	15,425	C
Indiana Wesleyan Univ	IN	31,815	VC
Iona College	NY	44,028	C
Iowa State Univ	IA	16,403	C
Ithaca College	NY	52,300	HC
James Madison Univ	VA	18,049	VC
John Carroll Univ	OH	44,560	C+
Johnson C. Smith Univ	NC	25,336	LC
Johnson State College	VT	16,721	C
Kentucky Christian Univ	KY	17,622	LC
Kentucky State Univ	KY	11,000	LC
Kutztown Univ of Pennsylvania	PA	16,909	LC
La Roche College	PA	34,802	LC
La Sierra Univ	CA	35,694	VC
Lasell College	MA	42,500	LC
Lewis Univ	IL	23,050	C
Lewis-Clark State College	ID	6,990	C
Liberty Univ	VA	19,101	C
Limestone College	SC	29,880	C
Lincoln Univ	MO	11,996	NC
Lindenwood Univ	MO	20,750	C
Lindsey Wilson College	KY	30,470	VC
Lipscomb Univ	TN	35,722	VC
Lock Haven Univ of Pennsylvania	PA	17,587	LC
Longwood Univ	VA	20,924	C
Louisiana State Univ	LA	18,677	VC+
Louisiana State Univ in Shreveport	LA	5,606	C
Louisiana Tech Univ	LA	8,000	C
Loyola Marymount Univ	CA	53,240	VC+
Loyola Univ New Orleans	LA	46,581	VC
MacMurray College	IL	20,755	C
Madonna Univ	MI	24,540	VC
Malone Univ	OH	34,334	C
Mansfield Univ	PA	19,468	LC

School	ST	$IS	SR
Marymount Manhattan College	NY	40,118	VC
Marymount Univ	VA	36,178	C
Maryville Univ of St. Louis	MO	34,920	VC
Mass College of Liberal Arts	MA	16,733	C
Mayville State Univ	ND	11,401	NC
McNeese State Univ	LA		C
Medaille College	NY	35,112	VC
Medgar Evers College / The CUNY	NY	4,920	NC
Mercy College	NY	29,996	C
Metropolitan State Univ	MN	5,923	SP
Mich Tech Univ	MI	22,105	VC
Middlebury College	VT	57,470	MC
Midway College	KY	20,150	C
Mills College	CA	54,119	HC
Minot State Univ	ND	10,915	C
Misericordia Univ	PA	39,840	C
Missouri Baptist Univ	MO	30,310	C
Missouri Southern State Univ	MO	11,910	C
Missouri Valley College	MO	22,200	C
Mitchell College	CT	40,983	C
Montana State Univ	MT	14,068	VC
Montana State Univ-Billings	MT	12,425	LC
Montana Tech of The Univ of Montana	MT	14,650	VC
Montreat College	NC	31,298	VC
Morehead State Univ	KY	10,900	C
Morris College	SC	16,006	LC
Mount Aloysius College	PA	27,970	C
Mount Ida College	MA	30,115	LC
Mount Mary Univ	WI	32,836	LC
Mount Olive College	NC	18,426	C
Mount St. Mary's College/ Chalon Campus	CA	43,897	VC+
Mountain State Univ	WV	14,330	NC
Murray State Univ	KY	14,944	C
National Univ	CA	14,730	SP
Neumann Univ	PA	31,078	LC
New Mexico Inst of Mining and Technology	NM	12,892	HC
Newman Univ	KS	30,380	C+
Niagara Univ	NY	39,800	C
Northern Arizona Univ	AZ	18,592	C
Northern Illinois Univ	IL	19,768	C
Northern Kentucky Univ	KY	15,302	LC
Northwest Nazarene Univ	ID	24,275	NC
Northwest Univ	WA	18,854	C
Northwestern State Univ of Louisiana	LA	14,368	C
Norwich Univ	VT	28,212	C
Notre Dame de Namur Univ	CA	41,610	LC
Notre Dame of Maryland Univ	MD	27,700	C
Oakland Univ	MI	19,391	VC
Ohio Dominican Univ	OH	38,380	C+
Okla Christian Univ	OK	24,975	VC
Okla City Univ	OK	33,546	VC
Okla State Univ	OK	14,310	VC
Okla Wesleyan Univ	OK	21,300	C
Oral Roberts Univ	OK	31,734	C
Oregon State Univ	OR	19,017	C+
Otterbein College	OH	32,214	C
Our Lady of Holy Cross College	LA	8,090	LC
Our Lady of the Lake Univ of San Antonio	TX	22,430	LC
Palm Beach Atlantic Univ	FL	33,882	LC
Park Univ	MO	17,525	C
Paul Quinn College	TX	25,350	LC
Penn State Univ/Altoona	PA	11,464	C
Penn State Univ/Univ Park	PA	25,404	VC
Pepperdine Univ	CA	55,372	HC+
Pittsburg State Univ	KS	12,032	C
Point Loma Nazarene Univ	CA	38,610	VC
Point Park Univ	PA	36,390	C
Polytechnic Inst of New York Univ	NY	53,064	HC+
Pontifical Catholic Univ of PR	PR	7,310	
Portland State Univ	OR	18,672	C
Post Univ	CT	35,750	LC
Prescott College	AZ	33,284	C+
Providence College	RI	55,995	HC
Purchase College / SUNY	NY	16,951	C
Purdue Univ/West Lafayette	IN	20,278	HC
Quinnipiac Univ	CT	53,580	VC
Ramapo College of New Jersey	NJ	24,938	C+
Regis College	MA	47,565	LC
Reinhardt College	GA	25,000	C
Rhode Island College	RI	17,132	LC
Richard Stockton College of New Jersey	NJ	20,000	VC
Rider Univ	NJ	45,720	C
Rivier College	NH	35,000	VC
Roberts Wesleyan College	NY	37,384	C+
Roosevelt Univ	IL	22,605	VC
Rosemont College	PA	42,350	C
Rowan Univ	NJ	23,570	VC
Rutgers, The State Univ of New Jersey/Camden Campus	NJ	24,254	C
Sacred Heart Univ	CT	48,564	VC

School	ST	$IS	SR
St. Anselm College	NH	48,324	VC
St. John's Univ	MN	46,146	C
St. Joseph's Univ	PA	52,272	VC
St. Leo Univ	FL	27,990	C
St. Louis Univ	MO	46,594	VC+
St. Mary's College of Calif	CA	53,550	C
St. Vincent College	PA	40,244	C
Salem International Univ	WV	18,020	C
Samford Univ	AL	35,700	VC+
San Diego Christian College	CA	31,012	C
San Diego State Univ	CA	20,578	VC
San Francisco State Univ	CA	18,514	C
Santa Clara Univ	CA	54,702	MC
Sarah Lawrence College	NY	48,000	HC
Schreiner Univ	TX	32,734	LC
Seattle Pacific Univ	WA	41,559	VC+
Seattle Univ	WA	47,010	VC+
Seton Hall Univ	NJ	45,902	C
Seton Hill Univ	PA	35,172	C
Shaw Univ	NC	15,488	LC
Shenandoah Univ	VA	39,268	C
Shimer College	IL	32,875	VC
Siena Heights Univ	MI	17,000	LC
Simpson Univ	CA	28,900	C
Skidmore College	NY	57,926	HC
Sonoma State Univ	CA	20,541	C
S Dak State Univ	SD	14,296	C
Southeastern Louisiana Univ	LA	13,325	C
Southern Illinois Univ Carbondale	IL	21,620	C
Southern Illinois Univ Edwardsville	IL	17,532	C
Southern Methodist Univ	TX	57,755	MC
Southern New Hampshire Univ	NH	38,100	C
Southern Oregon Univ	OR	17,874	C
Southern Vermont College	VT	30,740	LC
Southwestern College	KS	29,270	C
Spalding Univ	KY	31,850	LC
Spring Hill College	AL	42,130	VC
St. Edward's Univ	TX	44,674	VC
St. Francis College	NY	34,200	LC
St. John's College, Santa Fe	NM	54,998	HC+
St. John's College-Annapolis	MD	53,590	HC
St. John's Univ	NY	52,840	C+
St. Joseph's College, New York / Brooklyn Campus	NY	21,878	C
St. Joseph's College, New York / Suffolk Campus	NY	21,878	VC
St. Thomas Univ	FL	32,310	C+
SUNY Inst of Technology at Utica / Rome	NY	23,818	C
SUNY/Empire State College	NY	6,315	SP
Stephens College	MO	34,500	VC
Stony Brook Univ / SUNY	NY	19,359	HC
SUNY New Paltz	NY	15,010	C
Susquehanna Univ	PA	49,170	C
Sweet Briar College	VA	43,765	C+
Syracuse Univ	NY	54,512	HC
Taylor Univ	IN	36,742	VC+
Texas A&M Univ at Galveston	TX	11,258	C
Texas Southern Univ	TX	18,212	LC
Texas State Univ	TX	16,495	VC
Texas Tech Univ	TX	14,243	C
The Catholic Univ of America	DC	52,852	VC
The Masters College	CA	38,160	C+
Thomas Aquinas College	CA	32,450	HC+
Thomas Edison State College	NJ	5,700	SP
Thomas More College	KY	34,760	C
Thomas More College of Liberal Arts	NH	28,600	C
Thomas Univ	GA	11,520	NC
Touro College	NY	23,150	VC
Trinity International Univ	IL	31,070	C
Tulane Univ	LA	58,942	MC
Union College	NY		MC
Union Inst & Univ	OH	8,912	SP
Univ of Alaska Anchorage	AK	15,290	NC
Univ of Alaska Southeast	AK	11,493	C
Univ of Arkansas at Little Rock	AR		C
Univ of Arkansas at Monticello	AR	8,470	NC
Univ of Arkansas at Pine Bluff	AR	10,600	C
Univ of Calif at Riverside	CA	27,204	C
Univ of Central Florida	FL	15,711	VC+
Univ of Central Okla	OK	12,293	C
Univ of Charleston	WV	28,650	VC
Univ of Cincinnati	OH	20,199	VC
Univ of Dayton	OH	43,750	VC
Univ of Delaware	DE	22,728	VC
Univ of Detroit Mercy	MI	30,450	C
Univ of Evansville	IN	41,056	VC+
Univ of Hawaii at Hilo	HI	6,500	C
Univ of Houston	TX	19,184	VC
Univ of Illinois at Urbana-Champaign	IL	24,300	HC
Univ of Iowa	IA	17,481	VC
Univ of Kansas	KS	16,980	C+

School	ST	$IS	SR
Univ of La Verne	CA	47,010	VC
Univ of Louisiana at Monroe	LA	12,998	C
Univ of Louisville	KY	17,460	VC
Univ of Maine at Augusta	ME	6,855	C
Univ of Maine at Farmington	ME	17,841	C
Univ of Maine at Fort Kent	ME	14,975	LC
Univ of Maine at Machias	ME	10,523	C
Univ of Maine at Presque Isle	ME	15,011	LC
Univ of Mary	ND	16,714	C
Univ of Mary Washington	VA	19,484	VC
Univ of Maryland/Eastern Shore	MD	14,000	C
Univ of Maryland/Univ College	MD	6,168	SP
Univ of Mass Amherst	MA	23,697	VC+
Univ of Mass Dartmouth	MA	22,223	C
Univ of Mass Lowell	MA	19,316	C
Univ of Memphis	TN	15,094	C
Univ of Miami	FL	55,166	MC
Univ of Mich/Ann Arbor	MI	22,102	HC+
Univ of Mich/Dearborn	MI	9,885	VC
Univ of Minn/Morris	MN	17,150	VC
Univ of Miss	MS	15,482	VC
Univ of Missouri/Columbia	MO	18,201	MC
Univ of Missouri-Kansas City	MO	19,603	C
Univ of Missouri-St. Louis	MO	18,304	VC
Univ of Mobile	AL	27,870	VC
Univ of Montana	MT	13,670	C
Univ of Montana-Western	MT	9,753	LC
Univ of Nebr - Lincoln	NE	17,507	VC
Univ of Nebr at Omaha	NE	12,700	C
Univ of Nevada/Reno	NV	14,500	NC
Univ of New England	ME	46,145	C+
Univ of New Haven	CT	47,740	C
Univ of New Mexico	NM	15,300	C
Univ of North Alabama	AL	9,960	C
Univ of N Car at Asheville	NC	13,500	VC+
Univ of N Car at Charlotte	NC	15,847	C
Univ of N Car at Greensboro	NC	12,848	C
Univ of North Texas	TX	15,628	C
Univ of Northern Iowa	IA	14,776	C
Univ of Notre Dame	IN		MC
Univ of Okla	OK	17,634	VC+
Univ of Pittsburgh at Bradford	PA	21,316	LC
Univ of Pittsburgh at Pittsburgh	PA	27,800	HC+
Univ of PR Recinto de Rio Piedras	PR	5,750	
Univ of Redlands	CA	40,500	VC
Univ of St. Francis	IN	29,810	C
Univ of St. Mary	KS	28,400	C+
Univ of San Diego	CA	53,302	HC+
Univ of S Car Upstate	SC	17,673	LC
Univ of S Dak	SD	15,111	C
Univ of South Florida	FL	13,000	C
Univ of St. Francis	IL	36,490	C
Univ of St. Thomas - Houston	TX	36,490	VC
Univ of Tampa	FL	35,160	VC
Univ of Texas at Austin	TX	44,074	HC
Univ of Texas-Pan American	TX	12,432	LC
Univ of the Ozarks	AR	22,100	C
Univ of the Pacific	CA	52,146	VC
Univ of Virginia's College at Wise	VA	11,076	C
Univ of Washington	WA	14,722	VC
Univ of Wisc/Eau Claire	WI	15,430	VC
Univ of Wisc/Green Bay	WI	14,900	C
Univ of Wisc/Oshkosh	WI	10,426	LC
Univ of Wisc/Platteville	WI	14,274	C
Univ of Wisc/Stevens Point	WI	14,043	C
Univ of Wisc-Milwaukee	WI	18,436	C
Urbana Univ	OH	21,190	C
Utah State Univ	UT	11,803	C
Utica College	NY	44,734	C
Vanguard Univ of Southern Calif	CA	35,833	VC
Victory Univ	TN	19,118	C
Villanova Univ	PA	56,436	MC
Virginia Intermont College	VA	32,411	LC
Virginia Wesleyan College	VA	28,433	LC
Viterbo Univ	WI	30,070	C
Walsh Univ	OH	35,100	C
Warner Pacific College	OR	25,550	C
Washburn Univ	KS	12,165	NC
Washington Adventist Univ	MD	25,859	C+
Washington State Univ	WA	20,461	C
Wayne State Univ	MI	19,493	C
Wesley College	DE	31,115	LC
West Chester Univ of Pennsylvania	PA	16,836	C
West Texas A&M Univ	TX	13,478	C
West Virginia Univ	WV	15,794	C+
Western Carolina Univ	NC	13,965	C+
Western Conn State Univ	CT	18,327	C
Western Illinois Univ	IL	20,130	C
Western Kentucky Univ	KY	11,000	LC
Western New England Univ	MA	45,590	C
Westfield State Univ	MA	18,489	C
Westmont College	CA	41,500	HC
Wheeling Jesuit Univ	WV	34,668	C

School	ST	$IS	SR
Wichita State Univ	KS	12,539	C
Wilberforce Univ	OH	15,100	LC
Wiley College	TX		LC
Wilkes Univ	PA	42,786	C
William Carey Univ	MS	13,500	LC
William Peace Univ	NC	32,900	LC
Wilmington College	OH	29,784	C
Wingate Univ	NC	34,990	C
Wright State Univ	OH	16,983	C
Xavier Univ	OH	43,740	VC
York College	NE	19,475	C
York College / CUNY	NY	5,496	NC

LIBRARY SCIENCE

School	ST	$IS	SR
Ball State Univ	IN	17,850	C
Clarion Univ of Pennsylvania	PA	17,370	C
Kutztown Univ of Pennsylvania	PA	16,909	LC
Northwestern Okla State Univ	OK	7,275	NC
Southern Conn State Univ	CT	18,033	C
Univ of Arizona	AZ	20,105	C
Univ of Central Arkansas	AR	10,840	VC
Univ of Maine at Augusta	ME	6,855	C
Univ of Nebr at Omaha	NE	12,700	C

LIFE SCIENCE

School	ST	$IS	SR
Arizona State Univ	AZ	18,818	C+
Atlantic Union College	MA	21,600	LC
Baylor Univ	TX	46,720	HC
Biola Univ	CA	40,320	VC
Bowling Green State Univ	OH	18,970	C
East Texas Baptist Univ	TX	29,135	C
Indiana Univ East	IN	6,639	LC
Iowa Wesleyan College	IA	30,850	LC
Kansas State Univ	KS	15,497	VC
Kent State Univ	OH	19,352	C
Malone Univ	OH	34,334	C
McMurry Univ	TX	25,962	LC
Minn State Univ, Mankato	MN	14,900	C
Missouri Univ of Science and Technology	MO	18,655	VC+
Mount Vernon Nazarene Univ	OH	29,590	C
National Univ	CA	14,730	SP
New York Inst of Technology	NY	40,590	VC
Niagara Univ	NY	39,800	C
Northwest Univ	WA	18,854	C
Ohio Univ	OH	20,676	VC
Otterbein College	OH	32,214	C
Suffolk Univ	MA	46,548	C
United States Military Academy	NY		MC
Wayland Baptist Univ	TX	16,058	LC
Wayne State College	NE	11,764	NC
Western Washington Univ	WA	18,519	VC
Wright State Univ	OH	16,983	C
Xavier Univ	OH	43,740	VC

LIFE SCIENCE SECONDARY SCHOOL EDUCATION

School	ST	$IS	SR
Franklin College	IN	35,885	C
St. Mary's Univ of Minn	MN	37,015	C
Texas Christian Univ	TX	47,570	HC
Univ of Nebr - Lincoln	NE	17,507	VC

LINGUISTICS

School	ST	$IS	SR
Alabama A&M Univ	AL	96,100	C
Bard College at Simon's Rock	MA	58,963	HC+
Binghamton Univ / The SUNY	NY	20,832	HC+
Boston College	MA	58,506	MC
Boston Univ	MA	54,130	HC+
Brandeis Univ	MA	58,820	HC
Brigham Young Univ	UT	12,100	HC
Brown Univ	RI	56,150	MC
Bryn Mawr College	PA	57,760	MC
Cal State, Chico	CA	18,952	C
Cal State, Fresno	CA	17,405	C
Cal State, Fullerton	CA	25,188	C+
Cal State, Monterey Bay	CA	26,871	LC
Cal State, Northridge	CA	28,313	C
Calvin College	MI	37,585	VC+
Carleton College	MN	58,149	MC
Central College	IA	36,980	VC
CUNY/Brooklyn College	NY	5,884	C+
Cleveland State Univ	OH	21,357	C
College of William & Mary	VA	25,085	MC
Columbia Univ in the City of New York	NY	61,116	MC
Columbia Univ/Barnard College	NY	39,000	MC
Cornell Univ	NY	59,037	MC
Dartmouth College	NH	57,996	MC
DePauw Univ	IN	48,950	VC+
Duke Univ	NC	50,250	MC
Earlham College	IN	49,710	VC+
Eastern Mich Univ	MI	17,961	C
Emory Univ	GA	45,000	MC
Florida Atlantic Univ	FL	17,339	C
Florida State Univ	FL	15,238	HC
Georgetown Univ	DC	52,910	MC
Gordon College	MA	42,660	VC+
Hampshire College	MA	58,320	MC
Harvard Univ/Harvard College	MA	49,000	MC
Haverford College	PA	59,236	MC
Hofstra Univ	NY	48,020	VC+
Indiana Univ Bloomington	IN	19,358	HC
Iowa State Univ	IA	16,403	C
Lawrence Univ	WI	46,371	HC
Lehman College / The CUNY	NY	5,778	LC
Macalester College	MN	53,419	MC
Marlboro College	VT	35,980	VC
Mass Inst of Technology	MA	54,238	MC
Miami Univ	OH	24,191	HC
Mich State Univ	MI	13,689	VC
Montclair State Univ	NJ	22,614	C
New York Univ	NY	61,470	MC
Northeastern Illinois Univ	IL		C
Northeastern Univ	MA	55,296	MC
Northwestern Univ	IL	37,595	MC
Oakland Univ	MI	19,391	VC
Ohio Univ	OH	20,676	VC
Old Dominion Univ	VA	18,662	C
Oswego / SUNY	NY	20,009	VC
Pitzer College	CA	54,988	MC
Pomona College	CA	57,680	MC
Purdue Univ/West Lafayette	IN	20,278	HC
Queens College / The CUNY	NY	17,107	VC
Reed College	OR	57,780	MC
Rice Univ	TX	43,288	MC
Rutgers, The State Univ of New Jersey/New Brunswick	NJ	25,077	VC
San Diego State Univ	CA	20,578	VC
Seattle Pacific Univ	WA	41,559	VC+
Southern Illinois Univ Carbondale	IL	21,620	C
Stanford Univ	CA	56,411	MC
Stony Brook Univ / SUNY	NY	19,359	HC
Swarthmore College	PA	57,870	MC
Syracuse Univ	NY	54,512	HC
Temple Univ	PA	24,392	VC
Ohio State Univ	OH	19,887	MC
Truman State Univ	MO	13,546	HC
Tulane Univ	LA	58,942	MC
Univ at Albany / SUNY	NY	18,674	VC
Univ at Buffalo / The SUNY	NY	20,283	VC
Univ of Alaska Fairbanks	AK	13,955	C
Univ of Arizona	AZ	20,105	C
Univ of Calif at Berkeley	CA	23,322	MC
Univ of Calif at Davis	CA	24,482	HC
Univ of Calif at Los Angeles	CA	25,686	MC
Univ of Calif at Riverside	CA	27,204	C
Univ of Calif at San Diego	CA	21,000	VC
Univ of Calif at Santa Barbara	CA	27,551	HC
Univ of Calif at Santa Cruz	CA	27,807	VC
Univ of Chicago	IL	55,416	MC
Univ of Cincinnati	OH	20,199	VC
Univ of Colo Boulder	CO	22,605	VC+
Univ of Conn	CT	23,744	HC
Univ of Florida	FL	15,783	HC+
Univ of Georgia	GA	19,508	VC
Univ of Hawaii at Hilo	HI	6,500	C
Univ of Hawaii at Manoa	HI	19,379	VC
Univ of Illinois at Urbana-Champaign	IL	24,300	HC
Univ of Iowa	IA	17,481	VC
Univ of Kansas	KS	16,980	C+
Univ of Kentucky	KY	19,868	C
Univ of Louisville	KY	17,460	VC
Univ of Maryland	MD	18,801	HC
Univ of Maryland/Baltimore County	MD	18,000	VC
Univ of Mass Amherst	MA	23,697	VC+
Univ of Mich/Ann Arbor	MI	22,102	HC+
Univ of Minn/Twin Cities	MN		HC
Univ of Miss	MS	15,482	VC
Univ of Missouri/Columbia	MO	18,201	MC
Univ of New Hampshire	NH	24,702	VC
Univ of New Mexico	NM	15,300	C
Univ of N Car at Chapel Hill	NC	18,348	MC
Univ of Okla	OK	17,634	VC+
Univ of Oregon	OR	20,872	VC
Univ of Pennsylvania	PA	56,106	MC
Univ of Pittsburgh at Pittsburgh	PA	27,800	HC+
Univ of Rochester	NY	58,500	MC
Univ of Southern Calif	CA	56,903	MC
Univ of Texas at Austin	TX	44,074	HC
Univ of Texas at El Paso	TX	8,764	NC
Univ of Toledo	OH	18,464	C
Univ of Utah	UT	13,462	VC
Univ of Vermont	VT	26,120	VC+
Univ of Wisc/Madison	WI	18,757	HC
Univ of Wisc-Milwaukee	WI	18,436	C
Washington State Univ	WA	20,461	C
Washington Univ in St. Louis	MO	58,818	MC
Wayne State Univ	MI	19,493	C
Western Washington Univ	WA	18,519	VC
Yale Univ	CT	55,300	MC

LITERATURE

School	ST	$IS	SR
Adrian College	MI	33,800	C
American Jewish Univ	CA	32,600	C
American Univ	DC	54,829	HC+
Andrews Univ	MI	28,030	C+
Aquinas College	MI	33,060	C
Arizona State Univ	AZ	18,818	C+
Bard College	NY	59,872	HC
Bard College at Simon's Rock	MA	58,963	HC+
Baylor Univ	TX	46,720	HC
Beloit College	WI	49,970	HC
Benedictine Univ	IL	35,220	C
Bennington College	VT	56,990	HC+
Binghamton Univ / The SUNY	NY	20,832	HC+
Brigham Young Univ	UT	12,100	HC
Bryant Univ	RI	49,179	VC
Calif College of the Arts	CA	48,334	SP
Cal State, San Marcos	CA	14,576	C
Calvin College	MI	37,585	VC+
Castleton State College	VT	19,424	C
Claremont McKenna College	CA	58,065	MC
Coe College	IA	43,590	VC
College of the Holy Cross	MA	56,232	MC
Columbia Univ/School of General Studies	NY	54,083	MC
Cornerstone Univ and Grand Rapids Theological Seminary	MI	30,866	C
DePauw Univ	IN	48,950	VC+
Dordt College	IA	34,160	VC
Duke Univ	NC	50,250	MC
Duquesne Univ	PA	42,017	VC
Eastern Mich Univ	MI	17,961	C
Eastern Nazarene College	MA	30,000	C
Eastern Washington Univ	WA	16,388	C
Eckerd College	FL	43,902	VC
Elon Univ	NC	40,046	HC
Emory and Henry College	VA	387,460	C
Eugene Lang College - The New School for Liberal Arts	NY	55,650	VC
Fairleigh Dickinson Univ/ College at Florham	NJ	42,142	C
Fitchburg State Univ	MA	17,241	C
George Fox Univ	OR	40,750	C+
George Washington Univ	DC	57,108	MC
Goddard College	VT	16,418	VC
Gonzaga Univ	WA	44,247	HC
Graceland Univ	IA	28,020	C
Hampshire College	MA	58,320	MC
Harvard Univ/Harvard College	MA	49,000	MC
Hellenic College/Holy Cross Greek Orthodox School of Theology	MA	33,190	VC
John Carroll Univ	OH	44,520	C+
Kutztown Univ of Pennsylvania	PA	16,909	LC
Le Moyne College	NY	42,200	VC
Lycoming College	PA	43,636	C
Maharishi Univ of Management	IA	31,000	VC
Marshall Univ	WV	14,820	C
Mass Inst of Technology	MA	54,238	MC
Murray State Univ	KY	14,944	C
Nazareth College of Rochester	NY	41,590	VC
New College of Florida	FL	14,504	HC+
New York Univ	NY	61,470	MC
Northwestern College of Iowa	IA	34,848	C+
Ohio Northern Univ	OH	42,075	VC
Ohio Univ	OH	20,676	VC
Old Dominion Univ	VA	18,662	C
Oral Roberts Univ	OK	31,734	C
Pacific Univ	OR	42,815	C
Pittsburg State Univ	KS	12,032	C
Point Loma Nazarene Univ	CA	38,610	VC
Pomona College	CA	57,680	MC
Prescott College	AZ	33,284	C+
Purchase College / SUNY	NY	16,951	C
Ramapo College of New Jersey	NJ	24,938	C+
Reed College	OR	57,780	MC
Richard Stockton College of New Jersey	NJ	20,000	VC
Roanoke College	VA	47,996	C+
Rocky Mountain College	MT	32,242	C
Roosevelt Univ	IL	22,605	VC
St. Mary-of-the-Woods College	IN	37,722	LC
St. Mary's Univ of Minn	MN	37,015	C
San Jose State Univ	CA	19,707	C
Sarah Lawrence College	NY	48,000	HC
Seattle Pacific Univ	WA	41,559	VC+
Southwest Minn State Univ	MN	14,000	C
Stevens Inst of Technology	NJ	50,130	HC
Swarthmore College	PA	57,870	MC
The College of Idaho	ID	31,277	VC
The SUNY at Potsdam	NY	17,754	C
Touro College	NY	23,150	VC
Union College	NE	23,270	VC
United States Military Academy	NY		MC
Univ of Alaska Southeast	AK	11,493	C
Univ of Bridgeport	CT	39,030	LC
Univ of Calif at San Diego	CA	21,000	VC
Univ of Calif at Santa Barbara	CA	27,551	HC
Univ of Calif at Santa Cruz	CA	27,807	VC
Univ of Evansville	IN	41,056	VC+
Univ of Mich/Ann Arbor	MI	22,102	HC+
Univ of New Haven	CT	47,740	C
Univ of N Car at Asheville	NC	13,500	VC+
Univ of Texas at Dallas	TX	21,046	HC
Washington Univ in St. Louis	MO	58,818	MC
Waynesburg Univ	PA	29,100	C
West Chester Univ of Pennsylvania	PA	16,836	C
Wheaton College	MA	54,934	HC+
Wheeling Jesuit Univ	WV	34,668	C
Wilberforce Univ	OH	15,100	LC
Williams College	MA	58,900	MC
Wright State Univ	OH	16,983	C
Yale Univ	CT	55,300	MC
Youngstown State Univ	OH	16,374	LC

LOGISTICS

School	ST	$IS	SR
Bryant Univ	RI	49,179	VC
Central Mich Univ	MI	18,066	C
Georgia Southern Univ	GA	16,414	C
Inter-American Univ of PR/ Bayamon Univ College	PR	4,428	
John Carroll Univ	OH	44,520	C+
Missouri State Univ	MO	13,996	VC
Ohio State Univ	OH	19,887	MC
Univ of Alaska Anchorage	AK	15,290	NC
Univ of Illinois at Urbana-Champaign	IL	24,300	HC
Univ of Maryland	MD	18,801	HC
Univ of Memphis	TN	15,094	C
Univ of Missouri-St. Louis	MO	18,304	VC
Univ of North Texas	TX	15,628	C
Univ of Pennsylvania	PA	56,106	MC
Univ of St. Francis	IL	36,490	C
Univ of Tenn at Knoxville	TN	20,364	VC+

LUSO-BRAZILIAN STUDIES

School	ST	$IS	SR
New York Univ	NY	61,470	MC
Smith College	MA	57,524	MC

MANAGEMENT ENGINEERING

School	ST	$IS	SR
Appalachian State Univ	NC	12,919	VC
Claremont McKenna College	CA	58,065	MC
Pitzer College	CA	54,988	MC
Stanford Univ	CA	56,411	MC
Univ of PR/Bayamon	PR	1,600	
Western Kentucky Univ	KY	11,000	LC
Worcester Polytechnic Inst	MA	53,440	HC+

MANAGEMENT INFORMATION SYSTEMS

School	ST	$IS	SR
Adams State College	CO	13,358	LC
Adelphi Univ	NY	43,130	VC
Albertus Magnus College	CT	37,382	LC
Alverno College	WI	30,483	LC
Amridge Univ	AL	6,870	LC
Andrews Univ	MI	28,030	C+
Angelo State Univ	TX	15,049	NC
Aquinas College	MI	33,060	C
Arkansas State Univ	AR	14,980	C
Ashford Univ	IA	21,780	C
Ashland Univ	OH	25,000	C
Augsburg College	MN	35,142	C
Aurora Univ	IL	26,870	C
Barry Univ	FL	38,190	C
Baylor Univ	TX	46,720	HC
Benedictine Univ	IL	35,220	C
Bentley Univ	MA	54,555	HC+
Binghamton Univ / The SUNY	NY	20,832	HC+
Biola Univ	CA	40,320	VC
Boston Univ	MA	54,130	HC+
Bowling Green State Univ	OH	18,970	C
Bradley Univ	IL	31,874	VC
Brewton-Parker College	GA	33,388	LC
Bridgewater College	VA	39,880	C
Brigham Young Univ	UT	12,100	HC
Bryant Univ	RI	49,179	VC
Butler Univ	IN	45,898	VC+
Cal State, Chico	CA	18,952	C
Cal State, Long Beach	CA	17,534	C+
Cal State, Northridge	CA	28,313	C
Cal State, Sacramento	CA	16,200	C
Cal State, San Bernardino	CA	12,000	C
Canisius College	NY	45,602	VC
Cedarville Univ	OH	31,036	VC+
Central Conn State Univ	CT	19,212	C
Central Mich Univ	MI	18,066	C
Chatham Univ	PA	42,440	VC
Clarkson Univ	NY	53,538	HC
Cleveland State Univ	OH	21,357	C
Colo Christian Univ	CO	27,500	VC

ST = STATE **$IS** = IN-STATE COSTS **SR** = SELECTOR RATING

(continued)

School	ST	$IS	SR
Colo Mesa Univ	CO	16,669	LC
Colo Technical Univ	CO	10,500	LC
Columbus State Univ	GA	13,176	C
Creighton Univ	NE	44,058	VC+
Dallas Baptist Univ	TX	29,118	C
Daniel Webster College	NH	25,380	C
De Sales Univ	PA	42,670	C
DePaul Univ	IL	46,120	VC
Dordt College	IA	34,160	VC
Drury Univ	MO	30,319	VC
Duquesne Univ	PA	42,017	VC
East Carolina Univ	NC	14,169	C
Eastern Illinois Univ	IL	20,502	C
Eastern Mich Univ	MI	17,961	C
Elon Univ	NC	40,046	HC
Eureka College	IL	19,280	C
Excelsior College	NY	895	SP
Fayetteville State Univ	NC	10,816	C
Florida Atlantic Univ	FL	17,339	C
Florida Inst of Technology	FL	48,290	VC
Florida International Univ	FL	17,747	VC
Fort Hays State Univ	KS	11,354	C
Friends Univ	KS	29,100	C
Gannon Univ	PA	37,940	C
George Fox Univ	OR	40,750	C+
Georgetown College	KY	38,690	C
Georgia Regents Univ	GA		C
Georgia Southern Univ	GA	16,414	C
Georgia State Univ	GA	12,000	VC
Goldey-Beacom College	DE	27,493	C
Grace College and Theological Seminary	IN	28,800	C
Grand View Univ	IA	31,050	C
Greenville College	IL	27,012	C
Hofstra Univ	NY	48,020	VC+
Humphreys College	CA	17,000	NC
Idaho State Univ	ID	11,908	C
Indiana State Univ	IN	16,000	C
Indiana Univ East	IN	6,639	LC
Indiana Univ of Pennsylvania	PA	20,180	LC
Indiana Univ South Bend	IN	15,293	C
Inter-American Univ of PR/ Aguadilla Campus	PR	5,578	
Inter-American Univ of PR/ Bayamon Univ College	PR	4,428	
Inter-American Univ of PR/ Fajardo Campus	PR	4,200	
Inter-American Univ of PR/ Metropolitan Campus	PR	4,320	
Inter-American Univ of PR/ Ponce	PR	3,700	
John Carroll Univ	OH	44,520	C+
Johnson and Wales Univ/ Providence Campus	RI	34,668	C
Kansas State Univ	KS	15,497	VC
King Univ	TN	33,140	C
La Salle Univ	PA	50,270	C
Le Moyne College	NY	42,200	VC
Lenoir-Rhyne College	NC	35,984	C
LeTourneau Univ	TX	26,230	C
Lewis Univ	IL	23,050	C
Liberty Univ	VA	19,101	C
Lindenwood Univ	MO	20,750	C
Lipscomb Univ	TN	35,722	VC
Loras College	IA	37,432	VC
Loyola Univ Chicago	IL	49,560	VC+
MacMurray College	IL	20,755	C
Marietta College	OH	42,135	VC
Marquette Univ	WI	43,664	VC+
Marshall Univ	WV	14,820	C
McMurry Univ	TX	25,962	LC
Medgar Evers College / The CUNY	NY	4,920	NC
Menlo College	CA	49,002	C
Mercyhurst Univ	PA	40,700	C
Messiah College	PA	39,540	VC
Metropolitan State Univ	MN	5,923	SP
Miami Univ	OH	24,191	HC
Midland Univ	NE	34,000	C
Milwaukee School of Engineering	WI	39,948	VC+
Minot State Univ	ND	10,915	C
Missouri Southern State Univ	MO	11,910	C
Missouri Univ of Science and Technology	MO	18,655	VC+
Montclair State Univ	NJ	22,614	C
Morehead State Univ	KY	10,900	C
Morningside College	IA	32,620	C
Mount Aloysius College	PA	27,970	C
Mount Mercy Univ	IA	34,385	C
Mount Vernon Nazarene Univ	OH	29,590	C
New Mexico Highlands Univ	NM	9,720	NC
New Mexico State Univ	NM	13,955	LC
New York Univ	NY	61,470	MC
Newman Univ	KS	30,380	C+
Nichols College	MA	37,240	LC
N Dak State Univ	ND	14,642	C
Northeastern Univ	MA	55,296	MC
Northern Kentucky Univ	KY	15,302	LC
Northwest Christian Univ	OR	27,399	C
Northwestern College	MN	24,000	C
Northwood Univ	MI	26,331	LC
Oakland Univ	MI	19,391	VC
Ohio Dominican Univ	OH	38,380	C+
Ohio Univ	OH	20,676	VC
Okla State Univ	OK	14,310	VC
Old Dominion Univ	VA	18,662	C
Oral Roberts Univ	OK	31,734	C
Oregon Inst of Technology	OR	8,910	C
Oregon State Univ	OR	19,017	C+
Ottawa Univ	KS	15,000	VC
Our Lady of the Lake Univ of San Antonio	TX	22,430	LC
Park Univ	MO	17,525	C
Peirce College	PA	12,760	NC
Penn State Erie/The Behrend College	PA	16,256	C
Penn State Univ/Univ Park	PA	25,404	VC
Pennsylvania College of Technology	PA	25,653	NC
Philadelphia Univ	PA	44,160	C
Rensselaer Polytechnic Inst	NY	59,229	MC
Rivier College	NH	35,000	VC
Rochester Inst of Technology	NY	42,450	VC+
Rockford College	IL	31,000	C
Rutgers, The State Univ of New Jersey/New Brunswick	NJ	25,077	VC
St. Francis Univ	PA	30,029	LC
St. Joseph's Univ	PA	52,272	VC
St. Louis Univ	MO	46,594	VC+
St. Mary's College	IN	45,160	VC
Salisbury Univ	MD	18,368	VC
Santa Clara Univ	CA	54,702	MC
Savannah State Univ	GA	13,156	C
Schreiner Univ	TX	32,734	LC
Seton Hall Univ	NJ	45,902	C
Seton Hill Univ	PA	35,172	C
Shippensburg Univ of Pennsylvania	PA	17,064	LC
Simmons College	MA	48,770	VC
Southeastern Univ	FL	27,201	C+
Southern Illinois Univ Edwardsville	IL	17,532	C
Southern Methodist Univ	TX	57,755	MC
Southern Nazarene Univ	OK	24,354	NC
Southwestern Okla State Univ	OK	9,160	C
Spring Arbor Univ	MI	26,740	C
St. Bonaventure Univ	NY	38,831	C
St. Catherine Univ	MN	37,782	C+
St. John's Univ	NY	52,840	C+
SUNY/Empire State College	NY	6,315	SP
Stephen F. Austin State Univ	TX	14,668	C
Stetson Univ	FL	49,512	VC+
SUNY College at Old Westbury	NY	16,324	C
SUNY Plattsburgh / SUNY	NY	18,083	VC
Taylor Univ	IN	36,742	VC+
Temple Univ	PA	24,392	VC
Tenn Wesleyan College	TN	21,250	C
Texas A&M Univ at Corpus Christi	TX	11,544	LC
Texas Tech Univ	TX	14,243	C
Texas Wesleyan Univ	TX	29,886	C
Ohio State Univ	OH	19,887	MC
Thiel College	PA	31,378	LC
Thomas College	ME	26,270	LC
Trine Univ	IN	39,400	VC
Univ of Alabama at Tuscaloosa	AL	17,164	C+
Univ of Alaska Anchorage	AK	15,290	NC
Univ of Arizona	AZ	20,105	C
Univ of Arkansas at Monticello	AR	8,470	NC
Univ of Bridgeport	CT	39,030	LC
Univ of Central Okla	OK	12,293	C
Univ of Conn	CT	23,744	HC
Univ of Dayton	OH	43,750	VC
Univ of Delaware	DE	22,728	VC
Univ of Evansville	IN	41,056	VC+
Univ of Georgia	GA	19,508	VC
Univ of Hartford	CT	42,674	C
Univ of Hawaii at Manoa	HI	19,379	VC
Univ of Houston	TX	19,184	VC
Univ of Idaho	ID	14,558	C
Univ of Illinois at Urbana-Champaign	IL	24,300	HC
Univ of Indianapolis	IN	31,740	LC
Univ of Jamestown	ND	24,738	C
Univ of Kansas	KS	16,980	C+
Univ of Louisiana at Monroe	LA	12,998	C
Univ of Mary	ND	16,714	C
Univ of Maryland	MD	18,801	HC
Univ of Maryland/Univ College	MD	6,168	SP
Univ of Mass Dartmouth	MA	22,223	C
Univ of Memphis	TN	15,094	C
Univ of Mich/Dearborn	MI	9,885	VC
Univ of Minn/Duluth	MN	18,964	C+
Univ of Miss	MS	15,482	VC
Univ of Missouri-St. Louis	MO	18,304	VC
Univ of Montana-Western	MT	9,753	LC
Univ of Nebr at Omaha	NE	12,700	C
Univ of Nevada, Las Vegas	NV	17,303	C
Univ of N Car at Charlotte	NC	15,847	C
Univ of North Texas	TX	15,628	C
Univ of Northern Iowa	IA	14,776	C
Univ of Notre Dame	IN		MC
Univ of Okla	OK	17,634	VC+
Univ of Pennsylvania	PA	56,106	MC
Univ of San Francisco	CA	49,674	VC
Univ of South Florida	FL	13,000	C
Univ of Southern Indiana	IN	14,657	C
Univ of Tampa	FL	35,160	VC
Univ of Texas at Austin	TX	44,074	HC
Univ of Texas at El Paso	TX	8,764	NC
Univ of the Sacred Heart	PR	5,590	
Univ of Tulsa	OK	45,311	HC+
Univ of Utah	UT	13,462	VC
Univ of West Georgia	GA	14,852	LC
Univ of Wisc/Oshkosh	WI	10,426	LC
Univ of Wisc-Milwaukee	WI	18,436	C
Univ of Wyoming	WY	13,855	C+
Upper Iowa Univ	IA	30,426	NC
Ursuline College	OH	33,198	LC
Utah State Univ	UT	11,803	C
Villanova Univ	PA	56,436	MC
Virginia State Univ	VA	11,318	C+
Viterbo Univ	WI	30,070	C
Washington State Univ	WA	20,461	C
Wayland Baptist Univ	TX	16,058	LC
Wayne State Univ	MI	19,493	C
Western Conn State Univ	CT	18,327	C
Western Illinois Univ	IL	20,130	C
Western Kentucky Univ	KY	11,000	LC
Western Mich Univ	MI	19,042	C
Western New Mexico Univ	NM	8,500	LC
Western Washington Univ	WA	18,519	VC
Westminster College	MO	30,490	VC
Widener Univ	PA	50,368	C
Winona State Univ	MN	16,530	C
Winston-Salem State Univ	NC	9,418	LC
Worcester Polytechnic Inst	MA	53,440	HC+
Wright State Univ	OH	16,983	C
York College of Pennsylvania	PA	26,590	C
Youngstown State Univ	OH	16,374	LC

MANAGEMENT SCIENCE

School	ST	$IS	SR
Abilene Christian Univ	TX	38,400	VC
Alabama A&M Univ	AL	96,100	C
Anderson Univ	IN	35,390	C
Arkansas State Univ	AR	14,980	C
Aurora Univ	IL	26,870	C
Avila Univ	MO	26,900	C
Barry Univ	FL	38,190	C
Belmont Univ	TN	37,380	VC+
Bethany College	WV	35,282	C
Bethel Univ	TN	19,186	C
Binghamton Univ / The SUNY	NY	20,832	HC+
Biola Univ	CA	40,320	VC
Boston College	MA	58,506	MC
Boston Univ	MA	54,130	HC+
Bridgewater State Univ	MA	18,752	C
Brigham Young Univ	UT	12,100	HC
Bryant Univ	RI	49,179	VC
Caldwell College	NJ	35,602	LC
Cal State, Fullerton	CA	25,188	C+
Cal State, Monterey Bay	CA	26,871	LC
Cal State, San Bernardino	CA	12,000	C
Calif Univ of Pennsylvania	PA	14,217	C
Cambridge College	MA	13,392	NC
Canisius College	NY	45,602	VC
Cazenovia College	NY	30,800	C
Central Mich Univ	MI	18,066	C
Chaminade Univ of Honolulu	HI	31,664	C
Champlain College	VT	44,850	VC
Chicago State Univ	IL	5,482	C
CUNY/Baruch College	NY	15,831	VC
Claflin Univ	SC	22,368	C+
Clemson Univ	SC	19,136	HC
Cleveland State Univ	OH	21,357	C
College of St. Benedict	MN	47,570	VC
College of St. Scholastica	MN	39,960	C
Colo Christian Univ	CO	27,500	VC
Colo Technical Univ	CO	10,500	LC
Concordia Univ Wisc	WI	28,980	C
Coppin State Univ	MD	14,905	VC
Creighton Univ	NE	44,058	VC+
Cumberland Univ	TN	21,220	C
Davenport Univ	MI	21,002	LC
Davis and Elkins College	WV	33,742	C
Defiance College	OH	30,645	C
Delta State Univ	MS	12,292	LC
DePaul Univ	IL	46,120	VC
Drake Univ	IA	30,980	VC+
Duquesne Univ	PA	42,017	VC
East Tenn State Univ	TN	9,000	C
Eastern Mich Univ	MI	17,961	C
Eastern Washington Univ	WA	16,388	C
Eckerd College	FL	43,902	VC
Elmhurst College	IL	42,032	C+
Embry-Riddle Aeronautical Univ - Worldwide	FL	15,512	C
Evangel Univ	MO	23,090	C
Faulkner Univ	AL	22,530	LC
Fitchburg State Univ	MA	17,241	C
Florida State Univ	FL	15,238	HC
Franklin Pierce Univ	NH	41,598	C
Franklin Univ	OH	7,000	SP
George Fox Univ	OR	40,750	C+
Georgia College and State Univ	GA	18,216	VC
Goodwin College	CT	19,400	LC
Grand Canyon Univ	AZ	24,540	VC
Grand Valley State Univ	MI	17,998	VC
Granite State College	NH	6,195	SP
Gwynedd-Mercy College	PA	33,560	C
Hardin-Simmons Univ	TX	23,560	C+
Hawaii Pacific Univ	HI	36,690	C
Heidelberg Univ	OH	34,100	C
Hiram College	OH	37,300	VC
Hood College	MD	44,630	C
Idaho State Univ	ID	11,908	C
Illinois State Univ	IL	22,634	VC
Indiana Univ-Purdue Univ Fort Wayne	IN	15,425	C
Indiana Wesleyan Univ	IN	31,815	VC
Iona College	NY	44,028	C
Iowa State Univ	IA	16,403	C
Johnson and Wales Univ/ Denver Campus	CO	34,368	C
Kean Univ	NJ	22,060	LC
Kennesaw State Univ	GA	13,017	VC
Langston Univ	OK	3,000	LC
Lehman College / The CUNY	NY	5,778	LC
Lesley Univ	MA	46,350	C
Limestone College	SC	29,880	C
Louisiana State Univ	LA	18,677	VC+
Louisiana State Univ in Shreveport	LA	5,606	C
Louisiana Tech Univ	LA	8,000	C
Loyola Univ New Orleans	LA	46,581	VC
Luther College	IA	44,380	VC+
Lynchburg College	VA	42,645	C
Madonna Univ	MI	24,540	VC
Maharishi Univ of Management	IA	31,000	VC
Manhattanville College	NY	46,260	VC
Marian Univ	WI	30,980	LC
Marylhurst Univ	OR	18,945	NC
Mass Inst of Technology	MA	54,238	MC
Metropolitan State Univ of Denver	CO	4,835	LC
Miami Univ	OH	24,191	HC
Midwestern State Univ	TX	9,722	C
Millikin Univ	IL	37,462	C
Milwaukee School of Engineering	WI	39,948	VC+
Minn State Univ, Mankato	MN	14,900	C
Minn State Univ, Moorhead	MN	13,392	C
Minot State Univ	ND	10,915	C
Missouri Baptist Univ	MO	30,310	C
Missouri Southern State Univ	MO	11,910	C
Missouri State Univ	MO	13,996	VC
Morehead State Univ	KY	10,900	C
Mount Aloysius College	PA	27,970	C
Mount Vernon Nazarene Univ	OH	29,590	C
Murray State Univ	KY	14,944	C
National Louis Univ	IL	16,915	LC
National Univ	CA	14,730	SP
New Jersey Inst of Technology	NJ	26,490	VC
New York Univ	NY	61,470	MC
Northeastern Illinois Univ	IL		C
Northern Arizona Univ	AZ	18,592	C
Northern Kentucky Univ	KY	15,302	LC
Notre Dame College	OH	34,942	VC
Ohio Northern Univ	OH	42,075	VC
Ohio Univ	OH	20,676	VC
Okla City Univ	OK	33,546	VC
Oral Roberts Univ	OK	31,734	C
Oregon State Univ	OR	19,017	C+
Oswego / SUNY	NY	20,009	VC
Palm Beach Atlantic Univ	FL	33,882	LC
Pepperdine Univ	CA	55,372	HC+
Philadelphia Univ	PA	44,160	C
Point Park Univ	PA	36,390	C
Portland State Univ	OR	18,672	C
Post Univ	CT	35,750	C
Prescott College	AZ	33,284	C+
Quinnipiac Univ	CT	53,580	VC
Regis College	MA	47,565	LC
Rensselaer Polytechnic Inst	NY	59,229	MC
Rice Univ	TX	43,288	MC
Richard Stockton College of New Jersey	NJ	20,000	VC
Rider Univ	NJ	45,720	C
Rivier College	NH	35,000	VC
Rochester Inst of Technology	NY	42,450	VC+
Roger Williams Univ	RI	45,788	C
Roosevelt Univ	IL	22,605	VC
Rutgers, The State Univ of New Jersey/Camden Campus	NJ	24,254	C
Rutgers, The State Univ of New Jersey/New Brunswick	NJ	25,077	VC
Rutgers, The State Univ of New Jersey/Newark Campus	NJ	25,376	C
St. Francis Univ	PA	30,029	LC
St. John's Univ	MN	46,146	C

ST = STATE **$IS** = IN-STATE COSTS **SR** = SELECTOR RATING

School	ST	$IS	SR
St. Joseph College	CT	45,630	LC
St. Leo Univ	FL	27,990	C
Salve Regina Univ	RI	47,250	VC
Samford Univ	AL	35,700	VC+
San Francisco State Univ	CA	18,514	C
Southern Illinois Univ Carbondale	IL	21,620	C
Southern Methodist Univ	TX	57,755	MC
Southern Nazarene Univ	OK	24,354	NC
Southwestern Adventist Univ	TX	23,026	LC
Southwestern Okla State Univ	OK	9,160	C
St. Ambrose Univ	IA		C
St. Bonaventure Univ	NY	38,831	C
St. Francis College	NY	34,200	LC
St. John's Univ	NY	52,840	C+
SUNY/Empire State College	NY	6,315	SP
Stephen F. Austin State Univ	TX	14,668	C
Suffolk Univ	MA	46,548	C
SUNY Cortland / The SUNY	NY	19,117	C
Syracuse Univ	NY	54,512	HC
Tarleton State Univ	TX	13,489	LC
Taylor Univ	IN	36,742	VC+
Tenn Tech Univ	TN	11,310	C
Texas A&M Univ	TX	16,956	VC+
Texas A&M Univ at Kingsville	TX	7,500	LC
The Catholic Univ of America	DC	52,852	VC
The Lincoln Univ	PA	15,154	LC
Thomas College	ME	26,270	LC
Touro College	NY	23,150	VC
Trine Univ	IN	39,400	VC
Troy Univ	AL	10,650	C
Tulane Univ	LA	58,942	MC
Tusculum College	TN	24,295	C
Tuskegee Univ	AL	26,750	C
Union College	NE	23,270	VC
Union Univ	TN	28,260	VC
United States Air Force Academy	CO		MC
United States Coast Guard Academy	CT		HC
United States Military Academy	NY		MC
Universidad del Turabo	PR	4,110	
Universidad Metropolitana	PR		
Univ of Akron	OH	20,436	C
Univ of Arizona	AZ	20,105	C
Univ of Arkansas at Little Rock	AR		C
Univ of Bridgeport	CT	39,030	LC
Univ of Calif at Berkeley	CA	23,322	MC
Univ of Calif at Riverside	CA	27,204	C
Univ of Calif at San Diego	CA	21,000	VC
Univ of Central Florida	FL	15,711	VC+
Univ of Central Missouri	MO	14,605	C
Univ of Cincinnati	OH	20,199	VC
Univ of Colo Boulder	CO	22,605	VC+
Univ of Delaware	DE	22,728	VC
Univ of Florida	FL	15,783	HC+
Univ of Georgia	GA	19,508	VC
Univ of Great Falls	MT	27,970	C
Univ of Hartford	CT	42,674	C
Univ of Hawaii at Manoa	HI	19,379	VC
Univ of Illinois at Chicago	IL	24,293	VC
Univ of Illinois at Urbana-Champaign	IL	24,300	HC
Univ of Iowa	IA	17,481	VC
Univ of Louisiana at Lafayette	LA	6,130	C
Univ of Louisiana at Monroe	LA	12,998	C
Univ of Louisville	KY	17,460	VC
Univ of Maryland/Univ College	MD	6,168	SP
Univ of Mass Boston	MA	11,966	C
Univ of Memphis	TN	15,094	C
Univ of Miami	FL	55,166	MC
Univ of Mich/Dearborn	MI	9,885	VC
Univ of Minn/Morris	MN	17,150	VC
Univ of Minn/Twin Cities	MN		HC
Univ of Miss	MS	15,482	VC
Univ of Montevallo	AL	17,320	C
Univ of Nebr - Lincoln	NE	17,507	VC
Univ of Nebr at Omaha	NE	12,700	C
Univ of Nevada, Las Vegas	NV	17,303	C
Univ of Nevada/Reno	NV	14,500	NC
Univ of N Car at Chapel Hill	NC	18,348	MC
Univ of North Texas	TX	15,628	C
Univ of Northern Colo	CO	15,973	C
Univ of Northern Iowa	IA	14,776	C
Univ of Notre Dame	IN		MC
Univ of Pittsburgh at Greensburg	PA	17,640	C
Univ of PR Recinto de Rio Piedras	PR	5,750	
Univ of PR/Cayey	PR	1,504	
Univ of S Car at Columbia	SC	19,725	VC+
Univ of S Dak	SD	15,111	C
Univ of South Florida	FL	13,000	C
Univ of South Florida/St. Petersburg	FL	12,769	VC
Univ of St. Francis	IL	36,490	C
Univ of Tenn at Knoxville	TN	20,364	VC+
Univ of Tenn at Martin	TN	13,217	C
Univ of Texas at Arlington	TX	10,908	LC
Univ of Texas at Austin	TX	44,074	HC
Univ of Texas at El Paso	TX	8,764	NC
Univ of Texas at San Antonio	TX	18,372	C
Univ of Texas-Pan American	TX	12,432	LC
Univ of Tulsa	OK	45,311	HC+
Univ of Utah	UT	13,462	VC
Univ of Wisc/Stout	WI	23,942	C
Univ of Wyoming	WY	13,855	C+
Upper Iowa Univ	IA	30,426	NC
Valparaiso Univ	IN	43,040	VC+
Virginia Polytechnic Inst and State Univ	VA	14,629	HC
Viterbo Univ	WI	30,070	C
Waynesburg Univ	PA	29,100	C
Webber International Univ	FL	25,664	C
Webster Univ	MO	33,990	C+
West Liberty Univ	WV	9,142	LC
West Texas A&M Univ	TX	13,478	C
Western Carolina Univ	NC	13,965	C+
Western Kentucky Univ	KY	11,000	LC
Western New England Univ	MA	45,590	C
Western Washington Univ	WA	18,519	VC
Wheeling Jesuit Univ	WV	34,668	C
Wichita State Univ	KS	12,539	C
Wilberforce Univ	OH	15,100	LC
Wilmington College	OH	29,784	C
Wright State Univ	OH	16,983	C
Xavier Univ	OH	43,740	VC

MANUFACTURING ENGINEERING

School	ST	$IS	SR
Boston Univ	MA	54,130	HC+
Bradley Univ	IL	31,874	VC
Brigham Young Univ	UT	12,100	HC
Calif Polytechnic State Univ	CA	19,847	HC
Calif State Polytechnic Univ, Pomona	CA	18,932	C
Central State Univ	OH	9,010	C
Eastern Mich Univ	MI	17,961	C
Ferris State Univ	MI	19,698	C
Hofstra Univ	NY	48,020	VC+
Kansas State Univ	KS	15,497	VC
Miami Univ	OH	24,191	HC
Mich State Univ	MI	13,689	VC
Midwestern State Univ	TX	9,722	C
Missouri Univ of Science and Technology	MO	18,655	VC+
New Jersey Inst of Technology	NJ	26,490	VC
New York Inst of Technology	NY	40,590	VC
N Dak State Univ	ND	14,642	C
Northern Kentucky Univ	KY	15,302	LC
Northwestern Univ	IL	37,595	MC
Oregon State Univ	OR	19,017	C+
Pennsylvania College of Technology	PA	25,653	NC
Purdue Univ/West Lafayette	IN	20,278	HC
Robert Morris Univ	PA	36,699	C
Rochester Inst of Technology	NY	42,450	VC+
Southern Illinois Univ Edwardsville	IL	17,532	C
Southwestern Okla State Univ	OK	9,160	C
St. Cloud State Univ	MN	10,600	C
Tenn Tech Univ	TN	11,310	C
Texas State Univ	TX	16,495	VC
Univ of Arkansas at Little Rock	AR		C
Univ of Calif at Berkeley	CA	23,322	MC
Univ of Conn	CT	23,744	HC
Univ of Detroit Mercy	MI	30,450	C
Univ of Mass Dartmouth	MA	22,223	C
Univ of Memphis	TN	15,094	C
Univ of Mich/Dearborn	MI	9,885	VC
Univ of North Texas	TX	15,628	C
Univ of Texas-Pan American	TX	12,432	LC
Univ of Wisc/Stout	WI	23,942	C
Washington State Univ	WA	20,461	C
Western Mich Univ	MI	19,042	C
Wichita State Univ	KS	12,539	C

MANUFACTURING TECHNOLOGY

School	ST	$IS	SR
Alabama State Univ	AL	14,142	NC
Alfred State / SUNY College of Technology	NY	18,034	C
Arizona State Univ	AZ	18,818	C+
Arkansas State Univ	AR	14,980	C
Bradley Univ	IL	31,874	VC
Brigham Young Univ	UT	12,100	HC
Central Conn State Univ	CT	19,212	C
Central Mich Univ	MI	18,066	C
Eastern Kentucky Univ	KY	11,161	C
Eastern Mich Univ	MI	17,961	C
Edinboro Univ of Pennsylvania	PA	15,940	LC
Fairmont State Univ	WV	12,098	LC
Farmingdale State College	NY	18,985	C
Fitchburg State Univ	MA	17,241	C
Idaho State Univ	ID	11,908	C
Illinois Inst of Technology	IL	38,512	HC+
Indiana State Univ	IN	16,000	C
Lake Superior State Univ	MI	18,121	C
Minn State Univ, Mankato	MN	14,900	C
Missouri Southern State Univ	MO	11,910	C
Montana State Univ-Northern	MT	12,500	NC
Murray State Univ	KY	14,944	C
Nicholls State Univ	LA	7,095	C
Northern Kentucky Univ	KY	15,302	LC
Northern Mich Univ	MI	15,300	VC
Oregon Inst of Technology	OR	8,910	C
Pittsburg State Univ	KS	12,032	C
Purdue Univ/West Lafayette	IN	20,278	HC
Rochester Inst of Technology	NY	42,450	VC+
S Dak State Univ	SD	14,296	C
Southern Arkansas Univ	AR	14,316	C
Southwestern Okla State Univ	OK	9,160	C
Texas State Univ	TX	16,495	VC
Univ of Central Missouri	MO	14,605	C
Univ of Dayton	OH	43,750	VC
Univ of Northern Iowa	IA	14,776	C
Univ of Rio Grande	OH	8,750	NC
Univ of Southern Indiana	IN	14,657	C
Wayne State Univ	MI	19,493	C
Western Carolina Univ	NC	13,965	C+
Western Illinois Univ	IL	20,130	C
Western Mich Univ	MI	19,042	C
Western Washington Univ	WA	18,519	VC

MARINE BIOLOGY

School	ST	$IS	SR
Alaska Pacific Univ	AK	33,360	VC
Auburn Univ	AL	20,052	VC+
Barry Univ	FL	38,190	C
Brown Univ	RI	56,150	MC
Carroll Univ	WI	24,860	C
Central Methodist Univ	MO	28,240	VC
College of Charleston	SC	21,273	VC
Dowling College	NY	25,000	LC
Eastern Nazarene College	MA	30,000	C
Fairleigh Dickinson Univ/Metropolitan Campus	NJ	40,254	C
Florida Atlantic Univ	FL	17,339	C
Florida Inst of Technology	FL	48,290	VC
Florida International Univ	FL	17,747	VC
Florida Southern College	FL	38,240	VC
Florida State Univ	FL	15,238	HC
Hampshire College	MA	58,320	MC
Missouri Southern State Univ	MO	11,910	C
Monmouth Univ	NJ	42,252	C
New College of Florida	FL	14,504	HC+
Northeastern Univ	MA	55,296	MC
Nova Southeastern Univ	FL	34,016	VC
Ohio Univ	OH	20,676	VC
Old Dominion Univ	VA	18,662	C
Prescott College	AZ	33,284	C+
Roger Williams Univ	RI	45,788	C
Rollins College	FL	52,370	HC
St. Paul's College	VA	16,030	NC
San Francisco State Univ	CA	18,514	C
Savannah State Univ	GA	13,156	C
Seattle Univ	WA	47,010	VC+
Southwestern College	KS	29,270	C
Spring Hill College	AL	42,130	VC
Stetson Univ	FL	49,512	VC+
Stony Brook Univ / SUNY	NY	19,359	HC
Texas A&M Univ at Galveston	TX	11,258	C
Texas State Univ	TX	16,495	VC
Troy Univ	AL	10,650	C
Unity College	ME	34,054	C
Univ of Alaska Southeast	AK	11,493	C
Univ of Calif at Los Angeles	CA	25,686	MC
Univ of Calif at Santa Barbara	CA	27,551	HC
Univ of Calif at Santa Cruz	CA	27,807	VC
Univ of Hawaii at Manoa	HI	19,379	VC
Univ of Maine	ME	19,712	C+
Univ of Maine at Machias	ME	10,523	C
Univ of Mass Dartmouth	MA	22,223	C
Univ of Miami	FL	55,166	MC
Univ of New England	ME	46,145	C+
Univ of New Haven	CT	47,740	C
Univ of N Car at Wilmington	NC	13,572	VC+
Univ of Oregon	OR	20,872	VC
Univ of PR/Humacao	PR	1,877	
Univ of West Alabama	AL	9,415	C
Univ of West Florida	FL	14,656	C
Waynesburg Univ	PA	29,100	C
Western Washington Univ	WA	18,519	VC

MARINE ENGINEERING

School	ST	$IS	SR
Calif Maritime Academy	CA	15,496	C
Maine Maritime Academy	ME	21,073	C
Maritime College / SUNY	NY	16,020	C
Mass Maritime Academy	MA	15,340	C
Texas A&M Univ at Galveston	TX	11,258	C
United States Merchant Marine Academy	NY		HC+
United States Naval Academy	MD		MC
Univ of New Orleans	LA	9,224	VC

MARINE ENGINEERING SYSTEMS

School	ST	$IS	SR
United States Merchant Marine Academy	NY		HC+

MARINE ENGINEERING/ SHIPYARD MANAGEMENT

School	ST	$IS	SR
United States Merchant Marine Academy	NY		HC+

MARINE SCIENCE

School	ST	$IS	SR
Coastal Carolina Univ	SC	17,620	C
East Stroudsburg Univ of Pennsylvania	PA	16,636	C
Eckerd College	FL	40,902	VC
Florida Gulf Coast Univ	FL		C
Hawaii Pacific Univ	HI	36,690	C
Jacksonville Univ	FL	37,780	C
Kutztown Univ of Pennsylvania	PA	16,909	LC
Maritime College / SUNY	NY	16,020	C
Montclair State Univ	NJ	22,614	C
Nova Southeastern Univ	FL	34,016	VC
Prescott College	AZ	33,284	C+
Richard Stockton College of New Jersey	NJ	20,000	VC
Rider Univ	NJ	45,720	C
Rutgers, The State Univ of New Jersey/New Brunswick	NJ	25,077	VC
St. Paul's College	VA	16,030	NC
Samford Univ	AL	35,700	VC+
San Jose State Univ	CA	19,707	C
Suffolk Univ	MA	46,548	C
Texas A&M Univ at Galveston	TX	11,258	C
United States Coast Guard Academy	CT		HC
Univ of Alabama at Tuscaloosa	AL	17,164	C+
Univ of Conn	CT	23,744	HC
Univ of Georgia	GA	19,508	VC
Univ of Hawaii at Hilo	HI	6,500	C
Univ of Maine	ME	19,712	C+
Univ of Miami	FL	55,166	MC
Univ of Mobile	AL	27,870	VC
Univ of New England	ME	46,145	C+
Univ of N Car at Wilmington	NC	13,572	VC+
Univ of San Diego	CA	53,302	HC+
Univ of S Car at Columbia	SC	19,725	VC+
Univ of Tampa	FL	35,160	VC
West Chester Univ of Pennsylvania	PA	16,836	C
Western Washington Univ	WA	18,519	VC

MARINE TRANSPORTATION

School	ST	$IS	SR
United States Merchant Marine Academy	NY		HC+

MARITIME LOGISTICS & SECURITY

School	ST	$IS	SR
United States Merchant Marine Academy	NY		HC+

MARITIME SCIENCE

School	ST	$IS	SR
Calif Maritime Academy	CA	15,496	C
Maine Maritime Academy	ME	21,073	C
Maritime College / SUNY	NY	16,020	C
Texas A&M Univ at Galveston	TX	11,258	C

MARKETING

School	ST	$IS	SR
Arkansas State Univ	AR	14,980	C
Baldwin Wallace Univ	OH	36,980	VC
Bowling Green State Univ	OH	18,970	C
Bryant Univ	RI	49,179	VC
Cabrini College	PA	40,859	LC
Christopher Newport Univ	VA	21,050	VC
Corban Univ	OR	34,764	C
Elon Univ	NC	40,046	HC
Fairfield Univ	CT	55,850	VC
Ferris State Univ	MI	19,698	C
Hood College	MD	44,630	C
Indiana Univ Bloomington	IN	19,358	HC
Indiana Univ East	IN	6,639	LC

School	ST	$IS	SR
Indiana Univ Kokomo	IN	6,674	LC
Indiana Univ-Purdue Univ Indianapolis	IN	17,290	C
Limestone College	SC	29,880	C
McNeese State Univ	LA		C
Nova Southeastern Univ	FL	34,016	VC
Okla City Univ	OK	33,546	VC
Rutgers, The State Univ of New Jersey/New Brunswick	NJ	25,077	VC
Rutgers, The State Univ of New Jersey/Newark Campus	NJ	25,376	C
St. Louis Univ	MO	46,594	V₲
St. Mary's Univ of Minn	MN	37,015	C
Southern Oregon Univ	OR	17,874	C
Tiffin Univ	OH	30,273	LC
Univ of Evansville	IN	41,056	V₲
Univ of Georgia	GA	19,508	VC
Univ of Louisiana at Monroe	LA	12,998	C
Univ of Miami	FL	55,166	MC
Univ of N Car at Charlotte	NC	15,847	C
Univ of St. Thomas - Houston	TX	36,490	VC
Univ of Wisc/Eau Claire	WI	15,430	VC
Univ of Wyoming	WY	13,855	₲
Winona State Univ	MN	16,530	C

MARKETING AND DISTRIBUTION

School	ST	$IS	SR
Alvernia Univ	PA	39,250	C
Aquinas College	MI	33,060	C
Becker College	MA	41,420	LC
Bryant Univ	RI	49,179	VC
Caldwell College	NJ	35,602	LC
Central Mich Univ	MI	18,066	C
Clayton State Univ	GA	12,000	LC
Florida Gulf Coast Univ	FL		C
Fort Lewis College	CO	15,513	C
Franklin Univ	OH	7,000	SP
Georgia College and State Univ	GA	18,216	VC
Gwynedd-Mercy College	PA	33,560	C
Indiana State Univ	IN	16,000	C
Inter-American Univ of PR/ Arecibo Campus	PR	3,350	
Johnson and Wales Univ/ Charlotte Campus	NC	35,421	C
Johnson and Wales Univ/ Providence Campus	RI	34,668	C
Kent State Univ	OH	19,352	C
Lake Erie College	OH	35,704	C
Limestone College	SC	29,880	C
Metropolitan State Univ	MN	5,923	SP
Mountain State Univ	WV	14,330	NC
Murray State Univ	KY	14,944	C
Nazareth College of Rochester	NY	41,590	VC
Neumann Univ	PA	31,078	LC
New Mexico Highlands Univ	NM	9,720	NC
New York Inst of Technology	NY	40,590	VC
Northern Kentucky Univ	KY	15,302	LC
Our Lady of Holy Cross College	LA	8,090	LC
Salve Regina Univ	RI	47,250	VC
Simmons College	MA	48,770	VC
Southern Illinois Univ Edwardsville	IL	17,532	C
Southwest Baptist Univ	MO	24,710	C
SUNY/Empire State College	NY	6,315	SP
Tarleton State Univ	TX	13,489	LC
Texas Tech Univ	TX	14,243	C
The Catholic Univ of America	DC	52,852	VC
Ohio State Univ	OH	19,887	MC
Union College	NE	23,270	VC
Univ of Arizona	AZ	20,105	C
Univ of Houston	TX	19,184	VC
Univ of Illinois at Urbana-Champaign	IL	24,300	HC
Univ of South Florida/St. Petersburg	FL	12,769	VC
Univ of West Georgia	GA	14,852	LC
West Virginia Univ	WV	15,794	₲
Western Carolina Univ	NC	13,965	₲
Western Kentucky Univ	KY	11,000	LC
Wilkes Univ	PA	42,786	C
Wilmington College	OH	29,784	C

MARKETING AND DISTRIBUTION EDUCATION

School	ST	$IS	SR
Central Washington Univ	WA	11,730	C
Dakota State Univ	SD	13,811	C
East Carolina Univ	NC	14,169	C
Eastern Washington Univ	WA	16,388	C
Fayetteville State Univ	NC	10,816	C
Johnson and Wales Univ/ Providence Campus	RI	34,668	C
N Car State Univ	NC	16,202	HC
Rider Univ	NJ	45,720	C
Univ of Nebr - Lincoln	NE	17,507	VC
Univ of Tenn at Knoxville	TN	20,364	V₲
Univ of Wisc/Stout	WI	23,942	C
Western Kentucky Univ	KY	11,000	LC

MARKETING MANAGEMENT

School	ST	$IS	SR
Adrian College	MI	33,800	C
Alverno College	WI	30,483	LC
Aquinas College	MI	33,060	C
Ashford Univ	IA	21,780	C
Assumption College	MA	45,721	VC
Aurora Univ	IL	26,870	C
Averett Univ	VA	36,000	LC
Baker College of Flint	MI	7,800	NC
Benedictine Univ	IL	35,220	C
Berry College	GA	39,254	HC
Bethany College	KS	30,605	NC
Binghamton Univ / The SUNY	NY	20,832	H₲
Biola Univ	CA	40,320	VC
Brigham Young Univ	UT	12,100	HC
Bryant Univ	RI	49,179	VC
Campbellsville Univ	KY	27,720	C
Canisius College	NY	45,602	VC
Carthage College	WI	33,000	C
Case Western Reserve Univ	OH	55,178	MC
Catawba College	NC	37,105	C
Central Mich Univ	MI	18,066	C
Champlain College	VT	44,850	VC
Chatham Univ	PA	42,440	VC
CUNY/Baruch College	NY	15,831	VC
Clarke Univ	IA	36,400	C
Cleary Univ	MI	11,000	C
College of St. Scholastica	MN	39,960	C
College of the Ozarks	MO	5,605	VC
College of William & Mary	VA	25,085	MC
Columbia College Chicago	IL	30,940	LC
Concordia Univ St. Paul	MN	27,200	C
Corban Univ	OR	34,764	C
Cumberland Univ	TN	21,220	C
Daniel Webster College	NH	25,380	C
Davenport Univ	MI	21,002	LC
DePaul Univ	IL	46,120	VC
Dominican Univ	IL	37,628	C
Dordt College	IA	34,160	VC
Drake Univ	IA	30,980	V₲
Drury Univ	MO	30,319	VC
East Carolina Univ	NC	14,169	C
Eastern Mich Univ	MI	17,961	C
Elizabethtown College	PA	47,600	VC
Elon Univ	NC	40,046	HC
Emerson College	MA	50,246	HC
Endicott College	MA	42,390	C
Felician College	NJ	41,640	C
Fitchburg State Univ	MA	17,241	C
Florida Inst of Technology	FL	48,290	VC
Fontbonne Univ	MO	31,384	C
Fordham Univ	NY	58,927	HC
George Washington Univ	DC	57,108	MC
Goldey-Beacom College	DE	27,493	C
Grove City College	PA	22,988	HC
Hardin-Simmons Univ	TX	23,560	₲
Hawaii Pacific Univ	HI	36,690	C
Hofstra Univ	NY	48,020	V₲
Huntington Univ	IN	32,220	C
Indiana Univ Kokomo	IN	6,674	LC
Indiana Univ of Pennsylvania	PA	20,180	LC
Iona College	NY	44,028	C
Johnson and Wales Univ/ Charlotte Campus	NC	35,421	C
Johnson and Wales Univ/ North Miami Campus	FL	34,368	C
Johnson and Wales Univ/ Providence Campus	RI	34,668	C
Kean Univ	NJ	22,060	LC
Kent State Univ	OH	19,352	C
King Univ	TN	33,140	C
La Roche College	PA	34,802	LC
La Sierra Univ	CA	35,694	VC
Lakeland College	WI	22,990	C
Le Moyne College	NY	42,200	VC
Lehigh Univ	PA	55,080	MC
LeTourneau Univ	TX	26,230	C
LIM College	NY	41,575	LC
Linfield College-McMinnville Campus	OR	46,166	C
Lipscomb Univ	TN	35,722	VC
Lourdes Univ	OH	26,055	LC
Lynn Univ	FL	43,500	C
Mary Baldwin College	VA	37,110	C
Maryville Univ of St. Louis	MO	34,920	VC
Menlo College	CA	49,002	C
Mercer Univ	GA	44,201	V₲
Metropolitan State Univ	MN	5,923	SP
Mich State Univ	MI	13,689	VC
Missouri Baptist Univ	MO	30,310	C
Monmouth Univ	NJ	42,252	C
Montclair State Univ	NJ	22,614	C
Morehead State Univ	KY	10,900	C
Mount Aloysius College	PA	27,970	C
Murray State Univ	KY	14,944	C
New York Univ	NY	61,470	MC
Northern Arizona Univ	AZ	18,592	C
Northwestern College	MN	24,000	C
Northwood Univ	FL	30,746	LC
Northwood Univ	MI	26,331	LC
Northwood Univ	TX	25,296	LC
Ohio Univ	OH	20,676	VC
Old Dominion Univ	VA	18,662	C
Olivet College	MI	19,984	C
Oregon State Univ	OR	19,017	₲
Our Lady of the Lake Univ of San Antonio	TX	22,430	LC
Palm Beach Atlantic Univ	FL	33,882	LC
Park Univ	MO	17,525	C
Peirce College	PA	12,760	NC
Penn State Erie/The Behrend College	PA	16,256	C
Penn State Univ/Univ Park	PA	25,404	VC
Pennsylvania College of Technology	PA	25,653	NC
Pepperdine Univ	CA	55,372	H₲
Pittsburg State Univ	KS	12,032	C
Plymouth State Univ	NH	23,148	LC
Providence College	RI	55,995	HC
Purdue Univ/West Lafayette	IN	20,278	HC
Quinnipiac Univ	CT	53,580	VC
Rhode Island College	RI	17,132	LC
Rochester College	MI	18,320	C
Rochester Inst of Technology	NY	42,450	V₲
Sacred Heart Univ	CT	48,564	VC
Saginaw Valley State Univ	MI	16,869	C
St. Joseph's Univ	PA	52,272	VC
St. Leo Univ	FL	27,990	C
Samford Univ	AL	35,700	V₲
Santa Clara Univ	CA	54,702	MC
Seattle Univ	WA	47,010	V₲
Seton Hall Univ	NJ	45,902	C
Shippensburg Univ of Pennsylvania	PA	17,064	LC
Siena College	NY	43,863	VC
Simpson College	IA	36,086	VC
Southeast Missouri State Univ	MO	14,983	LC
Southern New Hampshire Univ	NH	38,100	C
Spring Hill College	AL	42,130	VC
St. Edward's Univ	TX	44,674	VC
St. John Fisher College	NY	39,370	₲
St. John's Univ	NY	52,840	₲
St. Joseph's College, New York / Brooklyn Campus	NY	21,878	C
St. Joseph's College, New York / Suffolk Campus	NY	21,878	VC
Stephen F. Austin State Univ	TX	14,668	C
Stevenson Univ	MD	39,572	C
Syracuse Univ	NY	54,512	HC
Taylor Univ	IN	36,742	V₲
Texas Christian Univ	TX	47,570	HC
Texas Wesleyan Univ	TX	29,886	C
The College at Brockport / SUNY	NY	18,362	VC
Thomas College	ME	26,270	LC
Troy Univ	AL	10,650	C
Tulane Univ	LA	58,942	MC
Union College	KY	28,775	C
Union Univ	TN	28,260	VC
Univ of Arkansas at Fayetteville	AR	16,860	VC
Univ of Colo Boulder	CO	22,605	V₲
Univ of Idaho	ID	14,558	C
Univ of Illinois at Urbana-Champaign	IL	24,300	HC
Univ of Iowa	IA	17,481	VC
Univ of Maryland	MD	18,801	HC
Univ of Maryland/Univ College	MD	6,168	SP
Univ of Mass Amherst	MA	23,697	V₲
Univ of Memphis	TN	15,094	C
Univ of Miami	FL	55,166	MC
Univ of Mich/Dearborn	MI	9,885	VC
Univ of Minn Crookston	MN	17,834	C
Univ of Missouri-St. Louis	MO	18,304	VC
Univ of Nebr - Lincoln	NE	17,507	VC
Univ of N Dak	ND	14,094	C
Univ of North Florida	FL	15,578	VC
Univ of PR Recinto de Rio Piedras	PR	5,750	
Univ of Rio Grande	OH	8,750	NC
Univ of San Diego	CA	53,302	H₲
Univ of S Car Upstate	SC	17,673	LC
Univ of Texas at Austin	TX	44,074	HC
Univ of Texas at Dallas	TX	21,046	HC
Univ of Texas at San Antonio	TX	18,372	C
Univ of the Sciences	PA	48,320	V₲
Univ of Utah	UT	13,462	VC
Univ of Wisc-Milwaukee	WI	18,436	C
Ursuline College	OH	33,198	LC
Virginia Polytechnic Inst and State Univ	VA	14,629	HC
Virginia State Univ	VA	11,318	₲
Walsh Univ	OH	35,100	C
Warner Univ	FL	18,000	C
Washington State Univ	WA	20,461	C
Washington Univ in St. Louis	MO	58,818	MC
Webber International Univ	FL	25,664	C
Webster Univ	MO	33,990	₲
West Chester Univ of Pennsylvania	PA	16,836	C
Western Conn State Univ	CT	18,327	C
Wheeling Jesuit Univ	WV	34,668	C
Whitworth Univ	WA	45,826	V₲
Wilmington College	OH	29,784	C
Wingate Univ	NC	34,990	C
Youngstown State Univ	OH	16,374	LC

MARKETING/RETAILING/ MERCHANDISING

School	ST	$IS	SR
Abilene Christian Univ	TX	38,400	VC
Adams State College	CO	13,358	LC
Alabama A&M Univ	AL	96,100	C
Alabama State Univ	AL	14,142	NC
Albany State Univ	GA	8,500	C
Alderson Broaddus Univ	WV	28,656	C
Alfred Univ	NY	40,392	VC
American International College	MA	36,100	LC
Anderson Univ	IN	35,390	C
Andrews Univ	MI	28,030	₲
Angelo State Univ	TX	15,049	NC
Appalachian State Univ	NC	12,919	VC
Arcadia Univ	PA	33,570	₲
Arizona State Univ	AZ	18,818	₲
Arkansas State Univ	AR	14,980	C
Ashland Univ	OH	25,000	C
Auburn Univ	AL	20,052	V₲
Auburn Univ at Montgomery	AL	12,120	C
Augsburg College	MN	35,142	C
Aurora Univ	IL	26,870	C
Avila Univ	MO	26,900	C
Azusa Pacific Univ	CA	39,946	C
Ball State Univ	IN	17,850	C
Barry Univ	FL	38,190	C
Bay Path College	MA	34,565	C
Baylor Univ	TX	46,720	HC
Belmont Univ	TN	37,380	V₲
Benedictine Univ	IL	35,220	C
Bentley Univ	MA	54,555	H₲
Berkeley College	NY	18,300	LC
Berkeley College/New Jersey	NJ	27,300	LC
Berkeley College/ Westchester Campus	NY	28,500	LC
Black Hills State Univ	SD	13,562	LC
Blackburn College	IL	21,350	C
Bluffton Univ	OH	37,864	C
Boise State Univ	ID	12,802	C
Boston College	MA	58,506	MC
Boston Univ	MA	54,130	H₲
Bradley Univ	IL	31,874	VC
Brenau Univ Women's College	GA	26,650	₲
Bryant Univ	RI	49,179	VC
Buena Vista Univ	IA	37,954	C
Butler Univ	IN	45,898	V₲
Calif Baptist Univ	CA	35,890	C
Cal State, Fullerton	CA	25,188	₲
Cal State, Long Beach	CA	17,534	₲
Cal State, Northridge	CA	28,313	C
Cal State, Sacramento	CA	16,200	C
Canisius College	NY	45,602	VC
Caribbean Univ	PR	10,375	
Carnegie Mellon Univ	PA	51,260	MC
Cedar Crest College	PA	43,240	C
Cedarville Univ	OH	31,036	V₲
Central Conn State Univ	CT	19,212	C
Central Mich Univ	MI	18,066	C
Central State Univ	OH	9,010	C
Central Univ of Bayamon	PR	3,350	
Central Washington Univ	WA	11,730	C
Chaminade Univ of Honolulu	HI	31,664	C
Chancellor Univ	OH	11,000	C
Chestnut Hill College	PA	39,785	LC
Chicago State Univ	IL	5,482	C
CUNY/Baruch College	NY	15,831	VC
City Univ of Seattle	WA	14,880	NC
Claflin Univ	SC	22,368	₲
Clarion Univ of Pennsylvania	PA	17,370	C
Clemson Univ	SC	19,136	HC
Cleveland State Univ	OH	21,357	C
Coastal Carolina Univ	SC	17,620	C
Colo State Univ-Fort Collins	CO	20,090	VC
Columbia College	MO	24,578	C
Columbus State Univ	GA	13,176	C
Concord Univ	WV	13,102	C
Concordia Univ Wisc	WI	28,980	C
Cornerstone Univ and Grand Rapids Theological Seminary	MI	30,866	C
Creighton Univ	NE	44,058	V₲
Dallas Baptist Univ	TX	29,118	C
Davis and Elkins College	WV	33,742	C
De Sales Univ	PA	42,670	C
Defiance College	OH	30,645	C
Delaware State Univ	DE	14,700	LC
Delaware Valley College	PA	29,944	C
Delta State Univ	MS	12,292	LC
Dominican College	NY	31,270	C
Dowling College	NY	25,000	LC
Drexel Univ	PA	51,920	HC
Duquesne Univ	PA	42,017	VC

School	ST	$IS	SR
East Carolina Univ	NC	14,169	C
East Tenn State Univ	TN	9,000	C
Eastern Illinois Univ	IL	20,502	C
Eastern Kentucky Univ	KY	11,161	C
Eastern Mich Univ	MI	17,961	C
Eastern New Mexico Univ	NM	10,682	C
Eastern Univ	PA	37,704	C
Eastern Washington Univ	WA	16,388	C
Elizabethtown College School of Continuing and Professional Studies	PA		VC
Elmhurst College	IL	42,032	C+
Elmira College	NY	49,950	C+
Elms College	MA	23,900	VC
Emory Univ	GA	45,000	MC
Emporia State Univ	KS	12,897	C
Evangel Univ	MO	23,090	C
Excelsior College	NY	895	SP
Fairleigh Dickinson Univ/ College at Florham	NJ	42,142	C
Fairleigh Dickinson Univ/ Metropolitan Campus	NJ	40,254	C
Fairmont State Univ	WV	12,098	LC
Fashion Inst of Technology/SUNY	NY	12,468	SP
Ferris State Univ	MI	19,698	C
Florida Atlantic Univ	FL	17,339	C
Florida International Univ	FL	17,747	VC
Florida State Univ	FL	15,238	HC
Fontbonne Univ	MO	31,384	C
Fort Hays State Univ	KS	11,354	C
Fort Valley State Univ	GA	11,200	VC
Francis Marion Univ	SC	16,464	LC
Franklin Pierce Univ	NH	41,598	C
Gannon Univ	PA	37,940	C
George Mason Univ	VA	15,724	VC
Georgetown College	KY	38,690	C
Georgetown Univ	DC	52,910	MC
Georgia Regents Univ	GA		C
Georgia Southern Univ	GA	16,414	C
Georgia Southwestern State Univ	GA	12,218	C
Georgia State Univ	GA	12,000	VC
Glenville State College	WV	11,348	NC
Grambling State Univ	LA	13,384	LC
Grand Canyon Univ	AZ	24,540	VC
Grand Valley State Univ	MI	17,998	VC
Greenville College	IL	27,012	C
Hampton Univ	VA	28,528	C
Harding Univ	AR	21,432	C+
Hillsdale College	MI	31,890	HC+
Holy Family Univ	PA	40,030	LC
Howard Univ	DC	35,957	C
Husson Univ	ME	23,386	LC
Huston-Tillotson Univ	TX	18,124	C+
Idaho State Univ	ID	11,908	C
Illinois State Univ	IL	22,634	VC
Indiana State Univ	IN	16,000	C
Indiana Univ-Purdue Univ Fort Wayne	IN	15,425	C
Indiana Wesleyan Univ	IN	31,815	VC
Inter-American Univ of PR/ Aguadilla Campus	PR	5,578	
Inter-American Univ of PR/ Bayamon Univ College	PR	4,428	
Inter-American Univ of PR/ Fajardo Campus	PR	4,200	
Inter-American Univ of PR/ Metropolitan Campus	PR	4,320	
Inter-American Univ of PR/ Ponce	PR	3,700	
Inter-American Univ of PR/ San Germán	PR	6,720	
Iowa State Univ	IA	16,403	C
Jackson State Univ	MS	13,512	LC
Jacksonville State Univ	AL	12,280	LC
Jacksonville Univ	FL	37,780	C
James Madison Univ	VA	18,049	VC
John Carroll Univ	OH	44,520	C+
Johnson and Wales Univ/ Charlotte Campus	NC	35,421	C
Johnson and Wales Univ/ Denver Campus	CO	34,368	C
Johnson and Wales Univ/ North Miami Campus	FL	34,368	C
Johnson and Wales Univ/ Providence Campus	RI	34,668	C
Juniata College	PA	49,340	VC
Kansas State Univ	KS	15,497	VC
Kennesaw State Univ	GA	13,017	VC
Keuka College	NY	30,300	C
King's College	PA	41,678	C
Kutztown Univ of Pennsylvania	PA	16,909	LC
La Salle Univ	PA	50,270	C
Lake Superior State Univ	MI	18,121	C
Lamar Univ	TX	6,820	LC
Lasell College	MA	42,500	LC
LeTourneau Univ	TX	26,230	C
Lewis Univ	IL	23,050	C
Lincoln Univ	MO	11,996	NC
Lindenwood Univ	MO	20,750	C
Lipscomb Univ	TN	35,722	VC
LIU/Brooklyn Campus	NY	26,500	C
LIU/C.W. Post Campus	NY	38,888	C
Loras College	IA	37,432	VC
Louisiana State Univ	LA	18,677	VC+
Louisiana State Univ in Shreveport	LA	5,606	C
Louisiana Tech Univ	LA	8,000	C
Loyola Marymount Univ	CA	53,240	VC+
Loyola Univ Chicago	IL	49,560	VC+
Loyola Univ New Orleans	LA	46,581	VC
Lynchburg College	VA	42,645	C
MacMurray College	IL	20,755	C
Madonna Univ	MI	24,540	VC
Manhattan College	NY	44,955	VC
Marian Univ	WI	30,980	LC
Marietta College	OH	42,135	VC
Marquette Univ	WI	43,664	VC+
Marshall Univ	WV	14,820	C
Martin Univ	IN	11,000	SP
Marywood Univ	PA	40,695	C
McKendree Univ	IL	29,920	C+
McMurry Univ	TX	25,962	LC
Mercyhurst Univ	PA	40,700	C
Merrimack College	MA	44,215	C
Messiah College	PA	39,540	VC
Methodist Univ	NC	37,185	C
Metropolitan State Univ of Denver	CO	4,835	LC
Miami Univ	OH	24,191	HC
Mich State Univ	MI	13,689	VC
MidAmerica Nazarene Univ	KS	28,000	C
Middle Tenn State Univ	TN	8,650	C
Midland Univ	NE	34,000	C
Midwestern State Univ	TX	9,722	C
Millikin Univ	IL	37,462	C
Minn State Univ, Mankato	MN	14,900	C
Minn State Univ, Moorhead	MN	13,392	C
Minot State Univ	ND	10,915	C
Misericordia Univ	PA	39,840	C
Miss College	MS	21,998	VC
Missouri Southern State Univ	MO	11,910	C
Missouri State Univ	MO	13,996	VC
Missouri Western State Univ	MO	12,260	NC
Morgan State Univ	MD	14,500	VC
Mount Ida College	MA	30,115	LC
Mount Mary Univ	WI	32,836	LC
Mount Mercy Univ	IA	34,385	C
Mount Vernon Nazarene Univ	OH	29,590	C
Mountain State Univ	WV	14,330	NC
Murray State Univ	KY	14,944	C
New Mexico Highlands Univ	NM	9,720	NC
New Mexico State Univ	NM	13,955	LC
New York Inst of Technology	NY	40,590	VC
New York Univ	NY	61,470	MC
Niagara Univ	NY	39,800	C
Nicholls State Univ	LA	7,095	C
Nichols College	MA	37,240	LC
North Central College	IL	38,343	VC
North Georgia College & State Univ	GA	8,500	C
North Park Univ	IL	30,130	C
Northeastern Illinois Univ	IL		C
Northeastern State Univ	OK	8,615	VC
Northern Illinois Univ	IL	19,768	C
Northern Kentucky Univ	KY	15,302	LC
Northern Mich Univ	MI	15,300	VC
Northern State Univ	SD	14,021	C
Northwest Missouri State Univ	MO	14,229	C
Notre Dame College	OH	34,942	VC
Notre Dame de Namur Univ	CA	41,610	LC
Notre Dame of Maryland Univ	MD	27,700	C
Oakland Univ	MI	19,391	VC
Okla Baptist Univ	OK	28,202	VC
Okla Christian Univ	OK	24,975	VC
Okla State Univ	OK	14,310	VC
Olivet Nazarene Univ	IL	29,990	C
Oral Roberts Univ	OK	31,734	C
Oregon State Univ	OR	19,017	C+
Oswego / SUNY	NY	20,009	VC
Pace Univ	NY	48,094	VC
Parsons The New School for Design	NY	56,610	SP
Peru State College	NE	8,600	NC
Philadelphia Univ	PA	44,160	C
Pontifical Catholic Univ of PR	PR	7,310	
Portland State Univ	OR	18,672	C
Post Univ	CT	35,750	C
Prairie View A&M Univ	TX	15,205	LC
Purdue Univ/Calumet	IN	14,336	C
Purdue Univ/West Lafayette	IN	20,278	HC
Quincy Univ	IL	34,980	LC
Quinnipiac Univ	CT	53,580	VC
Radford Univ	VA	17,132	LC
Regis Univ	CO	41,318	C
Rider Univ	NJ	45,720	C
Robert Morris Univ	PA	36,699	C
Roberts Wesleyan College	NY	37,384	C+
Roger Williams Univ	RI	45,788	C
Roosevelt Univ	IL	22,605	VC
Rowan Univ	NJ	23,570	VC
Rutgers, The State Univ of New Jersey/Camden Campus	NJ	24,254	C
Rutgers, The State Univ of New Jersey/New Brunswick	NJ	25,077	VC
Rutgers, The State Univ of New Jersey/Newark Campus	NJ	25,376	C
St. Joseph's Univ	PA	52,272	VC
St. Mary-of-the-Woods College	IN	37,722	LC
St. Mary's Univ	TX	33,854	C
St. Peter's College	NJ	44,240	C
St. Vincent College	PA	40,244	C
St. Xavier Univ	IL	32,840	C
Salem State College	MA	13,161	LC
Salisbury Univ	MD	18,368	VC
Sam Houston State Univ	TX	17,082	C
San Diego State Univ	CA	20,578	VC
San Francisco State Univ	CA	18,514	C
San Jose State Univ	CA	19,707	C
Savannah State Univ	GA	13,156	C
Seton Hill Univ	PA	35,172	C
Slippery Rock Univ of Pennsylvania	PA	10,360	LC
S Car State Univ	SC	6,700	LC
Southeastern Louisiana Univ	LA	13,325	C
Southeastern Univ	FL	27,201	C+
Southern Adventist Univ	TN	26,190	C
Southern Conn State Univ	CT	18,033	C
Southern Illinois Univ Carbondale	IL	21,620	C
Southern Methodist Univ	TX	57,755	MC
Southern Nazarene Univ	OK	24,354	NC
Southern New Hampshire Univ	NH	38,100	C
Southern Oregon Univ	OR	17,874	C
Southern Univ and A&M College	LA	9,761	C+
Southwest Minn State Univ	MN	14,000	C
Southwestern Okla State Univ	OK	9,160	C
St. Ambrose Univ	IA		C
St. Bonaventure Univ	NY	38,831	C
St. Catherine Univ	MN	37,782	C+
St. Cloud State Univ	MN	10,600	C
St. Thomas Aquinas College	NY	30,000	C
St. Thomas Univ	FL	32,310	C+
Stephen F. Austin State Univ	TX	14,668	C
Stetson Univ	FL	49,512	VC+
Stonehill College	MA	46,780	VC+
Suffolk Univ	MA	46,548	C
SUNY College at Old Westbury	NY	16,324	C
SUNY New Paltz	NY	15,010	C
SUNY Plattsburgh / SUNY	NY	18,083	VC
Tabor College	KS	29,010	LC
Tarleton State Univ	TX	13,489	LC
Temple Univ	PA	24,392	VC
Tenn Tech Univ	TN	11,310	C
Texas A&M Univ	TX	16,956	VC+
Texas A&M Univ at Commerce	TX	10,496	C
Texas A&M Univ at Corpus Christi	TX	11,544	LC
Texas A&M Univ at Kingsville	TX	7,500	LC
Texas Southern Univ	TX	18,212	LC
Texas State Univ	TX	16,495	VC
Texas Wesleyan Univ	TX	29,886	C
Texas Woman's Univ	TX	13,633	LC
Tiffin Univ	OH	30,273	LC
Touro College	NY	23,150	VC
Trevecca Nazarene Univ	TN	30,118	C
Trine Univ	IN	39,400	VC
Trinity International Univ	IL	31,070	C
Troy Univ	AL	10,650	C
Tuskegee Univ	AL	26,750	C
Union Univ	TN	28,260	VC
Universidad del Turabo	PR	4,110	
Univ of Akron	OH	20,436	C
Univ of Alabama at Birmingham	AL	18,484	C+
Univ of Alabama at Huntsville	AL	17,625	VC
Univ of Alaska Anchorage	AK	15,290	NC
Univ of Arkansas at Fayetteville	AR	16,860	VC
Univ of Arkansas at Little Rock	AR		C
Univ of Bridgeport	CT	39,030	LC
Univ of Central Arkansas	AR	10,840	VC
Univ of Central Florida	FL	15,711	VC+
Univ of Central Missouri	MO	14,605	C
Univ of Central Okla	OK	12,293	C
Univ of Cincinnati	OH	20,199	VC
Univ of Conn	CT	23,744	HC
Univ of Dayton	OH	43,750	VC
Univ of Delaware	DE	22,728	VC
Univ of Denver	CO	51,787	VC+
Univ of Findlay	OH	31,916	C
Univ of Florida	FL	15,783	HC+
Univ of Great Falls	MT	27,970	C
Univ of Hartford	CT	42,674	C
Univ of Hawaii at Manoa	HI	19,379	VC
Univ of Houston-Downtown	TX	6,267	LC
Univ of Idaho	ID	14,558	C
Univ of Illinois at Chicago	IL	24,293	VC
Univ of Illinois at Urbana-Champaign	IL	24,300	HC
Univ of Indianapolis	IN	31,740	LC
Univ of Kansas	KS	16,980	C+
Univ of Kentucky	KY	19,868	C
Univ of Louisiana at Lafayette	LA	6,130	C
Univ of Louisiana at Monroe	LA	12,998	C
Univ of Louisville	KY	17,460	VC
Univ of Maine at Machias	ME	10,523	C
Univ of Mary Hardin-Baylor	TX	31,950	C+
Univ of Mass Dartmouth	MA	22,223	C
Univ of Mich-Flint	MI	17,547	C+
Univ of Minn/Twin Cities	MN		HC
Univ of Miss	MS	15,482	VC
Univ of Missouri/Columbia	MO	18,201	MC
Univ of Montana	MT	13,670	C
Univ of Montevallo	AL	17,320	C
Univ of Nebr - Lincoln	NE	17,507	VC
Univ of Nebr at Kearney	NE	14,855	LC
Univ of Nebr at Omaha	NE	12,700	C
Univ of Nevada, Las Vegas	NV	17,303	C
Univ of Nevada/Reno	NV	14,500	NC
Univ of New Haven	CT	47,740	C
Univ of New Orleans	LA	9,224	VC
Univ of North Alabama	AL	9,960	C
Univ of N Car at Charlotte	NC	15,847	C
Univ of N Car at Greensboro	NC	12,848	C
Univ of N Car at Wilmington	NC	13,572	VC+
Univ of North Texas	TX	15,628	C
Univ of Northern Colo	CO	15,973	C
Univ of Northern Iowa	IA	14,776	C
Univ of Notre Dame	IN		MC
Univ of Okla	OK	17,634	VC+
Univ of Pennsylvania	PA	56,106	MC
Univ of Pittsburgh at Pittsburgh	PA	27,800	HC+
Univ of Portland	OR	47,874	VC
Univ of PR/Arecibo	PR	7,227	
Univ of PR/Bayamon	PR	1,600	
Univ of PR/Mayaguez	PR	1,250	
Univ of San Francisco	CA	49,674	VC
Univ of Scranton	PA	51,940	VC
Univ of Sioux Falls	SD	22,990	C
Univ of South Alabama	AL	13,510	C
Univ of S Car at Columbia	SC	19,725	VC+
Univ of South Florida	FL	13,000	C
Univ of Southern Indiana	IN	14,657	C
Univ of Southern Miss	MS	13,170	C
Univ of St. Francis	IL	36,490	C
Univ of St. Thomas - Houston	TX	36,490	VC
Univ of Tampa	FL	35,160	VC
Univ of Tenn at Martin	TN	13,217	C
Univ of Texas at Arlington	TX	10,908	LC
Univ of Texas at El Paso	TX	8,764	NC
Univ of Texas-Pan American	TX	12,432	LC
Univ of the District of Columbia	DC	7,244	LC
Univ of the Ozarks	AR	22,100	C
Univ of the Sacred Heart	PR	5,590	
Univ of Toledo	OH	18,464	C
Univ of Tulsa	OK	45,311	HC+
Univ of Utah	UT	13,462	VC
Univ of Washington	WA	14,722	VC
Univ of West Florida	FL	14,656	C
Univ of Wisc Whitewater	WI	13,314	C
Univ of Wisc/La Crosse	WI	14,755	VC
Univ of Wisc/Madison	WI	18,757	HC
Univ of Wisc/Oshkosh	WI	10,426	LC
Univ of Wisc/Stout	WI	23,942	C
Upper Iowa Univ	IA	30,426	NC
Utah State Univ	UT	11,803	C
Valparaiso Univ	IN	43,040	VC+
Vanguard Univ of Southern Calif	CA	35,833	VC
Villanova Univ	PA	56,436	MC
Virginia Commonwealth Univ	VA	18,633	C
Viterbo Univ	WI	30,070	C
Wartburg College	IA	41,055	VC
Washburn Univ	KS	12,165	NC
Washington Univ in St. Louis	MO	58,818	MC
Wayne State Univ	MI	19,493	C
Waynesburg Univ	PA	29,100	C
West Liberty Univ	WV	9,142	LC
West Texas A&M Univ	TX	13,478	C
West Virginia State Univ	WV	8,378	NC
West Virginia Wesleyan College	WV	26,880	C
Western Illinois Univ	IL	20,130	C
Western Mich Univ	MI	19,042	C
Western New England Univ	MA	45,590	C
Western New Mexico Univ	NM	8,500	LC
Western Washington Univ	WA	18,519	VC
Westminster College	PA	31,290	C+
Westminster College	UT	37,708	VC
Wichita State Univ	KS	12,539	C
Wilberforce Univ	OH	15,100	LC

School	ST	$IS	SR
Woodbury Univ	CA	34,500	LC
Wright State Univ	OH	16,983	C
Xavier Univ	OH	43,740	VC
Yeshiva Univ	NY	47,250	VC+
York College / CUNY	NY	5,496	NC
York College of Pennsylvania	PA	26,590	C
Youngstown State Univ	OH	16,374	LC

MATERIALS ENGINEERING

School	ST	$IS	SR
Alfred Univ	NY	40,392	VC
Auburn Univ	AL	20,052	VC+
Calif Polytechnic State Univ	CA	19,847	HC
Calif State Polytechnic Univ, Pomona	CA	18,932	C
Drexel Univ	PA	51,920	HC
Florida State Univ	FL	15,238	HC
Georgia Inst of Technology	GA	20,464	MC
Iowa State Univ	IA	16,403	C
Johns Hopkins Univ	MD	47,492	MC
Mass Inst of Technology	MA	54,238	MC
Mich State Univ	MI	13,689	VC
Mich Tech Univ	MI	22,105	VC
Missouri Univ of Science and Technology	MO	18,655	VC+
New Mexico Inst of Mining and Technology	NM	12,892	HC
Northwestern Univ	IL	37,595	MC
Ohio Univ	OH	20,676	VC
Rensselaer Polytechnic Inst	NY	59,229	MC
San Jose State Univ	CA	19,707	C
Ohio State Univ	OH	19,887	MC
Univ at Albany / SUNY	NY	18,674	VC
Univ of Alabama at Birmingham	AL	18,484	C+
Univ of Arizona	AZ	20,105	C
Univ of Calif at Berkeley	CA	23,322	MC
Univ of Calif at Davis	CA	24,482	HC
Univ of Calif at Irvine	CA	25,961	VC
Univ of Calif at Los Angeles	CA	25,686	MC
Univ of Calif at Riverside	CA	27,204	C
Univ of Cincinnati	OH	20,199	VC
Univ of Conn	CT	23,744	HC
Univ of Florida	FL	15,783	HC+
Univ of Idaho	ID	14,558	C
Univ of Illinois at Chicago	IL	24,293	VC
Univ of Illinois at Urbana-Champaign	IL	24,300	HC
Univ of Kentucky	KY	19,868	C
Univ of Maryland	MD	18,801	HC
Univ of Mich/Ann Arbor	MI	22,102	HC+
Univ of Minn/Twin Cities	MN		HC
Univ of Pennsylvania	PA	56,106	MC
Univ of Pittsburgh at Pittsburgh	PA	27,800	HC+
Univ of Tenn at Knoxville	TN	20,364	VC+
Univ of Utah	UT	13,462	VC
Univ of Wisc-Milwaukee	WI	18,436	C
Virginia Polytechnic Inst and State Univ	VA	14,629	HC
Washington State Univ	WA	20,461	C
Winona State Univ	MN	16,530	C
Worcester Polytechnic Inst	MA	53,440	HC+
Wright State Univ	OH	16,983	C

MATERIALS SCIENCE

School	ST	$IS	SR
Arizona State Univ	AZ	18,818	C+
Boise State Univ	ID	12,802	C
Calif Inst of Technology	CA	54,045	MC
Case Western Reserve Univ	OH	55,178	MC
Columbia Univ in the City of New York	NY	61,116	MC
Duke Univ	NC	50,250	MC
Georgia Inst of Technology	GA	20,464	MC
Illinois Inst of Technology	IL	38,512	HC+
Johns Hopkins Univ	MD	47,492	MC
Mass Inst of Technology	MA	54,238	MC
Missouri State Univ	MO	13,996	VC
N Car State Univ	NC	16,202	HC
Northwestern Univ	IL	37,595	MC
Penn State Univ/Univ Park	PA	25,404	VC
Purdue Univ/West Lafayette	IN	20,278	HC
Rochester Inst of Technology	NY	42,450	VC+
Stanford Univ	CA	56,411	MC
Ohio State Univ	OH	19,887	MC
Univ at Albany / SUNY	NY	18,674	VC
Univ of Arizona	AZ	20,105	C
Univ of Calif at Berkeley	CA	23,322	MC
Univ of Calif at Los Angeles	CA	25,686	MC
Univ of Denver	CO	51,787	VC+
Univ of Illinois at Urbana-Champaign	IL	24,300	HC
Univ of Mass Dartmouth	MA	22,223	C
Univ of Mich/Ann Arbor	MI	22,102	HC+
Univ of Minn/Twin Cities	MN		HC
Univ of Pittsburgh at Pittsburgh	PA	27,800	HC+
Univ of the Ozarks	AR	22,100	C
Univ of Utah	UT	13,462	VC
Univ of Washington	WA	14,722	VC
Univ of Wisc/Eau Claire	WI	15,430	VC
Univ of Wisc/Madison	WI	18,757	HC

MATERIALS SCIENCE AND ENGINEERING

School	ST	$IS	SR
Cornell Univ	NY	59,037	MC
Lehigh Univ	PA	55,080	MC
Rutgers, The State Univ of New Jersey/New Brunswick	NJ	25,077	VC

MATHEMATICS

School	ST	$IS	SR
Abilene Christian Univ	TX	38,400	VC
Adams State College	CO	13,358	LC
Adelphi Univ	NY	43,130	VC
Adrian College	MI	33,800	C
Agnes Scott College	GA	45,323	VC+
Alabama A&M Univ	AL	96,100	C
Alabama State Univ	AL	14,142	NC
Albany State Univ	GA	8,500	C
Albertus Magnus College	CT	37,382	LC
Albion College	MI	43,884	VC
Albright College	PA	46,660	C
Alcorn State Univ	MS	9,500	C
Alderson Broaddus Univ	WV	28,656	C
Alfred Univ	NY	40,392	VC
Allegheny College	PA	49,020	HC
Allen Univ	SC	16,124	NC
Alma College	MI	42,400	VC
Alvernia Univ	PA	39,250	C
Alverno College	WI	30,483	LC
American International College	MA	36,100	LC
American Univ	DC	54,829	HC+
Amherst College	MA	58,744	MC
Anderson Univ	IN	35,390	C
Andrews Univ	MI	28,030	C+
Angelo State Univ	TX	15,049	NC
Appalachian State Univ	NC	12,919	VC
Aquinas College	MI	33,060	C
Arcadia Univ	PA	33,570	C+
Arizona State Univ	AZ	18,818	C+
Arkansas State Univ	AR	14,980	C
Arkansas Tech Univ	AR	13,164	LC
Armstrong Atlantic State Univ	GA	16,276	C
Asbury Univ	KY	32,038	VC
Ashland Univ	OH	25,000	C
Assumption College	MA	45,721	VC
Atlantic Union College	MA	24,600	LC
Auburn Univ	AL	20,052	VC+
Auburn Univ at Montgomery	AL	12,120	C
Augsburg College	MN	35,142	C
Augustana College	IL	43,398	HC
Augustana College	SD	35,500	VC
Aurora Univ	IL	26,870	C
Austin College	TX	36,940	HC
Austin Peay State Univ	TN	14,650	C
Averett Univ	VA	36,000	LC
Avila Univ	MO	26,900	C
Azusa Pacific Univ	CA	39,946	C
Baker Univ	KS	33,350	C+
Baldwin Wallace Univ	OH	36,980	VC
Ball State Univ	IN	17,850	C
Bard College	NY	59,872	HC
Bard College at Simon's Rock	MA	58,963	HC+
Barry Univ	FL	38,190	C
Barton College	NC	27,660	C
Bates College	ME	58,950	MC
Baylor Univ	TX	46,720	HC
Belhaven Univ	MS	27,170	C
Bellarmine Univ	KY	42,950	VC
Belmont Abbey College	NC	37,716	C
Belmont Univ	TN	37,380	VC+
Beloit College	WI	49,970	HC
Bemidji State Univ	MN	13,500	C
Benedict College	SC	20,454	NC
Benedictine College	KS	29,180	VC
Benedictine Univ	IL	35,220	C
Bennett College	NC		LC
Bennington College	VT	56,990	HC+
Bentley Univ	MA	54,555	HC+
Berea College	KY	7,220	HC
Berry College	GA	39,254	HC
Bethany College	KS	30,605	NC
Bethany College	WV	35,282	C
Bethel College	IN	31,560	C
Bethel College	KS	29,100	C
Bethel Univ	MN	34,940	VC
Bethel Univ	TN	19,186	C
Bethune-Cookman Univ	FL	22,290	LC
Binghamton Univ / The SUNY	NY	20,832	HC+
Biola Univ	CA	40,320	VC
Birmingham-Southern College	AL	42,370	VC+
Black Hills State Univ	SD	13,562	LC
Blackburn College	IL	21,350	C
Bloomfield College	NJ	36,960	C
Bloomsburg Univ of Pennsylvania	PA	13,598	C
Blue Mountain College	MS	13,550	LC
Bluefield College	VA	17,230	C+
Bluffton Univ	OH	37,864	C
Boise State Univ	ID	12,802	C
Boston College	MA	58,506	MC
Boston Univ	MA	54,130	HC+
Bowdoin College	ME	57,834	MC
Bowie State Univ	MD	23,990	LC
Bowling Green State Univ	OH	18,970	C
Bradley Univ	IL	31,874	VC
Brandeis Univ	MA	58,820	HC
Brescia Univ	KY	26,140	VC+
Briar Cliff Univ	IA	29,514	C
Bridgewater College	VA	39,880	C
Bridgewater State Univ	MA	18,752	C
Brigham Young Univ	UT	12,100	HC
Brigham Young Univ/Hawaii	HI	0,614	VC
Brown Univ	RI	56,150	MC
Bryan College	TN	24,194	C
Bryant Univ	RI	49,179	VC
Bryn Mawr College	PA	57,760	MC
Bucknell Univ	PA	58,160	MC
Buena Vista Univ	IA	37,954	C
Buffalo State/State Univ of Buffalo	NY	15,733	C+
Butler Univ	IN	45,898	VC+
Cabrini College	PA	40,859	LC
Caldwell College	NJ	35,602	LC
Calif Baptist Univ	CA	35,890	C
Calif Inst of Technology	CA	54,045	MC
Calif Lutheran Univ	CA	47,640	C
Calif Polytechnic State Univ	CA	19,847	HC
Calif State Polytechnic Univ, Pomona	CA	18,932	C
Cal State, Bakersfield	CA	8,000	LC
Cal State, Chico	CA	18,952	C
Cal State, Dominguez Hills	CA	17,056	LC
Cal State, East Bay	CA	16,549	C
Cal State, Fresno	CA	17,405	C
Cal State, Fullerton	CA	25,188	C+
Cal State, Long Beach	CA	17,534	C+
Cal State, Los Angeles	CA	15,829	C
Cal State, Monterey Bay	CA	26,871	LC
Cal State, Northridge	CA	28,313	C
Cal State, Sacramento	CA	16,200	C
Cal State, San Bernardino	CA	12,000	C
Cal State, San Marcos	CA	14,576	C
Cal State, Stanislaus	CA	18,582	C
Calif Univ of Pennsylvania	PA	14,217	C
Calvin College	MI	37,585	VC+
Cameron Univ	OK	9,267	LC
Campbell Univ	NC	25,500	C
Campbellsville Univ	KY	27,720	C
Canisius College	NY	45,602	VC
Capital Univ	OH	39,824	VC
Cardinal Stritch Univ	WI	24,054	C
Caribbean Univ	PR	10,375	
Carleton College	MN	58,149	MC
Carlow Univ	PA	30,272	C
Carnegie Mellon Univ	PA	51,260	MC
Carroll College	MT	28,000	C
Carroll Univ	WI	24,860	C
Carthage College	WI	33,000	C
Case Western Reserve Univ	OH	55,178	MC
Castleton State College	VT	19,424	C
Catawba College	NC	37,105	C
Cedar Crest College	PA	43,240	C
Cedarville Univ	OH	31,036	VC+
Centenary College	NJ	38,618	LC
Centenary College of Louisiana	LA	39,070	C+
Central College	IA	36,980	VC
Central Conn State Univ	CT	19,212	C
Central Methodist Univ	MO	28,240	VC
Central Mich Univ	MI	18,066	C
Central State Univ	OH	9,010	C
Central Washington Univ	WA	11,730	C
Centre College	KY	35,000	HC+
Chadron State College	NE	7,400	NC
Chapman Univ	CA	56,019	VC+
Charleston Southern Univ	SC	22,420	C
Chatham Univ	PA	42,440	VC
Chestnut Hill College	PA	30,785	LC
Cheyney Univ of Pennsylvania	PA	20,372	LC
Chicago State Univ	IL	5,482	C
Christian Brothers Univ	TN	19,140	HC
Christopher Newport Univ	VA	21,050	VC
Citadel, The	SC		C
CUNY/Baruch College	NY	15,831	VC
CUNY/Brooklyn College	NY	5,884	C+
Claflin Univ	SC	22,368	C+
Claremont McKenna College	CA	58,065	MC
Clarion Univ of Pennsylvania	PA	17,370	C
Clark Atlanta Univ	GA	30,006	C
Clark Univ	MA	47,020	HC+
Clarke Univ	IA	36,400	C
Clarkson Univ	NY	53,538	HC
Clearwater Christian College	FL	23,720	C
Clemson Univ	SC	19,136	HC
Cleveland State Univ	OH	21,357	C
Coastal Carolina Univ	SC	17,620	C
Coe College	IA	43,590	VC
Coker College	SC	32,256	LC
Colby College	ME	57,510	MC
Colgate Univ	NY	50,930	MC
College of Staten Island / The CUNY	NY	16,778	NC
College of Charleston	SC	21,273	VC
College of Mount St. Joseph	OH	33,880	C
College of Mount St. Vincent	NY	41,040	MC
College of New Jersey	NJ	25,376	HC
College of St. Benedict	MN	47,570	VC
College of St. Elizabeth	NJ	43,839	LC
College of St. Mary	NE	34,004	C
College of St. Scholastica	MN	39,960	C
College of the Holy Cross	MA	56,232	MC
College of the Ozarks	MO	5,605	VC
College of William & Mary	VA	25,085	MC
College of Wooster	OH	52,600	VC
Colo College	CO	54,534	MC
Colo Mesa Univ	CO	16,669	LC
Colo School of Mines	CO	18,000	HC
Colo State Univ-Fort Collins	CO	20,090	VC
Colo State Univ-Pueblo	CO	13,532	LC
Columbia College	MO	24,578	C
Columbia College	SC	27,882	C
Columbia Univ in the City of New York	NY	61,116	MC
Columbia Univ/Barnard College	NY	39,000	MC
Columbia Univ/School of General Studies	NY	54,083	MC
Columbus State Univ	GA	13,176	C
Concord Univ	WV	13,102	C
Concordia College New York	NY	31,500	VC
Concordia College, Moorhead	MN	39,974	C+
Concordia Univ - Irvine	CA	35,390	VC
Concordia Univ Nebr	NE	26,000	VC
Concordia Univ St. Paul	MN	27,200	C
Concordia Univ Wisc	WI	28,980	C
Concordia Univ, Ann Arbor	MI	27,220	VC
Concordia Univ, River Forest	IL	26,300	C
Conn College	CT	54,970	MC
Converse College	SC	37,130	C
Coppin State Univ	MD	14,905	VC
Corban Univ	OR	34,764	C
Cornell College	IA	44,930	HC
Cornell Univ	NY	59,037	MC
Covenant College	GA		VC+
Creighton Univ	NE	44,058	VC+
Culver-Stockton College	MO	30,900	C
Cumberland Univ	TN	21,220	C
CUNY-City College	NY	19,576	HC+
Daemen College	NY	31,510	C
Dakota State Univ	SD	13,811	C
Dakota Wesleyan Univ	SD	23,000	C
Dallas Baptist Univ	TX	29,118	C
Dartmouth College	NH	57,996	MC
Davidson College	NC	54,683	MC
Davis and Elkins College	WV	33,742	C
De Sales Univ	PA	42,670	C
Defiance College	OH	30,645	C
Delaware State Univ	DE	14,700	LC
Delta State Univ	MS	12,292	LC
Denison Univ	OH	54,670	HC+
DePaul Univ	IL	46,120	VC
DePauw Univ	IN	48,950	VC+
Dickinson College	PA	57,662	HC+
Dickinson State Univ	ND	8,550	NC
Doane College	NE	33,730	VC
Dominican College	NY	31,270	C
Dominican Univ	IL	37,628	C
Dordt College	IA	34,160	VC
Dowling College	NY	25,000	LC
Drake Univ	IA	30,980	VC+
Drew Univ/College of Liberal Arts	NJ	55,862	VC
Drexel Univ	PA	51,920	HC
Drury Univ	MO	30,319	VC
Duke Univ	NC	50,250	MC
Duquesne Univ	PA	42,017	VC
D'Youville College	NY	29,850	C
Earlham College	IN	49,710	VC+
East Carolina Univ	NC	14,169	C
East Central Univ	OK	10,223	LC
East Stroudsburg Univ of Pennsylvania	PA	16,636	C
East Tenn State Univ	TN	9,000	C
East Texas Baptist Univ	TX	29,135	C
Eastern Conn State Univ	CT	20,584	C
Eastern Illinois Univ	IL	20,502	C
Eastern Kentucky Univ	KY	11,161	C
Eastern Mennonite Univ	VA	38,850	VC
Eastern Mich Univ	MI	17,961	C
Eastern Nazarene College	MA	30,000	C
Eastern New Mexico Univ	NM	10,682	C
Eastern Oregon Univ	OR	10,400	C
Eastern Univ	PA	37,704	C
Eastern Washington Univ	WA	16,388	C
Eckerd College	FL	43,902	VC
Edgewood College	WI	33,294	C
Edinboro Univ of Pennsylvania	PA	15,940	LC

School	ST	$IS	SR
Edward Waters College	FL	17,856	LC
Elizabeth City State Univ	NC	11,638	C
Elizabethtown College	PA	47,600	VC
Elmhurst College	IL	42,032	C+
Elmira College	NY	49,950	C+
Elms College	MA	23,900	VC
Elon Univ	NC	40,046	HC
Embry-Riddle Aeronautical Univ - Daytona Beach	FL	40,884	C+
Emmanuel College	MA	47,985	VC
Emory and Henry College	VA	387,460	C
Emory Univ	GA	45,000	MC
Emporia State Univ	KS	12,897	C
Endicott College	MA	42,390	C
Erskine College	SC	37,360	C
Eureka College	IL	19,280	C
Evangel Univ	MO	23,090	C
Excelsior College	NY	895	SP
Fairfield Univ	CT	55,850	VC
Fairleigh Dickinson Univ/ College at Florham	NJ	42,142	C
Fairleigh Dickinson Univ/ Metropolitan Campus	NJ	40,254	C
Fairmont State Univ	WV	12,098	LC
Faulkner Univ	AL	22,530	LC
Fayetteville State Univ	NC	10,816	C
Felician College	NJ	41,640	C
Ferrum College	VA	27,740	LC
Fisk Univ	TN	19,830	C
Fitchburg State Univ	MA	17,241	C
Florida A&M Univ	FL	14,935	LC
Florida Atlantic Univ	FL	17,300	C
Florida Gulf Coast Univ	FL		C
Florida Inst of Technology	FL	48,290	VC
Florida International Univ	FL	17,747	VC
Florida Memorial Univ	FL	20,716	LC
Florida Southern College	FL	38,240	VC
Florida State Univ	FL	15,238	HC
Fontbonne Univ	MO	31,384	C
Fordham Univ	NY	58,927	HC
Fort Hays State Univ	KS	11,354	C
Fort Lewis College	CO	15,513	C
Fort Valley State Univ	GA	11,200	VC
Framingham State Univ	MA	16,750	C
Francis Marion Univ	SC	16,464	LC
Franciscan Univ of Steubenville	OH	27,320	VC
Franklin and Marshall College	PA	58,295	MC
Franklin College	IN	35,885	C
Franklin Pierce Univ	NH	41,598	C
Freed-Hardeman Univ	TN	19,697	VC
Fresno Pacific Univ	CA	32,136	C
Friends Univ	KS	29,100	C
Frostburg State Univ	MD	15,264	LC
Furman Univ	SC	54,006	HC
Gallaudet Univ	DC	25,380	SP
Gannon Univ	PA	37,940	C
Gardner-Webb Univ	NC	34,375	C+
George Fox Univ	OR	40,750	C+
George Mason Univ	VA	15,724	VC
George Washington Univ	DC	57,108	MC
Georgetown College	KY	38,690	C
Georgetown Univ	DC	52,910	MC
Georgia College and State Univ	GA	18,216	VC
Georgia Inst of Technology	GA	20,464	MC
Georgia Regents Univ	GA		C
Georgia Southern Univ	GA	16,414	C
Georgia Southwestern State Univ	GA	12,218	C
Georgia State Univ	GA	12,000	VC
Georgian Court Univ	NJ	39,726	LC
Gettysburg College	PA	56,820	HC
Gonzaga Univ	WA	44,247	HC
Gordon College	MA	42,660	VC+
Goshen College	IN	35,900	VC
Goucher College	MD	50,252	VC+
Grace College and Theological Seminary	IN	28,800	C
Graceland Univ	IA	28,020	C
Grambling State Univ	LA	13,384	LC
Grand Valley State Univ	MI	17,998	VC
Grand View Univ	IA	31,050	C
Greensboro College	NC	28,740	LC
Greenville College	IL	27,012	C
Grinnell College	IA	53,654	HC
Grove City College	PA	22,988	HC
Guilford College	NC	35,340	C
Gustavus Adolphus College	MN	48,170	HC
Gwynedd-Mercy College	PA	33,560	C
Hamilton College	NY	55,620	MC
Hamline Univ	MN	44,198	VC
Hampden-Sydney College	VA	48,848	C
Hampshire College	MA	58,320	MC
Hampton Univ	VA	28,528	C
Hannibal-LaGrange Univ	MO	24,490	C
Hanover College	IN	41,450	VC
Harding Univ	AR	21,432	C+
Hardin-Simmons Univ	TX	23,560	C+
Harris-Stowe State Univ	MO	14,360	NC
Hartwick College	NY	49,815	C+
Harvard Univ/Harvard College	MA	49,000	MC
Harvey Mudd College	CA	61,660	MC
Hastings College	NE	27,782	C+
Haverford College	PA	59,236	MC
Hawaii Pacific Univ	HI	36,690	C
Heidelberg Univ	OH	34,100	C
Henderson State Univ	AR	13,634	C
Hendrix College	AR	48,436	HC+
Heritage Univ	WA	17,664	NC
High Point Univ	NC	39,800	C
Hillsdale College	MI	31,890	HC+
Hiram College	OH	37,300	VC
Hobart and William Smith Colleges	NY	43,000	VC
Hofstra Univ	NY	48,020	VC+
Hollins Univ	VA	43,295	VC
Holy Family Univ	PA	40,030	LC
Hood College	MD	44,630	C
Hope College	MI	36,320	VC+
Houghton College	NY	35,740	VC
Houston Baptist Univ	TX	23,815	C+
Howard Payne Univ	TX	17,115	C
Howard Univ	DC	35,957	C
Humboldt State Univ	CA	18,400	C
Hunter College / The CUNY	NY	14,429	VC
Huntingdon College	AL	31,850	C
Huntington Univ	IN	32,220	C
Huston-Tillotson Univ	TX	18,124	C+
Idaho State Univ	ID	11,908	C
Illinois College	IL	25,770	VC
Illinois State Univ	IL	22,634	VC
Immaculata Univ	PA	43,000	C
Indiana State Univ	IN	16,000	C
Indiana Univ Bloomington	IN	10,358	HC
Indiana Univ East	IN	6,639	LC
Indiana Univ Kokomo	IN	6,674	LC
Indiana Univ Northwest	IN	6,738	LC
Indiana Univ of Pennsylvania	PA	20,180	LC
Indiana Univ South Bend	IN	15,293	C
Indiana Univ Southeast	IN	15,807	LC
Indiana Univ-Purdue Univ Fort Wayne	IN	15,425	C
Indiana Univ-Purdue Univ Indianapolis	IN	17,290	C
Indiana Wesleyan Univ	IN	31,815	VC
Inter-American Univ of PR/ Bayamon Univ College	PR	4,428	
Inter-American Univ of PR/ Fajardo Campus	PR	4,200	
Inter-American Univ of PR/ Metropolitan Campus	PR	4,320	
Inter-American Univ of PR/ Ponce	PR	3,700	
Inter-American Univ of PR/ San Germán	PR	6,720	
Iona College	NY	44,028	C
Iowa State Univ	IA	16,403	C
Iowa Wesleyan College	IA	30,850	LC
Ithaca College	NY	52,300	HC
Jackson State Univ	MS	13,512	LC
Jacksonville State Univ	AL	12,280	LC
Jacksonville Univ	FL	37,780	C
James Madison Univ	VA	18,049	VC
Jarvis Christian College	TX	19,552	NC
John Brown Univ	AR	30,996	VC+
John Carroll Univ	OH	44,520	C+
Johns Hopkins Univ	MD	47,492	MC
Johnson C. Smith Univ	NC	25,336	LC
Johnson State College	VT	16,721	C
Judson College	AL	24,690	C
Judson Univ	IL	25,130	C
Juniata College	PA	49,340	VC
Kalamazoo College	MI	47,825	HC+
Kansas State Univ	KS	15,497	VC
Kansas Wesleyan Univ	KS	32,000	C
Kean Univ	NJ	22,060	LC
Keene State College	NH	21,538	C
Kennesaw State Univ	GA	13,017	VC
Kent State Univ	OH	19,352	C
Kentucky State Univ	KY	11,000	LC
Kenyon College	OH	56,810	MC
King Univ	TN	33,140	C
King's College	PA	41,678	C
Knox College	IL		VC
Kutztown Univ of Pennsylvania	PA	16,909	LC
La Roche College	PA	34,802	LC
La Salle Univ	PA	50,270	C
La Sierra Univ	CA	35,694	VC
Lafayette College	PA	57,050	HC+
LaGrange College	GA	34,480	C
Lake Erie College	OH	35,704	C
Lake Forest College	IL	45,580	VC
Lake Superior State Univ	MI	18,121	C
Lakeland College	WI	22,990	C
Lamar Univ	TX	6,820	LC
Lander Univ	SC	22,514	C+
Lane College	TN	11,212	C
Langston Univ	OK	3,000	LC
Lawrence Tech Univ	MI	37,630	VC
Lawrence Univ	WI	46,371	HC
Le Moyne College	NY	42,200	VC
Lebanon Valley College	PA	38,570	C
Lee Univ	TN	18,690	C+
Lees-McRae College	NC	33,624	C
Lehigh Univ	PA	55,080	MC
Lehman College / The CUNY	NY	5,778	LC
LeMoyne-Owen College	TN	13,100	C
Lenoir-Rhyne College	NC	35,984	C
LeTourneau Univ	TX	26,230	C
Lewis & Clark College	OR	52,656	VC
Lewis Univ	IL	23,050	C
Lewis-Clark State College	ID	6,990	C
Liberty Univ	VA	19,101	C
Limestone College	SC	29,880	C
Lincoln Memorial Univ	TN	18,144	C
Lincoln Univ	MO	11,996	NC
Lindenwood Univ	MO	20,750	C
Lindsey Wilson College	KY	30,470	VC
Linfield College- McMinnville Campus	OR	46,166	C
Lipscomb Univ	TN	35,722	VC
Livingstone College	NC	17,815	LC
Lock Haven Univ of Pennsylvania	PA	17,587	LC
LIU/Brooklyn Campus	NY	26,500	C
LIU/C.W. Post Campus	NY	38,888	C
Longwood Univ	VA	20,924	C
Loras College	IA	37,432	VC
Louisiana College	LA	15,746	C
Louisiana State Univ	LA	18,677	VC+
Louisiana State Univ in Shreveport	LA	5,606	C
Louisiana Tech Univ	LA	8,000	C
Loyola Marymount Univ	CA	53,240	VC+
Loyola Univ Chicago	IL	49,560	VC+
Loyola Univ Maryland	MD		VC
Loyola Univ New Orleans	LA	46,581	VC
Lubbock Christian Univ	TX	25,518	C
Luther College	IA	44,380	VC+
Lycoming College	PA	43,636	C
Lynchburg College	VA	42,645	C
Lyndon State College	VT	14,233	C
Lyon College	AR	30,246	VC
Macalester College	MN	53,419	MC
MacMurray College	IL	20,755	C
Madonna Univ	MI	24,540	VC
Maharishi Univ of Management	IA	31,000	VC
Malone Univ	OH	34,334	C
Manchester College	IN	35,070	C
Manhattan College	NY	44,955	VC
Manhattanville College	NY	46,260	VC
Mansfield Univ	PA	19,468	LC
Marian Univ	WI	30,980	LC
Marian Univ/Indianapolis	IN	37,058	C
Marietta College	OH	42,135	VC
Marist College	NY	35,500	C
Marlboro College	VT	35,980	VC
Marquette Univ	WI	43,664	VC+
Mars Hill College	NC	22,950	LC
Marshall Univ	WV	14,820	C
Martin Univ	IN	11,000	SP
Mary Baldwin College	VA	37,110	C
Marygrove College	MI	21,290	C
Marymount Univ	VA	36,178	C
Maryville College	TN	33,150	VC
Maryville Univ of St. Louis	MO	34,920	VC
Marywood Univ	PA	40,695	C
Mass College of Liberal Arts	MA	16,733	C
Mass Inst of Technology	MA	54,238	MC
Mayville State Univ	ND	11,401	NC
McDaniel College	MD	45,600	VC
McKendree Univ	IL	29,920	C+
McMurry Univ	TX	25,962	LC
McNeese State Univ	LA		C
McPherson College	KS	28,138	C
Medgar Evers College / The CUNY	NY	4,920	NC
Mercer Univ	GA	44,201	VC+
Mercy College	NY	29,996	C
Mercyhurst Univ	PA	40,700	C
Meredith College	NC	31,420	C
Merrimack College	MA	44,215	C
Messiah College	PA	39,540	VC
Methodist Univ	NC	37,185	C
Metropolitan State Univ of Denver	CO	4,835	LC
Miami Univ	OH	24,191	HC
Mich State Univ	MI	13,689	VC
Mich Tech Univ	MI	22,105	VC
MidAmerica Nazarene Univ	KS	28,000	C
Middle Tenn State Univ	TN	8,650	C
Middlebury College	VT	57,470	MC
Midland Univ	NE	34,000	C
Midway College	KY	20,150	C
Midwestern State Univ	TX	9,722	C
Miles College	AL	16,530	NC
Millersville Univ of Pennsylvania	PA	18,498	C
Milligan College	TN	27,510	C
Millikin Univ	IL	37,462	C
Mills College	CA	54,119	HC
Millsaps College	MS	43,888	VC+
Minn State Univ, Mankato	MN	14,900	C
Minn State Univ, Moorhead	MN	13,392	C
Minot State Univ	ND	10,915	C
Misericordia Univ	PA	39,840	C
Miss College	MS	21,998	VC
Miss Univ for Women	MS	7,400	LC
Miss Valley State Univ	MS	9,706	LC
Missouri Baptist Univ	MO	30,310	C
Missouri Southern State Univ	MO	11,910	C
Missouri State Univ	MO	13,996	VC
Missouri Univ of Science and Technology	MO	18,655	VC+
Missouri Valley College	MO	22,200	C
Missouri Western State Univ	MO	12,260	NC
Molloy College	NY	38,950	C
Monmouth College	IL	39,290	C
Monmouth Univ	NJ	42,252	C
Montana State Univ	MT	14,068	VC
Montana State Univ-Billings	MT	12,425	LC
Montana Tech of The Univ of Montana	MT	14,650	VC
Montclair State Univ	NJ	22,614	C
Montreat College	NC	31,298	VC
Moravian College	PA	36,381	VC
Morehead State Univ	KY	10,900	C
Morehouse College	GA	38,640	C
Morgan State Univ	MD	14,500	VC
Morningside College	IA	32,620	C
Morris College	SC	16,006	LC
Mount Holyoke College	MA	53,596	HC+
Mount Marty College	SD	29,638	C
Mount Mary Univ	WI	32,836	LC
Mount Mercy Univ	IA	34,385	C
Mount Olive College	NC	18,426	C
Mount St. Mary College	NY	39,540	C
Mount St. Mary's Univ	MD	46,158	C
Mount St. Mary's College/ Chalon Campus	CA	43,897	VC+
Mount Vernon Nazarene Univ	OH	29,590	C
Muhlenberg College	PA	52,837	HC
Murray State Univ	KY	14,944	C
Muskingum Univ	OH	30,502	C
National Louis Univ	IL	16,915	LC
National Univ	CA	14,730	SP
Nazareth College of Rochester	NY	41,590	VC
Nebr Wesleyan Univ	NE	29,774	C+
New College of Florida	FL	14,504	HC+
New England College	NH	45,930	LC
New Jersey City Univ	NJ	21,060	C+
New Jersey Inst of Technology	NJ	26,490	VC
New Mexico Highlands Univ	NM	9,720	NC
New Mexico Inst of Mining and Technology	NM	12,892	HC
New Mexico State Univ	NM	13,955	LC
New York Inst of Technology	NY	40,590	VC
New York Univ	NY	61,470	MC
Newberry College	SC	26,850	LC
Newman Univ	KS	30,380	C+
Niagara Univ	NY	39,800	C
Nicholls State Univ	LA	7,095	C
Nichols College	MA	37,240	LC
Norfolk State Univ	VA	10,531	LC
N Car Agricultural and Technical State Univ	NC	13,175	LC
N Car Central Univ	NC	9,000	LC
N Car State Univ	NC	16,202	HC
N Car Wesleyan College	NC	29,440	C
North Central College	IL	38,343	VC
N Dak State Univ	ND	14,642	C
North Georgia College & State Univ	GA	8,500	C
North Park Univ	IL	30,130	C
Northeastern Illinois Univ	IL		C
Northeastern State Univ	OK	8,615	VC
Northeastern Univ	MA	55,296	MC
Northern Arizona Univ	AZ	18,592	C
Northern Illinois Univ	IL	19,768	C
Northern Kentucky Univ	KY	15,302	LC
Northern Mich Univ	MI	15,300	VC
Northern State Univ	SD	14,021	C
Northland College	WI	26,680	C
Northwest Missouri State Univ	MO	14,229	C
Northwest Nazarene Univ	ID	24,275	NC
Northwestern College	MN	24,000	C
Northwestern College of Iowa	IA	34,848	C+
Northwestern Okla State Univ	OK	7,275	NC
Northwestern State Univ of Louisiana	LA	14,368	C
Northwestern Univ	IL	37,595	MC
Norwich Univ	VT	28,212	C
Notre Dame College	OH	34,942	VC
Notre Dame of Maryland Univ	MD	27,700	C
Nova Southeastern Univ	FL	34,016	VC
Nyack College	NY	32,000	C
Oakland City Univ	IN	24,500	NC
Oakland Univ	MI	19,391	VC
Oakwood Univ	AL	23,035	C
Oberlin College	OH	57,025	MC
Occidental College	CA	59,592	MC+
Oglethorpe Univ	GA	42,580	VC
Ohio Dominican Univ	OH	38,380	C+
Ohio Northern Univ	OH	42,075	VC
Ohio Univ	OH	20,676	VC
Ohio Valley Univ	WV	17,752	C
Ohio Wesleyan Univ	OH	49,460	C+
Okla Baptist Univ	OK	28,202	VC
Okla Christian Univ	OK	24,975	VC

ST = STATE **$IS** = IN-STATE COSTS **SR** = SELECTOR RATING

School	ST	$IS	SR
Okla City Univ	OK	33,546	VC
Okla Panhandle State Univ	OK	8,996	NC
Okla State Univ	OK	14,310	VC
Okla Wesleyan Univ	OK	21,300	C
Old Dominion Univ	VA	18,662	C
Olivet College	MI	19,984	C
Olivet Nazarene Univ	IL	29,990	C
Oral Roberts Univ	OK	31,734	C
Oregon State Univ	OR	19,017	₵
Oswego / SUNY	NY	20,009	VC
Ottawa Univ	KS	15,000	VC
Otterbein College	OH	32,214	C
Ouachita Baptist Univ	AR	29,010	VC
Our Lady of the Lake Univ of San Antonio	TX	22,430	LC
Pace Univ	NY	48,094	VC
Pacific Lutheran Univ	WA	44,840	VC
Pacific Union College	CA	28,150	VC
Pacific Univ	OR	42,815	C
Paine College	GA	18,594	LC
Palm Beach Atlantic Univ	FL	33,882	LC
Park Univ	MO	17,525	C
Penn State Erie/The Behrend College	PA	16,256	C
Penn State Univ/Altoona	PA	11,464	C
Penn State Univ/Univ Park	PA	25,404	VC
Pepperdine Univ	CA	55,372	H₵
Peru State College	NE	8,600	NC
Pfeiffer Univ	NC	33,700	C
Philander Smith College	AR	19,760	LC
Piedmont College	GA	29,260	C
Pittsburg State Univ	KS	12,032	C
Pitzer College	CA	54,988	MC
Plymouth State Univ	NH	23,148	LC
Point Loma Nazarene Univ	CA	38,610	VC
Polytechnic Inst of New York Univ	NY	53,064	H₵
Pomona College	CA	57,680	MC
Pontifical Catholic Univ of PR	PR	7,310	
Portland State Univ	OR	18,672	C
Prairie View A&M Univ	TX	15,205	LC
Presbyterian College	SC	42,678	VC
Prescott College	AZ	33,284	₵
Princeton Univ	NJ	53,795	MC
Principia College	IL	35,140	₵
Providence College	RI	55,995	HC
Purchase College / SUNY	NY	16,951	C
Purdue Univ/Calumet	IN	14,336	C
Purdue Univ/West Lafayette	IN	20,278	HC
Queens College / The CUNY	NY	17,107	VC
Queens Univ of Charlotte	NC	39,543	VC
Quincy Univ	IL	34,980	LC
Quinnipiac Univ	CT	53,580	VC
Radford Univ	VA	17,132	LC
Ramapo College of New Jersey	NJ	24,938	₵
Randolph College	VA	43,960	VC
Randolph-Macon College	VA	45,086	C
Reed College	OR	57,780	MC
Regis Univ	CO	41,318	C
Rensselaer Polytechnic Inst	NY	59,229	MC
Rhode Island College	RI	17,132	LC
Rhodes College	TN	47,596	H₵
Rice Univ	TX	43,288	MC
Richard Stockton College of New Jersey	NJ	20,000	VC
Rider Univ	NJ	45,720	C
Ripon College	WI	36,959	₵
Rivier College	NH	35,000	VC
Roanoke College	VA	47,996	₵
Roberts Wesleyan College	NY	37,384	₵
Rochester Inst of Technology	NY	42,450	V₵
Rockford College	IL	31,000	C
Rockhurst Univ	MO	20,625	C
Rocky Mountain College	MT	32,242	C
Roger Williams Univ	RI	45,788	C
Rollins College	FL	52,370	HC
Roosevelt Univ	IL	22,605	VC
Rose-Hulman Inst of Technology	IN	51,738	MC
Rosemont College	PA	42,350	C
Rowan Univ	NJ	23,570	VC
Russell Sage College	NY	39,370	C
Rust College	MS	10,600	C
Rutgers, The State Univ of New Jersey/Camden Campus	NJ	24,254	C
Rutgers, The State Univ of New Jersey/New Brunswick	NJ	25,077	VC
Rutgers, The State Univ of New Jersey/Newark Campus	NJ	25,376	C
Sacred Heart Univ	CT	48,564	VC
Saginaw Valley State Univ	MI	16,869	C
St. Anselm College	NH	48,324	VC
St. Augustine's Univ	NC	14,000	C
St. Francis Univ	PA	30,029	LC
St. John's Univ	MN	46,146	C
St. Joseph College	CT	45,630	LC
St. Joseph's College	IN	35,790	C
St. Joseph's College of Maine	ME	31,580	C
St. Joseph's Univ	PA	52,272	VC
St. Leo Univ	FL	27,990	C
St. Louis Univ	MO	46,594	V₵
St. Martin's Univ	WA	38,082	C
St. Mary-of-the-Woods College	IN	37,722	LC
St. Mary's College	IN	45,160	VC
St. Mary's College of Calif	CA	53,550	C
St. Mary's Univ	TX	33,854	C
St. Mary's Univ of Minn	MN	37,015	C
St. Michael's College	VT	48,740	VC
St. Paul's College	VA	16,030	NC
St. Peter's College	NJ	44,240	C
St. Vincent College	PA	40,244	C
St. Xavier Univ	IL	32,840	C
Salem College	NC	29,326	VC
Salem State College	MA	13,161	LC
Salisbury Univ	MD	18,368	VC
Salve Regina Univ	RI	47,250	VC
Sam Houston State Univ	TX	17,082	C
Samford Univ	AL	35,700	V₵
San Diego Christian College	CA	31,012	C
San Diego State Univ	CA	20,578	VC
San Francisco State Univ	CA	18,514	C
San Jose State Univ	CA	19,707	C
Santa Clara Univ	CA	54,702	MC
Sarah Lawrence College	NY	48,000	HC
Savannah State Univ	GA	13,156	C
Schreiner Univ	TX	32,734	LC
Scripps College	CA	54,900	MC
Seattle Pacific Univ	WA	41,559	V₵
Seattle Univ	WA	47,010	V₵
Seton Hall Univ	NJ	45,902	C
Seton Hill Univ	PA	35,172	C
Sewanee: The Univ of the South	TN	47,700	H₵
Shaw Univ	NC	15,488	LC
Shawnee State Univ	OH	16,545	NC
Shenandoah Univ	VA	39,268	C
Shepherd Univ	WV	14,996	C
Shippensburg Univ of Pennsylvania	PA	17,064	LC
Shorter Univ	GA	26,470	C
Siena College	NY	43,863	VC
Siena Heights Univ	MI	17,000	LC
Silver Lake College	WI	22,600	LC
Simmons College	MA	48,770	VC
Simpson College	IA	36,086	VC
Simpson Univ	CA	28,900	C
Skidmore College	NY	57,926	HC
Slippery Rock Univ of Pennsylvania	PA	10,360	LC
Smith College	MA	57,524	MC
Sonoma State Univ	CA	20,541	C
S Car State Univ	SC	6,700	LC
S Dak School of Mines and Technology	SD	15,260	VC
S Dak State Univ	SD	14,296	C
Southeast Missouri State Univ	MO	14,983	LC
Southeastern Louisiana Univ	LA	13,325	C
Southeastern Okla State Univ	OK	7,966	C
Southeastern Univ	FL	27,201	₵
Southern Adventist Univ	TN	26,190	C
Southern Arkansas Univ	AR	14,316	C
Southern Conn State Univ	CT	18,033	C
Southern Illinois Univ Carbondale	IL	21,620	C
Southern Illinois Univ Edwardsville	IL	17,532	C
Southern Methodist Univ	TX	57,755	MC
Southern Nazarene Univ	OK	24,354	NC
Southern Oregon Univ	OR	17,874	C
Southern Polytechnic State Univ	GA	13,958	VC
Southern Univ and A&M College	LA	9,761	₵
Southern Univ at New Orleans	LA	1,000	NC
Southern Wesleyan Univ	SC	25,600	C
Southwest Baptist Univ	MO	24,710	C
Southwest Minn State Univ	MN	14,000	C
Southwestern Adventist Univ	TX	23,026	LC
Southwestern College	KS	29,270	C
Southwestern Okla State Univ	OK	9,160	C
Southwestern Univ	TX	45,660	VC
Spelman College	GA	24,650	VC
Spring Arbor Univ	MI	26,740	C
Spring Hill College	AL	42,130	VC
Springfield College	MA	25,000	C
St. Ambrose Univ	IA		C
St. Bonaventure Univ	NY	38,831	C
St. Catherine Univ	MN	37,782	₵
St. Cloud State Univ	MN	10,600	C
St. Edward's Univ	TX	44,674	VC
St. Francis College	NY	34,200	LC
St. John Fisher College	NY	39,370	₵
St. John's College, Santa Fe	NM	54,998	H₵
St. John's Univ	NY	52,840	₵
St. Joseph's College, New York / Brooklyn Campus	NY	21,878	C
St. Joseph's College, New York / Suffolk Campus	NY	21,878	VC
St. Lawrence Univ	NY	53,740	HC
St. Mary's College of Maryland	MD	26,699	HC
St. Norbert College	WI	39,992	VC
St. Olaf College	MN	49,960	H₵
Stanford Univ	CA	56,411	MC
SUNY/Empire State College	NY	6,315	SP
Stephen F. Austin State Univ	TX	14,668	C
Sterling College	KS	27,216	C
Stetson Univ	FL	49,512	V₵
Stevens Inst of Technology	NJ	50,130	HC
Stevenson Univ	MD	39,572	C
Stillman College	AL	18,400	C
Stonehill College	MA	46,780	V₵
Stony Brook Univ / SUNY	NY	19,359	HC
Suffolk Univ	MA	46,548	C
Sul Ross State Univ	TX	13,410	LC
SUNY College at Geneseo	NY	18,055	H₵
SUNY College at Old Westbury	NY	16,324	C
SUNY Cortland / The SUNY	NY	19,117	C
SUNY Fredonia / The SUNY at Fredonia	NY	18,702	VC
SUNY New Paltz	NY	15,010	C
SUNY Oneonta / SUNY	NY	16,919	VC
SUNY Plattsburgh / SUNY	NY	18,083	VC
Susquehanna Univ	PA	49,170	C
Swarthmore College	PA	57,870	MC
Sweet Briar College	VA	43,765	₵
Syracuse Univ	NY	54,512	HC
Tabor College	KS	29,010	LC
Talladega College	AL	13,000	C
Tarleton State Univ	TX	13,489	LC
Taylor Univ	IN	36,742	V₵
Temple Univ	PA	24,392	VC
Tenn State Univ	TN	9,048	C
Tenn Tech Univ	TN	11,310	C
Tenn Wesleyan College	TN	21,250	C
Texas A&M Univ	TX	16,956	V₵
Texas A&M Univ at Commerce	TX	10,496	C
Texas A&M Univ at Corpus Christi	TX	11,544	LC
Texas A&M Univ at Kingsville	TX	7,500	LC
Texas Christian Univ	TX	47,570	HC
Texas Lutheran Univ	TX	34,070	C
Texas Southern Univ	TX	18,212	LC
Texas State Univ	TX	16,495	VC
Texas Tech Univ	TX	14,243	C
Texas Wesleyan Univ	TX	29,886	C
Texas Woman's Univ	TX	13,633	LC
The Catholic Univ of America	DC	52,852	VC
The College at Brockport / SUNY	NY	18,362	VC
The College of Idaho	ID	31,277	VC
The College of New Rochelle	NY	33,600	VC
The College of St. Rose	NY	26,750	C
The Lincoln Univ	PA	15,154	LC
The Masters College	CA	38,160	₵
Ohio State Univ	OH	19,887	MC
The SUNY at Potsdam	NY	17,754	C
Thiel College	PA	31,378	LC
Thomas Edison State College	NJ	5,700	SP
Thomas More College	KY	34,760	C
Tougaloo College	MS	15,275	NC
Touro College	NY	23,150	VC
Towson Univ	MD	16,000	VC
Transylvania Univ	KY	40,310	V₵
Trevecca Nazarene Univ	TN	30,118	C
Trine Univ	IN	39,400	VC
Trinity Christian College	IL	28,869	C
Trinity College	CT		H₵
Trinity International Univ	IL	31,070	C
Trinity Univ	TX	44,174	H₵
Trinity Washington Univ	DC	30,250	₵
Troy Univ	AL	10,650	C
Truman State Univ	MO	13,546	HC
Tufts Univ	MA	58,780	MC
Tulane Univ	LA	58,942	MC
Tusculum College	TN	24,295	C
Tuskegee Univ	AL	26,750	C
Union College	KY	28,775	C
Union College	NE	23,270	VC
Union College	NY		MC
Union Univ	TN	28,260	VC
United States Air Force Academy	CO		MC
United States Military Academy	NY		MC
United States Naval Academy	MD		MC
Universidad del Turabo	PR	4,110	
Univ at Albany / SUNY	NY	18,674	VC
Univ at Buffalo / The SUNY	NY	20,283	VC
Univ of Akron	OH	20,436	C
Univ of Alabama at Birmingham	AL	18,484	₵
Univ of Alabama at Huntsville	AL	17,625	VC
Univ of Alabama at Tuscaloosa	AL	17,164	₵
Univ of Alaska Anchorage	AK	15,290	NC
Univ of Alaska Fairbanks	AK	13,955	C
Univ of Alaska Southeast	AK	11,493	C
Univ of Arizona	AZ	20,105	C
Univ of Arkansas at Fayetteville	AR	16,860	VC
Univ of Arkansas at Little Rock	AR		C
Univ of Arkansas at Monticello	AR	8,470	NC
Univ of Arkansas at Pine Bluff	AR	10,600	C
Univ of Bridgeport	CT	39,030	LC
Univ of Calif at Berkeley	CA	23,322	MC
Univ of Calif at Davis	CA	24,482	HC
Univ of Calif at Irvine	CA	25,961	VC
Univ of Calif at Los Angeles	CA	25,686	MC
Univ of Calif at Riverside	CA	27,204	C
Univ of Calif at San Diego	CA	21,000	VC
Univ of Calif at Santa Barbara	CA	27,551	HC
Univ of Calif at Santa Cruz	CA	27,807	VC
Univ of Central Arkansas	AR	10,840	VC
Univ of Central Florida	FL	15,711	V₵
Univ of Central Missouri	MO	14,605	C
Univ of Central Okla	OK	12,293	C
Univ of Chicago	IL	55,416	MC
Univ of Cincinnati	OH	20,199	VC
Univ of Colo at Colo Springs	CO	15,000	VC
Univ of Colo Boulder	CO	22,605	V₵
Univ of Colo Denver	CO	17,904	C
Univ of Conn	CT	23,744	HC
Univ of Dallas	TX	43,510	V₵
Univ of Dayton	OH	43,750	VC
Univ of Delaware	DE	22,728	VC
Univ of Denver	CO	51,787	V₵
Univ of Detroit Mercy	MI	30,450	C
Univ of Evansville	IN	41,056	V₵
Univ of Findlay	OH	31,916	C
Univ of Florida	FL	15,783	H₵
Univ of Georgia	GA	19,508	VC
Univ of Great Falls	MT	27,970	C
Univ of Hartford	CT	42,674	C
Univ of Hawaii at Hilo	HI	6,500	C
Univ of Hawaii at Manoa	HI	19,379	VC
Univ of Houston	TX	19,184	VC
Univ of Houston-Downtown	TX	6,267	LC
Univ of Idaho	ID	14,558	C
Univ of Illinois at Chicago	IL	24,293	VC
Univ of Illinois at Urbana-Champaign	IL	24,300	HC
Univ of Indianapolis	IN	31,740	LC
Univ of Iowa	IA	17,481	VC
Univ of Jamestown	ND	24,738	C
Univ of Kansas	KS	16,980	₵
Univ of Kentucky	KY	19,868	C
Univ of La Verne	CA	47,010	VC
Univ of Louisiana at Lafayette	LA	6,130	C
Univ of Louisiana at Monroe	LA	12,998	C
Univ of Louisville	KY	17,460	VC
Univ of Maine	ME	19,712	₵
Univ of Maine at Farmington	ME	17,841	C
Univ of Mary	ND	16,714	C
Univ of Mary Hardin-Baylor	TX	31,950	₵
Univ of Mary Washington	VA	19,484	VC
Univ of Maryland	MD	18,801	HC
Univ of Maryland/Baltimore County	MD	18,000	VC
Univ of Maryland/Eastern Shore	MD	14,000	C
Univ of Mass Amherst	MA	23,697	V₵
Univ of Mass Boston	MA	11,966	C
Univ of Mass Dartmouth	MA	22,223	C
Univ of Mass Lowell	MA	19,316	C
Univ of Memphis	TN	15,094	C
Univ of Miami	FL	55,166	MC
Univ of Mich/Ann Arbor	MI	22,102	H₵
Univ of Mich/Dearborn	MI	9,885	VC
Univ of Mich-Flint	MI	17,547	₵
Univ of Minn/Duluth	MN	18,964	₵
Univ of Minn/Morris	MN	17,150	VC
Univ of Minn/Twin Cities	MN		HC
Univ of Miss	MS	15,482	VC
Univ of Missouri/Columbia	MO	18,201	MC
Univ of Missouri-Kansas City	MO	19,603	C
Univ of Missouri-St. Louis	MO	18,304	VC
Univ of Mobile	AL	27,870	VC
Univ of Montana	MT	13,670	C
Univ of Montana-Western	MT	9,753	LC
Univ of Montevallo	AL	17,320	C
Univ of Mount Union	OH	35,130	C
Univ of Nebr - Lincoln	NE	17,507	VC
Univ of Nebr at Kearney	NE	14,855	LC
Univ of Nebr at Omaha	NE	12,700	C
Univ of Nevada, Las Vegas	NV	17,303	C
Univ of Nevada/Reno	NV	14,500	NC
Univ of New England	ME	46,145	₵
Univ of New Hampshire	NH	24,702	VC
Univ of New Haven	CT	47,740	C
Univ of New Mexico	NM	15,300	C

ST = STATE **$IS** = IN-STATE COSTS **SR** = SELECTOR RATING

School	ST	$IS	SR
Univ of New Orleans	LA	9,224	VC
Univ of North Alabama	AL	9,960	C
Univ of N Car at Asheville	NC	13,500	VC+
Univ of N Car at Chapel Hill	NC	18,348	MC
Univ of N Car at Charlotte	NC	15,847	C
Univ of N Car at Greensboro	NC	12,848	C
Univ of N Car at Wilmington	NC	13,572	VC+
Univ of N Dak	ND	14,094	C
Univ of North Florida	FL	15,578	VC
Univ of North Texas	TX	15,628	C
Univ of Northern Colo	CO	15,973	C
Univ of Northern Iowa	IA	14,776	C
Univ of Notre Dame	IN		MC
Univ of Okla	OK	17,634	VC+
Univ of Oregon	OR	20,872	VC
Univ of Pennsylvania	PA	56,106	MC
Univ of Pikeville	KY	24,750	NC
Univ of Pittsburgh at Bradford	PA	21,316	LC
Univ of Pittsburgh at Johnstown	PA	20,862	LC
Univ of Pittsburgh at Pittsburgh	PA	27,800	HC+
Univ of Portland	OR	47,874	VC
Univ of PR/Cayey	PR	1,504	
Univ of PR/Humacao	PR	1,877	
Univ of PR/Mayaguez	PR	1,250	
Univ of Puget Sound	WA	52,648	HC+
Univ of Redlands	CA	40,500	VC
Univ of Rio Grande	OH	8,750	NC
Univ of Rochester	NY	58,500	MC
Univ of St. Francis	IN	29,810	C
Univ of St. Mary	KS	28,400	C+
Univ of San Diego	CA	53,302	HC+
Univ of San Francisco	CA	49,674	VC
Univ of Science and Arts of Okla	OK	10,560	VC
Univ of Scranton	PA	51,940	VC
Univ of Sioux Falls	SD	22,990	C
Univ of South Alabama	AL	13,510	C
Univ of S Car at Columbia	SC	19,725	VC+
Univ of S Car Upstate	SC	17,673	LC
Univ of S Dak	SD	15,111	C
Univ of South Florida	FL	13,000	C
Univ of Southern Calif	CA	56,903	MC
Univ of Southern Indiana	IN	14,657	C
Univ of Southern Maine	ME	16,576	C
Univ of Southern Miss	MS	13,170	C
Univ of St. Francis	IL	36,490	C
Univ of St. Thomas - Houston	TX	36,490	VC
Univ of Tampa	FL	35,160	VC
Univ of Tenn at Chattanooga	TN	16,883	C
Univ of Tenn at Knoxville	TN	20,364	VC+
Univ of Tenn at Martin	TN	13,217	C
Univ of Texas at Arlington	TX	10,908	LC
Univ of Texas at Austin	TX	44,074	HC
Univ of Texas at Dallas	TX	21,046	HC
Univ of Texas at El Paso	TX	8,764	NC
Univ of Texas at San Antonio	TX	18,372	C
Univ of Texas-Pan American	TX	12,432	LC
Univ of the Cumberlands	KY	27,500	LC
Univ of the District of Columbia	DC	7,244	LC
Univ of the Incarnate Word	TX	35,200	LC
Univ of the Ozarks	AR	22,100	C
Univ of the Pacific	CA	52,146	VC
Univ of the Sacred Heart	PR	5,590	
Univ of the Southwest	NM	15,000	C
Univ of Toledo	OH	18,464	C
Univ of Tulsa	OK	45,311	HC+
Univ of Utah	UT	13,462	VC
Univ of Vermont	VT	26,120	VC+
Univ of Virginia	VA	22,175	MC
Univ of Virginia's College at Wise	VA	11,076	C
Univ of Washington	WA	14,722	VC
Univ of West Alabama	AL	9,415	C
Univ of West Florida	FL	14,656	C
Univ of West Georgia	GA	14,852	LC
Univ of Wisc Whitewater	WI	13,314	C
Univ of Wisc/Eau Claire	WI	15,430	VC
Univ of Wisc/Green Bay	WI	14,900	C
Univ of Wisc/La Crosse	WI	14,755	VC
Univ of Wisc/Madison	WI	18,757	HC
Univ of Wisc/Oshkosh	WI	10,426	LC
Univ of Wisc/Parkside	WI	10,181	LC
Univ of Wisc/Platteville	WI	14,274	C
Univ of Wisc/River Falls	WI	9,722	LC
Univ of Wisc/Stevens Point	WI	14,043	C
Univ of Wisc/Superior	WI	14,106	C
Univ of Wisc-Milwaukee	WI	18,436	C
Univ of Wyoming	WY	13,855	C+
Upper Iowa Univ	IA	30,426	NC
Ursinus College	PA	55,630	VC+
Ursuline College	OH	33,198	LC
Utah State Univ	UT	11,803	C
Utica College	NY	44,734	C
Valley City State Univ	ND	12,286	LC
Valparaiso Univ	IN	43,040	VC+
Vanderbilt Univ	TN	57,072	MC
Vanguard Univ of Southern Calif	CA	35,833	VC
Vassar College	NY	59,070	MC
Villanova Univ	PA	56,436	MC
Virginia Commonwealth Univ	VA	18,633	C
Virginia Military Inst	VA	16,156	C
Virginia Polytechnic Inst and State Univ	VA	14,629	HC
Virginia State Univ	VA	11,318	C+
Virginia Union Univ	VA	18,432	C
Virginia Wesleyan College	VA	28,433	LC
Viterbo Univ	WI	30,070	C
Voorhees College	SC	18,126	C
Wabash College	IN	44,160	VC
Wagner College	NY	48,600	VC
Wake Forest Univ	NC	51,000	MC
Walla Walla Univ	WA	26,256	NC
Walsh Univ	OH	35,100	C
Warren Wilson College	NC	34,888	VC
Wartburg College	IA	41,055	VC
Washburn Univ	KS	12,165	NC
Washington Adventist Univ	MD	25,859	C+
Washington and Jefferson College	PA	49,990	VC
Washington and Lee Univ	VA	52,812	MC
Washington College	MD	48,768	VC
Washington State Univ	WA	20,461	C
Washington Univ in St. Louis	MO	58,818	MC
Wayland Baptist Univ	TX	16,058	LC
Wayne State College	NE	11,764	NC
Wayne State Univ	MI	19,493	C
Waynesburg Univ	PA	29,100	C
Webster Univ	MO	33,990	C+
Wellesley College	MA	49,848	MC
Wells College	NY	38,680	VC
Wesley College	DE	31,115	LC
Wesleyan College	GA	24,000	C+
Wesleyan Univ	CT	59,844	MC
West Chester Univ of Pennsylvania	PA	16,836	C
West Liberty Univ	WV	9,142	LC
West Texas A&M Univ	TX	13,478	C
West Virginia State Univ	WV	8,378	NC
West Virginia Univ	WV	15,794	C+
West Virginia Wesleyan College	WV	26,880	C
Western Carolina Univ	NC	13,965	C+
Western Conn State Univ	CT	18,327	C
Western Illinois Univ	IL	20,130	C
Western Kentucky Univ	KY	11,000	LC
Western Mich Univ	MI	19,042	C
Western New England Univ	MA	45,590	C
Western New Mexico Univ	NM	8,500	LC
Western Oregon Univ	OR	15,021	C
Western State Colo Univ	CO	16,135	C
Western Washington Univ	WA	18,519	VC
Westfield State Univ	MA	18,489	C
Westminster College	MO	30,490	VC
Westminster College	PA	31,290	C+
Westminster College	UT	37,708	VC
Westmont College	CA	41,500	HC
Wheaton College	IL	39,650	HC+
Wheaton College	MA	54,934	HC+
Wheeling Jesuit Univ	WV	34,668	C
Whitman College	WA	54,400	MC
Whittier College	CA	43,416	C
Whitworth Univ	WA	45,826	VC+
Wichita State Univ	KS	12,539	C
Widener Univ	PA	50,368	C
Wilberforce Univ	OH	15,100	LC
Wiley College	TX		LC
Wilkes Univ	PA	42,786	C
Willamette Univ	OR	56,450	VC+
William Carey Univ	MS	13,500	LC
William Jewell College	MO	31,000	VC+
William Paterson Univ of New Jersey	NJ	21,694	C
William Woods Univ	MO		C
Williams College	MA	58,900	MC
Wilmington College	OH	29,784	C
Wilson College	PA	27,660	C
Wingate Univ	NC	34,990	C
Winona State Univ	MN	16,530	C
Winston-Salem State Univ	NC	9,418	LC
Winthrop Univ	SC	21,120	VC
Wisc Lutheran College	WI	23,510	VC
Wittenberg Univ	OH	47,766	VC
Wofford College	SC	45,795	VC
Worcester Polytechnic Inst	MA	53,440	HC+
Worcester State Univ	MA	18,657	C
Wright State Univ	OH	16,983	C
Xavier Univ	OH	43,740	VC
Xavier Univ of Louisiana	LA	25,300	C
Yale Univ	CT	55,300	MC
Yeshiva Univ	NY	47,250	VC+
York College / CUNY	NY	5,496	NC
York College of Pennsylvania	PA	26,590	C
Youngstown State Univ	OH	16,374	LC

MATHEMATICS - ACTUARIAL CONCENTRATION

School	ST	$IS	SR
Bethany College	WV	35,282	C
Bryant Univ	RI	49,179	VC
Seattle Univ	WA	47,010	VC+
Texas Christian Univ	TX	47,570	HC
West Chester Univ of Pennsylvania	PA	16,836	C

MATHEMATICS – ECONOMICS

School	ST	$IS	SR
Baldwin Wallace Univ	OH	36,980	VC
Bethany College	WV	35,282	C
Bowdoin College	ME	57,834	MC
Bryant Univ	RI	49,179	VC
Fordham Univ	NY	58,927	HC
Gettysburg College	PA	56,820	HC
High Point Univ	NC	39,800	C
Ithaca College	NY	52,300	HC
New York Univ	NY	61,470	MC
Northern Kentucky Univ	KY	15,302	LC
Reed College	OR	57,780	MC
Southern Oregon Univ	OR	17,874	C
Temple Univ	PA	24,392	VC
Univ of Dayton	OH	43,750	VC
Univ of Miami	FL	55,166	MC
Univ of Pittsburgh at Pittsburgh	PA	27,800	HC+
Wake Forest Univ	NC	51,000	MC
Wheaton College	MA	54,934	HC+
Yale Univ	CT	55,300	MC

MATHEMATICS – PHILOSOPHY

School	ST	$IS	SR
Yale Univ	CT	55,300	MC

MATHEMATICS EDUCATION

School	ST	$IS	SR
Adams State College	CO	13,358	LC
Alfred Univ	NY	40,392	VC
Andrews Univ	MI	28,030	C+
Appalachian State Univ	NC	12,919	VC
Aquinas College	MI	33,060	C
Arkansas State Univ	AR	14,980	C
Asbury Univ	KY	32,038	VC
Auburn Univ	AL	20,052	VC+
Averett Univ	VA	36,000	LC
Baker Univ	KS	33,350	C+
Baylor Univ	TX	46,720	HC
Bennett College	NC		LC
Bennington College	VT	56,990	HC+
Berry College	GA	39,254	HC
Bethany College	KS	30,605	NC
Bethany College	WV	35,282	C
Bethel College	IN	31,560	C
Bethel Univ	MN	34,940	VC
Biola Univ	CA	40,320	VC
Blackburn College	IL	21,350	C
Blue Mountain College	MS	13,550	LC
Boston Univ	MA	54,130	HC+
Bowdoin College	ME	57,834	MC
Bowling Green State Univ	OH	18,970	C
Brigham Young Univ	UT	12,100	HC
Brigham Young Univ/ Hawaii	HI	8,614	VC
Bryant Univ	RI	49,179	VC
Calif Baptist Univ	CA	35,890	C
Cal State, Chico	CA	18,952	C
Cal State, Long Beach	CA	17,534	C+
Calvin College	MI	37,585	VC+
Cameron Univ	OK	9,267	LC
Canisius College	NY	45,602	VC
Carthage College	WI	33,000	C
Catawba College	NC	37,105	C
Cedarville Univ	OH	31,036	VC+
Central Washington Univ	WA	11,730	C
CUNY/Brooklyn College	NY	5,884	C+
Claflin Univ	SC	22,368	C+
Coker College	SC	32,256	LC
College of New Jersey	NJ	25,376	HC
College of the Ozarks	MO	5,605	VC
Colo State Univ-Fort Collins	CO	20,090	VC
Concordia College New York	NY	31,500	VC
Concordia College, Moorhead	MN	39,974	C+
Concordia Univ St. Paul	MN	27,200	C
Corban Univ	OR	34,764	C
Covenant College	GA		VC+
CUNY-City College	NY	19,576	HC+
Daemen College	NY	31,510	C
Dakota State Univ	SD	13,811	C
Defiance College	OH	30,645	C
Delta State Univ	MS	12,292	LC
Dominican College	NY	31,270	C
Dordt College	IA	34,160	VC
Drake Univ	IA	30,980	VC+
Duquesne Univ	PA	42,017	VC
East Carolina Univ	NC	14,169	C
East Central Univ	OK	10,223	LC
East Texas Baptist Univ	TX	29,135	C
Eastern Mich Univ	MI	17,961	C
Eastern Washington Univ	WA	16,388	C
Edinboro Univ of Pennsylvania	PA	15,940	LC
Elizabethtown College	PA	47,600	VC
Elmhurst College	IL	42,032	C+
Elon Univ	NC	40,046	HC
Emory and Henry College	VA	387,460	C
Faulkner Univ	AL	22,530	LC
Ferris State Univ	MI	19,698	C
Florida Gulf Coast Univ	FL		C
Florida Inst of Technology	FL	48,290	VC
Florida State Univ	FL	15,238	HC
Fontbonne Univ	MO	31,384	C
Fort Valley State Univ	GA	11,200	VC
Franklin College	IN	35,885	C
Fresno Pacific Univ	CA	32,136	C
Gannon Univ	PA	37,940	C
Geneva College	PA	27,280	C
Georgia Southwestern State Univ	GA	12,218	C
Glenville State College	WV	11,348	NC
Goshen College	IN	35,900	VC
Grace College and Theological Seminary	IN	28,800	C
Grambling State Univ	LA	13,384	LC
Greensboro College	NC	28,740	LC
Greenville College	IL	27,012	C
Gwynedd-Mercy College	PA	33,560	C
Hardin-Simmons Univ	TX	23,560	C+
Hofstra Univ	NY	48,020	VC+
Hood College	MD	44,630	C
Houghton College	NY	35,740	VC
Houston Baptist Univ	TX	23,815	C+
Humboldt State Univ	CA	18,400	C
Huntingdon College	AL	31,850	C
Huntington Univ	IN	32,220	C
Indiana Univ Northwest	IN	6,738	LC
Indiana Univ South Bend	IN	15,293	C
Indiana Univ Southeast	IN	15,807	LC
Indiana Univ Purdue Univ Fort Wayne	IN	15,425	C
Indiana Univ-Purdue Univ Indianapolis	IN	17,290	C
Indiana Wesleyan Univ	IN	31,815	VC
Ithaca College	NY	52,300	HC
Jackson State Univ	MS	13,512	LC
John Carroll Univ	OH	44,520	C+
Johnson State College	VT	16,721	C
Judson College	AL	24,690	C
Judson Univ	IL	25,130	C
Juniata College	PA	49,340	VC
Keene State College	NH	21,538	C
Kennesaw State Univ	GA	13,017	VC
Kentucky State Univ	KY	11,000	LC
Keystone College	PA	28,680	LC
Kutztown Univ of Pennsylvania	PA	16,909	LC
Langston Univ	OK	3,000	LC
Le Moyne College	NY	42,200	VC
Lee Univ	TN	18,690	C+
Limestone College	SC	29,880	C
Lincoln Univ	MO	11,996	NC
Lipscomb Univ	TN	35,722	VC
Louisiana College	LA	15,746	C
Loyola Marymount Univ	CA	53,240	VC+
Loyola Univ Chicago	IL	49,560	VC+
Mansfield Univ	PA	19,468	LC
Marian Univ	WI	30,980	LC
Mars Hill College	NC	22,950	LC
Marymount Univ	VA	36,178	C
Marywood Univ	PA	40,695	C
Mass College of Liberal Arts	MA	16,733	C
Mayville State Univ	ND	11,401	NC
Mercyhurst Univ	PA	40,700	C
Messiah College	PA	39,540	VC
MidAmerica Nazarene Univ	KS	28,000	C
Miles College	AL	16,530	NC
Millikin Univ	IL	37,462	C
Minn State Univ, Moorhead	MN	13,392	C
Minot State Univ	ND	10,915	C
Miss Valley State Univ	MS	9,706	LC
Missouri Southern State Univ	MO	11,910	C
Monmouth Univ	NJ	42,252	C
Montana State Univ-Billings	MT	12,425	LC
Morningside College	IA	32,620	C
Morris College	SC	16,006	LC
Mount Vernon Nazarene Univ	OH	29,590	C
Nazareth College of Rochester	NY	41,590	VC
New York City College of Technology / The CUNY	NY	5,769	NC
New York Univ	NY	61,470	MC
Niagara Univ	NY	39,800	C
N Car Agricultural and Technical State Univ	NC	13,175	LC
N Car State Univ	NC	16,202	HC
North Georgia College & State Univ	GA	8,500	C
Northwest Missouri State Univ	MO	14,229	C
Northwest Nazarene Univ	ID	24,275	NC
Northwestern College	MN	24,000	C
Northwestern Okla State Univ	OK	7,275	NC
Northwestern Univ	IL	37,595	MC
Oakwood Univ	AL	23,035	C
Ohio Univ	OH	20,676	VC
Ohio Valley Univ	WV	17,752	C
Okla Christian Univ	OK	24,975	VC
Okla Wesleyan Univ	OK	21,300	C
Old Dominion Univ	VA	18,662	C
Olivet Nazarene Univ	IL	29,990	C
Oral Roberts Univ	OK	31,734	C

School	ST	$IS	SR
Oswego / SUNY	NY	20,009	VC
Ouachita Baptist Univ	AR	29,010	VC
Palm Beach Atlantic Univ	FL	33,882	LC
Pepperdine Univ	CA	55,372	HC+
Piedmont College	GA	29,260	C
Pittsburg State Univ	KS	12,032	C
Pontifical Catholic Univ of PR	PR	7,310	
Providence College	RI	55,995	HC
Purdue Univ/West Lafayette	IN	20,278	HC
Regis College	MA	47,565	LC
Rider Univ	NJ	45,720	C
Rivier College	NH	35,000	VC
Roberts Wesleyan College	NY	37,384	C+
Rocky Mountain College	MT	32,242	C
Rust College	MS	10,600	C
Sacred Heart Univ	CT	48,564	VC
Saginaw Valley State Univ	MI	16,869	C
St. Augustine's Univ	NC	14,000	C
St. Mary-of-the-Woods College	IN	37,722	LC
St. Mary's Univ of Minn	MN	37,015	C
Salisbury Univ	MD	18,368	VC
Schreiner Univ	TX	32,734	LC
Seattle Pacific Univ	WA	41,559	VC+
Seattle Univ	WA	47,010	VC+
Seton Hill Univ	PA	35,172	C
Shaw Univ	NC	15,488	LC
Shepherd Univ	WV	14,996	C
Shippensburg Univ of Pennsylvania	PA	17,064	LC
Shorter Univ	GA	26,470	C
Simpson Univ	CA	28,900	C
Southeast Missouri State Univ	MO	14,983	LC
Southeastern Okla State Univ	OK	7,966	C
Southern Illinois Univ Edwardsville	IL	17,532	C
Southern Nazarene Univ	OK	24,354	NC
Southern Univ and A&M College	LA	9,761	C+
Southern Univ at New Orleans	LA	1,000	NC
Southern Wesleyan Univ	SC	25,600	C
Southwest Baptist Univ	MO	24,710	C
Southwest Minn State Univ	MN	14,000	C
Southwestern College	KS	29,270	C
Southwestern Okla State Univ	OK	9,160	C
St. Edward's Univ	TX	44,674	VC
St. John Fisher College	NY	39,370	C+
St. John's Univ	NY	52,840	C+
Suffolk Univ	MA	46,548	C
SUNY College at Old Westbury	NY	16,324	C
SUNY New Paltz	NY	15,010	C
SUNY Oneonta / SUNY	NY	16,919	VC
SUNY Plattsburgh / SUNY	NY	18,083	VC
Syracuse Univ	NY	54,512	HC
Taylor Univ	IN	36,742	VC+
Temple Univ	PA	24,392	VC
Texas Christian Univ	TX	47,570	HC
Texas Southern Univ	TX	18,212	LC
Texas Wesleyan Univ	TX	29,886	C
The Catholic Univ of America	DC	52,852	VC
The College of St. Rose	NY	26,750	C
The SUNY at Potsdam	NY	17,754	C
Tougaloo College	MS	15,275	NC
Trevecca Nazarene Univ	TN	30,118	C
Trine Univ	IN	39,400	VC
Troy Univ	AL	10,650	C
Union College	NE	23,270	VC
Universidad del Turabo	PR	4,110	
Univ of Arkansas at Pine Bluff	AR	10,600	C
Univ of Calif at Los Angeles	CA	25,686	MC
Univ of Calif at Riverside	CA	27,204	C
Univ of Calif at San Diego	CA	21,000	VC
Univ of Central Florida	FL	15,711	VC+
Univ of Central Missouri	MO	14,605	C
Univ of Central Okla	OK	12,293	C
Univ of Conn	CT	23,744	HC
Univ of Delaware	DE	22,728	VC
Univ of Evansville	IN	41,056	VC+
Univ of Georgia	GA	19,508	VC
Univ of Great Falls	MT	27,970	C
Univ of Idaho	ID	14,558	C
Univ of Illinois at Chicago	IL	24,293	VC
Univ of Illinois at Urbana-Champaign	IL	24,300	HC
Univ of Indianapolis	IN	31,740	LC
Univ of Iowa	IA	17,481	VC
Univ of Kentucky	KY	19,868	C
Univ of Louisiana at Lafayette	LA	6,130	C
Univ of Louisiana at Monroe	LA	12,998	C
Univ of Mary	ND	16,714	C
Univ of Mary Hardin-Baylor	TX	31,950	C+
Univ of Maryland/Eastern Shore	MD	14,000	C
Univ of Miami	FL	55,166	MC
Univ of Mich/Dearborn	MI	9,885	VC
Univ of Minn/Duluth	MN	18,964	C+
Univ of Minn/Twin Cities	MN		HC
Univ of Miss	MS	15,482	VC
Univ of Missouri/Columbia	MO	18,201	MC
Univ of Montana-Western	MT	9,753	LC
Univ of Nebr - Lincoln	NE	17,507	VC
Univ of New Hampshire	NH	24,702	VC
Univ of New Haven	CT	47,740	C
Univ of New Orleans	LA	9,224	VC
Univ of N Car at Charlotte	NC	15,847	C
Univ of N Car at Greensboro	NC	12,848	C
Univ of North Florida	FL	15,578	VC
Univ of Okla	OK	17,634	VC+
Univ of Pittsburgh at Bradford	PA	21,316	LC
Univ of Pittsburgh at Johnstown	PA	20,862	LC
Univ of Rio Grande	OH	8,750	NC
Univ of St. Francis	IN	29,810	C
Univ of S Car Upstate	SC	17,673	LC
Univ of South Florida	FL	13,000	C
Univ of Southern Indiana	IN	14,657	C
Univ of the Cumberlands	KY	27,500	LC
Univ of Vermont	VT	26,120	VC+
Univ of Wisc/Green Bay	WI	14,900	C
Univ of Wisc/Superior	WI	14,106	C
Utah State Univ	UT	11,803	C
Valparaiso Univ	IN	43,040	VC+
Viterbo Univ	WI	30,070	C
Wartburg College	IA	41,055	VC
Washington Adventist Univ	MD	25,859	C+
Washington Univ in St. Louis	MO	58,818	MC
Wayne State Univ	MI	19,493	C
Webster Univ	MO	33,990	C+
West Chester Univ of Pennsylvania	PA	16,836	C
West Texas A&M Univ	TX	13,478	C
West Virginia Univ	WV	15,794	C+
Western Carolina Univ	NC	13,965	C+
Westmont College	CA	41,500	HC
Wheeling Jesuit Univ	WV	34,668	C
Whitworth Univ	WA	45,826	VC+
Widener Univ	PA	50,368	C
Wiley College	TX		LC
Wilmington College	OH	29,784	C
Wingate Univ	NC	34,990	C
Winona State Univ	MN	16,530	C
Wright State Univ	OH	16,983	C
Xavier Univ of Louisiana	LA	25,300	C
York College of Pennsylvania	PA	26,590	C
Youngstown State Univ	OH	16,374	LC

MATHEMATICS/ COMPUTATIONAL

School	ST	$IS	SR
Abilene Christian Univ	TX	38,400	VC
Aquinas College	MI	33,060	C
Bryant Univ	RI	49,179	VC
Lawrence Tech Univ	MI	37,630	VC
Loyola Univ Chicago	IL	49,560	VC+
Northern Kentucky Univ	KY	15,302	LC
Southwestern Univ	TX	45,660	VC
Temple Univ	PA	24,392	VC
Univ of Illinois at Chicago	IL	24,293	VC
Univ of Miami	FL	55,166	MC
West Chester Univ of Pennsylvania	PA	16,836	C

MATHEMATICS/THEORETICAL

School	ST	$IS	SR
Aquinas College	MI	33,060	C
Biola Univ	CA	40,320	VC
Seattle Univ	WA	47,010	VC+

MECHANICAL DESIGN TECHNOLOGY

School	ST	$IS	SR
Pennsylvania College of Technology	PA	25,653	NC
Western Washington Univ	WA	18,519	VC

MECHANICAL ENGINEERING

School	ST	$IS	SR
Alabama A&M Univ	AL	96,100	C
Alfred Univ	NY	40,392	VC
Arizona State Univ	AZ	18,818	C+
Arkansas State Univ	AR	14,980	C
Arkansas Tech Univ	AR	13,164	LC
Auburn Univ	AL	20,052	VC+
Baylor Univ	TX	46,720	HC
Bethel College	IN	31,560	C
Binghamton Univ / The SUNY	NY	20,832	HC+
Boise State Univ	ID	12,802	C
Boston Univ	MA	54,130	HC+
Bradley Univ	IL	31,874	VC
Brigham Young Univ	UT	12,100	HC
Bucknell Univ	PA	58,160	MC
Calif Baptist Univ	CA	35,890	C
Calif Inst of Technology	CA	54,045	MC
Calif Maritime Academy	CA	15,496	C
Calif Polytechnic State Univ	CA	19,847	HC
Calif State Polytechnic Univ, Pomona	CA	18,932	C
Cal State, Chico	CA	18,952	C
Cal State, Fresno	CA	17,405	C
Cal State, Fullerton	CA	25,188	C+
Cal State, Long Beach	CA	17,534	C+
Cal State, Los Angeles	CA	15,829	C
Cal State, Sacramento	CA	16,200	C
Calvin College	MI	37,585	VC+
Carnegie Mellon Univ	PA	51,260	MC
Case Western Reserve Univ	OH	55,178	MC
Cedarville Univ	OH	31,036	VC+
Central Conn State Univ	CT	19,212	C
Central Mich Univ	MI	18,066	C
Central Washington Univ	WA	11,730	C
Christian Brothers Univ	TN	19,140	HC
Clarkson Univ	NY	53,538	HC
Clemson Univ	SC	19,136	HC
Cleveland State Univ	OH	21,357	C
College of New Jersey	NJ	25,376	HC
Colo State Univ-Fort Collins	CO	20,090	VC
Columbia Univ in the City of New York	NY	61,116	MC
Cooper Union for the Advancement of Science and Art	NY	55,600	MC
Cornell Univ	NY	59,037	MC
CUNY-City College	NY	19,576	HC+
Daniel Webster College	NH	25,380	C
Delaware State Univ	DE	14,700	LC
Dordt College	IA	34,160	VC
Drexel Univ	PA	51,920	HC
Duke Univ	NC	50,250	MC
Elizabethtown College	PA	47,600	VC
Embry-Riddle Aeronautical Univ - Daytona Beach	FL	40,884	C+
Embry-Riddle Aeronautical Univ - Prescott Campus	AZ	40,584	VC
Fairfield Univ	CT	55,850	VC
Florida A&M Univ	FL	14,935	LC
Florida Atlantic Univ	FL	17,339	C
Florida Inst of Technology	FL	48,290	VC
Florida International Univ	FL	17,747	VC
Florida State Univ	FL	15,238	HC
Franklin W. Olin College of Engineering	MA	57,500	SP
Gannon Univ	PA	37,940	C
George Washington Univ	DC	57,108	MC
Georgia Inst of Technology	GA	20,464	MC
Georgia Southern Univ	GA	16,414	C
Gonzaga Univ	WA	44,247	HC
Grove City College	PA	22,988	HC
Harding Univ	AR	21,432	C+
Hofstra Univ	NY	48,020	VC+
Howard Univ	DC	35,957	C
Idaho State Univ	ID	11,908	C
Illinois Inst of Technology	IL	38,512	HC+
Indiana Inst of Technology	IN	34,240	LC
Indiana Univ-Purdue Univ Fort Wayne	IN	15,425	C
Inter-American Univ of PR/ Bayamon Univ College	PR	4,428	
Iowa State Univ	IA	16,403	C
Jacksonville Univ	FL	37,780	C
Johns Hopkins Univ	MD	47,492	MC
Kansas State Univ	KS	15,497	VC
Kettering Univ	MI	31,456	HC
Lafayette College	PA	57,050	HC+
Lake Superior State Univ	MI	18,121	C
Lamar Univ	TX	6,820	LC
Lawrence Tech Univ	MI	37,630	VC
Lehigh Univ	PA	55,080	MC
LeTourneau Univ	TX	26,230	C
Lipscomb Univ	TN	35,722	VC
Louisiana State Univ	LA	18,677	VC+
Louisiana Tech Univ	LA	8,000	C
Loyola Marymount Univ	CA	53,240	VC+
Manhattan College	NY	44,955	VC
Marquette Univ	WI	43,664	VC+
Mass Inst of Technology	MA	54,238	MC
Miami Univ	OH	24,191	HC
Mich State Univ	MI	13,689	VC
Mich Tech Univ	MI	22,105	VC
Milwaukee School of Engineering	WI	39,948	VC+
Minn State Univ, Mankato	MN	14,900	C
Missouri Univ of Science and Technology	MO	18,655	VC+
Montana State Univ	MT	14,068	VC
New Jersey Inst of Technology	NJ	26,490	VC
New Mexico Inst of Mining and Technology	NM	12,892	HC
New Mexico State Univ	NM	13,955	LC
New York Inst of Technology	NY	40,590	VC
New York Univ	NY	61,470	MC
N Car Agricultural and Technical State Univ	NC	13,175	LC
N Car State Univ	NC	16,202	HC
N Dak State Univ	ND	14,642	C
Northeastern Univ	MA	55,296	MC
Northern Arizona Univ	AZ	18,592	C
Northern Illinois Univ	IL	19,768	C
Northwestern Univ	IL	37,595	MC
Norwich Univ	VT	28,212	C
Oakland Univ	MI	19,391	VC
Ohio Northern Univ	OH	42,075	VC
Ohio Univ	OH	20,676	VC
Okla Christian Univ	OK	24,975	VC
Okla State Univ	OK	14,310	VC
Old Dominion Univ	VA	18,662	C
Oral Roberts Univ	OK	31,734	C
Oregon State Univ	OR	19,017	C+
Penn State Univ/Univ Park	PA	25,404	VC
Pennsylvania College of Technology	PA	25,653	NC
Point Park Univ	PA	36,390	C
Polytechnic Inst of New York Univ	NY	53,064	HC+
Prairie View A&M Univ	TX	15,205	LC
Princeton Univ	NJ	53,795	MC
Purdue Univ/Calumet	IN	14,336	C
Purdue Univ/West Lafayette	IN	20,278	HC
Quinnipiac Univ	CT	53,580	VC
Rensselaer Polytechnic Inst	NY	59,229	MC
Rice Univ	TX	43,288	MC
Rochester Inst of Technology	NY	42,450	VC+
Rose-Hulman Inst of Technology	IN	51,738	MC
Rowan Univ	NJ	23,570	VC
Rutgers, The State Univ of New Jersey/New Brunswick	NJ	25,077	VC
Saginaw Valley State Univ	MI	16,869	C
St. Louis Univ	MO	46,594	VC+
St. Martin's Univ	WA	38,082	C
St. Mary's Univ	TX	33,854	C
San Diego State Univ	CA	20,578	VC
San Francisco State Univ	CA	18,514	C
San Jose State Univ	CA	19,707	C
Santa Clara Univ	CA	54,702	MC
Seattle Univ	WA	47,010	VC+
S Dak School of Mines and Technology	SD	15,260	VC
S Dak State Univ	SD	14,296	C
Southern Illinois Univ Carbondale	IL	21,620	C
Southern Illinois Univ Edwardsville	IL	17,532	C
Southern Methodist Univ	TX	57,755	MC
Southern Polytechnic State Univ	GA	13,958	VC
Southern Univ and A&M College	LA	9,761	C+
Stanford Univ	CA	56,411	MC
Stevens Inst of Technology	NJ	50,130	HC
Stony Brook Univ / SUNY	NY	19,359	HC
Syracuse Univ	NY	54,512	HC
Temple Univ	PA	24,392	VC
Tenn State Univ	TN	9,048	C
Tenn Tech Univ	TN	11,310	C
Texas A&M Univ	TX	16,956	VC+
Texas A&M Univ at Kingsville	TX	7,500	LC
Texas Christian Univ	TX	47,570	HC
Texas Tech Univ	TX	14,243	C
The Catholic Univ of America	DC	52,852	VC
Ohio State Univ	OH	19,887	MC
Trine Univ	IN	39,400	VC
Tufts Univ	MA	58,780	MC
Tuskegee Univ	AL	26,750	C
Union College	NY		MC
United States Air Force Academy	CO		MC
United States Coast Guard Academy	CT		HC
United States Military Academy	NY		MC
United States Naval Academy	MD		MC
Universidad Politecnica de PR	PR	19,252	
Univ at Buffalo / The SUNY	NY	20,283	VC
Univ of Akron	OH	20,436	C
Univ of Alabama at Birmingham	AL	18,484	C+
Univ of Alabama at Huntsville	AL	17,625	VC
Univ of Alabama at Tuscaloosa	AL	17,164	C+
Univ of Alaska Fairbanks	AK	13,955	C
Univ of Arizona	AZ	20,105	C
Univ of Arkansas at Fayetteville	AR	16,860	VC
Univ of Calif at Berkeley	CA	23,322	MC
Univ of Calif at Davis	CA	24,482	HC
Univ of Calif at Irvine	CA	25,961	VC
Univ of Calif at Los Angeles	CA	25,686	MC
Univ of Calif at Riverside	CA	27,204	C
Univ of Calif at San Diego	CA	21,000	VC
Univ of Calif at Santa Barbara	CA	27,551	HC
Univ of Central Florida	FL	15,711	VC+
Univ of Cincinnati	OH	20,199	VC
Univ of Colo Boulder	CO	22,605	VC+
Univ of Colo Denver	CO	17,904	C
Univ of Conn	CT	23,744	HC
Univ of Dayton	OH	43,750	VC
Univ of Delaware	DE	22,728	VC
Univ of Denver	CO	51,787	VC+
Univ of Detroit Mercy	MI	30,450	C

ST = STATE $IS = IN-STATE COSTS SR = SELECTOR RATING

School	ST	$IS	SR
Univ of Evansville	IN	41,056	VC+
Univ of Florida	FL	15,783	HC+
Univ of Georgia	GA	19,508	VC
Univ of Hartford	CT	42,674	C
Univ of Hawaii at Manoa	HI	19,379	VC
Univ of Houston	TX	19,184	VC
Univ of Idaho	ID	14,558	C
Univ of Illinois at Chicago	IL	24,293	VC
Univ of Illinois at Urbana-Champaign	IL	24,300	HC
Univ of Indianapolis	IN	31,740	LC
Univ of Iowa	IA	17,481	VC
Univ of Kansas	KS	16,980	C+
Univ of Kentucky	KY	19,868	C
Univ of Louisiana at Lafayette	LA	6,130	C
Univ of Louisville	KY	17,460	VC
Univ of Maine	ME	19,712	C+
Univ of Maryland	MD	18,801	HC
Univ of Maryland/Baltimore County	MD	18,000	VC
Univ of Mass Amherst	MA	23,697	VC+
Univ of Mass Dartmouth	MA	22,223	C
Univ of Mass Lowell	MA	19,316	C
Univ of Memphis	TN	15,094	C
Univ of Miami	FL	55,166	MC
Univ of Mich/Ann Arbor	MI	22,102	HC+
Univ of Mich/Dearborn	MI	9,885	VC
Univ of Minn/Duluth	MN	18,964	C+
Univ of Minn/Twin Cities	MN		HC
Univ of Miss	MS	15,482	VC
Univ of Missouri/Columbia	MO	18,201	MC
Univ of Missouri-Kansas City	MO	19,003	C
Univ of Missouri-St. Louis	MO	18,304	VC
Univ of Mount Union	OH	35,130	C
Univ of Nebr - Lincoln	NE	17,507	VC
Univ of Nevada, Las Vegas	NV	17,303	C
Univ of Nevada/Reno	NV	14,500	NC
Univ of New Hampshire	NH	24,702	VC
Univ of New Haven	CT	47,740	C
Univ of New Mexico	NM	15,300	C
Univ of New Orleans	LA	9,224	VC
Univ of N Car at Charlotte	NC	15,847	C
Univ of N Dak	ND	14,094	C
Univ of North Florida	FL	15,578	VC
Univ of North Texas	TX	15,628	C
Univ of Notre Dame	IN		MC
Univ of Okla	OK	17,634	VC+
Univ of Pittsburgh at Pittsburgh	PA	27,800	HC+
Univ of Portland	OR	47,874	VC
Univ of PR/Mayaguez	PR	1,250	
Univ of Rochester	NY	58,500	MC
Univ of San Diego	CA	53,302	HC+
Univ of South Alabama	AL	13,510	C
Univ of S Car at Columbia	SC	19,725	VC+
Univ of South Florida	FL	13,000	C
Univ of Southern Calif	CA	56,903	MC
Univ of Tenn at Chattanooga	TN	16,883	C
Univ of Tenn at Knoxville	TN	20,364	VC+
Univ of Texas at Arlington	TX	10,908	LC
Univ of Texas at Austin	TX	44,074	HC
Univ of Texas at Dallas	TX	21,046	HC
Univ of Texas at El Paso	TX	8,764	NC
Univ of Texas at San Antonio	TX	18,372	C
Univ of Texas-Pan American	TX	12,432	LC
Univ of the District of Columbia	DC	7,244	LC
Univ of the Pacific	CA	52,146	VC
Univ of Toledo	OH	18,464	C
Univ of Tulsa	OK	45,311	HC+
Univ of Utah	UT	13,462	VC
Univ of Vermont	VT	26,120	VC+
Univ of Virginia	VA	22,175	MC
Univ of Wisc/Madison	WI	18,757	HC
Univ of Wisc/Platteville	WI	14,274	C
Univ of Wisc-Milwaukee	WI	18,436	C
Univ of Wyoming	WY	13,855	C+
Utah State Univ	UT	11,803	C
Valparaiso Univ	IN	43,040	VC+
Vanderbilt Univ	TN	57,072	MC
Villanova Univ	PA	56,436	MC
Virginia Commonwealth Univ	VA	18,633	C
Virginia Military Inst	VA	16,156	C
Virginia Polytechnic Inst and State Univ	VA	14,629	HC
Washington State Univ	WA	20,461	C
Washington Univ in St. Louis	MO	58,818	MC
Wayne State Univ	MI	19,493	C
West Texas A&M Univ	TX	13,478	C
West Virginia Univ	WV	15,794	C+
West Virginia Univ Inst of Technology	WV	14,094	NC
Western Kentucky Univ	KY	11,000	LC
Western Mich Univ	MI	19,042	C
Western New England Univ	MA	45,590	C
Wichita State Univ	KS	12,539	C
Widener Univ	PA	50,368	C
Wilkes Univ	PA	42,786	C
Worcester Polytechnic Inst	MA	53,440	HC+
Wright State Univ	OH	16,983	C
Yale Univ	CT	55,300	MC
York College of Pennsylvania	PA	26,590	C
Youngstown State Univ	OH	16,374	LC

MECHANICAL ENGINEERING TECHNOLOGY

School	ST	$IS	SR
Alabama A&M Univ	AL	96,100	C
Alfred State / SUNY College of Technology	NY	18,034	C
Arizona State Univ	AZ	18,818	C+
Buffalo State/State Univ of Buffalo	NY	15,733	C+
Central Conn State Univ	CT	19,212	C
Central Mich Univ	MI	18,066	C
Cleveland State Univ	OH	21,357	C
Colo State Univ-Pueblo	CO	13,532	LC
Eastern Mich Univ	MI	17,961	C
Eastern Washington Univ	WA	16,388	C
Fairleigh Dickinson Univ/Metropolitan Campus	NJ	40,254	C
Fairmont State Univ	WV	12,098	LC
Farmingdale State College	NY	18,985	C
Ferris State Univ	MI	19,698	C
Indiana State Univ	IN	16,000	C
Indiana Univ-Purdue Univ Fort Wayne	IN	15,425	C
Indiana Univ-Purdue Univ Indianapolis	IN	17,290	C
Metropolitan State Univ of Denver	CO	4,835	LC
Mich Tech Univ	MI	22,105	VC
Montana State Univ	MT	14,068	VC
New York City College of Technology / The CUNY	NY	5,769	NC
Okla State Univ	OK	14,310	VC
Old Dominion Univ	VA	18,662	C
Oregon Inst of Technology	OR	8,910	C
Penn State Erie/The Behrend College	PA	16,256	C
Pennsylvania College of Technology	PA	25,653	NC
Pittsburg State Univ	KS	12,032	C
Point Park Univ	PA	36,390	C
Purdue Univ/Calumet	IN	14,336	C
Purdue Univ/West Lafayette	IN	20,278	HC
Rochester Inst of Technology	NY	42,450	VC+
S Car State Univ	SC	6,700	LC
Southern Polytechnic State Univ	GA	13,958	VC
SUNY Inst of Technology at Utica / Rome	NY	23,818	C
Texas A&M Univ at Corpus Christi	TX	11,544	LC
Texas A&M Univ at Galveston	TX	11,258	C
Texas Tech Univ	TX	14,243	C
Univ of Akron	OH	20,436	C
Univ of Arkansas at Little Rock	AR		C
Univ of Cincinnati	OH	20,199	VC
Univ of Dayton	OH	43,750	VC
Univ of Hartford	CT	42,674	C
Univ of Houston	TX	19,184	VC
Univ of Maine	ME	19,712	C+
Univ of N Car at Charlotte	NC	15,847	C
Univ of North Texas	TX	15,628	C
Univ of Pittsburgh at Johnstown	PA	20,862	LC
Univ of Southern Miss	MS	13,170	C
Vaughn College of Aeronautics and Technology	NY	31,360	SP
Wayne State Univ	MI	19,493	C
Wentworth Inst of Technology	MA	29,800	SP
Western Washington Univ	WA	18,519	VC
Youngstown State Univ	OH	16,374	LC

MECHATRONICS ENGINEERING

School	ST	$IS	SR
Cal State, Chico	CA	18,952	C
Southern Polytechnic State Univ	GA	13,958	VC
Univ of Denver	CO	51,787	VC+
Vaughn College of Aeronautics and Technology	NY	31,360	SP

MEDIA ARTS

School	ST	$IS	SR
Alverno College	WI	30,483	LC
Anna Maria College	MA	34,600	LC
Art Inst of Portland	OR	23,040	SP
Ashland Univ	OH	25,000	C
Baker Univ	KS	33,350	C+
Bentley Univ	MA	54,555	HC+
Briar Cliff Univ	IA	29,514	C
Brigham Young Univ	UT	12,100	HC
Brown Univ	RI	56,150	MC
Butler Univ	IN	45,898	VC+
Cal State, Chico	CA	18,952	C
Cal State, Fresno	CA	17,405	C
Cal State, Los Angeles	CA	15,829	C
Calumet College of St. Joseph	IN	15,000	LC
Calvin College	MI	37,585	VC+
Canisius College	NY	45,602	VC
Carleton College	MN	58,149	MC
Carlow Univ	PA	30,272	C
Champlain College	VT	44,850	VC
Chatham Univ	PA	42,440	VC
Claremont McKenna College	CA	58,065	MC
College of the Ozarks	MO	5,605	VC
Cornerstone Univ and Grand Rapids Theological Seminary	MI	30,866	C
Denison Univ	OH	54,670	HC+
DePaul Univ	IL	46,120	VC
Drury Univ	MO	30,319	VC
East Stroudsburg Univ of Pennsylvania	PA	16,636	C
Eastern Mich Univ	MI	17,961	C
Edinboro Univ of Pennsylvania	PA	15,940	LC
Elon Univ	NC	40,046	HC
Emerson College	MA	50,246	HC
Florida Atlantic Univ	FL	17,339	C
Goddard College	VT	16,418	VC
Greenville College	IL	27,012	C
Hampshire College	MA	58,320	MC
Harding Univ	AR	21,432	C+
Hofstra Univ	NY	48,020	VC+
Houghton College	NY	35,740	VC
Howard Univ	DC	35,957	C
Hunter College / The CUNY	NY	14,429	VC
Huntington Univ	IN	32,220	C
Illinois State Univ	IL	22,634	VC
Indiana Univ-Purdue Univ Indianapolis	IN	17,290	C
Ithaca College	NY	52,300	HC
James Madison Univ	VA	18,049	VC
Johns Hopkins Univ	MD	47,492	MC
Judson Univ	IL	25,130	C
Kean Univ	NJ	22,060	LC
Kendall College of Art and Design of Ferris State Univ	MI	21,048	SP
Lake Erie College	OH	35,704	C
Lasell College	MA	42,500	LC
Lawrence Tech Univ	MI	37,630	VC
Le Moyne College	NY	42,200	VC
Lindsey Wilson College	KY	30,470	VC
Loras College	IA	37,432	VC
Loyola Marymount Univ	CA	53,240	VC+
Loyola Univ Chicago	IL	49,560	VC+
Macalester College	MN	53,419	MC
Maine College of Art	ME	28,812	SP
Marquette Univ	WI	43,664	VC+
Maryland Inst College of Art	MD	39,500	SP
Marylhurst Univ	OR	18,945	NC
Mass College of Art and Design	MA	23,600	SP
Mass Inst of Technology	MA	54,238	MC
Mercer Univ	GA	44,201	VC+
Mercy College	NY	29,996	C
Miami Univ	OH	24,191	HC
Mills College	CA	54,119	HC
Montana State Univ	MT	14,068	VC
Mount Ida College	MA	30,115	LC
Mount St. Mary College	NY	39,540	C
New Jersey City Univ	NJ	21,060	C+
New York Univ	NY	61,470	MC
Northeastern Illinois Univ	IL		C
Ohio Univ	OH	20,676	VC
Olivet Nazarene Univ	IL	29,990	C
Pepperdine Univ	CA	55,372	HC+
Pitzer College	CA	54,988	MC
Point Loma Nazarene Univ	CA	38,610	VC
Point Park Univ	PA	36,390	C
Pomona College	CA	57,680	MC
Queens College / The CUNY	NY	17,107	VC
Radford Univ	VA	17,132	LC
Rensselaer Polytechnic Inst	NY	59,229	MC
Robert Morris Univ	PA	36,699	C
Rocky Mountain College of Art and Design	CO	22,470	NC
Roger Williams Univ	RI	45,788	C
Rollins College	FL	52,370	HC
Roosevelt Univ	IL	22,605	VC
Sacred Heart Univ	CT	48,564	VC
Salve Regina Univ	RI	47,250	VC
San Francisco Art Inst	CA	52,492	SP
Savannah College of Art and Design	GA	46,824	SP
Southern Illinois Univ Edwardsville	IL	17,532	C
Southern Methodist Univ	TX	57,755	MC
Southern Polytechnic State Univ	GA	13,958	VC
Spalding Univ	KY	31,850	LC
St. Catherine Univ	MN	37,782	C+
Suffolk Univ	MA	46,548	C
SUNY College at Old Westbury	NY	16,324	C
SUNY Fredonia / The SUNY at Fredonia	NY	18,702	VC
Swarthmore College	PA	57,870	MC
Syracuse Univ	NY	54,512	HC
Taylor Univ	IN	36,742	VC+
Temple Univ	PA	24,392	VC
Thiel College	PA	31,378	LC
Towson Univ	MD	16,000	VC
Tulane Univ	LA	58,942	MC
Univ at Buffalo / The SUNY	NY	20,283	VC
Univ of Akron	OH	20,436	C
Univ of Calif at Irvine	CA	25,961	VC
Univ of Chicago	IL	55,416	MC
Univ of Denver	CO	51,787	VC+
Univ of Georgia	GA	19,508	VC
Univ of Hartford	CT	42,674	C
Univ of Illinois at Urbana-Champaign	IL	24,300	HC
Univ of Maine	ME	19,712	C+
Univ of Maine at Farmington	ME	17,841	C
Univ of Missouri-St. Louis	MO	18,304	VC
Univ of Mount Union	OH	35,130	C
Univ of New Mexico	NM	15,300	C
Univ of N Car at Greensboro	NC	12,848	C
Univ of Pittsburgh at Pittsburgh	PA	27,800	HC+
Univ of Rochester	NY	58,500	MC
Univ of San Francisco	CA	49,674	VC
Univ of S Car at Columbia	SC	19,725	VC+
Univ of Texas at Dallas	TX	21,046	HC
Univ of the District of Columbia	DC	7,244	LC
Univ of Utah	UT	13,462	VC
Vassar College	NY	59,070	MC
Virginia Commonwealth Univ	VA	18,633	C
Washburn Univ	KS	12,165	NC
Wayne State Univ	MI	19,493	C
Webster Univ	MO	33,990	C+
Wesley College	DE	31,115	LC
Western Conn State Univ	CT	18,327	C
Widener Univ	PA	50,368	C
Wilkes Univ	PA	42,786	C
Wilmington Univ	DE	7,778	NC
Xavier Univ	OH	43,740	VC

MEDIA MANAGEMENT

School	ST	$IS	SR
San Diego State Univ	CA	20,578	VC

MEDICAL ANTHROPOLOGY

School	ST	$IS	SR
Creighton Univ	NE	44,058	VC+

MEDICAL IMAGING

School	ST	$IS	SR
Indiana Univ Kokomo	IN	6,674	LC
Indiana Univ Kokomo	IN	6,674	LC
Indiana Univ South Bend	IN	15,293	C
Indiana Univ-Purdue Univ Indianapolis	IN	17,290	C
Thomas Edison State College	NJ	5,700	SP
Univ of Louisiana at Monroe	LA	12,998	C

MEDICAL LABORATORY SCIENCE

School	ST	$IS	SR
Albany College of Pharmacy and Health Sciences	NY	38,900	SP
Allen College	IA	26,110	SP
Augustana College	SD	35,500	VC
Eastern Illinois Univ	IL	20,502	C
Eastern Mich Univ	MI	17,961	C
Idaho State Univ	ID	11,908	C
Marquette Univ	WI	43,664	VC+
Monmouth Univ	NJ	42,252	C
Oakland Univ	MI	19,391	VC
Saginaw Valley State Univ	MI	16,869	C
St. Louis Univ	MO	46,594	VC+
St. Mary's Univ of Minn	MN	37,015	C
S Dak State Univ	SD	14,296	C
St. Edward's Univ	TX	44,674	VC
Ohio State Univ	OH	19,887	MC
Univ of Iowa	IA	17,481	VC
Univ of Louisiana at Monroe	LA	12,998	C
Univ of Mass Dartmouth	MA	22,223	C
Univ of New Hampshire	NH	24,702	VC
Univ of Utah	UT	13,462	VC
Univ of Vermont	VT	26,120	VC+
Western Carolina Univ	NC	13,965	C+
Xavier Univ	OH	43,740	VC
York College of Pennsylvania	PA	26,590	C

MEDICAL LABORATORY TECHNOLOGY

School	ST	$IS	SR
Alabama A&M Univ	AL	96,100	C
American International College	MA	36,100	LC
Anderson Univ	IN	35,390	C
Andrews Univ	MI	28,030	C+
Angelo State Univ	TX	15,049	NC

School	ST	$IS	SR
Arkansas Tech Univ	AR	13,164	LC
Auburn Univ	AL	20,052	V₵
Avila Univ	MO	26,900	C
Ball State Univ	IN	17,850	C
Baylor Univ	TX	46,720	HC
Bemidji State Univ	MN	13,500	C
Blackburn College	IL	21,350	C
Bloomsburg Univ of Pennsylvania	PA	13,598	C
Brescia Univ	KY	26,140	V₵
Caldwell College	NJ	35,602	LC
Cal State, Northridge	CA	28,313	C
Cal State, Sacramento	CA	16,200	C
Calif Univ of Pennsylvania	PA	14,217	C
Campbellsville Univ	KY	27,720	C
Canisius College	NY	45,602	VC
Cheyney Univ of Pennsylvania	PA	20,372	LC
Clemson Univ	SC	19,136	HC
Coker College	SC	32,256	LC
College of St. Mary	NE	34,334	C
Columbia College	SC	27,882	C
Concord Univ	WV	13,102	C
Concordia Univ Nebr	NE	26,000	VC
Defiance College	OH	30,645	C
Dordt College	IA	34,160	VC
East Stroudsburg Univ of Pennsylvania	PA	16,636	C
Eastern Mennonite Univ	VA	38,850	VC
Eastern Mich Univ	MI	17,961	C
Eastern New Mexico Univ	NM	10,682	C
Eastern Washington Univ	WA	16,388	C
Edinboro Univ of Pennsylvania	PA	15,940	LC
Elmira College	NY	49,950	₵
Elms College	MA	23,900	VC
Eureka College	IL	19,280	C
Evangel Univ	MO	23,090	C
Fairleigh Dickinson Univ/ College at Florham	NJ	42,142	C
Fairleigh Dickinson Univ/ Metropolitan Campus	NJ	40,254	C
Fayetteville State Univ	NC	10,816	C
Florida Atlantic Univ	FL	17,339	C
George Washington Univ	DC	57,108	MC
Graceland Univ	IA	28,020	C
Grand Valley State Univ	MI	17,998	VC
Gwynedd-Mercy College	PA	33,560	C
Holy Family Univ	PA	40,030	LC
Hunter College / The CUNY	NY	14,429	VC
Illinois College	IL	25,770	VC
Illinois State Univ	IL	22,634	VC
Indiana State Univ	IN	16,000	C
Indiana Wesleyan Univ	IN	31,815	VC
Inter-American Univ of PR/ San Germán	PR	6,720	
Judson Univ	IL	25,130	C
Kent State Univ	OH	19,352	C
Keuka College	NY	30,300	C
King's College	PA	41,678	C
Kutztown Univ of Pennsylvania	PA	16,909	LC
Lake Superior State Univ	MI	18,121	C
Lamar Univ	TX	6,820	LC
Langston Univ	OK	3,000	LC
Lebanon Valley College	PA	38,570	C
Lee Univ	TN	18,690	₵
Lenoir-Rhyne College	NC	35,984	C
Lincoln Memorial Univ	TN	18,144	C
Lock Haven Univ of Pennsylvania	PA	17,587	LC
LIU/C.W. Post Campus	NY	38,888	C
Louisiana College	LA	15,746	C
Louisiana Tech Univ	LA	8,000	C
Madonna Univ	MI	24,540	VC
Malone Univ	OH	34,334	C
Manchester College	IN	35,070	C
Marshall Univ	WV	14,820	C
Mayville State Univ	ND	11,401	NC
McKendree Univ	IL	29,920	₵
Mercy College	NY	29,996	C
Mercyhurst Univ	PA	40,700	C
Mich State Univ	MI	13,689	VC
Midwestern State Univ	TX	9,722	C
Minn State Univ, Moorhead	MN	13,392	C
Misericordia Univ	PA	39,840	C
Missouri Southern State Univ	MO	11,910	C
Missouri Western State Univ	MO	12,260	NC
Monmouth Univ	NJ	42,252	C
Morgan State Univ	MD	14,500	VC
Mount Aloysius College	PA	27,970	C
Mount Mercy Univ	IA	34,385	C
National Louis Univ	IL	16,915	LC
N Car State Univ	NC	16,202	HC
North Park Univ	IL	30,130	C
Northeastern State Univ	OK	8,615	VC
Northern Mich Univ	MI	15,300	VC
Northern State Univ	SD	14,021	C
Northwestern College of Iowa	IA	34,848	₵
Northwestern Okla State Univ	OK	7,275	NC
Norwich Univ	VT	28,212	C
Okla Christian Univ	OK	24,975	VC
Oral Roberts Univ	OK	31,734	C
Pontifical Catholic Univ of PR	PR	7,310	
Purdue Univ/Calumet	IN	14,336	C
Purdue Univ/West Lafayette	IN	20,278	HC
Rutgers, The State Univ of New Jersey/Camden Campus	NJ	24,254	C
Rutgers, The State Univ of New Jersey/Newark Campus	NJ	25,376	C
St. Augustine's Univ	NC	14,000	C
St. Francis Univ	PA	30,029	LC
St. Peter's College	NJ	44,240	C
Salem College	NC	29,326	VC
Salem State College	MA	13,161	LC
Seton Hill Univ	PA	35,172	C
Shorter Univ	GA	26,470	C
Slippery Rock Univ of Pennsylvania	PA	10,360	LC
Southeastern Okla State Univ	OK	7,966	C
Southern Arkansas Univ	AR	14,316	C
Southern Wesleyan Univ	SC	25,600	C
St. Francis College	NY	34,200	LC
St. Thomas Aquinas College	NY	30,000	C
Stevenson Univ	MD	39,572	C
Suffolk Univ	MA	46,548	C
SUNY Fredonia / The SUNY at Fredonia	NY	18,702	VC
SUNY Plattsburgh / SUNY	NY	18,083	VC
Tarleton State Univ	TX	13,489	LC
Texas A&M Univ at Kingsville	TX	7,500	LC
The Catholic Univ of America	DC	52,852	VC
Thiel College	PA	31,378	LC
Thomas More College	KY	34,760	C
Towson Univ	MD	16,000	VC
Union College	NE	23,270	VC
Union Univ	TN	28,260	VC
Univ of Central Florida	FL	15,711	V₵
Univ of Central Missouri	MO	14,605	C
Univ of Cincinnati	OH	20,199	VC
Univ of Conn	CT	23,744	HC
Univ of Delaware	DE	22,728	VC
Univ of Hartford	CT	42,674	C
Univ of Hawaii at Manoa	HI	19,379	VC
Univ of Indianapolis	IN	31,740	LC
Univ of Iowa	IA	17,481	VC
Univ of Kansas	KS	16,980	₵
Univ of Louisville	KY	17,460	VC
Univ of Maine	ME	19,712	₵
Univ of Mich-Flint	MI	17,547	₵
Univ of Minn/Twin Cities	MN		HC
Univ of New Mexico	NM	15,300	C
Univ of North Texas	TX	15,628	C
Univ of Okla	OK	17,634	V₵
Univ of Pittsburgh at Johnstown	PA	20,862	LC
Univ of St. Francis	IN	29,810	C
Univ of Scranton	PA	51,940	VC
Univ of Sioux Falls	SD	22,990	C
Univ of Southern Miss	MS	13,170	C
Univ of Tenn at Chattanooga	TN	16,883	C
Univ of Texas at El Paso	TX	8,764	NC
Univ of the Cumberlands	KY	27,500	LC
Univ of Utah	UT	13,462	VC
Univ of Virginia's College at Wise	VA	11,076	C
Univ of Washington	WA	14,722	VC
Univ of West Florida	FL	14,656	C
Univ of Wisc/La Crosse	WI	14,755	VC
Univ of Wisc/Oshkosh	WI	10,426	LC
Utah State Univ	UT	11,803	C
Wartburg College	IA	41,055	VC
Wesley College	DE	31,115	LC
Western Conn State Univ	CT	18,327	C
Western New Mexico Univ	NM	8,500	LC
Wichita State Univ	KS	12,539	C
William Carey Univ	MS	13,500	LC
William Jewell College	MO	31,000	V₵
Winthrop Univ	SC	21,120	VC
Wright State Univ	OH	16,983	C
York College / CUNY	NY	5,496	NC

MEDICAL PHYSICS

School	ST	$IS	SR
Belmont Univ	TN	37,380	V₵
Oakland Univ	MI	19,391	VC
Oregon State Univ	OR	19,017	₵
Presbyterian College	SC	42,678	VC
Univ of Arizona	AZ	20,105	C
Univ of Notre Dame	IN		MC

MEDICAL RECORDS ADMINISTRATION/SERVICES

School	ST	$IS	SR
Dakota State Univ	SD	13,811	C
Davenport Univ	MI	21,002	LC
East Carolina Univ	NC	14,169	C
Ferris State Univ	MI	19,698	C
Georgian Court Univ	NJ	39,726	LC
LIU/C.W. Post Campus	NY	38,888	C
Louisiana Tech Univ	LA	8,000	C
Norfolk State Univ	VA	10,531	LC
Pennsylvania College of Technology	PA	25,653	NC
Southwestern Okla State Univ	OK	9,160	C
St. Catherine Univ	MN	37,782	₵
Tenn State Univ	TN	9,048	C
Texas State Univ	TX	16,495	VC
Univ of Alabama at Birmingham	AL	18,484	₵
Western Carolina Univ	NC	13,965	₵

MEDICAL SCIENCE

School	ST	$IS	SR
Southern Illinois Univ Edwardsville	IL	17,532	C
Univ of Arizona	AZ	20,105	C
Univ of Chicago	IL	55,416	MC
Univ of Colo Denver	CO	17,904	C
Univ of Louisville	KY	17,460	VC
Univ of Utah	UT	13,462	VC
Univ of Wisc/Madison	WI	18,757	HC

MEDICAL TECHNOLOGY

School	ST	$IS	SR
Armstrong Atlantic State Univ	GA	16,276	C
Austin Peay State Univ	TN	14,650	C
Ball State Univ	IN	17,850	C
Barry Univ	FL	38,190	C
Bellarmine Univ	KY	42,950	VC
Belmont Univ	TN	37,380	V₵
Blue Mountain College	MS	13,550	LC
Bradley Univ	IL	31,874	VC
Brescia Univ	KY	26,140	V₵
Briar Cliff Univ	IA	29,514	C
Cameron Univ	OK	9,267	LC
Catawba College	NC	37,105	C
Clarion Univ of Pennsylvania	PA	17,370	C
Cleveland State Univ	OH	21,357	C
College of Staten Island / The CUNY	NY	16,778	NC
College of the Ozarks	MO	5,605	VC
Colo State Univ-Pueblo	CO	13,532	LC
East Carolina Univ	NC	14,169	C
East Central Univ	OK	10,223	LC
Edgewood College	WI	33,294	C
Farmingdale State College	NY	18,985	C
Ferris State Univ	MI	19,698	C
Gannon Univ	PA	37,940	C
Gardner-Webb Univ	NC	34,375	₵
George Mason Univ	VA	15,724	VC
Georgia Regents Univ	GA		C
Gwynedd-Mercy College	PA	33,560	C
Harding Univ	AR	21,432	₵
Hartwick College	NY	49,815	₵
Henderson State Univ	AR	13,634	C
Houghton College	NY	35,740	VC
Idaho State Univ	ID	11,908	C
Indiana Univ-Purdue Univ Fort Wayne	IN	15,425	C
Inter-American Univ of PR/ Fajardo Campus	PR	4,200	
Inter-American Univ of PR/ Metropolitan Campus	PR	4,320	
Inter-American Univ of PR/ Ponce	PR	3,700	
Kansas State Univ	KS	15,497	VC
Kean Univ	NJ	22,060	LC
Kutztown Univ of Pennsylvania	PA	16,909	LC
Lincoln Univ	MO	11,996	NC
Lindenwood Univ	MO	20,750	C
Lipscomb Univ	TN	35,722	VC
Lubbock Christian Univ	TX	25,518	C
Mansfield Univ	PA	19,468	LC
Marist College	NY	35,500	C
Marywood Univ	PA	40,695	C
Morehead State Univ	KY	10,900	C
Morningside College	IA	32,620	C
Mount Aloysius College	PA	27,970	C
Mount Marty College	SD	29,638	C
Mount Vernon Nazarene Univ	OH	29,590	C
Norfolk State Univ	VA	10,531	LC
Oakwood Univ	AL	23,035	C
Ohio Northern Univ	OH	42,075	VC
Old Dominion Univ	VA	18,662	C
Oregon State Univ	OR	19,017	₵
Pittsburg State Univ	KS	12,032	C
Prairie View A&M Univ	TX	15,205	LC
Roosevelt Univ	IL	22,605	VC
Rutgers, The State Univ of New Jersey/New Brunswick	NJ	25,077	VC
Saginaw Valley State Univ	MI	16,869	C
St. Joseph's College	IN	35,790	C
St. Leo Univ	FL	27,990	C
St. Mary-of-the-Woods College	IN	37,722	LC
Salisbury Univ	MD	18,368	VC
Sam Houston State Univ	TX	17,082	C
Seattle Univ	WA	47,010	V₵
Southeast Missouri State Univ	MO	14,983	LC
Southern Adventist Univ	TN	26,190	C
Southern Illinois Univ Edwardsville	IL	17,532	C
Southwest Baptist Univ	MO	24,710	C
Southwest Minn State Univ	MN	14,000	C
Southwestern Adventist Univ	TX	23,026	LC
Southwestern Okla State Univ	OK	9,160	C
St. Joseph's College, New York / Brooklyn Campus	NY	21,878	C
St. Joseph's College, New York / Suffolk Campus	NY	21,878	VC
SUNY Plattsburgh / SUNY	NY	18,083	VC
Tenn State Univ	TN	9,048	C
Texas Southern Univ	TX	10,212	LC
Texas Woman's Univ	TX	13,633	LC
The Catholic Univ of America	DC	52,852	VC
The College at Brockport / SUNY	NY	18,362	VC
The College of St. Rose	NY	26,750	C
Ohio State Univ	OH	19,887	MC
Tusculum College	TN	24,295	C
Univ at Buffalo / The SUNY	NY	20,283	VC
Univ of Alabama at Birmingham	AL	18,484	₵
Univ of Bridgeport	CT	39,030	LC
Univ of Central Arkansas	AR	10,840	VC
Univ of Hawaii at Manoa	HI	19,379	VC
Univ of Idaho	ID	14,558	C
Univ of Mass Boston	MA	11,966	C
Univ of Miss	MS	15,482	VC
Univ of Montana	MT	13,670	C
Univ of Mount Union	OH	35,130	C
Univ of New Orleans	LA	9,224	VC
Univ of N Car at Charlotte	NC	15,847	C
Univ of Rio Grande	OH	8,750	NC
Univ of S Dak	SD	15,111	C
Univ of South Florida	FL	13,000	C
Univ of St. Francis	IL	36,490	C
Univ of Tenn at Knoxville	TN	20,364	V₵
Univ of Texas at Arlington	TX	10,908	LC
Univ of Texas at Austin	TX	44,074	HC
Univ of the Sacred Heart	PR	5,590	
Univ of the Sciences	PA	48,320	V₵
West Chester Univ of Pennsylvania	PA	16,836	C
West Texas A&M Univ	TX	13,478	C
West Virginia Univ	WV	15,794	₵
Western Illinois Univ	IL	20,130	C
Western Kentucky Univ	KY	11,000	LC
Wilkes Univ	PA	42,786	C
Winston-Salem State Univ	NC	9,418	LC

MEDIEVAL STUDIES

School	ST	$IS	SR
Bard College	NY	59,872	HC
Bates College	ME	58,950	MC
Binghamton Univ / The SUNY	NY	20,832	H₵
Brown Univ	RI	56,150	MC
College of the Holy Cross	MA	56,232	MC
College of William & Mary	VA	25,085	MC
Columbia Univ in the City of New York	NY	61,116	MC
Columbia Univ/Barnard College	NY	39,000	MC
Cornell College	IA	44,930	HC
Dickinson College	PA	57,662	H₵
Duke Univ	NC	50,250	MC
Emory Univ	GA	45,000	MC
Fordham Univ	NY	58,927	HC
Hanover College	IN	41,450	VC
Mount Holyoke College	MA	53,596	H₵
New College of Florida	FL	14,504	H₵
New York Univ	NY	61,470	MC
Penn State Univ/Univ Park	PA	25,404	VC
Pomona College	CA	57,680	MC
Purdue Univ/West Lafayette	IN	20,278	HC
Rice Univ	TX	43,288	MC
Rutgers, The State Univ of New Jersey/New Brunswick	NJ	25,077	VC
Rutgers, The State Univ of New Jersey/Newark Campus	NJ	25,376	C
Sewanee: The Univ of the South	TN	47,700	H₵
Smith College	MA	57,524	MC
Southern Methodist Univ	TX	57,755	MC
St. Olaf College	MN	49,960	H₵
Swarthmore College	PA	57,870	MC
The Catholic Univ of America	DC	52,852	VC
Ohio State Univ	OH	19,887	MC
Tulane Univ	LA	58,942	MC
Univ at Albany / SUNY	NY	18,674	VC
Univ of Calif at Davis	CA	24,482	HC
Univ of Calif at Santa Barbara	CA	27,551	HC
Univ of Chicago	IL	55,416	MC
Univ of Mich/Ann Arbor	MI	22,102	H₵
Univ of Nebr - Lincoln	NE	17,507	VC
Univ of Notre Dame	IN		MC
Univ of Oregon	OR	20,872	VC
Vassar College	NY	59,070	MC
Washington and Lee Univ	VA	52,812	MC

School	ST	$IS	SR
Wellesley College	MA	49,848	MC
Wesleyan Univ	CT	59,844	MC

MENTAL HEALTH/HUMAN SERVICES

School	ST	$IS	SR
Calif Univ of Pennsylvania	PA	14,217	C
Franciscan Univ of Steubenville	OH	27,320	VC
Indiana Univ-Purdue Univ Indianapolis	IN	17,290	C
Inter-American Univ of PR/ Aguadilla Campus	PR	5,578	
Metropolitan College of New York	NY	16,720	VC
Morgan State Univ	MD	14,500	VC
Northern Kentucky Univ	KY	15,302	LC
Pennsylvania College of Technology	PA	25,653	NC
Prescott College	AZ	33,284	C+
Sinte Gleska Univ	SD	2,300	NC
Southern Oregon Univ	OR	17,874	C
Univ of Maine at Augusta	ME	6,855	C
Univ of North Florida	FL	15,578	VC
Univ of the Sciences	PA	48,320	VC+

METAL/JEWELRY

School	ST	$IS	SR
Adams State College	CO	13,358	LC
Calif College of the Arts	CA	48,334	SP
Cleveland Inst of Art	OH	48,641	SP
College for Creative Studies	MI		SP
Hofstra Univ	NY	48,020	VC+
Kendall College of Art and Design of Ferris State Univ	MI	21,048	SP
Maine College of Art	ME	28,812	SP
Mass College of Art and Design	MA	23,600	SP
Memphis College of Art	TN	33,550	SP
Pittsburg State Univ	KS	12,032	C
Rhode Island School of Design	RI	55,204	SP
Rochester Inst of Technology	NY	42,450	VC+
Savannah College of Art and Design	GA	46,824	SP
SUNY New Paltz	NY	15,010	C
Syracuse Univ	NY	54,512	HC
Temple Univ	PA	24,392	VC
Univ of Iowa	IA	17,481	VC
Univ of Kansas	KS	16,980	C+
Univ of Mass Dartmouth	MA	22,223	C
Univ of Mich/Ann Arbor	MI	22,102	HC+
Univ of Oregon	OR	20,872	VC

METALLURGICAL ENGINEERING

School	ST	$IS	SR
Colo School of Mines	CO	18,000	HC
Columbia Univ in the City of New York	NY	61,116	MC
Illinois Inst of Technology	IL	38,512	HC+
Missouri Univ of Science and Technology	MO	18,655	VC+
Montana Tech of The Univ of Montana	MT	14,650	VC
Oregon State Univ	OR	19,017	C+
S Dak School of Mines and Technology	SD	15,260	VC
Univ of Alabama at Tuscaloosa	AL	17,164	C+
Univ of Cincinnati	OH	20,199	VC
Univ of Illinois at Urbana-Champaign	IL	24,300	HC
Univ of Minn/Twin Cities	MN		HC
Univ of Nevada/Reno	NV	14,500	NC
Univ of Texas at El Paso	TX	8,764	NC
Univ of Utah	UT	13,462	VC

MEXICAN-AMERICAN/ CHICANO STUDIES

School	ST	$IS	SR
Arizona State Univ	AZ	18,818	C+
Cal State, Dominguez Hills	CA	17,056	LC
Cal State, Fresno	CA	17,405	C
Cal State, Fullerton	CA	25,188	C+
Cal State, Los Angeles	CA	15,829	C
Cal State, Northridge	CA	28,313	C
Concordia Univ Texas	TX	23,640	C
Metropolitan State Univ of Denver	CO	4,835	LC
Our Lady of the Lake Univ of San Antonio	TX	22,430	LC
Pitzer College	CA	54,988	MC
Pomona College	CA	57,680	MC
San Diego State Univ	CA	20,578	VC
San Jose State Univ	CA	19,707	C
Scripps College	CA	54,900	MC
Sonoma State Univ	CA	20,541	C
Southern Methodist Univ	TX	57,755	MC
Univ of Arizona	AZ	20,105	C
Univ of Calif at Davis	CA	24,482	HC
Univ of Calif at Los Angeles	CA	25,686	MC
Univ of Calif at Riverside	CA	27,204	C
Univ of Calif at Santa Barbara	CA	27,551	HC
Univ of Mich/Ann Arbor	MI	22,102	HC+
Univ of Minn/Twin Cities	MN		HC
Univ of New Mexico	NM	15,300	C
Univ of Northern Colo	CO	15,973	C
Univ of Texas at El Paso	TX	8,764	NC
Univ of Texas at San Antonio	TX	18,372	C
Univ of Texas-Pan American	TX	12,432	LC

MICROBIOLOGY

School	ST	$IS	SR
Albany College of Pharmacy and Health Sciences	NY	38,900	SP
Arizona State Univ	AZ	18,818	C+
Auburn Univ	AL	20,052	VC+
Brigham Young Univ	UT	12,100	HC
Calif Polytechnic State Univ	CA	19,847	HC
Cal State, Chico	CA	18,952	C
Cal State, Los Angeles	CA	15,829	C
Cal State, Northridge	CA	28,313	C
Cal State, Sacramento	CA	16,200	C
Clemson Univ	SC	19,136	HC
Colo State Univ-Fort Collins	CO	20,090	VC
Eastern Kentucky Univ	KY	11,161	C
Eastern Washington Univ	WA	16,388	C
Howard Univ	DC	35,067	C
Idaho State Univ	ID	11,908	C
Indiana Univ Bloomington	IN	19,358	HC
Inter-American Univ of PR/ Aguadilla Campus	PR	5,578	
Inter-American Univ of PR/ Arecibo Campus	PR	3,350	
Iowa State Univ	IA	16,403	C
Kansas State Univ	KS	15,497	VC
Kutztown Univ of Pennsylvania	PA	16,909	LC
Louisiana State Univ	LA	18,677	VC+
Marlboro College	VT	35,980	VC
Miami Univ	OH	24,191	HC
Mich State Univ	MI	13,689	VC
Mills College	CA	54,119	HC
Miss Univ for Women	MS	7,400	LC
Missouri Southern State Univ	MO	11,910	C
Montana State Univ	MT	14,068	VC
New Mexico State Univ	NM	13,955	LC
New York Univ	NY	61,470	MC
N Car State Univ	NC	16,202	HC
N Dak State Univ	ND	14,642	C
Northern Arizona Univ	AZ	18,592	C
Northern Mich Univ	MI	15,300	VC
Ohio Univ	OH	20,676	VC
Ohio Wesleyan Univ	OH	49,460	C+
Okla State Univ	OK	14,310	VC
Oregon State Univ	OR	19,017	C+
Purdue Univ/Calumet	IN	14,336	C
Purdue Univ/West Lafayette	IN	20,278	HC
Quinnipiac Univ	CT	53,580	VC
Rutgers, The State Univ of New Jersey/New Brunswick	NJ	25,077	VC
San Diego State Univ	CA	20,578	VC
San Francisco State Univ	CA	18,514	C
San Jose State Univ	CA	19,707	C
S Dak State Univ	SD	14,296	C
Southern Illinois Univ Carbondale	IL	21,620	C
SUNY / College of Environmental Science and Forestry	NY	18,351	HC
Texas A&M Univ	TX	16,956	VC+
Texas State Univ	TX	16,495	VC
Texas Tech Univ	TX	14,243	C
Ohio State Univ	OH	19,887	MC
Univ of Alabama at Tuscaloosa	AL	17,164	C+
Univ of Arizona	AZ	20,105	C
Univ of Calif at Berkeley	CA	23,322	MC
Univ of Calif at Davis	CA	24,482	HC
Univ of Calif at Irvine	CA	25,961	VC
Univ of Calif at Los Angeles	CA	25,686	MC
Univ of Calif at Riverside	CA	27,204	C
Univ of Calif at San Diego	CA	21,000	VC
Univ of Calif at Santa Barbara	CA	27,551	HC
Univ of Florida	FL	15,783	HC+
Univ of Georgia	GA	19,508	VC
Univ of Great Falls	MT	27,970	C
Univ of Hawaii at Manoa	HI	19,379	VC
Univ of Houston-Downtown	TX	6,267	LC
Univ of Idaho	ID	14,558	C
Univ of Illinois at Urbana-Champaign	IL	24,300	HC
Univ of Iowa	IA	17,481	VC
Univ of Kansas	KS	16,980	C+
Univ of Maine	ME	19,712	C+
Univ of Maryland	MD	18,801	HC
Univ of Mass Amherst	MA	23,697	VC+
Univ of Memphis	TN	15,094	C
Univ of Miami	FL	55,166	MC
Univ of Mich/Ann Arbor	MI	22,102	HC+
Univ of Mich/Dearborn	MI	9,885	VC
Univ of Minn/Twin Cities	MN		HC
Univ of Missouri/Columbia	MO	18,201	MC
Univ of Montana	MT	13,670	C
Univ of Nebr - Lincoln	NE	17,507	VC
Univ of New Hampshire	NH	24,702	VC
Univ of Northern Iowa	IA	14,776	C
Univ of Okla	OK	17,634	VC+
Univ of Pittsburgh at Pittsburgh	PA	27,800	HC+
Univ of PR/Arecibo	PR	7,227	
Univ of PR/Humacao	PR	1,877	
Univ of PR/Mayaguez	PR	1,250	
Univ of Rochester	NY	58,500	MC
Univ of South Florida	FL	13,000	C
Univ of Texas at Arlington	TX	10,908	LC
Univ of Texas at Austin	TX	44,074	HC
Univ of Texas at El Paso	TX	8,764	NC
Univ of the Sciences	PA	48,320	VC+
Univ of Vermont	VT	26,120	VC+
Univ of Washington	WA	14,722	VC
Univ of Wisc/La Crosse	WI	14,755	VC
Univ of Wisc/Madison	WI	18,757	HC
Univ of Wisc/Oshkosh	WI	10,426	LC
Univ of Wisc-Milwaukee	WI	18,436	C
Univ of Wyoming	WY	13,855	C+
Utah State Univ	UT	11,803	C
Wagner College	NY	48,600	VC
Washington State Univ	WA	20,461	C
West Chester Univ of Pennsylvania	PA	16,836	C

MIDDLE EASTERN STUDIES

School	ST	$IS	SR
Appalachian State Univ	NC	12,919	VC
Bard College	NY	59,872	HC
Brandeis Univ	MA	58,820	HC
Brigham Young Univ	UT	12,100	HC
Brown Univ	RI	56,150	MC
Claremont McKenna College	CA	58,065	MC
Columbia Univ in the City of New York	NY	61,116	MC
Columbia Univ/Barnard College	NY	39,000	MC
Columbia Univ/School of General Studies	NY	54,083	MC
Dartmouth College	NH	57,996	MC
Dickinson College	PA	57,662	HC+
Eastern Mich Univ	MI	17,961	C
Emory and Henry College	VA	387,460	C
Emory Univ	GA	45,000	MC
Fordham Univ	NY	58,927	HC
George Washington Univ	DC	57,108	MC
Gettysburg College	PA	56,820	HC
Hampshire College	MA	58,320	MC
Harvard Univ/Harvard College	MA	49,000	MC
Hood College	MD	44,630	C
McDaniel College	MD	45,600	VC
Middlebury College	VT	57,470	MC
Mount Holyoke College	MA	53,596	HC+
New York Univ	NY	61,470	MC
Pomona College	CA	57,680	MC
Rutgers, The State Univ of New Jersey/New Brunswick	NJ	25,077	VC
Sacred Heart Univ	CT	48,564	VC
Smith College	MA	57,524	MC
Syracuse Univ	NY	54,512	HC
Texas State Univ	TX	16,495	VC
Tufts Univ	MA	58,780	MC
Univ of Arizona	AZ	20,105	C
Univ of Arkansas at Fayetteville	AR	16,860	VC
Univ of Calif at Berkeley	CA	23,322	MC
Univ of Calif at Los Angeles	CA	25,686	MC
Univ of Calif at Riverside	CA	27,204	C
Univ of Calif at Santa Barbara	CA	27,551	HC
Univ of Conn	CT	23,744	HC
Univ of Mass Amherst	MA	23,697	VC+
Univ of Mich/Ann Arbor	MI	22,102	HC+
Univ of Minn/Twin Cities	MN		HC
Univ of Pennsylvania	PA	56,106	MC
Univ of Texas at Austin	TX	44,074	HC
Univ of Utah	UT	13,462	VC
Washington Univ in St. Louis	MO	58,818	MC
Wellesley College	MA	49,848	MC
Yale Univ	CT	55,300	MC

MIDDLE SCHOOL EDUCATION

School	ST	$IS	SR
Alabama A&M Univ	AL	96,100	C
Albany State Univ	GA	8,500	C
Alice Lloyd College	KY	4,900	C
Alvernia Univ	PA	39,250	C
Alverno College	WI	30,483	LC
American International College	MA	36,100	LC
Appalachian State Univ	NC	12,919	VC
Arkansas State Univ	AR	14,980	C
Arkansas Tech Univ	AR	13,164	LC
Armstrong Atlantic State Univ	GA	16,276	C
Asbury Univ	KY	32,038	VC
Auburn Univ	AL	20,052	VC+
Augustana College	SD	35,500	VC
Averett Univ	VA	36,000	LC
Avila Univ	MO	26,900	C
Baldwin Wallace Univ	OH	36,980	VC
Barton College	NC	27,660	C
Bellarmine Univ	KY	42,950	VC
Belmont Univ	TN	37,380	VC+
Bemidji State Univ	MN	13,500	C
Bennett College	NC		LC
Bennington College	VT	56,990	HC+
Berry College	GA	39,254	HC
Bethany College	KS	30,605	NC
Bethany College	WV	35,282	C
Bethel Univ	MN	34,940	VC
Bloomsburg Univ of Pennsylvania	PA	13,598	C
Bluefield College	VA	17,230	C+
Bluefield State College	WV	3,140	LC
Bluffton Univ	OH	37,864	C
Bowling Green State Univ	OH	18,970	C
Brenau Univ Women's College	GA	26,650	C+
Butler Univ	IN	45,898	VC+
Cabrini College	PA	40,859	LC
Campbell Univ	NC	25,500	C
Campbellsville Univ	KY	27,720	C
Canisius College	NY	45,602	VC
Capital Univ	OH	39,824	VC
Cardinal Stritch Univ	WI	21,054	C
Caribbean Univ	PR	10,375	
Carlow Univ	PA	30,272	C
Carson-Newman Univ	TN	29,058	C+
Carthage College	WI	33,000	C
Catawba College	NC	37,105	C
Cedarville Univ	OH	31,036	VC+
Central Methodist Univ	MO	28,240	VC
Central Washington Univ	WA	11,730	C
Champlain College	VT	44,850	VC
City Univ of Seattle	WA	14,880	NC
Claflin Univ	SC	22,368	C+
Clark Atlanta Univ	GA	30,006	C
Clayton State Univ	GA	12,000	LC
Coastal Carolina Univ	SC	17,620	C
College of Charleston	SC	21,273	VC
College of Mount St. Joseph	OH	33,880	C
Columbia College	MO	24,578	C
Columbus State Univ	GA	13,176	C
Concord Univ	WV	13,102	C
Concordia Univ Nebr	NE	26,000	VC
Concordia Univ St. Paul	MN	27,200	C
Concordia Univ, River Forest	IL	26,300	C
Cornerstone Univ and Grand Rapids Theological Seminary	MI	30,866	C
Cumberland Univ	TN	21,220	C
Dickinson State Univ	ND	8,550	NC
Dordt College	IA	34,160	VC
Duquesne Univ	PA	42,017	VC
East Carolina Univ	NC	14,169	C
Eastern Illinois Univ	IL	20,502	C
Eastern Kentucky Univ	KY	11,161	C
Eastern Mich Univ	MI	17,961	C
Eastern Univ	PA	37,704	C
Eastern Washington Univ	WA	16,388	C
Edinboro Univ of Pennsylvania	PA	15,940	LC
Elizabeth City State Univ	NC	11,638	C
Elms College	MA	23,900	VC
Elon Univ	NC	40,046	HC
Fairmont State Univ	WV	12,098	LC
Fayetteville State Univ	NC	10,816	C
Fitchburg State Univ	MA	17,241	C
Florida Inst of Technology	FL	48,290	VC
Fontbonne Univ	MO	31,384	C
Fort Valley State Univ	GA	11,200	VC
Francis Marion Univ	SC	16,464	LC
Freed-Hardeman Univ	TN	19,697	VC
Frostburg State Univ	MD	15,264	LC
Gannon Univ	PA	37,940	C
Gardner-Webb Univ	NC	34,375	C+
Georgetown College	KY	38,690	C
Georgia College and State Univ	GA	18,216	VC
Georgia Regents Univ	GA		C
Georgia Southern Univ	GA	16,414	C
Georgia Southwestern State Univ	GA	12,218	C
Glenville State College	WV	11,348	NC
Goddard College	VT	16,418	VC
Gordon College	MA	42,660	VC+
Goshen College	IN	35,900	VC
Grand Valley State Univ	MI	17,998	VC
Greensboro College	NC	28,740	LC
Grove City College	PA	22,988	HC
Gustavus Adolphus College	MN	48,170	HC
Hardin-Simmons Univ	TX	23,560	C+
Harris-Stowe State Univ	MO	14,360	NC
Heidelberg Univ	OH	34,100	C
Henderson State Univ	AR	13,634	C
High Point Univ	NC	39,800	C
Hillsdale College	MI	31,890	HC+
Humboldt State Univ	CA	18,400	C

School	ST	$IS	SR
Hunter College / The CUNY	NY	14,429	VC
Illinois State Univ	IL	22,634	VC
Immaculata Univ	PA	43,000	C
Indiana State Univ	IN	16,000	C
Indiana Univ-Purdue Univ Fort Wayne	IN	15,425	C
Ithaca College	NY	52,300	HC
John Brown Univ	AR	30,996	VǤ
John Carroll Univ	OH	44,520	Ǥ
Johnson State College	VT	16,721	C
Kean Univ	NJ	22,060	LC
Kennesaw State Univ	GA	13,017	VC
Kent State Univ	OH	19,352	C
Kentucky Christian Univ	KY	17,622	LC
Kentucky Wesleyan College	KY	27,440	VǤ
King's College	PA	41,678	C
Lake Erie College	OH	35,704	C
Lee Univ	TN	18,690	Ǥ
Lenoir-Rhyne College	NC	35,984	C
Lesley Univ	MA	46,350	C
Lincoln Memorial Univ	TN	18,144	C
Lipscomb Univ	TN	35,722	VC
Lubbock Christian Univ	TX	25,518	C
Malone Univ	OH	34,334	C
Manchester College	IN	35,070	C
Manhattan College	NY	44,955	VC
Marian Univ	WI	30,980	LC
Mars Hill College	NC	22,950	LC
Marshall Univ	WV	14,820	C
Maryville Univ of St. Louis	MO	34,920	VC
Mass College of Liberal Arts	MA	16,733	C
McMurry Univ	TX	25,962	LC
Medaille College	NY	35,112	VC
Methodist Univ	NC	37,185	C
Miami Univ	OH	24,191	HC
Midland Univ	NE	34,000	C
Millersville Univ of Pennsylvania	PA	18,498	C
Missouri Baptist Univ	MO	30,310	C
Missouri Southern State Univ	MO	11,910	C
Missouri State Univ	MO	13,996	VC
Montana State Univ-Billings	MT	12,425	LC
Montclair State Univ	NJ	22,614	C
Morehead State Univ	KY	10,900	C
Mount Aloysius College	PA	27,970	C
Mount Mercy Univ	IA	34,385	C
Mount Olive College	NC	18,426	C
Mount Vernon Nazarene Univ	OH	29,590	C
Nazareth College of Rochester	NY	41,590	VC
Nebr Wesleyan Univ	NE	29,774	Ǥ
New York Inst of Technology	NY	40,590	VC
Niagara Univ	NY	39,800	C
N Car Central Univ	NC	9,000	LC
N Car State Univ	NC	16,202	HC
N Car Wesleyan College	NC	29,440	C
North Georgia College & State Univ	GA	8,500	C
Northern Kentucky Univ	KY	15,302	LC
Northern State Univ	SD	14,021	C
Northland College	WI	26,680	C
Northwest Missouri State Univ	MO	14,229	C
Northwest Univ	WA	18,854	C
Northwestern College of Iowa	IA	34,848	Ǥ
Notre Dame College	OH	34,942	VC
Nova Southeastern Univ	FL	34,016	VC
Oakland City Univ	IN	24,500	NC
Ohio Dominican Univ	OH	38,380	Ǥ
Ohio Northern Univ	OH	42,075	VC
Ohio Wesleyan Univ	OH	49,460	Ǥ
Okla Christian Univ	OK	24,975	VC
Okla Wesleyan Univ	OK	21,300	C
Ouachita Baptist Univ	AR	29,010	VC
Paine College	GA	18,594	LC
Philander Smith College	AR	19,760	LC
Piedmont College	GA	29,260	C
Presbyterian College	SC	42,678	VC
Prescott College	AZ	33,284	Ǥ
Rhode Island College	RI	17,132	LC
Ripon College	WI	36,959	Ǥ
Sacred Heart Univ	CT	48,564	VC
St. Joseph's College	IN	35,790	C
St. Leo Univ	FL	27,990	C
St. Louis Univ	MO	46,594	VǤ
St. Vincent College	PA	40,244	C
St. Xavier Univ	IL	32,840	C
Schreiner Univ	TX	32,734	LC
Shippensburg Univ of Pennsylvania	PA	17,064	LC
Shorter Univ	GA	26,470	C
Southeast Missouri State Univ	MO	14,983	LC
Southeastern Louisiana Univ	LA	13,325	C
Southeastern Univ	FL	27,201	Ǥ
Southern Arkansas Univ	AR	14,316	C
Southern Univ and A&M College	LA	9,761	Ǥ
Southwest Baptist Univ	MO	24,710	C
Springfield College	MA	25,000	C
St. Francis College	NY	34,200	LC
St. John Fisher College	NY	39,370	Ǥ
St. John's Univ	NY	52,840	Ǥ
Stevenson Univ	MD	39,572	C
SUNY College at Old Westbury	NY	16,324	C
SUNY Cortland / The SUNY	NY	19,117	C
SUNY Fredonia / The SUNY at Fredonia	NY	18,702	VC
SUNY New Paltz	NY	15,010	C
Syracuse Univ	NY	54,512	HC
Tabor College	KS	29,010	LC
Texas Christian Univ	TX	47,570	HC
Texas Tech Univ	TX	14,243	C
Ohio State Univ	OH	19,887	MC
Thomas More College	KY	34,760	C
Thomas Univ	GA	11,520	NC
Toccoa Falls College	GA	23,210	C
Transylvania Univ	KY	40,310	VǤ
Tusculum College	TN	24,295	C
Union College	KY	28,775	C
Union Univ	TN	28,260	VC
Univ of Akron	OH	20,436	C
Univ of Arizona	AZ	20,105	C
Univ of Arkansas at Fayetteville	AR	16,860	VC
Univ of Arkansas at Monticello	AR	8,470	NC
Univ of Arkansas at Pine Bluff	AR	10,600	C
Univ of Central Arkansas	AR	10,840	VC
Univ of Central Missouri	MO	14,605	C
Univ of Cincinnati	OH	20,199	VC
Univ of Detroit Mercy	MI	30,450	C
Univ of Findlay	OH	31,916	C
Univ of Georgia	GA	19,508	VC
Univ of Great Falls	MT	27,970	C
Univ of Indianapolis	IN	31,740	LC
Univ of Iowa	IA	17,481	VC
Univ of Kansas	KS	16,980	Ǥ
Univ of Kentucky	KY	19,868	C
Univ of Louisiana at Monroe	LA	12,998	C
Univ of Louisville	KY	17,460	VC
Univ of Mary Hardin-Baylor	TX	31,950	Ǥ
Univ of Maryland	MD	18,801	HC
Univ of Minn/Duluth	MN	18,964	Ǥ
Univ of Missouri/Columbia	MO	18,201	MC
Univ of Missouri-Kansas City	MO	19,603	C
Univ of Montana-Western	MT	9,753	LC
Univ of Mount Union	OH	35,130	C
Univ of Nebr at Kearney	NE	14,855	LC
Univ of N Car at Chapel Hill	NC	18,348	MC
Univ of N Car at Charlotte	NC	15,847	C
Univ of N Car at Greensboro	NC	12,848	C
Univ of N Car at Wilmington	NC	13,572	VǤ
Univ of N Dak	ND	14,094	C
Univ of North Florida	FL	15,578	VC
Univ of Northern Iowa	IA	14,776	C
Univ of Pikeville	KY	24,750	NC
Univ of San Francisco	CA	49,674	VC
Univ of Sioux Falls	SD	22,990	C
Univ of S Car at Aiken	SC	16,278	C
Univ of S Car at Columbia	SC	19,725	VǤ
Univ of S Car Upstate	SC	17,673	LC
Univ of Southern Indiana	IN	14,657	C
Univ of Southern Miss	MS	13,170	C
Univ of the Cumberlands	KY	27,500	LC
Univ of the Ozarks	AR	22,100	C
Univ of Vermont	VT	26,120	VǤ
Univ of West Alabama	AL	9,415	C
Univ of West Florida	FL	14,656	C
Univ of Wisc Whitewater	WI	13,314	C
Univ of Wisc/Green Bay	WI	14,900	C
Univ of Wisc/Platteville	WI	14,274	C
Urbana Univ	OH	21,190	C
Ursuline College	OH	33,198	LC
Victory Univ	TN	19,118	C
Wagner College	NY	48,600	VC
Walsh Univ	OH	35,100	C
Washington Univ in St. Louis	MO	58,818	MC
Wayne State College	NE	11,764	NC
Waynesburg Univ	PA	29,100	C
Webster Univ	MO	33,990	Ǥ
Wesleyan College	GA	24,000	Ǥ
West Chester Univ of Pennsylvania	PA	16,836	C
West Liberty Univ	WV	9,142	LC
Western Carolina Univ	NC	13,965	Ǥ
Western Kentucky Univ	KY	11,000	LC
Western Mich Univ	MI	19,042	C
Westminster College	MO	30,490	VC
Wheeling Jesuit Univ	WV	34,668	C
Wilkes Univ	PA	42,786	C
William Woods Univ	MO		C
Wilmington College	OH	29,784	C
Wingate Univ	NC	34,990	C
Winthrop Univ	SC	21,120	VC
Wittenberg Univ	OH	47,766	VC
Wright State Univ	OH	16,983	C
Xavier Univ	OH	43,740	VC
Xavier Univ of Louisiana	LA	25,300	C
York College	NE	19,475	C
Youngstown State Univ	OH	16,374	LC

MILITARY SCIENCE

School	ST	$IS	SR
Campbell Univ	NC	25,500	C
Columbia College	MO	24,578	C
Eastern Mich Univ	MI	17,961	C
Eastern Washington Univ	WA	16,388	C
Florida Inst of Technology	FL	48,290	VC
Hawaii Pacific Univ	HI	36,690	C
Norfolk State Univ	VA	10,531	LC
Norwich Univ	VT	28,212	C
Rochester Inst of Technology	NY	42,450	VǤ
United States Air Force Academy	CO		MC
United States Military Academy	NY		MC

MILITARY TECHNOLOGY LEADERSHIP

School	ST	$IS	SR
Thomas Edison State College	NJ	5,700	SP

MILLING SCIENCE

School	ST	$IS	SR
Kansas State Univ	KS	15,497	VC

MINING AND MINERAL ENGINEERING

School	ST	$IS	SR
Colo School of Mines	CO	18,000	HC
Columbia Univ in the City of New York	NY	61,116	MC
Missouri Univ of Science and Technology	MO	18,655	VǤ
Montana Tech of The Univ of Montana	MT	14,650	VC
Mountain State Univ	WV	14,330	NC
New Mexico Inst of Mining and Technology	NM	12,892	HC
Penn State Univ/Univ Park	PA	25,404	VC
S Dak School of Mines and Technology	SD	15,260	VC
Southern Illinois Univ Carbondale	IL	21,620	C
Univ of Alaska Fairbanks	AK	13,955	C
Univ of Arizona	AZ	20,105	C
Univ of Kentucky	KY	19,868	C
Univ of Nevada/Reno	NV	14,500	NC
Univ of Utah	UT	13,462	VC
Virginia Polytechnic Inst and State Univ	VA	14,629	HC
West Virginia Univ	WV	15,794	Ǥ

MINISTRIES

School	ST	$IS	SR
Abilene Christian Univ	TX	38,400	VC
American Indian College	AZ	16,702	C
Amridge Univ	AL	6,870	LC
Asbury Univ	KY	32,038	VC
Atlantic Union College	MA	24,600	LC
Azusa Pacific Univ	CA	39,946	C
Belmont Univ	TN	37,380	VǤ
Bethel College	IN	31,560	C
Biola Univ	CA	40,320	VC
Bluffton Univ	OH	37,864	C
Clearwater Christian College	FL	23,720	C
Concordia Univ Wisc	WI	28,980	C
Corban Univ	OR	34,764	C
Dallas Baptist Univ	TX	29,118	C
Dominican Univ	IL	37,628	C
Dordt College	IA	34,160	VC
East Texas Baptist Univ	TX	29,135	C
Eastern Mennonite Univ	VA	38,850	VC
Eastern Nazarene College	MA	30,000	C
Freed-Hardeman Univ	TN	19,697	VC
Fresno Pacific Univ	CA	32,136	C
Geneva College	PA	27,280	C
George Fox Univ	OR	40,750	Ǥ
Greenville College	IL	27,012	C
Harding Univ	AR	21,432	Ǥ
Hardin-Simmons Univ	TX	23,560	Ǥ
Hope International Univ	CA	34,650	C
Houghton College	NY	35,740	VC
Huntington Univ	IN	32,220	C
Indiana Wesleyan Univ	IN	31,815	VC
John Brown Univ	AR	30,996	VǤ
Kentucky Christian Univ	KY	17,622	LC
Lee Univ	TN	18,690	Ǥ
Lindenwood Univ	MO	20,750	C
Lindsey Wilson College	KY	30,470	VC
Lubbock Christian Univ	TX	25,518	C
Malone Univ	OH	34,334	C
Marylhurst Univ	OR	18,945	NC
Messiah College	PA	39,540	VC
MidAmerica Nazarene Univ	KS	28,000	C
Missouri Baptist Univ	MO	30,310	C
Mount Olive College	NC	18,426	C
Mount Vernon Nazarene Univ	OH	29,590	C
North Central Univ	MN	20,946	C
Northwest Christian Univ	OR	27,399	C
Northwest Nazarene Univ	ID	24,275	NC
Northwest Univ	WA	18,854	C
Northwestern College	MN	24,000	C
Notre Dame College	OH	34,942	VC
Oakwood Univ	AL	23,035	C
Okla Christian Univ	OK	24,975	VC
Olivet Nazarene Univ	IL	29,990	C
Oral Roberts Univ	OK	31,734	C
Ouachita Baptist Univ	AR	29,010	VC
Palm Beach Atlantic Univ	FL	33,882	LC
Point Loma Nazarene Univ	CA	38,610	VC
Rochester College	MI	18,320	C
St. Joseph's College	IN	35,790	C
Simpson Univ	CA	28,900	C
Southeastern Univ	FL	27,201	Ǥ
Southwest Baptist Univ	MO	24,710	C
Tabor College	KS	29,010	LC
Taylor Univ	IN	30,742	VǤ
Tenn Wesleyan College	TN	21,250	C
Toccoa Falls College	GA	23,210	C
Trinity Bible College	ND		
Trinity Christian College	IL	28,869	C
Union College	KY	28,775	C
Union Univ	TN	28,260	VC
Univ of Mary	ND	16,714	C
Univ of Mary Hardin-Baylor	TX	31,950	Ǥ
Univ of St. Francis	IN	29,810	C
Valparaiso Univ	IN	43,040	VǤ
Vanguard Univ of Southern Calif	CA	35,833	VC
Warner Pacific College	OR	25,550	C
Waynesburg Univ	PA	29,100	C

MISSIONS

School	ST	$IS	SR
Asbury Univ	KY	32,038	VC
Bethel College	IN	31,560	C
Biola Univ	CA	40,320	VC
Cedarville Univ	OH	31,036	VǤ
Dordt College	IA	34,160	VC
East Texas Baptist Univ	TX	29,135	C
Eastern Univ	PA	37,704	C
Evangel Univ	MO	23,090	C
Fresno Pacific Univ	CA	32,136	C
Grace Bible College	MI	20,770	C
Hannibal-LaGrange Univ	MO	24,490	C
Harding Univ	AR	21,432	Ǥ
Hardin-Simmons Univ	TX	23,560	Ǥ
Lipscomb Univ	TN	35,722	VC
Lubbock Christian Univ	TX	25,518	C
MidAmerica Nazarene Univ	KS	28,000	C
Mount Vernon Nazarene Univ	OH	29,590	C
Northwest Nazarene Univ	ID	24,275	NC
Northwest Univ	WA	18,854	C
Okla Christian Univ	OK	24,975	VC
Olivet Nazarene Univ	IL	29,990	C
Simpson Univ	CA	28,900	C
Southern Nazarene Univ	OK	24,354	NC
Southwest Baptist Univ	MO	24,710	C
Spring Arbor Univ	MI	26,740	C
Trinity Bible College	ND		
Union Univ	TN	28,260	VC
Vanguard Univ of Southern Calif	CA	35,833	VC

MODERN DANCE

School	ST	$IS	SR
Texas Christian Univ	TX	47,570	HC

MODERN JEWISH STUDIES

School	ST	$IS	SR
San Diego State Univ	CA	20,578	VC

MODERN LANGUAGE

School	ST	$IS	SR
Anna Maria College	MA	34,600	LC
Aquinas College	MI	33,060	C
Augustana College	SD	35,500	VC
Averett Univ	VA	36,000	LC
Beloit College	WI	49,970	HC
Bethune-Cookman Univ	FL	22,290	LC
Bryant Univ	RI	49,179	VC
Calif Polytechnic State Univ	CA	19,847	HC
Canisius College	NY	45,602	VC
Clemson Univ	SC	19,136	HC
College of Mount St. Vincent	NY	41,040	MC
College of William & Mary	VA	25,085	MC
Converse College	SC	37,130	C
Duquesne Univ	PA	42,017	VC
Elizabethtown College	PA	47,600	VC
Emory and Henry College	VA	387,460	C
Emporia State Univ	KS	12,897	C
Fairfield Univ	CT	55,850	VC
Fort Hays State Univ	KS	11,354	C
Framingham State Univ	MA	16,750	C
Francis Marion Univ	SC	16,464	LC
Georgia Southern Univ	GA	16,414	C
Graceland Univ	IA	28,020	C
Hobart and William Smith Colleges	NY	43,000	VC
Ithaca College	NY	52,300	HC
James Madison Univ	VA	18,049	VC
John Carroll Univ	OH	44,520	Ǥ
Kansas State Univ	KS	15,497	VC
Kennesaw State Univ	GA	13,017	VC

School	ST	$IS	SR
Kenyon College	OH	56,810	MC
King Univ	TN	33,140	C
Knox College	IL		VC
Longwood Univ	VA	20,924	C
Loyola Marymount Univ	CA	53,240	VC+
Merrimack College	MA	44,215	C
Metropolitan State Univ of Denver	CO	4,835	LC
MidAmerica Nazarene Univ	KS	28,000	C
Mills College	CA	54,119	HC
Miss College	MS	21,998	VC
Monmouth Univ	NJ	42,252	C
Montana State Univ	MT	14,068	VC
Northern Arizona Univ	AZ	18,592	C
Notre Dame of Maryland Univ	MD	27,700	C
Ohio Univ	OH	20,676	VC
Pace Univ	NY	48,094	VC
Presbyterian College	SC	42,678	VC
St. Francis Univ	PA	30,029	LC
St. Peter's College	NJ	44,240	C
Seton Hall Univ	NJ	45,902	C
St. Lawrence Univ	NY	53,740	HC
Sweet Briar College	VA	43,765	C+
Syracuse Univ	NY	54,512	HC
Trinity College	CT		HC+
Union College	NY		MC
Univ of Arkansas at Monticello	AR	8,470	NC
Univ of Louisiana at Monroe	LA	12,998	C
Univ of Maine	ME	19,712	C+
Univ of Maryland/Baltimore County	MD	18,000	VC
Univ of Mass Lowell	MA	19,316	C
Univ of Miami	FL	55,166	MC
Univ of Texas at San Antonio	TX	18,372	C
Univ of Wisc/River Falls	WI	9,722	LC
Warren Wilson College	NC	34,888	VC
Wayne State College	NE	11,764	NC
Westmont College	CA	41,500	HC
Widener Univ	PA	50,368	C
Winthrop Univ	SC	21,120	VC
Wright State Univ	OH	16,983	C
Xavier Univ	OH	43,740	VC

MOLECULAR BIOLOGY

School	ST	$IS	SR
Adams State College	CO	13,358	LC
Alverno College	WI	30,483	LC
Andrews Univ	MI	28,030	C+
Appalachian State Univ	NC	12,919	VC
Arizona State Univ	AZ	18,818	C+
Assumption College	MA	45,721	VC
Auburn Univ	AL	20,052	VC+
Bellarmine Univ	KY	42,950	VC
Benedictine Univ	IL	35,220	C
Bethel Univ	MN	34,940	VC
Binghamton Univ / The SUNY	NY	20,832	HC+
Bradley Univ	IL	31,874	VC
Brigham Young Univ	UT	12,100	HC
Brown Univ	RI	56,150	MC
Calif Baptist Univ	CA	35,890	C
Cedarville Univ	OH	31,036	VC+
Centre College	KY	35,000	HC+
Chestnut Hill College	PA	39,785	LC
Claremont McKenna College	CA	58,065	MC
Clarion Univ of Pennsylvania	PA	17,370	C
Clarkson Univ	NY	53,538	HC
Coe College	IA	43,590	VC
Coker College	SC	32,256	LC
Colgate Univ	NY	50,930	MC
Florida Inst of Technology	FL	48,290	VC
Florida Southern College	FL	38,240	VC
Florida State Univ	FL	15,238	HC
Goshen College	IN	35,900	VC
Hardin-Simmons Univ	TX	23,560	C+
Houston Baptist Univ	TX	23,815	C+
Illinois Inst of Technology	IL	38,512	HC+
John Carroll Univ	OH	44,520	C+
Johns Hopkins Univ	MD	47,492	MC
Kenyon College	OH	56,810	MC
Kutztown Univ of Pennsylvania	PA	16,909	LC
Lawrence Tech Univ	MI	37,630	VC
Lehigh Univ	PA	55,080	MC
Lipscomb Univ	TN	35,722	VC
LIU/C.W. Post Campus	NY	38,888	C
Mansfield Univ	PA	19,468	LC
Marquette Univ	WI	43,664	VC+
Marshall Univ	WV	14,820	C
Messiah College	PA	39,540	VC
Middlebury College	VT	57,470	MC
Millikin Univ	IL	37,462	C
Mills College	CA	54,119	HC
Milwaukee School of Engineering	WI	39,948	VC+
Montclair State Univ	NJ	22,614	C
Muskingum Univ	OH	30,502	C
Nebr Wesleyan Univ	NE	29,774	C+
Northwest Nazarene Univ	ID	24,275	NC
Northwestern Univ	IL	37,595	MC
Ohio Northern Univ	OH	42,075	VC
Ohio Univ	OH	20,676	VC
Okla State Univ	OK	14,310	VC
Otterbein College	OH	32,214	C
Pittsburg State Univ	KS	12,032	C
Polytechnic Inst of New York Univ	NY	53,064	HC+
Pomona College	CA	57,680	MC
Princeton Univ	NJ	53,795	MC
Purdue Univ/West Lafayette	IN	20,278	HC
Rhodes College	TN	47,596	HC+
Rutgers, The State Univ of New Jersey/New Brunswick	NJ	25,077	VC
Salem International Univ	WV	18,020	C
Scripps College	CA	54,900	MC
SUNY / College of Environmental Science and Forestry	NY	18,351	HC
Stetson Univ	FL	49,512	VC+
Texas Tech Univ	TX	14,243	C
The Lincoln Univ	PA	15,154	LC
Ohio State Univ	OH	19,887	MC
Towson Univ	MD	16,000	VC
Tulane Univ	LA	58,942	MC
Univ at Albany / SUNY	NY	18,674	VC
Univ of Arizona	AZ	20,105	C
Univ of Calif at Berkeley	CA	23,322	MC
Univ of Calif at Los Angeles	CA	25,686	MC
Univ of Calif at San Diego	CA	21,000	VC
Univ of Calif at Santa Barbara	CA	27,551	HC
Univ of Calif at Santa Cruz	CA	27,807	VC
Univ of Colo Boulder	CO	22,605	VC+
Univ of Conn	CT	23,744	HC
Univ of Denver	CO	51,787	VC+
Univ of Great Falls	MT	27,970	C
Univ of Idaho	ID	14,558	C
Univ of Illinois at Urbana-Champaign	IL	24,300	HC
Univ of Kansas	KS	16,980	C+
Univ of Maine	ME	19,712	C+
Univ of Miami	FL	55,166	MC
Univ of Mich/Ann Arbor	MI	22,102	HC+
Univ of Minn/Duluth	MN	18,964	C+
Univ of New Hampshire	NH	24,702	VC
Univ of Pittsburgh at Pittsburgh	PA	27,800	HC+
Univ of Puget Sound	WA	52,648	HC+
Univ of Rochester	NY	58,500	MC
Univ of Texas at Austin	TX	44,074	HC
Univ of Texas at Dallas	TX	21,046	HC
Univ of Vermont	VT	26,120	VC+
Univ of Wisc/Madison	WI	18,757	HC
Univ of Wisc-Milwaukee	WI	18,436	C
Univ of Wyoming	WY	13,855	C+
Vanderbilt Univ	TN	57,072	MC
Wells College	NY	38,680	VC
Wesleyan Univ	CT	59,844	MC
West Chester Univ of Pennsylvania	PA	16,836	C
Western Washington Univ	WA	18,519	VC
Westminster College	PA	31,290	C+
Yale Univ	CT	55,300	MC

MOVEMENT SCIENCE

School	ST	$IS	SR
Texas Christian Univ	TX	47,570	HC
Univ of Idaho	ID	14,558	C
Winona State Univ	MN	16,530	C

MULTIMEDIA

School	ST	$IS	SR
Abilene Christian Univ	TX	38,400	VC
Academy of Art Univ	CA		
American Univ	DC	54,829	HC+
Arizona State Univ	AZ	18,818	C+
Art Inst of Atlanta	GA	24,000	SP
Art Inst of Portland	OR	23,040	SP
Belmont Univ	TN	37,380	VC+
Bennington College	VT	56,990	HC+
Bethel Univ	MN	34,940	VC
Bradley Univ	IL	31,874	VC
Calif Lutheran Univ	CA	47,640	C
Cameron Univ	OK	9,267	LC
Cedarville Univ	OH	31,036	VC+
Champlain College	VT	44,850	VC
CUNY/Brooklyn College	NY	5,884	C+
College of New Jersey	NJ	25,376	HC
Columbia College Chicago	IL	30,940	LC
CUNY-City College	NY	19,576	HC+
Dakota Wesleyan Univ	SD	23,000	C
Duquesne Univ	PA	42,017	VC
Florida Atlantic Univ	FL	17,339	C
George Fox Univ	OR	40,750	C+
George Washington Univ	DC	57,108	MC
Georgia Southern Univ	GA	16,414	C
Hawaii Pacific Univ	HI	36,690	C
Howard Payne Univ	TX	17,115	C
Kendall College of Art and Design of Ferris State Univ	MI	21,048	SP
La Salle Univ	PA	50,270	C
Lasell College	MA	42,500	LC
Lewis Univ	IL	23,050	C
Louisiana College	LA	15,746	C
Lyndon State College	VT	14,233	C
Lynn Univ	FL	43,500	C
McMurry Univ	TX	25,962	LC
Minot State Univ	ND	10,915	C
National Univ	CA	14,730	SP
Northeastern Univ	MA	55,296	MC
Ohio Univ	OH	20,676	VC
Rider Univ	NJ	45,720	C
St. Leo Univ	FL	27,990	C
San Diego State Univ	CA	20,578	VC
Simpson College	IA	36,086	VC
Univ of Mary Hardin-Baylor	TX	31,950	C+
Univ of New Haven	CT	47,740	C
Univ of N Car at Asheville	NC	13,500	VC+
Univ of the Arts	PA	38,450	SP
Washington State Univ	WA	20,461	C
Waynesburg Univ	PA	29,100	C
Western Washington Univ	WA	18,519	VC
Wilmington Univ	DE	7,778	NC

MUSEUM STUDIES

School	ST	$IS	SR
Baylor Univ	TX	46,720	HC
Juniata College	PA	49,340	VC
Tusculum College	TN	24,295	C
Univ of Central Okla	OK	12,293	C
Univ of Illinois at Chicago	IL	24,293	VC
Walsh Univ	OH	35,100	C

MUSIC

School	ST	$IS	SR
Abilene Christian Univ	TX	38,400	VC
Adams State College	CO	13,358	LC
Adelphi Univ	NY	43,130	VC
Adrian College	MI	33,800	C
Agnes Scott College	GA	45,323	VC+
Alabama State Univ	AL	14,142	NC
Albany State Univ	GA	8,500	C
Albion College	MI	43,884	VC
Alcorn State Univ	MS	9,500	C
Alderson Broaddus Univ	WV	28,656	C
Allegheny College	PA	49,020	HC
Allen Univ	SC	16,124	NC
Alma College	MI	42,400	VC
Alverno College	WI	30,483	LC
American Univ	DC	54,829	HC+
Amherst College	MA	58,744	MC
Andrews Univ	MI	28,030	C+
Angelo State Univ	TX	15,049	NC
Anna Maria College	MA	34,600	LC
Aquinas College	MI	33,060	C
Arizona State Univ	AZ	18,818	C+
Arkansas State Univ	AR	14,980	C
Arkansas Tech Univ	AR	13,164	LC
Armstrong Atlantic State Univ	GA	16,276	C
Asbury Univ	KY	32,038	VC
Ashland Univ	OH	25,000	C
Assumption College	MA	45,721	VC
Atlantic Union College	MA	24,600	LC
Augsburg College	MN	35,142	C
Augustana College	IL	43,398	HC
Augustana College	SD	35,500	VC
Austin College	TX	36,940	HC
Austin Peay State Univ	TN	14,650	C
Averett Univ	VA	36,000	LC
Avila Univ	MO	26,900	C
Azusa Pacific Univ	CA	39,946	C
Baker Univ	KS	33,350	C+
Baldwin Wallace Univ	OH	36,980	VC
Ball State Univ	IN	17,850	C
Bard College	NY	59,872	HC
Bard College at Simon's Rock	MA	58,963	HC+
Bates College	ME	58,950	MC
Baylor Univ	TX	46,720	HC
Belhaven Univ	MS	27,170	C
Bellarmine Univ	KY	42,950	VC
Belmont Univ	TN	37,380	VC+
Beloit College	WI	49,970	HC
Bemidji State Univ	MN	13,500	C
Benedict College	SC	20,454	NC
Benedictine College	KS	29,180	VC
Benedictine Univ	IL	35,220	C
Bennett College	NC		LC
Bennington College	VT	56,990	HC+
Berea College	KY	7,220	HC
Berklee College of Music	MA	47,100	SP
Berry College	GA	39,254	HC
Bethany College	KS	30,605	NC
Bethel College	KS	29,100	C
Bethel Univ	MN	34,940	VC
Bethel Univ	TN	19,186	C
Bethune-Cookman Univ	FL	22,290	LC
Binghamton Univ / The SUNY	NY	20,832	HC+
Biola Univ	CA	40,320	VC
Birmingham-Southern College	AL	42,370	VC+
Black Hills State Univ	SD	13,562	LC
Bloomsburg Univ of Pennsylvania	PA	13,598	C
Blue Mountain College	MS	13,550	LC
Bluefield College	VA	17,230	C+
Bluffton Univ	OH	37,864	C
Boise State Univ	ID	12,802	C
Boston College	MA	58,506	MC
Boston Conservatory	MA	56,380	SP
Boston Univ	MA	54,130	HC+
Bowdoin College	ME	57,834	MC
Bowling Green State Univ	OH	18,970	C
Bradley Univ	IL	31,874	VC
Brandeis Univ	MA	58,820	HC
Briar Cliff Univ	IA	29,514	C
Bridgewater College	VA	39,880	C
Bridgewater State Univ	MA	18,752	C
Brigham Young Univ	UT	12,100	HC
Brigham Young Univ/Hawaii	HI	8,614	VC
Brown Univ	RI	56,150	MC
Bryan College	TN	24,194	C
Bryn Mawr College	PA	57,760	MC
Bucknell Univ	PA	58,160	MC
Buena Vista Univ	IA	37,954	C
Buffalo State/State Univ of Buffalo	NY	15,733	C+
Butler Univ	IN	45,898	VC+
Cabrini College	PA	40,859	LC
Cairn Univ	PA	31,255	C
Caldwell College	NJ	35,602	LC
Calif Baptist Univ	CA	35,890	C
Calif Lutheran Univ	CA	47,640	C
Calif Polytechnic State Univ	CA	19,847	HC
Calif State Polytechnic Univ, Pomona	CA	18,932	C
Cal State, Bakersfield	CA	8,000	LC
Cal State, Chico	CA	18,952	C
Cal State, Dominguez Hills	CA	17,056	LC
Cal State, East Bay	CA	16,549	C
Cal State, Fresno	CA	17,405	C
Cal State, Fullerton	CA	25,188	C+
Cal State, Long Beach	CA	17,534	C+
Cal State, Los Angeles	CA	15,829	C
Cal State, Monterey Bay	CA	26,871	LC
Cal State, Northridge	CA	28,313	C
Cal State, Sacramento	CA	16,200	C
Cal State, San Bernardino	CA	12,000	C
Cal State, Stanislaus	CA	18,582	C
Calvin College	MI	37,585	VC+
Cameron Univ	OK	9,267	LC
Campbell Univ	NC	25,500	C
Campbellsville Univ	KY	27,720	C
Canisius College	NY	45,602	VC
Capital Univ	OH	39,824	VC
Cardinal Stritch Univ	WI	24,054	C
Carleton College	MN	58,149	MC
Carnegie Mellon Univ	PA	51,260	MC
Carroll Univ	WI	24,860	C
Carson-Newman Univ	TN	29,058	C+
Carthage College	WI	33,000	C
Case Western Reserve Univ	OH	55,178	MC
Castleton State College	VT	19,424	C
Catawba College	NC	37,105	C
Cedar Crest College	PA	43,240	C
Cedarville Univ	OH	31,036	VC+
Centenary College of Louisiana	LA	39,070	C+
Central College	IA	36,980	VC
Central Conn State Univ	CT	19,212	C
Central Methodist Univ	MO	28,240	VC
Central Mich Univ	MI	18,066	C
Central State Univ	OH	9,010	C
Central Washington Univ	WA	11,730	C
Centre College	KY	35,000	HC+
Chadron State College	NE	7,400	NC
Chapman Univ	CA	56,019	VC+
Charleston Southern Univ	SC	22,420	C
Chatham Univ	PA	42,440	VC
Chestnut Hill College	PA	39,785	LC
Cheyney Univ of Pennsylvania	PA	20,372	LC
Chicago State Univ	IL	5,482	C
Christopher Newport Univ	VA	21,050	VC
CUNY/Baruch College	NY	15,831	VC
CUNY/Brooklyn College	NY	5,884	C+
Claflin Univ	SC	22,368	C+
Clark Atlanta Univ	GA	30,006	C
Clark Univ	MA	47,020	HC+
Clarke Univ	IA	36,400	C
Clayton State Univ	GA	12,000	LC
Clearwater Christian College	FL	23,720	C
Cleveland Inst of Music	OH	56,882	SP
Cleveland State Univ	OH	21,357	C
Coastal Carolina Univ	SC	17,620	C
Coe College	IA	43,590	VC
Coker College	SC	32,256	LC
Colby College	ME	57,510	MC
Colgate Univ	NY	50,930	MC
College of Staten Island / The CUNY	NY	16,778	NC
College of Charleston	SC	21,273	VC
College of Mount St. Joseph	OH	33,880	C
College of New Jersey	NJ	25,376	HC
College of St. Benedict	MN	47,570	VC
College of St. Elizabeth	NJ	43,839	LC
College of St. Scholastica	MN	39,960	C
College of the Holy Cross	MA	56,232	MC
College of the Ozarks	MO	5,605	VC
College of William & Mary	VA	25,085	MC
College of Wooster	OH	52,600	VC
Colo Christian Univ	CO	27,500	VC

School	ST	$IS	SR
Colo College	CO	54,534	MC
Colo Mesa Univ	CO	16,669	LC
Colo State Univ-Fort Collins	CO	20,090	VC
Columbia College	SC	27,882	C
Columbia College Chicago	IL	30,940	LC
Columbia Univ in the City of New York	NY	61,116	MC
Columbia Univ/Barnard College	NY	39,000	MC
Columbia Univ/School of General Studies	NY	54,083	MC
Columbus State Univ	GA	13,176	C
Concordia College New York	NY	31,500	VC
Concordia College, Moorhead	MN	39,974	C+
Concordia Univ - Irvine	CA	35,390	VC
Concordia Univ Nebr	NE	26,000	VC
Concordia Univ St. Paul	MN	27,200	C
Concordia Univ Texas	TX	23,640	C
Concordia Univ Wisc	WI	28,980	C
Concordia Univ, Ann Arbor	MI	27,220	VC
Concordia Univ, River Forest	IL	26,300	C
Conn College	CT	54,970	MC
Converse College	SC	37,130	C
Corban Univ	OR	34,764	C
Cornell College	IA	44,930	HC
Cornell Univ	NY	59,037	MC
Cornerstone Univ and Grand Rapids Theological Seminary	MI	30,866	C
Cornish College of the Arts	WA	21,200	SP
Covenant College	GA		VC+
Creighton Univ	NE	44,058	VC+
Culver-Stockton College	MO	30,900	C
Cumberland Univ	TN	21,220	C
CUNY-City College	NY	19,576	HC+
Curtis Inst of Music	PA		SP
Dakota Wesleyan Univ	SD	23,000	C
Dallas Baptist Univ	TX	29,118	C
Dartmouth College	NH	57,996	MC
Davidson College	NC	54,683	MC
Davis and Elkins College	WV	33,742	C
Delaware State Univ	DE	14,700	LC
Delta State Univ	MS	12,292	LC
Denison Univ	OH	54,670	HC+
DePaul Univ	IL	46,120	VC
DePauw Univ	IN	48,950	VC+
Dickinson College	PA	57,662	HC+
Dickinson State Univ	ND	8,550	NC
Dillard Univ	LA	20,940	VC
Doane College	NE	33,730	VC
Dominican Univ	IL	37,628	C
Dominican Univ of Calif	CA	51,250	C
Dordt College	IA	34,160	VC
Dowling College	NY	25,000	LC
Drake Univ	IA	30,980	VC+
Drew Univ/College of Liberal Arts	NJ	55,862	VC
Drury Univ	MO	30,319	VC
Duke Univ	NC	50,250	MC
Earlham College	IN	49,710	VC+
East Central Univ	OK	10,223	LC
East Stroudsburg Univ of Pennsylvania	PA	16,636	C
East Tenn State Univ	TN	9,000	C
East Texas Baptist Univ	TX	29,135	C
Eastern Conn State Univ	CT	20,584	C
Eastern Illinois Univ	IL	20,502	C
Eastern Kentucky Univ	KY	11,161	C
Eastern Mennonite Univ	VA	38,850	VC
Eastern Mich Univ	MI	17,961	C
Eastern Nazarene College	MA	30,000	C
Eastern New Mexico Univ	NM	10,682	C
Eastern Oregon Univ	OR	10,400	C
Eastern Univ	PA	37,704	C
Eastern Washington Univ	WA	16,388	C
Eastman School of Music	NY	58,802	SP
Eckerd College	FL	43,902	VC
Edgewood College	WI	33,294	C
Edinboro Univ of Pennsylvania	PA	15,940	LC
Elizabeth City State Univ	NC	11,638	C
Elizabethtown College	PA	47,600	VC
Elmhurst College	IL	42,032	C+
Elmira College	NY	49,950	C+
Elon Univ	NC	40,046	HC
Emory Univ	GA	45,000	MC
Emporia State Univ	KS	12,897	C
Erskine College	SC	37,360	C
Eugene Lang College - The New School for Liberal Arts	NY	55,650	VC
Eureka College	IL	19,280	C
Evangel Univ	MO	23,090	C
Excelsior College	NY	895	SP
Faulkner Univ	AL	22,530	LC
Felician College	NJ	41,640	C
Fisk Univ	TN	19,830	C
Florida A&M Univ	FL	14,935	LC
Florida Atlantic Univ	FL	17,339	C
Florida Gulf Coast Univ	FL		C
Florida International Univ	FL	17,747	VC
Florida Memorial Univ	FL	20,716	LC
Florida Southern College	FL	38,240	VC
Florida State Univ	FL	15,238	HC

School	ST	$IS	SR
Fordham Univ	NY	58,927	HC
Fort Hays State Univ	KS	11,354	C
Fort Lewis College	CO	15,513	C
Francis Marion Univ	SC	16,464	LC
Franklin and Marshall College	PA	58,295	MC
Franklin College	IN	35,885	C
Franklin Pierce Univ	NH	41,598	C
Fresno Pacific Univ	CA	32,136	C
Friends Univ	KS	29,100	C
Frostburg State Univ	MD	15,264	LC
Furman Univ	SC	54,006	HC
Gardner-Webb Univ	NC	34,375	C+
Geneva College	PA	27,280	C
George Fox Univ	OR	40,750	C+
George Mason Univ	VA	15,724	VC
George Washington Univ	DC	57,108	MC
Georgetown College	KY	38,690	C
Georgia College and State Univ	GA	18,216	VC
Georgia Regents Univ	GA		C
Georgia Southern Univ	GA	16,414	C
Georgia Southwestern State Univ	GA	12,218	C
Georgia State Univ	GA	12,000	VC
Gettysburg College	PA	56,820	HC
Gonzaga Univ	WA	44,247	HC
Gordon College	MA	42,660	VC+
Goshen College	IN	35,900	VC
Goucher College	MD	50,252	VC+
Grace Bible College	MI	20,770	C
Grace College and Theological Seminary	IN	28,800	C
Graceland Univ	IA	28,020	C
Grambling State Univ	LA	13,384	LC
Grand Canyon Univ	AZ	24,540	VC
Grand Valley State Univ	MI	17,998	VC
Grand View Univ	IA	31,050	C
Greensboro College	NC	28,740	LC
Greenville College	IL	27,012	C
Grinnell College	IA	53,654	HC
Grove City College	PA	22,988	HC
Guilford College	NC	35,340	C
Gustavus Adolphus College	MN	48,170	HC
Hamilton College	NY	55,620	MC
Hamline Univ	MN	44,198	VC
Hampshire College	MA	58,320	MC
Hampton Univ	VA	28,528	C
Hannibal-LaGrange Univ	MO	24,490	C
Hanover College	IN	41,450	VC
Harding Univ	AR	21,432	C+
Hardin-Simmons Univ	TX	23,560	C+
Hartwick College	NY	49,815	C+
Harvard Univ/Harvard College	MA	49,000	MC
Hastings College	NE	27,782	C+
Haverford College	PA	59,236	MC
Heidelberg Univ	OH	34,100	C
Henderson State Univ	AR	13,634	C
Hendrix College	AR	48,436	HC+
High Point Univ	NC	39,800	C
Hillsdale College	MI	31,890	HC+
Hiram College	OH	37,300	VC
Hobart and William Smith Colleges	NY	43,000	VC
Hofstra Univ	NY	48,020	VC
Hollins Univ	VA	43,295	VC
Holy Names Univ	CA	40,310	NC
Hood College	MD	44,630	C
Hope College	MI	36,320	VC+
Hope International Univ	CA	34,650	C
Houghton College	NY	35,740	VC
Houston Baptist Univ	TX	23,815	C+
Howard Payne Univ	TX	17,115	C
Howard Univ	DC	35,957	C
Humboldt State Univ	CA	18,400	C
Hunter College / The CUNY	NY	14,429	VC
Huntingdon College	AL	31,850	C
Huston-Tillotson Univ	TX	18,124	C+
Idaho State Univ	ID	11,908	C
Illinois College	IL	25,770	VC
Illinois State Univ	IL	22,634	VC
Illinois Wesleyan Univ	IL	48,452	VC+
Immaculata Univ	PA	43,000	C
Indiana State Univ	IN	16,000	C
Indiana Univ Bloomington	IN	19,358	HC
Indiana Univ of Pennsylvania	PA	20,180	LC
Indiana Univ South Bend	IN	15,293	C
Indiana Univ Southeast	IN	15,807	LC
Indiana Univ-Purdue Univ Fort Wayne	IN	15,425	C
Indiana Wesleyan Univ	IN	31,815	VC
Inter-American Univ of PR/ San Germán	PR	6,720	
Iowa State Univ	IA	16,403	C
Iowa Wesleyan College	IA	30,850	LC
Ithaca College	NY	52,300	HC
Jacksonville State Univ	AL	12,280	LC
Jacksonville Univ	FL	37,780	C
James Madison Univ	VA	18,049	VC
John Brown Univ	AR	30,996	VC+
Johnson State College	VT	16,721	C
Judson Univ	IL	25,130	C
Juilliard School	NY	44,460	SP

School	ST	$IS	SR
Kalamazoo College	MI	47,825	HC+
Kansas State Univ	KS	15,497	VC
Kansas Wesleyan Univ	KS	32,000	C
Kean Univ	NJ	22,060	LC
Keene State College	NH	21,538	C
Kennesaw State Univ	GA	13,017	VC
Kent State Univ	OH	19,352	C
Kentucky Christian Univ	KY	17,622	LC
Kentucky Wesleyan College	KY	27,440	VC+
Kenyon College	OH	56,810	MC
Knox College	IL		VC
Kutztown Univ of Pennsylvania	PA	16,909	LC
La Salle Univ	PA	50,270	C
La Sierra Univ	CA	35,694	VC
Lafayette College	PA	57,050	HC+
LaGrange College	GA	34,480	C
Lake Forest College	IL	45,580	VC
Lakeland College	WI	22,990	C
Lamar Univ	TX	6,820	LC
Lander Univ	SC	22,514	C+
Lane College	TN	11,212	C
Langston Univ	OK	3,000	LC
Le Moyne College	NY	42,200	VC
Lebanon Valley College	PA	38,570	C
Lee Univ	TN	18,690	C+
Lehigh Univ	PA	55,080	MC
Lehman College / The CUNY	NY	5,778	LC
LeMoyne-Owen College	TN	13,100	C
Lenoir-Rhyne College	NC	35,984	C
Lewis & Clark College	OR	52,656	VC
Lewis Univ	IL	23,050	C
Liberty Univ	VA	19,101	C
Limestone College	SC	29,880	C
Lindenwood Univ	MO	20,750	C
Linfield College-McMinnville Campus	OR	46,166	C
Lipscomb Univ	TN	35,722	VC
Livingstone College	NC	17,815	LC
Lock Haven Univ of Pennsylvania	PA	17,587	LC
LIU/Brooklyn Campus	NY	26,500	C
LIU/C.W. Post Campus	NY	38,888	C
Longwood Univ	VA	20,924	C
Loras College	IA	37,432	VC
Louisiana College	LA	15,746	C
Louisiana State Univ	LA	18,677	VC+
Louisiana Tech Univ	LA	8,000	C
Loyola Marymount Univ	CA	53,240	VC+
Loyola Univ Chicago	IL	49,560	VC+
Loyola Univ New Orleans	LA	46,581	VC
Lubbock Christian Univ	TX	25,518	C
Luther College	IA	44,380	VC+
Lycoming College	PA	43,636	C
Lynchburg College	VA	42,645	C
Lyon College	AR	30,246	VC
Macalester College	MN	53,419	MC
MacMurray College	IL	20,755	C
Madonna Univ	MI	24,540	VC
Malone Univ	OH	34,334	C
Manchester College	IN	35,070	C
Manhattan School of Music	NY	55,850	SP
Manhattanville College	NY	46,260	VC
Mannes College New School for Music	NY	44,500	C
Mansfield Univ	PA	19,468	LC
Marian Univ	WI	30,980	LC
Marian Univ/Indianapolis	IN	37,058	C
Marietta College	OH	42,135	VC
Marlboro College	VT	35,980	VC
Mars Hill College	NC	22,950	LC
Marshall Univ	WV	14,820	C
Martin Univ	IN	11,000	SP
Mary Baldwin College	VA	37,110	C
Marygrove College	MI	21,290	C
Marylhurst Univ	OR	18,945	NC
Maryville College	TN	33,150	VC
Mass Inst of Technology	MA	54,238	MC
McDaniel College	MD	45,600	VC
McKendree Univ	IL	29,920	C+
McMurry Univ	TX	25,962	LC
McNeese State Univ	LA		C
McPherson College	KS	28,138	C
Mercer Univ	GA	44,201	VC+
Mercy College	NY	29,996	C
Mercyhurst Univ	PA	40,700	C
Meredith College	NC	31,420	C
Messiah College	PA	39,540	VC
Methodist Univ	NC	37,185	C
Miami Univ	OH	24,191	HC
Mich State Univ	MI	13,689	VC
MidAmerica Nazarene Univ	KS	28,000	C
Middle Tenn State Univ	TN	8,650	C
Middlebury College	VT	57,470	MC
Midland Univ	NE	34,000	C
Midwestern State Univ	TX	9,722	C
Millersville Univ of Pennsylvania	PA	18,498	C
Milligan College	TN	27,510	C
Millikin Univ	IL	37,462	C
Mills College	CA	54,119	HC
Millsaps College	MS	43,888	VC+
Minn State Univ, Mankato	MN	14,900	C
Minn State Univ, Moorhead	MN	13,392	C
Minot State Univ	ND	10,915	C

School	ST	$IS	SR
Miss College	MS	21,998	VC
Miss Univ for Women	MS	7,400	LC
Missouri Baptist Univ	MO	30,310	C
Missouri Southern State Univ	MO	11,910	C
Missouri State Univ	MO	13,996	VC
Missouri Western State Univ	MO	12,260	NC
Molloy College	NY	38,950	C
Monmouth College	IL	39,290	C
Monmouth Univ	NJ	42,252	C
Montana State Univ	MT	14,068	VC
Montana State Univ-Billings	MT	12,425	LC
Montana State Univ-Northern	MT	12,500	NC
Montclair State Univ	NJ	22,614	C
Moravian College	PA	36,381	VC
Morehead State Univ	KY	10,900	C
Morehouse College	GA	38,640	C
Morgan State Univ	MD	14,500	VC
Morningside College	IA	32,620	C
Mount Holyoke College	MA	53,596	HC+
Mount Marty College	SD	29,638	C
Mount Mercy Univ	IA	34,385	C
Mount Olive College	NC	18,426	C
Mount St. Mary's College/ Chalon Campus	CA	43,897	VC+
Mount Vernon Nazarene Univ	OH	29,590	C
Muhlenberg College	PA	52,837	HC
Murray State Univ	KY	14,944	C
Muskingum Univ	OH	30,502	C
Naropa Univ	CO	37,875	SP
Nazareth College of Rochester	NY	41,590	VC
Nebr Wesleyan Univ	NE	29,774	C+
New College of Florida	FL	14,504	HC+
New England Conservatory of Music	MA	52,550	SP
New Jersey City Univ	NJ	21,060	C+
New Mexico Highlands Univ	NM	9,720	NC
New Mexico State Univ	NM	13,955	LC
New York Univ	NY	61,470	MC
Newberry College	SC	26,850	LC
Nicholls State Univ	LA	7,095	C
N Car Agricultural and Technical State Univ	NC	13,175	LC
N Car Central Univ	NC	9,000	LC
North Central College	IL	38,343	VC
N Dak State Univ	ND	14,642	C
North Georgia College & State Univ	GA	8,500	C
North Park Univ	IL	30,130	C
Northeastern Illinois Univ	IL		C
Northeastern State Univ	OK	8,615	VC
Northeastern Univ	MA	55,296	MC
Northern Arizona Univ	AZ	18,592	C
Northern Illinois Univ	IL	19,768	C
Northern Kentucky Univ	KY	15,302	LC
Northern Mich Univ	MI	15,300	VC
Northern State Univ	SD	14,021	C
Northwest Christian Univ	OR	27,399	C
Northwest Missouri State Univ	MO	14,229	C
Northwest Nazarene Univ	ID	24,275	NC
Northwest Univ	WA	18,854	C
Northwestern College	MN	24,000	C
Northwestern College of Iowa	IA	34,848	C+
Northwestern Okla State Univ	OK	7,275	NC
Northwestern State Univ of Louisiana	LA	14,368	C
Northwestern Univ	IL	37,595	MC
Notre Dame de Namur Univ	CA	41,610	LC
Notre Dame of Maryland Univ	MD	27,700	C
Nova Southeastern Univ	FL	34,016	VC
Nyack College	NY	32,000	C
Oakland City Univ	IN	24,500	NC
Oakland Univ	MI	19,391	VC
Oakwood Univ	AL	23,035	C
Oberlin College	OH	57,025	MC
Occidental College	CA	59,592	MC+
Ohio Northern Univ	OH	42,075	VC
Ohio Univ	OH	20,676	VC
Ohio Wesleyan Univ	OH	49,460	C+
Okla Baptist Univ	OK	28,202	VC
Okla Christian Univ	OK	24,975	VC
Okla City Univ	OK	33,546	VC
Okla Panhandle State Univ	OK	8,996	NC
Okla State Univ	OK	14,310	VC
Okla Wesleyan Univ	OK	21,300	C
Old Dominion Univ	VA	18,662	C
Olivet Nazarene Univ	IL	29,990	C
Oral Roberts Univ	OK	31,734	C
Oregon State Univ	OR	19,017	C+
Oswego / SUNY	NY	20,009	VC
Ottawa Univ	KS	15,000	VC
Otterbein College	OH	32,214	C
Ouachita Baptist Univ	AR	29,010	VC
Our Lady of the Lake Univ of San Antonio	TX	22,430	LC
Pacific Lutheran Univ	WA	44,840	VC
Pacific Union College	CA	28,150	VC
Pacific Univ	OR	42,815	C

INDEX OF COLLEGE MAJORS

ST = STATE $IS = IN-STATE COSTS SR = SELECTOR RATING

School	ST	$IS	SR
Western Kentucky Univ	KY	11,000	LC
Western Mich Univ	MI	19,042	C
Western New Mexico Univ	NM	8,500	LC
Western Oregon Univ	OR	15,021	C
Western State Colo Univ	CO	16,135	C
Western Washington Univ	WA	18,519	VC
Westfield State Univ	MA	18,489	C
Westminster Choir College	NJ	36,000	SP
Westminster College	PA	31,290	C+
Westminster College	UT	37,708	VC
Westmont College	CA	41,500	HC
Wheaton College	IL	39,650	HC+
Wheaton College	MA	54,934	HC+
Whitman College	WA	54,400	MC
Whittier College	CA	43,416	C
Whitworth Univ	WA	45,826	VC+
Wichita State Univ	KS	12,539	C
Wilberforce Univ	OH	15,100	LC
Wiley College	TX		LC
Willamette Univ	OR	56,450	VC+
William Carey Univ	MS	13,500	LC
William Jewell College	MO	31,000	VC+
William Paterson Univ of New Jersey	NJ	21,694	C
Williams Baptist College	AR	20,070	C
Williams College	MA	58,900	MC
Wilmington College	OH	29,784	C
Wingate Univ	NC	34,990	C
Winona State Univ	MN	16,530	C
Winthrop Univ	SC	21,120	VC
Wisc Lutheran College	WI	23,510	VC
Wittenberg Univ	OH	47,766	VC
Wright State Univ	OH	16,983	C
Xavier Univ	OH	43,740	VC
Xavier Univ of Louisiana	LA	25,300	C
Yale Univ	CT	55,300	MC
Yeshiva Univ	NY	47,250	VC+
York College / CUNY	NY	5,496	NC
York College of Pennsylvania	PA	26,590	C
Youngstown State Univ	OH	16,374	LC

MUSIC BUSINESS MANAGEMENT

School	ST	$IS	SR
Albright College	PA	46,660	C
Anderson Univ	IN	35,390	C
Appalachian State Univ	NC	12,919	VC
Aquinas College	MI	33,060	C
Belmont Univ	TN	37,380	VC+
Berklee College of Music	MA	47,100	SP
Berry College	GA	39,254	HC
Bethel Univ	TN	19,186	C
Bradley Univ	IL	31,874	VC
Central Washington Univ	WA	11,730	C
College of the Ozarks	MO	5,605	VC
Columbia College Chicago	IL	30,940	LC
Concordia Univ St. Paul	MN	27,200	C
Dallas Baptist Univ	TX	29,118	C
Delta State Univ	MS	12,292	LC
DePaul Univ	IL	46,120	VC
DePauw Univ	IN	48,950	VC+
Dillard Univ	LA	20,940	VC
Drake Univ	IA	30,980	VC+
Elmhurst College	IL	42,032	C+
Five Towns College	NY	34,550	SP
Florida Southern College	FL	38,240	VC
Geneva College	PA	27,280	C
Georgia State Univ	GA	12,000	VC
Greenville College	IL	27,012	C
Grove City College	PA	22,988	HC
Hardin-Simmons Univ	TX	23,560	C+
Hofstra Univ	NY	48,020	VC+
Howard Univ	DC	35,957	C
Huntington Univ	IN	32,220	C
Indiana Univ Southeast	IN	15,807	LC
Johnson C. Smith Univ	NC	25,336	LC
Johnson State College	VT	16,721	C
Kentucky Christian Univ	KY	17,622	LC
Kentucky Wesleyan College	KY	27,440	VC+
Lebanon Valley College	PA	38,570	C
Lee Univ	TN	18,690	C+
Lewis Univ	IL	23,050	C
Loyola Univ New Orleans	LA	46,581	VC
Mansfield Univ	PA	19,468	LC
Marian Univ	WI	30,980	LC
Marywood Univ	PA	40,695	C
McKendree Univ	IL	29,920	C+
Messiah College	PA	39,540	VC
Middle Tenn State Univ	TN	8,650	C
Millikin Univ	IL	37,462	C
Minn State Univ, Mankato	MN	14,900	C
Monmouth Univ	NJ	42,252	C
Montreat College	NC	31,298	VC
Nazareth College of Rochester	NY	41,590	VC
New York Univ	NY	61,470	MC
Northwest Univ	WA	18,854	C
Northwestern State Univ of Louisiana	LA	14,368	C
Oakwood Univ	AL	23,035	C
Ohio Northern Univ	OH	42,075	VC
Old Dominion Univ	VA	18,662	C
Peru State College	NE	8,600	NC
St. Augustine's Univ	NC	14,000	C
St. Joseph's College	IN	35,790	C
S Car State Univ	SC	6,700	LC
Southern Illinois Univ Edwardsville	IL	17,532	C
Southern Nazarene Univ	OK	24,354	NC
Southern Oregon Univ	OR	17,874	C
SUNY Oneonta / SUNY	NY	16,919	VC
Syracuse Univ	NY	54,512	HC
The SUNY at Potsdam	NY	17,754	C
Tiffin Univ	OH	30,273	LC
Trevecca Nazarene Univ	TN	30,118	C
Univ of Evansville	IN	41,056	VC+
Univ of Hartford	CT	42,674	C
Univ of Memphis	TN	15,094	C
Univ of Miami	FL	55,166	MC
Univ of New Haven	CT	47,740	C
Univ of the Incarnate Word	TX	35,200	LC
Univ of the Pacific	CA	52,146	VC
Winston-Salem State Univ	NC	9,418	LC

MUSIC COMPOSITION

School	ST	$IS	SR
Baldwin Wallace Univ	OH	36,980	VC
Biola Univ	CA	40,320	VC
Cairn Univ	PA	31,255	C
Cedarville Univ	OH	31,036	VC+
Georgia Southern Univ	GA	16,414	C
Indiana Univ South Bend	IN	15,293	C
Indiana Univ Southeast	IN	15,807	LC
Keene State College	NH	21,538	C
Lipscomb Univ	TN	35,722	VC
New York Univ	NY	61,470	MC
Okla City Univ	OK	33,546	VC
Ouachita Baptist Univ	AR	29,010	VC
San Francisco Conservatory of Music	CA	53,923	SP
Southern Oregon Univ	OR	17,874	C
Temple Univ	PA	24,392	VC
Univ of Georgia	GA	19,508	VC
Univ of Miami	FL	55,166	MC
Univ of West Georgia	GA	14,852	LC
Youngstown State Univ	OH	16,374	LC

MUSIC EDUCATION

School	ST	$IS	SR
Abilene Christian Univ	TX	38,400	VC
Adams State College	CO	13,358	LC
Alabama A&M Univ	AL	96,100	C
Alabama State Univ	AL	14,142	NC
Albany State Univ	GA	8,500	C
Alderson Broaddus Univ	WV	28,656	C
Anderson Univ	IN	35,390	C
Andrews Univ	MI	28,030	C+
Anna Maria College	MA	34,600	LC
Appalachian State Univ	NC	12,919	VC
Aquinas College	MI	33,060	C
Arcadia Univ	PA	33,570	C+
Arizona State Univ	AZ	18,818	C+
Arkansas State Univ	AR	14,980	C
Arkansas Tech Univ	AR	13,164	LC
Armstrong Atlantic State Univ	GA	16,276	C
Asbury Univ	KY	32,038	VC
Ashland Univ	OH	25,000	C
Atlantic Union College	MA	24,600	LC
Auburn Univ	AL	20,052	VC+
Augsburg College	MN	35,142	C
Augustana College	IL	43,398	HC
Augustana College	SD	35,500	VC
Azusa Pacific Univ	CA	39,946	C
Baker Univ	KS	33,350	C+
Baldwin Wallace Univ	OH	36,980	VC
Baylor Univ	TX	46,720	HC
Benedictine College	KS	29,180	VC
Bennett College	NC		LC
Berklee College of Music	MA	47,100	SP
Berry College	GA	39,254	HC
Bethany College	KS	30,605	NC
Bethel College	IN	31,560	C
Bethel Univ	MN	34,940	VC
Bethel Univ	TN	19,186	C
Bethune-Cookman Univ	FL	22,290	LC
Biola Univ	CA	40,320	VC
Birmingham-Southern College	AL	42,370	VC+
Black Hills State Univ	SD	13,562	LC
Blue Mountain College	MS	13,550	LC
Bluffton Univ	OH	37,864	C
Boise State Univ	ID	12,802	C
Boston Conservatory	MA	56,380	SP
Boston Univ	MA	54,130	HC+
Bowling Green State Univ	OH	18,970	C
Bradley Univ	IL	31,874	VC
Brenau Univ Women's College	GA	26,650	C+
Bridgewater State Univ	MA	18,752	C
Brigham Young Univ	UT	12,100	HC
Bucknell Univ	PA	58,160	MC
Buena Vista Univ	IA	37,954	C
Butler Univ	IN	45,898	VC+
Cairn Univ	PA	31,255	C
Calif Baptist Univ	CA	35,890	C
Cal State, Fresno	CA	17,405	C
Cal State, Fullerton	CA	25,188	C+
Cal State, San Bernardino	CA	12,000	C
Calvin College	MI	37,585	VC+
Cameron Univ	OK	9,267	LC
Campbellsville Univ	KY	27,720	C
Carnegie Mellon Univ	PA	51,260	MC
Carroll Univ	WI	24,860	C
Carson-Newman Univ	TN	29,058	C+
Carthage College	WI	33,000	C
Case Western Reserve Univ	OH	55,178	MC
Castleton State College	VT	19,424	C
Catawba College	NC	37,105	C
Cedarville Univ	OH	31,036	VC+
Centenary College of Louisiana	LA	39,070	C+
Central College	IA	36,980	VC
Central Conn State Univ	CT	19,212	C
Central Methodist Univ	MO	28,240	VC
Central Mich Univ	MI	18,066	C
Central State Univ	OH	9,010	C
Central Washington Univ	WA	11,730	C
Chapman Univ	CA	56,019	VC+
Charleston Southern Univ	SC	22,420	C
Chestnut Hill College	PA	39,785	LC
Chicago State Univ	IL	5,482	C
CUNY/Brooklyn College	NY	5,884	C+
Claflin Univ	SC	22,368	C+
Clarion Univ of Pennsylvania	PA	17,370	C
Clarke Univ	IA	36,400	C
Clearwater Christian College	FL	23,720	C
Cleveland Inst of Music	OH	56,882	SP
Coe College	IA	43,590	VC
Coker College	SC	32,256	LC
College of New Jersey	NJ	25,376	HC
College of the Ozarks	MO	5,605	VC
Colo Christian Univ	CO	27,500	VC
Colo State Univ-Fort Collins	CO	20,090	VC
Colo State Univ-Pueblo	CO	13,532	LC
Columbia College	SC	27,882	C
Columbus State Univ	GA	13,176	C
Concord Univ	WV	13,102	C
Concordia College New York	NY	31,500	VC
Concordia College, Moorhead	MN	39,974	C+
Concordia Univ Nebr	NE	26,000	VC
Concordia Univ St. Paul	MN	27,200	C
Concordia Univ, River Forest	IL	26,300	C
Converse College	SC	37,130	C
Corban Univ	OR	34,764	C
Cornell College	IA	44,930	HC
Cornerstone Univ and Grand Rapids Theological Seminary	MI	30,866	C
Culver-Stockton College	MO	30,900	C
Cumberland Univ	TN	21,220	C
Delaware State Univ	DE	14,700	LC
Delta State Univ	MS	12,292	LC
DePaul Univ	IL	46,120	VC
DePauw Univ	IN	48,950	VC+
Dickinson State Univ	ND	8,550	NC
Dordt College	IA	34,160	VC
Dowling College	NY	25,000	LC
Drake Univ	IA	30,980	VC+
Drury Univ	MO	30,319	VC
Duquesne Univ	PA	42,017	VC
East Carolina Univ	NC	14,169	C
East Central Univ	OK	10,223	LC
East Texas Baptist Univ	TX	29,135	C
Eastern Kentucky Univ	KY	11,161	C
Eastern Mich Univ	MI	17,961	C
Eastern Nazarene College	MA	30,000	C
Eastern New Mexico Univ	NM	10,682	C
Eastern Washington Univ	WA	16,388	C
Eastman School of Music	NY	58,802	SP
Edinboro Univ of Pennsylvania	PA	15,940	LC
Elizabethtown College	PA	47,600	VC
Elmhurst College	IL	42,032	C+
Elon Univ	NC	40,046	HC
Emporia State Univ	KS	12,897	C
Eureka College	IL	19,280	C
Evangel Univ	MO	23,090	C
Fairmont State Univ	WV	12,098	LC
Faulkner Univ	AL	22,530	LC
Fayetteville State Univ	NC	10,816	C
Fisk Univ	TN	19,830	C
Five Towns College	NY	34,550	SP
Florida A&M Univ	FL	14,935	LC
Florida Gulf Coast Univ	FL		C
Florida Southern College	FL	38,240	VC
Florida State Univ	FL	15,238	HC
Fort Hays State Univ	KS	11,354	C
Freed-Hardeman Univ	TN	19,697	VC
Fresno Pacific Univ	CA	32,136	C
Friends Univ	KS	29,100	C
Furman Univ	SC	54,006	HC
Gardner-Webb Univ	NC	34,375	C+
Geneva College	PA	27,280	C
George Fox Univ	OR	40,750	C+
Georgetown College	KY	38,690	C+
Georgia College and State Univ	GA	18,216	VC
Georgia Regents Univ	GA		C
Georgia Southern Univ	GA	16,414	C
Georgia Southwestern State Univ	GA	12,218	C
Gettysburg College	PA	56,820	HC
Glenville State College	WV	11,348	NC
Gonzaga Univ	WA	44,247	HC
Gordon College	MA	42,660	VC+
Goshen College	IN	35,900	VC
Grace College and Theological Seminary	IN	28,800	C
Graceland Univ	IA	28,020	C
Grand Canyon Univ	AZ	24,540	VC
Grand Valley State Univ	MI	17,998	VC
Grand View Univ	IA	31,050	C
Greensboro College	NC	28,740	LC
Greenville College	IL	27,012	C
Grove City College	PA	22,988	HC
Gustavus Adolphus College	MN	48,170	HC
Hamline Univ	MN	44,198	VC
Harding Univ	AR	21,432	C+
Hardin-Simmons Univ	TX	23,560	C+
Hartwick College	NY	49,815	C+
Hastings College	NE	27,782	C+
Heidelberg Univ	OH	34,100	C
Henderson State Univ	AR	13,634	C
Hillsdale College	MI	31,890	HC+
Hofstra Univ	NY	48,020	VC+
Hope College	MI	36,320	VC+
Houghton College	NY	35,740	VC
Houston Baptist Univ	TX	23,815	C+
Howard Univ	DC	35,957	C
Humboldt State Univ	CA	18,400	C
Hunter College / The CUNY	NY	14,429	VC
Huntingdon College	AL	31,850	C
Huntington Univ	IN	32,220	C
Idaho State Univ	ID	11,908	C
Illinois State Univ	IL	22,634	VC
Illinois Wesleyan Univ	IL	48,452	VC+
Immaculata Univ	PA	43,000	C
Indiana State Univ	IN	16,000	C
Indiana Univ Bloomington	IN	19,358	HC
Indiana Univ of Pennsylvania	PA	20,180	LC
Indiana Univ South Bend	IN	15,293	C
Indiana Univ-Purdue Univ Fort Wayne	IN	15,425	C
Indiana Wesleyan Univ	IN	31,815	VC
Inter-American Univ of PR/ Fajardo Campus	PR	4,200	
Inter-American Univ of PR/ Ponce	PR	3,700	
Inter-American Univ of PR/ San Germán	PR	6,720	
Iowa State Univ	IA	16,403	C
Iowa Wesleyan College	IA	30,850	LC
Ithaca College	NY	52,300	HC
Jackson State Univ	MS	13,512	LC
Jacksonville State Univ	AL	12,280	LC
Jacksonville Univ	FL	37,780	C
John Brown Univ	AR	30,996	VC+
Johnson State College	VT	16,721	C
Judson College	AL	24,690	LC
Judson Univ	IL	25,130	C
Kansas State Univ	KS	15,497	VC
Kansas Wesleyan Univ	KS	32,000	C
Kean Univ	NJ	22,060	LC
Keene State College	NH	21,538	C
Kennesaw State Univ	GA	13,017	VC
Kent State Univ	OH	19,352	C
Kentucky Christian Univ	KY	17,622	LC
Kentucky State Univ	KY	11,000	LC
Kentucky Wesleyan College	KY	27,440	VC+
King Univ	TN	33,140	C
La Sierra Univ	CA	35,694	VC
Lake Forest College	IL	45,580	VC
Lakeland College	WI	22,990	C
Lamar Univ	TX	6,820	LC
Lander Univ	SC	22,514	C+
Lawrence Univ	WI	46,371	HC
Lebanon Valley College	PA	38,570	C
Lee Univ	TN	18,690	C+
Lenoir-Rhyne College	NC	35,984	C
Limestone College	SC	29,880	C
Lincoln Univ	MO	11,996	NC
Lindenwood Univ	MO	20,750	C
Lindsey Wilson College	KY	30,470	VC
Linfield College-McMinnville Campus	OR	46,166	C
Lipscomb Univ	TN	35,722	VC
Livingstone College	NC	17,815	LC
LIU/Brooklyn Campus	NY	26,500	C
LIU/C.W. Post Campus	NY	38,888	C
Longwood Univ	VA	20,924	C
Louisiana College	LA	15,746	C
Louisiana State Univ	LA	18,677	VC+
Louisiana Tech Univ	LA	8,000	C
Loyola Univ New Orleans	LA	46,581	VC
Lubbock Christian Univ	TX	25,518	C
MacMurray College	IL	20,755	C
Madonna Univ	MI	24,540	VC
Malone Univ	OH	34,334	C
Mansfield Univ	PA	19,468	LC
Marian Univ	WI	30,980	LC
Marietta College	OH	42,135	VC
Mars Hill College	NC	22,950	LC
Marshall Univ	WV	14,820	C
Maryville College	TN	33,150	VC
Marywood Univ	PA	40,695	C

School	ST	$IS	SR
McKendree Univ	IL	29,920	₵
Mercer Univ	GA	44,201	V₵
Mercyhurst Univ	PA	40,700	C
Meredith College	NC	31,420	C
Messiah College	PA	39,540	VC
Methodist Univ	NC	37,185	C
Metropolitan State Univ of Denver	CO	4,835	LC
Miami Univ	OH	24,191	HC
Mich State Univ	MI	13,689	VC
MidAmerica Nazarene Univ	KS	28,000	C
Midland Univ	NE	34,000	C
Midwestern State Univ	TX	9,722	C
Millersville Univ of Pennsylvania	PA	18,498	C
Milligan College	TN	27,510	C
Millikin Univ	IL	37,462	C
Minn State Univ, Mankato	MN	14,900	C
Minn State Univ, Moorhead	MN	13,392	C
Minot State Univ	ND	10,915	C
Miss College	MS	21,998	VC
Miss Univ for Women	MS	7,400	LC
Miss Valley State Univ	MS	9,706	LC
Missouri Baptist Univ	MO	30,310	C
Missouri Southern State Univ	MO	11,910	C
Missouri Western State Univ	MO	12,260	NC
Monmouth Univ	NJ	42,252	C
Montana State Univ	MT	14,068	VC
Montana State Univ-Billings	MT	12,425	LC
Montclair State Univ	NJ	22,614	C
Moravian College	PA	36,381	VC
Morningside College	IA	32,620	C
Mount Mary Univ	WI	32,836	LC
Mount Vernon Nazarene Univ	OH	29,590	C
Murray State Univ	KY	14,944	C
Muskingum Univ	OH	30,502	C
Nazareth College of Rochester	NY	41,590	VC
Nebr Wesleyan Univ	NE	29,774	₵
New Jersey City Univ	NJ	21,060	₵
New Mexico State Univ	NM	13,955	LC
New York Univ	NY	61,470	MC
Newberry College	SC	26,850	LC
Nicholls State Univ	LA	7,095	C
Norfolk State Univ	VA	10,531	LC
N Car Agricultural and Technical State Univ	NC	13,175	LC
North Central College	IL	38,343	VC
N Dak State Univ	ND	14,642	C
North Georgia College & State Univ	GA	8,500	C
Northeastern Illinois Univ	IL		C
Northeastern State Univ	OK	8,615	VC
Northern Arizona Univ	AZ	18,592	C
Northern Illinois Univ	IL	19,768	C
Northern Mich Univ	MI	15,300	VC
Northern State Univ	SD	14,021	C
Northland College	WI	26,680	C
Northwest Missouri State Univ	MO	14,229	C
Northwest Nazarene Univ	ID	24,275	NC
Northwestern College	MN	24,000	C
Northwestern College of Iowa	IA	34,848	₵
Northwestern Okla State Univ	OK	7,275	NC
Northwestern State Univ of Louisiana	LA	14,368	C
Northwestern Univ	IL	37,595	MC
Notre Dame of Maryland Univ	MD	27,700	C
Nyack College	NY	32,000	C
Oakland City Univ	IN	24,500	NC
Oakland Univ	MI	19,391	VC
Oakwood Univ	AL	23,035	C
Oberlin College	OH	57,025	MC
Ohio Northern Univ	OH	42,075	VC
Ohio Univ	OH	20,676	VC
Ohio Wesleyan Univ	OH	49,460	₵
Okla Baptist Univ	OK	28,202	VC
Okla Christian Univ	OK	24,975	VC
Okla City Univ	OK	33,546	VC
Okla State Univ	OK	14,310	VC
Okla Wesleyan Univ	OK	21,300	C
Old Dominion Univ	VA	18,662	C
Olivet Nazarene Univ	IL	29,990	C
Oral Roberts Univ	OK	31,734	C
Otterbein College	OH	32,214	C
Ouachita Baptist Univ	AR	29,010	VC
Pacific Lutheran Univ	WA	44,840	VC
Palm Beach Atlantic Univ	FL	33,882	LC
Peru State College	NE	8,600	NC
Piedmont College	GA	29,260	C
Pittsburg State Univ	KS	12,032	C
Plymouth State Univ	NH	23,148	LC
Point Loma Nazarene Univ	CA	38,610	VC
Pontifical Catholic Univ of PR	PR	7,310	
Presbyterian College	SC	42,678	VC
Prescott College	AZ	33,284	₵
Providence College	RI	55,995	HC
Queens College / The CUNY	NY	17,107	VC
Quincy Univ	IL	34,980	LC
Rhode Island College	RI	17,132	LC

School	ST	$IS	SR
Rider Univ	NJ	45,720	C
Roberts Wesleyan College	NY	37,384	₵
Rocky Mountain College	MT	32,242	C
Roosevelt Univ	IL	22,605	VC
Rowan Univ	NJ	23,570	VC
Saginaw Valley State Univ	MI	16,869	C
St. Augustine's Univ	NC	14,000	C
St. Mary's Univ of Minn	MN	37,015	C
St. Xavier Univ	IL	32,840	C
San Diego State Univ	CA	20,578	VC
San Jose State Univ	CA	19,707	C
Schreiner Univ	TX	32,734	LC
Seattle Pacific Univ	WA	41,559	V₵
Seton Hill Univ	PA	35,172	C
Shenandoah Univ	VA	39,268	C
Shepherd Univ	WV	14,996	C
Shorter Univ	GA	26,470	C
Siena Heights Univ	MI	17,000	LC
Silver Lake College	WI	22,600	LC
Simpson College	IA	36,086	VC
Simpson Univ	CA	28,900	C
Slippery Rock Univ of Pennsylvania	PA	10,360	LC
S Car State Univ	SC	6,700	LC
S Dak State Univ	SD	14,296	C
Southeast Missouri State Univ	MO	14,983	LC
Southeastern Okla State Univ	OK	7,966	C
Southeastern Univ	FL	27,201	₵
Southern Adventist Univ	TN	26,190	C
Southern Arkansas Univ	AR	14,316	₵
Southern Illinois Univ Edwardsville	IL	17,532	C
Southern Methodist Univ	TX	57,755	MC
Southern Nazarene Univ	OK	24,354	NC
Southern Univ and A&M College	LA	9,761	₵
Southern Univ at New Orleans	LA	1,000	NC
Southern Wesleyan Univ	SC	25,600	C
Southwest Baptist Univ	MO	24,710	C
Southwest Minn State Univ	MN	14,000	C
Southwestern College	KS	29,270	C
Southwestern Okla State Univ	OK	9,160	C
Spring Arbor Univ	MI	26,740	C
St. Ambrose Univ	IA		C
St. Catherine Univ	MN	37,782	₵
St. Cloud State Univ	MN	10,600	C
St. Norbert College	WI	39,992	VC
St. Olaf College	MN	49,960	H₵
Sterling College	KS	27,216	C
Stetson Univ	FL	49,512	V₵
SUNY Fredonia / The SUNY at Fredonia	NY	18,702	VC
Susquehanna Univ	PA	49,170	C
Syracuse Univ	NY	54,512	HC
Tabor College	KS	29,010	LC
Talladega College	AL	13,000	C
Taylor Univ	IN	36,742	V₵
Temple Univ	PA	24,392	VC
Tenn Tech Univ	TN	11,310	C
Texas A&M Univ at Commerce	TX	10,496	C
Texas A&M Univ at Kingsville	TX	7,500	LC
Texas Christian Univ	TX	47,570	HC
The Catholic Univ of America	DC	52,852	VC
The College of St. Rose	NY	26,750	C
Ohio State Univ	OH	19,887	MC
The SUNY at Potsdam	NY	17,754	C
Toccoa Falls College	GA	23,210	C
Tougaloo College	MS	15,275	NC
Towson Univ	MD	16,000	VC
Trevecca Nazarene Univ	TN	30,118	C
Trinity Christian College	IL	28,869	C
Troy Univ	AL	10,650	C
Union College	NE	23,270	VC
Union Univ	TN	28,260	VC
Universidad Adventista de las Antillas	PR	7,360	
Univ of Akron	OH	20,436	C
Univ of Alabama at Tuscaloosa	AL	17,164	₵
Univ of Alaska Anchorage	AK	15,290	NC
Univ of Alaska Fairbanks	AK	13,955	C
Univ of Arizona	AZ	20,105	C
Univ of Arkansas at Fayetteville	AR	16,860	VC
Univ of Arkansas at Monticello	AR	8,470	NC
Univ of Arkansas at Pine Bluff	AR	10,600	C
Univ of Central Arkansas	AR	10,840	VC
Univ of Central Florida	FL	15,711	V₵
Univ of Central Missouri	MO	14,605	C
Univ of Central Okla	OK	12,293	C
Univ of Cincinnati	OH	20,199	VC
Univ of Colo Boulder	CO	22,605	V₵
Univ of Conn	CT	23,744	HC
Univ of Dayton	OH	43,750	VC
Univ of Delaware	DE	22,728	VC
Univ of Evansville	IN	41,056	V₵
Univ of Florida	FL	15,783	H₵
Univ of Georgia	GA	19,508	VC
Univ of Hartford	CT	42,674	C

School	ST	$IS	SR
Univ of Idaho	ID	14,558	C
Univ of Illinois at Urbana-Champaign	IL	24,300	HC
Univ of Indianapolis	IN	31,740	LC
Univ of Iowa	IA	17,481	VC
Univ of Kansas	KS	16,980	₵
Univ of Kentucky	KY	19,868	C
Univ of Louisiana at Lafayette	LA	6,130	C
Univ of Louisiana at Monroe	LA	12,998	C
Univ of Louisville	KY	17,460	VC
Univ of Maine	ME	19,712	₵
Univ of Mary	ND	16,714	C
Univ of Mary Hardin-Baylor	TX	31,950	₵
Univ of Maryland	MD	18,801	HC
Univ of Maryland/Eastern Shore	MD	14,000	C
Univ of Miami	FL	55,166	MC
Univ of Mich/Ann Arbor	MI	22,102	H₵
Univ of Mich-Flint	MI	17,547	₵
Univ of Minn/Duluth	MN	18,964	₵
Univ of Minn/Twin Cities	MN		HC
Univ of Missouri/Columbia	MO	18,201	MC
Univ of Missouri-Kansas City	MO	19,603	C
Univ of Missouri-St. Louis	MO	18,304	VC
Univ of Montana	MT	13,670	C
Univ of Montana-Western	MT	9,753	LC
Univ of Montevallo	AL	17,320	C
Univ of Mount Union	OH	35,130	C
Univ of Nebr - Lincoln	NE	17,507	VC
Univ of Nebr at Kearney	NE	14,855	LC
Univ of Nevada/Reno	NV	14,500	NC
Univ of New Hampshire	NH	24,702	VC
Univ of New Mexico	NM	15,300	C
Univ of New Orleans	LA	9,224	VC
Univ of North Alabama	AL	9,960	C
Univ of N Car at Charlotte	NC	15,847	C
Univ of N Car at Greensboro	NC	12,848	C
Univ of N Car at Wilmington	NC	13,572	V₵
Univ of N Dak	ND	14,094	C
Univ of North Florida	FL	15,578	VC
Univ of Northern Colo	CO	15,973	C
Univ of Northern Iowa	IA	14,776	C
Univ of Okla	OK	17,634	V₵
Univ of Oregon	OR	20,872	VC
Univ of Puget Sound	WA	52,648	H₵
Univ of Redlands	CA	40,500	VC
Univ of Rio Grande	OH	8,750	NC
Univ of Rochester	NY	58,500	MC
Univ of Sioux Falls	SD	22,990	C
Univ of S Car at Aiken	SC	16,278	C
Univ of S Car at Columbia	SC	19,725	V₵
Univ of S Dak	SD	15,111	C
Univ of South Florida	FL	13,000	C
Univ of Southern Maine	ME	16,576	C
Univ of Southern Miss	MS	13,170	C
Univ of St. Thomas - Houston	TX	36,490	VC
Univ of Tampa	FL	35,160	VC
Univ of Tenn at Chattanooga	TN	16,883	C
Univ of the Cumberlands	KY	27,500	LC
Univ of the Incarnate Word	TX	35,200	LC
Univ of the Pacific	CA	52,146	VC
Univ of Toledo	OH	18,464	C
Univ of Tulsa	OK	45,311	H₵
Univ of Vermont	VT	26,120	V₵
Univ of Washington	WA	14,722	VC
Univ of West Florida	FL	14,656	C
Univ of West Georgia	GA	14,852	LC
Univ of Wisc Whitewater	WI	13,314	C
Univ of Wisc/Green Bay	WI	14,900	C
Univ of Wisc/Madison	WI	18,757	HC
Univ of Wisc/Oshkosh	WI	10,426	LC
Univ of Wisc/Platteville	WI	14,274	C
Univ of Wisc/River Falls	WI	9,722	LC
Univ of Wisc/Stevens Point	WI	14,043	C
Univ of Wisc/Superior	WI	14,106	C
Univ of Wisc-Milwaukee	WI	18,436	C
Univ of Wyoming	WY	13,855	₵
Utah State Univ	UT	11,803	C
Valparaiso Univ	IN	43,040	V₵
VanderCook College of Music	IL	26,360	SP
Virginia Union Univ	VA	18,432	C
Viterbo Univ	WI	30,070	C
Walla Walla Univ	WA	26,256	NC
Warner Pacific College	OR	25,550	C
Warner Univ	FL	18,000	C
Wartburg College	IA	41,055	VC
Washburn Univ	KS	12,165	NC
Washington Adventist Univ	MD	25,859	₵
Wayland Baptist Univ	TX	16,058	LC
Wayne State College	NE	11,764	NC
Webster Univ	MO	33,990	₵
West Chester Univ of Pennsylvania	PA	16,836	C
West Liberty Univ	WV	9,142	LC
West Texas A&M Univ	TX	13,478	C
West Virginia Wesleyan College	WV	26,880	C
Western Carolina Univ	NC	13,965	₵
Western Conn State Univ	CT	18,327	C
Western Mich Univ	MI	19,042	C

School	ST	$IS	SR
Western State Colo Univ	CO	16,135	C
Western Washington Univ	WA	18,519	VC
Westminster Choir College	NJ	36,000	SP
Westminster College	PA	31,290	₵
Westmont College	CA	41,500	HC
Wheaton College	IL	39,650	H₵
Whitworth Univ	WA	45,826	V₵
Wichita State Univ	KS	12,539	C
Wiley College	TX		LC
Willamette Univ	OR	56,450	V₵
William Carey Univ	MS	13,500	LC
William Jewell College	MO	31,000	V₵
William Paterson Univ of New Jersey	NJ	21,694	C
Wingate Univ	NC	34,990	C
Winona State Univ	MN	16,530	C
Winston-Salem State Univ	NC	9,418	LC
Winthrop Univ	SC	21,120	VC
Wittenberg Univ	OH	47,766	VC
Wright State Univ	OH	16,983	C
Xavier Univ	OH	43,740	VC
Xavier Univ of Louisiana	LA	25,300	C
York College	NE	19,475	C
York College of Pennsylvania	PA	26,590	C
Youngstown State Univ	OH	16,374	LC

MUSIC HISTORY AND APPRECIATION

School	ST	$IS	SR
Aquinas College	MI	33,060	C
Baldwin Wallace Univ	OH	36,980	VC
Baylor Univ	TX	46,720	HC
Boston Univ	MA	54,130	H₵
Bowling Green State Univ	OH	18,970	C
Bucknell Univ	PA	58,160	MC
Cal State, San Bernardino	CA	12,000	C
Calvin College	MI	37,585	V₵
Central Mich Univ	MI	18,066	C
Florida State Univ	FL	15,238	HC
Hardin-Simmons Univ	TX	23,560	₵
Hofstra Univ	NY	48,020	V₵
Howard Univ	DC	35,957	C
Johnson State College	VT	16,721	C
McKendree Univ	IL	29,920	₵
Nazareth College of Rochester	NY	41,590	VC
New England Conservatory of Music	MA	52,550	SP
Oberlin College	OH	57,025	MC
Ohio Univ	OH	20,676	VC
Rice Univ	TX	43,288	MC
Roosevelt Univ	IL	22,605	VC
Southern Illinois Univ Edwardsville	IL	17,532	C
Suffolk Univ	MA	46,548	C
Syracuse Univ	NY	54,512	HC
Temple Univ	PA	24,392	VC
The Catholic Univ of America	DC	52,852	VC
Ohio State Univ	OH	19,887	MC
Univ of Akron	OH	20,436	C
Univ of Calif at Los Angeles	CA	25,686	MC
Univ of Calif at San Diego	CA	21,000	VC
Univ of Cincinnati	OH	20,199	VC
Univ of Hartford	CT	42,674	C
Univ of Idaho	ID	14,558	C
Univ of Illinois at Urbana-Champaign	IL	24,300	HC
Univ of Kansas	KS	16,980	₵
Univ of Mich/Ann Arbor	MI	22,102	H₵
Univ of Mich/Dearborn	MI	9,885	VC
Univ of North Texas	TX	15,628	C
Univ of the Pacific	CA	52,146	VC
Univ of Washington	WA	14,722	VC
Vanderbilt Univ	TN	57,072	MC
West Chester Univ of Pennsylvania	PA	16,836	C
Western Washington Univ	WA	18,519	VC
Wright State Univ	OH	16,983	C
Youngstown State Univ	OH	16,374	LC

MUSIC INDUSTRY

School	ST	$IS	SR
Cal State, Chico	CA	18,952	C
Drexel Univ	PA	51,920	HC
Ferris State Univ	MI	19,698	C
Mercy College	NY	29,996	C
St. Mary's Univ of Minn	MN	37,015	C
The College of St. Rose	NY	26,750	C

MUSIC PERFORMANCE

School	ST	$IS	SR
Adams State College	CO	13,358	LC
Adrian College	MI	33,800	C
Anderson Univ	IN	35,390	C
Andrews Univ	MI	28,030	₵
Anna Maria College	MA	34,600	LC
Appalachian State Univ	NC	12,919	VC
Aquinas College	MI	33,060	C
Arizona State Univ	AZ	18,818	₵
Arkansas State Univ	AR	14,980	C
Augustana College	IL	43,398	HC
Averett Univ	VA	36,000	LC
Baldwin Wallace Univ	OH	36,980	VC
Barry Univ	FL	38,190	C

School	ST	$IS	SR
Baylor Univ	TX	46,720	HC
Belmont Univ	TN	37,380	VC+
Bennington College	VT	56,990	HC+
Berklee College of Music	MA	47,100	SP
Bethel College	IN	31,560	C
Bethel Univ	MN	34,940	VC
Binghamton Univ / The SUNY	NY	20,832	HC+
Biola Univ	CA	40,320	VC
Blackburn College	IL	21,350	C
Boston Conservatory	MA	56,380	SP
Boston Univ	MA	54,130	HC+
Bowling Green State Univ	OH	18,970	C
Bradley Univ	IL	31,874	VC
Brenau Univ Women's College	GA	26,650	C+
Brigham Young Univ	UT	12,100	HC
Bucknell Univ	PA	58,160	MC
Butler Univ	IN	45,898	VC+
Cairn Univ	PA	31,255	C
Calif Baptist Univ	CA	35,890	C
Calif Inst of the Arts	CA	46,368	SP
Calif Lutheran Univ	CA	47,640	C
Cal State, Fresno	CA	17,405	C
Cal State, Fullerton	CA	25,188	C+
Cal State, Los Angeles	CA	15,829	C
Cal State, San Bernardino	CA	12,000	C
Cal State, Stanislaus	CA	18,582	C
Calvin College	MI	37,585	VC+
Campbellsville Univ	KY	27,720	C
Canisius College	NY	45,602	VC
Centenary College of Louisiana	LA	39,070	C+
Central Mich Univ	MI	18,066	C
Chapman Univ	CA	56,019	VC+
CUNY/Brooklyn College	NY	5,884	C+
Clayton State Univ	GA	12,000	LC
Colo State Univ-Fort Collins	CO	20,090	VC
Colo State Univ-Pueblo	CO	13,532	LC
Columbia College	SC	27,882	C
Columbus State Univ	GA	13,176	C
Concordia College, Moorhead	MN	39,974	C+
Corban Univ	OR	34,764	C
Cornerstone Univ and Grand Rapids Theological Seminary	MI	30,866	C
Covenant College	GA		VC+
Dallas Baptist Univ	TX	29,118	C
DePaul Univ	IL	46,120	VC
DePauw Univ	IN	48,950	VC+
Dillard Univ	LA	20,940	VC
Dordt College	IA	34,160	VC
Drake Univ	IA	30,980	VC+
Duquesne Univ	PA	42,017	VC
East Carolina Univ	NC	14,169	C
East Texas Baptist Univ	TX	29,135	C
Eastern Mich Univ	MI	17,961	C
Eastern Nazarene College	MA	30,000	C
Eastern Washington Univ	WA	16,388	C
Eastman School of Music	NY	58,802	SP
Elon Univ	NC	40,046	HC
Emory and Henry College	VA	387,460	C
Evangel Univ	MO	23,090	C
Five Towns College	NY	34,550	SP
Florida Southern College	FL	38,240	VC
Florida State Univ	FL	15,238	HC
Fort Hays State Univ	KS	11,354	C
Friends Univ	KS	29,100	C
Furman Univ	SC	54,006	HC
George Washington Univ	DC	57,108	MC
Georgia Southern Univ	GA	16,414	C
Gordon College	MA	42,660	VC+
Grand Canyon Univ	AZ	24,540	VC
Grove City College	PA	22,998	HC
Hamline Univ	MN	44,198	VC
Hannibal-LaGrange Univ	MO	24,490	C
Hardin-Simmons Univ	TX	23,560	C+
Hofstra Univ	NY	48,020	VC+
Houghton College	NY	35,740	VC
Houston Baptist Univ	TX	23,815	C+
Huntington Univ	IN	32,220	C
Idaho State Univ	ID	11,908	C
Illinois State Univ	IL	22,634	VC
Illinois Wesleyan Univ	IL	48,452	VC+
Indiana Univ Bloomington	IN	19,358	HC
Indiana Univ of Pennsylvania	PA	20,180	LC
Indiana Univ Southeast	IN	15,807	LC
Indiana Univ-Purdue Univ Fort Wayne	IN	15,425	C
Inter-American Univ of PR/ Metropolitan Campus	PR	4,320	
Ithaca College	NY	52,300	HC
Jacksonville Univ	FL	37,780	C
Johnson State College	VT	16,721	C
Kean Univ	NJ	22,060	LC
Keene State College	NH	21,538	C
Kennesaw State Univ	GA	13,017	VC
Kentucky Christian Univ	KY	17,622	LC
Kentucky State Univ	KY	11,000	LC
La Sierra Univ	CA	35,694	VC
Lawrence Univ	WI	46,371	HC
Lee Univ	TN	18,690	C+
Lenoir-Rhyne College	NC	35,984	C
Lipscomb Univ	TN	35,722	VC
Louisiana Tech Univ	LA	8,000	C
Loyola Univ New Orleans	LA	46,581	VC
Lynn Univ	FL	43,500	C
Manhattan School of Music	NY	55,850	SP
Mannes College New School for Music	NY	44,500	C
Mansfield Univ	PA	19,468	LC
Mars Hill College	NC	22,950	LC
Marshall Univ	WV	14,820	C
Maryville College	TN	33,150	VC
Marywood Univ	PA	40,695	C
Meredith College	NC	31,420	C
Messiah College	PA	39,540	VC
Methodist Univ	NC	37,185	C
Metropolitan State Univ of Denver	CO	4,835	LC
Miami Univ	OH	24,191	HC
Mich State Univ	MI	13,689	VC
MidAmerica Nazarene Univ	KS	28,000	C
Millikin Univ	IL	37,462	C
Missouri Baptist Univ	MO	30,310	C
Montana State Univ-Billings	MT	12,425	LC
Montclair State Univ	NJ	22,614	C
Montreat College	NC	31,298	VC
Nazareth College of Rochester	NY	41,590	VC
New England Conservatory of Music	MA	52,550	SP
New Mexico State Univ	NM	13,955	LC
New York Univ	NY	61,470	MC
Newberry College	SC	26,850	LC
Northern Arizona Univ	AZ	18,592	C
Northwestern College	MN	24,000	C
Northwestern Univ	IL	37,595	MC
Nyack College	NY	32,000	C
Oakwood Univ	AL	23,035	C
Oberlin College	OH	57,025	MC
Ohio Northern Univ	OH	42,075	VC
Ohio Univ	OH	20,676	VC
Old Dominion Univ	VA	18,662	C
Olivet Nazarene Univ	IL	29,990	C
Oral Roberts Univ	OK	31,734	C
Otterbein College	OH	32,214	C
Pacific Lutheran Univ	WA	44,840	VC
Palm Beach Atlantic Univ	FL	33,882	LC
Penn State Univ/Univ Park	PA	25,404	VC
Pittsburg State Univ	KS	12,032	C
Point Loma Nazarene Univ	CA	38,610	VC
Queens College / The CUNY	NY	17,107	VC
Rhode Island College	RI	17,132	LC
Rice Univ	TX	43,288	MC
Roberts Wesleyan College	NY	37,384	C+
Rockford College	IL	31,000	C
Rocky Mountain College	MT	32,242	C
Rollins College	FL	52,370	HC
Roosevelt Univ	IL	22,605	VC
St. Mary's Univ of Minn	MN	37,015	C
St. Vincent College	PA	40,244	C
Sam Houston State Univ	TX	17,082	C
Samford Univ	AL	35,700	VC+
San Diego State Univ	CA	20,578	VC
Santa Fe Univ of Art and Design	NM	39,666	SP
Shenandoah Univ	VA	39,268	C
Simpson College	IA	36,086	VC
Southern Illinois Univ Edwardsville	IL	17,532	C
Southern Methodist Univ	TX	57,755	MC
Southern Nazarene Univ	OK	24,354	NC
Southern Oregon Univ	OR	17,874	C
Southwestern College	KS	29,270	C
St. Olaf College	MN	49,960	HC+
Stetson Univ	FL	49,512	VC+
SUNY Fredonia / The SUNY at Fredonia	NY	18,702	VC
Susquehanna Univ	PA	49,170	C
Syracuse Univ	NY	54,512	HC
Talladega College	AL	13,000	C
Taylor Univ	IN	36,742	VC+
Temple Univ	PA	24,392	VC
Texas State Univ	TX	16,495	VC
Texas Tech Univ	TX	14,243	C
The Catholic Univ of America	DC	52,852	VC
Ohio State Univ	OH	19,887	MC
The SUNY at Potsdam	NY	17,754	C
Toccoa Falls College	GA	23,210	C
Tougaloo College	MS	15,275	NC
Trinity Christian College	IL	28,869	C
Truman State Univ	MO	13,546	HC
Union College	NE	23,270	VC
Union Univ	TN	28,260	VC
Univ of Akron	OH	20,436	C
Univ of Alaska Anchorage	AK	15,290	NC
Univ of Alaska Fairbanks	AK	13,955	C
Univ of Calif at Irvine	CA	25,961	VC
Univ of Calif at Santa Barbara	CA	27,551	HC
Univ of Central Florida	FL	15,711	VC+
Univ of Colo Boulder	CO	22,605	VC+
Univ of Dayton	OH	43,750	VC
Univ of Denver	CO	51,787	VC+
Univ of Evansville	IN	41,056	VC+
Univ of Georgia	GA	19,508	VC
Univ of Hartford	CT	42,674	C
Univ of Idaho	ID	14,558	C
Univ of Illinois at Chicago	IL	24,293	VC
Univ of Illinois at Urbana-Champaign	IL	24,300	HC
Univ of Indianapolis	IN	31,740	LC
Univ of Kansas	KS	16,980	C+
Univ of Kentucky	KY	19,868	C
Univ of Maine	ME	19,712	C+
Univ of Mary Hardin-Baylor	TX	31,950	C+
Univ of Maryland	MD	18,801	HC
Univ of Mass Amherst	MA	23,697	VC+
Univ of Mass Lowell	MA	19,316	C
Univ of Miami	FL	55,166	MC
Univ of Mich/Ann Arbor	MI	22,102	HC+
Univ of Minn/Duluth	MN	18,964	C+
Univ of Missouri-Kansas City	MO	19,603	C
Univ of Mobile	AL	27,870	VC
Univ of Montana	MT	13,670	C
Univ of Montevallo	AL	17,320	C
Univ of Mount Union	OH	35,130	C
Univ of New Hampshire	NH	24,702	VC
Univ of New Haven	CT	47,740	C
Univ of N Car at Chapel Hill	NC	18,348	MC
Univ of N Car at Charlotte	NC	15,847	C
Univ of N Car at Greensboro	NC	12,848	C
Univ of N Car at Wilmington	NC	13,572	VC+
Univ of N Dak	ND	14,094	C
Univ of North Florida	FL	15,578	VC
Univ of North Texas	TX	15,628	C
Univ of Northern Iowa	IA	14,776	C
Univ of Oregon	OR	20,872	VC
Univ of Puget Sound	WA	52,648	HC+
Univ of Rochester	NY	58,500	MC
Univ of S Car Upstate	SC	17,673	LC
Univ of S Dak	SD	15,111	C
Univ of Southern Calif	CA	56,903	MC
Univ of Southern Maine	ME	16,576	C
Univ of Tampa	FL	35,160	VC
Univ of the Arts	PA	38,450	SP
Univ of the Pacific	CA	52,146	VC
Univ of Tulsa	OK	45,311	HC+
Univ of Washington	WA	14,722	VC
Univ of West Georgia	GA	14,852	LC
Univ of Wisc/Madison	WI	18,757	HC
Univ of Wisc/Superior	WI	14,106	C
Univ of Wyoming	WY	13,855	C+
Valparaiso Univ	IN	43,040	VC+
Vanderbilt Univ	TN	57,072	MC
Virginia State Univ	VA	11,318	C+
Viterbo Univ	WI	30,070	C
Walla Walla Univ	WA	26,256	NC
Wartburg College	IA	41,055	VC
Washburn Univ	KS	12,165	NC
Washington Adventist Univ	MD	25,859	C+
Washington State Univ	WA	20,461	C
Webster Univ	MO	33,990	C+
West Chester Univ of Pennsylvania	PA	16,836	C
Western Conn State Univ	CT	18,327	C
Western Mich Univ	MI	19,042	C
Westminster College	PA	31,290	C+
Wiley College	TX		LC
Willamette Univ	OR	56,450	VC+
William Carey Univ	MS	13,500	LC
Winona State Univ	MN	16,530	C
Winthrop Univ	SC	21,120	VC
Xavier Univ of Louisiana	LA	25,300	C
York College	NE	19,475	C
Youngstown State Univ	OH	16,374	LC

MUSIC PRODUCTION/ RECORDING TECHNOLOGY

School	ST	$IS	SR
Shenandoah Univ	VA	39,268	C
Univ of Denver	CO	51,787	VC+

MUSIC TECHNOLOGY

School	ST	$IS	SR
Bellarmine Univ	KY	42,950	VC
Berklee College of Music	MA	47,100	SP
Brigham Young Univ	UT	12,100	HC
Cal State, San Bernardino	CA	12,000	C
Cogswell Polytechnical College	CA	30,531	C
Conn College	CT	54,970	MC
Duquesne Univ	PA	42,017	VC
Elon Univ	NC	40,046	HC
Indiana Univ Southeast	IN	15,807	LC
Indiana Univ-Purdue Univ Indianapolis	IN	17,290	C
Keene State College	NH	21,538	C
Malone Univ	OH	34,334	C
Mercy College	NY	29,996	C
Minn State Univ, Moorhead	MN	13,392	C
New York Univ	NY	61,470	MC
Northeastern Univ	MA	55,296	MC
Northwestern Univ	IL	37,595	MC
Santa Fe Univ of Art and Design	NM	39,666	SP
Shenandoah Univ	VA	39,268	C
Stevens Inst of Technology	NJ	50,130	HC
Univ of Calif at San Diego	CA	21,000	VC
Univ of Hartford	CT	42,674	C
Univ of Miami	FL	55,166	MC

School	ST	$IS	SR
Univ of Mich/Ann Arbor	MI	22,102	HC+
Univ of New Haven	CT	47,740	C
Univ of N Car at Asheville	NC	13,500	VC+
Univ of St. Francis	IN	29,810	C
York College of Pennsylvania	PA	26,590	C

MUSIC THEATRE ACCOMPANYING

School	ST	$IS	SR
Indiana Univ Bloomington	IN	19,358	HC
Shenandoah Univ	VA	39,268	C

MUSIC THEORY AND COMPOSITION

School	ST	$IS	SR
Adams State College	CO	13,358	LC
Aquinas College	MI	33,060	C
Arizona State Univ	AZ	18,818	C+
Baldwin Wallace Univ	OH	36,980	VC
Baylor Univ	TX	46,720	HC
Belmont Univ	TN	37,380	VC+
Bennington College	VT	56,990	HC+
Berklee College of Music	MA	47,100	SP
Biola Univ	CA	40,320	VC
Boston Conservatory	MA	56,380	SP
Boston Univ	MA	54,130	HC+
Bowling Green State Univ	OH	18,970	C
Bradley Univ	IL	31,874	VC
Brigham Young Univ	UT	12,100	HC
Bucknell Univ	PA	58,160	MC
Butler Univ	IN	45,898	VC+
Calif Baptist Univ	CA	35,890	C
Calif Inst of the Arts	CA	46,368	SP
Calvin College	MI	37,585	VC+
Central Mich Univ	MI	18,066	C
Central Washington Univ	WA	11,730	C
Chapman Univ	CA	56,019	VC+
CUNY/Brooklyn College	NY	5,884	C+
Clayton State Univ	GA	12,000	LC
Colo State Univ-Fort Collins	CO	20,090	VC
Colo State Univ-Pueblo	CO	13,532	LC
Concordia College, Moorhead	MN	39,974	C+
DePaul Univ	IL	46,120	VC
DePauw Univ	IN	48,950	VC+
Dordt College	IA	34,160	VC
East Carolina Univ	NC	14,169	C
Eastman School of Music	NY	58,802	SP
Elmhurst College	IL	42,032	C+
Emory and Henry College	VA	387,460	C
Five Towns College	NY	34,550	SP
Florida State Univ	FL	15,238	HC
Fordham Univ	NY	58,927	HC
Fort Hays State Univ	KS	11,354	C
Furman Univ	SC	54,006	HC
Hardin-Simmons Univ	TX	23,560	C+
Hofstra Univ	NY	48,020	VC+
Houghton College	NY	35,740	VC
Houston Baptist Univ	TX	23,815	C+
Huntington Univ	IN	32,220	C
Illinois Wesleyan Univ	IL	48,452	VC+
Indiana Wesleyan Univ	IN	31,815	VC
Ithaca College	NY	52,300	HC
Jacksonville Univ	FL	37,780	C
Lawrence Univ	WI	46,371	HC
Lehigh Univ	PA	55,080	MC
Loyola Univ New Orleans	LA	46,581	VC
Manhattan School of Music	NY	55,850	SP
Mannes College New School for Music	NY	44,500	C
Marshall Univ	WV	14,820	C
Mich State Univ	MI	13,689	VC
Miss College	MS	21,998	VC
Montclair State Univ	NJ	22,614	C
Nazareth College of Rochester	NY	41,590	VC
New England Conservatory of Music	MA	52,550	SP
New York Univ	NY	61,470	MC
Newberry College	SC	26,850	LC
North Park Univ	IL	30,130	C
Northwestern College	MN	24,000	C
Northwestern Univ	IL	37,595	MC
Nyack College	NY	32,000	C
Oberlin College	OH	57,025	MC
Ohio Northern Univ	OH	42,075	VC
Ohio Univ	OH	20,676	VC
Old Dominion Univ	VA	18,662	C
Olivet Nazarene Univ	IL	29,990	C
Oral Roberts Univ	OK	31,734	C
Pacific Lutheran Univ	WA	44,840	VC
Palm Beach Atlantic Univ	FL	33,882	LC
Point Loma Nazarene Univ	CA	38,610	VC
Rice Univ	TX	43,288	MC
Roosevelt Univ	IL	22,605	VC
Sam Houston State Univ	TX	17,082	C
Samford Univ	AL	35,700	VC+
Santa Fe Univ of Art and Design	NM	39,666	SP
Shenandoah Univ	VA	39,268	C
Southern Illinois Univ Edwardsville	IL	17,532	C
Southern Methodist Univ	TX	57,755	MC
St. Olaf College	MN	49,960	HC+
Stetson Univ	FL	49,512	VC+

School	ST	$IS	SR
SUNY Fredonia / The SUNY at Fredonia	NY	18,702	VC
Syracuse Univ	NY	54,512	HC
Taylor Univ	IN	36,742	VC+
Temple Univ	PA	24,392	VC
Texas Christian Univ	TX	47,570	HC
Texas Tech Univ	TX	14,243	C
The Catholic Univ of America	DC	52,852	VC
The College of Idaho	ID	31,277	VC
Ohio State Univ	OH	19,887	MC
The SUNY at Potsdam	NY	17,754	C
Union Univ	TN	28,260	VC
Univ of Akron	OH	20,436	C
Univ of Calif at Santa Barbara	CA	27,551	HC
Univ of Cincinnati	OH	20,199	VC
Univ of Dayton	OH	43,750	VC
Univ of Delaware	DE	22,728	VC
Univ of Georgia	GA	19,508	VC
Univ of Hartford	CT	42,674	C
Univ of Idaho	ID	14,558	C
Univ of Illinois at Urbana-Champaign	IL	24,300	HC
Univ of Kansas	KS	16,980	C+
Univ of Maryland	MD	18,801	HC
Univ of Mich/Ann Arbor	MI	22,102	HC+
Univ of Missouri-Kansas City	MO	19,603	C
Univ of New Hampshire	NH	24,702	VC
Univ of New Haven	CT	47,740	C
Univ of N Car at Greensboro	NC	12,848	C
Univ of North Texas	TX	15,628	C
Univ of Northern Iowa	IA	14,776	C
Univ of Oregon	OR	20,872	VC
Univ of Rochester	NY	58,500	MC
Univ of Texas at Austin	TX	44,074	HC
Univ of the Arts	PA	38,450	SP
Univ of the Pacific	CA	52,146	VC
Univ of Wyoming	WY	13,855	C+
Valparaiso Univ	IN	43,040	VC+
Vanderbilt Univ	TN	57,072	MC
Wartburg College	IA	41,055	VC
Washington State Univ	WA	20,461	C
Washington Univ in St. Louis	MO	58,818	MC
Webster Univ	MO	33,990	C+
West Chester Univ of Pennsylvania	PA	16,836	C
West Texas A&M Univ	TX	13,478	C
Western Mich Univ	MI	19,042	C
Westminster Choir College	NJ	36,000	SP
Westminster College	PA	31,290	C+
Willamette Univ	OR	56,450	VC+
Wright State Univ	OH	16,983	C
Youngstown State Univ	OH	16,374	LC

MUSIC THERAPY

School	ST	$IS	SR
Alverno College	WI	30,483	LC
Anna Maria College	MA	34,600	LC
Appalachian State Univ	NC	12,919	VC
Arizona State Univ	AZ	18,818	C+
Augsburg College	MN	35,142	C
Baldwin Wallace Univ	OH	36,980	VC
Berklee College of Music	MA	47,100	SP
Charleston Southern Univ	SC	22,420	C
Drury Univ	MO	30,319	VC
Duquesne Univ	PA	42,017	VC
East Carolina Univ	NC	14,169	C
Eastern Mich Univ	MI	17,961	C
Elizabethtown College	PA	47,600	VC
Florida State Univ	FL	15,238	HC
Georgia College and State Univ	GA	18,216	VC
Howard Univ	DC	35,957	C
Immaculata Univ	PA	43,000	C
Indiana Univ-Purdue Univ Fort Wayne	IN	15,425	C
Louisiana College	LA	15,746	C
Loyola Univ New Orleans	LA	46,581	VC
Marylhurst Univ	OR	18,945	NC
Maryville Univ of St. Louis	MO	34,920	VC
Marywood Univ	PA	40,695	C
Mich State Univ	MI	13,689	VC
Molloy College	NY	38,950	C
Montclair State Univ	NJ	22,614	C
Nazareth College of Rochester	NY	41,590	VC
New York Univ	NY	61,470	MC
Queens Univ of Charlotte	NC	39,543	VC
St. Mary-of-the-Woods College	IN	37,722	LC
Sam Houston State Univ	TX	17,082	C
Seton Hill Univ	PA	35,172	C
Shenandoah Univ	VA	39,268	C
Southern Methodist Univ	TX	57,755	MC
Southwestern Okla State Univ	OK	9,160	C
SUNY Fredonia / The SUNY at Fredonia	NY	18,702	VC
SUNY New Paltz	NY	15,010	C
Temple Univ	PA	24,392	VC
Texas Woman's Univ	TX	13,633	LC
Univ of Alabama at Tuscaloosa	AL	17,164	C+
Univ of Dayton	OH	43,750	VC
Univ of Evansville	IN	41,056	VC+
Univ of Georgia	GA	19,508	VC
Univ of Iowa	IA	17,481	VC
Univ of Kansas	KS	16,980	C+
Univ of Louisville	KY	17,460	VC
Univ of Miami	FL	55,166	MC
Univ of Minn/Twin Cities	MN		HC
Univ of Missouri-Kansas City	MO	19,603	C
Univ of N Dak	ND	14,094	C
Univ of the Incarnate Word	TX	35,200	LC
Univ of the Pacific	CA	52,146	VC
Univ of Wisc/Oshkosh	WI	10,426	LC
Utah State Univ	UT	11,803	C
Wartburg College	IA	41,055	VC
West Texas A&M Univ	TX	13,478	C
Western Mich Univ	MI	19,042	C
William Carey Univ	MS	13,500	LC

MUSICAL THEATER

School	ST	$IS	SR
Adrian College	MI	33,800	C
American Univ	DC	54,829	HC+
Aquinas College	MI	33,060	C
Ashland Univ	OH	25,000	C
Baldwin Wallace Univ	OH	36,980	VC
Belmont Univ	TN	37,380	VC+
Birmingham-Southern College	AL	42,370	VC+
Blackburn College	IL	21,350	C
Boston Conservatory	MA	56,380	SP
Brenau Univ Women's College	GA	26,650	C+
Brigham Young Univ	UT	12,100	HC
Cal State, Chico	CA	18,952	C
Catawba College	NC	37,105	C
Central Mich Univ	MI	18,066	C
Clarke Univ	IA	36,400	C
Coastal Carolina Univ	SC	17,620	C
Coker College	SC	32,256	LC
College of the Ozarks	MO	5,605	VC
Cornerstone Univ and Grand Rapids Theological Seminary	MI	30,866	C
Creighton Univ	NE	44,058	VC+
Culver-Stockton College	MO	30,900	C
Elon Univ	NC	40,046	HC
Emerson College	MA	50,246	HC
Faulkner Univ	AL	22,530	LC
Florida Southern College	FL	38,240	VC
Florida State Univ	FL	15,238	HC
Friends Univ	KS	29,100	C
Howard Univ	DC	35,957	C
Illinois Wesleyan Univ	IL	48,452	VC+
Indiana Univ Bloomington	IN	19,358	HC
Ithaca College	NY	52,300	HC
Kutztown Univ of Pennsylvania	PA	16,909	LC
Lees-McRae College	NC	33,624	C
Limestone College	SC	29,880	C
Lipscomb Univ	TN	35,722	VC
Mars Hill College	NC	22,950	LC
Marywood Univ	PA	40,695	C
Mercyhurst Univ	PA	40,700	C
Meredith College	NC	31,420	C
Messiah College	PA	39,540	VC
Millikin Univ	IL	37,462	C
Missouri Baptist Univ	MO	30,310	C
Missouri State Univ	MO	13,996	VC
Montclair State Univ	NJ	22,614	C
Nazareth College of Rochester	NY	41,590	VC
Northwestern State Univ of Louisiana	LA	14,368	C
Oswego / SUNY	NY	20,009	VC
Otterbein College	OH	32,214	C
Ouachita Baptist Univ	AR	29,010	VC
Pace Univ	NY	48,094	VC
Palm Beach Atlantic Univ	FL	33,882	LC
Piedmont College	GA	29,260	C
Roosevelt Univ	IL	22,605	VC
Russell Sage College	NY	39,370	C
Sam Houston State Univ	TX	17,082	C
Samford Univ	AL	35,700	VC+
Santa Fe Univ of Art and Design	NM	39,666	SP
Seton Hill Univ	PA	35,172	C
Shenandoah Univ	VA	39,268	C
Shorter Univ	GA	26,470	C
Southern Illinois Univ Edwardsville	IL	17,532	C
St. Catherine Univ	MN	37,782	C+
SUNY College at Geneseo	NY	18,055	HC+
SUNY Cortland / The SUNY	NY	19,117	C
SUNY Fredonia / The SUNY at Fredonia	NY	18,702	VC
Sweet Briar College	VA	43,765	C+
Syracuse Univ	NY	54,512	HC
Texas Christian Univ	TX	47,570	HC
Texas State Univ	TX	16,495	VC
The Catholic Univ of America	DC	52,852	VC
Univ at Buffalo / The SUNY	NY	20,283	VC
Univ of Akron	OH	20,436	C
Univ of Arizona	AZ	20,105	C
Univ of Calif at Irvine	CA	25,961	VC
Univ of Hartford	CT	42,674	C
Univ of Idaho	ID	14,558	C
Univ of Indianapolis	IN	31,740	LC
Univ of Miami	FL	55,166	MC
Univ of Mich/Ann Arbor	MI	22,102	HC+
Univ of N Dak	ND	14,094	C
Univ of North Texas	TX	15,628	C
Univ of Northern Colo	CO	15,973	C
Univ of Okla	OK	17,634	VC+
Univ of the Arts	PA	38,450	SP
Univ of Tulsa	OK	45,311	HC+
Webster Univ	MO	33,990	C+
West Chester Univ of Pennsylvania	PA	16,836	C
West Texas A&M Univ	TX	13,478	C
Western Illinois Univ	IL	20,130	C
Western Mich Univ	MI	19,042	C
Westminster Choir College	NJ	36,000	SP
Wilkes Univ	PA	42,786	C
William Peace Univ	NC	32,900	LC
Wright State Univ	OH	16,983	C
Youngstown State Univ	OH	16,374	LC

MUSICOLOGY/ ETHNOMUSICOLOGY

School	ST	$IS	SR
Cal State, San Bernardino	CA	12,000	C
Univ of Calif at Los Angeles	CA	25,686	MC
Univ of Kansas	KS	16,980	C+

NATIVE AMERICAN STUDIES

School	ST	$IS	SR
Colgate Univ	NY	50,930	MC
College of St. Scholastica	MN	39,960	C
Creighton Univ	NE	44,058	VC+
Dartmouth College	NH	57,996	MC
East Central Univ	OK	10,223	LC
Heritage Univ	WA	17,664	NC
Humboldt State Univ	CA	18,400	C
Montana State Univ-Northern	MT	12,500	NC
Northern Arizona Univ	AZ	18,592	C
Southern Oregon Univ	OR	17,874	C
Stanford Univ	CA	56,411	MC
Univ of Alaska Fairbanks	AK	13,955	C
Univ of Calif at Berkeley	CA	23,322	MC
Univ of Calif at Davis	CA	24,482	HC
Univ of Calif at Riverside	CA	27,204	C
Univ of Minn/Duluth	MN	18,964	C+
Univ of Montana	MT	13,670	C
Univ of New Mexico	NM	15,300	C
Univ of Okla	OK	17,634	VC+

NATURAL RESOURCE MANAGEMENT

School	ST	$IS	SR
Alaska Pacific Univ	AK	33,360	VC
Angelo State Univ	TX	15,049	NC
Arizona State Univ	AZ	18,818	C+
Ball State Univ	IN	17,850	C
Calif Polytechnic State Univ	CA	19,847	HC
Cal State, Sacramento	CA	16,200	C
Central Mich Univ	MI	18,066	C
Colo State Univ-Fort Collins	CO	20,090	VC
Delaware State Univ	DE	14,700	LC
DePauw Univ	IN	48,950	VC+
Drury Univ	MO	30,319	VC
Glenville State College	WV	11,348	NC
Grand Valley State Univ	MI	17,998	VC
Green Mountain College	VT	33,547	LC
Humboldt State Univ	CA	18,400	C
Johnson State College	VT	16,721	C
Keystone College	PA	28,680	LC
Louisiana State Univ	LA	18,677	VC+
Marshall Univ	WV	14,820	C
McNeese State Univ	LA		C
Mich State Univ	MI	13,689	VC
Montana State Univ	MT	14,068	VC
New Mexico Highlands Univ	NM	9,720	NC
New Mexico State Univ	NM	13,955	LC
N Car State Univ	NC	16,202	HC
N Dak State Univ	ND	14,642	C
Northland College	WI	26,680	C
Okla State Univ	OK	14,310	VC
Oregon State Univ	OR	19,017	C+
Penn State Univ/Univ Park	PA	25,404	VC
Purdue Univ/West Lafayette	IN	20,278	HC
Rutgers, The State Univ of New Jersey/New Brunswick	NJ	25,077	VC
San Francisco State Univ	CA	18,514	C
S Dak State Univ	SD	14,296	C
Southern Oregon Univ	OR	17,874	C
SUNY / College of Environmental Science and Forestry	NY	18,351	HC
Sul Ross State Univ	TX	13,410	LC
Texas A&M Univ at Galveston	TX	11,258	C
Ohio State Univ	OH	19,887	MC
Unity College	ME	34,054	C
Univ of Alaska Fairbanks	AK	13,955	C
Univ of Arizona	AZ	20,105	C
Univ of Conn	CT	23,744	HC
Univ of Delaware	DE	22,728	VC
Univ of Florida	FL	15,783	HC+
Univ of Hawaii at Manoa	HI	19,379	VC
Univ of Idaho	ID	14,558	C
Univ of Illinois at Urbana-Champaign	IL	24,300	HC
Univ of Maine	ME	19,712	C+
Univ of Maryland	MD	18,801	HC
Univ of Mass Amherst	MA	23,697	VC+
Univ of Minn Crookston	MN	17,834	C
Univ of Minn/Twin Cities	MN		HC
Univ of Montana-Western	MT	9,753	LC
Univ of Nebr - Lincoln	NE	17,507	VC
Univ of Nevada/Reno	NV	14,500	NC
Univ of Northern Colo	CO	15,973	C
Univ of PR Recinto de Rio Piedras	PR	5,750	
Univ of Tenn at Martin	TN	13,217	C
Univ of Vermont	VT	26,120	VC+
Univ of Wisc/Stevens Point	WI	14,043	C
Utah State Univ	UT	11,803	C
Washington State Univ	WA	20,461	C
Washington Univ in St. Louis	MO	58,818	MC
West Virginia Univ	WV	15,794	C+
Western Carolina Univ	NC	13,965	C+

NATURAL RESOURCE/ ENVIRONMENTAL ECONOMICS

School	ST	$IS	SR
Rutgers, The State Univ of New Jersey/New Brunswick	NJ	25,077	VC
Univ of Georgia	GA	19,508	VC
Univ of Nebr - Lincoln	NE	17,507	VC

NATURAL RESOURCES

School	ST	$IS	SR
Cornell Univ	NY	59,037	MC
Sewanee: The Univ of the South	TN	47,700	HC+
Univ of Georgia	GA	19,508	VC
Univ of Tenn at Knoxville	TN	20,364	VC+

NATURAL SCIENCES

School	ST	$IS	SR
Alderson Broaddus Univ	WV	28,656	C
Bard College at Simon's Rock	MA	58,963	HC+
Benedictine College	KS	29,180	VC
Bethel College	KS	29,100	C
Biola Univ	CA	40,320	VC
Cal State, Fresno	CA	17,405	C
Cal State, Los Angeles	CA	15,829	C
Calvin College	MI	37,585	VC+
Carthage College	WI	33,000	C
Case Western Reserve Univ	OH	55,178	MC
Castleton State College	VT	19,424	C
Central College	IA	36,980	VC
Charleston Southern Univ	SC	22,420	C
Christian Brothers Univ	TN	19,140	HC
Clarion Univ of Pennsylvania	PA	17,370	C
Colby-Sawyer College	NH	47,870	C
Colgate Univ	NY	50,930	MC
College of St. Benedict	MN	47,570	VC
College of St. Mary	NE	34,334	C
College of St. Scholastica	MN	39,960	C
Colo State Univ-Fort Collins	CO	20,090	VC
Concordia Univ Nebr	NE	26,000	VC
Concordia Univ, River Forest	IL	26,300	C
Daemen College	NY	31,510	C
Dallas Baptist Univ	TX	29,118	C
Doane College	NE	33,730	VC
Dominican Univ	IL	37,628	C
Dowling College	NY	25,000	LC
Edgewood College	WI	33,294	C
Edinboro Univ of Pennsylvania	PA	15,940	LC
Elms College	MA	23,900	VC
Erskine College	SC	37,360	C
Evergreen State College	WA	12,969	C+
Felician College	NJ	41,640	C
Fordham Univ	NY	58,927	HC
Fresno Pacific Univ	CA	32,136	C
Georgian Court Univ	NJ	39,726	LC
Gwynedd-Mercy College	PA	33,560	C
Indiana Univ of Pennsylvania	PA	20,180	LC
John Carroll Univ	OH	44,520	C+
Johns Hopkins Univ	MD	47,492	MC
Keystone College	PA	28,680	LC
LeMoyne-Owen College	TN	13,100	C
Lesley Univ	MA	46,350	C
Lewis-Clark State College	ID	6,990	C
Loyola Marymount Univ	CA	53,240	VC+
Lyndon State College	VT	14,233	C
Madonna Univ	MI	24,540	VC
Mercer Univ	GA	44,201	VC+
Missouri State Univ	MO	13,996	VC
Missouri Western State Univ	MO	12,260	NC

School	ST	$IS	SR
Muhlenberg College	PA	52,837	HC
New College of Florida	FL	14,504	H₵
Oakwood Univ	AL	23,035	C
Oregon State Univ	OR	19,017	₵
Our Lady of the Lake Univ of San Antonio	TX	22,430	LC
Pacific Union College	CA	28,150	VC
Park Univ	MO	17,525	C
Pepperdine Univ	CA	55,372	H₵
Prescott College	AZ	33,284	₵
Rocky Mountain College	MT	32,242	C
St. Anselm College	NH	48,324	VC
St. John's Univ	MN	46,146	C
St. Peter's College	NJ	44,240	C
San Jose State Univ	CA	19,707	C
Shawnee State Univ	OH	16,545	NC
Shimer College	IL	32,875	VC
Shorter Univ	GA	26,470	C
Siena Heights Univ	MI	17,000	LC
Southwestern Okla State Univ	OK	9,160	C
Spelman College	GA	24,650	VC
St. Mary's College of Maryland	MD	26,699	HC
St. Norbert College	WI	39,992	VC
SUNY College at Geneseo	NY	18,055	H₵
Tabor College	KS	29,010	LC
Taylor Univ	IN	36,742	V₵
Texas A&M Univ at Galveston	TX	11,258	C
The Masters College	CA	38,160	₵
Unity College	ME	34,054	C
Universidad del Turabo	PR	4,110	
Universidad Metropolitana	PR		
Univ of Akron	OH	20,436	C
Univ of Alabama at Birmingham	AL	18,484	₵
Univ of Alaska Anchorage	AK	15,290	NC
Univ of Arizona	AZ	20,105	C
Univ of Hawaii at Hilo	HI	6,500	C
Univ of La Verne	CA	47,010	VC
Univ of Maryland	MD	18,801	HC
Univ of New Haven	CT	47,740	C
Univ of N Dak	ND	14,094	C
Univ of Pittsburgh at Greensburg	PA	17,640	C
Univ of Pittsburgh at Pittsburgh	PA	27,800	H₵
Univ of PR/Cayey	PR	1,504	
Univ of Puget Sound	WA	52,648	H₵
Univ of Science and Arts of Okla	OK	10,560	VC
Univ of Wisc/Stevens Point	WI	14,043	C
Virginia Wesleyan College	VA	28,433	LC
Viterbo Univ	WI	30,070	C
Washington and Lee Univ	VA	52,812	MC
Western Oregon Univ	OR	15,021	C
Worcester State Univ	MA	18,657	C
Xavier Univ	OH	43,740	VC
York College	NE	19,475	C

NATURAL SCIENCES/ MATHEMATICS

School	ST	$IS	SR
Indiana Univ East	IN	6,639	LC
Thomas Edison State College	NJ	5,700	SP

NAVAL ARCHITECTURE AND MARINE ENGINEERING

School	ST	$IS	SR
Maritime College / SUNY	NY	16,020	C
Stevens Inst of Technology	NJ	50,130	HC
Texas A&M Univ at Galveston	TX	11,258	C
United States Coast Guard Academy	CT		HC
United States Naval Academy	MD		MC
Univ of Mich/Ann Arbor	MI	22,102	H₵
Univ of New Orleans	LA	9,224	VC
Univ of Wisc/Madison	WI	18,757	HC
Webb Inst	NY	7,550	MC

NEAR EASTERN STUDIES

School	ST	$IS	SR
Brandeis Univ	MA	58,820	HC
Brigham Young Univ	UT	12,100	HC
Cornell Univ	NY	59,037	MC
Creighton Univ	NE	44,058	V₵
Indiana Univ Bloomington	IN	19,358	HC
Johns Hopkins Univ	MD	47,492	MC
Oberlin College	OH	57,025	MC
Princeton Univ	NJ	53,795	MC
Univ of Calif at Berkeley	CA	23,322	MC
Univ of Calif at Los Angeles	CA	25,686	MC
Univ of Chicago	IL	55,416	MC
Univ of Mich/Ann Arbor	MI	22,102	H₵
Univ of Mount Union	OH	35,130	C
Univ of Pennsylvania	PA	56,106	MC
Univ of Washington	WA	14,722	VC
Univ of Wisc-Milwaukee	WI	18,436	C
Washington Univ in St. Louis	MO	58,818	MC
Wayne State Univ	MI	19,493	C
Yale Univ	CT	55,300	MC

NEUROSCIENCES

School	ST	$IS	SR
Agnes Scott College	GA	45,323	V₵
Alabama A&M Univ	AL	96,100	C
Allegheny College	PA	49,020	HC
Amherst College	MA	58,744	MC
Baldwin Wallace Univ	OH	36,980	VC
Bates College	ME	58,950	MC
Baylor Univ	TX	46,720	HC
Belmont Univ	TN	37,380	V₵
Binghamton Univ / The SUNY	NY	20,832	H₵
Boston Univ	MA	54,130	H₵
Bowdoin College	ME	57,834	MC
Bowling Green State Univ	OH	18,970	C
Brandeis Univ	MA	58,820	HC
Brigham Young Univ	UT	12,100	HC
Brown Univ	RI	56,150	MC
Bucknell Univ	PA	58,160	MC
Canisius College	NY	45,602	VC
Cedar Crest College	PA	43,240	C
Centenary College of Louisiana	LA	39,070	₵
Central Mich Univ	MI	18,066	C
Christopher Newport Univ	VA	21,050	VC
Claremont McKenna College	CA	58,065	MC
Coe College	IA	43,590	VC
Colby College	ME	57,510	MC
Colgate Univ	NY	50,930	MC
College of Mount St. Joseph	OH	33,880	C
College of William & Mary	VA	25,085	MC
Colo College	CO	54,534	MC
Columbia Univ in the City of New York	NY	61,116	MC
Conn College	CT	54,970	MC
Dartmouth College	NH	57,996	MC
Dickinson College	PA	57,662	H₵
Dominican Univ	IL	37,628	C
Drake Univ	IA	30,980	V₵
Drew Univ/College of Liberal Arts	NJ	55,862	VC
Earlham College	IN	49,710	V₵
Emmanuel College	MA	47,985	VC
Emory Univ	GA	45,000	MC
Fitchburg State Univ	MA	17,241	C
Fordham Univ	NY	58,927	HC
Franklin and Marshall College	PA	58,295	MC
Furman Univ	SC	54,006	HC
George Mason Univ	VA	15,724	VC
Hamilton College	NY	55,620	MC
Hiram College	OH	37,300	VC
Indiana Univ Bloomington	IN	19,358	HC
Indiana Univ-Purdue Univ Indianapolis	IN	17,290	C
Johns Hopkins Univ	MD	47,492	MC
Kenyon College	OH	56,810	MC
King Univ	TN	33,140	C
King's College	PA	41,678	C
Knox College	IL		VC
Lafayette College	PA	57,050	H₵
Lake Forest College	IL	45,580	VC
Macalester College	MN	53,419	MC
Mass Inst of Technology	MA	54,238	MC
Middlebury College	VT	57,470	MC
Millsaps College	MS	43,888	V₵
Montana State Univ	MT	14,068	VC
Moravian College	PA	36,381	VC
Mount Holyoke College	MA	53,596	H₵
Muhlenberg College	PA	52,837	HC
Muskingum Univ	OH	30,502	C
New College of Florida	FL	14,504	H₵
New York Univ	NY	61,470	MC
Northeastern Univ	MA	55,296	MC
Northwest Nazarene Univ	ID	24,275	NC
Northwestern Univ	IL	37,595	MC
Nova Southeastern Univ	FL	34,016	VC
Oberlin College	OH	57,025	MC
Ohio Univ	OH	20,676	VC
Pitzer College	CA	54,988	MC
Pomona College	CA	57,680	MC
Queens College / The CUNY	NY	17,107	VC
Quinnipiac Univ	CT	53,580	VC
Regis Univ	CO	41,318	C
Rhodes College	TN	47,596	H₵
Scripps College	CA	54,900	MC
Skidmore College	NY	57,926	HC
Smith College	MA	57,524	MC
St. Lawrence Univ	NY	53,740	HC
Stonehill College	MA	46,780	V₵
Swarthmore College	PA	57,870	MC
Syracuse Univ	NY	54,512	HC
Texas Christian Univ	TX	47,570	HC
Ohio State Univ	OH	19,887	MC
Thiel College	PA	31,378	LC
Transylvania Univ	KY	40,310	V₵
Trinity College	CT		H₵
Tulane Univ	LA	58,942	MC
Union College	NY		MC
Univ of Alabama at Birmingham	AL	18,484	₵
Univ of Arizona	AZ	20,105	C
Univ of Calif at Irvine	CA	25,961	VC
Univ of Calif at Los Angeles	CA	25,686	MC
Univ of Calif at Riverside	CA	27,204	C
Univ of Calif at Santa Cruz	CA	27,807	VC
Univ of Colo Boulder	CO	22,605	V₵
Univ of Evansville	IN	41,056	V₵
Univ of Georgia	GA	19,508	VC
Univ of Illinois at Chicago	IL	24,293	VC
Univ of Miami	FL	55,166	MC
Univ of Mich/Ann Arbor	MI	22,102	H₵
Univ of New Hampshire	NH	24,702	VC
Univ of Pittsburgh at Pittsburgh	PA	27,800	H₵
Univ of Rochester	NY	58,600	MC
Univ of Scranton	PA	51,940	VC
Univ of Southern Calif	CA	56,903	MC
Univ of Texas at Dallas	TX	21,046	HC
Univ of Vermont	VT	26,120	V₵
Univ of Washington	WA	14,722	VC
Ursinus College	PA	55,630	V₵
Vassar College	NY	59,070	MC
Washington and Lee Univ	VA	52,812	MC
Washington State Univ	WA	20,461	C
Washington Univ in St. Louis	MO	58,818	MC
Wellesley College	MA	49,848	MC
Wesleyan Univ	CT	59,844	MC
Western New England Univ	MA	45,590	C
Westminster College	UT	37,708	VC
Wheaton College	MA	54,934	H₵

NONPROFIT/PUBLIC ORGANIZATION MANAGEMENT

School	ST	$IS	SR
American Univ	DC	54,829	H₵
Aquinas College	MI	33,060	C
Arizona State Univ	AZ	18,818	₵
Bryant Univ	RI	49,179	VC
Duquesne Univ	PA	42,017	VC
High Point Univ	NC	39,800	C
Huntington Univ	IN	32,220	C
Indiana Univ Bloomington	IN	19,358	HC
Mount Aloysius College	PA	27,970	C
Prescott College	AZ	33,284	₵
Rockhurst Univ	MO	20,625	C
Southern Adventist Univ	TN	26,190	C
Univ of Georgia	GA	19,508	VC
Univ of S Car Upstate	SC	17,673	LC
Univ of Wisc/Madison	WI	18,757	HC
Wright State Univ	OH	16,983	C

NORWEGIAN

School	ST	$IS	SR
St. Olaf College	MN	49,960	H₵
Univ of N Dak	ND	14,094	C

NUCLEAR ENERGY ENGINEERING TECHNOLOGY

School	ST	$IS	SR
Thomas Edison State College	NJ	5,700	SP

NUCLEAR ENGINEERING

School	ST	$IS	SR
Georgia Inst of Technology	GA	20,464	MC
Idaho State Univ	ID	11,908	C
Mass Inst of Technology	MA	54,238	MC
Missouri Univ of Science and Technology	MO	18,655	V₵
N Car State Univ	NC	16,202	HC
Oregon State Univ	OR	19,017	₵
Penn State Univ/Univ Park	PA	25,404	VC
Purdue Univ/West Lafayette	IN	20,278	HC
Rensselaer Polytechnic Inst	NY	59,229	MC
Texas A&M Univ	TX	16,956	V₵
United States Military Academy	NY		MC
Univ of Calif at Berkeley	CA	23,322	MC
Univ of Cincinnati	OH	20,199	VC
Univ of Florida	FL	15,783	H₵
Univ of Illinois at Urbana-Champaign	IL	24,300	HC
Univ of Mich/Ann Arbor	MI	22,102	H₵
Univ of New Mexico	NM	15,300	C
Univ of Tenn at Chattanooga	TN	16,883	C
Univ of Tenn at Knoxville	TN	20,364	V₵
Univ of Wisc/Madison	WI	18,757	HC

NUCLEAR ENGINEERING TECHNOLOGY

School	ST	$IS	SR
Old Dominion Univ	VA	18,662	C
Thomas Edison State College	NJ	5,700	SP
Univ of Florida	FL	15,783	H₵
Univ of North Texas	TX	15,628	C

NUCLEAR MEDICAL TECHNOLOGY

School	ST	$IS	SR
Adventist Universtiy of Health Sciences	FL	16,344	NC
Allen College	IA	26,110	SP
Ashford Univ	IA	21,780	C
Barry Univ	FL	38,190	C
Benedictine Univ	IL	35,220	C
Cedar Crest College	PA	43,240	C
Edinboro Univ of Pennsylvania	PA	15,940	LC
Ferris State Univ	MI	19,698	C
George Washington Univ	DC	57,108	MC
Georgia Regents Univ	GA		C
Indiana Univ of Pennsylvania	PA	20,180	LC
Mass College of Pharmacy and Health Sciences	MA	36,450	SP
Mount Aloysius College	PA	27,970	C
North Central College	IL	38,343	VC
Old Dominion Univ	VA	18,662	C
Rhode Island College	RI	17,132	LC
Robert Morris Univ	PA	36,699	C
Roosevelt Univ	IL	22,605	VC
Univ at Buffalo / The SUNY	NY	20,283	VC
Univ of Alabama at Birmingham	AL	18,484	₵
Univ of Central Arkansas	AR	10,840	VC
Univ of Cincinnati	OH	20,199	VC
Univ of Findlay	OH	31,916	C
Univ of Iowa	IA	17,481	VC
Univ of Nevada, Las Vegas	NV	17,303	C
Univ of St. Francis	IL	36,490	C
Univ of the Incarnate Word	TX	35,200	LC
Univ of Vermont	VT	26,120	V₵
Univ of Wisc/La Crosse	WI	14,755	VC
Wheeling Jesuit Univ	WV	34,668	C
York College of Pennsylvania	PA	26,590	C

NUCLEAR MEDICINE

School	ST	$IS	SR
Thomas Edison State College	NJ	5,700	SP

NUCLEAR MEDICINE TECHNOLOGY

School	ST	$IS	SR
Indiana Univ-Purdue Univ Indianapolis	IN	17,290	C
St. Louis Univ	MO	46,594	V₵
St. Mary's Univ of Minn	MN	37,015	C
Thomas Edison State College	NJ	5,700	SP

NUCLEAR TECHNOLOGY

School	ST	$IS	SR
Excelsior College	NY	895	SP
Peru State College	NE	8,600	NC

NURSING

School	ST	$IS	SR
Abilene Christian Univ	TX	38,400	VC
Adams State College	CO	13,358	LC
Adelphi Univ	NY	43,130	VC
Adventist Universtiy of Health Sciences	FL	16,344	NC
Agnes Scott College	GA	45,323	V₵
Alabama A&M Univ	AL	96,100	C
Albany State Univ	GA	8,500	C
Alcorn State Univ	MS	9,500	C
Alderson Broaddus Univ	WV	28,656	C
Allen College	IA	26,110	SP
Alvernia Univ	PA	39,250	C
Alverno College	WI	30,483	LC
American International College	MA	36,100	LC
Anderson Univ	IN	35,390	C
Andrews Univ	MI	28,030	₵
Angelo State Univ	TX	15,049	NC
Anna Maria College	MA	34,600	LC
Appalachian State Univ	NC	12,919	VC
Aquinas College	TN	29,250	₵
Arizona State Univ	AZ	18,818	₵
Arkansas State Univ	AR	14,980	C
Arkansas Tech Univ	AR	13,164	LC
Armstrong Atlantic State Univ	GA	16,276	C
Atlantic Union College	MA	24,600	LC
Auburn Univ	AL	20,052	V₵
Auburn Univ at Montgomery	AL	12,120	C
Augustana College	SD	35,500	VC
Aurora Univ	IL	26,870	C
Austin Peay State Univ	TN	14,650	C
Avila Univ	MO	26,900	C
Azusa Pacific Univ	CA	39,946	C
Baker Univ	KS	33,350	₵
Baldwin Wallace Univ	OH	36,980	VC
Ball State Univ	IN	17,850	C
Barry Univ	FL	38,190	C
Barton College	NC	27,660	C
Baylor Univ	TX	46,720	HC
Becker College	MA	41,420	LC
Bellarmine Univ	KY	42,950	VC
Belmont Univ	TN	37,380	V₵

School	ST	$IS	SR
Bemidji State Univ	MN	13,500	C
Benedictine College	KS	29,180	VC
Benedictine Univ	IL	35,220	C
Berea College	KY	7,220	HC
Bethel College	IN	31,560	C
Bethel College	KS	29,100	C
Bethel Univ	MN	34,940	VC
Bethel Univ	TN	19,186	C
Bethune-Cookman Univ	FL	22,290	LC
Binghamton Univ / The SUNY	NY	20,832	HC+
Biola Univ	CA	40,320	VC
Bloomfield College	NJ	36,960	C
Bloomsburg Univ of Pennsylvania	PA	13,598	C
Bluefield State College	WV	3,140	LC
Boise State Univ	ID	12,802	C
Boston College	MA	58,506	MC
Bowie State Univ	MD	23,990	LC
Bowling Green State Univ	OH	18,970	C
Bradley Univ	IL	31,874	VC
Brenau Univ Women's College	GA	26,650	C+
Briar Cliff Univ	IA	29,514	C
Brigham Young Univ	UT	12,100	HC
Cabarrus College of Health Sciences	NC	10,000	SP
Caldwell College	NJ	35,602	LC
Calif Baptist Univ	CA	35,890	C
Cal State, Bakersfield	CA	8,000	LC
Cal State, Chico	CA	18,952	C
Cal State, Dominguez Hills	CA	17,056	LC
Cal State, East Bay	CA	16,549	C
Cal State, Fresno	CA	17,405	C
Cal State, Fullerton	CA	25,188	C+
Cal State, Los Angeles	CA	15,829	C
Cal State, Northridge	CA	28,313	C
Cal State, Sacramento	CA	16,200	C
Cal State, San Bernardino	CA	12,000	C
Cal State, San Marcos	CA	14,576	C
Cal State, Stanislaus	CA	18,582	C
Calif Univ of Pennsylvania	PA	14,217	C
Calvin College	MI	37,585	VC+
Campbellsville Univ	KY	27,720	C
Capital Univ	OH	39,824	VC
Cardinal Stritch Univ	WI	24,054	C
Caribbean Univ	PR	10,375	
Carlow Univ	PA	30,272	C
Carroll College	MT	28,000	C
Carroll Univ	WI	24,860	C
Carson-Newman Univ	TN	29,058	C+
Case Western Reserve Univ	OH	55,178	MC
Castleton State College	VT	19,424	C
Cedar Crest College	PA	43,240	C
Cedarville Univ	OH	31,036	VC+
Central Conn State Univ	CT	19,212	C
Central Methodist Univ	MO	28,240	VC
Central Univ of Bayamon	PR	3,350	
Chaminade Univ of Honolulu	HI	31,664	C
Charleston Southern Univ	SC	22,420	C
Chicago State Univ	IL	5,482	C
Clarion Univ of Pennsylvania	PA	17,370	C
Clarke Univ	IA	36,400	C
Clarkson College	NE	16,300	VC
Clayton State Univ	GA	12,000	LC
Clemson Univ	SC	19,136	HC
Cleveland State Univ	OH	21,357	C
Coastal Carolina Univ	SC	17,620	C
Coe College	IA	43,590	VC
Colby-Sawyer College	NH	47,870	C
College of Staten Island / The CUNY	NY	16,778	NC
College of Mount St. Joseph	OH	33,880	C
College of Mount St. Vincent	NY	41,040	MC
College of New Jersey	NJ	25,376	HC
College of St. Benedict	MN	47,570	VC
College of St. Elizabeth	NJ	43,839	LC
College of St. Mary	NE	34,334	C
College of St. Scholastica	MN	39,960	C
College of the Ozarks	MO	5,605	VC
Colo Mesa Univ	CO	16,669	LC
Colo State Univ-Pueblo	CO	13,532	LC
Columbia College	MO	24,578	C
Columbus State Univ	GA	13,176	C
Concordia College, Moorhead	MN	39,974	C+
Concordia Univ	OR	34,930	C
Concordia Univ Wisc	WI	28,980	C
Coppin State Univ	MD	14,905	VC
Cox College	MO	15,000	LC
Creighton Univ	NE	44,058	VC+
Culver-Stockton College	MO	30,900	C
Cumberland Univ	TN	21,220	C
Curry College	MA	47,545	LC
Daemen College	NY	31,510	C
Dakota Wesleyan Univ	SD	23,000	C
Davenport Univ	MI	21,002	LC
De Sales Univ	PA	42,670	C
Defiance College	OH	30,645	C
Delaware State Univ	DE	14,700	LC
Delta State Univ	MS	12,292	LC
DePaul Univ	IL	46,120	VC
Dickinson State Univ	ND	8,550	NC
Dillard Univ	LA	20,940	VC
Dominican College	NY	31,270	C
Dominican Univ	IL	37,628	C
Dominican Univ of Calif	CA	51,250	C
Dordt College	IA	34,160	VC
Drexel Univ	PA	51,920	HC
Duquesne Univ	PA	42,017	VC
D'Youville College	NY	29,850	C
East Carolina Univ	NC	14,169	C
East Central Univ	OK	10,223	LC
East Stroudsburg Univ of Pennsylvania	PA	16,636	C
East Tenn State Univ	TN	9,000	C
East Texas Baptist Univ	TX	29,135	C
Eastern Illinois Univ	IL	20,502	C
Eastern Kentucky Univ	KY	11,161	C
Eastern Mennonite Univ	VA	38,850	VC
Eastern Mich Univ	MI	17,961	C
Eastern New Mexico Univ	NM	10,682	C
Eastern Oregon Univ	OR	10,400	C
Eastern Univ	PA	37,704	C
Eastern Washington Univ	WA	16,388	C
Edgewood College	WI	33,294	C
Edinboro Univ of Pennsylvania	PA	15,940	LC
Elmhurst College	IL	42,032	C+
Elmira College	NY	49,950	C+
Elms College	MA	23,900	VC
Emmanuel College	MA	47,985	VC
Emory Univ	GA	45,000	MC
Emporia State Univ	KS	10,007	C
Endicott College	MA	42,390	C
Excelsior College	NY	895	SP
Fairfield Univ	CT	55,850	VC
Fairleigh Dickinson Univ/ College at Florham	NJ	42,142	C
Fairleigh Dickinson Univ/ Metropolitan Campus	NJ	40,254	C
Farmingdale State College	NY	18,985	C
Fayetteville State Univ	NC	10,816	C
Felician College	NJ	41,640	C
Ferris State Univ	MI	19,698	C
Fitchburg State Univ	MA	17,241	C
Florida A&M Univ	FL	14,935	LC
Florida Atlantic Univ	FL	17,339	C
Florida Gulf Coast Univ	FL		C
Florida Southern College	FL	38,240	VC
Florida State Univ	FL	15,238	HC
Fort Hays State Univ	KS	11,354	C
Framingham State Univ	MA	16,750	C
Francis Marion Univ	SC	16,464	LC
Franciscan Univ of Steubenville	OH	27,320	VC
Franklin Pierce Univ	NH	41,598	C
Frostburg State Univ	MD	15,264	LC
Gannon Univ	PA	37,940	C
Gardner-Webb Univ	NC	34,375	C+
George Fox Univ	OR	40,750	C+
George Mason Univ	VA	15,724	VC
Georgetown Univ	DC	52,910	MC
Georgia College and State Univ	GA	18,216	VC
Georgia Regents Univ	GA		C
Georgia Southern Univ	GA	16,414	C
Georgia Southwestern State Univ	GA	12,218	C
Georgia State Univ	GA	12,000	VC
Georgian Court Univ	NJ	39,726	LC
Glenville State College	WV	11,348	NC
Gonzaga Univ	WA	44,247	HC
Goodwin College	CT	19,400	LC
Goshen College	IN	35,900	VC
Graceland Univ	IA	28,020	C
Grambling State Univ	LA	13,384	LC
Grand Canyon Univ	AZ	24,540	VC
Grand Valley State Univ	MI	17,998	VC
Grand View Univ	IA	31,050	C
Gustavus Adolphus College	MN	48,170	HC
Gwynedd-Mercy College	PA	33,560	C
Hampton Univ	VA	28,528	C
Hannibal-LaGrange Univ	MO	24,490	C
Harding Univ	AR	21,432	C+
Hardin-Simmons Univ	TX	23,560	C+
Hartwick College	NY	49,815	C+
Hawaii Pacific Univ	HI	36,690	C
Henderson State Univ	AR	13,634	C
Hiram College	OH	37,300	VC
Holy Family Univ	PA	40,030	LC
Holy Names Univ	CA	40,310	NC
Hood College	MD	44,630	C
Hope College	MI	36,320	VC+
Houston Baptist Univ	TX	23,815	C+
Howard Univ	DC	35,957	C
Humboldt State Univ	CA	18,400	C
Hunter College / The CUNY	NY	14,429	VC
Huntington Univ	IN	32,220	C
Husson Univ	ME	23,386	LC
Idaho State Univ	ID	11,908	C
Illinois State Univ	IL	22,634	VC
Illinois Wesleyan Univ	IL	48,452	VC+
Immaculata Univ	PA	43,000	C
Indiana State Univ	IN	16,000	C
Indiana Univ Bloomington	IN	19,358	HC
Indiana Univ East	IN	6,639	LC
Indiana Univ Kokomo	IN	6,674	LC
Indiana Univ Northwest	IN	6,738	LC
Indiana Univ of Pennsylvania	PA	20,180	LC
Indiana Univ South Bend	IN	15,293	C
Indiana Univ Southeast	IN	15,807	LC
Indiana Univ-Purdue Univ Fort Wayne	IN	15,425	C
Indiana Univ-Purdue Univ Indianapolis	IN	17,290	C
Indiana Wesleyan Univ	IN	31,815	VC
Inter-American Univ of PR/ Aguadilla Campus	PR	5,578	
Inter-American Univ of PR/ Arecibo Campus	PR	3,350	
Inter-American Univ of PR/ Fajardo Campus	PR	4,200	
Inter-American Univ of PR/ Metropolitan Campus	PR	4,320	
Inter-American Univ of PR/ Ponce	PR	3,700	
Inter-American Univ of PR/ San Germán	PR	6,720	
Iowa Wesleyan College	IA	30,850	LC
Jacksonville State Univ	AL	12,280	LC
Jacksonville Univ	FL	37,780	C
James Madison Univ	VA	18,049	VC
Johnson C. Smith Univ	NC	25,336	LC
Judson College	AL	24,690	C
Judson Univ	IL	25,130	C
Kansas Wesleyan Univ	KS	32,000	C
Kean Univ	NJ	22,060	LC
Keene State College	NH	21,538	C
Kennesaw State Univ	GA	13,017	VC
Kent State Univ	OH	19,352	C
Kentucky Christian Univ	KY	17,622	LC
Kentucky State Univ	KY	11,000	LC
Keuka College	NY	30,300	C
King Univ	TN	33,140	C
Kutztown Univ of Pennsylvania	PA	16,909	LC
La Roche College	PA	34,802	LC
La Salle Univ	PA	50,270	C
LaGrange College	GA	34,480	C
Lake Superior State Univ	MI	18,121	C
Lamar Univ	TX	6,820	LC
Lander Univ	SC	22,514	C+
Langston Univ	OK	3,000	LC
Le Moyne College	NY	42,200	VC
Lehman College / The CUNY	NY	5,778	LC
Lenoir-Rhyne College	NC	35,984	C
Lewis Univ	IL	23,050	C
Lewis-Clark State College	ID	6,990	C
Liberty Univ	VA	19,101	C
Lincoln Memorial Univ	TN	18,144	C
Lincoln Univ	MO	11,996	NC
Lindsey Wilson College	KY	30,470	VC
Linfield College-McMinnville Campus	OR	46,166	C
Lipscomb Univ	TN	35,722	VC
LIU/Brooklyn Campus	NY	26,500	C
LIU/C.W. Post Campus	NY	38,888	C
Longwood Univ	VA	20,924	C
Louisiana College	LA	15,746	C
Lourdes Univ	OH	26,055	LC
Loyola Univ Chicago	IL	49,560	VC+
Loyola Univ New Orleans	LA	46,581	VC
Lubbock Christian Univ	TX	25,518	C
Luther College	IA	44,380	VC+
Lynchburg College	VA	42,645	C
MacMurray College	IL	20,755	C
Madonna Univ	MI	24,540	VC
Malone Univ	OH	34,334	C
Mansfield Univ	PA	19,468	LC
Marian Univ	WI	30,980	LC
Marian Univ/Indianapolis	IN	37,058	C
Marquette Univ	WI	43,664	VC+
Marshall Univ	WV	14,820	C
Marymount Univ	VA	36,178	C
Maryville College	TN	33,150	VC
Maryville Univ of St. Louis	MO	34,920	VC
Marywood Univ	PA	40,695	C
Mass College of Pharmacy and Health Sciences	MA	36,450	SP
McKendree Univ	IL	29,920	C+
McMurry Univ	TX	25,962	LC
McNeese State Univ	LA		C
Medgar Evers College / The CUNY	NY	4,920	NC
Mercy College	NY	29,996	C
Mercy College of Health Sciences	IA	14,460	SP
Messiah College	PA	39,540	VC
Methodist Univ	NC	37,185	C
Metropolitan State Univ	MN	5,923	SP
Metropolitan State Univ of Denver	CO	4,835	LC
Miami Univ	OH	24,191	HC
Mich State Univ	MI	13,689	VC
MidAmerica Nazarene Univ	KS	28,000	C
Middle Tenn State Univ	TN	8,650	C
Midland Univ	NE	34,000	C
Midway College	KY	20,150	C
Midwestern State Univ	TX	9,722	C
Millersville Univ of Pennsylvania	PA	18,498	C
Milligan College	TN	27,510	C
Millikin Univ	IL	37,462	C
Mills College	CA	54,119	HC
Milwaukee School of Engineering	WI	39,948	VC+
Minn State Univ, Mankato	MN	14,900	C
Minn State Univ, Moorhead	MN	13,392	C
Minot State Univ	ND	10,915	C
Misericordia Univ	PA	39,840	C
Miss College	MS	21,998	VC
Miss Univ for Women	MS	7,400	LC
Missouri Southern State Univ	MO	11,910	C
Missouri State Univ	MO	13,996	VC
Missouri Western State Univ	MO	12,260	NC
Molloy College	NY	38,950	C
Monmouth Univ	NJ	42,252	C
Montana State Univ	MT	14,068	VC
Montana State Univ-Northern	MT	12,500	NC
Montana Tech of The Univ of Montana	MT	14,650	VC
Moravian College	PA	36,381	VC
Morehead State Univ	KY	10,900	C
Morningside College	IA	32,620	C
Mount Aloysius College	PA	27,970	C
Mount Marty College	SD	29,638	C
Mount Mercy Univ	IA	34,385	C
Mount St. Mary College	NY	39,540	C
Mount St. Mary's College/ Chalon Campus	CA	43,897	VC+
Mount Vernon Nazarene Univ	OH	29,590	C
Mountain State Univ	WV	14,330	NC
Murray State Univ	KY	14,944	C
Muskingum Univ	OH	30,502	C
National Univ	CA	14,730	SP
Nazareth College of Rochester	NY	41,590	VC
Nebr Methodist College of Nursing and Allied Health	NE	22,872	SP
Nebr Wesleyan Univ	NE	29,774	C+
Neumann Univ	PA	31,078	LC
New Jersey City Univ	NJ	21,060	C+
New Mexico State Univ	NM	13,955	LC
New York City College of Technology / The CUNY	NY	5,769	NC
New York Inst of Technology	NY	40,590	VC
New York Univ	NY	61,470	MC
Newman Univ	KS	30,380	C+
Niagara Univ	NY	39,800	C
Nicholls State Univ	LA	7,095	C
Norfolk State Univ	VA	10,531	LC
N Car Agricultural and Technical State Univ	NC	13,175	LC
N Car Central Univ	NC	9,000	LC
N Dak State Univ	ND	14,642	C
North Georgia College & State Univ	GA	8,500	C
North Park Univ	IL	30,130	C
Northeastern State Univ	OK	8,615	VC
Northeastern Univ	MA	55,296	MC
Northern Arizona Univ	AZ	18,592	C
Northern Illinois Univ	IL	19,768	C
Northern Kentucky Univ	KY	15,302	LC
Northern Mich Univ	MI	15,300	VC
Northwest Nazarene Univ	ID	24,275	NC
Northwest Univ	WA	18,854	C
Northwestern College of Iowa	IA	34,848	C+
Northwestern Okla State Univ	OK	7,275	NC
Northwestern State Univ of Louisiana	LA	14,368	C
Norwich Univ	VT	28,212	C
Notre Dame College	OH	34,942	VC
Notre Dame de Namur Univ	CA	41,610	LC
Notre Dame of Maryland Univ	MD	27,700	C
Nova Southeastern Univ	FL	34,016	VC
Nyack College	NY	32,000	C
Oakland Univ	MI	19,391	VC
Oakwood Univ	AL	23,035	C
Ohio State Univ at Lima	OH	7,140	C
Ohio State Univ at Mansfield	OH	13,160	C
Ohio State Univ at Marion	OH	9,850	MC
Ohio State Univ at Newark	OH	17,510	C
Ohio Univ	OH	20,676	VC
Okla Baptist Univ	OK	28,202	VC
Okla City Univ	OK	33,546	VC
Okla Panhandle State Univ	OK	8,996	NC
Old Dominion Univ	VA	18,662	C
Olivet Nazarene Univ	IL	29,990	C
Oral Roberts Univ	OK	31,734	C
Otterbein College	OH	32,214	C
Our Lady of Holy Cross College	LA	8,090	LC
Pace Univ	NY	48,094	VC
Pacific Lutheran Univ	WA	44,840	VC
Pacific Union College	CA	28,150	VC
Palm Beach Atlantic Univ	FL	33,882	LC
Penn State Univ/Altoona	PA	11,464	C
Penn State Univ/Univ Park	PA	25,404	VC

School	ST	$IS	SR
Pennsylvania College of Technology	PA	25,653	NC
Pfeiffer Univ	NC	33,700	C
Piedmont College	GA	29,260	C
Pittsburg State Univ	KS	12,032	C
Plymouth State Univ	NH	23,148	LC
Point Loma Nazarene Univ	CA	38,610	VC
Pontifical Catholic Univ of PR	PR	7,310	
Prairie View A&M Univ	TX	15,205	LC
Presentation College	SD	14,800	LC
Purdue Univ/Calumet	IN	14,336	C
Purdue Univ/West Lafayette	IN	20,278	HC
Queens Univ of Charlotte	NC	39,543	VC
Quincy Univ	IL	34,980	LC
Quinnipiac Univ	CT	53,580	VC
Radford Univ	VA	17,132	LC
Ramapo College of New Jersey	NJ	24,938	C+
Regis College	MA	47,565	LC
Regis Univ	CO	41,318	C
Research College of Nursing	MO	33,190	SP
Rhode Island College	RI	17,132	LC
Richard Stockton College of New Jersey	NJ	20,000	VC
Rivier College	NH	35,000	VC
Robert Morris Univ	PA	36,699	C
Roberts Wesleyan College	NY	37,384	C+
Rockford College	IL	31,000	C
Rockhurst Univ	MO	20,625	C
Rowan Univ	NJ	23,570	VC
Russell Sage College	NY	39,370	C
Rutgers, The State Univ of New Jersey/Camden Campus	NJ	24,254	C
Rutgers, The State Univ of New Jersey/New Brunswick	NJ	25,077	VC
Rutgers, The State Univ of New Jersey/Newark Campus	NJ	25,376	C
Sacred Heart Univ	CT	48,564	VC
Saginaw Valley State Univ	MI	16,869	C
St. Anselm College	NH	48,324	VC
St. Francis Univ	PA	30,029	LC
St. John's Univ	MN	46,146	C
St. Joseph College	CT	45,630	LC
St. Joseph's College	IN	35,790	C
St. Joseph's College of Maine	ME	31,580	C
St. Louis Univ	MO	46,594	VC+
St. Martin's Univ	WA	38,082	C
St. Mary-of-the-Woods College	IN	37,722	LC
St. Mary's College	IN	45,160	VC
St. Peter's College	NJ	44,240	C
St. Xavier Univ	IL	32,840	C
Salem State College	MA	13,161	LC
Salisbury Univ	MD	18,368	VC
Salve Regina Univ	RI	47,250	VC
Samford Univ	AL	35,700	VC+
San Diego State Univ	CA	20,578	VC
San Francisco State Univ	CA	18,514	C
San Jose State Univ	CA	19,707	C
Schreiner Univ	TX	32,734	LC
Seattle Pacific Univ	WA	41,559	VC+
Seattle Univ	WA	47,010	VC+
Seton Hall Univ	NJ	45,902	C
Shawnee State Univ	OH	16,545	NC
Shenandoah Univ	VA	39,268	C
Shepherd Univ	WV	14,996	C
Shorter Univ	GA	26,470	C
Simmons College	MA	48,770	VC
Simpson Univ	CA	28,900	C
Slippery Rock Univ of Pennsylvania	PA	10,360	LC
Sonoma State Univ	CA	20,541	C
S Car State Univ	SC	6,700	LC
S Dak State Univ	SD	14,296	C
South Univ	GA		LC
Southeast Missouri State Univ	MO	14,983	LC
Southeastern Louisiana Univ	LA	13,325	C
Southern Adventist Univ	TN	26,190	C
Southern Conn State Univ	CT	18,033	C
Southern Illinois Univ Edwardsville	IL	17,532	C
Southern Nazarene Univ	OK	24,354	NC
Southern Oregon Univ	OR	17,874	C
Southern Univ and A&M College	LA	9,761	C+
Southern Vermont College	VT	30,740	LC
Southwest Baptist Univ	MO	24,710	C
Southwestern Adventist Univ	TX	23,026	LC
Southwestern Okla State Univ	OK	9,160	C
Spalding Univ	KY	31,850	LC
Spring Arbor Univ	MI	26,740	C
Spring Hill College	AL	42,130	VC
St. Catherine Univ	MN	37,782	C+
St. Francis College	NY	34,200	LC
St. John Fisher College	NY	39,370	C+
St. Joseph's College, New York / Brooklyn Campus	NY	21,878	C
St. Olaf College	MN	49,960	HC+
SUNY Inst of Technology at Utica / Rome	NY	23,818	C
SUNY/Empire State College	NY	6,315	SP
Stephen F. Austin State Univ	TX	14,668	C
Stevenson Univ	MD	39,572	C
Stony Brook Univ / SUNY	NY	19,359	HC
SUNY New Paltz	NY	15,010	C
SUNY Plattsburgh / SUNY	NY	18,083	VC
Tarleton State Univ	TX	13,489	LC
Temple Univ	PA	24,392	VC
Tenn State Univ	TN	9,048	C
Tenn Tech Univ	TN	11,310	C
Tenn Wesleyan College	TN	21,250	C
Texas A&M Univ at Corpus Christi	TX	11,544	LC
Texas A&M Univ at Kingsville	TX	7,500	LC
Texas Christian Univ	TX	47,570	HC
Texas State Univ	TX	16,495	VC
Texas Woman's Univ	TX	13,633	LC
The Catholic Univ of America	DC	52,852	VC
The College at Brockport / SUNY	NY	18,362	VC
The College of Idaho	ID	31,277	VC
The College of New Rochelle	NY	33,600	VC
Ohio State Univ	OH	19,887	MC
Thomas Edison State College	NJ	5,700	SP
Thomas More College	KY	34,760	C
Thomas Univ	GA	11,520	NC
Touro College	NY	23,150	VC
Towson Univ	MD	16,000	VC
Trevecca Nazarene Univ	TN	30,118	C
Trinity Christian College	IL	28,869	C
Trinity College of Nursing & Health Sciences	IL	53,138	SP
Trinity Washington Univ	DC	30,250	C+
Troy Univ	AL	10,650	C
Truman State Univ	MO	13,546	HC
Tuskegee Univ	AL	26,750	C
Union College	KY	28,775	C
Union College	NE	23,270	VC
Union Univ	TN	28,260	VC
Universidad Adventista de las Antillas	PR	7,360	
Universidad Metropolitana	PR		
Univ at Buffalo / The SUNY	NY	20,283	VC
Univ of Akron	OH	20,436	C
Univ of Alabama at Birmingham	AL	18,484	C+
Univ of Alabama at Huntsville	AL	17,625	VC
Univ of Alabama at Tuscaloosa	AL	17,164	C+
Univ of Alaska Anchorage	AK	15,290	NC
Univ of Arizona	AZ	20,105	C
Univ of Arkansas at Fayetteville	AR	16,860	VC
Univ of Arkansas at Little Rock	AR		C
Univ of Arkansas at Monticello	AR	8,470	NC
Univ of Arkansas at Pine Bluff	AR	10,600	C
Univ of Calif at Irvine	CA	25,961	VC
Univ of Calif at Los Angeles	CA	25,686	MC
Univ of Central Arkansas	AR	10,840	VC
Univ of Central Florida	FL	15,711	VC+
Univ of Central Missouri	MO	14,605	C
Univ of Central Okla	OK	12,293	C
Univ of Charleston	WV	28,650	C
Univ of Cincinnati	OH	20,199	VC
Univ of Colo at Colo Springs	CO	15,000	VC
Univ of Colo Denver	CO	17,904	C
Univ of Conn	CT	23,744	HC
Univ of Delaware	DE	22,728	VC
Univ of Detroit Mercy	MI	30,450	C
Univ of Dubuque	IA	30,200	C
Univ of Evansville	IN	41,056	VC+
Univ of Findlay	OH	31,916	C
Univ of Florida	FL	15,783	HC+
Univ of Hartford	CT	42,674	C
Univ of Hawaii at Hilo	HI	6,500	C
Univ of Hawaii at Manoa	HI	19,379	VC
Univ of Illinois at Chicago	IL	24,293	VC
Univ of Indianapolis	IN	31,740	LC
Univ of Iowa	IA	17,481	VC
Univ of Jamestown	ND	24,738	C
Univ of Kansas	KS	16,980	C+
Univ of Kentucky	KY	19,868	C
Univ of Louisiana at Lafayette	LA	6,130	C
Univ of Louisiana at Monroe	LA	12,998	C
Univ of Louisville	KY	17,460	VC
Univ of Maine	ME	19,712	C+
Univ of Maine at Augusta	ME	6,855	C
Univ of Maine at Fort Kent	ME	14,975	LC
Univ of Mary	ND	16,714	C
Univ of Mary Hardin-Baylor	TX	31,950	C+
Univ of Mass Amherst	MA	23,697	VC+
Univ of Mass Boston	MA	11,966	C
Univ of Mass Dartmouth	MA	22,223	C
Univ of Mass Lowell	MA	19,316	C
Univ of Memphis	TN	15,094	C
Univ of Miami	FL	55,166	MC
Univ of Mich/Ann Arbor	MI	22,102	HC+
Univ of Mich-Flint	MI	17,547	C+
Univ of Minn/Twin Cities	MN		HC
Univ of Missouri/Columbia	MO	18,201	MC
Univ of Missouri-Kansas City	MO	19,603	C
Univ of Missouri-St. Louis	MO	18,304	VC
Univ of Mobile	AL	27,870	VC
Univ of Nebr at Kearney	NE	14,855	LC
Univ of Nevada, Las Vegas	NV	17,303	C
Univ of Nevada/Reno	NV	14,500	NC
Univ of New England	ME	46,145	C+
Univ of New Hampshire	NH	24,702	VC
Univ of New Mexico	NM	15,300	C
Univ of North Alabama	AL	9,960	C
Univ of N Car at Chapel Hill	NC	18,348	MC
Univ of N Car at Charlotte	NC	15,847	C
Univ of N Car at Greensboro	NC	12,848	C
Univ of N Car at Wilmington	NC	13,572	VC+
Univ of N Dak	ND	14,094	C
Univ of North Florida	FL	15,578	VC
Univ of Northern Colo	CO	15,973	C
Univ of Pennsylvania	PA	56,106	MC
Univ of Pikeville	KY	24,750	NC
Univ of Pittsburgh at Bradford	PA	21,316	LC
Univ of Pittsburgh at Johnstown	PA	20,862	LC
Univ of Pittsburgh at Pittsburgh	PA	27,800	HC+
Univ of Portland	OR	47,874	VC
Univ of PR/Arecibo	PR	7,227	
Univ of PR/Humacao	PR	1,877	
Univ of PR/Mayaguez	PR	1,250	
Univ of Rio Grande	OH	8,750	NC
Univ of Rochester	NY	58,500	MC
Univ of St. Francis	IN	29,810	C
Univ of St. Mary	KS	28,400	C+
Univ of San Francisco	CA	49,674	VC
Univ of Scranton	PA	51,940	VC
Univ of South Alabama	AL	13,510	C
Univ of S Car at Aiken	SC	16,278	C
Univ of S Car at Columbia	SC	19,725	VC+
Univ of S Car Upstate	SC	17,673	LC
Univ of South Florida	FL	13,000	C
Univ of Southern Indiana	IN	14,657	C
Univ of Southern Maine	ME	16,576	C
Univ of Southern Miss	MS	13,170	C
Univ of St. Francis	IL	36,490	C
Univ of St. Thomas - Houston	TX	36,490	VC
Univ of Tampa	FL	35,160	VC
Univ of Tenn at Chattanooga	TN	16,883	C
Univ of Tenn at Knoxville	TN	20,364	VC+
Univ of Tenn at Martin	TN	13,217	C
Univ of Texas at Arlington	TX	10,908	LC
Univ of Texas at Austin	TX	44,074	HC
Univ of Texas at El Paso	TX	8,764	NC
Univ of Texas-Pan American	TX	12,432	LC
Univ of the District of Columbia	DC	7,244	LC
Univ of the Incarnate Word	TX	35,200	LC
Univ of the Sacred Heart	PR	5,590	
Univ of Toledo	OH	18,464	C
Univ of Tulsa	OK	45,311	HC+
Univ of Utah	UT	13,462	VC
Univ of Vermont	VT	26,120	VC+
Univ of Virginia	VA	22,175	MC
Univ of Virginia's College at Wise	VA	11,076	C
Univ of Washington	WA	14,722	VC
Univ of West Florida	FL	14,656	C
Univ of West Georgia	GA	14,852	LC
Univ of Wisc/Eau Claire	WI	15,430	VC
Univ of Wisc/Green Bay	WI	14,900	C
Univ of Wisc/Madison	WI	18,757	HC
Univ of Wisc/Oshkosh	WI	10,426	LC
Univ of Wisc-Milwaukee	WI	18,436	C
Univ of Wyoming	WY	13,855	C+
Ursuline College	OH	33,198	LC
Utica College	NY	44,734	C
Valparaiso Univ	IN	43,040	VC+
Vanguard Univ of Southern Calif	CA	35,833	VC
Villanova Univ	PA	56,436	MC
Virginia Commonwealth Univ	VA	18,633	C
Viterbo Univ	WI	30,070	C
Wagner College	NY	48,600	VC
Walla Walla Univ	WA	26,256	NC
Walsh Univ	OH	35,100	C
Washburn Univ	KS	12,165	NC
Washington Adventist Univ	MD	25,859	C+
Washington State Univ	WA	20,461	C
Wayland Baptist Univ	TX	16,058	LC
Wayne State Univ	MI	19,493	C
Waynesburg Univ	PA	29,100	C
Webster Univ	MO	33,990	C+
Wesley College	DE	31,115	LC
West Chester Univ of Pennsylvania	PA	16,836	C
West Liberty Univ	WV	9,142	LC
West Texas A&M Univ	TX	13,478	C
West Virginia Univ	WV	15,794	C+
West Virginia Univ Inst of Technology	WV	14,094	NC
West Virginia Wesleyan College	WV	26,880	C
Western Carolina Univ	NC	13,965	C+
Western Conn State Univ	CT	18,327	C
Western Illinois Univ	IL	20,130	C
Western Kentucky Univ	KY	11,000	LC
Western Mich Univ	MI	19,042	C
Western Washington Univ	WA	18,519	VC
Westfield State Univ	MA	18,489	C
Westminster College	MO	30,490	VC
Westminster College	UT	37,708	VC
Wheaton College	IL	39,650	HC+
Wheeling Jesuit Univ	WV	34,668	C
Whitworth Univ	WA	45,826	VC+
Wichita State Univ	KS	12,539	C
Widener Univ	PA	50,368	C
Wilkes Univ	PA	42,786	C
William Carey Univ	MS	13,500	LC
William Jewell College	MO	31,000	VC+
William Paterson Univ of New Jersey	NJ	21,694	C
Wilmington Univ	DE	7,778	NC
Wingate Univ	NC	34,990	C
Winona State Univ	MN	16,530	C
Winston-Salem State Univ	NC	9,418	LC
Worcester State Univ	MA	18,657	C
Wright State Univ	OH	16,983	C
Xavier Univ	OH	43,740	VC
York College / CUNY	NY	5,496	NC
York College of Pennsylvania	PA	26,590	C
Youngstown State Univ	OH	16,374	LC

NURSING EDUCATION

School	ST	$IS	SR
Allen College	IA	26,110	SP
Cal State, Northridge	CA	28,313	C
Indiana Wesleyan Univ	IN	31,815	VC
New York Univ	NY	61,470	MC
Seattle Pacific Univ	WA	41,559	VC+
Univ of St. Thomas - Houston	TX	36,490	VC

NURSING HOME ADMINISTRATION

School	ST	$IS	SR
Mount Aloysius College	PA	27,970	C
New York Univ	NY	61,470	MC
Ohio Univ	OH	20,676	VC
Univ of Louisiana at Monroe	LA	12,998	C
Youngstown State Univ	OH	16,374	LC

NUTRITION

School	ST	$IS	SR
Abilene Christian Univ	TX	38,400	VC
Alabama A&M Univ	AL	96,100	C
Alcorn State Univ	MS	9,500	C
Andrews Univ	MI	28,030	C+
Appalachian State Univ	NC	12,919	VC
Arizona State Univ	AZ	18,818	C+
Auburn Univ	AL	20,052	VC+
Baylor Univ	TX	46,720	HC
Benedictine Univ	IL	35,220	C
Boston Univ	MA	54,130	HC+
Bowling Green State Univ	OH	18,970	C
Bridgewater College	VA	39,880	C
Brigham Young Univ	UT	12,100	HC
Calif Polytechnic State Univ	CA	19,847	HC
Case Western Reserve Univ	OH	55,178	MC
Cedar Crest College	PA	43,240	C
College of St. Benedict	MN	47,570	VC
College of St. Elizabeth	NJ	43,839	LC
Colo State Univ-Fort Collins	CO	20,090	VC
Concordia College, Moorhead	MN	39,974	C+
Dominican Univ	IL	37,628	C
Drexel Univ	PA	51,920	HC
East Carolina Univ	NC	14,169	C
Eastern Mich Univ	MI	17,961	C
Florida State Univ	FL	15,238	HC
Fort Valley State Univ	GA	11,200	VC
Framingham State Univ	MA	16,750	C
Gannon Univ	PA	37,940	C
Georgia State Univ	GA	12,000	VC
Goddard College	VT	16,418	VC
Hampshire College	MA	58,320	MC
Howard Univ	DC	35,957	C
Hunter College / The CUNY	NY	14,429	VC
Indiana Univ of Pennsylvania	PA	20,180	LC
Iowa State Univ	IA	16,403	C
Johnson and Wales Univ/ Denver Campus	CO	34,368	C
Kansas State Univ	KS	15,497	VC

School	ST	$IS	SR
Keene State College	NH	21,538	C
Kent State Univ	OH	19,352	C
La Salle Univ	PA	50,270	C
Langston Univ	OK	3,000	LC
LIU/C.W. Post Campus	NY	38,888	C
Louisiana State Univ	LA	18,677	V₲
Madonna Univ	MI	24,540	VC
Marshall Univ	WV	14,820	C
Meredith College	NC	31,420	C
Messiah College	PA	39,540	VC
Miami Univ	OH	24,191	HC
Mich State Univ	MI	13,689	VC
Middle Tenn State Univ	TN	8,650	C
Montclair State Univ	NJ	22,614	C
Murray State Univ	KY	14,944	C
New Mexico State Univ	NM	13,955	LC
New York Inst of Technology	NY	40,590	VC
New York Univ	NY	61,470	MC
N Car Central Univ	NC	9,000	LC
N Dak State Univ	ND	14,642	C
Northern Illinois Univ	IL	19,768	C
Ohio Univ	OH	20,676	VC
Okla State Univ	OK	14,310	VC
Oregon State Univ	OR	19,017	₲
Pepperdine Univ	CA	55,372	H₲
Point Loma Nazarene Univ	CA	38,610	VC
Purdue Univ/West Lafayette	IN	20,278	HC
Queens College / The CUNY	NY	17,107	VC
Rochester Inst of Technology	NY	42,450	V₲
Russell Sage College	NY	39,370	C
Rutgers, The State Univ of New Jersey/New Brunswick	NJ	25,077	VC
St. John's Univ	MN	46,146	C
St. Joseph College	CT	45,630	LC
St. Louis Univ	MO	46,594	V₲
Samford Univ	AL	35,700	V₲
San Diego State Univ	CA	20,578	VC
S Car State Univ	SC	6,700	LC
S Dak State Univ	SD	14,296	C
St. Catherine Univ	MN	37,782	₲
Stephen F. Austin State Univ	TX	14,668	C
SUNY Plattsburgh / SUNY	NY	18,083	VC
Syracuse Univ	NY	54,512	HC
Texas Christian Univ	TX	47,570	HC
Texas Southern Univ	TX	18,212	LC
Texas State Univ	TX	16,495	VC
Texas Tech Univ	TX	14,243	C
Ohio State Univ	OH	19,887	MC
Univ of Arizona	AZ	20,105	C
Univ of Arkansas at Fayetteville	AR	16,860	VC
Univ of Calif at Berkeley	CA	23,322	MC
Univ of Calif at Davis	CA	24,482	HC
Univ of Central Okla	OK	12,293	C
Univ of Conn	CT	23,744	HC
Univ of Dayton	OH	43,750	VC
Univ of Delaware	DE	22,728	VC
Univ of Illinois at Chicago	IL	24,293	VC
Univ of Illinois at Urbana-Champaign	IL	24,300	HC
Univ of Maine	ME	19,712	₲
Univ of Maryland	MD	18,801	HC
Univ of Mass Amherst	MA	23,697	V₲
Univ of Minn/Twin Cities	MN		HC
Univ of Missouri/Columbia	MO	18,201	MC
Univ of Nebr - Lincoln	NE	17,507	VC
Univ of Nevada/Reno	NV	14,500	NC
Univ of New Hampshire	NH	24,702	VC
Univ of New Haven	CT	47,740	C
Univ of New Mexico	NM	15,300	C
Univ of N Car at Chapel Hill	NC	18,348	MC
Univ of N Car at Greensboro	NC	12,848	C
Univ of North Florida	FL	15,578	VC
Univ of Northern Colo	CO	15,973	C
Univ of Northern Iowa	IA	14,776	C
Univ of PR Recinto de Rio Piedras	PR	5,750	
Univ of Southern Indiana	IN	14,657	C
Univ of Tenn at Knoxville	TN	20,364	V₲
Univ of Tenn at Martin	TN	13,217	C
Univ of Texas at Austin	TX	44,074	HC
Univ of the Incarnate Word	TX	35,200	LC
Univ of Vermont	VT	26,120	V₲
Univ of Wisc/Madison	WI	18,757	HC
Univ of Wisc/Stevens Point	WI	14,043	C
Univ of Wisc-Milwaukee	WI	18,436	C
Virginia Polytechnic Inst and State Univ	VA	14,629	HC
Wayne State Univ	MI	19,493	C
West Chester Univ of Pennsylvania	PA	16,836	C
West Virginia Univ	WV	15,794	₲
West Virginia Wesleyan College	WV	26,880	C
Winthrop Univ	SC	21,120	VC
Youngstown State Univ	OH	16,374	LC

NUTRITION AND DIETETICS

School	ST	$IS	SR
Indiana Univ Bloomington	IN	19,358	HC
St. Louis Univ	MO	46,594	V₲
Thomas Edison State College	NJ	5,700	SP

NUTRITION EDUCATION

School	ST	$IS	SR
Calif Baptist Univ	CA	35,890	C
Ohio Univ	OH	20,676	VC
Univ of Cincinnati	OH	20,199	VC
Univ of Illinois at Chicago	IL	24,293	VC

NUTRITIONAL SCIENCES

School	ST	$IS	SR
Cornell Univ	NY	59,037	MC
Fontbonne Univ	MO	31,384	C
Georgia Southern Univ	GA	16,414	C
McNeese State Univ	LA		C
St. Louis Univ	MO	46,594	V₲
San Jose State Univ	CA	19,707	C
Univ of Georgia	GA	19,508	VC
Univ of Illinois at Chicago	IL	24,293	VC

OCCUPATIONAL SAFETY AND HEALTH

School	ST	$IS	SR
Embry-Riddle Aeronautical Univ - Worldwide	FL	15,512	C
Grand Valley State Univ	MI	17,998	VC
Howard Payne Univ	TX	17,115	C
Keene State College	NH	21,538	C
Madonna Univ	MI	24,540	VC
Marshall Univ	WV	14,820	C
Millersville Univ of Pennsylvania	PA	18,498	C
Montana Tech of The Univ of Montana	MT	14,650	VC
Mountain State Univ	WV	14,330	NC
Murray State Univ	KY	14,944	C
N Car Agricultural and Technical State Univ	NC	13,175	LC
Oakland Univ	MI	19,391	VC
Purdue Univ/West Lafayette	IN	20,278	HC
Southeastern Louisiana Univ	LA	13,325	C
Southeastern Okla State Univ	OK	7,966	C
Southwest Baptist Univ	MO	24,710	C
Univ of Central Missouri	MO	14,605	C
Univ of Findlay	OH	31,916	C
Univ of N Dak	ND	14,094	C

OCCUPATIONAL THERAPY

School	ST	$IS	SR
American International College	MA	36,100	LC
Augustana College	IL	43,398	HC
Baker College of Flint	MI	7,800	NC
Barry Univ	FL	38,190	C
Bay Path College	MA	34,565	C
Brenau Univ Women's College	GA	26,650	₲
Cal State, Dominguez Hills	CA	17,056	LC
Calvin College	MI	37,585	V₲
Cleveland State Univ	OH	21,357	C
College of St. Benedict	MN	47,570	VC
College of St. Mary	NE	34,334	C
Colo State Univ-Pueblo	CO	13,532	LC
Concordia Univ Wisc	WI	28,980	C
Dominican College	NY	31,270	C
Dominican Univ of Calif	CA	51,250	C
Duquesne Univ	PA	42,017	VC
East Carolina Univ	NC	14,169	C
Eastern Kentucky Univ	KY	11,161	C
Eastern Mich Univ	MI	17,961	C
Elizabethtown College	PA	47,600	VC
Florida A&M Univ	FL	14,935	LC
Florida Gulf Coast Univ	FL		C
Gannon Univ	PA	37,940	C
Howard Univ	DC	35,957	C
Husson Univ	ME	23,386	LC
Indiana Univ Kokomo	IN	6,674	LC
Ithaca College	NY	52,300	HC
Keuka College	NY	30,300	C
Lamar Univ	TX	6,820	LC
Lenoir-Rhyne College	NC	35,984	C
LIU/Brooklyn Campus	NY	26,500	C
Maryville Univ of St. Louis	MO	34,920	VC
Misericordia Univ	PA	39,840	C
Mount Aloysius College	PA	27,970	C
Mount Mary Univ	WI	32,836	LC
Mountain State Univ	WV	14,330	NC
New York Inst of Technology	NY	40,590	VC
New York Univ	NY	61,470	MC
Pennsylvania College of Technology	PA	25,653	NC
Quinnipiac Univ	CT	53,580	VC
Russell Sage College	NY	39,370	C
Sacred Heart Univ	CT	48,564	VC
St. Francis Univ	PA	30,029	LC
St. John's Univ	MN	46,146	C
St. Louis Univ	MO	46,594	V₲
St. Vincent College	PA	40,244	C
San Jose State Univ	CA	19,707	C
Spalding Univ	KY	31,850	LC
St. Catherine Univ	MN	37,782	₲
Stony Brook Univ / SUNY	NY	19,359	HC
Tenn State Univ	TN	9,048	C
Ohio State Univ	OH	19,887	MC
Touro College	NY	23,150	VC
Towson Univ	MD	16,000	VC
Tuskegee Univ	AL	26,750	C
Univ at Buffalo / The SUNY	NY	20,283	VC
Univ of Central Arkansas	AR	10,840	VC
Univ of Findlay	OH	31,916	C
Univ of Florida	FL	15,783	H₲
Univ of Hartford	CT	42,674	C
Univ of Illinois at Chicago	IL	24,293	VC
Univ of Kansas	KS	16,980	₲
Univ of Louisiana at Monroe	LA	12,998	C
Univ of Mary	ND	16,714	C
Univ of Minn/Twin Cities	MN		HC
Univ of Missouri/Columbia	MO	18,201	MC
Univ of New England	ME	46,145	₲
Univ of New Hampshire	NH	24,702	VC
Univ of Pittsburgh at Pittsburgh	PA	27,800	H₲
Univ of Scranton	PA	51,940	VC
Univ of Southern Calif	CA	56,903	MC
Univ of Southern Indiana	IN	14,657	C
Univ of the Sciences	PA	48,320	V₲
Univ of Utah	UT	13,462	VC
Univ of Wisc/La Crosse	WI	14,755	VC
Univ of Wisc-Milwaukee	WI	18,436	C
Utica College	NY	44,734	C
Wartburg College	IA	41,055	VC
West Virginia Univ	WV	15,794	₲
Western Mich Univ	MI	19,042	C
Worcester State Univ	MA	18,657	C
York College / CUNY	NY	5,496	NC

OCEAN ENGINEERING

School	ST	$IS	SR
Florida Atlantic Univ	FL	17,339	C
Florida Inst of Technology	FL	48,290	VC
Mass Inst of Technology	MA	54,238	MC
Texas A&M Univ at Galveston	TX	11,258	C
United States Naval Academy	MD		MC
Univ of Washington	WA	14,722	VC
Virginia Polytechnic Inst and State Univ	VA	14,629	HC

OCEANOGRAPHY

School	ST	$IS	SR
Bowdoin College	ME	57,834	MC
Central Mich Univ	MI	18,066	C
Florida Inst of Technology	FL	48,290	VC
Hawaii Pacific Univ	HI	36,690	C
Humboldt State Univ	CA	18,400	C
Maine Maritime Academy	ME	21,073	C
Millersville Univ of Pennsylvania	PA	18,498	C
Old Dominion Univ	VA	18,662	C
Prescott College	AZ	33,284	₲
Texas A&M Univ at Galveston	TX	11,258	C
United States Naval Academy	MD		MC
Univ of Mich/Ann Arbor	MI	22,102	H₲
Univ of Washington	WA	14,722	VC

OFFICE SUPERVISION AND MANAGEMENT

School	ST	$IS	SR
Adams State College	CO	13,358	LC
Alabama A&M Univ	AL	96,100	C
Albany State Univ	GA	8,500	C
Baker College of Flint	MI	7,800	NC
Campbellsville Univ	KY	27,720	C
Central Conn State Univ	CT	19,212	C
Chancellor Univ	OH	11,000	C
Concord Univ	WV	13,102	C
Eastern Mich Univ	MI	17,961	C
Fayetteville State Univ	NC	10,816	C
Fort Hays State Univ	KS	11,354	C
Fort Valley State Univ	GA	11,200	VC
Georgia State Univ	GA	12,000	VC
Inter-American Univ of PR/ Bayamon Univ College	PR	4,428	
Johnson and Wales Univ/ Providence Campus	RI	34,668	C
Middle Tenn State Univ	TN	8,650	C
Miss Valley State Univ	MS	9,706	LC
Northwestern Okla State Univ	OK	7,275	NC
Rider Univ	NJ	45,720	C
S Car State Univ	SC	6,700	LC
Southwestern Adventist Univ	TX	23,026	LC
Sul Ross State Univ	TX	13,410	LC
Tabor College	KS	29,010	LC
Tarleton State Univ	TX	13,489	LC
Universidad Adventista de las Antillas	PR	7,360	
Univ of S Car at Columbia	SC	19,725	V₲
Univ of the Cumberlands	KY	27,500	LC
Univ of the District of Columbia	DC	7,244	LC
Univ of Wisc Whitewater	WI	13,314	C
Valley City State Univ	ND	12,286	LC
Wiley College	TX		LC

OPERA

School	ST	$IS	SR
Boston Conservatory	MA	56,380	SP

OPERATIONS MANAGEMENT

School	ST	$IS	SR
Ball State Univ	IN	17,850	C
George Mason Univ	VA	15,724	VC
Kent State Univ	OH	19,352	C
Le Moyne College	NY	42,200	VC
Marquette Univ	WI	43,664	V₲
Metropolitan State Univ	MN	5,923	SP
Minn State Univ, Moorhead	MN	13,392	C
New York Univ	NY	61,470	MC
Oakland Univ	MI	19,391	VC
Oswego / SUNY	NY	20,009	VC
Santa Clara Univ	CA	54,702	MC
Ohio State Univ	OH	19,887	MC
Thomas Edison State College	NJ	5,700	SP
Univ of Arizona	AZ	20,105	C
Univ of Delaware	DE	22,728	VC
Univ of Idaho	ID	14,558	C
Univ of Maryland	MD	18,801	HC
Univ of Mass Amherst	MA	23,697	V₲
Univ of Mass Dartmouth	MA	22,223	C
Univ of Missouri-St. Louis	MO	18,304	VC
Univ of N Dak	ND	14,094	C
Univ of North Texas	TX	15,628	C
Univ of Pennsylvania	PA	56,106	MC
Univ of Portland	OH	47,874	VC
Univ of Scranton	PA	51,940	VC
Univ of Utah	UT	13,462	VC
Univ of Wisc/Madison	WI	18,757	HC
Univ of Wisc-Milwaukee	WI	18,436	C
Washington State Univ	WA	20,461	C
Western Washington Univ	WA	18,519	VC

OPERATIONS RESEARCH

School	ST	$IS	SR
Boston College	MA	58,506	MC
Boston Univ	MA	54,130	H₲
Canisius College	NY	45,602	VC
CUNY/Baruch College	NY	15,831	VC
Columbia Univ in the City of New York	NY	61,116	MC
Milwaukee School of Engineering	WI	39,948	V₲
New York Univ	NY	61,470	MC
Princeton Univ	NJ	53,795	MC
United States Air Force Academy	CO		MC
United States Coast Guard Academy	CT		HC
United States Military Academy	NY		MC
United States Naval Academy	MD		MC
Univ of Calif at Berkeley	CA	23,322	MC
Univ of Dayton	OH	43,750	VC
Univ of Illinois at Urbana-Champaign	IL	24,300	HC

OPERATIONS RESEARCH AND ENGINEERING

School	ST	$IS	SR
Cornell Univ	NY	59,037	MC
Indiana Univ Bloomington	IN	19,358	HC

OPHTHALMIC TECHNOLOGY

School	ST	$IS	SR
Old Dominion Univ	VA	18,662	C

OPTICAL ENGINEERING

School	ST	$IS	SR
Rose-Hulman Inst of Technology	IN	51,738	MC
Univ of Alabama at Huntsville	AL	17,625	VC
Univ of Arizona	AZ	20,105	C
Univ of Rochester	NY	58,500	MC

OPTICS

School	ST	$IS	SR
Capitol College	MD	21,250	C
Saginaw Valley State Univ	MI	16,869	C
Univ of Arizona	AZ	20,105	C
Univ of Rochester	NY	58,500	MC

OPTOMETRY

School	ST	$IS	SR
Baylor Univ	TX	46,720	HC
Ferris State Univ	MI	19,698	C
Gannon Univ	PA	37,940	C
Indiana Univ Bloomington	IN	19,358	HC
Oral Roberts Univ	OK	31,734	C
Purdue Univ/Calumet	IN	14,336	C
Univ of Calif at Berkeley	CA	23,322	MC

ORGAN PERFORMANCE

School	ST	$IS	SR
Houghton College	NY	35,740	VC
Indiana Univ South Bend	IN	15,293	C
Texas Christian Univ	TX	47,570	HC
Wright State Univ	OH	16,983	C

ORGANIZATIONAL BEHAVIOR

School	ST	$IS	SR
Assumption College	MA	45,721	VC
Benedictine Univ	IL	35,220	C
Boston Univ	MA	54,130	H¢
Carroll Univ	WI	24,860	C
Coe College	IA	43,590	VC
College of St. Scholastica	MN	39,960	C
DePaul Univ	IL	46,120	VC
Franklin Univ	OH	7,000	SP
Hannibal-LaGrange Univ	MO	24,490	C
Huntington Univ	IN	32,220	C
Ithaca College	NY	52,300	HC
La Salle Univ	PA	50,270	C
Methodist Univ	NC	37,185	C
Mountain State Univ	WV	14,330	NC
National Univ	CA	14,730	SP
New York Univ	NY	61,470	MC
Northern Kentucky Univ	KY	15,302	LC
Northwestern Univ	IL	37,595	MC
Oral Roberts Univ	OK	31,734	C
Penn State Univ/Univ Park	PA	25,404	VC
Pitzer College	CA	54,988	MC
Robert Morris Univ	PA	36,699	C
Rollins College	FL	52,370	HC
St. Louis Univ	MO	46,594	V¢
Southern Methodist Univ	TX	57,755	MC
The Lincoln Univ	PA	15,154	LC
Univ of Calif at Davis	CA	24,482	HC
Univ of Central Missouri	MO	14,605	C
Univ of Illinois at Urbana-Champaign	IL	24,300	HC
Univ of Mich/Ann Arbor	MI	22,102	H¢
Univ of Minn Crookston	MN	17,834	C
Univ of North Texas	TX	15,628	C
Univ of San Francisco	CA	49,674	VC
Univ of Tulsa	OK	45,311	H¢
Woodbury Univ	CA	34,500	LC

ORGANIZATIONAL LEADERSHIP AND MANAGEMENT

School	ST	$IS	SR
Adams State College	CO	13,358	LC
Alderson Broaddus Univ	WV	28,656	C
Aurora Univ	IL	26,870	C
Baldwin Wallace Univ	OH	36,980	VC
Blackburn College	IL	21,350	C
Bluffton Univ	OH	37,864	C
Cameron Univ	OK	9,267	LC
Claflin Univ	SC	22,368	¢
College of Mount St. Joseph	OH	33,880	C
College of St Joseph	VT	30,600	LC
Concordia Univ St. Paul	MN	27,200	C
Defiance College	OH	30,645	C
Drury Univ	MO	30,319	VC
Eastern Illinois Univ	IL	20,502	C
Eastern Univ	PA	37,704	C
George Fox Univ	OR	40,750	¢
Greenville College	IL	27,012	C
Hilbert College	NY	28,550	C
Indiana Univ-Purdue Univ Fort Wayne	IN	15,425	C
Indiana Univ-Purdue Univ Indianapolis	IN	17,290	C
Keystone College	PA	28,680	LC
Le Moyne College	NY	42,200	VC
Loyola Univ Chicago	IL	49,560	V¢
Lubbock Christian Univ	TX	25,518	C
Marquette Univ	WI	43,664	V¢
Maryville Univ of St. Louis	MO	34,920	VC
McNeese State Univ	LA		C
Millikin Univ	IL	37,462	C
Mount Aloysius College	PA	27,970	C
Mountain State Univ	WV	14,330	NC
National Univ	CA	14,730	SP
Northwestern State Univ of Louisiana	LA	14,368	C
Nyack College	NY	32,000	C
Ohio Valley Univ	WV	17,752	C
Palm Beach Atlantic Univ	FL	33,882	LC
Point Park Univ	PA	36,390	C
Prescott College	AZ	33,284	¢
Purdue Univ/West Lafayette	IN	20,278	HC
St. Joseph's Univ	PA	52,272	VC
Samford Univ	AL	35,700	V¢
Simpson Univ	CA	28,900	C
Spring Hill College	AL	42,130	VC
St. Joseph's College, New York / Brooklyn Campus	NY	21,878	C
St. Joseph's College, New York / Suffolk Campus	NY	21,878	VC
Thomas Edison State College	NJ	5,700	SP
Union College	KY	28,775	C
Univ of Delaware	DE	22,728	VC
Univ of Louisiana at Monroe	LA	12,998	C
Univ of Minn/Duluth	MN	18,964	¢
Univ of Nebr - Lincoln	NE	17,507	VC
Univ of North Texas	TX	15,628	C
Univ of St. Francis	IL	36,490	C
Univ of Wisc/Eau Claire	WI	15,430	VC
Univ of Wyoming	WY	13,855	¢
Viterbo Univ	WI	30,070	C
Voorhees College	SC	18,126	C
Washington Adventist Univ	MD	25,859	¢
Wayne State Univ	MI	19,493	C
Wheeling Jesuit Univ	WV	34,668	C
Wright State Univ	OH	16,983	C

OUTDOOR LEADERSHIP/ EDUCATION

School	ST	$IS	SR
Shenandoah Univ	VA	39,268	C

PACIFIC AREA STUDIES

School	ST	$IS	SR
Brigham Young Univ/ Hawaii	HI	0,014	VC
Hawaii Pacific Univ	HI	36,690	C
New York Univ	NY	61,470	MC
Univ of Hawaii at Manoa	HI	19,379	VC

PACKAGING

School	ST	$IS	SR
Univ of Wisc/Stout	WI	23,942	C

PAINTING

School	ST	$IS	SR
Adams State College	CO	13,358	LC
Andrews Univ	MI	28,030	¢
Aquinas College	MI	33,060	C
Art Academy of Cincinnati	OH	25,940	SP
Bard College at Simon's Rock	MA	58,963	H¢
Barton College	NC	27,660	C
Bennington College	VT	56,990	H¢
Biola Univ	CA	40,320	VC
Birmingham-Southern College	AL	42,370	V¢
Boston Univ	MA	54,130	H¢
Buffalo State/State Univ of Buffalo	NY	15,733	¢
Calif College of the Arts	CA	48,334	SP
Cal State, San Bernardino	CA	12,000	C
Cleveland Inst of Art	OH	48,641	SP
College for Creative Studies	MI		SP
College of Visual Arts - School is Closed	MN	24,310	SP
Columbia College	MO	24,578	C
Dominican Univ	IL	37,628	C
Escuela de Artes Plasticas de PR	PR	2,660	
Ferris State Univ	MI	19,698	C
Harding Univ	AR	21,432	¢
Hofstra Univ	NY	48,020	V¢
Howard Univ	DC	35,957	C
Indiana Univ South Bend	IN	15,293	C
Indiana Univ Southeast	IN	15,807	LC
Indiana Univ-Purdue Univ Fort Wayne	IN	15,425	C
Indiana Univ-Purdue Univ Indianapolis	IN	17,290	C
Indiana Wesleyan Univ	IN	31,815	VC
Kansas City Art Inst	MO	38,000	SP
Kendall College of Art and Design of Ferris State Univ	MI	21,048	SP
Kutztown Univ of Pennsylvania	PA	16,909	LC
Laguna College of Art and Design	CA	26,500	SP
Lewis Univ	IL	23,050	C
Maine College of Art	ME	28,812	SP
Marshall Univ	WV	14,820	C
Maryland Inst College of Art	MD	39,500	SP
Marywood Univ	PA	40,695	C
Mass College of Art and Design	MA	23,600	SP
Memphis College of Art	TN	33,550	SP
Milwaukee Inst of Art and Design	WI	31,938	SP
Minneapolis College of Art and Design	MN	36,700	SP
Montserrat College of Art	MA	31,000	SP
Moore College of Art and Design	PA	38,124	SP
Northwest Nazarene Univ	ID	24,275	NC
Ohio Univ	OH	20,676	VC
Otis College of Art and Design	CA	35,404	SP
Pacific Northwest College of Art	OR	38,494	SP
Pittsburg State Univ	KS	12,032	C
Providence College	RI	55,995	HC
Rhode Island School of Design	RI	55,204	SP
Ringling College of Art and Design	FL	46,130	SP
San Francisco Art Inst	CA	52,492	SP
Santa Fe Univ of Art and Design	NM	39,666	SP
Savannah College of Art and Design	GA	46,824	SP
School of the Art Inst of Chicago	IL	44,000	SP
SUNY Fredonia / The SUNY at Fredonia	NY	18,702	VC
SUNY New Paltz	NY	15,010	C
Syracuse Univ	NY	54,512	HC
Temple Univ	PA	24,392	VC
Texas Christian Univ	TX	47,570	HC
The Catholic Univ of America	DC	52,852	VC
Univ of Dallas	TX	43,510	V¢
Univ of Hartford	CT	42,674	C
Univ of Illinois at Chicago	IL	24,293	VC
Univ of Illinois at Urbana-Champaign	IL	24,300	HC
Univ of Iowa	IA	17,481	VC
Univ of Kansas	KS	16,980	¢
Univ of Mass Dartmouth	MA	22,223	C
Univ of Miami	FL	55,166	MC
Univ of Mich/Ann Arbor	MI	22,102	H¢
Univ of Oregon	OR	20,872	VC
Univ of San Francisco	CA	40,674	VC
Univ of the Arts	PA	38,450	SP
Univ of Washington	WA	14,722	VC
Virginia Commonwealth Univ	VA	18,633	C
Washington Univ in St. Louis	MO	58,818	MC
Webster Univ	MO	33,990	¢
Western Washington Univ	WA	18,519	VC
Youngstown State Univ	OH	16,374	LC

PALEONTOLOGY

School	ST	$IS	SR
Univ of Okla	OK	17,634	V¢

PAPER AND PULP SCIENCE

School	ST	$IS	SR
Miami Univ	OH	24,191	HC
N Car State Univ	NC	16,202	HC
SUNY / College of Environmental Science and Forestry	NY	18,351	HC
Univ of Maine	ME	19,712	¢
Univ of Washington	WA	14,722	VC
Univ of Wisc/Stevens Point	WI	14,043	C
Western Mich Univ	MI	19,042	C

PAPER ENGINEERING

School	ST	$IS	SR
SUNY / College of Environmental Science and Forestry	NY	18,351	HC
Western Mich Univ	MI	19,042	C

PARALEGAL STUDIES

School	ST	$IS	SR
Anna Maria College	MA	34,600	LC
Avila Univ	MO	26,900	C
Burlington College	VT	32,510	SP
Cal State, San Bernardino	CA	12,000	C
Calumet College of St. Joseph	IN	15,000	LC
Central Washington Univ	WA	11,730	C
Chancellor Univ	OH	11,000	C
College of Mount St. Joseph	OH	33,880	C
College of St. Mary	NE	34,334	C
Concordia Univ Wisc	WI	28,980	C
Daemen College	NY	31,510	C
Davenport Univ	MI	21,002	LC
Eastern Kentucky Univ	KY	11,161	C
Eastern Mich Univ	MI	17,961	C
Elms College	MA	23,900	VC
Hamline Univ	MN	44,198	VC
Hilbert College	NY	28,550	C
Hodges Univ	FL	12,000	LC
Humphreys College	CA	17,000	NC
Husson Univ	ME	23,386	LC
Idaho State Univ	ID	11,908	C
Johnson and Wales Univ/ North Miami Campus	FL	34,368	C
Johnson and Wales Univ/ Providence Campus	RI	34,668	C
Kaplan Univ	IA	14,025	NC
Kent State Univ	OH	19,352	C
Kutztown Univ of Pennsylvania	PA	16,909	LC
Lake Erie College	OH	35,704	C
Lake Superior State Univ	MI	18,121	C
Lasell College	MA	42,500	LC
Lock Haven Univ of Pennsylvania	PA	17,587	LC
Marymount Univ	VA	36,178	C
Maryville Univ of St. Louis	MO	34,920	VC
Mercy College	NY	29,996	C
Minn State Univ, Moorhead	MN	13,392	C
Miss College	MS	21,998	VC
Miss Univ for Women	MS	7,400	LC
Montclair State Univ	NJ	22,614	C
Morehead State Univ	KY	10,900	C
Mount Aloysius College	PA	27,970	C
Mountain State Univ	WV	14,330	NC
National American Univ	SD	16,712	NC
Nebr Wesleyan Univ	NE	29,774	¢
New York City College of Technology / The CUNY	NY	5,769	NC
Newbury College	MA	41,850	C
Nova Southeastern Univ	FL	34,016	VC
Peirce College	PA	12,760	NC
Pennsylvania College of Technology	PA	25,653	NC
Point Park Univ	PA	36,390	C
Quinnipiac Univ	CT	53,580	VC
Roger Williams Univ	RI	45,788	C
St. Mary-of-the-Woods College	IN	37,722	LC
Samford Univ	AL	35,700	V¢
Southern Illinois Univ Carbondale	IL	21,620	C
Stephen F. Austin State Univ	TX	14,668	C
Stevenson Univ	MD	39,572	C
Suffolk Univ	MA	46,548	C
Texas Wesleyan Univ	TX	29,886	C
Tiffin Univ	OH	30,273	LC
Tulane Univ	LA	58,942	MC
Univ of Detroit Mercy	MI	30,450	C
Univ of Great Falls	MT	27,970	C
Univ of La Verne	CA	47,010	VC
Univ of Louisville	KY	17,460	VC
Univ of Maryland/Univ College	MD	6,168	SP
Univ of Mass Boston	MA	11,966	C
Univ of Miss	MS	15,482	VC
Univ of Tenn at Chattanooga	TN	16,883	C
Virginia Intermont College	VA	32,411	LC
Washburn Univ	KS	12,165	NC
William Woods Univ	MO		C
Winona State Univ	MN	16,530	C
Woodbury Inst of Champlain College in Burlington	VT	15,150	LC

PARKS AND RECREATION MANAGEMENT

School	ST	$IS	SR
Alabama State Univ	AL	14,142	NC
Arizona State Univ	AZ	18,818	¢
Arkansas Tech Univ	AR	13,164	LC
Aurora Univ	IL	26,870	C
Belmont Abbey College	NC	37,716	C
Bemidji State Univ	MN	13,500	C
Cal State, Sacramento	CA	16,200	C
Calif Univ of Pennsylvania	PA	14,217	C
Central Mich Univ	MI	18,066	C
Central Washington Univ	WA	11,730	C
Cheyney Univ of Pennsylvania	PA	20,372	LC
Clemson Univ	SC	19,136	HC
Concord Univ	WV	13,102	C
Davenport Univ	MI	21,002	LC
Delaware State Univ	DE	14,700	LC
East Carolina Univ	NC	14,169	C
East Stroudsburg Univ of Pennsylvania	PA	16,636	C
Eastern Washington Univ	WA	16,388	C
Evangel Univ	MO	23,090	C
Florida International Univ	FL	17,747	VC
George Mason Univ	VA	15,724	VC
Houghton College	NY	35,740	VC
Humboldt State Univ	CA	18,400	C
Huntington Univ	IN	32,220	C
Illinois State Univ	IL	22,634	VC
Indiana Inst of Technology	IN	34,240	LC
Indiana State Univ	IN	16,000	C
Johnson and Wales Univ/ Charlotte Campus	NC	35,421	C
Johnson and Wales Univ/ North Miami Campus	FL	34,368	C
Johnson and Wales Univ/ Providence Campus	RI	34,668	C
Kansas State Univ	KS	15,497	VC
Lake Superior State Univ	MI	18,121	C
Marshall Univ	WV	14,820	C
Mich State Univ	MI	13,689	VC
Midland Univ	NE	34,000	C
Minn State Univ, Mankato	MN	14,900	C
Missouri Western State Univ	MO	12,260	NC
Montclair State Univ	NJ	22,614	C
Murray State Univ	KY	14,944	C
N Car State Univ	NC	16,202	HC
Northern Arizona Univ	AZ	18,592	C
Northern Mich Univ	MI	15,300	VC
Northland College	WI	26,680	C
Ohio Univ	OH	20,676	VC
Oregon State Univ	OR	19,017	¢
Penn State Univ/Univ Park	PA	25,404	VC
Prescott College	AZ	33,284	¢
Shorter Univ	GA	26,470	C
Slippery Rock Univ of Pennsylvania	PA	10,360	LC
S Dak State Univ	SD	14,296	C
Southwest Baptist Univ	MO	24,710	C
Springfield College	MA	25,000	C
St. Joseph's College, New York / Brooklyn Campus	NY	21,878	C
Stephen F. Austin State Univ	TX	14,668	C
Texas A&M Univ	TX	16,956	V¢
Unity College	ME	34,054	C
Univ of Arkansas at Pine Bluff	AR	10,600	C
Univ of Idaho	ID	14,558	C
Univ of Illinois at Urbana-Champaign	IL	24,300	HC
Univ of Iowa	IA	17,481	VC
Univ of Maine	ME	19,712	¢
Univ of Miss	MS	15,482	VC

ST = STATE $IS = IN-STATE COSTS SR = SELECTOR RATING

School	ST	$IS	SR
Univ of Missouri/Columbia	MO	18,201	MC
Univ of Nebr - Lincoln	NE	17,507	VC
Univ of N Car at Greensboro	NC	12,848	C
Univ of N Car at Wilmington	NC	13,572	VC+
Univ of Southern Miss	MS	13,170	C
Univ of Utah	UT	13,462	VC
Univ of Vermont	VT	26,120	VC+
Univ of Wisc/La Crosse	WI	14,755	VC
Utah State Univ	UT	11,803	C
Virginia Polytechnic Inst and State Univ	VA	14,629	HC
Virginia Wesleyan College	VA	28,433	LC
West Virginia Univ	WV	15,794	C+
Western Carolina Univ	NC	13,965	C+
Western Illinois Univ	IL	20,130	C
Western New England Univ	MA	45,590	C
Western Washington Univ	WA	18,519	VC
Wingate Univ	NC	34,990	C
York College of Pennsylvania	PA	26,590	C

PASTORAL STUDIES

School	ST	$IS	SR
Andrews Univ	MI	28,030	C+
Bethel College	IN	31,560	C
Brescia Univ	KY	26,140	VC+
Calif Baptist Univ	CA	35,890	C
Cedarville Univ	OH	31,036	VC+
Clearwater Christian College	FL	23,720	C
Concordia Univ Wisc	WI	28,980	C
Corban Univ	OR	34,764	C
Dallas Baptist Univ	TX	29,118	C
East Texas Baptist Univ	TX	29,135	C
Grace Bible College	MI	20,770	C
Greenville College	IL	27,012	C
Hope International Univ	CA	34,650	C
Houghton College	NY	35,740	VC
Kentucky Christian Univ	KY	17,622	LC
Loyola Univ Chicago	IL	49,560	VC+
Madonna Univ	MI	24,540	VC
Marian Univ/Indianapolis	IN	37,058	C
Morris College	SC	16,006	LC
Mount Vernon Nazarene Univ	OH	29,590	C
Newman Univ	KS	30,380	C+
North Central Univ	MN	20,946	C
Northwest Nazarene Univ	ID	24,275	NC
Northwest Univ	WA	18,854	C
Northwestern College	MN	24,000	C
Nyack College	NY	32,000	C
Okla Wesleyan Univ	OK	21,300	C
Olivet Nazarene Univ	IL	29,990	C
St. Mary's Univ of Minn	MN	37,015	C
Simpson Univ	CA	28,900	C
Southeastern Univ	FL	27,201	C+
Southwest Baptist Univ	MO	24,710	C
Tenn Wesleyan College	TN	21,250	C
Toccoa Falls College	GA	23,210	C
Trevecca Nazarene Univ	TN	30,118	C
Union College	NE	23,270	VC
Union Univ	TN	28,260	VC
Universidad Adventista de las Antillas	PR	7,360	
Univ of Mary	ND	16,714	C
Univ of St. Mary	KS	28,400	C+
Vanguard Univ of Southern Calif	CA	35,833	VC
Warner Univ	FL	18,000	C

PEACE STUDIES

School	ST	$IS	SR
Cal State, Dominguez Hills	CA	17,056	LC
Chapman Univ	CA	56,019	VC+
Colgate Univ	NY	50,930	MC
College of St. Benedict	MN	47,570	VC
College of St. Scholastica	MN	39,960	C
Creighton Univ	NE	44,058	VC+
DePaul Univ	IL	46,120	VC
DePauw Univ	IN	48,950	VC+
Earlham College	IN	49,710	VC+
Eastern Mennonite Univ	VA	38,850	VC
Goshen College	IN	35,900	VC+
Goucher College	MD	50,252	VC+
Guilford College	NC	35,340	C
Hamline Univ	MN	44,198	VC
Hampshire College	MA	58,320	MC
John Carroll Univ	OH	44,520	C+
Juniata College	PA	49,340	VC
Le Moyne College	NY	42,200	VC
Manchester College	IN	35,070	C
Manhattan College	NY	44,955	VC
Marquette Univ	WI	43,664	VC+
Messiah College	PA	39,540	VC
Naropa Univ	CO	37,875	SP
Nazareth College of Rochester	NY	41,590	VC
Northland College	WI	26,680	C
Norwich Univ	VT	28,212	C
Ohio Dominican Univ	OH	38,380	C+
Prescott College	AZ	33,284	C+
St. John's Univ	MN	46,146	C
Salisbury Univ	MD	18,368	VC
Swarthmore College	PA	57,870	MC
Tufts Univ	MA	58,780	MC
Univ of Calif at Berkeley	CA	23,322	MC
Univ of Hawaii at Manoa	HI	19,379	VC
Univ of N Car at Chapel Hill	NC	18,348	MC
Univ of Utah	UT	13,462	VC
Univ of Wisc-Milwaukee	WI	18,436	C
Warren Wilson College	NC	34,888	VC
Wartburg College	IA	41,055	VC
Wellesley College	MA	49,848	MC
Whitworth Univ	WA	45,826	VC+

PERCUSSION

School	ST	$IS	SR
Central Washington Univ	WA	11,730	C
Eastern Mich Univ	MI	17,961	C
Indiana Univ Bloomington	IN	19,358	HC
Indiana Univ-Purdue Univ Fort Wayne	IN	15,425	C
Marshall Univ	WV	14,820	C
Northwestern Univ	IL	37,595	MC
Roosevelt Univ	IL	22,605	VC
San Francisco Conservatory of Music	CA	53,923	SP
Syracuse Univ	NY	54,512	HC
Univ of Iowa	IA	17,481	VC
Univ of Kansas	KS	16,980	C+
Wright State Univ	OH	16,983	C
Youngstown State Univ	OH	16,374	LC

PERFORMING ARTS

School	ST	$IS	SR
Adelphi Univ	NY	43,130	VC
American Univ	DC	54,829	HC+
Appalachian State Univ	NC	12,919	VC
Aquinas College	MI	33,060	C
Arizona State Univ	AZ	18,818	C+
Averett Univ	VA	36,000	LC
Baylor Univ	TX	46,720	HC
Bennington College	VT	56,990	HC+
Bethel College	IN	31,560	C
Biola Univ	CA	40,320	VC
Blackburn College	IL	21,350	C
Boston Univ	MA	54,130	HC+
Bowling Green State Univ	OH	18,970	C
Brigham Young Univ	UT	12,100	HC
Brown Univ	RI	56,150	MC
Butler Univ	IN	45,898	VC+
Carroll College	MT	28,000	C
Carthage College	WI	33,000	C
Colby-Sawyer College	NH	47,870	C
College of the Ozarks	MO	5,605	VC
Colo State Univ-Fort Collins	CO	20,090	VC
Columbia College	SC	27,882	C
CUNY-City College	NY	19,576	HC+
De Sales Univ	PA	42,670	C
DePaul Univ	IL	46,120	VC
Dominican Univ	IL	37,628	C
Eastern Conn State Univ	CT	20,584	C
Eastern Kentucky Univ	KY	11,161	C
Eastern Mich Univ	MI	17,961	C
Edgewood College	WI	33,294	C
Elizabethtown College	PA	47,600	VC
Emerson College	MA	50,246	HC
Ferrum College	VA	27,740	LC
Fontbonne Univ	MO	31,384	C
Fordham Univ	NY	58,927	HC
Friends Univ	KS	29,100	C
Georgetown College	KY	38,690	C
Georgia Regents Univ	GA		C
Hampshire College	MA	58,320	MC
Huntington Univ	IN	32,220	C
Illinois Wesleyan Univ	IL	48,452	VC+
Ithaca College	NY	52,300	HC
Johnson State College	VT	16,721	C
Kean Univ	NJ	22,060	LC
Lees-McRae College	NC	33,624	C
Lindenwood Univ	MO	20,750	C
Mars Hill College	NC	22,950	LC
Mass College of Liberal Arts	MA	16,733	C
Missouri State Univ	MO	13,996	VC
Naropa Univ	CO	37,875	SP
Neumann Univ	PA	31,078	LC
New York Univ	NY	61,470	MC
N Dak State Univ	ND	14,642	C
Northern Kentucky Univ	KY	15,302	LC
Northwestern Univ	IL	37,595	MC
Oakland Univ	MI	19,391	VC
Ohio Univ	OH	20,676	VC
Old Dominion Univ	VA	18,662	C
Plymouth State Univ	NH	23,148	LC
Point Park Univ	PA	36,390	C
Prescott College	AZ	33,284	C+
Roosevelt Univ	IL	22,605	VC
Sacred Heart Univ	CT	48,564	VC
St. Mary's College of Calif	CA	53,550	C
Santa Fe Univ of Art and Design	NM	39,666	SP
Savannah College of Art and Design	GA	46,824	SP
Seton Hill Univ	PA	35,172	C
Shenandoah Univ	VA	39,268	C
Southern Methodist Univ	TX	57,755	MC
Southwest Baptist Univ	MO	24,710	C
Suffolk Univ	MA	46,548	C
SUNY College at Geneseo	NY	18,055	HC+
Temple Univ	PA	24,392	VC
Texas A&M Univ	TX	16,956	VC+
Texas Tech Univ	TX	14,243	C
Univ of Arizona	AZ	20,105	C
Univ of Florida	FL	15,783	HC+
Univ of Hartford	CT	42,674	C
Univ of Iowa	IA	17,481	VC
Univ of Mary Hardin-Baylor	TX	31,950	C+
Univ of Mich/Ann Arbor	MI	22,102	HC+
Univ of Missouri-Kansas City	MO	19,603	C
Univ of N Car School of the Arts	NC	7,401	SP
Univ of North Texas	TX	15,628	C
Univ of San Francisco	CA	49,674	VC
Univ of Southern Indiana	IN	14,657	C
Univ of Tampa	FL	35,160	VC
Univ of Tenn at Martin	TN	13,217	C
Univ of Texas-Pan American	TX	12,432	LC
Virginia Intermont College	VA	32,411	LC
Washington Univ in St. Louis	MO	58,818	MC
West Chester Univ of Pennsylvania	PA	16,836	C
West Texas A&M Univ	TX	13,478	C
Western Kentucky Univ	KY	11,000	LC
Western Mich Univ	MI	19,042	C
Youngstown State Univ	OH	16,374	LC

PERSONAL FINANCIAL PLANNING

School	ST	$IS	SR
Kansas State Univ	KS	15,497	VC
Univ of Wisc/Madison	WI	18,757	HC

PERSONNEL MANAGEMENT

School	ST	$IS	SR
Arcadia Univ	PA	33,570	C+
Auburn Univ	AL	20,052	VC+
Auburn Univ at Montgomery	AL	12,120	C
Ball State Univ	IN	17,850	C
Baylor Univ	TX	46,720	HC
Bellevue Univ	NE	4,600	NC
Cal State, Long Beach	CA	17,534	C+
CUNY/Baruch College	NY	15,831	VC
Dickinson State Univ	ND	8,550	NC
Eastern Mich Univ	MI	17,961	C
Eastern Washington Univ	WA	16,388	C
Faulkner Univ	AL	22,530	LC
Florida State Univ	FL	15,238	HC
Grand Valley State Univ	MI	17,998	VC
Hawaii Pacific Univ	HI	36,690	C
King's College	PA	41,678	C
Lamar Univ	TX	6,820	LC
Limestone College	SC	29,880	C
Louisiana Tech Univ	LA	8,000	C
Mansfield Univ	PA	19,468	LC
Mich State Univ	MI	13,689	VC
Nicholls State Univ	LA	7,095	C
Northern State Univ	SD	14,021	C
Oakland Univ	MI	19,391	VC
Our Lady of the Lake Univ of San Antonio	TX	22,430	LC
Portland State Univ	OR	18,672	C
Roosevelt Univ	IL	22,605	VC
Rowan Univ	NJ	23,570	VC
San Diego State Univ	CA	20,578	VC
San Francisco State Univ	CA	18,514	C
Seton Hill Univ	PA	35,172	C
Silver Lake College	WI	22,600	LC
St. Cloud State Univ	MN	10,600	C
Tarleton State Univ	TX	13,489	LC
Texas A&M Univ	TX	16,956	VC+
Troy Univ	AL	10,650	C
Univ of Illinois at Urbana-Champaign	IL	24,300	HC
Univ of Louisiana at Lafayette	LA	6,130	C
Univ of Montana	MT	13,670	C
Univ of Nebr at Kearney	NE	14,855	LC
Univ of PR Recinto de Rio Piedras	PR	5,750	
Univ of Southern Miss	MS	13,170	C
Univ of the Sacred Heart	PR	5,590	
Univ of Washington	WA	14,722	VC
Univ of Wisc Whitewater	WI	13,314	C
Utah State Univ	UT	11,803	C
Western Illinois Univ	IL	20,130	C
Wilmington Univ	DE	7,778	NC

PETROLEUM/NATURAL GAS ENGINEERING

School	ST	$IS	SR
Colo School of Mines	CO	18,000	HC
Louisiana State Univ	LA	18,677	VC+
Marietta College	OH	42,135	VC
Missouri Univ of Science and Technology	MO	18,655	VC+
Montana Tech of The Univ of Montana	MT	14,650	VC
New Mexico Inst of Mining and Technology	NM	12,892	HC
Nicholls State Univ	LA	7,095	C
Penn State Univ/Univ Park	PA	25,404	VC
Stanford Univ	CA	56,411	MC
Texas A&M Univ	TX	16,956	VC+
Texas A&M Univ at Kingsville	TX	7,500	LC
Univ of Alaska Fairbanks	AK	13,955	C
Univ of Houston	TX	19,184	VC
Univ of Kansas	KS	16,980	C+
Univ of Louisiana at Lafayette	LA	6,130	C
Univ of N Dak	ND	14,094	C
Univ of Okla	OK	17,634	VC+
Univ of Southern Calif	CA	56,903	MC
Univ of Texas at Austin	TX	44,074	HC
Univ of Tulsa	OK	45,311	HC+
Univ of Wyoming	WY	13,855	C+
West Virginia Univ	WV	15,794	C+

PHARMACEUTICAL CHEMISTRY

School	ST	$IS	SR
Lehigh Univ	PA	55,080	MC
Mich Tech Univ	MI	22,105	VC
Pittsburg State Univ	KS	12,032	C
Univ of Dayton	OH	43,750	VC
Univ of Mich/Ann Arbor	MI	22,102	HC+
Univ of the Sciences	PA	48,320	VC+

PHARMACEUTICAL SCIENCE

School	ST	$IS	SR
Albany College of Pharmacy and Health Sciences	NY	38,900	SP
Belmont Univ	TN	37,380	VC+
Cleveland State Univ	OH	21,357	C
De Sales Univ	PA	42,670	C
Duquesne Univ	PA	42,017	VC
Howard Univ	DC	35,957	C
Mass College of Pharmacy and Health Sciences	MA	36,450	SP
Northeastern Univ	MA	55,296	MC
Purdue Univ/West Lafayette	IN	20,278	HC
S Dak State Univ	SD	14,296	C
Ohio State Univ	OH	19,887	MC
Univ at Buffalo / The SUNY	NY	20,283	VC
Univ of Arizona	AZ	20,105	C
Univ of Calif at Irvine	CA	25,961	VC
Univ of Georgia	GA	19,508	VC
Univ of Houston	TX	19,184	VC
Univ of Louisiana at Monroe	LA	12,998	C
Univ of Mich/Ann Arbor	MI	22,102	HC+
Univ of Miss	MS	15,482	VC
Univ of N Car at Chapel Hill	NC	18,348	MC
Univ of Pittsburgh at Pittsburgh	PA	27,800	HC+
Univ of the Sciences	PA	48,320	VC+
West Chester Univ of Pennsylvania	PA	16,836	C
York College / CUNY	NY	5,496	NC

PHARMACOLOGY

School	ST	$IS	SR
Howard Univ	DC	35,957	C
New York Univ	NY	61,470	MC
Stony Brook Univ / SUNY	NY	19,359	HC
Univ at Buffalo / The SUNY	NY	20,283	VC
Univ of Arizona	AZ	20,105	C
Univ of Illinois at Chicago	IL	24,293	VC
Univ of Louisiana at Monroe	LA	12,998	C
Univ of the Sciences	PA	48,320	VC+
Univ of Wisc/Madison	WI	18,757	HC

PHARMACY

School	ST	$IS	SR
Butler Univ	IN	45,898	VC+
Cedarville Univ	OH	31,036	VC+
Drake Univ	IA	30,980	VC+
Duquesne Univ	PA	42,017	VC
Ferris State Univ	MI	19,698	C
Florida A&M Univ	FL	14,935	LC
Howard Univ	DC	35,957	C
Husson Univ	ME	23,386	LC
Johnson C. Smith Univ	NC	25,336	LC
Lamar Univ	TX	6,820	LC
LIU/Brooklyn Campus	NY	26,500	C
N Dak State Univ	ND	14,642	C
Northeastern Univ	MA	55,296	MC
Ohio Northern Univ	OH	42,075	VC
Presbyterian College	SC	42,678	VC
Regis Univ	CO	41,318	C
Roberts Wesleyan College	NY	37,384	C+
Rutgers, The State Univ of New Jersey/New Brunswick	NJ	25,077	VC
Seton Hill Univ	PA	35,172	C
S Dak State Univ	SD	14,296	C
St. John's Univ	NY	52,840	C+
The College of Idaho	ID	31,277	VC
Univ at Buffalo / The SUNY	NY	20,283	VC
Univ of Arizona	AZ	20,105	C
Univ of Calif at Santa Barbara	CA	27,551	HC
Univ of Cincinnati	OH	20,199	VC
Univ of Conn	CT	23,744	HC
Univ of Georgia	GA	19,508	VC

ST = STATE **$IS** = IN-STATE COSTS **SR** = SELECTOR RATING

School	ST	$IS	SR
Univ of Illinois at Chicago	IL	24,293	VC
Univ of Iowa	IA	17,481	VC
Univ of Kansas	KS	16,980	C
Univ of Louisiana at Monroe	LA	12,998	C
Univ of Mich/Ann Arbor	MI	22,102	HG
Univ of Minn/Twin Cities	MN		HC
Univ of Montana	MT	13,670	C
Univ of Texas at Austin	TX	44,074	HC
Univ of the Sciences	PA	48,320	VG
Univ of Toledo	OH	18,464	C
Univ of Utah	UT	13,462	VC
Washington Univ in St. Louis	MO	58,818	MC
West Virginia Univ	WV	15,794	G

PHILOSOPHY

School	ST	$IS	SR
Adelphi Univ	NY	43,130	VC
Adrian College	MI	33,800	C
Agnes Scott College	GA	45,323	VG
Albertus Magnus College	CT	37,382	LC
Albion College	MI	43,884	VC
Albright College	PA	46,660	C
Alfred Univ	NY	40,392	VC
Allegheny College	PA	49,020	HC
Alma College	MI	42,400	VC
Alvernia Univ	PA	39,250	C
Alverno College	WI	30,483	LC
American International College	MA	36,100	LC
American Univ	DC	54,829	HG
Amherst College	MA	58,744	MC
Anderson Univ	IN	35,390	C
Angelo State Univ	TX	15,049	NC
Appalachian State Univ	NC	12,919	VC
Aquinas College	MI	33,060	C
Aquinas College	TN	29,250	G
Arcadia Univ	PA	33,570	G
Arizona State Univ	AZ	18,818	G
Arkansas State Univ	AR	14,980	C
Asbury Univ	KY	32,038	VC
Ashland Univ	OH	25,000	C
Assumption College	MA	45,721	VC
Auburn Univ	AL	20,052	VG
Augsburg College	MN	35,142	C
Augustana College	IL	43,398	HC
Augustana College	SD	35,500	VC
Aurora Univ	IL	26,870	C
Austin College	TX	36,940	HC
Austin Peay State Univ	TN	14,650	C
Azusa Pacific Univ	CA	39,946	C
Baker Univ	KS	33,350	G
Baldwin Wallace Univ	OH	36,980	VC
Ball State Univ	IN	17,850	C
Bard College	NY	59,872	HC
Bard College at Simon's Rock	MA	58,963	HG
Barry Univ	FL	38,190	C
Bates College	ME	58,950	MC
Baylor Univ	TX	46,720	HC
Belhaven Univ	MS	27,170	C
Bellarmine Univ	KY	42,950	VC
Bellevue Univ	NE	4,600	NC
Belmont Abbey College	NC	37,716	C
Belmont Univ	TN	37,380	VG
Beloit College	WI	49,970	HC
Bemidji State Univ	MN	13,500	C
Benedict College	SC	20,454	NC
Benedictine College	KS	29,180	VC
Benedictine Univ	IL	35,220	C
Bennington College	VT	56,990	HG
Bentley Univ	MA	54,555	HG
Berea College	KY	7,220	HC
Berry College	GA	39,254	HC
Bethel College	IN	31,560	C
Bethel Univ	MN	34,940	VC
Binghamton Univ / The SUNY	NY	20,832	HG
Biola Univ	CA	40,320	VC
Birmingham-Southern College	AL	42,370	VG
Bloomfield College	NJ	36,960	C
Bloomsburg Univ of Pennsylvania	PA	13,598	C
Boise State Univ	ID	12,802	C
Boston College	MA	58,506	MC
Boston Univ	MA	54,130	HG
Bowdoin College	ME	57,834	MC
Bowling Green State Univ	OH	18,970	C
Bradley Univ	IL	31,874	VC
Brandeis Univ	MA	58,820	HC
Bridgewater College	VA	39,880	C
Bridgewater State Univ	MA	18,752	C
Brigham Young Univ	UT	12,100	HC
Brown Univ	RI	56,150	MC
Bryn Mawr College	PA	57,760	MC
Bucknell Univ	PA	58,160	MC
Buena Vista Univ	IA	37,954	C
Buffalo State/State Univ of Buffalo	NY	15,733	G
Butler Univ	IN	45,898	VG
Cabrini College	PA	40,859	LC
Calif Baptist Univ	CA	35,890	C
Calif Inst of Technology	CA	54,045	MC
Calif Lutheran Univ	CA	47,640	C
Calif Polytechnic State Univ	CA	19,847	HC
Calif State Polytechnic Univ, Pomona	CA	18,932	C
Cal State, Bakersfield	CA	8,000	LC
Cal State, Chico	CA	18,952	C
Cal State, Dominguez Hills	CA	17,056	LC
Cal State, East Bay	CA	16,549	C
Cal State, Fresno	CA	17,405	C
Cal State, Fullerton	CA	25,188	G
Cal State, Long Beach	CA	17,534	G
Cal State, Los Angeles	CA	15,829	C
Cal State, Northridge	CA	28,313	C
Cal State, Sacramento	CA	16,200	C
Cal State, San Bernardino	CA	12,000	C
Cal State, Stanislaus	CA	18,582	C
Calif Univ of Pennsylvania	PA	14,217	C
Calvin College	MI	37,585	VG
Canisius College	NY	45,602	VC
Capital Univ	OH	39,824	VC
Carleton College	MN	58,149	MC
Carlow Univ	PA	30,272	C
Carnegie Mellon Univ	PA	51,260	MC
Carroll College	MT	28,000	C
Carson-Newman Univ	TN	29,058	G
Carthage College	WI	33,000	C
Case Western Reserve Univ	OH	55,178	MC
Castleton State College	VT	19,424	C
Catawba College	NC	37,105	C
Cedarville Univ	OH	31,036	VG
Centenary College of Louisiana	LA	39,070	G
Central College	IA	36,980	VC
Central Conn State Univ	CT	19,212	C
Central Methodist Univ	MO	28,240	VC
Central Mich Univ	MI	18,066	C
Central Univ of Bayamon	PR	3,350	
Central Washington Univ	WA	11,730	C
Centre College	KY	35,000	HG
Chapman Univ	CA	56,019	VG
Christendom College	VA	28,120	VC
Christopher Newport Univ	VA	21,050	VC
CUNY/Baruch College	NY	15,831	VC
CUNY/Brooklyn College	NY	5,884	G
Claremont McKenna College	CA	58,065	MC
Clarion Univ of Pennsylvania	PA	17,370	C
Clark Atlanta Univ	GA	30,006	C
Clark Univ	MA	47,020	HG
Clarke Univ	IA	36,400	C
Clemson Univ	SC	19,136	HC
Cleveland State Univ	OH	21,357	C
Coastal Carolina Univ	SC	17,620	C
Coe College	IA	43,590	VC
Colby College	ME	57,510	MC
Colby-Sawyer College	NH	47,870	C
Colgate Univ	NY	50,930	MC
College of Staten Island / The CUNY	NY	16,778	NC
College of Charleston	SC	21,273	VC
College of Mount St. Vincent	NY	41,040	MC
College of New Jersey	NJ	25,376	HC
College of St. Benedict	MN	47,570	VC
College of St. Elizabeth	NJ	43,839	LC
College of St. Scholastica	MN	39,960	C
College of the Holy Cross	MA	56,232	MC
College of the Ozarks	MO	5,605	VC
College of William & Mary	VA	25,085	MC
College of Wooster	OH	52,600	VC
Colo College	CO	54,534	MC
Colo State Univ-Fort Collins	CO	20,090	VC
Columbia College	MO	24,578	C
Columbia Univ in the City of New York	NY	61,116	MC
Columbia Univ/Barnard College	NY	39,000	MC
Columbia Univ/School of General Studies	NY	54,083	MC
Concordia College, Moorhead	MN	39,974	G
Concordia Univ, Ann Arbor	MI	27,220	VC
Conn College	CT	54,970	MC
Cornell College	IA	44,930	HC
Cornell Univ	NY	59,037	MC
Cornerstone Univ and Grand Rapids Theological Seminary	MI	30,866	C
Covenant College	GA		VG
Creighton Univ	NE	44,058	VG
CUNY-City College	NY	19,576	HG
Curry College	MA	47,545	LC
Dallas Baptist Univ	TX	29,118	C
Dartmouth College	NH	57,996	MC
Davidson College	NC	54,683	MC
De Sales Univ	PA	42,670	C
Denison Univ	OH	54,670	HG
DePaul Univ	IL	46,120	VC
DePauw Univ	IN	48,950	VG
Dickinson College	PA	57,662	HG
Doane College	NE	33,730	VC
Dominican Univ	IL	37,628	C
Dordt College	IA	34,160	VC
Dowling College	NY	25,000	LC
Drake Univ	IA	30,980	VG
Drew Univ/College of Liberal Arts	NJ	55,862	VC
Drexel Univ	PA	51,920	HC
Drury Univ	MO	30,319	VC
Duke Univ	NC	50,250	MC
Duquesne Univ	PA	42,017	VC
D'Youville College	NY	29,850	C
Earlham College	IN	49,710	VG
East Carolina Univ	NC	14,169	C
East Stroudsburg Univ of Pennsylvania	PA	16,636	C
East Tenn State Univ	TN	9,000	C
Eastern Illinois Univ	IL	20,502	C
Eastern Kentucky Univ	KY	11,161	C
Eastern Mennonite Univ	VA	38,860	VC
Eastern Mich Univ	MI	17,961	C
Eastern Univ	PA	37,704	C
Eastern Washington Univ	WA	16,388	C
Eckerd College	FL	43,902	VC
Edinboro Univ of Pennsylvania	PA	15,940	LC
Edward Waters College	FL	17,856	LC
Elizabethtown College	PA	47,600	VC
Elmhurst College	IL	42,032	G
Elmira College	NY	49,950	G
Elon Univ	NC	40,046	HC
Emmanuel College	MA	47,985	VC
Emory and Henry College	VA	387,460	C
Emory Univ	GA	45,000	MC
Erskine College	SC	37,360	C
Eugene Lang College - The New School for Liberal Arts	NY	55,650	VC
Eureka College	IL	19,280	C
Excelsior College	NY	895	SP
Fairfield Univ	CT	55,850	VC
Fairleigh Dickinson Univ/ College at Florham	NJ	42,142	C
Fairleigh Dickinson Univ/ Metropolitan Campus	NJ	40,254	C
Felician College	NJ	41,640	C
Ferrum College	VA	27,740	LC
Fisk Univ	TN	19,830	C
Flagler College	FL	24,960	VC
Florida Atlantic Univ	FL	17,339	C
Florida Gulf Coast Univ	FL		C
Florida International Univ	FL	17,747	VC
Florida Memorial Univ	FL	20,716	LC
Florida Southern College	FL	38,240	VC
Florida State Univ	FL	15,238	HC
Fordham Univ	NY	58,927	HC
Fort Hays State Univ	KS	11,354	C
Fort Lewis College	CO	15,513	C
Franciscan Univ of Steubenville	OH	27,320	VC
Franklin and Marshall College	PA	58,295	MC
Franklin College	IN	35,885	C
Fresno Pacific Univ	CA	32,136	C
Frostburg State Univ	MD	15,264	LC
Furman Univ	SC	54,006	HC
Gallaudet Univ	DC	25,380	SP
Gannon Univ	PA	37,940	C
Geneva College	PA	27,280	C
George Fox Univ	OR	40,750	G
George Mason Univ	VA	15,724	VC
George Washington Univ	DC	57,108	MC
Georgetown College	KY	38,690	C
Georgetown Univ	DC	52,910	MC
Georgia College and State Univ	GA	18,216	VC
Georgia Southern Univ	GA	16,414	C
Georgia State Univ	GA	12,000	VC
Gettysburg College	PA	56,820	HC
Gonzaga Univ	WA	44,247	HC
Gordon College	MA	42,660	VG
Goucher College	MD	50,252	VG
Graceland Univ	IA	28,020	C
Grand Valley State Univ	MI	17,998	VC
Green Mountain College	VT	33,547	LC
Greenville College	IL	27,012	C
Grinnell College	IA	53,654	HC
Grove City College	PA	22,988	HC
Guilford College	NC	35,340	C
Gustavus Adolphus College	MN	48,170	HC
Hamilton College	NY	55,620	MC
Hamline Univ	MN	44,198	VC
Hampden-Sydney College	VA	48,848	C
Hampshire College	MA	58,320	MC
Hanover College	IN	41,450	VC
Hardin-Simmons Univ	TX	23,560	G
Hartwick College	NY	49,815	G
Harvard Univ/Harvard College	MA	49,000	MC
Hastings College	NE	27,782	G
Haverford College	PA	59,236	MC
Heidelberg Univ	OH	34,100	C
Hendrix College	AR	48,436	HG
High Point Univ	NC	39,800	C
Hiram College	OH	37,300	VC
Hobart and William Smith Colleges	NY	43,000	VC
Hofstra Univ	NY	48,020	VG
Hollins Univ	VA	43,295	VC
Holy Names Univ	CA	40,310	NC
Hood College	MD	44,630	C
Hope College	MI	36,320	VG
Houghton College	NY	35,740	VC
Howard Univ	DC	35,957	C
Humboldt State Univ	CA	18,400	C
Hunter College / The CUNY	NY	14,429	VC
Huntington Univ	IN	32,220	C
Idaho State Univ	ID	11,908	C
Illinois College	IL	25,770	VC
Illinois State Univ	IL	22,634	VC
Illinois Wesleyan Univ	IL	48,452	VG
Indiana State Univ	IN	16,000	C
Indiana Univ Bloomington	IN	19,358	HC
Indiana Univ Northwest	IN	6,738	LC
Indiana Univ of Pennsylvania	PA	20,180	LC
Indiana Univ South Bend	IN	15,293	C
Indiana Univ Southeast	IN	15,807	LC
Indiana Univ-Purdue Univ Fort Wayne	IN	15,425	C
Indiana Univ-Purdue Univ Indianapolis	IN	17,290	C
Iona College	NY	44,028	C
Iowa State Univ	IA	16,403	C
Ithaca College	NY	52,300	HC
Jacksonville Univ	FL	37,780	C
James Madison Univ	VA	18,049	VC
John Carroll Univ	OH	44,520	G
John Jay College of Criminal Justice / The CUNY	NY	6,059	C
Johns Hopkins Univ	MD	47,492	MC
Juniata College	PA	49,340	VC
Kalamazoo College	MI	47,825	HG
Kansas State Univ	KS	15,497	VC
Keene State College	NH	21,538	C
Kennesaw State Univ	GA	13,017	VC
Kent State Univ	OH	19,352	C
Kenyon College	OH	56,810	MC
King Univ	TN	33,140	C
King's College	PA	41,678	C
Knox College	IL		VC
Kutztown Univ of Pennsylvania	PA	16,909	LC
La Salle Univ	PA	50,270	C
Lafayette College	PA	57,050	HG
Lake Forest College	IL	45,580	VC
Lakeland College	WI	22,990	C
Lawrence Univ	WI	46,371	HC
Le Moyne College	NY	42,200	VC
Lebanon Valley College	PA	38,570	C
Lehigh Univ	PA	55,080	MC
Lehman College / The CUNY	NY	5,778	LC
Lenoir-Rhyne College	NC	35,984	C
Lewis & Clark College	OR	52,656	VC
Lewis Univ	IL	23,050	C
Linfield College-McMinnville Campus	OR	46,166	C
Lipscomb Univ	TN	35,722	VC
Lock Haven Univ of Pennsylvania	PA	17,587	LC
LIU/Brooklyn Campus	NY	26,500	C
LIU/C.W. Post Campus	NY	38,888	C
Loras College	IA	37,432	VC
Louisiana College	LA	15,746	C
Louisiana State Univ	LA	18,677	VG
Loyola Marymount Univ	CA	53,240	VG
Loyola Univ Chicago	IL	49,560	VG
Loyola Univ Maryland	MD		VC
Loyola Univ New Orleans	LA	46,581	VC
Luther College	IA	44,380	VG
Lycoming College	PA	43,636	C
Lynchburg College	VA	42,645	C
Macalester College	MN	53,419	MC
MacMurray College	IL	20,755	C
Malone Univ	OH	34,334	C
Manchester College	IN	35,070	C
Manhattan College	NY	44,955	VC
Manhattanville College	NY	46,260	VC
Mansfield Univ	PA	19,468	LC
Marian Univ/Indianapolis	IN	37,058	C
Marist College	NY	35,500	C
Marlboro College	VT	35,980	VC
Marquette Univ	WI	43,664	VG
Marshall Univ	WV	14,820	C
Mary Baldwin College	VA	37,110	C
Marymount Univ	VA	36,178	C
Marywood Univ	PA	40,695	C
Mass College of Liberal Arts	MA	16,733	C
Mass Inst of Technology	MA	54,238	MC
McDaniel College	MD	45,600	VC
McKendree Univ	IL	29,920	G
McPherson College	KS	28,138	C
Mercer Univ	GA	44,201	VG
Mercyhurst Univ	PA	40,700	C
Merrimack College	MA	44,215	C
Messiah College	PA	39,540	VC
Metropolitan State Univ	MN	5,923	SP
Metropolitan State Univ of Denver	CO	4,835	LC
Miami Univ	OH	24,191	HC
Mich State Univ	MI	13,689	VC
Middle Tenn State Univ	TN	8,650	C
Middlebury College	VT	57,470	MC
Millersville Univ of Pennsylvania	PA	18,498	C
Millikin Univ	IL	37,462	C

School	ST	$IS	SR
Mills College	CA	54,119	HC
Millsaps College	MS	43,888	VC+
Minn State Univ, Mankato	MN	14,900	C
Minn State Univ, Moorhead	MN	13,392	C
Misericordia Univ	PA	39,840	C
Missouri State Univ	MO	13,996	VC
Missouri Univ of Science and Technology	MO	18,655	VC+
Missouri Valley College	MO	22,200	C
Molloy College	NY	38,950	C
Monmouth College	IL	39,290	C
Montana State Univ	MT	14,068	VC
Montclair State Univ	NJ	22,614	C
Moravian College	PA	36,381	VC
Morehead State Univ	KY	10,900	C
Morehouse College	GA	38,640	C
Morgan State Univ	MD	14,500	VC
Morningside College	IA	32,620	C
Mount Holyoke College	MA	53,596	HC+
Mount Mary Univ	WI	32,836	LC
Mount Mercy Univ	IA	34,385	C
Mount St. Mary's Univ	MD	46,158	C
Mount St. Mary's College/ Chalon Campus	CA	43,897	VC+
Mount Vernon Nazarene Univ	OH	29,590	C
Muhlenberg College	PA	52,837	HC
Murray State Univ	KY	14,944	C
Muskingum Univ	OH	30,502	C
Nazareth College of Rochester	NY	41,590	VC
Nebr Wesleyan Univ	NE	29,774	C+
New College of Florida	FL	14,504	HC+
New England College	NH	45,930	LC
New Jersey City Univ	NJ	21,060	C+
New Mexico State Univ	NM	13,955	LC
New York Univ	NY	61,470	MC
Newberry College	SC	26,850	LC
Newman Univ	KS	30,380	C+
Niagara Univ	NY	39,800	C
N Car State Univ	NC	16,202	HC
North Central College	IL	38,343	VC
North Park Univ	IL	30,130	C
Northeastern Illinois Univ	IL		C
Northeastern Univ	MA	55,296	MC
Northern Arizona Univ	AZ	18,592	C
Northern Illinois Univ	IL	19,768	C
Northern Kentucky Univ	KY	15,302	LC
Northern Mich Univ	MI	15,300	VC
Northwest Missouri State Univ	MO	14,229	C
Northwest Univ	WA	18,854	C
Northwestern College of Iowa	IA	34,848	C+
Northwestern Univ	IL	37,595	MC
Notre Dame de Namur Univ	CA	41,610	LC
Nova Southeastern Univ	FL	34,016	VC
Nyack College	NY	32,000	C
Oakland Univ	MI	19,391	VC
Oberlin College	OH	57,025	MC
Occidental College	CA	59,592	MC+
Oglethorpe Univ	GA	42,580	VC
Ohio Dominican Univ	OH	38,380	C+
Ohio Northern Univ	OH	42,075	VC
Ohio Univ	OH	20,676	VC
Ohio Wesleyan Univ	OH	49,460	C+
Okla City Univ	OK	33,546	VC
Okla State Univ	OK	14,310	VC
Old Dominion Univ	VA	18,662	C
Olivet Nazarene Univ	IL	29,990	C
Oral Roberts Univ	OK	31,734	C
Oregon State Univ	OR	19,017	C+
Oswego / SUNY	NY	20,009	VC
Otterbein College	OH	32,214	C
Ouachita Baptist Univ	AR	29,010	VC
Our Lady of the Lake Univ of San Antonio	TX	22,430	LC
Pace Univ	NY	48,094	VC
Pacific Lutheran Univ	WA	44,840	VC
Pacific Univ	OR	42,815	C
Palm Beach Atlantic Univ	FL	33,882	LC
Penn State Univ/Univ Park	PA	25,404	VC
Pepperdine Univ	CA	55,372	HC+
Piedmont College	GA	29,260	C
Pitzer College	CA	54,988	MC
Plymouth State Univ	NH	23,148	LC
Point Loma Nazarene Univ	CA	38,610	VC
Pomona College	CA	57,680	MC
Pontifical Catholic Univ of PR	PR	7,310	
Portland State Univ	OR	18,672	C
Princeton Univ	NJ	53,795	MC
Principia College	IL	35,140	C+
Providence College	RI	55,995	HC
Purchase College / SUNY	NY	16,951	C
Purdue Univ/Calumet	IN	14,336	C
Purdue Univ/West Lafayette	IN	20,278	HC
Queens College / The CUNY	NY	17,107	VC
Queens Univ of Charlotte	NC	39,543	VC
Quinnipiac Univ	CT	53,580	VC
Randolph College	VA	43,960	VC
Randolph-Macon College	VA	45,086	C
Reed College	OR	57,780	MC
Regis Univ	CO	41,318	C
Rensselaer Polytechnic Inst	NY	59,229	MC
Rhode Island College	RI	17,132	LC
Rhodes College	TN	47,596	HC+
Rice Univ	TX	43,288	MC
Richard Stockton College of New Jersey	NJ	20,000	VC
Rider Univ	NJ	45,720	C
Ripon College	WI	36,959	C+
Roanoke College	VA	47,996	C+
Roberts Wesleyan College	NY	37,384	C+
Rochester Inst of Technology	NY	42,450	VC+
Rockford College	IL	31,000	C
Rockhurst Univ	MO	20,625	C
Rocky Mountain College	MT	32,242	C
Roger Williams Univ	RI	45,788	C
Rollins College	FL	52,370	HC
Roosevelt Univ	IL	22,605	VC
Rosemont College	PA	42,350	C
Rutgers, The State Univ of New Jersey/Camden Campus	NJ	24,254	C
Rutgers, The State Univ of New Jersey/New Brunswick	NJ	25,077	VC
Rutgers, The State Univ of New Jersey/Newark Campus	NJ	25,376	C
Sacred Heart Univ	CT	48,564	VC
St. Anselm College	NH	48,324	VC
St. Francis Univ	PA	30,029	LC
St. John's Univ	MN	46,146	C
St. Joseph College	CT	45,630	LC
St. Joseph's College	IN	35,790	C
St. Joseph's College of Maine	ME	31,580	C
St. Joseph's Univ	PA	52,272	VC
St. Louis Univ	MO	46,594	VC+
St. Mary's College	IN	45,160	VC
St. Mary's College of Calif	CA	53,550	C
St. Mary's Univ	TX	33,854	C
St. Mary's Univ of Minn	MN	37,015	C
St. Michael's College	VT	48,740	VC
St. Peter's College	NJ	44,240	C
St. Vincent College	PA	40,244	C
St. Xavier Univ	IL	32,840	C
Salem College	NC	29,326	VC
Salisbury Univ	MD	18,368	VC
Salve Regina Univ	RI	47,250	VC
Sam Houston State Univ	TX	17,082	C
Samford Univ	AL	35,700	VC+
San Diego State Univ	CA	20,578	VC
San Francisco State Univ	CA	18,514	C
San Jose State Univ	CA	19,707	C
Santa Clara Univ	CA	54,702	MC
Sarah Lawrence College	NY	48,000	HC
Schreiner Univ	TX	32,734	LC
Scripps College	CA	54,900	MC
Seattle Pacific Univ	WA	41,559	VC+
Seattle Univ	WA	47,010	VC+
Seton Hall Univ	NJ	45,902	C
Sewanee: The Univ of the South	TN	47,700	HC+
Siena College	NY	43,863	VC
Siena Heights Univ	MI	17,000	LC
Simmons College	MA	48,770	VC
Simpson College	IA	36,086	VC
Skidmore College	NY	57,926	HC
Slippery Rock Univ of Pennsylvania	PA	10,360	LC
Smith College	MA	57,524	MC
Sonoma State Univ	CA	20,541	C
Southeast Missouri State Univ	MO	14,983	LC
Southern Conn State Univ	CT	18,033	C
Southern Illinois Univ Carbondale	IL	21,620	C
Southern Illinois Univ Edwardsville	IL	17,532	C
Southern Methodist Univ	TX	57,755	MC
Southern Nazarene Univ	OK	24,354	NC
Southern Oregon Univ	OR	17,874	C
Southwestern Univ	TX	45,660	VC
Spelman College	GA	24,650	VC
Spring Arbor Univ	MI	26,740	C
Spring Hill College	AL	42,130	VC
St. Ambrose Univ	IA		C
St. Bonaventure Univ	NY	38,831	C
St. Catherine Univ	MN	37,782	C+
St. Cloud State Univ	MN	10,600	C
St. Edward's Univ	TX	44,674	VC
St. Francis College	NY	34,200	LC
St. John Fisher College	NY	39,370	C+
St. John's College, Santa Fe	NM	54,998	HC+
St. John's Univ	NY	52,840	C+
St. Lawrence Univ	NY	53,740	HC
St. Mary's College of Maryland	MD	26,699	HC
St. Norbert College	WI	39,992	VC
St. Olaf College	MN	49,960	HC+
St. Thomas Aquinas College	NY	30,000	C
Stanford Univ	CA	56,411	MC
Stephen F. Austin State Univ	TX	14,668	C
Stetson Univ	FL	49,512	VC+
Stevens Inst of Technology	NJ	50,130	HC
Stonehill College	MA	46,780	VC+
Stony Brook Univ / SUNY	NY	19,359	HC
Suffolk Univ	MA	46,548	C
SUNY College at Geneseo	NY	18,055	HC+
SUNY College at Old Westbury	NY	16,324	C
SUNY Cortland / The SUNY	NY	19,117	C
SUNY Fredonia / The SUNY at Fredonia	NY	18,702	VC
SUNY New Paltz	NY	15,010	C
SUNY Oneonta / SUNY	NY	16,919	VC
SUNY Plattsburgh / SUNY	NY	18,083	VC
Susquehanna Univ	PA	49,170	C
Swarthmore College	PA	57,870	MC
Sweet Briar College	VA	43,765	C+
Syracuse Univ	NY	54,512	HC
Tabor College	KS	29,010	LC
Taylor Univ	IN	36,742	VC+
Temple Univ	PA	24,392	VC
Texas A&M Univ	TX	16,956	VC+
Texas Christian Univ	TX	47,570	HC
Texas Lutheran Univ	TX	34,070	C
Texas State Univ	TX	16,495	VC
Texas Tech Univ	TX	14,243	C
The Catholic Univ of America	DC	52,852	VC
The College at Brockport / SUNY	NY	18,362	VC
The College of Idaho	ID	31,277	VC
The College of New Rochelle	NY	33,600	VC
The College of St. Rose	NY	26,750	C
The Lincoln Univ	PA	15,154	LC
Ohio State Univ	OH	19,887	MC
The SUNY at Potsdam	NY	17,754	C
Thiel College	PA	31,378	LC
Thomas Edison State College	NJ	5,700	SP
Thomas More College	KY	34,760	C
Toccoa Falls College	GA	23,210	C
Touro College	NY	23,150	VC
Towson Univ	MD	16,000	VC
Transylvania Univ	KY	40,310	VC+
Trinity Christian College	IL	28,869	C
Trinity College	CT		HC+
Trinity International Univ	IL	31,070	C
Trinity Univ	TX	44,174	HC+
Truman State Univ	MO	13,546	HC
Tufts Univ	MA	58,780	MC
Tulane Univ	LA	58,942	MC
Union College	NY		MC
Union Univ	TN	28,260	VC
United States Military Academy	NY		MC
Univ at Albany / SUNY	NY	18,674	VC
Univ at Buffalo / The SUNY	NY	20,283	VC
Univ of Akron	OH	20,436	C
Univ of Alabama at Birmingham	AL	18,484	C+
Univ of Alabama at Huntsville	AL	17,625	VC
Univ of Alabama at Tuscaloosa	AL	17,164	C+
Univ of Alaska Anchorage	AK	15,290	NC
Univ of Alaska Fairbanks	AK	13,955	C
Univ of Arizona	AZ	20,105	C
Univ of Arkansas at Fayetteville	AR	16,860	VC
Univ of Arkansas at Little Rock	AR		C
Univ of Calif at Davis	CA	24,482	HC
Univ of Calif at Irvine	CA	25,961	VC
Univ of Calif at Los Angeles	CA	25,686	MC
Univ of Calif at Riverside	CA	27,204	C
Univ of Calif at San Diego	CA	21,000	VC
Univ of Calif at Santa Barbara	CA	27,551	HC
Univ of Calif at Santa Cruz	CA	27,807	VC
Univ of Central Arkansas	AR	10,840	VC
Univ of Central Florida	FL	15,711	VC+
Univ of Central Okla	OK	12,293	C
Univ of Chicago	IL	55,416	MC
Univ of Cincinnati	OH	20,199	VC
Univ of Colo at Colo Springs	CO	15,000	VC
Univ of Colo Boulder	CO	22,605	VC+
Univ of Colo Denver	CO	17,904	C
Univ of Conn	CT	23,744	HC
Univ of Dallas	TX	43,510	VC+
Univ of Dayton	OH	43,750	VC
Univ of Delaware	DE	22,728	VC
Univ of Denver	CO	51,787	VC+
Univ of Detroit Mercy	MI	30,450	C
Univ of Dubuque	IA	30,200	C
Univ of Evansville	IN	41,056	VC+
Univ of Findlay	OH	31,916	C
Univ of Florida	FL	15,783	HC+
Univ of Georgia	GA	19,508	VC
Univ of Hartford	CT	42,674	C
Univ of Hawaii at Hilo	HI	6,500	C
Univ of Hawaii at Manoa	HI	19,379	VC
Univ of Houston	TX	19,184	VC
Univ of Houston-Downtown	TX	6,267	LC
Univ of Idaho	ID	14,558	C
Univ of Illinois at Chicago	IL	24,293	VC
Univ of Illinois at Urbana-Champaign	IL	24,300	HC
Univ of Indianapolis	IN	31,740	LC
Univ of Iowa	IA	17,481	VC
Univ of Kansas	KS	16,980	C+
Univ of Kentucky	KY	19,868	C
Univ of La Verne	CA	47,010	VC
Univ of Louisiana at Lafayette	LA	6,130	C
Univ of Louisville	KY	17,460	VC
Univ of Maine	ME	19,712	C+
Univ of Mary Washington	VA	19,484	VC
Univ of Maryland	MD	18,801	HC
Univ of Maryland/Baltimore County	MD	18,000	VC
Univ of Mass Amherst	MA	23,697	VC+
Univ of Mass Boston	MA	11,966	C
Univ of Mass Dartmouth	MA	22,223	C
Univ of Mass Lowell	MA	19,316	C
Univ of Memphis	TN	15,094	C
Univ of Miami	FL	55,166	MC
Univ of Mich/Ann Arbor	MI	22,102	HC+
Univ of Mich/Dearborn	MI	9,885	VC
Univ of Mich-Flint	MI	17,547	C+
Univ of Minn/Duluth	MN	18,964	C+
Univ of Minn/Morris	MN	17,150	VC
Univ of Minn/Twin Cities	MN		HC
Univ of Miss	MS	15,482	VC
Univ of Missouri/Columbia	MO	18,201	MC
Univ of Missouri-Kansas City	MO	19,603	C
Univ of Missouri-St. Louis	MO	18,304	VC
Univ of Montana	MT	13,670	C
Univ of Mount Union	OH	35,130	C
Univ of Nebr - Lincoln	NE	17,507	VC
Univ of Nebr at Omaha	NE	12,700	C
Univ of Nevada, Las Vegas	NV	17,303	C
Univ of Nevada/Reno	NV	14,500	NC
Univ of New England	ME	46,145	C+
Univ of New Hampshire	NH	24,702	VC
Univ of New Mexico	NM	15,300	C
Univ of New Orleans	LA	9,224	VC
Univ of N Car at Asheville	NC	13,500	VC+
Univ of N Car at Chapel Hill	NC	18,348	MC
Univ of N Car at Charlotte	NC	15,847	C
Univ of N Car at Greensboro	NC	12,848	C
Univ of N Dak	ND	14,094	C
Univ of North Florida	FL	15,578	VC
Univ of North Texas	TX	15,628	C
Univ of Northern Colo	CO	15,973	C
Univ of Northern Iowa	IA	14,776	C
Univ of Notre Dame	IN		MC
Univ of Okla	OK	17,634	VC+
Univ of Oregon	OR	20,872	VC
Univ of Pennsylvania	PA	56,106	MC
Univ of Pittsburgh at Pittsburgh	PA	27,800	HC+
Univ of Portland	OR	47,874	VC
Univ of PR Recinto de Rio Piedras	PR	5,750	
Univ of PR/Mayaguez	PR	1,250	
Univ of Puget Sound	WA	52,648	HC+
Univ of Redlands	CA	40,500	VC
Univ of Rochester	NY	58,500	MC
Univ of St. Francis	IN	29,810	C
Univ of San Diego	CA	53,302	HC+
Univ of San Francisco	CA	49,674	VC
Univ of Scranton	PA	51,940	VC
Univ of Sioux Falls	SD	22,990	C
Univ of South Alabama	AL	13,510	C
Univ of S Car at Columbia	SC	19,725	VC+
Univ of S Dak	SD	15,111	C
Univ of South Florida	FL	13,000	C
Univ of Southern Calif	CA	56,903	MC
Univ of Southern Indiana	IN	14,657	C
Univ of Southern Maine	ME	16,576	C
Univ of Southern Miss	MS	13,170	C
Univ of St. Thomas - Houston	TX	36,490	VC
Univ of Tampa	FL	35,160	VC
Univ of Tenn at Chattanooga	TN	16,883	C
Univ of Tenn at Knoxville	TN	20,364	VC+
Univ of Tenn at Martin	TN	13,217	C
Univ of Texas at Arlington	TX	10,908	LC
Univ of Texas at Austin	TX	44,074	HC
Univ of Texas at El Paso	TX	8,764	NC
Univ of Texas at San Antonio	TX	18,372	C
Univ of Texas-Pan American	TX	12,432	LC
Univ of the District of Columbia	DC	7,244	LC
Univ of the Incarnate Word	TX	35,200	LC
Univ of the Pacific	CA	52,146	VC
Univ of Toledo	OH	18,464	C
Univ of Tulsa	OK	45,311	HC+
Univ of Utah	UT	13,462	VC
Univ of Vermont	VT	26,120	VC+
Univ of Virginia	VA	22,175	MC
Univ of Washington	WA	14,722	VC
Univ of West Florida	FL	14,656	C
Univ of West Georgia	GA	14,852	LC
Univ of Wisc/Eau Claire	WI	15,430	VC
Univ of Wisc/Green Bay	WI	14,900	C
Univ of Wisc/La Crosse	WI	14,755	VC

School	ST	$IS	SR
Univ of Wisc/Madison	WI	18,757	HC
Univ of Wisc/Oshkosh	WI	10,426	LC
Univ of Wisc/Parkside	WI	10,181	LC
Univ of Wisc/Platteville	WI	14,274	C
Univ of Wisc/Stevens Point	WI	14,043	C
Univ of Wisc-Milwaukee	WI	18,436	C
Univ of Wyoming	WY	13,855	Ǥ
Urbana Univ	OH	21,190	C
Ursinus College	PA	55,630	VǤ
Ursuline College	OH	33,198	LC
Utah State Univ	UT	11,803	C
Utica College	NY	44,734	C
Valparaiso Univ	IN	43,040	VǤ
Vanderbilt Univ	TN	57,072	MC
Vassar College	NY	59,070	MC
Villanova Univ	PA	56,436	MC
Virginia Commonwealth Univ	VA	18,633	C
Virginia Polytechnic Inst and State Univ	VA	14,629	HC
Virginia Wesleyan College	VA	28,433	LC
Viterbo Univ	WI	30,070	C
Wabash College	IN	44,160	VC
Wagner College	NY	48,600	VC
Wake Forest Univ	NC	51,000	MC
Walsh Univ	OH	35,100	C
Warren Wilson College	NC	34,888	VC
Wartburg College	IA	41,055	VC
Washburn Univ	KS	12,165	NC
Washington and Jefferson College	PA	49,990	VC
Washington and Lee Univ	VA	52,812	MC
Washington College	MD	48,768	VC
Washington State Univ	WA	20,461	C
Washington Univ in St. Louis	MO	58,818	MC
Wayland Baptist Univ	TX	16,058	LC
Wayne State Univ	MI	19,493	C
Webster Univ	MO	33,990	Ǥ
Wellesley College	MA	49,848	MC
Wells College	NY	38,680	VC
Wesleyan College	GA	24,000	Ǥ
Wesleyan Univ	CT	59,844	MC
West Chester Univ of Pennsylvania	PA	16,836	C
West Virginia Univ	WV	15,794	Ǥ
West Virginia Wesleyan College	WV	26,880	C
Western Carolina Univ	NC	13,965	Ǥ
Western Illinois Univ	IL	20,130	C
Western Kentucky Univ	KY	11,000	LC
Western Mich Univ	MI	19,042	C
Western New England Univ	MA	45,590	C
Western Oregon Univ	OR	15,021	C
Western Washington Univ	WA	18,519	VC
Westminster College	MO	30,490	VC
Westminster College	PA	31,290	Ǥ
Westminster College	UT	37,708	VC
Westmont College	CA	41,500	HC
Wheaton College	IL	39,650	HǤ
Wheaton College	MA	54,934	HǤ
Wheeling Jesuit Univ	WV	34,668	C
Whitman College	WA	54,400	MC
Whittier College	CA	43,416	C
Whitworth Univ	WA	45,826	VǤ
Wichita State Univ	KS	12,539	C
Wiley College	TX		LC
Wilkes Univ	PA	42,786	C
Willamette Univ	OR	56,450	VǤ
William Jewell College	MO	31,000	VǤ
William Paterson Univ of New Jersey	NJ	21,694	C
Williams College	MA	58,900	MC
Wilmington College	OH	29,784	C
Wilson College	PA	27,660	C
Wingate Univ	NC	34,990	C
Winthrop Univ	SC	21,120	VC
Wittenberg Univ	OH	47,766	VC
Wofford College	SC	45,795	VC
Wright State Univ	OH	16,983	C
Xavier Univ	OH	43,740	VC
Xavier Univ of Louisiana	LA	25,300	C
Yale Univ	CT	55,300	MC
Yeshiva Univ	NY	47,250	VǤ
York College / CUNY	NY	5,496	NC
York College of Pennsylvania	PA	26,590	C
Youngstown State Univ	OH	16,374	LC

PHILOSOPHY AND RELIGION

School	ST	$IS	SR
Arizona State Univ	AZ	18,818	Ǥ
Augustana College	SD	35,500	VC
Bethel College	IN	31,560	C
Biola Univ	CA	40,320	VC
Cal State, Fresno	CA	17,405	C
Christian Brothers Univ	TN	19,140	HC
Claflin Univ	SC	22,368	Ǥ
Covenant College	GA		VǤ
Dakota Wesleyan Univ	SD	23,000	C
Dordt College	IA	34,160	VC
Friends Univ	KS	29,100	C
Hendrix College	AR	48,436	HǤ
Ithaca College	NY	52,300	HC
Kutztown Univ of Pennsylvania	PA	16,909	LC
Marymount Manhattan College	NY	40,118	VC
Mass College of Liberal Arts	MA	16,733	C
New York Univ	NY	61,470	MC
N Dak State Univ	ND	14,642	C
Northeastern Univ	MA	55,296	MC
Northern Kentucky Univ	KY	15,302	LC
Northwest Nazarene Univ	ID	24,275	NC
Nova Southeastern Univ	FL	34,016	VC
Nyack College	NY	32,000	C
Okla City Univ	OK	33,546	VC
Ouachita Baptist Univ	AR	29,010	VC
Pace Univ	NY	48,094	VC
Paine College	GA	18,594	LC
Philander Smith College	AR	19,760	LC
Point Loma Nazarene Univ	CA	38,610	VC
Prescott College	AZ	33,284	Ǥ
Radford Univ	VA	17,132	LC
Rowan Univ	NJ	23,570	VC
Shawnee State Univ	OH	16,545	NC
S Dak State Univ	SD	14,296	C
Southwestern College	KS	29,270	C
Spring Arbor Univ	MI	26,740	C
St. Joseph's College, New York / Brooklyn Campus	NY	21,878	C
St. Joseph's College, New York / Suffolk Campus	NY	21,878	VC
Taylor Univ	IN	36,742	VǤ
Univ of Maine at Farmington	ME	17,841	C
Univ of N Car at Wilmington	NC	13,572	VǤ
Univ of Notre Dame	IN		MC
Univ of Texas at San Antonio	TX	18,372	C
Virginia Commonwealth Univ	VA	18,633	C
Washington Adventist Univ	MD	25,859	Ǥ
Wesley College	DE	31,115	LC
West Chester Univ of Pennsylvania	PA	16,836	C
Wheeling Jesuit Univ	WV	34,668	C
Winthrop Univ	SC	21,120	VC
Youngstown State Univ	OH	16,374	LC

PHOTOGRAPHY

School	ST	$IS	SR
Academy of Art Univ	CA		
Adams State College	CO	13,358	LC
Andrews Univ	MI	28,030	Ǥ
Appalachian State Univ	NC	12,919	VC
Aquinas College	MI	33,060	C
Arcadia Univ	PA	33,570	Ǥ
Art Academy of Cincinnati	OH	25,940	SP
Art Center College of Design	CA	34,044	SP
Art Inst of Atlanta	GA	24,000	SP
Bard College	NY	59,872	HC
Bard College at Simon's Rock	MA	58,963	HǤ
Barry Univ	FL	38,190	C
Bellevue Univ	NE	4,600	NC
Bennington College	VT	56,990	HǤ
Biola Univ	CA	40,320	VC
Birmingham-Southern College	AL	42,370	VǤ
Brigham Young Univ	UT	12,100	HC
Buffalo State/State Univ of Buffalo	NY	15,733	Ǥ
Calif College of the Arts	CA	48,334	SP
Calif Inst of the Arts	CA	46,368	SP
Cal State, San Bernardino	CA	12,000	C
Central Mich Univ	MI	18,066	C
Cleveland Inst of Art	OH	48,641	SP
Coker College	SC	32,256	LC
College for Creative Studies	MI		SP
College of Art and Design at Lesley Univ	MA	39,730	SP
College of Visual Arts - School is Closed	MN	24,310	SP
Columbia College	MO	24,578	C
Columbia College Chicago	IL	30,940	LC
Columbus College of Art and Design	OH	37,732	SP
Corcoran College of Art and Design	DC	36,500	SP
Dominican Univ	IL	37,628	C
Drexel Univ	PA	51,920	HC
Endicott College	MA	42,390	C
Ferris State Univ	MI	19,698	C
Fitchburg State Univ	MA	17,241	C
Gallaudet Univ	DC	25,380	SP
Goddard College	VT	16,418	VC
Grand Valley State Univ	MI	17,998	VC
Hampshire College	MA	58,320	MC
Hofstra Univ	NY	48,020	VǤ
Howard Univ	DC	35,957	C
Indiana Univ South Bend	IN	15,293	C
Indiana Univ-Purdue Univ Fort Wayne	IN	15,425	C
Indiana Wesleyan Univ	IN	31,815	VC
Ithaca College	NY	52,300	HC
Kansas City Art Inst	MO	38,000	SP
Kendall College of Art and Design of Ferris State Univ	MI	21,048	SP
Kent State Univ	OH	19,352	C
King Univ	TN	33,140	C
Kutztown Univ of Pennsylvania	PA	16,909	LC
LIU/C.W. Post Campus	NY	38,888	C
Maine College of Art	ME	28,812	SP
Marlboro College	VT	35,980	VC
Marshall Univ	WV	14,820	C
Maryland Inst College of Art	MD	39,500	SP
Marywood Univ	PA	40,695	C
Mass College of Art and Design	MA	23,600	SP
Memphis College of Art	TN	33,550	SP
Milwaukee Inst of Art and Design	WI	31,938	SP
Minneapolis College of Art and Design	MN	36,700	SP
Montserrat College of Art	MA	31,000	SP
Morningside College	IA	32,620	C
New Jersey City Univ	NJ	21,060	Ǥ
New York Univ	NY	61,470	MC
Northern Arizona Univ	AZ	18,592	C
Notre Dame of Maryland Univ	MD	27,700	C
Ohio Univ	OH	20,676	VC
Okla City Univ	OK	33,546	VC
Otis College of Art and Design	CA	35,404	SP
Pacific Northwest College of Art	OR	38,494	SP
Pacific Union College	CA	28,150	VC
Parsons The New School for Design	NY	56,610	SP
Point Park Univ	PA	36,390	C
Pratt Inst	NY	49,520	SP
Prescott College	AZ	33,284	Ǥ
Providence College	RI	55,995	HC
Purdue Univ/West Lafayette	IN	20,278	HC
Rhode Island School of Design	RI	55,204	SP
Ringling College of Art and Design	FL	46,130	SP
Rochester Inst of Technology	NY	42,450	VǤ
Rocky Mountain College of Art and Design	CO	22,470	NC
Salem State College	MA	13,161	LC
Sam Houston State Univ	TX	17,082	C
San Francisco Art Inst	CA	52,492	SP
Santa Fe Univ of Art and Design	NM	39,666	SP
Savannah College of Art and Design	GA	46,824	SP
School of the Art Inst of Chicago	IL	44,000	SP
School of Visual Arts	NY	36,500	SP
Seattle Univ	WA	47,010	VǤ
Southeast Missouri State Univ	MO	14,983	LC
Southern Illinois Univ Carbondale	IL	21,620	C
St. Edward's Univ	TX	44,674	VC
St. John's Univ	NY	52,840	Ǥ
SUNY Fredonia / The SUNY at Fredonia	NY	18,702	VC
SUNY New Paltz	NY	15,010	C
Syracuse Univ	NY	54,512	HC
Temple Univ	PA	24,392	VC
Texas A&M Univ at Commerce	TX	10,496	C
Texas Christian Univ	TX	47,570	HC
Texas State Univ	TX	16,495	VC
Texas Tech Univ	TX	14,243	C
Thomas Edison State College	NJ	5,700	SP
Univ of Central Florida	FL	15,711	VǤ
Univ of Central Missouri	MO	14,605	C
Univ of Central Okla	OK	12,293	C
Univ of Dayton	OH	43,750	VC
Univ of Florida	FL	15,783	HǤ
Univ of Hartford	CT	42,674	C
Univ of Illinois at Chicago	IL	24,293	VC
Univ of Illinois at Urbana-Champaign	IL	24,300	HC
Univ of Iowa	IA	17,481	VC
Univ of La Verne	CA	47,010	VC
Univ of Mass Dartmouth	MA	22,223	C
Univ of Miami	FL	55,166	MC
Univ of Mich/Ann Arbor	MI	22,102	HǤ
Univ of Oregon	OR	20,872	VC
Univ of the Arts	PA	38,450	SP
Univ of Washington	WA	14,722	VC
Virginia Commonwealth Univ	VA	18,633	C
Virginia Intermont College	VA	32,411	LC
Washington Univ in St. Louis	MO	58,818	MC
Webster Univ	MO	33,990	Ǥ
Western Washington Univ	WA	18,519	VC
Youngstown State Univ	OH	16,374	LC

PHYSICAL ACTIVITY

School	ST	$IS	SR
Univ of Pittsburgh at Pittsburgh	PA	27,800	HǤ

PHYSICAL CHEMISTRY

School	ST	$IS	SR
Centre College	KY	35,000	HǤ
Union Univ	TN	28,260	VC
Univ of Calif at San Diego	CA	21,000	VC

PHYSICAL EDUCATION

School	ST	$IS	SR
Adams State College	CO	13,358	LC
Adelphi Univ	NY	43,130	VC
Adrian College	MI	33,800	C
Alabama A&M Univ	AL	96,100	C
Albany State Univ	GA	8,500	C
Albion College	MI	43,884	VC
Alderson Broaddus Univ	WV	28,656	C
Alice Lloyd College	KY	4,900	C
Anderson Univ	IN	35,390	C
Appalachian State Univ	NC	12,919	VC
Aquinas College	MI	33,060	C
Arkansas State Univ	AR	14,980	C
Arkansas Tech Univ	AR	13,164	LC
Armstrong Atlantic State Univ	GA	16,276	C
Asbury Univ	KY	32,038	VC
Ashland Univ	OH	25,000	C
Auburn Univ	AL	20,052	VǤ
Augsburg College	MN	35,142	C
Augustana College	IL	43,398	HC
Augustana College	SD	35,500	VC
Aurora Univ	IL	26,870	C
Averett Univ	VA	36,000	LC
Azusa Pacific Univ	CA	39,946	C
Baker Univ	KS	33,350	Ǥ
Baldwin Wallace Univ	OH	36,980	VC
Ball State Univ	IN	17,850	C
Barry Univ	FL	38,190	C
Barton College	NC	27,660	C
Baylor Univ	TX	46,720	HC
Bellevue Univ	NE	4,600	NC
Belmont Univ	TN	37,380	VǤ
Benedictine College	KS	29,180	C
Berea College	KY	7,220	HC
Berry College	GA	39,254	HC
Bethany College	KS	30,605	NC
Bethany College	WV	35,282	C
Bethel College	IN	31,560	C
Bethel Univ	MN	34,940	VC
Bethel Univ	TN	19,186	C
Bethune-Cookman Univ	FL	22,290	LC
Biola Univ	CA	40,320	VC
Black Hills State Univ	SD	13,562	LC
Blackburn College	IL	21,350	C
Blue Mountain College	MS	13,550	LC
Bluffton Univ	OH	37,864	C
Boise State Univ	ID	12,802	C
Boston Univ	MA	54,130	HǤ
Bowling Green State Univ	OH	18,970	C
Brewton-Parker College	GA	33,388	LC
Bridgewater College	VA	39,880	C
Bridgewater State Univ	MA	18,752	C
Bryan College	TN	24,194	C
Cal State, Dominguez Hills	CA	17,056	LC
Cal State, Los Angeles	CA	15,829	C
Cal State, Northridge	CA	28,313	C
Cal State, Stanislaus	CA	18,582	C
Calvin College	MI	37,585	VǤ
Cameron Univ	OK	9,267	LC
Campbellsville Univ	KY	27,720	C
Canisius College	NY	45,602	VC
Capital Univ	OH	39,824	VC
Carroll College	MT	28,000	C
Carroll Univ	WI	24,860	C
Carthage College	WI	33,000	C
Castleton State College	VT	19,424	C
Catawba College	NC	37,105	C
Cedarville Univ	OH	31,036	VǤ
Centenary College of Louisiana	LA	39,070	Ǥ
Central Conn State Univ	CT	19,212	C
Central Methodist Univ	MO	28,240	VC
Central Mich Univ	MI	18,066	C
Central State Univ	OH	9,010	C
Central Washington Univ	WA	11,730	C
Charleston Southern Univ	SC	22,420	C
Chicago State Univ	IL	5,482	C
Citadel, The	SC		C
CUNY/Brooklyn College	NY	5,884	Ǥ
Clark Atlanta Univ	GA	30,006	C
Clearwater Christian College	FL	23,720	C
Cleveland State Univ	OH	21,357	C
Coastal Carolina Univ	SC	17,620	C
Coe College	IA	43,590	VC
Coker College	SC	32,256	LC
College of Charleston	SC	21,273	VC
College of Mount St. Vincent	NY	41,040	MC
College of New Jersey	NJ	25,376	HC
College of the Ozarks	MO	5,605	VC
Concordia College, Moorhead	MN	39,974	Ǥ
Concordia Univ Nebr	NE	26,000	VC
Concordia Univ St. Paul	MN	27,200	C
Concordia Univ Wisc	WI	28,980	C
Concordia Univ, Ann Arbor	MI	27,220	VC

School	ST	$IS	SR
Concordia Univ, River Forest	IL	26,300	C
Corban Univ	OR	34,764	C
Cornerstone Univ and Grand Rapids Theological Seminary	MI	30,866	C
Culver-Stockton College	MO	30,900	C
Cumberland Univ	TN	21,220	C
Dakota Wesleyan Univ	SD	23,000	C
Dallas Baptist Univ	TX	29,118	C
Davis and Elkins College	WV	33,742	C
Defiance College	OH	30,645	C
Delaware State Univ	DE	14,700	LC
Denison Univ	OH	54,670	H₵
DePaul Univ	IL	46,120	VC
Doane College	NE	33,730	VC
Dordt College	IA	34,160	VC
Drury Univ	MO	30,319	VC
East Carolina Univ	NC	14,169	C
East Central Univ	OK	10,223	LC
East Tenn State Univ	TN	9,000	C
East Texas Baptist Univ	TX	29,135	C
Eastern Conn State Univ	CT	20,584	C
Eastern Kentucky Univ	KY	11,161	C
Eastern Mennonite Univ	VA	38,850	VC
Eastern Mich Univ	MI	17,961	C
Eastern New Mexico Univ	NM	10,682	C
Eastern Oregon Univ	OR	10,400	C
Eastern Washington Univ	WA	16,388	C
Edinboro Univ of Pennsylvania	PA	15,940	LC
Edward Waters College	FL	17,856	LC
Elizabeth City State Univ	NC	11,638	C
Elmhurst College	IL	42,032	₵
Elon Univ	NC	40,046	HC
Emory and Henry College	VA	387,460	C
Emporia State Univ	KS	12,897	C
Endicott College	MA	42,390	C
Erskine College	SC	37,360	C
Eureka College	IL	19,280	C
Evangel Univ	MO	23,090	C
Faulkner Univ	AL	22,530	LC
Ferrum College	VA	27,740	LC
Florida Atlantic Univ	FL	17,339	C
Florida International Univ	FL	17,747	VC
Florida Memorial Univ	FL	20,716	LC
Florida State Univ	FL	15,238	HC
Fort Hays State Univ	KS	11,354	C
Fort Valley State Univ	GA	11,200	VC
Franklin College	IN	35,885	C
Freed-Hardeman Univ	TN	19,697	VC
Fresno Pacific Univ	CA	32,136	C
Frostburg State Univ	MD	15,264	LC
Gallaudet Univ	DC	25,380	SP
Gardner-Webb Univ	NC	34,375	₵
George Mason Univ	VA	15,724	VC
Georgia State Univ	GA	12,000	VC
Glenville State College	WV	11,348	NC
Gonzaga Univ	WA	44,247	HC
Goshen College	IN	35,900	VC
Grace College and Theological Seminary	IN	28,800	C
Graceland Univ	IA	28,020	C
Grambling State Univ	LA	13,384	LC
Grand Canyon Univ	AZ	24,540	VC
Grand View Univ	IA	31,050	C
Greensboro College	NC	28,740	LC
Greenville College	IL	27,012	C
Hampton Univ	VA	28,528	C
Hardin-Simmons Univ	TX	23,560	₵
Heidelberg Univ	OH	34,100	C
Henderson State Univ	AR	13,634	C
High Point Univ	NC	39,800	C
Hillsdale College	MI	31,890	H₵
Hofstra Univ	NY	48,020	V₵
Houghton College	NY	35,740	VC
Houston Baptist Univ	TX	23,815	₵
Howard Univ	DC	35,957	C
Humboldt State Univ	CA	18,400	C
Huntingdon College	AL	31,850	C
Huntington Univ	IN	32,220	C
Husson Univ	ME	23,386	LC
Huston-Tillotson Univ	TX	18,124	₵
Idaho State Univ	ID	11,908	C
Illinois State Univ	IL	22,634	VC
Indiana Inst of Technology	IN	34,240	LC
Indiana State Univ	IN	16,000	C
Indiana Univ Bloomington	IN	19,358	HC
Indiana Univ of Pennsylvania	PA	20,180	LC
Indiana Wesleyan Univ	IN	31,815	VC
Inter-American Univ of PR/ Aguadilla Campus	PR	5,578	
Iowa State Univ	IA	16,403	C
Iowa Wesleyan College	IA	30,850	LC
Ithaca College	NY	52,300	HC
Jacksonville Univ	FL	37,780	C
John Brown Univ	AR	30,996	VC
John Carroll Univ	OH	44,520	₵
Johnson C. Smith Univ	NC	25,336	LC
Johnson State College	VT	16,721	C
Judson Univ	IL	25,130	C
Kansas Wesleyan Univ	KS	32,000	C
Kean Univ	NJ	22,060	LC
Keene State College	NH	21,538	C
Kennesaw State Univ	GA	13,017	VC
Kent State Univ	OH	19,352	C

School	ST	$IS	SR
Kentucky State Univ	KY	11,000	LC
Kentucky Wesleyan College	KY	27,440	V₵
King Univ	TN	33,140	C
La Sierra Univ	CA	35,694	VC
Lander Univ	SC	22,514	₵
Lane College	TN	11,212	C
Langston Univ	OK	3,000	LC
Lee Univ	TN	18,690	₵
LeTourneau Univ	TX	26,230	C
Liberty Univ	VA	19,101	C
Limestone College	SC	29,880	C
Lincoln Univ	MO	11,996	NC
Lindenwood Univ	MO	20,750	C
Linfield College-McMinnville Campus	OR	46,166	C
Lipscomb Univ	TN	35,722	VC
Lock Haven Univ of Pennsylvania	PA	17,587	LC
Longwood Univ	VA	20,924	C
Loras College	IA	37,432	VC
Louisiana Tech Univ	LA	8,000	C
Lubbock Christian Univ	TX	25,518	C
Luther College	IA	44,380	V₵
Lyndon State College	VT	14,233	C
MacMurray College	IL	20,755	C
Malone Univ	OH	34,334	C
Manhattan College	NY	44,955	VC
Marian Univ/Indianapolis	IN	37,058	C
Mars Hill College	NC	22,950	LC
Marshall Univ	WV	14,820	C
Maryville College	TN	33,150	VC
Marywood Univ	PA	40,095	C
Mayville State Univ	ND	11,401	NC
McDaniel College	MD	45,600	VC
McKendree Univ	IL	29,920	₵
McMurry Univ	TX	25,962	LC
McPherson College	KS	28,138	C
Messiah College	PA	39,540	VC
Methodist Univ	NC	37,185	C
Metropolitan State Univ of Denver	CO	4,835	LC
Mich State Univ	MI	13,689	VC
MidAmerica Nazarene Univ	KS	28,000	C
Middle Tenn State Univ	TN	8,650	C
Midwestern State Univ	TX	9,722	C
Millikin Univ	IL	37,462	C
Minn State Univ, Mankato	MN	14,900	C
Minn State Univ, Moorhead	MN	13,392	C
Minot State Univ	ND	10,915	C
Miss Valley State Univ	MS	9,706	LC
Missouri Baptist Univ	MO	30,310	C
Missouri Southern State Univ	MO	11,910	C
Missouri State Univ	MO	13,996	VC
Missouri Valley College	MO	22,200	C
Monmouth College	IL	39,290	C
Monmouth Univ	NJ	42,252	C
Montana State Univ-Billings	MT	12,425	LC
Montana State Univ-Northern	MT	12,500	NC
Montclair State Univ	NJ	22,614	C
Morehead State Univ	KY	10,900	C
Morgan State Univ	MD	14,500	VC
Mount Marty College	SD	29,638	C
Mount Vernon Nazarene Univ	OH	29,590	C
Muskingum Univ	OH	30,502	C
Nebr Wesleyan Univ	NE	29,774	₵
New England College	NH	45,930	LC
New Mexico State Univ	NM	13,955	LC
Newberry College	SC	26,850	LC
N Car Agricultural and Technical State Univ	NC	13,175	LC
N Car Central Univ	NC	9,000	LC
N Dak State Univ	ND	14,642	C
North Georgia College & State Univ	GA	8,500	C
Northeastern Illinois Univ	IL		C
Northern Illinois Univ	IL	19,768	C
Northern Kentucky Univ	KY	15,302	LC
Northern Mich Univ	MI	15,300	VC
Northern State Univ	SD	14,021	C
Northwest Missouri State Univ	MO	14,229	C
Northwest Nazarene Univ	ID	24,275	NC
Northwest Univ	WA	18,854	C
Northwestern College	MN	24,000	C
Northwestern College of Iowa	IA	34,848	₵
Northwestern Okla State Univ	OK	7,275	NC
Norwich Univ	VT	28,212	C
Nova Southeastern Univ	FL	34,016	VC
Oakwood Univ	AL	23,035	C
Ohio Northern Univ	OH	42,075	VC
Ohio Univ	OH	20,676	VC
Ohio Wesleyan Univ	OH	49,460	₵
Okla Baptist Univ	OK	28,202	VC
Okla Christian Univ	OK	24,975	VC
Okla Panhandle State Univ	OK	8,996	NC
Okla State Univ	OK	14,310	VC
Okla Wesleyan Univ	OK	21,300	C
Old Dominion Univ	VA	18,662	C
Olivet College	MI	19,984	C
Olivet Nazarene Univ	IL	29,990	C
Oral Roberts Univ	OK	31,734	C
Ottawa Univ	KS	15,000	VC

School	ST	$IS	SR
Otterbein College	OH	32,214	C
Pacific Lutheran Univ	WA	44,840	VC
Pacific Union College	CA	28,150	VC
Palm Beach Atlantic Univ	FL	33,882	LC
Pepperdine Univ	CA	55,372	H₵
Peru State College	NE	8,600	NC
Pfeiffer Univ	NC	33,700	C
Philander Smith College	AR	19,760	LC
Pittsburg State Univ	KS	12,032	C
Plymouth State Univ	NH	23,148	LC
Point Loma Nazarene Univ	CA	38,610	VC
Pontifical Catholic Univ of PR	PR	7,310	
Prairie View A&M Univ	TX	15,205	LC
Prescott College	AZ	33,284	₵
Queens College / The CUNY	NY	17,107	VC
Quincy Univ	IL	34,980	LC
Radford Univ	VA	17,132	LC
Randolph College	VA	43,960	VC
Rhode Island College	RI	17,132	LC
Roanoke College	VA	47,996	₵
Roberts Wesleyan College	NY	37,384	₵
Rockford College	IL	31,000	C
Rocky Mountain College	MT	32,242	C
Saginaw Valley State Univ	MI	16,869	C
St. Augustine's Univ	NC	14,000	C
St. Joseph's College	IN	35,790	C
St. Joseph's College of Maine	ME	31,580	C
St. Mary's College of Calif	CA	53,550	C
Salisbury Univ	MD	18,368	VC
Sam Houston State Univ	TX	17,082	C
San Diego State Univ	CA	20,578	VC
San Francisco State Univ	CA	18,514	C
Schreiner Univ	TX	32,734	LC
Seattle Pacific Univ	WA	41,559	V₵
Shaw Univ	NC	15,488	LC
Shepherd Univ	WV	14,996	C
Simpson College	IA	36,086	VC
S Car State Univ	SC	6,700	LC
S Dak State Univ	SD	14,296	C
Southeast Missouri State Univ	MO	14,983	LC
Southeastern Louisiana Univ	LA	13,325	C
Southeastern Okla State Univ	OK	7,966	C
Southern Adventist Univ	TN	26,190	C
Southern Conn State Univ	CT	18,033	C
Southern Illinois Univ Carbondale	IL	21,620	C
Southern Illinois Univ Edwardsville	IL	17,532	C
Southern Methodist Univ	TX	57,755	MC
Southern Nazarene Univ	OK	24,354	NC
Southern Oregon Univ	OR	17,874	C
Southern Univ at New Orleans	LA	1,000	NC
Southern Wesleyan Univ	SC	25,600	C
Southwest Baptist Univ	MO	24,710	C
Southwest Minn State Univ	MN	14,000	C
Southwestern Adventist Univ	TX	23,026	LC
Southwestern College	KS	29,270	C
Southwestern Okla State Univ	OK	9,160	C
Springfield College	MA	25,000	C
St. Ambrose Univ	IA		C
St. Andrews Univ	NC	32,050	LC
St. Bonaventure Univ	NY	38,831	C
St. Catherine Univ	MN	37,782	₵
St. Edward's Univ	TX	44,674	VC
St. Francis College	NY	34,200	LC
Stillman College	AL	18,460	C
SUNY Cortland / The SUNY	NY	19,117	C
Syracuse Univ	NY	54,512	HC
Tabor College	KS	29,010	LC
Tarleton State Univ	TX	13,489	LC
Taylor Univ	IN	36,742	V₵
Temple Univ	PA	24,392	VC
Tenn Tech Univ	TN	11,310	C
Tenn Wesleyan College	TN	21,250	C
Texas A&M Univ	TX	16,956	V₵
Texas A&M Univ at Kingsville	TX	7,500	LC
Texas Christian Univ	TX	47,570	HC
Texas Lutheran Univ	TX	34,070	C
Texas Southern Univ	TX	18,212	LC
Texas State Univ	TX	16,495	VC
Texas Wesleyan Univ	TX	29,886	C
The College at Brockport / SUNY	NY	18,362	VC
The College of Idaho	ID	31,277	VC
The Masters College	CA	38,160	₵
Ohio State Univ	OH	19,887	MC
Tougaloo College	MS	15,275	NC
Towson Univ	MD	16,000	VC
Trevecca Nazarene Univ	TN	30,118	C
Trine Univ	IN	39,400	VC
Trinity International Univ	IL	31,070	C
Troy Univ	AL	10,650	C
Truman State Univ	MO	13,546	HC
Tusculum College	TN	24,295	C
Tuskegee Univ	AL	26,750	C
Union College	KY	28,775	C
Union College	NE	23,270	VC

School	ST	$IS	SR
Union Univ	TN	28,260	VC
Universidad del Turabo	PR	4,110	
Univ of Akron	OH	20,436	C
Univ of Alabama at Birmingham	AL	18,484	₵
Univ of Alabama at Tuscaloosa	AL	17,164	₵
Univ of Alaska Anchorage	AK	15,290	NC
Univ of Arkansas at Monticello	AR	8,470	NC
Univ of Arkansas at Pine Bluff	AR	10,600	C
Univ of Calif at Davis	CA	24,482	HC
Univ of Central Arkansas	AR	10,840	VC
Univ of Central Missouri	MO	14,605	C
Univ of Central Okla	OK	12,293	C
Univ of Charleston	WV	28,650	C
Univ of Delaware	DE	22,728	VC
Univ of Dubuque	IA	30,200	C
Univ of Findlay	OH	31,916	C
Univ of Great Falls	MT	27,970	C
Univ of Hawaii at Manoa	HI	19,379	VC
Univ of Idaho	ID	14,558	C
Univ of Illinois at Chicago	IL	24,293	VC
Univ of Illinois at Urbana-Champaign	IL	24,300	HC
Univ of Indianapolis	IN	31,740	LC
Univ of Jamestown	ND	24,738	C
Univ of Kansas	KS	16,980	₵
Univ of Kentucky	KY	19,868	C
Univ of Louisville	KY	17,460	VC
Univ of Maine	ME	19,712	₵
Univ of Maine at Presque Isle	ME	15,011	LC
Univ of Mary	ND	16,714	C
Univ of Mary Hardin-Baylor	TX	31,950	₵
Univ of Maryland	MD	18,801	HC
Univ of Maryland/Eastern Shore	MD	14,000	C
Univ of Memphis	TN	15,094	C
Univ of Mich/Ann Arbor	MI	22,102	H₵
Univ of Minn/Duluth	MN	18,964	₵
Univ of Minn/Twin Cities	MN		HC
Univ of Missouri-St. Louis	MO	18,304	VC
Univ of Mobile	AL	27,870	VC
Univ of Montana	MT	13,670	C
Univ of Montana-Western	MT	9,753	LC
Univ of Montevallo	AL	17,320	C
Univ of Mount Union	OH	35,130	C
Univ of Nebr at Kearney	NE	14,855	LC
Univ of Nebr at Omaha	NE	12,700	C
Univ of Nevada, Las Vegas	NV	17,303	C
Univ of New Hampshire	NH	24,702	VC
Univ of New Mexico	NM	15,300	C
Univ of New Orleans	LA	9,224	VC
Univ of North Alabama	AL	9,960	C
Univ of N Car at Greensboro	NC	12,848	C
Univ of N Car at Wilmington	NC	13,572	V₵
Univ of N Dak	ND	14,094	C
Univ of North Florida	FL	15,578	VC
Univ of Northern Colo	CO	15,973	C
Univ of Northern Iowa	IA	14,776	C
Univ of PR/Arecibo	PR	7,227	
Univ of Rio Grande	OH	8,750	NC
Univ of Science and Arts of Okla	OK	10,560	VC
Univ of South Alabama	AL	13,510	C
Univ of S Car at Columbia	SC	19,725	V₵
Univ of S Car Upstate	SC	17,673	LC
Univ of S Dak	SD	15,111	C
Univ of South Florida	FL	13,000	C
Univ of Southern Indiana	IN	14,657	C
Univ of Texas at Arlington	TX	10,908	LC
Univ of the Cumberlands	KY	27,500	LC
Univ of the District of Columbia	DC	7,244	LC
Univ of the Incarnate Word	TX	35,200	LC
Univ of the Ozarks	AR	22,100	C
Univ of the Pacific	CA	52,146	VC
Univ of the Sacred Heart	PR	5,590	
Univ of Toledo	OH	18,464	C
Univ of Vermont	VT	26,120	V₵
Univ of West Alabama	AL	9,415	C
Univ of West Georgia	GA	14,852	LC
Univ of Wisc Whitewater	WI	13,314	C
Univ of Wisc/Eau Claire	WI	15,430	VC
Univ of Wisc/La Crosse	WI	14,755	VC
Univ of Wisc/Madison	WI	18,757	HC
Univ of Wisc/Oshkosh	WI	10,426	LC
Univ of Wisc/Platteville	WI	14,274	C
Univ of Wisc/River Falls	WI	9,722	LC
Univ of Wisc/Stevens Point	WI	14,043	C
Univ of Wisc/Superior	WI	14,106	C
Univ of Wyoming	WY	13,855	₵
Upper Iowa Univ	IA	30,426	NC
Utah State Univ	UT	11,803	C
Valley City State Univ	ND	12,286	LC
Valparaiso Univ	IN	43,040	V₵
Vanguard Univ of Southern Calif	CA	35,833	VC
Virginia State Univ	VA	11,318	₵
Walla Walla Univ	WA	26,256	NC
Walsh Univ	OH	35,100	C
Warner Pacific College	OR	25,550	C
Warner Univ	FL	18,000	C
Wartburg College	IA	41,055	VC

School	ST	$IS	SR
Washburn Univ	KS	12,165	NC
Washington Adventist Univ	MD	25,859	C+
Washington State Univ	WA	20,461	C
Wayland Baptist Univ	TX	16,058	LC
Wayne State Univ	MI	19,493	C
Wesley College	DE	31,115	LC
West Chester Univ of Pennsylvania	PA	16,836	C
West Liberty Univ	WV	9,142	LC
West Texas A&M Univ	TX	13,478	C
West Virginia Univ	WV	15,794	C+
West Virginia Wesleyan College	WV	26,880	C
Western Carolina Univ	NC	13,965	C+
Western Illinois Univ	IL	20,130	C
Western Kentucky Univ	KY	11,000	LC
Western Mich Univ	MI	19,042	C
Western New Mexico Univ	NM	8,500	LC
Western Washington Univ	WA	18,519	VC
Westminster College	MO	30,490	VC
Wichita State Univ	KS	12,539	C
Wiley College	TX		LC
William Carey Univ	MS	13,500	LC
William Paterson Univ of New Jersey	NJ	21,694	C
William Penn Univ	IA	26,000	C
William Woods Univ	MO		C
Williams Baptist College	AR	20,070	C
Wilmington College	OH	29,784	C
Wingate Univ	NC	34,990	C
Winona State Univ	MN	16,530	C
Winston-Salem State Univ	NC	9,418	LC
Winthrop Univ	SC	21,120	VC
Wright State Univ	OH	16,983	C
York College / CUNY	NY	5,496	NC
Youngstown State Univ	OH	16,374	LC

PHYSICAL FITNESS/ MOVEMENT

School	ST	$IS	SR
Ashland Univ	OH	25,000	C
Auburn Univ	AL	20,052	VC+
Augustana College	SD	35,500	VC
Baylor Univ	TX	46,720	HC
Boston Univ	MA	54,130	HC+
Brigham Young Univ/ Hawaii	HI	8,614	VC
Buena Vista Univ	IA	37,954	C
Calif State Polytechnic Univ, Pomona	CA	18,932	C
Cal State, East Bay	CA	16,549	C
Cal State, Fresno	CA	17,405	C
Cal State, Monterey Bay	CA	26,871	LC
Cal State, San Marcos	CA	14,576	C
Campbell Univ	NC	25,500	C
Capital Univ	OH	39,824	VC
Clarke Univ	IA	36,400	C
Colo Mesa Univ	CO	16,669	LC
Concordia Univ Nebr	NE	26,000	VC
Concordia Univ St. Paul	MN	27,200	C
Concordia Univ, River Forest	IL	26,300	C
Dallas Baptist Univ	TX	29,118	C
Defiance College	OH	30,645	C
DePauw Univ	IN	48,950	VC+
East Carolina Univ	NC	14,169	C
East Stroudsburg Univ of Pennsylvania	PA	16,636	C
East Texas Baptist Univ	TX	29,135	C
Eastern Nazarene College	MA	30,000	C
Eureka College	IL	19,280	C
George Washington Univ	DC	57,108	MC
Grand Canyon Univ	AZ	24,540	VC
Hope College	MI	36,320	VC+
Houston Baptist Univ	TX	23,815	C+
Humboldt State Univ	CA	18,400	C
Ithaca College	NY	52,300	HC
James Madison Univ	VA	18,049	VC
Johnson State College	VT	16,721	C
Kansas State Univ	KS	15,497	VC
Lakeland College	WI	22,990	C
Lasell College	MA	42,500	LC
Lewis-Clark State College	ID	6,990	C
Limestone College	SC	29,880	C
Louisiana State Univ	LA	18,677	VC+
Lubbock Christian Univ	TX	25,518	C
Lynchburg College	VA	42,645	C
Marshall Univ	WV	14,820	C
Marywood Univ	PA	40,695	C
Metropolitan State Univ of Denver	CO	4,835	LC
Miami Univ	OH	24,191	HC
Minot State Univ	ND	10,915	C
Miss Univ for Women	MS	7,400	LC
New England College	NH	45,930	LC
New Mexico Highlands Univ	NM	9,720	NC
New Mexico State Univ	NM	13,955	LC
N Dak State Univ	ND	14,642	C
Northern Illinois Univ	IL	19,768	C
Northern Kentucky Univ	KY	15,302	LC
Northern Mich Univ	MI	15,300	VC
Northern State Univ	SD	14,021	C
Northwestern College of Iowa	IA	34,848	C+
Notre Dame de Namur Univ	CA	41,610	LC
Oakwood Univ	AL	23,035	C
Occidental College	CA	59,592	MC+
Purdue Univ/West Lafayette	IN	20,278	HC
St. Augustine's Univ	NC	14,000	C
Sam Houston State Univ	TX	17,082	C
San Diego Christian College	CA	31,012	C
Seattle Pacific Univ	WA	41,559	VC+
Shenandoah Univ	VA	39,268	C
Sonoma State Univ	CA	20,541	C
Southern Methodist Univ	TX	57,755	MC
Southern Nazarene Univ	OK	24,354	NC
Spring Arbor Univ	MI	26,740	C
Springfield College	MA	25,000	C
St. Edward's Univ	TX	44,674	VC
Stephen F. Austin State Univ	TX	14,668	C
Sul Ross State Univ	TX	13,410	LC
Tarleton State Univ	TX	13,489	LC
Temple Univ	PA	24,392	VC
Texas Southern Univ	TX	18,212	LC
Texas Woman's Univ	TX	13,633	LC
Ohio State Univ	OH	19,887	MC
Truman State Univ	MO	13,546	HC
Union College	NE	23,270	VC
Univ of Central Okla	OK	12,293	C
Univ of Florida	FL	15,783	HC+
Univ of Illinois at Chicago	IL	24,293	VC
Univ of La Verne	CA	47,010	VC
Univ of Mass Boston	MA	11,966	C
Univ of Mich/Ann Arbor	MI	22,102	HC+
Univ of Nevada, Las Vegas	NV	17,303	C
Univ of New Hampshire	NH	24,702	VC
Univ of N Car at Charlotte	NC	15,847	C
Univ of North Texas	TX	15,628	C
Univ of Northern Colo	CO	15,973	C
Univ of Rio Grande	OH	8,750	NC
Univ of Texas at Austin	TX	44,074	HC
Univ of Texas at El Paso	TX	8,764	NC
Univ of Texas-Pan American	TX	12,432	LC
Univ of Toledo	OH	18,464	C
Upper Iowa Univ	IA	30,426	NC
Urbana Univ	OH	21,190	C
Virginia Polytechnic Inst and State Univ	VA	14,629	HC
West Liberty Univ	WV	9,142	LC
Western State Colo Univ	CO	16,135	C
Westfield State Univ	MA	18,489	C
Whittier College	CA	43,416	C
Winona State Univ	MN	16,530	C

PHYSICAL SCIENCE SECONDARY SCHOOL EDUCATION

School	ST	$IS	SR
Dordt College	IA	34,160	VC
Duquesne Univ	PA	42,017	VC
Keene State College	NH	21,538	C
Texas Christian Univ	TX	47,570	HC
Univ of Nebr - Lincoln	NE	17,507	VC
Youngstown State Univ	OH	16,374	LC

PHYSICAL SCIENCES

School	ST	$IS	SR
Arkansas Tech Univ	AR	13,164	LC
Asbury Univ	KY	32,038	VC
Auburn Univ at Montgomery	AL	12,120	C
Bennington College	VT	56,990	HC+
Bethany College	WV	35,282	C
Bethel College	IN	31,560	C
Biola Univ	CA	40,320	VC
Black Hills State Univ	SD	13,562	LC
Bluffton Univ	OH	37,864	C
Brescia Univ	KY	26,140	VC+
Cal State, Chico	CA	18,952	C
Cal State, East Bay	CA	16,549	C
Cal State, Sacramento	CA	16,200	C
Cal State, Stanislaus	CA	18,582	C
Calif Univ of Pennsylvania	PA	14,217	C
Central Conn State Univ	CT	19,212	C
Central Mich Univ	MI	18,066	C
Colgate Univ	NY	50,930	MC
Colo Mesa Univ	CO	16,669	LC
Colo State Univ-Fort Collins	CO	20,090	VC
Concordia Univ Nebr	NE	26,000	VC
Concordia Univ, Ann Arbor	MI	27,220	VC
Concordia Univ, River Forest	IL	26,300	C
Creighton Univ	NE	44,058	VC+
Dakota State Univ	SD	13,811	C
DePaul Univ	IL	46,120	VC
Doane College	NE	33,730	VC
Dordt College	IA	34,160	VC
East Stroudsburg Univ of Pennsylvania	PA	16,636	C
Embry-Riddle Aeronautical Univ - Daytona Beach	FL	40,884	C+
Emporia State Univ	KS	12,897	C
Eureka College	IL	19,280	C
Fort Hays State Univ	KS	11,354	C
Freed-Hardeman Univ	TN	19,697	VC
Harvard Univ/Harvard College	MA	49,000	MC
Indiana Univ Kokomo	IN	6,674	LC
Indiana Univ-Purdue Univ Fort Wayne	IN	15,425	C
Kansas State Univ	KS	15,497	VC
Kent State Univ	OH	19,352	C
Le Moyne College	NY	42,200	VC
Malone Univ	OH	34,334	C
Mayville State Univ	ND	11,401	NC
Mich State Univ	MI	13,689	VC
Minot State Univ	ND	10,915	C
Miss Univ for Women	MS	7,400	LC
Muhlenberg College	PA	52,837	HC
Northwestern State Univ of Louisiana	LA	14,368	C
Okla Panhandle State Univ	OK	8,996	NC
Olivet Nazarene Univ	IL	29,990	C
Peru State College	NE	6,000	NC
Ripon College	WI	36,959	C+
Rowan Univ	NJ	23,570	VC
St. Michael's College	VT	48,740	VC
Salisbury Univ	MD	18,368	VC
San Diego State Univ	CA	20,578	VC
St. John's Univ	NY	52,840	C+
Trine Univ	IN	39,400	VC
Union Univ	TN	28,260	VC
Univ of Arkansas at Monticello	AR	8,470	NC
Univ of Calif at Berkeley	CA	23,322	MC
Univ of Calif at Riverside	CA	27,204	C
Univ of Dayton	OH	43,750	VC
Univ of Great Falls	MT	27,970	C
Univ of Maryland	MD	18,801	HC
Univ of Mich-Flint	MI	17,547	C+
Univ of Pittsburgh at Bradford	PA	21,316	LC
Univ of Rio Grande	OH	8,750	NC
Univ of South Florida	FL	13,000	C
Univ of Southern Calif	CA	56,903	MC
Univ of Texas-Pan American	TX	12,432	LC
Univ of Wisc/Eau Claire	WI	15,430	VC
Univ of Wisc/Platteville	WI	14,274	C
Washington State Univ	WA	20,461	C
Washington Univ in St. Louis	MO	58,818	MC
Wayland Baptist Univ	TX	16,058	LC
Wesleyan College	GA	24,000	C+
Youngstown State Univ	OH	16,374	LC

PHYSICAL THERAPY

School	ST	$IS	SR
American International College	MA	36,100	LC
Armstrong Atlantic State Univ	GA	16,276	C
Biola Univ	CA	40,320	VC
Boston Univ	MA	54,130	HC+
Cal State, Northridge	CA	28,313	C
Cal State, Sacramento	CA	16,200	C
Carson-Newman Univ	TN	29,058	C+
Chatham Univ	PA	42,440	VC
Clarke Univ	IA	36,400	C
Cleveland State Univ	OH	21,357	C
Coe College	IA	43,590	VC
Duquesne Univ	PA	42,017	VC
Fairleigh Dickinson Univ/ Metropolitan Campus	NJ	40,254	C
Florida A&M Univ	FL	14,935	LC
Gannon Univ	PA	37,940	C
Gordon College	MA	42,660	VC+
Grand Valley State Univ	MI	17,998	VC
Gustavus Adolphus College	MN	48,170	HC
Howard Univ	DC	35,957	C
Hunter College / The CUNY	NY	14,429	VC
Husson Univ	ME	23,386	LC
Ithaca College	NY	52,300	HC
Lamar Univ	TX	6,820	LC
Langston Univ	OK	3,000	LC
Lewis Univ	IL	23,050	C
LIU/Brooklyn Campus	NY	26,500	C
Maryville Univ of St. Louis	MO	34,920	VC
Misericordia Univ	PA	39,840	C
Missouri Southern State Univ	MO	11,910	C
Missouri State Univ	MO	13,996	VC
Mount Aloysius College	PA	27,970	C
New York Inst of Technology	NY	40,590	VC
New York Univ	NY	61,470	MC
North Park Univ	IL	30,130	C
Northeastern Univ	MA	55,296	MC
Notre Dame College	OH	34,942	VC
Ohio Univ	OH	20,676	VC
Okla Baptist Univ	OK	28,202	VC
Purdue Univ/Calumet	IN	14,336	C
Quinnipiac Univ	CT	53,580	VC
Regis Univ	CO	41,318	C
Richard Stockton College of New Jersey	NJ	20,000	VC
Russell Sage College	NY	39,370	C
Sacred Heart Univ	CT	48,564	VC
St. Francis Univ	PA	30,029	LC
St. Vincent College	PA	40,244	C
Simmons College	MA	48,770	VC
Stony Brook Univ / SUNY	NY	19,359	HC
Tarleton State Univ	TX	13,489	LC
Tenn State Univ	TN	9,048	C
Ohio State Univ	OH	19,887	MC
Thiel College	PA	31,378	LC
Touro College	NY	23,150	VC
Trinity International Univ	IL	31,070	C
Truman State Univ	MO	13,546	HC
Univ at Buffalo / The SUNY	NY	20,283	VC
Univ of Akron	OH	20,436	C
Univ of Central Arkansas	AR	10,840	VC
Univ of Conn	CT	23,744	HC
Univ of Florida	FL	15,783	HC+
Univ of Hartford	CT	42,674	C
Univ of Illinois at Chicago	IL	24,293	VC
Univ of Kentucky	KY	19,868	C
Univ of Mary	ND	10,714	C
Univ of Maryland/Eastern Shore	MD	14,000	C
Univ of Mich-Flint	MI	17,547	C+
Univ of Minn/Twin Cities	MN		HC
Univ of Missouri/Columbia	MO	18,201	MC
Univ of N Car at Wilmington	NC	13,572	VC+
Univ of N Dak	ND	14,094	C
Univ of North Florida	FL	15,578	VC
Univ of the Sciences	PA	48,320	VC+
Univ of Toledo	OH	18,464	C
Univ of Utah	UT	13,462	VC
Utica College	NY	44,734	C
Vanguard Univ of Southern Calif	CA	35,833	VC
Virginia Polytechnic Inst and State Univ	VA	14,629	HC
Walsh Univ	OH	35,100	C
West Virginia Univ	WV	15,794	C+
Winston-Salem State Univ	NC	9,418	LC

PHYSICAL THERAPY ASSISTANT

School	ST	$IS	SR
Calif Univ of Pennsylvania	PA	14,217	C
Idaho State Univ	ID	11,908	C
Mount Aloysius College	PA	27,970	C

PHYSICIAN'S ASSISTANT

School	ST	$IS	SR
College of St. Mary	NE	34,334	C
Colo State Univ-Pueblo	CO	13,532	LC
CUNY-City College	NY	19,576	HC+
Daemen College	NY	31,510	C
De Sales Univ	PA	42,670	C
Duquesne Univ	PA	42,017	VC
D'Youville College	NY	29,850	C
Gannon Univ	PA	37,940	C
Gardner-Webb Univ	NC	34,375	C+
George Washington Univ	DC	57,108	MC
Grand Valley State Univ	MI	17,998	VC
Howard Univ	DC	35,957	C
King's College	PA	41,678	C
LIU/Brooklyn Campus	NY	26,500	C
Marietta College	OH	42,135	VC
Mars Hill College	NC	22,950	LC
Methodist Univ	NC	37,185	C
Missouri State Univ	MO	13,996	VC
Mount Aloysius College	PA	27,970	C
Mountain State Univ	WV	14,330	NC
New York Inst of Technology	NY	40,590	VC
Northern Mich Univ	MI	15,300	VC
Pennsylvania College of Technology	PA	25,653	NC
Philadelphia Univ	PA	44,160	C
Quinnipiac Univ	CT	53,580	VC
Rochester Inst of Technology	NY	42,450	VC+
St. Francis Univ	PA	30,029	LC
St. Vincent College	PA	40,244	C
Seton Hill Univ	PA	35,172	C
South Univ	GA		LC
Southern Illinois Univ Carbondale	IL	21,620	C
St. Francis College	NY	34,200	LC
St. John's Univ	NY	52,840	C+
Union College	NE	23,270	VC
Univ of Findlay	OH	31,916	C
Univ of Kentucky	KY	19,868	C
Univ of Miami	FL	55,166	MC
Univ of Texas-Pan American	TX	12,432	LC
Univ of the Sciences	PA	48,320	VC+
Univ of Wisc/La Crosse	WI	14,755	VC
Univ of Wisc/Madison	WI	18,757	HC
Wagner College	NY	48,600	VC
Wichita State Univ	KS	12,539	C

PHYSICS

School	ST	$IS	SR
Abilene Christian Univ	TX	38,400	VC
Adams State College	CO	13,358	LC
Adelphi Univ	NY	43,130	VC
Adrian College	MI	33,800	C
Agnes Scott College	GA	45,323	VC+
Alabama A&M Univ	AL	96,100	C
Alabama State Univ	AL	14,142	NC
Albion College	MI	43,884	VC
Albright College	PA	46,660	C
Alfred Univ	NY	40,392	VC
Allegheny College	PA	49,020	HC

INDEX OF COLLEGE MAJORS

School	ST	$IS	SR
Alma College	MI	42,400	VC
American Univ	DC	54,829	HC+
Amherst College	MA	58,744	MC
Anderson Univ	IN	35,390	C
Andrews Univ	MI	28,030	C+
Angelo State Univ	TX	15,049	NC
Appalachian State Univ	NC	12,919	VC
Arizona State Univ	AZ	18,818	C+
Arkansas State Univ	AR	14,980	C
Arkansas Tech Univ	AR	13,164	LC
Ashland Univ	OH	25,000	C
Auburn Univ	AL	20,052	VC+
Augsburg College	MN	35,142	C
Augustana College	IL	43,398	HC
Augustana College	SD	35,500	VC
Austin College	TX	36,940	HC
Austin Peay State Univ	TN	14,650	C
Azusa Pacific Univ	CA	39,946	C
Baker Univ	KS	33,350	C+
Baldwin Wallace Univ	OH	36,980	VC
Ball State Univ	IN	17,850	C
Bard College	NY	59,872	HC
Bard College at Simon's Rock	MA	58,963	HC+
Bates College	ME	58,950	MC
Baylor Univ	TX	46,720	HC
Bellarmine Univ	KY	42,950	VC
Belmont Univ	TN	37,380	VC+
Beloit College	WI	49,970	HC
Bemidji State Univ	MN	13,500	C
Benedict College	SC	20,454	NC
Benedictine College	KS	29,180	VC
Benedictine Univ	IL	35,220	C
Bennington College	VT	56,990	HC+
Berea College	KY	7,220	HC
Berry College	GA	39,254	HC
Bethel Univ	MN	34,940	VC
Binghamton Univ / The SUNY	NY	20,832	HC+
Biola Univ	CA	40,320	VC
Birmingham-Southern College	AL	42,370	VC+
Bloomsburg Univ of Pennsylvania	PA	13,598	C
Bluffton Univ	OH	37,864	C
Boise State Univ	ID	12,802	C
Boston College	MA	58,506	MC
Boston Univ	MA	54,130	HC+
Bowdoin College	ME	57,834	MC
Bowling Green State Univ	OH	18,970	C
Bradley Univ	IL	31,874	VC
Brandeis Univ	MA	58,820	HC
Bridgewater College	VA	39,880	C
Bridgewater State Univ	MA	18,752	C
Brigham Young Univ	UT	12,100	HC
Brown Univ	RI	56,150	MC
Bryn Mawr College	PA	57,760	MC
Bucknell Univ	PA	58,160	MC
Buena Vista Univ	IA	37,954	C
Buffalo State/State Univ of Buffalo	NY	15,733	C+
Butler Univ	IN	45,898	VC+
Calif Inst of Technology	CA	54,045	MC
Calif Lutheran Univ	CA	47,640	C
Calif Polytechnic State Univ	CA	19,847	HC
Calif State Polytechnic Univ, Pomona	CA	18,932	C
Cal State, Bakersfield	CA	8,000	LC
Cal State, Chico	CA	18,952	C
Cal State, Dominguez Hills	CA	17,056	LC
Cal State, East Bay	CA	16,549	C
Cal State, Fresno	CA	17,405	C
Cal State, Fullerton	CA	25,188	C+
Cal State, Long Beach	CA	17,534	C+
Cal State, Los Angeles	CA	15,829	C
Cal State, Northridge	CA	28,313	C
Cal State, Sacramento	CA	16,200	C
Cal State, San Bernardino	CA	12,000	C
Cal State, Stanislaus	CA	18,582	C
Calif Univ of Pennsylvania	PA	14,217	C
Calvin College	MI	37,585	VC+
Cameron Univ	OK	9,267	LC
Canisius College	NY	45,602	VC
Carleton College	MN	58,149	MC
Carnegie Mellon Univ	PA	51,260	MC
Carthage College	WI	33,000	C
Case Western Reserve Univ	OH	55,178	MC
Cedarville Univ	OH	31,036	VC+
Centenary College of Louisiana	LA	39,070	C+
Central College	IA	36,980	VC
Central Conn State Univ	CT	19,212	C
Central Methodist Univ	MO	28,240	VC
Central Mich Univ	MI	18,066	C
Central Washington Univ	WA	11,730	C
Centre College	KY	35,000	HC+
Chadron State College	NE	7,400	NC
Chapman Univ	CA	56,019	VC+
Chatham Univ	PA	42,440	VC
Chicago State Univ	IL	5,482	C
Christian Brothers Univ	TN	19,140	HC
Citadel, The	SC		C
CUNY/Brooklyn College	NY	5,884	C+
Claremont McKenna College	CA	58,065	MC
Clarion Univ of Pennsylvania	PA	17,370	C
Clark Atlanta Univ	GA	30,006	C
Clark Univ	MA	47,020	HC+
Clarkson Univ	NY	53,538	HC
Clemson Univ	SC	19,136	HC
Cleveland State Univ	OH	21,357	C
Coastal Carolina Univ	SC	17,620	C
Coe College	IA	43,590	VC
Colby College	ME	57,510	MC
Colgate Univ	NY	50,930	MC
College of Staten Island / The CUNY	NY	16,778	NC
College of Charleston	SC	21,273	VC
College of Mount St. Vincent	NY	41,040	MC
College of New Jersey	NJ	25,376	HC
College of St. Benedict	MN	47,570	VC
College of the Holy Cross	MA	56,232	MC
College of William & Mary	VA	25,085	MC
College of Wooster	OH	52,600	VC
Colo College	CO	54,534	MC
Colo School of Mines	CO	18,000	HC
Colo State Univ-Fort Collins	CO	20,090	VC
Colo State Univ-Pueblo	CO	13,532	LC
Columbia Univ in the City of New York	NY	61,116	MC
Columbia Univ/Barnard College	NY	39,000	MC
Columbia Univ/School of General Studies	NY	54,083	MC
Concordia College, Moorhead	MN	39,974	C+
Concordia Univ, Ann Arbor	MI	27,220	VC
Conn College	CT	54,970	MC
Cornell College	IA	44,930	HC
Cornell Univ	NY	59,037	MC
Covenant College	GA		VC+
Creighton Univ	NE	44,058	VC+
CUNY-City College	NY	19,576	HC+
Curry College	MA	47,545	LC
Dartmouth College	NH	57,996	MC
Davidson College	NC	54,683	MC
Delaware State Univ	DE	14,700	LC
Denison Univ	OH	54,670	HC+
DePaul Univ	IL	46,120	VC
DePauw Univ	IN	48,950	VC+
Dickinson College	PA	57,662	HC+
Dillard Univ	LA	20,940	VC
Doane College	NE	33,730	VC
Dordt College	IA	34,160	VC
Drake Univ	IA	30,980	VC+
Drew Univ/College of Liberal Arts	NJ	55,862	VC
Drexel Univ	PA	51,920	HC
Drury Univ	MO	30,319	VC
Duke Univ	NC	50,250	MC
Duquesne Univ	PA	42,017	VC
Earlham College	IN	49,710	VC+
East Carolina Univ	NC	14,169	C
East Central Univ	OK	10,223	LC
East Tenn State Univ	TN	9,000	C
Eastern Illinois Univ	IL	20,502	C
Eastern Mich Univ	MI	17,961	C
Eastern Nazarene College	MA	30,000	C
Eastern Oregon Univ	OR	10,400	C
Eastern Washington Univ	WA	16,388	C
Eckerd College	FL	43,902	VC
Edinboro Univ of Pennsylvania	PA	15,940	LC
Elizabeth City State Univ	NC	11,638	C
Elizabethtown College	PA	47,600	VC
Elmhurst College	IL	42,032	C+
Elon Univ	NC	40,046	HC
Emory and Henry College	VA	387,460	C
Emory Univ	GA	45,000	MC
Emporia State Univ	KS	12,897	C
Erskine College	SC	37,360	C
Excelsior College	NY	895	SP
Fairfield Univ	CT	55,850	VC
Fisk Univ	TN	19,830	C
Florida A&M Univ	FL	14,935	LC
Florida Atlantic Univ	FL	17,339	C
Florida Inst of Technology	FL	48,290	VC
Florida International Univ	FL	17,747	VC
Florida State Univ	FL	15,238	HC
Fordham Univ	NY	58,927	HC
Fort Hays State Univ	KS	11,354	C
Fort Lewis College	CO	15,513	C
Francis Marion Univ	SC	16,464	LC
Franklin and Marshall College	PA	58,295	MC
Frostburg State Univ	MD	15,264	LC
Furman Univ	SC	54,006	HC
Geneva College	PA	27,280	C
George Mason Univ	VA	15,724	VC
George Washington Univ	DC	57,108	MC
Georgetown College	KY	38,690	C
Georgetown Univ	DC	52,910	MC
Georgia College and State Univ	GA	18,216	VC
Georgia Inst of Technology	GA	20,464	MC
Georgia Regents Univ	GA		C
Georgia Southern Univ	GA	16,414	C
Georgia State Univ	GA	12,000	VC
Gettysburg College	PA	56,820	HC
Gonzaga Univ	WA	44,247	HC
Gordon College	MA	42,660	VC+
Goshen College	IN	35,900	VC
Goucher College	MD	50,252	VC+
Grambling State Univ	LA	13,384	LC
Grand Valley State Univ	MI	17,998	VC
Greenville College	IL	27,012	C
Grinnell College	IA	53,654	HC
Grove City College	PA	22,988	HC
Guilford College	NC	35,340	C
Gustavus Adolphus College	MN	48,170	HC
Hamilton College	NY	55,620	MC
Hamline Univ	MN	44,198	VC
Hampden-Sydney College	VA	48,848	C
Hampshire College	MA	58,320	MC
Hampton Univ	VA	28,528	C
Hanover College	IN	41,450	VC
Harding Univ	AR	21,432	C+
Hardin-Simmons Univ	TX	23,560	C+
Hartwick College	NY	49,815	C+
Harvard Univ/Harvard College	MA	49,000	MC
Harvey Mudd College	CA	61,660	MC
Hastings College	NE	27,782	C+
Haverford College	PA	59,236	MC
Heidelberg Univ	OH	34,100	C
Henderson State Univ	AR	13,634	C
Hendrix College	AR	48,436	HC+
Hillsdale College	MI	31,890	HC+
Hiram College	OH	37,300	VC
Hobart and William Smith Colleges	NY	43,000	VC
Hofstra Univ	NY	48,020	VC+
Hollins Univ	VA	43,295	VC
Hope College	MI	36,320	VC+
Houghton College	NY	35,740	VC
Houston Baptist Univ	TX	23,815	C+
Howard Univ	DC	35,957	C
Humboldt State Univ	CA	18,400	C
Hunter College / The CUNY	NY	14,429	VC
Huntington Univ	IN	32,220	C
Idaho State Univ	ID	11,908	C
Illinois College	IL	25,770	VC
Illinois Inst of Technology	IL	38,512	HC+
Illinois State Univ	IL	22,634	VC
Illinois Wesleyan Univ	IL	48,452	VC+
Indiana State Univ	IN	16,000	C
Indiana Univ Bloomington	IN	19,358	HC
Indiana Univ of Pennsylvania	PA	20,180	LC
Indiana Univ South Bend	IN	15,293	C
Indiana Univ-Purdue Univ Fort Wayne	IN	15,425	C
Indiana Univ-Purdue Univ Indianapolis	IN	17,290	C
Iona College	NY	44,028	C
Iowa State Univ	IA	16,403	C
Ithaca College	NY	52,300	HC
Jackson State Univ	MS	13,512	LC
Jacksonville State Univ	AL	12,280	LC
Jacksonville Univ	FL	37,780	C
James Madison Univ	VA	18,049	VC
John Carroll Univ	OH	44,520	C
Johns Hopkins Univ	MD	47,492	MC
Johnson C. Smith Univ	NC	25,336	LC
Juniata College	PA	49,340	VC
Kalamazoo College	MI	47,825	HC+
Kansas State Univ	KS	15,497	VC
Kansas Wesleyan Univ	KS	32,000	C
Keene State College	NH	21,538	C
Kent State Univ	OH	19,352	C
Kentucky Wesleyan College	KY	27,440	VC+
Kenyon College	OH	56,810	MC
King Univ	TN	33,140	C
King's College	PA	41,678	C
Knox College	IL		VC
Kutztown Univ of Pennsylvania	PA	16,909	LC
La Sierra Univ	CA	35,694	VC
Lafayette College	PA	57,050	HC+
Lake Forest College	IL	45,580	VC
Lamar Univ	TX	6,820	LC
Lane College	TN	11,212	C
Lawrence Tech Univ	MI	37,630	VC
Lawrence Univ	WI	46,371	HC
Le Moyne College	NY	42,200	VC
Lebanon Valley College	PA	38,570	C
Lehigh Univ	PA	55,080	MC
Lehman College / The CUNY	NY	5,778	LC
Lenoir-Rhyne College	NC	35,984	C
Lewis & Clark College	OR	52,656	VC
Lewis Univ	IL	23,050	C
Lincoln Univ	MO	11,996	NC
Linfield College-McMinnville Campus	OR	46,166	C
Lipscomb Univ	TN	35,722	VC
Lock Haven Univ of Pennsylvania	PA	17,587	LC
LIU/C.W. Post Campus	NY	38,888	C
Longwood Univ	VA	20,924	C
Louisiana State Univ	LA	18,677	VC+
Louisiana State Univ in Shreveport	LA	5,606	C
Louisiana Tech Univ	LA	8,000	C
Loyola Marymount Univ	CA	53,240	VC+
Loyola Univ Chicago	IL	49,560	VC+
Loyola Univ Maryland	MD		VC
Loyola Univ New Orleans	LA	46,581	VC
Luther College	IA	44,380	VC+
Lycoming College	PA	43,636	C
Lynchburg College	VA	42,645	C
Macalester College	MN	53,419	MC
MacMurray College	IL	20,755	C
Manchester College	IN	35,070	C
Manhattan College	NY	44,955	VC
Manhattanville College	NY	46,260	VC
Mansfield Univ	PA	19,468	LC
Marietta College	OH	42,135	VC
Marlboro College	VT	35,980	VC
Marquette Univ	WI	43,664	VC+
Marshall Univ	WV	14,820	C
Mary Baldwin College	VA	37,110	C
Mass College of Liberal Arts	MA	16,733	C
Mass Inst of Technology	MA	54,238	MC
McDaniel College	MD	45,600	VC
McMurry Univ	TX	25,962	LC
Mercer Univ	GA	44,201	VC+
Merrimack College	MA	44,215	C
Messiah College	PA	39,540	VC
Metropolitan State Univ of Denver	CO	4,835	LC
Miami Univ	OH	24,191	HC
Mich State Univ	MI	13,689	VC
Mich Tech Univ	MI	22,105	VC
MidAmerica Nazarene Univ	KS	28,000	C
Middle Tenn State Univ	TN	8,650	C
Middlebury College	VT	57,470	MC
Millersville Univ of Pennsylvania	PA	18,498	C
Millikin Univ	IL	37,462	C
Millsaps College	MS	43,888	VC+
Minn State Univ, Mankato	MN	14,900	C
Minn State Univ, Moorhead	MN	13,392	C
Minot State Univ	ND	10,915	C
Miss College	MS	21,998	VC
Missouri Southern State Univ	MO	11,910	C
Missouri Univ of Science and Technology	MO	18,655	VC+
Monmouth College	IL	39,290	C
Montana State Univ	MT	14,068	VC
Montclair State Univ	NJ	22,614	C
Moravian College	PA	36,381	VC
Morehead State Univ	KY	10,900	C
Morehouse College	GA	38,640	C
Morgan State Univ	MD	14,500	VC
Morningside College	IA	32,620	C
Mount Holyoke College	MA	53,596	HC+
Muhlenberg College	PA	52,837	HC
Murray State Univ	KY	14,944	C
Muskingum Univ	OH	30,502	C
Nebr Wesleyan Univ	NE	29,774	C+
New College of Florida	FL	14,504	HC+
New Jersey City Univ	NJ	21,060	C+
New Mexico Highlands Univ	NM	9,720	NC
New Mexico Inst of Mining and Technology	NM	12,892	HC
New Mexico State Univ	NM	13,955	LC
New York Inst of Technology	NY	40,590	VC
New York Univ	NY	61,470	MC
Norfolk State Univ	VA	10,531	LC
N Car Agricultural and Technical State Univ	NC	13,175	LC
N Car Central Univ	NC	9,000	LC
N Car State Univ	NC	16,202	HC
North Central College	IL	38,343	VC
N Dak State Univ	ND	14,642	C
North Georgia College & State Univ	GA	8,500	C
North Park Univ	IL	30,130	C
Northeastern Illinois Univ	IL		C
Northeastern Univ	MA	55,296	MC
Northern Arizona Univ	AZ	18,592	C
Northern Illinois Univ	IL	19,768	C
Northern Kentucky Univ	KY	15,302	LC
Northern Mich Univ	MI	15,300	VC
Northwest Missouri State Univ	MO	14,229	C
Northwest Nazarene Univ	ID	24,275	NC
Northwestern Okla State Univ	OK	7,275	NC
Northwestern Univ	IL	37,595	MC
Norwich Univ	VT	28,212	C
Notre Dame of Maryland Univ	MD	27,700	C
Oakland Univ	MI	19,391	VC
Oberlin College	OH	57,025	MC
Occidental College	CA	59,592	MC+
Oglethorpe Univ	GA	42,580	VC
Ohio Northern Univ	OH	42,075	VC
Ohio Univ	OH	20,676	VC
Ohio Wesleyan Univ	OH	49,460	C+
Okla Baptist Univ	OK	28,202	VC
Okla City Univ	OK	33,546	VC
Okla State Univ	OK	14,310	VC
Old Dominion Univ	VA	18,662	C
Oral Roberts Univ	OK	31,734	C
Oregon State Univ	OR	19,017	C+
Oswego / SUNY	NY	20,009	VC
Otterbein College	OH	32,214	C

School	ST	$IS	SR
Ouachita Baptist Univ	AR	29,010	VC
Pacific Lutheran Univ	WA	44,840	VC
Pacific Union College	CA	28,150	VC
Pacific Univ	OR	42,815	C
Penn State Erie/The Behrend College	PA	16,256	C
Penn State Univ/Univ Park	PA	25,404	VC
Pepperdine Univ	CA	55,372	HC+
Piedmont College	GA	29,260	C
Pittsburg State Univ	KS	12,032	C
Pitzer College	CA	54,988	MC
Point Loma Nazarene Univ	CA	38,610	VC
Polytechnic Inst of New York Univ	NY	53,064	HC+
Pomona College	CA	57,680	MC
Pontifical Catholic Univ of PR	PR	7,310	
Portland State Univ	OR	18,672	C
Prairie View A&M Univ	TX	15,205	LC
Presbyterian College	SC	42,678	VC
Princeton Univ	NJ	53,795	MC
Principia College	IL	35,140	C+
Purdue Univ/Calumet	IN	14,336	C
Purdue Univ/West Lafayette	IN	20,278	HC
Queens College / The CUNY	NY	17,107	VC
Radford Univ	VA	17,132	LC
Randolph College	VA	43,960	VC
Randolph-Macon College	VA	45,086	C
Reed College	OR	57,780	MC
Rensselaer Polytechnic Inst	NY	59,229	MC
Rhode Island College	RI	17,132	LC
Rhodes College	TN	47,596	HC+
Rice Univ	TX	43,288	MC
Richard Stockton College of New Jersey	NJ	20,000	VC
Rider Univ	NJ	45,720	C
Ripon College	WI	36,959	C+
Roanoke College	VA	47,996	C+
Roberts Wesleyan College	NY	37,384	C+
Rochester Inst of Technology	NY	42,450	VC+
Rockhurst Univ	MO	20,625	C
Rollins College	FL	52,370	HC
Rose-Hulman Inst of Technology	IN	51,738	MC
Rowan Univ	NJ	23,570	VC
Rutgers, The State Univ of New Jersey/Camden Campus	NJ	24,254	C
Rutgers, The State Univ of New Jersey/New Brunswick	NJ	25,077	VC
Rutgers, The State Univ of New Jersey/Newark Campus	NJ	25,376	C
Saginaw Valley State Univ	MI	16,869	C
St. John's Univ	MN	46,146	C
St. Joseph's Univ	PA	52,272	VC
St. Louis Univ	MO	46,594	VC+
St. Mary's College of Calif	CA	53,550	C
St. Mary's Univ	TX	33,854	C
St. Mary's Univ of Minn	MN	37,015	C
St. Michael's College	VT	48,740	VC
St. Peter's College	NJ	44,240	C
St. Vincent College	PA	40,244	C
Salisbury Univ	MD	18,368	VC
Sam Houston State Univ	TX	17,082	C
Samford Univ	AL	35,700	VC+
San Diego State Univ	CA	20,578	VC
San Francisco State Univ	CA	18,514	C
San Jose State Univ	CA	19,707	C
Santa Clara Univ	CA	54,702	MC
Scripps College	CA	54,900	MC
Seattle Pacific Univ	WA	41,559	VC+
Seattle Univ	WA	47,010	VC+
Seton Hall Univ	NJ	45,902	C
Seton Hill Univ	PA	35,172	C
Sewanee: The Univ of the South	TN	47,700	HC+
Shaw Univ	NC	15,488	LC
Shippensburg Univ of Pennsylvania	PA	17,064	LC
Siena College	NY	43,863	VC
Simmons College	MA	48,770	VC
Simpson College	IA	36,086	VC
Skidmore College	NY	57,926	HC
Slippery Rock Univ of Pennsylvania	PA	10,360	LC
Smith College	MA	57,524	MC
Sonoma State Univ	CA	20,541	C
S Car State Univ	SC	6,700	LC
S Dak School of Mines and Technology	SD	15,260	VC
S Dak State Univ	SD	14,296	C
Southeast Missouri State Univ	MO	14,983	LC
Southeastern Louisiana Univ	LA	13,325	C
Southeastern Okla State Univ	OK	7,966	C
Southern Adventist Univ	TN	26,190	C
Southern Conn State Univ	CT	18,033	C
Southern Illinois Univ Carbondale	IL	21,620	C
Southern Illinois Univ Edwardsville	IL	17,532	C
Southern Methodist Univ	TX	57,755	MC
Southern Nazarene Univ	OK	24,354	NC
Southern Oregon Univ	OR	17,874	C
Southern Polytechnic State Univ	GA	13,958	VC
Southern Univ and A&M College	LA	9,761	C+
Southern Univ at New Orleans	LA	1,000	NC
Southwestern Adventist Univ	TX	23,026	LC
Southwestern Okla State Univ	OK	9,160	C
Southwestern Univ	TX	45,660	VC
Spelman College	GA	24,650	VC
Spring Arbor Univ	MI	26,740	C
St. Ambrose Univ	IA		C
St. Bonaventure Univ	NY	38,831	C
St. Cloud State Univ	MN	10,600	C
St. John Fisher College	NY	39,370	C
St. John's Univ	NY	52,840	C+
St. Lawrence Univ	NY	53,740	HC
St. Mary's College of Maryland	MD	26,699	HC
St. Norbert College	WI	39,992	VC
St. Olaf College	MN	49,960	HC+
Stanford Univ	CA	56,411	MC
Stephen F. Austin State Univ	TX	14,668	C
Stetson Univ	FL	49,512	VC+
Stevens Inst of Technology	NJ	50,130	HC
Stonehill College	MA	46,780	VC+
Stony Brook Univ / SUNY	NY	19,359	HC
Suffolk Univ	MA	46,548	C
SUNY College at Geneseo	NY	18,055	HC+
SUNY Cortland / The SUNY	NY	19,117	C
SUNY Fredonia / The SUNY at Fredonia	NY	18,702	VC
SUNY New Paltz	NY	15,010	C
SUNY Oneonta / SUNY	NY	16,919	VC
SUNY Plattsburgh / SUNY	NY	18,083	VC
Susquehanna Univ	PA	49,170	C
Swarthmore College	PA	57,870	MC
Sweet Briar College	VA	43,765	C+
Syracuse Univ	NY	54,512	HC
Talladega College	AL	13,000	C
Tarleton State Univ	TX	13,489	LC
Taylor Univ	IN	36,742	VC+
Temple Univ	PA	24,392	VC
Tenn State Univ	TN	9,048	C
Tenn Tech Univ	TN	11,310	C
Texas A&M Univ	TX	16,956	VC+
Texas A&M Univ at Commerce	TX	10,496	C
Texas A&M Univ at Kingsville	TX	7,500	LC
Texas Christian Univ	TX	47,570	HC
Texas Lutheran Univ	TX	34,070	C
Texas State Univ	TX	16,495	VC
Texas Tech Univ	TX	14,243	C
The Catholic Univ of America	DC	52,852	VC
The College at Brockport / SUNY	NY	18,362	VC
The Lincoln Univ	PA	15,154	LC
Ohio State Univ	OH	19,887	MC
The SUNY at Potsdam	NY	17,754	C
Thiel College	PA	31,378	LC
Thomas More College	KY	34,760	C
Tougaloo College	MS	15,275	NC
Touro College	NY	23,150	VC
Towson Univ	MD	16,000	VC
Transylvania Univ	KY	40,310	VC+
Trevecca Nazarene Univ	TN	30,118	C
Trinity College	CT		HC+
Trinity Univ	TX	44,174	HC+
Truman State Univ	MO	13,546	HC
Tufts Univ	MA	58,780	MC
Tulane Univ	LA	58,942	MC
Tuskegee Univ	AL	26,750	C
Union College	NE	23,270	VC
Union College	NY		MC
Union Univ	TN	28,260	VC
United States Air Force Academy	CO		MC
United States Military Academy	NY		MC
United States Naval Academy	MD		MC
Univ at Albany / SUNY	NY	18,674	VC
Univ at Buffalo / The SUNY	NY	20,283	VC
Univ of Akron	OH	20,436	C
Univ of Alabama at Birmingham	AL	18,484	C+
Univ of Alabama at Huntsville	AL	17,625	VC
Univ of Alabama at Tuscaloosa	AL	17,164	C+
Univ of Alaska Fairbanks	AK	13,955	C
Univ of Arizona	AZ	20,105	C
Univ of Arkansas at Fayetteville	AR	16,860	VC
Univ of Arkansas at Little Rock	AR		C
Univ of Arkansas at Pine Bluff	AR	10,600	C
Univ of Calif at Berkeley	CA	23,322	MC
Univ of Calif at Davis	CA	24,482	HC
Univ of Calif at Irvine	CA	25,961	VC
Univ of Calif at Los Angeles	CA	25,686	MC
Univ of Calif at Riverside	CA	27,204	C
Univ of Calif at San Diego	CA	21,000	VC
Univ of Calif at Santa Barbara	CA	27,551	HC
Univ of Calif at Santa Cruz	CA	27,807	VC
Univ of Central Arkansas	AR	10,840	VC
Univ of Central Florida	FL	15,711	VC+
Univ of Central Missouri	MO	14,605	C
Univ of Chicago	IL	55,416	MC
Univ of Cincinnati	OH	20,199	VC
Univ of Colo at Colo Springs	CO	15,000	VC
Univ of Colo Boulder	CO	22,605	VC+
Univ of Colo Denver	CO	17,904	C
Univ of Conn	CT	23,744	HC
Univ of Dallas	TX	43,510	VC+
Univ of Dayton	OH	43,750	VC
Univ of Delaware	DE	22,728	VC
Univ of Denver	CO	51,787	VC+
Univ of Evansville	IN	41,056	VC+
Univ of Florida	FL	15,783	HC+
Univ of Georgia	GA	19,508	VC
Univ of Hartford	CT	42,674	C
Univ of Hawaii at Hilo	HI	6,500	C
Univ of Hawaii at Manoa	HI	19,379	VC
Univ of Houston	TX	19,184	VC
Univ of Idaho	ID	14,558	C
Univ of Illinois at Chicago	IL	24,293	VC
Univ of Illinois at Urbana-Champaign	IL	24,300	HC
Univ of Indianapolis	IN	31,740	LC
Univ of Iowa	IA	17,481	VC
Univ of Kansas	KS	16,980	C+
Univ of Kentucky	KY	19,868	C
Univ of La Verne	CA	47,010	VC
Univ of Louisiana at Lafayette	LA	6,130	C
Univ of Louisville	KY	17,460	VC
Univ of Maine	ME	19,712	C+
Univ of Mary Washington	VA	19,484	VC
Univ of Maryland	MD	18,801	HC
Univ of Maryland/Baltimore County	MD	18,000	VC
Univ of Mass Amherst	MA	23,697	VC+
Univ of Mass Boston	MA	11,966	C
Univ of Mass Dartmouth	MA	22,223	C
Univ of Mass Lowell	MA	19,316	C
Univ of Memphis	TN	15,094	C
Univ of Miami	FL	55,166	MC
Univ of Mich/Ann Arbor	MI	22,102	HC+
Univ of Mich/Dearborn	MI	9,885	VC
Univ of Mich-Flint	MI	17,547	C+
Univ of Minn/Duluth	MN	18,964	C+
Univ of Minn/Morris	MN	17,150	VC
Univ of Minn/Twin Cities	MN		HC
Univ of Miss	MS	15,482	VC
Univ of Missouri/Columbia	MO	18,201	MC
Univ of Missouri-Kansas City	MO	19,603	C
Univ of Missouri-St. Louis	MO	18,304	VC
Univ of Montana	MT	13,670	C
Univ of Mount Union	OH	35,130	C
Univ of Nebr - Lincoln	NE	17,507	VC
Univ of Nebr at Kearney	NE	14,855	LC
Univ of Nebr at Omaha	NE	12,700	C
Univ of Nevada, Las Vegas	NV	17,303	C
Univ of Nevada/Reno	NV	14,500	NC
Univ of New Hampshire	NH	24,702	VC
Univ of New Mexico	NM	15,300	C
Univ of New Orleans	LA	9,224	VC
Univ of North Alabama	AL	9,960	C
Univ of N Car at Asheville	NC	13,500	VC+
Univ of N Car at Chapel Hill	NC	18,348	MC
Univ of N Car at Charlotte	NC	15,847	C
Univ of N Car at Greensboro	NC	12,848	C
Univ of N Car at Wilmington	NC	13,572	VC+
Univ of N Dak	ND	14,094	C
Univ of North Florida	FL	15,578	VC
Univ of North Texas	TX	15,628	C
Univ of Northern Colo	CO	15,973	C
Univ of Northern Iowa	IA	14,776	C
Univ of Notre Dame	IN		MC
Univ of Okla	OK	17,634	VC+
Univ of Oregon	OR	20,872	VC
Univ of Pennsylvania	PA	56,106	MC
Univ of Pittsburgh at Pittsburgh	PA	27,800	HC+
Univ of Portland	OR	47,874	VC
Univ of PR/Humacao	PR	1,877	
Univ of PR/Mayaguez	PR	1,250	
Univ of Puget Sound	WA	52,648	HC+
Univ of Redlands	CA	40,500	VC
Univ of Rochester	NY	58,500	HC+
Univ of San Diego	CA	53,302	HC+
Univ of San Francisco	CA	49,674	VC
Univ of Science and Arts of Okla	OK	10,560	VC
Univ of Scranton	PA	51,940	VC
Univ of South Alabama	AL	13,510	C
Univ of S Car at Columbia	SC	19,725	VC+
Univ of S Dak	SD	15,111	C
Univ of South Florida	FL	13,000	C
Univ of Southern Calif	CA	56,903	MC
Univ of Southern Maine	ME	16,576	C
Univ of Southern Miss	MS	13,170	C
Univ of St. Thomas - Houston	TX	36,490	VC
Univ of Tenn at Chattanooga	TN	16,883	C
Univ of Tenn at Knoxville	TN	20,364	VC+
Univ of Texas at Arlington	TX	10,908	LC
Univ of Texas at Austin	TX	44,074	HC
Univ of Texas at Dallas	TX	21,046	HC
Univ of Texas at El Paso	TX	8,764	NC
Univ of Texas at San Antonio	TX	18,372	C
Univ of Texas-Pan American	TX	12,432	LC
Univ of the Cumberlands	KY	27,500	LC
Univ of the District of Columbia	DC	7,244	LC
Univ of the Pacific	CA	52,146	VC
Univ of the Sciences	PA	48,320	VC+
Univ of Toledo	OH	18,464	C
Univ of Tulsa	OK	45,311	HC+
Univ of Utah	UT	13,462	VC
Univ of Vermont	VT	26,120	VC+
Univ of Virginia	VA	22,175	MC
Univ of Washington	WA	14,722	VC
Univ of West Alabama	AL	9,415	C
Univ of West Florida	FL	14,656	C
Univ of West Georgia	GA	14,852	LC
Univ of Wisc Whitewater	WI	13,314	C
Univ of Wisc/Eau Claire	WI	15,430	VC
Univ of Wisc/La Crosse	WI	14,755	VC
Univ of Wisc/Madison	WI	18,757	HC
Univ of Wisc/Oshkosh	WI	10,426	LC
Univ of Wisc/Parkside	WI	10,181	LC
Univ of Wisc/Platteville	WI	14,274	C
Univ of Wisc/River Falls	WI	9,722	LC
Univ of Wisc/Stevens Point	WI	14,043	C
Univ of Wisc-Milwaukee	WI	18,436	C
Univ of Wyoming	WY	13,855	C+
Ursinus College	PA	55,630	VC+
Utah State Univ	UT	11,803	C
Utica College	NY	44,734	C
Valparaiso Univ	IN	43,040	VC+
Vanderbilt Univ	TN	57,072	MC
Vassar College	NY	59,070	MC
Villanova Univ	PA	56,436	MC
Virginia Commonwealth Univ	VA	18,633	C
Virginia Military Inst	VA	16,156	C
Virginia Polytechnic Inst and State Univ	VA	14,629	HC
Virginia State Univ	VA	11,318	C+
Wabash College	IN	44,160	VC
Wagner College	NY	48,600	VC
Wake Forest Univ	NC	51,000	MC
Walla Walla Univ	WA	26,256	NC
Wartburg College	IA	41,055	VC
Washburn Univ	KS	12,165	NC
Washington and Jefferson College	PA	49,990	VC
Washington and Lee Univ	VA	52,812	MC
Washington College	MD	48,768	VC
Washington State Univ	WA	20,461	C
Washington Univ in St. Louis	MO	58,818	MC
Wayne State Univ	MI	19,493	C
Wellesley College	MA	49,848	MC
Wells College	NY	38,680	VC
Wesleyan College	GA	24,000	C+
Wesleyan Univ	CT	59,844	MC
West Chester Univ of Pennsylvania	PA	16,836	C
West Texas A&M Univ	TX	13,478	C
West Virginia Univ	WV	15,794	C+
West Virginia Univ Inst of Technology	WV	14,094	NC
West Virginia Wesleyan College	WV	26,880	C
Western Illinois Univ	IL	20,130	C
Western Kentucky Univ	KY	11,000	LC
Western Mich Univ	MI	19,042	C
Western Washington Univ	WA	18,519	VC
Westminster College	MO	30,490	VC
Westminster College	PA	31,290	C+
Westminster College	UT	37,708	VC
Westmont College	CA	41,500	HC
Wheaton College	IL	39,650	HC+
Wheaton College	MA	54,934	HC+
Wheeling Jesuit Univ	WV	34,668	C
Whitman College	WA	54,400	MC
Whittier College	CA	43,416	C
Whitworth Univ	WA	45,826	VC+
Wichita State Univ	KS	12,539	C
Widener Univ	PA	50,368	C
Wiley College	TX		LC
Willamette Univ	OR	56,450	VC+
William Jewell College	MO	31,000	VC+
Williams College	MA	58,900	MC
Winona State Univ	MN	16,530	C
Wittenberg Univ	OH	47,766	VC
Wofford College	SC	45,795	VC
Worcester Polytechnic Inst	MA	53,440	HC+

School	ST	$IS	SR
Wright State Univ	OH	16,983	C
Xavier Univ	OH	43,740	VC
Xavier Univ of Louisiana	LA	25,300	C
Yale Univ	CT	55,300	MC
York College / CUNY	NY	5,496	NC
Youngstown State Univ	OH	16,374	LC

PHYSICS WITH ASTROPHYSICS OPTION

School	ST	$IS	SR
Univ of Nebr - Lincoln	NE	17,507	VC

PHYSIOLOGY

School	ST	$IS	SR
Boston Univ	MA	54,130	HC+
Brigham Young Univ	UT	12,100	HC
Cal State, Long Beach	CA	17,534	C+
Florida State Univ	FL	15,238	HC
Georgia Southern Univ	GA	16,414	C
Hampshire College	MA	58,320	MC
Howard Univ	DC	35,957	C
Marquette Univ	WI	43,664	VC+
Mich State Univ	MI	13,689	VC
Northern Mich Univ	MI	15,300	VC
Okla State Univ	OK	14,310	VC
Rutgers, The State Univ of New Jersey/New Brunswick	NJ	25,077	VC
San Francisco State Univ	CA	18,514	C
Southern Illinois Univ Carbondale	IL	21,620	C
Texas State Univ	TX	10,495	VC
Univ of Arizona	AZ	20,105	C
Univ of Calif at Davis	CA	24,482	HC
Univ of Calif at Los Angeles	CA	25,686	MC
Univ of Calif at San Diego	CA	21,000	VC
Univ of Calif at Santa Barbara	CA	27,551	HC
Univ of Colo Boulder	CO	22,605	VC+
Univ of Conn	CT	23,744	HC
Univ of Great Falls	MT	27,970	C
Univ of Illinois at Urbana-Champaign	IL	24,300	HC
Univ of Minn/Twin Cities	MN		HC
Univ of Montana-Western	MT	9,753	LC
Univ of Oregon	OR	20,872	VC
Univ of Wyoming	WY	13,855	C+

PIANO PEDAGOGY

School	ST	$IS	SR
Ithaca College	NY	52,300	HC
Samford Univ	AL	35,700	VC+
Texas Christian Univ	TX	47,570	HC

PIANO PERFORMANCE

School	ST	$IS	SR
Biola Univ	CA	40,320	VC
Dallas Baptist Univ	TX	29,118	C
Indiana Univ South Bend	IN	15,293	C
New York Univ	NY	61,470	MC
Ouachita Baptist Univ	AR	29,010	VC
Samford Univ	AL	35,700	VC+
Univ of Central Okla	OK	12,293	C
Webster Univ	MO	33,990	C+
West Chester Univ of Pennsylvania	PA	16,836	C
Youngstown State Univ	OH	16,374	LC

PIANO/ORGAN

School	ST	$IS	SR
Bennington College	VT	56,990	HC+
Boston Conservatory	MA	56,380	SP
Calif Baptist Univ	CA	35,890	C
Calvin College	MI	37,585	VC+
Central Mich Univ	MI	18,066	C
Central Washington Univ	WA	11,730	C
Columbia College	SC	27,882	C
East Central Univ	OK	10,223	LC
East Texas Baptist Univ	TX	29,135	C
Eastern Mich Univ	MI	17,961	C
Florida State Univ	FL	15,238	HC
Hardin-Simmons Univ	TX	23,560	C+
Illinois Wesleyan Univ	IL	48,452	VC+
Indiana Univ Bloomington	IN	19,358	HC
Indiana Univ-Purdue Univ Fort Wayne	IN	15,425	C
Jackson State Univ	MS	13,512	LC
Lenoir-Rhyne College	NC	35,984	C
Loyola Univ New Orleans	LA	46,581	VC
Manhattan School of Music	NY	55,850	SP
Mannes College New School for Music	NY	44,500	C
Marshall Univ	WV	14,820	C
Millikin Univ	IL	37,462	C
Miss College	MS	21,998	VC
Northwestern College	MN	24,000	C
Northwestern Univ	IL	37,595	MC
Nyack College	NY	32,000	C
Ohio Univ	OH	20,676	VC
Okla City Univ	OK	33,546	VC
Ouachita Baptist Univ	AR	29,010	VC
Pacific Lutheran Univ	WA	44,840	VC
Palm Beach Atlantic Univ	FL	33,882	LC
Point Loma Nazarene Univ	CA	38,610	VC
Rider Univ	NJ	45,720	C
Roosevelt Univ	IL	22,605	VC
Samford Univ	AL	35,700	VC+
San Francisco Conservatory of Music	CA	53,923	SP
Shenandoah Univ	VA	39,268	C
Shorter Univ	GA	26,470	C
Southern Methodist Univ	TX	57,755	MC
Stetson Univ	FL	49,512	VC+
Syracuse Univ	NY	54,512	HC
Temple Univ	PA	24,392	VC
The Catholic Univ of America	DC	52,852	VC
Ohio State Univ	OH	19,887	MC
Union Univ	TN	28,260	VC
Univ of Cincinnati	OH	20,199	VC
Univ of Iowa	IA	17,481	VC
Univ of Kansas	KS	16,980	C+
Univ of Tulsa	OK	45,311	HC+
Westminster Choir College	NJ	36,000	SP
Youngstown State Univ	OH	16,374	LC

PLANETARY AND SPACE SCIENCE

School	ST	$IS	SR
Boston Univ	MA	54,130	HC+
Calif Inst of Technology	CA	54,045	MC
Florida Inst of Technology	FL	48,290	VC
Univ of Arizona	AZ	20,105	C
Virginia Polytechnic Inst and State Univ	VA	14,629	HC
Wilmington College	OH	29,784	C

PLANT GENETICS

School	ST	$IS	SR
Brigham Young Univ	UT	12,100	HC
Purdue Univ/West Lafayette	IN	20,278	HC
SUNY / College of Environmental Science and Forestry	NY	18,351	HC
Univ of Calif at Berkeley	CA	23,322	MC
Univ of Calif at Riverside	CA	27,204	C
Washington State Univ	WA	20,461	C

PLANT PATHOLOGY

School	ST	$IS	SR
Iowa State Univ	IA	16,403	C
Mich State Univ	MI	13,689	VC
New Mexico State Univ	NM	13,955	LC
SUNY / College of Environmental Science and Forestry	NY	18,351	HC
Univ of Arizona	AZ	20,105	C
Univ of Calif at Riverside	CA	27,204	C
Univ of Delaware	DE	22,728	VC
Univ of Georgia	GA	19,508	VC
Univ of Wisc/Madison	WI	18,757	HC
Washington State Univ	WA	20,461	C

PLANT PHYSIOLOGY

School	ST	$IS	SR
Brigham Young Univ	UT	12,100	HC
Pittsburg State Univ	KS	12,032	C
Purdue Univ/West Lafayette	IN	20,278	HC
SUNY / College of Environmental Science and Forestry	NY	18,351	HC
Ohio State Univ	OH	19,887	MC
Univ of Illinois at Urbana-Champaign	IL	24,300	HC

PLANT PROTECTION (PEST MANAGEMENT)

School	ST	$IS	SR
Iowa State Univ	IA	16,403	C
N Dak State Univ	ND	14,642	C
Penn State Univ/Univ Park	PA	25,404	VC
Purdue Univ/West Lafayette	IN	20,278	HC
Texas Tech Univ	TX	14,243	C
Univ of Hawaii at Manoa	HI	19,379	VC
Washington State Univ	WA	20,461	C
West Texas A&M Univ	TX	13,478	C

PLANT SCIENCE

School	ST	$IS	SR
Arkansas State Univ	AR	14,980	C
Brigham Young Univ	UT	12,100	HC
Calif State Polytechnic Univ, Pomona	CA	18,932	C
Cal State, Fresno	CA	17,405	C
Cornell Univ	NY	59,037	MC
Florida State Univ	FL	15,238	HC
Fort Valley State Univ	GA	11,200	VC
Iowa State Univ	IA	16,403	C
Louisiana State Univ	LA	18,677	VC+
Middle Tenn State Univ	TN	8,650	C
Missouri State Univ	MO	13,996	VC
Montana State Univ	MT	14,068	VC
N Dak State Univ	ND	14,642	C
Okla State Univ	OK	14,310	VC
Pittsburg State Univ	KS	12,032	C
Purdue Univ/West Lafayette	IN	20,278	HC
Rutgers, The State Univ of New Jersey/New Brunswick	NJ	25,077	VC
S Dak State Univ	SD	14,296	C
Southeast Missouri State Univ	MO	14,983	LC
Southern Illinois Univ Carbondale	IL	21,620	C
SUNY / College of Environmental Science and Forestry	NY	18,351	HC
Tarleton State Univ	TX	13,489	LC
Tenn Tech Univ	TN	11,310	C
Texas A&M Univ at Kingsville	TX	7,500	LC
Ohio State Univ	OH	19,887	MC
The SUNY College of Agriculture and Tech at Cobleskill	NY	18,869	VC
Univ of Arizona	AZ	20,105	C
Univ of Calif at Davis	CA	24,482	HC
Univ of Calif at Santa Cruz	CA	27,807	VC
Univ of Delaware	DE	22,728	VC
Univ of Florida	FL	15,783	HC+
Univ of Georgia	GA	19,508	VC
Univ of Hawaii at Manoa	HI	19,379	VC
Univ of Idaho	ID	14,558	C
Univ of Maryland	MD	18,801	HC
Univ of Mass Amherst	MA	23,697	VC+
Univ of Missouri/Columbia	MO	18,201	MC
Univ of Nebr - Lincoln	NE	17,507	VC
Univ of New Hampshire	NH	24,702	VC
Univ of Tenn at Knoxville	TN	20,364	VC+
Univ of Tenn at Martin	TN	13,217	C
Univ of Vermont	VT	26,120	VC+
Utah State Univ	UT	11,803	C
Washington State Univ	WA	20,461	C
Washington Univ in St. Louis	MO	58,818	MC
West Texas A&M Univ	TX	13,478	C
West Virginia Univ	WV	15,794	C+

PLASTICS ENGINEERING

School	ST	$IS	SR
Ferris State Univ	MI	19,698	C
Pennsylvania College of Technology	PA	25,653	NC
Univ of Illinois at Urbana-Champaign	IL	24,300	HC
Univ of Mass Lowell	MA	19,316	C
Univ of Wisc/Stout	WI	23,942	C
Western Washington Univ	WA	18,519	VC

PLASTICS TECHNOLOGY

School	ST	$IS	SR
Eastern Mich Univ	MI	17,961	C
Penn State Erie/The Behrend College	PA	16,256	C
Pittsburg State Univ	KS	12,032	C
Shawnee State Univ	OH	16,545	NC

PLAYWRITING/ SCREENWRITING

School	ST	$IS	SR
Bennington College	VT	56,990	HC+
Biola Univ	CA	40,320	VC
Chapman Univ	CA	56,019	VC+
DePaul Univ	IL	46,120	VC
Goddard College	VT	16,418	VC
Howard Univ	DC	35,957	C
Metropolitan State Univ	MN	5,923	SP
Ohio Univ	OH	20,676	VC
Univ of Southern Calif	CA	56,903	MC
Webster Univ	MO	33,990	C+

POLICY ANALYSIS AND MANAGEMENT

School	ST	$IS	SR
Cornell Univ	NY	59,037	MC
Indiana Univ Bloomington	IN	19,358	HC

POLISH

School	ST	$IS	SR
Univ of Illinois at Chicago	IL	24,293	VC
Univ of Pittsburgh at Pittsburgh	PA	27,800	HC+
Univ of Wisc/Madison	WI	18,757	HC

POLITICAL SCIENCE/ GOVERNMENT

School	ST	$IS	SR
Abilene Christian Univ	TX	38,400	VC
Adams State College	CO	13,358	LC
Adelphi Univ	NY	43,130	VC
Adrian College	MI	33,800	C
Agnes Scott College	GA	45,323	VC+
Alabama A&M Univ	AL	96,100	C
Alabama State Univ	AL	14,142	NC
Albany State Univ	GA	8,500	C
Albertus Magnus College	CT	37,382	LC
Albion College	MI	43,884	VC
Albright College	PA	46,660	C
Alcorn State Univ	MS	9,500	C
Alderson Broaddus Univ	WV	28,656	C
Alfred Univ	NY	40,392	VC
Allegheny College	PA	49,020	HC
Allen Univ	SC	16,124	NC
Alma College	MI	42,400	VC
Alvernia Univ	PA	39,250	C
Alverno College	WI	30,483	LC
American International College	MA	36,100	LC
American Jewish Univ	CA	32,600	C
American Univ	DC	54,829	HC+
Amherst College	MA	58,744	MC
Anderson Univ	IN	35,390	C
Andrews Univ	MI	28,030	C+
Angelo State Univ	TX	15,049	NC
Anna Maria College	MA	34,600	LC
Appalachian State Univ	NC	12,919	VC
Aquinas College	MI	33,060	C
Arcadia Univ	PA	33,570	C+
Arizona State Univ	AZ	18,818	C+
Arkansas State Univ	AR	14,980	C
Arkansas Tech Univ	AR	13,164	LC
Armstrong Atlantic State Univ	GA	16,276	C
Asbury Univ	KY	32,038	VC
Ashland Univ	OH	25,000	C
Assumption College	MA	45,721	VC
Auburn Univ	AL	20,052	VC+
Auburn Univ at Montgomery	AL	12,120	C
Augsburg College	MN	35,142	C
Augustana College	IL	43,398	HC
Augustana College	SD	35,500	VC
Aurora Univ	IL	26,870	C
Austin College	TX	36,940	HC
Austin Peay State Univ	TN	14,650	C
Averett Univ	VA	36,000	LC
Avila Univ	MO	26,900	C
Azusa Pacific Univ	CA	39,946	C
Baldwin Wallace Univ	OH	36,980	VC
Ball State Univ	IN	17,850	C
Bard College	NY	59,872	HC
Bard College at Simon's Rock	MA	58,963	HC+
Barry Univ	FL	38,190	C
Barton College	NC	27,660	C
Bates College	ME	58,950	MC
Baylor Univ	TX	46,720	HC
Belhaven Univ	MS	27,170	C
Bellarmine Univ	KY	42,950	VC
Bellevue Univ	NE	4,600	NC
Belmont Abbey College	NC	37,716	C
Belmont Univ	TN	37,380	VC+
Beloit College	WI	49,970	HC
Bemidji State Univ	MN	13,500	C
Benedict College	SC	20,454	NC
Benedictine College	KS	29,180	VC
Benedictine Univ	IL	35,220	C
Bennett College	NC		LC
Bennington College	VT	56,990	HC+
Berea College	KY	7,220	HC
Berry College	GA	39,254	HC
Bethany College	WV	35,282	C
Bethel Univ	MN	34,940	VC
Bethune-Cookman Univ	FL	22,290	LC
Binghamton Univ / The SUNY	NY	20,832	HC+
Birmingham-Southern College	AL	42,370	VC+
Black Hills State Univ	SD	13,562	LC
Blackburn College	IL	21,350	C
Bloomfield College	NJ	36,960	C
Bloomsburg Univ of Pennsylvania	PA	13,598	C
Boise State Univ	ID	12,802	C
Boston College	MA	58,506	MC
Boston Univ	MA	54,130	HC+
Bowdoin College	ME	57,834	MC
Bowling Green State Univ	OH	18,970	C
Bradley Univ	IL	31,874	VC
Brandeis Univ	MA	58,820	HC
Brenau Univ Women's College	GA	26,650	C+
Brewton-Parker College	GA	33,388	LC
Briar Cliff Univ	IA	29,514	C
Bridgewater College	VA	39,880	C
Bridgewater State Univ	MA	18,752	C
Brigham Young Univ	UT	12,100	HC
Brigham Young Univ/ Hawaii	HI	8,614	VC
Brown Univ	RI	56,150	MC
Bryant Univ	RI	49,179	VC
Bryn Mawr College	PA	57,760	MC
Bucknell Univ	PA	58,160	MC
Buena Vista Univ	IA	37,954	C
Buffalo State/State Univ of Buffalo	NY	15,733	C+
Butler Univ	IN	45,898	VC+
Cabrini College	PA	40,859	LC
Caldwell College	NJ	35,602	LC
Calif Baptist Univ	CA	35,890	C
Calif Inst of Technology	CA	54,045	MC
Calif Lutheran Univ	CA	47,640	C
Calif Polytechnic State Univ	CA	19,847	HC
Calif State Polytechnic Univ, Pomona	CA	18,932	C
Cal State, Bakersfield	CA	8,000	LC
Cal State, Chico	CA	18,952	C
Cal State, Dominguez Hills	CA	17,056	LC
Cal State, East Bay	CA	16,549	C
Cal State, Fresno	CA	17,405	C
Cal State, Fullerton	CA	25,188	C+
Cal State, Long Beach	CA	17,534	C+
Cal State, Los Angeles	CA	15,829	C

School	ST	$IS	SR
Cal State, Northridge	CA	28,313	C
Cal State, San Bernardino	CA	12,000	C
Cal State, San Marcos	CA	14,576	C
Cal State, Stanislaus	CA	18,582	C
Calif Univ of Pennsylvania	PA	14,217	C
Calvin College	MI	37,585	VC+
Cameron Univ	OK	9,267	LC
Campbell Univ	NC	25,500	C
Campbellsville Univ	KY	27,720	C
Capital Univ	OH	39,824	VC
Carleton College	MN	58,149	MC
Carlow Univ	PA	30,272	C
Carnegie Mellon Univ	PA	51,260	MC
Carroll College	MT	28,000	C
Carroll Univ	WI	24,860	C
Carthage College	WI	33,000	C
Case Western Reserve Univ	OH	55,178	MC
Catawba College	NC	37,105	C
Cedar Crest College	PA	43,240	C
Cedarville Univ	OH	31,036	VC+
Centenary College	NJ	38,618	LC
Centenary College of Louisiana	LA	39,070	C+
Central College	IA	36,980	VC
Central Conn State Univ	CT	19,212	C
Central Methodist Univ	MO	28,240	VC
Central State Univ	OH	9,010	C
Central Washington Univ	WA	11,730	C
Centre College	KY	35,000	HC+
Chadron State College	NE	7,400	NC
Chapman Univ	CA	56,019	VC+
Charleston Southern Univ	SC	22,420	C
Chatham Univ	PA	42,440	VC
Chestnut Hill College	PA	39,785	LC
Cheyney Univ of Pennsylvania	PA	20,372	LC
Chicago State Univ	IL	5,482	C
Christendom College	VA	28,120	VC
Christopher Newport Univ	VA	21,050	VC
Citadel, The	SC		C
CUNY/Baruch College	NY	15,831	VC
CUNY/Brooklyn College	NY	5,884	C+
Claflin Univ	SC	22,368	C+
Claremont McKenna College	CA	58,065	MC
Clarion Univ of Pennsylvania	PA	17,370	C
Clark Atlanta Univ	GA	30,006	C
Clark Univ	MA	47,020	HC+
Clarke Univ	IA	36,400	C
Clarkson Univ	NY	53,538	HC
Clemson Univ	SC	19,136	HC
Cleveland State Univ	OH	21,357	C
Coastal Carolina Univ	SC	17,620	C
Coe College	IA	43,590	VC
Coker College	SC	32,256	LC
Colby College	ME	57,510	MC
Colgate Univ	NY	50,930	MC
College of Staten Island / The CUNY	NY	16,778	NC
College of Charleston	SC	21,273	VC
College of New Jersey	NJ	25,376	HC
College of St. Benedict	MN	47,570	VC
College of the Holy Cross	MA	56,232	MC
College of William & Mary	VA	25,085	MC
College of Wooster	OH	52,600	VC
Colo College	CO	54,534	MC
Colo Mesa Univ	CO	16,669	LC
Colo State Univ-Fort Collins	CO	20,090	VC
Colo State Univ-Pueblo	CO	13,532	LC
Columbia College	MO	24,578	C
Columbia College	SC	27,882	C
Columbia Univ in the City of New York	NY	61,116	MC
Columbia Univ/Barnard College	NY	39,000	MC
Columbia Univ/School of General Studies	NY	54,083	MC
Columbus State Univ	GA	13,176	C
Concord Univ	WV	13,102	C
Concordia College, Moorhead	MN	39,974	C+
Concordia Univ - Irvine	CA	35,390	VC
Concordia Univ, River Forest	IL	26,300	C
Conn College	CT	54,970	MC
Converse College	SC	37,130	C
Coppin State Univ	MD	14,905	VC
Corban Univ	OR	34,764	C
Cornell College	IA	44,930	HC
Creighton Univ	NE	44,058	VC+
Culver-Stockton College	MO	30,900	C
Cumberland Univ	TN	21,220	C
CUNY-City College	NY	19,576	HC+
Curry College	MA	47,545	LC
Daemen College	NY	31,510	C
Dallas Baptist Univ	TX	29,118	C
Davidson College	NC	54,683	MC
Davis and Elkins College	WV	33,742	C
De Sales Univ	PA	42,670	C
Delaware State Univ	DE	14,700	LC
Delta State Univ	MS	12,292	LC
Denison Univ	OH	54,670	HC+
DePaul Univ	IL	46,120	VC
DePauw Univ	IN	48,950	VC+
Dickinson College	PA	57,662	HC+
Dickinson State Univ	ND	8,550	NC
Dillard Univ	LA	20,940	VC
Doane College	NE	33,730	VC
Dominican Univ	IL	37,628	C
Dominican Univ of Calif	CA	51,250	C
Dordt College	IA	34,160	VC
Dowling College	NY	25,000	LC
Drake Univ	IA	30,980	VC+
Drew Univ/College of Liberal Arts	NJ	55,862	VC
Drexel Univ	PA	51,920	HC
Drury Univ	MO	30,319	VC
Duke Univ	NC	50,250	MC
Duquesne Univ	PA	42,017	VC
Earlham College	IN	49,710	VC+
East Carolina Univ	NC	14,169	C
East Central Univ	OK	10,223	LC
East Stroudsburg Univ of Pennsylvania	PA	16,636	C
East Tenn State Univ	TN	9,000	C
East Texas Baptist Univ	TX	29,135	C
Eastern Conn State Univ	CT	20,584	C
Eastern Illinois Univ	IL	20,502	C
Eastern Kentucky Univ	KY	11,161	C
Eastern Mich Univ	MI	17,961	C
Eastern New Mexico Univ	NM	10,682	C
Eastern Univ	PA	37,704	C
Eastern Washington Univ	WA	16,388	C
Eckerd College	FL	43,902	VC
Edgewood College	WI	33,294	C
Edinboro Univ of Pennsylvania	PA	15,940	LC
Edward Waters College	FL	17,856	LC
Elizabeth City State Univ	NC	11,638	C
Elizabethtown College	PA	47,600	VC
Elmhurst College	IL	42,032	C+
Elmira College	NY	49,950	C+
Elon Univ	NC	40,046	HC
Emmanuel College	MA	47,985	VC
Emory and Henry College	VA	387,460	C
Emory Univ	GA	45,000	MC
Emporia State Univ	KS	12,897	C
Endicott College	MA	42,390	C
Eugene Lang College - The New School for Liberal Arts	NY	55,650	VC
Eureka College	IL	19,280	C
Evangel Univ	MO	23,090	C
Excelsior College	NY	895	SP
Fairfield Univ	CT	55,850	VC
Fairleigh Dickinson Univ/College at Florham	NJ	42,142	C
Fairleigh Dickinson Univ/Metropolitan Campus	NJ	40,254	C
Fairmont State Univ	WV	12,098	LC
Fayetteville State Univ	NC	10,816	C
Ferris State Univ	MI	19,698	C
Ferrum College	VA	27,740	LC
Fisk Univ	TN	19,830	C
Fitchburg State Univ	MA	17,241	C
Flagler College	FL	24,960	VC
Florida A&M Univ	FL	14,935	LC
Florida Atlantic Univ	FL	17,339	C
Florida Gulf Coast Univ	FL		C
Florida International Univ	FL	17,747	VC
Florida Memorial Univ	FL	20,716	LC
Florida Southern College	FL	38,240	VC
Florida State Univ	FL	15,238	HC
Fordham Univ	NY	58,927	HC
Fort Hays State Univ	KS	11,354	C
Fort Lewis College	CO	15,513	C
Fort Valley State Univ	GA	11,200	VC
Framingham State Univ	MA	16,750	C
Francis Marion Univ	SC	16,464	LC
Franciscan Univ of Steubenville	OH	27,320	VC
Franklin and Marshall College	PA	58,295	MC
Franklin College	IN	35,885	C
Franklin Pierce Univ	NH	41,598	C
Friends Univ	KS	29,100	C
Frostburg State Univ	MD	15,264	LC
Furman Univ	SC	54,006	HC
Gallaudet Univ	DC	25,380	SP
Gannon Univ	PA	37,940	C
Geneva College	PA	27,280	C
George Fox Univ	OR	40,750	C+
George Mason Univ	VA	15,724	VC
George Washington Univ	DC	57,108	MC
Georgetown College	KY	38,690	C
Georgetown Univ	DC	52,910	MC
Georgia College and State Univ	GA	18,216	VC
Georgia Regents Univ	GA		C
Georgia Southern Univ	GA	16,414	C
Georgia Southwestern State Univ	GA	12,218	C
Georgia State Univ	GA	12,000	VC
Gettysburg College	PA	56,820	HC
Gonzaga Univ	WA	44,247	HC
Gordon College	MA	42,660	VC+
Goucher College	MD	50,252	VC+
Grambling State Univ	LA	13,384	LC
Grand Valley State Univ	MI	17,998	VC
Grand View Univ	IA	31,050	C
Greensboro College	NC	28,740	LC
Grinnell College	IA	53,654	HC
Grove City College	PA	22,988	HC
Guilford College	NC	35,340	C
Gustavus Adolphus College	MN	48,170	HC
Hamilton College	NY	55,620	MC
Hamline Univ	MN	44,198	VC
Hampden-Sydney College	VA	48,848	C
Hampshire College	MA	58,320	MC
Hampton Univ	VA	28,528	C
Hanover College	IN	41,450	VC
Harding Univ	AR	21,432	C+
Hardin-Simmons Univ	TX	23,560	C+
Hartwick College	NY	49,815	C+
Harvard Univ/Harvard College	MA	49,000	MC
Hastings College	NE	27,782	C+
Haverford College	PA	59,230	MC
Hawaii Pacific Univ	HI	36,690	C
Heidelberg Univ	OH	34,100	C
Henderson State Univ	AR	13,634	C
Hendrix College	AR	48,436	HC+
High Point Univ	NC	39,800	C
Hilbert College	NY	28,550	C
Hillsdale College	MI	31,890	HC+
Hiram College	OH	37,300	VC
Hobart and William Smith Colleges	NY	43,000	VC
Hofstra Univ	NY	48,020	VC+
Hollins Univ	VA	43,295	VC
Holy Family Univ	PA	40,030	LC
Hood College	MD	44,630	C
Hope College	MI	36,320	VC+
Houghton College	NY	35,740	VC
Houston Baptist Univ	TX	23,815	C+
Howard Payne Univ	TX	17,115	C
Howard Univ	DC	35,957	C
Humboldt State Univ	CA	18,400	C
Hunter College / The CUNY	NY	14,429	VC
Huntingdon College	AL	31,850	C
Huston-Tillotson Univ	TX	18,124	C+
Idaho State Univ	ID	11,908	C
Illinois College	IL	25,770	VC
Illinois Inst of Technology	IL	38,512	HC+
Illinois State Univ	IL	22,634	VC
Illinois Wesleyan Univ	IL	48,452	VC+
Indiana State Univ	IN	16,000	C
Indiana Univ Bloomington	IN	19,358	HC
Indiana Univ East	IN	6,639	LC
Indiana Univ Kokomo	IN	6,674	LC
Indiana Univ Northwest	IN	6,738	LC
Indiana Univ of Pennsylvania	PA	20,180	LC
Indiana Univ South Bend	IN	15,293	C
Indiana Univ Southeast	IN	15,807	LC
Indiana Univ-Purdue Univ Fort Wayne	IN	15,425	C
Indiana Univ-Purdue Univ Indianapolis	IN	17,290	C
Indiana Wesleyan Univ	IN	31,815	VC
Inter-American Univ of PR/Fajardo Campus	PR	4,200	
Inter-American Univ of PR/Metropolitan Campus	PR	4,320	
Inter-American Univ of PR/Ponce	PR	3,700	
Inter-American Univ of PR/San Germán	PR	6,720	
Iona College	NY	44,028	C
Iowa State Univ	IA	16,403	C
Ithaca College	NY	52,300	HC
Jackson State Univ	MS	13,512	LC
Jacksonville State Univ	AL	12,280	LC
Jacksonville Univ	FL	37,780	C
James Madison Univ	VA	18,049	VC
John Brown Univ	AR	30,996	VC+
John Carroll Univ	OH	44,520	C+
John Jay College of Criminal Justice / The CUNY	NY	6,059	C
Johns Hopkins Univ	MD	47,492	MC
Johnson C. Smith Univ	NC	25,336	LC
Johnson State College	VT	16,721	C
Judson Univ	IL	25,130	C
Juniata College	PA	49,340	VC
Kalamazoo College	MI	47,825	HC+
Kansas State Univ	KS	15,407	VC
Kean Univ	NJ	22,060	LC
Keene State College	NH	21,538	C
Kennesaw State Univ	GA	13,017	VC
Kent State Univ	OH	19,352	C
Kentucky State Univ	KY	11,000	LC
Kentucky Wesleyan College	KY	27,440	VC+
Kenyon College	OH	56,810	MC
Keuka College	NY	30,300	C
King Univ	TN	33,140	C
King's College	PA	41,678	C
Knox College	IL		VC
Kutztown Univ of Pennsylvania	PA	16,909	LC
La Salle Univ	PA	50,270	C
La Sierra Univ	CA	35,694	VC
Lafayette College	PA	57,050	HC+
LaGrange College	GA	34,480	C
Lake Erie College	OH	35,704	C
Lake Forest College	IL	45,580	VC
Lake Superior State Univ	MI	18,121	C
Lamar Univ	TX	6,820	LC
Lander Univ	SC	22,514	C+
Lawrence Univ	WI	46,371	HC
Le Moyne College	NY	42,200	VC
Lebanon Valley College	PA	38,570	C
Lee Univ	TN	18,690	C+
Lehigh Univ	PA	55,080	MC
Lehman College / The CUNY	NY	5,778	LC
LeMoyne-Owen College	TN	13,100	C
Lenoir-Rhyne College	NC	35,984	C
Lewis & Clark College	OR	52,656	VC
Lewis Univ	IL	23,050	C
Liberty Univ	VA	19,101	C
Lincoln Univ	MO	11,096	NC
Lindenwood Univ	MO	20,750	C
Linfield College-McMinnville Campus	OR	46,166	C
Lipscomb Univ	TN	35,722	VC
Livingstone College	NC	17,815	LC
Lock Haven Univ of Pennsylvania	PA	17,587	LC
LIU/Brooklyn Campus	NY	26,500	C
LIU/C.W. Post Campus	NY	38,888	C
Longwood Univ	VA	20,924	C
Loras College	IA	37,432	VC
Louisiana State Univ	LA	18,677	VC+
Louisiana Tech Univ	LA	8,000	C
Loyola Marymount Univ	CA	53,240	VC+
Loyola Univ Chicago	IL	49,560	VC+
Loyola Univ Maryland	MD		VC
Loyola Univ New Orleans	LA	46,581	VC
Luther College	IA	44,380	VC+
Lycoming College	PA	43,636	C
Lynchburg College	VA	42,645	C
Lynn Univ	FL	43,500	C
Lyon College	AR	30,246	VC
Macalester College	MN	53,419	MC
MacMurray College	IL	20,755	C
Malone Univ	OH	34,334	C
Manchester College	IN	35,070	C
Manhattan College	NY	44,955	VC
Manhattanville College	NY	46,260	VC
Mansfield Univ	PA	19,468	LC
Marian Univ/Indianapolis	IN	37,058	C
Marietta College	OH	42,135	VC
Marist College	NY	35,500	C
Marlboro College	VT	35,980	VC
Marquette Univ	WI	43,664	VC+
Mars Hill College	NC	22,950	LC
Marshall Univ	WV	14,820	C
Martin Univ	IN	11,000	SP
Mary Baldwin College	VA	37,110	C
Marygrove College	MI	21,290	C
Marymount Manhattan College	NY	40,118	VC
Marymount Univ	VA	36,178	C
Maryville College	TN	33,150	VC
Marywood Univ	PA	40,695	C
Mass College of Liberal Arts	MA	16,733	C
Mass Inst of Technology	MA	54,238	MC
McDaniel College	MD	45,600	VC
McKendree Univ	IL	29,920	C+
McMurry Univ	TX	25,962	LC
McNeese State Univ	LA		C
Mercer Univ	GA	44,201	VC+
Mercy College	NY	29,996	C
Mercyhurst Univ	PA	40,700	C
Meredith College	NC	31,420	C
Merrimack College	MA	44,215	C
Messiah College	PA	39,540	VC
Methodist Univ	NC	37,185	C
Metropolitan State Univ of Denver	CO	4,835	LC
Miami Univ	OH	24,191	HC
Mich State Univ	MI	13,689	VC
Middle Tenn State Univ	TN	8,650	C
Middlebury College	VT	57,470	MC
Midwestern State Univ	TX	9,722	C
Miles College	AL	16,530	NC
Millersville Univ of Pennsylvania	PA	18,498	C
Millikin Univ	IL	37,462	C
Mills College	CA	54,119	HC
Millsaps College	MS	40,000	VC+
Minn State Univ, Mankato	MN	14,900	C
Minn State Univ, Moorhead	MN	13,392	C
Miss College	MS	21,998	VC
Miss Univ for Women	MS	7,400	LC
Miss Valley State Univ	MS	9,706	LC
Missouri Southern State Univ	MO	11,910	C
Missouri State Univ	MO	13,996	VC
Missouri Valley College	MO	22,200	C
Missouri Western State Univ	MO	12,260	NC
Molloy College	NY	38,950	C
Monmouth College	IL	39,290	C
Monmouth Univ	NJ	42,252	C
Montana State Univ	MT	14,068	VC
Montana State Univ-Billings	MT	12,425	LC
Montclair State Univ	NJ	22,614	C
Moravian College	PA	36,381	VC
Morehead State Univ	KY	10,900	C
Morehouse College	GA	38,640	C
Morgan State Univ	MD	14,500	VC

ST = STATE $IS = IN-STATE COSTS SR = SELECTOR RATING

School	ST	$IS	SR
Morningside College	IA	32,620	C
Morris College	SC	16,006	LC
Mount Aloysius College	PA	27,970	C
Mount Holyoke College	MA	53,596	H₵
Mount Mercy Univ	IA	34,385	C
Mount St. Mary College	NY	39,540	C
Mount St. Mary's Univ	MD	46,158	C
Mount St. Mary's College/ Chalon Campus	CA	43,897	V₵
Mount Vernon Nazarene Univ	OH	29,590	C
Muhlenberg College	PA	52,837	HC
Murray State Univ	KY	14,944	C
Muskingum Univ	OH	30,502	C
Nazareth College of Rochester	NY	41,590	VC
Nebr Wesleyan Univ	NE	29,774	₵
Neumann Univ	PA	31,078	LC
New College of Florida	FL	14,504	H₵
New England College	NH	45,930	LC
New Jersey City Univ	NJ	21,060	₵
New Mexico Highlands Univ	NM	9,720	NC
New Mexico State Univ	NM	13,955	LC
New York Inst of Technology	NY	40,590	VC
New York Univ	NY	61,470	MC
Newberry College	SC	26,850	LC
Niagara Univ	NY	39,800	C
Nicholls State Univ	LA	7,095	C
Norfolk State Univ	VA	10,531	LC
N Car Agricultural and Technical State Univ	NC	13,175	LC
N Car Central Univ	NC	9,000	LC
N Car State Univ	NC	16,202	HC
N Car Wesleyan College	NC	29,440	C
North Central College	IL	38,343	VC
N Dak State Univ	ND	14,642	C
North Georgia College & State Univ	GA	8,500	C
North Park Univ	IL	30,130	C
Northeastern Illinois Univ	IL		C
Northeastern State Univ	OK	8,615	VC
Northeastern Univ	MA	55,296	MC
Northern Arizona Univ	AZ	18,592	C
Northern Illinois Univ	IL	19,768	C
Northern Kentucky Univ	KY	15,302	LC
Northern Mich Univ	MI	15,300	VC
Northern State Univ	SD	14,021	C
Northwest Missouri State Univ	MO	14,229	C
Northwest Nazarene Univ	ID	24,275	NC
Northwestern College of Iowa	IA	34,848	₵
Northwestern Okla State Univ	OK	7,275	NC
Northwestern Univ	IL	37,595	MC
Norwich Univ	VT	28,212	C
Notre Dame College	OH	34,942	VC
Notre Dame de Namur Univ	CA	41,610	LC
Notre Dame of Maryland Univ	MD	27,700	C
Nova Southeastern Univ	FL	34,016	VC
Oakland Univ	MI	19,391	VC
Oberlin College	OH	57,025	MC
Occidental College	CA	59,592	M₵
Oglethorpe Univ	GA	42,580	VC
Ohio Dominican Univ	OH	38,380	₵
Ohio Northern Univ	OH	42,075	VC
Ohio Univ	OH	20,676	VC
Ohio Wesleyan Univ	OH	49,460	₵
Okla Baptist Univ	OK	28,202	VC
Okla City Univ	OK	33,546	VC
Okla State Univ	OK	14,310	VC
Okla Wesleyan Univ	OK	21,300	C
Old Dominion Univ	VA	18,662	C
Olivet Nazarene Univ	IL	29,990	C
Oral Roberts Univ	OK	31,734	C
Oregon State Univ	OR	19,017	₵
Oswego / SUNY	NY	20,009	VC
Ottawa Univ	KS	15,000	VC
Otterbein College	OH	32,214	C
Ouachita Baptist Univ	AR	29,010	VC
Our Lady of the Lake Univ of San Antonio	TX	22,430	LC
Pace Univ	NY	48,094	VC
Pacific Lutheran Univ	WA	44,840	VC
Pacific Univ	OR	42,815	C
Palm Beach Atlantic Univ	FL	33,882	LC
Park Univ	MO	17,525	C
Paul Quinn College	TX	25,350	LC
Penn State Erie/The Behrend College	PA	16,256	C
Penn State Univ/Univ Park	PA	25,404	VC
Pepperdine Univ	CA	55,372	H₵
Pfeiffer Univ	NC	33,700	C
Philander Smith College	AR	19,760	LC
Piedmont College	GA	29,260	C
Pittsburg State Univ	KS	12,032	C
Pitzer College	CA	54,988	MC
Plymouth State Univ	NH	23,148	LC
Point Loma Nazarene Univ	CA	38,610	VC
Point Park Univ	PA	36,390	C
Pomona College	CA	57,680	MC
Pontifical Catholic Univ of PR	PR	7,310	
Portland State Univ	OR	18,672	C
Prairie View A&M Univ	TX	15,205	LC
Presbyterian College	SC	42,678	VC
Princeton Univ	NJ	53,795	MC
Principia College	IL	35,140	₵
Providence College	RI	55,995	HC
Purchase College / SUNY	NY	16,951	C
Purdue Univ/Calumet	IN	14,336	C
Purdue Univ/West Lafayette	IN	20,278	HC
Queens College / The CUNY	NY	17,107	VC
Queens Univ of Charlotte	NC	39,543	VC
Quincy Univ	IL	34,980	LC
Quinnipiac Univ	CT	53,580	VC
Radford Univ	VA	17,132	LC
Ramapo College of New Jersey	NJ	24,938	₵
Randolph College	VA	43,960	VC
Randolph-Macon College	VA	45,086	C
Reed College	OR	57,780	MC
Regis College	MA	47,565	LC
Regis Univ	CO	41,318	C
Rhode Island College	RI	17,132	LC
Rhodes College	TN	47,596	H₵
Rice Univ	TX	43,288	MC
Richard Stockton College of New Jersey	NJ	20,000	VC
Rider Univ	NJ	45,720	C
Ripon College	WI	36,959	₵
Rivier College	NH	35,000	VC
Roanoke College	VA	47,996	₵
Rockford College	IL	31,000	C
Rockhurst Univ	MO	20,625	C
Rocky Mountain College	MT	32,242	C
Roger Williams Univ	RI	45,788	C
Rollins College	FL	52,370	HC
Roosevelt Univ	IL	22,605	VC
Rosemont College	PA	42,350	C
Rowan Univ	NJ	23,570	VC
Russell Sage College	NY	39,370	C
Rust College	MS	10,600	C
Rutgers, The State Univ of New Jersey/Camden Campus	NJ	24,254	C
Rutgers, The State Univ of New Jersey/New Brunswick	NJ	25,077	VC
Rutgers, The State Univ of New Jersey/Newark Campus	NJ	25,376	C
Sacred Heart Univ	CT	48,564	VC
Saginaw Valley State Univ	MI	16,869	C
St. Anselm College	NH	48,324	VC
St. Augustine's Univ	NC	14,000	C
St. Francis Univ	PA	30,029	LC
St. John's Univ	MN	46,146	C
St. Joseph's College	IN	35,790	C
St. Joseph's Univ	PA	52,272	VC
St. Leo Univ	FL	27,990	C
St. Louis Univ	MO	46,594	V₵
St. Martin's Univ	WA	38,082	C
St. Mary's College	IN	45,160	VC
St. Mary's College of Calif	CA	53,550	C
St. Mary's Univ	TX	33,854	C
St. Mary's Univ of Minn	MN	37,015	C
St. Michael's College	VT	48,740	VC
St. Paul's College	VA	16,030	NC
St. Peter's College	NJ	44,240	C
St. Vincent College	PA	40,244	C
St. Xavier Univ	IL	32,840	C
Salisbury Univ	MD	18,368	VC
Salve Regina Univ	RI	47,250	VC
Sam Houston State Univ	TX	17,082	C
Samford Univ	AL	35,700	V₵
San Diego State Univ	CA	20,578	VC
San Francisco State Univ	CA	18,514	C
San Jose State Univ	CA	19,707	C
Santa Clara Univ	CA	54,702	MC
Sarah Lawrence College	NY	48,000	HC
Savannah State Univ	GA	13,156	C
Schreiner Univ	TX	32,734	LC
Scripps College	CA	54,900	MC
Seattle Pacific Univ	WA	41,559	V₵
Seattle Univ	WA	47,010	V₵
Seton Hall Univ	NJ	45,902	C
Seton Hill Univ	PA	35,172	C
Sewanee: The Univ of the South	TN	47,700	H₵
Shaw Univ	NC	15,488	LC
Shenandoah Univ	VA	39,268	C
Shepherd Univ	WV	14,996	C
Shippensburg Univ of Pennsylvania	PA	17,064	LC
Siena College	NY	43,863	VC
Simmons College	MA	48,770	VC
Simpson College	IA	36,086	VC
Skidmore College	NY	57,926	HC
Slippery Rock Univ of Pennsylvania	PA	10,360	LC
Smith College	MA	57,524	MC
Sonoma State Univ	CA	20,541	C
S Car State Univ	SC	6,700	LC
S Dak State Univ	SD	14,296	C
Southeast Missouri State Univ	MO	14,983	LC
Southeastern Louisiana Univ	LA	13,325	C
Southeastern Okla State Univ	OK	7,966	C
Southern Arkansas Univ	AR	14,316	C
Southern Conn State Univ	CT	18,033	C
Southern Illinois Univ Carbondale	IL	21,620	C
Southern Illinois Univ Edwardsville	IL	17,532	C
Southern Methodist Univ	TX	57,755	MC
Southern Nazarene Univ	OK	24,354	NC
Southern New Hampshire Univ	NH	38,100	C
Southern Oregon Univ	OR	17,874	C
Southern Polytechnic State Univ	GA	13,958	VC
Southern Univ and A&M College	LA	9,761	₵
Southern Univ at New Orleans	LA	1,000	NC
Southwest Baptist Univ	MO	24,710	C
Southwest Minn State Univ	MN	14,000	C
Southwestern Okla State Univ	OK	9,160	C
Southwestern Univ	TX	45,660	VC
Spelman College	GA	24,650	VC
Spring Hill College	AL	42,130	VC
Springfield College	MA	25,000	C
St. Ambrose Univ	IA		C
St. Bonaventure Univ	NY	38,831	C
St. Catherine Univ	MN	37,782	₵
St. Cloud State Univ	MN	10,600	C
St. Edward's Univ	TX	44,674	VC
St. Francis College	NY	34,200	LC
St. John Fisher College	NY	39,370	₵
St. John's Univ	NY	52,840	₵
St. Joseph's College, New York / Brooklyn Campus	NY	21,878	C
St. Joseph's College, New York / Suffolk Campus	NY	21,878	VC
St. Lawrence Univ	NY	53,740	HC
St. Mary's College of Maryland	MD	26,699	HC
St. Norbert College	WI	39,992	VC
St. Olaf College	MN	49,960	H₵
St. Thomas Univ	FL	32,310	₵
Stanford Univ	CA	56,411	MC
Stephen F. Austin State Univ	TX	14,668	C
Stetson Univ	FL	49,512	V₵
Stonehill College	MA	46,780	V₵
Stony Brook Univ / SUNY	NY	19,359	HC
Suffolk Univ	MA	46,548	C
Sul Ross State Univ	TX	13,410	LC
SUNY College at Geneseo	NY	18,055	H₵
SUNY College at Old Westbury	NY	16,324	C
SUNY Cortland / The SUNY	NY	19,117	C
SUNY Fredonia / The SUNY at Fredonia	NY	18,702	VC
SUNY New Paltz	NY	15,010	C
SUNY Oneonta / SUNY	NY	16,919	VC
SUNY Plattsburgh / SUNY	NY	18,083	VC
Susquehanna Univ	PA	49,170	C
Swarthmore College	PA	57,870	MC
Sweet Briar College	VA	43,765	₵
Syracuse Univ	NY	54,512	HC
Tarleton State Univ	TX	13,489	LC
Taylor Univ	IN	36,742	V₵
Temple Univ	PA	24,392	VC
Tenn State Univ	TN	9,048	C
Tenn Tech Univ	TN	11,310	C
Texas A&M Univ	TX	16,956	V₵
Texas A&M Univ at Commerce	TX	10,496	C
Texas A&M Univ at Corpus Christi	TX	11,544	LC
Texas A&M Univ at Kingsville	TX	7,500	LC
Texas Christian Univ	TX	47,570	HC
Texas Lutheran Univ	TX	34,070	C
Texas Southern Univ	TX	18,212	LC
Texas State Univ	TX	16,495	VC
Texas Tech Univ	TX	14,243	C
Texas Wesleyan Univ	TX	29,886	C
Texas Woman's Univ	TX	13,633	LC
The Catholic Univ of America	DC	52,852	VC
The College at Brockport / SUNY	NY	18,362	VC
The College of Idaho	ID	31,277	VC
The College of New Rochelle	NY	33,600	VC
The College of St. Rose	NY	26,750	C
The Lincoln Univ	PA	15,154	LC
The Masters College	CA	38,160	₵
Ohio State Univ	OH	19,887	MC
The SUNY at Potsdam	NY	17,754	C
Thiel College	PA	31,378	LC
Thomas Edison State College	NJ	5,700	SP
Thomas More College	KY	34,760	C
Tougaloo College	MS	15,275	NC
Touro College	NY	23,150	VC
Towson Univ	MD	16,000	VC
Transylvania Univ	KY	40,310	V₵
Trevecca Nazarene Univ	TN	30,118	C
Trinity College	CT		H₵
Trinity Univ	TX	44,174	H₵
Trinity Washington Univ	DC	30,250	₵
Troy Univ	AL	10,650	C
Truman State Univ	MO	13,546	HC
Tufts Univ	MA	58,780	MC
Tulane Univ	LA	58,942	MC
Tusculum College	TN	24,295	C
Tuskegee Univ	AL	26,750	C
Union College	NY		MC
Union Univ	TN	28,260	VC
United States Air Force Academy	CO		MC
United States Coast Guard Academy	CT		HC
United States Military Academy	NY		MC
United States Naval Academy	MD		MC
Univ at Albany / SUNY	NY	18,674	VC
Univ at Buffalo / The SUNY	NY	20,283	VC
Univ of Akron	OH	20,436	C
Univ of Alabama at Birmingham	AL	18,484	₵
Univ of Alabama at Huntsville	AL	17,625	VC
Univ of Alabama at Tuscaloosa	AL	17,164	₵
Univ of Alaska Anchorage	AK	15,290	NC
Univ of Alaska Fairbanks	AK	13,955	C
Univ of Alaska Southeast	AK	11,493	C
Univ of Arizona	AZ	20,105	C
Univ of Arkansas at Fayetteville	AR	16,860	VC
Univ of Arkansas at Little Rock	AR		C
Univ of Arkansas at Monticello	AR	8,470	NC
Univ of Arkansas at Pine Bluff	AR	10,600	C
Univ of Calif at Berkeley	CA	23,322	MC
Univ of Calif at Davis	CA	24,482	HC
Univ of Calif at Irvine	CA	25,961	VC
Univ of Calif at Los Angeles	CA	25,686	MC
Univ of Calif at Riverside	CA	27,204	C
Univ of Calif at San Diego	CA	21,000	VC
Univ of Calif at Santa Barbara	CA	27,551	HC
Univ of Calif at Santa Cruz	CA	27,807	VC
Univ of Central Arkansas	AR	10,840	VC
Univ of Central Florida	FL	15,711	V₵
Univ of Central Missouri	MO	14,605	C
Univ of Central Okla	OK	12,293	C
Univ of Charleston	WV	28,650	C
Univ of Chicago	IL	55,416	MC
Univ of Cincinnati	OH	20,199	VC
Univ of Colo at Colo Springs	CO	15,000	VC
Univ of Colo Boulder	CO	22,605	V₵
Univ of Colo Denver	CO	17,904	C
Univ of Conn	CT	23,744	HC
Univ of Dallas	TX	43,510	V₵
Univ of Dayton	OH	43,750	VC
Univ of Delaware	DE	22,728	VC
Univ of Denver	CO	51,787	V₵
Univ of Detroit Mercy	MI	30,450	C
Univ of Evansville	IN	41,056	V₵
Univ of Findlay	OH	31,916	C
Univ of Florida	FL	15,783	H₵
Univ of Georgia	GA	19,508	VC
Univ of Great Falls	MT	27,970	C
Univ of Hartford	CT	42,674	C
Univ of Hawaii at Hilo	HI	6,500	C
Univ of Hawaii at Manoa	HI	19,379	VC
Univ of Houston-Downtown	TX	6,267	LC
Univ of Idaho	ID	14,558	C
Univ of Illinois at Chicago	IL	24,293	VC
Univ of Illinois at Urbana-Champaign	IL	24,300	HC
Univ of Indianapolis	IN	31,740	LC
Univ of Iowa	IA	17,481	VC
Univ of Kansas	KS	16,980	₵
Univ of Kentucky	KY	19,868	C
Univ of La Verne	CA	47,010	VC
Univ of Louisiana at Lafayette	LA	6,130	C
Univ of Louisiana at Monroe	LA	12,998	C
Univ of Louisville	KY	17,460	VC
Univ of Maine	ME	19,712	₵
Univ of Maine at Farmington	ME	17,841	C
Univ of Mary Hardin-Baylor	TX	31,950	₵
Univ of Mary Washington	VA	19,484	VC
Univ of Maryland	MD	18,801	HC
Univ of Maryland/Baltimore County	MD	18,000	VC
Univ of Maryland/Univ College	MD	6,168	SP
Univ of Mass Amherst	MA	23,697	V₵
Univ of Mass Boston	MA	11,966	C
Univ of Mass Dartmouth	MA	22,223	C
Univ of Mass Lowell	MA	19,316	C
Univ of Memphis	TN	15,094	C
Univ of Miami	FL	55,166	MC
Univ of Mich/Ann Arbor	MI	22,102	H₵
Univ of Mich/Dearborn	MI	9,885	VC
Univ of Mich-Flint	MI	17,547	₵

ST = STATE **$IS** = IN-STATE COSTS **SR** = SELECTOR RATING

School	ST	$IS	SR
Univ of Minn/Duluth	MN	18,964	C+
Univ of Minn/Morris	MN	17,150	VC
Univ of Minn/Twin Cities	MN		HC
Univ of Miss	MS	15,482	VC
Univ of Missouri/Columbia	MO	18,201	MC
Univ of Missouri-Kansas City	MO	19,603	C
Univ of Missouri-St. Louis	MO	18,304	VC
Univ of Mobile	AL	27,870	VC
Univ of Montana	MT	13,670	C
Univ of Montana-Western	MT	9,753	LC
Univ of Montevallo	AL	17,320	C
Univ of Mount Union	OH	35,130	C
Univ of Nebr - Lincoln	NE	17,507	VC
Univ of Nebr at Kearney	NE	14,855	LC
Univ of Nebr at Omaha	NE	12,700	C
Univ of Nevada, Las Vegas	NV	17,303	C
Univ of Nevada/Reno	NV	14,500	NC
Univ of New England	ME	46,145	C+
Univ of New Hampshire	NH	24,702	VC
Univ of New Haven	CT	47,740	C
Univ of New Mexico	NM	15,300	C
Univ of New Orleans	LA	9,224	VC
Univ of North Alabama	AL	9,960	C
Univ of N Car at Asheville	NC	13,500	VC+
Univ of N Car at Chapel Hill	NC	18,348	MC
Univ of N Car at Charlotte	NC	15,847	C
Univ of N Car at Greensboro	NC	12,848	C
Univ of N Car at Wilmington	NC	13,572	VC+
Univ of N Dak	ND	14,094	C
Univ of North Florida	FL	15,578	VC
Univ of North Texas	TX	15,628	C
Univ of Northern Colo	CO	15,973	C
Univ of Northern Iowa	IA	14,776	C
Univ of Notre Dame	IN		MC
Univ of Okla	OK	17,634	VC+
Univ of Oregon	OR	20,872	VC
Univ of Pennsylvania	PA	56,106	MC
Univ of Pikeville	KY	24,750	NC
Univ of Pittsburgh at Greensburg	PA	17,640	C
Univ of Pittsburgh at Johnstown	PA	20,862	LC
Univ of Pittsburgh at Pittsburgh	PA	27,800	HC+
Univ of Portland	OR	47,874	VC
Univ of PR Recinto de Rio Piedras	PR	5,750	
Univ of PR/Mayaguez	PR	1,250	
Univ of Puget Sound	WA	52,648	HC+
Univ of Redlands	CA	40,500	VC
Univ of Rio Grande	OH	8,750	NC
Univ of Rochester	NY	58,500	MC
Univ of St. Mary	KS	28,400	C+
Univ of San Diego	CA	53,302	HC+
Univ of San Francisco	CA	49,674	VC
Univ of Science and Arts of Okla	OK	10,560	VC
Univ of Scranton	PA	51,940	VC
Univ of Sioux Falls	SD	22,990	C
Univ of South Alabama	AL	13,510	C
Univ of S Car at Aiken	SC	16,278	C
Univ of S Car at Columbia	SC	19,725	VC+
Univ of S Car Upstate	SC	17,673	LC
Univ of S Dak	SD	15,111	C
Univ of South Florida	FL	13,000	C
Univ of South Florida/St. Petersburg	FL	12,769	VC
Univ of Southern Calif	CA	56,903	MC
Univ of Southern Indiana	IN	14,657	C
Univ of Southern Maine	ME	16,576	C
Univ of Southern Miss	MS	13,170	C
Univ of St. Francis	IL	36,490	C
Univ of St. Thomas - Houston	TX	36,490	VC
Univ of Tampa	FL	35,160	VC
Univ of Tenn at Chattanooga	TN	16,883	C
Univ of Tenn at Knoxville	TN	20,364	VC+
Univ of Tenn at Martin	TN	13,217	C
Univ of Texas at Arlington	TX	10,908	LC
Univ of Texas at Austin	TX	44,074	HC
Univ of Texas at Dallas	TX	21,046	HC
Univ of Texas at El Paso	TX	8,764	NC
Univ of Texas at San Antonio	TX	18,372	C
Univ of Texas-Pan American	TX	12,432	LC
Univ of the Cumberlands	KY	27,500	LC
Univ of the District of Columbia	DC	7,244	LC
Univ of the Incarnate Word	TX	35,200	LC
Univ of the Ozarks	AR	22,100	C
Univ of the Pacific	CA	52,146	VC
Univ of Toledo	OH	18,464	C
Univ of Tulsa	OK	45,311	HC+
Univ of Utah	UT	13,462	VC
Univ of Vermont	VT	26,120	VC+
Univ of Virginia	VA	22,175	MC
Univ of Virginia's College at Wise	VA	11,076	C
Univ of Washington	WA	14,722	VC
Univ of West Florida	FL	14,656	C
Univ of West Georgia	GA	14,852	LC
Univ of Wisc Whitewater	WI	13,314	C
Univ of Wisc/Eau Claire	WI	15,430	VC
Univ of Wisc/Green Bay	WI	14,900	C
Univ of Wisc/La Crosse	WI	14,755	VC
Univ of Wisc/Madison	WI	18,757	HC
Univ of Wisc/Oshkosh	WI	10,426	LC
Univ of Wisc/Parkside	WI	10,181	LC
Univ of Wisc/Platteville	WI	14,274	C
Univ of Wisc/River Falls	WI	9,722	LC
Univ of Wisc/Stevens Point	WI	14,043	C
Univ of Wisc/Superior	WI	14,106	C
Univ of Wisc-Milwaukee	WI	18,436	C
Univ of Wyoming	WY	13,855	C+
Ursinus College	PA	55,630	VC+
Utah State Univ	UT	11,803	C
Utica College	NY	44,704	C
Valparaiso Univ	IN	43,040	VC+
Vanderbilt Univ	TN	57,072	MC
Vanguard Univ of Southern Calif	CA	35,833	VC
Vassar College	NY	59,070	MC
Villanova Univ	PA	56,436	MC
Virginia Commonwealth Univ	VA	18,633	C
Virginia Intermont College	VA	32,411	LC
Virginia Polytechnic Inst and State Univ	VA	14,629	HC
Virginia State Univ	VA	11,318	C+
Virginia Union Univ	VA	18,432	C
Virginia Wesleyan College	VA	28,433	LC
Wabash College	IN	44,160	VC
Wagner College	NY	48,600	VC
Wake Forest Univ	NC	51,000	MC
Walsh Univ	OH	35,100	C
Warren Wilson College	NC	34,888	VC
Wartburg College	IA	41,055	VC
Washburn Univ	KS	12,165	NC
Washington Adventist Univ	MD	25,859	C+
Washington and Jefferson College	PA	49,990	VC
Washington and Lee Univ	VA	52,812	MC
Washington College	MD	48,768	VC
Washington State Univ	WA	20,461	C
Washington Univ in St. Louis	MO	58,818	MC
Wayland Baptist Univ	TX	16,058	LC
Wayne State College	NE	11,764	NC
Wayne State Univ	MI	19,493	C
Webster Univ	MO	33,990	C+
Wellesley College	MA	49,848	MC
Wells College	NY	38,680	VC
Wesley College	DE	31,115	LC
Wesleyan College	GA	24,000	C+
Wesleyan Univ	CT	59,844	MC
West Chester Univ of Pennsylvania	PA	16,836	C
West Liberty Univ	WV	9,142	LC
West Texas A&M Univ	TX	13,478	C
West Virginia State Univ	WV	8,378	NC
West Virginia Univ	WV	15,794	C+
West Virginia Wesleyan College	WV	26,880	C
Western Carolina Univ	NC	13,965	C+
Western Conn State Univ	CT	18,327	C
Western Illinois Univ	IL	20,130	C
Western Kentucky Univ	KY	11,000	LC
Western Mich Univ	MI	19,042	C
Western New England Univ	MA	45,590	C
Western Oregon Univ	OR	15,021	C
Western State Colo Univ	CO	16,135	C
Western Washington Univ	WA	18,519	VC
Westfield State Univ	MA	18,489	C
Westminster College	MO	30,490	VC
Westminster College	PA	31,290	C+
Westminster College	UT	37,708	VC
Westmont College	CA	41,500	HC
Wheaton College	IL	39,650	HC+
Wheaton College	MA	54,934	HC+
Wheeling Jesuit Univ	WV	34,668	C
Whitman College	WA	54,400	MC
Whittier College	CA	43,416	C
Whitworth Univ	WA	45,826	VC+
Wichita State Univ	KS	12,539	C
Widener Univ	PA	50,368	C
Wilberforce Univ	OH	15,100	LC
Wilkes Univ	PA	42,786	C
Willamette Univ	OR	56,450	VC+
William Jewell College	MO	31,000	VC+
William Paterson Univ of New Jersey	NJ	21,694	C
William Peace Univ	NC	32,900	LC
William Penn Univ	IA	26,000	C
William Woods Univ	MO		C
Williams College	MA	58,900	MC
Wilmington College	OH	29,784	C
Wilson College	PA	27,660	C
Wingate Univ	NC	34,990	C
Winona State Univ	MN	16,530	C
Winston-Salem State Univ	NC	9,418	LC
Winthrop Univ	SC	21,120	VC
Wisc Lutheran College	WI	23,510	VC
Wittenberg Univ	OH	47,766	VC
Wofford College	SC	45,795	VC
Woodbury Univ	CA	34,500	LC
Wright State Univ	OH	16,983	C
Xavier Univ	OH	43,740	VC
Xavier Univ of Louisiana	LA	25,300	C
Yale Univ	CT	55,300	MC
Yeshiva Univ	NY	47,250	VC+
York College / CUNY	NY	5,496	NC
York College of Pennsylvania	PA	26,590	C
Youngstown State Univ	OH	16,374	LC

POLYMER SCIENCE

School	ST	$IS	SR
Case Western Reserve Univ	OH	55,178	MC
Eastern Mich Univ	MI	17,961	C
Georgia Inst of Technology	GA	20,464	MC
Pittsburg State Univ	KS	12,032	C
Rochester Inst of Technology	NY	42,450	VC+
SUNY / College of Environmental Science and Forestry	NY	18,351	HC
Univ of Calif at Davis	CA	24,482	HC
Univ of Southern Miss	MS	13,170	C
Western Washington Univ	WA	18,519	VC

PORTUGUESE

School	ST	$IS	SR
Brigham Young Univ	UT	12,100	HC
Brown Univ	RI	56,150	MC
Dartmouth College	NH	57,996	MC
Florida International Univ	FL	17,747	VC
Georgetown Univ	DC	52,910	MC
Harvard Univ/Harvard College	MA	49,000	MC
Indiana Univ Bloomington	IN	19,358	HC
New York Univ	NY	61,470	MC
Princeton Univ	NJ	53,795	MC
Rutgers, The State Univ of New Jersey/New Brunswick	NJ	25,077	VC
Rutgers, The State Univ of New Jersey/Newark Campus	NJ	25,376	C
Ohio State Univ	OH	19,887	MC
Tulane Univ	LA	58,942	MC
Univ of Calif at Los Angeles	CA	25,686	MC
Univ of Calif at Santa Barbara	CA	27,551	HC
Univ of Florida	FL	15,783	HC+
Univ of Illinois at Urbana-Champaign	IL	24,300	HC
Univ of Iowa	IA	17,481	VC
Univ of Mass Amherst	MA	23,697	VC+
Univ of Mass Dartmouth	MA	22,223	C
Univ of New Mexico	NM	15,300	C
Univ of Texas at Austin	TX	44,074	HC
Univ of Wisc/Madison	WI	18,757	HC
Yale Univ	CT	55,300	MC

POULTRY SCIENCE

School	ST	$IS	SR
Auburn Univ	AL	20,052	VC+
N Car State Univ	NC	16,202	HC
Stephen F. Austin State Univ	TX	14,668	C
Texas A&M Univ	TX	16,956	VC+
Univ of Arkansas at Fayetteville	AR	16,860	VC
Univ of Georgia	GA	19,508	VC
Univ of Maryland/Eastern Shore	MD	14,000	C
Univ of Wisc/Madison	WI	18,757	HC
Virginia Polytechnic Inst and State Univ	VA	14,629	HC

PREALLIED HEALTH

School	ST	$IS	SR
Biola Univ	CA	40,320	VC
Ithaca College	NY	52,300	HC
La Salle Univ	PA	50,270	C
Mount Aloysius College	PA	27,970	C
Northwest Nazarene Univ	ID	24,275	NC
Sacred Heart Univ	CT	48,564	VC
St. Michael's College	VT	48,740	VC
Xavier Univ	OH	43,740	VC

PRECISION PRODUCTION

School	ST	$IS	SR
Calif College of the Arts	CA	48,334	SP

PREDENTISTRY

School	ST	$IS	SR
Albertus Magnus College	CT	37,382	LC
Albion College	MI	43,884	VC
American International College	MA	36,100	LC
Arcadia Univ	PA	33,570	C+
Ashland Univ	OH	25,000	C
Auburn Univ	AL	20,052	VC+
Baldwin Wallace Univ	OH	36,980	VC
Ball State Univ	IN	17,850	C
Barry Univ	FL	38,190	C
Baylor Univ	TX	46,720	HC
Bellarmine Univ	KY	42,950	VC
Beloit College	WI	49,970	HC
Bemidji State Univ	MN	13,500	C
Bethel College	IN	31,560	C
Biola Univ	CA	40,320	VC
Boise State Univ	ID	12,802	C
Brigham Young Univ/Hawaii	HI	8,614	VC
Calif Lutheran Univ	CA	47,640	C
Calvin College	MI	37,585	VC+
Campbellsville Univ	KY	27,720	C
Canisius College	NY	45,602	VC
Capital Univ	OH	39,824	VC
Cardinal Stritch Univ	WI	24,054	C
Carroll College	MT	28,000	C
Chadron State College	NE	7,400	NC
Chicago State Univ	IL	5,482	C
Christopher Newport Univ	VA	21,050	VC
Clark Univ	MA	47,020	HC+
Clemson Univ	SC	19,136	HC
Coe College	IA	43,590	VC
College of St. Benedict	MN	47,570	VC
Colo State Univ-Pueblo	CO	13,532	LC
Concord Univ	WV	13,102	C
Concordia Univ Nebr	NE	26,000	VC
Concordia Univ, Ann Arbor	MI	27,220	VC
Converse College	SC	37,130	C
Corban Univ	OR	34,764	C
Cornerstone Univ and Grand Rapids Theological Seminary	MI	30,866	C
CUNY-City College	NY	19,576	HC+
Davis and Elkins College	WV	33,742	C
Dominican Univ	IL	37,628	C
Dordt College	IA	34,160	VC
Drury Univ	MO	30,319	VC
Eastern Washington Univ	WA	16,388	C
Eckerd College	FL	43,902	VC
Elizabethtown College	PA	47,600	VC
Elmira College	NY	49,950	C+
Elms College	MA	23,900	VC
Florida A&M Univ	FL	14,935	LC
Florida Southern College	FL	38,240	VC
Florida State Univ	FL	15,238	HC
Fontbonne Univ	MO	31,384	C
Freed-Hardeman Univ	TN	19,697	VC
George Fox Univ	OR	40,750	C+
Gettysburg College	PA	56,820	HC
Goshen College	IN	35,900	VC
Grace College and Theological Seminary	IN	28,800	C
Graceland Univ	IA	28,020	C
Grand Valley State Univ	MI	17,998	VC
Gustavus Adolphus College	MN	48,170	HC
Hardin-Simmons Univ	TX	23,560	C+
Heidelberg Univ	OH	34,100	C
Hillsdale College	MI	31,890	HC+
Hofstra Univ	NY	48,020	VC+
Houghton College	NY	35,740	VC
Howard Univ	DC	35,957	C
Humboldt State Univ	CA	18,400	C
Hunter College / The CUNY	NY	14,429	VC
Indiana Univ Kokomo	IN	6,674	LC
Indiana Univ-Purdue Univ Fort Wayne	IN	15,425	C
Iowa Wesleyan College	IA	30,850	LC
Ithaca College	NY	52,300	HC
Johnson C. Smith Univ	NC	25,336	LC
Judson Univ	IL	25,130	C
Kent State Univ	OH	19,352	C
Kentucky Wesleyan College	KY	27,440	VC+
Keuka College	NY	30,300	C
King's College	PA	41,678	C
Kutztown Univ of Pennsylvania	PA	16,909	LC
La Salle Univ	PA	50,270	C
Lake Superior State Univ	MI	18,121	C
Lamar Univ	TX	6,820	LC
Le Moyne College	NY	42,200	VC
Lehigh Univ	PA	55,080	MC
Lehman College / The CUNY	NY	5,778	LC
Lenoir-Rhyne College	NC	35,984	C
Lewis Univ	IL	23,050	C
Lincoln Memorial Univ	TN	18,144	C
Lipscomb Univ	TN	35,722	VC
Livingstone College	NC	17,815	LC
LIU/Brooklyn Campus	NY	26,500	C
LIU/C.W. Post Campus	NY	38,888	C
Louisiana College	LA	15,746	C
Loyola Univ New Orleans	LA	46,581	VC
MacMurray College	IL	20,755	C
Manhattan College	NY	44,955	VC
Mars Hill College	NC	22,950	LC
Marshall Univ	WV	14,820	C
Maryville College	TN	33,150	VC
Mercer Univ	GA	44,201	VC+
Mercyhurst Univ	PA	40,700	C
Merrimack College	MA	44,215	C
Methodist Univ	NC	37,185	C
Mich Tech Univ	MI	22,105	VC
Midland Univ	NE	34,000	C
Midwestern State Univ	TX	9,722	C
Millikin Univ	IL	37,462	C
Minn State Univ, Mankato	MN	14,900	C
Minn State Univ, Moorhead	MN	13,392	C
Missouri Southern State Univ	MO	11,910	C
Montclair State Univ	NJ	22,614	C
Mount Aloysius College	PA	27,970	C

School	ST	$IS	SR
Mount Mary Univ	WI	32,836	LC
New York Univ	NY	61,470	MC
Niagara Univ	NY	39,800	C
N Car State Univ	NC	16,202	HC
North Central College	IL	38,343	VC
North Georgia College & State Univ	GA	8,500	C
North Park Univ	IL	30,130	C
Northern Kentucky Univ	KY	15,302	LC
Northern Mich Univ	MI	15,300	VC
Northern State Univ	SD	14,021	C
Northwest Missouri State Univ	MO	14,229	C
Northwest Nazarene Univ	ID	24,275	NC
Northwestern College of Iowa	IA	34,848	C+
Notre Dame of Maryland Univ	MD	27,700	C
Ohio Univ	OH	20,676	VC
Ohio Wesleyan Univ	OH	49,460	C+
Okla Baptist Univ	OK	28,202	VC
Okla Wesleyan Univ	OK	21,300	C
Olivet College	MI	19,984	C
Oral Roberts Univ	OK	31,734	C
Oregon State Univ	OR	19,017	C+
Oswego / SUNY	NY	20,009	VC
Ouachita Baptist Univ	AR	29,010	VC
Pittsburg State Univ	KS	12,032	C
Quinnipiac Univ	CT	53,580	VC
Rhode Island College	RI	17,132	LC
Rivier College	NH	35,000	VC
Rochester Inst of Technology	NY	42,450	VC+
Roosevelt Univ	IL	22,605	VC
Rosemont College	PA	42,350	C
Sacred Heart Univ	CT	48,564	VC
Saginaw Valley State Univ	MI	16,869	C
St. Anselm College	NH	48,324	VC
St. John's Univ	MN	46,146	C
St. Joseph's College	IN	35,790	C
St. Mary-of-the-Woods College	IN	37,722	LC
St. Mary's Univ	TX	33,854	C
St. Peter's College	NJ	44,240	C
St. Vincent College	PA	40,244	C
St. Xavier Univ	IL	32,840	C
Seton Hill Univ	PA	35,172	C
Simpson College	IA	36,086	VC
Spring Hill College	AL	42,130	VC
Springfield College	MA	25,000	C
St. Cloud State Univ	MN	10,600	C
St. Edward's Univ	TX	44,674	VC
St. Thomas Univ	FL	32,310	C+
SUNY / College of Environmental Science and Forestry	NY	18,351	HC
SUNY Fredonia / The SUNY at Fredonia	NY	18,702	VC
SUNY Oneonta / SUNY	NY	16,919	VC
Syracuse Univ	NY	54,512	HC
Tarleton State Univ	TX	13,489	LC
Temple Univ	PA	24,392	VC
Texas A&M Univ at Commerce	TX	10,496	C
Texas A&M Univ at Kingsville	TX	7,500	LC
The Catholic Univ of America	DC	52,852	VC
Thiel College	PA	31,378	LC
Touro College	NY	23,150	VC
Trinity Christian College	IL	28,869	C
Truman State Univ	MO	13,546	HC
Union Univ	TN	28,260	VC
Univ at Albany / SUNY	NY	18,674	VC
Univ of Arkansas at Pine Bluff	AR	10,600	C
Univ of Bridgeport	CT	39,030	LC
Univ of Central Arkansas	AR	10,840	VC
Univ of Central Missouri	MO	14,605	C
Univ of Central Okla	OK	12,293	C
Univ of Cincinnati	OH	20,199	VC
Univ of Dayton	OH	43,750	VC
Univ of Detroit Mercy	MI	30,450	C
Univ of Evansville	IN	41,056	VC+
Univ of Great Falls	MT	27,970	C
Univ of Hartford	CT	42,674	C
Univ of Illinois at Chicago	IL	24,293	VC
Univ of Iowa	IA	17,481	VC
Univ of Mass Amherst	MA	23,697	VC+
Univ of Miami	FL	55,166	MC
Univ of Minn/Twin Cities	MN		HC
Univ of Nebr - Lincoln	NE	17,507	VC
Univ of Nebr at Kearney	NE	14,855	LC
Univ of New Haven	CT	47,740	C
Univ of N Car at Wilmington	NC	13,572	VC+
Univ of Notre Dame	IN		MC
Univ of Rio Grande	OH	8,750	NC
Univ of St. Francis	IN	29,810	C
Univ of Southern Miss	MS	13,170	C
Univ of St. Francis	IL	36,490	C
Univ of Tenn at Knoxville	TN	20,364	VC+
Univ of West Alabama	AL	9,415	C
Univ of West Florida	FL	14,656	C
Univ of Wisc/Eau Claire	WI	15,430	VC
Utah State Univ	UT	11,803	C
Virginia Polytechnic Inst and State Univ	VA	14,629	HC
Walsh Univ	OH	35,100	C
Washington Adventist Univ	MD	25,859	C+
Washington State Univ	WA	20,461	C
Washington Univ in St. Louis	MO	58,818	MC
Waynesburg Univ	PA	29,100	C
West Chester Univ of Pennsylvania	PA	16,836	C
West Liberty Univ	WV	9,142	LC
West Texas A&M Univ	TX	13,478	C
Western Carolina Univ	NC	13,965	C+
Western New Mexico Univ	NM	8,500	LC
Western State Colo Univ	CO	16,135	C
Westminster College	PA	31,290	C+
Wheeling Jesuit Univ	WV	34,668	C
Whitworth Univ	WA	45,826	VC+
Wingate Univ	NC	34,990	C
Winona State Univ	MN	16,530	C
Wright State Univ	OH	16,983	C
Youngstown State Univ	OH	16,374	LC

PREENGINEERING

School	ST	$IS	SR
Adams State College	CO	13,358	LC
Alice Lloyd College	KY	4,900	C
Aquinas College	MI	33,060	C
Asbury Univ	KY	32,038	VC
Augustana College	IL	43,398	HC
Baldwin Wallace Univ	OH	36,980	VC
Ball State Univ	IN	17,850	C
Bard College at Simon's Rock	MA	58,963	HC+
Barry Univ	FL	38,190	C
Bellarmine Univ	KY	42,950	VC
Bethel College	IN	31,560	C
Campbell Univ	NC	25,500	C
Campbellsville Univ	KY	27,720	C
Canisius College	NY	45,602	VC
Coe College	IA	43,590	VC
College of St. Benedict	MN	47,570	VC
College of the Ozarks	MO	5,605	VC
Colo State Univ-Pueblo	CO	13,532	LC
Concordia Univ, Ann Arbor	MI	27,220	VC
DePauw Univ	IN	48,950	VC+
Edgewood College	WI	33,294	C
Elizabethtown College	PA	47,600	VC
Elmhurst College	IL	42,032	C+
Embry-Riddle Aeronautical Univ - Worldwide	FL	15,512	C
Freed-Hardeman Univ	TN	19,697	VC
Furman Univ	SC	54,006	HC
Goshen College	IN	35,900	VC
Harvard Univ/Harvard College	MA	49,000	MC
Heidelberg Univ	OH	34,100	C
Houghton College	NY	35,740	VC
Hunter College / The CUNY	NY	14,429	VC
Iowa Wesleyan College	IA	30,850	LC
Johnson C. Smith Univ	NC	25,336	LC
Judson Univ	IL	25,130	C
Kentucky Wesleyan College	KY	27,440	VC+
Kutztown Univ of Pennsylvania	PA	16,909	LC
Le Moyne College	NY	42,200	VC
Lenoir-Rhyne College	NC	35,984	C
Lewis Univ	IL	23,050	C
Lipscomb Univ	TN	35,722	VC
LIU/C.W. Post Campus	NY	38,888	C
Loyola Univ New Orleans	LA	46,581	VC
MacMurray College	IL	20,755	C
Mansfield Univ	PA	19,468	LC
Marshall Univ	WV	14,820	C
Maryville College	TN	33,150	VC
Midwestern State Univ	TX	9,722	C
Millikin Univ	IL	37,462	C
Minn State Univ, Mankato	MN	14,900	C
Mount Vernon Nazarene Univ	OH	29,590	C
Niagara Univ	NY	39,800	C
North Central College	IL	38,343	VC
North Georgia College & State Univ	GA	8,500	C
Northern Kentucky Univ	KY	15,302	LC
Northwest Missouri State Univ	MO	14,229	C
Northwest Nazarene Univ	ID	24,275	NC
Notre Dame of Maryland Univ	MD	27,700	C
Oral Roberts Univ	OK	31,734	C
Oswego / SUNY	NY	20,009	VC
Peru State College	NE	8,600	NC
Pfeiffer Univ	NC	33,700	C
Pittsburg State Univ	KS	12,032	C
Providence College	RI	55,995	HC
Regis Univ	CO	41,318	C
Richard Stockton College of New Jersey	NJ	20,000	VC
Roberts Wesleyan College	NY	37,384	C+
Saginaw Valley State Univ	MI	16,869	C
St. John's Univ	MN	46,146	C
St. Mary's College of Calif	CA	53,550	C
St. Michael's College	VT	48,740	VC
Scripps College	CA	54,900	MC
Shaw Univ	NC	15,488	LC
Simpson College	IA	36,086	VC
Southern Oregon Univ	OR	17,874	C
St. Edward's Univ	TX	44,674	VC
Texas A&M Univ at Commerce	TX	10,496	C
The College of Idaho	ID	31,277	VC
Thiel College	PA	31,378	LC
Truman State Univ	MO	13,546	HC
Union Univ	TN	28,260	VC
Univ of Arkansas at Pine Bluff	AR	10,600	C
Univ of Central Arkansas	AR	10,840	VC
Univ of N Car at Wilmington	NC	13,572	VC+
Univ of Rio Grande	OH	8,750	NC
Wayland Baptist Univ	TX	16,058	LC
West Liberty Univ	WV	9,142	LC
West Texas A&M Univ	TX	13,478	C
Western Carolina Univ	NC	13,965	C+
Western New England Univ	MA	45,590	C
Western State Colo Univ	CO	16,135	C
Wheeling Jesuit Univ	WV	34,668	C
Widener Univ	PA	50,368	C
Wilberforce Univ	OH	15,100	LC
Wingate Univ	NC	34,990	C
Winona State Univ	MN	16,530	C
Yeshiva Univ	NY	47,250	VC+

PRE-HEALTH STUDIES

School	ST	$IS	SR
Asbury Univ	KY	32,038	VC
Bethel College	IN	31,560	C
Binghamton Univ / The SUNY	NY	20,832	HC+
Biola Univ	CA	40,320	VC
Cornerstone Univ and Grand Rapids Theological Seminary	MI	30,866	C
Elmhurst College	IL	42,032	C+
Hofstra Univ	NY	48,020	VC+
Ithaca College	NY	52,300	HC
Marshall Univ	WV	14,820	C
Mass College of Liberal Arts	MA	16,733	C
New York Univ	NY	61,470	MC
Oswego / SUNY	NY	20,009	VC
Point Park Univ	PA	36,390	C
Texas Christian Univ	TX	47,570	HC
Univ of Arizona	AZ	20,105	C
Univ of Illinois at Chicago	IL	24,293	VC
Univ of Miami	FL	55,166	MC
Valparaiso Univ	IN	43,040	VC+

PRELAW

School	ST	$IS	SR
Adams State College	CO	13,358	LC
Albertus Magnus College	CT	37,382	LC
American International College	MA	36,100	LC
Aquinas College	MI	33,060	C
Arcadia Univ	PA	33,570	C+
Ashland Univ	OH	25,000	C
Averett Univ	VA	36,000	LC
Ball State Univ	IN	17,850	C
Barry Univ	FL	38,190	C
Beloit College	WI	49,970	HC
Bemidji State Univ	MN	13,500	C
Bennington College	VT	56,990	HC+
Bethel College	IN	31,560	C
Biola Univ	CA	40,320	VC
Black Hills State Univ	SD	13,562	LC
Blackburn College	IL	21,350	C
Bryant Univ	RI	49,179	VC
Calif Lutheran Univ	CA	47,640	C
Calvin College	MI	37,585	VC+
Campbell Univ	NC	25,500	C
Campbellsville Univ	KY	27,720	C
Canisius College	NY	45,602	VC
Capital Univ	OH	39,824	VC
Cardinal Stritch Univ	WI	24,054	C
Carroll College	MT	28,000	C
Catawba College	NC	37,105	C
Cedarville Univ	OH	31,036	VC+
Central Washington Univ	WA	11,730	C
Chadron State College	NE	7,400	NC
Chicago State Univ	IL	5,482	C
Christopher Newport Univ	VA	21,050	VC
Clark Univ	MA	47,020	HC+
Clearwater Christian College	FL	23,720	C
Clemson Univ	SC	19,136	HC
Coe College	IA	43,590	VC
College of St. Benedict	MN	47,570	VC
College of the Ozarks	MO	5,605	VC
Colo State Univ-Pueblo	CO	13,532	LC
Concord Univ	WV	13,102	C
Concordia Univ Nebr	NE	26,000	VC
Concordia Univ, River Forest	IL	26,300	C
Converse College	SC	37,130	C
Corban Univ	OR	34,764	C
CUNY-City College	NY	19,576	HC+
Davis and Elkins College	WV	33,742	C
Dominican Univ	IL	37,628	C
Dordt College	IA	34,160	VC
Drury Univ	MO	30,319	VC
East Central Univ	OK	10,223	LC
Eastern Washington Univ	WA	16,388	C
Eckerd College	FL	43,902	VC
Edgewood College	WI	33,294	C
Edinboro Univ of Pennsylvania	PA	15,940	LC
Elmira College	NY	49,950	C+
Elms College	MA	23,900	VC
Faulkner Univ	AL	22,530	LC
Fitchburg State Univ	MA	17,241	C
Florida Inst of Technology	FL	48,290	VC
Florida State Univ	FL	15,238	HC
Fontbonne Univ	MO	31,384	C
Fresno Pacific Univ	CA	32,136	C
George Fox Univ	OR	40,750	C+
Gettysburg College	PA	56,820	HC
Grace College and Theological Seminary	IN	28,800	C
Grand Valley State Univ	MI	17,998	VC
Gustavus Adolphus College	MN	48,170	HC
Hamline Univ	MN	44,198	VC
Hardin-Simmons Univ	TX	23,560	C+
Heidelberg Univ	OH	34,100	C
Hillsdale College	MI	31,890	HC+
Houghton College	NY	35,740	VC
Humboldt State Univ	CA	18,400	C
Hunter College / The CUNY	NY	14,429	VC
Huntington Univ	IN	32,220	C
Illinois College	IL	25,770	VC
Immaculata Univ	PA	43,000	C
Indiana Inst of Technology	IN	34,240	LC
Indiana Univ Kokomo	IN	6,674	LC
Indiana Univ-Purdue Univ Fort Wayne	IN	15,425	C
Indiana Wesleyan Univ	IN	31,815	VC
Iowa Wesleyan College	IA	30,850	LC
Ithaca College	NY	52,300	HC
Johnson C. Smith Univ	NC	25,336	LC
Johnson State College	VT	16,721	C
Judson Univ	IL	25,130	C
Kansas Wesleyan Univ	KS	32,000	C
Kentucky Wesleyan College	KY	27,440	VC+
Keuka College	NY	30,300	C
King's College	PA	41,678	C
La Salle Univ	PA	50,270	C
Lafayette College	PA	57,050	HC+
Lake Superior State Univ	MI	18,121	C
Lamar Univ	TX	6,820	LC
Le Moyne College	NY	42,200	VC
Lehman College / The CUNY	NY	5,778	LC
Lenoir-Rhyne College	NC	35,984	C
LeTourneau Univ	TX	26,230	C
Lewis Univ	IL	23,050	C
Limestone College	SC	29,880	C
Lincoln Memorial Univ	TN	18,144	C
Lindenwood Univ	MO	20,750	C
Lipscomb Univ	TN	35,722	VC
Livingstone College	NC	17,815	LC
LIU/Brooklyn Campus	NY	26,500	C
LIU/C.W. Post Campus	NY	38,888	C
Louisiana College	LA	15,746	C
Lubbock Christian Univ	TX	25,518	C
MacMurray College	IL	20,755	C
Manchester College	IN	35,070	C
Manhattan College	NY	44,955	VC
Mansfield Univ	PA	19,468	LC
Marlboro College	VT	35,980	VC
Mars Hill College	NC	22,950	LC
Marshall Univ	WV	14,820	C
Maryville College	TN	33,150	VC
Marywood Univ	PA	40,695	C
Mayville State Univ	ND	11,401	NC
Mercer Univ	GA	44,201	VC+
Mercyhurst Univ	PA	40,700	C
Merrimack College	MA	44,215	C
Methodist Univ	NC	37,185	C
Metropolitan College of New York	NY	16,720	VC
Mich State Univ	MI	13,689	VC
Middle Tenn State Univ	TN	8,650	C
Midland Univ	NE	34,000	C
Midwestern State Univ	TX	9,722	C
Millikin Univ	IL	37,462	C
Mills College	CA	54,119	HC
Minn State Univ, Mankato	MN	14,900	C
Minn State Univ, Moorhead	MN	13,392	C
Missouri Univ of Science and Technology	MO	18,655	VC+
Monmouth Univ	NJ	42,252	C
Mount Aloysius College	PA	27,970	C
Mount Mary Univ	WI	32,836	LC
Mount Vernon Nazarene Univ	OH	29,590	C
National Univ	CA	14,730	SP
New York Inst of Technology	NY	40,590	VC
Newbury College	MA	41,850	C
Niagara Univ	NY	39,800	C
N Car State Univ	NC	16,202	HC
North Central College	IL	38,343	VC
North Georgia College & State Univ	GA	8,500	C
North Park Univ	IL	30,130	C
Northern Kentucky Univ	KY	15,302	LC
Northern Mich Univ	MI	15,300	VC
Northern State Univ	SD	14,021	C

School	ST	$IS	SR
Northwest Missouri State Univ	MO	14,229	C
Northwest Nazarene Univ	ID	24,275	NC
Northwestern College of Iowa	IA	34,848	C+
Notre Dame of Maryland Univ	MD	27,700	C
Oakland City Univ	IN	24,500	NC
Ohio Univ	OH	20,676	VC
Ohio Wesleyan Univ	OH	49,460	C+
Okla Baptist Univ	OK	28,202	VC
Okla Christian Univ	OK	24,975	VC
Okla City Univ	OK	33,546	VC
Okla Wesleyan Univ	OK	21,300	C
Olivet College	MI	19,984	C
Oral Roberts Univ	OK	31,734	C
Oswego / SUNY	NY	20,009	VC
Ouachita Baptist Univ	AR	29,010	VC
Palm Beach Atlantic Univ	FL	33,882	LC
Peru State College	NE	8,600	NC
Pittsburg State Univ	KS	12,032	C
Quinnipiac Univ	CT	53,580	VC
Regis Univ	CO	41,318	C
Rensselaer Polytechnic Inst	NY	59,229	MC
Rhode Island College	RI	17,132	LC
Rider Univ	NJ	45,720	C
Rivier College	NH	35,000	VC
Roberts Wesleyan College	NY	37,384	C+
Rochester Inst of Technology	NY	42,450	VC+
Roosevelt Univ	IL	22,605	VC
Rosemont College	PA	42,350	C
Sacred Heart Univ	CT	48,564	VC
Saginaw Valley State Univ	MI	16,869	C
St. Anselm College	NH	48,324	VC
St. Augustine's Univ	NC	14,000	C
St. John's Univ	MN	46,146	C
St. Joseph's College	IN	35,790	C
St. Mary-of-the-Woods College	IN	37,722	LC
St. Mary's Univ	TX	33,854	C
St. Michael's College	VT	48,740	VC
St. Peter's College	NJ	44,240	C
St. Vincent College	PA	40,244	C
St. Xavier Univ	IL	32,840	C
Schreiner Univ	TX	32,734	LC
Scripps College	CA	54,900	MC
Seattle Pacific Univ	WA	41,559	VC+
Seton Hill Univ	PA	35,172	C
Shawnee State Univ	OH	16,545	NC
Simpson College	IA	36,086	VC
Southern Oregon Univ	OR	17,874	C
Springfield College	MA	25,000	C
St. Cloud State Univ	MN	10,600	C
St. Edward's Univ	TX	44,674	VC
St. John's Univ	NY	52,840	C+
St. Thomas Aquinas College	NY	30,000	C
St. Thomas Univ	FL	32,310	C+
SUNY / College of Environmental Science and Forestry	NY	18,351	HC
Stephens College	MO	34,500	VC
Stetson Univ	FL	49,512	VC+
Stillman College	AL	18,460	C
SUNY Fredonia / The SUNY at Fredonia	NY	18,702	VC
SUNY Oneonta / SUNY	NY	16,919	VC
Syracuse Univ	NY	54,512	HC
Tarleton State Univ	TX	13,489	LC
Temple Univ	PA	24,392	VC
Texas A&M Univ at Commerce	TX	10,496	C
Texas A&M Univ at Kingsville	TX	7,500	LC
Texas Wesleyan Univ	TX	29,886	C
The Catholic Univ of America	DC	52,852	VC
Thiel College	PA	31,378	LC
Touro College	NY	23,150	VC
Trinity Christian College	IL	28,869	C
Truman State Univ	MO	13,546	HC
Union Univ	TN	28,260	VC
Univ at Albany / SUNY	NY	18,674	VC
Univ of Bridgeport	CT	39,030	LC
Univ of Central Missouri	MO	14,605	C
Univ of Cincinnati	OH	20,199	VC
Univ of Detroit Mercy	MI	30,450	C
Univ of Evansville	IN	41,056	VC+
Univ of Findlay	OH	31,916	C
Univ of Great Falls	MT	27,970	C
Univ of Illinois at Urbana-Champaign	IL	24,300	HC
Univ of Iowa	IA	17,481	VC
Univ of Mary	ND	16,714	C
Univ of Miami	FL	55,166	MC
Univ of Minn/Duluth	MN	18,964	C+
Univ of Minn/Morris	MN	17,150	VC
Univ of Minn/Twin Cities	MN		HC
Univ of Montana-Western	MT	9,753	LC
Univ of Nebr - Lincoln	NE	17,507	VC
Univ of Nebr at Kearney	NE	14,855	LC
Univ of N Car at Wilmington	NC	13,572	VC+
Univ of Pittsburgh at Pittsburgh	PA	27,800	HC+
Univ of Rio Grande	OH	8,750	NC
Univ of Sioux Falls	SD	22,990	C
Univ of Southern Miss	MS	13,170	C
Univ of the Incarnate Word	TX	35,200	LC
Univ of Tulsa	OK	45,311	HC+
Univ of West Alabama	AL	9,415	C
Univ of West Florida	FL	14,656	C
Univ of Wisc Whitewater	WI	13,314	C
Univ of Wisc/Eau Claire	WI	15,430	VC
Univ of Wisc/River Falls	WI	9,722	LC
Urbana Univ	OH	21,190	C
Ursuline College	OH	33,198	LC
Utah State Univ	UT	11,803	C
Valparaiso Univ	IN	43,040	VC+
Vassar College	NY	59,070	MC
Victory Univ	TN	19,118	C
Virginia Polytechnic Inst and State Univ	VA	14,629	HC
Walsh Univ	OH	35,100	C
Warren Wilson College	NC	34,888	VC
Washington Adventist Univ	MD	25,859	C+
Washington State Univ	WA	20,461	C
Wayland Baptist Univ	TX	16,058	LC
Waynesburg Univ	PA	29,100	C
Webber International Univ	FL	25,664	C
West Chester Univ of Pennsylvania	PA	16,836	C
West Liberty Univ	WV	9,142	LC
West Texas A&M Univ	TX	13,478	C
Western Carolina Univ	NC	13,965	C+
Western State Colo Univ	CO	16,135	C
Westminster College	PA	31,290	C+
Westminster College	UT	37,708	VC
Wheeling Jesuit Univ	WV	34,668	C
Whitworth Univ	WA	45,826	VC+
Wilberforce Univ	OH	15,100	LC
William Peace Univ	NC	32,900	LC
Wilmington College	OH	29,784	C
Wingate Univ	NC	34,990	C
Winona State Univ	MN	16,530	C
Wright State Univ	OH	16,983	C
Youngstown State Univ	OH	16,374	LC

PREMEDICINE

School	ST	$IS	SR
Adams State College	CO	13,358	LC
Albertus Magnus College	CT	37,382	LC
Albion College	MI	43,884	VC
American International College	MA	36,100	LC
American Jewish Univ	CA	32,600	C
Aquinas College	MI	33,060	C
Arcadia Univ	PA	33,570	C+
Ashland Univ	OH	25,000	C
Auburn Univ	AL	20,052	VC+
Augustana College	IL	43,398	HC
Avila Univ	MO	26,900	C
Baldwin Wallace Univ	OH	36,980	VC
Ball State Univ	IN	17,850	C
Bard College at Simon's Rock	MA	58,963	HC+
Barry Univ	FL	38,190	C
Baylor Univ	TX	46,720	HC
Bellarmine Univ	KY	42,950	VC
Beloit College	WI	49,970	HC
Bemidji State Univ	MN	13,500	C
Bennington College	VT	56,990	HC+
Bethel College	IN	31,560	C
Bethel Univ	TN	19,186	C
Biola Univ	CA	40,320	VC
Blackburn College	IL	21,350	C
Bluffton Univ	OH	37,864	C
Boise State Univ	ID	12,802	C
Brigham Young Univ/Hawaii	HI	8,614	VC
Cabrini College	PA	40,859	LC
Calif Lutheran Univ	CA	47,640	C
Cal State, San Bernardino	CA	12,000	C
Calvin College	MI	37,585	VC+
Campbellsville Univ	KY	27,720	C
Canisius College	NY	45,602	VC
Capital Univ	OH	39,824	VC
Cardinal Stritch Univ	WI	24,054	C
Carroll College	MT	28,000	C
Central Univ of Bayamon	PR	3,350	
Chadron State College	NE	7,400	NC
Chicago State Univ	IL	5,482	C
Christopher Newport Univ	VA	21,050	VC
Clark Univ	MA	47,020	HC+
Clearwater Christian College	FL	23,720	C
Clemson Univ	SC	19,136	HC
Cleveland State Univ	OH	21,357	C
Coe College	IA	43,590	VC
Coker College	SC	32,256	LC
College of St. Benedict	MN	47,570	VC
College of the Ozarks	MO	5,605	VC
Colo State Univ-Pueblo	CO	13,532	LC
Concord Univ	WV	13,102	C
Concordia Univ	OR	34,930	C
Concordia Univ Nebr	NE	26,000	VC
Concordia Univ, Ann Arbor	MI	27,220	VC
Concordia Univ, River Forest	IL	26,300	C
Converse College	SC	37,130	C
Corban Univ	OR	34,764	C
Cornerstone Univ and Grand Rapids Theological Seminary	MI	30,866	C
CUNY-City College	NY	19,576	HC+
Dakota State Univ	SD	13,811	C
Davis and Elkins College	WV	33,742	C
Dominican Univ	IL	37,628	C
Dominican Univ of Calif	CA	51,250	C
Dordt College	IA	34,160	VC
Drexel Univ	PA	51,920	HC
Drury Univ	MO	30,319	VC
Earlham College	IN	49,710	VC+
East Stroudsburg Univ of Pennsylvania	PA	16,636	C
Eastern Washington Univ	WA	16,388	C
Eckerd College	FL	43,902	VC
Edinboro Univ of Pennsylvania	PA	15,940	LC
Elizabethtown College	PA	47,600	VC
Elmhurst College	IL	42,032	C+
Elmira College	NY	49,950	C+
Elms College	MA	23,900	VC
Florida A&M Univ	FL	14,935	LC
Florida Inst of Technology	FL	48,290	VC
Florida Southern College	FL	38,240	VC
Florida State Univ	FL	15,238	HC
Fontbonne Univ	MO	31,384	C
Freed-Hardeman Univ	TN	19,697	VC
Fresno Pacific Univ	CA	32,136	C
Friends Univ	KS	29,100	C
George Fox Univ	OR	40,750	C+
George Washington Univ	DC	57,108	MC
Gettysburg College	PA	56,820	HC
Goshen College	IN	35,900	VC
Grace College and Theological Seminary	IN	28,800	C
Graceland Univ	IA	28,020	C
Grand Valley State Univ	MI	17,998	VC
Gustavus Adolphus College	MN	48,170	HC
Hamline Univ	MN	44,198	VC
Hampshire College	MA	58,320	MC
Hardin-Simmons Univ	TX	23,560	C+
Hawaii Pacific Univ	HI	36,690	C
Heidelberg Univ	OH	34,100	C
Hillsdale College	MI	31,890	HC+
Hofstra Univ	NY	48,020	VC+
Houghton College	NY	35,740	VC
Howard Univ	DC	35,957	C
Humboldt State Univ	CA	18,400	C
Hunter College / The CUNY	NY	14,429	VC
Huntington Univ	IN	32,220	C
Immaculata Univ	PA	43,000	C
Indiana Univ Kokomo	IN	6,674	LC
Indiana Univ-Purdue Univ Fort Wayne	IN	15,425	C
Indiana Univ-Purdue Univ Indianapolis	IN	17,290	C
Indiana Wesleyan Univ	IN	31,815	VC
Inter-American Univ of PR/ San Germán	PR	6,720	
Iowa Wesleyan College	IA	30,850	LC
Ithaca College	NY	52,300	HC
Jackson State Univ	MS	13,512	LC
Johnson C. Smith Univ	NC	25,336	LC
Johnson State College	VT	16,721	C
Judson Univ	IL	25,130	C
Kent State Univ	OH	19,352	C
Kentucky Wesleyan College	KY	27,440	VC+
Keuka College	NY	30,300	C
King's College	PA	41,678	C
Kutztown Univ of Pennsylvania	PA	16,909	LC
La Salle Univ	PA	50,270	C
Lake Superior State Univ	MI	18,121	C
Lamar Univ	TX	6,820	LC
Le Moyne College	NY	42,200	VC
Lees-McRae College	NC	33,624	C
Lehigh Univ	PA	55,080	MC
Lehman College / The CUNY	NY	5,778	LC
Lenoir-Rhyne College	NC	35,984	C
LeTourneau Univ	TX	26,230	C
Lewis Univ	IL	23,050	C
Lincoln Memorial Univ	TN	18,144	C
Lipscomb Univ	TN	35,722	VC
Livingstone College	NC	17,815	LC
LIU/Brooklyn Campus	NY	26,500	C
LIU/C.W. Post Campus	NY	38,888	C
Louisiana College	LA	15,746	C
Loyola Univ New Orleans	LA	46,581	VC
Lubbock Christian Univ	TX	25,518	C
MacMurray College	IL	20,755	C
Manhattan College	NY	44,955	VC
Marlboro College	VT	35,980	VC
Marquette Univ	WI	43,664	VC+
Mars Hill College	NC	22,950	LC
Marshall Univ	WV	14,820	C
Marymount Manhattan College	NY	40,118	VC
Maryville College	TN	33,150	VC
Marywood Univ	PA	40,695	C
Mass College of Pharmacy and Health Sciences	MA	36,450	SP
Mayville State Univ	ND	11,401	NC
Mercer Univ	GA	44,201	VC+
Mercy College of Health Sciences	IA	14,460	SP
Mercyhurst Univ	PA	40,700	C
Merrimack College	MA	44,215	C
Mich Tech Univ	MI	22,105	VC
Midland Univ	NE	34,000	C
Midwestern State Univ	TX	9,722	C
Milligan College	TN	27,510	C
Millikin Univ	IL	37,462	C
Minn State Univ, Mankato	MN	14,900	C
Minn State Univ, Moorhead	MN	13,392	C
Missouri Southern State Univ	MO	11,910	C
Missouri Univ of Science and Technology	MO	18,655	VC+
Monmouth Univ	NJ	42,252	C
Montclair State Univ	NJ	22,614	C
Mount Aloysius College	PA	27,970	C
Mount Mary Univ	WI	32,836	LC
Mount Vernon Nazarene Univ	OH	29,590	C
New York Univ	NY	61,470	MC
Niagara Univ	NY	39,800	C
N Car State Univ	NC	16,202	HC
N Car Wesleyan College	NC	29,440	C
North Central College	IL	38,343	VC
North Georgia College & State Univ	GA	8,500	C
North Park Univ	IL	30,130	C
Northern Kentucky Univ	KY	15,302	LC
Northern Mich Univ	MI	15,300	VC
Northern State Univ	SD	14,021	C
Northwest Missouri State Univ	MO	14,229	C
Northwest Nazarene Univ	ID	24,275	NC
Northwestern College of Iowa	IA	34,848	C+
Northwestern Univ	IL	37,595	MC
Notre Dame of Maryland Univ	MD	27,700	C
Oakland City Univ	IN	24,500	NC
Ohio Univ	OH	20,676	VC
Ohio Wesleyan Univ	OH	49,460	C+
Okla Baptist Univ	OK	28,202	VC
Okla Christian Univ	OK	24,975	VC
Okla City Univ	OK	33,546	VC
Okla Wesleyan Univ	OK	21,300	C
Olivet College	MI	19,984	C
Oral Roberts Univ	OK	31,734	C
Oregon State Univ	OR	19,017	C+
Oswego / SUNY	NY	20,009	VC
Ouachita Baptist Univ	AR	29,010	VC
Penn State Univ/Univ Park	PA	25,404	VC
Peru State College	NE	8,600	NC
Pfeiffer Univ	NC	33,700	C
Philadelphia Univ	PA	44,160	C
Pittsburg State Univ	KS	12,032	C
Point Park Univ	PA	36,390	C
Quinnipiac Univ	CT	53,580	VC
Regis Univ	CO	41,318	C
Rensselaer Polytechnic Inst	NY	59,229	MC
Rhode Island College	RI	17,132	LC
Rider Univ	NJ	45,720	C
Rivier College	NH	35,000	VC
Roberts Wesleyan College	NY	37,384	C+
Rochester Inst of Technology	NY	42,450	VC+
Roosevelt Univ	IL	22,605	VC
Rosemont College	PA	42,350	C
Sacred Heart Univ	CT	48,564	VC
Saginaw Valley State Univ	MI	16,869	C
St. Anselm College	NH	48,324	VC
St. Augustine's Univ	NC	14,000	C
St. John's Univ	MN	46,146	C
St. Joseph's College	IN	35,790	C
St. Mary-of-the-Woods College	IN	37,722	LC
St. Mary's Univ	TX	33,854	C
St. Peter's College	NJ	44,240	C
St. Vincent College	PA	40,244	C
St. Xavier Univ	IL	32,840	C
Sarah Lawrence College	NY	48,000	HC
Seton Hill Univ	PA	35,172	C
Shawnee State Univ	OH	16,545	NC
Siena Heights Univ	MI	17,000	LC
Simpson College	IA	36,086	VC
Southern Oregon Univ	OR	17,874	C
Spring Hill College	AL	42,130	VC
Springfield College	MA	25,000	C
St. Cloud State Univ	MN	10,600	C
St. Edward's Univ	TX	44,674	VC
St. John's Univ	NY	52,840	C+
St. Thomas Aquinas College	NY	30,000	C
St. Thomas Univ	FL	32,310	C+
SUNY / College of Environmental Science and Forestry	NY	18,351	HC
Stillman College	AL	18,460	C
SUNY Fredonia / The SUNY at Fredonia	NY	18,702	VC
SUNY Oneonta / SUNY	NY	16,919	VC
Syracuse Univ	NY	54,512	HC
Tarleton State Univ	TX	13,489	LC
Taylor Univ	IN	36,742	VC+
Temple Univ	PA	24,392	VC

School	ST	$IS	SR
Texas A&M Univ at Commerce	TX	10,496	C
Texas A&M Univ at Kingsville	TX	7,500	LC
The Catholic Univ of America	DC	52,852	VC
Thiel College	PA	31,378	LC
Touro College	NY	23,150	VC
Trine Univ	IN	39,400	VC
Trinity Christian College	IL	28,869	C
Trinity International Univ	IL	31,070	C
Truman State Univ	MO	13,546	HC
Tusculum College	TN	24,295	C
Union Univ	TN	28,260	VC
Univ at Albany / SUNY	NY	18,674	VC
Univ of Arkansas at Pine Bluff	AR	10,600	C
Univ of Bridgeport	CT	39,030	LC
Univ of Calif at Irvine	CA	25,961	VC
Univ of Central Arkansas	AR	10,840	VC
Univ of Central Missouri	MO	14,605	C
Univ of Central Okla	OK	12,293	C
Univ of Cincinnati	OH	20,199	VC
Univ of Dayton	OH	43,750	VC
Univ of Detroit Mercy	MI	30,450	C
Univ of Evansville	IN	41,056	VC+
Univ of Findlay	OH	31,916	C
Univ of Great Falls	MT	27,970	C
Univ of Hartford	CT	42,674	C
Univ of Illinois at Chicago	IL	24,293	VC
Univ of Iowa	IA	17,481	VC
Univ of Mary	ND	10,714	C
Univ of Mass Amherst	MA	23,697	VC+
Univ of Miami	FL	55,166	MC
Univ of Minn/Morris	MN	17,150	VC
Univ of Minn/Twin Cities	MN		HC
Univ of Nebr - Lincoln	NE	17,507	VC
Univ of Nebr at Kearney	NE	14,855	LC
Univ of New England	ME	46,145	C+
Univ of New Haven	CT	47,740	C
Univ of New Orleans	LA	9,224	VC
Univ of N Car at Wilmington	NC	13,572	VC+
Univ of Notre Dame	IN		MC
Univ of PR/Mayaguez	PR	1,250	C
Univ of Rio Grande	OH	8,750	NC
Univ of St. Francis	IN	29,810	C
Univ of Sioux Falls	SD	22,990	C
Univ of Southern Miss	MS	13,170	C
Univ of St. Francis	IL	36,490	C
Univ of Tenn at Knoxville	TN	20,364	VC+
Univ of Tulsa	OK	45,311	HC+
Univ of West Alabama	AL	9,415	C
Univ of West Florida	FL	14,656	C
Univ of Wisc/Eau Claire	WI	15,430	VC
Univ of Wisc/River Falls	WI	9,722	LC
Univ of Wisc-Milwaukee	WI	18,436	C
Urbana Univ	OH	21,190	C
Ursuline College	OH	33,198	LC
Utah State Univ	UT	11,803	C
Valparaiso Univ	IN	43,040	VC+
Vanguard Univ of Southern Calif	CA	35,833	VC
Vassar College	NY	59,070	MC
Virginia Intermont College	VA	32,411	LC
Virginia Polytechnic Inst and State Univ	VA	14,629	HC
Walsh Univ	OH	35,100	C
Warren Wilson College	NC	34,888	VC
Washington State Univ	WA	20,461	C
Washington Univ in St. Louis	MO	58,818	MC
Wayland Baptist Univ	TX	16,058	LC
Waynesburg Univ	PA	29,100	C
West Chester Univ of Pennsylvania	PA	16,836	C
West Liberty Univ	WV	9,142	LC
West Texas A&M Univ	TX	13,478	C
Western Carolina Univ	NC	13,965	C+
Western New Mexico Univ	NM	8,500	LC
Westminster College	PA	31,290	C+
Wheeling Jesuit Univ	WV	34,668	C
Whitworth Univ	WA	45,826	VC+
Wilmington College	OH	29,784	C
Wingate Univ	NC	34,990	C
Winona State Univ	MN	16,530	C
Wright State Univ	OH	16,983	C
Xavier Univ of Louisiana	LA	25,300	C
Youngstown State Univ	OH	16,374	LC

PREOPTOMETRY

School	ST	$IS	SR
Adams State College	CO	13,358	LC
Arcadia Univ	PA	33,570	C+
Ashland Univ	OH	25,000	C
Auburn Univ	AL	20,052	VC+
Ball State Univ	IN	17,850	C
Bethel College	IN	31,560	C
Calvin College	MI	37,585	VC+
Cardinal Stritch Univ	WI	24,054	C
Carroll College	MT	28,000	C
Christopher Newport Univ	VA	21,050	VC
College of St. Benedict	MN	47,570	VC
Colo State Univ-Pueblo	CO	13,532	LC
Corban Univ	OR	34,764	C
Dordt College	IA	34,160	VC
Drury Univ	MO	30,319	VC
Florida State Univ	FL	15,238	HC
Freed-Hardeman Univ	TN	19,697	VC
Hofstra Univ	NY	48,020	VC+
Houghton College	NY	35,740	VC
Indiana Univ-Purdue Univ Fort Wayne	IN	15,425	C
Iowa Wesleyan College	IA	30,850	LC
Ithaca College	NY	52,300	HC
Le Moyne College	NY	42,200	VC
Lehigh Univ	PA	55,080	MC
Lenoir-Rhyne College	NC	35,984	C
Lewis Univ	IL	23,050	C
Lipscomb Univ	TN	35,722	VC
Louisiana College	LA	15,746	C
Marshall Univ	WV	14,820	C
Millikin Univ	IL	37,462	C
Missouri Southern State Univ	MO	11,910	C
Mount Aloysius College	PA	27,970	C
Northwest Nazarene Univ	ID	24,275	NC
Oregon State Univ	OR	19,017	C+
Oswego / SUNY	NY	20,009	VC
Pittsburg State Univ	KS	12,032	C
St. John's Univ	MN	46,146	C
Simpson College	IA	36,086	VC
SUNY Fredonia / The SUNY at Fredonia	NY	18,702	VC
Trinity Christian College	IL	28,869	C
Univ of Central Arkansas	AR	10,840	VC
Univ of Central Okla	OK	12,293	C
Univ of Evansville	IN	41,056	VC+
Univ of Hartford	CT	42,674	C
Univ of Iowa	IA	17,481	VC
Univ of N Car at Wilmington	NC	13,572	VC+
Univ of St. Francis	IL	36,490	C
Univ of Wisc/Eau Claire	WI	15,430	VC
Walsh Univ	OH	35,100	C
Washington State Univ	WA	20,461	C
Western Carolina Univ	NC	13,965	C+
Wheeling Jesuit Univ	WV	34,668	C
Winona State Univ	MN	16,530	C
Youngstown State Univ	OH	16,374	LC

PREOSTEOPATHY

School	ST	$IS	SR
Colo State Univ-Pueblo	CO	13,532	LC
Drury Univ	MO	30,319	VC
Hofstra Univ	NY	48,020	VC+
Kent State Univ	OH	19,352	C
Marshall Univ	WV	14,820	C
Marywood Univ	PA	40,695	C
Mercyhurst Univ	PA	40,700	C
Mount Aloysius College	PA	27,970	C
New York Inst of Technology	NY	40,590	VC
Sacred Heart Univ	CT	48,564	VC
Seton Hill Univ	PA	35,172	C
Wheeling Jesuit Univ	WV	34,668	C
Youngstown State Univ	OH	16,374	LC

PREPHARMACY

School	ST	$IS	SR
Adams State College	CO	13,358	LC
Alabama A&M Univ	AL	96,100	C
Alice Lloyd College	KY	4,900	C
Baldwin Wallace Univ	OH	36,980	VC
Ball State Univ	IN	17,850	C
Barry Univ	FL	38,190	C
Biola Univ	CA	40,320	VC
Boise State Univ	ID	12,802	C
Calvin College	MI	37,585	VC+
Campbell Univ	NC	25,500	C
Campbellsville Univ	KY	27,720	C
Canisius College	NY	45,602	VC
Carroll College	MT	28,000	C
Christopher Newport Univ	VA	21,050	VC
Clemson Univ	SC	19,136	HC
College of St. Benedict	MN	47,570	VC
College of the Ozarks	MO	5,605	VC
Colo State Univ-Pueblo	CO	13,532	LC
Concord Univ	WV	13,102	C
Corban Univ	OR	34,764	C
Dominican Univ	IL	37,628	C
Dordt College	IA	34,160	VC
Drury Univ	MO	30,319	VC
Florida Southern College	FL	38,240	VC
Florida State Univ	FL	15,238	HC
Freed-Hardeman Univ	TN	19,697	VC
Goshen College	IN	35,900	VC
Houghton College	NY	35,740	VC
Huntington Univ	IN	32,220	C
Husson Univ	ME	23,386	LC
Indiana Univ Kokomo	IN	6,674	LC
Indiana Univ-Purdue Univ Fort Wayne	IN	15,425	C
Indiana Univ-Purdue Univ Indianapolis	IN	17,290	C
Le Moyne College	NY	42,200	VC
Lewis Univ	IL	23,050	C
Lipscomb Univ	TN	35,722	VC
LIU/C.W. Post Campus	NY	38,888	C
Lubbock Christian Univ	TX	25,518	C
Mars Hill College	NC	22,950	LC
Marshall Univ	WV	14,820	C
Mercer Univ	GA	44,201	VC+
Mercyhurst Univ	PA	40,700	C
Mich Tech Univ	MI	22,105	VC
Midwestern State Univ	TX	9,722	C
Millikin Univ	IL	37,462	C
Minn State Univ, Mankato	MN	14,900	C
Minn State Univ, Moorhead	MN	13,392	C
Missouri Southern State Univ	MO	11,910	C
Montclair State Univ	NJ	22,614	C
Mount Aloysius College	PA	27,970	C
Mount Vernon Nazarene Univ	OH	29,590	C
North Georgia College & State Univ	GA	8,500	C
Northern Kentucky Univ	KY	15,302	LC
Northwest Missouri State Univ	MO	14,229	C
Northwest Nazarene Univ	ID	24,275	NC
Notre Dame of Maryland Univ	MD	27,700	C
Ohio Univ	OH	20,676	VC
Oregon State Univ	OR	19,017	C+
Peru State College	NE	8,600	NC
Pittsburg State Univ	KS	12,032	C
Roberts Wesleyan College	NY	37,384	C+
Roosevelt Univ	IL	22,605	VC
Sacred Heart Univ	CT	48,564	VC
St. John's Univ	MN	46,146	C
St. Joseph's College of Maine	ME	31,580	C
St. Michael's College	VT	48,740	VC
St. Vincent College	PA	40,244	C
St. Xavier Univ	IL	32,840	C
Simpson College	IA	36,086	VC
Southern Oregon Univ	OR	17,874	C
SUNY / College of Environmental Science and Forestry	NY	18,351	HC
Tarleton State Univ	TX	13,489	LC
Texas A&M Univ at Commerce	TX	10,496	C
Texas A&M Univ at Kingsville	TX	7,500	LC
Thiel College	PA	31,378	LC
Truman State Univ	MO	13,546	HC
Union Univ	TN	28,260	VC
Univ of Arkansas at Pine Bluff	AR	10,600	C
Univ of Central Arkansas	AR	10,840	VC
Univ of Evansville	IN	41,056	VC+
Univ of Florida	FL	15,783	HC+
Univ of Illinois at Chicago	IL	24,293	VC
Univ of Iowa	IA	17,481	VC
Univ of Miami	FL	55,166	MC
Univ of Minn/Twin Cities	MN		HC
Univ of Nebr - Lincoln	NE	17,507	VC
Univ of New England	ME	46,145	C+
Univ of N Car at Wilmington	NC	13,572	VC+
Univ of St. Francis	IL	36,490	C
Univ of Tenn at Knoxville	TN	20,364	VC+
Univ of the Pacific	CA	52,146	VC
Univ of Wisc/Eau Claire	WI	15,430	VC
Univ of Wisc/River Falls	WI	9,722	LC
Walsh Univ	OH	35,100	C
Washington State Univ	WA	20,461	C
Washington Univ in St. Louis	MO	58,818	MC
West Liberty Univ	WV	9,142	LC
West Texas A&M Univ	TX	13,478	C
Western Carolina Univ	NC	13,965	C+
Western New Mexico Univ	NM	8,500	LC
Wheeling Jesuit Univ	WV	34,668	C
Wilkes Univ	PA	42,786	C
Wingate Univ	NC	34,990	C
Winona State Univ	MN	16,530	C
Xavier Univ	OH	43,740	VC

PREPHYSICAL THERAPY

School	ST	$IS	SR
Asbury Univ	KY	32,038	VC
Baldwin Wallace Univ	OH	36,980	VC
Bellarmine Univ	KY	42,950	VC
Bethany College	WV	35,282	C
Bethel College	IN	31,560	C
Biola Univ	CA	40,320	VC
Boise State Univ	ID	12,802	C
Calif Baptist Univ	CA	35,890	C
Calvin College	MI	37,585	VC+
Christopher Newport Univ	VA	21,050	VC
Coe College	IA	43,590	VC
College of St. Benedict	MN	47,570	VC
Corban Univ	OR	34,764	C
Dordt College	IA	34,160	VC
Drury Univ	MO	30,319	VC
Elizabethtown College	PA	47,600	VC
Elmhurst College	IL	42,032	C+
Florida Southern College	FL	38,240	VC
Fontbonne Univ	MO	31,384	C
Houghton College	NY	35,740	VC
Huntington Univ	IN	32,220	C
Indiana Univ Kokomo	IN	6,674	LC
Lubbock Christian Univ	TX	25,518	C
Marshall Univ	WV	14,820	C
Mich Tech Univ	MI	22,105	VC
Millikin Univ	IL	37,462	C
Mount Aloysius College	PA	27,970	C
Mount Vernon Nazarene Univ	OH	29,590	C
Northwest Nazarene Univ	ID	24,275	NC
Oregon State Univ	OR	19,017	C+
Oswego / SUNY	NY	20,009	VC
Pittsburg State Univ	KS	12,032	C
Sacred Heart Univ	CT	48,564	VC
Saginaw Valley State Univ	MI	16,869	C
St. John's Univ	MN	46,146	C
St. Mary's Univ of Minn	MN	37,015	C
Simpson College	IA	36,086	VC
Southern Oregon Univ	OR	17,874	C
St. Edward's Univ	TX	44,674	VC
Univ of Dayton	OH	43,750	VC
Univ of Iowa	IA	17,481	VC
Univ of Miami	FL	55,166	MC
Univ of N Car at Wilmington	NC	13,572	VC+
Univ of St. Francis	IL	36,490	C
Univ of Wisc/Eau Claire	WI	15,430	VC
Walsh Univ	OH	35,100	C
Washington State Univ	WA	20,461	C
Waynesburg Univ	PA	29,100	C
West Chester Univ of Pennsylvania	PA	16,836	C
Western Carolina Univ	NC	13,965	C+
Wheeling Jesuit Univ	WV	34,668	C
Widener Univ	PA	50,368	C
Winona State Univ	MN	16,530	C

PREPODIATRY

School	ST	$IS	SR
Colo State Univ-Pueblo	CO	13,532	LC
Hofstra Univ	NY	48,020	VC+
Le Moyne College	NY	42,200	VC
Marshall Univ	WV	14,820	C
Mount Aloysius College	PA	27,970	C
Oregon State Univ	OR	19,017	C+
Univ of Iowa	IA	17,481	VC
Univ of N Car at Wilmington	NC	13,572	VC+
Winona State Univ	MN	16,530	C

PREVENTIVE/WELLNESS HEALTH CARE

School	ST	$IS	SR
Appalachian State Univ	NC	12,919	VC
Arizona State Univ	AZ	18,818	C+
Daemen College	NY	31,510	C
Mount Aloysius College	PA	27,970	C
Murray State Univ	KY	14,944	C
Oakland Univ	MI	19,391	VC
St. Louis Univ	MO	46,594	VC+
Univ of New England	ME	46,145	C+

PREVETERINARY SCIENCE

School	ST	$IS	SR
Adams State College	CO	13,358	LC
Alabama A&M Univ	AL	96,100	C
Albertus Magnus College	CT	37,382	LC
Andrews Univ	MI	28,030	C+
Arcadia Univ	PA	33,570	C+
Ashland Univ	OH	25,000	C
Auburn Univ	AL	20,052	VC+
Baldwin Wallace Univ	OH	36,980	VC
Ball State Univ	IN	17,850	C
Becker College	MA	41,420	LC
Bellarmine Univ	KY	42,950	VC
Beloit College	WI	49,970	HC
Bethany College	WV	35,282	C
Boise State Univ	ID	12,802	C
Calvin College	MI	37,585	VC+
Canisius College	NY	45,602	VC
Cardinal Stritch Univ	WI	24,054	C
Carroll College	MT	28,000	C
Christopher Newport Univ	VA	21,050	VC
Clemson Univ	SC	19,136	HC
Coe College	IA	43,590	VC
College of St. Benedict	MN	47,570	VC
College of the Ozarks	MO	5,605	VC
Colo State Univ-Pueblo	CO	13,532	LC
Corban Univ	OR	34,764	C
Cornerstone Univ and Grand Rapids Theological Seminary	MI	30,866	C
Dordt College	IA	34,160	VC
Drury Univ	MO	30,319	VC
Eastern Washington Univ	WA	16,388	C
Elmhurst College	IL	42,032	C+
Florida State Univ	FL	15,238	HC
Freed-Hardeman Univ	TN	19,697	VC
George Fox Univ	OR	40,750	C+
Goshen College	IN	35,900	VC
Graceland Univ	IA	28,020	C
Hillsdale College	MI	31,890	HC+
Hofstra Univ	NY	48,020	VC
Houghton College	NY	35,740	VC
Indiana Univ-Purdue Univ Fort Wayne	IN	15,425	C
Indiana Univ-Purdue Univ Indianapolis	IN	17,290	C
Iowa Wesleyan College	IA	30,850	LC
Kansas State Univ	KS	15,497	VC
Kent State Univ	OH	19,352	C
Keuka College	NY	30,300	C
Le Moyne College	NY	42,200	VC
Lees-McRae College	NC	33,624	C
Lenoir-Rhyne College	NC	35,984	C
LeTourneau Univ	TX	26,230	C

School	ST	$IS	SR
Lewis Univ	IL	23,050	C
Louisiana College	LA	15,746	C
Loyola Univ New Orleans	LA	46,581	VC
MacMurray College	IL	20,755	C
Mars Hill College	NC	22,950	LC
Mercyhurst Univ	PA	40,700	C
Midwestern State Univ	TX	9,722	C
Millikin Univ	IL	37,462	C
Minn State Univ, Mankato	MN	14,900	C
Minn State Univ, Moorhead	MN	13,392	C
Missouri Southern State Univ	MO	11,910	C
Mount Aloysius College	PA	27,970	C
N Car State Univ	NC	16,202	HC
North Central College	IL	38,343	VC
N Dak State Univ	ND	14,642	C
North Georgia College & State Univ	GA	8,500	C
Northern Kentucky Univ	KY	15,302	LC
Northern Mich Univ	MI	15,300	VC
Northwest Missouri State Univ	MO	14,229	C
Northwest Nazarene Univ	ID	24,275	NC
Ohio Wesleyan Univ	OH	49,460	₲
Olivet College	MI	19,984	C
Oswego / SUNY	NY	20,009	VC
Penn State Univ/Univ Park	PA	25,404	VC
Peru State College	NE	8,600	NC
Pittsburg State Univ	KS	12,032	C
Rhode Island College	RI	17,132	LC
Rivier College	NH	35,000	VC
Roberts Wesleyan College	NY	37,384	₲
Rochester Inst of Technology	NY	42,450	V₲
Roosevelt Univ	IL	22,605	VC
Sacred Heart Univ	CT	48,564	VC
St. John's Univ	MN	46,146	C
St. Mary-of-the-Woods College	IN	37,722	LC
St. Vincent College	PA	40,244	C
Seton Hill Univ	PA	35,172	C
Simpson College	IA	36,086	VC
Spring Hill College	AL	42,130	VC
Syracuse Univ	NY	54,512	HC
Tarleton State Univ	TX	13,489	LC
Texas A&M Univ at Kingsville	TX	7,500	LC
The Catholic Univ of America	DC	52,852	VC
Thiel College	PA	31,378	LC
Truman State Univ	MO	13,546	HC
Univ of Central Arkansas	AR	10,840	VC
Univ of Central Missouri	MO	14,605	C
Univ of Evansville	IN	41,056	V₲
Univ of Findlay	OH	31,916	C
Univ of Illinois at Urbana-Champaign	IL	24,300	HC
Univ of Iowa	IA	17,481	VC
Univ of Maryland	MD	18,801	HC
Univ of Mass Amherst	MA	23,697	V₲
Univ of Miami	FL	55,166	MC
Univ of Minn/Twin Cities	MN		HC
Univ of Montana-Western	MT	9,753	LC
Univ of New Hampshire	NH	24,702	VC
Univ of New Haven	CT	47,740	C
Univ of New Orleans	LA	9,224	VC
Univ of N Car at Wilmington	NC	13,572	V₲
Univ of Rio Grande	OH	8,750	NC
Univ of St. Francis	IL	36,490	C
Univ of Tenn at Knoxville	TN	20,364	V₲
Univ of Wisc/Eau Claire	WI	15,430	VC
Virginia Intermont College	VA	32,411	LC
Walsh Univ	OH	35,100	C
Washington State Univ	WA	20,461	C
Washington Univ in St. Louis	MO	58,818	MC
Waynesburg Univ	PA	29,100	C
West Texas A&M Univ	TX	13,478	C
Western Carolina Univ	NC	13,965	₲
Wheeling Jesuit Univ	WV	34,668	C
Wilmington College	OH	29,784	C
Wingate Univ	NC	34,990	C
Winona State Univ	MN	16,530	C
Youngstown State Univ	OH	16,374	LC

PRINTING TECHNOLOGY

School	ST	$IS	SR
Pennsylvania College of Technology	PA	25,653	NC
Rochester Inst of Technology	NY	42,450	V₲

PRINTMAKING

School	ST	$IS	SR
Adams State College	CO	13,358	LC
Aquinas College	MI	33,060	C
Art Academy of Cincinnati	OH	25,940	SP
Bennington College	VT	56,990	H₲
Biola Univ	CA	40,320	VC
Birmingham-Southern College	AL	42,370	V₲
Buffalo State/State Univ of Buffalo	NY	15,733	₲
Calif College of the Arts	CA	48,334	SP
Cal State, San Bernardino	CA	12,000	C
Cleveland Inst of Art	OH	48,641	SP
College for Creative Studies	MI		SP
College of Visual Arts - School is Closed	MN	24,310	SP
Columbia College	MO	24,578	C
Drake Univ	IA	30,980	V₲
Escuela de Artes Plasticas de PR	PR	2,660	
Ferris State Univ	MI	19,698	C
Houghton College	NY	35,740	VC
Howard Univ	DC	35,957	C
Indiana Univ South Bend	IN	15,293	C
Indiana Univ Southeast	IN	15,807	LC
Indiana Univ-Purdue Univ Fort Wayne	IN	15,425	C
Indiana Univ-Purdue Univ Indianapolis	IN	17,290	C
Indiana Wesleyan Univ	IN	31,815	VC
Kansas City Art Inst	MO	38,000	SP
Kendall College of Art and Design of Ferris State Univ	MI	21,048	SP
Kutztown Univ of Pennsylvania	PA	16,909	LC
Maine College of Art	ME	28,812	SP
Maryland Inst College of Art	MD	39,500	SP
Mass College of Art and Design	MA	23,600	SP
Milwaukee Inst of Art and Design	WI	31,938	SP
Minneapolis College of Art and Design	MN	36,700	SP
Montserrat College of Art	MA	31,000	SP
Northwest Nazarene Univ	ID	24,275	NC
Ohio Univ	OH	20,676	VC
Pacific Northwest College of Art	OR	38,494	SP
Rhode Island School of Design	RI	55,204	SP
Ringling College of Art and Design	FL	46,130	SP
San Francisco Art Inst	CA	52,492	SP
Savannah College of Art and Design	GA	46,824	SP
School of the Art Inst of Chicago	IL	44,000	SP
Syracuse Univ	NY	54,512	HC
Temple Univ	PA	24,392	VC
Texas A&M Univ at Commerce	TX	10,496	C
Texas Christian Univ	TX	47,570	HC
Univ of Dallas	TX	43,510	V₲
Univ of Hartford	CT	42,674	C
Univ of Iowa	IA	17,481	VC
Univ of Kansas	KS	16,980	₲
Univ of Miami	FL	55,166	MC
Univ of Mich/Ann Arbor	MI	22,102	H₲
Univ of Oregon	OR	20,872	VC
Univ of the Arts	PA	38,450	SP
Washington Univ in St. Louis	MO	58,818	MC
Webster Univ	MO	33,990	₲
Youngstown State Univ	OH	16,374	LC

PRODUCTION AND OPERATIONS MANAGEMENT

School	ST	$IS	SR
San Diego State Univ	CA	20,578	VC

PROFESSIONAL PROGRAM IN ACCOUNTING

School	ST	$IS	SR
Texas Christian Univ	TX	47,570	HC
Univ of Louisiana at Monroe	LA	12,998	C

PROPERTY MANAGEMENT

School	ST	$IS	SR
New York Univ	NY	61,470	MC
Univ of Wisc/Stout	WI	23,942	C

PSYCHOBIOLOGY

School	ST	$IS	SR
Albright College	PA	46,660	C
Arcadia Univ	PA	33,570	₲
Binghamton Univ / The SUNY	NY	20,832	H₲
Centre College	KY	35,000	H₲
Florida Atlantic Univ	FL	17,339	C
Hamilton College	NY	55,620	MC
Houghton College	NY	35,740	VC
La Sierra Univ	CA	35,694	VC
Lebanon Valley College	PA	38,570	C
Lindsey Wilson College	KY	30,470	VC
Quinnipiac Univ	CT	53,580	VC
Ripon College	WI	36,959	₲
Simmons College	MA	48,770	VC
Swarthmore College	PA	57,870	MC
Tiffin Univ	OH	30,273	LC
Univ of Calif at Los Angeles	CA	25,686	MC
Univ of New England	ME	46,145	₲
Wilson College	PA	27,660	C

PSYCHOLOGY

School	ST	$IS	SR
Abilene Christian Univ	TX	38,400	VC
Adams State College	CO	13,358	LC
Adelphi Univ	NY	43,130	VC
Adrian College	MI	33,800	C
Agnes Scott College	GA	45,323	V₲
Alabama A&M Univ	AL	96,100	C
Alabama State Univ	AL	14,142	NC
Alaska Pacific Univ	AK	33,360	VC
Albany State Univ	GA	8,500	C
Albertus Magnus College	CT	37,382	LC
Albion College	MI	43,884	VC
Albright College	PA	46,660	C
Alcorn State Univ	MS	9,500	C
Alderson Broaddus Univ	WV	28,656	C
Alfred Univ	NY	40,392	VC
Allegheny College	PA	49,020	HC
Alma College	MI	42,400	VC
Alvernia Univ	PA	39,250	C
Alverno College	WI	30,483	LC
American International College	MA	36,100	LC
American Jewish Univ	CA	32,600	C
American Univ	DC	54,829	H₲
Amherst College	MA	58,744	MC
Anderson Univ	IN	35,390	C
Andrews Univ	MI	28,030	₲
Angelo State Univ	TX	15,049	NC
Anna Maria College	MA	34,600	LC
Appalachian State Univ	NC	12,919	VC
Aquinas College	MI	33,060	C
Arcadia Univ	PA	33,570	₲
Arizona State Univ	AZ	18,818	₲
Arkansas State Univ	AR	14,980	C
Arkansas Tech Univ	AR	13,164	LC
Armstrong Atlantic State Univ	GA	16,276	C
Asbury Univ	KY	32,038	VC
Ashford Univ	IA	21,780	C
Ashland Univ	OH	25,000	C
Assumption College	MA	45,721	VC
Atlantic Union College	MA	24,600	LC
Auburn Univ	AL	20,052	V₲
Auburn Univ at Montgomery	AL	12,120	C
Augsburg College	MN	35,142	C
Augustana College	IL	43,398	HC
Augustana College	SD	35,500	VC
Aurora Univ	IL	26,870	C
Austin College	TX	36,940	HC
Austin Peay State Univ	TN	14,650	C
Averett Univ	VA	36,000	LC
Avila Univ	MO	26,900	C
Azusa Pacific Univ	CA	39,946	C
Baker Univ	KS	33,350	₲
Baldwin Wallace Univ	OH	36,980	VC
Ball State Univ	IN	17,850	C
Bard College	NY	59,872	HC
Bard College at Simon's Rock	MA	58,963	H₲
Barry Univ	FL	38,190	C
Barton College	NC	27,660	C
Bates College	ME	58,950	MC
Bay Path College	MA	34,565	C
Baylor Univ	TX	46,720	HC
Becker College	MA	41,420	LC
Belhaven Univ	MS	27,170	C
Bellarmine Univ	KY	42,950	VC
Bellevue Univ	NE	4,600	NC
Belmont Abbey College	NC	37,716	C
Belmont Univ	TN	37,380	V₲
Beloit College	WI	49,970	HC
Bemidji State Univ	MN	13,500	C
Benedictine College	KS	29,180	VC
Benedictine Univ	IL	35,220	C
Bennett College	NC		LC
Bennington College	VT	56,990	H₲
Berea College	KY	7,220	HC
Berry College	GA	39,254	HC
Bethany College	KS	30,605	NC
Bethany College	WV	35,282	C
Bethel College	IN	31,560	C
Bethel College	KS	29,100	C
Bethel Univ	MN	34,940	VC
Bethel Univ	TN	19,186	C
Bethune-Cookman Univ	FL	22,290	LC
Binghamton Univ / The SUNY	NY	20,832	H₲
Biola Univ	CA	40,320	VC
Birmingham-Southern College	AL	42,370	V₲
Black Hills State Univ	SD	13,562	LC
Blackburn College	IL	21,350	C
Bloomfield College	NJ	36,960	C
Bloomsburg Univ of Pennsylvania	PA	13,598	C
Blue Mountain College	MS	13,550	LC
Bluefield College	VA	17,230	₲
Bluffton Univ	OH	37,864	C
Boise State Univ	ID	12,802	C
Boston College	MA	58,506	MC
Boston Univ	MA	54,130	H₲
Bowdoin College	ME	57,834	MC
Bowie State Univ	MD	23,990	LC
Bowling Green State Univ	OH	18,970	C
Bradley Univ	IL	31,874	VC
Brandeis Univ	MA	58,820	HC
Brenau Univ Women's College	GA	26,650	₲
Brescia Univ	KY	26,140	V₲
Brewton-Parker College	GA	33,388	LC
Briar Cliff Univ	IA	29,514	C
Bridgewater College	VA	39,880	C
Bridgewater State Univ	MA	18,752	C
Brigham Young Univ	UT	12,100	HC
Brigham Young Univ/ Hawaii	HI	8,614	VC
Brown Univ	RI	56,150	MC
Bryan College	TN	24,194	C
Bryant Univ	RI	49,179	VC
Bryn Athyn College	PA	27,984	C
Bryn Mawr College	PA	57,760	MC
Bucknell Univ	PA	58,160	MC
Buena Vista Univ	IA	37,954	C
Buffalo State/State Univ of Buffalo	NY	15,700	₲
Burlington College	VT	32,510	SP
Butler Univ	IN	45,898	V₲
Cabrini College	PA	40,859	LC
Cairn Univ	PA	31,255	C
Caldwell College	NJ	35,602	LC
Calif Baptist Univ	CA	35,890	C
Calif Lutheran Univ	CA	47,640	C
Calif Polytechnic State Univ	CA	19,847	HC
Calif State Polytechnic Univ, Pomona	CA	18,932	C
Cal State, Bakersfield	CA	8,000	LC
Cal State, Dominguez Hills	CA	17,056	LC
Cal State, East Bay	CA	16,549	C
Cal State, Fresno	CA	17,405	C
Cal State, Fullerton	CA	25,188	₲
Cal State, Long Beach	CA	17,534	₲
Cal State, Los Angeles	CA	15,829	C
Cal State, Monterey Bay	CA	26,871	LC
Cal State, Northridge	CA	28,313	C
Cal State, Sacramento	CA	16,200	C
Cal State, San Bernardino	CA	12,000	C
Cal State, San Marcos	CA	14,576	C
Cal State, Stanislaus	CA	18,582	C
Calif Univ of Pennsylvania	PA	14,217	C
Calumet College of St. Joseph	IN	15,000	LC
Calvin College	MI	37,585	V₲
Cambridge College	MA	13,392	NC
Cameron Univ	OK	9,267	LC
Campbell Univ	NC	25,500	C
Campbellsville Univ	KY	27,720	C
Canisius College	NY	45,602	VC
Capital Univ	OH	39,824	VC
Cardinal Stritch Univ	WI	24,054	C
Carleton College	MN	58,149	MC
Carlos Albizu Univ	FL	12,053	LC
Carlow Univ	PA	30,272	C
Carnegie Mellon Univ	PA	51,260	MC
Carroll College	MT	28,000	C
Carroll Univ	WI	24,860	C
Carson-Newman Univ	TN	29,058	₲
Carthage College	WI	33,000	C
Case Western Reserve Univ	OH	55,178	MC
Castleton State College	VT	19,424	C
Catawba College	NC	37,105	C
Cazenovia College	NY	30,800	C
Cedar Crest College	PA	43,240	C
Cedarville Univ	OH	31,036	V₲
Centenary College	NJ	38,618	LC
Centenary College of Louisiana	LA	39,070	₲
Central College	IA	36,980	VC
Central Conn State Univ	CT	19,212	C
Central Methodist Univ	MO	28,240	VC
Central Mich Univ	MI	18,066	C
Central State Univ	OH	9,010	C
Central Univ of Bayamon	PR	3,350	
Central Washington Univ	WA	11,730	C
Centre College	KY	35,000	H₲
Chadron State College	NE	7,400	NC
Chaminade Univ of Honolulu	HI	31,664	C
Champlain College	VT	44,850	VC
Chapman Univ	CA	56,019	V₲
Charleston Southern Univ	SC	22,420	C
Chatham Univ	PA	42,440	VC
Chestnut Hill College	PA	39,785	LC
Cheyney Univ of Pennsylvania	PA	20,372	LC
Chicago State Univ	IL	5,482	C
Christian Brothers Univ	TN	19,140	HC
Christopher Newport Univ	VA	21,050	VC
Citadel, The	SC		C
CUNY/Baruch College	NY	15,831	VC
CUNY/Brooklyn College	NY	5,884	₲
Claremont McKenna College	CA	58,065	MC
Clarion Univ of Pennsylvania	PA	17,370	C
Clark Atlanta Univ	GA	30,006	C
Clark Univ	MA	47,020	H₲
Clarke Univ	IA	36,400	C
Clarkson Univ	NY	53,538	HC
Clearwater Christian College	FL	23,720	C
Clemson Univ	SC	19,136	HC
Cleveland State Univ	OH	21,357	C
Coastal Carolina Univ	SC	17,620	C
Coe College	IA	43,590	VC

School	ST	$IS	SR
Coker College	SC	32,256	LC
Colby College	ME	57,510	MC
Colby-Sawyer College	NH	47,870	C
Colgate Univ	NY	50,930	MC
College of Staten Island / The CUNY	NY	16,778	NC
College of Charleston	SC	21,273	VC
College of Mount St. Joseph	OH	33,880	C
College of Mount St. Vincent	NY	41,040	MC
College of New Jersey	NJ	25,376	HC
College of St. Benedict	MN	47,570	VC
College of St. Elizabeth	NJ	43,839	LC
College of St. Mary	NE	34,334	C
College of St. Scholastica	MN	39,960	C
College of St Joseph	VT	30,600	LC
College of the Holy Cross	MA	56,232	MC
College of the Ozarks	MO	5,605	VC
College of William & Mary	VA	25,085	MC
College of Wooster	OH	52,600	VC
Colo Christian Univ	CO	27,500	VC
Colo College	CO	54,534	MC
Colo Mesa Univ	CO	16,669	LC
Colo State Univ-Fort Collins	CO	20,090	VC
Colo State Univ-Pueblo	CO	13,532	LC
Columbia College	MO	24,578	C
Columbia College	SC	27,882	C
Columbia Univ in the City of New York	NY	61,116	MC
Columbia Univ/Barnard College	NY	39,000	MC
Columbia Univ/School of General Studies	NY	54,000	MC
Columbus State Univ	GA	13,176	C
Concord Univ	WV	13,102	C
Concordia College, Moorhead	MN	39,974	C+
Concordia Univ	OR	34,930	C
Concordia Univ - Irvine	CA	35,390	VC
Concordia Univ Nebr	NE	26,000	VC
Concordia Univ St. Paul	MN	27,200	C
Concordia Univ Wisc	WI	28,980	C
Concordia Univ, Ann Arbor	MI	27,220	VC
Concordia Univ, River Forest	IL	26,300	C
Conn College	CT	54,970	MC
Converse College	SC	37,130	C
Coppin State Univ	MD	14,905	VC
Corban Univ	OR	34,764	C
Cornell College	IA	44,930	HC
Cornell Univ	NY	59,037	MC
Cornerstone Univ and Grand Rapids Theological Seminary	MI	30,866	C
Covenant College	GA		VC+
Creighton Univ	NE	44,058	VC+
Culver-Stockton College	MO	30,900	C
Cumberland Univ	TN	21,220	C
CUNY-City College	NY	19,576	HC+
Curry College	MA	47,545	LC
Daemen College	NY	31,510	C
Dakota Wesleyan Univ	SD	23,000	C
Dallas Baptist Univ	TX	29,118	C
Daniel Webster College	NH	25,380	C
Dartmouth College	NH	57,996	MC
Davidson College	NC	54,683	MC
Davis and Elkins College	WV	33,742	C
De Sales Univ	PA	42,670	C
Defiance College	OH	30,645	C
Delaware State Univ	DE	14,700	LC
Delta State Univ	MS	12,292	LC
Denison Univ	OH	54,670	HC+
DePaul Univ	IL	46,120	VC
DePauw Univ	IN	48,950	VC+
Dickinson College	PA	57,662	HC+
Dillard Univ	LA	20,940	VC
Doane College	NE	33,730	VC
Dominican College	NY	31,270	C
Dominican Univ	IL	37,628	C
Dominican Univ of Calif	CA	51,250	C
Dordt College	IA	34,160	VC
Dowling College	NY	25,000	LC
Drake Univ	IA	30,980	VC+
Drew Univ/College of Liberal Arts	NJ	55,862	VC
Drexel Univ	PA	51,920	HC
Drury Univ	MO	30,319	VC
Duke Univ	NC	50,250	MC
Duquesne Univ	PA	42,017	VC
D'Youville College	NY	29,850	C
Earlham College	IN	49,710	VC+
East Carolina Univ	NC	14,169	C
East Central Univ	OK	10,223	LC
East Stroudsburg Univ of Pennsylvania	PA	16,636	C
East Tenn State Univ	TN	9,000	C
East Texas Baptist Univ	TX	29,135	C
Eastern Conn State Univ	CT	20,584	C
Eastern Illinois Univ	IL	20,502	C
Eastern Kentucky Univ	KY	11,161	C
Eastern Mennonite Univ	VA	38,850	VC
Eastern Mich Univ	MI	17,961	C
Eastern Nazarene College	MA	30,000	C
Eastern New Mexico Univ	NM	10,682	C
Eastern Oregon Univ	OR	10,400	C
Eastern Univ	PA	37,704	C
Eastern Washington Univ	WA	16,388	C
Eckerd College	FL	43,902	VC
Edgewood College	WI	33,294	C
Edinboro Univ of Pennsylvania	PA	15,940	LC
Edward Waters College	FL	17,856	LC
Elizabeth City State Univ	NC	11,638	C
Elizabethtown College	PA	47,600	VC
Elmhurst College	IL	42,032	C+
Elmira College	NY	49,950	C+
Elms College	MA	23,900	VC
Elon Univ	NC	40,046	HC
Embry-Riddle Aeronautical Univ - Daytona Beach	FL	40,884	C+
Emmanuel College	MA	47,985	VC
Emory and Henry College	VA	387,460	C
Emory Univ	GA	45,000	MC
Emporia State Univ	KS	12,897	C
Endicott College	MA	42,390	C
Erskine College	SC	37,360	C
Eugene Lang College - The New School for Liberal Arts	NY	55,650	VC
Eureka College	IL	19,280	C
Evangel Univ	MO	23,090	C
Excelsior College	NY	895	SP
Fairfield Univ	CT	55,850	VC
Fairleigh Dickinson Univ/ College at Florham	NJ	42,142	C
Fairleigh Dickinson Univ/ Metropolitan Campus	NJ	40,254	C
Fairmont State Univ	WV	12,098	LC
Faulkner Univ	AL	22,530	LC
Fayetteville State Univ	NC	10,816	C
Felician College	NJ	41,640	C
Ferris State Univ	MI	19,698	C
Ferrum College	VA	27,740	LC
Fisk Univ	TN	19,830	C
Fitchburg State Univ	MA	17,241	C
Flagler College	FL	24,960	VC
Florida A&M Univ	FL	14,935	LC
Florida Atlantic Univ	FL	17,339	C
Florida Gulf Coast Univ	FL		C
Florida Inst of Technology	FL	48,290	VC
Florida International Univ	FL	17,747	VC
Florida Memorial Univ	FL	20,716	LC
Florida Southern College	FL	38,240	VC
Florida State Univ	FL	15,238	HC
Fontbonne Univ	MO	31,384	C
Fordham Univ	NY	58,927	HC
Fort Hays State Univ	KS	11,354	C
Fort Lewis College	CO	15,513	C
Fort Valley State Univ	GA	11,200	VC
Framingham State Univ	MA	16,750	C
Francis Marion Univ	SC	16,464	LC
Franciscan Univ of Steubenville	OH	27,320	VC
Franklin and Marshall College	PA	58,295	MC
Franklin College	IN	35,885	C
Franklin Pierce Univ	NH	41,598	C
Freed-Hardeman Univ	TN	19,697	VC
Fresno Pacific Univ	CA	32,136	C
Friends Univ	KS	29,100	C
Frostburg State Univ	MD	15,264	LC
Furman Univ	SC	54,006	HC
Gallaudet Univ	DC	25,380	SP
Gannon Univ	PA	37,940	C
Gardner-Webb Univ	NC	34,375	C+
Geneva College	PA	27,280	C
George Fox Univ	OR	40,750	C+
George Mason Univ	VA	15,724	VC
George Washington Univ	DC	57,108	MC
Georgetown College	KY	38,690	C
Georgetown Univ	DC	52,910	MC
Georgia College and State Univ	GA	18,216	VC
Georgia Inst of Technology	GA	20,464	MC
Georgia Regents Univ	GA		C
Georgia Southwestern State Univ	GA	12,218	C
Georgia State Univ	GA	12,000	VC
Georgian Court Univ	NJ	39,726	LC
Gettysburg College	PA	56,820	HC
Glenville State College	WV	11,348	NC
Goddard College	VT	16,418	VC
Goldey-Beacom College	DE	27,493	C
Gonzaga Univ	WA	44,247	HC
Gordon College	MA	42,660	VC+
Goshen College	IN	35,900	VC
Goucher College	MD	50,252	VC+
Grace College and Theological Seminary	IN	28,800	C
Graceland Univ	IA	28,020	C
Grambling State Univ	LA	13,384	LC
Grand Canyon Univ	AZ	24,540	VC
Grand Valley State Univ	MI	17,998	VC
Grand View Univ	IA	31,050	C
Green Mountain College	VT	33,547	LC
Greensboro College	NC	28,740	LC
Greenville College	IL	27,012	C
Grinnell College	IA	53,654	HC
Grove City College	PA	22,988	HC
Guilford College	NC	35,340	C
Gustavus Adolphus College	MN	48,170	HC
Gwynedd-Mercy College	PA	33,560	C
Hamilton College	NY	55,620	MC
Hamline Univ	MN	44,198	VC
Hampden-Sydney College	VA	48,848	C
Hampshire College	MA	58,320	MC
Hampton Univ	VA	28,528	C
Hannibal-LaGrange Univ	MO	24,490	C
Hanover College	IN	41,450	VC
Harding Univ	AR	21,432	C+
Hardin-Simmons Univ	TX	23,560	C+
Hartwick College	NY	49,815	C+
Harvard Univ/Harvard College	MA	49,000	MC
Hastings College	NE	27,782	C+
Haverford College	PA	59,236	MC
Hawaii Pacific Univ	HI	36,690	C
Heidelberg Univ	OH	34,100	C
Henderson State Univ	AR	13,634	C
Hendrix College	AR	48,436	HC+
Heritage Univ	WA	17,664	NC
High Point Univ	NC	39,800	C
Hilbert College	NY	28,550	C
Hillsdale College	MI	31,890	HC+
Hiram College	OH	37,300	VC
Hobart and William Smith Colleges	NY	43,000	VC
Hofstra Univ	NY	48,020	VC+
Hollins Univ	VA	43,295	VC
Holy Family Univ	PA	40,030	LC
Holy Names Univ	CA	40,310	NC
Hood College	MD	44,630	C
Hope College	MI	36,320	VC+
Hope International Univ	CA	34,650	C
Houghton College	NY	35,740	VC
Houston Baptist Univ	TX	23,815	C+
Howard Payne Univ	TX	17,115	C
Howard Univ	DC	35,957	C
Humboldt State Univ	CA	18,400	C
Hunter College / The CUNY	NY	14,429	VC
Huntingdon College	AL	31,850	C
Huntington Univ	IN	32,220	C
Husson Univ	ME	23,386	LC
Huston-Tillotson Univ	TX	18,124	C+
Idaho State Univ	ID	11,908	C
Illinois College	IL	25,770	VC
Illinois Inst of Technology	IL	38,512	HC+
Illinois State Univ	IL	22,634	VC
Illinois Wesleyan Univ	IL	48,452	VC+
Immaculata Univ	PA	43,000	C
Indiana Inst of Technology	IN	34,240	LC
Indiana State Univ	IN	16,000	C
Indiana Univ Bloomington	IN	19,358	HC
Indiana Univ East	IN	6,639	LC
Indiana Univ Kokomo	IN	6,674	LC
Indiana Univ Northwest	IN	6,738	LC
Indiana Univ of Pennsylvania	PA	20,180	LC
Indiana Univ South Bend	IN	15,293	C
Indiana Univ Southeast	IN	15,807	LC
Indiana Univ-Purdue Univ Fort Wayne	IN	15,425	C
Indiana Univ-Purdue Univ Indianapolis	IN	17,290	C
Indiana Wesleyan Univ	IN	31,815	VC
Inter-American Univ of PR/ Aguadilla Campus	PR	5,578	
Inter-American Univ of PR/ Fajardo Campus	PR	4,200	
Inter-American Univ of PR/ Metropolitan Campus	PR	4,320	
Inter-American Univ of PR/ Ponce	PR	3,700	
Inter-American Univ of PR/ San Germán	PR	6,720	
Iona College	NY	44,028	C
Iowa State Univ	IA	16,403	C
Iowa Wesleyan College	IA	30,850	LC
Ithaca College	NY	52,300	HC
Jackson State Univ	MS	13,512	LC
Jacksonville State Univ	AL	12,280	LC
Jacksonville Univ	FL	37,780	C
James Madison Univ	VA	18,049	VC
John Brown Univ	AR	30,996	VC+
John Carroll Univ	OH	44,520	C+
John Jay College of Criminal Justice / The CUNY	NY	6,059	C
Johns Hopkins Univ	MD	47,492	MC
Johnson C. Smith Univ	NC	25,336	LC
Johnson State College	VT	16,721	C
Judson College	AL	24,690	C
Judson Univ	IL	25,130	C
Juniata College	PA	49,340	VC
Kalamazoo College	MI	47,825	HC+
Kansas State Univ	KS	15,497	VC
Kansas Wesleyan Univ	KS	32,000	C
Kean Univ	NJ	22,060	LC
Keene State College	NH	21,538	C
Kennesaw State Univ	GA	13,017	VC
Kent State Univ	OH	19,352	C
Kentucky State Univ	KY	11,000	LC
Kentucky Wesleyan College	KY	27,440	VC+
Kenyon College	OH	56,810	MC
Keuka College	NY	30,300	C
Keystone College	PA	28,680	LC
King Univ	TN	33,140	C
King's College	PA	41,678	C
Knox College	IL		VC
Kutztown Univ of Pennsylvania	PA	16,909	LC
La Roche College	PA	34,802	LC
La Salle Univ	PA	50,270	C
La Sierra Univ	CA	35,694	VC
Lafayette College	PA	57,050	HC+
LaGrange College	GA	34,480	C
Lake Erie College	OH	35,704	C
Lake Forest College	IL	45,580	VC
Lake Superior State Univ	MI	18,121	C
Lakeland College	WI	22,990	C
Lamar Univ	TX	6,820	LC
Lander Univ	SC	22,514	C+
Langston Univ	OK	3,000	LC
Lasell College	MA	42,500	LC
Lawrence Tech Univ	MI	37,630	VC
Lawrence Univ	WI	46,371	HC
Le Moyne College	NY	42,200	VC
Lebanon Valley College	PA	38,570	C
Lee Univ	TN	18,690	C+
Lees-McRae College	NC	33,624	C
Lehigh Univ	PA	55,080	MC
Lehman College / The CUNY	NY	5,778	LC
Lenoir-Rhyne College	NC	35,984	C
Lesley Univ	MA	46,350	C
LeTourneau Univ	TX	26,230	C
Lewis & Clark College	OR	52,656	VC
Lewis Univ	IL	23,050	C
Lewis-Clark State College	ID	6,990	C
Liberty Univ	VA	19,101	C
Limestone College	SC	29,880	C
Lincoln Memorial Univ	TN	18,144	C
Lincoln Univ	MO	11,996	NC
Lindenwood Univ	MO	20,750	C
Lindsey Wilson College	KY	30,470	VC
Linfield College-McMinnville Campus	OR	46,166	C
Lipscomb Univ	TN	35,722	VC
Livingstone College	NC	17,815	LC
Lock Haven Univ of Pennsylvania	PA	17,587	LC
LIU/Brooklyn Campus	NY	26,500	C
LIU/C.W. Post Campus	NY	38,888	C
Longwood Univ	VA	20,924	C
Loras College	IA	37,432	VC
Louisiana College	LA	15,746	C
Louisiana State Univ	LA	18,677	VC+
Louisiana State Univ in Shreveport	LA	5,606	C
Louisiana Tech Univ	LA	8,000	C
Lourdes Univ	OH	26,055	LC
Loyola Marymount Univ	CA	53,240	VC+
Loyola Univ Chicago	IL	49,560	VC+
Loyola Univ Maryland	MD		VC
Loyola Univ New Orleans	LA	46,581	VC
Lubbock Christian Univ	TX	25,518	C
Luther College	IA	44,380	VC+
Lycoming College	PA	43,636	C
Lynchburg College	VA	42,645	C
Lyndon State College	VT	14,233	C
Lynn Univ	FL	43,500	C
Lyon College	AR	30,246	VC
Macalester College	MN	53,419	MC
MacMurray College	IL	20,755	C
Madonna Univ	MI	24,540	VC
Malone Univ	OH	34,334	C
Manchester College	IN	35,070	C
Manhattan College	NY	44,955	VC
Manhattanville College	NY	46,260	VC
Mansfield Univ	PA	19,468	LC
Marian Univ	WI	30,980	LC
Marian Univ/Indianapolis	IN	37,058	C
Marietta College	OH	42,135	VC
Marist College	NY	35,500	C
Marlboro College	VT	35,980	VC
Marquette Univ	WI	43,664	VC+
Mars Hill College	NC	22,950	LC
Marshall Univ	WV	14,820	C
Martin Univ	IN	11,000	SP
Mary Baldwin College	VA	37,110	C
Marygrove College	MI	21,290	C
Marylhurst Univ	OR	18,945	NC
Marymount Manhattan College	NY	40,118	VC
Marymount Univ	VA	36,178	C
Maryville College	TN	33,150	VC
Maryville Univ of St. Louis	MO	34,920	VC
Marywood Univ	PA	40,695	C
Mass College of Liberal Arts	MA	16,733	C
McDaniel College	MD	45,600	VC
McKendree Univ	IL	29,920	C+
McMurry Univ	TX	25,962	LC
McNeese State Univ	LA		C
McPherson College	KS	28,138	C
Medaille College	NY	35,112	VC
Medgar Evers College / The CUNY	NY	4,920	NC
Menlo College	CA	49,002	C
Mercer Univ	GA	44,201	VC+
Mercy College	NY	29,996	C
Mercyhurst Univ	PA	40,700	C
Meredith College	NC	31,420	C
Merrimack College	MA	44,215	C
Messiah College	PA	39,540	VC
Methodist Univ	NC	37,185	C

ST = STATE **$IS** = IN-STATE COSTS **SR** = SELECTOR RATING

School	ST	$IS	SR
Metropolitan College of New York	NY	16,720	VC
Metropolitan State Univ	MN	5,923	SP
Metropolitan State Univ of Denver	CO	4,835	LC
Miami Univ	OH	24,191	HC
Mich State Univ	MI	13,689	VC
Mich Tech Univ	MI	22,105	VC
MidAmerica Nazarene Univ	KS	28,000	C
Middle Tenn State Univ	TN	8,650	C
Middlebury College	VT	57,470	MC
Midland Univ	NE	34,000	C
Midway College	KY	20,150	C
Midwestern State Univ	TX	9,722	C
Millersville Univ of Pennsylvania	PA	18,498	C
Milligan College	TN	27,510	C
Millikin Univ	IL	37,462	C
Mills College	CA	54,119	HC
Millsaps College	MS	43,888	VC+
Minn State Univ, Mankato	MN	14,900	C
Minn State Univ, Moorhead	MN	13,392	C
Minot State Univ	ND	10,915	C
Misericordia Univ	PA	39,840	C
Miss College	MS	21,998	VC
Miss Univ for Women	MS	7,400	LC
Missouri Baptist Univ	MO	30,310	C
Missouri Southern State Univ	MO	11,910	C
Missouri Univ of Science and Technology	MO	18,655	VC+
Missouri Valley College	MO	22,200	C
Missouri Western State Univ	MO	12,260	NC
Mitchell College	CT	40,983	C
Molloy College	NY	38,950	C
Monmouth College	IL	39,290	C
Monmouth Univ	NJ	42,252	C
Montana State Univ	MT	14,068	VC
Montana State Univ-Billings	MT	12,425	LC
Montclair State Univ	NJ	22,614	C
Moravian College	PA	36,381	VC
Morehead State Univ	KY	10,900	C
Morehouse College	GA	38,640	C
Morgan State Univ	MD	14,500	VC
Morningside College	IA	32,620	C
Mount Aloysius College	PA	27,970	C
Mount Holyoke College	MA	53,596	HC+
Mount Mary Univ	WI	32,836	LC
Mount Mercy Univ	IA	34,385	C
Mount Olive College	NC	18,426	C
Mount St. Mary College	NY	39,540	C
Mount St. Mary's Univ	MD	46,158	C
Mount St. Mary's College/ Chalon Campus	CA	43,897	VC+
Mount Vernon Nazarene Univ	OH	29,590	C
Mount Washington College	NH	21,500	NC
Mountain State Univ	WV	14,330	NC
Muhlenberg College	PA	52,837	HC
Murray State Univ	KY	14,944	C
Muskingum Univ	OH	30,502	C
Naropa Univ	CO	37,875	SP
National Louis Univ	IL	16,915	LC
National Univ	CA	14,730	SP
Nazareth College of Rochester	NY	41,590	VC
Nebr Wesleyan Univ	NE	29,774	C+
Neumann Univ	PA	31,078	LC
New College of Florida	FL	14,504	HC+
New England College	NH	45,930	LC
New Jersey City Univ	NJ	21,060	C+
New Mexico Highlands Univ	NM	9,720	NC
New Mexico Inst of Mining and Technology	NM	12,892	HC
New Mexico State Univ	NM	13,955	LC
New York Univ	NY	61,470	MC
Newberry College	SC	26,850	LC
Newbury College	MA	41,850	C
Newman Univ	KS	30,380	C+
Niagara Univ	NY	39,800	C
Nicholls State Univ	LA	7,095	C
Nichols College	MA	37,240	LC
Norfolk State Univ	VA	10,531	LC
N Car Agricultural and Technical State Univ	NC	13,175	LC
N Car Central Univ	NC	9,000	LC
N Car State Univ	NC	16,202	HC
N Car Wesleyan College	NC	29,440	C
North Central College	IL	38,343	VC
N Dak State Univ	ND	14,642	C
North Georgia College & State Univ	GA	8,500	C
North Park Univ	IL	30,130	C
Northeastern Illinois Univ	IL		C
Northeastern Univ	MA	55,296	MC
Northern Arizona Univ	AZ	18,592	C
Northern Illinois Univ	IL	19,768	C
Northern Kentucky Univ	KY	15,302	LC
Northern Mich Univ	MI	15,300	VC
Northern State Univ	SD	14,021	C
Northland College	WI	26,680	C
Northwest Christian Univ	OR	27,399	C
Northwest Missouri State Univ	MO	14,229	C
Northwest Nazarene Univ	ID	24,275	NC
Northwest Univ	WA	18,854	C
Northwestern College	MN	24,000	C
Northwestern College of Iowa	IA	34,848	C+
Northwestern Okla State Univ	OK	7,275	NC
Northwestern State Univ of Louisiana	LA	14,368	C
Northwestern Univ	IL	37,595	MC
Norwich Univ	VT	28,212	C
Notre Dame College	OH	34,942	VC
Notre Dame de Namur Univ	CA	41,610	LC
Notre Dame of Maryland Univ	MD	27,700	C
Nova Southeastern Univ	FL	34,016	VC
Nyack College	NY	32,000	C
Oakland Univ	MI	19,391	VC
Oakwood Univ	AL	23,035	C
Oberlin College	OH	57,025	MC
Occidental College	CA	59,592	MC+
Oglethorpe Univ	GA	42,580	VC
Ohio Dominican Univ	OH	38,380	C+
Ohio Northern Univ	OH	42,075	VC
Ohio State Univ at Lima	OH	7,140	C
Ohio State Univ at Mansfield	OH	13,160	C
Ohio State Univ at Marion	OH	9,850	MC
Ohio State Univ at Newark	OH	17,510	C
Ohio Univ	OH	20,676	VC
Ohio Valley Univ	WV	17,752	C
Ohio Wesleyan Univ	OH	49,460	C+
Okla Baptist Univ	OK	28,202	VC
Okla Christian Univ	OK	24,975	VC
Okla City Univ	OK	33,546	VC
Okla Panhandle State Univ	OK	8,996	NC
Okla State Univ	OK	14,310	VC
Old Dominion Univ	VA	18,662	C
Olivet College	MI	19,984	C
Olivet Nazarene Univ	IL	29,990	C
Oral Roberts Univ	OK	31,734	C
Oregon State Univ	OR	19,017	C+
Oswego / SUNY	NY	20,009	VC
Ottawa Univ	KS	15,000	VC
Otterbein College	OH	32,214	C
Ouachita Baptist Univ	AR	29,010	VC
Our Lady of the Lake Univ of San Antonio	TX	22,430	LC
Pace Univ	NY	48,094	VC
Pacific Lutheran Univ	WA	44,840	VC
Pacific Union College	CA	28,150	VC
Pacific Univ	OR	42,815	C
Paine College	GA	18,594	LC
Palm Beach Atlantic Univ	FL	33,882	LC
Park Univ	MO	17,525	C
Paul Quinn College	TX	25,350	LC
Penn State Erie/The Behrend College	PA	16,256	C
Penn State Univ/Univ Park	PA	25,404	VC
Pepperdine Univ	CA	55,372	HC+
Peru State College	NE	8,600	NC
Pfeiffer Univ	NC	33,700	C
Philadelphia Univ	PA	44,160	C
Philander Smith College	AR	19,760	LC
Piedmont College	GA	29,260	C
Pine Manor College	MA	32,659	LC
Pittsburg State Univ	KS	12,032	C
Pitzer College	CA	54,988	MC
Plymouth State Univ	NH	23,148	LC
Point Loma Nazarene Univ	CA	38,610	VC
Point Park Univ	PA	36,390	C
Pomona College	CA	57,680	MC
Pontifical Catholic Univ of PR	PR	7,310	
Portland State Univ	OR	18,672	C
Post Univ	CT	35,750	C
Prairie View A&M Univ	TX	15,205	LC
Presbyterian College	SC	42,678	VC
Prescott College	AZ	33,284	C+
Princeton Univ	NJ	53,795	MC
Providence College	RI	55,995	HC
Purchase College / SUNY	NY	16,951	C
Purdue Univ/Calumet	IN	14,336	C
Purdue Univ/West Lafayette	IN	20,278	HC
Queens College / The CUNY	NY	17,107	VC
Queens Univ of Charlotte	NC	39,543	VC
Quincy Univ	IL	34,980	LC
Quinnipiac Univ	CT	53,580	VC
Radford Univ	VA	17,132	LC
Ramapo College of New Jersey	NJ	24,938	C+
Randolph College	VA	43,960	VC
Randolph-Macon College	VA	45,086	C
Reed College	OR	57,780	MC
Regis College	MA	47,565	LC
Regis Univ	CO	41,318	C
Rensselaer Polytechnic Inst	NY	59,229	MC
Rhode Island College	RI	17,132	LC
Rhodes College	TN	47,596	HC+
Rice Univ	TX	43,288	MC
Richard Stockton College of New Jersey	NJ	20,000	VC
Rider Univ	NJ	45,720	C
Ripon College	WI	36,959	C+
Rivier College	NH	35,000	VC
Roanoke College	VA	47,996	C+
Robert Morris Univ	PA	36,699	C
Roberts Wesleyan College	NY	37,384	C+
Rochester College	MI	18,320	C
Rochester Inst of Technology	NY	42,450	VC+
Rockford College	IL	31,000	C
Rockhurst Univ	MO	20,625	C
Rocky Mountain College	MT	32,242	C
Roger Williams Univ	RI	45,788	C
Rollins College	FL	52,370	HC
Roosevelt Univ	IL	22,605	VC
Rosemont College	PA	42,350	C
Rowan Univ	NJ	23,570	VC
Russell Sage College	NY	39,370	C
Rutgers, The State Univ of New Jersey/Camden Campus	NJ	24,254	C
Rutgers, The State Univ of New Jersey/New Brunswick	NJ	25,077	VC
Rutgers, The State Univ of New Jersey/Newark Campus	NJ	25,376	C
Sacred Heart Univ	CT	48,564	VC
Saginaw Valley State Univ	MI	16,869	C
St. Anselm College	NH	48,324	VC
St. Augustine's Univ	NC	14,000	C
St. Francis Univ	PA	30,029	LC
St. John's Univ	MN	46,146	C
St. Joseph College	CT	45,630	LC
St. Joseph's College	IN	35,790	C
St. Joseph's College of Maine	ME	31,580	C
St. Joseph's Univ	PA	52,272	VC
St. Leo Univ	FL	27,990	C
St. Louis Univ	MO	46,594	VC+
St. Martin's Univ	WA	38,082	C
St. Mary-of-the-Woods College	IN	37,722	LC
St. Mary's College	IN	45,160	VC
St. Mary's College of Calif	CA	53,550	C
St. Mary's Univ	TX	33,854	C
St. Mary's Univ of Minn	MN	37,015	C
St. Michael's College	VT	48,740	VC
St. Peter's College	NJ	44,240	C
St. Vincent College	PA	40,244	C
St. Xavier Univ	IL	32,840	C
Salem College	NC	29,326	VC
Salem State College	MA	13,161	LC
Salisbury Univ	MD	18,368	VC
Salve Regina Univ	RI	47,250	VC
Sam Houston State Univ	TX	17,082	C
Samford Univ	AL	35,700	VC+
San Diego Christian College	CA	31,012	C
San Diego State Univ	CA	20,578	VC
San Francisco State Univ	CA	18,514	C
San Jose State Univ	CA	19,707	C
Santa Clara Univ	CA	54,702	MC
Sarah Lawrence College	NY	48,000	HC
Schreiner Univ	TX	32,734	LC
Scripps College	CA	54,900	MC
Seattle Pacific Univ	WA	41,559	VC+
Seattle Univ	WA	47,010	VC+
Seton Hall Univ	NJ	45,902	C
Seton Hill Univ	PA	35,172	C
Sewanee: The Univ of the South	TN	47,700	HC+
Shaw Univ	NC	15,488	LC
Shawnee State Univ	OH	16,545	NC
Shenandoah Univ	VA	39,268	C
Shepherd Univ	WV	14,996	C
Shippensburg Univ of Pennsylvania	PA	17,064	LC
Shorter Univ	GA	26,470	C
Siena College	NY	43,863	VC
Siena Heights Univ	MI	17,000	LC
Silver Lake College	WI	22,600	LC
Simmons College	MA	48,770	VC
Simpson College	IA	36,086	VC
Simpson Univ	CA	28,900	C
Skidmore College	NY	57,926	HC
Slippery Rock Univ of Pennsylvania	PA	10,360	LC
Smith College	MA	57,524	MC
Sojourner-Douglass College	MD	9,160	LC
Sonoma State Univ	CA	20,541	C
S Car State Univ	SC	6,700	LC
S Dak State Univ	SD	14,296	C
Southeast Missouri State Univ	MO	14,983	LC
Southeastern Louisiana Univ	LA	13,325	C
Southeastern Okla State Univ	OK	7,966	C
Southeastern Univ	FL	27,201	C+
Southern Adventist Univ	TN	26,190	C
Southern Arkansas Univ	AR	14,316	C
Southern Conn State Univ	CT	18,033	C
Southern Illinois Univ Carbondale	IL	21,620	C
Southern Illinois Univ Edwardsville	IL	17,532	C
Southern Methodist Univ	TX	57,755	MC
Southern Nazarene Univ	OK	24,354	NC
Southern New Hampshire Univ	NH	38,100	C
Southern Oregon Univ	OR	17,874	C
Southern Polytechnic State Univ	GA	13,958	VC
Southern Univ and A&M College	LA	9,761	C+
Southern Univ at New Orleans	LA	1,000	NC
Southern Vermont College	VT	30,740	LC
Southern Wesleyan Univ	SC	25,600	C
Southwest Baptist Univ	MO	24,710	C
Southwest Minn State Univ	MN	14,000	C
Southwestern Adventist Univ	TX	23,026	LC
Southwestern College	KS	29,270	C
Southwestern Okla State Univ	OK	9,160	C
Southwestern Univ	TX	45,660	VC
Spalding Univ	KY	31,850	LC
Spelman College	GA	24,650	VC
Spring Arbor Univ	MI	26,740	C
Spring Hill College	AL	42,130	VC
Springfield College	MA	25,000	C
St. Ambrose Univ	IA		C
St. Andrews Univ	NC	32,050	LC
St. Bonaventure Univ	NY	38,831	C
St. Catherine Univ	MN	37,782	C+
St. Cloud State Univ	MN	10,600	C
St. Edward's Univ	TX	44,674	VC
St. Francis College	NY	34,200	LC
St. John Fisher College	NY	39,370	C+
St. John's Univ	NY	52,840	C+
St. Joseph's College, New York / Brooklyn Campus	NY	21,878	C
St. Joseph's College, New York / Suffolk Campus	NY	21,878	VC
St. Lawrence Univ	NY	53,740	HC
St. Mary's College of Maryland	MD	26,699	HC
St. Norbert College	WI	39,992	VC
St. Olaf College	MN	49,960	HC+
St. Thomas Aquinas College	NY	30,000	C
St. Thomas Univ	FL	32,310	C+
Stanford Univ	CA	56,411	MC
SUNY Inst of Technology at Utica / Rome	NY	23,818	C
SUNY/Empire State College	NY	6,315	SP
Stephen F. Austin State Univ	TX	14,668	C
Stetson Univ	FL	49,512	VC+
Stevenson Univ	MD	39,572	C
Stonehill College	MA	46,780	VC+
Stony Brook Univ / SUNY	NY	19,359	HC
Suffolk Univ	MA	46,548	C
Sul Ross State Univ	TX	13,410	LC
SUNY College at Geneseo	NY	18,055	HC+
SUNY College at Old Westbury	NY	16,324	C
SUNY Cortland / The SUNY	NY	19,117	C
SUNY Fredonia / The SUNY at Fredonia	NY	18,702	VC
SUNY New Paltz	NY	15,010	C
SUNY Oneonta / SUNY	NY	16,919	VC
SUNY Plattsburgh / SUNY	NY	18,083	VC
Susquehanna Univ	PA	49,170	C
Swarthmore College	PA	57,870	MC
Sweet Briar College	VA	43,765	C+
Syracuse Univ	NY	54,512	HC
Tabor College	KS	29,010	LC
Talladega College	AL	13,000	C
Taylor Univ	IN	36,742	VC+
Temple Univ	PA	24,392	VC
Tenn State Univ	TN	9,048	C
Tenn Tech Univ	TN	11,310	C
Tenn Wesleyan College	TN	21,250	C
Texas A&M Univ	TX	16,956	VC+
Texas A&M Univ at Commerce	TX	10,496	C
Texas A&M Univ at Corpus Christi	TX	11,544	LC
Texas A&M Univ at Kingsville	TX	7,500	LC
Texas Christian Univ	TX	47,570	HC
Texas Lutheran Univ	TX	34,070	C
Texas Southern Univ	TX	10,212	LC
Texas State Univ	TX	16,495	VC
Texas Tech Univ	TX	14,243	C
Texas Wesleyan Univ	TX	29,886	C
Texas Woman's Univ	TX	13,633	LC
The Catholic Univ of America	DC	52,852	VC
The College at Brockport / SUNY	NY	18,362	VC
The College of Idaho	ID	31,277	VC
The College of New Rochelle	NY	33,600	VC
The College of St. Rose	NY	26,750	C
Ohio State Univ	OH	19,887	MC
The SUNY at Potsdam	NY	17,754	C
Thiel College	PA	31,378	LC
Thomas College	ME	26,270	LC
Thomas Edison State College	NJ	5,700	SP
Thomas More College	KY	34,760	C
Thomas Univ	GA	11,520	NC
Tougaloo College	MS	15,275	NC

ST = STATE **$IS** = IN-STATE COSTS **SR** = SELECTOR RATING

School	ST	$IS	SR
Touro College	NY	23,150	VC
Towson Univ	MD	16,000	VC
Transylvania Univ	KY	40,310	VC+
Trevecca Nazarene Univ	TN	30,118	C
Trine Univ	IN	39,400	VC
Trinity Christian College	IL	28,869	C
Trinity College	CT		HC+
Trinity International Univ	IL	31,070	C
Trinity Univ	TX	44,174	HC+
Trinity Washington Univ	DC	30,250	C+
Troy Univ	AL	10,650	C
Truman State Univ	MO	13,546	HC
Tufts Univ	MA	58,780	MC
Tulane Univ	LA	58,942	MC
Tusculum College	TN	24,295	C
Tuskegee Univ	AL	26,750	C
Union College	KY	28,775	C
Union College	NE	23,270	VC
Union College	NY		MC
Union Inst & Univ	OH	8,912	SP
Union Univ	TN	28,260	VC
United States Air Force Academy	CO		MC
Universidad del Turabo	PR	4,110	
Universidad Metropolitana	PR		
Univ at Albany / SUNY	NY	18,674	VC
Univ at Buffalo / The SUNY	NY	20,283	VC
Univ of Akron	OH	20,436	C
Univ of Alabama at Birmingham	AL	18,484	C+
Univ of Alabama at Huntsville	AL	17,625	VC
Univ of Alabama at Tuscaloosa	AL	17,164	C+
Univ of Alaska Anchorage	AK	15,290	NC
Univ of Alaska Fairbanks	AK	13,955	C
Univ of Arizona	AZ	20,105	C
Univ of Arkansas at Fayetteville	AR	16,860	VC
Univ of Arkansas at Little Rock	AR		C
Univ of Arkansas at Monticello	AR	8,470	NC
Univ of Arkansas at Pine Bluff	AR	10,600	C
Univ of Bridgeport	CT	39,030	LC
Univ of Calif at Berkeley	CA	23,322	MC
Univ of Calif at Davis	CA	24,482	HC
Univ of Calif at Irvine	CA	25,961	VC
Univ of Calif at Los Angeles	CA	25,686	MC
Univ of Calif at Riverside	CA	27,204	C
Univ of Calif at San Diego	CA	21,000	VC
Univ of Calif at Santa Barbara	CA	27,551	HC
Univ of Calif at Santa Cruz	CA	27,807	VC
Univ of Central Arkansas	AR	10,840	VC
Univ of Central Florida	FL	15,711	VC+
Univ of Central Missouri	MO	14,605	C
Univ of Central Okla	OK	12,293	C
Univ of Charleston	WV	28,650	C
Univ of Chicago	IL	55,416	MC
Univ of Cincinnati	OH	20,199	VC
Univ of Colo at Colo Springs	CO	15,000	VC
Univ of Colo Boulder	CO	22,605	VC+
Univ of Colo Denver	CO	17,904	C
Univ of Conn	CT	23,744	HC
Univ of Dallas	TX	43,510	VC+
Univ of Dayton	OH	43,750	VC
Univ of Delaware	DE	22,728	VC
Univ of Denver	CO	51,787	VC+
Univ of Detroit Mercy	MI	30,450	C
Univ of Dubuque	IA	30,200	C
Univ of Evansville	IN	41,056	VC+
Univ of Findlay	OH	31,916	C
Univ of Florida	FL	15,783	HC+
Univ of Georgia	GA	19,508	VC
Univ of Great Falls	MT	27,970	C
Univ of Hartford	CT	42,674	C
Univ of Hawaii at Hilo	HI	6,500	C
Univ of Hawaii at Manoa	HI	19,379	VC
Univ of Houston-Downtown	TX	6,267	LC
Univ of Idaho	ID	14,558	C
Univ of Illinois at Chicago	IL	24,293	VC
Univ of Illinois at Urbana-Champaign	IL	24,300	HC
Univ of Indianapolis	IN	31,740	LC
Univ of Iowa	IA	17,481	VC
Univ of Jamestown	ND	24,738	C
Univ of Kansas	KS	16,980	C+
Univ of Kentucky	KY	19,868	C
Univ of La Verne	CA	47,010	VC
Univ of Louisiana at Lafayette	LA	6,130	C
Univ of Louisiana at Monroe	LA	12,998	C
Univ of Louisville	KY	17,460	VC
Univ of Maine	ME	19,712	C+
Univ of Maine at Farmington	ME	17,841	C
Univ of Mary	ND	16,714	C
Univ of Mary Hardin-Baylor	TX	31,950	C+
Univ of Mary Washington	VA	19,484	VC
Univ of Maryland	MD	18,801	HC
Univ of Maryland/Baltimore County	MD	18,000	VC
Univ of Maryland/Univ College	MD	6,168	SP
Univ of Mass Amherst	MA	23,697	VC+
Univ of Mass Boston	MA	11,966	C
Univ of Mass Dartmouth	MA	22,223	C
Univ of Mass Lowell	MA	19,316	C
Univ of Memphis	TN	15,094	C
Univ of Miami	FL	55,166	MC
Univ of Mich/Ann Arbor	MI	22,102	HC+
Univ of Mich/Dearborn	MI	9,885	VC
Univ of Mich-Flint	MI	17,547	C+
Univ of Minn/Duluth	MN	18,964	C+
Univ of Minn/Morris	MN	17,150	VC
Univ of Minn/Twin Cities	MN		HC
Univ of Miss	MS	15,482	VC
Univ of Missouri/Columbia	MO	18,201	MC
Univ of Missouri-Kansas City	MO	19,603	C
Univ of Missouri-St. Louis	MO	18,304	VC
Univ of Mobile	AL	27,870	VC
Univ of Montana	MT	13,670	C
Univ of Montevallo	AL	17,320	C
Univ of Mount Union	OH	35,130	C
Univ of Nebr - Lincoln	NE	17,507	VC
Univ of Nebr at Kearney	NE	14,855	LC
Univ of Nebr at Omaha	NE	12,700	C
Univ of Nevada, Las Vegas	NV	17,303	C
Univ of Nevada/Reno	NV	14,500	NC
Univ of New England	ME	46,145	C+
Univ of New Hampshire	NH	24,702	VC
Univ of New Haven	CT	47,740	C
Univ of New Mexico	NM	15,300	C
Univ of New Orleans	LA	9,224	VC
Univ of North Alabama	AL	9,960	C
Univ of N Car at Asheville	NC	13,500	VC+
Univ of N Car at Chapel Hill	NC	18,348	MC
Univ of N Car at Charlotte	NC	15,847	C
Univ of N Car at Greensboro	NC	12,848	C
Univ of N Car at Wilmington	NC	13,572	VC+
Univ of N Dak	ND	14,094	C
Univ of North Florida	FL	15,578	VC
Univ of North Texas	TX	15,628	C
Univ of Northern Colo	CO	15,973	C
Univ of Northern Iowa	IA	14,776	C
Univ of Notre Dame	IN		MC
Univ of Okla	OK	17,634	VC+
Univ of Oregon	OR	20,872	VC
Univ of Pennsylvania	PA	56,106	MC
Univ of Pikeville	KY	24,750	NC
Univ of Pittsburgh at Bradford	PA	21,316	LC
Univ of Pittsburgh at Greensburg	PA	17,640	C
Univ of Pittsburgh at Johnstown	PA	20,862	LC
Univ of Pittsburgh at Pittsburgh	PA	27,800	HC+
Univ of Portland	OR	47,874	VC
Univ of PR Recinto de Rio Piedras	PR	5,750	
Univ of PR/Cayey	PR	1,504	
Univ of PR/Mayaguez	PR	1,250	
Univ of Puget Sound	WA	52,648	HC+
Univ of Redlands	CA	40,500	VC
Univ of Rio Grande	OH	8,750	NC
Univ of Rochester	NY	58,500	MC
Univ of St. Francis	IN	29,810	C
Univ of St. Mary	KS	28,400	C+
Univ of San Diego	CA	53,302	HC+
Univ of San Francisco	CA	49,674	VC
Univ of Science and Arts of Okla	OK	10,560	VC
Univ of Scranton	PA	51,940	VC
Univ of Sioux Falls	SD	22,990	C
Univ of South Alabama	AL	13,510	C
Univ of S Car at Aiken	SC	16,278	C
Univ of S Car at Columbia	SC	19,725	VC+
Univ of S Car Upstate	SC	17,673	LC
Univ of S Dak	SD	15,111	C
Univ of South Florida	FL	13,000	C
Univ of South Florida/St. Petersburg	FL	12,769	VC
Univ of Southern Calif	CA	56,903	MC
Univ of Southern Indiana	IN	14,657	C
Univ of Southern Maine	ME	16,576	C
Univ of Southern Miss	MS	13,170	C
Univ of St. Francis	IL	36,490	C
Univ of St. Thomas - Houston	TX	36,490	VC
Univ of Tampa	FL	35,160	VC
Univ of Tenn at Chattanooga	TN	16,883	C
Univ of Tenn at Knoxville	TN	20,364	VC+
Univ of Tenn at Martin	TN	13,217	C
Univ of Texas at Arlington	TX	10,908	LC
Univ of Texas at Austin	TX	44,074	HC
Univ of Texas at Dallas	TX	21,046	HC
Univ of Texas at El Paso	TX	8,764	NC
Univ of Texas-Pan American	TX	12,432	LC
Univ of the Cumberlands	KY	27,500	LC
Univ of the District of Columbia	DC	7,244	LC
Univ of the Incarnate Word	TX	35,200	LC
Univ of the Ozarks	AR	22,100	C
Univ of the Pacific	CA	52,146	VC
Univ of the Sacred Heart	PR	5,590	
Univ of the Sciences	PA	48,320	VC+
Univ of the Southwest	NM	15,000	C
Univ of Toledo	OH	18,464	C
Univ of Tulsa	OK	45,311	HC+
Univ of Utah	UT	13,462	VC
Univ of Vermont	VT	26,120	VC+
Univ of Virginia	VA	22,175	MC
Univ of Virginia's College at Wise	VA	11,076	C
Univ of Washington	WA	14,722	VC
Univ of West Alabama	AL	9,415	C
Univ of West Florida	FL	14,656	C
Univ of West Georgia	GA	14,852	LC
Univ of Wisc Whitewater	WI	13,314	C
Univ of Wisc/Eau Claire	WI	15,430	VC
Univ of Wisc/Green Bay	WI	14,900	C
Univ of Wisc/La Crosse	WI	14,755	VC
Univ of Wisc/Madison	WI	18,757	HC
Univ of Wisc/Oshkosh	WI	10,426	LC
Univ of Wisc/Parkside	WI	10,181	LC
Univ of Wisc/Platteville	WI	14,274	C
Univ of Wisc/River Falls	WI	9,722	LC
Univ of Wisc/Stevens Point	WI	14,043	C
Univ of Wisc/Stout	WI	23,942	C
Univ of Wisc/Superior	WI	14,106	C
Univ of Wisc-Milwaukee	WI	18,436	C
Univ of Wyoming	WY	13,855	C+
Upper Iowa Univ	IA	30,426	NC
Urbana Univ	OH	21,190	C
Ursinus College	PA	55,630	VC+
Ursuline College	OH	33,198	LC
Utah State Univ	UT	11,803	C
Utica College	NY	44,734	C
Valparaiso Univ	IN	43,040	VC+
Vanderbilt Univ	TN	57,072	MC
Vanguard Univ of Southern Calif	CA	35,833	VC
Vassar College	NY	59,070	MC
Victory Univ	TN	19,118	C
Villanova Univ	PA	56,436	MC
Virginia Commonwealth Univ	VA	18,633	C
Virginia Intermont College	VA	32,411	LC
Virginia Military Inst	VA	16,156	C
Virginia Polytechnic Inst and State Univ	VA	14,629	HC
Virginia State Univ	VA	11,318	C+
Virginia Union Univ	VA	18,432	C
Virginia Wesleyan College	VA	28,433	LC
Viterbo Univ	WI	30,070	C
Wabash College	IN	44,160	VC
Wagner College	NY	48,600	VC
Wake Forest Univ	NC	51,000	MC
Walla Walla Univ	WA	26,256	NC
Walsh Univ	OH	35,100	C
Warner Univ	FL	18,000	C
Warren Wilson College	NC	34,888	VC
Wartburg College	IA	41,055	VC
Washburn Univ	KS	12,165	NC
Washington Adventist Univ	MD	25,859	C+
Washington and Jefferson College	PA	49,990	VC
Washington and Lee Univ	VA	52,812	MC
Washington College	MD	48,768	VC
Washington State Univ	WA	20,461	C
Washington Univ in St. Louis	MO	58,818	MC
Wayland Baptist Univ	TX	16,058	LC
Wayne State College	NE	11,764	NC
Wayne State Univ	MI	19,493	C
Waynesburg Univ	PA	29,100	C
Webster Univ	MO	33,990	C+
Wellesley College	MA	49,848	MC
Wells College	NY	38,680	VC
Wesley College	DE	31,115	LC
Wesleyan College	GA	24,000	C+
Wesleyan Univ	CT	59,844	MC
West Chester Univ of Pennsylvania	PA	16,836	C
West Liberty Univ	WV	9,142	LC
West Texas A&M Univ	TX	13,478	C
West Virginia State Univ	WV	8,378	NC
West Virginia Univ	WV	15,794	C+
West Virginia Wesleyan College	WV	26,880	C
Western Carolina Univ	NC	13,965	C+
Western Conn State Univ	CT	18,327	C
Western Illinois Univ	IL	20,130	C
Western Kentucky Univ	KY	11,000	LC
Western Mich Univ	MI	19,042	C
Western New England Univ	MA	45,590	C
Western New Mexico Univ	NM	8,500	LC
Western Oregon Univ	OR	15,021	C
Western State Colo Univ	CO	16,135	C
Western Washington Univ	WA	18,519	VC
Westfield State Univ	MA	18,489	C
Westminster College	MO	30,490	VC
Westminster College	PA	31,290	C+
Westminster College	UT	37,708	VC
Westmont College	CA	41,500	HC
Wheaton College	IL	39,650	HC+
Wheaton College	MA	54,934	HC+
Wheeling Jesuit Univ	WV	34,668	C
Whitman College	WA	54,400	MC
Whittier College	CA	43,416	C
Whitworth Univ	WA	45,826	VC+
Wichita State Univ	KS	12,539	C
Widener Univ	PA	50,368	C
Wilberforce Univ	OH	15,100	LC
Wilkes Univ	PA	42,786	C
Willamette Univ	OR	56,450	VC+
William Carey Univ	MS	13,500	LC
William Jewell College	MO	31,000	VC+
William Paterson Univ of New Jersey	NJ	21,694	C
William Peace Univ	NC	32,900	LC
William Penn Univ	IA	26,000	C
William Woods Univ	MO		C
Williams Baptist College	AR	20,070	C
Williams College	MA	58,900	MC
Wilmington College	OH	29,784	C
Wilson College	PA	27,660	C
Wingate Univ	NC	34,990	C
Winona State Univ	MN	16,530	C
Winston-Salem State Univ	NC	9,418	LC
Winthrop Univ	SC	21,120	VC
Wisc Lutheran College	WI	23,510	VC
Wittenberg Univ	OH	47,766	VC
Wofford College	SC	45,795	VC
Woodbury Univ	CA	34,500	LC
Worcester State Univ	MA	18,657	C
Wright State Univ	OH	16,983	C
Xavier Univ	OH	43,740	VC
Xavier Univ of Louisiana	LA	25,300	C
Yale Univ	CT	55,300	MC
Yeshiva Univ	NY	47,250	VC+
York College	NE	19,475	C
York College / CUNY	NY	5,490	NC
York College of Pennsylvania	PA	26,590	C
Youngstown State Univ	OH	16,374	LC

PSYCHOLOGY EDUCATION

School	ST	$IS	SR
Bethany College	WV	35,282	C
Eastern Mich Univ	MI	17,961	C
Kutztown Univ of Pennsylvania	PA	16,909	LC
Mount Holyoke College	MA	53,596	HC+
Nazareth College of Rochester	NY	41,590	VC
Pittsburg State Univ	KS	12,032	C
Rocky Mountain College	MT	32,242	C
St. Vincent College	PA	40,244	C
Tulane Univ	LA	58,942	MC
Univ of Arizona	AZ	20,105	C
Univ of Delaware	DE	22,728	VC
Univ of Rio Grande	OH	8,750	NC
Valparaiso Univ	IN	43,040	VC+
York College	NE	19,475	C

PUBLIC ADMINISTRATION

School	ST	$IS	SR
American International College	MA	36,100	LC
Aquinas College	MI	33,060	C
Auburn Univ	AL	20,052	VC+
Augustana College	IL	43,398	HC
Austin Peay State Univ	TN	14,650	C
Baylor Univ	TX	46,720	HC
Bentley Univ	MA	54,555	HC+
Blackburn College	IL	21,350	C
Brown Univ	RI	56,150	MC
Buena Vista Univ	IA	37,954	C
Cal State, Bakersfield	CA	8,000	LC
Cal State, Chico	CA	18,952	C
Cal State, Dominguez Hills	CA	17,056	LC
Cal State, Fresno	CA	17,405	C
Cal State, Fullerton	CA	25,188	C+
Cal State, Sacramento	CA	16,200	C
Cal State, San Bernardino	CA	12,000	C
Calvin College	MI	37,585	VC+
Carlow Univ	PA	30,272	C
Carnegie Mellon Univ	PA	51,260	MC
Carroll College	MT	28,000	C
Catawba College	NC	37,105	C
Cedarville Univ	OH	31,036	VC+
Central State Univ	OH	9,010	C
Central Washington Univ	WA	11,730	C
Chancellor Univ	OH	11,000	C
Dakota Wesleyan Univ	SD	23,000	C
DePaul Univ	IL	46,120	VC
Doane College	NE	33,730	VC
Dordt College	IA	34,160	VC
Eastern Mich Univ	MI	17,961	C
Edgewood College	WI	33,294	C
Elizabethtown College	PA	47,600	VC
Elizabethtown College School of Continuing and Professional Studies	PA		VC
Elon Univ	NC	40,046	HC
Evangel Univ	MO	23,090	C
Fayetteville State Univ	NC	10,816	C
Flagler College	FL	24,960	VC
Florida A&M Univ	FL	14,935	LC
Florida Atlantic Univ	FL	17,339	C
Florida International Univ	FL	17,747	VC
Florida Memorial Univ	FL	20,716	LC
George Mason Univ	VA	15,724	VC
Grambling State Univ	LA	13,384	LC
Grand Valley State Univ	MI	17,998	VC
Harding Univ	AR	21,432	C+

School	ST	$IS	SR
Hawaii Pacific Univ	HI	36,690	C
Heidelberg Univ	OH	34,100	C
Henderson State Univ	AR	13,634	C
Howard Univ	DC	35,957	C
Indiana Univ Kokomo	IN	6,674	LC
Indiana Univ-Purdue Univ Fort Wayne	IN	15,425	C
Inter-American Univ of PR/ Fajardo Campus	PR	4,200	
Inter-American Univ of PR/ Ponce	PR	3,700	
Inter-American Univ of PR/ San Germán	PR	6,720	
James Madison Univ	VA	18,049	VC
John Jay College of Criminal Justice / The CUNY	NY	6,059	C
Juniata College	PA	49,340	VC
Kean Univ	NJ	22,060	LC
Kentucky State Univ	KY	11,000	LC
Kutztown Univ of Pennsylvania	PA	16,909	LC
La Salle Univ	PA	50,270	C
Lakeland College	WI	22,990	C
Lamar Univ	TX	6,820	LC
LeTourneau Univ	TX	26,230	C
Lewis Univ	IL	23,050	C
Lincoln Univ	MO	11,996	NC
Lindenwood Univ	MO	20,750	C
LIU/C.W. Post Campus	NY	38,888	C
Louisiana College	LA	15,746	C
Mass College of Liberal Arts	MA	16,733	C
Medgar Evers College / The CUNY	NY	4,920	NC
Metropolitan State Univ	MN	5,923	SP
Miami Univ	OH	24,191	HC
Mich State Univ	MI	13,689	VC
Middle Tenn State Univ	TN	8,650	C
Mills College	CA	54,119	HC
Millsaps College	MS	43,888	VC+
Miss Valley State Univ	MS	9,706	LC
Missouri Valley College	MO	22,200	C
Mount Aloysius College	PA	27,970	C
Murray State Univ	KY	14,944	C
New York Univ	NY	61,470	MC
Norfolk State Univ	VA	10,531	LC
Northern Arizona Univ	AZ	18,592	C
Northern Kentucky Univ	KY	15,302	LC
Northern Mich Univ	MI	15,300	VC
Northland College	WI	26,680	C
Northwest Missouri State Univ	MO	14,229	C
Northwestern State Univ of Louisiana	LA	14,368	C
Nova Southeastern Univ	FL	34,016	VC
Oakland Univ	MI	19,391	VC
Ohio Univ	OH	20,676	VC
Park Univ	MO	17,525	C
Plymouth State Univ	NH	23,148	LC
Point Park Univ	PA	36,390	C
Pontifical Catholic Univ of PR	PR	7,310	
Rhode Island College	RI	17,132	LC
Roger Williams Univ	RI	45,788	C
Roosevelt Univ	IL	22,605	VC
Rutgers, The State Univ of New Jersey/Newark Campus	NJ	25,376	C
Saginaw Valley State Univ	MI	16,869	C
St. Francis Univ	PA	30,029	LC
St. Joseph's Univ	PA	52,272	VC
Samford Univ	AL	35,700	VC+
San Diego State Univ	CA	20,578	VC
Seattle Univ	WA	47,010	VC+
Shaw Univ	NC	15,488	LC
Shenandoah Univ	VA	39,268	C
Shippensburg Univ of Pennsylvania	PA	17,064	LC
Siena Heights Univ	MI	17,000	LC
Silver Lake College	WI	22,600	LC
Slippery Rock Univ of Pennsylvania	PA	10,360	LC
Sojourner-Douglass College	MD	9,160	LC
Southeastern Univ	FL	27,201	C+
Southern Adventist Univ	TN	26,190	C
Southwest Minn State Univ	MN	14,000	C
St. Ambrose Univ	IA		C
St. Cloud State Univ	MN	10,600	C
St. John's Univ	NY	52,840	C+
Stanford Univ	CA	56,411	MC
Stephen F. Austin State Univ	TX	14,668	C
Stonehill College	MA	46,780	VC+
Talladega College	AL	13,000	C
Texas A&M Univ at Kingsville	TX	7,500	LC
Texas State Univ	TX	16,495	VC
Thomas Edison State College	NJ	5,700	SP
Union Inst & Univ	OH	8,912	SP
Universidad del Turabo	PR	4,110	
Univ of Alaska Southeast	AK	11,493	C
Univ of Arizona	AZ	20,105	C
Univ of Arkansas at Fayetteville	AR	16,860	VC
Univ of Arkansas at Little Rock	AR		C
Univ of Central Arkansas	AR	10,840	VC
Univ of Central Florida	FL	15,711	VC+
Univ of Central Okla	OK	12,293	C
Univ of Georgia	GA	19,508	VC
Univ of Illinois at Chicago	IL	24,293	VC
Univ of Kansas	KS	16,980	C+
Univ of La Verne	CA	47,010	VC
Univ of Maine	ME	19,712	C+
Univ of Maine at Augusta	ME	6,855	C
Univ of Mich-Flint	MI	17,547	C+
Univ of Miss	MS	15,482	VC
Univ of Missouri/Columbia	MO	18,201	MC
Univ of Missouri-St. Louis	MO	18,304	VC
Univ of Nebr at Omaha	NE	12,700	C
Univ of Nevada, Las Vegas	NV	17,303	C
Univ of New Haven	CT	47,740	C
Univ of N Dak	ND	14,094	C
Univ of North Florida	FL	15,578	VC
Univ of Northern Iowa	IA	14,776	C
Univ of Oregon	OR	20,872	VC
Univ of Pennsylvania	PA	56,106	MC
Univ of Pittsburgh at Pittsburgh	PA	27,800	HC+
Univ of San Francisco	CA	49,674	VC
Univ of Tenn at Knoxville	TN	20,364	VC+
Univ of Tenn at Martin	TN	13,217	C
Univ of Texas at Dallas	TX	21,046	HC
Univ of Texas at San Antonio	TX	18,372	C
Univ of the District of Columbia	DC	7,244	LC
Univ of Virginia	VA	22,175	MC
Univ of Wisc Whitewater	WI	13,314	C
Univ of Wisc/Green Bay	WI	14,900	C
Univ of Wisc/La Crosse	WI	14,755	VC
Univ of Wisc/Stevens Point	WI	14,043	C
Univ of Wisc/Superior	WI	14,106	C
Virginia Intermont College	VA	32,411	LC
Virginia State Univ	VA	11,318	C+
Wagner College	NY	48,600	VC
Washburn Univ	KS	12,165	NC
West Texas A&M Univ	TX	13,478	C
West Virginia Univ Inst of Technology	WV	14,094	NC
Western New Mexico Univ	NM	8,500	LC
Western Oregon Univ	OR	15,021	C
Winona State Univ	MN	16,630	C
Winston-Salem State Univ	NC	9,418	LC

PUBLIC AFFAIRS

School	ST	$IS	SR
Albion College	MI	43,884	VC
Arizona State Univ	AZ	18,818	C+
Bryant Univ	RI	49,179	VC
Cal State, Chico	CA	18,952	C
Chatham Univ	PA	42,440	VC
CUNY/Baruch College	NY	15,831	VC
College of William & Mary	VA	25,085	MC
Columbia College	SC	27,882	C
DePaul Univ	IL	46,120	VC
Dickinson College	PA	57,662	HC+
Duke Univ	NC	50,250	MC
Emory and Henry College	VA	387,460	C
Georgia Inst of Technology	GA	20,464	MC
Hamilton College	NY	55,620	MC
Howard Univ	DC	35,957	C
Indiana Univ Bloomington	IN	19,358	HC
Indiana Univ Northwest	IN	6,738	LC
Indiana Univ-Purdue Univ Fort Wayne	IN	15,425	C
Indiana Univ-Purdue Univ Indianapolis	IN	17,290	C
Meredith College	NC	31,420	C
Mills College	CA	54,119	HC
Muskingum Univ	OH	30,502	C
New College of Florida	FL	14,504	HC+
Olivet Nazarene Univ	IL	29,990	C
Pomona College	CA	57,680	MC
Rice Univ	TX	43,288	MC
Rochester Inst of Technology	NY	42,450	VC+
St. Vincent College	PA	40,244	C
Southern Methodist Univ	TX	57,755	MC
Southern New Hampshire Univ	NH	38,100	C
St. Mary's College of Maryland	MD	26,699	HC
SUNY/Empire State College	NY	6,315	SP
Stevenson Univ	MD	39,572	C
Texas Southern Univ	TX	18,212	LC
Ohio State Univ	OH	19,887	MC
Trinity College	CT		HC+
Univ of Chicago	IL	55,416	MC
Univ of Denver	CO	51,787	VC+
Univ of Illinois at Chicago	IL	24,293	VC
Univ of Mich/Ann Arbor	MI	22,102	HC+
Univ of Missouri/Columbia	MO	18,201	MC
Univ of New Haven	CT	47,740	C
Univ of N Car at Chapel Hill	NC	18,348	MC
Univ of Okla	OK	17,634	VC+
Univ of Pittsburgh at Pittsburgh	PA	27,800	HC+
Vanderbilt Univ	TN	57,072	MC
Virginia Polytechnic Inst and State Univ	VA	14,629	HC
Washington and Lee Univ	VA	52,812	MC
Wayne State Univ	MI	19,493	C
Wells College	NY	38,680	VC
Western Washington Univ	WA	18,519	VC

PUBLIC HEALTH

School	ST	$IS	SR
Agnes Scott College	GA	45,323	VC+
Allegheny College	PA	49,020	HC
Allen College	IA	26,110	SP
American Univ	DC	54,829	HC+
Andrews Univ	MI	28,030	C+
Baldwin Wallace Univ	OH	36,980	VC
Benedict College	SC	20,454	NC
Bowling Green State Univ	OH	10,970	C
Calif Baptist Univ	CA	35,890	C
Cal State, Fresno	CA	17,405	C
Calvin College	MI	37,585	VC+
Central Mich Univ	MI	18,066	C
Central Washington Univ	WA	11,730	C
Colby-Sawyer College	NH	47,870	C
College of Charleston	SC	21,273	VC
Dillard Univ	LA	20,940	VC
East Carolina Univ	NC	14,169	C
East Tenn State Univ	TN	9,000	C
Edinboro Univ of Pennsylvania	PA	15,940	LC
Elon Univ	NC	40,046	HC
Fort Lewis College	CO	15,513	C
Howard Univ	DC	35,957	C
Hunter College / The CUNY	NY	14,429	VC
Indiana Univ Bloomington	IN	19,358	HC
Indiana Univ-Purdue Univ Indianapolis	IN	17,290	C
Ithaca College	NY	52,300	HC
Kent State Univ	OH	19,352	C
Malone Univ	OH	34,334	C
Marshall Univ	WV	14,820	C
Minn State Univ, Mankato	MN	14,900	C
Miss Univ for Women	MS	7,400	LC
Montclair State Univ	NJ	22,614	C
New Jersey City Univ	NJ	21,060	C+
New York Univ	NY	61,470	MC
Northeastern Illinois Univ	IL		C
Ohio Univ	OH	20,676	VC
Old Dominion Univ	VA	18,662	C
Oregon State Univ	OR	19,017	C+
Regis College	MA	47,565	LC
Richard Stockton College of New Jersey	NJ	20,000	VC
Rutgers, The State Univ of New Jersey/New Brunswick	NJ	25,077	VC
St. Louis Univ	MO	46,594	VC+
San Jose State Univ	CA	19,707	C
Santa Clara Univ	CA	54,702	MC
Shenandoah Univ	VA	39,268	C
Simmons College	MA	48,770	VC
Southern Conn State Univ	CT	18,033	C
St. Cloud State Univ	MN	10,600	C
St. Joseph's College, New York / Suffolk Campus	NY	21,878	VC
Syracuse Univ	NY	54,512	HC
Taylor Univ	IN	36,742	VC+
Temple Univ	PA	24,392	VC
Truman State Univ	MO	13,546	HC
Tulane Univ	LA	58,942	MC
Univ of Alabama at Birmingham	AL	18,484	C+
Univ of Arizona	AZ	20,105	C
Univ of Calif at Berkeley	CA	23,322	MC
Univ of Calif at Irvine	CA	25,961	VC
Univ of Colo Denver	CO	17,904	C
Univ of Evansville	IN	41,056	VC+
Univ of Georgia	GA	19,508	VC
Univ of Illinois at Chicago	IL	24,293	VC
Univ of Illinois at Urbana-Champaign	IL	24,300	HC
Univ of Mass Amherst	MA	23,697	VC+
Univ of Miami	FL	55,166	MC
Univ of Missouri/Columbia	MO	18,201	MC
Univ of N Car at Charlotte	NC	15,847	C
Univ of N Car at Greensboro	NC	12,848	C
Univ of Rochester	NY	58,500	MC
Univ of S Car at Columbia	SC	19,725	VC+
Univ of Tampa	FL	35,160	VC
Univ of the Cumberlands	KY	27,500	LC
Univ of Utah	UT	13,462	VC
Univ of Wisc/Eau Claire	WI	15,430	VC
Utah State Univ	UT	11,803	C
Wayne State Univ	MI	19,493	C
West Chester Univ of Pennsylvania	PA	16,836	C
Western Kentucky Univ	KY	11,000	LC
Western New Mexico Univ	NM	8,500	LC
Winona State Univ	MN	16,530	C
Youngstown State Univ	OH	16,374	LC

PUBLIC HISTORY/ARCHIVES

School	ST	$IS	SR
Arizona State Univ	AZ	18,818	C+
Arkansas Tech Univ	AR	13,164	LC
East Carolina Univ	NC	14,169	C
Northern Kentucky Univ	KY	15,302	LC

PUBLIC RELATIONS

School	ST	$IS	SR
Abilene Christian Univ	TX	38,400	VC
American Univ	DC	54,829	HC+
Andrews Univ	MI	28,030	C+
Appalachian State Univ	NC	12,919	VC
Auburn Univ	AL	20,052	VC+
Baldwin Wallace Univ	OH	36,980	VC
Barry Univ	FL	38,190	C
Belmont Univ	TN	37,380	VC+
Biola Univ	CA	40,320	VC
Bluffton Univ	OH	37,864	C
Boston Univ	MA	54,100	HC+
Brigham Young Univ	UT	12,100	HC
Butler Univ	IN	45,898	VC+
Calif Baptist Univ	CA	35,890	C
Cal State, Chico	CA	18,952	C
Cal State, Fresno	CA	17,405	C
Cal State, Fullerton	CA	25,188	C+
Capital Univ	OH	39,824	VC
Cardinal Stritch Univ	WI	24,054	C
Carroll College	MT	28,000	C
Central Mich Univ	MI	18,066	C
Central Washington Univ	WA	11,730	C
Champlain College	VT	44,850	VC
Chapman Univ	CA	56,019	VC+
Coe College	IA	43,590	VC
College of the Ozarks	MO	5,605	VC
Columbia College	MO	24,578	C
DePaul Univ	IL	46,120	VC
Drake Univ	IA	30,980	VC+
Drury Univ	MO	30,319	VC
Eastern Kentucky Univ	KY	11,161	C
Eastern Mich Univ	MI	17,961	C
Emerson College	MA	50,246	HC
Ferris State Univ	MI	19,698	C
Florida Southern College	FL	38,240	VC
Florida State Univ	FL	15,238	HC
Franklin College	IN	35,885	C
Freed-Hardeman Univ	TN	19,697	VC
George Washington Univ	DC	57,108	MC
Georgia Southern Univ	GA	16,414	C
Gonzaga Univ	WA	44,247	HC
Greenville College	IL	27,012	C
Gwynedd-Mercy College	PA	33,560	C
Hardin-Simmons Univ	TX	23,560	C+
Hawaii Pacific Univ	HI	36,690	C
Heidelberg Univ	OH	34,100	C
Hofstra Univ	NY	48,020	VC+
Howard Univ	DC	35,957	C
Huntington Univ	IN	32,220	C
Illinois State Univ	IL	22,634	VC
Indiana Univ South Bend	IN	15,293	C
Indiana Univ-Purdue Univ Indianapolis	IN	17,290	C
Ithaca College	NY	52,300	HC
John Brown Univ	AR	30,996	VC+
Kent State Univ	OH	19,352	C
Lasell College	MA	42,500	LC
Le Moyne College	NY	42,200	VC
Lee Univ	TN	18,690	C+
Lewis Univ	IL	23,050	C
LIU/C.W. Post Campus	NY	38,888	C
Loras College	IA	37,432	VC
Malone Univ	OH	34,334	C
Mansfield Univ	PA	19,468	LC
Marietta College	OH	42,135	VC
Marquette Univ	WI	43,664	VC+
Marshall Univ	WV	14,820	C
McKendree Univ	IL	29,920	C+
Mercyhurst Univ	PA	40,700	C
Messiah College	PA	39,540	VC
Middle Tenn State Univ	TN	8,650	C
Millikin Univ	IL	37,462	C
Minn State Univ, Moorhead	MN	13,392	C
Missouri Baptist Univ	MO	30,310	C
Montana State Univ-Billings	MT	12,425	LC
Montclair State Univ	NJ	22,614	C
Mount Mary Univ	WI	32,836	LC
Mount St. Mary College	NY	39,540	C
Mount Vernon Nazarene Univ	OH	29,590	C
Murray State Univ	KY	14,944	C
New York Univ	NY	61,470	MC
Northern Mich Univ	MI	15,300	VC
Northwest Missouri State Univ	MO	14,229	C
Northwestern College	MN	24,000	C
Northwestern College of Iowa	IA	34,848	C+
Northwestern Okla State Univ	OK	7,275	NC
Notre Dame College	OH	34,942	VC
Ohio Dominican Univ	OH	38,380	C+
Ohio Northern Univ	OH	42,075	VC
Ohio Univ	OH	20,676	VC
Okla City Univ	OK	33,546	VC
Oswego / SUNY	NY	20,009	VC
Otterbein College	OH	32,214	C
Pacific Union College	CA	28,150	VC
Park Univ	MO	17,525	C
Pepperdine Univ	CA	55,372	HC+
Pittsburg State Univ	KS	12,032	C
Point Park Univ	PA	36,390	C

School	ST	$IS	SR
Pontifical Catholic Univ of PR	PR	7,310	
Purdue Univ/Calumet	IN	14,336	C
Purdue Univ/West Lafayette	IN	20,278	HC
Quinnipiac Univ	CT	53,580	VC
Rider Univ	NJ	45,720	C
Roosevelt Univ	IL	22,605	VC
Rowan Univ	NJ	23,570	VC
St. Mary's Univ of Minn	MN	37,015	C
San Diego State Univ	CA	20,578	VC
San Jose State Univ	CA	19,707	C
Shorter Univ	GA	26,470	C
Southeast Missouri State Univ	MO	14,983	LC
Southeastern Univ	FL	27,201	C+
Southern Adventist Univ	TN	26,190	C
Southern Illinois Univ Edwardsville	IL	17,532	C
Southern Methodist Univ	TX	57,755	MC
Spring Hill College	AL	42,130	VC
St. John's Univ	NY	52,840	C+
Stephens College	MO	34,500	VC
Suffolk Univ	MA	46,548	C
SUNY Plattsburgh / SUNY	NY	18,083	VC
Syracuse Univ	NY	54,512	HC
Taylor Univ	IN	36,742	VC+
Temple Univ	PA	24,392	VC
Texas State Univ	TX	16,495	VC
Texas Tech Univ	TX	14,243	C
Union College	NE	23,270	VC
Union Univ	TN	28,260	VC
Univ of Akron	OH	20,430	C
Univ of Alabama at Tuscaloosa	AL	17,164	C+
Univ of Central Florida	FL	15,711	VC+
Univ of Central Missouri	MO	14,605	C
Univ of Central Okla	OK	12,293	C
Univ of Florida	FL	15,783	HC+
Univ of Georgia	GA	19,508	VC
Univ of Idaho	ID	14,558	C
Univ of Indianapolis	IN	31,740	LC
Univ of Louisiana at Lafayette	LA	6,130	C
Univ of Miami	FL	55,166	MC
Univ of Nebr - Lincoln	NE	17,507	VC
Univ of North Alabama	AL	9,960	C
Univ of Northern Iowa	IA	14,776	C
Univ of Okla	OK	17,634	VC+
Univ of Oregon	OR	20,872	VC
Univ of Pittsburgh at Bradford	PA	21,316	LC
Univ of Rio Grande	OH	8,750	NC
Univ of S Car at Columbia	SC	19,725	VC+
Univ of Southern Calif	CA	56,903	MC
Univ of Southern Indiana	IN	14,657	C
Univ of Tenn at Knoxville	TN	20,364	VC+
Univ of Texas at Austin	TX	44,074	HC
Univ of Wisc Whitewater	WI	13,314	C
Ursuline College	OH	33,198	LC
Utica College	NY	44,734	C
Wartburg College	IA	41,055	VC
Washington State Univ	WA	20,461	C
Wayne State Univ	MI	19,493	C
Waynesburg Univ	PA	29,100	C
Webster Univ	MO	33,990	C+
West Texas A&M Univ	TX	13,478	C
West Virginia Univ	WV	15,794	C+
West Virginia Wesleyan College	WV	26,880	C
Western Kentucky Univ	KY	11,000	LC
Western Mich Univ	MI	19,042	C
Western New England Univ	MA	45,590	C
Westminster College	PA	31,290	C+
William Penn Univ	IA	26,000	C
Wilmington College	OH	29,784	C
Wingate Univ	NC	34,990	C
Winthrop Univ	SC	21,120	VC
Xavier Univ	OH	43,740	VC
York College of Pennsylvania	PA	26,590	C
Youngstown State Univ	OH	16,374	LC

PUBLISHING

School	ST	$IS	SR
Benedictine Univ	IL	35,220	C
Biola Univ	CA	40,320	VC
Emerson College	MA	50,246	HC
Hofstra Univ	NY	48,020	VC+
New York Univ	NY	61,470	MC
Rochester Inst of Technology	NY	42,450	VC+
West Texas A&M Univ	TX	13,478	C

PUERTO RICAN STUDIES

School	ST	$IS	SR
CUNY/Brooklyn College	NY	5,884	C+
Rutgers, The State Univ of New Jersey/Newark Campus	NJ	25,376	C
Univ of Mich/Ann Arbor	MI	22,102	HC+

PURCHASING/INVENTORY MANAGEMENT

School	ST	$IS	SR
Arizona State Univ	AZ	18,818	C+
Central Mich Univ	MI	18,066	C
Univ of Illinois at Urbana-Champaign	IL	24,300	HC
Univ of North Texas	TX	15,628	C

QUANTITATIVE METHODS

School	ST	$IS	SR
Bard College at Simon's Rock	MA	58,963	HC+
Bucknell Univ	PA	58,160	MC
CUNY-City College	NY	19,576	HC+
James Madison Univ	VA	18,049	VC
Univ of Cincinnati	OH	20,199	VC
Univ of Washington	WA	14,722	VC
Whitworth Univ	WA	45,826	VC+

RADIATION PROTECTION

School	ST	$IS	SR
Thomas Edison State College	NJ	5,700	SP

RADIATION THERAPY

School	ST	$IS	SR
Benedictine Univ	IL	35,220	C
Georgia Regents Univ	GA		C
Gwynedd-Mercy College	PA	33,560	C
Howard Univ	DC	35,957	C
Indiana Univ-Purdue Univ Indianapolis	IN	17,290	C
Mount Aloysius College	PA	27,970	C
North Central College	IL	38,343	VC
Oregon State Univ	OR	19,017	C+
St. Louis Univ	MO	46,594	VC+
Texas State Univ	TX	16,495	VC
Thomas Edison State College	NJ	5,700	SP
Univ of Mich-Flint	MI	17,547	C+
Univ of St. Francis	IL	36,490	C
Univ of Vermont	VT	26,120	VC+
Univ of Wisc/La Crosse	WI	14,755	VC
Wayne State Univ	MI	19,493	C

RADIO/TELEVISION TECHNOLOGY

School	ST	$IS	SR
Arkansas State Univ	AR	14,980	C
Ball State Univ	IN	17,850	C
Biola Univ	CA	40,320	VC
Cal State, Fullerton	CA	25,188	C+
CUNY/Brooklyn College	NY	5,884	C+
Columbia College Chicago	IL	30,940	LC
De Sales Univ	PA	42,670	C
Drury Univ	MO	30,319	VC
Emerson College	MA	50,246	HC
Hardin-Simmons Univ	TX	23,560	C+
Hofstra Univ	NY	48,020	VC+
Le Moyne College	NY	42,200	VC
Lewis Univ	IL	23,050	C
Lyndon State College	VT	14,233	C
Marshall Univ	WV	14,820	C
Mount Ida College	MA	30,115	LC
New York Univ	NY	61,470	MC
Northern Kentucky Univ	KY	15,302	LC
Northwestern Univ	IL	37,595	MC
Ohio Univ	OH	20,676	VC
Pacific Union College	CA	28,150	VC
Rowan Univ	NJ	23,570	VC
San Francisco State Univ	CA	18,514	C
Southeast Missouri State Univ	MO	14,983	LC
Southern Illinois Univ Carbondale	IL	21,620	C
Southern Illinois Univ Edwardsville	IL	17,532	C
St. John's Univ	NY	52,840	C+
Stephen F. Austin State Univ	TX	14,668	C
Univ of Arkansas at Little Rock	AR		C
Univ of Central Florida	FL	15,711	VC+
Univ of Montana	MT	13,670	C
Univ of North Texas	TX	15,628	C
Univ of Southern Indiana	IN	14,657	C
Univ of Southern Miss	MS	13,170	C
Vanguard Univ of Southern Calif	CA	35,833	VC

RADIO/TV

School	ST	$IS	SR
San Diego State Univ	CA	20,578	VC

RADIOGRAPH MEDICAL TECHNOLOGY

School	ST	$IS	SR
Alderson Broaddus Univ	WV	28,656	C
Clarkson College	NE	16,300	VC
Howard Univ	DC	35,957	C
La Roche College	PA	34,802	LC
Misericordia Univ	PA	39,840	C
Mount Aloysius College	PA	27,970	C
Oregon Inst of Technology	OR	8,910	C
Pennsylvania College of Technology	PA	25,653	NC
Ohio State Univ	OH	19,887	MC
Univ of St. Francis	IL	36,490	C

RADIOLOGIC IMAGING MODALITIES

School	ST	$IS	SR
St. Louis Univ	MO	46,594	VC+
Thomas Edison State College	NJ	5,700	SP

RADIOLOGICAL SCIENCE

School	ST	$IS	SR
Adventist Universtiy of Health Sciences	FL	16,344	NC
Arkansas State Univ	AR	14,980	C
Armstrong Atlantic State Univ	GA	16,276	C
Concordia Univ St. Paul	MN	27,200	C
Friends Univ	KS	29,100	C
George Washington Univ	DC	57,108	MC
Idaho State Univ	ID	11,908	C
Indiana Univ Northwest	IN	6,738	LC
Manhattan College	NY	44,955	VC
Midwestern State Univ	TX	9,722	C
Missouri State Univ	MO	13,996	VC
Mount Aloysius College	PA	27,970	C
New York City College of Technology / The CUNY	NY	5,769	NC
Northwestern State Univ of Louisiana	LA	14,368	C
Purdue Univ/West Lafayette	IN	20,278	HC
Quinnipiac Univ	CT	53,580	VC
Regis College	MA	47,565	LC
Southern Vermont College	VT	30,740	LC
St. Francis College	NY	34,200	LC
St. John's Univ	NY	52,840	C+
Suffolk Univ	MA	46,548	C
Univ of Central Arkansas	AR	10,840	VC
Univ of Charleston	WV	28,650	C
Univ of Iowa	IA	17,481	VC
Univ of Mich/Ann Arbor	MI	22,102	HC+
Univ of Missouri/Columbia	MO	18,201	MC
Univ of New Mexico	NM	15,300	C
Univ of N Car at Chapel Hill	NC	18,348	MC
Univ of Pittsburgh at Bradford	PA	21,316	LC
Univ of South Alabama	AL	13,510	C
Univ of Southern Indiana	IN	14,657	C

RADIOLOGICAL TECHNOLOGY

School	ST	$IS	SR
Allen College	IA	26,110	SP
Austin Peay State Univ	TN	14,650	C
Avila Univ	MO	26,900	C
Bloomsburg Univ of Pennsylvania	PA	13,598	C
Boise State Univ	ID	12,802	C
Briar Cliff Univ	IA	29,514	C
Cal State, Northridge	CA	28,313	C
Champlain College	VT	44,850	VC
Clarion Univ of Pennsylvania	PA	17,370	C
Clarkson College	NE	16,300	VC
College of St Joseph	VT	30,600	LC
Concordia Univ Wisc	WI	28,980	C
Fairleigh Dickinson Univ/ College at Florham	NJ	42,142	C
Fairleigh Dickinson Univ/ Metropolitan Campus	NJ	40,254	C
Fort Hays State Univ	KS	11,354	C
Friends Univ	KS	29,100	C
Gwynedd-Mercy College	PA	33,560	C
Henderson State Univ	AR	13,634	C
Holy Family Univ	PA	40,030	LC
Howard Univ	DC	35,957	C
Inter-American Univ of PR/ Aguadilla Campus	PR	5,578	
Kent State Univ	OH	19,352	C
LIU/C.W. Post Campus	NY	38,888	C
Marian Univ	WI	30,980	LC
Mass College of Pharmacy and Health Sciences	MA	36,450	SP
McNeese State Univ	LA		C
Minot State Univ	ND	10,915	C
Mount Aloysius College	PA	27,970	C
Mount Marty College	SD	29,638	C
Mount Mary Univ	WI	32,836	LC
Mountain State Univ	WV	14,330	NC
Nebr Methodist College of Nursing and Allied Health	NE	22,872	SP
N Dak State Univ	ND	14,642	C
Presentation College	SD	14,800	LC
Purdue Univ/West Lafayette	IN	20,278	HC
Rhode Island College	RI	17,132	LC
Southern Illinois Univ Carbondale	IL	21,620	C
Univ of Hartford	CT	42,674	C
Univ of Jamestown	ND	24,738	C
Univ of Louisiana at Monroe	LA	12,998	C
Univ of Mary	ND	16,714	C
Univ of Nevada, Las Vegas	NV	17,303	C
Wayne State Univ	MI	19,493	C
William Carey Univ	MS	13,500	LC
Xavier Univ	OH	43,740	VC

RANCH MANAGEMENT

School	ST	$IS	SR
Texas Christian Univ	TX	47,570	HC
Univ of Nebr - Lincoln	NE	17,507	VC

RANGE/FARM MANAGEMENT

School	ST	$IS	SR
Colo State Univ-Fort Collins	CO	20,090	VC
Eastern Oregon Univ	OR	10,400	C
Lake Erie College	OH	35,704	C
New Mexico State Univ	NM	13,955	LC
N Dak State Univ	ND	14,642	C
Oregon State Univ	OR	19,017	C+
S Dak State Univ	SD	14,296	C
Tarleton State Univ	TX	13,489	LC
Texas A&M Univ	TX	16,956	VC+
Texas A&M Univ at Kingsville	TX	7,500	LC
Texas Tech Univ	TX	14,243	C
Unity College	ME	34,054	C
Univ of Calif at Davis	CA	24,482	HC
Univ of Idaho	ID	14,558	C
Univ of Illinois at Urbana-Champaign	IL	24,300	HC
Univ of Nebr - Lincoln	NE	17,507	VC
Univ of Wyoming	WY	13,855	C+
Utah State Univ	UT	11,803	C
Washington State Univ	WA	20,461	C
Wilmington College	OH	29,784	C

READING EDUCATION

School	ST	$IS	SR
Baylor Univ	TX	46,720	HC
Calif Univ of Pennsylvania	PA	14,217	C
Defiance College	OH	30,645	C
Eastern Mich Univ	MI	17,961	C
Florida State Univ	FL	15,238	HC
Georgia Southern Univ	GA	16,414	C
Hardin-Simmons Univ	TX	23,560	C+
Houston Baptist Univ	TX	23,815	C+
Howard Univ	DC	35,957	C
Missouri Southern State Univ	MO	11,910	C
Muskingum Univ	OH	30,502	C
Salisbury Univ	MD	18,368	VC
S Car State Univ	SC	6,700	LC
Univ of Arkansas at Little Rock	AR		C
Univ of Georgia	GA	19,508	VC
Univ of Great Falls	MT	27,970	C
Univ of Mary Hardin-Baylor	TX	31,950	C+
Univ of Rio Grande	OH	8,750	NC
West Texas A&M Univ	TX	13,478	C
Western Washington Univ	WA	18,519	VC
Wingate Univ	NC	34,990	C

REAL ESTATE

School	ST	$IS	SR
Angelo State Univ	TX	15,049	NC
Baylor Univ	TX	46,720	HC
Cal State, Sacramento	CA	16,200	C
Central Mich Univ	MI	18,066	C
Chancellor Univ	OH	11,000	C
CUNY/Baruch College	NY	15,831	VC
Clarion Univ of Pennsylvania	PA	17,370	C
Colo State Univ-Fort Collins	CO	20,090	VC
DePaul Univ	IL	46,120	VC
Florida Atlantic Univ	FL	17,339	C
Florida International Univ	FL	17,747	VC
Georgia State Univ	GA	12,000	VC
Indiana Univ Bloomington	IN	19,358	HC
La Roche College	PA	34,802	LC
Marquette Univ	WI	43,664	VC+
Marylhurst Univ	OR	18,945	NC
Menlo College	CA	49,002	C
Monmouth Univ	NJ	42,252	C
Morehead State Univ	KY	10,900	C
New York Univ	NY	61,470	MC
Old Dominion Univ	VA	18,662	C
Peirce College	PA	12,760	NC
San Diego State Univ	CA	20,578	VC
Southern Methodist Univ	TX	57,755	MC
Syracuse Univ	NY	54,512	HC
Temple Univ	PA	24,392	VC
Texas A&M Univ at Kingsville	TX	7,500	LC
Ohio State Univ	OH	19,887	MC
Thomas Edison State College	NJ	5,700	SP
Univ of Central Florida	FL	15,711	VC+
Univ of Cincinnati	OH	20,199	VC
Univ of Conn	CT	23,744	HC
Univ of Denver	CO	51,787	VC+
Univ of Georgia	GA	19,508	VC
Univ of Illinois at Chicago	IL	24,293	VC
Univ of Illinois at Urbana-Champaign	IL	24,300	HC
Univ of Miami	FL	55,166	MC
Univ of Miss	MS	15,482	VC
Univ of Missouri/Columbia	MO	18,201	MC
Univ of Nebr at Omaha	NE	12,700	C
Univ of Nevada, Las Vegas	NV	17,303	C
Univ of N Car at Charlotte	NC	15,847	C
Univ of North Texas	TX	15,628	C

School	ST	$IS	SR
Univ of Northern Iowa	IA	14,776	C
Univ of Pennsylvania	PA	56,106	MC
Univ of San Diego	CA	53,302	HC+
Univ of S Car at Columbia	SC	19,725	VC+
Univ of Texas at Arlington	TX	10,908	LC
Univ of West Georgia	GA	14,852	LC
Univ of Wisc/Madison	WI	18,757	HC
Univ of Wisc-Milwaukee	WI	18,436	C
Villanova Univ	PA	56,436	MC

REAL ESTATE FINANCE

School	ST	$IS	SR
Texas Christian Univ	TX	47,570	HC
Wright State Univ	OH	16,983	C

RECREATION ADMINISTRATION

School	ST	$IS	SR
San Diego State Univ	CA	20,578	VC

RECREATION AND LEISURE SERVICES

School	ST	$IS	SR
Alcorn State Univ	MS	9,500	C
Aquinas College	MI	33,060	C
Arizona State Univ	AZ	18,818	C+
Asbury Univ	KY	32,038	VC
Aurora Univ	IL	26,870	C
Brigham Young Univ	UT	12,100	HC
Calif Polytechnic State Univ	CA	19,847	HC
Cal State, East Bay	CA	16,549	C
Cal State, Northridge	CA	28,313	C
Calvin College	MI	37,585	VC+
Catawba College	NC	37,105	C
Central Washington Univ	WA	11,730	C
Chicago State Univ	IL	5,482	C
Colo State Univ-Pueblo	CO	13,532	LC
Cumberland Univ	TN	21,220	C
East Central Univ	OK	10,223	LC
Eastern Conn State Univ	CT	20,584	C
Eastern Washington Univ	WA	16,388	C
Emporia State Univ	KS	12,897	C
Ferrum College	VA	27,740	LC
Florida State Univ	FL	15,238	HC
Franklin College	IN	35,885	C
Frostburg State Univ	MD	15,264	LC
Gallaudet Univ	DC	25,380	SP
Georgia College and State Univ	GA	18,216	VC
Gordon College	MA	42,660	VC+
Graceland Univ	IA	28,020	C
Grambling State Univ	LA	13,384	LC
Green Mountain College	VT	33,547	LC
Greenville College	IL	27,012	C
Hannibal-LaGrange Univ	MO	24,490	C
Henderson State Univ	AR	13,634	C
Houghton College	NY	35,740	VC
Indiana Inst of Technology	IN	34,240	LC
Indiana State Univ	IN	16,000	C
Indiana Univ Bloomington	IN	19,358	HC
Ithaca College	NY	52,300	HC
James Madison Univ	VA	18,049	VC
Johnson and Wales Univ/ North Miami Campus	FL	34,368	C
Johnson and Wales Univ/ Providence Campus	RI	34,668	C
Kent State Univ	OH	19,352	C
Kutztown Univ of Pennsylvania	PA	16,909	LC
Lindsey Wilson College	KY	30,470	VC
Lyndon State College	VT	14,233	C
Mars Hill College	NC	22,950	LC
Maryville College	TN	33,150	VC
Metropolitan State Univ of Denver	CO	4,835	LC
Middle Tenn State Univ	TN	8,650	C
Missouri State Univ	MO	13,996	VC
Montclair State Univ	NJ	22,614	C
Morris College	SC	16,006	LC
Mount Olive College	NC	18,426	C
Murray State Univ	KY	14,944	C
New England College	NH	45,930	LC
New York Univ	NY	61,470	MC
N Car State Univ	NC	16,202	HC
N Dak State Univ	ND	14,642	C
North Georgia College & State Univ	GA	8,500	C
Northwest Missouri State Univ	MO	14,229	C
Northwest Nazarene Univ	ID	24,275	NC
Ohio Univ	OH	20,676	VC
Okla State Univ	OK	14,310	VC
Old Dominion Univ	VA	18,662	C
Olivet Nazarene Univ	IL	29,990	C
Oral Roberts Univ	OK	31,734	C
Ouachita Baptist Univ	AR	29,010	VC
Pacific Lutheran Univ	WA	44,840	VC
Pittsburg State Univ	KS	12,032	C
Plymouth State Univ	NH	23,148	LC
Radford Univ	VA	17,132	LC
Rensselaer Polytechnic Inst	NY	59,229	MC
Shaw Univ	NC	15,488	LC
Shepherd Univ	WV	14,996	C
Simpson Univ	CA	28,900	C
Southeast Missouri State Univ	MO	14,983	LC
Southeastern Okla State Univ	OK	7,966	C
Southern Conn State Univ	CT	18,033	C
Southern Illinois Univ Carbondale	IL	21,620	C
Southern Wesleyan Univ	SC	25,600	C
Southwest Baptist Univ	MO	24,710	C
St. Joseph's College, New York / Brooklyn Campus	NY	21,878	C
St. Joseph's College, New York / Suffolk Campus	NY	21,878	VC
St. Thomas Aquinas College	NY	30,000	C
Texas A&M Univ at Galveston	TX	11,258	C
The College at Brockport / SUNY	NY	18,362	VC
Tougaloo College	MS	15,275	NC
Trine Univ	IN	39,400	VC
Unity College	ME	34,054	C
Univ of Central Missouri	MO	14,605	C
Univ of Florida	FL	15,783	HC+
Univ of Georgia	GA	19,508	VC
Univ of Hawaii at Manoa	HI	19,379	VC
Univ of Idaho	ID	14,558	C
Univ of Illinois at Urbana-Champaign	IL	24,300	HC
Univ of Iowa	IA	17,481	VC
Univ of Maine at Machias	ME	10,523	C
Univ of Maine at Presque Isle	ME	15,011	LC
Univ of Memphis	TN	15,094	C
Univ of Minn/Twin Cities	MN		HC
Univ of Nebr at Omaha	NE	12,700	C
Univ of New Hampshire	NH	24,702	VC
Univ of North Texas	TX	15,628	C
Univ of Northern Colo	CO	15,973	C
Univ of Northern Iowa	IA	14,776	C
Univ of South Alabama	AL	13,510	C
Univ of S Dak	SD	15,111	C
Univ of Tenn at Chattanooga	TN	16,883	C
Univ of Toledo	OH	18,464	C
Univ of Utah	UT	13,462	VC
Univ of Wyoming	WY	13,855	C+
Upper Iowa Univ	IA	30,426	NC
Voorhees College	SC	18,126	C
Warren Wilson College	NC	34,888	VC
Wartburg College	IA	41,055	VC
West Virginia Univ	WV	15,794	C+
Western Kentucky Univ	KY	11,000	LC
Western Mich Univ	MI	19,042	C
Western State Colo Univ	CO	16,135	C
William Penn Univ	IA	26,000	C
Winona State Univ	MN	16,530	C
York College of Pennsylvania	PA	26,590	C

RECREATION EDUCATION

School	ST	$IS	SR
Alderson Broaddus Univ	WV	28,656	C
Baylor Univ	TX	46,720	HC
Benedict College	SC	20,454	NC
Campbellsville Univ	KY	27,720	C
Claflin Univ	SC	22,368	C+
College of the Ozarks	MO	5,605	VC
Eastern Illinois Univ	IL	20,502	C
Eastern Washington Univ	WA	16,388	C
Friends Univ	KS	29,100	C
Georgia Southern Univ	GA	16,414	C
Georgia Southwestern State Univ	GA	12,218	C
Johnson State College	VT	16,721	C
Lyndon State College	VT	14,233	C
Messiah College	PA	39,540	VC
Northeastern Illinois Univ	IL		C
Northwest Missouri State Univ	MO	14,229	C
Northwest Nazarene Univ	ID	24,275	NC
Oral Roberts Univ	OK	31,734	C
Plymouth State Univ	NH	23,148	LC
Prescott College	AZ	33,284	C+
St. Mary's College of Calif	CA	53,550	C
San Francisco State Univ	CA	18,514	C
San Jose State Univ	CA	19,707	C
Southern Adventist Univ	TN	26,190	C
Southern Oregon Univ	OR	17,874	C
Southern Univ at New Orleans	LA	1,000	NC
SUNY Cortland / The SUNY	NY	19,117	C
Toccoa Falls College	GA	23,210	C
Univ of Arkansas at Fayetteville	AR	16,860	VC
Univ of Conn	CT	23,744	HC
Univ of Idaho	ID	14,558	C
Univ of Maine	ME	19,712	C+
Univ of Minn/Duluth	MN	18,964	C+
Univ of Nevada, Las Vegas	NV	17,303	C
Univ of New Hampshire	NH	24,702	VC
Univ of Tenn at Knoxville	TN	20,364	VC+
Wayne State Univ	MI	19,493	C
Western Washington Univ	WA	18,519	VC

RECREATION THERAPY

School	ST	$IS	SR
Alderson Broaddus Univ	WV	28,656	C
Ashland Univ	OH	25,000	C
Cal State, Northridge	CA	28,313	C
Calvin College	MI	37,585	VC+
Catawba College	NC	37,105	C
Central Mich Univ	MI	18,066	C
East Carolina Univ	NC	14,169	C
Eastern Mich Univ	MI	17,961	C
Eastern Washington Univ	WA	16,388	C
Grand Valley State Univ	MI	17,998	VC
Green Mountain College	VT	33,547	LC
Hampton Univ	VA	28,528	C
Houghton College	NY	35,740	VC
Huntington Univ	IN	32,220	C
Indiana Inst of Technology	IN	34,240	LC
Indiana Univ Bloomington	IN	19,358	HC
Ithaca College	NY	52,300	HC
Lake Superior State Univ	MI	18,121	C
Longwood Univ	VA	20,924	C
Nova Southeastern Univ	FL	34,016	VC
Pittsburg State Univ	KS	12,032	C
Shaw Univ	NC	15,488	LC
Southern Univ and A&M College	LA	9,761	C+
Springfield College	MA	25,000	C
Temple Univ	PA	24,392	VC
Unity College	ME	34,054	C
Univ of Iowa	IA	17,481	VC
Univ of N Car at Wilmington	NC	13,572	VC+
Univ of Southern Maine	ME	16,576	C
Univ of Wisc/La Crosse	WI	14,755	VC
Univ of Wisc-Milwaukee	WI	18,436	C
Utica College	NY	44,734	C
West Virginia State Univ	WV	8,378	NC
Western Carolina Univ	NC	13,965	C+
Winston-Salem State Univ	NC	9,418	LC

RECREATIONAL FACILITIES MANAGEMENT

School	ST	$IS	SR
Alaska Pacific Univ	AK	33,360	VC
Alderson Broaddus Univ	WV	28,656	C
Appalachian State Univ	NC	12,919	VC
Aquinas College	MI	33,060	C
Ashland Univ	OH	25,000	C
Bluffton Univ	OH	37,864	C
Cal State, Fresno	CA	17,405	C
Carroll Univ	WI	24,860	C
Central Methodist Univ	MO	28,240	VC
Central Mich Univ	MI	18,066	C
Colo State Univ-Fort Collins	CO	20,090	VC
Dordt College	IA	34,160	VC
East Carolina Univ	NC	14,169	C
Eastern Mennonite Univ	VA	38,850	VC
Florida Gulf Coast Univ	FL		C
Florida State Univ	FL	15,238	HC
Glenville State College	WV	11,348	NC
Graceland Univ	IA	28,020	C
Green Mountain College	VT	33,547	LC
Houghton College	NY	35,740	VC
Indiana Wesleyan Univ	IN	31,815	VC
Johnson and Wales Univ/ Providence Campus	RI	34,668	C
Johnson State College	VT	16,721	C
Kean Univ	NJ	22,060	LC
Kent State Univ	OH	19,352	C
Millikin Univ	IL	37,462	C
Missouri Valley College	MO	22,200	C
Ohio Univ	OH	20,676	VC
Oregon State Univ	OR	19,017	C+
Oswego / SUNY	NY	20,009	VC
Pittsburg State Univ	KS	12,032	C
San Francisco State Univ	CA	18,514	C
Shorter Univ	GA	26,470	C
Sierra Nevada College	NV	32,700	VC
Southwestern Okla State Univ	OK	9,160	C
Texas State Univ	TX	16,495	VC
Trine Univ	IN	39,400	VC
Union College	KY	28,775	C
Univ of Iowa	IA	17,481	VC
Univ of Minn/Twin Cities	MN		HC
Univ of Nevada, Las Vegas	NV	17,303	C
Univ of N Car at Chapel Hill	NC	18,348	MC
Univ of St. Francis	IL	36,490	C
Univ of the Sciences	PA	48,320	VC+

REHABILITATION THERAPY

School	ST	$IS	SR
Assumption College	MA	45,721	VC
Boston Univ	MA	54,130	HC+
Cal State, Los Angeles	CA	15,829	C
Central Mich Univ	MI	18,066	C
Clarion Univ of Pennsylvania	PA	17,370	C
Coppin State Univ	MD	14,905	VC
East Carolina Univ	NC	14,169	C
Emporia State Univ	KS	12,897	C
Florida State Univ	FL	15,238	HC
Hilbert College	NY	28,550	C
Indiana Univ of Pennsylvania	PA	20,180	LC
Ithaca College	NY	52,300	HC
Maryville Univ of St. Louis	MO	34,920	VC
Montana State Univ-Billings	MT	12,425	LC
Penn State Univ/Univ Park	PA	25,404	VC
Shaw Univ	NC	15,488	LC
Southern Illinois Univ Carbondale	IL	21,620	C
Southern Univ and A&M College	LA	9,761	C+
Springfield College	MA	25,000	C
St. Catherine Univ	MN	37,782	C+
Stephen F. Austin State Univ	TX	14,668	C
Stetson Univ	FL	49,512	VC+
Thomas Univ	GA	11,520	NC
Troy Univ	AL	10,650	C
Univ of Arizona	AZ	20,105	C
Univ of Arkansas at Pine Bluff	AR	10,600	C
Univ of Florida	FL	15,783	HC+
Univ of Illinois at Urbana-Champaign	IL	24,300	HC
Univ of Maine at Farmington	ME	17,841	C
Univ of Maryland/Eastern Shore	MD	14,000	C
Univ of North Texas	TX	15,628	C
Univ of Northern Colo	CO	15,973	C
Univ of Pittsburgh at Pittsburgh	PA	27,800	HC+
Univ of Tenn at Chattanooga	TN	16,883	C
Univ of Texas-Pan American	TX	12,432	LC
Univ of Wisc/Stout	WI	23,942	C
Western Washington Univ	WA	18,519	VC
Wilberforce Univ	OH	15,100	LC
Wright State Univ	OH	16,983	C

RELIGION

School	ST	$IS	SR
Adrian College	MI	33,800	C
Agnes Scott College	GA	45,323	VC+
Albertus Magnus College	CT	37,382	LC
Albion College	MI	43,884	VC
Albright College	PA	46,660	C
Allegheny College	PA	49,020	HC
Alma College	MI	42,400	VC
Alverno College	WI	30,483	LC
Amherst College	MA	58,744	MC
Anderson Univ	IN	35,390	C
Andrews Univ	MI	28,030	C+
Anna Maria College	MA	34,600	LC
Appalachian State Univ	NC	12,919	VC
Aquinas College	MI	33,060	C
Arizona State Univ	AZ	18,818	C+
Arkansas Baptist College	AR	9,000	NC
Asbury Univ	KY	32,038	VC
Ashford Univ	IA	21,780	C
Ashland Univ	OH	25,000	C
Atlantic Union College	MA	24,600	LC
Augsburg College	MN	35,142	C
Augustana College	IL	43,398	HC
Augustana College	SD	35,500	VC
Aurora Univ	IL	26,870	C
Austin College	TX	36,940	HC
Averett Univ	VA	36,000	LC
Azusa Pacific Univ	CA	39,946	C
Baker Univ	KS	33,350	C+
Baldwin Wallace Univ	OH	36,980	VC
Ball State Univ	IN	17,850	C
Bard College	NY	59,872	HC
Barton College	NC	27,660	C
Baylor Univ	TX	46,720	HC
Belmont Univ	TN	37,380	VC+
Beloit College	WI	49,970	HC
Benedict College	SC	20,454	NC
Benedictine College	KS	29,180	VC
Berea College	KY	7,220	HC
Berry College	GA	39,254	HC
Bethany College	WV	35,282	C
Bethel College	IN	31,560	C
Bethel College	KS	29,100	C
Bethune-Cookman Univ	FL	22,290	LC
Birmingham-Southern College	AL	42,370	VC+
Bloomfield College	NJ	36,960	C
Bluefield College	VA	17,230	C+
Boston Univ	MA	54,130	HC+
Bowdoin College	ME	57,834	MC
Bradley Univ	IL	31,874	VC
Brescia Univ	KY	26,140	VC+
Bridgewater College	VA	39,880	C
Brown Univ	RI	56,150	MC
Bryan College	TN	24,194	C
Bryn Athyn College	PA	27,984	C
Bryn Mawr College	PA	57,760	MC
Bucknell Univ	PA	58,160	MC
Buena Vista Univ	IA	37,954	C
Butler Univ	IN	45,898	VC+
Calif Lutheran Univ	CA	47,640	C
Cal State, Bakersfield	CA	8,000	LC
Cal State, Fullerton	CA	25,188	C+
Cal State, Long Beach	CA	17,534	C+
Calumet College of St. Joseph	IN	15,000	LC

School	ST	$IS	SR
Calvin College	MI	37,585	VC+
Campbell Univ	NC	25,500	C
Capital Univ	OH	39,824	VC
Cardinal Stritch Univ	WI	24,054	C
Carleton College	MN	58,149	MC
Carroll College	MT	28,000	C
Carroll Univ	WI	24,860	C
Carson-Newman Univ	TN	29,058	C+
Carthage College	WI	33,000	C
Case Western Reserve Univ	OH	55,178	MC
Catawba College	NC	37,105	C
Centenary College of Louisiana	LA	39,070	C+
Central College	IA	36,980	VC
Central Methodist Univ	MO	28,240	VC
Central Mich Univ	MI	18,066	C
Central Univ of Bayamon	PR	3,350	
Centre College	KY	35,000	HC+
Chaminade Univ of Honolulu	HI	31,664	C
Chapman Univ	CA	56,019	VC+
Charleston Southern Univ	SC	22,420	C
CUNY/Brooklyn College	NY	5,884	C+
Claremont McKenna College	CA	58,065	MC
Clark Atlanta Univ	GA	30,006	C
Clarke Univ	IA	36,400	C
Cleveland State Univ	OH	21,357	C
Coe College	IA	43,590	VC
Colby College	ME	57,510	MC
Colgate Univ	NY	50,930	MC
College of Mount St. Joseph	OH	33,880	C
College of Mount St. Vincent	NY	41,040	MC
College of St. Scholastica	MN	39,960	C
College of the Holy Cross	MA	56,232	MC
College of the Ozarks	MO	5,605	VC
College of William & Mary	VA	25,085	MC
College of Wooster	OH	52,600	VC
Colo College	CO	54,534	MC
Columbia College	SC	27,882	C
Columbia Univ in the City of New York	NY	61,116	MC
Columbia Univ/Barnard College	NY	39,000	MC
Columbia Univ/School of General Studies	NY	54,083	MC
Concordia College New York	NY	31,500	VC
Concordia College, Moorhead	MN	39,974	C+
Concordia Univ St. Paul	MN	27,200	C
Concordia Univ Wisc	WI	28,980	C
Concordia Univ, Ann Arbor	MI	27,220	VC
Concordia Univ, River Forest	IL	26,300	C
Conn College	CT	54,970	MC
Converse College	SC	37,130	C
Cornell College	IA	44,930	HC
Cornerstone Univ and Grand Rapids Theological Seminary	MI	30,866	C
Culver-Stockton College	MO	30,900	C
Daemen College	NY	31,510	C
Dartmouth College	NH	57,996	MC
Davidson College	NC	54,683	MC
Davis and Elkins College	WV	33,742	C
Defiance College	OH	30,645	C
Denison Univ	OH	54,670	HC+
DePaul Univ	IL	46,120	VC
DePauw Univ	IN	48,950	VC+
Dickinson College	PA	57,662	HC+
Doane College	NE	33,730	VC
Dominican Univ	IL	37,628	C
Dominican Univ of Calif	CA	51,250	C
Dordt College	IA	34,160	VC
Drake Univ	IA	30,980	VC+
Drew Univ/College of Liberal Arts	NJ	55,862	VC
Drury Univ	MO	30,319	VC
Duke Univ	NC	50,250	MC
Earlham College	IN	49,710	VC+
East Texas Baptist Univ	TX	29,135	C
Eastern Mennonite Univ	VA	38,850	VC
Eastern Nazarene College	MA	30,000	C
Eastern New Mexico Univ	NM	10,682	C
Eckerd College	FL	43,902	VC
Edgewood College	WI	33,294	C
Edward Waters College	FL	17,856	LC
Elizabethtown College	PA	47,600	VC
Elizabethtown College School of Continuing and Professional Studies	PA		VC
Elmhurst College	IL	42,032	C+
Elms College	MA	23,900	VC
Emmanuel College	MA	47,985	VC
Emory and Henry College	VA	387,460	C
Emory Univ	GA	45,000	MC
Erskine College	SC	37,360	C
Eugene Lang College - The New School for Liberal Arts	NY	55,650	VC
Eureka College	IL	19,280	C
Evangel Univ	MO	23,090	C
Felician College	NJ	41,640	C
Ferrum College	VA	27,740	LC
Fisk Univ	TN	19,830	C
Flagler College	FL	24,960	VC
Florida International Univ	FL	17,747	VC
Florida Memorial Univ	FL	20,716	LC
Florida Southern College	FL	38,240	VC
Florida State Univ	FL	15,238	HC
Fontbonne Univ	MO	31,384	C
Fordham Univ	NY	58,927	HC
Franklin and Marshall College	PA	58,295	MC
Franklin College	IN	35,885	C
Fresno Pacific Univ	CA	32,136	C
Friends Univ	KS	29,100	C
Furman Univ	SC	54,006	HC
Gardner-Webb Univ	NC	34,375	C+
George Fox Univ	OR	40,750	C+
George Mason Univ	VA	15,724	VC
George Washington Univ	DC	57,108	MC
Georgetown College	KY	38,690	C
Georgetown Univ	DC	52,910	MC
Georgian Court Univ	NJ	39,726	LC
Gettysburg College	PA	56,820	HC
Gonzaga Univ	WA	44,247	HC
Goshen College	IN	35,900	VC
Goucher College	MD	50,252	VC+
Grace College and Theological Seminary	IN	28,800	C
Graceland Univ	IA	28,020	C
Greensboro College	NC	28,740	LC
Greenville College	IL	27,012	C
Grinnell College	IA	53,654	HC
Guilford College	NC	35,340	C
Gustavus Adolphus College	MN	48,170	HC
Hamilton College	NY	55,620	MC
Hamline Univ	MN	44,198	VC
Hampden-Sydney College	VA	48,848	C
Hampshire College	MA	58,320	MC
Harding Univ	AR	21,432	C+
Hartwick College	NY	49,815	C+
Harvard Univ/Harvard College	MA	49,000	MC
Hastings College	NE	27,782	C+
Haverford College	PA	59,236	MC
Heidelberg Univ	OH	34,100	C
Hellenic College/Holy Cross Greek Orthodox School of Theology	MA	33,190	VC
Hendrix College	AR	48,436	HC+
High Point Univ	NC	39,800	C
Hillsdale College	MI	31,890	HC+
Hiram College	OH	37,300	VC
Hobart and William Smith Colleges	NY	43,000	VC
Hofstra Univ	NY	48,020	VC+
Hollins Univ	VA	43,295	VC
Holy Family Univ	PA	40,030	LC
Holy Names Univ	CA	40,310	NC
Hood College	MD	44,630	C
Hope College	MI	36,320	VC+
Houghton College	NY	35,740	VC
Howard Univ	DC	35,957	C
Humboldt State Univ	CA	18,400	C
Hunter College / The CUNY	NY	14,429	VC
Huntingdon College	AL	31,850	C
Huntington Univ	IN	32,220	C
Illinois College	IL	25,770	VC
Illinois Wesleyan Univ	IL	48,452	VC+
Indiana Wesleyan Univ	IN	31,815	VC
Iona College	NY	44,028	C
Iowa State Univ	IA	16,403	C
Iowa Wesleyan College	IA	30,850	LC
James Madison Univ	VA	18,049	VC
Jarvis Christian College	TX	19,552	NC
John Carroll Univ	OH	44,520	C+
Judson College	AL	24,690	C
Kalamazoo College	MI	47,825	HC+
Kansas Wesleyan Univ	KS	32,000	C
La Roche College	PA	34,802	LC
La Salle Univ	PA	50,270	C
La Sierra Univ	CA	35,694	VC
Lafayette College	PA	57,050	HC+
LaGrange College	GA	34,480	C
Lake Forest College	IL	45,580	VC
Lakeland College	WI	22,990	C
Lane College	TN	11,212	C
Le Moyne College	NY	42,200	VC
Lebanon Valley College	PA	38,570	C
Lees-McRae College	NC	33,624	C
Lehigh Univ	PA	55,080	MC
Lenoir-Rhyne College	NC	35,984	C
Lewis & Clark College	OR	52,656	VC
Lewis Univ	IL	23,050	C
Liberty Univ	VA	19,101	C
Lindenwood Univ	MO	20,750	C
Linfield College-McMinnville Campus	OR	46,166	C
Loras College	IA	37,432	VC
Louisiana College	LA	15,746	C
Loyola Univ New Orleans	LA	46,581	VC
Luther College	IA	44,380	VC+
Lycoming College	PA	43,636	C
Lynchburg College	VA	42,645	C
Lyon College	AR	30,246	VC
Macalester College	MN	53,419	MC
MacMurray College	IL	20,755	C
Madonna Univ	MI	24,540	VC
Manchester College	IN	35,070	C
Manhattan College	NY	44,955	VC
Manhattanville College	NY	46,260	VC
Mars Hill College	NC	22,950	LC
Martin Univ	IN	11,000	SP
Mary Baldwin College	VA	37,110	C
Marygrove College	MI	21,290	C
Marylhurst Univ	OR	18,945	NC
Maryville College	TN	33,150	VC
Marywood Univ	PA	40,695	C
McDaniel College	MD	45,600	VC
McKendree Univ	IL	29,920	C+
McMurry Univ	TX	25,962	LC
McPherson College	KS	28,138	C
Mercer Univ	GA	44,201	VC+
Mercyhurst Univ	PA	40,700	C
Meredith College	NC	31,420	C
Merrimack College	MA	44,215	C
Methodist Univ	NC	37,185	C
Miami Univ	OH	24,191	HC
Mich State Univ	MI	13,689	VC
Middlebury College	VT	57,470	MC
Midland Univ	NE	34,000	C
Millsaps College	MS	43,888	VC+
Missouri Baptist Univ	MO	30,310	C
Missouri State Univ	MO	13,996	VC
Missouri Valley College	MO	22,200	C
Monmouth College	IL	39,290	C
Montclair State Univ	NJ	22,614	C
Montreat College	NC	31,298	VC
Moravian College	PA	36,381	VC
Morehouse College	GA	38,640	C
Morgan State Univ	MD	14,500	VC
Morningside College	IA	32,620	C
Mount Aloysius College	PA	27,970	C
Mount Holyoke College	MA	53,596	HC+
Mount Marty College	SD	29,638	C
Mount Mercy Univ	IA	34,385	C
Mount Olive College	NC	18,426	C
Mount St. Mary's College/Chalon Campus	CA	43,897	VC+
Mount Vernon Nazarene Univ	OH	29,590	C
Mountain State Univ	WV	14,330	NC
Muhlenberg College	PA	52,837	HC
Muskingum Univ	OH	30,502	C
Naropa Univ	CO	37,875	SP
Nazareth College of Rochester	NY	41,590	VC
Nebr Wesleyan Univ	NE	29,774	C+
New College of Florida	FL	14,504	HC+
New York Univ	NY	61,470	MC
Newberry College	SC	26,850	LC
Niagara Univ	NY	39,800	C
N Car State Univ	NC	16,202	HC
N Car Wesleyan College	NC	29,440	C
North Central College	IL	38,343	VC
North Central Univ	MN	20,946	C
Northeastern Univ	MA	55,296	MC
Northland College	WI	26,680	C
Northwest Univ	WA	18,854	C
Northwestern College of Iowa	IA	34,848	C+
Northwestern Univ	IL	37,595	MC
Notre Dame de Namur Univ	CA	41,610	LC
Notre Dame of Maryland Univ	MD	27,700	C
Nyack College	NY	32,000	C
Oakland City Univ	IN	24,500	NC
Oakwood Univ	AL	23,035	C
Oberlin College	OH	57,025	MC
Occidental College	CA	59,592	MC+
Ohio Northern Univ	OH	42,075	VC
Ohio Univ	OH	20,676	VC
Ohio Wesleyan Univ	OH	49,460	C+
Okla Baptist Univ	OK	28,202	VC
Okla City Univ	OK	33,546	VC
Okla Wesleyan Univ	OK	21,300	C
Olivet Nazarene Univ	IL	29,990	C
Oral Roberts Univ	OK	31,734	C
Ottawa Univ	KS	15,000	VC
Otterbein College	OH	32,214	C
Ouachita Baptist Univ	AR	29,010	VC
Our Lady of the Lake Univ of San Antonio	TX	22,430	LC
Pacific Lutheran Univ	WA	44,840	VC
Pacific Union College	CA	28,150	VC
Pepperdine Univ	CA	55,372	HC+
Pfeiffer Univ	NC	33,700	C
Piedmont College	GA	29,260	C
Point Loma Nazarene Univ	CA	38,610	VC
Pontifical Catholic Univ of PR	PR	7,310	
Presbyterian College	SC	42,678	VC
Prescott College	AZ	33,284	C+
Princeton Univ	NJ	53,795	MC
Principia College	IL	35,140	C+
Purdue Univ/West Lafayette	IN	20,278	HC
Queens College / The CUNY	NY	17,107	VC
Queens Univ of Charlotte	NC	39,543	VC
Randolph College	VA	43,960	C
Randolph-Macon College	VA	45,086	C
Reed College	OR	57,780	MC
Regis Univ	CO	41,318	C
Rhodes College	TN	47,596	HC+
Rice Univ	TX	43,288	MC
Ripon College	WI	36,959	C+
Roanoke College	VA	47,996	C+
Roberts Wesleyan College	NY	37,384	C+
Rocky Mountain College	MT	32,242	C
Rollins College	FL	52,370	HC
Rosemont College	PA	42,350	C
Rutgers, The State Univ of New Jersey/Camden Campus	NJ	24,254	C
Rutgers, The State Univ of New Jersey/New Brunswick	NJ	25,077	VC
Sacred Heart Univ	CT	48,564	VC
St. Francis Univ	PA	30,029	LC
St. Joseph College	CT	45,630	LC
St. Joseph's College	IN	35,790	C
St. Leo Univ	FL	27,990	C
St. Martin's Univ	WA	38,082	C
St. Mary's College	IN	45,160	VC
St. Mary's College of Calif	CA	53,550	C
St. Michael's College	VT	48,740	VC
St. Xavier Univ	IL	32,840	C
Salem College	NC	29,326	VC
Salve Regina Univ	RI	47,250	VC
Samford Univ	AL	35,700	VC+
San Francisco State Univ	CA	18,514	C
San Jose State Univ	CA	19,707	C
Santa Clara Univ	CA	54,702	MC
Sarah Lawrence College	NY	48,000	HC
Schreiner Univ	TX	32,734	LC
Scripps College	CA	61,000	MC
Seattle Univ	WA	47,010	VC+
Seton Hall Univ	NJ	45,902	C
Seton Hill Univ	PA	35,172	C
Sewanee: The Univ of the South	TN	47,700	HC+
Shaw Univ	NC	15,488	LC
Shenandoah Univ	VA	39,268	C
Shorter Univ	GA	26,470	C
Siena College	NY	43,863	VC
Siena Heights Univ	MI	17,000	LC
Silver Lake College	WI	22,600	LC
Simpson College	IA	36,086	VC
Simpson Univ	CA	28,900	C
Skidmore College	NY	57,926	HC
Smith College	MA	57,524	MC
Southeastern Univ	FL	27,201	C+
Southern Methodist Univ	TX	57,755	MC
Southern Wesleyan Univ	SC	25,600	C
Southwestern Adventist Univ	TX	23,026	LC
Southwestern Univ	TX	45,660	VC
Spelman College	GA	24,650	VC
St. Edward's Univ	TX	44,674	VC
St. Francis College	NY	34,200	LC
St. John Fisher College	NY	39,370	C+
St. Lawrence Univ	NY	53,740	HC
St. Mary's College of Maryland	MD	26,699	HC
St. Norbert College	WI	39,992	VC
St. Olaf College	MN	49,960	HC+
St. Thomas Aquinas College	NY	30,000	C
St. Thomas Univ	FL	32,310	C+
Stanford Univ	CA	56,411	MC
Stetson Univ	FL	49,512	VC+
Stillman College	AL	18,460	C
Stonehill College	MA	46,780	VC+
Stony Brook Univ / SUNY	NY	19,359	HC
SUNY College at Old Westbury	NY	16,324	C
Susquehanna Univ	PA	49,170	C
Swarthmore College	PA	57,870	MC
Sweet Briar College	VA	43,765	C+
Syracuse Univ	NY	54,512	HC
Tabor College	KS	29,010	LC
Temple Univ	PA	24,392	VC
Texas A&M Univ at Commerce	TX	10,496	C
Texas Christian Univ	TX	47,570	HC
Texas Wesleyan Univ	TX	29,886	C
The Catholic Univ of America	DC	52,852	VC
The College of Idaho	ID	31,277	VC
The College of New Rochelle	NY	33,600	VC
The College of St. Rose	NY	26,750	C
The Lincoln Univ	PA	15,154	LC
Thiel College	PA	31,378	LC
Thomas Edison State College	NJ	5,700	SP
Tougaloo College	MS	15,275	NC
Towson Univ	MD	16,000	VC
Transylvania Univ	KY	40,310	VC+
Trevecca Nazarene Univ	TN	30,118	C
Trinity College	CT		HC+
Trinity Univ	TX	44,174	HC+
Truman State Univ	MO	13,546	HC
Tufts Univ	MA	58,780	MC
Tulane Univ	LA	58,942	MC
Union College	KY	28,775	C
Union College	NE	23,270	VC
Union College	NY		MC
Union Univ	TN	28,260	VC

ST = STATE $IS = IN-STATE COSTS SR = SELECTOR RATING

School	ST	$IS	SR
Universidad Adventista de las Antillas	PR	7,360	
Univ at Albany / SUNY	NY	18,674	VC
Univ of Alabama at Tuscaloosa	AL	17,164	C+
Univ of Bridgeport	CT	39,030	LC
Univ of Calif at Berkeley	CA	23,322	MC
Univ of Calif at Davis	CA	24,482	HC
Univ of Calif at Irvine	CA	25,961	VC
Univ of Calif at Los Angeles	CA	25,686	MC
Univ of Calif at Riverside	CA	27,204	C
Univ of Calif at San Diego	CA	21,000	VC
Univ of Calif at Santa Barbara	CA	27,551	HC
Univ of Central Arkansas	AR	10,840	VC
Univ of Central Florida	FL	15,711	VC+
Univ of Chicago	IL	55,416	MC
Univ of Dayton	OH	43,750	VC
Univ of Denver	CO	51,787	VC+
Univ of Detroit Mercy	MI	30,450	C
Univ of Dubuque	IA	30,200	C
Univ of Findlay	OH	31,916	C
Univ of Florida	FL	15,783	HC+
Univ of Georgia	GA	19,508	VC
Univ of Great Falls	MT	27,970	C
Univ of Hawaii at Manoa	HI	19,379	VC
Univ of Illinois at Urbana-Champaign	IL	24,300	HC
Univ of Indianapolis	IN	31,740	LC
Univ of Iowa	IA	17,481	VC
Univ of Jamestown	ND	24,738	C
Univ of Kansas	KS	16,980	C+
Univ of La Verne	CA	47,010	VC
Univ of Mary Hardin-Baylor	TX	31,950	C+
Univ of Mary Washington	VA	19,484	VC
Univ of Miami	FL	55,166	MC
Univ of Mich/Ann Arbor	MI	22,102	HC+
Univ of Miss	MS	15,482	VC
Univ of Missouri/Columbia	MO	18,201	MC
Univ of Mobile	AL	27,870	VC
Univ of Mount Union	OH	35,130	C
Univ of New Mexico	NM	15,300	C
Univ of N Car at Asheville	NC	13,500	VC+
Univ of N Car at Chapel Hill	NC	18,348	MC
Univ of N Car at Charlotte	NC	15,847	C
Univ of N Car at Greensboro	NC	12,848	C
Univ of N Car at Wilmington	NC	13,572	VC+
Univ of N Dak	ND	14,094	C
Univ of North Florida	FL	15,578	VC
Univ of Northern Iowa	IA	14,776	C
Univ of Okla	OK	17,634	VC+
Univ of Oregon	OR	20,872	VC
Univ of Pennsylvania	PA	56,106	MC
Univ of Pikeville	KY	24,750	NC
Univ of Pittsburgh at Pittsburgh	PA	27,800	HC+
Univ of Puget Sound	WA	52,648	HC+
Univ of Redlands	CA	40,500	VC
Univ of Rochester	NY	58,500	MC
Univ of St. Francis	IN	29,810	C
Univ of San Francisco	CA	49,674	VC
Univ of Sioux Falls	SD	22,990	C
Univ of S Car at Columbia	SC	19,725	VC+
Univ of South Florida	FL	13,000	C
Univ of Southern Calif	CA	56,003	MC
Univ of St. Thomas - Houston	TX	36,490	VC
Univ of Tenn at Knoxville	TN	20,364	VC+
Univ of Texas at Austin	TX	44,074	HC
Univ of the Cumberlands	KY	27,500	LC
Univ of the Incarnate Word	TX	35,200	LC
Univ of the Ozarks	AR	22,100	C
Univ of the Pacific	CA	52,146	VC
Univ of Tulsa	OK	45,311	HC+
Univ of Vermont	VT	26,120	VC+
Univ of Virginia	VA	22,175	MC
Univ of Washington	WA	14,722	VC
Univ of West Florida	FL	14,656	C
Univ of Wisc/Madison	WI	18,757	HC
Univ of Wisc/Oshkosh	WI	10,426	LC
Univ of Wisc-Milwaukee	WI	18,436	C
Ursuline College	OH	33,198	LC
Valparaiso Univ	IN	43,040	VC+
Vanderbilt Univ	TN	57,072	MC
Vassar College	NY	59,070	MC
Villanova Univ	PA	56,436	MC
Virginia Commonwealth Univ	VA	18,633	C
Virginia Intermont College	VA	32,411	LC
Virginia Union Univ	VA	18,432	C
Virginia Wesleyan College	VA	28,433	LC
Wabash College	IN	44,160	VC
Wake Forest Univ	NC	51,000	MC
Walla Walla Univ	WA	26,256	NC
Warren Wilson College	NC	34,888	VC
Wartburg College	IA	41,055	VC
Washburn Univ	KS	12,165	NC
Washington Adventist Univ	MD	25,859	C+
Washington and Lee Univ	VA	52,812	MC
Washington State Univ	WA	20,461	C
Washington Univ in St. Louis	MO	58,818	MC
Wayland Baptist Univ	TX	16,058	LC
Webster Univ	MO	33,990	C+
Wellesley College	MA	49,848	MC
Wells College	NY	38,680	VC
Wesleyan College	GA	24,000	C+
Wesleyan Univ	CT	59,844	MC
West Virginia Wesleyan College	WV	26,880	C
Western Illinois Univ	IL	20,130	C
Western Kentucky Univ	KY	11,000	LC
Western Mich Univ	MI	19,042	C
Westminster College	MO	30,490	VC
Westminster College	PA	31,290	C+
Westmont College	CA	41,500	HC
Wheaton College	MA	54,934	HC+
Wheeling Jesuit Univ	WV	34,668	C
Whitman College	WA	54,400	MC
Whittier College	CA	43,416	C
Wiley College	TX		LC
Willamette Univ	OR	56,450	VC+
William Carey Univ	MS	13,500	LC
William Jewell College	MO	31,000	VC+
Williams Baptist College	AR	20,070	C
Williams College	MA	58,900	MC
Wilmington College	OH	29,784	C
Wilson College	PA	27,660	C
Wingate Univ	NC	34,990	C
Winthrop Univ	SC	21,120	VC
Wittenberg Univ	OH	47,766	VC
Wofford College	SC	45,795	VC
Wright State Univ	OH	16,983	C
Yale Univ	CT	55,300	MC
Yeshiva Univ	NY	47,250	VC+
Youngstown State Univ	OH	16,374	LC

RELIGIOUS EDUCATION

School	ST	$IS	SR
Andrews Univ	MI	28,030	C+
Baylor Univ	TX	46,720	HC
Cal State, Northridge	CA	28,313	C
Campbellsville Univ	KY	27,720	C
Clearwater Christian College	FL	23,720	C
College of Mount St. Joseph	OH	33,880	C
Concordia Univ St. Paul	MN	27,200	C
Cornerstone Univ and Grand Rapids Theological Seminary	MI	30,866	C
Dallas Baptist Univ	TX	29,118	C
East Texas Baptist Univ	TX	29,135	C
Georgia State Univ	GA	12,000	VC
Grace Bible College	MI	20,770	C
Houghton College	NY	35,740	VC
Indiana Wesleyan Univ	IN	31,815	VC
Kansas Wesleyan Univ	KS	32,000	C
La Roche College	PA	34,802	LC
Lenoir-Rhyne College	NC	35,984	C
Louisiana College	LA	15,746	C
Loyola Univ Chicago	IL	49,560	VC+
Loyola Univ New Orleans	LA	46,581	VC
Marian Univ/Indianapolis	IN	37,058	C
Mercyhurst Univ	PA	40,700	C
Morris College	SC	16,006	LC
Mount Vernon Nazarene Univ	OH	29,590	C
Muskingum Univ	OH	30,502	C
North Central Univ	MN	20,946	C
Northwest Univ	WA	18,854	C
Northwestern College	MN	24,000	C
Oakwood Univ	AL	23,035	C
Okla Christian Univ	OK	24,975	VC
Okla City Univ	OK	33,546	VC
Oral Roberts Univ	OK	31,734	C
Penn State Univ/Univ Park	PA	25,404	VC
Pfeiffer Univ	NC	33,700	C
Presbyterian College	SC	42,678	VC
St. Mary's Univ of Minn	MN	37,015	C
Simpson Univ	CA	28,900	C
Southern Adventist Univ	TN	26,190	C
Southwest Baptist Univ	MO	24,710	C
Sterling College	KS	27,216	C
Texas Wesleyan Univ	TX	29,886	C
Thiel College	PA	31,378	LC
Trinity Bible College	ND		
Union College	NE	23,270	VC
Univ of Arizona	AZ	20,105	C
Univ of Calif at Riverside	CA	27,204	C
Univ of Dayton	OH	43,750	VC
Univ of Jamestown	ND	24,738	C
Vanguard Univ of Southern Calif	CA	35,833	VC
Viterbo Univ	WI	30,070	C
Wayland Baptist Univ	TX	16,058	LC
West Virginia Wesleyan College	WV	26,880	C
Williams Baptist College	AR	20,070	C

RELIGIOUS MUSIC

School	ST	$IS	SR
Aquinas College	MI	33,060	C
Baylor Univ	TX	46,720	HC
Belhaven Univ	MS	27,170	C
Bethel Univ	MN	34,940	VC
Calvin College	MI	37,585	VC+
Campbellsville Univ	KY	27,720	C
Centenary College of Louisiana	LA	39,070	C+
Charleston Southern Univ	SC	22,420	C
Clearwater Christian College	FL	23,720	C
College of the Ozarks	MO	5,605	VC
Columbia College	SC	27,882	C
Concordia College New York	NY	31,500	VC
Concordia Univ St. Paul	MN	27,200	C
Concordia Univ Texas	TX	23,640	C
Concordia Univ Wisc	WI	28,980	C
Concordia Univ, Ann Arbor	MI	27,220	VC
Dallas Baptist Univ	TX	29,118	C
East Texas Baptist Univ	TX	29,135	C
Eastern Nazarene College	MA	30,000	C
Evangel Univ	MO	23,090	C
Franciscan Univ of Steubenville	OH	27,320	VC
Furman Univ	SC	54,006	HC
Gardner-Webb Univ	NC	34,375	C+
Georgetown College	KY	38,690	C
Grove City College	PA	22,988	HC
Hannibal-LaGrange Univ	MO	24,490	C
Hardin-Simmons Univ	TX	23,560	C+
Houghton College	NY	35,740	VC
Houston Baptist Univ	TX	23,815	C+
Huntington Univ	IN	32,220	C
Indiana Wesleyan Univ	IN	31,815	VC
Johnson C. Smith Univ	NC	25,336	LC
Kentucky Christian Univ	KY	17,622	LC
Lee Univ	TN	18,690	C+
Lenoir-Rhyne College	NC	35,984	C
Louisiana College	LA	15,746	C
Madonna Univ	MI	24,540	VC
Malone Univ	OH	34,334	C
McKendree Univ	IL	29,920	C+
Milligan College	TN	27,510	C
Miss College	MS	21,998	VC
Missouri Baptist Univ	MO	30,310	C
Mount Vernon Nazarene Univ	OH	29,590	C
North Central Univ	MN	20,946	C
Northwest Univ	WA	18,854	C
Northwestern College of Iowa	IA	34,848	C+
Nyack College	NY	32,000	C
Okla Wesleyan Univ	OK	21,300	C
Olivet Nazarene Univ	IL	29,990	C
Oral Roberts Univ	OK	31,734	C
Ouachita Baptist Univ	AR	29,010	VC
Pfeiffer Univ	NC	33,700	C
Samford Univ	AL	35,700	VC+
Seton Hill Univ	PA	35,172	C
Shenandoah Univ	VA	39,268	C
Shorter Univ	GA	26,470	C
Southeastern Univ	FL	27,201	C+
Southern Nazarene Univ	OK	24,354	NC
Southwest Baptist Univ	MO	24,710	C
St. Olaf College	MN	49,960	HC+
Union Univ	TN	28,260	VC
Univ of Mobile	AL	27,870	VC
Univ of the Cumberlands	KY	27,500	LC
Valparaiso Univ	IN	43,040	VC+
Warner Pacific College	OR	25,550	C
Warner Univ	FL	18,000	C
Wartburg College	IA	41,055	VC
Wayland Baptist Univ	TX	16,058	LC
Westminster College	PA	31,290	C+
William Carey Univ	MS	13,500	LC
Williams Baptist College	AR	20,070	C

RELIGIOUS STUDIES

School	ST	$IS	SR
Bates College	ME	58,950	MC
Biola Univ	CA	40,320	VC
Cabrini College	PA	40,859	LC
Cal State, Chico	CA	18,952	C
Cornell Univ	NY	59,037	MC
Dallas Baptist Univ	TX	29,118	C
Dordt College	IA	34,160	VC
Elon Univ	NC	40,046	HC
Fairfield Univ	CT	55,850	VC
Fontbonne Univ	MO	31,384	C
Houghton College	NY	35,740	VC
Indiana Univ Bloomington	IN	19,358	HC
Indiana Univ of Pennsylvania	PA	20,180	LC
Indiana Univ-Purdue Univ Indianapolis	IN	17,290	C
Kenyon College	OH	56,810	MC
New York Univ	NY	61,470	MC
Pomona College	CA	57,680	MC
St. Joseph's Univ	PA	52,272	VC
San Diego State Univ	CA	20,578	VC
San Jose State Univ	CA	19,707	C
Univ of Colo Boulder	CO	22,605	VC+
Univ of Miami	FL	55,166	MC
Univ of Nebr - Lincoln	NE	17,507	VC
Univ of N Car at Charlotte	NC	15,847	C
Univ of Wisc/Eau Claire	WI	15,430	VC
Univ of Wyoming	WY	13,855	C+
Viterbo Univ	WI	30,070	C
Webster Univ	MO	33,990	C+

RESPIRATORY THERAPY

School	ST	$IS	SR
Armstrong Atlantic State Univ	GA	16,276	C
Ball State Univ	IN	17,850	C
Bellarmine Univ	KY	42,950	VC
Boise State Univ	ID	12,802	C
Dakota State Univ	SD	13,811	C
Drury Univ	MO	30,319	VC
Gannon Univ	PA	37,940	C
Georgia Regents Univ	GA		C
Georgia State Univ	GA	12,000	VC
Gwynedd-Mercy College	PA	33,560	C
Indiana Univ of Pennsylvania	PA	20,180	LC
Indiana Univ-Purdue Univ Indianapolis	IN	17,290	C
La Roche College	PA	34,802	LC
Marshall Univ	WV	14,820	C
Midwestern State Univ	TX	9,722	C
Missouri State Univ	MO	13,996	VC
Nebr Methodist College of Nursing and Allied Health	NE	22,872	SP
N Dak State Univ	ND	14,642	C
Nova Southeastern Univ	FL	34,016	VC
Point Park Univ	PA	36,390	C
Salisbury Univ	MD	18,368	VC
Shenandoah Univ	VA	39,268	C
Southern Illinois Univ Carbondale	IL	21,620	C
St. Catherine Univ	MN	37,782	C+
Stony Brook Univ / SUNY	NY	19,359	HC
Tenn State Univ	TN	9,048	C
Texas Southern Univ	TX	18,212	LC
Texas State Univ	TX	16,495	VC
Ohio State Univ	OH	19,887	MC
Thomas Edison State College	NJ	5,700	SP
Univ of Akron	OH	20,436	C
Univ of Alabama at Birmingham	AL	18,484	C+
Univ of Indianapolis	IN	31,740	LC
Univ of Kansas	KS	16,980	C+
Univ of Mary	ND	16,714	C
Univ of Missouri/Columbia	MO	18,201	MC
Univ of N Car at Charlotte	NC	15,847	C
Univ of South Alabama	AL	13,510	C
Univ of the Ozarks	AR	22,100	C
Washington Adventist Univ	MD	25,859	C+
West Chester Univ of Pennsylvania	PA	16,836	C
Wheeling Jesuit Univ	WV	34,668	C
York College of Pennsylvania	PA	26,590	C
Youngstown State Univ	OH	16,374	LC

RETAILING

School	ST	$IS	SR
Central Mich Univ	MI	18,066	C
Chancellor Univ	OH	11,000	C
East Central Univ	OK	10,223	LC
Johnson and Wales Univ/Providence Campus	RI	34,668	C
Marywood Univ	PA	40,695	C
Montclair State Univ	NJ	22,614	C
Mount Ida College	MA	30,115	LC
Ohio Univ	OH	20,676	VC
Purdue Univ/West Lafayette	IN	20,278	HC
Siena Heights Univ	MI	17,000	LC
Simmons College	MA	48,770	VC
Southern New Hampshire Univ	NH	38,100	C
Syracuse Univ	NY	54,512	HC
Texas Tech Univ	TX	14,243	C
Univ of Arizona	AZ	20,105	C
Univ of Minn/Twin Cities	MN		HC
Univ of Pennsylvania	PA	56,106	MC
Univ of S Car at Columbia	SC	19,725	VC+
Univ of Tenn at Knoxville	TN	20,364	VC+
Univ of Wisc/Madison	WI	18,757	HC
Univ of Wisc/Stout	WI	23,942	C
Youngstown State Univ	OH	16,374	LC

ROMANCE LANGUAGES AND LITERATURE

School	ST	$IS	SR
Boston College	MA	58,506	MC
Bowdoin College	ME	57,834	MC
Bowling Green State Univ	OH	18,970	C
Bryn Mawr College	PA	57,760	MC
Carleton College	MN	58,149	MC
Christopher Newport Univ	VA	21,050	VC
Clark Univ	MA	47,020	HC+
Colo College	CO	54,534	MC
CUNY-City College	NY	19,576	HC+
Dartmouth College	NH	57,996	MC
DePauw Univ	IN	48,950	VC+
Dowling College	NY	25,000	LC
Haverford College	PA	59,236	MC
Johns Hopkins Univ	MD	47,492	MC
Mount Holyoke College	MA	53,596	HC+
New York Univ	NY	61,470	MC
Oberlin College	OH	57,025	MC
Point Loma Nazarene Univ	CA	38,610	VC
Pomona College	CA	57,680	MC
Queens Univ of Charlotte	NC	39,543	VC
Rockford College	IL	31,000	C
St. Thomas Aquinas College	NY	30,000	C
Truman State Univ	MO	13,546	HC

School	ST	$IS	SR
Univ of Chicago	IL	55,416	MC
Univ of Georgia	GA	19,508	VC
Univ of Maine	ME	19,712	¢
Univ of Maryland	MD	18,801	HC
Univ of Nevada, Las Vegas	NV	17,303	C
Univ of N Car at Chapel Hill	NC	18,348	MC
Univ of Notre Dame	IN		MC
Univ of Oregon	OR	20,872	VC
Univ of PR Recinto de Rio Piedras	PR	5,750	
Washington and Lee Univ	VA	52,812	MC
Washington Univ in St. Louis	MO	58,818	MC
Wayne State Univ	MI	19,493	C
Wesleyan Univ	CT	59,844	MC
Wheeling Jesuit Univ	WV	34,668	C

RURAL ECONOMICS

School	ST	$IS	SR
Univ of Alaska Fairbanks	AK	13,955	C
Univ of Idaho	ID	14,558	C

RURAL SOCIOLOGY

School	ST	$IS	SR
S Dak State Univ	SD	14,296	C
Univ of Missouri/Columbia	MO	18,201	MC
Univ of Wisc/Madison	WI	18,757	HC

RUSSIAN

School	ST	$IS	SR
American Univ	DC	54,829	H¢
Amherst College	MA	59,744	MC
Arizona State Univ	AZ	18,818	¢
Bard College	NY	59,872	HC
Bates College	ME	58,950	MC
Baylor Univ	TX	46,720	HC
Beloit College	WI	49,970	HC
Bowdoin College	ME	57,834	MC
Bowling Green State Univ	OH	18,970	C
Brigham Young Univ	UT	12,100	HC
Bryn Mawr College	PA	57,760	MC
Bucknell Univ	PA	58,160	MC
Carleton College	MN	58,149	MC
Central Washington Univ	WA	11,730	C
CUNY/Brooklyn College	NY	5,884	¢
Colgate Univ	NY	50,930	MC
College of the Holy Cross	MA	56,232	MC
Columbia Univ in the City of New York	NY	61,116	MC
Columbia Univ/Barnard College	NY	39,000	MC
Cornell College	IA	44,930	HC
Dartmouth College	NH	57,996	MC
Dickinson College	PA	57,662	H¢
Ferrum College	VA	27,740	LC
Florida State Univ	FL	15,238	HC
George Washington Univ	DC	57,108	MC
Georgetown Univ	DC	52,910	MC
Goucher College	MD	50,252	V¢
Grinnell College	IA	53,654	HC
Gustavus Adolphus College	MN	48,170	HC
Harvard Univ/Harvard College	MA	49,000	MC
Haverford College	PA	59,236	MC
Hofstra Univ	NY	48,020	V¢
Hunter College / The CUNY	NY	14,429	VC
Iowa State Univ	IA	16,403	C
Juniata College	PA	49,340	VC
La Salle Univ	PA	50,270	C
Lawrence Univ	WI	46,371	HC
Lehman College / The CUNY	NY	5,778	LC
Luther College	IA	44,380	V¢
Macalester College	MN	53,419	MC
Marlboro College	VT	35,980	VC
Miami Univ	OH	24,191	HC
Mich State Univ	MI	13,689	VC
Middlebury College	VT	57,470	MC
New York Univ	NY	61,470	MC
Northern Illinois Univ	IL	19,768	C
Oberlin College	OH	57,025	MC
Ohio Univ	OH	20,676	VC
Penn State Univ/Univ Park	PA	25,404	VC
Pomona College	CA	57,680	MC
Portland State Univ	OR	18,672	C
Purdue Univ/West Lafayette	IN	20,278	HC
Queens College / The CUNY	NY	17,107	VC
Rider Univ	NJ	45,720	C
Rutgers, The State Univ of New Jersey/New Brunswick	NJ	25,077	VC
San Diego State Univ	CA	20,578	VC
Sarah Lawrence College	NY	48,000	HC
Scripps College	CA	54,900	MC
Seattle Pacific Univ	WA	41,559	V¢
Sewanee: The Univ of the South	TN	47,700	H¢
Smith College	MA	57,524	MC
Southern Illinois Univ Carbondale	IL	21,620	C
Southern Methodist Univ	TX	57,755	MC
St. Olaf College	MN	49,960	H¢
Swarthmore College	PA	57,870	MC
Texas A&M Univ	TX	16,956	V¢
Ohio State Univ	OH	19,887	MC
Thomas Edison State College	NJ	5,700	SP
Trinity College	CT		H¢
Trinity Univ	TX	44,174	H¢
Truman State Univ	MO	13,546	HC
Tufts Univ	MA	58,780	MC
Tulane Univ	LA	58,942	MC
Univ of Alabama at Tuscaloosa	AL	17,164	¢
Univ of Arizona	AZ	20,105	C
Univ of Calif at Davis	CA	24,482	HC
Univ of Calif at Riverside	CA	27,204	C
Univ of Chicago	IL	55,416	MC
Univ of Denver	CO	51,787	V¢
Univ of Florida	FL	15,783	H¢
Univ of Georgia	GA	19,508	VC
Univ of Hawaii at Manoa	HI	19,379	VC
Univ of Illinois at Chicago	IL	24,293	VC
Univ of Iowa	IA	17,481	VC
Univ of Kentucky	KY	19,868	C
Univ of Maryland	MD	18,801	HC
Univ of Maryland/Baltimore County	MD	18,000	VC
Univ of Mich/Ann Arbor	MI	22,102	H¢
Univ of Minn/Twin Cities	MN		HC
Univ of Missouri/Columbia	MO	18,201	MC
Univ of Montana	MT	13,670	C
Univ of Nebr - Lincoln	NE	17,507	VC
Univ of New Hampshire	NH	24,702	VC
Univ of New Mexico	NM	15,300	C
Univ of N Car at Chapel Hill	NC	18,348	MC
Univ of Notre Dame	IN		MC
Univ of Okla	OK	17,634	V¢
Univ of Oregon	OR	20,872	VC
Univ of Pennsylvania	PA	56,106	MC
Univ of Pittsburgh at Pittsburgh	PA	27,800	H¢
Univ of Rochester	NY	58,500	MC
Univ of S Car at Columbia	SC	19,725	V¢
Univ of South Florida	FL	13,000	C
Univ of Southern Calif	CA	56,903	MC
Univ of Tenn at Knoxville	TN	20,364	V¢
Univ of Texas at Arlington	TX	10,908	LC
Univ of Texas at Austin	TX	44,074	HC
Univ of Utah	UT	13,462	VC
Univ of Vermont	VT	26,120	V¢
Univ of Wisc/Madison	WI	18,757	HC
Univ of Wyoming	WY	13,855	¢
Vanderbilt Univ	TN	57,072	MC
Wake Forest Univ	NC	51,000	MC
Wayne State Univ	MI	19,493	C
Wellesley College	MA	49,848	MC
West Chester Univ of Pennsylvania	PA	16,836	C
Western Washington Univ	WA	18,519	VC
Wheaton College	MA	54,934	H¢
Williams College	MA	58,900	MC
Wittenberg Univ	OH	47,766	VC
Yale Univ	CT	55,300	MC

RUSSIAN AND SLAVIC STUDIES

School	ST	$IS	SR
American Univ	DC	54,829	H¢
Augsburg College	MN	35,142	C
Bard College	NY	59,872	HC
Bard College at Simon's Rock	MA	58,963	H¢
Baylor Univ	TX	46,720	HC
Boston College	MA	58,506	MC
Brown Univ	RI	56,150	MC
Colgate Univ	NY	50,930	MC
College of the Holy Cross	MA	56,232	MC
College of Wooster	OH	52,600	VC
Colo College	CO	54,534	MC
Columbia Univ in the City of New York	NY	61,116	MC
Conn College	CT	54,970	MC
Cornell College	IA	44,930	HC
Dartmouth College	NH	57,996	MC
DePauw Univ	IN	48,950	V¢
Eastern Mich Univ	MI	17,961	C
Emory Univ	GA	45,000	MC
Florida State Univ	FL	15,238	HC
George Mason Univ	VA	15,724	VC
Grand Valley State Univ	MI	17,998	VC
Hamilton College	NY	55,620	MC
Harvard Univ/Harvard College	MA	49,000	MC
Hobart and William Smith Colleges	NY	43,000	VC
Indiana Univ Bloomington	IN	19,358	HC
Kent State Univ	OH	19,352	C
Lafayette College	PA	57,050	H¢
Middlebury College	VT	57,470	MC
Mount Holyoke College	MA	53,596	H¢
Muhlenberg College	PA	52,837	HC
New York Univ	NY	61,470	MC
Oakland Univ	MI	19,391	VC
Pomona College	CA	57,680	MC
Purdue Univ/West Lafayette	IN	20,278	HC
Rhodes College	TN	47,596	H¢
Rutgers, The State Univ of New Jersey/New Brunswick	NJ	25,077	VC
San Diego State Univ	CA	20,578	VC
Sarah Lawrence College	NY	48,000	HC
Smith College	MA	57,524	MC
Southern Methodist Univ	TX	57,755	MC
St. Olaf College	MN	49,960	H¢
Stetson Univ	FL	49,512	V¢
Syracuse Univ	NY	54,512	HC
Texas Tech Univ	TX	14,243	C
Tufts Univ	MA	58,780	MC
Tulane Univ	LA	58,942	MC
Univ of Alaska Fairbanks	AK	13,955	C
Univ of Calif at Los Angeles	CA	25,686	MC
Univ of Calif at Riverside	CA	27,204	C
Univ of Calif at San Diego	CA	21,000	VC
Univ of Illinois at Chicago	IL	24,293	VC
Univ of Illinois at Urbana-Champaign	IL	24,300	HC
Univ of Iowa	IA	17,481	VC
Univ of Kansas	KS	16,980	¢
Univ of Maryland	MD	18,801	HC
Univ of Mass Amherst	MA	23,697	V¢
Univ of Mich/Ann Arbor	MI	22,102	H¢
Univ of Minn/Twin Cities	MN		HC
Univ of N Car at Chapel Hill	NC	18,348	MC
Univ of Northern Iowa	IA	14,776	C
Univ of Okla	OK	17,634	V¢
Univ of Rochester	NY	58,500	MC
Univ of Texas at Austin	TX	44,074	HC
Univ of Tulsa	OK	45,311	H¢
Univ of Vermont	VT	26,120	V¢
Univ of Washington	WA	14,722	VC
Wesleyan Univ	CT	59,844	MC
Wheaton College	MA	54,934	H¢
Yale Univ	CT	55,300	MC

RUSSIAN LANGUAGES AND LITERATURE

School	ST	$IS	SR
Brandeis Univ	MA	58,820	HC
Colby College	ME	57,510	MC
Emory Univ	GA	45,000	MC
New College of Florida	FL	14,504	H¢
Oberlin College	OH	57,025	MC
Okla State Univ	OK	14,310	VC
Reed College	OR	57,780	MC
St. Louis Univ	MO	46,594	V¢
Stony Brook Univ / SUNY	NY	19,359	HC
Syracuse Univ	NY	54,512	HC
Univ of Calif at Los Angeles	CA	25,686	MC
Univ of Calif at Riverside	CA	27,204	C
Univ of Colo Boulder	CO	22,605	V¢
Univ of Illinois at Chicago	IL	24,293	VC
Univ of Illinois at Urbana-Champaign	IL	24,300	HC
Univ of Mich/Ann Arbor	MI	22,102	H¢
Univ of Wisc-Milwaukee	WI	18,436	C
Vassar College	NY	59,070	MC
Washington and Lee Univ	VA	52,812	MC
Wellesley College	MA	49,848	MC
Yale Univ	CT	55,300	MC

SAFETY AND SECURITY TECHNOLOGY

School	ST	$IS	SR
Davenport Univ	MI	21,002	LC
Embry-Riddle Aeronautical Univ - Daytona Beach	FL	40,884	¢
Farmingdale State College	NY	18,985	C
Georgetown College	KY	38,690	C
La Roche College	PA	34,802	LC
Lewis Univ	IL	23,050	C
Madonna Univ	MI	24,540	VC
Marshall Univ	WV	14,820	C
Univ of Wisc Whitewater	WI	13,314	C

SAFETY MANAGEMENT

School	ST	$IS	SR
Amridge Univ	AL	6,870	LC
Concordia Univ, Ann Arbor	MI	27,220	VC
Franklin Univ	OH	7,000	SP
Illinois State Univ	IL	22,634	VC
Indiana State Univ	IN	16,000	C
Indiana Univ-Purdue Univ Indianapolis	IN	17,290	C
John Jay College of Criminal Justice / The CUNY	NY	6,059	C
Marshall Univ	WV	14,820	C
Pittsburg State Univ	KS	12,032	C
S Dak State Univ	SD	14,296	C
Univ of Central Missouri	MO	14,605	C
Univ of Houston-Downtown	TX	6,267	LC

SAFETY SCIENCE

School	ST	$IS	SR
Central Washington Univ	WA	11,730	C
Embry-Riddle Aeronautical Univ - Daytona Beach	FL	40,884	¢
Embry-Riddle Aeronautical Univ - Prescott Campus	AZ	40,584	VC
Indiana Univ Bloomington	IN	19,358	HC
Indiana Univ of Pennsylvania	PA	20,180	LC
Virginia Commonwealth Univ	VA	18,633	C

SANSKRIT AND INDIAN STUDIES

School	ST	$IS	SR
Bard College	NY	59,872	HC
Harvard Univ/Harvard College	MA	49,000	MC
Univ of Iowa	IA	17,481	VC

SCANDINAVIAN LANGUAGES

School	ST	$IS	SR
Augsburg College	MN	35,142	C
Augustana College	IL	43,398	HC
Gustavus Adolphus College	MN	48,170	HC
Indiana Univ Bloomington	IN	19,358	HC
North Park Univ	IL	30,130	C
Pacific Lutheran Univ	WA	44,840	VC
Univ of Calif at Berkeley	CA	23,322	MC
Univ of Calif at Los Angeles	CA	25,686	MC
Univ of Minn/Twin Cities	MN		HC
Univ of Texas at Austin	TX	44,074	HC
Univ of Washington	WA	14,722	VC

SCANDINAVIAN STUDIES

School	ST	$IS	SR
Augsburg College	MN	35,142	C
Concordia College, Moorhead	MN	30,071	¢
Luther College	IA	44,380	V¢
Minn State Univ, Mankato	MN	14,900	C
Pacific Lutheran Univ	WA	44,840	VC
Univ of Wisc/Madison	WI	18,757	HC
Univ of Wisc-Milwaukee	WI	18,436	C

SCENIC AND LIGHTING DESIGN

School	ST	$IS	SR
Shenandoah Univ	VA	39,268	C
Webster Univ	MO	33,990	¢

SCHOOL PSYCHOLOGY

School	ST	$IS	SR
Adams State College	CO	13,358	LC
Calif Univ of Pennsylvania	PA	14,217	C
Eastern Mich Univ	MI	17,961	C
Howard Univ	DC	35,957	C
Lubbock Christian Univ	TX	25,518	C
New York Univ	NY	61,470	MC
Southwestern Okla State Univ	OK	9,160	C
Univ of Arizona	AZ	20,105	C
Univ of Georgia	GA	19,508	VC

SCIENCE

School	ST	$IS	SR
Alfred Univ	NY	40,392	VC
Alvernia Univ	PA	39,250	C
Alverno College	WI	30,483	LC
American International College	MA	36,100	LC
Arcadia Univ	PA	33,570	¢
Bennington College	VT	56,990	H¢
Bowling Green State Univ	OH	18,970	C
Buena Vista Univ	IA	37,954	C
Caribbean Univ	PR	10,375	
Cedar Crest College	PA	43,240	C
Central Mich Univ	MI	18,066	C
Cheyney Univ of Pennsylvania	PA	20,372	LC
Clarkson Univ	NY	53,538	HC
Coe College	IA	43,590	VC
Colo Christian Univ	CO	27,500	VC
Concordia Univ, Ann Arbor	MI	27,220	VC
Drexel Univ	PA	51,920	HC
East Stroudsburg Univ of Pennsylvania	PA	16,636	C
Eastern Mich Univ	MI	17,961	C
Eastern Nazarene College	MA	30,000	C
Fairleigh Dickinson Univ/ Metropolitan Campus	NJ	40,254	C
Fordham Univ	NY	58,927	HC
Fort Hays State Univ	KS	11,354	C
Gannon Univ	PA	37,940	C
Grace College and Theological Seminary	IN	28,800	C
Graceland Univ	IA	28,020	C
Grand Valley State Univ	MI	17,998	VC
Grinnell College	IA	53,654	HC
Hampshire College	MA	58,320	MC
Hawaii Pacific Univ	HI	36,690	C
Heritage Univ	WA	17,664	NC
Houghton College	NY	35,740	VC
Indiana Wesleyan Univ	IN	31,815	VC
John Brown Univ	AR	30,996	V¢
Johnson C. Smith Univ	NC	25,336	LC
Keene State College	NH	21,538	C
King's College	PA	41,678	C
La Salle Univ	PA	50,270	C
Le Moyne College	NY	42,200	VC
Lee Univ	TN	18,690	¢
LeMoyne-Owen College	TN	13,100	C

School	ST	$IS	SR
Linfield College-McMinnville Campus	OR	46,166	C
Loras College	IA	37,432	VC
Lyndon State College	VT	14,233	C
Madonna Univ	MI	24,540	VC
Marygrove College	MI	21,290	C
Marylhurst Univ	OR	18,945	NC
Maryville Univ of St. Louis	MO	34,920	VC
Marywood Univ	PA	40,695	C
Mayville State Univ	ND	11,401	NC
Middle Tenn State Univ	TN	8,650	C
Montana Tech of The Univ of Montana	MT	14,650	VC
Morehouse College	GA	38,640	C
Mount Aloysius College	PA	27,970	C
Mount St. Mary College	NY	39,540	C
National Louis Univ	IL	16,915	LC
Northwest Missouri State Univ	MO	14,229	C
Okla City Univ	OK	33,546	VC
Okla Wesleyan Univ	OK	21,300	C
Oregon State Univ	OR	19,017	C+
Penn State Erie/The Behrend College	PA	16,256	C
Penn State Univ/Altoona	PA	11,464	C
Piedmont College	GA	29,260	C
Pitzer College	CA	54,988	MC
Pomona College	CA	57,680	MC
Purdue Univ/West Lafayette	IN	20,278	HC
Rockford College	IL	31,000	C
Rutgers, The State Univ of New Jersey/Camden Campus	NJ	24,254	C
Samford Univ	AL	35,700	VC+
Seattle Univ	WA	47,010	VC+
Sierra Nevada College	NV	32,700	VC
Southern Nazarene Univ	OK	24,354	NC
Southern Oregon Univ	OR	17,874	C
St. John's College, Santa Fe	NM	54,998	HC+
SUNY/Empire State College	NY	6,315	SP
The Lincoln Univ	PA	15,154	LC
Tiffin Univ	OH	30,273	LC
Trevecca Nazarene Univ	TN	30,118	C
Troy Univ	AL	10,650	C
Tulane Univ	LA	58,942	MC
Union College	NE	23,270	VC
Union College	NY		MC
United States Air Force Academy	CO		MC
United States Naval Academy	MD		MC
Univ of Alabama at Huntsville	AL	17,625	VC
Univ of Alaska Fairbanks	AK	13,955	C
Univ of Denver	CO	51,787	VC+
Univ of Findlay	OH	31,916	C
Univ of Great Falls	MT	27,970	C
Univ of Mass Amherst	MA	23,697	VC+
Univ of Mich/Dearborn	MI	9,885	VC
Univ of Mich-Flint	MI	17,547	C+
Univ of N Dak	ND	14,094	C
Univ of Northern Iowa	IA	14,776	C
Univ of Oregon	OR	20,872	VC
Univ of St. Francis	IN	29,810	C
Univ of Texas at El Paso	TX	8,764	NC
Univ of Wisc/Parkside	WI	10,181	LC
Univ of Wisc/River Falls	WI	9,722	LC
Univ of Wisc/Stout	WI	23,942	C
Upper Iowa Univ	IA	30,426	NC
Urbana Univ	OH	21,190	C
Valley City State Univ	ND	12,286	LC
Villanova Univ	PA	56,436	MC
Virginia Commonwealth Univ	VA	18,633	C
Walsh Univ	OH	35,100	C
Washburn Univ	KS	12,165	NC
Washington State Univ	WA	20,461	C
Wayland Baptist Univ	TX	16,058	LC
West Virginia Univ	WV	15,794	C+
Western New Mexico Univ	NM	8,500	LC
Westfield State Univ	MA	18,489	C
Widener Univ	PA	50,368	C
Wilberforce Univ	OH	15,100	LC
Willamette Univ	OR	56,450	VC+
William Woods Univ	MO		C

SCIENCE AND MANAGEMENT

School	ST	$IS	SR
Claremont McKenna College	CA	58,065	MC
George Mason Univ	VA	15,724	VC
Philadelphia Univ	PA	44,160	C
Pitzer College	CA	54,988	MC
Scripps College	CA	54,900	MC
Texas A&M Univ at Galveston	TX	11,258	C

SCIENCE AND SOCIETY

School	ST	$IS	SR
Arizona State Univ	AZ	18,818	C+
Bard College	NY	59,872	HC
Brown Univ	RI	56,150	MC
Butler Univ	IN	45,898	VC+
College of Staten Island / The CUNY	NY	16,778	NC
Northwestern Univ	IL	37,595	MC
Ramapo College of New Jersey	NJ	24,938	C+
Rutgers, The State Univ of New Jersey/Newark Campus	NJ	25,376	C
Univ of Puget Sound	WA	52,648	HC+
Walsh Univ	OH	35,100	C
Wesleyan Univ	CT	59,844	MC

SCIENCE AND TECHNOLOGY STUDIES

School	ST	$IS	SR
Cornell Univ	NY	59,037	MC
Kean Univ	NJ	22,060	LC

SCIENCE EDUCATION

School	ST	$IS	SR
Adams State College	CO	13,358	LC
Alabama A&M Univ	AL	96,100	C
Albany State Univ	GA	8,500	C
Alfred Univ	NY	40,392	VC
Alverno College	WI	30,483	LC
American International College	MA	36,100	LC
Anderson Univ	IN	35,390	C
Andrews Univ	MI	28,030	C+
Appalachian State Univ	NC	12,919	VC
Aquinas College	MI	33,060	C
Arkansas State Univ	AR	14,980	C
Arkansas Tech Univ	AR	13,164	LC
Asbury Univ	KY	32,038	VC
Ashford Univ	IA	21,780	C
Ashland Univ	OH	25,000	C
Auburn Univ	AL	20,052	VC+
Averett Univ	VA	36,000	LC
Baker Univ	KS	33,350	C+
Baldwin Wallace Univ	OH	36,980	VC
Ball State Univ	IN	17,850	C
Baylor Univ	TX	46,720	HC
Bemidji State Univ	MN	13,500	C
Bennett College	NC		LC
Bethany College	KS	30,605	NC
Bethany College	WV	35,282	C
Bethel College	IN	31,560	C
Bethel Univ	MN	34,940	VC
Bethune-Cookman Univ	FL	22,290	LC
Black Hills State Univ	SD	13,562	LC
Blackburn College	IL	21,350	C
Blue Mountain College	MS	13,550	LC
Boston Univ	MA	54,130	HC+
Bowie State Univ	MD	23,990	LC
Bowling Green State Univ	OH	18,970	C
Brigham Young Univ	UT	12,100	HC
Brigham Young Univ/Hawaii	HI	8,614	VC
Bryan College	TN	24,194	C
Buena Vista Univ	IA	37,954	C
Buffalo State/State Univ of Buffalo	NY	15,733	C+
Cal State, Long Beach	CA	17,534	C+
Calvin College	MI	37,585	VC+
Cameron Univ	OK	9,267	LC
Canisius College	NY	45,602	VC
Caribbean Univ	PR	10,375	
Carroll Univ	WI	24,860	C
Carson-Newman Univ	TN	29,058	C+
Catawba College	NC	37,105	C
Cedarville Univ	OH	31,036	VC+
Central Univ of Bayamon	PR	3,350	
Central Washington Univ	WA	11,730	C
Chadron State College	NE	7,400	NC
Charleston Southern Univ	SC	22,420	C
CUNY/Brooklyn College	NY	5,884	C+
College of New Jersey	NJ	25,376	HC
Colo State Univ-Fort Collins	CO	20,090	VC
Concord Univ	WV	13,102	C
Concordia Univ Nebr	NE	26,000	VC
Concordia Univ St. Paul	MN	27,200	C
Concordia Univ, River Forest	IL	26,300	C
Converse College	SC	37,130	C
Cornell College	IA	44,930	HC
Cornerstone Univ and Grand Rapids Theological Seminary	MI	30,866	C
Covenant College	GA		VC+
Daemen College	NY	31,510	C
Defiance College	OH	30,645	C
Delaware State Univ	DE	14,700	LC
Dickinson State Univ	ND	8,550	NC
Dominican College	NY	31,270	C
Dordt College	IA	34,160	VC
East Carolina Univ	NC	14,169	C
East Texas Baptist Univ	TX	29,135	C
Eastern Illinois Univ	IL	20,502	C
Eastern Mich Univ	MI	17,961	C
Eastern Nazarene College	MA	30,000	C
Eastern Washington Univ	WA	16,388	C
Edgewood College	WI	33,294	C
Edinboro Univ of Pennsylvania	PA	15,940	LC
Elizabethtown College	PA	47,600	VC
Elmira College	NY	49,950	C+
Elms College	MA	23,900	VC
Elon Univ	NC	40,046	HC
Eureka College	IL	19,280	C
Evangel Univ	MO	23,090	C
Fairmont State Univ	WV	12,098	LC
Florida A&M Univ	FL	14,935	LC
Florida Inst of Technology	FL	48,290	VC
Florida International Univ	FL	17,747	VC
Florida State Univ	FL	15,238	HC
Franklin College	IN	35,885	C
Freed-Hardeman Univ	TN	19,697	VC
Fresno Pacific Univ	CA	32,136	C
Friends Univ	KS	29,100	C
Georgia Southwestern State Univ	GA	12,218	C
Gettysburg College	PA	56,820	HC
Glenville State College	WV	11,348	NC
Goshen College	IN	35,900	VC
Grace College and Theological Seminary	IN	28,800	C
Grand Valley State Univ	MI	17,998	VC
Greensboro College	NC	28,740	LC
Greenville College	IL	27,012	C
Gustavus Adolphus College	MN	48,170	HC
Gwynedd-Mercy College	PA	33,560	C
Hamline Univ	MN	44,198	VC
Hardin-Simmons Univ	TX	23,560	C+
Hastings College	NE	27,782	C+
Heidelberg Univ	OH	34,100	C
Heritage Univ	WA	17,664	NC
Hillsdale College	MI	31,890	HC+
Hofstra Univ	NY	48,020	VC+
Holy Family Univ	PA	40,030	LC
Hood College	MD	44,630	C
Hope College	MI	36,320	VC+
Houghton College	NY	35,740	VC
Humboldt State Univ	CA	18,400	C
Hunter College / The CUNY	NY	14,429	VC
Huntingdon College	AL	31,850	C
Huntington Univ	IN	32,220	C
Husson Univ	ME	23,386	LC
Illinois College	IL	25,770	VC
Immaculata Univ	PA	43,000	C
Indiana State Univ	IN	16,000	C
Indiana Univ-Purdue Univ Fort Wayne	IN	15,425	C
Indiana Wesleyan Univ	IN	31,815	VC
Inter-American Univ of PR/San Germán	PR	6,720	
Iowa Wesleyan College	IA	30,850	LC
John Brown Univ	AR	30,996	VC+
Johnson State College	VT	16,721	C
Judson College	AL	24,690	C
Judson Univ	IL	25,130	C
Juniata College	PA	49,340	VC
Keene State College	NH	21,538	C
King's College	PA	41,678	C
Kutztown Univ of Pennsylvania	PA	16,909	LC
La Salle Univ	PA	50,270	C
Lamar Univ	TX	6,820	LC
Langston Univ	OK	3,000	LC
Le Moyne College	NY	42,200	VC
Lehman College / The CUNY	NY	5,778	LC
Lenoir-Rhyne College	NC	35,984	C
LeTourneau Univ	TX	26,230	C
Lincoln Memorial Univ	TN	18,144	C
Lindenwood Univ	MO	20,750	C
Livingstone College	NC	17,815	LC
Lock Haven Univ of Pennsylvania	PA	17,587	LC
LIU/Brooklyn Campus	NY	26,500	C
LIU/C.W. Post Campus	NY	38,888	C
Louisiana College	LA	15,746	C
Loyola Univ Chicago	IL	49,560	VC+
Lubbock Christian Univ	TX	25,518	C
Lyndon State College	VT	14,233	C
MacMurray College	IL	20,755	C
Malone Univ	OH	34,334	C
Manhattan College	NY	44,955	VC
Mansfield Univ	PA	19,468	LC
Marian Univ	WI	30,980	LC
Mars Hill College	NC	22,950	LC
Maryville College	TN	33,150	VC
Marywood Univ	PA	40,695	C
Mayville State Univ	ND	11,401	NC
Mercyhurst Univ	PA	40,700	C
Messiah College	PA	39,540	VC
Miami Univ	OH	24,191	HC
MidAmerica Nazarene Univ	KS	28,000	C
Midland Univ	NE	34,000	C
Miles College	AL	16,530	NC
Minn State Univ, Mankato	MN	14,900	C
Minn State Univ, Moorhead	MN	13,392	C
Minot State Univ	ND	10,915	C
Miss Valley State Univ	MS	9,706	LC
Missouri Southern State Univ	MO	11,910	C
Missouri State Univ	MO	13,996	VC
Monmouth Univ	NJ	42,252	C
Montana State Univ-Billings	MT	12,425	LC
Montana State Univ-Northern	MT	12,500	NC
Morningside College	IA	32,620	C
Morris College	SC	16,006	LC
Mount Aloysius College	PA	27,970	C
Mount Mary Univ	WI	32,836	LC
Mount Vernon Nazarene Univ	OH	29,590	C
Muskingum Univ	OH	30,502	C
Nebr Wesleyan Univ	NE	29,774	C+
New Mexico Highlands Univ	NM	9,720	NC
New York Inst of Technology	NY	40,590	VC
New York Univ	NY	61,470	MC
Niagara Univ	NY	39,800	C
N Car State Univ	NC	16,202	HC
North Georgia College & State Univ	GA	8,500	C
Northeastern State Univ	OK	8,615	VC
Northern Kentucky Univ	KY	15,302	LC
Northern Mich Univ	MI	15,300	VC
Northern State Univ	SD	14,021	C
Northwest Missouri State Univ	MO	14,229	C
Northwest Nazarene Univ	ID	24,275	NC
Northwestern College of Iowa	IA	34,848	C+
Northwestern Okla State Univ	OK	7,275	NC
Notre Dame of Maryland Univ	MD	27,700	C
Nova Southeastern Univ	FL	34,016	VC
Oakland City Univ	IN	24,500	NC
Oakwood Univ	AL	23,035	C
Ohio Univ	OH	20,676	VC
Ohio Valley Univ	WV	17,752	C
Ohio Wesleyan Univ	OH	49,460	C+
Okla Baptist Univ	OK	28,202	VC
Okla Christian Univ	OK	24,975	VC
Okla Wesleyan Univ	OK	21,300	C
Old Dominion Univ	VA	18,662	C
Olivet Nazarene Univ	IL	29,990	C
Oral Roberts Univ	OK	31,734	C
Ouachita Baptist Univ	AR	29,010	VC
Palm Beach Atlantic Univ	FL	33,882	LC
Peru State College	NE	8,600	NC
Pfeiffer Univ	NC	33,700	C
Piedmont College	GA	29,260	C
Plymouth State Univ	NH	23,148	LC
Pontifical Catholic Univ of PR	PR	7,310	
Purdue Univ/Calumet	IN	14,336	C
Purdue Univ/West Lafayette	IN	20,278	HC
Queens College / The CUNY	NY	17,107	VC
Rhode Island College	RI	17,132	LC
Rider Univ	NJ	45,720	C
Rocky Mountain College	MT	32,242	C
Rowan Univ	NJ	23,570	VC
Rust College	MS	10,600	C
Sacred Heart Univ	CT	48,564	VC
Saginaw Valley State Univ	MI	16,869	C
St. Augustine's Univ	NC	14,000	C
St. Mary-of-the-Woods College	IN	37,722	LC
St. Mary's Univ	TX	33,854	C
St. Michael's College	VT	48,740	VC
St. Vincent College	PA	40,244	C
St. Xavier Univ	IL	32,840	C
Salem State College	MA	13,161	LC
Schreiner Univ	TX	32,734	LC
Seattle Pacific Univ	WA	41,559	VC+
Seton Hill Univ	PA	35,172	C
Shaw Univ	NC	15,488	LC
Shepherd Univ	WV	14,996	C
Slippery Rock Univ of Pennsylvania	PA	10,360	LC
Southeast Missouri State Univ	MO	14,983	LC
Southeastern Okla State Univ	OK	7,966	C
Southern Arkansas Univ	AR	14,316	C
Southern Conn State Univ	CT	18,033	C
Southern Illinois Univ Edwardsville	IL	17,532	C
Southern Nazarene Univ	OK	24,354	NC
Southern Univ at New Orleans	LA	1,000	NC
Southwest Minn State Univ	MN	14,000	C
Southwestern Okla State Univ	OK	9,160	C
Springfield College	MA	25,000	C
St. Cloud State Univ	MN	10,600	C
St. Edward's Univ	TX	44,674	VC
St. John Fisher College	NY	39,370	C+
St. John's Univ	NY	52,840	C+
St. Thomas Aquinas College	NY	30,000	C
SUNY / College of Environmental Science and Forestry	NY	18,351	HC
Suffolk Univ	MA	46,548	C
SUNY College at Old Westbury	NY	16,324	C
SUNY Fredonia / The SUNY at Fredonia	NY	18,702	VC
SUNY New Paltz	NY	15,010	C
SUNY Oneonta / SUNY	NY	16,919	VC
Syracuse Univ	NY	54,512	HC
Tabor College	KS	29,010	LC
Taylor Univ	IN	36,742	VC+

ST = STATE **$IS** = IN-STATE COSTS **SR** = SELECTOR RATING

School	ST	$IS	SR
Texas A&M Univ at Commerce	TX	10,496	C
Texas Christian Univ	TX	47,570	HC
Texas Tech Univ	TX	14,243	C
The College of St. Rose	NY	26,750	C
Toccoa Falls College	GA	23,210	C
Tougaloo College	MS	15,275	NC
Trevecca Nazarene Univ	TN	30,118	C
Trine Univ	IN	39,400	VC
Troy Univ	AL	10,650	C
Union College	KY	28,775	C
Universidad del Turabo	PR	4,110	
Univ of Arizona	AZ	20,105	C
Univ of Arkansas at Pine Bluff	AR	10,600	C
Univ of Calif at San Diego	CA	21,000	VC
Univ of Central Arkansas	AR	10,840	VC
Univ of Central Florida	FL	15,711	VC+
Univ of Central Missouri	MO	14,605	C
Univ of Central Okla	OK	12,293	C
Univ of Charleston	WV	28,650	C
Univ of Cincinnati	OH	20,199	VC
Univ of Conn	CT	23,744	HC
Univ of Delaware	DE	22,728	VC
Univ of Evansville	IN	41,056	VC+
Univ of Georgia	GA	19,508	VC
Univ of Great Falls	MT	27,970	C
Univ of Idaho	ID	14,558	C
Univ of Illinois at Urbana-Champaign	IL	24,300	HC
Univ of Indianapolis	IN	31,740	LC
Univ of Iowa	IA	17,481	VC
Univ of Kentucky	KY	19,868	C
Univ of Louisiana at Lafayette	LA	6,130	C
Univ of Louisville	KY	17,460	VC
Univ of Mary Hardin-Baylor	TX	31,950	C+
Univ of Maryland/Eastern Shore	MD	14,000	C
Univ of Mich/Dearborn	MI	9,885	VC
Univ of Minn/Duluth	MN	18,964	C+
Univ of Minn/Twin Cities	MN		HC
Univ of Miss	MS	15,482	VC
Univ of Missouri/Columbia	MO	18,201	MC
Univ of Montana	MT	13,670	C
Univ of Montana-Western	MT	9,753	LC
Univ of Nebr - Lincoln	NE	17,507	VC
Univ of Nebr at Kearney	NE	14,855	LC
Univ of New Hampshire	NH	24,702	VC
Univ of New Haven	CT	47,740	C
Univ of North Alabama	AL	9,960	C
Univ of N Car at Charlotte	NC	15,847	C
Univ of N Car at Greensboro	NC	12,848	C
Univ of North Florida	FL	15,578	VC
Univ of Northern Colo	CO	15,973	C
Univ of Northern Iowa	IA	14,776	C
Univ of Notre Dame	IN		MC
Univ of Okla	OK	17,634	VC+
Univ of Pittsburgh at Bradford	PA	21,316	LC
Univ of Pittsburgh at Johnstown	PA	20,862	LC
Univ of Rio Grande	OH	8,750	NC
Univ of St. Francis	IN	29,810	C
Univ of Sioux Falls	SD	22,990	C
Univ of South Florida	FL	13,000	C
Univ of Southern Indiana	IN	14,657	C
Univ of Southern Miss	MS	13,170	C
Univ of the Cumberlands	KY	27,500	LC
Univ of Toledo	OH	18,464	C
Univ of Vermont	VT	26,120	VC+
Univ of West Alabama	AL	9,415	C
Univ of Wisc Whitewater	WI	13,314	C
Univ of Wisc/Eau Claire	WI	15,430	VC
Univ of Wisc/La Crosse	WI	14,755	VC
Univ of Wisc/Oshkosh	WI	10,426	LC
Univ of Wisc/Stout	WI	23,942	C
Univ of Wisc/Superior	WI	14,106	C
Utah State Univ	UT	11,803	C
Valparaiso Univ	IN	43,040	VC+
Vanguard Univ of Southern Calif	CA	35,833	VC
Victory Univ	TN	19,118	C
Virginia Polytechnic Inst and State Univ	VA	14,629	HC
Viterbo Univ	WI	30,070	C
Warner Univ	FL	18,000	C
Wartburg College	IA	41,055	VC
Washington State Univ	WA	20,461	C
Washington Univ in St. Louis	MO	58,818	MC
Wayne State College	NE	11,764	NC
Wayne State Univ	MI	19,493	C
West Chester Univ of Pennsylvania	PA	16,836	C
West Liberty Univ	WV	9,142	LC
West Texas A&M Univ	TX	13,478	C
Western Carolina Univ	NC	13,965	C+
Western New Mexico Univ	NM	8,500	LC
Western State Colo Univ	CO	16,135	C
Western Washington Univ	WA	18,519	VC
Wheeling Jesuit Univ	WV	34,668	C
Whitworth Univ	WA	45,826	VC+
Widener Univ	PA	50,368	C
William Penn Univ	IA	26,000	C
Wilmington College	OH	29,784	C
Wingate Univ	NC	34,990	C
Winona State Univ	MN	16,530	C
Wittenberg Univ	OH	47,766	VC
Wright State Univ	OH	16,983	C
Xavier Univ	OH	43,740	VC
Xavier Univ of Louisiana	LA	25,300	C
York College	NE	19,475	C
York College of Pennsylvania	PA	26,590	C

SCIENCE OF EARTH SYSTEMS

School	ST	$IS	SR
Cornell Univ	NY	59,037	MC
Univ of Illinois at Chicago	IL	24,293	VC

SCIENCE OF NATURAL AND ENVIRONMENTAL SYSTEMS

School	ST	$IS	SR
Cornell Univ	NY	59,037	MC

SCIENCE TECHNOLOGY

School	ST	$IS	SR
Arizona State Univ	AZ	18,818	C+
Colby College	ME	57,510	MC
James Madison Univ	VA	18,049	VC
Lehigh Univ	PA	55,080	MC
Marshall Univ	WV	14,820	C
Mass Inst of Technology	MA	54,238	MC
Rensselaer Polytechnic Inst	NY	59,229	MC
Scripps College	CA	54,900	MC
Stevens Inst of Technology	NJ	50,130	HC
Univ of Pennsylvania	PA	56,106	MC

SCIENTIFIC/MEDICAL MARKETING

School	ST	$IS	SR
Carlow Univ	PA	30,272	C

SCULPTURE

School	ST	$IS	SR
Adams State College	CO	13,358	LC
Aquinas College	MI	33,060	C
Art Academy of Cincinnati	OH	25,940	SP
Bennington College	VT	56,990	HC+
Birmingham-Southern College	AL	42,370	VC+
Boston Univ	MA	54,130	HC+
Buffalo State/State Univ of Buffalo	NY	15,733	C+
Calif College of the Arts	CA	48,334	SP
Cal State, San Bernardino	CA	12,000	C
Cleveland Inst of Art	OH	48,641	SP
College for Creative Studies	MI		SP
College of Visual Arts - School is Closed	MN	24,310	SP
Escuela de Artes Plasticas de PR	PR	2,660	
Ferris State Univ	MI	19,698	C
Howard Univ	DC	35,957	C
Indiana Univ Bloomington	IN	19,358	HC
Indiana Univ South Bend	IN	15,293	C
Indiana Univ-Purdue Univ Fort Wayne	IN	15,425	C
Indiana Univ-Purdue Univ Indianapolis	IN	17,290	C
Kansas City Art Inst	MO	38,000	SP
Kendall College of Art and Design of Ferris State Univ	MI	21,048	SP
Kutztown Univ of Pennsylvania	PA	16,909	LC
Maine College of Art	ME	28,812	SP
Marshall Univ	WV	14,820	C
Maryland Inst College of Art	MD	39,500	SP
Marywood Univ	PA	40,695	C
Mass College of Art and Design	MA	23,600	SP
Milwaukee Inst of Art and Design	WI	31,938	SP
Minneapolis College of Art and Design	MN	36,700	SP
Montserrat College of Art	MA	31,000	SP
Moore College of Art and Design	PA	38,124	SP
Ohio Univ	OH	20,676	VC
Pacific Northwest College of Art	OR	38,494	SP
Providence College	RI	55,995	HC
Rhode Island School of Design	RI	55,204	SP
Ringling College of Art and Design	FL	46,130	SP
Rochester Inst of Technology	NY	42,450	VC+
San Francisco Art Inst	CA	52,492	SP
Santa Fe Univ of Art and Design	NM	39,666	SP
Savannah College of Art and Design	GA	46,824	SP
School of the Art Inst of Chicago	IL	44,000	SP
SUNY New Paltz	NY	15,010	C
Syracuse Univ	NY	54,512	HC
Temple Univ	PA	24,392	VC
Texas Christian Univ	TX	47,570	HC
Univ of Dallas	TX	43,510	VC+
Univ of Hartford	CT	42,674	C
Univ of Illinois at Chicago	IL	24,293	VC
Univ of Illinois at Urbana-Champaign	IL	24,300	HC
Univ of Iowa	IA	17,481	VC
Univ of Kansas	KS	16,980	C+
Univ of Mass Dartmouth	MA	22,223	C
Univ of Miami	FL	55,166	MC
Univ of Mich/Ann Arbor	MI	22,102	HC+
Univ of Oregon	OR	20,872	VC
Univ of the Arts	PA	38,450	SP
Univ of Washington	WA	14,722	VC
Virginia Commonwealth Univ	VA	18,633	C
Washington Univ in St. Louis	MO	58,818	MC
Webster Univ	MO	33,990	C+
Western Washington Univ	WA	18,519	VC

SECONDARY EDUCATION

School	ST	$IS	SR
Abilene Christian Univ	TX	38,400	VC
Adams State College	CO	13,358	LC
Adrian College	MI	33,800	C
Alabama A&M Univ	AL	96,100	C
Alabama State Univ	AL	14,142	NC
Albright College	PA	46,660	C
Alderson Broaddus Univ	WV	28,656	C
Alfred Univ	NY	40,392	VC
Alice Lloyd College	KY	4,900	C
Alma College	MI	42,400	VC
Alvernia Univ	PA	39,250	C
Alverno College	WI	30,483	LC
American International College	MA	36,100	LC
American Univ	DC	54,829	HC+
Andrews Univ	MI	28,030	C+
Appalachian State Univ	NC	12,919	VC
Aquinas College	MI	33,060	C
Aquinas College	TN	29,250	C+
Arcadia Univ	PA	33,570	C+
Arizona State Univ	AZ	18,818	C+
Armstrong Atlantic State Univ	GA	16,276	C
Asbury Univ	KY	32,038	VC
Ashland Univ	OH	25,000	C
Auburn Univ	AL	20,052	VC+
Auburn Univ at Montgomery	AL	12,120	C
Augsburg College	MN	35,142	C
Augustana College	IL	43,398	HC
Aurora Univ	IL	26,870	C
Averett Univ	VA	36,000	LC
Baker Univ	KS	33,350	C+
Baylor Univ	TX	46,720	HC
Bemidji State Univ	MN	13,500	C
Benedictine College	KS	29,180	VC
Bennington College	VT	56,990	HC+
Bethany College	KS	30,605	NC
Bethany College	WV	35,282	C
Bethel College	IN	31,560	C
Bethel Univ	MN	34,940	VC
Birmingham-Southern College	AL	42,370	VC+
Black Hills State Univ	SD	13,562	LC
Blackburn College	IL	21,350	C
Bloomsburg Univ of Pennsylvania	PA	13,598	C
Blue Mountain College	MS	13,550	LC
Bluefield College	VA	17,230	C+
Boise State Univ	ID	12,802	C
Boston College	MA	58,506	MC
Bowling Green State Univ	OH	18,970	C
Briar Cliff Univ	IA	29,514	C
Bucknell Univ	PA	58,160	MC
Buena Vista Univ	IA	37,954	C
Buffalo State/State Univ of Buffalo	NY	15,733	C+
Butler Univ	IN	45,898	VC+
Cabrini College	PA	40,859	LC
Calif Univ of Pennsylvania	PA	14,217	C
Calumet College of St. Joseph	IN	15,000	LC
Calvin College	MI	37,585	VC+
Capital Univ	OH	39,824	VC
Cardinal Stritch Univ	WI	24,054	C
Caribbean Univ	PR	10,375	
Carlow Univ	PA	30,272	C
Carroll College	MT	28,000	C
Carson-Newman Univ	TN	29,058	C+
Carthage College	WI	33,000	C
Centenary College	NJ	38,618	LC
Central State Univ	OH	9,010	C
Central Univ of Bayamon	PR	3,350	
Central Washington Univ	WA	11,730	C
Chadron State College	NE	7,400	NC
Chaminade Univ of Honolulu	HI	31,664	C
Champlain College	VT	44,850	VC
Chicago State Univ	IL	5,482	C
Citadel, The	SC		C
CUNY/Brooklyn College	NY	5,884	C+
Clarion Univ of Pennsylvania	PA	17,370	C
Clarke Univ	IA	36,400	C
Clearwater Christian College	FL	23,720	C
Clemson Univ	SC	19,136	HC
Cleveland State Univ	OH	21,357	C
Coe College	IA	43,590	VC
College of Staten Island / The CUNY	NY	16,778	NC
College of Charleston	SC	21,273	VC
College of St Joseph	VT	30,600	LC
College of the Ozarks	MO	5,605	VC
Colo Christian Univ	CO	27,500	VC
Columbia College	MO	24,578	C
Columbus State Univ	GA	13,176	C
Concord Univ	WV	13,102	C
Concordia College, Moorhead	MN	39,974	C+
Concordia Univ	OR	34,930	C
Concordia Univ Nebr	NE	26,000	VC
Concordia Univ St. Paul	MN	27,200	C
Concordia Univ Texas	TX	23,640	C
Concordia Univ Wisc	WI	28,980	C
Concordia Univ, Ann Arbor	MI	27,220	VC
Concordia Univ, River Forest	IL	26,300	C
Converse College	SC	37,130	C
Cornell College	IA	44,930	HC
Cornerstone Univ and Grand Rapids Theological Seminary	MI	30,866	C
Creighton Univ	NE	44,058	VC+
Cumberland Univ	TN	21,220	C
CUNY-City College	NY	19,576	HC+
Dakota State Univ	SD	13,811	C
Davis and Elkins College	WV	33,742	C
Defiance College	OH	30,645	C
Delaware Valley College	PA	29,944	C
DePaul Univ	IL	46,120	VC
Dickinson State Univ	ND	8,550	NC
Dominican College	NY	31,270	C
Dominican Univ	IL	37,628	C
Dordt College	IA	34,160	VC
Dowling College	NY	25,000	LC
Drake Univ	IA	30,980	VC+
Drury Univ	MO	30,319	VC
Duquesne Univ	PA	42,017	VC
East Stroudsburg Univ of Pennsylvania	PA	16,636	C
East Texas Baptist Univ	TX	29,135	C
Eastern Kentucky Univ	KY	11,161	C
Eastern Mennonite Univ	VA	38,850	VC
Eastern Mich Univ	MI	17,961	C
Eastern Washington Univ	WA	16,388	C
Edinboro Univ of Pennsylvania	PA	15,940	LC
Elizabethtown College	PA	47,600	VC
Elmhurst College	IL	42,032	C+
Elmira College	NY	49,950	C+
Elms College	MA	23,900	VC
Elon Univ	NC	40,046	HC
Emmanuel College	MA	47,985	VC
Emporia State Univ	KS	12,897	C
Eureka College	IL	19,280	C
Evangel Univ	MO	23,090	C
Fairmont State Univ	WV	12,098	LC
Faulkner Univ	AL	22,530	LC
Fayetteville State Univ	NC	10,816	C
Felician College	NJ	41,640	C
Fitchburg State Univ	MA	17,241	C
Flagler College	FL	24,960	VC
Florida Gulf Coast Univ	FL		C
Florida Memorial Univ	FL	20,716	LC
Florida Southern College	FL	38,240	VC
Fontbonne Univ	MO	31,384	C
Fort Valley State Univ	GA	11,200	VC
Franklin College	IN	35,885	C
Franklin Pierce Univ	NH	41,598	C
Freed-Hardeman Univ	TN	19,697	VC
Friends Univ	KS	29,100	C
Gallaudet Univ	DC	25,380	SP
Gannon Univ	PA	37,940	C
Gardner-Webb Univ	NC	34,375	C+
Georgia Southwestern State Univ	GA	12,218	C
Gettysburg College	PA	56,820	HC
Glenville State College	WV	11,348	NC
Goddard College	VT	16,418	VC
Gordon College	MA	42,660	VC+
Goshen College	IN	35,900	VC
Grace Bible College	MI	20,770	C
Grambling State Univ	LA	13,384	LC
Grand Canyon Univ	AZ	24,540	VC
Grand Valley State Univ	MI	17,998	VC
Grand View Univ	IA	31,050	C
Green Mountain College	VT	33,547	LC
Greensboro College	NC	28,740	LC
Gustavus Adolphus College	MN	48,170	HC
Gwynedd-Mercy College	PA	33,560	C
Hamline Univ	MN	44,198	VC
Hannibal-LaGrange Univ	MO	24,490	C
Harding Univ	AR	21,432	C+
Hardin-Simmons Univ	TX	23,560	C+
Harris-Stowe State Univ	MO	14,360	NC
Hastings College	NE	27,782	C+
Heidelberg Univ	OH	34,100	C
Heritage Univ	WA	17,664	NC
Hillsdale College	MI	31,890	HC+
Hofstra Univ	NY	48,020	VC+
Holy Family Univ	PA	40,030	LC
Hood College	MD	44,630	C

School	ST	$IS	SR
Hope College	MI	36,320	V₲
Hope International Univ	CA	34,650	C
Houghton College	NY	35,740	VC
Houston Baptist Univ	TX	23,815	₲
Howard Payne Univ	TX	17,115	C
Howard Univ	DC	35,957	C
Humboldt State Univ	CA	18,400	C
Hunter College / The CUNY	NY	14,429	VC
Huntington Univ	IN	32,220	C
Idaho State Univ	ID	11,908	C
Illinois College	IL	25,770	VC
Immaculata Univ	PA	43,000	C
Indiana State Univ	IN	16,000	C
Indiana Univ Bloomington	IN	19,358	HC
Indiana Univ East	IN	6,639	LC
Indiana Univ Kokomo	IN	6,674	LC
Indiana Univ Northwest	IN	6,738	LC
Indiana Univ South Bend	IN	15,293	C
Indiana Univ Southeast	IN	15,807	LC
Indiana Univ-Purdue Univ Fort Wayne	IN	15,425	C
Indiana Wesleyan Univ	IN	31,815	VC
Inter-American Univ of PR/ Aguadilla Campus	PR	5,578	
Inter-American Univ of PR/ Arecibo Campus	PR	3,350	
Inter-American Univ of PR/ Barranquitas	PR	3,350	
Inter-American Univ of PR/ Fajardo Campus	PR	4,200	
Inter-American Univ of PR/ Metropolitan Campus	PR	4,320	
Inter-American Univ of PR/ Ponce	PR	3,700	
Inter-American Univ of PR/ San Germán	PR	6,720	
Iowa State Univ	IA	16,403	C
Iowa Wesleyan College	IA	30,850	LC
Ithaca College	NY	52,300	HC
Jacksonville State Univ	AL	12,280	LC
Jarvis Christian College	TX	19,552	NC
John Brown Univ	AR	30,996	VC
John Carroll Univ	OH	44,520	₲
Johnson State College	VT	16,721	C
Judson Univ	IL	25,130	C
Juniata College	PA	49,340	VC
Kansas State Univ	KS	15,497	VC
Kansas Wesleyan Univ	KS	32,000	C
Kean Univ	NJ	22,060	LC
Keene State College	NH	21,538	C
Kentucky State Univ	KY	11,000	LC
Kentucky Wesleyan College	KY	27,440	V₲
Keuka College	NY	30,300	C
King Univ	TN	33,140	C
King's College	PA	41,678	C
Knox College	IL		VC
Kutztown Univ of Pennsylvania	PA	16,909	LC
La Salle Univ	PA	50,270	C
La Sierra Univ	CA	35,694	VC
Lake Superior State Univ	MI	18,121	C
Lakeland College	WI	22,990	C
Lamar Univ	TX	6,820	LC
Lasell College	MA	42,500	LC
Le Moyne College	NY	42,200	VC
Lehman College / The CUNY	NY	5,778	LC
Lenoir-Rhyne College	NC	35,984	C
LeTourneau Univ	TX	26,230	C
Lewis Univ	IL	23,050	C
Lewis-Clark State College	ID	6,990	C
Lincoln Memorial Univ	TN	18,144	C
Lindenwood Univ	MO	20,750	C
Lindsey Wilson College	KY	30,470	VC
Livingstone College	NC	17,815	LC
Lock Haven Univ of Pennsylvania	PA	17,587	LC
LIU/Brooklyn Campus	NY	26,500	C
LIU/C.W. Post Campus	NY	38,888	C
Louisiana College	LA	15,746	C
Louisiana State Univ in Shreveport	LA	5,606	C
Louisiana Tech Univ	LA	8,000	C
Loyola Univ Chicago	IL	49,560	V₲
Lubbock Christian Univ	TX	25,518	C
MacMurray College	IL	20,755	C
Madonna Univ	MI	24,540	VC
Malone Univ	OH	34,334	C
Manchester College	IN	35,070	C
Manhattan College	NY	44,955	VC
Mansfield Univ	PA	19,468	LC
Marian Univ	WI	30,980	LC
Marquette Univ	WI	43,664	V₲
Marshall Univ	WV	14,820	C
Maryville College	TN	33,150	VC
Maryville Univ of St. Louis	MO	34,920	VC
Marywood Univ	PA	40,695	C
Mass College of Liberal Arts	MA	16,733	C
Mayville State Univ	ND	11,401	NC
McMurry Univ	TX	25,962	LC
McPherson College	KS	28,138	C
Mercer Univ	GA	44,201	V₲
Mercyhurst Univ	PA	40,700	C
Merrimack College	MA	44,215	C
Methodist Univ	NC	37,185	C
Miami Univ	OH	24,191	HC
Mich Tech Univ	MI	22,105	VC
Midland Univ	NE	34,000	C
Miles College	AL	16,530	NC
Millikin Univ	IL	37,462	C
Minn State Univ, Mankato	MN	14,900	C
Missouri Baptist Univ	MO	30,310	C
Missouri Southern State Univ	MO	11,910	C
Missouri Univ of Science and Technology	MO	18,655	V₲
Missouri Western State Univ	MO	12,260	NC
Molloy College	NY	38,950	C
Monmouth College	IL	39,290	C
Monmouth Univ	NJ	42,252	C
Montana State Univ	MT	14,068	VC
Montana State Univ Billings	MT	12,425	LC
Montana State Univ-Northern	MT	12,500	NC
Moravian College	PA	36,381	VC
Mount Aloysius College	PA	27,970	C
Mount Marty College	SD	29,638	C
Mount Mary Univ	WI	32,836	LC
Mount Mercy Univ	IA	34,385	C
Mount Olive College	NC	18,426	C
Murray State Univ	KY	14,944	C
Muskingum Univ	OH	30,502	C
New England College	NH	45,930	LC
New Jersey City Univ	NJ	21,060	₲
New Mexico State Univ	NM	13,955	LC
New York Inst of Technology	NY	40,590	VC
New York Univ	NY	61,470	MC
Newman Univ	KS	30,380	₲
Niagara Univ	NY	39,800	C
Nicholls State Univ	LA	7,095	C
N Car State Univ	NC	16,202	HC
North Central College	IL	38,343	VC
N Dak State Univ	ND	14,642	C
North Georgia College & State Univ	GA	8,500	C
North Park Univ	IL	30,130	C
Northeastern Illinois Univ	IL		C
Northeastern State Univ	OK	8,615	VC
Northern Arizona Univ	AZ	18,592	C
Northern Kentucky Univ	KY	15,302	LC
Northern Mich Univ	MI	15,300	VC
Northern State Univ	SD	14,021	C
Northland College	WI	26,680	C
Northwest Missouri State Univ	MO	14,229	C
Northwest Nazarene Univ	ID	24,275	NC
Northwest Univ	WA	18,854	C
Northwestern College of Iowa	IA	34,848	₲
Northwestern Okla State Univ	OK	7,275	NC
Northwestern State Univ of Louisiana	LA	14,368	C
Northwestern Univ	IL	37,595	MC
Notre Dame College	OH	34,942	VC
Notre Dame of Maryland Univ	MD	27,700	C
Nova Southeastern Univ	FL	34,016	VC
Nyack College	NY	32,000	C
Oakland City Univ	IN	24,500	NC
Okla Baptist Univ	OK	28,202	VC
Okla City Univ	OK	33,546	VC
Okla State Univ	OK	14,310	VC
Okla Wesleyan Univ	OK	21,300	C
Old Dominion Univ	VA	18,662	C
Olivet College	MI	19,984	C
Oswego / SUNY	NY	20,009	VC
Ouachita Baptist Univ	AR	29,010	VC
Our Lady of Holy Cross College	LA	8,090	LC
Paine College	GA	18,594	LC
Palm Beach Atlantic Univ	FL	33,882	LC
Penn State Univ/Univ Park	PA	25,404	VC
Pepperdine Univ	CA	55,372	H₲
Peru State College	NE	8,600	NC
Pfeiffer Univ	NC	33,700	C
Pittsburg State Univ	KS	12,032	C
Point Park Univ	PA	36,390	C
Pontifical Catholic Univ of PR	PR	7,310	
Prescott College	AZ	33,284	₲
Providence College	RI	55,995	HC
Purdue Univ/Calumet	IN	14,336	C
Purdue Univ/West Lafayette	IN	20,278	HC
Quinnipiac Univ	CT	53,580	VC
Rhode Island College	RI	17,132	LC
Rider Univ	NJ	45,720	C
Ripon College	WI	36,959	₲
Rivier College	NH	35,000	VC
Roberts Wesleyan College	NY	37,384	₲
Rockhurst Univ	MO	20,625	C
Roger Williams Univ	RI	45,788	C
Roosevelt Univ	IL	22,605	VC
Rosemont College	PA	42,350	C
Rust College	MS	10,600	C
St. Anselm College	NH	48,324	VC
St. Francis Univ	PA	30,029	LC
St. Joseph's College	IN	35,790	C
St. Leo Univ	FL	27,990	C
St. Mary's Univ	TX	33,854	C
St. Mary's Univ of Minn	MN	37,015	C
St. Michael's College	VT	48,740	VC
St. Paul's College	VA	16,030	NC
St. Peter's College	NJ	44,240	C
St. Xavier Univ	IL	32,840	C
Salem International Univ	WV	18,020	C
Salem State College	MA	13,161	LC
Salve Regina Univ	RI	47,250	VC
Samford Univ	AL	35,700	V₲
Schreiner Univ	TX	32,734	LC
Seattle Pacific Univ	WA	41,559	V₲
Seton Hall Univ	NJ	45,902	C
Seton Hill Univ	PA	35,172	C
Shaw Univ	NC	15,488	LC
Shepherd Univ	WV	14,996	C
Shippensburg Univ of Pennsylvania	PA	17,004	LC
Silver Lake College	WI	22,600	LC
Simmons College	MA	48,770	VC
Simpson College	IA	36,086	VC
Simpson Univ	CA	28,900	C
Slippery Rock Univ of Pennsylvania	PA	10,360	LC
S Dak State Univ	SD	14,296	C
Southeast Missouri State Univ	MO	14,983	LC
Southeastern Okla State Univ	OK	7,966	C
Southeastern Univ	FL	27,201	₲
Southern Conn State Univ	CT	18,033	C
Southern New Hampshire Univ	NH	38,100	C
Southern Univ and A&M College	LA	9,761	₲
Southern Univ at New Orleans	LA	1,000	NC
Southwest Baptist Univ	MO	24,710	C
Southwestern Adventist Univ	TX	23,026	LC
Southwestern Okla State Univ	OK	9,160	C
Spring Hill College	AL	42,130	VC
Springfield College	MA	25,000	C
St. Ambrose Univ	IA		C
St. Catherine Univ	MN	37,782	₲
St. Cloud State Univ	MN	10,600	C
St. Francis College	NY	34,200	LC
St. John Fisher College	NY	39,370	₲
St. John's Univ	NY	52,840	₲
St. Joseph's College, New York / Brooklyn Campus	NY	21,878	C
St. Joseph's College, New York / Suffolk Campus	NY	21,878	VC
St. Thomas Aquinas College	NY	30,000	C
St. Thomas Univ	FL	32,310	₲
Stetson Univ	FL	49,512	V₲
SUNY College at Old Westbury	NY	16,324	C
SUNY Cortland / The SUNY	NY	19,117	C
SUNY Fredonia / The SUNY at Fredonia	NY	18,702	VC
SUNY New Paltz	NY	15,010	C
SUNY Oneonta / SUNY	NY	16,919	VC
Tabor College	KS	29,010	LC
Taylor Univ	IN	36,742	V₲
Temple Univ	PA	24,392	VC
Tenn Tech Univ	TN	11,310	C
Tenn Wesleyan College	TN	21,250	C
Texas A&M Univ	TX	16,956	V₲
Texas A&M Univ at Commerce	TX	10,496	C
Texas A&M Univ at Kingsville	TX	7,500	LC
Texas Christian Univ	TX	47,570	HC
The Catholic Univ of America	DC	52,852	VC
The Masters College	CA	38,160	₲
Thiel College	PA	31,378	LC
Thomas More College	KY	34,760	C
Thomas Univ	GA	11,520	NC
Trevecca Nazarene Univ	TN	30,118	C
Trine Univ	IN	39,400	VC
Trinity International Univ	IL	31,070	C
Troy Univ	AL	10,650	C
Tuskegee Univ	AL	26,750	C
Union College	KY	28,775	C
Union College	NE	23,270	VC
Union Univ	TN	28,260	VC
Unity College	ME	34,054	C
Universidad Adventista de las Antillas	PR	7,360	
Universidad del Turabo	PR	4,110	
Universidad Metropolitana	PR		
Univ of Alabama at Birmingham	AL	18,484	₲
Univ of Alabama at Tuscaloosa	AL	17,164	₲
Univ of Arizona	AZ	20,105	C
Univ of Arkansas at Little Rock	AR		C
Univ of Central Arkansas	AR	10,840	VC
Univ of Central Missouri	MO	14,605	C
Univ of Central Okla	OK	12,293	C
Univ of Cincinnati	OH	20,199	VC
Univ of Dayton	OH	43,750	VC
Univ of Delaware	DE	22,728	VC
Univ of Detroit Mercy	MI	30,450	C
Univ of Findlay	OH	31,916	C
Univ of Great Falls	MT	27,970	C
Univ of Hartford	CT	42,674	C
Univ of Hawaii at Manoa	HI	19,379	VC
Univ of Idaho	ID	14,558	C
Univ of Illinois at Chicago	IL	24,293	VC
Univ of Illinois at Urbana-Champaign	IL	24,300	HC
Univ of Indianapolis	IN	31,740	LC
Univ of Iowa	IA	17,481	VC
Univ of Kansas	KS	16,980	₲
Univ of Kentucky	KY	19,868	C
Univ of Louisiana at Lafayette	LA	6,130	C
Univ of Louisiana at Monroe	LA	12,998	C
Univ of Louisville	KY	17,460	VC
Univ of Maine	ME	19,712	₲
Univ of Maine at Farmington	ME	17,841	C
Univ of Maine at Fort Kent	ME	14,975	LC
Univ of Maine at Presque Isle	ME	15,011	LC
Univ of Mary Hardin-Baylor	TX	31,950	₲
Univ of Maryland	MD	18,801	HC
Univ of Maryland/Eastern Shore	MD	14,000	C
Univ of Miami	FL	55,166	MC
Univ of Mich/Dearborn	MI	9,885	VC
Univ of Mich-Flint	MI	17,547	₲
Univ of Minn/Duluth	MN	18,964	₲
Univ of Minn/Morris	MN	17,150	VC
Univ of Missouri/Columbia	MO	18,201	MC
Univ of Missouri-Kansas City	MO	19,603	C
Univ of Missouri-St. Louis	MO	18,304	VC
Univ of Montana	MT	13,670	C
Univ of Montana-Western	MT	9,753	LC
Univ of Nebr - Lincoln	NE	17,507	VC
Univ of Nebr at Kearney	NE	14,855	LC
Univ of Nebr at Omaha	NE	12,700	C
Univ of Nevada, Las Vegas	NV	17,303	C
Univ of Nevada/Reno	NV	14,500	NC
Univ of New England	ME	46,145	₲
Univ of New Haven	CT	47,740	C
Univ of New Mexico	NM	15,300	C
Univ of New Orleans	LA	9,224	VC
Univ of North Alabama	AL	9,960	C
Univ of N Car at Wilmington	NC	13,572	V₲
Univ of North Florida	FL	15,578	VC
Univ of Pikeville	KY	24,750	NC
Univ of Pittsburgh at Johnstown	PA	20,862	LC
Univ of Portland	OR	47,874	VC
Univ of PR Recinto de Rio Piedras	PR	5,750	
Univ of PR/Cayey	PR	1,504	
Univ of Rio Grande	OH	8,750	NC
Univ of St. Francis	IN	29,810	C
Univ of San Francisco	CA	49,674	VC
Univ of Scranton	PA	51,940	VC
Univ of Sioux Falls	SD	22,990	C
Univ of South Alabama	AL	13,510	C
Univ of S Car at Aiken	SC	16,278	C
Univ of S Car Upstate	SC	17,673	LC
Univ of S Dak	SD	15,111	C
Univ of Southern Indiana	IN	14,657	C
Univ of Southern Miss	MS	13,170	C
Univ of St. Francis	IL	36,490	C
Univ of Tampa	FL	35,160	VC
Univ of Tenn at Chattanooga	TN	16,883	C
Univ of Tenn at Martin	TN	13,217	C
Univ of the Incarnate Word	TX	35,200	LC
Univ of the Southwest	NM	15,000	C
Univ of Toledo	OH	18,464	C
Univ of Vermont	VT	26,120	V₲
Univ of West Alabama	AL	9,415	C
Univ of West Florida	FL	14,656	C
Univ of West Georgia	GA	14,852	LC
Univ of Wisc Whitewater	WI	13,314	C
Univ of Wisc/Green Bay	WI	14,900	C
Univ of Wisc/La Crosse	WI	14,755	VC
Univ of Wisc/Madison	WI	18,757	HC
Univ of Wisc/Oshkosh	WI	10,426	LC
Univ of Wisc/Platteville	WI	14,274	C
Univ of Wisc/River Falls	WI	9,722	LC
Univ of Wisc/Superior	WI	14,106	C
Univ of Wyoming	WY	13,855	₲
Urbana Univ	OH	21,190	C
Ursuline College	OH	33,198	LC
Utah State Univ	UT	11,803	C
Valparaiso Univ	IN	43,040	V₲
Vanderbilt Univ	TN	57,072	MC
Vanguard Univ of Southern Calif	CA	35,833	VC
Victory Univ	TN	19,118	C
Villanova Univ	PA	56,436	MC
Virginia Intermont College	VA	32,411	LC
Virginia Polytechnic Inst and State Univ	VA	14,629	HC
Virginia Union Univ	VA	18,432	C
Virginia Wesleyan College	VA	28,433	LC
Wagner College	NY	48,600	VC
Walsh Univ	OH	35,100	C
Wartburg College	IA	41,055	VC

School	ST	$IS	SR
Washburn Univ	KS	12,165	NC
Washington State Univ	WA	20,461	C
Washington Univ in St. Louis	MO	58,818	MC
Webster Univ	MO	33,990	C+
West Chester Univ of Pennsylvania	PA	16,836	C
West Liberty Univ	WV	9,142	LC
West Virginia State Univ	WV	8,378	NC
West Virginia Wesleyan College	WV	26,880	C
Western Carolina Univ	NC	13,965	C+
Western Conn State Univ	CT	18,327	C
Western Mich Univ	MI	19,042	C
Western New England Univ	MA	45,590	C
Western New Mexico Univ	NM	8,500	LC
Western State Colo Univ	CO	16,135	C
Western Washington Univ	WA	18,519	VC
Westfield State Univ	MA	18,489	C
Westminster College	MO	30,490	VC
Westminster College	PA	31,290	C+
Wheaton College	IL	39,650	HC+
Wheeling Jesuit Univ	WV	34,668	C
Whitworth Univ	WA	45,826	VC+
Wichita State Univ	KS	12,539	C
Wiley College	TX		LC
William Jewell College	MO	31,000	VC+
William Penn Univ	IA	26,000	C
Williams Baptist College	AR	20,070	C
Wilmington College	OH	29,784	C
Winona State Univ	MN	16,530	C
Winthrop Univ	SC	21,120	VC
Wittenberg Univ	OH	47,766	VC
Wright State Univ	OH	16,983	C
York College	NE	19,475	C
York College of Pennsylvania	PA	26,590	C
Youngstown State Univ	OH	16,374	LC

SECRETARIAL STUDIES/ OFFICE MANAGEMENT

School	ST	$IS	SR
Caribbean Univ	PR	10,375	
Chancellor Univ	OH	11,000	C
Dordt College	IA	34,160	VC
Inter-American Univ of PR/ Aguadilla Campus	PR	5,578	
Inter-American Univ of PR/ Barranquitas	PR	3,350	
Inter-American Univ of PR/ Bayamon Univ College	PR	4,428	
Inter-American Univ of PR/ Fajardo Campus	PR	4,200	
Inter-American Univ of PR/ Metropolitan Campus	PR	4,320	
Inter-American Univ of PR/ Ponce	PR	3,700	
Inter-American Univ of PR/ San Germán	PR	6,720	
Johnson and Wales Univ/ Providence Campus	RI	34,668	C
Southeastern Okla State Univ	OK	7,966	C
Southern Univ at New Orleans	LA	1,000	NC
Universidad del Turabo	PR	4,110	
Univ of PR Recinto de Rio Piedras	PR	5,750	
Univ of PR/Arecibo	PR	7,227	
Univ of PR/Cayey	PR	1,504	
Univ of PR/Humacao	PR	1,877	
Univ of the Sacred Heart	PR	5,590	

SLAVIC LANGUAGES

School	ST	$IS	SR
Columbia Univ/School of General Studies	NY	54,083	MC
Duke Univ	NC	50,250	MC
Indiana Univ Bloomington	IN	19,358	HC
New York Univ	NY	61,470	MC
Northwestern Univ	IL	37,595	MC
Princeton Univ	NJ	53,795	MC
Stanford Univ	CA	56,411	MC
Univ of Calif at Berkeley	CA	23,322	MC
Univ of Calif at Santa Barbara	CA	27,551	HC
Univ of Chicago	IL	55,416	MC
Univ of Illinois at Chicago	IL	24,293	VC
Univ of Kansas	KS	16,980	C+
Univ of Pittsburgh at Pittsburgh	PA	27,800	HC+
Univ of Texas at Austin	TX	44,074	HC
Univ of Virginia	VA	22,175	MC
Univ of Washington	WA	14,722	VC
Wayne State Univ	MI	19,493	C
Yale Univ	CT	55,300	MC

SMALL BUSINESS MANAGEMENT

School	ST	$IS	SR
Adams State College	CO	13,358	LC
Cal State, Chico	CA	18,952	C
Cal State, San Bernardino	CA	12,000	C
Carroll Univ	WI	24,860	C
Concord Univ	WV	13,102	C
Ferris State Univ	MI	19,698	C
Florida Atlantic Univ	FL	17,339	C
Florida State Univ	FL	15,238	HC
Hawaii Pacific Univ	HI	36,690	C
Huntington Univ	IN	32,220	C
Indiana Univ South Bend	IN	15,293	C
Johnson and Wales Univ/ Providence Campus	RI	34,668	C
Johnson State College	VT	16,721	C
Mount Aloysius College	PA	27,970	C
Mount Ida College	MA	30,115	LC
Northern Arizona Univ	AZ	18,592	C
Rowan Univ	NJ	23,570	VC
Stetson Univ	FL	49,512	VC+
Tusculum College	TN	24,295	C
Union College	NE	23,270	VC
Univ of Montana	MT	13,670	C
Univ of Montana-Western	MT	9,753	LC

SOCIAL FOUNDATIONS

School	ST	$IS	SR
Amridge Univ	AL	6,870	LC
Eastern Mich Univ	MI	17,961	C

SOCIAL PSYCHOLOGY

School	ST	$IS	SR
Bennington College	VT	56,990	HC+
Clarion Univ of Pennsylvania	PA	17,370	C
Florida Atlantic Univ	FL	17,339	C
Goddard College	VT	16,418	VC
Lehigh Univ	PA	55,080	MC
Mary Baldwin College	VA	37,110	C
Our Lady of Holy Cross College	LA	8,090	LC
Park Univ	MO	17,525	C
Univ of Calif at Irvine	CA	25,961	VC

SOCIAL SCIENCE

School	ST	$IS	SR
Adelphi Univ	NY	43,130	VC
Anna Maria College	MA	34,600	LC
Aquinas College	MI	33,060	C
Arizona State Univ	AZ	18,818	C+
Ashford Univ	IA	21,780	C
Ashland Univ	OH	25,000	C
Averett Univ	VA	36,000	LC
Azusa Pacific Univ	CA	39,946	C
Bellevue Univ	NE	4,600	NC
Bemidji State Univ	MN	13,500	C
Benedict College	SC	20,454	NC
Benedictine College	KS	29,180	VC
Benedictine Univ	IL	35,220	C
Bennington College	VT	56,990	HC+
Bethany College	KS	30,605	NC
Bethel College	IN	31,560	C
Biola Univ	CA	40,320	VC
Black Hills State Univ	SD	13,562	LC
Bluefield State College	WV	3,140	LC
Bluffton Univ	OH	37,864	C
Boise State Univ	ID	12,802	C
Bowling Green State Univ	OH	18,970	C
Brewton-Parker College	GA	33,388	LC
Buena Vista Univ	IA	37,954	C
Calif Lutheran Univ	CA	47,640	C
Cal State, Chico	CA	18,952	C
Cal State, Fresno	CA	17,405	C
Cal State, Los Angeles	CA	15,829	C
Cal State, Monterey Bay	CA	26,871	LC
Cal State, Sacramento	CA	16,200	C
Cal State, San Bernardino	CA	12,000	C
Cal State, San Marcos	CA	14,576	C
Cal State, Stanislaus	CA	18,582	C
Calif Univ of Pennsylvania	PA	14,217	C
Canisius College	NY	45,602	VC
Cardinal Stritch Univ	WI	24,054	C
Caribbean Univ	PR	10,375	
Carnegie Mellon Univ	PA	51,260	MC
Carroll College	MT	28,000	C
Carson-Newman Univ	TN	29,058	C+
Carthage College	WI	33,000	C
Castleton State College	VT	19,424	C
Cazenovia College	NY	30,800	C
Central Mich Univ	MI	18,066	C
Central Washington Univ	WA	11,730	C
Chadron State College	NE	7,400	NC
Chancellor Univ	OH	11,000	C
Charleston Southern Univ	SC	22,420	C
Cheyney Univ of Pennsylvania	PA	20,372	LC
Clarion Univ of Pennsylvania	PA	17,370	C
Clarkson Univ	NY	53,538	HC
Cleveland State Univ	OH	21,357	C
Colgate Univ	NY	50,930	MC
College of St. Benedict	MN	47,570	VC
College of St. Mary	NE	34,334	C
Colo Christian Univ	CO	27,500	VC
Colo Mesa Univ	CO	16,669	LC
Colo State Univ-Pueblo	CO	13,532	LC
Concord Univ	WV	13,102	C
Concordia Univ Wisc	WI	28,980	C
Concordia Univ, River Forest	IL	26,300	C
Coppin State Univ	MD	14,905	VC
Corban Univ	OR	34,764	C
Covenant College	GA		VC+
Cumberland Univ	TN	21,220	C
Daniel Webster College	NH	25,380	C
Delta State Univ	MS	12,292	LC
DePaul Univ	IL	46,120	VC
Dominican College	NY	31,270	C
Dominican Univ	IL	37,628	C
Dordt College	IA	34,160	VC
Dowling College	NY	25,000	LC
Eastern Conn State Univ	CT	20,584	C
Eastern Mennonite Univ	VA	38,850	VC
Eastern Washington Univ	WA	16,388	C
Edinboro Univ of Pennsylvania	PA	15,940	LC
Elizabeth City State Univ	NC	11,638	C
Emporia State Univ	KS	12,897	C
Eureka College	IL	19,280	C
Evangel Univ	MO	23,090	C
Fayetteville State Univ	NC	10,816	C
Felician College	NJ	41,640	C
Florida A&M Univ	FL	14,935	LC
Florida Atlantic Univ	FL	17,339	C
Florida State Univ	FL	15,238	HC
Fordham Univ	NY	58,927	HC
Fresno Pacific Univ	CA	32,136	C
Frostburg State Univ	MD	15,264	LC
Gardner-Webb Univ	NC	34,375	C+
George Fox Univ	OR	40,750	C+
Goddard College	VT	16,418	VC
Graceland Univ	IA	28,020	C
Grand Valley State Univ	MI	17,998	VC
Gustavus Adolphus College	MN	48,170	HC
Hamline Univ	MN	44,198	VC
Harding Univ	AR	21,432	C+
Harvard Univ/Harvard College	MA	49,000	MC
Hastings College	NE	27,782	C+
Hawaii Pacific Univ	HI	36,690	C
Heidelberg Univ	OH	34,100	C
Hillsdale College	MI	31,890	HC+
Hope International Univ	CA	34,650	C
Humboldt State Univ	CA	18,400	C
Hunter College / The CUNY	NY	14,429	VC
Illinois State Univ	IL	22,634	VC
Immaculata Univ	PA	43,000	C
Indiana Univ of Pennsylvania	PA	20,180	LC
Indiana Univ-Purdue Univ Fort Wayne	IN	15,425	C
James Madison Univ	VA	18,049	VC
Johns Hopkins Univ	MD	47,492	MC
Johnson C. Smith Univ	NC	25,336	LC
Kansas State Univ	KS	15,497	VC
Keene State College	NH	21,538	C
Keystone College	PA	28,680	LC
Lake Erie College	OH	35,704	C
Lake Superior State Univ	MI	18,121	C
Lamar Univ	TX	6,820	LC
Langston Univ	OK	3,000	LC
LeMoyne-Owen College	TN	13,100	C
Lesley Univ	MA	46,350	C
Lewis-Clark State College	ID	6,990	C
Liberty Univ	VA	19,101	C
Lincoln Memorial Univ	TN	18,144	C
Lindsey Wilson College	KY	30,470	VC
Lock Haven Univ of Pennsylvania	PA	17,587	LC
LIU/Brooklyn Campus	NY	26,500	C
Loyola Univ New Orleans	LA	46,581	VC
Lyndon State College	VT	14,233	C
Madonna Univ	MI	24,540	VC
Marlboro College	VT	35,980	VC
Marygrove College	MI	21,290	C
Marylhurst Univ	OR	18,945	NC
Maryville College	TN	33,150	VC
Marywood Univ	PA	40,695	C
Mayville State Univ	ND	11,401	NC
McKendree Univ	IL	29,920	C+
Medaille College	NY	35,112	VC
Mercer Univ	GA	44,201	VC+
Metropolitan State Univ	MN	5,923	SP
Mich State Univ	MI	13,689	VC
Mich Tech Univ	MI	22,105	VC
Midland Univ	NE	34,000	C
Minot State Univ	ND	10,915	C
Miss Univ for Women	MS	7,400	LC
Missouri Baptist Univ	MO	30,310	C
Missouri Southern State Univ	MO	11,910	C
Montana State Univ-Northern	MT	12,500	NC
Moravian College	PA	36,381	VC
Morehead State Univ	KY	10,900	C
Mount Marty College	SD	29,638	C
Mount St. Mary College	NY	39,540	C
Mount St. Mary's College/ Chalon Campus	CA	43,897	VC+
Muskingum Univ	OH	30,502	C
National Louis Univ	IL	16,915	LC
Nazareth College of Rochester	NY	41,590	VC
New College of Florida	FL	14,504	HC+
New York Univ	NY	61,470	MC
Niagara Univ	NY	39,800	C
N Car State Univ	NC	16,202	HC
North Central College	IL	38,343	VC
N Dak State Univ	ND	14,642	C
North Georgia College & State Univ	GA	8,500	LC
Northeastern State Univ	OK	8,615	VC
Northern Kentucky Univ	KY	15,302	LC
Northern State Univ	SD	14,021	C
Northwest Christian Univ	OR	27,399	C
Northwest Missouri State Univ	MO	14,229	C
Northwestern Okla State Univ	OK	7,275	NC
Notre Dame de Namur Univ	CA	41,610	LC
Ohio Wesleyan Univ	OH	49,460	C+
Okla Baptist Univ	OK	28,202	VC
Olivet Nazarene Univ	IL	29,990	C
Our Lady of Holy Cross College	LA	8,090	LC
Pace Univ	NY	48,094	VC
Pepperdine Univ	CA	55,372	HC+
Peru State College	NE	8,600	NC
Piedmont College	GA	29,260	C
Plymouth State Univ	NH	23,148	LC
Point Loma Nazarene Univ	CA	38,610	VC
Polytechnic Inst of New York Univ	NY	53,064	HC+
Pontifical Catholic Univ of PR	PR	7,310	
Prescott College	AZ	33,284	C+
Providence College	RI	55,995	HC
Quinnipiac Univ	CT	53,580	VC
Radford Univ	VA	17,132	LC
Ramapo College of New Jersey	NJ	24,938	C+
Rhode Island College	RI	17,132	LC
Robert Morris Univ	PA	36,699	C
Rockford College	IL	01,000	O
Roger Williams Univ	RI	45,788	C
Roosevelt Univ	IL	22,605	VC
Rosemont College	PA	42,350	C
St. John's Univ	MN	46,146	C
St. Mary's Univ of Minn	MN	37,015	C
St. Paul's College	VA	16,030	NC
St. Peter's College	NJ	44,240	C
St. Xavier Univ	IL	32,840	C
Salisbury Univ	MD	18,368	VC
San Diego State Univ	CA	20,578	VC
San Jose State Univ	CA	19,707	C
Seattle Pacific Univ	WA	41,559	VC+
Seton Hall Univ	NJ	45,902	C
Shawnee State Univ	OH	16,545	NC
Shenandoah Univ	VA	39,268	C
Shimer College	IL	32,875	VC
Shorter Univ	GA	26,470	C
Siena Heights Univ	MI	17,000	LC
Silver Lake College	WI	22,600	LC
Simpson Univ	CA	28,900	C
Skidmore College	NY	57,926	HC
Slippery Rock Univ of Pennsylvania	PA	10,360	LC
Southeastern Okla State Univ	OK	7,966	C
Southern Illinois Univ Carbondale	IL	21,620	C
Southern Methodist Univ	TX	57,755	MC
Southern New Hampshire Univ	NH	38,100	C
Southern Oregon Univ	OR	17,874	C
Southwestern Adventist Univ	TX	23,026	LC
Spring Arbor Univ	MI	26,740	C
Spring Hill College	AL	42,130	VC
St. Andrews Univ	NC	32,050	LC
St. Cloud State Univ	MN	10,600	C
St. Joseph's College, New York / Brooklyn Campus	NY	21,878	C
St. Joseph's College, New York / Suffolk Campus	NY	21,878	VC
St. Thomas Aquinas College	NY	30,000	C
Stetson Univ	FL	49,512	VC+
Stony Brook Univ / SUNY	NY	19,359	HC
Suffolk Univ	MA	46,548	C
Sul Ross State Univ	TX	13,410	LC
SUNY New Paltz	NY	15,010	C
Tabor College	KS	29,010	LC
Temple Univ	PA	24,392	VC
The Catholic Univ of America	DC	52,852	VC
Thomas Edison State College	NJ	5,700	SP
Thomas Univ	GA	11,520	NC
Touro College	NY	23,150	VC
Towson Univ	MD	16,000	VC
Trine Univ	IN	39,400	VC
Trinity International Univ	IL	31,070	C
Troy Univ	AL	10,650	C
Tulane Univ	LA	58,942	MC
Union College	NE	23,270	VC
Union College	NY		MC
Union Inst & Univ	OH	8,912	SP
United States Air Force Academy	CO		MC
Universidad del Turabo	PR	4,110	
Universidad Metropolitana	PR		
Univ at Buffalo / The SUNY	NY	20,283	VC
Univ of Akron	OH	20,436	C
Univ of Alaska Southeast	AK	11,493	C
Univ of Bridgeport	CT	39,030	LC
Univ of Calif at Berkeley	CA	23,322	MC
Univ of Calif at Davis	CA	24,482	HC

School	ST	$IS	SR
Univ of Calif at Irvine	CA	25,961	VC
Univ of Central Florida	FL	15,711	VC+
Univ of Chicago	IL	55,416	MC
Univ of Cincinnati	OH	20,199	VC
Univ of Denver	CO	51,787	VC+
Univ of Great Falls	MT	27,970	C
Univ of Houston-Downtown	TX	6,267	LC
Univ of Indianapolis	IN	31,740	LC
Univ of Iowa	IA	17,481	VC
Univ of La Verne	CA	47,010	VC
Univ of Maine at Augusta	ME	6,855	C
Univ of Maine at Fort Kent	ME	14,975	LC
Univ of Mary	ND	16,714	C
Univ of Maryland/Univ College	MD	6,168	SP
Univ of Mich/Ann Arbor	MI	22,102	HC+
Univ of Mich-Flint	MI	17,547	C+
Univ of Minn/Morris	MN	17,150	VC
Univ of Missouri/Columbia	MO	18,201	MC
Univ of Mobile	AL	27,870	VC
Univ of Montana-Western	MT	9,753	LC
Univ of Montevallo	AL	17,320	C
Univ of Mount Union	OH	35,130	C
Univ of Nebr at Kearney	NE	14,855	LC
Univ of Nevada, Las Vegas	NV	17,303	C
Univ of New England	ME	46,145	C+
Univ of N Dak	ND	14,094	C
Univ of North Texas	TX	15,628	C
Univ of Northern Colo	CO	15,973	C
Univ of Northern Iowa	IA	14,776	C
Univ of Oregon	OR	20,872	VC
Univ of Pittsburgh at Bradford	PA	21,316	LC
Univ of Pittsburgh at Greensburg	PA	17,640	C
Univ of Pittsburgh at Johnstown	PA	20,862	LC
Univ of Pittsburgh at Pittsburgh	PA	27,800	HC+
Univ of PR Recinto de Rio Piedras	PR	5,750	
Univ of PR/Mayaguez	PR	1,250	
Univ of South Florida	FL	13,000	C
Univ of South Florida/St. Petersburg	FL	12,769	VC
Univ of Southern Calif	CA	56,903	MC
Univ of Southern Miss	MS	13,170	C
Univ of the Ozarks	AR	22,100	C
Univ of the Pacific	CA	52,146	VC
Univ of Utah	UT	13,462	VC
Univ of Virginia's College at Wise	VA	11,076	C
Univ of West Alabama	AL	9,415	C
Univ of West Florida	FL	14,656	C
Univ of Wisc/Platteville	WI	14,274	C
Univ of Wisc/Stevens Point	WI	14,043	C
Univ of Wyoming	WY	13,855	C+
Upper Iowa Univ	IA	30,426	NC
Valley City State Univ	ND	12,286	LC
Valparaiso Univ	IN	43,040	VC+
Virginia Wesleyan College	VA	28,433	LC
Warner Pacific College	OR	25,550	C
Washington State Univ	WA	20,461	C
Washington Univ in St. Louis	MO	58,818	MC
Wayland Baptist Univ	TX	16,058	LC
Wayne State College	NE	11,764	NC
Waynesburg Univ	PA	29,100	C
Webster Univ	MO	33,990	C+
Wesleyan College	GA	24,000	C+
West Liberty Univ	WV	9,142	LC
West Texas A&M Univ	TX	13,478	C
West Virginia Wesleyan College	WV	26,880	C
Western Carolina Univ	NC	13,965	C+
Western Conn State Univ	CT	18,327	C
Western New Mexico Univ	NM	8,500	LC
Western Oregon Univ	OR	15,021	C
Westminster College	PA	31,290	C+
Westminster College	UT	37,708	VC
Westmont College	CA	41,500	HC
Wheaton College	IL	39,650	HC+
Wilberforce Univ	OH	15,100	LC
Wiley College	TX		LC
William Carey Univ	MS	13,500	LC
Wilmington College	OH	29,784	C
Wisc Lutheran College	WI	23,510	VC
Worcester Polytechnic Inst	MA	53,440	HC+

SOCIAL SCIENCE EDUCATION

School	ST	$IS	SR
Appalachian State Univ	NC	12,919	VC
Aquinas College	MI	33,060	C
Arkansas State Univ	AR	14,980	C
Armstrong Atlantic State Univ	GA	16,276	C
Auburn Univ	AL	20,052	VC+
Baylor Univ	TX	46,720	HC
Bethany College	WV	35,282	C
Bethune-Cookman Univ	FL	22,290	LC
Blackburn College	IL	21,350	C
Blue Mountain College	MS	13,550	LC
Boise State Univ	ID	12,802	C
Bowling Green State Univ	OH	18,970	C
Brigham Young Univ	UT	12,100	HC
Brigham Young Univ/Hawaii	HI	8,614	VC
Campbellsville Univ	KY	27,720	C
Central Methodist Univ	MO	28,240	VC
Coker College	SC	32,256	LC
Colby-Sawyer College	NH	47,870	C
College of New Jersey	NJ	25,376	HC
College of St. Scholastica	MN	39,960	C
Delta State Univ	MS	12,292	LC
Dordt College	IA	34,160	VC
Eastern Illinois Univ	IL	20,502	C
Eastern Nazarene College	MA	30,000	C
Eastern Washington Univ	WA	16,388	C
Fayetteville State Univ	NC	10,816	C
Florida Gulf Coast Univ	FL		C
Florida State Univ	FL	15,238	HC
Fresno Pacific Univ	CA	32,136	C
Friends Univ	KS	29,100	C
Georgia Southwestern State Univ	GA	12,218	C
Hope International Univ	CA	34,650	C
Humboldt State Univ	CA	18,400	C
Huntingdon College	AL	31,850	C
Illinois State Univ	IL	22,634	VC
Indiana Univ of Pennsylvania	PA	20,180	LC
Jackson State Univ	MS	13,512	LC
Knox College	IL		VC
Kutztown Univ of Pennsylvania	PA	16,909	LC
Lincoln Univ	MO	11,996	NC
Marian Univ	WI	30,980	LC
Marywood Univ	PA	40,695	C
Mayville State Univ	ND	11,401	NC
Mercyhurst Univ	PA	40,700	C
Miles College	AL	16,530	NC
Millikin Univ	IL	37,462	C
Miss Valley State Univ	MS	9,706	LC
Missouri Southern State Univ	MO	11,910	C
Montana State Univ-Billings	MT	12,425	LC
Montana State Univ-Northern	MT	12,500	NC
Nazareth College of Rochester	NY	41,590	VC
Nebr Wesleyan Univ	NE	29,774	C+
New York Univ	NY	61,470	MC
N Car Agricultural and Technical State Univ	NC	13,175	LC
N Dak State Univ	ND	14,642	C
North Georgia College & State Univ	GA	8,500	C
Northwest Nazarene Univ	ID	24,275	NC
Oakwood Univ	AL	23,035	C
Olivet Nazarene Univ	IL	29,990	C
Piedmont College	GA	29,260	C
Prescott College	AZ	33,284	C+
Rocky Mountain College	MT	32,242	C
Rust College	MS	10,600	C
Sacred Heart Univ	CT	48,564	VC
St. Mary-of-the-Woods College	IN	37,722	LC
Schreiner Univ	TX	32,734	LC
Seattle Pacific Univ	WA	41,559	VC+
Seton Hill Univ	PA	35,172	C
Simpson Univ	CA	28,900	C
Southeastern Louisiana Univ	LA	13,325	C
Southern Illinois Univ Edwardsville	IL	17,532	C
Southwestern Okla State Univ	OK	9,160	C
Stetson Univ	FL	49,512	VC+
SUNY Oneonta / SUNY	NY	16,919	VC
Texas Wesleyan Univ	TX	29,886	C
Trine Univ	IN	39,400	VC
Troy Univ	AL	10,650	C
Union College	NE	23,270	VC
Universidad del Turabo	PR	4,110	
Univ of Arkansas at Pine Bluff	AR	10,600	C
Univ of Central Florida	FL	15,711	VC+
Univ of Mary	ND	16,714	C
Univ of Maryland/Eastern Shore	MD	14,000	C
Univ of Miss	MS	15,482	VC
Univ of Montana-Western	MT	9,753	LC
Univ of Nebr - Lincoln	NE	17,507	VC
Univ of North Alabama	AL	9,960	C
Univ of N Car at Greensboro	NC	12,848	C
Univ of Northern Colo	CO	15,973	C
Univ of Pittsburgh at Johnstown	PA	20,862	LC
Univ of Rio Grande	OH	8,750	NC
Univ of Southern Indiana	IN	14,657	C
Univ of Utah	UT	13,462	VC
Univ of Wisc/Oshkosh	WI	10,426	LC
Univ of Wisc/Superior	WI	14,106	C
Valparaiso Univ	IN	43,040	VC+
Warner Univ	FL	18,000	C
Washington Univ in St. Louis	MO	58,818	MC
Western Carolina Univ	NC	13,965	C+
Westmont College	CA	41,500	HC
Wiley College	TX		LC
Wilmington College	OH	29,784	C
Wingate Univ	NC	34,990	C
Wright State Univ	OH	16,983	C
York College	NE	19,475	C
Youngstown State Univ	OH	16,374	LC

SOCIAL STUDIES

School	ST	$IS	SR
Andrews Univ	MI	28,030	C+
Aquinas College	MI	33,060	C
Arkansas Tech Univ	AR	13,164	LC
Barton College	NC	27,660	C
Bethany College	WV	35,282	C
Bethel Univ	MN	34,940	VC
Bluefield College	VA	17,230	C+
Bluffton Univ	OH	37,864	C
Brescia Univ	KY	26,140	VC+
Caldwell College	NJ	35,602	LC
Central Mich Univ	MI	18,066	C
Chaminade Univ of Honolulu	HI	31,664	C
Cleveland State Univ	OH	21,357	C
Concordia Univ, Ann Arbor	MI	27,220	VC
DePaul Univ	IL	46,120	VC
East Stroudsburg Univ of Pennsylvania	PA	16,636	C
Eastern Mich Univ	MI	17,961	C
Eastern Nazarene College	MA	30,000	C
Eastern New Mexico Univ	NM	10,682	C
Erskine College	SC	37,360	C
Ferrum College	VA	27,740	LC
Hamline Univ	MN	44,198	VC
Harvard Univ/Harvard College	MA	49,000	MC
Hiram College	OH	37,300	VC
Indiana Wesleyan Univ	IN	31,815	VC
Ithaca College	NY	52,300	HC
Mayville State Univ	ND	11,401	NC
McMurry Univ	TX	25,962	LC
Methodist Univ	NC	37,185	C
Minn State Univ, Mankato	MN	14,900	C
Miss College	MS	21,998	VC
Missouri Southern State Univ	MO	11,910	C
Mount Aloysius College	PA	27,970	C
Mount St. Mary's Univ	MD	46,158	C
New York Inst of Technology	NY	40,590	VC
New York Univ	NY	61,470	MC
Ohio Northern Univ	OH	42,075	VC
Okla Panhandle State Univ	OK	8,996	NC
Okla Wesleyan Univ	OK	21,300	C
Olivet College	MI	19,984	C
Our Lady of the Lake Univ of San Antonio	TX	22,430	LC
Pacific Union College	CA	28,150	VC
Pfeiffer Univ	NC	33,700	C
Purdue Univ/West Lafayette	IN	20,278	HC
S Car State Univ	SC	6,700	LC
Southern Wesleyan Univ	SC	25,600	C
Southwestern Adventist Univ	TX	23,026	LC
Spring Arbor Univ	MI	26,740	C
St. Catherine Univ	MN	37,782	C+
St. Francis College	NY	34,200	LC
St. John's Univ	NY	52,840	C+
Tulane Univ	LA	58,942	MC
Univ of Mich/Dearborn	MI	9,885	VC
Univ of Texas-Pan American	TX	12,432	LC
Univ of Wisc/Eau Claire	WI	15,430	VC
Univ of Wisc/Madison	WI	18,757	HC
Univ of Wisc/River Falls	WI	9,722	LC
Univ of Wisc/Superior	WI	14,106	C
Utica College	NY	44,734	C
Vassar College	NY	59,070	MC
Virginia Wesleyan College	VA	28,433	LC
Viterbo Univ	WI	30,070	C
Washington State Univ	WA	20,461	C
Wayland Baptist Univ	TX	16,058	LC
Wesleyan Univ	CT	59,844	MC
Western Kentucky Univ	KY	11,000	LC
Western Washington Univ	WA	18,519	VC
Youngstown State Univ	OH	16,374	LC

SOCIAL STUDIES EDUCATION

School	ST	$IS	SR
Adams State College	CO	13,358	LC
Alabama State Univ	AL	14,142	NC
Alfred Univ	NY	40,392	VC
Alice Lloyd College	KY	4,900	C
Anderson Univ	IN	35,390	C
Andrews Univ	MI	28,030	C+
Appalachian State Univ	NC	12,919	VC
Asbury Univ	KY	32,038	VC
Augustana College	SD	35,500	VC
Averett Univ	VA	36,000	LC
Baylor Univ	TX	46,720	HC
Bethany College	WV	35,282	C
Bethel College	IN	31,560	C
Bethel Univ	MN	34,940	VC
Biola Univ	CA	40,320	VC
Bloomsburg Univ of Pennsylvania	PA	13,598	C
Boston Univ	MA	54,130	HC+
Cameron Univ	OK	9,267	LC
Canisius College	NY	45,602	VC
Catawba College	NC	37,105	C
Cedarville Univ	OH	31,036	VC+
Centenary College of Louisiana	LA	39,070	C+
Central Washington Univ	WA	11,730	C
CUNY/Brooklyn College	NY	5,884	C+
Clearwater Christian College	FL	23,720	C
Colby-Sawyer College	NH	47,870	C
College of New Jersey	NJ	25,376	HC
College of the Ozarks	MO	5,605	VC
Concordia College New York	NY	31,500	VC
Concordia College, Moorhead	MN	39,974	C+
Concordia Univ St. Paul	MN	27,200	C
Corban Univ	OR	34,764	C
CUNY-City College	NY	19,576	HC+
Daemen College	NY	31,510	C
Defiance College	OH	30,645	C
Duquesne Univ	PA	42,017	VC
East Carolina Univ	NC	14,169	C
East Texas Baptist Univ	TX	29,135	C
Eastern Mich Univ	MI	17,961	C
Edgewood College	WI	33,294	C
Edinboro Univ of Pennsylvania	PA	15,940	LC
Elizabethtown College	PA	47,600	VC
Ferris State Univ	MI	19,698	C
Franklin College	IN	35,885	C
Gannon Univ	PA	37,940	C
Glenville State College	WV	11,348	NC
Grambling State Univ	LA	13,384	LC
Green Mountain College	VT	33,547	LC
Greensboro College	NC	28,740	LC
Gwynedd-Mercy College	PA	33,560	C
Hardin-Simmons Univ	TX	23,560	C+
Hofstra Univ	NY	48,020	VC+
Huntington Univ	IN	32,220	C
Indiana State Univ	IN	16,000	C
Indiana Univ Bloomington	IN	19,358	HC
Indiana Univ Northwest	IN	6,738	LC
Indiana Univ South Bend	IN	15,293	C
Indiana Univ Southeast	IN	15,807	LC
Indiana Univ-Purdue Univ Indianapolis	IN	17,290	C
Indiana Wesleyan Univ	IN	31,815	VC
Ithaca College	NY	52,300	HC
Judson College	AL	24,690	C
Juniata College	PA	49,340	VC
Kent State Univ	OH	19,352	C
Kentucky Christian Univ	KY	17,622	LC
Kentucky State Univ	KY	11,000	LC
Keystone College	PA	28,680	LC
Kutztown Univ of Pennsylvania	PA	16,909	LC
La Salle Univ	PA	50,270	C
Le Moyne College	NY	42,200	VC
Louisiana College	LA	15,746	C
Malone Univ	OH	34,334	C
Mansfield Univ	PA	19,468	LC
Mars Hill College	NC	22,950	LC
Marshall Univ	WV	14,820	C
Marygrove College	MI	21,290	C
Messiah College	PA	39,540	VC
MidAmerica Nazarene Univ	KS	28,000	C
Millersville Univ of Pennsylvania	PA	18,498	C
Minn State Univ, Moorhead	MN	13,392	C
Missouri Southern State Univ	MO	11,910	C
Missouri Valley College	MO	22,200	C
Montana State Univ-Billings	MT	12,425	LC
Morningside College	IA	32,620	C
Morris College	SC	16,006	LC
Mount Aloysius College	PA	27,970	C
Mount Vernon Nazarene Univ	OH	29,590	C
New York Univ	NY	61,470	MC
Niagara Univ	NY	39,800	C
N Car State Univ	NC	16,202	HC
Northwestern College	MN	24,000	C
Ohio Univ	OH	20,676	VC
Okla Christian Univ	OK	24,975	VC
Okla Wesleyan Univ	OK	21,300	C
Old Dominion Univ	VA	18,662	C
Oral Roberts Univ	OK	31,734	C
Oswego / SUNY	NY	20,009	VC
Ouachita Baptist Univ	AR	29,010	VC
Pfeiffer Univ	NC	33,700	C
Pittsburg State Univ	KS	12,032	C
Pontifical Catholic Univ of PR	PR	7,310	
Prescott College	AZ	33,284	C+
Providence College	RI	55,995	HC
Purdue Univ/West Lafayette	IN	20,278	HC
Rider Univ	NJ	45,720	C
Rivier College	NH	35,000	VC
Rocky Mountain College	MT	32,242	C
Sacred Heart Univ	CT	48,564	VC
Saginaw Valley State Univ	MI	16,869	C
St. Augustine's Univ	NC	14,000	C
St. Mary's Univ of Minn	MN	37,015	C
Shaw Univ	NC	15,488	LC
Shepherd Univ	WV	14,996	C
Shippensburg Univ of Pennsylvania	PA	17,064	LC
Southeast Missouri State Univ	MO	14,983	LC

School	ST	$IS	SR
Southeastern Okla State Univ	OK	7,966	C
Southern Nazarene Univ	OK	24,354	NC
Southern New Hampshire Univ	NH	38,100	C
Southern Univ and A&M College	LA	9,761	₲
Southern Univ at New Orleans	LA	1,000	NC
Southwest Baptist Univ	MO	24,710	C
St. Edward's Univ	TX	44,674	VC
St. John Fisher College	NY	39,370	₲
St. John's Univ	NY	52,840	₲
St. Olaf College	MN	49,960	H₲
St. Thomas Univ	FL	32,310	₲
SUNY College at Old Westbury	NY	16,324	C
SUNY New Paltz	NY	15,010	C
Syracuse Univ	NY	54,512	HC
Taylor Univ	IN	36,742	V₲
Texas Christian Univ	TX	47,570	HC
Texas Wesleyan Univ	TX	29,886	C
The SUNY at Potsdam	NY	17,754	C
Thomas More College	KY	34,760	C
Tiffin Univ	OH	30,273	LC
Union College	KY	28,775	C
Univ of Central Missouri	MO	14,605	C
Univ of Central Okla	OK	12,293	C
Univ of Charleston	WV	28,650	C
Univ of Conn	CT	23,744	HC
Univ of Evansville	IN	41,056	V₲
Univ of Georgia	GA	19,508	VC
Univ of Great Falls	MT	27,970	C
Univ of Indianapolis	IN	31,740	LC
Univ of Kentucky	KY	19,868	C
Univ of Louisiana at Lafayette	LA	6,130	C
Univ of Louisiana at Monroe	LA	12,998	C
Univ of Mary Hardin-Baylor	TX	31,950	₲
Univ of Mich/Dearborn	MI	9,885	VC
Univ of Minn/Duluth	MN	18,964	₲
Univ of Minn/Twin Cities	MN		HC
Univ of Missouri/Columbia	MO	18,201	MC
Univ of Montana-Western	MT	9,753	LC
Univ of N Car at Charlotte	NC	15,847	C
Univ of N Car at Greensboro	NC	12,848	C
Univ of North Florida	FL	15,578	VC
Univ of Okla	OK	17,634	V₲
Univ of Pittsburgh at Bradford	PA	21,316	LC
Univ of Rio Grande	OH	8,750	NC
Univ of St. Francis	IN	29,810	C
Univ of S Car Upstate	SC	17,673	LC
Univ of South Florida	FL	13,000	C
Univ of the Cumberlands	KY	27,500	LC
Univ of Vermont	VT	26,120	V₲
Univ of Wisc Whitewater	WI	13,314	C
Univ of Wisc/La Crosse	WI	14,755	VC
Valparaiso Univ	IN	43,040	V₲
Virginia Wesleyan College	VA	28,433	LC
Viterbo Univ	WI	30,070	C
Wartburg College	IA	41,055	VC
Washington State Univ	WA	20,461	C
Washington Univ in St. Louis	MO	58,818	MC
Wayne State Univ	MI	19,493	C
Webster Univ	MO	33,990	₲
West Chester Univ of Pennsylvania	PA	16,836	C
West Texas A&M Univ	TX	13,478	C
Wheeling Jesuit Univ	WV	34,668	C
Whitworth Univ	WA	45,826	V₲
Wilmington College	OH	29,784	C
Winona State Univ	MN	16,530	C
Xavier Univ of Louisiana	LA	25,300	C
York College of Pennsylvania	PA	26,590	C
Youngstown State Univ	OH	16,374	LC

SOCIAL STUDIES SECONDARY SCHOOL EDUCATION

School	ST	$IS	SR
Biola Univ	CA	40,320	VC
Concordia Univ St. Paul	MN	27,200	C
Elizabethtown College	PA	47,600	VC
Murray State Univ	KY	14,944	C
New York Univ	NY	61,470	MC
Ouachita Baptist Univ	AR	29,010	VC
Texas Christian Univ	TX	47,570	HC
The College of St. Rose	NY	26,750	C
Univ of Wisc/Superior	WI	14,106	C
Webster Univ	MO	33,990	₲

SOCIAL WORK

School	ST	$IS	SR
Abilene Christian Univ	TX	38,400	VC
Adams State College	CO	13,358	LC
Adelphi Univ	NY	43,130	VC
Adrian College	MI	33,800	C
Alabama A&M Univ	AL	96,100	C
Alabama State Univ	AL	14,142	NC
Albany State Univ	GA	8,500	C
Alcorn State Univ	MS	9,500	C
Alvernia Univ	PA	39,250	C
Anderson Univ	IN	35,390	C
Andrews Univ	MI	28,030	₲
Angelo State Univ	TX	15,049	NC
Anna Maria College	MA	34,600	LC
Appalachian State Univ	NC	12,919	VC
Arizona State Univ	AZ	18,818	₲
Arkansas State Univ	AR	14,980	C
Asbury Univ	KY	32,038	VC
Ashland Univ	OH	25,000	C
Atlantic Union College	MA	24,600	LC
Auburn Univ	AL	20,052	V₲
Augsburg College	MN	35,142	C
Augustana College	IL	43,398	HC
Aurora Univ	IL	26,870	C
Austin Peay State Univ	TN	14,650	C
Avila Univ	MO	26,900	C
Azusa Pacific Univ	CA	39,946	C
Ball State Univ	IN	17,850	C
Barton College	NC	27,660	C
Baylor Univ	TX	46,720	HC
Belhaven Univ	MS	27,170	C
Belmont Univ	TN	37,380	V₲
Bemidji State Univ	MN	13,500	C
Benedict College	SC	20,454	NC
Bennett College	NC		LC
Bethany College	WV	35,282	C
Bethel College	KS	29,100	C
Bethel Univ	MN	34,940	VC
Biola Univ	CA	40,320	VC
Bloomsburg Univ of Pennsylvania	PA	13,598	C
Bluffton Univ	OH	37,864	C
Boise State Univ	ID	12,802	C
Bowie State Univ	MD	23,990	LC
Bowling Green State Univ	OH	18,970	C
Bradley Univ	IL	31,874	VC
Brescia Univ	KY	26,140	V₲
Briar Cliff Univ	IA	29,514	C
Bridgewater State Univ	MA	18,752	C
Brigham Young Univ	UT	12,100	HC
Brigham Young Univ/Hawaii	HI	8,614	VC
Buena Vista Univ	IA	37,954	C
Buffalo State/State Univ of Buffalo	NY	15,733	₲
Cabrini College	PA	40,859	LC
Cairn Univ	PA	31,255	C
Cal State, Chico	CA	18,952	C
Cal State, Fresno	CA	17,405	C
Cal State, Los Angeles	CA	15,829	C
Cal State, Sacramento	CA	16,200	C
Cal State, San Bernardino	CA	12,000	C
Calif Univ of Pennsylvania	PA	14,217	C
Calvin College	MI	37,585	V₲
Campbell Univ	NC	25,500	C
Campbellsville Univ	KY	27,720	C
Capital Univ	OH	39,824	VC
Caribbean Univ	PR	10,375	
Carlow Univ	PA	30,272	C
Carthage College	WI	33,000	C
Castleton State College	VT	19,424	C
Cedar Crest College	PA	43,240	C
Cedarville Univ	OH	31,036	V₲
Central Conn State Univ	CT	19,212	C
Central Mich Univ	MI	18,066	C
Central State Univ	OH	9,010	C
Central Univ of Bayamon	PR	3,350	
Central Washington Univ	WA	11,730	C
Chadron State College	NE	7,400	NC
Champlain College	VT	44,850	VC
Chapman Univ	CA	56,019	V₲
Chatham Univ	PA	42,440	VC
Christopher Newport Univ	VA	21,050	VC
Clark Atlanta Univ	GA	30,006	C
Clarke Univ	IA	36,400	C
Cleveland State Univ	OH	21,357	C
Coker College	SC	32,256	LC
College of Staten Island / The CUNY	NY	16,778	NC
College of Mount St. Joseph	OH	33,880	C
College of St. Scholastica	MN	39,960	C
College of the Ozarks	MO	5,605	VC
Colo State Univ-Fort Collins	CO	20,090	VC
Colo State Univ-Pueblo	CO	13,532	LC
Columbia College	MO	24,578	C
Columbia College	SC	27,882	C
Concord Univ	WV	13,102	C
Concordia College New York	NY	31,500	VC
Concordia College, Moorhead	MN	39,974	₲
Concordia Univ	OR	34,930	C
Concordia Univ Wisc	WI	28,980	C
Concordia Univ, River Forest	IL	26,300	C
Coppin State Univ	MD	14,905	VC
Cornerstone Univ and Grand Rapids Theological Seminary	MI	30,866	C
Creighton Univ	NE	44,058	V₲
Daemen College	NY	31,510	C
Defiance College	OH	30,645	C
Delaware State Univ	DE	14,700	LC
Delta State Univ	MS	12,292	LC
Dickinson State Univ	ND	8,550	NC
Dominican College	NY	31,270	C
Dordt College	IA	34,160	VC
East Carolina Univ	NC	14,169	C
East Central Univ	OK	10,223	LC
East Tenn State Univ	TN	9,000	C
Eastern Conn State Univ	CT	20,584	C
Eastern Kentucky Univ	KY	11,161	C
Eastern Mennonite Univ	VA	38,850	VC
Eastern Mich Univ	MI	17,961	C
Eastern Nazarene College	MA	30,000	C
Eastern New Mexico Univ	NM	10,682	C
Eastern Univ	PA	37,704	C
Eastern Washington Univ	WA	16,388	C
Edinboro Univ of Pennsylvania	PA	15,940	LC
Elizabeth City State Univ	NC	11,638	C
Elizabethtown College	PA	47,600	VC
Elms College	MA	23,900	VC
Evangel Univ	MO	23,090	C
Fayetteville State Univ	NC	10,816	C
Ferris State Univ	MI	19,698	C
Ferrum College	VA	27,740	LC
Florida A&M Univ	FL	14,935	LC
Florida Atlantic Univ	FL	17,339	C
Florida Gulf Coast Univ	FL		C
Florida International Univ	FL	17,747	VC
Florida State Univ	FL	15,238	HC
Fontbonne Univ	MO	31,384	C
Fordham Univ	NY	58,927	HC
Fort Hays State Univ	KS	11,354	C
Fort Valley State Univ	GA	11,200	VC
Franciscan Univ of Steubenville	OH	27,320	VC
Franklin Pierce Univ	NH	41,598	C
Freed-Hardeman Univ	TN	19,697	VC
Fresno Pacific Univ	CA	32,136	C
Frostburg State Univ	MD	15,264	LC
Gallaudet Univ	DC	25,380	SP
Gannon Univ	PA	37,940	C
George Fox Univ	OR	40,750	₲
George Mason Univ	VA	15,724	VC
Georgia Regents Univ	GA		C
Georgia State Univ	GA	12,000	VC
Georgian Court Univ	NJ	39,726	LC
Gordon College	MA	42,660	V₲
Goshen College	IN	35,900	VC
Grace College and Theological Seminary	IN	28,800	C
Grambling State Univ	LA	13,384	LC
Grand Valley State Univ	MI	17,998	VC
Greenville College	IL	27,012	C
Gwynedd-Mercy College	PA	33,560	C
Harding Univ	AR	21,432	₲
Hardin-Simmons Univ	TX	23,560	₲
Hawaii Pacific Univ	HI	36,690	C
Heritage Univ	WA	17,664	NC
Hood College	MD	44,630	C
Hope College	MI	36,320	V₲
Howard Payne Univ	TX	17,115	C
Howard Univ	DC	35,957	C
Humboldt State Univ	CA	18,400	C
Huntington Univ	IN	32,220	C
Idaho State Univ	ID	11,908	C
Illinois State Univ	IL	22,634	VC
Indiana State Univ	IN	16,000	C
Indiana Univ Bloomington	IN	19,358	HC
Indiana Univ East	IN	6,639	LC
Indiana Univ Northwest	IN	6,738	LC
Indiana Univ South Bend	IN	15,293	C
Indiana Univ-Purdue Univ Indianapolis	IN	17,290	C
Indiana Wesleyan Univ	IN	31,815	VC
Inter-American Univ of PR/Aguadilla Campus	PR	5,578	
Inter-American Univ of PR/Arecibo Campus	PR	3,350	
Inter-American Univ of PR/Fajardo Campus	PR	4,200	
Inter-American Univ of PR/Metropolitan Campus	PR	4,320	
Inter-American Univ of PR/Ponce	PR	3,700	
Iona College	NY	44,028	C
Jackson State Univ	MS	13,512	LC
Jacksonville State Univ	AL	12,280	LC
James Madison Univ	VA	18,049	VC
Jarvis Christian College	TX	19,552	NC
Johnson C. Smith Univ	NC	25,336	LC
Judson College	AL	24,690	C
Juniata College	PA	49,340	VC
Kansas State Univ	KS	15,497	VC
Kentucky Christian Univ	KY	17,622	LC
Kentucky State Univ	KY	11,000	LC
Keuka College	NY	30,300	C
Kutztown Univ of Pennsylvania	PA	16,909	LC
La Salle Univ	PA	50,270	C
La Sierra Univ	CA	35,694	VC
Lamar Univ	TX	6,820	LC
Lehman College / The CUNY	NY	5,778	LC
LeMoyne-Owen College	TN	13,100	C
Lewis Univ	IL	23,050	C
Lewis-Clark State College	ID	6,990	C
Limestone College	SC	29,880	C
Lincoln Memorial Univ	TN	18,144	C
Lincoln Univ	MO	11,996	NC
Lindenwood Univ	MO	20,750	C
Lipscomb Univ	TN	35,722	VC
Livingstone College	NC	17,815	LC
Lock Haven Univ of Pennsylvania	PA	17,587	LC
LIU/Brooklyn Campus	NY	26,500	C
LIU/C.W. Post Campus	NY	38,888	C
Longwood Univ	VA	20,924	C
Loras College	IA	37,432	VC
Louisiana College	LA	15,746	C
Lourdes Univ	OH	26,055	LC
Loyola Univ Chicago	IL	49,560	V₲
Lubbock Christian Univ	TX	25,518	C
Luther College	IA	44,380	V₲
MacMurray College	IL	20,755	C
Madonna Univ	MI	24,540	VC
Malone Univ	OH	34,334	C
Manchester College	IN	35,070	C
Mansfield Univ	PA	19,468	LC
Marian Univ	WI	30,980	LC
Marist College	NY	35,500	C
Mars Hill College	NC	22,950	LC
Marshall Univ	WV	14,820	C
Mary Baldwin College	VA	37,110	C
Marygrove College	MI	21,290	C
Marywood Univ	PA	40,695	C
McDaniel College	MD	45,600	VC
McKendree Univ	IL	29,920	₲
Mercy College	NY	29,996	C
Mercyhurst Univ	PA	40,700	C
Meredith College	NC	31,420	C
Messiah College	PA	39,540	VC
Methodist Univ	NC	37,185	C
Metropolitan College of New York	NY	16,720	VC
Metropolitan State Univ	MN	5,923	SP
Metropolitan State Univ of Denver	CO	4,835	LC
Miami Univ	OH	24,191	HC
Mich State Univ	MI	13,689	VC
Middle Tenn State Univ	TN	8,650	C
Midwestern State Univ	TX	9,722	C
Miles College	AL	16,530	NC
Millersville Univ of Pennsylvania	PA	18,498	C
Minn State Univ, Mankato	MN	14,900	C
Minn State Univ, Moorhead	MN	13,392	C
Minot State Univ	ND	10,915	C
Misericordia Univ	PA	39,840	C
Miss College	MS	21,998	VC
Miss Valley State Univ	MS	9,706	LC
Missouri State Univ	MO	13,996	VC
Missouri Western State Univ	MO	12,260	NC
Molloy College	NY	38,950	C
Monmouth Univ	NJ	42,252	C
Morehead State Univ	KY	10,900	C
Morgan State Univ	MD	14,500	VC
Mount Mary Univ	WI	32,836	LC
Mount Mercy Univ	IA	34,385	C
Mount St. Mary College	NY	39,540	C
Mount St. Mary's College/Chalon Campus	CA	43,897	V₲
Mount Vernon Nazarene Univ	OH	29,590	C
Mountain State Univ	WV	14,330	NC
Murray State Univ	KY	14,944	C
Nazareth College of Rochester	NY	41,590	VC
Nebr Wesleyan Univ	NE	29,774	₲
New Mexico Highlands Univ	NM	9,720	NC
New Mexico State Univ	NM	13,955	LC
New York Univ	NY	61,470	MC
Niagara Univ	NY	39,800	C
N Car Agricultural and Technical State Univ	NC	13,175	LC
N Car Central Univ	NC	9,000	LC
N Car State Univ	NC	16,202	HC
Northeastern Illinois Univ	IL		C
Northeastern State Univ	OK	8,615	VC
Northern Arizona Univ	AZ	18,592	C
Northern Kentucky Univ	KY	15,302	LC
Northern Mich Univ	MI	15,300	VC
Northwest Nazarene Univ	ID	24,275	NC
Northwestern College of Iowa	IA	34,848	₲
Northwestern Okla State Univ	OK	7,275	NC
Northwestern State Univ of Louisiana	LA	14,368	C
Nyack College	NY	32,000	C
Oakland Univ	MI	19,391	VC
Oakwood Univ	AL	23,035	C
Oglethorpe Univ	GA	42,580	VC
Ohio Dominican Univ	OH	38,380	₲
Ohio Univ	OH	20,676	VC
Okla Baptist Univ	OK	28,202	VC
Olivet Nazarene Univ	IL	29,990	C
Oral Roberts Univ	OK	31,734	C
Our Lady of the Lake Univ of San Antonio	TX	22,430	LC
Pacific Lutheran Univ	WA	44,840	VC
Pacific Union College	CA	28,150	VC
Pacific Univ	OR	42,815	C
Park Univ	MO	17,525	C
Philander Smith College	AR	19,760	LC
Pittsburg State Univ	KS	12,032	C
Plymouth State Univ	NH	23,148	LC

School	ST	$IS	SR
Point Loma Nazarene Univ	CA	38,610	VC
Pontifical Catholic Univ of PR	PR	7,310	
Portland State Univ	OR	18,672	C
Prairie View A&M Univ	TX	15,205	LC
Prescott College	AZ	33,284	C+
Presentation College	SD	14,800	LC
Providence College	RI	55,995	HC
Purdue Univ/West Lafayette	IN	20,278	HC
Quincy Univ	IL	34,980	LC
Radford Univ	VA	17,132	LC
Ramapo College of New Jersey	NJ	24,938	C+
Regis College	MA	47,565	LC
Rhode Island College	RI	17,132	LC
Richard Stockton College of New Jersey	NJ	20,000	VC
Roberts Wesleyan College	NY	37,384	C+
Rust College	MS	10,600	C
Rutgers, The State Univ of New Jersey/Camden Campus	NJ	24,254	C
Rutgers, The State Univ of New Jersey/New Brunswick	NJ	25,077	VC
Rutgers, The State Univ of New Jersey/Newark Campus	NJ	25,376	C
Sacred Heart Univ	CT	48,564	VC
Saginaw Valley State Univ	MI	16,869	C
St. Francis Univ	PA	30,029	LC
St. Joseph College	CT	45,630	LC
St. Leo Univ	FL	27,990	C
St. Louis Univ	MO	46,594	VC+
St. Martin's Univ	WA	38,082	C
St. Mary's College	IN	45,160	VC
Salem State College	MA	13,161	LC
Salisbury Univ	MD	18,368	VC
Salve Regina Univ	RI	47,250	VC
San Diego State Univ	CA	20,578	VC
San Francisco State Univ	CA	18,514	C
San Jose State Univ	CA	19,707	C
Savannah State Univ	GA	13,156	C
Seattle Univ	WA	47,010	VC+
Seton Hall Univ	NJ	45,902	C
Seton Hill Univ	PA	35,172	C
Shaw Univ	NC	15,488	LC
Shepherd Univ	WV	14,996	C
Shippensburg Univ of Pennsylvania	PA	17,064	LC
Siena College	NY	43,863	VC
Siena Heights Univ	MI	17,000	LC
Skidmore College	NY	57,926	HC
Slippery Rock Univ of Pennsylvania	PA	10,360	LC
Sojourner-Douglass College	MD	9,160	LC
S Car State Univ	SC	6,700	LC
Southeast Missouri State Univ	MO	14,983	LC
Southeastern Louisiana Univ	LA	13,325	C
Southeastern Univ	FL	27,201	C+
Southern Adventist Univ	TN	26,190	C
Southern Conn State Univ	CT	18,033	C
Southern Illinois Univ Carbondale	IL	21,620	C
Southern Illinois Univ Edwardsville	IL	17,532	C
Southern Univ and A&M College	LA	9,761	C+
Southern Univ at New Orleans	LA	1,000	NC
Southwest Minn State Univ	MN	14,000	C
Southwestern Adventist Univ	TX	23,026	LC
Southwestern Okla State Univ	OK	9,160	C
Spalding Univ	KY	31,850	LC
Spring Arbor Univ	MI	26,740	C
St. Catherine Univ	MN	37,782	C+
St. Cloud State Univ	MN	10,600	C
St. Edward's Univ	TX	44,674	VC
St. Olaf College	MN	49,960	HC+
Stephen F. Austin State Univ	TX	14,668	C
Stony Brook Univ / SUNY	NY	19,359	HC
SUNY Fredonia / The SUNY at Fredonia	NY	18,702	VC
SUNY Plattsburgh / SUNY	NY	18,083	VC
Syracuse Univ	NY	54,512	HC
Talladega College	AL	13,000	C
Tarleton State Univ	TX	13,489	LC
Taylor Univ	IN	36,742	VC+
Temple Univ	PA	24,392	VC
Tenn State Univ	TN	9,048	C
Texas A&M Univ at Commerce	TX	10,496	C
Texas Christian Univ	TX	47,570	HC
Texas Southern Univ	TX	18,212	LC
Texas State Univ	TX	16,495	VC
Texas Tech Univ	TX	14,243	C
Texas Woman's Univ	TX	13,633	LC
The Catholic Univ of America	DC	52,852	VC
The College at Brockport / SUNY	NY	18,362	VC

School	ST	$IS	SR
The College of New Rochelle	NY	33,600	VC
The College of St. Rose	NY	26,750	C
Ohio State Univ	OH	19,887	MC
Thomas Univ	GA	11,520	NC
Trevecca Nazarene Univ	TN	30,118	C
Trinity Christian College	IL	28,869	C
Troy Univ	AL	10,650	C
Tuskegee Univ	AL	26,750	C
Union College	KY	28,775	C
Union College	NE	23,270	VC
Union Inst & Univ	OH	8,912	SP
Union Univ	TN	28,260	VC
Univ at Albany / SUNY	NY	18,674	VC
Univ of Akron	OH	20,436	C
Univ of Alabama at Birmingham	AL	18,484	C+
Univ of Alabama at Tuscaloosa	AL	17,164	C+
Univ of Alaska Anchorage	AK	15,290	NC
Univ of Alaska Fairbanks	AK	13,955	C
Univ of Arkansas at Fayetteville	AR	16,860	VC
Univ of Arkansas at Little Rock	AR		C
Univ of Arkansas at Monticello	AR	8,470	NC
Univ of Arkansas at Pine Bluff	AR	10,600	C
Univ of Calif at Berkeley	CA	23,322	MC
Univ of Central Florida	FL	15,711	VC+
Univ of Central Missouri	MO	14,605	C
Univ of Charleston	WV	28,650	C
Univ of Cincinnati	OH	20,199	VC
Univ of Detroit Mercy	MI	30,450	C
Univ of Findlay	OH	31,916	C
Univ of Georgia	GA	19,508	VC
Univ of Hawaii at Manoa	HI	19,379	VC
Univ of Houston-Downtown	TX	6,267	LC
Univ of Indianapolis	IN	31,740	LC
Univ of Iowa	IA	17,481	VC
Univ of Kansas	KS	16,980	C+
Univ of Kentucky	KY	19,868	C
Univ of Louisiana at Monroe	LA	12,998	C
Univ of Louisville	KY	17,460	VC
Univ of Maine	ME	19,712	C+
Univ of Maine at Presque Isle	ME	15,011	LC
Univ of Mary	ND	16,714	C
Univ of Mary Hardin-Baylor	TX	31,950	C+
Univ of Maryland/Baltimore County	MD	18,000	VC
Univ of Memphis	TN	15,094	C
Univ of Mich-Flint	MI	17,547	C+
Univ of Miss	MS	15,482	VC
Univ of Missouri/Columbia	MO	18,201	MC
Univ of Missouri-St. Louis	MO	18,304	VC
Univ of Montana	MT	13,670	C
Univ of Montevallo	AL	17,320	C
Univ of Nebr at Kearney	NE	14,855	LC
Univ of Nebr at Omaha	NE	12,700	C
Univ of Nevada, Las Vegas	NV	17,303	C
Univ of Nevada/Reno	NV	14,500	NC
Univ of New Hampshire	NH	24,702	VC
Univ of North Alabama	AL	9,960	C
Univ of N Car at Charlotte	NC	15,847	C
Univ of N Car at Greensboro	NC	12,848	C
Univ of N Car at Wilmington	NC	13,572	VC+
Univ of N Dak	ND	14,094	C
Univ of North Texas	TX	15,628	C
Univ of Northern Iowa	IA	14,776	C
Univ of Okla	OK	17,634	VC+
Univ of Pikeville	KY	24,750	NC
Univ of Pittsburgh at Pittsburgh	PA	27,800	HC+
Univ of Portland	OR	47,874	VC
Univ of PR Recinto de Rio Piedras	PR	5,750	
Univ of PR/Humacao	PR	1,877	
Univ of Rio Grande	OH	8,750	NC
Univ of St. Francis	IN	29,810	C
Univ of Sioux Falls	SD	22,990	C
Univ of South Alabama	AL	13,510	C
Univ of S Car at Columbia	SC	19,725	VC+
Univ of S Dak	SD	15,111	C
Univ of South Florida	FL	13,000	C
Univ of Southern Indiana	IN	14,657	C
Univ of Southern Maine	ME	16,576	C
Univ of Southern Miss	MS	13,170	C
Univ of St. Francis	IL	36,490	C
Univ of Tenn at Chattanooga	TN	16,883	C
Univ of Tenn at Knoxville	TN	20,364	VC+
Univ of Tenn at Martin	TN	13,217	C
Univ of Texas at Arlington	TX	10,908	LC
Univ of Texas at Austin	TX	44,074	HC
Univ of Texas at El Paso	TX	8,764	NC
Univ of Texas-Pan American	TX	12,432	LC
Univ of the Cumberlands	KY	27,500	LC
Univ of the District of Columbia	DC	7,244	LC
Univ of the Sacred Heart	PR	5,590	
Univ of Toledo	OH	18,464	C
Univ of Utah	UT	13,462	VC

School	ST	$IS	SR
Univ of Vermont	VT	26,120	VC+
Univ of Washington	WA	14,722	VC
Univ of West Florida	FL	14,656	C
Univ of Wisc Whitewater	WI	13,314	C
Univ of Wisc/Eau Claire	WI	15,430	VC
Univ of Wisc/Green Bay	WI	14,900	C
Univ of Wisc/Madison	WI	18,757	HC
Univ of Wisc/Oshkosh	WI	10,426	LC
Univ of Wisc/River Falls	WI	9,722	LC
Univ of Wisc/Stevens Point	WI	14,043	C
Univ of Wisc/Superior	WI	14,106	C
Univ of Wisc-Milwaukee	WI	18,436	C
Univ of Wyoming	WY	13,855	C+
Ursuline College	OH	33,198	LC
Utah State Univ	UT	11,803	C
Valparaiso Univ	IN	43,040	VC+
Virginia Commonwealth Univ	VA	18,633	C
Virginia Intermont College	VA	32,411	LC
Virginia State Univ	VA	11,318	C+
Virginia Union Univ	VA	18,432	C
Virginia Wesleyan College	VA	28,433	LC
Viterbo Univ	WI	30,070	C
Walla Walla Univ	WA	26,256	NC
Warner Univ	FL	18,000	C
Warren Wilson College	NC	34,888	VC
Wartburg College	IA	41,055	VC
Washburn Univ	KS	12,165	NC
Wayne State Univ	MI	19,493	C
West Chester Univ of Pennsylvania	PA	16,836	C
West Texas A&M Univ	TX	13,478	C
West Virginia State Univ	WV	8,378	NC
West Virginia Univ	WV	15,794	C+
Western Carolina Univ	NC	13,965	C+
Western Conn State Univ	CT	18,327	C
Western Illinois Univ	IL	20,130	C
Western Kentucky Univ	KY	11,000	LC
Western Mich Univ	MI	19,042	C
Western New England Univ	MA	45,590	C
Western New Mexico Univ	NM	8,500	LC
Westfield State Univ	MA	18,489	C
Wheelock College	MA	33,075	C
Whittier College	CA	43,416	C
Wichita State Univ	KS	12,539	C
Widener Univ	PA	50,368	C
Wilberforce Univ	OH	15,100	LC
William Woods Univ	MO		C
Wilmington College	OH	29,784	C
Winona State Univ	MN	16,530	C
Winthrop Univ	SC	21,120	VC
Wright State Univ	OH	16,983	C
Xavier Univ	OH	43,740	VC
York College / CUNY	NY	5,496	NC
Youngstown State Univ	OH	16,374	LC

SOCIOLOGY

School	ST	$IS	SR
Abilene Christian Univ	TX	38,400	VC
Adams State College	CO	13,358	LC
Adelphi Univ	NY	43,130	VC
Adrian College	MI	33,800	C
Agnes Scott College	GA	45,323	VC+
Alabama A&M Univ	AL	96,100	C
Alabama State Univ	AL	14,142	NC
Albany State Univ	GA	8,500	C
Albertus Magnus College	CT	37,382	LC
Albion College	MI	43,884	VC
Albright College	PA	46,660	C
Alcorn State Univ	MS	9,500	C
Alfred Univ	NY	40,392	VC
Allen Univ	SC	16,124	NC
Alma College	MI	42,400	VC
Alverno College	WI	30,483	LC
American International College	MA	36,100	LC
American Univ	DC	54,829	HC+
Amherst College	MA	58,744	MC
Anderson Univ	IN	35,390	C
Andrews Univ	MI	28,030	C+
Angelo State Univ	TX	15,049	NC
Anna Maria College	MA	34,600	LC
Appalachian State Univ	NC	12,919	VC
Aquinas College	MI	33,060	C
Arcadia Univ	PA	33,570	C+
Arizona State Univ	AZ	18,818	C+
Arkansas State Univ	AR	14,980	C
Arkansas Tech Univ	AR	13,164	LC
Asbury Univ	KY	32,038	VC
Ashland Univ	OH	25,000	C
Assumption College	MA	45,721	VC
Auburn Univ	AL	20,052	VC+
Auburn Univ at Montgomery	AL	12,120	C
Augsburg College	MN	35,142	C
Augustana College	IL	43,398	HC
Augustana College	SD	35,500	VC
Aurora Univ	IL	26,870	C
Austin College	TX	36,940	HC
Austin Peay State Univ	TN	14,650	C
Averett Univ	VA	36,000	LC
Avila Univ	MO	26,900	C
Azusa Pacific Univ	CA	39,946	C
Baker Univ	KS	33,350	C+
Baldwin Wallace Univ	OH	36,980	VC
Ball State Univ	IN	17,850	C
Bard College	NY	59,872	HC

School	ST	$IS	SR
Barry Univ	FL	38,190	C
Bates College	ME	58,950	MC
Baylor Univ	TX	46,720	HC
Bellarmine Univ	KY	42,950	VC
Bellevue Univ	NE	4,600	NC
Belmont Univ	TN	37,380	VC+
Beloit College	WI	49,970	HC
Bemidji State Univ	MN	13,500	C
Benedict College	SC	20,454	NC
Benedictine College	KS	29,180	VC
Benedictine Univ	IL	35,220	C
Bennington College	VT	56,990	HC+
Berea College	KY	7,220	HC
Berry College	GA	39,254	HC
Bethel College	IN	31,560	C
Bethel Univ	TN	19,186	C
Bethune-Cookman Univ	FL	22,290	LC
Binghamton Univ / The SUNY	NY	20,832	HC+
Biola Univ	CA	40,320	VC
Birmingham-Southern College	AL	42,370	VC+
Black Hills State Univ	SD	13,562	LC
Bloomfield College	NJ	36,960	C
Bloomsburg Univ of Pennsylvania	PA	13,598	C
Bluffton Univ	OH	37,864	C
Boise State Univ	ID	12,802	C
Boston College	MA	58,506	MC
Boston Univ	MA	54,130	HC+
Bowdoin College	ME	57,834	MC
Bowie State Univ	MD	23,990	LC
Bowling Green State Univ	OH	18,970	C
Bradley Univ	IL	31,874	VC
Brandeis Univ	MA	58,820	HC
Brewton-Parker College	GA	33,388	LC
Briar Cliff Univ	IA	29,514	C
Bridgewater College	VA	39,880	C
Bridgewater State Univ	MA	18,752	C
Brigham Young Univ	UT	12,100	HC
Brown Univ	RI	56,150	MC
Bryant Univ	RI	49,179	VC
Bryn Mawr College	PA	57,760	MC
Bucknell Univ	PA	58,160	MC
Buffalo State/State Univ of Buffalo	NY	15,733	C+
Butler Univ	IN	45,898	VC+
Cabrini College	PA	40,859	LC
Caldwell College	NJ	35,602	LC
Calif Baptist Univ	CA	35,890	C
Calif Lutheran Univ	CA	47,640	C
Calif Polytechnic State Univ	CA	19,847	HC
Calif State Polytechnic Univ, Pomona	CA	18,932	C
Cal State, Bakersfield	CA	8,000	LC
Cal State, Chico	CA	18,952	C
Cal State, Dominguez Hills	CA	17,056	LC
Cal State, East Bay	CA	16,549	C
Cal State, Fresno	CA	17,405	C
Cal State, Long Beach	CA	17,534	C+
Cal State, Los Angeles	CA	15,829	C
Cal State, Northridge	CA	28,313	C
Cal State, Sacramento	CA	16,200	C
Cal State, San Bernardino	CA	12,000	C
Cal State, San Marcos	CA	14,576	C
Cal State, Stanislaus	CA	18,582	C
Calvin College	MI	37,585	VC+
Cameron Univ	OK	9,267	LC
Campbellsville Univ	KY	27,720	C
Canisius College	NY	45,602	VC
Capital Univ	OH	39,824	VC
Cardinal Stritch Univ	WI	24,054	C
Carleton College	MN	58,149	MC
Carlow Univ	PA	30,272	C
Carroll College	MT	28,000	C
Carroll Univ	WI	24,860	C
Carson-Newman Univ	TN	29,058	C+
Carthage College	WI	33,000	C
Case Western Reserve Univ	OH	55,178	MC
Castleton State College	VT	19,424	C
Catawba College	NC	37,105	C
Cedarville Univ	OH	31,036	VC+
Centenary College	NJ	38,618	LC
Centenary College of Louisiana	LA	39,070	C+
Central College	IA	36,980	VC
Central Conn State Univ	CT	19,212	C
Central Methodist Univ	MO	28,240	VC
Central Mich Univ	MI	18,066	C
Central State Univ	OH	9,010	C
Central Univ of Bayamon	PR	3,350	
Central Washington Univ	WA	11,730	C
Centre College	KY	35,000	HC+
Chadron State College	NE	7,400	NC
Chapman Univ	CA	56,019	VC+
Charleston Southern Univ	SC	22,420	C
Chestnut Hill College	PA	39,785	LC
Chicago State Univ	IL	5,482	C
Christopher Newport Univ	VA	21,050	VC
CUNY/Baruch College	NY	15,831	VC
CUNY/Brooklyn College	NY	5,884	C+
Claflin Univ	SC	22,368	C+
Clarion Univ of Pennsylvania	PA	17,370	C
Clark Atlanta Univ	GA	30,006	C

School	ST	$IS	SR
Clark Univ	MA	47,020	HC+
Clarke Univ	IA	36,400	C
Clemson Univ	SC	19,136	HC
Cleveland State Univ	OH	21,357	C
Coastal Carolina Univ	SC	17,620	C
Coe College	IA	43,590	VC
Coker College	SC	32,256	LC
Colby College	ME	57,510	MC
Colby-Sawyer College	NH	47,870	C
Colgate Univ	NY	50,930	MC
College of Staten Island / The CUNY	NY	16,778	NC
College of Charleston	SC	21,273	VC
College of Mount St. Joseph	OH	33,880	C
College of Mount St. Vincent	NY	41,040	MC
College of New Jersey	NJ	25,376	HC
College of St. Benedict	MN	47,570	VC
College of St. Elizabeth	NJ	43,839	LC
College of the Holy Cross	MA	56,232	MC
College of the Ozarks	MO	5,605	VC
College of William & Mary	VA	25,085	MC
College of Wooster	OH	52,600	VC
Colo College	CO	54,534	MC
Colo Mesa Univ	CO	16,669	LC
Colo State Univ-Fort Collins	CO	20,090	VC
Colo State Univ-Pueblo	CO	13,532	LC
Columbia College	MO	24,578	C
Columbia College	SC	27,882	C
Columbia Univ in the City of New York	NY	61,116	MC
Columbia Univ/Barnard College	NY	39,000	MC
Columbia Univ/School of General Studies	NY	54,083	MC
Columbus State Univ	GA	13,176	C
Concord Univ	WV	13,102	C
Concordia College, Moorhead	MN	39,974	C+
Concordia Univ St. Paul	MN	27,200	C
Concordia Univ, Ann Arbor	MI	27,220	VC
Concordia Univ, River Forest	IL	26,300	C
Conn College	CT	54,970	MC
Cornell College	IA	44,930	HC
Cornell Univ	NY	59,037	MC
Covenant College	GA		VC+
Creighton Univ	NE	44,058	VC+
Cumberland Univ	TN	21,220	C
CUNY-City College	NY	19,576	HC+
Curry College	MA	47,545	LC
Dakota Wesleyan Univ	SD	23,000	C
Dallas Baptist Univ	TX	29,118	C
Dartmouth College	NH	57,996	MC
Davidson College	NC	54,683	MC
Davis and Elkins College	WV	33,742	C
Delaware State Univ	DE	14,700	LC
Denison Univ	OH	54,670	HC+
DePaul Univ	IL	46,120	VC
DePauw Univ	IN	48,950	VC+
Dickinson College	PA	57,662	HC+
Dickinson State Univ	ND	8,550	NC
Dillard Univ	LA	20,940	VC
Doane College	NE	33,730	VC
Dominican Univ	IL	37,628	C
Dordt College	IA	34,160	VC
Dowling College	NY	25,000	LC
Drake Univ	IA	30,980	VC+
Drew Univ/College of Liberal Arts	NJ	55,862	VC
Drexel Univ	PA	51,920	HC
Drury Univ	MO	30,319	VC
Duke Univ	NC	50,250	MC
Duquesne Univ	PA	42,017	VC
D'Youville College	NY	29,850	C
Earlham College	IN	49,710	VC+
East Carolina Univ	NC	14,169	C
East Central Univ	OK	10,223	LC
East Stroudsburg Univ of Pennsylvania	PA	16,636	C
East Tenn State Univ	TN	9,000	C
East Texas Baptist Univ	TX	29,135	C
Eastern Conn State Univ	CT	20,584	C
Eastern Illinois Univ	IL	20,502	C
Eastern Kentucky Univ	KY	11,161	C
Eastern Mennonite Univ	VA	38,850	VC
Eastern Mich Univ	MI	17,961	C
Eastern Nazarene College	MA	30,000	C
Eastern New Mexico Univ	NM	10,682	C
Eastern Oregon Univ	OR	10,400	C
Eastern Univ	PA	37,704	C
Eastern Washington Univ	WA	16,388	C
Eckerd College	FL	43,902	VC
Edgewood College	WI	33,294	C
Edward Waters College	FL	17,856	LC
Elizabeth City State Univ	NC	11,638	C
Elizabethtown College	PA	47,600	VC
Elmhurst College	IL	42,032	C+
Elmira College	NY	49,950	C+
Elms College	MA	23,900	VC
Elon Univ	NC	40,046	HC
Emmanuel College	MA	47,985	VC
Emory and Henry College	VA	387,460	C
Emory Univ	GA	45,000	MC
Emporia State Univ	KS	12,897	C

School	ST	$IS	SR
Eugene Lang College - The New School for Liberal Arts	NY	55,650	VC
Eureka College	IL	19,280	C
Evangel Univ	MO	23,090	C
Excelsior College	NY	895	SP
Fairfield Univ	CT	55,850	VC
Fairleigh Dickinson Univ/ College at Florham	NJ	42,142	C
Fairmont State Univ	WV	12,098	LC
Fayetteville State Univ	NC	10,816	C
Ferris State Univ	MI	19,698	C
Fisk Univ	TN	19,830	C
Fitchburg State Univ	MA	17,241	C
Flagler College	FL	24,960	VC
Florida A&M Univ	FL	14,935	LC
Florida Atlantic Univ	FL	17,339	C
Florida Gulf Coast Univ	FL		C
Florida International Univ	FL	17,747	VC
Florida Memorial Univ	FL	20,716	LC
Florida Southern College	FL	38,240	VC
Florida State Univ	FL	15,238	HC
Fontbonne Univ	MO	31,384	C
Fordham Univ	NY	58,927	HC
Fort Hays State Univ	KS	11,354	C
Fort Lewis College	CO	15,513	C
Fort Valley State Univ	GA	11,200	VC
Framingham State Univ	MA	16,750	C
Francis Marion Univ	SC	16,464	LC
Franciscan Univ of Steubenville	OH	27,320	VC
Franklin and Marshall College	PA	58,295	MC
Franklin College	IN	35,885	C
Frostburg State Univ	MD	15,264	LC
Furman Univ	SC	54,006	HC
Gallaudet Univ	DC	25,380	SP
Gardner-Webb Univ	NC	34,375	C+
Geneva College	PA	27,280	C
George Fox Univ	OR	40,750	C+
George Mason Univ	VA	15,724	VC
George Washington Univ	DC	57,108	MC
Georgetown College	KY	38,690	C
Georgetown Univ	DC	52,910	MC
Georgia College and State Univ	GA	18,216	VC
Georgia Regents Univ	GA		C
Georgia Southern Univ	GA	16,414	C
Georgia Southwestern State Univ	GA	12,218	C
Georgia State Univ	GA	12,000	VC
Gettysburg College	PA	56,820	HC
Gonzaga Univ	WA	44,247	HC
Gordon College	MA	42,660	VC+
Goshen College	IN	35,900	VC
Goucher College	MD	50,252	VC+
Grace College and Theological Seminary	IN	28,800	C
Graceland Univ	IA	28,020	C
Grambling State Univ	LA	13,384	LC
Grand Canyon Univ	AZ	24,540	VC
Grand Valley State Univ	MI	17,998	VC
Green Mountain College	VT	33,547	LC
Greensboro College	NC	28,740	LC
Greenville College	IL	27,012	C
Grinnell College	IA	53,654	HC
Guilford College	NC	35,340	C
Gustavus Adolphus College	MN	48,170	HC
Gwynedd-Mercy College	PA	33,560	C
Hamilton College	NY	55,620	MC
Hamline Univ	MN	44,198	VC
Hampshire College	MA	58,320	MC
Hampton Univ	VA	28,528	C
Hannibal-LaGrange Univ	MO	24,490	C
Hanover College	IN	41,450	VC
Hardin-Simmons Univ	TX	23,560	C+
Hartwick College	NY	49,815	C+
Harvard Univ/Harvard College	MA	49,000	MC
Hastings College	NE	27,782	C+
Haverford College	PA	59,236	MC
Hawaii Pacific Univ	HI	36,690	C
Henderson State Univ	AR	13,634	C
Hendrix College	AR	48,436	HC+
High Point Univ	NC	39,800	C
Hillsdale College	MI	31,890	HC+
Hiram College	OH	37,300	VC
Hobart and William Smith Colleges	NY	43,000	VC
Hofstra Univ	NY	48,020	VC+
Hollins Univ	VA	43,295	VC
Holy Family Univ	PA	40,030	LC
Holy Names Univ	CA	40,310	NC
Hood College	MD	44,630	C
Hope College	MI	36,320	VC+
Houghton College	NY	35,740	VC
Houston Baptist Univ	TX	23,815	C+
Howard Payne Univ	TX	17,115	C
Howard Univ	DC	35,957	C
Humboldt State Univ	CA	18,400	C
Hunter College / The CUNY	NY	14,429	VC
Huntington Univ	IN	32,220	C
Huston-Tillotson Univ	TX	18,124	C+
Idaho State Univ	ID	11,908	C
Illinois College	IL	25,770	VC
Illinois State Univ	IL	22,634	VC

School	ST	$IS	SR
Illinois Wesleyan Univ	IL	48,452	VC+
Immaculata Univ	PA	43,000	C
Indiana State Univ	IN	16,000	C
Indiana Univ Bloomington	IN	19,358	HC
Indiana Univ East	IN	6,639	LC
Indiana Univ Kokomo	IN	6,674	LC
Indiana Univ Northwest	IN	6,738	LC
Indiana Univ of Pennsylvania	PA	20,180	LC
Indiana Univ South Bend	IN	15,293	C
Indiana Univ Southeast	IN	15,807	LC
Indiana Univ-Purdue Univ Fort Wayne	IN	15,425	C
Indiana Univ-Purdue Univ Indianapolis	IN	17,290	C
Indiana Wesleyan Univ	IN	31,815	VC
Inter-American Univ of PR/ Fajardo Campus	PR	4,200	
Inter-American Univ of PR/ Metropolitan Campus	PR	4,320	
Inter-American Univ of PR/ Ponce	PR	3,700	
Inter-American Univ of PR/ San Germán	PR	6,720	
Iona College	NY	44,028	C
Iowa State Univ	IA	16,403	C
Iowa Wesleyan College	IA	30,850	LC
Ithaca College	NY	52,300	HC
Jackson State Univ	MS	13,512	LC
Jacksonville State Univ	AL	12,280	LC
Jacksonville Univ	FL	37,780	C
James Madison Univ	VA	18,049	VC
Jarvis Christian College	TX	19,552	NC
John Carroll Univ	OH	44,520	C+
Johns Hopkins Univ	MD	47,492	MC
Johnson C. Smith Univ	NC	25,336	LC
Johnson State College	VT	16,721	C
Judson Univ	IL	25,130	C
Juniata College	PA	49,340	VC
Kalamazoo College	MI	47,825	HC+
Kansas State Univ	KS	15,497	VC
Kansas Wesleyan Univ	KS	32,000	C
Kean Univ	NJ	22,060	LC
Kennesaw State Univ	GA	13,017	VC
Kent State Univ	OH	19,352	C
Kentucky State Univ	KY	11,000	LC
Kentucky Wesleyan College	KY	27,440	VC+
Kenyon College	OH	56,810	MC
Keuka College	NY	30,300	C
King's College	PA	41,678	C
Knox College	IL		VC
Kutztown Univ of Pennsylvania	PA	16,909	LC
La Roche College	PA	34,802	LC
La Salle Univ	PA	50,270	C
La Sierra Univ	CA	35,694	VC
Lafayette College	PA	57,050	HC+
LaGrange College	GA	34,480	C
Lake Forest College	IL	45,580	VC
Lake Superior State Univ	MI	18,121	C
Lakeland College	WI	22,990	C
Lamar Univ	TX	6,820	LC
Lander Univ	SC	22,514	C+
Lane College	TN	11,212	C
Langston Univ	OK	3,000	LC
Lasell College	MA	42,500	LC
Le Moyne College	NY	42,200	VC
Lebanon Valley College	PA	38,570	C
Lee Univ	TN	18,690	C+
Lehigh Univ	PA	55,080	MC
Lehman College / The CUNY	NY	5,778	LC
LeMoyne-Owen College	TN	13,100	C
Lenoir-Rhyne College	NC	35,984	C
Lewis & Clark College	OR	52,656	VC
Lewis Univ	IL	23,050	C
Lincoln Univ	MO	11,996	NC
Lindenwood Univ	MO	20,750	C
Linfield College-McMinnville Campus	OR	46,166	C
Livingstone College	NC	17,815	LC
Lock Haven Univ of Pennsylvania	PA	17,587	LC
LIU/Brooklyn Campus	NY	26,500	C
Longwood Univ	VA	20,924	C
Loras College	IA	37,432	VC
Louisiana College	LA	15,746	C
Louisiana State Univ	LA	18,677	VC+
Louisiana State Univ in Shreveport	LA	5,606	C
Louisiana Tech Univ	LA	8,000	C
Lourdes Univ	OH	26,055	LC
Loyola Marymount Univ	CA	53,240	VC+
Loyola Univ Chicago	IL	49,560	VC+
Loyola Univ Maryland	MD		VC
Loyola Univ New Orleans	LA	46,581	VC
Luther College	IA	44,380	VC+
Lycoming College	PA	43,636	C
Lynchburg College	VA	42,645	C
Macalester College	MN	53,419	MC
Madonna Univ	MI	24,540	VC
Manchester College	IN	35,070	C
Manhattan College	NY	44,955	VC
Manhattanville College	NY	46,260	VC
Mansfield Univ	PA	19,468	LC
Marian Univ/Indianapolis	IN	37,058	C
Marlboro College	VT	35,980	VC

School	ST	$IS	SR
Marquette Univ	WI	43,664	VC+
Mars Hill College	NC	22,950	LC
Marshall Univ	WV	14,820	C
Martin Univ	IN	11,000	SP
Mary Baldwin College	VA	37,110	C
Marymount Manhattan College	NY	40,118	VC
Marymount Univ	VA	36,178	C
Maryville College	TN	33,150	VC
Maryville Univ of St. Louis	MO	34,920	VC
Mass College of Liberal Arts	MA	16,733	C
McDaniel College	MD	45,600	VC
McKendree Univ	IL	29,920	C+
McMurry Univ	TX	25,962	LC
McNeese State Univ	LA		C
McPherson College	KS	28,138	C
Mercer Univ	GA	44,201	VC+
Mercy College	NY	29,996	C
Mercyhurst Univ	PA	40,700	C
Meredith College	NC	31,420	C
Merrimack College	MA	44,215	C
Messiah College	PA	39,540	VC
Methodist Univ	NC	37,185	C
Metropolitan State Univ of Denver	CO	4,835	LC
Miami Univ	OH	24,191	HC
Mich State Univ	MI	13,689	VC
MidAmerica Nazarene Univ	KS	28,000	C
Middle Tenn State Univ	TN	8,650	C
Middlebury College	VT	57,470	MC
Midland Univ	NE	34,000	C
Midwestern State Univ	TX	9,722	C
Millersville Univ of Pennsylvania	PA	18,498	C
Milligan College	TN	27,510	C
Millikin Univ	IL	37,462	C
Mills College	CA	54,119	HC
Millsaps College	MS	43,888	VC+
Minn State Univ, Mankato	MN	14,900	C
Minn State Univ, Moorhead	MN	13,392	C
Minot State Univ	ND	10,915	C
Miss College	MS	21,998	VC
Miss Valley State Univ	MS	9,706	LC
Missouri Southern State Univ	MO	11,910	C
Missouri State Univ	MO	13,996	VC
Missouri Valley College	MO	22,200	C
Molloy College	NY	38,950	C
Monmouth College	IL	39,290	C
Monmouth Univ	NJ	42,252	C
Montana State Univ	MT	14,068	VC
Montana State Univ-Billings	MT	12,425	LC
Montclair State Univ	NJ	22,614	C
Moravian College	PA	36,381	VC
Morehead State Univ	KY	10,900	C
Morehouse College	GA	38,640	C
Morgan State Univ	MD	14,500	VC
Morris College	SC	16,006	LC
Mount Holyoke College	MA	53,596	HC+
Mount Mercy Univ	IA	34,385	C
Mount St. Mary College	NY	39,540	C
Mount St. Mary's Univ	MD	46,158	C
Mount St. Mary's College/ Chalon Campus	CA	43,897	VC+
Mount Vernon Nazarene Univ	OH	29,590	C
Muhlenberg College	PA	52,837	HC
Murray State Univ	KY	14,944	C
Muskingum Univ	OH	30,502	C
National Univ	CA	14,730	SP
Nazareth College of Rochester	NY	41,590	VC
Nebr Wesleyan Univ	NE	29,774	C+
New College of Florida	FL	14,504	HC+
New England College	NH	45,930	LC
New Jersey City Univ	NJ	21,060	C+
New Mexico Highlands Univ	NM	9,720	NC
New Mexico State Univ	NM	13,955	LC
New York Inst of Technology	NY	40,590	VC
New York Univ	NY	61,470	MC
Newberry College	SC	26,850	LC
Newman Univ	KS	30,380	C+
Niagara Univ	NY	39,800	C
Nicholls State Univ	LA	7,095	C
Norfolk State Univ	VA	10,531	LC
N Car Agricultural and Technical State Univ	NC	13,175	LC
N Car Central Univ	NC	9,000	LC
N Car State Univ	NC	16,202	HC
N Car Wesleyan College	NC	29,440	C
North Central College	IL	38,343	VC
N Dak State Univ	ND	14,642	C
North Georgia College & State Univ	GA	8,500	C
North Park Univ	IL	30,130	C
Northeastern Illinois Univ	IL		C
Northeastern State Univ	OK	8,615	VC
Northeastern Univ	MA	55,296	MC
Northern Arizona Univ	AZ	18,592	C
Northern Illinois Univ	IL	19,768	C
Northern Kentucky Univ	KY	15,302	LC
Northern Mich Univ	MI	15,300	VC
Northern State Univ	SD	14,021	C
Northland College	WI	26,680	C

School	ST	$IS	SR
Northwest Missouri State Univ	MO	14,229	C
Northwestern College of Iowa	IA	34,848	C+
Northwestern Okla State Univ	OK	7,275	NC
Northwestern Univ	IL	37,595	MC
Notre Dame de Namur Univ	CA	41,610	LC
Nova Southeastern Univ	FL	34,016	VC
Nyack College	NY	32,000	C
Oakland Univ	MI	19,391	VC
Oberlin College	OH	57,025	MC
Occidental College	CA	59,592	MC+
Oglala Lakota College	SD	2,000	NC
Oglethorpe Univ	GA	42,580	VC
Ohio Dominican Univ	OH	38,380	C+
Ohio Northern Univ	OH	42,075	VC
Ohio Univ	OH	20,676	VC
Ohio Valley Univ	WV	17,752	C
Ohio Wesleyan Univ	OH	49,460	C+
Okla Baptist Univ	OK	28,202	VC
Okla City Univ	OK	33,546	VC
Okla State Univ	OK	14,310	VC
Okla Wesleyan Univ	OK	21,300	C
Old Dominion Univ	VA	18,662	C
Olivet College	MI	19,984	C
Olivet Nazarene Univ	IL	29,990	C
Oregon State Univ	OR	19,017	C+
Oswego / SUNY	NY	20,009	VC
Ottawa Univ	KS	15,000	VC
Otterbein College	OH	32,214	C
Ouachita Baptist Univ	AR	29,010	VC
Our Lady of the Lake Univ of San Antonio	TX	22,430	LC
Pace Univ	NY	48,094	VC
Pacific Lutheran Univ	WA	44,840	VC
Pacific Univ	OR	42,815	C
Paine College	GA	18,594	LC
Park Univ	MO	17,525	C
Penn State Univ/Univ Park	PA	25,404	VC
Pepperdine Univ	CA	55,372	HC+
Peru State College	NE	8,600	NC
Philander Smith College	AR	19,760	LC
Piedmont College	GA	29,260	C
Pittsburg State Univ	KS	12,032	C
Pitzer College	CA	54,988	MC
Point Loma Nazarene Univ	CA	38,610	VC
Pomona College	CA	57,680	MC
Pontifical Catholic Univ of PR	PR	7,310	
Portland State Univ	OR	18,672	C
Post Univ	CT	35,750	C
Prairie View A&M Univ	TX	15,205	LC
Presbyterian College	SC	42,678	VC
Prescott College	AZ	33,284	C+
Princeton Univ	NJ	53,795	MC
Principia College	IL	35,140	C+
Providence College	RI	55,995	HC
Purchase College / SUNY	NY	16,951	C
Purdue Univ/Calumet	IN	14,336	C
Purdue Univ/West Lafayette	IN	20,278	HC
Queens College / The CUNY	NY	17,107	VC
Queens Univ of Charlotte	NC	39,543	VC
Quinnipiac Univ	CT	53,580	VC
Radford Univ	VA	17,132	LC
Ramapo College of New Jersey	NJ	24,938	C+
Randolph College	VA	43,960	VC
Randolph-Macon College	VA	45,086	C
Reed College	OR	57,780	MC
Regis College	MA	47,565	LC
Regis Univ	CO	41,318	C
Rhode Island College	RI	17,132	LC
Rhodes College	TN	47,596	HC+
Rice Univ	TX	43,288	MC
Rider Univ	NJ	45,720	C
Ripon College	WI	36,959	C+
Rivier College	NH	35,000	VC
Roanoke College	VA	47,996	C+
Rockford College	IL	31,000	C
Rocky Mountain College	MT	32,242	C
Roger Williams Univ	RI	45,788	C
Rollins College	FL	52,370	HC
Roosevelt Univ	IL	22,605	VC
Rosemont College	PA	42,350	C
Rowan Univ	NJ	23,570	VC
Russell Sage College	NY	39,370	C
Rust College	MS	10,600	C
Rutgers, The State Univ of New Jersey/Camden Campus	NJ	24,254	C
Rutgers, The State Univ of New Jersey/New Brunswick	NJ	25,077	VC
Rutgers, The State Univ of New Jersey/Newark Campus	NJ	25,376	C
Sacred Heart Univ	CT	48,564	VC
Saginaw Valley State Univ	MI	16,869	C
St. Anselm College	NH	48,324	VC
St. Augustine's Univ	NC	14,000	C
St. Francis Univ	PA	30,029	LC
St. John's Univ	MN	46,146	C
St. Joseph's College	IN	35,790	C
St. Joseph's College of Maine	ME	31,580	C
St. Joseph's Univ	PA	52,272	VC
St. Leo Univ	FL	27,990	C
St. Louis Univ	MO	46,594	VC+
St. Martin's Univ	WA	38,082	C
St. Mary's College	IN	45,160	VC
St. Mary's College of Calif	CA	53,550	C
St. Mary's Univ	TX	33,854	C
St. Mary's Univ of Minn	MN	37,015	C
St. Michael's College	VT	48,740	VC
St. Paul's College	VA	16,030	NC
St. Peter's College	NJ	44,240	C
St. Vincent College	PA	40,244	C
St. Xavier Univ	IL	32,840	C
Salem College	NC	29,326	VC
Salem State College	MA	13,161	LC
Salisbury Univ	MD	18,368	VC
Salve Regina Univ	RI	47,250	VC
Sam Houston State Univ	TX	17,082	C
Samford Univ	AL	35,700	VC+
San Diego State Univ	CA	20,578	VC
San Francisco State Univ	CA	18,514	C
San Jose State Univ	CA	19,707	C
Santa Clara Univ	CA	54,702	MC
Sarah Lawrence College	NY	48,000	HC
Savannah State Univ	GA	13,156	C
Scripps College	CA	54,900	MC
Seattle Pacific Univ	WA	41,559	VC+
Seattle Univ	WA	47,010	VC+
Seton Hall Univ	NJ	45,902	C
Seton Hill Univ	PA	35,172	C
Shaw Univ	NC	15,488	LC
Shawnee State Univ	OH	16,545	NC
Shenandoah Univ	VA	39,268	C
Shepherd Univ	WV	14,996	C
Shippensburg Univ of Pennsylvania	PA	17,064	LC
Shorter Univ	GA	26,470	C
Siena College	NY	43,863	VC
Simmons College	MA	48,770	VC
Simpson College	IA	36,086	VC
Skidmore College	NY	57,926	HC
Slippery Rock Univ of Pennsylvania	PA	10,360	LC
Smith College	MA	57,524	MC
Sonoma State Univ	CA	20,541	C
S Car State Univ	SC	6,700	LC
S Dak State Univ	SD	14,296	C
Southeastern Louisiana Univ	LA	13,325	C
Southeastern Okla State Univ	OK	7,966	C
Southern Arkansas Univ	AR	14,316	C
Southern Conn State Univ	CT	18,033	C
Southern Illinois Univ Carbondale	IL	21,620	C
Southern Illinois Univ Edwardsville	IL	17,532	C
Southern Methodist Univ	TX	57,755	MC
Southern Nazarene Univ	OK	24,354	NC
Southern Oregon Univ	OR	17,874	C
Southern Univ and A&M College	LA	9,761	C+
Southern Univ at New Orleans	LA	1,000	NC
Southwest Baptist Univ	MO	24,710	C
Southwest Minn State Univ	MN	14,000	C
Southwestern Univ	TX	45,660	VC
Spelman College	GA	24,650	VC
Spring Arbor Univ	MI	26,740	C
Spring Hill College	AL	42,130	VC
Springfield College	MA	25,000	C
St. Ambrose Univ	IA		C
St. Bonaventure Univ	NY	38,831	C
St. Catherine Univ	MN	37,782	C+
St. Cloud State Univ	MN	10,600	C
St. Edward's Univ	TX	44,674	VC
St. Francis College	NY	34,200	LC
St. John Fisher College	NY	39,370	C+
St. John's Univ	NY	52,840	C+
St. Joseph's College, New York / Brooklyn Campus	NY	21,878	C
St. Joseph's College, New York / Suffolk Campus	NY	21,878	VC
St. Lawrence Univ	NY	53,740	HC
St. Mary's College of Maryland	MD	26,699	HC
St. Norbert College	WI	39,992	VC
St. Olaf College	MN	49,960	HC+
Stanford Univ	CA	56,411	MC
SUNY Inst of Technology at Utica / Rome	NY	23,818	C
SUNY/Empire State College	NY	6,315	SP
Stephen F. Austin State Univ	TX	14,668	C
Stetson Univ	FL	49,512	VC+
Stonehill College	MA	46,780	VC+
Stony Brook Univ / SUNY	NY	19,359	HC
Suffolk Univ	MA	46,548	C
SUNY College at Geneseo	NY	18,055	HC+
SUNY College at Old Westbury	NY	16,324	C
SUNY Cortland / The SUNY	NY	19,117	C
SUNY Fredonia / The SUNY at Fredonia	NY	18,702	VC
SUNY New Paltz	NY	15,010	C
SUNY Oneonta / SUNY	NY	16,919	VC
SUNY Plattsburgh / SUNY	NY	18,083	VC
Susquehanna Univ	PA	49,170	C
Swarthmore College	PA	57,870	MC
Sweet Briar College	VA	43,765	C+
Syracuse Univ	NY	54,512	HC
Tabor College	KS	29,010	LC
Talladega College	AL	13,000	C
Tarleton State Univ	TX	13,489	LC
Taylor Univ	IN	36,742	VC+
Temple Univ	PA	24,392	VC
Tenn State Univ	TN	9,048	C
Tenn Tech Univ	TN	11,310	C
Texas A&M Univ	TX	16,956	VC+
Texas A&M Univ at Commerce	TX	10,496	C
Texas A&M Univ at Corpus Christi	TX	11,544	LC
Texas A&M Univ at Kingsville	TX	7,500	LC
Texas Christian Univ	TX	47,570	HC
Texas Lutheran Univ	TX	34,070	C
Texas Southern Univ	TX	18,212	LC
Texas State Univ	TX	16,495	VC
Texas Tech Univ	TX	14,243	C
Texas Wesleyan Univ	TX	29,886	C
Texas Woman's Univ	TX	13,633	LC
The Catholic Univ of America	DC	52,852	VC
The College at Brockport / SUNY	NY	18,362	VC
The College of New Rochelle	NY	33,600	VC
The College of St. Rose	NY	26,750	C
The Lincoln Univ	PA	15,154	LC
Ohio State Univ	OH	19,887	MC
The SUNY at Potsdam	NY	17,754	C
Thiel College	PA	31,378	LC
Thomas Edison State College	NJ	5,700	SP
Thomas More College	KY	34,760	C
Tougaloo College	MS	15,275	NC
Touro College	NY	23,150	VC
Towson Univ	MD	16,000	VC
Transylvania Univ	KY	40,310	VC+
Trevecca Nazarene Univ	TN	30,118	C
Trinity Christian College	IL	28,869	C
Trinity College	CT		HC+
Trinity Univ	TX	44,174	HC+
Trinity Washington Univ	DC	30,250	C+
Troy Univ	AL	10,650	C
Truman State Univ	MO	13,546	HC
Tufts Univ	MA	58,780	MC
Tulane Univ	LA	58,942	MC
Tuskegee Univ	AL	26,750	C
Union College	KY	28,775	C
Union College	NY		MC
Union Univ	TN	28,260	VC
Universidad del Turabo	PR	4,110	
Universidad Metropolitana	PR		
Univ at Albany / SUNY	NY	18,674	VC
Univ at Buffalo / The SUNY	NY	20,283	VC
Univ of Akron	OH	20,436	C
Univ of Alabama at Birmingham	AL	18,484	C+
Univ of Alabama at Huntsville	AL	17,625	VC
Univ of Alaska Anchorage	AK	15,290	NC
Univ of Alaska Fairbanks	AK	13,955	C
Univ of Arizona	AZ	20,105	C
Univ of Arkansas at Fayetteville	AR	16,860	VC
Univ of Arkansas at Little Rock	AR		C
Univ of Arkansas at Pine Bluff	AR	10,600	C
Univ of Calif at Berkeley	CA	23,322	MC
Univ of Calif at Davis	CA	24,482	HC
Univ of Calif at Irvine	CA	25,961	VC
Univ of Calif at Los Angeles	CA	25,686	MC
Univ of Calif at Riverside	CA	27,204	C
Univ of Calif at San Diego	CA	21,000	VC
Univ of Calif at Santa Barbara	CA	27,551	HC
Univ of Calif at Santa Cruz	CA	27,807	VC
Univ of Central Arkansas	AR	10,840	VC
Univ of Central Florida	FL	15,711	VC+
Univ of Central Missouri	MO	14,605	C
Univ of Central Okla	OK	12,293	C
Univ of Chicago	IL	55,416	MC
Univ of Cincinnati	OH	20,199	VC
Univ of Colo at Colo Springs	CO	15,000	VC
Univ of Colo Boulder	CO	22,605	VC+
Univ of Colo Denver	CO	17,904	C
Univ of Conn	CT	23,744	HC
Univ of Dayton	OH	43,750	VC
Univ of Delaware	DE	22,728	VC
Univ of Denver	CO	51,787	VC+
Univ of Detroit Mercy	MI	30,450	C
Univ of Dubuque	IA	30,200	C
Univ of Evansville	IN	41,056	VC+
Univ of Findlay	OH	31,916	C
Univ of Florida	FL	15,783	HC+
Univ of Georgia	GA	19,508	VC
Univ of Great Falls	MT	27,970	C
Univ of Hartford	CT	42,674	C
Univ of Hawaii at Hilo	HI	6,500	C
Univ of Hawaii at Manoa	HI	19,379	VC
Univ of Houston-Downtown	TX	6,267	LC
Univ of Idaho	ID	14,558	C
Univ of Illinois at Chicago	IL	24,293	VC
Univ of Illinois at Urbana-Champaign	IL	24,300	HC
Univ of Indianapolis	IN	31,740	LC
Univ of Iowa	IA	17,481	VC
Univ of Kansas	KS	16,980	C+
Univ of Kentucky	KY	19,868	C
Univ of La Verne	CA	47,010	VC
Univ of Louisiana at Lafayette	LA	6,130	C
Univ of Louisiana at Monroe	LA	12,998	C
Univ of Louisville	KY	17,460	VC
Univ of Maine	ME	19,712	C+
Univ of Maine at Farmington	ME	17,841	C
Univ of Mary Hardin-Baylor	TX	31,950	C+
Univ of Mary Washington	VA	19,484	VC
Univ of Maryland	MD	18,801	HC
Univ of Maryland/Baltimore County	MD	18,000	VC
Univ of Maryland/Eastern Shore	MD	14,000	C
Univ of Mass Amherst	MA	23,697	VC+
Univ of Mass Boston	MA	11,966	C
Univ of Mass Dartmouth	MA	22,223	C
Univ of Mass Lowell	MA	19,316	C
Univ of Memphis	TN	15,094	C
Univ of Miami	FL	55,166	MC
Univ of Mich/Ann Arbor	MI	22,102	HC+
Univ of Mich/Dearborn	MI	9,885	VC
Univ of Mich-Flint	MI	17,547	C+
Univ of Minn/Duluth	MN	18,964	C+
Univ of Minn/Morris	MN	17,150	VC
Univ of Minn/Twin Cities	MN		HC
Univ of Miss	MS	15,482	VC
Univ of Missouri/Columbia	MO	18,201	MC
Univ of Missouri-Kansas City	MO	19,603	C
Univ of Missouri-St. Louis	MO	18,304	VC
Univ of Mobile	AL	27,870	VC
Univ of Montana	MT	13,670	C
Univ of Montana-Western	MT	9,753	LC
Univ of Montevallo	AL	17,320	C
Univ of Mount Union	OH	35,130	C
Univ of Nebr - Lincoln	NE	17,507	VC
Univ of Nebr at Kearney	NE	14,855	LC
Univ of Nebr at Omaha	NE	12,700	C
Univ of Nevada, Las Vegas	NV	17,303	C
Univ of Nevada/Reno	NV	14,500	NC
Univ of New England	ME	46,145	C+
Univ of New Hampshire	NH	24,702	VC
Univ of New Mexico	NM	15,300	C
Univ of New Orleans	LA	9,224	VC
Univ of North Alabama	AL	9,960	C
Univ of N Car at Asheville	NC	13,500	VC+
Univ of N Car at Chapel Hill	NC	18,348	MC
Univ of N Car at Charlotte	NC	15,847	C
Univ of N Car at Greensboro	NC	12,848	C
Univ of N Car at Wilmington	NC	13,572	VC+
Univ of N Dak	ND	14,094	C
Univ of North Florida	FL	15,578	VC
Univ of North Texas	TX	15,628	C
Univ of Northern Colo	CO	15,973	C
Univ of Northern Iowa	IA	14,776	C
Univ of Notre Dame	IN		MC
Univ of Okla	OK	17,634	VC+
Univ of Oregon	OR	20,872	VC
Univ of Pennsylvania	PA	56,106	MC
Univ of Pikeville	KY	24,750	NC
Univ of Pittsburgh at Bradford	PA	21,316	LC
Univ of Pittsburgh at Johnstown	PA	20,862	LC
Univ of Pittsburgh at Pittsburgh	PA	27,800	HC+
Univ of Portland	OR	47,874	VC
Univ of PR Recinto de Rio Piedras	PR	5,750	
Univ of PR/Mayaguez	PR	1,250	
Univ of Puget Sound	WA	52,648	HC+
Univ of Redlands	CA	40,500	VC
Univ of Rio Grande	OH	8,750	NC
Univ of St. Francis	IN	29,810	C
Univ of St. Mary	KS	28,400	C+
Univ of San Diego	CA	53,302	HC+
Univ of San Francisco	CA	49,674	VC
Univ of Science and Arts of Okla	OK	10,560	VC
Univ of Scranton	PA	51,940	VC
Univ of Sioux Falls	SD	22,990	C
Univ of South Alabama	AL	13,510	C
Univ of S Car at Aiken	SC	16,278	C
Univ of S Car at Columbia	SC	19,725	VC+
Univ of S Car Upstate	SC	17,673	LC
Univ of S Dak	SD	15,111	C
Univ of South Florida	FL	13,000	C
Univ of Southern Calif	CA	56,903	MC
Univ of Southern Indiana	IN	14,657	C
Univ of Southern Maine	ME	16,576	C

ST = STATE **$IS** = IN-STATE COSTS **SR** = SELECTOR RATING

School	ST	$IS	SR
Univ of Southern Miss	MS	13,170	C
Univ of Tampa	FL	35,160	VC
Univ of Tenn at Chattanooga	TN	16,883	C
Univ of Tenn at Knoxville	TN	20,364	VC+
Univ of Tenn at Martin	TN	13,217	C
Univ of Texas at Arlington	TX	10,908	LC
Univ of Texas at Austin	TX	44,074	HC
Univ of Texas at Dallas	TX	21,046	HC
Univ of Texas at El Paso	TX	8,764	NC
Univ of Texas at San Antonio	TX	18,372	C
Univ of Texas-Pan American	TX	12,432	LC
Univ of the District of Columbia	DC	7,244	LC
Univ of the Incarnate Word	TX	35,200	LC
Univ of the Ozarks	AR	22,100	C
Univ of the Pacific	CA	52,146	VC
Univ of the Southwest	NM	15,000	C
Univ of Toledo	OH	18,464	C
Univ of Tulsa	OK	45,311	HC+
Univ of Utah	UT	13,462	VC
Univ of Vermont	VT	26,120	VC+
Univ of Virginia	VA	22,175	MC
Univ of Washington	WA	14,722	VC
Univ of West Alabama	AL	9,415	C
Univ of West Georgia	GA	14,852	LC
Univ of Wisc Whitewater	WI	13,314	C
Univ of Wisc/Eau Claire	WI	15,430	VC
Univ of Wisc/La Crosse	WI	14,755	VC
Univ of Wisc/Madison	WI	18,757	HC
Univ of Wisc/Oshkosh	WI	10,426	LC
Univ of Wisc/Parkside	WI	10,181	LC
Univ of Wisc/River Falls	WI	9,722	LC
Univ of Wisc/Stevens Point	WI	14,043	C
Univ of Wisc/Superior	WI	14,106	C
Univ of Wisc-Milwaukee	WI	18,436	C
Univ of Wyoming	WY	13,855	C+
Upper Iowa Univ	IA	30,426	NC
Urbana Univ	OH	21,190	C
Ursinus College	PA	55,630	VC+
Ursuline College	OH	33,198	LC
Utah State Univ	UT	11,803	C
Utica College	NY	44,734	C
Valparaiso Univ	IN	43,040	VC+
Vanderbilt Univ	TN	57,072	MC
Vanguard Univ of Southern Calif	CA	35,833	VC
Vassar College	NY	59,070	MC
Villanova Univ	PA	56,436	MC
Virginia Commonwealth Univ	VA	18,633	C
Virginia Polytechnic Inst and State Univ	VA	14,629	HC
Virginia State Univ	VA	11,318	C+
Virginia Union Univ	VA	18,432	C
Virginia Wesleyan College	VA	28,433	LC
Viterbo Univ	WI	30,070	C
Voorhees College	SC	18,126	C
Wagner College	NY	48,600	VC
Wake Forest Univ	NC	51,000	MC
Walla Walla Univ	WA	26,256	NC
Walsh Univ	OH	35,100	C
Warner Pacific College	OR	25,550	C
Warren Wilson College	NC	34,888	VC
Wartburg College	IA	41,055	VC
Washburn Univ	KS	12,165	NC
Washington and Jefferson College	PA	49,990	VC
Washington and Lee Univ	VA	52,812	MC
Washington College	MD	48,768	VC
Washington State Univ	WA	20,461	C
Wayland Baptist Univ	TX	16,058	LC
Wayne State College	NE	11,764	NC
Wayne State Univ	MI	19,493	C
Waynesburg Univ	PA	29,100	C
Webster Univ	MO	33,990	C+
Wellesley College	MA	49,848	MC
Wells College	NY	38,680	VC
Wesleyan Univ	CT	59,844	MC
West Chester Univ of Pennsylvania	PA	16,836	C
West Liberty Univ	WV	9,142	LC
West Texas A&M Univ	TX	13,478	C
West Virginia State Univ	WV	8,378	NC
West Virginia Univ	WV	15,794	C+
West Virginia Wesleyan College	WV	26,880	C
Western Carolina Univ	NC	13,965	C+
Western Conn State Univ	CT	18,327	C
Western Illinois Univ	IL	20,130	C
Western Kentucky Univ	KY	11,000	LC
Western Mich Univ	MI	19,042	C
Western New England Univ	MA	45,590	C
Western New Mexico Univ	NM	8,500	LC
Western Oregon Univ	OR	15,021	C
Western State Colo Univ	CO	16,135	C
Western Washington Univ	WA	18,519	VC
Westfield State Univ	MA	18,489	C
Westminster College	MO	30,490	VC
Westminster College	PA	31,290	C+
Westminster College	UT	37,708	VC
Westmont College	CA	41,500	HC
Wheaton College	IL	39,650	HC+
Wheaton College	MA	54,934	HC+
Whitman College	WA	54,400	MC
Whittier College	CA	43,416	C
Whitworth Univ	WA	45,826	VC+
Wichita State Univ	KS	12,539	C
Widener Univ	PA	50,368	C
Wilberforce Univ	OH	15,100	LC
Wiley College	TX		LC
Wilkes Univ	PA	42,786	C
Willamette Univ	OR	56,450	VC+
William Paterson Univ of New Jersey	NJ	21,694	C
William Penn Univ	IA	26,000	C
Williams College	MA	58,900	MC
Wilmington College	OH	29,784	C
Wilson College	PA	27,660	C
Wingate Univ	NC	34,990	C
Winona State Univ	MN	16,530	C
Winston-Salem State Univ	NC	9,418	LC
Winthrop Univ	SC	21,120	VC
Wittenberg Univ	OH	47,766	VC
Wofford College	SC	45,795	VC
Worcester State Univ	MA	18,657	C
Wright State Univ	OH	16,983	C
Xavier Univ	OH	43,740	VC
Xavier Univ of Louisiana	LA	25,300	C
Yale Univ	CT	55,300	MC
Yeshiva Univ	NY	47,250	VC+
York College / CUNY	NY	5,496	NC
York College of Pennsylvania	PA	26,590	C
Youngstown State Univ	OH	16,374	LC

SOFTWARE ENGINEERING

School	ST	$IS	SR
Allegheny College	PA	49,020	HC
Arizona State Univ	AZ	18,818	C+
Auburn Univ	AL	20,052	VC+
Baldwin Wallace Univ	OH	36,980	VC
Butler Univ	IN	45,898	VC+
Calif Polytechnic State Univ	CA	19,847	HC
Central Washington Univ	WA	11,730	C
Champlain College	VT	44,850	VC
Chapman Univ	CA	56,019	VC+
Clarkson Univ	NY	53,538	HC
Drexel Univ	PA	51,920	HC
Embry-Riddle Aeronautical Univ - Daytona Beach	FL	40,884	C+
Embry-Riddle Aeronautical Univ - Prescott Campus	AZ	40,584	VC
Fairfield Univ	CT	55,850	VC
Florida Inst of Technology	FL	48,290	VC
Gannon Univ	PA	37,940	C
George Mason Univ	VA	15,724	VC
Indiana Inst of Technology	IN	34,240	LC
Keene State College	NH	21,538	C
Kutztown Univ of Pennsylvania	PA	16,909	LC
Lipscomb Univ	TN	35,722	VC
Loyola Univ Chicago	IL	49,560	VC+
Miami Univ	OH	24,191	HC
Mich Tech Univ	MI	22,105	VC
Milwaukee School of Engineering	WI	39,948	VC+
Monmouth Univ	NJ	42,252	C
National Univ	CA	14,730	SP
Okla City Univ	OK	33,546	VC
Oswego / SUNY	NY	20,009	VC
Purdue Univ/West Lafayette	IN	20,278	HC
Quinnipiac Univ	CT	53,580	VC
Rochester Inst of Technology	NY	42,450	VC+
Rose-Hulman Inst of Technology	IN	51,738	MC
San Jose State Univ	CA	19,707	C
Shippensburg Univ of Pennsylvania	PA	17,064	LC
S Dak State Univ	SD	14,296	C
Southern Polytechnic State Univ	GA	13,958	VC
Univ of Calif at Irvine	CA	25,961	VC
Univ of Mass Dartmouth	MA	22,223	C
Univ of Miami	FL	55,166	MC
Univ of Mich/Dearborn	MI	9,885	VC
Univ of Minn Crookston	MN	17,834	C
Univ of N Car at Charlotte	NC	15,847	C
Univ of Texas at Dallas	TX	21,046	HC
Univ of Wisc/Platteville	WI	14,274	C
Vermont Technical College	VT	15,751	C

SOIL SCIENCE

School	ST	$IS	SR
Alabama A&M Univ	AL	96,100	C
Auburn Univ	AL	20,052	VC+
Baylor Univ	TX	46,720	HC
Calif Polytechnic State Univ	CA	19,847	HC
Clemson Univ	SC	19,136	HC
Colo State Univ-Fort Collins	CO	20,090	VC
Eastern Oregon Univ	OR	10,400	C
Mich State Univ	MI	13,689	VC
New Mexico State Univ	NM	13,955	LC
N Car State Univ	NC	16,202	HC
N Dak State Univ	ND	14,642	C
Okla State Univ	OK	14,310	VC
Purdue Univ/West Lafayette	IN	20,278	HC
SUNY / College of Environmental Science and Forestry	NY	18,351	HC
Tenn Tech Univ	TN	11,310	C
Texas A&M Univ at Kingsville	TX	7,500	LC
Univ of Arizona	AZ	20,105	C
Univ of Arkansas at Fayetteville	AR	16,860	VC
Univ of Calif at Davis	CA	24,482	HC
Univ of Calif at Riverside	CA	27,204	C
Univ of Delaware	DE	22,728	VC
Univ of Florida	FL	15,783	HC+
Univ of Georgia	GA	19,508	VC
Univ of Hawaii at Manoa	HI	19,379	VC
Univ of Idaho	ID	14,558	C
Univ of Mass Amherst	MA	23,697	VC+
Univ of Missouri/Columbia	MO	18,201	MC
Univ of New Hampshire	NH	24,702	VC
Univ of Tenn at Knoxville	TN	20,364	VC+
Univ of Wisc/Madison	WI	18,757	HC
Univ of Wisc/Platteville	WI	14,274	C
Univ of Wisc/River Falls	WI	9,722	LC
Univ of Wisc/Stevens Point	WI	14,043	C
Utah State Univ	UT	11,803	C
Virginia Polytechnic Inst and State Univ	VA	14,629	HC
Washington State Univ	WA	20,461	C
West Texas A&M Univ	TX	13,478	C

SOUTH ASIAN STUDIES

School	ST	$IS	SR
Appalachian State Univ	NC	12,919	VC
Binghamton Univ / The SUNY	NY	20,832	HC+
Brown Univ	RI	56,150	MC
Middlebury College	VT	57,470	MC
Mount Holyoke College	MA	53,596	HC+
Oakland Univ	MI	19,391	VC
Univ of Calif at Berkeley	CA	23,322	MC
Univ of Calif at Los Angeles	CA	25,686	MC
Univ of Chicago	IL	55,416	MC
Univ of Minn/Twin Cities	MN		HC
Univ of Pennsylvania	PA	56,106	MC
Univ of Washington	WA	14,722	VC
Washington Univ in St. Louis	MO	58,818	MC
Yale Univ	CT	55,300	MC

SOUTHWEST AMERICAN STUDIES

School	ST	$IS	SR
Colo College	CO	54,534	MC
Fort Lewis College	CO	15,513	C
Southern Methodist Univ	TX	57,755	MC

SPANISH

School	ST	$IS	SR
Abilene Christian Univ	TX	38,400	VC
Adams State College	CO	13,358	LC
Adelphi Univ	NY	43,130	VC
Adrian College	MI	33,800	C
Agnes Scott College	GA	45,323	VC+
Alabama State Univ	AL	14,142	NC
Albany State Univ	GA	8,500	C
Albion College	MI	43,884	VC
Albright College	PA	46,660	C
Alfred Univ	NY	40,392	VC
Allegheny College	PA	49,020	HC
Alma College	MI	42,400	VC
American International College	MA	36,100	LC
American Univ	DC	54,829	HC+
Amherst College	MA	58,744	MC
Anderson Univ	IN	35,390	C
Andrews Univ	MI	28,030	C+
Angelo State Univ	TX	15,049	NC
Appalachian State Univ	NC	12,919	VC
Aquinas College	MI	33,060	C
Arizona State Univ	AZ	18,818	C+
Arkansas State Univ	AR	14,980	C
Armstrong Atlantic State Univ	GA	16,276	C
Asbury Univ	KY	32,038	VC
Ashland Univ	OH	25,000	C
Assumption College	MA	45,721	VC
Auburn Univ	AL	20,052	VC+
Augsburg College	MN	35,142	C
Augustana College	IL	43,398	HC
Augustana College	SD	35,500	VC
Aurora Univ	IL	26,870	C
Austin College	TX	36,940	HC
Azusa Pacific Univ	CA	39,946	C
Baker Univ	KS	33,350	C+
Baldwin Wallace Univ	OH	36,980	VC
Ball State Univ	IN	17,850	C
Bard College	NY	59,872	HC
Barry Univ	FL	38,190	C
Bates College	ME	58,950	MC
Baylor Univ	TX	46,720	HC
Bellarmine Univ	KY	42,950	VC
Belmont Univ	TN	37,380	VC+
Beloit College	WI	49,970	HC
Bemidji State Univ	MN	13,500	C
Benedictine College	KS	29,180	VC
Benedictine Univ	IL	35,220	C
Bennington College	VT	56,990	HC+
Berea College	KY	7,220	HC
Berry College	GA	39,254	HC
Bethany College	WV	35,282	C
Bethel College	IN	31,560	C
Bethel Univ	MN	34,940	VC
Binghamton Univ / The SUNY	NY	20,832	HC+
Biola Univ	CA	40,320	VC
Birmingham-Southern College	AL	42,370	VC+
Black Hills State Univ	SD	13,562	LC
Blackburn College	IL	21,350	C
Bloomsburg Univ of Pennsylvania	PA	13,598	C
Blue Mountain College	MS	13,550	LC
Bluffton Univ	OH	37,864	C
Boise State Univ	ID	12,802	C
Boston Univ	MA	54,130	HC+
Bowdoin College	ME	57,834	MC
Bowling Green State Univ	OH	18,970	C
Bradley Univ	IL	31,874	VC
Brandeis Univ	MA	58,820	HC
Brescia Univ	KY	26,140	VC+
Briar Cliff Univ	IA	29,514	C
Bridgewater College	VA	39,880	C
Bridgewater State Univ	MA	18,752	C
Brigham Young Univ	UT	12,100	HC
Bryan College	TN	24,194	C
Bryant Univ	RI	49,179	VC
Bryn Mawr College	PA	57,760	MC
Bucknell Univ	PA	58,160	MC
Buena Vista Univ	IA	37,954	C
Buffalo State/State Univ of Buffalo	NY	15,733	C+
Butler Univ	IN	45,898	VC+
Cabrini College	PA	40,859	LC
Caldwell College	NJ	35,602	LC
Calif Baptist Univ	CA	35,890	C
Calif Lutheran Univ	CA	47,640	C
Calif State Polytechnic Univ, Pomona	CA	18,932	C
Cal State, Bakersfield	CA	8,000	LC
Cal State, Chico	CA	18,952	C
Cal State, Dominguez Hills	CA	17,056	LC
Cal State, East Bay	CA	16,549	C
Cal State, Fresno	CA	17,405	C
Cal State, Fullerton	CA	25,188	C+
Cal State, Long Beach	CA	17,534	C+
Cal State, Los Angeles	CA	15,829	C
Cal State, Monterey Bay	CA	26,871	LC
Cal State, Northridge	CA	28,313	C
Cal State, Sacramento	CA	16,200	C
Cal State, San Bernardino	CA	12,000	C
Cal State, San Marcos	CA	14,576	C
Cal State, Stanislaus	CA	18,582	C
Calif Univ of Pennsylvania	PA	14,217	C
Calvin College	MI	37,585	VC+
Campbell Univ	NC	25,500	C
Canisius College	NY	45,602	VC
Capital Univ	OH	39,824	VC
Cardinal Stritch Univ	WI	24,054	C
Carleton College	MN	58,149	MC
Carlow Univ	PA	30,272	C
Carnegie Mellon Univ	PA	51,260	MC
Carroll College	MT	28,000	C
Carroll Univ	WI	24,860	C
Carson-Newman Univ	TN	29,058	C+
Carthage College	WI	33,000	C
Case Western Reserve Univ	OH	55,178	MC
Castleton State College	VT	19,424	C
Catawba College	NC	37,105	C
Cedarville Univ	OH	31,036	VC+
Centenary College of Louisiana	LA	39,070	C+
Central College	IA	36,980	VC
Central Conn State Univ	CT	19,212	C
Central Methodist Univ	MO	28,240	VC
Central Mich Univ	MI	18,066	C
Central Univ of Bayamon	PR	3,350	
Central Washington Univ	WA	11,730	C
Centre College	KY	35,000	HC+
Chapman Univ	CA	56,019	VC+
Charleston Southern Univ	SC	22,420	C
Chatham Univ	PA	42,440	VC
Chestnut Hill College	PA	39,785	LC
Chicago State Univ	IL	5,482	C
Christopher Newport Univ	VA	21,050	VC
Citadel, The	SC		C
CUNY/Baruch College	NY	15,831	VC
CUNY/Brooklyn College	NY	5,884	C+
Claremont McKenna College	CA	58,065	MC
Clarion Univ of Pennsylvania	PA	17,370	C
Clark Univ	MA	47,020	HC+
Clarke Univ	IA	36,400	C
Clemson Univ	SC	19,136	HC
Cleveland State Univ	OH	21,357	C
Coastal Carolina Univ	SC	17,620	C
Coe College	IA	43,590	VC
Coker College	SC	32,256	LC
Colby College	ME	57,510	MC
Colgate Univ	NY	50,930	MC
College of Staten Island / The CUNY	NY	16,778	NC

ST = STATE **$IS** = IN-STATE COSTS **SR** = SELECTOR RATING

School	ST	$IS	SR
College of Charleston	SC	21,273	VC
College of Mount St. Vincent	NY	41,040	MC
College of New Jersey	NJ	25,376	HC
College of St. Benedict	MN	47,570	VC
College of St. Elizabeth	NJ	43,839	LC
College of St. Mary	NE	34,334	C
College of the Holy Cross	MA	56,232	MC
College of the Ozarks	MO	5,605	VC
College of Wooster	OH	52,600	VC
Colo Mesa Univ	CO	16,669	LC
Colo State Univ-Fort Collins	CO	20,090	VC
Colo State Univ-Pueblo	CO	13,532	LC
Columbia College	SC	27,882	C
Columbia Univ in the City of New York	NY	61,116	MC
Columbia Univ/Barnard College	NY	39,000	MC
Columbia Univ/School of General Studies	NY	54,083	MC
Columbus State Univ	GA	13,176	C
Concordia College, Moorhead	MN	39,974	Ȼ
Concordia Univ Texas	TX	23,640	C
Concordia Univ Wisc	WI	28,980	C
Concordia Univ, Ann Arbor	MI	27,220	VC
Converse College	SC	37,130	C
Cornell College	IA	44,930	HC
Cornell Univ	NY	59,037	MC
Covenant College	GA		VȻ
CUNY-City College	NY	19,576	HȻ
Daemen College	NY	31,510	C
Dartmouth College	NH	57,996	MC
Davidson College	NC	54,683	MC
De Sales Univ	PA	42,670	C
Delaware State Univ	DE	14,700	LC
Denison Univ	OH	54,670	HȻ
DePaul Univ	IL	46,120	VC
DePauw Univ	IN	48,950	VȻ
Dickinson College	PA	57,662	HȻ
Dickinson State Univ	ND	8,550	NC
Doane College	NE	33,730	VC
Dominican College	NY	31,270	C
Dominican Univ	IL	37,628	C
Dordt College	IA	34,160	VC
Drew Univ/College of Liberal Arts	NJ	55,862	VC
Drury Univ	MO	30,319	VC
Duke Univ	NC	50,250	MC
Duquesne Univ	PA	42,017	VC
Earlham College	IN	49,710	VȻ
East Stroudsburg Univ of Pennsylvania	PA	16,636	C
East Texas Baptist Univ	TX	29,135	C
Eastern Conn State Univ	CT	20,584	C
Eastern Kentucky Univ	KY	11,161	C
Eastern Mennonite Univ	VA	38,850	VC
Eastern Mich Univ	MI	17,961	C
Eastern Nazarene College	MA	30,000	C
Eastern New Mexico Univ	NM	10,682	C
Eastern Univ	PA	37,704	C
Eastern Washington Univ	WA	16,388	C
Eckerd College	FL	43,902	VC
Edgewood College	WI	33,294	C
Elizabethtown College	PA	47,600	VC
Elmhurst College	IL	42,032	Ȼ
Elmira College	NY	49,950	Ȼ
Elms College	MA	23,900	VC
Elon Univ	NC	40,046	HC
Emmanuel College	MA	47,985	VC
Emory Univ	GA	45,000	MC
Evangel Univ	MO	23,090	C
Fayetteville State Univ	NC	10,816	C
Ferrum College	VA	27,740	LC
Fisk Univ	TN	19,830	C
Flagler College	FL	24,960	VC
Florida Atlantic Univ	FL	17,339	C
Florida Gulf Coast Univ	FL		C
Florida International Univ	FL	17,747	VC
Florida Southern College	FL	38,240	VC
Florida State Univ	FL	15,238	HC
Fordham Univ	NY	58,927	HC
Fort Hays State Univ	KS	11,354	C
Fort Lewis College	CO	15,513	C
Franciscan Univ of Steubenville	OH	27,320	VC
Franklin and Marshall College	PA	58,295	MC
Franklin College	IN	35,885	C
Fresno Pacific Univ	CA	32,136	C
Friends Univ	KS	29,100	C
Furman Univ	SC	54,006	HC
Gallaudet Univ	DC	25,380	SP
Gardner-Webb Univ	NC	34,375	Ȼ
Geneva College	PA	27,280	C
George Fox Univ	OR	40,750	Ȼ
George Mason Univ	VA	15,724	VC
George Washington Univ	DC	57,108	MC
Georgetown College	KY	38,690	C
Georgetown Univ	DC	52,910	MC
Georgia College and State Univ	GA	18,216	VC
Georgia Regents Univ	GA		C
Georgia State Univ	GA	12,000	VC
Georgian Court Univ	NJ	39,726	LC
Gettysburg College	PA	56,820	HC

School	ST	$IS	SR
Gonzaga Univ	WA	44,247	HC
Gordon College	MA	42,660	VȻ
Goshen College	IN	35,900	VC
Goucher College	MD	50,252	VȻ
Grace College and Theological Seminary	IN	28,800	C
Graceland Univ	IA	28,020	C
Grand Valley State Univ	MI	17,998	VC
Greensboro College	NC	28,740	LC
Greenville College	IL	27,012	C
Grinnell College	IA	53,654	HC
Grove City College	PA	22,988	HC
Guilford College	NC	35,340	C
Gustavus Adolphus College	MN	48,170	HC
Hamline Univ	MN	44,198	VC
Hampden-Sydney College	VA	48,848	C
Hanover College	IN	41,450	VC
Harding Univ	AR	21,432	Ȼ
Hardin-Simmons Univ	TX	23,560	Ȼ
Hartwick College	NY	49,815	Ȼ
Harvard Univ/Harvard College	MA	49,000	MC
Hastings College	NE	27,782	Ȼ
Haverford College	PA	59,236	MC
Heidelberg Univ	OH	34,100	C
Henderson State Univ	AR	13,634	C
Hendrix College	AR	48,436	HȻ
High Point Univ	NC	39,800	C
Hillsdale College	MI	31,890	HȻ
Hiram College	OH	37,300	VC
Hofstra Univ	NY	48,020	VȻ
Hollins Univ	VA	43,295	VC
Hood College	MD	44,630	C
Hope College	MI	36,320	VȻ
Houghton College	NY	35,740	VC
Houston Baptist Univ	TX	23,815	Ȼ
Howard Payne Univ	TX	17,115	C
Howard Univ	DC	35,957	C
Humboldt State Univ	CA	18,400	C
Hunter College / The CUNY	NY	14,429	VC
Idaho State Univ	ID	11,908	C
Illinois College	IL	25,770	VC
Illinois State Univ	IL	22,634	VC
Immaculata Univ	PA	43,000	C
Indiana State Univ	IN	16,000	C
Indiana Univ Bloomington	IN	19,358	HC
Indiana Univ Northwest	IN	6,738	LC
Indiana Univ of Pennsylvania	PA	20,180	LC
Indiana Univ South Bend	IN	15,293	C
Indiana Univ Southeast	IN	15,807	LC
Indiana Univ-Purdue Univ Fort Wayne	IN	15,425	C
Indiana Univ-Purdue Univ Indianapolis	IN	17,290	C
Indiana Wesleyan Univ	IN	31,815	VC
Inter-American Univ of PR/ Fajardo Campus	PR	4,200	
Inter-American Univ of PR/ Metropolitan Campus	PR	4,320	
Inter-American Univ of PR/ Ponce	PR	3,700	
Inter-American Univ of PR/ San Germán	PR	6,720	
Iona College	NY	44,028	C
Iowa State Univ	IA	16,403	C
Ithaca College	NY	52,300	HC
Jacksonville Univ	FL	37,780	C
John Brown Univ	AR	30,996	VȻ
John Carroll Univ	OH	44,520	Ȼ
Johns Hopkins Univ	MD	47,492	MC
Johnson C. Smith Univ	NC	25,336	LC
Judson College	AL	24,690	C
Juniata College	PA	49,340	VC
Kalamazoo College	MI	47,825	HȻ
Kansas Wesleyan Univ	KS	32,000	C
Kean Univ	NJ	22,060	LC
Keene State College	NH	21,538	C
Kent State Univ	OH	19,352	C
Kentucky Wesleyan College	KY	27,440	VȻ
Kenyon College	OH	56,810	MC
King Univ	TN	33,140	C
King's College	PA	41,678	C
Knox College	IL		VC
Kutztown Univ of Pennsylvania	PA	16,909	LC
La Roche College	PA	34,802	LC
La Salle Univ	PA	50,270	C
La Sierra Univ	CA	35,694	VC
Lafayette College	PA	57,050	HȻ
LaGrange College	GA	34,480	C
Lake Forest College	IL	45,580	VC
Lake Superior State Univ	MI	18,121	C
Lakeland College	WI	22,990	C
Lamar Univ	TX	6,820	LC
Lander Univ	SC	22,514	Ȼ
Lawrence Univ	WI	46,371	HC
Le Moyne College	NY	42,200	VC
Lebanon Valley College	PA	38,570	C
Lee Univ	TN	18,690	Ȼ
Lehigh Univ	PA	55,080	MC
Lehman College / The CUNY	NY	5,778	LC
Lenoir-Rhyne College	NC	35,984	C
Liberty Univ	VA	19,101	C

School	ST	$IS	SR
Lincoln Univ	MO	11,996	NC
Lindenwood Univ	MO	20,750	C
Linfield College-McMinnville Campus	OR	46,166	C
Lipscomb Univ	TN	35,722	VC
Lock Haven Univ of Pennsylvania	PA	17,587	LC
LIU/C.W. Post Campus	NY	38,888	C
Loras College	IA	37,432	VC
Louisiana State Univ	LA	18,677	VȻ
Louisiana Tech Univ	LA	8,000	C
Loyola Marymount Univ	CA	53,240	VȻ
Loyola Univ Chicago	IL	49,560	VȻ
Loyola Univ Maryland	MD		VC
Loyola Univ New Orleans	LA	46,581	VC
Luther College	IA	44,380	VȻ
Lycoming College	PA	40,036	C
Lynchburg College	VA	42,645	C
Lyon College	AR	30,246	VC
Macalester College	MN	53,419	MC
MacMurray College	IL	20,755	C
Madonna Univ	MI	24,540	VC
Malone Univ	OH	34,334	C
Manchester College	IN	35,070	C
Manhattan College	NY	44,955	VC
Manhattanville College	NY	46,260	VC
Mansfield Univ	PA	19,468	LC
Marian Univ	WI	30,980	LC
Marian Univ/Indianapolis	IN	37,058	C
Marietta College	OH	42,135	VC
Marist College	NY	35,500	C
Marlboro College	VT	35,980	VC
Marquette Univ	WI	43,664	VȻ
Mars Hill College	NC	22,950	LC
Marshall Univ	WV	14,820	C
Martin Univ	IN	11,000	SP
Mary Baldwin College	VA	37,110	C
Maryville College	TN	33,150	VC
Marywood Univ	PA	40,695	C
McDaniel College	MD	45,600	VC
McMurry Univ	TX	25,962	LC
McPherson College	KS	28,138	C
Mercer Univ	GA	44,201	VȻ
Mercy College	NY	29,996	C
Meredith College	NC	31,420	C
Messiah College	PA	39,540	VC
Methodist Univ	NC	37,185	C
Metropolitan State Univ of Denver	CO	4,835	LC
Miami Univ	OH	24,191	HC
Mich State Univ	MI	13,689	VC
MidAmerica Nazarene Univ	KS	28,000	C
Middle Tenn State Univ	TN	8,650	C
Middlebury College	VT	57,470	MC
Midwestern State Univ	TX	9,722	C
Millersville Univ of Pennsylvania	PA	18,498	C
Millikin Univ	IL	37,462	C
Mills College	CA	54,119	HC
Millsaps College	MS	43,888	VȻ
Minn State Univ, Mankato	MN	14,900	C
Minn State Univ, Moorhead	MN	13,392	C
Minot State Univ	ND	10,915	C
Miss College	MS	21,998	VC
Miss Univ for Women	MS	7,400	LC
Missouri Southern State Univ	MO	11,910	C
Missouri State Univ	MO	13,996	VC
Missouri Western State Univ	MO	12,260	NC
Molloy College	NY	38,950	C
Monmouth College	IL	39,290	C
Monmouth Univ	NJ	42,252	C
Montclair State Univ	NJ	22,614	C
Moravian College	PA	36,381	VC
Morehouse College	GA	38,640	C
Morningside College	IA	32,620	C
Mount Holyoke College	MA	53,596	HȻ
Mount Mary Univ	WI	32,836	LC
Mount St. Mary's Univ	MD	46,158	C
Mount St. Mary's College/ Chalon Campus	CA	43,897	VȻ
Mount Vernon Nazarene Univ	OH	29,590	C
Muhlenberg College	PA	52,837	HC
Murray State Univ	KY	14,944	C
Muskingum Univ	OH	30,502	C
Nazareth College of Rochester	NY	41,590	VC
Nebr Wesleyan Univ	NE	29,774	Ȼ
New College of Florida	FL	14,504	HȻ
New Jersey City Univ	NJ	21,060	Ȼ
New Mexico Highlands Univ	NM	9,720	NC
New York Univ	NY	61,470	MC
Newberry College	SC	26,850	LC
Niagara Univ	NY	39,800	C
N Car Central Univ	NC	9,000	LC
N Car State Univ	NC	16,202	HC
North Central College	IL	38,343	VC
N Dak State Univ	ND	14,642	C
North Georgia College & State Univ	GA	8,500	C
North Park Univ	IL	30,130	C
Northeastern Illinois Univ	IL		C
Northeastern State Univ	OK	8,615	VC
Northern Arizona Univ	AZ	18,592	C

School	ST	$IS	SR
Northern Illinois Univ	IL	19,768	C
Northern Kentucky Univ	KY	15,302	LC
Northern Mich Univ	MI	15,300	VC
Northern State Univ	SD	14,021	C
Northwest Missouri State Univ	MO	14,229	C
Northwest Nazarene Univ	ID	24,275	NC
Northwestern College	MN	24,000	C
Northwestern College of Iowa	IA	34,848	Ȼ
Northwestern Univ	IL	37,595	MC
Oakland Univ	MI	19,391	VC
Oakwood Univ	AL	23,035	C
Oberlin College	OH	57,025	MC
Occidental College	CA	59,592	MȻ
Oglethorpe Univ	GA	42,580	VC
Ohio Northern Univ	OH	42,075	VC
Ohio Univ	OH	20,676	VC
Ohio Wesleyan Univ	OH	49,460	Ȼ
Okla Baptist Univ	OK	28,202	VC
Okla Christian Univ	OK	24,975	VC
Okla City Univ	OK	33,546	VC
Okla State Univ	OK	14,310	VC
Old Dominion Univ	VA	18,662	C
Olivet Nazarene Univ	IL	29,990	C
Oral Roberts Univ	OK	31,734	C
Oregon State Univ	OR	19,017	Ȼ
Oswego / SUNY	NY	20,009	VC
Otterbein College	OH	32,214	C
Ouachita Baptist Univ	AR	29,010	VC
Our Lady of the Lake Univ of San Antonio	TX	22,430	LC
Pace Univ	NY	48,094	VC
Pacific Lutheran Univ	WA	44,840	VC
Pacific Union College	CA	28,150	VC
Pacific Univ	OR	42,815	C
Park Univ	MO	17,525	C
Penn State Univ/Univ Park	PA	25,404	VC
Pepperdine Univ	CA	55,372	HȻ
Piedmont College	GA	29,260	C
Pittsburg State Univ	KS	12,032	C
Pitzer College	CA	54,988	MC
Plymouth State Univ	NH	23,148	LC
Point Loma Nazarene Univ	CA	38,610	VC
Pomona College	CA	57,680	MC
Pontifical Catholic Univ of PR	PR	7,310	
Portland State Univ	OR	18,672	C
Prairie View A&M Univ	TX	15,205	LC
Presbyterian College	SC	42,678	VC
Prescott College	AZ	33,284	Ȼ
Princeton Univ	NJ	53,795	MC
Principia College	IL	35,140	Ȼ
Providence College	RI	55,995	HC
Purdue Univ/Calumet	IN	14,336	C
Purdue Univ/West Lafayette	IN	20,278	HC
Queens College / The CUNY	NY	17,107	VC
Queens Univ of Charlotte	NC	39,543	VC
Quinnipiac Univ	CT	53,580	VC
Randolph College	VA	43,960	VC
Randolph-Macon College	VA	45,086	C
Regis College	MA	47,565	LC
Regis Univ	CO	41,318	C
Rhode Island College	RI	17,132	LC
Rhodes College	TN	47,596	HȻ
Rider Univ	NJ	45,720	C
Ripon College	WI	36,959	Ȼ
Roanoke College	VA	47,996	Ȼ
Roberts Wesleyan College	NY	37,384	Ȼ
Rockford College	IL	31,000	C
Rockhurst Univ	MO	20,625	C
Rollins College	FL	52,370	HC
Roosevelt Univ	IL	22,605	VC
Rosemont College	PA	42,350	C
Rowan Univ	NJ	23,570	VC
Russell Sage College	NY	39,370	C
Rutgers, The State Univ of New Jersey/Camden Campus	NJ	24,254	C
Rutgers, The State Univ of New Jersey/New Brunswick	NJ	25,077	VC
Rutgers, The State Univ of New Jersey/Newark Campus	NJ	25,376	C
Sacred Heart Univ	CT	48,564	VC
Saginaw Valley State Univ	MI	16,869	C
St. Anselm College	NH	48,324	VC
St. Augustine's Univ	NC	14,000	C
St. Francis Univ	PA	30,029	LC
St. John's Univ	MN	46,146	C
St. Joseph College	CT	45,630	LC
St. Joseph's Univ	PA	52,272	VC
St. Louis Univ	MO	46,594	VȻ
St. Mary's College	IN	45,160	VC
St. Mary's College of Calif	CA	53,550	C
St. Mary's Univ	TX	33,854	C
St. Mary's Univ of Minn	MN	37,015	C
St. Michael's College	VT	48,740	VC
St. Peter's College	NJ	44,240	C
St. Vincent College	PA	40,244	C
St. Xavier Univ	IL	32,840	C
Salem College	NC	29,326	VC
Salisbury Univ	MD	18,368	VC
Salve Regina Univ	RI	47,250	VC
Sam Houston State Univ	TX	17,082	C

School	ST	$IS	SR
Samford Univ	AL	35,700	VC+
San Diego State Univ	CA	20,578	VC
San Francisco State Univ	CA	18,514	C
San Jose State Univ	CA	19,707	C
Sarah Lawrence College	NY	48,000	HC
Scripps College	CA	54,900	MC
Seattle Pacific Univ	WA	41,559	VC+
Seattle Univ	WA	47,010	VC+
Seton Hall Univ	NJ	45,902	C
Seton Hill Univ	PA	35,172	C
Sewanee: The Univ of the South	TN	47,700	HC+
Shenandoah Univ	VA	39,268	C
Shepherd Univ	WV	14,996	C
Shippensburg Univ of Pennsylvania	PA	17,064	LC
Shorter Univ	GA	26,470	C
Siena College	NY	43,863	VC
Siena Heights Univ	MI	17,000	LC
Simmons College	MA	48,770	VC
Simpson College	IA	36,086	VC
Skidmore College	NY	57,926	HC
Slippery Rock Univ of Pennsylvania	PA	10,360	LC
Smith College	MA	57,524	MC
Sonoma State Univ	CA	20,541	C
S Car State Univ	SC	6,700	LC
S Dak State Univ	SD	14,296	C
Southeastern Louisiana Univ	LA	13,325	C
Southern Arkansas Univ	AR	14,316	C
Southern Conn State Univ	CT	18,033	C
Southern Illinois Univ Carbondale	IL	21,620	C
Southern Illinois Univ Edwardsville	IL	17,532	C
Southern Methodist Univ	TX	57,755	MC
Southern Nazarene Univ	OK	24,354	NC
Southern Oregon Univ	OR	17,874	C
Southern Univ and A&M College	LA	9,761	C+
Southern Univ at New Orleans	LA	1,000	NC
Southwest Baptist Univ	MO	24,710	C
Southwest Minn State Univ	MN	14,000	C
Southwestern Univ	TX	45,660	VC
Spelman College	GA	24,650	VC
Spring Arbor Univ	MI	26,740	C
St. Ambrose Univ	IA		C
St. Bonaventure Univ	NY	38,831	C
St. Catherine Univ	MN	37,782	C+
St. Edward's Univ	TX	44,674	VC
St. Francis College	NY	34,200	LC
St. John Fisher College	NY	39,370	C+
St. John's Univ	NY	52,840	C+
St. Joseph's College, New York / Brooklyn Campus	NY	21,878	C
St. Joseph's College, New York / Suffolk Campus	NY	21,878	VC
St. Lawrence Univ	NY	53,740	HC
St. Norbert College	WI	39,992	VC
St. Olaf College	MN	49,960	HC+
St. Thomas Aquinas College	NY	30,000	C
Stanford Univ	CA	56,411	MC
Stephen F. Austin State Univ	TX	14,668	C
Stetson Univ	FL	49,512	VC+
Stonehill College	MA	46,780	VC+
Suffolk Univ	MA	46,548	C
Sul Ross State Univ	TX	13,410	LC
SUNY College at Geneseo	NY	18,055	HC+
SUNY College at Old Westbury	NY	16,324	C
SUNY Fredonia / The SUNY at Fredonia	NY	18,702	VC
SUNY New Paltz	NY	15,010	C
SUNY Oneonta / SUNY	NY	16,919	VC
SUNY Plattsburgh / SUNY	NY	18,083	VC
Susquehanna Univ	PA	49,170	C
Swarthmore College	PA	57,870	MC
Sweet Briar College	VA	43,765	C+
Tarleton State Univ	TX	13,489	LC
Taylor Univ	IN	36,742	VC+
Temple Univ	PA	24,392	VC
Tenn Tech Univ	TN	11,310	C
Texas A&M Univ	TX	16,956	VC+
Texas A&M Univ at Commerce	TX	10,496	C
Texas A&M Univ at Corpus Christi	TX	11,544	LC
Texas A&M Univ at Kingsville	TX	7,500	LC
Texas Christian Univ	TX	47,570	HC
Texas Lutheran Univ	TX	34,070	C
Texas Southern Univ	TX	18,212	LC
Texas State Univ	TX	16,495	VC
Texas Tech Univ	TX	14,243	C
Texas Wesleyan Univ	TX	29,886	C
The Catholic Univ of America	DC	52,852	VC
The College at Brockport / SUNY	NY	18,362	VC
The College of Idaho	ID	31,277	VC
The College of New Rochelle	NY	33,600	VC
The College of St. Rose	NY	26,750	C
The Lincoln Univ	PA	15,154	LC
Ohio State Univ	OH	19,887	MC
The SUNY at Potsdam	NY	17,754	C
Thomas Edison State College	NJ	5,700	SP
Thomas More College	KY	34,760	C
Towson Univ	MD	16,000	VC
Transylvania Univ	KY	40,310	VC+
Trinity Christian College	IL	28,869	C
Trinity College	CT		HC+
Trinity Univ	TX	44,174	HC+
Truman State Univ	MO	13,546	HC
Tufts Univ	MA	58,780	MC
Tulane Univ	LA	58,942	MC
Union College	NE	23,270	VC
Union Univ	TN	28,260	VC
Universidad Adventista de las Antillas	PR	7,360	
Universidad del Turabo	PR	4,110	
Univ at Albany / SUNY	NY	18,674	VC
Univ at Buffalo / The SUNY	NY	20,283	VC
Univ of Akron	OH	20,436	C
Univ of Alabama at Birmingham	AL	18,484	C+
Univ of Alabama at Tuscaloosa	AL	17,164	C+
Univ of Alaska Fairbanks	AK	13,955	C
Univ of Arizona	AZ	20,105	C
Univ of Arkansas at Fayetteville	AR	16,860	VC
Univ of Arkansas at Little Rock	AR		C
Univ of Calif at Berkeley	CA	23,322	MC
Univ of Calif at Davis	CA	24,102	HC
Univ of Calif at Irvine	CA	25,961	VC
Univ of Calif at Los Angeles	CA	25,686	MC
Univ of Calif at Riverside	CA	27,204	C
Univ of Calif at Santa Barbara	CA	27,551	HC
Univ of Central Arkansas	AR	10,840	VC
Univ of Central Florida	FL	15,711	VC+
Univ of Central Missouri	MO	14,605	C
Univ of Central Okla	OK	12,293	C
Univ of Cincinnati	OH	20,199	VC
Univ of Colo at Colo Springs	CO	15,000	VC
Univ of Colo Boulder	CO	22,605	VC+
Univ of Colo Denver	CO	17,904	C
Univ of Conn	CT	23,744	HC
Univ of Dallas	TX	43,510	VC+
Univ of Dayton	OH	43,750	VC
Univ of Denver	CO	51,787	VC+
Univ of Evansville	IN	41,056	VC+
Univ of Findlay	OH	31,916	C
Univ of Florida	FL	15,783	HC+
Univ of Georgia	GA	19,508	VC
Univ of Hawaii at Manoa	HI	19,379	VC
Univ of Houston	TX	19,184	VC
Univ of Houston-Downtown	TX	6,267	LC
Univ of Idaho	ID	14,558	C
Univ of Illinois at Chicago	IL	24,293	VC
Univ of Illinois at Urbana-Champaign	IL	24,300	HC
Univ of Indianapolis	IN	31,740	LC
Univ of Iowa	IA	17,481	VC
Univ of Jamestown	ND	24,738	C
Univ of Kansas	KS	16,980	C+
Univ of Kentucky	KY	19,868	C+
Univ of La Verne	CA	47,010	VC
Univ of Louisiana at Lafayette	LA	6,130	C
Univ of Louisiana at Monroe	LA	12,998	C
Univ of Louisville	KY	17,460	VC
Univ of Maine	ME	19,712	C+
Univ of Mary Hardin-Baylor	TX	31,950	C+
Univ of Mary Washington	VA	19,484	VC
Univ of Maryland	MD	18,801	HC
Univ of Maryland/Baltimore County	MD	18,000	VC
Univ of Maryland/Univ College	MD	6,168	SP
Univ of Mass Amherst	MA	23,697	VC+
Univ of Mass Boston	MA	11,966	C
Univ of Mass Dartmouth	MA	22,223	C
Univ of Miami	FL	55,166	MC
Univ of Mich/Ann Arbor	MI	22,102	HC+
Univ of Mich-Flint	MI	17,547	C+
Univ of Minn/Duluth	MN	18,964	C+
Univ of Minn/Morris	MN	17,150	VC
Univ of Minn/Twin Cities	MN		HC
Univ of Miss	MS	15,482	VC
Univ of Missouri/Columbia	MO	18,201	MC
Univ of Missouri-Kansas City	MO	19,603	C
Univ of Missouri-St. Louis	MO	18,304	VC
Univ of Montana	MT	13,670	C
Univ of Montevallo	AL	17,320	C
Univ of Mount Union	OH	35,130	C
Univ of Nebr - Lincoln	NE	17,507	VC
Univ of Nebr at Kearney	NE	14,855	LC
Univ of Nebr at Omaha	NE	12,700	C
Univ of Nevada, Las Vegas	NV	17,303	C
Univ of Nevada/Reno	NV	14,500	NC
Univ of New Hampshire	NH	24,702	VC
Univ of New Mexico	NM	15,300	C
Univ of New Orleans	LA	9,224	VC
Univ of North Alabama	AL	9,960	C
Univ of N Car at Asheville	NC	13,500	VC+
Univ of N Car at Charlotte	NC	15,847	C
Univ of N Car at Greensboro	NC	12,848	C
Univ of N Car at Wilmington	NC	13,572	VC+
Univ of N Dak	ND	14,094	C
Univ of North Florida	FL	15,578	VC
Univ of North Texas	TX	15,628	C
Univ of Northern Colo	CO	15,973	C
Univ of Northern Iowa	IA	14,776	C
Univ of Notre Dame	IN		MC
Univ of Okla	OK	17,634	VC+
Univ of Oregon	OR	20,872	VC
Univ of Pikeville	KY	24,750	NC
Univ of Pittsburgh at Pittsburgh	PA	27,800	HC+
Univ of Portland	OR	47,874	VC
Univ of Puget Sound	WA	52,648	HC+
Univ of Redlands	CA	40,500	VC
Univ of Rochester	NY	58,500	MC
Univ of San Diego	CA	53,302	HC+
Univ of San Francisco	CA	49,674	VC
Univ of Scranton	PA	51,940	VC
Univ of S Car at Columbia	SC	19,725	VC+
Univ of S Car Upstate	SC	17,673	LC
Univ of S Dak	SD	15,111	C
Univ of South Florida	FL	13,000	C
Univ of Southern Calif	CA	56,903	MC
Univ of Southern Indiana	IN	14,657	C
Univ of St. Thomas - Houston	TX	36,490	VC
Univ of Tampa	FL	35,160	VC
Univ of Tenn at Chattanooga	TN	16,883	C
Univ of Tenn at Martin	TN	13,217	C
Univ of Texas at Arlington	TX	10,908	LC
Univ of Texas at Austin	TX	44,074	HC
Univ of Texas at El Paso	TX	8,764	NC
Univ of Texas at San Antonio	TX	18,372	C
Univ of Texas-Pan American	TX	12,432	LC
Univ of the District of Columbia	DC	7,244	LC
Univ of the Incarnate Word	TX	35,200	LC
Univ of the Pacific	CA	52,146	VC
Univ of Toledo	OH	18,464	C
Univ of Tulsa	OK	45,311	HC+
Univ of Utah	UT	13,462	VC
Univ of Vermont	VT	26,120	VC+
Univ of Virginia	VA	22,175	MC
Univ of Virginia's College at Wise	VA	11,076	C
Univ of Washington	WA	14,722	VC
Univ of Wisc Whitewater	WI	13,314	C
Univ of Wisc/Eau Claire	WI	15,430	VC
Univ of Wisc/Green Bay	WI	14,900	C
Univ of Wisc/La Crosse	WI	14,755	VC
Univ of Wisc/Madison	WI	18,757	HC
Univ of Wisc/Oshkosh	WI	10,426	LC
Univ of Wisc/Parkside	WI	10,181	LC
Univ of Wisc/Platteville	WI	14,274	C
Univ of Wisc/Stevens Point	WI	14,043	C
Univ of Wyoming	WY	13,855	C+
Ursinus College	PA	55,630	VC+
Utah State Univ	UT	11,803	C
Valley City State Univ	ND	12,286	LC
Valparaiso Univ	IN	43,040	VC+
Vanderbilt Univ	TN	57,072	MC
Vanguard Univ of Southern Calif	CA	35,833	VC
Villanova Univ	PA	56,436	MC
Virginia Polytechnic Inst and State Univ	VA	14,629	HC
Virginia Wesleyan College	VA	28,433	LC
Viterbo Univ	WI	30,070	C
Wabash College	IN	44,160	VC
Wake Forest Univ	NC	51,000	MC
Walla Walla Univ	WA	26,256	NC
Walsh Univ	OH	35,100	C
Wartburg College	IA	41,055	VC
Washburn Univ	KS	12,165	NC
Washington and Jefferson College	PA	49,990	VC
Washington and Lee Univ	VA	52,812	MC
Washington College	MD	48,768	VC
Washington State Univ	WA	20,461	C
Washington Univ in St. Louis	MO	58,818	MC
Wayland Baptist Univ	TX	16,058	LC
Wayne State College	NE	11,764	NC
Webster Univ	MO	33,990	C+
Wellesley College	MA	49,848	MC
Wells College	NY	38,680	VC
Wesleyan College	GA	24,000	C+
West Chester Univ of Pennsylvania	PA	16,836	C
West Texas A&M Univ	TX	13,478	C
Western Carolina Univ	NC	13,965	C+
Western Conn State Univ	CT	18,327	C
Western Illinois Univ	IL	20,130	C
Western Kentucky Univ	KY	11,000	LC
Western Mich Univ	MI	19,042	C
Western New Mexico Univ	NM	8,500	LC
Western Oregon Univ	OR	15,021	C
Western State Colo Univ	CO	16,135	C
Western Washington Univ	WA	18,519	VC
Westfield State Univ	MA	18,489	C
Westminster College	MO	30,490	VC
Westminster College	PA	31,290	C+
Westmont College	CA	41,500	HC
Wheaton College	IL	39,650	HC+
Wheeling Jesuit Univ	WV	34,668	C
Whitman College	WA	54,400	MC
Whittier College	CA	43,416	C
Whitworth Univ	WA	45,826	VC+
Wichita State Univ	KS	12,539	C
Widener Univ	PA	50,368	C
Wilkes Univ	PA	42,786	C
Willamette Univ	OR	56,450	VC+
William Carey Univ	MS	13,500	LC
William Jewell College	MO	31,000	VC+
William Paterson Univ of New Jersey	NJ	21,694	C
Williams College	MA	58,900	MC
Wilmington College	OH	29,784	C
Wilson College	PA	27,660	C
Winona State Univ	MN	16,530	C
Winston-Salem State Univ	NC	9,418	LC
Winthrop Univ	SC	21,120	VC
Wisc Lutheran College	WI	23,510	VC
Wittenberg Univ	OH	47,766	VC
Wofford College	SC	45,795	VC
Worcester State Univ	MA	18,657	C
Wright State Univ	OH	16,983	C
Xavier Univ	OH	43,740	VC
Xavier Univ of Louisiana	LA	25,300	C
Yale Univ	CT	55,300	MC
York College / CUNY	NY	5,496	NC
York College of Pennsylvania	PA	26,590	C
Youngstown State Univ	OH	16,374	LC

SPANISH / ADOLESCENCE EDUCATION

School	ST	$IS	SR
Bethany College	WV	35,282	C
Indiana Univ Northwest	IN	6,738	LC
Indiana Univ of Pennsylvania	PA	20,180	LC
Indiana Univ-Purdue Univ Indianapolis	IN	17,290	C
Messiah College	PA	39,540	VC
Nazareth College of Rochester	NY	41,590	VC
Oswego / SUNY	NY	20,009	VC
SUNY Plattsburgh / SUNY	NY	18,083	VC
The College of St. Rose	NY	26,750	C

SPANISH AND HISPANIC STUDIES

School	ST	$IS	SR
Creighton Univ	NE	44,058	VC+

SPANISH STUDIES

School	ST	$IS	SR
American Univ	DC	54,829	HC+
Bard College	NY	59,872	HC
Bard College at Simon's Rock	MA	58,963	HC+
Barton College	NC	27,660	C
Bentley Univ	MA	54,555	HC+
Cal State, San Bernardino	CA	12,000	C
Cedar Crest College	PA	43,240	C
Coe College	IA	43,590	VC
Creighton Univ	NE	44,058	VC+
Dartmouth College	NH	57,996	MC
Drury Univ	MO	30,319	VC
Fairleigh Dickinson Univ/ College at Florham	NJ	42,142	C
Fairleigh Dickinson Univ/ Metropolitan Campus	NJ	40,254	C
Fordham Univ	NY	58,927	HC
Hobart and William Smith Colleges	NY	43,000	VC
Holy Names Univ	CA	40,310	NC
Howard Univ	DC	35,957	C
Lake Erie College	OH	35,704	C
Messiah College	PA	39,540	VC
Mills College	CA	54,119	HC
Minn State Univ, Moorhead	MN	13,392	C
Montana State Univ-Billings	MT	12,425	LC
New College of Florida	FL	14,504	HC+
Olivet Nazarene Univ	IL	29,990	C
Purdue Univ/West Lafayette	IN	20,278	HC
Ramapo College of New Jersey	NJ	24,938	C+
Reed College	OR	57,780	MC
Santa Clara Univ	CA	54,702	MC
Southeast Missouri State Univ	MO	14,983	LC
Southern Nazarene Univ	OK	24,354	NC
Spring Hill College	AL	42,130	VC
Stony Brook Univ / SUNY	NY	19,359	HC
Sweet Briar College	VA	43,765	C+
Syracuse Univ	NY	54,512	HC
The Catholic Univ of America	DC	52,852	VC
The SUNY at Potsdam	NY	17,754	C
Union College	NY		MC
Univ of Calif at Los Angeles	CA	25,686	MC
Univ of Calif at San Diego	CA	21,000	VC

School	ST	$IS	SR
Univ of Illinois at Chicago	IL	24,293	VC
Univ of Wisc-Milwaukee	WI	18,436	C
Vassar College	NY	59,070	MC
Westminster College	UT	37,708	VC
Winthrop Univ	SC	21,120	VC
Youngstown State Univ	OH	16,374	LC

SPECIAL EDUCATION

School	ST	$IS	SR
Abilene Christian Univ	TX	38,400	VC
Adams State College	CO	13,358	LC
Alabama A&M Univ	AL	96,100	C
Alabama State Univ	AL	14,142	NC
Albany State Univ	GA	8,500	C
Albright College	PA	46,660	C
Alcorn State Univ	MS	9,500	C
American International College	MA	36,100	LC
Appalachian State Univ	NC	12,919	VC
Aquinas College	MI	33,060	C
Arcadia Univ	PA	33,570	C+
Arizona State Univ	AZ	18,818	C+
Armstrong Atlantic State Univ	GA	16,276	C
Auburn Univ	AL	20,052	VC+
Augustana College	SD	35,500	VC
Aurora Univ	IL	26,870	C
Austin Peay State Univ	TN	14,650	C
Avila Univ	MO	26,900	C
Baylor Univ	TX	46,720	HC
Bellarmine Univ	KY	42,950	VC
Benedictine College	KS	29,180	VC
Benedictine Univ	IL	35,220	C
Bennett College	NC		LC
Black Hills State Univ	SD	13,562	LC
Bloomsburg Univ of Pennsylvania	PA	13,598	C
Bluffton Univ	OH	37,864	C
Boise State Univ	ID	12,802	C
Boston College	MA	58,506	MC
Boston Univ	MA	54,130	HC+
Bowling Green State Univ	OH	18,970	C
Bradley Univ	IL	31,874	VC
Brenau Univ Women's College	GA	26,650	C+
Brescia Univ	KY	26,140	VC+
Bridgewater State Univ	MA	18,752	C
Brigham Young Univ	UT	12,100	HC
Brigham Young Univ/ Hawaii	HI	8,614	VC
Buena Vista Univ	IA	37,954	C
Buffalo State/State Univ of Buffalo	NY	15,733	C+
Butler Univ	IN	45,898	VC+
Cabrini College	PA	40,859	LC
Cal State, Long Beach	CA	17,534	C+
Calif Univ of Pennsylvania	PA	14,217	C
Calvin College	MI	37,585	VC+
Canisius College	NY	45,602	VC
Cardinal Stritch Univ	WI	24,054	C
Caribbean Univ	PR	10,375	
Carlow Univ	PA	30,272	C
Cedarville Univ	OH	31,036	VC+
Central Methodist Univ	MO	28,240	VC
Central State Univ	OH	9,010	C
Central Washington Univ	WA	11,730	C
Cheyney Univ of Pennsylvania	PA	20,372	LC
Christian Brothers Univ	TN	19,140	HC
Clarion Univ of Pennsylvania	PA	17,370	C
Clarke Univ	IA	36,400	C
Clearwater Christian College	FL	23,720	C
Clemson Univ	SC	19,136	HC
Cleveland State Univ	OH	21,357	C
Coastal Carolina Univ	SC	17,620	C
College of Charleston	SC	21,273	VC
College of Mount St. Joseph	OH	33,880	C
College of Mount St. Vincent	NY	41,040	MC
College of New Jersey	NJ	25,376	HC
Columbia College	SC	27,882	C
Columbus State Univ	GA	13,176	C
Concord Univ	WV	13,102	C
Concordia Univ Nebr	NE	26,000	VC
Concordia Univ St. Paul	MN	27,200	C
Coppin State Univ	MD	14,905	VC
Cumberland Univ	TN	21,220	C
CUNY-City College	NY	19,576	HC+
Curry College	MA	47,545	LC
Dakota Wesleyan Univ	SD	23,000	C
Delaware State Univ	DE	14,700	LC
DePaul Univ	IL	46,120	VC
Doane College	NE	33,730	VC
Dominican College	NY	31,270	C
Dordt College	IA	34,160	VC
Dowling College	NY	25,000	LC
East Carolina Univ	NC	14,169	C
East Central Univ	OK	10,223	LC
East Stroudsburg Univ of Pennsylvania	PA	16,636	C
East Tenn State Univ	TN	9,000	C
Eastern Illinois Univ	IL	20,502	C
Eastern Kentucky Univ	KY	11,161	C
Eastern Mennonite Univ	VA	38,850	VC
Eastern Mich Univ	MI	17,961	C
Eastern New Mexico Univ	NM	10,682	C
Edinboro Univ of Pennsylvania	PA	15,940	LC
Elizabeth City State Univ	NC	11,638	C
Elmhurst College	IL	42,032	C+
Elms College	MA	23,900	VC
Elon Univ	NC	40,046	HC
Erskine College	SC	37,360	C
Evangel Univ	MO	23,090	C
Felician College	NJ	41,640	C
Fitchburg State Univ	MA	17,241	C
Florida Atlantic Univ	FL	17,339	C
Florida Gulf Coast Univ	FL		C
Florida International Univ	FL	17,747	VC
Fontbonne Univ	MO	31,384	C
Freed-Hardeman Univ	TN	19,607	VC
Gannon Univ	PA	37,940	C
Georgia College and State Univ	GA	18,216	VC
Georgia Regents Univ	GA		C
Georgia Southern Univ	GA	16,414	C
Georgia Southwestern State Univ	GA	12,218	C
Glenville State College	WV	11,348	NC
Gonzaga Univ	WA	44,247	HC
Gordon College	MA	42,660	VC+
Goucher College	MD	50,252	VC+
Grace College and Theological Seminary	IN	28,800	C
Grambling State Univ	LA	13,384	LC
Grand Valley State Univ	MI	17,998	VC
Green Mountain College	VT	33,547	LC
Greensboro College	NC	28,740	LC
Greenville College	IL	27,012	C
Grove City College	PA	22,988	HC
Gwynedd-Mercy College	PA	33,560	C
Hastings College	NE	27,782	C+
High Point Univ	NC	39,800	C
Holy Family Univ	PA	40,030	LC
Hood College	MD	44,630	C
Hope College	MI	36,320	VC+
Houghton College	NY	35,740	VC
Houston Baptist Univ	TX	23,815	C+
Illinois State Univ	IL	22,634	VC
Indiana State Univ	IN	16,000	C
Indiana Univ Bloomington	IN	19,358	HC
Indiana Univ of Pennsylvania	PA	20,180	LC
Indiana Univ South Bend	IN	15,293	C
Indiana Univ Southeast	IN	15,807	LC
Indiana Wesleyan Univ	IN	31,815	VC
Inter-American Univ of PR/ Aguadilla Campus	PR	5,578	
Inter-American Univ of PR/ Arecibo Campus	PR	3,350	
Inter-American Univ of PR/ Fajardo Campus	PR	4,200	
Inter-American Univ of PR/ Metropolitan Campus	PR	4,320	
Inter-American Univ of PR/ Ponce	PR	3,700	
Inter-American Univ of PR/ San Germán	PR	6,720	
Jackson State Univ	MS	13,512	LC
Jacksonville State Univ	AL	12,280	LC
Jarvis Christian College	TX	19,552	NC
Juniata College	PA	49,340	VC
Kansas Wesleyan Univ	KS	32,000	C
Kean Univ	NJ	22,060	LC
Keene State College	NH	21,538	C
King's College	PA	41,678	C
Kutztown Univ of Pennsylvania	PA	16,909	LC
La Salle Univ	PA	50,270	C
Lake Erie College	OH	35,704	C
Lamar Univ	TX	6,820	LC
Lander Univ	SC	22,514	C+
Le Moyne College	NY	42,200	VC
Lebanon Valley College	PA	38,570	C
Lee Univ	TN	18,690	C+
LeMoyne-Owen College	TN	13,100	C
Lesley Univ	MA	46,350	C
Lewis Univ	IL	23,050	C
Lincoln Univ	MO	11,996	NC
Lock Haven Univ of Pennsylvania	PA	17,587	LC
LIU/Brooklyn Campus	NY	26,500	C
Longwood Univ	VA	20,924	C
Loras College	IA	37,432	VC
Louisiana College	LA	15,746	C
Louisiana State Univ	LA	18,677	VC+
Louisiana Tech Univ	LA	8,000	C
Loyola Univ Chicago	IL	49,560	VC+
MacMurray College	IL	20,755	C
Malone Univ	OH	34,334	C
Manhattan College	NY	44,955	VC
Mansfield Univ	PA	19,468	LC
Marian Univ/Indianapolis	IN	37,058	C
Marist College	NY	35,500	C
Marshall Univ	WV	14,820	C
Marygrove College	MI	21,290	C
Marymount Univ	VA	36,178	C
Marywood Univ	PA	40,695	C
McPherson College	KS	28,138	C
Medgar Evers College / The CUNY	NY	4,920	NC
Mercer Univ	GA	44,201	VC+
Mercy College	NY	29,996	C
Mercyhurst Univ	PA	40,700	C
Methodist Univ	NC	37,185	C
Miami Univ	OH	24,191	HC
Mich State Univ	MI	13,689	VC
Middle Tenn State Univ	TN	8,650	C
Millersville Univ of Pennsylvania	PA	18,498	C
Minn State Univ, Moorhead	MN	13,392	C
Misericordia Univ	PA	39,840	C
Miss College	MS	21,998	VC
Missouri Southern State Univ	MO	11,910	C
Missouri State Univ	MO	13,996	VC
Molloy College	NY	38,950	C
Monmouth Univ	NJ	42,252	C
Montana State Univ-Billings	MT	12,425	LC
Morehead State Univ	KY	10,900	C
Morningside College	IA	32,620	C
Mount Marty College	SD	29,638	C
Mount Vernon Nazarene Univ	OH	29,590	C
Murray State Univ	KY	14,944	C
Muskingum Univ	OH	30,502	C
Nebr Wesleyan Univ	NE	29,774	C+
New England College	NH	45,930	LC
New Jersey City Univ	NJ	21,060	C+
New Mexico Highlands Univ	NM	9,720	NC
New Mexico State Univ	NM	13,955	LC
New York Univ	NY	61,470	MC
Niagara Univ	NY	39,800	C
Nicholls State Univ	LA	7,095	C
N Car Agricultural and Technical State Univ	NC	13,175	LC
North Georgia College & State Univ	GA	8,500	C
Northeastern Illinois Univ	IL		C
Northeastern State Univ	OK	8,615	VC
Northern Arizona Univ	AZ	18,592	C
Northern Illinois Univ	IL	19,768	C
Northern Kentucky Univ	KY	15,302	LC
Northern State Univ	SD	14,021	C
Northwest Missouri State Univ	MO	14,229	C
Northwest Univ	WA	18,854	C
Northwestern College of Iowa	IA	34,848	C+
Northwestern Okla State Univ	OK	7,275	NC
Notre Dame College	OH	34,942	VC
Notre Dame of Maryland Univ	MD	27,700	C
Ohio Dominican Univ	OH	38,380	C+
Ohio Univ	OH	20,676	VC
Okla Christian Univ	OK	24,975	VC
Old Dominion Univ	VA	18,662	C
Oral Roberts Univ	OK	31,734	C
Our Lady of the Lake Univ of San Antonio	TX	22,430	LC
Penn State Univ/Univ Park	PA	25,404	VC
Peru State College	NE	8,600	NC
Pfeiffer Univ	NC	33,700	C
Piedmont College	GA	29,260	C
Point Park Univ	PA	36,390	C
Pontifical Catholic Univ of PR	PR	7,310	
Prescott College	AZ	33,284	C+
Providence College	RI	55,995	HC
Purdue Univ/West Lafayette	IN	20,278	HC
Quincy Univ	IL	34,980	LC
Rhode Island College	RI	17,132	LC
Roberts Wesleyan College	NY	37,384	C+
Rockford College	IL	31,000	C
Saginaw Valley State Univ	MI	16,869	C
St. Joseph College	CT	45,630	LC
St. Joseph's Univ	PA	52,272	VC
St. Louis Univ	MO	46,594	VC+
St. Martin's Univ	WA	38,082	C
St. Mary-of-the-Woods College	IN	37,722	LC
Salve Regina Univ	RI	47,250	VC
Seattle Pacific Univ	WA	41,559	VC+
Seton Hall Univ	NJ	45,902	C
Seton Hill Univ	PA	35,172	C
Shaw Univ	NC	15,488	LC
Shawnee State Univ	OH	16,545	NC
Silver Lake College	WI	22,600	LC
Slippery Rock Univ of Pennsylvania	PA	10,360	LC
S Car State Univ	SC	6,700	LC
Southeastern Louisiana Univ	LA	13,325	C
Southern Conn State Univ	CT	18,033	C
Southern Illinois Univ Carbondale	IL	21,620	C
Southern Illinois Univ Edwardsville	IL	17,532	C
Southern New Hampshire Univ	NH	38,100	C
Southern Univ and A&M College	LA	9,761	C+
Southern Wesleyan Univ	SC	25,600	C
Southwestern Okla State Univ	OK	9,160	C
Spring Arbor Univ	MI	26,740	C
St. Bonaventure Univ	NY	38,831	C
St. John Fisher College	NY	39,370	C+
St. John's Univ	NY	52,840	C+
St. Joseph's College, New York / Brooklyn Campus	NY	21,878	C
St. Joseph's College, New York / Suffolk Campus	NY	21,878	VC
St. Thomas Aquinas College	NY	30,000	C
SUNY College at Geneseo	NY	18,055	HC+
SUNY College at Old Westbury	NY	16,324	C
SUNY Plattsburgh / SUNY	NY	18,083	VC
Syracuse Univ	NY	54,512	HC
Tabor College	KS	29,010	LC
Tenn State Univ	TN	9,048	C
Tenn Tech Univ	TN	11,310	C
Texas State Univ	TX	10,495	VC
The College of St. Rose	NY	26,750	C
Tougaloo College	MS	15,275	NC
Touro College	NY	23,150	VC
Towson Univ	MD	16,000	VC
Trevecca Nazarene Univ	TN	30,118	C
Trinity Christian College	IL	28,869	C
Troy Univ	AL	10,650	C
Tusculum College	TN	24,295	C
Tuskegee Univ	AL	26,750	C
Union College	KY	28,775	C
Union Univ	TN	28,260	VC
Universidad del Turabo	PR	4,110	
Univ of Akron	OH	20,436	C
Univ of Alabama at Birmingham	AL	18,484	C+
Univ of Alabama at Tuscaloosa	AL	17,164	C+
Univ of Arizona	AZ	20,105	C
Univ of Arkansas at Little Rock	AR		C
Univ of Arkansas at Pine Bluff	AR	10,600	C
Univ of Central Arkansas	AR	10,840	VC
Univ of Central Missouri	MO	14,605	C
Univ of Central Okla	OK	12,293	C
Univ of Charleston	WV	28,650	C
Univ of Cincinnati	OH	20,199	VC
Univ of Conn	CT	23,744	HC
Univ of Dayton	OH	43,750	VC
Univ of Delaware	DE	22,728	VC
Univ of Detroit Mercy	MI	30,450	C
Univ of Evansville	IN	41,056	VC+
Univ of Georgia	GA	19,508	VC
Univ of Great Falls	MT	27,970	C
Univ of Hartford	CT	42,674	C
Univ of Idaho	ID	14,558	C
Univ of Kentucky	KY	19,868	C
Univ of Louisiana at Lafayette	LA	6,130	C
Univ of Louisiana at Monroe	LA	12,998	C
Univ of Maine at Farmington	ME	17,841	C
Univ of Mary	ND	16,714	C
Univ of Mary Hardin-Baylor	TX	31,950	C+
Univ of Maryland	MD	18,801	HC
Univ of Memphis	TN	15,094	C
Univ of Mich/Dearborn	MI	9,885	VC
Univ of Miss	MS	15,482	VC
Univ of Missouri-St. Louis	MO	18,304	VC
Univ of Montana-Western	MT	9,753	LC
Univ of Nebr - Lincoln	NE	17,507	VC
Univ of Nebr at Kearney	NE	14,855	LC
Univ of Nevada, Las Vegas	NV	17,303	C
Univ of Nevada/Reno	NV	14,500	NC
Univ of New Mexico	NM	15,300	C
Univ of N Car at Charlotte	NC	15,847	C
Univ of N Car at Greensboro	NC	12,848	C
Univ of N Car at Wilmington	NC	13,572	VC+
Univ of North Florida	FL	15,578	VC
Univ of Northern Colo	CO	15,973	C
Univ of Northern Iowa	IA	14,776	C
Univ of Okla	OK	17,634	VC+
Univ of PR Recinto de Rio Piedras	PR	5,750	
Univ of PR/Cayey	PR	1,504	
Univ of St. Francis	IN	29,810	C
Univ of South Alabama	AL	13,510	C
Univ of S Car at Aiken	SC	16,278	C
Univ of S Car Upstate	SC	17,673	LC
Univ of S Dak	SD	15,111	C
Univ of South Florida	FL	13,000	C
Univ of Southern Indiana	IN	14,657	C
Univ of St. Francis	IL	36,490	C
Univ of Tenn at Chattanooga	TN	16,883	C
Univ of Tenn at Knoxville	TN	20,364	VC+
Univ of Tenn at Martin	TN	13,217	C
Univ of the Cumberlands	KY	27,500	LC
Univ of the Southwest	NM	15,000	C
Univ of Toledo	OH	18,464	C
Univ of Utah	UT	13,462	VC
Univ of Vermont	VT	26,120	VC+
Univ of West Alabama	AL	9,415	C
Univ of West Georgia	GA	14,852	LC
Univ of Wisc Whitewater	WI	13,314	C
Univ of Wisc/Eau Claire	WI	15,430	VC
Univ of Wisc/Madison	WI	18,757	HC
Univ of Wisc/Oshkosh	WI	10,426	LC

School	ST	$IS	SR
Univ of Wisc/Stout	WI	23,942	C
Univ of Wisc-Milwaukee	WI	18,436	C
Univ of Wyoming	WY	13,855	C+
Ursuline College	OH	33,198	LC
Utah State Univ	UT	11,803	C
Vanderbilt Univ	TN	57,072	MC
Virginia Union Univ	VA	18,432	C
Walla Walla Univ	WA	26,256	NC
Walsh Univ	OH	35,100	C
Washington State Univ	WA	20,461	C
Wayne State College	NE	11,764	NC
Wayne State Univ	MI	19,493	C
Waynesburg Univ	PA	29,100	C
Webster Univ	MO	33,990	C+
West Chester Univ of Pennsylvania	PA	16,836	C
West Liberty Univ	WV	9,142	LC
West Texas A&M Univ	TX	13,478	C
Western Carolina Univ	NC	13,965	C+
Western Illinois Univ	IL	20,130	C
Western Mich Univ	MI	19,042	C
Western New Mexico Univ	NM	8,500	LC
Western Washington Univ	WA	18,519	VC
Westfield State Univ	MA	18,489	C
Westminster College	UT	37,708	VC
Wheeling Jesuit Univ	WV	34,668	C
Wheelock College	MA	33,075	C
Wichita State Univ	KS	12,539	C
Widener Univ	PA	50,368	C
Wiley College	TX		LC
William Paterson Univ of New Jersey	NJ	21,694	C
William Penn Univ	IA	26,000	C
William Woods Univ	MO		C
Winona State Univ	MN	16,530	C
Winston-Salem State Univ	NC	9,418	LC
Winthrop Univ	SC	21,120	VC
Wittenberg Univ	OH	47,766	VC
Wright State Univ	OH	16,983	C
Xavier Univ	OH	43,740	VC
York College	NE	19,475	C
York College of Pennsylvania	PA	26,590	C
Youngstown State Univ	OH	16,374	LC

SPECIFIC LEARNING DISABILITIES

School	ST	$IS	SR
Aquinas College	MI	33,060	C
Baldwin Wallace Univ	OH	36,980	VC
Barton College	NC	27,660	C
Florida International Univ	FL	17,747	VC
Florida State Univ	FL	15,238	HC
Idaho State Univ	ID	11,908	C
Northwest Missouri State Univ	MO	14,229	C
Univ of South Florida	FL	13,000	C
Winona State Univ	MN	16,530	C

SPEECH CORRECTION

School	ST	$IS	SR
Columbia College	SC	27,882	C
East Texas Baptist Univ	TX	29,135	C
Ithaca College	NY	52,300	HC
Kutztown Univ of Pennsylvania	PA	16,909	LC
Lewis Univ	IL	23,050	C
MidAmerica Nazarene Univ	KS	28,000	C
New York Univ	NY	61,470	MC
Western Carolina Univ	NC	13,965	C+

SPEECH PATHOLOGY/AUDIOLOGY

School	ST	$IS	SR
Adelphi Univ	NY	43,130	VC
Alabama A&M Univ	AL	96,100	C
Andrews Univ	MI	28,030	C+
Appalachian State Univ	NC	12,919	VC
Arizona State Univ	AZ	18,818	C+
Arkansas State Univ	AR	14,980	C
Armstrong Atlantic State Univ	GA	16,276	C
Auburn Univ	AL	20,052	VC+
Augustana College	IL	43,398	HC
Ball State Univ	IN	17,850	C
Baylor Univ	TX	46,720	HC
Biola Univ	CA	40,320	VC
Bloomsburg Univ of Pennsylvania	PA	13,598	C
Boston Univ	MA	54,130	HC+
Brescia Univ	KY	26,140	VC+
Brigham Young Univ	UT	12,100	HC
Buffalo State/State Univ of Buffalo	NY	15,733	C+
Butler Univ	IN	45,898	VC+
Cal State, East Bay	CA	16,549	C
Cal State, Fresno	CA	17,405	C
Cal State, Fullerton	CA	25,188	C+
Cal State, Los Angeles	CA	15,829	C
Cal State, Northridge	CA	28,313	C
Cal State, Sacramento	CA	16,200	C
Calvin College	MI	37,585	VC+
Case Western Reserve Univ	OH	55,178	MC
Central Mich Univ	MI	18,066	C
CUNY/Brooklyn College	NY	5,884	C+
Clarion Univ of Pennsylvania	PA	17,370	C
Clemson Univ	SC	19,136	HC
Cleveland State Univ	OH	21,357	C
Colo State Univ-Pueblo	CO	13,532	LC
Delta State Univ	MS	12,292	LC
Duquesne Univ	PA	42,017	VC
East Carolina Univ	NC	14,169	C
East Stroudsburg Univ of Pennsylvania	PA	16,636	C
Eastern Illinois Univ	IL	20,502	C
Eastern Mich Univ	MI	17,961	C
Eastern New Mexico Univ	NM	10,682	C
Eastern Washington Univ	WA	16,388	C
Edinboro Univ of Pennsylvania	PA	15,940	LC
Elmhurst College	IL	42,032	C+
Elmira College	NY	49,950	C+
Elms College	MA	23,900	VC
Emerson College	MA	50,246	HC
Florida State Univ	FL	15,238	HC
Fontbonne Univ	MO	31,384	C
Fort Hays State Univ	KS	11,354	C
Geneva College	PA	27,280	C
George Washington Univ	DC	57,108	MC
Hampton Univ	VA	28,528	C
Harding Univ	AR	21,432	C+
Hardin-Simmons Univ	TX	23,560	C+
Hofstra Univ	NY	48,020	VC+
Howard Univ	DC	35,957	C
Idaho State Univ	ID	11,908	C
Illinois State Univ	IL	22,634	VC
Indiana State Univ	IN	16,000	C
Indiana Univ Bloomington	IN	19,358	HC
Indiana Univ of Pennsylvania	PA	20,180	LC
Indiana Univ South Bend	IN	15,293	C
Indiana Univ-Purdue Univ Fort Wayne	IN	15,425	C
Iona College	NY	44,028	C
Ithaca College	NY	52,300	HC
James Madison Univ	VA	18,049	VC
Kansas State Univ	KS	15,497	VC
Kean Univ	NJ	22,060	LC
Kent State Univ	OH	19,352	C
Kutztown Univ of Pennsylvania	PA	16,909	LC
La Salle Univ	PA	50,270	C
Lamar Univ	TX	6,820	LC
Lehman College / The CUNY	NY	5,778	LC
LIU/C.W. Post Campus	NY	38,888	C
Louisiana State Univ	LA	18,677	VC+
Louisiana Tech Univ	LA	8,000	C
Loyola Univ Maryland	MD		VC
Marquette Univ	WI	43,664	VC+
Marshall Univ	WV	14,820	C
Marymount Manhattan College	NY	40,118	VC
Marywood Univ	PA	40,695	C
Mercy College	NY	29,996	C
Miami Univ	OH	24,191	HC
Mich State Univ	MI	13,689	VC
Minn State Univ, Mankato	MN	14,900	C
Minn State Univ, Moorhead	MN	13,392	C
Minot State Univ	ND	10,915	C
Miss Univ for Women	MS	7,400	LC
Missouri State Univ	MO	13,996	VC
Molloy College	NY	38,950	C
Murray State Univ	KY	14,944	C
Nazareth College of Rochester	NY	41,590	VC
New Mexico State Univ	NM	13,955	LC
New York Univ	NY	61,470	MC
Nicholls State Univ	LA	7,095	C
N Car State Univ	NC	16,202	HC
Northeastern Univ	MA	55,296	MC
Northern Illinois Univ	IL	19,768	C
Northern Mich Univ	MI	15,300	VC
Northern State Univ	SD	14,021	C
Northwestern Univ	IL	37,595	MC
Nova Southeastern Univ	FL	34,016	VC
Ohio Univ	OH	20,676	VC
Okla State Univ	OK	14,310	VC
Old Dominion Univ	VA	18,662	C
Ouachita Baptist Univ	AR	29,010	VC
Our Lady of the Lake Univ of San Antonio	TX	22,430	LC
Pace Univ	NY	48,094	VC
Purdue Univ/West Lafayette	IN	20,278	HC
Queens College / The CUNY	NY	17,107	VC
Radford Univ	VA	17,132	LC
Richard Stockton College of New Jersey	NJ	20,000	VC
Rockhurst Univ	MO	20,625	C
St. Louis Univ	MO	46,594	VC+
St. Mary's College	IN	45,160	VC
St. Xavier Univ	IL	32,840	C
San Diego State Univ	CA	20,578	VC
San Francisco State Univ	CA	18,514	C
San Jose State Univ	CA	19,707	C
Shaw Univ	NC	15,488	LC
S Car State Univ	SC	6,700	LC
Southern Illinois Univ Carbondale	IL	21,620	C
Southern Illinois Univ Edwardsville	IL	17,532	C
Southern Methodist Univ	TX	57,755	MC
Southern Univ and A&M College	LA	9,761	C+
St. Cloud State Univ	MN	10,600	C
St. John's Univ	NY	52,840	C+
SUNY Cortland / The SUNY	NY	19,117	C
SUNY Fredonia / The SUNY at Fredonia	NY	18,702	VC
SUNY New Paltz	NY	15,010	C
Syracuse Univ	NY	54,512	HC
Tenn State Univ	TN	9,048	C
Texas A&M Univ at Kingsville	TX	7,500	LC
Texas Christian Univ	TX	47,570	HC
Texas State Univ	TX	16,495	VC
The College of Idaho	ID	31,277	VC
Ohio State Univ	OH	19,887	MC
Thiel College	PA	31,378	LC
Towson Univ	MD	16,000	VC
Truman State Univ	MO	13,546	HC
Univ at Buffalo / The SUNY	NY	20,283	VC
Univ of Akron	OH	20,436	C
Univ of Arizona	AZ	20,105	C
Univ of Arkansas at Little Rock	AR		C
Univ of Central Arkansas	AR	10,840	VC
Univ of Central Florida	FL	15,711	VC+
Univ of Central Missouri	MO	14,605	C
Univ of Central Okla	OK	12,293	C
Univ of Cincinnati	OH	20,199	VC
Univ of Colo Boulder	CO	22,605	VC+
Univ of Florida	FL	15,783	HC+
Univ of Hawaii at Manoa	HI	19,379	VC
Univ of Iowa	IA	17,481	VC
Univ of Louisiana at Lafayette	LA	6,130	C
Univ of Louisiana at Monroe	LA	12,998	C
Univ of Maine	ME	19,712	C+
Univ of Maryland	MD	18,801	HC
Univ of Mass Amherst	MA	23,697	VC+
Univ of Minn/Twin Cities	MN		HC
Univ of Miss	MS	15,482	VC
Univ of Montevallo	AL	17,320	C
Univ of Nebr - Lincoln	NE	17,507	VC
Univ of Nevada/Reno	NV	14,500	NC
Univ of New Hampshire	NH	24,702	VC
Univ of New Mexico	NM	15,300	C
Univ of N Car at Greensboro	NC	12,848	C
Univ of North Texas	TX	15,628	C
Univ of Northern Colo	CO	15,973	C
Univ of Northern Iowa	IA	14,776	C
Univ of Oregon	OR	20,872	VC
Univ of Science and Arts of Okla	OK	10,560	VC
Univ of South Alabama	AL	13,510	C
Univ of S Dak	SD	15,111	C
Univ of Southern Miss	MS	13,170	C
Univ of Texas at Austin	TX	44,074	HC
Univ of Texas at Dallas	TX	21,046	HC
Univ of Texas-Pan American	TX	12,432	LC
Univ of the District of Columbia	DC	7,244	LC
Univ of the Pacific	CA	52,146	VC
Univ of Toledo	OH	18,464	C
Univ of Tulsa	OK	45,311	HC+
Univ of Utah	UT	13,462	VC
Univ of Vermont	VT	26,120	VC+
Univ of Virginia	VA	22,175	MC
Univ of Washington	WA	14,722	VC
Univ of West Georgia	GA	14,852	LC
Univ of Wisc/Madison	WI	18,757	HC
Univ of Wisc/Oshkosh	WI	10,426	LC
Univ of Wisc/River Falls	WI	9,722	LC
Univ of Wisc/Stevens Point	WI	14,043	C
Univ of Wisc-Milwaukee	WI	18,436	C
Univ of Wyoming	WY	13,855	C+
Utah State Univ	UT	11,803	C
Washington State Univ	WA	20,461	C
Wayne State Univ	MI	19,493	C
West Chester Univ of Pennsylvania	PA	16,836	C
West Liberty Univ	WV	9,142	LC
West Texas A&M Univ	TX	13,478	C
West Virginia Univ	WV	15,794	C+
Western Illinois Univ	IL	20,130	C
Western Kentucky Univ	KY	11,000	LC
Western Mich Univ	MI	19,042	C
Western Washington Univ	WA	18,519	VC
Wichita State Univ	KS	12,539	C
Worcester State Univ	MA	18,657	C
Xavier Univ of Louisiana	LA	25,300	C

SPEECH THERAPY

School	ST	$IS	SR
Baylor Univ	TX	46,720	HC
Biola Univ	CA	40,320	VC
Cal State, Fresno	CA	17,405	C
Cleveland State Univ	OH	21,357	C
Ithaca College	NY	52,300	HC
Misericordia Univ	PA	39,840	C
Southern Univ and A&M College	LA	9,761	C+
Stephen F. Austin State Univ	TX	14,668	C
Temple Univ	PA	24,392	VC
Ohio State Univ	OH	19,887	MC
Univ of Miss	MS	15,482	VC

SPEECH/DEBATE/RHETORIC

School	ST	$IS	SR
Albany State Univ	GA	8,500	C
Albion College	MI	43,884	VC
Arkansas Tech Univ	AR	13,164	LC
Ashland Univ	OH	25,000	C
Auburn Univ	AL	20,052	VC+
Augsburg College	MN	35,142	C
Augustana College	IL	43,398	HC
Ball State Univ	IN	17,850	C
Bates College	ME	58,950	MC
Baylor Univ	TX	46,720	HC
Bellarmine Univ	KY	42,950	VC
Beloit College	WI	49,970	HC
Binghamton Univ / The SUNY	NY	20,832	HC+
Black Hills State Univ	SD	13,562	LC
Bloomsburg Univ of Pennsylvania	PA	13,598	C
Blue Mountain College	MS	13,550	LC
Bridgewater State Univ	MA	18,752	C
Buena Vista Univ	IA	37,954	C
Butler Univ	IN	45,898	VC+
Cal State, East Bay	CA	16,549	C
Cal State, Fresno	CA	17,405	C
Cal State, Fullerton	CA	25,188	C+
Cal State, Los Angeles	CA	15,820	C
Cal State, Northridge	CA	28,313	C
Calif Univ of Pennsylvania	PA	14,217	C
Canisius College	NY	45,602	VC
Capital Univ	OH	39,824	VC
Central Mich Univ	MI	18,066	C
Central Washington Univ	WA	11,730	C
Chadron State College	NE	7,400	NC
Charleston Southern Univ	SC	22,420	C
Chicago State Univ	IL	5,482	C
CUNY/Brooklyn College	NY	5,884	C+
Clarion Univ of Pennsylvania	PA	17,370	C
Clark Atlanta Univ	GA	30,006	C
Concordia Univ Nebr	NE	26,000	VC
Concordia Univ Wisc	WI	28,980	C
Cornerstone Univ and Grand Rapids Theological Seminary	MI	30,866	C
Denison Univ	OH	54,670	HC+
DePaul Univ	IL	46,120	VC
Dickinson State Univ	ND	8,550	NC
Dordt College	IA	34,160	VC
Dowling College	NY	25,000	LC
Drake Univ	IA	30,980	VC+
Duquesne Univ	PA	42,017	VC
East Carolina Univ	NC	14,169	C
East Central Univ	OK	10,223	LC
East Tenn State Univ	TN	9,000	C
East Texas Baptist Univ	TX	29,135	C
Eastern Kentucky Univ	KY	11,161	C
Eastern Mich Univ	MI	17,961	C
Eastern Nazarene College	MA	30,000	C
Eastern Washington Univ	WA	16,388	C
Emerson College	MA	50,246	HC
Evangel Univ	MO	23,090	C
Fairmont State Univ	WV	12,098	LC
Fayetteville State Univ	NC	10,816	C
Fisk Univ	TN	19,830	C
Florida State Univ	FL	15,238	HC
Freed-Hardeman Univ	TN	19,697	VC
Geneva College	PA	27,280	C
Georgia College and State Univ	GA	18,216	VC
Georgia State Univ	GA	12,000	VC
Gonzaga Univ	WA	44,247	HC
Graceland Univ	IA	28,020	C
Greenville College	IL	27,012	C
Gustavus Adolphus College	MN	48,170	HC
Hannibal-LaGrange Univ	MO	24,490	C
Hardin-Simmons Univ	TX	23,560	C+
Hastings College	NE	27,782	C+
Hillsdale College	MI	31,890	HC+
Hofstra Univ	NY	48,020	VC+
Humboldt State Univ	CA	18,400	C
Illinois College	IL	25,770	VC
Illinois State Univ	IL	22,634	VC
Indiana Univ-Purdue Univ Fort Wayne	IN	15,425	C
Iona College	NY	44,028	C
Iowa State Univ	IA	16,403	C
Jackson State Univ	MS	13,512	LC
James Madison Univ	VA	18,049	VC
Kansas Wesleyan Univ	KS	32,000	C
Kutztown Univ of Pennsylvania	PA	16,909	LC
Lamar Univ	TX	6,820	LC
Lander Univ	SC	22,514	C+
Langston Univ	OK	3,000	LC
Lehman College / The CUNY	NY	5,778	LC
Lock Haven Univ of Pennsylvania	PA	17,587	LC
LIU/Brooklyn Campus	NY	26,500	C

School	ST	$IS	SR
Louisiana College	LA	15,746	C
Louisiana Tech Univ	LA	8,000	C
Madonna Univ	MI	24,540	VC
Marietta College	OH	42,135	VC
McKendree Univ	IL	29,920	C+
McPherson College	KS	28,138	C
Metropolitan State Univ of Denver	CO	4,835	LC
Miami Univ	OH	24,191	HC
Minn State Univ, Mankato	MN	14,900	C
Minn State Univ, Moorhead	MN	13,392	C
Miss Valley State Univ	MS	9,706	LC
Missouri Southern State Univ	MO	11,910	C
Missouri State Univ	MO	13,996	VC
Missouri Valley College	MO	22,200	C
Missouri Western State Univ	MO	12,260	NC
Montclair State Univ	NJ	22,614	C
Morehead State Univ	KY	10,900	C
Morgan State Univ	MD	14,500	VC
Mount Mercy Univ	IA	34,385	C
Murray State Univ	KY	14,944	C
Muskingum Univ	OH	30,502	C
New York Univ	NY	61,470	MC
N Car Agricultural and Technical State Univ	NC	13,175	LC
North Central College	IL	38,343	VC
Northeastern State Univ	OK	8,615	VC
Northern Kentucky Univ	KY	15,302	LC
Northern Mich Univ	MI	15,300	VC
Northwest Missouri State Univ	MO	14,229	C
Northwest Nazarene Univ	ID	24,275	NC
Northwestern Okla State Univ	OK	7,275	NC
Ohio Univ	OH	20,676	VC
Okla Baptist Univ	OK	28,202	VC
Oral Roberts Univ	OK	31,734	C
Oregon State Univ	OR	19,017	C+
Otterbein College	OH	32,214	C
Ouachita Baptist Univ	AR	29,010	VC
Pepperdine Univ	CA	55,372	HC+
Portland State Univ	OR	18,672	C
Prairie View A&M Univ	TX	15,205	LC
Radford Univ	VA	17,132	LC
Rowan Univ	NJ	23,570	VC
St. Mary's Univ	TX	33,854	C
Sam Houston State Univ	TX	17,082	C
San Francisco State Univ	CA	18,514	C
San Jose State Univ	CA	19,707	C
Shippensburg Univ of Pennsylvania	PA	17,064	LC
Southeastern Okla State Univ	OK	7,966	C
Southern Illinois Univ Carbondale	IL	21,620	C
Southern Illinois Univ Edwardsville	IL	17,532	C
Southern Nazarene Univ	OK	24,354	NC
Southern Univ at New Orleans	LA	1,000	NC
Southwestern Adventist Univ	TX	23,026	LC
St. Ambrose Univ	IA		C
St. Catherine Univ	MN	37,782	C+
St. Cloud State Univ	MN	10,600	C
St. John's Univ	NY	52,840	C+
St. Joseph's College, New York / Brooklyn Campus	NY	21,878	C
St. Joseph's College, New York / Suffolk Campus	NY	21,878	VC
Stephen F. Austin State Univ	TX	14,668	C
Suffolk Univ	MA	46,548	C
SUNY New Paltz	NY	15,010	C
Syracuse Univ	NY	54,512	HC
Tarleton State Univ	TX	13,489	LC
Temple Univ	PA	24,392	VC
Tenn State Univ	TN	9,048	C
Texas A&M Univ	TX	16,956	VC+
Texas A&M Univ at Corpus Christi	TX	11,544	LC
Touro College	NY	23,150	VC
Trinity Univ	TX	44,174	HC+
Univ of Alaska Southeast	AK	11,493	C
Univ of Arkansas at Monticello	AR	8,470	NC
Univ of Arkansas at Pine Bluff	AR	10,600	C
Univ of Calif at Berkeley	CA	23,322	MC
Univ of Calif at Davis	CA	24,482	HC
Univ of Central Arkansas	AR	10,840	VC
Univ of Central Missouri	MO	14,605	C
Univ of Dubuque	IA	30,200	C
Univ of Florida	FL	15,783	HC+
Univ of Hawaii at Manoa	HI	19,379	VC
Univ of Illinois at Urbana-Champaign	IL	24,300	HC
Univ of Indianapolis	IN	31,740	LC
Univ of Iowa	IA	17,481	VC
Univ of Kansas	KS	16,980	C+
Univ of La Verne	CA	47,010	VC
Univ of Maine	ME	19,712	C+
Univ of Mary Hardin-Baylor	TX	31,950	C+
Univ of Mich/Ann Arbor	MI	22,102	HC+
Univ of Minn/Morris	MN	17,150	VC
Univ of Minn/Twin Cities	MN		HC
Univ of Nebr - Lincoln	NE	17,507	VC
Univ of Nebr at Kearney	NE	14,855	LC
Univ of Nebr at Omaha	NE	12,700	C
Univ of Nevada/Reno	NV	14,500	NC
Univ of N Car at Wilmington	NC	13,572	VC+
Univ of Northern Iowa	IA	14,776	C
Univ of Sioux Falls	SD	22,990	C
Univ of S Car at Columbia	SC	19,725	VC+
Univ of South Florida	FL	13,000	C
Univ of Southern Indiana	IN	14,657	C
Univ of Southern Miss	MS	13,170	C
Univ of Texas at Arlington	TX	10,908	LC
Univ of Texas at Austin	TX	44,074	HC
Univ of Texas at El Paso	TX	8,764	NC
Univ of Washington	WA	14,722	VC
Univ of Wisc Whitewater	WI	13,314	C
Univ of Wisc/La Crosse	WI	14,755	VC
Univ of Wisc/Oshkosh	WI	10,426	LC
Univ of Wisc/River Falls	WI	9,722	LC
Univ of Wisc/Superior	WI	14,106	C
Wabash College	IN	44,160	VC
Walla Walla Univ	WA	26,256	NC
Washburn Univ	KS	12,165	NC
Wayne State College	NE	11,764	NC
West Texas A&M Univ	TX	13,478	C
West Virginia Univ	WV	15,794	C+
West Virginia Wesleyan College	WV	26,880	C
Western Carolina Univ	NC	13,965	C+
Western Oregon Univ	OR	15,021	C
Whitman College	WA	54,400	MC
Whitworth Univ	WA	45,826	VC+
Willamette Univ	OR	56,450	VC+
Wilmington College	OH	29,784	C
Winona State Univ	MN	16,530	C
Yeshiva Univ	NY	47,250	VC+
York College / CUNY	NY	5,496	NC

SPORTS AND WELLNESS STUDIES

School	ST	$IS	SR
Adams State College	CO	13,358	LC
Aquinas College	MI	33,060	C
Averett Univ	VA	36,000	LC
Corban Univ	OR	34,764	C
Dakota Wesleyan Univ	SD	23,000	C
Ithaca College	NY	52,300	HC
Nova Southeastern Univ	FL	34,016	VC
St. Louis Univ	MO	46,594	VC+
Southwestern College	KS	29,270	C
SUNY Plattsburgh / SUNY	NY	18,083	VC
Univ of Illinois at Chicago	IL	24,293	VC
Univ of Montana-Western	MT	9,753	LC
Winthrop Univ	SC	21,120	VC

SPORTS MANAGEMENT

School	ST	$IS	SR
Adams State College	CO	13,358	LC
Alvernia Univ	PA	39,250	C
Anderson Univ	IN	35,390	C
Anna Maria College	MA	34,600	LC
Aquinas College	MI	33,060	C
Arkansas State Univ	AR	14,980	C
Asbury Univ	KY	32,038	VC
Ashford Univ	IA	21,780	C
Augustana College	SD	35,500	VC
Baker Univ	KS	33,350	C+
Baldwin Wallace Univ	OH	36,980	VC
Barry Univ	FL	38,190	C
Barton College	NC	27,660	C
Becker College	MA	41,420	LC
Belmont Abbey College	NC	37,716	C
Bethany College	KS	30,605	NC
Bethany College	WV	35,282	C
Bethel College	IN	31,560	C
Blackburn College	IL	21,350	C
Bluffton Univ	OH	37,864	C
Bowling Green State Univ	OH	18,970	C
Buena Vista Univ	IA	37,954	C
Cabrini College	PA	40,859	LC
Calif Univ of Pennsylvania	PA	14,217	C
Calvin College	MI	37,585	VC+
Cameron Univ	OK	9,267	LC
Campbell Univ	NC	25,500	C
Campbellsville Univ	KY	27,720	C
Canisius College	NY	45,602	VC
Castleton State College	VT	19,424	C
Catawba College	NC	37,105	C
Cedarville Univ	OH	31,036	VC+
Central Methodist Univ	MO	28,240	VC
Claflin Univ	SC	22,368	C+
Clarke Univ	IA	36,400	C
Coastal Carolina Univ	SC	17,620	C
Colby-Sawyer College	NH	47,870	C
College of Mount St. Joseph	OH	33,880	C
College of St Joseph	VT	30,600	LC
Columbia College	MO	24,578	C
Concordia Univ Nebr	NE	26,000	VC
Concordia Univ St. Paul	MN	27,200	C
Coppin State Univ	MD	14,905	VC
Corban Univ	OR	34,764	C
Cornerstone Univ and Grand Rapids Theological Seminary	MI	30,866	C
Culver-Stockton College	MO	30,900	C
Dakota Wesleyan Univ	SD	23,000	C
Dallas Baptist Univ	TX	29,118	C
Daniel Webster College	NH	25,380	C
De Sales Univ	PA	42,670	C
Defiance College	OH	30,645	C
Delaware Valley College	PA	29,944	C
Dordt College	IA	34,160	VC
Dowling College	NY	25,000	LC
Drexel Univ	PA	51,920	HC
Drury Univ	MO	30,319	VC
Eastern Conn State Univ	CT	20,584	C
Edinboro Univ of Pennsylvania	PA	15,940	LC
Elon Univ	NC	40,046	HC
Emmanuel College	MA	47,985	VC
Endicott College	MA	42,390	C
Erskine College	SC	37,380	C
Farmingdale State College	NY	18,985	C
Faulkner Univ	AL	22,530	LC
Ferrum College	VA	27,740	LC
Flagler College	FL	24,960	VC
Florida Inst of Technology	FL	48,290	VC
Florida State Univ	FL	15,238	HC
Fontbonne Univ	MO	31,384	C
Franklin Pierce Univ	NH	41,598	C
Fresno Pacific Univ	CA	32,136	C
Gannon Univ	PA	37,940	C
Gardner-Webb Univ	NC	34,375	C+
Georgia Southern Univ	GA	16,414	C
Glenville State College	WV	11,348	NC
Goldey-Beacom College	DE	27,493	C
Grand Canyon Univ	AZ	24,540	VC
Grand View Univ	IA	31,050	C
Guilford College	NC	35,340	C
Gwynedd-Mercy College	PA	33,560	C
Hampton Univ	VA	28,528	C
Harding Univ	AR	21,432	C+
Heidelberg Univ	OH	34,100	C
Hilbert College	NY	28,550	C
Holy Family Univ	PA	40,030	LC
Hope International Univ	CA	34,650	C
Howard Univ	DC	35,957	C
Huntingdon College	AL	31,850	C
Huntington Univ	IN	32,220	C
Husson Univ	ME	23,386	LC
Indiana Inst of Technology	IN	34,240	LC
Indiana State Univ	IN	16,000	C
Indiana Univ Bloomington	IN	19,358	HC
Indiana Univ-Purdue Univ Indianapolis	IN	17,290	C
Iowa Wesleyan College	IA	30,850	LC
Ithaca College	NY	52,300	HC
Johnson and Wales Univ/ Charlotte Campus	NC	35,421	C
Johnson and Wales Univ/ Denver Campus	CO	34,368	C
Johnson and Wales Univ/ North Miami Campus	FL	34,368	C
Johnson and Wales Univ/ Providence Campus	RI	34,668	C
Judson Univ	IL	25,130	C
Kent State Univ	OH	19,352	C
Kentucky Wesleyan College	KY	27,440	VC+
Keystone College	PA	28,680	LC
King Univ	TN	33,140	C
Lake Erie College	OH	35,704	C
Lasell College	MA	42,500	LC
Lees-McRae College	NC	33,624	C
Lenoir-Rhyne College	NC	35,984	C
Lewis Univ	IL	23,050	C
Liberty Univ	VA	19,101	C
Limestone College	SC	29,880	C
Lindenwood Univ	MO	20,750	C
Livingstone College	NC	17,815	LC
Louisiana State Univ	LA	18,677	VC+
Loyola Univ Chicago	IL	49,560	VC+
Lubbock Christian Univ	TX	25,518	C
Lynchburg College	VA	42,645	C
Lyndon State College	VT	14,233	C
Lynn Univ	FL	43,500	C
MacMurray College	IL	20,755	C
Madonna Univ	MI	24,540	VC
Malone Univ	OH	34,334	C
Marian Univ	WI	30,980	LC
Marian Univ/Indianapolis	IN	37,058	C
Marietta College	OH	42,135	VC
Marshall Univ	WV	14,820	C
Maryville Univ of St. Louis	MO	34,920	VC
Mayville State Univ	ND	11,401	NC
Medaille College	NY	35,112	VC
Menlo College	CA	49,002	C
Messiah College	PA	39,540	VC
Methodist Univ	NC	37,185	C
Miami Univ	OH	24,191	HC
MidAmerica Nazarene Univ	KS	28,000	C
Midway College	KY	20,150	C
Millikin Univ	IL	37,462	C
Misericordia Univ	PA	39,840	C
Miss Univ for Women	MS	7,400	LC
Missouri Baptist Univ	MO	30,310	C
Mitchell College	CT	40,983	C
Mount St. Mary's Univ	MD	46,158	C
Mount Vernon Nazarene Univ	OH	29,590	C
Nebr Wesleyan Univ	NE	29,774	C+
Neumann Univ	PA	31,078	LC
New England College	NH	45,930	LC
New York Univ	NY	61,470	MC
Newbury College	MA	41,850	C
Nichols College	MA	37,240	LC
North Central College	IL	38,343	VC
N Dak State Univ	ND	14,642	C
Northern Kentucky Univ	KY	15,302	LC
Northwood Univ	FL	30,746	LC
Northwood Univ	MI	26,331	LC
Ohio Dominican Univ	OH	38,380	C+
Ohio Northern Univ	OH	42,075	VC
Ohio Univ	OH	20,676	VC
Ohio Valley Univ	WV	17,752	C
Old Dominion Univ	VA	18,662	C
Olivet Nazarene Univ	IL	29,990	C
Peru State College	NE	8,600	NC
Pfeiffer Univ	NC	33,700	C
Piedmont College	GA	29,260	C
Point Park Univ	PA	36,390	C
Principia College	IL	35,140	C+
Queens Univ of Charlotte	NC	39,543	VC
Quincy Univ	IL	34,980	LC
Roanoke College	VA	47,996	C+
Robert Morris Univ	PA	36,699	C
Rochester College	MI	18,320	C
Sacred Heart Univ	CT	48,564	VC
St. Joseph's College	IN	35,790	C
St. Leo Univ	FL	27,990	C
St. Mary's Univ of Minn	MN	37,015	C
Salem International Univ	WV	18,020	C
Samford Univ	AL	35,700	VC+
Seton Hall Univ	NJ	45,902	C
Seton Hill Univ	PA	35,172	C
Shawnee State Univ	OH	16,545	NC
Shenandoah Univ	VA	39,268	C
Shorter Univ	GA	26,470	C
Simpson College	IA	36,086	VC
Southeast Missouri State Univ	MO	14,983	LC
Southeastern Louisiana Univ	LA	13,325	C
Southeastern Univ	FL	27,201	C+
Southern Nazarene Univ	OK	24,354	NC
Southern New Hampshire Univ	NH	38,100	C
Southern Vermont College	VT	30,740	LC
Southern Wesleyan Univ	SC	25,600	C
Southwest Baptist Univ	MO	24,710	C
Southwestern College	KS	29,270	C
Springfield College	MA	25,000	C
St. Ambrose Univ	IA		C
St. John Fisher College	NY	39,370	C+
St. John's Univ	NY	52,840	C+
St. Thomas Univ	FL	32,310	C+
Sterling College	KS	27,216	C
Stetson Univ	FL	49,512	VC+
SUNY Cortland / The SUNY	NY	19,117	C
SUNY Fredonia / The SUNY at Fredonia	NY	18,702	VC
Syracuse Univ	NY	54,512	HC
Taylor Univ	IN	36,742	VC+
Temple Univ	PA	24,392	VC
Tenn Wesleyan College	TN	21,250	C
Texas Wesleyan Univ	TX	29,886	C
The College at Brockport / SUNY	NY	18,362	VC
Thomas College	ME	26,270	LC
Towson Univ	MD	16,000	VC
Trevecca Nazarene Univ	TN	30,118	C
Trine Univ	IN	39,400	VC
Trinity International Univ	IL	31,070	C
Troy Univ	AL	10,650	C
Tusculum College	TN	24,295	C
Union College	KY	28,775	C
Union Univ	TN	28,260	VC
Univ of Arkansas at Little Rock	AR		C
Univ of Charleston	WV	28,650	C
Univ of Dayton	OH	43,750	VC
Univ of Delaware	DE	22,728	VC
Univ of Evansville	IN	41,056	VC+
Univ of Georgia	GA	19,508	VC
Univ of Idaho	ID	14,558	C
Univ of Indianapolis	IN	31,740	LC
Univ of Kansas	KS	16,980	C+
Univ of Louisville	KY	17,460	VC
Univ of Mary Hardin-Baylor	TX	31,950	C+
Univ of Mass Amherst	MA	23,697	VC+
Univ of Miami	FL	55,166	MC
Univ of Mich/Ann Arbor	MI	22,102	HC+
Univ of Minn Crookston	MN	17,834	C
Univ of Montana-Western	MT	9,753	LC
Univ of Mount Union	OH	35,130	C
Univ of New England	ME	46,145	C+
Univ of New Haven	CT	47,740	C
Univ of North Florida	FL	15,578	VC
Univ of Pittsburgh at Bradford	PA	21,316	LC
Univ of St. Mary	KS	28,400	C+
Univ of S Car at Columbia	SC	19,725	VC+
Univ of Southern Indiana	IN	14,657	C
Univ of Tampa	FL	35,160	VC
Univ of Tenn at Knoxville	TN	20,364	VC+
Univ of the Incarnate Word	TX	35,200	LC
Univ of Tulsa	OK	45,311	HC+
Univ of West Georgia	GA	14,852	LC

ST = STATE **$IS** = IN-STATE COSTS **SR** = SELECTOR RATING

School	ST	$IS	SR
Urbana Univ	OH	21,190	C
Valparaiso Univ	IN	43,040	V¢
Virginia Commonwealth Univ	VA	18,633	C
Virginia Intermont College	VA	32,411	LC
Viterbo Univ	WI	30,070	C
Warner Univ	FL	18,000	C
Washington State Univ	WA	20,461	C
Wayne State College	NE	11,764	NC
Webber International Univ	FL	25,664	C
Wesley College	DE	31,115	LC
West Virginia Univ	WV	15,794	¢
Western Carolina Univ	NC	13,965	¢
Western New England Univ	MA	45,590	C
Wheeling Jesuit Univ	WV	34,668	C
Wichita State Univ	KS	12,539	C
William Penn Univ	IA	26,000	C
Wilmington College	OH	29,784	C
Wilmington Univ	DE	7,778	NC
Wingate Univ	NC	34,990	C
Winston-Salem State Univ	NC	9,418	LC
Winthrop Univ	SC	21,120	VC
Xavier Univ	OH	43,740	VC
York College of Pennsylvania	PA	26,590	C

SPORTS MARKETING

School	ST	$IS	SR
Baylor Univ	TX	46,720	HC
Duquesne Univ	PA	42,017	VC
Indiana Univ Bloomington	IN	19,358	HC
Miami Univ	OH	24,191	HC
St. Joseph's Univ	PA	52,272	VC
Southern Nazarene Univ	OK	24,354	NC
Thomas More College	KY	34,760	C
Xavier Univ	OH	43,740	VC

SPORTS MEDIA

School	ST	$IS	SR
Bethany College	WV	35,282	C
Ithaca College	NY	52,300	HC
Lasell College	MA	42,500	LC
Marshall Univ	WV	14,820	C
Newman Univ	KS	30,380	¢
Southern Nazarene Univ	OK	24,354	NC
Texas Christian Univ	TX	47,570	HC

SPORTS MEDICINE

School	ST	$IS	SR
Alcorn State Univ	MS	9,500	C
Aquinas College	MI	33,060	C
Avila Univ	MO	26,900	C
Belhaven Univ	MS	27,170	C
Briar Cliff Univ	IA	29,514	C
Campbellsville Univ	KY	27,720	C
Canisius College	NY	45,602	VC
Capital Univ	OH	39,824	VC
Central Mich Univ	MI	18,066	C
Concordia Univ Wisc	WI	28,980	C
Eastern Mich Univ	MI	17,961	C
Eastern Nazarene College	MA	30,000	C
Elon Univ	NC	40,046	HC
Florida State Univ	FL	15,238	HC
Howard Univ	DC	35,957	C
Ithaca College	NY	52,300	HC
John Brown Univ	AR	30,996	V¢
King's College	PA	41,678	C
Lander Univ	SC	22,514	¢
Mercyhurst Univ	PA	40,700	C
Merrimack College	MA	44,215	C
Norwich Univ	VT	28,212	C
Ohio Univ	OH	20,676	VC
Pepperdine Univ	CA	55,372	H¢
Samford Univ	AL	35,700	V¢
Southern Oregon Univ	OR	17,874	C
Towson Univ	MD	16,000	VC
Trinity International Univ	IL	31,070	C
Tusculum College	TN	24,295	C
Union Univ	TN	28,260	VC
Univ of Detroit Mercy	MI	30,450	C
Univ of Kansas	KS	16,980	¢
Univ of Nevada, Las Vegas	NV	17,303	C
Univ of Pittsburgh at Bradford	PA	21,316	LC
Univ of Southern Maine	ME	16,576	C
Urbana Univ	OH	21,190	C
Western Carolina Univ	NC	13,965	¢

SPORTS PSYCHOLOGY

School	ST	$IS	SR
Texas Christian Univ	TX	47,570	HC

SPORTS STUDIES

School	ST	$IS	SR
Bethel College	IN	31,560	C
Brewton-Parker College	GA	33,388	LC
Bryant Univ	RI	49,179	VC
Eastern Illinois Univ	IL	20,502	C
Guilford College	NC	35,340	C
Huntington Univ	IN	32,220	C
Ithaca College	NY	52,300	HC
Lasell College	MA	42,500	LC
Messiah College	PA	39,540	VC
Miami Univ	OH	24,191	HC
Southern Nazarene Univ	OK	24,354	NC
St. Andrews Univ	NC	32,050	LC
St. Bonaventure Univ	NY	38,831	C
Trinity Christian College	IL	28,869	C
Univ of Iowa	IA	17,481	VC
Univ of Montana-Western	MT	9,753	LC
Vanguard Univ of Southern Calif	CA	35,833	VC

STATISTICS

School	ST	$IS	SR
American Univ	DC	54,829	H¢
Appalachian State Univ	NC	12,919	VC
Arizona State Univ	AZ	18,818	¢
Biola Univ	CA	40,320	VC
Bowling Green State Univ	OH	18,970	C
Brigham Young Univ	UT	12,100	HC
Brown Univ	RI	56,150	MC
Bryant Univ	RI	49,179	VC
Calif Baptist Univ	CA	35,890	C
Calif Polytechnic State Univ	CA	19,847	HC
Cal State, Chico	CA	18,952	C
Cal State, East Bay	CA	16,549	C
Cal State, Fullerton	CA	25,188	¢
Cal State, Long Beach	CA	17,534	¢
Carnegie Mellon Univ	PA	51,260	MC
Case Western Reserve Univ	OH	55,178	MC
Central Mich Univ	MI	18,066	C
CUNY/Baruch College	NY	15,831	VC
Colo State Univ-Fort Collins	CO	20,090	VC
Columbia Univ in the City of New York	NY	61,116	MC
Columbia Univ/Barnard College	NY	39,000	MC
Columbia Univ/School of General Studies	NY	54,083	MC
Cornell Univ	NY	59,037	MC
Eastern Kentucky Univ	KY	11,161	C
Eastern Mich Univ	MI	17,961	C
Elon Univ	NC	40,046	HC
Florida International Univ	FL	17,747	VC
Florida State Univ	FL	15,238	HC
Fordham Univ	NY	58,927	HC
George Washington Univ	DC	57,108	MC
Georgia State Univ	GA	12,000	VC
Grand Valley State Univ	MI	17,998	VC
Harvard Univ/Harvard College	MA	49,000	MC
Hunter College / The CUNY	NY	14,429	VC
Idaho State Univ	ID	11,908	C
Indiana Univ Bloomington	IN	19,358	HC
Indiana Univ-Purdue Univ Fort Wayne	IN	15,425	C
Iowa State Univ	IA	16,403	C
James Madison Univ	VA	18,049	VC
Kansas State Univ	KS	15,497	VC
Le Moyne College	NY	42,200	VC
Lehigh Univ	PA	55,080	MC
Loyola Univ Chicago	IL	49,560	V¢
Luther College	IA	44,380	V¢
Marquette Univ	WI	43,664	V¢
Miami Univ	OH	24,191	HC
Mich State Univ	MI	13,689	VC
Missouri Univ of Science and Technology	MO	18,655	V¢
Montana Tech of The Univ of Montana	MT	14,650	VC
Mount Holyoke College	MA	53,596	H¢
New York Univ	NY	61,470	MC
N Car State Univ	NC	16,202	HC
N Dak State Univ	ND	14,642	C
Northern Kentucky Univ	KY	15,302	LC
Northwest Missouri State Univ	MO	14,229	C
Northwestern Univ	IL	37,595	MC
Oakland Univ	MI	19,391	VC
Ohio Northern Univ	OH	42,075	VC
Ohio Univ	OH	20,676	VC
Okla State Univ	OK	14,310	VC
Old Dominion Univ	VA	18,662	C
Penn State Univ/Univ Park	PA	25,404	VC
Purdue Univ/West Lafayette	IN	20,278	HC
Rice Univ	TX	43,288	MC
Rochester Inst of Technology	NY	42,450	V¢
Roosevelt Univ	IL	22,605	VC
Rutgers, The State Univ of New Jersey/New Brunswick	NJ	25,077	VC
St. Mary's College	IN	45,160	VC
San Diego State Univ	CA	20,578	VC
San Francisco State Univ	CA	18,514	C
San Jose State Univ	CA	19,707	C
Southern Illinois Univ Edwardsville	IL	17,532	C
Southern Methodist Univ	TX	57,755	MC
St. Cloud State Univ	MN	10,600	C
St. John Fisher College	NY	39,370	¢
Stanford Univ	CA	56,411	MC
SUNY Oneonta / SUNY	NY	16,919	VC
Univ of Akron	OH	20,436	C
Univ of Arizona	AZ	20,105	C
Univ of Arkansas at Fayetteville	AR	16,860	VC
Univ of Calif at Berkeley	CA	23,322	MC
Univ of Calif at Davis	CA	24,482	HC
Univ of Calif at Los Angeles	CA	25,686	MC
Univ of Calif at Riverside	CA	27,204	C
Univ of Calif at Santa Barbara	CA	27,551	HC
Univ of Central Florida	FL	15,711	V¢
Univ of Chicago	IL	55,416	MC
Univ of Conn	CT	23,744	HC
Univ of Delaware	DE	22,728	VC
Univ of Denver	CO	51,787	V¢
Univ of Florida	FL	15,783	H¢
Univ of Georgia	GA	19,508	VC
Univ of Houston-Downtown	TX	6,267	LC
Univ of Illinois at Chicago	IL	24,293	VC
Univ of Illinois at Urbana-Champaign	IL	24,300	HC
Univ of Iowa	IA	17,481	VC
Univ of Louisiana at Lafayette	LA	6,130	C
Univ of Maryland/Baltimore County	MD	18,000	VC
Univ of Miami	FL	55,166	MC
Univ of Mich/Ann Arbor	MI	22,102	H¢
Univ of Minn/Duluth	MN	18,964	¢
Univ of Minn/Morris	MN	17,150	VC
Univ of Minn/Twin Cities	MN		HC
Univ of Missouri/Columbia	MO	18,201	MC
Univ of Nebr at Kearney	NE	14,855	LC
Univ of New Mexico	NM	15,300	C
Univ of N Car at Wilmington	NC	13,572	V¢
Univ of North Florida	FL	15,578	VC
Univ of Northern Colo	CO	15,973	C
Univ of Pennsylvania	PA	56,106	MC
Univ of Pittsburgh at Pittsburgh	PA	27,800	H¢
Univ of Rochester	NY	58,500	MC
Univ of S Car at Columbia	SC	19,725	V¢
Univ of Southern Miss	MS	13,170	C
Univ of Tenn at Knoxville	TN	20,364	V¢
Univ of Texas at El Paso	TX	8,764	NC
Univ of Texas at San Antonio	TX	18,372	C
Univ of Vermont	VT	26,120	V¢
Univ of Washington	WA	14,722	VC
Univ of West Florida	FL	14,656	C
Univ of Wisc/Madison	WI	18,757	HC
Univ of Wyoming	WY	13,855	¢
Utah State Univ	UT	11,803	C
Virginia Polytechnic Inst and State Univ	VA	14,629	HC
Washington Univ in St. Louis	MO	58,818	MC
West Chester Univ of Pennsylvania	PA	16,836	C
Western Mich Univ	MI	19,042	C
Winona State Univ	MN	16,530	C
Wright State Univ	OH	16,983	C
Xavier Univ of Louisiana	LA	25,300	C
Yale Univ	CT	55,300	MC
Youngstown State Univ	OH	16,374	LC

STRATEGIC COMMUNICATION

School	ST	$IS	SR
American Univ	DC	54,829	H¢
Calvin College	MI	37,585	V¢
Chapman Univ	CA	56,019	V¢
Concordia Univ St. Paul	MN	27,200	C
Elon Univ	NC	40,046	HC
Texas Christian Univ	TX	47,570	HC
Univ of Denver	CO	51,787	V¢

STRINGS

School	ST	$IS	SR
Bennington College	VT	56,990	H¢
Central Washington Univ	WA	11,730	C
Eastern Mich Univ	MI	17,961	C
Florida State Univ	FL	15,238	HC
Hardin-Simmons Univ	TX	23,560	¢
Indiana Univ-Purdue Univ Fort Wayne	IN	15,425	C
Manhattan School of Music	NY	55,850	SP
Mannes College New School for Music	NY	44,500	C
Marshall Univ	WV	14,820	C
Northwestern College	MN	24,000	C
Northwestern Univ	IL	37,595	MC
Roosevelt Univ	IL	22,605	VC
San Francisco Conservatory of Music	CA	53,923	SP
Seattle Univ	WA	47,010	V¢
Syracuse Univ	NY	54,512	HC
Texas Christian Univ	TX	47,570	HC
Univ of Iowa	IA	17,481	VC
Univ of Kansas	KS	16,980	¢
Wright State Univ	OH	16,983	C
Youngstown State Univ	OH	16,374	LC

STUDIO ART

School	ST	$IS	SR
Adrian College	MI	33,800	C
Agnes Scott College	GA	45,323	V¢
Allegheny College	PA	49,020	HC
American Univ	DC	54,829	H¢
Angelo State Univ	TX	15,049	NC
Anna Maria College	MA	34,600	LC
Appalachian State Univ	NC	12,919	VC
Assumption College	MA	45,721	VC
Augsburg College	MN	35,142	C
Augustana College	IL	43,398	HC
Baker Univ	KS	33,350	¢
Baldwin Wallace Univ	OH	36,980	VC
Bard College	NY	59,872	HC
Barton College	NC	27,660	C
Baylor Univ	TX	46,720	HC
Bellarmine Univ	KY	42,950	VC
Belmont Univ	TN	37,380	V¢
Beloit College	WI	49,970	HC
Benedict College	SC	20,454	NC
Benedictine Univ	IL	35,220	C
Bennington College	VT	56,990	H¢
Berry College	GA	39,254	HC
Bethel College	IN	31,560	C
Binghamton Univ / The SUNY	NY	20,832	H¢
Biola Univ	CA	40,320	VC
Birmingham-Southern College	AL	42,370	V¢
Bloomsburg Univ of Pennsylvania	PA	13,598	C
Boston College	MA	58,506	MC
Bowdoin College	ME	57,834	MC
Bradley Univ	IL	31,874	VC
Brandeis Univ	MA	58,820	HC
Brenau Univ Women's College	GA	26,650	¢
Brigham Young Univ	UT	12,100	HC
Cabrini College	PA	40,859	LC
Caldwell College	NJ	35,602	LC
Carleton College	MN	58,149	MC
Carthage College	WI	33,000	C
Cazenovia College	NY	30,800	C
Centenary College of Louisiana	LA	39,070	¢
Central Washington Univ	WA	11,730	C
Christian Brothers Univ	TN	19,140	HC
Clark Univ	MA	47,020	H¢
Clarke Univ	IA	36,400	C
Coastal Carolina Univ	SC	17,620	C
Colby College	ME	57,510	MC
Colby-Sawyer College	NH	47,870	C
Colgate Univ	NY	50,930	MC
College of Charleston	SC	21,273	VC
College of the Holy Cross	MA	56,232	MC
College of the Ozarks	MO	5,605	VC
Colo College	CO	54,534	MC
Columbia College	SC	27,882	C
Concordia Univ Nebr	NE	26,000	VC
Concordia Univ St. Paul	MN	27,200	C
Cornell College	IA	44,930	HC
Creighton Univ	NE	44,058	V¢
Dartmouth College	NH	57,996	MC
Denison Univ	OH	54,670	H¢
DePauw Univ	IN	48,950	V¢
Drake Univ	IA	30,980	V¢
East Carolina Univ	NC	14,169	C
Eastern Washington Univ	WA	16,388	C
Elizabethtown College	PA	47,600	VC
Emmanuel College	MA	47,985	VC
Endicott College	MA	42,390	C
Florida Southern College	FL	38,240	VC
Florida State Univ	FL	15,238	HC
Fordham Univ	NY	58,927	HC
Framingham State Univ	MA	16,750	C
Franklin and Marshall College	PA	58,295	MC
Gallaudet Univ	DC	25,380	SP
Georgia Regents Univ	GA		C
Georgia State Univ	GA	12,000	VC
Gettysburg College	PA	56,820	HC
Graceland Univ	IA	28,020	C
Hamilton College	NY	55,620	MC
Henderson State Univ	AR	13,634	C
Hiram College	OH	37,300	VC
Hobart and William Smith Colleges	NY	43,000	VC
Hollins Univ	VA	43,295	VC
Houghton College	NY	35,740	VC
Huntington Univ	IN	32,220	C
Indiana State Univ	IN	16,000	C
Indiana Univ Bloomington	IN	19,358	HC
Indiana Univ of Pennsylvania	PA	20,180	LC
Indiana Wesleyan Univ	IN	31,815	VC
Ithaca College	NY	52,300	HC
Jacksonville Univ	FL	37,780	C
Johnson State College	VT	16,721	C
Juniata College	PA	49,340	VC
Kansas Wesleyan Univ	KS	32,000	C
Kean Univ	NJ	22,060	LC
Keene State College	NH	21,538	C
Kentucky State Univ	KY	11,000	LC
Knox College	IL		VC
Kutztown Univ of Pennsylvania	PA	16,909	LC
Lawrence Univ	WI	46,371	HC
Lewis & Clark College	OR	52,656	VC
Lewis Univ	IL	23,050	C
Limestone College	SC	29,880	C
Lindenwood Univ	MO	20,750	C
Linfield College-McMinnville Campus	OR	46,166	C
Lipscomb Univ	TN	35,722	VC
Loras College	IA	37,432	VC
Louisiana College	LA	15,746	C

School	ST	$IS	SR
Louisiana State Univ	LA	18,677	VC+
Loyola Marymount Univ	CA	53,240	VC+
Loyola Univ Chicago	IL	49,560	VC+
Loyola Univ New Orleans	LA	46,581	VC
Lycoming College	PA	43,636	C
Marian Univ/Indianapolis	IN	37,058	C
Marietta College	OH	42,135	VC
Mary Baldwin College	VA	37,110	C
Maryville Univ of St. Louis	MO	34,920	VC
Marywood Univ	PA	40,695	C
Mass College of Art and Design	MA	23,600	SP
Memphis College of Art	TN	33,550	SP
Mercyhurst Univ	PA	40,700	C
Messiah College	PA	39,540	VC
Mich State Univ	MI	13,689	VC
Middle Tenn State Univ	TN	8,650	C
Middlebury College	VT	57,470	MC
Millikin Univ	IL	37,462	C
Mills College	CA	54,119	HC
Millsaps College	MS	43,888	VC+
Minneapolis College of Art and Design	MN	36,700	SP
Montclair State Univ	NJ	22,614	C
Moravian College	PA	36,381	VC
Mount Holyoke College	MA	53,596	HC+
Murray State Univ	KY	14,944	C
Nazareth College of Rochester	NY	41,590	VC
Nebr Wesleyan Univ	NE	29,774	C+
New York Univ	NY	61,470	MC
North Central College	IL	38,343	VC
Northeastern Univ	MA	55,296	MC
Northern Arizona Univ	AZ	18,592	C
Northern Illinois Univ	IL	19,768	C
Northern Kentucky Univ	KY	15,302	LC
Northwestern College	MN	24,000	C
Notre Dame College	OH	34,942	VC
Notre Dame of Maryland Univ	MD	27,700	C
Oakland Univ	MI	19,391	VC
Ohio Univ	OH	20,676	VC
Okla City Univ	OK	33,546	VC
Old Dominion Univ	VA	18,662	C
Oral Roberts Univ	OK	31,734	C
Parsons The New School for Design	NY	56,610	SP
Pomona College	CA	57,680	MC
Prescott College	AZ	33,284	C+
Principia College	IL	35,140	C+
Providence College	RI	55,995	HC
Queens College / The CUNY	NY	17,107	VC
Randolph-Macon College	VA	45,086	C
Rhode Island College	RI	17,132	LC
Rivier College	NH	35,000	VC
Roberts Wesleyan College	NY	37,384	C+
Rochester Inst of Technology	NY	42,450	VC+
Rollins College	FL	52,370	HC
St. Louis Univ	MO	46,594	VC+
St. Mary's Univ of Minn	MN	37,015	C
St. Vincent College	PA	40,244	C
Salem College	NC	29,326	VC
Salve Regina Univ	RI	47,250	VC
San Diego State Univ	CA	20,578	VC
Santa Clara Univ	CA	54,702	MC
Santa Fe Univ of Art and Design	NM	39,666	SP
Scripps College	CA	54,900	MC
Seton Hill Univ	PA	35,172	C
Silver Lake College	WI	22,600	LC
Smith College	MA	57,524	MC
Southern Conn State Univ	CT	18,033	C
Southern Illinois Univ Edwardsville	IL	17,532	C
Southern Methodist Univ	TX	57,755	MC
Southern Oregon Univ	OR	17,874	C
Spring Hill College	AL	42,130	VC
St. Lawrence Univ	NY	53,740	HC
St. Olaf College	MN	49,960	HC+
Stanford Univ	CA	56,411	MC
Stony Brook Univ / SUNY	NY	19,359	HC
SUNY New Paltz	NY	15,010	C
Susquehanna Univ	PA	49,170	C
Sweet Briar College	VA	43,765	C+
Texas Christian Univ	TX	47,570	HC
Texas State Univ	TX	16,495	VC
Texas Tech Univ	TX	14,243	C
The Catholic Univ of America	DC	52,852	VC
The College at Brockport / SUNY	NY	18,362	VC
The College of St. Rose	NY	26,750	C
The SUNY at Potsdam	NY	17,754	C
Transylvania Univ	KY	40,310	VC+
Trinity Christian College	IL	28,869	C
Trinity College	CT		HC+
Troy Univ	AL	10,650	C
Truman State Univ	MO	13,546	HC
Tulane Univ	LA	58,942	MC
Union College	NE	23,270	VC
Union College	NY		MC
Univ at Albany / SUNY	NY	18,674	VC
Univ at Buffalo / The SUNY	NY	20,283	VC
Univ of Akron	OH	20,436	C
Univ of Arizona	AZ	20,105	C
Univ of Calif at Davis	CA	24,482	HC
Univ of Calif at Irvine	CA	25,961	VC
Univ of Calif at San Diego	CA	21,000	VC
Univ of Central Missouri	MO	14,605	C
Univ of Colo Boulder	CO	22,605	VC+
Univ of Findlay	OH	31,916	C
Univ of Georgia	GA	19,508	VC
Univ of Houston	TX	19,184	VC
Univ of Idaho	ID	14,558	C
Univ of Illinois at Chicago	IL	24,293	VC
Univ of Indianapolis	IN	31,740	LC
Univ of Maine	ME	19,712	C+
Univ of Mary Washington	VA	19,484	VC
Univ of Maryland	MD	18,801	HC
Univ of Mass Amherst	MA	23,697	VC+
Univ of Miami	FL	55,166	MC
Univ of Minn/Duluth	MN	18,904	C+
Univ of Minn/Morris	MN	17,150	VC
Univ of Minn/Twin Cities	MN		HC
Univ of Missouri-Kansas City	MO	19,603	C
Univ of Missouri-St. Louis	MO	18,304	VC
Univ of Montevallo	AL	17,320	C
Univ of Nebr - Lincoln	NE	17,507	VC
Univ of New Hampshire	NH	24,702	VC
Univ of New Mexico	NM	15,300	C
Univ of New Orleans	LA	9,224	VC
Univ of N Car at Chapel Hill	NC	18,348	MC
Univ of N Car at Wilmington	NC	13,572	VC+
Univ of North Texas	TX	15,628	C
Univ of Northern Iowa	IA	14,776	C
Univ of Notre Dame	IN		MC
Univ of Pittsburgh at Pittsburgh	PA	27,800	HC+
Univ of Redlands	CA	40,500	VC
Univ of Rochester	NY	58,500	MC
Univ of St. Francis	IN	29,810	C
Univ of S Car at Columbia	SC	19,725	VC+
Univ of S Car Upstate	SC	17,673	LC
Univ of Southern Calif	CA	56,903	MC
Univ of St. Thomas - Houston	TX	36,490	VC
Univ of Tenn at Knoxville	TN	20,364	VC+
Univ of Texas at Arlington	TX	10,908	LC
Univ of Texas at Austin	TX	44,074	HC
Univ of the Pacific	CA	52,146	VC
Univ of Washington	WA	14,722	VC
Univ of West Florida	FL	14,656	C
Univ of Wisc/Stout	WI	23,942	C
Univ of Wisc/Superior	WI	14,106	C
Viterbo Univ	WI	30,070	C
Wake Forest Univ	NC	51,000	MC
Washington and Lee Univ	VA	52,812	MC
Washington Univ in St. Louis	MO	58,818	MC
Webster Univ	MO	33,990	C+
Wellesley College	MA	49,848	MC
Wesleyan College	GA	24,000	C+
Wesleyan Univ	CT	59,844	MC
West Chester Univ of Pennsylvania	PA	16,836	C
West Texas A&M Univ	TX	13,478	C
Wheaton College	MA	54,934	HC+
Whitman College	WA	54,400	MC
Wichita State Univ	KS	12,539	C
Willamette Univ	OR	56,450	VC+
William Paterson Univ of New Jersey	NJ	21,694	C
William Woods Univ	MO		C
Wofford College	SC	45,795	VC
Wright State Univ	OH	16,983	C
York College / CUNY	NY	5,496	NC
Youngstown State Univ	OH	16,374	LC

SUPPLY CHAIN MANAGEMENT

School	ST	$IS	SR
Arizona State Univ	AZ	18,818	C+
Arkansas State Univ	AR	14,980	C
Binghamton Univ / The SUNY	NY	20,832	HC+
Boise State Univ	ID	12,802	C
Bryant Univ	RI	49,179	VC
Cal State, Chico	CA	18,952	C
Clarkson Univ	NY	53,538	HC
Duquesne Univ	PA	42,017	VC
Eastern Mich Univ	MI	17,961	C
Elmhurst College	IL	42,032	C+
Embry-Riddle Aeronautical Univ - Worldwide	FL	15,512	C
Fontbonne Univ	MO	31,384	C
Hofstra Univ	NY	48,020	VC+
Howard Univ	DC	35,957	C
Indiana Univ Bloomington	IN	19,358	HC
Indiana Univ Southeast	IN	15,807	LC
Indiana Univ-Purdue Univ Indianapolis	IN	17,290	C
Lehigh Univ	PA	55,080	MC
Lipscomb Univ	TN	35,722	VC
Marquette Univ	WI	43,664	VC+
Miami Univ	OH	24,191	HC
Rutgers, The State Univ of New Jersey/Newark Campus	NJ	25,376	C
Shippensburg Univ of Pennsylvania	PA	17,064	LC
Southeastern Louisiana Univ	LA	13,325	C
SUNY Plattsburgh / SUNY	NY	18,083	VC
Syracuse Univ	NY	54,512	HC
Texas Christian Univ	TX	47,570	HC
Tuskegee Univ	AL	26,750	C
Univ of Houston	TX	19,184	VC
Univ of Houston-Downtown	TX	6,267	LC
Univ of Kansas	KS	16,980	C+
Univ of Maryland	MD	18,801	HC
Univ of Nebr - Lincoln	NE	17,507	VC
Univ of N Car at Charlotte	NC	15,847	C
Univ of Pittsburgh at Pittsburgh	PA	27,800	HC+
Univ of Wisc/Stout	WI	23,942	C
Wayne State Univ	MI	19,493	C
Western Illinois Univ	IL	20,130	C
Western Mich Univ	MI	19,042	C
Wright State Univ	OH	16,983	C

SURVEY AND MAPPING TECHNOLOGY

School	ST	$IS	SR
Alfred State / SUNY College of Technology	NY	18,034	C
East Tenn State Univ	TN	9,000	C
Glenville State College	WV	11,348	NC
Metropolitan State Univ of Denver	CO	4,835	LC
Southern Polytechnic State Univ	GA	13,958	VC
SUNY / College of Environmental Science and Forestry	NY	18,351	HC
Univ of Akron	OH	20,436	C
Univ of Alaska Anchorage	AK	15,290	NC

SURVEYING ENGINEERING

School	ST	$IS	SR
Cal State, Fresno	CA	17,405	C
Ferris State Univ	MI	19,698	C
Metropolitan State Univ of Denver	CO	4,835	LC
Mich Tech Univ	MI	22,105	VC
New Mexico State Univ	NM	13,955	LC
Oregon Inst of Technology	OR	8,910	C
Purdue Univ/West Lafayette	IN	20,278	HC
Universidad Metropolitana	PR		
Universidad Politecnica de PR	PR	19,252	
Univ of Arkansas at Little Rock	AR		C
Univ of Maine	ME	19,712	C+
Univ of PR/Mayaguez	PR	1,250	

SUSTAINABLE MANAGEMENT

School	ST	$IS	SR
American Univ	DC	54,829	HC+
Baldwin Wallace Univ	OH	36,980	VC
Catawba College	NC	37,105	C
Chatham Univ	PA	42,440	VC
Goddard College	VT	16,418	VC
Indiana Univ-Purdue Univ Indianapolis	IN	17,290	C
Kean Univ	NJ	22,060	LC
Lipscomb Univ	TN	35,722	VC
Marylhurst Univ	OR	18,945	NC
Messiah College	PA	39,540	VC
Univ of Wisc/Green Bay	WI	14,900	C
Univ of Wisc/Stout	WI	23,942	C
Univ of Wisc/Superior	WI	14,106	C
Viterbo Univ	WI	30,070	C
Xavier Univ	OH	43,740	VC

SYSTEMS ANALYSIS

School	ST	$IS	SR
Arizona State Univ	AZ	18,818	C+
Baldwin Wallace Univ	OH	36,980	VC
George Washington Univ	DC	57,108	MC
Johnson and Wales Univ/ Providence Campus	RI	34,668	C
Rochester Inst of Technology	NY	42,450	VC+

SYSTEMS ENGINEERING

School	ST	$IS	SR
Binghamton Univ / The SUNY	NY	20,832	HC+
Case Western Reserve Univ	OH	55,178	MC
Embry-Riddle Aeronautical Univ - Worldwide	FL	15,512	C
George Mason Univ	VA	15,724	VC
Missouri Univ of Science and Technology	MO	18,655	VC+
Point Park Univ	PA	36,390	C
Southern Nazarene Univ	OK	24,354	NC
Southern Polytechnic State Univ	GA	13,958	VC
Stanford Univ	CA	56,411	MC
Stevens Inst of Technology	NJ	50,130	HC
Taylor Univ	IN	36,742	VC+
Texas A&M Univ at Galveston	TX	11,258	C
United States Military Academy	NY		MC
United States Naval Academy	MD		MC
Univ of Arizona	AZ	20,105	C
Univ of New Haven	CT	47,740	C
Univ of N Car at Charlotte	NC	15,847	C
Univ of Southern Calif	CA	56,903	MC
Univ of Virginia	VA	22,175	MC
Washington Univ in St. Louis	MO	58,818	MC
West Virginia Univ	WV	15,794	C+
Wright State Univ	OH	16,983	C

SYSTEMS SCIENCE

School	ST	$IS	SR
Case Western Reserve Univ	OH	55,178	MC
Johnson and Wales Univ/ Providence Campus	RI	34,668	C
Stanford Univ	CA	56,411	MC
Washington Univ in St. Louis	MO	58,818	MC
Worcester Polytechnic Inst	MA	53,440	HC+

TEACHING ENGLISH AS A SECOND/FOREIGN LANGUAGE (TESOL/TEFOL)

School	ST	$IS	SR
Andrews Univ	MI	28,030	C+
Aquinas College	MI	33,060	C
Bethel Univ	MN	34,940	VC
Brigham Young Univ/ Hawaii	HI	8,614	VC
Campbellsville Univ	KY	27,720	C
Canisius College	NY	45,602	VC
Caribbean Univ	PR	10,375	
Carroll College	MT	28,000	C
Elms College	MA	23,900	VC
Goshen College	IN	35,900	VC
Hawaii Pacific Univ	HI	36,690	C
Houghton College	NY	35,740	VC
Houston Baptist Univ	TX	23,815	C+
Howard Payne Univ	TX	17,115	C
Huntington Univ	IN	32,220	C
Inter-American Univ of PR/ Arecibo Campus	PR	3,350	
Inter-American Univ of PR/ San Germán	PR	6,720	
Kent State Univ	OH	19,352	C
Le Moyne College	NY	42,200	VC
LIU/Brooklyn Campus	NY	26,500	C
Mercy College	NY	29,996	C
Missouri Southern State Univ	MO	11,910	C
Murray State Univ	KY	14,944	C
Northeastern Illinois Univ	IL		C
Nyack College	NY	32,000	C
Okla Christian Univ	OK	24,975	VC
Oswego / SUNY	NY	20,009	VC
Pontifical Catholic Univ of PR	PR	7,310	
Salisbury Univ	MD	18,368	VC
San Jose State Univ	CA	19,707	C
Seattle Pacific Univ	WA	41,559	VC+
Taylor Univ	IN	36,742	VC+
Texas Wesleyan Univ	TX	29,886	C
Union Univ	TN	28,260	VC
Univ of Arizona	AZ	20,105	C
Univ of Georgia	GA	19,508	VC
Univ of Louisville	KY	17,460	VC
Univ of Minn/Twin Cities	MN		HC
Univ of Nebr - Lincoln	NE	17,507	VC
Univ of Nebr at Kearney	NE	14,855	LC
Univ of Northern Iowa	IA	14,776	C
Univ of PR/Mayaguez	PR	1,250	
Univ of Utah	UT	13,462	VC
Western Carolina Univ	NC	13,965	C+
Winona State Univ	MN	16,530	C

TECHNICAL AND BUSINESS WRITING

School	ST	$IS	SR
Arizona State Univ	AZ	18,818	C+
Carlow Univ	PA	30,272	C
Cedarville Univ	OH	31,036	VC+
Champlain College	VT	44,850	VC
Clarkson Univ	NY	53,538	HC
Eastern Mich Univ	MI	17,961	C
Illinois Inst of Technology	IL	38,512	HC+
Indiana Univ-Purdue Univ Fort Wayne	IN	15,425	C
King Univ	TN	33,140	C
Lawrence Tech Univ	MI	37,630	VC
Madonna Univ	MI	24,540	VC
Metropolitan State Univ	MN	5,923	SP
Mich Tech Univ	MI	22,105	VC
Milwaukee School of Engineering	WI	39,948	VC+
Missouri Univ of Science and Technology	MO	18,655	VC+
Mount Mary Univ	WI	32,836	LC
New Jersey Inst of Technology	NJ	26,490	VC
New Mexico Inst of Mining and Technology	NM	12,892	HC
New York Inst of Technology	NY	40,590	VC
New York Univ	NY	61,470	MC

School	ST	$IS	SR
Pittsburg State Univ	KS	12,032	C
Saginaw Valley State Univ	MI	16,869	C
Taylor Univ	IN	36,742	VC+
Tenn Tech Univ	TN	11,310	C
Univ of Arkansas at Little Rock	AR		C
Univ of Findlay	OH	31,916	C
Univ of Hartford	CT	42,674	C
Univ of Houston-Downtown	TX	6,267	LC
Univ of Montana-Western	MT	9,753	LC
Univ of Washington	WA	14,722	VC
Valparaiso Univ	IN	43,040	VC+
Winthrop Univ	SC	21,120	VC
Worcester Polytechnic Inst	MA	53,440	HC+
Youngstown State Univ	OH	16,374	LC

TECHNICAL COMMUNICATION

School	ST	$IS	SR
Bowling Green State Univ	OH	18,970	C
Cedarville Univ	OH	31,036	VC+
Indiana Univ-Purdue Univ Indianapolis	IN	17,290	C
Mercer Univ	GA	44,201	VC+
Southern Polytechnic State Univ	GA	13,958	VC

TECHNICAL EDUCATION

School	ST	$IS	SR
Bowling Green State Univ	OH	18,970	C
Brigham Young Univ	UT	12,100	HC
Central Conn State Univ	CT	19,212	C
College of New Jersey	NJ	25,376	HC
Eastern Illinois Univ	IL	20,502	C
Eastern Kentucky Univ	KY	11,161	C
Eastern Mich Univ	MI	17,961	C
Eastern New Mexico Univ	NM	10,682	C
Elizabeth City State Univ	NC	11,638	C
Ferris State Univ	MI	19,698	C
Fitchburg State Univ	MA	17,241	C
Fort Hays State Univ	KS	11,354	C
Illinois State Univ	IL	22,634	VC
Millersville Univ of Pennsylvania	PA	18,498	C
Montana State Univ	MT	14,068	VC
Murray State Univ	KY	14,944	C
New York City College of Technology / The CUNY	NY	5,769	NC
New York Inst of Technology	NY	40,590	VC
Norfolk State Univ	VA	10,531	LC
N Car State Univ	NC	16,202	HC
Oswego / SUNY	NY	20,009	VC
Pittsburg State Univ	KS	12,032	C
Purdue Univ/West Lafayette	IN	20,278	HC
Rhode Island College	RI	17,132	LC
Rochester College	MI	18,320	C
S Dak State Univ	SD	14,296	C
Southwestern Okla State Univ	OK	9,160	C
Temple Univ	PA	24,392	VC
Texas State Univ	TX	16,495	VC
Ohio State Univ	OH	19,887	MC
Thomas Edison State College	NJ	5,700	SP
Tuskegee Univ	AL	26,750	C
Univ of Akron	OH	20,436	C
Univ of Arkansas at Fayetteville	AR	16,860	VC
Univ of Central Florida	FL	15,711	VC+
Univ of Idaho	ID	14,558	C
Univ of New Mexico	NM	15,300	C
Univ of Northern Iowa	IA	14,776	C
Univ of Southern Maine	ME	16,576	C
Univ of Wisc/Platteville	WI	14,274	C
Univ of Wisc/Stout	WI	23,942	C
Univ of Wyoming	WY	13,855	C+
Valley City State Univ	ND	12,286	LC
Wayne State Univ	MI	19,493	C
Western Kentucky Univ	KY	11,000	LC
Western Washington Univ	WA	18,519	VC

TECHNOLOGICAL MANAGEMENT

School	ST	$IS	SR
Alfred State / SUNY College of Technology	NY	18,034	C
Arkansas State Univ	AR	14,980	C
Brewton-Parker College	GA	33,388	LC
Clayton State Univ	GA	12,000	LC
Colo Technical Univ	CO	10,500	LC
Davenport Univ	MI	21,002	LC
Embry-Riddle Aeronautical Univ - Worldwide	FL	15,512	C
Excelsior College	NY	895	SP
Franklin Univ	OH	7,000	SP
Golden Gate Univ	CA	17,000	C
Johnson and Wales Univ/ Providence Campus	RI	34,668	C
Lawrence Tech Univ	MI	37,630	VC
Murray State Univ	KY	14,944	C
New Jersey Inst of Technology	NJ	26,490	VC
New York Inst of Technology	NY	40,590	VC
Northern Illinois Univ	IL	19,768	C
Ohio Northern Univ	OH	42,075	VC
Okla Panhandle State Univ	OK	8,996	NC
Oswego / SUNY	NY	20,009	VC
Pennsylvania College of Technology	PA	25,653	NC
Pittsburg State Univ	KS	12,032	C
Roger Williams Univ	RI	45,788	C
Southeast Missouri State Univ	MO	14,983	LC
Southern New Hampshire Univ	NH	38,100	C
Southern Univ at New Orleans	LA	1,000	NC
Stony Brook Univ / SUNY	NY	19,359	HC
The SUNY College of Agriculture and Tech at Cobleskill	NY	18,869	VC
Troy Univ	AL	10,650	C
Univ of Alaska Anchorage	AK	15,290	NC
Univ of Alaska Fairbanks	AK	13,955	C
Univ of Findlay	OH	31,916	C
Washburn Univ	KS	12,165	NC
Wayne State College	NE	11,764	NC
Wentworth Inst of Technology	MA	29,800	SP

TECHNOLOGY & SCIENCE EDUCATION

School	ST	$IS	SR
Colo State Univ-Fort Collins	CO	20,090	VC
Univ of Wisc/Stout	WI	23,942	C
Viterbo Univ	WI	30,070	C

TECHNOLOGY AND PUBLIC AFFAIRS

School	ST	$IS	SR
Georgia Inst of Technology	GA	20,464	MC
New Jersey Inst of Technology	NJ	26,490	VC
Pomona College	CA	57,680	MC
Vassar College	NY	59,070	MC
Washington Univ in St. Louis	MO	58,818	MC
Western Kentucky Univ	KY	11,000	LC
Western Washington Univ	WA	18,519	VC
Worcester Polytechnic Inst	MA	53,440	HC+

TELECOMMUNICATIONS

School	ST	$IS	SR
Alabama A&M Univ	AL	96,100	C
Baylor Univ	TX	46,720	HC
Bowling Green State Univ	OH	18,970	C
Cal State, Monterey Bay	CA	26,871	LC
Capitol College	MD	21,250	C
Colo Technical Univ	CO	10,500	LC
Concordia Univ Wisc	WI	28,980	C
Eastern Mich Univ	MI	17,961	C
Fort Hays State Univ	KS	11,354	C
Howard Univ	DC	35,957	C
Illinois State Univ	IL	22,634	VC
Indiana Univ Bloomington	IN	19,358	HC
Indiana Univ-Purdue Univ Fort Wayne	IN	15,425	C
Ithaca College	NY	52,300	HC
Kutztown Univ of Pennsylvania	PA	16,909	LC
Lee Univ	TN	18,690	C+
Mich State Univ	MI	13,689	VC
Morgan State Univ	MD	14,500	VC
Murray State Univ	KY	14,944	C
New York City College of Technology / The CUNY	NY	5,769	NC
New York Inst of Technology	NY	40,590	VC
Ohio Univ	OH	20,676	VC
Okla Baptist Univ	OK	28,202	VC
Pepperdine Univ	CA	55,372	HC+
Rochester Inst of Technology	NY	42,450	VC+
Roosevelt Univ	IL	22,605	VC
San Diego State Univ	CA	20,578	VC
Southern Methodist Univ	TX	57,755	MC
St. John's Univ	NY	52,840	C+
SUNY Inst of Technology at Utica / Rome	NY	23,818	C
Syracuse Univ	NY	54,512	HC
Temple Univ	PA	24,392	VC
Texas Tech Univ	TX	14,243	C
Univ of Alabama at Tuscaloosa	AL	17,164	C+
Univ of Florida	FL	15,783	HC+
Univ of Idaho	ID	14,558	C
Univ of Kentucky	KY	19,868	C
Univ of Louisiana at Lafayette	LA	6,130	C
Univ of Nebr at Kearney	NE	14,855	LC
Univ of North Texas	TX	15,628	C
Univ of Northern Colo	CO	15,973	C
Univ of PR/Arecibo	PR	7,227	
Univ of Texas at Dallas	TX	21,046	HC
Univ of the Sacred Heart	PR	5,590	
Univ of Wisc/Stout	WI	23,942	C
Western Mich Univ	MI	19,042	C
Youngstown State Univ	OH	16,374	LC

TELECOMMUNICATIONS ENGINEERING TECHNOLOGY

School	ST	$IS	SR
Farmingdale State College	NY	18,985	C
Jackson State Univ	MS	13,512	LC
Southern Polytechnic State Univ	GA	13,958	VC
Univ of Texas at Dallas	TX	21,046	HC

TEXTILE ENGINEERING

School	ST	$IS	SR
Auburn Univ	AL	20,052	VC+
N Car State Univ	NC	16,202	HC
Philadelphia Univ	PA	44,160	C

TEXTILE TECHNOLOGY

School	ST	$IS	SR
Clemson Univ	SC	19,136	HC
Fashion Inst of Technology/SUNY	NY	12,468	SP
Mich State Univ	MI	13,689	VC
Philadelphia Univ	PA	44,160	C
Univ of Wisc/Madison	WI	18,757	HC

TEXTILES AND CLOTHING

School	ST	$IS	SR
Albright College	PA	46,660	C
Auburn Univ	AL	20,052	VC+
Calif College of the Arts	CA	48,334	SP
College for Creative Studies	MI		SP
Eastern Mich Univ	MI	17,961	C
Fashion Inst of Technology/SUNY	NY	12,468	SP
Framingham State Univ	MA	16,750	C
Howard Univ	DC	35,957	C
Indiana State Univ	IN	16,000	C
Iowa State Univ	IA	16,403	C
Kansas State Univ	KS	15,497	VC
Lipscomb Univ	TN	35,722	VC
Louisiana State Univ	LA	18,677	VC+
Middle Tenn State Univ	TN	8,650	C
Moore College of Art and Design	PA	38,124	SP
New Mexico State Univ	NM	13,955	LC
N Car State Univ	NC	16,202	HC
N Dak State Univ	ND	14,642	C
Northern Illinois Univ	IL	19,768	C
Northwest Missouri State Univ	MO	14,229	C
Rhode Island School of Design	RI	55,204	SP
Univ of Calif at Davis	CA	24,482	HC
Univ of Central Missouri	MO	14,605	C
Univ of Idaho	ID	14,558	C
Univ of Illinois at Urbana-Champaign	IL	24,300	HC
Univ of Kentucky	KY	19,868	C
Univ of Minn/Twin Cities	MN		HC
Univ of Missouri/Columbia	MO	18,201	MC
Univ of Nebr - Lincoln	NE	17,507	VC
Univ of N Dak	ND	14,094	C
Univ of Texas at Austin	TX	44,074	HC
Univ of Wisc/Madison	WI	18,757	HC
Western Kentucky Univ	KY	11,000	LC
Western Mich Univ	MI	19,042	C

THEATER DESIGN

School	ST	$IS	SR
Adelphi Univ	NY	43,130	VC
Alabama A&M Univ	AL	96,100	C
Arcadia Univ	PA	33,570	C+
Arizona State Univ	AZ	18,818	C+
Baldwin Wallace Univ	OH	36,980	VC
Baylor Univ	TX	46,720	HC
Belmont Univ	TN	37,380	VC+
Bennington College	VT	56,990	HC+
Binghamton Univ / The SUNY	NY	20,832	HC+
Biola Univ	CA	40,320	VC
Boston Univ	MA	54,130	HC+
Calif Inst of the Arts	CA	46,368	SP
Cal State, Fresno	CA	17,405	C
Cal State, Fullerton	CA	25,188	C+
Central Mich Univ	MI	18,066	C
College of the Ozarks	MO	5,605	VC
Colo State Univ-Fort Collins	CO	20,090	VC
Cornish College of the Arts	WA	21,200	SP
DePaul Univ	IL	46,120	VC
Elon Univ	NC	40,046	HC
Emerson College	MA	50,246	HC
Eugene Lang College - The New School for Liberal Arts	NY	55,650	VC
Faulkner Univ	AL	22,530	LC
Florida Southern College	FL	38,240	VC
Florida State Univ	FL	15,238	HC
Fordham Univ	NY	58,927	HC
Grand Canyon Univ	AZ	24,540	VC
Hofstra Univ	NY	48,020	VC+
Huntington Univ	IN	32,220	C
Illinois Wesleyan Univ	IL	48,452	VC+
Ithaca College	NY	52,300	HC
Johnson State College	VT	16,721	C
Kean Univ	NJ	22,060	LC
Keene State College	NH	21,538	C
Lehigh Univ	PA	55,080	MC
Marshall Univ	WV	14,820	C
Mich Tech Univ	MI	22,105	VC
Millikin Univ	IL	37,462	C
Montclair State Univ	NJ	22,614	C
Ohio Univ	OH	20,676	VC
Okla City Univ	OK	33,546	VC
Old Dominion Univ	VA	18,662	C
Pace Univ	NY	48,094	VC
Palm Beach Atlantic Univ	FL	33,882	LC
Piedmont College	GA	29,260	C
Purchase College / SUNY	NY	16,951	C
Roosevelt Univ	IL	22,605	VC
Santa Fe Univ of Art and Design	NM	39,666	SP
Seton Hill Univ	PA	35,172	C
Shenandoah Univ	VA	39,268	C
Southern Illinois Univ Edwardsville	IL	17,532	C
Stephens College	MO	34,500	VC
SUNY College at Geneseo	NY	18,055	HC+
SUNY Fredonia / The SUNY at Fredonia	NY	18,702	VC
SUNY New Paltz	NY	15,010	C
Syracuse Univ	NY	54,512	HC
Temple Univ	PA	24,392	VC
Texas Christian Univ	TX	47,570	HC
Texas Tech Univ	TX	14,243	C
Texas Wesleyan Univ	TX	29,886	C
Ohio State Univ	OH	19,887	MC
Towson Univ	MD	16,000	VC
Tulane Univ	LA	58,942	MC
Univ of Central Missouri	MO	14,605	C
Univ of Central Okla	OK	12,293	C
Univ of Cincinnati	OH	20,199	VC
Univ of Conn	CT	23,744	HC
Univ of Florida	FL	15,783	HC+
Univ of Illinois at Chicago	IL	24,293	VC
Univ of Kansas	KS	16,980	C+
Univ of Maryland/Baltimore County	MD	18,000	VC
Univ of Miami	FL	55,166	MC
Univ of Mich/Ann Arbor	MI	22,102	HC+
Univ of Nebr - Lincoln	NE	17,507	VC
Univ of New Mexico	NM	15,300	C
Univ of N Car at Wilmington	NC	13,572	VC+
Univ of N Car School of the Arts	NC	7,401	SP
Univ of North Texas	TX	15,628	C
Univ of Northern Iowa	IA	14,776	C
Univ of Southern Calif	CA	56,903	MC
Vanderbilt Univ	TN	57,072	MC
Wagner College	NY	48,600	VC
Washburn Univ	KS	12,165	NC
Webster Univ	MO	33,990	C+
Western Mich Univ	MI	19,042	C
Western Washington Univ	WA	18,519	VC
Wright State Univ	OH	16,983	C

THEATER MANAGEMENT

School	ST	$IS	SR
Aquinas College	MI	33,060	C
Baldwin Wallace Univ	OH	36,980	VC
Barry Univ	FL	38,190	C
Benedictine College	KS	29,180	VC
Bethel Univ	TN	19,186	C
Biola Univ	CA	40,320	VC
Boston Univ	MA	54,130	HC+
Cal State, Fullerton	CA	25,188	C+
Catawba College	NC	37,105	C
CUNY/Brooklyn College	NY	5,884	C+
Colo Mesa Univ	CO	16,669	LC
DePaul Univ	IL	46,120	VC
Emerson College	MA	50,246	HC
Fitchburg State Univ	MA	17,241	C
Fontbonne Univ	MO	31,384	C
Grand Canyon Univ	AZ	24,540	VC
Hofstra Univ	NY	48,020	VC+
Illinois Wesleyan Univ	IL	48,452	VC+
Ithaca College	NY	52,300	HC
Johnson State College	VT	16,721	C
Marywood Univ	PA	40,695	C
Messiah College	PA	39,540	VC
New York Univ	NY	61,470	MC
Ohio Univ	OH	20,676	VC
Pace Univ	NY	48,094	VC
Roosevelt Univ	IL	22,605	VC
Salisbury Univ	MD	18,368	VC
Santa Fe Univ of Art and Design	NM	39,666	SP
Seton Hill Univ	PA	35,172	C
Shenandoah Univ	VA	39,268	C
Syracuse Univ	NY	54,512	HC
Temple Univ	PA	24,392	VC
Trinity College	CT		HC+
Univ of Akron	OH	20,436	C
Univ of Delaware	DE	22,728	VC
Univ of Evansville	IN	41,056	VC+
Univ of Hartford	CT	42,674	C
Univ of Idaho	ID	14,558	C
Univ of Miami	FL	55,166	MC
Univ of North Texas	TX	15,628	C
Univ of Southern Calif	CA	56,903	MC
Univ of Texas at El Paso	TX	8,764	NC

School	ST	$IS	SR
Wright State Univ	OH	16,983	C

THEATRE ACTING

School	ST	$IS	SR
Asbury Univ	KY	32,038	VC
Baldwin Wallace Univ	OH	36,980	VC
Bates College	ME	58,950	MC
Bethany College	WV	35,282	C
Biola Univ	CA	40,320	VC
Colo State Univ-Fort Collins	CO	20,090	VC
Dordt College	IA	34,160	VC
Eastern Conn State Univ	CT	20,584	C
Elon Univ	NC	40,046	HC
Eugene Lang College - The New School for Liberal Arts	NY	55,650	VC
Florida Southern College	FL	38,240	VC
Fontbonne Univ	MO	31,384	C
Fordham Univ	NY	58,927	HC
Nova Southeastern Univ	FL	34,016	VC
Okla City Univ	OK	33,546	VC
Oswego / SUNY	NY	20,009	VC
Pace Univ	NY	48,094	VC
Texas Christian Univ	TX	47,570	HC
The College at Brockport / SUNY	NY	18,362	VC
Univ of Central Okla	OK	12,293	C
Univ of Illinois at Chicago	IL	24,293	VC
Univ of Miami	FL	55,166	MC
Univ of Wyoming	WY	13,855	C+
Wright State Univ	OH	16,983	C
Youngstown State Univ	OH	16,374	LC

THEATRE ARTS

School	ST	$IS	SR
Adams State College	CO	13,358	LC
Alfred Univ	NY	40,392	VC
Alvernia Univ	PA	39,250	C
Angelo State Univ	TX	15,049	NC
Arkansas State Univ	AR	14,980	C
Augustana College	SD	35,500	VC
Bard College	NY	59,872	HC
Belmont Univ	TN	37,380	VC+
Berea College	KY	7,220	HC
Berry College	GA	39,254	HC
Bethany College	KS	30,605	NC
Bethany College	WV	35,282	C
Bethel College	IN	31,560	C
Binghamton Univ / The SUNY	NY	20,832	HC+
Biola Univ	CA	40,320	VC
Boise State Univ	ID	12,802	C
Bowdoin College	ME	57,834	MC
Brandeis Univ	MA	58,820	HC
Brescia Univ	KY	26,140	VC+
Butler Univ	IN	45,898	VC+
Calif Lutheran Univ	CA	47,640	C
Calif Polytechnic State Univ	CA	19,847	HC
Cal State, Chico	CA	18,952	C
Cal State, Fresno	CA	17,405	C
Calvin College	MI	37,585	VC+
Cameron Univ	OK	9,267	LC
Campbellsville Univ	KY	27,720	C
Canisius College	NY	45,602	VC
Catawba College	NC	37,105	C
Cedarville Univ	OH	31,036	VC+
Central Conn State Univ	CT	19,212	C
Christopher Newport Univ	VA	21,050	VC
Claremont McKenna College	CA	58,065	MC
Coe College	IA	43,590	VC
Colby College	ME	57,510	MC
College of Charleston	SC	21,273	VC
College of St. Benedict	MN	47,570	VC
Colo Mesa Univ	CO	16,669	LC
Concordia Univ St. Paul	MN	27,200	C
Cornell Univ	NY	59,037	MC
Creighton Univ	NE	44,058	VC+
DePaul Univ	IL	46,120	VC
Dickinson College	PA	57,662	HC+
Dominican Univ	IL	37,628	C
Dordt College	IA	34,160	VC
Drew Univ/College of Liberal Arts	NJ	55,862	VC
Elmhurst College	IL	42,032	C+
Elon Univ	NC	40,046	HC
Emporia State Univ	KS	12,897	C
Florida Southern College	FL	38,240	VC
Fontbonne Univ	MO	31,384	C
Franklin College	IN	35,885	C
Franklin Pierce Univ	NH	41,598	C
Gallaudet Univ	DC	25,380	SP
Georgia Southern Univ	GA	16,414	C
Goshen College	IN	35,900	VC
Goucher College	MD	50,252	VC+
Grand Canyon Univ	AZ	24,540	VC
Guilford College	NC	35,340	C
Hamline Univ	MN	44,198	VC
High Point Univ	NC	39,800	C
Howard Univ	DC	35,957	C
Huntington Univ	IN	32,220	C
Indiana Univ Bloomington	IN	19,358	HC
Indiana Univ of Pennsylvania	PA	20,180	LC
John Carroll Univ	OH	44,520	C+
Kean Univ	NJ	22,060	LC
Keene State College	NH	21,538	C
Kennesaw State Univ	GA	13,017	VC
King Univ	TN	33,140	C
LaGrange College	GA	34,480	C
Lake Forest College	IL	45,580	VC
Limestone College	SC	29,880	C
Linfield College-McMinnville Campus	OR	46,166	C
Lipscomb Univ	TN	35,722	VC
Loyola Univ Chicago	IL	49,560	VC+
Luther College	IA	44,380	VC+
Lynchburg College	VA	42,645	C
Marquette Univ	WI	43,664	VC+
Marshall Univ	WV	14,820	C
Missouri Baptist Univ	MO	30,010	C
Missouri State Univ	MO	13,996	VC
Monmouth Univ	NJ	42,252	C
Nazareth College of Rochester	NY	41,590	VC
North Central College	IL	38,343	VC
N Dak State Univ	ND	14,642	C
Northeastern Illinois Univ	IL		C
Northeastern Univ	MA	55,296	MC
Northern Arizona Univ	AZ	18,592	C
Occidental College	CA	59,592	MC+
Okla City Univ	OK	33,546	VC
Oswego / SUNY	NY	20,009	VC
Ouachita Baptist Univ	AR	29,010	VC
Pace Univ	NY	48,094	VC
Piedmont College	GA	29,260	C
Plymouth State Univ	NH	23,148	LC
Point Park Univ	PA	36,390	C
Pomona College	CA	57,680	MC
Quinnipiac Univ	CT	53,580	VC
Radford Univ	VA	17,132	LC
Rhodes College	TN	47,596	HC+
Roanoke College	VA	47,996	C+
Roger Williams Univ	RI	45,788	C
Rollins College	FL	52,370	HC
Rowan Univ	NJ	23,570	VC
St. John's Univ	MN	46,146	C
St. Joseph's College	IN	35,790	C
St. Joseph's Univ	PA	52,272	VC
St. Martin's Univ	WA	38,082	C
St. Mary's Univ of Minn	MN	37,015	C
Samford Univ	AL	35,700	VC+
San Diego State Univ	CA	20,578	VC
Santa Clara Univ	CA	54,702	MC
Schreiner Univ	TX	32,734	LC
Seattle Univ	WA	47,010	VC+
Seton Hall Univ	NJ	45,902	C
Sewanee: The Univ of the South	TN	47,700	HC+
Shenandoah Univ	VA	39,268	C
Southeast Missouri State Univ	MO	14,983	LC
Southern Oregon Univ	OR	17,874	C
Spring Hill College	AL	42,130	VC
St. Edward's Univ	TX	44,674	VC
St. Norbert College	WI	39,992	VC
St. Olaf College	MN	49,960	HC+
SUNY Fredonia / The SUNY at Fredonia	NY	18,702	VC
Swarthmore College	PA	57,870	MC
Taylor Univ	IN	36,742	VC+
Texas Christian Univ	TX	47,570	HC
Texas State Univ	TX	16,495	VC
The College of Idaho	ID	31,277	VC
Ohio State Univ	OH	19,887	MC
The SUNY at Potsdam	NY	17,754	C
Thomas Edison State College	NJ	5,700	SP
Transylvania Univ	KY	40,310	VC+
Univ at Buffalo / The SUNY	NY	20,283	VC
Univ of Alaska Fairbanks	AK	13,955	C
Univ of Arizona	AZ	20,105	C
Univ of Arkansas at Little Rock	AR		C
Univ of Calif at Riverside	CA	27,204	C
Univ of Central Florida	FL	15,711	VC+
Univ of Central Okla	OK	12,293	C
Univ of Colo Boulder	CO	22,605	VC+
Univ of Georgia	GA	19,508	VC
Univ of Illinois at Chicago	IL	24,293	VC
Univ of Iowa	IA	17,481	VC
Univ of Maryland	MD	18,001	HC
Univ of Miami	FL	55,166	MC
Univ of Miss	MS	15,482	VC
Univ of Nebr - Lincoln	NE	17,507	VC
Univ of New Haven	CT	47,740	C
Univ of N Car at Charlotte	NC	15,847	C
Univ of Oregon	OR	20,872	VC
Univ of Pittsburgh at Pittsburgh	PA	27,800	HC+
Univ of Rochester	NY	58,500	MC
Univ of San Diego	CA	53,302	HC+
Univ of Scranton	PA	51,940	VC
Univ of Southern Indiana	IN	14,657	C
Univ of Tenn at Knoxville	TN	20,364	VC+
Univ of Tulsa	OK	45,311	HC+
Univ of Utah	UT	13,462	VC
Univ of West Georgia	GA	14,852	LC
Univ of Wisc/Eau Claire	WI	15,430	VC
Univ of Wisc/Green Bay	WI	14,900	C
Univ of Wisc/Madison	WI	18,757	HC
Univ of Wisc/Superior	WI	14,106	C
Valparaiso Univ	IN	43,040	VC+
Vanguard Univ of Southern Calif	CA	35,833	VC
Warren Wilson College	NC	34,888	VC
Washington and Jefferson College	PA	49,990	VC
Wayne State Univ	MI	19,493	C
Whitman College	WA	54,400	MC
William Peace Univ	NC	32,900	LC
Winthrop Univ	SC	21,120	VC
Wofford College	SC	45,795	VC
Xavier Univ	OH	43,740	VC
Youngstown State Univ	OH	16,374	LC

THEATRE PRODUCTION

School	ST	$IS	SR
Bethany College	WV	35,282	C
Colo State Univ-Fort Collins	CO	20,090	VC
Elon Univ	NC	40,046	HC
Fontbonne Univ	MO	31,384	C
Fordham Univ	NY	58,927	HC
Okla City Univ	OK	33,546	VC
Oswego / SUNY	NY	20,009	VC
Southern Oregon Univ	OR	17,874	C
Texas Christian Univ	TX	47,570	HC
Univ of Illinois at Chicago	IL	24,293	VC
Youngstown State Univ	OH	16,374	LC

THEATRE STUDIES

School	ST	$IS	SR
Amherst College	MA	58,744	MC
Bowling Green State Univ	OH	18,970	C
Capital Univ	OH	39,824	VC
Chapman Univ	CA	56,019	VC+
Chatham Univ	PA	42,440	VC
Colo State Univ-Fort Collins	CO	20,090	VC
Elon Univ	NC	40,046	HC
Eugene Lang College - The New School for Liberal Arts	NY	55,650	VC
Indiana Univ Bloomington	IN	19,358	HC
Indiana Univ Northwest	IN	6,738	LC
Indiana Univ South Bend	IN	15,293	C
John Carroll Univ	OH	44,520	C+
Lindsey Wilson College	KY	30,470	VC
Malone Univ	OH	34,334	C
Southern Oregon Univ	OR	17,874	C
Texas Christian Univ	TX	47,570	HC
Univ of Central Florida	FL	15,711	VC+
Univ of Central Okla	OK	12,293	C
Univ of Denver	CO	51,787	VC+
Univ of Illinois at Chicago	IL	24,293	VC
Univ of New Mexico	NM	15,300	C
Viterbo Univ	WI	30,070	C
Wake Forest Univ	NC	51,000	MC
Wright State Univ	OH	16,983	C
Youngstown State Univ	OH	16,374	LC

THEOLOGICAL STUDIES

School	ST	$IS	SR
Alvernia Univ	PA	39,250	C
Andrews Univ	MI	28,030	C+
Aquinas College	MI	33,060	C
Aquinas College	TN	29,250	C+
Assumption College	MA	45,721	VC
Atlantic Union College	MA	24,600	LC
Avila Univ	MO	26,900	C
Bard College	NY	59,872	HC
Barry Univ	FL	38,190	C
Bellarmine Univ	KY	42,950	VC
Belmont Abbey College	NC	37,716	C
Benedictine Univ	IL	35,220	C
Bethel Univ	MN	34,940	VC
Boston College	MA	58,506	MC
Briar Cliff Univ	IA	29,514	C
Caldwell College	NJ	35,602	LC
Calif Lutheran Univ	CA	47,640	C
Calumet College of St. Joseph	IN	15,000	LC
Calvin College	MI	37,585	VC+
Carlow Univ	PA	30,272	C
Christendom College	VA	28,120	VC
College of St. Benedict	MN	47,570	VC
College of St. Elizabeth	NJ	43,839	LC
College of St. Mary	NE	34,334	C
Colo Christian Univ	CO	27,500	VC
Concordia Univ	OR	34,930	C
Concordia Univ - Irvine	CA	35,390	VC
Concordia Univ Nebr	NE	26,000	VC
Concordia Univ St. Paul	MN	27,200	C
Concordia Univ Wisc	WI	28,980	C
Concordia Univ, River Forest	IL	26,300	C
De Sales Univ	PA	42,670	C
Dominican Univ	IL	37,628	C
Duquesne Univ	PA	42,017	VC
Eastern Mennonite Univ	VA	38,850	VC
Eastern Univ	PA	37,704	C
Elmhurst College	IL	42,032	C+
Fordham Univ	NY	58,927	HC
Franciscan Univ of Steubenville	OH	27,320	VC
Gannon Univ	PA	37,940	C
Hanover College	IN	41,450	VC
Hardin-Simmons Univ	TX	23,560	C+
Immaculata Univ	PA	43,000	C
John Brown Univ	AR	30,996	VC+
John Carroll Univ	OH	44,520	C+
Juniata College	PA	49,340	VC
King's College	PA	41,678	C
Lenoir-Rhyne College	NC	35,984	C
Livingstone College	NC	17,815	LC
Lourdes Univ	OH	26,055	LC
Loyola Marymount Univ	CA	53,240	VC+
Loyola Univ Chicago	IL	49,560	VC+
Loyola Univ Maryland	MD		VC
Malone Univ	OH	34,334	C
Marian Univ/Indianapolis	IN	37,058	C
Marquette Univ	WI	43,664	VC+
Marymount Univ	VA	36,178	C
Messiah College	PA	39,540	VC
Molloy College	NY	38,950	C
Mount Mary Univ	WI	32,836	LC
Mount St. Mary's Univ	MD	46,158	C
Mount Vernon Nazarene Univ	OH	29,590	C
Newman Univ	KS	30,380	C+
Northwest Univ	WA	18,854	C
Notre Dame College	OH	34,942	VC
Nyack College	NY	32,000	C
Ohio Dominican Univ	OH	38,380	C+
Ouachita Baptist Univ	AR	29,010	VC
Pacific Union College	CA	28,150	VC
Pontifical Catholic Univ of PR	PR	7,310	
Providence College	RI	55,995	HC
Quincy Univ	IL	34,980	LC
Rockhurst Univ	MO	20,625	C
St. Anselm College	NH	48,324	VC
St. John's Univ	MN	46,146	C
St. Joseph's College of Maine	ME	31,580	C
St. Joseph's Univ	PA	52,272	VC
St. Louis Univ	MO	46,594	VC+
St. Mary-of-the-Woods College	IN	37,722	LC
St. Mary's Univ	TX	33,854	C
St. Peter's College	NJ	44,240	C
St. Vincent College	PA	40,244	C
Seattle Pacific Univ	WA	41,559	VC+
Seattle Univ	WA	47,010	VC+
Seton Hall Univ	NJ	45,902	C
Southern Adventist Univ	TN	26,190	C
Southern Nazarene Univ	OK	24,354	NC
Southwestern Adventist Univ	TX	23,026	LC
Spring Arbor Univ	MI	26,740	C
Spring Hill College	AL	42,130	VC
St. Ambrose Univ	IA		C
St. Bonaventure Univ	NY	38,831	C
St. Catherine Univ	MN	37,782	C+
St. John's Univ	NY	52,840	C+
Sterling College	KS	27,216	C
Texas Lutheran Univ	TX	34,070	C
The Catholic Univ of America	DC	52,852	VC
Thomas More College	KY	34,760	C
Trinity Christian College	IL	28,869	C
Union College	NE	23,270	VC
Universidad Adventista de las Antillas	PR	7,360	
Univ of Chicago	IL	55,416	MC
Univ of Dallas	TX	43,510	VC+
Univ of Evansville	IN	41,056	VC+
Univ of Great Falls	MT	27,970	C
Univ of Mary	ND	16,714	C
Univ of Mobile	AL	27,870	VC
Univ of Notre Dame	IN		MC
Univ of Portland	OR	47,874	VC
Univ of St. Mary	KS	28,400	C+
Univ of San Diego	CA	53,302	HC+
Univ of San Francisco	CA	49,674	VC
Univ of Scranton	PA	51,940	VC
Univ of St. Francis	IL	36,490	C
Univ of St. Thomas - Houston	TX	36,490	VC
Valparaiso Univ	IN	43,040	VC+
Vanguard Univ of Southern Calif	CA	35,833	VC
Villanova Univ	PA	56,436	MC
Walla Walla Univ	WA	26,256	NC
Walsh Univ	OH	35,100	C
Washington Adventist Univ	MD	25,859	C+
Wheeling Jesuit Univ	WV	34,668	C
Whitworth Univ	WA	45,826	VC+
Wisc Lutheran College	WI	23,510	VC
Xavier Univ	OH	43,740	VC
Xavier Univ of Louisiana	LA	25,300	C

THEOLOGY

School	ST	$IS	SR
Calvin College	MI	37,585	VC+
Creighton Univ	NE	44,058	VC+
St. Louis Univ	MO	46,594	VC+
St. Mary's Univ of Minn	MN	37,015	C

THERAPEUTIC RIDING

School	ST	$IS	SR
St. Andrews Univ	NC	32,050	LC

ST = STATE $IS = IN-STATE COSTS SR = SELECTOR RATING

THIRD WORLD STUDIES

School	ST	$IS	SR
Appalachian State Univ	NC	12,919	VC
Bethel Univ	MN	34,940	VC
Pitzer College	CA	54,988	MC
Univ of Calif at San Diego	CA	21,000	VC

TOTAL QUALITY MANAGEMENT (TQM)

School	ST	$IS	SR
Cal State, Dominguez Hills	CA	17,056	LC
San Diego State Univ	CA	20,578	VC

TOURISM

School	ST	$IS	SR
Arizona State Univ	AZ	18,818	₵
Bowling Green State Univ	OH	18,970	C
Brigham Young Univ	UT	12,100	HC
Brigham Young Univ/ Hawaii	HI	8,614	VC
Cal State, Dominguez Hills	CA	17,056	LC
Cal State, Fullerton	CA	25,188	₵
Central Washington Univ	WA	11,730	C
Coastal Carolina Univ	SC	17,620	C
Colo State Univ-Fort Collins	CO	20,090	VC
Dowling College	NY	25,000	LC
Eastern Mich Univ	MI	17,961	C
George Mason Univ	VA	15,724	VC
George Washington Univ	DC	57,108	MC
Hawaii Pacific Univ	HI	36,690	C
Indiana Univ Bloomington	IN	19,358	HC
Indiana Univ Kokomo	IN	6,674	LC
Indiana Univ-Purdue Univ Indianapolis	IN	17,290	C
James Madison Univ	VA	18,049	VC
Johnson and Wales Univ/ Charlotte Campus	NC	35,421	C
Johnson and Wales Univ/ North Miami Campus	FL	34,368	C
Johnson and Wales Univ/ Providence Campus	RI	34,668	C
Johnson State College	VT	16,721	C
Lasell College	MA	42,500	LC
Mich State Univ	MI	13,689	VC
Montclair State Univ	NJ	22,614	C
New Mexico State Univ	NM	13,955	LC
Niagara Univ	NY	39,800	C
Ohio Univ	OH	20,676	VC
Plymouth State Univ	NH	23,148	LC
Purdue Univ/West Lafayette	IN	20,278	HC
Rochester Inst of Technology	NY	42,450	V₵
Seton Hill Univ	PA	35,172	C
Sojourner-Douglass College	MD	9,160	LC
Southern New Hampshire Univ	NH	38,100	C
St. Joseph's College, New York / Suffolk Campus	NY	21,878	VC
St. Thomas Univ	FL	32,310	₵
Temple Univ	PA	24,392	VC
Texas State Univ	TX	16,495	VC
Univ of Central Missouri	MO	14,605	C
Univ of Hawaii at Manoa	HI	19,379	VC
Univ of Missouri/Columbia	MO	18,201	MC
Univ of Montana-Western	MT	9,753	LC
Univ of New Hampshire	NH	24,702	VC
Univ of New Haven	CT	47,740	C
Univ of New Orleans	LA	9,224	VC
Univ of the Sacred Heart	PR	5,590	
Virginia Polytechnic Inst and State Univ	VA	14,629	HC
West Liberty Univ	WV	9,142	LC
West Virginia Univ	WV	15,794	₵
Western Mich Univ	MI	19,042	C

TOXICOLOGY

School	ST	$IS	SR
Ashland Univ	OH	25,000	C
Nazareth College of Rochester	NY	41,590	VC
Penn State Univ/Univ Park	PA	25,404	VC
St. John's Univ	NY	52,840	₵
Univ of Calif at Davis	CA	24,482	HC
Univ of Georgia	GA	19,508	VC
Univ of Louisiana at Monroe	LA	12,998	C
Univ of the Sciences	PA	48,320	V₵

TOY DESIGN

School	ST	$IS	SR
Fashion Inst of Technology/SUNY	NY	12,468	SP
Otis College of Art and Design	CA	35,404	SP

TRADE AND INDUSTRIAL EDUCATION

School	ST	$IS	SR
Alabama A&M Univ	AL	96,100	C
Eastern Mich Univ	MI	17,961	C
Kent State Univ	OH	19,352	C
Missouri Southern State Univ	MO	11,910	C
New York Inst of Technology	NY	40,590	VC
Northern Kentucky Univ	KY	15,302	LC
Oswego / SUNY	NY	20,009	VC
Univ of Nevada, Las Vegas	NV	17,303	C
Univ of Wyoming	WY	13,855	₵
Virginia State Univ	VA	11,318	₵

TRADE AND INDUSTRIAL SUPERVISION AND MANAGEMENT

School	ST	$IS	SR
Cal State, Dominguez Hills	CA	17,056	LC
Eastern Mich Univ	MI	17,961	C
Metropolitan State Univ	MN	5,923	SP
Washington Univ in St. Louis	MO	58,818	MC

TRANSPORTATION AND TRAVEL MARKETING

School	ST	$IS	SR
Johnson and Wales Univ/ Providence Campus	RI	34,668	C
Northwood Univ	FL	30,746	LC
Northwood Univ	MI	26,331	LC

TRANSPORTATION ENGINEERING

School	ST	$IS	SR
Calif Polytechnic State Univ	CA	19,847	HC
Lawrence Tech Univ	MI	37,630	VC
Texas A&M Univ at Galveston	TX	11,258	C

TRANSPORTATION MANAGEMENT

School	ST	$IS	SR
Auburn Univ	AL	20,052	V₵
Calif Maritime Academy	CA	15,496	C
Dowling College	NY	25,000	LC
Embry-Riddle Aeronautical Univ - Daytona Beach	FL	40,884	₵
Embry-Riddle Aeronautical Univ - Worldwide	FL	15,512	C
Florida Memorial Univ	FL	20,716	LC
Iowa State Univ	IA	16,403	C
Maritime College / SUNY	NY	16,020	C
Mass Maritime Academy	MA	15,340	C
Niagara Univ	NY	39,800	C
Southern Univ at New Orleans	LA	1,000	NC
Texas A&M Univ at Galveston	TX	11,258	C
Ohio State Univ	OH	19,887	MC
Univ of Alaska Anchorage	AK	15,290	NC
Univ of Arkansas at Fayetteville	AR	16,860	VC
Univ of North Florida	FL	15,578	VC
Univ of Pennsylvania	PA	56,106	MC
Univ of Wisc/Superior	WI	14,106	C

TRANSPORTATION TECHNOLOGY

School	ST	$IS	SR
Maine Maritime Academy	ME	21,073	C

TURFGRASS AND LANDSCAPE MANAGEMENT

School	ST	$IS	SR
Univ of Georgia	GA	19,508	VC
Univ of Nebr - Lincoln	NE	17,507	VC

ULTRASOUND TECHNOLOGY

School	ST	$IS	SR
Barry Univ	FL	38,190	C
Mount Aloysius College	PA	27,970	C
Mountain State Univ	WV	14,330	NC
Newman Univ	KS	30,380	₵
Oregon Inst of Technology	OR	8,910	C
Rochester Inst of Technology	NY	42,450	V₵
Seattle Univ	WA	47,010	V₵
Washburn Univ	KS	12,165	NC

UNIVERSITY STUDIES

School	ST	$IS	SR
Shenandoah Univ	VA	39,268	C
Univ of Maine	ME	19,712	₵

URBAN DESIGN

School	ST	$IS	SR
New York Univ	NY	61,470	MC
Parsons The New School for Design	NY	56,610	SP
Univ at Albany / SUNY	NY	18,674	VC
Univ of Virginia	VA	22,175	MC

URBAN ECOLOGY

School	ST	$IS	SR
Hofstra Univ	NY	48,020	V₵
Seattle Univ	WA	47,010	V₵

URBAN PLANNING TECHNOLOGY

School	ST	$IS	SR
Ball State Univ	IN	17,850	C
Calif State Polytechnic Univ, Pomona	CA	18,932	C
Eastern Mich Univ	MI	17,961	C
Florida Atlantic Univ	FL	17,339	C
Mich State Univ	MI	13,689	VC
San Jose State Univ	CA	19,707	C
Texas State Univ	TX	16,495	VC
Univ of Nevada, Las Vegas	NV	17,303	C
Univ of Utah	UT	13,462	VC
Univ of Wisc-Milwaukee	WI	18,436	C
West Chester Univ of Pennsylvania	PA	16,836	C

URBAN STUDIES

School	ST	$IS	SR
Albertus Magnus College	CT	37,382	LC
Arizona State Univ	AZ	18,818	₵
Augsburg College	MN	35,142	C
Ball State Univ	IN	17,850	C
Baylor Univ	TX	46,720	HC
Bellevue Univ	NE	4,600	NC
Boston Univ	MA	54,130	H₵
Brown Univ	RI	56,150	MC
Bryn Mawr College	PA	57,760	MC
Buffalo State/State Univ of Buffalo	NY	15,733	₵
Calif State Polytechnic Univ, Pomona	CA	18,932	C
Cal State, Fresno	CA	17,405	C
Cal State, Northridge	CA	28,313	C
Calumet College of St. Joseph	IN	15,000	LC
Canisius College	NY	45,602	VC
Carnegie Mellon Univ	PA	51,260	MC
Cleveland State Univ	OH	21,357	C
College of Charleston	SC	21,273	VC
College of Mount St. Vincent	NY	41,040	MC
College of Wooster	OH	52,600	VC
Columbia Univ in the City of New York	NY	61,116	MC
Columbia Univ/Barnard College	NY	39,000	MC
Columbia Univ/School of General Studies	NY	54,083	MC
Conn College	CT	54,970	MC
Coppin State Univ	MD	14,905	VC
Cornell Univ	NY	59,037	MC
CUNY-City College	NY	19,576	H₵
DePaul Univ	IL	46,120	VC
Dillard Univ	LA	20,940	VC
Eastern Mich Univ	MI	17,961	C
Eastern Washington Univ	WA	16,388	C
Elmhurst College	IL	42,032	₵
Eugene Lang College - The New School for Liberal Arts	NY	55,650	VC
Fordham Univ	NY	58,927	HC
Furman Univ	SC	54,006	HC
Georgia State Univ	GA	12,000	VC
Hamline Univ	MN	44,198	VC
Hampshire College	MA	58,320	MC
Haverford College	PA	59,236	MC
Hobart and William Smith Colleges	NY	43,000	VC
Howard Univ	DC	35,957	C
Hunter College / The CUNY	NY	14,429	VC
Jackson State Univ	MS	13,512	LC
Langston Univ	OK	3,000	LC
Lipscomb Univ	TN	35,722	VC
Loyola Marymount Univ	CA	53,240	V₵
Manhattan College	NY	44,955	VC
Mass Inst of Technology	MA	54,238	MC
Metropolitan State Univ of Denver	CO	4,835	LC
Miami Univ	OH	24,191	HC
MidAmerica Nazarene Univ	KS	28,000	C
Minn State Univ, Mankato	MN	14,900	C
Morehouse College	GA	38,640	C
New College of Florida	FL	14,504	H₵
New York Univ	NY	61,470	MC
Northeastern Illinois Univ	IL		C
Northern Kentucky Univ	KY	15,302	LC
Northwestern College	MN	24,000	C
Northwestern Univ	IL	37,595	MC
Occidental College	CA	59,592	M₵
Queens College / The CUNY	NY	17,107	VC
Rhodes College	TN	47,596	H₵
Roosevelt Univ	IL	22,605	VC
Rutgers, The State Univ of New Jersey/Camden Campus	NJ	24,254	C
Rutgers, The State Univ of New Jersey/New Brunswick	NJ	25,077	VC
St. Augustine's Univ	NC	14,000	C
St. Louis Univ	MO	46,594	V₵
St. Peter's College	NJ	44,240	C
San Diego State Univ	CA	20,578	VC
San Francisco Art Inst	CA	52,492	SP
San Francisco State Univ	CA	18,514	C
Smith College	MA	57,524	MC
Southern Nazarene Univ	OK	24,354	NC
St. Cloud State Univ	MN	10,600	C
Stanford Univ	CA	56,411	MC
Trinity Univ	TX	44,174	H₵
Tufts Univ	MA	58,780	MC
Univ of Calif at Berkeley	CA	23,322	MC
Univ of Calif at Irvine	CA	25,961	VC
Univ of Calif at San Diego	CA	21,000	VC
Univ of Cincinnati	OH	20,199	VC
Univ of Conn	CT	23,744	HC
Univ of Illinois at Chicago	IL	24,293	VC
Univ of Mich/Dearborn	MI	9,885	VC
Univ of Mich-Flint	MI	17,547	₵
Univ of Minn/Duluth	MN	18,964	₵
Univ of Minn/Twin Cities	MN		HC
Univ of Missouri-Kansas City	MO	19,603	C
Univ of New Orleans	LA	9,224	VC
Univ of Pennsylvania	PA	56,106	MC
Univ of Pittsburgh at Pittsburgh	PA	27,800	H₵
Univ of Texas at Austin	TX	44,074	HC
Univ of the District of Columbia	DC	7,244	LC
Univ of the Sacred Heart	PR	5,590	
Univ of Utah	UT	13,462	VC
Univ of Wisc/Green Bay	WI	14,900	C
Univ of Wisc/Oshkosh	WI	10,426	LC
Univ of Wisc-Milwaukee	WI	18,436	C
Vanderbilt Univ	TN	57,072	MC
Vassar College	NY	59,070	MC
Virginia Commonwealth Univ	VA	18,633	C
Virginia Polytechnic Inst and State Univ	VA	14,629	HC
Washington Univ in St. Louis	MO	58,818	MC
Wayne State Univ	MI	19,493	C
Wheaton College	IL	39,650	H₵
Worcester State Univ	MA	18,657	C
Wright State Univ	OH	16,983	C

VASCULAR SONOGRAPHY

School	ST	$IS	SR
Thomas Edison State College	NJ	5,700	SP

VETERINARY SCIENCE

School	ST	$IS	SR
Becker College	MA	41,420	LC
Fort Valley State Univ	GA	11,200	VC
Lincoln Memorial Univ	TN	18,144	C
Medaille College	NY	35,112	VC
Mercy College	NY	29,996	C
Mich State Univ	MI	13,689	VC
Mount Ida College	MA	30,115	LC
Murray State Univ	KY	14,944	C
National American Univ	SD	16,712	NC
Newberry College	SC	26,850	LC
N Dak State Univ	ND	14,642	C
Penn State Univ/Univ Park	PA	25,404	VC
Tuskegee Univ	AL	26,750	C
Univ of Arizona	AZ	20,105	C
Univ of Georgia	GA	19,508	VC
Univ of Idaho	ID	14,558	C
Univ of Maryland	MD	18,801	HC
Univ of Missouri/Columbia	MO	18,201	MC
Univ of Montana-Western	MT	9,753	LC
Univ of Nebr - Lincoln	NE	17,507	VC
Utah State Univ	UT	11,803	C
West Virginia Univ	WV	15,794	₵
Wilson College	PA	27,660	C

VICTORIAN STUDIES

School	ST	$IS	SR
Bard College	NY	59,872	HC
Vassar College	NY	59,070	MC

VIDEO

School	ST	$IS	SR
American InterContinental Univ	GA	13,500	NC
Art Inst of Atlanta	GA	24,000	SP
Bennington College	VT	56,990	H₵
Calif Inst of the Arts	CA	46,368	SP
Calvin College	MI	37,585	V₵
Cornerstone Univ and Grand Rapids Theological Seminary	MI	30,866	C
CUNY-City College	NY	19,576	H₵
Drexel Univ	PA	51,920	HC
Fairleigh Dickinson Univ/ College at Florham	NJ	42,142	C
Fitchburg State Univ	MA	17,241	C
Five Towns College	NY	34,550	SP
George Mason Univ	VA	15,724	VC
Hampshire College	MA	58,320	MC
Hofstra Univ	NY	48,020	V₵
Ithaca College	NY	52,300	HC
Lasell College	MA	42,500	LC
Madonna Univ	MI	24,540	VC
Maryland Inst College of Art	MD	39,500	SP
Minneapolis College of Art and Design	MN	36,700	SP
New Mexico State Univ	NM	13,955	LC

School	ST	$IS	SR
Ohio Univ	OH	20,676	VC
Point Park Univ	PA	36,390	C
Rochester Inst of Technology	NY	42,450	VC+
School of the Art Inst of Chicago	IL	44,000	SP
School of Visual Arts	NY	36,500	SP
Southeast Missouri State Univ	MO	14,983	LC
Southern Methodist Univ	TX	57,755	MC
Spring Arbor Univ	MI	26,740	C
Stevenson Univ	MD	39,572	C
SUNY Fredonia / The SUNY at Fredonia	NY	18,702	VC
Syracuse Univ	NY	54,512	HC
Univ of Hartford	CT	42,674	C
Univ of Mich/Ann Arbor	MI	22,102	HC+
Univ of Okla	OK	17,634	VC+
Univ of Southern Calif	CA	56,903	MC
Webster Univ	MO	33,990	C+
Wilmington Univ	DE	7,778	NC

VISUAL AND PERFORMING ARTS

School	ST	$IS	SR
Albion College	MI	43,884	VC
Alderson Broaddus Univ	WV	28,656	C
Andrews Univ	MI	28,030	C+
Anna Maria College	MA	34,600	LC
Aquinas College	MI	33,060	C
Arizona State Univ	AZ	18,818	C+
Armstrong Atlantic State Univ	GA	16,276	C
Ashford Univ	IA	21,780	C
Belmont Univ	TN	37,380	VC+
Bennett College	NC		LC
Bennington College	VT	56,990	HC+
Bethel Univ	MN	34,940	VC
Binghamton Univ / The SUNY	NY	20,832	HC+
Bowling Green State Univ	OH	18,970	C
Brigham Young Univ	UT	12,100	HC
Brown Univ	RI	56,150	MC
Bucknell Univ	PA	58,160	MC
Burlington College	VT	32,510	SP
Calif Baptist Univ	CA	35,890	C
Calif College of the Arts	CA	48,334	SP
Calif Inst of the Arts	CA	46,368	SP
Cal State, Fullerton	CA	25,188	C+
Cal State, Monterey Bay	CA	26,871	LC
Cal State, San Marcos	CA	14,576	C
Central Mich Univ	MI	18,066	C
Central Washington Univ	WA	11,730	C
Chatham Univ	PA	42,440	VC
CUNY/Brooklyn College	NY	5,884	C+
Clark Univ	MA	47,020	HC+
Columbia Univ in the City of New York	NY	61,116	MC
Columbia Univ/School of General Studies	NY	54,083	MC
Columbus State Univ	GA	13,176	C
Coppin State Univ	MD	14,905	VC
Creighton Univ	NE	44,058	VC+
Curry College	MA	47,545	LC
Dordt College	IA	34,160	VC
Dowling College	NY	25,000	LC
Duke Univ	NC	50,250	MC
East Texas Baptist Univ	TX	29,135	C
Eastern Conn State Univ	CT	20,584	C
Eastern Mich Univ	MI	17,961	C
Eckerd College	FL	43,902	VC
Erskine College	SC	37,360	C
Fairfield Univ	CT	55,850	VC
Fayetteville State Univ	NC	10,816	C
Florida Atlantic Univ	FL	17,339	C
Fordham Univ	NY	58,927	HC
George Mason Univ	VA	15,724	VC
Goddard College	VT	16,418	VC
Grambling State Univ	LA	13,384	LC
Grand View Univ	IA	31,050	C
Green Mountain College	VT	33,547	LC
Guilford College	NC	35,340	C
Haverford College	PA	59,236	MC
Hofstra Univ	NY	48,020	VC+
Indiana Univ Bloomington	IN	19,358	HC
Inter-American Univ of PR/ Bayamon Univ College	PR	4,428	
Inter-American Univ of PR/ Fajardo Campus	PR	4,200	
Inter-American Univ of PR/ Ponce	PR	3,700	
Ithaca College	NY	52,300	HC
Johnson State College	VT	16,721	C
Kean Univ	NJ	22,060	LC
Kent State Univ	OH	19,352	C
Keystone College	PA	28,680	LC
King Univ	TN	33,140	C
Kutztown Univ of Pennsylvania	PA	16,909	LC
Lander Univ	SC	22,514	C+
Lees-McRae College	NC	33,624	C
Lesley Univ	MA	46,350	C
Lipscomb Univ	TN	35,722	VC
Longwood Univ	VA	20,924	C
Loras College	IA	37,432	VC
Loyola Univ New Orleans	LA	46,581	VC
Mass College of Liberal Arts	MA	16,733	C
Millikin Univ	IL	37,462	C
Naropa Univ	CO	37,875	SP
New England Conservatory of Music	MA	52,550	SP
New Mexico State Univ	NM	13,955	LC
Notre Dame College	OH	34,942	VC
Ohio Univ	OH	20,676	VC
Oregon State Univ	OR	19,017	C+
Otterbein College	OH	32,214	C
Ouachita Baptist Univ	AR	29,010	VC
Penn State Univ/Altoona	PA	11,464	C
Penn State Univ/Univ Park	PA	25,404	VC
Point Loma Nazarene Univ	CA	38,610	VC
Presbyterian College	SC	42,678	VC
Prescott College	AZ	33,284	C+
Purchase College / SUNY	NY	16,951	C
Purdue Univ/West Lafayette	IN	20,278	HC
Ramapo College of New Jersey	NJ	24,938	C+
Regis Univ	CO	41,318	C
Rice Univ	TX	43,288	MC
Roger Williams Univ	RI	45,788	C
Rutgers, The State Univ of New Jersey/New Brunswick	NJ	25,077	VC
Rutgers, The State Univ of New Jersey/Newark Campus	NJ	25,376	C
St. Augustine's Univ	NC	14,000	C
St. Mary's College	IN	45,160	VC
St. Peter's College	NJ	44,240	C
St. Vincent College	PA	40,244	C
Sarah Lawrence College	NY	48,000	HC
Savannah State Univ	GA	13,156	C
School of the Art Inst of Chicago	IL	44,000	SP
Schreiner Univ	TX	32,734	LC
Seattle Univ	WA	47,010	VC+
Shaw Univ	NC	15,488	LC
Siena College	NY	43,863	VC
Sonoma State Univ	CA	20,541	C
Southeast Missouri State Univ	MO	14,983	LC
Southern Oregon Univ	OR	17,874	C
Spring Arbor Univ	MI	26,740	C
St. Andrews Univ	NC	32,050	LC
St. Bonaventure Univ	NY	38,831	C
St. Lawrence Univ	NY	53,740	HC
St. Mary's College of Maryland	MD	26,699	HC
SUNY College at Old Westbury	NY	16,324	C
SUNY New Paltz	NY	15,010	C
Susquehanna Univ	PA	49,170	C
Taylor Univ	IN	36,742	VC+
Temple Univ	PA	24,392	VC
Texas Tech Univ	TX	14,243	C
The Lincoln Univ	PA	15,154	LC
The SUNY at Potsdam	NY	17,754	C
Univ of Alaska Anchorage	AK	15,290	NC
Univ of Arkansas at Little Rock	AR		C
Univ of Calif at Riverside	CA	27,204	C
Univ of Calif at San Diego	CA	21,000	VC
Univ of Chicago	IL	55,416	MC
Univ of Colo Denver	CO	17,904	C
Univ of Conn	CT	23,744	HC
Univ of Florida	FL	15,783	HC+
Univ of Hartford	CT	42,674	C
Univ of Illinois at Chicago	IL	24,293	VC
Univ of Maine at Farmington	ME	17,841	C
Univ of Maryland/Baltimore County	MD	18,000	VC
Univ of Montana-Western	MT	9,753	LC
Univ of New Haven	CT	47,740	C
Univ of N Dak	ND	14,094	C
Univ of North Texas	TX	15,628	C
Univ of Northern Colo	CO	15,973	C
Univ of Pennsylvania	PA	56,106	MC
Univ of San Diego	CA	53,302	HC+
Univ of San Francisco	CA	49,674	VC
Univ of Southern Calif	CA	56,903	MC
Univ of St. Francis	IL	36,490	C
Univ of Texas at Austin	TX	44,074	HC
Univ of Texas at Dallas	TX	21,046	HC
Univ of the Sacred Heart	PR	5,590	
Univ of Utah	UT	13,462	VC
Univ of Wisc/Platteville	WI	14,274	C
Univ of Wisc/Superior	WI	14,106	C
Virginia State Univ	VA	11,318	C+
Wagner College	NY	48,600	VC
Washington Univ in St. Louis	MO	58,818	MC
Wells College	NY	38,680	VC
West Chester Univ of Pennsylvania	PA	16,836	C
West Virginia Univ	WV	15,794	C+
Western Kentucky Univ	KY	11,000	LC
Western Washington Univ	WA	18,519	VC
Wichita State Univ	KS	12,539	C
Worcester State Univ	MA	18,657	C

VISUAL DESIGN

School	ST	$IS	SR
Art Academy of Cincinnati	OH	25,940	SP
Calif Inst of the Arts	CA	46,368	SP
Cal State, Fullerton	CA	25,188	C+
Cazenovia College	NY	30,800	C
Drury Univ	MO	30,319	VC
Eastern New Mexico Univ	NM	10,682	C
Farmingdale State College	NY	18,985	C
Indiana Univ-Purdue Univ Fort Wayne	IN	15,425	C
Kent State Univ	OH	19,352	C
Loyola Univ Chicago	IL	49,560	VC+
Nazareth College of Rochester	NY	41,590	VC
San Francisco State Univ	CA	18,514	C
Stevenson Univ	MD	39,572	C
Ohio State Univ	OH	19,887	MC
Truman State Univ	MO	13,546	HC
Univ of Dayton	OH	43,750	VC
Univ of Delaware	DE	22,728	VC
Univ of Mary Hardin-Baylor	TX	31,950	C+
Univ of Mass Dartmouth	MA	22,223	C
Univ of New Haven	CT	47,740	C

VISUAL EFFECTS

School	ST	$IS	SR
Academy of Art Univ	CA		
Otis College of Art and Design	CA	35,404	SP
Savannah College of Art and Design	GA	46,824	SP
School of Visual Arts	NY	36,500	SP

VITICULTURE AND ENOLOGY

School	ST	$IS	SR
Cornell Univ	NY	59,037	MC

VOCAL MUSIC EDUCATION

School	ST	$IS	SR
Calvin College	MI	37,585	VC+
Concordia Univ St. Paul	MN	27,200	C
Dordt College	IA	34,160	VC
Houghton College	NY	35,740	VC
Texas Christian Univ	TX	47,570	HC
Webster Univ	MO	33,990	C+
Youngstown State Univ	OH	16,374	LC

VOCAL PERFORMANCE

School	ST	$IS	SR
Dallas Baptist Univ	TX	29,118	C
Houghton College	NY	35,740	VC
New York Univ	NY	61,470	MC
Okla City Univ	OK	33,546	VC
Texas Christian Univ	TX	47,570	HC
Univ of Miami	FL	55,166	MC
Webster Univ	MO	33,990	C+
Wright State Univ	OH	16,983	C
Youngstown State Univ	OH	16,374	LC

VOCATIONAL EDUCATION

School	ST	$IS	SR
Auburn Univ	AL	20,052	VC+
Cal State, Los Angeles	CA	15,829	C
Cal State, San Bernardino	CA	12,000	C
Central Conn State Univ	CT	19,212	C
Chicago State Univ	IL	5,482	C
College of the Ozarks	MO	5,605	VC
Fitchburg State Univ	MA	17,241	C
Indiana Univ of Pennsylvania	PA	20,180	LC
Martin Univ	IN	11,000	SP
New York City College of Technology / The CUNY	NY	5,769	NC
N Car State Univ	NC	16,202	HC
Okla State Univ	OK	14,310	VC
Oswego / SUNY	NY	20,009	VC
Pittsburg State Univ	KS	12,032	C
San Diego State Univ	CA	20,578	VC
S Dak State Univ	SD	14,296	C
Southern Illinois Univ Carbondale	IL	21,620	C
Univ of Illinois at Urbana-Champaign	IL	24,300	HC
Univ of Toledo	OH	18,464	C
Univ of Wisc/Stout	WI	23,942	C
Valley City State Univ	ND	12,286	LC
Wayland Baptist Univ	TX	16,058	LC
Western Kentucky Univ	KY	11,000	LC
Western New Mexico Univ	NM	8,500	LC
Youngstown State Univ	OH	16,374	LC

VOICE

School	ST	$IS	SR
Baldwin Wallace Univ	OH	36,980	VC
Bennington College	VT	56,990	HC+
Butler Univ	IN	45,898	VC+
Calif Baptist Univ	CA	35,890	C
Calvin College	MI	37,585	VC+
Campbellsville Univ	KY	27,720	C
Central Mich Univ	MI	18,066	C
Central Washington Univ	WA	11,730	C
East Central Univ	OK	10,223	LC
East Texas Baptist Univ	TX	29,135	C
Eastern Mich Univ	MI	17,961	C
Florida State Univ	FL	15,238	HC
Hardin-Simmons Univ	TX	23,560	C+
Houghton College	NY	35,740	VC
Illinois Wesleyan Univ	IL	48,452	VC+
Indiana Univ Bloomington	IN	19,358	HC
Indiana Univ South Bend	IN	15,293	C
Indiana Univ-Purdue Univ Fort Wayne	IN	15,425	C
Loyola Univ New Orleans	LA	46,581	VC
Manhattan School of Music	NY	55,850	SP
Mannes College New School for Music	NY	44,500	C
Marshall Univ	WV	14,820	C
Millikin Univ	IL	37,462	C
Miss College	MS	21,998	VC
Mount Aloysius College	PA	27,970	C
New York Univ	NY	61,470	MC
Northwestern College	MN	24,000	C
Northwestern Univ	IL	37,595	MC
Nyack College	NY	32,000	C
Ohio Univ	OH	20,676	VC
Ouachita Baptist Univ	AR	29,010	VC
Pacific Lutheran Univ	WA	44,840	VC
Palm Beach Atlantic Univ	FL	33,882	LC
Point Loma Nazarene Univ	CA	38,610	VC
Rider Univ	NJ	45,720	C
Roosevelt Univ	IL	22,605	VC
Samford Univ	AL	35,700	VC+
San Francisco Conservatory of Music	CA	53,923	SP
Shorter Univ	GA	26,470	C
Stetson Univ	FL	49,512	VC+
Syracuse Univ	NY	54,512	HC
The Catholic Univ of America	DC	52,852	VC
Union Univ	TN	28,260	VC
Univ of Cincinnati	OH	20,199	VC
Univ of Illinois at Urbana-Champaign	IL	24,300	HC
Univ of Iowa	IA	17,481	VC
Univ of Kansas	KS	16,980	C+
Univ of Mobile	AL	27,870	VC
Univ of New Hampshire	NH	24,702	VC
Univ of Tulsa	OK	45,311	HC+
Valparaiso Univ	IN	43,040	VC+
Webster Univ	MO	33,990	C+
West Chester Univ of Pennsylvania	PA	16,836	C
Westminster Choir College	NJ	36,000	SP
York College	NE	19,475	C
Youngstown State Univ	OH	16,374	LC

WATER AND WASTEWATER TECHNOLOGY

School	ST	$IS	SR
Texas State Univ	TX	16,495	VC
Wright State Univ	OH	16,983	C

WATER RESOURCES

School	ST	$IS	SR
Central State Univ	OH	9,010	C
Colo State Univ-Fort Collins	CO	20,090	VC
Heidelberg Univ	OH	34,100	C
N Dak State Univ	ND	14,642	C
Northern Mich Univ	MI	15,300	VC
Prescott College	AZ	33,284	C+
SUNY Oneonta / SUNY	NY	16,919	VC
Tarleton State Univ	TX	13,489	LC
Texas A&M Univ at Galveston	TX	11,258	C
The College at Brockport / SUNY	NY	18,362	VC
Univ of Georgia	GA	19,508	VC
Univ of Nebr - Lincoln	NE	17,507	VC
Univ of New Hampshire	NH	24,702	VC

WEB SERVICES

School	ST	$IS	SR
Champlain College	VT	44,850	VC
Idaho State Univ	ID	11,908	C
Indiana Inst of Technology	IN	34,240	LC
Johnson and Wales Univ/ Providence Campus	RI	34,668	C
Limestone College	SC	29,880	C
Lipscomb Univ	TN	35,722	VC
Mercyhurst Univ	PA	40,700	C
Roger Williams Univ	RI	45,788	C
Southern Adventist Univ	TN	26,190	C
Taylor Univ	IN	36,742	VC+
Thiel College	PA	31,378	LC
Univ of Wisc/Stevens Point	WI	14,043	C
Univ of Wisc-Milwaukee	WI	18,436	C

WEB TECHNOLOGY

School	ST	$IS	SR
Belmont Univ	TN	37,380	VC+
Cogswell Polytechnical College	CA	30,531	C
Davenport Univ	MI	21,002	LC
Drexel Univ	PA	51,920	HC
Illinois Inst of Technology	IL	38,512	HC+
Lasell College	MA	42,500	LC
Limestone College	SC	29,880	C
Mercyhurst Univ	PA	40,700	C
Mount Aloysius College	PA	27,970	C
Pennsylvania College of Technology	PA	25,653	NC

School	ST	$IS	SR
Quinnipiac Univ	CT	53,580	VC
Roger Williams Univ	RI	45,788	C
Tenn Tech Univ	TN	11,310	C
Univ of St. Francis	IL	36,490	C

WELDING ENGINEERING

School	ST	$IS	SR
Ferris State Univ	MI	19,698	C
Idaho State Univ	ID	11,908	C
LeTourneau Univ	TX	26,230	C
Pennsylvania College of Technology	PA	25,653	NC
Ohio State Univ	OH	19,887	MC

WESTERN CIVILIZATION/ CULTURE

School	ST	$IS	SR
St. John's College-Annapolis	MD	53,590	HC
Univ of Montana-Western	MT	9,753	LC

WESTERN EUROPEAN STUDIES

School	ST	$IS	SR
Denison Univ	OH	54,670	HC+
St. John's College-Annapolis	MD	53,590	HC
Univ of Mich/Ann Arbor	MI	22,102	HC+
Washington Univ in St. Louis	MO	58,818	MC

WILDLIFE BIOLOGY

School	ST	$IS	SR
Adams State College	CO	13,358	LC
Auburn Univ	AL	20,052	VC+
Colo State Univ-Fort Collins	CO	20,090	VC
Friends Univ	KS	29,100	C
Humboldt State Univ	CA	18,400	C
Kansas State Univ	KS	15,497	VC
Lees-McRae College	NC	33,624	C
New Mexico State Univ	NM	13,955	LC
Ohio Univ	OH	20,676	VC
Oregon State Univ	OR	19,017	C+
Pittsburg State Univ	KS	12,032	C
Prescott College	AZ	33,284	C+
Purdue Univ/West Lafayette	IN	20,278	HC
S Dak State Univ	SD	14,296	C
SUNY / College of Environmental Science and Forestry	NY	18,351	HC
Tarleton State Univ	TX	13,489	LC
Texas State Univ	TX	16,495	VC
Unity College	ME	34,054	C
Univ of Alaska Fairbanks	AK	13,955	C
Univ of Calif at Davis	CA	24,482	HC
Univ of Florida	FL	15,783	HC+
Univ of Illinois at Urbana-Champaign	IL	24,300	HC
Univ of Minn/Twin Cities	MN		HC
Univ of Montana	MT	13,670	C
Univ of Montana-Western	MT	9,753	LC
Univ of Tenn at Knoxville	TN	20,364	VC+
Univ of Vermont	VT	26,120	VC+
Univ of Wisc/Madison	WI	18,757	HC
Univ of Wisc/Stevens Point	WI	14,043	C
Univ of Wyoming	WY	13,855	C+
Washington State Univ	WA	20,461	C
West Texas A&M Univ	TX	13,478	C

WILDLIFE MANAGEMENT

School	ST	$IS	SR
Arkansas State Univ	AR	14,980	C
Brigham Young Univ	UT	12,100	HC
Dakota Wesleyan Univ	SD	23,000	C
Delaware Valley College	PA	29,944	C
Eastern Kentucky Univ	KY	11,161	C
Eastern New Mexico Univ	NM	10,682	C
Frostburg State Univ	MD	15,264	LC
Kansas State Univ	KS	15,497	VC
Lake Superior State Univ	MI	18,121	C
Lincoln Memorial Univ	TN	18,144	C
Louisiana Tech Univ	LA	8,000	C
Mich State Univ	MI	13,689	VC
Mich Tech Univ	MI	22,105	VC
Missouri State Univ	MO	13,996	VC
Mountain State Univ	WV	14,330	NC
Murray State Univ	KY	14,944	C
Northwest Missouri State Univ	MO	14,229	C
Oregon State Univ	OR	19,017	C+
Peru State College	NE	8,600	NC
Prescott College	AZ	33,284	C+
Providence College	RI	55,995	HC
Stephen F. Austin State Univ	TX	14,668	C
Sul Ross State Univ	TX	13,410	LC
Tenn Tech Univ	TN	11,310	C
Texas A&M Univ at Commerce	TX	10,496	C
Texas Tech Univ	TX	14,243	C
The SUNY College of Agriculture and Tech at Cobleskill	NY	18,869	VC
Unity College	ME	34,054	C
Univ of Arkansas at Monticello	AR	8,470	NC
Univ of Delaware	DE	22,728	VC
Univ of Idaho	ID	14,558	C
Univ of Illinois at Urbana-Champaign	IL	24,300	HC
Univ of Maine	ME	19,712	C+
Univ of Nebr - Lincoln	NE	17,507	VC
Univ of New Hampshire	NH	24,702	VC
Univ of PR/Humacao	PR	1,877	
Utah State Univ	UT	11,803	C
Washington State Univ	WA	20,461	C

WINDS

School	ST	$IS	SR
Eastern Mich Univ	MI	17,961	C
Florida State Univ	FL	15,238	HC
Mannes College New School for Music	NY	44,500	C
Miss College	MS	21,998	VC
Northwestern Univ	IL	37,595	MC
Roosevelt Univ	IL	22,605	VC
San Francisco Conservatory of Music	CA	53,923	SP
Stetson Univ	FL	49,512	VC+
Syracuse Univ	NY	54,512	HC
Univ of Kansas	KS	16,980	C+
Univ of Mich/Ann Arbor	MI	22,102	HC+
Wright State Univ	OH	16,983	C
Youngstown State Univ	OH	16,374	LC

WINE AND VITICULTURE

School	ST	$IS	SR
Calif Polytechnic State Univ	CA	19,847	HC

WOMEN & GENDER STUDIES

School	ST	$IS	SR
Amherst College	MA	58,744	MC
Bates College	ME	58,950	MC
Cal State, Chico	CA	18,952	C
College of Staten Island / The CUNY	NY	16,778	NC
Duquesne Univ	PA	42,017	VC
Eastern Conn State Univ	CT	20,584	C
Goddard College	VT	16,418	VC
Illinois Wesleyan Univ	IL	48,452	VC+
Indiana Univ South Bend	IN	15,293	C
Keene State College	NH	21,538	C
Kenyon College	OH	56,810	MC
Lycoming College	PA	43,636	C
Mills College	CA	54,119	HC
New Jersey City Univ	NJ	21,060	C+
N Dak State Univ	ND	14,642	C
Northern Arizona Univ	AZ	18,592	C
Oswego / SUNY	NY	20,009	VC
Pace Univ	NY	48,094	VC
Seattle Univ	WA	47,010	VC+
Southern Oregon Univ	OR	17,874	C
Syracuse Univ	NY	54,512	HC
The College of St. Rose	NY	26,750	C
Univ of Colo Boulder	CO	22,605	VC+
Univ of Illinois at Chicago	IL	24,293	VC
Univ of Mass Dartmouth	MA	22,223	C
Univ of Nebr - Lincoln	NE	17,507	VC
Univ of Tulsa	OK	45,311	HC+
Univ of Wyoming	WY	13,855	C+
Winona State Univ	MN	16,530	C

WOMEN'S STUDIES

School	ST	$IS	SR
Agnes Scott College	GA	45,323	VC+
Albion College	MI	43,884	VC
Albright College	PA	46,660	C
Allegheny College	PA	49,020	HC
Alverno College	WI	30,483	LC
American Univ	DC	54,829	HC+
Appalachian State Univ	NC	12,919	VC
Arizona State Univ	AZ	18,818	C+
Augsburg College	MN	35,142	C
Augustana College	IL	43,398	HC
Ball State Univ	IN	17,850	C
Beloit College	WI	49,970	HC
Bennington College	VT	56,990	HC+
Berea College	KY	7,220	HC
Bowdoin College	ME	57,834	MC
Bowling Green State Univ	OH	18,970	C
Brandeis Univ	MA	58,820	HC
Bucknell Univ	PA	58,160	MC
Cal State, Fresno	CA	17,405	C
Cal State, Fullerton	CA	25,188	C+
Cal State, Long Beach	CA	17,534	C+
Cal State, Northridge	CA	28,313	C
Cal State, San Marcos	CA	14,576	C
Canisius College	NY	45,602	VC
Carleton College	MN	58,149	MC
Case Western Reserve Univ	OH	55,178	MC
Central Mich Univ	MI	18,066	C
Chatham Univ	PA	42,440	VC
CUNY/Brooklyn College	NY	5,884	C+
Clark Univ	MA	47,020	HC+
Cleveland State Univ	OH	21,357	C
Coe College	IA	43,590	VC
Colby College	ME	57,510	MC
Colgate Univ	NY	50,930	MC
College of Charleston	SC	21,273	VC
College of New Jersey	NJ	25,376	HC
College of William & Mary	VA	25,085	MC
College of Wooster	OH	52,600	VC
Colo College	CO	54,534	MC
Columbia Univ in the City of New York	NY	61,116	MC
Columbia Univ/Barnard College	NY	39,000	MC
Columbia Univ/School of General Studies	NY	54,083	MC
Cornell College	IA	44,930	HC
Dartmouth College	NH	57,996	MC
Denison Univ	OH	54,670	HC+
DePaul Univ	IL	46,120	VC
DePauw Univ	IN	48,950	VC+
Dickinson College	PA	57,662	HC+
Dominican Univ	IL	37,628	C
Dominican Univ of Calif	CA	51,250	C
Drew Univ/College of Liberal Arts	NJ	55,862	VC
Duke Univ	NC	50,250	MC
Earlham College	IN	49,710	VC+
East Carolina Univ	NC	14,169	C
Eastern Mich Univ	MI	17,961	C
Eckerd College	FL	43,902	VC
Emory Univ	GA	45,000	MC
Florida International Univ	FL	17,747	VC
Florida State Univ	FL	15,238	HC
Fordham Univ	NY	58,927	HC
Georgia State Univ	GA	12,000	VC
Gettysburg College	PA	56,820	HC
Goucher College	MD	50,252	VC+
Grinnell College	IA	53,654	HC
Guilford College	NC	35,340	C
Gustavus Adolphus College	MN	48,170	HC
Hamilton College	NY	55,620	MC
Hamline Univ	MN	44,198	VC
Hampshire College	MA	58,320	MC
Harvard Univ/Harvard College	MA	49,000	MC
Hobart and William Smith Colleges	NY	43,000	VC
Hofstra Univ	NY	48,020	VC+
Howard Univ	DC	35,957	C
Hunter College / The CUNY	NY	14,429	VC
Indiana Univ-Purdue Univ Fort Wayne	IN	15,425	C
John Carroll Univ	OH	44,520	C+
Kansas State Univ	KS	15,497	VC
Knox College	IL		VC
Lehigh Univ	PA	55,080	MC
Loyola Marymount Univ	CA	53,240	VC+
Loyola Univ Chicago	IL	49,560	VC+
Luther College	IA	44,380	VC+
Macalester College	MN	53,419	MC
Marshall Univ	WV	14,820	C
Mercer Univ	GA	44,201	VC+
Metropolitan State Univ	MN	5,923	SP
Miami Univ	OH	24,191	HC
Mich State Univ	MI	13,689	VC
Middlebury College	VT	57,470	MC
Minn State Univ, Mankato	MN	14,900	C
Minn State Univ, Moorhead	MN	13,392	C
Montclair State Univ	NJ	22,614	C
Mount Aloysius College	PA	27,970	C
Nazareth College of Rochester	NY	41,590	VC
Nebr Wesleyan Univ	NE	29,774	C+
New England College	NH	45,930	LC
New Mexico State Univ	NM	13,955	LC
Northeastern Illinois Univ	IL		C
Oakland Univ	MI	19,391	VC
Oberlin College	OH	57,025	MC
Ohio Univ	OH	20,676	VC
Ohio Wesleyan Univ	OH	49,460	C+
Old Dominion Univ	VA	18,662	C
Oregon State Univ	OR	19,017	C+
Oswego / SUNY	NY	20,009	VC
Pace Univ	NY	48,094	VC
Pacific Lutheran Univ	WA	44,840	VC
Penn State Univ/Univ Park	PA	25,404	VC
Pitzer College	CA	54,988	MC
Pomona College	CA	57,680	MC
Portland State Univ	OR	18,672	C
Prescott College	AZ	33,284	C+
Providence College	RI	55,995	HC
Purchase College / SUNY	NY	16,951	C
Purdue Univ/West Lafayette	IN	20,278	HC
Queens College / The CUNY	NY	17,107	VC
Randolph-Macon College	VA	45,086	C
Regis Univ	CO	41,318	C
Rhode Island College	RI	17,132	LC
Rice Univ	TX	43,288	MC
Roosevelt Univ	IL	22,605	VC
Rosemont College	PA	42,350	C
Rutgers, The State Univ of New Jersey/New Brunswick	NJ	25,077	VC
Rutgers, The State Univ of New Jersey/Newark Campus	NJ	25,376	C
Sacred Heart Univ	CT	48,564	VC
St. Joseph College	CT	45,630	LC
St. Louis Univ	MO	46,594	VC+
San Diego State Univ	CA	20,578	VC
San Francisco State Univ	CA	18,514	C
Santa Clara Univ	CA	54,702	MC
Sarah Lawrence College	NY	48,000	HC
Scripps College	CA	54,900	MC
Simmons College	MA	48,770	VC
Smith College	MA	57,524	MC
Sonoma State Univ	CA	20,541	C
Southwestern Univ	TX	45,660	VC
Spelman College	GA	24,650	VC
St. Bonaventure Univ	NY	38,831	C
St. Catherine Univ	MN	37,782	C+
St. Olaf College	MN	49,960	HC+
Stanford Univ	CA	56,411	MC
Stony Brook Univ / SUNY	NY	19,359	HC
Suffolk Univ	MA	46,548	C
SUNY Fredonia / The SUNY at Fredonia	NY	18,702	VC
SUNY New Paltz	NY	15,010	C
SUNY Plattsburgh / SUNY	NY	18,083	VC
Temple Univ	PA	24,392	VC
The College at Brockport / SUNY	NY	18,362	VC
The College of New Rochelle	NY	33,600	VC
Ohio State Univ	OH	19,887	MC
The SUNY at Potsdam	NY	17,754	C
Towson Univ	MD	16,000	VC
Trinity College	CT		HC+
Tufts Univ	MA	58,780	MC
Tulane Univ	LA	58,942	MC
Union College	NY		MC
Univ at Albany / SUNY	NY	18,674	VC
Univ at Buffalo / The SUNY	NY	20,283	VC
Univ of Arizona	AZ	20,105	C
Univ of Calif at Berkeley	CA	23,322	MC
Univ of Calif at Davis	CA	24,482	HC
Univ of Calif at Irvine	CA	25,961	VC
Univ of Calif at Los Angeles	CA	25,686	MC
Univ of Calif at Riverside	CA	27,204	C
Univ of Calif at Santa Barbara	CA	27,551	HC
Univ of Calif at Santa Cruz	CA	27,807	VC
Univ of Conn	CT	23,744	HC
Univ of Dayton	OH	43,750	VC
Univ of Delaware	DE	22,728	VC
Univ of Denver	CO	51,787	VC+
Univ of Georgia	GA	19,508	VC
Univ of Hawaii at Manoa	HI	19,379	VC
Univ of Illinois at Urbana-Champaign	IL	24,300	HC
Univ of Iowa	IA	17,481	VC
Univ of Kansas	KS	16,980	C+
Univ of Louisville	KY	17,460	VC
Univ of Maine	ME	19,712	C+
Univ of Maryland	MD	18,801	HC
Univ of Maryland/Baltimore County	MD	18,000	VC
Univ of Mass Amherst	MA	23,697	VC+
Univ of Mass Boston	MA	11,966	C
Univ of Miami	FL	55,166	MC
Univ of Mich/Ann Arbor	MI	22,102	HC+
Univ of Mich/Dearborn	MI	9,885	VC
Univ of Minn/Duluth	MN	18,964	C+
Univ of Minn/Morris	MN	17,150	VC
Univ of Minn/Twin Cities	MN		HC
Univ of Montana	MT	13,670	C
Univ of Montana-Western	MT	9,753	LC
Univ of Nebr at Omaha	NE	12,700	C
Univ of Nevada, Las Vegas	NV	17,303	C
Univ of New Hampshire	NH	24,702	VC
Univ of New Mexico	NM	15,300	C
Univ of N Car at Asheville	NC	13,500	VC+
Univ of N Car at Chapel Hill	NC	18,348	MC
Univ of N Car at Greensboro	NC	12,848	C
Univ of Okla	OK	17,634	VC+
Univ of Oregon	OR	20,872	VC
Univ of Pennsylvania	PA	56,106	MC
Univ of Rochester	NY	58,500	MC
Univ of Scranton	PA	51,940	VC
Univ of S Car at Columbia	SC	19,725	VC+
Univ of Southern Calif	CA	56,903	MC
Univ of Southern Maine	ME	16,576	C
Univ of Texas at San Antonio	TX	18,372	C
Univ of Toledo	OH	18,464	C
Univ of Utah	UT	13,462	VC
Univ of Washington	WA	14,722	VC
Univ of Wisc Whitewater	WI	13,314	C
Univ of Wisc/Eau Claire	WI	15,430	VC
Univ of Wisc/Green Bay	WI	14,900	C
Univ of Wisc/Madison	WI	18,757	HC
Univ of Wisc-Milwaukee	WI	18,436	C
Vassar College	NY	59,070	MC
Virginia Wesleyan College	VA	28,433	LC
Warren Wilson College	NC	34,888	VC
Washington State Univ	WA	20,461	C
Washington Univ in St. Louis	MO	58,818	MC
Wayne State Univ	MI	19,493	C
Webster Univ	MO	33,990	C+
Wellesley College	MA	49,848	MC
Wells College	NY	38,680	VC
West Chester Univ of Pennsylvania	PA	16,836	C

School	ST	$IS	SR
Western Illinois Univ	IL	20,130	C
Western Mich Univ	MI	19,042	C
Wheaton College	MA	54,934	H₵
Whitworth Univ	WA	45,826	V₵
Wichita State Univ	KS	12,539	C
Widener Univ	PA	50,368	C
Willamette Univ	OR	56,450	V₵
Williams College	MA	58,900	MC
Yale Univ	CT	55,300	MC

WOOD SCIENCE

School	ST	$IS	SR
N Car State Univ	NC	16,202	HC
Oregon State Univ	OR	19,017	₵
Pittsburg State Univ	KS	12,032	C
Purdue Univ/West Lafayette	IN	20,278	HC
SUNY / College of Environmental Science and Forestry	NY	18,351	HC
Univ of Maine	ME	19,712	₵
Univ of Mass Amherst	MA	23,697	V₵

WOODWORKING

School	ST	$IS	SR
Burlington College	VT	32,510	SP
Kendall College of Art and Design of Ferris State Univ	MI	21,048	SP
Pittsburg State Univ	KS	12,032	C
Rochester Inst of Technology	NY	42,450	V₵
SUNY New Paltz	NY	15,010	C
Univ of Rio Grande	OH	8,750	NC

WRITING

School	ST	$IS	SR
Calif College of the Arts	CA	48,334	SP
Calvin College	MI	37,585	V₵
Catawba College	NC	37,105	C
Coe College	IA	43,590	VC
Fontbonne Univ	MO	31,384	C
Georgia Southern Univ	GA	16,414	C
Houghton College	NY	35,740	VC
New York Univ	NY	61,470	MC
Savannah College of Art and Design	GA	46,824	SP
Syracuse Univ	NY	54,512	HC
Taylor Univ	IN	36,742	V₵
Texas Christian Univ	TX	47,570	HC
Univ of Wisc/Superior	WI	14,106	C

YIDDISH

School	ST	$IS	SR
Thomas Edison State College	NJ	5,700	SP

YOUTH MINISTRY

School	ST	$IS	SR
Andrews Univ	MI	28,030	₵
Asbury Univ	KY	32,038	VC
Benedictine College	KS	29,180	VC
Bethel College	IN	31,560	C
Bethel Univ	MN	34,940	VC
Bluffton Univ	OH	37,864	C
Cairn Univ	PA	31,255	C
Campbellsville Univ	KY	27,720	C
Cedarville Univ	OH	31,036	V₵
Charleston Southern Univ	SC	22,420	C
Colo Christian Univ	CO	27,500	VC
Concordia Univ	OR	34,930	C
Corban Univ	OR	34,764	C
Cornerstone Univ and Grand Rapids Theological Seminary	MI	30,866	C
Dordt College	IA	34,160	VC
East Texas Baptist Univ	TX	29,135	C
Eastern Univ	PA	37,704	C
Florida Southern College	FL	38,240	VC
Gordon College	MA	42,660	V₵
Goshen College	IN	35,900	VC
Grace Bible College	MI	20,770	C
Grace College and Theological Seminary	IN	28,800	C
Greenville College	IL	27,012	C
Harding Univ	AR	21,432	₵
Hardin-Simmons Univ	TX	23,560	₵
Hope International Univ	CA	34,650	C
Huntingdon College	AL	31,850	C
Huntington Univ	IN	32,220	C
John Brown Univ	AR	30,996	V₵
Judson Univ	IL	25,130	C
Kentucky Christian Univ	KY	17,622	LC
King Univ	TN	33,140	C
Lee Univ	TN	18,690	₵
Lenoir-Rhyne College	NC	35,984	C
Lipscomb Univ	TN	35,722	VC
Lubbock Christian Univ	TX	25,518	C
MacMurray College	IL	20,755	C
Malone Univ	OH	34,334	C
MidAmerica Nazarene Univ	KS	28,000	C
Mount Vernon Nazarene Univ	OH	29,590	C
North Park Univ	IL	30,130	C
Northwest Nazarene Univ	ID	24,275	NC
Northwest Univ	WA	18,854	C
Northwestern College	MN	24,000	C
Northwestern College of Iowa	IA	34,848	₵
Nyack College	NY	32,000	C
Ohio Northern Univ	OH	42,075	VC
Okla Christian Univ	OK	24,975	VC
Okla Wesleyan Univ	OK	21,300	C
Olivet Nazarene Univ	IL	29,990	C
Ouachita Baptist Univ	AR	29,010	VC
Rochester College	MI	18,320	C
St. Mary's Univ of Minn	MN	37,015	C
Simpson Univ	CA	28,900	C
Southern Nazarene Univ	OK	24,354	NC
Spring Arbor Univ	MI	26,740	C
Toccoa Falls College	GA	23,210	C
Trinity International Univ	IL	31,070	C
Union Univ	TN	28,260	VC
Univ of Indianapolis	IN	31,740	LC
Vanguard Univ of Southern Calif	CA	35,833	VC
Victory Univ	TN	19,118	C
York College	NE	19,475	C

ZOOLOGY

School	ST	$IS	SR
Alabama A&M Univ	AL	96,100	C
Andrews Univ	MI	28,030	₵
Auburn Univ	AL	20,052	V₵
Bennington College	VT	56,990	H₵
Cal State, Long Beach	CA	17,534	₵
Canisius College	NY	45,602	VC
Colo State Univ-Fort Collins	CO	20,090	VC
Delaware Valley College	PA	29,944	C
Florida State Univ	FL	15,238	HC
Fort Valley State Univ	GA	11,200	VC
Friends Univ	KS	29,100	C
Humboldt State Univ	CA	18,400	C
Idaho State Univ	ID	11,908	C
Kent State Univ	OH	19,352	C
Kentucky Wesleyan College	KY	27,440	V₵
Malone Univ	OH	34,334	C
Mars Hill College	NC	22,950	LC
Miami Univ	OH	24,191	HC
Mich State Univ	MI	13,689	VC
N Car State Univ	NC	16,202	HC
N Dak State Univ	ND	14,642	C
Northern Mich Univ	MI	15,300	VC
Northwest Missouri State Univ	MO	14,229	C
Ohio Univ	OH	20,676	VC
Ohio Wesleyan Univ	OH	49,460	₵
Okla State Univ	OK	14,310	VC
Olivet Nazarene Univ	IL	29,990	C
Oregon State Univ	OR	19,017	₵
Oswego / SUNY	NY	20,009	VC
Rutgers, The State Univ of New Jersey/Newark Campus	NJ	25,376	C
San Diego State Univ	CA	20,578	VC
San Francisco State Univ	CA	18,514	C
San Jose State Univ	CA	19,707	C
Southern Illinois Univ Carbondale	IL	21,620	C
Texas A&M Univ	TX	16,956	V₵
Texas State Univ	TX	16,495	VC
Texas Tech Univ	TX	14,243	C
Ohio State Univ	OH	19,887	MC
Univ of Calif at Davis	CA	24,482	HC
Univ of Calif at Santa Barbara	CA	27,551	HC
Univ of Florida	FL	15,783	H₵
Univ of Hawaii at Manoa	HI	19,379	VC
Univ of Kentucky	KY	19,868	C
Univ of Maine	ME	19,712	₵
Univ of Montana	MT	13,670	C
Univ of New Hampshire	NH	24,702	VC
Univ of Okla	OK	17,634	V₵
Univ of Vermont	VT	26,120	V₵
Univ of Washington	WA	14,722	VC
Univ of Wisc/Madison	WI	18,757	HC
Univ of Wyoming	WY	13,855	₵
Washington State Univ	WA	20,461	C
Western New Mexico Univ	NM	8,500	LC

ST = STATE **$IS** = IN-STATE COSTS **SR** = SELECTOR RATING

PART IV

A CLOSE LOOK AT THE COLLEGES

This section will help you understand the college Profiles that are at the heart of this directory, so you can get the most out of them.

The College Admissions Selector explains Barron's unique system of comparing every school's degree of admissions competitiveness. Colleges are rated from Most Competitive to Less Competitive, and more.

Explanations of the ratings are followed by an in-depth look at the college capsule and essay.

Next comes the Profiles—some 1700 four-year accredited colleges and universities in the United States—followed by encapsulated descriptions of about fifty religious schools. Universities outside the boundaries of this country are profiled here, too, including Canadian, European, an more.

COLLEGE ADMISSIONS SELECTOR

This index groups all the colleges listed in this book according to degree of admissions competitiveness. The *Selector* is not a rating of colleges by academic standards or quality of education; it is rather an attempt to describe, in general terms, the situation a prospective student will meet when applying for admission.

THE CRITERIA USED

The factors used in determining the category for each college were: median entrance examination scores for the 2013–2014 freshman class (the SAT score used was derived by averaging the median critical reading, math, and writing scores; the ACT score used was the median composite score); percentages of 2013–2014 freshmen scoring 500 and above and 600 and above on the critical reading, math, and writing sections of the SAT; percentages of 2013–2014 freshmen scoring 21 and above and 27 and above on the ACT; percentage of 2013–2014 freshmen who ranked in the upper fifth and the upper two-fifths of their high school graduating classes; minimum class rank and grade point average required for admission (if any); and percentage of applicants to the 2013–2014 freshman class who were accepted. The *Selector* cannot and does not take into account all the other factors that each college considers when making admissions decisions. Colleges place varying degrees of emphasis on the factors that comprise each of these categories.

USING THE SELECTOR

To use the *Selector* effectively, the prospective student's records should be compared realistically with the freshmen enrolled by the colleges in each category, as shown by the SAT or ACT scores, the quality of high school record emphasized by the colleges in each category, and the kinds of risks that the applicant wishes to take.

The student should also be aware of what importance a particular school places on various nonacademic factors; when available, this information is presented in the profile of the school. If a student has unusual qualifications that may compensate for exam scores or high school record, the student should examine admissions policies of the colleges in the next higher category than the one that encompasses his or her score and consider those colleges that give major consideration to factors other than exam scores and high school grades. The "safety" college should usually be chosen from the next lower category, where the student can be reasonably sure that his or her scores and high school record will fall above the median scores and records of the freshmen enrolled in the college.

The listing within each category is alphabetical and not in any qualitative order. State-supported institutions have been classified according to the requirements for state residents, but standards for admission of out-of-state students are usually higher. Colleges that are experimenting with the admission of students of higher potential but lower achievement may appear in a less competitive category because of this fact.

A WORD OF CAUTION

The *Selector* is intended primarily for preliminary screening, to eliminate the majority of colleges that are not suitable for a particular student. Be sure to examine the admissions policies spelled out in the *Admissions* section of each profile. And remember that many colleges have to reject *qualified* students; the *Selector* will tell you what your chances are, not which college will accept you.

MOST COMPETITIVE

Even superior students will encounter a great deal of competition for admission to the colleges in this category. In general, these colleges require high school rank in the top 10% to 20% and grade averages of A to B+. Median freshman test scores at these colleges are generally between 655 and 800 on the SAT and 29 and above on the ACT. In addition, many of these colleges admit only a small percentage of those who apply—usually fewer than one third.

Amherst College, MA
Bates College, ME
Boston College, MA
Bowdoin College, ME
Brown University, RI
Bryn Mawr College, PA
Bucknell University, PA
California Institute of Technology, CA
Carleton College, MN
Carnegie Mellon University, PA
Case Western Reserve University, OH
Claremont McKenna College, CA
Colby College, ME
Colgate University, NY
College of Mount Saint Vincent, NY
College of the Holy Cross, MA
College of William & Mary, VA
Colorado College, CO
Columbia University in the City of New York, NY
Columbia University/Barnard College, NY
Columbia University/School of General Studies, NY
Connecticut College, CT
Cooper Union for the Advancement of Science and Art, NY
Cornell University, NY
Dartmouth College, NH
Davidson College, NC
Duke University, NC
Emory University, GA
Franklin and Marshall College, PA
George Washington University, DC
Georgetown University, DC
Georgia Institute of Technology, GA
Hamilton College, NY
Hampshire College, MA
Harvard University/Harvard College, MA
Harvey Mudd College, CA
Haverford College, PA
Johns Hopkins University, MD
Kenyon College, OH
Lehigh University, PA
Macalester College, MN
Massachusetts Institute of Technology, MA
Middlebury College, VT
New York University, NY
Northeastern University, MA
Northwestern University, IL
Oberlin College, OH
Occidental College, CA
The Ohio State University, OH
Ohio State University at Marion, OH
Pitzer College, CA
Pomona College, CA
Princeton University, NJ
Reed College, OR
Rensselaer Polytechnic Institute, NY
Rice University, TX
Rose-Hulman Institute of Technology, IN
Santa Clara University, CA
Scripps College, CA
Smith College, MA
Southern Methodist University, TX
Stanford University, CA
Swarthmore College, PA
Tufts University, MA
Tulane University, LA
Union College, NY

United States Air Force Academy, CO
United States Military Academy, NY
United States Naval Academy, MD
University of California at Berkeley, CA
University of California at Los Angeles, CA
University of Chicago, IL
University of Miami, FL
University of Missouri/Columbia, MO
University of North Carolina at Chapel Hill, NC
University of Notre Dame, IN
University of Pennsylvania, PA
University of Richmond, VA
University of Rochester, NY
University of Southern California, CA
University of Virginia, VA
Vanderbilt University, TN
Vassar College, NY
Villanova University, PA
Wake Forest University, NC
Washington and Lee University, VA
Washington University in St. Louis, MO
Webb Institute, NY
Wellesley College, MA
Wesleyan University, CT
Whitman College, WA
Williams College, MA
Yale University, CT

HIGHLY COMPETITIVE

Colleges in this group generally look for students with grade averages of B+ to B and accept most of their students from the top 20% to 35% of the high school class. Median freshman test scores at these colleges generally range from 620 to 654 on the SAT and 27 or 28 on the ACT. These schools generally accept between one third and one half of their applicants.

To provide for finer distinctions within this admissions category, a plus (+) symbol has been placed before some entries. These are colleges with median freshman scores of 645 or more on the SAT or 28 or more on the ACT (depending on which test the college prefers), and colleges that accept fewer than one quarter of their applicants.

Allegheny College, PA
+American University, DC
Augustana College, IL
Austin College, TX
Babson College, MA
Bard College, NY
+Bard College at Simon's Rock, MA
Baylor University, TX
Beloit College, WI
+Bennington College, VT
+Bentley University, MA
Berea College, KY
Berry College, GA
+Binghamton University / The State University of New York, NY
+Boston University, MA
Brandeis University, MA
Brigham Young University, UT
California Polytechnic State University, CA
+Centre College, KY
Christian Brothers University, TN
+Clark University, MA
Clarkson University, NY
Clemson University, SC
College of New Jersey, NJ
+College of the Atlantic, ME
Colorado School of Mines, CO
Cornell College, IA
+CUNY-City College, NY
+Denison University, OH
+Dickinson College, PA
Drexel University, PA
Elon University, NC
Emerson College, MA
Florida State University, FL
Fordham University, NY
Furman University, SC
Gettysburg College, PA
Gonzaga University, WA
Grinnell College, IA
Grove City College, PA
Gustavus Adolphus College, MN
+Hendrix College, AR
+Hillsdale College, MI
+Illinois Institute of Technology, IL
Indiana University Bloomington, IN
Ithaca College, NY
+Kalamazoo College, MI
Kettering University, MI
+Lafayette College, PA
Lawrence University, WI
Miami University, OH
Mills College, CA
+Mount Holyoke College, MA
Muhlenberg College, PA
+New College of Florida, FL
New Mexico Institute of Mining and Technology, NM
North Carolina State University, NC
+Pepperdine University, CA
+Polytechnic Institute of New York University, NY
Providence College, RI
Purdue University/West Lafayette, IN
+Rhodes College, TN
Rollins College, FL
Sarah Lawrence College, NY
+Sewanee: The University of the South, TN
Skidmore College, NY
+St. John's College, Santa Fe, NM
St. John's College-Annapolis, MD
St. Lawrence University, NY
St. Mary's College of Maryland, MD
+St. Olaf College, MN
State University of New York / College of Environmental Science and Forestry, NY
Stevens Institute of Technology, NJ
Stony Brook University / State University of New York, NY
+SUNY College at Geneseo , NY
Syracuse University, NY
Texas Christian University, TX
+Thomas Aquinas College, CA
+Trinity College, CT
+Trinity University, TX
Truman State University, MO
United States Coast Guard Academy, CT
+United States Merchant Marine Academy, NY
University of California at Davis, CA
University of California at Santa Barbara, CA
University of Connecticut, CT
+University of Florida, FL
University of Illinois at Urbana-Champaign, IL
University of Maryland, MD
+University of Michigan/Ann Arbor, MI
University of Minnesota/Twin Cities, MN
+University of Pittsburgh at Pittsburgh, PA
+University of Puget Sound, WA
+University of San Diego, CA
University of Texas at Austin, TX
University of Texas at Dallas, TX
+University of Tulsa, OK
University of Wisconsin/Madison, WI
Virginia Polytechnic Institute and State University, VA
Westmont College, CA
+Wheaton College, IL
+Wheaton College, MA
+Worcester Polytechnic Institute, MA

VERY COMPETITIVE

The colleges in this category generally admit students whose averages are no less than B- and who rank in the top 35% to 50% of their graduating class. They generally report median freshman test scores in the 573 to 619 range on the SAT and from 24 to 26 on the ACT. These schools generally accept between one half and three quarters of their applicants.

The plus (+) has been placed before colleges with median freshman scores of 610 or above on the SAT or 26 or better on the ACT (depending on which test the college prefers), and colleges that accept fewer than one third of their applicants.

Abilene Christian University, TX
Adelphi University, NY
+Agnes Scott College, GA
Alaska Pacific University, AK
Albion College, MI
Alfred University, NY
Alma College, MI
Appalachian State University, NC
Asbury University, KY
Assumption College, MA
+Auburn University, AL
Augustana College, SD
Baldwin Wallace University, OH
Bellarmine University, KY
+Belmont University, TN
Benedictine College, KS
Bethel University, MN
Biola University, CA
+Birmingham-Southern College, AL
Bradley University, IL
+Brescia University, KY
Brigham Young University/Hawaii, HI
Bryant University, RI
+Butler University, IN
+Calvin College, MI
Canisius College, NY
Capital University, OH
The Catholic University of America, DC
+Cedarville University, OH
Central College, IA
Central Methodist University, MO
Champlain College, VT
+Chapman University, CA
Chatham University, PA
Christendom College, VA
Christopher Newport University, VA
City University of New York/Baruch College, NY
Clarkson College, NE
Coe College, IA
The College at Brockport / State University of New York, NY
College of Charleston, SC
The College of Idaho, ID
The College of New Rochelle, NY
College of New Rochelle - School of New Resources, NY
College of Saint Benedict , MN
College of the Ozarks, MO
College of Wooster, OH
Colorado Christian University, CO
Colorado State University-Fort Collins, CO
Concordia College New York, NY
Concordia University - Irvine, CA
Concordia University Nebraska, NE
Concordia University, Ann Arbor, MI
Coppin State University, MD
+Covenant College, GA
+Creighton University, NE
DePaul University, IL
+DePauw University, IN
Dillard University, LA
Doane College, NE
Dordt College, IA
+Drake University, IA
Drew University/College of Liberal Arts, NJ
Drury University, MO
Duquesne University, PA
+Earlham College, IN
Eastern Mennonite University, VA
Eckerd College, FL
Elizabethtown College, PA
Elizabethtown College School of Continuing and Professional Studies, PA
Elms College, MA
Embry-Riddle Aeronautical University - Prescott Campus, AZ
Emmanuel College, MA
Eugene Lang College - The New School for Liberal Arts, NY
Fairfield University, CT
Flagler College, FL
Florida Institute of Technology, FL
Florida International University, FL
Florida Southern College, FL
Fort Valley State University, GA
Franciscan University of Steubenville, OH
Freed-Hardeman University, TN
George Mason University, VA
Georgia College and State University, GA
Georgia State University, GA
Goddard College, VT
+Gordon College, MA
Goshen College, IN
+Goucher College, MD
Grand Canyon University, AZ
Grand Valley State University, MI
Hamline University, MN
Hanover College, IN
Hellenic College/Holy Cross Greek Orthodox School of Theology, MA
Hiram College, OH
Hobart and William Smith Colleges, NY
+Hofstra University, NY
Hollins University, VA
+Hope College, MI
Houghton College, NY
Hunter College / The City University of New York, NY
Illinois College, IL
Illinois State University, IL
+Illinois Wesleyan University, IL
Indiana Wesleyan University, IN
James Madison University, VA
+John Brown University, AR
Juniata College, PA
Kansas State University, KS
Kennesaw State University, GA
+Kentucky Wesleyan College, KY
Knox College, IL
La Sierra University, CA
Lake Forest College, IL
Lawrence Technological University, MI
Le Moyne College, NY
Lewis & Clark College, OR
Lindsey Wilson College, KY
Lipscomb University, TN
Loras College, IA
+Louisiana State University, LA
+Loyola Marymount University, CA
+Loyola University Chicago, IL
Loyola University Maryland, MD
Loyola University New Orleans, LA
+Luther College, IA
Lyon College, AR
Madonna University, MI
Maharishi University of Management, IA
Manhattan College, NY
Manhattanville College, NY
Marietta College, OH
Marlboro College, VT
+Marquette University, WI
Marymount Manhattan College, NY
Maryville College, TN

Maryville University of Saint Louis, MO
McDaniel College, MD
Medaille College, NY
+Mercer University, GA
Messiah College, PA
Metropolitan College of New York, NY
Michigan State University, MI
Michigan Technological University, MI
+Millsaps College, MS
+Milwaukee School of Engineering, WI
Mississippi College, MS
Missouri State University, MO
+Missouri University of Science and Technology, MO
Montana State University, MT
Montana Tech of The University of Montana, MT
Montreat College, NC
Moravian College, PA
Morgan State University, MD
+Mount St. Mary's College/Chalon Campus, CA
Nazareth College of Rochester, NY
New Jersey Institute of Technology, NJ
New York Institute of Technology, NY
North Central College, IL
Northeastern State University, OK
Northern Michigan University, MI
Notre Dame College, OH
Nova Southeastern University, FL
Oakland University, MI
Oglethorpe University, GA
Ohio Northern University, OH
Ohio University, OH
Oklahoma Baptist University, OK
Oklahoma Christian University, OK
Oklahoma City University, OK
Oklahoma State University, OK
Oswego / State University of New York, NY
Ottawa University, KS
Ouachita Baptist University, AR
Pace University, NY
Pacific Lutheran University, WA
Pacific Union College, CA
Penn State University/University Park , PA
Point Loma Nazarene University, CA
Presbyterian College, SC
Queens College / The City University of New York, NY
Queens University of Charlotte, NC
Quinnipiac University, CT
Randolph College, VA
Richard Stockton College of New Jersey, NJ
Rivier College, NH
+Rochester Institute of Technology, NY
Roosevelt University, IL
Rowan University, NJ
Rutgers, The State University of New Jersey/New Brunswick, NJ
Sacred Heart University, CT
Saint Anselm College, NH
Saint Joseph's University, PA
+Saint Louis University, MO
Saint Mary's College, IN
Saint Michael's College, VT
Salem College, NC
Salisbury University, MD
Salve Regina University, RI
+Samford University, AL
San Diego State University, CA
+Seattle Pacific University, WA
+Seattle University, WA
Shimer College, IL
Siena College, NY
Sierra Nevada College, NV
Simmons College, MA
Simpson College, IA
South Dakota School of Mines and Technology, SD
Southern Polytechnic State University, GA
Southwestern University, TX
Spelman College, GA
Spring Hill College, AL
St. Edward's University, TX
St. Joseph's College, New York / Suffolk Campus, NY
St. Norbert College, WI
The State University of New York College of Agriculture and Tech at Cobleskill, NY
Stephens College, MO
+Stetson University, FL
+Stonehill College, MA
SUNY Fredonia / The State University of New York at Fredonia, NY
SUNY Oneonta / State University of New York, NY
SUNY Plattsburgh / State University of New York, NY
+Taylor University, IN
Temple University, PA
+Texas A&M University, TX
Texas State University, TX
Touro College, NY
Towson University, MD
+Transylvania University, KY
Trine University, IN
Union College, NE
Union University, TN
University at Albany / SUNY, NY
University at Buffalo / The State University of New York, NY
University of Alabama at Huntsville, AL
University of Arkansas at Fayetteville, AR
University of California at Irvine, CA
University of California at San Diego, CA
University of California at Santa Cruz, CA
University of Central Arkansas, AR
+University of Central Florida, FL
University of Cincinnati, OH
University of Colorado at Colorado Springs, CO
+University of Colorado Boulder, CO
+University of Dallas, TX
University of Dayton, OH
University of Delaware, DE
+University of Denver, CO
+University of Evansville, IN
University of Georgia, GA
University of Hawaii at Manoa, HI
University of Houston, TX
University of Illinois at Chicago, IL
University of Iowa, IA
University of La Verne, CA
University of Louisville, KY
University of Mary Washington, VA
University of Maryland/Baltimore County, MD
+University of Massachusetts Amherst, MA
University of Michigan/Dearborn, MI
University of Minnesota/Morris, MN
University of Mississippi, MS
University of Missouri-St. Louis, MO
University of Mobile, AL
University of Nebraska - Lincoln, NE
University of New Hampshire, NH
University of New Orleans, LA
+University of North Carolina at Asheville, NC
+University of North Carolina at Wilmington, NC
University of North Florida, FL
+University of Oklahoma, OK
University of Oregon, OR
University of Portland, OR
University of Redlands, CA
University of Saint Thomas, MN
University of San Francisco, CA
University of Science and Arts of Oklahoma, OK
University of Scranton, PA
+University of South Carolina at Columbia, SC
University of South Florida/St. Petersburg, FL
University of St. Thomas - Houston, TX
University of Tampa, FL
+University of Tennessee at Knoxville, TN
University of the Pacific, CA
+University of the Sciences , PA
University of Utah, UT
+University of Vermont, VT
University of Washington, WA
University of Wisconsin/Eau Claire, WI
University of Wisconsin/La Crosse, WI
+Ursinus College, PA
+Valparaiso University, IN
Vanguard University of Southern California, CA
Wabash College, IN
Wagner College, NY
Warren Wilson College, NC
Wartburg College, IA

Washington and Jefferson College, PA
Washington College, MD
Wells College, NY
Western Washington University, WA
Westminster College, MO
Westminster College, UT
+Whitworth University, WA
+Willamette University, OR
+William Jewell College, MO
Winthrop University, SC
Wisconsin Lutheran College, WI
Wittenberg University, OH
Wofford College, SC
Xavier University, OH
+Yeshiva University, NY

COMPETITIVE

This category is a very broad one, covering colleges that generally have median freshman test scores between 500 and 572 on the SAT and between 21 and 23 on the ACT. Some of these colleges require that students have high school averages of B- or better, although others state a minimum of C+ or C. Generally, these colleges prefer students in the top 50% to 65% of the graduating class and accept between 75% and 85% of their applicants.

Colleges with a plus (+) are those with median freshman SAT scores of 563 or more or median freshman ACT scores of 24 or more (depending on which test the colleges prefers), and those that admit fewer than half of their applicants.

Adrian College, MI
Alabama Agricultural and Mechanical University, AL
Albany State University, GA
Albright College, PA
Alcorn State University, MS
Alderson Broaddus University, WV
Alfred State / SUNY College of Technology , NY
Alice Lloyd College, KY
Alvernia University, PA
American Indian College , AZ
American Jewish University , CA
Anderson University, IN
+Andrews University, MI
Aquinas College, MI
+Aquinas College, TN
+Arcadia University, PA
+Arizona State University, AZ
Arkansas State University, AR
Armstrong Atlantic State University, GA
Ashford University, IA
Ashland University, OH
Auburn University at Montgomery, AL
Augsburg College, MN
Aurora University, IL
Austin Peay State University, TN
Avila University, MO
Azusa Pacific University, CA
+Baker University, KS
Ball State University, IN
Barry University, FL
Barton College, NC
Bay Path College, MA
Beacon College, FL
Belhaven University, MS
Belmont Abbey College, NC
Bemidji State University, MN
Benedictine University, IL
Bethany College, WV
Bethel College, IN
Bethel College, KS
Bethel University, TN
Blackburn College, IL
Bloomfield College, NJ
Bloomsburg University of Pennsylvania, PA
+Bluefield College, VA
Bluffton University, OH
Boise State University, ID
Boricua College, NY
Bowling Green State University, OH
+Brenau University Women's College, GA
Briar Cliff University, IA
Bridgewater College, VA
Bridgewater State University, MA
Bryan College, TN
Bryn Athyn College , PA
Buena Vista University, IA
+Buffalo State/State University of Buffalo, NY
Cairn University, PA
California Baptist University, CA
California Lutheran University, CA
California Maritime Academy, CA
California State Polytechnic University, Pomona, CA
California State University, Chico, CA
California State University, East Bay, CA
California State University, Fresno, CA
+California State University, Fullerton, CA
+California State University, Long Beach, CA
California State University, Los Angeles, CA
California State University, Northridge, CA
California State University, Sacramento, CA
California State University, San Bernardino, CA
California State University, San Marcos, CA
California State University, Stanislaus, CA
California University of Pennsylvania, PA
Campbell University, NC
Campbellsville University, KY
Capitol College, MD
Cardinal Stritch University, WI
Carlow University, PA
Carroll College, MT
Carroll University, WI
+Carson-Newman University, TN
Carthage College, WI
Castleton State College, VT
Catawba College, NC
Cazenovia College, NY
Cedar Crest College, PA
+Centenary College of Louisiana, LA
Central Connecticut State University, CT
Central Michigan University, MI
Central State University, OH
Central Washington University, WA
Chaminade University of Honolulu, HI
Chancellor University, OH
Charleston Southern University, SC
Chicago State University, IL
Citadel, The, SC
+City University of New York/Brooklyn College, NY
+Claflin University, SC
Clarion University of Pennsylvania, PA
Clark Atlanta University, GA
Clarke University, IA
Clearwater Christian College, FL
Cleary University, MI
Cleveland State University, OH
Coastal Carolina University, SC
Cogswell Polytechnical College, CA
Colby-Sawyer College, NH
College of Mount Saint Joseph, OH
College of Saint Mary, NE
The College of Saint Rose, NY
College of Saint Scholastica, MN
Columbia College, MO
Columbia College, SC

Columbus State University, GA
Concord University, WV
+Concordia College, Moorhead, MN
Concordia University, OR
Concordia University Saint Paul, MN
Concordia University Texas, TX
Concordia University Wisconsin, WI
Concordia University, River Forest, IL
Converse College, SC
Corban University, OR
Cornerstone University and Grand Rapids Theological Seminary, MI
Culver-Stockton College, MO
Cumberland University, TN
Daemen College, NY
Dakota State University, SD
Dakota Wesleyan University, SD
Dallas Baptist University, TX
Daniel Webster College, NH
Davis and Elkins College, WV
De Sales University, PA
Defiance College, OH
Delaware Valley College, PA
Dominican College, NY
Dominican University, IL
Dominican University of California, CA
D'Youville College, NY
East Carolina University, NC
East Stroudsburg University of Pennsylvania, PA
East Tennessee State University, TN
East Texas Baptist University, TX
Eastern Connecticut State University, CT
Eastern Illinois University, IL
Eastern Kentucky University, KY
Eastern Michigan University, MI
Eastern Nazarene College, MA
Eastern New Mexico University, NM
Eastern Oregon University, OR
Eastern University, PA
Eastern Washington University, WA
East-West University, IL
Edgewood College, WI
Elizabeth City State University, NC
+Elmhurst College, IL
+Elmira College, NY
+Embry-Riddle Aeronautical University - Daytona Beach, FL
Embry-Riddle Aeronautical University - Worldwide, FL
Emory and Henry College, VA
Emporia State University, KS
Endicott College, MA
Erskine College, SC
Eureka College, IL
Evangel University, MO
+Evergreen State College, WA
Fairleigh Dickinson University/College at Florham, NJ
Fairleigh Dickinson University/Metropolitan Campus, NJ
Farmingdale State College, NY
Fayetteville State University, NC
Felician College, NJ
Ferris State University, MI
Fisk University, TN
Fitchburg State University, MA
Florida Atlantic University, FL
Florida Gulf Coast University, FL
Fontbonne University, MO
Fort Hays State University, KS
Fort Lewis College, CO
Framingham State University, MA
Franklin College, IN
Franklin Pierce University, NH
Fresno Pacific University, CA
Friends University, KS
Gannon University, PA
+Gardner-Webb University, NC
Geneva College, PA
+George Fox University, OR
Georgetown College, KY
Georgia Regents University, GA
Georgia Southern University, GA
Georgia Southwestern State University, GA
Golden Gate University, CA
Goldey-Beacom College, DE
Grace Bible College, MI
Grace College and Theological Seminary, IN
Graceland University, IA
Grand View University, IA
Greenville College, IL
Guilford College, NC
Gwynedd-Mercy College, PA
Hampden-Sydney College, VA
Hampton University, VA
Hannibal-LaGrange University, MO
+Harding University, AR
+Hardin-Simmons University, TX
+Hartwick College, NY
+Hastings College, NE
Hawaii Pacific University, HI
Heidelberg University, OH
Henderson State University, AR
High Point University, NC
Hilbert College, NY
Hood College, MD
Hope International University, CA
+Houston Baptist University, TX
Howard Payne University, TX
Howard University, DC
Humboldt State University, CA
Huntingdon College, AL
Huntington University, IN
+Huston-Tillotson University, TX
Idaho State University, ID
Immaculata University, PA
Indiana State University, IN
Indiana University South Bend, IN
Indiana University-Purdue University Fort Wayne, IN
Indiana University-Purdue University Indianapolis, IN
Iona College, NY
Iowa State University, IA
Jacksonville University, FL
+John Carroll University, OH
John Jay College of Criminal Justice / The City University of New York, NY
Johnson and Wales University/Charlotte Campus, NC
Johnson and Wales University/Denver Campus, CO
Johnson and Wales University/North Miami Campus, FL
Johnson and Wales University/Providence Campus, RI
Johnson State College, VT
Judson College, AL
Judson University, IL
Kansas Wesleyan University, KS
Keene State College, NH
Kent State University, OH
Keuka College, NY
King University, TN
King's College, PA
La Salle University, PA
LaGrange College, GA
Lake Erie College, OH
Lake Superior State University, MI
Lakeland College, WI
+Lander University, SC
Lane College, TN
Lebanon Valley College, PA
+Lee University, TN
Lees-McRae College, NC
LeMoyne-Owen College, TN
Lenoir-Rhyne College, NC
Lesley University, MA
LeTourneau University, TX
Lewis University, IL
Lewis-Clark State College, ID
Liberty University, VA
Limestone College, SC
Lincoln Memorial University, TN
Lindenwood University, MO
Linfield College-McMinnville Campus, OR
Long Island University/Brooklyn Campus, NY
Long Island University/C.W. Post Campus, NY
Longwood University, VA
Louisiana College, LA
Louisiana State University in Shreveport, LA
Louisiana Tech University, LA
Lubbock Christian University, TX
Lycoming College, PA

Lynchburg College, VA
Lyndon State College, VT
Lynn University, FL
MacMurray College, IL
Maine Maritime Academy, ME
Malone University, OH
Manchester College, IN
Mannes College New School for Music, NY
Marian University/Indianapolis, IN
Marist College, NY
Maritime College / State University of New York, NY
Marshall University, WV
Mary Baldwin College, VA
Marygrove College, MI
Marymount University, VA
Marywood University, PA
Massachusetts College of Liberal Arts, MA
Massachusetts Maritime Academy, MA
+The Masters College, CA
+McKendree University, IL
McNeese State University, LA
McPherson College, KS
Menlo College, CA
Mercy College, NY
Mercyhurst University, PA
Meredith College, NC
Merrimack College, MA
Methodist University, NC
MidAmerica Nazarene University, KS
Middle Tennessee State University, TN
Midland University, NE
Midway College, KY
Midwestern State University, TX
Millersville University of Pennsylvania, PA
Milligan College, TN
Millikin University, IL
Minnesota State University, Mankato, MN
Minnesota State University, Moorhead, MN
Minot State University, ND
Misericordia University, PA
Mississippi State University, MS
Missouri Baptist University, MO
Missouri Southern State University, MO
Missouri Valley College, MO
Mitchell College, CT
Molloy College, NY
Monmouth College, IL
Monmouth University, NJ
Monroe College, NY
Montclair State University, NJ
Morehead State University, KY
Morehouse College, GA
Morningside College, IA
Mount Aloysius College, PA
Mount Marty College, SD
Mount Mercy University, IA
Mount Olive College, NC
Mount Saint Mary College, NY
Mount Saint Mary's University, MD
Mount Vernon Nazarene University, OH
Murray State University, KY
Muskingum University, OH
+Nebraska Wesleyan University, NE
+New Jersey City University, NJ
Newbury College, MA
+Newman University, KS
Niagara University, NY
Nicholls State University, LA
North Carolina Wesleyan College, NC
North Central University, MN
North Dakota State University, ND
North Georgia College & State University, GA
North Park University, IL
Northeastern Illinois University, IL
Northern Arizona University, AZ
Northern Illinois University, IL
Northern State University, SD
Northland College, WI
Northwest Christian University, OR
Northwest Missouri State University, MO
Northwest University, WA
Northwestern College, MN
+Northwestern College of Iowa, IA
Northwestern State University of Louisiana, LA
Norwich University, VT
Notre Dame of Maryland University, MD
Nyack College, NY
Oakwood University, AL
+Ohio Dominican University, OH
Ohio State University at Lima, OH
Ohio State University at Mansfield, OH
Ohio State University at Newark, OH
Ohio Valley University, WV
+Ohio Wesleyan University, OH
Oklahoma Wesleyan University, OK
Old Dominion University, VA
Olivet College, MI
Olivet Nazarene University, IL
Oral Roberts University, OK
Oregon Institute of Technology, OR
+Oregon State University, OR
Otterbein College, OH
Pacific University, OR
Park University, MO
Penn State Erie/The Behrend College, PA
Penn State University/Altoona, PA
Pfeiffer University, NC
Philadelphia University, PA
Piedmont College, GA
Pittsburg State University, KS
Point Park University, PA
Portland State University, OR
Post University, CT
+Prescott College, AZ
+Principia College, IL
Purchase College / State University of New York , NY
Purdue University/Calumet, IN
+Ramapo College of New Jersey, NJ
Randolph-Macon College, VA
Regis University, CO
Reinhardt College, GA
Rider University, NJ
+Ripon College, WI
+Roanoke College, VA
Robert Morris University, PA
+Roberts Wesleyan College, NY
Rochester College, MI
Rockford College, IL
Rockhurst University, MO
Rocky Mountain College, MT
Roger Williams University, RI
Rosemont College, PA
Russell Sage College, NY
Rust College, MS
Rutgers, The State University of New Jersey/Camden Campus, NJ
Rutgers, The State University of New Jersey/Newark Campus, NJ
Saginaw Valley State University, MI
Saint Augustine's University, NC
Saint John's University, MN
Saint Joseph's College, IN
Saint Joseph's College of Maine, ME
Saint Leo University, FL
Saint Martin's University, WA
Saint Mary's College of California, CA
Saint Mary's University , TX
Saint Mary's University of Minnesota, MN
Saint Peter's College, NJ
Saint Vincent College, PA
Saint Xavier University, IL
Salem International University, WV
Sam Houston State University, TX
San Diego Christian College, CA
San Francisco State University, CA
San Jose State University, CA
Savannah State University, GA
Seton Hall University, NJ
Seton Hill University, PA
Shenandoah University, VA
Shepherd University, WV
Shorter University, GA
Simpson University, CA
Sonoma State University, CA

South Dakota State University, SD
Southeastern Louisiana University, LA
Southeastern Oklahoma State University, OK
+Southeastern University, FL
Southern Adventist University, TN
Southern Arkansas University, AR
Southern Connecticut State University, CT
Southern Illinois University Carbondale, IL
Southern Illinois University Edwardsville, IL
Southern New Hampshire University, NH
Southern Oregon University, OR
+Southern University and A&M College, LA
Southern Utah University, UT
Southern Wesleyan University, SC
Southwest Baptist University, MO
Southwest Minnesota State University, MN
Southwestern College, KS
Southwestern Oklahoma State University, OK
Spring Arbor University, MI
Springfield College, MA
St. Ambrose University, IA
St. Bonaventure University, NY
+St. Catherine University, MN
St. Cloud State University, MN
+St. John Fisher College, NY
+St. John's University, NY
St. Joseph's College, New York / Brooklyn Campus, NY
St. Thomas Aquinas College, NY
+St. Thomas University, FL
The State University of New York at Potsdam, NY
State University of New York Institute of Technology at Utica / Rome, NY
Stephen F. Austin State University, TX
Sterling College, KS
Sterling College, VT
Stevenson University, MD
Stillman College, AL
Suffolk University, MA
SUNY College at Old Westbury, NY
SUNY Cortland / The State University of New York, NY
SUNY New Paltz, NY
Susquehanna University, PA
+Sweet Briar College, VA
Talladega College, AL
Tennessee State University, TN
Tennessee Technological University, TN
Tennessee Wesleyan College, TN
Texas A&M University at Commerce, TX
Texas A&M University at Galveston, TX
Texas Lutheran University, TX
Texas Tech University, TX
Texas Wesleyan University, TX
Thomas More College, KY
Thomas More College of Liberal Arts, NH
Toccoa Falls College, GA
Trevecca Nazarene University, TN
Trinity Christian College, IL
Trinity International University, IL
+Trinity Washington University, DC
Troy University, AL
Tusculum College, TN
Tuskegee University, AL
Union College, KY
Unity College, ME
University of Akron, OH
+University of Alabama at Birmingham, AL
+University of Alabama at Tuscaloosa, AL
University of Alaska Fairbanks, AK
University of Alaska Southeast, AK
University of Arizona, AZ
University of Arkansas at Little Rock, AR
University of Arkansas at Pine Bluff, AR
University of California at Riverside, CA
University of Central Missouri, MO
University of Central Oklahoma, OK
University of Charleston, WV
University of Colorado Denver , CO
University of Detroit Mercy, MI
University of Dubuque, IA
University of Findlay, OH
University of Great Falls, MT
University of Hartford, CT
University of Hawaii at Hilo, HI
University of Idaho, ID
University of Jamestown, ND
+University of Kansas, KS
University of Kentucky, KY
University of Louisiana at Lafayette, LA
University of Louisiana at Monroe, LA
+University of Maine, ME
University of Maine at Augusta, ME
University of Maine at Farmington, ME
University of Maine at Machias, ME
University of Mary, ND
+University of Mary Hardin-Baylor, TX
University of Maryland/Eastern Shore, MD
University of Massachusetts Boston, MA
University of Massachusetts Dartmouth, MA
University of Massachusetts Lowell, MA
University of Memphis, TN
+University of Michigan-Flint, MI
University of Minnesota Crookston, MN
+University of Minnesota/Duluth, MN
University of Missouri-Kansas City, MO
University of Montana, MT
University of Montevallo, AL
University of Mount Union , OH
University of Nebraska at Omaha, NE
University of Nevada, Las Vegas, NV
+University of New England, ME
University of New Haven, CT
University of New Mexico, NM
University of North Alabama, AL
University of North Carolina at Charlotte, NC
University of North Carolina at Greensboro, NC
University of North Carolina at Pembroke, NC
University of North Dakota, ND
University of North Texas, TX
University of Northern Colorado, CO
University of Northern Iowa, IA
University of Pittsburgh at Greensburg, PA
+University of Rhode Island, RI
University of Saint Francis, IN
+University of Saint Mary, KS
University of Sioux Falls, SD
University of South Alabama, AL
University of South Carolina at Aiken, SC
University of South Dakota, SD
University of South Florida, FL
University of Southern Indiana, IN
University of Southern Maine, ME
University of Southern Mississippi, MS
University of St. Francis, IL
University of Tennessee at Chattanooga, TN
University of Tennessee at Martin, TN
University of Texas at San Antonio, TX
University of the Ozarks, AR
University of the Southwest, NM
University of Toledo, OH
University of Virginia's College at Wise, VA
University of West Alabama, AL
University of West Florida, FL
University of Wisconsin Whitewater, WI
University of Wisconsin/Green Bay, WI
University of Wisconsin/Platteville, WI
University of Wisconsin/Stevens Point, WI
University of Wisconsin/Stout, WI
University of Wisconsin/Superior, WI
University of Wisconsin-Milwaukee, WI
+University of Wyoming, WY
Urbana University, OH
Utah State University, UT
Utica College, NY
Valdosta State University, GA
Vermont Technical College, VT
Victory University, TN
Virginia Commonwealth University, VA
Virginia Military Institute, VA
+Virginia State University, VA
Virginia Union University, VA
Viterbo University, WI
Voorhees College, SC
Walsh University, OH
Warner Pacific College, OR

Warner University, FL
+Washington Adventist University, MD
Washington State University, WA
Wayne State University, MI
Waynesburg University, PA
Webber International University, FL
+Webster University, MO
+Wesleyan College, GA
West Chester University of Pennsylvania, PA
West Texas A&M University, TX
+West Virginia University, WV
West Virginia Wesleyan College, WV
+Western Carolina University, NC
Western Connecticut State University, CT
Western Illinois University, IL
Western Michigan University, MI
Western New England University, MA
Western Oregon University, OR
Western State Colorado University, CO
Westfield State University, MA
+Westminster College, PA
Wheeling Jesuit University, WV
Wheelock College, MA
Whittier College, CA
Wichita State University, KS
Widener University, PA
Wilkes University, PA
William Paterson University of New Jersey, NJ
William Penn University, IA
William Woods University, MO
Williams Baptist College, AR
Wilmington College, OH
Wilson College, PA
Wingate University, NC
Winona State University, MN
Worcester State University, MA
Wright State University, OH
Xavier University of Louisiana, LA
York College, NE
York College of Pennsylvania, PA

LESS COMPETITIVE

Included in this category are colleges with median freshman test scores generally below 500 on the SAT and below 21 on the ACT; some colleges that require entrance examinations but do not report median scores; and colleges that admit students with averages generally below C who rank in the top 65% of the graduating class. These colleges usually admit 85% or more of their applicants.

Adams State College, CO
Albertus Magnus College, CT
Alverno College, WI
American International College, MA
Amridge University, AL
Anna Maria College, MA
Arkansas Tech University, AR
Atlantic Union College, MA
Averett University, VA
Becker College, MA
Bennett College, NC
Berkeley College, NY
Berkeley College/New Jersey, NJ
Berkeley College/Westchester Campus, NY
Bethune-Cookman University, FL
Black Hills State University, SD
Blue Mountain College, MS
Bluefield State College, WV
Bowie State University, MD
Brewton-Parker College, GA
Cabrini College, PA
Caldwell College, NJ
California State University, Bakersfield, CA
California State University, Dominguez Hills, CA
California State University, Monterey Bay, CA
Calumet College of St. Joseph, IN
Cameron University, OK
Carlos Albizu University, FL
Centenary College, NJ
Chestnut Hill College, PA
Cheyney University of Pennsylvania, PA
Clayton State University, GA
Coker College, SC
College of Saint Elizabeth, NJ
College of St Joseph, VT
Colorado Mesa University, CO
Colorado State University-Pueblo, CO
Colorado Technical University, CO
Columbia College Chicago, IL
Cox College, MO
Curry College, MA
Davenport University, MI
Delaware State University, DE
Delta State University, MS
Dowling College, NY
East Central University, OK
Edinboro University of Pennsylvania, PA
Edward Waters College, FL
Fairmont State University, WV
Faulkner University, AL
Ferrum College, VA
Florida Agricultural and Mechanical University, FL
Florida Memorial University, FL
Francis Marion University, SC
Frostburg State University, MD
Georgian Court University, NJ
Goodwin College, CT
Grambling State University, LA
Green Mountain College, VT
Greensboro College, NC
Hodges University, FL
Holy Family University, PA
Husson University, ME
Indiana Institute of Technology, IN
Indiana University East, IN
Indiana University Kokomo, IN
Indiana University Northwest, IN
Indiana University of Pennsylvania, PA
Indiana University Southeast, IN
Iowa Wesleyan College, IA
Jackson State University, MS
Jacksonville State University, AL
Johnson C. Smith University, NC
Kean University, NJ
Kentucky Christian University, KY
Kentucky State University, KY
Keystone College, PA
Kutztown University of Pennsylvania, PA
La Roche College, PA
Lamar University, TX
Langston University, OK
Lasell College, MA
Lehman College / The City University of New York, NY
LIM College, NY
The Lincoln University, PA
Livingstone College, NC
Lock Haven University of Pennsylvania, PA
Lourdes University, OH
Mansfield University, PA
Marian University, WI
Mars Hill College, NC
McMurry University, TX

Metropolitan State University of Denver, CO
Mississippi University for Women, MS
Mississippi Valley State University, MS
Montana State University-Billings, MT
Morris College, SC
Mount Ida College, MA
Mount Mary University, WI
National Louis University, IL
Neumann University, PA
New England College, NH
New Mexico State University, NM
Newberry College, SC
Nichols College, MA
Norfolk State University, VA
North Carolina Agricultural and Technical State University, NC
North Carolina Central University, NC
Northern Kentucky University, KY
Northwood University, FL
Northwood University, MI
Northwood University, TX
Notre Dame de Namur University, CA
Our Lady of Holy Cross College, LA
Our Lady of the Lake University of San Antonio, TX
Paine College, GA
Palm Beach Atlantic University, FL
Paul Quinn College, TX
Philander Smith College, AR
Pine Manor College, MA
Plymouth State University, NH
Prairie View A&M University, TX
Presentation College, SD
Quincy University, IL
Radford University, VA
Regis College, MA
Rhode Island College, RI
Saint Francis University, PA
Saint Joseph College, CT
Saint Mary-of-the-Woods College, IN
Salem State College, MA
Schreiner University, TX
Shaw University, NC
Shippensburg University of Pennsylvania, PA
Siena Heights University, MI
Silver Lake College, WI
Slippery Rock University of Pennsylvania, PA
Sojourner-Douglass College, MD
South Carolina State University, SC
South University, GA
Southeast Missouri State University, MO
Southern Vermont College, VT
Southwestern Adventist University, TX
Spalding University, KY
St. Andrews University, NC
St. Francis College, NY
Sul Ross State University, TX
Tabor College, KS
Tarleton State University, TX
Texas A&M University at Corpus Christi, TX
Texas A&M University at Kingsville, TX
Texas Southern University, TX
Texas Woman's University, TX
Thiel College, PA
Thomas College, ME
Tiffin University, OH
University of Bridgeport, CT
University of Houston-Downtown, TX
University of Indianapolis, IN
University of Maine at Fort Kent, ME
University of Maine at Presque Isle, ME
University of Montana-Western, MT
University of Nebraska at Kearney, NE
University of Pittsburgh at Bradford, PA
University of Pittsburgh at Johnstown, PA
University of South Carolina Upstate, SC
University of Texas at Arlington, TX
University of Texas-Pan American, TX
University of the Cumberlands, KY
University of the District of Columbia, DC
University of the Incarnate Word, TX
University of West Georgia, GA
University of Wisconsin/Oshkosh, WI
University of Wisconsin/Parkside, WI
University of Wisconsin/River Falls, WI
Ursuline College, OH
Valley City State University, ND
Virginia Intermont College, VA
Virginia Wesleyan College, VA
Wayland Baptist University, TX
Wesley College, DE
West Liberty University, WV
Western Kentucky University, KY
Western New Mexico University, NM
Wilberforce University, OH
Wiley College, TX
William Carey University, MS
William Peace University, NC
Winston-Salem State University, NC
Woodbury Institute of Champlain College in Burlington, VT
Woodbury University, CA
Youngstown State University, OH

NONCOMPETITIVE

The colleges in this category generally only require evidence of graduation from an accredited high school (although they may also require completion of a certain number of high school units). Some require that entrance examinations be taken for placement purposes only, or only by graduates of unaccredited high schools or only by out-of-state students. In some cases, insufficient capacity may compel a college in this category to limit the number of students that are accepted; generally, however, if a college accepts 98% or more of its applicants, it automatically falls in this category. Colleges are also rated Noncompetitive if they admit all state residents, but have some requirements for nonresidents.

Adventist Universtiy of Health Sciences, FL
Alabama State University, AL
Allen University, SC
American InterContinental University, GA
Angelo State University, TX
Arkansas Baptist College, AR
Baker College of Flint, MI
Bellevue University, NE
Benedict College, SC
Bethany College, KS
Cambridge College, MA
Chadron State College, NE
City University of Seattle, WA
College of Staten Island / The City University of New York, NY
Concordia College - Alabama, AL
Dickinson State University, ND
Glenville State College, WV
Harris-Stowe State University, MO
Heritage University, WA
Holy Names University, CA
Humphreys College, CA
Jarvis Christian College, TX
Kaplan University, IA
Kendall College, IL
Lincoln University, MO
Marylhurst University, OR
Mayville State University, ND
Medgar Evers College / The City University of New York, NY
Miles College, AL
Missouri Western State University, MO
Montana State University-Northern, MT
Mount Washington College, NH
Mountain State University, WV
National American University, SD
New Mexico Highlands University, NM
New York City College of Technology / The City University of New York, NY
Northwest Nazarene University, ID
Northwestern Oklahoma State University, OK
Oakland City University, IN
Oglala Lakota College, SD
Oklahoma Panhandle State University, OK
Peirce College, PA
Pennsylvania College of Technology, PA
Peru State College, NE
Rocky Mountain College of Art and Design, CO
Saint Paul's College, VA
Shawnee State University, OH
Sinte Gleska University, SD
Southern Nazarene University, OK
Southern University at New Orleans, LA
St. Gregory's University, OK
Thomas University, GA
Tougaloo College, MS
University of Alaska Anchorage, AK
University of Arkansas at Monticello, AR
University of Nevada/Reno, NV
University of Pikeville, KY
University of Rio Grande, OH
University of Texas at El Paso, TX
Upper Iowa University, IA
Walla Walla University, WA
Washburn University, KS
Wayne State College, NE
Weber State University, UT
West Virginia State University, WV
West Virginia University Institute of Technology, WV
Wilmington University, DE
York College / City University of New York, NY

SPECIAL

Listed here are colleges whose programs of study are specialized; professional schools of art, music, nursing, and other disciplines. In general, the admissions requirements are not based primarily on academic criteria, but on evidence of talent or special interest in the field. Many other colleges and universities offer special-interest programs *in addition* to regular academic curricula, but such institutions have been given a regular competitive rating based on academic criteria. Schools oriented toward working adults have also been assigned this rating.

Albany College of Pharmacy and Health Sciences, NY
Allen College, IA
Art Academy of Cincinnati, OH
Art Center College of Design, CA
Art Institute of Atlanta, GA
Art Institute of Portland, OR
Benjamin Franklin Institute of Technology, MA
Berklee College of Music, MA
Boston Architectural College, MA
Boston Conservatory, MA
Burlington College, VT
Cabarrus College of Health Sciences, NC
California College of the Arts, CA
California Institute of the Arts, CA
Chamberlain College of Nursing, MO
Charter Oak State College, CT
Cincinnati College of Mortuary Science, OH
Cleveland Institute of Art, OH
Cleveland Institute of Music, OH
College for Creative Studies, MI
College of Art and Design at Lesley University, MA
College of Visual Arts - School is Closed, MN
Columbus College of Art and Design, OH
Corcoran College of Art and Design, DC
Cornish College of the Arts, WA
Curtis Institute of Music, PA
Eastman School of Music, NY
Excelsior College, NY
Fashion Institute of Technology/State University of New York, NY
Five Towns College, NY
Franklin University, OH
Franklin W. Olin College of Engineering, MA
Gallaudet University, DC
Granite State College, NH
Juilliard School, NY
Kansas City Art Institute, MO
Kendall College of Art and Design of Ferris State University, MI
Laguna College of Art and Design, CA
Maine College of Art, ME
Manhattan School of Music, NY
Martin University, IN
Maryland Institute College of Art, MD
Massachusetts College of Art and Design, MA
Massachusetts College of Pharmacy and Health Sciences, MA
Memphis College of Art, TN
Mercy College of Health Sciences, IA
Metropolitan State University, MN
Milwaukee Institute of Art and Design, WI
Minneapolis College of Art and Design, MN
Montserrat College of Art, MA
Moore College of Art and Design, PA
Naropa University, CO
National University, CA
Nebraska Methodist College of Nursing and Allied Health, NE
New England Conservatory of Music, MA
Otis College of Art and Design, CA
Pacific Northwest College of Art, OR
Parsons The New School for Design, NY
Pratt Institute, NY
Research College of Nursing, MO
Rhode Island School of Design, RI
Ringling College of Art and Design, FL
San Francisco Art Institute, CA
San Francisco Conservatory of Music, CA
Santa Fe University of Art and Design, NM
Savannah College of Art and Design, GA
School of the Art Institute of Chicago, IL
School of Visual Arts, NY
State University of New York/Empire State College, NY
Thomas Edison State College, NJ
Trinity College of Nursing & Health Sciences, IL
Union Institute & University, OH
University of Maryland/University College, MD
University of North Carolina School of the Arts, NC
University of the Arts, PA
VanderCook College of Music, IL
Vaughn College of Aeronautics and Technology, NY
Wentworth Institute of Technology, MA
Westminster Choir College, NJ

AN EXPLANATION OF THE COLLEGE ENTRIES

THE BASICS

Some 1700 U.S. colleges and universities, public and private college systems, and Canadian and other foreign universities are described in detail in the Profiles that follow.

The Choice of Schools

Colleges and universities in this country may achieve recognition from a number of professional organizations, but we have based our choice of U.S. colleges on accreditation from the U.S. regional accrediting associations.

Accreditation amounts to a stamp of approval given to a college. The accreditation process evaluates institutions and programs to determine whether they meet established standards of educational quality. The regional associations listed below supervise an aspect of the accrediting procedure—the study of a detailed report submitted by the institution applying for accreditation, and then an inspection visit by members of the accrediting agency. The six agencies are associated with the Commission on Recognition of Postsecondary Accreditation (CORPA). They include:

Middle States Association of Colleges and Schools
New England Association of Schools and Colleges
North Central Association of Colleges and Schools
Northwest Commission on Colleges and Universities
Southern Association of Colleges and Schools
Western Association of Schools and Colleges

Getting accreditation for the first time can take a school several years. To acknowledge that schools have begun this process, the agencies accord them candidate status. Most candidates eventually are awarded full accreditation.

The U.S. schools included in this book are fully accredited or are candidates for that status. If the latter is the case, it is indicated below the address of the school. Because the U.S. regional accrediting bodies do not officially accredit Canadian colleges and universities, and because there is no equivalent accrediting system in Canada, we have chosen to include only the larger, English-language Canadian schools—those with total full-time undergraduate enrollment of more than 10,000. It should be understood that size in no way relates to quality; there are many excellent Canadian colleges and universities with fewer than 10,000 students.

Four-Year Colleges Only

This book presents Profiles for all accredited four-year colleges that grant bachelor's degrees and admit freshmen with no previous college experience. Most of these colleges also accept transfer students. Profiles of upper-division schools, which offer only the junior or senior year of undergraduate study, are not included, nor are junior or community colleges.

Consistent Entries

Each Profile of a U.S. college is organized in the same way; the only Profiles that vary are those of Canada, schools abroad, and religious schools. The following discussion applies to the U.S. college Profiles, but refers to the other Profiles as well.

Every Profile begins with a capsule and is followed by separate sections covering the campus environment, student life, programs of study, admissions, financial aid, information for international students, computers, graduates, and the admissions contact. These categories are always introduced in the same sequence, so you can find data and compare specific points easily. The following commentary will help you evaluate and interpret the information given for each college.

Data Collection

Barron's *Profiles of American Colleges* was first published in 1964. Since then, it has been revised every year online; comprehensive revisions are undertaken every two years for the print edition. Such frequent updating is necessary because so much information about colleges—particularly enrollment figures, costs, programs of study, and admissions standards—changes rapidly.

The facts in the capsule portion of each Profile in this edition were gathered in the fall of 2013 and apply to the 2013–2014 academic year. Figures on tuition and room-and-board costs generally change soon after the book is published. For the most up-to-date information on such items, you should always check with the colleges. Other information—such as the basic nature of the school, its campus, and the educational goals of its students—changes less rapidly. A few new programs of study might be added or new services made available, but the basic educational offerings generally will remain constant.

THE CAPSULE

The capsule of each Profile provides basic information about the college at a glance. An explanation of the standard capsule is shown in the accompanying box.

All toll-free phone numbers are presumed to be out-of-state or both in-state and out-of-state, unless noted.

A former name is given if the name has been changed recently. To use the map code to the right of the college name, turn to the appropriate college-locator map at the beginning of each chapter. Wherever "n/av" is used in the capsule, it means the information was not available. The abbreviation "n/app" means not applicable.

Full-time, Part-time, Graduate

Enrollment figures are the clearest indication of the size of a college, and show whether or not it is coeducational and what the

COMPLETE NAME OF SCHOOL **MAP CODE**
(Former Name, if any)
City, State, Zip Code **Fax and Phone Numbers**

Full-time: Full-time undergraduate enrollment
Part-time: Part-time undergraduate enrollment
Graduate: Graduate enrollment
Year: Semesters, quarters, summer sessions
Application Deadline: Fall admission deadline

Faculty: Number of full-time faculty; AAUP category of school, salary-level symbol
Ph.D.s: Percentage of faculty holding Ph.D.
Student/Faculty: Full-time student/full-time faculty ratio
Tuition: Yearly tuition and fees (out-of-state if different)
Room & Board: Yearly room-and-board costs

Freshman Class: Number of students who applied, number accepted, number enrolled
SAT: Median Critical Reading, Median Math, Median Writing (abbreviated CR/M/W)
ACT: Median composite ACT

ADMISSIONS SELECTOR RATING

male-female ratio is. Graduate enrollment is presented to give a better idea of the size of the entire student body; some schools have far more graduate students enrolled than undergraduates.

Year
Some of the more innovative college calendars include the 4-1-4, 3-2-3, 3-3-1, and 1-3-1-4-3 terms. College administrators sometimes utilize various intersessions or interims—special short terms—for projects, independent study, short courses, or travel programs. The early semester calendar, which allows students to finish spring semesters earlier than those of the traditional semester calendar, gives students a head start on finding summer jobs. A modified semester (4-1-4) system provides a January or winter term, approximately four weeks long, for special projects that usually earn the same credit as one semester-long course. The trimester calendar divides the year into three equal parts; students may attend college during all three but generally take a vacation during any one. The quarter calendar divides the year into four equal parts; students usually attend for three quarters each year. The capsule also indicates schools that offer a summer session.

Application Deadline
Indicated here is the deadline for applications for admission to the fall semester. If there are no specific deadlines, it will say "open." Application deadlines for admission to other semesters are, where available, given in the admissions section of the profile.

Faculty
The first number given refers to the number of full-time faculty members at the college or university.

The Roman numeral and symbol that follow represent the salary level of faculty at the entire institution as compared with faculty salaries nationally. This information is based on the salary report* published by the American Association of University Professors (AAUP). The Roman numeral refers to the AAUP category to which the particular college or university is assigned. (This allows for comparison of faculty salaries at the same types of schools.) Category I includes "institutions that offer the doctorate degree, and that conferred in the most recent three years an annual average of fifteen or more earned doctorates covering a minimum of three nonrelated disciplines." Category IIA includes "institutions awarding degrees above the baccalaureate, but not included in Category I." Category IIB includes "institutions awarding only the baccalaureate or equivalent degree." Category III includes "institutions with academic ranks, mostly two-year institutions." Category IV includes "institutions without academic ranks." (With the exception of a few liberal arts colleges, this category includes mostly two-year institutions.)

The symbol that follows the Roman numeral indicates into which percentile range the average salary of professors, associate professors, assistant professors, and instructors at the school falls, as compared with other schools in the same AAUP category. The symbols used in this book represent the following:

++$	95th percentile and above
+$	80th–94.9th percentile
av$	60th–79.9th percentile
–$	40th–59.9th percentile
––$	39.9th percentile and below

If the school is not a member of AAUP, nothing will appear.

Ph.D.s
The figure here indicates the percentage of full-time faculty who have Ph.D.s or the highest terminal degree.

*Source: Annual Report on the Economic Status of the Profession published in the March-April 2013 issue of *Academe*: Bulletin of the AAUP, American Association of University Professors, 1133 Nineteeneth Street N.W., Suite 200, Washington, DC 20036

Student/Faculty
Student/faculty ratios may be deceptive because the faculties of many large universities include scholars and scientists who do little or no teaching. Nearly every college has some large lecture classes, usually in required or popular subjects, and many small classes in advanced or specialized fields. Here, the ratio reflects full-time students and full-time faculty, and some colleges utilize the services of a large part-time faculty. Additionally, some institutions factor in an FTE component in determining this ratio. We do not, and thus the Student/Faculty ratio that we report may differ somewhat from what the college reports. In general, a student/faculty ratio of 10 to 1 is very good.

If the faculty and student body are both mostly part-time, the entry will say "n/app."

Tuition
It is important to remember that tuition costs change continually and that in many cases, these changes are substantial. Particularly heavy increases have occurred recently and will continue to occur. On the other hand, some smaller colleges are being encouraged to lower tuitions, in order to make higher education more affordable. Students are therefore urged to contact individual colleges for the most current tuition figures.

The figure given here includes tuition and student fees for the school's standard academic year. If costs differ for state residents and out-of-state residents, the figure for nonresidents is given in parentheses. Where tuition costs are listed per credit hour (p/c), per course (p/course), or per unit (p/unit), student fees are not included. In some university systems, tuition is the same for all schools. However, student fees, and therefore the total tuition figure, may vary from school to school.

Room and Board
It is suggested that students check with individual schools for the most current room-and-board figures because, like tuition figures, they increase continually. The room-and-board figures given here represent the annual cost of a double room and all meals. The word "none" indicates that the college does not charge for room and board; "n/app" indicates that room and board are not provided.

Freshman Class
The numbers apply to the number of students who applied, were accepted, and enrolled in the 2013–2014 freshman class or in a recent class.

SAT, ACT
Whenever available, the median SAT scores—Critical Reading, Math, and Writing—and the median ACT composite score for the 2013–2014 freshman class are given. If the school has not reported median SAT or ACT scores, the capsule indicates whether the SAT or ACT is required. Note: Test scores are reported for mainstream students.

Admissions Selector Rating
The College Admissions Selector Rating indicates the degree of competitiveness of admission to the college.

THE GENERAL DESCRIPTION

The Introductory Paragraph

This paragraph indicates, in general, what types of programs the college offers, when it was founded, whether it is public or private, and its religious affiliation. Baccalaureate program accreditation and information on the size of the school's library collection are also provided.

In evaluating the size of the collection, keep in mind the difference between college and university libraries: A university's graduate and professional schools require many specialized books that would be of no value to an undergraduate. For a university, a ratio of one undergraduate to 500 books generally means an outstanding library, one to 200 an adequate library, one to 100 an inferior library. For a college, a ratio of one to 400 is outstanding, one to 300 superior, one to 200 adequate, one to 50 inferior.

These figures are somewhat arbitrary, because a large university with many professional schools or campuses requires more books than a smaller university. Furthermore, a recently founded college would be expected to have fewer books than an older school, since it has not inherited from the past what might be a great quantity of outdated and useless books. Most libraries can make up for deficiencies through interlibrary loans.

The ratio of students to the number of subscriptions to periodicals is less meaningful, and again, a university requires more periodicals than a college. But for a university, subscription to more than 15,000 periodicals is outstanding, and 6000 is generally more than adequate. For a college, 1500 subscriptions is exceptional, 700 very good, and 400 adequate. Subscription to fewer than 200 periodicals generally implies an inferior library with a very tight budget. Microform items are assuming greater importance within a library's holdings, and this information is included when available. Services of a Learning Resource Center and special facilities, such as a museum, radio or TV station, and Internet access are also described in this paragraph.

This paragraph also provides information on the campus: its size, the type of area in which it is located, and its proximity to a large city.

At most institutions, the existence of classrooms, administrative offices, and dining facilities may be taken for granted, and they generally are not mentioned in the entries unless they have been recently constructed or are considered exceptional.

Student Life

This section, with subdivisions that detail housing, campus activities, sports, facilities for disabled students, services offered to students, and campus safety concentrates on the everyday life of students.

The introductory paragraph, which includes various characteristics of the student body, gives an idea of the mix of attitudes and backgrounds. It includes, where available, percentages of students from out-of-state and from private or public high schools. It also indicates what percentage of the students belong to minority groups and what percentages are Protestant, Catholic, and Jewish. Finally, it tells the average age of all enrolled freshmen and of all undergraduates, and gives data on the freshman dropout rate and the percentage of freshmen who remain to graduate.

Housing. Availability of on-campus housing is described here. If you plan to live on campus, note the type, quantity, and capacity of the dormitory accommodations. Some colleges provide dormitory rooms for freshmen, but require upperclass students to make their own arrangements to live in fraternity or sorority houses, off-campus apartments, or rented rooms in private houses. Some small colleges require all students who do not live with parents or other relatives to live on campus. And some colleges have no residence halls.

This paragraph tells whether special housing is available and whether campus housing is single-sex or coed. It gives the percentage of those who live on campus and those who remain on campus on weekends. Finally, it states if alcohol is not permitted on campus and whether students may keep cars on campus.

Activities. Campus organizations play a vital part in students' social lives. This subsection lists types of activities, including student government, special interest or academic clubs, fraternities and sororities, and cultural and popular campus events sponsored at the college.

Sports. Sports are important on campus, so we indicate the extent of the athletic program by giving the number of intercollegiate and intramural sports offered for men and for women. We have also included the athletic and recreation facilities and campus stadium seating capacity.

Disabled Students. The colleges' own estimates of how accessible their campuses are to the physically disabled are provided. This information should be considered along with the specific kinds of special facilities available. If a Profile does not include a subsection on the disabled, the college did not provide the information.

Services. Services that may be available to students—free or for a fee—include counseling, tutoring, remedial instruction, and reader service for the blind.

Safety. This section lists the safety and security measures that are in place on the campus. These vary among schools, but may include 24-hour foot and vehicle patrol, self-defense education, security escort services, shuttle buses, informal discussions, pamphlets/posters/films, emergency telephones, and lighted pathways/sidewalks.

Programs of Study

Listed here are the bachelor's degrees granted, strongest and most popular majors, and whether associate, master's, and doctoral degrees are awarded. Major areas of study have been included under broader general areas (shown in capital letters in the profiles) for quicker reference; however, the general areas do not necessarily correspond to the academic divisions of the college or university but are more career-oriented.

Required. Wherever possible, information on specific required courses and distribution requirements is supplied, in addition to the number of credits or hours required for graduation. If the college requires students to maintain a certain grade point average (GPA) or pass comprehensive exams to graduate, that also is given.

Special. Special programs are described here. Students at almost every college now have the opportunity to study abroad, either through their college or through other institutions. Internships with businesses, schools, hospitals, and public agencies permit students to gain work experience as they learn. The pass/fail grading option, now quite prevalent, allows students to take courses in unfamiliar areas without threatening their academic average. Many schools offer students the opportunity to earn a combined B.A.-B.S. degree, pursue a general studies (no major) degree, or design their own major. Frequently students may take advantage of a cooperative program offered by two or more universities. Such a program might be referred to, for instance, as a 3-2 engineering program; a student in this program would spend three years at one institution and two at another. The number of national honor societies represented on campus is included. Schools also may conduct honors programs for qualified students, either university-wide or in specific major fields, and these also are listed.

Faculty/Classroom. The percentage of male and female faculty is mentioned here if provided by the college, along with the percentage of introductory courses taught by graduate students (if any). The average class size in an introductory lecture, laboratory, and regular class offering may also be indicated.

Admissions

The admissions section gives detailed information on standards so you can evaluate your chances for acceptance. Where the SAT or ACT scores of the 2013–2014 freshman class are broken down, you may compare your own scores. Because the role of standardized tests in the admissions process has been subject to criticism, more colleges are considering other factors such as recommendations from high school officials, leadership record, special talents, extracurricular activities, and advanced placement or honors courses completed. A few schools may consider education of parents, ability to pay for college, and relationship to alumni. Some give preference to state residents; others seek a geographically diverse student body.

If a college indicates that it follows an open admissions policy, it is noncompetitive and generally accepts all applicants who meet certain basic requirements, such as graduation from an accredited high school. If a college has rolling admissions, it decides on each application as soon as possible if the applicant's file is complete and does not specify a notification deadline. As a general rule, it is best to submit applications as early as possible.

Some colleges offer special admissions programs for nontraditional applicants. Early admissions programs allow students to begin college either during the summer before their freshman year or during what would have been their last year of high school; in the latter case, a high school diploma is not required. These programs are designed for students who are emotionally and educationally prepared for college at an earlier age than usual.

Deferred admissions plans permit students to spend a year at another activity, such as working or traveling, before beginning college. Students who take advantage of this option can relax during the year off, because they already have been accepted at a college and have a space reserved. During the year off from study, many students become clearer about their educational goals, and they perform better when they do begin study.

Early decision plans allow students to be notified by their first-choice school during the first term of the senior year. This plan may eliminate the anxiety of deciding whether or not to send a deposit to a second-choice college that offers admission before the first-choice college responds.

Requirements. This subsection specifies the minimum high school class rank and GPA, if any, required by the college for freshman applicants. It indicates what standardized tests (if any) are required, specifically the SAT or ACT, or for Puerto Rican schools, the CEEB (the Spanish-language version of the SAT). Additional requirements are given such as whether an essay, interview, or audition is necessary, and if AP*/CLEP credit is given. If a college accepts applications on computer disk or on-line, those facts are so noted and described. Other factors used by the school in the admissions decision are also listed.

Procedure. This subsection indicates when you should take entrance exams, the application deadlines for various sessions, the application fee, and when students are notified of the admissions decision. Some schools note that their application deadlines are open; this can mean either that they will consider applications until a class is filled, or that applications are considered right up until registration for the term in which the student wishes to enroll. If a waiting list is an active part of the admissions procedure, the college may indicate the number of applicants placed on that list and the number of wait-listed applicants accepted.

Transfer. Nearly every college admits some transfer students. These students may have earned associate degrees at two-year colleges and want to continue their education at a four-year college or wish to attend a different school. One important thing to consider when transferring is how many credits earned at one school will be accepted at another, so entire semesters won't be spent making up lost work. Because most schools require students to spend a specified number of hours in residence to earn a degree, it is best not to wait too long to transfer if you decide to do so.

Visiting. Some colleges hold special orientation programs for prospective students to give them a better idea of what the school is like. Many also will provide guides for informal visits, often allowing students to spend a night in the residence halls. You should make arrangements with the college before visiting.

Financial Aid

This paragraph in each Profile describes the availability of financial aid. It includes the percentage of freshmen and continuing students who receive aid, the average freshman award, and average and maximum amounts for various types of need-based and non-need-based financial aid. Aid application deadlines and required forms are also indicated.

International Students

This section begins by telling how many of the school's students come from outside the United States. It tells which English proficiency exam, if any, applicants must take. Any necessary college entrance exams, including SAT Subject tests, are listed.

Computers

This section details the scope of computerized facilities that are available for academic use. Limitations (if any) on student use of computer facilities are outlined. It also gives information on the required or recommended ownership of a PC.

Graduates

This section gives the number of graduates in the 2012–2013 class, the most popular majors and percentage of graduates earning degrees in those fields, and the percentages of graduates in the 2013 class who enrolled in graduate school or found employment within 6 months of graduation.

Admissions Contact

This is the name or title of the person to whom all correspondence regarding your application should be sent. Internet addresses are included here, along with the availability of a video of the campus.

---

* Advanced Placement and AP are registered trademarks owned by the College Entrance Examination Board. No endorsement of this product is implied or given.

PROFILES OF AMERICAN COLLEGES

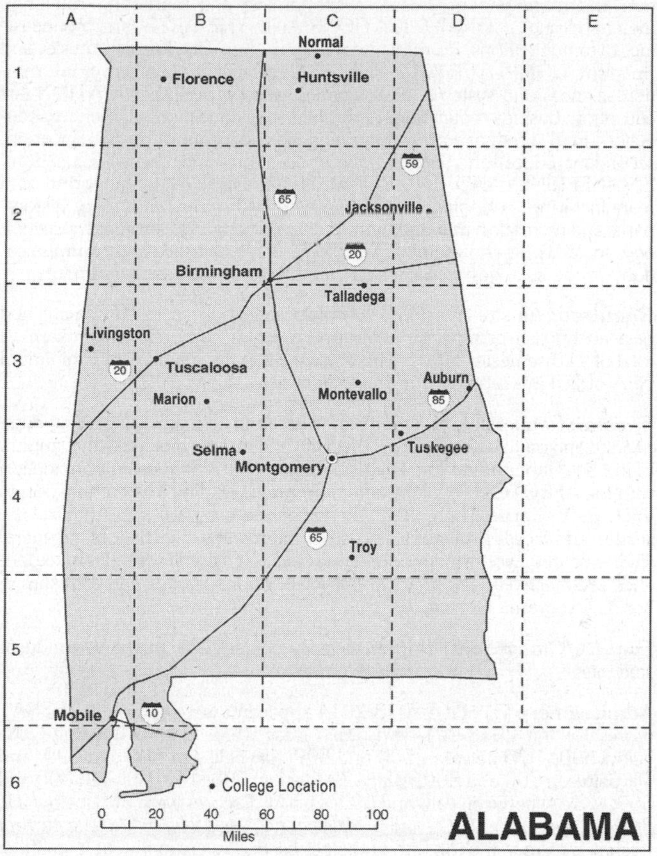

ALABAMA AGRICULTURAL AND MECHANICAL UNIVERSITY C-1

Normal, AL 35762

(256) 372-5245
(800) 553-0816; (256) 372-9747

Full-time: 2015 men, 2015 women
Part-time: 180 men, 205 women
Graduate: 385 men, 810 women
Year: semesters, summer session
Application Deadline: July 15
Freshman Class: n/av
SAT or ACT: required

Faculty: n/av
Ph.D.s: 70%
Student/Faculty: n/av
Tuition: $5010 ($9010)
Room & Board: $5600

COMPETITIVE

Alabama Agricultural and Mechanical University, founded in 1875, is a public land-grant institution offering undergraduate and graduate studies in agriculture, home economics, arts and sciences, business, education, engineering, and technology. The figures in the above capsule and in this profile are approximate. There are 5 undergraduate schools and one graduate school. In addition to regional accreditation, A&M has baccalaureate program accreditation with ABET, ADA, AHEA, CSWE, FIDER, and NCATE. The library contains 253,620 volumes, 48,300 microform items, and 3,010 audio/video tapes/CDs/DVDs, and subscribes to 2,070 periodicals including electronic. Computerized library services include interlibrary loans and database searching. Special learning facilities include an art gallery, radio station, TV station, state black archives. The 2001-acre campus is in a suburban area 90 miles north of Birmingham and 95 miles south of Nashville. Including any residence halls, there are 55 buildings.

Student Life: 70% of undergraduates are from Alabama. Others are from 42 states, 29 foreign countries, and Canada. 90% are from public schools. 90% are African American. 98% are Protestant. The average age of freshmen is 18; all undergraduates, 20. 30% do not continue beyond their first year; 60% remain to graduate.

Housing: 3100 students can be accommodated in college housing, which includes single-sex dorms. On-campus housing is guaranteed for all 4 years. 60% of students live on campus; of those, 60% remain on campus on weekends. Alcohol is not permitted. All students may keep cars.

Activities: 7% of men belong to 4 national fraternities; 9% of women belong to 4 national sororities. There are 109 groups on campus, including band, cheerleading, choir, chorus, computers, dance, debate, drama, drill team, ethnic, forensics, gay, honors, international, jazz band, marching band, newspaper, orchestra, pep band, political, professional, radio and TV, religious, social, student government, symphony, and yearbook. Popular campus events include Magic City Classic, Women's Week and Men's Week.

Sports: There are 7 intercollegiate sports for men and 7 for women, and 7 intramural sports for men and 7 for women. Facilities include a 7000-seat gym, an Olympic-size pool, track and playing fields, and a 21,000-seat stadium/health education complex.

Disabled Students: 85% of the campus is accessible. Facilities include wheelchair ramps, elevators, special parking, specially equipped restrooms, and lowered drinking fountains.

Services: Counseling and information services are available, as is tutoring in most subjects. There is a reader service for the blind.

Campus Safety and Security: Measures include 24-hour foot and vehicle patrol, self-defense education, and security escort services. There are lighted pathways/sidewalks.

Programs of Study: A&M confers B.A., B.S., B.S.C.E., B.S.E.E., B.S.E.T., B.S.M.E. and B.S.W. degrees. Associate, master's, and doctoral degrees are also awarded. Bachelor's degrees are awarded in AGRICULTURE (agricultural business management, agricultural economics, agronomy, animal science, forestry and related sciences, horticulture, and soil science), BIOLOGICAL SCIENCE (biology/biological science, neurosciences, nutrition, and zoology), BUSINESS (accounting, banking and finance, business administration and management, management science, marketing/retailing/merchandising, and office supervision and management), COMMUNICATIONS AND THE ARTS (art, classics, dramatic arts, English, French, German, graphic design, jazz, journalism, linguistics, telecommunications, and theater design), COMPUTER AND PHYSICAL SCIENCE (chemistry, computer science, mathematics, and physics), EDUCATION (agricultural education, art education, early childhood education, elementary education, home economics education, industrial arts education, middle school education, music education, physical education, science education, secondary education, special education, and trade and industrial education), ENGINEERING AND ENVIRONMENTAL DESIGN (city/community/regional planning, civil engineering, civil engineering technology, drafting and design technology, electrical/electronics engineering, electrical/electronics engineering technology, environmental engineering, industrial engineering, industrial engineering technology, mechanical engineering, and mechanical engineering technology), HEALTH PROFESSIONS (medical laboratory technology, nursing, prepharmacy, preveterinary science, and speech pathology/audiology), SOCIAL SCIENCE (criminology, economics, family/consumer studies, food science, history, human development, humanities and social science, political science/government, psychology, social work, and sociology). Physics, food science, and teacher education are the strongest academically. Business administration, education, and computer science have the largest enrollments.

Required: All students are required to take at least 52 hours of general studies, including phys ed, music, and art, and to maintain a minimum GPA of 2.0. Students must complete a total of 120 to 126 credit hours, with 30 to 36 in the major. A comprehensive exam is required for some majors.

Special: Co-op programs with Georgia Institute of Technology and Tuskegee University, cross-registration with the University of Alabama in Huntsville, Oakwood College, Calhoun Community College, and Athens State College, internships with various government agencies, dual majors, and work-study programs are available. There is a 3-2 engineering degree program with Georgia Institute of Technology. There are 5 national honor societies, a freshman honors program, and 5 departmental honors programs.

Faculty/Classroom: 70% of faculty are male; 30% are female. 50% teach undergraduates, 30% do research, and 30% do both. No introductory courses are taught by graduate students. The average class size in an introductory lecture is 90; in a laboratory is 20; and in a regular course is 30.

Requirements: The SAT or ACT is required, with a satisfactory score on the ACT. Applicants must have 4 years each of English, math, science, social studies, and history. An interview is recommended. The GED is accepted. A GPA of 2.0 is required. AP and CLEP credits are accepted. Important factors in the admissions decision are advanced placement or honors courses, leadership record, and recommendations by school officials.

Procedure: Freshmen are admitted to all sessions. There are early decision, early admissions, deferred admissions, and rolling admissions plans. Applications should be filed by July 15 for fall entry; December 1 for spring entry; and May 15 for summer entry. The fall 2013 application fee was $25. Applications are accepted online.

Transfer: Transfer students must have a minimum GPA of 2.0 and have earned at least 12 semester credit hours. 30 of 128 credits required for the bachelor's degree must be completed at A&M.

Visiting: There are regularly scheduled orientations for prospective students, consisting of sessions in June, July, and November. There are guides for informal visits and visitors may stay overnight. To schedule a visit, contact the Director of Admissions.

Financial Aid: In 2013-2014, 72% of all full-time freshmen and 68% of continuing full-time students received some form of financial aid. 75% of all full-time freshmen and 61% of continuing full-time students received need-based aid. The average freshman award was $12,018. Need-based scholarships or need-based grants averaged $11,937 ($14,450 maximum); need-based self-help aid (loans and jobs) averaged $2,884 ($2,884 maximum); and non-need-based athletic scholarships averaged $2,659 ($3,250 maximum). 50% of undergraduate students work part-time. Average annual earnings from campus work are $3600. The average financial indebtedness of the 2013 graduate was $6,060. The CCS/Profile, or FAFSA, or FFS, or SFS and the college's own financial statement are required. Check with the school for current application deadlines.

International Students: The school actively recruits these students. They must take the TOEFL.

Computers: 24 hours a day may access the system. There are no time limits. The fee is $50.

Admissions Contact: A. Boyle, Director of Admissions. E-Mail: *aboyle@asnaam.aamu.edu* Web: *www.aamu.edu*

ALABAMA STATE UNIVERSITY — C-4

Montgomery, AL 36101 — (334) 229-4291 (800) 253-5037; (334) 229-4984

Full-time: 1975 men, 2897 women	**Faculty:** n/av
Part-time: 212 men, 271 women	**Ph.D.s:** n/av
Graduate: 211 men, 508 women	**Student/Faculty:** n/av
Year: semesters, summer session	**Tuition:** $8720 ($15,656)
Application Deadline: July 30	**Room & Board:** $5422
Freshman Class: 7446 applied, 4036 accepted, 1542 enrolled	
SAT CR/M: 434/430 **ACT:** 17	**NONCOMPETITIVE**

Alabama State University, founded in 1867, is a state-assisted institution offering undergraduate programs in liberal arts and sciences, business administration, education, music, social work, aerospace studies, and health science. There are 7 undergraduate schools and one graduate school. In addition to regional accreditation, ASU has baccalaureate program accreditation with ACBSP, CSWE, NASDTEC, NASM, and NCATE. The library contains 433,939 volumes, 2.7 million microform items, and 44,679 audio/video tapes/CDs/DVDs, and subscribes to 4,506 periodicals including electronic. Computerized library services include interlibrary loans, database searching, and Internet access. Special learning facilities include an art gallery and radio station. The 253-acre campus is in a small town 91 miles south of Birmingham. Including any residence halls, there are 84 buildings.

Student Life: 70% of undergraduates are from Alabama. Others are from 41 states, 17 foreign countries, and Canada. 95% are African American. The average age of freshmen is 19; all undergraduates, 22. 70% do not continue beyond their first year; 30% remain to graduate.

Housing: 2113 students can be accommodated in college housing, which includes single-sex and coed dorms, on-campus apartments, off-campus apartments, and married student housing. In addition, there are honors houses. On-campus housing is available on a first-come and first-served basis. 55% of students commute. Alcohol is not permitted. All students may keep cars.

Activities: There are 79 groups on campus, including art, band, cheerleading, choir, chorus, dance, debate, drama, drill team, drum and bugle corps, forensics, honors, international, jazz band, marching band, musical theater, newspaper, orchestra, pep band, photography, political, professional, radio and TV, religious, social, social service, student government, symphony, and yearbook. Popular campus events include Spring and Fall Commencements, Founders Day Convocation, Fall Convocation and Honors Day Program.

Sports: There are 8 intercollegiate sports for men and 9 for women, and 6 intramural sports for men and 5 for women. Facilities include an 8000-seat acadome, a 26,500 seat stadium, a gym, 12 tennis courts, a swimming pool, an 8-lane indoor track, softball and baseball field and 3 weight rooms.

Disabled Students: 80% of the campus is accessible. Facilities include wheelchair ramps, elevators, special parking, specially equipped restrooms, special class scheduling, lowered drinking fountains, lowered telephones.

Services: Counseling and information services are available, as is tutoring in some subjects, Math, and English There is remedial math, reading, and writing.

Campus Safety and Security: Measures include 24-hour foot and vehicle patrol, emergency notification system, self-defense education, and security escort services. There are emergency telephones, lighted pathways/sidewalks, campus police.

Programs of Study: ASU confers B.A., B.S., B.M.E. and B.S.W. degrees. Master's and doctoral degrees are also awarded. Bachelor's degrees are awarded in BIOLOGICAL SCIENCE (biology/biological science), BUSINESS (accounting, banking and finance, business administration and management, business economics, and marketing/retailing/merchandising), COMMUNICATIONS AND THE ARTS (art, broadcasting, communications, dramatic arts, English, fine arts, French, music, and Spanish), COMPUTER AND PHYSICAL SCIENCE (chemistry, information sciences and systems, mathematics, and physics), EDUCATION (art education, business education, early childhood education, elementary education, English education, foreign languages education, music education, secondary education, social studies education, and special education), ENGINEERING AND ENVIRONMENTAL DESIGN (engineering and manufacturing technology), SOCIAL SCIENCE (criminal justice, history, parks and recreation management, political science/government, psychology, social work, and sociology). Biology, criminal justice and communication are the strongest acedemically, and have the largest enrollments.

Required: All students must complete a 42-hour core curriculum and pass an English proficiency exam and a senior comprehensive exam. A total of 120 semester hours, with at least 27 in the major, and a minimum GPA of 2.0 are required for graduation.

Special: Cooperative programs are offered in all majors, including engineering and math with Auburn University and marine biology with Dauphin Island Sea Laboratory. The Division of Aerospace Studies, in conjunction with the AFROTC curriculum, offers programs leading to a commission in the U.S. Air Force. There is a 3-2 engineering program with Auburn University, and cross enrollment is possible. Internships, dual majors, a general studies degree, work study, nondegree study, and credit for military experience are available. There are 8 national honor societies and a freshman honors program.

Faculty/Classroom: No introductory courses are taught by graduate students.

Admissions: 54% of the 2013-2014 applicants were accepted. The SAT scores for the 2013-2014 freshman class were: Critical Reading--79% below 500, 16% between 500 and 599, 4% between 600 and 699, and 1% between 700 and 800; Math--79% below 500, 14% between 500 and 599, and 6% between 600 and 699. The ACT scores were 60% below 21, 34% between 21 and 23, and 5% between 24 and 26. 36% of the current freshmen were in the top fifth of their class; 56% were in the top two fifths.

Requirements: The SAT or ACT is recommended. Applicants should be high school graduates with at least 3 units of English and 8 units combined in math, natural sciences, social sciences, and foreign languages. An interview is recommended. ASU requires applicants to be in the upper 30% of their class. A GPA of 2.2 is required. AP and CLEP credits are accepted.

Procedure: Freshmen are admitted fall, spring, and summer. Entrance exams should be taken in the fall of the senior year. There are early decision, early admissions, deferred admissions, and rolling admissions plans. Applications should be filed by July 30 for fall entry; December 30 for spring entry; and May 20 for summer entry. The fall 2013 application fee was $25. Applications are accepted online.

Transfer: 192 transfer students enrolled in 2012-2013. A minimum college GPA of 2.0 is required. An interview is recommended. No more than 64 semester hours are accepted for credit from 2-year colleges. 30 of 120 credits required for the bachelor's degree must be completed at ASU.

Visiting: There are regularly scheduled orientations for prospective students, including visits for spring, January and fall, July, and August . There are guides for informal visits. To schedule a visit, contact Freddie Williams at (334) 229-4291.

Financial Aid: ASU is a member of CSS. The FAFSA is required. The priority date for freshman financial aid applications for fall entry is April 1.

International Students: There are 108 international students enrolled. They must take the TOEFL, or complete ESL Level 112. They must also take the SAT or ACT.

Computers: All students may access the system 24 hours a day. There are no time limits and no fees.

Graduates: From July 1, 2012 to June 30, 2013, 600 bachelor's degrees were awarded. The most popular majors were elementary education (10%), computer information systems (9%), and social work (8%). 336 companies recruited on campus in 2012-2013. In an average class, 11% graduate in 4 years or less, 1% graduate in 5 years or less, and 26% graduate in 6 years or less.

Admissions Contact: Freddie Williams Jr., Director of Admissions. E-Mail: *fwilliams@alasu.edu* Web: *www.alasu.edu*

AMRIDGE UNIVERSITY C-4

Montgomery, AL 36117 (334) 387-7569
(800) 351-4040; (334) 387-3878

Full-time: 74 men, 127 women	**Faculty:** n/av
Part-time: 52 men, 69 women	**Ph.D.s:** 60%
Graduate: 139 men, 174 women	**Student/Faculty:** n/av
Year: semesters, summer session	**Tuition:** $11,520
Application Deadline: open	**Room & Board:** n/app
Freshman Class: n/av	

LESS COMPETITIVE

Amridge University, founded in 1967 and affiliated with the Church of Christ, merges traditional and online education, 90% of its students access Amridge University's programs via Distance Learning. There are 2 undergraduate schools and 3 graduate schools. The library contains 80,000 volumes, 500 microform items, and 800 audio/video tapes/CDs/DVDs, and subscribes to 1,200 periodicals including electronic. Computerized library services include interlibrary loans, database searching, and Internet access. The 9-acre campus is in an urban area in Montgomery, Alabama. Including any residence halls, there is 1 building.

Student Life: 53% of undergraduates are from out of state, mostly the South. Students are from 44 states, 1 foreign countries, and Canada. 39% are African American; 30% White; 28% race unknown. 77% are Baptist, Christian, Lutheran, and Methodist. The average age of freshmen is 27; all undergraduates, 35.

Housing: Alcohol is not permitted. All students commute. All students may keep cars.

Activities: There are no fraternities or sororities. Groups on campus include student government.

Disabled Students: Facilities include wheelchair ramps, special parking. All classrooms and the learning resource center are accessible.

Services: Counseling and information services are available, as is tutoring in most subjects.

Campus Safety and Security: Measures include emergency notification system and security escort services. There are lighted pathways/sidewalks.

Programs of Study: confers B.A., and B.S. degrees. Associate, master's, and doctoral degrees are also awarded. Bachelor's degrees are awarded in BUSINESS (business administration and management, human resources, and management information systems), EDUCATION (social foundations), SOCIAL SCIENCE (biblical studies, human development, law enforcement and corrections, liberal arts/general studies, ministries, and safety management). Human and Social Development, General Business, and Ministry/Bible have the largest enrollment.

Required: Students must complete at least 128 credit hours, with 40 in the major and a minimum GPA of 2.0.

Special: All undergraduate programs are available via distance learning

Faculty/Classroom: 74% of faculty are male; 26% are female. No introductory courses are taught by graduate students.

Requirements: All first time, entry-level undergraduate students are required to provide official SAT or ACT scores, official AFQT scores, or to take the ACCUPLACER assessment test (which is a proctored test provided by the University at no cost to the student.) Based on the test scores, the student may be required to take developmental courses. Admission status for first-time-in-college students may also be impacted by test scores. Undergraduate Entry-Level College Admission (First-time Freshmen)

Unconditional: 1. Admission to Amridge University's baccalaureate programs (four-year) will be granted to high school diploma graduates who score 17 or above on the American College Test (ACT) or 700 or above on the Scholastic Aptitude Test (SAT) of the College Entrance Examination Board, or the 50th percentile or higher on the Armed Forces Qualification Test (AFQT.). Applicants must present an official high school transcript or official proof of a GED and provide ACT or SAT scores to the Admissions Office at Amridge University. An occupational high school diploma, or a lesser diploma, will not be accepted as a valid high school diploma as documented by the respective official high school transcript. 2. Applicants who are 20 years of age or older and whose high school or GED transcript reflects at least an overall "B" (3.000 on 4.0 scale) average for all courses or a grade of "B" (or 80% passing score for GED) for 12th grade English and basic algebra may be accepted without taking an aptitude test. 3. Applicants who have not completed high school may be admitted on the basis of a GED. 4. Home-schooled applicants who have a composite ACT test score of 17, or an SAT score of 700 or the 50% percentile or higher on the AFQT may be admitted as unconditional students. Additionally, in accordance with Section 668.32 of Title 34 of the code of Federal Regulations, home-schooled students must obtain a secondary school completion credential for home school provided for under their respective State law. If the State law does not require a home-schooled student to obtain such credential, the student must submit documentation of a completed secondary school education in a home school setting that qualifies as an exemption from compulsory attendance requirements under State law. In addition, an interview with the student will be conducted by the Vice President of Academic Affairs or his or her designee. 5. Applicants from non-accredited high schools who have a composite ACT test score of 17 or an SAT score of 700 may be admitted as unconditional students. Graduates of non-accredited high schools must provide an official high school transcript and have completed a minimum of fifteen Carnegie Units. An occupational high school diploma, or a lesser diploma, will not be accepted as a valid high school diploma as documented by the respective official high school transcript. In accordance with Section 668.32 of Title 34 of the code of Federal Regulations, home-schooled students must obtain a secondary school completion credential for home school provided for under their respective State law. If the State law does not require a home-schooled student to obtain such credential, the student must submit documentation of a completed secondary school education in a home school setting that qualifies as an exemption from compulsory attendance requirements under State law. Also, an interview with the student will be conducted by the Vice President of Academic Affairs or his or her designee. 6. Students admitted unconditionally based on composite ACT/SAT scores but whose sub-report in English or math indicate a deficiency may be required to take developmental courses. Undergraduate Entry-Level College Admission Conditional: Applicants who fail to meet unconditional admission requirements may be approved for admission by special permission. The Admissions Office will consider students who show potential for college work in accordance with the following provisions: 1. Applicants whose composite ACT score equals 14 - 16 or an SAT score of 650 or the 31st - 49th percentile on the Armed Forces Qualification Test (AFQT) may be admitted to attend Amridge University as conditional students and may be required to take developmental courses. 2. Applicants from non-accredited high schools and/or home schooling who have a composite ACT test score of 14 - 16 or an SAT score of 650 or the 31st - 49th percentile on the AFQT may be admitted as conditional students and may be required to take developmental courses. An occupational high school diploma, or a lesser diploma, will not be accepted as a valid high school diploma as documented by the respective official high school transcript. In accordance with Section 668.32 of Title 34 of the code of Federal Regulations, home-schooled students must obtain a secondary school completion credential for home school provided for under their respective State law. If the State law does not require a home-schooled student to obtain such credential, the student must submit documentation of a completed secondary school education in a home school setting that qualifies as an exemption from compulsory attendance requirements under State law. In addition, an interview with the student will be conducted by the Vice President of Academic Affairs or his or her designee. 3. Entry-Level students without ACT or SAT scores will be required to take a proctored ACCUPLACER assessment and, based on the results, may be required to take developmental courses. 4. The applicant must complete all of the admission process. This includes providing all supporting documents, such as: an official high school transcript or GED, application, application fee, and ACCUPLACER assessment scores, ACCUPLACER assessment fee, etc., as required. 5. Students whose ACT, SAT or ACCUPLACER scores indicate a need for developmental reading courses will not be admitted to Amridge University because the University does not teach remedial reading. Students will be given guidance regarding remedial reading opportunities in their geographic location, and will be welcome to reapply to Amridge once reading issues have been addressed. UNDERGRADUATE TRANSFER STUDENT ADMISSION REQUIREMENTS Undergraduate Transfer Students Admission Unconditional: A transfer student will be eligible for unconditional admission with a cumulative grade point average (CGPA) of 2.0 on a 4.0 scale on all previously completed undergraduate coursework. Nontraditional credit will not be factored into the CGPA, such as: CLEP, DANTES, etc. Undergraduate Transfer Students Admission Conditional: 1. Transfer students who do not meet the above conditions may be eligible for conditional admission. Criteria for conditional admission may include one of the following: 2. When the student's record indicates a cumulative grade point average (CGPA) between 1.5 and 1.9 on a 4.0 scale on all previously completed coursework the newly enrolled student must earn a 2.0 grade point average on 24 semester hours attempted at Amridge University. 3. Students with a cumulative transfer grade point average below the 1.5 average (CGPA) must obtain approval of the Vice President of Academic Affairs for consideration for admission. Special consideration may be given to students who are over the age of 24. 4. A conditionally admitted transfer student will be permitted to take a maximum of 12 semester hours per semester until he or she has cleared the conditional status. 5. Those students transferring less than 64 semester hours may be required to take specified courses to enhance basic skills. CLEP credits are accepted.

Procedure: Freshmen are admitted to all sessions. There are deferred admissions and rolling admissions plans. Application deadlines are open. Application fee is $50. Notification is sent on a rolling basis. Applications are accepted online.

Transfer: 1000 transfer students enrolled in 2012-2013. Unconditional admission requires a 2.0 GPA on prior course work; below 2.0, students are admitted on a conditional basis. 40 of 128 credits required for the bachelor's degree must be completed at.

Financial Aid: In 2013-2014, 100% of all full-time freshmen and 100%

of continuing full-time students received some form of financial aid. 80% of all full-time freshmen and 80% of continuing full-time students received need-based aid. The FAFSA and the college's own financial statement are required. Check with the school for current application deadlines.

International Students: They must take the TOEFL with a minimum score of 440 on the paper-based TOEFL (PBT) or 65 on the Internet-based version (iBT). They must also take the SAT or ACT.

Computers: All students may access the system.

Graduates: From July 1, 2012 to June 30, 2013, 68 bachelor's degrees were awarded. The most popular majors were management communication (25%), human development (22%), and Ministry/Bible (20%).

Admissions Contact: Carl Byrd, Advising/Recruiting Services Coordinator. E-Mail: *carlbyrd@ambridgeuniversity.edu* Web: *www.amridgeuniversity.edu*

AUBURN UNIVERSITY SYSTEM

The Auburn University System, established in 1856, is a land-grant system in Alabama. It is governed by a board of trustees, whose chief administrator is the president. The primary goal of the system is to provide outstanding, economical instruction to its undergraduate, graduate, and professional students. The main priorities are to expand and diversify overall research efforts, and to disseminate and apply knowledge through extension and public service programs. The total student enrollment is usually 29,960 with 1701 faculty members. Altogether there are 120 baccalaureate, 75 master's, and 42 doctoral programs offered in the Auburn University System. Profiles of the 4-year campuses are included in this section.

AUBURN UNIVERSITY D-3

Auburn, AL 36849 **(334) 844-4080; (334) 844-4773**

Full-time: 8973 men, 9038 women	**Faculty:** n/av; I, --$
Part-time: 1135 men, 653 women	**Ph.D.s:** 95%
Graduate: 2520 men, 2545 women	**Student/Faculty:** 18 to 1
Year: semesters, summer session	**Tuition:** $9446 ($25,190)
Application Deadline: February 1	**Room & Board:** $10,606
Freshman Class: 15745 applied, 13027 accepted, 3726 enrolled	
SAT CR/M/W: 560/590/570 **ACT:** 27	**VERY COMPETITIVE+**

Auburn University, founded in 1856, is a state-supported land grant institution offering undergraduate, first professional, and graduate degrees in agriculture, business, education, engineering, liberal arts, sciences and math, veterinary medicine, architecture/design and construction, forestry, human sciences, nursing, and pharmacy. There are 11 undergraduate schools and one graduate school. In addition to regional accreditation, Auburn has baccalaureate program accreditation with AACSB, ABET, ACEJMC, ACPE, ADA, AHEA, ASLA, CSAB, CSWE, FIDER, NAAB, NASAD, NASM, NCATE, NLN, and SAF. The 3 libraries contain 4.3 million volumes, 2.7 million microform items, and 122,201 audio/video tapes/CDs/DVDs, and subscribe to 65,771 periodicals including electronic. Computerized library services include interlibrary loans, database searching, Internet access, and Wi-Fi capability. Special learning facilities include an art gallery, radio station, TV station, a nuclear science center, arboretum, electron microscope laboratory, MRI research center and a museum of fine arts. The 1875-acre campus is in a small town 110 miles southwest of Atlanta, GA. Including any residence halls, there are 322 buildings.

Student Life: 63% of undergraduates are from Alabama. Others are from 49 states, 82 foreign countries, and Canada. 86% are from public schools. 85% are White. The average age of freshmen is 18; all undergraduates, 20. 10% do not continue beyond their first year; 68% remain to graduate.

Housing: 3986 students can be accommodated in college housing, which includes single-sex and coed dorms, on-campus apartments, and married student housing. In addition, there are honors houses, fraternity houses, learning communities. On-campus housing is available on a first-come and first-served basis. 79% of students commute. Alcohol is not permitted. All students may keep cars.

Activities: 18% of men belong to 31 national fraternities; 29% of women belong to 19 national sororities. There are 340 groups on campus, including art, band, cheerleading, chess, choir, chorale, chorus, computers, dance, drama, drill team, environmental, ethnic, film, gay, honors, international, jazz band, literary magazine, marching band, musical theater, newspaper, opera, orchestra, pep band, photography, political, professional, radio and TV, religious, social, social service, student government, symphony, and yearbook. Popular campus events include A Day, Pep Rallies and Tiger Nights.

Sports: There are 8 intercollegiate sports for men and 11 for women, and 15 intramural sports for men and 15 for women. Facilities include an 87,451-seat stadium, a 10,500-seat coliseum, baseball and softball stadiums, a women's athletics center, a tennis center, an aquatics center, a soccer complex, a track, intramural field houses, a golf course, 2 equestrian arenas, and a student activities center with a volleyball arena, racquetball, tennis, and basketball courts, a fitness/weight room, and an aerobics/cardio theater.

Disabled Students: All of the campus is accessible. Facilities include wheelchair ramps, elevators, special parking, specially equipped restrooms, special class scheduling, lowered drinking fountains, special housing. elevators with Braille controls, wheelchair lifts and assistive technology lab.

Services: Counseling and information services are available, as is tutoring in most subjects. There is a reader service for the blind, and remedial writing. Auburn's Academic Support Services provides supplemental instruction and study partners through regularly scheduled peer-review sessions by students selected by the faculty.

Campus Safety and Security: Measures include 24-hour foot and vehicle patrol, emergency notification system, self-defense education, and security escort services. There are shuttle buses, emergency telephones, lighted pathways/sidewalks, and controlled access to dorms/residences.

Programs of Study: Auburn confers B.A., B.S., B.A.E., B.Arch., B.B.S.E., B.C.E., B.Che.E., B.E.E., B.F.A., B.Int. Arch., B.Int.Design, B.I.S.E., B.M.E., B.Mus.Ed., B.M., B.W.E, B.Mtl.E., B.P.F.E., B.SW.E. and B.B.S.E. B.A., B.S., B.A.E., B.Arch., B.B.E., B.C.E., B.Che.E., B.E.E., B.F.A., B.Int.Arch., B.Int Design, B.I.S.E., B.M.E., B.Mus.ED., B.Mtl.E., B.P.F.E., B.Sw.E. and B.W.E. Master's and doctoral degrees are also awarded. Bachelor's degrees are awarded in AGRICULTURE (agricultural business management, agricultural communications, agricultural economics, agriculture, agronomy, animal science, equine science, fishing and fisheries, forest engineering, forestry production and processing, horticulture, poultry science, and soil science), BIOLOGICAL SCIENCE (biochemistry, biology/biological science, botany, cell biology, marine biology, microbiology, molecular biology, nutrition, wildlife biology, and zoology), BUSINESS (accounting, apparel and accessories marketing, banking and finance, business administration and management, business economics, fashion merchandising, hotel/motel and restaurant management, international business management, marketing/retailing/merchandising, personnel management, and transportation management), COMMUNICATIONS AND THE ARTS (apparel design, art, communications, design, dramatic arts, English, fine arts, French, German, graphic design, industrial design, journalism, languages, public relations, Spanish, and speech/debate/rhetoric), COMPUTER AND PHYSICAL SCIENCE (actuarial science, applied mathematics, chemistry, computer science, geology, mathematics, physics, and software engineering), EDUCATION (business education, early childhood education, education, education administration, elementary education, English education, foreign languages education, health education, home economics education, industrial arts education, mathematics education, middle school education, music education, physical education, science education, secondary education, social science education, special education, and vocational education), ENGINEERING AND ENVIRONMENTAL DESIGN (aeronautical engineering, agricultural engineering, architecture, aviation administration/management, chemical engineering, civil engineering, computer engineering, construction management, electrical/electronics engineering, environmental science, industrial engineering, interior design, landscape architecture/design, materials engineering, mechanical engineering, and textile engineering), HEALTH PROFESSIONS (biomedical science, health care administration, medical laboratory technology, nursing, predentistry, premedicine, preoptometry, preveterinary science, and speech pathology/audiology), SOCIAL SCIENCE (anthropology, criminology, economics, food science, geography, history, home furnishings and equipment management/production/services, human development, philosophy, physical fitness/movement, political science/government, psychology, public administration, social work, sociology, and textiles and clothing). Engineering, education and architecture are the strongest academically. Engineering, business and liberal arts have the largest enrollments.

Required: Auburn University's Core Curriculum sets a foundation for learning by requiring students to complete 41-2 credit hours in courses that provide a broad-based academic foundation and that ensure students receive grounding in the competencies articulated in our general education student learning outcomes. The Core Curriculum consists of an 8 hour sequence in science, a six-hour sequence in English composition, a three-four hour course in mathematics, twelve hours of social science (including at least three hours in history), and twelve hours of humanities (including at least three hours of fine arts and three hours of literature). Each student is also required to complete a six-hour sequence in either literature or history. Students must also choose a major curriculum and complete its requirements and those of the college or school with at least a 2.0 GPA. The total number of credit hours required is at least 120; some majors require more.

Special: Opportunities are available for co-op programs, internships, work-study, and dual majors on a program-by-program basis; students should contact their advisers for specific information. 3-2 engineering degrees are offered with numerous other liberal arts colleges or with Auburn's colleges of Agriculture, Liberal Arts, or Sciences and Mathematics. Other options available to students include study abroad in more than 47 countries, credit by exam, non degree study, and pass/fail grading on select courses. There are 42 national honor societies, including Phi Beta Kappa, a freshman honors program, and 26 departmental honors programs.

Faculty/Classroom: 63% of faculty are male; 37% are female. Graduate students teach 17% of introductory courses.

Admissions: 83% of the 2013-2014 applicants were accepted. The SAT scores for the 2013-2014 freshman class were: Critical Reading--13% below 500, 52% between 500 and 599, 27% between 600 and 699, and 8% between 700 and 800; Math--10% below 500, 41% between 500 and 599, 37% between 600 and 699, and 12% between 700 and 800; Writing--19% below 500, 45% between 500 and 599, 30% between 600 and 699, and 6% between 700 and 800. The ACT scores were 3% below 21, 16% between 21 and 23, 30% between 24 and 26, 16% between 27 and 28, and 35% above 28. 51% of the current freshmen were in the top fifth of their class; 78% were in the top two fifths. There were 68 National Merit finalists.

Requirements: The SAT or ACT is required. Favorable consideration for admission will be given to accredited secondary school graduates whose college ability test scores and high school grades give promise of the greatest level of success in college courses. Secondary school students planning to apply for admission are required to complete 4 years of English, 3 years each of social studies and math, and 2 years of science. Applicants of a mature age who are not high school graduates may be considered for admission if their educational attainments are shown through testing to be equivalent to those of high school graduates. Tests include the USAFI General Education Development Test, the American College Test, or other tests recommended by the Admissions Committee. AP credits are accepted.

Procedure: Freshmen are admitted to all sessions. There are deferred admissions and rolling admissions plans. Applications should be filed by February 1 for fall entry; October 1 for spring entry; and February 1 for summer entry, along with a $50 fee. Notification is sent on a rolling basis. Applications are accepted online.

Transfer: 1052 transfer students enrolled in 2012-2013. Transfer applicants must provide official transcripts from each college attended. A satisfactory citizenship record, a minimum 2.5 GPA on all college work, and eligibility to re enter the institution last attended are required for transfer admission. All transfer students who have attempted 32 semester hours of college work must have earned a cumulative 2.5 GPA in at least 20 semester hours of standard academic courses, in addition to the overall 2.5 cumulative average. These 20 semester hours must include at least 1 course in English (college-level composition or literature) and 1 in natural science with a lab. 30 of 120 credits required for the bachelor's degree must be completed at Auburn.

Visiting: There are regularly scheduled orientations for prospective students, including War Eagle Days, held in the fall and spring and offering students and their families an opportunity to meet with representatives from admissions, financial aid, housing, residence life, and various academic departments. There are guides for informal visits and visitors may sit in on classes. To schedule a visit, contact the Office of Admissions at admissions@auburn.edu.

Financial Aid: In 2013-2014, 76% of all full-time freshmen and 69% of continuing full-time students received some form of financial aid. 37% of all full-time freshmen and 39% of continuing full-time students received need-based aid. The average freshman award was $12,249. Need-based scholarships or need-based grants averaged $6,883 ; need-based self-help aid (loans and jobs) averaged $3,666; and non-need-based athletic scholarships averaged $26,406. 13% of undergraduate students work part-time. Average annual earnings from campus work are $4500. The average financial indebtedness of the 2013 graduate was $26,640. Auburn is a member of CSS. The FAFSA is required. The deadline for filing freshman financial aid applications for fall entry is March 1.

International Students: There are 179 international students enrolled. The school actively recruits these students. They must take the TOEFL with a minimum score of 550 on the paper-based TOEFL (PBT) or 79 on the Internet-based version (iBT). They must also take the SAT or ACT.

Computers: All students may access the system. 24 hours a day. There are no time limits and no fees.

Graduates: From July 1, 2012 to June 30, 2013, 4278 bachelor's degrees were awarded. The most popular majors were business (19%), engineering (15%), and education (11%). 326 companies recruited on campus in 2012-2013. In an average class, 1% graduate in 3 years or less, 38% graduate in 4 years or less, 63% graduate in 5 years or less, and 68% graduate in 6 years or less. Of the 2012 graduating class, 42% were enrolled in graduate school within 6 months of graduation, and 77% were employed.

Admissions Contact: Dr. Wayne Alderman, Dean of Enrollment Services. E-Mail: *admissions@auburn.edu* Web: *www.auburn.edu*

AUBURN UNIVERSITY AT MONTGOMERY C-4

Montgomery, AL 36124 **(334) 244-3615; (334) 244-3795**

Full-time: 1158 men, 1748 women	**Faculty:** 168
Part-time: 535 men, 784 women	**Ph.D.s:** 82%
Graduate: 229 men, 535 women	**Student/Faculty:** 16 to 1
Year: semesters, summer session	**Tuition:** $8150 ($23,375)
Application Deadline: August 1	**Room & Board:** $3970
Freshman Class: 1739 applied, 1286 accepted, 567 enrolled	
SAT: required	**ACT:** 22 **COMPETITIVE**

Auburn University Montgomery, founded in 1967, is a public institution. The mission of Auburn University at Montgomery is to provide quality and diverse educational opportunities at the undergraduate and graduate levels through use of traditional and electronic delivery systems, and to foster and support an environment conducive to teaching, research, scholarship, and collaboration with government agencies, our community, and other educational institutions. There are 5 undergraduate schools and 5 graduate schools. In addition to regional accreditation, AUM has baccalaureate program accreditation with AACSB and NCATE. The library contains 386,660 volumes, 2.4 million microform items, and 25,965 audio/video tapes/CDs/DVDs, and subscribes to 725 periodicals including electronic. Computerized library services include interlibrary loans, database searching, Internet access, and Wi-Fi capability. Special learning facilities include an art gallery, TV station, A graphic arts center, and a mass communication lab., and a multimedia tlevision studio. The 500-acre campus is in a suburban area 7 miles east of downtown Montgomery. Including any residence halls, there are 16 buildings.

Student Life: 92% of undergraduates are from Alabama. Others are from 35 states, 31 foreign countries, and Canada. 53% are White; 30% African American. The average age of freshmen is 19; all undergraduates, 24. 42% do not continue beyond their first year; 32% remain to graduate.

Housing: 700 students can be accommodated in college housing, which includes single-sex and coed dorms, on-campus apartments, and married student housing. On-campus housing is available on a first-come and first-served basis. 88% of students commute. All students may keep cars.

Activities: 1% of men belong to 5 national fraternities; 2% of women belong to 6 national sororities. There are 54 groups on campus, including and campus activities board, art, cheerleading, computers, environmental, ethnic, gay, honors, international, musical theater, newspaper, professional, radio and TV, religious, social, social service, and student government. Popular campus events include AUM Fest, Welcome Week and Spring Fest.

Sports: There are 5 intercollegiate sports for men and 5 for women, and 15 intramural sports for men and 15 for women. Facilities include a multipurpose gym-auditorium, an indoor jogging and walking track, baseball and soccer fields, tennis courts, and softball field. A newly completed wellness center is available as part of students fees.

Disabled Students: 95% of the campus is accessible. Facilities include wheelchair ramps, elevators, special parking, specially equipped restrooms, special class scheduling, lowered drinking fountains, lowered telephones, and special housing.

Services: Counseling and information services are available, as is tutoring in every subject. There is a reader service for the blind, and remedial math, reading, and writing. Help with study skills is also available.

Campus Safety and Security: Measures include 24-hour foot and vehicle patrol and security escort services. There are emergency telephones and lighted pathways/sidewalks.

Programs of Study: AUM confers B.A., B.S., B.L.A., B.S.B.A. and B.S.N. degrees. Master's and doctoral degrees are also awarded. Bachelor's degrees are awarded in BIOLOGICAL SCIENCE (biology/biological science), BUSINESS (accounting, banking and finance, business administration and management, business economics, marketing/retailing/merchandising, and personnel management), COMMUNICATIONS AND THE ARTS (communications, English, and fine arts), COMPUTER AND PHYSICAL SCIENCE (information sciences and systems, mathematics, and physical sciences), EDUCATION (elementary education and secondary education), HEALTH PROFESSIONS (nursing), SOCIAL SCIENCE (criminal justice, history, international studies, liberal arts/general studies, political science/government, psychology, and sociology). Education, and liberal arts are the strongest academically. Political science, general business and elementary education have the largest enrollments.

Required: To graduate, students must complete a minimum of 120 credit hours with a minimum GPA of 2.0 in the major and overall. All students must fulfill English composition requirements and liberal education program requirements. All students must complete five writing intensive courses.

Special: AUM offers co-op programs in some majors, cross-registration with Huntingdon College and Faulkner University, and study abroad in South Korea. There are 7 national honor societies, a freshman honors program, and 10 departmental honors programs.

Faculty/Classroom: 50% of faculty are male; 50% are female. 98% teach undergraduates, and 98% do both. No introductory courses are taught by graduate students. The average class size in a laboratory is 24 and in a regular course is 32.

Admissions: 74% of the 2013-2014 applicants were accepted.

Requirements: The SAT or ACT is required. In addition, High school preparation should include English, math, social studies, science, and foreign language. The GED may be used for admission. A GPA of 2.3 is required. AP and CLEP credits are accepted.

Procedure: Freshmen are admitted to all sessions. Entrance exams should be taken in the junior year. There are early decision, early admissions, deferred admissions, and rolling admissions plans. Applications should be filed by August 1 for fall entry, along with a $25 fee. Applications are accepted online.

Transfer: Applicants for transfer must have a C average and be in good standing at their last school. 30 of 120 credits required for the bachelor's degree must be completed at AUM.

Visiting: There are regularly scheduled orientations for prospective students, including meetings with faculty, staff, advising, and registration. There are guides for informal visits and visitors may sit in on classes.

Financial Aid: In 2013-2014, 62% of all full-time freshmen and of continuing full-time students received some form of financial aid. 51% of all full-time freshmen and of continuing full-time students received need-based aid. The average freshman award was $8,094. Need-based scholarships or need-based grants averaged $4,738 ($6,150 maximum); and need-based self-help aid (loans and jobs) averaged $3,490 ($8,000 maximum). The FAFSA is required. The priority date for freshman financial aid applications for fall entry is March 1.

International Students: There are 186 international students enrolled. The school actively recruits these students. They must take the TOEFL with a minimum score of 500 on the paper-based TOEFL (PBT) or 61 on the Internet-based version (iBT). They must also take the SAT or ACT, scoring 18.

Computers: All students may access the system. from 7 a.m. to 1 a.m. There are no time limits and no fees.

Graduates: From July 1, 2012 to June 30, 2013, 640 bachelor's degrees were awarded. The most popular majors were business (31%), sciences (26%), and education (15%). 65 companies recruited on campus in 2012-2013. In an average class, 33% graduate in 6 years or less.

Admissions Contact: Valerie Crawford, Director Admissions. E-Mail: *admitme@aum.edu* Web: *www.aum.edu*

BIRMINGHAM-SOUTHERN COLLEGE C-2

Birmingham, AL 35254 **(205) 226-4696**
(800) 523-5793; (205) 523-3074

Full-time: 632 men, 535 women	**Faculty:** 111; IIB, -$
Part-time: 11 men, 10 women	**Ph.D.s:** 92%
Year: 4-1-4, summer session	**Student/Faculty:** 13 to 1
Application Deadline: February 1	**Tuition:** $30,690
	Room & Board: $12,280

Freshman Class: 1638 applied, 931 accepted, 356 enrolled
SAT CR/M/W: 570/580/570 **ACT:** 26 **VERYCOMPETITIVE+**

Birmingham-Southern College, founded in 1856, is a private liberal arts college affiliated with the United Methodist Church. There is one undergraduate school and one graduate school. In addition to regional accreditation, BSC has baccalaureate program accreditation with NASM and NCATE. The library contains 263,024 volumes, 90,675 microform items, and 38,261 audio/video tapes/CDs/DVDs, and subscribes to 40,000 periodicals including electronic. Computerized library services include interlibrary loans, database searching, Internet access, and Wi-Fi capability. Special learning facilities include an art gallery, planetarium, an environmental center, and an outdoor educational center. The 201-acre campus is in an urban area 3 miles west of downtown Birmingham. Including any residence halls, there are 45 buildings.

Student Life: 75% of undergraduates are from Alabama. Others are from 31 states, and 12 foreign countries. 65% are from public schools. 83% are White. 54% are Protestant; 16% claim no religious affiliation; 13% Catholic. The average age of freshmen is 18; all undergraduates, 21. 19% do not continue beyond their first year; 71% remain to graduate.

Housing: 1429 students can be accommodated in college housing, which includes single-sex dorms, on-campus apartments, and married student housing. In addition, there are fraternity houses, sorority houses, international, community service, and environmental areas in residence halls. On-campus housing is guaranteed for all 4 years. 84% of students live on campus; of those, 55% remain on campus on weekends. All students may keep cars.

Activities: 43% of men belong to 6 national fraternities; 52% of women belong to 7 national sororities. There are 79 groups on campus, including art, cheerleading, choir, chorale, chorus, computers, dance, drama, environmental, ethnic, gay, honors, international, jazz band, literary magazine, marching band, musical theater, newspaper, opera, orchestra, pep band, political, professional, religious, social, social service, student government, symphony, and yearbook. Popular campus events include Honors Day, Halloween on the Hilltop and Entertainment Fest.

Sports: There are 11 intercollegiate sports for men and 11 for women, and 19 intramural sports for men and 19 for women. Facilities include a football stadium, an urban environmental park, a coliseum, a baseball field, racquetball and tennis courts, 2 soccer fields, a weight room, an intramural athletic field, an indoor pool, a game room, an indoor jogging track, 3 gyms, and an aerobics studio.

Disabled Students: 90% of the campus is accessible. Facilities include wheelchair ramps, elevators, special parking, specially equipped restrooms, special class scheduling, lowered drinking fountains, lowered telephones, and special housing.

Services: Counseling and information services are available, as is tutoring in some subjects, math, English, and computer science. Through the use of peer tutors and one-on-one assistance, the Academic Resource Center also promotes the Foundation's general education goal of collaborative learning and peer-teaching.

Campus Safety and Security: Measures include 24-hour foot and vehicle patrol, emergency notification system, self-defense education, and security escort services. There are shuttle buses, emergency telephones, and lighted pathways/sidewalks.

Programs of Study: BSC confers B.A., B.F.A., B.Mus., B.Mus.Ed. and B.S. degrees. Bachelor's degrees are awarded in AGRICULTURE (environmental studies), BIOLOGICAL SCIENCE (biology/biological science), BUSINESS (accounting, business administration and management, and international business management), COMMUNICATIONS AND THE ARTS (art history and appreciation, dance, dramatic arts, English, French, German, music, musical theater, painting, photography, printmaking, sculpture, Spanish, and studio art), COMPUTER AND PHYSICAL SCIENCE (chemistry, computer science, mathematics, and physics), EDUCATION (art education, collaborative education, dance education, education services, music education, and secondary education), SOCIAL SCIENCE (Asian/Oriental studies, biopsychology, economics, history, interdisciplinary studies, international studies, Latin American studies, philosophy, political science/government, psychology, religion, and sociology). Biology, English, and psychology are the strongest academically. Business administration, accounting, and history have the largest enrollment.

Required: All students must complete 32 regular units with courses in English composition and literature, lab sciences, math, fine arts, foreign language, social sciences, history, and philosophy or religion as well as 4 (January) interim projects. A total of 128 credits with a GPA of at least 2.0 is required to graduate.

Special: There is cross-registration with the University of Alabama at Birmingham, Miles College, the University of Montevallo, and Samford University. Student-designed, dual, and interdisciplinary majors, internships, work-study programs, and study abroad are offered. There is a 3-2 nursing program with Vanderbilt University and a 3-2 environmental studies program wih Duke University. A 3-2 engineering degree is offered with the University of Alabama at Birmingham, Auburn University, Columbia University, and Washington University. There are 19 national honor societies, including Phi Beta Kappa, a freshman honors program, and 5 departmental honors programs.

Faculty/Classroom: 57% of faculty are male; 43% are female. 92% teach undergraduates. No introductory courses are taught by graduate students. The average class size in an introductory lecture is 17 and in a laboratory is 20.

Admissions: 18% of the 2013-2014 applicants were accepted. The SAT scores for the 2013-2014 freshman class were: Critical Reading--18% below 500, 44% between 500 and 599, 32% between 600 and 699, and 6% between 700 and 800; Math--12% below 500, 44% between 500 and 599, 32% between 600 and 699, and 11% between 700 and 800; Writing--16% below 500, 45% between 500 and 599, 28% between 600 and 699, and 12% between 700 and 800. The ACT scores were 4% below 21, 23% between 21 and 23, 27% between 24 and 26, 19% between 27 and 28, and 25% above 28. 40% of the current freshmen were in the top fifth of their class; 81% were in the top two fifths. There was 1 National Merit finalist. 5 freshmen graduated first in their class.

Requirements: The SAT or ACT is required. The minimum SAT score should be 970 combined, and the minimum ACT score, 21. Applicants should have graduated from an accredited secondary school with 4 courses in English, 4 each in math, science, and social studies, and a recommended 2 in foreign language. The GED is also accepted. An essay is required and an interview is recommended. Fine arts majors are advised to submit a portfolio or arrange an interview with the fine arts department. BSC requires applicants to be in the upper 50% of their class. A GPA of 2.3 is required. AP and CLEP credits are accepted. Important factors in the admissions decision are advanced placement or honors courses, leadership record, and recommendations by school officials.

Procedure: Freshmen are admitted fall, spring, and summer. Entrance exams should be taken in the spring of the junior year. There are early admissions and deferred admissions plans. Applications should be filed by February 1 for fall entry; December 15 for winter entry; January 15 for spring entry; and May 1 for summer entry, along with a $50 fee. Notification is sent on a rolling basis. Applications are accepted online.

Transfer: 27 transfer students enrolled in 2012-2013. Transfer applicants must have a minimum GPA of 2.0 and leave their former school in good standing. An essay and a school recommendation are required. An interview is recommended. 72 of 144 credits required for the bachelor's degree must be completed at BSC.

Visiting: There are regularly scheduled orientations for prospective students, including preview and scholarship days, and individual visits. There are guides for informal visits, visitors may sit in on classes, and stay overnight. To schedule a visit, contact Becky Baxter at bbaxter@bsc.edu.

Financial Aid: In 2013-2014, 99% of all full-time freshmen and 99% of continuing full-time students received some form of financial aid. 51% of all full-time freshmen and 51% of continuing full-time students received need-based aid. The average freshman award was $26,844. Need based scholarships or need-based grants averaged $6,290 ($16,000 maximum); need-based self-help aid (loans and jobs) averaged $2,549 ($6,500 maximum); and other non-need-based awards and non-need-based scholarships averaged $18,005 ($45,162 maximum). 28% of undergraduate students work part-time. Average annual earnings from campus work are $972. The average financial indebtedness of the 2013 graduate was $32,250. The FAFSA is required. The priority date for freshman financial aid applications for fall entry is March 1.

International Students: There are 36 international students enrolled. The school actively recruits these students. They must take the TOEFL with a minimum score of 500 on the paper-based TOEFL (PBT) or 61 on the Internet-based version (iBT). The SAT or ACT is required instead of the TOEFL for students whose primary language is English, with minimum English or verbal scores of 21 or 475.

Computers: All students may access the system 24 hours a day. There are no time limits. The fee is $660.

Graduates: From July 1, 2012 to June 30, 2013, 239 bachelor's degrees were awarded. The most popular majors were business administration (18%), biology (11%), and English (9%). 200 companies recruited on campus in 2012-2013. In an average class, 1% graduate in 3 years or less, 58% graduate in 4 years or less, 68% graduate in 5 years or less, and 72% graduate in 6 years or less.

Admissions Contact: Sheri S. Salmon, Assoc. VP for Enrollment Management. E-Mail: *admission@bsc.edu* Web: *www.bsc.edu*

CONCORDIA COLLEGE - ALABAMA — B-4

Selma, AL 36701 — **(334) 874-5700; (334) 874-5755**

Full-time: 350 men, 200 women
Part-time: 10 men, 40 women
Year: semesters
Application Deadline:
Freshman Class: n/av
ACT: recommended

Faculty: n/av
Ph.D.s: 20%
Student/Faculty: 3 to 1
Tuition: $8700
Room & Board: $4500

NONCOMPETITIVE

Concordia College Alabama, founded in 1922, is one of ten postsecondary institutions in the Concordia University System of the Luutheran Church-Missouri Synod. It is a private, historically black, four-year, coeducational institution. It's mission is to "prepare students through a Christ-centered education for lives of responsible service to the church, community and the world." There is one undergraduate school. The library contains 54,162 volumes, 4,405 microform items, and 2,015 audio/video tapes/CDs/DVDs, and subscribes to 348 periodicals including electronic. Computerized library services include interlibrary loans, database searching, Internet access, and Wi-Fi capability. The 22-acre campus is in a small town 50 miles west of Montgomery, AL. Including any residence halls, there are 13 buildings.

Student Life: 67% of undergraduates are from Alabama. Others are from 16 states, and 6 foreign countries. 92% are African American. 57% are Baptist; 17% claim no religious affiliation. The average age of freshmen is 18; all undergraduates, 21.

Housing: 350 students can be accommodated in college housing, which includes single-sex dorms. On-campus housing is guaranteed for all 4 years. 79% of students commute. Alcohol is not permitted. All students may keep cars.

Activities: There are no fraternities or sororities. There are 11 groups on campus, including cheerleading, choir, dance, drama, international, marching band, professional, religious, social service, and student government. Popular campus events include Spiritual Enrichment Activities and Homecoming.

Sports: There are 5 intercollegiate sports for men and 3 for women, and 3 intramural sports for men and 2 for women. Facilities include gymnasiums, swimming pool, health and fitness center, a game room, and playing field.

Disabled Students: 80% of the campus is accessible. Facilities include wheelchair ramps, elevators, special parking, specially equipped restrooms, lowered drinking fountains, and lowered telephones.

Services: Counseling and information services are available, as is tutoring in most subjects, and requested subjects. There is remedial math, reading, and writing.

Campus Safety and Security: Measures include 24-hour foot and vehicle patrol. There are lighted pathways/sidewalks, security guards, and security gates.

Programs of Study: CCA confers B.S. degrees. Associate degrees are also awarded. Bachelor's degrees are awarded in BUSINESS (business administration and management), EDUCATION (early childhood education and elementary education). Business administration and management, and elementary education are the strongest academically.

Required: To graduate, students must complete 126 to 137 credit hours, depending on the major, with a minium 2.0 GPA and pass comprehensive exams. General education requirements include 18 hours of humanities, 12 of social sciences, 9 of math, 6 of religion, 3 each of computer science and health/phys ed, and 1 of orientation to college.

Special: There are 1 national honor societies and a freshman honors program.

Faculty/Classroom: 45% of faculty are male; 55% are female. All teach undergraduates. No introductory courses are taught by graduate students. The average class size in an introductory lecture is 25; in a laboratory is 15; and in a regular course is 30.

Admissions: 4 freshmen graduated first in their class.

Requirements: The ACT is recommended. Applicants must have earned a high school diploma or GED. AP and CLEP credits are accepted. Important factors in the admissions decision are advanced placement or honors courses, evidence of special talent, and leadership record.

Procedure: Freshmen are admitted fall and spring. Entrance exams should be taken by the spring of their junior year. There is a deferred admissions plan. Check with the school for current application deadlines. The application fee is $10. Applications are accepted online.

Transfer: 122 transfer students enrolled in 2012-2013. Courses completed with a passing grade of C or better at an accredited post secondary institution will be accepted for transfer, but only work at Concordia is included in the cumulative GPA. 126 of 126 credits required for the bachelor's degree must be completed at CCA.

Visiting: There are regularly scheduled orientations for prospective students. There are guides for informal visits, visitors may sit in on classes, and stay overnight. To schedule a visit, contact Director of Enrollment Management at (334) 874-5700.

Financial Aid: In 2013-2014, 100% of all full-time freshmen and 100% of continuing full-time students received some form of financial aid. 100% of all full-time freshmen and 100% of continuing full-time students received need-based aid. The average freshman award was $4,410. 15% of undergraduate students work part-time. Average annual earnings from campus work are $700. The FAFSA is required. Check with the school for current application deadlines.

International Students: There are 12 international students enrolled. They must take the TOEFL and the college's own test. They must also take the SAT or ACT, and the college's own entrance exam.

Computers: All students may access the system. There are no time limits. The fee is $20.

Graduates: From July 1, 2012 to June 30, 2013, 42 bachelor's degrees were awarded. The most popular majors were business administration (48%), elementary education (40%), and early childhood education (12%). Of the 2012 graduating class, 62% were enrolled in graduate school within 6 months of graduation, and 50% were employed.

Admissions Contact: Gwendolyn Moore, Director of Enrollment Management. E-Mail: *gmoore@concordiaselma.edu* Web: *www.concordiaselma.edu*

FAULKNER UNIVERSITY — C-4

Montgomery, AL 36109 — **(334) 386-7200**
(800) 879-9816; (334) 386-7137

Full-time: 801 men, 1192 women
Part-time: 234 men, 536 women
Graduate: 241 men, 323 women
Year: semesters, summer session
Application Deadline:
Freshman Class: 388 enrolled
SAT CR/M/W: 460/460/430

Faculty: n/av
Ph.D.s: 39%
Student/Faculty: 15 to 1
Tuition: $15,880
Room & Board: $6650

ACT: 19 — **LESS COMPETITIVE**

Faulkner University, founded in 1942, is a private, multicampus university affiliated with the Church of Christ, offering undergraduate programs in Bible studies, business, education, and liberal arts and sciences. The figures in the above capsule and in this profile are in a recent year. There are 4 undergraduate schools and 4 graduate schools. In addition to regional accreditation, Faulkner has baccalaureate program accreditation with NCATE. The 2 libraries contain 329,835 volumes, 367,272 microform items, and 3,480 audio/video tapes/CDs/DVDs, and subscribe to 41,553 periodicals including electronic. Computerized library services include interlibrary loans, database searching, Internet access, and Wi-Fi capability. The 92-acre campus is in an urban area located 6.4 miles east of the Alabama State Capital in Montgomery, AL. Including any residence halls, there are 22 buildings.

Student Life: 85% of undergraduates are from Alabama. Others are from

37 states, 29 foreign countries, and Canada. 76% are from public schools. 50% are African American; 41% White. 64% are Protestant; 21% claim no religious affiliation; 11% Non-denominational. The average age of freshmen is 21; all undergraduates, 28. 32% do not continue beyond their first year; 26% remain to graduate.

Housing: 652 students can be accommodated in college housing, which includes single-sex dorms and on-campus apartments. On-campus housing is available on a first-come and first-served basis. Priority is given to out-of-town students. 81% of students commute. Alcohol is not permitted. All students may keep cars.

Activities: 15% of men belong to 5 local fraternities; 9% of women belong to 5 local sororities. There are 26 groups on campus, including band, cheerleading, chorus, drama, honors, jazz band, literary magazine, marching band, musical theater, newspaper, pep band, religious, social, social service, student government, and yearbook. Popular campus events include Annual Bible Lectureship, Jamboree and Fall Visitation Weekend.

Sports: There are 5 intercollegiate sports for men and 3 for women, and 16 intramural sports for men and 16 for women. Facilities include a gym, multiplex, a weight room, athletic weight room, walk/run track, exercise room, aerobics room, racquetball courts, game room, baseball and softball fields, and lighted tennis courts.

Disabled Students: All of the campus is accessible. Facilities include wheelchair ramps, elevators, special parking, specially equipped restrooms, special class scheduling, special housing. special needs are met.

Services: Counseling and information services are available, as is tutoring in most subjects, attempts are made to fulfill all requests for tutoring, sometimes with peers. There is a reader service for the blind, and remedial math, reading, and writing.

Campus Safety and Security: Measures include 24-hour foot and vehicle patrol, emergency notification system, and security escort services. There are lighted pathways/sidewalks and controlled access to dorms/residences.

Programs of Study: Faulkner confers B.A., and B.S. degrees. Associate, master's, and doctoral degrees are also awarded. Bachelor's degrees are awarded in BIOLOGICAL SCIENCE (biology/biological science), BUSINESS (accounting, business administration and management, human resources, management science, personnel management, and sports management), COMMUNICATIONS AND THE ARTS (English, music, musical theater, and theater design), COMPUTER AND PHYSICAL SCIENCE (computer science, information sciences and systems, and mathematics), EDUCATION (elementary education, English education, mathematics education, music education, physical education, and secondary education), SOCIAL SCIENCE (biblical studies, counseling/psychology, criminal justice, criminology, history, legal studies, liberal arts/general studies, prelaw, and psychology). Business, criminal justice and education have the largest enrollments.

Required: Students must complete a 52-semester-hour core curriculum, including courses in Bible, history, social science, English composition, literature, speech communication, physical and natural science, math, computer literacy, and phys ed. B.A. students must take 2 semesters of foreign language. At least 120 semester hours with a minimum GPA of 2.0 are required to graduate.

Special: A second bachelor's degree in a separate major may be completed with a minimum of 24 semester hours earned beyond the first degree. Cross-registration with Auburn University at Montgomery and Huntingdon College, dual majors, credit for life/military/work experience, and nondegree study are offered. Internships in education, psychology, criminal justice, Bible, and sports management are available, as are accelerated degree programs in some majors. There are 8 national honor societies, including Phi Beta Kappa, and 1 departmental honors programs.

Faculty/Classroom: 62% of faculty are male; 38% are female. 68% teach undergraduates. No introductory courses are taught by graduate students. The average class size in an introductory lecture is 20; in a laboratory is 15; and in a regular course is 15.

Admissions: The SAT scores for the 2013-2014 freshman class were: Critical Reading--65% below 500, 28% between 500 and 599, 4% between 600 and 699, and 4% between 700 and 800; Math--61% below 500, 32% between 500 and 599, 4% between 600 and 699, and 4% between 700 and 800; Writing--79% below 500, 16% between 500 and 599, 5% between 600 and 699, and % between 700 and 800. The ACT scores were 57% below 21, 22% between 21 and 23, 7% between 24 and 26, 3% between 27 and 28, and 2% above 28. 19% of the current freshmen were in the top fifth of their class; 46% were in the top two fifths. 1 freshman graduated first in the class.

Requirements: The ACT is required. The SAT is recommended. The ACT is required with a satisfactory score. Candidates must be graduates of an accredited secondary school, or have the GED equivalent, with a minimum of 15 academic units, including 3 in English. A GPA of 2.0 is required. AP and CLEP credits are accepted. Important factors in the admissions decision are leadership record, extracurricular activities record, recommendations by alumni, recommendations by school officials, advanced placement or honors courses, parents or siblings attended your school, and personality/intangible qualities.

Procedure: Freshmen are admitted fall, spring, and summer. There is a rolling admissions plan. Application deadlines are open. Application fee is $25. Notification is sent on a rolling basis. Applications are accepted online.

Transfer: Applicants must be in good academic standing from another accredited college. 30 of 120 credits required for the bachelor's degree must be completed at Faulkner.

Visiting: There are regularly scheduled orientations for prospective students. There are guides for informal visits, visitors may sit in on classes, and stay overnight. To schedule a visit, contact the Admissions Office.

Financial Aid: Faulkner is a member of CSS. The FAFSA, FFS, and the college's own financial statement are required. Check with the school for current application deadlines.

International Students: There are 66 international students enrolled. They must take the TOEFL. They must also take the SAT or ACT, scoring 18.

Computers: All students may access the system. There are no time limits and no fees.

Graduates: From July 1, 2012 to June 30, 2013, 575 bachelor's degrees were awarded. The most popular majors were business/marketing (63%), homeland security, law enforcement (20%), and education (3%). 25 companies recruited on campus in 2012-2013.

Admissions Contact: Neil Scott, Director of Admissions. E-Mail: *nscott@faulkner.edu* Web: *www.faulkner.edu*

HUNTINGDON COLLEGE C-4

Montgomery, AL 36106 **(334) 833-4497**
(800) 763-0313; (334) 833-4347

Full-time: 491 men, 411 women	**Faculty:** 42; IIB, --$
Part-time: 62 men, 146 women	**Ph.D.s:** 93%
Year: semesters, summer session	**Student/Faculty:** 22 to 1
Application Deadline:	**Tuition:** $23,500
	Room & Board: $8350

Freshman Class: 1720 applied, 1031 accepted, 261 enrolled
SAT CR/M: 455/455 **ACT:** 21 **COMPETITIVE**

Huntingdon College, founded in 1854 and affiliated with the United Methodist Church, is a private institution offering a liberal arts curriculum that focuses on the development of critical thinking skills. Through its Huntingdon Plan, the college provides hands-on experience through internships, service, and student-faculty research and exploration of the world through travel/study with faculty and fellow students in the junior or senior year; each student is also provided with a laptop computer. Huntingdon offers more than 20 majors and 14 intercollegiate NCAA Division III athletic teams. There is one undergraduate school. In addition to regional accreditation, Huntingdon has baccalaureate program accreditation with NASM. The library contains 113,364 volumes, 61,551 microform items, 4,421 audio/video tapes/CDs/DVDs, and subscribes to 191 periodicals including electronic. Computerized library services include interlibrary loans, database searching, Internet access, and Wi-Fi capability. Special learning facilities include an art gallery, Huntingdon College has four additional facilities, including The Bowman Ecological Center, where students collect and study samples of plants, trees, and aquatic life. Sybil Smith Hall a fully equipped music facility, with recital hall, reception hall, faculty offices and extensive music collection; The Dr. Laurie. Jean Weil Center for Human Performance, an on-campus athletic training/physical therapy clinic, adjacent to the College's main training/fitness facility for athletes; and The Methodist Archives Center, a depository for archival and historical records of the Alabama-West Florida Conference of the United Methodist Church and Huntingdon College. The 71-acre campus is in a suburban area 90 miles south of Birmingham. Including any residence halls, there are 21 buildings.

Student Life: 81% of undergraduates are from Alabama. Others are from 27 states, and 3 foreign countries. 76% are from public schools. 58% are White; 19% African American; 16% race unknown. 35% are Protestant; 25% claim no religious affiliation; 15% Mormon, nondenominational and Christian. The average age of freshmen is 18; all undergraduates, 23. 38% do not continue beyond their first year; 46% remain to graduate.

Housing: 545 students can be accommodated in college housing, which includes single-sex and coed dorms. In addition, there are fraternity houses, Special housing for disabled students. On-campus housing is guaranteed for all 4 years. 59% of students live on campus; of those, 65% remain on campus on weekends. Alcohol is not permitted. All students may keep cars.

Activities: 12% of men belong to 4 national fraternities; 18% of women belong to 3 national sororities. There are 50 groups on campus, including art, band, cheerleading, choir, chorale, chorus, drama, environmental, ethnic, honors, international, literary magazine, marching band, newspaper, pep band, political, professional, religious, social, social service, student government, and yearbook. Popular campus events include Stallworth Lecture Series, Luau on the Green, Service of Lessons and Carols, CloverJam, and Sports Extravaganzas.

Sports: There are 7 intercollegiate sports for men and 7 for women, and

7 intramural sports for men and 7 for women. Facilities include a multipurpose student center with a refurbished gym for basketball and a fitness training facility with fixed and free weight machines; an athletic center with a gym used primarily for volleyball; sports medicine and athletic training facilities; a 3,000-seat football stadium; and state-of-the-art weight training and conditioning facilities. There are also outdoor tennis courts, softball, baseball, and soccer fields, an outdoor basketball court and a sand volleyball court.

Disabled Students: 85% of the campus is accessible. Facilities include wheelchair ramps, elevators, special parking, specially equipped restrooms, special class scheduling, lowered drinking fountains, lowered telephones, and special housing.

Services: Counseling and information services are available, as is tutoring in some subjects, writing, mathematics, sciences and religion.

Campus Safety and Security: Measures include 24-hour foot and vehicle patrol, emergency notification system, self-defense education, and security escort services. There are emergency telephones, lighted pathways/sidewalks, controlled access to dorms/residences, weather alert broadcasts.

Programs of Study: Huntingdon confers B.A. and B.S. (B.S. degrees can be earned in the Adult Degree Completion Program (ADCP) only) degrees. Bachelor's degrees are awarded in BIOLOGICAL SCIENCE (biochemistry, biology/biological science, and cell biology), BUSINESS (accounting, business administration and management, and sports management), COMMUNICATIONS AND THE ARTS (art, communications, English, and music), COMPUTER AND PHYSICAL SCIENCE (chemistry and mathematics), EDUCATION (athletic training, Christian education, elementary education, English education, mathematics education, music education, physical education, science education, and social science education), HEALTH PROFESSIONS (exercise science), SOCIAL SCIENCE (history, political science/government, psychology, religion, and youth ministry). Biology and Chemistry are the strongest academically. Sport Studies, Biology and Business Administration have the largest enrollments.

Required: Huntingdon's core curriculum includes 36 hours of required courses, including 9 hours of religion/history of the church, 6 hours of writing/communication, and 3 hours each of fine art appreciation, history, literature, mathematics, natural sciences, social science and critical thinking (PACT). Students must maintain a minimum GPA of 2.0 over 120 credits for the bachelor's degree. Major requirements range from 30 to 60+ hours.

Special: Huntingdon currently offers more than 20 majors, the opportunity for travel/study experiences offered as part of regular educational costs, hands-on learning experiences in every program of study, dual majors, internships, and preprofessional advising. Cross-registration is available with Auburn University Montgomery, Faulkner University, and the Marine Environmental Sciences Consortium in Dauphin Island, Alabama. Work-study options are also available to qualifying students. There are 15 national honor societies and a freshman honors program.

Faculty/Classroom: 56% of faculty are male; 44% are female. All teach undergraduates. No introductory courses are taught by graduate students. The average class size in an introductory lecture is 19; in a laboratory is 14; and in a regular course is 12.

Admissions: 60% of the 2013-2014 applicants were accepted. The SAT scores for the 2013-2014 freshman class were: Critical Reading--72% below 500, 26% between 500 and 599, and 2% between 600 and 699; Math--67% below 500, 26% between 500 and 599, and 7% between 600 and 699. The ACT scores were 45% below 21, 28% between 21 and 23, 17% between 24 and 26, 7% between 27 and 28, and 3% above 28. 34% of the current freshmen were in the top fifth of their class; 61% were in the top two fifths. 1 freshman graduated first in the class.

Requirements: The SAT or ACT is required. In addition, prospective students must have received a high school diploma or its equivalency. AP, CLEP, IB and dual enrollment credits are considered for acceptance. AP and CLEP credits are accepted.

Procedure: Freshmen are admitted fall, spring, and summer. Entrance exams should be taken in the spring of the junior year. There are deferred admissions and rolling admissions plans. Check with the school for current application deadlines. Applications are accepted online.

Transfer: 77 transfer students enrolled in 2012-2013. Transfer students must have successfully completed 24 semester hours of nonremedial courses at a regionally accredited college or university and be in good standing at previously attended institutions; otherwise, students must meet the regular freshman admission requirements. Transfer admission to the Adult Degree Completion Program (ADCP) should be referenced in the college catalog. 30 of 120 credits required for the bachelor's degree must be completed at Huntingdon.

Visiting: There are regularly scheduled orientations for prospective students, The Office of Admissions offers personal campus visits during the week (Monday-Friday) and select Saturdays. There are guides for informal visits, visitors may sit in on classes, and stay overnight. To schedule a visit, contact the Office of Admission.

Financial Aid: In 2013-2014, 100% of all full-time freshmen and 100% of continuing full-time students received some form of financial aid. 79% of all full-time freshmen and 76% of continuing full-time students received need-based aid. The average freshman award was $16,902. Need-based scholarships or need-based grants averaged $13,975; need-based self-help aid (loans and jobs) averaged $3,816; and other non-need-based awards and non-need-based scholarships averaged $11,235. 22% of undergraduate students work part-time. Average annual earnings from campus work are $1000. The average financial indebtedness of the 2013 graduate was $20,375. The FAFSA and the college's own financial statement are required. The priority date for freshman financial aid applications for fall entry is March 1. The deadline for filing freshman financial aid applications for fall entry is rolling.

International Students: There are 4 international students enrolled. They must take the TOEFL with a minimum score of 500 on the paper-based TOEFL (PBT) or 45 on the Internet-based version (iBT). They must also take the SAT or ACT, scoring SAT Comp 930/Verb min 490; ACT Comp 20/Eng min 20.

Computers: All students may access the system 24 hours a day, 7 days a week. There are no time limits and no fees.

Graduates: From July 1, 2012 to June 30, 2013, 225 bachelor's degrees were awarded. The most popular majors were business administration/business management (44%), biology/cell biology (8%), and human performance/sport studies (6%).

Admissions Contact: Laura Duncan, VP of Enrollment Management. E-Mail: *admiss@huntingdon.edu* Web: *http:/www.huntingdon.edu/futureStudentsMain.aspx?id=1582*

JACKSONVILLE STATE UNIVERSITY — D-2

Jacksonville, AL 36265 — **(256) 782-5400**
(800) 231-5291; (256) 782-5121

Full-time: 2580 men, 3380 women	**Faculty:** n/av
Part-time: 750 men, 1185 women	**Ph.D.s:** n/av
Graduate: 525 men, 960 women	**Student/Faculty:** n/av
Year: semesters, summer session	**Tuition:** $7280 ($14,060)
Application Deadline: open	**Room & Board:** $6000
Freshman Class: n/av	
SAT or ACT: required	

LESS COMPETITIVE

Jacksonville State University, founded in 1883, is a public institution offering programs in business, arts and sciences, criminal justice, education, and nursing. There are 4 undergraduate schools and one graduate school. In addition to regional accreditation, JSU has baccalaureate program accreditation with AACSB, ABET, ADA, CSWE, NASAD, NASM, NCATE, and NLN. The library contains 701,687 volumes, 1.4 million microform items, and 37,515 audio/video tapes/CDs/DVDs, and subscribes to 30,982 periodicals including electronic. Computerized library services include interlibrary loans, database searching, and Internet access. Special learning facilities include a planetarium, radio station, TV station, a stellar observatory. The 459-acre campus is in a small town. Including any residence halls, there are 59 buildings.

Student Life: 78% of undergraduates are from Alabama. Others are from 43 states, 71 foreign countries, and Canada. 95% are from public schools. 64% are White; 29% African American. The average age of freshmen is 20; all undergraduates, 23. 31% do not continue beyond their first year; 38% remain to graduate.

Housing: 1703 students can be accommodated in college housing, which includes single-sex and coed dorms, on-campus apartments, off-campus apartments, and married student housing. In addition, there are honors houses, language houses, special-interest houses, fraternity houses, sorority houses, There is an international house available for students on Rotary Club International scholarships. On-campus housing is available on a first-come and first-served basis. 83% of students commute. Alcohol is not permitted. All students may keep cars.

Activities: 10% of men belong to 9 national fraternities; 10% of women belong to 8 national sororities. There are 100 groups on campus, including art, band, cheerleading, chess, choir, chorale, chorus, computers, dance, drama, drill team, drum and bugle corps, ethnic, honors, international, jazz band, marching band, musical theater, opera, orchestra, pep band, political, professional, radio and TV, religious, social, social service, student government, and symphony. Popular campus events include Visitation Day, and Parents Day.

Sports: There are 7 intercollegiate sports for men and 8 for women, and 15 intramural sports for men and 15 for women. Facilities include a 15,000-seat football stadium, indoor and outdoor courts, athletic fields, a 5,000-seat indoor gym, an indoor pool, a weight room, and a fitness center.

Disabled Students: 85% of the campus is accessible. Facilities include wheelchair ramps, elevators, special parking, specially equipped restrooms, lowered drinking fountains, and lowered telephones.

Services: Counseling and information services are available, as is tutoring in most subjects. There is remedial math, reading, and writing.

Campus Safety and Security: Measures include 24-hour foot and

vehicle patrol, emergency notification system, and security escort services. There are shuttle buses, emergency telephones, and lighted pathways/sidewalks.

Programs of Study: JSU confers B.A., B.S., B.F.A., B.S.Ed. and B.S.W. degrees. Master's degrees are also awarded. Bachelor's degrees are awarded in BIOLOGICAL SCIENCE (biology/biological science), BUSINESS (accounting, banking and finance, and marketing/retailing/merchandising), COMMUNICATIONS AND THE ARTS (communications, dramatic arts, English, and music), COMPUTER AND PHYSICAL SCIENCE (chemistry, computer science, mathematics, and physics), EDUCATION (early childhood education, elementary education, health education, home economics education, music education, secondary education, and special education), HEALTH PROFESSIONS (nursing), SOCIAL SCIENCE (criminal justice, economics, geography, history, political science/government, psychology, social work, and sociology). Elementary education, criminal justice, and nursing are the strongest academically.

Required: All students are required to complete a core curriculum of 46 semester hours, including 15 hours in fine arts and humanities, 8 each in communications and natural sciences, 6 each in analysis and social sciences, and 3 in wellness. English competency and courses in computer literacy are required. A total of 128 semester hours, with at least 52 hours in courses numbered 300 or above and a minimum GPA of 2.0, is required to graduate. At least 32 semester hours must be completed in residence at JSU with no more than 12 hours in correspondence work.

Special: Co-op programs with major area employees are available. JSU has cross-registration with the Marine Environmental Sciences Consortium and internships in education, political science, communication, journalism, and criminal justice. Work-study programs, dual majors in most programs, and credit for military experience are offered. There are 13 national honor societies and 1 departmental honors programs.

Faculty/Classroom: 48% of faculty are male; 52% are female. 82% teach undergraduates. No introductory courses are taught by graduate students. The average class size in a laboratory is 25 and in a regular course is 25.

Requirements: The SAT or ACT is required. In addition, applicants should be graduates of an accredited high school; the GED is also accepted. 19 on the ACT or a satisfactory score on the SAT is required for unconditional admission; 16 to 18 on the ACT or a minimum satisfactory score on the SAT is required for conditional admission. AP and CLEP credits are accepted.

Procedure: Freshmen are admitted to all sessions. There is a rolling admissions plan. Application deadlines are open. The fall 2013 application fee was $30. Applications are accepted online.

Transfer: 714 transfer students enrolled in 2012-2013. Transfer applicants must be eligible to return to the last institution attended. 32 of 128 credits required for the bachelor's degree must be completed at JSU.

Visiting: There are regularly scheduled orientations for prospective students, consisting of 2-day orientations scheduled during the summer. There are guides for informal visits.

Financial Aid: The FAFSA is required. Check with the school for current application deadlines.

International Students: They must take the TOEFL with a minimum score of 500 on the paper-based TOEFL (PBT) or 61 on the Internet-based version (iBT). They must also take the SAT or ACT. The SAT or ACT may be substituted with satisfactory scores (19 on the ACT).

Computers: All students may access the system. during specific lab hours. There are no time limits and no fees.

Admissions Contact: Martha Mitchell, Director of Admissions. E-Mail: *info@jsu.edu* Web: *www.jsu.edu*

JUDSON COLLEGE — B-3

Marion, AL 36756 (334) 683-5110
(800) 447-9472; (334) 683-5282

Full-time: 1 men, 261 women	**Faculty:** 31
Part-time: 15 men, 70 women	**Ph.D.s:** 81%
Year: semesters, summer session	**Student/Faculty:** 9 to 1
Application Deadline: open	**Tuition:** $15,630
	Room & Board: $9060

Freshman Class: 268 applied, 198 accepted, 68 enrolled
SAT or ACT: required

COMPETITIVE

Judson College, founded in 1838, is a private women's liberal arts college affiliated with the Alabama Baptist Convention. Men are accepted only in the Distance Learning division of the college. There is one undergraduate school. In addition to regional accreditation, Judson has baccalaureate program accreditation with NASM. The library contains 59,096 volumes, 2,012 microform items, and 1,359 audio/video tapes/CDs/DVDs, and subscribes to 32,679 periodicals including electronic. Computerized library services include interlibrary loans, database searching, Internet access, and Wi-Fi capability. The 118-acre campus is in a small town 75 miles southwest of Birmingham. Including any residence halls, there are 18 buildings.

Student Life: 82% of undergraduates are from Alabama. Others are from 19 states, and 4 foreign countries. 77% are from public schools. 75% are White; 14% African American. 90% are Protestant. The average age of freshmen is 18; all undergraduates, 25. 39% do not continue beyond their first year; 37% remain to graduate.

Housing: 264 students can be accommodated in college housing, which includes single-sex dorms. On-campus housing is guaranteed for all 4 years. 57% of students live on campus; of those, 25% remain on campus on weekends. Alcohol is not permitted. All students may keep cars.

Activities: There are no fraternities or sororities. There are 26 groups on campus, including art, band, choir, chorale, chorus, computers, Departmental Clubs, drama, environmental, honors, literary magazine, marching band, musical theater, newspaper, orchestra, photography, political, professional, religious, social, social service, student government, and yearbook. Popular campus events include Hockey Day, Junior-Sophomore Dance, Pageant, Christmas Tea and Vespers, and Rose Sunday.

Sports: There are 6 intercollegiate sports for women, and 3 intramural sports for women. Facilities include an indoor swimming pool, equine center with class rooms, tack rooms, stalls, and a covered riding arena, tennis courts, a wellness center, a gym with an aerobics room and weight training facility, a hockey field, a softball field, a soccer field, and a game room.

Disabled Students: 75% of the campus is accessible. Facilities include wheelchair ramps, elevators, special parking, specially equipped restrooms, lowered drinking fountains, lowered telephones, and special housing.

Services: Counseling and information services are available, as is tutoring in most subjects, Math, English, History, Business and others on request There is remedial math and writing.

Campus Safety and Security: Measures include 24-hour foot and vehicle patrol, emergency notification system, self-defense education, and security escort services. There are emergency telephones, lighted pathways/sidewalks, controlled access to dorms/residences, Card access systems are on classroom and administrative buildings.

Programs of Study: Judson confers B.A, B.Min., B.S. and B.S.W. degrees. Associate degrees are also awarded. Bachelor's degrees are awarded in AGRICULTURE (equine science), BIOLOGICAL SCIENCE (biology/biological science), BUSINESS (business administration and management), COMMUNICATIONS AND THE ARTS (applied music, art, English, and Spanish), COMPUTER AND PHYSICAL SCIENCE (chemistry and mathematics), EDUCATION (elementary education, English education, mathematics education, music education, science education, and social studies education), HEALTH PROFESSIONS (nursing), SOCIAL SCIENCE (criminal justice, history, interdisciplinary studies, psychology, religion, and social work). Biology, education, business, nursing, art, and English are the strongest academically. Biology, nursing, and psychology have the largest enrollments.

Required: All students are required to complete courses in English, history, multicultural studies, speech, religion, social science, math, science, humanities, computer literacy, health/phys ed, and women's studies. A total of 128 credit hours, with a minimum GPA of 2.0 (2.5 for education majors) is required to graduate. B.A. students must also complete at least 6 hours of foreign languages at the 200-level or above; B.S. students must complete at least 12 hours of math or science electives in addition to the core competency. A passing score is required on the English Language Usage Test and on the senior essay that meets the requirements of the Judson Quality Enhancement Plan.

Special: Cross-registration with the Marion Military Institute is available for ROTC students. B.A.-B.S. degrees are offered in criminal justice, math, business, biology, psychology, and chemistry. Students study abroad in such places as Salzburg, China, India, Oxford, Uganda, Australia, Latin America, and the Middle East. Dual majors, an equine science program, an accelerated degree program, an interdisciplinary major, work-study programs, and internships are offered. Students may combine their Associate Degree in Nursing with Biology for a B.S. degree. There are preprofessional programs in health areas, engineering, and law. The Distance Learning program offers credit for prior learning experience and provides individually paced instruction leading to a baccalaureate degree. There are 7 national honor societies, a freshman honors program, and 19 departmental honors programs.

Faculty/Classroom: 53% of faculty are male; 47% are female. All teach undergraduates. No introductory courses are taught by graduate students. The average class size in an introductory lecture is 23; in a laboratory is 12; and in a regular course is 7.

Admissions: 74% of the 2013-2014 applicants were accepted. 42% of the current freshmen were in the top fifth of their class; 67% were in the top two fifths.

Requirements: The SAT or ACT is required, with a minimum composite score of 18 on the ACT (SAT), applicants should have completed 17 high school credits, including 4 in English. Non-high school graduates must provide the GED equivalent. A GPA of 2.0 is required. AP and CLEP credits are accepted.

Procedure: Freshmen are admitted fall, winter, and summer. Entrance exams should be taken in the spring of the junior year. There are early admissions, deferred admissions, and rolling admissions plans. Application deadlines are open. The fall 2013 application fee was $35. Notification is sent on a rolling basis. Applications are accepted online.

Transfer: 56 transfer students enrolled in 2012-2013. Transfer students must have a minimum GPA of 2.0 and be eligible to return to the school from which they transfer. 32 of 128 credits required for the bachelor's degree must be completed at Judson.

Visiting: There are regularly scheduled orientations for prospective students, consisting of 3 college Scholarship Days, 1 in September, 1 in November and 1 in February, and a Junior Day in May. Activities include scholarship testing, an equine show, campus tours, faculty meetings, and financial aid planning. There are guides for informal visits, visitors may sit in on classes, and stay overnight. To schedule a visit, contact the Admissions Office.

Financial Aid: In 2013-2014, 100% of all full-time freshmen and 99% of continuing full-time students received some form of financial aid. 89% of all full-time freshmen and 87% of continuing full-time students received need-based aid. The average freshman award was $10,512. Need-based scholarships or need-based grants averaged $5,812 ($35,222 maximum); need-based self-help aid (loans and jobs) averaged $7,416 ($26,250 maximum); non-need-based athletic scholarships averaged $3,990 ($9,000 maximum); and other non-need-based awards and non-need-based scholarships averaged $8,037 ($35,222 maximum). 31% of undergraduate students work part-time. Average annual earnings from campus work are $899. The average financial indebtedness of the 2013 graduate was $24,374. The FAFSA is required. The priority date for freshman financial aid applications for fall entry is March 1. The deadline for filing freshman financial aid applications for fall entry is July 1.

International Students: There are 4 international students enrolled. The school actively recruits these students. They must take the TOEFL with a minimum score of 500 on the paper-based TOEFL (PBT) or 61 on the Internet-based version (iBT) and the college's own test.

Computers: All students may access the system. There are no time limits. The fee is $400.

Graduates: From July 1, 2012 to June 30, 2013, 58 bachelor's degrees were awarded. The most popular majors were nursing (34%), biology (12%), and English (9%). 10 companies recruited on campus in 2012-2013. In an average class, 3% graduate in 3 years or less, 10% graduate in 4 years or less, 68% graduate in 5 years or less, and 19% graduate in 6 years or less. Of the 2012 graduating class, 9% were enrolled in graduate school within 6 months of graduation, and 47% were employed.

Admissions Contact: Layne Calhoun, Executive Director of Enrollment Service. E-Mail: *admissions@judson.edu* Web: *www.judson.edu*

MILES COLLEGE C-2

Birmingham, AL 35208

(205) 929-1657
(800) 445-0708; (205) 929-1668

Full-time: 750 men, 950 women
Part-time: 40 men, 75 women
Year: semesters, summer session
Application Deadline: open
Faculty: n/av
Ph.D.s: n/av
Student/Faculty: n/av
Tuition: $11,014
Room & Board: $5516
Freshman Class: n/av
SAT or ACT: recommended

NONCOMPETITIVE

Miles College a senior, liberal arts, church related college with roots in the Christian Methodist Episcopal Church and in the tradition of the Historically Black College- motivates and directs its students to seek holistic development that leads to intellectual, ethical, spiritual and service-oriented lives. Guided by these core values, the Miles College education involves students in rigorous study of the liberal arts as preparation for work and life-long learning, in the acquisition of verbal, technological and cultural literacy, and in critical community participation; all as a prelude to responsible citizenship in the global society which they will help to shape. There are 6 undergraduate schools. Computerized library services include interlibrary loans, database searching, and Internet access. Special learning facilities include an art gallery, radio station, TV station, an Afro-American materials center, and a media center. The 81-acre campus is in an urban area 7 miles from downtown Birmingham. Including any residence halls, there are 33 buildings.

Housing: 750 students can be accommodated in college housing, which includes single-sex dorms, on-campus apartments, and off-campus apartments. On-campus housing is available on a first-come and first-served basis. Priority is given to out-of-town students. Alcohol is not permitted. All students may keep cars.

Activities: Groups on campus include band, cheerleading, choir, communications, dance, debate, drama, drill team, ethnic, honors, international, jazz band, marching band, musical theater, newspaper, professional, radio and TV, religious, social service, student government, and yearbook. Popular campus events include Senior Class Day, Spring Cultural and Arts Festival, Honors Day, and Intelligence Community Center of Academic Excellence Annual Colloquium.

Sports: There are 5 intercollegiate sports for men and 5 for women. Facilities include a 6,500-seat football field with state of the art synthetic turf and fieldhouse, a 1500-seat gym, a weight room, and a baseball field.

Disabled Students: Facilities include wheelchair ramps, elevators, special parking, specially equipped restrooms, special class scheduling, and lowered drinking fountains.

Services: Counseling and information services are available, as is tutoring in every subject. There is remedial math, reading, and writing. Miles offers educational support programs for students in pursuit of collegiate education at all ability levels.

Campus Safety and Security: Measures include 24-hour foot and vehicle patrol and security escort services. There are lighted pathways/sidewalks and controlled access to dorms/residences.

Programs of Study: Miles confers B.A., B.S. and B.S.W. degrees. Bachelor's degrees are awarded in BIOLOGICAL SCIENCE (biology/biological science), BUSINESS (accounting and business administration and management), COMMUNICATIONS AND THE ARTS (communications, English, and language arts), COMPUTER AND PHYSICAL SCIENCE (chemistry, computer science, and mathematics), EDUCATION (early childhood education, elementary education, mathematics education, science education, secondary education, and social science education), ENGINEERING AND ENVIRONMENTAL DESIGN (environmental science), SOCIAL SCIENCE (criminal justice, history, political science/government, and social work). Business is the strongest academically. Criminal justice has the largest enrollment.

Required: To graduate, all students must complete general education requirements. A minimum of 120 credit hours is required for a bachelor's degree in some programs, with a minimum GPA of 2.0 in the major. All students must pass English proficiency and exit exams.

Special: Miles offers co-op programs in all majors, internships, federal work-study, and cross-registration with the University of Alabama at Birmingham and other area colleges and universities. There are cooperative programs in allied health sciences with the University of Alabama at Birmingham, and in engineering, physics, veterinary medicine, and Asian studies. There is 1 national honor society and a freshman honors program.

Faculty/Classroom: All teach undergraduates. No introductory courses are taught by graduate students. The average class size in a regular course is 12.

Requirements: The SAT or ACT and ACT Writing Test are recommended. Students should be graduates of an accredited high school or hold a GED. A personal interview is recommended. A GPA of 2.0 is required.

Procedure: Freshmen are admitted to all sessions. Application deadlines are open. The fall 2013 application fee was $25.

Transfer: To qualify for admission as a transfer, student must be in good standing at the last accredited institution attended and submit official transcripts. 32 of 120 credits required for the bachelor's degree must be completed at Miles.

Visiting: There are guides for informal visits and visitors may sit in on classes. To schedule a visit, contact the Admissions Office.

Financial Aid: Miles is a member of CSS. The FAFSA is required. Check with the school for current application deadlines.

International Students: They must take the TOEFL or MELAB. They must also take the SAT or ACT.

Computers: All students may access the system. There are no time limits and no fees.

Graduates: From July 1, 2012 to June 30, 2013, 222 bachelor's degrees were awarded. The most popular majors were business administration and management (18%), criminal justice/law enforcement (16%), and communications/journalism (11%).

Admissions Contact: Christopher Robertson, Director of Admissions. E-Mail: *admissions@miles.edu* Web: *www.miles.edu*

OAKWOOD UNIVERSITY C-1

Huntsville, AL 35896

(256) 726-7000
(800) 824-5312; (256) 726-7154

Full-time: 690 men, 915 women
Part-time: 110 men, 110 women
Year: semesters, summer session
Application Deadline: open
Faculty: n/av
Ph.D.s: 54%
Student/Faculty: n/av
Tuition: $14,472
Room & Board: $9563
Freshman Class: n/av
SAT or ACT: recommended

COMPETITIVE

Oakwood University, founded in 1896, is a private, historically black, Seventh-day Adventist institution offering undergraduate programs in business and education, humanities, natural sciences and math, religion and theology, and social sciences. The figures in the above capsule and in this profile are approximate. In addition to regional accreditation, Oakwood has baccalaureate program accreditation with ACBSP, ADA, CSWE, and NCATE. The library contains 125,373 volumes, 2,140 microform items, and 4,816 audio/video tapes/CDs/DVDs, and subscribes to 630 periodicals including electronic. Computerized library services include database searching. Special learning facilities include a radio station, and a black history museum. The 105-acre campus is in a suburban area 5 miles northwest of Huntsville. Including any residence halls, there are 30 buildings.

Student Life: 79% of undergraduates are from out of state, mostly the South. Students are from 39 states, 22 foreign countries, and Canada. 52% are from public schools. 79% are African American; 12% Foreign. The average age of freshmen is 19; all undergraduates, 23. 27% do not continue beyond their first year.

Housing: 1173 students can be accommodated in college housing, which includes single-sex dorms and married student housing. On-campus housing is available on a first-come and first-served basis. Priority is given to out-of-town students. 71% of students live on campus; of those, 98% remain on campus on weekends. Alcohol is not permitted. Upperclassmen may keep cars.

Activities: There are no fraternities or sororities. There are 20 groups on campus, including band, choir, chorale, drama, honors, international, newspaper, professional, radio and TV, religious, student government, and yearbook. Popular campus events include Convocations, Arts and Lecture Series and Centennial.

Sports: There are 4 intramural sports for men and 3 for women. Facilities include a gym, skating rink, an Olympic-size pool, tennis courts, playing fields, racquetball courts, and a weight room.

Disabled Students: 80% of the campus is accessible. Facilities include wheelchair ramps, elevators, special parking, and specially equipped restrooms.

Services: Counseling and information services are available, as is tutoring in most subjects. There is remedial math, reading, and writing. Testing, counseling, and developmental guidance services are available through the counseling center.

Campus Safety and Security: Measures include 24-hour foot and vehicle patrol and security escort services. There are lighted pathways/sidewalks.

Programs of Study: Oakwood confers B.A., B.S., B.B.A., B.M. and B.S.W. degrees. Associate degrees are also awarded. Bachelor's degrees are awarded in BIOLOGICAL SCIENCE (biochemistry and biology/biological science), BUSINESS (accounting and business administration and management), COMMUNICATIONS AND THE ARTS (communications, English, French, music, music business management, music performance, and Spanish), COMPUTER AND PHYSICAL SCIENCE (chemistry, computer mathematics, computer science, information sciences and systems, mathematics, and natural sciences), EDUCATION (business education, elementary education, English education, home economics education, mathematics education, music education, physical education, science education, and social science education), HEALTH PROFESSIONS (medical technology and nursing), SOCIAL SCIENCE (dietetics, family/consumer studies, history, home economics, human development, international studies, ministries, physical fitness/movement, psychology, religion, religious education, and social work). Biochemistry, chemistry, and nursing are the strongest academically. Business and biology have the largest enrollments.

Required: To graduate, students must complete 128 semester hours, including 30 in the major and 40 in upper-division courses, with a GPA of 2.0. Regular chapel attendance is required. All students must complete a liberal arts core, and must meet English oral and written proficiency requirements.

Special: Students may cross-register with Alabama A&M, Athens State, or the University of Alabama at Huntsville. The college offers a student missionary abroad program as well as a study abroad program through the Adventist College Consortium. Internships, work-study, dual majors, independent study, life experience credit, and pass/fail options are also available. A second bachelor's degree is offered to students completing at least 160 semester credits. There are 1 national honor societies and 2 departmental honors programs.

Faculty/Classroom: 51% of faculty are male; 49% are female. All teach undergraduates. No introductory courses are taught by graduate students. The average class size in an introductory lecture is 30; in a laboratory is 30; and in a regular course is 40.

Requirements: The SAT or ACT is recommended. Applicants should be high school graduates with a minimum GPA of 2.0 and at least 11 academic units, distributed as follows: 4 in English, 2 each in math, science, and social studies, and 1 in typing. The GED is accepted. Two character references are required. Students with GPAs between 1.7 and 2.0 may be admitted on probation. Applicants admitted without test scores must take the ACT during freshman orientation. A GPA of 2.0 is required. AP and CLEP credits are accepted. Important factors in the admissions decision are recommendations by school officials, ability to finance college education, and leadership record.

Procedure: Freshmen are admitted to all sessions. Entrance exams should be taken before high school graduation. There are early decision and rolling admissions plans. Application deadlines are open. Application fee is $20.

Transfer: Applicants must submit a college transcript and a statement of honorable dismissal. Grades of C minus or better transfer for credit. 32 of 128 credits required for the bachelor's degree must be completed at Oakwood.

Visiting: There are guides for informal visits, visitors may sit in on classes, and stay overnight. To schedule a visit, contact the Enrollment Management.

Financial Aid: Oakwood is a member of CSS. The FAFSA and the college's own financial statement, and student and parent federal income tax returns are required. Check with the school for current application deadlines.

International Students: They must take the TOEFL and the college's own test. They must also take the SAT or ACT. Students may take the ACT on campus prior to registration.

Computers: There are no time limits, and fees vary.

Admissions Contact: Fred Pullins, Enrollment Management Director. E-Mail: *admission@oakwood.edu* Web: *www.oakwood.edu*

SAMFORD UNIVERSITY — C-2

Birmingham, AL 35229 — (205) 726-2871; (800) 888-7218; (205) 726-2171

Full-time: 998 men, 1852 women	**Faculty:** 197
Part-time: 49 men, 114 women	**Ph.D.s:** 87%
Graduate: 779 men, 1041 women	**Student/Faculty:** 14 to 1
Year: 4-1-4, summer session	**Tuition:** $26,328
Application Deadline: open	**Room & Board:** $9372
Freshman Class: 3447 applied, 2653 accepted, 765 enrolled	
SAT: CR/M/W: 565/565/560	**ACT:** 25 **VERY COMPETITIVE+**

Samford University is consistently ranked as one of the top universities in the South, with students from 44 states and 22 countries. Located in suburban Birmingham, Alabama, Samford was founded in 1841 and has 10 academic schools: arts, arts and sciences, business, divinity, education, health professions, law, nursing, pharmacy and public health. There are 7 undergraduate schools and 8 graduate schools. In addition to regional accreditation, Samford has baccalaureate program accreditation with AACSB, ADA, NASM, and NCATE. The 6 libraries contain 1.1 million volumes, 1.4 million microform items, and 51,132 audio/video tapes/CDs/DVDs, and subscribe to 46,629 periodicals including electronic. Computerized library services include interlibrary loans, database searching, Internet access, and Wi-Fi capability. Special learning facilities include an art gallery, planetarium, radio station, Global center, Drug information center, Nursing school state-of-the-art human simulation center, Business school investment trading room and conservatory. The 318-acre campus is in a suburban area 4 miles south of Birmingham, AL. Including any residence halls, there are 104 buildings.

Student Life: 64% of undergraduates are from out of state, mostly the South. Students are from 40 states, 15 foreign countries, and Canada. 52% are from public schools. 81% are White. 25% claim no religious affiliation; 22% Protestant. The average age of freshmen is 18; all undergraduates, 21. 13% do not continue beyond their first year; 70% remain to graduate.

Housing: 2301 students can be accommodated in college housing, which includes single-sex dorms and on-campus apartments. In addition, there are fraternity houses, sorority houses, a university-owned facility for study in England, and special housing accommodations for disabled and international students. On-campus housing is guaranteed for the freshman year only, is available on a first-come, and first-served basis. 71% of students live on campus. Alcohol is not permitted. All students may keep cars.

Activities: 10% of men belong to 6 national fraternities; 32% of women belong to 8 national sororities. There are 101 groups on campus, including Academic Organizations/Clubs and University Sponsored Organizations/Clubs, art, band, cheerleading, choir, chorale, chorus, computers, dance, debate, drama, environmental, ethnic, film, honors, international, jazz band, literary magazine, marching band, musical theater, newspaper, opera, orchestra, pep band, photography, political, professional, radio and TV, religious, social, social service, student government, symphony, and yearbook. Popular campus events include Homecoming, Family Weekend, Hanging of the Green, Lighting of the Way, Step Sing, NCAA Division I Athletics, Samford Gives Back, Shiloh (Campus Weekly Worship), Spring Fling, Greek Week, Harry's Coffeehouse Series, and Leadership Lunches.

Sports: There are 7 intercollegiate sports for men and 8 for women, and 22 intramural sports for men and 22 for women. Facilities include a variety of athletics and recreational (outdoor and indoor) facilities available for students at Samford University; a 6700-seat football stadium, a 4000-seat basketball gym, and a state-of-the-art student fitness/wellness center that has 8 treadmills, 8 elliptical machines, and 4 Lifecycles, all with personal televisions. The Samford University Track and Soccer Stadium is an outdoor recreation complex which includes track, sand volleyball, outdoor basketball, and 2 grass fields. Also available, is a 50ft high climbing wall offering more than 35 different climbing routes with varying degrees of challenge involved.

Disabled Students: All of the campus is accessible. Facilities include

wheelchair ramps, elevators, special parking, specially equipped restrooms, special class scheduling, lowered drinking fountains, lowered telephones.

Services: Counseling and information services are available, as is tutoring in most subjects. There is a reader service for the blind.

Campus Safety and Security: Measures include 24-hour foot and vehicle patrol, emergency notification system, self-defense education, and security escort services. There are emergency telephones, lighted pathways/sidewalks, and controlled access to dorms/residences.

Programs of Study: Samford confers B.S.B.A., B.S.E., B.S.N., B.A., B.F.A., B.M., B.M.E., and B.S degrees. Master's and doctoral degrees are also awarded. Bachelor's degrees are awarded in BIOLOGICAL SCIENCE (biochemistry, biology/biological science, marine science, and nutrition), BUSINESS (accounting, entrepreneurial studies, finance, management science, marketing management, organizational leadership and management, and sports management), COMMUNICATIONS AND THE ARTS (art, church music, classics, communications, English, French, German, graphic design, Greek, journalism, language arts, languages, Latin, music, music performance, music theory and composition, musical theater, piano/organ, piano pedagogy, piano performance, Spanish, theatre arts, and voice), COMPUTER AND PHYSICAL SCIENCE (chemistry, computer science, environmental geology, mathematics, physics, and science), EDUCATION (athletic training, early childhood education, English education, and secondary education), ENGINEERING AND ENVIRONMENTAL DESIGN (engineering physics, environmental science, and interior design), HEALTH PROFESSIONS (exercise science, health promotion, nursing, and sports medicine), SOCIAL SCIENCE (counseling/psychology, dietetics, economics, geography, history, human development, international relations, international studies, Latin American studies, liberal arts/general studies, paralegal studies, philosophy, political science/government, psychology, public administration, religion, religious music, and sociology). Pharmacy, law, nursing, business, and liberal arts are the strongest academically. Pharmacy, nursing, and law have the largest enrollments.

Required: The University Core and General Education curricula are designed to provide an academic foundation for work toward the major field of study and should be completed as early as possible. All undergraduates are required to take the University Core Curriculum at Samford (22 credits).

Special: The Department of Physics offers a dual-degree engineering program jointly with the following universities: University of Alabama at Birmingham, Auburn University, and Mercer University (Georgia). The five-year program leads to two degrees: a bachelor of science degree from Samford with a major in engineering physics, and a bachelor of engineering degree from the participating university. Students in this five-year program will first pursue a three-year general curriculum at Samford, followed by a two-year general technical curriculum at one of the participating engineering schools. Samford University cooperates with the University of Alabama at Birmingham (UAB), Miles College, University of Montevallo, and Birmingham-Southern College in a student exchange program known as the Birmingham Area Consortium for Higher Education (BACHE). The program is designed to expand the undergraduate educational opportunities for students at these institutions. As part of its commitment to internationalization of the curriculum, Samford University provides a special opportunity for students and faculty to live and study in one of the most cosmopolitan and culturally rich cities of the world—London. Daniel House, Samford's London Study Centre, serves as home and classroom to students and faculty throughout the year in a variety of academic programs. Samford offers opportunities to travel and study in foreign countries for credit. The purpose of these programs is to prepare Samford students for global citizenship in the 21st century. More specifically, Samford seeks to expose students and faculty to the peoples and cultures of other nations; to provide on-site observation of historical, scientific, and cultural phenomena; and to provide opportunities for foreign language study within the cultural context of the target languages. There are 23 national honor societies, a freshman honors program, and 21 departmental honors programs.

Faculty/Classroom: 49% of faculty are male; 51% are female. 62% teach undergraduates. No introductory courses are taught by graduate students. The average class size in an introductory lecture is 21 and in a laboratory is 11.

Admissions: 77% of the 2013-2014 applicants were accepted. The SAT scores for the 2013-2014 freshman class were: Critical Reading--18% below 500, 43% between 500 and 599, 32% between 600 and 699, and 7% between 700 and 800; Math--18% below 500, 47% between 500 and 599, 29% between 600 and 699, and 6% between 700 and 800; Writing--23% below 500, 48% between 500 and 599, 26% between 600 and 699, and 3% between 700 and 800. The ACT scores were 7% below 21, 26% between 21 and 23, 27% between 24 and 26, 17% between 27 and 28, and 23% above 28. There were 5 National Merit finalists.

Requirements: The SAT or ACT is required. In addition, Samford University seeks to enroll students capable of success in a challenging academic environment. Every applicant is evaluated individually on the basis of academic preparedness and potential, as well as personal fit with the mission and purpose of the university. The Admission Committee considers factors such as the rigor of the high school curriculum, grade point average, standardized test scores, and recommendations. AP and CLEP credits are accepted. Important factors in the admissions decision are recommendations by school officials, advanced placement or honors courses, and leadership record.

Procedure: Freshmen are admitted fall, spring, and summer. Entrance exams should be taken in the junior year. There are deferred admissions and rolling admissions plans. Application deadlines are open. Application fee is $40. Notifications are sent November 1. 33 applicants were on the 2013 waiting list; 4 were admitted. Applications are accepted online.

Transfer: 174 transfer students enrolled in 2012-2013. Transfer students generally receive favorable admission review when they present a minimum cumulative 2.50 grade point average on all college-level course-work, provided they have attempted at least 24 credits, or 36 quarter credits, at institutions accredited by one of the regional accrediting agencies. 64 of 128 credits required for the bachelor's degree must be completed at Samford.

Visiting: There are regularly scheduled orientations for prospective students, including campus tours offered 6 days a week. Tours last 90-minutes followed by a 30-minute information session. Special arrangements can be made for overnight stay, class visitation, and/or meeting with Admission and Financial Aid counselors. There are guides for informal visits, visitors may sit in on classes, and stay overnight. To schedule a visit, contact Office of Admission.

Financial Aid: In 2013-2014, 97% of all full-time freshmen and 91% of continuing full-time students received some form of financial aid. 50% of all full-time freshmen and 42% of continuing full-time students received need-based aid. The average freshman award was $19,376. Need-based scholarships or need-based grants averaged $3,766 ($34,285 maximum); need-based self-help aid (loans and jobs) averaged $3,115 ($26,573 maximum); non-need-based athletic scholarships averaged $13,412 ($35,790 maximum); and other non-need-based awards and non-need-based scholarships averaged $4,916 ($30,900 maximum). 18% of undergraduate students work part-time. Average annual earnings from campus work are $1880. The average financial indebtedness of the 2013 graduate was $27,623. The FAFSA and the state aid form are required. The priority date for freshman financial aid applications for fall entry is March 1.

International Students: There are 85 international students enrolled. The school actively recruits these students. They must take the TOEFL with a minimum score of 575 on the paper-based TOEFL (PBT) or 90 on the Internet-based version (iBT), TOEFL requirement may be waived if submitting the SAT or ACT. They must also take the SAT or ACT. SAT or ACT is required if available for student in country of residence.

Computers: All students may access the system. There are no time limits and no fees.

Graduates: From July 1, 2012 to June 30, 2013, 714 bachelor's degrees were awarded. The most popular majors were business and marketing (19%), health professions and related sciences (15%), and communication and journalism (9%). 144 companies recruited on campus in 2012-2013. In an average class, 49% graduate in 4 years or less, 64% graduate in 5 years or less, and 69% graduate in 6 years or less.

Admissions Contact: Jason E. Black, Dean of Admission. E-Mail: *admission@samford.edu* Web: *www.samford.edu*

SOUTHERN CHRISTIAN UNIVERSITY (See Amridge University)

SPRING HILL COLLEGE — A-5

Mobile, AL 36608 — (251) 380-3030; (800) 742-6704; (251) 460-2186

Full-time: 496 men, 730 women	**Faculty:** 78; IIA, --$
Part-time: 33 men, 60 women	**Ph.D.s:** 96%
Graduate: 43 men, 87 women	**Student/Faculty:** 16 to 1
Year: semesters, summer session	**Tuition:** $30,834
Application Deadline: July 15	**Room & Board:** $11,296
Freshman Class: 6596 applied, 3052 accepted, 431 enrolled	
SAT CR/M/W: 530/550/540 — **ACT:** 24	**VERY COMPETITIVE**

Founded in 1830, Spring Hill College is the oldest Catholic college in the Southeast as well as the third oldest Jesuit college and fifth oldest Catholic college in the United States. Ranked among the top 20 Southern colleges and universities "America's Best Colleges," its mission is to form students to become responsible leaders in service to others. There are 8 undergraduate schools and 5 graduate schools. The 2 libraries contain 183,372 volumes, 314,001 microform items, and 3,345 audio/video tapes/CDs/DVDs, and subscribe to 574 periodicals including electronic. Computerized library services include interlibrary loans, database searching, Internet access, and Wi-Fi capability. Special learning facilities include an art gallery, radio station, a theater. The 381-acre campus is in a suburban area in Mobile, Alabama. Including any residence halls, there are 33 buildings.

Student Life: 60% of undergraduates are from out of state, mostly the

South. Students are from 37 states, 11 foreign countries, and Canada. 66% are White; 15% African American. 51% are Catholic; 27% Protestant; 22% claim no religious affiliation. The average age of freshmen is 18; all undergraduates, 21. 24% do not continue beyond their first year; 56% remain to graduate.

Housing: 1048 students can be accommodated in college housing, which includes coed dorms and on-campus apartments. In addition, there are special-interest houses. On-campus housing is guaranteed for all 4 years. 78% of students live on campus. All students may keep cars.

Activities: 20% of men belong to 3 national fraternities; 28% of women belong to 5 national sororities. There are 39 groups on campus, including art, cheerleading, chorale, communications, computers, dance, drama, environmental, ethnic, film, gay, honors, international, literary magazine, newspaper, photography, political, professional, religious, social, social service, and student government. Popular campus events include Weeks of Welcome/Badger Expo, Christmas on the Hill, Late Night Breakfast, Free Art Fridays, Mardi Gras Week/Ball, Badger Brawl, International Service Immersion Trips, Crawfish Boil and Stress Free Zone (free massages).

Sports: There are 7 intercollegiate sports for men and 8 for women, and 12 intramural sports for men and 12 for women. Facilities include 18-hole golf course; basketball courts; outdoor sand volleyball area; baseball, softball, rugby, and soccer fields. A recreation center houses the intercollegiate basketball arena, racquetball courts, weight-training and exercise facilities, an aerobic exercise room, and a running track.

Disabled Students: 90% of the campus is accessible. Facilities include wheelchair ramps, elevators, special parking, specially equipped restrooms, special class scheduling, and special housing.

Services: Counseling and information services are available, as is tutoring in some subjects, English, theology, math, languages, philosophy, economics, biology, chemistry, psychology, history and accounting There is remedial math, reading, and writing.

Campus Safety and Security: Measures include 24-hour foot and vehicle patrol, emergency notification system, self-defense education, and security escort services. There are emergency telephones, lighted pathways/sidewalks, and controlled access to dorms/residences.

Programs of Study: Spring Hill confers B.A., B.S. and B.S.N. degrees. Master's degrees are also awarded. Bachelor's degrees are awarded in BIOLOGICAL SCIENCE (biochemistry, biology/biological science, and marine biology), BUSINESS (accounting, business administration and management, international business management, marketing management, and organizational leadership and management), COMMUNICATIONS AND THE ARTS (arts administration/management, communications, digital communications, English, English Writing, graphic design, journalism, public relations, studio art, and theatre arts), COMPUTER AND PHYSICAL SCIENCE (chemistry, computer science, and mathematics), EDUCATION (early childhood education, elementary education, and secondary education), ENGINEERING AND ENVIRONMENTAL DESIGN (engineering), HEALTH PROFESSIONS (nursing, predentistry, premedicine, and preveterinary science), SOCIAL SCIENCE (biopsychology, economics, history, humanities, international studies, liberal arts/general studies, philosophy, political science/government, psychology, social science, sociology, Spanish studies, and theological studies). Business, biology, and psychology have the largest enrollments.

Required: All students must take core curriculum courses in English composition and literature, history, philosophy, theology, math, science, social science, fine art, and foreign language. Students must also take: (1) one cultural diversity course; (2) at least 3 writing-enriched courses (including one in the major) beyond the required 4 core curriculum English courses; and (3) one LEAP (Learning, Engagement and Awareness, Personal Growth) course. Graduation requirements include completion of a minimum of 128 semester hours with a minimum GPA of 2.0 and 30 to 36 upper-division semester hours in the major with a minimum grade of C/C- (see department policy) in each of the major courses and prerequisites.

Special: SHC offers 3-2 engineering programs with the University of Alabama-Birmingham, Auburn University, the University of Florida, Marquette University, and Texas A & M University. The college is a member of the Marine Environmental Sciences Consortium and offers marine biology courses at the Dauphin Island Sea Lab. The college offers a study-abroad experience at its Italy Center in Bologna, Italy; other study abroad options are available through the CCSA (Cooperative Center for Study Abroad) consortium and the foreign study programs of other American Jesuit and non-Jesuit colleges and universities. Internships are available in many majors. There are 16 national honor societies and a freshman honors program.

Faculty/Classroom: 54% of faculty are male; 46% are female. 97% teach undergraduates. No introductory courses are taught by graduate students. The average class size in an introductory lecture is 23; in a laboratory is 14; and in a regular course is 17.

Admissions: 46% of the 2013-2014 applicants were accepted. The SAT scores for the 2013-2014 freshman class were: Critical Reading--39% below 500, 33% between 500 and 599, 20% between 600 and 699, and 8% between 700 and 800; Math--27% below 500, 43% between 500 and 599, 26% between 600 and 699, and 4% between 700 and 800; Writing--29% below 500, 40% between 500 and 599, 23% between 600 and 699, and 8% between 700 and 800. The ACT scores were 15% below 21, 33% between 21 and 23, 25% between 24 and 26, 15% between 27 and 28, and 12% above 28. 39% of the current freshmen were in the top fifth of their class; 66% were in the top two fifths. 5 freshmen graduated first in their class.

Requirements: The SAT or ACT is required. The ACT is preferred. Applicants should have completed at least 16 high school units, including 4 in English; 3 each in math, science, and social studies; 2 in foreign languages; and 1 academic elective. The GED equivalent is accepted. AP and CLEP credits are accepted.

Procedure: Freshmen are admitted fall, spring, and summer. Entrance exams should be taken in spring of the junior year or fall of the senior year. There are deferred admissions and rolling admissions plans. Applications should be filed by July 15 for fall entry; December 1 for spring entry, along with a $25 fee. Notification is sent on a rolling basis. Applications are accepted online.

Transfer: 42 transfer students enrolled in 2012-2013. Transfer applicants must have at least 20 semester hours of college credit, a minimum college cumulative GPA of 2.5, good academic standing at the last college or university attended, and satisfactory recommendations. 32 of 128 credits required for the bachelor's degree must be completed at Spring Hill.

Visiting: There are regularly scheduled orientations for prospective students, campus tour, faculty appointment, attending a class, interview with an admission counselor. There are guides for informal visits; visitors may sit in on classes, and stay overnight. To schedule a visit, contact the Office of Admissions at (800) 742-6704.

Financial Aid: Spring Hill is a member of CSS. The FAFSA and the state aid form are required. The priority date for freshman financial aid applications for fall entry is March 1.

International Students: There are 17 international students enrolled. The school actively recruits these students. They must take the TOEFL with a minimum score of 550 on the paper-based TOEFL (PBT) or 80 on the Internet-based version (iBT) or take the MELAB, IELTS; Cambridge CPE or CAE. students whose first language is English must take the ACT or SAT.

Computers: All students may access the system. Anytime. There are no time limits and no fees.

Graduates: From July 1, 2012 to June 30, 2013, 212 bachelor's degrees were awarded. The most popular majors were business (23%), psychology (10%), and nursing (8%). In an average class, 47% graduate in 4 years or less, 55% graduate in 5 years or less, and 56% graduate in 6 years or less.

Admissions Contact: Robert Stewart, Vice Pres for Admissions & Financial Aid. E-Mail: *admit@shc.edu* Web: *www.shc.edu/admissions*

STILLMAN COLLEGE B-3

Tuscaloosa, AL 35403 (404) 679-4501
(800) 841-5722; (205) 366-8817

Full-time: 700 men, 800 women	**Faculty:** n/av
Part-time: 40 men, 40 women	**Ph.D.s:** 70%
Year: semesters, summer session	**Student/Faculty:** n/av
Application Deadline:	**Tuition:** $13,526
	Room & Board: $5934
Freshman Class: n/av	
SAT or ACT: required	

COMPETITIVE

Stillman College, founded in 1876, is a small, private liberal arts institution affiliated with the Presbyterian Church. Figures in the above capsule and in this profile are approximate. The library contains 113,120 volumes, 7,240 microform items, and 3,550 audio/video tapes/CDs/DVDs, and subscribes to 360 periodicals including electronic. Computerized library services include interlibrary loans and database searching. Special learning facilities include an art gallery and radio station. The 100-acre campus is in a small town 60 miles from Birmingham and 105 miles from Montgomery. Including any residence halls, there are 26 buildings.

Student Life: 70% of undergraduates are from Alabama. Others are from 27 states, and 8 foreign countries. 95% are from public schools. 98% are African American. 99% are Protestant. The average age of freshmen is 19.

Housing: 750 students can be accommodated in college housing, which includes single-sex dorms and off-campus apartments. On-campus housing is available on a first-come and first-served basis. 50% of students commute. Alcohol is not permitted. All students may keep cars.

Activities: 10% of men belong to 4 national fraternities; 20% of women belong to 4 national sororities. There are 19 groups on campus, including art, band, cheerleading, choir, chorus, dance, debate, drama, honors, international, jazz band, marching band, newspaper, pep band, radio and TV, religious, social, social service, student government, and yearbook.

Sports: There are 6 intercollegiate sports for men and 6 for women. Facilities include a college center, tennis courts, stress center, bowling lanes, billiards, a swimming pool, a gym, a football field, and a weight room.

Disabled Students: Facilities include wheelchair ramps, elevators, special parking, and specially equipped restrooms.

Services: Counseling and information services are available, as is tutoring in some subjects, reading, writing, math, physics, and chemistry There is remedial math, reading, and writing.

Campus Safety and Security: Measures include 24-hour foot and vehicle patrol, self-defense education, and security escort services. There are lighted pathways/sidewalks.

Programs of Study: Stillman confers B.A., and B.S. degrees. Bachelor's degrees are awarded in BIOLOGICAL SCIENCE (biology/biological science), BUSINESS (business administration and management), COMMUNICATIONS AND THE ARTS (art, English, and music), COMPUTER AND PHYSICAL SCIENCE (computer science and mathematics), EDUCATION (elementary education and physical education), HEALTH PROFESSIONS (premedicine), SOCIAL SCIENCE (history, prelaw, and religion).

Required: To graduate, students must complete a minimum of 124 credit hours, with at least 30 in the major, and maintain a minimum GPA of 2.0 overall and in the major. The 53-credit-hour general education core includes courses in religion, logic, English composition, public speaking, african heritage, African American experience, history, social science, physical and life sciences, math, computer literacy, health, and phys ed. All students must submit a senior thesis and take a senior departmental exam.

Special: Stillman offers local, national, and international opportunites for cooperative education and internships. Cross-registration is possible with the University of Alabama at Birmingham, with which there also are cooperative degree programs in nursing and allied health. Federal work-study is available on and off campus, and students may earn credit for prior learning experiences. There are 3 national honor societies.

Faculty/Classroom: 40% of faculty are male; 60% are female. All teach undergraduates. No introductory courses are taught by graduate students. The average class size in an introductory lecture is 40; in a laboratory is 40; and in a regular course is 35.

Requirements: The SAT or ACT is required. Applicants should be high school graduates or have earned the GED. Secondary preparation should include 4 units of English and 1 unit each of math, science, and history. All applicants must have an interview. Music majors must audition. A GPA of 2.0 is required. AP and CLEP credits are accepted.

Procedure: Freshmen are admitted to all sessions. There is a rolling admissions plan. Check with the school for current application deadlines. The fall 2013 application fee was $25.

Transfer: Transfer applicants should present at least a C average in previous college work and must plan to spend at least a year in residence. 64 of 124 credits required for the bachelor's degree must be completed at Stillman.

Visiting: There are regularly scheduled orientations for prospective students. To schedule a visit, contact the Director of Recruitment.

Financial Aid: The CCS/Profile, or FAFSA, or FFS, or SFS and the college's own financial statement are required. Check with the school for current application deadlines.

International Students: The school actively recruits these students. They must take the TOEFL. They must also take the SAT or ACT.

Computers: All students may access the system. 8 a.m. to 9 p.m. Monday through Saturday. Students are limited to 69 hours per week. There are no fees.

Admissions Contact: Lu Ann Baker, Director of Admissions. E-Mail: *admissions@stillman.edu* Web: *www.stillman.edu*

TALLADEGA COLLEGE C-2

Talladega, AL 35160 **(256) 761-6416; (800) 633-2440**

Full-time: 270 men, 420 women	**Faculty:** n/av
Part-time: 20 men, 30 women	**Ph.D.s:** 60%
Year: semesters	**Student/Faculty:** n/av
Application Deadline: open	**Tuition:** $8500
	Room & Board: $5500
Freshman Class: n/av	
SAT or ACT: required	

COMPETITIVE

Talladega College, founded in 1867, is a private liberal arts institution offering emphases on business, sciences, and social work. The figures in above capsule and in this profile are approximate. In addition to regional accreditation, Dega has baccalaureate program accreditation with CSWE. The library contains 87,960 volumes, and 350 audio/video tapes/CDs/DVDs, and subscribes to 330 periodicals including electronic. Computerized library services include interlibrary loans. Special learning facilities include an art gallery, science drop-in center, curriculum and writing labs, and financial computer lab. The 130-acre campus is in a small town 55 miles east of Birmingham and 115 miles west of Atlanta. Including any residence halls, there are 42 buildings.

Student Life: 60% of undergraduates are from Alabama. Others are from 29 states, and 2 foreign countries. 99% are African American. 90% are Protestant. The average age of freshmen is 18; all undergraduates, 20. 22% do not continue beyond their first year; 45% remain to graduate.

Housing: 580 students can be accommodated in college housing, which includes single-sex dorms and on-campus apartments. In addition, there are honors houses. On-campus housing is guaranteed for all 4 years. 70% of students live on campus; of those, 90% remain on campus on weekends. Alcohol is not permitted. All students may keep cars.

Activities: 14% of men belong to 4 national fraternities; 40% of women belong to 4 national sororities. There are 23 groups on campus, including art, cheerleading, choir, chorus, computers, dance, drama, honors, jazz band, newspaper, professional, social, student government, and yearbook. Popular campus events include Spring Concert, Carnival and Coronation.

Sports: There are 4 intercollegiate sports for men and 4 for women, and 8 intramural sports for men and 3 for women. Facilities include a swimming pool, a 150-seat gym, lounges, game rooms, tennis courts, and a baseball field.

Disabled Students: 50% of the campus is accessible. Facilities include wheelchair ramps, elevators, special parking, and specially equipped restrooms.

Services: Counseling and information services are available, as is tutoring in every subject. There is remedial math, reading, and writing.

Campus Safety and Security: Measures include 24-hour foot and vehicle patrol and security escort services. There are lighted pathways/sidewalks.

Programs of Study: Dega confers B.A. degrees. Bachelor's degrees are awarded in BIOLOGICAL SCIENCE (biology/biological science), BUSINESS (accounting, banking and finance, and business administration and management), COMMUNICATIONS AND THE ARTS (English and music performance), COMPUTER AND PHYSICAL SCIENCE (chemistry, computer science, mathematics, and physics), EDUCATION (music education), SOCIAL SCIENCE (economics, history, psychology, public administration, social work, and sociology). Business, biology, and chemistry are the strongest academically. Biology has the largest enrollment.

Required: To graduate, students must maintain a minimum GPA of 2.5 while taking 124 to 127 total semester hours, including 60 in the major and completion of a core curriculum. Distribution requirements at the freshman level include 8 semester hours in natural sciences, 6 each in communications, social sciences, and humanities, 2 in phys ed, and 1 in freshman orientation; additional hours in these subjects vary by major at the sophomore level.

Special: Talladega offers co-op programs with other schools through individual departments, a 3-2 engineering degree with Auburn University, internships involving historic preservation work, work-study plans with Adopt-a-Family and Adult Literacy, and B.A.-B.S. degrees in biology, business administration, chemistry, and computer science. There are dual majors available in law, nursing, engineering, and allied health. There are 4 national honor societies.

Faculty/Classroom: 60% of faculty are male; 40% are female. All teach undergraduates, and 25% do both. No introductory courses are taught by graduate students. The average class size in an introductory lecture is 30; in a laboratory is 20; and in a regular course is 18.

Requirements: The SAT or ACT is required. Applicants must be graduates of an accredited secondary school with 22 academic units, including 4 in English, 3 in social studies, and 2 each in math, science, health/phys ed, and electives. The GED is considered. An essay and interview are recommended. An audition is required for music majors. A GPA of 2.5 is required. CLEP credits are accepted. Important factors in the admissions decision are advanced placement or honors courses, recommendations by school officials, and recommendations by alumni.

Procedure: Freshmen are admitted fall and spring. Entrance exams should be taken in the junior year. There are deferred admissions and rolling admissions plans. Application deadlines are open. The fall 2013 application fee was $25. Applications are accepted online.

Transfer: Applicants must have a cumulative GPA of 2.0 in college work. The SAT or ACT is recommended. 60 of 124 credits required for the bachelor's degree must be completed at Dega.

Visiting: There are guides for informal visits, visitors may sit in on classes, and stay overnight. To schedule a visit, contact the Admissions Office.

Financial Aid: The FAFSA, CCS/Profile, or FAFSA, or FFS, or SFS, and the college's own financial statement are required. Check with the school for current application deadlines.

International Students: The school actively recruits these students. They must take the TOEFL and the college's own test. They must also take the SAT or ACT.

Computers: All students may access the system from 8 a.m. to 4:30 p.m. and 7 p.m. to 10 p.m. daily. There are no time limits and no fees.

Admissions Contact: Monroe Thornton, Admissions Office. E-Mail: *admissions@talladega.edu* Web: *www.talladega.edu*

TROY UNIVERSITY C-4

Troy, AL 36082 (334) 670-3179
(800) 551-9716; (334) 670-3733

Full-time: 4050 men, 6300 women
Part-time: 5550 men, 6000 women
Graduate: 2575 men, 5260 women
Year: semesters, summer session
Application Deadline: open
Freshman Class: n/av
SAT or ACT: required
Faculty: n/av;IIA, --$
Ph.D.s: n/av
Student/Faculty: n/av
Tuition: $5150 ($10,050)
Room & Board: $6500

COMPETITIVE

Troy University, founded in 1887, is a public institution composed of a network of campuses throughout Alabama and worldwide. International in scope, Troy University provides a variety of educational programs at the undergraduate and graduate levels for a diverse student body. Academic programs are offered in traditional, nontraditional and emerging electronic formats. Information in this profile applies to the Troy, Phenix City, Dothan, and Montgomery campuses and University College sites. The figures in the above capsule and in this profile are approximate. There are 5 undergraduate schools and 5 graduate schools. In addition to regional accreditation, Troy has baccalaureate program accreditation with ACBSP, CSWE, NASM, NCATE, and NLN. The 4 libraries contain 594,716 volumes, 2.1 million microform items, and 19,532 audio/video tapes/CDs/DVDs, and subscribe to 3,263 periodicals including electronic. Computerized library services include interlibrary loans, database searching, Internet access, and Wi-Fi capability. Special learning facilities include an art gallery, planetarium, radio station, TV station, an arboretum, the Davis theater, and the Rosa L. Parks Library, and Museum and Children's Annex. The 768-acre campus is in a rural area Troy campus is 50 miles south of Montgomery. Including any residence halls, there are 111 buildings.

Student Life: 48% are White; 40% African American.

Housing: 1525 students can be accommodated in college housing, which includes single-sex and coed dorms, on-campus apartments, off-campus apartments, and married student housing. In addition, there are honors houses, special-interest houses, fraternity houses, sorority houses, an international house, and substance-free housing. On-campus housing is guaranteed for all 4 years. 66% of students commute. Alcohol is not permitted. All students may keep cars.

Activities: 19% of men belong to 12 national fraternities; 18% of women belong to 9 national sororities. There are 147 groups on campus, including art, band, cheerleading, choir, chorale, chorus, computers, dance, debate, drama, drill team, ethnic, film, forensics, gay, honors, international, jazz band, literary magazine, marching band, musical theater, newspaper, opera, orchestra, pep band, photography, political, professional, radio and TV, religious, social, social service, student government, and symphony. Popular campus events include ISCO Festival, Spring Picnic and Heritage Week.

Sports: There are 7 intercollegiate sports for men and 9 for women, and 11 intramural sports for men and 11 for women. Facilities include a 150-seat auditorium, a 3,000-square-foot weight training center, the 2,250-seat Pace-Riddle baseball stadium, a 9-hole golf course, the 30,000-seat Movie Gallery Veteran's Stadium, and 2 football practice fields. Other nearby facilities include a softball and soccer/track complex. The 4,000-seat Trojan Arena is home to both basketball teams and the volleyball team. Also available for student use is the natatorium with an indoor swimming pool, the recreational gym with an outdoor swimming pool and fitness centers, and intramural fields.

Disabled Students: 95% of the campus is accessible. Facilities include wheelchair ramps, elevators, special parking, specially equipped restrooms, special class scheduling, lowered drinking fountains, lowered telephones.

Services: Counseling and information services are available, as is tutoring in some subjects. There is a reader service for the blind, and remedial math, reading, and writing. Tutors may be provided for students upon request.

Campus Safety and Security: Measures include 24-hour foot and vehicle patrol, self-defense education, and security escort services. There are lighted pathways/sidewalks, and foot and vehicle patrols during class hours.

Programs of Study: Troy confers B.A., B.S., B.A.B.A., B.A.Ed., B.Applied Sc., B.F.A., B.M.Ed., B.S.B.A., B.S.Ed. and B.S.N. degrees. Associate and master's degrees are also awarded. Bachelor's degrees are awarded in BIOLOGICAL SCIENCE (biology/biological science and marine biology), BUSINESS (accounting, banking and finance, business administration and management, business economics, insurance, management science, marketing management, marketing/retailing/merchandising, personnel management, and sports management), COMMUNICATIONS AND THE ARTS (art, art history and appreciation, broadcasting, communications, design, dramatic arts, English, journalism, and studio art), COMPUTER AND PHYSICAL SCIENCE (chemistry, computer science, information sciences and systems, mathematics, and science), EDUCATION (art education, athletic training, collaborative education, early childhood education, elementary education, English education, health education, mathematics education, music education, physical education, science education, secondary education, social science education, and special education), ENGINEERING AND ENVIRONMENTAL DESIGN (environmental science and technological management), HEALTH PROFESSIONS (nursing and rehabilitation therapy), SOCIAL SCIENCE (criminal justice, history, human services, political science/government, psychology, social science, social work, and sociology). Business and education is the strongest academically. Business has the largest enrollment.

Required: All students must maintain a minimum GPA of 2.0 while taking 120 to 140 semester credit hours, 54 of which must be in their major field. Distribution requirements include 48 hours of general studies, covering such subjects as English, math, history, science, and fine arts.

Special: Cross-registration with the Marine Biological Consortium, internships in education, journalism, and nursing, study abroad in 5 countries, work-study programs at the university, and student-designed majors in public relations, advertising, and other fields are offered. Credit for life experience and nondegree study are also offered. There is a dual-degree program with Vyatka State University of Humanities in Kirov, Russia. There are 28 national honor societies, including Phi Beta Kappa, a freshman honors program, and 14 departmental honors programs.

Faculty/Classroom: All teach undergraduates. No introductory courses are taught by graduate students.

Requirements: The SAT or ACT is required. Applicants must have earned at least 15 Carnegie units, with 11 in academic courses and 3 to 4 in English. An interview is recommended, along with a portfolio or audition for some programs. The GED is accepted. A GPA of 2.0 is required. AP and CLEP credits are accepted. Important factors in the admissions decision are ability to finance college education, evidence of special talent, and extracurricular activities record.

Procedure: Freshmen are admitted fall, spring, and summer. Entrance exams should be taken in the spring of junior year of high school. There is a rolling admissions plan. Application deadlines are open. Application fee is $30. Applications are accepted online.

Transfer: Transfer applicants need 20 semester hours attempted at their previous institution, with a GPA of 2.0.

Visiting: There are regularly scheduled orientations for prospective students, including a campus tour, classroom visitation, academic consultation, and interviews. There are guides for informal visits and visitors may sit in on classes. To schedule a visit, contact the Office of Enrollment Services.

Financial Aid: Average annual earnings from campus work are $2050. The FAFSA and the college's own financial statement are required. Check with the school for current application deadlines.

International Students: The school actively recruits these students. They must take the TOEFL with a minimum score of 500 on the paper-based TOEFL (PBT) or 61 on the Internet-based version (iBT), or take the IELTS or the SAT. They must also take the SAT, scoring 18.

Computers: All students may access the system 7 days a week. There are no time limits and no fees.

Admissions Contact: Buddy Starling, Dean of Enrollment Services. E-Mail: *bstar@troy.edu* Web: *www.troy.edu*

TUSKEGEE UNIVERSITY D-4

Tuskegee, AL 36088 (334) 727-8289
(800) 622-6531; (334) 727 5750

Full-time: 1085 men, 1436 women
Part-time: 38 men, 39 women
Graduate: 161 men, 358 women
Year: semesters, summer session
Application Deadline: open
Faculty: 280; IIA, --$
Ph.D.s: 70%
Student/Faculty: 12 to 1
Tuition: $18,800
Room & Board: $7950
Freshman Class: 5147 applied, 3519 accepted, 650 enrolled
SAT CR/M: 500/480 **ACT:** 21

COMPETITIVE

Tuskegee University, founded in 1881 by Booker T. Washington, is an independent professional and technical institution offering degree programs in liberal arts and sciences, agriculture, architecture, business, education, engineering, and health professions. There are 7 undergraduate schools and 4 graduate schools. In addition to regional accreditation, Tuskegee has baccalaureate program accreditation with ABET, CSWE, NAAB, NCATE, and NLN. The 4 libraries contain 380,000 volumes, 2,500 microform items, and 3,000 audio/video tapes/CDs/DVDs, and subscribe to 1,150 periodicals including electronic. Computerized library services include interlibrary loans, database searching, Internet access, and Wi-Fi capability. Special learning facilities include a The 5200-acre campus is in a rural area 40 miles east of Montgomery, AL and 20 miles west of Auburn, AL. Including any residence halls, there are 160 buildings.

Student Life: 67% of undergraduates are from out of state, mostly the South. Students are from 42 states, 31 foreign countries, and Canada. 90% are from public schools. 80% are African American. The average age of freshmen is 19; all undergraduates, 22. 22% do not continue beyond their first year; 46% remain to graduate.

Housing: 2300 students can be accommodated in college housing, which

includes single-sex dorms, on-campus apartments, and married student housing. In addition, there are honors houses. On-campus housing is guaranteed for the freshman year only, is available on a first-come, and first-served basis. Alcohol is not permitted. All students may keep cars.

Activities: 4% of men belong to 6 local and 4 national fraternities; 4% of women belong to 5 local and 4 national sororities. There are 60 groups on campus, including band, cheerleading, choir, chorus, drama, honors, international, jazz band, marching band, newspaper, orchestra, religious, social service, and student government. Popular campus events include Spring Pageant, Campus All-Star Challenge and Student Leadership Retreat.

Sports: There are 5 intercollegiate sports for men and 5 for women, and 7 intramural sports for men and 6 for women. Facilities include a 10,000-seat stadium, a 5000-seat arena, a student center, tennis courts, a rifle range, playing fields, and an Olympic-size natatorium.

Disabled Students: Facilities include wheelchair ramps, elevators, special parking, specially equipped restrooms, special class scheduling, lowered drinking fountains, and lowered telephones.

Services: Counseling and information services are available, as is tutoring in some subjects. There is a reader service for the blind.

Campus Safety and Security: Measures include 24-hour foot and vehicle patrol and security escort services. There are lighted pathways/sidewalks.

Programs of Study: Tuskegee confers B.A., B.S. and B.S.N. degrees. Master's and doctoral degrees are also awarded. Bachelor's degrees are awarded in AGRICULTURE (agricultural economics, animal science, and horticulture), BIOLOGICAL SCIENCE (biology/biological science), BUSINESS (accounting, banking and finance, business administration and management, business economics, hospitality management services, management science, marketing/retailing/merchandising, and supply chain management), COMMUNICATIONS AND THE ARTS (English), COMPUTER AND PHYSICAL SCIENCE (chemistry, computer science, mathematics, and physics), EDUCATION (early childhood education, elementary education, physical education, secondary education, special education, and technical education), ENGINEERING AND ENVIRONMENTAL DESIGN (aeronautical engineering, architecture, biomedical engineering, chemical engineering, construction management, electrical/electronics engineering, electrical/electronics engineering technology, and mechanical engineering), HEALTH PROFESSIONS (allied health, nursing, occupational therapy, and veterinary science), SOCIAL SCIENCE (dietetics, economics, food science, history, political science/government, psychology, social work, and sociology). Engineering, nursing, veterinary science and business are the strongest academically. Engineering, biology, and veterinary science have the largest enrollments.

Required: All students must complete a general education curriculum, including courses in history, sociology, philosophy, art, English, humanities, political science, math, natural sciences, and phys ed. A minimum of 124 semester credits with a GPA of 2.0 is required for graduation.

Special: Cooperative programs, internships, work-study programs, dual majors, nondegree study, and a B.A.-B.S. degree are offered. There are 17 national honor societies, a freshman honors program, and 9 departmental honors programs.

Faculty/Classroom: 70% of faculty are male; 30% are female. No introductory courses are taught by graduate students.

Admissions: 68% of the 2013-2014 applicants were accepted. The SAT scores for the 2013-2014 freshman class were: Critical Reading--67% below 500, 27% between 500 and 599, and 4% between 600 and 699; Math--64% below 500, 26% between 500 and 599, and 8% between 600 and 699. The ACT scores were 17% below 21, 61% between 21 and 23, 15% between 24 and 26, 6% between 27 and 28, and 1% above 28. 60% of the current freshmen were in the top fifth of their class; 80% were in the top two fifths.

Requirements: The SAT or ACT is required. A GPA of 3.0 is recommended. Applicants should be graduates of an accredited secondary school or hold the GED. They should have completed 4 units of English, 3 each of social science and math, and 1 each of physical science and biological science. SAT: Subject tests in mathematics (level I or II) and 1 other subject are recommended. An essay is not required. A GPA of 3.0 is required. AP and CLEP credits are accepted. Important factors in the admissions decision are advanced placement or honors courses, ability to finance college education, and geographical diversity.

Procedure: Freshmen are admitted to all sessions. Entrance exams should be taken starting in the junior year. There are early admissions and rolling admissions plans. Application deadlines are open. Application fee is $25. Applications are accepted online.

Transfer: 166 transfer students enrolled in 2012-2013. Applicants must be in good standing at all previously attended institutions and have completed 12 or more semester hours with a GPA of 2.5. 44 of 124 credits required for the bachelor's degree must be completed at Tuskegee.

Visiting: There are guides for informal visits, visitors may sit in on classes, and stay overnight. To schedule a visit, contact the Office of Admissions.

Financial Aid: In 2013-2014, 87% of all full-time freshmen and 91% of continuing full-time students received some form of financial aid. 71% of all full-time freshmen and 74% of continuing full-time students received need-based aid. The average freshman award was $19,250. Need-based scholarships or need-based grants averaged $2,500 ($5,550 maximum); need-based self-help aid (loans and jobs) averaged $2,400 ($5,500 maximum); non-need-based athletic scholarships averaged $12,000 ($25,000 maximum); and other non-need-based awards and non-need-based scholarships averaged $3,500 ($10,000 maximum). 59% of undergraduate students work part-time. Average annual earnings from campus work are $2610. The average financial indebtedness of the 2013 graduate was $20,000. Tuskegee is a member of CSS. The CSS/Profile, and and federal tax returns is required. The priority date for freshman financial aid applications for fall entry is March 31. The deadline for filing freshman financial aid applications for fall entry is March 31.

International Students: There are 27 international students enrolled. They must take the TOEFL with a minimum score of 500 on the paper-based TOEFL (PBT) or 62 on the Internet-based version (iBT). They must also take the SAT or ACT, scoring 1000.

Computers: All students may access the system. There are no time limits and no fees.

Graduates: From July 1, 2012 to June 30, 2013, 356 bachelor's degrees were awarded. The most popular majors were engineering (11%), biology (11%), and business (8%). 87 companies recruited on campus in 2012-2013. In an average class, 17% graduate in 4 years or less, 28% graduate in 5 years or less, and 43% graduate in 6 years or less.

Admissions Contact: Elizabeth Dadzie, Associate VP of Admissions. E-Mail: *admissions@tuskegee.edu* Web: *www.tuskegee.edu*

UNIVERSITY OF ALABAMA SYSTEM

The University of Alabama System, established in 1900, is a public system in Alabama. It is governed by a board of trustees, whose chief administrator is the chancellor. The primary goal of the system is to serve all the people of the state through teaching, research, and public service. The main priorities are to promote the economic, cultural, and social welfare of Alabama through higher education; to educate and train the leasers and citizens of tomorrow; and to conduct research in all fields that address the critical needs of mankind. The total student enrollment for all three campuses is usually 44,500 with 3400 faculty members. Altogether there are 194 baccalaureate, 169 master's, 93 doctoral programs offered in the University of Alabama System. Profiles of the 4-year campuses are included in this section.

UNIVERSITY OF ALABAMA AT BIRMINGHAM C-2

Birmingham, AL 35294 **(205) 934-8221**
(800) 421-8743; (205) 975-7114

Full-time: 3501 men, 4856 women	**Faculty:** n/av
Part-time: 1279 men, 1866 women	**Ph.D.s:** 87%
Graduate: 2529 men, 4537 women	**Student/Faculty:** 18 to 1
Year: semesters, summer session	**Tuition:** $8904 ($20,394)
Application Deadline: June 1	**Room & Board:** $9580
Freshman Class: 5689 applied, 4934 accepted, 1773 enrolled	
SAT: required **ACT:** 25	**COMPETITIVE+**

The University of Alabama at Birmingham, founded in 1969, is a public institution offering degrees in the arts and sciences, business, dentistry, education, engineering, health professions, joint health sciences, medicine, nursing, optometry and public health. There are 8 undergraduate schools and 11 graduate schools. In addition to regional accreditation, UAB has baccalaureate program accreditation with AACSB, ABET, CAHEA, CSWE, NASAD, NASM, NCATE, and NLN. The 2 libraries contain 1.4 million volumes, 1.3 million microform items, and 35,976 audio/video tapes/CDs/DVDs, and subscribe to 36,371 periodicals including electronic. Computerized library services include interlibrary loans, database searching, Internet access, and Wi-Fi capability. Special learning facilities include an art gallery, radio station, TV station, Reynolds historical library, and Alabama museum of the health sciences. The 323-acre campus is in an urban area in Birmingham, Alabama. Including any residence halls, there are 204 buildings.

Student Life: 90% of undergraduates are from Alabama. Others are from 48 states, 53 foreign countries, and Canada. 92% are from public schools. 64% are White; 21% African American. The average age of freshmen is 18; all undergraduates, 24. 20% do not continue beyond their first year; 48% remain to graduate.

Housing: 2260 students can be accommodated in college housing, which includes single-sex and coed dorms, on-campus apartments, and married student housing. housing for disabled students. On-campus housing is available on a first-come and first-served basis. 78% of students commute. Alcohol is not permitted. All students may keep cars.

Activities: 4% of men belong to 10 national fraternities; 4% of women belong to 10 national sororities. There are 150 groups on campus, including band, cheerleading, chess, choir, chorale, chorus, computers, dance, drama, environmental, ethnic, gay, honors, international, jazz band, literary magazine, marching band, musical theater, newspaper, opera, orchestra, pep band, political, professional, radio and TV, religious, social, social service, and student government. Popular campus events include Springfest.

Sports: There are 6 intercollegiate sports for men and 11 for women, and 35 intramural sports for men and 35 for women. Facilities include a 150,000-square-foot recreation center with 4 basketball/volleyball courts, 5 racquetball courts (1 of which can be converted to squash and 4 for wallyball), 4 aerobics studios, 18,000 square feet of weight and cardio-fitness areas, a game room, a KidsZone, an aquatics center with both lap and leisure components, a gym used for indoor soccer, floor hockey, and badminton, a juice bar, an indoor track, and a climbing wall.

Disabled Students: All of the campus is accessible. Facilities include wheelchair ramps, elevators, special parking, specially equipped restrooms, lowered drinking fountains, lowered telephones, and special housing.

Services: Counseling and information services are available, as is tutoring in most subjects. There is a reader service for the blind, and remedial math, reading, and writing.

Campus Safety and Security: Measures include 24-hour foot and vehicle patrol, emergency notification system, self-defense education, and security escort services. There are shuttle buses, emergency telephones, lighted pathways/sidewalks, the school's officers patroling, mountain bikes, T-3 mobile electric transports, and motorcycles.

Programs of Study: UAB confers B.A., B.S., B.F.A., B.S.B.M.E., B.S.C.E., B.S.E.E., B.S.M.E., B.S.Mt.E., B.S.N. and B.S.S.W. degrees. Master's and doctoral degrees are also awarded. Bachelor's degrees are awarded in BIOLOGICAL SCIENCE (biology/biological science and neurosciences), BUSINESS (accounting, banking and finance, and marketing/retailing/merchandising), COMMUNICATIONS AND THE ARTS (art, communications, dramatic arts, English, French, music, and Spanish), COMPUTER AND PHYSICAL SCIENCE (chemistry, computer science, information sciences and systems, mathematics, natural sciences, and physics), EDUCATION (early childhood education, elementary education, health education, physical education, secondary education, and special education), ENGINEERING AND ENVIRONMENTAL DESIGN (biomedical engineering, civil engineering, electrical/electronics engineering, industrial administration/management, materials engineering, and mechanical engineering), HEALTH PROFESSIONS (cytotechnology, health science, medical records administration/services, medical technology, nuclear medical technology, nursing, public health, and respiratory therapy), SOCIAL SCIENCE (African American studies, anthropology, criminal justice, economics, history, international studies, philosophy, political science/government, psychology, social work, and sociology). Biology, psychology, and accounting are the largest.

Required: All students must complete a core curriculum that includes courses in math, computers, English, history, science and technology, social sciences, philosophy, fine arts, foreign language or culture, and literature. To receive a bachelor's degree, students must complete 128 semester hours for most programs, with a GPA of at least 2.0.

Special: UAB offers student-designed majors, cross-registration with the Birmingham Area Consortium for Higher Education, internships, study abroad in 32 countries, work-study programs, nondegree study, pass/fail options, and credit by exam and for life experience. Cooperative education programs in the student's area of interest provide full- or part-time work. Additionally, there are several special programs such as the Industrial Scholars Program (provides financial support and industry experience for engineering students), Fifth Year Master of Science program in biology, Mathematics Fast Track Program, and the Early Medical School Acceptance Program. There are 36 national honor societies, a freshman honors program, and 25 departmental honors programs.

Faculty/Classroom: 50% of faculty are male; 49% are female. No introductory courses are taught by graduate students.

Admissions: 87% of the 2013-2014 applicants were accepted. The ACT scores were 15% below 21, 25% between 21 and 23, 25% between 24 and 26, 14% between 27 and 28, and 21% above 28. 46% of the current freshmen were in the top fifth of their class; 74% were in the top two fifths. There were 11 National Merit finalists.

Requirements: The SAT or ACT is required. Applicants should have completed 17 Carnegie units and a college prep diploma, including 4 units in English, 3 each in math, science, and social studies, 1 in foreign language, and 3 in electives. The GED is accepted. A GPA of 2.0 is required. AP and CLEP credits are accepted.

Procedure: Freshmen are admitted to all sessions. Entrance exams should be taken by the beginning of the senior year. There are early admissions, deferred admissions, and rolling admissions plans. Applications should be filed by June 1 for fall entry, along with a $30 fee. Notification is sent on a rolling basis. Applications are accepted online.

Transfer: 1397 transfer students enrolled in 2012-2013. Transfer applicants must have a GPA of 2.0 after completing 24 semester hours (or 36 quarter hours) of college-level work. College transcripts are required of all students. Applicants who have completed fewer than 24 semester hours must meet the requirements of beginning freshmen.

Visiting: There are regularly scheduled orientations for prospective students, including a question-and-answer session, academic advising, sessions for parents, and presentations on student life, financial aid, housing, and student development. There are guides for informal visits and visitors may sit in on classes.

Financial Aid: In 2013-2014, 61% of all full-time freshmen students received some form of financial aid. 36% of all full-time freshmen students received need-based aid. The average freshman award was $9,710. Need-based scholarships or need-based grants averaged $4,968; need-based self-help aid (loans and jobs) averaged $4,766; non-need-based athletic scholarships averaged $18,022; and other non-need-based awards and non-need-based scholarships averaged $6,585. The average financial indebtedness of the 2013 graduate was $28,430. The FAFSA is required. The priority date for freshman financial aid applications for fall entry is March 1.

International Students: There are 180 international students enrolled. The school actively recruits these students. They must take the TOEFL with a minimum score of 500 on the paper-based TOEFL (PBT) or 77 on the Internet-based version (iBT). They must also take the SAT or ACT.

Computers: All students may access the system. There are no time limits and no fees.

Graduates: From July 1, 2012 to June 30, 2013, 2195 bachelor's degrees were awarded. The most popular majors were health professions and related programs (19%), business/marketing (18%), and education (11%). 254 companies recruited on campus in 2012-2013. In an average class, 25% graduate in 4 years or less, 42% graduate in 5 years or less, and 48% graduate in 6 years or less.

Admissions Contact: Kirk Kluver, Director of Admissions. E-Mail: *chooseuab@uab.edu* Web: *http:/www.uab.edu/apply*

UNIVERSITY OF ALABAMA AT HUNTSVILLE C-1

Huntsville, AL 35899 **(256) 824-2773**
(800) UAH-CALL; (256) 824-6073

Full-time: 2331 men, 1906 women	**Faculty:** 309; I, --$
Part-time: 846 men, 613 women	**Ph.D.s:** 86%
Graduate: 959 men, 721 women	**Student/Faculty:** 14 to 1
Year: semesters, summer session	**Tuition:** $9192 ($21,506)
Application Deadline: June 1	**Room & Board:** $8433
Freshman Class: 2054 applied, 1656 accepted, 651 enrolled	
SAT CR/M: 570/570	**ACT:** 26 **VERYCOMPETITIVE**

The University of Alabama in Huntsville, founded in 1950 and part of the University of Alabama system, is a public institution offering programs in Liberal Arts, Sciences, Business Administration, Nursing, and Engineering. There are 5 undergraduate schools and one graduate school. In addition to regional accreditation, UAHuntsville has baccalaureate program accreditation with AACSB, ABET, ACCE, CSAB, NASAD, NASM, and NCATE. The library contains 289,500 volumes, 571,000 microform items, and 1,489 audio/video tapes/CDs/DVDs, and subscribes to 339 periodicals including electronic. Computerized library services include interlibrary loans, database searching, Internet access, and Wi-Fi capability. Special learning facilities include an art gallery, radio station, an optical observatory and a radio telescope; the National Space Science and Technology Center located on our campus, shared between UAHuntsville, NASA and the National Weather Service; a rooftop greenhouse used for research and laboratory experiences. The 400-acre campus is in a suburban area 100 miles north of Birmingham and 90 miles south of Nashville. Including any residence halls, there are 59 buildings.

Student Life: 91% of undergraduates are from Alabama. Others are from 39 states, 66 foreign countries, and Canada. 90% are from public schools. 70% are White; 13% African American. 72% are Protestant; 11% Catholic. The average age of freshmen is 18; all undergraduates, 24. 19% do not continue beyond their first year; 48% remain to graduate.

Housing: 1680 students can be accommodated in college housing, which includes coed dorms, on-campus apartments, and married student housing. In addition, there are honors houses, fraternity houses, sorority houses, athletics teammates, freshman leadership and involvement, engineering, academic success and discovery. On-campus housing is guaranteed for the freshman year only, is available on a first-come, and first-served basis. 81% of students commute. Alcohol is not permitted. All students may keep cars.

Activities: 6% of men belong to 6 national fraternities. There are 125 groups on campus, including community service, honor societies, multicultural, special interest, academic, art, band, cheerleading, choir, chorale, chorus, computers, dance, drama, environmental, ethnic, gay, honors, international, jazz band, musical theater, newspaper, opera, pep band, political, professional, religious, social, social service, student government, and symphony. Popular campus events include Week of Welcome, Homecoming, Family Weekend, Late Night Breakfast, ChargerCon, The Big Event, Sandella Sounds, and Spring Fling.

Sports: There are 8 intercollegiate sports for men and 8 for women, and

11 intramural sports for men and 11 for women. Facilities include a 2800-seat gym, a swimming pool, racquetball and tennis courts, disc golf course, soccer fields, softball diamonds, and a fitness center with cardio equipment, indoor track, weight room, fitness classes, aquatics, sand volleyball, basketball courts and a sports nutrition center.

Disabled Students: 98% of the campus is accessible. Facilities include wheelchair ramps, elevators, special parking, specially equipped restrooms, special class scheduling, lowered drinking fountains, special housing, a swimming pool lift, and sign language interpreters.

Services: Counseling and information services are available, as is tutoring in most subjects, Tutoring services are available for most 100-200 level classes, most undergraduate math classes, and undergraduate writing in any discipline.

Campus Safety and Security: Measures include 24-hour foot and vehicle patrol, emergency notification system, self-defense education, and security escort services. There are emergency telephones, lighted pathways/sidewalks, controlled access to dorms/residences, emergency management plan, 911 system and digitally recorded security cameras.

Programs of Study: UAHuntsville confers B.A., B.F.A., B.S., B.S.B.A., B.S.A.E., B.S.Che.E., B.S.C.E., B.S.Cp.E., B.S.E.E., B.S.M.E., B.S.I.S.E., B.S.O.E., and B.S.N. degrees. Master's and doctoral degrees are also awarded. Bachelor's degrees are awarded in BIOLOGICAL SCIENCE (biology/biological science), BUSINESS (accounting, banking and finance, business administration and management, economics – statistics, and marketing/retailing/merchandising), COMMUNICATIONS AND THE ARTS (art, communications, English, languages, and music), COMPUTER AND PHYSICAL SCIENCE (chemistry, computer science, earth science, information sciences and systems, mathematics, physics, and science), EDUCATION (elementary education), ENGINEERING AND ENVIRONMENTAL DESIGN (chemical engineering, civil engineering, computer engineering, electrical/electronics engineering, industrial engineering, mechanical engineering, and optical engineering), HEALTH PROFESSIONS (nursing), SOCIAL SCIENCE (history, philosophy, political science/government, psychology, and sociology). Nursing, mechanical engineering and biological sciences. have the largest enrollments.

Required: All students must earn a minimum GPA of 2.0 over 120 to 134 credit hours, including 21 to 36 in their major. The core curriculum includes courses in English composition, literature, world history, foreign language and communications, fine arts, math, science, and social sciences.

Special: UAH offers co-op programs in all majors, cross-registration with Alabama Agricultural and Mechanical University, Athens State University, and Calhoun Community College, and internships in business, communications, education, and political science. A 3-2 engineering degree is available with Oakwood College. Dual majors, B.A.-B.S. degrees in math and biology, study abroad in 28 countries, nondegree study, and a pass/fail option are also offered. Joint Undergraduate Masters Program (JUMP) available in ten majors including Atmospheric Science, Biology, Business, Chemistry, Civil Engineering, Computer Science, Earth Systems Science, Electrical and Computer Engineering, Math and Physics. There are 15 national honor societies and a freshman honors program.

Faculty/Classroom: 58% of faculty are male; 42% are female. All teach and do research. Graduate students teach 7% of introductory courses. The average class size in an introductory lecture is 29; in a laboratory is 21; and in a regular course is 26.

Admissions: 81% of the 2013-2014 applicants were accepted. The SAT scores for the 2013-2014 freshman class were: Critical Reading--19% below 500, 42% between 500 and 599, 21% between 600 and 699, and 18% between 700 and 800; Math--17% below 500, 40% between 500 and 599, 31% between 600 and 699, and 12% between 700 and 800. The ACT scores were 16% below 21, 13% between 21 and 23, 25% between 24 and 26, 17% between 27 and 28, and 29% above 28. 45% of the current freshmen were in the top fifth of their class; 71% were in the top two fifths. There were 15 National Merit finalists. 10 freshmen graduated first in their class.

Requirements: The SAT or ACT is required. A sliding scale with the GPA determines the minimum test score needed. The GED is accepted. Students should present a minimum of 20 Carnegie units, including 4 years of English and social studies, and 3 each of math and science. A GPA of 2.0 is required. AP and CLEP credits are accepted.

Procedure: Freshmen are admitted fall, spring, and summer. Entrance exams should be taken during the junior year. There are early admissions, deferred admissions, and rolling admissions plans. Applications should be filed by June 1 for fall entry; December 15 for spring entry; and May 15 for summer entry, along with a $30 fee. Applications are accepted online.

Transfer: 776 transfer students enrolled in 2012-2013. Applicants need a minimum cumulative GPA of 2.0, over at least 24 hours of credit from a regionally accredited college or university. 32 of 128 credits required for the bachelor's degree must be completed at UAHuntsville.

Visiting: There are regularly scheduled orientations for prospective students, Info sessions on academics, campus life, financial aid and other important topics are provided as well as time dedicated to advising and class registration. Social activities are available for participants to meet both new and current students. There are guides for informal visits, visitors may sit in on classes, and stay overnight. To schedule a visit, contact Vangie Harris at (800) 824-2773.

Financial Aid: In 2013-2014, 84% of all full-time freshmen and 73% of continuing full-time students received some form of financial aid. 53% of all full-time freshmen and 56% of continuing full-time students received need-based aid. The average freshman award was $9,952. Need-based scholarships or need-based grants averaged $7,336 ($23,245 maximum); need-based self-help aid (loans and jobs) averaged $6,116 ($22,500 maximum); non-need-based athletic scholarships averaged $12,605 ($32,282 maximum); and other non-need-based awards and non-need-based scholarships averaged $7,103 ($36,509 maximum). 13% of undergraduate students work part-time. Average annual earnings from campus work are $3410. The average financial indebtedness of the 2013 graduate was $27,281. The FAFSA is required. The priority date for freshman financial aid applications for fall entry is April 1. The deadline for filing freshman financial aid applications for fall entry is July 31.

International Students: There are 202 international students enrolled. The school actively recruits these students. They must take the TOEFL with a minimum score of 500 on the paper-based TOEFL (PBT) or 62 on the Internet-based version (iBT) and the college's own test. They must also take the SAT or ACT.

Computers: All students may access the system 24 hours a day. There are no time limits and no fees.

Graduates: From July 1, 2012 to June 30, 2013, 1099 bachelor's degrees were awarded. The most popular majors were nursing (17%), mechanical engineering (11%), and biology (9%). 183 companies recruited on campus in 2012-2013. In an average class, 16% graduate in 4 years or less, 37% graduate in 5 years or less, and 48% graduate in 6 years or less.

Admissions Contact: Sandra Barinowski, Director of Admissions. E-Mail: *admitme@uah.edu* Web: *www.uah.edu./landing/prospective.php*

UNIVERSITY OF ALABAMA AT TUSCALOOSA — B-3

Tuscaloosa, AL 35487 — **(205) 348-6010**
(800) 933-BAMA; (205) 348-9046

Full-time: 11253 men, 12692 women	**Faculty:** n/av;I, -$
Part-time: 1022 men, 1267 women	**Ph.D.s:** n/av
Graduate: 2244 men, 3169 women	**Student/Faculty:** 19 to 1
Year: semesters, summer session	**Tuition:** $8600 ($21,900)
Application Deadline: March 1	**Room & Board:** $8564

Freshman Class: 22136 applied, 9636 accepted, 5728 enrolled
SAT or ACT: required

COMPETITIVE+

The University of Alabama, the state of Alabama's first public university is a senior comprehensive doctoral level institution. The university was established by constitutional provision under statutory mandates and authorizations. Its mission is to advance the intellectual and social condition of the people of the state through quality programs of teaching, research and service. There are 9 undergraduate schools and 11 graduate schools. In addition to regional accreditation, UA has baccalaureate program accreditation with AACSB, ABET, ACEJMC, ADA, CSWE, FIDER, NASAD, NASM, and NCATE. The 10 libraries contain 2.5 million volumes, 4.0 million microform items, and 526,856 audio/video tapes/CDs/DVDs, and subscribe to 23,222 periodicals including electronic. Computerized library services include interlibrary loans, database searching, and Internet access. Special learning facilities include an art gallery, natural history museum, radio station, TV station, special collections department, map library, observatory, specialized computer labs, and archeological site. The 1000-acre campus is in a suburban area 50 miles southwest of Birmingham. Including any residence halls, there are 216 buildings.

Student Life: 50% of undergraduates are from out of state, mostly the South. Students are from 50 states, 79 foreign countries, and Canada. 89% are from public schools. 81% are White; 12% African American. 56% are Protestant; 32% claim no religious affiliation. The average age of freshmen is 18; all undergraduates, 21. 14% do not continue beyond their first year; 87% remain to graduate.

Housing: 5800 students can be accommodated in college housing, which includes single-sex and coed dorms, on-campus apartments, and married student housing. In addition, there are honors houses, language houses, special-interest houses, fraternity houses, and sorority houses. On-campus housing is guaranteed for the freshman year only, is available on a first-come, and first-served basis. 92% of students live on campus; of those, 35% remain on campus on weekends. All students may keep cars.

Activities: 28% of men belong to 1 local and 26 national fraternities; 43% of women belong to 1 local and 20 national sororities. There are 391 groups on campus, including academic service, leadership and other national honoraries, art, band, cheerleading, chess, choir, chorale, chorus, computers, dance, debate, drama, drill team, ethnic, film, forensics, gay, honors, international, jazz band, literary magazine, marching band, musical theater, newspaper, opera, orchestra, pep band, photography, political, professional, radio and TV, religious, social, social service, student government, symphony, and yearbook. Popular campus events include Honors Week, Get on Board Day and Family Weekend.

Sports: There are 9 intercollegiate sports for men and 12 for women, and 17 intramural sports for men and 16 for women. Facilities include an 83,000-seat football stadium, a 15,000-seat basketball arena, a track and field facility, a 6,100-seat baseball stadium, a 1,600-foot softball stadium, an indoor football practice facility, lighted varsity and public tennis courts, an aquatic complex with Olympic-size and standard pools and a weightlifting facility, a soccer field, racquetball, basketball, and volleyball courts, weight and exercise rooms, an indoor/outdoor pool, and an 18-hole golf course with clubhouse and driving range.

Disabled Students: 90% of the campus is accessible. Facilities include wheelchair ramps, elevators, special parking, specially equipped restrooms, special class scheduling, lowered drinking fountains, lowered telephones, special housing. automatic doors, TDD, adaptive technology, and areas of rescue assistance.

Services: Counseling and information services are available, as is tutoring in some subjects, statistics math, chemistry, physics, computer science, accounting, finance, economics, and foreign languages There is a reader service for the blind, and remedial math, reading, and writing. a center for teaching and learning, a writing lab, a career center, computer-based self-tutoring, and a math computer lab. Many departments and colleges offer tutorial services or tutorial references.

Campus Safety and Security: Measures include 24-hour foot and vehicle patrol, self-defense education, and security escort services. There are emergency telephones, lighted pathways/sidewalks, community-oriented police service, UA police bike patrol, educational awareness for personal safety, alcohol awareness, child seat installations and domestic violence awareness programs.

Programs of Study: UA confers B.A., B.S., B.A.Com., B.F.A., B.M., B.S.A.E., B.S.C.B.A., B.S.C.E., B.S.Che.E., B.S.Chem., B.S.C.S., B.S.Ed., B.S.E.E., B.S.Geo., B.S.H.E.S., B.S.I.E., B.S.M.E., B.S.Met., B.S. Micr., B.S.N. and B.S.W. degrees. Master's and doctoral degrees are also awarded. Bachelor's degrees are awarded in BIOLOGICAL SCIENCE (biology/biological science, marine science, and microbiology), BUSINESS (accounting and management information systems), COMMUNICATIONS AND THE ARTS (advertising, art history and appreciation, classics, communications, dance, English, French, German, journalism, music, public relations, Russian, Spanish, and telecommunications), COMPUTER AND PHYSICAL SCIENCE (chemistry, computer science, geology, mathematics, and physics), EDUCATION (athletic training, early childhood education, elementary education, music education, physical education, secondary education, and special education), ENGINEERING AND ENVIRONMENTAL DESIGN (aerospace studies, chemical engineering, civil engineering, electrical/electronics engineering, environmental science, industrial administration/management, industrial engineering, interior design, mechanical engineering, and metallurgical engineering), HEALTH PROFESSIONS (music therapy and nursing), SOCIAL SCIENCE (American studies, anthropology, clothing and textiles management/production/services, criminal justice, economics, food science, geography, history, human development, interdisciplinary studies, international studies, philosophy, political science/government, psychology, religion, and social work). Advertising, accounting, and engineering are the strongest academically. Business, elementary education and nursing have the largest enrollments.

Required: To graduate, all students must complete a minimum of 120 semester hours, including at least 27 in the major, with a minimum GPA of 2.0. Core curriculum requirements include 12 hours each of humanities/fine arts and history/social science, 11 of natural science/math, 6 of computer studies or a foreign language, 6 of English composition, and 6 of upper-level courses with a writing component.

Special: UA offers cross-registration with Stillman College and Shelton State Community College, internships, international study programs, a Washington semester, a 3-week May-June interim term, exchange study within the United States, work-study, co-op programs, accelerated programs, B.A.-B.S. degrees, dual majors, student-designed majors, interdisciplinary majors in the New College arts and sciences program, credit for life experiences, nondegree study, and pass/fail options. There are 27 national honor societies, including Phi Beta Kappa, a freshman honors program, and 17 departmental honors programs.

Faculty/Classroom: 60% of faculty are male; 40% are female. 71% teach undergraduates, 5% do research, and 4% do both. Graduate students teach 28% of introductory courses. The average class size in an introductory lecture is 52; in a laboratory is 19; and in a regular course is 26.

Admissions: 44% of the 2013-2014 applicants were accepted.

Requirements: The SAT or ACT is required. A minimum GPA of 2.0 is required; admission is based on a sliding scale of test scores and high school GPA. The GED is accepted. High school preparation should include 4 units each of English and social studies, 3 each of math and science, 1 of foreign language, and history and 5 of academic electives. Students with a 3.0 cumulative GPA and a satisfactory ACT or SAT (verbal and math only) score will generally be admitted. A GPA of 2.0 is required. AP and CLEP credits are accepted. Important factors in the admissions decision are advanced placement or honors courses, evidence of special talent, and leadership record.

Procedure: Freshmen are admitted fall, spring, and summer. Entrance exams should be taken in the spring of the junior year. There are early admissions and rolling admissions plans. Applications should be filed by March 1 for fall entry; December 1 for spring entry; and March 1 for summer entry, along with a $40 fee. Notification is sent on a rolling basis. Applications are accepted online.

Transfer: 1463 transfer students enrolled in 2012-2013. Applicants need an overall minimum GPA of 2.0 with at least 24 semester hours earned. Those with fewer than 24 hours must meet freshman standards. 30 of 120 credits required for the bachelor's degree must be completed at UA.

Visiting: There are regularly scheduled orientations for prospective students, consisting of a campus tour followed by meetings with admissions counselors and faculty and staff. Customized visits to suit student and parent needs are possible. University Day (4 times a year) offers tours and information sessions. There are guides for informal visits, visitors may sit in on classes, and stay overnight. To schedule a visit, contact Office of Undergraduate Admissions.

Financial Aid: The average freshman award was $10,780. Need-based scholarships or need-based grants averaged $8,500; need-based self-help aid (loans and jobs) averaged $3,614; non-need-based athletic scholarships averaged $22,990; and other non-need-based awards and non-need-based scholarships averaged $8,495. The average financial indebtedness of the 2013 graduate was $26,714. The FAFSA is required. Check with the school for current application deadlines.

International Students: The school actively recruits these students. They must take the TOEFL, or earn a proficiency certificate from the university's English Language Institute. They must also take the SAT or ACT.

Computers: All students may access the system 24 hours a day. There are no time limits and no fees.

Graduates: From July 1, 2012 to June 30, 2013, 4463 bachelor's degrees were awarded. The most popular majors were business/marketing (29%), health professions and related programs (10%), and communication/journalism (9%). In an average class, 59% graduate in 3 years or less, 24% graduate in 5 years or less, and 67% graduate in 6 years or less. Of the 2012 graduating class, 87% were enrolled in graduate school within 6 months of graduation.

Admissions Contact: Mary K. Spiegel, Director of Undergraduate Admissions. E-Mail: *admissions@ua.edu* Web: *www.ua.edu*

UNIVERSITY OF MOBILE — A-5

Mobile, AL 36613 — **(251) 442-2249**
(800) 946-7267; (251) 675-6329

Full-time: 456 men, 801 women	**Faculty:** 83
Part-time: 33 men, 191 women	**Ph.D.s:** 64%
Graduate: 24 men, 105 women	**Student/Faculty:** 12 to 1
Year: semesters, summer session	**Tuition:** $18,540
Application Deadline: August 1	**Room & Board:** $9330

Freshman Class: 866 applied, 617 accepted, 259 enrolled
ACT: 23

VERY COMPETITIVE

University of Mobile, founded in 1961, is a private liberal arts institution affiliated with the Southern Baptists. There are 7 undergraduate schools and 5 graduate schools. In addition to regional accreditation, UMobile has baccalaureate program accreditation with ACBSP and NASM. The library contains 110,005 volumes, and 1,733 audio/video tapes/CDs/DVDs, and subscribes to 258 periodicals including electronic. Computerized library services include interlibrary loans, database searching, Internet access, and Wi-Fi capability. Special learning facilities include an art gallery. The 880-acre campus is in a suburban area 10 miles northwest of Mobile. Including any residence halls, there are 47 buildings.

Student Life: 76% of undergraduates are from Alabama. Others are from 29 states, 26 foreign countries, and Canada. 65% are White; 22% African American. The average age of freshmen is 18; all undergraduates, 24. 23% do not continue beyond their first year; 46% remain to graduate.

Housing: 710 students can be accommodated in college housing, which includes single-sex dorms and on-campus apartments. On-campus housing is guaranteed for the freshman year only, is available on a first-come, and first-served basis. 56% of students commute. Alcohol is not permitted. All students may keep cars.

Activities: There are no fraternities or sororities. There are 52 groups on campus, including art, band, cheerleading, choir, chorale, chorus, computers, dance, drama, drum and bugle corps, honors, international, jazz band, musical theater, opera, orchestra, pep band, political, professional, religious, social, social service, student government, and symphony. Popular campus events include College Preview Day, Upper Room Theater and Christmas Spectacular.

Sports: There are 6 intercollegiate sports for men and 7 for women, and 7 intramural sports for men and 6 for women. Facilities include An 800-seat gym, a tennis complex with 10 courts, a swimming pool, a track, baseball, softball, and 2 soccer fields, and a golf driving range with 2 putting greens.

Disabled Students: All of the campus is accessible. Facilities include wheelchair ramps, elevators, special parking, specially equipped restrooms, special class scheduling, and lowered drinking fountains.

Services: Counseling and information services are available, as is tutoring in some subjects, writing, English and math There is remedial math, reading, and writing.

Campus Safety and Security: Measures include 24-hour foot and vehicle patrol and emergency notification system. There are lighted pathways/sidewalks, controlled access to dorms/residences, a professional campus security service is available 24 hours per day.

Programs of Study: UMobile confers B.A., B.S., B.B.A., B.M. and B.S.N. degrees. Master's degrees are also awarded. Bachelor's degrees are awarded in AGRICULTURE (environmental studies), BIOLOGICAL SCIENCE (biology/biological science and marine science), BUSINESS (accounting and business administration and management), COMMUNICATIONS AND THE ARTS (art, communications, English, music, music performance, and voice), COMPUTER AND PHYSICAL SCIENCE (information sciences and systems and mathematics), EDUCATION (athletic training, early childhood education, elementary education, and physical education), HEALTH PROFESSIONS (nursing), SOCIAL SCIENCE (history, humanities, liberal arts/general studies, political science/government, psychology, religion, religious music, social science, sociology, and theological studies). Education, nursing, and worship leadership are the strongest academically. Business administration, elementary education, and nursing have the largest enrollments.

Required: All students are required to complete 127 credit hours, with at least 30 in their major field, and earn a minimum GPA of 2.0. Distribution requirements include 12 hours in English, 8 hours in lab science, 6 hours each in Christian ministries and history, 6 hours from among the subjects of business, computer information systems, economics, political science, psychology, and sociology, 3 hours each in speech/Philosophy and math, and 3 hours in art or music. Computer literacy must be demonstrated. Chapel attendance is also required.

Special: A variety of internships and work-study programs, B.A.-B.S. degrees, adult programs, and dual majors are available, as is a 3-2 engineering degree with the University of South Alabama. There are 13 national honor societies, a freshman honors program, and 1 departmental honors programs.

Faculty/Classroom: 48% of faculty are male; 52% are female. All teach undergraduates. No introductory courses are taught by graduate students. The average class size in an introductory lecture is 16; in a laboratory is 15; and in a regular course is 16.

Admissions: 71% of the 2013-2014 applicants were accepted. The SAT scores for the 2013-2014 freshman class were: Critical Reading--37% below 500, 38% between 500 and 599, 25% between 600 and 699, Math--38% below 500, 40% between 500 and 599, 19% between 600 and 699, and 3% between 700 and 800. 50% of the current freshmen were in the top fifth of their class; 84% were in the top two fifths.

Requirements: Applicants must have 22 Carnegie units and a minimum composite score of 21 on the ACT. The GED is accepted. The ACT is not required of applicants over age 25. A GPA of 2.8 is required. AP and CLEP credits are accepted. Important factors in the admissions decision are advanced placement or honors courses, ability to finance college education, and leadership record.

Procedure: Freshmen are admitted fall, spring, and summer. Entrance exams should be taken in August before the junior year. There are deferred admissions and rolling admissions plans. Applications should be filed by August 1 for fall entry; January 4 for spring entry; and May 1 for summer entry. The fall 2013 application fee was $25. Notification is sent on a rolling basis. Applications are accepted online.

Transfer: 128 transfer students enrolled in 2012-2013. Transfer students need to have earned a minimum GPA of 2.0 for previous college work. If fewer than 24 semester hours are accepted, a minimum score of 21 on the ACT and a high school transcript, or GED, are required. 32 of 127 credits required for the bachelor's degree must be completed at UMobile.

Visiting: There are regularly scheduled orientations for prospective students, including financial aid seminars, academic seminars, faculty advising, campus tours, and admissions counseling. There are guides for informal visits, visitors may sit in on classes, and stay overnight. To schedule a visit, contact Justin McGehee at (251) 442-2638.

Financial Aid: In 2013-2014, 85% of all full-time freshmen and 71% of continuing full-time students received some form of financial aid. 76% of all full-time freshmen and 64% of continuing full-time students received need-based aid. The average freshman award was $16,963. Need-based scholarships or need-based grants averaged $5,238; need-based self-help aid (loans and jobs) averaged $5,789; non-need-based athletic scholarships averaged $7,857; and other non-need-based awards and non-need-based scholarships averaged $6,985. The FAFSA, the state aid form, and the college's own financial statement are required. The deadline for filing freshman financial aid applications for fall entry is August 1.

International Students: There are 45 international students enrolled. The school actively recruits these students. They must take the TOEFL with a minimum score of 500 on the paper-based TOEFL (PBT) or 61 on the Internet-based version (iBT). They must also take the SAT or ACT, scoring 21.

Computers: All students may access the system 8 a.m. to 9 p.m. Monday through Friday and a half day Saturday. There are no time limits. The fee is $60 per semester.

Graduates: From July 1, 2012 to June 30, 2013, 286 bachelor's degrees were awarded. The most popular majors were education (22%), business (20%), and nursing (14%). In an average class, 30% graduate in 4 years or less, 12% graduate in 5 years or less, and 46% graduate in 6 years or less. Of the 2012 graduating class, 26% were enrolled in graduate school within 6 months of graduation, and 72% were employed.

Admissions Contact: Justin McGehee, Assistant Director of Enrollment. E-Mail: *jmcgehee@mail.umobile.edu* Web: *www.umobile.edu*

UNIVERSITY OF MONTEVALLO C-3

Montevallo, AL 35115 (205) 665-6034; (205) 665-6032

Full-time: 2350 men and women	**Faculty:** n/av; IIA, --$
Part-time: 270 men and women	**Ph.D.s:** n/av
Graduate: 446 men and women	**Student/Faculty:** 16 to 1
Year: semesters, summer session	**Tuition:** $10,000 ($19,690)
Application Deadline: August 1	**Room & Board:** $7320
Freshman Class: 531 enrolled	
ACT: 23	**SAT:** required **COMPETITIVE**

The University of Montevallo, founded in 1896, is a public, liberal arts institution offering courses in business, fine arts, music, teacher preparation and preprofessional training. There are 4 undergraduate schools and 2 graduate schools. In addition to regional accreditation, UM has baccalaureate program accreditation with AACSB, ADA, AHEA, CSWE, NASAD, NASM, and NCATE. The library contains 266,236 volumes, 795,344 microform items, 4,673 audio/video tapes/CDs/DVDs, and subscribes to 27,962 periodicals including electronic. Computerized library services include interlibrary loans and database searching. Special learning facilities include an art gallery, TV station, All-Steinway Music Department, Center for Innovative Teaching and Technology and Digital Cafe, distance learning classroom, glass-blowing studio, painting and drawing studios, Ebeneezer Swamp Ecological Preserve, speech and hearing center, and traffic safety center. The 160-acre campus is in a small town 35 miles south of Birmingham. Including any residence halls, there are 40 buildings.

Student Life: 95% of undergraduates are from Alabama. Others are from 6 states, 17 foreign countries, and Canada. 74% are White; 14% African American. The average age of freshmen is 18; all undergraduates, 20. 26% do not continue beyond their first year; 47% remain to graduate.

Housing: 1253 students can be accommodated in college housing, which includes single-sex and coed dorms and on-campus apartments. In addition, there are fraternity houses. On-campus housing is available on a first-come and first-served basis. 53% of students commute. All students may keep cars.

Activities: 19% of men belong to 7 national fraternities; 24% of women belong to 8 national sororities. There are 93 groups on campus, including art, cheerleading, choir, chorus, computers, dance, debate, drama, environmental, ethnic, forensics, gay, honors, international, jazz band, literary magazine, musical theater, newspaper, pep band, photography, political, professional, radio and TV, religious, social, social service, student government, and yearbook. Popular campus events include College Night, and Honors Day.

Sports: There are 4 intercollegiate sports for men and 6 for women, and 7 intramural sports for men and 4 for women. Facilities include a 97,000-square-foot Student Activity Center with a 6-lane collegiate competition size pool, a 6000-square-foot weight training and cardio-conditioning theater, and a 3500-seat arena; several athletic fields; tennis courts, sand volleyball facility, a lake, and camping area; and an 18-hole golf course and driving range.

Disabled Students: Facilities include wheelchair ramps, elevators, special parking, specially equipped restrooms, special class scheduling, lowered drinking fountains, and lowered telephones.

Services: Counseling and information services are available, as is tutoring in some subjects, study skills There is a reader service for the blind, and remedial math, reading, and writing.

Campus Safety and Security: Measures include 24-hour foot and vehicle patrol, emergency notification system, self-defense education, and security escort services. There are emergency telephones, lighted pathways/sidewalks, controlled access to dorms/residences, campus lighting, and electronic access into residence halls.

Programs of Study: UM confers B.A., B.S., B.B.A., B.F.A., B.M. and

B.M.E. degrees. Master's degrees are also awarded. Bachelor's degrees are awarded in BIOLOGICAL SCIENCE (biology/biological science), BUSINESS (accounting, banking and finance, business administration and management, management science, and marketing/retailing/merchandising), COMMUNICATIONS AND THE ARTS (art, communications, dramatic arts, English, French, German, journalism, music, music performance, Spanish, and studio art), COMPUTER AND PHYSICAL SCIENCE (chemistry and mathematics), EDUCATION (art education, education of the deaf and hearing impaired, elementary education, home economics education, music education, and physical education), ENGINEERING AND ENVIRONMENTAL DESIGN (environmental science), HEALTH PROFESSIONS (speech pathology/audiology), SOCIAL SCIENCE (family/consumer studies, history, political science/government, psychology, social science, social work, and sociology). Elementary/early childhood education, business, and art have the largest enrollments.

Required: To graduate, students must complete a minimum of 130 semester hours with an overall 2.0 GPA while meeting core, major, and minor requirements. Core requirements include 12 hours of writing reinforcement courses (usually met with literature and major/minor courses), 7 hours of sciences (2 branches), 6 hours each in foundations in writing, world literature, world civilizations, and institutions and issues courses, 4 hours of health/phys ed, 3 hours each of oral communications, math, computer science, fine arts, and humanities, and 1 additional fine arts or humanity elective.

Special: A 3-2 engineering degree is offered with Auburn University, the University of Alabama at Birmingham, and the University of Alabama at Tuscaloosa. Internships are required for some majors. Study abroad, B.A.-B.S. degrees, dual degrees, a Washington semester, and pass/fail options are available. There are 26 national honor societies, a freshman honors program, and 1 departmental honors program.

Faculty/Classroom: 99% teach undergraduates. No introductory courses are taught by graduate students. The average class size in an introductory lecture is 24; in a laboratory is 23; and in a regular course is 24.

Requirements: The SAT or ACT is required. The ACT is preferred. In addition, applicants must present a high school transcript with a minimum GPA of 2.5 and successful completion of a minimum of 16 academic or college-preparatory credits from 9th to 12th grade, including 4 units each of English, social studies, and math, 2 units of science, and 4 units of foreign language or electives. Applicants who have earned a GED should have an official copy of their score report sent in lieu of a high school transcript. A GPA of 2.0 is required. AP and CLEP credits are accepted. Important factors in the admissions decision are advanced placement or honors courses, evidence of special talent, and geographical diversity.

Procedure: Freshmen are admitted to all sessions. Entrance exams should be taken in spring of the junior year or fall of the senior year. There are deferred admissions and rolling admissions plans. Applications should be filed by August 1 for fall entry; December 1 for spring entry; and May 1 for summer entry. The fall 2013 application fee was $25. Notification is sent on a rolling basis. Applications are accepted online.

Transfer: 192 transfer students enrolled in 2012-2013. A minimum of a cumulative C average on all college-level study attempted must have been attained. This is a cumulative GPA of 2.0 or better on a 4.0 scale. Applicants must be a student in good standing - neither probation nor suspension can be in effect at the previous or current college of university attended. Transcripts of all previous study attempted must be submitted and evaluated before an application review can be conducted. Collegiate work from post-secondary institutions not accredited nor in candidacy status for accreditation by a regional accrediting association is not transferable to the University of Montevallo. Students who have completed less than 24 semester hours (or 36 quarter hours) of college-level study must also submit a secondary-school transcript and either an ACT or SAT score report and must satisfy all requirements for freshman admission. A maximum of 64 semester hours (or 96 quarter hours) may be transferred for credit from either a community or junior college. 33 of 130 credits required for the bachelor's degree must be completed at Montevallo.

Visiting: There are regularly scheduled orientations for prospective students, consisting of a program of orientation, advising, and academic counseling prior to enrollment. There are guides for informal visits, visitors may sit in on classes, and stay overnight. To schedule a visit, contact the Office of Admissions.

Financial Aid: 17% of undergraduate students work part-time. Average annual earnings from campus work are $4640. The FAFSA is required. The priority date for freshman financial aid applications for fall entry is March 1.

International Students: There are 35 international students enrolled. They must take the TOEFL with a minimum score of 525 on the paper-based TOEFL (PBT) or 71 on the Internet-based version (iBT). They must also take the SAT or ACT.

Computers: All students may access the system. Network access in the residence halls is available whenever those buildings are open. There are no time limits and no fees.

Graduates: From July 1, 2012 to June 30, 2013, 326 bachelor's degrees were awarded. The most popular majors were business/marketing (17%), education (13%), and visual and performing arts (12%). In an average class, 21% graduate in 4 years or less, 41% graduate in 5 years or less, and 47% graduate in 6 years or less.

Admissions Contact: Greg Embry, Director of Admissions. E-Mail: *admissions@montevallo.edu* Web: *go.montevallo.edu*

UNIVERSITY OF NORTH ALABAMA — B-1

Florence, AL 35632-0001 — **(256) 765-4608**, **(800) TALKUNA; (256) 765-4960**

Full-time: 2170 men, 2885 women
Part-time: 429 men, 677 women
Graduate: 443 men, 605 women
Year: semesters, summer session
Application Deadline: open
Freshman Class: n/av
ACT: required

Faculty: 269; IIA, --$
Ph.D.s: 68%
Student/Faculty: 18 to 1
Tuition: $6000 ($10,000)
Room & Board: $4960

COMPETITIVE

The University of North Alabama, founded in 1872, is a public institution offering degree programs in arts and sciences, business, education, and nursing. Figures in the above capsule and in this profile are approximate. There are 4 undergraduate schools and 3 graduate schools. In addition to regional accreditation, UNA has baccalaureate program accreditation with AACSB, ABET, ACBSP, CSWE, NASAD, NASM, NCATE, and NLN. The 3 libraries contain 405,406 volumes, 1.1 million microform items, and 14,236 audio/video tapes/CDs/DVDs, and subscribe to 3,711 periodicals including electronic. Computerized library services include interlibrary loans, database searching, Internet access, and laptop Internet portals. Special learning facilities include a learning resource center, art gallery, planetarium, and radio station. The 200-acre campus is in an urban area 116 miles north of Birmingham. Including any residence halls, there are 77 buildings.

Student Life: 74% of undergraduates are from Alabama. Others are from 36 states, 53 foreign countries, and Canada. 89% are from public schools. 69% are white. The average age of freshmen is 20; all undergraduates, 23. 32% do not continue beyond their first year; 56% remain to graduate.

Housing: 1563 students can be accommodated in college housing, which includes single-sex and coed dorms, on-campus apartments, off-campus apartments, and married student housing. In addition, there are fraternity houses, and an international house. On-campus housing is available on a first-come and first-served basis. 77% of students commute. Alcohol is not permitted. All students may keep cars.

Activities: 7% of men belong to 8 national fraternities; 13% of women belong to 7 national sororities. There are 91 groups on campus, including band, cheerleading, choir, chorus, computers, debate, drama, drill team, ethnic, film, honors, international, jazz band, literary magazine, marching band, musical theater, newspaper, pep band, photography, political, professional, radio and TV, religious, social, social service, and student government. Popular campus events include Spring Fling and George Lindsey Film Festival.

Sports: There are 6 intercollegiate sports for men and 6 for women, and 20 intramural sports for men and 20 for women. Facilities include a 13,500-seat football stadium, a 4000-seat gym, baseball and softball fields, an outdoor track, an indoor swimming pool, tennis courts, a fitness center with a cardio theater, weights and machines, an aerobics studio, and a gaming lounge, and an intramural field with 3 multipurpose courts, a 2-lane track, and equipment checkout.

Disabled Students: 96% of the campus is accessible. Facilities include wheelchair ramps, elevators, special parking, specially equipped restrooms, special class scheduling, lowered drinking fountains, and lowered telephones.

Services: Counseling and information services are available, as is tutoring in some subjects, math, English, history, biology, chemistry, accounting, finance, and economics There is a reader service for the blind, and remedial math and writing. and an academic resource center that features computer-assisted tutoring and faculty mentoring.

Campus Safety and Security: Measures include 24-hour foot and vehicle patrol and emergency notification system. There are shuttle buses, emergency telephones, lighted pathways/sidewalks, and controlled access to dorms/residences.

Programs of Study: UNA confers B.A., B.S., B.A.M., B.B.A., B.F.A., B.G.S., B.S.Ed., B.S.M., B.S.N., and B.S.W. degrees. Master's degrees are also awarded. Bachelor's degrees are awarded in BIOLOGICAL SCIENCE (biology/biological science and environmental biology), BUSINESS (accounting, banking and finance, business economics, and marketing/retailing/merchandising), COMMUNICATIONS AND THE ARTS (art, communications, dramatic arts, English, French, German, journalism, music, public relations, and Spanish), COMPUTER AND PHYSICAL SCIENCE (chemistry, computer science, geology, information sciences and systems, mathematics, and physics), EDUCATION (art education, business education, early childhood education, elementary education, foreign languages education, home economics education, music education, physical education, science education, secondary education, and social science education), ENGINEERING AND ENVIRONMENTAL DESIGN (interior design), HEALTH PROFESSIONS (industrial hygiene and nursing), SOCIAL SCIENCE (criminal justice, geography, history, liberal arts/general studies, political science/government, psychology, social work, and sociology). Physical sciences, biological sciences, and math are the strongest academically. Management, accounting, and marketing have the largest enrollments.

Required: Students must complete a core curriculum, which includes 12 semester hours in history, social and behavioral sciences, humanities, and fine arts, 11 in natural sciences and math, and 6 in language composition. Total number of hours in majors vary. Passing grades in 1 writing emphasis and 1 computer course also are needed. A minimum of 128 semester hours and a minimum GPA of 2.0 are required to graduate.

Special: UNA offers cooperative programs in all majors, work-study programs, various B.A.-B.S. degrees, dual majors, and a general studies degree. Nondegree study is possible. There are 13 national honor societies, including Phi Beta Kappa, a freshman honors program, and 2 departmental honors programs.

Faculty/Classroom: 53% of faculty are male; 47% are female. All teach undergraduates. No introductory courses are taught by graduate students.

Requirements: The ACT is required. In addition, applicants should be graduates of an accredited high school or have earned a GED. A GPA of 2.0 is required. AP and CLEP credits are accepted.

Procedure: Freshmen are admitted fall, spring, and summer. Entrance exams should be taken in the senior year. There are deferred admissions and rolling admissions plans. Application deadlines are open. The fall application fee was $25. Applications are accepted online.

Transfer: In a recent year, 707 transfer students enrolled. Applicants should be eligible to return to the school last attended. 30 of 128 credits required for the bachelor's degree must be completed at UNA.

Visiting: There are regularly scheduled orientations for prospective students, including orientation programs conducted each summer prior to the fall semester. There are guides for informal visits. To schedule a visit, contact the Office of Admissions.

Financial Aid: In a recent year, 59% of all full-time freshmen and 62% of continuing full-time students received some form of financial aid. 47% of all full-time freshmen and 52% of continuing full-time students received need-based aid. The average freshman award was $6,254. Need-based scholarships or need-based grants averaged $4,237; need-based self-help aid (loans and jobs) averaged $3,034; and non-need-based athletic scholarships averaged $2,598. 8% of undergraduate students work part-time. Average annual earnings from campus work are $2250. The FAFSA is required. Check with the school for current application deadlines.

International Students: I a recent year, 259 international students enrolled. The school actively recruits these students. They must take the TOEFL with a minimum score of 500 on the paper-based TOEFL (PBT).

Computers: Wireless access is available. All students may access the system. There are no time limits and no fees. It is strongly recommended that all students have a personal computer.

Graduates: In a recent year, 915 bachelor's degrees were awarded. The most popular majors were business (30%), education (18%), and nursing (17%). In an average class, 17% graduate in 4 years or less, 34% graduate in 5 years or less, and 39% graduate in 6 years or less.

Admissions Contact: Kim Mauldin, Director of Admissions. E-Mail: *admissions@una.edu* Web: *www.una.edu*

UNIVERSITY OF SOUTH ALABAMA — A-5

Mobile, AL 36688 — (251) 460-6141; (800) 872-5247; (251) 460-7023

Full-time: 3895 men, 4813 women	**Faculty:** 437; IIA, --$
Part-time: 1077 men, 1530 women	**Ph.D.s:** 76%
Graduate: 809 men, 2512 women	**Student/Faculty:** 21 to 1
Year: semesters, summer session	**Tuition:** $6360 ($12,720)
Application Deadline: August 10	**Room & Board:** $7150

Freshman Class: 4770 applied, 4159 accepted, 1944 enrolled

SAT CR/M/W: 514/513/501 — **ACT:** 23 — **COMPETITIVE**

The University of South Alabama, a state-supported institution established in 1963, offers undergraduate and graduate degrees in the allied health professions, arts and sciences, business and management studies, education, engineering, nursing, computer and information sciences, and medicine. There are 9 undergraduate schools and 9 graduate schools. In addition to regional accreditation, USA has baccalaureate program accreditation with AACSB, ABET, AHEA, APTA, CAHEA, CSAB, NASAD, NASM, NCATE, and NLN. The 2 libraries contain 515,914 volumes, 723,399 microform items, and 14,413 audio/video tapes/CDs/DVDs. Computerized library services include interlibrary loans and database searching. Special learning facilities include an art gallery, radio station, TV station, the Dauphin Island Sea Lab. The 1224-acre campus is in a suburban area 150 miles east of New Orleans. Including any residence halls, there are 111 buildings.

Student Life: 79% of undergraduates are from Alabama. Others are from 50 states, 87 foreign countries, and Canada. 67% are White; 19% African American. The average age of all undergraduates is 23. 34% do not continue beyond their first year; 37% remain to graduate.

Housing: 3098 students can be accommodated in college housing, which includes coed dorms, on-campus apartments, and married student housing. In addition, there are special-interest houses and fraternity houses. On-campus housing is available on a first-come and first-served basis. 75% of students commute. Alcohol is not permitted. All students may keep cars.

Activities: There are 155 groups on campus, including art, band, cheerleading, chess, choir, chorale, chorus, computers, dance, debate, drama, ethnic, film, gay, honors, international, jazz band, literary magazine, marching band, musical theater, newspaper, opera, orchestra, pep band, political, professional, radio and TV, religious, social, social service, student government, and symphony. Popular campus events include Club South, Greek Week and Chi Omega Songfest.

Sports: There are 7 intercollegiate sports for men and 8 for women, and 15 intramural sports for men and 15 for women. Facilities include a 10,000-seat arena; a 49,000-square-foot student recreation center, including 6 handball courts, fitness rooms, 2 basketball/volleyball courts, and an indoor track; several intramural fields; and an outdoor swimming pool.

Disabled Students: 90% of the campus is accessible. Facilities include wheelchair ramps, elevators, special parking, specially equipped restrooms, lowered drinking fountains, and lowered telephones.

Services: Counseling and information services are available, as is tutoring in some subjects. There is a reader service for the blind, and remedial math, reading, and writing.

Campus Safety and Security: Measures include 24-hour foot and vehicle patrol, emergency notification system, self-defense education, and security escort services. There are emergency telephones and lighted pathways/sidewalks.

Programs of Study: USA confers B.A., B.S., B.F.A., B.Mus., B.S.B.A., B.S.Cardioresp.Sc., B.S.C.E., B.S.Ch.E., B.S.C.L.S., B.S.Comp.Eng., B.S.Ed., B.S.E.E., B.S.M.E., B.S.N., B.S.Preprof.Hlth.Sc., B.S.R.S. and B.S.Sp.Hear.Sc. degrees. Master's and doctoral degrees are also awarded. Bachelor's degrees are awarded in BIOLOGICAL SCIENCE (biology/biological science), BUSINESS (accounting, banking and finance, business administration and management, business economics, marketing/retailing/merchandising, and recreation and leisure services), COMMUNICATIONS AND THE ARTS (communications, dramatic arts, English, fine arts, languages, and music), COMPUTER AND PHYSICAL SCIENCE (atmospheric sciences and meteorology, chemistry, computer science, geology, mathematics, and physics), EDUCATION (early childhood education, education, elementary education, health education, physical education, secondary education, and special education), ENGINEERING AND ENVIRONMENTAL DESIGN (chemical engineering, civil engineering, computer engineering, electrical/electronics engineering, and mechanical engineering), HEALTH PROFESSIONS (biomedical science, emergency medical technologies, nursing, radiological science, respiratory therapy, and speech pathology/audiology), SOCIAL SCIENCE (anthropology, criminal justice, geography, history, international studies, philosophy, political science/government, psychology, social work, and sociology). Business administration, nursing and elementary education have the largest enrollments.

Required: General education requirements consist of 12 hours in written composition, 12 hours in humanities and fine arts, at least 12 hours in history and the social and behavioral sciences, and 11 hours in natural science and math. A minimum of 128 semester hours, with a minimum GPA of 2.0, are required for graduation.

Special: USA offers co-op programs in most majors, federal work-study, internships, study abroad in many countries, dual majors, an adult degree program, and a personalized studies program. There are 43 national honor societies and a freshman honors program.

Faculty/Classroom: 51% of faculty are male; 49% are female. No introductory courses are taught by graduate students.

Admissions: 87% of the 2013-2014 applicants were accepted. The ACT scores were 33% below 21, 26% between 21 and 23, 23% between 24 and 26, 9% between 27 and 28, and 9% above 28.

Requirements: The ACT is required. Applicants should be high school graduates or have a GED certificate. A minimum ACT score of 19 is required for regular admission. AP and CLEP credits are accepted.

Procedure: Freshmen are admitted to all sessions. Entrance exams should be taken during the junior year or early in the senior year. There are early admissions and rolling admissions plans. Applications should be filed by August 10 for fall entry; December 1 for spring entry; and May 1 for summer entry. The fall 2013 application fee was $35.

Transfer: 1002 transfer students enrolled in 2012-2013. Transfer applicants must have at least a 2.0 GPA on all college work attempted for regular admission. 32 of 128 credits required for the bachelor's degree must be completed at USA.

Visiting: There are regularly scheduled orientations for prospective students, including 3 Saturday visiting days in November, February and April.

There are guides for informal visits and visitors may sit in on classes. To schedule a visit, contact Director of Admissions.

Financial Aid: The FAFSA and the college's own financial statement are required. Check with the school for current application deadlines.

International Students: There are 377 international students enrolled. The school actively recruits these students. They must take the TOEFL with a minimum score of 61 on the Internet-based version (iBT) and the college's own test.

Computers: All students may access the system. at various times.

Graduates: From July 1, 2012 to June 30, 2013, 1669 bachelor's degrees were awarded. The most popular majors were nursing (20%), elementary education (7%), and interdisciplinary studies (6%). In an average class, 14% graduate in 4 years or less, 30% graduate in 5 years or less, and 37% graduate in 6 years or less.

Admissions Contact: Norma Jean Tanner, Director of Admissions. E-Mail: *admiss@.usouthal.edu* Web: *www.southalabama.edu*

UNIVERSITY OF WEST ALABAMA A-3

Livingston, AL 35470 (205) 652-3400
(888) 636-8800; (205) 652-3522

Full-time: 700 men, 825 women	**Faculty:** n/av; IIA, --$
Part-time: 60 men, 110 women	**Ph.D.s:** n/av
Graduate: 90 men, 205 women	**Student/Faculty:** n/av
Year: semesters, summer session	**Tuition:** $6280 ($11,340)
Application Deadline: open	**Room & Board:** $4133
Freshman Class: n/av	
SAT or ACT: required	

COMPETITIVE

University of West Alabama, founded in 1835, is a state-controlled institution offering programs in liberal arts and sciences, business and commerce, general studies, and education. The figures in the above capsule and in this profile are approximate. There are 5 undergraduate schools and one graduate school. In addition to regional accreditation, UWA has baccalaureate program accreditation with NCATE and NLN. The 2 libraries contain 135,000 volumes, 500,000 microform items, and 7,500 audio/video tapes/CDs/DVDs, and subscribe to 700 periodicals including electronic. Computerized library services include interlibrary loans and database searching. Special learning facilities include an art gallery and TV station. The 600-acre campus is in a small town 35 miles east of Meridian, Mississippi. Including any residence halls, there are 36 buildings.

Student Life: 80% of undergraduates are from Alabama. Others are from 21 states, 9 foreign countries, and Canada. 88% are from public schools. 61% are White; 37% African American. The average age of freshmen is 18; all undergraduates, 22. 39% do not continue beyond their first year.

Housing: 903 students can be accommodated in college housing, which includes single-sex dorms, on-campus apartments, and married student housing. In addition, there are honors houses. On-campus housing is guaranteed for all 4 years. 37% of students commute. Alcohol is not permitted. All students may keep cars.

Activities: 10% of men belong to 6 national fraternities; 6% of women belong to 4 national sororities. There are 30 groups on campus, including band, cheerleading, choir, chorus, drama, drill team, ethnic, honors, international, jazz band, marching band, newspaper, pep band, photography, political, professional, radio and TV, religious, social, student government, symphony, and yearbook. Popular campus events include Springfest and Club Luie.

Sports: There are 5 intercollegiate sports for men and 5 for women, and 8 intramural sports for men and 8 for women. Facilities include an 800-seat gym, a 7500-seat football stadium, a baseball field, tennis and racquetball courts, a pool, weight rooms, a lake, and hiking trails.

Disabled Students: 95% of the campus is accessible. Facilities include wheelchair ramps, elevators, special parking, specially equipped restrooms, special class scheduling, and lowered drinking fountains.

Services: Counseling and information services are available, as is tutoring in most subjects. There is remedial math, reading, and writing.

Campus Safety and Security: Measures include 24-hour foot and vehicle patrol. There are lighted pathways/sidewalks.

Programs of Study: UWA confers B.A., B.S., B.B.A. and B.T. degrees. Associate and master's degrees are also awarded. Bachelor's degrees are awarded in BIOLOGICAL SCIENCE (biology/biological science and marine biology), BUSINESS (accounting and business administration and management), COMMUNICATIONS AND THE ARTS (English), COMPUTER AND PHYSICAL SCIENCE (chemistry, computer science, mathematics, and physics), EDUCATION (athletic training, early childhood education, elementary education, middle school education, physical education, science education, secondary education, and special education), ENGINEERING AND ENVIRONMENTAL DESIGN (environmental science and industrial engineering technology), HEALTH PROFESSIONS (predentistry and premedicine), SOCIAL SCIENCE (history, prelaw, psychology, social science, and sociology). English, business, and sciences are the strongest academically. Education and business have the largest enrollments.

Required: To graduate, all students must complete at least 120 semester hours with a minimum GPA of 2.0.

Special: There is a 3-2 engineering program with Auburn University and the University of Alabama at Birmingham. The 2-year technical division offers programs leading to a possible B.T. degree. B.A.-B.S. degrees, a co-op program in environmental science, and an accelerated degree are available. Nondegree study is possible. There are 5 national honor societies, a freshman honors program, and 4 departmental honors programs.

Faculty/Classroom: 60% of faculty are male; 40% are female. 90% teach undergraduates. Graduate students teach 4% of introductory courses. The average class size in an introductory lecture is 30; in a laboratory is 18; and in a regular course is 15.

Requirements: The SAT or ACT is required, with a minimum composite score of 18 on the ACT for unconditional admission. In addition, applicants should have completed 15 high school credits or the GED equivalent. Applications are accepted online. AP and CLEP credits are accepted.

Procedure: Freshmen are admitted to all sessions. Entrance exams should be taken during the junior or senior year. There are early admissions, deferred admissions, and rolling admissions plans. Application deadlines are open. Notification is sent on a rolling basis. Applications are accepted online.

Transfer: Transfer applicants must have maintained a minimum GPA of 2.0 in all previous college courses. 30 of 120 credits required for the bachelor's degree must be completed at UWA.

Visiting: There are regularly scheduled orientations for prospective students. There are guides for informal visits, visitors may sit in on classes, and stay overnight. To schedule a visit, contact the Admissions Office.

Financial Aid: The FAFSA and CCS/Profile, or FAFSA, or FFS, or SFS are required. Check with the school for current application deadlines.

International Students: They must take the TOEFL. They must also take the SAT or ACT, scoring 18.

Computers: All students may access the system. There are no time limits. The fee is $20.

Admissions Contact: Richard Hester, Director of Admissions. E-Mail: *admissions@uwa.edu* Web: *www.uwa.edu*

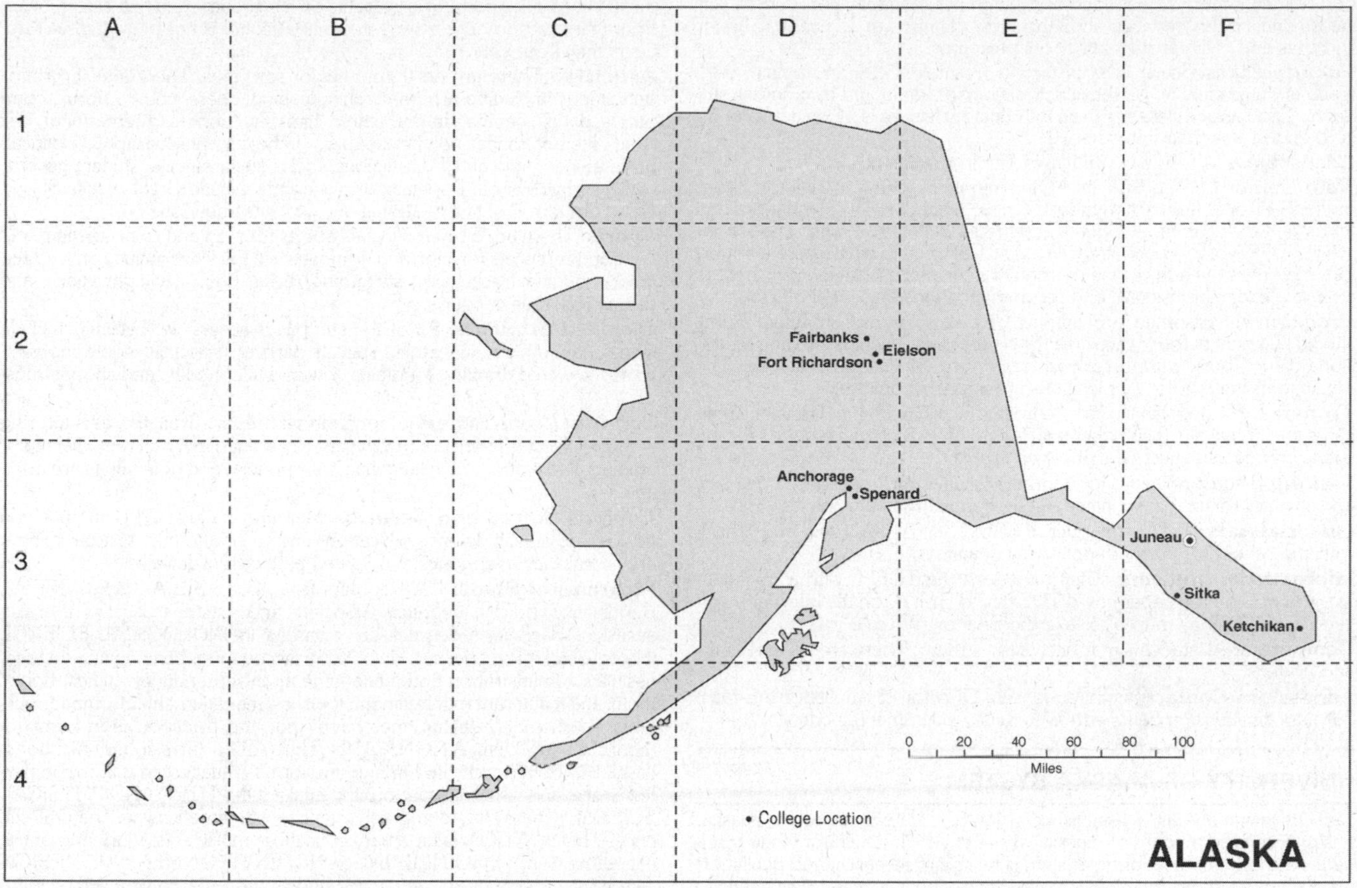

ALASKA PACIFIC UNIVERSITY D-3

Anchorage, AK 99508

(907) 564-8248
(800) 252-7528; (907) 564-8317

Full-time: 125 men, 200 women
Part-time: 60 men, 160 women
Graduate: 85 men, 190 women
Year: 4-1-4, summer session
Application Deadline:
Freshman Class: n/av
SAT or ACT: required

Faculty: n/av
Ph.D.s: 60%
Student/Faculty: 10 to 1
Tuition: $23,360
Room & Board: $10,000

VERY COMPETITIVE

Alaska Pacific University, founded in 1957 and affiliated with the United Methodist Church, is a private institution offering undergraduate, graduate, and adult degree-completion programs. There are 6 undergraduate schools and 6 graduate schools. The library contains 891,103 volumes, 627,916 microform items, and 13,324 audio/video tapes/CDs/DVDs, and subscribes to 3,840 periodicals including electronic. Computerized library services include interlibrary loans and Internet access. Special learning facilities include an art gallery, radio station, TV station, the Alaskana collection located in the Consortium Library. The 170-acre campus is in a suburban area in midtown Anchorage. Including any residence halls, there are 13 buildings.

Student Life: 73% of undergraduates are from Alaska. Others are from 37 states, and 2 foreign countries. 68% are White; 18% American Indian/Alaska Native. The average age of freshmen is 25; all undergraduates, 30. 25% do not continue beyond their first year; 36% remain to graduate.

Housing: 170 students can be accommodated in college housing, which includes coed dorms and on-campus apartments. In addition, there are special-interest houses. On-campus housing is guaranteed for the freshman year only, is available on a first-come, first-served basis, and is available on a lottery system for upperclassmen. 73% of students commute. Alcohol is not permitted. All students may keep cars.

Activities: There are no fraternities or sororities. There are 18 groups on campus, including departmental, art, band, chorus, drama, ethnic, international, newspaper, photography, professional, religious, social service, student government, and students in free enterprise. Popular campus events include Earth Day, Spring Honors Convocation and Fall Academic Convocation.

Sports: There is no sports program at APU. Facilities include a 300-seat sports center, an indoor swimming pool, cross-country skiing and running trails, a climbing wall, a soccer field, a lake for boating, and a weight/exercise room.

Disabled Students: 75% of the campus is accessible. Facilities include wheelchair ramps, elevators, special parking, specially equipped restrooms, lowered drinking fountains, and lowered telephones.

Services: Counseling and information services are available, as is tutoring in some subjects, math, writing, and other subjects as needed. There is remedial math and writing.

Campus Safety and Security: Measures include 24-hour foot and vehicle patrol, self-defense education, and security escort services. There are emergency telephones, lighted pathways/sidewalks, safety signs are posted as needed.

Programs of Study: APU confers B.A., and B.S. degrees. Associate and master's degrees are also awarded. Bachelor's degrees are awarded in AGRICULTURE (environmental studies and natural resource management), BIOLOGICAL SCIENCE (marine biology), BUSINESS (business administration and management and recreational facilities management), COMPUTER AND PHYSICAL SCIENCE (earth science), EDUCATION (elementary education), ENGINEERING AND ENVIRONMENTAL DESIGN (environmental science), HEALTH PROFESSIONS (health care administration), SOCIAL SCIENCE (human services, liberal arts/general studies, and psychology). Environmental science, outdoor studies, and psychology have the largest enrollments.

Required: All students must complete at least 128 semester hours, with 39 to 61 in the major, and maintain a minimum GPA of 2.0. Distribution requirements include 4 semester hours each in Orientation to Active Learning, a lab science, a course in social/behavioral science, and a course in ethics or religion; 2 courses in humanities; a sophomore seminar in the major; and a world language course that includes American Sign Language. Courses to meet writing, speech, and quantitative skills competencies are also required, as well as a 3-semester-hour practicum, portfolio, and senior project.

Special: Internships are required, and study abroad, student-designed majors, and B.A.-B.S. degrees in earth sciences, environmental science, and marine biology are possible. Accelerated degrees are offered through the Degree Completion Program for working adults in business administration management, accounting information for management, human services, and health services administration. There are 2 national honor societies and 2 departmental honors programs.

Faculty/Classroom: 42% of faculty are male; 58% are female. 98% teach undergraduates. No introductory courses are taught by graduate students. The average class size in an introductory lecture is 12; in a laboratory is 9; and in a regular course is 10.

Admissions: 1 freshman graduated first in the class.

Requirements: The SAT or ACT is required, with a satisfactory score on the SAT or at least 19 on the ACT. Two teacher recommendations and an essay are required. A GED is acceptable in lieu of a high school transcript. A GPA of 2.5 is required. AP and CLEP credits are accepted. Important factors in the admissions decision are advanced placement or honors courses, leadership record, and recommendations by school officials.

Procedure: Freshmen are admitted to all sessions. Entrance exams should be taken before January of the senior year. There is a rolling admissions plan. Check with the school for current application deadlines. The application fee is $25. Applications are accepted online.

Transfer: 80 transfer students enrolled in 2012-2013. Transfer applicants must have a 2.0 cumulative GPA. 32 of 128 credits required for the bachelor's degree must be completed at APU.

Visiting: There are guides for informal visits, visitors may sit in on classes, and stay overnight. To schedule a visit, contact the Admissions Office.

Financial Aid: APU is a member of CSS. The FAFSA is required. Check with the school for current application deadlines.

International Students: They must take the TOEFL with a minimum score of 550 on the paper-based TOEFL (PBT) or 79 on the Internet-based version (iBT). They must also take the SAT or ACT.

Computers: All students may access the system. There are no time limits and no fees.

Admissions Contact: Jennifer Jensen, Director of Admissions. E-Mail: *admissions@alaskapacific.edu* Web: *www.alaskapacific.edu*

UNIVERSITY OF ALASKA SYSTEM

The University of Alaska, established in 1975, is a private system in Alaska. It is governed by a board of regents whose chief administrator is the president. The primary goal of the system is teaching, research, and public service. The main priorities are maintaining open access to students to prepare them for and provide rigorus postsecondary programs; providing the cultural populations of Alaska with appropriate vocational and academic education; and conducting research with emphasis on arctic areas and isssues. The total student enrollment is usually about 27,500 with 2000 faculty members. Altogether there are 120 baccalaureate, 85 master's, 13 doctoral programs offered in the University of Alaska System. Profiles of the 4-year campuses are included in this section.

UNIVERSITY OF ALASKA ANCHORAGE — D-3

Anchorage, AK 99508 — **(907) 786-1480; (907) 786-4888**

Full-time: 2750 men, 3800 women	**Faculty:** n/av; IIA, av$
Part-time: 1500 men, 2775 women	**Ph.D.s:** 51%
Graduate: 315 men, 590 women	**Student/Faculty:** n/av
Year: semesters, summer session	**Tuition:** $5147 ($15,206)
Application Deadline:	**Room & Board:** $10,143
Freshman Class: n/av	
SAT or ACT: required	

NONCOMPETITIVE

The University of Alaska Anchorage, founded in 1954, is a public institution and a major unit of the University of Alaska statewide system. Its baccalaureate programs are administered through the Colleges of Arts and Sciences, Business and Public Policy, Health, Education, and Social Welfare, and the School of Engineering, and the Community and Technical College. There are 5 undergraduate schools and 5 graduate schools. In addition to regional accreditation, UAA has baccalaureate program accreditation with AACSB, ABET, ACEJMC, ADA, CAHEA, CSWE, NASAD, NASDTEC, and NLN. The library contains 676,750 volumes, 574,010 microform items, and 7,080 audio/video tapes/CDs/DVDs, and subscribes to 3,480 periodicals including electronic. Computerized library services include interlibrary loans and database searching. Special learning facilities include an art gallery, radio station, TV station, a dental clinic, a welding lab, an auto-diesel garage, a theater, photography labs, and a student art museum show case. The 428-acre campus is in a small town 3 miles from downtown Anchorage. Including any residence halls, there are 27 buildings.

Student Life: 98% of undergraduates are from Alaska. Others are from states. 66% are White; 11% American Indian/Alaska Native. The average age of freshmen is 20; all undergraduates, 29. 29% do not continue beyond their first year; 26% remain to graduate.

Housing: College-sponsored housing includes coed dorms and on-campus apartments. In addition, there are honors houses, language houses, floors for Alaska natives studying engineering, nursing students, first-year students under age 20, healthy lifestyle, quiet lifestyle and cultures. On-campus housing is available on a first-come and first-served basis. Priority is given to out-of-town students. Alcohol is not permitted. All students may keep cars.

Activities: There are no fraternities or sororities. There are 75 groups on campus, including art, band, cheerleading, chess, choir, chorus, computers, dance, debate, drama, ethnic, film, gay, honors, international, jazz band, literary magazine, newspaper, orchestra, photography, political, professional, radio and TV, religious, social, social service, student government, and yearbook. Popular campus events include Great Alaska Shoot-Out, Northern Lights Invitational and Student Showcase.

Sports: There are 5 intercollegiate sports for men and 6 for women, and 4 intramural sports for men and 4 for women. Facilities include an ice rink, indoor jogging track, gym, swimming/diving pool, a weight room, and racquetball/squash courts.

Disabled Students: All of the campus is accessible. Facilities include wheelchair ramps, elevators, special parking, specially equipped restrooms, lowered drinking fountains, lowered telephones, and special housing.

Services: Counseling and information services are available, as is tutoring in most subjects. There is a reader service for the blind, and remedial math, reading, and writing. Sign language, interpreters, and note takers are available.

Campus Safety and Security: Measures include 24-hour foot and vehicle patrol, self-defense education, and security escort services. There are emergency telephones and lighted pathways/sidewalks.

Programs of Study: UAA confers B.A., B.S., B.B.A., B.Ed., B.F.A., B.Mus. and B.S.W. degrees. Associate and master's degrees are also awarded. Bachelor's degrees are awarded in BIOLOGICAL SCIENCE (biology/biological science), BUSINESS (accounting, banking and finance, business administration and management, entrepreneurial studies, hotel/motel and restaurant management, logistics, management information systems, marketing/retailing/merchandising, and transportation management), COMMUNICATIONS AND THE ARTS (art, communications, dramatic arts, English, fine arts, journalism, languages, music, music performance, and visual and performing arts), COMPUTER AND PHYSICAL SCIENCE (chemistry, computer science, mathematics, and natural sciences), EDUCATION (elementary education, music education, and physical education), ENGINEERING AND ENVIRONMENTAL DESIGN (aeronautical technology, aerospace studies, air traffic control, airline piloting and navigation, civil engineering, electrical/electronics engineering, survey and mapping technology, and technological management), HEALTH PROFESSIONS (nursing), SOCIAL SCIENCE (anthropology, culinary arts, economics, history, human services, interdisciplinary studies, liberal arts/general studies, philosophy, political science/government, psychology, social work, and sociology). Education, nursing, and social sciences are the strongest academically. Elementary education, accounting, and nursing have the largest enrollments.

Required: General education requirements include 7 credits in natural science, 6 each in written communications, humanities, and social sciences, and 3 each in oral communication, quantitative skills, and fine arts. A total of 120 to 132 credits, with 48 upper-division courses, and a minimum GPA of 2.0 are required to graduate.

Special: UAA participates in the National Student Exchange Program and offers study abroad. UAA also offers B.A.-B.S. degrees, student-designed and dual majors, internships, pass/fail options, a 3-2 electrical engineering degree, a general studies degree, nondegree study, and credit for life experience. The Community and Technical College provides educational and vocational courses for career development. There are 2 national honor societies and 3 departmental honors programs.

Faculty/Classroom: 48% of faculty are male; 52% are female. No introductory courses are taught by graduate students. The average class size in an introductory lecture is 50; in a laboratory is 20; and in a regular course is 35.

Requirements: The SAT or ACT is required. In addition, applicants should be graduates of an accredited secondary school or have a high school or GED certificate. A GPA of 2.5 is required. AP and CLEP credits are accepted.

Procedure: Freshmen are admitted to all sessions. Entrance exams should be taken by May of the senior year. There are deferred admissions and rolling admissions plans. Check with the school for current application deadlines. The fall 2013 application fee was $40. Applications are accepted online.

Transfer: Applicants must meet admission requirements and must have a minimum GPA of 2.5 and at least 30 credit hours earned at an accredited post secondary institution. 30 of 120 credits required for the bachelor's degree must be completed at UAA.

Visiting: There are regularly scheduled orientations for prospective students, consisting of registration orientation, application process, campus tours, student appointments, and classes. There are guides for informal visits and visitors may sit in on classes. To schedule a visit, contact the Office of Admissions.

Financial Aid: UAA is a member of CSS. The FAFSA and the college's own financial statement are required. Check with the school for current application deadlines.

International Students: They must take the TOEFL. They must also take the SAT or ACT.

Computers: All students may access the system. There are no time limits and no fees.

Admissions Contact: Enrollment Services E-Mail: *enroll@uaa.alaska.edu* Web: *www.uaa.alaska.edu*

UNIVERSITY OF ALASKA FAIRBANKS D-2

Fairbanks, AK 99775 (907) 474-7500
(800) 478-1823; (907) 474-7097

Full-time: 1824 men, 1830 women	**Faculty:** 368; I, av$
Part-time: 1610 men, 2814 women	**Ph.D.s:** 66%
Graduate: 481 men, 697 women	**Student/Faculty:** 7 to 1
Year: semesters, summer session	**Tuition:** $6505 ($19,735)
Application Deadline: June 15	**Room & Board:** $7450
Freshman Class: 1150 applied, 783 accepted, 497 enrolled	
SAT CR/M/W: 560/560/520 **ACT:** 24	**COMPETITIVE**

The University of Alaska Fairbanks, founded in 1917 is the nation's northernmost Land, Sea, and Space Grant university and international research center. The institution advances and disseminates knowledge through teaching, research, and public service with an emphasis on Alaska and circumpolar regions. There are 8 undergraduate schools and 8 graduate schools. In addition to regional accreditation, UAF has baccalaureate program accreditation with AACSB, ABET, ACEJMC, CSAB, CSWE, NASM, NCATE, and SAF. The 3 libraries contain 1.2 million volumes, 133,755 microform items, and 95,528 audio/video tapes/CDs/DVDs, and subscribe to 55,685 periodicals including electronic. Computerized library services include interlibrary loans, database searching, Internet access, and Wi-Fi capability. Special learning facilities include an art gallery, natural history museum, radio station, TV station, several research institutes and labs for study in the physical and natural sciences are associated with the university. The 2250-acre campus is in a small town 4 miles northwest of Fairbanks. Including any residence halls, there are 66 buildings.

Student Life: 81% of undergraduates are from Alaska. Others are from 46 states, 16 foreign countries, and Canada. 50% are White; 27% race unknown. The average age of freshmen is 18; all undergraduates, 23. 23% do not continue beyond their first year; 37% remain to graduate.

Housing: 1390 students can be accommodated in college housing, which includes coed dorms, on-campus apartments, and married student housing. first-year experience residence, Alaska native cultural housing. On-campus housing is available on a first-come and first-served basis. 56% of students commute. All students may keep cars.

Activities: There are 160 groups on campus, including art, band, chess, choir, chorus, communications, computers, dance, drama, environmental, ethnic, film, gay, honors, international, jazz band, literary magazine, newspaper, orchestra, photography, political, professional, radio and TV, religious, social, student government, and symphony. Popular campus events include Starvation Gulch, All-Campus Day, and Meltdown.

Sports: There are 5 intercollegiate sports for men and 6 for women, and 5 intramural sports for men and 5 for women. Facilities include a 4500-seat arena, a 2000-seat gym, a 1500-seat skating rink, 2 racquetball courts, 2 weight rooms, 4 basketball courts, an Olympic-size swimming pool, a small-bore rifle range, and a lighted 30-mile ski trail.

Disabled Students: 90% of the campus is accessible. Facilities include wheelchair ramps, elevators, special parking, specially equipped restrooms, special class scheduling, lowered drinking fountains, lowered telephones, special housing, a shuttle bus, and a swimming pool equipped with hydraulic lifts.

Services: Counseling and information services are available, as is tutoring in some subjects, chemistry, calculus, languages, biology, math, physics, geology and English. There is a reader service for the blind, and remedial math, reading, and writing.

Campus Safety and Security: Measures include 24-hour foot and vehicle patrol, emergency notification system, self-defense education, and security escort services. There are shuttle buses, emergency telephones, lighted pathways/sidewalks, controlled access to dorms/residences, a 24-hour crisis line, evening patrols inside dorms.

Programs of Study: UAF confers B.A., B.S., B.B.A., B.A.S., B.E.M., B.F.A., B.M. and B.T. degrees. Associate, master's, and doctoral degrees are also awarded. Bachelor's degrees are awarded in AGRICULTURE (fishing and fisheries and natural resource management), BIOLOGICAL SCIENCE (biology/biological science and wildlife biology), BUSINESS (accounting and business administration and management), COMMUNICATIONS AND THE ARTS (art, communications, English, Eskimo, film arts, French, German, journalism, linguistics, music, music performance, Spanish, and theatre arts), COMPUTER AND PHYSICAL SCIENCE (applied physics, chemistry, computer science, earth science, geology, geoscience, mathematics, physics, and science), EDUCATION (early childhood education, elementary education, and music education), ENGINEERING AND ENVIRONMENTAL DESIGN (civil engineering, computer engineering, electrical/electronics engineering, emergency/disaster science, geological engineering, mechanical engineering, mining and mineral engineering, petroleum/natural gas engineering, and technological management), SOCIAL SCIENCE (anthropology, area studies, criminal justice, economics, ethnic studies, geography, history, homeland security, interdisciplinary studies, Japanese studies, Native American studies, philosophy, political science/government, psychology, rural economics, Russian and Slavic studies, social work, and sociology). Engineering, fisheries, and biology are the strongest academically. Biological sciences, business administration, and engineering have the largest enrollments.

Required: All students must complete core courses in English and oral communication, library skills, humanities, social science, natural science, and math. A minimum of 120 credit hours, with 27 to 30 in the major, and a 2.0 GPA are required for graduation.

Special: The university's Office of eLearning and Distance Education offers satellite education programs to Alaska residents to reach students at remote sites. Study abroad is offered in 42 countries. Internships are offered through the Rural Alaska Honors Institute. Student-designed majors, credit/no credit options, nondegree study, and credit for life, military, and work experience are also available. There are 10 national honor societies and a freshman honors program.

Faculty/Classroom: 59% of faculty are male; 41% are female. 54% teach undergraduates, 75% do research, and 40% do both. No introductory courses are taught by graduate students. The average class size in an introductory lecture is 20; in a laboratory is 15; and in a regular course is 18.

Admissions: 68% of the 2013-2014 applicants were accepted. The SAT scores for the 2013-2014 freshman class were: Critical Reading--26% below 500, 43% between 500 and 599, 27% between 600 and 699, and 4% between 700 and 800; Math--23% below 500, 41% between 500 and 599, 30% between 600 and 699, and 6% between 700 and 800; Writing--37% below 500, 43% between 500 and 599, 18% between 600 and 699, and 2% between 700 and 800. The ACT scores were 24% below 21, 23% between 21 and 23, 25% between 24 and 26, 13% between 27 and 28, and 15% above 28. 46% of the current freshmen were in the top fifth of their class; 76% were in the top two fifths. 32 freshmen graduated first in their class.

Requirements: The SAT or ACT is required. In addition, applicants should be graduates of an accredited secondary school with 16 academic credits, including 4 in English and 3 each in math, natural or physical sciences, and social sciences, with a minimum GPA of 2.5 in these courses. Applicants should have an overall high school GPA of at least 3.0 or an overall GPA of at least 2.5 along with an ACT Plus Writing score of at least 18 or SAT total score of at least 1290. The GED is not accepted. A GPA of 2.5 is required. AP and CLEP credits are accepted.

Procedure: Freshmen are admitted fall, spring, and summer. Entrance exams should be taken during one year of applying. There are early admissions, deferred admissions, and rolling admissions plans. Applications should be filed by June 15 for fall entry; November 1 for spring entry; and May 1 for summer entry, along with a $50 fee. Notification is sent on a rolling basis. Applications are accepted online.

Transfer: 238 transfer students enrolled in 2012-2013. A GPA of 2.0 in all previous college work and an honorable dismissal from all schools attended are required. Applicants with fewer than 30 semester hours of transferable credit also must have a high school GPA of 2.0. 30 of 120 credits required for the bachelor's degree must be completed at UAF.

Visiting: There are regularly scheduled orientations for prospective students, tours generally include academic facilities, dorms, and student recreation center, and may also include meeting with an admissions counselor, professors, advisors, and students, and classroom visits. There are guides for informal visits, visitors may sit in on classes, and stay overnight. To schedule a visit, contact UAF Office of Admissions.

Financial Aid: In 2013-2014, 89% of all full-time freshmen and 76% of continuing full-time students received some form of financial aid. 46% of all full-time freshmen and 51% of continuing full-time students received need-based aid. The average freshman award was $9,041. Need-based scholarships or need-based grants averaged $6,898 ($22,506 maximum); need-based self-help aid (loans and jobs) averaged $6,126 ($11,780 maximum); non-need-based athletic scholarships averaged $15,337 ($35,307 maximum); and other non-need-based awards and non-need-based scholarships averaged $8,950 ($41,002 maximum). 19% of undergraduate students work part-time. Average annual earnings from campus work are $5320. The average financial indebtedness of the 2013 graduate was $30,115. The FAFSA is required. The priority date for freshman financial aid applications for fall entry is February 15. The deadline for filing freshman financial aid applications for fall entry is June 30.

International Students: There are 51 international students enrolled. The school actively recruits these students. They must take the TOEFL with

a minimum score of 550 on the paper-based TOEFL (PBT) or 79 on the Internet-based version (iBT), IELTS. They must also take the SAT or ACT.

Computers: All students may access the system 24 hours per day. There are no time limits and no fees.

Graduates: From July 1, 2012 to June 30, 2013, 550 bachelor's degrees were awarded. The most popular majors were biological sciences (8%), psychology (7%), and business administration (6%). 89 companies recruited on campus in 2012-2013. In an average class, 2% graduate in 3 years or less, 14% graduate in 4 years or less, 32% graduate in 5 years or less, and 37% graduate in 6 years or less.

Admissions Contact: Libby Eddy, Registrar and Director of Admissions. E-Mail: *admissions@uaf.edu* Web: *http:/www.uaf.edu/admissions/*

UNIVERSITY OF ALASKA SOUTHEAST F-3

Juneau, AK 99801 **(907) 465-6457**
(877) 465-4827; (907) 465-6365

Full-time: 270 men, 325 women	**Faculty:** n/av; IIA, -$
Part-time: 625 men, 875 women	**Ph.D.s:** n/av
Graduate: 70 men, 80 women	**Student/Faculty:** n/av
Year: semesters, summer session	**Tuition:** $5693
Application Deadline: open	**Room & Board:** $8317
Freshman Class: n/av	
SAT or ACT: recommended	

COMPETITIVE

The University of Alaska Southeast, a multicampus institution founded in 1972, is part of the University of Alaska statewide system, with baccalaureate programs offered in business and public administration, education, and liberal arts and science. There are 3 undergraduate schools and 2 graduate schools. The library contains 250,000 volumes, 250,000 microform items, and 1,850 audio/video tapes/CDs/DVDs, and subscribes to 1,500 periodicals including electronic. Computerized library services include interlibrary loans and database searching. Special learning facilities include a The 198-acre campus is in a suburban area 10 miles north of Juneau. Including any residence halls, there are 18 buildings.

Student Life: 75% of undergraduates are from Alaska. Others are from 37 states, 12 foreign countries, and Canada. 95% are from public schools. 70% are White; 17% American Indian/Alaska Native. The average age of freshmen is 18; all undergraduates, 24.

Housing: 250 students can be accommodated in college housing, which includes single-sex dorms, on-campus apartments, and married student housing. On-campus housing is available on a first-come and first-served basis. Priority is given to out-of-town students. 90% of students commute. All students may keep cars.

Activities: There are no fraternities or sororities. There are 16 groups on campus, including choir, ethnic, gay, honors, literary magazine, newspaper, political, professional, religious, and student government. Popular campus events include Ski Day, Whale-watching, and Eagle Preserve Field Trips.

Sports: There are 3 intramural sports for men and 3 for women. Facilities include a community gym and pool, an activity center, and access to health club facilities.

Disabled Students: 95% of the campus is accessible. Facilities include wheelchair ramps, elevators, special parking, specially equipped restrooms, lowered drinking fountains, and lowered telephones.

Services: Counseling and information services are available, as is tutoring in most subjects. There is a reader service for the blind, and remedial math, reading, and writing.

Campus Safety and Security: There are shuttle buses, emergency telephones, lighted pathways/sidewalks, and late-night security at student housing.

Programs of Study: UAS confers B.A., B.S., B.B.A., B.Ed. and B.L.A. degrees. Associate and master's degrees are also awarded. Bachelor's degrees are awarded in BIOLOGICAL SCIENCE (biology/biological science and marine biology), BUSINESS (accounting and business administration and management), COMMUNICATIONS AND THE ARTS (art, communications, literature, and speech/debate/rhetoric), COMPUTER AND PHYSICAL SCIENCE (mathematics), EDUCATION (elementary education), ENGINEERING AND ENVIRONMENTAL DESIGN (environmental science), SOCIAL SCIENCE (liberal arts/general studies, political science/government, public administration, and social science). Accounting, marine biology, and environmental science are the strongest academically. Liberal arts has the largest enrollment.

Required: All students are required to complete general education courses, including 15 credits in humanities and social science, 10 in math and natural sciences, 6 in written communication skills, and 3 in speech. A total of 120 semester credits, with at least 36 in the major, and a minimum GPA of 2.0 are required in order to graduate. In the liberal arts program, a portfolio is required.

Special: UAS offers cross-registration through the National Student Exchange, and internships with federal and state agencies. Study abroad, work-study, dual and student-designed majors, credit/no credit options, and credit for military experience are also available. The School of Career and Continuing Education offers courses and certificate programs in technological skills.

Faculty/Classroom: 98% teach undergraduates. No introductory courses are taught by graduate students. The average class size in an introductory lecture is 20 and in a laboratory is 12.

Requirements: The SAT or ACT is recommended. Applicants should be graduates of an accredited secondary school or have the GED. A GPA of 2.0 is required. AP and CLEP credits are accepted.

Procedure: Freshmen are admitted fall and spring. There are early admissions, deferred admissions, and rolling admissions plans. Application deadlines are open. The fall 2013 application fee was $35.

Transfer: A minimum GPA of 2.0 from an accredited institution is required. 30 of 120 credits required for the bachelor's degree must be completed at UAS.

Visiting: There are regularly scheduled orientations for prospective students. There are guides for informal visits and visitors may sit in on classes.

Financial Aid: UAS is a member of CSS. The FAFSA and the college's own financial statement are required. Check with the school for current application deadlines.

International Students: They must take the TOEFL. They must also take the SAT or ACT.

Computers: All students may access the system. There are no time limits and no fees.

Admissions Contact: Greg Wagner, Director of Admissions. E-Mail: *jyuas@alaska.edu* Web: *www.usa.alaska.edu*

ARIZONA

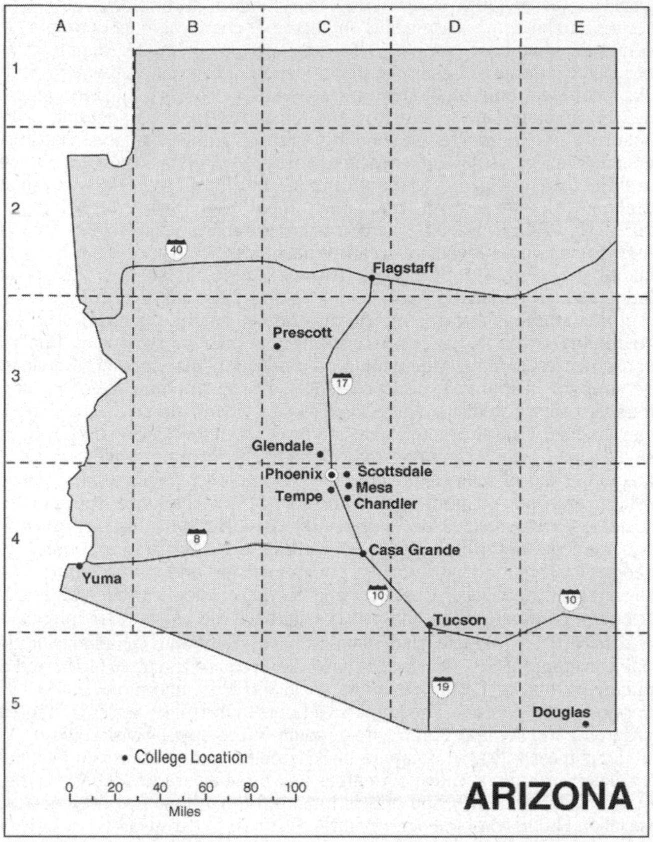

AMERICAN INDIAN COLLEGE C-4

Phoenix, AZ 85021 (602) 944-3335, ext.235
(800) 933-3828; (602) 943-8299

Full-time: 50 men, 45 women
Part-time: 15 men, 20 women
Year: semesters
Application Deadline: open
Freshman Class: n/av
SAT or ACT: required
Faculty: n/av
Ph.D.s: n/av
Student/Faculty: n/av
Tuition: $10,500
Room & Board: $6202

COMPETITIVE

American Indian College of the Assemblies of God, founded in 1957, is a Christian college with a specific mission of preparing American Indians for leadership in churches, education, and the community. The figures in the above capsule and in this profile are approximate. The library contains 20,000 volumes, and 35 audio/video tapes/CDs/DVDs, and subscribes to 102 periodicals including electronic. Computerized library services include Internet access. The 10-acre campus is in a small town in north Phoenix, just east of I17 and the Metrocenter area. Including any residence halls, there are 9 buildings.

Student Life: 72% of undergraduates are from Arizona. Others are from 10 states, and 1 foreign country. 85% are from public schools. 67% are American Indian/Alaska Native; 18% White. 100% are Protestant. The average age of freshmen is 23; all undergraduates, 26.

Housing: 80 students can be accommodated in college housing, which includes single-sex dorms and off-campus apartments. 52% of students live on campus; of those, 100% remain on campus on weekends. Alcohol is not permitted. All students may keep cars.

Activities: There are no fraternities or sororities. Groups on campus include band, cheerleading, drama, ethnic, religious, student government, and yearbook. Popular campus events include Missions Conventions, and College Days.

Sports: There is no sports program at AIC. Facilities include a full-size gym with a locker room and a weight room.

Disabled Students: All of the campus is accessible. Facilities include wheelchair ramps, special parking, specially equipped restrooms, and lowered drinking fountains.

Services: Counseling and information services are available, as is tutoring in most subjects. There is remedial math, reading, and writing.

Campus Safety and Security: There are lighted pathways/sidewalks, and night security.

Programs of Study: AIC confers B.A. degrees. Associate degrees are also awarded. Bachelor's degrees are awarded in EDUCATION (elementary education), SOCIAL SCIENCE (ministries).

Required: To graduate, all students must maintain a GPA of 2.0 and complete 128 total credits. Students must complete courses in history, science, math, computer, and bible studies. A comprehensive bible exam is required.

Special: Internships and dual majors are available.

Faculty/Classroom: 65% of faculty are male; 35% are female. All teach undergraduates. No introductory courses are taught by graduate students. The average class size in an introductory lecture is 11; in a laboratory is 6; and in a regular course is 6.

Requirements: The SAT or ACT is required. Transcripts from high school and any other secondary schools attended are required along with a pastor's reference form. Applicants are required to take placement tests with satisfactory results. A 2.0 GPA is required and the GED is accepted. A GPA of 2.0 is required. AP and CLEP credits are accepted. Important factors in the admissions decision are advanced placement or honors courses, evidence of special talent, and extracurricular activities record.

Procedure: Freshmen are admitted to all sessions. Entrance exams should be taken prior to acceptance. There are early decision, early admissions, and deferred admissions plans. Application deadlines are open.

Transfer: Official transcripts from high school and each college attended, plus a pastor's reference form are required. Students must demonstrate proficiency in English, writing, math, and reading. 30 of 128 credits required for the bachelor's degree must be completed at AIC.

Visiting: There are regularly scheduled orientations for prospective students, Consisting of College Days in the fall and spring semesters that include class visits, overnight stays in dorms, and meals in the cafeteria for 2 days. There are guides for informal visits, visitors may sit in on classes, and stay overnight. To schedule a visit, contact the Admissions Office.

Financial Aid: The FAFSA is required. Check with the school for current application deadlines.

International Students: They must take the TOEFL. They must also take the SAT or ACT.

Computers: All students may access the system. There are no time limits and no fees.

Admissions Contact: Sandra Ticeahkie, Director of Admissions. E-Mail: *aicadm@aicag.edu* Web: *www.aicag.edu*

ARIZONA BOARD OF REGENTS

The Arizona Board of Regents, established in 1945, is a private system in Arizona. It is governed by a board of regents, whose chief administrator is the executive director and chief executive officer. The primary goal of the system is teaching, research, and service. The main priorities are to provide strong undergraduate instruction programs; to conduct extensive research and graduate instruction programs; and to ensure access for qualified Arizona residents, especially underrepresented ethnic minorities. The total student enrollment is usually about 100,100 with 3550 faculty members. Altogether there are 325 baccalaureate, 250 masters, and 140 doctoral programs offered in the Arizona Board of Regents. Profiles of the 4-year campuses are included in this section.

ARIZONA STATE UNIVERSITY C-4

Tempe, AZ 85287 (480) 965-7788; (480) 965-3610

Full-time: 24992 men, 24953 women
Part-time: 4511 men, 4926 women
Graduate: 6898 men, 7098 women
Year: semesters, summer session
Application Deadline: February 1
Faculty: n/av; I, -$
Ph.D.s: 87%
Student/Faculty: 23 to 1
Tuition: $9724 ($22,977)
Room & Board: $9094
Freshman Class: 30696 applied, 26986 accepted, 9265 enrolled
SAT CR/M: 540/560 **ACT:** 24 **COMPETITIVE+**

Arizona State University is a public, comprehensive university. Founded as a normal school in 1885, it gained university status in 1958. Each of the four distinctive ASU campuses in metropolitan Phoenix offers a unique experience, while providing the same high academic quality. State-of-the-art facilities at the Downtown Phoenix campus create strong learning and career connections for students with media, health care, corporate and government organizations. Students at the Polytechnic campus, located in Mesa in the East Valley, explore professional and technical programs in thousands of square feet of new laboratory space. The historic Tempe campus is home to the Sun Devil athletic complex, performing arts facilities and high tech research space, creating a dynamic and engaging learning environment. With its award winning architecture and lush landscaping in a closely knit learning community, the West campus in northwest Phoenix offers business, education, and interdisciplinary arts and science programs. There are 15 undergraduate schools and 15 graduate schools. In addition to regional accreditation, ASU has baccalaureate program accreditation with AACSB, ABET, ACCE, ACEJMC, ADA, CSWE, NASAD, and NASM. The 8 libraries contain 4.6 million volumes, 7.7 million microform items, and 108,491 audio/video tapes/CDs/DVDs, and subscribe to 90,772 periodicals including electronic. Computerized library services include interlibrary loans, database searching, and Internet access. Special learning facilities include an art gallery, planetarium, radio station, TV station, museums, galleries, collections, research labs, digital labs, art, dance and development studios. The 1952-acre campus is in an urban area in metropolitan Phoenix. Including any residence halls, there are 390 buildings.

Student Life: 73% of undergraduates are from Arizona. Others are from 50 states, 93 foreign countries, and Canada. 93% are from public schools. 60% are White; 19% Hispanic. The average age of freshmen is 18; all undergraduates, 23. 20% do not continue beyond their first year; 57% remain to graduate.

Housing: 11214 students can be accommodated in college housing, which includes coed dorms, on-campus apartments, and married student housing. In addition, there are honors houses, special-interest houses, residence is available for freshmen and students in particular academic areas. On-campus housing is guaranteed for the freshman year only, is available on a first-come, and first-served basis. 81% of students commute. Alcohol is not permitted. All students may keep cars.

Activities: 6% of men belong to 1 local and 33 national fraternities; 7% of women belong to 25 national sororities. There are 850 groups on campus, including health, technology and sports, art, band, cheerleading, chess, choir, chorale, chorus, communications, computers, dance, debate, drama, drill team, entrepreneurship, environmental, ethnic, film, gay, honors, international, jazz band, literary magazine, marching band, musical theater, newspaper, orchestra, pep band, photography, political, professional, radio and TV, religious, social, social service, student government, and symphony. Popular campus events include Sun Devil Week, Cesar Chavez Service Day , Devilpalooza, Pitchfork Awards, Club Carnival, Fall Forward Leadership Conf, Finals Breakfast, Global Café, Homecoming, MLK Day of Service, Passport to ASU, Sun Devil 101, Welcome Week and World Festival.

Sports: There are 8 intercollegiate sports for men and 11 for women, and 20 intramural sports for men and 20 for women. Facilities include 5 stadiums (including football, baseball, softball, track, and soccer), a basketball, volleyball, gymnastics and wrestling arena, tennis facilities, an aquatic complex, a golf course, athletic and activity centers, and student recreation complexes.

Disabled Students: 99% of the campus is accessible. Facilities include wheelchair ramps, elevators, special parking, specially equipped restrooms, special class scheduling, lowered drinking fountains, lowered telephones. there are flashing alarms for the deaf, braille maps, modified residence hall rooms and an adaptive exercise program and facility.

Services: Counseling and information services are available, as is tutoring in most subjects, Over 200 different courses and writing tutoring. There is a reader service for the blind. Face-to-face and online tutoring are free to students on all campuses. Academic success courses and graduate test preparation are also available. Disability Resource Centers support the learning needs of students with documented disabilities.

Campus Safety and Security: Measures include security escort services. There are shuttle buses, emergency telephones, lighted pathways/sidewalks, controlled access to dorms/residences, a text messaging alert system (limited to those who sign up); surveillance cameras may be located in residence halls.

Programs of Study: ASU confers B.A., B.A.E., B.A.S., B.F.A., B.G.S., B.I.S., B.L.S., B.Mus., B.S., B.S.D., B.S.E., B.S.LA., B.S.N., B.S.P. and B.S.W. degrees. Master's and doctoral degrees are also awarded. Bachelor's degrees are awarded in AGRICULTURE (agricultural business management, conservation and regulation, and natural resource management), BIOLOGICAL SCIENCE (biochemistry, biology/biological science, life science, microbiology, molecular biology, and nutrition), BUSINESS (accounting, banking and finance, business administration and management, business communications, business law, business statistics, marketing/retailing/merchandising, nonprofit/public organization management, purchasing/inventory management, recreation and leisure services, supply chain management, and tourism), COMMUNICATIONS AND THE ARTS (art history, art, ceramic art and design, communications, dance, design, dramatic arts, English, film arts, fine arts, French, German, graphic design, industrial design, Italian, journalism, literature, multimedia, music, music performance, music theory and composition, performing arts, Russian, Spanish, technical and business writing, theater design, and visual and performing arts), COMPUTER AND PHYSICAL SCIENCE (applied mathematics, applied science, chemistry, computer mathematics, computer programming, computer science, digital arts/technology, earth science, geology, information sciences and systems, mathematics, physics, science technology, software engineering, statistics, and systems analysis), EDUCATION (early childhood education, education, elementary education, foreign languages education, music education, secondary education, and special education), ENGINEERING AND ENVIRONMENTAL DESIGN (aeronautical engineering, aeronautical technology, air traffic control, architecture, biomedical engineering, chemical engineering, city/community/regional planning, civil engineering, computer engineering, computer graphics, construction engineering, construction management, electrical/electronics engineering, electrical/electronics engineering technology, engineering, engineering and applied science, engineering management, environmental engineering, graphic arts technology, industrial engineering, industrial engineering technology, interior design, landscape architecture/design, manufacturing technology, materials science, mechanical engineering, and mechanical engineering technology), HEALTH PROFESSIONS (exercise science, health, health science, music therapy, nursing, preventive/wellness health care, and speech pathology/audiology), SOCIAL SCIENCE (African American studies, American Indian studies, American studies, anthropology, applied psychology, architectural studies, Asian/American studies, Asian/Oriental studies, counseling/psychology, criminal justice, economics, ethnic studies, family/consumer resource management, food production/management/services, geography, Hispanic American studies, history, human development, interdisciplinary studies, international studies, Judaic studies, Latin American studies, liberal arts/general studies, Mexican-American/Chicano studies, parks and recreation management, philosophy, philosophy and religion, political science/government, psychology, public affairs, public history/archives, religion, science and society, social science, social work, sociology, urban studies, and women's studies). Business, history, psychology, geology, anthropology, music, landscape architecture, accountancy, geography, engineering, nursing, communication and journalism are the strongest academically. Business, engineering, biological sciences, social sciences, communication and psychology have the largest enrollments.

Required: To graduate, students must have a minimum cumulative grade point average of 2.0 (some programs may require a higher GPA) and a minimum total of 120 credit hours, including a minimum of 45 hours in upper-division courses. The number of hours in the major varies by degree program, and some programs may require more upper-division work. All students must satisfy a minimum of 35 credit hours of approved General Studies course work in five core areas and three awareness areas: mathematics studies; literacy and critical inquiry; humanities, fine arts, design, social and behavioral sciences; natural sciences; global awareness; historical awareness, and cultural diversity in the United States.

Special: ASU offers internships in many disciplines, study abroad programs in over 60 countries, work-study programs, accelerated degree programs and a variety of interdisciplinary undergraduate programs. Students may participate in educational programs supported by a variety of centers and institutes, such as the Biodesign Institute, L. William Seidman Research Institute and the Knight Center for Digital Media Entrepreneurship. Also available are continuing education programs and summer math, science, and journalism programs for high school students. Students who attend Barrett, the Honors College, can choose from more than 275 majors and concentrations. Commencing Spring 2012 ASU has Semesters (15-week schedule) and Sessions (7.5 week schedule). There are 29 national honor societies, including Phi Beta Kappa, and a freshman honors program.

Faculty/Classroom: 56% of faculty are male; 44% are female. No introductory courses are taught by graduate students. The average class size in an introductory lecture is 52; in a laboratory is 23; and in a regular course is 35.

Admissions: 88% of the 2013-2014 applicants were accepted. The SAT scores for the 2013-2014 freshman class were: Critical Reading--28% below 500, 42% between 500 and 599, 24% between 600 and 699, and 6% between 700 and 800; Math--23% below 500, 39% between 500 and 599, 30% between 600 and 699, and 8% between 700 and 800. The ACT scores were 18% below 21, 26% between 21 and 23, 27% between 24 and 26, 13% between 27 and 28, and 16% above 28. 51% of the current freshmen were in the top fifth of their class; 78% were in the top two fifths. There were 97 National Merit finalists.

Requirements: The SAT or ACT is recommended. Applicants must successfully complete ASU competency requirement. * English - 4 years (composition/literature based) * Math - 4 years - Algebra I, Geometry, Algebra II and one course requiring Algebra II as a prerequisite. * Laboratory Science - 3 years total (1 year each from any of the following areas are accepted: Biology, Chemistry, Earth Science, Integrated Sciences, and Physics) * Social Science - 2 years (including one year American History) * Foreign Language - 2 years (same language) * Fine Arts - 1 year Applicants must also meet at least one of the following: * Top 25% in high school graduating class * 3.0 GPA in competency courses (4.0 = A) * ACT 22 (24 nonresidents)* * SAT Reasoning 1040 (1110 nonresidents)* All students who don't meet the above standards will be evaluated through a process called Individual Review. Through this process Undergraduate Admissions will review all available information about a student's application, carefully considering all aspects of a student's academic background and accomplishments. Submission of an ACT or SAT test score is highly recommended. In some cases, additional information might be requested. ASU welcomes home school students and recognizes the unique academic experiences they contribute to our rich community of scholars. A GPA of 3.0 is required. AP and CLEP credits are accepted.

Procedure: Freshmen are admitted fall and spring. There is a rolling admissions plan. Applications should be filed by February 1 for fall entry; December 1 for spring entry, along with a $50 fee. Notification is sent on a rolling basis. Applications are accepted online.

Transfer: 6776 transfer students enrolled in 2012-2013. All transfer students must meet ASU's graduation requirement by providing one of the following: official high school transcript with high school graduation date; GED with acceptable score of 500 or above; official college transcript with Associate degree posted (including award date); official college transcript with Associate degree in progress posted (including expected award date). Transfer applicants must meet at least one of the following requirements for admission to ASU. Please note that some ASU colleges and schools have higher requirements for admission to their majors. Arizona transfer students must meet one of the following requirements: Associate degree with a 2.00 cumulative GPA or higher (4.00=A); Arizona General Education Curriculum (AGEC) with a 2.50 cumulative GPA or higher (4.00=A); complete a transfer pathway program through an accredited Arizona community college. Nonresident transfer students must meet one of the following requirements: Associate degree with a 2.50 cumulative GPA or higher (4.00=A); AGEC with a 2.50 cumulative GPA or higher (4.00=A). (For those students transferring from a California community college, ASU accepts the Intersegmental General Education Transfer Curriculum/ California State University General Education [IGETC/CSU GE] patterns). Students with fewer than 24 transferable credit hours must have a minimum 2.50 cumulative GPA and meet freshman aptitude requirements to be considered through individual review. See freshman admission requirements. Some ASU colleges and schools have higher requirements for admission to their majors. See degree search for detailed admission information for your desired program of study. 30 of 120 credits required for the bachelor's degree must be completed at ASU.

Visiting: There are regularly scheduled orientations for prospective students. There are guides for informal visits and visitors may sit in on classes. To schedule a visit, contact the START Desk at (480) 727-7013.

Financial Aid: The FAFSA is required. The priority date for freshman financial aid applications for fall entry is March 1.

International Students: There are 2258 international students enrolled. The school actively recruits these students. They must take the TOEFL with a minimum score of 500 on the paper-based TOEFL (PBT) or 61 on the Internet-based version (iBT), IELTS. SAT or ACT is required for the W.P. Carey school of business.

Computers: All students may access the system. There are no time limits and no fees.

Graduates: From July 1, 2012 to June 30, 2013, 13210 bachelor's degrees were awarded. The most popular majors were business (15%), social sciences (8%), and education (8%). 1628 companies recruited on campus in 2012-2013. In an average class, 1% graduate in 3 years or less, 34% graduate in 4 years or less, 52% graduate in 5 years or less, and 57% graduate in 6 years or less. Of the 2012 graduating class, 15% were enrolled in graduate school within 6 months of graduation, and 80% were employed.

Admissions Contact: David Burge, Executive Director Undergrad Admissions. E-Mail: *admissions@asu.edu* Web: *https:/students.asu.edu/admission*

EMBRY-RIDDLE AERONAUTICAL UNIVERSITY - PRESCOTT CAMPUS C-3

Prescott, AZ 86301 **(928) 777-6600; (800) 888-3728**

Full-time: 1320 men, 367 women	**Faculty:** 98; IIB, av$
Part-time: 99 men, 27 women	**Ph.D.s:** 58%
Graduate: 32 men, 10 women	**Student/Faculty:** 15 to 1
Year: semesters, summer session	**Tuition:** $31,034
Application Deadline: July 1	**Room & Board:** $9550
Freshman Class: 1689 applied, 1334 accepted, 448 enrolled	
SAT CR/M/W: 570/600/530	**ACT:** 26 **VERY COMPETITIVE**

Embry-Riddle Aeronautical University, founded in 1926, is a private institution offering undergraduate programs in aviation, engineering, business, and professional training on 2 campuses: the Prescott campus, founded in 1978, and the Daytona Beach, Florida, campus. Graduate programs are also offered at both campuses. There are 3 undergraduate schools and one graduate school. In addition to regional accreditation, ERAU has baccalaureate program accreditation with ABET and ACBSP. The library contains 31,300 volumes, 105,309 microform items, and 2,164 audio/video tapes/CDs/DVDs, and subscribes to 197 periodicals including electronic. Computerized library services include interlibrary loans, database searching, Internet access, and Wi-Fi capability. Special learning facilities include a radio station, 4 wind tunnels, an aviation safety center, and an aircraft structures lab. The Flight Training Center at Ernest A. Love Field offers a simulator lab and flight operations center. The 539-acre campus is in a rural area 100 miles north of Phoenix. Including any residence halls, there are 28 buildings.

Student Life: 76% of undergraduates are from out of state, mostly the Southwest. Students are from 48 states, and 30 foreign countries. 60% are White. The average age of freshmen is 18; all undergraduates, 21. 21% do not continue beyond their first year; 59% remain to graduate.

Housing: 849 students can be accommodated in college housing, which includes coed dorms and on-campus apartments. On-campus housing is guaranteed for the freshman year only, is available on a first-come, and first-served basis. 50% of students commute. Alcohol is not permitted. All students may keep cars.

Activities: 9% of men belong to 5 national fraternities; 13% of women belong to 2 national sororities. There are 85 groups on campus, including chess, dance, debate, drill team, environmental, ethnic, gay, honors, international, jazz band, literary magazine, newspaper, political, professional, radio and TV, religious, social, social service, and student government. Popular campus events include Hypnotist, Casino Night, and Octoberwest.

Sports: There are 4 intercollegiate sports for men and 5 for women, and 16 intramural sports for men and 15 for women. Facilities include An activity center with 3 basketball courts and 3 volleyball courts, a gym/weight room, a multipurpose athletic playing field, a game room, a swimming pool complex, and a fitness facility.

Disabled Students: 95% of the campus is accessible. Facilities include wheelchair ramps, special parking, specially equipped restrooms, special class scheduling, lowered drinking fountains, lowered telephones, special housing. pneumatic doors.

Services: Counseling and information services are available, as is tutoring in most subjects. There is remedial math, reading, and writing.

Campus Safety and Security: Measures include 24-hour foot and vehicle patrol, emergency notification system, self-defense education, and security escort services. There are shuttle buses, emergency telephones, and lighted pathways/sidewalks.

Programs of Study: ERAU confers B.S. degrees. Master's degrees are also awarded. Bachelor's degrees are awarded in BIOLOGICAL SCIENCE (forensic science), COMMUNICATIONS AND THE ARTS (communications), COMPUTER AND PHYSICAL SCIENCE (astronomy, atmospheric sciences and meteorology, and software engineering), ENGINEERING AND ENVIRONMENTAL DESIGN (aeronautical science, aerospace studies, aviation administration/management, aviation maintenance management, computer engineering, electrical/electronics engineering, and mechanical engineering), SOCIAL SCIENCE (interdisciplinary studies and safety science). Aerospace engineering is the strongest academically. Aeronautical science has the largest enrollment.

Required: All students must complete 36 credits of general education requirements, including courses in communication skills, technical report writing, humanities/social sciences, math, physical science, economics, and computer science. A total of 120 to 136 credit hours with a minimum GPA of 2.0 is required to graduate.

Special: Cooperative and work-study programs, nondegree study, internships in all majors, and study abroad in 21 countries are offered. Flight training may be taken in conjunction with aeronautical science and other degree programs. Credit is given for life and military experience. There are 1 national honor societies and a freshman honors program.

Faculty/Classroom: 75% of faculty are male; 25% are female. All teach undergraduates. No introductory courses are taught by graduate students. The average class size in an introductory lecture is 23; in a laboratory is 16; and in a regular course is 23.

Admissions: 79% of the 2013-2014 applicants were accepted. The SAT scores for the 2013-2014 freshman class were: Critical Reading--19% below 500, 42% between 500 and 599, 31% between 600 and 699, and 8% between 700 and 800; Math--13% below 500, 35% between 500 and 599, 43% between 600 and 699, and 9% between 700 and 800; Writing--29% below 500, 44% between 500 and 599, 25% between 600 and 699, and 2% between 700 and 800. The ACT scores were 6% below 21, 19% between 21 and 23, 27% between 24 and 26, 16% between 27 and 28, and 32% above 28. 50% of the current freshmen were in the top fifth of their class; 78% were in the top two fifths.

Requirements: The SAT or ACT is recommended. AP and CLEP credits are accepted.

Procedure: Freshmen are admitted fall, spring, and summer. Entrance exams should be taken during the fall of the senior year. There are deferred admissions and rolling admissions plans. Early decision applications should be filed by December 1; regular applications, by July 1 for fall entry; November 1 for spring entry; and April 1 for summer entry, along with a $50 fee. Notification is sent on a Rolling basis. Applications are accepted online.

Transfer: 109 transfer students enrolled in 2012-2013. A G.P.A. of 2.5 is preferred. 30 of 120 credits required for the bachelor's degree must be completed at Embry-Riddle Aeronautical University.

Visiting: There are regularly scheduled orientations for prospective students. There are guides for informal visits. To schedule a visit, contact the Admissions Office.

Financial Aid: In 2013-2014, 95% of all full-time freshmen and 87% of

continuing full-time students received some form of financial aid. 86% of all full-time freshmen and 81% of continuing full-time students received need-based aid. The average freshman award was $17,904. Need-based scholarships or need-based grants averaged $12,046; need-based self-help aid (loans and jobs) averaged $4,810; and non-need-based athletic scholarships averaged $9,124. 33% of undergraduate students work part-time. Average annual earnings from campus work are $2106. The FAFSA is required. The priority date for freshman financial aid applications for fall entry is March 1.

International Students: There are 148 international students enrolled. The school actively recruits these students. They must take the TOEFL with a minimum score of 550 on the paper-based TOEFL (PBT) or 79 on the Internet-based version (iBT). They must also take the SAT or ACT.

Computers: All students may access the system at any time. There are no time limits and no fees.

Graduates: The most popular majors were aeronautical science, aerospace engineering, and aeronautics.

Admissions Contact: Bryan Dougherty, Dean, Enrollment Management. E-Mail: *pradmit@erau.edu* Web: *www.erau.edu*

GRAND CANYON UNIVERSITY C-4

Phoenix, AZ 85017

Full-time: 1767 men, 3568 women	**Faculty:** 223
Part-time: 4997 men, 17348 women	**Ph.D.s:** 19%
Graduate: 3052 men, 10025 women	**Student/Faculty:** 25 to 1
Year: semesters, summer session	**Tuition:** $16,640
Application Deadline: open	**Room & Board:** $7900
Freshman Class: n/av	
SAT or ACT: recommended	**VERY COMPETITIVE**

Grand Canyon University, founded in 1949, is a small, private, publically traded nonsectarian liberal arts institution. There are 5 undergraduate schools and 5 graduate schools. In addition to regional accreditation, GCU has baccalaureate program accreditation with ACBSP. The library contains 140,456 volumes, 53,459 microform items, and 527 audio/video tapes/CDs/DVDs, and subscribes to 9,502 periodicals including electronic. Computerized library services include interlibrary loans, database searching, Internet access, and Wi-Fi capability. Special learning facilities include an art gallery. The 100-acre campus is in a suburban area in Phoenix. Including any residence halls, there are 50 buildings.

Student Life: 73% of undergraduates are from out of state, mostly the Southwest. Students are from 50 states, 12 foreign countries, and Canada. 41% are White; 25% African American. 98% claim no religious affiliation. The average age of freshmen is 18; all undergraduates, 33.

Housing: 1600 students can be accommodated in college housing, which includes single-sex dorms, on-campus apartments, and married student housing. On-campus housing is available on a first-come and first-served basis. 52% of students commute. Alcohol is not permitted. All students may keep cars.

Activities: There are no fraternities or sororities. There are 12 groups on campus, including art, band, cheerleading, choir, chorale, chorus, dance, drama, ethnic, film, honors, international, literary magazine, musical theater, newspaper, pep band, photography, political, professional, religious, social, social service, and student government. Popular campus events include Spiritual Emphasis Week, Harvest Festival and Spring Formal.

Sports: There are 10 intercollegiate sports for men and 11 for women, and 6 intramural sports for men and 6 for women. Facilities include 5,000 seat arena, Intramural Fields, a 1500-seat baseball stadium, a 1550-seat gymnasium, athlete performance center, a 300-seat soccer/track & field venue, a 150-seat softball venue, 55,000 square foot student recreation center (includes recreational basketball courts-2; student fitness center, aerobics/dance room, cardio/weight facilities, locker facilities, wrestling and basketball intercollegiate training areas).

Disabled Students: 99% of the campus is accessible. Facilities include wheelchair ramps, elevators, special parking, specially equipped restrooms, lowered drinking fountains, and special housing.

Services: Counseling and information services are available, as is tutoring in every subject. There is remedial math, reading, and writing. Tutors are also trained in test-taking techniques, study skills, and time management.

Campus Safety and Security: Measures include 24-hour foot and vehicle patrol, emergency notification system, self-defense education, and security escort services. There are emergency telephones, lighted pathways/sidewalks, and controlled access to dorms/residences.

Programs of Study: GCU confers B.A., B.S. and B.S.N. degrees. Master's and doctoral degrees are also awarded. Bachelor's degrees are awarded in BIOLOGICAL SCIENCE (biology/biological science), BUSINESS (accounting, business administration and management, entrepreneurial studies, management science, marketing/retailing/merchandising, and sports management), COMMUNICATIONS AND THE ARTS (communications, communications technology, English, music, music performance, theatre arts, theater design, and theater management), COMPUTER AND PHYSICAL SCIENCE (digital arts/technology), EDUCATION (athletic training, dance education, education, elementary education, music education, physical education, and secondary education), HEALTH PROFESSIONS (exercise science, health science, and nursing), SOCIAL SCIENCE (addiction studies, Christian studies, forensic studies, history, interdisciplinary studies, international studies, physical fitness/movement, psychology, and sociology). Education, business, and nursing are the strongest academically, and have the largest enrollments.

Required: All students are required to complete 40 hours of general studies, including 12 hours each in Effective Communication and Critical Thinking, 8 hours in Global Awareness, and 4 hours each in University Foundation and Christian Worldview. A total of 120 semester hours, with a minimum GPA of 2.0, are required to graduate.

Special: Internships are ofered for most majors through organizatons, corporations, and agencies in the Phoenix area. Study abroad in 5 countries and a Washington semester are possible. There are 3 national honor societies and a freshman honors program.

Faculty/Classroom: 85% teach undergraduates. No introductory courses are taught by graduate students. The average class size in an introductory lecture is 18; in a laboratory is 14; and in a regular course is 18.

Requirements: The SAT or ACT is recommended. Applicants need to be graduates of an accredited high school or have a GED. A GPA of 3.0 is required. AP and CLEP credits are accepted. Important factors in the admissions decision are evidence of special talent, extracurricular activities record, and leadership record.

Procedure: Freshmen are admitted to all sessions. Entrance exams should be taken during the junior or senior year of high school. There are early decision and rolling admissions plans. Application deadlines are open. Applications are accepted online.

Transfer: 30 of 120 credits required for the bachelor's degree must be completed at GCU.

Visiting: There are regularly scheduled orientations for prospective students, including student orientation and registration in the summer. There are guides for informal visits, visitors may sit in on classes, and stay overnight. To schedule a visit, contact the Admission Office at (800) 800-9776.

Financial Aid: 14% of undergraduate students work part-time. Average annual earnings from campus work are $4800. Check with the school for current application deadlines.

International Students: There are 102 international students enrolled. The school actively recruits these students. They must take the TOEFL with a minimum score of 500 on the paper-based TOEFL (PBT) or 61 on the Internet-based version (iBT) and the college's own test.

Computers: All students may access the system. There are no time limits and no fees.

Graduates: From July 1, 2012 to June 30, 2013, 2279 bachelor's degrees were awarded. The most popular majors were nusing (17%), curriculum and instruction (5%), and special education (4%). 100 companies recruited on campus in 2012-2013.

Admissions Contact: E-Mail: *admissiononline@gcu.edu* Web: *www.gcu.edu*

NORTHERN ARIZONA UNIVERSITY C-2

Flagstaff, AZ 86011 **(928) 523-1428; (888) 628-2968**

Full-time: 8057 men, 10712 women	**Faculty:** n/av; I, --$	
Part-time: 1439 men, 2462 women	**Ph.D.s:** n/av	
Graduate: 1306 men, 2630 women	**Student/Faculty:** n/av	
Year: semesters, summer session	**Tuition:** $9738 ($22,093)	
Application Deadline:	**Room & Board:** $8854	
Freshman Class: 33989 applied, 31059 accepted, 4772 enrolled		
SAT CR/M/W: 520/520/200	**ACT:** 23	**COMPETITIVE**

Northern Arizona University, founded in 1899, is a comprehensive public university in the heart of the southern Colorado Plateau. At Northern Arizona University, we fully prepare students for meaningful life and work through our commitment to learning and teaching in an unparalleled environment. Through our main campus in Flagstaff and our distance-education opportunities throughout Arizona and online, we offer excellence in teaching, research, and public service to the citizens of Arizona and beyond. Northern Arizona University is a doctoral-intensive institution with undergraduate education at our core and significant research opportunities as well as select master's and doctoral programs. We offer undergraduate and graduate degrees in a full range of disciplines from liberal arts and sciences to professional and career-related fields. Our commitment to high-quality education at all levels is exemplified by small class size and close interaction between students and faculty. There are 8 undergraduate schools and one graduate school. In addition to regional accreditation, NAU has baccalaureate program accreditation with AACSB, ABET, ACBSP, ACCE, ADA, CSWE, NASM, NCATE, NRPA, and SAF. The library contains 786,389 volumes, and subscribes to 63,429 periodicals including electronic. Computerized library services include interlibrary loans, database searching, Internet access, and Wi-Fi capability. Special learning facilities include an art gallery, radio station, TV station, an observatory, research centers, and the Centennial Forest. The 740-acre campus is in a rural area 140 miles north of Flagstaff and 80 miles from the Grand Canyon's South Rim. Including any residence halls, there are 109 buildings.

Student Life: 71% of undergraduates are from Arizona. Others are from 50 states, 65 foreign countries, and Canada. 64% are White; 18% Hispanic. The average age of freshmen is 18; all undergraduates, 23. 28% do not continue beyond their first year; 72% remain to graduate.

Housing: 7500 students can be accommodated in college housing, which includes single-sex and coed dorms, on-campus apartments, and married student housing. In addition, there are honors houses, fraternity houses, and sorority houses. On-campus housing is guaranteed for the freshman year only, is available on a first-come, and first-served basis. 68% of students commute. All students may keep cars.

Activities: There are 337 groups on campus, including art, band, cheerleading, chess, choir, chorale, chorus, computers, dance, debate, drama, environmental, ethnic, film, forensics, gay, honors, international, jazz band, literary magazine, marching band, musical theater, newspaper, opera, orchestra, pep band, photography, political, professional, radio and TV, religious, social, social service, student government, and symphony. Popular campus events include Welcome Week, Family Weekend and Homecoming.

Sports: There are 6 intercollegiate sports for men and 9 for women, and 11 intramural sports for men and 9 for women. Facilities include Facilities include the Skydome for football, basketball, and indoor track and field; three recreation centers with basketball and racquetball courts and weight rooms, a 50-meter indoor swimming pool with diving facilities, and numerous outdoor grass fields for soccer, rugby, and lacrosse. The Health and Learning Center. The 272,000 square foot HLC engages students in holistic learning by integrating recreation, health services, athletics, and academics into one central location.

Disabled Students: 90% of the campus is accessible. Facilities include wheelchair ramps, elevators, special parking, specially equipped restrooms, special class scheduling, lowered drinking fountains, lowered telephones, and special housing.

Services: Counseling and information services are available, as is tutoring in most subjects. There is a reader service for the blind, and remedial math, reading, and writing.

Campus Safety and Security: Measures include 24-hour foot and vehicle patrol, emergency notification system, self-defense education, and security escort services. There are shuttle buses, emergency telephones, lighted pathways/sidewalks, and controlled access to dorms/residences.

Programs of Study: NAU confers B.A., B.A.S., B.B.A., B.F.A., B.M.Ed., B.Mus., B.P.S., B.S., B.S.Accy., B.S.B.A., B.S.C.S., B.S.D.H., B.S.E., B.S.Ed., B.S.F., B.S.Jour., B.S.N., B.S.S., B.S.W. and B.U.S. degrees. Master's and doctoral degrees are also awarded. Bachelor's degrees are awarded in AGRICULTURE (environmental studies and forestry and related sciences), BIOLOGICAL SCIENCE (biology/biological science and microbiology), BUSINESS (accounting, business administration and management, business economics, finance, hotel/motel and restaurant management, management science, marketing management, and small business management), COMMUNICATIONS AND THE ARTS (communications, English, film, television and digital media, journalism, modern language, music, music performance, photography, Spanish, studio art, and theatre arts), COMPUTER AND PHYSICAL SCIENCE (applied science, astronomy, chemistry, computer information technology, computer science, geology, mathematics, and physics), EDUCATION (early childhood education, elementary education, music education, secondary education, and special education), ENGINEERING AND ENVIRONMENTAL DESIGN (civil engineering, construction management, electrical and computer engineering, environmental engineering, environmental science, interior design, and mechanical engineering), HEALTH PROFESSIONS (biomedical science, dental hygiene, exercise science, health science, and nursing), SOCIAL SCIENCE (anthropology, criminal justice, criminology, crosscultural studies, geography, history, interdisciplinary studies, international relations, liberal arts/general studies, Native American studies, parks and recreation management, philosophy, political science/government, psychology, public administration, social work, sociology, and women and gender studies). Biology, elementary education, and nursing have the largest enrollments.

Required: To receive a bachelor's degree at Northern Arizona University, you must complete at least 120 units of credit. Within those total units, you must complete: all of Northern Arizona University's liberal studies requirements; all requirements for your specific academic plan(s); at least 30 units of upper-division courses, which may include transfer work; at least 30 units taken through Northern Arizona University, of which at least 18 must be upper-division courses (300 level or above); and a cumulative grade point average of at least 2.0 on all work attempted at Northern Arizona University.

Special: NAU offers co-op programs in business and hotel/restaurant management, cross-registration with many universities through the National Student Exchange, and internships in most majors. Legislative internships are offered through the Arizona State Senate and House of Representatives. Students may study abroad in over 50 countries. Work-study programs are available in numerous fields, including engineering, business, and park services. NAU now also offers a Personalized Learning program. There are a freshman honors program.

Faculty/Classroom: No introductory courses are taught by graduate students.

Admissions: 91% of the 2013-2014 applicants were accepted. The SAT scores for the 2013-2014 freshman class were: Critical Reading--37% below 500, 44% between 500 and 599, 17% between 600 and 699, and 2% between 700 and 800; Math--36% below 500, 44% between 500 and 599, 18% between 600 and 699, and 2% between 700 and 800; Writing--46% below 500, 40% between 500 and 599, 13% between 600 and 699, and 1% between 700 and 800. The ACT scores were 29% below 21, 30% between 21 and 23, 23% between 24 and 26, 10% between 27 and 28, and 7% above 28.

Requirements: The SAT or ACT is recommended. Students will be offered admission if they meet the following: 3.0 or higher core GPA*, or top 50 percent class rank and have no deficiencies in the required college preparatory courses. Home school students must meet aptitude requirements through ACT or SATI composite test scores. ACT score of 22 (Arizona resident) or 24 (non-resident) or SATI score of 1040 (Arizona resident) or 1110 (non-resident). *GPA is calculated using only the 16 core courses listed under course requirements. NAU requires applicants to be in the upper 50% of their class. A GPA of 3.0 is required. AP and CLEP credits are accepted.

Procedure: Freshmen are admitted fall, spring, and summer. Entrance exams should be taken Before the last semester of the senior year. There are deferred admissions and rolling admissions plans. Application deadlines are open. Application fee is $25. Applications are accepted online.

Transfer: 2482 transfer students enrolled in 2012-2013. Transfer students will be offered admission if they have earned more than 12 college credits and the Arizona General Education Curriculum (AGEC) or the California inter-segmental General Education Transfer Curriculum (IEGTC) with a cumulative GPA of 2.0; or earn an associate's degree with a cumulative GPA of 2.0. Transfer students must be eligible to re-enter the institution they last attended. 30 of 120 credits required for the bachelor's degree must be completed at NAU.

Visiting: There are regularly scheduled orientations for prospective students. There are guides for informal visits and visitors may sit in on classes. To schedule a visit, contact Office of Undergraduate Admissions and Orientation at (928) 523-0922.

Financial Aid: The FAFSA is required. The priority date for freshman financial aid applications for fall entry is February 14.

International Students: There are 776 international students enrolled. The school actively recruits these students. They must take the TOEFL with a minimum score of 525 on the paper-based TOEFL (PBT) or 70 on the Internet-based version (iBT).

Computers: All students may access the system. There are no time limits and no fees.

Graduates: From July 1, 2012 to June 30, 2013, 4450 bachelor's degrees were awarded. The most popular majors were elementary education (7%), psychology (5%), and nursing (5%). 200 companies recruited on campus in 2012-2013. In an average class, 2% graduate in 3 years or less, 33% graduate in 4 years or less, 48% graduate in 5 years or less, and 49% graduate in 6 years or less.

Admissions Contact: Anika Olsen, Director of Admissions. E-Mail: *Anika.Olsen@nau.edu* Web: *nau.edu*

PRESCOTT COLLEGE C-3

Prescott, AZ 86301 (928) 350-2100
(800) 628-6364; (928) 776-5242

Full-time: 204 men, 240 women — **Faculty:** 60
Part-time: 40 men, 61 women — **Ph.D.s:** 58%
Graduate: 90 men, 308 women — **Student/Faculty:** 9 to 1
Year: semesters, summer session — **Tuition:** $26,819
Application Deadline: August 15 — **Room & Board:** $6465
Freshman Class: 399 applied, 291 accepted, 49 enrolled
SAT CR/M/W: 565/520/534 — **ACT:** 23 — **COMPETITIVE+**

Prescott College, founded in 1966, is a private liberal arts institution offering a nontraditional undergraduate program complemented with experiential learning focused on sustainability, the environment, and social justice. The curriculum is organized into multidisciplinary courses that allow students to pursue individual areas of competency. Evaluations of a student's work are conducted through a portfolio/contract system and an ongoing series of student self-evaluations. Grades are optional. There are 2 undergraduate schools and 2 graduate schools. In addition to regional accreditation, Prescott has baccalaureate program accreditation with NASDTEC. The library contains 131,524 volumes, 155 microform items, and 1,732 audio/video tapes/CDs/DVDs, and subscribes to 31,330 periodicals including electronic. Computerized library services include interlibrary loans, database searching, Internet access, and Wi-Fi capability. Special learning facilities include an art gallery, a library annexes at Kino Bay, Mexico and Tucson Center; an experimental agroecology farm, a field station in Kino Bay, Mexico, a GIS station, state of the art visual arts classrooms and a functioning gallery, equipment gear warehouse, and a recycling center. In the library, access to 96,521 electronic books and a learning commons for writing and math help. The 13-acre campus is in a small town 100 miles northwest of Phoenix. Including any residence halls, there are 29 buildings.

Student Life: 75% of undergraduates are from out of state, mostly the West. Students are from 42 states, 6 foreign countries, and Canada. 73% are White; 12% race unknown. The average age of freshmen is 19; all undergraduates, 23. 27% do not continue beyond their first year; 37% remain to graduate.

Housing: 120 students can be accommodated in college housing, which includes coed dorms. On-campus houses, coed dorms, and coed housing. On-campus housing is guaranteed for the freshman year only, is available on a first-come, and first-served basis. 80% of students commute. Alcohol is not permitted. All students may keep cars.

Activities: There are no fraternities or sororities. There are 12 groups on campus, including and bicycle, agriculture, art, dance, drama, environmental, film, gay, international, literary magazine, newspaper, photography, political, social, social service, and student government. Popular campus events include Earth Day, and Southwest Writers Series.

Sports: There is no sports program or facilities at Prescott. Students have access to the local community pool, a weight room, gym, and city league sports.

Disabled Students: 90% of the campus is accessible. Facilities include wheelchair ramps, elevators, special parking, specially equipped restrooms, and special housing.

Services: Counseling and information services are available, as is tutoring in every subject. There is a learning specialist on staff, and untimed tests are available. There are recordings for the blind and dyslexic.

Campus Safety and Security: Measures include emergency notification system and security escort services. There are emergency telephones, controlled access to dorms/residences, after hours patrol.

Programs of Study: Prescott confers B.A., B.S. and B.F.A degrees. Master's and doctoral degrees are also awarded. Bachelor's degrees are awarded in AGRICULTURE (agriculture, environmental studies, forestry and related sciences, and wildlife management), BIOLOGICAL SCIENCE (biology/biological science, ecology, environmental biology, marine biology, marine science, and wildlife biology), BUSINESS (management science, nonprofit/public organization management, and organizational leadership and management), COMMUNICATIONS AND THE ARTS (art, arts administration/management, communications, creative writing, dance, dramatic arts, English, fine arts, journalism, literature, music, performing arts, photography, Spanish, studio art, and visual and performing arts), COMPUTER AND PHYSICAL SCIENCE (earth science, environmental geology, geology, mathematics, natural sciences, and oceanography), EDUCATION (agricultural education, art education, early childhood education, education, education of the emotionally handicapped, education of the exceptional child, education of the mentally handicapped, elementary education, environmental education, foreign languages education, guidance education, middle school education, music education, physical education, recreation education, secondary education, social science education, social studies education, and special education), ENGINEERING AND ENVIRONMENTAL DESIGN (environmental design, environmental science, and land use management and reclamation), HEALTH PROFESSIONS (art therapy, community health work, and mental health/human services), SOCIAL SCIENCE (addiction studies, anthropology, archeology, area studies, community services, counseling/psychology, economics, ethics, politics, and social policy, experimental psychology, gender studies, geography, history, human development, human ecology, human services, humanities, humanities and social science, international relations, international studies, Latin American studies, liberal arts/general studies, parks and recreation management, peace studies, philosophy and religion, psychology, religion, social science, social work, sociology, water resources, and women's studies). Environmental studies, and adventure education are the strongest academically. Environmental studies has the largest enrollment.

Required: Students must complete an orientation course, fulfill a minimum residency requirement, demonstrate proficiency in college-level writing and math, and meet course and credit requirements. Students design an individual program of studies within 7 multidisciplinary areas: adventure education, arts and letters, cultural and regional studies, education, environmental studies, humanities, and human development. Each student is required to submit a graduation proposal at the end of the junior year to a graduation review committee.

Special: Cross-registration with Eco-League colleges and the Consortium for Innovative Environments in Learning is possible. Student-coordinated internships, study abroad in almost any country, dual majors, a general studies degree, pass/fail options, and credit for life experience are offered. All majors are student-designed.

Faculty/Classroom: 44% of faculty are male; 56% are female. 82% teach undergraduates. No introductory courses are taught by graduate students. The average class size in an introductory lecture is 12; in a laboratory is 12; and in a regular course is 12.

Admissions: 73% of the 2013-2014 applicants were accepted. The SAT scores for the 2013-2014 freshman class were: Critical Reading--29% below 500, 41% between 500 and 599, 18% between 600 and 699, and 12% between 700 and 800; Math--44% below 500, 26% between 500 and 599, 24% between 600 and 699, and 6% between 700 and 800; Writing--33% below 500, 50% between 500 and 599, 11% between 600 and 699, and 6% between 700 and 800. The ACT scores were 8% below 21, 42% between 21 and 23, 33% between 27 and 28, and 17% above 28.

Requirements: The SAT is required. The ACT is recommended. In addition, a high school diploma is required, the GED is accepted. The school requires a completed application form, 1 essay, official transcripts, and 1 letter of recommendation. Students may also submit portfolios and writing samples. A GPA of 2.0 is required. AP and CLEP credits are accepted. Important factors in the admissions decision are extracurricular activities record, leadership record, and evidence of special talent.

Procedure: Freshmen are admitted fall and spring. There are early decision, deferred admissions, and rolling admissions plans. Early decision applications should be filed by December 1; regular applications, by August 15 for fall entry; and December 15 for spring entry. Notification of early decision is sent December 15; regular decision, on a rolling basis. 11 early decision candidates were accepted for the 2013-2014 class. Applications are accepted online.

Transfer: 119 transfer students enrolled in 2012-2013. Transfer applicants must meet the same requirements as entering freshmen and must also submit official college transcripts and an essay or personal statement. Students who successfully completed 2 years of college work (60 semester hours or 90 quarter credits) need not submit high school transcripts. There is a 2-year residency requirement. 60 of 120 credits required for the bachelor's degree must be completed at Prescott.

Visiting: There are regularly scheduled orientations for prospective students, including a campus tour, an interview with an admissions counselor, opportunities to sit in classes, faculty interviews, and informational meetings with financial aid and library staff. There are guides for informal visits and visitors may sit in on classes. To schedule a visit, contact the Admissions Office at admissions@prescott.edu.

Financial Aid: In 2013-2014, 78% of all full-time freshmen and 70% of continuing full-time students received some form of financial aid. 77% of all full-time freshmen and 69% of continuing full-time students received need-based aid. The average freshman award was $19,706. Need-based scholarships or need-based grants averaged $14,569; need-based self-help aid (loans and jobs) averaged $5,493; other non-need-based awards and non-need-based scholarships averaged $8,642; and $4,821 from other forms of aid. 31% of undergraduate students work part-time. Average annual earnings from campus work are $800. The average financial indebtedness of the 2013 graduate was $27,213. The FAFSA is required. The priority date for freshman financial aid applications for fall entry is March 1.

International Students: There are 8 international students enrolled. They must take the TOEFL with a minimum score of 500 on the paper-based TOEFL (PBT) or 61 on the Internet-based version (iBT).

Computers: All students may access the system. 24 hours a day, 7 days a week. There are no time limits and no fees.

Graduates: From July 1, 2012 to June 30, 2013, 196 bachelor's degrees were awarded. The most popular majors were human development (23%), environmental studies/natural resources (22%), and education (16%). In an average class, 23% graduate in 4 years or less, 34% graduate in 5 years or less, and 37% graduate in 6 years or less.

Admissions Contact: Nancy Simmons, Receptionist. E-Mail: *admissions@prescott.edu* Web: *www.prescott.edu*

UNIVERSITY OF ARIZONA D-4

Tucson, AZ 85721 **(520) 621-3705**

Full-time: 13623 men, 15212 women	**Faculty:** 1469; I, -$
Part-time: 1488 men, 1347 women	**Ph.D.s:** 92%
Graduate: 4409 men, 4542 women	**Student/Faculty:** 23 to 1
Year: semesters, summer session	**Tuition:** $10,391 ($27,073)
Application Deadline:	**Room & Board:** $9714
Freshman Class: n/av	
SAT or ACT: recommended	

COMPETITIVE

The University of Arizona, founded in 1885, is a public land-grant institution controlled by the state of Arizona. Undergraduate programs are offered in agriculture, architecture, arts and sciences, business and public administration, education, engineering and mines, nursing, pharmacy, and other health-related professions. There are 41 undergraduate schools and one graduate school. In addition to regional accreditation, UA has baccalaureate program accreditation with ACPE, ADA, NASAD, and NASM. The 7 libraries contain 6.6 million volumes, 5.8 million microform items, and 648,621 audio/video tapes/CDs/DVDs, and subscribe to 104,646 periodicals including electronic. Computerized library services include interlibrary loans, database searching, Internet access, and Wi-Fi capability. Special learning facilities include an art gallery, natural history museum, planetarium, radio station, TV station, the Ansel Adams Center for Creative Photography, and the Integrated Learning Center. The 392-acre campus is in an urban area in Tucson. Including any residence halls, there are 103 buildings.

Student Life: 68% of undergraduates are from Arizona. Others are from 50 states, 108 foreign countries, and Canada. 54% are White; 21% Hispanic. The average age of freshmen is 18; all undergraduates, 21.

Housing: 7216 students can be accommodated in college housing, which includes single-sex and coed dorms, on-campus apartments, and off-campus apartments. In addition, there are honors houses, special-interest houses, fraternity houses, and sorority houses. On-campus housing is available on a first-come and first-served basis. 80% of students commute. Alcohol is not permitted. All students may keep cars.

Activities: There are 672 groups on campus, including art, band, cheerleading, chess, choir, chorale, chorus, computers, dance, debate, drama, drill team, environmental, ethnic, film, gay, honors, international, jazz band, literary magazine, marching band, musical theater, newspaper, orchestra, pep band, photography, political, professional, radio and TV, religious, social, student government, and yearbook. Popular campus events include Spring Fling Carnival, Cultural Programs and Family Weekend.

Sports: There are 7 intercollegiate sports for men and 10 for women. Facilities include an athletic center, stadium, arena, and a student recreation facility with a weight room, a wave-less swimming pool, two gyms, aerobics facilities, treadmills, stair climbers, stationary bicycles, racquetball, squash, and handball courts. Hiking, backpacking, and skiing trails as well as facilities for kayaking, caving, and scuba diving are available.

Disabled Students: 85% of the campus is accessible. Facilities include wheelchair ramps, elevators, special parking, specially equipped restrooms, lowered drinking fountains, lowered telephones, special housing. physical therapy, counseling, interpreters, equipment maintenance and an adaptive athletics program.

Services: Counseling and information services are available, as is tutoring in most subjects. There is a reader service for the blind, and remedial math, reading, and writing.

Campus Safety and Security: Measures include 24-hour foot and vehicle patrol, emergency notification system, self-defense education, and security escort services. There are shuttle buses, emergency telephones, lighted pathways/sidewalks, and controlled access to dorms/residences.

Programs of Study: UA confers B.A., B.A.E., B.Arch., B.A.S., B.E.S., B.F.A., B.G.S., B.Mu., B.S., B.S.Ae.E, B.S.B.A., B.S.Bm.E., B.S.Bs.E., B.S.Ch.E., B.S.Cv.E., B.S.E., B.S.E.C.E., B.S.E.Mg., B.S.H.S., B.S.In.E., B.S.Me.E., B.S.Mn.E., B.S.M.S.E., B.S.N., B.S.O.S.E., B.S.S.B.E., B.S.S.Ed. and B.S.Sy.E. degrees. Master's and doctoral degrees are also awarded. Bachelor's degrees are awarded in AGRICULTURE (agricultural business management, agricultural economics, animal science, environmental studies, natural resource management, plant science, and soil science), BIOLOGICAL SCIENCE (biochemistry, biology/biological science, biometrics and biostatistics, cell biology, ecology, entomology, genetics, microbiology, molecular biology, neurosciences, nutrition, physiology, and plant pathology), BUSINESS (accounting, business administration and management, business economics, entrepreneurial studies, finance, management information systems, management science, marketing and distribution, operations management, and retailing), COMMUNICATIONS AND THE ARTS (art history, art, classics, communications, creative writing, dance, English, English as a second/foreign language, film arts, fine arts, French, Italian, journalism, linguistics, music, musical theater, performing arts, Russian, Spanish, studio art, and theatre arts), COMPUTER AND PHYSICAL SCIENCE (applied mathematics, applied science, astronomy, atmospheric sciences and meteorology, chemistry, computer science, geology, geoscience, hydrology, information sciences and systems, mathematics, medical physics, natural sciences, optics, physics, planetary and space science, and statistics), EDUCATION (agricultural education, art education, early childhood education, education, elementary education, library science, middle school education, music education, psychology education, school psychology, science education, secondary education, special education, and teaching English as a second/foreign language (TESOL/TEFOL)), ENGINEERING AND ENVIRONMENTAL DESIGN (aeronautical engineering, agricultural engineering, architecture, biomedical engineering, chemical engineering, civil engineering, electrical/electronics engineering, engineering, environmental engineering, environmental science, industrial engineering, landscape architecture/design, materials engineering, materials science, mechanical engineering, mining and mineral engineering, optical engineering, and systems engineering), HEALTH PROFESSIONS (environmental health science, medical science, nursing, pharmaceutical science, pharmacology, pharmacy, Pre Health Studies, public health, rehabilitation therapy, speech pathology/audiology, and veterinary science), SOCIAL SCIENCE (African studies, American Indian studies, anthropology, counseling/psychology, East Asian studies, economics, family/consumer studies, gender studies, geography, German area studies, history, human development, interdisciplinary studies, Judaic studies, Latin American studies, law, Mexican-American/Chicano studies, Middle Eastern studies, philosophy, political science/government, psychology, public administration, religious education, sociology, and women's studies). Sciences, social sciences and business administration are the strongest academically. Business and sciences have the largest enrollments.

Required: All students must complete a core curriculum of courses in natural sciences, traditions and cultures, individuals and societies, math, English, art, and a foreign language. A total of 120 credits, with a minimum GPA of 2.0, is required to graduate.

Special: Co-op programs are available in almost all majors. Internships in almost all disciplines. Washington semester for certain internships related to government. Accelerated Masters programs-MBA, MIS, and Entrepreneurship programs. 119 B.A.-B.S. degrees, dual majors, interdisciplinary degrees such as engineering-math and theater arts-education, a 3-2 arts and sciences-business degree, and student designed majors are offered. Study abroad in numerous countries, work-study programs on campus, a general studies degree, and pass/fail options are offered. Nondegree study is possible. There are 33 national honor societies, including Phi Beta Kappa, and a freshman honors program.

Faculty/Classroom: 62% of faculty are male; 38% are female. No introductory courses are taught by graduate students.

Admissions: There were 63 National Merit finalists.

Requirements: The SAT or ACT is recommended. Applicants should have completed 4 years each in high school English and math, 3 in science, 2 of a foreign language, and 1 each in history, fine arts, and social studies. A GED may be considered in place of a high school diploma. Some fine arts programs require auditions prior to admission. A GPA of 2.0 is required. AP and CLEP credits are accepted. Important factors in the admissions decision are advanced placement or honors courses, leadership record, and extracurricular activities record.

Procedure: Freshmen are admitted to all sessions. There is a rolling admissions plan. Check with the school for current application deadlines. The fall 2013 application fee was $50. Notification is sent on a rolling basis. Applications are accepted online.

Transfer: 1964 transfer students enrolled in 2012-2013. Resident transfer applicants must have a minimum GPA of 2.00; and nonresidents must have a minimum GPA of 2.5. Some university divisions have higher requirements. Admission is competitive for out-of-state students. 30 of 120 credits required for the bachelor's degree must be completed at UA.

Visiting: There are regularly scheduled orientations for prospective students, Consisting of an admissions presentation and tour. There are guides for informal visits and visitors may sit in on classes. To schedule a visit, contact the Admissions Office at (520) 621-6953.

Financial Aid: UA is a member of CSS. The FAFSA is required. Check with the school for current application deadlines.

International Students: There are 1753 international students enrolled. The school actively recruits these students. They must take the TOEFL with a minimum score of 550 on the paper-based TOEFL (PBT) or 70 on the Internet-based version (iBT) and the Comprehensive English Language Test. They must also take the SAT or ACT, scoring 1110. only if the applicant is a graduate of a U.S. high school.

Computers: All students may access the system, 24 hours a day. There are no time limits and no fees.

Graduates: From July 1, 2012 to June 30, 2013, 6494 bachelor's degrees were awarded.

Admissions Contact: Kasey Urquidez, Dean of Undergraduate Admissions . E-Mail: *admissions@arizona.edu* Web: *www.arizona.edu*

ARKANSAS

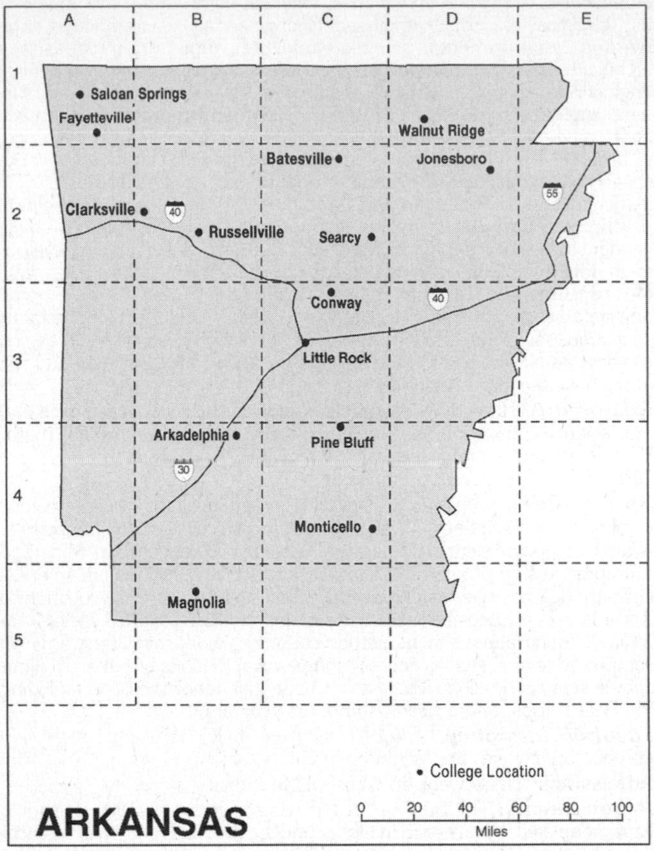

ARKANSAS BAPTIST COLLEGE C-3

Little Rock, AR 72202 **(501) 374-7856, ext. 19; (501) 375-9257**

Full-time: n/av	**Faculty:** n/av
Part-time: n/av	**Ph.D.s:** n/av
Graduate: n/av	**Student/Faculty:** n/av
Year: semesters, summer session	**Tuition:** $4500
Application Deadline:	**Room & Board:** $5500
Freshman Class: n/av	
	NONCOMPETITIVE

Arkansas Baptist College, founded in 1884, is a private liberal arts institution affiliated with American Baptist Churches. The figures in the above above capsule and in this profile are approximate. The library contains 32,000 volumes, 10,000 microform items, and 2,000 audio/video tapes/CDs/DVDs, and subscribes to 75 periodicals including electronic. Computerized library services include interlibrary loans, database searching, and Internet access. The campus is in a small town in downtown Little Rock. Including any residence halls, there are 9 buildings.

Student Life: 90% of undergraduates are from Arkansas. 100% are African American. 100% are Protestant. The average age of freshmen is 18; all undergraduates, 22.

Housing: 160 students can be accommodated in college housing, which includes single-sex dorms. On-campus housing is guaranteed for all 4 years. 50% of students commute. Alcohol is not permitted. All students may keep cars.

Activities: 10% of men belong to 3 local fraternities; 10% of women belong to 2 local sororities. There are 5 groups on campus, including cheerleading, computers, religious, social, and student government. Popular campus events include Ms. ABC and Mr. ABC Pageants.

Sports: There are 2 intercollegiate sports for men and 2 for women. Facilities include a gym.

Disabled Students: 40% of the campus is accessible. Facilities include wheelchair ramps and special parking.

Services: There is remedial math, reading, and writing.

Campus Safety and Security: Measures include 24-hour foot and vehicle patrol. There are lighted pathways/sidewalks.

Programs of Study: ABC confers B.A., and B.S. degrees. Associate degrees are also awarded. Bachelor's degrees are awarded in BUSINESS (accounting and business administration and management), COMPUTER AND PHYSICAL SCIENCE (computer science), EDUCATION (elementary education), SOCIAL SCIENCE (human services and religion). Business administration is the strongest academically and has the largest enrollment.

Required: Students must complete a minimum of 124 credit hours, with 45 in upper-division courses, and must maintain a minimum GPA of 2.0 overall and in the major. Required courses include the Old Testament, theology, humanities, liberal arts, and art or music appreciation.

Special: The college offers a co-op program with Ouachita Baptist University, work-study programs, combined B.A.-B.S. degrees, dual majors, and 1 general studies degree.

Faculty/Classroom: No introductory courses are taught by graduate students.

Requirements: For unconditional admission, applicants must be graduates of an accredited high school or have a GED. Others may be admitted conditionally. A GPA of 2.0 is required. Important factors in the admissions decision are ability to finance college education, evidence of special talent, and parents or siblings attended your school.

Procedure: Freshmen are admitted fall, spring, and summer. Entrance exams should be taken during the registration/orientation period of each semester. Check with the school for current application deadlines. The application fee is $25.

Transfer: For unconditional admission, transfer applicants must have a cumulative GPA of 2.0 and not have been suspended from the previously attended institution. Others may be admitted conditionally. 124 of 124 credits required for the bachelor's degree must be completed at ABC.

Visiting: There are regularly scheduled orientations for prospective students, tour of campus. There are guides for informal visits and visitors may sit in on classes. To schedule a visit, contact the Admissions and Enrollment Office.

Financial Aid: The FAFSA is required. Check with the school for current application deadlines.

International Students: They must take the TOEFL.

Computers: All students may access the system.

Admissions Contact: Freddie M. Fox E-Mail: *ffox@arbaptcol.edu or adm-info@mail.armstrong.edu* Web: *www.arkansasbaptist.edu*

ARKANSAS STATE UNIVERSITY D-2

State University, AR 72467 **(870) 972-2782; (870) 972-3545**

Full-time: 3289 men, 4356 women	**Faculty:** 438; IIA, --$
Part-time: 990 men, 1463 women	**Ph.D.s:** 82%
Graduate: 1107 men, 2347 women	**Student/Faculty:** 18 to 1
Year: semesters, summer session	**Tuition:** $7510 ($13,120)
Application Deadline: August 18	**Room & Board:** $7470
Freshman Class: 4838 applied, 3653 accepted, 1619 enrolled	
SAT CR/M/W: 470/509/445 **ACT:** 23	**COMPETITIVE**

Arkansas State University, founded in 1909 and part of the Arkansas State University System, is a state-supported institution offering undergraduate and graduate degrees in agriculture, humanities and social sciences, business, communications, education, engineering, sciences and mathematics, fine arts, nursing and health professions. There are 11 undergraduate schools and one graduate school. In addition to regional accreditation, ASU has baccalaureate program accreditation with AACSB, ABET, ACEJMC, ADA, ASLA, CSAB, CSWE, NASAD, NASM, NCATE, and NLN. The library contains 1.1 million volumes, and 30,520 audio/video tapes/CDs/DVDs, and subscribes to 33,889 periodicals including electronic. Computerized library services include interlibrary loans, database searching, Internet access, and Wi-Fi capability. Special learning facilities include an art gallery, natural history museum, radio station, TV station, facilities for agriculture and environmental ecotoxicology research, the Arkansas Biosciences Institute, the Fowler Center for Performing Arts, distance learning, the Hemingway-Pfeiffer Museum and Educational Center,a geographic information system facility, an electron microscope lab, and the Delta Studies Center. The 1376-acre campus is in a small town 70 miles west of Memphis, TN. Including any residence halls, there are 152 buildings.

Student Life: 85% of undergraduates are from Arkansas. Others are from 39 states, 50 foreign countries, and Canada. 93% are from public schools. 74% are White; 14% African American. The average age of freshmen is 18; all undergraduates, 23. 27% do not continue beyond their first year; 44% remain to graduate.

Housing: 3163 students can be accommodated in college housing, which includes single-sex and coed dorms, on-campus apartments, and married student housing. In addition, there are special-interest houses, fraternity houses, sorority houses, living learning communities (Honors, STEM, ROTC) and first-year residential experience wing. On-campus housing is available on a first-come and first-served basis. 72% of students commute. Alcohol is not permitted. All students may keep cars.

Activities: 12% of men belong to 11 national fraternities; 10% of women belong to 7 national sororities. There are 147 groups on campus, including academic, art, cheerleading, choir, computers, dance, debate, drama, drill team, ethnic, forensics, gay, honors, international, jazz band, marching band, musical theater, newspaper, pep band, photography, political, professional, radio and TV, religious, social, social service, student government, symphony, and yearbook. Popular campus events include Welcome Week, Order of the Pack, Homecoming, Mardi Gras Celebration, Springfest and MLK Celebration.

Sports: There are 7 intercollegiate sports for men and 9 for women, and 11 intramural sports for men and 11 for women. Facilities include a 10,563-seat convocation center for basketball games or 10,704-seats for concerts, a 30,708-seat football stadium, a 1,200-seat baseball complex, a 400-seat track facility, and a 500-seat soccer field.

Disabled Students: 90% of the campus is accessible. Facilities include wheelchair ramps, elevators, special parking, specially equipped restrooms, special class scheduling, lowered drinking fountains, lowered telephones.

Services: Counseling and information services are available, as is tutoring in most subjects. There is a reader service for the blind, and remedial math, reading, and writing. Tutoring is provided in virtually all general education subjects. Student Support Services tries to provide as much tutoring as possible for upper level courses when tutors are available for the subject areas.

Campus Safety and Security: Measures include 24-hour foot and vehicle patrol, emergency notification system, self-defense education, and security escort services. There are shuttle buses, emergency telephones, and lighted pathways/sidewalks.

Programs of Study: ASU confers B.A., B.S., B.A.S., B.F.A., B.M., B.M.E., B.S.A., B.S.E., B.S.C.E., B.S.E.E., B.S.M.E., B.S.N., B.S.E.N., B.S.R.S. and B.S.W. degrees. Associate, master's, and doctoral degrees are also awarded. Bachelor's degrees are awarded in AGRICULTURE (agricultural business management, agriculture, animal science, plant science, and wildlife management), BIOLOGICAL SCIENCE (biology/biological science and biotechnology), BUSINESS (accounting, banking and finance, business administration and management, business economics, international business, management information systems, management science, marketing, marketing/retailing/merchandising, sports management, and supply chain management), COMMUNICATIONS AND THE ARTS (art, communications, digital communications, English, fine arts, French, graphic design, information technology, journalism, music, music performance, radio/television technology, Spanish, and theatre arts), COMPUTER AND PHYSICAL SCIENCE (chemistry, clinical laboratory science, computer science, digital arts/technology, information sciences and systems, informatics and computer science, mathematics, and physics), EDUCATION (athletic training, business education, early childhood education, English education, foreign languages education, mathematics education, middle school education, music education, physical education, science education, and social science education), ENGINEERING AND ENVIRONMENTAL DESIGN (civil engineering technology, electrical/electronics engineering, emergency/disaster science, engineering, manufacturing technology, mechanical engineering, and technological management), HEALTH PROFESSIONS (exercise science, health promotion, nursing, radiological science, and speech pathology/audiology), SOCIAL SCIENCE (criminology, dietetics, economics, forensic studies, geography, history, interdisciplinary studies, philosophy, political science/government, psychology, social work, and sociology). Engineering, nursing, and biological sciences are the strongest academically. Nursing, early childhood education, and interdisciplinary studies have the largest enrollments.

Required: All students must complete a 35 hour credit distribution of general education courses. A total of at least 120 credits, with a minimum GPA of 2.0, is required to graduate.

Special: An interdisciplinary studies degree, study abroad, and work-study programs are offered. Dual majors and internships are available in many areas. Non-degree study is possible. There are 31 national honor societies and a freshman honors program.

Faculty/Classroom: 45% of faculty are male; 55% are female. 90% teach undergraduates, 20% do research, and 20% do both. Graduate students teach 5% of introductory courses. The average class size in an introductory lecture is 30; in a laboratory is 24; and in a regular course is 28.

Admissions: 76% of the 2013-2014 applicants were accepted. The SAT scores for the 2013-2014 freshman class were: Critical Reading--67% below 500, 25% between 500 and 599, 8% between 600 and 699; Math--47% below 500, 33% between 500 and 599, 7% between 600 and 699, and 13% between 700 and 800; Writing--75% below 500, 25% between 500 and 599. The ACT scores were 24% below 21, 31% between 21 and 23, 24% between 24 and 26, 12% between 27 and 28, and 8% above 28. 43% of the current freshmen were in the top fifth of their class; 66% were in the top two fifths. 48 freshmen graduated first in their class.

Requirements: The SAT or ACT is required. ASSET, or COMPASS scores are required, with ACT scores recommended. Applicants should have completed 14 academic high school units, including 4 each in English and math, 3 in social studies, 3 in science (must be labs), and it is recommended to take 2 in 1 foreign language. Applicants must have an ACT composite score of 21 and a high school GPA of 2.75 for unconditional admission. A GPA of 2.8 is required. AP and CLEP credits are accepted.

Procedure: Freshmen are admitted fall, spring, and summer. Entrance exams should be taken before April 1 of the high school senior year. There are early admissions and rolling admissions plans. Applications should be filed by August 18 for fall entry; January 13 for spring entry; and June 2 for summer entry, along with a $15 fee. Applications are accepted online.

Transfer: 886 transfer students enrolled in 2012-2013. Transfer applicants should have a minimum GPA of 2.0. Those having completed 12 or fewer credit hours will be admitted on the same basis as freshmen. Official transcripts from every institution attended are required. 32 of 120 credits required for the bachelor's degree must be completed at ASU.

Visiting: There are regularly scheduled orientations for prospective students, Consisting of various sessions held throughout the year. There are guides for informal visits, visitors may sit in on classes, and stay overnight. To schedule a visit, contact the Office of Recruitment at (870) 972-2782.

Financial Aid: In 2013-2014, 93% of all full-time freshmen and 75% of continuing full-time students received some form of financial aid. 82% of all full-time freshmen and 74% of continuing full-time students received need-based aid. The average freshman award was $13,000. Need-based scholarships or need-based grants averaged $7,800 ($9,000 maximum); need-based self-help aid (loans and jobs) averaged $6,200 ($8,500 maximum); non-need-based athletic scholarships averaged $9,500 ($10,000 maximum); and other non-need-based awards and non-need-based scholarships averaged $6,000 ($12,000 maximum). 9% of undergraduate students work part-time. Average annual earnings from campus work are $5880. The average financial indebtedness of the 2013 graduate was $25,000. ASU is a member of CSS. The FAFSA and the college's own financial statement are required. The priority date for freshman financial aid applications for fall entry is February 15. The deadline for filing freshman financial aid applications for fall entry is July 1.

International Students: There are 513 international students enrolled. The school actively recruits these students. They must take the TOEFL with a minimum score of 500 on the paper-based TOEFL (PBT) or 61 on the Internet-based version (iBT) or take the MELAB.

Computers: All students may access the system. during the day and evenings, weekdays and weekends. A schedule is posted online on the doors of the computer labs. There are no time limits and no fees.

Graduates: From July 1, 2012 to June 30, 2013, 1721 bachelor's degrees were awarded. The most popular majors were interdisciplinary studies (10%), early childhood education (8%), and nursing (6%). 216 companies recruited on campus in 2012-2013. In an average class, 11% graduate in 3 years or less, 28% graduate in 4 years or less, 37% graduate in 5 years or less, and 39% graduate in 6 years or less. Of the 2012 graduating class, 19% were enrolled in graduate school within 6 months of graduation, and 34% were employed.

Admissions Contact: Tammy Fowler, Director of Recruitment. E-Mail: *recruitment@astate.edu* Web: *www.astate.edu*

ARKANSAS TECH UNIVERSITY B-2

Russellville, AR 72801 (479) 968-0343
(800) 582-6953; (479) 964-0522

Full-time: 3334 men, 3729 women	**Faculty:** 317; IIB, --$
Part-time: 1455 men, 1964 women	**Ph.D.s:** 63%
Graduate: 265 men, 622 women	**Student/Faculty:** 18 to 1
Year: semesters, summer session	**Tuition:** $6918 ($12,888)
Application Deadline: open	**Room & Board:** $6246
Freshman Class: 3849 applied, 3272 accepted, 1755 enrolled	
SAT CR/M: 420/470 **ACT:** 21	**LESS COMPETITIVE**

Arkansas Tech University, founded in 1909, is a state-supported institution offering undergraduate instruction in arts and humanities, business, education, natural and health sciences, information technology, applied sciences, and other technical fields. Graduate instruction is offered in education, arts and humanities, instructional technology, information technology, fisheries and wildlife, nursing, emergency management, business administration, and engineering. There are 7 undergraduate schools and one graduate school. In addition to regional accreditation, Tech has baccalaureate program accreditation with AACSB, ABET, CAHEA, NASM, NCATE, NLN, and NRPA. The library contains 299,283 volumes, 902,193 microform items, and 15,369 audio/video tapes/CDs/DVDs, and subscribes to 756 periodicals including electronic. Computerized library services include interlibrary loans, database searching, Internet access, and Wi-Fi capability. Special learning facilities include an art gallery, radio station, TV station, an energy center, and a library with distance learning classrooms, satellite downlink, and 400 data drops for laptop computers. The 559-acre campus is in a small town 75 miles west of Little Rock. Including any residence halls, there are 111 buildings.

Student Life: 93% of undergraduates are from Arkansas. Others are from 40 states, 34 foreign countries, and Canada. 79% are White. The average

age of freshmen is 19; all undergraduates, 23. 34% do not continue beyond their first year; 43% remain to graduate.

Housing: 2886 students can be accommodated in college housing, which includes single-sex and coed dorms, on-campus apartments, and off-campus apartments. In addition, there are sorority houses. 70% of students commute. Alcohol is not permitted. All students may keep cars.

Activities: 5% of men belong to 7 national fraternities; 7% of women belong to 4 national sororities. There are 110 groups on campus, including art, band, cheerleading, choir, chorale, chorus, computers, dance, debate, drama, drill team, environmental, ethnic, honors, international, jazz band, literary magazine, marching band, newspaper, opera, orchestra, pep band, political, professional, radio and TV, religious, social, social service, and student government. Popular campus events include Greek Week, Family Day and Spring Fling.

Sports: There are 4 intercollegiate sports for men and 6 for women, and 20 intramural sports for men and 20 for women. Facilities include a coliseum, fields, racquetball courts, and a 10,000-seat stadium.

Disabled Students: All of the campus is accessible. Facilities include wheelchair ramps, elevators, special parking, specially equipped restrooms, special class scheduling, lowered drinking fountains, lowered telephones, and special housing.

Services: Counseling and information services are available, as is tutoring in most subjects. There is a reader service for the blind, and remedial math, reading, and writing.

Campus Safety and Security: Measures include 24-hour foot and vehicle patrol, emergency notification system, self-defense education, and security escort services. There are emergency telephones, lighted pathways/sidewalks, and controlled access to dorms/residences.

Programs of Study: Tech confers B.A., B.F.A., B.M.E., B.P.S., B.S., B.S.B.A., B.S.E.E., B.S.M.E. and B.S.N degrees. Associate and master's degrees are also awarded. Bachelor's degrees are awarded in AGRICULTURE (agricultural business management), BIOLOGICAL SCIENCE (biology/biological science), BUSINESS (accounting and hospitality management services), COMMUNICATIONS AND THE ARTS (art, communications, creative writing, English literature, journalism, languages, music, and speech/debate/rhetoric), COMPUTER AND PHYSICAL SCIENCE (chemistry, computer science, geology, information sciences and systems, mathematics, physical sciences, and physics), EDUCATION (agricultural education, art education, business education, early childhood education, education, elementary education, English education, foreign languages education, health education, health information management, middle school education, music education, physical education, and science education), ENGINEERING AND ENVIRONMENTAL DESIGN (electrical/electronics engineering, emergency/disaster science, engineering physics, and mechanical engineering), HEALTH PROFESSIONS (medical laboratory technology and nursing), SOCIAL SCIENCE (economics, history, international studies, parks and recreation management, political science/government, psychology, public history/archives, social studies, and sociology).

Required: Students must complete at least 120 semester hours, including 40 hours of upper-level courses to fulfill a major, and maintain a minimum GPA of 2.0. General education requirements include 15 hours of social sciences, fine arts, and humanities, 8 of science, 6 of English, and 3 of math. No more than four semester hours of activity credit may be counted toward graduation.

Special: Special academic features include internships and work-study programs, as well as study abroad, accelerated programs, B.A.-B.S. degrees, and dual degree. Independent study is available to seniors. Off-campus courses and online telecourses are also offered. There are 4 national honor societies and a freshman honors program.

Faculty/Classroom: 45% of faculty are male; 55% are female. No introductory courses are taught by graduate students.

Admissions: 85% of the 2013-2014 applicants were accepted. The SAT scores for the 2013-2014 freshman class were: Critical Reading--79% below 500, 11% between 500 and 599, 11% between 600 and 699; Math--71% below 500, 29% between 500 and 599. The ACT scores were 42% below 21, 22% between 21 and 23, 22% between 24 and 26, 10% between 27 and 28, and 5% above 28. 27% of the current freshmen were in the top fifth of their class; 50% were in the top two fifths. 3 freshmen graduated first in their class.

Requirements: The ACT is required. The SAT is recommended. Composite ACT score of 15 or above, composite SAT score of 1060 or above, or a composite COMPASS score of 47 (averaging scores in algebra, writing, and reading) or above for students who graduate from a public secondary school; composite ACT score of 19 or above, composite SAT score of 1330 or above, or a composite COMPASS score of 68 (averaging scores in algebra, writing, and reading) or above for students who graduate from a private secondary school, home school, or received a GED. Note: The ACT Writing exam is not required for admission purposes. A GPA of 2.0 is required. AP and CLEP credits are accepted.

Procedure: Freshmen are admitted to all sessions. Entrance exams should be taken no later than the second semester of the senior year of high school. There are deferred admissions and rolling admissions plans. Application deadlines are open. Notification is sent on a rolling basis. Applications are accepted online.

Transfer: 647 transfer students enrolled in 2012-2013. Transfer students making application for admission to Arkansas Tech University must submit official transcripts from all colleges/universities where they have been officially registered. Students seeking transfer of credit from other institutions may be asked to provide a catalog or course description from the transfer institution. Students with fewer than 24 semester hours of earned college-level credit must also submit a high school transcript and must request current transferable ACT or SAT scores be sent to the University. ACT, SAT, or COMPASS scores will not be required if the English and mathematics general education requirements have been satisfied with grades of "C" or better. In the event that receipt of a student's transcript is unavoidably delayed, as may frequently occur at midyear, a transfer student may be admitted provisionally pending receipt of the official transcript. However, the University reserves the right to require immediate withdrawal if the previous record does not meet admission requirements. Applicants for transfer must have earned a GPA of 2.00 (on a 4.00 scale) on all college-level courses attempted and be eligible to re-enroll at the last college or university attended. 30 of 120 credits required for the bachelor's degree must be completed at Tech.

Visiting: There are regularly scheduled orientations for prospective students. There are guides for informal visits and visitors may sit in on classes. To schedule a visit, contact the Admissions Office.

Financial Aid: In 2013-2014, 66% of all full-time freshmen and 69% of continuing full-time students received some form of financial aid. 57% of all full-time freshmen and 56% of continuing full-time students received need-based aid. The average freshman award was $9,142. Need-based scholarships or need-based grants averaged $4,345; need-based self-help aid (loans and jobs) averaged $2,837; and non-need-based athletic scholarships averaged $3,747. The average financial indebtedness of the 2013 graduate was $24,409. The FAFSA and the college's own financial statement are required. The deadline for filing freshman financial aid applications for fall entry is May 1.

International Students: There are 351 international students enrolled. The school actively recruits these students. They must take the TOEFL with a minimum score of 500 on the paper-based TOEFL (PBT) or 61 on the Internet-based version (iBT), or IELTS or EIKEN. They must also take the SAT or ACT, scoring 15.

Computers: All students may access the system. There are no time limits and no fees.

Graduates: From July 1, 2012 to June 30, 2013, 1277 bachelor's degrees were awarded. The most popular majors were professional studies (18%), nursing (9%), and early childhood education (8%).

Admissions Contact: Shauna Donnell, Director of Enrollment Management. E-Mail: *tech.enroll@atu.edu* Web: *www.atu.edu*

HARDING UNIVERSITY C-2

Searcy, AR 72149 **(501) 279-4407**
(800) 477-4407; (501) 279-4129

Full-time: 1868 men, 2227 women	**Faculty:** 215
Part-time: 163 men, 132 women	**Ph.D.s:** 68%
Graduate: 620 men, 1190 women	**Student/Faculty:** 17 to 1
Year: semesters, summer session	**Tuition:** $15,240
Application Deadline: June 1	**Room & Board:** $6192

Freshman Class: 2180 applied, 1663 accepted, 1041 enrolled
SAT CR/M: 560/550 **ACT:** 25 **COMPETITIVE+**

Harding University, founded in 1924, is a private Christian institution comprised of the Colleges of Allied Health, Arts and Humanities, Sciences, Bible and Religion, Business, Education, Nursing, and Pharmacy. There are 7 undergraduate schools and 5 graduate schools. In addition to regional accreditation, Harding has baccalaureate program accreditation with ABET, ACBSP, CSWE, NASM, NCATE, and NLN. The library contains 365,658 volumes, 241,437 microform items, and 11,315 audio/video tapes/CDs/DVDs, and subscribes to 75,942 periodicals including electronic. Computerized library services include interlibrary loans, database searching, Internet access, and Wi-Fi capability. Special learning facilities include an art gallery, radio station, and TV station. The 350-acre campus is in a small town 50 miles northeast of Little Rock and 105 miles west of Memphis, TN. Including any residence halls, there are 52 buildings.

Student Life: 71% of undergraduates are from out of state, mostly the South. Students are from 50 states, 47 foreign countries, and Canada. 65% are from public schools. 83% are White. 93% are Protestant. The average age of freshmen is 18; all undergraduates, 21. 18% do not continue beyond their first year; 64% remain to graduate.

Housing: 3136 students can be accommodated in college housing, which includes single-sex dorms, on-campus apartments, off-campus apartments, and married student housing. On-campus housing is guaranteed for all 4 years, is available on a first-come, and first-served basis. 72% of students live on campus; of those, 75% remain on campus on weekends. Alcohol is not permitted. All students may keep cars.

Activities: 46% of men belong to 13 local fraternities; 54% of women belong to 16 local sororities. There are 100 groups on campus, including art, band, cheerleading, choir, chorale, chorus, computers, debate, drama, ethnic, film, honors, international, jazz band, literary magazine, marching band, musical theater, newspaper, orchestra, pep band, photography, political, professional, radio and TV, religious, social, social service, student government, symphony, and yearbook. Popular campus events include Spring Sing, Homecoming, Bison Daze and Lectureship.

Sports: There are 8 intercollegiate sports for men and 8 for women, and 11 intramural sports for men and 9 for women. Facilities include Baseball and softball fields, racquetball, handball, and tennis courts, a football stadium, an indoor and outdoor track, a golf practice range, a gymnastics room, weight rooms, an Olympic-size swimming pool, and 2 gyms. The Football and Athletic Training Complex provides state of the art weight room, locker room, office space, as well as rehabilitation area and hydrotherapy area. Harding owns a 2000-acre camp in the Ozark Mountains with horses, 25 rustic cabins, streams, and hiking trails.

Disabled Students: 95% of the campus is accessible. Facilities include wheelchair ramps, elevators, special parking, specially equipped restrooms, special class scheduling, lowered drinking fountains, lowered telephones, and special housing.

Services: Counseling and information services are available, as is tutoring in most subjects. There is a reader service for the blind, and remedial math, reading, and writing.

Campus Safety and Security: Measures include 24-hour foot and vehicle patrol, emergency notification system, self-defense education, and security escort services. There are emergency telephones, lighted pathways/sidewalks, and controlled access to dorms/residences.

Programs of Study: Harding confers B.A., B.S., B.B.A., B.F.A., B.M.E., B.M.N., B.S.M.T., B.S.N. and B.S.W. degrees. Master's and doctoral degrees are also awarded. Bachelor's degrees are awarded in BIOLOGICAL SCIENCE (biochemistry and biology/biological science), BUSINESS (accounting, banking and finance, business administration and management, fashion merchandising, international business management, marketing/retailing/merchandising, and sports management), COMMUNICATIONS AND THE ARTS (advertising, art, broadcasting, communications, design, dramatic arts, English, fine arts, French, graphic design, journalism, media arts, music, painting, and Spanish), COMPUTER AND PHYSICAL SCIENCE (chemistry, computer science, information sciences and systems, mathematics, and physics), EDUCATION (athletic training, Christian education, early childhood education, elementary education, foreign languages education, music education, and secondary education), ENGINEERING AND ENVIRONMENTAL DESIGN (biomedical engineering, computer engineering, electrical/electronics engineering, interior design, and mechanical engineering), HEALTH PROFESSIONS (exercise science, health, health care administration, health science, medical technology, nursing, and speech pathology/audiology), SOCIAL SCIENCE (American studies, biblical languages, biblical studies, child care/child and family studies, criminal justice, dietetics, economics, history, home economics, humanities, international studies, legal studies, liberal arts/general studies, ministries, missions, political science/government, psychology, public administration, religion, social science, social work, and youth ministry). Engineering, premedicine and nursing are the strongest academically. Business, education and nursing have the largest enrollments.

Required: All students must complete 53 hours of general education courses, including religion, English composition, history, speech communications, social sciences, biology, physical science, math, Western literature, music and art appreciation, and phys ed. A total of 128 semester hours, with a minimum GPA of 2.0, is required to graduate. 32 hours must be completed in residence and 45 must be upper-level.

Special: The Harding campus in Florence, Italy, and programs in Greece, England, Latin America, France/Switzerland, Australia, and Zambia offer international studies. Internships are given in social work, teaching, nursing, and international missions. Co-op programs in all majors, work-study programs, dual majors, a general studies degree, and non-degree study are available. There are 11 national honor societies and a freshman honors program.

Faculty/Classroom: 60% of faculty are male; 40% are female. 78% teach undergraduates. No introductory courses are taught by graduate students. The average class size in an introductory lecture is 18 and in a laboratory is 14.

Admissions: 76% of the 2013-2014 applicants were accepted. The SAT scores for the 2013-2014 freshman class were: Critical Reading--25% below 500, 40% between 500 and 599, 26% between 600 and 699, and 9% between 700 and 800; Math--24% below 500, 38% between 500 and 599, 30% between 600 and 699, and 8% between 700 and 800. The ACT scores were 16% below 21, 23% between 21 and 23, 23% between 24 and 26, 15% between 27 and 28, and 23% above 28. 28% of the current freshmen were in the top fifth of their class; 44% were in the top two fifths. There were 7 National Merit finalists.

Requirements: The SAT or ACT is required. A lower GPA can be offset by higher test scores. Applicants should be graduates of an accredited secondary school and have completed 15 high school hours, including 4 in English, 3 each in math, and social studies, 3 in art, history, or music, and 2 in a science. An interview is highly recommended. AP and CLEP credits are accepted. Important factors in the admissions decision are leadership record, recommendations by school officials, and advanced placement or honors courses.

Procedure: Freshmen are admitted to all sessions. Entrance exams should be taken in the junior year or early in the senior year. There are early admissions, deferred admissions, and rolling admissions plans. Applications should be filed by June 1 for fall entry; November 1 for spring entry, along with a $40 fee. Notifications are sent May 1. Applications are accepted online.

Transfer: 220 transfer students enrolled in 2012-2013. Applicants with a minimum GPA of 2.0 and at least 14 semester hours earned are considered for admission. An interview is highly recommended. 32 of 128 credits required for the bachelor's degree must be completed at Harding.

Visiting: There are regularly scheduled orientations for prospective students. There are guides for informal visits, visitors may sit in on classes, and stay overnight. To schedule a visit, contact the Admissions Office.

Financial Aid: In 2013-2014, 96% of all full-time freshmen and 92% of continuing full-time students received some form of financial aid. The average freshman award was $13,461. 35% of undergraduate students work part-time. Average annual earnings from campus work are $1700. The average financial indebtedness of the 2013 graduate was $34,048. The FAFSA is required. The priority date for freshman financial aid applications for fall entry is February 15. The deadline for filing freshman financial aid applications for fall entry is April 1.

International Students: There are 291 international students enrolled. The school actively recruits these students. They must take the TOEFL with a minimum score of 550 on the paper-based TOEFL (PBT) or 79 on the Internet-based version (iBT). They must also take the SAT or ACT.

Computers: All students may access the system. There are no time limits. The fee is $480.

Graduates: From July 1, 2012 to June 30, 2013, 841 bachelor's degrees were awarded. The most popular majors were business/marketing (15%), early childhood licensure (13%), and health professions and related programs (13%). 251 companies recruited on campus in 2012-2013. In an average class, 42% graduate in 4 years or less, 61% graduate in 5 years or less, and 64% graduate in 6 years or less. Of the 2012 graduating class, 30% were enrolled in graduate school within 6 months of graduation.

Admissions Contact: Glen Dillard, Assistant Vice President for Enrollment Management. E-Mail: *gdillard@harding.edu* Web: *www.harding.edu*

HENDERSON STATE UNIVERSITY B-4

Arkadelphia, AR 71999	**(870) 230-5028; (870) 230-5066**
Full-time: 1268 men, 1610 women	**Faculty:** 167; IIA, --$
Part-time: 142 men, 179 women	**Ph.D.s:** 67%
Graduate: 122 men, 262 women	**Student/Faculty:** 17 to 1
Year: semesters, summer session	**Tuition:** $7284 ($13,404)
Application Deadline: open	**Room & Board:** $6350
Freshman Class: 3388 applied, 2106 accepted, 705 enrolled	
SAT CR/M: 500/536 **ACT:** 21	**COMPETITIVE**

Henderson State University, founded in 1890 as Arkadelphia Methodist College, became a state institution in 1929 and offers liberal arts courses. There are 3 undergraduate schools and 1 graduate school. In addition to regional accreditation, HSU has baccalaureate program accreditation with AACSB, ADA, NASM, and NCATE. The library contains 269,000 volumes, 213,000 microform items, and 20,600 audio/video tapes/CDs/DVDs. Computerized library services include interlibrary loans, database searching, and Internet access. Special learning facilities include an art gallery, planetarium, radio station, and TV station. The 152-acre campus is in a small town 60 miles southwest of Little Rock. Including any residence halls, there are 61 buildings.

Student Life: 96% of undergraduates are from Arkansas. Others are from 24 states, 23 foreign countries, and Canada. 66% are White; 24% African American. The average age of freshmen is 18; all undergraduates, 22. 45% do not continue beyond their first year; 29% remain to graduate.

Housing: 1378 students can be accommodated in college housing, which includes single-sex and coed dorms and off-campus apartments. In addition, there are honors houses, International student housing and apartments on campus that are managed by an outside group. On-campus housing is available on a first-come and first-served basis. 59% of students commute. Alcohol is not permitted. All students may keep cars.

Activities: There are 90 groups on campus, including art, band, cheerleading, choir, chorale, chorus, dance, debate, drama, ethnic, gay, honors, international, jazz band, marching band, musical theater, newspaper, pep band, political, professional, radio and TV, religious, social, social service, student government, and yearbook. Popular campus events include Spring Fling, Orientation and Family Day.

Sports: There are 5 intercollegiate sports for men and 7 for women. Facilities include a 9600-seat football stadium, a gym, an auxiliary gym, a weight room, an intramural practice field for football, a swimming pool, 6 tennis courts, baseball and softball fields, and a track.

Disabled Students: 90% of the campus is accessible. Facilities include wheelchair ramps, elevators, special parking, specially equipped restrooms, special class scheduling, lowered drinking fountains, and lowered telephones.

Services: Counseling and information services are available, as is tutoring in most subjects. There is a reader service for the blind.

Campus Safety and Security: Measures include 24-hour foot and vehicle patrol and emergency notification system. There are lighted pathways/sidewalks and controlled access to dorms/residences.

Programs of Study: HSU confers B.A., B.S., B.B.A., B.F.A., B.G.S., B.M., B.S.E. and B.S.N. degrees. Master's degrees are also awarded. Bachelor's degrees are awarded in BIOLOGICAL SCIENCE (biology/biological science), BUSINESS (accounting, business administration and management, and recreation and leisure services), COMMUNICATIONS AND THE ARTS (communications, dramatic arts, English, music, Spanish, and studio art), COMPUTER AND PHYSICAL SCIENCE (chemistry, computer science, information sciences and systems, mathematics, physics, and radiological technology), EDUCATION (art education, athletic training, business education, early childhood education, education, middle school education, music education, and physical education), ENGINEERING AND ENVIRONMENTAL DESIGN (aviation administration/management and engineering physics), HEALTH PROFESSIONS (medical technology and nursing), SOCIAL SCIENCE (criminal justice, family/consumer studies, history, human services, political science/government, psychology, public administration, and sociology). Education, business administration, and biology have the largest enrollments.

Required: All students must complete a total of 120 credit hours, including 30 in the major, with a minimum GPA of 2.0. Core requirements include 12 semester hours in social science, 11 in natural science, 9 in English, 6 in humanities, 3 each in non-Western culture, math, and oral communication, and 2 in phys ed or military science. Students must take the comprehensive Rising Junior Examination.

Special: HSU offers co-op programs and cross-registration with Ouachita Baptist University, internships in business, psychology, political science, recreation, and education, work-study programs, credit for military experience, nondegree study, and pass/fail options. There is a freshman honors program.

Faculty/Classroom: 49% of faculty are male; 51% are female. 95% teach undergraduates. No introductory courses are taught by graduate students. The average class size in an introductory lecture is 50; in a laboratory is 20; and in a regular course is 30.

Admissions: 62% of the 2013-2014 applicants were accepted. The SAT scores for the 2013-2014 freshman class were: Critical Reading--58% below 500, and 42% between 500 and 599; Math--37% below 500, 42% between 500 and 599, and 21% between 600 and 699. The ACT scores were 45% below 21, 26% between 21 and 23, 19% between 24 and 26, 6% between 27 and 28, and 4% above 28. 26% of the current freshmen were in the top fifth of their class; 52% were in the top two fifths. 8 freshmen graduated first in their class.

Requirements: The SAT or ACT is required. The ACT is recommended. Applicants need at least 15 academic credits or 15 Carnegie units. Students with a predicted GPA of 1.5 or below will be admitted conditionally. 4 units of English, 3 of history, civics, or American government, 2 each of natural science, math, and foreign language, and a half unit of computer science are recommended. AP and CLEP credits are accepted.

Procedure: Freshmen are admitted fall, spring, and summer. Entrance exams should be taken during the senior year. There is a rolling admissions plan. Application deadlines are open. Applications are accepted online.

Transfer: 297 transfer students enrolled in 2012-2013. Applicants with a cumulative GPA below 2.0 will be admitted conditionally. The entire academic record is considered. 30 of 124 credits required for the bachelor's degree must be completed at Henderson.

Visiting: There are regularly scheduled orientations for prospective students, Campus tours are given Monday through Friday at 10 a.m. and 1 p.m. Give us a call at 800-228-7333 or register for the tour online. There are guides for informal visits and visitors may stay overnight. To schedule a visit, contact the Admissions Office at admissions@hsu.edu.

Financial Aid: The FAFSA and FFS are required. Check with the school for current application deadlines.

International Students: There are 28 international students enrolled. The school actively recruits these students. They must take the TOEFL with a minimum score of 500 on the paper-based TOEFL (PBT) or 61 on the Internet-based version (iBT) or take the MELAB. They must also take the SAT or ACT, scoring 19.

Computers: All students may access the system. There are no time limits and no fees.

Graduates: From July 1, 2012 to June 30, 2013, 486 bachelor's degrees were awarded. The most popular majors were education (22%), business administration (14%), and general studies (13%). 75 companies recruited on campus in 2012-2013. In an average class, 18% graduate in 4 years or less, 30% graduate in 5 years or less, and 35% graduate in 6 years or less.

Admissions Contact: Vikita Hardwrick, Director of University Relations/Admissions. E-Mail: *admissions@hsu.edu* Web: *www.hsu.edu*

HENDRIX COLLEGE C-3

Conway, AR 72032 (501) 450-1362
(800) 277-9017; (501) 450-3843

Full-time: 631 men, 779 women
Part-time: 5 men, 1 women
Graduate: 9 men, 7 women
Year: semesters
Application Deadline:
Faculty: 105; IIB, -$
Ph.D.s: 92%
Student/Faculty: 11 to 1
Tuition: $37,816
Room & Board: $10,620
Freshman Class: 1928 applied, 1550 accepted, 436 enrolled
SAT CR/M: 606/598 **ACT:** 29 **HIGHLY COMPETITIVE+**

Hendrix College, founded in 1876, is a private liberal arts college affiliated with the United Methodist Church. There is one graduate school. In addition to regional accreditation, Hendrix has baccalaureate program accreditation with NASM and NCATE. The library contains 262,461 volumes, 67,202 microform items, and 4,029 audio/video tapes/CDs/DVDs, and subscribes to 46,126 periodicals including electronic. Computerized library services include interlibrary loans, database searching, Internet access, and Wi-Fi capability. Special learning facilities include an art gallery, radio station, a writing lab. The 180-acre campus is in a suburban area 25 miles northwest of Little Rock. Including any residence halls, there are 65 buildings.

Student Life: 55% of undergraduates are from out of state, mostly the South. Students are from 33 states, and 21 foreign countries. 79% are from public schools. 79% are White. 50% claim no religious affiliation; 23% Protestant. The average age of freshmen is 18; all undergraduates, 20. 12% do not continue beyond their first year; 68% remain to graduate.

Housing: 1208 students can be accommodated in college housing, which includes single-sex and coed dorms and on-campus apartments. In addition, there are language houses, a substance-free house. On-campus housing is guaranteed for all 4 years, is available on a first-come, first-served basis, and is available on a lottery system for upperclassmen. 88% of students live on campus; of those, 80% remain on campus on weekends. All students may keep cars.

Activities: There are no fraternities or sororities. There are 70 groups on campus, including art, band, cheerleading, chess, choir, chorale, chorus, dance, debate, drama, environmental, ethnic, film, gay, honors, international, jazz band, literary magazine, musical theater, newspaper, orchestra, pep band, photography, political, professional, radio and TV, religious, social, social service, student government, Ultimate Frisbee, and yearbook. Popular campus events include Kampus Kitty, Themed Dance Parties, Shirttails, and Dance Competition.

Sports: There are 10 intercollegiate sports for men and 11 for women, and 12 intramural sports for men and 12 for women. The Wellness and Athletic center is a 100,000 square foot building which includes a 1,200 seat competition gym, a fitness center with free weights/weight equipment as well as cardiovascular machines, an indoor climbing wall, a dance/movement studio and an indoor track. In addition, there is an indoor 25 meter pool with diving boards and a retractable roof, baseball, softball and soccer fields, a multi-purpose turf field and 5 outdoor tennis courts. Several athletic facilities were opened including a 1,500 seat stadium, a multi-purpose field house with additional locker rooms and a weight room, an additional multi-purpose turf field and a tennis bubble with three indoor courts.

Disabled Students: 90% of the campus is accessible. Facilities include wheelchair ramps, elevators, special parking, specially equipped restrooms, lowered drinking fountains, and push-button door openers.

Services: Counseling and information services are available, as is tutoring in some subjects, math, biology, writing, chemistry, foreign languanges, accounting, physics, genetics and zoology.

Campus Safety and Security: Measures include 24-hour foot and vehicle patrol, emergency notification system, self-defense education, and security escort services. There are emergency telephones, lighted pathways/sidewalks, and controlled access to dorms/residences.

Programs of Study: Hendrix confers B.A. degrees. Master's degrees are also awarded. Bachelor's degrees are awarded in AGRICULTURE (environmental studies), BIOLOGICAL SCIENCE (biochemistry and biology/biological science), BUSINESS (accounting and business economics), COMMUNICATIONS AND THE ARTS (art, classics, dramatic arts, English, French, German, music, and Spanish), COMPUTER AND PHYSICAL SCIENCE (chemical physics, chemistry, computer science, mathematics, and physics), HEALTH PROFESSIONS (allied health and exercise science), SOCIAL SCIENCE (American studies, anthropology, economics, history, interdisciplinary studies, international relations, philosophy, philosophy and religion, political science/government, psychology, religion, and sociology). Psychology, chemistry and philosophy are the strongest academically. Psychology, biology and biochemstry/molecular biology have the largest enrollments.

Required: The Collegiate Center is the general education program at Hendrix College and it has four distinct parts: (1) First-Year Experience (consists of The Engaged Citizen course that is grouped in faculty dyads and an Explorations seminar that meets weekly); (2) Capacities (consists of a bi-level writing program, foreign language (equivalent to two semesters), a quantitative skills course, and two physical activities); (3) Learning Domains (consists of 7 courses across 7 disciplines) including one course in Expressive Arts, one course in Historical Perspectives, one course in Literary Studies, two courses (one a lab) in Natural Science Inquiry, one course in Social and Behavioral Analysis, and one course in Values, Beliefs and Ethics; and (4) The Odyssey Program (consists of 3 reflective, engaged experiences across the six categories of Artistic Creativity, Global Awareness, Professional & Leadership Development, Service to the World, Undergraduate Research, and Special Programs). All majors include a senior capstone experience that varies by major and 32 courses are required for graduation.

Special: Internships and work-study may be arranged in all fields. The college offers 3-2 engineering programs with Columbia, Vanderbilt, and Washington Universities. Also available are a Washington semester, study abroad, dual majors, and student-designed interdisciplinary studies. Students can pursue minors in all academic departments, as well as African studies, art history, Asian studies, dance, secondary education, gender studies, international business, medical humanities, neuroscience, and public health. There are 12 national honor societies and including Phi Beta Kappa.

Faculty/Classroom: 49% of faculty are male; 51% are female. All teach undergraduates, 75% do research, and 75% do both. No introductory courses are taught by graduate students. The average class size in an introductory lecture is 20; in a laboratory is 19; and in a regular course is 17.

Admissions: 80% of the 2013-2014 applicants were accepted. The SAT scores for the 2013-2014 freshman class were: Critical Reading--14% below 500, 31% between 500 and 599, 34% between 600 and 699, and 21% between 700 and 800; Math--9% below 500, 44% between 500 and 599, 32% between 600 and 699, and 15% between 700 and 800. The ACT scores were 1% below 21, 12% between 21 and 23, 15% between 24 and 26, 19% between 27 and 28, and 53% above 28. 67% of the current freshmen were in the top fifth of their class; 89% were in the top two fifths. There was 1 National Merit finalist. 27 freshmen graduated first in their class.

Requirements: The SAT or ACT is required. Hendrix recommends that applicants have completed 4 high school units in English, 3 to 4 each in math and social studies, 2 or more in science, and 2 or more in a foreign language. The GED is accepted. AP and CLEP credits are accepted. Important factors in the admissions decision are extracurricular activities record, advanced placement or honors courses, and leadership record.

Procedure: Freshmen are admitted fall and spring. Entrance exams should be taken during the junior and senior years. There is an early admissions plan. Check with the school for current application deadlines. The application fee is $40. Notification of early decision is sent December 15; regular decision, March 1. Applications are accepted online.

Transfer: 19 transfer students enrolled in 2012-2013. Complete the Common Application online for free, or mail a completed Common Application along with $40 nonrefundable applicaiton fee. Submit an offical transcript starting in 9th grade. Request your ACT or SAT scores be sent to Hendrix. Have each college or university previously or currently attended send official transcript and a Dean of Student Affairs Recommendation Form. 16 of 32 credits required for the bachelor's degree must be completed at Hendrix.

Visiting: There are regularly scheduled orientations for prospective students, Student visits include attending a class, visits with current students and faculty, a campus tour, and a luncheon with speakers. Students may also stay overnight in a residence hall. There are guides for informal visits, visitors may sit in on classes, and stay overnight. To schedule a visit, contact the Office of Admission at (501) 450-1362.

Financial Aid: In 2013-2014, 100% of all full-time freshmen and 100% of continuing full-time students received some form of financial aid. 68% of all full-time freshmen and 61% of continuing full-time students received need-based aid. The average freshman award was $30,315. Need-based scholarships or need-based grants averaged $26,641 ($48,436 maximum); and need-based self-help aid (loans and jobs) averaged $5,137 ($7,500 maximum). 40% of undergraduate students work part-time. Average annual earnings from campus work are $1131. The average financial indebtedness of the 2013 graduate was $24,939. The FAFSA is required. The priority date for freshman financial aid applications for fall entry is March 1.

International Students: There are 69 international students enrolled. The school actively recruits these students. They must take the TOEFL with a minimum score of 550 on the paper-based TOEFL (PBT) or 79 on the Internet-based version (iBT).

Computers: All students may access the system, 24 hours a day, 7 days a week. There are no time limits and no fees.

Graduates: From July 1, 2012 to June 30, 2013, 309 bachelor's degrees were awarded. The most popular majors were biology (13%), psychology (11%), and English (7%). 65 companies recruited on campus in 2012-2013. In an average class, 63% graduate in 4 years or less, 67% graduate in 5 years or less, and 68% graduate in 6 years or less. Of the 2012 graduating class, 34% were enrolled in graduate school within 6 months of graduation.

Admissions Contact: Karen Foust, EVP Strategic Initiatives and VP Enrollment. Web: *www.hendrix.edu*

JOHN BROWN UNIVERSITY — A-1

Siloam Springs, AR 72761 — (479) 524-7150; (877) JBU-INFO; (479) 524-4196

Full-time: 705 men, 866 women	**Faculty:** n/av
Part-time: 99 men, 131 women	**Ph.D.s:** 51%
Graduate: 180 men, 336 women	**Student/Faculty:** 15 to 1
Year: semesters, summer session	**Tuition:** $22,734
Application Deadline: May 1	**Room & Board:** $8262
Freshman Class: 1143 applied, 798 accepted, 303 enrolled	
SAT CR/M/W: 586/581/562 **ACT:** 27	**VERY COMPETITIVE+**

John Brown University, founded in 1919, is a private, interdenominational Christian university offering nearly 50 undergraduate degree programs, 3 degree completion programs, and 9 graduate degree programs. There are 2 undergraduate schools and 2 graduate schools. In addition to regional accreditation, JBU has baccalaureate program accreditation with ABET, ACBSP, ACCE, and NCATE. The library contains 118,980 volumes, 67,000 microform items, and 5,437 audio/video tapes/CDs/DVDs. Computerized library services include interlibrary loans, database searching, and Internet access. Special learning facilities include an art gallery, radio station, TV station, a wellness assessment laboratory. The 200-acre campus is in a small town JBU is located in Siloam Springs, Arkansas, which is 25 mile west of Rogers, Arkansas and 80 mile east of Tulsa, Oklahoma. Including any residence halls, there are 33 buildings.

Student Life: 60% of undergraduates are from out of state, mostly the Mid-West. Students are from 42 states, 44 foreign countries, and Canada. 80% are White. 90% are Protestant. The average age of freshmen is 19; all undergraduates, 21. 20% do not continue beyond their first year; 70% remain to graduate.

Housing: 1100 students can be accommodated in college housing, which includes single-sex and coed dorms, on-campus apartments, off-campus apartments, and married student housing. On-campus housing is guaranteed for all 4 years. 69% of students live on campus; of those, 65% remain on campus on weekends. Alcohol is not permitted. All students may keep cars.

Activities: There are no fraternities or sororities. Groups on campus include art, cheerleading, choir, chorale, chorus, dance, debate, drama, ethnic, forensics, honors, international, jazz band, musical theater, newspaper, orchestra, pep band, photography, radio and TV, religious, student government, and yearbook. Popular campus events include Fall Breakway, Christmas Candlelight Service and Toilet Paper Game.

Sports: There are 6 intercollegiate sports for men and 6 for women, and 10 intramural sports for men and 8 for women. Facilities include a 2000-seat gym, soccer and softball fields, a baseball diamond, a training room, and a swimming pool. The Lifetime Health Complex includes an indoor track, 4 racquetball courts, a Nautilus fitness center, an aerobics room, tennis courts, a rugby pitch, and a 3-court recreation center.

Disabled Students: 95% of the campus is accessible. Facilities include wheelchair ramps, elevators, special parking, specially equipped restrooms, special class scheduling, lowered drinking fountains, lowered telephones, and special housing.

Services: Counseling and information services are available, as is tutoring in most subjects. There is remedial math, reading, and writing.

Campus Safety and Security: Measures include 24-hour foot and vehicle patrol, emergency notification system, self-defense education, and security escort services. There are lighted pathways/sidewalks and controlled access to dorms/residences.

Programs of Study: JBU confers B.A., B.S., B.Mus.Ed., B.S.E. and B.S.Eng. degrees. Associate and master's degrees are also awarded. Bachelor's degrees are awarded in BIOLOGICAL SCIENCE (biochemistry and biology/biological science), BUSINESS (accounting and business administration and management), COMMUNICATIONS AND THE ARTS (broadcasting, design, English, graphic design, illustration, journalism, music, public relations, and Spanish), COMPUTER AND PHYSICAL SCIENCE (chemistry, computer science, digital arts/technology, mathematics, and science), EDUCATION (early childhood education, elementary education, middle school education, music education, physical education, science education, and secondary education), ENGINEERING AND ENVIRONMENTAL DESIGN (construction management, electrical/electronics engineering, engineering, and environmental science), HEALTH PROFESSIONS (community health work and sports medicine), SOCIAL SCIENCE (biblical studies, crosscultural studies, family and community services, history, interdisciplinary studies, international studies, ministries, political science/government, psychology, theological studies, and youth ministry). Engineering, teacher education, visual arts and business are the strongest academically. Business, digital media, engineering and graphic design have the largest enrollments.

Required: All students must complete 25 hours of lower-level core courses, 19 to 22 of elective courses in wellness, natural science, mathematics, philosophy, arts, social studies, and global studies, and 8 hours in upper-level core courses. A total of 142 to 145 credit hours (includes hours for minor) with a minimum GPA of 2.25 (2.5 in profession education, teaching, and other state-required courses) is required to graduate. Students must complete an exit assessment before graduation.

Special: Internships or field experiences are available in most majors. Study abroad in 15 countries, a Washington semester, work-study, and accelerated degree programs in organizational management and early childhood education are offered. There are a freshman honors program and 12 departmental honors programs.

Faculty/Classroom: 67% of faculty are male; 33% are female. No introductory courses are taught by graduate students. The average class size in an introductory lecture is 22; in a laboratory is 15; and in a regular course is 20.

Admissions: 70% of the 2013-2014 applicants were accepted. The SAT scores for the 2013-2014 freshman class were: Critical Reading--20% below 500, 33% between 500 and 599, 35% between 600 and 699, and 12% between 700 and 800; Math--15% below 500, 41% between 500 and 599, 34% between 600 and 699, and 10% between 700 and 800; Writing--29% below 500, 34% between 500 and 599, 29% between 600 and 699, and 8% between 700 and 800. The ACT scores were 1% below 21, 28% between 21 and 23, 25% between 24 and 26, 25% between 27 and 28, and 18% above 28. 33% of the current freshmen were in the top fifth of their class; 60% were in the top two fifths.

Requirements: The SAT or ACT is recommended. Applicants should have completed 14 high school units, including 4 in English, 3 in math, 2 each in science, social studies, and foreign language, and 1 in history. 2 references are required: 1 from a high school counselor or teacher, the other from a pastor or church leader. An essay and an interview are recommended. Applicants 21 years of age or older may be admitted without ACT or SAT scores. A GPA of 2.5 is required. AP and CLEP credits are accepted.

Procedure: Freshmen are admitted fall and spring. Entrance exams should be taken during the spring of the junior year or fall of the senior year. There is a rolling admissions plan. Applications should be filed by May 1 for fall entry, along with a $25 fee. Applications are accepted online.

Transfer: 65 transfer students enrolled in 2012-2013. Transfer applicants must have completed at least 12 units of college work, with a minimum 2.5 GPA. 39 of 124 credits required for the bachelor's degree must be completed at JBU.

Visiting: There are regularly scheduled orientations for prospective students, including campus tours, consultations with faculty and coaches, and examination of financial aid opportunities. There are guides for informal visits, visitors may sit in on classes, and stay overnight. To schedule a visit, contact the Admissions Office.

Financial Aid: The CSS/Profile, FAFSA, and FFS are required. The priority date for freshman financial aid applications for fall entry is March 1.

International Students: They must take the TOEFL.

Computers: All students may access the system Monday - Thursday, 7:30 a.m. to 12 a.m. , Friday 7:30 a.m. to 5 p.m. , Saturday 12 p.m. to 5 p.m. and Sunday 3 p.m. to 11 p.m. There are no time limits and no fees.

Graduates: From July 1, 2012 to June 30, 2013, 466 bachelor's degrees were awarded. The most popular majors were business/marketing (50%), Education (10%), and Visual and Performing Art (7%). 63 companies recruited on campus in 2012-2013. In an average class, 1% graduate in 3 years or less, 66% graduate in 4 years or less, 58% graduate in 5 years or less, and 68% graduate in 6 years or less. Of the 2012 graduating class, 27% were enrolled in graduate school within 6 months of graduation, and 98% were employed.

Admissions Contact: Don Crandall, Vice President for Enrollment. E-Mail: *jbuinfo@jbu.edu* Web: *www.jbu.edu*

LYON COLLEGE C-2

Batesville, AR 72501 (870) 307-7250
(800) 423-2542; (870) 307-7542

Full-time: 273 men, 304 women	**Faculty:** 41; IIB, --$
Part-time: 7 men, 16 women	**Ph.D.s:** 95%
Graduate: n/av	**Student/Faculty:** 11 to 1
Year: semesters, summer session	**Tuition:** $23,406
Application Deadline: August 1	**Room & Board:** $7840
Freshman Class: n/av	

VERY COMPETITIVE

Lyon College, founded in 1872, is a selective, private, residential, liberal arts college affiliated with the Presbyterian Church. There is one undergraduate school. In addition to regional accreditation, Lyon has baccalaureate program accreditation with NCATE. The library contains 169,177 volumes, 2,928 microform items, and 6,921 audio/video tapes/CDs/DVDs, and subscribes to 31,799 periodicals including electronic. Computerized library services include interlibrary loans, database searching, Internet access, and Wi-Fi capability. Special learning facilities include an art gallery, a language lab, a math and science tutoring lab, and a computer lab. The 136-acre campus is in a small town 90 miles north of Little Rock. Including any residence halls, there are 30 buildings.

Student Life: 77% of undergraduates are from Arkansas. Others are from 21 states, and 13 foreign countries. 75% are White. The average age of freshmen is 18; all undergraduates, 21. 28% do not continue beyond their first year; 50% remain to graduate.

Housing: 492 students can be accommodated in college housing, which includes single-sex and coed dorms and on-campus apartments. In addition, there are special-interest houses, freshman-only housing. On-campus housing is guaranteed for all 4 years. 77% of students live on campus; of those, 70% remain on campus on weekends. All students may keep cars.

Activities: 28% of men belong to 3 national fraternities; 28% of women belong to 2 national sororities. There are 40 groups on campus, including art, bagpipe, band, cheerleading, choir, drama, ethnic, gay, honors, international, literary magazine, newspaper, orchestra, political, professional, religious, social, social service, student government, and yearbook. Popular campus events include Arkansas Scottish Festival, Service Day and Baccalaureate.

Sports: There are 4 intercollegiate sports for men and 5 for women, and 14 intramural sports for men and 14 for women. Facilities include an 1100-seat gym, softball, baseball, and soccer fields, a cross-country trail, an indoor swimming pool, 6 tennis courts, an indoor baseball practice facility, and a weight room.

Disabled Students: 80% of the campus is accessible. Facilities include wheelchair ramps, elevators, special parking, specially equipped restrooms, and special housing.

Services: Counseling and information services are available, as is tutoring in some subjects, foreign language and chemistry. writing and math labs are available.

Campus Safety and Security: Measures include 24-hour foot and vehicle patrol, emergency notification system, and security escort services. There are lighted pathways/sidewalks.

Programs of Study: Lyon confers B.A., and B.S. degrees. Bachelor's degrees are awarded in AGRICULTURE (environmental studies), BIOLOGICAL SCIENCE (biology/biological science), BUSINESS (accounting and business administration and management), COMMUNICATIONS AND THE ARTS (art, dramatic arts, English, music, and Spanish), COMPUTER AND PHYSICAL SCIENCE (chemistry and mathematics), EDUCATION (early childhood education), SOCIAL SCIENCE (economics, history, political science/government, psychology, and religion). English, biology, and psychology have the largest enrollments.

Required: All students are required to demonstrate proficiency in English composition, math, and foreign language; meet distribution requirements in social sciences, arts and literature, natural science and math, and religion and philosophy; take the 2-semester Western Tradition course sequence; complete the freshman orientation program; and take 1 semester of phys ed in each of the 4 years. The core curriculum requires 31 to 49 credit hours. A total of 120 credits, with a minimum GPA of 2.0, is required to graduate.

Special: Internships are offered as is cross-registration (for certain courses) with the University of Arkansas Community College at Batesville. A 2-2 engineering program is offered with the University of Missouri in Rolla, and a 3-2 program is offered with the University of Arkansas at Fayetteville. Work-study courses, study abroad in 4 countries, dual majors, student-designed majors, pass/fail options, a Washington semester, and credit for military experience are available. A 3-2 program is available with the University of Minnesota. There are 14 national honor societies.

Faculty/Classroom: 52% of faculty are male; 48% are female. All teach and do research. No introductory courses are taught by graduate students. The average class size in an introductory lecture is 23; in a laboratory is 19; and in a regular course is 17.

Admissions: 56% of the current freshmen were in the top fifth of their class; 79% were in the top two fifths. 12 freshmen graduated first in their class.

Requirements: The SAT or ACT is required. In addition, applicants should have completed a minimum of 16 high school units, including 4 in English, 3 each in science, math, and social sciences, and 2 in a foreign language. A letter of recommendation and an admission interview are recommended. AP credits are accepted.

Procedure: Freshmen are admitted fall and spring. Entrance exams should be taken in spring of the junior year and fall of the senior year. There are deferred admissions and rolling admissions plans. Applications should be filed by August 1 for fall entry; January 1 for spring entry, along with a $25 fee. Notification is sent on a rolling basis. Applications are accepted online.

Transfer: 61 transfer students enrolled in 2012-2013. Transfer applicants with 24 or more semester hours must submit a transcript and statement of good standing from each institution attended. Students with fewer than 24 semester hours must submit their final high school transcript and ACT or SAT scores. 30 of 120 credits required for the bachelor's degree must be completed at Lyon.

Visiting: There are regularly scheduled orientations for prospective students, consisting of a campus tour, admission and financial aid orientation, and information sessions with faculty and students. There are guides for informal visits and visitors may sit in on classes. To schedule a visit, contact the Admission Office.

Financial Aid: In 2013-2014, 100% of all full-time freshmen and 99% of continuing full-time students received some form of financial aid. 63% of all full-time freshmen and 62% of continuing full-time students received need-based aid. The average freshman award was $26,559. Need-based scholarships or need-based grants averaged $6,262 ($8,500 maximum); need-based self-help aid (loans and jobs) averaged $7,243 ($10,500 maximum); non-need-based athletic scholarships averaged $13,322 ($31,154 maximum); and other non-need-based awards and non-need-based scholarships averaged $13,416 ($61,154 maximum). 26% of undergraduate students work part-time. Average annual earnings from campus work are $998. The average financial indebtedness of the 2013 graduate was $17,179. The FAFSA is required. The priority date for freshman financial aid applications for fall entry is March 1.

International Students: There are 27 international students enrolled. The school actively recruits these students. They must take the TOEFL with a minimum score of 550 on the paper-based TOEFL (PBT) or 79 on the Internet-based version (iBT), IESLS. They must also take the SAT or ACT.

Computers: All students may access the system. There are no time limits and no fees.

Graduates: From July 1, 2012 to June 30, 2013, 100 bachelor's degrees were awarded. The most popular majors were psychology (21%), biology (12%), and English (11%). 30 companies recruited on campus in 2012-2013. In an average class, 43% graduate in 4 years or less, 49% graduate in 5 years or less, and 47% graduate in 6 years or less.

Admissions Contact: Josh Manning, Director of Enrollment Services. E-Mail: *admissions@lyon.edu* Web: *www.lyon.edu*

OUACHITA BAPTIST UNIVERSITY B-4

Arkadelphia, AR 71998 **(870) 245-5110**
(800) 342-5628; (870) 245-5500

Full-time: 704 men, 803 women	**Faculty:** 108; IIB, --$
Part-time: 22 men, 14 women	**Ph.D.s:** 82%
Year: semesters, summer session	**Student/Faculty:** 12 to 1
Application Deadline: open	**Tuition:** $22,370
	Room & Board: $6640

Freshman Class: 1740 applied, 1220 accepted, 393 enrolled
SAT CR/M: 517/535 **ACT:** 24 **VERY COMPETITIVE**

Ouachita Baptist University, founded in 1886, is a private liberal arts institution affiliated with the Arkansas Baptist State Convention. There are 7 undergraduate schools. In addition to regional accreditation, Ouachita has baccalaureate program accreditation with AACSB, ADA, NASM, and NCATE. The 2 libraries contain 845,042 volumes, 325,022 microform items, and 3,525 audio/video tapes/CDs/DVDs, and subscribe to 9,321 periodicals including electronic. Computerized library services include interlibrary loans and database searching. Special learning facilities include an art gallery and planetarium. The 200-acre campus is in a small town 65 miles southwest of Little Rock. Including any residence halls, there are 35 buildings.

Student Life: 61% of undergraduates are from Arkansas. Others are from 29 states, 34 foreign countries, and Canada. 90% are from public schools. 84% are White. 80% are Protestant; 15% Unknown. The average age of freshmen is 18; all undergraduates, 21. 20% do not continue beyond their first year; 60% remain to graduate.

Housing: 1598 students can be accommodated in college housing, which includes single-sex dorms, on-campus apartments, off-campus apartments, and married student housing. On-campus housing is guaranteed for all 4 years. 94% of students live on campus; of those, 50% remain on campus on weekends. Alcohol is not permitted. All students may keep cars.

Activities: 20% of men belong to 4 local fraternities; 35% of women belong to 5 local sororities. There are 60 groups on campus, including band, cheerleading, choir, chorale, chorus, computers, drama, drill team, ethnic, film, honors, international, jazz band, literary magazine, marching band, musical theater, newspaper, opera, orchestra, pep band, photography, political, professional, radio and TV, religious, social, social service, student government, and yearbook. Popular campus events include International Student Fair, Tiger Tunes and Tiger Traks.

Sports: There are 8 intercollegiate sports for men and 8 for women, and 5 intramural sports for men and 5 for women. Facilities include a 6000-seat football stadium; an indoor/outdoor tennis center; an indoor complex featuring a 2500-seat basketball arena, a swimming pool, a weight room, racquetball courts, and volleyball courts.

Disabled Students: 95% of the campus is accessible. Facilities include wheelchair ramps, elevators, special parking, specially equipped restrooms, special class scheduling, and lowered drinking fountains.

Services: Counseling and information services are available, as is tutoring in most subjects. There is a reader service for the blind, and remedial math, reading, and writing.

Campus Safety and Security: Measures include 24-hour foot and vehicle patrol and emergency notification system. There are emergency telephones, lighted pathways/sidewalks, and controlled access to dorms/residences.

Programs of Study: Ouachita confers B.A., B.S., B.M. and B.M.E. degrees. Bachelor's degrees are awarded in BIOLOGICAL SCIENCE (biology/biological science), BUSINESS (accounting, business administration and management, and recreation and leisure services), COMMUNICATIONS AND THE ARTS (applied music, art, church music, communications, dramatic arts, English, graphic design, instrumental performance, instrumental music education, keyboard - piano concentration, music, music composition, musical theater, piano/organ, piano performance, Spanish, speech/debate/rhetoric, theatre arts, visual and performing arts, and voice), COMPUTER AND PHYSICAL SCIENCE (chemistry, computer science, mathematics, and physics), EDUCATION (art education, business education, early childhood education, elementary education, foreign languages education, mathematics education, middle school education, music education, science education, secondary education, social studies education, and social studies secondary school education), HEALTH PROFESSIONS (predentistry, premedicine, and speech pathology/audiology), SOCIAL SCIENCE (biblical languages, biblical studies, Christian studies, dietetics, history, ministries, philosophy, philosophy and religion, political science/government, prelaw, psychology, religion, religious music, sociology, theological studies, and youth ministry). Biology, business administration, and Christian studies have the largest enrollments.

Required: All students must fulfill 48 semester hours of general education courses, including 2 semesters of 1 foreign language and 7 chapel credits. A total of 120 semester hours, with a minimum GPA of 2.0, is required for graduation.

Special: Ouachita offers cross registration with Henderson State University, a Washington semester for political science majors, internships for business majors and some mass communications and Christian studies majors, B.A.-B.S. degrees, dual majors, pass/fail options, and non-degree study. Study-abroad opportunities are available in Germany, England, France, Italy, Russia, Japan, China, Hong Kong, Australia, Austria, Belize, Scotland, Spain, South Africa, Costa Rica, and Morocco. There are 8 national honor societies and a freshman honors program.

Faculty/Classroom: 59% of faculty are male; 41% are female. All teach undergraduates, 45% do research, and 45% do both. No introductory courses are taught by graduate students. The average class size in an introductory lecture is 30; in a laboratory is 12; and in a regular course is 19.

Admissions: 70% of the 2013-2014 applicants were accepted. The SAT scores for the 2013-2014 freshman class were: Critical Reading--45% below 500, 38% between 500 and 599, 11% between 600 and 699, and 6% between 700 and 800; Math--34% below 500, 42% between 500 and 599, 21% between 600 and 699, and 3% between 700 and 800. The ACT scores were 10% below 21, 33% between 21 and 23, 22% between 24 and 26, 18% between 27 and 28, and 17% above 28. 50% of the current freshmen were in the top fifth of their class; 70% were in the top two fifths. There were 15 National Merit finalists. 17 freshmen graduated first in their class.

Requirements: The SAT or ACT is required. Applicants should have completed 19 high school units, including 4 in English, 3 in social science, and 2 each in natural science and math. 2 in a foreign language and 1/2 in computer science are also recommended. A GPA of 2.8 is required. AP and CLEP credits are accepted.

Procedure: Freshmen are admitted fall, spring, and summer. Entrance exams should be taken in the junior year. There are deferred admissions and rolling admissions plans. Application deadlines are open. Applications are accepted online.

Transfer: 46 transfer students enrolled in 2012-2013. Applicants must be eligible to return to their previous school. 60 of 120 credits required for the bachelor's degree must be completed at Ouachita.

Visiting: There are regularly scheduled orientations for prospective students, include a campus tour, a question-and-answer session, and meetings with professors and students. There are guides for informal visits, visitors may sit in on classes, and stay overnight. To schedule a visit, contact the Admissions Counseling Office.

Financial Aid: In 2013-2014, 99% of all full-time freshmen and 97% of continuing full-time students received some form of financial aid. 72% of all full-time freshmen and 81% of continuing full-time students received need-based aid. The average freshman award was $19,418. Need-based scholarships or need-based grants averaged $13,758; need-based self-help aid (loans and jobs) averaged $3,466; non-need-based athletic scholarships averaged $7,922; and other non-need-based awards and non-need-based scholarships averaged $9,338. 50% of undergraduate students work part-time. Average annual earnings from campus work are $1800. The average financial indebtedness of the 2013 graduate was $24,367. The FAFSA and the college's own financial statement are required. The priority date for freshman financial aid applications for fall entry is January 15.

International Students: There are 33 international students enrolled. The school actively recruits these students. They must take the TOEFL with a minimum score of 550 on the paper-based TOEFL (PBT) or 80 on the Internet-based version (iBT).

Computers: All students may access the system. There are no time limits. The fee is $80.

Graduates: From July 1, 2012 to June 30, 2013, 293 bachelor's degrees were awarded. The most popular majors were business (14%), visual and performing arts (13%), and biology (12%). 35 companies recruited on campus in 2012-2013. In an average class, 1% graduate in 3 years or less, 50% graduate in 4 years or less, 58% graduate in 5 years or less, and 69% graduate in 6 years or less. Of the 2012 graduating class, 45% were enrolled in graduate school within 6 months of graduation, and 92% were employed.

Admissions Contact: Lori Motl, Director of Admissions Counseling. E-Mail: *admissions@alpha.obu.edu* Web: *www.obu.edu*

PHILANDER SMITH COLLEGE C-3

Little Rock, AR 72202 (501) 370-5221
(800) 446-6772; (501) 370-5225

Full-time: 236 men, 444 women
Part-time: 22 men, 30 women
Year: semesters, summer session
Application Deadline: July 15
Faculty: 42
Ph.D.s: 55%
Student/Faculty: 15 to 1
Tuition: $12,260
Room & Board: $8500
Freshman Class: 2906 applied, 1976 accepted, 197 enrolled
SAT CR/M/W: 450/439/437 **ACT:** 18 **LESS COMPETITIVE**

Philander Smith College, founded in 1877, is affiliated with the United Methodist Church. The college offers undergraduate degrees in education, humanities, natural and physical sciences, business, and social science. The figures in the above capsule and in this profile are approximate. In addition to regional accreditation, PSC has baccalaureate program accreditation with ACBSP, CSWE, and NCATE. The library contains 83,000 volumes, 2,000 microform items, and 1,100 audio/video tapes/CDs/DVDs, and subscribes to 1,283 periodicals including electronic. Computerized library services include interlibrary loans, database searching, Internet access, and Wi-Fi capability. The 25-acre campus is in an urban area in Little Rock. Including any residence halls, there are 16 buildings.

Student Life: 52% of undergraduates are from out of state, mostly the Mid-West. Students are from 30 states, and 4 foreign countries. 92% are African American. 61% are Protestant; 31% claim no religious affiliation. The average age of freshmen is 18; all undergraduates, 24. 40% do not continue beyond their first year; 32% remain to graduate.

Housing: 392 students can be accommodated in college housing, which includes coed dorms. In addition, there are honors houses. On-campus housing is guaranteed for the freshman year only, is available on a first-come, and first-served basis. 53% of students live on campus. Alcohol is not permitted. All students may keep cars.

Activities: 4% of men belong to 4 national fraternities; 2% of women belong to 4 national sororities. There are 50 groups on campus, including cheerleading, chess, choir, dance, gay, honors, opera, pep band, political, professional, religious, social, social service, and student government. Popular campus events include Homecoming, Religous Emphasis Week, Sex Week, Greek Step Shows and First Thursdays.

Sports: There are 1 intercollegiate sports for men and 2 for women, and 1 intramural sports for men and 1 for women. Facilities include a complete gym with racquetball court and weight rooms.

Disabled Students: 90% of the campus is accessible. Facilities include wheelchair ramps, elevators, special parking, specially equipped restrooms, and lowered drinking fountains.

Services: Counseling and information services are available, as is tutoring in every subject. There is remedial math, reading, and writing.

Campus Safety and Security: Measures include 24-hour foot and vehicle patrol, emergency notification system, and security escort services. There are lighted pathways/sidewalks and controlled access to dorms/residences.

Programs of Study: PSC confers B.A., B.S., B.B.A. and B.S.W. degrees. Bachelor's degrees are awarded in BIOLOGICAL SCIENCE (biology/biological science), BUSINESS (business administration and management), COMMUNICATIONS AND THE ARTS (English and music), COMPUTER AND PHYSICAL SCIENCE (chemistry, computer science, and mathematics), EDUCATION (business education, early childhood education, middle school education, and physical education), SOCIAL SCIENCE (philosophy and religion, political science/government, psychology, social work, and sociology). Biology, computer science, math, chemistry, and education are the strongest academically. Biology, and business administration have the largest enrollments.

Required: To graduate, all students must complete at least 124 credit hours with a minimum 2.0 GPA and satisfy general education requirements, which include courses in speech, English composition, literature, philosophy and religion, physical and life science, math, computing, psychology, political science or sociology, economics, U.S. history, phys ed, and health.

Special: Internships in science, business administration, political science, social work, and other fields are available. There are 2 national honor societies.

Faculty/Classroom: 52% of faculty are male; 48% are female. All teach undergraduates, 3% do research, and 3% do both. No introductory courses are taught by graduate students. The average class size in an introductory lecture is 30; in a laboratory is 15; and in a regular course is 20.

Admissions: In a recent year, 68% applicants were accepted. The SAT scores in a recent year freshman class were: Critical Reading--67% below 500, 29% between 500 and 599, 5% between 600 and 699, Math--62% below 500, 38% between 500 and 599, Writing--76% below 500, 24% between 500 and 599. The ACT scores were 81% below 21, 9% between 21 and 23, 8% between 24 and 26, 1% between 27 and 28, and 1% above 28. There were 2 National Merit finalists. 2 freshmen graduated first in their class.

Requirements: The ACT is required. The SAT is accepted. Applicants must be graduates of an accredited secondary school or have a GED certificate. A GPA of 2.0 is required for unconditional admission. Students should have completed 16 academic credits, including 4 units of English, 2 of math, and 2 from 2 of the following: foreign language, science, or social studies. A GPA of 2.0 is required. AP and CLEP credits are accepted. Important factors in the admissions decision are ability to finance college education, leadership record, advanced placement or honors courses, personality/intangible qualities, geographical diversity, parents or siblings attended your school, evidence of special talent, extracurricular activities record, recommendations by alumni, and recommendations by school officials.

Procedure: Freshmen are admitted fall, spring, and summer. Entrance exams should be taken by July 15th. There are early admissions, deferred admissions, and rolling admissions plans. Early decision applications should be filed by March 15; regular applications, by July 15 for fall entry, along with a $25 fee. Notification of early decision is sent March 15; regular decision. Applications are accepted online.

Transfer: 59 transfer students enrolled in 2012-2013. 2.0 GPA 22 of 124 credits required for the bachelor's degree must be completed at PSC.

Visiting: There are regularly scheduled orientations for prospective students, presentation with handouts and question and answer and campus tour. There are guides for informal visits and visitors may sit in on classes.

Financial Aid: In a recent year, 97% of all full-time freshmen and 97% of continuing full-time students received some form of financial aid. 95% of all full-time freshmen and 96% of continuing full-time students received need-based aid. The average freshman award was $18,447. Need-based scholarships or need-based grants averaged $7,411 ($4,588 maximum); need-based self-help aid (loans and jobs) averaged $10,741 ($18,000 maximum); non-need-based athletic scholarships averaged $3,819 ($14,150 maximum); and other non-need-based awards and non-need-based scholarships averaged $1,800 ($5,175 maximum). 1% of undergraduate students work part-time. Average annual earnings from campus work are $2300. The average financial indebtedness of the 2013 graduate was $35,813. The FAFSA and the college's own financial statement are required. Check with the school for filing freshman financial aid applications.

International Students: There are 35 international students enrolled. The school actively recruits these students. They must take the TOEFL with a minimum score of 500 on the paper-based TOEFL (PBT), or IELP, or present an ESL certificate. They must also take the SAT or ACT.

Computers: All students may access the system. There are no time limits and no fees.

Graduates: In a recent year, 98 bachelor's degrees were awarded. The most popular majors were business admnistration (19%), organizational management (10%), and biology (10%). In an average class, 21% graduate in 4 years or less, 30% graduate in 5 years or less, and 32% graduate in 6 years or less. In a recent graduating class, 39% were enrolled in graduate school within 6 months of graduation.

Admissions Contact: C. Young, Office Manager. E-Mail: *cyoung@philander.edu* Web: *www.philander.edu*

SOUTHERN ARKANSAS UNIVERSITY B-5

Magnolia, AR 71754 (870) 235-4040
(800) 332-SAUM; (870) 235-4931

Full-time: 1130 men, 1450 women	**Faculty:** n/av; IIB, --$
Part-time: 150 men, 400 women	**Ph.D.s:** n/av
Graduate: 65 men, 225 women	**Student/Faculty:** n/av
Year: semesters, summer session	**Tuition:** $10,116
Application Deadline: open	**Room & Board:** $5200
Freshman Class: n/av	
ACT: required	**COMPETITIVE**

Southern Arkansas University, founded in 1909, is a state-supported liberal arts institution offering degrees in business administration, education, liberal and performing arts, and science and technology. The figures in the above capsule and in this profile are approximate. There are 4 undergraduate schools and one graduate school. In addition to regional accreditation, SAU has baccalaureate program accreditation with CSWE, NASAD, NASM, NCATE, and NLN. The library contains 150,341 volumes, 669,721 microform items, and 12,214 audio/video tapes/CDs/DVDs, and subscribes to 725 periodicals including electronic. Computerized library services include interlibrary loans, database searching, and Internet access. Special learning facilities include an art gallery, radio station, biological field station, and university farm. The 781-acre campus is in a small town. Including any residence halls, there are 27 buildings.

Student Life: 71% of undergraduates are from Arkansas. Others are from 22 states, 40 foreign countries, and Canada. 97% are from public schools. 69% are White; 24% African American. The average age of freshmen is 18; all undergraduates, 28. 32% do not continue beyond their first year.

Housing: 1043 students can be accommodated in college housing, which includes single-sex and coed dorms. In addition, there are honors houses, and an International house. On-campus housing is guaranteed for all 4 years. 66% of students commute. Alcohol is not permitted. All students may keep cars.

Activities: 6% of men belong to 7 national fraternities; 5% of women belong to 7 national sororities. There are 80 groups on campus, including art, band, cheerleading, choir, chorale, computers, dance, drama, drill team, ethnic, honors, international, jazz band, literary magazine, marching band, musical theater, newspaper, pep band, photography, political, professional, radio and TV, religious, social, and student government. Popular campus events include Spring Fling and Celebration of Lights (Christmas).

Sports: There are 8 intercollegiate sports for men and 8 for women, and 7 intramural sports for men and 7 for women. Facilities include a 6500-seat stadium, a 1450-seat gym, 10 lighted tennis courts, baseball and softball fields, a track, an indoor pool, a dance studio, a multipurpose building with basketball and volleyball courts, and a wellness center.

Disabled Students: 95% of the campus is accessible. Facilities include wheelchair ramps, elevators, special parking, specially equipped restrooms, special class scheduling, lowered drinking fountains, lowered telephones.

Services: Counseling and information services are available, as is tutoring in most subjects. There is remedial math, reading, and writing. and supplemental instruction in courses with high drop/failure rates.

Campus Safety and Security: Measures include 24-hour foot and vehicle patrol and security escort services. There are emergency telephones and lighted pathways/sidewalks.

Programs of Study: SAU confers B.A., B.S., B.A.S., B.B.A., B.M.E., B.S.E. and B.S.W. degrees. Associate and master's degrees are also awarded. Bachelor's degrees are awarded in AGRICULTURE (agricultural business management and agriculture), BIOLOGICAL SCIENCE (biology/biological science), BUSINESS (accounting and business administration and management), COMMUNICATIONS AND THE ARTS (art, broadcasting, communications, English, journalism, and Spanish), COMPUTER AND PHYSICAL SCIENCE (chemistry, computer science, and mathematics), EDUCATION (agricultural education, art education, business education, elementary education, health education, middle school education, music education, and science education), ENGINEERING AND ENVIRONMENTAL DESIGN (manufacturing technology), HEALTH PROFESSIONS (medical laboratory technology), SOCIAL SCIENCE (community services, history, political science/government, psychology, and sociology). Accounting and physical science is the strongest academically. Business administration and health education/kinesiology have the largest enrollments.

Required: All students must complete 43 semester hours of general education courses, including 18 in humanities, 12 in social sciences, 4 each in biological and physical science, 3 in math, and 2 to 3 in physical and health education. A minimum of 124 total semester hours, with a minimum GPA of 2.0, is required to graduate.

Special: Work-study programs at SAU, business and Spanish internships, study abroad in Russia and Mexico, and a general studies degree are offered. There are 1 national honor society, a freshman honors program, and 6 departmental honors programs.

Faculty/Classroom: 56% of faculty are male; 44% are female. 97% teach undergraduates, 10% do research, and 10% do both. No introductory courses are taught by graduate students. The average class size in an introductory lecture is 23; in a laboratory is 18; and in a regular course is 20.

Requirements: The ACT is required, with a minimum composite of 19. Applicants should have completed 4 high school units in English, 3 each in math and social studies, and 2 each in natural science and a foreign language. The GED is accepted. AP and CLEP credits are accepted.

Procedure: Freshmen are admitted to all sessions. Entrance exams should be taken in the fall prior to enrollment. There are deferred admissions and rolling admissions plans. Application deadlines are open. Notification is sent on a rolling basis. Applications are accepted online.

Transfer: Applicants must be eligible to return to their previous school and meet GPA requirements. Those with fewer than 24 credit hours must submit ACT or SAT scores and a high school transcript or GED. 30 of 124 credits required for the bachelor's degree must be completed at SAU.

Visiting: There are regularly scheduled orientations for prospective students. There are guides for informal visits, visitors may sit in on classes, and stay overnight. To schedule a visit, contact the Admissions Office.

Financial Aid: The FAFSA is required. Check with the school for current application deadlines.

International Students: The school actively recruits these students. They must take the TOEFL. They must also take the ACT.

Computers: All students may access the system. There are no time limits and no fees.

Admissions Contact: Sarah Jennings, Dean of Enrollment Services. E-Mail: *sejennings@saumag.edu* Web: *www.saumag.edu*

UNIVERSITY OF ARKANSAS SYSTEM

The University of Arkansas System, established in 1871, is a system in Arkansas. It is governed by a board of trustees, whose chief administrator is the president. The primary goal of the system is teaching, research, and public service. The student enrollment for all five campuses is usually 33,000 with 2500 faculty members. Altogether there are 240 baccalaureate, 112 master's, and 30 doctoral programs offered in the University of Arkansas System. Profiles of the 4-year campuses are included in this section.

UNIVERSITY OF ARKANSAS AT FAYETTEVILLE A-1

Fayetteville, AR 72701 (479) 575-5346
(800) 377-8632; (479) 575-7515

Full-time: 9044 men, 9521 women	**Faculty:** n/av; I, --$
Part-time: 1303 men, 1141 women	**Ph.D.s:** 75%
Graduate: 2244 men, 2078 women	**Student/Faculty:** 19 to 1
Year: semesters, summer session	**Tuition:** $7818 ($19,074)
Application Deadline: August 1	**Room & Board:** $9042
Freshman Class: 18908 applied, 11066 accepted, 4339 enrolled	
SAT CR/M: 540/560 **ACT:** 25	**VERY COMPETITIVE**

The University of Arkansas at Fayetteville, founded in 1871, is a land-grant institution offering undergraduate and graduate programs in liberal arts and sciences, agricultural, food, social and natural sciences, life sciences, business administration, engineering, architecture, education, law, and human environmental sciences. There are 8 undergraduate schools and 2 graduate schools. In addition to regional accreditation, U of A has baccalaureate program accreditation with AACSB, ABET, ACEJMC, ADA, CSWE, FIDER, NAAB, NASM, and NCATE. The 4 libraries contain 2.0 million volumes, 5.8 million microform items, and 37,256 audio/video tapes/CDs/DVDs, and subscribe to 27,518 periodicals including electronic. Computerized library services include interlibrary loans, database searching, Internet access, and Wi-Fi capability. Special learning facilities include a planetarium, radio station, TV station, numerous research centers. The 510-acre campus is in an urban area 190 miles northwest of Little Rock. Including any residence halls, there are 189 buildings.

Student Life: 58% of undergraduates are from Arkansas. Others are from 50 states, 119 foreign countries, and Canada. 85% are from public schools. 77% are White. The average age of freshmen is 18; all undergraduates, 21. 18% do not continue beyond their first year; 60% remain to graduate.

Housing: 5652 students can be accommodated in college housing, which includes single-sex and coed dorms and on-campus apartments. In addition, there are honors houses, special-interest houses, fraternity houses, sorority houses, international living/learning community and First-year experience program. On-campus housing is guaranteed for the freshman year only, is available on a first-come, and first-served basis. 75% of students commute. All students may keep cars.

Activities: 23% of men belong to 19 national fraternities; 36% of women belong to 14 national sororities. There are 469 groups on campus, including art, band, cheerleading, chess, choir, chorale, chorus, computers, dance, drama, drill team, ethnic, gay, honors, international, jazz band, literary magazine, marching band, musical theater, newspaper, opera, orchestra, pep band, photography, political, professional, radio and TV, religious, social, social service, student government, symphony, and yearbook. Popular campus events include Academic Festival, International Banquet and Fashion Show, and Martin Luther King Jr. Event.

Sports: There are 8 intercollegiate sports for men and 11 for women, and 56 intramural sports for men and 56 for women. Facilities include a 72,000-seat stadium, a 20,000-seat basketball arena, a 10,700-seat baseball stadium, a 9000-seat volleyball arena, a 1500-seat soccer stadium, 4 gyms, indoor and outdoor jogging tracks, 2 dance studios, 10 racquetball courts, a fitness and weight training center, a swimming pool, an outdoor recreation center, 10 outdoor and 6 indoor tennis courts, 10 multipurpose playing fields, an indoor practice football field, a 5000-seat indoor running track, a 7,000 seat outdoor track, a 1,500-seat softball stadium, and a gym/weight training and conditioning facility.

Disabled Students: All of the campus is accessible. Facilities include wheelchair ramps, elevators, special parking, specially equipped restrooms, special class scheduling, lowered drinking fountains, lowered telephones.

Services: Counseling and information services are available, as is tutoring in some subjects, Mathematical sciences and statistics, biological sciences, physics, chemistry, biochemistry, geosciences, anthropology, political science, sustainability, and world languages There is a reader service for the blind, and remedial math, reading, and writing. There is a math resource center and a writing center. Student Support Services and individual colleges have labs and other facilities.

Campus Safety and Security: Measures include 24-hour foot and vehicle patrol, emergency notification system, self-defense education, and security escort services. There are shuttle buses, emergency telephones, lighted pathways/sidewalks, controlled access to dorms/residences, crime prevention lectures, rape defense program, property engraving, bicycle patrol, and electronic card access in residence halls.

Programs of Study: U of A confers B.A., B.S., B.Arch., B.E.A., B.I.D., B.L.A., B.M., B.S.A., B.S.B.A., B.S.B.E., B.S.C.E., B.S.Ch.E., B.S.C.S.E., B.S.Cmp.E., B.S.E., B.S.E.E., B.S.H.E.S., B.S.I.B., B.S.I.E., B.S.M.E., B.S.N. and B.S.P.A. degrees. Master's and doctoral degrees are also awarded. Bachelor's degrees are awarded in AGRICULTURE (agricultural business management, agricultural communications, agricultural economics, animal science, horticulture, poultry science, and soil science), BIOLOGICAL SCIENCE (biology/biological science and nutrition), BUSINESS (accounting, apparel and accessories marketing, banking and finance, business administration and management, business economics, business information systems, finance, hospitality management services, human resources, international business management, marketing management, marketing/retailing/merchandising, and transportation management), COMMUNICATIONS AND THE ARTS (advertising, art, communication, dramatic arts, English, French, German, journalism, music, and Spanish), COMPUTER AND PHYSICAL SCIENCE (chemistry, computer science, earth science, geology, mathematics, physics, and statistics), EDUCATION (agricultural education, business education, (Education) Childhood Education, career, technical education & training, childhood education: 1-6, early childhood education, elementary education, middle school education, music education, recreation education, and technical education), ENGINEERING AND ENVIRONMENTAL DESIGN (architecture, bioengineering, chemical engineering, civil engineering, computer engineering, electrical/electronics engineering, environmental science, industrial engineering, interior design, landscape architecture, landscape architecture/design, and mechanical engineering), HEALTH PROFESSIONS (exercise science, health science, and nursing), SOCIAL SCIENCE (African studies, African American studies, American studies, anthropology, architectural studies, asian studies, classical/ancient civilization, criminal justice, dietetics, economics, European studies, food science, geography, history, human development, international relations, Latin American studies, Middle Eastern studies, philosophy, political science/government, psychology, public administration, social work, and sociology). Business, chemical and electrical engineering, and computer science are the strongest academically. Nursing, kinesiology, and biology have the largest enrollments.

Required: To graduate, all students must complete 35 hours of general education courses, including 9 in social sciences, 8 in science, 6 in English, and 3 each in fine arts, math, humanities, and history/government. No more than 25% of the minimum total of 120 hours may be D or below.

Special: Co-op programs and internships are available, as well as dual majors and B.A.-B.S. degrees in many majors, and study abroad in 47 countries. There are 3-2 engineering degrees with several universities, a combined medical/dental degree, and a 6-year B.S./J.D. degree for highly qualified students. Non-degree study is possible. There are 40 national honor societies, including Phi Beta Kappa, a freshman honors program, and 84 departmental honors programs.

Faculty/Classroom: 64% of faculty are male; 36% are female. 93% teach undergraduates. Graduate students teach 42% of introductory courses. The average class size in an introductory lecture is 39; in a laboratory is 16; and in a regular course is 31.

Admissions: 59% of the 2013-2014 applicants were accepted. The SAT scores for the 2013-2014 freshman class were: Critical Reading--21% below 500, 48% between 500 and 599, 25% between 600 and 699, and 6% between 700 and 800; Math--15% below 500, 45% between 500 and 599, 34% between 600 and 699, and 6% between 700 and 800. The ACT scores were 5% below 21, 21% between 21 and 23, 33% between 24 and 26, 16% between 27 and 28, and 25% above 28. 58% of the current freshmen were in the top fifth of their class; 87% were in the top two fifths.

Requirements: The SAT or ACT is required. In addition, U of A recommends 4 years of English and math and 3 years each of social science and natural science. AP and honors level courses will enhance the applicant's opportunity for admission. A GPA of 3.0 is required. AP and CLEP credits are accepted. Important factors in the admissions decision are advanced placement or honors courses, leadership record, and extracurricular activities record.

Procedure: Freshmen are admitted fall, spring, and summer. Entrance exams should be taken in the junior year or early in the senior year. There are early admissions, deferred admissions, and rolling admissions plans. Applications should be filed by August 1 for fall entry; December 20 for spring entry; and May 1 for summer entry, along with a $40 fee. Notification of early decision is sent 12 15; regular decision, on a rolling basis. Applications are accepted online.

Transfer: 1383 transfer students enrolled in 2012-2013. Applicants must present a GPA of 2.0 on all college course work attempted and be in good standing at the last institution attended. Those with fewer than 24 transferable semester credits must meet the requirements of entering freshmen in addition to those of transfer students. 30 of 120 credits required for the bachelor's degree must be completed at U of A.

Visiting: There are regularly scheduled orientations for prospective students, The visit consists of individual or group campus tours, meetings with an academic adviser, residence hall tours, and a meeting with an admissions counselor. Appointments are strongly encouraged for the best experience but not required. There are guides for informal visits and visitors may sit in on classes. To schedule a visit, contact Kristen Davidson at visit@uark.edu.

Financial Aid: In 2013-2014, 81% of all full-time freshmen and 66% of continuing full-time students received some form of financial aid. 40% of all full-time freshmen and 37% of continuing full-time students received need-based aid. The average freshman award was $10,004. Need-based scholarships or need-based grants averaged $7,547; need-based self-help aid (loans and jobs) averaged $3,954; non-need-based athletic scholarships averaged $9,007; and other non-need-based awards and non-need-based scholarships averaged $4,494. 5% of undergraduate students work part-time. Average annual earnings from campus work are $1301. The average financial indebtedness of the 2013 graduate was $22,695. The FAFSA is required. The priority date for freshman financial aid applications for fall entry is March 15.

International Students: There are 619 international students enrolled. The school actively recruits these students. They must take the TOEFL with a minimum score of 550 on the paper-based TOEFL (PBT) or 79 on the Internet-based version (iBT) and the college's own test. They must also take the SAT or ACT.

Computers: All students may access the system, 24 hours daily. There are no time limits and no fees.

Graduates: From July 1, 2012 to June 30, 2013, 3363 bachelor's degrees were awarded. The most popular majors were kinesiology (5%), marketing (5%), and finance (4%). 265 companies recruited on campus in 2012-2013. In an average class, 37% graduate in 4 years or less, 55% graduate in 5 years or less, and 60% graduate in 6 years or less.

Admissions Contact: Suzanne McCray, Vice Provost of Enrollment. E-Mail: *uofa@uark.edu* Web: *www.arkansas.edu*

UNIVERSITY OF ARKANSAS AT LITTLE ROCK C-3

Little Rock, AR 72204 **(501) 569-3492**
(800) 482-8892; (501) 569-8956

Full-time: 2457 men, 3095 women	**Faculty:** 408; IIA, --$
Part-time: 1678 men, 2740 women	**Ph.D.s:** 66%
Graduate: 894 men, 1513 women	**Student/Faculty:** 15 to 1
Year: semesters, summer session	**Tuition:** $7094 ($16,871)
Application Deadline: open	**Room & Board:** $9701
Freshman Class: 1344 applied, 864 accepted, 589 enrolled	
SAT CR/M: 395/485 **ACT:** 22	**COMPETITIVE**

The University of Arkansas at Little Rock began in 1927 as Little Rock Junior College, took the name of Little Rock University in 1957, and joined the University of Arkansas system in 1969. There are 7 undergraduate schools and 2 graduate schools. In addition to regional accreditation, UALR has baccalaureate program accreditation with AACSB, ABET, ACEJMC, ASLA, CSWE, NASAD, NASM, NCATE, and NLN. The library contains 674,979 volumes, 179,770 microform items, 11,682 audio/video tapes/CDs/DVDs, and subscribes to 95,870 periodicals including electronic. Computerized library services include interlibrary loans and database searching. Special learning facilities include an art gallery, planetarium, radio station, TV station, speech and hearing clinic. The 229-acre campus is in an urban area The main campus and law school are located in Little Rock. A second campus located in Benton, Arkansas. Including any residence halls, there are 56 buildings.

Student Life: 92% of undergraduates are from Arkansas. Others are from 49 states, 62 foreign countries, and Canada. 91% are from public schools. 52% are White; 23% African American. The average age of freshmen is 19; all undergraduates, 19. 41% do not continue beyond their first year; 21% remain to graduate.

Housing: 1376 students can be accommodated in college housing, which includes coed dorms, on-campus apartments, off-campus apartments, and married student housing, university-owned rental houses, special housing for disabled students. On-campus housing is available on a first-come and first-served basis. 85% of students commute. Alcohol is not permitted. All students may keep cars.

Activities: 2% of men belong to 5 national fraternities; 1% of women belong to 6 national sororities. There are 151 groups on campus, including student government and international students, art, cheerleading, chess, chorale, dance, drama, ethnic, honors, international, jazz band, literary magazine, musical theater, newspaper, opera, pep band, political, professional, radio and TV, religious, social, social service, student government, and university program council. Popular campus events include International Week, Sunshine Days and Art Spree.

Sports: There are 6 intercollegiate sports for men and 7 for women, and 18 intramural sports for men and 18 for women. Facilities include an 8,500-seat gym, swimming pool, tennis courts, baseball and intramural fields, soccer field/stadium, indoor/outdoor track facility, fitness and weight room, indoor jogging track, basketball, volleyball, and racquetball courts, steam room, and sauna.

Disabled Students: 85% of the campus is accessible. Facilities include wheelchair ramps, elevators, special parking, specially equipped restrooms, special class scheduling, lowered drinking fountains and study rooms.

Services: Counseling and information services are available, as is tutoring in every subject. There is a reader service for the blind, and remedial math, reading, and writing. Also available are a braille dictionary, typewriter, and reading machine and interpreters.

Campus Safety and Security: Measures include 24-hour foot and vehicle patrol, emergency notification system, self-defense education, and security escort services. There are shuttle buses, emergency telephones, lighted pathways/sidewalks, controlled access to dorms/residences, emergency phones, and a student patrol crime prevention unit.

Programs of Study: UALR confers B.A., B.S., B.B.A., B.S.W., B.A.T., B.F.A., B.S.E. and B.S.N. degrees. Associate, master's, and doctoral degrees are also awarded. Bachelor's degrees are awarded in BIOLOGICAL SCIENCE (bioinformatics, biology/biological science, and (Biological) Pre-Health Studies), BUSINESS (accounting, banking and finance, business administration and management, management science, marketing/retailing/merchandising, and sports management), COMMUNICATIONS AND THE ARTS (advertising, American Sign Language, art, art history and appreciation, dance, dramatic arts, English, French, journalism, music, radio/television technology, Spanish, technical and business writing, theatre arts, and visual and performing arts), COMPUTER AND PHYSICAL SCIENCE (applied mathematics, chemistry, computer programming, computer science, geology, information sciences and systems, mathematics, and physics), EDUCATION (early childhood education, education administration, education of the deaf and hearing impaired, elementary education, health education, reading education, secondary education, and special education), ENGINEERING AND ENVIRONMENTAL DESIGN (computer technology, construction engineering, construction management, construction technology, electrical/electronics engineering technology, engineering mechanics, engineering technology, industrial administration/management, manufacturing engineering, mechanical engineering technology, and surveying engineering), HEALTH PROFESSIONS (environmental health science, health science, nursing, and speech pathology/audiology), SOCIAL SCIENCE (criminal justice, economics, history, international studies, interpreter for the deaf, law, liberal arts/general studies, philosophy, political science/government, psychology, public administration, social work, and sociology). Systems engineering, construction management, computer science and management are the strongest academically. Psychology, management and criminal justice have the largest enrollments.

Required: All students must complete a minimum of 124 credit hours, including 45 at the upper level, while maintaining a GPA of 2.0. A minimum 44-hour core curriculum must be completed. Required categories include: English/Communications (9 hours), Math/Statistics (3 hours), Fine Arts/Humanities (9 hours), World Humanities (3 hours), Science (8 hours), and Social Sciences (15 hours). A second language requirement applies to students seeking a B.A. degree. Students must complete 30 hours in residence. Each student must complete a major and a minor or a double major.

Special: The University coordinates study abroad programs in China, Germany, Ghana, Great Britain, India, Norway, Poland, Romania, Taiwan, Turkey, Mexico, France, Spain, Hong Kong and Austria. UALR has exchange relationships with more than 30 countries. In addition, more than 100 internships and work-study positions are available in various academic departments. Cross-registration with the University of Arkansas Medical School in the area of Communication Disorders is offered at the graduate level. B.A. and B.S. degrees, a general studies degree, student-designed majors, nondegree study, and pass/fail options are offered. UALR offers Accelerated Online courses/degree programs and regular semester online degree programs. There are 3 national honor societies, a freshman honors program, and 5 departmental honors programs.

Faculty/Classroom: 52% of faculty are male; 48% are female. 80% teach undergraduates, all do research, and all teach and do research. Graduate students teach 4% of introductory courses. The average class size in an introductory lecture is 30; in a laboratory is 20; and in a regular course is 27.

Admissions: 64% of the 2013-2014 applicants were accepted. The SAT scores for the 2013-2014 freshman class were: Critical Reading--95% below 500, and 5% between 500 and 599; Math--5% below 500, 58% between 500 and 599, and 11% between 600 and 699. The ACT scores were 10% below 21, 55% between 21 and 23, and 35% above 28. 2 freshmen graduated first in their class.

Requirements: The SAT or ACT is required. In addition, two or more of the following criteria must be met: a high school GPA of at least 2.5 or a passing GED test score; an ACT composite score of at least 21 or a combined verbal/math SAT I score of 990 taken within the past 5 years; completion of a college preparatory core in high school that includes 4 units of English, 3 each of math and social studies, and 2 each of natural science and a single foreign language. Students with test subscores below the state minimum requirement will be placed in the appropriate development courses. A GPA of 2.5 is required. AP and CLEP credits are accepted.

Procedure: Freshmen are admitted to all sessions. Entrance exams should be taken during the fall of the senior year. There are early admissions, deferred admissions, and rolling admissions plans. Application deadlines are open. Application fee is $40. Applications are accepted online.

Transfer: 1183 transfer students enrolled in 2012-2013. Applicants must have a minimum college GPA of 2.0. Applicants must submit official transcripts from each college previously attended. Students who have 12 or fewer acceptable transfer credits must meet all the admission requirements for entering freshmen. 30 of 124 credits required for the bachelor's degree must be completed at UA-Little Rock.

Visiting: There are regularly scheduled orientations for prospective students, Orientation takes place before each semester attendance is required. Online orientation is offered. There are guides for informal visits and visitors may sit in on classes. To schedule a visit, contact the Admissions Office at (501) 569-3035.

Financial Aid: In 2013-2014, 82% of all full-time freshmen and 84% of continuing full-time students received some form of financial aid. 60% of all full-time freshmen and 51% of continuing full-time students received need-based aid. The average freshman award was $5,700. The FAFSA is required. Check with the school for current application deadlines.

International Students: There are 279 international students enrolled. They must take the TOEFL with a minimum score of 525 on the paper-based TOEFL (PBT) or 71 on the Internet-based version (iBT) and the college's own test, Test of Written English, with a score of at least 4 points. for entering freshmen and transfers with less than 12 credit hours, ACT, SAT or COMPASS is required for placement only.

Computers: All students may access the system 24 hours daily. There are no time limits and no fees.

Graduates: From July 1, 2012 to June 30, 2013, 1310 bachelor's degrees were awarded. The most popular majors were health professions and related programs (15%), homeland security, law enforcement, firefighting, and protective services (9%), and psychology (7%). In an average class, 12% graduate in 4 years or less, 11% graduate in 5 years or less, and 21% graduate in 6 years or less. Of the 2012 graduating class, 6% were enrolled in graduate school within 6 months of graduation.

Admissions Contact: Tammy Harrison, Director. E-Mail: *admissions@ualr.edu* Web: *www.ualr.edu*

UNIVERSITY OF ARKANSAS AT MONTICELLO C-4

Monticello, AR 71656 **(870) 460-1026; (870) 460-1933**

Full-time: 1120 men, 1361 women	**Faculty:** n/av
Part-time: 279 men, 603 women	**Ph.D.s:** 52%
Graduate: 35 men, 81 women	**Student/Faculty:** n/av
Year: semesters, summer session	**Tuition:** $5100 ($9270)
Application Deadline:	**Room & Board:** $4370

Freshman Class: 1794 applied, 1223 accepted, 795 enrolled
SAT or ACT: required

NONCOMPETITIVE

The University of Arkansas at Monticello was established in 1909 as the Fourth District Agricultural School. Made part of the public University of

Arkansas System in 1971, UAM offers liberal arts undergraduate courses and graduate programs. The figures in the above capsule and in this profile are approximate. There are 13 undergraduate schools and 2 graduate schools. In addition to regional accreditation, UAM has baccalaureate program accreditation with CSWE, NASM, NCATE, NLN, and SAF. The library contains 155,808 volumes, 285,552 microform items, and 675 audio/video tapes/CDs/DVDs, and subscribes to 994 periodicals including electronic. Computerized library services include interlibrary loans and database searching. Special learning facilities include a natural history museum, planetarium, a university forest, and a university farm. The 1844-acre campus is in a small town 90 miles south of Little Rock. Including any residence halls, there are 37 buildings.

Student Life: 89% of undergraduates are from Arkansas. Others are from 20 states, 6 foreign countries, and Canada. 99% are from public schools. 67% are White; 30% African American. The average age of freshmen is 21; all undergraduates, 24. 47% do not continue beyond their first year; 32% remain to graduate.

Housing: 800 students can be accommodated in college housing, which includes single-sex dorms, on-campus apartments, and married student housing. On-campus housing is guaranteed for all 4 years. 75% of students commute. Alcohol is not permitted. All students may keep cars.

Activities: 5% of men belong to 8 national fraternities; 3% of women belong to 5 national sororities. There are 61 groups on campus, including art, band, cheerleading, chess, choir, chorus, computers, debate, ethnic, gay, honors, international, jazz band, literary magazine, marching band, musical theater, newspaper, photography, political, professional, religious, social, social service, student government, and yearbook. Popular campus events include Forestry Festival, Special Olympics and Greek Week.

Sports: There are 5 intercollegiate sports for men and 5 for women, and 20 intramural sports for men and 20 for women. Facilities include a 4000-seat stadium, a 2500-seat gym, a swimming pool, baseball and softball fields, tennis and racquetball courts, and facilities for numerous intramural sports.

Disabled Students: All of the campus is accessible. Facilities include wheelchair ramps, elevators, special parking, specially equipped restrooms, special class scheduling, lowered drinking fountains, lowered telephones.

Services: Counseling and information services are available, as is tutoring in some subjects, general education There is a reader service for the blind, and remedial math, reading, and writing.

Campus Safety and Security: Measures include 24-hour foot and vehicle patrol. There are emergency telephones and lighted pathways/sidewalks.

Programs of Study: UAM confers B.A., B.S., B.A.S., B.B.A., B.G.S., B.S.N. and B.S.W degrees. Associate and master's degrees are also awarded. Bachelor's degrees are awarded in AGRICULTURE (agriculture, forestry and related sciences, and wildlife management), BIOLOGICAL SCIENCE (biology/biological science), BUSINESS (accounting, business administration and management, and management information systems), COMMUNICATIONS AND THE ARTS (art, English, modern language, music, and speech/debate/rhetoric), COMPUTER AND PHYSICAL SCIENCE (applied science, chemistry, geodetic science, information sciences and systems, mathematics, and physical sciences), EDUCATION (early childhood education, health education, middle school education, music education, and physical education), HEALTH PROFESSIONS (exercise science and nursing), SOCIAL SCIENCE (criminal justice, history, liberal arts/general studies, political science/government, psychology, and social work). Forestry and sciences is the strongest academically. Nursing, business administration, and P-4 early childhood special education have the largest enrollments.

Required: All students are required to complete 124 total semester hours, approximately 30 within their major, and maintain a minimum GPA of 2.0 (2.75 in education). Distribution requirements include 11 hours in basic sciences, 6 hours each in composition and humanities, and 3 hours each in fine arts, speech, U.S. history or government, psychology or sociology, social science, and math.

Special: A general studies degree, cross-registration within the University of Arkansas system, credit for military experience, dual majors, and nondegree study are available. There are 6 national honor societies.

Faculty/Classroom: 54% of faculty are male; 46% are female. All teach undergraduates, and 11% do research and teach. No introductory courses are taught by graduate students. The average class size in an introductory lecture is 26; in a laboratory is 21; and in a regular course is 20.

Admissions: In a recent year, 68% of the applicants were accepted. The ACT scores were 63% below 21, 19% between 21 and 23, 13% between 24 and 26, 3% between 27 and 28, and 2% above 28.

Requirements: The SAT or ACT is required. Applicants must have earned a high school diploma or GED. The Arkansas high school core curriculum is recommended. State law requires proof of immunization. AP and CLEP credits are accepted.

Procedure: Freshmen are admitted to all sessions. Entrance exams should be taken by December of the senior year. There are early admissions and rolling admissions plans. Application deadlines are open. Applications are accepted online.

Transfer: In a recent year, 291 transfer students enrolled. Transfer students must be in good academic standing at the previous college. ACT or SAT test scores are required only if the student has not successfully completed Freshman Composition I and College Algebra. 30 of 124 credits required for the bachelor's degree must be completed at UAM.

Visiting: There are regularly scheduled orientations for prospective students, including a review of admission requirements and financial aid opportunities and a visit to academic departments and faculty in the field of interest. There are guides for informal visits, visitors may sit in on classes, and stay overnight. To schedule a visit, contact the Office of Admissions.

Financial Aid: In a recent year, 99% of all full-time freshmen and 70% of continuing full-time students received some form of financial aid. 77% of all full-time freshmen and 49% of continuing full-time students received need-based aid. 11% of undergraduate students work part-time. Average annual earnings from campus work are $1711. In a recent year, the average financial indebtedness was $1,300. UAM is a member of CSS. The FAFSA is required. The priority date for freshman financial aid applications for fall entry is April 1. Check with the school for the deadline for filing freshman financial aid applications.

International Students: There are 5 international students enrolled. They must take the TOEFL with a minimum score of 550 on the paper-based TOEFL (PBT) or 80 on the Internet-based version (iBT). They must also take the SAT or ACT.

Computers: All students may access the system. There are no time limits and no fees.

Graduates: In a recent year, 264 bachelor's degrees were awarded. The most popular majors were business administration (17%), nursing (11%), and psychology (8%). In an average class, 11% graduate in 4 years or less, 21% graduate in 5 years or less, and 24% graduate in 6 years or less.

Admissions Contact: Mary Whiting, Director of Admissions. E-Mail: *whitingm@uamont.edu* Web: *www.uamont.edu*

UNIVERSITY OF ARKANSAS AT PINE BLUFF — C-4

Pine Bluff, AR 71601 — **(870) 575-8492; (870) 543-8014**

Full-time: 1260 men, 1520 women	**Faculty:** n/av
Part-time: 130 men, 205 women	**Ph.D.s:** n/av
Graduate: 50 men, 135 women	**Student/Faculty:** n/av
Year: semesters, summer session	**Tuition:** $5100 ($8600)
Application Deadline:	**Room & Board:** $6500
Freshman Class: n/av	
SAT or ACT: required	

COMPETITIVE

The University of Arkansas at Pine Bluff, established in 1873, is a historically black land-grant institution providing a liberal arts education as part of the public University of Arkansas system. The figures in the above capsule and in this profile are approximate. There are 5 undergraduate schools and one graduate school. In addition to regional accreditation, UAPB has baccalaureate program accreditation with AHEA, CSWE, NASM, NCATE, and NLN. The library contains 271,547 volumes, 119,205 microform items, and 4,299 audio/video tapes/CDs/DVDs, and subscribes to 1,050 periodicals including electronic. Computerized library services include interlibrary loans and database searching. Special learning facilities include an art gallery, radio station, and TV station. The 318-acre campus is in a small town 40 miles southeast of Little Rock and approximately 142 miles southwest of Memphis. Including any residence halls, there are 49 buildings.

Student Life: 80% of undergraduates are from Arkansas. Others are from 28 states, 17 foreign countries, and Canada. 94% are African American. The average age of freshmen is 18; all undergraduates, 22. 61% do not continue beyond their first year.

Housing: 1099 students can be accommodated in college housing, which includes single-sex dorms. honors clusters in the dorms. On-campus housing is guaranteed for all 4 years. 65% of students commute. Alcohol is not permitted. All students may keep cars.

Activities: There are 65 groups on campus, including art, band, cheerleading, choir, computers, drama, drill team, honors, jazz band, marching band, newspaper, orchestra, photography, political, professional, radio and TV, religious, social, social service, student government, and yearbook. Popular campus events include Founders Day, Spring Emphasis, and Unity Fest.

Sports: There are 7 intercollegiate sports for men and 8 for women, and 20 intramural sports for men and 19 for women. Facilities include a phys ed complex that provides activities such as flag football, basketball, volleyball, softball, tennis, handball, racquetball, track and field, and badminton. There is also a swimming pool and a 6,000-seat football stadium.

Disabled Students: 98% of the campus is accessible. Facilities include wheelchair ramps, elevators, special parking, specially equipped restrooms, special class scheduling, lowered drinking fountains, and lowered telephones.

Services: Counseling and information services are available, as is tutoring

in most subjects. There is a reader service for the blind, and remedial math, reading, and writing.

Campus Safety and Security: Measures include 24-hour foot and vehicle patrol, self-defense education, and security escort services. There are emergency telephones, lighted pathways/sidewalks, There is a department of public safety and security on campus.

Programs of Study: UAPB confers B.A., and B.S. degrees. Associate and master's degrees are also awarded. Bachelor's degrees are awarded in AGRICULTURE (agriculture, conservation and regulation, and fishing and fisheries), BIOLOGICAL SCIENCE (biology/biological science), BUSINESS (accounting and business administration and management), COMMUNICATIONS AND THE ARTS (art, English, journalism, music, and speech/debate/rhetoric), COMPUTER AND PHYSICAL SCIENCE (applied mathematics, chemistry, computer science, mathematics, and physics), EDUCATION (agricultural education, art education, business education, early childhood education, English education, home economics education, industrial arts education, mathematics education, middle school education, music education, physical education, science education, social science education, and special education), ENGINEERING AND ENVIRONMENTAL DESIGN (industrial engineering technology and preengineering), HEALTH PROFESSIONS (nursing, predentistry, premedicine, prepharmacy, and rehabilitation therapy), SOCIAL SCIENCE (criminal justice, family/consumer studies, gerontology, history, liberal arts/general studies, parks and recreation management, political science/government, psychology, social work, and sociology). Business administration, biology and computer science are the strongest academically and have the largest enrollments.

Required: All students must complete at least 124 hours of credit, including 30 hours in their major, while earning an overall 2.0 GPA (2.5 for teacher education majors) and a C or better in all major courses. Distribution requirements include English, math, social and natural science, and phys ed courses. Students must pass a comprehensive exam in their major.

Special: The university offers formal co-op education and work-study programs, concurrent registration with members of the University of Arkansas system, internships, B.A.-B.S. degrees, and dual and student-designed majors. Also offered are credit for military experience, nondegree study, individualized programs of study for honors college students, and study abroad. There are 4 national honor societies, a freshman honors program, and 6 departmental honors programs.

Faculty/Classroom: 54% of faculty are male; 46% are female. No introductory courses are taught by graduate students. The average class size in a laboratory is 20 and in a regular course is 21.

Requirements: The SAT or ACT is required. The ACT, with a satisfactory score is preferred. Applicants must have earned 15 credits, including 4 units of English and 3 each in social studies, math, and science. The GED is accepted. Students not meeting these requirements may apply for conditional admission. A GPA of 2.0 is required. AP and CLEP credits are accepted.

Procedure: Freshmen are admitted fall, spring, and summer. Entrance exams should be taken during the junior or senior year. There are early admissions, deferred admissions, and rolling admissions plans. Check with the school for current application deadlines.

Transfer: Transfer students must have a minimum GPA of 2.0. Applicants with fewer than 60 semester hours of college credit must submit an application, ACT or SAT I scores, and all college transcripts. 30 of 124 credits required for the bachelor's degree must be completed at UAPB.

Visiting: There are regularly scheduled orientations for prospective students. There are guides for informal visits, visitors may sit in on classes, and stay overnight. To schedule a visit, contact the Director of Recruitment at (501) 575-8961 or (800) 525-5272.

Financial Aid: UAPB is a member of CSS. The FAFSA is required. Check with the school for current application deadlines.

International Students: They must take the TOEFL. They must also take the SAT or ACT. The ACT is preferred. SAT scores may be used.

Computers: All students may access the system. 7 a.m. to 11 p.m. Monday through Friday, and during special weekend hours. There are no time limits. The fee is a $15 laboratory fee.

Admissions Contact: Erica Fulton, Director of Admissions and Academic Records. E-Mail: *fulton_e@4500.uapb.edu* Web: *www.uapb.edu*

UNIVERSITY OF CENTRAL ARKANSAS C-3

Conway, AR 72035 **(501) 450-3663; (800) 243-8245**

Full-time: 3396 men, 4740 women	**Faculty:** n/av; IIA, --$
Part-time: 683 men, 785 women	**Ph.D.s:** n/av
Graduate: 400 men, 1103 women	**Student/Faculty:** n/av
Year: semesters, summer session	**Tuition:** $7332 ($12,830)
Application Deadline:	**Room & Board:** $5270
Freshman Class: n/av	
SAT or ACT: required	

VERY COMPETITIVE

The University of Central Arkansas, established in 1907, is a comprehensive public institution offering undergraduate and graduate degrees in liberal arts, business, health-related sciences, and education. The figures given in the above capsule and in this profile are approximate. There are 7 undergraduate schools and one graduate school. In addition to regional accreditation, UCA has baccalaureate program accreditation with AACSB, ADA, APTA, CAHEA, NASAD, NASM, NCATE, and NLN. The library contains 440,376 volumes, 611,411 microform items, and 8,024 audio/video tapes/CDs/DVDs, and subscribes to 17,277 periodicals including electronic. Computerized library services include interlibrary loans, database searching, Internet access, and Wi-Fi capability. Special learning facilities include an art gallery, planetarium, radio station, and TV station. The 350-acre campus is in a small town 29 miles north of Little Rock. Including any residence halls, there are 118 buildings.

Student Life: 90% of undergraduates are from Arkansas. Others are from 42 states, 60 foreign countries, and Canada. 96% are from public schools. 69% are White; 16% African American. The average age of freshmen is 18; all undergraduates, 22. 29% do not continue beyond their first year; 55% remain to graduate.

Housing: 3870 students can be accommodated in college housing, which includes single-sex and coed dorms, on-campus apartments, off-campus apartments, and married student housing. In addition, there are honors houses, international students' residence hall, as well as residential colleges. On-campus housing is guaranteed for all 4 years. Alcohol is not permitted. All students may keep cars.

Activities: 10% of men belong to 12 national fraternities; 10% of women belong to 8 national sororities. There are 158 groups on campus, including art, band, cheerleading, choir, chorale, chorus, computers, dance, debate, drama, environmental, ethnic, film, forensics, gay, honors, international, jazz band, literary magazine, marching band, musical theater, newspaper, orchestra, pep band, photography, political, professional, radio and TV, religious, social, social service, student government, symphony, and yearbook. Popular campus events include Bear Facts Day, Greek God and Miss UCA.

Sports: There are 7 intercollegiate sports for men and 8 for women, and 10 intramural sports for men and 10 for women. Facilities include a gym, a swimming pool, a fitness center, racquetball and tennis courts, a track, soccer fields, a football field, a basketball court, and an indoor athletic facility.

Disabled Students: 98% of the campus is accessible. Facilities include wheelchair ramps, elevators, special parking, specially equipped restrooms, special class scheduling, lowered drinking fountains, lowered telephones, and special housing.

Services: Counseling and information services are available, as is tutoring in some subjects, biology, chemistry, physics, algebra, trigonometry, calculus, geometry, sociology, writing, literature, Spanish, accounting, business statistics, French, German, writing and technology. There is a reader service for the blind, and remedial math, reading, and writing.

Campus Safety and Security: Measures include 24-hour foot and vehicle patrol, emergency notification system, self-defense education, and security escort services. There are shuttle buses, emergency telephones, lighted pathways/sidewalks, and controlled access to dorms/residences.

Programs of Study: UCA confers B.A., B.S., B.S.E., B.P.S., B.B.A., B.F.A., B.M. and B.S.N. degrees. Associate, master's, and doctoral degrees are also awarded. Bachelor's degrees are awarded in BIOLOGICAL SCIENCE (biology/biological science), BUSINESS (accounting, banking and finance, business administration and management, business economics, insurance and risk management, and marketing/retailing/merchandising), COMMUNICATIONS AND THE ARTS (communications, English, French, journalism, music, Spanish, and speech/debate/rhetoric), COMPUTER AND PHYSICAL SCIENCE (applied mathematics, chemistry, computer science, information sciences and systems, mathematics, and physics), EDUCATION (art education, athletic training, early childhood education, education of the exceptional child, elementary education, foreign languages education, guidance education, library science, middle school education, music education, physical education, science education, secondary education, and special education), ENGINEERING AND ENVIRONMENTAL DESIGN (environmental science, interior design, and preengineering), HEALTH PROFESSIONS (exercise science, health care administration, health science, medical technology, nuclear medical technology, nursing, occupational therapy, physical therapy, predentistry, premedicine, preoptometry, prepharmacy, preveterinary science, radiological science, and speech pathology/audiology), SOCIAL SCIENCE (African American studies, dietetics, economics, family/consumer studies, geography, gerontology, history, philosophy, political science/government, psychology, public administration, religion, and sociology). Business, health-related sciences, and education are the strongest academically. Health professions and related sciences, business/marketing, and education have the largest enrollments.

Required: All students must earn a minimum of 124 semester hours, including 40 in upper-division courses. A minimum GPA of 2.25 is needed for the B.B.A., 2.5 for most education programs. Minimum requirements also include 3 semester hours in phys ed.

Special: Study abroad, work-study programs, a B.S.-B.A. degree, a 3-2 engineering degree with the University of Arkansas at Fayetteville, dual majors, nondegree study, and pass/fail options are available. Co-op programs in business, computer science, and health sciences and internships in education are also possible. There are 11 national honor societies, a freshman honors program, and 25 departmental honors programs.

Faculty/Classroom: No introductory courses are taught by graduate students.

Requirements: The SAT or ACT is required. AP and CLEP credits are accepted. Important factors in the admissions decision are advanced placement or honors courses, evidence of special talent, and recommendations by school officials.

Procedure: Freshmen are admitted to all sessions. There is a rolling admissions plan. Application deadlines are open. Applications are accepted online.

Transfer: 596 transfer students enrolled in 2012-2013. Applicants need, on UCA's scale, a minimum cumulative GPA of 2.0. 15 of 124 credits required for the bachelor's degree must be completed at UCA.

Visiting: There are regularly scheduled orientations for prospective students, including tours at 11 a.m. and 2 p.m.; departments and dormitories may be visited. There are also special visitation days that include a campus tour, departmental session, lunch, parents' session, optional residence hall tour, and classroom visit or planetarium show. Visitors may sit in on classes. To schedule a visit, contact the Admissions Office at admissions@uca.edu.

Financial Aid: The FAFSA is required. Check with the school for current application deadlines.

International Students: The school actively recruits these students. They must take the TOEFL.

Computers: All students may access the system. There are no time limits and no fees.

Graduates: From July 1, 2012 to June 30, 2013, 1554 bachelor's degrees were awarded. The most popular majors were health professions and related sciences (21%), business/marketing (21%), and education (9%).

Admissions Contact: Amber Hall, Director of Institutional Research. E-Mail: *amberh@uca.edu* Web: *www.uca.edu*

UNIVERSITY OF THE OZARKS B-2

Clarksville, AR 72830 (479) 979-1227
(800) 264-8636; (479) 979-1417

Full-time: 280 men, 325 women	**Faculty:** n/av; IIB, --$
Part-time: 20 men, 35 women	**Ph.D.s:** n/av
Year: semesters, summer session	**Student/Faculty:** n/av
Application Deadline: April 1	**Tuition:** $17,000
	Room & Board: $6100
Freshman Class: n/av	
SAT or ACT: required	

COMPETITIVE

The University of the Ozarks, founded in 1834, is a private, comprehensive liberal arts institution affiliated with the Presbyterian Church. The figures in the above capsule and in this profile are approximate. There are 4 undergraduate schools. In addition to regional accreditation, Ozarks has baccalaureate program accreditation with NCATE. The library contains 69,960 volumes, 6,927 microform items, and 2,955 audio/video tapes/CDs/DVDs, and subscribes to 611 periodicals including electronic. Computerized library services include interlibrary loans, database searching, Internet access, and Wi-Fi capability. Special learning facilities include an art gallery, radio station, TV station, the Jones Learning Center for students with diagnosed learning disabilities. The 35-acre campus is in a small town 100 miles northwest of Little Rock. Including any residence halls, there are 16 buildings.

Student Life: 51% of undergraduates are from Arkansas. Others are from 22 states, 20 foreign countries, and Canada. 93% are from public schools. 69% are White; 18% Foreign. 60% are Protestant; 20% claim no religious affiliation; 18% Catholic. The average age of freshmen is 18; all undergraduates, 20. 33% do not continue beyond their first year; 46% remain to graduate.

Housing: 550 students can be accommodated in college housing, which includes single-sex and coed dorms. On-campus housing is guaranteed for the freshman year only, is available on a first-come, and first-served basis. Priority is given to out-of-town students. 64% of students live on campus; of those, 51% remain on campus on weekends. Alcohol is not permitted. All students may keep cars.

Activities: There are no fraternities or sororities. There are 30 groups on campus, including art, cheerleading, choir, chorale, chorus, dance, debate, drama, environmental, film, forensics, honors, international, literary magazine, newspaper, political, professional, radio and TV, religious, social, social service, and student government. Popular campus events include International Fair and Banquet, Family Weekend and Freshman Matriculation Ceremony.

Sports: There are 5 intercollegiate sports for men and 5 for women, and 6 intramural sports for men and 5 for women. Facilities include a sports complex housing racquetball courts, a pool, and a 2,200-seat basketball arena. In addition, there are softball, soccer, and baseball fields, tennis courts, and a 700-seat soccer stadium.

Disabled Students: 90% of the campus is accessible. Facilities include elevators, special parking, specially equipped restrooms, special class scheduling, and lowered drinking fountains.

Services: Counseling and information services are available, as is tutoring in every subject. There is remedial math, reading, and writing.

Campus Safety and Security: Measures include 24-hour foot and vehicle patrol. There are emergency telephones and lighted pathways/sidewalks.

Programs of Study: Ozarks confers B.A., B.S. and B.G.S. degrees. Bachelor's degrees are awarded in BIOLOGICAL SCIENCE (biology/biological science), BUSINESS (accounting, business administration and management, and marketing/retailing/merchandising), COMMUNICATIONS AND THE ARTS (art, communications, dramatic arts, English, and music), COMPUTER AND PHYSICAL SCIENCE (chemistry and mathematics), EDUCATION (business education, early childhood education, middle school education, and physical education), ENGINEERING AND ENVIRONMENTAL DESIGN (environmental science and materials science), HEALTH PROFESSIONS (respiratory therapy), SOCIAL SCIENCE (economics, history, liberal arts/general studies, political science/government, psychology, religion, social science, and sociology). Business and biology have the largest enrollments.

Required: Students are required to earn 124 hours, with 30 to 54 in the major, and maintain a minimum GPA of 2.0. Distribution requirements include 9 hours in civic awareness and social science, 7 to 10 hours in math and science, 4 hours in phys ed and wellness, 3 hours in literature, fine arts, and religion, and up to 6 hours in global awareness.

Special: Internships, study abroad in 8 countries including Japan, numerous work-study programs, dual majors, a general studies degree, and a 3-2 engineering degree with the University of Arkansas are available. There are 3 national honor societies.

Faculty/Classroom: 70% of faculty are male; 30% are female. All teach undergraduates. No introductory courses are taught by graduate students. The average class size in an introductory lecture is 14; in a laboratory is 11; and in a regular course is 15.

Requirements: The SAT or ACT is required, with a satisfactory score on the SAT or on the ACT. An interview is recommended. The GED is accepted. A GPA of 2.0 is required. AP and CLEP credits are accepted. Important factors in the admissions decision are personality/intangible qualities, advanced placement or honors courses, and evidence of special talent.

Procedure: Freshmen are admitted to all sessions. Entrance exams should be taken as early as possible. There are deferred admissions and rolling admissions plans. Applications should be filed by April 1 for fall entry; December 1 for spring entry, along with a $30 fee. Applications are accepted online.

Transfer: 41 transfer students enrolled in 2012-2013. A GPA of 2.0 and college transcripts are required. Applicants with a GPA of less than 2.0 or fewer than 30 hours of college work must furnish high school transcripts and ACT or SAT results. 30 of 124 credits required for the bachelor's degree must be completed at Ozarks.

Visiting: There are regularly scheduled orientations for prospective students, including a campus tour and meetings with faculty and students, admissions, and financial aid. In most cases, prospective students may meet with the president and coaches as requested. There are guides for informal visits, visitors may sit in on classes, and stay overnight. To schedule a visit, contact the Admissions Office.

Financial Aid: In 2013-2014, 99% of all full-time freshmen and 91% of continuing full-time students received some form of financial aid. 66% of all full-time freshmen and 47% of continuing full-time students received need-based aid. The average freshman award was $11,800. 41% of undergraduate students work part-time. Average annual earnings from campus work are $1700. The average financial indebtedness of the 2013 graduate was $16,000. The FAFSA is required. Check with the school for current application deadlines.

International Students: There are 118 international students enrolled. The school actively recruits these students. They must take the TOEFL and the college's own test.

Computers: All students may access the system. There are no time limits. The fee is $150.

Graduates: From July 1, 2012 to June 30, 2013, 106 bachelor's degrees were awarded. The most popular majors were business administration/management (15%), biology (13%), and marketing (11%). 50 companies recruited on campus in 2012-2013. In an average class, 32% graduate in 4 years or less, 45% graduate in 5 years or less, and 46% graduate in 6 years or less. Of the 2012 graduating class, 11% were enrolled in graduate school within 6 months of graduation, and 68% were employed.

Admissions Contact: Emma Lee Morrow, Admissions Coordinator. E-Mail: *emorrow@ozarks.edu*. Web: *www.ozarks.edu*

WILLIAMS BAPTIST COLLEGE D-1

Walnut Ridge, AR 72476 (870) 759-4121
(800) 722-4434; (870) 886-3924

Full-time: 170 men, 294 women	**Faculty:** 29
Part-time: 50 men, 60 women	**Ph.D.s:** 55%
Graduate: none	**Student/Faculty:** 13 to 1
Year: semesters, summer session	**Tuition:** $13,750
Application Deadline:	**Room & Board:** $6320
Freshman Class: n/av	
SAT: required	

COMPETITIVE

Williams Baptist College, founded in 1941, is a private liberal arts institution providing undergraduate education in business, education, humanities, natural sciences, religion, and social sciences. WBC is affiliated with the Southern Baptist Church and is sponsored by the Arkansas Baptist Convention. In addition to regional accreditation, WBC has baccalaureate program accreditation with NCATE. The library contains 59,614 volumes, 160 microform items, and 20 audio/video tapes/CDs/DVDs, and subscribes to 61 periodicals including electronic. Computerized library services include interlibrary loans, database searching, Internet access, and Wi-Fi capability. Special learning facilities include an art gallery, an education curriculum lab. The 180-acre campus is in a rural area 100 miles northwest of Memphis, TN and 125 miles north of Little Rock. Including any residence halls, there are 41 buildings.

Student Life: 77% of undergraduates are from Arkansas. Others are from 16 states, and 5 foreign countries. 90% are from public schools. 88% are White. 91% are Protestant. The average age of freshmen is 18; all undergraduates, 24. 40% do not continue beyond their first year; 43% remain to graduate.

Housing: 473 students can be accommodated in college housing, which includes single-sex dorms, on-campus apartments, and married student housing. On-campus housing is guaranteed for all 4 years. 70% of students live on campus; of those, 50% remain on campus on weekends. Alcohol is not permitted. All students may keep cars.

Activities: There are no fraternities or sororities. There are 32 groups on campus, including art, cheerleading, choir, chorale, drama, international, literary magazine, professional, religious, social, social service, and student government. Popular campus events include Harvest Fest, Christmas in the Cove, and Spring Fling.

Sports: There are 3 intercollegiate sports for men and 4 for women, and 4 intramural sports for men and 4 for women. Facilities include a gym, a weight room, racquetball and tennis courts, a jogging track, sand volleyball, disc golf, and a student center.

Disabled Students: 90% of the campus is accessible. Facilities include wheelchair ramps, elevators, special parking, specially equipped restrooms, and lowered drinking fountains.

Services: Counseling and information services are available, as is tutoring in most subjects. There is remedial math.

Campus Safety and Security: Measures include 24-hour foot and vehicle patrol and emergency notification system. There are lighted pathways/sidewalks and controlled access to dorms/residences.

Programs of Study: WBC confers B.A., and B.S. degrees. Associate degrees are also awarded. Bachelor's degrees are awarded in BIOLOGICAL SCIENCE (biology/biological science), BUSINESS (business administration and management), COMMUNICATIONS AND THE ARTS (art, English, and music), COMPUTER AND PHYSICAL SCIENCE (computer science), EDUCATION (elementary education, physical education, and secondary education), SOCIAL SCIENCE (counseling/psychology, history, psychology, religion, religious education, and religious music). Education, psychology, and biology are the largest.

Required: To graduate, all students must follow a core curriculum including humanities, social science and religion, natural science and math, and physical activity. Chapel attendance is mandatory. A total of 123 credits, with 36 to 64 hours in the major, and a minimum GPA of 2.0 are required to graduate.

Special: WBC offers study abroad in England, Latin America, the Middle East, and Russia, a Washington semester through the American Studies Program, and a general studies major. There are 9 national honor societies and 10 departmental honors programs.

Faculty/Classroom: 51% of faculty are male; 49% are female. All teach and do research. No introductory courses are taught by graduate students.

Requirements: The SAT or ACT is required. First-time freshmen must have a minimum composite score of 19 and 2.5 cumulative high school GPA for unconditional admission. A GPA of 2.5 is required. AP and CLEP credits are accepted.

Procedure: Freshmen are admitted to all sessions. There is a rolling admissions plan. Application deadlines are open. Application fee is $20. Applications are accepted online. Application fees are waived if application is completed online.

Transfer: 47 transfer students enrolled in 2012-2013. Transfer students must have a GPA of 2.0 for unconditional admission. 32 of 123 credits required for the bachelor's degree must be completed at WBC.

Visiting: There are regularly scheduled orientations for prospective students. There are guides for informal visits, visitors may sit in on classes, and stay overnight. To schedule a visit, contact Andrew Watson at (800) 722-4434.

Financial Aid: In 2013-2014, 100% of all full-time freshmen and 99% of continuing full-time students received some form of financial aid. 66% of all full-time freshmen and 72% of continuing full-time students received need-based aid. The average freshman award was $16,492. Need-based scholarships or need-based grants averaged $5,040 ($7,246 maximum); need-based self-help aid (loans and jobs) averaged $4,753 ($9,996 maximum); non-need-based athletic scholarships averaged $4,288 ($16,000 maximum); and other non-need-based awards and non-need-based scholarships averaged $8,268 ($21,911 maximum). 40% of undergraduate students work part-time. Average annual earnings from campus work are $1392. The average financial indebtedness of the 2013 graduate was $20,046. The FAFSA is required. The priority date for freshman financial aid applications for fall entry is February 1. The deadline for filing freshman financial aid applications for fall entry is May 1.

International Students: There are 17 international students enrolled. They must take the TOEFL with a minimum score of 500 on the paper-based TOEFL (PBT) or 61 on the Internet-based version (iBT). They must also take the SAT or ACT, scoring 19.

Computers: All students may access the system. There are no time limits. The fee is $135.

Graduates: From July 1, 2012 to June 30, 2013, 101 bachelor's degrees were awarded. The most popular majors were psychology (23%), liberal arts (17%), and early childhood education (16%). In an average class, 24% graduate in 4 years or less, 36% graduate in 5 years or less, and 40% graduate in 6 years or less.

Admissions Contact: Angela Flippo, Director of Admissions. E-Mail: *admissions@wbclab.edu* Web: *www.wbcoll.edu*

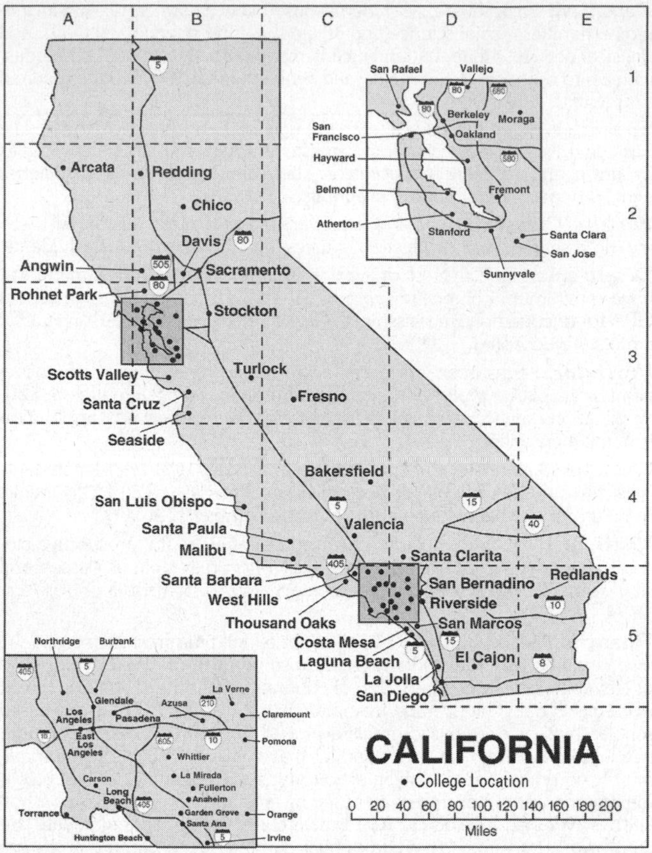

AMERICAN JEWISH UNIVERSITY C-5

Los Angeles, CA 90077 (310) 476-9777, ext. 250
(877) GO-2-AJULA; (310) 471-3657

Full-time: 40 men, 60 women
Part-time: 5 men, 5 women
Graduate: 65 men, 75 women
Year: semesters
Application Deadline: May 31
Freshman Class: n/av
SAT or ACT: required
Faculty: n/av; IIB, av$
Ph.D.s: 100%
Student/Faculty: n/av
Tuition: $24,200
Room & Board: $14,950

COMPETITIVE

The College of Arts and Sciences at American Jewish University is distinguished by its core curriculum integrating the study of Western and Jewish civilizations. It prepares students for careers and graduate studies in law, business, psychology, education, and other fields. The figures in the above capsule and in this profile are approximate. There are 3 graduate schools. The library contains 105,000 volumes, and subscribes to 400 periodicals including electronic. Computerized library services include interlibrary loans. Special learning facilities include an art gallery. The 28-acre campus is in a suburban area in Los Angeles. Including any residence halls, there are 9 buildings.

Student Life: 71% of undergraduates are from California. Others are from 22 states, and 2 foreign countries. 70% are from public schools. 81% are White. 94% are Jewish. The average age of freshmen is 18; all undergraduates, 23. 5% do not continue beyond their first year; 90% remain to graduate.

Housing: 192 students can be accommodated in college housing, which includes coed dorms, on-campus apartments, and married student housing. On-campus housing is guaranteed for all 4 years. 70% of students live on campus; of those, 70% remain on campus on weekends. All students may keep cars.

Activities: There are no fraternities or sororities. There are 15 groups on campus, including and Tikkum Olam, bioethics, Hillel, peer mentoring, psychology, art, choir, dance, drama, Israel Action, literary magazine, newspaper, political, radio and TV, religious, social, social service, and student government. Popular campus events include Israel Memorial Day (Yom Hazikaron), and Israel Independence Day (Yom Ha'atzmaut).

Sports: There is no sports program at AJU. Facilities include a gym, a basketball court, and a soccer field at the Familian campus in Los Angeles and horseback riding, swimming pools, and a ropes course at the Brandeis-Bardin campus in Simi Valley.

Disabled Students: All of the campus is accessible. Facilities include elevators, special parking, specially equipped restrooms, lowered drinking fountains, lowered telephones, and specially equipped dorm rooms.

Services: Counseling and information services are available, as is tutoring in most subjects. There is remedial math and writing.

Campus Safety and Security: Measures include 24-hour foot and vehicle patrol, self-defense education, and security escort services. There are emergency telephones and lighted pathways/sidewalks.

Programs of Study: AJU confers B.A. degrees. Master's degrees are also awarded. Bachelor's degrees are awarded in BUSINESS (business administration and management), COMMUNICATIONS AND THE ARTS (journalism and literature), HEALTH PROFESSIONS (premedicine), SOCIAL SCIENCE (ethics, politics, and social policy, Judaic studies, liberal arts/general studies, political science/government, and psychology).

Required: All students must complete a core curriculum combining the study of Jewish and Western civilizations, as well as courses in communications and foreign language and 1 in computer science. There are distribution requirements in math, natural and behavioral sciences, English, and fine arts. Other requirements vary according to the major, with at least 32 to 36 upper-division credits needed. A total of 120 semester units, with a minimum GPA of 2.0, is required to graduate.

Special: There is a 5-year joint business management program with American Jewish University's Lieber School of Graduate Studies and a 5-year joint master's degree in Jewish education with AJU's Fingerhut School of Education. Student designed and dual majors are available. Internships in all available majors, study abroad, work-study programs, accelerated degree programs, and pass/fail options are offered. Students may apply for independent study projects. There are 1 national honor societies.

Faculty/Classroom: 45% of faculty are male; 55% are female. All teach and do research. No introductory courses are taught by graduate students. The average class size in an introductory lecture is 7 and in a laboratory is 7.

Requirements: The SAT or ACT is required. Applicants must be graduates of an accredited secondary school or have a GED. A visit and an interview are recommeded for all students. 2 letters of recommendation, an autobiographical essay, and official high school transcripts are required. A GPA of 2.0 is required. AP credits are accepted. Important factors in the admissions decision are extracurricular activities record.

Procedure: Freshmen are admitted fall and spring. Entrance exams should be taken no later than November of the year prior to enrollment. There are early decision, deferred admissions, and rolling admissions plans. Applications should be filed by May 31 for fall entry; November 30 for spring entry. The fall 2013 application fee was $35. Notification is sent on a rolling basis. Applications are accepted online.

Transfer: In a recent year, 19 transfer students enrolled. Previous college work should be at the B level to transfer. Students with fewer than 60 college credits should also have a minimum 3.0 high school GPA, at least 1700 on the SAT or 24 on the ACT, recommendations, and an autobiographical essay. The SAT or ACT requirement is waived if the applicant has 60 or more transferable credits. A visit and an interview are recommended. 34 of 120 credits required for the bachelor's degree must be completed at AJU.

Visiting: There are regularly scheduled orientations for prospective students, including meeting with admissions representatives, department chairs, and the Dean of the College of Arts and Sciences, sitting in on classes, sleeping over in the doms, eating meals in the Berg dining hall, meeting current students and touring the campus. There are guides for informal visits, visitors may sit in on classes, and stay overnight. To schedule a visit, contact the Director of Undergraduate Admissions.

Financial Aid: The FAFSA and the college's own financial statement, and tax returns, and W2s are required. Check with the school for current application deadlines.

International Students: They must take the TOEFL with a minimum score of 79 on the Internet-based version (iBT). They must also take the SAT or ACT, scoring 1700.

Computers: All students may access the system. There are no time limits and no fees.

Admissions Contact: Director of Undergraduate Admissions E-Mail: *mdavidson@ajula.edu* Web: *www.ajula.edu*

ART CENTER COLLEGE OF DESIGN C-5

Pasadena, CA 91103 **(626) 396-2373; (626) 795-0578**

Full-time: 800 men, 540 women
Part-time: 125 men, 100 women
Graduate: 80 men, 65 women
Year: trimesters, summer session
Application Deadline: open
Freshman Class: n/av
SAT or ACT: required
Faculty: n/av
Ph.D.s: n/av
Student/Faculty: n/av
Tuition: $34,544
Room & Board: n/av

SPECIAL

Art Center College of Design, founded in 1930, is a private institution offering programs in fine arts and design. The figures in the above capsule and in this profile are approximate. There is one graduate school. In addition to regional accreditation, Art Center has baccalaureate program accreditation with NASAD. The library contains 64,000 volumes, 60,000 microform items, and 4,000 audio/video tapes/CDs/DVDs, and subscribes to 400 periodicals including electronic. Computerized library services include database searching and Internet access. Special learning facilities include an art gallery. The 175-acre campus is in a suburban area 10 miles northwest of Los Angeles. Including any residence halls, there are 2 buildings.

Student Life: 63% of undergraduates are from California. Others are from 46 states, 34 foreign countries, and Canada. 45% are Asian American; 42% White; 21% Foreign. The average age of freshmen is 23; all undergraduates, 24. 5% do not continue beyond their first year; 89% remain to graduate.

Housing: Alcohol is not permitted. All students commute. All students may keep cars.

Activities: There are no fraternities or sororities. There are 20 groups on campus, including ethnic, gay, international, religious, social, and student government.

Sports: There is no sports program at Art Center. Facilities include Students have access to athletic facilities at Occidental College and California Institute of Technology.

Disabled Students: All of the campus is accessible. Facilities include wheelchair ramps, elevators, special parking, specially equipped restrooms, lowered drinking fountains, and lowered telephones.

Services: Counseling and information services are available, as is tutoring in some subjects, some art classes.

Campus Safety and Security: Measures include 24-hour foot and vehicle patrol, emergency notification system, and security escort services. There are emergency telephones and lighted pathways/sidewalks.

Programs of Study: Art Center confers B.S., and B.F.A. degrees. Master's degrees are also awarded. Bachelor's degrees are awarded in COMMUNICATIONS AND THE ARTS (advertising, design, film arts, fine arts, graphic design, illustration, industrial design, and photography), ENGINEERING AND ENVIRONMENTAL DESIGN (environmental design). Illustration, graphic design, and industrial design are the largest.

Required: To graduate, students must complete a total of 135 credit hours, with 90 in the major, and 45 units of liberal arts and sciences. Course requirements vary by the program. A minimum GPA of 2.5 and a core curriculum of English Composition and Introduction to Modernism are also required.

Special: The college offers cross-registration with Occidental College, the California Institute of Technology, and the Southern California Institute of Architecture, internships, nondegree study, and study abroad in Sweden, Japan, and Germany.

Faculty/Classroom: 74% of faculty are male; 26% are female. 99% teach undergraduates. No introductory courses are taught by graduate students. The average class size in an introductory lecture is 22 and in a regular course is 30.

Requirements: The SAT or ACT is required. The ACT Optional Writing test is also required. Applicants must be graduates of an accredited secondary school or have a GED. Official transcripts and a portfolio must be submitted. An interview is recommended. AP credits are accepted. Important factors in the admissions decision are evidence of special talent, advanced placement or honors courses, and extracurricular activities record.

Procedure: Freshmen are admitted fall, spring, and summer. Entrance exams should be taken in the senior year. There is a rolling admissions plan. Application deadlines are open. Application fee is $50.

Transfer: 489 transfer students enrolled in 2012-2013. Transfer applicants must have a minimum 2.5 GPA and provide official transcripts from all colleges attended. Up to 60 units of liberal arts and studio credits may be transferred. Portfolios are required, and interviews are recommended. Up to 32 of the 45 liberal arts and science units required for graduation may be transferred. There is a 4-semester residency requirement. 75 of 135 credits required for the bachelor's degree must be completed at Art Center.

Visiting: There are regularly scheduled orientations for prospective students. There are guides for informal visits. To schedule a visit, contact the Admissions Office.

Financial Aid: In 2013-2014, 73% of all full-time freshmen and 76% of continuing full-time students received some form of financial aid. 70% of all full-time freshmen and 74% of continuing full-time students received need-based aid. The average freshman award was $12,000. Need-based scholarships or need-based grants averaged $7,000 ($10,000 maximum); and need-based self-help aid (loans and jobs) averaged $5,500 ($8,600 maximum). 30% of undergraduate students work part-time. Average annual earnings from campus work are $1500. The average financial indebtedness of the 2013 graduate was $70,000. Art Center is a member of CSS. The FAFSA is required. Check with the school for current application deadlines.

International Students: There are 275 international students enrolled. The school actively recruits these students. They must take the TOEFL with a minimum score of 80 on the Internet-based version (iBT) and the college's own test.

Computers: All students may access the system. There are no time limits and no fees.

Graduates: From July 1, 2012 to June 30, 2013, 376 bachelor's degrees were awarded. The most popular majors were Illustration (20%), graphic design (19%), and product design (16%). 200 companies recruited on campus in 2012-2013. In an average class, 70% graduate in 4 years or less and 77% graduate in 5 years or less. Of the 2012 graduating class, 89% were employed within 6 months of graduation.

Admissions Contact: Kit Baron, Vice President of Admissions. E-Mail: *admissions@artcenter.edu* Web: *www.artcenter.edu*

AZUSA PACIFIC UNIVERSITY D-5

Azusa, CA 91702 **(626) 812-3016**
(800) TALK-APU; (626) 812-3096

Full-time: 2056 men, 3627 women
Part-time: 331 men, 529 women
Graduate: 1247 men, 2965 women
Year: semesters, summer session
Application Deadline: May 1
Freshman Class: 5105 applied, 4201 accepted, 1225 enrolled
SAT or ACT: required
Faculty: n/av; IIA, -$
Ph.D.s: 74%
Student/Faculty: 14 to 1
Tuition: $32,306
Room & Board: $7640

COMPETITIVE

Azusa Pacific University, founded in 1899, is a private (non-profit), interdenominational Christian institution offering undergraduate and graduate programs in the liberal arts and emphasizing spiritual growth. There are 7 undergraduate schools and 8 graduate schools. In addition to regional accreditation, APU has baccalaureate program accreditation with CSWE, NASAD, NASM, and NLN. The 3 libraries contain 254,337 volumes, 703,979 microform items, and 24,911 audio/video tapes/CDs/DVDs, and subscribe to 56,262 periodicals including electronic. Computerized library services include interlibrary loans, database searching, and Internet access. Special learning facilities include an art gallery, radio station, and TV station. The 60-acre campus is in a small town 26 miles east of Los Angeles. Including any residence halls, there are 67 buildings.

Student Life: 82% of undergraduates are from California. 50% are White; 23% Hispanic. 43% are Protestant. The average age of freshmen is 18; all undergraduates, 22. 17% do not continue beyond their first year; 63% remain to graduate.

Housing: College-sponsored housing includes single-sex and coed dorms, on-campus apartments, and off-campus apartments. In addition, there are honors houses and special-interest houses. On-campus housing is available on a first-come, first-served basis, and is available on a lottery system for upperclassmen. 91% of students live on campus. Alcohol is not permitted. All students may keep cars.

Activities: There are no fraternities or sororities. There are 48 groups on campus, including art, band, cheerleading, choir, chorale, chorus, computers, dance, debate, drama, ethnic, film, honors, international, jazz band, literary magazine, marching band, musical theater, newspaper, opera, orchestra, pep band, photography, political, radio and TV, religious, social, social service, student government, and yearbook. Popular campus events include Missions Week, Mega Weekend-Homecoming/Dinner Rally and Night of Champions.

Sports: There are 8 intercollegiate sports for men and 10 for women, and 7 intramural sports for men and 7 for women. Facilities include an all-weather track, a 3000-seat football stadium, a baseball field, a 1200-seat gym, a residence hall lounge,turf recreation field, sand volleyball courts, indoor/outdoor basketball courts, and a recreation room.

Disabled Students: All of the campus is accessible. Facilities include wheelchair ramps, elevators, special parking, specially equipped restrooms, lowered drinking fountains, lowered telephones, and special housing.

Services: Counseling and information services are available, as is tutoring in most subjects. There is remedial math, reading, and writing.

Campus Safety and Security: Measures include 24-hour foot and vehicle patrol, emergency notification system, self-defense education, and security escort services. There are shuttle buses, emergency telephones, lighted pathways/sidewalks, and controlled access to dorms/residences.

Programs of Study: APU confers B.A., B.S., B.M., B.F.A, B.S.N. and

B.S.W. degrees. Master's and doctoral degrees are also awarded. Bachelor's degrees are awarded in BIOLOGICAL SCIENCE (biochemistry and biology/biological science), BUSINESS (accounting, business administration and management, and marketing/retailing/merchandising), COMMUNICATIONS AND THE ARTS (communications, English, music, and Spanish), COMPUTER AND PHYSICAL SCIENCE (chemistry, computer science, information sciences and systems, mathematics, and physics), EDUCATION (art education, music education, and physical education), HEALTH PROFESSIONS (nursing), SOCIAL SCIENCE (biblical studies, history, international studies, liberal arts/general studies, ministries, philosophy, political science/government, psychology, religion, social science, social work, and sociology). Nursing, education, and religion are the strongest academically. Business, nursing, psychology have the largest enrollments.

Required: All students must take 120 semester units and earn a minimum GPA of 2.0. 18 units of Bible courses, 120 hours of community ministry, and 2 units of health are required. General education requirements include courses in public speaking, fine arts, religion and philosophy, English, algebra, foreign language, and phys ed. Heritage and Institution, Identity and Relationships, and Nature are also required courses.

Special: Internships in ministerial and American studies, study abroad in Japan, Latin America, Taiwan, England, Australia, China, Tanzania, Italy, Israel, France, Lithuania, Spain, Uganda, and South Africa, and a Washington semester are available. In addition work study with the university, a B.A.-B.S. degree, dual majors in all programs, and a 3-2 engineering degree are offered. Accelerated degree programs are available in Christian leadership, computer information systems, management information systems, human development, and organizational leadership; there is also a Registered Nurse to Bachelor of Science in Nursing Program. APU awards credit for life experience and allows nondegree study. There are 2 national honor societies and a freshman honors program.

Faculty/Classroom: 48% of faculty are male; 52% are female. No introductory courses are taught by graduate students.

Admissions: 82% of the 2013-2014 applicants were accepted. The SAT scores for the 2013-2014 freshman class were: Critical Reading--25% below 500, 50% between 500 and 599, 23% between 600 and 699, and 2% between 700 and 800; Math--25% below 500, 47% between 500 and 599, 24% between 600 and 699, and 4% between 700 and 800; Writing--25% below 500, 51% between 500 and 599, 21% between 600 and 699, and 3% between 700 and 800.

Requirements: The SAT or ACT is required. An essay is required. A portfolio and an interview are recommended for certain programs. The GED is accepted. A GPA of 2.8 is required. AP and CLEP credits are accepted. Important factors in the admissions decision are personality/intangible qualities, evidence of special talent, and advanced placement or honors courses.

Procedure: Freshmen are admitted to all sessions. Entrance exams should be taken prior to enrollment. There are early admissions, deferred admissions, and rolling admissions plans. Early decision applications should be filed by February 15; regular applications, by May 1 for fall entry, along with a $45 fee. Notification of early decision is sent October 1; regular decision, April 1. applicants were on the 2013 waiting list; were admitted. Applications are accepted online. Application fees are waived if application is completed online.

Transfer: 658 transfer students enrolled in 2012-2013. Applicants must have a minimum GPA of 2.20 on previous college work. The SAT or ACT is not required if 30 or more semester units have been completed. An associate degree and an interview are recommended. 30 of 120 credits required for the bachelor's degree must be completed at APU.

Visiting: There are regularly scheduled orientations for prospective students, including Seniors Only Day in November, and a brother/sister weekend in February that is open to both juniors and seniors. There are guides for informal visits, visitors may sit in on classes, and stay overnight. To schedule a visit, contact the Admissions Office.

Financial Aid: In 2013-2014, 66% of all full-time freshmen and 63% of continuing full-time students received some form of financial aid. 66% of all full-time freshmen and 62% of continuing full-time students received need-based aid. The average freshman award was $19,088. Need-based scholarships or need-based grants averaged $15,616; need-based self-help aid (loans and jobs) averaged $9,705; non-need-based athletic scholarships averaged $8,810; and other non-need-based awards and non-need-based scholarships averaged $7,380. 20% of undergraduate students work part-time. The average financial indebtedness of the 2013 graduate was $23,070. The FAFSA and the college's own financial statement are required. Check with the school for current application deadlines.

International Students: There are 121 international students enrolled. The school actively recruits these students. They must take the TOEFL.

Computers: All students may access the system. Monday through Friday 8 a.m. to 11 p.m., Saturday 8:30 a.m. to 8 p.m., and Sunday 1 p.m. to 6 p.m. There are no time limits and no fees.

Graduates: From July 1, 2012 to June 30, 2013, 1600 bachelor's degrees were awarded. The most popular majors were business/marketing (22%), health professions and related programs (17%), and liberal arts (12%). In an average class, 47% graduate in 4 years or less, 62% graduate in 5 years or less, and 65% graduate in 6 years or less.

Admissions Contact: David Burke, Director of Undergraduate Admissions. E-Mail: *admissions@apu.edu* Web: *www.apu.edu*

BIOLA UNIVERSITY — D-5

La Mirada, CA 90639 — **(562) 903-4752** / **(800) OK-BIOLA; (562) 903-4709**

Full-time: 1582 men, 2575 women	**Faculty:** n/av; IIA, av$
Part-time: 88 men, 92 women	**Ph.D.s:** 74%
Graduate: 1294 men, 671 women	**Student/Faculty:** 16 to 1
Year: 4-1-4, summer session	**Tuition:** $32,142
Application Deadline: March 1	**Room & Board:** $9316
Freshman Class: 3528 applied, 2634 accepted, 930 enrolled	
SAT CR/M/W: 556/559/550	**ACT:** 24 **VERY COMPETITIVE**

Biola University, founded in 1908, is a private, Interdenominational Christian institution offering undergraduate and graduate degrees in arts and sciences, psychology, theology, intercultural studies, and business. Figures in the above capsule and in this profile are approximate. There are 7 undergraduate schools and 6 graduate schools. In addition to regional accreditation, Biola has baccalaureate program accreditation with ACBSP, NASAD, NASM, and NLN. The library contains 315,000 volumes, 580,000 microform items, and 9,232 audio/video tapes/CDs/DVDs, and subscribes to 30,000 periodicals including electronic. Computerized library services include interlibrary loans, database searching, Internet access, and Wi-Fi capability. Special learning facilities include an art gallery, radio station, TV station, film studio and a 3-D art facility, MIDI lab for music composition majors, electronic piano lab, listening lab with music archives, physical science labs, and scanning electron microscope, archeological dig-site on. The 95-acre campus is in a suburban area 22 miles southeast of Los Angeles. Including any residence halls, there are 53 buildings.

Student Life: 78% of undergraduates are from California. Others are from 40 states, 28 foreign countries, and Canada. 69% are from public schools. 56% are White; 17% Hispanic; 15% Asian American. 99% are Protestant. The average age of freshmen is 18; all undergraduates, 20. 14% do not continue beyond their first year; 65% remain to graduate.

Housing: 2307 students can be accommodated in college housing, which includes single-sex and coed dorms, on-campus apartments, and off-campus apartments. On-campus housing is guaranteed for the freshman year only, is available on a first-come, first-served basis, and is available on a lottery system for upperclassmen. 61% of students live on campus; of those, 73% remain on campus on weekends. Alcohol is not permitted. All students may keep cars.

Activities: There are no fraternities or sororities. There are 52 groups on campus, including dance clubs, gospel choir, missionary and ministries groups, Adventure club, art, band, cheerleading, chess, choir, chorale, dance, debate, drama, environmental, ethnic, film, forensics, honors, international, jazz band, literary magazine, musical theater, newspaper, opera, orchestra, political, professional, radio and TV, religious, social, social service, student government, symphony, and yearbook. Popular campus events include Multicultural Week, Christmas Celebration, Biola Weekend, Missions Conference and Torrey Conference.

Sports: There are 12 intercollegiate sports for men and 12 for women, and 10 intramural sports for men and 10 for women. Facilities include a gym/swimming complex, a 450-seat auditorium, athletic fields, including 1 for soccer, a quarter-mile track, a baseball diamond, tennis, sand volleyball, and basketball courts, and a fitness center.

Disabled Students: 90% of the campus is accessible. Facilities include wheelchair ramps, elevators, special parking, specially equipped restrooms, special class scheduling, lowered drinking fountains, and lowered telephones.

Services: Counseling and information services are available, as is tutoring in most subjects. There is a reader service for the blind. A Writing Center is available to all students.

Campus Safety and Security: Measures include 24-hour foot and vehicle patrol, emergency notification system, self-defense education, and security escort services. There are shuttle buses, emergency telephones, lighted pathways/sidewalks, controlled access to dorms/residences, Bicycle patrol, and Segway patrol.

Programs of Study: Biola confers B.A., B.S., B.F.A. and B.M. degrees. Master's and doctoral degrees are also awarded. Bachelor's degrees are awarded in BIOLOGICAL SCIENCE (biochemistry, biology/adolescence education, biology/biological science, and life science), BUSINESS (accounting, business administration and management, business communications, business economics, business information systems, economics – statistics, international business management, management information systems, management science, and marketing management), COMMUNICATIONS AND THE ARTS (advertising, American literature, American Sign Language, art, broadcasting, communications, dramatic arts, drawing, English, film arts, fine arts, graphic design, journalism, music, music composition, music performance, music theory and composition, painting, performing arts, photography, piano performance, playwriting/screenwriting, printmaking, public relations, publishing, radio/television technology, Spanish, studio art, theatre acting, theatre arts, theater design, and theater management), COMPUTER AND PHYSICAL SCIENCE (applied mathematics, chemistry, computer mathematics, computer information technology, computer science, information sciences and systems, mathematics, mathematics/theoretical, natural sciences, physical sciences, physics, and statistics), EDUCATION (Christian education, early childhood education, mathematics education, music education, physical education, social studies education, and social studies secondary school education), ENGINEERING AND ENVIRONMENTAL DESIGN (computational sciences, computer technology, engineering, and environmental science), HEALTH PROFESSIONS (nursing, physical therapy, preallied health, Pre-Health Studies, predentistry, premedicine, prepharmacy, prephysical therapy, speech pathology/audiology, and speech therapy), SOCIAL SCIENCE (anthropology, applied psychology, archeology, biblical studies, counseling/psychology, crosscultural studies, early childhood studies, economics, history, humanities, liberal arts/general studies, ministries, missions, philosophy, philosophy and religion, prelaw, psychology, religious studies, social science, social work, and sociology). Biblical studies, business administration, journalism/communication, and psychology are the strongest academically. Biblical studies, business, psychology have the largest enrollments.

Required: To graduate, students must pass a writing competency exam, complete 30 units of biblical studies and theology, and fulfill the general education and phys ed requirements. At least 130 semester hours must be completed, with 30 hours in the major and 24 of these in upper-division work. Other requirements vary by major. A minimum 2.0 GPA is required.

Special: Cross-registration with the Au Sable Institute of Environmental Studies is possible. Biola offers internships, summer travel tours, study abroad in 11 countries, and an American studies program in Washington D.C., sponsored by the Christian College Coalition. Special programs include L.A. Film Studies, a semester in Hollywood working in the film industry; Biola Baja, a 3-week program at Vermillion Sea Field, Baja; a family studies course at Focus on the Family Institute in Colorado Springs; a China studies program at Fudan University in Shanghai, China; and a development theory studies program in Honduras. Also available are on- and off-campus work-study programs, a B.A.- B.S. degree, a 3-2 engineering degree with the University of Southern California, dual majors, and nondegree study. There are several preprofessional programs available, including prelaw, prephysical therapy, and prechiropractic. A 3-1 program with Los Angeles College of Chiropractic is offered. Students can also attend a semester at Martha's Vineyard with the Contemporary Music Center and explore the many areas of the Christian music industry. There are 2 national honor societies, a freshman honors program, and 7 departmental honors programs.

Faculty/Classroom: 63% of faculty are male; 37% are female. No introductory courses are taught by graduate students.

Admissions: 75% of the 2013-2014 applicants were accepted. The SAT scores for the 2013-2014 freshman class were: Critical Reading--24% below 500, 42% between 500 and 599, 27% between 600 and 699, and 7% between 700 and 800; Math--26% below 500, 42% between 500 and 599, 29% between 600 and 699, and 3% between 700 and 800; Writing--25% below 500, 44% between 500 and 599, 25% between 600 and 699, and 6% between 700 and 800. The ACT scores were 7% below 21, 35% between 21 and 23, 28% between 24 and 26, 19% between 27 and 28, and 11% above 28.

Requirements: The SAT or ACT is required. Applicants need not be graduates of an accredited secondary school. The GED is accepted. Students should have completed 15 academic credits, including 4 years of English and foreign language, 3 years of math, and 2 each of social studies and science. All students must be evangelical Christians who can demonstrate Christian character, leadership ability, and the aptitude for possible success in college. Applicants must submit 1 reference from their pastor or someone on the pastoral staff. A personal essay is required. A GPA of 3.0 is required. AP and CLEP credits are accepted. Important factors in the admissions decision are personality/intangible qualities, recommendations by school officials, and leadership record.

Procedure: Freshmen are admitted to all sessions. There are early decision and rolling admissions plans. Early decision applications should be filed by November 15; regular applications, by March 1 for fall entry; and November 15 for spring entry, along with a $45 fee. Notification of early decision is sent January 15; regular decision, April 1. Applications are accepted online.

Transfer: 322 transfer students enrolled in 2012-2013. Applicants with fewer than 15 credit hours must submit both college transcripts and SAT scores. All students must provide high school transcripts. A minimum 2.0 GPA and an interview are required. 30 of 130 credits required for the bachelor's degree must be completed at Biola.

Visiting: There are regularly scheduled orientations for prospective students, including class visits; orientation with the departments of admissions, financial aid, and student affairs; chapel; a sporting event; and a Disneyland or Knott's Berry Farm visit. There are guides for informal visits, visitors may sit in on classes, and stay overnight. To schedule a visit, contact the Admissions Office at admissions@biola.edu.

Financial Aid: In 2013-2014, 69% of all full-time freshmen and 70% of continuing full-time students received some form of financial aid. 68% of all full-time freshmen and 67% of continuing full-time students received need-based aid. The average freshman award was $16,773. Need-based scholarships or need-based grants averaged $12,990; need-based self-help aid (loans and jobs) averaged $7,011; non-need-based athletic scholarships averaged $11,165; and other non-need-based awards and non-need-based scholarships averaged $6,523. 34% of undergraduate students work part-time. The average financial indebtedness of the 2013 graduate was $34,587. Biola is a member of CSS. The FAFSA and the college's own financial statement, and California residents should submit the Cal Grant GPA verification form. are required. The priority date for freshman financial aid applications for fall entry is May 15. The deadline for filing freshman financial aid applications for fall entry is June 15.

International Students: There are 180 international students enrolled. The school actively recruits these students. They must take the TOEFL with a minimum score of 600 on the paper-based TOEFL (PBT) or 100 on the Internet-based version (iBT). They must also take the SAT or ACT.

Computers: All students may access the system, 24 hours a day 7 days a week. There are no time limits and no fees.

Graduates: From July 1, 2012 to June 30, 2013, 898 bachelor's degrees were awarded. The most popular majors were business/marketing (19%), theology and religious vocations (14%), and visual and performing arts (11%). In an average class, 47% graduate in 4 years or less, 62% graduate in 5 years or less, and 65% graduate in 6 years or less. Of the 2012 graduating class, 50% were employed within 6 months of graduation.

Admissions Contact: André Stephens, Director of Undergraduate Admissions. E-Mail: *admissions@biola.edu* Web: *undergrad.biola.edu*

CALIFORNIA BAPTIST UNIVERSITY — D-5

Riverside, CA 92504 — (951) 343-4212; (877) 228-8866; (951) 343-4525

Full-time: 1633 men, 2709 women	**Faculty:** 215
Part-time: 196 men, 416 women	**Ph.D.s:** 70%
Graduate: 266 men, 811 women	**Student/Faculty:** 20 to 1
Year: semesters, summer session	**Tuition:** $26,900
Application Deadline: rolling	**Room & Board:** $8990
Freshman Class: 2916 applied, 2137 accepted, 909 enrolled	
SAT CR/M/W: 480/490/480 **ACT:** 21	**COMPETITIVE**

California Baptist University (CBU) is one of the top private Christian colleges and universities in Southern California. CBU offers bachelor's, master's and credential programs in Riverside, San Bernardino and online. California Baptist University believes each person has been created for a purpose. CBU strives to help students understand and engage this purpose by providing a Christ-centered educational experience that integrates academics with spiritual and social development opportunities. Graduates are challenged to become individuals whose skills, integrity and sense of purpose glorify God and distinguish them in the workplace and in the world. There are 11 undergraduate schools and 8 graduate schools. In addition to regional accreditation, CBU has baccalaureate program accreditation with ABET, ACBSP, and NASM. The library contains 232,039 volumes, 54,853 microform items, and 9,079 audio/video tapes/CDs/DVDs, and subscribes to 24,506 periodicals including electronic. Computerized library services include interlibrary loans, database searching, and Internet access. Special learning facilities include an art gallery, Music Production and Recording Studios, Language Lab, Digital Design and Photography Studio, Theater Arts Stage Production Workshop, Bourns Engineering Laboratories, Athletic Performance Center, Recreation and Fitness Center, Aquatic Center. The 131-acre campus is in a suburban area The California Baptist University campus is located 60 miles east of Los Angeles. Including any residence halls, there are 138 buildings.

Student Life: 92% of undergraduates are from California. Others are from 40 states, 26 foreign countries, and Canada. 90% are from public schools. 47% are White; 27% Hispanic. 51% are Protestant. The average age of freshmen is 19; all undergraduates, 23. 22% do not continue beyond their first year; 58% remain to graduate.

Housing: 2448 students can be accommodated in college housing, which includes single-sex and coed dorms, on-campus apartments, off-campus apartments, and married student housing. On-campus housing is available on a first-come and first-served basis. 56% of students commute. Alcohol is not permitted. All students may keep cars.

Activities: There are no fraternities or sororities. There are 34 groups on campus, including Caihong Campus Ministry and Bible Study, art, band, cheerleading, choir, chorale, chorus, communications, computers, debate, drama, drill team, environmental, ethnic, FAITH Club, film, forensics, honors, international, jazz band, literary magazine, musical theater, newspaper, orchestra, pep band, photography, political, professional, religious, social, social service, student government, and yearbook. Popular campus events include Twirp Week, Octoberfest, CBU CRAZIES, Annual Yule, Intramural Sports, and Spiritual Emphasis Week.

Sports: There are 10 intercollegiate sports for men and 9 for women, and 6 intramural sports for men and 6 for women. Facilities include 1,100-seat gym; 40,682-square-foot Recreation Center with indoor basketball courts, racquetball courts, climbing wall, and rooftop running track and soccer field; Aquatics Center with Olympic-size pool; Outdoor Athletic Complex with baseball, softball, and soccer fields; Athletic Performance Center; Athletic Training Clinic; Tennis Center; Sand volleyball courts.

Disabled Students: 95% of the campus is accessible. Facilities include wheelchair ramps, elevators, special parking, specially equipped restrooms, and lowered drinking fountains.

Services: Counseling and information services are available, as is tutoring in most subjects. There is remedial math, reading, and writing.

Campus Safety and Security: Measures include 24-hour foot and vehicle patrol, emergency notification system, self-defense education, and security escort services. There are emergency telephones, lighted pathways/sidewalks, and controlled access to dorms/residences.

Programs of Study: CBU confers B.A., B.S., B.S.C.E., B.S.E.C.E., B.S.E., B.S.M.E., B.S.N., B.A.T. and B.M. degrees. Master's degrees are also awarded. Bachelor's degrees are awarded in BIOLOGICAL SCIENCE (biochemistry, biology/biological science, and molecular biology), BUSINESS (accounting, business administration and management, and marketing/retailing/merchandising), COMMUNICATIONS AND THE ARTS (communications, dramatic arts, English, film arts, graphic design, journalism, music, music performance, music theory and composition, piano/organ, public relations, Spanish, visual and performing arts, and voice), COMPUTER AND PHYSICAL SCIENCE (chemistry, digital arts/technology, mathematics, and statistics), EDUCATION (health education, mathematics education, music education, and nutrition education), ENGINEERING AND ENVIRONMENTAL DESIGN (applied aviation, aviation administration/management, civil engineering, computer engineering, construction management, electrical/electronics engineering, engineering, environmental science, and mechanical engineering), HEALTH PROFESSIONS (exercise science, health care administration, health science, nursing, prephysical therapy, and public health), SOCIAL SCIENCE (anthropology, behavioral science, Christian studies, criminal justice, early childhood studies, history, interdisciplinary studies, international studies, liberal arts/general studies, pastoral studies, philosophy, political science/government, psychology, and sociology). Engineering, nursing, business administration, psychology, and education are the strongest academically. Nursing, business administration, psychology, and kinesiology have the largest enrollment.

Required: All students must be proficient in English and complete courses in English, Communication Arts, Math, Behavioral/social science, Art or Music, Philosophy, U.S. History, Study Abroad or Non-U.S. History, Political Science, laboratory science, science or kinesiology, and Christian Studies. A total of 124 units, with a minimum GPA of 2.0, is required to graduate.

Special: CBU offers accelerated programs in accounting, business administration, christian ministries, communication studies, criminal justice, early childhood studies, English, interdisciplinary studies, kinesiology, liberal studies, organizational leadership, political science, psychology, public administration, public relations, and sociology. Study abroad, internships, work-study programs, a Washington semester, B.A.-B.S. degrees, dual majors, and credit for military/work experience are available. There are 2 national honor societies, a freshman honors program, and 10 departmental honors programs.

Faculty/Classroom: 51% of faculty are male; 49% are female. 95% teach undergraduates, 10% do research, and 10% do both. No introductory courses are taught by graduate students. The average class size in an introductory lecture is 26 and in a laboratory is 13.

Admissions: 73% of the 2013-2014 applicants were accepted. The SAT scores for the 2013-2014 freshman class were: Critical Reading--56% below 500, 34% between 500 and 599, 9% between 600 and 699, and 1% between 700 and 800; Math--54% below 500, 33% between 500 and 599, 12% between 600 and 699, and 1% between 700 and 800; Writing--58% below 500, 32% between 500 and 599, 9% between 600 and 699, and 1% between 700 and 800. The ACT scores were 44% below 21, 31% between 21 and 23, 16% between 24 and 26, 5% between 27 and 28, and 4% above 28. 37% of the current freshmen were in the top fifth of their class; 67% were in the top two fifths. 12 freshmen graduated first in their class.

Requirements: The SAT or ACT is required. Applicants should be graduates of an accredited high school or have a GED. Required academic units: English-4, mathematics-3, Lab Science-2; foreign language-2, social studies-2, history-2. An essay and interview are recommended, and two references, preferably from a church leader and an official of an academic institution, are required. A GPA of 2.0 is required. AP and CLEP credits are accepted. Important factors in the admissions decision are recommendations by school officials, leadership record, and advanced placement or honors courses.

Procedure: Freshmen are admitted fall, spring, and summer. Entrance exams should be taken during the junior year. There are deferred admissions and rolling admissions plans. Early decision applications should be filed by December 15, along with a $45 fee. Notification of early decision is sent January 31; regular decision, Nov 9. Applications are accepted online.

Transfer: 1050 transfer students enrolled in 2012-2013. Applicants must have a minimum GPA of 2.0 if they are transferring at least 30 transferable semester units. Only courses with a grade of C- or better may transfer. Applicants transferring less than 30 units must have a high school GPA of at least 2.5 and must submit SAT or ACT scores. 36 of 124 credits required for the bachelor's degree must be completed at CBU.

Visiting: There are regularly scheduled orientations for prospective students, consisting of a welcome, orientation, academic fair, and tours. There are guides for informal visits, visitors may sit in on classes, and stay overnight. To schedule a visit, contact Admissions Office at (877) 228-8866.

Financial Aid: In 2013-2014, 65% of all full-time freshmen and 67% of continuing full-time students received some form of financial aid. 64% of all full-time freshmen and 68% of continuing full-time students received need-based aid. The average freshman award was $16,593. Need-based scholarships or need-based grants averaged $13,871; need-based self-help aid (loans and jobs) averaged $9,796; non-need-based athletic scholarships averaged $14,726; and other non-need-based awards and non-need-based scholarships averaged $6,437. 20% of undergraduate students work part-time. Average annual earnings from campus work are $3900. The average financial indebtedness of the 2013 graduate was $32,591. The FAFSA is required. The priority date for freshman financial aid applications for fall entry is March 2.

International Students: There are 149 international students enrolled. The school actively recruits these students. They must take the TOEFL with a minimum score of 71 on the Internet-based version (iBT), . They must also take the SAT or ACT, scoring 920.

Computers: All students may access the system. during open lab and library hours and any time from ports in student housing. There are no time limits and no fees.

Graduates: From July 1, 2012 to June 30, 2013, 850 bachelor's degrees were awarded. The most popular majors were business administration (14%), psychology (12%), and nursing and liberal arts (10%). 50 companies recruited on campus in 2012-2013. In an average class, 9% graduate in 3 years or less, 40% graduate in 4 years or less, 54% graduate in 5 years or less, and 58% graduate in 6 years or less.

Admissions Contact: Allen Johnson, Dean of Undergraduate Enrollment Srvcs. E-Mail: *admissions@calbaptist.edu* Web: *http:/www.calbaptist.edu/admissions/*

CALIFORNIA COLLEGE OF THE ARTS — B-3

San Francisco, CA 94107 — (415) 703-9532; (800) 447-1ART; (415) 703-9539

Full-time: 534 men, 871 women	**Faculty:** 81
Part-time: 27 men, 47 women	**Ph.D.s:** 64%
Graduate: 173 men, 274 women	**Student/Faculty:** 9 to 1
Year: semesters, summer session	**Tuition:** $40,334
Application Deadline:	**Room & Board:** $8000
Freshman Class: 1231 applied, 1113 accepted, 233 enrolled	
SAT CR/M/W: 520/570/520	**ACT:** 24 — **SPECIAL**

California College of the Arts, founded in 1907, offers 21 undergraduate programs and 11 graduate majors in the areas of fine arts, architecture, design, and writing. There are 2 undergraduate schools and 7 graduate schools. In addition to regional accreditation, CCA has baccalaureate program accreditation with FIDER, NAAB, and NASAD. The 2 libraries contain 89,109 volumes, and 4,271 audio/video tapes/CDs/DVDs, and subscribe to 577 periodicals including electronic. Computerized library services include interlibrary loans and database searching. Special learning facilities include an art gallery, new materials library. The 4-acre campus is in a small town San Francisco and Oakland. Including any residence halls, there are 18 buildings.

Student Life: 68% of undergraduates are from California. Others are from 41 states, 46 foreign countries, and Canada. 51% are from public schools. 33% are White; 22% Foreign; 16% Asian American; 14% Hispanic. The average age of freshmen is 18; all undergraduates, 22. 17% do not continue beyond their first year; 83% remain to graduate.

Housing: 363 students can be accommodated in college housing, which includes coed dorms and on-campus apartments. coed dorms, theme housing, and apartments for single students. On-campus housing is available on a first-come, first-served basis, and is available on a lottery system for upperclassmen. Priority is given to out-of-town students. 80% of students commute. Upperclassmen may keep cars.

Activities: There are 16 groups on campus, including art, environmental, ethnic, film, gay, honors, international, literary magazine, photography, professional, religious, social, and student government. Popular campus events include Holiday Luncheon, Art and Craft Fair, Career Expo, Oakland and SF Art Murmur, Art Receptions, and Artist Lectures.

Sports: There is no sports program at CCA.

Disabled Students: 91% of the campus is accessible. Facilities include

wheelchair ramps, elevators, special parking, specially equipped restrooms, special class scheduling, lowered drinking fountains, lowered telephones, and special housing.

Services: Counseling and information services are available, as is tutoring in most subjects, humanities and sciences, writing, math, and visual studies.

Campus Safety and Security: Measures include emergency notification system and security escort services. There are shuttle buses, lighted pathways/sidewalks, and controlled access to dorms/residences.

Programs of Study: CCA confers B.Arch, B.A. and B.F.A. degrees. Master's degrees are also awarded. Bachelor's degrees are awarded in COMMUNICATIONS AND THE ARTS (animation, art, ceramic art and design, communications technology, creative writing, drawing, English, film arts, glass, graphic design, illustration, industrial design, literature, metal/jewelry, painting, photography, printmaking, sculpture, visual and performing arts, and writing), COMPUTER AND PHYSICAL SCIENCE (digital arts/technology), ENGINEERING AND ENVIRONMENTAL DESIGN (architecture, furniture design, interior design, and precision production), SOCIAL SCIENCE (fashion design and technology and textiles and clothing). Graphic design, and architecture have the largest enrollments.

Required: Students must successfully complete 126 credits for the B.F.A. and B.A., and 165 for the B.Arch. All students must complete 12 credits from the First-Year Core division and one Diversity Studies studio course. Distribution requirements for the B.F.A. are 51 credits in humanities and science plus 75 credits combining major and additional studio courses. The B.A. requires 45 credits in humanities and science plus 81 credits in the major and additional studio courses. The B'Arch requires 45 credits in humanities and science plus 120 credits in the major and additional studio courses. All students must maintain a minimum GPA of 2.0.

Special: Cross-registration is permitted with Mills and Holy Names Colleges in Oakland. Internships are required for some majors and strongly encouraged for others. Exchange program for study abroad in 13 countries and Mobility program through The Association of Independent Colleges of Art and Design are offered. Student-designed majors, and non-degree study are possible. Summer English + Art Studio course for international students is available. In addition to the B.A degrees in Writing and Literature and Visual Studies, we also offer minors in both programs.

Faculty/Classroom: 57% of faculty are male; 43% are female. 89% teach undergraduates. No introductory courses are taught by graduate students. The average class size in an introductory lecture is 15 and in a regular course is 15.

Admissions: 90% of the 2013-2014 applicants were accepted. The SAT scores for the 2013-2014 freshman class were: Critical Reading--40% below 500, 37% between 500 and 599, 21% between 600 and 699, and 2% between 700 and 800; Math--31% below 500, 35% between 500 and 599, 28% between 600 and 699, and 6% between 700 and 800; Writing--41% below 500, 39% between 500 and 599, 20% between 600 and 699. The ACT scores were 24% below 21, 24% between 21 and 23, 39% between 24 and 26, 3% between 27 and 28, and 9% above 28.

Requirements: The SAT or ACT is recommended. Application, personal essay, high school transcripts (or college transcripts), 2 letters of recommendation, portfolio of creative work. International students must also show proof of English proficiency (TOEFL, IELTS, or PTE). A GPA of 2.0 is required. AP credits are accepted. Important factors in the admissions decision are evidence of special talent, recommendations by school officials, and extracurricular activities record.

Procedure: Freshmen are admitted to all sessions. There are early admissions, deferred admissions, and rolling admissions plans. Application deadlines are open. Application fee is $60. Notification is sent on a rolling basis. Applications are accepted online.

Transfer: 190 transfer students enrolled in 2012-2013. Applicants must submit a portfolio, previous college transcripts, high school transcripts, and 2 letters of recommendation. 30 of 126 credits required for the bachelor's degree must be completed at CCA.

Visiting: There are regularly scheduled orientations for prospective students, including daily tours, fall preview day, admitted student day, virtual information sessions and March madness. There are guides for informal visits and visitors may sit in on classes. To schedule a visit, contact the Office of Enrollment Services.

Financial Aid: In 2013-2014, 78% of all full-time freshmen and 77% of continuing full-time students received some form of financial aid. 78% of all full-time freshmen and 77% of continuing full-time students received need-based aid. The average freshman award was $26,584. Need-based scholarships or need-based grants averaged $22,962; need-based self-help aid (loans and jobs) averaged $3,893; and other non-need-based awards and non-need-based scholarships averaged $8,900. 100% of undergraduate students work part-time. Average annual earnings from campus work are $3000. The average financial indebtedness of the 2013 graduate was $29,625. The FAFSA and the state aid form are required. The priority date for freshman financial aid applications for fall entry is February 1.

International Students: There are 326 international students enrolled. The school actively recruits these students. They must take the TOEFL with a minimum score of 550 on the paper-based TOEFL (PBT) or 79 on the Internet-based version (iBT), Pearson Test of English, or IELTS. The SAT or ACT is recommended.

Computers: All students may access the system. There are no time limits and no fees.

Graduates: From July 1, 2012 to June 30, 2013, 293 bachelor's degrees were awarded. The most popular majors were graphic design, architecture, and illustration. 110 companies recruited on campus in 2012-2013. In an average class, 31% graduate in 4 years or less, 49% graduate in 5 years or less, and 61% graduate in 6 years or less. Of the 2012 graduating class, 59% were employed within 6 months of graduation.

Admissions Contact: Robynne Royster, Director of Undergraduate Admissions. E-Mail: *rroyster@cca.edu* Web: *www.cca.edu*

CALIFORNIA INSTITUTE OF TECHNOLOGY C-5

Pasadena, CA 91125 **(626) 395-6341; (626) 683-3026**

Full-time: 615 men, 382 women	**Faculty:** 302
Part-time: n/av	**Ph.D.s:** 97%
Graduate: 888 men, 358 women	**Student/Faculty:** 3 to 1
Year: quarters	**Tuition:** $41,538
Application Deadline: January 3	**Room & Board:** $12,507

Freshman Class: 5535 applied, 587 accepted, 249 enrolled
SAT or ACT: required

MOST COMPETITIVE

California Institute of Technology, founded in 1891, is a private institution offering programs in engineering, science, and math. There are 6 graduate schools. In addition to regional accreditation, Caltech has baccalaureate program accreditation with ABET. The 7 libraries contain 624,136 volumes, 10,586 microform items, and 3,033 audio/video tapes/CDs/DVDs, and subscribe to 2,641 periodicals including electronic. Computerized library services include interlibrary loans, database searching, and Internet access. The 124-acre campus is in a suburban area 12 miles northeast of Los Angeles. Including any residence halls, there are 105 buildings.

Student Life: 69% of undergraduates are from out of state, mostly the West. Students are from 46 states, 28 foreign countries, and Canada. 85% are from public schools. 40% are Asian American; 31% White; 11% Foreign. The average age of freshmen is 18; all undergraduates, 20. 2% do not continue beyond their first year; 90% remain to graduate.

Housing: 879 students can be accommodated in college housing, which includes coed dorms, off-campus apartments, and married student housing. On-campus housing is guaranteed for the freshman year only. Alcohol is not permitted. All students may keep cars.

Activities: There are no fraternities or sororities. There are 150 groups on campus, including art, band, cheerleading, chess, choir, chorale, chorus, computers, dance, drama, ethnic, film, gay, honors, international, jazz band, literary magazine, musical theater, newspaper, opera, orchestra, pep band, photography, political, professional, religious, social, social service, student government, symphony, and yearbook. Popular campus events include Ditch Day, International Day, and Pre-Frosh Weekend.

Sports: There are 9 intercollegiate sports for men and 8 for women, and 19 intramural sports for men and 15 for women. Facilities include 2 Olympic-size swimming pools, a 300-seat gym, a 440-meter track, a football field, 4 baseball fields, and 8 tennis courts. Another athletic facility includes a gym, a 4000-square-foot exercise room with equipment, and racquetball courts.

Disabled Students: 98% of the campus is accessible. Facilities include wheelchair ramps, elevators, special parking, specially equipped restrooms, and lowered telephones.

Services: Counseling and information services are available, as is tutoring in every subject. There is a reader service for the blind.

Campus Safety and Security: Measures include 24-hour foot and vehicle patrol, emergency notification system, self-defense education, and security escort services. There are emergency telephones, lighted pathways/sidewalks, and controlled access to dorms/residences.

Programs of Study: Caltech confers B.S. degrees. Master's and doctoral degrees are also awarded. Bachelor's degrees are awarded in BIOLOGICAL SCIENCE (biology/biological science), BUSINESS (business administration and management), COMPUTER AND PHYSICAL SCIENCE (applied mathematics, astrophysics, chemistry, computer mathematics, computer science, geochemistry, geology, geophysics and seismology, mathematics, physics, and planetary and space science), ENGINEERING AND ENVIRONMENTAL DESIGN (chemical engineering, computer engineering, electrical/electronics engineering, engineering and applied science, materials science, and mechanical engineering), HEALTH PROFESSIONS (environmental health science), SOCIAL SCIENCE (economics, history, history of science, philosophy, and political science/government). Engineering, physical science, computer science have the largest enrollments.

Required: Caltech's core curriculum consists of the following: -three terms (27 units) of mathematics Ma 1 abc: Calculus of One and Several Variables and Linear Algebra. Review of calculus. Complex numbers,

Taylor polynomials, infinite series. Comprehensive presentation of linear algebra. Derivatives of vector functions, multiple integrals, line and path integrals, theorems of Green and Stokes. -three terms (27 units) of physics Ph 1 abc: Classical Mechanics and Electromagnetism. Newtonian mechanics, electricity and magnetism, special relativity. Emphasis on physical insight and problem solving. -two terms (15 units) of chemistry Ch 1 ab: General Chemistry. Lectures and recitations dealing with the principles of chemistry. -one term (9 units) of biology a topical course introducing a variety of tools and concepts of modern biology. May be fulfilled with: Bi 1: Principles of Biology OR Bi 1 x. The Great Ideas of Biology: An Introduction through Experimentation OR Bi 8. Introduction to Molecular Biology: Organization and Expression of Genetic Information. -one term (9 units) freshman menu course menu courses include astronomy, geology, energy science, environmental science and engineering, or information science. -two terms (12 units) of introductory lab courses freshman chem lab, plus one other lab chosen from offerings in applied physics, biology, chemistry, engineering, or physics. -one term (3 units) of scientific writing students research, write, and revise a 3,000-word paper on a science or engineering topic, which is then published in an online journal established for that purpose. Students work with a faculty mentor on the content of the paper and receive editorial guidance from science writing instructors. -twelve terms (108 units) of humanities courses -two terms of Freshman Humanities, two terms of introductory social-science, -two terms of advanced humanities, two terms of advanced social-science. The remaining four courses may be chosen from any of the humanities or social-science offerings. Three writing intensive courses must be taken on grades. -three terms (9 units) Physical Education this requirement may be satisfied entirely or in part by participation in intercollegiate athletics, or successful completion of physical-education class course work. All grades are issued pass/fail.

Special: Caltech offers cross-registration with Scripps College, Occidental College, and Art Center College of Design, various work-study programs, including those with NASA's Jet Propulsion Laboratory, dual majors in any major, and independent studies degrees with faculty-approved student-designed majors. A 3-2 engineering degree is possible with several institutions. Pass/fail options are available for freshmen. A summer undergraduate research fellowship program is offered. Study abroad at University College in London, Cambridge University, and University of Copenhagen, in Denmark.

Faculty/Classroom: 82% of faculty are male; 18% are female. All teach and do research. No introductory courses are taught by graduate students. The average class size in an introductory lecture is 200 and in a regular course is 15.

Admissions: 11% of the 2013-2014 applicants were accepted. The SAT scores for the 2013-2014 freshman class were: Critical Reading--1% between 500 and 599, 20% between 600 and 699, and 79% between 700 and 800; Math--1% between 600 and 699, and 99% between 700 and 800; Writing--22% between 600 and 699, and 78% between 700 and 800. The ACT scores were 100% above 28. 100% of the current freshmen were in the top fifth of their class.

Requirements: The SAT or ACT is required. SAT II: Subject tests in math level II and one in physics, biology, or chemistry are required. Applicants should have completed 4 years of high school math (including a year of calculus), 3 years of English, 1 year of chemistry, 1 year of physics, and 1 year of U.S. History or Government (waived for international students) Important factors in the admissions decision are advanced placement or honors courses, recommendations by school officials, and evidence of special talent.

Procedure: Freshmen are admitted fall. Entrance exams should be taken through December of the senior year. There are early admissions and deferred admissions plans. Early decision applications should be filed by November 1; regular applications, by January 3 for fall entry, along with a $65 fee. Notification of early decision is sent December 15; regular decision, April 1. 556 applicants were on the 2013 waiting list; 40 were admitted. Applications are accepted online.

Transfer: 8 transfer students enrolled in 2012-2013. Transfers, admitted only into sophomore and junior classes, need a minimum GPA of 3.0. Applicants must have completed 1 year (2 years for juniors) of calculus and calculus-based physics, and must take Caltech's entrance exams in math and physics. Chemistry or chemical engineering majors also should have completed 1 year of chemistry and must take an additional entrance exam. 216 of 780 credits required for the bachelor's degree must be completed at Caltech.

Visiting: There are regularly scheduled orientations for prospective students, Visits include a student-led campus tour followed by an information session. There are guides for informal visits and visitors may sit in on classes. To schedule a visit, contact the Undergraduate Admissions Office.

Financial Aid: In 2013-2014, 56% of all full-time freshmen and 54% of continuing full-time students received some form of financial aid. 56% of all full-time freshmen and 54% of continuing full-time students received need-based aid. The average financial indebtedness of the 2013 graduate was $9,561. Caltech is a member of CSS. The CSS/Profile, FAFSA, the state aid form, and the college's own financial statement are required. The deadline for filing freshman financial aid applications for fall entry is Febuary 1.

International Students: There are 116 international students enrolled. The school actively recruits these students. They must also take the SAT or ACT.

Computers: All students may access the system any time. There are no time limits and no fees.

Graduates: From July 1, 2012 to June 30, 2013, 192 bachelor's degrees were awarded. The most popular majors were engineering (34%), physical sciences (25%), and mathematics (18%). 85 companies recruited on campus in 2012-2013. In an average class, 82% graduate in 4 years or less and 89% graduate in 6 years or less. Of the 2012 graduating class, 55% were enrolled in graduate school within 6 months of graduation.

Admissions Contact: Jarrid Whitney, Executive Director of Admissions and Fin. E-Mail: *ugadmissions@caltech.edu* Web: *admissions.caltech .edu*

CALIFORNIA INSTITUTE OF THE ARTS C-5

Valencia, CA 91355 **(661) 255-1050**
(800) 545-ARTS; (661) 253-7710

Full-time: 450 men, 437 women	**Faculty:** n/av
Part-time: 6 men, 2 women	**Ph.D.s:** n/av
Graduate: 251 men, 308 women	**Student/Faculty:** n/av
Year: semesters	**Tuition:** $37,242
Application Deadline: January 5	**Room & Board:** $10,123

Freshman Class: 1686 applied, 549 accepted, 258 enrolled

SPECIAL

California Institute of the Arts, founded in 1961, is a private institution offering undergraduate and graduate programs in art, dance, film and video, music, and theater, and graduate majors in directing, integrated media, and writing. There are 6 undergraduate schools and 6 graduate schools. In addition to regional accreditation, CalArts has baccalaureate program accreditation with NASAD and NASM. The library contains 203,471 volumes, 4,124 microform items, and 32,804 audio/video tapes/CDs/DVDs, and subscribes to 665 periodicals including electronic. Computerized library services include interlibrary loans, database searching, and Internet access. Special learning facilities include a learning resource center, art gallery, radio station, TV station, movie theater, sound stages, scenery construction shops, and slide and film libraries. The 60-acre campus is in a suburban area 30 miles north of Los Angeles. Including any residence halls, there are 3 buildings. The figures in the above capsule and in this profile are approximate.

Student Life: 51% of undergraduates are from out of state, mostly the Northeast. Students are from 42 states, 23 foreign countries, and Canada. 56% are white; 12% Hispanic; 11% Asian American. The average age of freshmen is 18; all undergraduates, 21. 23% do not continue beyond their first year.

Housing: 450 students can be accommodated in college housing, which includes coed dorms and on-campus apartments. On-campus housing is available on a first-come, first-served basis, and is available on a lottery system for upperclassmen. Priority is given to out-of-town students. 60% of students commute. All students may keep cars.

Activities: There are no fraternities or sororities. There are 21 groups on campus, including art, chess, dance, drama, ethnic, film, gay, international, jazz band, literary magazine, musical theater, newspaper, opera, orchestra, photography, political, radio and TV, religious, social service, sports clubs, student government, and symphony. Popular campus events include music festivals, theater productions, and poetry readings.

Sports: There is no sports program at CalArts. Facilities include tennis courts, sand volleyball courts, and a swimming pool.

Disabled Students: 95% of the campus is accessible. Facilities include wheelchair ramps, elevators, special parking, specially equipped restrooms, special class scheduling, lowered drinking fountains, lowered telephones, and special housing.

Services: Counseling and information services are available, as is tutoring in some subjects, ESL There is a reader service for the blind. All computerized media systems are used in the 6 major departments, and other subjects, which vary each year.

Campus Safety and Security: Measures include 24-hour foot and vehicle patrol, emergency notification system, and security escort services. There are lighted pathways/sidewalks.

Programs of Study: CalArts confers B.F.A. degrees. Master's degrees are also awarded. Bachelor's degrees are awarded in COMMUNICATIONS AND THE ARTS (animation, dance, dramatic arts, fine arts, music performance, music theory and composition, photography, theater design, video, visual and performing arts, and visual design). Art, music, and acting are the strongest academically. Art, film/video, and theater are the largest.

Required: To graduate, all students must complete a total of 120 semester units, with 46 in critical studies, and must satisfy all curriculum and degree requirements of the particular school.

Special: Cal Arts offers internships with local and national companies, student-designed majors, interdisciplinary studies, study abroad in 6 countries, and a cooperative education program.

Faculty/Classroom: 60% of faculty are male; 40% are female. No

introductory courses are taught by graduate students. The average class size in an introductory lecture is 25 and in a regular course is 14.

Requirements: Applicants must be graduates of an accredited secondary school or have a GED certificate. They must subbit an official transcript and an essay. Portfolios and auditions are required and an interview is recommended for some programs. AP credits are accepted. Important factors in the admissions decision are evidence of special talent and advanced placement or honors courses.

Procedure: Freshmen are admitted fall and spring. Applications should be filed by January 5 for fall entry; November 15 for spring entry, along with a $70 fee. Notifications are sent April 1. In a recent year, 63 applicants were on the waiting list; 8 were admitted.

Visiting: There are regularly scheduled orientations for prospective students, Campus tours are held Monday through Friday at 12 p.m. throughout the academic year. Visitors may sit in on classes. To schedule a visit, contact the Office of Admissions.

Financial Aid: In a recent year, 80% of all full-time freshmen and 80% of continuing full-time students received some form of financial aid. 73% of all full-time freshmen and 72% of continuing full-time students received need-based aid. Need-based scholarships or need-based grants averaged $16,642 ($36,166 maximum); and need-based self-help aid (loans and jobs) averaged $8,773. 27% of undergraduate students work part-time. CalArts is a member of CSS. The FAFSA is required. Check with the school for priority date for freshman financial aid applications.

International Students: There are 66 international students enrolled. They must take the TOEFL with a minimum score of 530 on the paper-based TOEFL (PBT) or 80 on the Internet-based version (iBT).

Computers: Wireless access is available. Students have access to the Institute network from their dorm rooms, studios, and in the library. They also have access to wireless in key locations within the main building of the Institute. All students may access the system. There are no time limits and no fees. Students enrolled in graphic design must have a personal computer.

Graduates: The most popular majors were music performance (19%), animation (14%), and technical theater/stagecraft (10%).

Admissions Contact: Molly Ryan, Director of Admissions. E-Mail: *mryan@calarts.edu* Web: *www.calarts.edu*

CALIFORNIA LUTHERAN UNIVERSITY C-5

Thousand Oaks, CA 91360 **(805) 493-3049**
(877) 258-3678; (805) 493-3645

Full-time: 1232 men, 1485 women	**Faculty:** 127; IIA, av$
Part-time: 70 men, 101 women	**Ph.D.s:** 94%
Graduate: 561 men, 833 women	**Student/Faculty:** 15 to 1
Year: semesters, summer session	**Tuition:** $35,720
Application Deadline: January 15	**Room & Board:** $11,920
Freshman Class: 6920 applied, 3323 accepted, 540 enrolled	
SAT CR/M/W: 540/560/540 **ACT:** 24	**COMPETITIVE**

California Lutheran University is a diverse, scholarly community dedicated to excellence in the liberal arts and sciences and professional studies. Rooted in the Lutheran tradition of Christian faith, the University encourages critical inquiry into matters of both faith and reason. The mission of the University is to educate leaders for a global society who are strong in character and judgment, confident in their identity and vocation, and committed to service and justice. There are 2 undergraduate schools and 3 graduate schools. The library contains 325,503 volumes, 22,000 microform items, and 2,926 audio/video tapes/CDs/DVDs, and subscribes to 152 periodicals including electronic. Computerized library services include interlibrary loans, database searching, Internet access, and Wi-Fi capability. Special learning facilities include an art gallery, radio station, TV station, Human Performance Lab, SEEd Project Garden. The 225-acre campus is in a suburban area 45 miles north of downtown Los Angeles in Ventura County, 50 miles south of Santa Barbara. Including any residence halls, there are 53 buildings.

Student Life: 83% of undergraduates are from California. Others are from 40 states, 45 foreign countries, and Canada. 75% are from public schools. 48% are White; 23% Hispanic; 12% Foreign. 25% are Catholic; 25% Protestant. The average age of freshmen is 18; all undergraduates, 20. 15% do not continue beyond their first year; 70% remain to graduate.

Housing: 1409 students can be accommodated in college housing, which includes coed dorms and on-campus apartments. On-campus housing is guaranteed for all 4 years. 53% of students live on campus; of those, 60% remain on campus on weekends. Alcohol is not permitted. All students may keep cars.

Activities: There are no fraternities or sororities. There are 80 groups on campus, including and Model United Nations, art, band, cheerleading, choir, chorale, chorus, computers, dance, debate, drama, environmental, ethnic, film, forensics, gay, honors, international, jazz band, literary magazine, musical theater, newspaper, orchestra, pep band, photography, political, professional, radio and TV, religious, social, social service, student alumni, student government, symphony, and yearbook. Popular campus events include Santa Lucia, Scandinavian Festival, Chinese New Year, World Fair and Service Day.

Sports: There are 10 intercollegiate sports for men and 10 for women, and 10 intramural sports for men and 10 for women. Facilities include The Gilbert Sports and Fitness Center includes Gilbert Arena for home basketball and volleyball games, Soiland Recreation Center for all students and staff, the Forrest Fitness Center, a dance studio, a training room and the CLU Athletic Hall of Fame. William Rolland Stadium is the new home of the CLU football and soccer teams. The Samuelson Aquatics Center features a 50-meter pool used by college and Olympic athletes as well as the CLU Community Pool. Other athletic facilities include the Poulson Tennis Center, George "Sparky" Anderson Field and Ullman Stadium used by the baseball team and Hutton Field used by the softball team.

Disabled Students: 95% of the campus is accessible. Facilities include wheelchair ramps, elevators, special parking, specially equipped restrooms, lowered drinking fountains, lowered telephones, and special housing.

Services: Counseling and information services are available, as is tutoring in every subject, The learning resources and writing centers offer help with study and writing skills. There is a reader service for the blind, and remedial math, reading, and writing. A student support services program helps low-income first-generation students adapt to the academic and social life of the campus. We have a coordinator for students with disabilities.

Campus Safety and Security: Measures include 24-hour foot and vehicle patrol, emergency notification system, self-defense education, and security escort services. There are emergency telephones, lighted pathways/sidewalks, controlled access to dorms/residences, All residence halls are equipped with security systems.

Programs of Study: Cal Lutheran confers B.A., and B.S. degrees. Master's and doctoral degrees are also awarded. Bachelor's degrees are awarded in AGRICULTURE (environmental studies), BIOLOGICAL SCIENCE (biochemistry and biology/biological science), BUSINESS (accounting and business administration and management), COMMUNICATIONS AND THE ARTS (art, communications, English, French, German, multimedia, music, music performance, Spanish, and theatre arts), COMPUTER AND PHYSICAL SCIENCE (chemistry, computer science, geology, information sciences and systems, mathematics, and physics), HEALTH PROFESSIONS (exercise science, predentistry, and premedicine), SOCIAL SCIENCE (criminal justice, economics, history, interdisciplinary studies, international studies, liberal arts/general studies, philosophy, political science/government, prelaw, psychology, religion, social science, sociology, and theological studies). Biology, accounting and economics are the strongest academically. Business, communication, and psychology have the largest enrollments.

Required: To graduate, all students must complete a core curriculum including 16 to 20 units in social science, 8 each in religion, foreign language, and science, 7 in English, 4 to 6 in creative arts, 4 in math, and 1 in phys ed. Students must also fulfill content requirements of a freshman cluster and take one course of each: writing-intensive, speaking intensive, global studies, U.S diversity, and senior level capstone. Also needed are a total of 124 units, 40 of which must be upper division with 32 hours in the major for a B.A. and a minimum of 36 hours for a B.S. The final 30 credits before graduation must be completed at CLU. Students must have a minimum 2.0 GPA.

Special: CLU offers co-op programs, internships, a Washington semester, and study abroad in over 70 countries. Also available are work-study and student-designed interdisciplinary degree majors, redit for experiential learning, special student status for non degree study, pass/fail options and continuing education. A bachelor's degree for professionals program offers accelerated degrees in accounting, business, computer science, communication, liberal studies, organizational leadership and psychology. There are 9 national honor societies and a freshman honors program.

Faculty/Classroom: 58% of faculty are male; 42% are female. 77% teach undergraduates. No introductory courses are taught by graduate students. The average class size in an introductory lecture is 18; in a laboratory is 15; and in a regular course is 17.

Admissions: 48% of the 2013-2014 applicants were accepted. The SAT scores for the 2013-2014 freshman class were: Critical Reading--24% below 500, 53% between 500 and 599, 21% between 600 and 699, and 2% between 700 and 800; Math--17% below 500, 51% between 500 and 599, 29% between 600 and 699, and 3% between 700 and 800; Writing--25% below 500, 53% between 500 and 599, 19% between 600 and 699, and 3% between 700 and 800. The ACT scores were 8% below 21, 32% between 21 and 23, 37% between 24 and 26, 12% between 27 and 28, and 11% above 28. 75% of the current freshmen were in the top fifth of their class; 20% were in the top two fifths.

Requirements: The SAT or ACT is required. Applicants must be graduates of an accredited secondary school and have completed a minimum of four years of English, two years of math, and two years each of foreign language, social studies, and lab science. The GED is accepted. An essay is required and an interview is recommended. AP and CLEP credits are accepted.

Procedure: Freshmen are admitted fall and spring. Entrance exams should be taken during spring of junior year, or early fall of senior year.

There is an early admissions plan. Early decision applications should be filed by November 15; regular applications, by January 15 for fall entry; and December 15 for spring entry, along with a $45 fee. Notification of early decision is sent January 15; regular decision, on a Rolling basis. 495 applicants were on the 2013 waiting list; 146 were admitted. Applications are accepted online.

Transfer: 335 transfer students enrolled in 2012-2013. Transfers should have at least a 2.75 transferable GPA and 28 transferable units. An application is required. An interview is recommended. Applicants must be in good standing at the previous college and may submit a recommendation from a college professor in lieu of a high school recommendation. 30 of 124 credits required for the bachelor's degree must be completed at Cal Lutheran.

Visiting: There are regularly scheduled orientations for prospective students, including an admission and financial aid interview, a tour, visits with faculty or coaches, and lunch. There are guides for informal visits, visitors may sit in on classes, and stay overnight. To schedule a visit, contact the Presidential Host Coordinators at prehost@callutheran.edu.

Financial Aid: In 2013-2014, 98% of all full-time freshmen and 93% of continuing full-time students received some form of financial aid. 70% of all full-time freshmen and 68% of continuing full-time students received need-based aid. The average freshman award was $25,700. Need-based scholarships or need-based grants averaged $22,550 ($41,370 maximum); need-based self-help aid (loans and jobs) averaged $2,700 ($13,500 maximum); and other non-need-based awards and non-need-based scholarships averaged $16,400 ($48,440 maximum). 55% of undergraduate students work part-time. Average annual earnings from campus work are $2500. The average financial indebtedness of the 2013 graduate was $24,120. The FAFSA is required. The priority date for freshman financial aid applications for fall entry is March 1.

International Students: There are 115 international students enrolled. The school actively recruits these students. They must take the TOEFL with a minimum score of 550 on the paper-based TOEFL (PBT) or 79 on the Internet-based version (iBT). They must also take the SAT or ACT.

Computers: All students may access the system any time. There are no time limits and no fees.

Graduates: From July 1, 2012 to June 30, 2013, 745 bachelor's degrees were awarded. The most popular majors were business (16%), psychology (12%), and communication (10%). 72 companies recruited on campus in 2012-2013. In an average class, 4% graduate in 3 years or less, 61% graduate in 4 years or less, 69% graduate in 5 years or less, and 70% graduate in 6 years or less. Of the 2012 graduating class, 36% were enrolled in graduate school within 6 months of graduation, and 56% were employed.

Admissions Contact: Michael Elgarico, Director of Undergraduate Admissions. E-Mail: *elgarico@callutheran.edu* Web: *www.callutheran.edu*

CALIFORNIA MARITIME ACADEMY B-3

Vallejo, CA 94590-0644 **(707) 654-1330**
(800) 561-1945; (707) 654-1336

Full-time: 705 men, 134 women	**Faculty:** 49; IIB, +$
Part-time: 17 men, 12 women	**Ph.D.s:** 50%
Graduate: n/av	**Student/Faculty:** 12 to 1
Year: semesters, summer session	**Tuition:** $6636 ($17,796)
Application Deadline: open	**Room & Board:** $9860

Freshman Class: 908 applied, 766 accepted, 260 enrolled
SAT or ACT: required

COMPETITIVE

California Maritime Academy, founded in 1929, is a public college that awards undergraduate degrees in marine transportation, business, engineering, and technology. In addition to regional accreditation, Cal Maritime has baccalaureate program accreditation with ABET. The library contains 30,000 volumes, 15,000 microform items, and subscribes to 300 periodicals including electronic. Computerized library services include interlibrary loans, database searching, and Internet access. Special learning facilities include a learning resource center, a training ship; navigation, steam plant, and diesel engine simulators; a fluid dynamics lab with wind tunnels and a miniature jet turbine engine; and a maritime simulation center for deck and engineering cadets. The 87-acre campus is in a suburban area 30 miles northeast of San Francisco. Including any residence halls, there are 39 buildings. The figures in the above capsule and in this profile are approximate.

Student Life: 87% of undergraduates are from California. Others are from 16 states, and 5 foreign countries. 70% are from public schools. 55% are white; 13% Asian American. The average age of freshmen is 19; all undergraduates, 22. 7% do not continue beyond their first year; 58% remain to graduate.

Housing: 680 students can be accommodated in college housing, which includes single-sex and coed dorms. 24-hour quiet residences. On-campus housing is guaranteed for all 4 years. 70% of students live on campus; of those, 30% remain on campus on weekends. Alcohol is not permitted. All students may keep cars.

Activities: There are no fraternities or sororities. There are 26 groups on campus, including business, engineering, yoga club, auto shop, chorale, drill team, ethnic, international, jazz band, newspaper, photography, professional, religious, social, social service, and student government. Popular campus events include movie nights, cultural dinner nights, and semiformal dance.

Sports: There are 7 intercollegiate sports for men and 5 for women, and 10 intramural sports for men and 8 for women. Facilities include a gym, a weight room, physical therapy and exercise rooms, a 25-meter pool, tennis and racquetball courts, and a sports field.

Disabled Students: 70% of the campus is accessible. Facilities include wheelchair ramps, special parking, specially equipped restrooms, lowered drinking fountains, and lowered telephones.

Services: Counseling and information services are available, as is tutoring in some subjects, math, English, engineering, and science. There is remedial math, reading, and writing.

Campus Safety and Security: Measures include 24-hour foot and vehicle patrol, self-defense education, and security escort services. There are lighted pathways/sidewalks, and surveillance cameras.

Programs of Study: Cal Maritime confers B.A., B.S. degrees. Bachelor's degrees are awarded in BUSINESS (business administration and management and transportation management), ENGINEERING AND ENVIRONMENTAL DESIGN (engineering technology, marine engineering, maritime science, and mechanical engineering). Mechanical engineering is the strongest academically. Marine transportation has the largest enrollment.

Required: Graduation requirements for all students include a minimum 2.0 GPA and completion of English composition, American government, U.S. history, algebra and trigonometry, computer science, and survival swimming courses. All students must participate in at least one 2-month training cruise.

Special: The academy has simulator training and requires a 2-month session aboard the academy's ship. Lab time is a major part of each program. Industry internships are available during the summer. Dual majors and co-op programs are available, as is cross-registration with other Cal State institutions. There are B.A.- B.S. degrees in mechanical engineering, business, marine transportation, facilities engineering, global studies, and marine engineering.

Faculty/Classroom: 85% of faculty are male; 15% are female. All teach undergraduates. No introductory courses are taught by graduate students. The average class size in an introductory lecture is 35; in a laboratory is 9; and in a regular course is 20.

Admissions: 84% of the 2011-2012 applicants were accepted.

Requirements: The SAT or ACT is required. In addition, secondary school courses must include 4 years of English, 3 each of math and electives, 2 of language, and 1 each of lab science, history, and a visual or performing art. A GPA of 2.0 is required. AP and CLEP credits are accepted. Important factors in the admissions decision are leadership record, advanced placement or honors courses, and evidence of special talent.

Procedure: Freshmen are admitted fall. Entrance exams should be taken by December of the senior year. There is a rolling admissions plan. Early decision applications should be filed by November 30, along with a $55 fee. Notifications are sent in January. Applications are accepted online.

Transfer: In a recent year, 98 transfer students enrolled. Applicants must have a 2.0 GPA, provide SAT or ACT scores, and be in good standing at the last institution attended. 30 of 120 credits required for the bachelor's degree must be completed at Cal Maritime.

Visiting: There are regularly scheduled orientations for prospective students. There are guides for informal visits. To schedule a visit, contact the Admissions Office.

Financial Aid: In a recent year, 81% of all full-time freshmen and 78% of continuing full-time students received some form of financial aid. 34% of all full-time freshmen and 32% of continuing full-time students received need-based aid. 40% of undergraduate students work part-time. Average annual earnings from campus work are $1018. The FAFSA is required. The priority date for freshman financial aid applications for fall entry is March 2. Check with the school for the deadline for filing freshman financial aid applications.

International Students: There are 11 international students enrolled. They must take the TOEFL with a minimum score of 500 on the paper-based TOEFL (PBT) or 61 on the Internet-based version (iBT), or the SAT or ACT.

Computers: All students may access the system. There are no time limits and no fees.

Graduates: In a recent year, 158 bachelor's degrees were awarded. The most popular majors were marine transportation (39%), global studies and maritime affairs (19%), and mechanical engineering (16%). In an average class, 2% graduate in 3 years or less, 51% graduate in 4 years or less, 59% graduate in 5 years or less, and 62% graduate in 6 years or less. In a recent graduating class, 1% were enrolled in graduate school within 6 months of graduation, and 10% were employed.

Admissions Contact: Director of Admissions and Enrollment Services. E-Mail:*admission@csum.edu Web: www.csum.edu*

CALIFORNIA POLYTECHNIC STATE UNIVERSITY B-4

San Luis Obispo, CA 93407 (805) 756-2311; (805) 756-5400

Full-time: 9836 men, 8222 women **Faculty:** 800; IIA, ++$
Part-time: 427 men, 254 women **Ph.D.s:** 82%
Graduate: 509 men, 455 women **Student/Faculty:** 21 to 1
Year: quarters, summer session **Tuition:** $8724 ($19,884)
Application Deadline: November 30 **Room & Board:** $11,123
Freshman Class: 40402 applied, 13953 accepted, 4871 enrolled
SAT CR/M: 595/630 **ACT:** 28 **HIGHLY COMPETITIVE**

California Polytechnic State University, founded in 1901, is a public institution that is part of the California State University system. It offers programs in agriculture, architecture and environmental design, business, education, engineering, liberal arts, sciences and math, and preprofessional studies. There are 6 undergraduate schools. In addition to regional accreditation, Cal Poly has baccalaureate program accreditation with AACSB, ABET, ACCE, ASLA, NAAB, NASAD, NASM, NRPA, and SAF. The library contains 795,216 volumes, 1.8 million microform items, 3,000 audio/video tapes/CDs/DVDs, and subscribes to 60,000 periodicals including electronic. Computerized library services include interlibrary loans, database searching, Internet access, and Wi-Fi capability. Special learning facilities include an art gallery, radio station, and TV station. The 6000-acre campus is in a suburban area 200 miles north of Los Angeles, and 230 miles south of San Francisco. Including any residence halls, there are 125 buildings.

Student Life: 90% of undergraduates are from California. Others are from states. 60% are White; 15% Hispanic; 11% Asian American. The average age of freshmen is 17; all undergraduates, 19. 7% do not continue beyond their first year.

Housing: 6239 students can be accommodated in college housing, which includes single-sex and coed dorms and on-campus apartments. In addition, there are honors houses, special-interest houses, Living/learning residence halls with an academic theme affiliated with University's six academic colleges (Engineering, Science & Math, Architecture, Agriculture, Liberal Arts, Business). On-campus apartment-style housing, with programmatic themes, special housing for international students, coed dorms. On-campus housing is available on a first-come, first-served basis, and is available on a lottery system for upperclassmen. 62% of students commute. Alcohol is not permitted. All students may keep cars.

Activities: 13% of men belong to 1 local and 21 national fraternities; 18% of women belong to 13 national sororities. There are 400 groups on campus, including art, band, cheerleading, chess, choir, chorale, chorus, computers, dance, debate, drama, environmental, ethnic, film, gay, honors, international, jazz band, literary magazine, marching band, musical theater, newspaper, opera, orchestra, pep band, photography, political, professional, radio and TV, religious, social, social service, student government, symphony, and various engineering clubs. Popular campus events include Rose Float, Open House, Week of Welcome, and SOAR.

Sports: There are 10 intercollegiate sports for men and 10 for women, and 7 intramural sports for men and 7 for women. Facilities include Outdoor track, outdoor swimming pools, indoor and sand volleyball, tennis, indoor and outdoor basketball and racquetball courts, weight rooms, cardio exercise rooms, martial arts room, synthetic and natural turf playing fields, baseball stadium, softball stadium, and football/soccer stadium.

Disabled Students: 80% of the campus is accessible. Facilities include wheelchair ramps, elevators, special parking, specially equipped restrooms, special class scheduling, lowered drinking fountains, lowered telephones, special housing.

Services: Counseling and information services are available, as is tutoring in most subjects. There is a reader service for the blind. Writing skills lab and test office. Psychological and career services are available.

Campus Safety and Security: Measures include 24-hour foot and vehicle patrol, emergency notification system, self-defense education, and security escort services. There are emergency telephones, lighted pathways/sidewalks, and controlled access to dorms/residences.

Programs of Study: Cal Poly confers B.A., B.S., B.Arch., B.F.A. and B.L.A. degrees. Master's degrees are also awarded. Bachelor's degrees are awarded in AGRICULTURE (agricultural business management, agricultural communications, agricultural mechanics, agricultural sciences, agronomy, animal science, dairy science, forestry and related sciences, natural resource management, soil science, and wine and viticulture), BIOLOGICAL SCIENCE (biochemistry, biology/biological science, microbiology, and nutrition), BUSINESS (business administration and management and recreation and leisure services), COMMUNICATIONS AND THE ARTS (art and design, communication studies, English, graphic communications, journalism, modern language, music, and theatre arts), COMPUTER AND PHYSICAL SCIENCE (chemistry, computer science, earth science, industrial technology, mathematics, physics, software engineering, and statistics), EDUCATION (agricultural education and education), ENGINEERING AND ENVIRONMENTAL DESIGN (aeronautical engineering, architectural engineering, architecture, biomedical engineering, bioresource engineering, city/community/regional planning, civil engineering, computer engineering, construction management, electrical/electronics engineering, engineering science, environmental engineering, environmental science, industrial engineering, landscape architecture, manufacturing engineering, materials engineering, mechanical engineering, and transportation engineering), HEALTH PROFESSIONS (kinesiology), SOCIAL SCIENCE (anthropology, child psychology/development, economics, ethnic studies, food science, history, interdisciplinary studies, liberal arts/general studies, liberal arts/engineering studies, philosophy, political science/government, psychology, and sociology).

Required: Students must have a minimum 2.0 GPA, 72 quarter units of general education, a minimum of 180 total units, a United States Cultural Pluralism course, completion of the Graduation Writing Requirement, a minimum of 50 units in residence and a senior project are required.

Special: Cal Poly offers work-study programs, co-op programs in numerous majors, study abroad, and dual majors. Credit for military experience and pass/fail options are available. There is a freshman honors program.

Faculty/Classroom: 62% of faculty are male; 38% are female. No introductory courses are taught by graduate students.

Admissions: 35% of the 2013-2014 applicants were accepted. The SAT scores for the 2013-2014 freshman class were: Critical Reading--8% below 500, 43% between 500 and 599, 39% between 600 and 699, and 10% between 700 and 800; Math--2% below 500, 29% between 500 and 599, 48% between 600 and 699, and 21% between 700 and 800. The ACT scores were 14% between 21 and 23, 59% between 24 and 26, and 27% above 28. 83% of the current freshmen were in the top fifth of their class; 98% were in the top two fifths.

Requirements: The SAT or ACT is required. In addition, applicants must be graduates of an accredited high school or have a GED. Required are 15 academic credits, including 4 years of English, 3 of math, 2 of science (2 lab), 2 of foreign language, and 1 each of social studies, history, visual and performing arts, and academic electives. AP and CLEP credits are accepted.

Procedure: Freshmen are admitted fall. Entrance exams should be taken mid-June every year. There are early decision and early admissions plans. Early decision applications should be filed by October 31; regular applications, by November 30 for fall entry, along with a $55 fee. Notification of early decision is sent December 15; regular decision, April 1. 1343 early decision candidates were accepted for the 2013-2014 class. 1603 applicants were on the 2013 waiting list; 15 were admitted. Applications are accepted online.

Transfer: 947 transfer students enrolled in 2012-2013. Applicants must meet general education and breadth requirements and submit college transcripts with a minimum GPA of 2.0 50 of 180 credits required for the bachelor's degree must be completed at Cal Poly.

Visiting: There are regularly scheduled orientations for prospective students, Campus tours are offered Monday through Friday at 11:10 AM. Admissions presentations for all freshmen and transfer prospective students are offered Monday through Friday at 1:00 PM. There are guides for informal visits. To schedule a visit, contact Admissions Office at admissions@calpoly.edu.

Financial Aid: The average freshman award was $10,129. Need-based scholarships or need-based grants averaged $3,567; need-based self-help aid (loans and jobs) averaged $3,773; non-need-based athletic scholarships averaged $5,029; other non-need-based awards and non-need-based scholarships averaged $1,946; and $3,854 from other forms of aid. The FAFSA is required. The priority date for freshman financial aid applications for fall entry is March 2.

International Students: There are 211 international students enrolled. The school actively recruits these students. They must take the TOEFL with a minimum score of 550 on the paper-based TOEFL (PBT) or 80 on the Internet-based version (iBT).

Computers: All students may access the system. There are no time limits and no fees.

Graduates: From July 1, 2012 to June 30, 2013, 3997 bachelor's degrees were awarded. The most popular majors were engineering technologies (27%), business/marketing (13%), and agriculture (12%). Of the 2012 graduating class, 13% were enrolled in graduate school within 6 months of graduation, and 73% were employed.

Admissions Contact: James L. Maraviglia, Assoc. VP, Marketing & Enroll. Develop.. E-Mail: *admissions@calpoly.edu* Web: *http:/admissions.calpoly.edu/*

CALIFORNIA STATE POLYTECHNIC UNIVERSITY, POMONA D-5

Pomona, CA 91768 **(909) 869-3427; (909) 869-5315**

Full-time: 10253 men, 8160 women **Faculty:** n/av; IIA, +$
Part-time: 1608 men, 931 women **Ph.D.s:** 82%
Graduate: 723 men, 826 women **Student/Faculty:** 25 to 1
Year: quarters, summer session **Tuition:** $6350 ($17,510)
Application Deadline: November 1 **Room & Board:** $12,582
Freshman Class: 47096 applied, 25048 accepted, 3257 enrolled
SAT CR/M: 500/540 **ACT:** 23 **COMPETITIVE**

California State Polytechnic University, Pomona, an occupationally oriented institution founded in 1938, is part of the state-supported university system. It offers undergraduate and graduate programs in agriculture, liberal arts and sciences, business, engineering, and technical and professional training. There are 8 undergraduate schools and 7 graduate schools. In addition to regional accreditation, Cal Poly Pomona has baccalaureate program accreditation with AACSB, ABET, ADA, ASLA, CSAB, and NAAB. The library contains 855,565 volumes, 1.4 million microform items, and 11,390 audio/video tapes/CDs/DVDs, and subscribes to 89,315 periodicals including electronic. Computerized library services include interlibrary loans, database searching, and Internet access. Special learning facilities include an art gallery, TV station, an interactive TV studio. The 1438-acre campus is in a suburban area 30 miles east of Los Angeles. Including any residence halls, there are 80 buildings.

Student Life: 99% of undergraduates are from California. Others are from 32 states, 44 foreign countries, and Canada. 90% are from public schools. 37% are Hispanic; 25% Asian American; 22% White. The average age of freshmen is 18; all undergraduates, 22. 8% do not continue beyond their first year; 51% remain to graduate.

Housing: 3500 students can be accommodated in college housing, which includes coed dorms and off-campus apartments. In addition, there are special-interest houses, Center for regenerative studies. On-campus housing is available on a first-come and first-served basis. 88% of students commute. All students may keep cars.

Activities: 2% of men belong to 6 local and 12 national fraternities; 1% of women belong to 4 local and 8 national sororities. There are 288 groups on campus, including art, band, cheerleading, choir, chorale, chorus, computers, drama, ethnic, film, gay, honors, international, jazz band, literary magazine, musical theater, newspaper, opera, orchestra, pep band, photography, political, professional, religious, social, social service, and student government. Popular campus events include Rose Float, Broncofest and Founders Day.

Sports: There are 6 intercollegiate sports for men and 6 for women. Facilities include a 5000-seat stadium, tennis and racquetball courts, basketball and volleyball courts, soccer, baseball, and softball fields, a track, swimming pool, gymnastics and weight rooms, a horse arena, and dance studios.

Disabled Students: 96% of the campus is accessible. Facilities include wheelchair ramps, elevators, special parking, specially equipped restrooms, special class scheduling, lowered drinking fountains, lowered telephones, and specialized tram, van and shuttle transportation.

Services: Counseling and information services are available, as is tutoring in most subjects. There is a reader service for the blind, and remedial math and writing.

Campus Safety and Security: Measures include 24-hour foot and vehicle patrol, emergency notification system, self-defense education, and security escort services. There are shuttle buses, emergency telephones, lighted pathways/sidewalks, vehicle assists, and crime prevention programs.

Programs of Study: Cal Poly Pomona confers B.A., B.S., BArch. and B.F.A. degrees. Master's and doctoral degrees are also awarded. Bachelor's degrees are awarded in AGRICULTURE (agricultural business management, agriculture, animal science, and plant science), BIOLOGICAL SCIENCE (biology/biological science and biotechnology), BUSINESS (apparel and accessories marketing, business administration and management, hotel/motel and restaurant management, human resources, and international business management), COMMUNICATIONS AND THE ARTS (art, communications, dramatic arts, English, graphic design, music, and Spanish), COMPUTER AND PHYSICAL SCIENCE (chemistry, computer science, geology, information sciences and systems, mathematics, and physics), ENGINEERING AND ENVIRONMENTAL DESIGN (architecture, chemical engineering, civil engineering, computer technology, construction technology, electrical/electronics engineering, engineering, engineering technology, industrial engineering, landscape architecture/design, manufacturing engineering, materials engineering, mechanical engineering, and urban planning technology), SOCIAL SCIENCE (anthropology, economics, food science, gender studies, geography, history, liberal arts/general studies, philosophy, physical fitness/movement, political science/government, psychology, sociology, and urban studies). Engineering, architecture and business are the strongest academically. Mechanical engineering, hospitality management and accounting (BUS) have the largest enrollment.

Required: All students must complete general education requirements, including courses in written and oral communications, critical thinking, math, humanities, natural sciences, and social sciences, and must pass a graduation writing test. A total of 180 (B.A.) to 246 (B.S.) quarter units with a minimum GPA of 2.0 is required to graduate.

Special: Cross-registration is possible with any California State University school. Internships and co-op programs are available in agriculture, business, environmental design, engineering, science, political science, behavioral science, and phys ed. An international study program in 17 countries, work-study programs, B.A.-B.S. degrees, a liberal studies degree, credit for military experience, an external degree program, and credit/no credit options are offered. Nondegree study is possible. There are 30 national honor societies and a freshman honors program.

Faculty/Classroom: 60% of faculty are male; 40% are female. No introductory courses are taught by graduate students. The average class size in an introductory lecture is 37; in a laboratory is 22; and in a regular course is 37.

Admissions: 53% of the 2013-2014 applicants were accepted. The SAT scores for the 2013-2014 freshman class were: Critical Reading--44% below 500, 40% between 500 and 599, 15% between 600 and 699, and 2% between 700 and 800; Math--30% below 500, 37% between 500 and 599, 27% between 600 and 699, and 6% between 700 and 800. The ACT scores were 28% below 21, 28% between 21 and 23, 24% between 24 and 26, 10% between 27 and 28, and 9% above 28.

Requirements: The SAT or ACT is recommended. In addition, applicants must be graduates of an accredited secondary school or have a GED equivalent. Secondary school courses must include 4 years of high school English, 3 each of math and electives, 2 of foreign language, and 1 each of science, history, and art. A GPA of 2.0 is required. AP and CLEP credits are accepted.

Procedure: Freshmen are admitted fall. Entrance exams should be taken during the fall of the senior year. There is a rolling admissions plan. Applications should be filed by November 1 for fall entry; June 1 for winter entry; August 1 for spring entry; and February 1 for summer entry, along with a $55 fee. Notification is sent on a rolling basis. Applications are accepted online.

Transfer: 2141 transfer students enrolled in 2012-2013. Applicants must have completed 56 semester or 90 quarter units including college preparatory subjects. A 2.0 GPA (2.4 for nonresidents) is required. 50 of 180 credits required for the bachelor's degree must be completed at Cal Poly Pomona.

Visiting: There are regularly scheduled orientations for prospective students, consisting of tours of the campus led by current undergraduate students and a 90-minute walking tour. There are guides for informal visits, visitors may sit in on classes, and stay overnight. To schedule a visit, contact the Admissions and Outreach at (909) 869-3529.

Financial Aid: In 2013-2014, 66% of all full-time freshmen and 64% of continuing full-time students received some form of financial aid. 48% of all full-time freshmen and 55% of continuing full-time students received need-based aid. The average freshman award was $10,998. Need-based scholarships or need-based grants averaged $9,650; need-based self-help aid (loans and jobs) averaged $3,432; non-need-based athletic scholarships averaged $1,639; and other non-need-based awards and non-need-based scholarships averaged $2,125. Average annual earnings from campus work are $2000. The average financial indebtedness of the 2013 graduate was $19,175. The FAFSA is required. The deadline for filing freshman financial aid applications for fall entry is March 2.

International Students: There are 802 international students enrolled. They must take the TOEFL with a minimum score of 525 on the paper-based TOEFL (PBT) or 70 on the Internet-based version (iBT). They must also take the SAT or ACT.

Computers: All students may access the system 24 hours per day. There are no time limits and no fees.

Graduates: From July 1, 2012 to June 30, 2013, 4203 bachelor's degrees were awarded. The most popular majors were hotel and restaurant management (7%), civil engineering (6%), and management and human resources (6%). 230 companies recruited on campus in 2012-2013. In an average class, 11% graduate in 4 years or less, 35% graduate in 5 years or less, and 53% graduate in 6 years or less.

Admissions Contact: Deborah L. Brandon, Executive Director, Admissions & Records. E-Mail: *dlbrandon@csupomona.edu* Web: *www.csupomona.edu*

CALIFORNIA STATE UNIVERSITY SYSTEM

The California State University System, established in 1961, is a public system in California. It is governed by a board of trustees, whose chief administrator is the chancellor. The primary goal of the system is teaching. The main priorities are to emphasize quality in instruction; to provide an environment in which scholarship, research, creative, artistic, and professional activity are valued and supported; and to stress the importance of the liberal arts and sciences. The total student enrollment is usually about 377,000 with about 22,000 faculty members. Altogether there are 965 baccalaureate, 600 master's, and 10 doctoral programs offered in the California State University System. Profiles of the 4-year campuses are included in this section.

CALIFORNIA STATE UNIVERSITY, BAKERSFIELD C-4

Bakersfield, CA 93311-1099 **(661) 664-2160; (661) 664-3389**

Full-time: 1500 men, 2750 women
Part-time: 410 men, 710 women
Graduate: 585 men, 1310 women
Year: trimesters, summer session
Application Deadline: open
Freshman Class: n/av
SAT or ACT: required
Faculty: n/av; IIA, +$
Ph.D.s: n/av
Student/Faculty: n/av
Tuition: $7182 ($11,500)
Room & Board: $7620

LESS COMPETITIVE

California State University/Bakersfield, founded in 1965, is part of the California State University System. It offers graduate and undergraduate programs in liberal arts and sciences, business, public administration, education, health fields, preengineering, and preprofessional training. Figures given in the above capsule and in this profile are approximate. There are 3 undergraduate schools and 10 graduate schools. In addition to regional accreditation, Cal State Bakersfield has baccalaureate program accreditation with AACSB, NCATE, and NLN. The library contains 339,900 volumes, 603,300 microform items, and 5,180 audio/video tapes/CDs/DVDs, and subscribes to 2,700 periodicals including electronic. Computerized library services include interlibrary loans and database searching. Special learning facilities include a learning resource center, art gallery, natural history museum, geological data sample repository, archeological information center, an instructional television network, applied research center, and animal care and treatment facility. The 375-acre campus is in a small town in southwest Bakersfield. Including any residence halls, there are 30 buildings. The figures in the above capsule and in this profile are approximate.

Student Life: 98% of undergraduates are from California. Others are from 25 states, 50 foreign countries, and Canada. 98% are from public schools. 51% are white; 25% Hispanic. The average age of freshmen is 19; all undergraduates, 25. 15% do not continue beyond their first year.

Housing: 330 students can be accommodated in college housing, which includes single-sex and coed dorms. On-campus housing is guaranteed for all 4 years. 98% of students commute. Alcohol is not permitted. All students may keep cars.

Activities: 2% of men belong to 3 national fraternities; 2% of women belong to 4 national sororities. There are 74 groups on campus, including art, band, cheerleading, chess, choir, chorale, computers, dance, drama, ethnic, film, gay, honors, international, jazz band, literary magazine, musical theater, newspaper, opera, orchestra, pep band, photography, political, professional, radio and TV, religious, social, social service, student government, and symphony. Popular campus events include Cinco de Mayo, Open Campus, and Jazz Festival.

Sports: There are 7 intercollegiate sports for men and 6 for women, and 12 intramural sports for men and 12 for women. Facilities include a 4000-seat gym, a wrestling sport center, an aquatic center, tennis and racquetball courts, and softball and soccer fields.

Disabled Students: Facilities include wheelchair ramps, elevators, special parking, specially equipped restrooms, special class scheduling, lowered drinking fountains, and lowered telephones.

Services: Counseling and information services are available, as is tutoring in most subjects, as well as in study skills There is a reader service for the blind, and remedial math, reading, and writing.

Campus Safety and Security: Measures include 24-hour foot and vehicle patrol, self-defense education, and security escort services. There are emergency telephones and lighted pathways/sidewalks.

Programs of Study: Cal State Bakersfield confers B.A. and B.S. degrees. Master's degrees are also awarded. Bachelor's degrees are awarded in BIOLOGICAL SCIENCE (biology/biological science), BUSINESS (business administration and management), COMMUNICATIONS AND THE ARTS (art, communications, dramatic arts, English, music, and Spanish), COMPUTER AND PHYSICAL SCIENCE (chemistry, computer science, geology, mathematics, and physics), ENGINEERING AND ENVIRONMENTAL DESIGN (land use management and reclamation), HEALTH PROFESSIONS (clinical science and nursing), SOCIAL SCIENCE (anthropology, child psychology/development, criminal justice, economics, history, liberal arts/general studies, philosophy, political science/government, psychology, public administration, religion, and sociology). Business, education, and public administration are the strongest academically. Business has the largest enrollment.

Required: All students must complete 72 quarter units of general education requirements in basic skills, Western civilization, non-Western culture, philosophy, fine arts, literature, technology, and physical, social, and life sciences. They must also take a comprehensive writing examination or complete an upper-division writing course with a grade of C or better, demonstrate understanding of American history and government institutions, and complete a senior seminar. A total of 186 quarter units with a minimum GPA of 2.0 is required in order to graduate.

Special: Cal State Bakersfield offers co-op programs in education and business administration, cross-registration through the National Student Exchange Program, study abroad at 36 universities in 16 countries, a 3-2 engineering degree with California Polytechnic State University/San Luis Obispo, and student-designed majors. Credit for life experience, pass/fail options, and nondegree study are available. Students may also earn credits as interns and participate in work-study programs on and off campus. There are a freshman honors program.

Faculty/Classroom: 62% of faculty are male, 38% are female. All teach and do research. No introductory courses are taught by graduate students. The average class size in an introductory lecture is 40; in a laboratory is 24; and in a regular course is 30.

Requirements: The SAT or ACT is required, if the GPA is below 3.0. (3.6 for nonresidents). Admission is based on an eligibility index that weights the GPA and standardized test scores. Applicants must be graduates of an accredited secondary school or GED equivalent, and have a total of 15 academic units, including 4 years of English, 3 of math, 2 of foreign language, 1 each of lab science, U.S. history/government, and visual and performing arts, and 3 of electives. A GPA of 2.0 is required. AP and CLEP credits are accepted.

Procedure: Freshmen are admitted fall, winter, and spring. Entrance exams should be taken by December of the senior year. There are early decision, early admissions, deferred admissions, and rolling admissions plans. Application deadlines are open. Application fee is $55.

Transfer: A 2.0 GPA (2.4 for nonresidents) is required in a minimum of 56 semester or 84 quarter units earned, including English and math. 45 of 186 credits required for the bachelor's degree must be completed at Cal State Bakersfield.

Visiting: There are regularly scheduled orientations for prospective students, consisting of a day-long orientation that includes meetings with faculty advisers and school deans. There are guides for informal visits and visitors may sit in on classes. To schedule a visit, contact the Office of Outreach Services.

Financial Aid: Cal State Bakersfield is a member of CSS. The FAFSA is required. Check with the school for current application deadlines.

International Students: The school actively recruits these students. They must take the TOEFL. The SAT or ACT is required if the GPA is below 3.0.

Computers: All students may access the system. There are no time limits and no fees.

Admissions Contact: Dr. Homer Montalvo, Dean of Admissions. E-Mail: *hmontalvo@csubak.edu* Web: *www.csub.edu*

CALIFORNIA STATE UNIVERSITY, CHICO B-2

Chico, CA 95929 **(530) 898-4428**
(800) 542-4426; (530) 898-6456

Full-time: 6806 men, 7403 women
Part-time: 543 men, 540 women
Graduate: 336 men, 728 women
Year: semesters, summer session
Application Deadline: November 30
Faculty: 496; IIA, av$
Ph.D.s: 84%
Student/Faculty: 24 to 1
Tuition: $8472 ($19,632)
Room & Board: $10,480
Freshman Class: 19217 applied, 12905 accepted, 2340 enrolled
SAT CR/M: 501/512 **ACT:** 21 **COMPETITIVE**

California State University, Chico, founded in 1887, is a public institution offering undergraduate programs in behavioral and social sciences, business, communication and education, engineering, computer science and technology, humanities and fine arts, natural sciences, agriculture, and nursing. The university offers Web-based classes. There are 7 undergraduate schools and one graduate school. In addition to regional accreditation, Chico State has baccalaureate program accreditation with AACSB, ABET, ACCE, ACEJMC, ADA, CSAB, CSWE, NASAD, NASM, and NRPA. The library contains 924,410 volumes, 1.2 million microform items, and 25,744 audio/video tapes/CDs/DVDs, and subscribes to 515 periodicals including electronic. Computerized library services include interlibrary loans, database searching, and Internet access. Special learning facilities include an art gallery, planetarium, radio station, an instructional media center, a university farm, a biological field station, an anthropology museum, a media preparation lab, a computer graphics lab, a recording arts studio, a writing center, and distributed learning technologies, anthropology museum, science museum. The 130-acre campus is in a small town 90 miles north of Sacramento, and 174 miles northeast of San Francisco. Including any residence halls, there are 77 buildings.

Student Life: 97% of undergraduates are from California. Others are from 36 states, 47 foreign countries, and Canada. 91% are from public schools. 52% are White; 22% Hispanic. The average age of freshmen is 18; all undergraduates, 24. 15% do not continue beyond their first year; 85% remain to graduate.

Housing: 2000 students can be accommodated in college housing, which includes coed dorms, on-campus apartments, and off-campus apartments.

In addition, there are honors houses, language houses, special-interest houses, fraternity houses, sorority houses, and thematic housing for minorities in engineering and science, math, and business. Theme floors include community service, recreational sports, leadership, adventure outings, and sustainability. On-campus housing is available on a first-come and first-served basis. 99% of students commute. Alcohol is not permitted. All students may keep cars.

Activities: 1% of men belong to 3 local and 11 national fraternities; 1% of women belong to 1 local and 11 national sororities. There are 186 groups on campus, including art, band, cheerleading, choir, chorale, chorus, computers, dance, debate, drama, environmental, ethnic, film, forensics, gay, honors, international, jazz band, literary magazine, musical theater, newspaper, opera, orchestra, pep band, political, professional, radio and TV, religious, social, social service, student government, symphony, and yearbook. Popular campus events include International Festival, Greek Week Community Challenge, and Up 'Til Dawn St. Jude Hospital Fund-raiser.

Sports: There are 6 intercollegiate sports for men and 7 for women, and 8 intramural sports for men and 8 for women. Facilities include 2 gyms, athletic training rooms, a dance studio, swimming and diving pools, a par course, putting greens and sand trap, handball/racquetball courts, baseball/softball fields, an all-weather track, a soccer stadium, a 7500-seat football stadium, and a residence hall sports center. A recreation center includes a climbing wall, a pool, fitness and weight rooms, a concert/events facility, and a computer lab.

Disabled Students: 95% of the campus is accessible. Facilities include wheelchair ramps, elevators, special parking, specially equipped restrooms, special class scheduling, lowered drinking fountains, lowered telephones, special housing.

Services: Counseling and information services are available, as is tutoring in most subjects, accounting, anthropology, Arabic, business administration, biology, chemistry, economics, finance, French, German, history, Italian, Japanese, math, management information systems, music, philosophy, physics, political science, psychology There is a reader service for the blind, and remedial math and writing. A student learning center offers a tutorial program, study skills development, learning assistance workshops, and writing resources.

Campus Safety and Security: Measures include 24-hour foot and vehicle patrol, emergency notification system, self-defense education, and security escort services. There are shuttle buses, emergency telephones, lighted pathways/sidewalks, controlled access to dorms/residences, a freshman safe start program, a victim awareness program, and crime prevention workshops.

Programs of Study: Chico State confers B.A., B.S., and B.F.A. degrees. Master's degrees are also awarded. Bachelor's degrees are awarded in AGRICULTURE (agricultural business management, agriculture, animal science, and horticulture), BIOLOGICAL SCIENCE (biochemistry, biology/biological science, botany, ecology, and microbiology), BUSINESS (accounting, business administration and management, finance, international economics, management information systems, small business management, and supply chain management), COMMUNICATIONS AND THE ARTS (art history, art, communication design , communication, communications, communication rhetoric/communication, communication science, English, English literature, fine arts, German, graphic design, journalism, linguistics, media arts, music, music industry, musical theater, public relations, Spanish, and theatre arts), COMPUTER AND PHYSICAL SCIENCE (applied mathematics, atmospheric sciences and meteorology, chemistry, computer science, geology, geoscience, mathematics, physical sciences, physics, and statistics), EDUCATION (agricultural education, art education, education, English education, health education, and mathematics education), ENGINEERING AND ENVIRONMENTAL DESIGN (civil engineering, computer engineering, computer graphics, construction management, electrical/electronics engineering, environmental science, interior design, mechanical engineering, and Mechatronics Engineering), HEALTH PROFESSIONS (environmental health science, health care administration, health science, and nursing), SOCIAL SCIENCE (anthropology, applied psychology, asian studies, child psychology/development, communication sciences & disorders, community services, criminal justice, dietetics, economics, French studies, geography, gerontology, history, humanities, international relations, Latin American studies, legal studies, liberal arts/general studies, philosophy, political science/government, public administration, public affairs, religious studies, social science, social work, sociology, and women & gender studies). Business administration, nursing, and psychology are the strongest academically, and have the largest enrollments.

Required: Graduation requirements include: complete a total of 120 to 132 units; 40 units of upper division coursework; a minimum of 12 units must be in their major;30 units in residence at California State University, Chico; 48 units of prescribed General Education (9 units as a resident at Chico State); minimum of two courses with focus on cultural diversity; demonstrate competent understanding of the Constitution of the United States, U.S. History, mathematics and writing; complete an approved major; and have a G.P.A of 2.0 or better. General education coursework includes: oral communications, writing, critical thinking, mathematics, two laboratory sciences (one physical science and one in the life sciences), US History, US Governmental Institutions, four writing intensive courses, and a GE Capstone course. In addition, each student must complete a Pathway, which consists of 18 units of lower division and 9 units of upper division coursework.

Special: The university offers co-op programs and cross-registration as part of the National Student Exchange. In addition, internships, distance learning, teacher certification, study abroad in 32 countries, work-study, student-designed majors, independent study, credit for experience, nondegree study, and pass/fail options are available. Chico State has a nationally recognized sustainability program and an established Institute for Sustainable Development. There are 15 national honor societies, including Phi Beta Kappa, a freshman honors program, and 40 departmental honors programs.

Faculty/Classroom: 52% of faculty are male; 48% are female. 97% teach undergraduates, and 21% do research. No introductory courses are taught by graduate students. The average class size in an introductory lecture is 25; in a laboratory is 21; and in a regular course is 22.

Admissions: 67% of the 2013-2014 applicants were accepted. The SAT scores for the 2013-2014 freshman class were: Critical Reading--39% below 500, 42% between 500 and 599, 10% between 600 and 699, and 1% between 700 and 800; Math--33% below 500, 45% between 500 and 599, 14% between 600 and 699, and 1% between 700 and 800.

Requirements: The SAT or ACT is required. An index combining GPA and SAT and ACT scores is used to determine eligibility for admission. Applicants must be graduates of a secondary school or have a GED and have completed 4 years of English, 3 years of math, 2 years of lab sciences (1 physical and 1 life), 2 years of the same foreign language, 2 years of social science, 1 year of a visual or performing art course, and 1 year of electives. A GPA of 2.0 is required. AP and CLEP credits are accepted.

Procedure: Freshmen are admitted fall and spring. Entrance exams should be taken in fall of the senior year. There are deferred admissions and rolling admissions plans. Early decision applications should be filed by October 30; regular applications, by November 30 for fall entry, along with a $55 fee. Notifications are sent March 1. Applications are accepted online.

Transfer: 1601 transfer students enrolled in 2012-2013. Transfer students who are California residents must have a minimum 2.0 GPA, and nonresidents need 2.4. Students must have made up any missing college preparatory subjects and provide a statement of good standing and transcripts from prior institutions. 30 of 124 credits required for the bachelor's degree must be completed at Chico State.

Visiting: There are regularly scheduled orientations for prospective students, consisting of a 1-hour tour given at 11:30 a.m. Monday through Saturday. There are guides for informal visits and visitors may sit in on classes. To schedule a visit, contact the Office of Admissions.

Financial Aid: In 2013-2014, 41% of all full-time freshmen and 44% of continuing full-time students received some form of financial aid. 25% of all full-time freshmen and 32% of continuing full-time students received need-based aid. The average freshman award was $10,851. Need-based scholarships or need-based grants averaged $7,387; need-based self-help aid (loans and jobs) averaged $4,581; non-need-based athletic scholarships averaged $2,710; and other non-need-based awards and non-need-based scholarships averaged $5,711. The FAFSA, and scholarship application form is required. The priority date for freshman financial aid applications for fall entry is March 2. The deadline for filing freshman financial aid applications for fall entry is on a rolling basis.

International Students: There are 515 international students enrolled. The school actively recruits these students. They must take the TOEFL with a minimum score of 500 on the paper-based TOEFL (PBT) or 61 on the Internet-based version (iBT), the IELTS. They must also take the SAT or ACT.

Computers: All students may access the system. There are no time limits and no fees.

Graduates: From July 1, 2012 to June 30, 2013, 3495 bachelor's degrees were awarded. The most popular majors were business administration (17%), health professions (9%), and social sciences (9%). 480 companies recruited on campus in 2012-2013. In an average class, 21% graduate in 4 years or less, 48% graduate in 5 years or less, and 56% graduate in 6 years or less.

Admissions Contact: Allan Bee, Director of Admissions. E-Mail: *info@csuchico.edu* Web: *www.csuchico.edu*

CALIFORNIA STATE UNIVERSITY, DOMINGUEZ HILLS C-5

Carson, CA 90747 (310) 243-3645

Full-time: 3179 men, 5386 women
Part-time: 1300 men, 2558 women
Graduate: 571 men, 1676 women
Year: semesters, summer session
Application Deadline: November 30
Freshman Class: 9719 applied, 7766 accepted, 1556 enrolled
SAT or ACT: required
Faculty: 182; IIA, av$
Ph.D.s: 71%
Student/Faculty: 47 to 1
Tuition: $6100 ($17,260)
Room & Board: $10,956

LESS COMPETITIVE

California State University, Dominguez Hills, founded in 1960 as part of the state-supported university system, offers graduate and undergraduate programs in liberal arts and sciences, business, fine arts, health sciences, and technology to a primarily commuter student body. There are 6 undergraduate schools and 6 graduate schools. In addition to regional accreditation, CSU Dominguez Hills has baccalaureate program accreditation with AACSB, ABET, CAHEA, CSWE, NASAD, NASM, NCATE, and NLN. The library contains 451,000 volumes, 741,446 microform items, and 4,295 audio/video tapes/CDs/DVDs, and subscribes to 666 periodicals including electronic. Computerized library services include interlibrary loans, database searching, and Internet access. Special learning facilities include an art gallery, radio station, and TV station. The 350-acre campus is in a suburban area 13 miles south of Los Angeles. Including any residence halls, there are 84 buildings.

Student Life: 99% of undergraduates are from California. Others are from 17 states, 93 foreign countries, and Canada. 96% are from public schools. 53% are Hispanic; 17% African American. The average age of freshmen is 18; all undergraduates, 25. 21% do not continue beyond their first year; 79% remain to graduate.

Housing: 655 students can be accommodated in college housing, which includes single-sex and coed on-campus apartments. On-campus housing is available on a first-come and first-served basis. 95% of students commute. All students may keep cars.

Activities: 1% of men belong to 6 national fraternities; 1% of women belong to 7 national sororities. There are 80 groups on campus, including art, band, cheerleading, choir, chorale, computers, dance, drama, drill team, ethnic, forensics, gay, honors, international, jazz band, literary magazine, musical theater, newspaper, political, professional, radio and TV, religious, social, social service, and student government. Popular campus events include Welcome Week, Toro Days and Unityfest.

Sports: There are 4 intercollegiate sports for men and 7 for women, and 12 intramural sports for men and 11 for women. Facilities include an 8,000-seat Toro Stadium with a soccer field, 400-meter track, 4,200-seat Torodome with 4 basketball and 4 volleyball courts, baseball, softball, and activity fields, a 6-lane pool, and a fitness center.

Disabled Students: All of the campus is accessible. Facilities include wheelchair ramps, elevators, special parking, specially equipped restrooms, lowered drinking fountains, lowered telephones, and special housing.

Services: Counseling and information services are available, as is tutoring in most subjects. There is a reader service for the blind, and remedial math, reading, and writing.

Campus Safety and Security: Measures include 24-hour foot and vehicle patrol and security escort services. There are emergency telephones and lighted pathways/sidewalks.

Programs of Study: CSU Dominguez Hills confers B.A., and B.S. degrees. Master's degrees are also awarded. Bachelor's degrees are awarded in BIOLOGICAL SCIENCE (biochemistry and biology/biological science), BUSINESS (business administration and management, labor studies, total quality management (TQM), tourism, and trade and industrial supervision and management), COMMUNICATIONS AND THE ARTS (art, communications, dramatic arts, English, music, and Spanish), COMPUTER AND PHYSICAL SCIENCE (chemistry, computer science, digital arts/technology, geology, mathematics, and physics), EDUCATION (physical education), ENGINEERING AND ENVIRONMENTAL DESIGN (computer technology), HEALTH PROFESSIONS (clinical science, health science, nursing, and occupational therapy), SOCIAL SCIENCE (African studies, anthropology, behavioral science, child psychology/development, criminal justice, geography, history, human services, interdisciplinary studies, liberal arts/general studies, Mexican-American/Chicano studies, peace studies, philosophy, political science/government, psychology, public administration, and sociology). Nursing is the strongest academically. Business ddministration, psychology, and criminal justice administration have the largest enrollments.

Required: To graduate, students must complete 120 to 132 semester units, including 54 to 60 units in general education, 40 units in upper-division courses, and specific courses or proficiency tests in U.S. history and politics, math, and writing. A minimum GPA of 2.0 must be maintained.

Special: Cross-registration is offered with 7 other California State University schools. Study abroad in 24 countries, on-campus work-study, internships, B.A.-B.S. degrees, dual and student-designed majors, credit for life experience, and pass/fail options are available. A B.A. in interdisciplinary studies, in which an accelerated degree is possible, and in liberal studies is offered. Many majors have evening programs. There are 5 national honor societies, a freshman honors program, and 34 departmental honors programs.

Faculty/Classroom: 47% of faculty are male; 53% are female. 88% teach undergraduates. No introductory courses are taught by graduate students. The average class size in an introductory lecture is 45; in a laboratory is 22; and in a regular course is 37.

Admissions: 80% of the 2013-2014 applicants were accepted.

Requirements: The SAT or ACT is required. Applicants must meet the CSU Eligibility Index, except those with a GPA of at least 3.0 (3.6 for nonresidents). Students must be high school graduates with a GPA of at least 2.0 and 15 academic units, including 4 in English, 3 in math, 2 in foreign language, 2 in social science, 2 in lab science, and 1 each in visual and performing arts and electives. The GED is accepted. A GPA of 2.0 is required. AP and CLEP credits are accepted.

Procedure: Freshmen are admitted fall, spring, and summer. Entrance exams should be taken prior to submitting an application. There are early admissions and rolling admissions plans. Applications should be filed by November 30 for fall entry; August 31 for spring entry; and February 28 for summer entry. The fall 2013 application fee was $55. Notification is sent on a rolling basis. Applications are accepted online.

Transfer: 2701 transfer students enrolled in 2012-2013. Applicants should have a college GPA of at least 2.0 (2.4 for nonresidents) and submit SAT or ACT scores if transferring fewer than 60 semester or 90 quarter units. 30 of 120 credits required for the bachelor's degree must be completed at CSU Dominguez Hills.

Visiting: There are regularly scheduled orientations for prospective students. There are guides for informal visits and visitors may sit in on classes. To schedule a visit, contact the Outreach Office at (310) 516-3696.

Financial Aid: In 2013-2014, 88% of all full-time freshmen and 74% of continuing full-time students received some form of financial aid. 75% of all full-time freshmen and 63% of continuing full-time students received need-based aid. The average freshman award was $5,698. Need-based scholarships or need-based grants averaged $5,216; need-based self-help aid (loans and jobs) averaged $1,769; and non-need-based athletic scholarships averaged $3,070. The average financial indebtedness of the 2013 graduate was $10,662. The FAFSA is required. The deadline for filing freshman financial aid applications for fall entry is March 2.

International Students: There are 211 international students enrolled. The school actively recruits these students. They must take the TOEFL with a minimum score of 550 on the paper-based TOEFL (PBT) or 80 on the Internet-based version (iBT). They must also take the SAT or ACT.

Computers: All students may access the system. There are no time limits and no fees.

Graduates: From July 1, 2012 to June 30, 2013, 2481 bachelor's degrees were awarded. The most popular majors were business administration (19%), psychology (10%), and nursing (9%). 210 companies recruited on campus in 2012-2013. In an average class, 5% graduate in 4 years or less, 20% graduate in 5 years or less, and 30% graduate in 6 years or less.

Admissions Contact: Admissions and Records E-Mail: *info@csudh.edu* Web: *www.csudh.edu*

CALIFORNIA STATE UNIVERSITY, EAST BAY B-3

Hayward, CA 94542 (510) 885-2310

Full-time: 3985 men, 6313 women
Part-time: 617 men, 938 women
Graduate: 738 men, 1260 women
Year: quarters, summer session
Application Deadline:
Freshman Class: n/av
SAT or ACT: recommended
Faculty: n/av; IIA, +$
Ph.D.s: n/av
Student/Faculty: n/av
Tuition: $6549 ($15,477)
Room & Board: $10,000

COMPETITIVE

California State University, Hayward, founded in 1957, is part of the California State University system. The institution offers degree programs in the arts, sciences, business and economics, and education to a primarily commuter student body. There are 4 undergraduate schools and 4 graduate schools. In addition to regional accreditation, Cal. State East Bay has baccalaureate program accreditation with AACSB, NASAD, NASM, NCATE, and NLN. The 2 libraries contain 912,912 volumes, 873,177 microform items, and 29,768 audio/video tapes/CDs/DVDs, and subscribe to 2,000 periodicals including electronic. Computerized library services include interlibrary loans, database searching, Internet access, and Wi-Fi capability. Special learning facilities include an art gallery, natural history museum, radio station, TV station, marine biology lab, and geology summer field camp. The 342-acre campus is in a small town 20 miles southeast of San Francisco in the Hayward Hills. Including any residence halls, there are 19 buildings.

Student Life: 92% of undergraduates are from California. Others are from 31 states, 63 foreign countries, and Canada. 85% are from public schools. 23% are Asian American; 23% Hispanic; 21% White; 11% African American. The average age of all undergraduates is 25. 25% do not continue beyond their first year; 50% remain to graduate.

Housing: 1300 students can be accommodated in college housing, which includes coed on-campus apartments. In addition, there are special-interest houses. On-campus housing is available on a first-come and first-served basis. 90% of students commute. All students may keep cars.

Activities: 1% of men belong to 4 national fraternities; 1% of women belong to 3 national sororities. There are 90 groups on campus, including art, cheerleading, choir, chorale, chorus, computers, dance, drama, environmental, ethnic, film, gay, honors, international, jazz band, literary magazine, musical theater, newspaper, opera, orchestra, pep band, photography, political, professional, radio and TV, religious, social, social service, student government, and symphony. Popular campus events include Science Fair, Leadership Conferences and Al Fresco.

Sports: There are 5 intercollegiate sports for men and 8 for women. Facilities include a tennis and racquetball courts, 2 swimming pools, a track, a soccer field, a martial arts facility, a dance studio, baseball and softball diamonds, a 9000-seat stadium, a 500-seat gym, and a 500-seat theater.

Disabled Students: 95% of the campus is accessible. Facilities include wheelchair ramps, elevators, special parking, specially equipped restrooms, special class scheduling, lowered drinking fountains, lowered telephones, special housing. The Disabled Student Services Center provides scribe, interpretive, and translation services.

Services: Counseling and information services are available, as is tutoring in most subjects. There is a reader service for the blind, and remedial math, reading, and writing.

Campus Safety and Security: Measures include 24-hour foot and vehicle patrol, self-defense education, and security escort services. There are shuttle buses, emergency telephones, and lighted pathways/sidewalks.

Programs of Study: Cal. State East Bay confers B.A., and B.S. degrees. Master's and doctoral degrees are also awarded. Bachelor's degrees are awarded in AGRICULTURE (environmental studies), BIOLOGICAL SCIENCE (biology/biological science), BUSINESS (accounting, business administration and management, and recreation and leisure services), COMMUNICATIONS AND THE ARTS (advertising, art, communications, dramatic arts, English, music, Spanish, and speech/debate/rhetoric), COMPUTER AND PHYSICAL SCIENCE (chemistry, computer science, geology, mathematics, physical sciences, physics, and statistics), ENGINEERING AND ENVIRONMENTAL DESIGN (engineering, environmental science, and industrial engineering), HEALTH PROFESSIONS (health science, nursing, and speech pathology/audiology), SOCIAL SCIENCE (anthropology, criminal justice, economics, ethnic studies, geography, history, human development, international studies, Latin American studies, liberal arts/general studies, philosophy, physical fitness/movement, political science/government, psychology, and sociology).

Required: In order to graduate, students must fulfill the university writing skills requirement, have a 2.0 minimum GPA, and complete 186 quarter units.

Special: Cal. State East Bay offers cross-registration with local community colleges, other CSU campuses, and the University of California, Berkeley. Internships, study abroad in 20 countries, work-study programs, and student-designed majors are also available. The PACE program provides degree opportunities in liberal studies, hospitality and leisure services, and in human development to working adults. There are 1 national honor societies, a freshman honors program, and 1 departmental honors programs.

Faculty/Classroom: 45% of faculty are male; 55% are female. No introductory courses are taught by graduate students.

Requirements: The SAT or ACT is recommended. All students must meet the eligibility index, a combination of the high school GPA and SAT or ACT scores. Applicants must be graduates of an accredited secondary school or have a GED certificate. Secondary school courses must include 4 years of English, 3 of math, 2 each of a language other than English, social science, and science with a lab, and 1 elective. A GPA of 2.0 is required. AP and CLEP credits are accepted.

Procedure: Freshmen are admitted to all sessions. Entrance exams should be taken prior to orientation. There is a rolling admissions plan. Check with the school for current application deadlines. The fall 2013 application fee was $55. Notification is sent on a rolling basis. Applications are accepted online.

Transfer: Applicants must have a minimum 2.0 GPA (2.45 for nonresidents), be in good standing at the last college attended, and either meet freshman admission requirements or have completed at least 56 transferable semester (84 quarter) units. 45 of 186 credits required for the bachelor's degree must be completed at Cal. State East Bay.

Visiting: There are regularly scheduled orientations for prospective students. There are guides for informal visits and visitors may sit in on classes. To schedule a visit, contact Welcome Center at admissions@csueastbay.edu.

Financial Aid: Cal. State East Bay is a member of CSS. The FAFSA is required. Check with the school for current application deadlines.

International Students: The school actively recruits these students. They must take the TOEFL. They must also take the SAT or ACT.

Computers: All students may access the system on a 24-hour basis from home and 16 hours per day on campus. There are no time limits and no fees.

Graduates: From July 1, 2012 to June 30, 2013, 2700 bachelor's degrees were awarded. The most popular majors were business administration (30%), health sciences (7%), and nursing (7%). In an average class, 25% graduate in 4 years or less, 35% graduate in 5 years or less, and 45% graduate in 6 years or less.

Admissions Contact: Director of Graduate Programs E-Mail: *annette.walker@csueastbay.edu* Web: *www.csueastbay.edu*

CALIFORNIA STATE UNIVERSITY, FRESNO C-3

Fresno, CA 93740 **(559) 278-6067; (559) 278-4812**

Full-time: 7314 men, 9836 women
Part-time: 1186 men, 1368 women
Graduate: 969 men, 1892 women
Year: semesters, summer session
Application Deadline: November 30
Freshman Class: 16242 applied, 9444 accepted, 3139 enrolled
SAT or ACT: required
Faculty: n/av; IIA, av$
Ph.D.s: n/av
Student/Faculty: n/av
Tuition: $6762 ($14,400)
Room & Board: $10,192

COMPETITIVE

California State University, Fresno, founded in 1911, is part of the state-supported university system. The school offers undergraduate and graduate programs in agriculture and technology, liberal arts and sciences, business administration, education, engineering, health fields, and preprofessional training. The figures given in the above capsule and in this profile are approximate. There are 8 undergraduate schools and 8 graduate schools. In addition to regional accreditation, Fresno State has baccalaureate program accreditation with AACSB, ABET, ACCE, ACEJMC, ADA, APTA, ASLA, CSWE, FIDER, NCATE, NLN, and NRPA. The library contains 1.2 million volumes, 1.6 million microform items, and 92,426 audio/video tapes/CDs/DVDs, and subscribes to 25,534 periodicals including electronic. Computerized library services include interlibrary loans, database searching, and Internet access. Special learning facilities include an art gallery, planetarium, radio station, various farm lab units. The 388-acre campus is in an urban area 200 miles southeast of San Francisco in the Central Valley of California.

Student Life: 97% of undergraduates are from California. Others are from 32 states, 53 foreign countries, and Canada. 98% are from public schools. 39% are Hispanic; 29% White; 15% Asian American. The average age of freshmen is 18; all undergraduates, 22. 17% do not continue beyond their first year; 83% remain to graduate.

Housing: 1100 students can be accommodated in college housing, which includes single-sex and coed dorms. In addition, there are special-interest houses. On-campus housing is available on a first-come and first-served basis. 95% of students commute. Alcohol is not permitted. All students may keep cars.

Activities: There are 413 groups on campus, including art, band, cheerleading, chess, choir, chorale, chorus, computers, dance, drama, drill team, ethnic, film, gay, honors, international, jazz band, marching band, musical theater, newspaper, opera, orchestra, pep band, photography, political, professional, radio and TV, religious, social, social service, student government, and symphony. Popular campus events include Vintage Days, International Week and Black History Month.

Sports: There are 7 intercollegiate sports for men and 11 for women. Facilities include Bulldog Stadium, home of the football and women's soccer teams, has a 41,031-seat capacity. Beiden Field, a 5,422-seat baseball stadium, is considered one of the finest collegiate complexes in the country and home to the 2008 NCAA National Champion baseball team. Bulldog Diamond, home of the 1998 NCAA champion Fresno State softball team, seats 3,288 and is the finest on-campus facility of its kind in the nation. Fresno State has track and field facilities, two gymnasiums, and putting greens and driving areas complete with sand traps for golf. The strength and conditioning center is one of the best weight rooms on the West Coast with 10,800 square feet, and the resplendent Spalding G. Wathen Tennis Center is home to the men's and women's tennis teams. In 2003, Fresno State opened the Save Mart Center, the largest on-campus arena on the West Coast with a capacity of 15,596. In 2005, the Ricchiuti Academic Center was constructed during the same time the Duncan Building was expanded to house the new football offices and locker room.

Disabled Students: All of the campus is accessible. Facilities include wheelchair ramps, elevators, special parking, specially equipped restrooms, special class scheduling, lowered drinking fountains, and lowered telephones.

Services: Counseling and information services are available, as is tutoring in most subjects. There is a reader service for the blind, and remedial math, reading, and writing.

Campus Safety and Security: Measures include 24-hour foot and

vehicle patrol, emergency notification system, self-defense education, and security escort services. There are emergency telephones, lighted pathways/sidewalks, closed circuit television cameras, and bicycle safety patrols.

Programs of Study: Fresno State confers B.A. and B.S. degrees. Master's and doctoral degrees are also awarded. Bachelor's degrees are awarded in AGRICULTURE (agricultural business management, agricultural communications, animal science, dairy science, and plant science), BIOLOGICAL SCIENCE (biology/biological science and biophysics), BUSINESS (accounting, business administration and management, business data processing, business law, and recreational facilities management), COMMUNICATIONS AND THE ARTS (art, communications, dramatic arts, English, French, German, graphic design, jazz, journalism, linguistics, media arts, music, music performance, public relations, Spanish, speech/debate/rhetoric, theatre arts, and theater design), COMPUTER AND PHYSICAL SCIENCE (chemistry, Computer Engineering Technology, computer science, geology, mathematics, natural sciences, and physics), EDUCATION (agricultural education and music education), ENGINEERING AND ENVIRONMENTAL DESIGN (civil engineering, civil engineering technology, computer engineering, construction management, electrical/electronics engineering, furniture design, industrial engineering, industrial engineering technology, interior design, mechanical engineering, and surveying engineering), HEALTH PROFESSIONS (health science, nursing, public health, speech pathology/audiology, and speech therapy), SOCIAL SCIENCE (African American studies, anthropology, child care/child and family studies, child psychology/development, counseling/psychology, criminology, economics, family/consumer studies, food science, forensic studies, French studies, geography, gerontology, history, home economics, humanities, Latin American studies, liberal arts/general studies, Mexican-American/Chicano studies, philosophy, philosophy and religion, physical fitness/movement, political science/government, psychology, public administration, social science, social work, sociology, urban studies, and women's studies). Business and liberal arts have the largest enrollments.

Required: All students must complete general education requirements. A minimum of 120 semester units, with a GPA of 2.0, is required to graduate. The number of required hours in the major varies.

Special: Study abroad in 17 countries, including England, New Zealand, China, and the South Pacific, co-op programs, internships, work-study programs, B.A.-B.S. degrees, dual majors, and student-designed majors are offered. A liberal studies major, credit for military experience, pass/fail options, and nondegree study are available. There are 10 national honor societies, including Phi Beta Kappa, a freshman honors program, and 4 departmental honors programs.

Faculty/Classroom: 53% of faculty are male; 47% are female. All teach undergraduates, all do research, and all teach and do research. No introductory courses are taught by graduate students.

Admissions: 58% of the 2013-2014 applicants were accepted. The SAT scores for the 2013-2014 freshman class were: Critical Reading--68% below 500, 24% between 500 and 599, 6% between 600 and 699, and 1% between 700 and 800; Math--61% below 500, 24% between 500 and 599, 6% between 600 and 699, and 1% between 700 and 800; Writing--69% below 500, 25% between 500 and 599, 5% between 600 and 699, and 1% between 700 and 800.

Requirements: The SAT or ACT is required. Only students with a GPA below 3.0 are required to submit the SAT or ACT scores. Applicants must be graduates of an accredited secondary school or have a GED. Secondary school courses must include 15 academic credits: 4 years of high school English, 3 each of math and electives, 2 of a foreign language, and 1 each of science, history/government, and visual/performing arts. A GPA of 2.0 is required. AP and CLEP credits are accepted.

Procedure: Freshmen are admitted fall and spring. Entrance exams should be taken as early as possible, by the first semester of the senior year. There is a rolling admissions plan. Applications should be filed by November 30 for fall entry, along with a $55 fee. Applications are accepted online.

Transfer: 2574 transfer students enrolled in 2012-2013. Transfer applicants must have a minimum GPA of 2.0 and 56 transferable semester units earned, including English and math. 30 of 124 credits required for the bachelor's degree must be completed at Fresno State.

Visiting: There are regularly scheduled orientations for prospective students, including 1- and 2-day overnight programs for entering students. There are guides for informal visits and visitors may stay overnight. To schedule a visit, contact the University Outreach Services at (559) 278-7533.

Financial Aid: In 2013-2014, 69% of all full-time freshmen received some form of financial aid. 76% of all full-time freshmen received need-based aid. The average freshman award was $11,194. Need-based scholarships or need-based grants averaged $1,024; need-based self-help aid (loans and jobs) averaged $3,243; non-need-based athletic scholarships averaged $14,332; and other non-need-based awards and non-need-based scholarships averaged $3,421. The average financial indebtedness of the 2013 graduate was $16,100. Fresno State is a member of CSS. The FAFSA is required. The priority date for freshman financial aid applications for fall entry is March 3.

International Students: There are 255 international students enrolled. The school actively recruits these students. They must take the TOEFL. They must also take the SAT or ACT.

Computers: All students may access the system anytime. There are no time limits and no fees.

Graduates: From July 1, 2012 to June 30, 2013, 3441 bachelor's degrees were awarded. The most popular majors were liberal studies-blended program (8%), psychology (6%), and criminology-law enforcement option (5%). In an average class, 15% graduate in 4 years or less, 36% graduate in 5 years or less, and 48% graduate in 6 years or less.

Admissions Contact: Tina Beddall, Interim Director of Admissions. E-Mail: *tinab@csufresno.edu* Web: *www.csufresno.edu*

CALIFORNIA STATE UNIVERSITY, FULLERTON D-5

Fullerton, CA 92834 **(657) 278-2371; (657) 278-2356**

Full-time: 11721 men, 14931 women	**Faculty:** 891; IIA, av$
Part-time: 2999 men, 3435 women	**Ph.D.s:** 87%
Graduate: 2104 men, 3105 women	**Student/Faculty:** 26 to 1
Year: semesters, summer session	**Tuition:** $6186 ($17,346)
Application Deadline: November 30	**Room & Board:** $12,816

Freshman Class: 41013 applied, 19614 accepted, 4667 enrolled

SAT CR/M: 490/520 **ACT:** 21 **COMPETITIVE+**

California State University, Fullerton, founded in 1957, is part of the California State University system. The school offers programs in the arts, business and economics, communications, engineering and computer science, education, health and human development, humanities and social science, natural science and math. The institution provides a comprehensive teaching credential program. There are 8 undergraduate schools and 8 graduate schools. In addition to regional accreditation, Cal State Fullerton has baccalaureate program accreditation with AACSB, ABET, ACEJMC, NASAD, NASM, NCATE, and NLN. The library contains 2.3 million volumes, 1.2 million microform items, and 65,305 audio/video tapes/CDs/DVDs, and subscribes to 80,890 periodicals including electronic. Computerized library services include interlibrary loans, database searching, Internet access, and Wi-Fi capability. Special learning facilities include an art gallery, radio station, TV station, a wildlife sanctuary, an arboretum, a desert studies center, a demographic research center, and a number of centers for studies in economics and business, the environment, aging, education, land use, oral and public history, and religion in American life. The 240-acre campus is in a suburban area 30 miles southeast of Los Angeles. Including any residence halls, there are 29 buildings.

Student Life: 98% of undergraduates are from California. Others are from 36 states, 59 foreign countries, and Canada. 95% are from public schools. 37% are Hispanic; 26% White; 22% Asian American. The average age of freshmen is 18; all undergraduates, 22. 11% do not continue beyond their first year; 89% remain to graduate.

Housing: 2000 students can be accommodated in college housing, which includes coed on-campus apartments and off-campus apartments. In addition, there are fraternity houses and sorority houses. On-campus housing is available on a first-come and first-served basis. 94% of students commute. All students may keep cars.

Activities: 2% of men belong to 5 local and 13 national fraternities; 2% of women belong to 1 local and 8 national sororities. There are 250 groups on campus, including art, band, cheerleading, choir, chorus, communications, computers, dance, debate, drama, ethnic, film, forensics, gay, honors, international, jazz band, literary magazine, musical theater, newspaper, opera, orchestra, pep band, photography, political, professional, radio and TV, religious, social, social service, and student government. Popular campus events include Block Party, Spring Concert, and Snow Day.

Sports: There are 6 intercollegiate sports for men and 9 for women, and 15 intramural sports for men and 11 for women. Facilities include a gym, a swimming pool, tennis and racquetball courts, baseball/softball, track, and soccer fields, a bowling alley, and a stadium.

Disabled Students: All of the campus is accessible. Facilities include wheelchair ramps, elevators, special parking, specially equipped restrooms, lowered drinking fountains, lowered telephones.

Services: Counseling and information services are available, as is tutoring in most subjects. There is a reader service for the blind, and remedial math, reading, and writing.

Campus Safety and Security: Measures include 24-hour foot and vehicle patrol, emergency notification system, self-defense education, and security escort services. There are shuttle buses, emergency telephones, and lighted pathways/sidewalks.

Programs of Study: Cal State Fullerton confers B.A., B.S., B.F.A. and B.M. degrees. Master's and doctoral degrees are also awarded. Bachelor's degrees are awarded in BIOLOGICAL SCIENCE (biochemistry and biology/biological science), BUSINESS (business administration and management, business economics, entrepreneurial studies, finance, international business management, management science, marketing/retailing/merchandising, and tourism), COMMUNICATIONS AND THE ARTS (advertising, art history, art, communications, comparative literature, dance, dramatic arts, English, fine arts, French, Japanese, journalism, linguistics, music, music performance, public relations, radio/television technology, Spanish, speech/debate/rhetoric, theater design, theater management, visual and performing arts, and visual design), COMPUTER AND PHYSICAL SCIENCE (applied mathematics, chemistry, computer science, geology, information sciences and systems, mathematics, physics, and statistics), EDUCATION (athletic training and music education), ENGINEERING AND ENVIRONMENTAL DESIGN (civil engineering, computer engineering, electrical/electronics engineering, engineering and applied science, and mechanical engineering), HEALTH PROFESSIONS (exercise science, health science, kinesiology, nursing, and speech pathology/audiology), SOCIAL SCIENCE (African American studies, American studies, anthropology, Asian/American studies, child care/child and family studies, criminal justice, economics, ethnic studies, European studies, geography, history, human services, Latin American studies, liberal arts/general studies, Mexican-American/Chicano studies, philosophy, political science/government, psychology, public administration, religion, and women's studies). Business, economics and teacher credential program are the strongest academically. Business and economics, humanities and social sciences, and health and human development have the largest enrollments.

Required: Graduation requirements for all students include completion of a minimum of 51 units of general education courses, a 2.0 GPA, and an upper-division writing course designated by the major department. 120 to 135 credit hours must be completed for graduation.

Special: The university offers distance learning, honors program, freshman program, internships and co-op programs in 45 academic areas, study abroad in 18 countries, and work-study programs both on and off campus. Double majors, and pass/fail options, teacher credential programs, and service learning are also available. There is a freshman honors program.

Faculty/Classroom: 50% of faculty are male; 50% are female. All teach and do research. No introductory courses are taught by graduate students. The average class size in an introductory lecture is 35; in a laboratory is 20; and in a regular course is 33.

Admissions: 48% of the 2013-2014 applicants were accepted. The SAT scores for the 2013-2014 freshman class were: Critical Reading--51% below 500, 39% between 500 and 599, 9% between 600 and 699, and 1% between 700 and 800; Math--38% below 500, 45% between 500 and 599, 15% between 600 and 699, and 2% between 700 and 800. The ACT scores were 43% below 21, 32% between 21 and 23, 19% between 24 and 26, 4% between 27 and 28, and 3% above 28. 49% of the current freshmen were in the top fifth of their class; 88% were in the top two fifths. 2 freshmen graduated first in their class.

Requirements: The SAT or ACT is required. Applicants must be graduates of an accredited secondary school or have a GED certificate. Secondary school courses must include 4 years of English, 3 of math, 2 each of a foreign language, science, and history, and 1 of visual or performing arts. Admission is based on the Qualifiable Eligibility Index, a combination of the high school GPA and either the SAT or ACT score. Auditions are required for music majors. A GPA of 2.0 is required. AP and CLEP credits are accepted.

Procedure: Freshmen are admitted fall. Entrance exams should be taken during the senior year of high school. There is a rolling admissions plan. Applications should be filed by November 30 for fall entry, along with a $55 fee. Notification is sent on a rolling basis. Applications are accepted online.

Transfer: 4752 transfer students enrolled in 2012-2013. Applicants must have a minimum 2.0 GPA. The SAT or ACT is required for students with fewer than 60 transferable units earned. Students with 60 transferable units or more must have 30 units of general education completed with a C or better, including English composition, math, speech, and critical thinking. 30 of 120 credits required for the bachelor's degree must be completed at Cal State Fullerton.

Visiting: There are regularly scheduled orientations for prospective students, consisting of daily campus tours and information on academic colleges, student services, student life, and the history of Cal State Fullerton. There are guides for informal visits. To schedule a visit, contact New Student & Parent Programs at (657) 278-2501.

Financial Aid: In 2013-2014, 60% of all full-time freshmen and 60% of continuing full-time students received some form of financial aid. 49% of all full-time freshmen and 47% of continuing full-time students received need-based aid. The average freshman award was $11,010. Need-based scholarships or need-based grants averaged $6,635; need-based self-help aid (loans and jobs) averaged $5,756; non-need-based athletic scholarships averaged $5,177; and other non-need-based awards and non-need-based scholarships averaged $7,301. The average financial indebtedness of the 2013 graduate was $14,983. The FAFSA is required. The priority date for freshman financial aid applications for fall entry is March 2. The deadline for filing freshman financial aid applications for fall entry is June 6.

International Students: There are 791 international students enrolled. They must take the TOEFL with a minimum score of 500 on the paper-based TOEFL (PBT) or 61 on the Internet-based version (iBT).

Computers: All students may access the system 24 hours a day. There are no time limits and no fees.

Graduates: From July 1, 2012 to June 30, 2013, 7472 bachelor's degrees were awarded. The most popular majors were business/marketing (24%), communication/journalism (13%), and health professions and related programs (8%). In an average class, 14% graduate in 4 years or less, 40% graduate in 5 years or less, and 53% graduate in 6 years or less.

Admissions Contact: Admissions Office E-Mail: *admissions@fullerton.edu* Web: *www.fullerton.edu*

CALIFORNIA STATE UNIVERSITY, LONG BEACH D-5

Long Beach, CA 90840-0106	(562) 985-5471; (562) 985-4973
Full-time: 10221 men, 14401 women	**Faculty:** n/av; IIA, +$
Part-time: 2039 men, 2626 women	**Ph.D.s:** 88%
Graduate: 2132 men, 3451 women	**Student/Faculty:** 24 to 1
Year: semesters, summer session	**Tuition:** $6740 ($17,900)
Application Deadline: November 30	**Room & Board:** $11,794
Freshman Class: 49767 applied, 15122 accepted, 3987 enrolled	
SAT CR/M: 500/530	**ACT:** 21 **COMPETITIVE+**

California State University, Long Beach, founded in 1949, is a nonprofit institution that is part of the California State University system. The commuter university offers undergraduate programs through the Colleges of Health and Human Services, Liberal Arts, Natural Sciences and Math, Business Administration, Engineering, the Arts,and Education. There are 7 undergraduate schools and 7 graduate schools. In addition to regional accreditation, CSULB has baccalaureate program accreditation with AACSB, ABET, ACEJMC, AHEA, APTA, CSWE, FIDER, NASAD, NASM, NLN, and NRPA. The library contains 2.0 million volumes, 1.5 million microform items, and 29,948 audio/video tapes/CDs/DVDs, and subscribes to 21,002 periodicals including electronic. Computerized library services include interlibrary loans, database searching, and Internet access. The figures in the above capsule and in this profile are approximate. Learning facilities include a learning resource center, art gallery, radio station, and TV station. The 322-acre campus is in a suburban area 25 miles southeast of Los Angeles. Including any residence halls, there are 84 buildings.

Student Life: 97% of undergraduates are from California. Others are from 46 states, 83 foreign countries, and Canada. 31% are Hispanic; 26% white; 23% Asian American. The average age of freshmen is 18; all undergraduates, 23. 12% do not continue beyond their first year; 53% remain to graduate.

Housing: 2400 students can be accommodated in college housing, which includes single-sex and coed dorms. On-campus housing is available on a first-come and first-served basis. 93% of students commute. All students may keep cars.

Activities: 4% of men belong to 17 national fraternities; 4% of women belong to 14 national sororities. There are 150 groups on campus, including art, band, cheerleading, choir, chorale, chorus, computers, dance, drama, drill team, ethnic, film, gay, honors, international, jazz band, literary magazine, musical theater, newspaper, opera, orchestra, pep band, photography, political, professional, radio and TV, religious, social, social service, student government, and symphony. Popular campus events include Kaleidoscope Spring Festival, Engineering Day, and Blues Festival.

Sports: There are 10 intercollegiate sports for men and 9 for women, and 14 intramural sports for men and 12 for women. Facilities include the Long Beach Arena (seats 11,500 for basketball), a baseball field (seats 1500), the Pyramid Sports Arena (seats 5000), and an indoor gym (seats 2000).

Disabled Students: 99% of the campus is accessible. Facilities include wheelchair ramps, elevators, special parking, specially equipped restrooms, special class scheduling, lowered drinking fountains, lowered telephones. The university also offers registration and mobility assistance, adaptive equipment, counseling, community referrals, and services to the learning-disabled.

Services: Counseling and information services are available, as is tutoring in most subjects. There is a reader service for the blind, and remedial math, reading, and writing.

Campus Safety and Security: Measures include 24-hour foot and vehicle patrol and security escort services. There are shuttle buses, emergency telephones, and lighted pathways/sidewalks.

Programs of Study: CSULB confers B.A., B.S., B.F.A., B.M., and B.Voc.Ed. degrees. Master's degrees are also awarded. Bachelor's degrees are awarded in BIOLOGICAL SCIENCE (biochemistry, biology/biological science, botany, cell biology, ecology, physiology, and zoology), BUSINESS (accounting, banking and finance, business administration and management, international business management, management information systems, marketing/retailing/merchandising, and personnel management), COMMUNICATIONS AND THE ARTS (art, communications, comparative literature, dance, design, dramatic arts, English, film arts, French, German, Japanese, journalism, music, and Spanish), COMPUTER AND PHYSICAL SCIENCE (applied mathematics, chemistry, computer science, earth science, geology, mathematics, physics, and statistics), EDUCATION (elementary education, mathematics education, science education, and special education), ENGINEERING AND ENVIRONMENTAL DESIGN (aerospace studies, chemical engineering, civil engineering, computer engineering, electrical/electronics engineering, engineering technology, and mechanical engineering), HEALTH PROFESSIONS (health care administration and health science), SOCIAL SCIENCE (African American studies, anthropology, Asian/Oriental studies, economics, geography, Hispanic American studies, history, human development, interdisciplinary studies, international studies, philosophy, political science/government, psychology, religion, sociology, and women's studies). Art, biological sciences, and music are the strongest academically. Business administration, psychology, and liberal studies are the largest.

Required: Graduation requirements for all students include the completion of 51 units in general education (45 for engineering majors), 40 units of upper-division course work, and 30 units in residence at the university. Students must have a minimum 2.0 GPA and a total of 124 to 140 credit hours, depending on the major. Required courses include University 100: "The University in Your Future."

Special: The university offers cross-registration with California State University, Dominguez Hills, for courses not offered at CSULB. Internships, study abroad in 22 countries, dual majors in engineering, a 3-2 engineering degree, student-designed majors, and pass/fail options are also available. There are 23 national honor societies, including Phi Beta Kappa, and a freshman honors program.

Faculty/Classroom: 50% of faculty are male; 50% are female. No introductory courses are taught by graduate students.

Admissions: In a recent year, 30% applicants were accepted. The SAT scores in a recent freshman class were: Critical Reading--47% below 500, 38% between 500 and 599, 14% between 600 and 700, and 1% above 700; Math--39% below 500, 37% between 500 and 599, 21% between 600 and 700, and 3% above 700. The ACT scores were 42% below 21, 25% between 21 and 23, 20% between 24 and 26, 7% between 27 and 28, and 6% above 28.

Requirements: The SAT or ACT is required. In addition, applicants must be graduates of an accredited secondary school and have completed 4 years of English, 3 years each of math and electives, 2 years of foreign language, and 1 year each of lab science, U.S. history or U.S. history and government, and 1 visual and performing arts. Students are admitted on the basis of the eligibility index, which is computed from the secondary school GPA and the SAT or ACT scores. California residents with a minimum 3.0 GPA are automatically admissible. A portfolio is required for art and design students. An audition is required for dance, music, and theater students. A GPA of 2.0 is required. AP and CLEP credits are accepted.

Procedure: Freshmen are admitted fall and spring. Entrance exams should be taken during the fall semester of the senior year. There is a rolling admissions plan. Applications should be filed by November 30 for fall entry; August 31 for spring entry. The fall 2011 application fee was $55. Applications are accepted online.

Transfer: In a recent year, 2077 transfer students enrolled. Upper-division students must have completed a minimum of 60 semester units and have a minimum 2.0 GPA; lower-division students must meet the same requirements as entering freshmen. 30 of 120 credits required for the bachelor's degree must be completed at CSULB.

Visiting: There are regularly scheduled orientations for prospective students, consisting of Student Orientation, Advising, and Registration (SOAR) sessions. Students may participate in SOAR I, which consists of advising and registration, or SOAR II, which involves a campus tour and an orientation to activities. There are guides for informal visits. To schedule a visit, contact the Office of School Relations at (562) 985-5358.

Financial Aid: CSULB is a member of CSS. The FAFSA is required. Check with the school for filing freshman financial aid applications.

International Students: The school actively recruits these students. They must take the TOEFL with a minimum score of 500 on the paper-based TOEFL (PBT) or 61 on the Internet-based version (iBT).

Computers: All students may access the system during open lab hours, which vary across campus. There are no time limits and no fees.

Graduates: In a recent year, 6746 bachelor's degrees were awarded. The most popular majors were business (19%), visual and performing arts (10%), and English (9%). In an average class, 12% graduate in 4 years or less and 53% graduate in 6 years or less.

Admissions Contact: Tom Enders, Associate Vice Pres. Enrollment Services. E-Mail: *tenders@csulb.edu* Web: *www.csulb.edu*

CALIFORNIA STATE UNIVERSITY, LOS ANGELES C-5

Los Angeles, CA 90032 **(323) 343-3940; (323) 343-3945**

Full-time: 6045 men, 8946 women	**Faculty:** n/av; IIA, +$
Part-time: 1318 men, 1765 women	**Ph.D.s:** 56%
Graduate: 1295 men, 2386 women	**Student/Faculty:** n/av
Year: quarters, summer session	**Tuition:** $6101 ($17,759)
Application Deadline: June 15	**Room & Board:** $9728
Freshman Class: 24218 applied, 16812 accepted, 2473 enrolled	
SAT CR/M/W: 430/440/430 **ACT:** 17	**COMPETITIVE**

California State University at Los Angeles, founded in 1947 as part of the state system, offers undergraduate and graduate programs in liberal arts and sciences, business education, engineering, health science, and professional training. There are 6 undergraduate schools and 6 graduate schools. In addition to regional accreditation, Cal State, LA has baccalaureate program accreditation with AACSB, ABET, ADA, CSWE, NASAD, NASM, NCATE, and NLN. The library contains 2.1 million volumes, 1.1 million microform items, and 34,477 audio/video tapes/CDs/DVDs, and subscribes to 648 periodicals including electronic. Computerized library services include interlibrary loans, database searching, and Internet access. Special learning facilities include an art gallery and TV station. The 173-acre campus is in a small town 5 miles east of downtown Los Angeles. Including any residence halls, there are 22 buildings.

Student Life: 95% of undergraduates are from California. Others are from 48 states, 76 foreign countries, and Canada. 80% are from public schools. 58% are Hispanic; 17% Asian American. The average age of freshmen is 18; all undergraduates, 25. 17% do not continue beyond their first year; 35% remain to graduate.

Housing: 1000 students can be accommodated in college housing, which includes single-sex dorms, on-campus apartments, and off-campus apartments. In addition, there are special-interest houses, and an international house. On-campus housing is guaranteed for the freshman year only, is available on a first-come, and first-served basis. 95% of students commute. All students may keep cars.

Activities: 1% of men belong to 8 national fraternities; 1% of women belong to 9 national sororities. There are 108 groups on campus, including band, chess, choir, chorale, chorus, computers, dance, drama, ethnic, forensics, gay, honors, international, jazz band, literary magazine, musical theater, newspaper, opera, orchestra, political, professional, radio and TV, religious, social, social service, student government, and symphony. Popular campus events include Christmas Toy, Food Drive and Earth Week.

Sports: There are 6 intercollegiate sports for men and 6 for women, and 9 intramural sports for men and 7 for women. Facilities include a 4,800-seat stadium, a 5,500-seat gym, a swimming pool, tennis and racquetball courts, a track, and athletic fields.

Disabled Students: 95% of the campus is accessible. Facilities include wheelchair ramps, elevators, special parking, specially equipped restrooms, and lowered telephones.

Services: Counseling and information services are available, as is tutoring in most subjects. There is a reader service for the blind, and remedial math, reading, and writing.

Campus Safety and Security: Measures include 24-hour foot and vehicle patrol, self-defense education, and security escort services. There are shuttle buses, emergency telephones, and lighted pathways/sidewalks.

Programs of Study: Cal State, LA confers B.A., B.M., B.S. and B.Voc.Ed. degrees. Master's and doctoral degrees are also awarded. Bachelor's degrees are awarded in BIOLOGICAL SCIENCE (biochemistry, biology/biological science, and microbiology), BUSINESS (business administration and management), COMMUNICATIONS AND THE ARTS (dramatic arts, English, French, graphic design, Japanese, media arts, music, music performance, Spanish, and speech/debate/rhetoric), COMPUTER AND PHYSICAL SCIENCE (chemistry, computer science, geology, information sciences and systems, mathematics, natural sciences, and physics), EDUCATION (industrial arts education, physical education, and vocational education), ENGINEERING AND ENVIRONMENTAL DESIGN (civil engineering, electrical/electronics engineering, engineering, industrial engineering technology, and mechanical engineering), HEALTH PROFESSIONS (health science, nursing, rehabilitation therapy, and speech pathology/audiology), SOCIAL SCIENCE (African American studies, anthropology, child psychology/development, criminal justice, dietetics, economics, fire protection, geography, history, interdisciplinary studies, Latin American studies, liberal arts/general studies, Mexican-American/Chicano studies, philosophy, political science/government, psychology, social science, social work, and sociology). Child development, psychology, and business administration have the largest enrollment.

Required: To graduate, students must complete 186 to 203 quarter units, with a minimum 2.0 GPA, and must demonstrate skills in math and oral and written communications. General education requirements include 72 quarter units in the social sciences, natural sciences, and humanities.

Special: Cross-registration is offered with other California State University schools. The school, as part of the state university system, is part of the California Desert Studies Consortium, which provides a field facility in the Mojave Desert to develop desert studies educational programs. It is also part of the Ocean Studies Institute, which facilitates marine educational and research activities. Students may design their own majors. Internships, study-abroad in 17 countries, work-study programs, B.A.-B.S. degrees, dual majors, pass/fail options, and credit for life experience are available. An accelerated degree program in nursing and computer science is offered. There are 25 national honor societies, a freshman honors program, and 5 departmental honors programs.

Faculty/Classroom: 51% of faculty are male; 49% are female. All teach undergraduates. No introductory courses are taught by graduate students. The average class size in an introductory lecture is 32; in a laboratory is 20; and in a regular course is 28.

Admissions: 69% of the 2013-2014 applicants were accepted. The SAT scores for the 2013-2014 freshman class were: Critical Reading--77% below 500, 19% between 500 and 599, 3% between 600 and 699, and 1% between 700 and 800; Math--72% below 500, 22% between 500 and 599, 5% between 600 and 699, and 1% between 700 and 800; Writing--77% below 500, 19% between 500 and 599, 3% between 600 and 699, and 1% between 700 and 800. The ACT scores were 79% below 21, 12% between 21 and 23, 6% between 24 and 26, 2% between 27 and 28, and 1% above 28.

Requirements: The SAT or ACT is required. The SAT or ACT and ACT Writing Test are recommended. Applicants should be graduates of accredited secondary schools or have a GED equivalent. 15 academic credits are required, including 4 years of English, 3 of math, 2 of the same foreign language, 1 each of biological and physical science with lab, 1 each of U.S. history and social science, and 1 year in electives and the visual and performing arts. A GPA of 2.0 is required. AP and CLEP credits are accepted.

Procedure: Freshmen are admitted to all sessions. Entrance exams should be taken during the junior year or senior year. There is a rolling admissions plan. Applications should be filed by June 15 for fall entry; October 1 for winter entry; February 1 for spring entry; and April 1 for summer entry. The fall 2013 application fee was $55. Applications are accepted online.

Transfer: 2499 transfer students enrolled in 2012-2013. Applicants must have 56 semester units (84 quarter units), a 2.0 GPA (2.4 GPA for nonresidents), and have completed the CSU graduation requirements in English composition, speech communication, critical thinking, and quantitative reasoning. 45 of 186 credits required for the bachelor's degree must be completed at Cal State, LA.

Visiting: There are guides for informal visits.

Financial Aid: In 2013-2014, 70% of all full-time freshmen and 77% of continuing full-time students received some form of financial aid. 70% of all full-time freshmen and 77% of continuing full-time students received need-based aid. The average freshman award was $10,884. Need-based scholarships or need-based grants averaged $9,665; need-based self-help aid (loans and jobs) averaged $3,716; non-need-based athletic scholarships averaged $10,876; and other non-need-based awards and non-need-based scholarships averaged $575. The CSS/Profile and FAFSA, and and the SAAC (in-state) are required. The deadline for filing freshman financial aid applications for fall entry is March 1.

International Students: There are 645 international students enrolled. They must take the TOEFL with a minimum score of 500 on the paper-based TOEFL (PBT) or 61 on the Internet-based version (iBT). They must also take the SAT or ACT.

Computers: All students may access the system. 24 hours a day. There is a 2-hour limit in the open access labs during peak demand periods. There are no fees.

Graduates: From July 1, 2012 to June 30, 2013, 3742 bachelor's degrees were awarded. The most popular majors were psychology (7%), social work (6%), and business administration/accounting (6%). 376 companies recruited on campus in 2012-2013. In an average class, 9% graduate in 4 years or less, 24% graduate in 5 years or less, and 37% graduate in 6 years or less.

Admissions Contact: Joan Woosley, Director of Admission and University Registrar. E-Mail: *admission@calstatela.edu* Web: *www.calstate.edu*

CALIFORNIA STATE UNIVERSITY, MONTEREY BAY B-3

Seaside, CA 93955 **(831) 582-5100; (831) 582-5110**

Full-time: 1893 men, 3061 women	**Faculty:** 113; IIA, -$
Part-time: 141 men, 213 women	**Ph.D.s:** 86%
Graduate: 123 men, 301 women	**Student/Faculty:** 28 to 1
Year: semesters, summer session	**Tuition:** $17,123
Application Deadline: March 15	**Room & Board:** $9748

Freshman Class: 13803 applied, 6161 accepted, 866 enrolled

SAT CR/M/W: 485/495/485 **ACT:** 21 **LESSCOMPETITIVE**

California State University, Monterey Bay, founded in 1994, is a public institution with 13 undergraduate divisions, including arts and sciences, communications, education and professional training, and science and technology. There are 5 undergraduate schools and 4 graduate schools. The library contains 87,595 volumes, 681 microform items, and 3,085 audio/video tapes/CDs/DVDs, and subscribes to 61,712 periodicals including electronic. Computerized library services include interlibrary loans, database searching, Internet access, and Wi-Fi capability. The 1387-acre campus is in a suburban area 90 miles south of San Francisco. Including any residence halls, there are 65 buildings.

Student Life: 97% of undergraduates are from California. Others are from 39 states, 29 foreign countries, and Canada. 92% are from public schools. 46% are White; 30% Hispanic. The average age of freshmen is 19; all undergraduates, 22. 33% do not continue beyond their first year; 39% remain to graduate.

Housing: 2450 students can be accommodated in college housing, which includes single-sex and coed dorms, on-campus apartments, and married student housing. Coed dorms, disabled students housing, international, theme and wellness housing, and six-person suite-style housing with living areas and kitchenette; substance-free residence hall. On-campus housing is guaranteed for the freshman year only, is available on a first-come, and first-served basis. 85% of students live on campus; of those, 60% remain on campus on weekends. All students may keep cars.

Activities: 2% of men belong to 4 local fraternities; 1% of women belong to 4 local sororities. There are 50 groups on campus, including cheerleading, choir, chorus, computers, dance, drama, ethnic, film, gay, international, musical theater, newspaper, pep band, photography, political, professional, radio and TV, religious, social, social service, student government, and yearbook. Popular campus events include Capstone Festival, Diversity Days, and Spring Formal.

Sports: There are 4 intercollegiate sports for men and 5 for women, and 5 intramural sports for men and 5 for women. Facilities include 3 racquetball courts, a 2500-square-foot fitness room, saunas, and a 10,000-square-foot gym with facilities for basketball, volleyball, badminton, indoor soccer, aerobics, and dance. There is also a soccer complex, an aquatic center, a disc golf course, a stadium track, and a baseball field.

Disabled Students: All of the campus is accessible. Facilities include wheelchair ramps, elevators, special parking, specially equipped restrooms, special class scheduling, lowered drinking fountains, lowered telephones, special housing. any official campus program can accommodate, with notice.

Services: Counseling and information services are available, as is tutoring in some subjects, computer skills and others by demand. There is a reader service for the blind, and remedial math, reading, and writing.

Campus Safety and Security: Measures include 24-hour foot and vehicle patrol, self-defense education, and security escort services. There are shuttle buses, emergency telephones, and lighted pathways/sidewalks.

Programs of Study: CSUMB confers B.A., and B.S. degrees. Master's degrees are also awarded. Bachelor's degrees are awarded in BIOLOGICAL SCIENCE (biology/biological science), BUSINESS (business administration and management and management science), COMMUNICATIONS AND THE ARTS (communications technology, linguistics, music, Spanish, telecommunications, and visual and performing arts), COMPUTER AND PHYSICAL SCIENCE (computer science, earth science, and mathematics), EDUCATION (education), HEALTH PROFESSIONS (health), SOCIAL SCIENCE (behavioral science, human services, humanities, international studies, liberal arts/general studies, physical fitness/movement, psychology, and social science). Computer science, technology, and business administration are the strongest academically. Business administraion, liberal studies, and human communication have the largest enrollments.

Required: To graduate, students must complete 120 to 132 credit hours, including general education requirements and at least 24 hours in the major. Courses in physical education, technology, foreign language, and service learning are also required.

Special: Study abroad in 18 countries, internships, work-study programs, and an integrated studies major are available.

Faculty/Classroom: 52% of faculty are male; 48% are female. All teach undergraduates. No introductory courses are taught by graduate students. The average class size in an introductory lecture is 23; in a laboratory is 17; and in a regular course is 22.

Admissions: 45% of the 2013-2014 applicants were accepted. The SAT scores for the 2013-2014 freshman class were: Critical Reading--53% below 500, 36% between 500 and 599, 10% between 600 and 699, and 1% between 700 and 800; Math--52% below 500, 36% between 500 and 599, 11% between 600 and 699, and 1% between 700 and 800; Writing--56% below 500, 35% between 500 and 599, and 8% between 600 and 699. The ACT scores were 21% below 21, 54% between 21 and 23, % between 24 and 26, 24% between 27 and 28, and 1% above 28. 46% of the current freshmen were in the top fifth of their class; 87% were in the top two fifths.

Requirements: CSUMB requires applicants to be in the upper 70% of their class. A GPA of 2.0 is required. AP and CLEP credits are accepted. Important factors in the admissions decision are leadership record, recommendations by school officials, advanced placement or honors courses, parents or siblings attended your school, evidence of special talent, personality/intangible qualities, extracurricular activities record, recommendations by alumni, and geographical diversity.

Procedure: Freshmen are admitted fall and spring. Entrance exams should be taken March, April, or May of each year. Applications should be filed by March 15 for fall entry; November 30 for spring entry, along with a $55 fee. Notifications are sent November 30. Applications are accepted online.

Transfer: 744 transfer students enrolled in 2012-2013. Transfer requirements include a college GPA of 2.0 (residents) or 2.4 (non-residents) and 60 transferable baccalaureate semester units, including 30 units of general education courses. 30 credits required for the bachelor's degree must be completed at CSUMB.

Visiting: There are regularly scheduled orientations for prospective students, including onsite academic advising and registration, campus tours, and campus fair. There are guides for informal visits, visitors may sit in on classes, and stay overnight. To schedule a visit, contact the Office of Admissions.

Financial Aid: In 2013-2014, 46% of all full-time freshmen and 47% of continuing full-time students received some form of financial aid. 32% of all full-time freshmen and 61% of continuing full-time students received need-based aid. The average freshman award was $10,686. Need-based scholarships or need-based grants averaged $9,282; need-based self-help aid (loans and jobs) averaged $4,264; non-need-based athletic scholarships averaged $3,241; other non-need-based awards and non-need-based scholarships averaged $4,241; and $2,937 from other forms of aid. Average annual earnings from campus work are $3000. The average financial indebtedness of the 2013 graduate was $15,305. The FAFSA and the state aid form are required. The priority date for freshman financial aid applications for fall entry is March 2. The deadline for filing freshman financial aid applications for fall entry is June 21.

International Students: There are 36 international students enrolled. They must take the TOEFL with a minimum score of 500 on the paper-based TOEFL (PBT) or 61 on the Internet-based version (iBT). They must also take the SAT or ACT.

Computers: All students may access the system. There are no time limits and no fees.

Graduates: From July 1, 2012 to June 30, 2013, 1055 bachelor's degrees were awarded. The most popular majors were liberal arts/general studies/and business/marketing (17%), psychology (12%), and social sciences/parks and recreation (9%). In an average class, 1% graduate in 3 years or less, 40% graduate in 4 years or less, 30% graduate in 5 years or less, and 39% graduate in 6 years or less.

Admissions Contact: Veronica Chuckwuemeka, Director. E-Mail: *veronica_chukwuemeka@csumb.edu* Web: *www.csumb.edu*

CALIFORNIA STATE UNIVERSITY, NORTHRIDGE C-5

Northridge, CA 91330	**(818) 677-3700; (818) 677-3766**
Full-time: 12569 men, 15424 women	**Faculty:** n/av; IIA, av$
Part-time: 2624 men, 2781 women	**Ph.D.s:** n/av
Graduate: 1827 men, 3085 women	**Student/Faculty:** 27 to 1
Year: semesters, summer session	**Tuition:** $17,685
Application Deadline:	**Room & Board:** $10,628
Freshman Class: 30903 applied, 18947 accepted, 5818 enrolled	
SAT CR/M: 455/465 **ACT:** 19	**COMPETITIVE**

California State University, Northridge, founded in 1958, is part of the state-supported university system offering degree programs in the liberal arts and sciences, business administration, education, engineering, music, health fields, and fine arts. There are 8 undergraduate schools and 1 graduate school. In addition to regional accreditation, CSUN has baccalaureate program accreditation with AACSB, ABET, ACEJMC, AHEA, APTA, CAHEA, CSAB, NASAD, NASM, NCATE, and NRPA. The library contains 1.4 million volumes, 3.2 million microform items, 14,074 audio/video tapes/CDs/DVDs, and subscribes to 2,110 periodicals including electronic. Computerized library services include interlibrary loans and database searching. Special learning facilities include an art gallery, planetarium, radio station, TV station, observatory, anthropological museum, botanical gardens, urban archives center, natural center on deafness, center for the study of cancer and development biology. The 356-acre campus is in an urban area 20 miles north of Los Angeles, and 25 miles to the Los Angeles airport. Including any residence halls, there are 76 buildings.

Student Life: 93% of undergraduates are from California. Others are from 46 states, and Canada. 93% are from public schools. 68% are Hispanic; 43% White; 19% Asian American; 19% American Indian/Alaska Native; 13% Foreign. The average age of freshmen is 18; all undergraduates, 24.

Housing: 2400 students can be accommodated in college housing, which includes coed on-campus apartments and off-campus apartments. In addition, there are fraternity houses, sorority houses, and an international house. On-campus housing is guaranteed for all 4 years, is available on a first-come, and first-served basis. All students may keep cars.

Activities: There are 181 groups on campus, including art, band, cheerleading, choir, chorale, chorus, computers, dance, drama, ethnic, film, gay, honors, international, jazz band, literary magazine, marching band, musical theater, newspaper, opera, orchestra, photography, political, professional, radio and TV, religious, social, social service, student government, symphony, and yearbook. Popular campus events include International Student Days, Campus Community Day and Welcome Week.

Sports: There are 8 intercollegiate sports for men and 10 for women, and 9 intramural sports for men and 9 for women. Facilities include 2 gyms, 2 swimming pools, softball and soccer fields, handball, racquetball, tennis courts, baseball field, a track and field, volleyball, waterpolo, and cross county golf.

Disabled Students: 98% of the campus is accessible. Facilities include wheelchair ramps, elevators, special parking, specially equipped restrooms, special class scheduling, lowered drinking fountains, lowered telephones. electric doors, adaptive equipment, braille services, interpreters for hearing impaired, note-taking services, oral test, priority registration, reader services, reading machines, talking/taped books, tape recorders, TTY, academic coaching and skills enhancement, application assistance, and job placement services.

Services: Counseling and information services are available, as is tutoring in some subjects, English and math There is a reader service for the blind, and remedial math, reading, and writing. Student tutors are available for other selected subjects as well.

Campus Safety and Security: Measures include 24-hour foot and vehicle patrol and security escort services. There are shuttle buses, emergency telephones, and lighted pathways/sidewalks.

Programs of Study: CSUN confers B.A., B.S. and B.M. degrees. Master's degrees are also awarded. Bachelor's degrees are awarded in BIOLOGICAL SCIENCE (biochemistry, biology/biological science, environmental biology, genetics, and microbiology), BUSINESS (accounting, banking and finance, business administration and management, management information systems, marketing/retailing/merchandising, and recreation and leisure services), COMMUNICATIONS AND THE ARTS (African languages, art, dance, dramatic arts, English, film arts, French, German, journalism, languages, linguistics, music, Spanish, and speech/debate/rhetoric), COMPUTER AND PHYSICAL SCIENCE (astrophysics, chemistry, computer science, earth science, geology, mathematics, physics, and radiological technology), EDUCATION (business education, education of the deaf and hearing impaired, home economics education, journalism education, nursing education, and physical education), ENGINEERING AND ENVIRONMENTAL DESIGN (engineering), HEALTH PROFESSIONS (biomedical science, exercise science, health, health care administration, medical laboratory technology, nursing, physical therapy, recreation therapy, and speech pathology/audiology), SOCIAL SCIENCE (African American studies, anthropology, Asian/American studies, child psychology/development, criminology, economics, family/consumer resource management, family/consumer studies, French studies, geography, German area studies, history, humanities, liberal arts/general studies, Mexican-American/Chicano studies, philosophy, political science/government, psychology, religious education, sociology, urban studies, and women's studies). Liberal studies is the strongest academically. Business administration and economics, social and behavioral sciences and arts, media and communication hace the largest enrollments.

Required: All students must complete 52 units of general education requirements in 6 areas, including courses in American history, U.S. Constitution, state and local government, English, math, logic, and oral and written communication. A total of 124 semester units for the B.A., 128 to 132 for the B.S., and 132 for the B.M., with a minimum GPA of 2.0, is required to graduate. At least 30 semester units must be completed in residence.

Special: Cross-registration is offered through the Intra System Visitor Program. Study abroad in 16 countries, internships, university work-study programs, dual majors, student-designed majors, credit for military experience, and pass/fail options for elective courses are offered. There are 4 national honor societies, a freshman honors program, and 5 departmental honors programs.

Faculty/Classroom: 60% of faculty are male; 40% are female. All teach undergraduates. Graduate students teach 12% of introductory courses. The average class size in an introductory lecture is 33 and in a laboratory is 20.

Admissions: 61% of the 2013-2014 applicants were accepted. The SAT scores for the 2013-2014 freshman class were: Critical Reading--69% below 500, and 26% between 500 and 599; Math--63% below 500, 28% between 500 and 599, and 8% between 600 and 699.

Requirements: The SAT or ACT is required. Applicants should have completed 4 years of high school English, 3 of math and 1 academic electives, 2 of foreign language, and 1 each of lab science, social studies, U.S. history/government, and visual/performing arts. A GPA of 2.0 is required. AP and CLEP credits are accepted. Important factors in the admissions decision are recommendations by school officials, evidence of special talent, and leadership record.

Procedure: Freshmen are admitted fall and spring. Entrance exams

should be taken by December of the senior year. There are early decision and rolling admissions plans. Check with the school for current application deadlines. The application fee is $55. Notification is sent on a rolling basis. Applications are accepted online.

Transfer: 5248 transfer students enrolled in 2012-2013. A GPA of 2.0 (2.4 for nonresidents) is required in a minimum of 56 transferable semester units. Basic courses in writing, math, speech, and logic must be completed with a grade of C or better. 30 of 124 credits required for the bachelor's degree must be completed at CSUN.

Visiting: There are regularly scheduled orientations for prospective students, held in June and July for fall entrance and in November for spring entrance. There are guides for informal visits, visitors may sit in on classes, and stay overnight. To schedule a visit, contact Student Outreach and Recruitment at (818) 677-2879.

Financial Aid: In 2013-2014, 48% of all full-time freshmen students received some form of financial aid. 48% of all full-time freshmen students received need-based aid. The average freshman award was $19,329. Need-based scholarships or need-based grants averaged $15,946; need-based self-help aid (loans and jobs) averaged $6,532; non-need-based athletic scholarships averaged $13,550; other non-need-based awards and non-need-based scholarships averaged $1,855; and $6,400 from other forms of aid. The average financial indebtedness of the 2013 graduate was $17,534. CSUN is a member of CSS. The FAFSA, and SAAC is required. The priority date for freshman financial aid applications for fall entry is March 2.

International Students: They must take the TOEFL.

Computers: All students may access the system 24 hours a day, 7 days a week.

Graduates: From July 1, 2012 to June 30, 2013, 6885 bachelor's degrees were awarded. The most popular majors were education (26%), protective services/public asministration (23%), and health professions and related programs (11%). Of the 2012 graduating class, 75% were enrolled in graduate school within 6 months of graduation.

Admissions Contact: Patricia Lord, Director of Admissions and Records. E-Mail: *amy.matsubara@csun.edu* Web: *www.csum.edu*

CALIFORNIA STATE UNIVERSITY, SACRAMENTO B-3

Sacramento, CA 95819 **(916) 278-7362**
(800) 722-4748; (916) 278-5603

Full-time: 8697 men, 11713 women
Part-time: 1971 men, 2320 women
Graduate: 1071 men, 2244 women
Year: semesters, summer session
Application Deadline: November 30
Freshman Class: 18617 applied, 12496 accepted, 4671 enrolled
SAT or ACT: required
Faculty: n/av; IIA, av$
Ph.D.s: n/av
Student/Faculty: n/av
Tuition: $7072 ($18,232)
Room & Board: $10,128

COMPETITIVE

California State University, Sacramento is an integral part of the community, committed to access, excellence and diversity. California State University, Sacramento is dedicated to the life-altering potential of learning that balances a liberal arts education with depth of knowledge in a discipline. We are committed to providing an excellent education to all eligible applicants who aspire to expand their knowledge and prepare themselves for meaningful lives, careers, and service to their community. Reflecting the metropolitan character of the area, California State University, Sacramento is a richly diverse community. As such, the University is committed to fostering in all its members a sense of inclusiveness, respect for human differences, and concern for others. In doing so, we strive to create a pluralistic community in which members participate collaboratively in all aspects of university life. There are 7 undergraduate schools and 7 graduate schools. In addition to regional accreditation, Sacramento State has baccalaureate program accreditation with AACSB, ABET, ACBSP, ACCE, ADA, AHEA, APTA, ASLA, CSWE, FIDER, NASAD, NASM, NCATE, NLN, NRPA, and TEAC. The library contains 1.4 million volumes, 2.4 million microform items, and 53,515 audio/video tapes/CDs/DVDs, and subscribes to 2,171 periodicals including electronic. Computerized library services include interlibrary loans, database searching, and Internet access. Special learning facilities include a learning resource center, art gallery, radio station, an aquatic center, an anthropology museum, several art galleries, and a brand new wellness center. The 300-acre campus is in a suburban area 90 miles northeast of San Francisco. Including any residence halls, there are 52 buildings.

Student Life: 99% of undergraduates are from California. Others are from 37 states, 36 foreign countries, and Canada. 96% are from public schools. 44% are white; 18% Asian American; 14% Hispanic.

Housing: 1100 students can be accommodated in college housing, which includes coed dorms and off-campus apartments. On-campus housing is available on a first-come and first-served basis. 95% of students commute. All students may keep cars.

Activities: 7% of men belong to 3 local and 18 national fraternities; 5% of women belong to 1 local and 20 national sororities. There are 230 groups on campus, including art, band, cheerleading, chess, choir, chorale, chorus, computers, dance, debate, drama, ethnic, film, gay, honors, international, jazz band, literary magazine, marching band, musical theater, newspaper, opera, orchestra, pep band, photography, political, professional, radio and TV, religious, social, social service, student government, and symphony. Popular campus events include Greek Week, Festival of New American Music, and River City Days.

Sports: Facilities include a 17000-seat stadium, 2 gyms, 2 swimming pools, an all-weather outdoor track, 16 tennis courts, baseball, softball, and soccer fields, and an aquatic center, with sailing, wind-surfing, rowing, and canoeing.

Disabled Students: 90% of the campus is accessible. Facilities include wheelchair ramps, elevators, special parking, specially equipped restrooms, special class scheduling, lowered drinking fountains, and lowered telephones.

Services: Counseling and information services are available, as is tutoring in most subjects. There is a reader service for the blind, and remedial math, reading, and writing.

Campus Safety and Security: Measures include 24-hour foot and vehicle patrol, self-defense education, and security escort services. There are shuttle buses, emergency telephones, and lighted pathways/sidewalks.

Programs of Study: Sacramento State confers B.A., B.S., B.M., and B.V.E. degrees. Master's and doctoral degrees are also awarded. Bachelor's degrees are awarded in AGRICULTURE (natural resource management), BIOLOGICAL SCIENCE (biology/biological science and microbiology), BUSINESS (accounting, banking and finance, business administration and management, insurance, international business management, management information systems, marketing/retailing/merchandising, and real estate), COMMUNICATIONS AND THE ARTS (communications, dramatic arts, English, French, German, journalism, music, and Spanish), COMPUTER AND PHYSICAL SCIENCE (chemistry, computer science, geology, mathematics, physical sciences, and physics), EDUCATION (business education, early childhood education, and health education), ENGINEERING AND ENVIRONMENTAL DESIGN (civil engineering, computer engineering, electrical/electronics engineering, engineering technology, and mechanical engineering), HEALTH PROFESSIONS (environmental health science, medical laboratory technology, nursing, physical therapy, and speech pathology/audiology), SOCIAL SCIENCE (anthropology, criminal justice, economics, geography, history, homeland security, international relations, parks and recreation management, philosophy, psychology, public administration, social science, social work, and sociology). Nursing, criminal justice, and business administration are the strongest academically. Business administration, and communications have the largest enrollments.

Required: In order to graduate, students must complete a minimum of 120 semester hours, including 30 to 86 hours in the major, with a minimum 2.0 GPA. Students must complete 51 units in general education requirements and take proficiency exams in writing and a foreign language. Distribution requirements include 15 units in the individual and society; 12 each in arts and humanities and physical universe/life forms, 9 in English language communication, and 3 in understanding personal development. A course in race and ethnicity in American society is required.

Special: The university offers cross-registration with other California State University schools, co-op programs in many academic programs, internships, a Washington semester, study abroad in 12 countries, and dual and student-designed majors. A joint Ph.D. program in public history is available with the university of California at Santa Barbara. There are including Phi Beta Kappa and a freshman honors program.

Faculty/Classroom: 51% of faculty are male; 49% are female. All teach and do research. No introductory courses are taught by graduate students. The average class size in an introductory lecture is 38; in a laboratory is 19; and in a regular course is 34.

Admissions: In a recent year, 67% applicants were accepted.

Requirements: The SAT or ACT is required of applicants with a high school GPA below 3.0. Applicants should have completed 4 years of high school English, 3 years of math, 2 years of a foreign language, 1 year each of lab science, history, and visual/performing arts and 3 years of college preparatory electives. A GPA of 2.0 is required. AP and CLEP credits are accepted.

Procedure: Freshmen are admitted fall and spring. Entrance exams should be taken before December of the senior year. There are deferred admissions and rolling admissions plans. Applications should be filed by November 30 for fall entry. The fall 2011 application fee was $55. Notifications are sent November 1. Applications are accepted online.

Transfer: In a recent year, 3556 transfer students enrolled. Applicants must have a 2.0 GPA and 56 transferable semester units, including 30 units of specific general education courses to include oral and written communication, critical thinking, and math. 30 of 120 credits required for the bachelor's degree must be completed at Sacramento State.

Visiting: There are regularly scheduled orientations for prospective students. There are guides for informal visits and visitors may sit in on classes. To schedule a visit, contact the University Outreach Services Office.

Financial Aid: Sacramento State is a member of CSS. The FAFSA, and SAAC is required. Check with the school for current application deadlines.

International Students: There are 333 international students enrolled. The school actively recruits these students. They must take the TOEFL. They must also take the SAT or ACT.

Computers: All students may access the system. There are no time limits and no fees. It is strongly recommended that all students have a personal computer.

Graduates: In a recent year, 5075 bachelor's degrees were awarded. The most popular majors were business/marketing (21%), homeland security (11%), and communication/journalism (8%).

Admissions Contact: Emiliano Diaz, Director of University Outreach Services. E-Mail: *outreach@csus.edu* Web: *www.csus.edu*

CALIFORNIA STATE UNIVERSITY, SAN BERNARDINO D-5

San Bernardino, CA 92407-2397 **(909) 537-5188; (909) 537-7034**

Full-time: 4817 men, 8163 women	**Faculty:** n/av; IIA, av$
Part-time: 707 men, 1045 women	**Ph.D.s:** n/av
Graduate: 919 men, 1599 women	**Student/Faculty:** n/av
Year: quarters, summer session	**Tuition:** $6953 ($12,150)
Application Deadline: open	**Room & Board:** $10,296
Freshman Class: n/av	
	COMPETITIVE

California State University, San Bernardino, founded in 1965, is a public, comprehensive regional university offering programs in business and public administration, natural sciences, education, arts and letters, and social and behavioral sciences. The figures given in the above capsule and in this profile are approximate. There are 5 undergraduate schools and 19 graduate schools. In addition to regional accreditation, CSUSB has baccalaureate program accreditation with AACSB, ABET, ADA, CSAB, CSWE, NASAD, NASM, NCATE, and NLN. Computerized library services include interlibrary loans and database searching. Special learning facilities include a learning resource center, art gallery, and radio station. The 430-acre campus is in a suburban area 60 miles east of Los Angeles and 60 miles west of Palm Springs. Including any residence halls, there are 45 buildings.

Student Life: 99% of undergraduates are from California. 46% are Hispanic; 24% white. The average age of freshmen is 18; all undergraduates, 22. 18% do not continue beyond their first year; 82% remain to graduate.

Housing: College-sponsored housing includes single-sex and coed dorms and on-campus apartments. In addition, there are special-interest houses, 1 all-women dorm. On-campus housing is available on a first-come and first-served basis. All students may keep cars.

Activities: 4% of men belong to 1 local and 8 national fraternities; 3% of women belong to 6 national sororities. There are 80 groups on campus, including art, cheerleading, choir, chorale, chorus, computers, dance, drama, ethnic, gay, honors, international, jazz band, musical theater, newspaper, orchestra, political, professional, radio and TV, religious, social, social service, and student government. Popular campus events include Annual Picnic and California Indian Cultural Awareness Conference.

Sports: There are 4 intercollegiate sports for men and 7 for women. Facilities include an arena for basketball and volleyball, baseball, softball, and soccer fields, tennis courts, swimming pools for water polo and recreational swimming, and a gym for recreational workouts.

Disabled Students: 95% of the campus is accessible. Facilities include wheelchair ramps, elevators, special parking, specially equipped restrooms, lowered drinking fountains, lowered telephones.

Services: Counseling and information services are available, as is tutoring in most subjects. There is a reader service for the blind, and remedial math and writing.

Campus Safety and Security: Measures include 24-hour foot and vehicle patrol, self-defense education, and security escort services. There are emergency telephones, lighted pathways/sidewalks, e-mail and web site alerts.

Programs of Study: CSUSB confers B.A., B.S., and B.V.E. degrees. Master's degrees are also awarded. Bachelor's degrees are awarded in AGRICULTURE (environmental studies), BIOLOGICAL SCIENCE (biochemistry and biology/biological science), BUSINESS (accounting, banking and finance, business administration and management, business economics, human resources, international business management, management information systems, management science, and small business management), COMMUNICATIONS AND THE ARTS (art, art history and appreciation, ceramic art and design, communications, dance, dramatic arts, English, French, graphic design, music, music history and appreciation, music performance, music technology, musicology/ethnomusicology, painting, photography, printmaking, sculpture, and Spanish), COMPUTER AND PHYSICAL SCIENCE (applied physics, chemistry, computer science, geology, mathematics, and physics), EDUCATION (bilingual/bicultural education, health education, music education, and vocational education), HEALTH PROFESSIONS (environmental health science, exercise science, health care administration, health science, nursing, and premedicine), SOCIAL SCIENCE (American studies, anthropology, child psychology/development, criminal justice, economics, ethnic studies, food science, geography, gerontology, history, human development, human services, humanities, liberal arts/general studies, paralegal studies, philosophy, political science/government, psychology, public administration, social science, social work, sociology, and Spanish studies). Liberal studies, nursing, and psychology have the largest enrollments.

Required: To graduate, students must complete 180 to 198 quarter hours, including 60 in upper-division courses and requirements for the major, with a minimum GPA of 2.0. The 82-credit general education program includes courses in basic skills, natural sciences, humanities, social and behavioral sciences, lifelong understanding, upper-division writing, multicultural/gender studies, and electives. Students must also demonstrate an understanding of the U.S. Constitution, American history, and California government.

Special: The university offers cross-registration with other CSU campuses and study abroad in 18 countries. Also available are internships, accelerated study, campus and community work-study programs, B.A.-B.S. degrees, dual and student-designed majors, credit for vocational education and military experience, and nondegree study. There are 3 national honor societies, including Phi Beta Kappa, and a freshman honors program.

Faculty/Classroom: No introductory courses are taught by graduate students. The average class size in an introductory lecture is 40; in a laboratory is 18; and in a regular course is 24.

Requirements: Applicants must be graduates of an accredited secondary school. Preparatory work should include 4 years of English, 3 of math, 2 of foreign language, 1 each of U.S. history/government, lab science, and visual and performing arts, and 3 of electives. Admission is based on an eligibility index that weighs the high school GPA and the SAT or ACT score. Students with GPAs of 3.0 or better (3.6 for nonresidents) are exempt from test score requirements. AP and CLEP credits are accepted. Important factors in the admissions decision are advanced placement or honors courses, recommendations by school officials, and leadership record.

Procedure: Freshmen are admitted to all sessions. Entrance exams should be taken prior to applying. There is a rolling admissions plan. Application deadlines are open. Check with the school for the application fee. Notification is sent on a rolling basis. Applications are accepted online.

Transfer: In a recent year, 1676 transfer students enrolled. Applicants must have a minimum college GPA of 2.0 (2.4 for nonresidents) and be in good standing at the previously attended institution. Those with fewer than 56 transferable semester units must submit ACT or SAT scores. 45 of 180 credits required for the bachelor's degree must be completed at CSUSB.

Visiting: There are regularly scheduled orientations for prospective students, including sessions on admissions requirements, financial aid information, and campus (student) life information. There are guides for informal visits, visitors may sit in on classes, and stay overnight. To schedule a visit, contact the Outreach Services Office.

Financial Aid: The FAFSA is required. Check with the school for current application deadlines.

International Students: There are 557 international students enrolled. The school actively recruits these students.

Computers: All students may access the system. There are no time limits and no fees.

Graduates: In a recent year, 2868 bachelor's degrees were awarded. The most popular majors were psychology (10%), criminal justice (7%), and liberal studies (7%).

Admissions Contact: Olivia Rosas, Director. A campus DVD is available. Web: *www.csusb.edu*

CALIFORNIA STATE UNIVERSITY, SAN MARCOS D-5

San Marcos, CA 92096-0001 **(760) 750-4848**

Full-time: 2853 men, 4459 women	**Faculty:** n/av; IIA, av$
Part-time: 912 men, 1258 women	**Ph.D.s:** n/av
Graduate: 229 men, 555 women	**Student/Faculty:** n/av
Year: semesters, summer session	**Tuition:** $7096 ($8865)
Application Deadline: November 30	**Room & Board:** $8480
Freshman Class: n/av	
SAT CR/M: 470/490	**ACT:** recommended **COMPETITIVE**

California State University, San Marcos, founded in 1989, is a public commuter institution that is part of the California State University system. There are 4 undergraduate schools and 3 graduate schools. In addition to regional accreditation, Cal State San Marcos has baccalaureate program accreditation with NCATE. The library contains 257,816 volumes, 957,916 microform items, and 9,613 audio/video tapes/CDs/DVDs, and subscribes to 2,708 periodicals including electronic. Computerized library services include interlibrary loans and database searching. Special learning facilities include a learning resource center. The 304-acre campus is in a suburban area 32 miles northeast of San Diego. Including any residence halls, there are 10 buildings. The figures in the above capsule and in this profile are approximate.

Student Life: 98% of undergraduates are from California. 42% are white; 30% Hispanic. The average age of freshmen is 18; all undergraduates, 23.

Housing: College-sponsored housing includes coed on-campus apartments. 93% of students commute. Alcohol is not permitted.

Activities: There are 84 groups on campus, including chorale, computers, dance, drama, ethnic, gay, honors, international, newspaper, political, professional, religious, social, and student government. Popular campus events include Admissions Day, San Marcos Grand Festival, and Preview Day.

Sports: There are 5 intercollegiate sports for men and 5 for women. Facilities include an Olympic-quality track, Softball Field, Baseball Field, Disc Golf Course, Multi Purpose Gym.

Disabled Students: All of the campus is accessible. Facilities include wheelchair ramps, elevators, special parking, specially equipped restrooms, special class scheduling, lowered drinking fountains, and lowered telephones.

Services: There is a reader service for the blind, and remedial math, reading, and writing, a writing center, and math, accounting, and computer labs.

Campus Safety and Security: Measures include 24-hour foot and vehicle patrol and security escort services. There are emergency telephones and lighted pathways/sidewalks.

Programs of Study: Cal State San Marcos confers B.A. and B.S. degrees. Master's and doctoral degrees are also awarded. Bachelor's degrees are awarded in BIOLOGICAL SCIENCE (biochemistry, biology/biological science, and biotechnology), BUSINESS (business administration and management), COMMUNICATIONS AND THE ARTS (communications, literature, Spanish, and visual and performing arts), COMPUTER AND PHYSICAL SCIENCE (chemistry, computer science, and mathematics), HEALTH PROFESSIONS (nursing), SOCIAL SCIENCE (criminology, economics, history, human development, liberal arts/general studies, physical fitness/movement, political science/government, psychology, social science, sociology, and women's studies). Business administration, liberal studies, and communications have the largest enrollments.

Required: To graduate, students must attain foreign language proficiency at the intermediate level, fulfill a writing requirement, and maintain a GPA of 2.0. A minimum of 120 credits is required depending on the major.

Special: There is cross-registration with other CSU campuses. Internships, student-designed majors (special major) study abroad in 16 countries, and work-study programs are available. There are 6 national honor societies and 6 departmental honors programs.

Faculty/Classroom: 40% of faculty are male; 60% are female. No introductory courses are taught by graduate students. The average class size in an introductory lecture is 24; in a laboratory is 19; and in a regular course is 24.

Admissions: The SAT scores in a recent year, freshman class were: Critical Reading--60% below 500, 32% between 500 and 599, 7% between 600 and 700, and 1% above 700; Math--52% below 500, 37% between 500 and 599, 10% between 600 and 700, and 1% above 700.

Requirements: The SAT or ACT is recommended. In addition, summary of requirements and recommendations, including academic and Carnegie credits, test scores, essay, interview, audition or portfolio, GED acceptance, and any special circumstances are required. A GPA of 2.0 is required. AP and CLEP credits are accepted.

Procedure: Freshmen are admitted fall and spring. Applications should be filed by November 30 for fall entry; August 31 for spring entry, along with a $55 fee. Notifications are sent November 1. Applications are accepted online.

Transfer: In a recent year, 1165 transfer students enrolled. Requirements include 60 units completed and a 2.0 GPA for California residents, 2.4 for nonresidents. Applicants must have completed a minimum of 30 semester units in general education courses and be in good standing at their last institution of attendance. 50 of 120 credits required for the bachelor's degree must be completed at Cal State San Marcos.

Visiting: There are regularly scheduled orientations for prospective students, including workshops and a campus tour. There are guides for informal visits and visitors may sit in on classes. To schedule a visit, contact the Office of Admissions.

Financial Aid: Cal State San Marcos is a member of CSS. The FAFSA is required. Check with the school for deadline for filing freshman financial aid applications.

International Students: The school actively recruits these students. They must take the TOEFL with a minimum score of 550 on the paper-based TOEFL (PBT) or 80 on the Internet-based version (iBT).

Computers: There are 1400 institutionally owned computers and workstations with 110 computer labs and classrooms. All students may access the system. There are no time limits and no fees. It is strongly recommended that all students have a personal computer.

Graduates: In a recent year, 1665 bachelor's degrees were awarded.

Admissions Contact: Nathan Evans, Director of Admissions and Recruitment. E-Mail: *apply@csusm.edu* Web: *www.csusm.edu*

CALIFORNIA STATE UNIVERSITY, STANISLAUS B-3

Turlock, CA 95382 **(209) 667-3070; (209) 667-3788**

Full-time: 1610 men, 3010 women	**Faculty:** n/av; IIA, av$
Part-time: 665 men, 1355 women	**Ph.D.s:** n/av
Graduate: 520 men, 1190 women	**Student/Faculty:** n/av
Year: semesters, summer session	**Tuition:** $7082 ($16,000)
Application Deadline: open	**Room & Board:** $12,500
Freshman Class: n/av	

COMPETITIVE

California State University, Stanislaus, founded in 1957, is a state-supported institution offering undergraduate and graduate programs in liberal and fine arts, business, health science, and teacher preparation. Figures in the above capsule and in this profile are approximate. There are 3 undergraduate schools and 1 graduate school. In addition to regional accreditation, CSU Stanislaus has baccalaureate program accreditation with AACSB, CSWE, NASAD, NASM, and NCATE. The library contains 363,479 volumes, 1.3 million microform items, and 4,288 audio/video tapes/CDs/DVDs, and subscribes to 1,398 periodicals including electronic. Computerized library services include interlibrary loans, database searching, Internet access, and laptop Internet portals. Special learning facilities include a learning resource center, art gallery, radio station, laser lab, marine sciences station, greenhouse, art gallery, main stage theater, recital hall, observatory, art complex, and distance learning studios. The 228-acre campus is in a suburban area in the San Joaquin Valley, about 100 miles south of San Francisco. Including any residence halls, there are 26 buildings.

Student Life: 94% of undergraduates are from California. Others are from 21 states, 46 foreign countries, and Canada. 95% are from public schools. 43% are white; 27% Hispanic; 11% Asian American. The average age of freshmen is 18; all undergraduates, 25. 18% do not continue beyond their first year; 50% remain to graduate.

Housing: 650 students can be accommodated in college housing, which includes coed dorms and on-campus apartments. On-campus housing is available on a first-come and first-served basis. 90% of students commute. All students may keep cars.

Activities: 3% of men belong to 1 local and 4 national fraternities; 3% of women belong to 5 local and 3 national sororities. There are 64 groups on campus, including art, band, cheerleading, choir, chorale, chorus, computers, dance, drama, ethnic, gay, honors, international, jazz band, newspaper, opera, orchestra, photography, political, professional, radio and TV, religious, social, social service, student government, and symphony. Popular campus events include Warrior Day, College Day, and Wellness Day.

Sports: There are 6 intercollegiate sports for men and 6 for women, and 9 intramural sports for men and 9 for women. Facilities include a field house, a 2300-seat gym, softball and baseball diamonds, a soccer field, tennis courts, an all-weather track, a swimming pool, and a weight room.

Disabled Students: 99% of the campus is accessible. Facilities include wheelchair ramps, elevators, special parking, specially equipped restrooms, lowered drinking fountains, lowered telephones, special housing.

Services: Counseling and information services are available, as is tutoring in most subjects. There is a reader service for the blind, and remedial math, reading, and writing.

Campus Safety and Security: Measures include 24-hour foot and vehicle patrol, self-defense education, and security escort services. There are shuttle buses, emergency telephones, lighted pathways/sidewalks, CPR and first-aid training.

Programs of Study: CSU Stanislaus confers B.A., B.S., B.F.A., and B.M. degrees. Master's degrees are also awarded. Bachelor's degrees are awarded in AGRICULTURE (agriculture), BIOLOGICAL SCIENCE (biology/biological science), BUSINESS (business administration and management), COMMUNICATIONS AND THE ARTS (art, art history and appreciation, communications, dramatic arts, English, fine arts, French, music, music performance, and Spanish), COMPUTER AND PHYSICAL SCIENCE (applied physics, chemistry, computer science, geology, information sciences and systems, mathematics, physical sciences, and physics), EDUCATION (health education and physical education), HEALTH PROFESSIONS (nursing), SOCIAL SCIENCE (anthropology, child psychology/development, cognitive science, criminal justice, developmental psychology, economics, ethnic studies, geography, history, interdisciplinary studies, liberal arts/general studies, philosophy, political science/government, psychology, social science, and sociology). Liberal studies, business administration, and psychology have the largest enrollments.

Required: To graduate, students must complete at least 120 semester units, including 51 in the general education program and 40 in upper-division courses, with a minimum GPA of 2.0. Distribution requirements consist of 12 units of Social, Economic, and Political Institutions and Human Behavior; 9 each of Communication Skills, Natural Sciences and Mathematics, and Humanities; and 3 of Individual Resources for Modern Living.

Special: Numerous co-op programs and internships are offered. Cross-registration with the Higher Education Consortium of Central California, study abroad, work-study programs, nondegree study, an accelerated degree program, B.A.-B.S. degrees, dual majors, student-designed majors, and pass/fail options are also available. There are 10 national honor societies, including Phi Beta Kappa, a freshman honors program, and 99 departmental honors programs.

Faculty/Classroom: 53% of faculty are male; 47% are female. All teach undergraduates. No introductory courses are taught by graduate students.

Requirements: Admission is based on an eligibility index that weights GPA and the SAT or ACT scores. Applicants with a GPA of 3.0 (3.4 for nonresidents) are exempt from test score requirements. Applicants should be graduates of an accredited secondary school. Preparatory course work should include 4 years of English, 3 of math, 2 each of foreign language, history/social sciences, and lab science, 1 of visual and performing arts, and 1 academic elective. A GPA of 3.0 is required. AP and CLEP credits are accepted. Important factors in the admissions decision are advanced placement or honors courses, evidence of special talent, and geographical diversity.

Procedure: Freshmen are admitted to all sessions. Entrance exams should be taken in fall of the senior year. There is a rolling admissions plan. Check with the school for current application deadlines. The application fee is $55. Notification is sent on a rolling basis. Applications are accepted online.

Transfer: Applicants must have a college GPA of 2.0 (2.4 for nonresidents) and have completed their lower-division general education English and math courses. Those with fewer than 60 transferable semester credits must meet freshman entrance requirements. 30 of 120 credits required for the bachelor's degree must be completed at CSU Stanislaus.

Visiting: There are regularly scheduled orientations for prospective students. There are guides for informal visits and visitors may sit in on classes. To schedule a visit, contact University Outreach.

Financial Aid: The FAFSA, and the SAAC for California residents is required. Check with the school for current application deadlines.

International Students: They must take the TOEFL. They must also take the SAT or ACT.

Computers: Wireless access is available. All students may access the system. There are no time limits and no fees.

Admissions Contact: Lisa Bernardo, Director of Admissions and Records. A campus DVD is available. E-Mail: *outreach_help_desk@csustan.edu* Web: *www.csustan.edu*

CHAPMAN UNIVERSITY — D-5

Orange, CA 92866 — **(714) 997-6711**
(888) CU-APPLY; (714) 997-6713

Full-time: 2331 men, 3422 women	**Faculty:** 319; IIA, ++$
Part-time: 142 men, 110 women	**Ph.D.s:** 85%
Graduate: 796 men, 1091 women	**Student/Faculty:** 14 to 1
Year: 4-1-4, summer session	**Tuition:** $43,573
Application Deadline: January 15	**Room & Board:** $12,446

Freshman Class: 11750 applied, 5253 accepted, 1289 enrolled
SAT CR/M/W: 590/610/610 **ACT:** 26 **VERYCOMPETITIVE+**

Chapman University, founded in 1861, is one of the oldest, most prestigious private universities in California. Chapman's picturesque campus is located in the heart of Orange County, one of the nation's most exciting centers of arts, business, science and technology, and draws outstanding students from across the United States and around the world. Known for its blend of liberal arts and professional programs, Chapman University encompasses seven schools and colleges. The university's mission is to provide personalized education of distinction that leads to inquiring, ethical and productive lives as global citizens. There are 6 undergraduate schools and 7 graduate schools. In addition to regional accreditation, Chapman has baccalaureate program accreditation with AACSB and NASM. The 2 libraries contain 309,464 volumes, 689,109 microform items, and 24,188 audio/video tapes/CDs/DVDs, and subscribe to 62,680 periodicals including electronic. Computerized library services include interlibrary loans, database searching, Internet access, and Wi-Fi capability. Special learning facilities include an art gallery, radio station, food science sensory lab and economic sciences lab. The 78-acre campus is in a suburban area 35 miles southeast of Los Angeles. Including any residence halls, there are 40 buildings.

Student Life: 71% of undergraduates are from California. Others are from 49 states, 59 foreign countries, and Canada. 60% are White; 14% Hispanic. 31% are Catholic; 31% Protestant; 14% claim no religious affiliation; 14% Buddhist, Baha'i, Eastern Orthodox, Hindu, and Muslim. The average age of freshmen is 18; all undergraduates, 20. 9% do not continue beyond their first year; 76% remain to graduate.

Housing: 1958 students can be accommodated in college housing, which includes coed dorms, on-campus apartments, and married student housing. In addition, there are special-interest houses. On-campus housing is guaranteed for the freshman year only, is available on a first-come, first-served basis, and is available on a lottery system for upperclassmen. Priority is given to out-of-town students. 68% of students commute. All students may keep cars.

Activities: 28% of men belong to 9 national fraternities; 38% of women belong to 8 national sororities. Groups on campus include art, band, cheerleading, choir, chorale, chorus, computers, dance, debate, drama, environmental, ethnic, film, forensics, gay, honors, international, jazz band, literary magazine, musical theater, newspaper, opera, orchestra, pep band, photography, political, professional, radio and TV, religious, social, social service, student government, symphony, and yearbook. Popular campus events include Lunchtime Concerts, Spring Sizzle and All University Formal.

Sports: There are 9 intercollegiate sports for men and 10 for women, and 4 intramural sports for men and 4 for women. Facilities include gym, weight room, soccer/football field, aquatic center, and tennis courts; baseball and softball fields are also available for student use nearby in the city of Orange.

Disabled Students: 75% of the campus is accessible. Facilities include wheelchair ramps, elevators, special parking, specially equipped restrooms, special class scheduling, lowered drinking fountains, lowered telephones, and special housing.

Services: Counseling and information services are available, as is tutoring in most subjects. There is a reader service for the blind, and remedial math, reading, and writing. there are note takers, readers, and tapes for deaf, blind, and international students; special study skills workshops; and help for the learning disabled.

Campus Safety and Security: Measures include 24-hour foot and vehicle patrol, emergency notification system, self-defense education, and security escort services. There are emergency telephones, lighted pathways/sidewalks, controlled access to dorms/residences, rape awareness, and victim assistance programs.

Programs of Study: Chapman confers B.A., B.S., B.F.A. and B.M. degrees. Master's and doctoral degrees are also awarded. Bachelor's degrees are awarded in BIOLOGICAL SCIENCE (biochemistry and biology/biological science), BUSINESS (accounting and business administration and management), COMMUNICATIONS AND THE ARTS (acting, art, art history and appreciation, broadcasting, communications, creative writing, dance, dramatic arts, English, film arts, film, television and digital media, French, graphic design, keyboard - piano concentration, music, music performance, music theory and composition, playwriting/screenwriting, public relations, Spanish, strategic communication, and theatre studies), COMPUTER AND PHYSICAL SCIENCE (chemistry, computer science, digital arts/technology, information sciences and systems, mathematics, physics, and software engineering), EDUCATION (athletic training, education, and music education), ENGINEERING AND ENVIRONMENTAL DESIGN (environmental science), HEALTH PROFESSIONS (health science and kinesiology), SOCIAL SCIENCE (economics, history, peace studies, philosophy, political science/government, psychology, religion, social work, and sociology). Business, computational science, and history are the strongest academically. Business, film production, and communication studies have the largest enrollments.

Required: Students in the baccalaureate program must complete a total of 124 credits with at least a 2.0 GPA. The general education program includes courses in artistic inquiry, natural science inquiry, quantitative inquiry, social inquiry, values and ethical inquiry, and written inquiry. Freshman foundation, global citizenship, and interdisciplinary courses are also required.

Special: Internship programs are available. Students are encouraged to study abroad for a semester or spend a semester in Washington, D.C. Dual and student-designed majors are possible. A general studies degree, B.A.-B.S. degrees, nondegree study options, and pass/fail options are also permitted. A 3-2 engineering degree with the University of California, Irvine, is possible. There are 13 national honor societies and a freshman honors program.

Faculty/Classroom: 58% of faculty are male; 42% are female. 89% teach undergraduates. No introductory courses are taught by graduate students. The average class size in an introductory lecture is 24 and in a laboratory is 20.

Admissions: 45% of the 2013-2014 applicants were accepted. The SAT scores for the 2013-2014 freshman class were: Critical Reading--7% below 500, 43% between 500 and 599, 41% between 600 and 699, and 9% between 700 and 800; Math--4% below 500, 36% between 500 and 599, 50% between 600 and 699, and 10% between 700 and 800; Writing--4% below 500, 39% between 500 and 599, 46% between 600 and 699, and 11% between 700 and 800. The ACT scores were 2% below 21, 11% between 21 and 23, 31% between 24 and 26, 25% between 27 and 28, and 30% above 28. 80% of the current freshmen were in the top fifth of their class; 97% were in the top two fifths.

Requirements: The SAT or ACT is required. The ACT Optional Writing test is also required. Applicants should be graduates of accredited high schools or have earned the GED. Secondary preparation should include 4 years of English, foreign language, math, and social science; and 2 years of science. Prospective art or music majors should show some preparation in those fields. A personal essay is required. An on-campus interview is recommended. Entry to the film school requires portfolio acceptance. Dance performance and theater performance require audition. AP and CLEP credits are accepted. Important factors in the admissions decision are advanced placement or honors courses, evidence of special talent, and leadership record.

Procedure: Freshmen are admitted fall and spring. Entrance exams should be taken by fall of the senior year. Applications should be filed by January 15 for fall entry; November 1 for spring entry, along with a $65 fee. Notifications are sent March 15. 377 applicants were on the 2013 waiting list; 90 were admitted. Applications are accepted online.

Transfer: 394 transfer students enrolled in 2012-2013. Transfer applicants should have completed at least 12 credits of transferable college work with a 2.25 minimum GPA. High school records and SAT or ACT scores should be submitted if fewer than 30 transferable credits have been completed. 48 of 124 credits required for the bachelor's degree must be completed at Chapman.

Visiting: There are regularly scheduled orientations for prospective students, consisting of Fall and Spring Campus Exploration Day events. Weekday appointments and campus tours are also available. There are guides for informal visits and visitors may sit in on classes. To schedule a visit, contact the Office of Admissions.

Financial Aid: Chapman is a member of CSS. The FAFSA and the state aid form are required. The priority date for freshman financial aid applications for fall entry is March 2.

International Students: There are 217 international students enrolled. The school actively recruits these students. They must take the TOEFL with a minimum score of 550 on the paper-based TOEFL (PBT) or 79 on the Internet-based version (iBT). They must also take the SAT or ACT.

Computers: All students may access the system 24 hours, 7 days a week. There are no time limits and no fees.

Graduates: From July 1, 2012 to June 30, 2013, 1300 bachelor's degrees were awarded. The most popular majors were business administration (15%), film production (14%), and communication studies (9%). In an average class, 2% graduate in 3 years or less, 59% graduate in 4 years or less, 73% graduate in 5 years or less, and 76% graduate in 6 years or less.

Admissions Contact: Mike Drummy, Assistant Vice President and Chief Admission Officer. E-Mail: *admit@chapman.edu* Web: *www.chapman .edu*

CLAREMONT COLLEGES, THE

The Claremont Colleges, established in 1925, is a private system in California. It is governed by the council of the Claremont Colleges, whose chief administrator is the chief executive officer. The primary goal of the system is to provide outstanding instruction to its undergraduate, graduate, and professional students. The total student enrollment is usually 6,500 and 1,010 faculty members. Altogether there are 194 baccalaureate, 24 master's, and 15 doctoral programs offered in Claremont Colleges. Profiles of the 4-year campuses are included in this section.

CLAREMONT MCKENNA COLLEGE — D-5

Claremont, CA 91711 — **(909) 621-8088; (909) 621-8516**

Full-time: 660 men, 600 women	**Faculty:** 138; IIB, ++$
Part-time: 1 men, 3 women	**Ph.D.s:** 96%
Graduate: 25 men, 6 women	**Student/Faculty:** n/av
Year: semesters, summer session	**Tuition:** $44,085
Application Deadline: January 2	**Room & Board:** $13,980
Freshman Class: 5058 applied, 688 accepted, 291 enrolled	
SAT CR/M/W: 700/720/710 **ACT:** 31	**MOST COMPETITIVE**

Established in 1946, Claremont McKenna College (CMC) is a highly selective, independent, coeducational, residential, undergraduate liberal arts college with a curricular emphasis on economics, government, and public affairs. Unlike so many other colleges, which champion either a traditional liberal arts education or the acquisition of professional and technical skills, CMC builds bridges between the two. By combining the intellectual breadth of the liberal arts with the more pragmatic concerns of public affairs, based on principles established by founding President George C. S. Benson, CMC helps students acquire the vision, skills, and values they will need to lead society. As expressed in the College's mission statement CMC seeks to "educate its students for thoughtful and productive lives and responsible leadership in business, government, and the professions, and to support faculty and student scholarship that contribute to intellectual vitality and the understanding of public policy issues." The library contains 1.4 million volumes, 980,340 microform items, and 10,287 audio/video tapes/CDs/ DVDs, and subscribes to 22,978 periodicals including electronic. Computerized library services include interlibrary loans, database searching, and Internet access. The 69-acre campus is in a suburban area 35 miles east of downtown Los Angeles.

Student Life: 61% of undergraduates are from out of state. Students are from 45 states, 32 foreign countries, and Canada. 45% are White; 13% race unknown; 12% Foreign; 11% Asian American. The average age of freshmen is 18; all undergraduates, 20. 5% do not continue beyond their first year; 92% remain to graduate.

Housing: 1129 students can be accommodated in college housing, which includes single-sex and coed dorms and on-campus apartments. All are substance-free. On-campus housing is guaranteed for the freshman year only. 94% of students live on campus. Upperclassmen may keep cars.

Activities: There are no fraternities or sororities. Groups on campus include debate, religious, social service, and student government.

Sports: There are 10 intercollegiate sports for men and 11 for women. Facilities include basketball courts, a weight room, a fitness center, a track and football field, an aquatic center, tennis courts, baseball, softball, lacrosse, and soccer fields, an archery range, and squash and volleyball courts.

Disabled Students: Facilities include wheelchair ramps, elevators, special parking, specially equipped restrooms. the campus complies with ADA requirements and reasonably accommodates students with physical disabilities as necessary to meet their access needs.

Services: The Center for Writing and Public Discourse offers writing assistance and specialized workshops.

Campus Safety and Security: Measures include 24-hour foot and vehicle patrol, emergency notification system, and security escort services. There are emergency telephones, lighted pathways/sidewalks, and controlled access to dorms/residences.

Programs of Study: CMC confers B.A. degrees. Master's degrees are also awarded. Bachelor's degrees are awarded in AGRICULTURE (environmental studies), BIOLOGICAL SCIENCE (biochemistry, biology/ biological science, biophysics, molecular biology, and neurosciences), BUSINESS (accounting and management engineering), COMMUNICATIONS AND THE ARTS (classics, film arts, French, literature, media arts, Spanish, and theatre arts), COMPUTER AND PHYSICAL SCIENCE (chemistry, mathematics, physics, and science and management), ENGINEERING AND ENVIRONMENTAL DESIGN (environmental science), SOCIAL SCIENCE (American studies, Asian/Oriental studies, economics, Hispanic American studies, history, interdisciplinary studies, international relations, legal studies, Middle Eastern studies, philosophy, political science/government, psychology, and religion).

Required: All students must complete 32 courses (128 semester hours), including General Education, major and grade-point requirements.

Special: Internships, Washington DC and Silicon Valley programs, BA/ MA program in Finance, 3-2 engineering degree, cross registration with the Claremont Colleges, study abroad programs, ten research institutes, and the Robert Day Scholars program. There are including Phi Beta Kappa.

Faculty/Classroom: 65% of faculty are male; 35% are female. No introductory courses are taught by graduate students. The average class size in a regular course is 18.

Admissions: 14% of the 2013-2014 applicants were accepted. The SAT scores for the 2013-2014 freshman class were: Critical Reading--7% between 500 and 599, 43% between 600 and 699, and 51% between 700 and 800; Math--3% between 500 and 599, 38% between 600 and 699, and 60% between 700 and 800; Writing--7% between 500 and 599, 36% between 600 and 699, and 57% between 700 and 800.

Requirements: The SAT or ACT is required. The ACT Optional Writing test is also required. AP credits are accepted. Important factors in the admissions decision are advanced placement or honors courses, leadership record, and extracurricular activities record.

Procedure: Freshmen are admitted fall. Entrance exams should be taken no later than fall of senior year. There is a early decision plan. Early decision applications should be filed by November 1; regular applications, by January 2 for fall entry; and November 1 for spring entry, along with a $60 fee. Notification of early decision is sent December 15; regular decision, April 1. 152 early decision candidates were accepted for the 2013-2014 class. 549 applicants were on the 2013 waiting list; 54 were admitted. Applications are accepted online.

Transfer: 34 transfer students enrolled in 2012-2013. 64 of 128 credits required for the bachelor's degree must be completed at CMC.

Visiting: There are regularly scheduled orientations for prospective students. There are guides for informal visits, visitors may sit in on classes, and stay overnight. To schedule a visit, contact the Office of Admission.

Financial Aid: In 2013-2014, 49% of all full-time freshmen and 47% of continuing full-time students received some form of financial aid. 46% of all full-time freshmen and 41% of continuing full-time students received need-based aid. The average freshman award was $39,953. CMC is a member of CSS. The CSS/Profile, FAFSA, and the state aid form are required. The priority date for freshman financial aid applications for fall entry is February 1. The deadline for filing freshman financial aid applications for fall entry is February 1.

International Students: There are 152 international students enrolled. The school actively recruits these students. They must take the TOEFL with a minimum score of 600 on the paper-based TOEFL (PBT) or 100 on the Internet-based version (iBT). They must also take the SAT or ACT.

Computers: All students may access the system. There are no time limits and no fees.

Graduates: From July 1, 2012 to June 30, 2013, 317 bachelor's degrees were awarded. The most popular majors were economics (30%), government (15%), and psychology (15%). 150 companies recruited on campus in 2012-2013. In an average class, 80% graduate in 4 years or less, 91% graduate in 5 years or less, and 92% graduate in 6 years or less.

Admissions Contact: Georgette R. DeVeres, AVP and Dean of Admission & Fin Aid. E-Mail: *admission@cmc.edu* Web: *www.cmc.edu*

COGSWELL POLYTECHNICAL COLLEGE B-3

Sunnyvale, CA 94089 (408) 541-0100, ext.147 (800)-264-7955; (408) 747-0764

Full-time: 142 men, 45 women	**Faculty:** 11
Part-time: 87 men, 14 women	**Ph.D.s:** 35%
Graduate: n/av	**Student/Faculty:** 12 to 1
Year: semesters, summer session	**Tuition:** $20,168
Application Deadline: open	**Room & Board:** $11,363
Freshman Class: 146 applied, 79 accepted, 45 enrolled	
SAT or ACT: recommended	

COMPETITIVE

Strategically located in Silicon Valley and with over one hundred and twenty years of academic history, Cogswell College provides accredited higher education that empowers students to innovate through the integration of art, engineering and entrepreneurship. There is 1 undergraduate school and 1 graduate school. The library contains 103,000 volumes, 250 microform items, and 831 audio/video tapes/CDs/DVDs, and subscribes to 16 periodicals including electronic. Computerized library services include database searching. Special learning facilities include an art gallery, radio station, drawing and sculpture studios, digital arts labs, audio labs, and a recording studio. The 4-acre campus is in a suburban area 40 miles south of San Francisco in California's Silicon Valley. Including any residence halls, there is 1 building. The figures in the above capsule and in this profile are approximate.

Student Life: 88% of undergraduates are from California. Others are from 13 states, and 2 foreign countries. 65% are from public schools. 49% are white; 15% Hispanic. The average age of freshmen is 19; all undergraduates, 28. 29% do not continue beyond their first year; 71% remain to graduate.

Housing: 70 students can be accommodated in college housing, which includes off-campus apartments. Arrangements can be made to accommodate students in private houses or at nearby corporate apartments. Alcohol is not permitted. All students commute. All students may keep cars.

Activities: There are no fraternities or sororities. Groups on campus include art, computers, honors, international, jazz band, radio and TV, and student government. Popular campus events include Founders Day, club competitions, and Friday concerts.

Sports: There is no sports program at Cogswell College. Facilities include a game room, a student lounge, and access to community athletic facilities.

Disabled Students: Facilities include wheelchair ramps, special parking, specially equipped restrooms, special class scheduling, lowered drinking fountains, and lowered telephones.

Services: There is remedial math and writing. On campus tutoring is available if needed for any subjects.

Campus Safety and Security: Measures include emergency notification system. There are emergency telephones, lighted pathways/sidewalks, controlled access to dorms/residences, an emergency evacuation plan, and maps in the classrooms.

Programs of Study: Cogswell College confers B.A.D.A.A., B.S.D.A.T., B.S.D.A.E., B.S.(Comp Eng), B.S.S.E., B.S.F.A., B.S.F.P.T., B.A.E.I. degrees. Master's degrees are also awarded. Bachelor's degrees are awarded in BUSINESS (entrepreneurial studies), COMMUNICATIONS AND THE ARTS (animation, audio technology, and music technology), COMPUTER AND PHYSICAL SCIENCE (computer programming, digital arts/technology, and web technology), ENGINEERING AND ENVIRONMENTAL DESIGN (computer engineering and computer graphics), SOCIAL SCIENCE (fire control and safety technology and fire protection). Digital Art and Animation and, Digital Audio Technology, have the strongest and largest enrollments.

Required: To graduate, students must complete a total of 120 to 131 credits with 18 to 27 in the major and have a 2.0 GPA. 45 to 56 credits in general education core courses are required, depending on the major, and include courses in English, math, natural sciences, social sciences, and humanities.

Special: Cogswell offers various internships and work-study programs. The college administers the Degree at a Distance Program (DDP) for the Fire Service program for Arizona, California, and Nevada, through which nonresident students can earn a B.S. in Fire Administration or Fire Prevention and Technology. There is a freshman honors program.

Faculty/Classroom: 65% of faculty are male; 35% are female. No introductory courses are taught by graduate students. The average class size in an introductory lecture is 15; in a laboratory is 8; and in a regular course is 25.

Admissions: In a recent year, 54% of applicants were accepted.

Requirements: The SAT or ACT is recommended. Applicants must be high school graduates or have the GED. Secondary preparation must include 3 years of English, 2 to 3 of math, including algebra, geometry, and trigonometry, and 1 year of science. Cogswell requires a personal essay and recommends a personal interview. A portfolio is required for computer and video imaging programs. A GPA of 2.7 is required. AP and CLEP credits are accepted. Important factors in the admissions decision are evidence of special talent, recommendations by school officials, and ability to finance college education.

Procedure: Freshmen are admitted to all sessions. There is a rolling admissions plan. Application deadlines are open. Applications are accepted online.

Transfer: Applicants must have completed at least 12 college credits with a 2.2 GPA. An interview is recommended. 40 of 120 credits required for the bachelor's degree must be completed at Cogswell College.

Visiting: Visitors may sit in on classes. To schedule a visit, contact Admissions.

Financial Aid: In a recent year, 77% of all full-time freshmen and 75% of continuing full-time students received some form of financial aid. 75% of all full-time freshmen and 72% of continuing full-time students received need-based aid. 4% of undergraduate students work part-time. The average financial indebtedness of a recent graduate class was $22,352. Cogswell College is a member of CSS. The FAFSA and the college's own financial statement are required. Check with the school for current application deadlines.

International Students: There are 11 international students enrolled. They must take the TOEFL with a minimum score of 525 on the paper-based TOEFL (PBT).

Computers: All students may access the system. There are no time limits and no fees. It is strongly recommended that all students have a personal computer.

Graduates: In a recent year, 47 bachelor's degrees were awarded. The most popular majors were digital art and animation (43%), fire administration (34%), and digital audio technology (15%). In an average class, 33% graduate in 4 years or less, 44% graduate in 5 years or less, and 55% graduate in 6 years or less.

Admissions Contact: Abraham Chacko, Director of Admissions. E-Mail: *admissions@cogswell.edu Web: www.cogswell.edu*

CONCORDIA UNIVERSITY - IRVINE D-5

Irvine, CA 92612 (949) 854-8002, ext. 1118 (800) 229-1200; (949) 854-6894

Full-time: 618 men, 974 women	**Faculty:** n/av
Part-time: 39 men, 107 women	**Ph.D.s:** n/av
Graduate: 837 men, 944 women	**Student/Faculty:** n/av
Year: semesters, summer session	**Tuition:** $26,800
Application Deadline:	**Room & Board:** $8590
Freshman Class: n/av	
SAT or ACT: required	

VERY COMPETITIVE

Concordia University, founded in 1972, is a private liberal arts college affiliated with the Lutheran Church-Missouri Synod. There are 5 undergraduate schools and 4 graduate schools. The library contains 82,600 volumes, 54,550 microform items, and 2,000 audio/video tapes/CDs/DVDs, and subscribes to 10,513 periodicals including electronic. Computerized library services include interlibrary loans, database searching, and Internet access. Special learning facilities include an art gallery, newspaper. The 70-acre campus is in a suburban area 40 miles south of Los Angeles. Including any residence halls, there are 26 buildings.

Student Life: 89% of undergraduates are from California. Others are from 34 states, 18 foreign countries, and Canada. 66% are White; 13% Hispanic. 16% are Catholic; 15% Non-denominational. The average age of freshmen is 18; all undergraduates, 22. 73% remain to graduate.

Housing: 1077 students can be accommodated in college housing, which includes single-sex dorms. On-campus housing is guaranteed for all 4 years. 69% of students live on campus; of those, 95% remain on campus on weekends. All students may keep cars.

Activities: There are no fraternities or sororities. There are 20 groups on campus, including art, choir, chorale, chorus, communications, dance, debate, drama, ethnic, film, forensics, honors, literary magazine, newspaper, political, radio and TV, religious, social, social service, student government, and yearbook. Popular campus events include Closing Banquet, Christmas Dance and Oktoberfest.

Sports: There are 9 intercollegiate sports for men and 10 for women, and 7 intramural sports for men and 6 for women. Facilities include a 1800-seat gym, a soccer field, a baseball/softball diamond, volleyball, tennis, and racquetball courts, a track field, a weight room, a dance room, team rooms, and locker rooms.

Disabled Students: 90% of the campus is accessible. Facilities include wheelchair ramps, elevators, special parking, and specially equipped restrooms.

Services: Counseling and information services are available, as is tutoring

in some subjects, math, chemistry, critical thinking, Spanish, biology and calculus.

Campus Safety and Security: Measures include 24-hour foot and vehicle patrol and security escort services. There are lighted pathways/sidewalks.

Programs of Study: Concordia Irvine confers B.A. degrees. Associate and master's degrees are also awarded. Bachelor's degrees are awarded in BIOLOGICAL SCIENCE (biology/biological science), BUSINESS (business administration and management), COMMUNICATIONS AND THE ARTS (art, communications, dramatic arts, English, film arts, and music), COMPUTER AND PHYSICAL SCIENCE (chemistry and mathematics), EDUCATION (Christian education and early childhood education), HEALTH PROFESSIONS (exercise science), SOCIAL SCIENCE (behavioral science, biblical languages, history, humanities, international studies, liberal arts/general studies, political science/government, psychology, and theological studies). Business administration, education and social science are the strongest academically.

Required: All students must complete 49 semester hours of general education requirements, including courses in humanities and fine arts, math and science, social science, religion, and exercise and sport science. A total of 128 credits is required to graduate. A GPA of 2.0 in major and program course work must be maintained. For the CU Accelerate program, 120 semester units are required to graduate.

Special: Cross-registration is possible with 9 Concordia University institutions nationwide. An accelerated degree program in either applied liberal arts or business administration and leadership. Internships, study abroad, and dual and student-designed majors are available. There are 6 national honor societies, a freshman honors program, and 2 departmental honors programs.

Faculty/Classroom: 63% of faculty are male; 37% are female. No introductory courses are taught by graduate students.

Requirements: The SAT or ACT is required. Applicants should be high school graduates with 4 years of English, 3 each of math and science, and 2 each of social studies and a foreign language. The GED is accepted. A school reference is also required. A GPA of 2.8 is required. AP and CLEP credits are accepted.

Procedure: Freshmen are admitted fall and spring. Entrance exams should be taken by the fall of the senior year. There are deferred admissions and rolling admissions plans. Check with the school for current application deadlines. The fall 2013 application fee was $50. Notification is sent on a rolling basis. Applications are accepted online.

Transfer: A GPA of 2.3 is required in a minimum of 24 semester or 36 quarter units completed. An academic reference is required, as are official high school transcripts. 32 of 128 credits required for the bachelor's degree must be completed at Concordia Irvine.

Visiting: There are regularly scheduled orientations for prospective students. There are guides for informal visits, visitors may sit in on classes, and stay overnight. To schedule a visit, contact the Admission Office.

Financial Aid: The FAFSA and the college's own financial statement are required. Check with the school for current application deadlines.

International Students: The school actively recruits these students. They must take the TOEFL. They must also take the SAT or ACT.

Computers: All students may access the system. There are no time limits and no fees.

Admissions Contact: Scott Rhodes, Executive Director of Admissions.
E-Mail: *scott.rhodes@cui.edu* Web: *www.cui.edu*

DOMINICAN UNIVERSITY OF CALIFORNIA — B-3

San Rafael, CA 94901-2298 — **(888) 323-6763**
(888) 323-6763; (415) 485-3214

Full-time: 350 men, 1000 women	**Faculty:** n/av
Part-time: 75 men, 200 women	**Ph.D.s:** 74%
Graduate: 215 men, 500 women	**Student/Faculty:** n/av
Year: semesters, summer session	**Tuition:** $37,850
Application Deadline: open	**Room & Board:** $14,400
Freshman Class: n/av	
SAT or ACT: required	

COMPETITIVE

Dominican University of California, founded in 1890, is an independent, international, learner-centered university of Catholic heritage. The figures in the above capsule and in this profile are approximate. There are 4 undergraduate schools and 4 graduate schools. In addition to regional accreditation, Dominican has baccalaureate program accreditation with NLN. The library contains 92,536 volumes, 3,500 microform items, and 1,640 audio/video tapes/CDs/DVDs, and subscribes to 597 periodicals including electronic. Computerized library services include interlibrary loans, database searching, Internet access, and laptop Internet portals. Special learning facilities include a learning resource center, art gallery, radio station, music library, and art history slide and print collection. The 80-acre campus is in a suburban area 12 miles north of San Francisco. Including any residence halls, there are 25 buildings.

Student Life: 91% of undergraduates are from California. Others are from 31 states, 15 foreign countries, and Canada. 48% are from public schools. 33% are white; 25% Asian American; 18% Hispanic. 38% are Catholic. The average age of freshmen is 18; all undergraduates, 24. 16% do not continue beyond their first year; 34% remain to graduate.

Housing: 600 students can be accommodated in college housing, which includes coed dorms. On-campus housing is available on a first-come, first-served basis, and is available on a lottery system for upperclassmen. 55% of students commute. Upperclassmen may keep cars.

Activities: There are no fraternities or sororities. There are 27 groups on campus, including art, band, cheerleading, choir, chorale, dance, drama, environmental, ethnic, film, gay, honors, international, jazz band, literary magazine, musical theater, newspaper, orchestra, photography, political, professional, radio and TV, religious, social service, and student government. Popular campus events include Shield Day (welcoming the freshman class), Boat Dance, and Penguin Ball.

Sports: There are 5 intercollegiate sports for men and 7 for women, and 5 intramural sports for men and 5 for women. Facilities include a gym, a fitness center, a 6-lane swimming pool, 2 full-sized basketball courts, a multipurpose room for dance and exercise classes, tennis courts, and a soccer field.

Disabled Students: 50% of the campus is accessible. Facilities include wheelchair ramps, elevators, special parking, specially equipped restrooms, special class scheduling, and lowered drinking fountains.

Services: Counseling and information services are available, as is tutoring in most subjects, writing, math, chemistry, economics, time management, study skills, anatomy, physiology, algebra, and physics. There is a reader service for the blind, and remedial math and writing.

Campus Safety and Security: Measures include 24-hour foot and vehicle patrol, emergency notification system, and security escort services. There are emergency telephones, lighted pathways/sidewalks, and controlled access to dorms/residences.

Programs of Study: Dominican confers B.A., B.S., B.F.A., and B.S.N. degrees. Master's degrees are also awarded. Bachelor's degrees are awarded in AGRICULTURE (environmental studies), BIOLOGICAL SCIENCE (biology/biological science), BUSINESS (business administration and management and international business management), COMMUNICATIONS AND THE ARTS (art, art history and appreciation, communications, creative writing, dance, English literature, graphic design, and music), HEALTH PROFESSIONS (nursing, occupational therapy, and premedicine), SOCIAL SCIENCE (history, humanities, international studies, liberal arts/general studies, political science/government, psychology, religion, and women's studies). Nursing, biology, psychology, and business management have the largest enrollments.

Required: All students must complete 124 credit hours including at least 24 in upper-division work, with a minimum 2.0 GPA. Core requirements include a cultural heritage colloquium of 9 units, 6 units each in religion and first-year interdisciplinary studies, 3 to 4 units each of math and quantitative reasoning, natural science, social science, moral philosophy and ethics, and creative and performing arts, and 1 unit of information and research. Students must pass a computer competency test, and a senior thesis, project, recital, or comprehensive exam is required.

Special: There is a semester interchange program with colleges in Michigan, Florida, or New York. Dominican also offers study abroad, dual majors for students with a 3.0 GPA or better, B.A.-B.S. degrees, student-designed majors, a Washington semester, internships, pass/fail options outside of major and general education courses, and an evening/weekend bachelor's degree program. There are 3 national honor societies, including Phi Beta Kappa, a freshman honors program, and 3 departmental honors programs.

Faculty/Classroom: 47% of faculty are male; 53% are female. All teach undergraduates, 75% do research, and 75% do both. No introductory courses are taught by graduate students. The average class size in an introductory lecture is 19; in a laboratory is 15; and in a regular course is 15.

Requirements: The SAT or ACT is required. In addition, applicants must be graduates of an accredited high school or have earned the GED. Secondary preparation must include 4 years of English, 2 each of math and a foreign language, and 1 each of lab science and history. An essay and a recommendation are required. An interview and a visit to the campus are highly recommended. Prospective music majors are encouraged to schedule an audition. AP and CLEP credits are accepted. Important factors in the admissions decision are recommendations by school officials, extracurricular activities record, and evidence of special talent.

Procedure: Freshmen are admitted fall and spring. Entrance exams should be taken in the late fall or early spring of the senior year. There are deferred admissions and rolling admissions plans. Application deadlines are open. Application fee is $50. Applications are accepted online.

Transfer: In a recent year, 110 transfer students enrolled. Applicants must have a 2.0 GPA at an accredited college. They must also submit official high school and college transcripts and a letter of recommendation from a professor, academic dean, or counselor. 30 of 124 credits required for the bachelor's degree must be completed at Dominican.

Visiting: There are regularly scheduled orientations for prospective stu-

dents, including financial aid conferences, lunch on campus, meeting with the prospective academic adviser, and a campus tour. There are guides for informal visits and visitors may sit in on classes. To schedule a visit, contact the Admissions Office.

Financial Aid: In a recent year, 97% of all full-time freshmen and 85% of continuing full-time students received some form of financial aid. 70% of all full-time freshmen and 72% of continuing full-time students received need-based aid. Need-based scholarships or need-based grants averaged $14,006 ($28,922 maximum); need-based self-help aid (loans and jobs) averaged $4,646 ($7,375 maximum); non-need-based athletic scholarships averaged $2,567 ($6,000 maximum); and other non-need based awards and non-need-based scholarships averaged $7,660 ($15,500 maximum). 17% of undergraduate students work part-time. The average financial indebtedness of a recent graduate class was $19,092. Dominican is a member of CSS. The FAFSA and the college's own financial statement are required. Check with the school for current application deadlines.

International Students: There are 30 international students enrolled. The school actively recruits these students. They must take the TOEFL with a minimum score of 550 on the paper-based TOEFL (PBT) or 80 on the Internet-based version (iBT). They must also take the SAT or ACT.

Computers: All students may access the system. There is a 2-hour time limit only when other students are waiting. There are no fees.

Graduates: In a recent year, 283 bachelor's degrees were awarded. The most popular majors were nursing (27%), psychology (15%), and business (11%). In an average class, 44% graduate in 4 years or less, 46% graduate in 5 years or less, and 51% graduate in 6 years or less.

Admissions Contact: Rebecca Finn Kenney, Asst. VP of Undergraduate Admissions. E-Mail: *enroll@dominican.edu* Web: *www.dominican.edu*

FRESNO PACIFIC UNIVERSITY C-3

Fresno, CA 93702 (559) 453-2039
(800) 660-6089; (559) 453-2007

Full-time: 701 men, 1448 women	**Faculty:** n/av; IIA, --$
Part-time: 108 men, 182 women	**Ph.D.s:** n/av
Graduate: 320 men, 701 women	**Student/Faculty:** n/av
Year: semesters, summer session	**Tuition:** $25,236
Application Deadline:	**Room & Board:** $6900
Freshman Class: n/av	
SAT or ACT: required	

COMPETITIVE

Fresno Pacific University, founded in 1944, is a private Christian liberal arts college offering both undergraduate and graduate degrees, affiliated with the Mennonite Brethren. There are 4 undergraduate schools and 5 graduate schools. The library contains 197,532 volumes, 315,000 microform items, and 7,840 audio/video tapes/CDs/DVDs, and subscribes to 3,200 periodicals including electronic. Computerized library services include interlibrary loans, database searching, and Internet access. Special learning facilities include a The 42-acre campus is in a suburban area 150 miles southeast of San Francisco. Including any residence halls, there are 20 buildings.

Student Life: 97% of undergraduates are from California. Others are from 14 states, 12 foreign countries, and Canada. 86% are from public schools. 50% are White; 29% Hispanic. 79% are Protestant; 15% Catholic. The average age of freshmen is 20; all undergraduates, 21. 20% do not continue beyond their first year; 62% remain to graduate.

Housing: 550 students can be accommodated in college housing, which includes single-sex dorms, on-campus apartments, and off-campus apartments. In addition, there are special-interest houses. On-campus housing is available on a first-come, first-served basis, and is available on a lottery system for upperclassmen. Priority is given to out-of-town students. 51% of students commute. Alcohol is not permitted. All students may keep cars.

Activities: There are no fraternities or sororities. There are 20 groups on campus, including art, cheerleading, choir, chorale, chorus, communications, dance, drama, ethnic, honors, international, jazz band, newspaper, pep band, political, professional, religious, social, social service, and student government. Popular campus events include Carol Sing, Winter Ball, and Junior/Senior Banquet.

Sports: There are 8 intercollegiate sports for men and 8 for women, and 9 intramural sports for men and 9 for women. Facilities include a gym, 3 soccer fields, a swimming pool, a track and field facility, a weight room, 2 racquetball courts, and 7 tennis courts.

Disabled Students: All of the campus is accessible. Facilities include wheelchair ramps, elevators, special parking, specially equipped restrooms, lowered drinking fountains, lowered telephones, and special housing.

Services: Counseling and information services are available, as is tutoring in every subject. There is a reader service for the blind, and remedial math, reading, and writing. audio books

Campus Safety and Security: Measures include 24-hour foot and vehicle patrol, self-defense education, and security escort services. There are shuttle buses, emergency telephones, lighted pathways/sidewalks, 24-hour CCTV monitored in real-time closed-circuit security cameras. 16 cameras create a virtual perimeter patrol of the campus with 5 emergency telephones and 8 regular telephones.

Programs of Study: FPU confers B.A., and B.S. degrees. Associate and master's degrees are also awarded. Bachelor's degrees are awarded in BIOLOGICAL SCIENCE (biology/biological science), BUSINESS (accounting, business administration and management, and sports management), COMMUNICATIONS AND THE ARTS (English, music, and Spanish), COMPUTER AND PHYSICAL SCIENCE (chemistry, mathematics, and natural sciences), EDUCATION (English education, mathematics education, music education, physical education, science education, and social science education), ENGINEERING AND ENVIRONMENTAL DESIGN (environmental science), HEALTH PROFESSIONS (premedicine), SOCIAL SCIENCE (history, ministries, missions, philosophy, prelaw, psychology, religion, social science, and social work). Business, education and religion are the strongest academically. Business, education and psychology are the largest.

Required: Students must complete 124 semester units, 40 of which are in upper-division courses, with at least a 2.0 GPA. General education requirements include a biblical studies/world civilization series, and 2 courses each in humanities, natural sciences, social sciences, and phys ed and math. Students are required to attend College Hour, a twice-weekly program of lectures, films, and concerts. Students are encouraged to volunteer 2 hours of community service per week. Several majors require internships.

Special: Accelerated degrees and internships are available as is a 1-semester cooperative program with the University of California, Davis. Cross-registration is possible with San Joaquin College of Law and California State University, Fresno. A B.A. in management and organizational development is offered to working adults. Other off-campus learning opportunities include programs in American studies in Washington, D.C., urban studies in Chicago, and study abroad in Israel, Japan, and Costa Rica, and at Brethren Colleges in England, Spain, France, Germany, or China. There are 2 national honor societies, a freshman honors program, and 1 departmental honors programs.

Faculty/Classroom: 66% of faculty are male; 34% are female. 78% teach undergraduates. No introductory courses are taught by graduate students. The average class size in a laboratory is 14 and in a regular course is 18.

Admissions: 4 freshmen graduated first in their class.

Requirements: The SAT or ACT is required. Applicants should be graduates of an accredited high school or have the GED. Required secondary preparation includes 4 years of college prep English, 2 years of social studies, algebra 1 and 2, and geometry, and at least 1 year of a lab science. The college recommends that applicants also take courses in art, music, and 2 years of the same foreign language, all with a grade of C or better. An essay is required, and an audition is recommended for prospective music majors. A GPA of 3.1 is required. AP and CLEP credits are accepted. Important factors in the admissions decision are recommendations by school officials, advanced placement or honors courses, and extracurricular activities record.

Procedure: Freshmen are admitted fall and spring. Entrance exams should be taken During the fall of their senior year. There are early admissions and rolling admissions plans. Check with the school for current application deadlines. The application fee is $40. Notification is sent on a rolling basis. Applications are accepted online.

Transfer: Applicants should have completed at least 24 transferable units of college work with a 2.4 GPA. Those with fewer credits may apply any time but must meet freshman admission requirements. The SAT or ACT scores are recommended. 30 of 124 credits required for the bachelor's degree must be completed at FPU.

Visiting: There are regularly scheduled orientations for prospective students. There are guides for informal visits, visitors may sit in on classes, and stay overnight. To schedule a visit, contact the Admissions Office.

Financial Aid: The FAFSA is required. Check with the school for current application deadlines.

International Students: The school actively recruits these students. They must take the TOEFL.

Computers: All students may access the system 24 hours/per day. There are no time limits and no fees.

Admissions Contact: Yammilette Rodriguez, Undergraduate College Admission. E-Mail: *ugadmis@fresno.edu* Web: *www.fresno.edu*

GOLDEN GATE UNIVERSITY B-3

San Francisco, CA 94105 (415) 442-7800 (800) 448-4968; (415) 442-7807

Full-time: 85 men, 110 women
Part-time: 215 men, 235 women
Graduate: 1555 men, 1795 women
Year: varies, summer session
Application Deadline:
Freshman Class: n/av
Faculty: n/av
Ph.D.s: n/av
Student/Faculty: n/av
Tuition: $17,500
Room & Board: n/av
COMPETITIVE

Golden Gate University, founded in 1901, is a private, independent, commuter institution offering undergraduate and graduate degrees in business administration, accounting, human and social sciences, and special programs. The figures given in the above capsule and in this profile are approximate. There are 3 undergraduate schools and 4 graduate schools. The 2 libraries contain 300,000 volumes, and subscribe to 2,500 periodicals including electronic. Computerized library services include interlibrary loans and database searching. Special learning facilities include a The 1-acre campus is in an urban area in San Francisco. Including any residence halls, there are 2 buildings.

Student Life: 51% are White; 19% Asian American; 18% Foreign. The average age of freshmen is 21; all undergraduates, 37. 12% do not continue beyond their first year.

Housing: College-sponsored housing includes Alcohol is not permitted. All students commute.

Activities: There are no fraternities or sororities. There are 5 groups on campus, including ethnic, international, newspaper, professional, and social. Popular campus events include Commencement Ball.

Sports: There is no sports program at Golden Gate.

Disabled Students: All of the campus is accessible. Facilities include wheelchair ramps, elevators, special parking, and specially equipped restrooms.

Services: Counseling and information services are available, as is tutoring in some subjects. There is remedial math, reading, and writing.

Campus Safety and Security: Measures include security escort services.

Programs of Study: Golden Gate confers B.S., and B.B.A. degrees. Master's and doctoral degrees are also awarded. Bachelor's degrees are awarded in BUSINESS (accounting, banking and finance, human resources, and international business management), ENGINEERING AND ENVIRONMENTAL DESIGN (technological management). Accounting, finance, and information systems are the strongest academically. Finance, accounting, and management are the largest.

Required: A total of 123 trimester hours, with 21 to 33 in the major, are required to graduate. A minimum GPA of 2.0 is also required.

Special: The university offers cooperative programs, cross-registration with the San Francisco Consortium, internships, an accelerated degree program, dual majors, credit for military experience, nondegree study, and credit/no credit options. Also available are weekend classes and 10-week terms.

Faculty/Classroom: All teach undergraduates. No introductory courses are taught by graduate students. The average class size in an introductory lecture is 25; in a laboratory is 15; and in a regular course is 20.

Requirements: Applicants must be graduates of an accredited secondary school or have a GED. A GPA of 3.0 is required. AP and CLEP credits are accepted.

Procedure: Freshmen are admitted fall, spring, and summer. There is a rolling admissions plan. Check with the school for current application deadlines. Notification is sent on a rolling basis. Applications are accepted online.

Transfer: At least 24 transferable units and a 2.0 overall GPA are required. A minimum of 30 units out of 123, including 21 in the major, must be completed at GGU.

Visiting: Visitors may sit in on classes. To schedule a visit, contact the Student Affairs Office.

Financial Aid: The FAFSA is required. Check with the school for current application deadlines.

International Students: The school actively recruits these students. They must take the TOEFL.

Computers: All students may access the system at designated hours. There are no time limits and no fees.

Admissions Contact: Office of Admissions and Student Affairs E-Mail: *info@ggu.edu* Web: *www.ggu.edu*

HARVEY MUDD COLLEGE D-5

Claremont, CA 91711 (909) 621-8011; (909) 607-7046

Full-time: 427 men, 374 women
Part-time: 1 men, 1 women
Graduate: n/av
Year: semesters
Application Deadline: January 1
Faculty: 93; IIB, ++$
Ph.D.s: 100%
Student/Faculty: 9 to 1
Tuition: $46,509
Room & Board: $15,151
Freshman Class: 3336 applied, 643 accepted, 217 enrolled
SAT CR/M/W: 730/770/720 **ACT:** 34 **MOST COMPETITIVE**

Harvey Mudd College, founded in 1955, is one of the Claremont Colleges. It is a private college specializing in a math, science, and engineering education within a liberal arts tradition. There are 5 undergraduate schools and 2 graduate schools. In addition to regional accreditation, Harvey Mudd has baccalaureate program accreditation with ABET. The library contains 2.0 million volumes, and subscribes to 70,000 periodicals including electronic. Computerized library services include interlibrary loans, database searching, Internet access, and Wi-Fi capability. Special learning facilities include an art gallery, planetarium, and radio station. The 33-acre campus is in a suburban area 35 miles east of Los Angeles. Including any residence halls, there are 18 buildings.

Student Life: 62% of undergraduates are from out of state, mostly the Middle Atlantic. Students are from 42 states, 20 foreign countries, and Canada. 68% are from public schools. 47% are White; 22% Asian American; 11% Foreign. The average age of freshmen is 18; all undergraduates, 20. 1% do not continue beyond their first year; 88% remain to graduate.

Housing: 782 students can be accommodated in college housing, which includes single-sex and coed dorms, on-campus apartments, and off-campus apartments. On-campus housing is guaranteed for all 4 years. 97% of students live on campus; of those, 97% remain on campus on weekends. Upperclassmen may keep cars.

Activities: There are no fraternities or sororities. There are 65 groups on campus, including art, band, chess, choir, chorale, chorus, computers, dance, drama, environmental, ethnic, film, gay, international, jazz band, literary magazine, musical theater, newspaper, orchestra, photography, political, professional, radio and TV, religious, social, social service, student government, symphony, and yearbook. Popular campus events include 5-class Competition Relay Races, Wednesday Night Performance Series and Friday Film Nights.

Sports: There are 10 intercollegiate sports for men and 10 for women, and 10 intramural sports for men and 10 for women. Facilities include Claremont, Mudd, and Scripps shared athletic facility housing 2 gym floors, a weight room, a 400-meter track, a swimming pool, 9 tennis courts, and sports fields. The HMC campus recreation facility houses a full-size gym floor, an aerobics/dance room, and a fitness room with cardio and weight equipment.

Disabled Students: Facilities include wheelchair ramps, elevators, special parking, specially equipped restrooms, special class scheduling, and lowered drinking fountains.

Services: Counseling and information services are available, as is tutoring in most subjects. Additional support is offered on a case-by-case basis in coordination with Associate Dean of Academic Affairs, the Associate Dean of Student Life, the Academic Excellence Program and our faculty.

Campus Safety and Security: Measures include 24-hour foot and vehicle patrol, emergency notification system, self-defense education, and security escort services. There are emergency telephones, lighted pathways/sidewalks, and controlled access to dorms/residences.

Programs of Study: Harvey Mudd confers B.S. degrees. Bachelor's degrees are awarded in BIOLOGICAL SCIENCE (biology/biological science), COMPUTER AND PHYSICAL SCIENCE (chemistry, computer science, mathematics, and physics), ENGINEERING AND ENVIRONMENTAL DESIGN (engineering). Physics, chemistry, biology, engineering, math and computer science are the strongest academically. Engineering, computer science and math are the largest.

Required: The required curriculum, as revised by the College in January, 2010, is divided into three components: the Common Core, which provides the foundation for advanced study; the program in Humanities, Social Sciences, and the Arts, which completes the liberal arts nature of a Harvey Mudd College education by providing humanistic, social scientific, and aesthetic perspectives; and the Major, which builds depth and technical competence. Unifying all of these is an emphasis on strong oral and written communications, the development of computational skills, and direct experience with a research or design project. In order to be recommended by the faculty for the Bachelor of Science degree, students are required to complete satisfactorily a minimum of 128 credit hours of courses (including approved transfer credits for courses taken at other colleges). Students must also complete all of the requirements of each of the three curricular components as well as a physical education requirement.

Special: Students may cross-register at any of the other Claremont Colleges. Industry sponsored projects (The Clinic Program) are available for all students and Engineering and Computer Science majors are required to participate in Clinic. All students may choose to study abroad and an on campus office supports these students We have dual and special majors in Computer Science and Math, Mathematical and Computational Biology, Chemistry and Biolgy and student-designed majors are available. A 3-2 engineering degree with Claremont McKenna College or Scripps College is possible. The first semester for freshmen is taken on a pass/fail basis. There are 1 national honor societies and 7 departmental honors programs.

Faculty/Classroom: 63% of faculty are male; 37% are female. All teach undergraduates, all do research, and all teach and do research. No introductory courses are taught by graduate students. The average class size in an introductory lecture is 65; in a laboratory is 20; and in a regular course is 20.

Admissions: 19% of the 2013-2014 applicants were accepted. The SAT scores for the 2013 2014 freshman class were: Critical Reading--3% between 500 and 599, 32% between 600 and 699, and 65% between 700 and 800; Math--9% between 600 and 699, and 91% between 700 and 800; Writing--5% between 500 and 599, 31% between 600 and 699, and 64% between 700 and 800. The ACT scores were 2% between 27 and 28, and 98% above 28. 100% of the current freshmen were in the top fifth of their class. There were 54 National Merit finalists. 18 freshmen graduated first in their class.

Requirements: The SAT or ACT is required. The ACT Optional Writing test is also required. The ACT is recommended. In addition, applicants must have completed 4 years each of English and math (including algebra, demonstrative and analytic geometry, trigonometry, and calculus), 3 years of science (including 1 year each of physics and chemistry) and 1 year of hisoty. The college strongly recommends that applicants take 2 years of a foreign language and 2 additional years each of history and social sciences. Students are required to take the SAT or ACT and SAT subject tests in math (level 2) and 1 other subject are required. Letters of recommendation are required from the student's counselor, a math or science teacher, and an English, social science, or foreign language teacher. Applicants must submit 2 personal essays and are encouraged to seek an interview. Important factors in the admissions decision are advanced placement or honors courses, recommendations by school officials, and extracurricular activities record.

Procedure: Freshmen are admitted fall. Entrance exams should be taken RD-Jan test date, ED I-Nov test date, ED II-Dec test date. There are early decision and deferred admissions plans. Early decision applications should be filed by November 15; regular applications, by January 1 for fall entry, along with a $70 fee. Notification of early decision is sent December 15; regular decision, April 1. 66 early decision candidates were accepted for the 2013-2014 class. 563 applicants were on the 2013 waiting list. Applications are accepted online.

Transfer: 2 transfer students enrolled in 2012-2013. Applicants must submit SAT subject test scores, transcripts, course descriptions, and references from a college math, science, or engineering teacher and from a counselor. Students should aim to complete courses equivalent to the courses in our core curriculum. 64 of 128 credits required for the bachelor's degree must be completed at Harvey Mudd.

Visiting: There are regularly scheduled orientations for prospective students, including tours and interviews conducted Monday through Friday and some Saturday mornings in the fall. There are guides for informal visits, visitors may sit in on classes, and stay overnight. To schedule a visit, contact the Office of Admission at (909) 621-8011.

Financial Aid: In 2013-2014, 75% of all full-time freshmen and 74% of continuing full-time students received some form of financial aid. 50% of all full-time freshmen and 48% of continuing full-time students received need-based aid. The average freshman award was $33,644. Need-based scholarships or need-based grants averaged $39,885 ($60,025 maximum); need-based self-help aid (loans and jobs) averaged $6,267 ($11,225 maximum); and other non-need-based awards and non-need-based scholarships averaged $8,859 ($21,345 maximum). 67% of undergraduate students work part-time. Average annual earnings from campus work are $1000. The average financial indebtedness of the 2013 graduate was $28,255. Harvey Mudd is a member of CSS. The CSS/Profile, FAFSA, and the state aid form are required. The deadline for filing freshman financial aid applications for fall entry is February 1.

International Students: There are 99 international students enrolled. The school actively recruits these students. They must take the TOEFL with a minimum score of 600 on the paper-based TOEFL (PBT) or 100 on the Internet-based version (iBT), or IELTS if English has not been their primary language of instruction for the last 5 years. They must also take the SAT or ACT. For the ACT the optional writing section must be taken.

Computers: All students may access the system 24 hours a day. There are no time limits and no fees.

Graduates: From July 1, 2012 to June 30, 2013, 189 bachelor's degrees were awarded. The most popular majors were engineering (41%), computer science (14%), and math and physics (TIE) (10%). 142 companies recruited on campus in 2012-2013. In an average class, 83% graduate in 4 years or less, 88% graduate in 5 years or less, and 88% graduate in 6 years or less. Of the 2012 graduating class, 30% were enrolled in graduate school within 6 months of graduation, and 63% were employed.

Admissions Contact: Peter Osgood, Director of Admission. E-Mail: *admission@hmc.edu* Web: *www.hmc.edu*

HOLY NAMES UNIVERSITY — B-3

Oakland, CA 94619 — (510) 436-1351, (800) 430-1321; (510) 436-1325

Full-time: 110 men, 310 women	**Faculty:** n/av
Part-time: 35 men, 185 women	**Ph.D.s:** n/av
Graduate: 75 men, 310 women	**Student/Faculty:** n/av
Year: semesters, summer session	**Tuition:** $30,050
Application Deadline: open	**Room & Board:** $10,260
Freshman Class: n/av	
SAT or ACT: required	

NON COMPETITIVE

Holy Names University, founded in 1868, is an independent college affiliated with the Roman Catholic Church. It offers education in the liberal arts and preparation for some professions. There is 1 graduate school. In addition to regional accreditation, Holy Names has baccalaureate program accreditation with NASM and NLN. The library contains 111,472 volumes, 50,931 microform items, and 5,142 audio/video tapes/CDs/ DVDs, and subscribes to 190 periodicals including electronic. Computerized library services include database searching and Internet access. Special learning facilities include a learning resource center, art gallery, a performing arts center, a 400-seat theater, and a black box theater. The 60-acre campus is in an urban area 20 miles east of San Francisco. Including any residence halls, there are 15 buildings. The figures in the above capsule and in this profile are approximate.

Student Life: 96% of undergraduates are from California. Others are from 14 states, 12 foreign countries, and Canada. 62% are from public schools. 32% are African American; 28% white; 16% Hispanic. The average age of freshmen is 18; all undergraduates, 32. 38% do not continue beyond their first year; 46% remain to graduate.

Housing: 351 students can be accommodated in college housing, which includes coed dorms. On-campus housing is guaranteed for all 4 years. 67% of students commute. All students may keep cars.

Activities: There are no fraternities or sororities. There are 10 groups on campus, including choir, chorale, computers, drama, ethnic, gay, honors, international, orchestra, religious, social service, and student government. Popular campus events include Humanistic Studies Days and Founders Day.

Sports: There are 4 intercollegiate sports for men and 4 for women. Facilities include a gym, a pool, a fitness center, locker rooms and training rooms, and an outdoor fitness course.

Disabled Students: 60% of the campus is accessible. Facilities include elevators, special parking, specially equipped restrooms, lowered drinking fountains, lowered telephones, a learning disability program, and special accomodations based on student need and eligibility.

Services: Counseling and information services are available, as is tutoring in most subjects. There is remedial math and writing. Note takers and extended time for tests may be arranged.

Campus Safety and Security: Measures include self-defense education and security escort services. There are lighted pathways/sidewalks, a 24-hour manned entrance gate and nighttime foot patrol.

Programs of Study: Holy Names confers B.A., B.S., B.Mus., and B.S.N. degrees. Master's degrees are also awarded. Bachelor's degrees are awarded in BIOLOGICAL SCIENCE (biology/biological science), BUSINESS (business administration and management and human resources), COMMUNICATIONS AND THE ARTS (communications, English, English as a second/foreign language, and music), COMPUTER AND PHYSICAL SCIENCE (computer science), HEALTH PROFESSIONS (nursing), SOCIAL SCIENCE (history, human services, humanities, liberal arts/general studies, philosophy, psychology, religion, sociology, and Spanish studies). Business administration, nursing, and psychology have the largest enrollments.

Required: Students must have a 2.0 GPA and complete at least 120 hours with 24 to 36 in the major and 20 upper-division hours taken outside the major field. Students must complete a core curriculum, including foundation courses in critical thinking and communication, and courses in disciplinary studies, integrative studies across cultures, and writing across the curriculum. In some cases these requirements may be satisfied by secondary record, advanced placement, or challenge test. All students must take multidisciplinary courses in humanistic studies and a senior colloquium.

Special: Students may cross-register for 1 course per semester at any of 9 members of the Regional Association of East Bay Colleges and Universities. Internships, study abroad, and cooperative exchange programs with Central College in Iowa, Anna Maria College in Massachusetts, the Center for Bilingual Multicultural Studies in Mexico, and Kansai University of Foreign Studies in Japan are available. Dual and student-designed majors and interdisciplinary majors, including business administration and communication and business administration and philosophy are offered. Accelerated degrees are available in all B.A. programs. A weekend college for adults, limited nondegree study, and pass/fail options are available. There are 10 national honor societies and 1 departmental honors program.

Faculty/Classroom: 36% of faculty are male; 64% are female. 61%

teach undergraduates. No introductory courses are taught by graduate students. The average class size in an introductory lecture is 22; in a laboratory is 13; and in a regular course is 15.

Requirements: The SAT or ACT is required. In addition, applicants must be graduates of an accredited secondary school or have earned the GED. Secondary preparation should include at least 4 years of English, 3 years of math, 2 years of a single foreign language, 1 year each of lab science and U.S. history, 1 additional year of advanced courses in math, lab science, or foreign language, and 3 other 1-year college preparatory electives. In addition, the college requires a personal essay. Music auditions are required for scholarship applicants and recommended for others. AP and CLEP credits are accepted. Important factors in the admissions decision are advanced placement or honors courses, leadership record, and recommendations by school officials.

Procedure: Freshmen are admitted fall and spring. Entrance exams should be taken during the fall of the senior year. There are deferred admissions and rolling admissions plans. Check with the school for current application deadlines. The application fee is $35. Applications are accepted online.

Transfer: Applicants must have at least a 2.2 GPA in college work or a minimum of 30 transferable units. They must submit college records, a letter of recommendation from a college teacher or counselor, and a personal statement of their educational goals. 24 of 120 credits required for the bachelor's degree must be completed at Holy Names.

Visiting: There are guides for informal visits, visitors may sit in on classes, and stay overnight. To schedule a visit, contact the Admissions Office.

Financial Aid: The FAFSA is required. Check with the school for current application deadlines.

International Students: The school actively recruits these students. They must take the TOEFL or MELAB.

Computers: All students may access the system 8 a.m. to 10 p.m. daily in the labs. Network access is available 24 hours a day. There are no time limits and no fees.

Admissions Contact: Jeffrey Miller, Vice President for Enrollment Management. E-Mail: *admissions@hnc.edu* Web: *www.hnc.edu*

HOPE INTERNATIONAL UNIVERSITY — D-5

Fullerton, CA 92831 — **(714) 879-3901; (800) 762-1294; (714) 524-0231**

Full-time: 300 men, 374 women	**Faculty:** n/av
Part-time: 112 men, 138 women	**Ph.D.s:** 85%
Graduate: 174 men, 258 women	**Student/Faculty:** 13 to 1
Year: 4-1-4, summer session	**Tuition:** $26,050
Application Deadline:	**Room & Board:** $8600
Freshman Class: n/av	
SAT or ACT: required	

COMPETITIVE

Hope International University, founded in 1928, is a small, private liberal arts institution affiliated with the Independent Christian Church/Churches of Christ. There are 5 undergraduate schools and 5 graduate schools. The library contains 95,600 volumes, 100 microform items, and 2,115 audio/video tapes/CDs/DVDs, and subscribes to 500 periodicals including electronic. Computerized library services include interlibrary loans, database searching, Internet access, and Wi-Fi capability. The 15-acre campus is in an urban area 45 miles southeast of Los Angeles. Including any residence halls, there are 9 buildings. The figures in the above capsule and in this profile are approximate.

Student Life: 74% of undergraduates are from California. Others are from 27 states, 11 foreign countries, and Canada. 88% are from public schools. 44% are White; 16% Hispanic; 12% two or more races; 11% race unknown. 92% are Protestant. The average age of freshmen is 18; all undergraduates, 21. 25% do not continue beyond their first year; 45% remain to graduate.

Housing: 530 students can be accommodated in college housing, which includes single-sex dorms and on-campus apartments. On-campus housing is guaranteed for all 4 years. 53% of students commute. Alcohol is not permitted. All students may keep cars.

Activities: There are no fraternities or sororities. There are 17 groups on campus, including cheerleading, choir, chorale, chorus, communications, drama, international, jazz band, literary magazine, musical theater, newspaper, orchestra, religious, social service, student government, Students participate in Model UN at Harvard and Security Council at Yale, and yearbook. Popular campus events include Sadie Hawkins, Spring Formal, and Happy House (community Halloween outreach).

Sports: There are 6 intercollegiate sports for men and 7 for women, and 6 intramural sports for men and 6 for women. Facilities include 2500-seat gym with basketball and volleyball courts, fitness center, swimming pool, and recreation room.

Disabled Students: 95% of the campus is accessible. Facilities include elevators, special parking, specially equipped restrooms. Priority is given to disabled students for first-floor housing.

Services: Counseling and information services are available, as is tutoring in most subjects. There is a reader service for the blind, and remedial math, reading, and writing.

Campus Safety and Security: Measures include 24-hour foot and vehicle patrol, emergency notification system, and security escort services. There are emergency telephones, lighted pathways/sidewalks, and controlled access to dorms/residences.

Programs of Study: HIU confers B.A., B.S., B.Mus. degrees. Associate and master's degrees are also awarded. Bachelor's degrees are awarded in BUSINESS (accounting, business administration and management, and sports management), COMMUNICATIONS AND THE ARTS (church music, communications, English literature, and music), EDUCATION (education, secondary education, and social science education), HEALTH PROFESSIONS (health science), SOCIAL SCIENCE (biblical studies, child psychology/development, crosscultural studies, human development, human services, liberal arts/general studies, ministries, pastoral studies, psychology, social science, and youth ministry). Ministry/Biblical studies, psychology and counseling, and business are the largest.

Required: Regular attendance at chapel and participation in Christian service is required. To graduate, students must complete at least 124 credit units with 36 to 51 in the major. A minimum GPA of 2.0 must be maintained. The core curriculum includes required and elective courses in biblical studies, leadership, written and oral communication, social sciences, humanities, natural sciences, and math.

Special: Hope International offers co-op programs and cross-registration with California State University, Fullerton. Internships, study abroad in 7 countries, work-study programs, dual and student-designed majors, nondegree study, pass/fail options, and credit for life, military, and work experience are also offered. There is 1 departmental honors program.

Faculty/Classroom: 57% of faculty are male; 43% are female. All teach undergraduates. No introductory courses are taught by graduate students. The average class size in an introductory lecture is 33; in a laboratory is 20; and in a regular course is 30.

Requirements: The SAT or ACT is required. Applicants must be high school graduates. The GED is accepted. A personal essay and references from a church leader and an academic counselor are required. AP and CLEP credits are accepted.

Procedure: Freshmen are admitted fall and spring. Entrance exams should be taken before enrolling. There are deferred admissions and rolling admissions plans. Check with the school for current application deadlines. The fall 2013 application fee was $40. Applications are accepted online.

Transfer: Transfer students must submit copies of college transcripts and SAT or ACT scores if fewer than 30 college units have been completed. A minimum GPA of 2.0 is required. 30 of 124 credits required for the bachelor's degree must be completed at HIU.

Visiting: There are regularly scheduled orientations for prospective students. There are guides for informal visits, visitors may sit in on classes, and stay overnight. To schedule a visit, contact the Admissions Office.

Financial Aid: The FAFSA and the college's own financial statement are required. Check with the school for current application deadlines.

International Students: There are 22 international students enrolled. The school actively recruits these students. They must take the TOEFL with a minimum score of 83 on the Internet-based version (iBT).

Computers: All students may access the system at any time. There are no time limits and no fees.

Graduates: From July 1, 2012 to June 30, 2013, 143 bachelor's degrees were awarded. The most popular majors were psychology, social science and human services (41%), ministries and biblical studies (27%), and business (19%). In an average class, 29% graduate in 4 years or less, 38% graduate in 5 years or less, and 44% graduate in 6 years or less.

Admissions Contact: Dionne Butler, Director of Undergraduate Admissions. E-Mail: *dkbutler@hiu.edu* Web: *www.hiu.edu*

HUMBOLDT STATE UNIVERSITY — A-1

Arcata, CA 95521-8299 — **(707) 826-4402; (866) 850-9556; (707) 826-6194**

Full-time: 2855 men, 3255 women	**Faculty:** n/av; IIA, av$
Part-time: 355 men, 365 women	**Ph.D.s:** n/av
Graduate: 415 men, 635 women	**Student/Faculty:** n/av
Year: semesters, summer session	**Tuition:** $8900 ($16,700)
Application Deadline: open	**Room & Board:** $10,500
Freshman Class: n/av	
SAT or ACT: recommended	

COMPETITIVE

Humboldt State University, founded in 1913, is a liberal arts institution and the northernmost campus of the California State University system. There are 3 undergraduate schools and 1 graduate school. In addition to regional accreditation, Humboldt has baccalaureate program accreditation with ABET, CSWE, NASAD, NASM, NLN, and SAF. The library contains 566,531 volumes, 610,992 microform items, and 21,955 audio/video tapes/CDs/DVDs, and subscribes to 1,413 periodicals including electronic. Computerized library services include interlibrary loans, database searching, Internet access, and laptop Internet portals. Special learning facilities include a learning resource center, art gallery, natural history museum, radio station, observatory, greenhouse, solar hydrogen project, wildlife sanctuaries, the Center for Appropriate Technology, child development lab, ceramics lab, jewelry lab, marine lab, marine research vessel, fish hatchery, and wildlife care center. The 161-acre campus is in a small town 275 miles north of San Francisco. Including any residence halls, there are 93 buildings.

Student Life: 83% of undergraduates are from California. Others are from 50 states, 28 foreign countries, and Canada. 95% are from public schools. 53% are white. The average age of freshmen is 19; all undergraduates, 24. 25% do not continue beyond their first year; 49% remain to graduate.

Housing: 1400 students can be accommodated in college housing, which includes single-sex and coed dorms and on-campus apartments. In addition, there are special-interest houses, and living learning houses. On-campus housing is available on a first-come and first-served basis. 82% of students commute. All students may keep cars.

Activities: There are 178 groups on campus, including art, band, cheerleading, chorale, chorus, computers, dance, debate, drama, environmental, ethnic, film, gay, honors, international, jazz band, literary magazine, marching band, musical theater, newspaper, opera, orchestra, pep band, photography, political, professional, radio and TV, religious, social, social service, student government, and symphony. Popular campus events include Campus Dialogue on Race, International Education week, and International Cultural Festival.

Sports: There are 5 intercollegiate sports for men and 7 for women, and 4 intramural sports for men and 4 for women. Facilities include a 7000-seat stadium, an all-weather track, a swimming pool, tennis and racquetball courts, playing fields, 2 gyms, a student recreation center with exercise equipment and weight room, and a rock-climbing wall.

Disabled Students: 60% of the campus is accessible. Facilities include wheelchair ramps, elevators, special parking, specially equipped restrooms, special class scheduling, lowered drinking fountains, lowered telephones. wheelchair accessible transportation, and a study center.

Services: Counseling and information services are available, as is tutoring in every subject. There is a reader service for the blind, and remedial math, reading, and writing.

Campus Safety and Security: Measures include 24-hour foot and vehicle patrol, emergency notification system, self-defense education, and security escort services. There are emergency telephones, lighted pathways/sidewalks, emergency transportation services.

Programs of Study: Humboldt confers B.A. and B.S. degrees. Master's degrees are also awarded. Bachelor's degrees are awarded in AGRICULTURE (fishing and fisheries, forestry and related sciences, and natural resource management), BIOLOGICAL SCIENCE (biology/biological science, botany, wildlife biology, and zoology), BUSINESS (business administration and management and business economics), COMMUNICATIONS AND THE ARTS (art, communications, dramatic arts, English, fine arts, French, German, journalism, music, Spanish, and speech/debate/rhetoric), COMPUTER AND PHYSICAL SCIENCE (chemistry, geology, information sciences and systems, mathematics, oceanography, and physics), EDUCATION (business education, elementary education, English education, industrial arts education, mathematics education, middle school education, music education, physical education, science education, secondary education, and social science education), ENGINEERING AND ENVIRONMENTAL DESIGN (environmental engineering, environmental science, industrial engineering technology, and land use management and reclamation), HEALTH PROFESSIONS (nursing, predentistry, and premedicine), SOCIAL SCIENCE (anthropology, child psychology/development, geography, history, liberal arts/general studies, Native American studies, parks and recreation management, philosophy, physical fitness/movement, political science/government, prelaw, psychology, religion, social science, social work, and sociology). Environmental resources engineering, natural resources, and performing arts are the strongest academically. Biological sciences has the largest enrollment.

Required: To graduate, students must complete 120 to 132 semester credits, including 48 in general education courses, 24 to 36 in the major, and up to 40 in electives, with a minimum overall GPA of 2.0. Requirements include freshman reading and composition, diversity and common ground course work, and U.S. history course work as required by the California legislature.

Special: HSU offers campus work-study programs and co-op programs with a variety of public and private agencies, fisheries, biology, geology, botany, engineering, soil science, hydrology, and range and soil conservation. Internships and study abroad in 25 countries, with semesters in London, China, and Greece, are also offered. Dual majors, student-designed majors, credit for life and military experience, and credit/no credit grading options are also available.

Faculty/Classroom: 53% of faculty are male; 47% are female. All teach undergraduates. No introductory courses are taught by graduate students. The average class size in an introductory lecture is 33; in a laboratory is 21; and in a regular course is 24.

Requirements: The SAT or ACT is recommended. In addition, applicants must be high school graduates with a minimum of 15 academic credits, to include 4 years in English, 3 years in college prep math, 2 years each in foreign language, social science, and lab science, including 1 year physical and 1 year life science, and 1 year each of U.S. history/government and visual and performing arts. The GED is accepted. HSU uses an eligibility index that combines GPA and ACT or SAT scores for admission. Requirements are higher for out-of-state applicants. Contact the Office of Admissions for further information. A GPA of 2.0 is required. AP and CLEP credits are accepted.

Procedure: Freshmen are admitted fall and spring. Entrance exams should be taken prior to admission. There are early decision and rolling admissions plans. Check with the school for current application deadlines. The application fee is $55. Notification is sent on a rolling basis. Applications are accepted online.

Transfer: Applicants must have a minimum college GPA of 2.0 (2.4 for nonresidents). To enter, students need 30 general education units with a grade of C or better, including courses in written and speech communication, critical thinking, and math. Students with fewer than 56 transferable semester units must meet freshman requirements. 30 of 132 credits required for the bachelor's degree must be completed at Humboldt.

Visiting: There are regularly scheduled orientations for prospective students, including Preview Day in the spring and mandatory summer orientation for new students, which provides peer and academic counseling, registration, and a variety of social activities. There are guides for informal visits, visitors may sit in on classes, and stay overnight. To schedule a visit, contact the Office of Admissions.

Financial Aid: The FAFSA is required. Check with the school for current application deadlines.

International Students: There are 61 international students enrolled. The school actively recruits these students. They must take the TOEFL.

Computers: Wireless access is available. There are 10 computer labs with a total of 193 PCs and 71 Macs available for student use. Additionally, there are 585 computers available for use within specific disciplines. All students may access the system 24 hours a day, 7 days a week. There are no time limits and no fees. It is strongly recommended that all students have a personal computer.

Admissions Contact: Rebecca Kalal, Assistant Director of Admissions. A campus DVD is available. E-Mail: *hsuinfo@.humboldt.edu* Web: *www.humboldt.edu*

HUMPHREYS COLLEGE B-3

Stockton, CA 95207 **(209) 478-0800; (209) 478-8721**

Full-time: n/av	**Faculty:** n/av
Part-time: n/av	**Ph.D.s:** n/av
Graduate: n/av	**Student/Faculty:** n/av
Year: trimesters, summer session	**Tuition:** $10,500
Application Deadline: open	**Room & Board:** $7500
Freshman Class: n/av	

NON COMPETITIVE

Humphreys College, founded in 1896, is an independent institution offering undergraduate degrees in business management, accounting, paralegal studies, computer management, law, early childhood education, and liberal arts to a primarily commuter student body. The figures given in the above capsule and in this profile are approximate. There is 1 graduate school. The 2 libraries contain 21,000 volumes, and 1,000 audio/video tapes/CDs/DVDs, and subscribe to 110 periodicals including electronic. Computerized library services include database searching. The 10-acre campus is in a suburban area 40 miles south of Sacramento. Including any residence halls, there are 9 buildings.

Student Life: 97% of undergraduates are from California. Others are from 4 states, and 5 foreign countries. 97% are from public schools. 70% are white; 17% Hispanic. The average age of freshmen is 23; all undergraduates, 25. 20% do not continue beyond their first year; 50% remain to graduate.

Housing: 64 students can be accommodated in college housing, which includes single-sex on-campus apartments and married student housing. On-campus housing is available on a first-come and first-served basis. Priority is given to out-of-town students. 90% of students commute. Alcohol is not permitted. All students may keep cars.

Activities: There are no fraternities or sororities. There are 4 groups on campus, including professional and student government. Popular campus events include a Halloween party, a Christmas dinner, and a quarterly Hot Dog Day barbecue.

Sports: There is no sports program at Humphreys. Facilities include a swimming pool, a basketball court, a tennis court, and sports fields.

Disabled Students: All of the campus is accessible. Facilities include wheelchair ramps, special parking, specially equipped restrooms, special class scheduling, lowered drinking fountains, and lowered telephones.

Services: Counseling and information services are available, as is tutoring in some subjects, accounting There is remedial math and writing.

Campus Safety and Security: Measures include 24-hour foot and

vehicle patrol and security escort services. There are lighted pathways/ sidewalks.

Programs of Study: Humphreys confers B.S. degrees. Associate and doctoral degrees are also awarded. Bachelor's degrees are awarded in BUSINESS (accounting, business administration and management, court reporting, and management information systems), EDUCATION (early childhood education), SOCIAL SCIENCE (community services and paralegal studies). Paralegal studies is the largest.

Required: To graduate, students must complete a total of 180 quarter units, including 56 in the major and 72 in general education courses, with a minimum GPA of 2.0.

Special: Local internship positions are available for students of paralegal studies and business administration. Dual majors in business studies are possible.

Faculty/Classroom: 51% of faculty are male; 49% are female. All teach undergraduates. No introductory courses are taught by graduate students. The average class size in an introductory lecture is 17.

Requirements: Applicants must be graduates of an accredited secondary school or have earned a GED. AP and CLEP credits are accepted.

Procedure: Freshmen are admitted to all sessions. Entrance exams should be taken at any time. There are deferred admissions and rolling admissions plans. Application deadlines are open. Check with the school for the Application fee.

Transfer: Applicants must submit official transcripts and have a GPA of at least 2.0. 36 of 180 credits required for the bachelor's degree must be completed at Humphreys.

Visiting: There are regularly scheduled orientations for prospective students, including a campus tour, classroom visits, and meetings with admissions, financial aid, and academic advisers. There are guides for informal visits and visitors may sit in on classes. To schedule a visit, contact Santa Lopez in Admissions.

Financial Aid: Humphreys is a member of CSS. The FAFSA is required. Check with the school for current application deadlines.

International Students: They must take the TOEFL or MELAB.

Computers: All students may access the system when a lab aide or instructor is present or with an instructor's permission. There are no time limits and no fees.

Admissions Contact: Santa Lopez-Minatre, Director of Admissions. E-Mail: *ugadmission@humphreys.edu* Web: *www.humphreys.edu*

LA SIERRA UNIVERSITY D-5

Riverside, CA 92515 (951) 785-2957
(800) 874-5587; (951) 785-2447

Full-time: 615 men, 865 women	**Faculty:** n/av
Part-time: 90 men, 110 women	**Ph.D.s:** n/av
Graduate: 160 men, 175 women	**Student/Faculty:** n/av
Year: trimesters, summer session	**Tuition:** $28,314
Application Deadline:	**Room & Board:** $7380
Freshman Class: n/av	
SAT or ACT: required	
	VERY COMPETITIVE

La Sierra University, founded originally as La Sierra Academy in 1922, is a Seventh-day Adventist, private university, offering undergraduate and graduate programs in applied and liberal arts and sciences, business and management, religion, and education. There are 5 undergraduate schools and 4 graduate schools. In addition to regional accreditation, La Sierra has baccalaureate program accreditation with ABET, CSWE, and NASM. The library contains 262,554 volumes, and 648,664 microform items, and subscribes to 825 periodicals including electronic. Computerized library services include interlibrary loans, database searching, Internet access, and Wi-Fi capability. Special learning facilities include an art gallery, natural history museum, observatory, missionary museum, and arboretum. The 300-acre campus is in a suburban area 40 miles east of Los Angeles. Including any residence halls, there are 48 buildings.

Student Life: 20% of undergraduates are from California. Others are from 34 states, 58 foreign countries, and Canada. 39% are from public schools. 35% are White; 31% Asian American; 19% Hispanic. 90% are Protestant; 12% claim no religious affiliation. The average age of freshmen is 19; all undergraduates, 22.

Housing: 650 students can be accommodated in college housing, which includes single-sex dorms, on-campus apartments, off-campus apartments, and married student housing. In addition, there are honors houses. On-campus housing is guaranteed for all 4 years, is guaranteed for the freshman year only, is available on a first-come, and first-served basis. Priority is given to out-of-town students. 56% of students commute. Alcohol is not permitted. All students may keep cars.

Activities: There are no fraternities or sororities. There are 30 groups on campus, including art, band, choir, chorale, chorus, computers, debate, drama, environmental, ethnic, film, honors, international, literary magazine, newspaper, orchestra, photography, professional, religious, social service, student government, symphony, and yearbook. Popular campus events include University Experience, Academic Expo and Community Service Day.

Sports: There are 3 intercollegiate sports for men and 3 for women, and 9 intramural sports for men and 9 for women. Facilities include a gym, soccer and flag football fields, a running track, a swimming pool, and a fitness center.

Disabled Students: 99% of the campus is accessible. Facilities include wheelchair ramps, elevators, special parking, specially equipped restrooms, and special class scheduling.

Services: Counseling and information services are available, as is tutoring in most subjects. There is a reader service for the blind, and remedial math, reading, and writing. and a learning support center.

Campus Safety and Security: Measures include 24-hour foot and vehicle patrol, emergency notification system, and security escort services. There are emergency telephones, lighted pathways/sidewalks, and controlled access to dorms/residences.

Programs of Study: La Sierra confers B.A., B.S., B.F.A., B.Mus. and B.S.W. degrees. Master's and doctoral degrees are also awarded. Bachelor's degrees are awarded in BIOLOGICAL SCIENCE (biochemistry, biology/biological science, biometrics and biostatistics, and biophysics), BUSINESS (accounting, banking and finance, business administration and management, electronic business, international business management, and marketing management), COMMUNICATIONS AND THE ARTS (art, communications, English, English as a second/foreign language, fine arts, graphic design, music, music performance, and Spanish), COMPUTER AND PHYSICAL SCIENCE (chemistry, computer science, information sciences and systems, mathematics, and physics), EDUCATION (elementary education, music education, physical education, and secondary education), HEALTH PROFESSIONS (exercise science and health science), SOCIAL SCIENCE (history, liberal arts/general studies, political science/ government, psychobiology, psychology, religion, social work, and sociology). Biology, criminal justice and business have the largest enrollments.

Required: To graduate, students must complete 190 units, at least 60 of which must be upper-division, with a GPA of 2.0. All students must complete a University Studies curriculum requirements and 3 community service courses.

Special: Cross-registration with Walla Walla College is necessary for engineering students. Study abroad is available in 3 countries through the Adventist Colleges Abroad Consortium. Liberal studies students work with an adviser to design their own major. There are a freshman honors program.

Faculty/Classroom: All teach undergraduates, 70% do research, and 70% do both. Graduate students teach 1% of introductory courses. The average class size in an introductory lecture is 30; in a laboratory is 21; and in a regular course is 20.

Requirements: The SAT or ACT is required. In addition, prospective students should have a high school diploma or equivalent. Completion of college preparatory work is required. A recommendation is also required. A GPA of 2.5 is required. AP and CLEP credits are accepted. Important factors in the admissions decision are recommendations by school officials, leadership record, and evidence of special talent.

Procedure: Freshmen are admitted to all sessions. Entrance exams should be taken during the senior year. There are deferred admissions and rolling admissions plans. Check with the school for current application deadlines. The fall 2013 application fee was $30.

Transfer: Transcripts from all previous colleges are required. 36 of 190 credits required for the bachelor's degree must be completed at La Sierra.

Visiting: There are regularly scheduled orientations for prospective students, including a tour and meetings with faculty and administrators. There are guides for informal visits, visitors may sit in on classes, and stay overnight. To schedule a visit, contact the Admissions Department.

Financial Aid: La Sierra is a member of CSS. The FAFSA is required. Check with the school for current application deadlines.

International Students: There are 283 international students enrolled. The school actively recruits these students. They must take the TOEFL with a minimum score of 500 on the paper-based TOEFL (PBT). They must also take the SAT or ACT.

Computers: All students may access the system 24 hours a day. There are no time limits and no fees.

Graduates: From July 1, 2012 to June 30, 2013, 208 bachelor's degrees were awarded. The most popular majors were biomedical science (9%), management (7%), and exercise science: scientific basis (5%). In an average class, 35% graduate in 4 years or less and 45% graduate in 6 years or less.

Admissions Contact: Ivy Tejeda, Associate Director of Admissions. E-Mail: *admissions@lasierra.edu* Web: *www.lasierra.edu*

LAGUNA COLLEGE OF ART AND DESIGN D-5

Laguna Beach, CA 92651 (949) 376-6000
(800) 255-0762; (949) 376-6009

Full-time: 193 men, 273 women
Part-time: 15 men, 33 women
Graduate: 12 men, 19 women
Year: semesters, summer session
Application Deadline:
Freshman Class: n/av
SAT or ACT: required
Faculty: 15
Ph.D.s: n/av
Student/Faculty: 13 to 1
Tuition: $26,500
Room & Board: n/app
SPECIAL

Laguna College of Art and Design, founded in 1961, is a independent, institution offering full-and part-time undergraduate art programs leading to a Certficate of Arts, Bachelor of Fine Arts, Post-Baccalaureate and Master of Fine Arts degrees. There is 1 undergraduate school and 1 graduate school. In addition to regional accreditation, LCAD has baccalaureate program accreditation with NASAD. The library contains 17,128 volumes and 1,643 audio/video tapes/CDs/DVDs, and subscribes to 95 periodicals including electronic. Computerized library services include interlibrary loans, database searching, Internet access, and Wi-Fi capability. Special learning facilities include an art gallery. The 9-acre campus is in a small town 47 miles southeast of Los Angeles, and 65 miles north of San Diego. Including any residence halls, there are 15 buildings.

Student Life: 85% of undergraduates are from California. Others are from 33 states, 13 foreign countries, and Canada. 90% are from public schools. 45% are White; 18% race unknown; 15% Asian American; 15% Hispanic. The average age of freshmen is 19; all undergraduates, 23. 15% do not continue beyond their first year; 60% remain to graduate.

Housing: 54 students can be accommodated in college housing, which includes single-sex dorms. The institute will assist in the location of off-campus housing. Priority is given to out-of-town students. 89% of students commute. Alcohol is not permitted. All students may keep cars.

Activities: There are no fraternities or sororities. There are 2 groups on campus, including art and student government.

Sports: There is no sports program at LCAD.

Disabled Students: 90% of the campus is accessible. Facilities include special parking, specially equipped restrooms, special class scheduling, and lowered drinking fountains.

Services: There is remedial reading and writing.

Campus Safety and Security: Measures include security escort services. The institute will assist in the location of off-campus housing.

Programs of Study: LCAD confers B.F.A. degrees. Master's degrees are also awarded. Bachelor's degrees are awarded in COMMUNICATIONS AND THE ARTS (animation, drawing, graphic design, illustration, and painting).

Required: All students must complete 122 credit hours, with approximately 55 in the major, including studio electives. General education requirements include 30 hours in liberal arts and 15 in art history. 22 hours of studio foundation courses are required, in which students explore all artistic medium.

Special: Internships are possible, and work-study is available on campus. Students may petition the registrar if they wish to attempt more than 15 semester units.

Faculty/Classroom: 64% of faculty are male; 36% are female. All teach undergraduates. No introductory courses are taught by graduate students. The average class size in an introductory lecture is 15 and in a regular course is 12.

Requirements: The SAT or ACT is required. Students must be high school graduates or hold an equivalent GED. A personal essay and letter of recommendation are required, as is a personal or telephone interview, and a 12-18 piece portfolio. A GPA of 2.5 is required. AP and CLEP credits are accepted. Important factors in the admissions decision are evidence of special talent, recommendations by school officials, and ability to finance college education.

Procedure: Freshmen are admitted fall and spring. There are deferred admissions and rolling admissions plans. Check with the school for current application deadlines. The application fee is $35. Applications are accepted online.

Transfer: 65 transfer students enrolled in 2012-2013. In addition to freshman requirements, transfer students must submit all prior college transcripts. 45 of 122 credits required for the bachelor's degree must be completed at LCAD.

Visiting: There are regularly scheduled orientations for prospective students, consisting of national portfolio days and open house. There are guides for informal visits and visitors may sit in on classes. To schedule a visit, contact the Admissions Office at (949) 376-6000 x248.

Financial Aid: In 2013-2014, 99% of all full-time freshmen and 85% of continuing full-time students received some form of financial aid. 65% of all full-time freshmen and 70% of continuing full-time students received need-based aid. The average freshman award was $15,500. 4% of undergraduate students work part-time. Average annual earnings from campus work are $1500. The average financial indebtedness of the 2013 graduate was $26,323. The FAFSA is required. Check with the school for current application deadlines.

International Students: There are 19 international students enrolled. They must take the TOEFL with a minimum score of 550 on the paper-based TOEFL (PBT) or 79 on the Internet-based version (iBT) and the college's own test.

Computers: All students may access the system. There are no time limits and no fees.

Graduates: From July 1, 2012 to June 30, 2013, 51 bachelor's degrees were awarded. The most popular majors were drawing and painting (23%), game art (12%), and graphic design (12%).

Admissions Contact: Christopher Brown, Director of Admissions + Financial Aid. E-Mail: *admissions@lcad.edu* Web: *www.lcad.edu*

LOYOLA MARYMOUNT UNIVERSITY C-5

Los Angeles, CA 90045 (310) 338-2750
(800) LMU-INFO; (310) 338-2797

Full-time: 2521 men, 3414 women
Part-time: 154 men, 116 women
Graduate: 1351 men, 2105 women
Year: semesters, summer session
Application Deadline: January 15
Freshman Class: 11472 applied, 6209 accepted, 1341 enrolled
SAT CR/M/W: 593/603/597
Faculty: 544
Ph.D.s: 96%
Student/Faculty: 11 to 1
Tuition: $40,040
Room & Board: $13,200
ACT: 27
VERYCOMPETITIVE+

Loyola Marymount University is one of the largest Catholic universities in the West and one of 28 Jesuit universities in the United States. LMU, founded in 1911, is a comprehensive university offering 60 major programs and 56 minor programs for undergraduates. LMU's 142-acre campus, designated as one of the country's most beautiful, is situated on a bluff overlooking Los Angeles and the Pacific Ocean. There are 5 undergraduate schools and 2 graduate schools. In addition to regional accreditation, LMU has baccalaureate program accreditation with AACSB, ABET, NASAD, NASM, and NCATE. The library contains 598,443 volumes, 130,185 microform items, and 29,700 audio/video tapes/CDs/DVDs. Computerized library services include interlibrary loans, database searching, Internet access, and Wi-Fi capability. Special learning facilities include an art gallery, radio station, TV station, the Burns Fine Arts Center, and the Little Theatre. The 142-acre campus is in a suburban area 15 miles southwest of downtown Los Angeles. Including any residence halls, there are 60 buildings.

Student Life: 78% of undergraduates are from California. Others are from 48 states, 66 foreign countries, and Canada. 50% are from public schools. 49% are White; 22% Hispanic. 44% are Catholic; 28% claim no religious affiliation; 25% Christian, Muslim, Buddhist and Hindu. The average age of freshmen is 18; all undergraduates, 20. 9% do not continue beyond their first year; 76% remain to graduate.

Housing: 3210 students can be accommodated in college housing, which includes single-sex and coed dorms and on campus apartments. In addition, there are honors houses and special-interest houses. On-campus housing is guaranteed for the freshman year only and is available on a lottery system for upperclassmen. 52% of students live on campus. All students may keep cars.

Activities: 16% of men belong to 7 national fraternities; 33% of women belong to 10 national sororities. There are 140 groups on campus, including art, cheerleading, chess, choir, chorale, chorus, computers, dance, debate, drama, ethnic, film, gay, honors, international, literary magazine, newspaper, orchestra, pep band, political, professional, radio and TV, religious, social, social service, student government, and yearbook. Popular campus events include College Fest, Madness at Midnight, Charity Ball and Club Fest.

Sports: There are 8 intercollegiate sports for men and 10 for women, and 5 intramural sports for men and 5 for women. Facilities include an athletic pavilion, a 4166-seat gym, a swimming pool, tennis, handball, and racquetball courts, a baseball stadium, a floating crew shell house, soccer, rugby, and football fields, and a recreation center.

Disabled Students: 95% of the campus is accessible. Facilities include wheelchair ramps, elevators, special parking, specially equipped restrooms, special class scheduling, lowered drinking fountains, lowered telephones, special housing. special test and registration arrangements, and hearing aid equipment in the library.

Services: Counseling and information services are available, as is tutoring in most subjects. There is a reader service for the blind, and remedial math, reading, and writing. There is an extensive learning resource center with full-time specialists in reading, writing, and study skills, as well as a peer tutoring staff and computer-aided instruction.

Campus Safety and Security: Measures include 24-hour foot and vehicle patrol, emergency notification system, and security escort services. There are emergency telephones, lighted pathways/sidewalks, and controlled access to dorms/residences.

Programs of Study: LMU confers B.A., B.S., B.B.A., B.S.A. and B.S.E.

degrees. Master's and doctoral degrees are also awarded. Bachelor's degrees are awarded in BIOLOGICAL SCIENCE (biochemistry and biology/biological science), BUSINESS (accounting, business administration and management, entrepreneurial studies, and marketing/retailing/merchandising), COMMUNICATIONS AND THE ARTS (animation, art history and appreciation, classics, communications, dance, dramatic arts, English, French, Greek, Latin, media arts, modern language, music, Spanish, and studio art), COMPUTER AND PHYSICAL SCIENCE (chemistry, computer science, mathematics, natural sciences, and physics), EDUCATION (athletic training and mathematics education), ENGINEERING AND ENVIRONMENTAL DESIGN (civil engineering, electrical/electronics engineering, engineering physics, environmental science, and mechanical engineering), HEALTH PROFESSIONS (health science), SOCIAL SCIENCE (African American studies, Asian/Oriental studies, classical/ancient civilization, economics, European studies, Hispanic American studies, history, humanities, liberal arts/general studies, philosophy, political science/government, psychology, sociology, theological studies, urban studies, and women's studies). Engineering, entrepreneurship, school of film and television are the strongest academically. Psychology, communication studies, and marketing have the largest enrollment.

Required: Regardless of major, all undergraduates must take courses in the following core areas: American cultures; college writing; communication/critical thinking; critical and creative arts; history; literature, math, science, and technology; philosophy; social sciences, and theological studies. A minimum 2.0 GPA is required, as are at least 120 semester hours, with at least 45 semester hours in upper-division courses. At least 30 of the last 36 semester hours of academic work and at least two thirds of the upper-division semester hours of the major must be completed at LMU.

Special: LMU offers internships and volunteer work experience with local firms, study abroad in over 20 countries, a Washington semester, dual majors, work-study, student-designed and individualized studies majors, a general studies degree, non-degree study, and some pass/fail options for electives. There are 20 national honor societies and a freshman honors program.

Faculty/Classroom: 54% of faculty are male; 46% are female. All teach and do research. Graduate students teach 4% of introductory courses. The average class size in an introductory lecture is 23 and in a laboratory is 53.

Admissions: 54% of the 2013-2014 applicants were accepted. The SAT scores for the 2013-2014 freshman class were: Critical Reading--9% below 500, 42% between 500 and 599, 42% between 600 and 699, and 7% between 700 and 800; Math--7% below 500, 38% between 500 and 599, 47% between 600 and 699, and 8% between 700 and 800; Writing--7% below 500, 43% between 500 and 599, 43% between 600 and 699, and 7% between 700 and 800. The ACT scores were 4% below 21, 12% between 21 and 23, 31% between 24 and 26, 24% between 27 and 28, and 29% above 28.

Requirements: The SAT is required. The ACT is recommended. Prospective students must be graduates of an accredited secondary school and have completed 4 years of English, 3 each of a foreign language, math, and social studies, 2 of science, and 1 of an academic elective. A recommendation from an official of a previous school and essays are required. An interview is recommended. AP credits are accepted. Important factors in the admissions decision are advanced placement or honors courses, evidence of special talent, and personality/intangible qualities.

Procedure: Freshmen are admitted fall and spring. Entrance exams should be taken during the spring of the junior year or fall of senior year. There are early admissions, deferred admissions, and rolling admissions plans. Applications should be filed by January 15 for fall entry; October 15 for spring entry, along with a $60 fee. 387 applicants were on the 2013 waiting list; 79 were admitted. Applications are accepted online.

Transfer: 438 transfer students enrolled in 2012-2013. Applicants must have a minimum 3.00 GPA in college work and most recent college work. Students who were not academically eligible for admission as freshmen must have at least 30 semester hours of college work. Grades below C (2.0) do not transfer. No minimum credit hours are necessary for students who meet freshman requirements. The SAT I is required for those with fewer than 30 transfer hours, and letters of recommendation are recommended for all transfer students. 30 of 120 credits required for the bachelor's degree must be completed at LMU.

Visiting: There are regularly scheduled orientations for prospective students. Student visits consist of an open house in the fall. There are guides for informal visits and visitors may sit in on classes. To schedule a visit, contact the Admissions Office.

Financial Aid: In 2013-2014, 90% of all full-time freshmen and 85% of continuing full-time students received some form of financial aid. 58% of all full-time freshmen and 60% of continuing full-time students received need-based aid. The average freshman award was $25,105. Need-based scholarships or need-based grants averaged $6,877 ($49,558 maximum); need-based self-help aid (loans and jobs) averaged $4,159 ($52,707 maximum); non-need-based athletic scholarships averaged $1,460 ($67,521 maximum); other non-need-based awards and non-need-based scholarships averaged $6,753 ($56,859 maximum); and $5,856 from other forms of aid. 54% of undergraduate students work part-time. Average annual earnings from campus work are $1235. The average financial indebtedness of the 2013 graduate was $32,746. The FAFSA and the college's own financial statement are required. Check with the school for current application deadlines.

International Students: There are 313 international students enrolled. The school actively recruits these students. They must take the TOEFL with a minimum score of 550 on the paper-based TOEFL (PBT) or 80 on the Internet-based version (iBT). They must also take the SAT or ACT.

Computers: All students may access the system. Labs are available more than 60 hours per week. There are no time limits and no fees.

Graduates: From July 1, 2012 to June 30, 2013, 1524 bachelor's degrees were awarded. The most popular majors were communication studies (12%), English (6%), and psycology (6%). 140 companies recruited on campus in 2012-2013. In an average class, 1% graduate in 3 years or less, 67% graduate in 4 years or less, 74% graduate in 5 years or less, and 76% graduate in 6 years or less. Of the 2012 graduating class, 29% were enrolled in graduate school within 6 months of graduation, and 50% were employed.

Admissions Contact: Matthew Fissinger, Director of Undergraduate Admissions. E-Mail: *admissions@lmu.edu* Web: *http:/admission.lmu.edu/*

MENLO COLLEGE B-3

Atherton, CA 94027 **(650) 543-3910**
(800) 55-MENLO; (650) 543-4476

Full-time: 438 men, 266 women	**Faculty:** 32
Part-time: 7 men, 2 women	**Ph.D.s:** 88%
Graduate: n/av	**Student/Faculty:** 22 to 1
Year: semesters, summer session	**Tuition:** $37,100
Application Deadline: Open	**Room & Board:** $11,902
Freshman Class: 1717 applied, 1519 accepted, 139 enrolled	
SAT CR/M/W: 470/500/480 **ACT:** 20	**COMPETITIVE**

Menlo College, founded in 1927, is a private college offering programs in business management and psychology with a strong liberal arts foundation. There is one undergraduate school. The library contains 60,600 volumes, and 1,020 audio/video tapes/CDs/DVDs, and subscribes to 41,050 periodicals including electronic. Computerized library services include interlibrary loans, database searching, Internet access, and Wi-Fi capability. Special learning facilities include an art gallery, dedicated computer labs, social media labs, academic success center, writing lab, math lab, and study slam sessions. The 45-acre campus is in a suburban area 30 miles south of San Francisco and 30 miles north of San Jose. Including any residence halls, there are 13 buildings.

Student Life: 69% of undergraduates are from California. Others are from 23 states, 30 foreign countries, and Canada. 35% are White; 21% Hispanic; 13% Foreign. The average age of freshmen is 18; all undergraduates, 21. 18% do not continue beyond their first year; 55% remain to graduate.

Housing: 503 students can be accommodated in college housing, which includes single-sex and coed dorms. On-campus housing is guaranteed for the freshman year only. 61% of students live on campus; of those, 80% remain on campus on weekends. All students may keep cars.

Activities: There are no fraternities or sororities. There are 35 groups on campus, including art, band, cheerleading, chess, chorale, communications, computers, environmental, ethnic, film, Finance/Investment club, gay, honors, international, photography, political, professional, religious, social, social service, and student government. Popular campus events include School of Business Administration Day, Luau, Homecoming and Mystery Dance.

Sports: There are 8 intercollegiate sports for men and 8 for women, and 2 intramural sports for men and 2 for women. Facilities include 2 swimming pools, soccer and football fields, tennis courts, a track, a 600-seat gym, a fitness center, a weight facility, and a baseball diamond. The campus stadium seats 1000, the largest auditorium/arena.

Disabled Students: 95% of the campus is accessible. Facilities include wheelchair ramps, elevators, special parking, specially equipped restrooms, lowered drinking fountains, lowered telephones, and special housing.

Services: Counseling and information services are available, as is tutoring in most subjects. There is a reader service for the blind, and remedial math, reading, and writing.

Campus Safety and Security: Measures include 24-hour foot and vehicle patrol, emergency notification system, and security escort services. There are emergency telephones, lighted pathways/sidewalks, and controlled access to dorms/residences.

Programs of Study: Menlo confers B.A. in Business and B.A in Psychology and B.S. in Business degrees. Bachelor's degrees are awarded in BUSINESS (accounting, entrepreneurial studies, finance, human resources, international business management, management information systems, marketing management, real estate, and sports management), SOCIAL

SCIENCE (psychology). Business and psychology are the strongest academically. Business has the largest enrollment.

Required: Students must complete 124 units with a cumulative GPA above 2.0 to earn a Bachelor's degree. All students must complete 49 credit hours of general education courses and 39-63 hours of major courses depending on the specific major. The remaining courses are free electives.

Special: Business students are required to earn 6 credits through internships. Menlo also offers study abroad in Spain, China, Chile,and Japan; dual and student-designed majors, B.A.-B.S. degrees. There are 2 national honor societies and 1 departmental honors programs.

Faculty/Classroom: 55% of faculty are male; 45% are female. All teach undergraduates, and 88% do both. No introductory courses are taught by graduate students. The average class size in an introductory lecture is 19; in a laboratory is 27; and in a regular course is 19.

Admissions: 88% of the 2013-2014 applicants were accepted. The SAT scores for the 2013-2014 freshman class were: Critical Reading--63% below 500, 33% between 500 and 599, 3% between 600 and 699, and 1% between 700 and 800; Math--46% below 500, 43% between 500 and 599, 9% between 600 and 699, and 2% between 700 and 800; Writing--64% below 500, 30% between 500 and 599, 6% between 600 and 699. The ACT scores were 50% below 21, 12% between 21 and 23, 25% between 24 and 26, 10% between 27 and 28, and 3% above 28. 1 freshman graduated first in the class.

Requirements: The SAT or ACT is required. A personal essay and letter of recommendation should be submitted. The GED is accepted. A GPA of 2.5 is required. AP and CLEP credits are accepted. Important factors in the admissions decision are advanced placement or honors courses, evidence of special talent, and leadership record.

Procedure: Freshmen are admitted fall and spring. Entrance exams should be taken During a junior or a senior year of high school. There are early admissions, deferred admissions, and rolling admissions plans. Early decision applications should be filed by December 1, along with a $40 fee. Notification of early decision is sent December 15; regular decision, on a Rolling basis. Applications are accepted online.

Transfer: 89 transfer students enrolled in 2012-2013. Transfer applicants must show potential for success indicated by a 2.0 GPA at the college level. Those with fewer than 12 credits must meet freshman requirements. 30 of 124 credits required for the bachelor's degree must be completed at Menlo.

Visiting: There are regularly scheduled orientations for prospective students, There are two Open Houses, one in early Fall and one in early Spring, where prospective students can meet with key faculty and staff and tour the campus. In late Spring there is a Preview Day interactive event culminating with the Student Luau. There are guides for informal visits, visitors may sit in on classes, and stay overnight. To schedule a visit, contact the Office of Admissions.

Financial Aid: In 2013-2014, 98% of all full-time freshmen and 97% of continuing full-time students received some form of financial aid. 64% of all full-time freshmen and 63% of continuing full-time students received need-based aid. The average freshman award was $28,041. Need-based scholarships or need-based grants averaged $24,979 ($36,500 maximum); need-based self-help aid (loans and jobs) averaged $3,585 ($4,500 maximum); non-need-based athletic scholarships averaged $5,591 ($21,527 maximum); and other non-need-based awards and non-need-based scholarships averaged $14,014 ($19,000 maximum). 52% of undergraduate students work part-time. Average annual earnings from campus work are $1800. The average financial indebtedness of the 2013 graduate was $28,972. The FAFSA is required. The priority date for freshman financial aid applications for fall entry is March 2.

International Students: There are 96 international students enrolled. The school actively recruits these students. They must take the TOEFL with a minimum score of 500 on the paper-based TOEFL (PBT) or 61 on the Internet-based version (iBT), or take the SAT or ACT if English is their first language.

Computers: All students may access the system 24 hours a day, 7 days a week. There are no time limits and no fees.

Graduates: From July 1, 2012 to June 30, 2013, 139 bachelor's degrees were awarded. The most popular majors were management (42%), marketing (14%), and accounting (7%). In an average class, 55% graduate in 6 years or less. Of the 2012 graduating class, 87% were employed within 6 months of graduation.

Admissions Contact: Holly Dalton, Dean of Enrollment Management.
E-Mail: *holly.dalton@menlo.edu* Web: *www.menlo.edu*

MILLS COLLEGE B-3

Oakland, CA 94613 (510) 430-2135
(800) 87-MILLS; (510) 430-3314

Full-time: 922 women	**Faculty:** 94; IIA, ++$
Part-time: 63 women	**Ph.D.s:** 92%
Graduate: 126 men, 484 women	**Student/Faculty:** 9 to 1
Year: semesters	**Tuition:** $41,494
Application Deadline: February 1	**Room & Board:** $12,625
Freshman Class: 1827 applied, 1242 accepted, 217 enrolled	
SAT CR/M/W: 000/560/570	**ACT:** 26 **HIGHLY COMPETITIVE**

Located in the heart of the San Francisco Bay Area, Mills College has shaped women's lives for more than 160 years. Offering a progressive liberal arts and sciences curriculum taught by renowned faculty, Mills gives students the personal attention that leads to extraordinary learning. There is one undergraduate school and 4 graduate schools. The library contains 244,110 volumes, 28,315 microform items, and 14,057 audio/video tapes/CDs/DVDs, and subscribes to 50,202 periodicals including electronic. Computerized library services include interlibrary loans, database searching, Internet access, and Wi-Fi capability. Special learning facilities include an art gallery, a children's school, a small book press, an electronic/computer music studio, a botanical garden, a computer learning studio, and a radio broadcasting room. The 135-acre campus is in an urban area in the San Francisco Bay area, 12 miles east of San Francisco and 8 miles from Berkeley. Including any residence halls, there are 64 buildings.

Student Life: 82% of undergraduates are from California. Others are from 48 states, and 12 foreign countries. 84% are from public schools. 47% are White; 22% Hispanic; 12% Asian American. 52% claim no religious affiliation; 17% Buddhist, Hindu, and Muslim; 14% Catholic; 13% Protestant. The average age of freshmen is 18; all undergraduates, 22. 19% do not continue beyond their first year; 62% remain to graduate.

Housing: 810 students can be accommodated in college housing, which includes single-sex and coed dorms, on-campus apartments, and married student housing. In addition, there are language houses, special-interest houses, Married-student housing is offered on an equal basis to domestic partners of lesbian and gay students, and a student co-op house is available for juniors and seniors. On-campus housing is guaranteed for all 4 years, is available on a first-come, and first-served basis. 58% of students live on campus; of those, 77% remain on campus on weekends. All students may keep cars.

Activities: There are no fraternities or sororities. There are 63 groups on campus, including art, cheerleading, choir, dance, drama, environmental, ethnic, film, gay, honors, international, literary magazine, newspaper, political, professional, religious, social, social service, student government, and yearbook. Popular campus events include Black and White Ball, Spring Fling, Heritage Months, Fetish Ball, Choir Winter Celebration, Vagina Monologues, Final Snacks & Midnight Breakfast, Final Fridays, and Second Saturdays.

Sports: There are 6 intercollegiate sports for women, and 9 intramural sports for women. Facilities include Mills College athletic and recreational facilities include a multi-purpose gymnasium, fitness center with a complete array of cardio-fitness and strength training equipment, staffed and equipped training room, activity rooms, dance studios, state-of-the-art aquatic center and therapy spa, 6 newly refurbished lighted tennis courts, grass soccer field, and on-campus running trail. Just minutes away are miles of wooded trails for hiking and running, and the Mills boathouse at Briones Reservoir provides for year-round rowing.

Disabled Students: All of the campus is accessible. Facilities include wheelchair ramps, elevators, special parking, specially equipped restrooms, special class scheduling, lowered drinking fountains, lowered telephones, and special housing.

Services: Counseling and information services are available, as is tutoring in every subject. There is a reader service for the blind, and remedial writing.

Campus Safety and Security: Measures include 24-hour foot and vehicle patrol, emergency notification system, self-defense education, and security escort services. There are shuttle buses, emergency telephones, lighted pathways/sidewalks, controlled access to dorms/residences, AED units, vehicle jumps.

Programs of Study: Mills confers B.A. and B.S. degrees. Master's and doctoral degrees are also awarded. Bachelor's degrees are awarded in AGRICULTURE (environmental studies), BIOLOGICAL SCIENCE (biochemistry, biology/biological science, microbiology, and molecular biology), BUSINESS (business economics), COMMUNICATIONS AND THE ARTS (art history, comparative literature, creative writing, dance, English, English literature, English Writing, French, media arts, modern language, music, Spanish, and studio art), COMPUTER AND PHYSICAL SCIENCE (chemistry, computer science, and mathematics), ENGINEERING AND ENVIRONMENTAL DESIGN (environmental science), HEALTH PROFESSIONS (nursing), SOCIAL SCIENCE (American studies, anthropology, biopsychology, child psychology/development, early childhood studies, economics, ethnic studies, government, French studies, Hispanic American studies, history, international relations, liberal arts/general studies, philosophy, political science/government, prelaw, psychology, public administration, public affairs, sociology, Spanish studies, and women and gender studies). English, psychology, political, legal, economic analysis, and computer science are the strongest academically. Psychology, English, and biology have the largest enrollments.

Required: To graduate, students must fulfill general education requirements, earn a total of 34 semester course credits, with 10 to 17 in the major, and maintain a minimum GPA of 2.0. Required courses include English, a second-semester writing course, and 1 course in the following: quantitative and computational reasoning, information literacy/ information technology, interdisciplinary perspectives, women and gender, multicultural perspectives, creation and criticism in the arts, historical perspectives, natural sciences, and human institutions and behavior.

Special: There is cross-registration with the University of California at Berkeley, California State University, and California College of the Arts, among others. Mills offers co-op programs, internships, study abroad, a Washington semester, work-study programs, dual majors, student-designed majors, and interdisciplinary majors, including political, legal, and economic analysis. Accelerated degree programs include 3-2 engineering, 4+1 M.B.A., 4+1 M.P.P., a 4+1 B.A./M.A. program in which students graduate in 5 years with a bachelor's degree in psychology and a master's in infant mental health, and a 4+1 program in which students earn a B.A., an M.A. in education, and complete a program qualifying them for a teaching credential. A general studies degree, credit by exam, and pass/fail options are also available. Mills also offers a a 3-2 engineering degree with USC and a prenursing program leading to a bachelor's degree in nursing at Samuel Merritt College. There are 5 national honor societies including Phi Beta Kappa.

Faculty/Classroom: 30% of faculty are male; 70% are female. All teach and do research. No introductory courses are taught by graduate students. The average class size in an introductory lecture is 25; in a laboratory is 15; and in a regular course is 16.

Admissions: 68% of the 2013-2014 applicants were accepted. The SAT scores for the 2013-2014 freshman class were: Critical Reading--13% below 500, 36% between 500 and 599, 40% between 600 and 699, and 11% between 700 and 800; Math--22% below 500, 45% between 500 and 599, 30% between 600 and 699, and 3% between 700 and 800; Writing--20% below 500, 38% between 500 and 599, 37% between 600 and 699, and 5% between 700 and 800. The ACT scores were 7% below 21, 33% between 21 and 23, 16% between 24 and 26, 26% between 27 and 28, and 18% above 28. 62% of the current freshmen were in the top fifth of their class; 91% were in the top two fifths. 3 freshmen graduated first in their class.

Requirements: The SAT or ACT is required. Students are required to submit a high school transcript, two letters of recommendation, a school report, official SAT or ACT test scores, and a writing sample or personal statement. Interviews are recommended but not required. GED or High School Proficiency are accepted in lieu of a High School Transcript. We recommend a cumulative GPA of 3.0 or higher and SAT scores above 1500 combined. AP and CLEP credits are accepted. Important factors in the admissions decision are advanced placement or honors courses, personality/intangible qualities, and recommendations by school officials.

Procedure: Freshmen are admitted fall and spring. Entrance exams should be taken at least 1 month prior to application. There are early decision and deferred admissions plans. Early decision applications should be filed by November 15; regular applications, by February 1 for fall entry; and November 1 for spring entry, along with a $50 fee. Notification of early decision is sent December 1; regular decision, February 15. 496 early decision candidates were accepted for the 2013-2014 class. Applications are accepted online.

Transfer: 117 transfer students enrolled in 2012-2013. A writing sample, two letters of recommendation, a high school transcript, and official transcripts from all colleges attended are required.The recommended minimum GPA to apply to Mills is 3.0. We consider other factors such as writing skills, strength of curriculum, and number of credit hours. 12 of 34 credits required for the bachelor's degree must be completed at Mills.

Visiting: There are regularly scheduled orientations for prospective students, Consisting of class visits, campus tours, lunch with faculty, financial aid workshops, an admissions interview, and an overnight stay. There are guides for informal visits, visitors may sit in on classes, and stay overnight. To schedule a visit, contact Kathleen Mulvey at kmulvey@mills.edu.

Financial Aid: In 2013-2014, 99% of all full-time freshmen and 95% of continuing full-time students received some form of financial aid. 88% of all full-time freshmen and 84% of continuing full-time students received need-based aid. The average freshman award was $40,894. Need-based scholarships or need-based grants averaged $27,603; and need-based self-help aid (loans and jobs) averaged $6,297. 104% of undergraduate students work part-time. Average annual earnings from campus work are $2292. The average financial indebtedness of the 2013 graduate was $29,349. The FAFSA and the college's own financial statement are required. The priority date for freshman financial aid applications for fall entry is January 15. The deadline for filing freshman financial aid applications for fall entry is February 15.

International Students: There are 14 international students enrolled. They must take the TOEFL with a minimum score of 550 on the paper-based TOEFL (PBT) or 80 on the Internet-based version (iBT).

Computers: All students may access the system 24 hours a day, year-round. There are no time limits. The fee is $180.

Graduates: From July 1, 2012 to June 30, 2013, 240 bachelor's degrees were awarded. The most popular majors were English (40%), psychology (25%), and biology (18%). 63 companies recruited on campus in 2012-2013. In an average class, 53% graduate in 4 years or less, 61% graduate in 5 years or less, and 64% graduate in 6 years or less. Of the 2012 graduating class, 20% were enrolled in graduate school within 6 months of graduation, and 36% were employed.

Admissions Contact: Belinda Zazueta, Director of Undergraduate Admission . E-Mail: *admission@mills.edu* Web: *www.mills.edu*

MOUNT ST. MARY'S COLLEGE/CHALON CAMPUS C-5

Los Angeles, CA 90049 (310) 954-4250
(800) 999-9893; (310) 954-4259

Full-time: 91 men, 1712 women	**Faculty:** 88
Part-time: 83 men, 402 women	**Ph.D.s:** 61%
Graduate: 126 men, 448 women	**Student/Faculty:** 12 to 1
Year: semesters	**Tuition:** $33,367
Application Deadline: February 15	**Room & Board:** $10,530
Freshman Class: 1799 applied, 309 accepted, 528 enrolled	
SAT or ACT: required	
	VERY COMPETITIVE+

Mount Saint Mary's College, founded in 1925 and affiliated with the Catholic Church, is a private, primarily women's institution that offers programs in the liberal arts and sciences. There is one undergraduate school and one graduate school. In addition to regional accreditation, The Mount has baccalaureate program accreditation with NLN. The 2 libraries contain 140,000 volumes, and 2,520 audio/video tapes/CDs/DVDs, and subscribe to 25,000 periodicals including electronic. Computerized library services include interlibrary loans, database searching, Internet access, and Wi-Fi capability. Special learning facilities include an art gallery, and a Film Studio. The 72-acre campus is in an urban area 10 miles west of Los Angeles. Including any residence halls, there are 31 buildings.

Student Life: 97% of undergraduates are from California. Others are from 19 states, 5 foreign countries, and Canada. 70% are from public schools. 49% are Hispanic; 17% Asian American; 15% White. 53% are Catholic; 14% Protestant; 13% claim no religious affiliation. The average age of freshmen is 18; all undergraduates, 23. 16% do not continue beyond their first year; 84% remain to graduate.

Housing: 668 students can be accommodated in college housing, which includes single-sex dorms. On-campus housing is available on a first-come and first-served basis. 71% of students commute. All students may keep cars.

Activities: There are no fraternities; 1% of women belong to 2 local and 1 national sororities. There are 28 groups on campus, including art, choir, drama, environmental, ethnic, film, gay, Greek cultural, honors, international, newspaper, political, professional, religious, social, social service, student government, and yearbook. Popular campus events include Leadership Boot Camp, Charity Ball and Spring Carnival.

Sports: There are 1 intramural sports for men and 2 for women. Facilities include a basketball court, tennis courts, volleyball court, swimming pool, fitness workout room, and dance studio.

Disabled Students: All of the campus is accessible. Facilities include wheelchair ramps, elevators, special parking, specially equipped restrooms, lowered drinking fountains, lowered telephones, and special housing.

Services: Counseling and information services are available, as is tutoring in most subjects. A peer tutoring program is available.

Campus Safety and Security: Measures include 24-hour foot and vehicle patrol, emergency notification system, self-defense education, and security escort services. There are shuttle buses, emergency telephones, lighted pathways/sidewalks, and controlled access to dorms/residences.

Programs of Study: The Mount confers B.A., B.S. and B.S.N. degrees. Associate, master's, and doctoral degrees are also awarded. Bachelor's degrees are awarded in BIOLOGICAL SCIENCE (biochemistry and biology/biological science), BUSINESS (business administration and management), COMMUNICATIONS AND THE ARTS (art, English, film arts, French, music, and Spanish), COMPUTER AND PHYSICAL SCIENCE (chemistry and mathematics), EDUCATION (elementary education), HEALTH PROFESSIONS (health care administration and nursing), SOCIAL SCIENCE (American studies, child psychology/development, counseling/psychology, gerontology, history, liberal arts/general studies, philosophy, political science/government, psychology, religion, social science, social work, and sociology). Nursing is the strongest academically and has the largest enrollment.

Required: To graduate, students must complete at least 124 semester units with a GPA of 2.0 (C average); a minimum of 45 semester units must be in upper-division work. The total number of hours students must complete in their major varies. All students must satisfy a senior residence requirement and complete a general studies program. Freshmen entering the college with fewer than 24 units must complete Introduction to College Studies. Students must file a graduation application in the Registrar's Office by the end of the term prior to the term of projected completion.

Special: The Mount offers cross-registration with UCLA, the University of Judaism, internships, study abroad in 17 countries, a Washington semester through American University, dual and student-designed majors, work-study programs, and an accelerated degree program in nursing. There are 20 national honor societies, including Phi Beta Kappa, and a freshman honors program.

Faculty/Classroom: 27% of faculty are male; 73% are female. 92% teach undergraduates. No introductory courses are taught by graduate students. The average class size in an introductory lecture is 23; in a laboratory is 18; and in a regular course is 23.

Admissions: 17% of the 2013-2014 applicants were accepted.

Requirements: The SAT or ACT is required. Applicants must be graduates of an accredited secondary school or have earned the GED, with 16 academic credits and 16 Carnegie units, including 4 years of English literature and composition, 2 or 3 years each of math, science, and social studies, and 1 or 2 years of history. An essay is required, and an interview is recommended. A GPA of 2.5 is required. AP and CLEP credits are accepted. Important factors in the admissions decision are advanced placement or honors courses, extracurricular activities record, and leadership record.

Procedure: Freshmen are admitted fall and spring. Entrance exams should be taken at the end of the junior year or the beginning of the senior year. There is a rolling admissions plan. Applications should be filed by February 15 for fall entry; November 1 for spring entry, along with a $50 fee. Notification is sent on a rolling basis. Applications are accepted online.

Transfer: 254 transfer students enrolled in 2012-2013. Transfer students must have a minimum 2.40 GPA with at least 24 completed credit hours. 30 of 124 credits required for the bachelor's degree must be completed at The Mount.

Visiting: There are regularly scheduled orientations for prospective students, including workshops, student panels, tours, class visits, and faculty presentations. There are guides for informal visits, visitors may sit in on classes, and stay overnight. To schedule a visit, contact the Admissions Office.

Financial Aid: In 2013-2014, 92% of all full-time freshmen and 80% of continuing full-time students received some form of financial aid. 86% of all full-time freshmen and 77% of continuing full-time students received need-based aid. The average freshman award was $29,900. Need-based scholarships or need-based grants averaged $11,000; and need-based self-help aid (loans and jobs) averaged $5,500 ($12,000 maximum). 45% of undergraduate students work part-time. Average annual earnings from campus work are $2723. The average financial indebtedness of the 2013 graduate was $26,500. The Mount is a member of CSS. The FAFSA and the college's own financial statement are required. The priority date for freshman financial aid applications for fall entry is February 15.

International Students: There are 22 international students enrolled. They must take the TOEFL with a minimum score of 530 on the paper-based TOEFL (PBT) or 75 on the Internet-based version (iBT). They must also take the SAT or ACT.

Computers: All students may access the system anytime. There are no time limits and no fees.

Graduates: From July 1, 2012 to June 30, 2013, 360 bachelor's degrees were awarded. The most popular majors were nursing (50%), sociology (13%), and business (11%). In an average class, 54% graduate in 4 years or less, 59% graduate in 5 years or less, and 62% graduate in 6 years or less. Of the 2012 graduating class, 26% were enrolled in graduate school within 6 months of graduation, and 31% were employed.

Admissions Contact: Yvonne Berumen, Director of Admissions. E-Mail: *admissions@msmc.la.edu* Web: *www.msmc.la.edu*

NATIONAL UNIVERSITY

D-5

La Jolla, CA 92037

800-NAT-UNIV
(800) NAT-UNIV; (858) 642-8709

Full-time: 670 men, 1000 women	**Faculty:** n/av
Part-time: 2020 men, 2230 women	**Ph.D.s:** n/av
Graduate: 7700 men, 12275 women	**Student/Faculty:** n/av
Year: trimesters, summer session	**Tuition:** n/av
Application Deadline: open	**Room & Board:** n/app
Freshman Class: n/av	**SPECIAL**

National University is a private institution that makes lifelong learning opportunities accessible to nontraditional learners in 11 major cities. Courses are offered in an accelerated 1 course per month format. National also offers more than 30 degrees and 300 courses online. The figures given in the above capsule and in this profile are approximate. There are 6 undergraduate schools and 6 graduate schools. The library contains 250,916 volumes, and 7,459 audio/video tapes/CDs/DVDs, and subscribes to 14,111 periodicals including electronic. Computerized library services include interlibrary loans, database searching, Internet access, and laptop Internet portals. Special learning facilities include a learning resource center and TV station. The 15-acre campus is in an urban area 3 miles northeast of downtown San Diego.

Student Life: 94% of undergraduates are from California. Others are from 47 states, 76 foreign countries, and Canada. 55% are white; 17% Hispanic. The average age of freshmen is 29; all undergraduates, 32. 71% remain to graduate.

Housing: There are no residence halls. All students commute.

Activities: There are no fraternities or sororities. There is 1 group on campus, including honors.

Sports: There is no sports program at National.

Disabled Students: All of the campus is accessible. Facilities include wheelchair ramps, elevators, special parking, specially equipped restrooms, special class scheduling, lowered drinking fountains, and lowered telephones.

Services: There is remedial math, reading, and writing.

Campus Safety and Security: Measures include 24-hour foot and vehicle patrol. There are lighted pathways/sidewalks.

Programs of Study: National confers B.A., B.S., B.B.A., and B.S.N. degrees. Associate and master's degrees are also awarded. Bachelor's degrees are awarded in BIOLOGICAL SCIENCE (life science), BUSINESS (accounting, banking and finance, management science, organizational behavior, and organizational leadership and management), COMMUNICATIONS AND THE ARTS (design, English, and multimedia), COMPUTER AND PHYSICAL SCIENCE (computer science, earth science, information sciences and systems, mathematics, and software engineering), ENGINEERING AND ENVIRONMENTAL DESIGN (construction engineering, construction management, and environmental science), HEALTH PROFESSIONS (allied health and nursing), SOCIAL SCIENCE (behavioral science, criminal justice, early childhood studies, history, interdisciplinary studies, international studies, liberal arts/general studies, prelaw, psychology, and sociology). Computer science, accounting, and psychology are the strongest academically. Criminal justice, psychology, and interdisciplinary studies have the largest enrollments.

Required: To graduate, students must complete 180 quarter units, including 36 upper-division quarter units with a minimum GPA of 2.0. A minimum of 45 quarter units in the major and 70.5 in the core curriculum are required.

Special: Cross-registration with California Community Colleges is possible. National offers all degree programs in an accelerated format of 1 course per month. There are 3 national honor societies.

Faculty/Classroom: 67% of faculty are male; 33% are female. All teach and do research. No introductory courses are taught by graduate students. The average class size in an introductory lecture is 18 and in a regular course is 18.

Requirements: Graduation from an accredited secondary school or satisfactory scores on the GED are required for admission. A GPA of 2.0 is required. AP and CLEP credits are accepted.

Procedure: Freshmen are admitted to all sessions. There are deferred admissions and rolling admissions plans. Application deadlines are open. Application fee is $60. Applications are accepted online.

Transfer: Transfer applicants must have a minimum GPA of 2.0. Transcripts from all previous institutions attended must be submitted and an interview is required. 45 of 180 credits required for the bachelor's degree must be completed at National.

Visiting: There are guides for informal visits and visitors may sit in on classes. To schedule a visit, contact Megan Magee at advisor@nu.edu.

Financial Aid: The CSS/Profile, FAFSA, and the college's own financial statement are required. The deadline for filing freshman financial aid applications for fall entry is rolling.

International Students: The school actively recruits these students. They must take the TOEFL or MELAB.

Computers: Wireless access is available. Computers are available to all students. Computer equipment and network access for student use is provided in the computer center, labs, and library. All students may access the system Monday through Friday, 8 a.m. to 9 p.m., and Saturday, 8 a.m. to 2 p.m. There are no time limits and no fees.

Admissions Contact: Admissions Office. E-Mail: *admissions@nu.edu* Web: *www.nu.edu*

NOTRE DAME DE NAMUR UNIVERSITY B-3

Belmont, CA 94002 **(650) 508-3600**
(800) 263-0545; (650) 508-3426

Full-time: 278 men, 467 women	**Faculty:** 47; IIA, -$
Part-time: 115 men, 287 women	**Ph.D.s:** 90%
Graduate: 219 men, 601 women	**Student/Faculty:** 17 to 1
Year: semesters, summer session	**Tuition:** $29,930
Application Deadline:	**Room & Board:** $11,680

Freshman Class: 1789 applied, 1270 accepted, 177 enrolled
SAT CR/M/W: 470/470/480 **ACT:** 20 **LESS COMPETITIVE**

Notre Dame de Namur University is a fully accredited, private, independent, Catholic, co-educational institution serving undergraduate and graduate students. NDNU was founded as College of Notre Dame in 1851 in San Jose, California by the Sisters of Notre Dame de Namur and moved to Belmont, California in 1923. There are 3 undergraduate schools and one graduate school. The library contains 108,006 volumes, and 9,603 audio/video tapes/CDs/DVDs. Computerized library services include interlibrary loans, database searching, Internet access, and Wi-Fi capability. Special learning facilities include an art gallery. The 50-acre campus is in a suburban area 24 miles south of San Francisco. Including any residence halls, there are 24 buildings.

Student Life: 89% of undergraduates are from California. Others are from 24 states, 22 foreign countries, and Canada. 70% are from public schools. 40% are White; 19% Hispanic. 26% are Catholic. The average age of freshmen is 19; all undergraduates, 27. 28% do not continue beyond their first year; 55% remain to graduate.

Housing: 475 students can be accommodated in college housing, which includes coed dorms and on-campus apartments. On-campus housing is available on a first-come and first-served basis. 60% of students commute. All students may keep cars.

Activities: There are no fraternities or sororities. There are 20 groups on campus, including science and medical careers, academic, art, cheerleading, choir, computers, dance, drama, environmental, ethnic, gay, honors, international, musical theater, newspaper, professional, religious, social, social service, and student government. Popular campus events include Collaborations Day, Halloween Dance, and Thanksgiving in the Park.

Sports: There are 5 intercollegiate sports for men and 6 for women. Facilities include a gym, tennis courts, a soccer/lacrosse field, weight room, swimming pool, an arcade, and pool tables.

Disabled Students: 90% of the campus is accessible. Facilities include wheelchair ramps, elevators, special parking, specially equipped restrooms, and special class scheduling.

Services: Counseling and information services are available, as is tutoring in most subjects. There is remedial math, reading, and writing.

Campus Safety and Security: Measures include 24-hour foot and vehicle patrol, emergency notification system, and security escort services. There are shuttle buses and lighted pathways/sidewalks.

Programs of Study: NDNU confers B.A., B.S. and B.F.A. degrees. Master's degrees are also awarded. Bachelor's degrees are awarded in BIOLOGICAL SCIENCE (biochemistry and biology/biological science), BUSINESS (accounting, business administration and management, international business management, and marketing/retailing/merchandising), COMMUNICATIONS AND THE ARTS (art, communications, dramatic arts, English, fine arts, graphic design, and music), COMPUTER AND PHYSICAL SCIENCE (computer science and information sciences and systems), HEALTH PROFESSIONS (nursing), SOCIAL SCIENCE (history, human services, humanities, liberal arts/general studies, philosophy, physical fitness/movement, political science/government, psychology, religion, social science, and sociology). Biology, pre-medicine, and English are the strongest academically. Business administration, liberal studies, and psychology have the largest enrollments.

Required: All students must complete 34 to 36 units in common core requirements, 18 units in breadth requirements, and 3 units of career development. They must also satisfy 5 core competency requirements through courses that may also satisfy other requirements. American history is required for students who have not completed such a course in an American high school or an American international school. A total of 124 semester units with an overall GPA of 2.0 is required to graduate.

Special: The college offers a Washington semester through American University and Trinity College as well as an exchange program with Emmanuel College in Boston. Internships, accelerated degree programs in business administration, human service, and liberal studies, B.A.-B.S. degree in biology, dual and student-designed majors, a general studies degree, credit for military experience, and pass/fail options are offered. Study abroad is available in 7 countries. Non-degree study is possible. There are 6 national honor societies.

Faculty/Classroom: 45% of faculty are male; 55% are female. 68% teach undergraduates. No introductory courses are taught by graduate students. The average class size in an introductory lecture is 20; in a laboratory is 12; and in a regular course is 16.

Admissions: 71% of the 2013-2014 applicants were accepted. The SAT scores for the 2013-2014 freshman class were: Critical Reading--60% below 500, 31% between 500 and 599, 8% between 600 and 699, and 1% between 700 and 800; Math--63% below 500, 28% between 500 and 599, 9% between 600 and 699; Writing--59% below 500, 37% between 500 and 599, and 4% between 600 and 699. The ACT scores were 54% below 21, 29% between 21 and 23, 12% between 24 and 26, 2% between 27 and 28, and 3% above 28. 33% of the current freshmen were in the top fifth of their class; 55% were in the top two fifths.

Requirements: The SAT is required. Applicants should have completed 16 Carnegie units, including 4 years of high school English, 2 each of math, history/social studies, foreign language, and 1 of lab science. In addition, students should have 1 year in 3 of these areas beyond the basic requirements. An essay is required. An audition is required for music programs. A GPA of 2.0 is required. AP and CLEP credits are accepted. Important factors in the admissions decision are advanced placement or honors courses, evidence of special talent, and leadership record.

Procedure: Freshmen are admitted fall, spring, and summer. Entrance exams should be taken by the December test date of the senior year. There are early admissions, deferred admissions, and rolling admissions plans. Application deadlines are open. Application fee is $50. Notification is sent on a rolling basis. Applications are accepted online.

Transfer: 194 transfer students enrolled in 2012-2013. Transfer applicants must have a 2.0 GPA to be considered for admission. 30 of 124 credits required for the bachelor's degree must be completed at NDNU.

Visiting: There are regularly scheduled orientations for prospective students, consisting of tours and information on student life, financial aid, academics, and registration. There are guides for informal visits and visitors may sit in on classes. To schedule a visit, contact the Admission Office.

Financial Aid: In 2013-2014, 97% of all full-time freshmen and 86% of continuing full-time students received some form of financial aid. 92% of all full-time freshmen and 85% of continuing full-time students received need-based aid. The average freshman award was $27,074. Need-based scholarships or need-based grants averaged $20,868; and need-based self-help aid (loans and jobs) averaged $4,218. The average financial indebtedness of the 2013 graduate was $27,280. NDNU is a member of CSS. The FAFSA is required. The priority date for freshman financial aid applications for fall entry is March 2.

International Students: There are 20 international students enrolled. The school actively recruits these students. They must take the TOEFL with a minimum score of 500 on the paper-based TOEFL (PBT) or 61 on the Internet-based version (iBT).

Computers: All students may access the system 7 days a week. There are no time limits and no fees.

Graduates: From July 1, 2012 to June 30, 2013, 196 bachelor's degrees were awarded. The most popular majors were business administration and management (30%), human services (15%), and psychology (12%). In an average class, 5% graduate in 3 years or less, 45% graduate in 4 years or less, 50% graduate in 5 years or less, and 55% graduate in 6 years or less.

Admissions Contact: Jason Murray, Director of Admissions. E-Mail: *admissions@ndnu.edu* Web: *www.ndnu.edu*

OCCIDENTAL COLLEGE C-5

Los Angeles, CA 90041 **(323) 259-2700**
(800) 825-5262; (323) 341-4875

Full-time: 924 men, 1189 women	**Faculty:** 163; IIB, +$
Part-time: 6 men, 9 women	**Ph.D.s:** 94%
Graduate: n/av	**Student/Faculty:** 12 to 1
Year: semesters, summer session	**Tuition:** $46,652
Application Deadline: January 10	**Room & Board:** $12,940

Freshman Class: 6072 applied, 2554 accepted, 552 enrolled
SAT CR/M/W: 650/650/660 **ACT:** 30 **MOSTCOMPETITIVE+**

Occidental College, founded in 1887, is a private nonsectarian school of liberal arts and sciences, one of the few top liberal arts colleges in an urban setting. There is one undergraduate school. The library contains 431,586 volumes, 6,839 microform items, and 12,338 audio/video tapes/CDs/DVDs, and subscribes to 55,322 periodicals including electronic. Computerized library services include interlibrary loans, database searching, Internet access, and Wi-Fi capability. Special learning facilities include an art gallery, radio station, student newspaper and yearbook, fully equipped theater, art studio and gallery, ornithology and geology collections, and physics, plasma, and optic labs. The 120-acre campus is in an urban area in the city of Los Angeles. Including any residence halls, there are 44 buildings.

Student Life: 51% of undergraduates are from California. Others are from 44 states, 24 foreign countries, and Canada. 58% are from public schools. 51% are White; 16% Hispanic; 13% Asian American. 35% are Protestant; 30% claim no religious affiliation; 19% Catholic; 11% Jewish. The average age of freshmen is 18; all undergraduates, 20. 7% do not continue beyond their first year; 88% remain to graduate.

Housing: 1565 students can be accommodated in college housing, which includes single-sex and coed dorms. In addition, there are special-interest houses, fraternity houses, multicultural, sustainability, food justice, pet, and gender neutral. On-campus housing is available on a lottery system for upperclassmen. 70% of students live on campus; of those, 60% remain on campus on weekends. All students may keep cars.

Activities: 10% of men belong to 5 national fraternities; 13% of women belong to 2 local and 2 national sororities. There are 116 groups on campus, including art, cheerleading, chess, choir, chorale, dance, drama, environmental, ethnic, film, gay, honors, international, jazz band, literary magazine, musical theater, newspaper, orchestra, photography, political, professional, radio and TV, religious, social, social service, student government, student investment fund; entrepreneurs, symphony, and yearbook. Popular campus events include Dance Production, New Play Festival, and Taste of Oxy.

Sports: There are 10 intercollegiate sports for men and 11 for women, and 6 intramural sports for men and 6 for women. Facilities include a football, soccer, baseball, and softball fields, an all-weather track, tennis courts, an outdoor pool, outdoor basketball courts, a dance studio, a sports medicine center, gym, weight room, and a fitness center.

Disabled Students: 80% of the campus is accessible. Facilities include wheelchair ramps, elevators, special parking, specially equipped restrooms, lowered drinking fountains, lowered telephones. Occidental has a hillside campus.

Services: Counseling and information services are available, as is tutoring in most subjects. Peer and faculty advisers are available through the Center for Academic Excellence

Campus Safety and Security: Measures include 24-hour foot and vehicle patrol, emergency notification system, and security escort services. There are shuttle buses, emergency telephones, lighted pathways/sidewalks, controlled access to dorms/residences, whistle alert program.

Programs of Study: Oxy confers A.B. degrees. Master's degrees are also awarded. Bachelor's degrees are awarded in BIOLOGICAL SCIENCE (biochemistry and biology/biological science), COMMUNICATIONS AND THE ARTS (art history, Chinese, English, French, Japanese, languages, music, Spanish, and theatre arts), COMPUTER AND PHYSICAL SCIENCE (chemistry, geology, mathematics, and physics), SOCIAL SCIENCE (American studies, asian studies, cognitive science, cultural studies/critical theory & analysis, East Asian studies, economics, history, international relations, Latin American studies, philosophy, physical fitness/movement, political science/government, psychology, religion, sociology, and urban studies). Social sciences, biology, and chemistry are the strongest academically. Social sciences, English, and diplomacy and world affairs have the largest enrollments.

Required: To graduate, students must complete 32 courses of 4 semester hours each and maintain a minimum GPA of 2.0. In addition, all students must fulfill core course requirements in foreign language, fine arts, writing proficiency; 12 units are required in science and mathematics, foreign language, and cultural studies. To graduate, all students must complete a comprehensive exam; some majors require a thesis.

Special: Cross-registration is permitted with the California Institute of Technology and the Art Center College of Design. Students may study abroad in 41 countries in Europe, Asia, Africa, and Latin America. Opportunities are provided for internships, a Washington semester, a U.N. semester in New York City, dual and student-designed majors, a 3-2 engineering degree with the California Institute of Technology, a 3-3 law program with Columbia, a 4-2 biotech program with Keck, and an exchange program with Spelman and Morehouse. There are 8 national honor societies including Phi Beta Kappa.

Faculty/Classroom: 56% of faculty are male; 44% are female. All teach and do research. No introductory courses are taught by graduate students. The average class size in an introductory lecture is 19; in a laboratory is 12; and in a regular course is 15.

Admissions: 42% of the 2013-2014 applicants were accepted. The SAT scores for the 2013-2014 freshman class were: Critical Reading--1% below 500, 20% between 500 and 599, 53% between 600 and 699, and 26% between 700 and 800; Math--1% below 500, 19% between 500 and 599, 54% between 600 and 699, and 27% between 700 and 800; Writing--1% below 500, 18% between 500 and 599, 53% between 600 and 699, and 28% between 700 and 800. The ACT scores were 34% above 28. 83% of the current freshmen were in the top fifth of their class.

Requirements: The SAT or ACT is required. Applicants should be high school graduates of high academic standing with 4 years of English, 4 of math, 3 each of foreign language and science, and 2 each of social studies and history. The GED is accepted. An essay is required and an interview is recommended. AP credits are accepted. Important factors in the admissions decision are extracurricular activities record, advanced placement or honors courses, and recommendations by school officials.

Procedure: Freshmen are admitted fall. Entrance exams should be taken no later than December of the senior year. There are early decision and deferred admissions plans. Early decision applications should be filed by November 15; regular applications, by January 10 for fall entry, along with a $60 fee. Notification of early decision is sent December 15; regular decision, April 1. 122 early decision candidates were accepted for the 2013-2014 class. 344 applicants were on the 2013 waiting list; 19 were admitted. Applications are accepted online.

Transfer: 34 transfer students enrolled in 2012-2013. Students must have at least a B average (3.0 GPA) in all courses submitted for transfer credit. The SAT or ACT is required. The application deadline is March 15 for the fall, October 15 for the spring. 64 of 128 credits required for the bachelor's degree must be completed at Oxy.

Visiting: There are regularly scheduled orientations for prospective students, including campus tours Monday through Friday at 10:15 a.m. and 1:30 p.m., followed by information sessions with an admission officer at 11:30 a.m. and 4 p.m. There are guides for informal visits, visitors may sit in on classes, and stay overnight. To schedule a visit, contact the Office of Admission at admission@oxy.edu.

Financial Aid: In 2013-2014, 66% of all full-time freshmen and 72% of continuing full-time students received some form of financial aid. 56% of all full-time freshmen and 58% of continuing full-time students received need-based aid. The average freshman award was $27,041. Need-based scholarships or need-based grants averaged $31,258 ($61,033 maximum); need-based self-help aid (loans and jobs) averaged $6,788 ($13,500 maximum); and other non-need-based awards and non-need-based scholarships averaged $8,222 ($49,918 maximum). 57% of undergraduate students work part-time. Average annual earnings from campus work are $1546. The average financial indebtedness of the 2013 graduate was $21,015. The CSS/Profile, FAFSA, and the state aid form, and noncustodial parent's statement are required. The deadline for filing freshman financial aid applications for fall entry is February 1.

International Students: There are 103 international students enrolled. The school actively recruits these students. They must take the TOEFL with a minimum score of 600 on the paper-based TOEFL (PBT). They must also take the SAT or ACT.

Computers: All students may access the system at any time. There are no time limits and no fees.

Graduates: From July 1, 2012 to June 30, 2013, 554 bachelor's degrees were awarded. The most popular majors were economics (14%), diplomacy and world affairs (11%), and biology (10%). 50 companies recruited on campus in 2012 2013. In an average class, 82% graduate in 4 years or less, 86% graduate in 5 years or less, and 88% graduate in 6 years or less. Of the 2012 graduating class, 30% were enrolled in graduate school within 6 months of graduation, and 65% were employed.

Admissions Contact: Sally Richmond, Director of Admissions. E-Mail: *admission@oxy.edu* Web: *www.oxy.edu*

OTIS COLLEGE OF ART AND DESIGN — C-5

Los Angeles, CA 90045 — (310) 665-6820; (800) 527-6847; (310) 665-6821

Full-time: 364 men, 781 women	**Faculty:** n/av
Part-time: 2 men, 11 women	**Ph.D.s:** 50%
Graduate: 18 men, 50 women	**Student/Faculty:** 22 to 1
Year: semesters, summer session	**Tuition:** $35,904
Application Deadline:	**Room & Board:** n/av
Freshman Class: 1204 applied, 1106 accepted, 318 enrolled	
SAT CR/M/W: 510/500/480 **ACT:** 19	**SPECIAL**

Otis College of Art and Design, founded in 1918, is a private college offering undergraduate programs in fine arts (painting, photo, and sculpture/new genres), advertising, graphic design and illustration, fashion design, toy design, product design, architecture/landscape/interiors, and digital media design. Graduate programs in fine arts, writing, public practice and graphic design. As part of their instruction, students work directly with professional artists, designers, critics, and writers. There are 7 undergraduate schools and 4 graduate schools. In addition to regional accreditation, Otis has baccalaureate program accreditation with NASAD. The library contains 42,000 volumes, and 2,500 audio/video tapes/CDs/DVDs, and subscribes to 150 periodicals including electronic. Computerized library services include database searching, Internet access, and Wi-Fi capability. Special learning facilities include an art gallery, a photographic darkroom, printmaking studios, a fine books press room, a woodworking studio, a digital imaging room, a metalworking shop, prototype shop, and multiuse studios. The 5-acre campus is in an urban area on the west side of Los Angeles. Including any residence halls, there are 3 buildings. The figures in the above capsule and in this profile are approximate.

Student Life: 74% of undergraduates are from California. Others are from 50 states, 32 foreign countries, and Canada. 75% are from public schools. 33% are Asian American; 23% White; 16% Foreign; 13% Hispanic. The average age of all undergraduates is 22. 31% do not continue beyond their first year.

Housing: 120 students can be accommodated in college housing, which includes single-sex off-campus apartments. On-campus housing is available on a first-come and first-served basis. Priority is given to out-of-town students. 90% of students commute. Alcohol is not permitted. All students may keep cars.

Activities: There are no fraternities or sororities. Groups on campus include art, gay, international, literary magazine, newspaper, religious, social, and student government. Popular campus events include Gallery Openings, Yearly Fashion Design Show, and Student Leadership Retreat.

Sports: There is no sports program at Otis.

Disabled Students: All of the campus is accessible. Facilities include wheelchair ramps, elevators, special parking, specially equipped restrooms, lowered drinking fountains, and lowered telephones.

Services: Counseling and information services are available, as is tutoring in most subjects. There is remedial math, reading, and writing.

Campus Safety and Security: Measures include 24-hour foot and vehicle patrol, emergency notification system, self-defense education, and security escort services. There are emergency telephones and lighted pathways/sidewalks.

Programs of Study: Otis confers B.F.A. degrees. Master's degrees are also awarded. Bachelor's degrees are awarded in COMMUNICATIONS AND THE ARTS (advertising, design, graphic design, illustration, industrial design, painting, photography, toy design, and visual effects), COMPUTER AND PHYSICAL SCIENCE (digital arts/technology), ENGINEERING AND ENVIRONMENTAL DESIGN (architecture), SOCIAL SCIENCE (fashion design and technology). Digital media design, communication arts (graphic design and illustration), and fashion design are the largest.

Required: The bachelor of fine arts is awarded to students in good academic standing who have successfully completed no less than 130 credits, of which a minimum of 30 are in the liberal arts, with 12 in the history of art and design. Graduation requirements include course work in computer literacy, English, humanities, math, biological or physical sciences, and social science.

Special: Study abroad is available in London, Paris, and Stockholm. Internships are available for many different companies, across majors. Independent study is also available. There are a freshman honors program.

Faculty/Classroom: 42% of faculty are male; 58% are female. All teach undergraduates. No introductory courses are taught by graduate students. The average class size in an introductory lecture is 20.

Admissions: 92% of the 2013-2014 applicants were accepted. The SAT scores for the 2013-2014 freshman class were: Critical Reading--46% below 500, 34% between 500 and 599, 17% between 600 and 699, and 3% between 700 and 800; Math--36% below 500, 38% between 500 and 599, 20% between 600 and 699, and 6% between 700 and 800; Writing--48% below 500, 35% between 500 and 599, 15% between 600 and 699, and 2% between 700 and 800. The ACT scores were 46% below 21, 31% between 21 and 23, 8% between 24 and 26, 8% between 27 and 28, and 7% above 28.

Requirements: The SAT or ACT is required. In addition, Applicants must be graduates of an accredited secondary school or have a GED certificate and submit a portfolio. Interviews are recommended for students, and essays are required. Applicants must have 4 units of English, 3 of math, 2 each of science (1 lab) and history, and 1 of social studies. A GPA of 2.5 is required. AP credits are accepted.

Procedure: Freshmen are admitted fall and spring. Entrance exams should be taken in the fall. There is a rolling admissions plan. Application deadlines are open. Application fee is $50. Applications are accepted online.

Transfer: 160 transfer students enrolled in 2012-2013. Transfer students must have a minimum 2.5 GPA and submit high school and college transcripts, an essay, and a statement of good standing from prior institutions. A portfolio is required. An interview is recommended. 62 of 130 credits required for the bachelor's degree must be completed at Otis.

Visiting: There are regularly scheduled orientations for prospective students, including a campus tour, portfolio evaluation, and financial aid information. There are guides for informal visits. To schedule a visit, contact the Admissions Office.

Financial Aid: The FAFSA and the state aid form are required. The priority date for freshman financial aid applications for fall entry is February 15.

International Students: There are 183 international students enrolled. The school actively recruits these students. They must take the TOEFL with a minimum score of 550 on the paper-based TOEFL (PBT) or 79 on the Internet-based version (iBT), iELTS or Pearson's Test of English. They must also take the SAT or ACT. students from countries where English is the official language should take the ACT or SAT instead of the TOEFL.

Computers: All students may access the system. There are no time limits and no fees.

Graduates: The most popular majors were visual arts (96%) and architecture (4%).

Admissions Contact: Yvette Sobky Shaffer, Assistant Director & Interim Dean Admiss. E-Mail: *admissions@otis.edu* Web: *www.otis.edu*

PACIFIC UNION COLLEGE — B-2

Angwin, CA 94508-9707 — (707) 965-6336; (800) 862-7080; (707) 965-6432

Full-time: 500 men, 575 women
Part-time: 135 men, 165 women
Graduate: n/av
Year: trimesters, summer session
Application Deadline: open
Freshman Class: n/av
SAT or ACT: recommended

Faculty: n/av
Ph.D.s: n/av
Student/Faculty: n/av
Tuition: $22,650
Room & Board: $6500

VERY COMPETITIVE

Pacific Union College, founded in 1888, is a private college affiliated with the Seventh-day Adventist Church, offering programs in liberal arts, religion, business, health science, and teacher preparation, among others. The figures given in the above capsule and in this profile are approximate. There is 1 graduate school. In addition to regional accreditation, PUC has baccalaureate program accreditation with CSWE, NASM, and NLN. The library contains 148,218 volumes, 125,268 microform items, and 6,623 audio/video tapes/CDs/DVDs, and subscribes to 10,637 periodicals including electronic. Computerized library services include interlibrary loans, database searching, Internet access, and laptop Internet portals. Special learning facilities include a learning resource center, art gallery, natural history museum, radio station, a video production studio, an observatory and a marine field station. The 1500-acre campus is in a rural area 70 miles north of San Francisco. Including any residence halls, there are 60 buildings.

Student Life: 76% of undergraduates are from California. Others are from 42 states, 26 foreign countries, and Canada. 40% are white; 29% Asian American; 15% Hispanic. The average age of freshmen is 19; all undergraduates, 21. 32% do not continue beyond their first year; 40% remain to graduate.

Housing: 1344 students can be accommodated in college housing, which includes single-sex dorms and married student housing. On-campus housing is guaranteed for the freshman year only. 76% of students live on campus. Alcohol is not permitted. All students may keep cars.

Activities: There are no fraternities or sororities. There are 50 groups on campus, including campus ministries, academic interest groups, art, band, chess, choir, chorale, computers, drama, ethnic, film, honors, jazz band, literary magazine, newspaper, orchestra, photography, political, radio and TV, religious, social, student government, symphony, and yearbook. Popular campus events include picnic and ski days, All-College Get-Acquainted Party, and Fall and Spring Festivals.

Sports: There are 3 intercollegiate sports for men and 3 for women, and 6 intramural sports for men and 6 for women. Facilities include a gym, a pool, lighted tennis courts, and 3 athletic fields for softball, soccer, volleyball, flag ball, and track and field.

Disabled Students: 95% of the campus is accessible. Facilities include wheelchair ramps, elevators, special parking, specially equipped restrooms, and special class scheduling.

Services: Counseling and information services are available, as is tutoring in most subjects. There is a reader service for the blind, and remedial math and writing.

Campus Safety and Security: Measures include 24-hour foot and vehicle patrol, emergency notification system, self-defense education, and security escort services. There are emergency telephones, lighted pathways/sidewalks, and a safety committee.

Programs of Study: PUC confers B.A., B.S., B.B.A., B.Mus., and B.S.W. degrees. Associate and master's degrees are also awarded. Bachelor's degrees are awarded in BIOLOGICAL SCIENCE (biology/biological science and biophysics), BUSINESS (business administration and management), COMMUNICATIONS AND THE ARTS (communications, English, fine arts, French, graphic design, journalism, music, photography, public relations, radio/television technology, and Spanish), COMPUTER AND PHYSICAL SCIENCE (applied mathematics, chemistry, computer science, mathematics, natural sciences, and physics), EDUCATION (early childhood education and physical education), ENGINEERING AND ENVIRONMENTAL DESIGN (airline piloting and navigation and graphic arts technology), HEALTH PROFESSIONS (nursing), SOCIAL SCIENCE (history, psychology, religion, social studies, social work, and theological studies). Sciences and behavioral science are the strongest academically. Nursing and business administration have the largest enrollments.

Required: To graduate, a student must complete a minimum of 192 quarter hours, including 60 in upper-level courses, maintain a minimum GPA of 2.0. Distribution requirements include courses in rhetoric, statistics, historic, philosophy, social science, foreign language, literature, visual and applied arts, music, math, science, and health and fitness. A religion course is required, as is a thesis in some programs.

Special: Students may study abroad in Austria, Spain, France, Argentina, and Italy, earn B.A.-B.S. degrees, take dual majors, and pursue a major in interdisciplinary studies. Internships, social work, education, and ministerial field experiences, and accelerated degree programs in business management and early childhood education are also offered. The college offers nondegree study and credit for life, military, and work experience. There are 2 national honor societies and a freshman honors program.

Faculty/Classroom: 56% of faculty are male; 44% are female. All teach undergraduates. No introductory courses are taught by graduate students. The average class size in an introductory lecture is 19; in a laboratory is 18; and in a regular course is 17.

Requirements: The SAT or ACT is recommended. Scores are used only for advising purposes. Candidates for admission should have completed 4 years of English, 2 of math, and 1 each of science and history. A GPA of 2.3 is required. AP and CLEP credits are accepted. Important factors in the admissions decision are recommendations by school officials, leadership record, and advanced placement or honors courses.

Procedure: Freshmen are admitted to all sessions. Entrance exams should be taken in the junior or senior year. There is a rolling admissions plan. Application deadlines are open. Application fee is $30. Applications are accepted online.

Transfer: Admission requirements are the same as for nontransfer students. 36 of 192 credits required for the bachelor's degree must be completed at PUC.

Visiting: There are regularly scheduled orientations for prospective students. There are guides for informal visits, visitors may sit in on classes, and stay overnight. To schedule a visit, contact the Admissions Office.

Financial Aid: In a recent year, 100% of all full-time freshmen and 99% of continuing full-time students received some form of financial aid. 95% of all full-time freshmen and 64% of continuing full-time students received need-based aid. 80% of undergraduate students work part-time. Average annual earnings from campus work are $1500. The FAFSA and the college's own financial statement are required. Check with the school for current application deadlines.

International Students: There are 92 international students enrolled. They must take the TOEFL. They must also take the SAT or ACT.

Computers: Wireless access is available. All dorms have an Ethernet port available. Wireless access is available in public areas such as dorm lobbies, dining commons, and the campus center. Labs providing Internet connectivity total approximately 175 computers. All students may access the system. at any time. There are no time limits and no fees. It is strongly recommended that all students have a personal computer.

Graduates: In a recent year, 325 bachelor's degrees were awarded. The most popular majors were nursing (36%), business (19%), and chemistry (5%). In an average class, 12% graduate in 4 years or less, 19% graduate in 5 years or less, and 36% graduate in 6 years or less.

Admissions Contact: Darren Hagen, Director of Enrollment Services. A campus DVD is available. E-Mail: *enroll@puc.edu* Web: *www.puc.edu*

PEPPERDINE UNIVERSITY C-4

Malibu, CA 90263	(310) 506-4369; (310) 506-4861
Full-time: 1262 men, 1824 women	**Faculty:** n/av; IIA, ++$
Part-time: 232 men, 170 women	**Ph.D.s:** 100%
Graduate: 1499 men, 2332 women	**Student/Faculty:** 15 to 1
Year: semesters, summer session	**Tuition:** $42,772
Application Deadline: January 5	**Room & Board:** $12,600
Freshman Class: 9222 applied, 3497 accepted, 777 enrolled	
SAT CR/M/W: 604/623/610	**ACT:** 29 **HIGHLY COMPETITIVE+**

Pepperdine University, founded in 1937, is a private liberal arts university affiliated with the Church of Christ. There is one undergraduate school and 4 graduate schools. In addition to regional accreditation, Pepperdine has baccalaureate program accreditation with AACSB and NCATE. The 4 libraries contain 551,502 volumes, 505,458 microform items, and 15,402 audio/video tapes/CDs/DVDs, and subscribe to 51,798 periodicals including electronic. Computerized library services include interlibrary loans, database searching, and Internet access. Special learning facilities include an art gallery, radio station, TV station, Writing Center, The Academic Center for Excellence. The 830-acre campus is in a suburban area 35 miles northwest of Los Angeles, overlooking the Pacific Ocean. Including any residence halls, there are 76 buildings.

Student Life: 53% of undergraduates are from California. Others are from 50 states, 60 foreign countries, and Canada. 65% are from public schools. 45% are White; 15% Hispanic; 12% Asian American. 16% are Catholic. The average age of freshmen is 18; all undergraduates, 20.

Housing: College-sponsored housing includes single-sex dorms, on-campus apartments, off-campus apartments, and married student housing. In addition, there are honors houses and special-interest houses. On-campus housing is guaranteed for the freshman year only and is available on a lottery system for upperclassmen. Alcohol is not permitted. All students may keep cars.

Activities: There are 60 groups on campus, including Hawaiian, women's leadership, art, band, cheerleading, chess, choir, chorale, chorus, computers, dance, debate, drama, environmental, ethnic, film, honors, international, jazz band, literary magazine, medical, musical theater, newspaper, opera, orchestra, pep band, photography, political, professional, radio and TV, religious, social, social service, student government, and symphony. Popular campus events include Waves Weekend, C2F (Culture and Club Fair), Songfest and REEL Stories Student Film Festival.

Sports: There are 8 intercollegiate sports for men and 9 for women, and 7 intramural sports for men and 7 for women. Facilities include a field house, a pool, a weight room, basketball, racquetball, tennis courts, playing fields, an all-weather track, an aerobics room, and a whirlpool/hot tub.

Disabled Students: 90% of the campus is accessible. Facilities include wheelchair ramps, elevators, special parking, specially equipped restrooms, special class scheduling, lowered drinking fountains, lowered telephones, and special housing.

Services: Counseling and information services are available, as is tutoring in most subjects.

Campus Safety and Security: Measures include 24-hour foot and vehicle patrol, emergency notification system, self-defense education, and security escort services. There are shuttle buses, emergency telephones, lighted pathways/sidewalks, in-room safes, guarded entrances to campus, security cameras, and a campus crimewatch program.

Programs of Study: Pepperdine confers B.A., B.S. and B.S.M. degrees. Master's and doctoral degrees are also awarded. Bachelor's degrees are awarded in BIOLOGICAL SCIENCE (biology/biological science and nutrition), BUSINESS (accounting, business administration and management, international business management, management science, and marketing management), COMMUNICATIONS AND THE ARTS (advertising, art, art history and appreciation, communications, creative writing, dramatic arts, English, film arts, French, German, Italian, journalism, media arts, music, public relations, Spanish, speech/debate/rhetoric, and telecommunications), COMPUTER AND PHYSICAL SCIENCE (chemistry, computer science, mathematics, natural sciences, and physics), EDUCATION (elementary education, mathematics education, physical education, and secondary education), ENGINEERING AND ENVIRONMENTAL DESIGN (engineering), HEALTH PROFESSIONS (sports medicine), SOCIAL SCIENCE (economics, Hispanic American studies, history, humanities, international studies, liberal arts/general studies, philosophy, political science/government, psychology, religion, social science, and sociology). Natural sciences (premedical), sports medicine, business administration, economics and political science are the strongest academically. Communication and business have the largest enrollments.

Required: To graduate, students must complete 128 units, including 64 units of general education requirements. 2 years of a broad liberal arts core curriculum are needed. Courses are required in English, religion, Western heritage, non-Western heritage, American heritage, behavioral science, foreign language, lab science, math, speech and rhetoric, freshman seminar, and phys ed. Students must take at least 40 upper-division units and complete a 28-unit residency requirement. Pepperdine requires a minimum GPA of 2.0 for graduation.

Special: Students may earn 1 to 4 units for an internship, available in most majors, participate in a Washington semester, and study abroad in 8 countries. The school offers a 3-2 engineering degree with Washington University in St. Louis and the University of Southern California. There are dual majors in any discipline, student-designed contract majors, federal work-study programs, nondegree study, and pass/fail options. There are 14 national honor societies and 6 departmental honors programs.

Faculty/Classroom: 58% of faculty are male; 42% are female. All teach and do research. No introductory courses are taught by graduate students. The average class size in an introductory lecture is 18; in a laboratory is 15; and in a regular course is 17.

Admissions: 38% of the 2013-2014 applicants were accepted. The SAT scores for the 2013-2014 freshman class were: Critical Reading--6% below 500, 39% between 500 and 599, 42% between 600 and 699, and 13% between 700 and 800; Math--5% below 500, 28% between 500 and 599, 46% between 600 and 699, and 21% between 700 and 800; Writing--5% below 500, 34% between 500 and 599, 43% between 600 and 699, and 18% between 700 and 800. The ACT scores were 6% below 21, 8% between 21 and 23, 19% between 24 and 26, 21% between 27 and 28, and 46% above 28. 74% of the current freshmen were in the top fifth of their class; 93% were in the top two fifths.

Requirements: The SAT or ACT is required. It is strongly recommended that candidates for admission present a college preparatory program that includes 4 years of English, 3 of math, 2 each of foreign language and science, and courses in speech communication, humanities, and social science. AP and CLEP credits are accepted. Important factors in the admissions decision are advanced placement or honors courses, recommendations by school officials, and evidence of special talent.

Procedure: Freshmen are admitted fall and spring. Entrance exams should be taken in the fall. There is a deferred admissions plan. Applications should be filed by January 5 for fall entry; October 15 for spring entry, along with a $65 fee. Notifications are sent April 1. Applications are accepted online.

Transfer: Transfer applicants should have a minimum GPA of 3.0 from an accredited college. SAT or ACT scores are required for applicants who have completed fewer than 30 transferable semester hours at an accredited college. 28 of 128 credits required for the bachelor's degree must be completed at Pepperdine.

Visiting: There are regularly scheduled orientations for prospective students, Information sessions, campus tours, classroom visits, admission counselor meetings, and meeting faculty member. . There are guides for informal visits, visitors may sit in on classes, and stay overnight. To schedule a visit, contact the Housing and Residence Life Office.

Financial Aid: In 2013-2014, 76% of all full-time freshmen and 73% of continuing full-time students received some form of financial aid. 53% of all full-time freshmen and 53% of continuing full-time students received need-based aid. The average freshman award was $33,178. Need-based scholarships or need-based grants averaged $29,916 ($54,172 maximum); need-based self-help aid (loans and jobs) averaged $9,208 ($55,296 maximum); non-need-based athletic scholarships averaged $40,028 ($54,272 maximum); other non-need-based awards and non-need-based scholarships averaged $22,857 ($46,816 maximum); and $9,102 from other forms of aid. 40% of undergraduate students work part-time. Average annual earnings from campus work are $2100. The average financial indebtedness of the 2013 graduate was $29,823. The FAFSA and the college's own financial statement, and the federal income tax form, the state scholarship/grant form (California residents), and W-2 wage statements are required. The priority date for freshman financial aid applications for fall entry is February 15.

International Students: There are 290 international students enrolled. The school actively recruits these students. They must take the TOEFL with a minimum score of 550 on the paper-based TOEFL (PBT) or 80 on the Internet-based version (iBT) and the college's own test. They must also take the SAT.

Computers: Students may access the system with permission from the faculty. Word processing labs are open to all students. There are no time limits and no fees.

Graduates: From July 1, 2012 to June 30, 2013, 891 bachelor's degrees were awarded. The most popular majors were business administration (9%), international business (6%), and advertising (4%). In an average class, 3% graduate in 3 years or less, 69% graduate in 4 years or less, 80% graduate in 5 years or less, and 81% graduate in 6 years or less.

Admissions Contact: Michael Truschke, Dean of Admission and Enrollment Management. E-Mail: *admission-seaver@pepperdine.edu* Web: *www.pepperdine.edu*

PITZER COLLEGE D-5

Claremont, CA 91711-6101 (909) 621-8129
(800) PITZER-1; (909) 621-8770

Full-time: 411 men, 647 women	**Faculty:** 74; IIB, +$
Part-time: 12 men, 29 women	**Ph.D.s:** 100%
Graduate: n/av	**Student/Faculty:** 12 to 1
Year: semesters, summer session	**Tuition:** $42,550
Application Deadline: January 1	**Room & Board:** $12,438
Freshman Class: 3743 applied, 903 accepted, 272 enrolled	
SAT CR/M: 652/641	**ACT:** 30 **MOST COMPETITIVE**

Pitzer College, founded in 1963, is a private liberal arts college that through an interdisciplinary approach emphasizes social justice, intercultural understanding, and environmental sensitivity. It is one of the Claremont Colleges. The library contains 250,000 volumes, 1.2 million microform items, and 17,000 audio/video tapes/CDs/DVDs, and subscribes to 35,000 periodicals including electronic. Computerized library services include interlibrary loans, database searching, Internet access, and laptop Internet portals. Special learning facilities include an art gallery, radio station, a social science lab, an arboretum, and a farm in Costa Rica. The 31-acre campus is in a suburban area 35 miles east of Los Angeles. Including any residence halls, there are 17 buildings.

Student Life: 50% of undergraduates are from out of state, mostly the Northwest. Students are from 42 states, 14 foreign countries, and Canada. 46% are white; 16% Hispanic. The average age of freshmen is 18; all undergraduates, 21. 7% do not continue beyond their first year; 80% remain to graduate.

Housing: 734 students can be accommodated in college housing, which includes coed dorms and off-campus apartments. In addition, there are special-interest houses, a quiet hall, an involvement tower, and food co-op, substance-free, and all-female floors. On-campus housing is guaranteed for the freshman year only. 75% of students live on campus; of those, 75% remain on campus on weekends. Upperclassmen may keep cars.

Activities: There are no fraternities or sororities. There are 50 groups on campus, including art, band, chess, choir, chorale, chorus, computers, dance, debate, drama, environmental, ethnic, film, gay, honors, international, jazz band, literary magazine, newspaper, orchestra, photography, political, professional, radio and TV, religious, social, social service, student government, and symphony. Popular campus events include the Kohoutek Festival, Hammock on the Mounds, and Reggae Festival.

Sports: There are 10 intercollegiate sports for men and 11 for women. Facilities include 3 gyms, 5 swimming pools, 20 tennis courts, numerous playing fields, and lighted volleyball courts. The campus stadium seats 1200. There are also shared intercollegiate sports with Pomona College. The Gold Student Center features a fitness room, lap pool, Frisbee field, and basketball and volleyball courts.

Disabled Students: 95% of the campus is accessible. Facilities include wheelchair ramps, elevators, special parking, specially equipped restrooms, lowered drinking fountains, lowered telephones, and special housing.

Services: Counseling and information services are available, as is tutoring in most subjects, and tutoring software and programs for the learning disabled. There is a reader service for the blind, and remedial writing.

Campus Safety and Security: Measures include 24-hour foot and vehicle patrol, emergency notification system, self-defense education, and security escort services. There are emergency telephones and lighted pathways/sidewalks.

Programs of Study: Pitzer confers B.A. degrees. Bachelor's degrees are awarded in BIOLOGICAL SCIENCE (biochemistry, biology/biological science, and neurosciences), BUSINESS (management engineering and organizational behavior), COMMUNICATIONS AND THE ARTS (art, classics, dance, dramatic arts, English, film arts, French, linguistics, media arts, music, and Spanish), COMPUTER AND PHYSICAL SCIENCE (chemistry, mathematics, physics, science, and science and management), ENGINEERING AND ENVIRONMENTAL DESIGN (environmental science), SOCIAL SCIENCE (African American studies, American studies, anthropology, Asian/American studies, Asian/Oriental studies, Caribbean studies, economics, European studies, history, international relations, Latin American studies, Mexican-American/Chicano studies, philosophy, political science/government, psychology, sociology, Third World studies, and women's studies). Social and behavioral sciences are the strongest academically and have the largest enrollments.

Required: Students must complete a total of 32 courses with a 2.0 GPA. Although requirements vary according to major, most students take introductory or preparatory courses in their first 2 years and courses in or related to their major in the last 2 years. All students must fulfill educational objectives in the following areas: interdisciplinary and intercultural exploration; social responsibility and the ethical implications of knowledge and action; breadth of knowledge; and written expression. More than 10 courses are required in the major.

Special: Students may cross-register at any of the other Claremont Colleges, or study abroad in 60 countries in Africa, Asia, Europe, Latin America, North America, or Oceania. There are co-op programs, work-study, internships, dual majors, student-designed majors, an extensive first-year seminar program, and interdisciplinary study offered in science and technology, and international or intercultural studies. Joint advanced degrees are offered in math, economics, M.I.S., psychology, and public policy, as is a 7-year B.A./D.O. program with the College of Western Health Sciences. There are independent study and limited pass/fail options. There are 1 national honor societies and 18 departmental honors programs.

Faculty/Classroom: 54% of faculty are male; 46% are female. All teach and do research. No introductory courses are taught by graduate students. The average class size in an introductory lecture is 20; in a laboratory is 18; and in a regular course is 18.

Admissions: 24% of the 2011-2012 applicants were accepted. The SAT scores for the 2011-2012 freshman class were: Critical Reading--15% between 500 and 599, 60% between 600 and 700, and 25% above 700; Math--24% between 500 and 599, 60% between 600 and 700, and 16% above 700. 75% of the current freshmen were in the top fifth of their class; 98% were in the top two fifths.

Requirements: Applicants must be graduates of an accredited secondary school or have earned the GED. Secondary school courses must include 4 years of English courses requiring extensive writing, and 3 years each of social and behavioral sciences including history, lab science, foreign language, and math. A personal essay is required and a personal interview is recommended. Students in the top 10% of their class or those with an unweighted GPA in academic subjects of 3.5 are not required to submit ACT or SAT scores. Students without these qualifications must submit either ACT or SAT scores, 2 SAT subject tests, 2 AP test scores of at least 4 (1 in English, 1 in math or science), 2 IB exams (English 1A and Mathematics Methods Standard Level or a higher-level course), or a recent analytical writing sample from a humanities or social science course and a math exam from a course at the algebra II level or higher, both including teacher's comments and grades. AP credits are accepted. Important factors in the admissions decision are advanced placement or honors courses, leadership record, and evidence of special talent.

Procedure: Freshmen are admitted fall and spring. Entrance exams should be taken by January 1. There are early decision and deferred admissions plans. Early decision applications should be filed by November 1; regular applications, by January 1 for fall entry; and October 15 for spring entry. The fall 2011 application fee was $50. Notifications are sent April 1. Applications are accepted online.

Transfer: In a recent year, 21 transfer students enrolled. No more than 2 years of previous credits may be transferred. 64 of 128 credits required for the bachelor's degree must be completed at Pitzer.

Visiting: There are regularly scheduled orientations for prospective students. There are guides for informal visits, visitors may sit in on classes, and stay overnight. To schedule a visit, contact the Office of Admissions.

Financial Aid: In a recent year, 34% of all full-time freshmen and 40% of continuing full-time students received some form of financial aid. 32% of all full-time freshmen and 39% of continuing full-time students received need-based aid. The average freshman award was $35,509. Need-based scholarships or need-based grants averaged $32,873; need-based self-help aid (loans and jobs) averaged $4,914; and other non-need-based awards and non-need-based scholarships averaged $5,000. Pitzer is a member of CSS. The CSS/Profile, FAFSA, and the state aid form are required. The deadline for filing freshman financial aid applications for fall entry is February 1.

International Students: There are 36 international students enrolled. The school actively recruits these students. They must take the TOEFL with a minimum score of 520 on the paper-based TOEFL (PBT) or 70 on the Internet-based version (iBT).

Computers: Wireless access is available. There are student computer labs, and all residential-life rooms are hardwired. All students may access the system. There are no time limits and no fees.

Graduates: In a recent year, 244 bachelor's degrees were awarded. The most popular majors were psychology (17%), political studies (11%), and sociology (11%). 25 companies recruited on campus in 2010-2011. In an average class, 75% graduate in 4 years or less, 80% graduate in 5 years or less, and 85% graduate in 6 years or less. Of a recent graduating class, 17% were enrolled in graduate school within 6 months of graduation, and 56% were employed.

Admissions Contact: Angel Perez, Vice President, Admission and Financial Aid. E-Mail: *admission@pitzer.edu* Web: *www.pitzer.edu*

POINT LOMA NAZARENE UNIVERSITY D-5

San Diego, CA 92106 (619) 849-2520
(800) 733-7770; (619) 849-2601

Full-time: 888 men, 1462 women	**Faculty:** n/av; IIB, +$
Part-time: 25 men, 40 women	**Ph.D.s:** 80%
Graduate: 206 men, 571 women	**Student/Faculty:** 14 to 1
Year: semesters, summer session	**Tuition:** $29,510
Application Deadline: March 1	**Room & Board:** $9100

Freshman Class: 3545 applied, 1983 accepted, 601 enrolled
SAT or ACT: required

VERY COMPETITIVE

Point Loma Nazarene University, founded in 1902, is a private liberal arts university affiliated with the Church of the Nazarene. There are 2 undergraduate schools and 5 graduate schools. In addition to regional accreditation, PLNU has baccalaureate program accreditation with ACBSP. The library contains 167,558 volumes, 129,478 microform items, and 4,995 audio/video tapes/CDs/DVDs, and subscribes to 6,600 periodicals including electronic. Computerized library services include interlibrary loans, database searching, and Internet access. Special learning facilities include an art gallery, radio station, TV station, a lab preschool. The 90-acre campus is in a suburban area in San Diego. Including any residence halls, there are 51 buildings.

Student Life: 80% of undergraduates are from California. Others are from 39 states, 15 foreign countries, and Canada. 66% are White; 19% Hispanic. 90% are Protestant. The average age of freshmen is 18; all undergraduates, 20. 17% do not continue beyond their first year; 75% remain to graduate.

Housing: 1657 students can be accommodated in college housing, which includes single-sex and coed dorms, on-campus apartments, off-campus apartments, and married student housing. On-campus housing is available on a first-come, first-served basis, and is available on a lottery system for upperclassmen. 68% of students live on campus. Alcohol is not permitted. Upperclassmen may keep cars.

Activities: There are 31 groups on campus, including art, band, cheerleading, choir, chorale, computers, debate, drama, ethnic, film, forensics, honors, international, jazz band, literary magazine, musical theater, newspaper, opera, orchestra, pep band, political, professional, radio and TV, religious, social, social service, student government, and yearbook. Popular campus events include Spiritual Emphasis Week and Christmas Messiah Concert.

Sports: There are 7 intercollegiate sports for men and 5 for women, and 18 intramural sports for men and 17 for women. Facilities include a gym, baseball and soccer fields, a track, tennis courts, dorm lounges, and table tennis and pool tables.

Disabled Students: All of the campus is accessible. Facilities include wheelchair ramps, elevators, special parking, specially equipped restrooms, special class scheduling, lowered drinking fountains, and lowered telephones.

Services: Counseling and information services are available, as is tutoring in most subjects. There is a reader service for the blind, and remedial math, reading, and writing.

Campus Safety and Security: Measures include 24-hour foot and vehicle patrol, self-defense education, and security escort services. There are shuttle buses, emergency telephones, and lighted pathways/sidewalks.

Programs of Study: PLNU confers B.A., B.S., B.Mus. and B.S.N. degrees. Master's degrees are also awarded. Bachelor's degrees are awarded in BIOLOGICAL SCIENCE (biology/biological science and nutrition), BUSINESS (accounting, business administration and management, and business communications), COMMUNICATIONS AND THE ARTS (broadcasting, communications, dramatic arts, graphic design, journalism, literature, media arts, music, music performance, music theory and composition, piano/organ, romance languages and literature, Spanish, visual and performing arts, and voice), COMPUTER AND PHYSICAL SCIENCE (chemistry, computer science, information sciences and systems, mathematics, and physics), EDUCATION (art education, athletic training, music education, and physical education), ENGINEERING AND ENVIRONMENTAL DESIGN (engineering physics and environmental science), HEALTH PROFESSIONS (exercise science and nursing), SOCIAL SCIENCE (biblical studies, child psychology/development, dietetics, family and community services, history, industrial and organizational psychology, international studies, liberal arts/general studies, ministries, philosophy, philosophy and religion, political science/government, psychology, religion, social science, social work, and sociology).

Required: To graduate, students must complete a minimum of 128 semester units. At least 24 upper-division semester units are needed for the major. A minimum GPA of 2.0 is required. Students must complete the general education requirements, though B.S.N. candidates need not take a foreign language. General education requirements include 9 courses in cultural studies, 5 in the sciences, 4 in cognitive studies, and 3 in religious studies. Students must demonstrate proficiency in writing and math.

Special: PLNU offers internships in the church, in state and national governments, in journalism, in small business, and in the film industry. Students may study abroad in several world capitals and in more than 40 countries. There are Washington and United Nations semester programs. Various dual or interdepartmental majors are offered, including biology-chemistry, graphic communications, human environmental science-business, and church music-youth ministries. There are pre-professional programs in medicine/dentistry, law, and engineering. A general studies degree in liberal studies is available, as is credit for life, military, and work experience for nursing students. There are 6 national honor societies, a freshman honors program, and 10 departmental honors programs.

Faculty/Classroom: 58% of faculty are male; 42% are female. No introductory courses are taught by graduate students.

Admissions: 56% of the 2013-2014 applicants were accepted. The SAT scores for the 2013-2014 freshman class were: Critical Reading--14% below 500, 44% between 500 and 599, 35% between 600 and 699, and 7% between 700 and 800; Math--14% below 500, 42% between 500 and 599, 37% between 600 and 699, and 7% between 700 and 800; Writing--16% below 500, 47% between 500 and 599, 31% between 600 and 699, and 6% between 700 and 800.

Requirements: The SAT or ACT is required. Candidates for admission should have completed 4 years of English, 3 of math, 2 each of a lab science and the same foreign language, and 1 of history. A GPA of 2.8 is required. AP and CLEP credits are accepted. Important factors in the admissions decision are personality/intangible qualities, leadership record, and advanced placement or honors courses.

Procedure: Freshmen are admitted fall and spring. Entrance exams should be taken in the junior year or early in the senior year. Applications should be filed by March 1 for fall entry. Notifications are sent April 1. 186 applicants were on the 2013 waiting list; 49 were admitted. Applications are accepted online.

Transfer: 134 transfer students enrolled in 2012-2013. Transfer students must have a minimum cumulative GPA of 2.0 (based on transferable units) to be considered for admission. Applicants with at least 36 transferable units at the time of application need only submit college transcripts (high school transcripts are not required for these applicants). 24 of 128 credits required for the bachelor's degree must be completed at PLNU.

Visiting: There are regularly scheduled orientations for prospective students, including campus tours and appointments with major advisers. There are guides for informal visits, visitors may sit in on classes, and stay overnight. To schedule a visit, contact the Admissions Office.

Financial Aid: PLNU is a member of CSS. The FAFSA is required. The priority date for freshman financial aid applications for fall entry is March 2.

International Students: There are 9 international students enrolled. They must take the TOEFL with a minimum score of 550 on the paper-based TOEFL (PBT) or 80 on the Internet-based version (iBT).

Computers: All students may access the system when computer labs are open. There are no time limits and no fees.

Graduates: From July 1, 2012 to June 30, 2013, 544 bachelor's degrees were awarded. The most popular majors were business/marketing (24%), health professions and related programs (13%), and visual and performing arts (8%). In an average class, 61% graduate in 4 years or less, 73% graduate in 5 years or less, and 75% graduate in 6 years or less.

Admissions Contact: Eric Groves, Director of Undergraduate Admissions. E-Mail: *admissions@pointloma.edu* Web: *www.pointloma.edu*

POMONA COLLEGE D-5

Claremont, CA 91711 (909) 621-8134; (909) 621-8952

Full-time: 766 men, 830 women **Faculty:** 190; IIB, ++$
Part-time: 7 men, 9 women **Ph.D.s:** 99%
Graduate: n/av **Student/Faculty:** 8 to 1
Year: semesters **Tuition:** $43,580
Application Deadline: January 1 **Room & Board:** $14,100
Freshman Class: 7153 applied, 996 accepted, 397 enrolled
SAT CR/M/W: 730/730/730 **ACT:** 33 **MOST COMPETITIVE**

Established in 1887, Pomona College is one of the nation's leading liberal arts colleges and the founding member of The Claremont Colleges, a consortium of five undergraduate and two graduate schools. The 3 libraries contain 2.0 million volumes, 1.4 million microform items, and 777 audio/video tapes/CDs/DVDs, and subscribe to 6,624 periodicals including electronic. Computerized library services include interlibrary loans, database searching, and Internet access. Special learning facilities include an art gallery, radio station, observatory, modern languages and international relations center, organic farm. The 140-acre campus is in a suburban area 35 miles east of Los Angeles, and 20 miles east of Pasadena. Including any residence halls, there are 63 buildings.

Student Life: 68% of undergraduates are from out of state, mostly the Northeast. Students are from 46 states, 24 foreign countries, and Canada. 65% are from public schools. 44% are White; 15% Hispanic; 12% Asian American. The average age of freshmen is 18; all undergraduates, 20. 3% do not continue beyond their first year; 96% remain to graduate.

Housing: 1500 students can be accommodated in college housing, which includes coed dorms and on-campus apartments. In addition, there are language houses. On-campus housing is guaranteed for all 4 years. 98% of students live on campus. Upperclassmen may keep cars.

Activities: There are 200 groups on campus, including the Outdoors Club of the Claremont Colleges, art, band, chess, choir, chorus, dance, debate, drama, environmental, ethnic, film, gay, honors, international, jazz band, literary magazine, musical theater, newspaper, On the Loose, orchestra, pep band, photography, political, professional, radio and TV, religious, social, social service, student government, symphony, and yearbook.

Sports: There are 10 intercollegiate sports for men and 11 for women, and 13 intramural sports for men and 13 for women. Facilities include an all-weather track, 2 swimming pools, a weight room, a fitness center, a dance studio, various playing fields, and courts for tennis, squash, racquetball, basketball, volleyball, and badminton.

Disabled Students: 80% of the campus is accessible. Facilities include wheelchair ramps, elevators, special parking, specially equipped restrooms, special class scheduling, lowered drinking fountains, and lowered telephones.

Services: Counseling and information services are available, as is tutoring in most subjects. There is a reader service for the blind.

Campus Safety and Security: Measures include 24-hour foot and vehicle patrol, emergency notification system, self-defense education, and security escort services. There are emergency telephones, lighted pathways/sidewalks, and controlled access to dorms/residences.

Programs of Study: Pomona confers B.A. degrees. Bachelor's degrees are awarded in AGRICULTURE (environmental studies), BIOLOGICAL SCIENCE (biology/biological science, molecular biology, and neurosciences), COMMUNICATIONS AND THE ARTS (art history and appreciation, Chinese, classics, dance, English, fine arts, French, Japanese, languages, linguistics, literature, media arts, music, romance languages and literature, Russian, Spanish, studio art, and theatre arts), COMPUTER AND PHYSICAL SCIENCE (chemistry, computer science, geology, mathematics, physics, and science), ENGINEERING AND ENVIRONMENTAL DESIGN (technology and public affairs), SOCIAL SCIENCE (africana studies, American studies, anthropology, Asian/American studies, Asian/Oriental studies, cognitive science, economics, German area studies, Hispanic American studies, history, international relations, Latin American studies, medieval studies, Mexican-American/Chicano studies, Middle Eastern studies, philosophy, political science/government, psychology, public affairs, religious studies, Russian and Slavic studies, sociology, and women's studies).

Required: The B.A. requires 32 credits, 30 of which must be completed post-matriculation. Students must satisfy the Breadth of Study requirement (one course in each of five areas), complete a first-year Critical Inquiry seminar, take one P.E. course in the first year, demonstrate proficiency in 3 semesters of the same foreign language, and satisfy the requirements for a major (including a senior exercise).

Special: Students may cross-register at any of The Claremont Colleges, which are on adjacent campuses and follow the same academic schedule. Study abroad is offered through 49 programs in 31 countries. The Pomona College Internship Program provides students with paid part-time internships in the greater Los Angeles area. Paid internship opportunities are also offered in the summer. The college's Summer Undergraduate Research Program enables students to conduct extended, focused research in close cooperation with a Pomona faculty member. SURP funding includes room and board, a supply budget, and a stipend. More than 200 students engaged in research in summer 2013. Other opportunities include spending a semester in Washington, D.C.; a 3-2 engineering program offered with the California Institute of Technology, Washington University in St. Louis, and Dartmouth College; spending one semester at Colby, Smith, Spelman, or Swarthmore colleges; independent study options; and dual and student-designed majors. There are including Phi Beta Kappa.

Faculty/Classroom: 54% of faculty are male; 46% are female. All teach undergraduates, all do research, and all teach and do research. No introductory courses are taught by graduate students. The average class size in a regular course is 15.

Admissions: 14% of the 2013-2014 applicants were accepted. 97% of the current freshmen were in the top fifth of their class; 100% were in the top two fifths. 21 freshmen graduated first in their class.

Requirements: The SAT or ACT is required. Although applicants need not be graduates of accredited high schools (some may be admitted after the junior year), most are, or have earned the GED. Secondary preparation must include 4 years of English, 3 years each of math and foreign languages, and 2 years each of lab and social sciences. An interview is strongly recommended. AP credits are accepted. Important factors in the admissions decision are advanced placement or honors courses, recommendations by school officials, and extracurricular activities record.

Procedure: Freshmen are admitted fall. Entrance exams should be taken before December of the senior year. There is a early decision plan. Early decision applications should be filed by November 1; regular applications, by January 1 for fall entry, along with a $70 fee. Notification of early decision is sent December 15; regular decision, April 1. 140 early decision candidates were accepted for the 2013-2014 class. 253 applicants were on the 2013 waiting list; 73 were admitted. Applications are accepted online.

Transfer: 13 transfer students enrolled in 2012-2013. Applicants must have completed at least 1 year (24 semester hours) of college-level courses at the time of enrollment. 16 of 32 credits required for the bachelor's degree must be completed at Pomona.

Visiting: There are regularly scheduled orientations for prospective students, including interviews, information sessions, and guided tours. Visitors may sit in on classes and stay overnight. To schedule a visit, contact the Office of Admissions.

Financial Aid: In 2013-2014, 57% of all full-time freshmen and 54% of continuing full-time students received some form of financial aid. 57% of all full-time freshmen and 54% of continuing full-time students received need-based aid. The average freshman award was $46,477. Need-based scholarships or need-based grants averaged $44,703 ; and need-based self-help aid (loans and jobs) averaged $1,774. The average financial indebtedness of the 2013 graduate was $13,441. Pomona is a member of CSS. The CSS/Profile and FAFSA are required. The priority date for freshman financial aid applications for fall entry is February 1. The deadline for filing freshman financial aid applications for fall entry is June 1.

International Students: There are 121 international students enrolled. The school actively recruits these students. They must take the TOEFL with a minimum score of 600 on the paper-based TOEFL (PBT) or 100 on the Internet-based version (iBT). They must also take the SAT or ACT.

Computers: All students may access the system. There are no time limits and no fees.

Graduates: From July 1, 2012 to June 30, 2013, 362 bachelor's degrees were awarded. The most popular majors were economics (13%), math (11%), and neuroscience (9%). 500 companies recruited on campus in 2012-2013. In an average class, 93% graduate in 4 years or less, 95% graduate in 5 years or less, and 96% graduate in 6 years or less. Of the 2012 graduating class, 20% were enrolled in graduate school within 6 months of graduation, and 35% were employed.

Admissions Contact: Seth Allen, Dean of Admissions. E-Mail: *admissions@pomona.edu* Web: *www.pomona.edu/admissions*

SAINT MARY'S COLLEGE OF CALIFORNIA B-3

Moraga, CA 94575 (925) 631-4224
(800) 800-4SMC; (925) 376-7193

Full-time: 1106 men, 1675 women **Faculty:** 194; IIA, +$
Part-time: 101 men, 153 women **Ph.D.s:** 95%
Graduate: 396 men, 797 women **Student/Faculty:** 14 to 1
Year: 4-1-4, summer session **Tuition:** $39,890
Application Deadline: February 1 **Room & Board:** $13,660
Freshman Class: 5256 applied, 3448 accepted, 623 enrolled
SAT CR/M: 552/558 **ACT:** 24 **COMPETITIVE**

Saint Mary's College of California, founded in 1863, is a private, independent, liberal arts college affiliated with the Roman Catholic Church. The school offers undergraduate and graduate programs in liberal arts, nursing, economics and business administration, education, and preprofessional studies. There are 4 undergraduate schools and 3 graduate schools. In addition to regional accreditation, SMC has baccalaureate program accreditation with NLN. The library contains 309,615 volumes, 446,888 microform items, and 9,611 audio/video tapes/CDs/DVDs, and subscribes to 58,339 periodicals including electronic. Computerized library services include interlibrary loans, database searching, Internet access, and Wi-Fi capability. Special learning facilities include an art gallery, radio station, Observatory. The 420-acre campus is in a suburban area 20 miles east of San Francisco. Including any residence halls, there are 77 buildings.

Student Life: 84% of undergraduates are from California. Others are from 40 states, 18 foreign countries, and Canada. 57% are from public schools. 48% are White; 24% Hispanic; 11% Asian American. 43% are Catholic; 39% claim no religious affiliation; 13% Protestant. The average age of freshmen is 19; all undergraduates, 21. 13% do not continue beyond their first year; 87% remain to graduate.

Housing: 1557 students can be accommodated in college housing, which includes single-sex and coed dorms, on-campus apartments, and off-campus apartments. In addition, there are honors houses, special-interest houses, Lasallian and Santiago living communities. On-campus housing is guaranteed for the freshman year only and is available on a lottery system for upperclassmen. 62% of students live on campus; of those, 50% remain on campus on weekends. All students may keep cars.

Activities: There are no fraternities or sororities. There are 41 groups on campus, including art, cheerleading, choir, chorale, chorus, dance, debate, drama, environmental, ethnic, forensics, gay, honors, international, jazz band, literary magazine, musical theater, newspaper, pep band, political, professional, radio and TV, religious, social, social service, and student government. Popular campus events include Cultural Nights, and Coffee House events.

Sports: There are 7 intercollegiate sports for men and 9 for women, and 7 intramural sports for men and 7 for women. Facilities include a gym, football, baseball and recreational fields, swimming pool, lighted tennis courts, soccer field and rugby pitch, weight room, and workout facility.

Disabled Students: 90% of the campus is accessible. Facilities include wheelchair ramps, elevators, special parking, specially equipped restrooms, special class scheduling, lowered drinking fountains, lowered telephones, and special housing.

Services: Counseling and information services are available, as is tutoring in most subjects. There is a reader service for the blind, and remedial writing. Tutoring is available in 1-on-1 sessions or group workshops. Readers, note takers, and other services are provided to learning or physically disabled students.

Campus Safety and Security: Measures include 24-hour foot and vehicle patrol, emergency notification system, and security escort services. There are emergency telephones, lighted pathways/sidewalks, controlled access to dorms/residences, late night transport/escort service.

Programs of Study: SMC confers B.A., and B.S. degrees. Master's and doctoral degrees are also awarded. Bachelor's degrees are awarded in AGRICULTURE (environmental studies), BIOLOGICAL SCIENCE (biology/biological science), BUSINESS (accounting and business administration and management), COMMUNICATIONS AND THE ARTS (art, classical languages, communications, English, French, performing arts, and Spanish), COMPUTER AND PHYSICAL SCIENCE (chemistry, computer science, mathematics, and physics), EDUCATION (health education, physical education, and recreation education), ENGINEERING AND ENVIRONMENTAL DESIGN (environmental science and preengineering), HEALTH PROFESSIONS (health science), SOCIAL SCIENCE (anthropology, economics, history, international studies, liberal arts/general studies, philosophy, political science/government, psychology, religion, and sociology). Business administration, communications and psychology have the largest enrollments.

Required: To graduate, students must complete 36 course credits, including 17 at the upper-division level, with a GPA of 2.0 overall and in the major. Specific requirements include a 4-course Great Books seminar and 2 courses each in religious studies, humanities, math/science, written English, and social sciences. All students must demonstrate proficiency in a second language.

Special: The college offers seminars in all fields, dual and student-designed majors, study abroad in 8 countries, a Washington semester, work-study, cross-registration with the Regional Association of East Bay Colleges and Universities, and B.A.-B.S. liberal arts degree. There are 3-2 engineering programs with Washington University, the University of Southern California, and Boston University. There are a freshman honors program and 2 departmental honors programs.

Faculty/Classroom: 48% of faculty are male; 52% are female. All teach and do research. No introductory courses are taught by graduate students. The average class size in an introductory lecture is 25; in a laboratory is 16; and in a regular course is 20.

Admissions: 66% of the 2013-2014 applicants were accepted. The SAT scores for the 2013-2014 freshman class were: Critical Reading--23% below 500, 49% between 500 and 599, 23% between 600 and 699, and 5% between 700 and 800; Math--23% below 500, 46% between 500 and 599, 29% between 600 and 699, and 4% between 700 and 800. The ACT scores were 13% below 21, 33% between 21 and 23, 27% between 24 and 26, 14% between 27 and 28, and 11% above 28. 51% of the current freshmen were in the top fifth of their class; 79% were in the top two fifths. 6 freshmen graduated first in their class.

Requirements: The SAT or ACT is required, with the SAT preferred. Candidates should be graduates of an accredited secondary school, with 16 academic units, including 4 in English and 1 each in algebra, advanced algebra, geometry, and U.S. history. It is recommended that the remaining units be made up of foreign language, lab science, and additional academic electives in the student's areas of strength. The GED is accepted. An essay is required. A GPA of 2.0 is required. AP and CLEP credits are accepted. Important factors in the admissions decision are recommendations by school officials, advanced placement or honors courses, and parents or siblings attended your school.

Procedure: Freshmen are admitted to all sessions. Entrance exams should be taken by December of the senior year. There are early admissions and deferred admissions plans. Early decision applications should be filed by November 15; regular applications, by February 1 for fall entry; and January 1 for spring entry, along with a $55 fee. Notification of early decision is sent December 15; regular decision, March 15. 894 applicants were on the 2013 waiting list; 167 were admitted. Applications are accepted online.

Transfer: 199 transfer students enrolled in 2012-2013. Applicants must have a GPA of 2.3 and a minimum of 23 transferable academic semester units. 9 of 36 credits required for the bachelor's degree must be completed at SMC.

Visiting: There are regularly scheduled orientations for prospective students, Weekdays: 9 a.m. presentation & 10 a.m. tour & 1 p.m. presentation & 2 p.m. tour. Weekends (Sept.-May): 10 a.m. presentation & 11 a.m. tour. There are guides for informal visits, visitors may sit in on classes, and stay overnight. To schedule a visit, contact Patrick Lorenzo at (925) 631-4106.

Financial Aid: In 2013-2014, 94% of all full-time freshmen and 96% of continuing full-time students received some form of financial aid. 89% of all full-time freshmen and 76% of continuing full-time students received need-based aid. The average freshman award was $31,979. Need-based scholarships or need-based grants averaged $24,082 ($31,200 maximum); need-based self-help aid (loans and jobs) averaged $6,640 ($7,500 maximum); non-need-based athletic scholarships averaged $36,486 ($59,470 maximum); and other non-need-based awards and non-need-based scholarships averaged $14,946 ($39,740 maximum). 60% of undergraduate students work part-time. Average annual earnings from campus work are $2007. The average financial indebtedness of the 2013 graduate was $33,000. SMC is a member of CSS. The FAFSA, and California GPA verification form for residents only is required. The priority date for freshman financial aid applications for fall entry is February 15.

International Students: There are 70 international students enrolled. The school actively recruits these students. They must take the TOEFL with a minimum score of 550 on the paper-based TOEFL (PBT) or 79 on the Internet-based version (iBT) and the Comprehensive English Language Test, Nonnative English speakers who submit a score ofor higher on the TOEFL may be admitted as full-time undergraduates. Others may be accepted conditionally and enrolled in the college's Intensive English rogram.

Computers: All students may access the system. There are no time limits and no fees.

Graduates: From July 1, 2012 to June 30, 2013, 598 bachelor's degrees were awarded. The most popular majors were business administration (19%), communication (12%), and psychology (10%). 92 companies recruited on campus in 2012-2013. In an average class, 52% graduate in 4 years or less, 56% graduate in 5 years or less, and 57% graduate in 6 years or less. Of the 2012 graduating class, 14% were enrolled in graduate school within 6 months of graduation, and 64% were employed.

Admissions Contact: Michael McKeon, Dean of Admissions. E-Mail: *smcadmit@stmarys-ca.edu* Web: *www.stmarys-ca.edu*

SAN DIEGO CHRISTIAN COLLEGE D-5
Christian Heritage College

El Cajon, CA 92019 **(619) 588-7747**
(800) 676-2242; (619) 590-1739

Full-time: n/av	**Faculty:** n/av
Part-time: n/av	**Ph.D.s:** n/av
Graduate: n/av	**Student/Faculty:** n/av
Year: semesters, summer session	**Tuition:** $23,190
Application Deadline: open	**Room & Board:** $8822
Freshman Class: n/av	
SAT or ACT: required	

COMPETITIVE

San Diego Christian College is a small, private institution founded in 1970 by the Scott Memorial Baptist Church of San Diego, with which it is still affiliated. It offers programs in the liberal arts, business, and education. Figures given in the above capsule and in this profile are approximate. There is one undergraduate school. The library contains 69,435 volumes, 80 microform items, and 61,522 audio/video tapes/CDs/DVDs, and subscribes to 30,475 periodicals including electronic. Computerized library services include interlibrary loans, database searching, and Internet access. Special learning facilities include a The 32-acre campus is in a suburban area 15 miles east of San Diego. Including any residence halls, there are 14 buildings.

Student Life: 80% of undergraduates are from California. Others are from states. 75% are from public schools. 70% are White. 100% are Protestant. The average age of freshmen is 18; all undergraduates, 21. 40% do not continue beyond their first year; 30% remain to graduate.

Housing: 200 students can be accommodated in college housing, which includes single-sex dorms and off-campus apartments. In addition, there are language houses. On-campus housing is guaranteed for all 4 years, is available on a first-come, and first-served basis. 50% of students commute. Alcohol is not permitted. All students may keep cars.

Activities: There are no fraternities or sororities. There are 16 groups on campus, including art, cheerleading, choir, chorale, chorus, computers, drama, honors, international, musical theater, newspaper, pep band, political, religious, social, student government, and yearbook. Popular campus events include Spring, Winter, and Valentine's Day Banquets and the Missions Conference.

Sports: There are 3 intercollegiate sports for men and 4 for women, and 5 intramural sports for men and 4 for women. Facilities include a swimming pool, a gym, outdoor courts for tennis, volleyball, and basketball, soccer and softball fields.

Disabled Students: 90% of the campus is accessible. Facilities include wheelchair ramps, elevators, special parking, and special class scheduling.

Services: Counseling and information services are available, as is tutoring in some subjects, Tutors recruited as needed for most general education courses There is remedial math, reading, and writing.

Campus Safety and Security: Measures include 24-hour foot and vehicle patrol and emergency notification system. There are lighted pathways/sidewalks, and a fenced campus.

Programs of Study: SDCC confers B.A., and B.S. degrees. Associate degrees are also awarded. Bachelor's degrees are awarded in BIOLOGICAL SCIENCE (biology/biological science), BUSINESS (business administration and management), COMMUNICATIONS AND THE ARTS (communications, English, and music), COMPUTER AND PHYSICAL SCIENCE (mathematics), EDUCATION (education), ENGINEERING AND ENVIRONMENTAL DESIGN (aviation administration/management), SOCIAL SCIENCE (biblical studies, history, human development, interdisciplinary studies, liberal arts/general studies, physical fitness/movement, and psychology). Counseling psychology, education, and business are the strongest academically. Business, education, and human development have the largest enrollments.

Required: The required credits for graduation vary by degree program and major. All students must take 46 to 52 credits in sciences and math, social science, and humanities; 20 credits in personal Christian development and biblical studies; and the balance in major field requirements and electives. A 2.0 GPA is required for graduation.

Special: Students attend chapel 3 times each week, participate in an annual Bible conference, and complete a student ministry assignment each semester. Independent study for 1 to 3 credits can be arranged. There are internships in psychology, pastoral studies, and education.

Faculty/Classroom: 60% of faculty are male; 40% are female. All teach undergraduates. No introductory courses are taught by graduate students. The average class size in an introductory lecture is 40; in a laboratory is 15; and in a regular course is 16.

Requirements: The SAT or ACT is required. The ACT is preferred. Applicants must have a high school diploma or the GED, or have successfully completed the California State High School Proficiency Exam. Secondary preparation should include 4 units of English, 3 each of math, natural science, and social studies, and 2 of a single foreign language. A personal essay is also required. In addition, applicants must meet certain spiritual requirements. A GPA of 2.3 is required. AP and CLEP credits are accepted. Important factors in the admissions decision are recommendations by school officials, leadership record, and extracurricular activities record.

Procedure: Freshmen are admitted fall and spring. Entrance exams should be taken during the junior year. There is a rolling admissions plan. Application deadlines are open. The fall 2013 application fee was $25. Notification is sent on a rolling basis.

Transfer: 30 of 124 credits required for the bachelor's degree must be completed at SDCC.

Visiting: There are regularly scheduled orientations for prospective students, including a campus tour, cafeteria meal, and class and chapel attendance. There are guides for informal visits, visitors may sit in on classes, and stay overnight. To schedule a visit, contact the Admissions Office.

Financial Aid: SDCC is a member of CSS. The FAFSA and the college's own financial statement are required. Check with the school for current application deadlines.

International Students: The school actively recruits these students. They must take the TOEFL and the college's own test. They must also take the SAT or ACT, scoring 900.

Computers: All students may access the system. There are no time limits and no fees.

Admissions Contact: Misty Chappelle, Director of Admissions. E-Mail: *chcadm@adm.christianheritage.edu* Web: *www.sdcc.edu*

SAN DIEGO STATE UNIVERSITY — D-5

San Diego, CA 92182 — **(619) 594-6336; (619) 594-1250**

Full-time: 10883 men, 13548 women	**Faculty:** n/av; IIA, +$
Part-time: 1573 men, 1805 women	**Ph.D.s:** 86%
Graduate: 1950 men, 3000 women	**Student/Faculty:** n/av
Year: semesters, summer session	**Tuition:** $6766 ($17,926)
Application Deadline: November 30	**Room & Board:** $13,812
Freshman Class: 54509 applied, 20292 accepted, 4760 enrolled	
SAT CR/M: 540/563	**ACT:** 24 **VERY COMPETITIVE**

San Diego State University, founded in 1897, is a public research university that is part of the California State University system. There are 8 undergraduate schools. In addition to regional accreditation, SDSU has baccalaureate program accreditation with AACSB, ABET, ACEJMC, CSWE, NASAD, and NRPA. The library contains 2.2 million volumes, 4.6 million microform items, 42,724 audio/video tapes/CDs/DVDs, and subscribes to 75,661 periodicals including electronic. Computerized library services include interlibrary loans, database searching, Internet access, and Wi-Fi capability. Special learning facilities include an art gallery, planetarium, radio station, TV station, a theater and a recital hall. The 282-acre campus is in an urban area 8 miles east of downtown San Diego. Including any residence halls, there are 56 buildings.

Student Life: 93% of undergraduates are from California. Others are from 50 states, 118 foreign countries, and Canada. 36% are White; 31% Hispanic; 14% Asian American. The average age of freshmen is 19; all undergraduates, 22. 12% do not continue beyond their first year.

Housing: 4107 students can be accommodated in college housing, which includes coed dorms and on-campus apartments. In addition, there are honors houses, language houses, special-interest houses, fraternity houses, sorority houses, gender neutral housing, international housing, a living/learning center, Aztec engineering residence, and substance-free and quiet-study housing. On-campus housing is guaranteed for the freshman year only, is available on a first-come, and first-served basis. 84% of students commute. All students may keep cars.

Activities: 7% of men belong to 22 national fraternities; 8% of women belong to 20 national sororities. There are 320 groups on campus, including art, band, cheerleading, choir, chorale, chorus, dance, debate, drama, drill team, environmental, ethnic, film, gay, honors, international, jazz band, literary magazine, marching band, musical theater, newspaper, opera, orchestra, pep band, political, professional, radio and TV, religious, social, social service, student government, and symphony. Popular campus events include Student Involvement Expo, Welcome Week, Aztec Nights and Midnight Breakfast Finals Week.

Sports: There are 6 intercollegiate sports for men and 14 for women, and 11 intramural sports for men and 11 for women. Facilities include a gym, basketball, racquetball, tennis, and volleyball courts, a swimming pool/aquaplex, a track, soccer, softball, baseball, and football fields, an aquatic center, a weight room, bowling and gymnastic equipment, a cardio room, and a 30-foot climbing wall.

Disabled Students: 99% of the campus is accessible. Facilities include wheelchair ramps, elevators, special parking, specially equipped restrooms, special class scheduling, lowered drinking fountains, lowered telephones.

Services: Counseling and information services are available, as is tutoring in most subjects. There is a reader service for the blind.

Campus Safety and Security: Measures include 24-hour foot and vehicle patrol, emergency notification system, self-defense education, and security escort services. There are shuttle buses, emergency telephones, lighted pathways/sidewalks, and controlled access to dorms/residences.

Programs of Study: SDSU confers B.A., B.S. and B.M. degrees. Master's and doctoral degrees are also awarded. Bachelor's degrees are awarded in AGRICULTURE (agricultural business management and environmental studies), BIOLOGICAL SCIENCE (biology/biological science, botany, ecology, microbiology, nutrition, and zoology), BUSINESS (accounting, business administration and management, finance, financial services, hospitality management services, insurance and risk management, international business management, international economics, international security/conflict resolution mgmt, marketing/retailing/merchandising, personnel management, real estate, total quality management (TQM), and production and operations management), COMMUNICATIONS AND THE ARTS (advertising, art history, art, classics, communication studies, communications, comparative literature, dance, English, French, German, graphic design, Japanese, journalism, linguistics, media management, multimedia, music, music performance, public relations, radio/tv, recreation administration, Russian, Spanish, studio art, telecommunications, and theatre arts), COMPUTER AND PHYSICAL SCIENCE (applied mathematics, astronomy, chemical physics, chemistry, computer science, geology, industrial technology, information sciences and systems, mathematics, physical sciences, physics, and statistics), EDUCATION (athletic training, industrial arts education, music education, physical education, and vocational education), ENGINEERING AND ENVIRONMENTAL DESIGN (aeronautical engineering, civil engineering, computer engineering, construction engineering, electrical/electronics engineering, engineering, environmental engineering, environmental science, interior design, and mechanical engineering), HEALTH PROFESSIONS (environmental health science, exercise science, health communication, health science, nursing, and speech pathology/audiology), SOCIAL SCIENCE (African American studies, American Indian studies, American studies, anthropology, Asian/Oriental studies, child psychology/development, criminal justice, economics, European studies, geography, gerontology, history, home economics, humanities, interdisciplinary studies, Latin American studies, liberal arts/general studies, Mexican-American/Chicano studies, modern jewish studies, philosophy, political science/government, psychology, public administration, religious studies, Russian and Slavic studies, social science, social work, sociology, urban studies, and women's studies). Business administration, psychology, and biology have the largest enrollments.

Required: To graduate, students must complete a minimum of 120 units, including 49 general education units. The number of units in the major varies by program. A 2.0 or higher GPA must be maintained, depending on the major. Students must demonstrate math and writing competency and fulfill requirements in upper-division writing and in American Institutions. Certain majors require a senior thesis.

Special: There are 30 national honor societies, including Phi Beta Kappa, a freshman honors program, and 24 departmental honors programs.

Faculty/Classroom: No introductory courses are taught by graduate students. The average class size in an introductory lecture is 77; in a laboratory is 15; and in a regular course is 54.

Admissions: 37% of the 2013-2014 applicants were accepted. The SAT scores for the 2013-2014 freshman class were: Critical Reading--27% below 500, 51% between 500 and 599, 20% between 600 and 699, and 2% between 700 and 800; Math--19% below 500, 46% between 500 and 599, 31% between 600 and 699, and 4% between 700 and 800. The ACT scores were 15% below 21, 27% between 21 and 23, 34% between 24 and 26, 15% between 27 and 28, and 9% above 28. 60% of the current freshmen were in the top fifth of their class; 91% were in the top two fifths.

Requirements: The SAT or ACT is required. Applicants must have a qualifying CSU eligibility index, based on a combination of GPA and standardized test scores. Candidates for admission should have completed 4 years of English, 3 of math, 2 each of science and a foreign language, and 1 each of social studies, U.S. history, and visual and performing arts, and 1 of electives. AP and CLEP credits are accepted.

Procedure: Freshmen are admitted fall. Entrance exams should be taken by October of the senior year. Applications should be filed by November 30 for fall entry, along with a $55 fee. Notifications are sent in March. Applications are accepted online.

Transfer: 3616 transfer students enrolled in 2012-2013. Transfer applicants are required to declare a major and have completed all preparation for the major courses and pre-major requirements if applicable. In addition, all lower division general education courses must be completed. Must have "C" grades in four required classes: Oral Communication, Written Communication, Critical Thinking, and Mathematics (above the level of intermediate Algebra). Different application policies apply for applicants in and out of SDSU service area and for applicants in impacted majors. Refer to the Office of Admission website for more information. 30 of 120 credits required for the bachelor's degree must be completed at SDSU.

Visiting: There are regularly scheduled orientations for prospective students, including tours that can be scheduled with SDSU ambassadors.

Financial Aid: The average freshman award was $8,300. SDSU is a member of CSS. The FAFSA and the state aid form are required. Check with the school for current application deadlines.

International Students: There are 2018 international students enrolled. The school actively recruits these students. They must take the TOEFL with a minimum score of 80 on the Internet-based version (iBT) and the college's own test, or take the IELTS, scoring 6.5 or higher. They must also take the SAT or ACT.

Computers: All students may access the system. There are no time limits and no fees.

Graduates: From July 1, 2012 to June 30, 2013, 6107 bachelor's degrees were awarded. The most popular majors were psychology (9%), criminal justice administration (6%), and business administration/management (5%). 619 companies recruited on campus in 2012-2013. In an average class, 33% graduate in 4 years or less, 60% graduate in 5 years or less, and 67% graduate in 6 years or less.

Admissions Contact: Bev Arata, Director of Admissions. E-Mail: *admissions@sdsu.edu* Web: *www.sdsu.edu/apply*

SAN FRANCISCO ART INSTITUTE B-3

San Francisco, CA 94133 415-749-4500
800-345-7324; 415-749-4592

Full-time: 195 men, 249 women	**Faculty:** 18
Part-time: 11 men, 23 women	**Ph.D.s:** 67%
Graduate: 78 men, 124 women	**Student/Faculty:** 25 to 1
Year: semesters, summer session	**Tuition:** $38,406
Application Deadline: February 1	**Room & Board:** $14,086
Freshman Class: n/av	
SAT CR/M/W: 560/500/540 **ACT:** 24	**SPECIAL**

San Francisco Art Institute, founded in 1871, is a private college devoted to the practice, theory, and criticism of fine art. In addition to regional accreditation, SFAI has baccalaureate program accreditation with NASAD. The library contains 32,500 volumes, and 3,370 audio/video tapes/CDs/DVDs, and subscribes to 210 periodicals including electronic. Computerized library services include interlibrary loans, database searching, Internet access, and Wi-Fi capability. Special learning facilities include an art gallery and radio station. The 4-acre campus is in an urban area The Russian Hill neighborhood of San Francisco. Including any residence halls, there are 6 buildings.

Student Life: 61% of undergraduates are from California. Others are from 26 states, 21 foreign countries, and Canada. 48% are White; 16% Hispanic; 13% Foreign. The average age of freshmen is 19; all undergraduates, 23. 35% do not continue beyond their first year; 29% remain to graduate.

Housing: 145 students can be accommodated in college housing, which includes coed dorms. On-campus housing is available on a first-come and first-served basis. 72% of students commute. Some may keep cars.

Activities: There are no fraternities or sororities. There are 14 groups on campus, including art, Art criticism, communications, ethnic, film, international, newspaper, photography, radio and TV, social, and student government. Popular campus events include Visiting Artists and Scholars Lecture Series; Graduate Lecture Series; openings for the Walter and McBean, Diego Rivera, Swell Galleries, Winter Art Sale, and Annual Art Party.

Sports: There is no sports program at SFAI.

Disabled Students: 70% of the campus is accessible. Facilities include wheelchair ramps, elevators, special parking, specially equipped restrooms, and special class scheduling.

Services: Counseling and information services are available, as is tutoring in every subject.

Campus Safety and Security: Measures include 24-hour foot and vehicle patrol and emergency notification system. There are emergency telephones, video security cameras.

Programs of Study: SFAI confers B.F.A., and B.A. degrees. Master's degrees are also awarded. Bachelor's degrees are awarded in COMMUNICATIONS AND THE ARTS (art history and appreciation, film arts, media arts, painting, photography, printmaking, and sculpture), COMPUTER AND PHYSICAL SCIENCE (digital arts/technology), SOCIAL SCIENCE (urban studies). Painting, photography, design and technology are the largest.

Required: For the BFA degree, the following majors are available: Design and Technology, Film, New Genres, Painting, Photography, Printmaking, and Sculpture. The BA degree has the following majors available: History and Theory of Contemporary Art, and Urban Studies. Degree-seeking undergraduates complete 120 units with a minimum 2.00 grade point average. BFA candidates complete 33 Liberal Arts units, 15 Art History units, 36 Major Studio units, and 36 Elective Studio units. BA candidates complete 33 Liberal Arts units and 33 General/Studio Elective units. History and Theory of Contemporary Art majors complete 15 Art History units and 39 Major Interdisciplinary units. Urban Studies majors complete 9 Art History units and 45 Major Interdisciplinary units. Entering freshmen require participation in the Contemporary Practices Seminar. Seniors in BA programs have a 6-unit, research and thesis requirement, while seniors in BFA programs participate in the Senior Review Seminar and Exhibition.

Special: The following special academic programs are available at SFAI: -Honors Interdisciplinary Studio for qualifying seniors -Internships, for college credit -Double majors for studio programs--any two of: Design and Technology, Film, New Genres, Painting, Photography, Printmaking, and Sculpture -one semester full-time registration at a participating school within the Association of Independent Colleges of Art & Design (AICAD) consortium, which includes participating schools from Canada, Ireland, and Japan -study abroad in the following countries: Czech Republic, Israel, England, France, Scotland, Holland, Germany, South Korea, and Sweden.

Faculty/Classroom: 51% of faculty are male; 49% are female. 83% teach undergraduates. No introductory courses are taught by graduate students. The average class size in an introductory lecture is 24; in a laboratory is 12; and in a regular course is 16.

Admissions: 83% of the 2013-2014 applicants were accepted. The SAT scores for the 2013-2014 freshman class were: Critical Reading--32% below 500, 39% between 500 and 599, 26% between 600 and 699, and

3% between 700 and 800; Math--48% below 500, 39% between 500 and 599, and 13% between 600 and 699; Writing--35% below 500, 32% between 500 and 599, and 32% between 600 and 699. The ACT scores were 13% below 21, 38% between 21 and 23, 13% between 24 and 26, 25% between 27 and 28, and 13% above 28.

Requirements: The SAT or ACT is recommended. In addition, Portfolio of artwork and an artist statement is required for BFA applicants, while a critical essay is required for BA applicants. BFA and BA applicants need to submit a letter of recommendation. The GED Certificate is accepted in lieu of a high school diploma. SAT and/or ACT test scores are strongly recommended. Interviews are recommended, but not required. A GPA of 2.0 is required. AP and CLEP credits are accepted. Important factors in the admissions decision are evidence of special talent, recommendations by school officials, and recommendations by alumni.

Procedure: Freshmen are admitted to all sessions. Entrance exams should be taken Fall of Senior Year. There are deferred admissions and rolling admissions plans. Applications should be filed by February 1 for fall entry; November 15 for spring entry, along with a $75 fee. Applications are accepted online.

Transfer: 88 transfer students enrolled in 2012-2013. Transfer students must have satisfactory prior college performance and a portfolio/artist statement (BFA applicants) or critical essay (BA applicants) appropriate to their level of experience. College transcripts are required, as well as a letter of recommendation. Interviews are recommended, but not required. 60 of 120 credits required for the bachelor's degree must be completed at SFAI.

Visiting: There are regularly scheduled orientations for prospective students, Portfolio reviews and an introduction to the school, its faculty, students, and alumni. There are guides for informal visits and visitors may sit in on classes. To schedule a visit, contact the Admissions Office at (415) 749-4500.

Financial Aid: 27% of undergraduate students work part-time. Average annual earnings from campus work are $1121. The average financial indebtedness of the 2013 graduate was $19,861. The FAFSA is required. The priority date for freshman financial aid applications for fall entry is February 1. The deadline for filing freshman financial aid applications for fall entry is March 1.

International Students: There are 61 international students enrolled. The school actively recruits these students. They must take the TOEFL with a minimum score of 550 on the paper-based TOEFL (PBT) or 79 on the Internet-based version (iBT), Academic IELTS accepted with a minimum score of 6.5.

Computers: All students may access the system. There are no time limits and no fees.

Graduates: From July 1, 2012 to June 30, 2013, 84 bachelor's degrees were awarded. The most popular majors were painting (44%), photography (17%), and film (9%). In an average class, 22% graduate in 4 years or less, 24% graduate in 5 years or less, and 29% graduate in 6 years or less. Of the 2012 graduating class, 12% were enrolled in graduate school within 6 months of graduation, and 65% were employed.

Admissions Contact: Jana Rumberger, Director of Admissions. E-Mail: *admissions@sfai.edu* Web: *www.sfai.edu*

SAN FRANCISCO CONSERVATORY OF MUSIC B-3

San Francisco, CA 94102	(415) 503-6231; (415) 503-6299
Full-time: 87 men, 85 women	**Faculty:** 30
Part-time: 2 men, 1 women	**Ph.D.s:** 30%
Graduate: 98 men, 130 women	**Student/Faculty:** 6 to 1
Year: semesters	**Tuition:** $41,923
Application Deadline: December 1	**Room & Board:** $12,000
Freshman Class: 275 applied, 118 accepted, 33 enrolled	
	SPECIAL

The San Francisco Conservatory of Music, founded in 1917, is a private institution offering undergraduate, graduate, and postgraduate programs in music performance. There is 1 undergraduate school and 1 graduate school. In addition to regional accreditation, SFCM has baccalaureate program accreditation with NASM. The library contains 36,755 volumes, and 20,585 audio/video tapes/CDs/DVDs, and subscribes to 70 periodicals including electronic. Computerized library services include interlibrary loans, database searching, Internet access, and Wi-Fi capability. Special learning facilities include a The 2-acre campus is in an urban area downtown in the Civic Center of San Francisco. Including any residence halls, there is 1 building.

Student Life: 51% of undergraduates are from out of state, mostly the Middle Atlantic. Students are from 37 states, 22 foreign countries, and Canada. 36% are White; 30% Foreign; 13% race unknown. The average age of freshmen is 19; all undergraduates, 21. 13% do not continue beyond their first year; 64% remain to graduate.

Housing: Alcohol is not permitted. All students commute. No one may keep cars.

Activities: There are no fraternities or sororities. There is 1 group on campus, including student government.

Sports: There is no sports program at SFCM.

Disabled Students: All of the campus is accessible. Facilities include wheelchair ramps, elevators, special parking, specially equipped restrooms, special class scheduling, lowered drinking fountains, and lowered telephones.

Services: Counseling and information services are available, as is tutoring in every subject.

Programs of Study: SFCM confers B.M. degrees. Master's degrees are also awarded. Bachelor's degrees are awarded in COMMUNICATIONS AND THE ARTS (guitar, music, music composition, percussion, piano/organ, strings, voice, and winds). Voice, piano, and violin are the largest.

Required: Students must complete 130 credit hours, 98 of which must be music related, and the remainder in general education courses, including courses in fine arts, English, history, and humanities . Specific required courses and total number of hours in the major vary by instrument. Students must also pass the senior recital and maintain a minimum GPA of 2.5.

Special: Work-study programs are available. There is a freshman honors program.

Faculty/Classroom: 70% of faculty are male; 30% are female. 98% teach undergraduates, and 1% do research. No introductory courses are taught by graduate students. The average class size in a regular course is 12.

Admissions: 43% of the 2013-2014 applicants were accepted.

Requirements: All applicants must have reached a high level of musical proficiency. An audition is required. A GPA of 2.5 is required. AP and CLEP credits are accepted. Important factors in the admissions decision are evidence of special talent, personality/intangible qualities, and extracurricular activities record.

Procedure: Freshmen are admitted fall and spring. Entrance exams should be taken by December 1. Applications should be filed by December 1 for fall entry; October 1 for spring entry, along with a $110 fee. Notifications are sent April 1. 74 applicants were on the 2013 waiting list; 27 were admitted. Applications are accepted online.

Transfer: 18 transfer students enrolled in 2012-2013. Transfer students must demonstrate a high level of musical proficiency, submit 2 letters of recommendation, and have a good academic record. An audition is required. 30 of 130 credits required for the bachelor's degree must be completed at SFCM.

Visiting: There are regularly scheduled orientations for prospective students, including individual tours and information sessions. There are guides for informal visits and visitors may sit in on classes. To schedule a visit, contact the Office of Music Admissions at admit@sfcm.edu.

Financial Aid: In 2013-2014, 97% of all full-time freshmen and 99% of continuing full-time students received some form of financial aid. 85% of all full-time freshmen and 95% of continuing full-time students received need-based aid. The average freshman award was $33,947. Need-based scholarships or need-based grants averaged $22,500 ($39,500 maximum); need-based self-help aid (loans and jobs) averaged $4,750 ($7,500 maximum); and other non-need-based awards and non-need-based scholarships averaged $15,000 ($35,000 maximum). 28% of undergraduate students work part-time. Average annual earnings from campus work are $1791. The average financial indebtedness of the 2013 graduate was $13,100. The CSS/Profile, FAFSA, and the college's own financial statement are required. The priority date for freshman financial aid applications for fall entry is February 1. The deadline for filing freshman financial aid applications for fall entry is March 1.

International Students: There are 50 international students enrolled. The school actively recruits these students. They must take the TOEFL with a minimum score of 500 on the paper-based TOEFL (PBT) or 61 on the Internet-based version (iBT). They must also take the SAT or ACT.

Computers: All students may access the system when the building is open. There are no time limits and no fees.

Graduates: From July 1, 2012 to June 30, 2013, 45 bachelor's degrees were awarded. The most popular majors were orchestral instruments (56%), voice (23%), and keyboard (11%). In an average class, 2% graduate in 3 years or less, 62% graduate in 4 years or less, and 64% graduate in 5 years or less.

Admissions Contact: Melissa Cocco-Mitten, Admissions Office. E-Mail: *admit@sfcm.edu* Web: *www.sfcm.edu*

SAN FRANCISCO STATE UNIVERSITY B-3

San Francisco, CA 94132	(415) 338-6486; (415) 338-3880
Full-time: 9399 men, 12712 women	**Faculty:** n/av
Part-time: 1951 men, 2094 women	**Ph.D.s:** 36%
Graduate: 1471 men, 2278 women	**Student/Faculty:** n/av
Year: semesters, summer session	**Tuition:** $6938 ($18,098)
Application Deadline: November 30	**Room & Board:** $11,576
Freshman Class: 34930 applied, 20889 accepted, 3612 enrolled	
SAT CR/M: 490/505	**ACT:** required **COMPETITIVE**

San Francisco State University, founded in 1899, is a public liberal arts institution offering graduate and undergraduate programs as part of the California State University system. There are 6 undergraduate schools and

6 graduate schools. In addition to regional accreditation, SF State, San Francsico State has baccalaureate program accreditation with AACSB, ACEJMC, ADA, AHEA, NASM, and NLN. The library contains 921,744 volumes, 1.7 million microform items, and 264,128 audio/video tapes/CDs/DVDs, and subscribes to 73,735 periodicals including electronic. Computerized library services include interlibrary loans, database searching, and Internet access. Special learning facilities include an art gallery, natural history museum, planetarium, radio station, TV station, a field campus, the labor archives and research center, a media access center, and an anthropology museum. The 142-acre campus is in an urban area in San Francisco. Including any residence halls, there are 23 buildings.

Student Life: 92% of undergraduates are from California. Others are from 37 states, 97 foreign countries, and Canada. 32% are Asian American; 27% White; 23% Hispanic. The average age of freshmen is 18; all undergraduates, 23.

Housing: 3200 students can be accommodated in college housing, which includes coed dorms, off-campus apartments, and married student housing. In addition, there are language houses, special-interest houses, Theme housing. On-campus housing is available on a first-come and first-served basis. 88% of students commute. Alcohol is not permitted. All students may keep cars.

Activities: 3% of men belong to 1 local and 10 national fraternities; 4% of women belong to 6 local and 10 national sororities. There are 200 groups on campus, including and Model UN, art, band, cheerleading, choir, chorale, chorus, communications, computers, dance, debate, drama, environmental, ethnic, film, forensics, gay, honors, international, jazz band, literary magazine, Music Ensembles, musical theater, newspaper, opera, orchestra, political, professional, radio and TV, religious, social, social service, student government, and symphony. Popular campus events include Activities Fair and Crafts Festival, Morrison Artists' Series Chamber Music Program and the Alexander String Quartet.

Sports: There are 5 intercollegiate sports for men and 6 for women, and 3 intramural sports for men and 3 for women. Facilities include a 6500-seat stadium, 2 gyms, an indoor pool, a weight room, a training room, wrestling and gymnastics areas, a dance studio, an all-weather track, 14 tennis courts, softball and baseball fields, and auxiliary practice fields.

Disabled Students: Facilities include wheelchair ramps, elevators, special parking, specially equipped restrooms, special class scheduling, lowered drinking fountains, lowered telephones, special housing.

Services: Counseling and information services are available, as is tutoring in every subject.

Campus Safety and Security: Measures include 24-hour foot and vehicle patrol, emergency notification system, self-defense education, and security escort services. There are shuttle buses, emergency telephones, lighted pathways/sidewalks, and controlled access to dorms/residences.

Programs of Study: San Francsico State confers B.A., B.S. and B.M. degrees. Master's and doctoral degrees are also awarded. Bachelor's degrees are awarded in AGRICULTURE (environmental studies and natural resource management), BIOLOGICAL SCIENCE (biochemistry, biology/biological science, botany, cell biology, ecology, marine biology, microbiology, physiology, and zoology), BUSINESS (accounting, banking and finance, business administration and management, electronic business, entrepreneurial studies, hospitality management services, hotel/motel and restaurant management, institutional management, international business management, labor studies, management science, marketing/retailing/merchandising, personnel management, and recreational facilities management), COMMUNICATIONS AND THE ARTS (apparel design, art, broadcasting, Chinese, classics, communications, comparative literature, creative writing, dance, design, dramatic arts, English, film arts, French, German, Italian, Japanese, journalism, languages, music, radio/television technology, Spanish, speech/debate/rhetoric, and visual design), COMPUTER AND PHYSICAL SCIENCE (applied mathematics, astronomy, astrophysics, atmospheric sciences and meteorology, chemistry, computer science, earth science, geology, information sciences and systems, mathematics, physics, and statistics), EDUCATION (elementary education, home economics education, industrial arts education, physical education, and recreation education), ENGINEERING AND ENVIRONMENTAL DESIGN (civil engineering, computer engineering, electrical/electronics engineering, industrial administration/management, industrial engineering technology, interior design, and mechanical engineering), HEALTH PROFESSIONS (clinical science, exercise science, health science, nursing, and speech pathology/audiology), SOCIAL SCIENCE (African studies, American studies, anthropology, Asian/American studies, clothing and textiles management/production/services, consumer services, criminal justice, dietetics, economics, family/consumer studies, geography, history, humanities, humanities and social science, interdisciplinary studies, international relations, Judaic studies, liberal arts/general studies, philosophy, political science/government, psychology, religion, social work, sociology, urban studies, and women's studies).

Required: To graduate, students must complete 120 to 132 credits with a minimum GPA of 2.0. The required general education core includes 27 credits in arts and sciences, 12 in basic skills subjects, and 9 in upper-division courses. English composition and U.S. history and government competency requirements may be fulfilled by either exam or course work.

Special: Students may cross-register with the California College of Podiatric Medicine, the City College of San Francisco, Cogswell College of Engineering, and several other area universities. Study abroad in 23 countries, a Washington semester, campus work-study, a general studies degree, dual and student-designed majors, credit for life experience, nondegree study, and pass/fail options are also offered. There are including Phi Beta Kappa, a freshman honors program, and 1 departmental honors programs.

Faculty/Classroom: 47% of faculty are male; 53% are female. No introductory courses are taught by graduate students.

Admissions: 60% of the 2013-2014 applicants were accepted. The SAT scores for the 2013-2014 freshman class were: Critical Reading--54% below 500, 35% between 500 and 599, 10% between 600 and 699, and 1% between 700 and 800; Math--46% below 500, 40% between 500 and 599, and 13% between 600 and 699.

Requirements: The SAT or ACT is required. In addition, Applicants should be graduates of an accredited secondary school with a minimum GPA of 2.0. The GED is accepted. High school courses should include 4 years of English, 3 of math, 2 of foreign language, and 1 each of U.S. history or government, lab science, and visual and performing arts. A GPA of 2.0 is required. AP and CLEP credits are accepted.

Procedure: Freshmen are admitted fall and spring. There is a rolling admissions plan. Applications should be filed by November 30 for fall entry, along with a $55 fee. Notification is sent on a rolling basis. Applications are accepted online.

Transfer: 3766 transfer students enrolled in 2012-2013. Applicants must have a college GPA of 2.0 (2.4 for nonresidents). Those with fewer than 56 transferable semester credits must meet freshman entrance requirements. 30 of 120 credits required for the bachelor's degree must be completed at SF State, San Francsico State.

Visiting: There are regularly scheduled orientations for prospective students. There are guides for informal visits and visitors may sit in on classes. To schedule a visit, contact the Student Outreach Services at (415) 338-2355.

Financial Aid: The average freshman award was $11,932. Need based scholarships or need-based grants averaged $10,404 ; need-based self-help aid (loans and jobs) averaged $4,242; non-need-based athletic scholarships averaged $3,449; and other non-need-based awards and non-need-based scholarships averaged $2,536. The average financial indebtedness of the 2013 graduate was $20,493. San Francsico State is a member of CSS. The FAFSA is required. The priority date for freshman financial aid applications for fall entry is March 2.

International Students: There are 1666 international students enrolled. The school actively recruits these students. They must take the TOEFL with a minimum score of 500 on the paper-based TOEFL (PBT) or 61 on the Internet-based version (iBT). They must also take the SAT or ACT.

Computers: All students may access the system 24 hours daily. There are no time limits and no fees.

Graduates: From July 1, 2012 to June 30, 2013, 6344 bachelor's degrees were awarded. The most popular majors were business/marketing (24%), social sciences (10%), and visual and performing arts (9%). In an average class, 34% graduate in 5 years or less and 46% graduate in 6 years or less.

Admissions Contact: John Pliska, Director. E-Mail: *ugadmit@sfsu.edu*
Web: *http:/www.sfsu.edu/*

SAN JOSE STATE UNIVERSITY B-3

San Jose, CA 95192 **408.283.7500**

Full-time: 10628 men, 10224 women	**Faculty:** n/av; IIA, +$
Part-time: 2580 men, 2430 women	**Ph.D.s:** n/av
Graduate: 2077 men, 2827 women	**Student/Faculty:** n/av
Year: semesters, summer session	**Tuition:** $7303 ($16,231)
Application Deadline:	**Room & Board:** $12,404
Freshman Class: n/av	
SAT or ACT: required	

COMPETITIVE

San Jose State University, founded in 1857 and part of the California State University system, is a public institution offering undergraduate and graduate programs in applied arts and science, social science, and social work to a primarily commuter student body. There are 8 undergraduate schools and 8 graduate schools. In addition to regional accreditation, SJSU has baccalaureate program accreditation with AACSB, ABET, ACEJMC, CSWE, NASAD, NASM, NCATE, and NRPA. The library contains 1.4 million volumes, 1.1 million microform items, and 36,288 audio/video tapes/CDs/DVDs, and subscribes to 111,317 periodicals including electronic. Computerized library services include interlibrary loans, database searching, Internet access, and Wi-Fi capability. Special learning facilities include an art gallery, radio station, and TV station. The 154-acre campus is in an urban area in the center of San Jose. Including any residence halls, there are 64 buildings.

Student Life: 96% of undergraduates are from California. Others are from states, and Canada. 32% are Asian American; 24% White; 22% Hispanic. The average age of freshmen is 19; all undergraduates, 23.

Housing: 4000 students can be accommodated in college housing, which includes coed dorms and on-campus apartments. In addition, there are special-interest houses, fraternity houses, sorority houses, and an international students center. On-campus housing is available on a first-come and first-served basis. Alcohol is not permitted. All students may keep cars.

Activities: Groups on campus include art, band, cheerleading, choir, chorale, chorus, communications, dance, drama, ethnic, film, gay, international, marching band, musical theater, newspaper, photography, political, radio and TV, social, student government, and symphony. Popular campus events include International Food Bazaar, Welcome Day, and National Collegiate Alcohol Awareness Week.

Sports: There are 6 intercollegiate sports for men and 10 for women. Facilities include a gym, pool, track, football field, baseball field, a recreation center with racquetball courts and a bowling alley.

Disabled Students: 98% of the campus is accessible. Facilities include wheelchair ramps, elevators, special parking, specially equipped restrooms, special class scheduling, lowered drinking fountains, lowered telephones, and preadmission assistance.

Services: Counseling and information services are available, as is tutoring in most subjects. There is a reader service for the blind, and remedial math and writing. There are also test accommodations, sign-language interpreters, liaisons to faculty, and note takers.

Campus Safety and Security: Measures include 24-hour foot and vehicle patrol, emergency notification system, self-defense education, and security escort services. There are shuttle buses, emergency telephones, lighted pathways/sidewalks, controlled access to dorms/residences, and a canine patrol.

Programs of Study: SJSU confers B.A., B.S., B.F.A. and B.Mus. degrees. Master's and doctoral degrees are also awarded. Bachelor's degrees are awarded in AGRICULTURE (environmental studies), BIOLOGICAL SCIENCE (biochemistry, biology/biological science, botany, forensic science, marine science, microbiology, nutritional sciences, and zoology), BUSINESS (accounting, banking and finance, business administration and management, international business management, and marketing/retailing/merchandising), COMMUNICATIONS AND THE ARTS (advertising, art history, broadcasting, Chinese, communication studies, dance, design, dramatic arts, English, film arts, fine arts, French, German, Japanese, jazz, journalism, literature, music, public relations, Spanish, and speech/debate/rhetoric), COMPUTER AND PHYSICAL SCIENCE (applied mathematics, chemistry, computer science, geology, mathematics, natural sciences, physics, software engineering, and statistics), EDUCATION (early childhood education, education administration, education of the deaf and hearing impaired, music education, recreation education, and teaching English as a second/foreign language (TESOL/TEFOL)), ENGINEERING AND ENVIRONMENTAL DESIGN (aeronautical engineering, biomedical engineering, chemical engineering, civil engineering, computer engineering, electrical/electronics engineering, engineering, industrial engineering, interior design, materials engineering, mechanical engineering, and urban planning technology), HEALTH PROFESSIONS (health science, nursing, occupational therapy, public health, and speech pathology/audiology), SOCIAL SCIENCE (anthropology, criminal justice, economics, food science, geography, history, Mexican-American/Chicano studies, philosophy, political science/government, psychology, religion, religious studies, social science, social work, and sociology). Accounting is the strongest academically. Psychology, accounting, electrical engineering have the largest enrollments.

Required: Students must complete 39 units of core general education, including 12 units of upper-division courses in residence and 6 units of American history and institutions. A minimum of 124 credits, with at least 24 in the major, a minimum GPA of 2.0, and the successful completion of writing, English, and entry-level math tests are required to graduate.

Special: SJSU has opportunities for cooperative programs in business, science, engineering, arts, and the humanities, work-study with many employers, internships (some required, some optional), study abroad in 16 countries, field experiences, and student teaching. An accelerated program is offered in nursing, and the B.A.-B.S. degree and dual majors are available in various areas of study. A general studies degree, student-designed majors, nondegree study, and credit/no-credit options are possible. There is a freshman honors program.

Faculty/Classroom: 50% of faculty are male; 50% are female. No introductory courses are taught by graduate students. The average class size in an introductory lecture is 30; in a laboratory is 20; and in a regular course is 25.

Requirements: The SAT or ACT is required. Scores are used to calculate an eligibility index rating, which determines qualification for admission. Graduation from an accredited secondary school is required; the GED is accepted. Applicants must have completed 4 years of English, 3 each of math and electives, 2 of a foreign language, and 1 each of history, science, and art. AP and CLEP credits are accepted. Important factors in the admissions decision are personality/intangible qualities, recommendations by alumni, and recommendations by school officials.

Procedure: Freshmen are admitted fall and spring. Entrance exams should be taken prior to the fall semester. There are deferred admissions and rolling admissions plans. Check with the school for current application deadlines. The fall 2013 application fee was $55. Applications are accepted online.

Transfer: Applicants must have a minimum GPA of 2.0. The student's rating in the eligibility index is also considered in determining qualification for transfer. 30 of 124 credits required for the bachelor's degree must be completed at SJSU.

Visiting: There are regularly scheduled orientations for prospective students. There are guides for informal visits and visitors may sit in on classes. To schedule a visit, contact the Office of Relations at (408) 924-2564.

Financial Aid: SJSU is a member of CSS. The FAFSA is required. Check with the school for current application deadlines.

International Students: The school actively recruits these students. They must take the TOEFL. They must also take the SAT or ACT.

Computers: All students may access the system 9 a.m. to 8 p.m. Monday through Friday and 9 a.m. to 5 p.m. Saturday. There are no time limits and no fees.

Graduates: From July 1, 2012 to June 30, 2013, 5206 bachelor's degrees were awarded. The most popular majors were psychology (5%), business management (5%), and accounting (4%).

Admissions Contact: Student Services Web: *http:/info.sjsu.edu/home/admission.html*

SANTA CLARA UNIVERSITY B-3

Santa Clara, CA 95053 **(408) 554-4700; (408) 554-5255**

Full-time: 2673 men, 2665 women	**Faculty:** 404; IIA, ++$
Part-time: 51 men, 46 women	**Ph.D.s:** 93%
Graduate: 1755 men, 1580 women	**Student/Faculty:** 12 to 1
Year: varies, summer session	**Tuition:** $42,156
Application Deadline: January 7	**Room & Board:** $12,546
Freshman Class: 14980 applied, 7456 accepted, 1291 enrolled	
SAT CR/M: 630/660 **ACT:** 29	**MOST COMPETITIVE**

Santa Clara University, a comprehensive Jesuit, Catholic university, offers its students rigorous undergraduate curricula in arts and sciences, business, and engineering, plus master's and law degrees and engineering Ph.D.s. Distinguished nationally by one of the highest graduation rates among all U.S. master's universities, California's oldest operating higher education institution demonstrates faith-inspired values of ethics and social justice. Founded in 1851 by the Society of Jesus, SCU was established on the site of Mission Santa Clara de Asis, the eighth of 21 California missions and strives to educate leaders of competence, conscience, and compassion. There are 3 undergraduate schools and 6 graduate schools. In addition to regional accreditation, has baccalaureate program accreditation with AACSB and ABET. The 2 libraries contain 1.3 million volumes, 2.5 million microform items, and 27,789 audio/video tapes/CDs/DVDs, and subscribe to 5,818 periodicals including electronic. Computerized library services include interlibrary loans, database searching, Internet access, and Wi-Fi capability. Special learning facilities include an art gallery, planetarium, radio station, A California Mission; archeology lab; Center for Nanostructures; Robotics Systems Lab; Satellite Mission Control Room; three interdisciplinary Centers of Distinction: Center for Science, Technology, and Society; Ignatian Center for Jesuit Education; and the Markkula Center for Applied Ethics; several centers of academic outreach in the business and legal disciplines. The 106-acre campus is in a suburban area 40 miles south of San Francisco, in the heart of Silicon Valley. Including any residence halls, there are 113 buildings.

Student Life: 62% of undergraduates are from California. Others are from 46 states, 42 foreign countries, and Canada. 50% are from public schools. 48% are White; 17% Hispanic; 14% Asian American. The average age of freshmen is 18; all undergraduates, 20.

Housing: 3103 students can be accommodated in college housing, which includes coed dorms, on-campus apartments, and off-campus apartments. All freshman students select 1 of 8 residential learning communities (RLC), which provide a holistic educational experience by bringing together the academic, residential, and social components of campus life. Themes for the RLCs include: civic engagement, international issues, leadership, science, social justice, social responsibility, sustainability and the arts, and Western culture. On-campus housing is guaranteed for the freshman year only, is available on a first-come, first-served basis, and is available on a lottery system for upperclassmen. 52% of students live on campus; of those, 50% remain on campus on weekends. Upperclassmen may keep cars.

Activities: There are no fraternities or sororities. There are 124 groups on campus, including major-specific, art, cheerleading, choir, chorale, chorus, communications, computers, dance, debate, drama, environmental, ethnic, film, forensics, gay, gospel choir, honors, international, jazz band, literary magazine, musical theater, newspaper, opera, orchestra, pep band, photography, political, professional, radio and TV, religious, social, social service, student government, symphony, and yearbook. Popular campus events include Bronco Week (Spirit Week), Cinco de Mayo, Family Weekend and Grand Reunion (alumni event).

Sports: There are 9 intercollegiate sports for men and 10 for women, and 9 intramural sports for men and 9 for women. The university's campus consists of six prominent athletic facilities: The Leavey Center, a 4,500-seat arena for basketball and volleyball with a weight room for the athletic teams; Buck Shaw Stadium, a 6,800-seat stadium for soccer; The Degheri Tennis Center which has nine lighted outdoor tennis courts that serve the men's and women's tennis teams and recreation for intramural sports or drop-in play; Stephen Schott Baseball Stadium, a 1,500-seat baseball facility; the Sullivan Aquatic Center, a shared athletics and recreation outdoor Olympic-size swimming pool with seating for 500 fans; the Pat Malley Fitness and Recreation Center, a 45,000-square-foot facility with three courts for basketball, volleyball or badminton, a weight room and multi-purpose room, and locker rooms with sauna; and Bellomy Field, a lighted six-acre, synthetic field that serves club sports, intramural sports and open recreation.

Disabled Students: 95% of the campus is accessible. Facilities include wheelchair ramps, elevators, special parking, specially equipped restrooms, special class scheduling, lowered drinking fountains, lowered telephones, special housing. Residence Halls are structured to allow access for disabled students. Note takers and voice recognition software are available as needed.

Services: Counseling and information services are available, as is tutoring in most subjects.

Campus Safety and Security: Measures include 24-hour foot and vehicle patrol, emergency notification system, self-defense education, and security escort services. There are emergency telephones, lighted pathways/sidewalks, and controlled access to dorms/residences.

Programs of Study: confers B.A., B.S. and B.S.C. degrees. Master's and doctoral degrees are also awarded. Bachelor's degrees are awarded in BIOLOGICAL SCIENCE (biochemistry and biology/biological science), BUSINESS (accounting, finance, management information systems, marketing management, and operations management), COMMUNICATIONS AND THE ARTS (art history and appreciation, communications, English, Greek, Latin, music, studio art, and theatre arts), COMPUTER AND PHYSICAL SCIENCE (chemistry, Computer Engineering Technology, computer science, mathematics, and physics), ENGINEERING AND ENVIRONMENTAL DESIGN (bioengineering, civil engineering, electrical/electronics engineering, engineering, engineering physics, environmental science, and mechanical engineering), HEALTH PROFESSIONS (public health), SOCIAL SCIENCE (anthropology, classical/ancient civilization, economics, ethnic studies, French studies, German area studies, history, Italian studies, Latin American studies, liberal arts/general studies, philosophy, political science/government, psychology, religion, sociology, Spanish studies, and women's studies). Communication, psychology, political science and finance are the strongest academically. Biology, psychology, communication have the largest enrollments.

Required: All students are required to maintain a GPA of at least 2.0 in both major and minor subjects. Students must take 175 quarter units for most bachelor's degrees. Core requirements include 17 courses--critical thinking and writing 1 and 2; cultures and ideas 1, 2; second language; mathematics; religion, theology, and culture 1, 2, and 3; ethics; civic engagement; diversity; arts; social science; natural science; science, technology and society--and advanced writing, experiential learning for social justice, and pathways requirements that often are embedded in other requirements for the core or for majors.

Special: Study abroad is offered in 55 countries through over 100 programs, many of which include academic internships and community based learning opportunities. A co-op program in engineering, dual majors, internships in business, government, and nonprofit agencies, a general studies degree, student-designed majors, work-study, The Washington Semester, and pass/fail options also are available. There are 24 national honor societies, including Phi Beta Kappa, and a freshman honors program.

Faculty/Classroom: 58% of faculty are male; 42% are female. 74% teach undergraduates, and all teach and do research. No introductory courses are taught by graduate students.

Admissions: 50% of the 2013-2014 applicants were accepted. The SAT scores for the 2013-2014 freshman class were: Critical Reading--4% below 500, 30% between 500 and 599, 48% between 600 and 699, and 18% between 700 and 800; Math--3% below 500, 18% between 500 and 599, 50% between 600 and 699, and 29% between 700 and 800. The ACT scores were 5% between 21 and 23, 16% between 24 and 26, 22% between 27 and 28, and 57% above 28. 75% of the current freshmen were in the top fifth of their class; 96% were in the top two fifths. 25 freshmen graduated first in their class.

Requirements: The SAT is required. Applicants should have 18 academic units, including 4 years each of English and math, 3 each of foreign language and science, 1 or 2 of which are a lab, 1 each in social studies and history, and 2 in electives. An essay is required. An audition is recommended for theater arts majors. The GED is accepted. AP credits are accepted. Important factors in the admissions decision are advanced placement or honors courses, recommendations by school officials, and leadership record.

Procedure: Freshmen are admitted fall. Entrance exams should be taken by December 1. There are early decision, early admissions, deferred admissions, and rolling admissions plans. Early decision applications should be filed by December 15; regular applications, by January 7 for fall entry, along with a $55 fee. 105 early decision candidates were accepted for the 2013-2014 class. 2436 applicants were on the 2013 waiting list; 142 were admitted. Applications are accepted online.

Transfer: 146 transfer students enrolled in 2012-2013. Arts and Sciences: 3.3 GPA, 2 English, 1 College level Math, 1 biological or physical science with lab. Business School: 3.5 GPA, 2 English, 2 Calculus, Financial Accounting, Managerial Accounting, Macroeconomics, Microeconomics. School of Engineering: 3.5 GPA, 2 English, 2 Calculus, 1 Chemistry, 2 Calculus based Physics. 87 of 176 credits required for the bachelor's degree must be completed at Santa Clara.

Visiting: There are regularly scheduled orientations for prospective students, Available Monday through Friday. There are guides for informal visits, visitors may sit in on classes, and stay overnight. To schedule a visit, contact the Office of Undergraduate Admission at Admission@scu.edu.

Financial Aid: In 2013-2014, 74% of all full-time freshmen received some form of financial aid. 65% of all full-time freshmen received need-based aid. The average freshman award was $28,699. Need-based scholarships or need-based grants averaged $23,527; need-based self-help aid (loans and jobs) averaged $3,879; non-need-based athletic scholarships averaged $35,731; and other non-need-based awards and non-need-based scholarships averaged $10,919. 45% of undergraduate students work part-time. Average annual earnings from campus work are $2975. The CSS/Profile and FAFSA are required. The priority date for freshman financial aid applications for fall entry is February 1.

International Students: There are 170 international students enrolled. The school actively recruits these students. They must take the TOEFL with a minimum score of 575 on the paper-based TOEFL (PBT) or 90 on the Internet-based version (iBT). They must also take the SAT or ACT.

Computers: All students may access the system. There are no time limits and no fees.

Graduates: From July 1, 2012 to June 30, 2013, 1155 bachelor's degrees were awarded. The most popular majors were finance (11%), communication (10%), and accounting (8%).

Admissions Contact: Sandra Hayes, Dean of Admissions. E-Mail: *Admission@scu.edu* Web: *www.scu.edu*

SCRIPPS COLLEGE D-5

Claremont, CA 91711 **(909) 621-8578**
(800) 770-1333; (909) 607-7508

Full-time: 940 women	**Faculty:** 81; IIB, +$
Part-time: 5 women	**Ph.D.s:** n/av
Graduate: 3 men, 14 women	**Student/Faculty:** 10 to 1
Year: semesters, summer session	**Tuition:** $41,950
Application Deadline: January 2	**Room & Board:** $12,950

Freshman Class: 2373 applied, 769 accepted, 235 enrolled
SAT or ACT: required

MOSTCOMPETITIVE

Scripps College, founded in 1926, is a private liberal arts institution for women. A member of the Claremont Colleges, Scripps emphasizes a challenging core curriculum based on interdisciplinary humanistic studies. There are 5 undergraduate schools. The library contains 2.6 million volumes, 980,340 microform items, and 4,597 audio/video tapes/CDs/DVDs, and subscribes to 15,588 periodicals including electronic. Computerized library services include interlibrary loans, database searching, Internet access, and Wi-Fi capability. Special learning facilities include an art gallery, radio station, humanities museum, and biological field station. The 37-acre campus is in a suburban area 35 miles east of Los Angeles. Including any residence halls, there are 27 buildings.

Student Life: 52% of undergraduates are from out of state, mostly the Northwest. Students are from states. 52% are White; 18% Asian American. The average age of freshmen is 18; all undergraduates, 20. 8% do not continue beyond their first year; 90% remain to graduate.

Housing: 836 students can be accommodated in college housing, which includes single-sex dorms, on-campus apartments, and off-campus apartments. foreign language corridors. On-campus housing is guaranteed for all 4 years. 95% of students live on campus. All students may keep cars.

Activities: There are no fraternities or sororities. There are 200 groups on campus, including art, chess, choir, chorale, chorus, computers, dance, debate, drama, environmental, ethnic, film, gay, honors, international, literary magazine, musical theater, newspaper, orchestra, photography, political, professional, radio and TV, radio only, religious, social, social service, student government, symphony, and yearbook. Popular campus events include Spring Fling Carnival, Levitt on the Lawn, Break Away Series, Scripps Outdoor Adventure Program and Holiday Dinner.

Sports: There are 11 intercollegiate sports for women, and 6 intramural sports for women. Facilities include the Sallie Tiernan Field House is a state-of-the art 24,000 square-foot facility with an aerobics studio, cardio machine room, weight room, and other spaces for fitness and health education. The facility also includes the swimming pool and soccer/lacrosse fields. There are also tennis courts, a climbing wall, an outdoor track, and fields for baseball and softball.

Disabled Students: 80% of the campus is accessible. Facilities include wheelchair ramps, elevators, special parking, specially equipped restrooms, special class scheduling, lowered drinking fountains, and special housing.

Services: Counseling and information services are available, as is tutoring in every subject. There is a reader service for the blind.

Campus Safety and Security: Measures include 24-hour foot and vehicle patrol, emergency notification system, self-defense education, and security escort services. There are emergency telephones, lighted pathways/sidewalks, and controlled access to dorms/residences.

Programs of Study: Scripps confers B.A. degrees. Bachelor's degrees are awarded in AGRICULTURE (environmental studies), BIOLOGICAL SCIENCE (biology/biological science, molecular biology, and neurosciences), COMMUNICATIONS AND THE ARTS (art history and appreciation, Chinese, classical languages, communications, dance, dramatic arts, English, Germanic languages and literature, Italian, Japanese, languages, music, Russian, Spanish, and studio art), COMPUTER AND PHYSICAL SCIENCE (chemistry, computer science, geology, mathematics, physics, science and management, and science technology), ENGINEERING AND ENVIRONMENTAL DESIGN (environmental science and preengineering), SOCIAL SCIENCE (African American studies, American studies, anthropology, Asian/American studies, Asian/Oriental studies, classical/ancient civilization, economics, European studies, French studies, German area studies, Hispanic American studies, history, humanities, Italian studies, Judaic studies, Latin American studies, law, Mexican-American/Chicano studies, philosophy, political science/government, prelaw, psychology, religion, sociology, and women's studies). Psychology, politics/international relations, economics, English, French studies are the strongest academically. Art and biology have the largest enrollments.

Required: Students must complete a total of 32 courses, or 128 units, with at least a C average. Requirements include a 3-semester humanities core, a first-year writing/critical thinking course, and 1 course each in fine arts, letters, natural science, social science, gender and women's studies, and race and ethnic studies. A senior thesis or project is also required.

Special: Students may cross-register with any of the other Claremont Colleges. Scripps also offers study abroad in 36 countries, a Washington semester, and student-designed, dual, and interdisciplinary majors, including organizational studies and science, technology, and society. Many courses are offered as seminars. There are 4-1 accelerated degree programs in the arts and business administration. A 3-2 engineering program (B.A.-B.S.) is offered with Harvey Mudd College, USC, UC Berkeley, Columbia, Stanford, Boston Universities, and others. There are 7 national honor societies including Phi Beta Kappa.

Faculty/Classroom: 41% of faculty are male; 59% are female. All teach and do research. No introductory courses are taught by graduate students. The average class size in an introductory lecture is 30; in a laboratory is 20; and in a regular course is 16.

Admissions: 32% of the 2013-2014 applicants were accepted. The SAT scores for the 2013-2014 freshman class were: 10% between 500 and 599, 47% between 600 and 699, and 44% between 700 and 800; Math--12% between 500 and 599, 6% between 600 and 699, and 29% between 700 and 800; Writing--5% between 500 and 599, 45% between 600 and 699, and 50% between 700 and 800.

Requirements: The SAT or ACT is required. Applicants must have completed 4 units each of high school English and math, 3 each of lab science and social studies, and either 3 of a single foreign language or 2 each of 2 languages. SAT Subject Tests and an interview are recommended. An essay and a graded writing assignment from the junior or senior year are required. A GPA of 3.5 is required. AP and CLEP credits are accepted. Important factors in the admissions decision are advanced placement or honors courses, evidence of special talent, and leadership record.

Procedure: Freshmen are admitted fall and spring. Entrance exams should be taken by December of the senior year. There are early decision, early admissions, and deferred admissions plans. Early decision applications should be filed by November 15; regular applications, by January 2 for fall entry; and November 1 for spring entry, along with a $60 fee. Notification of early decision is sent December 15; regular decision, April 1. 499 applicants were on the 2013 waiting list; 55 were admitted. Applications are accepted online.

Transfer: A cumulative college GPA of 3.0 is required.

Visiting: There are guides for informal visits, visitors may sit in on classes, and stay overnight. To schedule a visit, contact the Admission Office.

Financial Aid: Scripps is a member of CSS. The CSS/Profile, FAFSA, and the state aid form are required. The priority date for freshman financial aid applications for fall entry is February 1.

International Students: There are 45 international students enrolled. The school actively recruits these students. They must take the TOEFL with a minimum score of 600 on the paper-based TOEFL (PBT) or 100 on the Internet-based version (iBT). They must also take the SAT or ACT.

Computers: All students may access the system. There are no time limits and no fees.

Graduates: From July 1, 2012 to June 30, 2013, 278 bachelor's degrees were awarded. The most popular majors were psychology (16%), social sciences (14%), ethnic, and gender studies (13%). 300 companies recruited on campus in 2012-2013. In an average class, 2% graduate in 3 years or less, 85% graduate in 4 years or less, 89% graduate in 5 years or less, and 90% graduate in 6 years or less.

Admissions Contact: Victoria Romero, VP for Enrollment. E-Mail: *VRomero@scrippscollege.edu* Web: *www.scrippscollege.edu*

SIMPSON UNIVERSITY — B-2

Redding, CA 96003 — (530) 224-5600; (888) 9-SIMPSON; (530) 226-4861

Full-time: 322 men, 665 women	**Faculty:** 43
Part-time: 12 men, 20 women	**Ph.D.s:** 56%
Graduate: 102 men, 176 women	**Student/Faculty:** 15 to 1
Year: semesters, summer session	**Tuition:** $22,100
Application Deadline: open	**Room & Board:** $7800
Freshman Class: 533 applied, 317 accepted, 158 enrolled	
SAT CR/M/W: 500/500/490 **ACT:** 21	**COMPETITIVE**

Simpson University, founded in 1921, is a Christian university offering undergraduate, graduate, and teaching credential programs. Simpson University is an official institution of the Christian and Missionary Alliance, and the student population represents more than 25 evangelical denominations. There are no undergraduate schools and 3 graduate schools. The library contains 176,640 volumes, 242,910 microform items, and 3,253 audio/video tapes/CDs/DVDs, and subscribes to 24,334 periodicals including electronic. Computerized library services include interlibrary loans, database searching, Internet access, and Wi-Fi capability. The 92-acre campus is in a suburban area in the northeast city limits of Redding. Including any residence halls, there are 17 buildings.

Student Life: 87% of undergraduates are from California. Others are from 27 states, and 7 foreign countries. 59% are from public schools. 60% are White. 99% are Protestant. The average age of freshmen is 18; all undergraduates, 25. 35% do not continue beyond their first year; 45% remain to graduate.

Housing: 590 students can be accommodated in college housing, which includes single-sex dorms, off-campus apartments, and married student housing. In addition, there are special-interest houses, Gatehouse- Missionary Kid Housing. On-campus housing is guaranteed for all 4 years. 55% of students commute. Alcohol is not permitted. All students may keep cars.

Activities: There are no fraternities or sororities. There are 20 groups on campus, including Commuter Students Association, psychology, band, choir, chorale, computers, drama, ethnic, film, golf, international, jazz band, newspaper, orchestra, photography, professional, religious, social, social service, student government, symphony, and yearbook. Popular campus events include Spring Banquet, Missions Emphasis Week and Airband.

Sports: There are 5 intercollegiate sports for men and 6 for women, and 2 intramural sports for men and 1 for women. Facilities include a soccer field, a 1450-seat gym, weight and training rooms, a softball field, outdoor volleyball and basketball courts. Students have access to nearby facilities for swimming, boating, mountain climbing, and skiing.

Disabled Students: 95% of the campus is accessible. Facilities include wheelchair ramps, elevators, special parking, specially equipped restrooms, lowered drinking fountains, lowered telephones, and special housing.

Services: Counseling and information services are available, as is tutoring in every subject. There is remedial math and writing.

Campus Safety and Security: Measures include 24-hour foot and vehicle patrol, emergency notification system, and security escort services. There are emergency telephones, lighted pathways/sidewalks, controlled access to dorms/residences, emergency whistle program, local police patrols, and monthly campus safety meetings.

Programs of Study: Simpson confers B.A., and B.S. degrees. Associate and master's degrees are also awarded. Bachelor's degrees are awarded in BIOLOGICAL SCIENCE (biology/biological science), BUSINESS (accounting, business administration and management, human resources, organizational leadership and management, and recreation and leisure services), COMMUNICATIONS AND THE ARTS (communications, English, and music), COMPUTER AND PHYSICAL SCIENCE (mathematics), EDUCATION (elementary education, English education, mathematics education, music education, secondary education, and social science education), HEALTH PROFESSIONS (health care administration and nursing), SOCIAL SCIENCE (biblical studies, crosscultural studies, history, liberal arts/general studies, ministries, missions, pastoral studies, psychology, religion, religious education, social science, and youth ministry). Biology, nursing, and music are the strongest academically. Psychology, business administration, and liberal studies have the largest enrollments.

Required: Students must complete at least 124 credits, with a minimum of 36 upper-division credits and at least 42 major credits (of which 24 must be upper division). A minimum GPA of 2.0 must be maintained. Foundational studies requirements include 24 credits in biblical studies and theology and 41 credits in human expression, human history and behavior, and global environment.

Special: Off-campus educational programs are offered through the China Studies Program, Contemporary Music Program in Martha's Vineyard, Latin American Studies Program, Los Angeles Film Studies Center, Middle East Studies Program, Oxford Honors Program, and the Russian Studies Program. Students may study abroad in a variety of countries. Internships are available in Christian education, pastoral studies, youth ministries, business, and psychology. Work-study programs in elementary education and with the federal government are also available. There is also a 1-year, nondegree certificate program in Bible and contemporary church music. There are 2 national honor societies and 1 departmental honors programs.

Faculty/Classroom: 52% of faculty are male; 48% are female. 65% teach undergraduates. No introductory courses are taught by graduate students. The average class size in an introductory lecture is 42; in a laboratory is 11; and in a regular course is 11.

Admissions: 59% of the 2013-2014 applicants were accepted. The SAT scores for the 2013-2014 freshman class were: Critical Reading--35% below 500, 41% between 500 and 599, 22% between 600 and 699, and 2% between 700 and 800; Math--36% below 500, 50% between 500 and 599, and 14% between 600 and 699; Writing--42% below 500, 43% between 500 and 599, 15% between 600 and 699. The ACT scores were 44% below 21, 26% between 21 and 23, 13% between 24 and 26, 11% between 27 and 28, and 4% above 28. 53% of the current freshmen were in the top fifth of their class; 71% were in the top two fifths.

Requirements: The SAT or ACT is required. Applicants must be graduates of an accredited high school or have a GED. It is recommended that applicants have completed 4 years of high school English, 3 each of math, science, and social studies/history, and 2 of a foreign language. A GPA of 2.0 is required. AP and CLEP credits are accepted. Important factors in the admissions decision are leadership record, personality/intangible qualities, and recommendations by school officials.

Procedure: Freshmen are admitted to all sessions. Entrance exams should be taken during the junior year or in the fall of the senior year. There are deferred admissions and rolling admissions plans. Application deadlines are open. Application fee is $25. Notification is sent on a rolling basis. Applications are accepted online.

Transfer: 98 transfer students enrolled in 2012-2013. Transfer applicants with at least 30 semester college credits need not submit SAT or ACT scores. 30 of 124 credits required for the bachelor's degree must be completed at Simpson.

Visiting: There are regularly scheduled orientations for prospective students, Genesis Weekend. There are guides for informal visits, visitors may sit in on classes, and stay overnight. To schedule a visit, contact the Visit Coordinator at (530) 226-4769.

Financial Aid: In 2013-2014, 100% of all full-time freshmen and 99% of continuing full-time students received some form of financial aid. 91% of all full-time freshmen and 94% of continuing full-time students received need-based aid. The average freshman award was $14,815. Need-based scholarships or need-based grants averaged $15,600 ($25,400 maximum); need-based self-help aid (loans and jobs) averaged $4,300 ($9,000 maximum); non-need-based athletic scholarships averaged $7,227 ($9,000 maximum); and other non-need-based awards and non-need-based scholarships averaged $7,610 ($21,600 maximum). 27% of undergraduate students work part-time. Average annual earnings from campus work are $3452. The average financial indebtedness of the 2013 graduate was $17,524. Simpson is a member of CSS. The FAFSA and the college's own financial statement are required. The priority date for freshman financial aid applications for fall entry is March 2.

International Students: There are 7 international students enrolled. They must take the TOEFL with a minimum score of 500 on the paper-based TOEFL (PBT) or 79 on the Internet-based version (iBT). They must also take the SAT or ACT.

Computers: All students may access the system. There are no time limits. The fee is $80.

Graduates: From July 1, 2012 to June 30, 2013, 300 bachelor's degrees were awarded. The most popular majors were liberal arts (18%), psychology (18%), and human resources management (9%). In an average class, 1% graduate in 3 years or less, 32% graduate in 4 years or less, 43% graduate in 5 years or less, and 45% graduate in 6 years or less.

Admissions Contact: Kendell Kluttz, Director of Admissions. E-Mail: *admissions@simpsonu.edu* Web: *www.simpsonu.edu*

SONOMA STATE UNIVERSITY — B-3

Rohnert Park, CA 94928 — **(707) 664-2778**

Full-time: 2931 men, 4721 women	**Faculty:** 175; IIA, av$
Part-time: 311 men, 388 women	**Ph.D.s:** 60%
Graduate: 216 men, 553 women	**Student/Faculty:** 25 to 1
Year: semesters, summer session	**Tuition:** $8996 ($17,824)
Application Deadline: November 30	**Room & Board:** $11,545
Freshman Class: 14272 applied, 12870 accepted, 1807 enrolled	
SAT CR/M: 440/540	**ACT:** 23 — **COMPETITIVE**

Sonoma State University, founded in 1960 and part of the California State University system, offers undergraduate programs in business and economics, natural sciences, social sciences, and arts and humanities; and graduate programs in education, counseling, business, and other fields. There are 4 undergraduate schools and one graduate school. In addition to regional accreditation, Sonoma State has baccalaureate program accreditation with AACSB, NASAD, NASM, and NLN. The library contains 647,168 volumes, 1.7 million microform items, and 56,870 audio/video tapes/CDs/DVDs, and subscribes to 123,328 periodicals including electronic. Computerized library services include interlibrary loans, database searching, Internet access, and Wi-Fi capability. Special learning facilities include an art gallery, radio station, an observatory, and natural preserve. The 275-acre campus is in a suburban area 45 miles north of San Francisco. Including any residence halls, there are 62 buildings.

Student Life: 98% of undergraduates are from California. Others are from 31 states, 26 foreign countries, and Canada. 84% are from public schools. 59% are White; 19% Hispanic. The average age of freshmen is 21; all undergraduates, 21. 27% do not continue beyond their first year; 54% remain to graduate.

Housing: 3054 students can be accommodated in college housing, which includes single-sex and coed dorms and on-campus apartments. In addition, there are special-interest houses, and women-in-science, substance-free and intensive-study houses. On-campus housing is guaranteed for the freshman year only, is available on a first-come, and first-served basis. 63% of students commute. All students may keep cars.

Activities: 5% of men belong to 5 national fraternities; 11% of women belong to 9 national sororities. There are 100 groups on campus, including art, cheerleading, chess, choir, chorale, chorus, computers, dance, drama, ethnic, gay, honors, international, jazz band, literary magazine, musical theater, newspaper, orchestra, pep band, political, professional, radio and TV, religious, social, social service, student government, and video. Popular campus events include Science Night, Parents Day, and Unity Through Diversity Week.

Sports: There are 14 intercollegiate sports for men and 9 for women, and 8 intramural sports for men and 8 for women. Facilities include a 5,000-seat stadium, a 3,000-seat gym, a field house, tennis courts, a pool, a 500-seat auditorium, and various playing fields. The Sonoma State University Recreation Center, a 59,000 square-foot facility includes a two-court gymnasium, one-court gymnasium/soccer arena, fitness center, climbing wall, outdoor adventure resource and equipment rental area, game room, exercise studios, locker rooms, and spa.

Disabled Students: All of the campus is accessible. Facilities include wheelchair ramps, elevators, special parking, specially equipped restrooms, special class scheduling, lowered drinking fountains, lowered telephones. , a reading machine, phonic listening devices, PC and mainframe access, and interpreters are also available.

Services: Counseling and information services are available, as is tutoring in most subjects. There is a reader service for the blind, and remedial math, reading, and writing. Learning disability assessment is also available.

Campus Safety and Security: Measures include 24-hour foot and vehicle patrol, emergency notification system, self-defense education, and security escort services. There are emergency telephones and lighted pathways/sidewalks.

Programs of Study: Sonoma State confers B.A., B.F.A. and B.S. degrees. Master's degrees are also awarded. Bachelor's degrees are awarded in BIOLOGICAL SCIENCE (biochemistry and biology/biological science), BUSINESS (business administration and management), COMMUNICATIONS AND THE ARTS (art, communications, English, fine arts, French, music, Spanish, and visual and performing arts), COMPUTER AND PHYSICAL SCIENCE (chemistry, computer science, geology, mathematics, and physics), ENGINEERING AND ENVIRONMENTAL DESIGN (environmental science), HEALTH PROFESSIONS (nursing), SOCIAL SCIENCE (African American studies, American Indian studies, anthropology, criminal justice, economics, ethnic studies, gender studies, geography, history, human development, interdisciplinary studies, international studies, Latin American studies, liberal arts/general studies, Mexican-American/Chicano studies, philosophy, physical fitness/movement, political science/government, psychology, sociology, and women's studies). Liberal arts, physics and math are the strongest academically. Business, psychology and liberal studies have the largest enrollments.

Required: Undergraduate students must complete 120 to 132 units, depending on the degree program, consisting of 48 to 51 units of general education, a concentration of study in a specific major, and electives. General education programs require experience in oral and written communications, critical thinking, natural science and math, arts and humanities, social sciences, and personal integration. All students must take an ethnic studies course and the equivalent of courses in U.S. government, U.S. history, and California government.

Special: Students may cross-register at Mills College, Oakland, and University of California, Berkeley. Study-abroad programs are available in 17 countries. Community service internships, work-study, nondegree study through Open University, and pass/fail grading options are available. B.A. and B.S. options in biology, chemistry, environmental studies, geology, interdisciplinary studies, math, and physics are offered. The Hutchins School B.A. in liberal studies offers small seminar classes and an interdisciplinary curriculum. Distance learning programs in nursing are available at 3 off-site centers. There are 6 national honor societies and 5 departmental honors programs.

Faculty/Classroom: 46% of faculty are male; 54% are female. 87% teach undergraduates. Graduate students teach 1% of introductory courses. The average class size in an introductory lecture is 40; in a laboratory is 18; and in a regular course is 30.

Admissions: 90% of the 2013-2014 applicants were accepted. The SAT scores for the 2013-2014 freshman class were: Critical Reading--51% below 500, 39% between 500 and 599, 10% between 600 and 699, and 1% between 700 and 800; Math--51% below 500, 39% between 500 and 599, 10% between 600 and 699, and 1% between 700 and 800. The ACT scores were 44% below 21, 33% between 21 and 23, 15% between 24 and 26, 5% between 27 and 28, and 2% above 28.

Requirements: The SAT or ACT is required. Applicants should be graduates of accredited high schools or have earned the GED. Secondary school preparation should include 4 years each of arts and humanities, 3 years each of English, math, social science, and academic electives, and 1 each of music, history, and a lab science. A GPA of 2.0 is required. AP and CLEP credits are accepted. Important factors in the admissions decision are geographical diversity, parents or siblings attended the school, and evidence of special talent.

Procedure: Freshmen are admitted fall and spring. There is a rolling admissions plan. Applications should be filed by November 30 for fall entry; August 30 for spring entry, along with a $55 fee. Applications are accepted online.

Transfer: 1026 transfer students enrolled in 2012-2013. Applicants must have a minimum 2.0 GPA. The maximum number of transferable credits is 70. 30 of 120 credits required for the bachelor's degree must be completed at Sonoma State.

Visiting: There are regularly scheduled orientations for prospective students, consisting of programs in the spring and summer. There are guides for informal visits and visitors may sit in on classes. To schedule a visit, contact the Admissions Development Office at (707) 664-3032.

Financial Aid: In 2013-2014, 40% of all full-time freshmen and 20% of continuing full-time students received some form of financial aid. 36% of all full-time freshmen and 21% of continuing full-time students received need-based aid. The average freshman award was $9,613. Need-based scholarships or need-based grants averaged $10,295; need-based self-help aid (loans and jobs) averaged $3,535; non-need-based athletic scholarships averaged $1,596; and other non-need-based awards and non-need-based scholarships averaged $1,156. 15% of undergraduate students work part-time. Average annual earnings from campus work are $4373. The FAFSA is required. The priority date for freshman financial aid applications for fall entry is January 31.

International Students: There are 148 international students enrolled. The school actively recruits these students. They must take the TOEFL with a minimum score of 500 on the paper-based TOEFL (PBT) or 61 on the Internet-based version (iBT).

Computers: All students may access the system. There are no time limits and no fees.

Graduates: From July 1, 2012 to June 30, 2013, 1089 bachelor's degrees were awarded. The most popular majors were business administration (33%), psychology (15%), and liberal studies (11%). 720 companies recruited on campus in 2012-2013. In an average class, 23% graduate in 3 years or less, 28% graduate in 4 years or less, 22% graduate in 5 years or less, and 54% graduate in 6 years or less.

Admissions Contact: Gustavo Flores, Director of Admissions & Records. E-Mail: *student.outreach@sonoma.edu* Web: *www.sonoma.edu*

STANFORD UNIVERSITY B-3

Stanford, CA 94305 **(650) 723-2091; (650) 723-6050**

Full-time: 3706 men, 3274 women
Part-time: 23 men, 58 women
Graduate: 6550 men, 4525 women
Year: quarters, summer session
Application Deadline: January 15
Freshman Class: 38828 applied, 2208 accepted, 1677 enrolled
SAT or ACT: required

Faculty: n/av; I, ++$
Ph.D.s: 99%
Student/Faculty: 5 to 1
Tuition: $43,245
Room & Board: $13,166

MOST COMPETITIVE

Stanford is a research university, located in one of the most culturally dynamic and diverse areas of the nation with seven schools: Business, Earth Sciences, Education, Engineering, Humanities and Sciences, Law and Medicine. Stanford's campus is considered among the most beautiful worldwide. Stanford's entrepreneurial character draws from the legacy of its founders, Jane and Leland Stanford, and its relationship to Silicon Valley. Current faculty have won 22 Nobels and 5 Pulitzers. Areas of academic excellence cross disciplines, ranging from humanities to social sciences to engineering and the sciences. Students, distinguished by initiative, love of learning and commitment to public service, are talented in many areas, including academics, art, music and athletics. There are 3 undergraduate schools and 7 graduate schools. In addition to regional accreditation, Stanford has baccalaureate program accreditation with AACSB and ABET. The 20 libraries contain 9.3 million volumes, 6.0 million microform items, and 2.5 million audio/video tapes/CDs/DVDs, and subscribe to 77,000 periodicals including electronic. Computerized library services include interlibrary loans, database searching, Internet access, and Wi-Fi capability. Special learning facilities include an art gallery, radio station, TV station, an art museum, a biological preserve, a linear accelerator, an observatory. The 8180-acre campus is in a suburban area 30 miles south of San Francisco, and 20 miles north of San Jose. Including any residence halls, there are 700 buildings.

Student Life: 53% of undergraduates are from out of state, mostly the South. Students are from 50 states, 90 foreign countries, and Canada. 58% are from public schools. 41% are White; 22% Asian American; 14% Hispanic. The average age of freshmen is 18; all undergraduates, 20. 1% do not continue beyond their first year; 95% remain to graduate.

Housing: 6448 students can be accommodated in college housing, which includes single-sex and coed dorms, on-campus apartments, off-campus apartments, and married student housing. In addition, there are language houses, special-interest houses, fraternity houses, sorority houses, ethnic theme houses, substance free housing, academic interest. On-campus housing is guaranteed for all 4 years. 91% of students live on campus; of those, 95% remain on campus on weekends. Upperclassmen may keep cars.

Activities: 24% of men belong to 16 national fraternities; 28% of women belong to 14 national sororities. There are 625 groups on campus, including art, band, cheerleading, chess, choir, chorale, chorus, computers, dance, debate, drama, environmental, ethnic, film, gay, honors, international, jazz band, literary magazine, marching band, musical theater, newspaper, opera, orchestra, pep band, photography, political, professional, radio and TV, religious, social, social service, student government, symphony, There are 625 student organizations at Stanford., and yearbook. Popular campus events include the Big Game, Full Moon on the Quad, and Gaities.

Sports: There are 16 intercollegiate sports for men and 20 for women. Facilities include club sports, intramural sports, athletic fields, gyms, swimming pools, volleyball courts, lighted tennis courts, dance studios, climbing wall, weight rooms, an 18-hole golf course, a sailing facility, a rowing facility, handball, racquetball, squash courts, a baseball diamond, a football stadium, a softball stadium, a soccer stadium and field hockey and lacrosse fields.

Disabled Students: 98% of the campus is accessible. Facilities include wheelchair ramps, elevators, special parking, specially equipped restrooms, special class scheduling, lowered drinking fountains, lowered telephones, special housing. Stanford has a Diversity and Access Office and an Office of Accessible Education to provide help.

Services: Counseling and information services are available, as is tutoring in most subjects. There is a reader service for the blind. Schwab Learning Center offers services for students with learning disabilities and attention-deficit hyperactivity disorder.

Campus Safety and Security: Measures include 24-hour foot and vehicle patrol, emergency notification system, self-defense education, and security escort services. There are shuttle buses, emergency telephones, lighted pathways/sidewalks, controlled access to dorms/residences, AlertSU notifies students immediately of safety threats on campus.

Programs of Study: Stanford confers A.B., B.S. and B.A.S. degrees. Master's and doctoral degrees are also awarded. Bachelor's degrees are awarded in BIOLOGICAL SCIENCE (biology/biological science), BUSINESS (management engineering), COMMUNICATIONS AND THE ARTS (art, art history and appreciation, Chinese, classics, communications, comparative literature, dramatic arts, English, film arts, fine arts, French, Italian, Japanese, linguistics, music, Slavic languages, Spanish, and studio art), COMPUTER AND PHYSICAL SCIENCE (chemistry, computer science, earth science, geology, geophysics and seismology, geoscience, mathematics, physics, and statistics), ENGINEERING AND ENVIRONMENTAL DESIGN (aeronautical engineering, architectural engineering, bioengineering, chemical engineering, civil engineering, electrical/electronics engineering, engineering, engineering physics, environmental engineering, industrial engineering, materials science, mechanical engineering, petroleum/natural gas engineering, and systems engineering), SOCIAL SCIENCE (African American studies, American studies, anthropology, archeology, area studies, Asian/American studies, crosscultural studies, East Asian studies, economics, German area studies, Hispanic American studies, history, Iberian studies, international relations, Latin American studies, Native American studies, philosophy, political science/government, psychology, public administration, religion, sociology, systems science, urban studies, and women's studies). Computer science, human biology, and engineering have the largest enrollments.

Required: To graduate, students must complete 180 units, including requirements for the major, a writing requirement, and 1 year of a foreign language. General education requirements include the one-quarter freshman class Thinking Matters. Also required is Ways of Thinking, Ways of Doing, which includes eleven courses in eight subject areas, including aesthetic and interpretive inquiry, social inquiry, scientific analysis,formal reasoning, quantitative reasoning, engaging diversity, moral and ethical reasoning and creative expression.

Special: Internships, study abroad, a Washington semester, marine research center, semester at sea, 12 overseas study programs, dual majors, a B.A.-B.S. degree, research opportunities, honors programs and coterminal bachelor's and master's programs.

Faculty/Classroom: 73% of faculty are male; 27% are female. All teach undergraduates, all do research, and all teach and do research. No introductory courses are taught by graduate students.

Admissions: 6% of the 2013-2014 applicants were accepted. The SAT scores for the 2013-2014 freshman class were: Critical Reading--4% between 500 and 599, 27% between 600 and 699, and 70% between 700 and 800; Math--2% between 500 and 599, 21% between 600 and 699, and 77% between 700 and 800; Writing--3% between 500 and 599, 25% between 600 and 699, and 72% between 700 and 800. The ACT scores were 1% between 24 and 26, 13% between 27 and 28, and 86% above 28. 100% of the current freshmen were in the top fifth of their class.

Requirements: The SAT or ACT is required. The ACT Optional Writing test is also required. The SAT (Critical Reading, Math and Writing) or ACT Plus Writing is required. SAT Subject Tests are strongly recommended. The university recommends that applicants have strong preparation in high school English, math, a foreign language, science and social studies. If English is not your native language, we recommend, but do not require, the Test of English as a Foreign Language. Generally speaking, Stanford students have taken the most rigorous classes available to them. AP credits are accepted. Important factors in the admissions decision are advanced placement or honors courses, personality/intangible qualities, and recommendations by school officials.

Procedure: Freshmen are admitted fall. Entrance exams should be taken By Nov. 1 for early decision; Jan. 15 for regular admission. There are early decision and deferred admissions plans. Early decision applications should be filed by November 1; regular applications, by January 15 for fall entry, along with a $90 fee. Notification of early decision is sent December 15; regular decision, April 1. 725 early decision candidates were accepted for the 2013-2014 class. 576 applicants were on the 2013 waiting list; were admitted. Applications are accepted online.

Transfer: 28 transfer students enrolled in 2012-2013. Transfer students must complete 1 full year of academic work prior to enrollment. There is only fall quarter enrollment for transfer students. The application deadline is March 15. 90 of 180 credits required for the bachelor's degree must be completed at Stanford.

Visiting: There are regularly scheduled orientations for prospective students, including group information sessions and campus tours. There are guides for informal visits, visitors may sit in on classes, and stay overnight. To schedule a visit, contact the Office of Undergraduate Admission at admission@stanford.edu.

Financial Aid: In 2013-2014, 84% of continuing full-time students received some form of financial aid. 74% of all full-time freshmen and 67% of continuing full-time students received need-based aid. The average freshman award was $42,514. Need-based scholarships or need-based grants averaged $40,395; need-based self-help aid (loans and jobs) averaged $2,165; and non-need-based athletic scholarships averaged $31,334. The average financial indebtedness of the 2013 graduate was $16,640. Stanford is a member of CSS. The CSS/Profile and FAFSA are required. The priority date for freshman financial aid applications for fall entry is February 15.

International Students: There are 564 international students enrolled. The school actively recruits these students. They must also take the SAT or ACT. SAT Subject tests are strongly recommended.

Computers: All students may access the system. There are no time limits and no fees.

Graduates: From July 1, 2012 to June 30, 2013, 1660 bachelor's degrees were awarded. The most popular majors were social science (18%), interdisciplinary studies (16%), and engineering (15%). 350 companies recruited on campus in 2012-2013. In an average class, 90% graduate in 5 years or less and 95% graduate in 6 years or less.

Admissions Contact: Richard H. Shaw, Dean of Admissions. E-Mail: *admission@stanford.edu* Web: *www.stanford.edu*

THE MASTER'S COLLEGE — D-4

Santa Clarita, CA 91321 — (661) 362-2600; (800) 568-6248; (661) 362-2718

Full-time: 477 men, 490 women	**Faculty:** 58
Part-time: 98 men, 33 women	**Ph.D.s:** 74%
Graduate: 352 men, 35 women	**Student/Faculty:** 10 to 1
Year: semesters, summer session	**Tuition:** $28,800
Application Deadline: March 2	**Room & Board:** $9360
Freshman Class: 757 applied, 590 accepted, 256 enrolled	
SAT CR/M/W: 552/536/538 **ACT:** 24	**COMPETITIVE+**

The Master's College, founded in 1927, is a Christ centered liberal arts college that exists to advance the kingdom of God by equipping students for moral integrity and lives of service in strategic fields of ministry and vocation. Within this authentic and life-changing community students from around the globe gather to be challenged academically, culturally engaged and to embrace Biblical fidelity in all things. There is one undergraduate school and one graduate school. In addition to regional accreditation, TMC has baccalaureate program accreditation with ABHES and NASM. The library contains 193,130 volumes, 38,349 microform items, and 2,723 audio/video tapes/CDs/DVDs, and subscribes to 34,685 periodicals including electronic. Computerized library services include interlibrary loans, database searching, Internet access, and Wi-Fi capability. Special learning facilities include a The 110 acre campus is in a suburban area 35 miles north of Los Angeles. Including any residence halls, there are 32 buildings.

Student Life: 73% of undergraduates are from California. Others are from 43 states, 19 foreign countries, and Canada. 26% are from public schools. 66% are White. 100% are Protestant. The average age of freshmen is 19; all undergraduates, 20. 20% do not continue beyond their first year; 56% remain to graduate.

Housing: 808 students can be accommodated in college housing, which includes single-sex dorms and off-campus apartments. On-campus housing is guaranteed for all 4 years, is guaranteed for the freshman year only, is available on a first-come, and first-served basis. 75% of students live on campus; of those, 80% remain on campus on weekends. Alcohol is not permitted. All students may keep cars.

Activities: There are no fraternities or sororities. There are 15 groups on campus, including band, choir, chorale, drama, film, jazz band, musical theater, newspaper, opera, orchestra, pep band, political, radio and TV, religious, social service, and student government. Popular campus events include College View Weekend, Community Day, and Truth and Life Conference.

Sports: There are 6 intercollegiate sports for men and 5 for women, and 6 intramural sports for men and 6 for women. Facilities include a gym, a sports field, tennis and volleyball courts, an intramural field, a swimming pool, and a fitness facility.

Disabled Students: All of the campus is accessible. Facilities include wheelchair ramps, elevators, special parking, specially equipped restrooms, lowered drinking fountains, and lowered telephones.

Services: Counseling and information services are available, as is tutoring in most subjects. There is remedial math.

Campus Safety and Security: Measures include 24-hour foot and vehicle patrol, emergency notification system, and security escort services. There are shuttle buses and lighted pathways/sidewalks.

Programs of Study: TMC confers B.A., B.M. and B.S. degrees. Master's degrees are also awarded. Bachelor's degrees are awarded in BIOLOGICAL SCIENCE (biology/biological science), BUSINESS (business administration and management), COMMUNICATIONS AND THE ARTS (communications, English, and music), COMPUTER AND PHYSICAL SCIENCE (information sciences and systems, mathematics, and natural sciences), EDUCATION (elementary education, physical education, and secondary education), SOCIAL SCIENCE (biblical studies, history, home economics, liberal arts/general studies, and political science/government). Biological sciences, Biblical studies, and business administration are the strongest academically. Biblical studies, business administration, and communication have the largest enrollments.

Required: Students must complete at least 122 semester hours, including 78 distributed as follows: 24 hours in Biblical studies, 18 in social sciences, 9 in English, 7 in natural science, 6 in cross-cultural studies, and 3 each in communication, business, logical reasoning, and fine arts. Students must complete at least 40 semester hours in upper-division courses and at least 40 in the major and must maintain a minimum GPA of 2.0.

Special: Students may cross-register with the Coalition of Christian Colleges and Universities and may participate in a co-op program with the College of the Canyons. Internships are offered with local churches, radio stations, and newspapers. A Washington semester, study abroad, dual majors in music plus a second discipline, and a general studies degree are available. The Master's Institute, a 1-year certificate Bible program, is also offered.

Faculty/Classroom: 76% of faculty are male; 24% are female. All teach undergraduates. No introductory courses are taught by graduate students. The average class size in an introductory lecture is 30; in a laboratory is 11; and in a regular course is 14.

Admissions: 78% of the 2013-2014 applicants were accepted. The SAT scores for the 2013-2014 freshman class were: Critical Reading--24% below 500, 50% between 500 and 599, 17% between 600 and 699, and 7% between 700 and 800; Math--31% below 500, 37% between 500 and 599, 20% between 600 and 699, and 7% between 700 and 800; Writing--27% below 500, 38% between 500 and 599, 22% between 600 and 699, and 5% between 700 and 800. The ACT scores were 23% below 21, 32% between 21 and 23, 24% between 24 and 26, 6% between 27 and 28, and 15% above 28. 48% of the current freshmen were in the top fifth of their class; 73% were in the top two fifths. 2 freshmen graduated first in their class.

Requirements: The SAT or ACT is required. Applicants must have completed 4 years of English, 3 each of math and science, 2 of history, and 8 units of electives. A GPA of 2.8 is required. AP and CLEP credits are accepted. Important factors in the admissions decision are personality/intangible qualities, recommendations by school officials, and leadership record.

Procedure: Freshmen are admitted fall and spring. Entrance exams should be taken In the fall. There are early admissions and deferred admissions plans. Early decision applications should be filed by November 15; regular applications, by March 2 for fall entry, along with a $40 fee. Notification of early decision is sent December 22; regular decision, April 1. 303 early decision candidates were accepted for the 2013-2014 class. Applications are accepted online.

Transfer: 90 transfer students enrolled in 2012-2013. Applicants must meet freshman requirements. A maximum of 70 units can be transferred from a junior college and 94 units from a 4-year college. 28 of 122 credits required for the bachelor's degree must be completed at TMC.

Visiting: There are regularly scheduled orientations for prospective students, Including class visitation, meetings with faculty, interviews, athletic events, an overnight stay, and college activities. There are guides for informal visits, visitors may sit in on classes, and stay overnight. To schedule a visit, contact the Admissions Office.

Financial Aid: In 2013-2014, 98% of all full-time freshmen and 92% of continuing full-time students received some form of financial aid. 61% of all full-time freshmen and 41% of continuing full-time students received need-based aid. The average freshman award was $22,295. Need-based scholarships or need-based grants averaged $13,918 ($5,645 maximum); need-based self-help aid (loans and jobs) averaged $6,619 ($5,500 maximum); non-need-based athletic scholarships averaged $21,063 ($37,740 maximum); and other non-need-based awards and non-need-based scholarships averaged $7,893 ($14,000 maximum). 48% of undergraduate students work part-time. Average annual earnings from campus work are $2000. The average financial indebtedness of the 2013 graduate was $11,500. TMC is a member of CSS. The FAFSA and the college's own financial statement are required. Check with the school for current application deadlines.

International Students: There are 47 international students enrolled. The school actively recruits these students. They must take the TOEFL.

Computers: All students may access the system. There are no time limits and no fees.

Graduates: From July 1, 2012 to June 30, 2013, 224 bachelor's degrees were awarded. The most popular majors were Biblical studies (30%), business (13%), and liberal studies (11%). In an average class, 8% graduate in 3 years or less, 48% graduate in 4 years or less, 55% graduate in 5 years or less, and 56% graduate in 6 years or less. Of the 2012 graduating class, 10% were enrolled in graduate school within 6 months of graduation.

Admissions Contact: John Melcon, Director of Admissions. E-Mail: *admissions@masters.edu* Web: *www.masters.edu*

THOMAS AQUINAS COLLEGE C-4

Santa Paula, CA 93060 (800) 634-9797

(800) 634-9797; (805) 421-5905

Full-time: 185 men, 181 women	**Faculty:** 31
Part-time: n/av	**Ph.D.s:** 84%
Graduate: n/av	**Student/Faculty:** 11 to 1
Year: semesters	**Tuition:** $24,500
Application Deadline:	**Room & Board:** $7950

Freshman Class: 202 applied, 161 accepted, 103 enrolled

SAT CR/M/W: 650/610/630 **ACT:** 28 **HIGHLYCOMPETITIVE+**

Thomas Aquinas College, founded in 1971 and affiliated with the Roman Catholic Church, is a small, private, liberal arts college offering an integrated studies curriculum based on the Great Books. All classes are conducted as conversations directed by teachers using the Socratic method. There is one undergraduate school. The library contains 64,585 volumes, and 6,508 audio/video tapes/CDs/DVDs, and subscribes to 60 periodicals including electronic. Computerized library services include Internet access and Wi-Fi capability. The 131-acre campus is in a rural area 70 miles northwest of Los Angeles. Including any residence halls, there are 19 buildings.

Student Life: 62% of undergraduates are from out of state, mostly the Mid-West. Students are from 37 states, 4 foreign countries, and Canada. 15% are from public schools. 73% are White; 15% Hispanic. 98% are Catholic. The average age of freshmen is 18; all undergraduates, 20. 14% do not continue beyond their first year; 86% remain to graduate.

Housing: 398 students can be accommodated in college housing, which includes single-sex dorms. On-campus housing is guaranteed for all 4 years. 99% of students live on campus; of those, 90% remain on campus on weekends. Alcohol is not permitted. All students may keep cars.

Activities: There are no fraternities or sororities. There are 6 groups on campus, including Tocqueville Political Forum, choir, chorale, chorus, drama, literary magazine, Medical Society, and orchestra. Popular campus events include St. Thomas Aquinas Day, President's Day, St. Patrick's Day and Easter.

Sports: There are 7 intramural sports for men and 6 for women. Facilities include a tennis, basketball, and volleyball courts, a soccer field, swimming area, weight-lifting rooms, and a softball field.

Disabled Students: All of the campus is accessible. Facilities include wheelchair ramps, elevators, special parking, specially equipped restrooms, lowered drinking fountains, lowered telephones, and special housing.

Services: There is remedial writing. All students may be tutored by the full-time teaching faculty.

Programs of Study: TAC confers B.A. degrees. Bachelor's degrees are awarded in SOCIAL SCIENCE (liberal arts/general studies).

Required: The entire curriculum is required of all students: it includes four years each of Philosophy, Theology, Mathematics, Science and Seminar (Seminar covers philosophical works not covered in the Philosophy courses, Literature, History, and Social Science, among others), two years of Language (Latin), and one year of Music. Seniors are required to write and defend a thesis. A total of 146 semester hours, with a minimum GPA of 2.0, is required to graduate.

Faculty/Classroom: 89% of faculty are male; 11% are female. All teach undergraduates. No introductory courses are taught by graduate students. The average class size in a laboratory is 17 and in a regular course is 17.

Admissions: 80% of the 2013-2014 applicants were accepted. The SAT scores for the 2013-2014 freshman class were: Critical Reading--2% below 500, 26% between 500 and 599, 44% between 600 and 699, and 28% between 700 and 800; Math--2% below 500, 39% between 500 and 599, 46% between 600 and 699, and 12% between 700 and 800; Writing--9% below 500, 23% between 500 and 599, 51% between 600 and 699, and 18% between 700 and 800. The ACT scores were 30% between 21 and 23, 4% between 24 and 26, 15% between 27 and 28, and 52% above 28. 50% of the current freshmen were in the top fifth of their class; 88% were in the top two fifths. There were 8 National Merit finalists.

Requirements: The SAT or ACT is required. Candidates for Admission are expected to have completed four years of English and a minimum of two years of natural science, two years of a foreign language, two years of algebra, and one year of geometry. Additional work in science, mathematics and language study is recommended. Important factors in the admissions decision are personality/intangible qualities, advanced placement or honors courses, and recommendations by school officials.

Procedure: Freshmen are admitted fall. Entrance exams should be taken by November. There is a rolling admissions plan. Application deadlines are open. 27 applicants were on the 2013 waiting list; 16 were admitted. Applications are accepted online.

Transfer: The integrated nature of the program demands that all students start as freshmen, and so, regardless of past education we only admit students as freshmen. 15-20% of each freshman class has attended College elswhere prior to enrolling in Thomas Aquinas College. 146 of 146 credits required for the bachelor's degree must be completed at TAC.

Visiting: There are regularly scheduled orientations for prospective students, Includes a campus tour and the hosting of prospective students by current students. Visits are for up to 3 days and consist of observing classes, attending lectures and concerts, enjoying community meals and events. . There are guides for informal visits, visitors may sit in on classes, and stay overnight. To schedule a visit, contact the Admissions Office.

Financial Aid: In 2013-2014, 84% of all full-time freshmen and 81% of continuing full-time students received some form of financial aid. 83% of all full-time freshmen and 78% of continuing full-time students received need-based aid. The average freshman award was $22,262. Need-based scholarships or need-based grants averaged $15,509 ($23,794 maximum); need-based self-help aid (loans and jobs) averaged $6,109 ($9,136 maximum); and other non-need-based awards and non-need-based scholarships averaged $14 ($1,187 maximum). 81% of undergraduate students work part-time. Average annual earnings from campus work are $3873. The average financial indebtedness of the 2013 graduate was $14,088. TAC is a member of CSS. The FAFSA and the college's own financial statement, and parent and student federal tax returns are required. The deadline for filing freshman financial aid applications for fall entry is March 2.

International Students: There are 19 international students enrolled. They must take the TOEFL with a minimum score of 570 on the paper-based TOEFL (PBT). They must also take the SAT or ACT.

Computers: All students may access the system. Always in the dorms, in the career center by appointment and anytime the other buildings are open (library, mailroom). There are no time limits and no fees.

Graduates: From July 1, 2012 to June 30, 2013, 91 bachelor's degrees were awarded. The most popular majors were liberal arts (100%). 24 companies recruited on campus in 2012-2013. In an average class, 71% graduate in 4 years or less, 74% graduate in 5 years or less, and 76% graduate in 6 years or less. Of the 2012 graduating class, 99% were employed within 6 months of graduation.

Admissions Contact: Jonathan P. Daly, Director of Admissions. E-Mail: *admissions@thomasaquinas.edu* Web: *www.thomasaquinas.edu*

UNIVERSITY OF CALIFORNIA SYSTEM

The University of California System, established in 1868, is a public system in California. It is governed by a board of regents, whose chief administrator is the president. The primary goal of the system is teaching, research, and public service. The total enrollment in a recent year of all 10 campuses is about 230,000 with approximately 9500 faculty members. Altogether there are 565 baccalaureate, 250 master's, and 200 doctoral programs offered in the University of California System. 4-year campuses are located in Berkeley, Davis, Irvine, Los Angeles, Riverside, San Diego, Santa Barbara, Merced, and Santa Cruz. Profiles of the 4-year campuses are included in this section.

UNIVERSITY OF CALIFORNIA AT BERKELEY B-3

Berkeley, CA 94720 **(510) 642-2316**

Full-time: n/av	**Faculty:** n/av; I
Part-time: n/av	**Ph.D.s:** 99%
Graduate: n/av	**Student/Faculty:** n/av
Year: semesters, summer session	**Tuition:** $8938 ($31,665)
Application Deadline: November 30	**Room & Board:** $14,384
Freshman Class: 48650 applied, 10561 accepted, 4356 enrolled	
SAT CR/M/W: 660/700/670 **ACT:** 30	**MOST COMPETITIVE**

The University of California at Berkeley, founded in 1868, is a public institution offering a wide variety of programs in the social and physical sciences, liberal arts, and professional fields. It is the oldest campus of the University of California system. There are 7 undergraduate schools and 14 graduate schools. In addition to regional accreditation, Cal has baccalaureate program accreditation with AACSB, ABET, ADA, ASLA, and SAF. The 35 libraries contain 10.4 million volumes, 6.6 million microform items, and 46,162 audio/video tapes/CDs/DVDs, and subscribe to 82,151 periodicals including electronic. Computerized library services include interlibrary loans and database searching. Special learning facilities include an art gallery, natural history museum, radio station, TV station, a botanical garden, an anthropology museum, a hall of science, the University Art Museum and Pacific Film Archive, a seismographic station, an herbaria, the Hall for the Performing Arts, an observatory, and many off-campus facilities. The 1232-acre campus is in an urban area 10 miles east of San Francisco. Including any residence halls, there are 300 buildings.

Student Life: 90% of undergraduates are from California. Others are from 50 states, 80 foreign countries, and Canada. 85% are from public schools. 43% are Asian American; 32% White; 13% Hispanic. The average age of freshmen is 19; all undergraduates, 21. 4% do not continue beyond their first year; 90% remain to graduate.

Housing: 8800 students can be accommodated in college housing, which includes single-sex and coed dorms, off-campus apartments, and married student housing. In addition, there are honors houses, language houses, special-interest houses, fraternity houses, sorority houses, substance-free housing, an international house, theme housing, and co-ops. On-campus housing is guaranteed for the freshman year only and is available on a lottery system for upperclassmen. All students may keep cars.

Activities: There are 400 groups on campus, including art, band, cheerleading, chess, choir, chorale, chorus, computers, dance, debate, drama, ethnic, film, forensics, gay, honors, international, jazz band, literary magazine, marching band, musical theater, newspaper, orchestra, pep band, photography, political, professional, radio and TV, religious, social, social service, student government, and symphony. Popular campus events include The Big Game, Cal Performances, and E-Week.

Sports: Facilities include a football stadium, a track stadium, a basketball pavilion, 4 gyms, a martial arts room, 7 swimming pools, 3 weight rooms, squash, racquetball, handball, volleyball, and tennis courts, and baseball and softball fields.

Disabled Students: 95% of the campus is accessible. Facilities include wheelchair ramps, elevators, special parking, specially equipped restrooms, special class scheduling, lowered drinking fountains, and lowered telephones.

Services: Counseling and information services are available, as is tutoring in most subjects. There is a reader service for the blind.

Campus Safety and Security: Measures include 24-hour foot and vehicle patrol, emergency notification system, self-defense education, and security escort services. There are shuttle buses, emergency telephones, lighted pathways/sidewalks, controlled access to dorms/residences, a rape prevention peer education program, an earthquake emergency preparedness program, and safety, threats and alerts reports via computer.

Programs of Study: Cal confers A.B., and B.S. degrees. Master's and doctoral degrees are also awarded. Bachelor's degrees are awarded in AGRICULTURE (conservation and regulation and forestry and related sciences), BIOLOGICAL SCIENCE (biology/biological science, microbiology, molecular biology, nutrition, and plant genetics), BUSINESS (business administration and management, management science, and operations research), COMMUNICATIONS AND THE ARTS (art, art history and appreciation, Chinese, classical languages, communications, comparative literature, dance, dramatic arts, Dutch, English, film arts, French, German, Greek, Italian, Japanese, Latin, linguistics, music, Scandinavian languages, Slavic languages, Spanish, and speech/debate/rhetoric), COMPUTER AND PHYSICAL SCIENCE (applied mathematics, astrophysics, chemistry, computer science, earth science, mathematics, physical sciences, physics, and statistics), ENGINEERING AND ENVIRONMENTAL DESIGN (architecture, bioengineering, chemical engineering, civil engineering, computer engineering, electrical/electronics engineering, engineering and applied science, engineering physics, environmental engineering, environmental science, industrial engineering, landscape architecture/design, manufacturing engineering, materials engineering, materials science, mechanical engineering, and nuclear engineering), HEALTH PROFESSIONS (optometry and public health), SOCIAL SCIENCE (African American studies, American studies, anthropology, Asian/American studies, Asian/Oriental studies, Celtic studies, classical/ancient civilization, cognitive science, economics, ethnic studies, geography, Hispanic American studies, history, interdisciplinary studies, Latin American studies, law, Middle Eastern studies, Native American studies, Near Eastern studies, peace studies, political science/government, psychology, religion, social science, social work, sociology, South Asian studies, urban studies, and women's studies). Electrical engineering and computer science, political science, and economics have the largest enrollments.

Required: All undergraduate students are required to satisfy the general university requirements of English and writing proficiency and take integrative and comparative courses in American history, institutions, and cultures. Students must complete 120 units with a minimum GPA of 2.0.

Special: Co-op programs, cross-registration with many area schools, internships, work-study programs, and study abroad in 35 countries are available. Interdisciplinary majors are also available, as are pass/fail options, independent study, an independent research and undergraduate research program, and a freshman seminar program, in which 15 to 25 students meet with professors to explore a wide range of majors. There is a 3-2 engineering program with the University of California, Santa Cruz.

Faculty/Classroom: 65% of faculty are male; 35% are female. No introductory courses are taught by graduate students.

Admissions: 22% of the 2013-2014 applicants were accepted. The SAT scores for the 2013-2014 freshman class were: Critical Reading--8% below 500, 20% between 500 and 599, 43% between 600 and 699, and 29% between 700 and 800; Math--4% below 500, 14% between 500 and 599, 32% between 600 and 699, and 51% between 700 and 800; Writing--6% below 500, 18% between 500 and 599, 42% between 600 and 699, and 34% between 700 and 800.

Requirements: The SAT or ACT is required. Applicants must submit scores from 2 SAT Subject Tests. Also required are 4 years of English, 3 of math (4 recommended), 2 each of history/social sciences, lab science (3 recommended), foreign language (3 recommended), and college preparatory electives. AP credits are accepted. Important factors in the admissions decision are advanced placement or honors courses, evidence of special talent, and leadership record.

Procedure: Freshmen are admitted fall. Entrance exams should be taken no later than December test dates in the senior year. There is a deferred admissions plan. Applications should be filed by November 30 for fall entry, along with a $60 fee. Notifications are sent March 30. Applications are accepted online.

Transfer: 2012 transfer students enrolled in 2012-2013. 24 of 120 credits required for the bachelor's degree must be completed at Cal.

Visiting: There are regularly scheduled orientations for prospective students, including 1 1/2 hour student-led walking tours, usually followed by an admissions information presentation; self-guided tours are also available. There are guides for informal visits and visitors may sit in on classes. To schedule a visit, contact the Visitor Services at (510) 642-5215.

Financial Aid: In 2013-2014, 50% of all full-time freshmen and 49% of continuing full-time students received some form of financial aid. 48% of all full-time freshmen and 48% of continuing full-time students received need-based aid. The average freshman award was $17,250. Need-based scholarships or need-based grants averaged $12,651; need-based self-help aid (loans and jobs) averaged $6,037; non-need-based athletic scholarships averaged $12,873; and other non-need-based awards and non-need-based scholarships averaged $2,136. The average financial indebtedness of the 2013 graduate was $14,751. The FAFSA is required. The deadline for filing freshman financial aid applications for fall entry is March 2.

International Students: There are 1073 international students enrolled. They must take the TOEFL with a minimum score of 550 on the paper-based TOEFL (PBT) or 83 on the Internet-based version (iBT). They must also take the SAT or ACT.

Computers: All students may access the system. There are no time limits and no fees.

Graduates: From July 1, 2012 to June 30, 2013, 7247 bachelor's degrees were awarded. The most popular majors were molecular biology (10%), economics (7%), and political science (7%). 600 companies recruited on campus in 2012-2013. In an average class, 3% graduate in 3 years or less, 69% graduate in 4 years or less, 88% graduate in 5 years or less, and 90% graduate in 6 years or less.

Admissions Contact: Walter A. Robinson, Director of Undergraduate Admission. Web: *www.berkeley.edu*

UNIVERSITY OF CALIFORNIA AT DAVIS B-2

Davis, CA 95616-8507	**(530) 752-2971; (530) 752-1280**
Full-time: 11140 men, 13647 women	**Faculty:** n/av; I, ++$
Part-time: 142 men, 167 women	**Ph.D.s:** 98%
Graduate: 3292 men, 3344 women	**Student/Faculty:** 15 to 1
Year: quarters, summer session	**Tuition:** $14,360($37,238)
Application Deadline: November 30	**Room & Board:** $13,197
Freshman Class: 43295 applied, 19460 accepted, 4501 enrolled	
SAT CR/M/W: 600/640/600	**ACT:** 27 **HIGHLY COMPETITIVE**

University of California at Davis, founded in 1908, is a land-grant, comprehensive institution offering programs in arts and science, agricultural and environmental sciences, and engineering. There are 4 undergraduate schools and 5 graduate schools. In addition to regional accreditation, UC Davis has baccalaureate program accreditation with ABET, ADA, and ASLA. The 6 libraries contain 4.2 million volumes, 4.3 million microform items, and 19,581 audio/video tapes/CDs/DVDs, and subscribe to 74,836 periodicals including electronic. Computerized library services include database searching. Special learning facilities include a learning resource center, art gallery, radio station, an experimental farm, a 150-acre arboretum, a raptor center, an equestrian center, a primate research center, and the Crocker Nuclear Laboratory. The 5300-acre campus is in a suburban area 15 miles west of Sacramento, and 72 miles northeast of San Francisco. Including any residence halls, there are 186 buildings.

Student Life: 98% of undergraduates are from California. Others are from 47 states, 113 foreign countries, and Canada. 90% are from public schools. 38% are Asian American; 34% white; 15% Hispanic. The average age of freshmen is 18; all undergraduates, 21. 8% do not continue beyond their first year; 82% remain to graduate.

Housing: 5653 students can be accommodated in college housing, which includes single-sex and coed dorms, on-campus apartments, off-campus apartments, and married student housing. In addition, there are honors houses, language houses, and special-interest houses. On-campus housing is guaranteed for the freshman year only. 75% of students commute. Alcohol is not permitted. No one may keep cars.

Activities: There are 320 groups on campus, including art, band, cheerleading, chess, choir, chorus, computers, dance, debate, drama, ethnic, film, gay, honors, international, jazz band, literary magazine, marching band, musical theater, newspaper, orchestra, pep band, photography, political, professional, radio and TV, religious, social, social service, student government, and symphony. Popular campus events include Picnic Day, Whole Earth Festival, and Asian Pacific Cultural Week.

Sports: There are 9 intercollegiate sports for men and 14 for women. Facilities include a football stadium, tennis and basketball courts, equestrian trails, a track field, baseball, soccer, and softball fields, a recreation hall, 2 gyms, 2 swimming pools, bowling alleys, weight-training facilities, and an outdoor roller hockey rink.

Disabled Students: All of the campus is accessible. Facilities include wheelchair ramps, elevators, special parking, specially equipped restrooms, special class scheduling, lowered drinking fountains, lowered telephones.

Services: Counseling and information services are available, as is tutoring in most subjects. There is a reader service for the blind, and remedial math and writing.

Campus Safety and Security: Measures include 24-hour foot and vehicle patrol, emergency notification system, self-defense education, and security escort services. There are shuttle buses, emergency telephones, lighted pathways/sidewalks, There is also a rape prevention program, a crime prevention unit, a bike patrol unit, and a K-9 program.

Programs of Study: UC Davis confers B.S., A.B., and B.A.S. degrees. Master's and doctoral degrees are also awarded. Bachelor's degrees are awarded in AGRICULTURE (agricultural business management, agricultural economics, animal science, international agriculture, plant science, range/farm management, and soil science), BIOLOGICAL SCIENCE (avian sciences, bacteriology, biochemistry, biology/biological science, botany, ecology, entomology, environmental biology, genetics, microbiology, nutrition, physiology, toxicology, wildlife biology, and zoology), BUSINESS (organizational behavior), COMMUNICATIONS AND THE ARTS (art history and appreciation, Chinese, communications, comparative literature, design, dramatic arts, English, fine arts, French, German, Greek, Italian, Japanese, Latin, linguistics, music, Russian, Spanish, speech/debate/rhetoric, and studio art), COMPUTER AND PHYSICAL SCIENCE (atmospheric sciences and meteorology, chemistry, computer science, geology, hydrology, mathematics, physics, polymer science, and statistics), EDUCATION (physical education), ENGINEERING AND ENVIRONMENTAL DESIGN (aeronautical engineering, agricultural engineering, bioengineering, chemical engineering, civil engineering, computer engineering, electrical/electronics engineering, environmental design, environmental science, landscape architecture/design, materials engineering, and mechanical engineering), HEALTH PROFESSIONS (community health work and environmental health science), SOCIAL SCIENCE (African studies, American studies, anthropology, behavioral science, classical/ancient civilization, dietetics, East Asian studies, economics, food science, geography, history, human development, human ecology, international relations, medieval studies, Mexican-American/Chicano studies, Native American studies, philosophy, political science/government, psychology, religion, social science, sociology, textiles and clothing, and women's studies). Agricultural, biological, and biotechnical sciences are the strongest academically. Biological science, biochemistry, and psychology have the largest enrollments.

Required: General education requirements vary by college but are based on 3 components: topical breadth, social-cultural diversity, and writing experience. A minimum of 180 quarter units with a minimum GPA of 2.0 are required for graduation, as is proficiency in English composition and an American History and Institutions requirement.

Special: There are credit and noncredit internship programs. Study abroad in more than 32 countries and a Washington semester are offered. Students may participate in college work-study, federal work-study, and California work-study programs. Several A.B.-B.S. degrees are offered. Students may design their own majors, take dual majors, and elect pass/fail options. Interdisciplinary majors are offered in African American and African studies, American studies, Mexican American studies, comparative literature, East Asian studies, exercise science, international relations, linguistics, medieval studies, Native American studies, religious studies, and women's studies. There are 24 national honor societies, including Phi Beta Kappa, a freshman honors program, and 3 departmental honors programs.

Faculty/Classroom: 63% of faculty are male; 37% are female. No introductory courses are taught by graduate students.

Admissions: In a recent year, 45% applicants were accepted. The SAT scores for a recent freshman class were: Critical Reading--14% below 500, 34% between 500 and 599, 40% between 600 and 700, and 11% above 700; Math--8% below 500, 23% between 500 and 599, 46% between 600 and 700, and 22% above 700; Writing--12% below 500, 34% between 500 and 599, 40% between 600 and 700, and 13% above 700. 100% of the current freshmen were in the top fifth of their class.

Requirements: The SAT or ACT is required. In addition, candidates for admission should have completed 4 units of English, 3 of math, and 2 each of foreign language, history/social science, lab science, and college preparatory electives, for a total of 15 units. Two SAT Subject Tests are required in two different areas. A GPA of 3.0 is required. AP credits are accepted. Important factors in the admissions decision are advanced placement or honors courses, evidence of special talent, and leadership record.

Procedure: Freshmen are admitted fall, winter, and spring. Entrance exams should be taken by December of the senior year. There is a deferred admissions plan. Applications should be filed by November 30 for fall entry. The fall application fee was $60. Notifications are sent March 15. Applications are accepted online.

Transfer: 2756 transfer students enrolled in 2010-2011. Junior-level transfers have priority. Requirements vary by college, discipline, and major. 35 of 180 credits required for the bachelor's degree must be completed at UC Davis.

Visiting: There are regularly scheduled orientations for prospective students, including weekend tours of the campus, weekday tours by appointment, and drop-in counseling with staff and faculty. The campus also offers a 1-day preview for prospective students and their families. There are guides for informal visits, visitors may sit in on classes, and stay overnight. To schedule a visit, contact UC Davis Visitor Services.

Financial Aid: In a recent year, 54% of all full-time freshmen students received some form of financial aid. 51% of all full-time freshmen and continuing full-time students received need-based aid. The average freshman award was $15,811. Need-based scholarships or need-based grants averaged $12,361; need-based self-help aid (loans and jobs) averaged $5,305; non-need-based athletic scholarships averaged $10,804; and other non-need-based awards and non-need-based scholarships averaged $4,763. The average financial indebtedness of the 2011 graduate was $15,155. UC Davis is a member of CSS. The FAFSA is required. The deadline for filing freshman financial aid applications for fall entry is March 2.

International Students: They must take the TOEFL with a minimum score of 550 on the paper-based TOEFL (PBT) or 60 on the Internet-based version (iBT). They must also take the SAT or ACT.

Computers: Wireless access is available. All students may access the system. There are no time limits and no fees. It is strongly recommended that all students have a personal computer.

Graduates: In a recent year, 6369 bachelor's degrees were awarded. The most popular majors were psychology (10%), biological sciences (6%), and economics (6%). In an average class, 2% graduate in 3 years or less, 51% graduate in 4 years or less, 78% graduate in 5 years or less, and 82% graduate in 6 years or less. Of a recent graduating class, 38% were enrolled in graduate school within 6 months of graduation, and 79% were employed.

Admissions Contact: Walter Robinson, Director, Undergraduate Admissions. E-Mail: *undergraduateadmissions@ucdavis* Web: *www.ucdavis.edu*

UNIVERSITY OF CALIFORNIA AT IRVINE D-5

Irvine, CA 92697 **(949) 824-6703; (949) 824-2951**

Full-time: 9965 men, 11913 women	**Faculty:** 1467; I
Part-time: 196 men, 142 women	**Ph.D.s:** 98%
Graduate: 3108 men, 2155 women	**Student/Faculty:** 19 to 1
Year: quarters, summer session	**Tuition:** $14,226 ($37,104)
Application Deadline: November 30	**Room & Board:** $11,735
Freshman Class: 56508 applied, 23956 accepted, 5077 enrolled	
SAT CR/M/W: 540/610/550	**ACT:** required **VERY COMPETITIVE**

The University of California, Irvine, founded in 1965, is a public research university and part of the University of California System. There are 13 undergraduate schools and 15 graduate schools. In addition to regional accreditation, UCI has baccalaureate program accreditation with AACSB and ABET. The 4 libraries contain 3.2 million volumes, 2.2 million microform items, and 123,396 audio/video tapes/CDs/DVDs, and subscribe to 132,134 periodicals including electronic. Computerized library services include interlibrary loans, database searching, and Internet access. Special learning facilities include an art gallery, planetarium, radio station, a freshwater marsh reserve, an arboretum, a laser institute, and numerous research centers. The 1489-acre campus is in a suburban area 40 miles south of Los Angeles. Including any residence halls, there are 492 buildings.

Student Life: 91% of undergraduates are from California. Others are from 40 states, 70 foreign countries, and Canada. 86% are from public schools. 52% are Asian American; 20% Hispanic; 19% White. The average age of freshmen is 18; all undergraduates, 21. 7% do not continue beyond their first year; 93% remain to graduate.

Housing: 10199 students can be accommodated in college housing, which includes single-sex and coed dorms, on-campus apartments, and married student housing. In addition, there are honors houses, special-interest houses, fraternity houses, and sorority houses. On-campus housing is available on a first-come, first-served basis, and is available on a lottery system for upperclassmen. 62% of students commute. All students may keep cars.

Activities: 9% of men belong to 21 national fraternities; 10% of women belong to 3 local and 23 national sororities. There are 543 groups on campus, including art, band, cheerleading, chess, choir, chorus, communications, computers, dance, debate, drama, environmental, ethnic, film, gay, honors, international, jazz band, literary magazine, marching band, musical theater, newspaper, opera, orchestra, pep band, political, professional, radio and TV, religious, social, social service, student government, symphony, and yearbook. Popular campus events include Celebrate UCI, Shocktoberfest, Homecoming, Reggae and Wayzgoose Festivals, Welcome Week's All UCI Dance Battle.

Sports: There are 35 intercollegiate sports for men and 33 for women, and 23 intramural sports for men and 23 for women. Facilities include a 2500-seat track stadium, a 5000-seat events center, a 1000-seat soccer field, a 500-seat tennis stadium, baseball and other fields, a swimming pool, 6 indoor handball/racquetball/squash courts, and an activities hall with areas for badminton, basketball, volleyball, combatives, fencing, and weight training. A sailing and crew base is located in nearby Newport Beach.

Disabled Students: 95% of the campus is accessible. Facilities include wheelchair ramps, elevators, special parking, specially equipped restrooms, special class scheduling, lowered drinking fountains, lowered telephones, special housing.

Services: Counseling and information services are available, as is tutoring in some subjects, Varies by quarter There is a reader service for the blind, and remedial reading and writing.

Campus Safety and Security: Measures include 24-hour foot and vehicle patrol, emergency notification system, self-defense education, and security escort services. There are shuttle buses, emergency telephones, and lighted pathways/sidewalks.

Programs of Study: UCI confers B.A., B.S., B.F.A. and B.Mus. degrees. Master's and doctoral degrees are also awarded. Bachelor's degrees are awarded in AGRICULTURE (environmental studies), BIOLOGICAL SCIENCE (biochemistry, bioinformatics, biology/biological science, botany, cell biology, ecology, genetics, microbiology, and neurosciences), BUSINESS (business administration and management, business economics, and economics – statistics), COMMUNICATIONS AND THE ARTS (art history, classics, comparative literature, dance, dramatic arts, English, film arts, French, Japanese, journalism, Korean, media arts, music, music performance, musical theater, Spanish, and studio art), COMPUTER AND PHYSICAL SCIENCE (chemistry, computer science, earth science, environmental geology, geology, information sciences and systems, mathematics, physics, and software engineering), ENGINEERING AND ENVIRONMENTAL DESIGN (aeronautical engineering, biomedical engineering, chemical engineering, civil engineering, computer engineering, electrical/electronics engineering, engineering, environmental engineering, environmental science, materials engineering, and mechanical engineering), HEALTH PROFESSIONS (nursing, pharmaceutical science, premedicine, and public health), SOCIAL SCIENCE (African American studies, anthropology, Asian/American studies, Chinese Studies, classical/ancient civilization, criminology, East Asian studies, economics, European studies, German area studies, (Social Science) Global Studies, Hispanic American studies, history, humanities, interdisciplinary studies, international studies, philosophy, political science/government, psychology, religion, social psychology, social science, sociology, urban studies, and women's studies). Biological sciences, psychology and social behavior, and business economics have the largest enrollments.

Required: To graduate, students must maintain a GPA of at least 2.0, earn 180 quarter units, satisfy all the requirements for their majors, and fulfill requirements in English composition and in American history and institutions. Further, students must also meet the following General Education requirements: I. Writing (two lower-division plus one upper-division course) II. Science and Technology (three courses) III. Social and Behavioral Sciences (three courses) IV. Arts and Humanities (three courses) V. Quantitative, Symbolic, and Computational Reasoning(three courses that may also satisfy another GE category) VI. Language Other Than English (one course) VII. Multicultural Studies (one course that may also satisfy another GE category) VIII. International/Global Issues (one course that may also satisfy another GE category).

Special: Students may study abroad in dozens of locations. UCI also offers internships, a Washington semester, Semester at Sea, work-study programs with the university, B.A.-B.S. degrees, dual majors, and pass/fail options. There are 7 national honor societies, including Phi Beta Kappa, and a freshman honors program.

Faculty/Classroom: 64% of faculty are male; 36% are female. All teach and do research. No introductory courses are taught by graduate students. The average class size in an introductory lecture is 107; in a laboratory is 20; and in a regular course is 31.

Admissions: 42% of the 2013-2014 applicants were accepted. The SAT scores for the 2013-2014 freshman class were: Critical Reading--34% below 500, 37% between 500 and 599, 24% between 600 and 699, and 5% between 700 and 800; Math--15% below 500, 30% between 500 and 599, 40% between 600 and 699, and 15% between 700 and 800; Writing--27% below 500, 40% between 500 and 599, 28% between 600 and 699, and 5% between 700 and 800.

Requirements: The SAT or ACT is required. Required minimum scores are determined by an eligibility index. Applicants need 15 academic credits, including 4 years of English, 3 in math, and 2 each in foreign language, history/social science, lab science, and electives. An additional year each in foreign language, math, and science is recommended. An essay also is needed. The GED is accepted. AP credits are accepted.

Procedure: Freshmen are admitted fall. Entrance exams should be taken no later than December of the senior year. Applications should be filed by November 30 for fall entry, along with a $70 fee. Notifications are sent March 31. Applications are accepted online.

Transfer: 1727 transfer students enrolled in 2012-2013. UC requirements for admission as a tranfer applicant vary according to the high school record. Please see catalog for full details. 36 of 180 credits required for the bachelor's degree must be completed at UCI.

Visiting: There are regularly scheduled orientations for prospective students. There are guides for informal visits, visitors may sit in on classes, and stay overnight. To schedule a visit, contact the Visitor Center at (949) 824.4636.

Financial Aid: UCI is a member of CSS. The FAFSA, and GPA verification form to state agency is required. The priority date for freshman financial aid applications for fall entry is March 2. The deadline for filing freshman financial aid applications for fall entry is May 2.

International Students: There are 1292 international students enrolled. They must take the TOEFL with a minimum score of 550 on the paper-based TOEFL (PBT) or 80 on the Internet-based version (iBT). They must also take the SAT or ACT.

Computers: All students may access the system 24 hours a day. There are no time limits and no fees.

Graduates: From July 1, 2012 to June 30, 2013, 6766 bachelor's degrees were awarded. The most popular majors were biological sciences (14%), business economics (8%), and pyschology and social behavior (6%). In an average class, 4% graduate in 3 years or less, 68% graduate in 4 years or less, 84% graduate in 5 years or less, and 86% graduate in 6 years or less.

Admissions Contact: Brent Yunek, Assistant Vice Chancellor, Enrollment Se. E-Mail: *admissions@uci.edu* Web: *www.uci.edu*

UNIVERSITY OF CALIFORNIA AT LOS ANGELES C-5

Los Angeles, CA 90095 **(310) 825-3101; (310) 206-1206**

Full-time: 11378 men, 14056 women **Faculty:** n/av; I, +$
Part-time: 386 men, 342 women **Ph.D.s:** 98%
Graduate: 7128 men, 6303 women **Student/Faculty:** n/av
Year: quarters, summer session **Tuition:** $12,118($34,996)
Application Deadline: November 30 **Room & Board:** $14,468
Freshman Class: 57670 applied, 13088 accepted, 4636 enrolled
SAT CR/M/W: 640/680/660 **ACT:** 29 **MOST COMPETITIVE**

University of California at Los Angeles (UCLA), founded in 1919, is a public institution offering undergraduate and graduate degrees. Its disciplines include arts and sciences, engineering, applied science, health sciences, law, management, and theater, film, and television. There are 5 undergraduate schools and 12 graduate schools. In addition to regional accreditation, UCLA has baccalaureate program accreditation with AACSB, ABET, ADA, CSAB, CSWE, FIDER, NAAB, and NLN. The 13 libraries contain 9.2 million volumes, 6.2 million microform items, and 5.0 million audio/video tapes/CDs/DVDs, and subscribe to 78,463 periodicals including electronic. Computerized library services include interlibrary loans, database searching, and Internet access. Special learning facilities include a learning resource center, art gallery, natural history museum, planetarium, radio station, TV station, Air Photo Archives; Arts Library; Biomed Library; Young Research Library; Clark Memorial Library; College Library; Cuneiform Digital Library; Darling Biomedical Library; Darling Law Library; Film and Television Archive; Folklore and Mythology Archive; Ethnomusicology Archive; Institute for Social Science Library; Libraries of the Ethnic Studies Centers; Music Library; Rudolph East Asian Library; Rosenfeld Management Library; Science and Engineering Library; UES Gonda Library; University Archives; Performing Arts Special Collections. MUSEUMS--Fowler Museum, Hammer Museum of Art and Culture Center, Grunwald Center for Graphic Arts, New Wright Gallery; GARDENS--Mildred E. Mathias Botanical Garden, Franklin D. Murphy Sculpture Garden, Hannah Carter Japanese Garden; ART--Eli and Edythe Broad Art Center; DANCE--Glorya Kaufman Hall; THEATER--Geffen Playhouse, Macgowan Little Theater, Freud Playhouse, Billy Wilder Theater; MUSIC--Royce Hall, Schoenberg Hall, Pauley Pavilion, Los Angeles Tennis Center; FILM--James Bridges Theater. The 419-acre campus is in an urban area in Los Angeles. Including any residence halls, there are 190 buildings.

Student Life: 89% of undergraduates are from California. Others are from 46 states, 71 foreign countries, and Canada. 77% are from public schools. 36% are Asian American; 32% white; 16% Hispanic. The average age of freshmen is 18; all undergraduates, 21. 3% do not continue beyond their first year; 92% remain to graduate.

Housing: 13,300 students can be accommodated in college housing, which includes coed dorms, off-campus apartments, and married student housing. In addition, there are special-interest houses, fraternity houses, and sorority houses. On-campus housing is available on a lottery system for upperclassmen. 64% of students commute. Alcohol is not permitted. Some may keep cars.

Activities: 13% of men belong to 32 national fraternities; 13% of women belong to 33 national sororities. There are 1000 groups on campus, including art, band, cheerleading, chess, choir, chorale, chorus, computers, dance, debate, drama, environmental, ethnic, film, forensics, gay, honors, international, jazz band, literary magazine, marching band, musical theater, newspaper, opera, orchestra, pep band, photography, political, professional, radio and TV, religious, social, social service, student government, symphony, and yearbook. Popular campus events include Career Week, Casino Night, and Welcome Week.

Sports: There are 10 intercollegiate sports for men and 12 for women, and 21 intramural sports for men and 19 for women. Facilities include a pavilion, a stadium, a tennis center, and a recreation and sports center.

Disabled Students: All of the campus is accessible. Facilities include wheelchair ramps, elevators, special parking, specially equipped restrooms, special class scheduling, lowered drinking fountains, and lowered telephones.

Services: Counseling and information services are available, as is tutoring in most subjects. There is a reader service for the blind.

Campus Safety and Security: Measures include 24-hour foot and vehicle patrol, emergency notification system, self-defense education, and security escort services. There are shuttle buses, emergency telephones, lighted pathways/sidewalks, and controlled access to dorms/residences.

Programs of Study: UCLA confers B.A., and B.S degrees. Master's and doctoral degrees are also awarded. Bachelor's degrees are awarded in AGRICULTURE (environmental studies), BIOLOGICAL SCIENCE (biochemistry, biology/biological science, biophysics, cell biology, ecology, marine biology, microbiology, molecular biology, neurosciences, and physiology), BUSINESS (business economics), COMMUNICATIONS AND THE ARTS (American literature, Arabic, art, art history and appreciation, Chinese, classics, communications, dramatic arts, English, film arts, French, German, Greek, Hebrew, Italian, Japanese, Korean, Latin, linguistics, music, music history and appreciation, musicology/ethnomusicology, Portuguese, Russian languages and literature, Scandinavian languages, and Spanish), COMPUTER AND PHYSICAL SCIENCE (applied mathematics, astrophysics, atmospheric sciences and meteorology, chemistry, computer science, earth science, geology, geophysics and seismology, mathematics, physics, and statistics), EDUCATION (mathematics education), ENGINEERING AND ENVIRONMENTAL DESIGN (aeronautical engineering, aerospace studies, architecture, bioengineering, biomedical engineering, chemical engineering, civil engineering, computer engineering, electrical/electronics engineering, environmental science, geological engineering, materials engineering, materials science, and mechanical engineering), HEALTH PROFESSIONS (nursing), SOCIAL SCIENCE (African studies, African American studies, American Indian studies, anthropology, Asian/American studies, Asian/Oriental studies, classical/ancient civilization, cognitive science, East Asian studies, economics, European studies, French studies, geography, history, international studies, Italian studies, Judaic studies, Latin American studies, Mexican-American/Chicano studies, Middle Eastern studies, Near Eastern studies, philosophy, political science/government, psychobiology, psychology, religion, Russian and Slavic studies, sociology, South Asian studies, Spanish studies, and women's studies). Economics, psychology, and political science have the largest enrollments.

Required: Students must complete a minimum of 180 quarter units and maintain a minimum GPA of 2.0 in all courses. All students must demonstrate a proficiency in English composition, or take specific courses to achieve this proficiency, and must also meet course requirements in American history and institutions. Other requirements vary by major and college or school.

Special: Opportunities are provided for internships, work-study programs, study abroad in 33 countries, student-designed majors, dual majors, and interdisciplinary majors, including chemistry and materials science, Chicana and Chicano studies, and math and engineering. There is a Washington, D.C., program for 20 to 30 students selected each fall and spring. There are 21 national honor societies, including Phi Beta Kappa, a freshman honors program, and 100 departmental honors programs.

Faculty/Classroom: 65% of faculty are male; 35% are female. All teach and do research. No introductory courses are taught by graduate students.

Admissions: In a recent year, 23% applicants were accepted. The SAT scores for a recent freshman class were: Critical Reading--8% below 500, 24% between 500 and 599, 45% between 600 and 700, and 23% above 700; Math--6% below 500, 16% between 500 and 599, 36% between 600 and 700, and 42% above 700; Writing--6% below 500, 21% between 500 and 599, 40% between 600 and 700, and 33% above 700. The ACT scores were 8% below 21, 13% between 21 and 23, 16% between 24 and 26, 14% between 27 and 28, and 53% above 28.

Requirements: The SAT or ACT is required. The ACT Optional Writing test is also required. In addition, for freshmen applicants applying for admission to Fall Quarter 2012 or later, we will no longer require two SAT subject exams. (We will still review these exams if applicants choose to send them to us, and certain SAT subject exams may be recommended for some majors). We will continue to require either the SAT Reasoning or ACT with Writing examination. AP credits are accepted. Important factors in the admissions decision are advanced placement or honors courses, evidence of special talent, and leadership record.

Procedure: Freshmen are admitted fall. Entrance exams should be taken preferably in the junior year, but no later than December of the senior year. Applications should be filed by November 30 for fall entry. The fall 2011 application fee was $60. Notifications are sent March 15. Applications are accepted online.

Transfer: In a recent year, 3229 transfer students enrolled. For minimum requirements, transfer students must have earned 90 quarter units at the previous college and have completed preparatory courses for the selected major. Most students selected present a GPA of 3.0 or better. 68 of 180 credits required for the bachelor's degree must be completed at UCLA.

Visiting: There are regularly scheduled orientations for prospective students, including campus tours by current UCLA students, offered weekdays at 10:15 a.m. and 2:15 p.m. Reservations are required. Visitors may sit in on classes. To schedule a visit, contact the Undergraduate Admissions.

Financial Aid: In a recent year, 56% of all full-time freshmen and 55%

of continuing full-time students received some form of financial aid. 54% of all full-time freshmen and 52% of continuing full-time students received need-based aid. Need-based scholarships or need-based grants averaged $16,080; need-based self-help aid (loans and jobs) averaged $6,144; non-need-based athletic scholarships averaged $18,580; and other non-need-based awards and non-need-based scholarships averaged $5,493. The FAFSA and the college's own financial statement are required. The deadline for filing freshman financial aid applications for fall entry is March 2.

International Students: There are 1498 international students enrolled. They must take the TOEFL with a minimum score of 550 on the paper-based TOEFL (PBT) or 83 on the Internet-based version (iBT), IELTS, scoring at least 7. They must also take the SAT or ACT.

Computers: Wireless access is available. Technology at UCLA is highly decentralized and is typically managed at the local level: schools, divisions, subdivisions, and departments. Each has unique computing facilities responding to domain specific needs. In addition there are research data center facilities for high performance computing researchers, an extensive grid computing initiative, and a robust digital library program including ongoing digitization activities for special collections. All students may access the system 24 hours a day, 7 days a week. There are no fees.

Graduates: In a recent year, 7518 bachelor's degrees were awarded. The most popular majors were politicial science (9%), history (8%), and psychology (8%). In an average class, 3% graduate in 3 years or less, 70% graduate in 4 years or less, 87% graduate in 5 years or less, and 90% graduate in 6 years or less.

Admissions Contact: Vu Tran, Director of Undergraduate Admissions. E-Mail: *ugadm@saonet.ucla.edu* Web: *www.admissions.ucla.edu*

UNIVERSITY OF CALIFORNIA AT RIVERSIDE D-5

Riverside, CA 92521	**(951) 827-4531; (951) 827-6346**
Full-time: 8817 men, 9380 women	**Faculty:** 751; I, av$
Part-time: 248 men, 167 women	**Ph.D.s:** 98%
Graduate: 1470 men, 1206 women	**Student/Faculty:** 21 to 1
Year: quarters, summer session	**Tuition:** $14,004 ($36,882)
Application Deadline: November 30	**Room & Board:** $13,200
Freshman Class: 34816 applied, 20973 accepted, 4201 enrolled	
SAT CR/M/W: 540/540/580 **ACT:** 23	**COMPETITIVE**

The University of California at Riverside, founded in 1954, is a public research university with undergraduate and graduate programs in engineering, humanities, arts, social sciences, natural and agricultural sciences, medicine, public policy, health sciences, education and business. There are 3 undergraduate schools and 9 graduate schools. In addition to regional accreditation, UCR has baccalaureate program accreditation with AACSB and ABET. The 4 libraries contain 3.2 million volumes, 2.3 million microform items, and subscribe to 97,678 periodicals including electronic. Computerized library services include interlibrary loans, database searching, Internet access, and Wi-Fi capability. Special learning facilities include an art gallery, radio station, Culver Center for the Arts; Sweeney Art Gallery; UCR/California Museum of Photography; College of Engineering-Center for Environmental Research and Technology; Air Pollution Research Center; Agricultural Research Institute for Deserts; Citrus Variety Collection; Agricultural Experiment Station; Botanic Gardens; Entomology Museum; George E. Brown Salinity Lab; Core Instrumentation Facility for genomics research. The 1200-acre campus is in a suburban area 50 miles east of Los Angeles. Including any residence halls, there are 668 buildings.

Student Life: 98% of undergraduates are from California. Others are from 35 states, 43 foreign countries, and Canada. 92% are from public schools. 35% are Asian American; 32% Hispanic; 17% White. The average age of freshmen is 18; all undergraduates, 20.3. 11% do not continue beyond their first year; 89% remain to graduate.

Housing: 6045 students can be accommodated in college housing, which includes coed dorms, on-campus apartments, and married student housing. In addition, there are honors houses, special-interest houses, and an international village. On-campus housing is guaranteed for the freshman year only, is available on a first-come, first-served basis, and is available on a lottery system for upperclassmen. 70% of students commute. All students may keep cars.

Activities: 1% of men belong to 6 local and 14 national fraternities; 1% of women belong to 8 local and 12 national sororities. There are 470 groups on campus, including art, bagpipe, cheerleading, computers, dance, drama, ethnic, film, gay, honors, international, literary magazine, musical theater, newspaper, pep band, photography, political, professional, radio and TV, social, social service, and student government. Popular campus events include HEAT Festival, Block Party and Spring Splash.

Sports: There are 7 intercollegiate sports for men and 8 for women, and 8 intramural sports for men and 9 for women. UCR competes in the NCAA Division I. The campus has a heated Olympic-size pool, an 80,000 square foot student recreation center with a weight room/fitness center, 4 indoor multi-use courts, 4 racquetball courts, 1 squash court, 3 fitness studios, 10 tennis courts, a roller hockey rink, challenge ropes course, and a jogging trail.

Disabled Students: Facilities include wheelchair ramps, elevators, special parking, specially equipped restrooms, special class scheduling, lowered drinking fountains, lowered telephones, special housing, and automatic doors.

Services: Counseling and information services are available, as is tutoring in most subjects, individual and group tutoring. There is a reader service for the blind. There are also study skills classes, and preparation sessions for graduate entrance exams, study groups, individual counseling and lab work, and speed-reading classes.

Campus Safety and Security: Measures include 24-hour foot and vehicle patrol, emergency notification system, self-defense education, and security escort services. There are shuttle buses, emergency telephones, lighted pathways/sidewalks, off Campus Point to Point Shuttle Service; 24/7 University of California police department.

Programs of Study: UCR confers B.A., and B.S. degrees. Master's and doctoral degrees are also awarded. Bachelor's degrees are awarded in AGRICULTURE (soil science), BIOLOGICAL SCIENCE (biochemistry, biology/biological science, cell biology, entomology, genetics, microbiology, neurosciences, plant genetics, and plant pathology), BUSINESS (business administration and management, business economics, and management science), COMMUNICATIONS AND THE ARTS (art history, art, art history and appreciation, Chinese, classical languages, comparative literature, creative writing, dance, dramatic arts, English, film arts, French, German, Germanic languages and literature, Japanese, languages, linguistics, music, Russian, Russian languages and literature, Spanish, theatre arts, and visual and performing arts), COMPUTER AND PHYSICAL SCIENCE (chemistry, computer science, geology, geophysics and seismology, geoscience, information sciences and systems, mathematics, physical sciences, physics, and statistics), EDUCATION (mathematics education), ENGINEERING AND ENVIRONMENTAL DESIGN (bioengineering, chemical engineering, electrical/electronics engineering, engineering and applied science, engineering mechanics, environmental engineering, environmental science, materials engineering, and mechanical engineering), HEALTH PROFESSIONS (biomedical science), SOCIAL SCIENCE (African American studies, anthropology, Asian/American studies, Asian/Oriental studies, classical/ancient civilization, economics, ethnic studies, history, humanities and social science, interdisciplinary studies, Latin American studies, liberal arts/general studies, Mexican-American/Chicano studies, Middle Eastern studies, Native American studies, philosophy, political science/government, psychology, religion, religious education, Russian and Slavic studies, sociology, and women's studies). Engineering is the strongest academically. Business administration, biology and psychology have the largest enrollments.

Required: Students must demonstrate proficiency in English and a knowledge of American history and institutions. A total of 180 quarter credit hours with a minimum GPA of 2.0 is required in order to graduate. The number of hours in the major varies. All students must complete a 1-year sequence in English composition, in computers, math, or statistics, and in concepts/issues of ethnicity. There are breadth requirements in humanities, social sciences, and natural sciences/math for all students; the number of units/courses in each group depends on the student's college and major. A thesis is required for honors program students.

Special: Internships, work-study programs with various agencies and employers on and off campus, study abroad in 35 countries, and a semester in Washington are available. The campus has a School of Medicine now accepting students, and a School of Public Policy. Student-dual majors, opportunities for undergraduate research, and pass/fail options in elective subjects are possible. Grants are available for research, fieldwork, or other creative activity. Academic internships and co-op programs are offered in all majors. There are 14 national honor societies, including Phi Beta Kappa, a freshman honors program, and 13 departmental honors programs.

Faculty/Classroom: 65% of faculty are male; 35% are female. All teach undergraduates, 74% do research, and 74% do both. No introductory courses are taught by graduate students.

Admissions: 60% of the 2013-2014 applicants were accepted. The SAT scores for the 2013-2014 freshman class were: Critical Reading--26% below 500, 45% between 500 and 599, 22% between 600 and 699, and 6% between 700 and 800; Math--17% below 500, 39% between 500 and 599, 34% between 600 and 699, and 9% between 700 and 800; Writing--26% below 500, 48% between 500 and 599, 23% between 600 and 699, and 2% between 700 and 800. The ACT scores were 27% below 21, 29% between 21 and 23, 25% between 24 and 26, 10% between 27 and 28, and 9% above 28. 100% of the current freshmen were in the top fifth of their class.

Requirements: The SAT or ACT is required. The ACT Optional Writing test is also required. In addition, the minimum GPA varies depending on SAT or ACT scores. Candidates for admission should have completed 4 years of English, 3 of math, and 2 of foreign language, history, science, 1 visual/performing arts and electives. UCR requires applicants to be in the upper 25% of their class. AP credits are accepted.

Procedure: Freshmen are admitted fall. Entrance exams should be taken by December of the senior year. Applications should be filed by November 30 for fall entry, along with a $70 fee. Notifications are sent February 1.

3748 applicants were on the 2013 waiting list; 1412 were admitted. Applications are accepted online.

Transfer: 1235 transfer students enrolled in 2012-2013. Transfer students applying to selecting majors must meet major preparation and GPA requirements for that major. 45 of 180 credits required for the bachelor's degree must be completed at UCR.

Visiting: There are regularly scheduled orientations for prospective students, Discover Days; Highlander Day: College Week Live Virtual UCR Day; Chancellor's receptions in the spring, tours are available throughout the year on weekdays and some Saturdays. There are guides for informal visits, visitors may sit in on classes, and stay overnight. To schedule a visit, contact Griselda Rodriguez at (951) 827-4531.

Financial Aid: In 2013-2014, 89% of all full-time freshmen and 85% of continuing full-time students received some form of financial aid. 77% of all full-time freshmen and 78% of continuing full-time students received need-based aid. The average freshman award was $23,102. Need-based scholarships or need-based grants averaged $18,133; need-based self-help aid (loans and jobs) averaged $6,484; non-need-based athletic scholarships averaged $13,828; and other non-need-based awards and non-need-based scholarships averaged $2,882. 27% of undergraduate students work part-time. The average financial indebtedness of the 2013 graduate was $21,300. The FAFSA is required. The priority date for freshman financial aid applications for fall entry is March 2. The deadline for filing freshman financial aid applications for fall entry is May 1.

International Students: There are 586 international students enrolled. The school actively recruits these students. They must take the TOEFL with a minimum score of 550 on the paper-based TOEFL (PBT) or 80 on the Internet-based version (iBT), or IELTS. They must also take the SAT or ACT.

Computers: All students may access the system. There are no time limits and no fees.

Graduates: From July 1, 2012 to June 30, 2013, 4196 bachelor's degrees were awarded. The most popular majors were business/marketing (15%), psychology (10%), and biology (7%). 248 companies recruited on campus in 2012-2013. In an average class, 2% graduate in 3 years or less, 42% graduate in 4 years or less, 62% graduate in 5 years or less, and 69% graduate in 6 years or less. Of the 2012 graduating class, 39% were enrolled in graduate school within 6 months of graduation, and 78% were employed.

Admissions Contact: Emily Engelschall, Director, Undergraduate Admissions. E-Mail: *discover@ucr.edu* Web: *www.ucr.edu*

UNIVERSITY OF CALIFORNIA AT SAN DIEGO D-5

La Jolla, CA 92093 (858) 534-4831

Full-time: 9775 men, 10700 women	**Faculty:** n/av; I, +$
Part-time: n/av	**Ph.D.s:** n/av
Graduate: 2160 men, 1475 women	**Student/Faculty:** n/av
Year: trimesters, summer session	**Tuition:** $9500 ($22,500)
Application Deadline: November 30	**Room & Board:** $12,500
Freshman Class: n/av	
SAT or ACT: required	

VERY COMPETITIVE

University of California at San Diego, founded in 1960, is a public liberal arts institution. The figures given in the above capsule and in this profile are approximate. There are 6 undergraduate schools and 5 graduate schools. In addition to regional accreditation, UCSD has baccalaureate program accreditation with ABET. The 10 libraries contain 2.6 million volumes, 2.9 million microform items, and 87,625 audio/video tapes/CDs/DVDs, and subscribe to 24,986 periodicals including electronic. Computerized library services include interlibrary loans, database searching, and Internet access. Special learning facilities include an art gallery, radio station, TV station, aquarium-museum, supercomputer center, and theater. The 1976-acre campus is in a suburban area 12 miles north of downtown San Diego. Including any residence halls, there are 501 buildings.

Student Life: 95% of undergraduates are from California. Others are from states, 70 foreign countries, and Canada. 88% are from public schools. 41% are Asian American; 34% white. The average age of freshmen is 18; all undergraduates, 21. 7% do not continue beyond their first year; 93% remain to graduate.

Housing: 6352 students can be accommodated in college housing, which includes coed dorms, on-campus apartments, off-campus apartments, and married student housing. In addition, there are language houses, special-interest houses, international house. On-campus housing is available on a lottery system for upperclassmen. 64% of students commute. All students may keep cars.

Activities: 10% of men belong to 14 national fraternities; 10% of women belong to 19 national sororities. There are 450 groups on campus, including enterprise, academic, art, band, cheerleading, chess, choir, chorale, chorus, computers, dance, debate, drama, ethnic, film, gay, honors, international, jazz band, literary magazine, musical theater, newspaper, opera, orchestra, pep band, photography, political, professional, radio and TV, religious, social, social service, student government, symphony, and yearbook. Popular campus events include Fall Festival on the Green, Spring Sun God Festival, and Asian Pacific Awareness Week.

Sports: There are 12 intercollegiate sports for men and 12 for women, and 27 intramural sports for men and 23 for women. Facilities include a 9-lane, all-weather track, soccer and softball fields, an athletic training facility, 2 pools, a spa, a weight room, tennis courts, playing fields, and a golf driving range. An 188,000-square-foot recreation complex features a 5000-seat arena, 8 handball/racquetball courts, 2 squash courts, a 12,000-square-foot weight-training facility, a climbing wall, and basketball, volleyball, and badminton courts.

Disabled Students: 95% of the campus is accessible. Facilities include wheelchair ramps, elevators, special parking, specially equipped restrooms, special class scheduling, lowered drinking fountains, lowered telephones. special accommodations, and administrative support services.

Services: Counseling and information services are available, as is tutoring in most subjects. There is a reader service for the blind.

Campus Safety and Security: Measures include 24-hour foot and vehicle patrol, self-defense education, and security escort services. There are shuttle buses, emergency telephones, lighted pathways/sidewalks, a student safety awareness program, peer educators, and an on-campus police department.

Programs of Study: UCSD confers B.A. and B.S. degrees. Master's and doctoral degrees are also awarded. Bachelor's degrees are awarded in AGRICULTURE (animal science and environmental studies), BIOLOGICAL SCIENCE (biochemistry, bioinformatics, biology/biological science, biophysics, biotechnology, ecology, microbiology, molecular biology, and physiology), BUSINESS (management science), COMMUNICATIONS AND THE ARTS (art history and appreciation, Chinese, classics, communications, dance, dramatic arts, English literature, Germanic languages and literature, linguistics, literature, music, music history and appreciation, music technology, studio art, and visual and performing arts), COMPUTER AND PHYSICAL SCIENCE (applied mathematics, applied physics, chemistry, computer science, earth science, information sciences and systems, mathematics, physical chemistry, and physics), EDUCATION (mathematics education and science education), ENGINEERING AND ENVIRONMENTAL DESIGN (aerospace studies, bioengineering, chemical engineering, computer engineering, electrical/electronics engineering, engineering, engineering physics, environmental engineering, environmental science, and mechanical engineering), SOCIAL SCIENCE (anthropology, cognitive science, economics, ethnic studies, French studies, gender studies, history, human development, international studies, Italian studies, Japanese studies, Judaic studies, Latin American studies, philosophy, political science/government, psychology, religion, Russian and Slavic studies, sociology, Spanish studies, Third World studies, and urban studies). Sciences, engineering, and the arts are the strongest academically. Biology, economics, and psychology have the largest enrollments.

Required: Graduation requirements vary by undergraduate college but students must complete 180 to 184 total quarter units or 45 to 46 courses, with a minimum of 60 credit hours or 12 to 22 courses in the major. Students must maintain a minimum GPA of 2.0.

Special: Internships in many fields, work-study, study abroad in more than 30 countries, and a Washington semester are offered. B.A.-B.S. degrees, an accelerated degree, dual majors, student-designed majors, and exchange programs with Dartmouth College, Spelman College, and Morehouse College are available. Nondegree study, credit for military experience, and pass/fail options are possible. There are 2 national honor societies, including Phi Beta Kappa, a freshman honors program, and 14 departmental honors programs.

Faculty/Classroom: 73% of faculty are male; 27% are female. 98% teach undergraduates, and all do research. Graduate students teach 2% of introductory courses. The average class size in an introductory lecture is 300; in a laboratory is 40; and in a regular course is 100.

Requirements: The SAT or ACT is required. In addition, the SAT Reasoning Test with critical reading, math and writing, or ACT Assesment plus Writing, and 2 SAT Subject Tests in two different areas: history/social science, literature, math (Level 2 only), science or language other than English, are required. Tests must be taken by December of senior year. A GPA of 2.8 is required. AP credits are accepted. Important factors in the admissions decision are advanced placement or honors courses, leadership record, and extracurricular activities record.

Procedure: Freshmen are admitted fall. Entrance exams should be taken by December of the senior year. Applications should be filed by November 30 for fall entry, along with a $55 fee. Notifications are sent March 30. Applications are accepted online.

Transfer: California residents should have a competitive GPA; average 2004 GPA was 3.42. Transfers should have completed 90 quarter units. Preference is given to applicants from state community colleges. 36 of 180 credits required for the bachelor's degree must be completed at UCSD.

Visiting: There are regularly scheduled orientations for prospective students. There are guides for informal visits and visitors may sit in on classes. To schedule a visit, contact Campus Tours.

Financial Aid: UCSD is a member of CSS. The FAFSA and the state aid form are required. Check with the school for current application deadlines.

International Students: They must take the TOEFL, and the SAT or ACT.

Computers: All students may access the system 24 hours every day. There are no time limits and no fees. It is strongly recommended that all students have a personal computer.

Admissions Contact: Mae Brown, Assistant Vice Chancellor, Admissions and Enrollment. E-Mail: *admissionsinfo@sandiego.edu* Web: *www.sandiego.edu*

UNIVERSITY OF CALIFORNIA AT SANTA BARBARA C-5

Santa Barbara, CA 93106 (805) 893-2881; (805) 893-2676

Full-time: 9065 men, 10011 women
Part-time: 172 men, 114 women
Graduate: 1611 men, 1252 women
Year: quarters, summer session
Application Deadline: November 30
Faculty: 885; I, ++$
Ph.D.s: 100%
Student/Faculty: 17 to 1
Tuition: $13,746 ($35,767)
Room & Board: $13,805
Freshman Class: 62427 applied, 24813 accepted, 4624 enrolled
SAT CR/M/W: 610/640/630 **ACT:** 27 **HIGHLY COMPETITIVE**

The University of California at Santa Barbara, founded in 1909, is a public liberal arts institution offering programs in creative studies, engineering, and letters and science. There are 3 undergraduate schools and one graduate school. In addition to regional accreditation, UCSB has baccalaureate program accreditation with ABET and CSAB. The library contains 3.0 million volumes, 3.8 million microform items, and 5.5 million audio/video tapes/CDs/DVDs, and subscribes to 92,139 periodicals including electronic. Computerized library services include interlibrary loans, database searching, Internet access, and Wi-Fi capability. Special learning facilities include an art gallery, radio station, a language and learning lab, and numerous national and multicampus research institutes. The 1055-acre campus is in a suburban area 10 miles north of Santa Barbara. Including any residence halls, there are 399 buildings.

Student Life: 93% of undergraduates are from California. Others are from 48 states, 80 foreign countries, and Canada. 86% are from public schools. 40% are White; 24% Asian American; 24% Hispanic. The average age of freshmen is 18; all undergraduates, 20. 9% do not continue beyond their first year; 91% remain to graduate.

Housing: 6300 students can be accommodated in college housing, which includes coed dorms, on-campus apartments, off-campus apartments, and married student housing. In addition, there are special-interest houses, special interest floors. On-campus housing is guaranteed for the freshman year only, is available on a first-come, and first-served basis. 66% of students commute. All students may keep cars.

Activities: 8% of men belong to 20 national fraternities; 12% of women belong to 24 national sororities. There are 455 groups on campus, including art, band, cheerleading, chess, choir, chorale, chorus, computers, dance, drama, environmental, ethnic, film, gay, honors, international, jazz band, literary magazine, musical theater, newspaper, opera, pep band, photography, political, professional, radio and TV, religious, social, social service, student government, symphony, and yearbook. Popular campus events include Club Day, Activities Fair, and UCEN Cultural Festival, and Exxtravaganza.

Sports: There are 10 intercollegiate sports for men and 10 for women, and 19 intramural sports for men and 19 for women. Facilities include 4 gyms, a gymnastics facility, rock-climbing walls, indoor and outdoor basketball courts, outdoor tennis and sand volleyball courts, 3 swimming pools, including 1 Olympic-sized, a football/soccer stadium, softball diamond, baseball stadium, indoor/outdoor racquetball/squash courts, extensive playing fields, weight rooms, fitness center, and a synthetic track.

Disabled Students: All of the campus is accessible. Facilities include wheelchair ramps, elevators, special parking, specially equipped restrooms, special class scheduling, lowered drinking fountains, and lowered telephones.

Services: Counseling and information services are available, as is tutoring in most subjects. There is a reader service for the blind, and remedial reading and writing.

Campus Safety and Security: Measures include 24-hour foot and vehicle patrol, emergency notification system, self-defense education, and security escort services. There are emergency telephones and lighted pathways/sidewalks.

Programs of Study: UCSB confers B.A., B.F.A., B.M. and B.S. degrees. Master's and doctoral degrees are also awarded. Bachelor's degrees are awarded in BIOLOGICAL SCIENCE (biochemistry, biology/biological science, cell biology, ecology, evolutionary biology, marine biology, microbiology, molecular biology, physiology, and zoology), BUSINESS (accounting), COMMUNICATIONS AND THE ARTS (art, art history and appreciation, Chinese, classics, communications, comparative literature, dance, dramatic arts, English, film arts, French, German, Germanic languages and literature, Japanese, linguistics, literature, music, music performance, music theory and composition, Portuguese, Slavic languages, and Spanish), COMPUTER AND PHYSICAL SCIENCE (actuarial science, chemistry, computer science, earth science, geology, geophysics and seismology, hydrology, mathematics, physics, and statistics), ENGINEERING AND ENVIRONMENTAL DESIGN (chemical engineering, computer engineering, electrical/electronics engineering, environmental science, and mechanical engineering), HEALTH PROFESSIONS (pharmacy), SOCIAL SCIENCE (African American studies, anthropology, Asian/American studies, Asian/Oriental studies, biopsychology, economics, geography, history, interdisciplinary studies, international studies, Islamic studies, Italian studies, Latin American studies, medieval studies, Mexican-American/Chicano studies, Middle Eastern studies, philosophy, political science/government, psychology, religion, sociology, and women's studies). Economics, biological science and psychology have the largest enrollments.

Required: Graduation requirements vary by college. Generally, students will take one third of their distribution in the major subject, one third in general education courses, and one third in elective courses. General subject requirements include courses in English, foreign language, science/math/technology, social sciences, civilization and thought, literature, and the arts; specific subject requirements include 6 writing-intensive courses and 1 course each in non-Western culture, quantitative relationships, and ethnic studies. To graduate, students must earn at least 180 quarter units, with a minimum GPA of 2.0, and have completed the American History and Institutions requirement.

Special: A Washington semester, internships, cross-registration with all University of California campuses, study abroad in 34 countries, work-study programs, dual majors, student-designed majors, the B.A.-B.S. degree, and an accelerated degree program in electrical engineering are offered. There are 3 national honor societies, including Phi Beta Kappa, and a freshman honors program.

Faculty/Classroom: 63% of faculty are male; 37% are female. All teach and do research. No introductory courses are taught by graduate students. The average class size in an introductory lecture is 100; in a laboratory is 17; and in a regular course is 40.

Admissions: 40% of the 2013-2014 applicants were accepted. The SAT scores for the 2013-2014 freshman class were: Critical Reading--10% below 500, 32% between 500 and 599, 42% between 600 and 699, and 16% between 700 and 800; Math--6% below 500, 23% between 500 and 599, 45% between 600 and 699, and 27% between 700 and 800; Writing--6% below 500, 29% between 500 and 599, 45% between 600 and 699, and 19% between 700 and 800. The ACT scores were 7% below 21, 14% between 21 and 23, 21% between 24 and 26, 17% between 27 and 28, and 41% above 28. 100% of the current freshmen were in the top fifth of their class; 100% were in the top two fifths.

Requirements: The SAT is required. The ACT and ACT Writing Test are recommended. In addition, SAT Subject tests in math and 1 other choice. Candidates for admission must have completed 4 years of English, 3 of math, and 2 each of foreign language, lab science, history/social science, and college-preparatory electives. An additional year each in foreign language, math, and science is recommended. A GPA of 3.3 is required. AP credits are accepted.

Procedure: Freshmen are admitted fall. Entrance exams should be taken by December of the senior year. Applications should be filed by November 30 for fall entry, along with a $70 fee. Notifications are sent March 1. Applications are accepted online.

Transfer: 1651 transfer students enrolled in 2012-2013. High school transcripts, college transcripts, and an essay or personal statement are required for all transfer applicants. Standardized test scores are required of all lower division transfers. An applicant must be in good standing at prior institution but no statement to this request is required. Preference is given to students who have completed 90 quarter (60 a semester) units and who transfer from community colleges. California residents should have a minimum 2.0 GPA in transferable course work; nonresidents, a 2.8 GPA. Students with fewer than 12 quarter or semester units of transferable course work must provide standardized test scores. 35 of 180 credits required for the bachelor's degree must be completed at UCSB.

Visiting: There are regularly scheduled orientations for prospective students, consisting of a campus film, an information session, and a walking tour of the campus led by a student guide. There are guides for informal visits, visitors may sit in on classes, and stay overnight. To schedule a visit, contact the Office of Relations at (805) 893-2485.

Financial Aid: In 2013-2014, 62% of all full-time freshmen and 58% of continuing full-time students received some form of financial aid. 58% of all full-time freshmen and 53% of continuing full-time students received need-based aid. The average freshman award was $23,996. Need-based scholarships or need-based grants averaged $19,295; need-based self-help aid (loans and jobs) averaged $6,583; non-need-based athletic scholarships averaged $12,907; and other non-need-based awards and non-need-based scholarships averaged $10,886. 19% of undergraduate students work part-time. The average financial indebtedness of the 2013 graduate was $18,361. UCSB is a member of CSS. The FAFSA is required. The deadline for filing freshman financial aid applications for fall entry is March 2.

International Students: There are 552 international students enrolled. They must take the TOEFL with a minimum score of 550 on the paper-based TOEFL (PBT) or 80 on the Internet-based version (iBT). They must also take the SAT or ACT.

Computers: All students may access the system. at any time, if students have their own computer and modem. There are no time limits and no fees.
Graduates: From July 1, 2012 to June 30, 2013, 5775 bachelor's degrees were awarded. The most popular majors were biological sciences (15%), economics (9%), and psychology (8%). 475 companies recruited on campus in 2012-2013. In an average class, 69% graduate in 4 years or less, 83% graduate in 5 years or less, and 86% graduate in 6 years or less.
Admissions Contact: Office of Admissions E-Mail: *appinfo@sa.ucsb .edu* Web: *www.ucsb.edu*

UNIVERSITY OF CALIFORNIA AT SANTA CRUZ B-3

Santa Cruz, CA 95064 **(831) 459-4008; (831) 459-4452**

Full-time: 7197 men, 8253 women	**Faculty:** n/av; I, av$
Part-time: 114 men, 131 women	**Ph.D.s:** 98%
Graduate: 818 men, 690 women	**Student/Faculty:** 18 to 1
Year: trimesters, summer session	**Tuition:** $13,398 ($36,276)
Application Deadline: November 30	**Room & Board:** $14,409

Freshman Class: 38640 applied, 20039 accepted, 3303 enrolled
SAT CR/M/W: 550/560/550 **ACT:** 24 **VERY COMPETITIVE**

The University of California, Santa Cruz is a public university, one of 10 campuses in the University of California. Located 80 miles south of San Francisco in coastal community of Santa Cruz, the campus lies on 2,001 acres of rolling hills overlooking the Pacific Ocean and Monterey Bay. Founded in 1965,UC Santa Cruz began as a showcase for progressive, cross-disciplinary undergraduate education, innovative teaching methods and contemporary architecture. Since then, it has evolved into a modern research university with a wide variety of undergraduate and graduate programs, while retaining its reputation for strong undergraduate support and political activism. The residential college system, consisting of 10 small colleges, combines the student support of a small college with the resources of a major university. There are 10 undergraduate schools and one graduate school. In addition to regional accreditation, UCSC has baccalaureate program accreditation with ABET. The 2 libraries contain 2.3 million volumes, 68,573 microform items, and 56,757 audio/video tapes/CDs/ DVDs, and subscribe to 46,433 periodicals including electronic. Computerized library services include interlibrary loans, database searching, and Internet access. Special learning facilities include an art gallery, natural history museum, radio station, TV station, Agroecology Program - The Farm, Arboretum, Long Marine Lab, Seymour Marine Discovery Center, Lick Observatory on Mt. Hamilton, Silicon Valley Center, Digital Arts Research Center, Genome Bioinformatics Project, and a Computer Game Design. The campus is in a small town. Including any residence halls, there are 559 buildings.

Student Life: 96% of undergraduates are from California. Others are from 46 states, 79 foreign countries, and Canada. 90% are from public schools. 37% are White; 30% Hispanic; 20% Asian American. The average age of freshmen is 19; all undergraduates, 21. 9% do not continue beyond their first year; 75% remain to graduate.

Housing: 8415 students can be accommodated in college housing, which includes single-sex and coed dorms, on-campus apartments, off-campus apartments, and married student housing. In addition, there are language houses, special-interest houses, and multicultural residence halls. On-campus housing is available on a lottery system for upperclassmen. 53% of students commute. Alcohol is not permitted. Upperclassmen may keep cars.

Activities: 1% of men belong to 1% of women belong to There are 157 groups on campus, including art, band, cheerleading, chess, choir, chorale, chorus, computers, dance, debate, drama, ethnic, film, gay, honors, international, jazz band, literary magazine, musical theater, newspaper, opera, orchestra, photography, political, professional, radio and TV, religious, social, social service, student government, and symphony. Popular campus events include Multicultural Festival and Martin Luther King Convocation.

Sports: There are 5 intercollegiate sports for men and 7 for women, and 10 intramural sports for men and 6 for women. Facilities include a 50-meter pool, 2 playing fields, a weight room, an all-weather jogging track, fully equipped gyms, a fitness course, racquetball, tennis, and basketball courts, and a 12,000-square-foot fitness center.

Disabled Students: 90% of the campus is accessible. Facilities include wheelchair ramps, elevators, special parking, specially equipped restrooms, special class scheduling, lowered drinking fountains, lowered telephones. wheelchair lift-equipped transportation.

Services: Counseling and information services are available, as is tutoring in most subjects, writing There is a reader service for the blind. A learning center helps SAA/EOP students with math and writing skills. There is also a program to help any student who is having trouble with certain courses.

Campus Safety and Security: Measures include 24-hour foot and vehicle patrol, emergency notification system, self-defense education, and security escort services. There are shuttle buses, emergency telephones, lighted pathways/sidewalks, a rape prevention program, seminars for residential staff, and guards at each entrance from 8 p.m. until dawn.

Programs of Study: UCSC confers B.A., B.S. and B.M. degrees. Master's and doctoral degrees are also awarded. Bachelor's degrees are awarded in AGRICULTURE (environmental studies and plant science), BIOLOGICAL SCIENCE (biochemistry, bioinformatics, biology/biological science, cell biology, ecology, evolutionary biology, marine biology, molecular biology, and neurosciences), BUSINESS (business economics and international economics), COMMUNICATIONS AND THE ARTS (art, art history and appreciation, classical languages, dramatic arts, film arts, language arts, linguistics, literature, and music), COMPUTER AND PHYSICAL SCIENCE (chemistry, computer game design/development, computer science, earth science, geology, information sciences and systems, mathematics, and physics), ENGINEERING AND ENVIRONMENTAL DESIGN (computer engineering and electrical/electronics engineering), HEALTH PROFESSIONS (health science), SOCIAL SCIENCE (American studies, anthropology, community services, economics, German area studies, history, Italian studies, Latin American studies, law, philosophy, political science/government, psychology, sociology, and women's studies). Psychology, business management economics and biology have the largest enrollments.

Required: To graduate, all students must complete 36 full-credit courses (180 quarter units) with a minimum GPA of 2.0. Courses are required in arts, English, history, writing-intensive, U.S. ethnic minorities/ non-Western society, humanities, math, sciences, and social sciences. They must satisfy university requirements in U.S. history and institutions and in English composition, the residence requirement, the core course, and a comprehensive exam or equivalent body of work, or a senior thesis. Particular college requirements and those of an approved major vary. All students must also satisfy each of the UCSC general education requirements with a course graded C or better.

Special: Cross-registration is possible with other University of California campuses, Hampshire College, the University of New Hampshire, and the University of New Mexico. UCSC also offers work-study, a Washington semester, internships in many arenas, study abroad in 34 countries, student-designed majors, dual majors, and a B.A.-B.S. degree in earth sciences, chemistry, and computer science. There are including Phi Beta Kappa and a freshman honors program.

Faculty/Classroom: 58% of faculty are male; 42% are female. All teach and do research. Graduate students teach 1% of introductory courses.

Admissions: 52% of the 2013-2014 applicants were accepted. The SAT scores for the 2013-2014 freshman class were: Critical Reading--27% below 500, 36% between 500 and 599, 29% between 600 and 699, and 8% between 700 and 800; Math--21% below 500, 34% between 500 and 599, 33% between 600 and 699, and 11% between 700 and 800; Writing--26% below 500, 38% between 500 and 599, 30% between 600 and 699, and 6% between 700 and 800. The ACT scores were 23% below 21, 21% between 21 and 23, 24% between 24 and 26, 12% between 27 and 28, and 18% above 28. 100% of the current freshmen were in the top fifth of their class; 100% were in the top two fifths.

Requirements: The SAT or ACT is required. The ACT Optional Writing test is also required. In addition, Applicants must be graduates of an accredited secondary school or have a GED certificate. They should have completed 15 academic credits, including 4 years of English, 3 of math, and 2 each of foreign language, history, lab science, visual or performing arts, and college preparatory electives. Auditions are required for music majors, and portfolios are required for art majors. All students must submit a personal statement. Nonresidents must meet additional requirements. A GPA of 2.8 is required. AP credits are accepted. Important factors in the admissions decision are advanced placement or honors courses, evidence of special talent, and extracurricular activities record.

Procedure: Freshmen are admitted fall and winter. Entrance exams should be taken by December of the senior year. Applications should be filed by November 30 for fall entry, along with a $70 fee. Notifications are sent March 31. applicants were on the 2013 waiting list; were admitted. Applications are accepted online.

Transfer: 1005 transfer students enrolled in 2012-2013. Applicants should have completed 84 quarter credits, with a GPA of 2.4 required for California residents and 2.8 for nonresidents, and all subject areas must be completed. No senior transfers are accepted. 35 of 180 credits required for the bachelor's degree must be completed at UCSC.

Visiting: There are regularly scheduled orientations for prospective students. There are guides for informal visits and visitors may sit in on classes. To schedule a visit, contact the Office of Admissions at (831) 459-4008.

Financial Aid: In 2013-2014, 68% of continuing full-time students received some form of financial aid. 56% of continuing full-time students received need-based aid. The average freshman award was $23,293. Need-based scholarships or need-based grants averaged $18,108 ; need-based self-help aid (loans and jobs) averaged $6,663; and other non-need-based awards and non-need-based scholarships averaged $10,897. The average financial indebtedness of the 2013 graduate was $19,851. The FAFSA is required. The priority date for freshman financial aid applications for fall entry is January 1. The deadline for filing freshman financial aid applications for fall entry is March 2.

International Students: There are 806 international students enrolled.

They must take the TOEFL with a minimum score of 550 on the paper-based TOEFL (PBT) or 83 on the Internet-based version (iBT). They must also take the SAT or ACT.

Computers: All students may access the system. There are no time limits and no fees.

Graduates: From July 1, 2012 to June 30, 2013, 3958 bachelor's degrees were awarded. The most popular majors were biological and life sciences (16%), social sciences (15%), and psychology (13%). In an average class, 4% graduate in 3 years or less, 55% graduate in 4 years or less, 70% graduate in 5 years or less, and 74% graduate in 6 years or less.

Admissions Contact: Michael Mc Cawley, Director of Admissions. E-Mail: *admissions@ucsc.edu* Web: *www.uscs.edu*

UNIVERSITY OF LA VERNE D-5

La Verne, CA 91750 (909) 392-2800
(800) 876-4858; (909) 392-2714

Full-time: 1054 men, 1541 women	**Faculty:** 214
Part-time: 37 men, 50 women	**Ph.D.s:** 81%
Graduate: 961 men, 1468 women	**Student/Faculty:** 14 to 1
Year: 4-1-4, summer session	**Tuition:** $35,000
Application Deadline: February 1	**Room & Board:** $12,010
Freshman Class: 8264 applied, 2843 accepted, 563 enrolled	
SAT CR/M/W: 510/520/510	**ACT:** 22 **VERY COMPETITIVE**

Since 1891, the University of La Verne has been dedicated to the belief that a quality, values-based education enriches the human condition by engendering service, scholarly accomplishment, and professionalism. Though decades of growth have changed its appearance and reach, La Verne has retained its sense of purpose, seeking to provide students with individual attention to spark personal growth through intellectual challenge and development. The University takes pride in knowing its nearly 50,000 alumni worldwide have made a difference in their professions and communities. There are 3 undergraduate schools and 4 graduate schools. In addition to regional accreditation, La Verne has baccalaureate program accreditation with NCATE. The library contains 181,576 volumes, 1,068 microform items, and 1,640 audio/video tapes/CDs/DVDs, and subscribes to 37,287 periodicals including electronic. Computerized library services include interlibrary loans, database searching, Internet access, and Wi-Fi capability. Special learning facilities include an art gallery, natural history museum, radio station, TV station, a theater, archeology lab, and nuclear magnetic resonance (NMR) facility. The -acre campus is in a suburban area The University's main campus is located on the eastern edge of Los Angeles County, some 30 miles from downtown Los Angeles. Its 38-acre campus is located in the City of La Verne's historic Old Town district. Including any residence halls, there are 35 buildings.

Student Life: 97% of undergraduates are from California. Others are from 19 states, and 10 foreign countries. 51% are Hispanic; 26% White. The average age of freshmen is 18; all undergraduates, 20. 13% do not continue beyond their first year; 59% remain to graduate.

Housing: 837 students can be accommodated in college housing, which includes single-sex and coed dorms. In addition, there are special-interest houses. On-campus housing is available on a first-come, first-served basis, and is available on a lottery system for upperclassmen. Priority is given to out-of-town students. 68% of students commute. Alcohol is not permitted. All students may keep cars.

Activities: 7% of men belong to 1 local and 2 national fraternities; 16% of women belong to 2 local and 3 national sororities. There are 66 groups on campus, including art, band, choir, chorale, chorus, communications, computers, dance, debate, drama, environmental, ethnic, forensics, gay, honors, international, jazz band, literary magazine, musical theater, newspaper, pep band, photography, political, professional, radio and TV, religious, social, social service, and student government. Popular campus events include Homecoming, Club Day, and Greek Week.

Sports: There are 11 intercollegiate sports for men and 9 for women. Facilities include a football field, soccer field, and track. Indoor gym with a weight and fitness centers.

Disabled Students: Facilities include wheelchair ramps, elevators, special parking, specially equipped restrooms, lowered drinking fountains, and lowered telephones.

Services: Counseling and information services are available, as is tutoring in most subjects. There is a reader service for the blind, and remedial math and writing. Students may use the Learning Enhancement Center or schedule tutoring free of charge.

Campus Safety and Security: Measures include 24-hour foot and vehicle patrol, emergency notification system, and security escort services. There are shuttle buses, emergency telephones, lighted pathways/sidewalks, and controlled access to dorms/residences.

Programs of Study: La Verne confers B.A., and B.S. degrees. Associate, master's, and doctoral degrees are also awarded. Bachelor's degrees are awarded in BIOLOGICAL SCIENCE (biology/biological science and environmental biology), BUSINESS (accounting, business administration and management, business economics, electronic business, institutional management, and international business management), COMMUNICATIONS AND THE ARTS (art, art history and appreciation, broadcasting, communications, comparative literature, dramatic arts, English, French, German, journalism, music, photography, Spanish, and speech/debate/rhetoric), COMPUTER AND PHYSICAL SCIENCE (chemistry, computer science, mathematics, natural sciences, and physics), EDUCATION (athletic training and education), ENGINEERING AND ENVIRONMENTAL DESIGN (computer engineering and environmental science), HEALTH PROFESSIONS (health care administration), SOCIAL SCIENCE (anthropology, behavioral science, child psychology/development, criminology, history, international studies, liberal arts/general studies, paralegal studies, philosophy, physical fitness/movement, political science/government, psychology, public administration, religion, social science, and sociology). Business administration, natural science, education and psychology are the strongest academically. Business administration, organizational management, liberal studies, child development and psychology have the largest enrollments.

Required: 128 semester hours, 44 must be taken at La Verne. At least 16 semester hours of the last 32 must be taken at La Verne. The La Verne Experience integrates curricular, co-curricular, and community engagement activities for traditional undergraduates and spans throughout their four years at La Verne.

Special: Study abroad programs, work-study programs, student-designed majors, accelerated programs for adults. There are 9 national honor societies and a freshman honors program.

Faculty/Classroom: 50% of faculty are male; 50% are female. No introductory courses are taught by graduate students. The average class size in an introductory lecture is 17 and in a regular course is 17.

Admissions: 34% of the 2013-2014 applicants were accepted. The SAT scores for the 2013-2014 freshman class were: Critical Reading--42% below 500, 44% between 500 and 599, 14% between 600 and 699, and 1% between 700 and 800; Math--34% below 500, 51% between 500 and 599, 14% between 600 and 699, and 1% between 700 and 800; Writing--45% below 500, 44% between 500 and 599, 10% between 600 and 699, and 1% between 700 and 800. The ACT scores were 35% below 21, 35% between 21 and 23, 21% between 24 and 26, 7% between 27 and 28, and 3% above 28. 49% of the current freshmen were in the top fifth of their class; 80% were in the top two fifths. 3 freshmen graduated first in their class.

Requirements: The ACT Optional Writing test is required. The SAT or ACT is recommended. Applicants must be graduates of an accredited secondary school. To apply for admission to the University, the following documents must be submitted to the Office of Admission: Application for Admission and Application Fee (using the La Verne Application for Admission or the Common Application); Personal Statement; High School Transcripts; SAT I or ACT Test Scores; Letter of Recommendation. AP and CLEP credits are accepted.

Procedure: Freshmen are admitted fall and spring. Entrance exams should be taken during the junior or senior year. There are deferred admissions and rolling admissions plans. Applications should be filed by February 1 for fall entry; December 1 for spring entry, along with a $50 fee. Notifications are sent December 1. Applications are accepted online.

Transfer: 221 transfer students enrolled in 2012-2013. Transfer requirements include: 28 college semester units completed upon enrollment at La Verne, 2.7 GPA, College-level English and college-level math (typically college algebra or statistics or pre-calculus and higher). 44 of 128 credits required for the bachelor's degree must be completed at La Verne.

Visiting: There are regularly scheduled orientations for prospective students, Student visits include campus tours, faculty and student panels, and meals. There are guides for informal visits, visitors may sit in on classes, and stay overnight. To schedule a visit, contact the Admissions Office.

Financial Aid: In 2013-2014, 86% of all full-time freshmen and 83% of continuing full-time students received some form of financial aid. 82% of all full-time freshmen and 77% of continuing full-time students received need-based aid. The average freshman award was $29,569. Need-based scholarships or need-based grants averaged $9,600; and need-based self-help aid (loans and jobs) averaged $8,073. The average financial indebtedness of the 2013 graduate was $30,677. The FAFSA, and Cal Grant Application is required. The priority date for freshman financial aid applications for fall entry is March 2.

International Students: There are 123 international students enrolled. The school actively recruits these students. They must take the TOEFL with a minimum score of 550 on the paper-based TOEFL (PBT) or 80 on the Internet-based version (iBT), the Comprehensive English Language Test, and the college's own test, SAT critical reading score of 550, a minimum score of 6.5 on IELTS. They must also take the SAT or ACT.

Computers: All students may access the system 24 hours, 7 days a week. There are no time limits and no fees.

Graduates: From July 1, 2012 to June 30, 2013, 414 bachelor's degrees were awarded. The most popular majors were business administration (14%), psychology (10%), and liberal studies (10%). In an average class, 42% graduate in 4 years or less, 55% graduate in 5 years or less, and 59% graduate in 6 years or less.

Admissions Contact: Ana Liza V. Zell, Associate Dean of Undergraduate Admissions. E-Mail: *admission@laverne.edu* Web: *www.laverne.edu*

UNIVERSITY OF REDLANDS E-5

Redlands, CA 92373-0999 (909) 335-4074
(800) 455-5064; (909) 335-4089

Full-time: 975 men, 1375 women	**Faculty:** n/av; IIA, av$
Part-time: 10 men, 15 women	**Ph.D.s:** 86%
Graduate: 30 men, 20 women	**Student/Faculty:** n/av
Year: semesters	**Tuition:** $30,500
Application Deadline: open	**Room & Board:** $10,000
Freshman Class: n/av	
SAT or ACT: required	**VERY COMPETITIVE**

University of Redlands, founded in 1907, is a private institution that offers programs in liberal and fine arts, business, and teacher preparation. Figures in the above capsule and in this profile are approximate. There are 2 undergraduate schools and 4 graduate schools. The library contains 421,219 volumes, 317,465 microform items, and 6,091 audio/video tapes/CDs/DVDs, and subscribes to 12,800 periodicals including electronic. Computerized library services include interlibrary loans, database searching, and Internet access. Special learning facilities include an art gallery, radio station, a language lab, a computer center, and a geographic information systems lab. The 160-acre campus is in a suburban area 60 miles east of Los Angeles. Including any residence halls, there are 86 buildings.

Student Life: 71% of undergraduates are from California. Others are from 45 states, 8 foreign countries, and Canada. 60% are white; 12% Hispanic. The average age of freshmen is 18; all undergraduates, 20. 15% do not continue beyond their first year; 60% remain to graduate.

Housing: 1621 students can be accommodated in college housing, which includes single-sex and coed dorms, on-campus apartments, and off-campus apartments. In addition, there are honors houses, special-interest houses, fraternity houses, and sorority houses. On-campus housing is guaranteed for all 4 years. 70% of students live on campus. All students may keep cars.

Activities: 3% of men belong to 6 local fraternities; 6% of women belong to 5 local sororities. There are 105 groups on campus, including art, band, cheerleading, chess, choir, chorale, chorus, dance, debate, drama, drill team, ethnic, film, gay, honors, international, jazz band, literary magazine, musical theater, newspaper, opera, orchestra, pep band, photography, political, professional, radio and TV, religious, social, social service, student government, symphony, and yearbook. Popular campus events include Mayfest, Multicultural Festival, and Feast of Lights.

Sports: There are 10 intercollegiate sports for men and 10 for women, and 7 intramural sports for men and 7 for women. Facilities include a fitness center, an aquatic center, a football stadium, tennis courts, and baseball, softball, soccer, and lacrosse fields.

Disabled Students: 25% of the campus is accessible. Facilities include wheelchair ramps, elevators, special parking, specially equipped restrooms, special class scheduling, lowered drinking fountains, and lowered telephones.

Services: Counseling and information services are available, as is tutoring in every subject. There is a reader service for the blind.

Campus Safety and Security: Measures include 24-hour foot and vehicle patrol, self-defense education, and security escort services. There are shuttle buses, emergency telephones, lighted pathways/sidewalks, and safety whistles.

Programs of Study: Redlands confers B.A., B.S., and B.Mus. degrees. Master's degrees are also awarded. Bachelor's degrees are awarded in AGRICULTURE (environmental studies), BIOLOGICAL SCIENCE (biochemistry and biology/biological science), BUSINESS (accounting and business administration and management), COMMUNICATIONS AND THE ARTS (art, creative writing, dramatic arts, English, English literature, French, German, music, Spanish, and studio art), COMPUTER AND PHYSICAL SCIENCE (chemistry, computer science, information sciences and systems, mathematics, and physics), EDUCATION (music education), ENGINEERING AND ENVIRONMENTAL DESIGN (environmental science), SOCIAL SCIENCE (anthropology, Asian/Oriental studies, economics, history, interdisciplinary studies, international relations, liberal arts/general studies, philosophy, political science/government, psychology, religion, and sociology). Liberal arts is the strongest academically. Business has the largest enrollment.

Required: Requirements for graduation vary according to the degree and major. Students must complete at least 128 units with at least 32 in residence and maintain a minimum GPA of 2.0. Students pursuing a B.S. degree must fulfill an additional field requirement or a minor. A comprehensive exam is required for some programs. A liberal arts core curriculum, first-year seminar, community service, and participation in 2 May terms are required.

Special: Cross-registration with sister colleges, various internships, and study abroad in 50 countries are offered. A Washington semester, a Sacramento program, various work-study programs, B.A.-B.S. degrees, a liberal studies degree, dual majors, and accelerated degree programs are available. Students may pursue nondegree study, take advantage of pass/fail options, and receive credit for life or work experience. At the Johnston Center for Integrative Studies, students design their own majors and courses of study. There are 4 national honor societies, including Phi Beta Kappa, a freshman honors program, and 23 departmental honors programs.

Faculty/Classroom: 48% of faculty are male; 52% are female. All teach undergraduates. No introductory courses are taught by graduate students. The average class size in an introductory lecture is 20; in a laboratory is 10; and in a regular course is 12.

Requirements: The SAT or ACT is required. Applicants should complete at least 16 credits in academic areas, including 4 years of English, 3 years of math, up to and including Algebra II, and 2 to 3 years of foreign language, sciences, and social studies. AP and CLEP credits are accepted. Important factors in the admissions decision are advanced placement or honors courses, leadership record, and personality/intangible qualities.

Procedure: Freshmen are admitted fall and spring. Entrance exams should be taken prior to application. There are deferred admissions and rolling admissions plans. Check with the school for current application deadlines. The fall 2011 application fee was $45. Applications are accepted online.

Transfer: The SAT or the ACT may be required of transfer applicants, depending on how many units are accepted. 32 of 128 credits required for the bachelor's degree must be completed at Redlands.

Visiting: There are regularly scheduled orientations for prospective students, including campus tours at 10 a.m., 1 p.m., and 4 p.m., on weekdays and 11 a.m. and 1 p.m. on Saturdays during the school year, interviews with counselors, department heads, and coaches, and sitting in on classes. There are guides for informal visits, visitors may sit in on classes, and stay overnight. To schedule a visit, contact the Admissions office.

Financial Aid: The FAFSA and the college's own financial statement, and the GPA verification form for California residents are required. Check with the school for current application deadlines.

International Students: The school actively recruits these students. They must take the TOEFL. They must also take the SAT or ACT.

Computers: Wireless access is available. Housed within the Fletcher Jones Center are labs/classrooms, a hands-on lab, and a faculty technology center. All labs/classrooms are available when not being used for class. All students may access the system. There are no time limits and no fees.

Admissions Contact: Paul M. Driscoll, Dean of Admissions. E-Mail: *admissions@uor.edu* Web: *www.redlands.edu*

UNIVERSITY OF SAN DIEGO D-5

San Diego, CA 92110 (619) 260-4506
(800) 248-4873; (619) 260-6836

Full-time: 2459 men, 3027 women	**Faculty:** 299; I, av$
Part-time: 89 men, 90 women	**Ph.D.s:** 96%
Graduate: 1027 men, 1629 women	**Student/Faculty:** 15 to 1
Year: 4-1-4, summer session	**Tuition:** $41,392
Application Deadline: December 15	**Room & Board:** $11,910
Freshman Class: 16578 applied, 7060 accepted, 1074 enrolled	
SAT CR/M/W: 600/620/610	**ACT:** 28 **HIGHLY COMPETITIVE+**

The University of San Diego, founded in 1949, is a private, Catholic liberal arts university. There are 4 undergraduate schools and 6 graduate schools. In addition to regional accreditation, USD has baccalaureate program accreditation with AACSB, ABET, and NCATE. The 2 libraries contain 1.0 million volumes, 1.2 million microform items, 16,860 audio/video tapes/CDs/DVDs, and subscribe to 38,368 periodicals including electronic. Computerized library services include interlibrary loans, database searching, Internet access, and Wi-Fi capability. Special learning facilities include an art gallery, radio station, TV station, media center, child development center, greenhouse. The 180-acre campus is in an urban area 5 miles north of downtown San Diego. Including any residence halls, there are 85 buildings.

Student Life: 62% of undergraduates are from California. Others are from 50 states, 66 foreign countries, and Canada. 58% are from public schools. 48% are Catholic; 23% Protestant; 21% claim no religious affiliation. The average age of freshmen is 18; all undergraduates, 20. 10% do not continue beyond their first year; 75% remain to graduate.

Housing: 2500 students can be accommodated in college housing, which includes single-sex and coed dorms and on-campus apartments. In addition, there are honors houses and special-interest houses. On-campus housing is guaranteed for the freshman year only, is available on a first-come, first-served basis, and is available on a lottery system for upperclassmen. 56% of students commute. All students may keep cars.

Activities: 21% of men belong to 6 national fraternities; 36% of women belong to 8 national sororities. There are 75 groups on campus, including academic, art, cheerleading, choir, chorale, dance, debate, drama, environmental, ethnic, gay, honors, international, jazz band, musical theater, newspaper, pep band, political, professional, radio and TV, religious, social, social service, student government, and symphony. Popular campus events include Alcala bazaar, Orientation week, Sponsored Concerts and Events.

Sports: There are 8 intercollegiate sports for men and 10 for women, and 10 intramural sports for men and 10 for women. Facilities include a sports center, a 6000 seat stadium for football and soccer, tennis courts, swimming pools, newly renovated 1700 seat baseball facility, and the Mission Bay Aquatic Center.

Disabled Students: 85% of the campus is accessible. Facilities include wheelchair ramps, elevators, special parking, specially equipped restrooms, lowered drinking fountains. Individual needs can be accommodated.

Services: Counseling and information services are available, as is tutoring in most subjects.

Campus Safety and Security: Measures include 24-hour foot and vehicle patrol, emergency notification system, self-defense education, and security escort services. There are shuttle buses, emergency telephones, lighted pathways/sidewalks, and controlled access to dorms/residences.

Programs of Study: USD confers B.A., B.A./B.S., B.Acc. and B.B.A. degrees. Master's and doctoral degrees are also awarded. Bachelor's degrees are awarded in AGRICULTURE (environmental studies), BIOLOGICAL SCIENCE (biochemistry, biology/biological science, biophysics, and marine science), BUSINESS (accounting, business administration and management, business economics, finance, international business management, marketing management, and real estate), COMMUNICATIONS AND THE ARTS (art history, art and design, communications, English, French, music, Spanish, theatre arts, and visual and performing arts), COMPUTER AND PHYSICAL SCIENCE (chemistry, computer science, mathematics, and physics), ENGINEERING AND ENVIRONMENTAL DESIGN (electrical/electronics engineering, industrial engineering, and mechanical engineering), SOCIAL SCIENCE (anthropology, architectural studies, behavioral science, economics, ethnic studies, history, humanities, international relations, Italian studies, liberal arts/general studies, philosophy, political science/government, psychology, sociology, and theological studies). Business administration, finance and communication studies have the largest enrollments.

Required: All students must take 124 credit hours,including 36 to 72 in their major, while maintaining a minimum GPA of 2.0. Distribution requirements include 9 units each of religious studies and humanities and fine arts, 6 each of philosophy, natural sciences, and social sciences, 3 or 4 of math, 3 of composition and literature, 3 semesters of foreign language, as well as 3 units upper division writing and 3 units in diversity of the human experience.

Special: A B.A.-B.S. degree is offered in electrical, industrial and mechanical engineering. Internships in all disciplines, study abroad in 35 countries and work-study programs on campus are available. The Washington Center Academic Seminar takes place each January in Washington, DC. The Department of Political Science and International Relations offers an intersession course (PS434) which enables students to earn 3 units for attending the seminar. There are 22 national honor societies, including Phi Beta Kappa, and a freshman honors program.

Faculty/Classroom: 49% of faculty are male; 51% are female. No introductory courses are taught by graduate students. The average class size in a laboratory is 49 and in a regular course is 23.

Admissions: 43% of the 2013-2014 applicants were accepted. The SAT scores for the 2013-2014 freshman class were: Critical Reading--9% below 500, 39% between 500 and 599, 42% between 600 and 699, and 10% between 700 and 800; Math--7% below 500, 30% between 500 and 599, 49% between 600 and 699, and 14% between 700 and 800; Writing--8% below 500, 34% between 500 and 599, 46% between 600 and 699, and 12% between 700 and 800. The ACT scores were 3% below 21, 11% between 21 and 23, 19% between 24 and 26, 26% between 27 and 28, and 41% above 28. 69% of the current freshmen were in the top fifth of their class; 91% were in the top two fifths. 39 freshmen graduated first in their class.

Requirements: The SAT is required. In addition, applicants should present a well-balanced secondary school program of college preparatory courses in English, foreign language, math, laboratory science, history, and social science. Both the content of the academic program as well as the quality of performance is considered. In addition, SAT/ACT results are used to broaden understanding of the applicant's potential. Participation in extracurricular activities at the school and in the community or church is taken into consideration in the admission decision. AP and CLEP credits are accepted. Important factors in the admissions decision are advanced placement or honors courses, extracurricular activities record, and ability to finance college education.

Procedure: Freshmen are admitted fall, spring, and summer. Applications should be filed by December 15 for fall entry; October 1 for spring entry, along with a $55 fee. 1791 applicants were on the 2013 waiting list; 625 were admitted. Applications are accepted online.

Transfer: 534 transfer students enrolled in 2012-2013. Transfer students must have a minimum GPA of 3.0 and have earned 24 credit hours. 30 of 124 credits required for the bachelor's degree must be completed at USD.

Visiting: There are regularly scheduled orientations for prospective students, tours and information sessions offered by the Admissions Office Monday through Friday 10 a.m. and 1:30 p.m., and most Saturdays from November through April at 11:00 a.m. There are guides for informal visits, visitors may sit in on classes, and stay overnight. To schedule a visit, contact the Undergraduate Admissions Office.

Financial Aid: In 2013-2014, 76% of all full-time freshmen and 72% of continuing full-time students received some form of financial aid. 56% of all full-time freshmen and 53% of continuing full-time students received need-based aid. The average freshman award was $29,600. Need-based scholarships or need-based grants averaged $23,756; need-based self-help aid (loans and jobs) averaged $6,750; non-need-based athletic scholarships averaged $33,243; and other non-need-based awards and non-need-based scholarships averaged $12,914. 22% of undergraduate students work part-time. Average annual earnings from campus work are $2933. The average financial indebtedness of the 2013 graduate was $29,115. The FAFSA is required. The priority date for freshman financial aid applications for fall entry is March 2. The deadline for filing freshman financial aid applications for fall entry is March 2.

International Students: There are 391 international students enrolled. The school actively recruits these students. They must take the TOEFL with a minimum score of 550 on the paper-based TOEFL (PBT) or 80 on the Internet-based version (iBT). They must also take the SAT or ACT.

Computers: All students may access the system. There are no time limits and no fees.

Graduates: From July 1, 2012 to June 30, 2013, 1336 bachelor's degrees were awarded. The most popular majors were business administration (11%), finance (10%), and communication (9%). 116 companies recruited on campus in 2012-2013. In an average class, 66% graduate in 4 years or less, 75% graduate in 5 years or less, and 75% graduate in 6 years or less. Of the 2012 graduating class, 81% were enrolled in graduate school within 6 months of graduation, and 14% were employed.

Admissions Contact: Minh-Ha Hoang, Director of Admissions. E-Mail: *admissions@sandiego.edu* Web: *www.sandiego.edu/admissions/undergraduate*

UNIVERSITY OF SAN FRANCISCO B-3

San Francisco, CA 94117 **(415) 422-6563**
(800) CALL USF; (415) 422-2217

Full-time: 2247 men, 3830 women	**Faculty:** 480; I, av$
Part-time: 125 men, 142 women	**Ph.D.s:** 93%
Graduate: 1328 men, 2345 women	**Student/Faculty:** 15 to 1
Year: 4-1-4, summer session	**Tuition:** $37,924
Application Deadline:	**Room & Board:** $12,750

Freshman Class: 12029 applied, 6973 accepted, 1190 enrolled
SAT or ACT: required

VERY COMPETITIVE

The University of San Francisco, founded in 1855, is a private Roman Catholic institution run by the Jesuit Fathers and offering degree programs in the arts and sciences, business, education, nursing, and law. Figures in the above capsule and in this profile are approximate. There are 3 undergraduate schools and 5 graduate schools. In addition to regional accreditation, USF has baccalaureate program accreditation with AACSB, CSAB, and NLN. The 2 libraries contain 1,000,000 volumes, 900,000 microform items, and 6,000 audio/video tapes/CDs/DVDs, and subscribe to 2,500 periodicals including electronic. Computerized library services include interlibrary loans, database searching, Internet access, and Wi-Fi capability. Special learning facilities include an art gallery, radio station, TV station, rare book room, the Institute for Chinese-Western Cultural History, and the Center for Pacific Rim Studies. The 55-acre campus is in an urban area in the heart of the city. Including any residence halls, there are 17 buildings.

Student Life: 69% of undergraduates are from California. Others are from 50 states, 79 foreign countries, and Canada. 49% are from public schools. 37% are White; 24% Asian American; 18% Hispanic; 13% Foreign. 38% are Catholic; 13% Buddhist, Hindu, and Muslim. The average age of freshmen is 18; all undergraduates, 20. 14% do not continue beyond their first year; 70% remain to graduate.

Housing: 2250 students can be accommodated in college housing, which includes single-sex and coed dorms, on-campus apartments, and off-campus apartments. In addition, there are special-interest houses, a multicultural floor, an academic interest floor, a freshman experiences floor, and a quiet floor. On-campus housing is guaranteed for the freshman year only. 64% of students live on campus. Alcohol is not permitted. All students may keep cars.

Activities: 1% of men belong to 2 local and 1 national fraternities; 1% of women belong to 4 local and 2 national sororities. There are 100 groups on campus, including band, cheerleading, choir, chorale, chorus, computers, dance, drama, environmental, ethnic, honors, international, jazz band, literary magazine, musical theater, newspaper, orchestra, pep band, political, professional, radio and TV, religious, social, social service, student government, and yearbook. Popular campus events include Founders Day and International Week.

Sports: There are 7 intercollegiate sports for men and 7 for women, and 8 intramural sports for men and 8 for women. Facilities include a 600-seat soccer stadium, a recreation center with a 50-meter swimming pool, a multipurpose gym, a weight room, a dance and aerobics room, a martial arts room, and 5 racquetball/handball courts.

Disabled Students: 95% of the campus is accessible. Facilities include wheelchair ramps, elevators, special parking, specially equipped restrooms, lowered drinking fountains, and exam accommodations.

Services: Counseling and information services are available, as is tutoring in every subject. There is a reader service for the blind. There is a full-time counselor for learning-disabled students, as well as a learning and writing center for students in need of academic assistance.

Campus Safety and Security: Measures include 24-hour foot and vehicle patrol, emergency notification system, self-defense education, and security escort services. There are shuttle buses, emergency telephones, lighted pathways/sidewalks, and controlled access to dorms/residences.

Programs of Study: USF confers B.A., B.S., B.Arch., B.F.A., B.P.A., B.S.B.A. and B.S.N. degrees. Master's and doctoral degrees are also awarded. Bachelor's degrees are awarded in BIOLOGICAL SCIENCE (biology/biological science), BUSINESS (accounting, banking and finance, business administration and management, hospitality management services, hotel/motel and restaurant management, international business management, management information systems, marketing/retailing/ merchandising, and organizational behavior), COMMUNICATIONS AND THE ARTS (art history and appreciation, arts administration/ management, communications, drawing, English, fine arts, French, graphic design, illustration, media arts, painting, performing arts, Spanish, and visual and performing arts), COMPUTER AND PHYSICAL SCIENCE (chemistry, computer science, information sciences and systems, mathematics, and physics), EDUCATION (athletic training, elementary education, middle school education, and secondary education), ENGINEERING AND ENVIRONMENTAL DESIGN (architecture and environmental science), HEALTH PROFESSIONS (exercise science and nursing), SOCIAL SCIENCE (economics, history, Latin American studies, law enforcement and corrections, philosophy, political science/government, psychology, public administration, religion, sociology, and theological studies). Sciences and business are the strongest academically. Business, communications, nursing, and psychology have the largest enrollment.

Required: All students must maintain a GPA of at least 2.0 and take 128 credit hours, including 58 in upper-division courses. 36 to 58 hours are required in the major. The current general education requirements include 9 units each of basic skills and history/social science, 6 each of philosophy, religious studies, cultural perspectives, natural science, and literature and fine arts, and 3 of ethics.

Special: Cross-registration with the San Francisco Consortium, internships with local business, social services, and research opportunities are available. Study abroad in Europe and Japan, work-study programs on and off campus and with social service agencies, a B.A.-B.S. degree in exercise and sports science, dual majors in liberal arts and education, 3-2 engineering degrees with the University of Southern California, student-designed majors, nondegree study, and limited pass/fail options are also available. The College of Professional Studies is a degree completion program for working adults. There are 3 national honor societies, a freshman honors program, and 1 departmental honors programs.

Faculty/Classroom: 54% of faculty are male; 46% are female. 90% teach undergraduates, 75% do research, and 90% do both. No introductory courses are taught by graduate students. The average class size in an introductory lecture is 28; in a laboratory is 14; and in a regular course is 20.

Admissions: 58% of the 2013-2014 applicants were accepted. 47% of the current freshmen were in the top fifth of their class; 82% were in the top two fifths. 1 freshman graduated first in the class.

Requirements: The SAT or ACT is required. Applicants are required to have 20 academic units, based on 6 years of academic electives, 4 of English, 3 each of math and social studies, and 2 each of foreign language and lab science. An essay is required. The GED is accepted. A GPA of 3.0 is required. AP and CLEP credits are accepted. Important factors in the admissions decision are extracurricular activities record, evidence of special talent, and leadership record.

Procedure: Freshmen are admitted fall and spring. Entrance exams should be taken during the first half of the senior year. There are deferred admissions and rolling admissions plans. Check with the school for current application deadlines. The application fee is $55. Notification of early decision is sent January 15; regular decision, on a rolling basis. Applications are accepted online.

Transfer: 452 transfer students enrolled in 2012-2013. Applicants need a minimum GPA of 3.0, with minimum 2.0 in sciences. 45 of 128 credits required for the bachelor's degree must be completed at USF.

Visiting: There are regularly scheduled orientations for prospective students, including a tour of campus, academic buildings, library, residence halls, recreation centers, and a group information session hosted by an admissions staff member. There are guides for informal visits, visitors may sit in on classes, and stay overnight. To schedule a visit, contact the Office of Admissions.

Financial Aid: In 2013-2014, 77% of all full-time freshmen and 68% of continuing full-time students received some form of financial aid. 76% of all full-time freshmen and 64% of continuing full-time students received need-based aid. The average freshman award was $28,651. Need-based scholarships or need-based grants averaged $24,168 ($56,761 maximum); need-based self-help aid (loans and jobs) averaged $14,305 ($54,774 maximum); non-need-based athletic scholarships averaged $17,741 ($26,140 maximum); other non-need-based awards and non-need-based scholarships averaged $8,573 ($23,000 maximum); and $14,622 from other forms of aid. The average financial indebtedness of the 2013 graduate was $29,059. The FAFSA is required. The deadline for filing freshman financial aid applications for fall entry is February 1.

International Students: There are 731 international students enrolled. The school actively recruits these students. They must take the TOEFL with a minimum score of 550 on the paper-based TOEFL (PBT) or 79 on the Internet-based version (iBT). They must also take the SAT.

Computers: All students may access the system. There are no time limits and no fees.

Graduates: From July 1, 2012 to June 30, 2013, 1323 bachelor's degrees were awarded. The most popular majors were finance (7%) and nursing (12%). 100 companies recruited on campus in 2012-2013. In an average class, 1% graduate in 3 years or less, 45% graduate in 4 years or less, 65% graduate in 5 years or less, and 70% graduate in 6 years or less.

Admissions Contact: Michael Hughes, Director of Admissions. E-Mail: *admissions@usfca.edu* Web: *www.usfca.edu*

UNIVERSITY OF SOUTHERN CALIFORNIA C-5

Los Angeles, CA 90089 **(213) 740-1111; (213) 740-6364**

Full-time: 8637 men, 8982 women	**Faculty:** 1572; I
Part-time: 395 men, 302 women	**Ph.D.s:** 90%
Graduate: 10313 men, 11329 women	**Student/Faculty:** 9 to 1
Year: semesters, summer session	**Tuition:** $44,463
Application Deadline: January 10	**Room & Board:** $12,440

Freshman Class: 46104 applied, 9187 accepted, 3021 enrolled
SAT or ACT: required

MOST COMPETITIVE

University of Southern California, founded in 1880, is a private institution offering undergraduate and graduate programs in liberal arts, fine arts, education, business, law, dentistry, engineering, communications, and health professions. There are 13 undergraduate schools and 18 graduate schools. In addition to regional accreditation, USC has baccalaureate program accreditation with AACSB, ABET, ACEJMC, ACPE, ADA, APTA, CSWE, NAAB, NASM, and NLN. The 23 libraries contain 4.8 million volumes, 6.6 million microform items, and 84,953 audio/video tapes/CDs/ DVDs. Computerized library services include interlibrary loans, database searching, Internet access, and Wi-Fi capability. Special learning facilities include an art gallery, natural history museum, radio station, TV station, state-of-the-art cinema/film-making facilities, labs, wind tunnel, and marine science center. The 226-acre campus is in an urban area 3 miles south of the Los Angeles Civic Center. Including any residence halls, there are 166 buildings.

Student Life: 68% of undergraduates are from California. Others are from 50 states, and 87 foreign countries. 39% are White; 23% Asian American; 14% Hispanic; 12% Foreign. The average age of freshmen is 18; all undergraduates, 20. 3% do not continue beyond their first year; 97% remain to graduate.

Housing: 6990 students can be accommodated in college housing, which includes coed dorms, on-campus apartments, off-campus apartments, and married student housing. In addition, there are special-interest houses, fraternity houses, sorority houses, and a Greek honors house, African American, Jewish, Latino, LGBT, multicultural floors; substance-free housing; business, cinema, environmental, law and women in science and engineering floors; and an international residential hall. On-campus housing is guaranteed for the freshman year only, is available on a first-come, first-served basis, and is available on a lottery system for upperclassmen. 62% of students commute. All students may keep cars.

Activities: 25% of men belong to 6 local and 30 national fraternities; 21% of women belong to 7 local and 18 national sororities. There are 769 groups on campus, including art, band, cheerleading, chess, choir, chorale, chorus, computers, dance, debate, drama, drill team, environmental, ethnic, film, forensics, gay, honors, international, jazz band, literary magazine, marching band, musical theater, newspaper, opera, orchestra, pep band, photography, political, professional, radio and TV, religious, social, social service, student government, symphony, and yearbook. Popular campus events include Springfest, International Food and Cultural Fair and Spectrum Concert Series.

Sports: There are 10 intercollegiate sports for men and 12 for women, and 30 intramural sports for men and 23 for women. Facilities include a student athletic center, a track, a gym, 2 Olympic pools, and tennis, swimming, and baseball stadiums.

Disabled Students: 97% of the campus is accessible. Facilities include wheelchair ramps, elevators, special parking, specially equipped restrooms, special housing. shuttle service for students with temporary disabilities.

Services: Counseling and information services are available, as is tutoring in every subject. There is a reader service for the blind. Accommodations are made for students with disabilities.

Campus Safety and Security: Measures include 24-hour foot and vehicle patrol, emergency notification system, self-defense education, and security escort services. There are shuttle buses, emergency telephones, lighted pathways/sidewalks, The safety department responds to calls for service on and off campus.

Programs of Study: USC confers B.A., B.S., B.Arch., B.F.A., B.Land.Arch. and B.M. degrees. Master's and doctoral degrees are also awarded. Bachelor's degrees are awarded in AGRICULTURE (environmental studies), BIOLOGICAL SCIENCE (biology/biological science, biophysics, and neurosciences), BUSINESS (accounting, business administration and management, and international business management), COMMUNICATIONS AND THE ARTS (art history and appreciation, broadcasting, classics, communications, comparative literature, creative writing, dramatic arts, East Asian languages and literature, English, English literature, film arts, fine arts, French, Italian, jazz, journalism, linguistics, music, music performance, playwriting/screenwriting, public relations, Russian, Spanish, studio art, theater design, theater management, video, and visual and performing arts), COMPUTER AND PHYSICAL SCIENCE (applied mathematics, astronomy, chemistry, computer science, geology, mathematics, physical sciences, and physics), ENGINEERING AND ENVIRONMENTAL DESIGN (aeronautical engineering, aerospace studies, architecture, biomedical engineering, chemical engineering, civil engineering, computer engineering, construction engineering, electrical/electronics engineering, environmental engineering, environmental science, industrial engineering, mechanical engineering, petroleum/natural gas engineering, and systems engineering), HEALTH PROFESSIONS (dental hygiene, exercise science, and occupational therapy), SOCIAL SCIENCE (African American studies, American studies, anthropology, Asian/American studies, classical/ancient civilization, East Asian studies, economics, ethics, politics, and social policy, geography, gerontology, history, international relations, Judaic studies, Latin American studies, philosophy, political science/government, psychology, religion, social science, sociology, and women's studies). Business, communications and biological sciences have the largest enrollments.

Required: All students must satisfy requirements in foreign language, freshman writing, general education, and take 1 multicultural course. Graduation requirements include a minimum of 128 credit hours and a minimum GPA of 2.0.

Special: Cross-registration is permitted with Hebrew Union College and Howard University. Internships in various majors, a Washington semester, work-study programs, study abroad in 29 countries, dual majors, a general studies degree, student-designed majors, a 3-2 engineering degree, and pass/fail options are available. Students are encouraged to pursue interdisciplinary study linking core art and science disciplines to professional programs. There are 50 national honor societies, including Phi Beta Kappa, and a freshman honors program.

Faculty/Classroom: 60% of faculty are male; 40% are female. 84% teach undergraduates. No introductory courses are taught by graduate students.

Admissions: 20% of the 2013-2014 applicants were accepted. The SAT scores for the 2013-2014 freshman class were: Critical Reading--3% below 500, 14% between 500 and 599, 47% between 600 and 699, and 36% between 700 and 800; Math--1% below 500, 8% between 500 and 599, 34% between 600 and 699, and 57% between 700 and 800; Writing--1% below 500, 9% between 500 and 599, 39% between 600 and 699, and 50% between 700 and 800. There were 251 National Merit finalists.

Requirements: The SAT or ACT is required. The ACT Optional Writing test is also required. In addition, 3 SAT Subject Tests are recommended. Graduation from an accredited secondary school is required. Applicants must have completed at least 13 year-long courses in English, humanities, math, natural sciences, social sciences, and foreign languages, plus 3 additional year-long courses in those areas or in computer science and, with some exceptions, theater, fine arts, journalism, music or speech. AP credits are accepted. Important factors in the admissions decision are advanced placement or honors courses, recommendations by school officials, and evidence of special talent.

Procedure: Freshmen are admitted fall and spring. Entrance exams should be taken by November of the senior year for scholarship applicants; by December for all others. Applications should be filed by January 10 for fall entry, along with a $80 fee. Notifications are sent April 1. Applications are accepted online.

Transfer: 1658 transfer students enrolled in 2012-2013. Transfer applicants must submit 30 units of transferable work with a strong GPA in a rigorous selection of courses. SAT or ACT scores are considered if 30 units have not been completed. 64 of 128 credits required for the bachelor's degree must be completed at USC.

Visiting: There are regularly scheduled orientations for prospective students. There are guides for informal visits, visitors may sit in on classes, and stay overnight. To schedule a visit, contact the Admission Office.

Financial Aid: In 2013-2014, 74% of all full-time freshmen and 69% of continuing full-time students received some form of financial aid. 41% of all full-time freshmen and 45% of continuing full-time students received need-based aid. The average freshman award was $32,811. Need-based scholarships or need-based grants averaged $30,378; need-based self-help aid (loans and jobs) averaged $5,720; non-need-based athletic scholarships averaged $36,606; and other non-need-based awards and non-need-based scholarships averaged $19,924. The average financial indebtedness of the 2013 graduate was $28,575. USC is a member of CSS. The CSS/Profile and FAFSA, and Parent and Student Federal Income Tax forms and all schedules are required. The priority date for freshman financial aid applications for fall entry is February 2.

International Students: There are 2237 international students enrolled. The school actively recruits these students. They must take the TOEFL. Undergraduate students who score 500 or better on the verbal portion of the SAT are exempted from providing TOEFL scores. Upon arrival students with low TOEFL scores are required to take our local English proficiency examination. They must also take the SAT or ACT.

Computers: All students may access the system. There are no time limits and no fees.

Graduates: From July 1, 2012 to June 30, 2013, 4539 bachelor's degrees were awarded. The most popular majors were business (19%), communication (6%), and psychology (5%). In an average class, 3% graduate in 3 years or less, 75% graduate in 4 years or less, 89% graduate in 5 years or less, and 90% graduate in 6 years or less.

Admissions Contact: Timothy Brunold, Dean of Admission. E-Mail: *admdean@usc.edu* Web: *www.usc.edu*

UNIVERSITY OF THE PACIFIC — B-3

Stockton, CA 95211 — (209) 946-2211
(800) 959-2867; (209) 946-2413

Full-time: 1811 men, 1969 women	**Faculty:** n/av; IIA, +$
Part-time: 48 men, 49 women	**Ph.D.s:** 74%
Graduate: 1101 men, 1443 women	**Student/Faculty:** 14 to 1
Year: semesters, summer session	**Tuition:** $39,810
Application Deadline: February 15	**Room & Board:** $12,336
Freshman Class: 14222 applied, 10332 accepted, 958 enrolled	
SAT CR/M/W: 570/605/570	**ACT:** 25 — **VERY COMPETITIVE**

The University of the Pacific, founded in 1851, is a private institution that offers undergraduate and graduate programs in the arts and sciences, and professional programs in pharmacy, law, and dentistry. There are 8 undergraduate schools and one graduate school. In addition to regional accreditation, Pacific has baccalaureate program accreditation with AACSB, ABET, NASAD, NASM, and NCATE. The 2 libraries contain 381,686 volumes, 691,985 microform items, 12,732 audio/video tapes/CDs/DVDs, and subscribe to 12,732 periodicals including electronic. Computerized library services include interlibrary loans, database searching, and Internet access. Special learning facilities include an art gallery, radio station, the Brubeck Institute. The 175-acre campus is in a suburban area 80 miles east of San Francisco, and 40 miles south of Sacramento. Including any residence halls, there are 68 buildings.

Student Life: 85% of undergraduates are from California. The remaining 15% are from other states and Canada. 36% are Asian American; 35% White; 12% Hispanic. The average age of freshmen is 18; all undergraduates, 20. 13% do not continue beyond their first year; 82% remain to graduate.

Housing: 2208 students can be accommodated in college housing, which includes coed dorms, on-campus apartments, and married student housing. In addition, there are honors houses, special-interest houses, fraternity houses, sorority houses, intercultural, wellness, pharmacy, honors, and learning involvement theme houses. On-campus housing is guaranteed for the freshman year only, is available on a first-come, first-served basis, and is available on a lottery system for upperclassmen. Priority is given to out-of-town students. 57% of students live on campus. Alcohol is not permitted. All students may keep cars.

Activities: 15% of men belong to 1 local and 7 national fraternities; 22% of women belong to 1 local and 6 national sororities. There are 100 groups on campus, including intramurals, model UN, resident hall association and campus ministries, residential learning, band, cheerleading, choir, chorale, chorus, club sports, computers, dance, debate, drama, ethnic, forensics, gay, honors, international, jazz band, literary magazine, musical theater, newspaper, opera, orchestra, pep band, photography, political, professional, radio and TV, religious, social, social service, student government, symphony, and yearbook. Popular campus events include Alumni Weekend, Pacific Boardwalk Carnival and Cultural Diversity Week.

Sports: There are 7 intercollegiate sports for men and 9 for women, and 30 intramural sports for men and 30 for women. Facilities include a 6000-seat sports arena, an Olympic-size pool, tennis courts, a softball field, and a fitness center.

Disabled Students: 90% of the campus is accessible. Facilities include wheelchair ramps, elevators, special parking, specially equipped restrooms, special class scheduling, lowered drinking fountains, and lowered telephones.

Services: Counseling and information services are available, as is tutoring in every subject. There is a reader service for the blind, and remedial math, reading, and writing.

Campus Safety and Security: Measures include 24-hour foot and vehicle patrol and security escort services. There are emergency telephones and lighted pathways/sidewalks.

Programs of Study: Pacific confers B.A., B.S., B.F.A., B.M., B.S.B.A., B.S.B.E., B.S.C.E., B.S.E.E., B.S.E.M., B.S.E.P. and B.S.M.E. degrees. Master's and doctoral degrees are also awarded. Bachelor's degrees are awarded in BIOLOGICAL SCIENCE (biochemistry and biology/biological science), BUSINESS (business administration and management), COMMUNICATIONS AND THE ARTS (art, communications, dramatic arts, English, French, German, graphic design, Japanese, music, music business management, music history and appreciation, music performance, music theory and composition, Spanish, and studio art), COMPUTER AND PHYSICAL SCIENCE (applied mathematics, chemistry, computer science, geology, geophysics and seismology, information sciences and systems, mathematics, and physics), EDUCATION (education, music education, and physical education), ENGINEERING AND ENVIRONMENTAL DESIGN (civil engineering, computer engineering, electrical/electronics engineering, engineering management, engineering physics, environmental science, and mechanical engineering), HEALTH PROFESSIONS (music therapy, prepharmacy, and speech pathology/audiology), SOCIAL SCIENCE (economics, history, international relations, international studies, liberal arts/general studies, philosophy, political science/government, psychology, religion, social science, and sociology). Natural sciences and the professions is the strongest academically. Arts and sciences, pharmacy, and business have the largest enrollments.

Required: Students must complete at least 124 credit hours to graduate. The required general education program consists of 3 "mentor seminars" and 6 to 9 other courses chosen from categories such as the Individual and Society, Human Heritage, Natural World and Formal Systems of Thought.

Special: The engineering school requires and guarantees a co-op program for specialized training in the field. Internships for credit or pay in all majors, more than 230 study-abroad programs in more than 80 countries, a Washington semester, and more than 20 work-study programs also are available. Student-designed majors, B.A./B.S. degrees, dual majors in most disciplines, and pass/fail options are possible. There are 18 national honor societies, a freshman honors program, and 42 departmental honors programs.

Faculty/Classroom: 55% of faculty are male; 45% are female. All teach undergraduates. No introductory courses are taught by graduate students. The average class size in a regular course is 19.

Admissions: 73% of the 2013-2014 applicants were accepted. The SAT scores for the 2013-2014 freshman class were: Critical Reading--21% below 500, 38% between 500 and 599, 31% between 600 and 699, and 10% between 700 and 800; Math--15% below 500, 29% between 500 and 599, 34% between 600 and 699, and 22% between 700 and 800; Writing--23% below 500, 37% between 500 and 599, 29% between 600 and 699, and 11% between 700 and 800. The ACT scores were 4% below 21, 30% between 24 and 26, and 66% above 28.

Requirements: The SAT or ACT is required. Applicants must have 16 academic credits, including a recommended 4 years of high school English, 3 of math, 2 in the same foreign language, 2 of lab science, 1 of U.S history or government, 1 of fine or performing arts, and 4 additional academic courses. An essay is required and an interview is recommended. In addition, music students must audition. The GED is accepted plus one year of math and science for science and health related majors. A GPA of 2.5 is required. AP and CLEP credits are accepted. Important factors in the admissions decision are advanced placement or honors courses, leadership record, and extracurricular activities record.

Procedure: Freshmen are admitted fall and spring. Entrance exams should be taken in the spring of the junior year or fall of the senior year. There are early decision, early admissions, deferred admissions, and rolling admissions plans. Early decision applications should be filed by November 15; regular applications, by February 15 for fall entry; and November 15 for spring entry, along with a $35 fee. Notification of early decision is sent January 15; regular decision, March 15. 1100 applicants were on the 2013 waiting list; 34 were admitted. Applications are accepted online.

Transfer: 178 transfer students enrolled in 2012-2013. Applicants should have a minimum GPA of 3.0 and at least 16 credit hours. The SAT or ACT and high school transcripts are required if fewer than 30 units of college work have been completed. 32 of 124 credits required for the bachelor's degree must be completed at Pacific.

Visiting: There are regularly scheduled orientations for prospective students, Visiting students can take a tour, and schedule appointments with faculty, admissions, financial aid personnel, and class visits. There are guides for informal visits, visitors may sit in on classes, and stay overnight. To schedule a visit, contact the Admissions Office.

Financial Aid: The average freshman award was $29,290. Need-based scholarships or need-based grants averaged $21,932; need-based self-help aid (loans and jobs) averaged $8,630; non-need-based athletic scholarships averaged $35,468; and other non-need-based awards and non-need-based scholarships averaged $7,611. Pacific is a member of CSS. The FAFSA is required. The deadline for filing freshman financial aid applications for fall entry is February 15.

International Students: There are 125 international students enrolled. The school actively recruits these students. They must take the TOEFL. The SAT or ACT is required if the student has attended a U.S.-style high school.

Computers: All students may access the system any time. There are no time limits and no fees.

Graduates: From July 1, 2012 to June 30, 2013, 823 bachelor's degrees were awarded. The most popular majors were business/marketing (24%), biological/life sciences (16%), and engineering/engineering tech (8%).

Admissions Contact: Margaret Adkins, Director of Admissions. E-Mail: *madkins@pacific.edu* Web: *www.pacific.edu*

VANGUARD UNIVERSITY OF SOUTHERN CALIFORNIA D-5

Costa Mesa, CA 92626 (714) 556-3610
(800) 722-6279; (714) 966-5471

Full-time: 532 men, 962 women	**Faculty:** n/av
Part-time: 156 men, 391 women	**Ph.D.s:** 81%
Graduate: 79 men, 189 women	**Student/Faculty:** 19 to 1
Year: semesters, summer session	**Tuition:** $23,500
Application Deadline: March 2	**Room & Board:** $8433

Freshman Class: 1244 applied, 917 accepted, 412 enrolled
SAT or ACT: required

VERY COMPETITIVE

Vanguard University of Southern California, founded in 1920, is a private Christian comprehensive university of liberal arts and professional studies affiliated with the Assemblies of God. Figures in the above capsule and in this profile are approximate. There are 4 graduate schools. The library contains 175,877 volumes, 20,795 microform items, and 7,962 audio/video tapes/CDs/DVDs, and subscribes to 10,000 periodicals including electronic. Computerized library services include interlibrary loans, database searching, and Internet access. The 38-acre campus is in a suburban area 40 miles southeast of Los Angeles, and 5 miles north of Newport Beach. Including any residence halls, there are 25 buildings.

Student Life: 95% of undergraduates are from California. Others are from 29 states, 8 foreign countries, and Canada. 75% are from public schools. 56% are White; 27% Hispanic. 74% are Protestant; 22% Unknown. The average age of freshmen is 22; all undergraduates, 24. 25% do not continue beyond their first year; 55% remain to graduate.

Housing: 1074 students can be accommodated in college housing, which includes single-sex and coed dorms, on-campus apartments, off-campus apartments, and married student housing. On-campus housing is available on a first-come, first-served basis, and is available on a lottery system for upperclassmen. Priority is given to out-of-town students. 74% of students live on campus; of those, 75% remain on campus on weekends. Alcohol is not permitted. All students may keep cars.

Activities: There are no fraternities or sororities. There are 30 groups on campus, including art, band, choir, chorale, chorus, computers, dance, debate, drama, ethnic, film, forensics, international, jazz band, literary magazine, musical theater, newspaper, opera, orchestra, photography, political, professional, radio and TV, religious, social, social service, student government, student ministries, symphony, and yearbook. Popular campus events include Harvest Party, International Missions Week and Christmas Party.

Sports: There are 7 intercollegiate sports for men and 8 for women, and 4 intramural sports for men and 4 for women. Facilities include a gym, baseball, softball, and soccer fields, a weight room, and contracted off-campus tennis courts and track course.

Disabled Students: 95% of the campus is accessible. Facilities include wheelchair ramps, elevators, special parking, specially equipped restrooms, special class scheduling, and special housing.

Services: Counseling and information services are available, as is tutoring in most subjects.

Campus Safety and Security: Measures include 24-hour foot and vehicle patrol, emergency notification system, and security escort services. There are emergency telephones, lighted pathways/sidewalks, controlled access to dorms/residences, room and vehicle locks.

Programs of Study: VUSC confers B.A., and B.S. degrees. Associate and master's degrees are also awarded. Bachelor's degrees are awarded in BIOLOGICAL SCIENCE (biochemistry and biology/biological science), BUSINESS (accounting, business administration and management, international business management, and marketing/retailing/merchandising), COMMUNICATIONS AND THE ARTS (broadcasting, communications, digital communications, dramatic arts, English, music, radio/television technology, Spanish, and theatre arts), COMPUTER AND PHYSICAL SCIENCE (chemistry and mathematics), EDUCATION (athletic training, education, elementary education, physical education, science education, secondary education, and sports studies), HEALTH PROFESSIONS (exercise science, nursing, physical therapy, and premedicine), SOCIAL SCIENCE (anthropology, biblical studies, Christian studies, history, liberal arts/general studies, ministries, missions, pastoral studies, political science/government, psychology, religious education, sociology, theological studies, and youth ministry). Religion, social sciences and natural sciences, kinesiology are the strongest academically. Business, psychology and communication have the largest enrollments.

Required: Students must complete a minimum of 124 credits, with 40 to 70 in the major. General education requirements include 16 credits in religion, 15 in humanities and fine arts, 12 in social science, 7 in natural sciences and math, and 2 in phys ed.

Special: Study abroad in cooperation with Assemblies of God programs and programs in the CCCU with placement in over 100 countries, a general studies degree, work-study, accelerated degree programs in business, psychology, and religion, and pass/fail options are available. 3 summer sessions are offered. There are 9 national honor societies and 6 departmental honors programs.

Faculty/Classroom: 54% of faculty are male; 46% are female. 57% teach undergraduates. No introductory courses are taught by graduate students. The average class size in an introductory lecture is 40; in a laboratory is 12; and in a regular course is 19.

Admissions: 74% of the 2013-2014 applicants were accepted. There was 1 National Merit finalist. 5 freshmen graduated first in their class.

Requirements: The SAT or ACT is required. High school courses should include 4 years of English, 3 of social studies, and 2 of math and science. Applicants are required to write an application essay and submit 2 references--1 academic and 1 from a pastor/minister. A GPA of 2.8 is required. AP and CLEP credits are accepted. Important factors in the admissions decision are leadership record, advanced placement or honors courses, and evidence of special talent.

Procedure: Freshmen are admitted fall and spring. Entrance exams should be taken in the junior year. There is a rolling admissions plan. Early decision applications should be filed by December 1; regular applications, by March 2 for fall entry; and December 1 for spring entry, along with a $45 fee. applicants were on the 2013 waiting list; were admitted.

Transfer: 173 transfer students enrolled in 2012-2013. Transfer applicants must submit college transcripts and have a minimum college GPA of 2.5. 24 of 124 credits required for the bachelor's degree must be completed at VUSC.

Visiting: There are regularly scheduled orientations for prospective students, fall and spring university visit days with schedules for students and parents. There are guides for informal visits, visitors may sit in on classes, and stay overnight. To schedule a visit, contact Undergraduate Admissions at (714) 966-5496.

Financial Aid: In 2013-2014, 92% of all full-time freshmen received some form of financial aid. The FAFSA, and state scholarship/grant forms is required. Check with the school for current application deadlines.

International Students: They must take the TOEFL with a minimum score of 550 on the paper-based TOEFL (PBT) or 80 on the Internet-based version (iBT).

Computers: All students may access the system 24 hours a day 7 days a week. There are no time limits and no fees.

Graduates: From July 1, 2012 to June 30, 2013, 432 bachelor's degrees were awarded. The most popular majors were psychology (20%), business administration (17%), and communications (11%). In an average class, 45% graduate in 4 years or less and 54% graduate in 6 years or less.

Admissions Contact: Katy Neric, Assoc Director Admissions Marketing. E-Mail: *admissions@vanguard.edu* Web: *www.vanguard.edu*

WESTMONT COLLEGE C-5

Santa Barbara, CA 93108 — (805) 565-6005; (800) 777-9011; (805) 565-6234

Full-time: 515 men, 800 women	**Faculty:** n/av; IIB, +$
Part-time: 5 men, 20 women	**Ph.D.s:** 89%
Graduate: n/av	**Student/Faculty:** n/av
Year: semesters, summer session	**Tuition:** $32,000
Application Deadline:	**Room & Board:** $10,500
Freshman Class: n/av	
SAT or ACT: required	

HIGHLY COMPETITIVE

Westmont College, founded in 1937, is a private, nondenominational Christian institution offering undergraduate liberal arts degrees. Figures in the above capsule and in this profile are approximate. The library contains 162,274 volumes, 20,687 microform items, and 7,926 audio/video tapes/CDs/DVDs, and subscribes to 3,211 periodicals including electronic. Computerized library services include interlibrary loans, database searching, and Internet access. Special learning facilities include an art gallery, radio station, an observatory, a science center with a premedical center, and a physiology lab. The 111-acre campus is in a suburban area 90 miles north of Los Angeles. Including any residence halls, there are 30 buildings.

Student Life: 69% of undergraduates are from California. Others are from 41 states, 8 foreign countries, and Canada. 70% are from public schools. 69% are White. 95% are Protestant. The average age of freshmen is 18; all undergraduates, 20. 13% do not continue beyond their first year; 70% remain to graduate.

Housing: 1113 students can be accommodated in college housing, which includes single-sex and coed dorms and off-campus apartments. On-campus housing is guaranteed for all 4 years. 84% of students live on campus; of those, 65% remain on campus on weekends. Alcohol is not permitted. Upperclassmen may keep cars.

Activities: There are no fraternities or sororities. There are 50 groups on campus, including art, band, chess, choir, chorale, chorus, computers, dance, debate, drama, ethnic, film, honors, international, jazz band, leadership, literary magazine, musical theater, newspaper, opera, orchestra, pep band, photography, political, professional, radio and TV, religious, social, social service, student government, symphony, and yearbook. Popular campus events include Spring Sing Musical/Talent Show, Multicultural Fellowship Week, and Theatrical and Musical Productions.

Sports: There are 6 intercollegiate sports for men and 6 for women, and 10 intramural sports for men and 10 for women. Facilities include a 2133 seat gym, a soccer/baseball field, a swimming pool, a fitness room, a dance studio, a track, and volleyball, tennis, basketball, and racquetball courts.

Disabled Students: 60% of the campus is accessible. Facilities include wheelchair ramps, elevators, special parking, specially equipped restrooms, special class scheduling, lowered drinking fountains, lowered telephones, and special housing.

Services: Counseling and information services are available, as is tutoring in every subject. There is a reader service for the blind, and remedial math. A writers' corner supervised by tutors is available.

Campus Safety and Security: Measures include 24-hour foot and vehicle patrol, self-defense education, and security escort services. There are shuttle buses, emergency telephones, and lighted pathways/sidewalks.

Programs of Study: Westmont confers B.A., and B.S. degrees. Bachelor's degrees are awarded in BIOLOGICAL SCIENCE (biology/biological science), BUSINESS (business economics), COMMUNICATIONS AND THE ARTS (art, communications, dramatic arts, English, French, modern language, music, and Spanish), COMPUTER AND PHYSICAL SCIENCE (chemistry, computer science, mathematics, and physics), EDUCATION (art education, English education, mathematics education, music education, and social science education), ENGINEERING AND ENVIRONMENTAL DESIGN (engineering physics), HEALTH PROFESSIONS (exercise science), SOCIAL SCIENCE (European studies, history, liberal arts/general studies, philosophy, political science/government, psychology, religion, social science, and sociology). Biology, communication studies, and economics/business have the largest enrollments.

Required: Of the 124 semester units required for graduation, the college's general education requirements include 20 semester units of Common Context courses and 32 semester units of Common Inquiries courses. In addition, students must complete Common Skills courses and courses relating to Competent and Compassionate Action. Courses in religions studies and phys ed are required, as are courses in the history of Western civilization and English composition. Math proficiency is also required. There are distribution requirements in social sciences, humanities, and natural sciences. The total number of hours in the major varies from 36 to 66. A GPA of 2.0 must be maintained.

Special: Westmont offers cross-registration with 12 Christian colleges in the Christian College Consortium, internships in local businesses and social agencies, study abroad in 11 countries, and semesters in Washington, D.C., San Francisco, and Los Angeles. B.A.-B.S. degrees, student-designed majors, work-study programs, a 3-2 engineering program with several California universities, the University of Washington, and Boston University, and pass/fail options are also available. There are preprofessional programs in sports medicine, dentistry, engineering, law, medicine, ministry/missions, optometry, pharmacology, physical therapy, teaching, and veterinary medicine. There are 8 national honor societies, a freshman honors program, and 9 departmental honors programs.

Faculty/Classroom: 67% of faculty are male; 33% are female. All teach and do research. No introductory courses are taught by graduate students. The average class size in an introductory lecture is 30; in a laboratory is 15; and in a regular course is 20.

Requirements: The SAT or ACT is required. The ACT Optional Writing test is also required. In addition, Applicants need 16 academic credits, including 4 years of high school English, 3 of math, 2 each of a foreign language, social science, and physical science, and 1 each of history and biological science. Interviews are recommended. Essays are required. The

GED is accepted. AP and CLEP credits are accepted. Important factors in the admissions decision are advanced placement or honors courses, leadership record, and extracurricular activities record.

Procedure: Freshmen are admitted fall and spring. Entrance exams should be taken during the spring of the junior year or the beginning of the senior year. Check with the school for current application deadlines. The fall 2013 application fee was $35. applicants were on the 2013 waiting list; were admitted. Applications are accepted online.

Transfer: In a recent year, 55 transfer students enrolled. Transfer students from 2-year colleges should have a minimum GPA of 2.8 and students from 4-year colleges or universities, a 2.5. The college will not accept more than 64 transferable units from a community college; there is no maximum number of transferable units from a 4-year college. High school transcripts and test scores are required if the student has fewer than 24 transferable units. 32 of 124 credits required for the bachelor's degree must be completed at Westmont.

Visiting: There are regularly scheduled orientations for prospective students, consisting of meeting faculty and administrators and attending classes, academic seminars, student/parent panels, academic open houses, admission and financial aid sessions, student led small groups, campus tours, and various cultural events. There are guides for informal visits, visitors may sit in on classes, and stay overnight. To schedule a visit, contact Admissions/Campus Visit Coordinator.

Financial Aid: In a recent year, 83% of all full-time freshmen and 85% of continuing full-time students received some form of financial aid. 83% of all full-time freshmen and 85% of continuing full-time students received need-based aid. 54% of undergraduate students work part-time. Average annual earnings from campus work are $909. The FAFSA is required. Check with the school for current application deadlines.

International Students: There are 9 international students enrolled. The school actively recruits these students. They must take the TOEFL with a minimum score of 560 on the paper-based TOEFL (PBT) or 83 on the Internet-based version (iBT). They must also take the SAT or ACT.

Computers: All students may access the system. There are no time limits and no fees.

Graduates: From July 1, 2012 to June 30, 2013, 326 bachelor's degrees were awarded. The most popular majors were business/economics (14%), English (12%), and social sciences (9%). 50 companies recruited on campus in 2012-2013. In an average class, 54% graduate in 3 years or less, 68% graduate in 4 years or less, 70% graduate in 5 years or less, and 73% graduate in 6 years or less. Of the 2012 graduating class, 48% were enrolled in graduate school within 6 months of graduation, and 85% were employed.

Admissions Contact: Joyce M. Luy, Dean of Admissions. E-Mail: *admissions@westmont.edu* Web: *www.westmont.edu*

WHITTIER COLLEGE D-5

Whittier, CA 90608 **(562) 907-4238; (562) 907-4870**

Full-time: 634 men, 720 women	**Faculty:** 92; IIB, +$
Part-time: 7 men, 7 women	**Ph.D.s:** 100%
Graduate: 258 men, 286 women	**Student/Faculty:** 15 to 1
Year: semesters, summer session	**Tuition:** $34,368
Application Deadline: February 1	**Room & Board:** $10,048
Freshman Class: 1970 applied, 1639 accepted, 358 enrolled	
SAT CR/M: 526/532	**ACT:** 22 **COMPETITIVE**

Whittier College, founded in 1887 by the Society of Friends and chartered by the State of California in 1901, is an independent, secular, liberal arts institution. There is 1 undergraduate school and 2 graduate schools. In addition to regional accreditation, Whittier has baccalaureate program accreditation with CSWE. The library contains 127,410 volumes, 6,877 microform items, and 1,793 audio/video tapes/CDs/DVDs, and subscribes to 26,365 periodicals including electronic. Computerized library services include interlibrary loans, database searching, Internet access, and laptop Internet portals. Special learning facilities include a learning resource center, art gallery, radio station, performing arts center, and writing center. The 75-acre campus is in a suburban area 18 miles southeast of Los Angeles, in the foothills of the San Gabriel Mountains. Including any residence halls, there are 51 buildings. The figures in the above capsule and in this profile are approximate.

Student Life: 71% of undergraduates are from California. Others are from 25 states, 16 foreign countries, and Canada. 40% are white; 29% Hispanic. The average age of freshmen is 18; all undergraduates, 20. 26% do not continue beyond their first year; 54% remain to graduate.

Housing: 840 students can be accommodated in college housing, which includes coed dorms. In addition, there are special-interest houses. On-campus housing is guaranteed for all 4 years. 61% of students live on campus; of those, 85% remain on campus on weekends. All students may keep cars.

Activities: 13% of men belong to 4 local fraternities; 21% of women belong to 6 local sororities. There are 90 groups on campus, including art, band, cheerleading, choir, chorale, chorus, computers, dance, drama, ethnic, film, gay, honors, international, jazz band, literary magazine, musical theater, newspaper, photography, political, professional, radio and TV, religious, social, social service, and student government. Popular campus events include Helping Hands Day, Tardeada-Latino Cultural Celebration, and MLK Jr. Oratorical Contest.

Sports: There are 11 intercollegiate sports for men and 10 for women, and 5 intramural sports for men and 5 for women. Facilities include a 7000-seat stadium, a 2000-seat gym, 4 playing fields, an athletics center, an aquatics center, a fitness center, and tennis courts.

Disabled Students: 75% of the campus is accessible. Facilities include wheelchair ramps, elevators, special parking, specially equipped restrooms, special class scheduling, lowered drinking fountains, lowered telephones, and special housing.

Services: Counseling and information services are available, as is tutoring in every subject.

Campus Safety and Security: Measures include 24-hour foot and vehicle patrol, emergency notification system, self-defense education, and security escort services. There are emergency telephones and lighted pathways/sidewalks.

Programs of Study: Whittier confers B.A. degrees. Master's and doctoral degrees are also awarded. Bachelor's degrees are awarded in BIOLOGICAL SCIENCE (biochemistry and biology/biological science), BUSINESS (business administration and management), COMMUNICATIONS AND THE ARTS (art, Chinese, dramatic arts, English, French, music, and Spanish), COMPUTER AND PHYSICAL SCIENCE (chemistry, mathematics, and physics), ENGINEERING AND ENVIRONMENTAL DESIGN (environmental science), SOCIAL SCIENCE (child psychology/development, economics, history, international studies, philosophy, physical fitness/movement, political science/government, psychology, religion, social work, and sociology). Business administration, political science, and English have the largest enrollments.

Required: All students must take a total of 120 credits, including at least 30 in the major field, with a minimum GPA of 2.0. Distribution requirements include 4 courses in 4 distinct areas of communication, and a pair of courses in science and society.

Special: Internships are possible fall, spring, and summer. Study abroad is offered in 30 countries. The Whittier Scholars Program offers self-designed interdisciplinary curricula, and dual majors are possible in all majors. Nondegree study and pass/fail options are available. Whittier offers a 3-2 engineering program with the Universities of Southern California and Minnesota, and a 3-3 law degree with Whittier Law School. There are 17 national honor societies and 16 departmental honors programs.

Faculty/Classroom: 47% of faculty are male; 53% are female. All teach and do research. No introductory courses are taught by graduate students. The average class size in an introductory lecture is 20; in a laboratory is 24; and in a regular course is 22.

Admissions: In a recent year, 83% of the applicants were accepted. The SAT scores for a recent freshman class were: Critical Reading--38% below 500, 42% between 500 and 599, 17% between 600 and 700, and 3% above 700; Math--36% below 500, 41% between 500 and 599, 21% between 600 and 700, and 2% above 700; Writing--40% below 500, 42% between 500 and 599, 16% between 600 and 700, and 2% above 700. The ACT scores were 36% below 21, 27% between 21 and 23, 23% between 24 and 26, 8% between 27 and 28, and 6% above 28. 54% of the current freshmen were in the top fifth of their class; 75% were in the top two fifths. 16 freshmen graduated first in their class.

Requirements: The SAT or ACT is required. The SAT is preferred. The college recommends that applicants have 4 years of high school English, 3 years each of history, math, and science, and 2 years of a foreign language. An essay is required. An interview is recommended. A GPA of 2.5 is required. AP credits are accepted. Important factors in the admissions decision are advanced placement or honors courses, recommendations by school officials, and leadership record.

Procedure: Freshmen are admitted fall and spring. Entrance exams should be taken during the junior year or fall of the senior year. There are early admissions, deferred admissions, and rolling admissions plans. Early decision applications should be filed by December 1; regular applications, by February 1 for fall entry; and December 1 for spring entry, along with a $50 fee. Notification of early decision is sent December 29; regular decision, March 1. Applications are accepted online.

Transfer: In a recent year, 95 transfer students enrolled. Transfer applicants are considered on a case-by-case basis, but a minimum GPA of 2.5 is recommended in academic course work. The SAT or the ACT is required for students with fewer than 30 academic units. The GED is accepted for transfer applicants with at least 30 academic units. 30 of 120 credits required for the bachelor's degree must be completed at Whittier.

Visiting: There are regularly scheduled orientations for prospective students, consisting of an interview with an admission officer and a campus tour. Customized visits can be arranged to include faculty, coaches, extracurricular activities, class visits, and residence hall tours. There are guides for informal visits, visitors may sit in on classes, and stay overnight. To schedule a visit, contact the Office of Admissions.

Financial Aid: In a recent year, 83% of all full-time freshmen and 75%

of continuing full-time students received some form of financial aid. 67% of all full-time freshmen and 64% of continuing full-time students received need-based aid. 64% of undergraduate students work part-time. Whittier is a member of CSS. The FAFSA and the college's own financial statement are required. The deadline for filing freshman financial aid applications for fall entry is February 15.

International Students: There are 32 international students enrolled. The school actively recruits these students. They must take the TOEFL. They must also take the SAT or ACT.

Computers: All students may access the system 24 hours daily. There are no time limits and no fees.

Graduates: In a recent year, 259 bachelor's degrees were awarded. The most popular majors were business (12%), political science (10%), and English (10%). 38 companies recruited on campus in 2010-2011. In an average class, 49% graduate in 4 years or less, 62% graduate in 5 years or less, and 64% graduate in 6 years or less. In a recent year, 37% were enrolled in graduate school within 6 months of graduation, and 57% were employed.

Admissions Contact: Lisa Meyer, Vice President of Enrollment. E-Mail: *admission@whittier.edu* *Web: www.whittier.edu*

WOODBURY UNIVERSITY C-5

Burbank, CA 91510-7846 (818) 252-5221
(800) 784-9663; (818) 767-7520

Full-time: 465 men, 585 women	**Faculty:** n/av; IIA, av$
Part-time: 110 men, 145 women	**Ph.D.s:** 58%
Graduate: 110 men, 140 women	**Student/Faculty:** n/av
Year: semesters, summer session	**Tuition:** $26,000
Application Deadline: open	**Room & Board:** $9500
Freshman Class: n/av	
SAT: required	

LESS COMPETITIVE

Woodbury University, founded in 1884, is a private institution that emphasizes business and professional design education. Figures in the above capsule and in profile are approximate. There are 4 undergraduate schools and 3 graduate schools. In addition to regional accreditation, Woodbury has baccalaureate program accreditation with ACBSP, FIDER, and NAAB. The library contains 71,178 volumes, 93,770 microform items, and 20,065 audio/video tapes/CDs/DVDs, and subscribes to 358 periodicals including electronic. Computerized library services include interlibrary loans, database searching, and Internet access. Special learning facilities include a learning resource center, art gallery, architecture gallery, art/design gallery, and fashion center. The 22-acre campus is in a suburban area 17 miles north of Los Angeles. Including any residence halls, there are 22 buildings.

Student Life: Most undergraduates are from the West, 41 foreign countries, and Canada. 45% are white; 30% Hispanic. The average age of freshmen is 18; all undergraduates, 22. 24% do not continue beyond their first year; 53% remain to graduate.

Housing: 227 students can be accommodated in college housing, which includes single-sex and coed dorms and off-campus apartments. nonsmoking suites. On-campus housing is available on a first-come and first-served basis. 80% of students commute. Alcohol is not permitted. All students may keep cars.

Activities: 1% of men belong to 1 local and 1 national fraternities; 1% of women belong to 2 local and 1 national sororities. There are 25 groups on campus, including drama, ethnic, fashion, international, newspaper, professional, religious, social, social service, and student government. Popular campus events include University Gala, Winter Formal, and Springfest.

Sports: There are 4 intramural sports for men and 4 for women. Facilities include basketball and volleyball courts, weight training and aerobics rooms, an outdoor swimming pool, a quarter-mile track, and a field for soccer and other sports.

Disabled Students: 95% of the campus is accessible. Facilities include wheelchair ramps, elevators, special parking, specially equipped restrooms, special class scheduling, and special housing.

Services: Counseling and information services are available, as is tutoring in some subjects, accounting, physics, structures, economics, and math There is remedial math, reading, and writing. Books on tape are available for the blind.

Campus Safety and Security: Measures include 24-hour foot and vehicle patrol, self-defense education, and security escort services. There are emergency telephones and lighted pathways/sidewalks.

Programs of Study: Woodbury confers B.A., B.S., B.Arch., and B.F.A. degrees. Master's degrees are also awarded. Bachelor's degrees are awarded in BUSINESS (accounting, business administration and management, fashion merchandising, marketing/retailing/merchandising, and organizational behavior), COMMUNICATIONS AND THE ARTS (animation, communications, and graphic design), COMPUTER AND PHYSICAL SCIENCE (information sciences and systems), ENGINEERING AND ENVIRONMENTAL DESIGN (architecture and interior design), SOCIAL SCIENCE (fashion design and technology, history, interdisciplinary studies, political science/government, and psychology). Business and architecture are the strongest academically and have the largest enrollments.

Required: To graduate with a B.S., students must complete 126 semester units, including 61 to 66 in the major; with a B.A., 120 including 45 to 54 in the major; with a B.F.A., 128 including 68 in the major; and with a B.Arch., 160 semester units, including 98 in the major. All students must maintain a minimum GPA of 2.0 and take freshman composition, computer literacy, and public speaking courses. Course work in behavioral and social sciences, fine arts, humanities, physical and biological sciences, and math are also part of the curriculum.

Special: Internships or verified work experience is required for all majors with the exception of organizational leadership and interdisciplinary studies. Concurrent registration with area institutions, work-study programs, study abroad in France, Spain, China, Korea, England, and Germany, dual majors, and pass/fail options also are offered.

Faculty/Classroom: 51% of faculty are male; 49% are female. No introductory courses are taught by graduate students. The average class size in an introductory lecture is 25; in a laboratory is 15; and in a regular course is 15.

Requirements: The SAT is required. In addition, an application form, a essay, 2 academic references, official high school transcripts, and official SAT or ACT scores are required for all applicants. A GPA of 2.0 is required. AP and CLEP credits are accepted. Important factors in the admissions decision are advanced placement or honors courses, evidence of special talent, and recommendations by school officials.

Procedure: Freshmen are admitted fall, spring, and summer. Entrance exams should be taken prior to application. There are deferred admissions and rolling admissions plans. Application deadlines are open. Check with the school for current fees. Notification is sent on a rolling basis. Applications are accepted online.

Transfer: In a recent year, 152 transfer students enrolled. Applicants are required to have maintained a minimum GPA of 2.0 and to take the SAT or ACT if they have completed fewer than 30 semester units. 45 credits required for the bachelor's degree must be completed at Woodbury.

Visiting: There are regularly scheduled orientations for prospective students, consisting of meeting with admissions counselors, the president, faculty members, students, financial aid counselors, and student services staff. There are guides for informal visits, visitors may sit in on classes, and stay overnight. To schedule a visit, contact the Admissions Office.

Financial Aid: In a recent year, 88% of all full-time freshmen and 90% of continuing full-time students received some form of financial aid. 88% of all full-time freshmen and 88% of continuing full-time students received need-based aid. The average freshman award was $17,417. Need-based scholarships or need-based grants averaged $14,448; need-based self-help aid (loans and jobs) averaged $3,543; and other non-need-based awards and non-need-based scholarships averaged $12,706. 10% of undergraduate students work part-time. Average annual earnings from campus work are $1200. Woodbury is a member of CSS. The FAFSA and the college's own financial statement are required. Check with the school for current application deadlines.

International Students: There are 74 international students enrolled. The school actively recruits these students. They must take the TOEFL with a minimum score of 500 on the paper-based TOEFL (PBT). They must also take the SAT or ACT.

Computers: Wireless access is available. All students may access the system 24 hours a day. There are no time limits. The fee is $100. It is strongly recommended that all students have a personal computer.

Graduates: In a recent year, 233 bachelor's degrees were awarded. The most popular majors were architecture (30%), business management (16%), and fashion design (10%). In an average class, 34% graduate in 4 years or less, 49% graduate in 5 years or less, and 53% graduate in 6 years or less.

Admissions Contact: Ruth Lorenzana, Director of Admissions. E-Mail: *info@woodbury.edu* Web: *www.woodbury.edu*

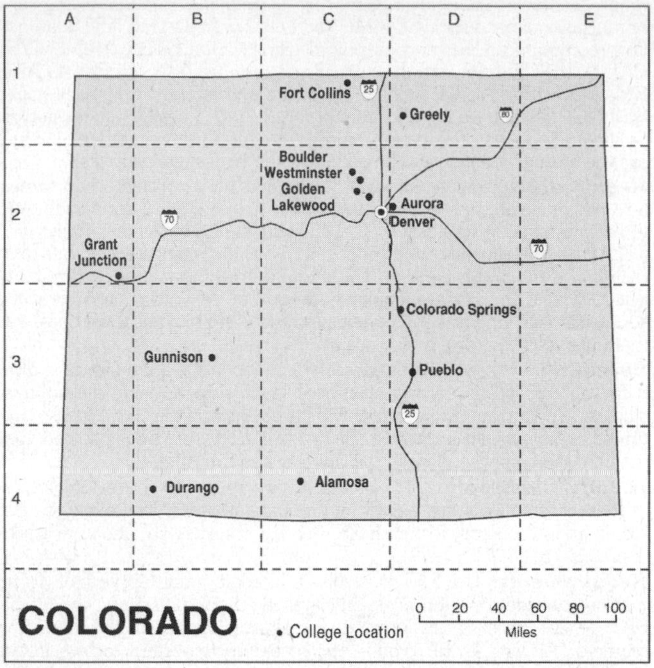

ADAMS STATE COLLEGE C-4

Alamosa, CO 81101 (719) 587-7802
(800) 824-6494; (719) 587-7522

Full-time: 974 men, 1041 women	**Faculty:** 102
Part-time: 296 men, 431 women	**Ph.D.s:** 70%
Graduate: 450 men, 1421 women	**Student/Faculty:** 17 to 1
Year: semesters, summer session	**Tuition:** $6127 ($16,375)
Application Deadline: August 1	**Room & Board:** $8231
Freshman Class: 2534 applied, 1613 accepted, 599 enrolled	
SAT CR/M/W: 480/500/460 **ACT:** 20	**LESS COMPETITIVE**

Adams State College, founded in 1921, is a public liberal arts college awarding undergraduate and graduate degrees. There are 6 undergraduate schools and 1 graduate school. In addition to regional accreditation, ASC has baccalaureate program accreditation with AACSB, NASM, and TEAC. The library contains 178,280 volumes, 20,000 microform items, and 2,800 audio/video tapes/CDs/DVDs, and subscribes to 56,886 periodicals including electronic. Computerized library services include interlibrary loans, database searching, Internet access, and laptop Internet portals. Special learning facilities include a learning resource center, art gallery, natural history museum, planetarium, radio station, geology museum, counseling lab, and nursing lab. The 90-acre campus is in a small town 220 miles south of Denver, and 200 miles north of Albuquerque. Including any residence halls, there are 55 buildings.

Student Life: 73% of undergraduates are from Colorado. Others are from 45 states, 10 foreign countries, and Canada. 56% are white; 33% Hispanic. The average age of freshmen is 19; all undergraduates, 24. 45% do not continue beyond their first year; 32% remain to graduate.

Housing: 1200 students can be accommodated in college housing, which includes single-sex and coed dorms, on-campus apartments, and married student housing. freshman interest-group housing, pledge learning community (pledge to stay drug and alcohol free), outdoor adventure community, and academic theme floors. On-campus housing is available on a first-come, first-served basis, and is available on a lottery system for upperclassmen. 60% of students commute. Alcohol is not permitted. All students may keep cars.

Activities: There are no fraternities or sororities. There are 50 groups on campus, including band, cheerleading, chess, choir, chorale, computers, dance, drama, environmental, ethnic, gay, honors, international, jazz band, literary magazine, marching band, newspaper, pep band, photography, political, professional, radio and TV, religious, social service, and student government. Popular events include Snow Daze and Spring Fest.

Sports: There are 5 intercollegiate sports for men and 7 for women, and 11 intramural sports for men and 11 for women. Facilities include a multipurpose gym, multi-purpose field house, swimming pool, outdoor handball, racquetball, and tennis courts, indoor and outdoor tracks, varsity softball field, intramural softball field, soccer field, football practice field, weight room, free weights and weight machines, an 1800-square-foot climbing wall, an aerobics studio, a cardiovascular area, and game facilities.

Disabled Students: 95% of the campus is accessible. Facilities include wheelchair ramps, elevators, special parking, specially equipped restrooms, special class scheduling, lowered drinking fountains, and lowered telephones.

Services: Counseling and information services are available, as is tutoring in every subject. There is a reader service for the blind, and remedial math, reading, and writing. Interpreters, note takers, and tapes for the blind are also available

Campus Safety and Security: Measures include emergency notification system, self-defense education, and security escort services. There are emergency telephones, lighted pathways/sidewalks, controlled access to dorms/residences, safety seminars with biannual staff/faculty training.

Programs of Study: ASC confers B.A., B.S., B.S.N., and B.F.A. degrees. Associate and master's degrees are also awarded. Bachelor's degrees are awarded in AGRICULTURE (agricultural business management), BIOLOGICAL SCIENCE (biochemistry, biology/biological science, cell biology, ecology, molecular biology, and wildlife biology), BUSINESS (accounting, banking and finance, business administration and management, business economics, business law, international business management, management information systems, marketing/retailing/merchandising, office supervision and management, organizational leadership and management, small business management, and sports management), COMMUNICATIONS AND THE ARTS (advertising, art, art history and appreciation, ceramic art and design, communications, creative writing, design, dramatic arts, drawing, English, fiber/textiles/weaving, graphic design, metal/jewelry, music, music performance, music theory and composition, painting, photography, printmaking, sculpture, Spanish, and theatre arts), COMPUTER AND PHYSICAL SCIENCE (chemical physics, chemistry, computer science, earth science, geology, mathematics, and physics), EDUCATION (art education, athletic training, business education, education, elementary education, English education, foreign languages education, mathematics education, music education, physical education, school psychology, science education, secondary education, social studies education, special education, and sports and wellness studies), ENGINEERING AND ENVIRONMENTAL DESIGN (preengineering), HEALTH PROFESSIONS (allied health, exercise science, health care administration, nursing, premedicine, preoptometry, prepharmacy, and preveterinary science), SOCIAL SCIENCE (corrections, counseling/psychology, criminology, economics, geography, history, interdisciplinary studies, law enforcement and corrections, liberal arts/general studies, political science/government, prelaw, psychology, social work, and sociology). Biology and allied health sciences are the strongest academically. Business and education have the largest enrollments.

Required: All students must maintain a GPA of at least 2.0 and complete 120 credit hours, including 24 in the major. General education requirements total 38 and include passing both a technology proficiency exam and a writing assessment.

Special: Cross-registration through the State Colleges of Colorado consortium is available. Work-study programs with the college, dual majors, a general studies degree, and student-designed majors are possible. Study abroad in association with the National Student Exchange and non-degree study are offered.

Faculty/Classroom: 45% of faculty are male; 55% are female. 93% teach undergraduates. No introductory courses are taught by graduate students. The average class size in a laboratory is 15. 16 in a regular course.

Admissions: 64% of a recent year applicants were accepted. The SAT scores for a recent freshman class were: Critical Reading--53% below 500, 37% between 500 and 599, 10% between 600 and 700; Math--49% below 500, 42% between 500 and 599, 9% between 600 and 700; Writing--64% below 500, 30% between 500 and 599, 6% between 600 and 700. The ACT scores were 62% below 21, 21% between 21 and 23, 10% between 24 and 26, 5% between 27 and 28, and 2% above 28. 24% of the current freshmen were in the top fifth of their class; 54% were in the top two fifths.

Requirements: The ACT is required. Applicants are required to have at least 15 academic credits with 4 in English, 3 in social science, 4each in math, 3 in science with 2 being lab-based, and a foreign language, and 2 academic electives. The GED is accepted. A GPA of 2.5 is required. AP and CLEP credits are accepted.

Procedure: Freshmen are admitted fall, spring, and summer. Entrance exams should be taken during the junior year. There are deferred admissions and rolling admissions plans. Applications should be filed by August 1 for fall entry; December 1 for spring entry, along with a $30 fee. Applications are accepted online.

Transfer: 492 transfer students enrolled in a recent year. Applicants must have a minimum GPA of 2.0. If they have fewer than 12 credits, the SAT or ACT test scores and official high school transcripts are also required. 30 of 120 credits required for the bachelor's degree must be completed at ASC.

Visiting: There are regularly scheduled orientations for prospective students, including a meeting with academic faculty, a campus tour, information on financial aid and housing, and a free ticket to an athletic event (when applicable). There are guides for informal visits, visitors may sit in on classes, and stay overnight. To schedule a visit, contact the Admissions Office.

Financial Aid: In a recent year, 97% of all full-time freshmen and 90% of continuing full-time students received some form of financial aid. 94% of all full-time freshmen and 88% of continuing full-time students received need-based aid. The average freshman award was $8,574. Need-based scholarships or need-based grants averaged $1,785 ($11,569 maximum); need-based self-help aid (loans and jobs) averaged $1,232 ($3,750 maximum); and other non-need-based awards and non-need-based scholarships averaged $3,413 ($14,250 maximum). 43% of undergraduate students work part-time. Average annual earnings from campus work are $1124. The FAFSA is required. The priority date for freshman financial aid applications for fall entry is March 15. The deadline for filing freshman financial aid applications for fall entry is April 15.

International Students: There are 42 international students enrolled. They must take the TOEFL with a minimum score of 550 on the paper-based TOEFL (PBT) or 79 on the Internet-based version (iBT). They must also take the SAT or ACT, scoring 19.

Graduates: In a recent year, 326 bachelor's degrees were awarded. The most popular majors were liberal arts (11%), business administration (7%), and management (6%). In an average class, 14% graduate in 4 years or less, 27% graduate in 5 years or less, and 32% graduate in 6 years or less.

Admissions Contact: Enrollment Management. A campus DVD is available. E-Mail: *ascadmit@adams.edu* Web: *www.adams.edu*

COLORADO CHRISTIAN UNIVERSITY C-2

Lakewood, CO 80226-7499 (303) 963-3207
(800) 44 FAITH; (303) 963-3401

Full-time: 425 men, 700 women	**Faculty:** n/av
Part-time: 175 men, 175 women	**Ph.D.s:** 85%
Graduate: 55 men, 80 women	**Student/Faculty:** n/av
Year: semesters, summer session	**Tuition:** $20,500
Application Deadline: open	**Room & Board:** $8000
Freshman Class: n/av	
SAT or ACT: required	**VERY COMPETITIVE**

Colorado Christian University, founded in 1914, is a private, Christian interdenominational institution offering undergraduate and graduate programs in the arts and sciences, biblical studies, music, and education. The figures in the above capsule are approximate. There are 4 undergraduate schools and 3 graduate schools. The library contains 53,532 volumes, 281,234 microform items, and 3,917 audio/video tapes/CDs/DVDs, and subscribes to 415 periodicals including electronic. Computerized library services include interlibrary loans, database searching, and Internet access. Special learning facilities include a learning resource center and art gallery. The 29-acre campus is in a suburban area 10 miles west of Denver. Including any residence halls, there are 21 buildings.

Student Life: 59% of undergraduates are from Colorado. Others are from 44 states, 16 foreign countries, and Canada. 81% are white. 99% are Protestant. The average age of freshmen is 19; all undergraduates, 20. 33% do not continue beyond their first year.

Housing: 732 students can be accommodated in college housing, which includes single-sex dorms, on-campus apartments, off-campus apartments, and married student housing. In addition, there are special-interest houses. On-campus housing is guaranteed for the freshman year only, is available on a first-come, first-served basis, and is available on a lottery system for upperclassmen. Priority is given to out-of-town students. 65% of students live on campus; of those, 38% remain on campus on weekends. Alcohol is not permitted. All students may keep cars.

Activities: There are no fraternities or sororities. There are 21 groups on campus, including band, cheerleading, choir, chorus, computers, drama, honors, international, jazz band, literary magazine, musical theater, newspaper, orchestra, photography, professional, religious, social, social service, student government, symphony, and yearbook. Popular campus events include Preview Days, Spring Retreat, and New Student Retreat.

Sports: There are 5 intercollegiate sports for men and 5 for women, and 6 intramural sports for men and 6 for women. Facilities include a gym and soccer and practice fields.

Disabled Students: 85% of the campus is accessible. Facilities include wheelchair ramps, special parking, specially equipped restrooms, special class scheduling, lowered drinking fountains, lowered telephones, and special housing.

Services: Counseling and information services are available, as is tutoring in every subject. There is remedial math, reading, and writing.

Campus Safety and Security: Measures include 24-hour foot and vehicle patrol and security escort services. There are emergency telephones and lighted pathways/sidewalks.

Programs of Study: CCU confers B.A., B.S., and B.M. degrees. Associate and master's degrees are also awarded. Bachelor's degrees are awarded in BIOLOGICAL SCIENCE (biology/biological science), BUSINESS (accounting, business administration and management, human resources, management information systems, and management science), COMMUNICATIONS AND THE ARTS (art, communications, English, and music), COMPUTER AND PHYSICAL SCIENCE (computer management and science), EDUCATION (elementary education, music education, and secondary education), SOCIAL SCIENCE (biblical studies, history, liberal arts/general studies, psychology, social science, theological studies, and youth ministry). Science, biology, and education are the strongest academically. Human resources management, computer/information technology, and liberal arts have the largest enrollments.

Required: To graduate, students must complete at least 128 semester hours, including the 48-hour general education requirement and courses specified for the major, with a minimum cumulative GPA of 2.0, 2.5 in the major. The university requires 4 semesters of Christian service and regular chapel attendance. All students must complete 12 credits in biblical studies.

Special: The school offers an ROTC program in cooperation with CU Boulder, cross-registration with the Focus on the Family Institute, internships, study abroad in 7 countries, a Washington semester, and work-study programs. Accelerated degree programs are available in Christian leadership, organizational management, and management of information systems. Dual and student-designed majors, nondegree study, pass/fail options, and credit for life, military, and work experience are also available. There are 2 national honor societies, a freshman honors program, and 1 departmental honors programs.

Faculty/Classroom: 65% of faculty are male; 35% are female. No introductory courses are taught by graduate students. The average class size in an introductory lecture is 25; in a laboratory is 18; and in a regular course is 30.

Requirements: The SAT or ACT is required. Applicants must be graduates of an accredited secondary school. The GED is accepted. An essay is required. A campus visit is recommended. A GPA of 2.8 is required. AP and CLEP credits are accepted.

Procedure: Freshmen are admitted to all sessions. There are deferred admissions and rolling admissions plans. Check with the school for current application deadlines. Check with the school for the current application fee. Applications are accepted online.

Transfer: Applicants for transfer should have completed 12 college credits with a minimum GPA of 2.0. 30 of 128 credits required for the bachelor's degree must be completed at CCU.

Visiting: There are regularly scheduled orientations for prospective students. There are guides for informal visits, visitors may sit in on classes, and stay overnight. To schedule a visit, contact the Office of Admissions.

Financial Aid: The FAFSA is required. Check with the school for current application deadlines.

International Students: The school actively recruits these students. They must take the TOEFL and the college's own test. They must also take the SAT or ACT.

Admissions Contact: Director of Admissions. A campus DVD is available. Web: *www.ccu.edu*

COLORADO COLLEGE D-3

Colorado Springs, CO 80903 (719) 389-6344
(800) 542-7214; (719) 389-6816

Full-time: 914 men, 1111 women	**Faculty:** n/av; IIB, +$
Part-time: 6 men, 9 women	**Ph.D.s:** 99%
Graduate: 7 men, 13 women	**Student/Faculty:** 10 to 1
Year: other, summer session	**Tuition:** $44,222
Application Deadline: January 15	**Room & Board:** $10,312
Freshman Class: 5780 applied, 1288 accepted, 522 enrolled	
SAT CR/M/W: 660/660/660 **ACT:** 30	**MOST COMPETITIVE**

Colorado College, founded in 1874, is an independent liberal arts and sciences institution. The academic year is based on a block plan, under which students take only 1 course during each of the 8 3-1/2-week-long blocks of study; there is also a 9-week 3-block summer session. There is one undergraduate school and one graduate school. The 2 libraries contain 574,541 volumes, 137,029 microform items, and 41,768 audio/video tapes/CDs/DVDs, and subscribe to 42,159 periodicals including electronic. Computerized library services include interlibrary loans, database searching, Internet access, and Wi-Fi capability. Special learning facilities include an art gallery, radio station, an electronic music studio, music library, a telescope dome, a multimedia computer lab, the Colorado College Press, an herbarium, a Fourier transform nuclear magnetic resonance spectrometer, a scanning electronic microscope and transmission electronic microscope, an environmental service van equipped for field research, petrographic microscopes, an X-ray diffractometer, a sedimentology lab, metabolic equipment, hydrostatic weighing equipment, and a cadaver study in sports science. The 90-acre campus is in an urban area in Colorado Springs, 70 miles south of Denver. Including any residence halls, there are 77 buildings.

Student Life: 81% of undergraduates are from out of state, mostly the Middle Atlantic. Students are from 49 states, 59 foreign countries, and Canada. 69% are White. The average age of freshmen is 18; all undergraduates, 20. 4% do not continue beyond their first year; 96% remain to graduate.

Housing: 1546 students can be accommodated in college housing, which includes single-sex and coed dorms, on-campus apartments, and off-campus apartments. In addition, there are language houses, special-interest houses, fraternity houses, substance-free, smoke-free, diversity, community arts, arts and crafts, and sustainable living houses. On-campus housing is guaranteed for all 4 years. 76% of students live on campus. Upperclassmen may keep cars.

Activities: 7% of men belong to 3 national fraternities; 11% of women belong to 3 national sororities. There are 144 groups on campus, including and health awareness, science, art, band, chess, choir, chorale, chorus, communications, computers, dance, debate, drama, environmental, ethnic, film, forensics, gay, honors, international, jazz band, literary magazine, musical theater, newspaper, orchestra, outdoor, photography, political, professional, religious, social, social service, student government, symphony, and yearbook. Popular campus events include Afternoon and Evening Blues, Rock, Folk, Jazz, and World Music Concerts and an Annual Arts and Crafts Sale, Winter Ball and Homecoming.

Sports: There are 8 intercollegiate sports for men and 8 for women, and 14 intramural sports for men and 14 for women. Facilities include a sports center with 2 gyms, weight and exercise rooms, squash, tennis, and racquetball courts, a pool, an ice rink, and playing fields.

Disabled Students: College staff members work closely with students who have documented disabilities requiring accommodation to ensure equal access to the college's programs, activities, and services.

Services: Colorado College offers a variety of services and resources to help students succeed.

Campus Safety and Security: Measures include 24-hour foot and vehicle patrol, emergency notification system, self-defense education, and security escort services. There are emergency telephones, lighted pathways/sidewalks, controlled access to dorms/residences, whistle stop program, and fire safety inspections.

Programs of Study: CC confers B.A. degrees. Master's degrees are also awarded. Bachelor's degrees are awarded in BIOLOGICAL SCIENCE (biochemistry, biology/biological science, and neurosciences), BUSINESS (international economics), COMMUNICATIONS AND THE ARTS (art history and appreciation, classics, comparative literature, creative writing, dance, dramatic arts, English, film arts, Germanic languages and literature, music, romance languages and literature, and studio art), COMPUTER AND PHYSICAL SCIENCE (chemistry, computer mathematics, computer science, geology, mathematics, and physics), EDUCATION (education), ENGINEERING AND ENVIRONMENTAL DESIGN (environmental science), SOCIAL SCIENCE (anthropology, Asian/Oriental studies, economics, French studies, gender studies, Hispanic American studies, history, history of philosophy, interdisciplinary studies, Italian studies, liberal arts/general studies, philosophy, political science/government, psychology, religion, Russian and Slavic studies, sociology, Southwest American studies, and women's studies). Economics, biology, organisms, ecology, evolution, and sociology are the largest.

Required: To graduate, students must have a GPA of 2.0. No major may require more than 14 units in any one department and no more than 16 overall (including prerequisites). Students must take and pass at least 1 full unit in each academic division. They must complete a Critical Perspectives requirement, consisting of "West in Time" units (one two-block course, 2 units); a "Global Cultures" unit (1 unit); a "Social Inequality" unit (1 unit); Scientific Investigation of the Natural World (2 units, including at least one lab or field course); Quantitative Reasoning (1 unit). Courses may meet more than one designation (for example, a course may be designated both "West in Time" and "Global Cultures") but students must choose one designation or the other, except in the case of "Quantitative Reasoning," which may be fulfilled along with any of the other Critical Perspectives requirements. Basic competency in a foreign language is also required, as is 2 units of a First Year Experience course.

Special: CC offers study abroad in many countries, a Washington semester, student-designed majors, 3-3 law program opportunity with Columbia University School of Law, and 3-2/4-2 engineering degrees with Columbia University, Rensselaer Polytechnic Institute, University of Southern California, and Washington University. There are 12 national honor societies and including Phi Beta Kappa.

Faculty/Classroom: 57% of faculty are male; 43% are female. All teach undergraduates. No introductory courses are taught by graduate students. The average class size in a regular course is 15.

Admissions: 22% of the 2013-2014 applicants were accepted. The SAT scores for the 2013-2014 freshman class were: Critical Reading--2% below 500, 20% between 500 and 599, 48% between 600 and 699, and 31% between 700 and 800; Math--2% below 500, 15% between 500 and 599, 50% between 600 and 699, and 33% between 700 and 800; Writing--2% below 500, 16% between 500 and 599, 55% between 600 and 699, and 28% between 700 and 800. The ACT scores were 1% below 21, 2% between 21 and 23, 16% between 24 and 26, 17% between 27 and 28, and 64% above 28. 87% of the current freshmen were in the top fifth of their class; 98% were in the top two fifths. 21 freshmen graduated first in their class.

Requirements: Applicants should have completed at least 16 (18 to 20 recommended) high school academic credits. The GED is accepted. An essay is required. Colorado College has adopted a new flexible testing policy which allows applicants an expanded set of choices for meeting standardized test requirements. AP credits are accepted. Important factors in the admissions decision are advanced placement or honors courses, extracurricular activities record, and evidence of special talent.

Procedure: Freshmen are admitted fall and spring. Entrance exams should be taken by January 15 for fall entry. There are early decision, early admissions, and deferred admissions plans. Early decision applications should be filed by November 15; regular applications, by January 15 for fall entry; and November 1 for spring entry, along with a $60 fee. Notification of early decision is sent December 15; regular decision, April 1. 204 early decision candidates were accepted for the 2013-2014 class. 872 applicants were on the 2013 waiting list; 43 were admitted. Applications are accepted online.

Transfer: 37 transfer students enrolled in 2012-2013. 64 of 128 credits required for the bachelor's degree must be completed at CC.

Visiting: There are regularly scheduled orientations for prospective students, including a class visit, an information session with an admissions director, and a student-led tour. There are guides for informal visits, visitors may sit in on classes, and stay overnight. To schedule a visit, contact the Admission Office.

Financial Aid: CC is a member of CSS. The CSS/Profile and FAFSA, and noncustodial parents' form, parent and student tax return are required. The priority date for freshman financial aid applications for fall entry is November 15. The deadline for filing freshman financial aid applications for fall entry is February 15.

International Students: There are 124 international students enrolled. The school actively recruits these students. Applicants must submit either the SAT Reasoning, ACT test, or three exams of the applicant's choice chosen from a list.

Graduates: From July 1, 2012 to June 30, 2013, 547 bachelor's degrees were awarded. The most popular majors were sociology (7%), economics (6%), and biology (general) (6%). 30 companies recruited on campus in 2012-2013. In an average class, 1% graduate in 3 years or less, 79% graduate in 4 years or less, 86% graduate in 5 years or less, and 87% graduate in 6 years or less.

Admissions Contact: Roberto Garcia, Director of Admissions. E-Mail: *admission@coloradocollege.edu* Web: *www.coloradocollege.edu*

COLORADO MESA UNIVERSITY — A-2
Mesa State College

Grand Junction, CO 81501 — (970) 248-1613; (800)982-6372; (970) 248-1973

Full-time: 3371 men, 3660 women	**Faculty:** n/av
Part-time: 929 men, 1454 women	**Ph.D.s:** n/av
Graduate: 25 men, 64 women	**Student/Faculty:** 24 to 1
Year: semesters, summer session	**Tuition:** $7206 ($17,944)
Application Deadline:	**Room & Board:** $9643
Freshman Class: n/av	

LESS COMPETITIVE

A comprehensive university located in the center of western Colorado, Colorado Mesa University (formerly Mesa State College), is dedicated to providing an exceptional educational experience in a student-centered environment featuring small class sizes and a high level of student/faculty interaction. As western Colorado's largest university, with enrollment exceeding 9,000 students, the University serves as the primary intellectual and cultural center of western Colorado and promotes the exchange of ideas that are of regional, national and international importance. Founded in 1925, the University offers professional and technical programs at the undergraduate and graduate level. The main campus is located in the heart of Grand Junction, nestled between mountains and high-desert canyons, and is minutes away from the best outdoor recreation in the country. Professors are dedicated to teaching and providing educational opportunities and tools that help students succeed in today's interconnected world. With low student-to-teacher ratios, students and professors have the opportunity to build one-on-one relationships. The University remains one of the most affordable universities in Colorado. Additionally, campus expansion has resulted in the renovation and addition of state-of-the-art learning facilities. Athletics are an integral part of the collegiate experience. Student athletes compete in 23 NCAA Division II athletic teams as members of the Rocky

Mountain Athletic Conference, and have regularly achieved national rankings. With all that has changed in the institution's history, dedication to providing the highest quality education in a student-centered environment has always remained. It is this principle that will continue to guide the University into the future. In addition to regional accreditation, CMU has baccalaureate program accreditation with NASM. The library contains 330,121 volumes, 1.0 million microform items, and 19,089 audio/video tapes/CDs/DVDs, and subscribes to 431 periodicals including electronic. Computerized library services include interlibrary loans, database searching, Internet access, and Wi-Fi capability. Special learning facilities include an art gallery and radio station. The 78-acre campus is in a small town 250 miles west of Denver and 300 miles East of Salt Lake City. Including any residence halls, there are 26 buildings.

Student Life: 88% of undergraduates are from Colorado. Others are from 45 states, 14 foreign countries, and Canada. 72% are White; 14% Hispanic. The average age of freshmen is 20; all undergraduates, 24. 35% do not continue beyond their first year; 30% remain to graduate.

Housing: 2251 students can be accommodated in college housing, which includes coed dorms and on-campus apartments. On-campus housing is available on a first-come and first-served basis. 79% of students commute. Alcohol is not permitted. All students may keep cars.

Activities: There are no fraternities or sororities. There are 50 groups on campus, including art, cheerleading, choir, chorale, chorus, computers, dance, drama, ethnic, film, gay, honors, international, jazz band, literary magazine, marching band, musical theater, newspaper, outdoor program and club sports, political, professional, radio and TV, religious, social, social service, and student government. Popular campus events include Unity Fest and Art Shows.

Sports: There are 11 intercollegiate sports for men and 10 for women, and 5 intramural sports for men and 5 for women. Facilities include a weight room, tennis courts, a swimming pool, and a recreation center with climbing walls, racquetball courts, an elevated running track, and workout facilities.

Disabled Students: All of the campus is accessible. Facilities include wheelchair ramps, elevators, special parking, specially equipped restrooms, special class scheduling, lowered drinking fountains, lowered telephones, and special housing.

Services: Counseling and information services are available, as is tutoring in every subject. There is a reader service for the blind, and remedial math, reading, and writing.

Campus Safety and Security: Measures include 24-hour foot and vehicle patrol, emergency notification system, self-defense education, and security escort services. There are emergency telephones, lighted pathways/sidewalks, and controlled access to dorms/residences.

Programs of Study: CMU confers B.A., B.S., B.A.S., B.B.A., B.F.A. and B.S.N. degrees. Associate, master's, and doctoral degrees are also awarded. Bachelor's degrees are awarded in BIOLOGICAL SCIENCE (biology/biological science), BUSINESS (accounting, business administration and management, and management information systems), COMMUNICATIONS AND THE ARTS (art, communications, English, music, Spanish, theatre arts, and theater management), COMPUTER AND PHYSICAL SCIENCE (computer science, mathematics, and physical sciences), ENGINEERING AND ENVIRONMENTAL DESIGN (engineering technology, environmental science, and graphic arts technology), HEALTH PROFESSIONS (nursing), SOCIAL SCIENCE (history, liberal arts/general studies, physical fitness/movement, political science/government, psychology, social science, and sociology). Physics, environmental science and technology. are the strongest academically. Kinesiology, business, and nursing have the largest enrollments.

Required: To graduate, students must complete a minimum of 120 credits, with 40 hours in upper-level courses in the emphasis area and a minimum GPA of 2.0. All students must take 33 hours of general education courses and 3 hours of physical education.

Special: CMU offers internships in many of its programs, including one in the state legislature, a Washington semester, work-study programs, and the B.A.-B.S. degree in several majors. Nondegree study for students over 20 years of age and credit for life, military, and work experience are available. There are 10 national honor societies, a freshman honors program, and 5 departmental honors programs.

Faculty/Classroom: All teach undergraduates. No introductory courses are taught by graduate students. The average class size in an introductory lecture is 25; in a laboratory is 15; and in a regular course is 20.

Admissions: 22% of the current freshmen were in the top fifth of their class; 45% were in the top two fifths.

Requirements: The SAT or ACT is required. In addition, applicants must be graduates of an accredited secondary school or hold the GED. The college prefers that students complete 4 years of high school English and math, 3 of science, 2 of social studies and electives, 1 of a foreign language, and 1 of history. An essay, an interview, or an audition is recommended for some majors. A GPA of 2.0 is required. AP and CLEP credits are accepted.

Procedure: Freshmen are admitted to all sessions. Entrance exams should be taken late in the junior year or early in the senior year. There are deferred admissions and rolling admissions plans. Application deadlines are open. Application fee is $30. Applications are accepted online.

Transfer: 652 transfer students enrolled in 2012-2013. Applicants must have a minimum GPA of 2.3 with 13 semester hours; otherwise, they must meet the criteria for entering freshmen. 28 of 120 credits required for the bachelor's degree must be completed at CMU.

Visiting: There are regularly scheduled orientations for prospective students. There are guides for informal visits and visitors may sit in on classes. To schedule a visit, contact The Admissions Office at (970) 248-1875.

Financial Aid: The FAFSA is required. Check with the school for current application deadlines.

International Students: They must take the TOEFL with a minimum score of 525 on the paper-based TOEFL (PBT) or 50 on the Internet-based version (iBT). They must also take the SAT or ACT.

Graduates: From July 1, 2012 to June 30, 2013, 727 bachelor's degrees were awarded. The most popular majors were business administration (13%), nursing (8%), and kinesiology (6%). 150 companies recruited on campus in 2012-2013. In an average class, 1% graduate in 3 years or less, 13% graduate in 4 years or less, 29% graduate in 5 years or less, and 29% graduate in 6 years or less.

Admissions Contact: Jared Meier, Director of Admissions. E-Mail: *admissions@coloradomesa.edu* Web: *www.coloradomesa.edu*

COLORADO SCHOOL OF MINES C-2

Golden, CO 80401 (303) 273-3220
(888) 446-9489; (303) 273-3509

Full-time: 2125 men, 590 women	**Faculty:** n/av; I, -$
Part-time: 470 men, 135 women	**Ph.D.s:** 90%
Graduate: 635 men, 270 women	**Student/Faculty:** n/av
Year: semesters, summer session	**Tuition:** $11,000 ($24,000)
Application Deadline:	**Room & Board:** $8000
Freshman Class: n/av	
SAT or ACT: required	

HIGHLY COMPETITIVE

The Colorado School of Mines, founded in 1874, is a public institution offering programs in math, science, economics, and engineering. In addition to regional accreditation, Mines has baccalaureate program accreditation with ABET. The library contains 356,000 volumes, 236,000 microform items, and subscribes to 2,700 periodicals including electronic. Computerized library services include interlibrary loans, database searching, and Internet access. Special learning facilities include a The 373-acre campus is in a small town 20 miles west of Denver. Including any residence halls, there are 40 buildings.

Student Life: 76% of undergraduates are from Colorado. Others are from 44 states, 52 foreign countries, and Canada. 90% are from public schools. 79% are White. 52% are Protestant; 21% Catholic; 20% claim no religious affiliation. The average age of freshmen is 18; all undergraduates, 20. 14% do not continue beyond their first year; 67% remain to graduate.

Housing: 855 students can be accommodated in college housing, which includes single-sex and coed dorms, on-campus apartments, and married student housing. In addition, there are fraternity houses. On-campus housing is guaranteed for the freshman year only, is available on a first-come, and first-served basis. 10% of students commute. All students may keep cars.

Activities: 19% of men belong to 7 national fraternities; 19% of women belong to 3 national sororities. There are 95 groups on campus, including band, cheerleading, choir, chorus, computers, drama, ethnic, honors, international, jazz band, literary magazine, marching band, musical theater, newspaper, political, professional, religious, social, social service, student government, and yearbook. Popular campus events include International Day and Parents Day.

Sports: There are 9 intercollegiate sports for men and 7 for women, and 20 intramural sports for men and 20 for women. Facilities include a 10,000-seat stadium, a recreation center, a gym, numerous intramural fields, tennis courts, and a field house.

Disabled Students: All of the campus is accessible. Facilities include wheelchair ramps, elevators, special parking, specially equipped restrooms, special class scheduling, lowered drinking fountains, lowered telephones, and special housing.

Services: Counseling and information services are available, as is tutoring in most subjects. There is a reader service for the blind, and remedial math and writing.

Campus Safety and Security: Measures include 24-hour foot and vehicle patrol, emergency notification system, and self-defense education. There are emergency telephones and lighted pathways/sidewalks.

Programs of Study: Mines confers B.S. degrees. Master's and doctoral degrees are also awarded. Bachelor's degrees are awarded in COMPUTER AND PHYSICAL SCIENCE (chemistry, mathematics, and physics), ENGINEERING AND ENVIRONMENTAL DESIGN (chemical engineering, engineering, geological engineering, geophysical engineering, metallurgical engineering, mining and mineral engineering, and petroleum/natural gas engineering), SOCIAL SCIENCE (economics). Chemical engineering, geological engineering, and petroleum engineering are the strongest academically. General engineering, chemical engineering, and engineering physics have the largest enrollments.

Required: Students must complete 138 to 148 credit hours, with 35 to 40 hours in the major and a GPA of 2.0. Required courses include humanities, calculus, physics, computer science, chemistry, and phys ed.

Special: Co-op programs, internships in the McBride honors program in the humanities, accelerated degree programs in all majors, dual majors, study abroad in 20 countries, and nondegree study are offered. There are 1 national honor societies, a freshman honors program, and 3 departmental honors programs.

Faculty/Classroom: 80% of faculty are male; 20% are female. 93% teach undergraduates, 50% do research, and 50% do both. No introductory courses are taught by graduate students. The average class size in an introductory lecture is 100; in a laboratory is 22; and in a regular course is 29.

Admissions: 75 freshmen graduated first in their class.

Requirements: The SAT or ACT is required. Applicants must be graduates of an accredited secondary school. The GED is accepted. Students should have completed 16 high school academic credits, including 4 credits each of English and math, 3 of science, 2 of social studies, and 3 academic electives. AP credits are accepted. Important factors in the admissions decision are advanced placement or honors courses, leadership record, and recommendations by school officials.

Procedure: Freshmen are admitted to all sessions. Entrance exams should be taken by late in the junior year or early in the senior year. There are deferred admissions and rolling admissions plans. Check with the school for current application deadlines. The fall 2013 application fee was $45. Applications are accepted online.

Transfer: 79 transfer students enrolled in 2012-2013. Transfer applicants must have a minimum GPA of 2.75 30 of 138 credits required for the bachelor's degree must be completed at Mines.

Visiting: There are regularly scheduled orientations for prospective students, including a half day-long visitation program twice each fall where students may visit departments and talk with faculty. Sessions in admissions and financial aid also are given. There are guides for informal visits and visitors may sit in on classes. To schedule a visit, contact the Admissions Office.

Financial Aid: In 2013-2014, 85% of all full-time freshmen and 85% of continuing full-time students received some form of financial aid. 74% of all full-time freshmen and 74% of continuing full-time students received need-based aid. The average freshman award was $15,540. Need-based scholarships or need-based grants averaged $8,350; and need-based self-help aid (loans and jobs) averaged $7,190. 70% of undergraduate students work part-time. Average annual earnings from campus work are $900. The average financial indebtedness of the 2013 graduate was $18,500. Mines is a member of CSS. The FAFSA is required. Check with the school for current application deadlines.

International Students: There are 204 international students enrolled. The school actively recruits these students. They must take the TOEFL and the Comprehensive English Language Test.

Graduates: From July 1, 2012 to June 30, 2013, 563 bachelor's degrees were awarded. The most popular majors were general engineering (34%), petroleum engineering (12%), and chemical engineering (11%). 267 companies recruited on campus in 2012-2013. In an average class, 1% graduate in 3 years or less, 40% graduate in 4 years or less, 66% graduate in 5 years or less, and 69% graduate in 6 years or less. Of the 2012 graduating class, 20% were enrolled in graduate school within 6 months of graduation, and 95% were employed.

Admissions Contact: Bruce Goetz, Director of Admissions. E-Mail: *admit@mines.edu* Web: *www.mines.edu*

COLORADO STATE UNIVERSITY-FORT COLLINS C-1

Fort Collins, CO 80523	**(970) 491-6909; (970) 491-7799**
Full-time: 10202 men, 10774 women	**Faculty:** 984; I, -$
Part-time: 865 men, 724 women	**Ph.D.s:** 99%
Graduate: 2058 men, 2411 women	**Student/Faculty:** 17 to 1
Year: semesters, summer session	**Tuition:** $9314 ($25,167)
Application Deadline: February 1	**Room & Board:** $10,776
Freshman Class: 17970 applied, 13914 accepted, 4443 enrolled	
SAT CR/M: 560/580	**ACT:** 25 **VERY COMPETITIVE**

Colorado State University, founded in 1870 and part of the Colorado State University system, is a public, land-grant institution offering 70 undergraduate degrees in 62 departments within 8 colleges. There are 8 undergraduate schools and one graduate school. In addition to regional accreditation, Colorado State has baccalaureate program accreditation with AACSB, ABET, ACCE, ACEJMC, CSWE, NASM, and SAF. The 2 libraries contain 2.8 million volumes, 86,614 microform items, and 2,890 audio/video tapes/CDs/DVDs, and subscribe to 77,181 periodicals including electronic. Computerized library services include interlibrary loans, database searching, Internet access, and Wi-Fi capability. Special learning facilities include an art gallery, radio station, TV station, Colorado State can boast many unique state-of-the-art learning facilities including a concert hall, thrust theatre, music hall, engineering research center, equine center, veterinary teaching hospital, environmental learning center, and a plant environmental research center. These are just a few of the cutting-edge learning facilities that serve the many disciplines at CSU. The 586-acre campus is in a suburban area about 65 miles north of Denver. Including any residence halls, there are 157 buildings.

Student Life: 77% of undergraduates are from Colorado. Others are from 50 states, 76 foreign countries, and Canada. 72% are White. The average age of freshmen is 18; all undergraduates, 21. 14% do not continue beyond their first year; 65% remain to graduate.

Housing: 6699 students can be accommodated in college housing, which includes coed dorms, on-campus apartments, off-campus apartments, and married student housing. honors floors, and more than 10 different residential learning communities. On-campus housing is guaranteed for the freshman year only, is available on a first-come, and first-served basis. 75% of students commute. All students may keep cars.

Activities: 7% of men belong to 21 national fraternities; 9% of women belong to 16 national sororities. There are 590 groups on campus, including art, band, cheerleading, choir, chorale, chorus, computers, dance, drama, drill team, environmental, ethnic, film, gay, honors, international, jazz band, literary magazine, marching band, musical theater, newspaper, opera, orchestra, pep band, photography, political, professional, radio and TV, religious, social, social service, student government, and symphony. Popular campus events include Homecoming, Ag Day, President's Annual Address and Picnic.

Sports: There are 5 intercollegiate sports for men and 9 for women, and 22 intramural sports for men and 22 for women. Athletic and recreation facilities include a renovated 30,000-seat stadium, an 8745-seat arena, indoor and outdoor tracks, tennis courts, intramural fields, indoor swimming pools, a comprehensive student recreation center (featuring free weights, state-of-the-art fitness equipment, and sports courts), and a ropes course.

Disabled Students: 98% of the campus is accessible. Facilities include wheelchair ramps, elevators, special parking, specially equipped restrooms, special class scheduling, lowered drinking fountains, lowered telephones, special housing.

Services: Counseling and information services are available, as is tutoring in most subjects. There is a reader service for the blind. Interpreters and note takers are available.

Campus Safety and Security: Measures include 24-hour foot and vehicle patrol, emergency notification system, self-defense education, and security escort services. There are shuttle buses, emergency telephones, lighted pathways/sidewalks, controlled access to dorms/residences, lectures by campus police on a variety of safety issues, a crime victim support unit and a bike patrol.

Programs of Study: Colorado State confers B.A., B.S., B.F.A., B.S.W. and B.M. degrees. Master's and doctoral degrees are also awarded. Bachelor's degrees are awarded in AGRICULTURE (agricultural business management, agricultural economics, animal science, equine science, fishing and fisheries, forestry and related sciences, horticulture, natural resource management, range/farm management, and soil science), BIOLOGICAL SCIENCE (biochemistry, biology/biological science, botany, ecology, microbiology, nutrition, wildlife biology, and zoology), BUSINESS (apparel and accessories marketing, banking and finance, business administration and management, hospitality management services, hotel/motel and restaurant management, marketing/retailing/merchandising, real estate, recreational facilities management, and tourism), COMMUNICATIONS AND THE ARTS (apparel design, art, art history and appreciation, communications, creative writing, dance, dramatic arts, English, fine arts, French, German, journalism, languages, music, music performance, music theory and composition, performing arts, Spanish, theatre acting, theater design, theatre production, and theatre studies), COMPUTER AND PHYSICAL SCIENCE (applied mathematics, chemistry, computer science, geology, information sciences and systems, mathematics, natural sciences, physical sciences, physics, and statistics), EDUCATION (agricultural education, art education, education, English education, foreign languages education, mathematics education, music education, science education, and technology & science education), ENGINEERING AND ENVIRONMENTAL DESIGN (bioengineering, biomedical engineering, chemical engineering, civil engineering, computer engineering, computer technology, construction management, electrical/electronics engineering, engineering, engineering and applied science, engineering physics, environmental engineering, interior design, landscape architecture/design, and mechanical engineering), HEALTH PROFESSIONS (biomedical science, environmental health science, exercise science, and health science), SOCIAL SCIENCE (anthropology, economics, ethnic studies, family/consumer studies, fire services administration, food science, history, human development, interdisciplinary studies, international studies, liberal arts/general studies, philosophy, political science/government, psychology, social work, sociology, and water resources). Biomedical sciences, chemical and biological engineering, and mechanical engineering are the strongest academically. Business, biology, health and exercise science have the largest enrollments.

Required: To graduate, students must complete at least 120 credit hours (more for some programs) of which 42 must be upper division. The minimum GPA for graduation is 2.0. Students must complete the All University Core and all curricular requirements as described in the current catalog.

Special: Colorado State offers a co-op program in Engineering. Study abroad, a semester at sea, work-study programs, internships, B.A.-B.S. degrees, dual majors, and pass/fail options are available. Teaching certification students receive a bachelor's degree in their chosen subject and also complete a certification sequence through the School of Education. There are 32 national honor societies, including Phi Beta Kappa, a freshman honors program, and 19 departmental honors programs.

Faculty/Classroom: 64% of faculty are male; 36% are female. All teach and do research. Graduate students teach 18% of introductory courses. The average class size in an introductory lecture is 59; in a laboratory is 23; and in a regular course is 39.

Admissions: 77% of the 2013-2014 applicants were accepted. The SAT scores for the 2013-2014 freshman class were: Critical Reading--20% below 500, 46% between 500 and 599, 30% between 600 and 699, and 5% between 700 and 800; Math--17% below 500, 43% between 500 and 599, 35% between 600 and 699, and 5% between 700 and 800. The ACT scores were 11% below 21, 28% between 21 and 23, 30% between 24 and 26, 14% between 27 and 28, and 16% above 28. 42% of the current freshmen were in the top fifth of their class; 76% were in the top two fifths. There were 7 National Merit finalists. 69 freshmen graduated first in their class.

Requirements: The SAT or ACT is required. Graduation from secondary school is required, but the GED is accepted. Priority consideration is given to applicants who have earned a minimum 3.25 GPA with no D/F grades and who will have successfully satisfied our academic course work standards before enrolling at CSU. Applicants with a GPA below 3.25, occasional D/F grades, and/or fewer than the 18 recommended high school units are encouraged to apply, since many factors are considered in the holistic review process. Please see our Admissions website (http:/admissions.colostate.edu/) for detailed information. The 18 recommended high school credits are to include 4 English, 4 math (algebra I and II, geometry, and an advanced math), 3 natural sciences (at least 2 must include a lab), 2 social studies, 1 history, 2 foreign language (must be the same language), and 2 academic electives. An essay (minimum 250 words) and 1 recommendation are required. The most recent freshman class entered with an average: GPA of 3.61; ACT Composite score of 24.7; SAT Critical Reading score of 566; and SAT Math score of 574. AP and CLEP credits are accepted.

Procedure: Freshmen are admitted to all sessions. Entrance exams should be taken During the junior year or early fall of the senior year. There are deferred admissions and rolling admissions plans. Applications should be filed by February 1 for fall entry; November 1 for spring entry, along with a $50 fee. Notification is sent on a rolling basis. Applications are accepted online.

Transfer: 1447 transfer students enrolled in 2012-2013. Strong candidates for transfer admission have earned a minimum 2.5 cumulative GPA in 30 or more college-level academic semester credits and have satisfied the transfer admissions requirement in mathematics (see admissions website for details), http:/admissions.colostate.edu/. Students holding an Associate Degree from an accredited Colorado institution are guaranteed admission provided that it is the last institution attended and that a cumulative 2.0 GPA has been achieved from all institutions attended. Specific majors may require additional course work and a higher GPA. 30 of 120 credits required for the bachelor's degree must be completed at Colorado State.

Visiting: There are regularly scheduled orientations for prospective students, Regularly scheduled visit days provide specialized information for particular groups including high school seniors and juniors, transfer students, special interests and others. A daily information session and campus tour are presented each weekday. There are guides for informal visits and visitors may sit in on classes. To schedule a visit, contact the Office of Admissions.

Financial Aid: In 2013-2014, 60% of all full-time freshmen and 64% of continuing full-time students received some form of financial aid. 48% of all full-time freshmen and 52% of continuing full-time students received need-based aid. The average freshman award was $11,492. Need-based scholarships or need-based grants averaged $9,670; need-based self-help aid (loans and jobs) averaged $5,126; non-need-based athletic scholarships averaged $20,734; and other non-need-based awards and non-need-based scholarships averaged $4,059. 30% of undergraduate students work part-time. Average annual earnings from campus work are $3566. The average financial indebtedness of the 2013 graduate was $21,185. The FAFSA is required. The priority date for freshman financial aid applications for fall entry is March 1. The deadline for filing freshman financial aid applications for fall entry is March 1.

International Students: There are 630 international students enrolled. The school actively recruits these students. They must take the TOEFL with a minimum score of 550 on the paper-based TOEFL (PBT) or 79 on the Internet-based version (iBT), Scores from other English language proficiency exams may be considered in lieu of the TOEFL. They must also take the SAT and ACT.

Graduates: From July 1, 2012 to June 30, 2013, 4879 bachelor's degrees were awarded. The most popular majors were business administration (14%), human development and family studies (9%), and social sciences (9%). 662 companies recruited on campus in 2012-2013. In an average class, 2% graduate in 3 years or less, 36% graduate in 4 years or less, 60% graduate in 5 years or less, and 65% graduate in 6 years or less. Of the 2012 graduating class, 13% were enrolled in graduate school within 6 months of graduation, and 54% were employed.

Admissions Contact: Bryan Whish, Director of Undergraduate Admission. E-Mail: *admissions@colostate.edu* Web: *http:/admissions.colostate.edu/*

COLORADO STATE UNIVERSITY-PUEBLO D-3

Pueblo, CO 81001-4901 (719) 549-2462
(877) 872-9653; (719) 549-2419

Full-time: 1550 men, 1900 women
Part-time: 800 men, 1250 women
Graduate: 85 men, 140 women
Year: semesters, summer session
Application Deadline: open
Freshman Class: n/av
SAT or ACT: required

Faculty: n/av
Ph.D.s: 70%
Student/Faculty: n/av
Tuition: $6222 ($18,744)
Room & Board: $8260

LESS COMPETITIVE

Colorado State University - Pueblo, founded in 1933, is part of the Colorado State University System. The public institution offers undergraduate programs in humanities and social sciences, business administration, nursing, applied science, technology, engineering, and education. The figures in the above capsule and in this profile are approximate. There are 5 undergraduate schools and 3 graduate schools. In addition to regional accreditation, USC has baccalaureate program accreditation with ABET, CSWE, NASM, and NLN. The library contains 180,000 volumes, 10,000 microform items, and 16,862 audio/video tapes/CDs/DVDs, and subscribes to 1,327 periodicals including electronic. Computerized library services include interlibrary loans and database searching. Special learning facilities include a learning resource center, art gallery, radio station, TV station, and nature center. The 275-acre campus is in an urban area 100 miles south of Denver, 50 miles south of Colorado Springs, 100 miles north of New Mexico. Including any residence halls, there are 15 buildings.

Student Life: 87% of undergraduates are from Colorado. Others are from 41 states, 32 foreign countries, and Canada. 59% are white; 26% Hispanic. The average age of freshmen is 19; all undergraduates, 26. 39% do not continue beyond their first year; 27% remain to graduate.

Housing: 652 students can be accommodated in college housing, which includes coed dorms and on-campus apartments. On-campus housing is guaranteed for the freshman year only, is available on a first-come, and first-served basis. 81% of students commute. Alcohol is not permitted. All students may keep cars.

Activities: 1% of men belong to 2 national fraternities; 1% of women belong to 1 local sororities. There are 68 groups on campus, including art, cheerleading, choir, chorale, computers, drama, ethnic, gay, honors, international, jazz band, literary magazine, newspaper, pep band, political, professional, radio and TV, religious, social, social service, student government, and symphony. Popular campus events include the Town and Gown series, Teacher Career Fair, and departmental lecture series.

Sports: There are 5 intercollegiate sports for men and 5 for women, and 5 intramural sports for men and 3 for women. Facilities include an arena with an indoor swimming pool, a weight room, a rock-climbing wall, and racquetball, basketball, and volleyball courts; a sports complex with tennis courts, and baseball, softball, and soccer fields; bike trails; a rope course; and a nature center.

Disabled Students: All of the campus is accessible. Facilities include wheelchair ramps, elevators, special parking, specially equipped restrooms, special class scheduling, lowered drinking fountains, and lowered telephones.

Services: Counseling and information services are available, as is tutoring in most subjects. Remedial math and English are available on-campus from a local community college

Campus Safety and Security: Measures include 24-hour foot and vehicle patrol, self-defense education, and security escort services. There are emergency telephones and lighted pathways/sidewalks.

Programs of Study: USC confers B.A., B.S., B.S.B.A., B.S.C.E.T., B.S.E.E.T., B.S.I.En., B.S.M.E.T., B.S.N., and B.S.W. degrees. Master's degrees are also awarded. Bachelor's degrees are awarded in BIOLOGICAL SCIENCE (biochemistry, biology/biological science, and biotechnology), BUSINESS (accounting, business administration and management, and recreation and leisure services), COMMUNICATIONS AND THE

ARTS (art, broadcasting, communications, English, journalism, music performance, music theory and composition, and Spanish), COMPUTER AND PHYSICAL SCIENCE (chemistry, information sciences and systems, mathematics, and physics), EDUCATION (music education), ENGINEERING AND ENVIRONMENTAL DESIGN (automotive technology, civil engineering technology, electrical/electronics engineering technology, industrial administration/management, industrial engineering, mechanical engineering technology, and preengineering), HEALTH PROFESSIONS (chiropractic, environmental health science, exercise science, medical technology, nursing, occupational therapy, physician's assistant, predentistry, premedicine, preoptometry, preosteopathy, prepharmacy, prepodiatry, preveterinary science, and speech pathology/audiology), SOCIAL SCIENCE (criminology, economics, history, political science/government, prelaw, psychology, social science, social work, and sociology). Business, engineering technology, and nursing are the strongest academically. Accounting, biology, and management have the largest enrollments.

Required: To graduate, all students must complete at least 120 semester hours, including 40 in upper-division courses and 30 to 48 in the major, with a minimum GPA of 2.0. General education requirements include a 14-credit skills component of courses in communication, computer literacy, and quantitative skills, as well as a 19-credit knowledge component of courses in humanities, social sciences, and science and technology. Other requirements vary with the major.

Special: USC offers co-op programs, internships, study abroad in 8 countries, and on-campus work-study programs. Also available are 5-year combined B.S.B.A./M.B.A. degrees, a 3-2 engineering degree with Colorado State University, dual majors, nondegree study, and preprofessional programs in forestry, physical therapy, and wildlife management. USC is a member of the National Student Exchange. There are 10 national honor societies, including Phi Beta Kappa, a freshman honors program, and 10 departmental honors programs.

Faculty/Classroom: 60% of faculty are male; 39% are female. 99% teach undergraduates, 10% do research, and 4% do both. No introductory courses are taught by graduate students. The average class size in an introductory lecture is 70; in a laboratory is 24; and in a regular course is 22.

Requirements: The SAT or ACT is required. Applicants must be graduates of an accredited secondary school or have a GED certificate with a minimum score of 45. USC computes a CCHE admission index, comprised of the high school GPA and SAT or ACT scores. Students scoring below the minimum will still be considered by an admissions committee. Academic preparation should consist of 4 years of English, 3 of math including algebra and geometry, 2 of natural science including physical science, 3 years of social studies including American government, and 1 year of a foreign language. AP and CLEP credits are accepted. Important factors in the admissions decision are advanced placement or honors courses, leadership record, and recommendations by school officials.

Procedure: Freshmen are admitted to all sessions. Entrance exams should be taken during spring of the junior year or fall of the senior year. There is a rolling admissions plan. Check with the school for current application deadlines. Notification is sent on a rolling basis.

Transfer: A minimum GPA of 2.0 and official transcripts of previous college work are required. Applicants with fewer than 30 credit hours must submit ACT or SAT scores and high school transcripts. 30 of 120 credits required for the bachelor's degree must be completed at USC.

Visiting: There are regularly scheduled orientations for prospective students, including a tour, lunch, and mini-sessions on financial aid, athletics, scholarships, and student services. There are guides for informal visits and visitors may sit in on classes. To schedule a visit, contact the Admissions Office.

Financial Aid: The FAFSA is required. Check with the school for current application deadlines.

International Students: The school actively recruits these students. They must take the TOEFL or MELAB.

Admissions Contact: Director of Admissions and Records E-Mail: *info@uscolo.edu* Web: *www.colostate-pueblo.edu*

FORT LEWIS COLLEGE — B-4

Durango, CO 81301 — **(970) 247-7180; (970) 247-7179**

Full-time: 1881 men, 1817 women	**Faculty:** 158; IIB, --$
Part-time: 185 men, 145 women	**Ph.D.s:** 87%
Graduate: 7 men, 30 women	**Student/Faculty:** 21 to 1
Year: varies, summer session	**Tuition:** $6923 ($17,763)
Application Deadline: August 1	**Room & Board:** $8590
Freshman Class: 2560 applied, 2240 accepted, 876 enrolled	
ACT: 22	**SAT:** required — **COMPETITIVE**

Fort Lewis College, founded in 1911, is a public institution with undergraduate programs in arts and sciences, business and education. There are 2 undergraduate schools and one graduate school. In addition to regional accreditation, FLC has baccalaureate program accreditation with AACSB, ABET, NASM, and TEAC. The library contains 257,653 volumes, 344,803 microform items, and 10,300 audio/video tapes/CDs/DVDs, and subscribes to 26,820 periodicals including electronic. Computerized library services include interlibrary loans, database searching, Internet access, and Wi-Fi capability. Special learning facilities include an art gallery, radio station, a center for Southwest studies. The 362-acre campus is in a small town Durango Colorado, is in the southwestern corner of Colorado, about 330 southwest of Denver. Including any residence halls, there are 58 buildings.

Student Life: 59% of undergraduates are from Colorado. Others are from 50 states, 20 foreign countries, and Canada. 85% are from public schools. 60% are White; 20% American Indian/Alaska Native. The average age of freshmen is 18; all undergraduates, 21. 35% do not continue beyond their first year; 38% remain to graduate.

Housing: 1572 students can be accommodated in college housing, which includes coed dorms, on-campus apartments, and married student housing. Living learning, and faculty in residence programs. On-campus housing is guaranteed for the freshman year only, is available on a first-come, and first-served basis. 63% of students commute. Alcohol is not permitted. All students may keep cars.

Activities: There are no fraternities or sororities. There are 65 groups on campus, including art, band, cheerleading, choir, chorale, chorus, computers, dance, drama, environmental, ethnic, gay, honors, international, jazz band, literary magazine, newspaper, pep band, political, professional, radio and TV, religious, social, social service, student government, and symphony. Popular campus events include Fiesta on the Mesa, Fall Blaze, Homecoming and Hozhoni Days.

Sports: There are 5 intercollegiate sports for men and 6 for women, and 16 intramural sports for men and 16 for women. Facilities include a field house, an outdoor sports complex, an indoor swimming pool, and a student life center, which includes a 3-court gym, racquetball court, aerobic/dance studio, track, climbing wall, and cardio/weight area.

Disabled Students: All of the campus is accessible. Facilities include wheelchair ramps, elevators, special parking, specially equipped restrooms, special class scheduling, lowered drinking fountains, lowered telephones, special housing, and workstations modified for individual needs.

Services: Counseling and information services are available, as is tutoring in most subjects. There is a reader service for the blind, and remedial math, reading, and writing.

Campus Safety and Security: Measures include 24-hour foot and vehicle patrol, emergency notification system, self-defense education, and security escort services. There are shuttle buses, emergency telephones, lighted pathways/sidewalks, and controlled access to dorms/residences.

Programs of Study: FLC confers B.A., and B.S. degrees. Master's degrees are also awarded. Bachelor's degrees are awarded in AGRICULTURE (environmental studies), BIOLOGICAL SCIENCE (biochemistry and biology/biological science), BUSINESS (accounting, business administration and management, business economics, and marketing and distribution), COMMUNICATIONS AND THE ARTS (art, dramatic arts, English, music, and Spanish), COMPUTER AND PHYSICAL SCIENCE (chemistry, geology, mathematics, and physics), EDUCATION (athletic training), HEALTH PROFESSIONS (exercise science and public health), SOCIAL SCIENCE (American Indian studies, anthropology, economics, gender studies, history, humanities, interdisciplinary studies, philosophy, political science/government, psychology, sociology, and Southwest American studies). Business, psychology and biology have the largest enrollments.

Required: To graduate, students must complete 120 semester hours with 30 to 40 hours in the major, 50 credits outside the major, and a minimum GPA of 2.0 overall and in the major. A total of 32 to 44 hours in general distribution courses is required.

Special: The college offers cooperative programs in most majors, numerous internships, a Washington semester for political science majors, study abroad in 32 countries, student-designed majors, a general studies degree, nondegree study, pass/fail option, and B.A.-B.S. degrees. There are 3-2 engineering degrees with 4 universities and a preforestry degree with Colorado State and Northern Arizona Universities. There are 5 national honor societies and a freshman honors program.

Faculty/Classroom: 50% of faculty are male; 50% are female. All teach undergraduates. No introductory courses are taught by graduate students. The average class size in an introductory lecture is 21; in a laboratory is 20; and in a regular course is 21.

Admissions: 88% of the 2013-2014 applicants were accepted. The SAT scores for the 2013-2014 freshman class were: Critical Reading--38% below 500, 44% between 500 and 599, 14% between 600 and 699, and 3% between 700 and 800; Math--33% below 500, 48% between 500 and 599, 17% between 600 and 699, and 1% between 700 and 800; Writing--43% below 500, 39% between 500 and 599, 16% between 600 and 699. The ACT scores were 37% below 21, 30% between 21 and 23, 21% between 24 and 26, 8% between 27 and 28, and 5% above 28. 32% of the current freshmen were in the top fifth of their class; 65% were in the top two fifths.

Requirements: The SAT or ACT is required. Applicants must be graduates of an accredited secondary school or have a GED certificate. An interview is recommended. AP and CLEP credits are accepted.

Procedure: Freshmen are admitted to all sessions. Entrance exams

should be taken in spring of the junior year. There are deferred admissions and rolling admissions plans. Early decision applications should be filed by January 15; regular applications, by August 1 for fall entry. The fall 2013 application fee was $40. Notification is sent on a rolling basis. Applications are accepted online.

Transfer: 416 transfer students enrolled in 2012-2013. Applicants for transfer should have completed a minimum of 12 credit hours and have a GPA of 2.40. Courses completed with a grade of C- or better may transfer. An interview is recommended. 30 of 120 credits required for the bachelor's degree must be completed at FLC.

Visiting: There are regularly scheduled orientations for prospective students. There are guides for informal visits, visitors may sit in on classes, and stay overnight. To schedule a visit, contact the Office of Admission.

Financial Aid: In 2013-2014, 95% of all full-time freshmen and 80% of continuing full-time students received some form of financial aid. 65% of all full-time freshmen and 60% of continuing full-time students received need-based aid. The average freshman award was $12,131. Need-based scholarships or need-based grants averaged $5,840 ($16,000 maximum); need-based self-help aid (loans and jobs) averaged $4,304 ($5,500 maximum); non-need-based athletic scholarships averaged $10,635 ($16,000 maximum); other non-need-based awards and non-need-based scholarships averaged $6,000 ($16,000 maximum); and $1,400 from other forms of aid. 90% of undergraduate students work part-time. The average financial indebtedness of the 2013 graduate was $25,313. FLC is a member of CSS. The FAFSA is required. The priority date for freshman financial aid applications for fall entry is February 15.

International Students: There are 61 international students enrolled. They must take the TOEFL with a minimum score of 500 on the paper-based TOEFL (PBT) or 61 on the Internet-based version (iBT).

Graduates: From July 1, 2012 to June 30, 2013, 697 bachelor's degrees were awarded. The most popular majors were business administration (16%), biology (7%), and psychology (7%). 140 companies recruited on campus in 2012-2013. In an average class, 17% graduate in 4 years or less, 33% graduate in 5 years or less, and 37% graduate in 6 years or less. Of the 2012 graduating class, 17% were enrolled in graduate school within 6 months of graduation.

Admissions Contact: Andy Burns, Director of Admissions. E-Mail: *admission@fortlewis.edu* Web: *www.explore.fortlewis.edu*

JOHNSON AND WALES UNIVERSITY/DENVER CAMPUS C-2

Denver, CO 80220 **1-877-598-3368; (303) 256-9333**

Full-time: 618 men, 916 women	**Faculty:** 48
Part-time: 62 men, 76 women	**Ph.D.s:** n/av
Graduate: n/av	**Student/Faculty:** 24 to 1
Year: quarters, summer session	**Tuition:** $25,507
Application Deadline: open	**Room & Board:** $9761

Freshman Class: 3019 applied, 1920 accepted, 397 enrolled

COMPETITIVE

Johnson & Wales University/Denver Campus, founded in 2000, offers degree programs in its College of Business, College of Culinary Arts, Hospitality College, and School of Education. There are 4 undergraduate schools. The figures in the above capsule and in this profile are approximate. The library contains 29,000 volumes, and 1,200 audio/video tapes/CDs/DVDs, and subscribes to 215 periodicals including electronic. Computerized library services include interlibrary loans, database searching, Internet access, and laptop Internet portals. Special learning facilities include a learning resource center. The 26-acre campus is in a suburban area. Including any residence halls, there are 19 buildings.

Student Life: 60% of undergraduates are from out of state, mostly the West. Students are from 50 states, 11 foreign countries, and Canada. 48% are white; 11% Hispanic. The average age of freshmen is 18; all undergraduates, 18. 67% remain to graduate.

Housing: College-sponsored housing includes coed dorms and on-campus apartments. On-campus housing is available on a lottery system for upperclassmen. 69% of students commute. Alcohol is not permitted. All students may keep cars.

Activities: There are no fraternities; 1% of women belong to 1 national sorority. There are 26 groups on campus, including Leadership Academy, Campus Activities Board, cheerleading, dance, drama, gay, international, literary magazine, musical theater, newspaper, professional, social, student government, and yearbook. Popular campus events include Winter Week, Love Fest, and Spring Fling.

Sports: Facilities include a gym, a weight room, a cardio room, a sand volleyball pit, and an outdoor basketball court.

Disabled Students: All of the campus is accessible. Facilities include wheelchair ramps, elevators, special parking, specially equipped restrooms, special class scheduling, lowered drinking fountains, and lowered telephones.

Services: Counseling and information services are available, as is tutoring in every subject.

Campus Safety and Security: Measures include 24-hour foot and vehicle patrol and security escort services. There are shuttle buses and emergency telephones.

Programs of Study: JWU confers B.S. degrees. Associate degrees are also awarded. Bachelor's degrees are awarded in BIOLOGICAL SCIENCE (nutrition), BUSINESS (accounting, banking and finance, entrepreneurial studies, hotel/motel and restaurant management, international business management, management science, marketing/retailing/merchandising, and sports management), SOCIAL SCIENCE (criminal justice and food production/management/services). Culinary, sports entertainment event management, and food service management have the largest enrollments.

Required: To graduate, students must complete 180 quarter credit hours, including at least 36 in the major, with a minimum GPA of 2.0. Required classes include English, math, history, psychology, sociology, economics, science, and professional development.

Special: The university offers co-op programs, accelerated degree programs, dual majors, study abroad, and worldwide work-study opportunities in business, hospitality, technology, and culinary arts; Most majors require 11-week internships. There are a freshman honors program.

Faculty/Classroom: No introductory courses are taught by graduate students.

Admissions: 64% of a recent year applicants were accepted.

Requirements: Although SAT and ACT scores are required only for students applying for honors admissions, students who have taken these tests are encouraged to submit their scores. A GPA of 2.0 is required. AP and CLEP credits are accepted. Important factors in the admissions decision are advanced placement or honors courses, extracurricular activities record, parents or siblings who attended this school, and recommendations by school officials.

Procedure: Freshmen are admitted to all sessions. There are deferred admissions and rolling admissions plans. Application deadlines are open. Applications are accepted online.

Transfer: 162 transfer students enrolled in a recent year. Applicants are required to submit official high school and college transcripts and must have earned a minimum college GPA of 2.0. 45 of 180 credits required for the bachelor's degree must be completed at JWU.

Visiting: There are guides for informal visits. Visitors may sit in on classes and stay overnight. To schedule a visit, contact Admissions.

Financial Aid: JWU is a member of CSS. The FAFSA is required. The priority date for freshman financial aid applications for fall entry is March 1.

International Students: The school actively recruits these students.

Admissions Contact: Director of Admissions. A campus DVD is available. E-Mail: *admissions.den@jwu.edu* Web: *www.jwu.edu*

METROPOLITAN STATE UNIVERSITY OF DENVER C-2

Denver, CO 80217-3362 **(303) 556-3058; (303) 556-6345**

Full-time: 5900 men, 7500 women	**Faculty:** n/av
Part-time: 3725 men, 4850 women	**Ph.D.s:** n/av
Graduate: n/av	**Student/Faculty:** n/av
Year: semesters, summer session	**Tuition:** $5335 ($13,000)
Application Deadline: open	**Room & Board:** n/app

Freshman Class: n/av

SAT or ACT: required

LESS COMPETITIVE

Metropolitan State College of Denver, founded in 1963, is a public commuter institution offering degree programs in the liberal arts and sciences, business, and professional studies, as well as individualized degree programs. The figures in the above capsule and in this profile are approximate. There are 3 undergraduate schools. In addition to regional accreditation, Metro State has baccalaureate program accreditation with AACSB, ABET, CSWE, NASAD, NASM, NCATE, NLN, and NRPA. The library contains 692,677 volumes, 1.1 million microform items, and 16,975 audio/video tapes/CDs/DVDs, and subscribes to 4,150 periodicals including electronic. Computerized library services include interlibrary loans and database searching. Special learning facilities include a learning resource center, art gallery, radio station, TV station, a world indoor airport, a writing center, and student support services. The 175-acre campus is in an urban area in Denver. Including any residence halls, there are 38 buildings.

Student Life: 96% of undergraduates are from Colorado. Others are from 46 states, 44 foreign countries, and Canada. 96% are from public schools. 68% are white; 13% Hispanic. The average age of freshmen is 19; all undergraduates, 26. 38% do not continue beyond their first year.

Housing: There are no residence halls. All students commute.

Activities: There are no fraternities or sororities. There are 100 groups on campus, including art, band, cheerleading, chess, choir, chorale, chorus, computers, debate, drama, ethnic, gay, honors, international, jazz band, literary magazine, musical theater, newspaper, orchestra, political, professional, radio and TV, religious, social, social service, student government, and symphony. Popular campus events include Club Day, World Friendship Festival, and Family Night.

Sports: There are 6 intercollegiate sports for men and 7 for women, and

10 intramural sports for men and 6 for women. Facilities include playing fields, volleyball, basketball, badminton, racquetball, handball, squash, and tennis courts, a swimming pool, a dance studio, a weight room, a fitness center and green room, a 3500-seat events center, an auxiliary gym, and a 3/4-mile jogging path.

Disabled Students: 90% of the campus is accessible. Facilities include wheelchair ramps, elevators, special parking, specially equipped restrooms, special class scheduling, lowered drinking fountains, lowered telephones.

Services: Counseling and information services are available, as is tutoring in most subjects. ESL services and an adult learning services office are available.

Campus Safety and Security: Measures include 24-hour foot and vehicle patrol, self-defense education, and security escort services. There are shuttle buses, emergency telephones, lighted pathways/sidewalks, bicycle registration, and date/acquaintance rape education seminars.

Programs of Study: Metro State confers B.A., B.S., and B.F.A. degrees. Bachelor's degrees are awarded in BIOLOGICAL SCIENCE (biology/biological science), BUSINESS (accounting, banking and finance, hospitality management services, management science, marketing/retailing/merchandising, and recreation and leisure services), COMMUNICATIONS AND THE ARTS (art, communications, English, fine arts, industrial design, journalism, modern language, music performance, Spanish, and speech/debate/rhetoric), COMPUTER AND PHYSICAL SCIENCE (atmospheric sciences and meteorology, chemistry, computer management, computer science, information sciences and systems, mathematics, and physics), EDUCATION (music education and physical education), ENGINEERING AND ENVIRONMENTAL DESIGN (airline piloting and navigation, aviation administration/management, aviation computer technology, civil engineering technology, electrical/electronics engineering technology, environmental science, industrial administration/management, industrial engineering technology, land use management and reclamation, mechanical engineering technology, survey and mapping technology, and surveying engineering), HEALTH PROFESSIONS (health care administration and nursing), SOCIAL SCIENCE (African American studies, anthropology, behavioral science, criminal justice, economics, history, human services, Mexican-American/Chicano studies, philosophy, physical fitness/movement, political science/government, psychology, social work, sociology, and urban studies). Criminal justice, psychology, and management have the largest enrollments.

Required: To graduate, students must complete at least 120 credit hours, 40 of which must be upper division and 30 in the major, with a minimum overall GPA of 2.0. There are 3 levels of general studies requirements, totaling 33 hours and including a multicultural requirement and a senior experience.

Special: Metro State offers co-op and service-learning programs in most majors and cross-registration with a consortium of state colleges and the University of Colorado at Denver. Internships, study abroad, work-study programs, dual majors, student-designed majors, an accelerated degree program in nursing, nondegree study, and pass/fail options are available. There are 9 national honor societies, a freshman honors program, and 10 departmental honors programs.

Faculty/Classroom: 56% of faculty are male; 44% are female. All teach undergraduates. No introductory courses are taught by graduate students. The average class size in an introductory lecture is 25; in a laboratory is 14; and in a regular course is 19.

Requirements: The SAT or ACT is required. Applicants should be graduates of an accredited secondary school, with 15 Carnegie units. The GED is accepted. AP and CLEP credits are accepted. Important factors in the admissions decision are recommendations by school officials, extracurricular activities record, and evidence of special talent.

Procedure: Freshmen are admitted to all sessions. Entrance exams should be taken prior to application. There is a rolling admissions plan. Check with the school for current application deadlines. The fall 2011 application fee was $25. Applications are accepted online.

Transfer: Applicants must have a 2.0 GPA and be in good standing at their previous school. Some probationary transfers are considered. 30 of 120 credits required for the bachelor's degree must be completed at Metro State.

Visiting: There are regularly scheduled orientations for prospective students, including class scheduling and registration, college services and resources, transfer of credit, academic advising, choice of major, career counseling, and assessment testing if needed. There are guides for informal visits and visitors may sit in on classes. To schedule a visit, contact the Office of Admissions.

Financial Aid: Metro State is a member of CSS. The FAFSA is required. Check with the school for current application deadlines.

International Students: They must take the TOEFL. The SAT or ACT is required if the applicant is under 20 and has graduated from a U.S. high school.

Admissions Contact: Office of Admissions, Director. A campus DVD is available. E-Mail: *askmetro@mscd.edu* Web: *www.mscd.edu*

NAROPA UNIVERSITY — C-2

Boulder, CO 80302 — (303) 546-5295; (800) 772-6951; (303) 546-3572

Full-time: 123 men, 236 women	**Faculty:** 24; IIA, --$
Part-time: 15 men, 9 women	**Ph.D.s:** 61%
Graduate: 190 men, 419 women	**Student/Faculty:** 11 to 1
Year: semesters	**Tuition:** $28,970
Application Deadline: January 15	**Room & Board:** $8905
Freshman Class: 79 applied, 63 accepted, 38 enrolled	**SPECIAL**

Naropa University, founded in 1974, is a private nonsectarian Buddhist-inspired, experiential liberal arts institution. It offers undergraduate and graduate degrees in the arts, social sciences, and the humanities. There are 4 undergraduate schools and one graduate school. The library contains 35,853 volumes, and 5,794 audio/video tapes/CDs/DVDs, and subscribes to 52 periodicals including electronic. Computerized library services include interlibrary loans, database searching, Internet access, and Wi-Fi capability. Special learning facilities include an art gallery, meditation halls, a writing center, a community arts center, career and community engagement center, on-campus counseling center. The 12-acre campus is in an urban area in Boulder, Colorado. Including any residence halls, there are 14 buildings.

Student Life: 66% of undergraduates are from out of state, mostly the West. Students are from 40 states, 8 foreign countries, and Canada. 65% are White; 12% race unknown. The average age of freshmen is 21; all undergraduates, 25.

Housing: 103 students can be accommodated in college housing, which includes coed on-campus apartments. On-campus housing is guaranteed for the freshman year only, is available on a first-come, first-served basis, and is available on a lottery system for upperclassmen. 81% of students commute. Alcohol is not permitted. All students may keep cars.

Activities: There are no fraternities or sororities. There are 35 groups on campus, including art, chorus, dance, drama, environmental, ethnic, gay, international, literary magazine, political, professional, religious, social, social service, and student government. Popular campus events include Open Mic Coffee House Night, Sustainability/Earth Days, Community Practice Day, and Shambhala Day.

Sports: There is no sports program at Naropa.

Disabled Students: 85% of the campus is accessible. Facilities include wheelchair ramps, elevators, special parking, specially equipped restrooms, special class scheduling, lowered drinking fountains, and lowered telephones.

Services: Counseling and information services are available, as is tutoring in some subjects. There is a reader service for the blind.

Campus Safety and Security: Measures include emergency notification system, self-defense education, and security escort services. There are lighted pathways/sidewalks, controlled access to dorms/residences, evening foot and vehicle patrol, 24 hour on-call liaison to local police/fire department.

Programs of Study: Naropa confers B.A., and B.F.A. degrees. Master's degrees are also awarded. Bachelor's degrees are awarded in AGRICULTURE (environmental studies), COMMUNICATIONS AND THE ARTS (English, music, performing arts, and visual and performing arts), EDUCATION (early childhood education), SOCIAL SCIENCE (interdisciplinary studies, peace studies, psychology, and religion). Psychology, interdisciplinary studies and English have the largest enrollments.

Required: Students must complete 120 credits, 36 to 37 in the major, with a 2.0 average GPA. An extensive core curriculum includes courses in contemplative practices, world wisdom studies, cultural and historical studies, artistic process, scientific inquiry, diversity, humanities, and civic engagement.

Special: Cross-registration with the University of Colorado, work-study programs, internships, dual majors, study abroad (Bhutan, China, Andes and Amazon, India, Nepal, Indonesia, Mekong, Central America and the Middle East), and student-designed majors are available. Volunteer opportunities are also available.

Faculty/Classroom: 38% of faculty are male; 62% are female. 61% teach undergraduates. No introductory courses are taught by graduate students. The average class size in an introductory lecture is 15 and in a regular course is 14.

Admissions: 80% of the 2013-2014 applicants were accepted.

Requirements: A high school transcript, an interview, 2 recommendations, and 3 essays are required. The GED is accepted. AP and CLEP credits are accepted.

Procedure: Freshmen are admitted fall and spring. There are deferred admissions and rolling admissions plans. Applications should be filed by January 15 for fall entry; October 15 for spring entry, along with a $50 fee. Notification is sent on a rolling basis. Applications are accepted online.

Transfer: 91 transfer students enrolled in 2012-2013. Official college transcripts for each academic institution attended. Creative work (writing samples, art slides, music samples) are accepted. 60 of 120 credits required for the bachelor's degree must be completed at Naropa.

Visiting: There are regularly scheduled orientations for prospective students, including daily tours, class visitation, meetings with counselors, and 2 Preview Weekends (fall and spring). There are guides for informal visits and visitors may sit in on classes. To schedule a visit, contact The Visitation Coordinator at (303) 546-3572.

Financial Aid: In 2013-2014, 59% of all full-time freshmen and 67% of continuing full-time students received some form of financial aid. 59% of all full-time freshmen and 67% of continuing full-time students received need-based aid. The average freshman award was $26,978. Need-based scholarships or need-based grants averaged $17,922; need-based self-help aid (loans and jobs) averaged $10,032; and other non-need-based awards and non-need-based scholarships averaged $5,500. The FAFSA is required. The priority date for freshman financial aid applications for fall entry is March 1.

International Students: There are 11 international students enrolled. They must take the TOEFL with a minimum score of 550 on the paper-based TOEFL (PBT) or 80 on the Internet-based version (iBT).

Graduates: From July 1, 2012 to June 30, 2013, 114 bachelor's degrees were awarded. The most popular majors were psychology (29%), interdisciplinary studies (22%), and writing and literature (9%).

Admissions Contact: Janet Erickson, Dean of Admissions. E-Mail: *admissions@naropa.edu* Web: *www.naropa.edu*

REGIS UNIVERSITY C-2

Denver, CO 80221-1099 (303) 458-4900
(800) 388-2366; (303) 964-5534

Full-time: 530 men, 940 women	**Faculty:** 100
Part-time: 25 men, 25 women	**Ph.D.s:** 95%
Graduate: n/av	**Student/Faculty:** n/av
Year: semesters, summer session	**Tuition:** $31,888
Application Deadline: open	**Room & Board:** $9430

Freshman Class: 1946 applied, 1546 accepted, 377 enrolled
SAT: required **ACT:** 23 **COMPETITIVE**

Regis University, founded in 1877, is a private, Roman Catholic liberal arts institution operated by the Society of Jesus, the Jesuits. The figures in the above capsule and in this profile are approximate. There are 3 undergraduate schools. In addition to regional accreditation, Regis has baccalaureate program accreditation with CAHEA, NCATE, and NLN. The library contains 425,000 volumes, 140,000 microform items, and 110,000 audio/video tapes/CDs/DVDs, and subscribes to 4,000 periodicals including electronic. Computerized library services include interlibrary loans, database searching, Internet access, and laptop Internet portals. Special learning facilities include a learning resource center, art gallery, radio station, nursing labs, physical therapy labs, cadaver lab, music labs, classrooms in residence halls. The 90-acre campus is in a suburban area in north Denver. Including any residence halls, there are 16 buildings.

Student Life: 58% of undergraduates are from Colorado. Others are from 45 states, 6 foreign countries, and Canada. 55% are from public schools. 75% are white; 16% Hispanic. 43% are Catholic; 11% Protestant. The average age of freshmen is 18; all undergraduates, 21. 20% do not continue beyond their first year; 65% remain to graduate.

Housing: 680 students can be accommodated in college housing, which includes coed dorms and on-campus apartments. In addition, there are honors houses, special-interest houses, service to others. On-campus housing is guaranteed for all 4 years. 60% of students live on campus; of those, 80% remain on campus on weekends. All students may keep cars.

Activities: There are no fraternities or sororities. There are 54 groups on campus, including art, cheerleading, chess, choir, chorus, dance, debate, environmental, ethnic, forensics, gay, honors, international, jazz band, leadership, literary magazine, musical theater, newspaper, orchestra, photography, political, professional, radio and TV, religious, social, social service, student government, and yearbook. Popular campus events include Mistletoe Madness, Ranger Week, and Hall Olympics.

Sports: There are 5 intercollegiate sports for men and 7 for women, and 8 intramural sports for men and 7 for women. Facilities include a 2800-seat gym, a pool, and playing fields.

Disabled Students: 80% of the campus is accessible. Facilities include wheelchair ramps, elevators, special parking, specially equipped restrooms, special class scheduling, lowered drinking fountains, and lowered telephones.

Services: Counseling and information services are available, as is tutoring in every subject. There is a reader service for the blind.

Campus Safety and Security: Measures include 24-hour foot and vehicle patrol, emergency notification system, self-defense education, and security escort services. There are shuttle buses, emergency telephones, lighted pathways/sidewalks, and controlled access to dorms/residences.

Programs of Study: Regis confers B.A., B.S., and B.S.N. degrees. Master's and doctoral degrees are also awarded. Bachelor's degrees are awarded in AGRICULTURE (environmental studies), BIOLOGICAL SCIENCE (biochemistry, biology/biological science, and neurosciences), BUSINESS (accounting, business administration and management, business economics, international business management, and marketing/retailing/merchandising), COMMUNICATIONS AND THE ARTS (communications, English, French, music, Spanish, and visual and performing arts), COMPUTER AND PHYSICAL SCIENCE (chemistry, computer science, and mathematics), EDUCATION (education), ENGINEERING AND ENVIRONMENTAL DESIGN (preengineering), HEALTH PROFESSIONS (nursing, pharmacy, physical therapy, and premedicine), SOCIAL SCIENCE (economics, history, philosophy, political science/government, prelaw, psychology, religion, sociology, and women's studies). Business has the largest enrollment.

Required: Students must complete 128 credit hours with a minimum GPA of 2.0. Required courses include 58 credit hours in the core curriculum, of which 12 are seminars, 7 to 8 are math and natural science, 6 are in literature/humanities, social science, religious studies, and philosophy, and 3 each are in economics, communication arts, and fine arts.

Special: Cross-registration is possible with Denver University and Metropolitan State. Internships, study abroad, and work-study programs with Regis are available. The college offers B.A.-B.S. degrees, dual majors, student-designed majors, a 3-2 engineering degree with Washington University, and pass/fail options. An accelerated degree program in nursing is also offered. There are 3 national honor societies and a freshman honors program.

Faculty/Classroom: 52% of faculty are male; 48% are female. All teach and do research. No introductory courses are taught by graduate students. The average class size in an introductory lecture is 26 and in a laboratory is 16.

Admissions: 79% of a recent year applicants were accepted. The SAT scores for the 2011-2012 freshman class were: Critical Reading--32% below 500, 42% between 500 and 599, 22% between 600 and 700, and 4% above 700; Math--31% below 500, 40% between 500 and 599, 25% between 600 and 700, and 4% above 700. The ACT scores were 23% below 21, 27% between 21 and 23, 26% between 24 and 26, 12% between 27 and 28, and 12% above 28. 48% of the current freshmen were in the top fifth of their class; 74% were in the top two fifths. 30 freshmen graduated first in their class.

Requirements: The SAT or ACT is required. Applicants should be graduates of an accredited secondary school. The GED is accepted. Students should have completed 16 high school academic credits, including 4 years of English, 3 each of math, science, and history, 2 of a foreign language, and 1 to 2 of social studies. A recommendation from the high school counselor and an essay are required. An interview is recommended. A GPA of 2.3 is required. AP and CLEP credits are accepted. Important factors in the admissions decision are recommendations by school officials, leadership record, and extracurricular activities record.

Procedure: Freshmen are admitted fall and spring. Entrance exams should be taken in the fall. There are deferred admissions and rolling admissions plans. Application deadlines are open. Application fee is $40. Notification is sent on a rolling basis. Applications are accepted online.

Transfer: 81 transfer students enrolled in a recent year. Applicants must have a GPA of 2.5. All previous college work is considered. The college reviews each applicant individually. 30 of 128 credits required for the bachelor's degree must be completed at Regis.

Visiting: There are guides for informal visits, visitors may sit in on classes, and stay overnight. To schedule a visit, contact the Admissions Office.

Financial Aid: In a recent year, 90% of all full-time freshmen and 90% of continuing full-time students received some form of financial aid. 63% of all full-time freshmen and 65% of continuing full-time students received need-based aid. The FAFSA and the college's own financial statement are required. Check with the school for current application deadlines.

International Students: The school actively recruits these students. They must take the TOEFL or MELAB, and the ELS/ALA.

Graduates: In a recent year, 279 bachelor's degrees were awarded. In an average class, 47% graduate in 4 years or less, 62% graduate in 5 years or less, and 65% graduate in 6 years or less.

Admissions Contact: Director of Admissions. A campus DVD is available. E-Mail: *regisadm@regis.edu* Web: *www.regis.edu*

ROCKY MOUNTAIN COLLEGE OF ART AND DESIGN C-2

Denver, CO 80214 (800) 888-2787

Full-time: 206 men, 354 women	**Faculty:** 44
Part-time: 38 men, 72 women	**Ph.D.s:** 8%
Graduate: 8 men, 19 women	**Student/Faculty:** 13 to 1
Year: semesters, summer session	**Tuition:** $22,470
Application Deadline:	**Room & Board:** n/app

Freshman Class: n/av
SAT or ACT: required **SPECIAL**

Rocky Mountain College of Art and Design, founded in 1963, is a private institution. In addition to regional accreditation, RMCAD has baccalaureate program accreditation with NASAD. The 2 libraries contain 15,500 volumes, and 2,100 audio/video tapes/CDs/DVDs, and subscribe to 30 periodicals including electronic. Computerized library services include database searching, Internet access, and Wi-Fi capability. Special learning facilities include an art gallery. The 23-acre campus is in a suburban area 5 miles west of downtown Denver. Including any residence halls, there are 18 buildings.

Student Life: 73% of undergraduates are from Colorado. Others are from 46 states. 63% are White; 17% race unknown. The average age of freshmen is 23; all undergraduates, 24. 31% do not continue beyond their first year; 44% remain to graduate.

Housing: Alcohol is not permitted. All students commute. All students may keep cars.

Activities: There are no fraternities or sororities. There are 13 groups on campus, including art, computers, dance, gay, professional, religious, social, and student government. Popular campus events include Welcome Back Week and Graduation exhibit.

Sports: There is no sports program at RMCAD.

Disabled Students: 95% of the campus is accessible. Facilities include wheelchair ramps, elevators, special parking, specially equipped restrooms, special class scheduling, and lowered drinking fountains.

Services: Counseling and information services are available, as is tutoring in every subject. There is remedial math and writing.

Campus Safety and Security: Measures include emergency notification system, self-defense education, and security escort services. There are shuttle buses, emergency telephones, and lighted pathways/sidewalks.

Programs of Study: RMCAD confers B.F.A., and B.A. degrees. Master's degrees are also awarded. Bachelor's degrees are awarded in COMMUNICATIONS AND THE ARTS (animation, fine arts, game design and development, graphic design, illustration, media arts, and photography), EDUCATION (art education), ENGINEERING AND ENVIRONMENTAL DESIGN (interior design). Illustration, graphic design, and fine art are the largest.

Required: All students must take 39 credits of liberal studies, including 6 credits in communication and critical thought, 12 credits in art and design history, 9 credits in humanities and contemporary thought seminars, and 3 credits each in social and behavioral sciences, physical and natural sciences, and math. A total of 120 credit hours is required with a 2.0 GPA (2.5 for art education). All majors must take courses in visual design, drawing, life drawing, and digital image drawing.

Special: The college offers an accelerated B.F.A. degree program. A 3-credit internship is required for interior design and communication design majors. Others may participate in noncredit internships.

Faculty/Classroom: 44% of faculty are male; 56% are female. All teach undergraduates. No introductory courses are taught by graduate students.

Requirements: The SAT or ACT is required. Applicants must submit ACT or SAT scores and high school transcripts. An interview and portfolio are required. A GPA of 2.0 is required. AP and CLEP credits are accepted. Important factors in the admissions decision are evidence of special talent, ability to finance college education, personality/intangible qualities, extracurricular activities record, leadership record, advanced placement or honors courses, parents or siblings attended your school, recommendations by alumni, geographical diversity, and recommendations by school officials.

Procedure: Freshmen are admitted fall, spring, and summer. There are deferred admissions and rolling admissions plans. Application deadlines are open. Application fee is $50. Applications are accepted online.

Transfer: 103 transfer students enrolled in 2012-2013. The last 15 credits must be taken in residence, and no transfer credit may be taken in the final term. Transfer students who have an associate's degree or higher from a regionally accredited institution in the United States automatically receive credit for all liberal studies except art history. 60 of 120 credits required for the bachelor's degree must be completed at RMCAD.

Visiting: There are regularly scheduled orientations for prospective students, consisting of a campus tour and meetings with an admissions counselor and financial aid advisor. Drop-in tours are hosted twice a month. There are guides for informal visits and visitors may sit in on classes. To schedule a visit, contact the Admissions Office.

Financial Aid: The FAFSA is required. Check with the school for current application deadlines.

International Students: There are 6 international students enrolled. They must take the TOEFL with a minimum score of 550 on the paper-based TOEFL (PBT) or 80 on the Internet-based version (iBT), IELTS (minimum score of 7) or other proof of English proficiency, such as successful completion of a U.S. ESL program. They must also take the SAT or ACT.

Graduates: From July 1, 2012 to June 30, 2013, 132 bachelor's degrees were awarded. The most popular majors were illustration (26%), fine art (20%), and graphic design (17%). In an average class, 33% graduate in 4 years or less and 44% graduate in 6 years or less.

Admissions Contact: Admissions Department E-Mail: *admissions@rmcad.edu* Web: *www.rmcad.edu*

UNITED STATES AIR FORCE ACADEMY D-3

Colorado Springs, CO 80840-5025 **(719) 333-2520 (800) 443-9266; (719) 333-3012**

Full-time: 3635 men, 835 women	**Faculty:** n/av
Part-time: n/app	**Ph.D.s:** 49%
Graduate: n/app	**Student/Faculty:** n/av
Year: semesters, summer session	**Tuition:** see profile
Application Deadline: open	**Room & Board:** see profile
Freshman Class: n/av	
SAT or ACT: required	

MOST COMPETITIVE

The United States Air Force Academy, was founded in 1954 and is a public institution. Graduates receive the B.S. degree and a second lieutenant's commission in the regular Air Force. All graduates are obligated to serve at least 5 years of active duty military service. Tuition, room, board, medical, and dental expenses are paid by the U.S. government. Each cadet receives a monthly salary from which to pay for uniforms, supplies, and personal expenses. Entering freshmen are required to deposit $2,500 to defray the initial costs of uniforms and personal expenses incurred upon entry. Students who are unable to submit the full deposit will receive a reduced monthly cash allotment until prescribed levels are reached. Figures in the above capsule are approximate. In addition to regional accreditation, USAFA has baccalaureate program accreditation with ABET and CSAB. The 2 libraries contain 551,476 volumes, 729,880 microform items, and 3,643 audio/video tapes/CDs/DVDs, and subscribe to 36,252 periodicals including electronic. Computerized library services include interlibrary loans, database searching, Internet access, and laptop Internet portals. Special learning facilities include a learning resource center, art gallery, planetarium, radio station, TV station, a field engineering and readiness lab, and an aeronautics lab/aeronautical research center. The 18000-acre campus is in a suburban area 70 miles south of downtown Denver and 8 miles north of downtown Colorado Springs. Including any residence halls, there are 13 buildings.

Student Life: 95% of undergraduates are from out of state, mostly the South. Others are from 30 foreign countries. 77% are white. 58% are Protestant; 30% Catholic. The average age of freshmen is 18; all undergraduates, 20. 15% do not continue beyond their first year; 85% remain to graduate.

Housing: 4550 students can be accommodated in college housing, which includes coed dorms. On-campus housing is guaranteed for all 4 years. Alcohol is not permitted. Upperclassmen may keep cars.

Activities: There are no fraternities or sororities. There are 87 groups on campus, including show choir, band, chamber music, cheerleading, chess, choir, chorale, chorus, computers, drama, drill team, drum and bugle corps, ethnic, film, forensics, honors, marching band, musical theater, pep band, photography, professional, radio and TV, religious, social, social service, and student government. Popular campus events include Acceptance Parade and Christmas events.

Sports: There are 17 intercollegiate sports for men and 10 for women, and 14 intramural sports for men and 13 for women. Facilities include a 47,000-seat stadium, a cadet gym, a field house, 143 acres of athletic facilities and recreational areas, 3 basketball gyms, 4 indoor tennis courts, an Olympic-size swimming pool, a water polo pool, 3 squash and 19 racquetball/handball courts, 3 weight-training rooms, and 2 18-hole golf courses.

Disabled Students: All of the campus is accessible. Facilities include wheelchair ramps, elevators, special parking, specially equipped restrooms, and lowered drinking fountains.

Services: Counseling and information services are available, as is tutoring in every subject. There is remedial math, reading, and writing.

Campus Safety and Security: Measures include 24-hour foot and vehicle patrol, self-defense education, and security escort services. There are emergency telephones and lighted pathways/sidewalks.

Programs of Study: USAFA confers B.S. degrees. Bachelor's degrees are awarded in BIOLOGICAL SCIENCE (biology/biological science), BUSINESS (management science and operations research), COMMUNICATIONS AND THE ARTS (English), COMPUTER AND PHYSICAL SCIENCE (atmospheric sciences and meteorology, chemistry, computer science, mathematics, physics, and science), ENGINEERING AND ENVIRONMENTAL DESIGN (aeronautical engineering, aerospace studies, civil engineering, computer engineering, electrical/electronics engineering, engineering, engineering and applied science, engineering mechanics, environmental engineering, mechanical engineering, and military science), SOCIAL SCIENCE (behavioral science, economics, geography, history, humanities, international studies, law, political science/government, psychology, and social science). Engineering and basic sciences is the strongest academically. Engineering, management, and social sciences have the largest enrollments.

Required: Cadets must complete the requirements for the core curriculum and for an academic major. They must be proficient in phys ed and military training and demonstrate an aptitude for commissioned service and leadership. A total of 145 to 161 semester hours is required, with a minimum GPA of 2.0, to graduate. The required curriculum includes 9 hours of military arts and sciences, 6 hours of phys ed, and 1 hour of aviation.

Special: All cadets receive orientation flights in Air Force aircraft and take aviation science courses. A semester exchange program is available with the French Air Force Academy and U.S. Army, Naval, and Coast Guard academies. Freshman classes start in June, and basic cadet training must be completed before academics begin in August. Work-study programs are available, and dual majors are possible in all areas. There is an interdisciplinary space operations major. There are 2 national honor societies and a freshman honors program.

Faculty/Classroom: 85% of faculty are male; 15% are female. All teach undergraduates, and 10% do research. No introductory courses are taught by graduate students. The average class size in an introductory lecture is 17; in a laboratory is 17; and in a regular course is 17.

Admissions: 45 freshmen graduated first in their class.

Requirements: The SAT or ACT is required. Candidates must be U.S. citizens between 17 and 22 years of age, unmarried and with no dependents, and nominated from a legal source. Students should have completed 4 years each of English, math, and lab sciences and 2 years each of social sciences and foreign languages. A computer course is recommended. A personal interview is required, as is an essay and a drug and alcohol abuse certificate. A GPA of 2.0 is required. AP credits are accepted. Important factors in the admissions decision are advanced placement or honors courses, leadership record, and personality/intangible qualities.

Procedure: Freshmen are admitted summer. Entrance exams should be taken in the spring of the junior year. Check with the school for current application deadlines. Applications are accepted online.

Transfer: All students must enter as freshmen and attend 4 years. 145 of 145 credits required for the bachelor's degree must be completed at USAFA.

Visiting: There are regularly scheduled orientations for prospective students, consisting of a 2-day orientation held in March and April. Students are given briefings by the superintendent, the commandant of cadets, the dean of cadets, and the director of athletics. Students stay overnight in the dormitories and shadow their escort cadets the second day, attending classes, training, and meals. There is also a daily tour. There are guides for informal visits. To schedule a visit, contact the Director of Admissions.

Financial Aid: Check with the school for current application deadlines.

International Students: There are 52 international students enrolled. They must also take the SAT or ACT.

Graduates: In a recent year, 986 bachelor's degrees were awarded. The most popular majors were social sciences (36%), engineering (35%), and basic sciences (15%). In an average class, 71% graduate in 4 years or less and 77% graduate in 5 years or less. Of the recent graduating class, 3% were enrolled in graduate school within 6 months of graduation, and 97% were employed.

Admissions Contact: Associate Director, Admissions/Selections. Web: *www.academyadmissions.com*

UNIVERSITY OF COLORADO SYSTEM

The University of Colorado System, established in 1876, is a private system in Colorado. It is governed by a board of regents whose chief administrator is the president. The primary goal of the system is comprehensive research. The main priorities are research, teaching, and public service. The total student enrollment for all four campuses is usually about 45,000 with 4750 faculty members. Profiles of the 4-year campuses are included in this section.

UNIVERSITY OF COLORADO AT COLORADO SPRINGS D-3

Colorado Springs, CO 80918 **(719) 262-3383; (800) 990-8227**

Full-time: 1900 men, 3500 women	**Faculty:** n/av; IIA, --$
Part-time: 550 men, 800 women	**Ph.D.s:** 64%
Graduate: 630 men, 900 women	**Student/Faculty:** n/av
Year: semesters, summer session	**Tuition:** $6500 ($18,000)
Application Deadline: open	**Room & Board:** $9500
Freshman Class: n/av	
SAT or ACT: required	

VERY COMPETITIVE

The University of Colorado at Colorado Springs, established in 1965, is a public institution, with programs in liberal arts, business, engineering, education, and nursing. The figures in the above capsule and in this profile are approximate. There are 4 undergraduate schools and 5 graduate schools. In addition to regional accreditation, UCCS has baccalaureate program accreditation with AACSB, ABET, CSAB, NCATE, and NLN. The library contains 669,757 volumes, 432,872 microform items, and 5,979 audio/video tapes/CDs/DVDs, and subscribes to 2,247 periodicals including electronic. Computerized library services include interlibrary loans, database searching, and Internet access. Special learning facilities include a learning resource center, art gallery, a center for excellence in oral communication, a math learning center, a science learning center, a writing center, and a language technology center. The 504-acre campus is in a small town 70 miles south of Denver. Including any residence halls, there are 24 buildings.

Student Life: 92% of undergraduates are from Colorado. Others are from 48 states, 35 foreign countries, and Canada. 76% are white. The average age of freshmen is 18; all undergraduates, 28. 35% do not continue beyond their first year; 40% remain to graduate.

Housing: 900 students can be accommodated in college housing, which includes single-sex and coed dorms and on-campus apartments. On-campus housing is available on a first-come and first-served basis. 88% of students commute. All students may keep cars.

Activities: 1% of men belong to 1 national fraternity; 1% of women belong to 1 local sorority. There are 50 groups on campus, including art, choir, computers, dance, drama, ethnic, film, gay, honors, international, literary magazine, newspaper, photography, political, professional, radio and TV, religious, social, and student government. Popular campus events include Winter Holiday Festival, and Comedy Night.

Sports: There are 5 intercollegiate sports for men and 5 for women, and 13 intramural sports for men and 12 for women. Facilities include a gym, softball and soccer fields, a multipurpose field, tennis and volleyball courts, and a fitness center.

Disabled Students: 95% of the campus is accessible. Facilities include wheelchair ramps, elevators, special parking, specially equipped restrooms, lowered drinking fountains, and lowered telephones.

Services: Counseling and information services are available, as is tutoring in most subjects. There is a reader service for the blind.

Campus Safety and Security: Measures include 24-hour foot and vehicle patrol, self-defense education, and security escort services. There are shuttle buses, emergency telephones, and lighted pathways/sidewalks.

Programs of Study: UCCS confers B.A. and B.S. degrees. Master's and doctoral degrees are also awarded. Bachelor's degrees are awarded in BIOLOGICAL SCIENCE (biology/biological science), BUSINESS (business administration and management), COMMUNICATIONS AND THE ARTS (communications, English, fine arts, and Spanish), COMPUTER AND PHYSICAL SCIENCE (chemistry, computer science, mathematics, and physics), ENGINEERING AND ENVIRONMENTAL DESIGN (electrical/electronics engineering), HEALTH PROFESSIONS (health care administration and nursing), SOCIAL SCIENCE (anthropology, economics, geography, history, philosophy, political science/government, psychology, and sociology). Business, engineering, and psychology are the strongest academically.

Required: To graduate, students must complete 124 credit hours, with at least 30 of them in the major, with a minimum GPA of 2.0. All students must take English and a computer literacy course. Other requirements vary with the program.

Special: The university offers work-study, dual majors, nondegree study, and pass/fail options. There are 3 national honor societies including Phi Beta Kappa.

Faculty/Classroom: 51% of faculty are male; 49% are female. 93% teach undergraduates, 80% do research, and 80% do both. Graduate students teach 1% of introductory courses. The average class size in an introductory lecture is 32; in a laboratory is 45; and in a regular course is 22.

Requirements: The SAT or ACT is required. Applicants must be graduates of an accredited secondary school. The GED is accepted. Secondary school courses must include 15 high school credits, including 4 years of English, 3 years each of math and science, 2 years each of foreign language and social studies, and 1 academic elective. AP and CLEP credits are accepted. Important factors in the admissions decision are advanced placement or honors courses, evidence of special talent, and recommendations by school officials.

Procedure: Freshmen are admitted to all sessions. Entrance exams should be taken during the senior year. There are deferred admissions and rolling admissions plans. Check with the school for current application deadlines. Applications are accepted online.

Transfer: Applicants must have a minimum GPA of 2.5 and a minimum of 12 credit hours earned. 30 of 124 credits required for the bachelor's degree must be completed at UCCS.

Visiting: There are regularly scheduled orientations for prospective students. There are guides for informal visits and visitors may sit in on classes. To schedule a visit, contact the Marketing Office.

Financial Aid: The FAFSA is required. Check with the school for current application deadlines.

International Students: They must take the TOEFL. They must also take the SAT or ACT.

Admissions Contact: Admissions Office E-Mail: *admrec@uccs.edu* Web: *www.uccs.edu*

UNIVERSITY OF COLORADO BOULDER C-2

Boulder, CO 80309 **(303) 492-6301; (303) 492-7115**

Full-time: 12960 men, 10799 women	**Faculty:** 1382; I, -$
Part-time: 1016 men, 686 women	**Ph.D.s:** 90%
Graduate: 2096 men, 2217 women	**Student/Faculty:** 17 to 1
Year: semesters, summer session	**Tuition:** $10,347 ($32,115)
Application Deadline: January 15	**Room & Board:** $12,258

Freshman Class: 22477 applied, 19710 accepted, 5846 enrolled

SAT CR/M: 570/600 **ACT:** 27 **VERY COMPETITIVE+**

The University of Colorado Boulder, established in 1876, is a public institution offering undergraduate and graduate programs in arts and sciences, business, engineering, environmental design, music, education, journalism and mass communication, and law. There are 5 undergraduate schools and 3 graduate schools. In addition to regional accreditation, CU-Boulder has baccalaureate program accreditation with AACSB, ABET, ACEJMC, NASM, and NCATE. The 7 libraries contain 6.5 million volumes, 9.1 million microform items, and 95,046 audio/video tapes/CDs/DVDs. Computerized library services include interlibrary loans, database searching, Internet access, and Wi-Fi capability. Special learning facilities include an art gallery, natural history museum, planetarium, radio station, interactive foreign language video center, mountain research station, integrated teaching and learning lab in engineering, and multidisciplinary information technology center. The 600-acre campus is in a suburban area 30 miles northwest of Denver. Including any residence halls, there are 200 buildings.

Student Life: 63% of undergraduates are from Colorado. Others are from 50 states, 100 foreign countries, and Canada. 91% are from public schools. 74% are White. The average age of freshmen is 18; all undergraduates, 21. 15% do not continue beyond their first year; 70% remain to graduate.

Housing: 7392 students can be accommodated in college housing, which includes coed dorms, on-campus apartments, off-campus apartments, and married student housing. In addition, there are honors houses, special-interest houses, 14 residential academic programs that include housing in the dorms. On-campus housing is guaranteed for the freshman year only, is available on a first-come, and first-served basis. 72% of students commute. All students may keep cars.

Activities: 11% of men belong to 21 national fraternities; 17% of women belong to 2 local and 14 national sororities. There are 400 groups on campus, including art, band, cheerleading, chess, choir, chorale, chorus, communications, computers, dance, debate, drama, drill team, environmental, ethnic, film, gay, honors, international, jazz band, literary magazine, marching band, musical theater, newspaper, opera, orchestra, pep band, photography, political, professional, radio and TV, religious, social, social service, student government, and symphony. Popular campus events include Conference on World Affairs, Colorado Shakespeare Festival, Holiday Festival (orchestra, choir, and other musical group performances), Football Games, International Festival, and Global Jam.

Sports: There are 6 intercollegiate sports for men and 9 for women, and 13 intramural sports for men and 13 for women. CU-Boulder has a 53,500-seat stadium, an 8,700-seat events center, 4 outdoor lighted basketball courts, and five outdoor recreational fields to accommodate rugby, ultimate frisbee, and soccer. The student recreation center is undergoing extensive renovation, scheduled for completion in April 2014. New features include expanded weight training and cardio space; fitness and wellness amenities that include a wellness suite, massage studio, private area for health screenings, and five fitness studios including mind body, indoor cycling, and functional training; a new ice rink with cutting edge 200X85 sheet and stadium seating; three outdoor tennis courts on the roof of the ice rink (in addition to five other courts on campus); a buffalo-shaped, 2-yard, 2-lane outdoor leisure pool; state-of-the-art climbing wall; and new locker rooms with dry heat saunas. Rec center facilities also include an 8-lane swimming pool; diving pool; two large general purpose gyms; three indoor basketball courts; a 1/10th-mile indoor running track; courts for handball, racquetball, and squash; and aerobics studio. Additionally, four program areas are offered instruction, outdoor program, intramurals, and club sports that provide organized sports and classes.

Disabled Students: 85% of the campus is accessible. Facilities include wheelchair ramps, elevators, special parking, specially equipped restrooms, special class scheduling, lowered drinking fountains, lowered telephones, special housing. power-assisted doors, assisted classroom listening devices, TTY phone support systems, and an assistive technology lab to enable students with disabilities to access computer systems, information resources, and online services.

Services: Counseling and information services are available, as is tutoring in most subjects. There is a reader service for the blind, and remedial writing. Academic Excellence Program/Student Support Services offers a number of services supportive of low-income and first-generation college students and individuals with disabilities. Services include academic skill building, tutoring, technology and computer skill building, and study groups.

Campus Safety and Security: Measures include 24-hour foot and vehicle patrol, emergency notification system, self-defense education, and security escort services. There are shuttle buses, emergency telephones, lighted pathways/sidewalks, controlled access to dorms/residences, Campus police are academy-trained and commissioned officers of the Boulder police force.

Programs of Study: CU-Boulder confers B.A., B.Envd., B.F.A., B.A.Mus., B.Mus., B.Mus.Ed., B.S., and I.B.A. degrees. Master's and doctoral degrees are also awarded. Bachelor's degrees are awarded in BIOLOGICAL SCIENCE (biochemistry, ecology, evolutionary biology, molecular biology, neurosciences, and physiology), BUSINESS (accounting, business administration and management, finance, management science, and marketing management), COMMUNICATIONS AND THE ARTS (advertising, art history, art history and appreciation, broadcasting, Chinese, classics, communications, dance, English, film arts, fine arts, French, Italian, Japanese, journalism, linguistics, music, music performance, Russian languages and literature, Spanish, studio art, and theatre arts), COMPUTER AND PHYSICAL SCIENCE (applied mathematics, astronomy, chemistry, computer science, geology, mathematics, and physics), EDUCATION (music education), ENGINEERING AND ENVIRONMENTAL DESIGN (aeronautical engineering, architectural engineering, bioengineering, chemical engineering, civil engineering, computer engineering, electrical/electronics engineering, engineering physics, environmental design, environmental engineering, environmental science, and mechanical engineering), HEALTH PROFESSIONS (speech pathology/audiology), SOCIAL SCIENCE (anthropology, Asian/Oriental studies, asian studies, economics, ethnic studies, geography, German area studies, history, humanities, international relations, Judaic studies, philosophy, political science/government, psychology, religious studies, sociology, and women & gender studies). Psychology, integrative physiology, and communication have the largest enrollments.

Required: Undergraduate degree requirements (e.g., number of credits overall and in the major, minimum GPA, core curriculum requirements) vary by degree program (e.g., B.A., B.F.A) and by undergraduate college and program.

Special: Fourteen residential programs for freshmen and sophomores offer a small liberal arts college atmosphere while taking advantage of the resources of a major university. Student-designed and dual majors, internships, 5-year B.A.-M.A. degrees, and cooperative programs in engineering and computer science are available. Study abroad in 65 countries, work-study programs in federal labs, internships, and cross-registration with other University of Colorado campuses are also offered. There are 27 national honor societies, including Phi Beta Kappa, a freshman honors program, and 60 departmental honors programs.

Faculty/Classroom: 62% of faculty are male; 38% are female. 89% teach undergraduates, and all do research. Graduate students teach 11% of introductory courses. The average class size in an introductory lecture is 37; in a laboratory is 20; and in a regular course is 23.

Admissions: 88% of the 2013-2014 applicants were accepted. The SAT scores for the 2013-2014 freshman class were: Critical Reading--16% below 500, 44% between 500 and 599, 32% between 600 and 699, and 9% between 700 and 800; Math--11% below 500, 38% between 500 and 599, 39% between 600 and 699, and 12% between 700 and 800. The ACT scores were 4% below 21, 16% between 21 and 23, 29% between 24 and 26, 19% between 27 and 28, and 32% above 28. 46% of the current freshmen were in the top fifth of their class; 77% were in the top two fifths. There were 13 National Merit finalists. 123 freshmen graduated first in their class.

Requirements: The SAT or ACT is required. Applicants must send an official score report for either the SAT or the ACT and either an official high school transcript or an official copy of certificate of high school equivalency and official GED scores. They are expected to have completed 17 credits of high school work as identified by the CU-Boulder Minimum Academic Preparation Standards. Required application materials include 2 short-answer essay questions and one academic letter of recommendation. Interviews are not used in the decision-making process. Auditions are required for consideration to the College of Music. Portfolios are discouraged. A GPA of 2.0 is required. AP and CLEP credits are accepted.

Procedure: Freshmen are admitted fall, spring, and summer. Entrance exams should be taken no later than December of the senior year. There are early admissions and deferred admissions plans. Early decision applications should be filed by November 15; regular applications, by January 15 for fall entry; October 1 for spring entry; and January 15 for summer entry, along with a $50 fee. Notification of early decision is sent February 1; regular decision, April 1. 469 applicants were on the 2013 waiting list. Applications are accepted online.

Transfer: 1219 transfer students enrolled in 2012-2013. Transfer applicants must submit official high school and college transcripts. Students who have completed fewer than 24 semester hours of transferable college work must also submit SAT or ACT results. Required application materials include 2 short-answer essay questions. Starting with Spring 2014 applications, one academic letter of recommendation will be required. College of Music applicants must also complete a College of Music application after their admission application has been submitted, provide a letter of reference, and schedule an audition. 45 of 120 credits required for the bachelor's degree must be completed at CU-Boulder.

Visiting: There are regularly scheduled orientations for prospective students, Visit includes a 1-hour information session hosted by an admission representative, followed by a student-led, 90-minute walking tour of campus. CU-Boulder also offers all-day visit programs. There are guides for informal visits and visitors may sit in on classes. To schedule a visit, contact the Admissions Office.

Financial Aid: In 2013-2014, 72% of all full-time freshmen and 58% of continuing full-time students received some form of financial aid. 44% of all full-time freshmen and 36% of continuing full-time students received need-based aid. The average freshman award was $22,860. Need-based scholarships or need-based grants averaged $14,303 ($61,290 maximum); need-based self-help aid (loans and jobs) averaged $9,972 ($33,600 maximum); non-need-based athletic scholarships averaged $42,120 ($99,578 maximum); and other non-need-based awards and non-need-based scholarships averaged $6,879 ($50,500 maximum). 18% of undergraduate students work part-time. Average annual earnings from campus work are $4410. The average financial indebtedness of the 2013 graduate was $24,880. The FAFSA and tax returns are required. The priority date for freshman financial aid applications for fall entry is March 1.

International Students: There are 918 international students enrolled. The school actively recruits these students.

Graduates: From July 1, 2012 to June 30, 2013, 5729 bachelor's degrees were awarded. The most popular majors were psychology (11%), integrative physiology (5%), and communcation (4%). 614 companies recruited on campus in 2012-2013. In an average class, 44% graduate in 4 years or less, 66% graduate in 5 years or less, and 70% graduate in 6 years or less. Of the 2012 graduating class, 20% were enrolled in graduate school within 6 months of graduation, and 74% were employed.

Admissions Contact: Director of Admissions. E-Mail: *apply@colorado.edu* Web: *http:/admissions.colorado.edu/undergraduate*

UNIVERSITY OF COLORADO DENVER C-2

Denver, CO 80217	**(303) 556-3287; (303) 556-4838**
Full-time: 3625 men, 4116 women	**Faculty:** n/av; I, --$
Part-time: 2436 men, 2926 women	**Ph.D.s:** 72%
Graduate: 3671 men, 5622 women	**Student/Faculty:** 17 to 1
Year: semesters, summer session	**Tuition:** $7494 ($21,006)
Application Deadline: July 22	**Room & Board:** $10,410
Freshman Class: 3075 applied, 2333 accepted, 991 enrolled	
SAT CR/M: 540/540 **ACT:** 23	**COMPETITIVE**

The University of Colorado at Denver, formerly known as the University of Colorado at Denver and Health Sciences Center, is a public institution that was established in 1912. The University has two campuses. The downtown Denver campus is a commuter school with programs in the liberal arts and sciences, business, engineering and applied sciences, music, architecture and planning, and education. The Anschutz Medical Campus is a commuter school with programs in medicine, nursing, pharmacy, and dentistry. There are 5 undergraduate schools and 7 graduate schools. In addition to regional accreditation, CU Denver has baccalaureate program accreditation with AACSB, ABET, NAAB, NASM, and NCATE. The library contains 683,089 volumes, 1.0 million microform items, and 15,491 audio/video tapes/CDs/DVDs, and subscribes to 93,559 periodicals including electronic. Computerized library services include interlibrary loans, database searching, Internet access, and Wi-Fi capability. Special learning facilities include an art gallery, a writing center. The 151-acre campus is in an urban area in downtown Denver.

Student Life: 93% of undergraduates are from Colorado. Others are from 50 states, 67 foreign countries, and Canada. 52% are White; 15% Hispanic. The average age of freshmen is 18; all undergraduates, 24. 29% do not continue beyond their first year; 45% remain to graduate.

Housing: 685 students can be accommodated in college housing, which includes coed dorms and off-campus apartments. On-campus housing is guaranteed for the freshman year only. 95% of students commute. Alcohol is not permitted. All students may keep cars.

Activities: There are no fraternities or sororities. There are 228 groups on campus, including art, cheerleading, chorale, computers, dance, drama, environmental, ethnic, film, gay, honors, international, jazz band, Men's Club Hockey, musical theater, newspaper, political, professional, radio and TV, religious, social, social service, and student government. Popular campus events include Fall Festival.

Sports: There are 10 intramural sports for men and 12 for women. Facilities include a facility that includes a diving well, a weight room, squash, racquetball/handball, and tennis courts and a basketball half-court, a dance studio, 3 gym arenas, a fitness center and a green room, a 400-meter track, a football/rugby/lacrosse field, softball fields, a baseball field, a soccer field, and a sand volleyball court.

Disabled Students: All of the campus is accessible. Facilities include wheelchair ramps, elevators, special parking, specially equipped restrooms, special class scheduling, lowered drinking fountains, lowered telephones, a transit system, and an adaptive computer lab.

Services: Counseling and information services are available, as is tutoring in most subjects. There is a reader service for the blind. There are ESL classes and study skills courses.

Campus Safety and Security: Measures include 24-hour foot and vehicle patrol, emergency notification system, self-defense education, and security escort services. There are shuttle buses, emergency telephones, lighted pathways/sidewalks, crime prevention programs, and emergency response.

Programs of Study: CU Denver confers B.A., B.S. and B.F.A degrees. Master's and doctoral degrees are also awarded. Bachelor's degrees are awarded in BIOLOGICAL SCIENCE (biology/biological science), BUSINESS (business administration and management), COMMUNICATIONS AND THE ARTS (communications, English, English Writing, fine arts, French, music, Spanish, and visual and performing arts), COMPUTER AND PHYSICAL SCIENCE (chemistry, computer science, mathematics, and physics), EDUCATION (education), ENGINEERING AND ENVIRONMENTAL DESIGN (architecture, bioengineering, civil engineering, electrical/electronics engineering, and mechanical engineering), HEALTH PROFESSIONS (medical science, nursing, and public health), SOCIAL SCIENCE (anthropology, criminal justice, economics, ethnic studies, geography, history, interdisciplinary studies, international studies, philosophy, political science/government, psychology, and sociology). Business, Nursing and psychology are the strongest academically. Business administration, biology, and psychology have the largest enrollments.

Required: To graduate, students must complete 120 credit hours with a minimum GPA of 2.0. All students must complete the core curriculum courses in addition to the requirements for the major.

Special: Students can cross-register with Metropolitan State College, Community College of Denver, and Red Rocks Community College. Concurrent enrollment with any University of Colorado campus is possible. Cooperative programs, 1-semester internships, study abroad in 12 countries, work-study programs, an accelerated degree program in Liberal Arts and Arts and Media, and B.A.-B.S. degrees are available. The university offers dual majors, a general studies degree, non-degree study, and pass/fail options. There are small individualized classes, peer advocates, and workshops. There are 10 national honor societies and a freshman honors program.

Faculty/Classroom: 48% of faculty are male; 52% are female. No introductory courses are taught by graduate students. The average class size in an introductory lecture is 27; in a laboratory is 20; and in a regular course is 27.

Admissions: 76% of the 2013-2014 applicants were accepted. The SAT scores for the 2013-2014 freshman class were: Critical Reading--26% below 500, 47% between 500 and 599, 21% between 600 and 699, and 6% between 700 and 800; Math--30% below 500, 40% between 500 and 599, 23% between 600 and 699, and 7% between 700 and 800. 47% of the current freshmen were in the top fifth of their class; 75% were in the top two fifths.

Requirements: The SAT or ACT is required. Preference for admission is given to applicants who rank in the top 30% of their high school graduating class and present a composite score of 21 or higher on the ACT, or a combined score of 950 or higher on the SAT. CU Denver requires applicants to be in the upper 30% of their class. A GPA of 2.5 is required. AP and CLEP credits are accepted. Important factors in the admissions decision are advanced placement or honors courses, evidence of special talent, and extracurricular activities record.

Procedure: Freshmen are admitted fall, spring, and summer. Entrance exams should be taken in the junior or senior year of high school. There are deferred admissions and rolling admissions plans. Applications should be filed by July 22 for fall entry; December 1 for spring entry; and May 3 for summer entry, along with a $50 fee. Notification is sent on a rolling basis. Applications are accepted online.

Transfer: 1531 transfer students enrolled in 2012-2013. Students transferring less than 30 approved college credits are required to submit standardized test scores and high school GPA and rank. Students transferring 30 approved credits or more from an accredited college only need to submit their current college transcript and proof of good-standing. 60 of 120 credits required for the bachelor's degree must be completed at CU Denver.

Visiting: There are regularly scheduled orientations for prospective students, Student visits include a mini-lecture, campus tour, and financial aid and academic advising. There are guides for informal visits and visitors may sit in on classes. To schedule a visit, contact the Office of Admissions.

Financial Aid: In 2013-2014, 60% of all full-time freshmen and 58% of continuing full-time students received some form of financial aid. 51% of all full-time freshmen and 45% of continuing full-time students received need-based aid. The average freshman award was $8,120. Need-based scholarships or need-based grants averaged $7,500; need-based self-help aid (loans and jobs) averaged $3,343; and other non-need-based awards and non-need-based scholarships averaged $3,125. The average financial indebtedness of the 2013 graduate was $19,480. The FAFSA and the college's own financial statement, and and tax returns are required. The priority date for freshman financial aid applications for fall entry is April 1.

International Students: There are 1017 international students enrolled. The school actively recruits these students. They must take the TOEFL with a minimum score of 537 on the paper-based TOEFL (PBT) or 75 on the Internet-based version (iBT). They must also take the SAT or ACT.
Graduates: From July 1, 2012 to June 30, 2013, 2184 bachelor's degrees were awarded. The most popular majors were business administration (16%), nursing (11%), and psychology (10%). In an average class, 18% graduate in 4 years or less, 39% graduate in 5 years or less, and 45% graduate in 6 years or less.
Admissions Contact: Chris Dowen, Director of Admissions. E-Mail: *admissions@cudenver.edu* Web: *www.ucdenver.edu*

UNIVERSITY OF DENVER C-2

Denver, CO 80208 **(303) 871-2036; (303) 871-3301**

Full-time: 2353 men, 2776 women	**Faculty:** 480; I, --$
Part-time: 146 men, 242 women	**Ph.D.s:** 90%
Graduate: 2628 men, 3633 women	**Student/Faculty:** 10 to 1
Year: quarters, summer session	**Tuition:** $40,707
Application Deadline: January 15	**Room & Board:** $11,080
Freshman Class: 13735 applied, 10539 accepted, 1399 enrolled	
SAT CR/M/W: 610/610/580	**ACT:** 28 **VERYCOMPETITIVE+**

The University of Denver, established in 1864, is a private institution offering degrees in arts and sciences, fine arts, music, business, engineering, and education. There are 8 undergraduate schools and 10 graduate schools. In addition to regional accreditation, DU has baccalaureate program accreditation with AACSB, ABET, NASAD, and NASM. The 2 libraries contain 2.3 million volumes, 1.1 million microform items, and 24,425 audio/video tapes/CDs/DVDs, and subscribe to 282,209 periodicals including electronic. Computerized library services include interlibrary loans, database searching, Internet access, and Wi-Fi capability. Special learning facilities include an art gallery, radio station, a high-altitude lab, an observatory, and an elementary and early learning center. The 125-acre campus is in an urban area 8 miles south of downtown Denver. Including any residence halls, there are 74 buildings.
Student Life: 59% of undergraduates are from out of state, mostly the Mid-West. Students are from 50 states, 47 foreign countries, and Canada. 68% are White. The average age of freshmen is 18; all undergraduates, 21. 14% do not continue beyond their first year; 78% remain to graduate.
Housing: 2422 students can be accommodated in college housing, which includes single-sex and coed dorms, on-campus apartments, off-campus apartments, and married student housing. In addition, there are honors houses, special-interest houses, fraternity houses, sorority houses, 5 living and learning communities, a pioneer leadership program floor, and an honors floor. On-campus housing is guaranteed for the freshman year only and is available on a lottery system for upperclassmen. 55% of students commute. All students may keep cars.
Activities: 24% of men belong to 9 national fraternities; 28% of women belong to 5 national sororities. There are 160 groups on campus, including art, band, cheerleading, chess, choir, chorale, chorus, communications, computers, dance, debate, drama, drum and bugle corps, environmental, ethnic, film, forensics, gay, honors, international, jazz band, literary magazine, musical theater, newspaper, opera, orchestra, pep band, photography, political, professional, radio and TV, religious, social, social service, student government, and symphony. Popular campus events include Winter Carnival, May Days, and Festival of Nations Celebration.
Sports: There are 8 intercollegiate sports for men and 9 for women. Facilities include a sports and wellness center housing 2 ice arenas, a gym, a multipurpose field house, an Olympic-size swimming pool, a fitness center, racquetball courts, studios for yoga, dance, cycling, and karate, a 25-foot climbing wall, a health clinic, a soccer field, a lacrosse stadium, and a tennis pavilion.
Disabled Students: 85% of the campus is accessible. Facilities include wheelchair ramps, elevators, special parking, specially equipped restrooms, special class scheduling, lowered drinking fountains, lowered telephones, and special housing.
Services: Counseling and information services are available, as is tutoring in most subjects. There is a reader service for the blind.
Campus Safety and Security: Measures include 24-hour foot and vehicle patrol, emergency notification system, self-defense education, and security escort services. There are shuttle buses, emergency telephones, lighted pathways/sidewalks, controlled access to dorms/residences, and in-room safes.
Programs of Study: DU confers B.A., B.S., B.B.A., B.F.A., B.M., B.S.A.C.C., B.S.B.A., B.S.C.H., B.S.C.P.E., B.S.E.E. and B.S.M.E. degrees. Master's and doctoral degrees are also awarded. Bachelor's degrees are awarded in BIOLOGICAL SCIENCE (biochemistry, bioinformatics, biology/biological science, ecology, and molecular biology), BUSINESS (accounting, banking and finance, business administration and management, business economics, business statistics, finance, hospitality management services, international business management, marketing/retailing/merchandising, and real estate), COMMUNICATIONS AND THE ARTS (animation, art history, art, art/art studies, art history and appreciation, communication studies, dramatic arts, English, film arts, French, German, Italian, jazz, journalism, languages, media arts, music, music production/recording technology, music performance, Russian, Spanish, strategic communication, and theatre studies), COMPUTER AND PHYSICAL SCIENCE (chemistry, computer game design/development, computer science, digital arts/technology, environmental chemistry, information sciences and systems, mathematics, physics, science, and statistics), ENGINEERING AND ENVIRONMENTAL DESIGN (bioengineering, computer engineering, construction management, electrical and computer engineering, electrical/electronics engineering, environmental science, materials science, mechanical engineering, and Mechatronics Engineering), HEALTH PROFESSIONS (biology), SOCIAL SCIENCE (anthropology, Asian/American studies, cognitive science, criminology, economics, geography, history, interdisciplinary studies, international studies, Judaic studies, philosophy, political science/government, psychology, public affairs, religion, social science, sociology, and women's studies). Information technology studies, real estate and construction management, and accounting are the strongest academically. Management, biology, and general business have the largest enrollments.
Required: For graduation, students must complete 183 to 194 quarter hours, including 40 to 135 in the major, with a minimum GPA of 2.0. They must fulfill foundational requirements in the freshman and sophomore years, and with junior standing take core courses in communities and environments, self and identities, and change and continuity, and must complete a writing-intensive course. Distribution requirements include 12 quarter hours each of English, natural sciences, arts and humanities, and social sciences, 8 of math and computer science, and 4 of oral communication.
Special: DU offers co-op programs, study abroad through more than 59 programs, internships across the country and internationally, a Washington quarter, work-study programs, accelerated degree programs, and dual majors. Non-degree study and pass/fail options are also available. There are 19 national honor societies, including Phi Beta Kappa, and a freshman honors program.
Faculty/Classroom: 53% of faculty are male; 47% are female. 71% teach undergraduates, 70% do research, and 53% do both. Graduate students teach 5% of introductory courses. The average class size in an introductory lecture is 23; in a laboratory is 18; and in a regular course is 19.
Admissions: 77% of the 2013-2014 applicants were accepted. The SAT scores for the 2013-2014 freshman class were: Critical Reading--12% below 500, 34% between 500 and 599, 42% between 600 and 699, and 12% between 700 and 800; Math--5% below 500, 36% between 500 and 599, 48% between 600 and 699, and 11% between 700 and 800; Writing--15% below 500, 44% between 500 and 599, 35% between 600 and 699, and 6% between 700 and 800. The ACT scores were 2% below 21, 10% between 21 and 23, 26% between 24 and 26, 20% between 27 and 28, and 42% above 28. 70% of the current freshmen were in the top fifth of their class; 92% were in the top two fifths. 22 freshmen graduated first in their class.
Requirements: The SAT or ACT is required. Applicants must be graduates of an accredited secondary school. The GED is accepted. DU recommends that applicants have 4 years in English, 3 to 4 in math, and 2 to 4 each in foreign language, social sciences, and natural sciences (2 with lab). An essay and a counselor recommendation are required, and a Hyde interview is strongly encouraged. AP and CLEP credits are accepted. Important factors in the admissions decision are advanced placement or honors courses, personality/intangible qualities, and evidence of special talent.
Procedure: Freshmen are admitted to all sessions. Entrance exams should be taken by January of the senior year. There are early admissions and deferred admissions plans. Early decision applications should be filed by November 1; regular applications, by January 15 for fall entry; December 1 for winter entry; February 15 for spring entry; and May 1 for summer entry, along with a $60 fee. Notification of early decision is sent January 15; regular decision, March 15. 1659 applicants were on the 2013 waiting list; 108 were admitted. Applications are accepted online.
Transfer: 182 transfer students enrolled in 2012-2013. Applicants must submit an official transcript from all colleges attended. Those students with fewer than 30 semester hours of college credit must submit a high school transcript and test scores. A minimum GPA of 2.0 is required, but a GPA of 3.0 is recommended. 45 of 183 credits required for the bachelor's degree must be completed at DU.
Visiting: There are regularly scheduled orientations for prospective students, including tours and information sessions throughout the year, and 2 day-long open houses in the fall. Visitors may sit in on classes and stay overnight. To schedule a visit, contact the Office of Undergraduate Admission at admission@du.edu.
Financial Aid: In 2013-2014, 79% of all full-time freshmen and 81% of continuing full-time students received some form of financial aid. 44% of all full-time freshmen and 42% of continuing full-time students received need-based aid. The average freshman award was $32,229. Need-based scholarships or need-based grants averaged $27,121; need-based self-help aid (loans and jobs) averaged $7,368; non-need-based athletic scholarships

averaged $33,742; and other non-need-based awards and non-need-based scholarships averaged $14,880. Average annual earnings from campus work are $3000. The average financial indebtedness of the 2013 graduate was $22,106. DU is a member of CSS. The CSS/Profile and FAFSA are required. The deadline for filing freshman financial aid applications for fall entry is March 1.

International Students: There are 475 international students enrolled. The school actively recruits these students. They must take the TOEFL with a minimum score of 550 on the paper-based TOEFL (PBT) or 80 on the Internet-based version (iBT), IELTS, Intensive English Language Program. They must also take the SAT or ACT.

Graduates: From July 1, 2012 to June 30, 2013, 1223 bachelor's degrees were awarded. The most popular majors were finance (11%), international studies (7%), and international business (6%). 200 companies recruited on campus in 2012-2013. In an average class, 2% graduate in 3 years or less, 66% graduate in 4 years or less, 76% graduate in 5 years or less, and 78% graduate in 6 years or less.

Admissions Contact: Office of Admission E-Mail: *admission@du.edu* Web: *www.du.edu*

UNIVERSITY OF NORTHERN COLORADO D-1

Greeley, CO 80639 (970) 351-2881 (888) 700-4UNC; (970) 351-2984

Full-time: 3584 men, 5715 women	**Faculty:** 428; I, --$
Part-time: 321 men, 611 women	**Ph.D.s:** n/av
Graduate: 609 men, 1759 women	**Student/Faculty:** 22 to 1
Year: semesters, summer session	**Tuition:** $69230($18,245)
Application Deadline: August 1	**Room & Board:** $10,050
Freshman Class: 8092 applied, 5939 accepted, 2274 enrolled	
SAT CR/M/W: 531/533/516	**ACT:** 23 **COMPETITIVE**

The University of Northern Colorado, founded in 1890, is a state-supported public institution offering undergraduate and graduate programs in liberal arts and sciences, business, education, health and human sciences, and performing and visual arts. There are 6 undergraduate schools and 1 graduate school. In addition to regional accreditation, UNC has baccalaureate program accreditation with AACSB, ADA, NASM, NCATE, and NLN. The 2 libraries contain 1.1 million volumes, 2.1 million microform items, and 36,009 audio/video tapes/CDs/DVDs, and subscribe to 40,304 periodicals including electronic. Computerized library services include interlibrary loans, database searching, Internet access, and laptop Internet portals. Special learning facilities include a learning resource center, art gallery, radio station, more than 30 partner schools. The 260-acre campus is in a suburban area 50 miles north of Denver. Including any residence halls, there are 86 buildings.

Student Life: 88% of undergraduates are from Colorado. Others are from 50 states, 23 foreign countries, and Canada. 55% are white; 13% Hispanic. The average age of freshmen is 18; all undergraduates, 22.

Housing: 3176 students can be accommodated in college housing, which includes single-sex and coed dorms, on-campus apartments, and married student housing. off-campus houses, graduate women's houses, and special-interest floors. On-campus housing is guaranteed for the freshman year only, is available on a first-come, first-served basis, and is available on a lottery system for upperclassmen. 68% of students commute. All students may keep cars.

Activities: 6% of men belong to 11 national fraternities; 7% of women belong to 9 national sororities. There are 138 groups on campus, including art, band, cheerleading, chess, choir, chorale, chorus, computers, dance, drama, drill team, ethnic, film, gay, honors, international, jazz band, literary magazine, marching band, musical theater, newspaper, opera, orchestra, pep band, photography, political, professional, radio and TV, religious, social, social service, student government, and symphony. Popular campus events include Hawaiian Luau, Academic Excellence Week, and International Dinner.

Sports: There are 8 intercollegiate sports for men and 9 for women, and 16 intramural sports for men and 16 for women. Maxcy Hall is the center of the sports world on campus. It's a modern facility that's got it all. 50-foot rock climbing wall, full high ropes course and bouldering cave an 8,000 square-foot fitness center, $300,000 worth of treadmills, spin cycles, ellipticals, strength equipment and free weights, 4,000-seat gymnasium, 2,200-seat hockey rink, Olympic-size swimming pool with a diving well, 33,000 square-foot field house, complete with indoor track, basketball, volleyball and indoor lacrosse courts, 6 racquetball courts and 3 squash courts, dance studio, and a physical therapy/training room. Maxcy is surrounded by 50 acres of athletic fields and courts for tennis and basketball and a quarter-mile track. Plus, there is a new field for softball and a modern turf field for soccer, lacrosse and intramural competition.

Disabled Students: All of the campus is accessible. Facilities include wheelchair ramps, elevators, special parking, specially equipped restrooms, special class scheduling, lowered drinking fountains, lowered telephones. academic support services such as note taking, transportation, interpreters, adaptive computer instruction, and library assistance.

Services: Counseling and information services are available, as is tutoring in most subjects. There is a reader service for the blind, and remedial math, reading, and writing.

Campus Safety and Security: Measures include 24-hour foot and vehicle patrol, emergency notification system, and security escort services. There are shuttle buses, emergency telephones, and lighted pathways/sidewalks.

Programs of Study: UNC confers B.A., B.M., B.M.E., and B.S. degrees. Master's and doctoral degrees are also awarded. Bachelor's degrees are awarded in AGRICULTURE (natural resource management), BIOLOGICAL SCIENCE (biology/biological science and nutrition), BUSINESS (business administration and management, management science, marketing/retailing/merchandising, and recreation and leisure services), COMMUNICATIONS AND THE ARTS (American Sign Language, art, communications, English, fine arts, French, German, graphic design, journalism, music, musical theater, Spanish, telecommunications, and visual and performing arts), COMPUTER AND PHYSICAL SCIENCE (chemistry, earth science, geology, information sciences and systems, mathematics, physics, and statistics), EDUCATION (athletic training, education, music education, physical education, science education, social science education, and special education), HEALTH PROFESSIONS (exercise science, nursing, rehabilitation therapy, and speech pathology/audiology), SOCIAL SCIENCE (African American studies, anthropology, Asian/American studies, criminal justice, dietetics, economics, ethics, politics, and social policy, geography, gerontology, history, human services, interdisciplinary studies, international relations, Mexican-American/Chicano studies, philosophy, physical fitness/movement, political science/government, psychology, social science, and sociology). Business, music, and nursing are the strongest academically. Business, interdisciplinary studies, and sport and exercise science have the largest enrollments.

Required: Students must earn a minimum of 120 semester hours (some majors require additional hours) with a minimum GPA of 2.0. All students must complete 40 semester hours in required general education courses and meet all degree requirements in the major.

Special: UNC offers internships and co-op programs in many majors and study abroad in England, Australia, Spain, France, and Germany or through the International Student Exchange Program. Dual majors, student designed majors, credit by exam, and pass/fail options are also available. There are 7 national honor societies and a freshman honors program.

Faculty/Classroom: 45% of faculty are male; 55% are female. All teach and do research. Graduate students teach 17% of introductory courses. The average class size in an introductory lecture is 46; in a laboratory is 27; and in a regular course is 28.

Admissions: 73% of a recent year applicants were accepted. The SAT scores for a recent year freshman class were: Critical Reading--33% below 500, 46% between 500 and 599, 18% between 600 and 700, and 3% above 700; Math--34% below 500, 43% between 500 and 599, 20% between 600 and 700, and 3% above 700; Writing--43% below 500, 36% between 500 and 599, 21% between 600 and 700. The ACT scores were 47% below 21, 57% between 21 and 23, 18% between 24 and 26, 15% between 27 and 28, and 3% above 28. 32% of the current freshmen were in the top fifth of their class; 69% were in the top two fifths. 29 freshmen graduated first in their class.

Requirements: The SAT or ACT is required. Admission standards are set by the Colorado Commission on Higher Education, but each applicant is evaluated on an individual basis. In general, an ACT score of 22, or an SAT composite score of 1000, and a cumulative GPA of 2.9, are required. Graduation from an accredited high school is required. A GPA of 3.2 is required. AP and CLEP credits are accepted. Important factors in the admissions decision are recommendations by school officials, evidence of special talent, and advanced placement or honors courses.

Procedure: Freshmen are admitted fall, spring, and summer. Entrance exams should be taken as early as possible. There are deferred admissions and rolling admissions plans. Applications should be filed by August 1 for fall entry; December 20 for spring entry; and May 1 for summer entry, along with a $45 fee. Applications are accepted online.

Transfer: 817 transfer students enrolled in 2010-2011. Transfer students who have completed 12 or fewer hours of college must meet the same criteria for admission as entering freshmen. Transfers with 13 or more semester hours must have a minimum 2.4 GPA. 30 of 120 credits required for the bachelor's degree must be completed at UNC.

Visiting: There are regularly scheduled orientations for prospective students, including academic advising, registration, tours, and special activities. There are guides for informal visits and visitors may sit in on classes. To schedule a visit, contact the UNC Visitors Center.

Financial Aid: In a recent year, 56% of all full-time freshmen and 72% of continuing full-time students received some form of financial aid. 36% of all full-time freshmen and 50% of continuing full-time students received need-based aid. The average freshman award was $2,238. Need-based scholarships or need-based grants averaged $2,097; need-based self-help aid (loans and jobs) averaged $1,659; non-need-based athletic scholarships averaged $5,434; and other non-need-based awards and non-need-based scholarships averaged $838. The FAFSA is required. The deadline for filing freshman financial aid applications for fall entry is March 1.

International Students: There are 130 international students enrolled. They must take the TOEFL with a minimum score of 520 on the paper-based TOEFL (PBT) or 70 on the Internet-based version (iBT) or take the MELAB. They must also take the SAT or ACT.

Graduates: In a recent year, 1921 bachelor's degrees were awarded. The most popular majors were interdisciplinary studies (15%), business administration (12%), and nursing (7%). 469 companies recruited on campus in a recent year. In an average class, 87% graduate in 4 years or less, 92% graduate in 5 years or less, and 94% graduate in 6 years or less. Of a recent year graduating class, 3% were enrolled in graduate school within 6 months of graduation, and 87% were employed.

Admissions Contact: Director of Admissions. A campus DVD is available. E-Mail: *admissions.help@unco.edu* Web: *www.unco.edu*

WESTERN STATE COLORADO UNIVERSITY B-3

Gunnison, CO 81231 (970) 943-2119
(800) 876-5309; (970) 943-2212

Full-time: 1113 men, 753 women	**Faculty:** 109; IIB, --$
Part-time: 150 men, 169 women	**Ph.D.s:** n/av
Graduate: 60 men, 150 women	**Student/Faculty:** 16 to 1
Year: semesters, summer session	**Tuition:** $7343 ($17,284)
Application Deadline: June 1	**Room & Board:** $8792
Freshman Class: 1523 applied, 1406 accepted, 469 enrolled	
SAT CR/M: 509/516	**ACT:** 22 **COMPETITIVE**

Western State Colorado University, founded in 1901, is a public institution offering undergraduate programs in liberal arts and sciences, business, recreation, and education. There are 8 undergraduate schools and 2 graduate schools. In addition to regional accreditation, Western has baccalaureate program accreditation with NASM. The library contains 252,757 volumes, 105,363 microform items, and 10,268 audio/video tapes/CDs/DVDs, and subscribes to 211 periodicals including electronic. Computerized library services include interlibrary loans and database searching. Special learning facilities include an art gallery, radio station, TV station, a greenhouse, W mountain archeological site, and media production studio. The 228-acre campus is in a rural area 210 miles southwest of Denver. Including any residence halls, there are 31 buildings.

Student Life: 75% of undergraduates are from Colorado. Others are from 50 states, 8 foreign countries, and Canada. 85% are from public schools. 65% are White. The average age of freshmen is 18; all undergraduates, 21. 32% do not continue beyond their first year; 39% remain to graduate.

Housing: 1234 students can be accommodated in college housing, which includes single-sex and coed dorms, on-campus apartments, and married student housing. In addition, there are special-interest houses, theme floors on art, science, and outdoor pursuits. On-campus housing is guaranteed for the freshman year only, is available on a first-come, and first-served basis. 55% of students commute. Alcohol is not permitted. All students may keep cars.

Activities: There are no fraternities or sororities. There are 60 groups on campus, including adventure race team, alpine ski, and wilderness pursuits, baseball, climbing, English performance poetry club, hockey, men's and women's rugby, men's and women's soccer, mountain bike/road cycling, art, band, cheerleading, choir, chorale, chorus, dance, drama, environmental, ethnic, gay, honors, international, jazz band, literary magazine, marching band, musical theater, newspaper, nordic, opera, orchestra, pep band, photography, political, professional, radio and TV, religious, social, social service, student government, and symphony. Popular campus events include Family Weekend, Spring Carnival and Winter Fest.

Sports: There are 15 intercollegiate sports for men and 14 for women, and 9 intramural sports for men and 9 for women. Facilities include a fitness center, 2 gyms, a 5000-seat football stadium, an all-weather track, a number of playing fields, a weight room, an indoor swimming pool, a games/pool area, and tennis and volleyball courts.

Disabled Students: 90% of the campus is accessible. Facilities include wheelchair ramps, elevators, special parking, specially equipped restrooms, special class scheduling, lowered drinking fountains, lowered telephones, special housing. screen reader programs available on all student lab computers, ADA compliant rooms in residence halls, and an audio device that increases telephone volume.

Services: Counseling and information services are available, as is tutoring in most subjects. There is a reader service for the blind, and remedial math and writing.

Campus Safety and Security: Measures include 24-hour foot and vehicle patrol and security escort services. There are emergency telephones, lighted pathways/sidewalks, special event van shuttle service.

Programs of Study: Western confers B.A., and B.F.A. degrees. Master's degrees are also awarded. Bachelor's degrees are awarded in AGRICULTURE (environmental studies), BIOLOGICAL SCIENCE (biology/biological science), BUSINESS (accounting, business administration and management, and recreation and leisure services), COMMUNICATIONS AND THE ARTS (art, communications, dramatic arts, English, fine arts, music, and Spanish), COMPUTER AND PHYSICAL SCIENCE (chemistry, computer science, geology, and mathematics), EDUCATION (art education, elementary education, foreign languages education, music education, science education, and secondary education), ENGINEERING AND ENVIRONMENTAL DESIGN (preengineering), HEALTH PROFESSIONS (predentistry), SOCIAL SCIENCE (anthropology, economics, history, physical fitness/movement, political science/government, prelaw, psychology, and sociology). Business, biological sciences and communications are the strongest academically. Exercise and sports science, recreation and outdoor education have the largest enrollments.

Required: To be eligible to graduate, students must complete 120 credit hours and attain a minimum GPA of 2.0. Students must complete 35 core curriculum credits, 26 of which must be fulfilled through liberal arts credits in human relationships, natural sciences, and creative arts, as well as completing competencies in written expression, oral communication, and math.

Special: The Department of Business and Accounting offers a co-op program. Study abroad, internships, work-study programs, an accelerated degree program in teacher education, dual and student-designed majors, and credit for military and work experience are available. There are 9 national honor societies and a freshman honors program.

Faculty/Classroom: 51% of faculty are male; 49% are female. All teach and do research. No introductory courses are taught by graduate students. The average class size in an introductory lecture is 22, in a laboratory is 15; and in a regular course is 19.

Admissions: 92% of the 2013-2014 applicants were accepted. The SAT scores for the 2013-2014 freshman class were: Critical Reading--47% below 500, 42% between 500 and 599, 11% between 600 and 699; Math--52% below 500, 39% between 500 and 599, 9% between 600 and 699. The ACT scores were 43% below 21, 28% between 21 and 23, 17% between 24 and 26, 8% between 27 and 28, and 4% above 28. 20% of the current freshmen were in the top fifth of their class; 43% were in the top two fifths. 1 freshman graduated first in the class.

Requirements: The SAT or ACT is required. An essay required and interview is recommended. Applicants must be graduates of an accredited secondary school. Western recommends that in high school students complete 4 units of English, 4 units of math, 3 units of laboratory science, 3 units of social science, and at least 1 unit of foreign language. Western requires applicants to be in the upper 40% of their class. A GPA of 2.5 is required. AP and CLEP credits are accepted. Important factors in the admissions decision are advanced placement or honors courses, leadership record, and extracurricular activities record.

Procedure: Freshmen are admitted to all sessions. Entrance exams should be taken during spring of junior year or fall of senior year. There are deferred admissions and rolling admissions plans. Applications should be filed by June 1 for fall entry; November 1 for spring entry, along with a $30 fee. Notification is sent on a rolling basis. Applications are accepted online.

Transfer: 159 transfer students enrolled in 2012-2013. Transfer applicants must have a minimum GPA of 2.0, and may be asked to submit SAT or ACT test scores. 30 of 120 credits required for the bachelor's degree must be completed at Western.

Visiting: There are regularly scheduled orientations for prospective students, Campus tours, and meetings with faculty, coaches, and admissions counselors are available. There are guides for informal visits and visitors may sit in on classes. To schedule a visit, contact the Admissions Office.

Financial Aid: In 2013-2014, 82% of all full-time freshmen and 74% of continuing full-time students received some form of financial aid. 82% of all full-time freshmen and 74% of continuing full-time students received need-based aid. The average freshman award was $11,666. Need-based scholarships or need-based grants averaged $5,480 ($7,058 maximum); need-based self-help aid (loans and jobs) averaged $4,097 ($5,600 maximum); and non-need-based athletic scholarships averaged $2,484 ($4,128 maximum). 21% of undergraduate students work part-time. Average annual earnings from campus work are $600. The average financial indebtedness of the 2013 graduate was $22,431. The FAFSA is required. The priority date for freshman financial aid applications for fall entry is March 1.

International Students: There are 14 international students enrolled. They must take the TOEFL with a minimum score of 550 on the paper-based TOEFL (PBT) or 96 on the Internet-based version (iBT).

Graduates: From July 1, 2012 to June 30, 2013, 362 bachelor's degrees were awarded. The most popular majors were business (23%), parks and recreation (14%), and social sciences (11%). 45 companies recruited on campus in 2012-2013. In an average class, 1% graduate in 3 years or less, 26% graduate in 4 years or less, 37% graduate in 5 years or less, and 39% graduate in 6 years or less. Of the 2012 graduating class, 12% were enrolled in graduate school within 6 months of graduation, and 25% were employed.

Admissions Contact: Dale Gaubatz, Director of Admissions. E-Mail: *dgaubatz@western.edu* Web: *www.western.edu*

CONNECTICUT

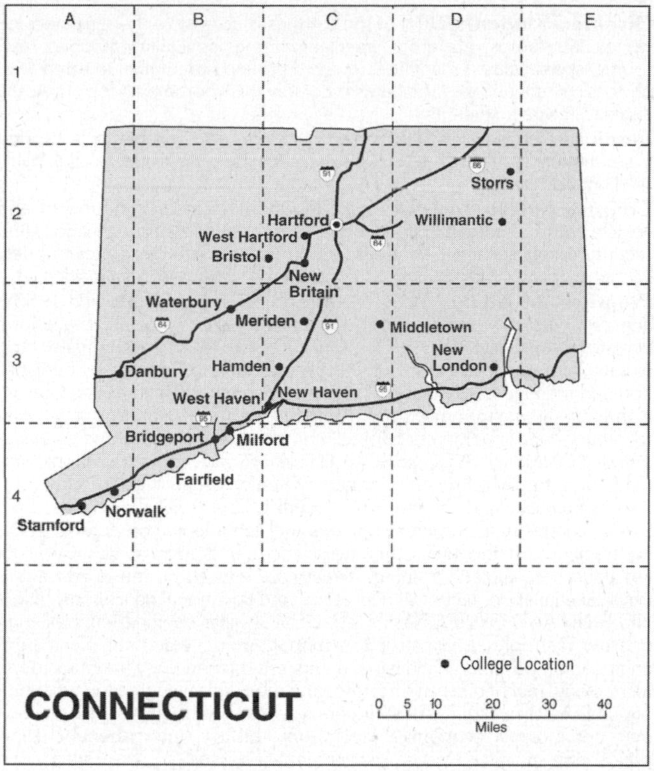

ALBERTUS MAGNUS COLLEGE C-3

New Haven, CT 06511-1189 (203) 773-8501
(800) 578-9160; (203) 773-9539

Full-time: 474 men, 902 women
Part-time: 74 men, 154 women
Graduate: 120 men, 286 women
Year: semesters, summer session
Application Deadline: open
Faculty: 42; IIB, av$
Ph.D.s: 92%
Student/Faculty: 13 to 1
Tuition: $26,784
Room & Board: $11,588
Freshman Class: 619 applied, 499 accepted, 134 enrolled
SAT CR/M/W: 456/448/472

LESS COMPETITIVE

Albertus Magnus College, founded in 1925, is a private college affiliated with the Roman Catholic Church and sponsored by the Dominican Sisters of Peace. The college offers undergraduate and graduate degrees in the liberal arts and sciences and in business. There are 3 undergraduate schools and 2 graduate schools. The library contains 100,000 volumes, 7,500 microform items, and 2,000 audio/video tapes/CDs/DVDs, and subscribes to 32,000 periodicals including electronic. Computerized library services include interlibrary loans, database searching, and Internet access. Special learning facilities include a learning resource center, art gallery, a theater, an academic skill center, and computer centers. The 55-acre campus is in a suburban area 80 miles from New York City. Including any residence halls, there are 17 buildings. The figures in the above capsule and in this profile are approximate.

Student Life: 95% of undergraduates are from Connecticut. Others are from 6 states, and 2 foreign countries. 85% are from public schools. 45% are white; 22% African American; 11% Hispanic. 55% are Catholic; 18% claim no religious affiliation; 17% Protestant. The average age of freshmen is 18; all undergraduates, 22. 24% do not continue beyond their first year; 64% remain to graduate.

Housing: 320 students can be accommodated in college housing, which includes single-sex and coed dorms. Residence halls are mainly old mansions that have been converted into student housing. Each building houses 15 to 65 students. On-campus housing is guaranteed for all 4 years. 50% of students commute. All students may keep cars.

Activities: There are no fraternities or sororities. There are 20 groups on campus, including business, criminal justice, art, computers, dance, drama, English, ethnic, gay, honors, international, literary magazine, musical theater, photography, political, professional, religious, social, social service, and student government. Popular campus events include Fall Candlelight Ceremony, Christmas events, and Laurel Day.

Sports: There are 7 intercollegiate sports for men and 7 for women. Facilities include an Olympic-size pool, a gym, indoor and outdoor tracks, racquetball and volleyball courts, weight and dance rooms, 4 tennis courts, a game room, and soccer and softball fields.

Disabled Students: All of the campus is accessible. Facilities include wheelchair ramps, elevators, special parking, specially equipped restrooms, special class scheduling, lowered drinking fountains, and lowered telephones.

Services: Counseling and information services are available, as is tutoring in every subject, math, English, science, statistics, writing; eTutoring is available in several additional subjects as well. There is remedial math, reading, and writing.

Campus Safety and Security: Measures include 24-hour foot and vehicle patrol, emergency notification system, and security escort services. There are emergency telephones, lighted pathways/sidewalks, and controlled access to dorms/residences.

Programs of Study: Albertus Magnus confers B.A., B.S., and B.F.A. degrees. Associate and master's degrees are also awarded. Bachelor's degrees are awarded in BIOLOGICAL SCIENCE (biology/biological science), BUSINESS (accounting, business administration and management, and management information systems), COMMUNICATIONS AND THE ARTS (communications, dramatic arts, English, and fine arts), COMPUTER AND PHYSICAL SCIENCE (mathematics), EDUCATION (education), HEALTH PROFESSIONS (art therapy, predentistry, premedicine, and preveterinary science), SOCIAL SCIENCE (criminology, history, human services, humanities, industrial and organizational psychology, liberal arts/general studies, philosophy, political science/government, prelaw, psychology, religion, sociology, and urban studies). English, psychology, business, science, and art therapy are the strongest academically. Business management, sociology/criminal justice, and psychology have the largest enrollments.

Required: To graduate, all students must complete at least 120 credit-hours, including 60 outside the major and at least 30 in the major. General education requirements, including 6 credits each in English and humanities, and 3 each in fine arts, math, science, and senior humanities, must be fulfilled. Distribution requirements include 3 credits each of history, social science, philosophy, religion, and literature. Service learning or career explorations are also required. A minimum 2.0 GPA is required.

Special: The college offers junior- and senior-year internships allowing up to 12 credits, study abroad, a Washington semester, work-study programs, and accelerated degree programs in business and information technology, psychology, criminal justice, communications, English, humanities, and general studies. Also available are dual and student-designed majors, nondegree study, pass/fail options, independent study, and preprofessional programs. Students may take accelerated degree programs in the evening or take weekend courses. The college also offers a teacher certification program, including placement for the student teaching. There are 5 national honor societies, a freshman honors program, and 12 departmental honors programs.

Faculty/Classroom: 54% of faculty are male; 46% are female. All teach and do research. No introductory courses are taught by graduate students. The average class size in an introductory lecture is 20; in a laboratory is 10; and in a regular course is 15.

Admissions: In a recent year, 81% of applicants were accepted. The SAT scores for a recent freshman class were: Critical Reading--43% below 500, 41% between 500 and 599, 14% between 600 and 700, and 2% above 700; Math--53% below 500, 30% between 500 and 599, 15% between 600 and 700, and 1% above 700; Writing--48% below 500, 36% between 500 and 599, 15% between 600 and 700, and 1% above 700. 23% of the current freshmen were in the top fifth of their class; 45% were in the top two fifths.

Requirements: The SAT is required, with a minimum recommended composite score of 800. Applicants must be graduates of an accredited secondary school or have a GED certificate and have completed 16 academic credits, including 4 years of English, 2 or 3 years each of foreign language, math, and science, 2 years of history, and 1 year of social studies. High school transcripts, rank, and 2 letters of recommendation are required. An interview is recommended. Albertus Magnus requires applicants to be in the upper 50% of their class. A GPA of 2.5 is required. AP and CLEP credits are accepted. Important factors in the admissions decision are advanced placement or honors courses, recommendations by school officials, and leadership record.

Procedure: Freshmen are admitted to all sessions. Entrance exams should be taken between April of the junior year and November of the senior year. There are deferred admissions and rolling admissions plans. Application deadlines are open. Application fee is $35. Notifications are sent December 15. Applications are accepted online.

Transfer: 52 transfer students enrolled in 2010-2011. Transfer students must present a minimum 2.0 overall GPA and a 2.0 GPA for all transferable, compatible course work. 30 of 120 credits required for the bachelor's degree must be completed at Albertus Magnus.

Visiting: There are regularly scheduled orientations for prospective students, consisting of registration, a general introduction, a financial aid/major introduction, lunch, a campus tour, and an interview. There are guides for informal visits and visitors may sit in on classes. To schedule a visit, contact the Admissions Office.

Financial Aid: In a recent year, 85% of all full-time freshmen and 80% of continuing full-time students received some form of financial aid. 80% of all full-time freshmen and 68% of continuing full-time students received need-based aid. The average freshman award was $24,415. Need-based scholarships or need-based grants averaged $13,084 ($27,600 maximum); need-based self-help aid (loans and jobs) averaged $3,515 ($8,500 maximum); other non-need-based awards and non-need-based scholarships averaged $7,572 ($45,500 maximum); and $244 from other forms of aid. 9% of undergraduate students work part-time. Average annual earnings from campus work are $1804. The average financial indebtedness of a recent graduate was $32,323. The FAFSA and the college's own financial statement are required. The priority date for freshman financial aid applications for fall entry is February 28.

International Students: There is 1 international student enrolled. The school actively recruits these students. They must take the TOEFL with a minimum score of 550 on the paper-based TOEFL (PBT) or 79 on the Internet-based version (iBT).

Computers: Access to the wireless network is available to all students in all buildings on campus and it can be used to access all internet-based services, including the College Portal, the Learning Management System, and all library resources. In addition to the wireless network, 90 desktop computers are available to students to access internet-based services; these computers are located in several computer labs in academic and administrative buildings, and the library. All students may access the system 24/7. There are no time limits and no fees. It is strongly recommended that all students have a personal computer.

Graduates: In a recent year, 372 bachelor's degrees were awarded. The most popular majors were management (62%), sociology (13%), and psychology (7%). 28 companies recruited on campus in 2010-2011. In an average class, 48% graduate in 4 years or less, 63% graduate in 5 years or less, and 63% graduate in 6 years or less. Of the 2010 graduating class, 25% were enrolled in graduate school within 6 months of graduation, and 70% were employed.

Admissions Contact: Dean of Admissions and Financial Aid. E-Mail: *admissions@albertus.edu* Web: *www.albertus.edu*

CENTRAL CONNECTICUT STATE UNIVERSITY C-2

New Britain, CT 06050 **(860) 832-2278**
(888) 733-2278; (860) 832-2522

Full-time: 4003 men, 3621 women	**Faculty:** 434; IIA, +$
Part-time: 1105 men, 1042 women	**Ph.D.s:** 83%
Graduate: 750 men, 1374 women	**Student/Faculty:** 16 to 1
Year: semesters, summer session	**Tuition:** $8706 ($20,211)
Application Deadline:	**Room & Board:** $10,506

Freshman Class: 5551 applied, 3560 accepted, 1293 enrolled
SAT CR/M/W: 500/508/504

COMPETITIVE

There are 4 undergraduate schools and one graduate school. In addition to regional accreditation, CCSU has baccalaureate program accreditation with AACSB, ABET, CSAB, CSWE, NCATE, and NLN. The library contains 588,278 volumes, 84,556 microform items, and 10,987 audio/video tapes/CDs/DVDs, and subscribes to 46,750 periodicals including electronic. Computerized library services include interlibrary loans, database searching, Internet access, and Wi-Fi capability. Special learning facilities include an art gallery, planetarium, radio station, TV station, including writing and math centers. The 294-acre campus is in a suburban area 10 miles west of Hartford. Including any residence halls, there are 39 buildings.

Student Life: 96% of undergraduates are from Connecticut. Others are from 44 states, 53 foreign countries, and Canada. 70% are White. The average age of freshmen is 18; all undergraduates, 23. 23% do not continue beyond their first year; 52% remain to graduate.

Housing: 2090 students can be accommodated in college housing, which includes single-sex and coed dorms. On-campus housing is guaranteed for all 4 years, is available on a first-come, and first-served basis. 79% of students commute. All students may keep cars.

Activities: 1% of men belong to 2 national fraternities; 1% of women belong to 1 national sorority. There are 100 groups on campus, including art, band, cheerleading, choir, chorale, chorus, computers, dance, drama, ethnic, gay, honors, international, jazz band, literary magazine, marching band, newspaper, orchestra, pep band, photography, political, professional, radio and TV, religious, social, social service, student government, and symphony. Popular campus events include Winter and Spring Weekends, First Week and Vance Lectures.

Sports: There are 7 intercollegiate sports for men and 8 for women. Facilities include a 3,800-seat gym, 8 tennis courts, a 6,000-seat football stadium, a 37,000-square-foot air-supported recreation facility, a natatorium, weight training rooms, and softball, baseball, touch football, and soccer fields.

Disabled Students: 90% of the campus is accessible. Facilities include wheelchair ramps, elevators, special parking, specially equipped restrooms, special class scheduling, lowered drinking fountains, lowered telephones. personal care attendants who serve as roommates for physically disabled resident students.

Services: Counseling and information services are available, as is tutoring in some subjects. There is a reader service for the blind, and remedial math, reading, and writing.

Campus Safety and Security: Measures include 24-hour foot and vehicle patrol, emergency notification system, self-defense education, and security escort services. There are shuttle buses, emergency telephones, lighted pathways/sidewalks, and controlled access to dorms/residences.

Programs of Study: CCSU confers B.A., B.S., B.F.A. and B.S.N. degrees. Master's and doctoral degrees are also awarded. Bachelor's degrees are awarded in BIOLOGICAL SCIENCE (biochemistry and biology/biological science), BUSINESS (accounting, business administration and management, finance, hospitality management services, international business management, management information systems, marketing/retailing/merchandising, and office supervision and management), COMMUNICATIONS AND THE ARTS (art, communications, dramatic arts, English, French, German, graphic design, Italian, journalism, music, Spanish, and theatre arts), COMPUTER AND PHYSICAL SCIENCE (chemistry, Computer Engineering Technology, computer science, earth science, mathematics, physical sciences, and physics), EDUCATION (art education, athletic training, elementary education, music education, physical education, technical education, and vocational education), ENGINEERING AND ENVIRONMENTAL DESIGN (civil engineering, civil engineering technology, construction management, electrical/electronics engineering technology, industrial engineering technology, manufacturing technology, mechanical engineering, and mechanical engineering technology), HEALTH PROFESSIONS (nursing), SOCIAL SCIENCE (anthropology, criminology, economics, geography, history, international studies, philosophy, political science/government, psychology, social work, and sociology). Psychology, criminology, and communication have the largest enrollments.

Required: To graduate, all students must complete at least 122 to 130 credit hours, depending on the major, with a minimum GPA of 2.0. General education requirements total 44 to 46 credits in arts and humanities, sciences, math, communications, and fitness/wellness studies. Students must also demonstrate foreign language proficiency, complete 6 credits in courses with a global context, and satisfy a First-Year Experience requirement.

Special: The university offers co-op programs and cross-registration with several other Connecticut educational institutions, study abroad in more than 45 countries, internships in most departments, work-study programs, dual majors, and student-designed majors. There are 7 national honor societies, a freshman honors program, and 1 departmental honors programs.

Faculty/Classroom: 56% of faculty are male; 44% are female. All teach undergraduates. No introductory courses are taught by graduate students.

Admissions: 64% of the 2013-2014 applicants were accepted. The SAT scores for the 2013-2014 freshman class were: Critical Reading--50% below 500, 41% between 500 and 599, 9% between 600 and 699, and 1% between 700 and 800; Math--46% below 500, 43% between 500 and 599, 11% between 600 and 699, and 1% between 700 and 800; Writing--47% below 500, 42% between 500 and 599, 11% between 600 and 699, and 1% between 700 and 800.

Requirements: The SAT is required. The ACT Optional Writing test is also required. Applicants must be graduates of an accredited secondary school or have earned a GED. An interview is recommended. CCSU also recommends that applicants have 14 academic credits: 4 in English, 3 each in math and a foreign language, and 2 each in science and social sciences, including 1 in U.S. history. AP and CLEP credits are accepted. Important factors in the admissions decision are extracurricular activities record, recommendations by school officials, and advanced placement or honors courses.

Procedure: Freshmen are admitted fall and spring. Entrance exams should be taken in May of the junior year or November of the senior year. There are deferred admissions and rolling admissions plans. Check with the school for current application deadlines. The application fee is $50. Notifications are sent April 1. 110 applicants were on the 2013 waiting list; were admitted. Applications are accepted online.

Transfer: 1072 transfer students enrolled in 2012-2013. Applicants must have a minimum of 12 transferable credits and a GPA of 2.0, and must submit official transcripts from previous schools attended. 30 of 122 credits required for the bachelor's degree must be completed at CCSU.

Visiting: There are regularly scheduled orientations for prospective students, including a fall open house in October and daily and select Saturday visits throughout the fall and spring. There are guides for informal visits and visitors may sit in on classes. To schedule a visit, contact the Admissions Office at (860) 832-2278.

Financial Aid: In 2013-2014, 79% of all full-time freshmen and 74% of continuing full-time students received some form of financial aid. 75% of all full-time freshmen and 65% of continuing full-time students received need-based aid. The average freshman award was $12,600. Need-based scholarships or need-based grants averaged $5,674 ($8,500 maximum); need-based self-help aid (loans and jobs) averaged $6,926 ($7,000 maximum); non-need-based athletic scholarships averaged $11,500 ($12,000 maximum); and other non-need-based awards and non-need-based scholarships averaged $2,019 ($3,000 maximum). 80% of undergraduate students work part time. Average annual earnings from campus work are $2500. CCSU is a member of CSS. The FAFSA, and federal income tax returns is required. The priority date for freshman financial aid applications for fall entry is March 1.

International Students: There are 101 international students enrolled. The school actively recruits these students. They must take the TOEFL with a minimum score of 500 on the paper-based TOEFL (PBT).

Computers: All students may access the system. 8:30 a.m. to 12 p.m., Monday to Thursday; 8:30 a.m. to 6 p.m., Friday; 9 a.m. to 6 p.m., Saturday; and 1 p.m. to 10 p.m., Sunday. There are no time limits and no fees.

Graduates: The most popular majors were business/marketing (25%), social sciences (16%), and education (8%). In an average class, 25% graduate in 4 years or less, 45% graduate in 5 years or less, and 54% graduate in 6 years or less.

Admissions Contact: Larry Hall, Director of Recruitment and Admissions. E-Mail: *admissions@ccsu.edu* Web: *www.ccsu.edu*

CHARTER OAK STATE COLLEGE — C-2

New Britain, CT 06053 — **860-515-3701; 860-760-6047**

Full-time: 96 men, 205 women	**Faculty:** n/av
Part-time: 446 men, 834 women	**Ph.D.s:** n/av
Graduate: none	**Student/Faculty:** 14 to 1
Year: semesters, summer session	**Tuition:** $8280 ($10,890)
Application Deadline:	**Room & Board:** n/app
Freshman Class: n/av	**SPECIAL**

Charter Oak State College, founded in 1973, is a public online college offering degree programs for adult students. Credits may be earned by taking online courses at Charter Oak or by other means, such as transfer, testing, portfolio review, or contract learning. The campus is in a suburban area. Charter Oak State College is an online college. Its administrative offices are located 13 miles southwest of Hartford, CT. Including any residence halls, there are 2 buildings.

Student Life: 73% of undergraduates are from Connecticut. Others are from 43 states, and Canada. 60% are White; 16% African American. The average age of all undergraduates is 39.

Activities: There are no fraternities or sororities. Groups on campus include student government.

Sports: There is no sports program at Charter Oak.

Disabled Students: All of the campus is accessible. Facilities include wheelchair ramps, elevators, special parking, specially equipped restrooms. Academic programs are all done online. Services can be obtained by phone, fax, email, and Internet.

Services: Counseling and information services are available, as is tutoring in some subjects. Tutoring is available online.

Programs of Study: Charter Oak confers B.A., and B.S. degrees. Associate degrees are also awarded. Bachelor's degrees are awarded in COMPUTER AND PHYSICAL SCIENCE (computer security and information assurance), EDUCATION (health information management), HEALTH PROFESSIONS (health care administration), SOCIAL SCIENCE (liberal arts/general studies).

Required: Bachelor's degree completion requires at least 120 credits, including transfer credits. The total must consist of at least 90 liberal arts credits for a B.A. or 60 liberal arts credits for a B.S. Students must have a GPA of at least 2.0 to graduate. Additional general education and major/concentration requirements also apply.

Faculty/Classroom: 43% of faculty are male; 57% are female. All teach undergraduates. No introductory courses are taught by graduate students.

Requirements: Charter Oak State College requires applicants to have earned at least 9 college credits and be at least 16 years of age. A high school diploma or GED is required to qualify for federal financial aid. Charter Oak accepts transfer students only. AP and CLEP credits are accepted.

Procedure: Freshmen are admitted to all sessions. There are deferred admissions and rolling admissions plans. Application deadlines are open. Application fee is $75. Applications are accepted online.

Transfer: At least 9 credits of transfer work. 6 of 120 credits required for the bachelor's degree must be completed at Charter Oak.

Visiting: There are regularly scheduled orientations for prospective students.

Financial Aid: The FAFSA is required. Check with the school for current application deadlines.

International Students: They must take the college's own test, International students must fulfill Charter Oak's written communication general education requirement before admission.

Computers: All students may access the system. There are no time limits and no fees.

Graduates: From July 1, 2012 to June 30, 2013, 429 bachelor's degrees were awarded.

Admissions Contact: Director of Admissions. E-Mail: *admissions@charteroak.edu* Web: *www.charteroak.edu*

CONNECTICUT COLLEGE — D-3

New London, CT 06320-4196 — **(860) 439-2200; (860) 439-4301**

Full-time: 722 men, 1133 women	**Faculty:** 178; IIB, +$
Part-time: 13 men, 28 women	**Ph.D.s:** 92%
Graduate: 2 men, 5 women	**Student/Faculty:** 9 to 1
Year: n/av	**Tuition:** $44,490
Application Deadline: January 1	**Room & Board:** $11,480
Freshman Class: 5241 applied, 1804 accepted, 509 enrolled	
SAT CR/M/W: 660/660/680 **ACT:** 29	**MOST COMPETITIVE**

Situated on the coast of southern New England, Connecticut College is a highly selective private liberal arts college with about 1,900 students from all across the country and throughout the world. On the college's 750-acre arboretum campus overlooking Long Island Sound, students and faculty create a vibrant social, cultural and intellectual community enriched by diverse perspectives. The college, founded in 1911, is known for its unique combination of interdisciplinary studies, international programs, funded internships, student-faculty research and service learning. There is 1 graduate school. The 2 libraries contain 616,590 volumes, 151,979 microform items, and 98,432 audio/video tapes/CDs/DVDs, and subscribe to 5,599 periodicals including electronic. Computerized library services include interlibrary loans, database searching, Internet access, and laptop Internet portals. Special learning facilities include an art gallery, radio station, 750-acre arboretum, greenhouse, ion accelerator, refracting telescope and observatory, scanning and transmission electron microscopes, nuclear magnetic resonance spectrometer, tunable diode laser spectroscopy laboratory, center for electronic and digital sound, neuroscience and animal behavior laboratories, clinical and social psychology research observation suites. The 750-acre campus is in a small town midway between Boston and New York City. Including any residence halls, there are 103 buildings. The figures in the above capsule and in this profile are approximate.

Student Life: 85% of undergraduates are from out of state, mostly the Northeast. Students are from 42 states, 46 foreign countries, and Canada. 50% are from public schools. 74% are white. 27% are Protestant; 26% Catholic; 17% claim no religious affiliation; 14% Jewish. The average age of freshmen is 18; all undergraduates, 20. 10% do not continue beyond their first year; 85% remain to graduate.

Housing: 1790 students can be accommodated in college housing, which includes coed dorms and on-campus apartments. In addition, there are language houses, special-interest houses, quiet housing, theme housing, substance-free housing, gender-neutral housing. On-campus housing is guaranteed for all 4 years and is available on a lottery system for upperclassmen. 99% of students live on campus. All students may keep cars.

Activities: There are no fraternities or sororities. There are 55 groups on campus, including a cappella, art, band, chess, choir, chorale, chorus, computers, dance, drama, environmental, ethnic, film, gay, honors, international, jazz band, literary magazine, newspaper, opera, orchestra, photography, political, professional, radio and TV, religious, social, social service, student government, and symphony. Popular campus events include Eclipse Weekend, Harvestfest, and Floralia.

Sports: There are 12 intercollegiate sports for men and 14 for women, and 12 intramural sports for men and 10 for women. The Connecticut College athletics complex includes the Charles B. Luce Field House, Dayton Arena, a new 10,000-square-foot fitness/wellness center, Lott Natatorium, an artificial-turf field, an eight-lane all weather track, new tennis courts, and playing fields on Tempel Green at the center of campus.

Disabled Students: All of the campus is accessible. Facilities include wheelchair ramps, elevators, special parking, specially equipped restrooms, special class scheduling, lowered drinking fountains, and lowered telephones.

Services: Counseling and information services are available, as is tutoring in some subjects, math, writing, and biological sciences.

Campus Safety and Security: Measures include 24-hour foot and vehicle patrol, emergency notification system, and security escort services. There are shuttle buses, emergency telephones, lighted pathways/sidewalks, controlled access to dorms/residences, Campus-wide emergency communications system.

Programs of Study: Connecticut College confers B.A. degrees. Master's degrees are also awarded. Bachelor's degrees are awarded in BIOLOGICAL SCIENCE (biochemistry, biology/biological science, botany, and neurosciences), COMMUNICATIONS AND THE ARTS (art, art history and appreciation, Chinese, classics, dance, dramatic arts, English, film arts,

French, German, Japanese, music, and music technology), COMPUTER AND PHYSICAL SCIENCE (astrophysics, chemistry, mathematics, and physics), ENGINEERING AND ENVIRONMENTAL DESIGN (architecture and environmental science), SOCIAL SCIENCE (African studies, American studies, anthropology, East Asian studies, economics, gender studies, Hispanic American studies, history, human development, international relations, Italian studies, Latin American studies, philosophy, political science/government, psychology, religion, Russian and Slavic studies, sociology, and urban studies). Economics, English, government, international relations, psychology, biological sciences, environmental studies, history have the largest enrollments.

Required: To graduate, students must complete at least 128 credit hours with a minimum GPA of 2.0. Distribution requirements cover 7 courses from 7 academic areas, plus a foreign language and 2 writing-intensive courses.

Special: Cross-registration with 12 area colleges, internships in government, human services, and other fields, a Washington semester at American University, dual majors, student-designed majors, a 3-2 engineering degree with Washington University in St. Louis and Boston University, non-degree study, and satisfactory/unsatisfactory options are available. One third of the junior class studies abroad. An international studies certificate program is available, which combines competency in a foreign language, an internship, and study abroad. There are also certificate programs in museum studies, community action and public policy, conservation biology and environmental studies, arts and technology, and teaching. There are 5 national honor societies including Phi Beta Kappa.

Faculty/Classroom: 52% of faculty are male; 48% are female. All teach undergraduates and all do research. No introductory courses are taught by graduate students. The average class size in an introductory lecture is 25; in a laboratory is 13; and in a regular course is 19.

Admissions: In a recent year, 34% of applicants were accepted. The SAT scores for a recent freshman class were: Critical Reading--1% below 500, 8% between 500 and 599, 63% between 600 and 700, and 28% above 700; Math--10% between 500 and 599, 64% between 600 and 700, and 26% above 700; Writing--1% below 500, 10% between 500 and 599, 50% between 600 and 700, and 39% above 700.

Requirements: The submission of standardized tests is optional, although students whose primary language is not English are required to submit the TOEFL or its equivalent. In addition, applicants must be graduates of an accredited secondary school. An essay is required and an interview is recommended. AP credits are accepted.

Procedure: Freshmen are admitted fall and spring. Entrance exams should be taken by January of the senior year. There are early decision and deferred admissions plans. Early decision applications should be filed by November 15; regular applications, by January 1 for fall entry; and December 1 for spring entry, along with a $60 fee. Notification of early decision is sent December 15; regular decision, April 1. Applications are accepted online.

Transfer: 18 transfer students enrolled in a recent year. Applicants must have a minimum college GPA of 3.0 and be in good standing at the previous school attended. SAT or ACT scores are required and an interview is recommended. 64 of 128 credits required for the bachelor's degree must be completed at Connecticut College.

Visiting: There are regularly scheduled orientations for prospective students, Student visits include an introduction to the college, student perspectives, academic programs, a luncheon for parents and students, tours, and a reception. There are guides for informal visits, visitors may sit in on classes, and stay overnight. To schedule a visit, contact the Admission Office.

Financial Aid: In a recent year, 48% of all full-time freshmen and 48% of continuing full-time students received some form of financial aid. 48% of all full-time freshmen and 48% of continuing full-time students received need-based aid. The average freshman award was $32,993. The average financial indebtedness of the 2011 graduate was $22,790. Connecticut College is a member of CSS. The CSS/Profile and FAFSA, and parent and student tax forms, including noncustodial parent's statement, are required. The deadline for filing freshman financial aid applications for fall entry is January 15.

International Students: There are 90 international students enrolled. The school actively recruits these students. They must take the TOEFL with a minimum score of 600 on the paper-based TOEFL (PBT) or 100 on the Internet-based version (iBT), APIEL, IELTS, MELAB, ELPT or equivalent.

Computers: The campus has 84 wireless access points in academic buildings and all residence halls, with 3100 network drops. The college owns and supports about 1,600 computers, some for faculty/staff, others in student labs. All students may access the system 24 hours a day. There are no time limits and no fees. It is strongly recommended that all students have a personal computer.

Graduates: In a recent year, 453 bachelor's degrees were awarded. The most popular majors were economics (16%), government (10%), and international relations (8%). In an average class, 83% graduate in 4 years or less, 85% graduate in 5 years or less, and 85% graduate in 6 years or less. Of the 2010 graduating class, 25% were enrolled in graduate school within 6 months of graduation, and 75% were employed.

Admissions Contact: Dean of Admissions. E-Mail: *admission@conncoll.edu* Web: *www.connecticutcollege.edu*

CONNECTICUT STATE UNIVERSITY SYSTEM

The Connecticut State University System, established in 1983, is a public system in Connecticut. It is governed by a board of trustees, whose chief administrator is the president. The primary goal of the system is teaching. The main priorities are access, with emphasis on a multi-cultural experience; quality, within a context of curriculum diversity and a range of delivery systems; and public service, including linkages with schools, state government, and private enterprise. CSUS is the largest public university system in Connecticut, and offers 90 baccalaureate, 77 graduate and numerous professional degrees. The total student enrollment is about 38,000 with 2,005 faculty members. Profiles of the 4-year campuses are included in this section.

EASTERN CONNECTICUT STATE UNIVERSITY — D-2

Willimantic, CT 06226 — **(860) 465-5286**

Full-time: 2023 men, 2372 women	**Faculty:** 194
Part-time: 373 men, 411 women	**Ph.D.s:** 94%
Graduate: 48 men, 141 women	**Student/Faculty:** 22 to 1
Year: semesters, summer session	**Tuition:** $9376 ($21,241)
Application Deadline: May 1	**Room & Board:** $11,208
Freshman Class: 5112 applied, 3299 accepted, 985 enrolled	
SAT CR/M/W: 510/510/520	**ACT:** 22 **COMPETITIVE**

Eastern Connecticut State University, founded in 1889, is the state's public liberal arts university. There are 3 undergraduate schools and one graduate school. In addition to regional accreditation, Eastern has baccalaureate program accreditation with CSWE and NCATE. The library contains 408,479 volumes, 973,594 microform items, and 9,006 audio/video tapes/CDs/DVDs, and subscribes to 44,778 periodicals including electronic. Computerized library services include interlibrary loans, database searching, Internet access, and Wi-Fi capability. Special learning facilities include an art gallery, planetarium, radio station, TV station, an arboretum, Child and Family Development Resource Center, Church Farm Center for the Arts and Sciences. The 182-acre campus is in a small town 29 miles east of Hartford and 90 miles southwest of Boston. Including any residence halls, there are 54 buildings.

Student Life: 95% of undergraduates are from Connecticut. Others are from 24 states, 50 foreign countries, and Canada. 95% are from public schools. 70% are White. The average age of freshmen is 18; all undergraduates, 22. 22% do not continue beyond their first year; 51% remain to graduate.

Housing: 2655 students can be accommodated in college housing, which includes coed dorms and on-campus apartments. In addition, there are honors houses and special-interest houses. 53% of students live on campus. Alcohol is not permitted. Upperclassmen may keep cars.

Activities: There are no fraternities or sororities. There are 77 groups on campus, including and ice hockey, fencing, football, art, cheerleading, club sports include rugby, computers, dance, debate, drama, environmental, ethnic, gay, honors, international, newspaper, photography, political, professional, radio and TV, religious, social, social service, student government, and yearbook. Popular campus events include Open Rec Night, Springfest and Arts and Lecture Series.

Sports: There are 7 intercollegiate sports for men and 10 for women, and 15 intramural sports for men and 15 for women. Facilities include a student center with theaters, café, billiards, fitness center, a 2800-seat field house, a 6-lane swimming pool, soccer field, baseball complex, softball stadium, 400 meter 8-lane track, field hockey field, intramural field, tennis, basketball, racquetball, and squash courts, weight room, matted rooms for yoga and martial arts, and trails in an arboretum.

Disabled Students: Facilities include wheelchair ramps, elevators, special parking, specially equipped restrooms, special class scheduling, and lowered drinking fountains.

Services: Counseling and information services are available, as is tutoring in every subject.

Campus Safety and Security: Measures include 24-hour foot and vehicle patrol, emergency notification system, and security escort services. There are shuttle buses, emergency telephones, lighted pathways/sidewalks, and controlled access to dorms/residences.

Programs of Study: Eastern confers B.A., B.S. and B.G.S. degrees. Associate and master's degrees are also awarded. Bachelor's degrees are awarded in BIOLOGICAL SCIENCE (biochemistry and biology/biological science), BUSINESS (accounting, business administration and management, industrial and labor relations, recreation and leisure services, and sports management), COMMUNICATIONS AND THE ARTS (communications, English, music, performing arts, Spanish, theatre acting, and visual and performing arts), COMPUTER AND PHYSICAL SCIENCE (computer science, information sciences and systems, and mathematics), EDUCATION (early childhood education, elementary education, and physical education), ENGINEERING AND ENVIRONMENTAL DESIGN (environmental science), SOCIAL SCIENCE (economics, history, liberal arts/general studies, political science/government, psychology, social science, social work, sociology, and women & gender studies). Business administration, psychology, and social sciences have the largest enrollments.

Required: To graduate, students must complete 120 credit hours, including the requirements of an academic major, with a GPA of 2.0. Liberal Arts Core Curriculum requirements include 26 credits in Methods and Concepts, 15 in Synthesis and Application, and 3 credits in Independent Inquiry.

Special: The University Honors Program promotes undergraduate scholarship by providing academically talented students with opportunities to participate in specially designed courses that prepare them to conduct independent research and/or scholarly activity under the oversight of a faculty mentor. The Individualized Major Plan is a student's self-designed interdisciplinary plan of study, which consists of courses from two or more disciplines and results in a B.A. or B.S. degree. The self-designed plan of study allows the student to take courses in areas that naturally complement each other in today's workplace and to develop a strong educational base in at least one subject to facilitate entrance into a graduate program. There are 8 national honor societies and a freshman honors program.

Faculty/Classroom: 51% of faculty are male; 49% are female. 98% teach undergraduates. No introductory courses are taught by graduate students. The average class size in an introductory lecture is 23.

Admissions: 65% of the 2013-2014 applicants were accepted. The SAT scores for the 2013-2014 freshman class were: Critical Reading--44% below 500, 45% between 500 and 599, 9% between 600 and 699, and 2% between 700 and 800; Math--42% below 500, 45% between 500 and 599, 12% between 600 and 699, and 1% between 700 and 800; Writing--39% below 500, 46% between 500 and 599, 13% between 600 and 699, and 1% between 700 and 800. The ACT scores were 32% below 21, 41% between 21 and 23, 20% between 24 and 26, 6% between 27 and 28, and 1% above 28. 23% of the current freshmen were in the top fifth of their class; 56% were in the top two fifths. 3 freshmen graduated first in their class.

Requirements: The SAT or ACT is required. Applicants must be graduates of an accredited secondary school or have a GED. They should have completed 15 high school academic credits, including 4 years of English, 4 of math, and 2 each of foreign language, social studies, and science (including 1 of lab science). While interviews are not generally required of students applying for admission, the Admission staff may request an interview with certain applicants to obtain additional information or clarify information. AP and CLEP credits are accepted. Important factors in the admissions decision are advanced placement or honors courses, personality/intangible qualities, and extracurricular activities record.

Procedure: Freshmen are admitted fall and spring. Entrance exams should be taken in November or December of the senior year. There are deferred admissions and rolling admissions plans. Applications should be filed by May 1 for fall entry, along with a $50 fee. Notification is sent on a rolling basis. applicants were on the 2013 waiting list; were admitted. Applications are accepted online.

Transfer: 499 transfer students enrolled in 2012-2013. Official college and high school transcripts are required. 30 of 120 credits required for the bachelor's degree must be completed at Eastern.

Visiting: There are regularly scheduled orientations for prospective students, including small group discussions, a tour of the campus, and a personal interview. There are guides for informal visits and visitors may sit in on classes. To schedule a visit, contact the Office of Admissions at admissions@easternct.edu.

Financial Aid: Eastern is a member of CSS. The FAFSA is required. The deadline for filing freshman financial aid applications for fall entry is March 15.

International Students: The school actively recruits these students. They must take the TOEFL. They must also take the SAT or ACT.

Computers: All students may access the system. There are no time limits and no fees.

Admissions Contact: Ned Harris, Director of Enrollment Management. E-Mail: *admissions@easternct.edu* Web: *http:/www1.easternct.edu/admissions/*

FAIRFIELD UNIVERSITY B-4

Fairfield, CT 06824 **(203) 254-4100; (203) 254-4199**

Full-time: 1426 men, 2120 women **Faculty:** 231; IIA, +$
Part-time: 140 men, 187 women **Ph.D.s:** 89%
Graduate: 339 men, 707 women **Student/Faculty:** 15 to 1
Year: semesters, summer session **Tuition:** $42,920
Application Deadline: January 15 **Room & Board:** $12,930
Freshman Class: 9582 applied, 6742 accepted, 963 enrolled
SAT CR/M/W: 570/590/590 **ACT:** 26 **VERY COMPETITIVE**

Founded in 1942, Fairfield University is a Catholic, Jesuit University that is rooted in one of the world's oldest intellectual and spiritual traditions. Located near the Connecticut shoreline just 60 miles northeast of New York City, Fairfield has over 3,500 undergraduate, 1,100 graduate and 400 part-time students from 32 states, 28 foreign countries, and Puerto Rico who are enrolled in the University's five schools; the College of Arts & Sciences, the Charles F. Dolan School of Business, Graduate School of Education and Allied Professions, the School of Engineering and the School of Nursing. Fairfield has a faculty student ratio of 11:1 and offers a comprehensive core curriculum, more than 40 undergraduate majors,16 interdisciplinary minors, 41 graduate programs, 20 NCAA Division I athletic teams, and a wide range of opportunities for service and civic engagement. Committed to the Jesuit ideals of broad intellectual inquiry, Fairfield University fosters a strong sense of community among its students and offers an educational experience that encourages the pursuit of social justice, and cultivation of the whole person: body, mind, and spirit. Fairfield's graduates from the Class of 2012 reported 96% had secured full-time employment, were admitted to graduate school or chose to participate in volunteer service within six months of graduation. There are 4 undergraduate schools and 5 graduate schools. In addition to regional accreditation, Fairfield has baccalaureate program accreditation with AACSB, ABET, NCATE, and NLN. The library contains 376,085 volumes, 945,121 microform items, and 15,670 audio/video tapes/CDs/DVDs, and subscribes to 68,690 periodicals including electronic. Computerized library services include interlibrary loans, database searching, Internet access, and Wi-Fi capability. Special learning facilities include an art gallery, radio station, TV station, a media center, 750-seat concert hall/theater, a rehearsal and improvisation theater, language learning lab, Business Education Simulation Training (BEST) classroom, SIM/simulated hospital environment and human patient simulators in the nursing facility, an art gallery and an art museum. The 200-acre campus is in a suburban, residential community 60 miles northeast of New York City and one mile from Long Island Sound. Including any residence halls, there are 48 buildings.

Student Life: 73% of undergraduates are from out of state, mostly the Northeast. Students are from 32 states, 28 foreign countries, and Canada. 55% are from public schools. 73% are White; 11% race unknown. The average age of freshmen is 18; all undergraduates, 21. 13% do not continue beyond their first year; 81% remain to graduate.

Housing: 2910 students can be accommodated in college housing, which includes single-sex and coed dorms and on-campus apartments. In addition, there are special-interest houses, and a substance-free floor. On-campus housing is guaranteed for all 4 years and is available on a lottery system for upperclassmen. 80% of students live on campus. Upperclassmen may keep cars.

Activities: There are no fraternities or sororities. There are 92 groups on campus, including art, band, cheerleading, chess, choir, chorale, chorus, communications, computers, dance, debate, drama, environmental, ethnic, film, gay, honors, international, jazz band, literary magazine, musical theater, newspaper, orchestra, pep band, photography, political, professional, radio and TV, religious, social, social service, student government, and yearbook. Popular campus events include Presidential Ball, Midnight Breakfast, Fall Concert, Relay for Life, Glee Club Pops Concert, Hunger Clean-up, Noche Caliente, Pride and Purpose, Rep Ya Flag, and Remixx Showcase.

Sports: There are 9 intercollegiate sports for men and 11 for women, and 13 intramural sports for men and 10 for women. Facilities include The Leslie C. Quick Jr. Recreation Complex, otherwise known as the RecPlex, is primarily used for open recreation, physical conditioning, and intramural sports. Numerous classes are coordinated within the RecPlex such as; fitness classes, tennis, Pilates, yoga, swimming in Fairfield's 25-meter pool, jazz dance, and aqua aerobics. The RecPlex also contains areas for cardio, weight training, three racquetball courts, saunas, whirlpools, and a field house that houses four courts interchangeable used for basketball, tennis, and volleyball. Membership is included in tuition and fees for all full-time undergraduates. Fairfield also sponsors 20 varsity sports which all compete in the NCAA's Division I. Varsity programs include nine men's and 11 women's sports teams. The Walsh Athletic Center offers a high-tech academic study center, a multimedia recruitment center, equipment rooms, strength and conditioning center, practice courts, and indoor batting cages. Additionally, Fairfield has two artificial surface fields, a grass soccer field, baseball and softball fields, state of the art tennis courts, an on campus basketball facility as well as an off campus basketball arena, rowing facility and golf facility.

Disabled Students: All of the campus is accessible. Facilities include

wheelchair ramps, elevators, special parking, specially equipped restrooms, special class scheduling, lowered drinking fountains, lowered telephones, special housing. Accommodations for seeing-eye dogs and a library computer station for physically challenged students are also available.

Services: Counseling and information services are available, as is tutoring in some subjects, Group Based peer tutoring is offered in the following courses: Chemistry, Biology, Physics, Psychology, and Nursing as well as Modern Languages courses in French, Italian and Spanish. Additional tutoring is offered in Accounting, Economics and Engineering There is a reader service for the blind. Fairfield University also offers tutoring at both the writing and math center.

Campus Safety and Security: Measures include 24-hour foot and vehicle patrol, emergency notification system, self-defense education, and security escort services. There are shuttle buses, emergency telephones, lighted pathways/sidewalks, controlled access to dorms/residences, EMT Public Safety officers, bike patrol, closed circuit television system, crime prevention seminars and information via campus television network.

Programs of Study: Fairfield confers B.A., B.S., B.S.E. and B.S.N. degrees. Master's and doctoral degrees are also awarded. Bachelor's degrees are awarded in BIOLOGICAL SCIENCE (biochemistry and biology/biological science), BUSINESS (accounting, business administration and management, finance, and marketing), COMMUNICATIONS AND THE ARTS (communication, English, modern language, and visual and performing arts), COMPUTER AND PHYSICAL SCIENCE (chemistry, computer science, information sciences and systems, mathematics, physics, and software engineering), ENGINEERING AND ENVIRONMENTAL DESIGN (computer engineering, electrical/electronics engineering, and mechanical engineering), HEALTH PROFESSIONS (nursing), SOCIAL SCIENCE (American studies, economics, history, international studies, philosophy, political science/government, psychology, religious studies, and sociology). Accounting, finance, biology, communication, and nursing are the strongest academically. Nursing, communication, and psychology have the largest enrollments.

Required: To graduate, students must complete 120 credits and completed at least 38 three or four credit courses with a minimum GPA of 2.0 both overall and in the major. Sixty of the 120 credits are in general education core requirements. Distribution requirements include 15 credits in philosophy, religious studies, and ethics, 15 credits in English and fine arts, 12 credits in math and natural sciences, 12 credits in history and social sciences, and 6 credits in foreign languages. Students are also required to take courses in US and world diversity.

Special: Fairfield administers its own study abroad program in several countries and has affiliations with 17 programs, a Washington semester, a federal work-study program, B.A.-B.S. degrees in economics, international studies, and psychology, student-designed majors, and dual majors in all subjects. The University offers 5th year graduate degree programs in education, psychology, and engineering. Fairfield University offers a four year Honors Program across the University open, by special admission, to all undergraduates regardless of the school in which they are enrolled. A bachelor of Arts/Sciences in Professional Studies is offered for part time students through the College of Arts and Sciences. Internships, both credit and noncredit, are offered at area corporations, publications, banks, and other organizations. Interdisciplinary minors include women's studies, entrepreneurship, marine science, Black studies, environmental studies, jazz, classical performance, Italian studies, Russian and Eastern European studies, Catholic studies and Judaic studies, applied ethics, Asian studies, Irish studies, Latin American and Caribbean studies, and peace and justice. Fairfield University offers a comprehensive study abroad program through our office of International Programs which includes: Italy, France, Spain, Ireland, Nicaragua, Tanzania, Australia, and Brazil. There are 22 national honor societies, including Phi Beta Kappa, and a freshman honors program.

Faculty/Classroom: 49% of faculty are male; 51% are female. 86% teach undergraduates. No introductory courses are taught by graduate students. The average class size in an introductory lecture is 22 and in a laboratory is 15.

Admissions: 70% of the 2013-2014 applicants were accepted. The SAT scores for the 2013-2014 freshman class were: Critical Reading--9% below 500, 53% between 500 and 599, 34% between 600 and 699, and 4% between 700 and 800; Math--6% below 500, 48% between 500 and 599, 41% between 600 and 699, and 5% between 700 and 800; Writing--6% below 500, 45% between 500 and 599, 43% between 600 and 699, and 7% between 700 and 800. The ACT scores were 2% below 21, 15% between 21 and 23, 39% between 24 and 26, 21% between 27 and 28, and 24% above 28.

Requirements: Fairfield has test optional admission. There is no additional information required if students choose not to submit test scores. There is no required grade point average, although most admitted students have a B average or better in a solid college preparatory program, which should include some advanced and/or honors classes. Students should have completed 15 academic credits, including 4 credits of English, 3 to 4 credits each of history, math, and lab science, and 2 to 4 credits of a foreign language. AP and CLEP credits are accepted. Important factors in the admissions decision are advanced placement or honors courses, recommendations by school officials, and extracurricular activities record.

Procedure: Freshmen are admitted fall. Entrance exams should be taken In the spring of the junior year or fall of the senior year. There are early decision, early admissions, and deferred admissions plans. Early decision applications should be filed by November 15; regular applications, by January 15 for fall entry, along with a $60 fee. Notification of early decision is sent January 1; regular decision, April 1. 57 early decision candidates were accepted for the 2013-2014 class. 1745 applicants were on the 2013 waiting list; 67 were admitted. Applications are accepted online.

Transfer: 38 transfer students enrolled in 2012-2013. Common Application for Transfer Students, Fairfield University Application Supplement, Application fee, Official high school transcript, Official college transcript from all universities attended (whether or not credit was earned), Mid-term Grade Progress Report, Dean of Students Certification Form. 60 of 120 credits required for the bachelor's degree must be completed at Fairfield.

Visiting: There are regularly scheduled orientations for prospective students, information sessions and tours offered weekdays and some weekends. Individualized class visits are available. There are guides for informal visits, visitors may sit in on classes, and stay overnight. To schedule a visit, contact The Office of Admission.

Financial Aid: In 2013-2014, 87% of all full-time freshmen and 85% of continuing full-time students received some form of financial aid. 55% of all full-time freshmen and 52% of continuing full-time students received need-based aid. The average freshman award was $18,436. Need-based scholarships or need-based grants averaged $22,926 ($42,920 maximum); need-based self-help aid (loans and jobs) averaged $3,723 ($7,750 maximum); non-need-based athletic scholarships averaged $19,890 ($56,425 maximum); and other non-need-based awards and non-need-based scholarships averaged $7,864 ($42,920 maximum). 85% of undergraduate students work part-time. Average annual earnings from campus work are $1560. The average financial indebtedness of the 2013 graduate was $38,052. Fairfield is a member of CSS. The CSS/Profile and FAFSA are required. The priority date for freshman financial aid applications for fall entry is February 15.

International Students: There are 64 international students enrolled. The school actively recruits these students. They must take the TOEFL with a minimum score of 550 on the paper-based TOEFL (PBT) or 80 on the Internet-based version (iBT), IELTS (International English Language Testing System).

Computers: All students may access the system 24 hours a day, 7 days a week. There are no time limits and no fees.

Graduates: From July 1, 2012 to June 30, 2013, 855 bachelor's degrees were awarded. The most popular majors were nursing (15%), communication (11%), and accounting (8%). 161 companies recruited on campus in 2012-2013. In an average class, 79% graduate in 4 years or less, 81% graduate in 5 years or less, and 82% graduate in 6 years or less. Of the 2012 graduating class, 28% were enrolled in graduate school within 6 months of graduation, and 65% were employed.

Admissions Contact: Karen Pellegrino, Dean of Enrollment. E-Mail: *admis@fairfield.edu* Web: *www.fairfield.edu*

GOODWIN COLLEGE

East Hartford, CT 06118 **860-528-4111; 800-889-3282**

Full-time: 131 men, 462 women	**Faculty:** 83
Part-time: 450 men, 2345 women	**Ph.D.s:** 37%
Graduate: n/av	**Student/Faculty:** 10 to 1
Year: semesters, summer session	**Tuition:** $19,400
Application Deadline:	**Room & Board:** n/app
Freshman Class: 604 applied, 250 enrolled	

LESS COMPETITIVE

Goodwin College, founded in 1999, is a private, four-year institution located in East Hartford, Connecticut. There is one undergraduate school. In addition to regional accreditation, Goodwin College has baccalaureate program accreditation with ABHES and NLN. Computerized library services include interlibrary loans, database searching, Internet access, and Wi-Fi capability. Special learning facilities include an art gallery. The 600-acre campus is in a suburban area. Including any residence halls, there are 7 buildings.

Student Life: 2% of undergraduates are from out of state, mostly the Northeast. Students are from 10 states, and 4 foreign countries. 52% are White; 23% African American; 20% Hispanic. The average age of freshmen is 25; all undergraduates, 30. 46% do not continue beyond their first year; 20% remain to graduate.

Housing: Alcohol is not permitted. All students commute. All students may keep cars.

Activities: There are no fraternities or sororities. Groups on campus include choral groups, environmental, ethnic, political, professional, social service, and student government.

Sports: There are 2 intramural sports for men and 1 for women.

Disabled Students: All of the campus is accessible. Facilities include

wheelchair ramps, elevators, special parking, specially equipped restrooms, and lowered drinking fountains.

Services: Counseling and information services are available, as is tutoring in most subjects. There is remedial math, reading, and writing.

Campus Safety and Security: Measures include emergency notification system and security escort services. There are shuttle buses, emergency telephones, and lighted pathways/sidewalks.

Programs of Study: Goodwin College confers B.S. degrees. Associate degrees are also awarded. Bachelor's degrees are awarded in AGRICULTURE (environmental studies), BUSINESS (business administration and management and management science), HEALTH PROFESSIONS (health science and nursing), SOCIAL SCIENCE (child care/child and family studies and human services). Nursing is the strongest academically. Health science is the largest.

Required: Satisfactory completion of all course requirement with a minimum GPA of 2.0; 25% of credits granted by the college; last 12 credits on transcript granted by the college;fullfilment of all financial obiligations. For Bachelor of Science degree, in addition to above, 15 credits in major core must be completed at the college; minimum of 45 credits at the 200 level or above; minimum of 30 credits at the 300 level or above; 20 hours of community service.

Special: Internships, field work or practica for all bachelors degree and some associate degree programs

Faculty/Classroom: 33% of faculty are male; 67% are female. All teach undergraduates. No introductory courses are taught by graduate students. The average class size in a regular course is 18.

Requirements: AP and CLEP credits are accepted.

Procedure: Freshmen are admitted fall, spring, and summer. There are early admissions, deferred admissions, and rolling admissions plans. Application deadlines are open. Application fee is $50. Applications are accepted online.

Transfer: 708 transfer students enrolled in 2012-2013. Grade of C or better 30 of 120 credits required for the bachelor's degree must be completed at Goodwin College.

Visiting: There are regularly scheduled orientations for prospective students, only for the AS Nursing program. There are guides for informal visits. To schedule a visit, contact Nicholas Lentino at (860) 528 4111.

Financial Aid: The FAFSA, CCS/Profile, or FAFSA, or FFS, or SFS, and the college's own financial statement are required. Check with the school for current application deadlines.

International Students: There are 4 international students enrolled.

Computers: All students may access the system. There are no time limits and no fees.

Graduates: From July 1, 2012 to June 30, 2013, 26 bachelor's degrees were awarded. The most popular majors were nursing (26%), health sciences (22%), and medical assisting (13%). In an average class, 20% graduate in 6 years or less. Of the 2012 graduating class, 70% were employed within 6 months of graduation.

Admissions Contact: Nicholas Lentino, Assistant Vice President/ Admissions. E-Mail: *nlentino@goodwin.edu* Web: *www.goodwin.edu*

MITCHELL COLLEGE D-3

New London, CT 06320 **(800) 443-2811**
(800) 443-2811; (860) 444-1209

Full-time: 395 men, 336 women	**Faculty:** 35
Part-time: 59 men, 68 women	**Ph.D.s:** 74%
Graduate: n/av	**Student/Faculty:** 14 to 1
Year: semesters, summer session	**Tuition:** $28,491
Application Deadline: rolling	**Room & Board:** $12,492
Freshman Class: n/av	

COMPETITIVE

Mitchell College, founded in 1938, is a private institution offering associate and bachelor degree programs in the liberal arts and professional areas. The figures in the above capsule and in this profile are approximate. The library contains 94,542 volumes, and 1,658 audio/video tapes/CDs/ DVDs, and subscribes to 90 periodicals including electronic. Computerized library services include interlibrary loans, database searching, Internet access, and Wi-Fi capability. Special learning facilities include a radio station. The 68-acre campus is in a suburban area in southeastern Connecticut, on the shore of the Thames River where it meets Long Island Sound. Including any residence halls, there are 26 buildings.

Student Life: 54% of undergraduates are from Connecticut. Others are from 26 states, and 5 foreign countries. 50% are from public schools. 66% are White; 12% Hispanic. 61% claim no religious affiliation; 18% Catholic; 12% Protestant. The average age of freshmen is 19; all undergraduates, 20. 43% do not continue beyond their first year; 47% remain to graduate.

Housing: 598 students can be accommodated in college housing, which includes single-sex and coed dorms and on-campus apartments. On-campus housing is guaranteed for all 4 years. 80% of students live on campus; of those, 60% remain on campus on weekends. All students may keep cars.

Activities: There are no fraternities or sororities. There are 35 groups on campus, including Behavioral Sciences), Academic (Education, art, cheerleading, choir, chorus, computers, dance, drama, ethnic, gay, honors, international, professional, radio and TV, religious, social, social service, and student government.

Sports: There are 8 intercollegiate sports for men and 7 for women, and 4 intramural sports for men and 4 for women. Facilities include basketball court, fitness center, two beaches, woods with natural and groomed trails, tennis courts, and athletic fields for all varsity teams.

Disabled Students: 50% of the campus is accessible. Facilities include wheelchair ramps, elevators, special parking, specially equipped restrooms, and special class scheduling.

Services: Counseling and information services are available, as is tutoring in most subjects. There is a reader service for the blind.

Campus Safety and Security: Measures include 24-hour foot and vehicle patrol, emergency notification system, and security escort services. There are shuttle buses, emergency telephones, lighted pathways/ sidewalks, and controlled access to dorms/residences.

Programs of Study: confers B.A. and B.S. degrees. Associate degrees are also awarded. Bachelor's degrees are awarded in AGRICULTURE (environmental studies), BUSINESS (business administration and management, hospitality management services, and sports management), COMMUNICATIONS AND THE ARTS (communications), EDUCATION (early childhood education), SOCIAL SCIENCE (criminal justice, homeland security, human development, liberal arts/general studies, and psychology). Early childhood education is the strongest academically. Business administration, criminal justice, sport and fitness management have the largest enrollments.

Required: To graduate: bachelor-degree-seeking students must complete 120 credits (associate-degree-seeking 60 credits) with a minimum GPA of 2.0 (2.67 for early childhood education). Required general education curriculum. Several majors contain a cumulating experience (a capstone, senior project, or internship).

Special: Internships are available through Academic Department Chairs. Liberal and Prefessional Studies offers an Individualized (student-designed) option. Work study jobs are available. Bachelor degrees (BA or BS) offered. There are 8 national honor societies, including Phi Beta Kappa, and 1 departmental honors program.

Faculty/Classroom: 49% of faculty are male; 51% are female. All teach undergraduates. No introductory courses are taught by graduate students. The average class size in an introductory lecture is 14; in a laboratory is 10; and in a regular course is 14.

Requirements: The GED is accepted. A recommendation and a personal statement are required. A personal interview is recommended but not required. A GPA of 2.0 is required. AP and CLEP credits are accepted. Important factors in the admissions decision are personality/intangible qualities, recommendations by school officials, and extracurricular activities record.

Procedure: Freshmen are admitted fall and spring. Entrance exams should be taken during summer orientation. There are early decision, deferred admissions, and rolling admissions plans. Early decision applications should be filed by November 15, along with a $30 fee. Notification of early decision is sent December 15; regular decision, on a Rolling basis. Applications are accepted online.

Transfer: 74 transfer students enrolled in 2012-2013. In addition to fulfilling regular application requirements, transfer applicants must submit official college transcripts from all colleges/universities attended. 30 of 120 credits required for the bachelor's degree must be completed at Mitchell.

Visiting: There are regularly scheduled orientations for prospective students, includes a student-guided tour and an interview with an admissions counselor. There are guides for informal visits and visitors may sit in on classes. To schedule a visit, contact Visit Coordinator, Admissions Office at (800) 443-2811.

Financial Aid: In 2013-2014, 83% of all full-time freshmen and 73% of continuing full-time students received some form of financial aid. 83% of all full-time freshmen and 73% of continuing full-time students received need-based aid. The average freshman award was $20,235. Need-based scholarships or need-based grants averaged $16,739; need-based self-help aid (loans and jobs) averaged $7,281; and other non-need-based awards and non-need-based scholarships averaged $7,636. The FAFSA is required. The priority date for freshman financial aid applications for fall entry is April 1.

International Students: There are 7 international students enrolled. The school actively recruits these students. They must take the TOEFL with a minimum score of 500 on the paper-based TOEFL (PBT), APIEL.

Computers: All students may access the system. at all times. There are no time limits and no fees.

Graduates: From July 1, 2012 to June 30, 2013, 190 bachelor's degrees were awarded. The most popular majors were liberal and pressional studies (23%), business administration (22%), and criminal justice (18%).

Admissions Contact: Gregg Gorneault, Director of Admissions. E-Mail: *gorneault_g@mitchell.edu* Web: *www.mitchell.edu*

POST UNIVERSITY B-3

Waterbury, CT 06723-2540 (203) 596-4520
(800) 345-2562; (203) 756-5810

Full-time: 325 men, 400 women	**Faculty:** n/av
Part-time: 200 men, 350 women	**Ph.D.s:** 61%
Graduate: n/av	**Student/Faculty:** n/av
Year: semesters, summer session	**Tuition:** $26,400
Application Deadline: open	**Room & Board:** $10,350
Freshman Class: n/av	
SAT or ACT: required	**COMPETITIVE**

Post University, founded in 1890, is a private institution offering liberal arts and business programs. The figures in the above capsule and in this profile are approximate. There are 2 undergraduate schools. The library contains 85,000 volumes, 75,158 microform items, and 1,027 audio/video tapes/CDs/DVDs, and subscribes to 427 periodicals including electronic. Computerized library services include interlibrary loans and database searching. Special learning facilities include a learning resource center, a tutorial center. The 70-acre campus is in an urban area 1 mile west of Waterbury. Including any residence halls, there are 13 buildings.

Student Life: 83% of undergraduates are from Connecticut. Others are from 12 states, 20 foreign countries, and Canada. 75% are from public schools. 63% are white; 17% African American. The average age of freshmen is 19; all undergraduates, 26. 23% do not continue beyond their first year; 39% remain to graduate.

Housing: 424 students can be accommodated in college housing, which includes coed dorms and off-campus apartments. On-campus housing is guaranteed for all 4 years. 58% of students live on campus; of those, 60% remain on campus on weekends. All students may keep cars.

Activities: There are no fraternities or sororities. There are 30 groups on campus, including cheerleading, chorale, chorus, computers, drama, ethnic, gay, honors, international, literary magazine, musical theater, social, social service, student government, and yearbook. Popular campus events include dances, concerts, and international food festivals.

Sports: There are 5 intercollegiate sports for men and 5 for women, and 4 intramural sports for men and 4 for women. Facilities include a soccer field, a fitness center, a weight room, a racquetball court, a swimming pool, and tennis courts.

Disabled Students: 70% of the campus is accessible. Facilities include wheelchair ramps, elevators, special parking, specially equipped restrooms, and special class scheduling.

Services: Counseling and information services are available, as is tutoring in most subjects. There is a reader service for the blind, and remedial math, reading, and writing.

Campus Safety and Security: Measures include 24-hour foot and vehicle patrol, self-defense education, and security escort services. There are shuttle buses and lighted pathways/sidewalks.

Programs of Study: TPU confers B.A. and B.S. degrees. Associate degrees are also awarded. Bachelor's degrees are awarded in BUSINESS (accounting, banking and finance, business administration and management, management science, and marketing/retailing/merchandising), COMMUNICATIONS AND THE ARTS (English), SOCIAL SCIENCE (criminal justice, history, liberal arts/general studies, psychology, and sociology). Biology is the strongest academically. Management and general studies are the largest.

Required: To graduate, all students must maintain a minimum GPA of 2.0, earn a total of 120 credits, including at least 33 in the major, and take a computer course.

Special: Co-op programs in all majors, cross-registration with Naugatuck Valley Community College, study abroad in England, the Netherlands, and Japan, internships with area businesses, general studies degrees, accelerated degree programs, B.A.-B.S. degrees, and credit for life experience are available. There are 2 national honor societies and 1 departmental honors program.

Faculty/Classroom: 57% of faculty are male; 43% are female. All teach undergraduates. No introductory courses are taught by graduate students. The average class size in an introductory lecture is 20; in a laboratory is 15; and in a regular course is 35.

Requirements: The SAT or ACT is required. Applicants must be graduates of an accredited secondary school, with 4 years of English and at least 16 total academic credits. The GED is accepted. A GPA of 2.0 is required. AP and CLEP credits are accepted. Important factors in the admissions decision are personality/intangible qualities, extracurricular activities record, and recommendations by school officials.

Procedure: Freshmen are admitted to all sessions. There are early admissions, deferred admissions, and rolling admissions plans. Check with the school for current application deadlines. In a recent year the application fee was $40. Notification is sent on a rolling basis. Applications are accepted online.

Transfer: Applicants must have a minimum college GPA of 2.0, submit an official college transcript, and have an interview. The SAT is recommended. 30 of 120 credits required for the bachelor's degree must be completed at PU.

Visiting: There are regularly scheduled orientations for prospective students, including tours, interviews with admissions counselors, and meetings with faculty and students. There are guides for informal visits, visitors may sit in on classes, and stay overnight. To schedule a visit, contact the Admissions Office.

Financial Aid: In a recent year, 100% of all full-time freshmen and 98% of continuing full-time students received some form of financial aid. 53% of all full-time freshmen and 54% of continuing full-time students received need-based aid. The average freshman award was $14,491. Need-based scholarships or need-based grants averaged $14,491; need-based self-help aid (loans and jobs) averaged $4,684; and non-need-based athletic scholarships averaged $10,890. The FAFSA and the college's own financial statement, and parent and student federal tax returns, are required. Check with the school for current application deadlines.

International Students: There are 48 international students enrolled. The school actively recruits these students. They must take the TOEFL with a minimum score of 500 on the paper-based TOEFL (PBT) or 79 on the Internet-based version (iBT).

Computers: All students may access the system. There are no time limits and no fees. It is strongly recommended that all students have a personal computer.

Admissions Contact: Dean of Admissions. A campus DVD is available.
E-Mail: *tpuadmis@teikyopost.edu* Web: *www.post.edu*

QUINNIPIAC UNIVERSITY C-3

Hamden, CT 06518 (203) 582-8600
(800) 462-1944; (203) 582-8906

Full-time: 2404 men, 3903 women	**Faculty:** 345; IIA
Part-time: 92 men, 143 women	**Ph.D.s:** 86%
Graduate: 779 men, 1482 women	**Student/Faculty:** 18 to 1
Year: semesters, summer session	**Tuition:** $39,330
Application Deadline: February 1	**Room & Board:** $14,250
Freshman Class: 20698 applied, 13913 accepted, 1800 enrolled	
SAT CR/M/W: 540/560/550 **ACT:** 25	**VERY COMPETITIVE**

Quinnipiac University, founded in 1929, is a private institution offering 58+ undergraduate majors and 22 graduate programs through the Schools of health sciences, nursing, business and engineering, communications, education, law, medicine and the college of arts and sciences. Located in Hamden, CT, mid-way between New York City and Boston and 8 miles north of New Haven on a stunning New England campus - home to 6400 undergraduate and 2200 graduate students. There are 5 undergraduate schools and 8 graduate schools. In addition to regional accreditation, Quinnipiac has baccalaureate program accreditation with AACSB, ABET, APTA, CAHEA, NCATE, and NLN. The 3 libraries contain 311,000 volumes, 592,900 microform items, and 6,000 audio/video tapes/CDs/DVDs, and subscribe to 44,700 periodicals including electronic. Computerized library services include interlibrary loans, database searching, Internet access, and Wi-Fi capability. Special learning facilities include an art gallery, radio station, TV station, An Gorta Mor: an exhibit on the Irish famine, part of Quinnipiac's Ireland's Great Hunger Museum which is located on Whitney Avenue. The 600-acre campus is in a suburban area Quinnipiac has three settings which make up the University. Located in Hamden, CT, just 8 miles north of New Haven, in a suburban setting. The Mount Carmel (main) campus of 250 acres with academic/recreation/library/residence buildings with housing for freshmen and sophomores. The nearby York Hill 250 acre campus provides suite-style housing for juniors and seniors, a 'lodge-like' student center, additional student parking and the TD Bank Sports Center. The North Haven 106 acre campus. Including any residence halls, there are 70 buildings.

Student Life: 77% of undergraduates are from out of state, mostly the Middle Atlantic. Students are from 28 states, 30 foreign countries, and Canada. 75% are from public schools. 78% are White. 51% are Catholic; 26% Protestant. The average age of freshmen is 19; all undergraduates, 21. 12% do not continue beyond their first year; 78% remain to graduate.

Housing: 5007 students can be accommodated in college housing, which includes coed dorms, on-campus apartments, and off-campus apartments. In addition, there are honors houses, special-interest houses, wellness housing. On-campus housing is guaranteed for all 4 years. 80% of students live on campus; of those, 75% remain on campus on weekends. Upperclassmen may keep cars.

Activities: 12% of men belong to 6 national fraternities; 11% of women belong to 7 national sororities. There are 120 groups on campus, including cheerleading, choir, chorus, dance, drama, environmental, ethnic, film, gay, honors, international, literary magazine, newspaper, pep band, political, professional, radio and TV, religious, social, social service, student government, and yearbook. Popular campus events include Siblings Weekend, Parents Weekend, Holiday party, and Fall and Spring Concerts.

Sports: There are 7 intercollegiate sports for men and 14 for women, and 6 intramural sports for men and 6 for women. Facilities include a sports

center with twin arenas, each seating more than 3000 for ice hockey and basketball, more than 20 acres of playing fields, and a recreation center with a weight training room, a steam room, a large multipurpose room for indoor tennis, basketball, volleyball, and aerobics, and a suspended indoor track.
Disabled Students: All of the campus is accessible. Facilities include wheelchair ramps, elevators, special parking, specially equipped restrooms, special class scheduling, and lowered drinking fountains.
Services: Counseling and information services are available, as is tutoring in most subjects, all freshman-level courses and others by request. Special workshops on work study skills, library resources, and time management are available.
Campus Safety and Security: Measures include 24-hour foot and vehicle patrol, emergency notification system, self-defense education, and security escort services. There are shuttle buses, emergency telephones, lighted pathways/sidewalks, controlled access to dorms/residences, perimeter security in the form of contract security officers at all entrances, and vehicle and occupant check-in identification.
Programs of Study: Quinnipiac confers B.A., B.S., and B.F.A. degrees. Master's and doctoral degrees are also awarded. Bachelor's degrees are awarded in BIOLOGICAL SCIENCE (biochemistry, biology/biological science, biotechnology, microbiology, and neurosciences), BUSINESS (accounting, banking and finance, business administration and management, business economics, entrepreneurial studies, finance, international business management, management science, marketing management, and marketing/retailing/merchandising), COMMUNICATIONS AND THE ARTS (advertising, communications, dramatic arts, English, journalism, public relations, Spanish, and theatre arts), COMPUTER AND PHYSICAL SCIENCE (chemistry, computer science, digital arts/technology, mathematics, software engineering, and web technology), EDUCATION (athletic training, elementary education, and secondary education), ENGINEERING AND ENVIRONMENTAL DESIGN (civil engineering, engineering, industrial engineering, and mechanical engineering), HEALTH PROFESSIONS (biomedical science, health science, nursing, occupational therapy, physical therapy, physician's assistant, predentistry, premedicine, and radiological science), SOCIAL SCIENCE (criminal justice, economics, gerontology, history, liberal arts/general studies, paralegal studies, philosophy, political science/government, prelaw, psychobiology, psychology, social science, and sociology). Psychology, physical therapy and nursing are the strongest academically. Communications, physical therapy and management have the largest enrollments.
Required: All students must complete 46 semester hours of the core curriculum, which includes a series of 3 seminars that explore community as it relates to the individual and the world, plus English, math, fine arts, social sciences, humanities and science. To graduate, students must maintain a GPA of 2.0 over 120 total semester hours.
Special: Internships or clinical placements are available in all majors. Students can choose to study abroad in more than 25 countries - particularly Ireland and Australia. A 6 or 7-year freshman entry-level doctorate (BS/DPT) in physical therapy and a 5 1/2 year freshman entry-level master's (BS/MOT) in occupational therapy are offered, as well as a 6-year BS in Health Sciences/MHS in a physician assistant master's program, and for those interested in teaching elementary or secondary education, a 5-year BA in an academic major plus a master of arts in teaching (MAT)which includes student teaching. An innovative BS/MBA is offered to academically talented business students in a 3+1 format to complete both degrees in 4 years. There are 20 national honor societies, a freshman honors program, and 20 departmental honors programs.
Faculty/Classroom: 48% of faculty are male; 52% are female. 85% teach undergraduates, 30% do research, and 30% do both. No introductory courses are taught by graduate students. The average class size in an introductory lecture is 24; in a laboratory is 15; and in a regular course is 22.
Admissions: 67% of the 2013-2014 applicants were accepted. The SAT scores for the 2013-2014 freshman class were: Critical Reading--22% below 500, 58% between 500 and 599, 18% between 600 and 699, and 2% between 700 and 800; Math--19% below 500, 51% between 500 and 599, 27% between 600 and 699, and 3% between 700 and 800; Writing--20% below 500, 57% between 500 and 599, 20% between 600 and 699, and 3% between 700 and 800. The ACT scores were 10% below 21, 18% between 21 and 23, 34% between 24 and 26, 28% between 27 and 28, and 10% above 28. 55% of the current freshmen were in the top fifth of their class; 89% were in the top two fifths. 30 freshmen graduated first in their class.
Requirements: The SAT or ACT is required. The ACT Optional Writing test is also required. A minimum composite score of 1050 on the SAT (critical reading plus math) or 23 composite on the ACT is recommended. The scores are used for admission and scholarship purposes. All students must have completed 16 academic credits, including 4 in English, 3 in math, 2 each in science and social studies, and 5 in electives. The GED is accepted. An interview is recommended, and an essay and at least one letter of recommendation are required. For majors in the health sciences, 4 years each of math and science are required. Quinnipiac requires applicants to be in the upper 40% of their class. A GPA of 2.9 is required. AP and CLEP credits are accepted. Important factors in the admissions decision are advanced placement or honors courses, extracurricular activities record, and personality/intangible qualities.
Procedure: Freshmen are admitted fall and spring. Entrance exams should be taken in the junior year and early in the senior year. There are early decision, deferred admissions, and rolling admissions plans. Early decision applications should be filed by November 1; regular applications, by February 1 for fall entry; and December 15 for spring entry, along with a $45 fee. Notification of early decision is sent December 1; regular decision, December 15. 170 early decision candidates were accepted for the 2013-2014 class. 1650 applicants were on the 2013 waiting list; 250 were admitted. Applications are accepted online.
Transfer: 178 transfer students enrolled in 2012-2013. Transfer students must have a minimum college GPA of 2.5 (some programs require a minimum of 3.0) and must submit SAT scores and high school or college transcripts if they have not received an associate degree prior to enrollment. An interview is recommended. 45 of 120 credits required for the bachelor's degree must be completed at Quinnipiac.
Visiting: There are regularly scheduled orientations for prospective students, consisting of interviews, a group information session, student-guided tours, financial aid sessions, an opportunity to speak with faculty, and open houses. Visitors may sit in on classes. To schedule a visit, contact the Admissions Office at (800) 462-1944.
Financial Aid: In 2013-2014, 91% of all full-time freshmen and 81% of continuing full-time students received some form of financial aid. 62% of all full-time freshmen and 58% of continuing full-time students received need-based aid. The average freshman award was $22,995. Need-based scholarships or need-based grants averaged $19,707 ($55,780 maximum); need-based self-help aid (loans and jobs) averaged $4,808 ($11,000 maximum); non-need-based athletic scholarships averaged $29,231 ($57,734 maximum); and other non-need-based awards and non-need-based scholarships averaged $14,959 ($38,000 maximum). 28% of undergraduate students work part-time. Average annual earnings from campus work are $2078. The average financial indebtedness of the 2013 graduate was $43,398. Quinnipiac is a member of CSS. The CSS/Profile and FAFSA are required. The priority date for freshman financial aid applications for fall entry is March 1. The deadline for filing freshman financial aid applications for fall entry is April 1.
International Students: There are 125 international students enrolled. The school actively recruits these students. They must take the TOEFL with a minimum score of 550 on the paper-based TOEFL (PBT) or 80 on the Internet-based version (iBT), IELTS . They must also take the SAT or ACT. only if the language of instruction is in English.
Computers: All students may access the system 24 hours a day. There are no time limits and no fees.
Graduates: From July 1, 2012 to June 30, 2013, 1484 bachelor's degrees were awarded. The most popular majors were health professions (30%), business (21%), and communications (19%). 250 companies recruited on campus in 2012-2013. In an average class, 71% graduate in 4 years or less, 75% graduate in 5 years or less, and 77% graduate in 6 years or less. Of the 2012 graduating class, 22% were enrolled in graduate school within 6 months of graduation, and 72% were employed.
Admissions Contact: Joan Isaac Mohr, Dean of Admissions. E-Mail: *admissions@quinnipiac.edu* Web: *www.quinnipiac.edu*

SACRED HEART UNIVERSITY B-4

Fairfield, CT 06825 **(203) 365-7560; (203) 365-7607**

Full-time: 1408 men, 2365 women	**Faculty:** 231
Part-time: 213 men, 503 women	**Ph.D.s:** 74%
Graduate: 644 men, 1850 women	**Student/Faculty:** 14 to 1
Year: semesters, summer session	**Tuition:** $35,050
Application Deadline: rolling	**Room & Board:** $13,514

Freshman Class: 7908 applied, 4800 accepted, 1267 enrolled

VERY COMPETITIVE

Sacred Heart University, founded in 1963, is a private Catholic institution that offers majors within health sciences, liberal arts and sciences, business, education, and information technology. There are 5 undergraduate schools and 3 graduate schools. In addition to regional accreditation, SHU has baccalaureate program accreditation with AACSB, APTA, CSWE, NCATE, and NLN. The 2 libraries contain 128,640 volumes, 223,036 microform items, and 1,237 audio/video tapes/CDs/DVDs, and subscribe to 41,089 periodicals including electronic. Computerized library services include interlibrary loans, database searching, and Internet access. Special learning facilities include a radio station, TV station, an Edgerton Center for Performing Arts, a Media Studies Lab, a Fashion Design Studio, and a Jandrisevits Learning Center. The 77-acre campus is in a suburban area 60 minutes from Manhattan and 150 minutes from Boston. The University also has domestic satellite campuses located in Stamford and Griswold, Connecticut. Including any residence halls, there are 22 buildings.
Student Life: 59% of undergraduates are from out of state, mostly the Northeast. Students are from 37 states, 17 foreign countries, and Canada.

68% are from public schools. 66% are White; 21% two or more races. 66% are Catholic. The average age of freshmen is 18; all undergraduates, 20. 19% do not continue beyond their first year; 81% remain to graduate.

Housing: 2634 students can be accommodated in college housing, which includes coed dorms, on-campus apartments, and off-campus apartments. In addition, there are honors houses, special-interest houses, living and learning communities with themes such as honors, business, wellness and community service. On-campus housing is guaranteed for all 4 years, is available on a first-come, first-served basis, and is available on a lottery system for upperclassmen. 54% of students live on campus. Upperclassmen may keep cars.

Activities: 19% of men belong to 26% of women belong to Groups on campus include ONE Campaign, WHRT Radio and Spectrum Newspaper, art, bagpipe, band, cheerleading, choir, chorale, chorus, computers, dance, debate, drama, drill team, environmental, ethnic, film, gay, Habitat for Humanity, honors, international, jazz band, literary magazine, marching band, musical theater, newspaper, orchestra, pep band, photography, political, professional, radio and TV, religious, social, social service, student government, and yearbook. Popular campus events include Fall and Spring Concerts, Student Affairs Lecture Series, Family Weekend and Pack the Pitt.

Sports: There are 14 intercollegiate sports for men and 17 for women, and 19 intramural sports for men and 18 for women. Facilities include The William H. Pitt Health and Recreation center with 4 multipurpose athletic courts, seating for 2,200, and a fitness center. There is a turf football field, an all-weather track, 6 championship tennis courts, and a new softball stadium.

Disabled Students: Facilities include wheelchair ramps, elevators, special parking, specially equipped restrooms, special class scheduling, lowered drinking fountains, lowered telephones, special housing. Special housing rooms are equipped with special audible alarms for students with hearing disabilities and other special accommodations can be made through Res Life.

Services: Counseling and information services are available, as is tutoring in every subject. There is a reader service for the blind, and remedial math, reading, and writing.

Campus Safety and Security: Measures include 24-hour foot and vehicle patrol, emergency notification system, self-defense education, and security escort services. There are shuttle buses, emergency telephones, lighted pathways/sidewalks, controlled access to dorms/residences. All campus-owned residence halls have sprinklers and alarms and are designated nonsmoking.

Programs of Study: SHU confers B.A., B.S., B.S.W. and B.S.N. degrees. Associate, master's, and doctoral degrees are also awarded. Bachelor's degrees are awarded in BIOLOGICAL SCIENCE (biology/biological science and ecology), BUSINESS (accounting, banking and finance, business administration and management, business economics, fashion merchandising, marketing management, and sports management), COMMUNICATIONS AND THE ARTS (communications, communications technology, creative writing, English, graphic design, media arts, performing arts, and Spanish), COMPUTER AND PHYSICAL SCIENCE (chemistry, computer science, computer security and information assurance, information sciences and systems, and mathematics), EDUCATION (athletic training, business education, education, elementary education, English education, foreign languages education, mathematics education, middle school education, science education, social science education, and social studies education), ENGINEERING AND ENVIRONMENTAL DESIGN (computer graphics), HEALTH PROFESSIONS (exercise science, health science, nursing, occupational therapy, physical therapy, preallied health, predentistry, premedicine, preosteopathy, prepharmacy, prephysical therapy, and preveterinary science), SOCIAL SCIENCE (criminal justice, history, Latin American studies, liberal arts/general studies, Middle Eastern studies, philosophy, political science/government, prelaw, psychology, religion, social work, sociology, and women's studies). Nursing, exercise science and health science are the strongest academically. Psychology, business, and nursing have the largest enrollments.

Required: At the undergraduate level, Sacred Heart University offers two baccalaureate degrees: Bachelor of Arts (BA) or Bachelor of Science (BS) depending upon the nature of the discipline of the major. The University offers 30 majors. The University also offers Associate in Arts (AA) and Associate in Science (AS) degrees. A central component of undergraduate study is the University's Core Curriculum, which embodies the University's commitment to academic excellence, social responsibility, and ethical awareness. All candidates for the baccalaureate degree must complete at least 120 credits, with a minimum of 30 credits taken at Sacred Heart University. A minimum cumulative grade point average (GPA) of 2.0 is required.

Special: SHU offers co-op programs in all majors, paid and unpaid internships at local, regional, and national organizations, including Fortune 500 and 1000 companies, hospitals, media outlets, social service agencies, and schools. Study abroad opportunities exist worldwide and year-round, and on-campus employment is available through the University's work-study program. There are 10 national honor societies, a freshman honors program, and 1 departmental honors program.

Faculty/Classroom: 47% of faculty are male; 53% are female. 93% teach undergraduates. No introductory courses are taught by graduate students. The average class size in an introductory lecture is 25; in a laboratory is 17; and in a regular course is 20.

Admissions: 61% of the 2013-2014 applicants were accepted. 31% of the current freshmen were in the top fifth of their class. 2 freshmen graduated first in their class.

Requirements: In addition, a completed application, essay, and 1 letter of recommendation are required. An interview is required for early decision candidates and recommended for all other candidates. Required are 4 years of English and 3 years of math, science, history, and language, with 4 years preferred. A GPA of 3.0 is required. AP and CLEP credits are accepted. Important factors in the admissions decision are recommendations by school officials, leadership record, and advanced placement or honors courses.

Procedure: Freshmen are admitted fall and spring. Entrance exams should be taken in May of the junior year and/or November of the senior year. There are early decision, deferred admissions, and rolling admissions plans. Early decision applications should be filed by December 1. The fall 2013 application fee was $50. Notification of early decision is sent December 15; regular decision, February 1. 197 early decision candidates were accepted for the 2013-2014 class. Applications are accepted online.

Transfer: 102 transfer students enrolled in 2012-2013. A minimum GPA of 2.0 is required. 30 of 120 credits required for the bachelor's degree must be completed at SHU.

Visiting: There are regularly scheduled orientations for prospective students, including Monday-Friday tours and interviews, weekend tours, interviews and information sessions, and open house programs during the academic year and summer. There are guides for informal visits, visitors may sit in on classes, and stay overnight. To schedule a visit, contact the Office of Undergraduate Admissions at (203) 365-7880.

Financial Aid: In 2013-2014, 73% of all full-time freshmen and 72% of continuing full-time students received some form of financial aid. 60% of all full-time freshmen and 59% of continuing full-time students received need-based aid. The average freshman award was $20,244. Need-based scholarships or need-based grants averaged $16,225 ; need-based self-help aid (loans and jobs) averaged $4,874; non-need-based athletic scholarships averaged $16,942; and other non-need-based awards and non-need-based scholarships averaged $11,738. Average annual earnings from campus work are $1120. The average financial indebtedness of the 2013 graduate was $24,390. SHU is a member of CSS. The CSS/Profile and FAFSA are required. The priority date for freshman financial aid applications for fall entry is February 15.

International Students: There are 108 international students enrolled. The school actively recruits these students. They must take the TOEFL with a minimum score of 570 on the paper-based TOEFL (PBT) or 92 on the Internet-based version (iBT). Test-Optional Admissions Policy.

Computers: All students may access the system 24 hours a day. There are no time limits and no fees.

Graduates: From July 1, 2012 to June 30, 2013, 843 bachelor's degrees were awarded. The most popular majors were psychology (32%), business administration (23%), and nursing (22%). 102 companies recruited on campus in 2012-2013. In an average class, 1% graduate in 3 years or less, 58% graduate in 4 years or less, 62% graduate in 5 years or less, and 63% graduate in 6 years or less. Of the 2012 graduating class, 18% were enrolled in graduate school within 6 months of graduation.

Admissions Contact: E-Mail: *enroll@sacredheart.edu* Web: *www.sacredheart.edu*

SAINT JOSEPH COLLEGE C-2

West Hartford, CT 06117 **(860) 231-5223; (866) 442-8752**

Full-time: 10 men, 810 women	**Faculty:** n/av; IIA, -$
Part-time: 15 men, 225 women	**Ph.D.s:** n/av
Graduate: 215 men, 1350 women	**Student/Faculty:** n/av
Year: semesters, summer session	**Tuition:** $32,000
Application Deadline: open	**Room & Board:** $14,630

Freshman Class: 1335 applied, 1047 accepted, 158 enrolled
SAT CR/M: 500/500

LESS COMPETITIVE

Saint Joseph College is a private institution consisting of an undergraduate women's program, a coed bachelor's degree completion program for adults, and a coed graduate school. The figures in the above capsule and in this profile are approximate. Computerized library services include interlibrary loans, database searching, Internet access, and laptop Internet portals. Special learning facilities include a learning resource center and art gallery. The 84-acre campus is in a suburban area 3 miles from Hartford, CT. Including any residence halls, there are 17 buildings.

Student Life: 94% of undergraduates are from Connecticut. Others are from states. 76% are white. The average age of freshmen is 18; all undergraduates, 25. 25% do not continue beyond their first year.

Housing: College-sponsored housing includes single-sex dorms. On-campus housing is available on a first-come and first-served basis. 60% of students commute. All students may keep cars.

Activities: There are no fraternities or sororities. Groups on campus include dance, drama, ethnic, gay, honors, international, political, professional, religious, social, social service, and student government.

Sports: There are 8 intercollegiate sports for women. Facilities include fitness center, basketball court, pool, indoor and outdoor tracks, tennis courts, softball field, soccer field, and dance studio.

Disabled Students: All of the campus is accessible. Facilities include wheelchair ramps, elevators, special parking, specially equipped restrooms, special class scheduling, and special housing.

Services: Counseling and information services are available, as is tutoring in most subjects.

Campus Safety and Security: Measures include 24-hour foot and vehicle patrol, emergency notification system, and security escort services. There are shuttle buses, emergency telephones, lighted pathways/sidewalks, and controlled access to dorms/residences.

Programs of Study: SJC confers B.A., and B.S. degrees. Master's and doctoral degrees are also awarded. Bachelor's degrees are awarded in BIOLOGICAL SCIENCE (biochemistry, biology/biological science, and nutrition), BUSINESS (accounting and management science), COMMUNICATIONS AND THE ARTS (art history and appreciation, English, and Spanish), COMPUTER AND PHYSICAL SCIENCE (chemistry and mathematics), EDUCATION (special education), HEALTH PROFESSIONS (nursing), SOCIAL SCIENCE (child psychology/development, family/consumer studies, history, international studies, philosophy, psychology, religion, social work, and women's studies). Nursing has the largest enrollment.

Required: To earn a bachelor's degree, students must have a minimum 2.0 GPA and 120 earned credits. In addition, requirements must be fulfilled in the general education curriculum and major area of study.

Special: Saint Joseph College offers cross-registration at member colleges through the Hartford Consortium for Higher Education. Internship opportunities, study abroad, double majors, and student-designed majors are also available. There is also a freshman honors program.

Faculty/Classroom: No introductory courses are taught by graduate students.

Admissions: 78% of the applicants were accepted. The SAT scores for a recent year freshman class were: Critical Reading--46% below 500, 44% between 500 and 599, 10% between 600 and 700; Math--49% below 500, 39% between 500 and 599, and 12% between 600 and 700.

Requirements: The SAT is required. SAT scores and high school GPA are important considerations for admission. A high school plan of study focused on college preparation is strongly suggested. AP and CLEP credits are accepted.

Procedure: Freshmen are admitted fall and spring. There are deferred admissions and rolling admissions plans. Application deadlines are open. Application fee is $50. Applications are accepted online.

Transfer: 45 of 120 credits required for the bachelor's degree must be completed at SJC.

Visiting: There are regularly scheduled orientations for prospective students. There are guides for informal visits, visitors may sit in on classes, and stay overnight. To schedule a visit, contact Director of Admissions.

Financial Aid: In a recent year, 90% of all full-time freshmen received some form of financial aid. 90% of all full-time freshmen students received need-based aid. The average freshman award was $23,527. Need-based scholarships or need-based grants averaged $19,320; and need-based self-help aid (loans and jobs) averaged $4,666. SJC is a member of CSS. The FAFSA is required. The priority date for freshman financial aid applications for fall entry is February 15.

International Students: They must take the TOEFL. They must also take the SAT or ACT.

Computers: Wireless access is available. All students may access the system. There are no time limits and no fees.

Admissions Contact: Director of Admissions. E-Mail: *admissions@sjc.edu* Web: *www.sjc.edu*

SOUTHERN CONNECTICUT STATE UNIVERSITY C-3

New Haven, CT 06515 (203) 392-5644
888-500-7378; (203) 392-5727

Full-time: 2801 men, 4488 women	**Faculty:** n/av; IIA, av$
Part-time: 575 men, 661 women	**Ph.D.s:** 83%
Graduate: 651 men, 1941 women	**Student/Faculty:** 14 to 1
Year: semesters, summer session	**Tuition:** $8050 ($17,047)
Application Deadline: April 1	**Room & Board:** $9983

Freshman Class: 4978 applied, 3756 accepted, 1360 enrolled
SAT CR/M/W: 470/470/480 **ACT:** 20 **COMPETITIVE**

Southern Connecticut State University, founded in 1893, provides undergraduate and graduate liberal arts programs in the arts, business, education, professional studies, and the sciences. It is part of the Connecticut State University system. The figures in the above capsule and this profile are approximate. There are 4 undergraduate schools and one graduate school. In addition to regional accreditation, SCSU has baccalaureate program accreditation with CSWE and NLN. The library contains 557,737 volumes, 51,608 microform items, and 10,312 audio/video tapes/CDs/DVDs, and subscribes to 4,727 periodicals including electronic. Computerized library services include interlibrary loans, database searching, and Internet access. Special learning facilities include an art gallery, planetarium, radio station, and TV station. The 168-acre campus is in an urban area 35 miles south of Hartford and 90 miles from New York City. Including any residence halls, there are 28 buildings.

Student Life: 95% of undergraduates are from Connecticut. Others are from 37 states, 10 foreign countries, and Canada. 90% are from public schools. 66% are White; 14% African American. The average age of freshmen is 18; all undergraduates, 22. 27% do not continue beyond their first year; 47% remain to graduate.

Housing: 2610 students can be accommodated in college housing, which includes single-sex dorms and on-campus apartments. On-campus housing is available on a first-come and first-served basis. 69% of students commute. Upperclassmen may keep cars.

Activities: 1% of men belong to 3 local and 3 national fraternities; 1% of women belong to 1 local and 2 national sororities. There are 149 groups on campus, including art, band, cheerleading, choir, chorale, chorus, computers, dance, drama, drill team, environmental, ethnic, gay, honors, international, jazz band, literary magazine, marching band, musical theater, newspaper, orchestra, pep band, photography, political, professional, radio and TV, religious, social, social service, student government, and yearbook. Popular campus events include Homecoming.

Sports: There are 9 intercollegiate sports for men and 8 for women. Facilities include a 6000-seat artificial-surface playing complex for football, soccer, field hockey, and track; a field house and gym facilities for basketball, gymnastics, badminton, tennis, track and field, volleyball, and indoor baseball; and an 8-lane swimming pool.

Disabled Students: 99% of the campus is accessible. Facilities include wheelchair ramps, elevators, special parking, specially equipped restrooms, special class scheduling, lowered drinking fountains, lowered telephones, and special computer facilities.

Services: Counseling and information services are available, as is tutoring in every subject. There is a reader service for the blind, and remedial math, reading, and writing.

Campus Safety and Security: Measures include 24-hour foot and vehicle patrol, emergency notification system, self-defense education, and security escort services. There are shuttle buses, emergency telephones, lighted pathways/sidewalks, controlled access to dorms/residences, Campus security is provided by a campus-based police force.

Programs of Study: SCSU confers B.A., B.S., B.S. in Business Administration degrees. Master's degrees are also awarded. Bachelor's degrees are awarded in BIOLOGICAL SCIENCE (biochemistry and biology/biological science), BUSINESS (accounting, banking and finance, business administration and management, business economics, marketing/retailing/merchandising, and recreation and leisure services), COMMUNICATIONS AND THE ARTS (art history and appreciation, communications, dramatic arts, English, fine arts, French, German, Italian, journalism, Spanish, and studio art), COMPUTER AND PHYSICAL SCIENCE (chemistry, computer science, earth science, mathematics, and physics), EDUCATION (art education, early childhood education, elementary education, foreign languages education, health education, library science, physical education, science education, secondary education, and special education), HEALTH PROFESSIONS (nursing and public health), SOCIAL SCIENCE (economics, geography, history, philosophy, political science/government, psychology, social work, and sociology). Psychology, liberal studies and elementary education have the largest enrollments.

Required: All students must complete distribution requirements that include 6 credits each in English composition and speech, natural sciences, and social sciences, 3 credits each in American politics, fine arts, foreign languages, math, literature, philosophy, and Western civilization, and 1 credit each in phys ed and health. Students must take 122 total credits, with a minimum of 30 hours in the major field, and maintain a minimum overall GPA of 2.0.

Special: SCSU offer co-op programs in all academic majors, internships in many departments, study abroad in a variety of countries, a combined B.A.-B.S. degree, dual majors, a general studies degree, student-designed majors in liberal studies, and pass/fail options. There are 2 national honor societies, a freshman honors program, and 1 departmental honors programs.

Faculty/Classroom: 51% of faculty are male; 49% are female. No introductory courses are taught by graduate students. The average class size in an introductory lecture is 21; in a laboratory is 17; and in a regular course is 18.

Admissions: 75% of the 2013-2014 applicants were accepted. The SAT scores for the 2013-2014 freshman class were: Critical Reading--62% below 500, 30% between 500 and 599, 7% between 600 and 699, and

1% between 700 and 800; Math--64% below 500, 30% between 500 and 599, 6% between 600 and 699; Writing--58% below 500, 34% between 500 and 599, and 8% between 600 and 699. The ACT scores were 56% below 21, 24% between 21 and 23, 16% between 24 and 26, 3% between 27 and 28, and 1% above 28. 18% of the current freshmen were in the top fifth of their class; 48% were in the top two fifths.

Requirements: The SAT is required. Applicants should be in the upper 50% of their high school class and should graduate with 4 years in English, 3 in math, and 2 each in natural sciences and social sciences, including American history. The GED is accepted. 2 years of foreign language are recommended. An essay is also required. A GPA of 2.5 is required. AP and CLEP credits are accepted.

Procedure: Freshmen are admitted fall and spring. There is a rolling admissions plan. Applications should be filed by April 1 for fall entry; December 1 for spring entry, along with a $50 fee. Applications are accepted online.

Transfer: 840 transfer students enrolled in 2012-2013. Transfer applicants must have a minimum of 6 college credits with a grade of C or better and an overall GPA of 2.0. The SAT is required for applicants with fewer than 24 college credits. 30 of 122 credits required for the bachelor's degree must be completed at SCSU.

Visiting: There are regularly scheduled orientations for prospective students, Extensive campus tour. There are guides for informal visits. To schedule a visit, contact the Admissions Office at (203) 392-5656.

Financial Aid: In 2013-2014, 82% of all full-time freshmen and 79% of continuing full-time students received some form of financial aid. 68% of all full-time freshmen and 64% of continuing full-time students received need-based aid. The average financial indebtedness of the 2013 graduate was $23,663. SCSU is a member of CSS. The FAFSA and the college's own financial statement are required. The priority date for freshman financial aid applications for fall entry is March 5. The deadline for filing freshman financial aid applications for fall entry is March 9.

International Students: There are 40 international students enrolled. They must take the TOEFL with a minimum score of 525 on the paper-based TOEFL (PBT) or 72 on the Internet-based version (iBT), International English Language Testing System (IELTS). They must also take the SAT or ACT.

Computers: All students may access the system. There are no time limits and no fees.

Graduates: From July 1, 2012 to June 30, 2013, 1660 bachelor's degrees were awarded. The most popular majors were health professions and related programs (13%) and psychology (12%). In an average class, 19% graduate in 4 years or less, 38% graduate in 5 years or less, and 44% graduate in 6 years or less.

Admissions Contact: Kimberly M. Crone, AVP for Academic Student Services. Web: *www.southernct.edu*

TRINITY COLLEGE C-2

Hartford, CT 06106 **(860) 297-2180; (860) 297-2287**

Full-time: 1145 men, 1069 women	**Faculty:** 198; IIB, +$
Part-time: 51 men, 43 women	**Ph.D.s:** 92%
Graduate: 42 men, 49 women	**Student/Faculty:** 9 to 1
Year: semesters	**Tuition:** n/av
Application Deadline: January 1	**Room & Board:** n/app

Freshman Class: 7653 applied, 2432 accepted, 604 enrolled

SAT CR/M/W: 610/650/630 **ACT:** 28 **HIGHLY COMPETITIVE+**

Founded in 1823, Trinity College in Hartford is an independent, nonsectarian liberal arts college. There is one graduate school. In addition to regional accreditation, Trinity has baccalaureate program accreditation with ABET. The library contains 992,817 volumes, 399,394 microform items, and 225,477 audio/video tapes/CDs/DVDs, and subscribes to 2,438 periodicals including electronic. Computerized library services include interlibrary loans, database searching, Internet access, and Wi-Fi capability. Special learning facilities include an art gallery, radio station, and TV station. The 100-acre campus is in an urban area southwest of downtown Hartford. Including any residence halls, there are 78 buildings.

Student Life: 83% of undergraduates are from out of state, mostly the Northeast. Students are from 49 states, 57 foreign countries, and Canada. 42% are from public schools. 65% are White. 30% claim no religious affiliation; 28% Protestant; 27% Catholic. The average age of freshmen is 18; all undergraduates, 20. 9% do not continue beyond their first year; 86% remain to graduate.

Housing: 2000 students can be accommodated in college housing, which includes coed dorms, on-campus apartments, and off-campus apartments. In addition, there are special-interest houses. On-campus housing is guaranteed for all 4 years. 90% of students live on campus; of those, 70% remain on campus on weekends. Upperclassmen may keep cars.

Activities: 20% of men belong to 5 local and 2 national fraternities. There are no sororities. There are 120 groups on campus, including art, bagpipe, band, cheerleading, chess, choir, chorale, chorus, dance, debate, drama, ethnic, film, gay, honors, international, jazz band, literary magazine, musical theater, newspaper, pep band, photography, political, professional, radio and TV, religious, social, social service, student government, and yearbook. Popular campus events include Human Rights Lecture Series, Black History Month and Latino Heritage Week.

Sports: There are 15 intercollegiate sports for men and 13 for women, and 14 intramural sports for men and 14 for women. Facilities include a pool, outdoor and indoor tracks, playing fields, a weight room, a fitness center, and tennis, squash, and basketball courts.

Disabled Students: 60% of the campus is accessible. Facilities include wheelchair ramps, elevators, special parking, specially equipped restrooms, special class scheduling, lowered drinking fountains, and lowered telephones.

Services: Counseling and information services are available, as is tutoring in every subject. There is a reader service for the blind. The writing center offers instruction in all forms of writing, and the math center provides individual tutoring on topics related to math and other courses involving quantitative reasoning.

Campus Safety and Security: Measures include 24-hour foot and vehicle patrol, self-defense education, and security escort services. There are shuttle buses, emergency telephones, and lighted pathways/sidewalks.

Programs of Study: Trinity confers B.A., and B.S. degrees. Master's degrees are also awarded. Bachelor's degrees are awarded in BIOLOGICAL SCIENCE (biochemistry, biology/biological science, and neurosciences), COMMUNICATIONS AND THE ARTS (art history and appreciation, classics, comparative literature, dance, dramatic arts, English, fine arts, French, German, Italian, modern language, music, Russian, Spanish, studio art, and theater management), COMPUTER AND PHYSICAL SCIENCE (chemistry, computer science, mathematics, and physics), EDUCATION (education), ENGINEERING AND ENVIRONMENTAL DESIGN (engineering and environmental science), SOCIAL SCIENCE (American studies, anthropology, classical/ancient civilization, economics, history, interdisciplinary studies, international studies, Judaic studies, philosophy, political science/government, psychology, public affairs, religion, sociology, and women's studies). Political science, economics, English and psychology have the largest enrollments.

Required: All students must complete 36 course credits, including 10 to 15 in the major and 1 from each of 5 distribution areas: arts, humanities, natural sciences, numerical and symbolic reasoning, and social sciences. Students must maintain at least a C average overall.

Special: Trinity offers special freshman programs for exceptional students, including interdisciplinary programs in the sciences and the humanities. There is an intensive study program under which students can devote a semester to 1 subject. Cross-registration through such programs as the Hartford Consortium and the Twelve-College Exchange Program, hundreds of internships (some with Connecticut Public Radio and TV on campus), study abroad virtually worldwide, including Rome, South Africa, Trinidad, Russia, and Nepal, a Washington semester, dual majors in all disciplines, student-designed majors, nondegree study, and pass/fail options also are offered. A 5-year advanced degree in electrical or mechanical engineering with Rensselaer Polytechnic Institute is available. There are 4 national honor societies and including Phi Beta Kappa.

Faculty/Classroom: 55% of faculty are male; 45% are female. All teach undergraduates, all do research, and all teach and do research. No introductory courses are taught by graduate students. The average class size in an introductory lecture is 20; in a laboratory is 16; and in a regular course is 13.

Admissions: 32% of the 2013-2014 applicants were accepted. The SAT scores for the 2013-2014 freshman class were: Critical Reading--2% below 500, 22% between 500 and 599, 49% between 600 and 699, and 27% between 700 and 800; Math--3% below 500, 32% between 500 and 599, 48% between 600 and 699, and 17% between 700 and 800; Writing--4% below 500, 25% between 500 and 599, 54% between 600 and 699, and 16% between 700 and 800. The ACT scores were 1% below 21, 11% between 21 and 23, 24% between 24 and 26, 34% between 27 and 28, and 30% above 28.

Requirements: The SAT or ACT is required. In addition, Trinity strongly emphasizes individual character and personal qualities in admission. Consequently, an interview and essay are recommended. The college requires 4 years of English, 2 years each in foreign language and algebra, and 1 year each in geometry, history, and lab science. AP credits are accepted. Important factors in the admissions decision are advanced placement or honors courses, extracurricular activities record, and evidence of special talent.

Procedure: Freshmen are admitted fall. Entrance exams should be taken in the fall of the senior year. There are early decision and deferred admissions plans. Early decision applications should be filed by November 15; regular applications, by January 1 for fall entry, along with a $60 fee. Notification of early decision is sent December 15; regular decision, April 1. 311 early decision candidates were accepted for the 2013-2014 class. Applications are accepted online.

Transfer: 15 transfer students enrolled in 2012-2013. Transfer applicants must take the SAT or ACT. A minimum college GPA of 3.0 is recommended. 18 of 36 credits required for the bachelor's degree must be completed at Trinity.

Visiting: There are regularly scheduled orientations for prospective students. There are guides for informal visits, visitors may sit in on classes, and stay overnight. To schedule a visit, contact the Admissions Office.

Financial Aid: In 2013-2014, 42% of all full-time freshmen and 42% of continuing full-time students received some form of financial aid. 40% of all full-time freshmen and 39% of continuing full-time students received need-based aid. The average freshman award was $39,282. Need-based scholarships or need-based grants averaged $35,580 ($62,350 maximum); need-based self-help aid (loans and jobs) averaged $10,121 ($11,000 maximum); and other non-need-based awards and non-need-based scholarships averaged $25,810 ($60,810 maximum). 29% of undergraduate students work part-time. Average annual earnings from campus work are $2500. The average financial indebtedness of the 2013 graduate was $4,538. Trinity is a member of CSS. The CSS/Profile and FAFSA are required. The priority date for freshman financial aid applications for fall entry is February 1. The deadline for filing freshman financial aid applications for fall entry is March 1.

International Students: There are 195 international students enrolled. The school actively recruits these students. They must take the TOEFL. They must also take the SAT or ACT.

Computers: All students may access the system. 24 hours a day. There are no time limits and no fees.

Graduates: From July 1, 2012 to June 30, 2013, 543 bachelor's degrees were awarded. The most popular majors were economics (16%), political science (12%), and history (7%). 200 companies recruited on campus in 2012-2013. In an average class, 81% graduate in 4 years or less, 83% graduate in 5 years or less, and 86% graduate in 6 years or less.

Admissions Contact: Larry R. Dow, Dean of Admissions/Financial Aid. E-Mail: *admissions.office@mail.trincoll.edu* Web: *www.trincoll.edu*

UNITED STATES COAST GUARD ACADEMY — D-3

New London, CT 06320 — (860) 444-8500; (800) 883-8724; (860) 701-6700

Full-time: n/av	**Faculty:** n/av
Part-time: n/av	**Ph.D.s:** 30%
Graduate: n/av	**Student/Faculty:** n/av
Year: semesters, summer session	**Tuition:** n/app
Application Deadline:	**Room & Board:** n/app
Freshman Class: n/av	
SAT or ACT: required	**HIGHLY COMPETITIVE**

The U.S. Coast Guard Academy, founded in 1876, is an Armed Forces Service Academy for men and women. Appointments are made solely on the basis of an annual nationwide competition. Except for an entrance fee of $3,000, the federal government covers all cadet expenses by providing a yearly allowance of $11,150. The figures in the above capsule and in this profile are approximate. In addition to regional accreditation, USCGA has baccalaureate program accreditation with ABET. The library contains 150,000 volumes, 60,000 microform items, and 1,500 audio/video tapes/CDs/DVDs, and subscribes to 850 periodicals including electronic. Computerized library services include interlibrary loans and database searching. The 110-acre campus is in a suburban area 45 miles southeast of Hartford. Including any residence halls, there are 25 buildings.

Student Life: 93% of undergraduates are from out of state, mostly the Northeast. Students are from 50 states, and 14 foreign countries. 79% are White. 33% are Catholic; 30% claim no religious affiliation; 29% Protestant. The average age of freshmen is 18; all undergraduates, 21. 21% do not continue beyond their first year; 67% remain to graduate.

Housing: 1000 students can be accommodated in college housing, which includes coed dorms. On-campus housing is guaranteed for all 4 years. Alcohol is not permitted. Upperclassmen may keep cars.

Activities: There are no fraternities or sororities. Groups on campus include bagpipe, band, cheerleading, choir, chorale, chorus, dance, debate, drama, drill team, drum and bugle corps, ethnic, international, jazz band, marching band, musical theater, newspaper, pep band, political, professional, religious, social, social service, student government, and yearbook. Popular campus events include Parents Weekend, Coast Guard Day, and Hispanic Heritage and Black History month.

Sports: There are 13 intercollegiate sports for men and 11 for women, and 13 intramural sports for men and 13 for women. Facilities include a field house with 3 basketball courts, a 6-lane swimming pool, 5 racquetball courts, and facilities for track meets, tennis matches, and baseball and softball games; an additional athletic facility with wrestling and weight rooms, basketball courts, gymnastics areas, a swimming pool, and saunas; a 4500-seat stadium; and practice and playing fields, outdoor tennis courts, and rowing and seamanship-sailing centers.

Disabled Students: 24% of the campus is accessible. Facilities include wheelchair ramps, elevators, special parking, and specially equipped restrooms.

Services: Counseling and information services are available, as is tutoring in every subject.

Campus Safety and Security: Measures include 24-hour foot and vehicle patrol and self-defense education. There are lighted pathways/sidewalks.

Programs of Study: USCGA confers B.S. degrees. Bachelor's degrees are awarded in BIOLOGICAL SCIENCE (marine science), BUSINESS (management science and operations research), ENGINEERING AND ENVIRONMENTAL DESIGN (civil engineering, electrical/electronics engineering, mechanical engineering, and naval architecture and marine engineering), SOCIAL SCIENCE (political science/government). Political science/government is the largest.

Required: To graduate, cadets must pass at least 37 courses, of which 25 are core; accumulate a minimum of 126 credit hours, with at least 90 credits of C or better, exclusive of phys ed; complete the academic requirements for one of the approved majors and attain a minimum GPA of 2.0 in all required upper-division courses in the major; successfully complete all professional development and phys ed requirements; and maintain a high sense of integrity.

Special: Cross-registration with Connecticut College, summer cruises to foreign ports, 6-week internships with various government agencies and some engineering and science organizations, and a 1-semester exchange program with the 3 other military academies are available. All graduates are commissioned in the U.S. Coast Guard. There are 2 national honor societies, a freshman honors program, and 3 departmental honors programs.

Faculty/Classroom: 90% of faculty are male; 10% are female. No introductory courses are taught by graduate students. The average class size in an introductory lecture is 28; in a laboratory is 18; and in a regular course is 20.

Requirements: The SAT or ACT is required. The ACT Optional Writing test is also required. In addition, Applicants must have reached the age of 17 but not the age of 23 by July 1 of the year of admission, be citizens of the United States, and be single at the time of appointment and remain single while attending the academy. Required secondary school courses include 4 years each of English and math.

Procedure: Freshmen are admitted fall. There are early admissions and rolling admissions plans. Check with the school for current application deadlines. Notification is sent on a rolling basis. Applications are accepted online.

Transfer: All transfer students must meet the same standards as incoming freshmen and must begin as freshmen no matter how many semesters or years of college they have completed.

Visiting: There are regularly scheduled orientations for prospective students, including an admissions briefing and tour of the academy every Monday, Wednesday, and Friday from 1 p.m. To schedule a visit, contact the Admissions Receptionist.

Financial Aid: Check with the school for current application deadlines.

International Students: They must take the TOEFL. They must also take the SAT or ACT.

Computers: All students may access the system 24 hours a day. There are no time limits and no fees.

Admissions Contact: Director of Admissions. E-Mail: *admissions@uscga.edu* Web: *www.usca.mil*

UNIVERSITY OF BRIDGEPORT — B-4

Bridgeport, CT 06604 — (203) 576-4552; (800) EXCEL-UB; (203) 576-4941

Full-time: 638 men, 1046 women	**Faculty:** 80
Part-time: 152 men, 667 women	**Ph.D.s:** 93%
Graduate: 1067 men, 1235 women	**Student/Faculty:** 15 to 1
Year: semesters, summer session	**Tuition:** $27,330
Application Deadline: April 1	**Room & Board:** $11,700
Freshman Class: 5595 applied, 3171 accepted, 403 enrolled	
SAT CR/M/W: 468/472/457 **ACT:** 20	**LESS COMPETITIVE**

The University of Bridgeport, founded in 1927, is a private, independent, nonsectarian university offering programs in the arts, humanities, and social sciences, business, engineering and design, natural sciences, human services, dental hygiene, chiropractic and naturopathic medicine, and teacher preparation. There are 7 undergraduate schools and 9 graduate schools. In addition to regional accreditation, UB has baccalaureate program accreditation with ABET, ADA, and NASAD. The library contains 275,000 volumes, 1.1 million microform items, and 3,342 audio/video tapes/CDs/DVDs, and subscribes to 45,712 periodicals including electronic. Computerized library services include interlibrary loans, database searching, and Internet access. Special learning facilities include a learning resource center and art gallery. The 86-acre campus is in a small town 60 miles northeast of New York City. Including any residence halls, there are 30 buildings.

Student Life: 56% of undergraduates are from Connecticut. Others are from 44 states, 74 foreign countries, and Canada. 89% are from public schools. 37% are African American; 28% white; 19% Hispanic. The average age of freshmen is 19; all undergraduates, 26. 47%.do not continue beyond their first year; 34% remain to graduate.

Housing: 1439 students can be accommodated in college housing, which

includes coed dorms. In addition, there are special-interest houses, and alcohol- and tobacco-free buildings. On-campus housing is guaranteed for all 4 years. 53% of students commute. All students may keep cars.

Activities: 1% of men belong to 2 local fraternities; 2% of women belong to 1 local sorority. There are 45 groups on campus, including art, cheerleading, choir, chorale, computers, debate, ethnic, gay, honors, international, literary magazine, newspaper, photography, political, professional, radio and TV, religious, social, social service, and student government. Popular campus events include International Festival, Winter Prelude, and Wisteria Ball.

Sports: There are 5 intercollegiate sports for men and 8 for women, and 8 intramural sports for men and 8 for women. Facilities include a gym, athletic fields, tennis and racquetball courts, and a recreation center with an indoor pool.

Disabled Students: 80% of the campus is accessible. Facilities include wheelchair ramps, elevators, special parking, specially equipped restrooms, and special class scheduling.

Services: Counseling and information services are available, as is tutoring in every subject. There is a reader service for the blind, and remedial math, reading, and writing.

Campus Safety and Security: Measures include 24-hour foot and vehicle patrol, emergency notification system, and security escort services. There are shuttle buses, emergency telephones, lighted pathways/sidewalks, controlled access to dorms/residencescampus security systems.

Programs of Study: UB confers B.A., B.F.A., B.M., and B.S. degrees. Associate, master's, and doctoral degrees are also awarded. Bachelor's degrees are awarded in BIOLOGICAL SCIENCE (biology/biological science), BUSINESS (accounting, banking and finance, business administration and management, fashion merchandising, international business management, international economics, management information systems, management science, and marketing/retailing/merchandising), COMMUNICATIONS AND THE ARTS (communications, English, graphic design, illustration, industrial design, journalism, literature, and music), COMPUTER AND PHYSICAL SCIENCE (computer science and mathematics), ENGINEERING AND ENVIRONMENTAL DESIGN (computer engineering and interior design), HEALTH PROFESSIONS (dental hygiene, medical technology, predentistry, and premedicine), SOCIAL SCIENCE (criminal justice, human development, human services, interdisciplinary studies, international studies, prelaw, psychology, religion, and social science). Computer science/engineering, business, and dental hygiene are the strongest academically. Dental hygiene, psychology, and computer science/engineering have the largest enrollments.

Required: All students are required to complete at least 120 credit hours, including at least 30 in the major field. A minimum GPA of 2.0 is necessary. Distribution requirements cover 33 core credits and are composed of skills, heritage, and capstone sections, including 3 hours each in English composition and quantitative skills, and 24 semester hours consisting of 6 hours each in humanities, natural science, and social science, and 3 each in integrated studies and fine arts.

Special: UB offers co-op programs with several local institutions, cross-registration with Sacred Heart and Fairfield Universities, internships in many degree programs, study abroad in England, Switzerland, or Spain, a Washington semester, and work-study programs. In addition, a general studies accelerated degree program, dual majors, student-designed majors, and B.A.-B.S. degrees are available. Credit for life experience, nondegree study, and pass/fail options are offered. There are 11 national honor societies and 1 departmental honors program.

Faculty/Classroom: 61% of faculty are male; 39% are female. All teach and do research. No introductory courses are taught by graduate students. The average class size in an introductory lecture is 17; in a laboratory is 10; and in a regular course is 16.

Admissions: 57% of a recent year applicants were accepted. The SAT scores for a recent year freshman class were: Critical Reading--67% below 500, 27% between 500 and 599, 6% between 600 and 700; Math--70% below 500, 23% between 500 and 599, and 6% between 600 and 700, and 1% above 700; Writing--74% below 500, 23% between 500 and 599, 3% between 600 and 700. 18% of the current freshmen were in the top fifth of their class; 50% were in the top two fifths. 1 freshman graduated first in the class.

Requirements: The SAT or ACT is required. Applicants are required to have 16 academic credits or Carnegie units, including 4 units of English, 3 of math, 2 in social studies, 2 in a lab science, and 5 electives. A portfolio is required for B.F.A. students and an audition for B.M. candidates. UB requires applicants to be in the upper 40% of their class. A GPA of 2.0 is required. AP and CLEP credits are accepted. Important factors in the admissions decision are advanced placement or honors courses, extracurricular activities record, and recommendations by school officials.

Procedure: Freshmen are admitted fall and spring. Entrance exams should be taken during the senior year. There are early decision, early admissions, deferred admissions, and rolling admissions plans. Applications should be filed by April 1 for fall entry; December 1 for spring entry. The fall application fee in a recent year was $50. Applications are accepted online.

Transfer: 170 transfer students enrolled in a recent year. Transfer applicants need a minimum GPA of 2.5 and at least 12 earned credit hours. The SAT or ACT and an interview are recommended. 30 of 120 credits required for the bachelor's degree must be completed at UB.

Visiting: There are regularly scheduled orientations for prospective students. There are guides for informal visits, visitors may sit in on classes, and stay overnight. To schedule a visit, contact the Admissions Office.

Financial Aid: In a recent year, 97% of all full-time freshmen and 97% of continuing full-time students received some form of financial aid. UB is a member of CSS. The FAFSA and the college's own financial statement are required. The deadline for filing freshman financial aid applications for fall entry is April 15.

International Students: There are 213 international students enrolled. The school actively recruits these students. They must take the TOEFL with a minimum score of 500 on the paper-based TOEFL (PBT) or 61 on the Internet-based version (iBT). They must also take the SAT or ACT.

Computers: All dorm rooms have access to the Internet. PCs are located in the library and various labs. All students may access the system 8 a.m. to 11 p.m. daily. UBnet is available 24 hours a day from dorm rooms or dial-ups. There are no time limits and no fees.

Graduates: In a recent year, 365 bachelor's degrees were awarded. The most popular majors were general studies (24%), business administration (20%), and psychology (14%). In an average class, 27% graduate in 4 years or less, 29% graduate in 5 years or less, and 30% graduate in 6 years or less. Of a recent year graduating class, 10% were enrolled in graduate school within 6 months of graduation, and 60% were employed.

Admissions Contact: Bryan Gross, Associate VP Enrollment Management. A campus DVD is available. E-Mail: *admit@bridgeport.edu* Web: *www.bridgeport.edu*

UNIVERSITY OF CONNECTICUT — D-2

Storrs, CT 06269 — **(860) 486-3137; (860) 486-1476**

Full-time: 8464 men, 8272 women	**Faculty:** n/av; I, +$
Part-time: 465 men, 327 women	**Ph.D.s:** 94%
Graduate: 3859 men, 4096 women	**Student/Faculty:** 17 to 1
Year: semesters, summer session	**Tuition:** $12,022 ($30,970)
Application Deadline:	**Room & Board:** $11,722
Freshman Class: 29966 applied, 13397 accepted, 3114 enrolled	
SAT CR/M: 597/629	**ACT:** 27 **HIGHLY COMPETITIVE**

The University of Connecticut, founded in 1881, is a public, land-grant, sea-grant, multicampus research institution offering degree programs in liberal arts and sciences and professional studies. There are 9 undergraduate schools and 5 graduate schools. In addition to regional accreditation, UConn has baccalaureate program accreditation with AACSB, ABET, ACPE, ADA, APTA, ASLA, CSAB, NASAD, NASM, NCATE, and NLN. The library contains 3.3 million volumes, 3.2 million microform items, and 106,017 audio/video tapes/CDs/DVDs, and subscribes to 424,922 periodicals including electronic. Computerized library services include interlibrary loans, database searching, and Internet access. Special learning facilities include an art gallery, natural history museum, planetarium, radio station, and TV station. The 4067-acre campus is in a rural area 25 miles east of Hartford. Including any residence halls, there are 350 buildings.

Student Life: 79% of undergraduates are from Connecticut. Others are from 46 states, 60 foreign countries, and Canada. 87% are from public schools. 64% are White. The average age of freshmen is 18; all undergraduates, 20. 7% do not continue beyond their first year; 82% remain to graduate.

Housing: 12076 students can be accommodated in college housing, which includes single-sex and coed dorms, on-campus apartments, off-campus apartments, and married student housing. In addition, there are honors houses, language houses, special-interest houses, fraternity houses, sorority houses, living and learning communities, business connections, Eco-house, global house, humanities house, public health house, women in math, science, and engineering. On-campus housing is guaranteed for the freshman year only. 72% of students live on campus; of those, 70% remain on campus on weekends. Upperclassmen may keep cars.

Activities: 10% of men belong to 16 national fraternities; 13% of women belong to 16 national sororities. There are 582 groups on campus, including art, band, cheerleading, chess, choir, chorale, chorus, computers, dance, debate, drama, drill team, environmental, ethnic, film, gay, honors, international, jazz band, literary magazine, marching band, musical theater, newspaper, opera, orchestra, pep band, photography, political, professional, radio and TV, religious, social, social service, student government, symphony, and yearbook. Popular campus events include Husky WOW (Week of Welcome,) Homecoming, Winter Weekend/One Ton Sundae, Lipsync, Oozeball, Huskymania/Midnight Madness, Family Weekend, UConn Late Night, and Midnight Breakfast.

Sports: There are 11 intercollegiate sports for men and 13 for women, and 29 intramural sports for men and 28 for women. Facilities include a sports center, a field house, a 16,000-seat football stadium, a 10,000-seat basketball stadium, and a student, faculty, and staff workout center.

Disabled Students: 90% of the campus is accessible. Facilities include

wheelchair ramps, elevators, special parking, specially equipped restrooms, special class scheduling, lowered drinking fountains, lowered telephones, special housing, a tactile map, and 4 specially equipped transportation vans.

Services: Counseling and information services are available, as is tutoring in most subjects. There is a reader service for the blind. Also available are a Braille printer, a Kurzweil reading machine and Mac computer with voice synthesizer, a machine to enlarge printed material, a talking calculator, and a TDD.

Campus Safety and Security: Measures include 24-hour foot and vehicle patrol, emergency notification system, self-defense education, and security escort services. There are shuttle buses, emergency telephones, and lighted pathways/sidewalks.

Programs of Study: UConn confers B.A., B.S., B.F.A., B.G.S., B.Mus., B.S.E., B.S.N. and B.S.Pharm. degrees. Associate, master's, and doctoral degrees are also awarded. Bachelor's degrees are awarded in AGRICULTURE (agricultural economics, agriculture, agronomy, animal science, horticulture, and natural resource management), BIOLOGICAL SCIENCE (biology/biological science, biophysics, evolutionary biology, genetics, marine science, molecular biology, nutrition, and physiology), BUSINESS (accounting, banking and finance, business administration and management, insurance and risk management, management information systems, marketing/retailing/merchandising, and real estate), COMMUNICATIONS AND THE ARTS (art, art history and appreciation, classics, communications, dramatic arts, English, French, German, journalism, linguistics, music, Spanish, theater design, and visual and performing arts), COMPUTER AND PHYSICAL SCIENCE (chemistry, computer science, geology, mathematics, physics, and statistics), EDUCATION (agricultural education, athletic training, education, elementary education, English education, foreign languages education, mathematics education, music education, recreation education, science education, social studies education, and special education), ENGINEERING AND ENVIRONMENTAL DESIGN (biomedical engineering, chemical engineering, civil engineering, computer engineering, electrical/electronics engineering, environmental engineering, environmental science, landscape architecture/design, manufacturing engineering, materials engineering, and mechanical engineering), HEALTH PROFESSIONS (cytotechnology, exercise science, health care administration, medical laboratory technology, nursing, pharmacy, and physical therapy), SOCIAL SCIENCE (anthropology, dietetics, economics, geography, history, human development, Italian studies, Latin American studies, Middle Eastern studies, philosophy, political science/government, psychology, sociology, urban studies, and women's studies). Biological sciences, psychology, and political science have the largest enrollments.

Required: To graduate, students must complete 120 credits with a GPA of 2.0. There are general education requirements in foreign language, expository writing, math, literature and the arts, culture and modern society, philosophical and ethical analysis, social scientific and comparative analysis, and science and technology. Students must complete a course that provides hands-on experience in a major computer application.

Special: UConn offers co-op programs in most majors, internships, more than 200 study-abroad programs in 65 countries, dual majors, general studies degrees, student-designed majors, work-study programs, nondegree study, and pass/fail options. There are 31 national honor societies, including Phi Beta Kappa, a freshman honors program, and 8 departmental honors programs.

Faculty/Classroom: 63% of faculty are male; 37% are female. Graduate students teach 33% of introductory courses. The average class size in an introductory lecture is 48; in a laboratory is 20; and in a regular course is 38.

Admissions: 45% of the 2013-2014 applicants were accepted. The SAT scores for the 2013-2014 freshman class were: Critical Reading--9% below 500, 38% between 500 and 599, 43% between 600 and 699, and 10% between 700 and 800; Math--5% below 500, 25% between 500 and 599, 50% between 600 and 699, and 20% between 700 and 800; Writing--9% below 500, 36% between 500 and 599, 44% between 600 and 699, and 11% between 700 and 800. 49 freshmen graduated first in their class.

Requirements: The SAT or ACT is required. Applicants must be graduates of an approved secondary school and should rank in the upper range of their class. The GED is accepted. Students must complete 16 high school academic units, including 4 years of English, 3 of math, 2 each of foreign language, science, and social studies, and 3 of electives. An essay is required. An audition is required for music and theater students and a portfolio for art students. AP credits are accepted. Important factors in the admissions decision are advanced placement or honors courses, evidence of special talent, and leadership record.

Procedure: Freshmen are admitted fall and spring. Entrance exams should be taken in the spring of the junior year or fall of the senior year. There are deferred admissions and rolling admissions plans. Check with the school for current application deadlines. The application fee is $70. Notifications are sent in March . 1600 applicants were on the 2013 waiting list; 436 were admitted. Applications are accepted online.

Transfer: 855 transfer students enrolled in 2012-2013. Applicants should have a minimum GPA of 2.7 and submit official transcripts from all colleges previously attended, the high school transcript, and SAT or ACT scores as needed. An associate degree or a minimum of 54 credit hours is recommended. 30 of 120 credits required for the bachelor's degree must be completed at UConn.

Visiting: There are regularly scheduled orientations for prospective students, including daily tours and information sessions. Visitors may sit in on classes. To schedule a visit, contact Lodewick Visitors Center at (860) 486-4900.

Financial Aid: In 2013-2014, 53% of all full-time freshmen and 55% of continuing full time students received some form of financial aid. 61% of all full-time freshmen and 64% of continuing full-time students received need-based aid. The average freshman award was $12,086. 49% of undergraduate students work part-time. Average annual earnings from campus work are $2025. The average financial indebtedness of the 2013 graduate was $24,373. The FAFSA is required. The priority date for freshman financial aid applications for fall entry is March 1.

International Students: There are 632 international students enrolled. The school actively recruits these students. They must take the TOEFL with a minimum score of 550 on the paper-based TOEFL (PBT) or 79 on the Internet-based version (iBT) and the college's own test. They must also take the SAT or ACT.

Computers: All students may access the system. 24 hours weekdays; 8 a.m. to 12 p.m. weekends. There are no time limits and no fees.

Graduates: From July 1, 2012 to June 30, 2013, 5149 bachelor's degrees were awarded. The most popular majors were social sciences (12%), business, management, marketing, and related support services (12%), and health professions and related programs (11%). In an average class, 67% graduate in 4 years or less, 81% graduate in 5 years or less, and 82% graduate in 6 years or less. Of the 2012 graduating class, 30% were enrolled in graduate school within 6 months of graduation, and 82% were employed.

Admissions Contact: Nathan Fuerst, Director of Admissions. E-Mail: *beahusky@uconn.edu* Web: *www.uconn.edu*

UNIVERSITY OF HARTFORD — C-2

West Hartford, CT 06117 — (860) 243-4296; (800) 947-4303; (860) 768-4961

Full-time: 2295 men, 2301 women	**Faculty:** 347; IIA, -$
Part-time: 298 men, 456 women	**Ph.D.s:** 86%
Graduate: 700 men, 975 women	**Student/Faculty:** 12 to 1
Year: semesters, summer session	**Tuition:** $31,254
Application Deadline: open	**Room & Board:** $12,420
Freshman Class: 11996 applied, 8208 accepted, 1331 enrolled	
SAT CR/M: 521/530	**ACT:** 22 — **COMPETITIVE**

The University of Hartford, founded in 1877, is an independent, nonsectarian institution offering extensive undergraduate and graduate programs ranging from liberal arts to business. There are 7 undergraduate schools and 6 graduate schools. In addition to regional accreditation, has baccalaureate program accreditation with AACSB, ABET, APTA, CAHEA, NASAD, NASM, NCATE, and NLN. The 3 libraries contain 579,177 volumes, 383,386 microform items, and 5,921 audio/video tapes/CDs/DVDs, and subscribe to 37,393 periodicals including electronic. Computerized library services include interlibrary loans, database searching, Internet access, and laptop Internet portals. Special learning facilities include a learning resource center, art gallery, radio station, TV station, the Museum of American Political Life. The 320-acre campus is in a suburban area 4 miles northwest of Hartford. Including any residence halls, there are 32 buildings.

Student Life: 57% of undergraduates are from out of state, mostly the Northeast. Students are from 45 states, 37 foreign countries, and Canada. 80% are from public schools. 61% are white; 14% African American. 91% claim no religious affiliation. The average age of freshmen is 18; all undergraduates, 22. 27% do not continue beyond their first year; 57% remain to graduate.

Housing: 3530 students can be accommodated in college housing, which includes coed dorms and on-campus apartments. In addition, there are honors houses, special-interest houses, the Residential College for the Arts, and the International Residential College. On-campus housing is guaranteed for all 4 years. 61% of students live on campus; of those, 85% remain on campus on weekends. All students may keep cars.

Activities: 17% of men belong to 7 national fraternities; 21% of women belong to 7 national sororities. There are 45 groups on campus, including art, band, cheerleading, choir, chorale, chorus, computers, drama, ethnic, gay, honors, international, jazz band, literary magazine, musical theater, newspaper, opera, orchestra, pep band, political, professional, radio and TV, religious, social, social service, student government, and symphony. Popular campus events include Welcome Weekend, Spring Weekend, and Winter Carnival.

Sports: There are 9 intercollegiate sports for men and 9 for women, and 15 intramural sports for men and 15 for women. Facilities include playing fields, a 25-meter outdoor pool, tennis courts, golf practice cages, a fitness trail, and a sports center with a 4,600-seat multipurpose court, an 8-lane swimming pool, a weight room, racquetball courts, a squash court, and saunas.

Disabled Students: All of the campus is accessible. Facilities include wheelchair ramps, elevators, special parking, specially equipped restrooms, lowered drinking fountains, lowered telephones, and special housing.

Services: Counseling and information services are available, as is tutoring in most subjects. There is a reader service for the blind, and remedial math, reading, and writing. The health education office offers peer counseling and workshops on health-related topics. Professional counseling is available.

Campus Safety and Security: Measures include 24-hour foot and vehicle patrol, emergency notification system, self-defense education, and security escort services. There are shuttle buses, emergency telephones, lighted pathways/sidewalks, and a bicycle patrol.

Programs of Study: confers B.A., B.F.A., B.Mus., B.S., B.S.A.E.T., B.S.B.A., B.S.C.E., B.S.Comp.E., B.S.Ed., B.S.E.E., and B.S.M.E. degrees. Associate, master's, and doctoral degrees are also awarded. Bachelor's degrees are awarded in BIOLOGICAL SCIENCE (biology/biological science), BUSINESS (accounting, banking and finance, business administration and management, entrepreneurial studies, insurance, management information systems, management science, and marketing/retailing/merchandising), COMMUNICATIONS AND THE ARTS (art history and appreciation, audio technology, ceramic art and design, communications, dance, design, dramatic arts, drawing, English, film arts, illustration, jazz, languages, media arts, music, music business management, music history and appreciation, music performance, music technology, music theory and composition, musical theater, painting, performing arts, photography, printmaking, sculpture, technical and business writing, theater management, video, and visual and performing arts), COMPUTER AND PHYSICAL SCIENCE (chemistry, computer science, information sciences and systems, mathematics, physics, and radiological technology), EDUCATION (early childhood education, elementary education, music education, secondary education, and special education), ENGINEERING AND ENVIRONMENTAL DESIGN (architectural engineering, biomedical engineering, chemical engineering technology, civil engineering, computer engineering, electrical/electronics engineering, electrical/electronics engineering technology, engineering, engineering technology, mechanical engineering, and mechanical engineering technology), HEALTH PROFESSIONS (health science, medical laboratory technology, nursing, occupational therapy, physical therapy, predentistry, premedicine, and preoptometry), SOCIAL SCIENCE (criminal justice, economics, history, human services, interdisciplinary studies, international studies, Judaic studies, law, philosophy, political science/government, psychology, and sociology). Accounting, management, and engineering are the strongest academically. Communication, architectural engineering and psychology have the largest enrollments.

Required: To graduate, students must complete at least 120 credit hours, fulfill the university's core curriculum requirements, and maintain an overall GPA of 2.0. Specific core and course requirements vary with the major.

Special: Cross-registration with the Greater Hartford Consortium, internships in all majors, study abroad, a Washington semester, work-study programs, credit for life experience, nondegree study, and pass/fail options are available. In addition, students may pursue accelerated degrees, B.A.-B.S. degrees, dual majors, or their own individually designed majors. There are interdisciplinary majors in acoustics and music and in experimental studio combining performing, literary, and visual arts. Also available are preprofessional programs in biology/preoptometry with the New England College of Optometry, predentistry with the New York University School of Dentistry, prechiropractic with the New York Chiropractic College, preosteopathic with the University of New England College of Osteopathic Medicine, and prepodiatry with the New York College of Podiatric Medicine. There are 19 national honor societies, a freshman honors program, and 7 departmental honors programs.

Faculty/Classroom: 61% of faculty are male; 39% are female. All teach undergraduates, and 97% do research. No introductory courses are taught by graduate students. The average class size in an introductory lecture is 43; in a laboratory is 21; and in a regular course is 24.

Admissions: In a recent year, 68% of applicants were accepted. The SAT scores for the 2011-2012 freshman class were: Critical Reading--46% below 500, 39% between 500 and 599, 14% between 600 and 700, and 1% above 700; Math--44% below 500, 37% between 500 and 599, 17% between 600 and 700, and 2% above 700. The ACT scores were 38% below 21, 28% between 21 and 23, 20% between 24 and 26, 6% between 27 and 28, and 8% above 28. 12% of the current freshmen were in the top fifth of their class; 27% were in the top two fifths.

Requirements: The SAT is required. Applicants should have 16 academic high school credits and 16 Carnegie units, including 4 units in English, 3 in math (3.5 for B.S. candidates), and 2 each in foreign language, science, and social studies. A portfolio and an audition are required for B.F.A. and B.Mus. candidates, respectively. A personal statement is required, and an interview is recommended for all students. AP and CLEP credits are accepted. Important factors in the admissions decision are advanced placement or honors courses, recommendations by school officials, and leadership record.

Procedure: Freshmen are admitted fall and spring. Entrance exams should be taken in the spring of the junior year or the fall of the senior year. There are deferred admissions and rolling admissions plans. Application deadlines are open. Notification is sent on a rolling basis. Applications are accepted online. Check with the school for current fee.

Transfer: 232 transfer students enrolled in a recent year. Transfer students must have a minimum college GPA of 2.25, with 2.5 recommended, and must submit SAT or ACT scores if they have fewer than 30 transferable college-level credits. An interview is also recommended. 30 of 120 credits required for the bachelor's degree must be completed at UH.

Visiting: There are regularly scheduled orientations for prospective students. There are guides for informal visits, visitors may sit in on classes, and stay overnight. To schedule a visit, contact the Office of Admissions.

Financial Aid: In a recent year, 94% of all full-time freshmen and 97% of continuing full-time students received some form of financial aid. 80% of all full-time freshmen and 78% of continuing full-time students received need-based aid. The average freshman award was $9,592. Need-based scholarships or need-based grants averaged $6,798; need-based self-help aid (loans and jobs) averaged $11,618; non-need-based athletic scholarships averaged $16,123; and other non-need-based awards and non-need-based scholarships averaged $3,578. 22% of undergraduate students work part-time. Average annual earnings from campus work are $3200. The FAFSA is required. The priority date for freshman financial aid applications for fall entry is February 1.

International Students: There are 195 international students enrolled. The school actively recruits these students. They must take the TOEFL with a minimum score of 550 on the paper-based TOEFL (PBT). The SAT or the ACT is required.

Computers: Wireless access is available. There is access at the main library and PC connections in each dorm room. All students may access the system. There are no time limits and no fees. It is strongly recommended that all students have a personal computer.

Graduates: In a recent year, 1072 bachelor's degrees were awarded. The most popular majors were communications (7%), psychology (4%), and architectural engineering tech. (4%). 182 companies recruited on campus in 2010-2011. In an average class, 53% graduate in 4 years or less, 58% graduate in 5 years or less, and 59% graduate in 6 years or less. Of a recent graduating class, 35% were enrolled in graduate school within 6 months of graduation, and 75% were employed.

Admissions Contact: Dean of Admissions. E-Mail: *admission@hartford.edu* Web: *www.hartford.edu*

UNIVERSITY OF NEW HAVEN — C-3

West Haven, CT 06516 (203) 932-7319
(800) 342-5864 ext. 7319; (203) 931-6093

Full-time: 2203 men, 2204 women	**Faculty:** n/av; IIA, av$
Part-time: 254 men, 203 women	**Ph.D.s:** 81%
Graduate: 843 men, 848 women	**Student/Faculty:** n/av
Year: 4-1-4, summer session	**Tuition:** $33,740
Application Deadline: open	**Room & Board:** $14,000
Freshman Class: 10169 applied, 7567 accepted, 1174 enrolled	
SAT CR/M/W: 510/520/510	**ACT:** 22 — **COMPETITIVE**

The University of New Haven is a private, top-tier comprehensive institution recognized as a national leader in experiential education. Founded in 1920, the University provides its students with a unique combination of a solid liberal arts education and real-world, hands-on career and research opportunities. There are 4 undergraduate schools and 4 graduate schools. In addition to regional accreditation, UNH has baccalaureate program accreditation with ABET, ADA, and NCATE. The library contains 362,563 volumes, 405,255 microform items, and 1,417 audio/video tapes/CDs/DVDs, and subscribes to 40,883 periodicals including electronic. Computerized library services include interlibrary loans, database searching, Internet access, and Wi-Fi capability. Special learning facilities include an art gallery, radio station, TV station, Institute of Forensic Science, crime scene training and technology center, nutrition lab, dental center, finance and technology center, communication studios, and music and sound recording facilities. The 82-acre campus is in a suburban area.

Student Life: 55% of undergraduates are from out of state, mostly the Northeast. Students are from 38 states, 36 foreign countries, and Canada. 52% are White; 20% race unknown. The average age of freshmen is 18; all undergraduates, 21. 24% do not continue beyond their first year; 55% remain to graduate.

Housing: 2579 students can be accommodated in college housing, which includes coed dorms, on-campus apartments, and off-campus apartments. On-campus housing is available on a first-come, first-served basis, and is available on a lottery system for upperclassmen. 51% of students live on campus. Upperclassmen may keep cars.

Activities: There are 165 groups on campus, including fire science, forensic science and chemistry, music and entertainment industry, band, cheerleading, choir, chorus, computers, criminal justice, dance, debate, drama, ethnic, film, forensics, gay, honors, international, jazz band, literary magazine, marching band, newspaper, orchestra, pep band, photography, political, professional, radio and TV, religious, social, social service, student government, symphony, and yearbook. Popular campus events include Homecoming, Snow Ball Formal, and Spring Weekend.

Sports: There are 7 intercollegiate sports for men and 9 for women, and 11 intramural sports for men and 11 for women. Facilities include Baseball, softball, and intramural playing fields; tennis courts; a gym with basketball courts, a weight training room, and a racquetball court; a 56000-square-foot recreation center; an outdoor stadium for football, soccer, and lacrosse.

Disabled Students: 6% of the campus is accessible. Facilities include wheelchair ramps, elevators, special parking, specially equipped restrooms, special class scheduling, lowered drinking fountains, lowered telephones, special housing, and special door handles.

Services: Counseling and information services are available, as is tutoring in every subject. There is a reader service for the blind, and remedial math, reading, and writing. Campus Access Services, Center for Learning Resources, and Office of Academic Services

Campus Safety and Security: Measures include 24-hour foot and vehicle patrol, emergency notification system, self-defense education, and security escort services. There are shuttle buses, emergency telephones, lighted pathways/sidewalks, controlled access to dorms/residences, required programs during orientation for new students as well as crime prevention program.

Programs of Study: UNH confers B.A., and B.S. degrees. Associate, master's, and doctoral degrees are also awarded. Bachelor's degrees are awarded in BIOLOGICAL SCIENCE (biochemistry, biology/biological science, biotechnology, marine biology, and nutrition), BUSINESS (accounting, banking and finance, business administration and management, hospitality management services, hotel/motel and restaurant management, marketing/retailing/merchandising, sports management, and tourism), COMMUNICATIONS AND THE ARTS (advertising, art, audio technology, communications, communications technology, creative writing, design, English, graphic design, journalism, literature, multimedia, music, music business management, music performance, music technology, music theory and composition, theatre arts, visual and performing arts, and visual design), COMPUTER AND PHYSICAL SCIENCE (applied mathematics, chemistry, computer management, computer mathematics, computer programming, computer science, mathematics, and natural sciences), EDUCATION (mathematics education, science education, and secondary education), ENGINEERING AND ENVIRONMENTAL DESIGN (chemical engineering, civil engineering, computer engineering, electrical/electronics engineering, engineering, environmental science, fire protection engineering, interior design, mechanical engineering, and systems engineering), HEALTH PROFESSIONS (dental hygiene, predentistry, premedicine, and preveterinary science), SOCIAL SCIENCE (behavioral science, clinical psychology, community psychology, corrections, counseling/psychology, criminal justice, criminology, dietetics, economics, family and community services, family/juvenile justice, fire control and safety technology, fire protection, fire science, fire services administration, forensic studies, (Social Science) Global Studies, history, international public service, international relations, international studies, law enforcement and corrections, legal studies, liberal arts/general studies, political science/government, psychology, public administration, and public affairs). Criminal justice, forensic science, and psychology have the largest enrollments.

Required: To graduate, all students must maintain a GPA of 2.0, pass a writing proficiency exam, and complete a total of 120 to 132 credits, depending on the major. Students must complete at least 40 credits from the university core curriculum, including a total of 28 credits in lab science, social sciences, history, literature or philosophy, and art, music, or theater, 9 credits in communication skills, and 3 credits each in quantitative skills, computers, and scientific methodology.

Special: UNH offers co-op programs in some majors, internships in all majors, work-study programs, interdisciplinary majors, fast-track business programs leading to bachelor's degrees in 3 years, 5-year B.S.-M.S. programs in education and in environmental science, and nondegree study programs. Study-abroad programs are available. There are a freshman honors program.

Faculty/Classroom: 69% of faculty are male; 31% are female. No introductory courses are taught by graduate students.

Admissions: 74% of the 2013-2014 applicants were accepted. The SAT scores for the 2013-2014 freshman class were: Critical Reading--40% below 500, 47% between 500 and 599, 12% between 600 and 699, and 1% between 700 and 800; Math--37% below 500, 43% between 500 and 599, 19% between 600 and 699, and 1% between 700 and 800; Writing--43% below 500, 45% between 500 and 599, 11% between 600 and 699, and 1% between 700 and 800. The ACT scores were 31% below 21, 31% between 21 and 23, 24% between 24 and 26, 10% between 27 and 28, and 4% above 28.

Requirements: The SAT or ACT is required. Applicants should be graduates of an accredited secondary school. The GED is accepted. An interview is recommended. A letter of recommendation is required along with a personal essay. AP and CLEP credits are accepted. Important factors in the admissions decision are advanced placement or honors courses, extracurricular activities record, and recommendations by school officials.

Procedure: Freshmen are admitted fall and spring. Entrance exams should be taken in the fall or winter of the senior year. There are early admissions and rolling admissions plans. Application deadlines are open. Application fee is $25. applicants were on the 2013 waiting list; were admitted. Applications are accepted online.

Transfer: 350 transfer students enrolled in 2012 2013. Applicants should have a minimum college GPA of 2.3 and should submit all official transcripts. An interview is recommended, and the SAT is required for students with fewer than 24 college credits. 30 of 120 credits required for the bachelor's degree must be completed at UNH.

Visiting: There are regularly scheduled orientations for prospective students, including daily information sessions, Open Houses, Accepted Student Days, Charger Days, and Summer Preview Days. There are guides for informal visits, visitors may sit in on classes, and stay overnight. To schedule a visit, contact Office of Undergraduate Admissions at admissions@newhaven.edu.

Financial Aid: UNH is a member of CSS. The FAFSA, and and copies of the student's and parents' 1040 tax forms and W-2 forms is required. Check with the school for current application deadlines.

International Students: There are 351 international students enrolled. The school actively recruits these students. They must take the TOEFL with a minimum score of 75 on the Internet-based version (iBT). They must also take the SAT or ACT. English-speaking students may submit the SAT or ACT scores instead.

Computers: All students may access the system. 24 hours a day. There are no time limits and no fees.

Graduates: From July 1, 2012 to June 30, 2013, 990 bachelor's degrees were awarded. The most popular majors were criminal justice (28%), forensic sciences (9%), and psychology (5%). In an average class, 44% graduate in 4 years or less, 53% graduate in 5 years or less, and 55% graduate in 6 years or less.

Admissions Contact: Kevin J. Phillips, Associate Vice President for Enrollment. E-Mail: *admissions@newhaven.edu* Web: *www.newhaven.edu*

WESLEYAN UNIVERSITY C-3

Middletown, CT 06459	**(860) 685-3000; (860) 685-3001**
Full-time: 1401 men, 1498 women	**Faculty:** 338; IIA, ++$
Part-time: 1 men, 6 women	**Ph.D.s:** 95%
Graduate: 137 men, 162 women	**Student/Faculty:** 9 to 1
Year: semesters, summer session	**Tuition:** $46,944
Application Deadline: January 1	**Room & Board:** $12,940
Freshman Class: 10690 applied, 2181 accepted, 741 enrolled	
SAT CR/M/W: 710/700/720	**ACT:** 32 **MOST COMPETITIVE**

Wesleyan University, founded in 1831, is a private institution offering programs in the liberal arts and sciences. There is one undergraduate school and one graduate school. The 3 libraries contain 1.6 million volumes, 295,419 microform items, and 64,776 audio/video tapes/CDs/DVDs, and subscribe to 23,675 periodicals including electronic. Computerized library services include interlibrary loans, database searching, Internet access, and Wi-Fi capability. Special learning facilities include an art gallery, radio station, an Observatory. The 316-acre campus is in a suburban area 15 miles south of Hartford, and 2 hours from both Boston and New York City. Including any residence halls, there are 301 buildings.

Student Life: 92% of undergraduates are from out of state, mostly the Northeast. Students are from 49 states, 52 foreign countries, and Canada. 50% are from public schools. 53% are White. The average age of freshmen is 19; all undergraduates, 20. 5% do not continue beyond their first year; 95% remain to graduate.

Housing: 2919 students can be accommodated in college housing, which includes single-sex and coed dorms, on-campus apartments, and off-campus apartments. In addition, there are language houses, special-interest houses, and fraternity houses. On-campus housing is guaranteed for all 4 years. 98% of students live on campus; of those, 99% remain on campus on weekends. All students may keep cars.

Activities: 4% of men belong to 6 local fraternities; 1% of women belong to 1 local sororities. There are 230 groups on campus, including art, band, cheerleading, chess, choir, chorale, chorus, communications, computers, dance, debate, drama, environmental, ethnic, film, gay, honors, international, jazz band, literary magazine, musical theater, newspaper, orchestra, pep band, photography, political, professional, radio and TV, religious, social, social service, student government, symphony, and yearbook. Popular campus events include Cultural Shows, and Spring Fling.

Sports: There are 15 intercollegiate sports for men and 14 for women, and 6 intramural sports for men and 6 for women. Facilities include a 5000-seat stadium, a 1200-seat gym, 50-meter Olympic-size pool, 400-

meter outdoor track, cross-country trail, hockey arena, strength and fitness center, 12 outdoor tennis courts, eight squash courts, three soccer fields, two football practice fields, rugby pitch, boathouse, baseball diamond, softball diamond, and two artificial turf fields. The field house contains a 200-meter indoor track, four indoor tennis courts, three recreational basketball courts, three volleyball courts, and three badminton courts.

Disabled Students: 53% of the campus is accessible. Facilities include wheelchair ramps, elevators, special parking, specially equipped restrooms, special class scheduling, lowered drinking fountains, lowered telephones, special housing.

Services: Counseling and information services are available, as is tutoring in most subjects. Peer advisor assistance in time management and academic skills development, writing tutors, math tutoring, quantitative skills and quantitative analysis, as well as supplemental instruction in biology and chemistry are available for students.

Campus Safety and Security: Measures include 24-hour foot and vehicle patrol, emergency notification system, self-defense education, and security escort services. There are shuttle buses, emergency telephones, lighted pathways/sidewalks, and controlled access to dorms/residences.

Programs of Study: Wesleyan confers B.A. degrees. Master's and doctoral degrees are also awarded. Bachelor's degrees are awarded in AGRICULTURE (environmental studies), BIOLOGICAL SCIENCE (biology/biological science, molecular biology, and neurosciences), COMMUNICATIONS AND THE ARTS (art history and appreciation, classics, dance, dramatic arts, English, English literature, film arts, music, romance languages and literature, and studio art), COMPUTER AND PHYSICAL SCIENCE (astronomy, chemistry, computer science, earth science, mathematics, and physics), SOCIAL SCIENCE (African American studies, American studies, anthropology, archeology, classical/ancient civilization, East Asian studies, economics, French studies, gender studies, German area studies, Hispanic American studies, history, Italian studies, Latin American studies, medieval studies, philosophy, political science/government, psychology, religion, Russian and Slavic studies, science and society, social studies, and sociology). Sciences, economics and history. are the strongest academically. Psychology, chemistry, and music have the largest enrollments.

Required: To graduate, all students must complete 128 credit hours. All students are expected, but not required to take courses each in humanities and arts, social and behavioral sciences, and natural science and math. A minimum academic average of 74 must be maintained, with at least 6 semesters of full-time residency.

Special: Wesleyan offers exchange programs with 11 northeastern colleges, cross-registration with 2 area colleges, study abroad in 45 countries on 6 continents, internships, dual and student-designed majors, and pass/fail options. 3-2 engineering programs with Cal Tech and Columbia University are also available. There are 2 national honor societies, including Phi Beta Kappa, and 48 departmental honors programs.

Faculty/Classroom: 52% of faculty are male; 48% are female. All teach and do research. No introductory courses are taught by graduate students. The average class size in an introductory lecture is 49; in a laboratory is 40; and in a regular course is 19.

Admissions: 20% of the 2013-2014 applicants were accepted. The SAT scores for the 2013-2014 freshman class were: Critical Reading--7% between 500 and 599, 33% between 600 and 699, and 60% between 700 and 800; Math--6% between 500 and 599, 39% between 600 and 699, and 55% between 700 and 800; Writing--6% between 500 and 599, 33% between 600 and 699, and 61% between 700 and 800. The ACT scores were 1% between 21 and 23, 3% between 24 and 26, 7% between 27 and 28, and 88% above 28. 97% of the current freshmen were in the top fifth of their class.

Requirements: The SAT or ACT is required. Applicants must submit the common application, transcript, recommendations, and either the ACT or SAT and 2 subject tests. Students should have a minimum of 20 academic credits, including 4 years each of English, foreign language, math, science, and social studies. AP credits are accepted. Important factors in the admissions decision are personality/intangible qualities, advanced placement or honors courses, and recommendations by school officials.

Procedure: Freshmen are admitted fall. Entrance exams should be taken in the spring of the junior year or the fall of the senior year. There are early decision, early admissions, and deferred admissions plans. Early decision applications should be filed by November 15; regular applications, by January 1 for fall entry, along with a $55 fee. Notification of early decision is sent December 15; regular decision, April 1. 372 early decision candidates were accepted for the 2013-2014 class. 954 applicants were on the 2013 waiting list; 48 were admitted. Applications are accepted online.

Transfer: 74 transfer students enrolled in 2012-2013. Applicants need a strong academic record and either SAT or ACT scores. An interview is recommended. 64 of 128 credits required for the bachelor's degree must be completed at Wesleyan.

Visiting: There are regularly scheduled orientations for prospective students, consisting of student visits include hour-long campus tours and group information sessions. There are guides for informal visits, visitors may sit in on classes, and stay overnight. To schedule a visit, contact The Office of Admission at (860) 685-3000.

Financial Aid: In 2013-2014, 48% of all full-time freshmen and 50% of continuing full-time students received some form of financial aid. 42% of all full-time freshmen and 45% of continuing full-time students received need-based aid. The average freshman award was $44,152. Need-based scholarships or need-based grants averaged $40,009; and need-based self-help aid (loans and jobs) averaged $5,057. 48% of undergraduate students work part-time. Average annual earnings from campus work are $935. The average financial indebtedness of the 2013 graduate was $17,808. Wesleyan is a member of CSS. The CSS/Profile and FAFSA, and Parent and student 1040 forms, W-2s, business tax returns are required. The priority date for freshman financial aid applications for fall entry is February 15. The deadline for filing freshman financial aid applications for fall entry is February 15.

International Students: There are 239 international students enrolled. The school actively recruits these students. They must take the TOEFL with a minimum score of 100 on the Internet-based version (iBT), or take the IELTS. They must also take the SAT or ACT.

Computers: All students may access the system. There are no time limits and no fees.

Graduates: From July 1, 2012 to June 30, 2013, 785 bachelor's degrees were awarded. The most popular majors were psychology (9%), English (7%), and government (6%). 548 companies recruited on campus in 2012-2013. In an average class, 86% graduate in 4 years or less, 91% graduate in 5 years or less, and 92% graduate in 6 years or less. Of the 2012 graduating class, 14% were enrolled in graduate school within 6 months of graduation, and 52% were employed.

Admissions Contact: Nancy Hargrave-Meislahn, Dean of Admissions and Financial Aid. E-Mail: *www.wesleyan.edu* Web: *www.wesleyan.edu/admission*

WESTERN CONNECTICUT STATE UNIVERSITY A-3

Danbury, CT 06810-6855 (203) 837-9000
(877) 837-9278; (203) 837-8338

Full-time: 2210 men, 2553 women	**Faculty:** n/av; IIA, +$
Part-time: 458 men, 594 women	**Ph.D.s:** 77%
Graduate: 203 men, 389 women	**Student/Faculty:** 16 to 1
Year: semesters, summer session	**Tuition:** $8104 ($18,728)
Application Deadline: May 1	**Room & Board:** $10,223
Freshman Class: n/av	
SAT: required	

COMPETITIVE

Western Connecticut State University, founded in 1903, is a public institution offering programs in business, arts and sciences, professional studies, and visual and performing arts. It is part of the Connecticut State University system. There are 4 undergraduate schools and 1 graduate school. In addition to regional accreditation, West Conn has baccalaureate program accreditation with CSWE and NASM. The 2 libraries contain 215,096 volumes, 513,783 microform items, and 13,100 audio/video tapes/CDs/DVDs, and subscribe to 1,010 periodicals including electronic. Computerized library services include interlibrary loans, database searching, Internet access, and laptop Internet portals. Special learning facilities include a learning resource center, art gallery, planetarium, radio station, TV station, an observatory, electron microscope, and photography studio. The 398-acre campus is in a suburban area 65 miles north of New York City. Including any residence halls, there are 25 buildings. The figures in the above capsule and in this profile are approximate.

Student Life: 92% of undergraduates are from Connecticut. Others are from 18 states, and 8 foreign countries. 96% are from public schools. 76% are white. The average age of freshmen is 18; all undergraduates, 22. 28% do not continue beyond their first year; 40% remain to graduate.

Housing: 1601 students can be accommodated in college housing, which includes single-sex and coed dorms, on-campus apartments, and married student housing. On-campus housing is available on a first-come and first-served basis. 71% of students commute. All students may keep cars.

Activities: 4% of men belong to 3 national fraternities; 4% of women belong to 4 national sororities. There are 82 groups on campus, including art, band, cheerleading, chess, choir, chorale, chorus, computers, dance, debate, drama, environmental, ethnic, film, gay, honors, international, jazz band, literary magazine, musical theater, newspaper, opera, orchestra, photography, political, professional, radio and TV, religious, social, social service, student government, and symphony. Popular campus events include West Fest, Midnight Breakfast, and Student Leadership Banquet.

Sports: There are 6 intercollegiate sports for men and 8 for women, and 6 intramural sports for men and 2 for women. Facilities include 2 gyms, a weight training area, 4 tennis courts, 5 playing fields, an indoor swimming pool, and a field house with an indoor running track.

Disabled Students: All of the campus is accessible. Facilities include wheelchair ramps, elevators, special parking, specially equipped restrooms, special class scheduling, lowered drinking fountains, and lowered telephones.

Services: Counseling and information services are available, as is tutoring

in every subject. There is a reader service for the blind, and remedial math, reading, and writing. a computer science clinic, a math clinic, and a writing lab.

Campus Safety and Security: Measures include 24-hour foot and vehicle patrol, emergency notification system, and security escort services. There are shuttle buses, emergency telephones, lighted pathways/sidewalks, and controlled access to dorms/residences.

Programs of Study: West Conn confers B.A., B.S., B.S. Ed., B.B.A., and B.Mus. degrees. Associate, master's, and doctoral degrees are also awarded. Bachelor's degrees are awarded in BIOLOGICAL SCIENCE (biology/biological science), BUSINESS (accounting, banking and finance, business administration and management, management information systems, and marketing management), COMMUNICATIONS AND THE ARTS (art, communications, dramatic arts, English, illustration, media arts, music, music performance, photography, Spanish, and studio art), COMPUTER AND PHYSICAL SCIENCE (atmospheric sciences and meteorology, chemistry, computer science, earth science, and mathematics), EDUCATION (elementary education, health education, music education, and secondary education), ENGINEERING AND ENVIRONMENTAL DESIGN (environmental science), HEALTH PROFESSIONS (community health work, health care administration, health science, medical laboratory technology, and nursing), SOCIAL SCIENCE (American studies, anthropology, criminal justice, economics, history, law enforcement and corrections, liberal arts/general studies, paralegal studies, political science/government, psychology, social science, social work, and sociology). Education, business, justice and law administration have the largest enrollments.

Required: To graduate, students must complete 122 credit hours, with a minimum GPA of 2.0 or higher for some programs. All students must also fulfill the general education distribution requirements, including phys ed, and the foreign language requirement. In addition, at least 30 credits and at least half of the major requirements must be completed at West-Conn.

Special: The university offers co-op programs with local corporations and the New England Regional Student Program. Student-designed majors, dual majors, study abroad, and pass/fail options are available. Nondegree study is offered at the University Center for Adult Education. There are 11 national honor societies, a freshman honors program, and 2 departmental honors programs.

Faculty/Classroom: 55% of faculty are male; 45% are female. All teach undergraduates, 25% do research, and 25% do both. No introductory courses are taught by graduate students. The average class size in an introductory lecture is 26 and in a laboratory is 17.

Requirements: The SAT is required. The ACT is accepted in lieu of SAT scores. Applicants must be graduates of an accredited secondary school. The GED is accepted. Students should have completed 13 high school academic credits, including 4 in English, 3 in math, 2 to 3 in foreign language, 2 in science, and 1 each in history and social studies. Additional credits in art, music, and computer science are highly recommended. An essay and an interview are recommended. A GPA of 2.7 is required. AP and CLEP credits are accepted. Important factors in the admissions decision are advanced placement or honors courses, evidence of special talent, and recommendations by school officials.

Procedure: Freshmen are admitted fall and spring. Entrance exams should be taken by December of the senior year. There are early admissions, deferred admissions, and rolling admissions plans. Applications should be filed by May 1 for fall entry, along with a $50 fee. Notifications are sent December 15. Applications are accepted online.

Transfer: 454 transfer students enrolled in 2010-2011. Transfers must have a minimum of 12 college credits. Applicants must have a cumulative GPA of 2.0 for all college course work. A higher GPA is required for some programs. 30 of 122 credits required for the bachelor's degree must be completed at West Conn.

Visiting: There are regularly scheduled orientations for prospective students, including campus tours on weekdays when classes are in session. There is an Open House on a Sunday in early November. There are guides for informal visits and visitors may sit in on classes. To schedule a visit, contact the Office of Admissions.

Financial Aid: In a recent year, 62% of all full-time freshmen and 59% of continuing full-time students received some form of financial aid. 58% of all full-time freshmen and 54% of continuing full-time students received need-based aid. The average freshman award was $11,405. Need-based scholarships or need-based grants averaged $4,781 ($10,229 maximum); need-based self-help aid (loans and jobs) averaged $4,221 ($27,489 maximum); and other non-need-based awards and non-need-based scholarships averaged $5,337 ($6,551 maximum). 3% of undergraduate students work part-time. Average annual earnings from campus work are $2258. West Conn is a member of CSS. The FAFSA and the college's own financial statement are required. Check with the school for current application deadlines.

International Students: They must take the TOEFL. They must also take the SAT.

Computers: There are a total of 1,021 wired computers available to all students. The wireless network accommodates 5,000 simultaneous users. All students may access the system at any time. There are no time limits and no fees.

Graduates: In a recent year, 807 bachelor's degrees were awarded. The most popular majors were management (10%), justice and law administration (9%), and psychology (8%).

Admissions Contact: Director of Admissions. E-Mail: *admissions@wcsu.edu* Web: *www.wcsu.ctstate.edu*

YALE UNIVERSITY C-3

New Haven, CT 06520 **(203) 432-9316; (203) 432-9370**

Full-time: 2710 men, 2683 women	**Faculty:** 885; I, +$
Part-time: 8 men, 4 women	**Ph.D.s:** 92%
Graduate: 3275 men, 3226 women	**Student/Faculty:** 6 to 1
Year: semesters, summer session	**Tuition:** $42,300
Application Deadline: December 31	**Room & Board:** $13,000
Freshman Class: 28977 applied, 2043 accepted, 1356 enrolled	
SAT CR/M/W: 750/750/760 **ACT:** 33	**MOST COMPETITIVE**

Yale University, founded in 1701, is a private liberal arts institution. There is one undergraduate school and 13 graduate schools. In addition to regional accreditation, Yale has baccalaureate program accreditation with AACSB, ABET, CAHEA, NAAB, NASM, NLN, and SAF. The 15 libraries contain 15.0 million volumes, 10.0 million microform items, and 400,000 audio/video tapes/CDs/DVDs, and subscribe to 450,000 periodicals including electronic. Computerized library services include interlibrary loans, database searching, Internet access, and Wi-Fi capability. Special learning facilities include an art gallery, natural history museum, planetarium, radio station, Yale Center for British Art, Beinecke Rare Book and Manuscript Library,Film Study Center, Center for Engineering Innovation and Design, Marsh Botanical Gardens and Yale Natural Preserves, and numerous research centers. The 342-acre campus is in an urban area 75 miles northeast of New York City. Including any residence halls, there are 440 buildings.

Student Life: 93% of undergraduates are from out of state, mostly the West. Students are from 49 states, 74 foreign countries, and Canada. 57% are from public schools. 53% are White; 17% Asian American; 11% Hispanic. The average age of freshmen is 18; all undergraduates, 20. 1% do not continue beyond their first year; 96% remain to graduate.

Housing: College-sponsored housing includes coed dorms. Students are ramdomly assigned to 1 of 12 residential colleges where they live, eat, socialize, and pursue varius academic and extracurricular activities. All undergraduate housing is provided through the residential college system. On-campus housing is guaranteed for the freshman year only and is available on a lottery system for upperclassmen. 88% of students live on campus. All students may keep cars.

Activities: There are 400 groups on campus, including art, band, cheerleading, chess, choir, chorale, chorus, communications, computers, dance, debate, drama, environmental, ethnic, film, gay, honors, international, jazz band, literary magazine, marching band, musical theater, newspaper, opera, orchestra, pep band, photography, political, professional, radio and TV, religious, social, social service, student government, symphony, and yearbook. Popular campus events include Freshman Dinner, Spring Fling Concert, Fall Show, Yale Symphony Orchestra Halloween Show, Yale Top Chef Competition, Yale-Harvard Football Game and special cultural dinners in the residential colleges.

Sports: There are 16 intercollegiate sports for men and 18 for women, and 25 intramural sports for men and 21 for women. Facilities include 71,000-seat Yale Bowl (football), sports complex, gymnasium, 2 swimming pools, fitness center, ice rink, sailing center, squash center, tennis center, golf course, boathouse.

Disabled Students: Facilities include wheelchair ramps, elevators, special parking, specially equipped restrooms, special class scheduling, lowered drinking fountains, lowered telephones, a door-to-door lift-van service.

Services: Counseling and information services are available, as is tutoring in every subject. There is a reader service for the blind.

Campus Safety and Security: Measures include 24-hour foot and vehicle patrol, emergency notification system, self-defense education, and security escort services. There are shuttle buses, emergency telephones, lighted pathways/sidewalks, and controlled access to dorms/residences.

Programs of Study: Yale confers B.A., and B.S. degrees. Master's and doctoral degrees are also awarded. Bachelor's degrees are awarded in AGRICULTURE (environmental studies), BIOLOGICAL SCIENCE (biochemistry, biology/biological science, biophysics, evolutionary biology, and molecular biology), COMMUNICATIONS AND THE ARTS (art history, art, Chinese, classics, dramatic arts, East Asian languages and literature, English, film arts, French, Germanic languages and literature, Italian, Japanese, linguistics, literature, music, Portuguese, Russian, Russian languages and literature, Slavic languages, and Spanish), COMPUTER AND PHYSICAL SCIENCE (applied mathematics, applied physics, astronomy, chemistry, computer science, geology, mathematics, mathematics – economics, mathematics – philosophy, physics, and statistics), ENGINEERING AND ENVIRONMENTAL DESIGN (architecture, biomedical engineering, chemical engineering, electrical/electronics engineering, engineering, engineering and applied science, environmental engineering, and mechanical engineering), SOCIAL SCIENCE (African studies, African American studies, American studies, anthropology, archeology, classical/ancient civilization, cognitive science, East Asian studies, Eastern European studies, economics, ethics, politics, and social policy, ethnic studies, German area studies, history, history of science, humanities, international studies, Judaic studies, Latin American studies, Middle Eastern studies, Near Eastern studies, philosophy, political science/government, psychology, religion, Russian and Slavic studies, sociology, South Asian studies, and women's studies). History, political science, and economics have the largest enrollments.

Required: To graduate, students must complete at least 36 semester courses, including 2 course credits in the humanities, 2 in the social sciences and 2 in the sciences; 2 writing courses; 2 in quantitative reasoning; and courses to further proficiency in a foreign language. All students complete requirements for an academic major. Yale does not have a 'minor' program but students may have two majors.

Special: The university runs a study abroad program in England and offers opportunities for term-time or summer study in many other countries. It also offers an accelerated degree program, B.A.-B.S. degrees, dual majors, and student-designed majors. Directed Studies, a special freshman program in the humanities, affords outstanding students the opportunity to survey the Western cultural tradition. Perspectives on Science is a special freshmen program for students who are especially strong in science and mathematics. Freshmen Seminars offer the opportunity for first-year students the opportunity to enroll in small classes with some of Yale's most distinguished faculty members. The STARS (Science, Technology and Research Scholars) program offers research opportunities, mentoring and support to students historically under-represented in fields of natural science and quantitative reasoning.

Faculty/Classroom: 64% of faculty are male; 36% are female. All teach undergraduates. No introductory courses are taught by graduate students.

Admissions: 7% of the 2013-2014 applicants were accepted. The SAT scores for the 2013-2014 freshman class were: Critical Reading--2% between 500 and 599, 22% between 600 and 699, and 76% between 700 and 800; Math--2% between 500 and 599, 7% between 600 and 699, and 81% between 700 and 800; Writing--2% between 500 and 599, 16% between 600 and 699, and 81% between 700 and 800.

Requirements: The SAT or ACT is required. The ACT Optional Writing test is also required. In addition, only those applicants submitting SAT scores must also take any 2 SAT Subject tests. ACT submitters must take the ACT with Writing. Most successful applicants rank in the top 10% of their high school class. All students must have completed a rigorous high school program encompassing all academic disciplines. 2 essays, 2 teacher recommendations and a counselor letter are required, and an interview is recommended. Yale offers a non-binding Single Choice Early Action option (not Early Decision.) AP credits are accepted. Important factors in the admissions decision are leadership record, extracurricular activities record, and advanced placement or honors courses.

Procedure: Freshmen are admitted fall. Entrance exams should be taken at any time up to and including the January test date in the year of application. There is a deferred admissions plan. Early decision applications should be filed by November 1; regular applications, by December 31 for fall entry, along with a $75 fee. Notifications are sent April 1. 617 applicants were on the 2013 waiting list; 70 were admitted. Applications are accepted online.

Transfer: 22 transfer students enrolled in 2012-2013. Applicants must take either the SAT or ACT and have 1 full year of credit. An essay and 3 letters of recommendation are required. (One Yale credit = one semester-long course.) 18 of 36 credits required for the bachelor's degree must be completed at Yale.

Visiting: There are regularly scheduled orientations for prospective students, Flexible: admissions information sessions, campus tours, in summer Student Forums. There are guides for informal visits and visitors may sit in on classes. To schedule a visit, contact the Receptionist Office at (203) 432-9300.

Financial Aid: In 2013-2014, 50% of all full-time freshmen and 55% of continuing full-time students received some form of financial aid. 50% of all full-time freshmen and 55% of continuing full-time students received need-based aid. The average freshman award was $46,530. Need-based scholarships or need-based grants averaged $41,230 ($55,900 maximum); and need-based self-help aid (loans and jobs) averaged $2,700 ($2,700 maximum). 56% of undergraduate students work part-time. Average annual earnings from campus work are $1433. The average financial indebtedness of the 2013 graduate was $12,626. Yale is a member of CSS. The CSS/Profile and FAFSA, and Student and parent tax returns; CSS divorced/separated parents statement and business/farm supplement if appropriate. are required. The deadline for filing freshman financial aid applications for fall entry is March 1.

International Students: There are 555 international students enrolled. The school actively recruits these students. They must take the TOEFL with a minimum score of 600 on the paper-based TOEFL (PBT) or 100 on the Internet-based version (iBT), IELTS or Pearson Test of English, the SAT, and 2 SAT Subject tests, or the ACT with Writing.

Computers: All students may access the system 24 hours a day. There are no time limits and no fees.

Graduates: From July 1, 2012 to June 30, 2013, 1285 bachelor's degrees were awarded. The most popular majors were political science (14%), economics (12%), and history (10%). In an average class, 96% graduate in 6 years or less. Of the 2012 graduating class, 21% were enrolled in graduate school within 6 months of graduation, and 75% were employed.

Admissions Contact: Margit Dahl, Director of Admissions. E-Mail: *student.questions@yale.edu* Web: *http:/admissions.yale.edu*

DELAWARE

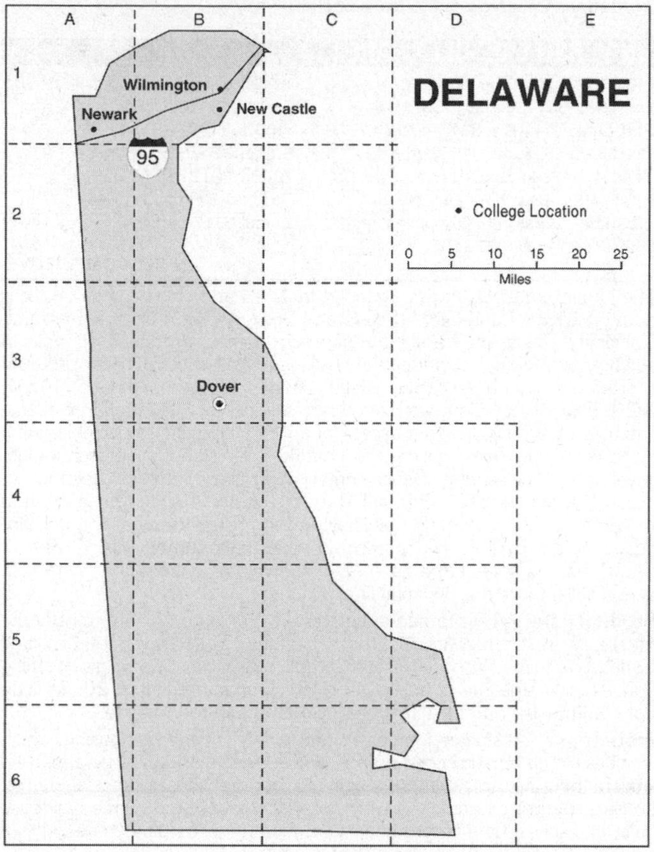

DELAWARE STATE UNIVERSITY B-3

Dover, DE 19901 **(302) 739-4917**

Full-time: 1000 men, 1350 women
Part-time: 250 men, 450 women
Graduate: 95 men, 185 women
Year: semesters, summer session
Application Deadline: open
Freshman Class: n/av
SAT or ACT: required
Faculty: n/av
Ph.D.s: 74%
Student/Faculty: n/av
Tuition: $6980 ($14,242)
Room & Board: $9386

LESS COMPETITIVE

Delaware State University, founded in 1891, is a publicly assisted institution. There are 4 undergraduate schools and 1 graduate school. In addition to regional accreditation, DSU has baccalaureate program accreditation with ACBSP and NCATE. Computerized library services include interlibrary loans and database searching. Special learning facilities include a learning resource center, art gallery, planetarium, and radio station. The 400-acre campus is in a suburban area 45 miles south of Wilmington. Including residence halls, there are 31 buildings.

Student Life: 56% of undergraduates are from Delaware. Others are from 29 states, 40 foreign countries, and Canada. 90% are from public schools. 64% are African American; 32% white. 18% claim no religious affiliation The average age of freshmen is 18; all undergraduates, 21. 32% do not continue beyond their first year; 28% remain to graduate.

Housing: 1334 students can be accommodated in college housing, which includes single-sex dorms. On-campus housing is available on a first-come and first-served basis. 54% of students commute. Alcohol is not permitted. All students may keep cars.

Activities: 50% of men belong to 4 national fraternities; 50% of women belong to 4 national sororities. There are 53 groups on campus, including cheerleading, choir, drama, ethnic, honors, international, jazz band, marching band, newspaper, pep band, radio and TV, religious, social service, student government, and yearbook. Popular campus events include Parents Day, Annual Career Fair, and Annual Pride Day.

Sports: There are 8 intercollegiate sports for men and 7 for women, and 20 intramural sports for men and 20 for women. Facilities include an indoor swimming pool, dance studio, racquetball & handball courts, 2 gyms, football stadium, baseball field, outdoor track, and tennis courts.

Disabled Students: All of the campus is accessible.

Services: Counseling and information services are available, as is tutoring in every subject, including remedial math, reading, and writing. A university tutoring program includes tutoring lab and tutorial service available in residence halls. A supplemental instruction program is available for challenging courses.

Campus Safety and Security: Measures include 24-hour foot and vehicle patrol. There are shuttle buses, emergency telephones, and lighted pathways/sidewalks.

Programs of Study: DSU confers B.A., B.S., B.S.W., and B.Tech. degrees. Master's degrees are also awarded. Bachelor's degrees are awarded in AGRICULTURE (agricultural business management, fish and game management, and natural resource management), BIOLOGICAL SCIENCE (biology/biological science and botany), BUSINESS (accounting, business administration and management, fashion merchandising, hotel/motel & restaurant management, marketing/retailing/merchandising), COMMUNICATIONS AND THE ARTS (English, French, journalism, music, Spanish), COMPUTER AND PHYSICAL SCIENCE (chemistry, computer science, mathematics, and physics), EDUCATION (agricultural education, art education, business education, early childhood education, elementary education, health education, home economics education, music education, physical education, science education, and special education), ENGINEERING AND ENVIRONMENTAL DESIGN (chemical engineering, civil engineering, electrical/electronics engineering, and mechanical engineering), HEALTH PROFESSIONS (community health work, environmental health science, and nursing), SOCIAL SCIENCE (economics, history, parks and recreation management, political science/government, psychology, social work, and sociology). Education is strongest academically. Business administration, education, English and mass communications have the largest enrollments.

Required: 52 hours of general education requirements must be completed, distributed as follows: 16 hours, core courses; 3 hours, arts and humanities; 6 hours, foreign languages; 6 hours, literature; 6 hours, math; 6 hours, natural sciences, and a minimum 3-hour Senior Capstone Experience course. A total of 121 credit hours and minimum GPA of 2.0 are required.

Special: The university offers accelerated degrees, combined B.A.-B.S. degrees, student-designed majors, and a 3-2 engineering program with the University of Delaware. There are assisted internships in airway science and nursing and co-op programs in business, education, home economics, social work, and agriculture. There are 6 national honor societies, including Phi Beta Kappa, and a freshman honors program.

Faculty/Classroom: 61% of faculty are male; 39% are female. No introductory courses are taught by graduate students. The average class size in a regular course is 16.

Requirements: The SAT or ACT is required. Applicants should graduate from an accredited secondary school or have a GED. 16 academic credits are required, including 4 units of English and 3 of math, of which 2 must be in algebra and 1 must be in geometry, 3 of science courses with a lab, 2 of history and/or social studies, and 4 of electives, including foreign language or computer science courses. A GPA of 2.0 is required. CLEP credits are accepted. Important factors in the admissions decision are extracurricular activities record, advanced placement or honors courses, and recommendations by school officials.

Procedure: Freshmen are admitted fall and spring. There are early admissions and rolling admissions plans.

Transfer: Applicants must submit a statement of honorable withdrawal and high school and college transcripts. 30 of 121 credits required for the bachelor's degree must be completed at DSU.

Visiting: There are regularly scheduled orientations for prospective students, including a High School Day Program, and guides for informal visits.

Financial Aid: DSU is a member of CSS. The CSS/Profile and FFS are required. Check with the school for current application deadlines.

International Students: They must take TOEFL & SAT or ACT.

Admissions Contact: Jethro Williams, Admissions Director. E-Mail: *jwilliams@dsc.edu Web: www.desu.edu*

GOLDEY-BEACOM COLLEGE B-1

Wilmington, DE 19808 **(302) 225-6248**
(800) 833-4877; (302) 996-5408

Full-time: 208 men, 254 women
Part-time: 70 men, 93 women
Graduate: 458 men, 269 women
Year: semesters, summer session
Application Deadline:
Freshman Class: 717 applied, 385 accepted, 128 enrolled
SAT: required
Faculty: 18
Ph.D.s: 100%
Student/Faculty: 24 to 1
Tuition: $22,140
Room & Board: $5353

COMPETITIVE

Goldey-Beacom College, founded in 1886, is a private coeducational college. There is one undergraduate school and one graduate school. In addition to regional accreditation. Goldey-Beacom College has baccalaureate program accreditation with ACBSP. Computerized library services include interlibrary loans, database searching, Internet access, and Wi-Fi capability. The 24-acre campus is in a suburban area Goldey-Beacom College is located in the Pike Creek Valley suburb of Wilmington, Delaware. Including any residence halls, there are 6 buildings.

Student Life: 67% of undergraduates are from Delaware. Others are from 19 states, 60 foreign countries, and Canada. 75% are from public schools. 41% are White; 28% Foreign; 15% African American. The average age of freshmen is 19; all undergraduates, 21. 24% do not continue beyond their first year; 62% remain to graduate.

Housing: 271 students can be accommodated in housing, which includes coed on-campus apartments, as well as special-interest houses. On-campus housing is guaranteed for all 4 years, and is available on a first-come, first-served basis. 64% of students commute. Students may keep cars.

Activities: No fraternities or sororities. There are 14 groups, including computers, drama, ethnic, honors, international, newspaper, professional, religious, social service, and student government. Campus events include Spring Fest, Karaoke Night, Casino Night and Homecoming.

Sports: There are 4 intercollegiate sports for men and 6 for women. Facilities include soccer & softball fields, tennis & handball courts, gym with basketball & volleyball courts, and fitness center available to all students & staff. When student interest, an intermural sports team is established.

Disabled Students: All of the campus is accessible.

Services: Counseling and information services are available, as is tutoring in most subjects. There is a reader service for the blind, and remedial math, reading, and writing. and computer-based tutorials.

Campus Safety and Security: Measures include 24-hour foot and vehicle patrol, emergency notification system, self-defense education, and security escort services. There are lighted pathways/sidewalks and controlled access to dorms/residences.

Programs of Study: confers B.A., and B.S. degrees. Associate and master's degrees are also awarded. Bachelor's degrees are awarded in BUSINESS (accounting, banking and finance, business administration and management, human resources, international business management, management information systems, marketing management, and sports management), COMPUTER AND PHYSICAL SCIENCE (information sciences and systems), SOCIAL SCIENCE (economics and psychology). Accounting, economics, and finance are the strongest academically. Accounting, management, and business administration have the largest enrollments.

Required: To graduate, students must complete 136 credit hours with GPA of 2.0. Also fulfill the College's degree requirements.

Special: A 5-year B.S/M.B.A degree, dual majors, internships, and work-study programs are available. There are 1 national honor societies, a freshman honors program, and 1 departmental honors programs.

Faculty/Classroom: 59% of faculty are male; 41% are female. 89% teach undergraduates. No introductory courses are taught by graduate students. The average class size in an introductory lecture is 28 and in a regular course is 21.

Admissions: 54% of the 2013-2014 applicants were accepted.

Requirements: The SAT is required. Applicants must be high school graduates or have a GED and submit their official high school transcripts and SAT scores A GPA of 2.0 is required. AP and CLEP credits are accepted. Important factors in the admissions decision are advanced placement or honors courses, extracurricular activities record, and recommendations by school officials.

Procedure: Freshmen are admitted to all sessions. There are early admissions, deferred admissions, and rolling admissions plans. Application deadlines are open. Applications are accepted online.

Transfer: 77 transfer students enrolled in 2012-2013. Transfer applicants must submit high school and college transcripts.

Visiting: There are regularly scheduled orientations for prospective students. A meeting with an admissions representative also includes a campus tour. There are guides for informal visits, visitors may sit in on classes, and stay overnight. To schedule a visit, contact the College's Admissions Office.

Financial Aid: In 2013-2014, 100% of all full-time freshmen and 80% of continuing full-time students received some form of financial aid. 99% of all full-time freshmen and 90% of undergraduate students work part-time. Average annual earnings from campus work are $1200. is a member of CSS. The FAFSA is required. The priority date for freshman financial aid applications for fall entry is April 15. The deadline for filing freshman financial aid applications for fall entry is July 15.

International Students: There are 55 international students enrolled. They must take the TOEFL with a minimum score of 500 on the paper-based TOEFL (PBT) or 60 on the Internet-based version (iBT), IELTS. They must also take the SAT or ACT, scoring 1200.

Graduates: From July 1, 2012 to June 30, 2013, 119 bachelor's degrees were awarded. The most popular majors were business administration (63%), accounting (26%), and psychology (5%). 81 companies recruited on campus in 2012-2013. In an average class, 41% graduate in 6 years or less. Of the 2012 graduating class, 45% were enrolled in graduate school within 6 months of graduation, and 90% were employed.

Admissions Contact: Larry Eby, Director of Admissions. E-Mail: *admissions@gbc.edu* Web: *www.gbc.edu*

UNIVERSITY OF DELAWARE — A-1

Newark, DE 19716 — **(302) 831-8123; (302) 831-6905**

Full-time: 6744 men, 9155 women — **Faculty:** 1165; I, av$
Part-time: 704 men, 824 women — **Ph.D.s:** 86%
Graduate: 1812 men, 1842 women — **Student/Faculty:** 13 to 1
Year: 4-1-4, summer session — **Tuition:** $11,682 ($28,772)
Application Deadline: January 15 — **Room & Board:** $11,046
Freshman Class: 26225 applied, 14829 accepted, 3817 enrolled
SAT CR/M/W: 599/610/595

VERY COMPETITIVE

The University of Delaware, founded in 1743 and chartered in 1833, is a state-assisted, Land-Grant, Sea-Grant, Space-Grant, Carnegie Research University. There are 7 undergraduate schools and 7 graduate schools. In addition to regional accreditation, Delaware has baccalaureate program accreditation with AACSB, ABET, ADA, APTA, CAHEA, NASM, NCATE, and NLN. Computerized library services include interlibrary loans, database searching, Internet access, and Wi-Fi capability. Special learning facilities include an art gallery, radio station, TV station, a preschool lab, development ice skating science center, computer-controlled greenhouse, nursing practice labs, physical therapy clinic, 400-acre agricultural research complex, exercise physiology biomechanics labs, foreign language media center, and composite materials center. The 969-acre campus is in a small town 12 miles southwest of Wilmington. With residence halls, there are 347 buildings.

Student Life: 64% of undergraduates are from out of state, mostly the Middle Atlantic. Students are from 47 states, 77 foreign countries, and Canada. 77% are White. 36% are Catholic; 26% claim no religious affiliation. The average age of freshmen is 18; all undergraduates, 20. 10% do not continue beyond their first year; 80% remain to graduate.

Housing: 7214 students can be accommodated in college housing, which includes single-sex and coed dorms, on-campus apartments, and married student housing. In addition, there are honors houses, special-interest houses, fraternity houses, sorority houses, alcohol/smoke-free residence halls, and suites. On-campus housing is guaranteed for all 4 years. 54% of students commute. All students may keep cars.

Activities: 15% of men belong to 20 national fraternities; 17% of women belong to 15 national sororities. There are 310 groups on campus, including art, band, cheerleading, chess, choir, chorale, chorus, computers, dance, debate, drama, drill team, drum and bugle corps, environmental, ethnic, film, gay, honors, international, jazz band, literary magazine, marching band, musical theater, newspaper, opera, orchestra, pep band, political, professional, radio and TV, religious, social service, student government, and symphony. Popular campus events include Greek Week, Convocation and Commencement.

Sports: There are 11 intercollegiate sports for men and 12 for women, and 32 intramural sports for men and 32 for women. Facilities include a 23,000-seat football stadium, 3 multipurpose gyms, 6 outdoor multipurpose fields, 8 outdoor basketball courts, 1 squash court, 15 racquetball courts, 21 outdoor tennis courts, indoor and outdoor pools, a universal weight room, a 5,000-seat basketball arena, a rock-climbing wall, a high-ropes challenge course, 4 student fitness centers, a strength and conditioning room with free weights, outdoor and indoor tracks, softball, baseball, lacrosse, and soccer fields, 2 ice arenas, and an outdoor hockey rink.

Disabled Students: 95% of the campus is accessible.

Services: Counseling and information services are available, as is tutoring in every subject. There is a reader service for the blind, and remedial math, reading, and writing. There is also a writing center, a math center, an academic services center for assistance with academic self-management development, critical thinking, and problem solving, as well as individual assistance for learning-disabled students.

Campus Safety and Security: Measures include 24-hour foot and vehicle patrol, emergency notification system, self-defense education, and security escort services. There are shuttle buses, emergency telephones, lighted pathways/sidewalks, controlled access to dorms/residences, ongoing student-awareness programs in the residence halls, community policing, and keycard access to residence halls.

Programs of Study: Delaware confers B.A., B.S., B.A.E.S., B.A. Liberal Studies, B.C.E., B.Ch.E., B.C.P.E., B.E.E., B.En. E., B.F.A., B.M.E., B.Mus., B.R.N., B.S.Ed. and B.S.N. degrees. Associate, master's, and doctoral degrees are also awarded. Bachelor's degrees are awarded in AGRICULTURE (agricultural business management, agricultural economics, agriculture, animal science, natural resource management, plant science, soil science, and wildlife management), BIOLOGICAL SCIENCE (biochemistry, biology/biological science, biotechnology, entomology, nutrition, and plant pathology), BUSINESS (accounting, banking and finance, business administration and management, hotel/motel and restaurant management, management information systems, management science, marketing/retailing/merchandising, operations management, organizational leadership and management, and sports management), COMMUNICATIONS AND THE ARTS (apparel design, applied music, art, art history and appreciation, communications, comparative literature, English, fine arts, historic preservation, Italian, journalism, languages, music, music theory and composition, theater management, and visual design), COMPUTER AND PHYSICAL SCIENCE (astronomy, chemistry, computer science, geology, information sciences and systems, mathematics, physics, and statistics), EDUCATION (athletic training, early childhood education, education, elementary education, English education, foreign languages education, mathematics education, music education, physical education, psychology education, science education, secondary education, and special education), ENGINEERING AND ENVIRONMENTAL DESIGN (bioengineering, chemical engineering, civil engineering, computer engineering, electrical/electronics engineering, engineering, engineering technology, environmental engineering, environmental science, landscape architecture/design, and mechanical engineering), HEALTH PROFESSIONS (health, health science, medical laboratory technology, and nursing), SOCIAL SCIENCE (anthropology, criminal justice, dietetics, East Asian studies, economics, European studies, family and community services, fashion design and technology, food production/management/services, food science, geography, history, human development, human services, interdisciplinary studies, international relations, Latin American studies, liberal arts/general studies, philosophy, political science/government, psychology, sociology, and women's studies). Biological sciences, psychology, and nursing have the largest enrollments.

Required: For graduation, students must complete at least 120 credits with a minimum GPA of 2.0. All students must take freshman English and 3 credits of course work with multicultural, ethnic, and/or gender-related content. Most majors require more than 120 credits. Most degree programs require that half of the courses be in the major field of study. Students must also have 1 incoming semester of First Year Experience (FYE) and 3 credits of Discovery Learning Experience (DLE).

Special: Students may participate in cooperative programs, internships, study abroad in 55 countries, a Washington semester, and work-study programs. The university offers accelerated degree programs, B.A.and B.S. degrees, dual majors, minors, student-designed majors (Bachelor of Arts in Liberal Studies), and pass/fail options. There are 4-1 degree programs in engineering, and hotel/restaurant management. Non-degree study is available through the Division of Continuing Education. There is an extensive undergraduate research program. Students may earn an enriched degree through the University Honors Program. There are 35 national honor societies, including Phi Beta Kappa, and a freshman honors program.

Faculty/Classroom: 61% of faculty are male; 39% are female. All teach undergraduates. No introductory courses are taught by graduate students. The average class size in a laboratory is 18 and in a regular course is 35.

Admissions: 57% of the 2013-2014 applicants were accepted. The SAT scores for the 2013-2014 freshman class were: Critical Reading--8% below 500, 42% between 500 and 599, 38% between 600 and 699, and 12% between 700 and 800; Math--7% below 500, 34% between 500 and 599, 46% between 600 and 699, and 13% between 700 and 800; Writing--9% below 500, 41% between 500 and 599, 41% between 600 and 699, and 9% between 700 and 800. The ACT scores were 1% below 21, 21% between 21 and 23, 62% between 24 and 26, and 16% between 27 and 28. 97 freshmen graduated first in their class.

Requirements: The SAT is required. The ACT Optional Writing test is also required. Applicants should be graduates of an accredited secondary school. The GED is accepted. Students should have completed a minimum of 18 high school academic units, including 4 units of English, 3 units of math, 3 units of science with 2 lab units, 2 units each of foreign language, history, and social studies, and 2 units of academic course electives. SAT Subject Tests are recommended, especially for honors program applicants. A writing sample and at least 1 letter of recommendation are required for all. AP credits are accepted. Important factors in the admissions decision are advanced placement or honors courses, recommendations by school officials, and personality/intangible qualities.

Procedure: Freshmen are admitted fall and spring. Entrance exams should be taken by their junior year or the beginning of the senior year. There are early admissions and deferred admissions plans. Applications should be filed by January 15 for fall entry; December 15 for spring entry, along with a $75 fee. Notifications are sent in mid-March.

Transfer: 488 transfer students enrolled in 2012-2013. Applicants for transfer should have completed at least 24 credits with a minimum GPA of 2.5 for most majors. Some majors require a GPA of 3.0 or better and/or specific course work. All transfer students must submit high school and college transcripts, an essay, and a statement of good standing from their prior institution. In some cases, an interview and standardized test scores are required. 30 of 120 credits required for the bachelor's degree must be completed at Delaware.

Visiting: There are regularly scheduled orientations for prospective students, consisting of 40-minute admissions session and 90-minute tour of campus. There are guides for informal visits and visitors may sit in on classes. To schedule a visit, contact the Admissions Office.

Financial Aid: In 2013-2014, 56% of all full-time freshmen and 49% of continuing full-time students received some form of financial aid. 31% of all full-time freshmen and 37% of continuing full-time students received need-based aid. The average freshman award was $14,427. Need-based scholarships or need-based grants averaged $8,756; need-based self-help aid (loans and jobs) averaged $6,719; non-need-based athletic scholarships averaged $15,631; other non-need-based awards and non-need-based scholarships averaged $6,569; and $6,408 from other forms of aid. The average financial indebtedness of the 2013 graduate was $33,649. The FAFSA is required. The priority date for freshman financial aid applications for fall entry is February 1. The deadline for filing freshman financial aid applications for fall entry is March 15.

International Students: There are 716 international students enrolled. The school actively recruits these students. They must take the TOEFL with a minimum score of 550 on the paper-based TOEFL (PBT) or 80 on the Internet-based version (iBT), or take the IELTS. The SAT is recommended.

Graduates: From July 1, 2012 to June 30, 2013, 3535 bachelor's degrees were awarded. The most popular majors were business/marketing (18%), social sciences (12%), and education (9%). 491 companies recruited on campus in 2012-2013. In an average class, 67% graduate in 5 years or less and 80% graduate in 6 years or less. Of the 2012 graduating class, 15% were enrolled in graduate school within 6 months of graduation, and 75% were employed.

Admissions Contact: Lou Hirsh, Director of Admissions. E-Mail: *admissions@udel.edu* Web: *http:/admissions.udel.edu/*

WESLEY COLLEGE B-3

Dover, DE 19901 (302) 736-2529; (800) 937-5398

Full-time: 657 men, 683 women	**Faculty:** n/av
Part-time: 130 men, 133 women	**Ph.D.s:** 75%
Graduate: 40 men, 91 women	**Student/Faculty:** n/av
Year: semesters, summer session	**Tuition:** $21,215
Application Deadline: open	**Room & Board:** $9940
Freshman Class: n/av	

LESS COMPETITIVE

Wesley College, founded in 1873, is a private liberal arts institution affiliated with the United Methodist Church. There are 4 graduate schools. In addition to regional accreditation, Wesley has baccalaureate program accreditation with NCATE and NLN. Computerized library services include interlibrary loans, database searching, and Internet access. The 26-acre campus is in a small town 75 miles south of Philadelphia. Including any residence halls, there are 20 buildings.

Student Life: 55% of undergraduates are from out of state, mostly the Middle Atlantic. Students are from 26 states, 4 foreign countries, and Canada. 85% are from public schools. 53% are White; 37% African American. 60% are Protestant; 22% Catholic; 17% claim no religious affiliation. The average age of freshmen is 18; all undergraduates, 20. 23% do not continue beyond their first year; 53% remain to graduate.

Housing: 778 students can be accommodated in college housing, which includes single-sex and coed dorms and on-campus apartments. In addition, there are honors houses. On-campus housing is guaranteed for all 4 years. 62% of students live on campus; of those, 30% remain on campus on weekends. Alcohol is not permitted. All students may keep cars.

Activities: 15% of men belong to 3 national fraternities; 15% of women belong to 3 local sororities. There are 30 groups on campus, including band, cheerleading, choir, chorale, chorus, communications, drama, ethnic, gay, honors, international, jazz band, literary magazine, newspaper, photography, political, professional, religious, social, social service, student government, and yearbook. Popular campus events include Family Day, International Fair and Spring Fling.

Sports: There are 8 intercollegiate sports for men and 8 for women, and 4 intramural sports for men and 4 for women. Facilities include a swimming pool, tennis courts, a football stadium, athletic fields, a gym, a game room, and an exercise room.

Disabled Students: 65% of the campus is accessible.

Services: Counseling and information services are available, as is tutoring in every subject. There is remedial math, reading, and writing.

Campus Safety and Security: Measures include 24-hour foot and vehicle patrol, emergency notification system, and security escort services. There are emergency telephones and lighted pathways/sidewalks.

Programs of Study: B.A.and B.S. degrees, associate and master's degrees are awarded. Bachelor's degrees are awarded in BIOLOGICAL SCIENCE (biology/biological science), BUSINESS (accounting, business administration and management, and sports management), COMMUNICATIONS AND THE ARTS (English, media arts, and music), COMPUTER AND PHYSICAL SCIENCE (mathematics), EDUCATION (elementary education and physical education), ENGINEERING AND ENVIRONMENTAL DESIGN (environmental science), HEALTH PROFESSIONS (exercise science, medical laboratory technology, and nursing), SOCIAL SCIENCE (American studies, history, international studies, legal studies, liberal arts/general studies, philosophy and religion, political science/

government, and psychology). Education, psychology, and business are strongest academically and have the largest enrollments.

Required: For graduation, students must complete 124 credit hours, with at least 15 hours in the major and a minimum GPA of 2.0. 50 hours of core courses including English, religion, science, math, American culture, non-American culture, and phys ed are required.

Special: Wesley offers internships in business and industry, environmental science, medical technology, and government agencies. Study abroad in 5 countries, work-study programs, dual majors, pass/fail options, and credit for life, military, and work experience are available. There are 2 national honor societies and 1 departmental honors programs.

Faculty/Classroom: 58% of faculty are male; 42% are female. All teach undergraduates, 3% do research, and 3% do both. No introductory courses are taught by graduate students. The average class size in an introductory lecture is 20; in a laboratory is 12; and in a regular course is 20.

Requirements: The SAT is required. Applicants must be graduates of an accredited secondary school; the GED is accepted. Students should complete 12 academic credits or 16 Carnegie units, including 4 units of English and 2 units each of math, history, science, and social studies. An interview is recommended. A GPA of 2.2 is required. AP and CLEP credits are accepted. Important factors in admissions decision are recommendations by school officials, extracurricular activities record, and leadership.

Procedure: Freshmen are admitted fall and winter. Entrance exams should be taken in the junior year. There are early decision, deferred admissions, and rolling admissions plans. Application deadlines are open. Application fee is $50.

Transfer: Applicants must have a minimum GPA of 2.0 and a minimum composite SAT score of 800. 36 of 124 credits required for the bachelor's degree must be completed at Wesley.

Visiting: There are regularly scheduled orientations for prospective students. There are guides for informal visits, visitors may sit in on classes, and stay overnight. To schedule a visit, contact the Office of Admissions.

Financial Aid: The FAFSA, SFS, and the college's own financial statement are required. Check with the school for current application deadlines.

International Students: The school actively recruits these students. They must take the TOEFL. They must also take the SAT.

Graduates: In a recent year, 272 bachelor's degrees were awarded. The most popular majors were business administration (41%), nursing (16%), and psychology (5%).

Admissions Contact: Howard Ballentine, Dean of Enrollment Management. E-Mail: *howard.ballentine@wesley.edu* Web: *www.wesley.edu*

WILMINGTON UNIVERSITY — B-1

New Castle, DE 19720 — **877-967-5464**

Full-time: 2017 men, 3188 women	**Faculty:** n/av
Part-time: 833 men, 2077 women	**Ph.D.s:** 55%
Graduate: 1378 men, 2973 women	**Student/Faculty:** n/av
Year: semesters, summer session	**Tuition:** $7778
Application Deadline:	**Room & Board:** n/app
Freshman Class: n/av	

NON COMPETITIVE

Wilmington University is a private, university that offers both undergraduate and graduate degree programs in a wide range of career areas. The University began with a charter class of 194 students in 1968 and now enrolls a diverse student body numbering more than 17,000 annually. There are 6 undergraduate schools and 6 graduate schools. In addition to regional accreditation, Wilmington has baccalaureate program accreditation with NASDTEC and NCATE. Computerized library services include interlibrary loans, database searching, and Internet access. Special learning facilities include a radio station and TV station. The 18-acre campus is in an urban area New Castle Site: 7 miles south of Wilmington. Including any residence halls, there are 9 buildings.

Student Life: 73% of undergraduates are from Delaware. Others are from 44 states, 21 foreign countries, and Canada. 85% are from public schools. 45% are White; 12% African American. The average age of freshmen is 25; all undergraduates, 33. 36% do not continue beyond their first year; 34% remain to graduate.

Housing: The college provides a list of housing accommodations in the community and makes recommendations for off-campus apartments. Alcohol is not permitted. All students commute. All students may keep cars.

Activities: There are no fraternities or sororities. There are 11 groups on campus, including behavioral science division club, criminal justice club, cheerleading, film, honors, International reading association, newspaper, photography, radio and TV, student government, and yearbook.

Sports: There are 4 intercollegiate sports for men and 5 for women. Facilities include a 20,000 square foot sports complex. Home of the men's and women's basketball, women's lacrosse, men's and women's soccer, and volleyball teams.

Disabled Students: All of the campus is accessible.

Services: Counseling and information services are available, as is tutoring in most subjects. There is remedial math, reading, and writing.

Campus Safety and Security: Measures include 24-hour foot and vehicle patrol, emergency notification system, and security escort services. There are emergency telephones and lighted pathways/sidewalks.

Programs of Study: Wilmington confers B.A., B.S. and B.S.N. degrees. Associate, master's, and doctoral degrees are also awarded. Bachelor's degrees are awarded in BUSINESS (accounting, banking and finance, business administration and management, personnel management, and sports management), COMMUNICATIONS AND THE ARTS (communications technology, media arts, multimedia, and video), EDUCATION (early childhood education and elementary education), ENGINEERING AND ENVIRONMENTAL DESIGN (aeronautical science and aviation administration/management), HEALTH PROFESSIONS (nursing), SOCIAL SCIENCE (behavioral science and criminal justice). Nursing and education are the strongest academically. Business, social/behavioral sciences and nursing have the largest enrollments.

Required: To graduate, students must complete a total of 120 hours with a minimum GPA of 2.0. 54 hours are required in the major. The 36-hour general studies core requirement includes 12 hours of social science, 9 each of English and humanities, and 3 each of math and science. At least 45 credit hours of upper-division course work are required, as is demonstrated competence in verbal and written communication and computational skills. At least 3 credits must be taken in computer operations. Nursing students must also submit official transcripts verifying graduation from a diploma or associate degree nursing program. Candidates for the B.S.N. degree must possess an R.N. license.

Special: The school offers practicums for education students, co-op programs, work-study programs with area employers, internships, a general studies degree, an accelerated degree program, dual majors, pass/fail options, credit for life experience, and by-challenge exam. There are 1 national honor societies and 2 departmental honors programs.

Faculty/Classroom: 70% of faculty are male; 30% are female. 66% teach undergraduates. No introductory courses are taught by graduate students. The average class size in an introductory lecture is 25; in a laboratory is 10; and in a regular course is 17.

Requirements: Graduation from an accredited secondary school or satisfactory scores on the GED are required for admission. An interview may be required of some students, and an essay is recommended. A GPA of 2.0 is required. AP and CLEP credits are accepted.

Procedure: Freshmen are admitted to all sessions. There are deferred admissions and rolling admissions plans. Application deadlines are open. Application fee is $25.

Transfer: 3013 transfer students enrolled in 2012-2013. Applicants must have a 2.0 GPA; those with lower GPA must have an interview. Applicants may be required to submit SAT I or ACT scores. Those with fewer than 15 semester credits must submit high school transcripts. No more than 75 semester credits will be accepted for transfer credit. 45 of 120 credits for Bachelor's degree must be completed at Wilmington.

Visiting: There are guides for informal visits and visitors may sit in on classes. To schedule a visit, contact the Admissions Office.

Financial Aid: In 2013-2014, 60% of all full-time freshmen received some form of financial aid. 50% of all full-time freshmen received need-based aid. The FAFSA is required.

International Students: They must take the TOEFL, or they may submit a transcript of successful completion of at least 12 credit hours from a U.S. institution of higher education.

Graduates: From July 1, 2012 to June 30, 2013, 1547 bachelor's degrees were awarded. The most popular majors were business management (13%), behavioral science (12%), and nursing (12%). In an average class, 34% graduate in 6 years or less.

Admissions Contact: Laura Morris, Director of Admissions. E-Mail: *infocenter@wilmu.edu* Web: *www.wilmu.edu/admission*

DISTRICT OF COLUMBIA

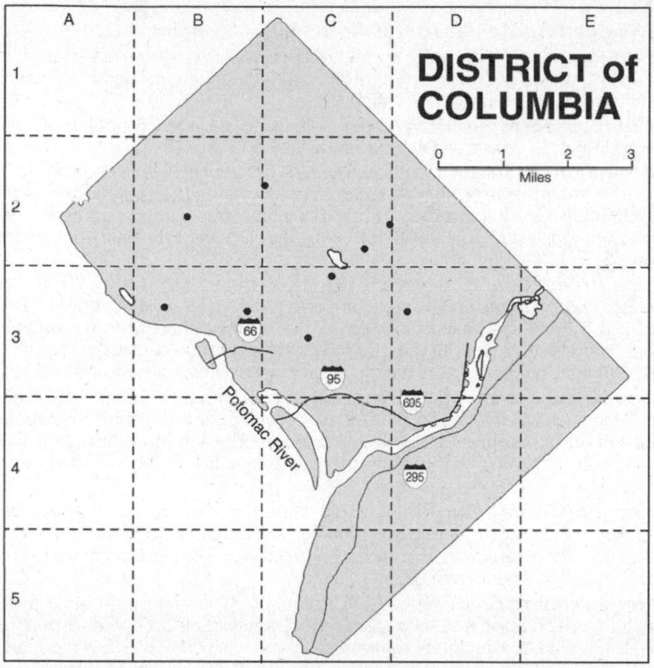

AMERICAN UNIVERSITY A-2

Washington, DC 20016 **(202) 885-6000; (202) 885-1025**

Full-time: 2715 men, 4271 women	**Faculty:** n/av; I, av$
Part-time: 171 men, 184 women	**Ph.D.s:** n/av
Graduate: 2156 men, 3322 women	**Student/Faculty:** n/av
Year: semesters, summer session	**Tuition:** $40,649
Application Deadline: January 15	**Room & Board:** $14,180

Freshman Class: 17545 applied, 7565 accepted, 1627 enrolled

SAT CR/M/W: 640/620/630 **ACT:** 28 **HIGHLY COMPETITIVE+**

American University is a private doctoral institution situated in a residential neighborhood of northwest Washington, D.C. There are 6 undergraduate schools and 6 graduate schools. In addition to regional accreditation, AU has baccalaureate program accreditation with AACSB, ACEJMC, NASDTEC, NASM, and NCATE. Computerized library services include interlibrary loans, database searching, Internet access, and Wi-Fi capability. Special learning facilities include an art gallery, radio station, TV station, American University's Washington College of Law Library, a state-of-the-art language resource center, multimedia design and development labs, science and computer science labs, and well-equipped buildings for art and the performing arts, National Public Radio station (WAMU 88.5FM). The 84-acre campus is in a suburban area 5 miles northwest of downtown Washington D.C. Including any residence halls, there are 53 buildings.

Student Life: 81% of undergraduates are from out of state, mostly the Middle Atlantic. Students are from 50 states, 112 foreign countries, and Canada. 55% are White. The average age of freshmen is 18; all undergraduates, 20. 12% do not continue beyond their first year; 80% remain to graduate.

Housing: 4000 students can be accommodated in college housing, which includes coed dorms and off-campus apartments. In addition, there are honors houses, special-interest houses, international-intercultural hall, honors hall, living learning community halls and floors, housing for students with disabilities handled on an individual basis. On-campus housing is guaranteed for the freshman year only, is available on a first-come, and first-served basis. Alcohol is not permitted. Upperclassmen may keep cars.

Activities: 21% of men belong to 15 national fraternities; 19% of women belong to 11 national sororities. There are 200 groups on campus, including art, band, cheerleading, chess, choir, chorale, chorus, computers, dance, debate, drama, environmental, ethnic, film, gay, honors, international, jazz band, literary magazine, musical theater, newspaper, opera, orchestra, pep band, photography, political, professional, radio and TV, religious, social, social service, student government, symphony, various athletic clubs, and yearbook. Popular campus events include Family Weekend, Founders Day Ball and Campus Beautification Day.

Sports: There are 6 intercollegiate sports for men and 8 for women. Facilities include a 6,000-seat sports arena, main fitness center, 2 swimming pools, hockey and soccer fields, a softball diamond, an all-purpose field, cardiovascular and strength training equipment, weight rooms, courts for tennis, basketball, and volleyball, an aerobics studio, an indoor jogging track, an outdoor 6-lane tartan track, and fitness centers within residence halls.

Disabled Students: 95% of the campus is accessible.

Services: Counseling and information services are available, as is tutoring in every subject. There is a reader service for the blind, and remedial math, reading, and writing. the Academic Support and Access Center is avaiable to help students develop the tools needed for college success. In addition, a math and statistics tutoring lab, a writing center, and a foreign language resource center are available.

Campus Safety and Security: Measures include 24-hour foot and vehicle patrol, emergency notification system, self-defense education, and security escort services. There are shuttle buses, emergency telephones, lighted pathways/sidewalks, controlled access to dorms/residences, crime prevention programs, building alarms, video surveillance, posted crime alerts, online annual crime reports, escorts, laptop security protocols, RAD courses, emergency preparedness protocols and alerting system.

Programs of Study: AU confers B.A., B.F.A., B.S. and B.S.B.A. degrees. Associate, master's, and doctoral degrees are also awarded. Bachelor's degrees are awarded in AGRICULTURE (environmental studies), BIOLOGICAL SCIENCE (biochemistry and biology/biological science), BUSINESS (business administration and management, international business management, nonprofit/public organization management, and sustainable management), COMMUNICATIONS AND THE ARTS (American literature, Arabic, art history and appreciation, audio technology, Chinese, communication, communications, creative writing, dramatic arts, film arts, fine arts, French, German, graphic design, Hebrew, Italian, Japanese, journalism, Korean, literature, multimedia, music, musical theater, performing arts, public relations, Russian, Spanish, strategic communication, and studio art), COMPUTER AND PHYSICAL SCIENCE (applied mathematics, chemistry, computer science, mathematics, physics, and statistics), EDUCATION (early childhood education, elementary education, foreign languages education, and secondary education), ENGINEERING AND ENVIRONMENTAL DESIGN (environmental science), HEALTH PROFESSIONS (health science and public health), SOCIAL SCIENCE (American studies, anthropology, area studies, clinical psychology, criminal justice, economics, government, French studies, gender studies, German area studies, history, interdisciplinary studies, international studies, Judaic studies, Latin American studies, law, philosophy, political science/government, psychology, Russian and Slavic studies, sociology, Spanish studies, and women's studies). International studies, business administration and political science have the largest enrollments.

Required: To graduate, students must complete 120 credit hours with a minimum GPA of 2.0. In addition, students must complete 31 credit hours of general education requirements in 5 curricular areas and fulfill the school's competency requirements in English composition and mathematics by either passing an exam or taking a course in each area. Please see program specific websites for additional requirements.

Special: AU offers co-op programs and internships in all majors, over 155 distinct study abroad programs in more than 45 countries, and the Washington Semester and Gateway programs. Work-study is available on campus and with local community service agencies. Dual majors, interdisciplinary programs, student-designed majors, 3-year B.A. degree programs, 3-2 engineering degrees, and B.A./B.S.degrees are also available. Combined bachelor's/master's programs are available in most majors. Cross-registration may be arranged through the Consortium of Universities of the Washington Metropolitan Area. Credit for life experience, nondegree study, and pass/fail options are available. There are preprofessional programs in engineering, law, and medicine (the medical program is aimed at strengthening credentials for applying to programs in medicine, dentistry, optometry, podiatry, oral survey, veterinary medicine, and public health). There are 12 national honor societies, including Phi Beta Kappa, and a freshman honors program.

Faculty/Classroom: No introductory courses are taught by graduate students.

Admissions: 43% of the 2013-2014 applicants were accepted. The SAT scores for the 2013-2014 freshman class were: Critical Reading--3% below 500, 23% between 500 and 599, 50% between 600 and 699, and 24% between 700 and 800; Math--4% below 500, 33% between 500 and 599, 51% between 600 and 699, and 12% between 700 and 800; Writing--3% below 500, 27% between 500 and 599, 52% between 600 and 699, and 18% between 700 and 800. The ACT scores were 1% below 21, 7% between 21 and 23, 22% between 24 and 26, 24% between 27 and 28, and 46% above 28.

Requirements: The SAT or ACT is required. Students must have graduated from an accredited secondary school with at least 16 Carnegie units, including at least 4 units in English, 3 units in college preparatory math (including the equivalent of 2 units in algebra), 3 units in science, 2 units in social sciences, and 2 units in foreign language(s). Applicants who have satisfactory scores on the GED may also apply. All students must submit an essay and 2 letters of recommendation. American University (AU) is continuing its test-optional pilot program for the 2014 fall semester. This program is open to all applicants (Early Decision and Regular Decision) for fall 2014. A GPA of 2.0 is required. AP and CLEP credits are accepted. Important factors in the admissions decision are advanced placement or honors courses, recommendations by school officials, and extracurricular activities record.

Procedure: Freshmen are admitted to all sessions. Entrance exams should be taken in the spring of the junior year or the fall of the senior year. There are early decision and deferred admissions plans. Early decision applications should be filed by November 15; regular applications, by January 15 for fall entry; December 1 for spring entry; and April 1 for summer entry, along with a $70 fee. Notification of early decision is sent December 31; regular decision, April 1. 650 early decision candidates were accepted for the 2013-2014 class. 1465 applicants were on the 2013 waiting list; 64 were admitted. Applications are accepted online.

Transfer: 317 transfer students enrolled in 2012-2013. Transfer applicants who wish to be considered competitive candidates should have a cumulative GPA of at least 2.5 from all schools attended. All applicants with a cumulative GPA of 2.0 or above will be considered. 45 of 120 credits required for the bachelor's degree must be completed at AU.

Visiting: There are regularly scheduled orientations for prospective students, including student-led daily tours and information sessions, open houses, and overnight programs. There are guides for informal visits, visitors may sit in on classes, and stay overnight. To schedule a visit, contact the Admissions Office Tours and Infromation Program at admissions@american.edu.

Financial Aid: In 2013-2014, 82% of all full-time freshmen and 68% of continuing full-time students received some form of financial aid. 71% of all full-time freshmen and 85% of continuing full-time students received need-based aid. The average freshman award was $27,900. Need-based scholarships or need-based grants averaged $26,081; need-based self-help aid (loans and jobs) averaged $4,858; non-need-based athletic scholarships averaged $33,328; and other non-need-based awards and non-need-based scholarships averaged $13,503. The FAFSA and the college's own financial statement are required. The deadline for filing freshman financial aid applications for fall entry is February 15.

International Students: There are 588 international students enrolled. The school actively recruits these students. They must take the TOEFL with a minimum score of 550 on the paper-based TOEFL (PBT) or 80 on the Internet-based version (iBT) and the college's own test, May also take the IELTS Composite with a score 6.5 or higher, or the Pearson Test of English with score 53 or higher.

Graduates: From July 1, 2012 to June 30, 2013, 1776 bachelor's degrees were awarded. The most popular majors were international studies (25%), business administration (15%), and political science (9%). In an average class, 5% graduate in 3 years or less, 76% graduate in 4 years or less, 79% graduate in 5 years or less, and 80% graduate in 6 years or less.

Admissions Contact: Greg Grauman, Asst Vice Provost. E-Mail: *admissions@american.edu* Web: *www.american.edu*

CORCORAN COLLEGE OF ART AND DESIGN — C-3

Washington, DC 20006 — (202) 639-1814; (888) CORCORAN; (202) 639-1830

Full-time: 130 men, 225 women	**Faculty:** n/av
Part-time: 25 men, 40 women	**Ph.D.s:** n/av
Graduate: 25 men, 75 women	**Student/Faculty:** n/av
Year: semesters, summer session	**Tuition:** $26,000
Application Deadline: open	**Room & Board:** $11,500
Freshman Class: n/av	
SAT or ACT: required	

SPECIAL

Established in 1890, the Corcoran College of Art and Design is a private professional art college offering undergraduate programs in fine art, design, and photography. There is 1 graduate school. In addition to regional accreditation, Corcoran has baccalaureate program accreditation with NASAD. Computerized library services include interlibrary loans, Internet access, and laptop Internet portals. Special learning facilities include a learning resource center and art gallery. The 7-acre campus is in an urban area in Washington, D.C. Including any residence halls, there are 3 buildings.

Student Life: 73% of undergraduates are from out of state, mostly the Middle Atlantic. Students are from 24 states, 32 foreign countries, and Canada. 75% are from public schools. 64% are white; 21% foreign nationals. The average age of freshmen is 18; all undergraduates, 22. 3% do not continue beyond their first year; 60% remain to graduate.

Housing: 110 students can be accommodated in college housing, which includes coed off-campus apartments. On-campus housing is guaranteed for the freshman year only, is available on a first-come, and first-served basis. 73% of students commute. Alcohol is not permitted. No cars.

Activities: There are no fraternities or sororities. There are 4 groups on campus, including art, literary magazine, newspaper, and student government.

Sports: There is no sports program at Corcoran.

Disabled Students: 70% of the campus is accessible.

Services: Counseling and information services are available, as is tutoring in most subjects, art history, writing, humanities, and general academic subjects. There is remedial writing.

Campus Safety and Security: Measures include 24-hour foot and vehicle patrol. There are lighted pathways/sidewalks.

Programs of Study: Corcoran confers B.F.A. degrees. Associate and master's degrees are also awarded. Bachelor's degrees are awarded in COMMUNICATIONS AND THE ARTS (fine arts, graphic design, and photography), EDUCATION (art education). Fine arts has the largest enrollment.

Required: Students must complete 126 credits, with 65 to 70 in the major and 23 in the core curriculum, and must maintain a minimum GPA of 2.0. Course distribution involves the disciplines of art history, humanities, liberal arts, and writing. Required curricula include courses in drawing, design, idea resources, and media. Seniors must present thesis exhibitions.

Special: Cooperative programs are permitted with the ACE and AICA art college consortiums. Opportunities are provided for internships in graphic design and photography, credit by exam, work-study programs with the Corcoran gallery of art, and nondegree study. B.F.A.-M.A.T. degree is offered.

Faculty/Classroom: 45% of faculty are male; 55% are female. All teach undergraduates. No introductory courses are taught by graduate students. The average class size in an introductory lecture is 23; in a laboratory is 10; and in a regular course is 10.

Requirements: The SAT or ACT is required. Applicants must have graduated from an approved secondary school; the GED is accepted. A portfolio is required, and an interview is recommended. A GPA of 2.5 is required. AP and CLEP credits are accepted. Important factors in the admissions decision are evidence of special talent, personality/intangible qualities, and advanced placement or honors courses.

Procedure: Freshmen are admitted fall and spring. Entrance exams should be taken prior to January 30 of the senior year. There are deferred admissions and rolling admissions plans. Application deadlines are open. The fall 2011 application fee was $40. Applications are accepted online.

Transfer: A review of studio art transcripts is considered for the level of entry of transfer students. A portfolio review is the final determining factor. 48 of 126 credits required for the bachelor's degree must be completed at Corcoran.

Visiting: There are regularly scheduled orientations for prospective students, including an introduction to staff, faculty, and the city and an overview of activities and housing. There are guides for informal visits and visitors may sit in on classes. To schedule a visit, contact the Admissions Department.

Financial Aid: Corcoran is a member of CSS. The FAFSA and the college's own financial statement are required. Check with the school for current application deadlines.

International Students: The school actively recruits these students. They must take the TOEFL. They must also take the SAT or ACT.

Computers: Wireless access is available. All students may access the system. There are no fees. Students enrolled in Graphic Design (sophomore year) must have a personal computer.

Admissions Contact: Elizabeth S. Paladino, Director of Admissions. E-Mail: *admissions@corcoran.org* Web: *www.corcoran.edu*

GALLAUDET UNIVERSITY — D-3

Washington, DC 20002 — (202) 651-5750; (800) 995-0550; (202) 651-5744

Full-time: 467 men, 539 women	**Faculty:** n/av; IIA, +$
Part-time: 33 men, 38 women	**Ph.D.s:** n/av
Graduate: 122 men, 362 women	**Student/Faculty:** n/av
Year: semesters, summer session	**Tuition:** $13,800
Application Deadline: open	**Room & Board:** $11,580
Freshman Class: 521 applied, 341 accepted, 201 enrolled	

SPECIAL

Gallaudet University, founded in 1864 as a university designed exclusively for deaf and hard-of-hearing students. There are 2 undergraduate schools and 2 graduate schools. In addition to regional accreditation, Gallaudet has baccalaureate program accreditation with ACBSP, CSWE, and NCATE. Computerized library services include interlibrary loans, database searching, and Internet access. Special learning facilities include an art gallery and TV station. The 99-acre campus is in an urban area in Washington, D.C. Including any residence halls, there are 35 buildings.

Student Life: 97% of undergraduates are from out of state, mostly the Middle Atlantic. Students are from 49 states, 19 foreign countries, and Canada. 60% are White; 14% Hispanic; 11% African American. The average age of freshmen is 19; all undergraduates, 23. 23% do not continue beyond their first year; 47% remain to graduate.

Housing: 1169 students can be accommodated in college housing, which includes single-sex and coed dorms, on-campus apartments, and married student housing. In addition, there are special-interest houses. On-campus housing is guaranteed for the freshman year only, is available on a first-come, and first-served basis. 75% of students live on campus. Alcohol is not permitted. All students may keep cars.

Activities: There are 28 groups on campus, including art, cheerleading, computers, dance, drama, ethnic, gay, honors, international, literary magazine, newspaper, political, religious, social, social service, student government, and yearbook. Popular campus events include Rockfest.

Sports: There are 6 intercollegiate sports for men and 7 for women, and 6 intramural sports for men and 6 for women. Facilities include field house, football field, baseball field, softball field, swimming pool, track, fitness complex, athletic training room, and team meeting rooms.

Disabled Students: All of the campus is accessible.

Services: Counseling and information services are available, as is tutoring in every subject, throughout the tutorial, English, and writing centers. There is remedial math, reading, and writing.

Campus Safety and Security: Measures include 24-hour foot and vehicle patrol, emergency notification system, self-defense education, and security escort services. There are shuttle buses, emergency telephones, and lighted pathways/sidewalks.

Programs of Study: Gallaudet confers B.A., and B.S. degrees. Master's and doctoral degrees are also awarded. Bachelor's degrees are awarded in BIOLOGICAL SCIENCE (biology/biological science), BUSINESS (accounting, business administration and management, and recreation and leisure services), COMMUNICATIONS AND THE ARTS (American Sign Language, art history and appreciation, communications, English, graphic design, photography, Spanish, studio art, and theatre arts), COMPUTER AND PHYSICAL SCIENCE (chemistry, computer science, digital arts/technology, information sciences and systems, and mathematics), EDUCATION (early childhood education, elementary education, physical education, and secondary education), SOCIAL SCIENCE (child care/child and family studies, economics, family/consumer studies, history, international studies, interpreter for the deaf, liberal arts/general studies, philosophy, political science/government, psychology, social work, and sociology). Interpretation, business administration, communication studies, physical education, and social work are the largest.

Required: The general studies program requires students to take 40 credits in general studies courses. All courses in the new curriculum emphasize skill development in critical thinking, language, and communication. These abilities are the heart of every course students take. The General Studies curriculum includes three components: Freshman Foundation courses (4 courses, total 12 credits) Integrated courses (6 courses, total 24 credits) Capstone Experience (1 course, total 4 credits)

Special: Honors program, first year study tour, study abroad programs, and self-directed majors There are 5 national honor societies, a freshman honors program, and 5 departmental honors programs.

Admissions: 65% of the 2013-2014 applicants were accepted.

Requirements: Applicants must submit a recent audiogram. SAT or ACT scores may be submitted. High school transcripts, letters of recommendation, and writing samples are required. The GED is accepted. AP and CLEP credits are accepted. Important factors in the admissions decision are advanced placement or honors courses, recommendations by school officials, and leadership record.

Procedure: Freshmen are admitted fall and spring. Entrance exams should be taken in October or November of the senior year. There are deferred admissions and rolling admissions plans. Application deadlines are open. Application fee is $50.

Transfer: 85 transfer students enrolled in 2012-2013. Deaf and hard-of-hearing transfer applicants must submit a recent audiogram, official college transcripts from all schools attended, and at least 2 letters of recommendation. Students should have completed 12 or more credit hours with at least a 2.0 GPA; those who do not meet these requirements must submit recent SAT or ACT scores and a final high school transcript.

Visiting: There are regularly scheduled orientations for prospective students, including a continential breakfast, tour of campus, academic fair, student panel, student/parent connections (infomation sessions), and lunch with faculty and students classroom observations, and interviews with selected offices and programs. There are guides for informal visits, visitors may sit in on classes, and stay overnight. To schedule a visit, contact the Gallaudet University Visitor's Coordinator at (202) 651-5750.

Financial Aid: In 2013-2014, 80% of all full-time freshmen and 23% of continuing full-time students received some form of financial aid. 80% of all full-time freshmen and 79% of continuing full-time students received need-based aid. The average freshman award was $18,747. Need-based scholarships or need-based grants averaged $17,643; and need-based self-help aid (loans and jobs) averaged $2,909. The FAFSA and the college's own financial statement are required. The priority date for freshman financial aid applications for fall entry is July 1.

International Students: There are 75 international students enrolled. They must take the TOEFL. They must also take the SAT or ACT, and the college's own entrance exam.

Graduates: From July 1, 2012 to June 30, 2013, 240 bachelor's degrees were awarded. The most popular majors were foreign languages, literatures, and linguistics (10%), business/marketing (9%), and visual and performing arts (9%). In an average class, 10% graduate in 4 years or less, 41% graduate in 5 years or less, and 47% graduate in 6 years or less.

Admissions Contact: Charity Reedy-Hines, Chief Enrollment Management Officer. E-Mail: *admissions.office@gallaudet.edu* Web: *admissions.gallaudet.edu*

GEORGE WASHINGTON UNIVERSITY B-3

Washington, DC 20052 (202) 994-6040
(800) 447-3765; (202) 994-0325

Full-time: 4215 men, 5533 women	**Faculty:** n/av; I, +$
Part-time: 343 men, 352 women	**Ph.D.s:** n/av
Graduate: 6521 men, 8296 women	**Student/Faculty:** 13 to 1
Year: semesters, summer session	**Tuition:** $44,648
Application Deadline:	**Room & Board:** $13,460
Freshman Class: n/av	
SAT or ACT: required	

MOST COMPETITIVE

George Washington University, founded in 1821, is a private institution providing degree programs. There are 7 undergraduate schools and 10 graduate schools. In addition to regional accreditation, GW has baccalaureate program accreditation with AACSB, ABET, CAHEA, CSAB, NASAD, NASM, and NCATE. Computerized library services include interlibrary loans and database searching. Special learning facilities include an art gallery, radio station, and TV station. The 37-acre campus is in an urban area 3 blocks west of the White House. Including any residence halls, there are 123 buildings.

Student Life: 98% of undergraduates are from out of state, mostly the Middle Atlantic. Students are from 50 states, 137 foreign countries, and Canada. 70% are from public schools. 65% are White. The average age of freshmen is 18; all undergraduates, 20. 7% do not continue beyond their first year; 81% remain to graduate.

Housing: 8245 students can be accommodated in college housing, which includes coed dorms and on-campus apartments. In addition, there are special-interest houses, fraternity houses, sorority houses, and sorority floors. On-campus housing is available on a lottery system for upperclassmen. 70% of students live on campus. All students may keep cars.

Activities: 23% of men belong to 11 national fraternities; 23% of women belong to 7 national sororities. There are 257 groups on campus, including and folk life, art, band, cheerleading, chess, choir, chorale, chorus, computers, dance, debate, drama, ethnic, film, forensics, gay, geology, honors, international, jazz band, literary magazine, marching band, musical theater, newspaper, opera, orchestra, pep band, photography, political, professional, radio and TV, religious, social, social service, and student government. Popular campus events include Spring Fling, Fall Fest and a yearly Benefit Auction.

Sports: There are 9 intercollegiate sports for men and 8 for women, and 16 intramural sports for men and 16 for women. Facilities include a 5000-seat gym with 2 auxiliary gyms, an AAU swimming pool, weight rooms, a jogging track, squash and racquetball courts, and soccer and baseball fields.

Disabled Students: 95% of the campus is accessible.

Services: Counseling and information services are available, as is tutoring in every subject. There is a reader service for the blind.

Campus Safety and Security: Measures include 24-hour foot and vehicle patrol, self-defense education, and security escort services. There are emergency telephones, lighted pathways/sidewalks, a bike patrol.

Programs of Study: GW confers B.A., B.S., B.Accy., B.B.A., B.Mus., B.S.C.E., B.S.C.Eng., B.S.C.S., B.S.E.E., B.S.H.S., B.S.M.E. and B.S.S.A. degrees. Associate, master's, and doctoral degrees are also awarded. Bachelor's degrees are awarded in BIOLOGICAL SCIENCE (biology/biological science), BUSINESS (accounting, banking and finance, business administration and management, business economics, human resources, international business management, marketing management, and tourism), COMMUNICATIONS AND THE ARTS (art history and appreciation, broadcasting, Chinese, classics, communications, dance, dramatic arts, English, fine arts, French, German, Japanese, journalism, literature, multimedia, music, music performance, public relations, Russian, and Spanish), COMPUTER AND PHYSICAL SCIENCE (applied mathematics, chemistry, computer science, geology, information sciences and systems, mathematics, physics, statistics, and systems analysis), ENGINEERING AND ENVIRONMENTAL DESIGN (civil engineering, computer engineering, electrical/electronics engineering, engineering, environmental science, and mechanical engineering), HEALTH PROFESSIONS (clinical science, emergency medical technologies, medical laboratory technology, nuclear medical technology, physician's assistant, premedicine, radiological science, and speech pathology/audiology), SOCIAL SCIENCE (American studies, anthropology, archeology, criminal justice, East Asian studies, economics, European studies, geography, history, human services, humanities, interdisciplinary studies, international relations,

Judaic studies, Latin American studies, liberal arts/general studies, Middle Eastern studies, philosophy, physical fitness/movement, political science/government, psychology, religion, and sociology). Political communication, international affairs, and biological sciences are the strongest academically. Psychology, and political science have the largest enrollments.

Required: Students must complete 120 semester hours with a minimum GPA of 2.0 for most majors. Arts and sciences majors must meet general curriculum requirements that include literacy, quantitative and logical reasoning, natural sciences, social and behavioral sciences, creative and performing arts, literature, Western civilization, and foreign languages or culture. Other requirements vary with divisions of the university.

Special: Cross-registration is available through the Consortium of Colleges and Universities. There are co-op programs in education, business, engineering, arts and sciences, and international affairs and internships in the Washington metropolitan area. Study abroad in locations throughout the world, work-study programs, dual majors, student-designed majors, and a 3-2 engineering degree program with 8 colleges are also available. Nondegree study, a general studies degree, credit by exam, and pass/fail options are possible. There are 12 national honor societies, including Phi Beta Kappa, a freshman honors program, and 21 departmental honors programs.

Faculty/Classroom: 61% of faculty are male; 39% are female. No introductory courses are taught by graduate students.

Requirements: The SAT or ACT is required. Students must have successfully completed a strong academic program in high school. SAT: Subject tests are strongly recommended. An essay, 1 teacher recommendation, and 1 counselor recommendation are required. An interview is encouraged. AP and CLEP credits are accepted. Important factors in the admissions decision are advanced placement or honors courses, recommendations by school officials, and leadership record.

Procedure: Freshmen are admitted to all sessions. Entrance exams should be taken in the junior year and the fall semester of the senior year. There are early decision and deferred admissions plans. Check with the school for current application deadlines. The fall 2013 application fee was $60. Applications are accepted online.

Transfer: In addition to a record of high grades and exam scores, applicants must submit official transcripts of all postsecondary work. Minimum GPA requirements vary from 2.5 to 3.0, depending on the major. The SAT or ACT is required, and an interview is encouraged. 30 of 120 credits required for the bachelor's degree must be completed at GW.

Visiting: There are regularly scheduled orientations for prospective students, including group information sessions and campus tours. Class visitation, lunch with current students, and other activities can be arranged, if requested in advance. There are guides for informal visits, visitors may sit in on classes, and stay overnight. To schedule a visit, contact the University Visitor Center at (202) 994-6602.

Financial Aid: GW is a member of CSS. The CSS/Profile and FAFSA are required. Check with the school for current application deadlines.

International Students: The school actively recruits these students. They must take the TOEFL and the college's own test. They must also take the SAT or ACT.

Admissions Contact: Dr. Kathryn M. Napper, Executive Dean for Admissions. E-Mail: *gwadm@gwu.edu* Web: *www.gwu.edu*

GEORGETOWN UNIVERSITY — B-3

Washington, DC 20057 — **(202) 687-3600; (202) 687-5084**

Full-time: 3212 men, 4030 women	**Faculty:** n/av; I, +$
Part-time: 142 men, 168 women	**Ph.D.s:** 74%
Graduate: 4798 men, 5007 women	**Student/Faculty:** 12 to 1
Year: semesters, summer session	**Tuition:** $41,893
Application Deadline: January 10	**Room & Board:** $13,017

Freshman Class: 20115 applied, 3413 accepted, 1570 enrolled

SAT or ACT: required

MOST COMPETITIVE

Georgetown University, founded in 1789, is a private institution affiliated with the Roman Catholic Church and offers programs in arts and sciences, business administration, foreign service, languages and linguistics, and nursing. There are 4 undergraduate schools and 3 graduate schools. In addition to regional accreditation, Georgetown has baccalaureate program accreditation with AACSB. Computerized library services include interlibrary loans, database searching, Internet access, and Wi-Fi capability. Special learning facilities include an art gallery, planetarium, radio station, and TV station. The 104-acre campus is in an urban area 1.5 miles northwest of downtown Washington D.C. Including any residence halls, there are 64 buildings.

Student Life: 96% of undergraduates are from out of state, mostly the Middle Atlantic. Students are from 50 states, 91 foreign countries, and Canada. 46% are from public schools. 60% are White; 11% Foreign. 42% are Catholic; 21% Protestant. The average age of freshmen is 18; all undergraduates, 21. 4% do not continue beyond their first year; 94% remain to graduate.

Housing: 5053 students can be accommodated in college housing, which includes coed dorms and on-campus apartments. Special interest floors are available in some residence halls. On-campus housing is available on a lottery system for upperclassmen. 63% of students live on campus. No one may keep cars.

Activities: There are no fraternities or sororities. There are 171 groups on campus, including art, band, cheerleading, chess, choir, chorale, chorus, computers, dance, debate, drama, ethnic, film, gay, honors, international, jazz band, literary magazine, musical theater, newspaper, orchestra, pep band, photography, political, professional, radio and TV, religious, social, social service, student government, and symphony. Popular campus events include GU Day, Career Week and Senior Salute.

Sports: There are 11 intercollegiate sports for men and 12 for women. Facilities include a 5,000-seat gym for basketball and volleyball, along with sports medicine and training room facilities, a 2,500-seat multi-sport field for football and lacrosse, and a 4-level sports and recreation faciltity that houses a swimming pool, basketball courts, aerobics rooms, a weight area, cardiovascular equipment, a wellness center, locker rooms, and racquetball courts.

Disabled Students: 94% of the campus is accessible.

Services: Counseling and information services are available, as is tutoring in some subjects, accounting, finance, biological sciences, math, Spanish, French and Arabic There is a reader service for the blind.

Campus Safety and Security: Measures include 24-hour foot and vehicle patrol, emergency notification system, and security escort services. There are shuttle buses, emergency telephones, lighted pathways/sidewalks, controlled access to dorms/residences, laptop computer registration, bicycle registration, and off-campus security assesments.

Programs of Study: Georgetown confers A.B., B.S., B.A.L.S., B.S.B.A., B.S.F.S. and B.S.N. degrees. Master's and doctoral degrees are also awarded. Bachelor's degrees are awarded in BIOLOGICAL SCIENCE (biochemistry, biology/biological science, and environmental biology), BUSINESS (accounting, banking and finance, business administration and management, finance, international business management, and marketing/retailing/merchandising), COMMUNICATIONS AND THE ARTS (Arabic, art history, art, Chinese, classics, comparative literature, English, fine arts, French, German, Italian, Japanese, linguistics, Portuguese, Russian, and Spanish), COMPUTER AND PHYSICAL SCIENCE (chemistry, computer science, mathematics, and physics), HEALTH PROFESSIONS (health and nursing), SOCIAL SCIENCE (American studies, anthropology, economics, history, interdisciplinary studies, international relations, philosophy, political science/government, psychology, religion, and sociology). International politics, government, and international politics have the largest enrollments.

Required: Students must complete 120 credits and maintain a minimum GPA of 2.0. A core of liberal arts courses is required, consisting of 2 courses each in philosophy and theology. Additional requirements are specific to undergraduate school as well as major concentration.

Special: Cross-registration is available with a consortium of universities in the Washington metropolitan area. Opportunities are provided for internships, study abroad in 30 countries, work-study programs, student-designed majors, and dual majors. A liberal studies degree, B.A. and B.S. degrees, non-degree study, credit by examination, and pass/fail options are also offered.

Faculty/Classroom: 62% of faculty are male; 38% are female. All teach and do research. No introductory courses are taught by graduate students.

Admissions: 17% of the 2013-2014 applicants were accepted. The SAT scores for the 2013-2014 freshman class were: Critical Reading--1% below 500, 9% between 500 and 599, 33% between 600 and 699, and 57% between 700 and 800; Math--1% below 500, 8% between 500 and 599, 36% between 600 and 699, and 56% between 700 and 800.

Requirements: The SAT or ACT is required. Graduation from an accredited secondary school is required, including 4 years of English, a minimum of 2 each of a foreign language, math, and social studies, and 1 of natural science. An additional 2 years each of math and science is required for students intending to major in math, science, nursing, or business. SAT subject tests are strongly recommended. AP credits are accepted. Important factors in the admissions decision are recommendations by school officials, leadership record, and advanced placement or honors courses.

Procedure: Freshmen are admitted fall. Entrance exams should be taken in the junior year and again at the beginning of the senior year. There is a deferred admissions plan. Early decision applications should be filed by November 1; regular applications, by January 10 for fall entry, along with a $70 fee. Notification of early decision is sent December 15; regular decision, April 1. Applications are accepted online.

Transfer: 168 transfer students enrolled in 2012-2013. Transfer students must have successfully completed a minimum of 12 credit hours with a minimum GPA of 3.0. Either the SAT or the ACT is required. An interview is recommended. Transfers must complete their last 2 years at Georgetown. 60 of 120 credits required for the bachelor's degree must be completed at Georgetown.

Visiting: There are regularly scheduled orientations for prospective stu-

dents, throughout the year, including a question and answer period led by an admissions officer, followed by a campus tour led by a student guide. There are guides for informal visits and visitors may sit in on classes. To schedule a visit, contact the Office of Undergraduate Admissions.

Financial Aid: Georgetown is a member of CSS. The CSS/Profile and FAFSA, and non-custodial profile, business/farm supplement, and tax returns are required. The deadline for filing freshman financial aid applications for fall entry is February 1.

International Students: There are 781 international students enrolled. The school actively recruits these students. They must take the TOEFL. They must also take the SAT or ACT.

Graduates: From July 1, 2012 to June 30, 2013, 1871 bachelor's degrees were awarded. The most popular majors were government (11%), international politics (9%), and nursing (9%). In an average class, 90% graduate in 4 years or less, 93% graduate in 5 years or less, and 94% graduate in 6 years or less.

Admissions Contact: Charles A. Deacon, Dean of Admissions. E-Mail: *guadmiss@georgetown.edu* Web: *www.georgetown.edu*

HOWARD UNIVERSITY C-3

Washington, DC 20059 (202) 806-2755
(800) 822-6363; (202) 806-2740

Full-time: 2058 men, 4212 women	**Faculty:** 608; I, --$
Part-time: 178 men, 240 women	**Ph.D.s:** 81%
Graduate: 1288 men, 2026 women	**Student/Faculty:** 10 to 1
Year: semesters, summer session	**Tuition:** $22,683
Application Deadline: February 1	**Room & Board:** $15,906
Freshman Class: 11687 applied, 5762 accepted, 1394 enrolled	
SAT CR/M/W: 540/530/530	**ACT:** 23 **COMPETITIVE**

Howard University, founded in 1867, is the largest predominantly Black university in the United States. There are 6 undergraduate schools and 12 graduate schools. In addition to regional accreditation, Howard has baccalaureate program accreditation with AACSB, ABET, ACEJMC, ACPE, ADA, APTA, CSWE, NAAB, NASAD, NASDTEC, NASM, and NCATE. Computerized library services include interlibrary loans, database searching, Internet access, and Wi-Fi capability. Special learning facilities include an art gallery, radio station, TV station, History and culture research centers (e.g. Moorland-Spingarn Research Center (MSRC); Ralph Bunche International Center; E. Frankin Frazier Reading Room). The 256-acre campus is in an urban area in Northwest Washington, D.C. Including any residence halls, there are 124 buildings.

Student Life: 96% of undergraduates are from out of state, mostly the Middle Atlantic. Students are from 44 states, 37 foreign countries, and Canada. 92% are African American. The average age of freshmen is 17; all undergraduates, 21. 24% do not continue beyond their first year; 72% remain to graduate.

Housing: 4600 students can be accommodated in college housing, which includes single-sex and coed dorms, on-campus apartments, and off-campus apartments. In addition, there are honors houses and special-interest houses. On-campus housing is available on a first-come, first-served basis, and is available on a lottery system for upperclassmen. 50% of students commute. Alcohol is not permitted. All students may keep cars.

Activities: There are 308 groups on campus, including programming boards (residence halls and activities); step teams; entertainment industry clubs, art, band, cheerleading, chess, choir, chorus, communications, community service; youth/peer mentorship; residence hall councils, computers, dance, debate, drama, drill team, drum and bugle corps, environmental, ethnic, film, forensics, gay, honors, international, jazz band, literary magazine, marching band, musical theater, newspaper, opera, orchestra, photography, political, professional, radio and TV, religious, social, social service, student government, and yearbook. Popular campus events include Orientation, Freshman Welcome Pep Rally and Pinning Ceremony, Opening Convocation, Charter Day Dinner, Global Community Week, Howard Homecoming, Spring Black Arts Festival (Springfest), MLK Day of Service and Student Leadership Conference.

Sports: There are 8 intercollegiate sports for men and 11 for women, and 5 intramural sports for men and 4 for women. Facilities include Greene Stadium (outdoor track, football/soccer/lacrosse field); Burr Gymnasium (basketball courts, swimming pool, indoor track, classrooms, weight room, cardio fitness center); Blackburn Recreational Center (bowling alley and pool hall); and several practice fields.

Disabled Students: All of the campus is accessible.

Services: Counseling and information services are available, as is tutoring in most subjects. There is a reader service for the blind, and remedial math, reading, and writing. Tutoring is also available in many subjects.

Campus Safety and Security: Measures include 24-hour foot and vehicle patrol, emergency notification system, self-defense education, and security escort services. There are shuttle buses, emergency telephones, lighted pathways/sidewalks and controlled access to dorms/residences.

Programs of Study: Howard confers B.B.A., B.A., B.S. and B.F.A. degrees. Master's and doctoral degrees are also awarded. Bachelor's degrees are awarded in BIOLOGICAL SCIENCE (anatomy, biochemistry, biology/biological science, genetics, microbiology, nutrition, and physiology), BUSINESS (accounting, banking and finance, business administration and management, fashion merchandising, international business management, labor studies, marketing/retailing/merchandising, sports management, and supply chain management), COMMUNICATIONS AND THE ARTS (advertising, Arabic, art history and appreciation, broadcasting, ceramic art and design, communications, communication science, dance, design, dramatic arts, English, film arts, French, graphic design, jazz, journalism, media arts, music, music business management, music history and appreciation, musical theater, painting, photography, playwriting/screenwriting, printmaking, public relations, sculpture, Spanish, telecommunications, and theatre arts), COMPUTER AND PHYSICAL SCIENCE (atmospheric sciences and meteorology, chemistry, Computer Engineering Technology, computer science, mathematics, physics, and radiological technology), EDUCATION (art education, early childhood education, education, education administration, elementary education, health education, music education, physical education, reading education, school psychology, and secondary education), ENGINEERING AND ENVIRONMENTAL DESIGN (architecture, chemical engineering, civil engineering, computer engineering, electrical/electronics engineering, environmental science, interior design, and mechanical engineering), HEALTH PROFESSIONS (allied health, clinical science, community health work, dental hygiene, health care administration, health science, music therapy, nursing, occupational therapy, pharmaceutical science, pharmacology, pharmacy, physical therapy, physician's assistant, predentistry, premedicine, public health, radiation therapy, radiograph medical technology, speech pathology/audiology, and sports medicine), SOCIAL SCIENCE (administration of justice , African studies, African American studies, anthropology, child psychology/development, classical/ancient civilization, counseling/psychology, criminal justice, economics, fashion design and technology, geography, history, human development, interdisciplinary studies, law, legal studies, philosophy, political science/government, psychology, public administration, public affairs, religion, social work, sociology, Spanish studies, textiles and clothing, urban studies, and women's studies). Biology, psychology, political science, journalism, and radio-TV-film have the largest enrollments.

Required: To graduate, students must (1) complete a total of 120 semester hours, exclusive of courses taken through the Center for Academic Reinforcement (CAR); (2) maintain grades of C or better in all courses used to satisfy the minimum credit-hour requirement for departmental majors; (3) maintain grades higher than C for courses used to satisfy requirements for departmental majors in any department stipulating this requirement; and (4) maintain a cumulative grade point average of 2.0 or better in departmental majors, as well as in the minor fields of concentration.

Special: Cross-registration is available with the Consortium of Universities in the Washington Metropolitan Area. Opportunities are also provided for internships, work-study, co-op programs, study abroad in 5 countries in Europe and Africa, B.A.-B.S. degrees in engineering and business, student-designed majors, pass/fail options, and accelerated degree programs in medicine and dentistry. There are 23 national honor societies, including Phi Beta Kappa, and a freshman honors program.

Faculty/Classroom: 56% of faculty are male; 44% are female. 63% teach undergraduates, 55% do research, and 33% do both. No introductory courses are taught by graduate students. The average class size in an introductory lecture is 36; in a laboratory is 20; and in a regular course is 20.

Admissions: 49% of the 2013-2014 applicants were accepted. The SAT scores for the 2013-2014 freshman class were: Critical Reading--26% below 500, 51% between 500 and 599, 21% between 600 and 699, and 2% between 700 and 800; Math--30% below 500, 47% between 500 and 599, 21% between 600 and 699, and 2% between 700 and 800; Writing--34% below 500, 48% between 500 and 599, 16% between 600 and 699, and 2% between 700 and 800. The ACT scores were 21% below 21, 33% between 21 and 23, 25% between 24 and 26, 12% between 27 and 28, and 10% above 28. 46% of the current freshmen were in the top fifth of their class; 74% were in the top two fifths.

Requirements: The SAT or ACT is required. The ACT Optional Writing test is also required. In addition, To be admitted into the College of Arts and Sciences, students must have taken the courses listed below with the unit requirements: English (4) Mathematics (2) Foreign language (2) Natural science (2) Social science (2) Any other academic courses counted toward graduation (4) Freshmen applicants must be in the upper half of the graduating class or submit a GED Certificate; have a minimum SAT score of 1000 or ACT composite score of 20. Two letters of recommendation from the high school are required. Transfer applicants from regionally accredited institutions must have a minimum GPA of 2.5 on a 4.0 scale on 15 hours which shall include one English and one college-level Mathematics course. A GPA of 3.0 is required. AP and CLEP credits are accepted. Important factors in the admissions decision are leadership record, advanced placement or honors courses, and personality/intangible qualities.

Procedure: Freshmen are admitted fall, spring, and summer. Entrance exams should be taken by January of senior year. There are early decision and rolling admissions plans. Early decision applications should be filed by November 1; regular applications, by February 1 for fall entry; November 1 for spring entry; and April 1 for summer entry, along with a $45 fee. Notification of early decision is sent December 20; regular decision, January 15. Applications are accepted online.

Transfer: 321 transfer students enrolled in 2012-2013. (1)15 transferrable credit hours (30 credit hours for the School of Business) from a regionally accredited postsecondary institution; (2) Earned a 2.5 cumulative GPA (3.0 GPA for the School of Business) and received a passing grade of C or better in both a college-level English and college-level math course; (3) Additional credentials such as a high school transcript and SAT scores may be requested for admission. 30 of 120 credits required for the bachelor's degree must be completed at Howard.

Visiting: There are regularly scheduled orientations for prospective students, Verbal presentation by Admission staff member, followed by walking guided tour. There are guides for informal visits and visitors may sit in on classes. To schedule a visit, contact the Office of Admissions.

Financial Aid: In 2013-2014, 97% of all full-time freshmen and 94% of continuing full-time students received some form of financial aid. 70% of all full-time freshmen and 79% of continuing full-time students received need-based aid. The average freshman award was $19,058. Need-based scholarships or need-based grants averaged $8,492 ($36,100 maximum); need-based self-help aid (loans and jobs) averaged $3,431 ($5,000 maximum); non-need-based athletic scholarships averaged $19,595 ($35,364 maximum); and other non-need-based awards and non-need-based scholarships averaged $14,189 ($39,000 maximum). 6% of undergraduate students work part-time. Average annual earnings from campus work are $2012. The average financial indebtedness of the 2013 graduate was $7,260. The FAFSA is required. The priority date for freshman financial aid applications for fall entry is February 1. The deadline for filing freshman financial aid applications for fall entry is May 17.

International Students: There are 167 international students enrolled. The school actively recruits these students. They must take the TOEFL with a minimum score of 550 on the paper-based TOEFL (PBT) or 79 on the Internet-based version (iBT), In lieu of the TOEFL (if not offered in your country), applicants may submit results from IELTS. They must also take the SAT or ACT.

Graduates: From July 1, 2012 to June 30, 2013, 1321 bachelor's degrees were awarded. The most popular majors were biology (8%), political science (7%), and psychology (7%). In an average class, 48% graduate in 4 years or less, 65% graduate in 5 years or less, and 69% graduate in 6 years or less.

Admissions Contact: Linda Sander-Hawkins, Office of Admissions. E-Mail: *admission@howard.edu* Web: *www.howard.edu*

THE CATHOLIC UNIVERSITY OF AMERICA C-2

Washington, DC 20064 **(202) 319-5305**
(800) 673-2772; (202) 319-6533

Full-time: 1601 men, 1972 women	**Faculty:** 270; I, -$
Part-time: 102 men, 124 women	**Ph.D.s:** 98%
Graduate: n/av	**Student/Faculty:** 10 to 1
Year: semesters, summer session	**Tuition:** $38,526
Application Deadline: February 15	**Room & Board:** $14,326
Freshman Class: n/av	
SAT or ACT: required	

VERY COMPETITIVE

The Catholic University of America, founded in 1887 and affiliated with the Roman Catholic Church, offers undergraduate programs in arts and sciences, engineering, architecture, nursing, philosophy, social service, and music and through the Metropolitan College. Only miles from the heart of Washington, DC, CUA's location provides a unique college experience and a wide spectrum of internship opportunities. There are 8 undergraduate schools and 11 graduate schools. In addition to regional accreditation, CUA has baccalaureate program accreditation with AACSB, ABET, ACPE, CSWE, NAAB, NASM, NCATE, and NLN. Computerized library services include interlibrary loans, database searching, Internet access, and Wi-Fi capability. Special learning facilities include an art gallery and radio station. The 180-acre campus is in an urban area in Washington, DC. Including any residence halls, there are 52 buildings.

Student Life: 96% of undergraduates are from out of state, mostly the Middle Atlantic. Students are from 50 states, 90 foreign countries, and Canada. 56% are from public schools. 62% are White. 80% are Catholic. The average age of freshmen is 18; all undergraduates, 20. 20% do not continue beyond their first year; 73% remain to graduate.

Housing: College-sponsored housing includes single-sex dorms and on-campus apartments. In addition, there are honors houses, special-interest houses, a freshman residential college, and a residential college for upperclassmen, living and learning communities based on common interest. On-campus housing is available on a first-come, first-served basis, and is available on a lottery system for upperclassmen. 62% of students live on campus. Upperclassmen may keep cars.

Activities: 1% of men belong to 2 national fraternities. There are 90 groups on campus, including art, cheerleading, choir, chorale, chorus, computers, dance, debate, drama, ethnic, film, honors, international, jazz band, literary magazine, musical theater, newspaper, opera, orchestra, pep band, political, professional, radio and TV, religious, social, social service, student government, symphony, and yearbook. Popular campus events include Luaupalooza, Movies on the Mall, Fall Fiesta, Beaux Arts Ball and Mistletoe Ball.

Sports: There are 10 intercollegiate sports for men and 11 for women, and 9 intramural sports for men and 9 for women. The DuFour Athletic Center houses 4 basketball and 5 handball/racquetball courts, a 6-lane, 25-meter swimming pool, a weight training room, an aerobics room, men's and women's saunas, 2 dance studios, an indoor jogging track, and 3 volleyball courts. Outdoor facilities include Cardinal Stadium made with state-of-the-art FieldTurf, adjoining grass playing fields, baseball and softball facilities, and 6 tennis courts.

Disabled Students: 78% of the campus is accessible.

Services: Counseling and information services are available, as is tutoring in most subjects. Center for Academic Success: Drop-in tutoring, individual tutoring, Smart-thinking online service, and Writing Center. There is a reader service for the blind, and remedial math, reading, and writing. Taped books/scanned books, assistive technology, including reading software and screen readers, test accommodations, and sign language interpreters are available.

Campus Safety and Security: Measures include 24-hour foot and vehicle patrol, emergency notification system, self-defense education, and security escort services. There are shuttle buses, emergency telephones, lighted pathways/sidewalks, controlled access to dorms/residences, fixed security posts, emergency whistles, watch captains in every building, and an access control system.

Programs of Study: CUA confers B.A., B.S., B.A.G.S., B.Arch., B.B.E., B.C.E., B.E.E., B.M., B.M.E., B.S.Arch., B.S.N. and B.S.B.A. degrees. Master's and doctoral degrees are also awarded. Bachelor's degrees are awarded in BIOLOGICAL SCIENCE (biochemistry, biology/biological science, and biotechnology), BUSINESS (accounting, banking and finance, business administration and management, finance, international economics, management science, and marketing and distribution), COMMUNICATIONS AND THE ARTS (art history, art, art history and appreciation, ceramic art and design, classics, communications, dramatic arts, English, English literature, French, German, Greek (classical), Italian, Latin, music, music history and appreciation, music performance, music theory and composition, musical theater, painting, piano/organ, Spanish, studio art, and voice), COMPUTER AND PHYSICAL SCIENCE (chemical physics, chemistry, computer science, elementary particle physics, mathematics, and physics), EDUCATION (art education, drama education, early childhood education, education, elementary education, English education, mathematics education, music education, and secondary education), ENGINEERING AND ENVIRONMENTAL DESIGN (architecture, biomedical engineering, civil engineering, computer engineering, construction engineering, electrical/electronics engineering, engineering, environmental engineering, environmental science, and mechanical engineering), HEALTH PROFESSIONS (medical laboratory technology, medical technology, nursing, predentistry, premedicine, and preveterinary science), SOCIAL SCIENCE (anthropology, economics, French studies, history, liberal arts/general studies, medieval studies, philosophy, political science/government, prelaw, psychology, religion, social science, social work, sociology, Spanish studies, and theological studies). Politics is the strongest academically. Architecture has the largest enrollment.

Required: To graduate, students must complete 120 credit hours, including 36 to 42 hours in the major, with a minimum GPA of 2.0. Courses must meet distribution requirements in theology and religious studies, philosophy, English composition, humanities, language and literature, math and natural sciences, and social and behavioral sciences. A comprehensive exam is required in most majors.

Special: Cross-registration is available with the Consortium of Universities of the Washington Metropolitan Area. Opportunities are also provided for internships, accelerated degree programs, dual majors, B.A.-B.S. degrees, work study, pass/fail options, and study abroad in 13 countries. There are 15 national honor societies, including Phi Beta Kappa, and a freshman honors program.

Faculty/Classroom: 70% teach undergraduates, and all do research. No introductory courses are taught by graduate students. The average class size in an introductory lecture is 21; in a laboratory is 20; and in a regular course is 19.

Requirements: The SAT or ACT is required. Applicants must be graduates of an accredited secondary school. Students should present 17 academic credits, including 4 each in English and social studies, 3 each in math and science, 2 in foreign languages, and 1 in fine arts or humanities. An essay is required, one letter of recommendation, official high school transcripts, and either an SAT or ACT score. An audition is required for music applicants, and a portfolio for architecture applicants is recommended. A GPA of 3.0 is required. AP credits are accepted. Important factors in the admissions decision are extracurricular activities record, leadership record, and advanced placement or honors courses.

Procedure: Freshmen are admitted fall and spring. Entrance exams

should be taken by February of the senior year of high school. There are early admissions and deferred admissions plans. Early decision applications should be filed by November 15; regular applications, by February 15 for fall entry. The fall 2013 application fee was $55. Notification of early decision is sent December 20; regular decision, March 15. Applications are accepted online.

Transfer: Applicants must submit a high school transcript, SAT or ACT scores, and a college transcript. A letter of recommendation and an essay are required. Terms of admission are finalized by the dean of the appropriate school. 60 of 120 credits required for the bachelor's degree must be completed at CUA.

Visiting: There are regularly scheduled orientations for prospective students, Visits include an information session with an admissions counselor and a guided campus tour. There are guides for informal visits, visitors may sit in on classes, and stay overnight. To schedule a visit, contact The Admissions Office.

Financial Aid: In 2013-2014, 90% of all full-time freshmen students received some form of financial aid. CUA is a member of CSS. The FAFSA is required. The priority date for freshman financial aid applications for fall entry is February 15.

International Students: There are 66 international students enrolled. The school actively recruits these students. They must take the TOEFL. They must also take the SAT or ACT.

Graduates: The most popular majors were architecture, nursing, and politics. In an average class, 62% graduate in 4 years or less and 68% graduate in 6 years or less. Of the 2012 graduating class, 36% were enrolled in graduate school within 6 months of graduation.

Admissions Contact: Christine Mica, Dean of University Admissions. E-Mail: *cua-admissions@cua.edu* Web: *www.cua.edu*

TRINITY WASHINGTON UNIVERSITY — C-2

Washington, DC 20017 — (202) 884-9400; (800) 492-6882; (202) 884-9403

Full-time: 17 men, 841 women	**Faculty:** 48; IIB, --$
Part-time: 45 men, 488 women	**Ph.D.s:** 98%
Graduate: 107 men, 515 women	**Student/Faculty:** 12 to 1
Year: semesters	**Tuition:** $21,540
Application Deadline:	**Room & Board:** $9710
Freshman Class: n/av	
SAT or ACT: recommended	

COMPETITIVE+

Trinity Washington University, founded in 1897, is a private, women's liberal arts college in the nation's capital. The school year consists of traditional semesters plus 1-week courses during January and May. The School of Professional Studies and School of Education are both co-ed and offer adult students bachelor's and master's degrees with evening and weekend classes. There are 4 undergraduate schools and 2 graduate schools. In addition to regional accreditation, Trinity has baccalaureate program accreditation with NCATE. Computerized library services include interlibrary loans, database searching, and Internet access. Special learning facilities include an art gallery. The 26-acre campus is in an urban area 2 1/2 miles north of the U.S. Capitol. Including any residence halls, there are 7 buildings.

Student Life: 51% of undergraduates are from out of state, mostly the Middle Atlantic. Students are from 21 states, and 2 foreign countries. 90% are from public schools. 68% are African American. 52% claim no religious affiliation; 35% Protestant; 12% Catholic. The average age of freshmen is 18; all undergraduates, 22. 30% do not continue beyond their first year; 50% remain to graduate.

Housing: 275 students can be accommodated in college housing, which includes single-sex dorms. On-campus housing is available on a first-come, first-served basis, and is available on a lottery system for upperclassmen. Priority is given to out-of-town students. 75% of students commute. Alcohol is not permitted. All students may keep cars.

Activities: There are no fraternities or sororities. There are 23 groups on campus, including choir, computers, dance, debate, drama, ethnic, honors, international, literary magazine, newspaper, political, professional, religious, social, social service, student government, and yearbook. Popular campus events include Founders Day, Class Days, Junior Ring Day, and Cap and Gown.

Sports: There are 5 intercollegiate sports for women, and 2 intramural sports for women. Facilities include 2 athletic fields for soccer and lacrosse, a fitness center, 6 tennis courts, and a state-of-the-art sports center with pool, weight room, and basketball court and volleyball court.

Disabled Students: 85% of the campus is accessible.

Services: Counseling and information services are available, as is tutoring in every subject. There is a reader service for the blind. and signing for hearing-impaired students.

Campus Safety and Security: Measures include 24-hour foot and vehicle patrol, self-defense education, and security escort services. There are shuttle buses, emergency telephones, lighted pathways/sidewalks, and controlled access to dorms/residences.

Programs of Study: Trinity confers B.A., and B.S. degrees. Associate and master's degrees are also awarded. Bachelor's degrees are awarded in BIOLOGICAL SCIENCE (biochemistry and biology/biological science), BUSINESS (business administration and management and business economics), COMMUNICATIONS AND THE ARTS (communications and English), COMPUTER AND PHYSICAL SCIENCE (chemistry and mathematics), EDUCATION (early childhood education, education, and elementary education), HEALTH PROFESSIONS (exercise science and nursing), SOCIAL SCIENCE (criminal justice, economics, history, human services, international studies, political science/government, psychology, and sociology). Nursing, exercise science, biology, chemistry, and biochemistry are the strongest academically. Psychology, business administration, nursing, and criminal justice have the largest enrollments.

Required: To graduate, students must complete a total of 128 credit hours with a minimum GPA of 2.0. Between 42 and 60 hours are required in the major. All students must take the courses required in the general education curriculum and must complete a senior seminar.

Special: Cross-registration is offered through the Consortium of Universities of the Washington Metropolitan Area. Trinity offers internships in all majors and minors, as well as work-study programs. Students may study in France, Italy, and various other countries by arrangement with their faculty adviser. B.A.-B.S. degrees, a 5-year accelerated degree in teaching, dual and student-designed majors, a general studies degree, credit for life experience, nondegree study, and pass/fail options are also available. There are 7 national honor societies, including Phi Beta Kappa, and a freshman honors program.

Faculty/Classroom: 35% of faculty are male; 65% are female. 72% teach undergraduates. No introductory courses are taught by graduate students. The average class size in an introductory lecture is 16; in a laboratory is 16; and in a regular course is 13.

Admissions: 2 freshmen graduated first in their class.

Requirements: The SAT or ACT is recommended. Graduation from an accredited secondary school or satisfactory scores on the GED are required for admission. A total of 16 academic credits is required, including 4 years of English and 3 to 4 years each of a foreign language, history, math, and science. An essay or graded writing sample is required, as are two letters of recommendation from faculty/guidance counselor. An interview is optional, but may be required of some applicants. Standardized tests are not required, but are recommended. A GPA of 2.0 is required. AP and CLEP credits are accepted. Important factors in the admissions decision are leadership record, extracurricular activities record, and recommendations by school officials.

Procedure: Freshmen are admitted fall and spring. Entrance exams should be taken junior year is preferred. There are deferred admissions and rolling admissions plans. Application deadlines are open. Application fee is $40. Applications are accepted online.

Transfer: 130 transfer students enrolled in 2012-2013. Transfer applicants must have a GPA of 2.5. An interview is recommended, and an essay and recommendation are required. 45 of 128 credits required for the bachelor's degree must be completed at Trinity.

Visiting: There are regularly scheduled orientations for prospective students, consisting of a half-day program, including an overview of the college, the curriculum, and financing. There are guides for informal visits, visitors may sit in on classes, and stay overnight. To schedule a visit, contact the Office of Admissions.

Financial Aid: In 2013-2014, 98% of all full-time freshmen and 95% of continuing full-time students received some form of financial aid. 83% of all full-time freshmen and 82% of continuing full-time students received need-based aid. The average freshman award was $23,280. Need-based scholarships or need-based grants averaged $14,000; need-based self-help aid (loans and jobs) averaged $7,000; and other non-need-based awards and non-need-based scholarships averaged $2,280. 7% of undergraduate students work part-time. Average annual earnings from campus work are $1400. The average financial indebtedness of the 2013 graduate was $17,000. Trinity is a member of CSS. The FAFSA is required. The priority date for freshman financial aid applications for fall entry is March 1.

International Students: There are 2 international students enrolled. They must take the TOEFL with a minimum score of 543 on the paper-based TOEFL (PBT) or 76 on the Internet-based version (iBT).

Graduates: From July 1, 2012 to June 30, 2013, 130 bachelor's degrees were awarded. The most popular majors were psychology (36%), business administration (15%), and English (10%).

Admissions Contact: Kelly Gosnell, Vice President of Admissions. E-Mail: *admissions@trinitydc.edu* Web: *www.trinitydc.edu*

UNIVERSITY OF THE DISTRICT OF COLUMBIA C-2

Washington, DC 20008 **(202) 274-6069; (202) 274-6341**

Full-time: 878 men, 1286 women
Part-time: 1238 men, 1709 women
Graduate: 60 men, 193 women
Year: semesters, summer session
Application Deadline:
Freshman Class: n/av
ACT: required

Faculty: 178; IIA, av$
Ph.D.s: 70%
Student/Faculty: 13 to 1
Tuition: $7244 ($14,540)
Room & Board: n/app

LESS COMPETITIVE

The University of the District of Columbia, founded in 1977, is a publicly funded, land-grant commuter institution offering programs in liberal arts, business, education, and technical fields. There are 5 undergraduate schools and one graduate school. In addition to regional accreditation, UDC has baccalaureate program accreditation with ABET, CAHEA, CSWE, NASDTEC, NASM, and NLN. Computerized library services include database searching and Wi-Fi capability. Special learning facilities include an art gallery, TV station, early childhood learning center. The 22-acre campus is in a suburban area in northwest Washington, D.C. Including any residence halls, there are 11 buildings.

Student Life: 66% of undergraduates are from District of Columbia. Others are from 44 states, and 108 foreign countries. 85% are from public schools. 72% are African American. The average age of freshmen is 25; all undergraduates, 31. 20% do not continue beyond their first year; 65% remain to graduate.

Housing: Alcohol is not permitted. All students commute.

Activities: 2% of men belong to 7 national fraternities; 2% of women belong to 5 national sororities. There are 139 groups on campus, including art, band, cheerleading, chess, choir, chorale, computers, dance, drama, drum and bugle corps, ethnic, film, honors, international, jazz band, marching band, newspaper, orchestra, pep band, photography, political, professional, radio and TV, religious, social, social service, student government, and yearbook. Popular campus events include the Cross-Cultural Extended Family Program and International Multicultural Recognition Day.

Sports: There are 6 intercollegiate sports for men and 6 for women, and 8 intramural sports for men and 6 for women. Facilities include a 3000-seat gym, a swimming pool, a weight room, and racquetball and tennis courts.

Disabled Students: All of the campus is accessible.

Services: Counseling and information services are available, as is tutoring in every subject. There is a reader service for the blind, and remedial math and reading.

Campus Safety and Security: Measures include 24-hour foot and vehicle patrol, emergency notification system, and security escort services. There are emergency telephones and lighted pathways/sidewalks.

Programs of Study: UDC confers B.A., and B.S. degrees. Associate and master's degrees are also awarded. Bachelor's degrees are awarded in BIOLOGICAL SCIENCE (biology/biological science), BUSINESS (accounting, banking and finance, business administration and management, marketing/retailing/merchandising, and office supervision and management), COMMUNICATIONS AND THE ARTS (dramatic arts, English, fine arts, French, media arts, music, and Spanish), COMPUTER AND PHYSICAL SCIENCE (chemistry, computer science, mathematics, and physics), EDUCATION (early childhood education, elementary education, health education, and physical education), ENGINEERING AND ENVIRONMENTAL DESIGN (architecture, aviation administration/management, civil engineering, construction engineering, electrical/electronics engineering, electromechanical technology, environmental science, and mechanical engineering), HEALTH PROFESSIONS (nursing and speech pathology/audiology), SOCIAL SCIENCE (criminal justice, economics, fire science, food science, geography, history, philosophy, political science/government, psychology, public administration, social work, sociology, and urban studies). Business is the strongest academically. Fine arts has the largest enrollment.

Required: To graduate, students must complete 120 to 130 semester hours with a minimum GPA of 2.0. All students must take 6 hours each of English composition, literature and advanced writing, foreign language, social science, math, and natural sciences; 4 of personal and community health; and 3 each of philosophy and fine arts.

Special: Cross-registration may be arranged through the Consortium of Universities of the Washington Metropolitan Area. Co-op programs with the federal government, internships, study abroad in 4 countries, work-study programs, and B.A.-B.S. degrees in administration of justice, chemistry, and physics are offered. Nondegree study and credit for life experience are also available. There are 4 national honor societies and a freshman honors program.

Faculty/Classroom: 68% of faculty are male; 32% are female. 89% teach undergraduates, 3% do research, and 20% do both. No introductory courses are taught by graduate students. The average class size in an introductory lecture is 23; in a laboratory is 23; and in a regular course is 23.

Requirements: The ACT is required. A High school diploma or GED is required for admission, along with an interview. High school courses must include 4 years of English and 2 each of foreign language, social science, lab science, and math (algebra and geometry). AP and CLEP credits are accepted. Important factors in the admissions decision are ability to finance college education, advanced placement or honors courses, and recommendations by school officials.

Procedure: Freshmen are admitted to all sessions. Entrance exams should be taken prior semester. Application deadlines are open. Notification is sent on a rolling basis.

Transfer: Applicants must have a minimum GPA of 2.0. Those with fewer than 30 hours of college credit must submit a high school transcript along with college records. 30 of 120 credits required for the bachelor's degree must be completed at UDC.

Visiting: There are guides for informal visits and visitors may sit in on classes. To schedule a visit, contact the Office of Student Recruitment.

Financial Aid: UDC is a member of CSS. The CSS/Profile and FFS are required. Check with the school for current application deadlines.

International Students: They must take the TOEFL. the university's own English, math, and reading tests.

Admissions Contact: LaVerne Hill-Flanagan, Director of Recruitment and Admissions. E-Mail: *lflanagan@udc.edu* Web: *www.udc.edu*

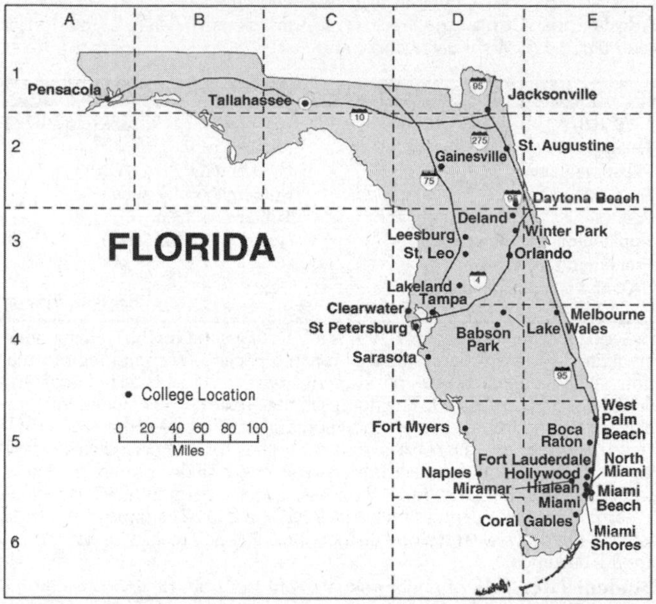

ADVENTIST UNIVERSITY OF HEALTH SCIENCES D-3

Orlando, FL 32803 (407) 303-9798
(800) 500-7747; (407) 303-9408

Full-time: 130 men, 464 women
Part-time: 387 men, 1595 women
Graduate: 27 men, 68 women
Year: trimesters, summer session
Application Deadline: July 1
Freshman Class: 830 applied, 817 accepted, 297 enrolled
SAT CR/M: 455/440 **ACT:** 19 **NONCOMPETITIVE**
Faculty: n/av
Ph.D.s: 43%
Student/Faculty: 15 to 1
Tuition: $10,780
Room & Board: $5564

Adventist University of Health Sciences, founded in 1992 and affiliated with the Seventh-Day Adventist Church, is a private institution offering associate and baccalaureate degrees in nursing and allied health, and masters in nurse anesthesia and occupational therapy. Students can also take a variety of general education and prerequisite courses and then transfer to an institution offering degrees that ADU does not offer. There is one undergraduate school and one graduate school. In addition to regional accreditation, ADU has baccalaureate program accreditation with NLN. The library contains 69,847 volumes, and 5,770 audio/video tapes/CDs/DVDs, and subscribes to 39,156 periodicals including electronic. Computerized library services include interlibrary loans, database searching, and Internet access. The 9-acre campus is in an urban area in Orlando. Including any residence halls, there are 6 buildings.

Student Life: 52% are White; 17% Hispanic; 15% African American. 31% are Protestant; 14% Catholic. The average age of freshmen is 30.

Housing: 184 students can be accommodated in college housing, which includes single-sex off-campus apartments. On-campus housing is available on a first-come and first-served basis. Priority is given to out-of-town students. Alcohol is not permitted. No one may keep cars.

Activities: There are no fraternities or sororities. Groups on campus include drama, newspaper, religious, and student government.

Sports: There is no sports program at ADU.

Disabled Students: All of the campus is accessible. Facilities include wheelchair ramps, elevators, special parking, specially equipped restrooms, special class scheduling, lowered drinking fountains, lowered telephones, and special housing.

Services: Counseling and information services are available, as is tutoring in most subjects. There is remedial math and writing.

Campus Safety and Security: Measures include 24-hour foot and vehicle patrol, emergency notification system, and security escort services. There are shuttle buses and lighted pathways/sidewalks.

Programs of Study: ADU confers B.S. degrees. Associate and master's degrees are also awarded. Bachelor's degrees are awarded in HEALTH PROFESSIONS (biomedical science, health science, nuclear medical technology, nursing, and radiological science).

Required: Professional program graduation requirements vary. They are all delineated in the Academic Bulletin and on the University's website.

Faculty/Classroom: 26% of faculty are male; 74% are female. All teach undergraduates. No introductory courses are taught by graduate students. The average class size in an introductory lecture is 27; in a laboratory is 24; and in a regular course is 27.

Admissions: 98% of the 2013-2014 applicants were accepted. The SAT scores for the 2013-2014 freshman class were: Critical Reading--72% below 500, 23% between 500 and 599, 5% between 600 and 699; Math--73% below 500, 24% between 500 and 599, 3% between 600 and 699. The ACT scores were 71% below 21, 21% between 21 and 23, 4% between 24 and 26, 2% between 27 and 28, and 2% above 28.

Requirements: The SAT or ACT is required. A GPA of 2.5 is required. AP and CLEP credits are accepted. Important factors in the admissions decision are advanced placement or honors courses, recommendations by school officials, and personality/intangible qualities.

Procedure: Freshmen are admitted fall, spring, and summer. There are early decision and rolling admissions plans. Early decision applications should be filed by February 1; regular applications, by July 1 for fall entry; November 1 for spring entry; and March 1 for summer entry, along with a $20 fee. Notification is sent on a rolling basis. applicants were on the 2013 waiting list; were admitted. Applications are accepted online.

Transfer: 1262 transfer students enrolled in 2012-2013. Applicants must submit the required data for general college admissions. Transfer credits must be submitted on an official transcript from a regionally accredited institution.

Visiting: There are regularly scheduled orientations for prospective students, including fall and spring open houses. There are guides for informal visits and visitors may sit in on classes. To schedule a visit, contact Sahira Gomez at (407) 303-8192.

Financial Aid: In 2013-2014, 89% of all full-time freshmen students received some form of financial aid. 74% of all full-time freshmen students received need-based aid. The average freshman award was $1,181. Need-based scholarships or need-based grants averaged $377 ($1,500 maximum); need-based self-help aid (loans and jobs) averaged $1,557 ($5,473 maximum); and other non-need-based awards and non-need-based scholarships averaged $1,610 ($20,295 maximum). 29% of undergraduate students work part-time. The FAFSA and the college's own financial statement are required. Check with the school for current application deadlines.

International Students: There are 8 international students enrolled. They must take the TOEFL. They must also take the SAT or ACT.

Computers: All students may access the system during regular hours of operation. There are no time limits and no fees.

Graduates: From July 1, 2012 to June 30, 2013, 446 bachelor's degrees were awarded. The most popular majors were radiologic sciences (48%), nursing (38%), and health sciences (6%).

Admissions Contact: Janet Calderon, Director of Admissions. E-Mail: *janet.calderon@adu.edu* Web: *www.adu.edu*

BARRY UNIVERSITY E-5

Miami Shores, FL 33161 (305) 899-3134
(800) 695-2279; (305) 899-2971

Full-time: 1270 men, 2900 women
Part-time: 350 men, 630 women
Graduate: 1270 men, 2400 women
Year: semesters, summer session
Application Deadline: open
Freshman Class: n/av
SAT or ACT: required
Faculty: n/av; IIA, --$
Ph.D.s: 80%
Student/Faculty: n/av
Tuition: $28,560
Room & Board: $9530
COMPETITIVE

Barry University is an independent Roman Catholic institution of liberal arts and professional studies. The figures in the above capsule and in this profile are approximate. There are 6 undergraduate schools and 10 graduate schools. In addition to regional accreditation, Barry has baccalaureate program accreditation with CAHEA and NLN. The library contains 322,079 volumes, 617,792 microform items, and 7,706 audio/video tapes/CDs/DVDs, and subscribes to 1,851 periodicals including electronic. Computerized library services include interlibrary loans and database searching. Special learning facilities include a learning resource center, art gallery, radio station, human performance lab, biotechnology lab, photography studios, TV studio, theater, biomechanics lab, and multimedia business classrooms. The 122-acre campus is in a suburban area 14 miles from Fort Lauderdale and 7 miles north of downtown Miami. Including any residence halls, there are 26 buildings.

Student Life: 63% of undergraduates are from Florida. Others are from 47 states, 81 foreign countries, and Canada. 80% are from public schools. 31% are Hispanic; 26% white; 24% African American. 24% are Catholic. The average age of freshmen is 18; all undergraduates, 23.

Housing: 750 students can be accommodated in college housing, which

includes single-sex and coed dorms and off-campus apartments. In addition, there are special-interest houses. On-campus housing is guaranteed for the freshman year only, is available on a first-come, first-served basis, and is available on a lottery system for upperclassmen. Priority is given to out-of-town students. 65% of students commute. All students may keep cars.

Activities: 11% of men belong to 3 national fraternities; 6% of women belong to 2 national sororities. There are 85 groups on campus, including cheerleading, chorale, computers, dance, drama, ethnic, honors, international, literary magazine, musical theater, newspaper, photography, political, professional, radio and TV, religious, social, social service, and student government. Popular campus events include Halloween Dance, Festival of Nations, and World AIDS Day.

Sports: There are 5 intercollegiate sports for men and 7 for women. Facilities include baseball, softball, and soccer fields, a health and sports center with an indoor gym, outdoor basketball courts, and racquetball and tennis courts, an outdoor swimming pool, a strength and conditioning center, an athletic training room, a human performance lab, and a biomechanics lab.

Disabled Students: 85% of the campus is accessible. Facilities include wheelchair ramps, elevators, special parking, specially equipped restrooms, special class scheduling, lowered drinking fountains, and lowered telephones.

Services: Counseling and information services are available, as is tutoring in most subjects. There is remedial math, reading, and writing.

Campus Safety and Security: Measures include 24-hour foot and vehicle patrol, self-defense education, and security escort services. There are shuttle buses, emergency telephones, and lighted pathways/sidewalks.

Programs of Study: Barry confers B.A., B.S., B.F.A., B.L.S., B.P.A., B.P.S., B.S.L.S., B.S.N., B.S.T., and B.S.W. degrees. Master's and doctoral degrees are also awarded. Bachelor's degrees are awarded in BIOLOGICAL SCIENCE (biology/biological science and marine biology), BUSINESS (accounting, international business management, management information systems, management science, marketing/retailing/merchandising, and sports management), COMMUNICATIONS AND THE ARTS (advertising, art, broadcasting, communications, dramatic arts, English, French, music performance, photography, public relations, Spanish, and theater management), COMPUTER AND PHYSICAL SCIENCE (chemistry, computer science, and mathematics), EDUCATION (early childhood education and physical education), ENGINEERING AND ENVIRONMENTAL DESIGN (preengineering), HEALTH PROFESSIONS (cytotechnology, medical technology, nuclear medical technology, nursing, occupational therapy, predentistry, premedicine, prepharmacy, and ultrasound technology), SOCIAL SCIENCE (criminology, economics, history, international studies, liberal arts/general studies, philosophy, political science/government, prelaw, psychology, sociology, and theological studies). Biology, chemistry, and elementary and early childhood education are the strongest academically. Nursing, elementary and early childhood education, and biology are the largest.

Required: To graduate, students must complete 120 credit hours, including at least 48 in upper-division courses, 40 to 60 in the major, and 45 distributed in these curricular divisions: theology and philosophy, written and oral communication, physical or natural science and math, social and behavior sciences, and humanities and the arts. A minimum GPA of 2.0 must be maintained.

Special: Barry offers junior- or senior-year internships, a Washington semester for prelaw/political science students, on-campus work-study programs in all departments, dual majors, a liberal studies degree, an accelerated degree program in nursing, nondegree study, and pass/fail options. Students may study in 25 European countries. Barry is a member of the College Consortium for International Studies; students can participate in more than 50 programs offered by members. There are 15 national honor societies and a freshman honors program.

Faculty/Classroom: 49% of faculty are male; 51% are female. 72% teach undergraduates. No introductory courses are taught by graduate students. The average class size in an introductory lecture is 17; in a laboratory is 14; and in a regular course is 17.

Requirements: The SAT or ACT is required. Graduation from an accredited secondary school or satisfactory scores on the GED are required for admission. A GPA of 2.0 is required. AP and CLEP credits are accepted.

Procedure: Freshmen are admitted to all sessions. Entrance exams should be taken as early as possible. There is a rolling admissions plan. Application deadlines are open. Applications are accepted online.

Transfer: Applicants must have earned at least 12 acceptable credit hours with a minimum GPA of 2.0. 30 of 120 credits required for the bachelor's degree must be completed at Barry.

Visiting: There are guides for informal visits and visitors may sit in on classes. To schedule a visit, contact the Undergraduate Admissions.

Financial Aid: Barry is a member of CSS. The FAFSA is required. Check with the school for current application deadlines.

International Students: The school actively recruits these students. They must take the TOEFL.

Computers: Wireless access is available. All students may access the system 24 hours a day. There are no time limits and no fees. It is strongly recommended that all students have a personal computer. Students enrolled in anesthesiology program (graduate degree) must have a personal computer. An IBM ThinkPad or Dell is recommended.

Admissions Contact: Director of Admissions. E-Mail: *admissions@mail.barry.edu* Web: *www.barry.edu*

BEACON COLLEGE D-3

Leesburg, FL 34748 (352) 787-7249; (352) 787-0721

Full-time: 80 men, 60 women	**Faculty:** n/av
Part-time: n/av	**Ph.D.s:** n/av
Graduate: n/av	**Student/Faculty:** n/av
Year: semesters, summer session	**Tuition:** $30,500
Application Deadline: open	**Room & Board:** $8500
Freshman Class: n/av	
SAT or ACT: recommended	

COMPETITIVE

Beacon College, founded in 1989, is a private institution that offers undergraduate degrees in liberal studies, human services, and computer information systems exclusively for students with language-based learning disabilities and/or ADHD. The figures in the above capsule and in this profile are approximate. The library contains 20,075 volumes, and 554 audio/video tapes/CDs/DVDs, and subscribes to 182 periodicals including electronic. Computerized library services include interlibrary loans, database searching, and Internet access. Special learning facilities include a learning resource center and art gallery. The 2-acre campus is in a small town in the downtown historic district. Including any residence halls, there are 11 buildings.

Student Life: 84% of undergraduates are from out of state, mostly the South. Students are from 25 states, and 1 foreign countries. 48% are from public schools. 81% are white; 14% African American. The average age of freshmen is 21. 23% do not continue beyond their first year; 76% remain to graduate.

Housing: 130 students can be accommodated in college housing, which includes coed on-campus apartments and off-campus apartments. On-campus housing is guaranteed for all 4 years. Alcohol is not permitted. All students may keep cars.

Activities: 38% of women belong to 1 local sorority. There are 15 groups on campus, including art, choir, computers, drama, literary magazine, musical theater, newspaper, social, social service, student government, and yearbook.

Disabled Students: 90% of the campus is accessible. Facilities include wheelchair ramps, special parking, specially equipped restrooms, special class scheduling, and special housing.

Services: Counseling and information services are available, as is tutoring in every subject. There is remedial math, reading, and writing. There is an academic mentoring program.

Campus Safety and Security: Measures include emergency notification system. There are lighted pathways/sidewalks, and school van transportation.

Programs of Study: Beacon confers B.A., and B.S. degrees. Associate degrees are also awarded. Bachelor's degrees are awarded in COMPUTER AND PHYSICAL SCIENCE (information sciences and systems), SOCIAL SCIENCE (human services and liberal arts/general studies). Information sciences and systems and liberal studies are the largest.

Required: To graduate, students must have 120 credit hours, including 33 credit hours of general education and at least 63 credit hours in their major, and a 2.0 GPA. Students in the liberal studies program must write a thesis and take a comprehensive exam.

Special: Internships, B.A.-B.S. degrees, dual majors, and study abroad are possible.

Faculty/Classroom: All teach undergraduates, 15% do research, and 15% do both. No introductory courses are taught by graduate students. The average class size in an introductory lecture is 8; in a laboratory is 10; and in a regular course is 8.

Requirements: Required testing and documentation include a clear diagnosis of learning disability or ADHD; Wechsler scales (WAIS-III are preferred) with full scale, cluster, and subtest scores; and Woodcock Johnson Test of Achievement with age- or grade-equivalency scores in reading, writing, and math; and average or above average IQ range with diagnosed learning disability. Although ACT and SAT scores are not required, the information is usual for placement and it is highly recommended that students take either the ACT or the SAT. Interviews may be required. CLEP credits are accepted. Important factors in the admissions decision are evidence of special talent, extracurricular activities record, and geographical diversity.

Procedure: Freshmen are admitted fall and spring. Entrance exams should be taken within 3 years prior to application. There is a rolling admissions plan. Application deadlines are open. Application fee is $50.

Transfer: Transfer students must meet the same requirements as all incoming students. 60 of 120 credits required for the bachelor's degree must be completed at Beacon.

Visiting: There are regularly scheduled orientations for prospective students. There are guides for informal visits. To schedule a visit, contact Admissions.

Financial Aid: The FAFSA and the college's own financial statement are required. Check with the school for current application deadlines.

International Students: There is 1 international student enrolled. They must take the TOEFL and WAIS subtests with the GLE in reading, writing, and math. The SAT or ACT is recommended.

Computers: Wireless access is available. All students may access the system. during school hours. There are no time limits and no fees. It is strongly recommended that all students have a personal computer.

Admissions Contact: Enrollment and Admissions Office. E-Mail: *admissions@beaconcollege.edu* Web: *www.beaconcollege.edu*

BETHUNE-COOKMAN UNIVERSITY D-2

Daytona Beach, FL 32114-3099 **(386) 481-2600**
(800) 448-0228; (386) 481-2601

Full-time: 1305 men, 2013 women	**Faculty:** 183; IIB, --$
Part-time: 101 men, 108 women	**Ph.D.s:** 58%
Graduate: 28 men, 23 women	**Student/Faculty:** 17 to 1
Year: semesters, summer session	**Tuition:** $14,490
Application Deadline: July 30	**Room & Board:** $8800

Freshman Class: 4707 applied, 3152 accepted, 886 enrolled

LESS COMPETITIVE

Bethune-Cookman University, founded in 1904, is a private liberal arts institution affiliated with the United Methodist Church. There are 6 undergraduate schools and 2 graduate schools. In addition to regional accreditation, B-CC or B-CU has baccalaureate program accreditation with NCATE. The library contains 127,930 volumes, 45,000 microform items, and 6,345 audio/video tapes/CDs/DVDs, and subscribes to 118 periodicals including electronic. Computerized library services include interlibrary loans, database searching, Internet access, and laptop Internet portals. Special learning facilities include a learning resource center, art gallery, radio station, TV station, observatory and founders' home and gravesite. The 84-acre campus is in a small town 65 miles east of Orlando. Including any residence halls, there are 63 buildings.

Student Life: 67% of undergraduates are from Florida. Others are from 39 states, 21 foreign countries, and Canada. 90% are from public schools. 92% are African American. 56% are Protestant; 28% Seventh Day Adventist, Muslim, and Jehovah Witness. The average age of freshmen is 18; all undergraduates, 21. 31% do not continue beyond their first year; 69% remain to graduate.

Housing: 1961 students can be accommodated in college housing, which includes single-sex and coed dorms. In addition, there are honors houses, Leadership House. On-campus housing is guaranteed for the freshman year only, is available on a first-come, and first-served basis. Priority is given to out-of-town students. 53% of students commute. Alcohol is not permitted. Upperclassmen may keep cars.

Activities: 25% of men belong to 5 national fraternities; 35% of women belong to 4 national sororities. There are 60 groups on campus, including band, cheerleading, choir, chorale, computers, dance, drama, drill team, honors, international, jazz band, literary magazine, marching band, newspaper, pep band, political, professional, radio and TV, religious, social, social service, student government, symphony, and yearbook. Popular campus events include Religious Outreach, Career Day, and Founders Day.

Sports: There are 8 intercollegiate sports for men and 9 for women, and 6 intramural sports for men and 8 for women. Facilities include a gym, weight-rooms, and practice fields.

Disabled Students: 35% of the campus is accessible. Facilities include wheelchair ramps, elevators, special parking, specially equipped restrooms, special class scheduling, lowered drinking fountains, and lowered telephones.

Services: Counseling and information services are available, as is tutoring in most subjects. There is remedial math, reading, and writing.

Campus Safety and Security: Measures include 24-hour foot and vehicle patrol and security escort services. There are lighted pathways/sidewalks, controlled access to dorms/residences, surveillance cameras and auto-lock door.

Programs of Study: B-CC or B-CU confers B.A., and B.S. degrees. Master's degrees are also awarded. Bachelor's degrees are awarded in BIOLOGICAL SCIENCE (biology/biological science), BUSINESS (accounting, business administration and management, hotel/motel and restaurant management, and international business management), COMMUNICATIONS AND THE ARTS (communications, dramatic arts, English, modern language, and music), COMPUTER AND PHYSICAL SCIENCE (chemistry, computer science, information sciences and systems, and mathematics), EDUCATION (business education, education, education of the exceptional child, elementary education, English education, music education, physical education, science education, and social science education), ENGINEERING AND ENVIRONMENTAL DESIGN (computer engineering), HEALTH PROFESSIONS (clinical science and nursing), SOCIAL SCIENCE (criminal justice, gerontology, history, international studies, liberal arts/general studies, political science/government, psychology, religion, and sociology). Business administration, education, and nursing are the strongest academically. Criminal justice has the largest enrollment.

Required: To graduate, students must have a minimum of 120 credit hours with a minimum GPA of 2.0. All students must complete a total of 39 hours in general education requirements, and pass at a specified level a senior exit exam that may include a standardized exam and/or senior area comprehensive exam. They must also complete a senior seminar and senior research paper, and must have 1 year residency, especially the last semester of study at B-CU.

Special: Students may take courses at other institutions with the approval of the area adviser or registrar. B-CU offers cooperative courses in all divisions, internships related to the student's major, work-study programs, an accelerated degree program in business administration, non-degree-study, and 3-2 engineering degrees. Study abroad is available in South Africa, Ghana, Cuba, Brazil and Zimbabwe. There are 11 national honor societies, a freshman honors program, and 1 departmental honors program.

Faculty/Classroom: 46% of faculty are male; 54% are female. No introductory courses are taught by graduate students. The average class size in an introductory lecture is 20; in a laboratory is 20; and in a regular course is 25.

Admissions: 67% of the 2011-2012 applicants were accepted.

Requirements: The SAT or ACT is required. Graduation from an accredited secondary school or satisfactory scores on the GED are required for admission. High school courses must include 24 credits with 4 of English, 3 each of math and science, 3 of social science and history, and 6 electives; 2 years of a modern language and 1 year of computer literacy are strongly recommended. Students must submit an essay and a letter of recommendation. A GPA of 2.3 is required. AP and CLEP credits are accepted. Important factors in the admissions decision are recommendations by school officials, leadership record, and geographical diversity.

Procedure: Freshmen are admitted to all sessions. Entrance exams should be taken during the fall prior to application. There are deferred admissions and rolling admissions plans. Applications should be filed by July 30 for fall entry; November 30 for spring entry; and April 30 for summer entry, along with a $25 fee. Notification is sent on a rolling basis.

Transfer: 108 transfer students enrolled in a recent year. Applicants must submit transcripts from previous institutions attended and a statement of good standing and eligibility to return. A minimum GPA of 2.25 is required. Students having fewer than 24 credit hours must meet the requirements for entering freshmen. 30 of 120 credits required for the bachelor's degree must be completed at B-CC or B-CU.

Visiting: There are guides for informal visits and visitors may sit in on classes. To schedule a visit, contact Office of Admissions.

Financial Aid: In a recent year, 82% of all full-time freshmen and 92% of continuing full-time students received some form of financial aid. 80% of all full-time freshmen and 89% of continuing full-time students received need-based aid. The average freshman award was $13,190. Need-based scholarships or need-based grants averaged $9,903 ($19,000 maximum); need-based self-help aid (loans and jobs) averaged $3,796 ($5,500 maximum); non-need-based athletic scholarships averaged $10,338 ($22,300 maximum); and other non-need-based awards and non-need-based scholarships averaged $8,380 ($20,000 maximum). 23% of undergraduate students work part-time. Average annual earnings from campus work are $2100. The average financial indebtedness of a recent graduate was $21,435. The FAFSA is required. The priority date for freshman financial aid applications for fall entry is April 1.

International Students: There are 70 international students enrolled. The school actively recruits these students. They must take the TOEFL with a minimum score of 550 on the paper-based TOEFL (PBT) or 73 on the Internet-based version (iBT). They must also take the SAT or ACT.

Computers: Computing labs available in all academic buildings, Library/Learning Resources Center, and all residential rooms have access to Internet and e-mail. All students may access the system. There are no time limits and no fees.

Graduates: In a recent year, 561 bachelor's degrees were awarded. The most popular majors were education (15%), criminal justice (14%), and business administration (12%). In an average class, 2% graduate in 3 years or less, 15% graduate in 4 years or less, 31% graduate in 5 years or less, and 37% graduate in 6 years or less. Of the recent graduating class, 20% were enrolled in graduate school within 6 months of graduation, and 17% were employed.

Admissions Contact: Director of Admissions. A campus DVD is available. *Web: www.cookman.edu*

CARLOS ALBIZU UNIVERSITY E-5

Miami, FL 33172 (305) 593-1223 ext 3259
(800) 672-3246; (305) 593-1854

Full-time: 65 men, 193 women
Part-time: 35 men, 138 women
Graduate: 146 men, 592 women
Year: varies, summer session
Application Deadline:
Freshman Class: 58 applied, 21 accepted, 16 enrolled
Faculty: 6
Ph.D.s: 87%
Student/Faculty: 11 to 1
Tuition: $12,553
Room & Board: n/app

LESS COMPETITIVE

Carlos Albizu University is a private, nonprofit, specialized institution of higher learning offering degrees at the undergraduate, graduate, and doctoral levels. CAU has campuses in San Juan, Puerto Rico, and Miami, Florida, founded in 1966 and 1980, respectively. There are 3 undergraduate schools and 3 graduate schools. The library contains 25,198 volumes, and 1,000 audio/video tapes/CDs/DVDs, and subscribes to 5,365 periodicals including electronic. Computerized library services include interlibrary loans, database searching, and Internet access. The 18-acre campus is in a small town in Miami. Including any residence halls, there are 2 buildings.

Student Life: 98% of undergraduates are from Florida. Others are from 22 states, 42 foreign countries, and Canada. 87% are Hispanic. The average age of freshmen is 28; all undergraduates, 35. 1% do not continue beyond their first year; 37% remain to graduate.

Housing: Alcohol is not permitted. All students commute. All students may keep cars.

Activities: There are no fraternities or sororities. There are 4 groups on campus, including dance, ethnic, gay, honors, newsletter, and student government. Popular campus events include Student Awards Banquet, Student Council Initiation Event, and Hispanic Heritage Month Event.

Sports: There is no sports program at CAU.

Disabled Students: All of the campus is accessible. Facilities include wheelchair ramps, special parking, specially equipped restrooms, and lowered drinking fountains.

Services: Counseling and information services are available, as is tutoring in most subjects. There is a mentoring program and student support services center.

Campus Safety and Security: Measures include 24-hour foot and vehicle patrol and security escort services. There are emergency telephones, lighted pathways/sidewalks, campus crime report.

Programs of Study: CAU confers B.A., B.S. and B.B.A. degrees. Master's and doctoral degrees are also awarded. Bachelor's degrees are awarded in BUSINESS (business administration and management), EDUCATION (elementary education), SOCIAL SCIENCE (psychology). Psychology has the largest enrollment.

Required: To graduate, students must earn 120 to 124 credits, with 39 to 67 in the major. Foundation courses include English composition, oral communication, math, behavioral life, physical sciences, humanities, cross-cultural studies, literature, liberal arts, and computing, for a total of 48 credits. A GPA of 2.5 is required.

Special: CAU offers cross-registration with other area colleges, internships or practicums in psychology and elementary education, federal work-study, an accelerated degree program in business administration, and dual majors in psychology and elementary education. There are 2 national honor societies and 2 departmental honors programs.

Faculty/Classroom: 39% of faculty are male; 61% are female. 47% teach undergraduates. No introductory courses are taught by graduate students. The average class size in an introductory lecture is 12; in a laboratory is 10; and in a regular course is 15.

Admissions: 36% of the 2013-2014 applicants were accepted.

Requirements: A GPA of 2.5 is required. AP and CLEP credits are accepted. Important factors in the admissions decision are advanced placement or honors courses and ability to finance college education.

Procedure: Freshmen are admitted fall, spring, and summer. There is a rolling admissions plan. Application deadlines are open. Application fee is $25. Notification is sent on a rolling basis. Applications are accepted online.

Transfer: 66 transfer students enrolled in 2012-2013. Transfer applicants must have an overall GPA of 2.5 and must submit official transcripts from all colleges/universities previously attended. 30 of 120 credits required for the bachelor's degree must be completed at CAU.

Visiting: There are regularly scheduled orientations for prospective students, new student orientation and 2 open houses per session. There are guides for informal visits and visitors may sit in on classes.

Financial Aid: In 2013-2014, 7% of all full-time freshmen students received some form of financial aid. 6% of all full-time freshmen and % of continuing full-time students received need-based aid. The average freshman award was $3,896. Need-based scholarships or need-based grants averaged $2,919 ($2,919 maximum); need-based self-help aid (loans and jobs) averaged $1,475 ($1,750 maximum); other non-need-based awards and non-need-based scholarships averaged $1,100 ($1,500 maximum); and $960 from other forms of aid. 4% of undergraduate students work part-time. Average annual earnings from campus work are $3600. The FAFSA and the college's own financial statement are required. The priority date for freshman financial aid applications for fall entry is April 15. The deadline for filing freshman financial aid applications for fall entry is June 1.

International Students: There are 12 international students enrolled. They must take the MELAB.

Computers: All students may access the system. from 10 a.m. to 9 p.m. Monday through Friday, and Saturdays from 9 a.m. to 3 p.m. There are no time limits and no fees.

Graduates: From July 1, 2012 to June 30, 2013, 108 bachelor's degrees were awarded. The most popular majors were psychology (54%), business (31%), and education (15%). Of the 2012 graduating class, 69% were enrolled in graduate school within 6 months of graduation, and 11% were employed.

Admissions Contact: Elery Rojas, Admissions Officer. E-Mail: *erojas@albizu.edu* Web: *www.albizu.edu*

CLEARWATER CHRISTIAN COLLEGE D-4

Clearwater, FL 33759 (727) 726-1153, ext. 220
(800) 348-4463; (727) 726-8597

Full-time: 290 men, 280 women
Part-time: 10 men, 10 women
Graduate: 5 men, 10 women
Year: semesters, summer session
Application Deadline: July 1
Freshman Class: n/av
SAT or ACT: required
Faculty: 32
Ph.D.s: 63%
Student/Faculty: 17 to 1
Tuition: $16,750
Room & Board: $7970

COMPETITIVE

Clearwater Christian College, founded in 1966, is a private, nondenominational institution offering 30 majors in graduate and undergraduate programs. The figures in the above capsule and in this profile are approximate. There are 6 undergraduate schools and 1 graduate school. The library contains 113,000 volumes, 100,000 microform items, and 7,570 audio/video tapes/CDs/DVDs, and subscribes to 12,000 periodicals including electronic. Computerized library services include interlibrary loans, database searching, Internet access, and laptop Internet portals. Special learning facilities include a learning resource center. The 138-acre campus is in a rural area 10 miles west of Tampa. Including any residence halls, there are 8 buildings.

Student Life: 55% of undergraduates are from out of state, mostly the South. Students are from 37 states, 9 foreign countries, and Canada. 25% are from public schools. 89% are white. 100% are Protestant. The average age of freshmen is 19; all undergraduates, 20. 30% do not continue beyond their first year; 44% remain to graduate.

Housing: 600 students can be accommodated in college housing, which includes single-sex dorms. On-campus housing is guaranteed for all 4 years. 79% of students live on campus; of those, 67% remain on campus on weekends. Alcohol is not permitted. All students may keep cars.

Activities: There are 20 groups on campus, including band, cheerleading, choir, chorale, chorus, drama, film, honors, newspaper, orchestra, pep band, political, professional, religious, social, social service, student government, symphony, and yearbook. Popular campus events include Junior Senior Banquet, film festival, and Midnight Madness.

Sports: There are 4 intercollegiate sports for men and 4 for women, and 4 intramural sports for men and 3 for women. Facilities include a 12,000-square-foot gym, a lighted outdoor soccer field, and outdoor basketball and tennis courts.

Disabled Students: All of the campus is accessible. Facilities include wheelchair ramps, elevators, special parking, and specially equipped restrooms.

Services: There is a reader service for the blind, and remedial math, reading, and writing as needed.

Campus Safety and Security: Measures include 24-hour foot and vehicle patrol and emergency notification system. There are lighted pathways/sidewalks.

Programs of Study: CCC confers B.A. and B.S. degrees. Associate and master's degrees are also awarded. Bachelor's degrees are awarded in BIOLOGICAL SCIENCE (biology/biological science), BUSINESS (accounting and business administration and management), COMMUNICATIONS AND THE ARTS (communications, English, and music), COMPUTER AND PHYSICAL SCIENCE (mathematics), EDUCATION (elementary education, music education, physical education, secondary education, social studies education, and special education), HEALTH PROFESSIONS (premedicine), SOCIAL SCIENCE (biblical studies, history, humanities, ministries, pastoral studies, prelaw, psychology, religious education, and religious music). Biology and premed are the strongest academically. Education and business have the largest enrollments.

Required: Students must complete courses in computer science, English, humanities, math, science, social science, and theology/Bible. A total of

128 credit hours is required, including more than 60 in the major, with a minimum GPA of 2.0. Students may have no grade lower than a C- in any major course.

Special: Students may cross-register for ROTC with the University of Florida. The college also offers internships, study abroad in 14 countries, and student-designed majors in interdisciplinary studies. There is 1 national honor society.

Faculty/Classroom: 69% of faculty are male; 31% are female. All teach undergraduates. No introductory courses are taught by graduate students. The average class size in an introductory lecture is 42; in a laboratory is 10; and in a regular course is 12.

Admissions: 8 freshmen graduated first in their class.

Requirements: The SAT or ACT is required, with a minimum score of 870 on the SAT or 18 composite on the ACT. Applicants must be high school graduates or have a GED certificate. An essay is required, and an interview is recommended. A GPA of 2.0 is required. AP and CLEP credits are accepted. Important factors in the admissions decision are personality/intangible qualities, recommendations by school officials, leadership record, parents or siblings attended the school, extracurricular activities record, ability to finance college education, advanced placement or honors courses, evidence of special talent, recommendations by alumni, and geographical diversity.

Procedure: Freshmen are admitted fall, spring, and summer. Entrance exams should be taken during the junior or senior year. There are deferred admissions and rolling admissions plans. Applications should be filed by July 1 for fall entry; December 1 for spring entry, along with a $35 fee. Applications are accepted online.

Transfer: 65 transfer students enrolled in a recent year. Transfer applicants must submit transcripts from all postsecondary schools attended. Grades of C or better transfer. Applicants must have a minimum cumulative postsecondary GPA of 2.0. 30 of 128 credits required for the bachelor's degree must be completed at CCC.

Visiting: There are regularly scheduled orientations for prospective students, consisting of campus tours, classroom visits, sessions on admissions and financial aid, lunch, and meeting administrators, faculty, and coaches. There are guides for informal visits, visitors may sit in on classes, and stay overnight. To schedule a visit, contact the Admissions Office.

Financial Aid: In a recent year, 99% of all full-time freshmen and 95% of continuing full-time students received some form of financial aid. The average freshman award was $13,609. 45% of undergraduate students work part-time. Average annual earnings from campus work are $1600. The average financial indebtedness of the 2011 graduate was $13,051. The CSS/Profile, FAFSA, and FFS are required. Check with the school for current application deadlines.

International Students: There are 17 international students enrolled. They must take the TOEFL. Applicants must also submit a Foreign Student Data Form. They must also take the SAT or ACT.

Computers: Residence halls have network connections and there are 50 computers in the library and computer lab for general use. All of the campus has wireless Internet connectivity. All students may access the system. There are no time limits. The fee is $62. It is strongly recommended that all students have a personal computer.

Graduates: In a recent year, 123 bachelor's degrees were awarded. The most popular majors were general studies (15%), education (14%), and psychology (11%). 60 companies recruited on campus in 2010-2011. In an average class, 3% graduate in 3 years or less, 37% graduate in 4 years or less, 42% graduate in 5 years or less, and 42% graduate in 6 years or less. Of the recent graduating class, 25% were enrolled in graduate school within 6 months of graduation, and 82% were employed.

Admissions Contact: Director of Admissions. A campus DVD is available. E-Mail: *admissions@clearwater.edu* Web: *www.clearwater.edu*

ECKERD COLLEGE D-4

St. Petersburg, FL 33711 (727) 864-8331
(800) 456-9009; (727) 866-2304

Full-time: 755 men, 1094 women	**Faculty:** 117; IIB, av$
Part-time: 17 men, 27 women	**Ph.D.s:** 93%
Graduate: n/av	**Student/Faculty:** 13 to 1
Year: 4-1-4, summer session	**Tuition:** $34,546
Application Deadline: April 1	**Room & Board:** $9652
Freshman Class: 3910 applied, 2776 accepted, 532 enrolled	
SAT CR/M: 565/550	**ACT:** 25 **VERY COMPETITIVE**

Eckerd College, founded in 1958, is a private liberal arts institution affiliated with the Presbyterian Church. Interdisciplinary programs are an important part of the school's curriculum, thus faculty are organized into collegia, rather than into traditional departments. The library contains 181,031 volumes, 14,338 microform items, and 3,415 audio/video tapes/CDs/DVDs, and subscribes to 6,775 periodicals including electronic. Computerized library services include interlibrary loans, database searching, and Internet access. Special learning facilities include an art gallery and radio station. The 188-acre campus is in a suburban area on 1 1/4 miles of Waterfront, 5 miles south of St. Petersburg. Including any residence halls, there are 87 buildings.

Student Life: 76% of undergraduates are from out of state, mostly the Middle Atlantic. Students are from 45 states, 35 foreign countries, and Canada. 79% are White. 61% claim no religious affiliation; 13% Catholic. The average age of freshmen is 18; all undergraduates, 20. 19% do not continue beyond their first year; 60% remain to graduate.

Housing: 1501 students can be accommodated in college housing, which includes single-sex and coed dorms and on-campus apartments. In addition, there are language houses, community service, pet dorms and substance free houses. On-campus housing is guaranteed for the freshman year only, is available on a first-come, first-served basis, and is available on a lottery system for upperclassmen. 81% of students live on campus; of those, 92% remain on campus on weekends. All students may keep cars.

Activities: There are no fraternities or sororities. There are 90 groups on campus, including art, cheerleading, chess, choir, chorale, chorus, communications, computers, dance, drama, environmental, ethnic, film, gay, honors, international, literary magazine, musical theater, newspaper, photography, political, professional, radio and TV, religious, social, social service, student government, water search and rescue, and yearbook. Popular campus events include Festival of Hope, EC Surreal-fest in partnership with the Dali Museum, Festival of Cultures and Earth Fest.

Sports: There are 5 intercollegiate sports for men and 6 for women, and 13 intramural sports for men and 13 for women. Facilities include a gym, a baseball and softball complex, soccer fields, tennis courts, an open-air multi-purpose sports pavilion, a weight room, a renovated and modernized fitness room, a swimming pool, and waterfront facilities.

Disabled Students: 95% of the campus is accessible. Facilities include wheelchair ramps, elevators, special parking, specially equipped restrooms, special class scheduling, lowered drinking fountains, and lowered telephones.

Services: Counseling and information services are available, as is tutoring in some subjects, math, sciences and foreign languages.

Campus Safety and Security: Measures include 24-hour foot and vehicle patrol, emergency notification system, and security escort services. There are emergency telephones and lighted pathways/sidewalks.

Programs of Study: Eckerd confers B.A., and B.S. degrees. Bachelor's degrees are awarded in AGRICULTURE (environmental studies), BIOLOGICAL SCIENCE (biochemistry, biology/biological science, and marine science), BUSINESS (business administration and management, international business management, and management science), COMMUNICATIONS AND THE ARTS (communications, comparative literature, creative writing, dramatic arts, French, literature, music, Spanish, and visual and performing arts), COMPUTER AND PHYSICAL SCIENCE (chemistry, computer science, geoscience, mathematics, and physics), HEALTH PROFESSIONS (predentistry and premedicine), SOCIAL SCIENCE (American studies, anthropology, classical/ancient civilization, East Asian studies, economics, history, human development, humanities, international relations, philosophy, political science/government, prelaw, psychology, religion, sociology, and women's studies). Marine science, environmental studies, psychology have the largest enrollments.

Required: To graduate, students must complete a total of 36 courses or 126 semester hours with a minimum GPA of 2.0. Required courses include 1 each in the arts, humanities, natural and social sciences, and environmental and global perspectives. Students must also demonstrate competencies in writing, speaking, foreign language, computation, and technology and must take a comprehensive exam or submit a thesis or project in the senior year.

Special: Eckerd offers internships, study abroad, work-study programs, and dual majors in all subjects, interdisciplinary majors in international relations and environmental studies, student-designed majors, nondegree study, and pass/fail options. Students may earn B.A.-B.S. degrees in biology, chemistry, and marine science. A 3-2 engineering degree is offered with Washington and Columbia Universities. There are 8 national honor societies, including Phi Beta Kappa, and a freshman honors program.

Faculty/Classroom: 58% of faculty are male; 42% are female. All teach and do research. No introductory courses are taught by graduate students. The average class size in an introductory lecture is 20; in a laboratory is 15; and in a regular course is 20.

Admissions: 71% of the 2013-2014 applicants were accepted. The SAT scores for the 2013-2014 freshman class were: Critical Reading--20% below 500, 45% between 500 and 599, 27% between 600 and 699, and 8% between 700 and 800; Math--25% below 500, 41% between 500 and 599, 30% between 600 and 699, and 4% between 700 and 800. The ACT scores were 14% below 21, 24% between 21 and 23, 29% between 24 and 26, 16% between 27 and 28, and 18% above 28.

Requirements: The SAT or ACT is required. Graduation from an accredited secondary school or satisfactory scores on the GED is required. High school courses must include 4 years of English, 3 each of math and science, 2 each of a foreign language and social studies, and 1 of history. SAT: Subject tests in writing, literature, and math are recommended. An essay is required and an interview is recommended. A GPA of 2.0 is required. AP and CLEP credits are accepted. Important factors in the admissions decision are advanced placement or honors courses, leadership record, and personality/intangible qualities.

Procedure: Freshmen are admitted fall, winter, and spring. Entrance exams should be taken in October, November or December. There are early admissions, deferred admissions, and rolling admissions plans. Applications should be filed by April 1 for fall entry; December 1 for winter entry; and December 1 for spring entry, along with a $40 fee. 111 applicants were on the 2013 waiting list; 34 were admitted. Applications are accepted online.

Transfer: 66 transfer students enrolled in 2012-2013. Applicants must have a minimum GPA of 2.5. The SAT or ACT is required. An interview is recommended. A faculty recommendation is required. 63 of 126 credits required for the bachelor's degree must be completed at Eckerd.

Visiting: There are regularly scheduled orientations for prospective students, consisting of an interview and a tour. There are guides for informal visits, visitors may sit in on classes, and stay overnight. To schedule a visit, contact the Admissions Office.

Financial Aid: The FAFSA is required. The priority date for freshman financial aid applications for fall entry is March 1.

International Students: There are 83 international students enrolled. The school actively recruits these students. They must take the TOEFL with a minimum score of 550 on the paper-based TOEFL (PBT) or 79 on the Internet-based version (iBT). They must also take the SAT or ACT.

Computers: All students may access the system at any time. There are no time limits and no fees.

Graduates: From July 1, 2012 to June 30, 2013, 439 bachelor's degrees were awarded. The most popular majors were marine science (10%), environmental studies (10%), and biology (8%). 120 companies recruited on campus in 2012-2013. In an average class, 60% graduate in 6 years or less. Of the 2012 graduating class, 35% were enrolled in graduate school within 6 months of graduation, and 60% were employed.

Admissions Contact: John Sullivan, Dean of Admissions and Financial Aid. E-Mail: *admissions@eckerd.edu* Web: *www.eckerd.edu*

EDWARD WATERS COLLEGE D-1

Jacksonville, FL 32209 (904) 470-8202 (888) 898-3191; (904) 470-8048

Full-time: 680 men, 620 women	**Faculty:** n/av
Part-time: 50 men, 50 women	**Ph.D.s:** 18%
Graduate: n/av	**Student/Faculty:** n/av
Year: semesters, summer session	**Tuition:** $11,494
Application Deadline: open	**Room & Board:** $7092
Freshman Class: n/av	

LESS COMPETITIVE

Edward Waters College, founded in 1866, is the oldest independent institution of higher learning in Florida. The college offers programs in the arts and sciences, business, and education. The figures in the above capsule and in this profile are approximate. There are 3 graduate schools. The library contains 65,798 volumes, and 2,900 audio/video tapes/CDs/DVDs, and subscribes to 1,350 periodicals including electronic. Computerized library services include interlibrary loans, database searching, and Internet access. Special learning facilities include a learning resource center, art gallery, a museum of African art. The 50-acre campus is in an urban area in Jacksonville. Including any residence halls, there are 25 buildings.

Student Life: 90% of undergraduates are from Florida. Others are from 12 states, 4 foreign countries, and Canada. 90% are from public schools. 95% are African American. The average age of freshmen is 18; all undergraduates, 20. 40% do not continue beyond their first year; 60% remain to graduate.

Housing: 584 students can be accommodated in college housing, which includes single-sex dorms. In addition, there are honors houses. 53% of students live on campus; of those, 45% remain on campus on weekends. Alcohol is not permitted. All students may keep cars.

Activities: 20% of men belong to 4 national fraternities; 35% of women belong to 4 national sororities. There are 20 groups on campus, including band, cheerleading, choir, chorus, dance, drama, drill team, honors, international, jazz band, marching band, newspaper, pep band, photography, political, professional, religious, social service, student government, and yearbook. Popular campus events include Fall and Spring Convocations, Religious Emphasis Week, and African American History Celebration.

Sports: There are 6 intercollegiate sports for men and 5 for women, and 3 intramural sports for men and 3 for women.

Disabled Students: 75% of the campus is accessible. Facilities include wheelchair ramps, elevators, special parking, specially equipped restrooms, and lowered drinking fountains.

Services: Counseling and information services are available, as is tutoring in every subject. There is remedial math, reading, and writing. There is a student support services program for students who are academically disadvantaged. Academic career counseling employment services are available.

Campus Safety and Security: Measures include 24-hour foot and vehicle patrol and security escort services. There are emergency telephones and lighted pathways/sidewalks.

Programs of Study: EWC confers B.A., B.S., and B.B.A. degrees. Bachelor's degrees are awarded in BIOLOGICAL SCIENCE (biology/biological science), BUSINESS (accounting and business administration and management), COMMUNICATIONS AND THE ARTS (communications and English), COMPUTER AND PHYSICAL SCIENCE (computer science and mathematics), EDUCATION (early childhood education, elementary education, and physical education), SOCIAL SCIENCE (criminal justice, history, philosophy, political science/government, psychology, religion, and sociology). Education is the strongest academically. Business administration has the largest enrollment.

Required: To graduate, all students must complete at least 120 credit hours, including 30 in the major, with a 2.0 GPA overall and in the major. Weekly chapel service attendance is required.

Special: EWC offers co-op programs, internships in communications, political science, education, and criminal justice, dual and student-designed majors, and work-study programs. A dual law degree with Florida Coastal School of Law and a 3-2 engineering degree with Florida A&M University are offered. There is a freshman honors program.

Faculty/Classroom: 50% of faculty are male; 50% are female. All teach undergraduates. No introductory courses are taught by graduate students.

Requirements: SAT or ACT scores are necessary for unconditional admission. Applicants must be graduates of an accredited secondary school or have a GED certificate and have taken the California Achievement Test. A GPA of 2.0 is required. AP and CLEP credits are accepted. Important factors in the admissions decision are advanced placement or honors courses, ability to finance college education, and recommendations by school officials.

Procedure: Freshmen are admitted fall and spring. There is a rolling admissions plan. Check with the school for current application deadlines. Applications are accepted online.

Transfer: 30 of 120 credits required for the bachelor's degree must be completed at EWC.

Visiting: There are guides for informal visits. To schedule a visit, contact the Admissions Office.

Financial Aid: EWC is a member of CSS. The FAFSA is required. The priority date for freshman financial aid applications for fall entry is March 1.

International Students: The school actively recruits these students.

Computers: All students may access the system. There are no time limits and no fees.

Admissions Contact: Director of Enrollment. A campus DVD is available. Web: *www.ewc.edu*

EMBRY-RIDDLE AERONAUTICAL UNIVERSITY - DAYTONA BEACH D-2

Daytona Beach, FL 32114 386-226-6100; (800) 862-2416

Full-time: 3619 men, 740 women	**Faculty:** 328; IIA, av$
Part-time: 266 men, 54 women	**Ph.D.s:** 65%
Graduate: 438 men, 162 women	**Student/Faculty:** 13 to 1
Year: semesters, summer session	**Tuition:** $31,334
Application Deadline: July 1	**Room & Board:** $9550

Freshman Class: 4074 applied, 3017 accepted, 944 enrolled

SAT CR/M/W: 530/580/510 **ACT:** 24 **COMPETITIVE+**

Embry-Riddle Aeronautical University, founded in 1926, is a private institution offering undergraduate programs in aviation, engineering, and business on 2 campuses: one in Daytona Beach and the other, founded in 1978, in Prescott, Arizona. There are 4 undergraduate schools and one graduate school. In addition to regional accreditation, ERAU has baccalaureate program accreditation with ABET and ACBSP. The library contains 102,374 volumes, 308,127 microform items, and 5,331 audio/video tapes/CDs/DVDs, and subscribes to 1,039 periodicals including electronic. Computerized library services include interlibrary loans, database searching, Internet access, and Wi-Fi capability. Special learning facilities include a radio station, State-of-the-Art Advanced Flight Simulation Center; Chandler Titus Engine Repair Station (AMS Engine Test); Clean Energy Systems Lab; Electrical Engineering Laboratory; Airport Technology and Operations Lab; Applied Aviation Simulation Lab; Business Process Lab; Radio-Frequency Identification Lab; Transportation and Logistics Lab . The 185-acre campus is in an urban area 48 miles northeast of Orlando. Including any residence halls, there are 45 buildings.

Student Life: 65% of undergraduates are from out of state, mostly the South. Students are from 50 states, 97 foreign countries, and Canada. 53% are White; 16% Foreign. The average age of freshmen is 18; all undergraduates, 21.

Housing: 1994 students can be accommodated in college housing, which includes coed dorms, on-campus apartments, and off-campus apartments. On-campus housing is guaranteed for the freshman year only, is available on a first-come, first-served basis, and is available on a lottery system for upperclassmen. 64% of students commute. All students may keep cars.

Activities: There are 140 groups on campus, including cheerleading, chess, chorale, computers, dance, debate, drama, drill team, environmental, ethnic, film, gay, honors, international, literary magazine, musical theater, newspaper, pep band, photography, political, professional, radio and TV, religious, social, social service, and student government. Popular campus events include Homecoming, Touch-n-Go events that includes Bands, Comedians, Magicians, Movies every Thursday night, Student Activities Fair and Annual Arts & Letters Shakespeare Production.

Sports: There are 7 intercollegiate sports for men and 8 for women. The ICI Center is a 50,000+ square-foot facility that is home to the Eagle's Men's Basketball and Women's Volleyball teams and is the centerpiece for campus recreation, athletics and some University functions; state-of-the-art Eagle Fitness Center; Swimming Pool with shower and locker room facilities; Tennis and Basketball Courts, Crotty Tennis Complex; Racquetball courts; Intercollegiate Soccer Stadium and Softball Fields; Sliwa Baseball Stadium; new state-of-the-art NCAA-approved Track & Field Complex.

Disabled Students: 95% of the campus is accessible. Facilities include wheelchair ramps, elevators, special parking, specially equipped restrooms, lowered drinking fountains, lowered telephones.

Services: Counseling and information services are available, as is tutoring in some subjects, First year math, physics, chemistry and writing (composition) There is remedial math, reading, and writing. Lower level engineering courses

Campus Safety and Security: Measures include 24-hour foot and vehicle patrol, emergency notification system, self-defense education, and security escort services. There are emergency telephones, lighted pathways/sidewalks, controlled access to dorms/residences, and in room safes.

Programs of Study: ERAU confers B.S. degrees. Associate, master's, and doctoral degrees are also awarded. Bachelor's degrees are awarded in BUSINESS (business administration and management and transportation management), COMMUNICATIONS AND THE ARTS (communications), COMPUTER AND PHYSICAL SCIENCE (atmospheric sciences and meteorology, computer science, mathematics, physical sciences, and software engineering), ENGINEERING AND ENVIRONMENTAL DESIGN (aeronautical engineering, aeronautical science, aerospace studies, air traffic control, airline piloting and navigation, aviation maintenance management, civil engineering, computer engineering, electrical/electronics engineering, engineering, engineering physics, engineering technology, and mechanical engineering), SOCIAL SCIENCE (psychology, safety and security technology, and safety science). Aerospace Engineering is the strongest academically. Aerospace Engineering, Aeronautical science (flight), and Aeronautics have the largest enrollments.

Required: To graduate, students must complete a total of 120 to 136 credit hours, including 60 in the major, with a minimum GPA of 2.0. All students must complete 36 credits of general education requirements, including courses in communication skills, technical report writing, humanities/social sciences, math, physical science, economics, and computer science.

Special: ERAU offers co-op programs and internships in all majors, study abroad in 21 countries, work-study programs, accelerated degree programs in aerospace engineering and engineering physics, credit for life experience, and non-degree study. There are 9 national honor societies and a freshman honors program.

Faculty/Classroom: 73% of faculty are male; 27% are female. All teach undergraduates. No introductory courses are taught by graduate students. The average class size in an introductory lecture is 28; in a laboratory is 15; and in a regular course is 23.

Admissions: 74% of the 2013-2014 applicants were accepted. The SAT scores for the 2013-2014 freshman class were: Critical Reading--33% below 500, 43% between 500 and 599, 21% between 600 and 699, and 3% between 700 and 800; Math--19% below 500, 40% between 500 and 599, 31% between 600 and 699, and 10% between 700 and 800; Writing--41% below 500, 40% between 500 and 599, 17% between 600 and 699, and 13% between 700 and 800. The ACT scores were 19% below 21, 24% between 21 and 23, 24% between 24 and 26, 14% between 27 and 28, and 19% above 28. 43% of the current freshmen were in the top fifth of their class; 70% were in the top two fifths.

Requirements: The SAT or ACT is recommended. Students should complete a competitive academic program in high school, including 16 Carnegie units with at least 3 years of math. Admissions decisions are based on the strength of the academic record, rank in class, standardized test scores, recommendations, and the written statement. A GPA of 2.0 is required. AP and CLEP credits are accepted. Important factors in the admissions decision are advanced placement or honors courses, recommendations by school officials, and evidence of special talent.

Procedure: Freshmen are admitted fall, spring, and summer. Entrance exams should be taken During spring of the junior year or fall of the senior year. There are deferred admissions and rolling admissions plans. Early decision applications should be filed by December 1; regular applications, by July 1 for fall entry; November 1 for spring entry; and April 1 for summer entry, along with a $50 fee. Notification is sent on a rolling basis. Applications are accepted online.

Transfer: 1003 transfer students enrolled in 2012-2013. A GPA of 2.5 is preferred. 30 of 120 credits required for the bachelor's degree must be completed at ERAU.

Visiting: There are regularly scheduled orientations for prospective students. There are guides for informal visits and visitors may sit in on classes. To schedule a visit, contact the Admissions Office at (386) 226-6100.

Financial Aid: In 2013-2014, 79% of all full-time freshmen and 81% of continuing full-time students received some form of financial aid. 80% of all full-time freshmen and 81% of continuing full-time students received need-based aid. The average freshman award was $16,066. Need-based scholarships or need-based grants averaged $11,732; need-based self help aid (loans and jobs) averaged $4,068; and non-need-based athletic scholarships averaged $15,298. 32% of undergraduate students work part-time. Average annual earnings from campus work are $2436. The FAFSA is required. The priority date for freshman financial aid applications for fall entry is March 1.

International Students: There are 698 international students enrolled. The school actively recruits these students. They must take the TOEFL with a minimum score of 550 on the paper-based TOEFL (PBT) or 79 on the Internet-based version (iBT). They must also take the SAT or ACT.

Computers: All students may access the system at any time. There are no time limits and no fees.

Graduates: From July 1, 2012 to June 30, 2013, 818 bachelor's degrees were awarded. The most popular majors were aerospace engineering and aeronautics. 120 companies recruited on campus in 2012-2013.

Admissions Contact: Robert J. Adams, Director of Undergraduate Admissions. E-Mail: *dbadmit@db.erau.edu* Web: *www.erau.edu*

EMBRY-RIDDLE AERONAUTICAL UNIVERSITY - WORLDWIDE

Daytona Beach, FL 32114 **800-522-6787 Option #2; 386-226-6984**

Full-time: 2655 men, 357 women	**Faculty:** n/av
Part-time: 6530 men, 870 women	**Ph.D.s:** 51%
Graduate: 4151 men, 848 women	**Student/Faculty:** n/av
Year: other, summer session	**Tuition:** $7032
Application Deadline:	**Room & Board:** $8480
Freshman Class: n/av	
ACT: recommended	

COMPETITIVE

Embry-Riddle Aeronautical University – Worldwide has a distinctive mission and history that set us apart from other universities. Worldwide has grown from humble beginnings at Fort Rucker in 1970, with 20 students and a single location, to over 150 locations in the United States, Canada, Europe, the Middle East and Asia, with more than 27,000 students and 90,000 annual registrations. There are 4 undergraduate schools. In addition to regional accreditation, ERAU - Worldwide has baccalaureate program accreditation with ACBSP. The library contains 102,374 volumes, 308,127 microform items, and 5,331 audio/video tapes/CDs/DVDs, and subscribes to 1,039 periodicals including electronic. Computerized library services include interlibrary loans, database searching, Internet access, and Wi-Fi capability. Special learning facilities include a radio station. Embry-Riddle Aeronautical University-Worldwide is made up of over 150 locations in the United States, Europe, the Middle East, and Asia.

Student Life: 50% are White; 25% race unknown.

Housing: College-sponsored housing includes

Activities: There are no fraternities or sororities.

Sports: There is no sports program at ERAU - Worldwide.

Services: There is remedial math and writing.

Campus Safety and Security: Measures include emergency notification system.

Programs of Study: ERAU - Worldwide confers B.S. degrees. Associate, master's, and doctoral degrees are also awarded. Bachelor's degrees are awarded in BUSINESS (business administration and management, management science, supply chain management, and transportation management), ENGINEERING AND ENVIRONMENTAL DESIGN (aeronautical science, aircraft mechanics, occupational safety and health, preengineering, systems engineering, and technological management), SOCIAL SCIENCE (fire science). Aeronautics, aeronautical science, and technical management are the strongest academically. Aeronautics, technical management and master of aeronautical science have the largest enrollments.

Required: Graduate students are required to complete all graduate course work with ERAU with a maximum of 12 credit hours of transfer work permitted. For undergraduate degree completion, at least 25 percent of semester credit hours must be earned through ERAU instruction. Students pursuing any undergraduate degree must earn a minimum cumulative grade point average (CGPA) of 2.00 for all work completed within the degree program at the University. Students pursuing any graduate degree must earn a minimum cumulative grade point average (CGPA) of 3.00 for all work completed within the degree program at the University. Students must complete the general graduation requirements as prescribed by the

University, as well as all degree requirements specified in the degree program being pursued. Graduation requirements are not subject to petition or waiver. Students must initiate an application for graduation through the student information system, and follow up by completing a Graduation Information Sheet in ERNIE. A qualified student will not be graduated by ERAU until a graduation application and information sheet have been received and processed by the University, and the graduation fee has been remitted.

Special: Embry-Riddle Aeronautical University is the world's oldest and largest fully accredited university specializing in aviation and aerospace. With more than 150 campuses,Embry-Riddle Worldwide's online and web-based EagleVision Home courses provide you the flexibility you need to complete your studies no matter where you are, day or night. Members of the military don't have to worry about getting transferred and starting over – they can take their studies with them.

Faculty/Classroom: 75% of faculty are male; 25% are female. No introductory courses are taught by graduate students.

Requirements: The ACT is recommended. In addition, Undergraduate Admissions Embry-Riddle considers all aspects of a student's qualifications and offers admission to the most competitive applicants building a talented and diverse population of students motivated toward careers in aviation and aerospace. Applications for admission are valid for one year from date received. Admitted students must enroll and maintain enrollment beyond the add/drop period within one year of admission or must reapply. High School Graduates Under the Age of 20 require extensive documentation to be considered. To learn more, visit the college website. In addition, a GPA of 2.0 is required. AP and CLEP credits are accepted.

Procedure: Freshmen are admitted to all sessions. There are deferred admissions and rolling admissions plans. Application deadlines are open. Application fee is $50. Applications are accepted online.

Transfer: 1003 transfer students enrolled in 2012-2013. Applicants who graduated from high school and subsequently completed a minimum of 12 semester hours of college level credit from an accredited degree granting institution are considered transfer students. Embry-Riddle considers each application for transfer admission individually, reviewing the student's academic record, grades received in all college-level courses, completion of fundamental studies in English and Mathematics, and the rigor of the student's academic program. To be considered for admission a transfer applicant must have a minimum of a 2.0 cumulative grade point average (CGPA) on a 4.0 scale from an accredited degree granting institution. When an applicant has attended more than one institution, a cumulative average for all previous college work attempted will be calculated to determine the overall CGPA. • Official transcripts from all colleges and universities (postsecondary) accredited degree-granting institutions attended • Military documents, if applicable

Financial Aid: In 2013-2014, 29% of all full-time freshmen and 36% of continuing full-time students received some form of financial aid. 89% of all full-time freshmen and 75% of continuing full-time students received need-based aid. The average freshman award was $6,702. Need-based scholarships or need-based grants averaged $5,037; and need-based self-help aid (loans and jobs) averaged $3,375. The FAFSA is required. The priority date for freshman financial aid applications for fall entry is March 1.

International Students: There are 295 international students enrolled. The school actively recruits these students. They must take the TOEFL with a minimum score of 550 on the paper-based TOEFL (PBT) or 79 on the Internet-based version (iBT).

Computers: All students may access the system. There are no time limits and no fees.

Graduates: From July 1, 2012 to June 30, 2013, 1885 bachelor's degrees were awarded. The most popular majors were aeronautics (69%), technical management (26%), and aviation business administration (2%).

Admissions Contact: E-Mail: *worldwide@erau.edu* Web: *http:/worldwide.erau.edu/admissions/index.html*

FLAGLER COLLEGE D-2

St. Augustine, FL 32084 **(904) 829-6481** **(800) 304-4208; (904) 826-0094**

Full-time: 1145 men, 1642 women	**Faculty:** 222; IIB, -$
Part-time: 50 men, 41 women	**Ph.D.s:** 71%
Graduate: n/av	**Student/Faculty:** 25 to 1
Year: semesters, summer session	**Tuition:** $16,180
Application Deadline: March 1	**Room & Board:** $8780
Freshman Class: 5396 applied, 2691 accepted, 708 enrolled	
SAT CR/M/W: 562/554/549	**ACT:** required **VERY COMPETITIVE**

Flagler College, founded in 1968, is an independent liberal arts college that emphasizes undergraduate education in select liberal and preprofessional studies. There is one undergraduate school. The library contains 248,589 volumes, 1,830 microform items, and 5,176 audio/video tapes/CDs/DVDs, and subscribes to 465 periodicals including electronic. Computerized library services include interlibrary loans, database searching, Internet access, and Wi-Fi capability. Special learning facilities include an art gallery, radio station, the Learning Center for assistance in writing, mathematics and study skills. The 32-acre campus is in a small town 35 miles south of Jacksonville and 45 miles north of Daytona Beach. Including any residence halls, there are 30 buildings.

Student Life: 63% of undergraduates are from Florida. Others are from 44 states, 38 foreign countries, and Canada. 78% are from public schools. 75% are White. The average age of freshmen is 18; all undergraduates, 21. 34% do not continue beyond their first year; 64% remain to graduate.

Housing: 1034 students can be accommodated in college housing, which includes single-sex dorms. On-campus housing is guaranteed for the freshman year only, is available on a first-come, and first-served basis. 62% of students live on campus; of those, 60% remain on campus on weekends. Alcohol is not permitted. All students may keep cars.

Activities: There are no fraternities or sororities. There are 36 groups on campus, including art, cheerleading, choir, chorus, dance, drama, environmental, ethnic, film, gay, honors, international, literary magazine, musical theater, newspaper, photography, political, professional, radio and TV, religious, social, social service, and student government. Popular campus events include De-Stress Day, Bachelor Bids, and Hogwarts House Parties.

Sports: There are 6 intercollegiate sports for men and 7 for women, and 44 intramural sports for men and 44 for women. Facilities include a 20-acre complex for baseball and soccer, 6 tennis courts, a swimming pool, a multipurpose gym, and an outdoor volleyball court.

Disabled Students: 90% of the campus is accessible. Facilities include wheelchair ramps, elevators, special parking, specially equipped restrooms, special class scheduling, lowered drinking fountains, lowered telephones, and special housing.

Services: There is a reader service for the blind, and remedial math, reading, and writing.

Campus Safety and Security: Measures include 24-hour foot and vehicle patrol, emergency notification system, self-defense education, and security escort services. There are shuttle buses, emergency telephones, lighted pathways/sidewalks, controlled access to dorms/residences, uniformed police officer from 6 pm to 6 am.

Programs of Study: Flagler confers B.A., B.S. and B.F.A. degrees. Bachelor's degrees are awarded in BUSINESS (accounting, business administration and management, and sports management), COMMUNICATIONS AND THE ARTS (art history, communications, dramatic arts, English, fine arts, graphic design, and Spanish), EDUCATION (art education, education of the deaf and hearing impaired, education of the exceptional child, elementary education, and secondary education), ENGINEERING AND ENVIRONMENTAL DESIGN (environmental science), SOCIAL SCIENCE (economics, history, Latin American studies, liberal arts/general studies, philosophy, political science/government, psychology, public administration, religion, and sociology). Business, education, communication, coastal environmental science and prelaw are the strongest academically. Psychology, communications, and business have the largest enrollments.

Required: To graduate a student must complete 120 semester hours with at least a 2.0 grade point average. Completion of one major in accordance with the requirements set forth by the academic department. Completion of 36 hours in General Education. Students are required to take a minimum of five courses designated Writing Intensive within the General Education curriculum.

Special: The school offers internships, work-study, and dual majors. Students may participate in study-abroad programs in almost any country. Students majoring in deaf education can work directly with students at the Florida State School for the Deaf and Blind. There are 12 national honor societies and 7 departmental honors programs.

Faculty/Classroom: 51% of faculty are male; 48% are female. All teach undergraduates. No introductory courses are taught by graduate students. The average class size in an introductory lecture is 22; in a laboratory is 20; and in a regular course is 20.

Admissions: 50% of the 2013-2014 applicants were accepted. The SAT scores for the 2013-2014 freshman class were: Critical Reading--10% below 500, 69% between 500 and 599, 18% between 600 and 699, and 1% between 700 and 800; Math--11% below 500, 76% between 500 and 599, 11% between 600 and 699, and 1% between 700 and 800; Writing--14% below 500, 71% between 500 and 599, 11% between 600 and 699, and 1% between 700 and 800.

Requirements: The SAT or ACT is required. The ACT Optional Writing test is also required. In addition, Student must have graduated from an accredited secondary school or have a satisfactory score on the GED. Students must have a total of 19 academic credits. High school courses must include 4 credits of English, 3 credits each of math and science, and 2 credits of a foreign language. An essay is required, and an interview is recommended. A GPA of 2.5 is required. AP and CLEP credits are accepted. Important factors in the admissions decision are advanced placement or honors courses, leadership record, and extracurricular activities record.

Procedure: Freshmen are admitted fall and spring. Entrance exams should be taken during the fall of the senior year at the latest. There are early decision and deferred admissions plans. Early decision applications should be filed by January 15; regular applications, by March 1 for fall entry; and December 15 for spring entry, along with a $50 fee. Notification of early decision is sent February 1; regular decision, March 15. 393 early decision candidates were accepted for the 2013-2014 class. 129 applicants were on the 2013 waiting list; 31 were admitted. Applications are accepted online.

Transfer: 191 transfer students enrolled in 2012-2013. Transfer students must have a minimum of 24 semester hours with a satisfactory GPA. Transfers must also present satisfactory scores from the SAT or ACT. 45 of 120 credits required for the bachelor's degree must be completed at Flagler.

Visiting: There are regularly scheduled orientations for prospective students, visitation weekend. There are guides for informal visits and visitors may sit in on classes. To schedule a visit, contact the Office of Admissions at admissions@flagler.edu.

Financial Aid: In 2013-2014, 92% of all full-time freshmen and 87% of continuing full-time students received some form of financial aid. 56% of all full-time freshmen and 44% of continuing full-time students received need-based aid. The average freshman award was $12,178. Need-based scholarships or need-based grants averaged $9,095; need-based self-help aid (loans and jobs) averaged $3,399; non-need-based athletic scholarships averaged $6,797; and other non-need-based awards and non-need-based scholarships averaged $961. 69% of undergraduate students work part-time. Average annual earnings from campus work are $1400. The average financial indebtedness of the 2013 graduate was $24,526. The FAFSA and the college's own financial statement are required. The deadline for filing freshman financial aid applications for fall entry is April 1.

International Students: There are 93 international students enrolled. They must take the TOEFL with a minimum score of 550 on the paper-based TOEFL (PBT) or 79 on the Internet-based version (iBT). They must also take the SAT or ACT. IELTS.

Computers: All students may access the system. Internet is available 24 hours a day. There are no time limits and no fees.

Graduates: From July 1, 2012 to June 30, 2013, 644 bachelor's degrees were awarded. The most popular majors were business (16%), art (14%), and communications (14%). In an average class, 50% graduate in 4 years or less, 63% graduate in 5 years or less, and 65% graduate in 6 years or less.

Admissions Contact: Marc G. Williar, Vice President of Enrollment Management. E-Mail: *admiss@flagler.edu* Web: *www.flagler.edu*

FLORIDA AGRICULTURAL AND MECHANICAL UNIVERSITY C-1

Tallahassee, FL 32307 **(850) 599-3796; (850) 599-3069**

Full-time: 3498 men, 5588 women	**Faculty:** 396; IIA, av$
Part-time: 409 men, 558 women	**Ph.D.s:** 73%
Graduate: 726 men, 1278 women	**Student/Faculty:** 19 to 1
Year: semesters, summer session	**Tuition:** $5785 ($17,725)
Application Deadline: May 15	**Room & Board:** $9150
Freshman Class: 5747 applied, 2795 accepted, 1364 enrolled	
SAT CR/M/W: 470/470/460 **ACT:** 20	**LESS COMPETITIVE**

Florida Agricultural and Mechanical University, founded in 1887 and a public institution within the state university system of Florida, offers undergraduate programs in agriculture, allied health science, architecture, the arts and sciences, business and industry, education, engineering, journalism, pharmacy and pharmaceutical sciences, upper-level nursing, and technology. There are 12 undergraduate schools and one graduate school. In addition to regional accreditation, Florida A&M has baccalaureate program accreditation with AACSB, ABET, ACEJMC, ACPE, APTA, CSWE, NAAB, NCATE, and NLN. The 4 libraries contain 1.1 million volumes, 509,940 microform items, and 77,145 audio/video tapes/CDs/DVDs, and subscribe to 201,405 periodicals including electronic. Computerized library services include interlibrary loans, database searching, Internet access, and Wi-Fi capability. Special learning facilities include an art gallery, radio station, TV station, black archives, and an observatory. The 422-acre campus is in an urban area 169 miles west of Jacksonville, Florida. Including any residence halls, there are 211 buildings.

Student Life: 84% of undergraduates are from Florida. Others are from 42 states, 50 foreign countries, and Canada. 94% are African American. The average age of freshmen is 18; all undergraduates, 22. 20% do not continue beyond their first year; 40% remain to graduate.

Housing: 2697 students can be accommodated in college housing, which includes single-sex dorms, on-campus apartments, and married student housing. On-campus housing is guaranteed for the freshman year only, is available on a first-come, and first-served basis. Priority is given to out-of-town students. 73% of students commute. Alcohol is not permitted. Upperclassmen may keep cars.

Activities: 2% of men belong to 4 national fraternities; 3% of women belong to 4 national sororities. There are 135 groups on campus, including cheerleading, choir, chorus, dance, drama, drill team, ethnic, honors, international, jazz band, marching band, newspaper, orchestra, pep band, political, professional, radio and TV, religious, social, social service, student government, and symphony. Popular campus events include FAMU Essen-Theater, FAMU Orchesis Dance Theater and Ebony Fashion Fair.

Sports: There are 8 intercollegiate sports for men and 8 for women. Facilities include a 3,300-seat gym, a 1,600-seat auditorium, a 25,559-seat football stadium, swimming pools, baseball diamonds, softball and track fields, tennis courts, a bowling alley, a pool hall, a student activities center, and a fitness center.

Disabled Students: 90% of the campus is accessible. Facilities include wheelchair ramps, elevators, special parking, and specially equipped restrooms.

Services: Counseling and information services are available, as is tutoring in some subjects, math, English and reading There is remedial math, reading, and writing.

Campus Safety and Security: Measures include 24-hour foot and vehicle patrol, emergency notification system, self-defense education, and security escort services. There are shuttle buses, emergency telephones, and lighted pathways/sidewalks.

Programs of Study: Florida A&M confers B.A., B.Arch., B.C.J., B.S., B.S.Arch. and Constr.E.T., B.S.Arch.E.T., B.S.Studies., B.S.C.E., B.S.C.E.T., B.S.Ch.E., B.S.Constr.E.T., B.S.E.E., B.S.Elect.E.T., B.S.H.C.M., B.S.I.E., B.S.J., B.S.M.E., B.S.M.R.A., B.S.N., B.S.Pharm., B.S.P.T., B.S.R.T., B.S.T. and B.S.W. degrees. Associate, master's, and doctoral degrees are also awarded. Bachelor's degrees are awarded in AGRICULTURE (animal science and horticulture), BIOLOGICAL SCIENCE (biology/biological science), BUSINESS (accounting, banking and finance, business administration and management, and business economics), COMMUNICATIONS AND THE ARTS (dramatic arts, English, fine arts, journalism, and music), COMPUTER AND PHYSICAL SCIENCE (actuarial science, chemistry, computer science, mathematics, and physics), EDUCATION (art education, business education, early childhood education, elementary education, industrial arts education, music education, and science education), ENGINEERING AND ENVIRONMENTAL DESIGN (chemical engineering, civil engineering, electrical/electronics engineering, engineering technology, industrial engineering, and mechanical engineering), HEALTH PROFESSIONS (nursing, occupational therapy, pharmacy, physical therapy, predentistry, and premedicine), SOCIAL SCIENCE (criminal justice, economics, history, political science/government, psychology, public administration, social science, social work, and sociology). Business, engineering and pharmacy are the strongest academically. Business administration, management, and biology bological sciences have the largest enrollments.

Required: General education requirements include 36 credit hours in English, humanities, social science, natural science, American history, foreign language, and math at the college algebra level or above. In order to graduate, students must complete at least 120 credit hours, including 30 in a major field, with a minimum GPA of 2.0.

Special: Cooperative programs and cross-registration are offered in conjunction with Florida State University. Internships are available either on or off campus. Florida A&M also offers a Washington semester for architecture majors, a B.A.-B.S. degree, credit for life experience, and pass/fail options. Nondegree study is possible. There is a freshman honors program.

Faculty/Classroom: 53% of faculty are male; 47% are female. 72% teach undergraduates, 72% do research, and 72% do both. No introductory courses are taught by graduate students.

Admissions: 49% of the 2013-2014 applicants were accepted. The SAT scores for the 2013-2014 freshman class were: Critical Reading--64% below 500, 27% between 500 and 599, 7% between 600 and 699, and 1% between 700 and 800; Math--66% below 500, 27% between 500 and 599, 6% between 600 and 699, and 1% between 700 and 800; Writing--72% below 500, 24% between 500 and 599, and 3% between 600 and 699. The ACT scores were 55% below 21, 29% between 21 and 23, 10% between 24 and 26, 4% between 27 and 28, and 2% above 28.

Requirements: The SAT or ACT is required, with a satisfactory score on the SAT, or 19 on the ACT. Applicants must be graduates of accredited secondary schools or have earned a GED. The university requires 19 academic credits, including 4 each in English and academic electives, 3 each in math, science, and social studies, and 2 in foreign language. A GPA of 2.5 is required. AP and CLEP credits are accepted. Important factors in the admissions decision are recommendations by school officials, extracurricular activities record, and evidence of special talent.

Procedure: Freshmen are admitted to all sessions. Entrance exams should be taken by the fall of the senior year. There are deferred admissions and rolling admissions plans. Applications should be filed by May 15 for fall entry; November 15 for spring entry; and April 1 for summer entry, along with a $30 fee. Applications are accepted online.

Transfer: 442 transfer students enrolled in 2012-2013. Applicants must present a minimum GPA of 2.0 in at least 60 semester hours or 90 quarter hours earned. 30 of 120 credits required for the bachelor's degree must be completed at Florida A&M.

Visiting: There are regularly scheduled orientations for prospective students. There are guides for informal visits and visitors may sit in on classes.

Financial Aid: The FAFSA is required. The priority date for freshman financial aid applications for fall entry is March 1.

International Students: There are 80 international students enrolled. They must take the TOEFL with a minimum score of 500 on the paper-based TOEFL (PBT) or 61 on the Internet-based version (iBT). They must also take the SAT or ACT.

Computers: All students may access the system. There are no time limits and no fees.

Graduates: From July 1, 2012 to June 30, 2013, 1470 bachelor's degrees were awarded. The most popular majors were health (20%), business administration and management (14%), and criminal justice (11%). 76 companies recruited on campus in 2012-2013. In an average class, 11% graduate in 4 years or less, 27% graduate in 5 years or less, and 40% graduate in 6 years or less. Of the 2012 graduating class, 33% were enrolled in graduate school within 6 months of graduation.

Admissions Contact: Barbara Cox, Director. E-Mail: *barbara.cox@famu.edu* Web: *www.famu.edu*

FLORIDA ATLANTIC UNIVERSITY E-5

Boca Raton, FL 33431 (561) 297-3040
(800) 299-4FAU; (561) 297-2758

Full-time: 7085 men, 8508 women
Part-time: 3843 men, 5387 women
Graduate: 1991 men, 3224 women
Year: semesters, summer session
Application Deadline: May 1
Freshman Class: 27888 applied, 10876 accepted, 3237 enrolled
Faculty: 875; I, --$
Ph.D.s: 90%
Student/Faculty: 20 to 1
Tuition: $5986 ($21,543)
Room & Board: $11,353

COMPETITIVE

When it opened in 1964, FAU was one of the few universities in the country to offer only upper-division and graduate-level work, on the theory that freshmen and sophomores could be served by the community college system. Located in rapidly growing Southeast Florida, the University responded to the need to provide increased access to educational opportunities by opening its doors to freshmen in 1984. Today, with its well developed system of distributed campuses and sites that offer students high-quality degree programs at seven locations, FAU serves as a model for America's urban, regional universities. FAU offers a comprehensive array of undergraduate and graduate programs, enrolling more than 29,000 students who bring rich cultural diversity to campus life. There are 9 undergraduate schools and 8 graduate schools. In addition to regional accreditation, FAU has baccalaureate program accreditation with AACSB, ABET, CSAB, CSWE, NAAB, NASM, NCATE, and NLN. The 4 libraries contain 206,615 volumes, 2.1 million microform items, and 22,414 audio/video tapes/CDs/DVDs, and subscribe to 12,549 periodicals including electronic. Computerized library services include interlibrary loans, database searching, Internet access, and Wi-Fi capability. Special learning facilities include an art gallery, planetarium, radio station, TV station, engineering research labs, a marine sciences research center, a K-12 developmental research school, a nonnative fish research lab, and an environmental sciences center, medical school. The 850-acre campus is in a suburban area 17 miles north of Ft. Lauderdale, 45 miles north of Miami, and 22 miles south of Palm Beach. Including any residence halls, there are 160 buildings.

Student Life: 96% of undergraduates are from Florida. Others are from 49 states, 135 foreign countries, and Canada. 73% are from public schools. 50% are White; 22% Hispanic; 18% African American. The average age of freshmen is 18; all undergraduates, 24. 22% do not continue beyond their first year; 43% remain to graduate.

Housing: 3750 students can be accommodated in college housing, which includes single-sex and coed dorms and on-campus apartments. In addition, there are honors houses, special-interest houses, Living- Learning Communities. On-campus housing is guaranteed for the freshman year only, is available on a first-come, and first-served basis. 85% of students commute. All students may keep cars.

Activities: 1% of men belong to 11 national fraternities; 1% of women belong to 8 national sororities. There are 250 groups on campus, including art, band, cheerleading, chess, choir, chorale, chorus, computers, dance, debate, drama, drill team, environmental, ethnic, film, forensics, gay, honors, international, jazz band, literary magazine, marching band, musical theater, newspaper, opera, orchestra, pep band, photography, political, professional, radio and TV, religious, social, social service, and student government. Popular campus events include Luau, African American Festival, Festival of Nations and Homecoming.

Sports: There are 8 intercollegiate sports for men and 9 for women, and 10 intramural sports for men and 10 for women. Facilities include a 54,000 sq. ft. facility that houses weight rooms, training rooms, lighted baseball, softball, and soccer stadiums: arena for volleyball and basketball, cross country and track field complex; football practice field; aquatic center tennis courts, fitness center with cardio; outdoor basketball courts, practice fields, and a football stadium.

Disabled Students: All of the campus is accessible. Facilities include wheelchair ramps, elevators, special parking, specially equipped restrooms, lowered drinking fountains, and lowered telephones.

Services: Counseling and information services are available, as is tutoring in most subjects. There is a reader service for the blind. Remedial work must be taken at the community college level.

Campus Safety and Security: Measures include 24-hour foot and vehicle patrol, emergency notification system, self-defense education, and security escort services. There are shuttle buses, emergency telephones, lighted pathways/sidewalks, and controlled access to dorms/residences.

Programs of Study: FAU confers B.A., B.S., B.A.E., B.Arch., B.B.A., B.E.C.E. B.F.A., B.H.S., B.I.E.T., B.Mus., B.P.M., B.S.C.E., B.S.C.V., B.S.E., B.S.E.E., B.S.G.E., B.S.H.S., B.S.M.E., B.S.M.T., B.S.N., B.S.O.E., B.S.W. and B.U.R.P. degrees. Associate, master's, and doctoral degrees are also awarded. Bachelor's degrees are awarded in BIOLOGICAL SCIENCE (biology/biological science and marine biology), BUSINESS (accounting, banking and finance, business administration and management, business economics, hospitality management services, human resources, international business management, management information systems, marketing/retailing/merchandising, real estate, and small business management), COMMUNICATIONS AND THE ARTS (art, communications, dramatic arts, English, fine arts, French, German, graphic design, Italian, jazz, journalism, linguistics, media arts, multimedia, music, Spanish, and visual and performing arts), COMPUTER AND PHYSICAL SCIENCE (chemistry, computer science, computer security and information assurance, geology, information sciences and systems, mathematics, and physics), EDUCATION (education of the exceptional child, elementary education, English education, foreign languages education, physical education, and special education), ENGINEERING AND ENVIRONMENTAL DESIGN (architecture, civil engineering, computer engineering, electrical/electronics engineering, engineering, mechanical engineering, ocean engineering, and urban planning technology), HEALTH PROFESSIONS (health care administration, health science, medical laboratory technology, and nursing), SOCIAL SCIENCE (anthropology, criminal justice, economics, geography, history, interdisciplinary studies, Judaic studies, liberal arts/general studies, philosophy, political science/government, psychobiology, psychology, public administration, social psychology, social science, social work, and sociology). Engineering, education and business are the strongest academically. biological science, psychology and elementary education have the largest enrollments.

Required: All students must take the College Level Academic Skills Test (CLAST) required by the state. To graduate, students must complete a total of 120 credit hours, with a minimum GPA of 2.0. All students must take the required courses in the core curriculum, including 9 credits each of humanities and social sciences, and 6 each of math, communication, and natural sciences, and must demonstrate proficiency in a foreign language.

Special: FAU offers cooperative programs and internships in most majors. Work-study programs, dual and student-designed majors, a general studies degree, credit for military experience, nondegree study, and pass/fail options are available. The school offers a Washington semester, study abroad through all state university system of Florida programs. There are 21 national honor societies, a freshman honors program, and 9 departmental honors programs.

Faculty/Classroom: 54% of faculty are male; 46% are female. All teach and do research. Graduate students teach 5% of introductory courses. The average class size in an introductory lecture is 38; in a laboratory is 21; and in a regular course is 29.

Admissions: 39% of the 2013-2014 applicants were accepted. 51% of the current freshmen were in the top fifth of their class; 80% were in the top two fifths. There were 2 National Merit finalists.

Requirements: The SAT or ACT is required, with a satisfactory score on the SAT Critical Reading and Math sections or on the ACT. In addition, graduation from an accredited secondary school or satisfactory scores on the GED are required. Students must have 19 academic credits, including 4 units of English, 3 each of math (algebra I and higher), science (including 2 with substantial lab work), and social studies, and 2 of a foreign language, plus 4 of electives in computer science, fine arts, or humanities. A portfolio or an audition may be requested by individual departments. An essay and an interview are required. A GPA of 2.0 is required. AP and CLEP credits are accepted. Important factors in the admissions decision are advanced placement or honors courses, evidence of special talent, and recommendations by school officials.

Procedure: Freshmen are admitted fall, spring, and summer. There are early decision, early admissions, deferred admissions, and rolling admissions plans. Applications should be filed by May 1 for fall entry; October 15 for spring entry; and March 15 for summer entry, along with a $30 fee. Applications are accepted online.

Transfer: 3425 transfer students enrolled in 2012-2013. Students must have a minimum GPA of 2.0, submit official transcripts from the previous schools attended, and be in good standing at those institutions. Applicants from a community or junior college in Florida with an associate degree are automatically admitted. Students with fewer than 60 transferable hours must meet the same criteria as entering freshmen. 30 of 120 credits required for the bachelor's degree must be completed at FAU.

Visiting: There are regularly scheduled orientations for prospective stu-

dents, consisting of a group tour. There are guides for informal visits. To schedule a visit, contact the Admissions Office.

Financial Aid: In 2013-2014, 63% of all full-time freshmen and 65% of continuing full-time students received some form of financial aid. 58% of all full-time freshmen and 49% of continuing full-time students received need-based aid. The average freshman award was $6,000. Need-based scholarships or need-based grants averaged $6,078 ; need-based self-help aid (loans and jobs) averaged $5,356; and non-need-based athletic scholarships averaged $9,892. FAU is a member of CSS. The FAFSA is required. The deadline for filing freshman financial aid applications for fall entry is March 1.

International Students: There are 268 international students enrolled. The school actively recruits these students. They must take the TOEFL with a minimum score of 550 on the paper-based TOEFL (PBT). They must also take the SAT or ACT.

Computers: All students may access the system. Hours vary depending on the lab. There are no time limits and no fees.

Graduates: From July 1, 2012 to June 30, 2013, 4892 bachelor's degrees were awarded. The most popular majors were elementary education (8%), accounting (8%), and criminal justice (7%). 200 companies recruited on campus in 2012-2013. In an average class, 17% graduate in 4 years or less, 35% graduate in 5 years or less, and 43% graduate in 6 years or less.

Admissions Contact: Barbar Pletcher, Director of Admissions. E-Mail: *Admissions@fau.edu* Web: *https:/www.discover-fau.org/transferapply/splitter.htm*

FLORIDA GULF COAST UNIVERSITY D-5

Fort Myers, FL 33965 (239) 590-7891
(888) 889-1095; (239) 590-7894

Full-time: 4429 men, 5709 women	**Faculty:** n/av; IIA, --$
Part-time: 1291 men, 1432 women	**Ph.D.s:** 72%
Graduate: 401 men, 836 women	**Student/Faculty:** 23 to 1
Year: semesters, summer session	**Tuition:** n/av
Application Deadline: May 1	**Room & Board:** n/app

Freshman Class: 10804 applied, 7108 accepted, 2761 enrolled
SAT: required

COMPETITIVE

Florida Gulf Coast University, founded in 1991, is part of the State University System of Florida. There are 5 undergraduate schools. In addition to regional accreditation, FGCU has baccalaureate program accreditation with AACSB, APTA, CSWE, and NLN. The library contains 276,638 volumes, 843,772 microform items, and 319,258 audio/video tapes/CDs/DVDs, and subscribes to 409,967 periodicals including electronic. Computerized library services include interlibrary loans, database searching, Internet access, and Wi-Fi capability. Special learning facilities include an art gallery, radio station, TV station, chickee huts, computer labs, and a family resource center. The 760-acre campus is in a suburban area in southwest Florida in southern Lee County. Including any residence halls, there are 112 buildings.

Student Life: 93% of undergraduates are from Florida. Others are from 46 states, 87 foreign countries, and Canada. 67% are White; 19% Hispanic. The average age of freshmen is 18; all undergraduates, 22.

Housing: 4200 students can be accommodated in college housing, which includes coed dorms, on-campus apartments, and off-campus apartments. On-campus housing is available on a first-come and first-served basis. 67% of students commute. Alcohol is not permitted. Some may keep cars.

Activities: 1% of men belong to 7 national fraternities; 7% of women belong to 5 national sororities. There are 125 groups on campus, including art, cheerleading, chess, computers, dance, debate, drama, environmental, ethnic, film, gay, honors, international, literary magazine, musical theater, newspaper, political, professional, religious, social, social service, and student government. Popular campus events include Eagle Expo, and President's Lecture Series.

Sports: There are 6 intercollegiate sports for men and 8 for women, and 9 intramural sports for men and 9 for women. Facilities include a fitness center, a lakefront, a 4500-seat teaching gym, 2 playing fields, 12 tennis courts, softball complex seating 2500, baseball field, Swanson Stadium seating 2500, and Aquatics Center with a 50-meter Olympic sized pool and 25 yard recreational pool.

Disabled Students: All of the campus is accessible. Facilities include wheelchair ramps, elevators, special parking, specially equipped restrooms, special class scheduling, lowered drinking fountains, lowered telephones, and special housing.

Services: Counseling and information services are available, as is tutoring in most subjects.

Campus Safety and Security: Measures include 24-hour foot and vehicle patrol, self-defense education, and security escort services. There are shuttle buses, emergency telephones, and lighted pathways/sidewalks.

Programs of Study: FGCU confers B.A., and B.S. degrees. Associate, master's, and doctoral degrees are also awarded. Bachelor's degrees are awarded in AGRICULTURE (environmental studies), BIOLOGICAL SCIENCE (biology/biological science, biotechnology, and marine science), BUSINESS (accounting, banking and finance, marketing and distribution, and recreational facilities management), COMMUNICATIONS AND THE ARTS (art, communications, English, music, and Spanish), COMPUTER AND PHYSICAL SCIENCE (applied science, chemistry, computer science, and mathematics), EDUCATION (athletic training, early childhood education, elementary education, mathematics education, music education, secondary education, social science education, and special education), ENGINEERING AND ENVIRONMENTAL DESIGN (civil engineering and environmental engineering), HEALTH PROFESSIONS (clinical science, community health work, exercise science, health science, nursing, and occupational therapy), SOCIAL SCIENCE (anthropology, child psychology/development, counseling/psychology, criminal justice, criminology, economics, forensic studies, history, law, liberal arts/general studies, philosophy, political science/government, psychology, social work, and sociology). Management, communication, and psychology have the largest enrollments.

Required: To graduate, students must have a 2.0 minimum GPA and 120 credit hours that include courses in phys ed, computer science, general education, service learning, and university colloquium.

Special: The university offers cross-registration with the University of Central Florida, study abroad in China, a Washington semester, accelerated degree in biology, and work-study programs. There is 1 national honor society, including Phi Beta Kappa, a freshman honors program, and 1 departmental honors programs.

Faculty/Classroom: 55% of faculty are male; 45% are female. All teach and do research. No introductory courses are taught by graduate students. The average class size in a regular course is 25.

Admissions: 66% of the 2013-2014 applicants were accepted. The SAT scores for the 2013-2014 freshman class were: Critical Reading--43% below 500, 46% between 500 and 599, 10% between 600 and 699, and 1% between 700 and 800; Math--41% below 500, 46% between 500 and 599, 12% between 600 and 699, and 1% between 700 and 800; Writing--52% below 500, 40% between 500 and 599, 7% between 600 and 699, and 1% between 700 and 800. The ACT scores were 5% below 21, 70% between 21 and 23, 23% between 27 and 28, and 2% above 28. 27% of the current freshmen were in the top fifth of their class; 61% were in the top two fifths. 4 freshmen graduated first in their class.

Requirements: The SAT is required. The ACT Optional Writing test is also required. SAT or ACT A GPA of 2.0 is required. AP and CLEP credits are accepted.

Procedure: Freshmen are admitted fall, spring, and summer. Entrance exams should be taken in the junior year. There is a deferred admissions plan. Applications should be filed by May 1 for fall entry; November 9 for spring entry; and February 1 for summer entry, along with a $30 fee. Applications are accepted online.

Transfer: 1058 transfer students enrolled in 2012-2013. Lower level transfers must meet the same requirements as regular admissions. Upper level transfers must have a 2.0 GPA and 60 hours of transferable credit, and be in good standing at their last institution. 30 of 120 credits required for the bachelor's degree must be completed at FGCU.

Visiting: There are regularly scheduled orientations for prospective students. There are guides for informal visits and visitors may sit in on classes. To schedule a visit, contact the Admissions Office.

Financial Aid: In 2013-2014, 57% of all full-time freshmen students received some form of financial aid. 36% of all full-time freshmen students received need-based aid. The average freshman award was $9,135. Need-based scholarships or need-based grants averaged $5,080; need-based self-help aid (loans and jobs) averaged $6,887; and non-need-based athletic scholarships averaged $6,774. The average financial indebtedness of the 2013 graduate was $23,863. FGCU is a member of CSS. The FAFSA is required. The deadline for filing freshman financial aid applications for fall entry is March 1.

International Students: There are 206 international students enrolled. The school actively recruits these students. They must take the TOEFL with a minimum score of 550 on the paper-based TOEFL (PBT) or 79 on the Internet-based version (iBT). They must also take the SAT or ACT, scoring 440.

Computers: All students may access the system any time. There are no time limits and no fees.

Graduates: From July 1, 2012 to June 30, 2013, 1873 bachelor's degrees were awarded. The most popular majors were communication/journalism (10%), management (8%), and psychology (6%). In an average class, 47% graduate in 6 years or less.

Admissions Contact: Marc Maviolette, Director of Admissions. E-Mail: *oar@fgcu.edu* Web: *www.fgcu.edu*

FLORIDA INSTITUTE OF TECHNOLOGY E-4

Melbourne, FL 32901-6975 (321) 674-8030
(800) 888-4348; (321) 723-9468

Full-time: 1750 men, 750 women
Part-time: 120 men, 80 women
Graduate: 1550 men, 1000 women
Year: semesters, summer session
Application Deadline: open
Freshman Class: n/av
SAT or ACT: required

Faculty: n/av
Ph.D.s: 89%
Student/Faculty: n/av
Tuition: $31,370
Room & Board: $8500

VERY COMPETITIVE

Florida Institute of Technology, founded in 1958, offers undergraduate degrees in engineering, science, business, psychology, liberal arts, and aeronautics. Figures in the above capsule and in this profile are approximate. There are 5 undergraduate schools and 6 graduate schools. In addition to regional accreditation, Florida Tech has baccalaureate program accreditation with ABET and CSAB. The library contains 425,251 volumes, 318,552 microform items, and 9,167 audio/video tapes/CDs/DVDs, and subscribes to 25,474 periodicals including electronic. Computerized library services include interlibrary loans, database searching, Internet access, and laptop Internet portals. Special learning facilities include a learning resource center, radio station, and TV station. The 130-acre campus is in a suburban area 70 miles east of Orlando. Including any residence halls, there are 75 buildings.

Student Life: 46% of undergraduates are from out of state, mostly the Middle Atlantic. Students are from 49 states, 81 foreign countries, and Canada. 56% are from public schools. 49% are white; 21% foreign nationals. The average age of freshmen is 19; all undergraduates, 20. 25% do not continue beyond their first year; 54% remain to graduate.

Housing: 1390 students can be accommodated in college housing, which includes single-sex and coed dorms and on-campus apartments. On-campus housing is guaranteed for the freshman year only, is available on a first-come, and first-served basis. 51% of students commute. All students may keep cars.

Activities: 15% of men belong to 6 national fraternities; 14% of women belong to 3 national sororities. There are 99 groups on campus, including cheerleading, chess, chorus, computers, dance, drama, drill team, ethnic, film, honors, international, literary magazine, newspaper, pep band, political, professional, radio and TV, religious, social, social service, and student government. Popular campus events include International Festival and Big Man on Campus.

Sports: There are 6 intercollegiate sports for men and 8 for women, and 9 intramural sports for men and 9 for women. Facilities include a sports and recreation center with 2 basketball courts, a racquetball court, and a 5000-square-foot weight and fitness area with cardiovascular machines, free weights, and specialized weight equipment.

Disabled Students: 90% of the campus is accessible. Facilities include wheelchair ramps, elevators, special parking, specially equipped restrooms, special class scheduling, lowered drinking fountains, and lowered telephones.

Services: Counseling and information services are available, as is tutoring in every subject. There is a reader service for the blind, and remedial math, reading, and writing.

Campus Safety and Security: Measures include 24-hour foot and vehicle patrol, self-defense education, and security escort services. There are emergency telephones, lighted pathways/sidewalks.

Programs of Study: Florida Tech confers B.A. and B.S. degrees. Master's and doctoral degrees are also awarded. Bachelor's degrees are awarded in AGRICULTURE (environmental studies), BIOLOGICAL SCIENCE (biochemistry, biology/biological science, ecology, marine biology, and molecular biology), BUSINESS (accounting, business administration and management, electronic business, international business management, and management information systems), COMMUNICATIONS AND THE ARTS (communications), COMPUTER AND PHYSICAL SCIENCE (applied mathematics, astronomy, atmospheric sciences and meteorology, chemistry, computer science, oceanography, physics, planetary and space science, and software engineering), EDUCATION (mathematics education, middle school education, and science education), ENGINEERING AND ENVIRONMENTAL DESIGN (aeronautical engineering, aeronautical science, aviation administration/management, aviation computer technology, chemical engineering, civil engineering, computer engineering, construction engineering, electrical/electronics engineering, environmental science, mechanical engineering, military science, and ocean engineering), HEALTH PROFESSIONS (premedicine), SOCIAL SCIENCE (forensic studies, humanities, interdisciplinary studies, and psychology). Engineering, science, and aeronautics are the strongest academically. Aerospace engineering, mechanical engineering, and aviation have the largest enrollments.

Required: To graduate, students must have a minimum 2.0 GPA and 120 to 135 credit hours. The required number of hours in the major varies. All students must take 9 hours in communication and humanities and 3 in English composition. The core curriculum also requires 6 credit hours each in physical or life sciences and math and 3 hours in computer science and social sciences.

Special: Florida Tech offers co-op programs in all majors. Students may choose to pursue more than 1 degree by completing degree requirements for each major. Internships are available in the senior year for many majors, including psychology, engineering, and aeronautics. Study abroad and work-study programs are available. There are 8 national honor societies and 1 departmental honors program.

Faculty/Classroom: 79% of faculty are male; 21% are female. 7% teach undergraduates, 5% do research, and 88% do both. Graduate students teach 9% of introductory courses. The average class size in an introductory lecture is 22; in a laboratory is 18; and in a regular course is 20.

Admissions: 6 freshmen graduated first in their class.

Requirements: The SAT or ACT is required. Applicants must be graduates of an accredited secondary school or have a GED certificate. At least 18 academic credits or Carnegie units are required, including 4 years each of English, math, and science. An experiential essay is required and an interview is recommended. A GPA of 2.8 is required. AP and CLEP credits are accepted. Important factors in the admissions decision are advanced placement or honors courses, recommendations by school officials, and extracurricular activities record.

Procedure: Freshmen are admitted fall and spring. Entrance exams should be taken during the junior year or the beginning of the senior year of high school. There are deferred admissions and rolling admissions plans. Application deadlines are open. Application fee is $50. Applications are accepted online.

Transfer: Applicants must have a minimum 2.5 GPA. If transfer students have fewer than 30 semester hours, high school transcripts and SAT or ACT scores are required. A personal statement is recommended. 25 credits required for the bachelor's degree must be completed at Florida Tech.

Visiting: There are regularly scheduled orientations for prospective students, including tours and interviews with admissions staff, faculty, or department heads upon request. There are guides for informal visits and visitors may sit in on classes. To schedule a visit, contact The Office of Undergraduate Admission.

Financial Aid: The FAFSA is required. Check with the school for current application deadlines.

International Students: The school actively recruits these students. They must take the TOEFL, and a math entrance qualifying exam. If students score below 550 on the (paper-based), they take language courses on campus.

Computers: Wireless access is available. All students may access the system 24 hours per day. There are no time limits and no fees.

Admissions Contact: Michael J. Perry, Director, Undergraduate Admissions. A campus DVD is available. E-Mail: *perrymj@fit.edu* Web: *www.fit.edu*

FLORIDA INTERNATIONAL UNIVERSITY E-5

Miami, FL 33199 (305) 348-3675; (305) 348-3648

Full-time: 10521 men, 13480 women
Part-time: 6192 men, 7275 women
Graduate: 3699 men, 5094 women
Year: semesters, summer session
Application Deadline: January 18

Faculty: n/av; I, --$
Ph.D.s: 87%
Student/Faculty: n/av
Tuition: $6417 ($18,816)
Room & Board: $11,330

Freshman Class: 15863 applied, 6418 accepted, 2636 enrolled
SAT CR/M/W: 571/569/563 **ACT:** 25 **VERY COMPETITIVE**

Florida International University (FIU) is a multi-campus public research university offering a broad array of undergraduate, graduate, and professional programs. FIU offers more than 180 baccalaureate, masters, professional and research doctorate programs and conducts basic and applied research. Interdisciplinary centers and institutes conduct collaborative research to seek innovative solutions to economic, technological, and social problems. FIU is dynamic. We have a can-do spirit that you will feel on our campuses. This vibrancy is reflected in the campus through modern architecture and the energy of our students. There are 10 undergraduate schools. In addition to regional accreditation, FIU has baccalaureate program accreditation with AACSB, ABET, ACCE, ACEJMC, APTA, ASLA, CSWE, NAAB, NASAD, NASM, NCATE, NLN, and NRPA. The 5 libraries contain 2.2 million volumes, 4.3 million microform items, and 57,466 audio/video tapes/CDs/DVDs, and subscribe to 61,891 periodicals including electronic. Computerized library services include interlibrary loans, database searching, Internet access, and Wi-Fi capability. Special learning facilities include an art gallery, radio station, Frost Art Museum, Nature Preserve, Biscayne Bay Preserve, Wolfsonian Art Museum. The university has two main campuses, the 344-acre Modesto A. Maidique campus in western Miami-Dade County, and the 200-acre Biscayne Bay Campus in northeast Miami-Dade County. Including any residence halls, there are 129 buildings.

Student Life: 93% of undergraduates are from Florida. Others are from 50 states, 146 foreign countries, and Canada. 62% are Hispanic; 13% White; 13% African American. The average age of freshmen is 18; all undergraduates, 23.

Housing: 3011 students can be accommodated in college housing, which includes coed dorms, on-campus apartments, and married student housing. In addition, there are fraternity houses. On-campus housing is available on a first-come and first-served basis. 93% of students commute. All students may keep cars.

Activities: There are 192 groups on campus, including band, cheerleading, chorus, drama, environmental, ethnic, gay, honors, international, jazz band, marching band, newspaper, opera, political, professional, radio and TV, religious, social, social service, student government, and symphony. Popular campus events include Welcome Week, Homecoming and Dance Marathon.

Sports: There are 5 intercollegiate sports for men and 9 for women, and 14 intramural sports for men and 15 for women. Facilities include a 20,000 seat football stadium, a 5000-seat arena with basketball and racquetball courts, an aquatic center, baseball and soccer fields, a fitness center with Nautilus machines, and a racquet sports center with lighted tennis and racquetball courts.

Disabled Students: All of the campus is accessible. Facilities include wheelchair ramps, elevators, special parking, specially equipped restrooms, special class scheduling, lowered drinking fountains, lowered telephones. There is also accessible computer equipment for visually impaired students, including talking and large-print computers.

Services: Counseling and information services are available, as is tutoring in most subjects. There is a reader service for the blind, and remedial math, reading, and writing. Note taking, adapted testing, and special registration may be arranged for disabled students.

Campus Safety and Security: Measures include 24-hour foot and vehicle patrol, emergency notification system, and security escort services. There are emergency telephones and lighted pathways/sidewalks.

Programs of Study: FIU confers B.A., B.S., B.Ac., B.B.A., B.F.A., B.H.S.A., B.M., B.P.A. and B.S.N. degrees. Master's and doctoral degrees are also awarded. Bachelor's degrees are awarded in BIOLOGICAL SCIENCE (biology/biological science and marine biology), BUSINESS (accounting, banking and finance, business administration and management, hospitality management services, international business management, management information systems, marketing/retailing/merchandising, and real estate), COMMUNICATIONS AND THE ARTS (art, art history and appreciation, dramatic arts, English, fine arts, French, Italian, music, Portuguese, and Spanish), COMPUTER AND PHYSICAL SCIENCE (chemistry, computer science, geology, mathematics, physics, and statistics), EDUCATION (art education, early childhood education, education, elementary education, physical education, science education, special education, and specific learning disabilities), ENGINEERING AND ENVIRONMENTAL DESIGN (architecture, biomedical engineering, civil engineering, computer engineering, construction engineering, construction technology, electrical/electronics engineering, environmental engineering, environmental science, interior design, landscape architecture/design, and mechanical engineering), HEALTH PROFESSIONS (exercise science and health care administration), SOCIAL SCIENCE (Asian/Oriental studies, criminal justice, dietetics, economics, geography, history, international relations, liberal arts/general studies, parks and recreation management, philosophy, political science/government, psychology, public administration, religion, social work, sociology, and women's studies).

Required: To graduate, students must complete between 120 and 152 hours with a 2.0 GPA. There are also general education and writing requirements.

Special: FIU offers co-op and work-study programs, and study abroad in 30 countries. Accelerated degree programs, nondegree study, dual majors, and several combined bachelor's-master's programs. There are 40 national honor societies, including Phi Beta Kappa, and a freshman honors program.

Faculty/Classroom: 54% of faculty are male; 46% are female. No introductory courses are taught by graduate students.

Admissions: 40% of the 2013-2014 applicants were accepted. The SAT scores for the 2013-2014 freshman class were: Critical Reading--6% below 500, 63% between 500 and 599, 28% between 600 and 699, and 3% between 700 and 800; Math--9% below 500, 58% between 500 and 599, 31% between 600 and 699, and 2% between 700 and 800; Writing--10% below 500, 64% between 500 and 599, 24% between 600 and 699, and 2% between 700 and 800. The ACT scores were 1% below 21, 24% between 21 and 23, 46% between 24 and 26, 16% between 27 and 28, and 13% above 28.

Requirements: The SAT or ACT is required. FRESHMAN APPLICANTS in addition to the application, must have the following credentials: 1. Official secondary school transcripts and appropriate test scores: Scholastic Aptitude Test (SAT) or the American College Test (ACT with writing). 2. Proof of graduation from an accredited secondary school must be submitted before enrolling. 3. High School diplomas accepted for undergraduate degree-seeking admission to FIU must be completed at a secondary institution accredited by a regional accrediting body or at an institution accredited by a national accrediting agency recognized by the United States Department of Education. 4. Eighteen academic units in college preparatory courses are required as follows: 4 English; 4 Mathematics; 3 Natural Science; 3 Social Science; 2 Foreign Languages; 2 Academic Electives (see notes). Freshman admission decisions are made based on the student's strong academic preparation. Competition for placement in the freshman class includes a review of all academic credentials and a completed file. Applicants are encouraged to complete the MyMajorMatch assessment to match their interest with FIU majors, find an appropriate major, and explore possible careers. Students who apply to majors in Theatre and Music must meet University academic standards and receive the approval of the respective department through an audition. Students should contact the specific department for audition dates. Notes: 1.Two units in the same foreign language are required. 2 Academic Electives are from the fields of mathematics, English, natural science, social science, and a foreign language. The academic grade point average will be computed only on the units listed above. Grades in honors courses, International Baccalaureate (IB), and advanced placement (AP) courses will be given additional weight. Admission to the University is a selective process and satisfying the general requirements does not guarantee acceptance. A GPA of 2.0 is required. AP and CLEP credits are accepted. Important factors in the admissions decision are advanced placement or honors courses, evidence of special talent, and recommendations by school officials.

Procedure: Freshmen are admitted fall, spring, and summer. Entrance exams should be taken during the spring of the junior year. There is a rolling admissions plan. Application deadlines are open. Application fee is $30. Applications are accepted online.

Transfer: 4248 transfer students enrolled in 2012-2013. Degree seeking transfer applicants with fewer than 60 semester hours of transfer credits must meet the same requirements as beginning freshmen students. In addition, they must demonstrate satisfactory performance in their college work. Applicants who receive an Associate in Arts (A.A.) degree from a Florida Public Community College or State University in Florida will be considered for admission without restriction except for published limited access programs within the University. Students transferring from independent Florida and out-of-state colleges into the University's upper division must have maintained a minimum 2.0 grade point average using a 4.0 scale (with the exception of some limited access programs). All applicants must meet the criteria published for limited access programs and should consult the specific college and major for requirements. 30 of 120 credits required for the bachelor's degree must be completed at FIU.

Visiting: There are regularly scheduled orientations for prospective students, Tours are available on both the Modesto Maidique campus and Biscayne Bay campuses. There are guides for informal visits and visitors may sit in on classes. To schedule a visit, contact the Undgergraduate Admissions.

Financial Aid: FIU is a member of CSS. The FAFSA is required. The deadline for filing freshman financial aid applications for fall entry is March 1.

International Students: There are 1461 international students enrolled. The school actively recruits these students. They must take the TOEFL with a minimum score of 500 on the paper-based TOEFL (PBT) or 63 on the Internet-based version (iBT). They must also take the SAT or ACT.

Computers: All students may access the system 8 a.m. to 4 a.m. There are no time limits and no fees.

Graduates: From July 1, 2012 to June 30, 2013, 7077 bachelor's degrees were awarded. The most popular majors were business administration (35%), social sciences (9%), and psychology (8%).

Admissions Contact: Barry Taylor, Admissions Director. E-Mail: *admissions@fiu.edu* Web: *www.fiu.edu*

FLORIDA MEMORIAL UNIVERSITY E-5

Miami, FL 33054 (305) 626-3750
(800) 822-1362; (305) 626-3769

Full-time: n/av	**Faculty:** 80
Part-time: n/av	**Ph.D.s:** 40%
Graduate: n/av	**Student/Faculty:** 18 to 1
Year: n/app	**Tuition:** $14,604
Application Deadline: open	**Room & Board:** $6112
Freshman Class: n/av	
SAT or ACT: required	

LESS COMPETITIVE

Florida Memorial University, founded in 1879, is a private liberal arts institution affiliated with the American Baptist Church. The figures in the above capsule and in this profile are approximate. There are 6 undergraduate schools. The library contains 88,000 volumes, and subscribes to 400 periodicals including electronic. Special learning facilities include a The 77-acre campus is in an urban area in northwestern Miami. Including any residence halls, there are 12 buildings.

Activities: There are no fraternities or sororities.

Sports: There is no sports program at Florida Memorial.

Disabled Students: All of the campus is accessible.

Programs of Study: Florida Memorial confers B.A., and B.S. degrees.

Bachelor's degrees are awarded in BIOLOGICAL SCIENCE (biology/biological science), BUSINESS (accounting, business administration and management, and transportation management), COMMUNICATIONS AND THE ARTS (English, fine arts, and music), COMPUTER AND PHYSICAL SCIENCE (chemistry, computer science, and mathematics), EDUCATION (elementary education, physical education, and secondary education), ENGINEERING AND ENVIRONMENTAL DESIGN (air traffic control, aviation administration/management, and aviation computer technology), SOCIAL SCIENCE (criminal justice, philosophy, political science/government, psychology, public administration, religion, and sociology).

Required: To graduate, all students must complete at least 124 credit hours, including 62 hours of general education requirements, with a minimum overall GPA of 2.0. Students must successfully complete all 4 subtests of the Florida College-Level Academic Skills Test by junior year.

Special: Private sector and college internships, work-study, and a 3-2 engineering program with the University of Miami are available. Pass/fail credit and nondegree options are possible. There is a freshman honors program.

Faculty/Classroom: No introductory courses are taught by graduate students.

Requirements: The SAT or ACT is required. Applicants must be graduates of an accredited secondary school or have a GED certificate. 1 faculty and 2 personal recommendations, an autobiography, and a health certificate are required. Up to 20% of a freshman class may be admitted for 1 semester on a conditional basis to demonstrate their abilities. A GPA of 2.0 is required.

Procedure: Freshmen are admitted fall and spring. Application deadlines are open.

Transfer: Transcripts must be submitted for all previous college work, as well as high school transcripts for students with fewer than 3 credits. The SAT or ACT is required. 30 of 124 credits required for the bachelor's degree must be completed at Florida Memorial.

Financial Aid: The CSS/Profile and FFS are required. Check with the school for current application deadlines.

International Students: They must take the TOEFL.

Computers: All students may access the system. There are no time limits and no fees.

Admissions Contact: Peggy Martin, Director of Admissions. E-Mail: *pmartin@fmuniv.edu Web: www.fmuniv.edu*

FLORIDA SOUTHERN COLLEGE D-3

Lakeland, FL 33801 **(863) 680-4131**
(800) 274-4131; (863) 680-4120

Full-time: 860 men, 1258 women	**Faculty:** 119; IIB
Part-time: 32 men, 40 women	**Ph.D.s:** 80%
Graduate: 67 men, 136 women	**Student/Faculty:** 14 to 1
Year: semesters, summer session	**Tuition:** $28,580
Application Deadline: May 1	**Room & Board:** $9660
Freshman Class: 4963 applied, 2476 accepted, 633 enrolled	
SAT CR/M/W: 540/540/530	**ACT:** 25 **VERY COMPETITIVE**

Founded in 1885, Florida Southern College, is a private, comprehensive college that maintains its commitment to academic excellence through 50 undergraduate programs and distinctive graduate programs in business administration, education, and nursing. Florida Southern has a 13:1 student/faculty ratio; is a national leader in engaged learning; and boasts 27 NCAA Division II National Championships. Located on scenic Lake Hollingsworth in Central Florida, FSC is home to the world's largest single-site collection of Frank Lloyd Wright architecture. There are 4 undergraduate schools and 3 graduate schools. In addition to regional accreditation, Florida Southern has baccalaureate program accreditation with AACSB and NASM. The 2 libraries contain 542,183 volumes, 448,346 microform items, and 7,226 audio/video tapes/CDs/DVDs, and subscribe to 7,591 periodicals including electronic. Computerized library services include interlibrary loans, database searching, Internet access, and Wi-Fi capability. Special learning facilities include an art gallery, planetarium, TV station, a special learning facilities include the Rinker Technology Center; numerous computer labs across campus, including the popular TuTu's Cyber Café; the recently dedicated Christoverson Humanities Building with a film studies theater and modern language lab; the state-of-the-art Blanton Nursing Building with high-tech classrooms and a learning lab featuring a full complement of patient simulators; the McKay Archives Center, which houses the College's original Frank Lloyd Wright drawings and documents, the Florida Citrus Hall of Fame, and the Center for Florida History; and the Davis Performing Arts Center, including the nationally renowned Branscomb Auditorium, modern Buckner Theatre, and Melvin Art Gallery. The campus also is home to the Roberts Center for Learning and Literacy and the Roberts Academy, a transitional school for gifted elementary-age students with dyslexia. Construction has begun for two new facilities: a cutting-edge building that will include a simulated trading floor as well as high-tech classrooms and a dedicated career center for students in the Barney Barnett School of Business and Free Enterprise and the 4,700-square-foot Wynee Warden Dance Studio, offering stunning lake views and plentiful natural light through a soaring glass half-rotunda. In addition, the majority of the campus provides WiFi access. The 113-acre campus is in a suburban area Located off Interstate 4, FSC is 30 miles east of Tampa, 40 miles west of Orlando, with easy access to two international airports. Including any residence halls, there are 83 buildings.

Student Life: 64% of undergraduates are from Florida. Others are from 45 states, 49 foreign countries, and Canada. 82% are from public schools. 73% are White. 37% are Protestant; 29% claim no religious affiliation; 22% Catholic. The average age of freshmen is 18; all undergraduates, 21. 22% do not continue beyond their first year; 55% remain to graduate.

Housing: 1712 students can be accommodated in college housing, which includes single-sex and coed dorms, off-campus apartments, and married student housing. In addition, there are honors houses, special-interest houses, fraternity houses, and sorority houses. On-campus housing is guaranteed for all 4 years. 79% of students live on campus; of those, 90% remain on campus on weekends. Alcohol is not permitted. All students may keep cars.

Activities: 37% of men belong to 7 national fraternities; 32% of women belong to 7 national sororities. There are 83 groups on campus, including community service, extracurricular, Greek and honor's., art, band, cheerleading, chess, choir, chorale, chorus, Clubs and organizations include a variety of campus ministries, dance, drama, environmental, ethnic, film, forensics, honors, international, jazz band, literary magazine, musical theater, newspaper, opera, orchestra, pep band, photography, political, professional, radio and TV, religious, social, social service, student government, symphony, and yearbook. Popular campus events include Graduating Class Water Dome Splash, Greek Week, Flick 'n' Float movies in the pool, FSC's Got Talent, Flap Jack Fling, annual Carnival and Festival, Homecoming, Festival of Fine Arts, and Founders Day.

Sports: There are 10 intercollegiate sports for men and 11 for women, and 25 intramural sports for men and 25 for women. Florida Southern's campus provides a variety of outdoor recreational areas, including intramural fields for softball, soccer, lacrosse, flag football, and Frisbee golf; gardens and plazas; a waterfront program offering water-skiing, canoeing, and kayaking; and a 3-mile walk/run path around Lake Hollingsworth. The Hollis Wellness Center provides a fully-equipped weight room with personal trainers; an aerobics, Pilates, and yoga studio; a large gymnasium for basketball and volleyball and other intramural sports; and a heated competition-size swimming pool. The College's recently renovated 1,800-seat Jenkins Field House is used for intercollegiate basketball and volleyball, and features locker rooms, weight rooms, and athletic training facilities. Facilities for baseball, lacrosse, and golf are conveniently located near campus. The Warden Tennis Center with a grandstand, two championship courts and eight tournament courts opened in fall 2012, around the same time as the debut of Mr. George's Green, a 2.3-acre central open space ideal for recreational and social events. With 27 national championships, the College's NCAA Division II athletic program is among the best in the nation, and we were ranked number 9 in the nation for "Everybody Plays Intramural Sports" by The Princeton Review.

Disabled Students: 68% of the campus is accessible. Facilities include wheelchair ramps, elevators, special parking, specially equipped restrooms, special class scheduling, lowered drinking fountains, lowered telephones, and special housing.

Services: Counseling and information services are available, as is tutoring in most subjects. The Student Solutions Center provides tutoring in various subjects Monday through Friday as well as peer-assisted study sessions in select areas. The center also offers support for navigating financial aid, academic advising, student life, and billing. Additional resources include the Center for English Proficiency and Academic Success to assist international students.

Campus Safety and Security: Measures include 24-hour foot and vehicle patrol, emergency notification system, self-defense education, and security escort services. There are shuttle buses, emergency telephones, lighted pathways/sidewalks, controlled access to dorms/residences, hand held buttons that students can use in emergency.

Programs of Study: Florida Southern confers B.A., B.S., B.F.A., B.M., B.M.E. and B.S.N. degrees. Master's degrees are also awarded. Bachelor's degrees are awarded in AGRICULTURE (agricultural business management, agriculture, environmental studies, and horticulture), BIOLOGICAL SCIENCE (biochemistry, biology/biological science, marine biology, and molecular biology), BUSINESS (accounting and business administration and management), COMMUNICATIONS AND THE ARTS (advertising, art history and appreciation, broadcasting, communications, communication rhetoric/communication, creative writing, dance, digital communications, dramatic arts, English, graphic design, journalism, music, music business management, music performance, musical theater, public relations, Spanish, studio art, theatre acting, theatre arts, and theater design), COMPUTER AND PHYSICAL SCIENCE (chemistry, computer mathematics, computer science, and mathematics), EDUCATION (art education, athletic training, elementary education, music education, and secondary education), ENGINEERING AND ENVIRONMENTAL DESIGN (landscape architecture/design), HEALTH PROFESSIONS (nursing, predentistry, premedicine, prepharmacy, and prephysical therapy), SOCIAL SCIENCE (criminology, economics, history, humanities, philosophy, political science/government, psychology, religion, sociology, and youth ministry). Biological sciences, nursing, business, communication, and psychology are the strongest academically. Business administration, biology, psychology, and nursing have the largest enrollments.

Required: To gradate, a student needs a minimum of 124 semester credit hours from Florida Southern College and other regionally accredited colleges or universities. A maximum 62 of the required semester credit hours may have been earned at a junior/community college. After completing 96 hours, a student must finish the remaining credits at Florida Southern College. Some degree programs require more than 124 semester hours.

Special: Florida Southern College offers a dynamic, transformational curriculum complemented by a variety of exciting experiential opportunities, including guaranteed internships for all students, numerous travel-study programs, student-faculty research, service learning, and music/theater performances. FSC is the only private college in the state affiliated with the prestigious Washington Center, a D.C.-based internship provider supporting students to study and work in the nation's capital, as well as other major cities around the world. The Honors Program offers innovative curriculum options to talented students seeking extraordinary inter-disciplinary learning opportunities. Honors students receive priority registration and are able to take course overloads without paying additional fees. An agreement with the University of South Florida's School of Medicine guarantees admission to all Honors Students who complete the undergraduate requirements. A self-designed major provides motivated students with the option to create a degree program to suit a unique interest or career path, such as Art Therapy, Politics and Justice, Technology Management, and more. All FSC students are encouraged to participate in an international or domestic travel-study experience at little to no additional cost as part of their educational journey. Month-long and semester internships have taken FSC students to England, France, Italy, Spain, China, the Bahamas, Peru, Greece, and Turkey. The College also offers year-long study through Regent's College in London and a popular modern language school in Spain. In fall 2013, the College launched the Hollingsworth Scholars program, a full-tuition scholarship offered to select students of extraordinary academic talent and vision. There are 22 national honor societies, a freshman honors program, and 8 departmental honors programs.

Faculty/Classroom: 57% of faculty are male; 43% are female. All teach undergraduates, and 35% do both. No introductory courses are taught by graduate students. The average class size in an introductory lecture is 22; in a laboratory is 17; and in a regular course is 18.

Admissions: 50% of the 2013-2014 applicants were accepted. The SAT scores for the 2013-2014 freshman class were: Critical Reading--23% below 500, 54% between 500 and 599, 19% between 600 and 699, and 4% between 700 and 800; Math--18% below 500, 57% between 500 and 599, 23% between 600 and 699, and 2% between 700 and 800; Writing--33% below 500, 47% between 500 and 599, 19% between 600 and 699, and 3% between 700 and 800. The ACT scores were 5% below 21, 30% between 21 and 23, 35% between 24 and 26, 14% between 27 and 28, and 16% above 28. 46% of the current freshmen were in the top fifth of their class; 73% were in the top two fifths.

Requirements: The SAT or ACT is required. Applicants are expected to have earned credit in at least 18 units of college preparatory courses and graduated from an accredited secondary school. It is recommended that students have a 3.0 GPA. An essay is required, and an interview is recommended. Applicants must submit either the SAT or ACT. A GPA of 2.0 is required. AP and CLEP credits are accepted. Important factors in the admissions decision are leadership record, geographical diversity, and recommendations by school officials.

Procedure: Freshmen are admitted to all sessions. Entrance exams should be taken starting in the junior year of high school. There are early decision, early admissions, deferred admissions, and rolling admissions plans. Early decision applications should be filed by December 1; regular applications, by May 1 for fall entry; and December 1 for spring entry, along with a $30 fee. Notification of early decision is sent December 15; regular decision, on a rolling basis. 50 early decision candidates were accepted for the 2013-2014 class. Applications are accepted online.

Transfer: 111 transfer students enrolled in 2012-2013. Students who have successfully completed work at a regionally accredited college or university may apply for admission to Florida Southern College. Applicants should submit SAT or ACT scores, if available, along with a personal statement indicating the reason for the transfer. Official transcripts are required from each postsecondary institution attended. Transfer students must have a minimum 2.5 GPA in all college work attempted. An associate degree and an interview are recommended. 32 of 128 credits required for the bachelor's degree must be completed at Florida Southern.

Visiting: There are regularly scheduled orientations for prospective students, including meeting with faculty, a campus tour, and class visits, as well as special programming for parents, with a brief history of Frank Lloyd Wright, who was the campus architect. There are guides for informal visits, visitors may sit in on classes, and stay overnight. To schedule a visit, contact the Admissions Office at fscadm@flsouthern.edu.

Financial Aid: In 2013-2014, 99% of all full-time freshmen and 98% of continuing full-time students received some form of financial aid. 73% of all full-time freshmen and 73% of continuing full-time students received need-based aid. The average freshman award was $26,728. Need-based scholarships or need-based grants averaged $17,154 ($44,724 maximum); need-based self-help aid (loans and jobs) averaged $1,751 ($5,400 maximum); non-need-based athletic scholarships averaged $12,867 ($39,190 maximum); and other non-need-based awards and non-need-based scholarships averaged $14,377 ($42,255 maximum). 65% of undergraduate students work part-time. Average annual earnings from campus work are $1750. The average financial indebtedness of the 2013 graduate was $33,191. The FAFSA and the college's own financial statement, and the parents' and student's tax returns are required. The priority date for freshman financial aid applications for fall entry is March 1. The deadline for filing freshman financial aid applications for fall entry is July 1.

International Students: There are 123 international students enrolled. The school actively recruits these students. They must take the TOEFL with a minimum score of 550 on the paper-based TOEFL (PBT) or 79 on the Internet-based version (iBT). They must also take the SAT or ACT.

Computers: All students may access the system 24 hours daily. There are no time limits and no fees.

Graduates: From July 1, 2012 to June 30, 2013, 501 bachelor's degrees were awarded. The most popular majors were business (26%), nursing (11%), and education (10%). 312 companies recruited on campus in 2012-2013. In an average class, 48% graduate in 4 years or less, 57% graduate in 5 years or less, and 58% graduate in 6 years or less. Of the 2012 graduating class, 24% were enrolled in graduate school within 6 months of graduation, and 70% were employed.

Admissions Contact: Erin Ervin, Director of Admissions. E-Mail: *fscadm@flsouthern.edu* Web: *http:/www.flsouthern.edu*

FLORIDA STATE UNIVERSITY — C-1

Tallahassee, FL 32306 — **(850) 644-6200; (850) 644-0197**

Full-time: 12669 men, 16421 women	**Faculty:** 747; I, --$
Part-time: 1958 men, 1660 women	**Ph.D.s:** 92%
Graduate: 3780 men, 4601 women	**Student/Faculty:** 22 to 1
Year: semesters, summer session	**Tuition:** $5826 ($20,992)
Application Deadline: January 25	**Room & Board:** $9412
Freshman Class: 30040 applied, 16124 accepted, 5738 enrolled	
SAT CR/M/W: 600/595/600	**ACT:** 27 **HIGHLY COMPETITIVE**

Florida State University, a public institution founded in 1851, is a residential university designated as a Doctoral Research (Extensive) University by the Carnegie Foundation for the Advancement of Teaching. There are 15 undergraduate schools and 16 graduate schools. In addition to regional accreditation, FSU has baccalaureate program accreditation with AACSB, ABET, ADA, AHEA, ASLA, CSWE, FIDER, NASAD, NASM, NCATE, NLN, and NRPA. The 8 libraries contain 3.0 million volumes, 9.8 million microform items, and 257,419 audio/video tapes/CDs/DVDs, and subscribe to 72,825 periodicals including electronic. Computerized library services include interlibrary loans, database searching, and Internet access. Special learning facilities include an art gallery, planetarium, radio station, TV station, nuclear accelerator, x-ray emission lab, marine lab, supercomputers, and the National High Magnetic Field Laboratory. The 452-acre campus is in a suburban area 163 miles west of Jacksonville. Including any residence halls, there are 237 buildings.

Student Life: 88% of undergraduates are from Florida. Others are from 50 states, 128 foreign countries, and Canada. 81% are from public schools. 70% are White; 16% Hispanic; 11% African American. The average age of freshmen is 18; all undergraduates, 21. 9% do not continue beyond their first year; 91% remain to graduate.

Housing: 6111 students can be accommodated in college housing, which includes single-sex and coed dorms, on-campus apartments, and married student housing. In addition, there are honors houses, special-interest houses, fraternity houses, sorority houses, living and learning centers, music residence, scholarship houses, and academic discipline houses, wellness housing, Cooperative living through the southern scholarship foundation and several private residence halls. On-campus housing is available on a first-come and first-served basis. 75% of students live on campus. All students may keep cars.

Activities: 16% of men belong to 31 national fraternities; 19% of women belong to 26 national sororities. There are 628 groups on campus, including art, band, cheerleading, chess, choir, chorale, chorus, computers, dance, debate, drama, drill team, ethnic, forensics, gay, honors, international, jazz band, literary magazine, marching band, musical theater, newspaper, opera, orchestra, pep band, political, professional, radio and TV, religious, social, social service, student government, and symphony. Popular campus events include Twelve Days of Dance, Parents Weekend and Seven Days of Opening Nights.

Sports: There are 9 intercollegiate sports for men and 10 for women, and 27 intramural sports for men and 27 for women. Facilities include an

80,000-seat stadium, an aquatic center with a heated outdoor swimming pool, a golf course, a track, courts for basketball, tennis, racquetball, and handball, a student recreation center with an indoor Olympic-size swimming pool, 2 Jacuzzis, a steam room, a sauna, 10 racquetball courts, a squash court, a multipurpose gym, a 3-lane jogging track, aerobic rooms, aerobic exercise machines, free and fixed weights, and a lakefront recreation area for outdoor water sports.

Disabled Students: 99% of the campus is accessible. Facilities include wheelchair ramps, elevators, special parking, specially equipped restrooms, special class scheduling, lowered drinking fountains, and lowered telephones.

Services: Counseling and information services are available, as is tutoring in most subjects. There is a reader service for the blind, and remedial math, reading, and writing.

Campus Safety and Security: Measures include 24-hour foot and vehicle patrol, emergency notification system, self-defense education, and security escort services. There are shuttle buses, emergency telephones, lighted pathways/sidewalks, a full-time police force, a bicycle identification program, a valuables identification program, and a victim advocate program.

Programs of Study: FSU confers B.A., B.S., B.S.N., B.F.A, B.M. and B.M.Ed. degrees. Associate, master's, and doctoral degrees are also awarded. Bachelor's degrees are awarded in AGRICULTURE (environmental studies and plant science), BIOLOGICAL SCIENCE (biochemistry, biology/biological science, cell biology, ecology, evolutionary biology, genetics, marine biology, molecular biology, nutrition, physiology, and zoology), BUSINESS (accounting, banking and finance, business administration and management, entrepreneurial studies, fashion merchandising, hotel/motel and restaurant management, insurance and risk management, international business management, management science, marketing/retailing/merchandising, personnel management, recreation and leisure services, recreational facilities management, small business management, and sports management), COMMUNICATIONS AND THE ARTS (advertising, American literature, apparel design, art history and appreciation, broadcasting, classics, communications, creative writing, dance, dramatic arts, English, fiber/textiles/weaving, film arts, French, German, Greek, Italian, jazz, Latin, linguistics, music, music history and appreciation, music performance, music theory and composition, musical theater, piano/organ, public relations, Russian, Spanish, speech/debate/rhetoric, strings, studio art, theater design, voice, and winds), COMPUTER AND PHYSICAL SCIENCE (actuarial science, applied mathematics, atmospheric sciences and meteorology, chemical technology, chemistry, computer science, geology, information sciences and systems, mathematics, physics, and statistics), EDUCATION (art education, athletic training, early childhood education, education of the emotionally handicapped, education of the mentally handicapped, education of the visually handicapped, elementary education, English education, foreign languages education, health education, home economics education, mathematics education, music education, physical education, reading education, science education, social science education, and specific learning disabilities), ENGINEERING AND ENVIRONMENTAL DESIGN (bioengineering, biomedical engineering, chemical engineering, civil engineering, computer engineering, electrical/electronics engineering, environmental engineering, environmental science, graphic arts technology, industrial engineering, interior design, materials engineering, and mechanical engineering), HEALTH PROFESSIONS (community health work, music therapy, nursing, predentistry, premedicine, preoptometry, prepharmacy, preveterinary science, rehabilitation therapy, speech pathology/audiology, and sports medicine), SOCIAL SCIENCE (American studies, anthropology, Asian/Oriental studies, Caribbean studies, child care/child and family studies, classical/ancient civilization, clothing and textiles management/production/services, criminology, dietetics, Eastern European studies, economics, family/consumer studies, fashion design and technology, food science, geography, history, home economics, humanities, international relations, Latin American studies, philosophy, political science/government, prelaw, psychology, religion, Russian and Slavic studies, social science, social work, sociology, and women's studies). Biology, meteorology, and physics are the strongest academically. Psychology, and business have the largest enrollments.

Required: Students must satisfy the Florida College-Level Academic Skills (CLAS) requirement or an approved alternative. The required core curriculum includes 6 semester hours in Mathematics, 6 in English composition, 6 to 12 in history/social science, 5 to 11 humanities/fine arts, and 7 in natural sciences. Students must satisfy major requirements of their chosen degree program, including additional requirements set by the college offering the degree. All academic areas require at least 120 semester hours for graduation. Additional information is available in the General Bulletin.

Special: Cross-registration with Florida Agricultural and Mechanical University and Tallahassee Community College is possible, as is study at FSU centers in London or Florence and in programs in Costa Rica, France, Russia, Spain, Switzerland, and Vietnam, among other countries. FSU offers cooperative programs in Engineering, Computer Science, Business, and Communication, work-study programs, general studies and combined B.A.-B.S. degrees, dual majors, and accelerated degree programs. Internships are required in Criminology, Human Science, Education, Nursing, Business (PMG), and Social Work. There are pre-professional programs in Health and Law. There are 34 national honor societies, including Phi Beta Kappa, a freshman honors program, and 60 departmental honors programs.

Faculty/Classroom: 59% of faculty are male; 41% are female. Graduate students teach 49% of introductory courses. The average class size in an introductory lecture is 40; in a laboratory is 18; and in a regular course is 36.

Admissions: 54% of the 2013-2014 applicants were accepted. The SAT scores for the 2013-2014 freshman class were: Critical Reading--2% below 500, 48% between 500 and 599, 42% between 600 and 699, and 8% between 700 and 800; Math--3% below 500, 46% between 500 and 599, 43% between 600 and 699, and 6% between 700 and 800; Writing--3% below 500, 49% between 500 and 599, 43% between 600 and 699, and 5% between 700 and 800. The ACT scores were 6% between 21 and 23, and 94% above 28. 88% of the current freshmen were in the top fifth of their class. There were 13 National Merit finalists.

Requirements: The SAT or ACT is required. In addition, It is recommended that in-state students have at least an A-/B+ weighted average and a satisfactory SAT or ACT score. Out-of-state students must meet higher standards. Applicants should have at least the following high school units; 4 in English and math, 3 in natural science, and social science, and 2 in a foreign language. Other factors include the number of honors, AP, and IB classes, strength of academic curriculum, class rank, among others. FSU requires applicants to be in the upper 77% of their class. A GPA of 3.9 is required. AP and CLEP credits are accepted. Important factors in the admissions decision are advanced placement or honors courses, evidence of special talent, and recommendations by school officials.

Procedure: Freshmen are admitted fall, spring, and summer. Entrance exams should be taken beginning in the second semester of the junior year. There is a rolling admissions plan. Applications should be filed by January 25 for fall entry; November 1 for spring entry; and February 13 for summer entry, along with a $30 fee. Applications are accepted online.

Transfer: 2115 transfer students enrolled in 2012-2013. Transfer applicants should present at least a 3.0 cumulative college GPA unless transferring from a Florida public community college with an associate in arts degree, in which case the minimum college GPA needed varies according to major. Applicants with less than 60 semester hours of transferable credit must also meet freshman admission requirements. All transfers must have completed 2 years of the same foreign language in high school or have 8 semester hours at the college level. Students must pass the Florida CLAST. 30 of 120 credits required for the bachelor's degree must be completed at FSU.

Visiting: There are regularly scheduled orientations for prospective students, including campus tours several times daily on weekdays. Walking and riding tours are available and tours are coordinated around an 11:00 admissions information session. There are guides for informal visits and visitors may sit in on classes. To schedule a visit, contact the Visitor Services at visitorservices@admin.fsu.edu.

Financial Aid: In 2013-2014, 95% of all full-time freshmen and 88% of continuing full-time students received some form of financial aid. 45% of all full-time freshmen and 53% of continuing full-time students received need-based aid. The average freshman award was $7,093. Need-based scholarships or need-based grants averaged $4,756 ($11,512 maximum); need-based self-help aid (loans and jobs) averaged $3,128 ($4,150 maximum); non-need-based athletic scholarships averaged $5,587 ($5,587 maximum); and other non-need-based awards and non-need-based scholarships averaged $4,426 ($7,400 maximum). 3% of undergraduate students work part-time. Average annual earnings from campus work are $1964. The average financial indebtedness of the 2013 graduate was $21,532. The FAFSA and the college's own financial statement are required. The priority date for freshman financial aid applications for fall entry is January 15.

International Students: There are 407 international students enrolled. They must take the TOEFL with a minimum score of 550 on the paper-based TOEFL (PBT) or 80 on the Internet-based version (iBT). They must also take the SAT or ACT.

Computers: All students may access the system, although use of some machines is restricted to particular majors or graduate students. There are no time limits and no fees.

Graduates: From July 1, 2012 to June 30, 2013, 7938 bachelor's degrees were awarded. The most popular majors were business/marketing (19%), social sciences (18%), and psychology and English (6%). In an average class, 4% graduate in 3 years or less, 50% graduate in 4 years or less, 71% graduate in 5 years or less, and 74% graduate in 6 years or less. Of the 2012 graduating class, 48% were enrolled in graduate school within 6 months of graduation, and 63% were employed.

Admissions Contact: Andrew Brady, Statistical Coodinator. E-Mail: *abrady@fsu.edu* Web: *www.fsu.edu*

HODGES UNIVERSITY D-5

Naples, FL 34119-7932 (239) 513-1122
(800) 466-8017; (239) 513-9054

Full-time: 375 men, 765 women
Part-time: 120 men, 255 women
Graduate: 100 men, 140 women
Year: semesters, summer session
Application Deadline: open
Freshman Class: n/av
Faculty: n/av
Ph.D.s: 66%
Student/Faculty: n/av
Tuition: $12,500
Room & Board: n/app

LESS COMPETITIVE

Hodges University, founded in 1990, is a private institution offering undergraduate and graduate degree programs in business and public administration, accounting, criminal justice, health administration and allied health, interdisciplinary studies, applied psychology, information systems management, computer technology, and paralegal studies. The figures in the above capsule and in this profile are approximate. There are 4 undergraduate schools and 3 graduate schools. The library contains 39,808 volumes, and 836 audio/video tapes/CDs/DVDs, and subscribes to 31,019 periodicals including electronic. Computerized library services include interlibrary loans, database searching, and Internet access. Special learning facilities include an art gallery. The 10-acre campus is in a suburban area 100 miles west of Fort Lauderdale. Including any residence halls, there is 1 building.

Student Life: 99% of undergraduates are from Florida. Others are from 7 states, and 3 foreign countries. 57% are white; 23% Hispanic; 16% African American. The average age of freshmen is 31; all undergraduates, 31.

Housing: There are no residence halls. All students commute.

Activities: There are no fraternities or sororities. Groups on campus include literary magazine and student government.

Disabled Students: All of the campus is accessible. Facilities include elevators, special parking, specially equipped restrooms, and lowered drinking fountains.

Services: There is remedial math and writing.

Campus Safety and Security: Measures include security escort services. There are lighted pathways/sidewalks.

Programs of Study: Hodges confers B.S. degrees. Associate and master's degrees are also awarded. Bachelor's degrees are awarded in BUSINESS (accounting and business administration and management), COMPUTER AND PHYSICAL SCIENCE (information sciences and systems), ENGINEERING AND ENVIRONMENTAL DESIGN (computer technology), HEALTH PROFESSIONS (health and health care administration), SOCIAL SCIENCE (criminal justice, interdisciplinary studies, and paralegal studies). Management and interdisiplinary studies are the largest.

Required: To graduate, students must complete a minimum of 122 semester hours, with at least 60 in the major and a minimum GPA of 2.0. At least 48 hours must be upper-division courses. A comprehensive exam is required.

Special: Dual majors, internships, work study, online classes, and credit for life experience are possible. There is 1 departmental honors program.

Faculty/Classroom: 64% of faculty are male; 36% are female. 94% teach undergraduates. No introductory courses are taught by graduate students. The average class size in an introductory lecture is 14 and in a regular course is 14.

Requirements: AP and CLEP credits are accepted.

Procedure: Freshmen are admitted fall, winter, and summer. Entrance exams should be taken any time. There is a rolling admissions plan. Application deadlines are open. The fall 2011 application fee was $20. Notification is sent on a rolling basis. Applications are accepted online.

Transfer: Applicants must submit previous transcripts. Only credits completed with a C or better will transfer. 32 of 122 credits required for the bachelor's degree must be completed at Hodges.

Visiting: There are regularly scheduled orientations for prospective students. Orientations for undergraduates are held 3 days prior to start of the term.

Financial Aid: The FAFSA is required. Check with the school for current application deadlines.

International Students: The school actively recruits these students. They must take the TOEFL, CPAT and COMPASS.

Computers: Wireless access is available. The network and/or wireless system is available in computer labs, classrooms, the library, and student lounges. All students may access the system. There are no time limits and no fees.

Admissions Contact: Rita Lampus, VP of Student Enrollment. E-Mail: *rlampus@hodges.edu* Web: *www.hodges.edu*

JACKSONVILLE UNIVERSITY D-1

Jacksonville, FL 32211 (904) 256-7000
(800) 225-2027; (904) 256-7012

Full-time: 1075 men, 1125 women
Part-time: 165 men, 675 women
Graduate: 190 men, 295 women
Year: semesters, summer session
Application Deadline: open
Freshman Class: n/av
SAT or ACT: required
Faculty: n/av; IIA, --$
Ph.D.s: 78%
Student/Faculty: n/av
Tuition: $28,400
Room & Board: $10,380

COMPETITIVE

Jacksonville University, founded in 1934, is a private institution offering undergraduate and graduate degree programs in the arts and sciences, fine arts, and business. The figures in the above capsule and in this profile are approximate. There are 3 undergraduate schools and 4 graduate schools. In addition to regional accreditation, JU has baccalaureate program accreditation with NASAD, NASM, and NLN. The library contains 385,016 volumes, 253,284 microform items, and 24,919 audio/video tapes/CDs/DVDs, and subscribes to 19,740 periodicals including electronic. Computerized library services include interlibrary loans, database searching, and Internet access. Special learning facilities include a learning resource center, art gallery, planetarium, radio station, TV station, a chemistry research lab, and a marine science center. The 198-acre campus is in a suburban area 10 minutes from downtown Jacksonville, near the St. Johns River. Including any residence halls, there are 48 buildings.

Student Life: 60% of undergraduates are from Florida. Others are from 45 states, 50 foreign countries, and Canada. 56% are white; 20% African American. 35% claim no religious affiliation; 18% Protestant; 16% Catholic. The average age of freshmen is 19; all undergraduates, 22. 35% do not continue beyond their first year; 49% remain to graduate.

Housing: 1342 students can be accommodated in college housing, which includes single-sex dorms and on-campus apartments. On-campus housing is guaranteed for the freshman year only, is available on a first-come, first-served basis, and is available on a lottery system for upperclassmen. 59% of students live on campus; of those, 60% remain on campus on weekends. All students may keep cars.

Activities: 20% of men belong to 8 national fraternities; 15% of women belong to 7 national sororities. There are 100 groups on campus, including art, band, cheerleading, choir, chorale, chorus, computers, dance, debate, drama, drill team, environmental, ethnic, film, gay, honors, international, jazz band, literary magazine, musical theater, newspaper, orchestra, pep band, photography, political, professional, radio and TV, religious, social, social service, student government, and symphony. Popular campus events include FIN Fest and Campus Movie Fest.

Sports: There are 8 intercollegiate sports for men and 9 for women. Facilities include a 1500-seat stadium, a gym, a swimming pool, a boathouse, baseball and softball diamonds, soccer and football fields, and an archery range. There are also tennis, basketball, handball/racquetball, volleyball, and shuffleboard courts, an all-purpose playing field, a 440-yard track, a 540-seat auditorium, a 220-seat recital hall, and a dance pavilion.

Disabled Students: All of the campus is accessible. Facilities include wheelchair ramps, elevators, special parking, specially equipped restrooms, special class scheduling, lowered drinking fountains. Accommodation is made for all students regardless of disability.

Services: Counseling and information services are available, as is tutoring in most subjects. There is a reader service for the blind, and remedial math, reading, and writing. There also is a writer service for note taking in class.

Campus Safety and Security: Measures include 24-hour foot and vehicle patrol, self-defense education, and security escort services. There are emergency telephones and lighted pathways/sidewalks.

Programs of Study: JU confers B.A., B.S., B.B.A., B.F.A., B.G.S., B.Mus., B.Mus.Ed., and B.S.N. degrees. Master's degrees are also awarded. Bachelor's degrees are awarded in BIOLOGICAL SCIENCE (biology/biological science and marine science), BUSINESS (accounting, banking and finance, business administration and management, international business management, and marketing/retailing/merchandising), COMMUNICATIONS AND THE ARTS (art history and appreciation, communications, dance, dramatic arts, English, French, music, music performance, music theory and composition, Spanish, and studio art), COMPUTER AND PHYSICAL SCIENCE (chemistry, computer science, information sciences and systems, mathematics, and physics), EDUCATION (art education, dance education, education of the exceptional child, elementary education, music education, and physical education), ENGINEERING AND ENVIRONMENTAL DESIGN (aviation administration/management, computer graphics, electrical/electronics engineering, engineering physics, environmental science, and mechanical engineering), HEALTH PROFESSIONS (nursing), SOCIAL SCIENCE (economics, geography, history, humanities, international studies, philosophy, political science/government, psychology, and sociology). Business administration, nursing, and biology have the largest enrollments.

Required: All students must complete a core curriculum, which provides the liberal arts foundation for all bachelor's degrees. The core includes 4 hours of lab science and 3 hours each of English composition, world literature, economics, fine arts, global studies, humanities, modern world history, math, philosophy, social science, and technology. The B.A. degree requires completion of a foreign language component in place of 3 hours of global studies. A minimum of 120 credit hours, with a minimum GPA of 2.0, is needed to graduate.

Special: Internships and work-study are available, as are student-designed majors and a dual major in music and business. There is a co-op program in art, and a 3-2 engineering degree is available with 7 other universities and technological institutes. There is a Washington semester and study abroad in 12 countries. Credit is granted for military experience. There are 16 national honor societies, including Phi Beta Kappa, and a freshman honors program.

Faculty/Classroom: 53% of faculty are male; 47% are female. No introductory courses are taught by graduate students. The average class size in an introductory lecture is 18; in a laboratory is 16; and in a regular course is 14.

Requirements: The SAT or ACT is required. Applicants must be graduates of an accredited secondary school and provide an official copy of their secondary school transcripts or have a GED. At least 18 academic credits are required, including 4 in English, 3 each in math, natural science, and social sciences, and 2 of the same foreign language. Art students must submit a portfolio. Music, theater, and dance students must audition. A GPA of 2.0 is required. AP and CLEP credits are accepted. Important factors in the admissions decision are advanced placement or honors courses, extracurricular activities record, and leadership record.

Procedure: Freshmen are admitted to all sessions. Entrance exams should be taken in the spring of the junior year or the fall or spring of the senior year. There are early admissions, deferred admissions, and rolling admissions plans. Application deadlines are open. The application fee in a recent year was $30. Applications are accepted online.

Transfer: Transfer students must submit official transcripts from all colleges attended. Art students must submit a portfolio; music and dance students must audition. Transfer applicants must have completed at least 1 semester at an accredited college or university, be in good standing at the last institution attended, and have a minimum GPA of 2.0. 30 of 120 credits required for the bachelor's degree must be completed at JU.

Visiting: There are regularly scheduled orientations for prospective students, consisting of an interview, a campus tour, advisement, area presentations, registration, a parents program, and mock classes. There are guides for informal visits, visitors may sit in on classes, and stay overnight. To schedule a visit, contact the Admissions Office.

Financial Aid: JU is a member of CSS. The FAFSA, the college's own financial statement, a federal tax return and W-2 are required. Check with the school for current application deadlines.

International Students: The school actively recruits these students. They must take the TOEFL with a minimum score of 540 on the paper-based TOEFL (PBT) or 76 on the Internet-based version (iBT). They must also take the SAT or ACT.

Computers: All students may access the system. during lab hours, 7 days a week. There is also dial-in-access. There are no time limits and no fees. It is strongly recommended that all students have a personal computer.

Admissions Contact: Lisa Hannasch, Director of Admissions. E-Mail: *admissions@ju.edu* *Web: www.ju.edu*

JOHNSON AND WALES UNIVERSITY/NORTH MIAMI CAMPUS — E-5

North Miami, FL 33181 — **(305) 892-7020**

Full-time: 870 men, 1194 women	**Faculty:** 58
Part-time: 48 men, 41 women	**Ph.D.s:** n/av
Graduate: n/av	**Student/Faculty:** 32 to 1
Year: trimesters	**Tuition:** $25,107
Application Deadline: open	**Room & Board:** $9261
Freshman Class: n/av	
SAT or ACT: recommended	**COMPETITIVE**

Johnson & Wales University/North Miami Campus, founded in 1992, offers degree programs in its College of Culinary Arts, College of Business, and Hospitality College. There are 3 undergraduate schools. The library contains 12,525 volumes, and 2,301 audio/video tapes/CDs/DVDs, and subscribes to 232 periodicals including electronic. Computerized library services include interlibrary loans, database searching, Internet access, and laptop Internet portals. Special learning facilities include a learning resource center, a university-owned/operated hotel. The campus is in the heart of North Miami, between Miami and Fort Lauderdale. Including any residence halls, there are 13 buildings.

Student Life: 52% of undergraduates are from Florida. Others are from 44 states, 54 foreign countries, and Canada. 24% are African American; 23% white; 21% Hispanic. The average age of freshmen is 19; all undergraduates, 20.

Housing: 1184 students can be accommodated in college housing, which includes coed dorms and on-campus apartments. On-campus housing is available on a lottery system for upperclassmen. All students may keep cars.

Activities: Groups on campus include cheerleading, dance, ethnic, gay, honors, international, music ensembles and campus ministries, newspaper, pep band, professional, religious, social, and student government.

Sports: There are 4 intercollegiate sports for men and 4 for women, and 5 intramural sports for men and 5 for women. Facilities include a fitness center located in Biscayne Commons residence hall. The center is equipped with cardio machines, free weights, universal machines, treadmills, and so on and is open 7 days a week.

Disabled Students: All of the campus is accessible. Facilities include wheelchair ramps, elevators, special parking, specially equipped restrooms, special class scheduling, lowered drinking fountains, lowered telephones, and special housing.

Services: Counseling and information services are available, as is tutoring in every subject.

Campus Safety and Security: Measures include 24-hour foot and vehicle patrol and security escort services. There are shuttle buses and emergency telephones.

Programs of Study: JWU confers B.S. degrees. Associate degrees are also awarded. Bachelor's degrees are awarded in BUSINESS (accounting, business administration and management, entrepreneurial studies, hospitality management services, hotel/motel and restaurant management, marketing management, marketing/retailing/merchandising, recreation and leisure services, sports management, and tourism), ENGINEERING AND ENVIRONMENTAL DESIGN (electrical/electronics engineering and food services technology), SOCIAL SCIENCE (clothing and textiles management/production/services, criminal justice, food production/management/services, paralegal studies, and parks and recreation management).

Required: To graduate, students must complete 180 quarter credit hours, including at least 36 in the major, with a minimum GPA of 2.0. Required classes include English, math history, economics, science, psychology, sociology, and professional development.

Special: The university offers co-op programs, accelerated degree programs, dual majors, study abroad, and worldwide work-study opportunities in business, hospitality, technology, and culinary arts. Most majors require 11-week internships.

Faculty/Classroom: 61% of faculty are male; 37% are female. No introductory courses are taught by graduate students.

Requirements: Although SAT and ACT scores are required only for students applying for honors admissions, students who have taken these test are encouraged to submit their scores. A GPA of 2.0 is required. AP and CLEP credits are accepted. Important factors in the admissions decision are advanced placement or honors courses, extracurricular activities record, and recommendations by school officials.

Procedure: Freshmen are admitted to all sessions. There are deferred admissions and rolling admissions plans. Application deadlines are open.

Transfer: 125 transfer students enrolled in 2010-2011. Applicants are required to submit official high school and college transcripts and must have earned a minimum college GPA of 2.0.

Visiting: There are regularly scheduled orientations for prospective students, including an introduction to the academic and social aspects of the campus experience through interactive sessions. There are guides for informal visits, visitors may sit in on classes, and stay overnight. To schedule a visit, contact Admissions.

Financial Aid: JWU is a member of CSS. The FAFSA is required. Check with the school for current application deadlines.

International Students: There are 192 international students enrolled. The school actively recruits these students. They must take the TOEFL.

Computers: There are general-purpose labs and labs equipped with specialized software applications. The computer labs offer free Internet access, e-mail access, and black-and-white printing. All students may access the system.

Graduates: The most popular majors were marketing (24%), food service management (8%), and business administration (6%).

Admissions Contact: Director of Admissions. A campus DVD is available. E-Mail: *admissions.fla@jwu.edu* Web: *www.jwu.edu*

LYNN UNIVERSITY — E-5

Boca Raton, FL 33431 — **(561) 237-7831** / **(800) 888-LYNN; (561) 237-7100**

Full-time: 796 men, 703 women	**Faculty:** 93
Part-time: 69 men, 89 women	**Ph.D.s:** 67%
Graduate: 202 men, 238 women	**Student/Faculty:** 16 to 1
Year: varies, summer session	**Tuition:** $32,600
Application Deadline:	**Room & Board:** $10,900
Freshman Class: 2162 applied, 2047 accepted, 415 enrolled	
SAT CR/M/W: 450/460/450 — **ACT:** 20	**COMPETITIVE**

Lynn University was founded in 1962 and is a private, coeducational institution with a solid reputation for academic quality and educational innovation, providing academic programs that reflect societal needs and encourage collaborative approaches to the challenges our students will face in the workplace and in the world. Lynn's nationally recognized Institute for Achievement and Learning is committed to providing the highest quality, empirically based resources and academic support to both non-traditional and traditional learners. The student body is comprised of students from 87 countries and 45 states/territories. There are 5 undergraduate schools and 5 graduate schools. In addition to regional accreditation, LU has baccalaureate program accreditation with NASM. The library contains 67,989 volumes, and 8,545 audio/video tapes/CDs/DVDs, and subscribes to 197,354 periodicals including electronic. Computerized library services include interlibrary loans, database searching, and Internet access. Special learning facilities include a radio station, TV station, The TV station is Internet delivery/streaming capable. The radio station streams live on the Internet 24/7. The 123-acre campus is in a suburban area Midway between Fort Lauderdale and Palm Beach. Including any residence halls, there are 20 buildings.

Student Life: 58% of undergraduates are from out of state, mostly the Northeast. Students are from 45 states, 87 foreign countries, and Canada. 43% are White; 23% Foreign; 17% Asian American. The average age of freshmen is 18; all undergraduates, 21. 31% do not continue beyond their first year; 40% remain to graduate.

Housing: 913 students can be accommodated in college housing, which includes single-sex and coed dorms. Conservatory of music students housed in the same building with one another. On-campus housing is available on a first-come, first-served basis, and is available on a lottery system for upperclassmen. 52% of students commute. All students may keep cars.

Activities: 3% of men belong to 2 national fraternities; 9% of women belong to 2 national sororities. There are 40 groups on campus, including International Affairs Society, Campus Crusades for Christ, Chabad, Gay-Straight Alliance, Hillel, Knights of the Roundtable, Newman Club, Black Student Union, cheerleading, dance, drama, ethnic, gay, honors, international, Organization of Latin American Students, political, professional, religious, social, social service, and student government. Popular campus events include Founders Day, Multicultural Day, Knights Unite Day of Caring, Relay for Life and SpringFest Week.

Sports: There are 6 intercollegiate sports for men and 8 for women, and 5 intramural sports for men and 5 for women. All sports, except men's and women's golf, play on campus. Facilities include the Perper Tennis Complex, the DeHoernle Sports and Cultural Center (basketball and volleyball), the McCusker Sports Complex (baseball, soccer, and softball).

Disabled Students: 90% of the campus is accessible. Facilities include wheelchair ramps, elevators, special parking, specially equipped restrooms, special class scheduling, lowered drinking fountains, and special housing.

Services: Counseling and information services are available, as is tutoring in most subjects, There are services for learning-disabled students. There is a reader service for the blind, and remedial math, reading, and writing.

Campus Safety and Security: Measures include 24-hour foot and vehicle patrol, emergency notification system, self-defense education, and security escort services. There are shuttle buses, lighted pathways/sidewalks, in-room safes, SAFERIDE within 10 mile radius of campus.

Programs of Study: LU confers B.A., B.S., B.M. and B.P.S. degrees. Master's and doctoral degrees are also awarded. Bachelor's degrees are awarded in AGRICULTURE (environmental studies), BIOLOGICAL SCIENCE (biology/biological science), BUSINESS (entrepreneurial studies, fashion merchandising, hotel/motel and restaurant management, international business management, investments and securities, marketing management, and sports management), COMMUNICATIONS AND THE ARTS (advertising, communications, dramatic arts, film arts, multimedia, and music performance), EDUCATION (elementary education), ENGINEERING AND ENVIRONMENTAL DESIGN (aviation administration/management), SOCIAL SCIENCE (criminal justice, forensic studies, political science/government, and psychology). Business Administration, Psychology,Hospitality Management,Sports Management,Criminal Justice have the largest enrollments.

Required: Undergraduate: 120 credits and 2.0 minimum GPA Graduate: 30 credits and 3.0 minimum GPA Doctoral (EdD): 51 credits and 3.25 minimum GPA

Special: Opportunities are provided for internships, which are required in many majors. Study abroad includes semester-long opportunities offered through program providers in 30 cities in 19 countries as well as short-term faculty-led programs (2-8 weeks). Countries: Argentina, Australia, Austria, Brazil, Chile, China, Czech Republic, Denmark, England, France, Germany, Greece, Ireland, Italy, Netherlands, New Zealand, South Africa, Spain, Turkey. There are 5 national honor societies.

Faculty/Classroom: 59% of faculty are male; 41% are female. All teach undergraduates. No introductory courses are taught by graduate students. The average class size in a regular course is 18.

Admissions: 95% of the 2013-2014 applicants were accepted. The SAT scores for the 2013-2014 freshman class were: Critical Reading--74% below 500, 20% between 500 and 599, 5% between 600 and 699, and 1% between 700 and 800; Math--66% below 500, 27% between 500 and 599, and 7% between 600 and 699; Writing--75% below 500, 18% between 500 and 599, 6% between 600 and 699, and 1% between 700 and 800. The ACT scores were 65% below 21, 18% between 21 and 23, 9% between 24 and 26, 6% between 27 and 28, and 2% above 28.

Requirements: The SAT or ACT is required. Graduation from an accredited secondary school is required; the GED is accepted. Applicants must have a minimum high school GPA of 2.0. An essay and an interview are recommended. A GPA of 2.5 is required. AP and CLEP credits are accepted. Important factors in the admissions decision are recommendations by school officials, personality/intangible qualities, and extracurricular activities record.

Procedure: Freshmen are admitted fall and spring. Entrance exams should be taken during the junior or senior year. There are early admissions, deferred admissions, and rolling admissions plans. Application deadlines are open. Application fee is $45. Notification is sent on a rolling basis. Applications are accepted online.

Transfer: 160 transfer students enrolled in 2012-2013. Transfer students must submit an official transcript from each previous college attended, plus a recommendation from the dean of students. The student must have maintained a minimum GPA of 2.0. An interview is recommended. Most complete an essay and a personal statement. 30 of 120 credits required for the bachelor's degree must be completed at LU.

Visiting: There are 2 orientations held for prospective students 1 for fall and 1 for spring enrollment. Orientation agendas include a university welcome, overview of policies & important info, advising, move-in to residence halls & student activities. There are guides for informal visits, visitors may sit in on classes, and stay overnight. To schedule a visit, contact The Office of Admission.

Financial Aid: In 2013-2014, 78% of all full-time freshmen and 74% of continuing full-time students received some form of financial aid. 45% of all full-time freshmen and 44% of continuing full-time students received need-based aid. The average freshman award was $21,550. Need-based scholarships or need-based grants averaged $10,108 ($21,584 maximum); need-based self-help aid (loans and jobs) averaged $20,234 ($57,486 maximum); non-need-based athletic scholarships averaged $26,536 ($44,550 maximum); and other non-need-based awards and non-need-based scholarships averaged $12,355 ($45,539 maximum). The average financial indebtedness of the 2013 graduate was $33,742. LU is a member of CSS. The FAFSA is required. The priority date for freshman financial aid applications for fall entry is March 1.

International Students: There are 361 international students enrolled. The school actively recruits these students. They must take the TOEFL with a minimum score of 525 on the paper-based TOEFL (PBT) or 71 on the Internet-based version (iBT), IELTS and Pearson's. They must also take the SAT or ACT.

Computers: All students may access the system. There are no time limits and no fees.

Graduates: From July 1, 2012 to June 30, 2013, 379 bachelor's degrees were awarded. The most popular majors were business administration (40%), hospitality (11%), and criminal justice (9%). 40 companies recruited on campus in 2012-2013. In an average class, 3% graduate in 3 years or less, 28% graduate in 4 years or less, 40% graduate in 5 years or less, and 43% graduate in 6 years or less. Of the 2012 graduating class, 70% were employed within 6 months of graduation.

Admissions Contact: Stefano Papaleo, Director of Undergraduate Admission. E-Mail: *admission@lynn.edu* Web: *www.lynn.edu*

NEW COLLEGE OF FLORIDA D-4

Sarasota, FL 34243 **(941) 487-5000; (941) 487-5010**

Full-time: 320 men, 481 women	**Faculty:** 71; IIB, av$
Part-time: n/av	**Ph.D.s:** 97%
Graduate: n/av	**Student/Faculty:** 10 to 1
Year: semesters	**Tuition:** $6532 ($28,949)
Application Deadline: February 15	**Room & Board:** $8972

Freshman Class: 1414 applied, 751 accepted, 183 enrolled

SAT CR/M/W: 680/620/640 **ACT:** 29 **HIGHLY COMPETITIVE+**

New College of Florida, established in 1960, is the honors college for the liberal arts and sciences of the State University System of Florida. There is 1 undergraduate school. The library contains 281,794 volumes, 198,287 microform items, and 6,001 audio/video tapes/CDs/DVDs, and subscribes to 1,086 periodicals including electronic. Computerized library services include interlibrary loans, database searching, Internet access, and laptop Internet portals. Special learning facilities include a learning resource center, art gallery, a media and educational technology center, public archaeology lab, writing resource center, quantitative resource center, language resource center, marine biology research center, black box theater, fine arts complex, and a living ecosystem teaching and research aquarium. The 119-acre campus is in a suburban area of Florida, 50 miles south of Tampa, and is located on Sarasota Bay. Including any residence halls, there are 53 buildings.

Student Life: 83% of undergraduates are from Florida. Others are from 40 states, 22 foreign countries, and Canada. 83% are from public schools. 76% are white; 13% Hispanic. The average age of freshmen is 18; all undergraduates, 20. 18% do not continue beyond their first year; 68% remain to graduate.

Housing: 636 students can be accommodated in college housing, which includes coed dorms and on-campus apartments. Specialized housing options may be arranged in response to student interest. On-campus housing is guaranteed for all 4 years. 76% of students live on campus. All students may keep cars.

Activities: There are no fraternities or sororities. There are 60 groups on campus, including art, chess, chorale, chorus, computers, dance, debate, drama, environmental, ethnic, film, gay, international, jazz band, literary magazine, newspaper, photography, political, radio and TV, religious, social, social service, and student government. Popular campus events include Halloween and graduation parties, a diversity discussion service, and a kickball tournament.

Sports: There are 1 intercollegiate sports for men and 1 for women, and 20 intramural sports for men and 20 for women. Facilities include a soccer field, a softball diamond, a fitness path, outdoor tennis and basketball courts, a volleyball pit, playground equipment, a swimming pool, and a fitness center with Cybex equipment and indoor facilities for racquetball, aerobics, dance, and yoga.

Disabled Students: 80% of the campus is accessible. Facilities include wheelchair ramps, elevators, special parking, specially equipped restrooms, special class scheduling, lowered drinking fountains, lowered telephones, and special housing.

Services: There is a reader service for the blind. A writing resouce center provides assistance in developing writing skills and strategies. A Quantitative Resource center provides assistance in math and statistics as well as the technology needed in these fields.

Campus Safety and Security: Measures include 24-hour foot and vehicle patrol, emergency notification system, self-defense education, and security escort services. There are emergency telephones, lighted pathways/sidewalks, controlled access to dorms/residences, 24-hour dispatch/information services, and fire/smoke alarm systems in all dorms.

Programs of Study: New College confers B.A. degrees. Bachelor's degrees are awarded in AGRICULTURE (environmental studies), BIOLOGICAL SCIENCE (biochemistry, biology/biological science, marine biology, and neurosciences), COMMUNICATIONS AND THE ARTS (art, art history and appreciation, Chinese, classics, English, French, Germanic languages and literature, literature, music, Russian languages and literature, and Spanish), COMPUTER AND PHYSICAL SCIENCE (applied mathematics, chemistry, mathematics, natural sciences, and physics), ENGINEERING AND ENVIRONMENTAL DESIGN (computational sciences), SOCIAL SCIENCE (anthropology, economics, French studies, gender studies, German area studies, history, humanities, international studies, Latin American studies, medieval studies, philosophy, political science/government, psychology, public affairs, religion, social science, sociology, Spanish studies, and urban studies). Biology, psychology, economics, anthropology, English, political science have the largest enrollments.

Required: An academic credit system is not used. To qualify for graduation, students must complete 7 semester contracts, which are designed by the student in consultation with faculty; 3 independent study projects completed during January each year, between the fall and spring semesters; a senior thesis, that involves original research or creative work and includes working closely with a faculty committee of the student's choice; and an oral baccalaureate exam, which is primarily a defense of the senior thesis. To fulfill the liberal arts curriculum requirements, students must complete 8 LAC-designated courses, including 1 each in humanities, natural sciences, and social sciences. Exemptions from the LAC requirements are possible through AP exam scores of 3 or above, IB exam scores of 5 to 7, and transferable college course work at the general education level. Students also must use online training to sign up for a college e-mail account and complete the College Level Academic Skills Test or be exempted by appropriate college courses work or SAT or ACT scores.

Special: Domestic and international internships, study abroad, accelerated degree programs, student-designed interdisciplinary and dual majors, and independent study are available. There is a freshman honors program.

Faculty/Classroom: 47% of faculty are male; 53% are female. 30% teach undergraduates. No introductory courses are taught by graduate students. The average class size in an introductory lecture is 22; in a laboratory is 14; and in a regular course is 22.

Admissions: In a recent year, 53% of applicants were accepted. The SAT scores for the recent freshman class were: Critical Reading--1% below 500, 8% between 500 and 599, 48% between 600 and 700, and 43% above 700; Math--2% below 500, 28% between 500 and 599, 54% between 600 and 700, and 17% above 700; Writing--1% below 500, 21% between 500 and 599, 57% between 600 and 700, and 21% above 700. The ACT scores were 4% between 21 and 23, 14% between 24 and 26, 24% between 27 and 28, and 58% above 28. 74% of the current freshmen were in the top fifth of their class; 91% were in the top two fifths. There were 21 National Merit finalists. 3 freshmen graduated first in their class.

Requirements: The SAT or ACT is required. The ACT Optional Writing test is also required. Graduation from an accredited secondary school (preferred) or the GED. High school students should pursue at least 5 academic courses each year, at the most rigorous level available, with a minimum distribution of 4 years of English and Mathematics; 3 years each of sciences and social sciences; 2 consecutive years of the same foreign language; and 3 other academic courses. Application essays must be submitted. AP credits are accepted. Important factors in the admissions decision are advanced placement or honors courses, evidence of special talent, and recommendations by school officials.

Procedure: Freshmen are admitted fall and spring. Entrance exams should be taken by fall of the senior year. There is a deferred admissions plan. Applications should be filed by February 15 for fall entry; December 15 for spring entry, along with a $30 fee. Notifications are sent April 1. 56 applicants were on the 2011 waiting list; 22 were admitted. Applications are accepted online.

Transfer: 38 transfer students enrolled in 2010-2011. Transfers must be in good academic and financial standing with their previous college(s). Transfers with less than 60 semester hours must submit SAT or ACT scores.

Visiting: There are regularly scheduled orientations for prospective students, Including a campus tour, admissions information session, and/or class visits, which must be scheduled individually by the student through Admissions. Visitors may sit in on classes. To schedule a visit, contact Campus Visit Facilitator.

Financial Aid: In a recent year, 100% of all full-time freshmen and 98% of continuing full-time students received some form of financial aid. 36% of all full-time freshmen and 43% of continuing full-time students received need-based aid. The average freshman award was $10,521. Need-based scholarships or need-based grants averaged $1,929 ($23,300 maximum); need-based self-help aid (loans and jobs) averaged $888 ($7,000 maximum); and other non-need-based awards and non-need-based scholarships averaged $7,704 ($40,199 maximum). 21% of undergraduate students work part-time. Average annual earnings from campus work are $2449. The average financial indebtedness of the 2011 graduate was $15,438. The FAFSA is required. The priority date for freshman financial aid applications for fall entry is February 15.

International Students: There are 31 international students enrolled. The school actively recruits these students. They must take the TOEFL with a minimum score of 560 on the paper-based TOEFL (PBT) or 83 on the Internet-based version (iBT). They must also take the SAT or ACT.

Computers: Wireless access is available. All students may use the network, either on-campus or through a proxy off-campus. Wireless is available in many locations on campus. There are PCs available in the library and in a computer lab. An Apple computer lab is also available to students. All students may access the system 24 hours a day. There are no time limits and no fees.

Graduates: In a recent year, 153 bachelor's degrees were awarded. The most popular majors were biology (12%), psychology (10%), and economics (9%). In an average class, 1% graduate in 3 years or less, 57% graduate in 4 years or less, 67% graduate in 5 years or less, and 68% graduate in 6 years or less. Of the 2010 graduating class, 29% were enrolled in graduate school within 6 months of graduation.

Admissions Contact: Admissions and Financial Aid. E-Mail: *admissions@ncf.edu* Web: *www.ncf.edu*

NORTHWOOD UNIVERSITY E-5

West Palm Beach, FL 33409-2911 **(561) 478-5500 (800) 458-8325; (561) 640-3328**

Full-time: 350 men, 210 women	**Faculty:** 16
Part-time: 15 men, 10 women	**Ph.D.s:** 37%
Graduate: n/av	**Student/Faculty:** 35 to 1
Year: semesters, summer session	**Tuition:** $19,830
Application Deadline: open	**Room & Board:** $8126
Freshman Class: n/av	
SAT or ACT: required	

LESS COMPETITIVE

Northwood University, founded in 1959, is a private institution offering undergraduate degrees in business administration and management. Campuses are located in Florida, Michigan, and Texas. The Florida campus opened in 1982. The figures in the above capsule and in this profile are approximate. There is 1 graduate school. The library contains 13,341 volumes, and 250 audio/video tapes/CDs/DVDs, and subscribes to 60 periodicals including electronic. Computerized library services include interlibrary loans, database searching, Internet access, and laptop Internet portals. Special learning facilities include a learning resource center, art gallery, the Ethics Center for Business. The 96-acre campus is in a suburban area 70 miles north of Miami. Including any residence halls, there are 10 buildings.

Student Life: 50% of undergraduates are from out of state, mostly the

South. Students are from 36 states, 46 foreign countries, and Canada. 70% are from public schools. 43% are white; 34% foreign nationals. The average age of freshmen is 18; all undergraduates, 21. 44% do not continue beyond their first year; 40% remain to graduate.

Housing: 432 students can be accommodated in college housing, which includes single-sex on-campus apartments. On-campus housing is guaranteed for the freshman year only. 63% of students commute. All students may keep cars.

Activities: There are no fraternities or sororities. There are 12 groups on campus, including art, cheerleading, chess, computers, dance, debate, drama, ethnic, film, honors, international, musical theater, newspaper, photography, political, professional, religious, social, social service, and student government. Popular campus events include Spring Fling, Winter Carnival, and Movies on the Lawn.

Sports: There are 5 intercollegiate sports for men and 5 for women, and 5 intramural sports for men and 5 for women. Facilities include baseball, softball, and soccer fields, a student center, and a recreation center with an outdoor swimming pool and basketball, tennis, and handball/racquetball courts.

Disabled Students: 80% of the campus is accessible. Facilities include wheelchair ramps, elevators, special parking, specially equipped restrooms, special class scheduling, lowered drinking fountains, and lowered telephones.

Services: Counseling and information services are available, as is tutoring in some subjects, accounting, math, and English. There is remedial math and writing.

Campus Safety and Security: Measures include 24-hour foot and vehicle patrol, emergency notification system, and security escort services. There are shuttle buses, emergency telephones, lighted pathways/sidewalks, and controlled access to dorms/residences.

Programs of Study: Northwood confers B.B.A. degrees. Associate degrees are also awarded. Bachelor's degrees are awarded in BUSINESS (accounting, banking and finance, business administration and management, hotel/motel and restaurant management, international business management, marketing management, sports management, and transportation and travel marketing), COMMUNICATIONS AND THE ARTS (advertising). Accounting and management information systems are the strongest academically. Business management and automotive marketing are the largest.

Required: To graduate, all students must complete a minimum of 123 credit hours with 24 credit hours in the major. A minimum GPA of 2.0 must be maintained. Requirements include a general studies core and 3 credit hours in computer science. Internships are required in some majors.

Special: Northwood offers cooperative programs and cross-registration with Georgian College in Canada, internships with various automotive and fashion marketing corporations, study abroad in 15 countries, and various work-study programs. Internships are available for all programs and required in 4. Also available are an accelerated degree program in all majors, dual majors, and credit for military experience.

Faculty/Classroom: 56% of faculty are male; 44% are female. All teach undergraduates. No introductory courses are taught by graduate students. The average class size in an introductory lecture is 16; in a laboratory is 13; and in a regular course is 16.

Requirements: The SAT or ACT is required. Applicants must be graduates of an accredited secondary school or have a GED certificate. An interview is recommended. A GPA of 2.0 is required. AP and CLEP credits are accepted. Important factors in the admissions decision are advanced placement or honors courses, leadership record, and evidence of special talent.

Procedure: Freshmen are admitted to all sessions. Entrance exams should be taken in the fall of the senior year. There are deferred admissions and rolling admissions plans. Check with the school for current application deadlines. The application fee is $25. Notification is sent on a rolling basis. Applications are accepted online.

Transfer: 136 transfer students enrolled in a recent year. Applicants must have a minimum 2.0 GPA, with at least 15 credit hours earned and official transcripts of all completed college-level work. Good academic and social standing are required. An interview is recommended. 31 of 123 credits required for the bachelor's degree must be completed at Northwood.

Visiting: There are regularly scheduled orientations for prospective students, including a fall and spring open house, campus tours, and meetings with students and financial aid and academic staff. There are guides for informal visits, visitors may sit in on classes, and stay overnight. To schedule a visit, contact the Admissions Office.

Financial Aid: In a recent year, 60% of all full-time freshmen and 45% of continuing full-time students received some form of financial aid. 53% of all full-time freshmen and 36% of continuing full-time students received need-based aid. The average freshman award was $17,741. Need-based scholarships or need-based grants averaged $6,941; need-based self-help aid (loans and jobs) averaged $4,212; non-need-based athletic scholarships averaged $7,736; and other non-need-based awards and non-need-based scholarships averaged $9,392. 10% of undergraduate students work part-time. Average annual earnings from campus work are $1743. The average financial indebtedness of a recent graduate was $19,293. The FAFSA and the state aid form are required. Check with the school for current application deadlines.

International Students: There are 194 international students enrolled. The school actively recruits these students. They must take the TOEFL with a minimum score of 500 on the paper-based TOEFL (PBT) or 61 on the Internet-based version (iBT). They must also take the SAT or ACT.

Computers: Wireless access is available. All students may access the system. There are no time limits and no fees.

Graduates: In a recent year, 174 bachelor's degrees were awarded. The most popular majors were automotive marketing (25%), international business (21%), and management (18%). In an average class, 30% graduate in 4 years or less, 36% graduate in 5 years or less, and 40% graduate in 6 years or less. Of the 2010 graduating class, 95% were employed within 6 months of graduation.

Admissions Contact: Admissions Office. A campus DVD is available.
E-Mail: *fladmit@northwood.edu* Web: *www.northwood.edu*

NOVA SOUTHEASTERN UNIVERSITY — E-5

Fort Lauderdale, FL 33314 — **(954) 262-8000; (800) 338-4723**

Full-time: 1109 men, 2343 women	**Faculty:** n/av
Part-time: 406 men, 1298 women	**Ph.D.s:** 75%
Graduate: 6329 men, 14185 women	**Student/Faculty:** 18 to 1
Year: trimesters, summer session	**Tuition:** $24,500 ($25,430)
Application Deadline: open	**Room & Board:** $10,130
Freshman Class: 4328 applied, 2487 accepted, 673 enrolled	
SAT CR/M: 520/530	**ACT:** 23 **VERY COMPETITIVE**

Nova Southeastern University, founded in 1964, is an independent institution offering degree programs in liberal arts, sciences, business, health sciences, education, and preprofessional studies. The university also offers graduate and first-professional programs. There are 5 undergraduate schools and 10 graduate schools. In addition to regional accreditation, NSU has baccalaureate program accreditation with NCATE and NLN. The 5 libraries contain 823,797 volumes, 2.3 million microform items, and 62,388 audio/video tapes/CDs/DVDs, and subscribe to 50,033 periodicals including electronic. Computerized library services include interlibrary loans, database searching, Internet access, and Wi-Fi capability. Special learning facilities include an art gallery, radio station, Center of Excellence for Coral Reef Ecosystems Science, Dryland Training. Palm Beach Student Educational Center, Nursing Simulation Labs, The Huizenga Sales Institute, Neuro Immune Medicine Clinic, Health professions division museum, hall of fame, performing arts center, oceanographic center, law center, family village center, Preschool. The 300-acre campus is in a suburban area 10 miles west of downtown Fort Lauderdale. Including any residence halls, there are 39 buildings.

Student Life: 79% of undergraduates are from Florida. Others are from 48 states, 71 foreign countries, and Canada. 32% are Hispanic; 31% White; 21% African American. The average age of freshmen is 19; all undergraduates, 27. 28% do not continue beyond their first year; 42% remain to graduate.

Housing: 1472 students can be accommodated in college housing, which includes coed dorms, on-campus apartments, and married student housing. Theme housing, Leadership, CoED Greek and Quiet. On-campus housing is guaranteed for all 4 years. 82% of students commute. All students may keep cars.

Activities: 7% of men belong to 6 national fraternities; 10% of women belong to 6 national sororities. There are 316 groups on campus, including band, cheerleading, chorale, chorus, computers, dance, drama, environmental, ethnic, gay, honors, international, literary magazine, musical theater, newspaper, orchestra, political, professional, radio and TV, religious, social, social service, and student government. Popular campus events include Hollywood Squares, Life 101, Sharkapalooza and Student Life Achievement Awards.

Sports: There are 7 intercollegiate sports for men and 9 for women, and 7 intramural sports for men and 7 for women. Facilities include baseball and soccer fields and a recreational complex with a swimming pool and basketball and tennis courts.

Disabled Students: All of the campus is accessible. Facilities include wheelchair ramps, elevators, special parking, specially equipped restrooms, special class scheduling, lowered drinking fountains, and special housing.

Services: Counseling and information services are available, as is tutoring in some subjects, science, math, and writing.

Campus Safety and Security: Measures include 24-hour foot and vehicle patrol, emergency notification system, and security escort services. There are shuttle buses, emergency telephones, lighted pathways/sidewalks, and controlled access to dorms/residences.

Programs of Study: NSU confers B.A., B.H.Sc., B.S., B.B.A. and B.S.N. degrees. Associate, master's, and doctoral degrees are also awarded. Bachelor's degrees are awarded in BIOLOGICAL SCIENCE (marine biology, marine science, and neurosciences), BUSINESS (accounting, business administration and management, finance, and marketing), COMMUNICATIONS AND THE ARTS (communication studies, dance, dramatic arts, fine arts, music, and theatre acting), COMPUTER AND PHYSICAL SCIENCE (chemistry, Computer Engineering Technology, computer information systems, computer science, and mathematics), EDUCATION (art education, education, education of the exceptional child, elementary education, English education, general studies, middle school education, physical education, science education, secondary education, and sports and wellness studies), ENGINEERING AND ENVIRONMENTAL DESIGN (computer engineering and environmental science), HEALTH PROFESSIONS (biology, diagnostic medical sonography, exercise science, health promotion, kinesiology, nursing, recreation therapy, respiratory therapy, and speech pathology/audiology), SOCIAL SCIENCE (anthropology, behavioral science, criminal justice, human development, human services, international relations, legal studies, paralegal studies, philosophy, philosophy and religion, political science/government, psychology, public administration, and sociology). Biology, nursing, and business, have the largest enrollments.

Required: To graduate, all students must complete at least 120 credit hours, at least 30 of the credits must be earned at NSU and at least 50% of the credits in the major area must be earned at NSU. A minimum 2.25 GPA is needed for courses in the major, and a 2.0 for all other courses.

Special: NSU offers internships, study abroad, work-study, accelerated degree programs, nondegree study, Washington Semester, Undergraduate Honors Program, and undergraduate research experience . Combined bachelor-professional degree programs and a dual admission program are also available. There are 9 national honor societies and a freshman honors program.

Faculty/Classroom: 47% of faculty are male; 53% are female. No introductory courses are taught by graduate students. The average class size in a regular course is 14.

Admissions: 57% of the 2013-2014 applicants were accepted. The SAT scores for the 2013-2014 freshman class were: Critical Reading--37% below 500, 39% between 500 and 599, 20% between 600 and 699, and 4% between 700 and 800; Math--31% below 500, 43% between 500 and 599, 22% between 600 and 699, and 5% between 700 and 800. The ACT scores were 23% below 21, 27% between 21 and 23, 18% between 24 and 26, 18% between 27 and 28, and 13% above 28. 11 freshmen graduated first in their class.

Requirements: The SAT or ACT is required. Applicants must be graduates of an accredited secondary school or have a GED certificate. An interview is recommended. AP and CLEP credits are accepted. Important factors in the admissions decision are advanced placement or honors courses, leadership record, recommendations by alumni, and recommendations by school officials.

Procedure: Freshmen are admitted to all sessions. Entrance exams should be taken by June 15 for the fall semester. There are deferred admissions and rolling admissions plans. Application deadlines are open. Application fee is $50. Notification is sent on a rolling basis. Applications are accepted online.

Transfer: 813 transfer students enrolled in 2012-2013. Applicants must have a minimum 2.6 GPA from a regionally accredited institution. An interview is recommended. At least 50% of credits in the major or specialty must be earned at NSU. 30 of 120 credits required for the bachelor's degree must be completed at NSU.

Visiting: There are regularly scheduled orientations for prospective students. There are guides for informal visits and visitors may sit in on classes.

Financial Aid: Check with the school for current application deadlines.

International Students: There are 335 international students enrolled. The school actively recruits these students. They must take the TOEFL with a minimum score of 550 on the paper-based TOEFL (PBT) or 79 on the Internet-based version (iBT), IELTS. They must also take the SAT or ACT, scoring 1000.

Computers: All students may access the system. There are no time limits and no fees.

Graduates: From July 1, 2012 to June 30, 2013, 1538 bachelor's degrees were awarded. The most popular majors were health professions (31%), biological/life sciences (21%), and business/marketing (20%). In an average class, 2% graduate in 3 years or less, 25% graduate in 4 years or less, 37% graduate in 5 years or less, and 41% graduate in 6 years or less.

Admissions Contact: Maria Dillard, Undergraduate Admissions. E-Mail: *admissions@nova.edu* Web: *www.nova.edu*

PALM BEACH ATLANTIC UNIVERSITY E-5

West Palm Beach, FL 33416 (561) 803-2101
(888) GO TO PBA; (561) 803-2115

Full-time: 815 men, 1543 women	**Faculty:** 128
Part-time: 243 men, 286 women	**Ph.D.s:** 81%
Graduate: 292 men, 585 women	**Student/Faculty:** 18 to 1
Year: semesters, summer session	**Tuition:** $25,532
Application Deadline:	**Room & Board:** $8350

Freshman Class: 1618 applied, 1361 accepted, 578 enrolled
SAT or ACT: required

LESS COMPETITIVE

Founded in 1968, Palm Beach Atlantic University, is an interdenominational Christian university with some 48 undergraduate majors (including nursing). Graduate degrees in business, leadership, counseling psychology, divinity and pharmacy are offered. Located in West Palm Beach of southeast Florida, PBA is an ideal place to grow and explore your faith with young people of many races, nationalities, and creeds. There are 9 undergraduate schools and 4 graduate schools. In addition to regional accreditation, PBA has baccalaureate program accreditation with ACPE and NASM. The library contains 265,745 volumes, 5,925 audio/video tapes/CDs/DVDs, and subscribes to 28,841 periodicals including electronic. Computerized library services include interlibrary loans, database searching, Internet access, and Wi-Fi capability. Special learning facilities include an art gallery, Center for Writing Excellence (writing assistance); Student Success Center (peer tutorting, First Year Experience, and ADA accomodations). The 96-acre campus is in an urban area 60 miles north of Miami, 180 miles south of Orlando.

Student Life: 68% of undergraduates are from Florida. Others are from 50 states, 45 foreign countries, and Canada. 59% are White; 14% African American; 14% Hispanic. 14% are Catholic; 11% claim no religious affiliation. The average age of freshmen is 18; all undergraduates, 23. 27% do not continue beyond their first year; 48% remain to graduate.

Housing: 1108 students can be accommodated in college housing, which includes single-sex and coed dorms and on-campus apartments. In addition, there are honors houses and special-interest houses. On-campus housing is available on a first-come and first-served basis. 53% of students commute. Alcohol is not permitted. All students may keep cars.

Activities: There are no fraternities or sororities. There are 39 groups on campus, including and music ensembles, Campus Ministries, concert band, International organizations, Army ROTC, art, band, choir, chorale, chorus, communications, computers, dance, drama, environmental, ethnic, film, honors, international, jazz band, literary magazine, musical theater, newspaper, orchestra, pep band, photography, political, professional, radio and TV, religious, social, social service, student government, and symphony. Popular campus events include American Free Enterprise Day and Christival.

Sports: There are 4 intercollegiate sports for men and 6 for women, and 9 intramural sports for men and 9 for women. PBA's home of athletics & Recreation is housed in the 65,000 Square Foot Facility known as the Greene Complex for Sports & Recreation. The Greene complex houses the Rubin Arena, locker rooms, athletic training facility, fitness center, and recreational space for both its Varsity and club level sports programs. Currently, PBA is constructing the Rinker Athletic Complex which will house all of PBA's outside sports including Baseball, Softball, Tennis and Soccer.

Disabled Students: There are 4 intercollegiate sports for men and 6 for women, and 9 intramural sports for men and 9 for women. Facilities include PBA's home of athletics & Recreation is housed in the 65,000 Square Foot Facility known as the Greene Complex for Sports & Recreation. The Greene complex houses the Rubin Arena, locker rooms, athletic training facility, fitness center, and recreational space for both its Varsity and club level sports programs. Currently, PBA is constructing the Rinker Athletic Complex which will house all of PBA's outside sports including Baseball, Softball, Tennis and Soccer. Facilities include wheelchair ramps, elevators, special parking, specially equipped restrooms, and special class scheduling.

Services: Counseling and information services are available, as is tutoring in most subjects. There is a reader service for the blind, and remedial math and writing. Center for Writing Excellence

Campus Safety and Security: Measures include 24-hour foot and vehicle patrol, emergency notification system, self-defense education, and security escort services. There are emergency telephones, lighted pathways/sidewalks, controlled access to dorms/residences, closed circuit television system.

Programs of Study: PBA confers B.A., B.S., B.G.S., B.Mus. and B.S.N. degrees. Associate, master's, and doctoral degrees are also awarded. Bachelor's degrees are awarded in BIOLOGICAL SCIENCE (biology/biological science), BUSINESS (banking and finance, business administration and management, international business management, management science, marketing management, and organizational leadership and management), COMMUNICATIONS AND THE ARTS (art, communications, dance, English, film arts, graphic design, journalism, music, music performance, music theory and composition, musical theater, piano/organ, theater design, and voice), COMPUTER AND PHYSICAL SCIENCE (chemistry, computer science, and mathematics), EDUCATION (art education, athletic training, elementary education, English education, mathematics education, music education, physical education, science education, and secondary education), HEALTH PROFESSIONS (exercise science and nursing), SOCIAL SCIENCE (biblical studies, crosscultural studies, history, interdisciplinary studies, liberal arts/general studies, ministries, philosophy, political science/government, prelaw, and psychology). English, biology, and medicinal and biological chemistry are the strongest academically. Business, pharmacy, and psychology have the largest enrollments.

Required: Students must complete general education requirements and a minimum of 120 credit hours. Students must complete 42 credit hours in courses numbered 3000 or above (Bachelor of Music students, 33 hours). The last 32 credit hours must be completed at PBA and a minimum 2.0 GPA is required.

Special: PBA offers work-study, internships, a student-designed interdisciplinary major, accelerated degree programs in organizational management (evening program only) and ministry, a London semester, study abroad through the Coalition of Christian Colleges and Universities, and teacher certification. There is a freshman honors program.

Faculty/Classroom: 52% of faculty are male; 48% are female. 79% teach undergraduates. No introductory courses are taught by graduate students.

Admissions: 84% of the 2013-2014 applicants were accepted. There was 1 National Merit finalist.

Requirements: The SAT or ACT is required. Applicants must be graduates of an accredited secondary school or have a GED certificate, and have completed 18 academic credits: 4 in English, 3 in math, science, 2 in a foreign language, and 5 in electives. An essay and an interview are required. A portfolio is recommended for art students. A GPA of 2.0 is required. AP and CLEP credits are accepted. Important factors in the admissions decision are advanced placement or honors courses, leadership record, and personality/intangible qualities.

Procedure: Freshmen are admitted to all sessions. Entrance exams should be taken in the junior year of high school. There are deferred admissions and rolling admissions plans. Application deadlines are open. Application fee is $50. Notifications are sent September 1. 105 applicants were on the 2013 waiting list; 58 were admitted. Applications are accepted online.

Transfer: 332 transfer students enrolled in 2012-2013. Transfer students must have a minimum 2.5 GPA on at least 12 semester hours, 300-500 word essay, and 2 letters of recommendation. An interview is required. 32 of 120 credits required for the bachelor's degree must be completed at PBA.

Visiting: There are regularly scheduled orientations for prospective students, including a general open house and a school-specific open house. There are guides for informal visits, visitors may sit in on classes, and stay overnight. To schedule a visit, contact the Admissions Office.

Financial Aid: In 2013-2014, 100% of all full-time freshmen and 100% of continuing full-time students received some form of financial aid. 74% of all full-time freshmen and 76% of continuing full-time students received need-based aid. The average freshman award was $24,499. Need-based scholarships or need-based grants averaged $5,816 ($16,106 maximum); need-based self-help aid (loans and jobs) averaged $3,338 ($6,000 maximum); non-need-based athletic scholarships averaged $13,379 ($32,425 maximum); and other non-need-based awards and non-need-based scholarships averaged $15,418 ($37,763 maximum). 100% of undergraduate students work part-time. Average annual earnings from campus work are $1097. The average financial indebtedness of the 2013 graduate was $28,520. The FAFSA and the state aid form are required. The priority date for freshman financial aid applications for fall entry is May 1.

International Students: There are 98 international students enrolled. The school actively recruits these students. They must take the TOEFL with a minimum score of 79 on the Internet-based version (iBT). They must also take the SAT or ACT.

Computers: All students may access the system. There are no time limits and no fees.

Graduates: From July 1, 2012 to June 30, 2013, 429 bachelor's degrees were awarded. The most popular majors were business/marketing (30%), ministry (11%), and music and fine arts (10%). 111 companies recruited on campus in 2012-2013. In an average class, 38% graduate in 4 years or less, 46% graduate in 5 years or less, and 48% graduate in 6 years or less.

Admissions Contact: Jamie Zugelder, Director of Admissions. E-Mail: *admissions_admissions@pba.edu* Web: *www.pba.edu*

RINGLING COLLEGE OF ART AND DESIGN — D-4

Sarasota, FL 34234 (941) 351-5100
(800) 255-7695; (941) 359-7517

Full-time: 475 men, 737 women
Part-time: 11 men, 30 women
Graduate: n/av
Year: semesters
Application Deadline: open
Faculty: 92
Ph.D.s: 60%
Student/Faculty: 13 to 1
Tuition: $34,840 ($38,540)
Room & Board: $12,670
Freshman Class: 1225 applied, 898 accepted, 257 enrolled
SPECIAL

Ringling College of Art and Design, founded in 1931, is a private art college. In addition to regional accreditation, Ringling College (RCAD) has baccalaureate program accreditation with FIDER and NASAD. The library contains 58,565 volumes, 10,335 audio/video tapes/CDs/DVDs, and subscribes to 375 periodicals including electronic. Computerized library services include interlibrary loans, database searching, Internet access, and Wi-Fi capability. Special learning facilities include an art gallery, a total of 65,000 slides and 78,800 digital images in house. The 49-acre campus is in an urban area 50 miles south of Tampa. Including any residence halls, there are 108 buildings.

Student Life: 59% of undergraduates are from out of state, mostly the Northeast. Students are from 44 states, 50 foreign countries, and Canada. 54% are White; 15% Hispanic; 13% Foreign. The average age of freshmen is 18; all undergraduates, 21. 22% do not continue beyond their first year; 65% remain to graduate.

Housing: 849 students can be accommodated in college housing, which includes single-sex and coed dorms, on-campus apartments, and married student housing. On-campus housing is available on a first-come, first-served basis, and is available on a lottery system for upperclassmen. Priority is given to out-of-town students. 65% of students live on campus; of those, 100% remain on campus on weekends. All students may keep cars.

Activities: There are no fraternities or sororities. There are 32 groups on campus, including art, computers, environmental, ethnic, film, gay, honors, international, photography, professional, religious, social, social service, and student government. Popular campus events include Welcome Back Bash Admissions Fall Open House, Avant Garde, and Digital Film Speaker Series.

Sports: Facilities include a recreation room with pool tables and ping pong tables, a fitness center with aerobic studio, cardio vascular machines and weights, and a green space used for soccer, football, and quidditch in addition to a lighted basketball court.

Disabled Students: 80% of the campus is accessible. Facilities include wheelchair ramps, elevators, special parking, specially equipped restrooms, special class scheduling, lowered drinking fountains.

Services: Counseling and information services are available, as is tutoring in some subjects, English, art history, and history There is remedial writing. Text-to-speech conversion as well as speech-to-text conversion.

Campus Safety and Security: Measures include 24-hour foot and vehicle patrol, emergency notification system, self-defense education, and security escort services. There are emergency telephones, lighted pathways/sidewalks, controlled access to dorms/residences, blue light phone towers for general and emergency Public Safety assistance.

Programs of Study: Ringling College: RCAD confers B.A., and B.F.A. degrees. Bachelor's degrees are awarded in COMMUNICATIONS AND THE ARTS (advertising, art, fine arts, graphic design, illustration, painting, photography, printmaking, and sculpture), COMPUTER AND PHYSICAL SCIENCE (digital arts/technology), ENGINEERING AND ENVIRONMENTAL DESIGN (computer graphics and interior design). Illustration and computer animation are the strongest academically and have the largest enrollments.

Required: To graduate, all students must complete 120 semester hours with a distribution of 66 hours of studio art within each major, 30 hours of liberal arts, 12 hours of art history and 15 hours of electives. A minimum 2.0 GPA and courses in drawing, 2-and 3-dimensional design, art history, and written communication are required.

Special: The college offers cross-registration with the Association of Independent colleges of Art and Design (AICAD) and study abroad in France, England, and Ireland. Also available are credit by portfolio, and a nondegree continuing education program.

Faculty/Classroom: 70% of faculty are male; 30% are female. All teach undergraduates. No introductory courses are taught by graduate students. The average class size in an introductory lecture is 25 and in a regular course is 17.

Admissions: 73% of the 2013-2014 applicants were accepted.

Requirements: Applicants must have received either a standard high school diploma from an accredited secondary school or a GED. Admission is based on the academic record, letters of recommendation, and a portfolio. An essay is required and an interview is recommended. A GPA of 2.0 is required. AP and CLEP credits are accepted. Important factors in the admissions decision are evidence of special talent, advanced placement or honors courses, and recommendations by school officials.

Procedure: Freshmen are admitted fall. There is a rolling admissions plan. Check with the school for current application deadlines. The application fee is $70. Applications are accepted online.

Transfer: 103 transfer students enrolled in 2012-2013. Transfer students must meet the same criteria as freshmen and must also submit college transcripts. 45 of 120 credits required for the bachelor's degree must be completed at Ringling College: RCAD.

Visiting: There are guides for informal visits and visitors may sit in on classes. To schedule a visit, contact Gregg Prigerson at gprigers@ringling.edu.

Financial Aid: In 2013-2014, 77% of all full-time freshmen and 79% of continuing full-time students received some form of financial aid. 63% of all full-time freshmen and 60% of continuing full-time students received need-based aid. The average freshman award was $17,037. Need-based scholarships or need-based grants averaged $10,870; need-based self-help aid (loans and jobs) averaged $6,909; and other non-need-based awards and non-need-based scholarships averaged $13,257. 25% of undergraduate students work part-time. Average annual earnings from campus work are $1907. The average financial indebtedness of the 2013 graduate was $67,373. The FAFSA and the college's own financial statement are required. The priority date for freshman financial aid applications for fall entry is March 1.

International Students: There are 159 international students enrolled. The school actively recruits these students. They must take the TOEFL with a minimum score of 500 on the paper-based TOEFL (PBT) or 61 on the Internet based version (iBT).

Computers: All students may access the system. There are no time limits and no fees.

Graduates: From July 1, 2012 to June 30, 2013, 319 bachelor's degrees were awarded. The most popular majors were illustration (31%), computer animation (16%), and graphic design (11%). 60 companies recruited on campus in 2012-2013. In an average class, 61% graduate in 4 years or less, 63% graduate in 5 years or less, and 65% graduate in 6 years or less. Of the 2012 graduating class, 8% were enrolled in graduate school within 6 months of graduation, and 70% were employed.

Admissions Contact: James H. Dean, Dean of Admissions. E-Mail: *admissions@ringling.edu* Web: *www.ringling.edu*

ROLLINS COLLEGE — D-3

Winter Park, FL 32789 — **(407) 691-2573; 407-646-2351**

Full-time: 765 men, 1119 women	**Faculty:** n/av; IIA, av$
Part-time: none	**Ph.D.s:** 90%
Graduate: 262 men, 313 women	**Student/Faculty:** 10 to 1
Year: semesters	**Tuition:** $39,900
Application Deadline: February 15	**Room & Board:** $12,470
Freshman Class: 4542 applied, 2533 accepted, 518 enrolled	
	HIGHLY COMPETITIVE

Founded through innovation, focused on excellence, fueled by dedication to pragmatic liberal arts - Rollins College has transformed lives by educating responsible, global citizens since 1885. Located in Winter Park, Florida, Rollins provides small-town community and proximity to neighboring Orlando, a premier international destination. Beneath Spanish moss and inside the arched doorways of Spanish Mediterranean buildings, students experience small classes led by faculty nationally recognized for innovative teaching and scholarship. There are 2 graduate schools. In addition to regional accreditation, Rollins has baccalaureate program accreditation with AACSB and NASM. The library contains 366,684 volumes, including 494 microform items. Computerized library services include interlibrary loans, database searching, Internet access, and Wi-Fi capability. Special learning facilities include an art gallery, radio station, TV station, art museum, theaters, writing center, and student resource center. The 80-acre campus is in a suburban area 5 miles north of Orlando.

Student Life: 54% of undergraduates are from Florida. Others are from 42 states, 49 foreign countries, and Canada. 54% are from public schools. 69% are White; 13% Hispanic. The average age of freshmen is 18; all undergraduates, 20. 16% do not continue beyond their first year; 62% remain to graduate.

Housing: 1264 students can be accommodated in college housing, which includes single-sex and coed dorms and on-campus apartments. In addition, there are honors houses, special-interest houses, fraternity houses, and sorority houses. On-campus housing is guaranteed for the freshman year only. 68% of students live on campus. Upperclassmen may keep cars.

Activities: 29% of men belong to 1 local and 4 national fraternities; 35% of women belong to 1 local and 6 national sororities. There are 121 groups on campus, including art, band, cheerleading, chess, choir, chorale, chorus, computers, dance, debate, drama, drum and bugle corps, environmental, ethnic, film, gay, honors, international, jazz band, literary magazine, musical theater, newspaper, orchestra, pep band, photography, political, professional, radio and TV, religious, social, social service, student government, symphony, and yearbook. Popular campus events include WPRK 91.5 Marathon, Civic Engagement Week and Sexual Assault Awareness Week.

Sports: There are 11 intercollegiate sports for men and 12 for women, and 9 intramural sports for men and 10 for women. Facilities include a 2500-seat auditorium, a 600-seat stadium, tennis courts, baseball and soccer fields, a field house with a gym that seats 2500, a weight room, a boat house, and a swimming pool.

Disabled Students: 80% of the campus is accessible. Facilities include wheelchair ramps, elevators, special parking, specially equipped restrooms, special class scheduling, lowered drinking fountains, lowered telephones, and special housing.

Services: Counseling and information services are available, as is tutoring in every subject. There is a reader service for the blind, and remedial math, reading, and writing.

Campus Safety and Security: Measures include 24-hour foot and vehicle patrol, emergency notification system, self-defense education, and security escort services. There are shuttle buses, emergency telephones, lighted pathways/sidewalks, controlled access to dorms/residences, 24-hour locked residential units.

Programs of Study: Rollins confers A.B. degrees. Master's degrees are also awarded. Bachelor's degrees are awarded in BIOLOGICAL SCIENCE (biochemistry, biology/biological science, and marine biology), BUSINESS (international business management and organizational behavior), COMMUNICATIONS AND THE ARTS (art history and appreciation, communications, dramatic arts, English, French, media arts, music, music performance, Spanish, studio art, and theatre arts), COMPUTER AND PHYSICAL SCIENCE (chemistry, computer science, mathematics, and physics), EDUCATION (elementary education), ENGINEERING AND ENVIRONMENTAL DESIGN (environmental science), SOCIAL SCIENCE (anthropology, Asian/Oriental studies, classical/ancient civilization, crosscultural studies, economics, history, humanities, international relations, Latin American studies, philosophy, political science/government, psychology, religion, and sociology). International business, psychology, and economics have the largest enrollments.

Required: Students must complete a minimum of 140 semester hours of academic work, of which at least sixty-four (64) semester hours must be outside a single departmental prefix. All students must complete a minimum of sixteen (16) semester hours that are not used to meet either a general education curriculum or major requirement. Students must earn a minimum academic average of a 2.00 ('C') for all courses taken at Rollins and achieve a minimum academic average of a 2.00 ('C') for all courses taken to fulfill major requirements.

Special: Rollins offers cross-registration with the evening studies division, co-op programs with American University in Washington, D.C., and Duke University School of Forestry and Environmental Studies. Departmental and professional internships, study abroad in 9 countries, and a Washington semester are also options. Also available are an accelerated (3-2) MBA program, a B.A.-B.S. degree in preengineering with Washington University (St. Louis), Auburn, and Columbia Universities, an interdepartmental biochemistry/molecular biology major, dual majors in any combination, and student-designed majors. Nondegree study and pass/fail options are possible. There are 5 national honor societies, a freshman honors program, and 30 departmental honors programs.

Faculty/Classroom: 57% of faculty are male; 43% are female. No introductory courses are taught by graduate students.

Admissions: 56% of the 2013-2014 applicants were accepted. The SAT scores for the 2013-2014 freshman class were: Critical Reading--5% below 500, 46% between 500 and 599, 41% between 600 and 699, and 9% between 700 and 800; Math--7% below 500, 39% between 500 and 599, 43% between 600 and 699, and 9% between 700 and 800; Writing--9% below 500, 46% between 500 and 599, 35% between 600 and 699, and 9% between 700 and 800.

Requirements: Applicants must be graduates of an accredited secondary school or have a GED certificate and have completed 4 years of English, 3 of math, and 2 each of foreign language, science, and social studies. An essay is required. SAT Subject tests in writing, math, and foreign language and an interview are recommended. AP and CLEP credits are accepted. Important factors in the admissions decision are advanced placement or honors courses, evidence of special talent, and extracurricular activities record.

Procedure: Freshmen are admitted fall and spring. Entrance exams should be taken by the first semester of the senior year. There are early decision and deferred admissions plans. Early decision applications should be filed by November 15; regular applications, by February 15 for fall entry; and November 1 for spring entry. The fall 2013 application fee was $40. Notification of early decision is sent December 15; regular decision, April 1. 200 early decision candidates were accepted for the 2013-2014 class. 188 applicants were on the 2013 waiting list; 13 were admitted. Applications are accepted online.

Transfer: 62 transfer students enrolled in 2012-2013. Transfer students must satisfy all regular admission requirements and submit official transcripts of college and high school work and SAT or ACT scores. A recommended 3.0 GPA and a year's worth of credit hours earned are required. An interview is recommended. 64 of 140 credits required for the bachelor's degree must be completed at Rollins.

Visiting: There are regularly scheduled orientations for prospective stu-

dents, as well as Fall Open House. There are guides for informal visits and visitors may sit in on classes. To schedule a visit, contact The Office of Admissions.

Financial Aid: In 2013-2014, 77% of all full-time freshmen and 83% of continuing full-time students received some form of financial aid. 54% of all full-time freshmen and 62% of continuing full-time students received need-based aid. The average freshman award was $29,800. The average financial indebtedness of the 2013 graduate was $24,096. Rollins is a member of CSS. The FAFSA and the college's own financial statement are required. The priority date for freshman financial aid applications for fall entry is March 1.

International Students: There are 101 international students enrolled. The school actively recruits these students. They must take the TOEFL with a minimum score of 550 on the paper-based TOEFL (PBT) or 80 on the Internet-based version (iBT). They must also take the SAT or ACT.

Computers: All students may access the system. There are no time limits and no fees.

Graduates: From July 1, 2012 to June 30, 2013, 389 bachelor's degrees were awarded. The most popular majors were economics (12%), psychology (10%), and English (8%). In an average class, 62% graduate in 4 years or less, 70% graduate in 5 years or less, and 71% graduate in 6 years or less.

Admissions Contact: Udeth Lugo, Director of Institutional Research. E-Mail: *ir@rollins.edu* Web: *www.rollins.edu*

SAINT LEO UNIVERSITY D-3

Saint Leo, FL 33574 (352) 588-8283
(800) 334-5532; (352) 588-8257

Full-time: 1049 men, 1049 women	**Faculty:** 111
Part-time: 35 men, 34 women	**Ph.D.s:** 83%
Graduate: 1223 men, 1993 women	**Student/Faculty:** 19 to 1
Year: semesters, summer session	**Tuition:** $18,870
Application Deadline: August 15	**Room & Board:** $9120
Freshman Class: 2648 applied, 2245 accepted, 635 enrolled	
SAT CR/M/W: 510/510/480 **ACT:** 21	**COMPETITIVE**

Saint Leo University, founded in 1889, has undergraduate students who benefit from an education that integrates caring faculty, state-of-the-art technology and active learning as they choose from more than 50 academic programs and endorsements. There are 3 undergraduate schools and 5 graduate schools. In addition to regional accreditation, Saint Leo has baccalaureate program accreditation with CSWE. The library contains 275,049 volumes, 26,208 microform items, and 3,164 audio/video tapes/CDs/DVDs, and subscribes to 148,546 periodicals including electronic. Computerized library services include interlibrary loans, database searching, Internet access, and Wi-Fi capability. Special learning facilities include a radio station and TV station. The 259-acre campus is in a rural area 40 miles north of Tampa. Including any residence halls, there are 33 buildings.

Student Life: 72% of undergraduates are from Florida. Others are from 44 states, 56 foreign countries, and Canada. 77% are from public schools. 61% are White; 14% Hispanic; 11% African American. 45% claim no religious affiliation; 32% Catholic; 19% Protestant. The average age of freshmen is 19; all undergraduates, 21. 33% do not continue beyond their first year; 45% remain to graduate.

Housing: 1297 students can be accommodated in college housing, which includes single-sex and coed dorms, on-campus apartments, and off-campus apartments. On-campus housing is guaranteed for all 4 years. 62% of students live on campus; of those, 85% remain on campus on weekends. All students may keep cars.

Activities: 17% of men belong to 2 local and 4 national fraternities; 16% of women belong to 4 national sororities. There are 80 groups on campus, including and Caribbean student association, the Quest, campus activities board, cheerleading, chorus, drama, environmental, ethnic, honors, international, literary magazine, musical theater, newspaper, political, professional, radio and TV, religious, social, social service, student government, and yearbook. Popular campus events include Spring Fling, Winter Formal, and Family Fall Festival.

Sports: There are 8 intercollegiate sports for men and 9 for women, and 10 intramural sports for men and 10 for women. Facilities include a 1500-seat indoor gym, a fitness center, an outdoor swimming pool, a golf course, soccer, softball, baseball, and practice fields, basketball, volleyball, racquetball, and lighted tennis courts, turf field, sailing, and canoeing.

Disabled Students: 95% of the campus is accessible. Facilities include wheelchair ramps, elevators, special parking, specially equipped restrooms, lowered drinking fountains, special housing. Accommodations for persons with disabilities are available on a case-by-case basis with proper documentation.

Services: Counseling and information services are available, as is tutoring in most subjects. There is a reader service for the blind, and remedial math and writing.

Campus Safety and Security: Measures include 24-hour foot and vehicle patrol, emergency notification system, and security escort services. There are shuttle buses, emergency telephones, lighted pathways/sidewalks, and controlled access to dorms/residences.

Programs of Study: Saint Leo confers B.A., B.S., B.A.S. and B.S.W. degrees. Associate and master's degrees are also awarded. Bachelor's degrees are awarded in BIOLOGICAL SCIENCE (biology/biological science), BUSINESS (accounting, business administration and management, business communications, hospitality management services, human resources, management science, marketing management, and sports management), COMMUNICATIONS AND THE ARTS (English and multimedia), COMPUTER AND PHYSICAL SCIENCE (information sciences and systems and mathematics), EDUCATION (elementary education, middle school education, and secondary education), ENGINEERING AND ENVIRONMENTAL DESIGN (environmental science), HEALTH PROFESSIONS (health care administration and medical technology), SOCIAL SCIENCE (criminal justice, history, human services, international studies, liberal arts/general studies, political science/government, psychology, religion, social work, and sociology). Accounting, biology, and education are the strongest academically. Biology, criminal justice, and psychology have the largest enrollments.

Required: To graduate, all students must complete a minimum of 120 academic credits with 30 to 60 hours in the major, all the requirements of their division and major, and 53 to 56 hours in the general education program. The honors program may be substituted for general education requirements. A minimum 2.0 GPA and capstone course are required, and there is a 30-hour residency requirement.

Special: Saint Leo offers internships in most majors, study abroad in 11 countries, work-study programs on campus, dual majors, and credit for military experience. There is a prelaw program, preprofessional programs in medicine, dentistry, and veterinary science, learning enhancement for academic progress, and Air Force and Army ROTC programs. Saint Leo also offers articulation agreements with Nova Southeastern University (osteopathy, dental, pharmacy, and nursing), University of St. Augustine for Health Sciences (occupational and physical therapy), Life Chiropractic School, and an affiliation agreement with Bayfront Medical Center (St. Petersburg). There are 18 national honor societies, a freshman honors program, and 1 departmental honors programs.

Faculty/Classroom: 56% of faculty are male; 44% are female. All teach undergraduates. No introductory courses are taught by graduate students. The average class size in a laboratory is 14 and in a regular course is 18.

Admissions: 85% of the 2013-2014 applicants were accepted. The SAT scores for the 2013-2014 freshman class were: Critical Reading--39% below 500, 49% between 500 and 599, 11% between 600 and 699, and 1% between 700 and 800; Math--37% below 500, 52% between 500 and 599, 10% between 600 and 699, and 1% between 700 and 800; Writing--61% below 500, 31% between 500 and 599, 7% between 600 and 699, and 1% between 700 and 800. The ACT scores were 34% below 21, 42% between 21 and 23, 15% between 24 and 26, 5% between 27 and 28, and 4% above 28. 20% of the current freshmen were in the top fifth of their class; 46% were in the top two fifths. 3 freshmen graduated first in their class.

Requirements: The SAT or ACT is recommended. Applicants must be graduates of an accredited secondary school or have a GED certificate and have completed 4 credits in English, 3 each in math and social studies, and 2 each in science, foreign language, and electives. A GPA of 2.7 is required. AP and CLEP credits are accepted. Important factors in the admissions decision are advanced placement or honors courses, personality/intangible qualities, and recommendations by school officials.

Procedure: Freshmen are admitted fall and spring. Entrance exams should be taken by the fall of the senior year. There are deferred admissions and rolling admissions plans. Applications should be filed by August 15 for fall entry. The fall 2013 application fee was $40. Notification is sent on a rolling basis. Applications are accepted online.

Transfer: 150 transfer students enrolled in 2012-2013. Applicants must submit an official transcript from each previously attended college, a recommendation from the dean of students of the last institution attended, and a writing sample. A minimum 2.5 GPA is required. If transferring fewer than 24 academic credits, high school transcript (or GED) and standardized test scores are required. 30 of 120 credits required for the bachelor's degree must be completed at Saint Leo.

Visiting: There are regularly scheduled orientations for prospective students, consisting of overnight campus visitation programs. There are guides for informal visits, visitors may sit in on classes, and stay overnight. To schedule a visit, contact the Office of Admission at (352) 334-5532.

Financial Aid: In 2013-2014, 93% of all full-time freshmen and 93% of continuing full-time students received some form of financial aid. 93% of all full-time freshmen and 90% of continuing full-time students received need-based aid. The average freshman award was $21,994. Need-based scholarships or need-based grants averaged $9,599 ($26,329 maximum); need-based self-help aid (loans and jobs) averaged $4,452 ($7,000 maximum); non-need-based athletic scholarships averaged $9,867 ($22,000 maximum); and other non-need-based awards and non-need-based scholarships averaged $3,666 ($23,000 maximum). 32% of undergraduate students work part-time. Average annual earnings from campus work are $2000. The average financial indebtedness of the 2013 graduate was $19,749. Saint Leo is a member of CSS. The FAFSA is required. The priority date for freshman financial aid applications for fall entry is March 1.

International Students: There are 277 international students enrolled. The school actively recruits these students. They must take the TOEFL with a minimum score of 550 on the paper-based TOEFL (PBT) or 80 on the Internet-based version (iBT), An SAT Verbal (minimum score 450 required) or IELTS (minimum score 6 required) may be substituted for TOEFL.

Computers: All students may access the system. There are no time limits and no fees.

Graduates: From July 1, 2012 to June 30, 2013, 202 bachelor's degrees were awarded. The most popular majors were business/marketing (36%), protective services (16%), and psychology (11%). 20 companies recruited on campus in 2012-2013. In an average class, 32% graduate in 4 years or less, 41% graduate in 5 years or less, and 43% graduate in 6 years or less. Of the 2012 graduating class, 33% were enrolled in graduate school within 6 months of graduation, and 73% were employed.

Admissions Contact: Dana Davies, Associate Vice President of Enrollment. E-Mail: *admission@saintleo.edu* Web: *www.saintleo.edu*

SOUTHEASTERN UNIVERSITY — D-3

Lakeland, FL 33801 — (863) 667-5018; (800) 500-8760; (863) 667-5200

Full-time: 896 men, 1210 women	**Faculty:** 93; IIB, -$
Part-time: 184 men, 158 women	**Ph.D.s:** 67%
Graduate: 106 men, 149 women	**Student/Faculty:** 22 to 1
Year: semesters, summer session	**Tuition:** $18,596
Application Deadline:	**Room & Board:** $8605
Freshman Class: 1442 applied, 707 accepted, 592 enrolled	
SAT CR/M/W: 509/487/494 **ACT:** 21	**COMPETITIVE+**

Southeastern University, founded in 1935, is a Christian liberal arts institution offering 43 degree programs that equip students to serve in both professional careers and ministry-related fields. There are 5 undergraduate schools and 4 graduate schools. The 2 libraries contain 131,072 volumes, 2,163 microform items, and 8,046 audio/video tapes/CDs/DVDs, and subscribe to 1,223 periodicals including electronic. Computerized library services include interlibrary loans, database searching, and Internet access. Special learning facilities include a radio station, TV station, Pentecostal Research Library. The 88-acre campus is in a suburban area 30 miles east of Tampa and 45 miles west of Orlando. Including any residence halls, there are 30 buildings.

Student Life: 65% of undergraduates are from Florida. Others are from 47 states, 21 foreign countries, and Canada. 67% are White; 13% Hispanic; 99% are Protestant. The average age of freshmen is 20; all undergraduates, 23. 36% do not continue beyond their first year; 39% remain to graduate.

Housing: 1355 students can be accommodated in college housing, which includes single-sex dorms and on-campus apartments. On-campus housing is available on a first-come and first-served basis. 51% of students live on campus; of those, 60% remain on campus on weekends. Alcohol is not permitted. All students may keep cars.

Activities: There are no fraternities or sororities. There are 30 groups on campus, including band, cheerleading, choir, chorale, chorus, communications, computers, drama, ethnic, honors, international, jazz band, musical theater, newspaper, opera, orchestra, political, professional, radio and TV, religious, social, social service, student government, symphony, and yearbook.

Sports: There are 6 intercollegiate sports for men and 7 for women, and 8 intramural sports for men and 8 for women. Facilities include a gym, baseball and soccer fields, tennis, racquetball, and beach volleyball courts, a weight room, and intramural fields.

Disabled Students: 90% of the campus is accessible. Facilities include wheelchair ramps, elevators, special parking, specially equipped restrooms, special class scheduling, and lowered drinking fountains.

Services: Counseling and information services are available, as is tutoring in most subjects, Science, English, Math, Religion, History, Music, Communication There is remedial math, reading, and writing.

Campus Safety and Security: Measures include 24-hour foot and vehicle patrol, emergency notification system, and security escort services. There are emergency telephones, lighted pathways/sidewalks, controlled access to dorms/residences, and a main entrance security booth attendant.

Programs of Study: Southeastern confers B.A., B.S., B.M. and B.S.W. degrees. Associate, master's, and doctoral degrees are also awarded. Bachelor's degrees are awarded in BIOLOGICAL SCIENCE (biology/biological science), BUSINESS (accounting, banking and finance, business administration and management, management information systems, marketing/retailing/merchandising, and sports management), COMMUNICATIONS AND THE ARTS (broadcasting, communications, dramatic arts, English, journalism, music, and public relations), COMPUTER AND PHYSICAL SCIENCE (mathematics), EDUCATION (education of the exceptional child, elementary education, middle school education, music education, and secondary education), SOCIAL SCIENCE (biblical studies, criminal justice, history, interdisciplinary studies, ministries, pastoral studies, psychology, public administration, religion, religious music, and social work). Religion, education, and business are the strongest academically. Religion and business have the largest enrollments.

Required: Every degree student must complete 125 to 130 hours, including 36 hours of general education and up to 20 hours of religion (transfer students may have fewer required, based on transfer hours). Distribution requirements include 6 to 12 hours each in arts and communications, human adjustment, science and math, social sciences, and humanities and fine arts. A minimum GPA of 2.0 must be maintained.

Special: Internships are available in communications, education, ministry, psychology, pastoral studies, Christian education, and business. There are accelerated degree programs in church leadership and in business and professional leadership, study abroad in 7 countries, and a Washington semester. There are 2 national honor societies, a freshman honors program, and 2 departmental honors programs.

Faculty/Classroom: 66% of faculty are male; 34% are female. All teach undergraduates. No introductory courses are taught by graduate students. The average class size in an introductory lecture is 60; in a laboratory is 20; and in a regular course is 32.

Admissions: 49% of the 2013-2014 applicants were accepted. The SAT scores for the 2013-2014 freshman class were: Critical Reading--45% below 500, 39% between 500 and 599, 15% between 600 and 699, and 2% between 700 and 800; Math--53% below 500, 35% between 500 and 599, 12% between 600 and 699, and 1% between 700 and 800; Writing--52% below 500, 35% between 500 and 599, 12% between 600 and 699, and 2% between 700 and 800. The ACT scores were 50% below 21, 22% between 21 and 23, 18% between 24 and 26, 6% between 27 and 28, and 4% above 28.

Requirements: The SAT or ACT is required. The GED is accepted. A GPA of 1.5 is required. AP and CLEP credits are accepted. Important factors in the admissions decision are extracurricular activities record, recommendations by school officials, and personality/intangible qualities.

Procedure: Freshmen are admitted to all sessions. Entrance exams should be taken prior to enrollment. There is a rolling admissions plan. Check with the school for current application deadlines. The application fee is $40. Applications are accepted online.

Transfer: 257 transfer students enrolled in 2012-2013. Admission requirements for transfer applicants are the same as for first-time students. 30 of 124 credits required for the bachelor's degree must be completed at Southeastern.

Visiting: There are regularly scheduled orientations for prospective students, Preview Days (fall and spring), which consist of a 24-hour overview of campus life with class visits, faculty reception, admission/financial aid workshops, student panel discussion, and a worship service. There are guides for informal visits, visitors may sit in on classes, and stay overnight. To schedule a visit, contact the Admission Office at (800) 500-8760.

Financial Aid: The FAFSA and the college's own financial statement are required. Check with the school for current application deadlines.

International Students: The school actively recruits these students. They must take the TOEFL. They must also take the SAT or ACT.

Computers: All students may access the system during designated lab hours or from residence halls. There are no time limits and no fees.

Admissions Contact: Omar Rashed, Director of Admissions. E-Mail: *admission@seuniversity.edu* Web: *www.seuniversity.edu*

ST. THOMAS UNIVERSITY — E-5

Miami, FL 33054 — (305) 628-6546; (800) 367-9010; (305) 628-6591

Full-time: 500 men, 645 women	**Faculty:** 113
Part-time: n/av	**Ph.D.s:** n/av
Graduate: 601 men, 755 women	**Student/Faculty:** n/av
Year: semesters, summer session	**Tuition:** $23,910
Application Deadline: open	**Room & Board:** $8400
Freshman Class: 1646 applied, 780 accepted, 270 enrolled	
SAT CR/M/W: 440/440/430 **ACT:** 17	**COMPETITIVE+**

St.Thomas University, founded in 1961, is a private, liberal arts university affiliated with the Roman Catholic church and sponsored by the archdiocese of Miami. There are 5 undergraduate schools and 4 graduate schools. The 2 libraries contain 200,000 volumes, and subscribe to 1,000 periodicals including electronic. Computerized library services include interlibrary loans, database searching, Internet access, and laptop Internet portals. Special learning facilities include a learning resource center and TV station. The figures in the above capsule and in this profile are approximate. The 140-acre campus is in a suburban area 10 miles from Miami and Fort Lauderdale. Including any residence halls, there are 15 buildings.

Student Life: 85% of undergraduates are from Florida. Others are from 25 states, 45 foreign countries, and Canada. 70% are from public schools.

39% are Hispanic; 23% African American; 21% white; 18% foreign nationals. 55% are Catholic; 12% claim no religious affiliation. The average age of freshmen is 19; all undergraduates, 25. 30% do not continue beyond their first year; 42% remain to graduate.

Housing: 300 students can be accommodated in college housing, which includes coed dorms. On-campus housing is guaranteed for all 4 years. 80% of students commute. All students may keep cars.

Activities: There are no fraternities or sororities. There are 30 groups on campus, including art, choir, chorus, computers, debate, drama, ethnic, gay, honors, international, literary magazine, newspaper, photography, political, professional, radio and TV, religious, social, social service, and student government. Popular campus events include Senior Capping Ceremony, Freshman Investiture Ceremony, and Land and Water Olympics.

Sports: There are 6 intercollegiate sports for men and 6 for women, and 5 intramural sports for men and 5 for women. Facilities include Wellness Center, basketball courts, baseball fields, soccer, softball fields, tennis courts, a weight room, and a swimming pool.

Disabled Students: 90% of the campus is accessible. Facilities include wheelchair ramps, elevators, special parking, specially equipped restrooms, special class scheduling, lowered drinking fountains, lowered telephones, and special housing.

Services: Counseling and information services are available, as is tutoring in most subjects. There is remedial math, reading, and writing. Computer-assisted instruction is available.

Campus Safety and Security: Measures include 24-hour foot and vehicle patrol, self-defense education, and security escort services. There are emergency telephones and lighted pathways/sidewalks.

Programs of Study: STU confers B.A., and B.B.A. degrees. Master's degrees are also awarded. Bachelor's degrees are awarded in BIOLOGICAL SCIENCE (biology/biological science), BUSINESS (accounting, banking and finance, business administration and management, hospitality management services, international business management, marketing/retailing/merchandising, sports management, and tourism), COMMUNICATIONS AND THE ARTS (communications and English), COMPUTER AND PHYSICAL SCIENCE (computer programming and computer science), EDUCATION (elementary education, secondary education, and social studies education), HEALTH PROFESSIONS (predentistry and premedicine), SOCIAL SCIENCE (criminal justice, history, human services, international relations, liberal arts/general studies, political science/government, prelaw, psychology, and religion). Sports administration, accounting, and biology are the strongest academically. Business management, psychology, and criminal justice have the largest enrollments.

Required: All students must complete at least 120 semester credits with 30 to 60 in the major and specific courses including 12 credits in English, 9 each in math/physical science, philosophy, and religion, and 6 each in history, social science, and humanities. Students must maintain a 2.0 overall GPA and a 2.25 GPA in the major subject.

Special: Communication arts, hospitality management, and sports administration internships, study abroad in Spain, work-study, and a general studies degree are available. The university grants credit for life, military, and work experience via the Life Experience Portfolio. There is a freshman honors program and 1 departmental honors program.

Faculty/Classroom: 45% of faculty are male; 55% are female. No introductory courses are taught by graduate students.

Admissions: 47% of the 2011-2012 applicants were accepted. The SAT scores for the 2011-2012 freshman class were: Critical Reading--78% below 500, 20% between 500 and 599, and 2% between 600 and 700; Math--80% below 500, 18% between 500 and 599, and 2% between 600 and 700; Writing--79% below 500, 19% between 500 and 599, and 2% between 600 and 700. The ACT scores were 83% below 21, 13% between 21 and 23, and 4% between 24 and 26.

Requirements: The SAT or ACT is required. Applicants should have completed 18 high school units including 4 units in English, 3 each in math and social science, and 2 in science. STU requires applicants to be in the upper 50% of their class. A GPA of 2.5 is required. AP and CLEP credits are accepted. Important factors in the admissions decision are recommendations by school officials, advanced placement or honors courses, and evidence of special talent.

Procedure: Freshmen are admitted to all sessions. Entrance exams should be taken during December of the senior year of high school. There are deferred admissions and rolling admissions plans. Application deadlines are open. Application fee is $40.

Transfer: Maximum credit hours accepted are 60 from a junior college and 90 from a 4-year institution. No grade of D is acceptable in courses beyond sophomore level or in the major. Students with fewer than 30 credits must submit a high school transcript and SAT or ACT scores. 30 of 120 credits required for the bachelor's degree must be completed at STU.

Visiting: There are regularly scheduled orientations for prospective students. There are guides for informal visits, visitors may sit in on classes, and stay overnight. To schedule a visit, contact the Admissions Office.

Financial Aid: In 2011-2012, 90% of all full-time freshmen students received some form of financial aid. 15% of undergraduate students work part-time. Average annual earnings from campus work are $4000. The CSS/Profile, FAFSA, and the college's own financial statement are required. The priority date for freshman financial aid applications for fall entry is April 1.

International Students: There are 200 international students enrolled. The school actively recruits these students. They must take the TOEFL with a minimum score of 527 on the paper-based TOEFL (PBT) or 71 on the Internet-based version (iBT) and the college's own test IELTS. They must also take the SAT or ACT, and the college's own entrance exam.

Computers: Wireless access is available. All students may access the system any time. There are no time limits and no fees. It is strongly recommended that all students have a personal computer.

Admissions Contact: Andre Lightbourn, Dean of Enrollment Management. A campus DVD is available. E-Mail: *alightbo@stu.edu* Web: *www.stu.edu*

STATE UNIVERSITY SYSTEM OF FLORIDA

The State University System of Florida, established in 1906, is a public system in Florida. It is governed by a constitutional board of governors, whose chief administrator is the chancellor. The primary goal of the system is teaching, research, and public service. The main priorities are to improve the quality of undergraduate education, to solve critical state problems, to forge public-private partnerships, and to increase the efficiency of the system. The total student enrollment of all 11 campuses is usually about 321,135 with 17377 faculty members. Altogether there are 746 baccalaureate, 677 master's, and 292 doctoral programs offered in the State University System of Florida. 4-year campuses are located in Gainesville, Tallahassee, Tampa, Boca Raton, Pensacola, Orlando, Jacksonville, Miami, Fort Myers, and Sarasota. Profiles of the 4-year campuses are included in this section.

STETSON UNIVERSITY

D-3

DeLand, FL 32723

(386) 822-7100
(800) 688-0101; (386) 822-7112

Full-time: 1158 men, 1534 women	**Faculty:** 168; IIA, +$
Part-time: 24 men, 13 women	**Ph.D.s:** 95%
Graduate: 610 men, 705 women	**Student/Faculty:** 12 to 1
Year: semesters, summer session	**Tuition:** $38,330
Application Deadline: March 15	**Room & Board:** $11,182
Freshman Class: 10509 applied, 6227 accepted, 852 enrolled	
SAT CR/M/W: 584/577/562	**ACT:** 26 **VERY COMPETITIVE+**

Stetson University is the oldest private university in the State of Florida. Located in DeLand with a second campus in Gulfport and two satellite centers -- one in Celebration and the other in Tampa -- Stetson spans Central Florida from coast to coast. Founded in 1883 by Henry A. DeLand as the DeLand Academy and later renamed Stetson University to honor its benefactor, John B. Stetson, the university has a storied history of leadership, values and significance. The university is home to many Florida firsts, including the first collegiate newspaper, the first chapter of Phi Beta Kappa (the nation's oldest and most prestigious undergraduate honor society), the oldest schools of business administration and music and the first college of law. Stetson also was Florida's first private university to integrate. Stetson is about more than the buildings and those who helped build them; it's really about a vibrant, growing institution where students are prepared to lead lives of significance. The university is led by its ninth president, Wendy B. Libby and is home to 73 undergraduate academic programs in law, music, arts and sciences and business with graduate studies offered in business and education. The university is accredited by numerous agencies, including the Southern Association of Colleges and Schools Commission on Colleges, and curriculum is closely aligned with the marketplace to prepare students for life after Stetson. Undergraduate leadership, research, social justice, advocacy and volunteer service, and participatory activities flourish at all four of the university's locations. There are 3 undergraduate schools and 2 graduate schools. In addition to regional accreditation, Stetson has baccalaureate program accreditation with AACSB, NASM, and NCATE. The 3 libraries contain 477,894 volumes, 305,161 microform items, 18,876 audio/video tapes/CDs/DVDs, and subscribe to 79,078 periodicals including electronic. Computerized library services include interlibrary loans, database searching, Internet access, and Wi-Fi capability. Special learning facilities include an art gallery, a museum of minerals. The 155-acre campus is in a small town 35 miles north of Orlando and 25 miles west of Daytona Beach. Including any residence halls, there are 93 buildings.

Student Life: 74% of undergraduates are from Florida. Others are from 41 states, 51 foreign countries, and Canada. 78% are from public schools. 65% are White; 14% Hispanic. 51% claim no religious affiliation; 21% Protestant; 19% Catholic. The average age of freshmen is 18; all undergraduates, 20. 22% do not continue beyond their first year; 64% remain to graduate.

Housing: 1900 students can be accommodated in college housing, which includes single-sex and coed dorms and on-campus apartments. In addi-

tion, there are honors houses, language houses, special-interest houses, fraternity houses, sorority houses, Family & Partnered housing, gender-neutral housing, Pet-friendly options (pets allowed), Living-Learning Communities: First-Year Experience, Women's Leadership, Wellness, and Honors Houses. On-campus housing is guaranteed for all 4 years. 68% of students live on campus; of those, 60% remain on campus on weekends. All students may keep cars.

Activities: 28% of men belong to 6 national fraternities; 24% of women belong to 5 national sororities. There are 134 groups on campus, including band, cheerleading, chess, choir, chorale, chorus, computers, dance, drama, ethnic, gay, honors, international, jazz band, literary magazine, Model UN, musical theater, newspaper, opera, orchestra, pep band, political, professional, radio and TV, religious, social, social service, student government, symphony, and yearbook. Popular campus events include Undergraduate Research Showcase, Greenfeather Service Week, and Homecoming.

Sports: There are 8 intercollegiate sports for men and 10 for women, and 19 intramural sports for men and 19 for women. Facilities include weightroom and exercise facilities, fieldhouse, basketball courts, volleyball courts, tennis courts, handball courts, softball fields, soccer fields, baseball fields, running trail, swimming pool.

Disabled Students: 80% of the campus is accessible. Facilities include wheelchair ramps, elevators, special parking, specially equipped restrooms, special class scheduling, lowered drinking fountains, and lowered telephones.

Services: Counseling and information services are available, as is tutoring in most subjects. There is a reader service for the blind, and remedial writing.

Campus Safety and Security: Measures include 24-hour foot and vehicle patrol, emergency notification system, self-defense education, and security escort services. There are emergency telephones, lighted pathways/sidewalks, and controlled access to dorms/residences.

Programs of Study: Stetson confers B.A., B.S., B.B.A., B.M. and B.M.E. degrees. Master's degrees are also awarded. Bachelor's degrees are awarded in BIOLOGICAL SCIENCE (biochemistry, biology/biological science, marine biology, and molecular biology), BUSINESS (accounting, banking and finance, business administration and management, business economics, international business management, management information systems, marketing/retailing/merchandising, small business management, and sports management), COMMUNICATIONS AND THE ARTS (art, communications, dramatic arts, English, French, German, guitar, music, music performance, music theory and composition, piano/organ, Spanish, voice, and winds), COMPUTER AND PHYSICAL SCIENCE (chemistry, computer science, digital arts/technology, mathematics, and physics), EDUCATION (elementary education, music education, secondary education, and social science education), ENGINEERING AND ENVIRONMENTAL DESIGN (environmental science), HEALTH PROFESSIONS (health science and rehabilitation therapy), SOCIAL SCIENCE (American studies, economics, geography, history, humanities, international studies, philosophy, political science/government, prelaw, psychology, religion, Russian and Slavic studies, social science, and sociology). Biology, chemistry, physics, finance, mathematics, computer science, and music are the strongest academically. Psychology, business administration, integrative health science and biology are the largest.

Required: Stetson's curriculum is designed to provide its students with a high quality liberal education. To graduate, all students must complete 32 units/courses, equivalent to 128 credits.

Special: Stetson offers co-op programs in preengineering, prelaw, premedicine, forestry, environmental studies, internships in most disciplines, study abroad in Argentina, Australia, Austria, Belize, Brazil, Bulgaria, Cayman Islands, China, Cuba, Ecuador, Egypt, France, Germany, Greece, Guatemala, Hong Kong, Hungary, Israel, Italy, Japan, Jordan, Korea, Mexico, Netherlands, Panama, Peru, Poland, Puerto Rico, Russia, South Africa, Spain, Switzerland, Tanzania, Thailand, Turkey, Uruguay, United Kingdom (Scotland and England), Vietnam, and New Zealand and a Washington semester at American University. B.A.- B.S. degrees, dual majors, student-designed majors through the honors programs, 3-2 engineering degrees, a 3-3 law degree with Stetson College of Law, and pass/fail options are also offered. There is also the Leadership Development Program, the Roland George Investments Program, in which students manage an actual investment portfolio worth nearly 3 million, and the Family Business Center. There are 27 national honor societies, including Phi Beta Kappa, and a freshman honors program.

Faculty/Classroom: 57% of faculty are male; 43% are female. All teach undergraduates. No introductory courses are taught by graduate students. The average class size in an introductory lecture is 21; in a laboratory is 19; and in a regular course is 19.

Admissions: 59% of the 2013-2014 applicants were accepted. The SAT scores for the 2013-2014 freshman class were: Critical Reading--13% below 500, 45% between 500 and 599, 36% between 600 and 699, and 7% between 700 and 800; Math--12% below 500, 46% between 500 and 599, 38% between 600 and 699, and 4% between 700 and 800; Writing--19% below 500, 48% between 500 and 599, 31% between 600 and 699, and 2% between 700 and 800. The ACT scores were 17% below 21, 24% between 21 and 23, 27% between 24 and 26, 17% between 27 and 28, and 19% above 28. 51% of the current freshmen were in the top fifth of their class; 81% were in the top two fifths. 14 freshmen graduated first in their class.

Requirements: The SAT or ACT is required. Applicants must be graduates of an accredited secondary school or have a GED, and have completed 4 years of English, 3 of math and science, and 2 each of foreign language, social sciences, and electives. Auditions are required for music students. A GPA of 2.0 is required. AP and CLEP credits are accepted. Important factors in the admissions decision are advanced placement or honors courses, leadership record, and evidence of special talent.

Procedure: Freshmen are admitted fall, spring, and summer. Entrance exams should be taken in the spring of the junior year or the fall of the senior year. There are early decision, deferred admissions, and rolling admissions plans. Application deadlines are open. Application fee is $50. Notification is sent on a rolling basis. 35 early decision candidates were accepted for the 2013-2014 class. Applications are accepted online.

Transfer: 130 transfer students enrolled in 2012-2013. Transfer students must have completed a semester of academic work in good standing at an accredited college with a minimum 2.0 GPA. A 2.8 GPA and an interview are recommended. They must submit high school and college transcripts and also an essay or personal statement. 64 of 128 credits required for the bachelor's degree must be completed at Stetson.

Visiting: There are regularly scheduled orientations for prospective students, consisting of a campus tour and orientation, interviews, class visits, and presentations. There are guides for informal visits, visitors may sit in on classes, and stay overnight. To schedule a visit, contact the Admissions Office.

Financial Aid: In 2013-2014, 100% of all full-time freshmen and 98% of continuing full-time students received some form of financial aid. 79% of all full-time freshmen and 75% of continuing full-time students received need-based aid. The average freshman award was $36,568. Need-based scholarships or need-based grants averaged $26,931 ($52,675 maximum); need-based self-help aid (loans and jobs) averaged $4,684 ($9,964 maximum); non-need-based athletic scholarships averaged $21,222 ($37,980 maximum); and other non-need-based awards and non-need-based scholarships averaged $21,325 ($50,134 maximum). 37% of undergraduate students work part-time. Average annual earnings from campus work are $2205. The average financial indebtedness of the 2013 graduate was $33,278. Stetson is a member of CSS. The FAFSA is required. The priority date for freshman financial aid applications for fall entry is March 15.

International Students: There are 134 international students enrolled. The school actively recruits these students. They must take the TOEFL with a minimum score of 550 on the paper-based TOEFL (PBT) or 79 on the Internet-based version (iBT), Student may take either the TOEFL or the IELTS. Minimum score for IELTS is 6.0. They must also take the SAT or ACT.

Computers: All students may access the system. There are no time limits and no fees.

Graduates: From July 1, 2012 to June 30, 2013, 457 bachelor's degrees were awarded. The most popular majors were business (25%), visual/performing arts (11%), and social sciences (10%). 66 companies recruited on campus in 2012-2013. In an average class, 3% graduate in 3 years or less, 56% graduate in 4 years or less, 63% graduate in 5 years or less, and 64% graduate in 6 years or less. Of the 2012 graduating class, 25% were enrolled in graduate school within 6 months of graduation, and 35% were employed.

Admissions Contact: Rodney San Jose, Executive Director of Admissions. E-Mail: *admissions@stetson.edu* Web: *www.stetson.edu*

UNIVERSITY OF CENTRAL FLORIDA — D-3

Orlando, FL 32816	**(407) 823-3000; (407) 823-5625**
Full-time: 16480 men, 19680 women	**Faculty:** n/av; I, --$
Part-time: 6797 men, 8312 women	**Ph.D.s:** 79%
Graduate: 3646 men, 4825 women	**Student/Faculty:** 31 to 1
Year: semesters, summer session	**Tuition:** $6317 ($22,415)
Application Deadline: May 1	**Room & Board:** $9394
Freshman Class: 31850 applied, 15572 accepted, 6068 enrolled	
SAT CR/M/W: 585/595/560 **ACT:** 26	**VERY COMPETITIVE+**

The University of Central Florida, founded in 1963, is the nation's second-largest university. Located in Orlando, Florida, UCF and its 12 colleges provide opportunities to 59,740 students, offering 177 bachelor's and master's degrees and 30 doctoral programs. Students come from all 50 states and 148 countries. Kiplinger and The Princeton Review ranked a UCF education as one of the best values in the country in 2012-13. There are 10 undergraduate schools and 11 graduate schools. In addition to regional accreditation, UCF has baccalaureate program accreditation with AACSB, ABET, CAHEA, CSWE, NASM, and NCATE. The library contains 2.5 million volumes, 3.2 million microform items, and 55,793 audio/video tapes/CDs/DVDs, and subscribes to 43,381 periodicals including electronic. Computerized library services include interlibrary loans, database searching, Internet access, and Wi-Fi capability. Special learning facilities include an art gallery, radio station, TV station, University Writing Center, Robinson Observatory, an arboretum, Townes Laser Institute, Florida Energy Center, Morgridge International Reading Center, Center for Research & Education in Optics and Lasers, Toni Jennings Exceptional Education Institute, Communication Disorders Clinic, Institute for Simulation & Training, Florida Solar Energy Center, Biomolecular Science Center, fine art research facility and non-profit publisher, Florida Space Institute, Community Counseling and Research Center, Florida Photonics Center of Excellence, Institute for Diversity and Ethics in Sport, Blackstone LaunchPad at UCF, Center for Advanced Turbomachinery and Energy Research, Center for Computer Vision, Coastal Dynamics of Sea Level Research Cluster of Excellence, Dick Pope Sr. Institute for Tourism Studies, Lou Frey Institute of Politics and Government, NanoScience Technology Center, Advanced Materials Processing and Analysis Center, and a partnership with one of the nation's largest research parks located adjacent to campus. The 1415-acre campus is in a suburban area 13 miles northeast of downtown Orlando. Including any residence halls, there are 173 buildings.

Student Life: 95% of undergraduates are from Florida. Others are from 50 states, 147 foreign countries, and Canada. 57% are White; 22% Hispanic. The average age of freshmen is 18; all undergraduates, 22. 13% do not continue beyond their first year; 67% remain to graduate.

Housing: 11605 students can be accommodated in college housing, which includes single-sex and coed dorms, on-campus apartments, and off-campus apartments. In addition, there are honors houses, special-interest houses, fraternity houses, and sorority houses. On-campus housing is available on a first-come and first-served basis. 82% of students commute. All students may keep cars.

Activities: 6% of men belong to 24 national fraternities; 7% of women belong to 22 national sororities. There are 550 groups on campus, including and sports, pre-professional medical society, art, band, cheerleading, chess, choir, chorus, communications, computers, dance, debate, drama, drill team, environmental, ethnic, film, forensics, gay, honors, international, jazz band, literary magazine, marching band, musical theater, newspaper, opera, orchestra, pep band, photography, political, professional, radio and TV, religious, social, social service, student government, symphony, and volunteer UCF. Popular campus events include Homecoming Events, Spirit Splash, Greek Extravaganza, Symphony Under the Stars, Concerts, Comedians and Movies on the Plaza.

Sports: There are 6 intercollegiate sports for men and 9 for women, and 17 intramural sports for men and 17 for women. Facilities include Football stadium and arena, Baseball stadium, Softball stadium, Lake Pickett Rowing Complex, 7 tennis courts, an outdoor adventure challenge course, 8 sand volleyball courts, 3 outdoor basketball courts, a disc golf course, 2 swimming pools, exercise/multipurpose rooms, spin studio, a 14,000-square-foot fitness space, a 3-lane track, a weight floor, cardio floor, a climbing tower, 4 indoor basketball/volleyball courts, baseball/softball field, 2 multi-purpose grass fields, Lake Claire outdoor recreational space, 6 turf fields, 2 multi-purpose indoor courts, 4 racquetball courts.

Disabled Students: 97% of the campus is accessible. Facilities include wheelchair ramps, elevators, special parking, specially equipped restrooms, special class scheduling, lowered drinking fountains, lowered telephones.

Services: Counseling and information services are available, as is tutoring in some subjects, Biology and Microbio, Chemistry (inc- Organic & Biochem), Genetics, Human Anatomy and Physiology, Astronomy, Accounting, Finance, Statistics, C Programming, Object-oriented Programming, Computer Engineering Statics and Dynamics, Thermodynamics, Physics.

Campus Safety and Security: Measures include 24-hour foot and vehicle patrol, emergency notification system, self-defense education, and security escort services. There are shuttle buses, emergency telephones, lighted pathways/sidewalks, controlled access to dorms/residences, including a college-sponsored transportation system that buses students to and from apartment complexes within a 2- or 3-mile radius of the school.

Programs of Study: UCF confers B.A., B.S., B.A.B.A., B.A.S., B.F.A., B.M., B.M.E., B.S.A.E., B.S.B.A., B.S.C.E., B.S.Con.E., B.S.Cp.E., B.S.E.E., B.S.E.E.T., B.S.Env.E., B.S.E.T., B.S.I.E., B.S.M.E., B.S.N., B.Des., B.S.P.S.E., and B.S.W. degrees. Associate, master's, and doctoral degrees are also awarded. Bachelor's degrees are awarded in BIOLOGICAL SCIENCE (biology/biological science and biotechnology), BUSINESS (accounting, banking and finance, business administration and management, business economics, hospitality management services, management science, marketing/retailing/merchandising, and real estate), COMMUNICATIONS AND THE ARTS (advertising, art, broadcasting, communications, dramatic arts, English, film arts, fine arts, French, information technology, journalism, languages, music, music performance, photography, public relations, radio/television technology, Spanish, theatre arts, and theatre studies), COMPUTER AND PHYSICAL SCIENCE (applied science, chemistry, computer science, digital arts/technology, information sciences and systems, mathematics, physics, and statistics), EDUCATION (art education, athletic training, business education, early childhood education, education of the exceptional child, elementary education, English education, foreign languages education, health information management, mathematics education, music education, science education, social science education, and technical education), ENGINEERING AND ENVIRONMENTAL DESIGN (aeronautical engineering, aerospace studies, architecture, civil engineering, computer engineering, construction engineering, electrical/electronics engineering, environmental engineering, food services technology, industrial engineering, and mechanical engineering), HEALTH PROFESSIONS (biomedical science, exercise science, health care administration, health science, medical laboratory technology, nursing, and speech pathology/audiology), SOCIAL SCIENCE (anthropology, criminal justice, economics, food production/management/services, forensic studies, (Social Science) Global Studies, history, humanities, interdisciplinary studies, international studies, Latin American studies, legal studies, liberal arts/general studies, philosophy, political science/government, psychology, public administration, religion, social science, social work, and sociology). Engineering, business administration and computer science are the strongest academically. Psychology, biomedical sciences, and health related fields have the largest enrollments.

Required: To graduate, students must complete at least 120 semester hours, with 36 hours in general education program courses, including 9 each in communication foundations and cultural and historical foundations and 6 each in math foundations, science foundations, and social foundations. Students must maintain a minimum GPA of 2.0. There is a 30-hour residency requirement, and the last semester is required in residence.

Special: Internships are available in most majors through UCF's extensive partnerships with area businesses and industries such as NASA, Disney, Universal Studios, and AT&T. Students may participate in study abroad and co-op and work-study programs, earn B.A.-B.S. degrees or a liberal studies degree, or pursue dual majors. Nondegree study and pass/fail options are available. There are 24 national honor societies, a freshman honors program, and 55 departmental honors programs.

Faculty/Classroom: 55% of faculty are male; 45% are female. 69% teach undergraduates, 66% do research, and 39% do both. Graduate students teach 11% of introductory courses. The average class size in an introductory lecture is 44; in a laboratory is 16; and in a regular course is 44.

Admissions: 49% of the 2013-2014 applicants were accepted. The SAT scores for the 2013-2014 freshman class were: Critical Reading--9% below 500, 50% between 500 and 599, 33% between 600 and 699, and 8% between 700 and 800; Math--7% below 500, 45% between 500 and 599, 40% between 600 and 699, and 8% between 700 and 800; Writing--18% below 500, 52% between 500 and 599, 26% between 600 and 699, and 4% between 700 and 800. The ACT scores were 2% below 21, 26% between 21 and 23, 36% between 24 and 26, 18% between 27 and 28, and 18% above 28. 60% of the current freshmen were in the top fifth of their class; 92% were in the top two fifths. There were 61 National Merit finalists. 51 freshmen graduated first in their class.

Requirements: The SAT or ACT is required. The ACT Optional Writing test is also required. GPA and standardized test scores are rated on a sliding scale. A high school diploma or GED is required. Applicants should have completed 4 units of English, 4 each of math, 3 units of science (2 with labs), and social studies, and 2 of a foreign language, plus 2 of academic electives. A GPA of 2.0 is required. AP and CLEP credits are accepted. Important factors in the admissions decision are advanced placement or honors courses, evidence of special talent, and leadership record.

Procedure: Freshmen are admitted fall, spring, and summer. Entrance exams should be taken during the junior year or the first semester of the senior year. There is a rolling admissions plan. Applications should be filed by May 1 for fall entry; November 1 for spring entry; and March 1 for summer entry, along with a $30 fee. Notification is sent on a rolling basis. 908 applicants were on the 2013 waiting list; 554 were admitted. Applications are accepted online.

Transfer: 10452 transfer students enrolled in 2012-2013. A minimum GPA of 2.0 is required in all college work. Either the SAT or the ACT is required of applicants with fewer than 60 credit hours. Other transfer requirements vary widely. 30 of 120 credits required for the bachelor's degree must be completed at UCF.

Visiting: There are regularly scheduled orientations for prospective students, including tours offered twice a day, Monday through Friday, followed by a group information session or personal interview. There are guides for informal visits and visitors may sit in on classes. To schedule a visit, contact the Undergraduate Admissions Office.

Financial Aid: In 2013-2014, 95% of all full-time freshmen and 86% of continuing full-time students received some form of financial aid. 49% of all full-time freshmen and 58% of continuing full-time students received need-based aid. The average freshman award was $7,816. Need-based scholarships or need-based grants averaged $4,572 ($13,500 maximum); need-based self-help aid (loans and jobs) averaged $3,531 ($10,472 maximum); non-need-based athletic scholarships averaged $8,915 ($23,083 maximum); and other non-need-based awards and non-need-based scholarships averaged $3,189 ($30,625 maximum). Average annual earnings from campus work are $6000. The average financial indebtedness of the 2013 graduate was $23,186. The FAFSA is required. The priority date for freshman financial aid applications for fall entry is March 1. The deadline for filing freshman financial aid applications for fall entry is June 30.

International Students: There are 546 international students enrolled. They must take the TOEFL with a minimum score of 550 on the paper-based TOEFL (PBT) or 80 on the Internet-based version (iBT). They must also take the SAT or ACT. Students with fewer than 60 semester hours of college credit must take either the SAT or the ACT.

Computers: All students may access the system at all times. There are no time limits and no fees.

Graduates: From July 1, 2012 to June 30, 2013, 12525 bachelor's degrees were awarded. The most popular majors were business (23%), health professions (13%), and psychology (10%). 759 companies recruited on campus in 2012-2013. In an average class, 2% graduate in 3 years or less, 36% graduate in 4 years or less, 61% graduate in 5 years or less, and 67% graduate in 6 years or less. Of the 2012 graduating class, 21% were enrolled in graduate school within 6 months of graduation, and 69% were employed.

Admissions Contact: Undergraduate Admissions E-Mail: *admission@ucf.edu* Web: *www.admissions.ucf.edu*

UNIVERSITY OF FLORIDA — D-2

Gainesville, FL 32611 — **(352) 294 3683**

Full-time: 13427 men, 16887 women	**Faculty:** 3146
Part-time: 1552 men, 1302 women	**Ph.D.s:** 83%
Graduate: 8049 men, 8661 women	**Student/Faculty:** n/av
Year: semesters, summer session	**Tuition:** $6263 ($28,541)
Application Deadline: November 1	**Room & Board:** $9520

Freshman Class: 28144 applied, 12591 accepted, 6383 enrolled

SAT CR/M/W: 625/638/624 **ACT:** 28 **HIGHLY COMPETITIVE+**

The University of Florida, founded in 1853, is a public liberal arts institution that is part of the state university system of Florida. There are 16 undergraduate schools. In addition to regional accreditation, UF has baccalaureate program accreditation with AACSB, ABET, ACCE, ACEJMC, ACPE, ADA, APTA, ASLA, FIDER, NAAB, NASAD, NASM, NCATE, and SAF. The 7 libraries contain 4.9 million volumes, 6.6 million microform items, and 84,716 audio/video tapes/CDs/DVDs, and subscribe to 165,339 periodicals including electronic. Computerized library services include interlibrary loans, database searching, Internet access, and Wi-Fi capability. Special learning facilities include an art gallery, natural history museum, radio station, TV station, performing arts center, and a teaching hospital. The 1955-acre campus is in a suburban area 75 miles from Jacksonville, FL. Including any residence halls, there are 904 buildings.

Student Life: 94% of undergraduates are from Florida. Others are from 50 states, 153 foreign countries, and Canada. 58% are White; 19% Hispanic. The average age of freshmen is 18; all undergraduates, 21.

Housing: 8894 students can be accommodated in college housing, which includes coed dorms, on-campus apartments, off-campus apartments, and married student housing. In addition, there are honors houses, special-interest houses, fraternity houses, sorority houses, Honors residential college, career exploration community, wellness communities, faculty-in-residence communities, first-year experience program, engineering community, fine arts living learning community, global living learning community, sophomore experience program, pre-health community, ROTC community, and a international house. On-campus housing is available on a first-come and first-served basis. All students may keep cars.

Activities: 23% of men belong to 38 national fraternities; 20% of women belong to 26 national sororities. There are 980 groups on campus, including art, band, cheerleading, chess, choir, chorale, chorus, computers, dance, debate, drama, environmental, ethnic, film, gay, honors, international, jazz band, literary magazine, marching band, newspaper, opera, orchestra, pep band, photography, political, professional, radio and TV, religious, social, social service, student government, and symphony. Popular campus events include Homecoming Parade, Annual Dance Marathon and ACCENT Speaker's Bureau, Gator Growl Student Run Pep Rally, and Florida Invitational Step Show.

Sports: There are 31 intercollegiate sports for men and 31 for women, and 45 intramural sports for men and 45 for women. Facilities include A 12,000-seat athletic center, tennis, volleyball, and basketball courts, a 60,000-square-foot fitness park, an Olympic-size swimming pool, a running track, weight rooms, intramural fields, an 83,000-seat stadium, and lakefront facilities. An expanded recreational facility opened in 2010 with 140,000 square feet of space for cardio, strength, group fitness, basketball, indoor soccer, racquetball and other activities.

Disabled Students: 95% of the campus is accessible. Facilities include wheelchair ramps, elevators, special parking, specially equipped restrooms, special class scheduling, lowered drinking fountains, lowered telephones. computer access for the blind and visually impaired students.

Services: Counseling and information services are available, as is tutoring in every subject. There is a reader service for the blind. There is a Counseling and Wellness Center, in addition to free tutoring through Broward Teaching Center

Campus Safety and Security: Measures include 24-hour foot and vehicle patrol, emergency notification system, self-defense education, and security escort services. There are shuttle buses, emergency telephones, lighted pathways/sidewalks, and controlled access to dorms/residences.

Programs of Study: UF confers B.A., and B.S. degrees. Associate, master's, and doctoral degrees are also awarded. Bachelor's degrees are awarded in AGRICULTURE (agricultural business management, agronomy, animal science, dairy science, forestry and related sciences, horticulture, natural resource management, plant science, and soil science), BIOLOGICAL SCIENCE (botany, entomology, microbiology, wildlife biology, and zoology), BUSINESS (accounting, banking and finance, business administration and management, human resources, insurance, management science, marketing/retailing/merchandising, and recreation and leisure services), COMMUNICATIONS AND THE ARTS (advertising, art, art history and appreciation, dance, East Asian languages and literature, English, French, German, graphic design, journalism, linguistics, music, performing arts, photography, Portuguese, public relations, Russian, Spanish, speech/debate/rhetoric, telecommunications, theater design, and visual and performing arts), COMPUTER AND PHYSICAL SCIENCE (astronomy, chemistry, computer science, earth science, geology, information sciences and systems, mathematics, physics, and statistics), EDUCATION (agricultural education, art education, elementary education, health education, and music education), ENGINEERING AND ENVIRONMENTAL DESIGN (aeronautical engineering, agricultural engineering, architecture, chemical engineering, civil engineering, computer engineering, construction engineering, electrical/electronics engineering, emergency/disaster science, engineering and applied science, environmental engineering, industrial engineering technology, interior design, landscape architecture/design, materials engineering, mechanical engineering, nuclear engineering, and nuclear engineering technology), HEALTH PROFESSIONS (allied health, exercise science, health science, nursing, occupational therapy, physical therapy, prepharmacy, rehabilitation therapy, and speech pathology/audiology), SOCIAL SCIENCE (American studies, anthropology, Asian/Oriental studies, classical/ancient civilization, criminology, economics, food science, geography, history, home economics, interdisciplinary studies, Judaic studies, philosophy, physical fitness/movement, political science/government, psychology, religion, and sociology). Psychology, biology and political science are the strongest academically. Biology, psychology and mechanical engineering are the largest.

Required: UNDERGRADUATE: Requirements for graduation vary depending on the major elected, but all students are required to complete a minimum of 120 credits and maintain a minimum 2.0 GPA, including 36 credits of general education courses. GRADUATE: All graduate degrees require the minimum stipulated number of credits for the type of degree, and a 3.0 GPA in the major, in the minor if applicable, and overall. Master's Degrees Most require a minimum of 30 credits, with curriculum and requirements dictated by each degree program.

Special: Co-Op programs Cross-registration; None Internships vary by majors. Students should consult their major department. For internships not in the major, students should contact the Honors Program (www.honors.ufl.edu) Study Abroad; Yes. International Center (https:/www.ufic.ufl.edu/SAS/OutboundStudents.html) Washington Semester: Yes The Washington Experience and the Capital Semester in Washington – Journalism Track Work Study Program Yes. Accelerated degree programs vary by major. Dual majors vary by colleges. Student-designed majors: Interdisciplinary Studies in the College of Liberal Arts and Sciences Innovation Academy at UF: A groundbreaking living/learning community that offers a flexible spring-summer cohort, enlightening guest speakers, diverse internship opportunities, co-curricular environment, and a minor in Innovation. 3-2 engineering degree with the University of the Virgin Islands There are 100 national honor societies, including Phi Beta Kappa, a freshman honors program, and 100 departmental honors programs.

Faculty/Classroom: 65% of faculty are male; 35% are female. No introductory courses are taught by graduate students.

Admissions: 45% of the 2013-2014 applicants were accepted. The SAT scores for the 2013-2014 freshman class were: Critical Reading--4% below 500, 29% between 500 and 599, 48% between 600 and 699, and 18% between 700 and 800; Math--3% below 500, 22% between 500 and 599, 52% between 600 and 699, and 22% between 700 and 800; Writing--6% below 500, 27% between 500 and 599, 49% between 600 and 699, and 18% between 700 and 800. The ACT scores were 3% below 21, 6% between 21 and 23, 16% between 24 and 26, 23% between 27 and 28, and 51% above 28.

Requirements: The SAT or ACT is required. The ACT Optional Writing test is also required. A satisfactory score on the SAT and a minimum score of 19 on the ACT are required. Candidates should have graduated from an accredited secondary school or have a GED, and have completed 4 years of English, 4 years of math, 3 science, and 3 social studies, 2 years of a foreign language, and 4 units of academic electives. A GPA of 2.5 is required. AP and CLEP credits are accepted. Important factors in the admissions decision are advanced placement or honors courses, extracurricular activities record, and evidence of special talent.

Procedure: Freshmen are admitted to all sessions. Entrance exams should be taken in the junior year. Applications should be filed by November 1 for fall entry; November 1 for spring entry; and November 1 for summer entry, along with a $30 fee. Notifications are sent February 13. Applications are accepted online.

Transfer: 2445 transfer students enrolled in 2012-2013. Admission requirements for transfer students vary by college. Students must have 60 hours or AA degree. 30 of 120 credits required for the bachelor's degree must be completed at UF.

Visiting: There are regularly scheduled orientations for prospective students, refer to the Welcome Center calendar for tour time, as tours are based on time of year. There are guides for informal visits, visitors may sit in on classes, and stay overnight. To schedule a visit, contact the UF Welcome Center.

Financial Aid: In 2013-2014, 99% of all full-time freshmen and 98% of continuing full-time students received some form of financial aid. 41% of all full-time freshmen and 42% of continuing full-time students received need-based aid. The average freshman award was $11,325. Need-based scholarships or need-based grants averaged $7,361; need-based self-help aid (loans and jobs) averaged $3,964; non-need-based athletic scholarships averaged $15,625; and other non-need-based awards and non-need-based scholarships averaged $5,163. 12% of undergraduate students work part-time. Average annual earnings from campus work are $1506. The average financial indebtedness of the 2013 graduate was $20,708. UF is a member of CSS. The FAFSA is required. The priority date for freshman financial aid applications for fall entry is March 15.

International Students: There are 325 international students enrolled. The school actively recruits these students. They must take the TOEFL with a minimum score of 550 on the paper-based TOEFL (PBT) or 80 on the Internet-based version (iBT), IELTS. They must also take the SAT or ACT. Freshmen and lower-division transfers must take the SAT or ACT.

Computers: All students may access the system. There are no time limits and no fees.

Graduates: From July 1, 2012 to June 30, 2013, 8244 bachelor's degrees were awarded. The most popular majors were psychology (6%), biology (5%), and political science (4%). In an average class, 5% graduate in 3 years or less, 67% graduate in 4 years or less, 83% graduate in 5 years or less, and 85% graduate in 6 years or less.

Admissions Contact: Zina Evans, Vice President for Enrollment Management. Web: *www.ufl.edu*

UNIVERSITY OF MIAMI E-6

Coral Gables, FL 33124 **(305) 284-4323; (305) 284-6605**

Full-time: 5229 men, 5408 women	**Faculty:** n/av; I, av$
Part-time: 304 men, 439 women	**Ph.D.s:** 91%
Graduate: 2735 men, 2820 women	**Student/Faculty:** 12 to 1
Year: semesters, summer session	**Tuition:** $42,852
Application Deadline: January 1	**Room & Board:** $12,314
Freshman Class: 28907 applied, 11691 accepted, 2140 enrolled	
SAT CR/M/W: 640/680/640	**ACT:** 30 **MOST COMPETITIVE**

The mission of the University of Miami encompasses two primary goals: empowering the discoveries that enhance civilization and preparing our students for success in their careers and in life. A brilliant faculty corps draws exceptional students, and the cumulative impact of the two has made the University one of the fastest-rising research universities in the nation. Dynamic courses are offered in more than 180 majors and programs and students have the freedom to cross disciplines and carve an educational path unique to their aptitudes and interests. At UM, a student can construct learning around individual strengths, interests, curiosities, passions, and goals by taking advantage of an array of learning options in our nine undergraduate schools and two graduate professional schools. The Cognates Program of General Education allows a student to use those options to create an education that is both broad and deep and that displays who the student is and what the student cares about. Our approach nurtures curiosity and exploration of the world outside the classroom while also bringing the world to the University of Miami campus. The value of a University of Miami education is the ability to become part of this vast and renewable resource, gaining knowledge, inspiration, camaraderie and connections that will prove invaluable for years to come. There are 9 undergraduate schools and 3 graduate schools. In addition to regional accreditation, UM has baccalaureate program accreditation with AACSB, ABET, APTA, NAAB, NASM, and TEAC. The 10 libraries contain 3.5 million volumes, 4.1 million microform items, and 106,136 audio/video tapes/CDs/DVDs, and subscribe to 92,958 periodicals including electronic. Computerized library services include interlibrary loans, database searching, Internet access, and Wi-Fi capability. Special learning facilities include an art gallery, radio station, TV station, Cinema, observatory, palmetum, marine science research vessels, broadcasting studios, concert hall, arboretum, performing arts theater, film studios, sound stage, museum, wellness center and state-of-the-art student activities center. The 239-acre campus is in a suburban area 7 miles from Miami International Airport. Including any residence halls, there are 130 buildings.

Student Life: 54% of undergraduates are from out of state, mostly the Middle Atlantic. Students are from 50 states, 105 foreign countries, and Canada. 61% are from public schools. 43% are White; 22% Hispanic; 14% Foreign. 40% are Protestant; 33% Catholic; 15% Hindu, Muslim, Buddhism and unknown. ; 12% Jewish. The average age of freshmen is 18; all undergraduates, 21. 9% do not continue beyond their first year; 91% remain to graduate.

Housing: 4310 students can be accommodated in college housing, which includes single-sex and coed dorms and on-campus apartments. In addition, there are special-interest houses, fraternity houses, Freshmen are required to live on campus, and they live in residential colleges with live-in resident faculty. On-campus housing is guaranteed for the freshman year only, is available on a first-come, first-served basis, and is available on a lottery system for upperclassmen. 62% of students commute. Some may keep cars.

Activities: 14% of men belong to 21 national fraternities; 17% of women belong to 15 national sororities. There are 260 groups on campus, including art, athletic organizations, band, cheerleading, chess, choir, chorale, chorus, computers, dance, debate, drama, environmental, ethnic, film, gay, honors, international, jazz band, literary magazine, marching band, musical theater, newspaper, opera, orchestra, pep band, political, professional, radio and TV, religious, social, social service, student government, symphony, and yearbook. Popular campus events include Homecoming, Alumni Weekend, 'Canes Spirit Day, International Week, SportsFest, Miami International Film Festival, CaneFest, Hug the Lake, and Thanksgiving Day Matchup Program.

Sports: There are 8 intercollegiate sports for men and 10 for women, and 28 intramural sports for men and 28 for women. Facilities include The Cobb Stadium, a soccer and track & field facility; the BankUnited Center, home of UM's basketball program and the University's first large-capacity venue for other educational, cultural and community events; Hecht Center Athletic Training Facility, equipped with the latest in diagnostic and rehabilitative equipment and serves as the main lab for the Athletic Training Major; Schwartz Center for Athletic Excellence, serves the University's more than 400 student-athletes with resources such as a new academic center and expanded training facilities; Mark Light Baseball Stadium, home to UM's baseball program; Alex Rodriguez Park, the newly renovated facility at Mark Light Baseball Stadium; Neil Schiff Tennis Center, 16-court facility with seating for 1,000 spectators; University Center Pool, this double-Olympic-size swimming pool is home to UM's swimming and diving teams and is enjoyed recreationally by UM students and faculty; Sun Life Stadium, a world-class sports and entertainment facility that hosts a wide variety of events, including the Miami Hurricanes football games; Herbert Wellness Center, a premier fitness, recreation and wellness facility that includes a fitness room, aerobic classes, indoor track, gymnasium with basketball, volleyball and badminton courts, racquetball and squash courts, tennis, indoor pool, spa, sauna and community and cooking classes.

Disabled Students: Facilities include wheelchair ramps, elevators, special parking, specially equipped restrooms, special class scheduling, lowered drinking fountains, lowered telephones, special housing, and lowered elevator controls.

Services: Counseling and information services are available, as is tutoring in some subjects. There is a reader service for the blind.

Campus Safety and Security: Measures include 24-hour foot and vehicle patrol, emergency notification system, self-defense education, and security escort services. There are shuttle buses, emergency telephones, lighted pathways/sidewalks, controlled access to dorms/residences, There has been a comprehensive crime prevention program since 1981.

Programs of Study: UM confers A.B., B.A., B.S., B.A.M., B.A.M.A., B.Arch., B.B.A., B.F.A., B.G.S., B.L.A., B.M., B.S.A.E., B.S.A.S.E., B.S.B.A., B.S.B.E., B.S.C., B.S.C.E., B.S.Cp.E., B.S.Ed., B.S.E.E., B.S.E.S., B.S.En.E., B.S.H.S., B.S.I.E., B.S.M.A.S., B.S.M.E., B.S.N. and B.S.P.H. degrees. Master's and doctoral degrees are also awarded. Bachelor's degrees are awarded in BIOLOGICAL SCIENCE (biochemistry, marine biology, marine science, microbiology, molecular biology, and neurosciences), BUSINESS (accounting, entrepreneurial studies, finance, human resources/organizational mgmt, international finance, international marketing, management science, marketing, marketing management, real estate, and sports management), COMMUNICATIONS AND THE ARTS (advertising, art history, art, ceramic art and design, classical languages, classics, communication, communication studies, English, film arts, fine arts, French, German, graphic design, Greek (classical), instrumental performance, jazz, journalism, modern language, music, music business management, music composition, music performance, music technology, musical theater, painting, photography, printmaking, public relations, sculpture, Spanish, studio art, theatre acting, theatre arts, theater design, theater management, and vocal performance), COMPUTER AND PHYSICAL SCIENCE (applied mathematics, atmospheric sciences and meteorology, chemistry, computer game design/development, computer information systems, computer science, geology, geoscience, mathematics, mathematics/computational, mathematics – economics, physics, software engineering, and statistics), EDUCATION (athletic training, education of the exceptional child, elementary education, mathematics education, music education, and secondary education), ENGINEERING AND ENVI-

RONMENTAL DESIGN (aerospace studies, architectural engineering, architecture, biomedical engineering, civil engineering, computer engineering, computer graphics, electrical/electronics engineering, engineering science, environmental engineering, environmental science, industrial engineering, and mechanical engineering), HEALTH PROFESSIONS (biology, exercise science, health administration and policy, health care administration, health science, music therapy, nursing, physician's assistant, Pre-Health Studies, predentistry, premedicine, prepharmacy, prephysical therapy, preveterinary science, and public health), SOCIAL SCIENCE (africana studies, American studies, anthropology, classical/ancient civilization, criminology, economics, gender studies, geography, history, human development, interdisciplinary studies, international studies, Judaic studies, Latin American studies, legal studies, liberal arts/general studies, philosophy, political science/government, prelaw, psychology, religion, religious studies, sociology, and women's studies). Business/marketing, biological/life sciences, and social sciences. are the largest.

Required: To receive a Bachelor's degree from the University, the student must earn at least 120 semester hours of credit, more in some schools, with a C average or better as well as a C average for all work done at the University of Miami. The student must fulfill the general education requirements as well as meet all of the degree requirements of their respective school or college. Each student must complete the final 45 credits that are applied to his or her baccalaureate degree in residence at the University of Miami. In addition, each student must complete at least half of the credits specified for his or her major in residence at the University of Miami.

Special: Our internships, work-study programs, and study-abroad programs provide the opportunity for UM students to acquire an expansive perspective in their academic career. Opportunities to learn and grow flourish through our special programs such as our accelerated degree programs as well as our dual degree programs. There are 52 national honor societies, including Phi Beta Kappa, and a freshman honors program.

Faculty/Classroom: 62% of faculty are male; 38% are female. No introductory courses are taught by graduate students.

Admissions: 40% of the 2013-2014 applicants were accepted. The SAT scores for the 2013-2014 freshman class were: Critical Reading--4% below 500, 21% between 500 and 599, 49% between 600 and 699, and 26% between 700 and 800; Math--2% below 500, 12% between 500 and 599, 48% between 600 and 699, and 38% between 700 and 800; Writing--3% below 500, 23% between 500 and 599, 50% between 600 and 699, and 24% between 700 and 800. The ACT scores were 74% above 28. 89% of the current freshmen were in the top fifth of their class; 96% were in the top two fifths. There were 51 National Merit finalists. 53 freshmen graduated first in their class.

Requirements: The SAT or ACT is required. It is recommended that applicants have completed 4 units of English, 4 units of Mathematics, 3 units of Science with 2 of the 3 units being in lab, 2 units of Foreign Language, 3 units of Social Studies, 2 units of History, and 2 units of Academic Electives with 1 unit being in Computer Science and 1 unit being in Visual/Performing Arts. Applicants are based on the strength of their high school curriculum and grades earned, standardized test scores, letters of recommendation, essay, extracurricular activities and awards/achievements. The GED is accepted. Portfolios are required for the Arts and Architecture programs. Auditions are required for the Music and Theatre Programs. Supplemental applications are required for the Frost School of Music, BFA Theatre, BFA Art, Architecture, and Dual Degree Programs. AP and CLEP credits are accepted. Important factors in the admissions decision are extracurricular activities record, recommendations by school officials, and advanced placement or honors courses.

Procedure: Freshmen are admitted fall and spring. Entrance exams should be taken the summer before the senior year in high school. There are early decision, early admissions, and deferred admissions plans. Early decision applications should be filed by November 1; regular applications, by January 1 for fall entry; and November 1 for spring entry, along with a $70 fee. Notification of early decision is sent December 20; regular decision, April 15. 157 early decision candidates were accepted for the 2013-2014 class. Applications are accepted online.

Transfer: 599 transfer students enrolled in 2012-2013. Only credits from a regionally accredited institution are transferable to the University of Miami. The average accepted transfer student has a 3.4 GPA. Courses with a grade lower than a C will not transfer, however these grades will still be used to compute an admission GPA. If the student has fewer than 30 college credits when submitting the application, official high school transcripts, the Common Application Secondary School Final Report and SAT/ACT scores must be submitted in addition to the core application documents. Portfolios are required for BFA Art and Architecture programs. Supplemental applications are required for the Frost School of Music, BFA Theatre, BFA Art and Architecture programs. 45 of 120 credits required for the bachelor's degree must be completed at UM.

Visiting: There are regularly scheduled orientations for prospective students, Several open house programs that enable students to tour the campus and meet with representatives from admission, financial aid, and various university departments. Daily information sessions are offered on campus as well as walking tours. There are guides for informal visits and visitors may sit in on classes.

Financial Aid: In 2013-2014, 79% of all full-time freshmen and 72% of continuing full-time students received some form of financial aid. 50% of all full-time freshmen and 45% of continuing full-time students received need-based aid. The average freshman award was $33,811. Need-based scholarships or need-based grants averaged $26,119 ($61,603 maximum); need-based self-help aid (loans and jobs) averaged $7,760 ($39,392 maximum); non-need-based athletic scholarships averaged $33,262 ($60,906 maximum); other non-need-based awards and non-need-based scholarships averaged $18,404 ($60,960 maximum); and $22,872 from other forms of aid. 56% of undergraduate students work part-time. Average annual earnings from campus work are $2000. The average financial indebtedness of the 2013 graduate was $27,827. UM is a member of CSS. The CSS/Profile and FAFSA are required. The priority date for freshman financial aid applications for fall entry is February 1.

International Students: There are 1510 international students enrolled. The school actively recruits these students. They must take the TOEFL with a minimum score of 550 on the paper-based TOEFL (PBT) or 80 on the Internet-based version (iBT), All students whose native language is not English are required to submit official results of the TOEFL or IELTS. They must also take the SAT or ACT. SAT/ACTnot required and shouldn't be submitted for admission consideration from applicants attending school outside U.S.

Computers: All students may access the system. 24 hours a day. There are no time limits and no fees.

Graduates: From July 1, 2012 to June 30, 2013, 2451 bachelor's degrees were awarded. The most popular majors were psychology (6%), biology (6%), and finance (5%). 362 companies recruited on campus in 2012-2013. In an average class, 4% graduate in 3 years or less, 71% graduate in 4 years or less, 81% graduate in 5 years or less, and 82% graduate in 6 years or less. Of the 2012 graduating class, 28% were enrolled in graduate school within 6 months of graduation, and 59% were employed.

Admissions Contact: Deanna L. Voss, Executive Director of Admission. E-Mail: *admission@miami.edu* Web: *www.miami.edu/ug*

UNIVERSITY OF NORTH FLORIDA D-1

Jacksonville, FL 32224 **(904) 620-2624; (904) 620-2414**

Full-time: 4464 men, 5624 women	**Faculty:** 381; IIA, --$
Part-time: 1937 men, 2238 women	**Ph.D.s:** 92%
Graduate: 692 men, 1128 women	**Student/Faculty:** 20 to 1
Year: semesters, summer session	**Tuition:** $6353 ($20,756)
Application Deadline: May 10	**Room & Board:** $9225

Freshman Class: 7199 applied, 3189 accepted, 807 enrolled
SAT CR/M: 611/604 **ACT:** 26 **VERY COMPETITIVE**

The University of North Florida, founded in 1965, is a public university that is part of the state university system. There are 5 undergraduate schools and 5 graduate schools. In addition to regional accreditation, UNF has baccalaureate program accreditation with AACSB, ABET, ACCE, NASM, NCATE, and NLN. The library contains 864,706 volumes, 1.5 million microform items, and 35,263 audio/video tapes/CDs/DVDs, and subscribes to 37,919 periodicals including electronic. Computerized library services include interlibrary loans, database searching, Internet access, and Wi-Fi capability. Special learning facilities include an art gallery, radio station, TV station, a theater, auditorium, nature preserve, Museum of Science and History (MOSH). The 1300-acre campus is in an urban area 12 miles southeast of downtown Jacksonville. Including any residence halls, there are 84 buildings.

Student Life: 95% of undergraduates are from Florida. Others are from 43 states, 113 foreign countries, and Canada. 70% are White. 99% claim no religious affiliation. The average age of freshmen is 18; all undergraduates, 23. 18% do not continue beyond their first year; 48% remain to graduate.

Housing: 2900 students can be accommodated in college housing, which includes coed dorms and on-campus apartments. In addition, there are honors houses. On-campus housing is guaranteed for the freshman year only, is available on a first-come, and first-served basis. 79% of students commute. All students may keep cars.

Activities: 3% of men belong to 11 national fraternities; 5% of women belong to 9 national sororities. There are 196 groups on campus, including art, band, cheerleading, choir, chorale, chorus, computers, dance, drama, drum and bugle corps, environmental, ethnic, film, gay, honors, international, jazz band, literary magazine, newspaper, photography, political, professional, radio and TV, religious, social, social service, and student government. Popular campus events include Clubfest, Spring Bash and Earth Music Fest.

Sports: There are 7 intercollegiate sports for men and 10 for women, and 11 intramural sports for men and 11 for women. Facilities include a baseball stadium, softball, soccer, and multipurpose fields, a 9800-seat soccer stadium, an aquatic center, a fitness center, jogging trails, racquetball, basketball, volleyball, and tennis courts, a 6000-seat multipurpose arena, and lakes for canoeing and fishing. New Student Wellness Complex contains 34' climbing wall, 200m indoor 3-lane rubbger track, 3 dedicated group fitness rooms, and wheelchair-accessible equipmet including Cybex Total Access weight machines.

Disabled Students: Facilities include wheelchair ramps, elevators, special parking, specially equipped restrooms, special class scheduling, lowered drinking fountains, lowered telephones, special housing. The Disability Resource Center provides specialized assistance and equipment, including priority registration, interpreters for the hearing impaired, and proctored testing.

Services: Counseling and information services are available, as is tutoring in some subjects, accounting, American sign language, biology, chemistry, comping science, economics, English for academic purposes, history, mathematics, physics, psychology, world languages and writing.

Campus Safety and Security: Measures include 24-hour foot and vehicle patrol, emergency notification system, self-defense education, and security escort services. There are shuttle buses, emergency telephones, lighted pathways/sidewalks, and university police presentations at new student orientation.

Programs of Study: UNF confers B.A., B.S., B.A.E., B.B.A., B.F.A., B.H.A., B.M., B.M.E., B.S.A.T., B.S.E.E., B.S.H. and B.S.N. degrees. Associate, master's, and doctoral degrees are also awarded. Bachelor's degrees are awarded in BIOLOGICAL SCIENCE (biology/biological science and nutrition), BUSINESS (accounting, banking and finance, business administration and management, business economics, finance, global/general management, international business management, marketing management, sports management, and transportation management), COMMUNICATIONS AND THE ARTS (American Sign Language, art, communications, English, English literature, fine arts, jazz, music, music performance, and Spanish), COMPUTER AND PHYSICAL SCIENCE (applied mathematics, chemistry, computer science, information sciences and systems, mathematics, physics, and statistics), EDUCATION (art education, athletic training, elementary education, English education, mathematics education, middle school education, music education, physical education, science education, secondary education, social studies education, and special education), ENGINEERING AND ENVIRONMENTAL DESIGN (civil engineering, construction engineering, construction management, electrical/electronics engineering, and mechanical engineering), HEALTH PROFESSIONS (health care administration, health science, mental health/human services, nursing, and physical therapy), SOCIAL SCIENCE (anthropology, counseling/psychology, criminal justice, dietetics, economics, ethnic studies, French studies, history, interdisciplinary studies, philosophy, political science/government, psychology, public administration, religion, and sociology). Nursing, fine arts, and elementary education are the strongest academically. Psychology, communication and business have the largest enrollments.

Required: Students are required to take general education distribution requirements, including 9 hours of composition and humanities and 6 each of natural science, math, and social science. There is a core curriculum in Western civilization and cultural diversity. A minimum 2.0 GPA and 120 credit hours, with a minimum of 60 hours in the major, are needed for graduation.

Special: There are cooperative programs and internships in most majors and work-study programs with several Jacksonville businesses. Study abroad, an accelerated degree program in nursing, B.A.-B.S. degrees in math, statistics, and psychology, dual majors, and student-designed majors also are available. Credit is given for military experience. There are 6 national honor societies, a freshman honors program, and 14 departmental honors programs.

Faculty/Classroom: 54% of faculty are male; 46% are female. 91% teach undergraduates, 58% do research, and 50% do both. Graduate students teach 19% of introductory courses. The average class size in an introductory lecture is 36; in a laboratory is 20; and in a regular course is 34.

Admissions: 44% of the 2013-2014 applicants were accepted. The SAT scores for the 2013-2014 freshman class were: Critical Reading--1% below 500, 40% between 500 and 599, 52% between 600 and 699, and 7% between 700 and 800; Math--1% below 500, 43% between 500 and 599, 52% between 600 and 699, and 4% between 700 and 800; Writing--11% below 500, 53% between 500 and 599, 33% between 600 and 699, and 3% between 700 and 800. The ACT scores were 10% between 21 and 23, 56% between 24 and 26, 16% between 27 and 28, and 18% above 28. 49% of the current freshmen were in the top fifth of their class; 79% were in the top two fifths.

Requirements: The SAT or ACT is required. The Office of Admissions will recalculate a grade point average (GPA) based on the following eighteen (18) academic units in college preparatory courses. Additional weight is given to grades of "C" or higher earned in honors, Dual Enrollment, Advanced Placement, IB, or AICE courses. While students may not have completed all the required courses at the time an application is submitted, they are required to complete them prior to high school graduation and entrance into UNF. The State of Florida has implemented new minimum admission standards for freshmen applicants to all state universities. In order to be considered, students must have a minimum 2.5 recalculated GPA, on a 4.0 scale, and meet minimum test score requirements (460 SAT Critical Reading, 460 SAT Math, 440 SAT Writing; or 19 ACT Reading, 19 ACT Math, 18 ACT English/Writing). Please keep in mind that these standards only outline potential eligibility for admission to a state university. UNF's admission criteria depend on the applicant pool and will be higher than these minimums. A GPA of 2.5 is required. AP and CLEP credits are accepted. Important factors in the admissions decision are advanced placement or honors courses, recommendations by school officials, and evidence of special talent.

Procedure: Freshmen are admitted to all sessions. Entrance exams should be taken during the spring of the junior year or the fall of the senior year. There is a deferred admissions plan. Applications should be filed by May 10 for fall entry; October 18 for spring entry; and Feb 8 for summer entry, along with a $30 fee. Notification is sent on a rolling basis. Applications are accepted online.

Transfer: 3108 transfer students enrolled in 2012-2013. Upper-level transfer students are defined as those with at least 60 transferable credit hours or an Associate of Arts degree from a Florida public or postsecondary institution. Admission requirements will vary by major, term, and space-availability. In order to be considered, applicants must meet or exceed a cumulative college GPA of 2.0 or higher, including a "C" or higher average and "good standing" status at the most recent college attended. Listed below are the minimum required materials for upper-level students to submit in order to be evaluated for a decision. Additional requirements will exist for students applying to limited access/selective admission programs or as international students. 30 of 120 credits required for the bachelor's degree must be completed at UNF.

Visiting: There are regularly scheduled orientations for prospective students, consisting of open houses which include tours of the campus and housing, a general information session, financial aid sessions, academic advising, and personal interviews by request. There are guides for informal visits. To schedule a visit, contact the Admissions Office.

Financial Aid: In 2013-2014, 92% of all full-time freshmen and 80% of continuing full-time students received some form of financial aid. 47% of all full-time freshmen and 53% of continuing full-time students received need-based aid. The average freshman award was $8,514. Need-based scholarships or need-based grants averaged $6,613 ($16,372 maximum); need-based self-help aid (loans and jobs) averaged $3,071 ($7,625 maximum); non-need-based athletic scholarships averaged $7,381 ($21,000 maximum); and other non-need-based awards and non-need-based scholarships averaged $5,059 ($32,412 maximum). 6% of undergraduate students work part-time. The average financial indebtedness of the 2013 graduate was $15,712. The FAFSA is required. The deadline for filing freshman financial aid applications for fall entry is April 1.

International Students: There are 242 international students enrolled. The school actively recruits these students. They must take the TOEFL. They must also take the SAT or ACT.

Computers: All students may access the system. The general purpose labs are open more than 100 hours per week. There are no time limits and no fees.

Graduates: From July 1, 2012 to June 30, 2013, 3113 bachelor's degrees were awarded. The most popular majors were psychology (10%), communications (9%), and business administration and management (6%). 281 companies recruited on campus in 2012-2013. In an average class, 1% graduate in 3 years or less, 19% graduate in 4 years or less, 40% graduate in 5 years or less, and 47% graduate in 6 years or less.

Admissions Contact: Chad Learch, Director of Admissions. E-Mail: *osprey@unf.edu* Web: *www.unf.edu*

UNIVERSITY OF SOUTH FLORIDA D-4

Tampa, FL 33620 **(813) 974-3350; (813) 974-9689**

Full-time: 10100 men, 14575 women	**Faculty:** n/av; I, --$
Part-time: 4390 men, 5920 women	**Ph.D.s:** 90%
Graduate: 3850 men, 6400 women	**Student/Faculty:** n/av
Year: semesters, summer session	**Tuition:** $4500 ($17,500)
Application Deadline: open	**Room & Board:** $9500
Freshman Class: n/av	
SAT or ACT: required	

COMPETITIVE

The University of South Florida, founded in 1956, is a comprehensive public institution and part of the Florida Division of Colleges and Universities, offering programs in liberal and fine arts, business, engineering, health science, and education. USF also maintains campuses at Lakeland, Sarasota, and St. Petersburg. The figures in the above capsule and in this profile are approximate. There are 6 undergraduate schools and 11 graduate schools. In addition to regional accreditation, USF has baccalaureate program accreditation with AACSB, ABET, ACEJMC, ASLA, CSAB, CSWE, NAAB, NASAD, NASM, NCATE, and NLN. The 5 libraries contain 2.3 million volumes, 4.4 million microform items, and 55,762 audio/video tapes/CDs/DVDs, and subscribe to 32,423 periodicals including electronic. Computerized library services include interlibrary loans, database searching, and Internet access. Special learning facilities include a learning resource center, art gallery, radio station, TV station, mock broadcasting studio, anthropology museum, and botanical gardens. The 1941-acre campus is in an urban area 10 miles northeast of downtown Tampa. Including any residence halls, there are 434 buildings.

Student Life: 96% of undergraduates are from Florida. Others are from 50 states, 132 foreign countries, and Canada. 91% are from public schools. 65% are white; 13% African American; 13% Hispanic. The average age of freshmen is 19; all undergraduates, 22. 18% do not continue beyond their first year; 47% remain to graduate.

Housing: 4326 students can be accommodated in college housing, which includes single-sex and coed dorms, on-campus apartments, and married student housing. In addition, there are honors houses, special-interest houses, fraternity houses, sorority houses, graduate students only, medical students, and an international hall. On-campus housing is available on a first-come and first-served basis. 87% of students commute. All students may keep cars.

Activities: 7% of men belong to 19 national fraternities; 6% of women belong to 11 national sororities. There are 200 groups on campus, including art, band, cheerleading, chess, choir, chorale, chorus, computers, dance, drama, drill team, ethnic, film, gay, honors, international, jazz band, literary magazine, marching band, musical theater, newspaper, opera, orchestra, pep band, photography, political, professional, radio and TV, religious, social, social service, student government, and symphony. Popular campus events include minority events, international events, and the University Lecture Series.

Sports: There are 9 intercollegiate sports for men and 9 for women, and 20 intramural sports for men and 19 for women. Facilities include a 10,000-seat multipurpose arena, 4 pools, tennis and indoor racquetball courts, a track, a jogging course, an indoor recreation center with weight training and aerobics rooms, a soccer stadium, a softball complex, a baseball stadium, and an 18-hole golf course.

Disabled Students: All of the campus is accessible. Facilities include wheelchair ramps, elevators, special parking, specially equipped restrooms, special class scheduling, lowered drinking fountains, and lowered telephones.

Services: Counseling and information services are available, as is tutoring in most subjects. There is a reader service for the blind.

Campus Safety and Security: Measures include 24-hour foot and vehicle patrol, self-defense education, and security escort services. There are shuttle buses, emergency telephones, lighted pathways/sidewalks, and university police.

Programs of Study: USF confers B.A., B.S., B.F.A., B.I.S., B.M., and B.S.W. degrees. Associate, master's, and doctoral degrees are also awarded. Bachelor's degrees are awarded in BIOLOGICAL SCIENCE (biology/biological science and microbiology), BUSINESS (accounting, banking and finance, business administration and management, business economics, management information systems, management science, and marketing/retailing/merchandising), COMMUNICATIONS AND THE ARTS (classics, communications, dance, dramatic arts, English literature, French, German, Italian, music, Russian, Spanish, and speech/debate/rhetoric), COMPUTER AND PHYSICAL SCIENCE (chemistry, geology, mathematics, physical sciences, and physics), EDUCATION (art education, business education, education, education of the emotionally handicapped, education of the mentally handicapped, elementary education, English education, foreign languages education, mathematics education, music education, physical education, science education, social studies education, special education, and specific learning disabilities), ENGINEERING AND ENVIRONMENTAL DESIGN (chemical engineering, civil engineering, computer engineering, electrical/electronics engineering, engineering, environmental science, industrial engineering, and mechanical engineering), HEALTH PROFESSIONS (medical technology and nursing), SOCIAL SCIENCE (African American studies, American studies, anthropology, criminology, economics, geography, gerontology, history, humanities, international relations, liberal arts/general studies, philosophy, political science/government, psychology, religion, social science, social work, and sociology). Education, business, and arts and sciences are the strongest academically. Business and education have the largest enrollments.

Required: To graduate, all students are required to complete at least 120 credit hours, including 36 distributed among English, math, science, social science, historical perspectives, fine arts, and humanities and 9 of exit requirements in major works/major issues and literature/writing. The number of hours required for each major varies. Students must maintain a minimum GPA of 2.0.

Special: USF offers co-op programs in business and engineering, study abroad, cross-registration, work-study programs, accelerated degree programs in public health and medicine, internships, a Washington semester, dual and student-designed majors, a liberal arts degree, nondegree study, and pass/fail options for some courses. There are 21 national honor societies, a freshman honors program, and 18 departmental honors programs.

Faculty/Classroom: 57% of faculty are male; 43% are female. 48% teach undergraduates, and 16% do research. No introductory courses are taught by graduate students. The average class size in an introductory lecture is 39; in a laboratory is 21; and in a regular course is 26.

Admissions: There were 12 National Merit finalists.

Requirements: The SAT or ACT is required. Candidates for admission should have completed 4 units each of English and academic electives, 3 each of math, science, and social studies, and 2 of a foreign language. The GED is accepted. Applicants who do not meet minimum requirements but have important attributes, special talents, or unique circumstances are considered for admission by an academic faculty committee. A GPA of 2.0 is required. AP and CLEP credits are accepted. Important factors in the admissions decision are advanced placement or honors courses, evidence of special talent, and recommendations by school officials.

Procedure: Freshmen are admitted to all sessions. Entrance exams should be taken at the end of the junior year or the beginning of the senior year. There is a rolling admissions plan. Check with the school for current application deadlines. The fall application fee was $30. Notification is sent on a rolling basis. Applications are accepted online.

Transfer: Applicants must have a cumulative college GPA of 2.0 and be in good standing at their last institution. 30 of 120 credits required for the bachelor's degree must be completed at USF.

Visiting: There are regularly scheduled orientations for prospective students, including a 2-day program. There are guides for informal visits and visitors may sit in on classes. To schedule a visit, contact the Admissions Office/New Student Orientation.

Financial Aid: The FAFSA is required. Check with the school for current application deadlines.

International Students: The school actively recruits these students. They must take the TOEFL. They must also take the SAT or ACT.

Computers: Wireless access is available. All students may access the system. There are no time limits and no fees.

Admissions Contact: Director of Admissions. A campus DVD is available. E-Mail: *dhollema@admin.usf.edu* Web: *www.usf.edu*

UNIVERSITY OF SOUTH FLORIDA/ST. PETERSBURG D-4

St. Petersburg, FL 33701 **727-873-4142; 727-873-4525**

Full-time: 1134 men, 1654 women	**Faculty:** 107; I, --$
Part-time: 462 men, 756 women	**Ph.D.s:** n/av
Graduate: 155 men, 303 women	**Student/Faculty:** 24 to 1
Year: semesters, summer session	**Tuition:** $5199 ($14,387)
Application Deadline: March 15	**Room & Board:** $7570

Freshman Class: 1996 applied, 914 accepted, 474 enrolled

SAT CR/M/W: 530/530/510 **ACT:** 23 **VERY COMPETITIVE**

USF St. Petersburg offers master's level and undergraduate programs in the arts and sciences, business and education within a student-centered environment. The figures in the above capsule and in this profile are approximate. The first regional institution in the USF System with separate accreditation, USFSP distinguishes itself by its urban waterfront location in downtown St. Petersburg and its focus on undergraduate research, civic engagement and small classes. Most faculty members hold the highest degree in their field and teach courses from the freshman to graduate level. USFSP retains its separate identity and mission while contributing to and benefiting from the associations, cooperation, and shared resources of a premier national research university. There are 3 undergraduate schools and one graduate school. In addition to regional accreditation, USF St. Petersburg has baccalaureate program accreditation with AACSB, ACEJMC, and NCATE. The library contains 236,793 volumes, 899,329 microform items, and 10,329 audio/video tapes/CDs/DVDs, and subscribes to 52,812 periodicals including electronic. Computerized library services include interlibrary loans, database searching, Internet access, and Wi-Fi capability. The waterfront campus is located on Bayboro Harbor in downtown St. Petersburg.

Student Life: 97% of undergraduates are from Florida. 74% are White; 13% Hispanic.

Housing: 600 students can be accommodated in college housing, which includes coed dorms. On-campus housing is guaranteed for the freshman year only. Priority is given to out-of-town students. 85% of students commute. Alcohol is not permitted. All students may keep cars.

Activities: There are no fraternities or sororities. There are 100 groups on campus, including debate, environmental, ethnic, gay, newspaper, professional, religious, social service, and student government. Popular campus events include Welcome Week, Homecoming Week, Spring Fling and Leadership Retreats.

Sports: There are 5 intramural sports for men and 5 for women. Facilities include Recreation center, aquatics center and waterfront activities; sailing, kayaking and paddle boarding.

Disabled Students: Facilities include wheelchair ramps, elevators, special parking, specially equipped restrooms, special class scheduling, lowered drinking fountains, lowered telephones, and special housing.

Services: Counseling and information services are available, as is tutoring in some subjects. There is remedial math and writing.

Campus Safety and Security: Measures include 24-hour foot and vehicle patrol, emergency notification system, and security escort services. There are emergency telephones, lighted pathways/sidewalks, and controlled access to dorms/residences.

Programs of Study: USF St. Petersburg confers B.A., B.S. and B.F.A. degrees. Master's degrees are also awarded. Bachelor's degrees are awarded in BIOLOGICAL SCIENCE (biology/biological science), BUSINESS (accounting, business administration and management, entrepreneurial studies, finance, global/general management, management science, and marketing and distribution), COMMUNICATIONS AND THE ARTS (communications, English, and graphic design), COMPUTER AND PHYSICAL SCIENCE (information sciences and systems), EDUCATION (education), ENGINEERING AND ENVIRONMENTAL DESIGN (environmental science), HEALTH PROFESSIONS (health science), SOCIAL SCIENCE (anthropology, criminology, economics, history, political science/government, psychology, and social science).

Special: There are 7 national honor societies, a freshman honors program, and 3 departmental honors programs.

Faculty/Classroom: 48% of faculty are male; 52% are female. No introductory courses are taught by graduate students. The average class size in an introductory lecture is 36 and in a laboratory is 23.

Admissions: 46% of the 2013-2014 applicants were accepted. 6% of the current freshmen were in the top fifth of their class.

Requirements: The SAT or ACT is required. The ACT Optional Writing test is also required. AP and CLEP credits are accepted.

Procedure: Freshmen are admitted fall and spring. Entrance exams should be taken Junior year in high school. There are deferred admissions and rolling admissions plans. Applications should be filed by March 15 for fall entry; November 15 for spring entry, along with a $30 fee. Applications are accepted online.

Transfer: 582 transfer students enrolled in 2012-2013. Courses taken at a regionally accredited school, minimum GPA of 2.5 (or a GPA of 2.0 if holding an AA degree).

Visiting: There are regularly scheduled orientations for prospective students. There are guides for informal visits. To schedule a visit, contact Prospective Student Outreach at (727) USF-4802.

Financial Aid: In 2013-2014, 73% of all full-time freshmen and 70% of continuing full-time students received some form of financial aid. 38% of all full-time freshmen and 43% of continuing full-time students received need-based aid. The average freshman award was $6,932. Need-based scholarships or need-based grants averaged $5,024 ; need-based self-help aid (loans and jobs) averaged $3,098; and other non-need-based awards and non-need-based scholarships averaged $2,058. The average financial indebtedness of the 2013 graduate was $23,665. The FAFSA is required. Check with the school for current application deadlines.

International Students: They must take the TOEFL.

Computers: All students may access the system. There are no time limits and no fees.

Graduates: From July 1, 2012 to June 30, 2013, 705 bachelor's degrees were awarded. The most popular majors were accounting (15%), psychology (10%), and general business (10%). In an average class, 11% graduate in 4 years or less, 26% graduate in 5 years or less, and 33% graduate in 6 years or less.

Admissions Contact: Holly Kickliter, Director, Admissions and Marketing. E-Mail: *admissions@mail.usf.edu* Web: *www.usfsp.edu/enrollment*

UNIVERSITY OF TAMPA D-4

Tampa, FL 33606 (813) 257-1808
(888) 646-2738; (813) 258-7398

Full-time: 2759 men, 3429 women	**Faculty:** 277; IIA, av$
Part-time: 151 men, 160 women	**Ph.D.s:** 87%
Graduate: 364 men, 397 women	**Student/Faculty:** n/av
Year: semesters, summer session	**Tuition:** $25,772
Application Deadline:	**Room & Board:** $9388

Freshman Class: 15345 applied, 8011 accepted, 1590 enrolled
SAT CR/M/W: 525/540/520 **ACT:** 24 **VERY COMPETITIVE**

The University of Tampa, founded in 1931, is a comprehensive, independent institution that offers degree programs in more than 100 undergraduate and preprofessional areas of study and graduate and evening programs. There are 4 undergraduate schools and one graduate school. In addition to regional accreditation, UT has baccalaureate program accreditation with AACSB, NASM, and NLN. The library contains 238,320 volumes, 68,718 microform items, and 13,938 audio/video tapes/CDs/DVDs, and subscribes to 56,657 periodicals including electronic. Computerized library services include interlibrary loans, database searching, Internet access, and Wi-Fi capability. Special learning facilities include an art gallery, radio station, TV station, a fully equipped research vessel for marine science studies, a music facility, writing and language labs, an academic center for excellence, a graphic design studio, a marine science lab, and art studios. The 105-acre campus is in an urban area in Tampa. Including any residence halls, there are 54 buildings.

Student Life: 70% of undergraduates are from out of state, mostly the Northeast. Students are from 50 states, 122 foreign countries, and Canada. 59% are White; 12% Hispanic. The average age of freshmen is 18; all undergraduates, 21. 26% do not continue beyond their first year; 57% remain to graduate.

Housing: 3747 students can be accommodated in college housing, which includes single-sex and coed dorms and on-campus apartments. a special honors floor, a nontraditional floor, a leadership floor and a substance-free floor. 59% of students live on campus; of those, 75% remain on campus on weekends. All students may keep cars.

Activities: 10% of men belong to 11 national fraternities; 21% of women belong to 10 national sororities. There are 180 groups on campus, including leadership, media and special interest., academic, art, band, cheerleading, chess, chorale, chorus, computers, dance, drama, ethnic, gay, honors, international, jazz band, literary magazine, musical theater, newspaper, orchestra, pep band, political, professional, religious, social, social service, student government, symphony, and yearbook. Popular campus events include Into the Streets (volunteer program), Greek Sing and Leadership Awards Night.

Sports: There are 8 intercollegiate sports for men and 11 for women, and 22 intramural sports for men and 22 for women. Facilities include Campus Recreation Facilities: McNiff Fitness Center; two outdoor basketball courts; two outdoor sand volleyball courts Athletic Facilities (shared with Campus Recreation): Intramural Field (1 field); The Art and Poly Pepin Stadium (1 field); Bob Martinez Athletic Center (3 courts/locker rooms/academic study lounge); softball field (1 field); Cass Gymnasium (1 court); Naimoli and Young Family Tennis Complex (6 courts); Aquatic Center (pool); Naimoli Family Athletic and Intramural Complex (1 field plus side practice field) Athletic Department (Exclusive): Bailey Baseball Field; McNeel Boathouse.

Disabled Students: All of the campus is accessible. Facilities include wheelchair ramps, elevators, special parking, specially equipped restrooms, lowered drinking fountains, lowered telephones, and special housing.

Services: Counseling and information services are available, as is tutoring in every subject. There is remedial math, reading, and writing.

Campus Safety and Security: Measures include 24-hour foot and vehicle patrol, emergency notification system, self-defense education, and security escort services. There are shuttle buses, emergency telephones, lighted pathways/sidewalks, and a full-service, and on-campus security office.

Programs of Study: UT confers B.A., B.S., B.F.A., B.L.S., B.M. and B.S.N. degrees. Associate and master's degrees are also awarded. Bachelor's degrees are awarded in BIOLOGICAL SCIENCE (biochemistry, biology/biological science, and marine science), BUSINESS (accounting, banking and finance, business administration and management, business economics, entrepreneurial studies, international business management, management information systems, marketing/retailing/merchandising, and sports management), COMMUNICATIONS AND THE ARTS (advertising, art, communications, creative writing, dramatic arts, English, film arts, graphic design, music, music performance, performing arts, and Spanish), COMPUTER AND PHYSICAL SCIENCE (chemistry, digital arts/technology, and mathematics), EDUCATION (athletic training, elementary education, music education, and secondary education), ENGINEERING AND ENVIRONMENTAL DESIGN (computer graphics and environmental science), HEALTH PROFESSIONS (exercise science, nursing, and public health), SOCIAL SCIENCE (criminology, economics, forensic studies, history, international studies, liberal arts/general studies, philosophy, political science/government, psychology, and sociology). Performing arts, mathematics and philosophy are the strongest academically. Management, communication and psychology have the largest enrollments.

Required: To graduate, students must maintain a minimum GPA of 2.0 in at least 124 credit hours, including the 2-year learning community, 11 hours each in humanities/fine arts and social science, 6 in natural science, global issues, nonWestern studies, and art/aesthetics as well as writing-intensive course work. The requirements for individual majors vary.

Special: Students may participate in internships, work-study programs on campus, study abroad in 14 countries, a Washington Center internship, and an Oxford semester program. UT also offers summer marine science courses at the Gulf Coast Research Laboratory, nondegree study, pass/fail options, dual majors, accelerated degree programs, and credit for life, military, and work experience. There are 19 national honor societies, a freshman honors program, and 16 departmental honors programs.

Faculty/Classroom: 42% of faculty are male; 58% are female. All teach undergraduates. No introductory courses are taught by graduate students. The average class size in an introductory lecture is 24; in a laboratory is 16; and in a regular course is 22.

Admissions: 52% of the 2013-2014 applicants were accepted. The SAT scores for the 2013-2014 freshman class were: Critical Reading--32% below 500, 54% between 500 and 599, 13% between 600 and 699, and 1% between 700 and 800; Math--24% below 500, 55% between 500 and 599, 19% between 600 and 699, and 1% between 700 and 800; Writing--37% below 500, 49% between 500 and 599, 13% between 600 and 699, and 2% between 700 and 800. The ACT scores were 15% below 21, 36% between 21 and 23, 30% between 24 and 26, 13% between 27 and 28, and 6% above 28. 32% of the current freshmen were in the top fifth of their class; 74% were in the top two fifths.

Requirements: The SAT or ACT is required. Candidates for admission should have completed 4 credits in English, 3 each in math, science, and social studies, and 3 in college-preparatory electives. Of the science units, 2 must be labs. The GED is accepted. A portfolio or an audition is required for specific art and music programs. A GPA of 2.5 is required. AP and CLEP credits are accepted. Important factors in the admissions decision are recommendations by school officials, evidence of special talent, and personality/intangible qualities.

Procedure: Freshmen are admitted fall, spring, and summer. Entrance exams should be taken by the end of the junior year or early in the senior year. There are deferred admissions and rolling admissions plans. Application deadlines are open. Application fee is $40. Notifications are sent October 1. 1290 applicants were on the 2013 waiting list; 56 were admitted. Applications are accepted online.

Transfer: 471 transfer students enrolled in 2012-2013. Applicants should have earned 17 or more college credits with a minimum GPA of 2.0. 31 of 124 credits required for the bachelor's degree must be completed at UT.

Visiting: There are regularly scheduled orientations for prospective students, including a campus tour and an interview with an admissions counselor, faculty, and others as requested. There are guides for informal visits, visitors may sit in on classes, and stay overnight. To schedule a visit, contact the Admissions Office.

Financial Aid: In 2013-2014, 93% of all full-time freshmen and 90% of continuing full-time students received some form of financial aid. 63% of all full-time freshmen and 59% of continuing full-time students received need-based aid. The average freshman award was $15,712. Need-based scholarships or need-based grants averaged $10,912 ($43,645 maximum); need-based self-help aid (loans and jobs) averaged $7,566 ($32,008 maximum); non-need-based athletic scholarships averaged $8,323 ($34,018 maximum); and other non-need-based awards and non-need-based scholarships averaged $6,766 ($40,739 maximum). 21% of undergraduate students work part-time. Average annual earnings from campus work are $1701. The average financial indebtedness of the 2013 graduate was $23,977. The FAFSA is required. The priority date for freshman financial aid applications for fall entry is February 1.

International Students: There are 673 international students enrolled. The school actively recruits these students. They must take the TOEFL with a minimum score of 550 on the paper-based TOEFL (PBT) or 79 on the Internet-based version (iBT).

Computers: All students may access the system. There are no time limits and no fees.

Graduates: From July 1, 2012 to June 30, 2013, 1319 bachelor's degrees were awarded. The most popular majors were business/marketing (26%), social sciences (12%), and communications (12%). 328 companies recruited on campus in 2012-2013. In an average class, 2% graduate in 3 years or less, 51% graduate in 4 years or less, 60% graduate in 5 years or less, and 61% graduate in 6 years or less. Of the 2012 graduating class, 16% were enrolled in graduate school within 6 months of graduation, and 85% were employed.

Admissions Contact: Dennis Nostrand, Vice President for Enrollment. E-Mail: *admissions@ut.edu* Web: *www.ut.edu*

UNIVERSITY OF WEST FLORIDA — A-1

Pensacola, FL 32514 — **(850) 474-2230**
(800) 263-1074; (850) 474-3360

Full-time: 3227 men, 4332 women	**Faculty:** n/av; IIA, --$
Part-time: 1164 men, 1609 women	**Ph.D.s:** n/av
Graduate: 836 men, 1483 women	**Student/Faculty:** 24 to 1
Year: semesters, summer session	**Tuition:** $6238 ($19,120)
Application Deadline: June 30	**Room & Board:** $8418

Freshman Class: 13623 applied, 8284 accepted, 1797 enrolled
SAT or ACT: required

COMPETITIVE

The University of West Florida, founded in 1967, is a public, regional comprehensive institution, that is part of the State University System of Florida. There are 3 undergraduate schools and 3 graduate schools. In addition to regional accreditation, UWF has baccalaureate program accreditation with AACSB, ABET, CSWE, NASM, NCATE, and NLN. The library contains 767,633 volumes, 1.2 million microform items, and 5,224 audio/video tapes/CDs/DVDs, and subscribes to 5,056 periodicals including electronic. Computerized library services include interlibrary loans and database searching. Special learning facilities include an art gallery, radio station, TV station, an archeology museum. The 1600-acre campus is in a suburban area 10 miles north of downtown Pensacola. Including any residence halls, there are 205 buildings.

Student Life: 95% of undergraduates are from Florida. Others are from 48 states, 70 foreign countries, and Canada. 70% are White; 12% African American. The average age of freshmen is 19; all undergraduates, 24. 16% do not continue beyond their first year; 74% remain to graduate.

Housing: 1800 students can be accommodated in college housing, which includes coed dorms and on-campus apartments. In addition, there are honors houses. On-campus housing is available on a first-come and first-served basis. 82% of students commute. All students may keep cars.

Activities: There are 158 groups on campus, including art, band, cheerleading, chess, choir, chorale, chorus, communications, computers, dance, debate, drama, environmental, ethnic, film, forensics, gay, honors, international, jazz band, literary magazine, musical theater, newspaper, orchestra, political, professional, radio and TV, religious, social, social service, student government, and symphony.

Sports: There are 6 intercollegiate sports for men and 8 for women, and 12 intramural sports for men and 12 for women. Facilities include facilities for baseball, track, tennis, racquetball, handball, softball, soccer, swimming, diving, weight lifting, and aerobics.

Disabled Students: 80% of the campus is accessible. Facilities include wheelchair ramps, elevators, special parking, specially equipped restrooms, special class scheduling, lowered drinking fountains, and special housing.

Services: Counseling and information services are available, as is tutoring in most subjects. There is remedial math. Remedial courses are offered on campus by the local community college.

Campus Safety and Security: Measures include 24-hour foot and vehicle patrol, emergency notification system, self-defense education, and security escort services. There are emergency telephones, lighted pathways/sidewalks, and a trolley system.

Programs of Study: UWF confers B.A., B.S., B.F.A., B.S.B.A., B.S.C.E., B.S.E.E. and B.S.N degrees. Associate, master's, and doctoral degrees are also awarded. Bachelor's degrees are awarded in BIOLOGICAL SCIENCE (biology/biological science and marine biology), BUSINESS (accounting, banking and finance, business administration and management, business economics, and marketing/retailing/merchandising), COMMUNICATIONS AND THE ARTS (communications, English, music, and studio art), COMPUTER AND PHYSICAL SCIENCE (chemistry, computer science, mathematics, physics, and statistics), EDUCATION (art education, early childhood education, elementary education, health education, middle school education, music education, and secondary education), ENGINEERING AND ENVIRONMENTAL DESIGN (computer engineering and electrical/electronics engineering), HEALTH PROFESSIONS (medical laboratory technology, nursing, predentistry, and premedicine), SOCIAL SCIENCE (criminal justice, history, philosophy, political science/government, prelaw, psychology, religion, social science, and social work). Accounting, communication arts and management are the strongest academically. Communication arts, psychology and business have the largest enrollments.

Required: To graduate, students must maintain a 2.0 GPA and complete 120 semester hours with a minimum of 24 hours in the major and 24 hours in upper-division courses.

Special: Internships are arranged on an individual basis through a student's major department. The college offers pass/fail options and credit for military experience. A 3-2 engineering degree is also offered. There are 5 national honor societies and a freshman honors program.

Faculty/Classroom: 53% of faculty are male; 47% are female. No introductory courses are taught by graduate students. The average class size in an introductory lecture is 34; in a laboratory is 21; and in a regular course is 26.

Admissions: 61% of the 2013-2014 applicants were accepted. The SAT scores for the 2013-2014 freshman class were: Critical Reading--44% below 500, 44% between 500 and 599, 10% between 600 and 699, and 1% between 700 and 800; Math--49% below 500, 41% between 500 and 599, 9% between 600 and 699, and 1% between 700 and 800; Writing--60% below 500, 34% between 500 and 599, 5% between 600 and 699, and 1% between 700 and 800. The ACT scores were 8% below 21, 56% between 21 and 23, 32% between 24 and 26, 2% between 27 and 28, and 2% above 28. 4 freshmen graduated first in their class.

Requirements: The SAT or ACT is required. Students must have completed 4 years of English, 3 each of math (algebra 1 and higher), science, and social studies, and 2 of a foreign language. A GPA of 2.0 is required. AP and CLEP credits are accepted. Important factors in the admissions decision are advanced placement or honors courses, evidence of special talent, and geographical diversity.

Procedure: Freshmen are admitted to all sessions. Entrance exams should be taken by the fall of the senior year. There are early admissions and rolling admissions plans. Early decision applications should be filed by June 30; regular applications, by June 30 for fall entry, along with a $30 fee. Applications are accepted online.

Transfer: Applicants must have a 2.0 GPA and a 2.0 at their last institution. Transfer students with fewer than 60 semester hours of transferable credit must meet freshman admission requirements. 30 of 120 credits required for the bachelor's degree must be completed at UWF.

Visiting: There are regularly scheduled orientations for prospective students, including 5 Open House Programs per year. There are guides for informal visits and visitors may sit in on classes. To schedule a visit, contact the Admissions Office.

Financial Aid: In 2013-2014, 23% of all full-time freshmen and 54% of

continuing full-time students received some form of financial aid. 15% of all full-time freshmen and 57% of continuing full-time students received need-based aid. The average freshman award was $2,034. Need-based scholarships or need-based grants averaged $1,735 ($4,000 maximum); need-based self-help aid (loans and jobs) averaged $2,352 ($3,500 maximum); non-need-based athletic scholarships averaged $626 ($1,500 maximum); and other non-need-based awards and non-need-based scholarships averaged $2,276 ($10,900 maximum). The FAFSA and the college's own financial statement are required. Check with the school for current application deadlines.

International Students: There are 228 international students enrolled. They must take the TOEFL with a minimum score of 525 on the paper-based TOEFL (PBT) or 69 on the Internet-based version (iBT) or take the MELAB, . They must also take the SAT or ACT, scoring 970.

Computers: All students may access the system. There are no time limits and no fees.

Graduates: From July 1, 2012 to June 30, 2013, 2082 bachelor's degrees were awarded. The most popular majors were psychology (8%), nursing (5%), and criminal justice (5%).

Admissions Contact: Katherine Condon, Interim Director of Admissions. E-Mail: *admissions@uwf.edu* Web: *www.uwf.edu*

WARNER UNIVERSITY D-4

Lake Wales, FL 33859 (863) 638-7212
(800) 309-9563; (863) 638-7290

Full-time: 340 men, 450 women	**Faculty:** 52
Part-time: 65 men, 235 women	**Ph.D.s:** 54%
Graduate: 40 men, 20 women	**Student/Faculty:** 15 to 1
Year: semesters, summer session	**Tuition:** $12,000
Application Deadline: open	**Room & Board:** $6000
Freshman Class: n/av	
SAT or ACT: required	

COMPETITIVE

Warner University is a Christian college in the liberal arts tradition committed to the search for truth in the context of Christian faith and academic excellence. There are 2 undergraduate schools and 1 graduate school. The library contains 74,000 volumes, 7,267 microform items, and 15,200 audio/video tapes/CDs/DVDs, and subscribes to 178 periodicals including electronic. Computerized library services include interlibrary loans, database searching, and Internet access. Special learning facilities include a learning resource center. The 380-acre campus is in a rural area 5 miles south of Lake Wales. Including any residence halls, there are 20 buildings.

Student Life: 88% of undergraduates are from Florida. Others are from 26 states, 18 foreign countries, and Canada. 68% are white; 17% African American. 61% are Protestant; 29% claim no religious affiliation. The average age of freshmen is 19; all undergraduates, 22. 62% do not continue beyond their first year; 50% remain to graduate.

Housing: 235 students can be accommodated in college housing, which includes single-sex dorms and off-campus apartments. On-campus housing is guaranteed for all 4 years. 58% of students commute. Alcohol is not permitted. All students may keep cars.

Activities: There are no fraternities or sororities. There are 14 groups on campus, including band, cheerleading, choir, chorale, chorus, computers, honors, newspaper, pep band, photography, religious, social, social service, and student government. Popular campus events include Christmas banquet, Barn Party, and Spring banquet.

Sports: There are 7 intercollegiate sports for men and 8 for women, and 4 intramural sports for men and 3 for women. Facilities include the Turner Athletic Center.

Disabled Students: 90% of the campus is accessible. Facilities include wheelchair ramps, special parking, specially equipped restrooms, lowered drinking fountains, and lowered telephones.

Services: Counseling and information services are available, as is tutoring in most subjects. There is remedial math, reading, and writing.

Campus Safety and Security: Measures include 24-hour foot and vehicle patrol and security escort services. There are shuttle buses, emergency telephones, lighted pathways/sidewalks, and special training in CPR/First Aid and emergency response.

Programs of Study: WU confers B.A. degrees. Associate and master's degrees are also awarded. Bachelor's degrees are awarded in BIOLOGICAL SCIENCE (biology/biological science), BUSINESS (accounting, banking and finance, business administration and management, business law, institutional management, marketing management, and sports management), COMMUNICATIONS AND THE ARTS (communications and English), COMPUTER AND PHYSICAL SCIENCE (information sciences and systems), EDUCATION (business education, education of the exceptional child, elementary education, English education, music education, physical education, science education, and social science education), HEALTH PROFESSIONS (exercise science), SOCIAL SCIENCE (biblical studies, history, pastoral studies, psychology, religious music, and social work). Biblical studies, social work, and teacher education are the strongest academically. Organizational management, church ministry, and teacher education have the largest enrollments.

Required: To graduate, students must complete 128 credit hours with a GPA of 2.0 to 2.5, depending on the major. 30 to 80 hours are required in the major. 48 hours of upper-division courses are required, as is a computer application course in the major.

Special: Internships are required in many majors, including teacher education, social work, sports management, and church ministry. An accelerated degree program is available in organizational management. HEART (Hunger Education and Resoure Training) is a missionary training program designed to equip students to serve in missions, community development work, or crosscultural assignments in developing countries. There are 5 national honor societies and 1 departmental honors program.

Faculty/Classroom: 72% of faculty are male; 28% are female. All teach undergraduates, 20% do research, and 20% do both. No introductory courses are taught by graduate students. The average class size in an introductory lecture is 28; in a laboratory is 20; and in a regular course is 18.

Admissions: There is 1 National Merit finalist. 2 freshmen graduated first in their class.

Requirements: The SAT or ACT is required. A GPA of 2.3 is required. AP and CLEP credits are accepted.

Procedure: Freshmen are admitted fall and spring. Entrance exams should be taken in the junior or senior year. There are early admissions, deferred admissions, and rolling admissions plans. Application deadlines are open. Application fee is $20. Applications are accepted online.

Transfer: 39 transfer students enrolled in 2010-2011. Applicants may transfer 24 or more hours from a regionally accredited school and must present a GPA of 2.0 or higher. 36 of 128 credits required for the bachelor's degree must be completed at WU.

Visiting: There are regularly scheduled orientations for prospective students, consisiting of Warner Weekend held in the spring. There are guides for informal visits, visitors may sit in on classes, and stay overnight. To schedule a visit, contact Admissions.

Financial Aid: In 2011-2012, 93% of all full-time freshmen and 98% of continuing full-time students received some form of financial aid. 91% of all full-time freshmen and 52% of continuing full-time students received need-based aid. 47% of undergraduate students work part-time. Average annual earnings from campus work are $1528. The FAFSA and the state aid form are required. The priority date for freshman financial aid applications for fall entry is May 10. The deadline for filing freshman financial aid applications for fall entry is October 1.

International Students: There are 31 international students enrolled. The school actively recruits these students. They must take the TOEFL. They must also take the SAT or ACT.

Computers: All students may access the system 7:30 a.m. to 10:45 p.m., Monday to Friday, and some weekend hours. There are no time limits and no fees. It is strongly recommended that all students have a personal computer. Students enrolled in online majors must have a personal computer.

Graduates: From July 1, 2010 to June 30, 2011, 368 bachelor's degrees were awarded. The most popular majors were organizational management (63%), elementary education (6%), and business administration (3%). In an average class, 25% graduate in 4 years or less, 32% graduate in 5 years or less, and 35% graduate in 6 years or less.

Admissions Contact: Jason Roe, Director of Admissions. E-Mail: *admissions@warner.edu* Web: *www.warner.edu*

WEBBER INTERNATIONAL UNIVERSITY D-4

Babson Park, FL 33827 (863) 638-2910
(800) 741-1844; (863) 638-1591

Full-time: 426 men, 202 women	**Faculty:** 20
Part-time: 16 men, 11 women	**Ph.D.s:** 60%
Graduate: 28 men, 34 women	**Student/Faculty:** 31 to 1
Year: semesters, summer session	**Tuition:** $20,418
Application Deadline: August 1	**Room & Board:** $5246
Freshman Class: 461 applied, 322 accepted, 183 enrolled	
SAT or ACT: required	

COMPETITIVE

Webber International University, founded in 1927, is a privately endowed, institution offering undergraduate and graduate degrees in business. There is one undergraduate school and one graduate school. The library contains 15,000 volumes, 200 audio/video tapes/CDs/DVDs, and subscribes to 2 periodicals including electronic. Computerized library services include interlibrary loans, database searching, Internet access, and Wi-Fi capability. The 110-acre campus is in a small town 50 miles east of Tampa and 50 miles south of Orlando. Including any residence halls, there are 12 buildings.

Student Life: 69% of undergraduates are from Florida. Others are from 24 states, 41 foreign countries, and Canada. 41% are White; 24% African American; 23% Foreign. The average age of freshmen is 19; all undergraduates, 22. 14% do not continue beyond their first year; 86% remain to graduate.

Housing: 419 students can be accommodated in college housing, which

includes single-sex and coed dorms and off-campus apartments. On-campus housing is guaranteed for the freshman year only, is available on a first-come, and first-served basis. 53% of students live on campus. All students may keep cars.

Activities: There are no fraternities or sororities. There are 11 groups on campus, including cheerleading, debate, honors, international, marching band, newspaper, pep band, photography, political, professional, religious, social, social service, and student government. Popular campus events include Webber Weekend, International Day, and End-of-the-Year Beach Party.

Sports: There are 9 intercollegiate sports for men and 9 for women, and 6 intramural sports for men and 6 for women. Facilities include a gym, 2 weight rooms, 6 tennis courts, a football practice field, a swimming pool, softball, baseball, and soccer fields, 4 beach volleyball courts, and a pier for fishing on the lake.

Disabled Students: 90% of the campus is accessible. Facilities include wheelchair ramps, special parking, specially equipped restrooms, special class scheduling, and special housing.

Services: Counseling and information services are available, as is tutoring in most subjects. There is remedial math, reading, and writing.

Campus Safety and Security: Measures include 24-hour foot and vehicle patrol, emergency notification system, self-defense education, and security escort services. There are lighted pathways/sidewalks, , and a security patrol nights and all weekend.

Programs of Study: Webber confers B.S. degrees. Associate and master's degrees are also awarded. Bachelor's degrees are awarded in BUSINESS (accounting, banking and finance, business administration and management, business communications, hospitality management services, management science, marketing management, and sports management), COMPUTER AND PHYSICAL SCIENCE (computer security and information assurance and information sciences and systems), SOCIAL SCIENCE (prelaw). General business studies is the strongest academically and has the largest enrollment.

Required: To graduate, all students must complete 120 credit hours, including courses in their major, a 36-credit general curriculum, and a 36-credit business core, 18-credit tailored electives, and 30-credit area of concentration. A GPA of 2.0 or better must be maintained. Students must pass the college's required English courses and meet its writing requirements. All students must take at least 3 computer courses.

Special: Cross-registration with Warner Southern College, South Florida Community College, and Polk State College is available. Internships, study abroad in 5 countries, work study, and B.S. degrees are offered. Any combination of majors requires an additional 30 credit hours for a total of 150 to graduate.

Faculty/Classroom: 56% of faculty are male; 44% are female. All teach undergraduates. No introductory courses are taught by graduate students. The average class size in a regular course is 21.

Admissions: 70% of the 2013-2014 applicants were accepted. The SAT scores for the 2013-2014 freshman class were: Critical Reading--68% below 500, 29% between 500 and 599, 3% between 600 and 699; Math--63% below 500, 32% between 500 and 599, 4% between 600 and 699, and 1% between 700 and 800. The ACT scores were 70% below 21, 20% between 21 and 23; 1% between 27 and 28.

Requirements: The SAT or ACT is required. Applicants should be graduates of accredited secondary schools and have completed 3 years each of English, math, and science and 2 years of social studies. An essay is also required. The GED is accepted. A GPA of 2.0 is required. AP and CLEP credits are accepted.

Procedure: Freshmen are admitted to all sessions. Entrance exams should be taken during the senior year. There are deferred admissions and rolling admissions plans. Applications should be filed by August 1 for fall entry; December 1 for spring entry; and April 1 for summer entry, along with a $35 fee. Applications are accepted online.

Transfer: Applicants must have a minimum GPA of 2.0 with 15 credit hours and leave their previous institution in good academic standing. Students with fewer than 15 credits must meet freshman requirements. 30 of 120 credits required for the bachelor's degree must be completed at Webber.

Visiting: There are regularly scheduled orientations for prospective students, including a campus tour and individual attention from admission counselors and other office representatives such as financial aid, coaches, and professors. There are guides for informal visits, visitors may sit in on classes, and stay overnight. To schedule a visit, contact the Vice President Enrollment Management.

Financial Aid: In 2013-2014, 98% of all full-time freshmen and 99% of continuing full-time students received some form of financial aid. 62% of all full-time freshmen and 60% of continuing full-time students received need-based aid. The average freshman award was $18,697. Need-based scholarships or need-based grants averaged $15,812 ($24,550 maximum); need-based self-help aid (loans and jobs) averaged $3,139 ($11,000 maximum); non-need-based athletic scholarships averaged $3,755 ($12,000 maximum); and other non-need-based awards and non-need-based scholarships averaged $12,973 ($16,000 maximum). 40% of undergraduate students work part-time. Average annual earnings from campus work are $1300. The average financial indebtedness of the 2013 graduate was $26,676. Webber is a member of CSS. The FAFSA is required. The priority date for freshman financial aid applications for fall entry is April 1. The deadline for filing freshman financial aid applications for fall entry is August 1.

International Students: There are 170 international students enrolled. The school actively recruits these students. They must take the TOEFL. we consider each application on a case by case basis.

Computers: All students may access the system. There are no time limits and no fees.

Graduates: From July 1, 2012 to June 30, 2013, 131 bachelor's degrees were awarded. The most popular majors were general business studies (73%), sport management (18%), and communications (1%). 40 companies recruited on campus in 2012-2013. In an average class, 1% graduate in 3 years or less, 33% graduate in 4 years or less, 48% graduate in 5 years or less, and 50% graduate in 6 years or less.

Admissions Contact: Jeff Bennett, Vice President Enrollment Management. E-Mail: *admissions@webber.edu* Web: *www.webber.edu*

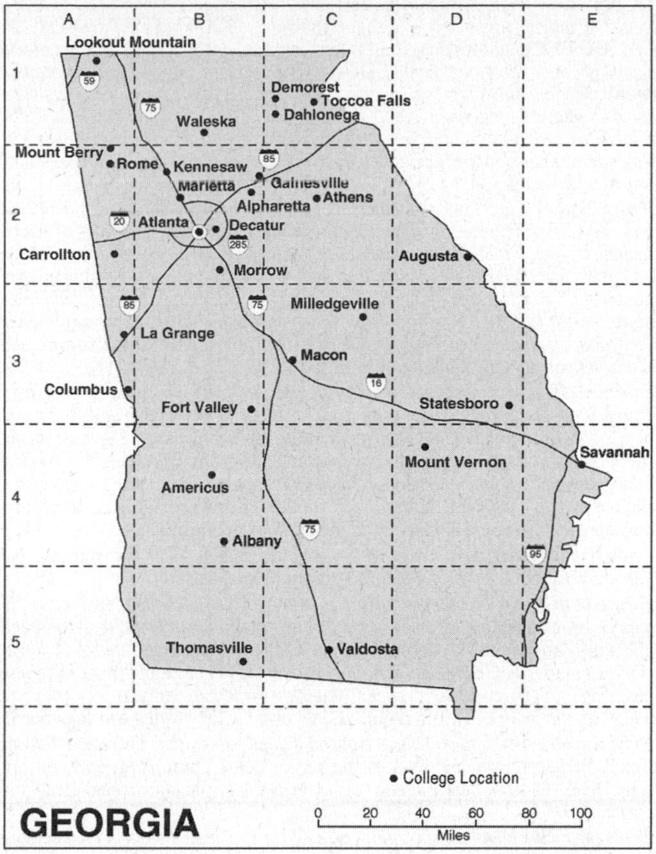

AGNES SCOTT COLLEGE B-2

Decatur, GA 30030 (404) 471-6423
(800) 868-8602; (404) 471-6414

Full-time: 8 men, 889 women **Faculty:** 70
Part-time: 2 men, 16 women **Ph.D.s:** 97%
Graduate: n/av **Student/Faculty:** 11 to 1
Year: semesters, summer session **Tuition:** $34,788
Application Deadline: March 1 **Room & Board:** $10,535
Freshman Class: 1340 applied, 896 accepted, 254 enrolled
SAT CR/M/W: 590/570/570 **ACT:** 26 **VERY COMPETITIVE+**

Agnes Scott College, founded in 1889, is an independent liberal arts college for women and is affiliated with the Presbyterian Church. There is one undergraduate school. Computerized library services include interlibrary loans, database searching, Internet access, and Wi-Fi capability. Special learning facilities include an art gallery, planetarium, TV station, an educational technology center, multimedia classrooms, and centers for writing and speaking. The 100-acre campus is in an urban area 6 miles from downtown Atlanta. Including any residence halls, there are 27 buildings.

Student Life: 63% of undergraduates are from Georgia. Others are from 37 states, and 32 foreign countries. 75% are from public schools. 33% are African American; 31% White; 12% Foreign. 38% are Protestant. The average age of freshmen is 18; all undergraduates, 20. 17% do not continue beyond their first year; 72% remain to graduate.

Housing: 795 students can be accommodated in college housing, which includes single-sex dorms and on-campus apartments. In addition, there are special-interest houses, language wings within residence halls for French and German and CHOICE housing (Choosing Healthy Options In a Community Environment). On-campus housing is guaranteed for all 4 years. 82% of students live on campus; of those, 70% remain on campus on weekends. All students may keep cars.

Activities: There are no fraternities or sororities. There are 81 groups on campus, including art, cheerleading, choir, chorale, chorus, dance, drama, environmental, ethnic, gay, honors, international, literary magazine, musical theater, newspaper, orchestra, pep band, photography, political, professional, religious, social, social service, student government, and yearbook. Popular campus events include Black Cat, Holiday Parties and Senior Investiture.

Sports: There are 6 intercollegiate sports for women, and 3 intramural sports for women. Facilities include a fitness center, a gym with a regulation basketball court, an 8-lane indoor pool, a soccer field, a tennis facility, a weight room, a track, an aerobics room, and dance studios.

Disabled Students: 90% of the campus is accessible.

Services: Counseling and information services are available, as is tutoring in some subjects, classical languages, English, math, physics, biology, psychology, chemistry, economics and foreign languages There is a reader service for the blind. Center for writing and speaking, and a resource center for math and science.

Campus Safety and Security: Measures include 24-hour foot and vehicle patrol, emergency notification system, self-defense education, and security escort services. There are emergency telephones, lighted pathways/sidewalks, controlled access to dorms/residences, reimbursement for emergency taxi service.

Programs of Study: Agnes Scott confers B.A., B.S. degrees. Bachelor's degrees are awarded in BIOLOGICAL SCIENCE (biochemistry, biology/biological science, and neurosciences), BUSINESS (business administration and management), COMMUNICATIONS AND THE ARTS (art history and appreciation, classical languages, creative writing, dance, dramatic arts, English literature, French, German, music, Spanish, and studio art), COMPUTER AND PHYSICAL SCIENCE (astrophysics, chemistry, computer science, mathematics, and physics), ENGINEERING AND ENVIRONMENTAL DESIGN (engineering), HEALTH PROFESSIONS (nursing and public health), SOCIAL SCIENCE (African studies, anthropology, classical/ancient civilization, economics, history, international relations, philosophy, political science/government, psychology, religion, sociology, and women's studies). Psychology, English literature-creative writing, and economics have the largest enrollments.

Required: Requirements for graduation include first-year seminar and courses in English composition and reading, foreign language, and phys ed, as well as courses in literature and fine arts, religious or philosophical thought, historical studies or classical civilization, natural science, math, social science, and social and cultural analysis. Students must complete 128 credit hours, including 32 to 52 in the major, with a 2.0 GPA.

Special: There is cross-registration through ARCHE (a 19-member consortium), and more than 300 credit and noncredit internships are available. There is a 3-2 engineering program with the Georgia Institute of Technology, a Computer Science dual-degree program with Emory University, a 3-2 nursing program with Emory University and the college also offers student-designed interdisciplinary majors. Pass/fail options are also available. Opportunities for study abroad include exchange programs, a Global Awareness program, and Global Connections. Also offered are a Washington semester, the PLEN Public Policy Semester, the Mills College Exchange, and work-study programs. B.A. degree requirements may be completed in 3 years. There are 14 national honor societies, including Phi Beta Kappa, and 13 departmental honors programs.

Faculty/Classroom: 37% of faculty are male; 63% are female. All teach and do research. No introductory courses are taught by graduate students. The average class size in a regular course is 21.

Admissions: 67% of the 2013-2014 applicants were accepted. The SAT scores for the 2013-2014 freshman class were: Critical Reading--17% below 500, 38% between 500 and 599, 33% between 600 and 699, and 12% between 700 and 800; Math--19% below 500, 40% between 500 and 599, 27% between 600 and 699, and 14% between 700 and 800; Writing--16% below 500, 40% between 500 and 599, 36% between 600 and 699, and 8% between 700 and 800. The ACT scores were 16% below 21, 19% between 21 and 23, 26% between 24 and 26, 16% between 27 and 28, and 23% above 28. 60% of the current freshmen were in the top fifth of their class; 83% were in the top two fifths. 3 freshmen graduated first in their class.

Requirements: Applications must include at least one of the following: SAT/ACT scores; an interview with an Agnes Scott College representative; a graded writing sample. All home-schooled students must submit SAT I or ACT scores and SAT II Subject tests. All applicants (except early admission) must graduate from an accredited secondary school or have a GED. A total of 16 academic credits is recommended, including 4 years of English, 3 of math, and 2 each of a foreign language, science, and social studies. An essay is required, and an interview is recommended. An audition is required for those seeking a music scholarship. AP credits are accepted. Important factors in the admissions decision are leadership record, recommendations by school officials, and advanced placement or honors courses.

Procedure: Freshmen are admitted fall and spring. Entrance exams should be taken late in the junior year or by January of the senior year. There are early admissions and deferred admissions plans. Early decision applications should be filed by November 15; regular applications, by March 1 for fall entry; and November 1 for spring entry, along with a $35 fee. Notification of early decision is sent December 15; regular decision, March 1. Applications are accepted online. Application fees are waived if application is completed online.

Transfer: 14 transfer students enrolled in 2012-2013. A minimum college GPA of 3.0 is required, as is an interview and a letter of recommendation from a professor. 64 of 128 credits required for the bachelor's degree must be completed at Agnes Scott.

Visiting: There are regularly scheduled orientations for prospective students, including tours, interviews, residence hall experiences, and informational sessions. There are guides for informal visits, visitors may sit in on classes, and stay overnight. To schedule a visit, contact the Admissions Office at admission@agnesscott.edu.

Financial Aid: In 2013-2014, 100% of all full-time freshmen and 99% of continuing full-time students received some form of financial aid. 73% of all full-time freshmen and 78% of continuing full-time students received need-based aid. The average freshman award was $32,641. Need-based scholarships or need-based grants averaged $27,030; need-based self-help aid (loans and jobs) averaged $4,285; and other non-need-based awards and non-need-based scholarships averaged $20,681. 90% of undergraduate students work part-time. Average annual earnings from campus work are $2000. The average financial indebtedness of the 2013 graduate was $30,139. Agnes Scott is a member of CSS. The FAFSA and the college's own financial statement, and previous year's tax return are required. The priority date for freshman financial aid applications for fall entry is February 15. The deadline for filing freshman financial aid applications for fall entry is May 1.

International Students: There are 105 international students enrolled. The school actively recruits these students. They must take the TOEFL, with a score of 600 recommended. They must also take the SAT or ACT.

Computers: All students may access the system. There are no time limits and no fees.

Graduates: From July 1, 2012 to June 30, 2013, 175 bachelor's degrees were awarded. The most popular majors were psychology (17%), economics and organizational management (7%), and English lit-creative writing (6%). 55 companies recruited on campus in 2012-2013. In an average class, 2% graduate in 3 years or less, 70% graduate in 4 years or less, 66% graduate in 5 years or less, and 72% graduate in 6 years or less. Of the 2012 graduating class, 21% were enrolled in graduate school within 6 months of graduation, and 46% were employed.

Admissions Contact: Alexa Gaeta, Director of Admissions. E-Mail: *admission@agnesscott.edu* Web: *www.agnesscott.edu*

ALBANY STATE UNIVERSITY — B-4

Albany, GA 31705-2796 — (229) 430-4646; (800) 822-RAMS; (229) 430-4105

Full-time: 855 men, 1610 women	**Faculty:** n/av
Part-time: 150 men, 410 women	**Ph.D.s:** 52%
Graduate: 115 men, 330 women	**Student/Faculty:** n/av
Year: semesters, summer session	**Tuition:** $3500 ($10,500)
Application Deadline: open	**Room & Board:** $5000
Freshman Class: n/av	
SAT or ACT: required	

COMPETITIVE

Albany State University, founded in 1903, is a state-supported institution within the University System of Georgia, offering programs in liberal arts, business, health fields, and teacher education. The figures in the above capsule and in this profile are approximate. There are 4 undergraduate schools and 1 graduate school. In addition to regional accreditation, Albany State has baccalaureate program accreditation with ACBSP, NCATE, and NLN. Computerized library services include interlibrary loans and database searching. Special learning facilities include a radio station. The 144-acre campus is in an urban area 175 miles south of Atlanta. Including any residence halls, there are 28 buildings.

Student Life: 98% of undergraduates are from Georgia. 91% are African American. The average age of all undergraduates is 24.

Housing: College-sponsored housing includes single-sex dorms. On-campus housing is available on a first-come, first-served basis, and is available on a lottery system for upperclassmen. Alcohol is not permitted. All students may keep cars.

Activities: Groups on campus include art, band, cheerleading, choir, chorale, computers, dance, debate, drama, drill team, honors, jazz band, marching band, musical theater, pep band, political, professional, religious, social, social service, student government, and yearbook. Popular campus events include Honors Day and Founders Day.

Sports: There are 5 intercollegiate sports for men and 6 for women, and 2 intramural sports for men and 1 for women. Facilities include tennis courts, baseball and softball fields, an Olympic-size pool, a recreation room, and an all-weather track.

Disabled Students: 90% of the campus is accessible.

Services: There is remedial math, reading, and writing.

Campus Safety and Security: Measures include 24-hour foot and vehicle patrol and security escort services. There are emergency telephones and lighted pathways/sidewalks.

Programs of Study: Associate and master's degrees are also awarded. Bachelor's degrees are awarded in BIOLOGICAL SCIENCE (biology/biological science), BUSINESS (accounting, marketing/retailing/merchandising, and office supervision and management), COMMUNICATIONS AND THE ARTS (art, dramatic arts, English, fine arts, French, music, Spanish, and speech/debate/rhetoric), COMPUTER AND PHYSICAL SCIENCE (chemistry, computer science, information sciences and systems, and mathematics), EDUCATION (early childhood education, health education, middle school education, music education, physical education, science education, and special education), HEALTH PROFESSIONS (allied health and nursing), SOCIAL SCIENCE (criminal justice, forensic studies, history, political science/government, psychology, social work, and sociology).

Required: To graduate, all students must complete 120 semester hours, including 30 in the major. The core curriculum includes 12 hours of social science, 10 to 11 of science/math/technology, 9 of essential composition and math skills, 6 of humanities/fine arts, 5 of leadership and global awareness, and 3 of phys ed. Most majors require a minimum GPA of 2.25. Students must take a Regents exam to assess English language skills competency, pass a comprehensive exam in their major, and/or score satisfactorily on the aptitude section of the GRE.

Special: The university offers co-op programs in all majors, 2+2 programs with Darton College, dual majors in social sciences, and 3-2 engineering degrees with the Georgia Institute of Technology. Several work-study programs and a gerontology training program are available. Albany State participates in the Georgian Intern Programs. All language majors are eligible to study abroad. There are 5 national honor societies, a freshman honors program, and 4 departmental honors programs.

Faculty/Classroom: 56% of faculty are male; 44% are female. No introductory courses are taught by graduate students.

Requirements: The SAT or ACT is required. Applicants must be graduates of an accredited secondary school and have completed 4 years each of English and math, 3 each of science and social sciences, and 2 of a foreign language. A GED is accepted; however, GED students must take and pass SAT: Subject tests in areas where college-preparatory courses are deficient. A GPA of 2.0 is required. AP and CLEP credits are accepted.

Procedure: Freshmen are admitted to all sessions. Entrance exams should be taken by December of the senior year. There is an early admissions plan. Check with the school for current application deadlines, and application fees.

Transfer: Students must provide official transcripts of all previous college work. Students with fewer than 30 transferable semester hours must meet freshman requirements. 30 of 120 credits required for the bachelor's degree must be completed at Albany State.

Visiting: There are regularly scheduled orientations for prospective students, consisting of summer and fall orientations and planned campus visitations. There are guides for informal visits and visitors may sit in on classes. To schedule a visit, contact the Office of Student Affairs.

Financial Aid: The FAFSA is required. Check with the school for current application deadlines.

International Students: They must take the TOEFL. They must also take the SAT or ACT, and the college's own entrance exam.

Computers: All students may access the system. There are no time limits and no fees.

Graduates: From July 1, 2010 to June 30, 2011, 485 bachelor's degrees were awarded. The most popular majors were criminal justice (9%), sociology (7%), and allied health science (6%).

Admissions Contact: Fred Suttles, Assistant Director of Recruitment. A campus DVD is available. E-Mail: *fsuttles@asurams.edu* Web: *www.albany.edu*

AMERICAN INTERCONTINENTAL UNIVERSITY — B-2

Atlanta, GA 30326 — (404) 965-5721; (800) 999-4248; (404) 965-5701

Full-time: 290 men, 720 women	**Faculty:** n/av
Part-time: n/av	**Ph.D.s:** 99%
Graduate: n/av	**Student/Faculty:** n/av
Year: trimesters, summer session	**Tuition:** $14,000
Application Deadline: open	**Room & Board:** n/av
Freshman Class: n/av	

NONCOMPETITIVE

American InterContinental University, founded in 1977, is a private institution offering undergraduate programs in interior design, visual communication, fashion design, fashion marketing, business, video production, and information technology. The figures in the above capsule and in this profile are approximate. In addition to regional accreditation, AIU has baccalaureate program accreditation with FIDER. Computerized library services include interlibrary loans and database searching. Special learning facilities include a learning resource center and art gallery. The 1-acre campus is in an urban area in north Atlanta. Including any residence halls, there is 1 building.

Student Life: 62% of undergraduates are from out of state, mostly the

South. Students are from 40 states, 54 foreign countries, and Canada. 45% are white; 25% African American; 25% foreign nationals. The average age of freshmen is 19; all undergraduates, 24.

Housing: There are no residence halls. All students commute.

Activities: There are no fraternities or sororities. There are 6 groups on campus, including newspaper, professional, social, and student government. Popular campus events include International Day, Career Days, and Fashion Association Bazaar.

Sports: There is no sports program at AIU.

Disabled Students: All of the campus is accessible.

Services: There is remedial math, reading, and writing.

Campus Safety and Security: Measures include 24-hour foot and vehicle patrol and security escort services. There are emergency telephones and lighted pathways/sidewalks.

Programs of Study: AIU confers B.B.A. and B.F.A. degrees. Associate degrees are also awarded. Bachelor's degrees are awarded in BUSINESS (business administration and management and fashion merchandising), COMMUNICATIONS AND THE ARTS (video), COMPUTER AND PHYSICAL SCIENCE (information sciences and systems), ENGINEERING AND ENVIRONMENTAL DESIGN (commercial art and interior design), SOCIAL SCIENCE (fashion design and technology). Interior design and visual communication are the strongest academically and have the largest enrollments.

Required: Requirements for individual programs of study, all students must complete 25 credit hours each in humanities and social sciences and 5 credit hours in math. Students may substitute 10 hours of a foreign language for 10 hours of social science. 190 quarter credit hours are required to graduate, with 140 in the major and a minimum GPA of 2.0.

Special: Students may earn up to 20 credit hours in internships. Study abroad in London and Dubai is offered. All majors offer accelerated degree opportunities. A dual major in fashion marketing and design is available. There is a freshman honors program.

Faculty/Classroom: 39% of faculty are male; 61% are female. All teach undergraduates. No introductory courses are taught by graduate students. The average class size in an introductory lecture is 25; in a laboratory is 16; and in a regular course is 18.

Requirements: Applicants should be graduates of a secondary school and should submit 2 personal references. The GED is accepted. A GPA of 2.0 is required. AP and CLEP credits are accepted. Important factors in the admissions decision are personality/intangible qualities, leadership record, and evidence of special talent.

Procedure: Freshmen are admitted to all sessions. There is an early admissions plan. Application deadlines are open. Check with the school for current application fee.

Transfer: Transfer students must have a minimum 2.0. GPA. 2 personal references must be submitted. 60 of 190 credits required for the bachelor's degree must be completed at AIU.

Visiting: There are regularly scheduled orientations for prospective students. There are guides for informal visits and visitors may sit in on classes. To schedule a visit, contact Admissions.

Financial Aid: AIU is a member of CSS. The CSS/Profile, FAFSA, and the college's own financial statement are required. Check with the school for current application deadlines.

International Students: The school actively recruits these students. They must take the TOEFL and the college's own test.

Computers: All students may access the system. There are no time limits and no fees.

Admissions Contact: Tina Rowe, Director of Admissions. E-Mail: *trowe@aiuniv.edu* Web: *www.aiuniv.edu*

ARMSTRONG ATLANTIC STATE UNIVERSITY — E-4

Savannah, GA 31419 — **912-344-2503**
(800) 633-2349; (912) 344-3417

Full-time: 1570 men, 3129 women	**Faculty:** 237
Part-time: 563 men, 1115 women	**Ph.D.s:** n/av
Graduate: 159 men, 565 women	**Student/Faculty:** 20 to 1
Year: semesters, summer session	**Tuition:** $6010 ($18,212)
Application Deadline: July 15	**Room & Board:** $10,266
Freshman Class: 2719 applied, 1944 accepted, 1016 enrolled	
SAT CR/M/W: 500/490/480 — **ACT:** 21	**COMPETITIVE**

Armstrong Atlantic State University is "teaching-centered and student-focused, providing diverse learning experiences and professional programs grounded in the liberal arts." Armstrong is governed by the Board of Regents of the University System of Georgia. Recognized as a state university, Armstrong offers more than 100 academic programs and majors in the College of Education, College of Health Professions, College of Liberal Arts, College of Science and Technology, and Graduate Studies. The academic community includes more than 7,100 students from nearly every state and 70 different countries, and more than 580 faculty and staff members. The university grants more than 60 academic credentials including undergraduate and graduate certificates, as well as associate, bachelor, and master's degrees. Armstrong offered its first Doctor of Physical Therapy degree in May 2010. Armstrong Atlantic State University has been accredited as a senior institution by the Southern Association of Colleges and Schools since January 1, 1968, and was most recently reaccredited in December 2002. There are 4 undergraduate schools and 4 graduate schools. In addition to regional accreditation, Armstrong has baccalaureate program accreditation with ABET, NASM, and NCATE. Computerized library services include interlibrary loans, database searching, Internet access, and Wi-Fi capability. Special learning facilities include an art gallery. The 267-acre campus is in a suburban area 250 miles from Atlanta and 150 miles from Jacksonville, FL. Including any residence halls, there are 27 buildings.

Student Life: 92% of undergraduates are from Georgia. Others are from 44 states, 70 foreign countries, and Canada. 61% are White; 24% African American. The average age of freshmen is 19; all undergraduates, 24. 33% do not continue beyond their first year; 31% remain to graduate.

Housing: 1411 students can be accommodated in college housing, which includes coed dorms and on-campus apartments. On-campus housing is guaranteed for the freshman year only, is available on a first-come, first-served basis, and is available on a lottery system for upperclassmen. 81% of students commute. Alcohol is not permitted. All students may keep cars.

Activities: There are 80 groups on campus, including band, cheerleading, choir, chorus, computers, dance, debate, drama, ethnic, gay, honors, international, jazz band, literary magazine, musical theater, newspaper, political, professional, religious, social, social service, and student government. Popular campus events include Celebrate Armstrong, International Week and HOLA (Hispanic Outreach and Leadership), Treasure Savannah.

Sports: There are 5 intercollegiate sports for men and 6 for women, and 29 intramural sports for men and 29 for women. Facilities include Outdoor soccer, softball and baseball fields. The ARC houses the volleyball program where our volleyball team practices and competes, the facility seats approximately 800 people. The Alumni Arena has a full court basketball court where both the men's and women's teams practice and compete. Alumni Arena seats approximately 3,500. Student Recreation Center: 38,000 square feet. 2 Basketball courts, 1 multipurpose room, 1 weight room area, 2 locker rooms. 1 Outdoor Field space: 4 acre lighted area, can hold 3 flag football fields or 2 softball fields.

Services: Counseling and information services are available, as is tutoring in most subjects. There is a reader service for the blind, and remedial math, reading, and writing.

Campus Safety and Security: Measures include 24-hour foot and vehicle patrol, emergency notification system, self-defense education, and security escort services. There are emergency telephones, lighted pathways/sidewalks, and controlled access to dorms/residences.

Programs of Study: Armstrong confers B.A., B.S., B.F.A., B.H.S., B.I.T., B.L.S., B.M.E., B.S.Ed., B.S.I.T., B.S.M.L.S., B.S.N., B.S.N.C., B.S.P. and B.S.R.S. degrees. Associate, master's, and doctoral degrees are also awarded. Bachelor's degrees are awarded in BIOLOGICAL SCIENCE (biology/biological science), COMMUNICATIONS AND THE ARTS (art, dramatic arts, English, music, Spanish, and visual and performing arts), COMPUTER AND PHYSICAL SCIENCE (applied physics, chemistry, computer science, information sciences and systems, and mathematics), EDUCATION (art education, elementary education, middle school education, music education, physical education, secondary education, social science education, and special education), HEALTH PROFESSIONS (health science, medical technology, nursing, physical therapy, radiological science, respiratory therapy, and speech pathology/audiology), SOCIAL SCIENCE (criminal justice, economics, history, liberal arts/general studies, political science/government, and psychology). Biology, nursing and health sciences have the largest enrollments.

Required: The core curriculum consists of 60 hours in humanities, math, natural sciences, and social sciences and 3 in phys ed. A minimum GPA of 2.0 overall and a grade of C or better in each major course is required. Each student must complete 123 hours, with 29 hours in the major, and must take a comprehensive exam.

Special: There are 11 national honor societies and a freshman honors program.

Faculty/Classroom: 41% of faculty are male; 59% are female. 94% teach undergraduates. No introductory courses are taught by graduate students. The average class size in an introductory lecture is 24; in a laboratory is 20; and in a regular course is 20.

Admissions: 71% of the 2013-2014 applicants were accepted. The SAT scores for the 2013-2014 freshman class were: Critical Reading--45% below 500, 44% between 500 and 599, 9% between 600 and 699, and 1% between 700 and 800; Math--53% below 500, 39% between 500 and 599, 9% between 600 and 699; Writing--57% below 500, 36% between 500 and 599, 7% between 600 and 699. The ACT scores were 49% below 21, 32% between 21 and 23, 13% between 24 and 26, 5% between 27 and 28, and 2% above 28.

Requirements: The SAT or ACT is required. Applicants should graduate from an accredited secondary school. A GED may be accepted. College preparatory work should include 4 units of English and science, 3 units of math, and social studies, and 2 of foreign language. Art students must submit a portfolio. A GPA of 2.5 is required. AP and CLEP credits are accepted.

Procedure: Freshmen are admitted to all sessions. There are deferred admissions and rolling admissions plans. Applications should be filed by July 15 for fall entry; December 15 for spring entry; and May 1 for summer entry, along with a $25 fee. Applications are accepted online.

Transfer: 619 transfer students enrolled in 2012-2013. Transfer applicants must submit all transcripts and must be in good standing at the last college attended. 30 of 123 credits required for the bachelor's degree must be completed at Armstrong.

Visiting: There are regularly scheduled orientations for prospective students, including a tour of the campus and departments. There are guides for informal visits. To schedule a visit, contact Campus Tours at (912) 344-2503.

Financial Aid: The FAFSA is required. The priority date for freshman financial aid applications for fall entry is March 15. The deadline for filing freshman financial aid applications for fall entry is April 20.

International Students: There are 191 international students enrolled. They must take the TOEFL with a minimum score of 523 on the paper-based TOEFL (PBT) or 70 on the Internet-based version (iBT). They must also take the SAT or ACT.

Computers: All students may access the system. There are no time limits and no fees.

Graduates: From July 1, 2012 to June 30, 2013, 975 bachelor's degrees were awarded. The most popular majors were nursing (16%), liberal studies (12%), and health sciences (9%). In an average class, 11% graduate in 4 years or less, 26% graduate in 5 years or less, and 31% graduate in 6 years or less.

Admissions Contact: Linc Morris, Interim Director of Admissions. E-Mail: *adm-info@armstrong.edu* Web: *www.armstrong.edu*

ART INSTITUTE OF ATLANTA B-2

Atlanta, GA 30328 **(770) 394-8300**
(800) 275-4242; (770) 394-0008

Full-time: 1250 men, 1105 women	**Faculty:** n/av
Part-time: 180 men, 185 women	**Ph.D.s:** 51%
Graduate: n/av	**Student/Faculty:** n/av
Year: trimesters, summer session	**Tuition:** $17,500
Application Deadline: open	**Room & Board:** $7500
Freshman Class: n/av	**SPECIAL**

The Art Institute of Atlanta, founded in 1949, is a private institution that offers bachelor's degree programs in advertising, media arts and animation, digital media production, game art and design, graphic design, interior design, multimedia and web design, photographic imaging, and culinary arts management. Figures in the above capsule are approximate. In addition to regional accreditation, The Art Institute has baccalaureate program accreditation with FIDER. Computerized library services include interlibrary loans, database searching, and Internet access. Special learning facilities include a learning resource center, art gallery, an academic support center. The 7-acre campus is in a suburban area in the metro-Atlanta community of Dunwoody, approximately 5 miles north of the city limits. Including any residence halls, there are 2 buildings.

Student Life: 73% of undergraduates are from Georgia. Others are from 44 states, 38 foreign countries, and Canada. 49% are white; 34% African American. The average age of freshmen is 20; all undergraduates, 23.

Housing: College-sponsored housing includes coed off-campus apartments. On-campus housing is guaranteed for all 4 years. All students commute. All students may keep cars.

Activities: There are no fraternities or sororities. There are 16 groups on campus, including art, dance, gay, international, photography, professional, social service, and student government. Popular campus events include gallery openings, Quarterly Welcome Week, and Quarterly Portfolio Show.

Sports: There is no sports program at The Art Institute. Facilities include basketball courts and fields for touch football, a swimming pool, and a weight room in student housing.

Disabled Students: All of the campus is accessible.

Services: Counseling and information services are available, as is tutoring in most subjects. There is remedial math, reading, and writing. Tutoring is available in computer classes.

Campus Safety and Security: Measures include 24-hour foot and vehicle patrol and self-defense education. There are shuttle buses and lighted pathways/sidewalks.

Programs of Study: The Art Institute confers B.A., B.S., and B.F.A. degrees. Associate degrees are also awarded. Bachelor's degrees are awarded in COMMUNICATIONS AND THE ARTS (advertising, animation, graphic design, multimedia, photography, and video), ENGINEERING AND ENVIRONMENTAL DESIGN (computer graphics and interior design), SOCIAL SCIENCE (culinary arts). Graphic design, culinary arts, and video production are the largest.

Required: The Art Institute requires 192 credit hours for the B.F.A., with a minimum GPA of 2.0. Students in design-based majors complete a portfolio of work prior to graduation. The core curriculum includes foundation art, English, art history, humanties, math, and science courses. Foundation art classes are not required for culinary arts students.

Special: Internships in all programs, independent study, work-study programs, and study abroad are possible. There are 1 departmental honors programs.

Faculty/Classroom: 53% of faculty are male; 47% are female. All teach undergraduates. No introductory courses are taught by graduate students. The average class size in a regular course is 16.

Requirements: Students must submit SAT, ACT, ASSET, or COMPASS test scores. (COMPASS testing is offered free at the college to any applicant needing it). Preference is given to applicants with GPAs of 3.0 or above; a minimum GPA of 2.5 for bachelor's degree applicants is highly recommended. An official transcript showing high school GPA is required; the GED is accepted. An essay and an interview are required. AP and CLEP credits are accepted.

Procedure: Freshmen are admitted to all sessions. Entrance exams should be taken prior to the application closing date. There are early admissions, deferred admissions, and rolling admissions plans. Application deadlines are open. The application fee is $50. Applications are accepted online.

Transfer: In addition to fulfilling general admission requirements, transfer students must also submit all previous college transcripts. 96 of 192 credits required for the bachelor's degree must be completed at The Art Institute.

Visiting: There are regularly scheduled orientations for prospective students, including individual tours and interviews. There are guides for informal visits and visitors may sit in on classes. To schedule a visit, contact the Office of Admissions.

Financial Aid: The FAFSA and the state aid form are required. Check with the school for current application deadlines.

International Students: The school actively recruits these students. They must take the TOEFL. ASSET, COMPASS, SAT, or ACT scores can be submitted instead.

Computers: All students may access the system. There are no time limits and no fees.

Admissions Contact: Brooke Simpson, Director of Admissions. A campus DVD is available. E-Mail: *aiaadm@aii.edu* Web: *www.artinstitutes.edu*

BERRY COLLEGE A-2

Mount Berry, GA 30149 **(706) 236-2215**
(800) BERRYGA; (706) 290-2178

Full-time: 798 men, 1309 women	**Faculty:** 165; IIA, --$
Part-time: 11 men, 23 women	**Ph.D.s:** 89%
Graduate: 22 men, 60 women	**Student/Faculty:** 13 to 1
Year: semesters, summer session	**Tuition:** $29,090
Application Deadline: February 1	**Room & Board:** $10,164
Freshman Class: 3901 applied, 2353 accepted, 672 enrolled	
SAT CR/M/W: 590/580/550	**ACT:** 26 **HIGHLY COMPETITIVE**

Berry College, founded in 1902, is a private nonsectarian college offering programs in fine and liberal arts and preprofessional programs in education and business. There are 4 undergraduate schools and 2 graduate schools. In addition to regional accreditation, Berry has baccalaureate program accreditation with AACSB, NASM, and NCATE. Computerized library services include interlibrary loans, database searching, Internet access, and Wi-Fi capability. Special learning facilities include an art gallery, an observatory, an equine center, a forestry center, beef-and-dairy-cattle operations, BOLD (Berry Outdoor Leadership Development), Wildlife Management Area, Longleaf Pine Project, student-only campsites, and a trail system for hiking, biking, and horseback riding. The 27000-acre campus is in a suburban area north of Rome on U.S. 27 in northwest Georgia, 72 miles northwest of Atlanta and 75 miles from Chattanooga, TN. Including any residence halls, there are 47 buildings.

Student Life: 68% of undergraduates are from Georgia. Others are from 33 states, 13 foreign countries, and Canada. 76% are from public schools. 84% are White. The average age of freshmen is 19; all undergraduates, 20. 21% do not continue beyond their first year; 60% remain to graduate.

Housing: 1843 students can be accommodated in college housing, which includes single-sex and coed dorms and on-campus apartments. On-campus housing is guaranteed for all 4 years. 86% of students live on campus; of those, 60% remain on campus on weekends. Alcohol is not permitted. All students may keep cars.

Activities: There are no fraternities or sororities. There are 80 groups on campus, including art, cheerleading, chess, choir, chorus, communications, computers, dance, drama, environmental, ethnic, forensics, honors, international, jazz band, literary magazine, musical theater, newspaper, orchestra, pep band, political, professional, religious, social, social service, student government, symphony, and yearbook. Popular campus events include Mountain Day, Conson Wilson Lecture Series and BCTC Theatre Season.

Sports: There are 11 intercollegiate sports for men and 12 for women, and 21 intramural sports for men and 21 for women. Facilities include Athletic and recreational facility with six-lane 25-yard competitive swimming pool, multipurpose athletic court, basketball court, racquetball courts, and a performance gym in a 1,900+ seat arena; tennis courts; equine center; baseball, softball, and soccer/lacrosse fields; numerous running and biking trails; 6 camping pads, including 1 ADA pad; an 18-hole disc golf course; and 10 tennis courts.

Disabled Students: 80% of the campus is accessible.

Services: Counseling and information services are available, as is tutoring in most subjects. There is a reader service for the blind, and remedial writing.

Campus Safety and Security: Measures include 24-hour foot and vehicle patrol and emergency notification system. There are emergency telephones, lighted pathways/sidewalks, controlled access to dorms/residences, and a gated campus, mobile police patrols, identification of valuables, limited access to campus.

Programs of Study: Berry confers B.A., B.S., B.Mus. and B.S.N. degrees. Master's degrees are also awarded. Bachelor's degrees are awarded in AGRICULTURE (animal science), BIOLOGICAL SCIENCE (biochemistry and biology/biological science), BUSINESS (accounting, business administration and management, finance, and marketing management), COMMUNICATIONS AND THE ARTS (art, art history and appreciation, communications, English, English literature, French, German, music, music business management, Spanish, studio art, and theatre arts), COMPUTER AND PHYSICAL SCIENCE (chemistry, mathematics, and physics), EDUCATION (art education, early childhood education, mathematics education, middle school education, music education, and physical education), ENGINEERING AND ENVIRONMENTAL DESIGN (environmental science), HEALTH PROFESSIONS (exercise science), SOCIAL SCIENCE (anthropology, economics, history, interdisciplinary studies, international studies, philosophy, political science/government, psychology, religion, and sociology). Animal science, psychology and biology have the largest enrollments.

Required: General education requirements include 5 courses in the humanities and fine arts, 3 each in behavioral science, math and natural sciences, communication, and health and phys ed, and 2 in electives. A 2.0 GPA and a total of 124 credits, including at least 30 hours in the major, are required for graduation. All students are also required to attend at least 3 approved cultural events per semester and pass a comprehensive exam or other senior assessment in the major.

Special: The college offers internships, study abroad in more than 20 countries, work-study programs, student-designed majors, co-op programs, cross-registration with Shorter College, dual majors, credit by exam, and nondegree study. There are 3-2 engineering degrees and dual-degree programs in several fields with the Georgia Institute of Technology. There is also a dual-degree program in nursing with Emory University. There are 12 national honor societies, a freshman honors program, and 20 departmental honors programs.

Faculty/Classroom: 57% of faculty are male; 43% are female. 99% do both. No introductory courses are taught by graduate students. The average class size in an introductory lecture is 19 and in a laboratory is 17.

Admissions: 60% of the 2013-2014 applicants were accepted. The SAT scores for the 2013-2014 freshman class were: Critical Reading--8% below 500, 46% between 500 and 599, 38% between 600 and 699, and 8% between 700 and 800; Math--7% below 500, 52% between 500 and 599, 36% between 600 and 699, and 4% between 700 and 800; Writing--18% below 500, 51% between 500 and 599, 27% between 600 and 699, and 4% between 700 and 800. The ACT scores were 1% below 21, 22% between 21 and 23, 30% between 24 and 26, 18% between 27 and 28, and 28% above 28. 58% of the current freshmen were in the top fifth of their class; 86% were in the top two fifths. There was 1 National Merit finalist. 19 freshmen graduated first in their class.

Requirements: The SAT or ACT is required. Applicants should be graduates of an accredited high school or have a GED. 20 academic credits are required, including 4 units each of English and math (to include algebra I, algebra II, and either geometry or trigonometry), 3 each of science and social studies, and 2 of a foreign language. AP credits are accepted. Important factors in the admissions decision are advanced placement or honors courses, leadership record, and recommendations by school officials.

Procedure: Freshmen are admitted to all sessions. Entrance exams should be taken by the fall of the senior year. There is a rolling admissions plan. Applications should be filed by February 1 for fall entry. Notifications are sent November 1. 33 applicants were on the 2013 waiting list; 1 was admitted. Applications are accepted online.

Transfer: 40 transfer students enrolled in 2012-2013. Applicants must submit official transcripts from all colleges previously attended, have a minimum GPA of 2.5, and be in good standing at the last school attended. 62 of 124 credits required for the bachelor's degree must be completed at Berry.

Visiting: There are regularly scheduled orientations for prospective students, including weekdays and Saturday mornings. Students should schedule campus visits in advance. . There are guides for informal visits, visitors may sit in on classes, and stay overnight. To schedule a visit, contact The Office of Admissions.

Financial Aid: In 2013-2014, 100% of all full-time freshmen and 99% of continuing full-time students received some form of financial aid. 77% of all full-time freshmen and 73% of continuing full-time students received need-based aid. The average freshman award was $23,432. Need-based scholarships or need-based grants averaged $20,093; need-based self-help aid (loans and jobs) averaged $4,296; and other non-need-based awards and non-need-based scholarships averaged $11,140. 91% of undergraduate students work part time. Average annual earnings from campus work are $2358. The average financial indebtedness of the 2013 graduate was $25,335. The FAFSA is required. The priority date for freshman financial aid applications for fall entry is March 1.

International Students: There are 19 international students enrolled. The school actively recruits these students. They must take the TOEFL with a minimum score of 550 on the paper-based TOEFL (PBT) or 80 on the Internet-based version (iBT), IELTS. They must also take the SAT or ACT. if the student is from an English-speaking country.

Computers: All students may access the system. There are no time limits and no fees.

Graduates: From July 1, 2012 to June 30, 2013, 406 bachelor's degrees were awarded. The most popular majors were biology/ biological sciences and general (13%), animal science, general (10%), and psychology (10%). 90 companies recruited on campus in 2012-2013. In an average class, 2% graduate in 3 years or less, 55% graduate in 4 years or less, 61% graduate in 5 years or less, and 60% graduate in 6 years or less.

Admissions Contact: Brett Kennedy, Director of Admissions. E-Mail: *admissions@berry.edu* Web: *www.berry.edu*

BRENAU UNIVERSITY WOMEN'S COLLEGE B-2

Gainesville, GA 30501 (770) 534-6100
(800) 252-5119; (770) 538-4701

Full-time: 798 women	**Faculty:** 70
Part-time: 69 women	**Ph.D.s:** 73%
Graduate: 49 women	**Student/Faculty:** 10 to 1
Year: semesters, summer session	**Tuition:** $17,700
Application Deadline: open	**Room & Board:** $8950
Freshman Class: n/av	
SAT or ACT: required	

COMPETITIVE+

Brenau University Women's College, founded in 1878, is a private undergraduate and graduate liberal arts institution for women. Coeducational programs are offered as part of the university, in an evening and weekend format. There are 4 undergraduate schools. In addition to regional accreditation, Brenau has baccalaureate program accreditation with FIDER, NCATE, and NLN. Computerized library services include interlibrary loans, database searching, Internet access, and laptop Internet portals. Special learning facilities include a learning resource center, art gallery, natural history museum, radio station, and TV station. The 57-acre campus is in a suburban area 50 miles northeast of Atlanta. Including any residence halls, there are 65 buildings.

Student Life: 88% of undergraduates are from Georgia. Others are from 19 states, 12 foreign countries, and Canada. 55% are white; 19% African American. The average age of freshmen is 18; all undergraduates, 22.

Housing: 498 students can be accommodated in college housing, which includes single-sex dorms and on-campus apartments. In addition, there are honors houses, special-interest houses, sorority houses, Honors (for freshmen students apart of the academic honors programs), Special interest (for athletes). On-campus housing is guaranteed for all 4 years. 57% of students live on campus. Alcohol is not permitted. All students may keep cars.

Activities: There are no fraternities; 19% of women belong to 8 national sororities. There are 48 groups on campus, including art, cheerleading, choir, chorale, chorus, crew team, dance, debate, drama, environmental, ethnic, honors, international, literary magazine, musical theater, newspaper, opera, photography, political, professional, radio and TV, religious, social, social service, student government, symphony, and yearbook. Popular campus events include Remember All the Traditions Week, May Day, and Spade Hunt.

Sports: There are 8 intercollegiate sports for women, and facilities include a tennis center, a recreation field, a gym, fitness center, and a natatorium. Soccer and softball are played at off-campus facilities.

Disabled Students: 90% of the campus is accessible.

Services: Counseling and information services are available, as is tutoring in every subject. There is remedial math, reading, and writing. and professional degreed tutors for diagnosed learning-disabled students and physically disabled students for a fee. Free exam proctoring for learning and physically disabled students.

Campus Safety and Security: Measures include 24-hour foot and

vehicle patrol, emergency notification system, self-defense education, and security escort services. There are lighted pathways/sidewalks.

Programs of Study: Brenau confers B.A., B.S., B.B.A., B.F.A., B.Mus., and B.S.N. degrees. Master's degrees are also awarded. Bachelor's degrees are awarded in AGRICULTURE (environmental studies), BIOLOGICAL SCIENCE (biology/biological science), BUSINESS (accounting, business administration and management, fashion merchandising, and marketing/retailing/merchandising), COMMUNICATIONS AND THE ARTS (arts administration/management, communications, dance, dramatic arts, English, fine arts, music performance, musical theater, and studio art), EDUCATION (art education, dance education, early childhood education, middle school education, music education, and special education), ENGINEERING AND ENVIRONMENTAL DESIGN (commercial art, graphic and printing production, and interior design), HEALTH PROFESSIONS (nursing and occupational therapy), SOCIAL SCIENCE (history, international studies, liberal arts/general studies, political science/government, and psychology). Nursing, occupational therapy, and performing arts have the largest enrollments.

Required: To graduate, all students must complete at least 120 semester hours of work including 48 to 69 hours in the major. Requirements for each degree vary, but students must maintain a 2.0 GPA overall and a 2.5 GPA in course work required by the major. Most majors either require or encourage internships. In addition to specific requirements, students must take courses in women's health, lifetime fitness, and leisure studies.

Special: Cross-registration is possible with the Atlanta Regional Consortium for Higher Education. Students may study abroad in 10 foreign countries. Brenau offers B.A.-B.S. degrees, work study programs, internships, a general studies degree, and student-designed majors. Students may receive credit for life, military, and work experience. There are 11 national honor societies, a freshman honors program, and 5 departmental honors programs.

Faculty/Classroom: 39% of faculty are male; 61% are female. All teach undergraduates. No introductory courses are taught by graduate students.

Requirements: The SAT or ACT is required. Candidates for admission should meet current graduation requirements for the state of Georgia. A GPA of 2.0 is required. AP and CLEP credits are accepted. Important factors in the admissions decision are advanced placement or honors courses, extracurricular activities record, and evidence of special talent.

Procedure: Freshmen are admitted fall and spring. Entrance exams should be taken in the fall of the senior year or the spring of the junior year. There are deferred admissions and rolling admissions plans. Application deadlines are open. Check with the school for the current application fee. Notifications are sent October 1. Applications are accepted online.

Transfer: 108 transfer students enrolled in a recent year. A minimum GPA of 2.0 on transfer credits is required, and transfer students must submit high school transcripts and SAT scores if fewer than 30 hours were earned. The last 45 semester hours, including at least 30 in the major, must be taken at Brenau. Students must maintain a minimum GPA of 2.0 and 2.5 in the major. 45 of 120 credits required for the bachelor's degree must be completed at Brenau.

Visiting: There are regularly scheduled orientations for prospective students, consisting of a campus tour, information sessions, and an interview. There are guides for informal visits, visitors may sit in on classes, and stay overnight. To schedule a visit, contact the Admissions Office.

Financial Aid: In a recent year, 78% of all full-time freshmen and 71% of continuing full-time students received some form of financial aid. 78% of all full-time freshmen and 71% of continuing full-time students received need-based aid. The average freshman award was $17,242. Need-based scholarships or need-based grants averaged $14,631; need-based self-help aid (loans and jobs) averaged $3,900; non-need-based athletic scholarships averaged $14,060; and other non-need-based awards and non-need-based scholarships averaged $8,938. The FAFSA and the state aid form are required. The priority date for freshman financial aid applications for fall entry is April 1.

International Students: There are 35 international students enrolled. The school actively recruits these students. They must take the TOEFL with a minimum score of 500 on the paper-based TOEFL (PBT), or completion of Level 109 at an ELS Language Center. They must also take the SAT or ACT, scoring 900. only if the TOEFL is not taken.

Computers: Wireless access is available. The Student Lab is provided for students to do homework and check e-mail. The lab has 32 computers, 3-networked laser printers, a large format inkjet printer, and 8 scanners. Current software on these computers includes Microsoft Office 2007 plus selected software specific to individual classes. Additional computers for e-mail and homework are available in the Commuter Lounge as well as most residence halls. Kiosk computers with Internet-only access are available in The Brenau Tea Room and the Jacobs Building. Women's College residential students have the option to connect to the Brenau "RapidConnect" residential network. RapidConnect is a FAST and FREE Internet access connection provided by the university for use in most campus housing so that residential students can access the university's online resources and accomplish academic goals. All students may access the system 24 hours per day. There are no time limits. The fee is $250 per year. Students enrolled in Interior Design must have a personal computer.

Graduates: In a recent year, 205 bachelor's degrees were awarded. The most popular majors were visual and performing arts (28%), health profession (23%), and teacher education (19%).

Admissions Contact: Christina White, Associate VP of Enrollment Management and Dean. A campus DVD is available. E-Mail: *cwhite@brenau.edu* Web: *www.brenau.edu*

BREWTON-PARKER COLLEGE — D-4

Mt. Vernon, GA 30445-0197 — (912) 583-3247; (800) 342-1087; (912) 583-4498

Full-time: 237 men, 231 women	**Faculty:** 31
Part-time: 79 men, 82 women	**Ph.D.s:** 45%
Graduate: n/av	**Student/Faculty:** 9 to 1
Year: semesters, summer session	**Tuition:** $26,080
Application Deadline: open	**Room & Board:** $7308
Freshman Class: n/av	
SAT: required	

LESS COMPETITIVE

Brewton-Parker College is a four-year Christian college located on the main campus in Mount Vernon, Georgia, and one external site in Newnan. Affiliated with the Georgia Baptist Convention, the College offers four baccalaureate degrees in a caring, Christian environment that nurtures the whole student. Students enjoy challenging academic programs in an unapologetically Christian setting. Residential students participate in a comprehensive campus life program involving student organizations, intramural sports, campus ministry opportunities, and weekend activities. In addition to regional accreditation, BPC has baccalaureate program accreditation with NCATE. The library contains 98,045 volumes, 1,562 microform items, and 6,941 audio/video tapes/CDs/DVDs, and subscribes to 132 periodicals including electronic. Computerized library services include interlibrary loans, database searching, Internet access, and laptop Internet portals. Special learning facilities include a learning resource center, a living history museum, nature trail, greenhouse. The 270-acre campus is in a rural located on Hwy 280 in the adjoining towns of Mt. Vernon and Ailey, GA. Including any residence halls, there are 36 buildings.

Student Life: 95% of undergraduates are from Georgia. The average age of freshmen is 20; all undergraduates, 26.

Housing: 410 students can be accommodated in college housing, which includes single-sex dorms. On-campus housing is guaranteed for all 4 years. 50% of students commute. Alcohol is not permitted. All students may keep cars.

Activities: There are no fraternities or sororities. There are 22 groups on campus, including cheerleading, choir, Circle K, film, honors, international, professional, religious, social, social service, and student government. Popular campus events include Homecoming, Alumni Weekend, Fall Festival.

Sports: There are 4 intercollegiate sports for men and 5 for women, and 8 intramural sports for men and 8 for women. Facilities include softball, baseball, and soccer fields, tennis courts, a swimming pool, a gym, a track, an intramural field, an outdoor volleyball court, a physical fitness building, a game room, and a campus lake.

Disabled Students: 80% of the campus is accessible. Facilities include wheelchair ramps, special parking, specially equipped restrooms, and special housing.

Services: Counseling and information services are available, as is tutoring in most subjects. There is remedial math, reading, and writing. Tutoring in Spanish is available.

Campus Safety and Security: There are lighted pathways/sidewalks, controlled access to dorms/residences, evening security guard on campus.

Programs of Study: BPC confers B.A., B.S., and B.Min. degrees. Associate degrees are also awarded. Bachelor's degrees are awarded in BIOLOGICAL SCIENCE (biology/biological science), BUSINESS (accounting, business administration and management, and management information systems), COMMUNICATIONS AND THE ARTS (communications, dramatic arts, and English), COMPUTER AND PHYSICAL SCIENCE (information sciences and systems), EDUCATION (early childhood education, physical education, and sports studies), ENGINEERING AND ENVIRONMENTAL DESIGN (technological management), SOCIAL SCIENCE (Christian studies, history, human services, liberal arts/general studies, political science/government, psychology, social science, and sociology). Business, education, and psychology have the largest enrollments.

Required: The required core curriculum consists of humanities, math, natural science, social science, phys ed, and computer science. Students must maintain a minimum 2.0 GPA with half of the major taken at BPC.

Special: The college offers internships, a general studies degree, B.A.-B.S. degrees, B.Min. degree, and non-degree study. There are 3 national honor societies.

Faculty/Classroom: 54% of faculty are male; 46% are female. No introductory courses are taught by graduate students. The average class

size in an introductory lecture is 20; in a laboratory is 24; and in a regular course is 17.

Admissions: The SAT scores for the 2011-2012 freshman class were: Critical Reading--65% below 500, 29% between 500 and 599, 5% between 600 and 700, and 1% above 700; Math--65% below 500, 29% between 500 and 599, 6% between 600 and 700; Writing--65% below 500, 29% between 500 and 599, 6% between 600 and 700. The ACT scores were 87% between 21 and 23, 11% between 27 and 28, and 2% above 28.

Requirements: The SAT is required. The ACT and ACT Writing Test are recommended. A GED is accepted. Students should prepare with 4 years of English, 3 of social studies, and 2 each of foreign language, math, and science. A GPA of 2.0 is required. AP and CLEP credits are accepted. Important factors in the admissions decision are personality/intangible qualities, leadership record, and advanced placement or honors courses.

Procedure: Freshmen are admitted to all sessions. Entrance exams should be taken during the senior year of high school. There is a deferred admissions plan. Application deadlines are open. Application fee is $25. Applications are accepted online.

Transfer: 81 transfer students enrolled in 2010-2011. Applicants must submit transcripts from previously attended institutions, along with high school transcripts, if they have completed fewer than 30 semester hours.

Visiting: There are regularly scheduled orientations for prospective students, consisting of a campus tour and academic and financial aid sessions. There are guides for informal visits, visitors may sit in on classes, and stay overnight. To schedule a visit, contact the Office of Admissions.

Financial Aid: In a recent year, 95% of all full-time freshmen and 95% of continuing full-time students received some form of financial aid. BPC is a member of CSS. The FAFSA and the college's own financial statement are required. Check with the school for current application deadlines.

International Students: There are 13 international students enrolled. They must also take the SAT, scoring 880.

Computers: There are 104 computers available for student use in classrooms and labs. Wireless network is available in several buildings throughout campus. All students may access the system. There are no time limits and no fees.

Graduates: In a recent year, 124 bachelor's degrees were awarded. The most popular majors were early childhood education (10%), business (9%), and psychology (8%).

Admissions Contact: Director of Admissions. E-Mail: *admissions@bpc.edu* Web: *www.bpc.edu*

CLARK ATLANTA UNIVERSITY

B-2

Atlanta, GA 30314

(404) 880-8043
(800) 668-3228; (404) 880-6174

Full-time: 611 men, 1903 women	**Faculty:** n/av; IIB, --$
Part-time: 40 men, 75 women	**Ph.D.s:** 79%
Graduate: 227 men, 602 women	**Student/Faculty:** 15 to 1
Year: semesters, summer session	**Tuition:** $21,100
Application Deadline:	**Room & Board:** $8906
Freshman Class: 5873 applied, 3336 accepted, 781 enrolled	
SAT CR/M: 430/420	**ACT:** 18 **COMPETITIVE**

Clark Atlanta University was formed in 1988 from the consolidation of Clark College (1869) and Atlanta University (1865). A private, predominantly black college affiliated with the United Methodist Church, CAU offers programs in arts and sciences, business administration, education, and social work. There are 5 undergraduate schools and 4 graduate schools. In addition to regional accreditation, CAU has baccalaureate program accreditation with AACSB, CAHEA, CSWE, and NCATE. The library contains 647,162 volumes, 841,341 microform items, and 7,860 audio/video tapes/CDs/DVDs, and subscribes to 1,996 periodicals including electronic. Computerized library services include interlibrary loans and database searching. Special learning facilities include an art gallery, radio station, TV station, a distance learning instructional technology education center. The 113-acre campus is in an urban area 3 miles southwest of Atlanta. Including any residence halls, there are 30 buildings.

Student Life: 63% of undergraduates are from out of state, mostly the South. Students are from 41 states, and 14 foreign countries. 87% are African American. The average age of freshmen is 18; all undergraduates, 20. 36% do not continue beyond their first year; 39% remain to graduate.

Housing: 2448 students can be accommodated in college housing, which includes single-sex and coed dorms, on-campus apartments, and off-campus apartments. On-campus housing is available on a first-come, first-served basis, and is available on a lottery system for upperclassmen. 62% of students live on campus. Alcohol is not permitted. All students may keep cars.

Activities: 2% of men belong to 4 national fraternities; 3% of women belong to 4 national sororities. There are 77 groups on campus, including art, band, cheerleading, choir, chorale, chorus, computers, dance, drama, drill team, ethnic, film, honors, international, jazz band, marching band, musical theater, newspaper, orchestra, pep band, photography, political, professional, radio and TV, religious, social, social service, student government, and symphony. Popular campus events include Commencement and Alumni Weekend, Founders Week and Convocations.

Sports: There are 7 intercollegiate sports for men and 7 for women, and 6 intramural sports for men and 6 for women. Facilities include a gym, a stadium, and a student center.

Disabled Students: 70% of the campus is accessible. Facilities include wheelchair ramps, elevators, special parking, and specially equipped restrooms.

Services: Counseling and information services are available, as is tutoring in every subject. There is remedial math, reading, and writing.

Campus Safety and Security: Measures include 24-hour foot and vehicle patrol and security escort services. There are shuttle buses, emergency telephones, and lighted pathways/sidewalks.

Programs of Study: CAU confers B.A., B.S. and B.S.W. degrees. Master's and doctoral degrees are also awarded. Bachelor's degrees are awarded in BIOLOGICAL SCIENCE (biology/biological science), BUSINESS (accounting and business administration and management), COMMUNICATIONS AND THE ARTS (art, communications, English, languages, music, and speech/debate/rhetoric), COMPUTER AND PHYSICAL SCIENCE (chemistry, computer science, mathematics, and physics), EDUCATION (business education, early childhood education, middle school education, and physical education), SOCIAL SCIENCE (economics, history, philosophy, political science/government, psychology, religion, social work, and sociology). Business administration, physical and biological sciences and communications are the strongest academically. Business, communications and psychology have the largest enrollments.

Required: To graduate, students must complete a minimum of 122 hours of course work, including a prescribed major sequence, with a minimum 2.0 GPA. Beyond the general education core requirements, at least 60% of courses must represent work at or above the 300 level.

Special: Clark Atlanta offers co-op programs, public and private internships, study abroad in 12 countries, accelerated degree programs in biology, chemistry, physics, computer science, math, religion, and accounting, and a Washington semester. There is cross-registration with Atlanta University Center, Georgia Institute of Technology, Georgia State University, and Paine College. B.A.-B.S. degrees may be obtained in business and management, education, and social and natural sciences. Dual majors in allied health and engineering and a 3-2 engineering degree with 7 universities are also available. There are 10 national honor societies and a freshman honors program.

Faculty/Classroom: 53% of faculty are male; 47% are female. 81% teach undergraduates. No introductory courses are taught by graduate students. The average class size in an introductory lecture is 16; in a laboratory is 15; and in a regular course is 16.

Admissions: 57% of the 2013-2014 applicants were accepted. The SAT scores for the 2013-2014 freshman class were: Critical Reading--83% below 500, 17% between 500 and 599; Math--82% below 500, 17% between 500 and 599, 1% between 600 and 699. The ACT scores were 74% below 21, 16% between 21 and 23, 8% between 24 and 26, 2% between 27 and 28. 23% of the current freshmen were in the top fifth of their class; 49% were in the top two fifths.

Requirements: The SAT or ACT is required. Applicants must be high school graduates or hold the GED. A letter of recommendation is required. A GPA of 2.5 is required. AP and CLEP credits are accepted. Important factors in the admissions decision are advanced placement or honors courses and recommendations by school officials.

Procedure: Freshmen are admitted fall and spring. Entrance exams should be taken by January. There are early admissions, deferred admissions, and rolling admissions plans. Check with the school for current application deadlines. The fall 2013 application fee was $35. Notification is sent on a rolling basis. Applications are accepted online.

Transfer: Applicants must have a 2.3 GPA, be in good standing at the institution previously attended, and have completed at least 12 semester hours. 30 of 122 credits required for the bachelor's degree must be completed at CAU.

Visiting: There are regularly scheduled orientations for prospective students. There are guides for informal visits and visitors may sit in on classes. To schedule a visit, contact the Admission Counselor.

Financial Aid: The FAFSA is required. Check with the school for current application deadlines.

International Students: There are 22 international students enrolled. The school actively recruits these students. They must take the TOEFL.

Computers: Those students with assigned user identification codes may access the system. any time. There are no time limits and no fees.

Graduates: From July 1, 2012 to June 30, 2013, 479 bachelor's degrees were awarded. The most popular majors were communication (23%), business/marketing (23%), and psychology (12%). In an average class, 21% graduate in 4 years or less, 14% graduate in 5 years or less, and 4% graduate in 6 years or less.

Admissions Contact: Sanchez Dwight , Director of Admissions. E-Mail: *dsanchez@cau.edu* Web: *www.cau.edu*

CLAYTON STATE UNIVERSITY B-2

Morrow, GA 30260-0285 (770) 961-5100; (770) 961-3752

Full-time: 825 men, 1615 women
Part-time: 915 men, 1875 women
Graduate: n/av
Year: semesters, summer session
Application Deadline: open
Freshman Class: n/av
SAT or ACT: required
Faculty: n/av; IIB, -$
Ph.D.s: 51%
Student/Faculty: n/av
Tuition: $4000 ($13,200)
Room & Board: $8000

LESS COMPETITIVE

Clayton State University, founded in 1969 as a public junior college, has been a 4-year undergraduate college in the University System of Georgia since 1985. The first baccalaureate degrees were awarded in 1989. There are 4 undergraduate schools and 1 graduate school. In addition to regional accreditation, Clayton State has baccalaureate program accreditation with ADA, NCATE, and NLN. The library contains 97,835 volumes, 254,014 microform items, and 5,113 audio/video tapes/CDs/DVDs, and subscribes to 750 periodicals including electronic. Computerized library services include interlibrary loans and database searching. Special learning facilities include a learning resource center, a concert facility. The 160-acre campus is in a suburban area 17 miles south of downtown Atlanta near Hartsfield International Airport. Including any residence halls, there are 12 buildings.

Student Life: 92% of undergraduates are from Georgia. Others are from 28 states, 42 foreign countries, and Canada. The average age of all undergraduates is 28. 37% do not continue beyond their first year.

Housing: Alcohol is not permitted. All students may keep cars.

Activities: There are 20 groups on campus, including art, band, cheerleading, choir, chorale, chorus, computers, drama, ethnic, gay, honors, international, jazz band, musical theater, newspaper, professional, religious, social, social service, and student government. Popular campus events include Southern Crescent Festival and Spring Fling.

Sports: There are 4 intercollegiate sports for men and 4 for women. Facilities include a gym, jogging trails, a circuit training facility, a weight room, soccer fields, and tennis, badminton, volleyball, and basketball courts.

Disabled Students: All of the campus is accessible. Facilities include wheelchair ramps, elevators, special parking, specially equipped restrooms, special class scheduling, lowered drinking fountains, and lowered telephones.

Services: Counseling and information services are available, as is tutoring in most subjects. There is remedial math, reading, and writing.

Campus Safety and Security: Measures include 24-hour foot and vehicle patrol, self-defense education, and security escort services. There are emergency telephones and lighted pathways/sidewalks.

Programs of Study: Clayton State confers B.A., B.S., B.A.S., B.B.A., B.M., and B.S.N. degrees. Associate degrees are also awarded. Bachelor's degrees are awarded in BUSINESS (accounting, business administration and management, and marketing and distribution), COMMUNICATIONS AND THE ARTS (music, music performance, and music theory and composition), COMPUTER AND PHYSICAL SCIENCE (information sciences and systems), EDUCATION (middle school education), ENGINEERING AND ENVIRONMENTAL DESIGN (technological management), HEALTH PROFESSIONS (allied health, dental hygiene, health care administration, and nursing), SOCIAL SCIENCE (history and interdisciplinary studies). Nursing, middle school education, and music performance are the strongest academically. Management has the largest enrollment.

Required: Students in the baccalaureate program must complete 120 to 126 semester hours, including a 60-hour core curriculum in English and humanities, math or sciences, and social sciences. A 2.0 minimum GPA is required for graduation.

Special: Co-op programs and internships can be arranged in all majors except middle school education. The B.A.S. career program enables associate degree holders to complete the baccalaureate degree. Cross-registration is offered through the University Center Consortium. Dual majors, B.A.-B.S. degrees, study abroad, student-designed majors, and work-study programs are offered. Distance learning opportunities are possible. There are 2 national honor societies and a freshman honors program.

Faculty/Classroom: 51% of faculty are male; 49% are female. All teach undergraduates. No introductory courses are taught by graduate students.

Requirements: The SAT or ACT is required. Applicants should be graduates of accredited secondary schools. High school preparation should include 4 courses each in English and math, 3 each in science, history, and social studies, and 2 in a foreign language. Students may also be admitted on the strength of their high school academic records. AP and CLEP credits are accepted.

Procedure: Freshmen are admitted to all sessions. Entrance exams should be taken before registration. There are early admissions, deferred admissions, and rolling admissions plans. Check with the school for current application deadlines. Check with the school for the current application. Notification is sent on a rolling basis. Applications are accepted online.

Transfer: Applicants with fewer than 30 semester hours or 45 quarter credits must meet the same criteria as entering freshmen. 30 of 120 credits required for the bachelor's degree must be completed at Clayton State.

Visiting: There are regularly scheduled orientations for prospective students, including tours of the campus and the opportunity to meet faculty and staff and learn about the athletic programs, the notebook computers, and campus life. There are guides for informal visits and visitors may sit in on classes. To schedule a visit, contact the Office of Admissions.

Financial Aid: Clayton State is a member of CSS. The FAFSA and the college's own financial statement are required. Check with the school for current application deadlines.

International Students: The school actively recruits these students. They must take the TOEFL, Georgia State Test for English Proficiency (G-STEP). They must also take the SAT or ACT.

Computers: All students may access the system. All students are required to have a personal computer.

Admissions Contact: Scott Burke, Director of Admissions. E-Mail: *ccsu-info@mail.clayton.edu* Web: *www.clayton.edu*

COLUMBUS STATE UNIVERSITY A-3

Columbus, GA 31907-5645 (706) 507-8800; (866) 264-2035; (706) 568-2462

Full-time: 1917 men, 3078 women
Part-time: 895 men, 1179 women
Graduate: 503 men, 720 women
Year: semesters, summer session
Application Deadline: June 30
Freshman Class: 3454 applied, 2075 accepted, 1240 enrolled
SAT CR/M/W: 508/496/490
ACT: 21
Faculty: 265
Ph.D.s: 78%
Student/Faculty: 19 to 1
Tuition: $6396 ($18,372)
Room & Board: $7780

COMPETITIVE

Columbus State University, established in 1958, is a public liberal arts institution within the University System of Georgia. There are 4 undergraduate schools and 1 graduate school. The figures in the above capsule and in this profile are approximate. In addition to regional accreditation, Columbus State has baccalaureate program accreditation with AACSB, APTA, NASAD, NASM, NCATE, and NLN. The 2 libraries contain 263,110 volumes, 1.1 million microform items, and 12,122 audio/video tapes/CDs/DVDs, and subscribe to 1,394 periodicals including electronic. Computerized library services include interlibrary loans, database searching, and Internet access. Special learning facilities include a learning resource center, art gallery, planetarium, archives. The 150-acre campus is in a suburban area in Columbus, Georgia, 100 miles south of Atlanta. Including any residence halls, there are 55 buildings.

Student Life: 86% of undergraduates are from Georgia. Others are from 40 states, 41 foreign countries, and Canada. 55% are white; 35% African American. The average age of freshmen is 19; all undergraduates, 24. 32% do not continue beyond their first year; 32% remain to graduate.

Housing: 1200 students can be accommodated in college housing, which includes single-sex on-campus apartments and off-campus apartments. In addition, there are special-interest houses. On-campus housing is guaranteed for all 4 years. 81% of students commute. Alcohol is not permitted. All students may keep cars.

Activities: 2% of men belong to 1 local and 8 national fraternities; 2% of women belong to 3 local and 5 national sororities. There are 51 groups on campus, including art, band, cheerleading, choir, chorale, chorus, computers, dance, debate, drama, drill team, environmental, ethnic, film, honors, international, jazz band, literary magazine, musical theater, newspaper, orchestra, pep band, photography, political, professional, religious, social, social service, student government, and symphony. Popular campus events include Black History Month, Halloween, and Greek Week.

Sports: There are 6 intercollegiate sports for men and 7 for women, and 16 intramural sports for men and 16 for women. Facilities include A recently completed state of the Art Student Recreation Center with physical fitness rooms, racketball courts, swimming pools, basketball courts climbing wall, etc. Also, tennis courts, baseball, soccer, softball, and intramural multipurpose fields, a walking trail, volleyball and basketball courts.

Disabled Students: All of the campus is accessible. Facilities include wheelchair ramps, elevators, special parking, specially equipped restrooms, special class scheduling, lowered drinking fountains, lowered telephones.

Services: Counseling and information services are available, as is tutoring in most subjects. There is a reader service for the blind, and remedial math, reading, and writing. Scribe and braille services are also available.

Campus Safety and Security: Measures include 24-hour foot and vehicle patrol, emergency notification system, self-defense education, and security escort services. There are shuttle buses, emergency telephones, lighted pathways/sidewalks, and shuttles for evening students.

Programs of Study: Columbus State confers B.A., B.S.. B.B.A., B.M., B.S.Ed. and B.S.N. degrees. Associate, master's, and doctoral degrees are also awarded. Bachelor's degrees are awarded in BIOLOGICAL SCIENCE (biology/biological science), BUSINESS (accounting, banking and finance, business administration and management, management information systems, and marketing/retailing/merchandising), COMMUNICATIONS

AND THE ARTS (art, communications, dramatic arts, English, French, music, music performance, Spanish, and visual and performing arts), COMPUTER AND PHYSICAL SCIENCE (chemistry, computer science, earth science, and mathematics), EDUCATION (art education, drama education, early childhood education, foreign languages education, health education, middle school education, music education, secondary education, and special education), HEALTH PROFESSIONS (exercise science, health science, and nursing), SOCIAL SCIENCE (criminal justice, history, political science/government, psychology, and sociology). Nursing, biology, and music are the strongest academically. Nursing, business, and early childhood education have the largest enrollments.

Required: To graduate, all students must maintain a 2.0 GPA and complete a minimum of 123 semester hours, 63 of them in a core curriculum and 60 in the major. Three semester hours of phys ed are required. All students must complete English 1101, English 1102, and Math 1111 with a C or better, and satisfy the Georgia History and Constitution and U.S. History and Constitution requirement by taking specified courses at a University System of Georgia institution or, for transfers from outside the system, by passing an exemption test. Some majors require a comprehensive exam.

Special: Internships, a Washington semester, work-study, and study abroad in 14 countries is possible. A 3-2 engineering degree with the Georgia Institute of Technology and a B.A.-B.S. degree in biology, chemistry, math, or psychology are also available. There are 19 national honor societies and a freshman honors program.

Faculty/Classroom: 53% of faculty are male; 47% are female. 98% teach undergraduates. No introductory courses are taught by graduate students. The average class size in an introductory lecture is 27; in a laboratory is 17; and in a regular course is 26.

Admissions: In a recent year, 60% of applicants were accepted. The SAT scores for a current freshman class were: Critical Reading--48% below 500, 38% between 500 and 599, 13% between 600 and 700, and 1% above 700; Math--54% below 500, 36% between 500 and 599, 9% between 600 and 700, and 1% above 700; Writing--57% below 500, 34% between 500 and 599, 8% between 600 and 700, and 1% above 700. The ACT scores were 59% below 21, 25% between 21 and 23, 12% between 24 and 26, 3% between 27 and 28, and 1% above 28.

Requirements: The SAT or ACT is required. The SAT is preferred, with a minimum Critical Reading score of 440 and Math score of 410. A minimum ACT score of 17 English and 17 math is accepted. Applicants must be graduates of accredited secondary schools. 16 academic credits are required, including 4 each in English and math, 3 each in science and social studies, and 2 in a foreign language. A GPA of 2.3 is required. AP and CLEP credits are accepted.

Procedure: Freshmen are admitted to all sessions. Entrance exams should be taken in the fall of the senior year. There are early admissions and rolling admissions plans. Applications should be filed by June 30 for fall entry; November 1 for spring entry; and March 1 for summer entry, along with a $30 fee. Applications are accepted online.

Transfer: 604 transfer students enrolled in a recent year. Transfer students with fewer than 30 hours of credit must meet the same requirements as entering freshmen. Transfer students must have a 2.0 GPA and be eligible to return to the institution last attended. 30 of 123 credits required for the bachelor's degree must be completed at Columbus State.

Visiting: There are regularly scheduled orientations for prospective students. During the fall and spring semesters, there are college visitation programs. Prospective students may arrange a tour on any weekday. There are guides for informal visits and visitors may sit in on classes. To schedule a visit, contact the Admissions Office.

Financial Aid: In a recent year, 88% of all full-time freshmen and 83% of continuing full-time students received some form of financial aid. 58% of all full-time freshmen and 58% of continuing full-time students received need-based aid. The average freshman award was $10,477. Need-based scholarships or need-based grants averaged $4,926; need-based self-help aid (loans and jobs) averaged $3,228; non-need-based athletic scholarships averaged $4,486; and other non-need-based awards and non-need-based scholarships averaged $5,433. The average financial indebtedness of a recent graduate was $21,486. The FAFSA is required. The priority date for freshman financial aid applications for fall entry is May 1.

International Students: There are 68 international students enrolled. The school actively recruits these students. They must take the TOEFL with a minimum score of 550 on the paper-based TOEFL (PBT) or 79 on the Internet-based version (iBT). They must also take the SAT or ACT.

Computers: Wireless access is available. All students may access the system. There are no time limits. The fee is $66.

Graduates: In a recent year, 872 bachelor's degrees were awarded. The most popular majors were nursing (11%), management (8%), and criminal justice (8%). In an average class, 12% graduate in 4 years or less, 23% graduate in 5 years or less, and 33% graduate in 6 years or less.

Admissions Contact: Susan Lovell, Director of Enrollment Services. A campus DVD is available. E-Mail: *lovell_susan@colstate.edu* Web: *www.colstate.edu*

COVENANT COLLEGE — A-1

Lookout Mountain, GA 30750 — (706) 820-2398
(888) 451-2683; (706) 820-0893

Full-time: 451 men, 599 women	**Faculty:** 62; IIB, --$
Part-time: 22 men, 22 women	**Ph.D.s:** 90%
Graduate: 117 men, 53 women	**Student/Faculty:** 14 to 1
Year: semesters, summer session	**Tuition:** $29,100
Application Deadline: May 1	**Room & Board:** $8530
Freshman Class: 1109 applied, 629 accepted, 295 enrolled	
SAT CR/M/W: 595/575/590	**ACT:** 26 **VERY COMPETITIVE+**

Covenant College, founded in 1955, is a private liberal arts college affiliated with the Presbyterian Church in America. There is one graduate school. The library contains 90,629 volumes, 125,000 microform items, 4,214 audio/video tapes/CDs/DVDs, and subscribes to 525 periodicals including electronic. Computerized library services include interlibrary loans, database searching, and Internet access. Special learning facilities include an art gallery and radio station. The 350-acre campus is in a suburban area 12 miles southwest of Chattanooga, Tennessee. Including any residence halls, there are 13 buildings.

Student Life: 77% of undergraduates are from out of state, mostly the South. Students are from 45 states, 21 foreign countries, and Canada. 89% are White. 99% are Protestant. The average age of freshmen is 18; all undergraduates, 20. 21% do not continue beyond their first year; 55% remain to graduate.

Housing: 917 students can be accommodated in college housing, which includes single-sex dorms and on-campus apartments, and theme housing. On-campus housing is guaranteed for all 4 years. 98% of students live on campus. Alcohol is not permitted. All students may keep cars.

Activities: There are no fraternities or sororities. There are 43 groups on campus, including campus ministries, music ensembles and student-run film society, cheerleading, chorale, concert band, dance, drama, honors, international, jazz band, literary magazine, musical theater, newspaper, photography, professional, radio and TV, religious, social, social service, student government, and yearbook. Popular campus events include Madrigal Dinner, Spring Banquet and Kilter Night.

Sports: There are 6 intercollegiate sports for men and 7 for women, and 5 intramural sports for men and 5 for women. Facilities include a gym, a weight room, a swimming pool, tennis courts, 3 soccer fields, running trails, an aerobics room, and a wellness room equipped with a variety of fitness machines.

Disabled Students: All of the campus is accessible. Facilities include wheelchair ramps, elevators, special parking, specially equipped restrooms, lowered drinking fountains, lowered telephones, and special doors for wheelchair access.

Services: Counseling and information services are available, as is tutoring in some subjects, math and writing.

Campus Safety and Security: Measures include emergency notification system. There are lighted pathways/sidewalks, and a watchman who maintains campus security at night.

Programs of Study: Covenant confers B.A., B.S. and B.Mus. degrees. Associate and master's degrees are also awarded. Bachelor's degrees are awarded in BIOLOGICAL SCIENCE (biology/biological science), BUSINESS (business administration and management), COMMUNICATIONS AND THE ARTS (art, dramatic arts, English, French, music, music performance, and Spanish), COMPUTER AND PHYSICAL SCIENCE (chemistry, computer science, mathematics, and physics), EDUCATION (elementary education, English education, mathematics education, and science education), SOCIAL SCIENCE (biblical studies, economics, history, interdisciplinary studies, philosophy, philosophy and religion, psychology, social science, and sociology). English, history, sociology and education have the largest enrollments.

Required: All students must complete 55 to 63 hours of core and distribution requirements, including course work in Bible studies, interdisciplinary studies, English composition, cross-cultural experience, language, phys ed, lab science, social science, and history. A minimum total of 126 credits and a GPA of 2.0 are required for graduation. All students must also complete an oral interview and a senior integration project, in which they explore a problem in their major field in light of Christian philosophy.

Special: Cross-registration is possible with the Council for Christian Colleges and Universities (CCCU). Students may study abroad in 9 countries or spend a semester in Washington. There is a 3-2 engineering program with Georgia Tech and other universities and technical institutes. Juniors and seniors may take classes on a pass/fail basis. There are 4 national honor societies and 4 departmental honors programs.

Faculty/Classroom: 75% of faculty are male; 26% are female. All teach undergraduates. No introductory courses are taught by graduate students. The average class size in an introductory lecture is 19; in a laboratory is 16; and in a regular course is 18.

Admissions: 57% of the 2013-2014 applicants were accepted. The SAT scores for the 2013-2014 freshman class were: Critical Reading--10% below 500, 40% between 500 and 599, 37% between 600 and 699, and

13% between 700 and 800; Math--12% below 500, 50% between 500 and 599, 29% between 600 and 699, and 9% between 700 and 800; Writing--14% below 500, 41% between 500 and 599, 34% between 600 and 699, and 11% between 700 and 800. The ACT scores were 2% below 21, 29% between 21 and 23, and 69% above 28. 40% of the current freshmen were in the top fifth of their class; 72% were in the top two fifths.

Requirements: The SAT or ACT is required. Students must submit the following: application for admission, application fee, Christian testimony, official high school transcript, minimum GPA of 2.50, a combined SAT score of at least 1000 (sum of critical reading and math section scores) or composite ACT score of at least 21, academic references, and a church reference. Applicants must graduate from an accredited high school or have a GED. Applicants should have 14 total units, including 4 years of high school English, 3 years of math, and 2 years each of history, science, and social studies. An essay and an interview are required. A GPA of 2.5 is required. AP and CLEP credits are accepted. Important factors in the admissions decision are advanced placement or honors courses, extracurricular activities record, and leadership record.

Procedure: Freshmen are admitted fall and spring. Entrance exams should be taken by January of the senior year. There is a rolling admissions plan. Applications should be filed by May 1 for fall entry; November 1 for spring entry, along with a $35 fee. Notification of early decision is sent August 1.

Transfer: 26 transfer students enrolled in 2012-2013. Transfer applicants must take either the SAT, with a minimum satisfactory score, or the ACT, with a minimum composite of 21. Courses with a grade of C or better that apply toward the selected Covenant program will receive transfer credit. 32 of 126 credits required for the bachelor's degree must be completed at Covenant.

Visiting: There are regularly scheduled orientations for prospective students, consisting of a campus preview weekend during which high school students stay in dormitories and attend classes, seminars, and other college activities. There are guides for informal visits, visitors may sit in on classes, and stay overnight.

Financial Aid: In 2013-2014, 100% of all full-time freshmen and 87% of continuing full-time students received some form of financial aid. 87% of all full-time freshmen and 84% of continuing full-time students received need-based aid. The average freshman award was $23,826. Need-based scholarships or need-based grants averaged $17,26; need-based self-help aid (loans and jobs) averaged $8,003; other non-need-based awards and non-need-based scholarships averaged $10,837; and $6,448 from other forms of aid. 53% of undergraduate students work part-time. Average annual earnings from campus work are $2560. The average financial indebtedness of the 2013 graduate was $22,790. The FAFSA, the state aid form, and the college's own financial statement are required. The priority date for freshman financial aid applications for fall entry is March 1. The deadline for filing freshman financial aid applications for fall entry is March 31.

International Students: There are 16 international students enrolled. The school actively recruits these students. They must take the TOEFL with a minimum score of 540 on the paper-based TOEFL (PBT) or 76 on the Internet-based version (iBT). Applicants are encouraged to take the SAT or ACT if it is available in their country.

Computers: All students may access the system 8 a.m. to 12 a.m. Monday through Thursday and Saturday and 8 a.m. to 6 p.m. on Friday. There are no time limits. The fee is $80.

Graduates: From July 1, 2012 to June 30, 2013, 203 bachelor's degrees were awarded. The most popular majors were education (20%), business/marketing (12%), and social sciences (11%).

Admissions Contact: Sarah Ocando, Assoc. Director of Admissions. E-Mail: *admissions@covenant.edu* Web: *www.covenant.edu*

EMORY UNIVERSITY B-2

Atlanta, GA 30322 (404) 727-6036

Full-time: 2400 men, 3230 women	**Faculty:** n/av; I, +$
Part-time: 15 men, 30 women	**Ph.D.s:** 100%
Graduate: 2250 men, 3030 women	**Student/Faculty:** n/av
Year: semesters, summer session	**Tuition:** $35,000
Application Deadline: open	**Room & Board:** $10,000
Freshman Class: n/av	
SAT or ACT: required	

MOST COMPETITIVE

Emory University, founded in 1836, is a private institution affiliated with the United Methodist Church. The figures in the above capsule and in this profile are approximate. There are 4 undergraduate schools and 7 graduate schools. The 8 libraries contain 3.0 million volumes, 272,000 microform items, and 53,575 audio/video tapes/CDs/DVDs, and subscribe to 54,000 periodicals including electronic. Computerized library services include interlibrary loans, database searching, Internet access, and laptop Internet portals. Special learning facilities include a learning resource center, art gallery, planetarium, radio station, TV station, the Michael C. Carlos Museum, and the Carter Center. The 634-acre campus is in a suburban area 5 miles northeast of downtown Atlanta. Including any residence halls, there are 150 buildings.

Student Life: 80% of undergraduates are from out of state, mostly the South. Students are from 50 states, 47 foreign countries, and Canada. 65% are from public schools. 60% are white; 16% Asian American. 13% claim no religious affiliation; 11% Jewish. The average age of freshmen is 18; all undergraduates, 20. 6% do not continue beyond their first year; 89% remain to graduate.

Housing: 4014 students can be accommodated in college housing, which includes single-sex and coed dorms, on-campus apartments, and married student housing. In addition, there are honors houses, language houses, special-interest houses, fraternity houses, sorority houses, and theme housing. On-campus housing is guaranteed for all 4 years. 70% of students live on campus; of those, 95% remain on campus on weekends. Upperclassmen may keep cars.

Activities: 31% of men belong to 12 national fraternities; 33% of women belong to 13 national sororities. There are 220 groups on campus, including art, bagpipe, band, cheerleading, chess, choir, chorale, chorus, computers, dance, debate, drama, ethnic, film, gay, honors, international, jazz band, literary magazine, musical theater, newspaper, orchestra, pep band, photography, political, professional, radio and TV, religious, social, social service, student government, symphony, and yearbook. Popular campus events include Heritage Ball, Dooley's Week, and Festival of Nine Lessons.

Sports: There are 8 intercollegiate sports for men and 8 for women, and 20 intramural sports for men and 20 for women. Facilities include a recreation center, which contains a 3000-seat gym with 4 basketball courts, 5 volleyball courts, an Olympic-size swimming pool, indoor track, 2 Nautilus weight rooms, a sheer rock wall, and tennis, racquetball, and squash courts. In addition, there is a soccer field and a 400-meter track, with seating for 2000 spectators.

Disabled Students: 90% of the campus is accessible. Facilities include wheelchair ramps, elevators, special parking, specially equipped restrooms, special class scheduling, lowered drinking fountains, lowered telephones, and special housing.

Services: Counseling and information services are available, as is tutoring in most subjects. There is a reader service for the blind.

Campus Safety and Security: Measures include 24-hour foot and vehicle patrol, self-defense education, and security escort services. There are shuttle buses, emergency telephones, lighted pathways/sidewalks, The campus patrol is a fully accredited police department.

Programs of Study: Emory confers B.A., B.S., B.B.A., and B.S.N. degrees. Associate, master's, and doctoral degrees are also awarded. Bachelor's degrees are awarded in AGRICULTURE (environmental studies), BIOLOGICAL SCIENCE (biology/biological science and neurosciences), BUSINESS (accounting, banking and finance, business administration and management, business economics, and marketing/retailing/merchandising), COMMUNICATIONS AND THE ARTS (art, art history and appreciation, Chinese, classics, comparative literature, creative writing, dance, dramatic arts, English, film arts, fine arts, French, Greek, Italian, Japanese, journalism, Latin, linguistics, music, Russian languages and literature, and Spanish), COMPUTER AND PHYSICAL SCIENCE (chemistry, computer science, mathematics, and physics), EDUCATION (educational statistics and research), HEALTH PROFESSIONS (nursing), SOCIAL SCIENCE (African studies, African American studies, American studies, anthropology, Asian/American studies, Asian/Oriental studies, Caribbean studies, classical/ancient civilization, economics, French studies, German area studies, history, interdisciplinary studies, international studies, Italian studies, Judaic studies, Latin American studies, medieval studies, Middle Eastern studies, philosophy, political science/government, psychology, religion, Russian and Slavic studies, sociology, and women's studies).

Required: To graduate, students must complete 132 semester hours, including courses during the first 2 years in English, science, math, history, the social sciences, health, and phys ed. Students must have a GPA of 1.9 for the first 3 years and 2.0 in the senior year. The number of hours required for the major varies by department. A thesis is required for students in honors or dual B.A.-M.A. or B.S.-M.S. programs.

Special: Special academic programs include cross-registration with Atlanta area colleges and universities, departmental internships, work-study programs, dual majors, 3-2 and 4-2 engineering degrees with Georgia Tech, and pass/fail options. A Washington semester and B.A.-B.S. degrees are available, and students may study abroad in many countries. There are accelerated degree programs offered in biology, chemistry, math, physics, English, history, philosophy, political science, sociology, and computer science. There are 30 national honor societies and including Phi Beta Kappa.

Faculty/Classroom: 59% of faculty are male; 41% are female. 58% teach undergraduates, 65% do research. Graduate students teach 10% of introductory courses. The average class size in an introductory lecture is 27; in a laboratory is 27; and in a regular course is 20.

Requirements: The SAT or ACT is required. In addition, students must submit a hight school transcript. Students may submit SAT results, but they are not required unless a student is homeschooled. A recommendation from a high school counselor and up to 2 additional letters of recommendation are required. The student must have acquired 16 academic credits in secondary school, including 4 years of English, 3 years of math, and 2 years each of history, science, and foreign language. AP credits are accepted. Important factors in the admissions decision are advanced placement or honors courses, recommendations by school officials, and extracurricular activities record.

Procedure: Freshmen are admitted fall. Entrance exams should be taken prior to applying. There are early decision, early admissions, and deferred admissions plans. Check with the school for current application deadlines. The fall application fee was $50. Applications are accepted online.

Transfer: Applicants must have taken the SAT or ACT and completed at least 1 year of college, with a GPA of 3.0. 64 of 132 credits required for the bachelor's degree must be completed at Emory.

Visiting: There are regularly scheduled orientations for prospective students, including a student-led campus tour and an informational focus session led by a member of our Admission staff. Prospective students may also arrange to sit in on classes, as well as meet with faculty or athletic coaches. There are guides for informal visits and visitors may sit in on classes. To schedule a visit, contact Office of Undergraduate Admission.

Financial Aid: Emory is a member of CSS. The CSS/Profile and FAFSA are required. Check with the school for current application deadlines.

International Students: The school actively recruits these students. They must take the TOEFL. They must also take the SAT or ACT.

Computers: Wireless access is available. All students may access the system. 24 hours a day. There are no time limits and no fees.

Admissions Contact: Admissions Department, Dean of Admissions. A campus DVD is available. E-Mail: *admiss@learnlink.emory.edu* Web: *www.emory.edu/admissions*

FORT VALLEY STATE UNIVERSITY B-3

Fort Valley, GA 31030 **(478) 825-6307; (478) 825-6169**

Full-time: 1313 men, 1688 women
Part-time: 175 men, 245 women
Graduate: 64 men, 86 women
Year: semesters, summer session
Application Deadline:
Faculty: 153
Ph.D.s: 64%
Student/Faculty: 20 to 1
Tuition: $5012 ($16,626)
Room & Board: $6188
Freshman Class: 5343 applied, 2161 accepted, 960 enrolled
SAT or ACT: required

VERY COMPETITIVE

Fort Valley State University, founded in 1895, is a public land-grant member of the University System of Georgia. The university offers undergraduate programs in the arts and sciences, business, education, agriculture, engineering, and other vocational and technical fields. Graduate programs are offered in early childhood, middle grades education, mental health and rehabilitation counseling, and guidance counseling. The figures in the above capsule and in this profile is approximate. There are 3 undergraduate schools and 1 graduate school. In addition to regional accreditation, FVSU has baccalaureate program accreditation with NCATE. The library contains 250,000 volumes, 172,000 microform items, and subscribes to 1,168 periodicals including electronic. Computerized library services include interlibrary loans and database searching. Special learning facilities include a radio station, TV station, experimental agricultural plots, animal research centers, and greenhouse complex. The 1375-acre campus is in a rural area 30 miles southwest of Macon. Including any residence halls, there are 35 buildings.

Student Life: 96% of undergraduates are from Georgia. Others are from 29 states, and 5 foreign countries. 92% are African American. The average age of freshmen is 19; all undergraduates, 21. 27% do not continue beyond their first year; 39% remain to graduate.

Housing: 1450 students can be accommodated in college housing, which includes single-sex and coed dorms and on-campus apartments. On-campus housing is guaranteed for the freshman year only, is available on a first-come, and first-served basis. 62% of students live on campus. Alcohol is not permitted. All students may keep cars.

Activities: 5% of men belong to 4 national fraternities; 2% of women belong to 5 national sororities. There are 73 groups on campus, including band, cheerleading, choir, chorus, dance, drama, honors, international, jazz band, marching band, newspaper, opera, orchestra, political, radio and TV, religious, social service, and student government. Popular campus events include Black History month.

Sports: There are 5 intercollegiate sports for men and 6 for women, and 3 intramural sports for men and 3 for women. Facilities include a stadium, a gym, a baseball field, lighted tennis courts, an indoor swimming pool, indoor and outdoor tracks, and shuffleboard courts.

Disabled Students: All of the campus is accessible. Facilities include wheelchair ramps, elevators, special parking, specially equipped restrooms, and special housing.

Services: Counseling and information services are available, as is tutoring in most subjects. There is remedial math, reading, and writing.

Campus Safety and Security: Measures include 24-hour foot and vehicle patrol. There are emergency telephones.

Programs of Study: FVSU confers B.A., B.S., B.B.A. and B.S.W. degrees. Associate and master's degrees are also awarded. Bachelor's degrees are awarded in AGRICULTURE (agricultural economics, animal science, horticulture, and plant science), BIOLOGICAL SCIENCE (biology/biological science, nutrition, and zoology), BUSINESS (accounting, business administration and management, marketing/retailing/merchandising, and office supervision and management), COMMUNICATIONS AND THE ARTS (communications and English), COMPUTER AND PHYSICAL SCIENCE (chemistry, computer science, information sciences and systems, and mathematics), EDUCATION (agricultural education, early childhood education, home economics education, mathematics education, middle school education, physical education, and secondary education), ENGINEERING AND ENVIRONMENTAL DESIGN (agricultural engineering technology, commercial art, and electrical/electronics engineering technology), HEALTH PROFESSIONS (veterinary science), SOCIAL SCIENCE (child psychology/development, criminal justice, economics, political science/government, psychology, social work, and sociology).

Required: Students must complete a minimum of 120 credit hours, plus 5 additional hours to satisfy requirements for freshmen orientation and for military science or phys ed. General education requirements include courses in humanities, social science, and math/science, and courses in the major. The bachelor's degree requires a minimum GPA of 2.0 and no grade below C in the major.

Special: Students may participate in cooperative work-study programs with local industries, cross-register for courses at Robins Residence Center, and study abroad. FVSU also offers a 3-2 dual degree program in chemistry/geosciences with University of Oklahoma, in engineering or other technical fields with Georgia Institute of Technology, and a 3-2 engineering degree with University of Nevada, Las Vegas. There are 5 national honor societies and a freshman honors program.

Faculty/Classroom: 50% of faculty are male; 50% are female. No introductory courses are taught by graduate students. The average class size in a regular course is 25.

Admissions: 40% of the 2013-2014 applicants were accepted.

Requirements: The SAT or ACT is required. Applicants must be graduates of an accredited secondary school or have earned a GED. The university requires at least 17 academic units of study, including 4 in English, 3 in social science, 3 each in math and science, and 2 of foreign language. A GPA of 2.7 is required. AP and CLEP credits are accepted.

Procedure: Freshmen are admitted to all sessions. There are early admissions, deferred admissions, and rolling admissions plans. Check with the school for current application deadlines. The application fee is $30. Applications are accepted online.

Transfer: 135 transfer students enrolled in 2012-2013. In addition to meeting standard admission requirements, transfers must submit transcripts from all colleges previously attended. Transfer credit is accepted based on a 2.0 minimum GPA, and only courses with a C or better will be accepted. 45 of 125 credits required for the bachelor's degree must be completed at FVSU.

Visiting: There are regularly scheduled orientations for prospective students, including an overview, an introduction of administration and faculty, and a tour. There are guides for informal visits and visitors may sit in on classes. To schedule a visit, contact the Office of Enrollment Management.

Financial Aid: In 2013-2014, 94% of all full-time freshmen students received some form of financial aid. 8% of all full-time freshmen students received need-based aid. The average freshman award was $2,300. Need-based scholarships or need-based grants averaged $2,300; need-based self-help aid (loans and jobs) averaged $2,425; and other non-need-based awards and non-need-based scholarships averaged $1,850. The FAFSA is required. Check with the school for current application deadlines.

International Students: There are 23 international students enrolled. They must take the TOEFL and the college's own test. They must also take the SAT or ACT.

Computers: There are no time limits and no fees.

Graduates: From July 1, 2012 to June 30, 2013, 230 bachelor's degrees were awarded. The most popular majors were mathmatics (43%), visual/performing arts (17%), and psychology (10%). In an average class, 13% graduate in 4 years or less, 33% graduate in 5 years or less, and 39% graduate in 6 years or less.

Admissions Contact: Donovan Coley, Interim Director of Admissions. Web: *www.fvsu.edu*

GEORGIA COLLEGE AND STATE UNIVERSITY C-3

Milledgeville, GA 31061 **(478) 445-1283; (478) 445-1914**

Full-time: 2091 men, 3173 women **Faculty:** 317; IIA, --$
Part-time: 203 men, 262 women **Ph.D.s:** n/av
Graduate: 279 men, 543 women **Student/Faculty:** 17 to 1
Year: semesters, summer session **Tuition:** $8790 ($26,690)
Application Deadline: April 1 **Room & Board:** $9426
Freshman Class: 4056 applied, 2754 accepted, 1392 enrolled
SAT CR/M/W: 573/570/557 **ACT:** 24 **VERY COMPETITIVE**

Georgia College and State University, founded in 1889, is the public liberal arts university of Georgia. There are 4 undergraduate schools and one graduate school. In addition to regional accreditation, Georgia College has baccalaureate program accreditation with AACSB and NCATE. The library contains 210,609 volumes, 24,459 microform items, and 12,963 audio/video tapes/CDs/DVDs, and subscribes to 42,613 periodicals including electronic. Computerized library services include interlibrary loans, database searching, Internet access, and Wi-Fi capability. Special learning facilities include an art gallery, natural history museum, planetarium, radio station, TV station, Campus Theatre -an art deco theatre adjacent to the campus serves as a performance space and bookstore for both the college and the community. The 602-acre campus is in a small town 30 miles from Macon. Including any residence halls, there are 91 buildings.

Student Life: 98% of undergraduates are from Georgia. Others are from 23 states, 42 foreign countries, and Canada. 85% are White. The average age of freshmen is 18; all undergraduates, 20. 15% do not continue beyond their first year; 85% remain to graduate.

Housing: 2237 students can be accommodated in college housing, which includes single-sex and coed dorms and off-campus apartments. In addition, there are honors houses and special-interest houses. On-campus housing is guaranteed for the freshman year only, is available on a first-come, and first-served basis. 65% of students commute. All students may keep cars.

Activities: 19% of men belong to 9 national fraternities; 34% of women belong to 10 national sororities. There are 145 groups on campus, including band, cheerleading, choir, chorale, chorus, dance, debate, drama, ethnic, gay, honors, international, jazz band, literary magazine, musical theater, photography, political, professional, radio and TV, religious, residence student association, social, social service, student government, and yearbook. Popular campus events include Week of Welcome, Progressive Dinner and International Week.

Sports: There are 5 intercollegiate sports for men and 6 for women, and 13 intramural sports for men and 13 for women. Georgia College Wellness & recreation Center is LEED Silver certified and encompasses 101,000 square feet. Reflecting the university's commitment to a holistic approach to health and wellness, the center combines fitness and recreation activities, health education programs and formal wellness courses with health services and counseling services - all in one centralized location.

Disabled Students: 90% of the campus is accessible. Facilities include wheelchair ramps, elevators, special parking, specially equipped restrooms, special class scheduling, lowered drinking fountains, lowered telephones, and special housing.

Services: Counseling and information services are available, as is tutoring in some subjects such as math, calculus, statistics, economics, chemistry, biology, physics, accounting, and management.

Campus Safety and Security: Measures include 24-hour foot and vehicle patrol, emergency notification system, self-defense education, and security escort services. There are shuttle buses, emergency telephones, lighted pathways/sidewalks, and controlled access to dorms/residences.

Programs of Study: Georgia College confers B.A., B.S., B.B.A., B.M.E., B.M.T. and B.S.N. degrees. Master's and doctoral degrees are also awarded. Bachelor's degrees are awarded in BIOLOGICAL SCIENCE (biology/biological science), BUSINESS (accounting, business administration and management, management science, marketing and distribution, and recreation and leisure services), COMMUNICATIONS AND THE ARTS (art, dramatic arts, English, French, journalism, music, Spanish, and speech/debate/rhetoric), COMPUTER AND PHYSICAL SCIENCE (chemistry, computer science, information sciences and systems, mathematics, and physics), EDUCATION (athletic training, early childhood education, middle school education, music education, and special education), ENGINEERING AND ENVIRONMENTAL DESIGN (environmental science), HEALTH PROFESSIONS (community health work, exercise science, music therapy, and nursing), SOCIAL SCIENCE (criminal justice, economics, geography, history, liberal arts/general studies, philosophy, political science/government, psychology, and sociology). Biology, nursing, and management are the largest.

Required: To graduate, students must complete at least 120 semester hours, of which 40 must be completed in residence. Complete 21 of the last 30 credit hours at the upper level. All B.A. candidates and some B.S. candidates must demonstrate a foreign language proficiency. All students must pass an exam on the history and Constitution of both the United States and Georgia, the reading and writing sections of the Regents exam, and a senior exit exam in the major. They must also earn a C or better in English 1101.

Special: GCSU has study-abroad agreements with institutions worldwide, a Washington semester, co-op programs, internships, work-study programs, dual majors, independent study, and student-designed majors. There is a 3-2 engineering degree program with the Georgia Institute of Technology. There is a freshman honors program.

Faculty/Classroom: 45% of faculty are male; 55% are female. All teach undergraduates. No introductory courses are taught by graduate students.

Admissions: 68% of the 2013-2014 applicants were accepted. The SAT scores for the 2013-2014 freshman class were: Critical Reading--11% below 500, 55% between 500 and 599, 30% between 600 and 699, and 4% between 700 and 800; Math--13% below 500, 51% between 500 and 599, 33% between 600 and 699, and 3% between 700 and 800; Writing--18% below 500, 53% between 500 and 599, 26% between 600 and 699, and 2% between 700 and 800. The ACT scores were 9% below 21, 29% between 21 and 23, 42% between 24 and 26, 14% between 27 and 28, and 6% above 28.

Requirements: The SAT or ACT is required. The ACT Optional Writing test is also required. In addition, Applicants must be graduates of an accredited or recognized secondary school and must complete the Georgia college preparatory curriculum requirements, including 4 units each of English and math (with math I or algebra I being the minimum level for consideration), 4 of science, (including 2 lab sciences), 2 of the same foreign language, and 3 of social science. A GPA of 2.0 is required. AP and CLEP credits are accepted. Important factors in the admissions decision are advanced placement or honors courses, extracurricular activities record, and evidence of special talent.

Procedure: Freshmen are admitted to all sessions. Entrance exams should be taken reg admission, ACT in Feb & SAT in March. There are early admissions, deferred admissions, and rolling admissions plans. Applications should be filed by April 1 for fall entry; November 1 for spring entry; and May 1 for summer entry, along with a $35 fee. Notification is sent on a rolling basis. Applications are accepted online.

Transfer: 415 transfer students enrolled in 2012-2013. To transfer applicants must submit official transcripts from all colleges attended and be eligible to return to their previous institution. Those who have completed fewer than 30 semester hours must meet all freshman admissions requirements. Applicants' transfer GPA is determined by number of credit hours being transferred. 40 of 120 credits required for the bachelor's degree must be completed at Georgia College.

Visiting: There are regularly scheduled orientations for prospective students, includes receptions, tours, school meetings, information sessions, and academic and cocurricular advising and registration. There are guides for informal visits and visitors may sit in on classes. To schedule a visit, contact the Office of Admissions at admissions@gcsu.edu.

Financial Aid: The average freshman award was $7,686. Need-based scholarships or need-based grants averaged $4,173; need-based self-help aid (loans and jobs) averaged $3,299; and non-need-based athletic scholarships averaged $2,792. 15% of undergraduate students work part-time. Average annual earnings from campus work are $7810. The average financial indebtedness of the 2013 graduate was $18,195. The FAFSA is required. The priority date for freshman financial aid applications for fall entry is March. The deadline for filing freshman financial aid applications for fall entry is July 1.

International Students: There are 72 international students enrolled. The school actively recruits these students. They must take the TOEFL with a minimum score of 500 on the paper-based TOEFL (PBT) or 61 on the Internet-based version (iBT), SAT Verbal score of 440, ACT English score of 17, or IELTS score of 6.0. To comply with NCAA regulations, international students who will compete in intercollegiate athletics must take either the SAT or ACT.

Computers: All students may access the system. Lab hours vary. There are no time limits. The fee is $68.

Graduates: From July 1, 2012 to June 30, 2013, 1183 bachelor's degrees were awarded. The most popular majors were psychology (10%), management (9%), and nursing (8%). In an average class, 33% graduate in 4 years or less, 51% graduate in 5 years or less, and 57% graduate in 6 years or less.

Admissions Contact: Stephen Lazawski, Director of Admissions. E-Mail: *admissions@gcsu.edu* Web: *www.gcsu.edu*

GEORGIA INSTITUTE OF TECHNOLOGY B-2

Atlanta, GA 30332 **(404) 894-4154; (404) 894-9511**

Full-time: 8837 men, 4454 women **Faculty:** n/av; I, +$
Part-time: 888 men, 379 women **Ph.D.s:** 84%
Graduate: 5121 men, 1792 women **Student/Faculty:** 18 to 1
Year: semesters, summer session **Tuition:** $10,650 ($29,954)
Application Deadline: January 10 **Room & Board:** $9814
Freshman Class: 17669 applied, 7265 accepted, 2673 enrolled
SAT CR/M/W: 660/710/670 **ACT:** 31 **MOST COMPETITIVE**

Georgia Institute of Technology, founded in 1885, is a public technological institution offering programs in architecture, management, policy, international affairs, engineering, computing, and science. There are 6 undergraduate schools and 6 graduate schools. In addition to regional accreditation, Georgia Tech has baccalaureate program accreditation with AACSB, ABET, ACCE, NAAB, and NASAD. The library contains 2.5 million volumes, 4.8 million microform items, and 327,587 audio/video tapes/CDs/DVDs, and subscribes to 24,736 periodicals including electronic. Computerized library services include interlibrary loans, database searching, Internet access, and Wi-Fi capability. Special learning facilities include an art gallery, radio station, TV station, G. Wayne Clough Undergraduate Learning Commons, Center for Academic Enrichment, Center for Academic Success, Center for the Enhancement of Teaching and Learning, Communication Center. The 400-acre campus is in an urban area in Atlanta, GA. Including any residence halls, there are 239 buildings.

Student Life: 64% of undergraduates are from Georgia. Others are from 48 states, 86 foreign countries, and Canada. 55% are White; 18% Asian American; 11% Foreign. The average age of freshmen is 18; all undergraduates, 20. 4% do not continue beyond their first year; 79% remain to graduate.

Housing: 9744 students can be accommodated in college housing, which includes single-sex and coed dorms, on-campus apartments, and married student housing. In addition, there are honors houses, language houses, special-interest houses, fraternity houses, sorority houses, freshman experience. On-campus housing is available on a first-come and first-served basis. 52% of students live on campus; of those, 74% remain on campus on weekends. Alcohol is not permitted. All students may keep cars.

Activities: 23% of men belong to 35 national fraternities; 29% of women belong to 15 national sororities. There are 529 groups on campus, including athletic and outdoor., cultural, art, band, cheerleading, chess, choir, chorale, chorus, communications, computers, debate, departmental, drama, drill team, environmental, ethnic, film, gay, honors, international, jazz band, literary magazine, marching band, newspaper, orchestra, pep band, photography, political, professional, radio and TV, religious, social, social service, student government, symphony, and yearbook. Popular campus events include Team Buzz, Into the Streets, MLK Day of Service, Relay for Life and Tech Beautification Day.

Sports: There are 9 intercollegiate sports for men and 8 for women, and 7 intramural sports for men and 7 for women. Facilities include a 4,000-seat baseball stadium, a 55,000-seat football stadium, softball fields, an 8,600-seat basketball arena, a golf practice facility, an 88,000-square-foot football practice facility, a basketball practice center with a 2,000-square-foot weight room, an Olympic aquatic center for swimming and diving, a state-of-the-art 6-court indoor tennis complex that seats 232 spectators, outdoor tennis courts, and outdoor turf field featuring flag football fields, 2 outdoor sand volleyball courts, and a 300,659 square foot recreation center with 6 multipurpose indoor courts, strength training and cardio-fitness, 4 racquetball/wallyball/squash courts, a running track, a climbing wall, co-ed sauna, 3 studios for aerobic fitness programs.

Disabled Students: 75% of the campus is accessible. Facilities include wheelchair ramps, elevators, special parking, specially equipped restrooms, special class scheduling, lowered drinking fountains, special housing. visual alarms in housing, assistive listening devices, and adaptable living space.

Services: Counseling and information services are available, as is tutoring in most subjects. There is a reader service for the blind, and remedial math, reading, and writing. The Learning Assistance Program provides tutors for calculus, chemistry, and physics through call-in Tutor-Vision, which airs live on the GT Cable Network. One to One Tutoring is offered in addition to success workshops, Peer Led Undergraduate Study (PLUS), walk-in tutoring and academic coaching.

Campus Safety and Security: Measures include 24-hour foot and vehicle patrol, emergency notification system, self-defense education, and security escort services. There are shuttle buses, emergency telephones, lighted pathways/sidewalks, controlled access to dorms/residences, foot patrol, bike patrol, limited access to dorms, mobile security patrol, video cameras, K-9 force, and bike and laptop registration is offered.

Programs of Study: Georgia Tech confers B.S. degrees. Master's and doctoral degrees are also awarded. Bachelor's degrees are awarded in BIOLOGICAL SCIENCE (biochemistry and biology/biological science), BUSINESS (business administration and management and international economics), COMMUNICATIONS AND THE ARTS (industrial design), COMPUTER AND PHYSICAL SCIENCE (applied mathematics, applied physics, chemistry, computer science, earth science, mathematics, physics, and polymer science), ENGINEERING AND ENVIRONMENTAL DESIGN (aeronautical engineering, architecture, biomedical engineering, chemical engineering, civil engineering, computer engineering, construction management, electrical/electronics engineering, environmental engineering, industrial engineering, materials engineering, materials science, mechanical engineering, nuclear engineering, and technology and public affairs), SOCIAL SCIENCE (economics, history of science, international relations, psychology, and public affairs). Engineering, management and computer science are the strongest academically. Mechanical engineering, biomedical engineering and industrial engineering have the largest enrollments.

Required: All students must fulfill the core curriculum requirements and maintain a 2.0 GPA for their entire academic program. Core curriculum requirements include 12 hours of science, math, and technology; 12 hours of social sciences, 13 hours of essential skills courses (English composition, calculus, and computing), 6 hours of humanities, and 5 or more hours of electives depending on the major. Other course requirements include a U.S. and Georgia history/constitution course, a global perspectives course, a U.S perspectives course, an ethics course, and a wellness course.

Special: Extensive co-op programs, cross-registration with other Atlanta-area colleges, internships, and undergraduate research opportunities are available. Numerous study abroad opportunities available. An engineering transfer program is offered within the university system, and a liberal arts-engineering dual degree program serves area colleges and institutions nationwide. Students have access to multidisciplinary and certificate programs outside their major field of study. The College of Engineering offers the opportunity to transfer to Georgia Tech via the Dual Degree Engineering Program (DDEP) and the Regional Engineering Transfer Program (RETP). There are 25 national honor societies, a freshman honors program, and 11 departmental honors programs.

Faculty/Classroom: 74% of faculty are male; 26% are female. No introductory courses are taught by graduate students. The average class size in an introductory lecture is 39; in a laboratory is 17; and in a regular course is 33.

Admissions: 41% of the 2013-2014 applicants were accepted. The SAT scores for the 2013-2014 freshman class were: Critical Reading--1% below 500, 12% between 500 and 599, 52% between 600 and 699, and 34% between 700 and 800; Math--3% between 500 and 599, 36% between 600 and 699, and 61% between 700 and 800; Writing--1% below 500, 11% between 500 and 599, 54% between 600 and 699, and 34% between 700 and 800. The ACT scores were 1% below 21, 1% between 21 and 23, 7% between 24 and 26, 11% between 27 and 28, and 80% above 28. There were 119 National Merit finalists.

Requirements: The SAT or ACT is required. The ACT Optional Writing test is also required. Candidates for admission must have completed 4 units each of English and Math; 3 units of Social Studies; 4 units of Science, including 2 units of lab sciences; and 2 units of a foreign language. An essay is required. AP credits are accepted.

Procedure: Freshmen are admitted fall and summer. Entrance exams should be taken by the end of the junior year. There are early admissions and deferred admissions plans. Applications should be filed by January 10 for fall entry; January 10 for summer entry. The fall 2013 application fee was $75. Notifications are sent March 15. 1655 applicants were on the 2013 waiting list; 270 were admitted. Applications are accepted online.

Transfer: 817 transfer students enrolled in 2012-2013. Transfer applicants must have completed a minimum of 30 semester hours or 45 quarter hours of course work. All of the specifically required courses on the course requirements chart for the prospective major must be completed. Grades and academic standing must be satisfactory for the last term of enrollment at the prior college. The minimum transfer GPA requirement for most majors is 3.00. Some programs require a higher transfer GPA. 36 of 122 credits required for the bachelor's degree must be completed at Georgia Tech.

Visiting: There are regularly scheduled orientations for prospective students, the session is conducted by a counselor from the Office of Undergraduate Admission who discusses the admission process, majors, opportunities outside of the classroom, campus activities, and student life. There are guides for informal visits, visitors may sit in on classes, and stay overnight. To schedule a visit, contact the Office of Undergraduate Admissions.

Financial Aid: In 2013-2014, 42% of all full-time freshmen and 45% of continuing full-time students received some form of financial aid. 40% of all full-time freshmen and 39% of continuing full-time students received need-based aid. The average freshman award was $17,497. Need-based scholarships or need-based grants averaged $10,096; need-based self-help aid (loans and jobs) averaged $6,055; non-need-based athletic scholarships averaged $17,541; and other non need-based awards and non-need-based scholarships averaged $3,796. The average financial indebtedness of the 2013 graduate was $25,027. The FAFSA and the college's own financial statement are required. The deadline for filing freshman financial aid applications for fall entry is February 15.

International Students: There are 1544 international students enrolled. They must also take the SAT or ACT, scoring 430.

Computers: All students may access the system. There are no time limits and no fees.

Graduates: From July 1, 2012 to June 30, 2013, 3122 bachelor's degrees were awarded. The most popular majors were mechanical engineering (13%), management (10%), and industrial engineering (10%). 819 companies recruited on campus in 2012-2013. In an average class, 40% graduate in 4 years or less, 75% graduate in 5 years or less, and 82% graduate in 6 years or less. Of the 2012 graduating class, 20% were enrolled in graduate school within 6 months of graduation, and 70% were employed.

Admissions Contact: Rick Clark, Director of Undergraduate Admissions. E-Mail: *admission@gatech.edu* Web: *www.gatech.edu*

GEORGIA REGENTS UNIVERSITY D-2

Augusta, GA 30904-2200 (706) 737-1632; (706) 667-4355

Full-time: 1600 men, 2562 women
Part-time: 682 men, 1117 women
Graduate: 209 men, 571 women
Year: semesters, summer session
Application Deadline: July 21
Freshman Class: n/av
SAT or ACT: required

Faculty: n/av; IIA, --$
Ph.D.s: n/av
Student/Faculty: n/av
Tuition: $4634 ($16,248)
Room & Board: n/av

COMPETITIVE

Georgia Regents University, founded in 1925, is a liberal arts institution within the University System of Georgia. There are 3 undergraduate schools and 3 graduate schools. In addition to regional accreditation, has baccalaureate program accreditation with AACSB, CSWE, NASAD, NASM, NCATE, and NLN. The figures in the above capsule and in this profile are approximate. The library contains 765,268 volumes, 1.3 million microform items, and 6,876 audio/video tapes/CDs/DVDs, and subscribes to 35,705 periodicals including electronic. Computerized library services include interlibrary loans, database searching, Internet access, and laptop Internet portals. Special learning facilities include a learning resource center, art gallery, radio station, History Walk and Guardhouse Museum. The 316-acre campus is in a small town 140 miles east of Atlanta on the Georgia-South Carolina border. Including any residence halls, there are 35 buildings.

Student Life: 89% of undergraduates are from Georgia. Others are from 45 states, 60 foreign countries, and Canada. 95% are from public schools. 56% are white; 27% African American. The average age of freshmen is 19; all undergraduates, 24. 32% do not continue beyond their first year; 25% remain to graduate.

Housing: All students commute. All students may keep cars.

Activities: 1% of men belong to 3 national fraternities; 1% of women belong to 3 national sororities. There are 64 groups on campus, including art, band, cheerleading, choir, chorus, drama, ethnic, film, gay, honors, international, jazz band, literary magazine, musical theater, newspaper, orchestra, pep band, photography, political, professional, radio and TV, religious, social, social service, student government, and symphony. Popular campus events include Homecoming, Lyceum Series, Family Fun Days, and Pig Out.

Sports: There are 5 intercollegiate sports for men and 6 for women, and 2 intramural sports for men and 2 for women. Facilities include a 2000-seat gym and fitness center; baseball, soccer, and softball fields; a tennis center; an 18-hole golf course with club house; golf house; fitness center in the student activites center.

Disabled Students: 90% of the campus is accessible. Facilities include wheelchair ramps, elevators, special parking, specially equipped restrooms, special class scheduling, lowered drinking fountains, and lowered telephones.

Services: Counseling and information services are available, as is tutoring in most subjects. There is a reader service for the blind, and remedial math, reading, and writing.

Campus Safety and Security: Measures include 24-hour foot and vehicle patrol, emergency notification system, and security escort services. There are shuttle buses, emergency telephones, lighted pathways/sidewalks, controlled access to dorms/residences, controlled access to labs after hours.

Programs of Study: confers B.A., B.S., B.B.A., B.F.A., B.M., B.S.Ed., B.S.W., B.S.N, and B.S.K degrees. Associate and master's degrees are also awarded. Bachelor's degrees are awarded in BIOLOGICAL SCIENCE (biology/biological science), BUSINESS (accounting, banking and finance, business administration and management, management information systems, and marketing/retailing/merchandising), COMMUNICATIONS AND THE ARTS (art, communications, English, French, music, performing arts, Spanish, and studio art), COMPUTER AND PHYSICAL SCIENCE (chemistry, computer science, mathematics, and physics), EDUCATION (elementary education, foreign languages education, health education, middle school education, music education, and special education), HEALTH PROFESSIONS (nursing), SOCIAL SCIENCE (criminal justice, history, political science/government, psychology, social work, and sociology). Biology, nursing, psychology, management, and early childhood education have the largest enrollments.

Required: Students must complete 125 hours with a minimum GPA of 2.0. All students are required to take 6 courses in phys ed., pass the Regents test in reading and composition, and demonstrate, through course completion or exam, a knowledge of U.S. and Georgia history and their constitutions.

Special: The school offers co-op programs and internships with area companies, work-study programs, dual majors, nondegree study, and cross-registration with Paine College. There are 5 national honor societies, a freshman honors program, and 7 departmental honors programs.

Faculty/Classroom: No introductory courses are taught by graduate students. The average class size in an introductory lecture is 30; in a laboratory is 19; and in a regular course is 27.

Requirements: The SAT or ACT is required. In addition, applicants must have at least a 2.0 HSGPA,with a verbal score of 430 and math score of 400 on the SAT or a comparable score on the ACT. Applicants must be graduates of an accredited secondary school. The GED is accepted. Secondary school courses must include 4 units each of English and math, 3 each of science and social science, and 2 of a foreign language. A GPA of 2.0 is required. AP and CLEP credits are accepted.

Procedure: Freshmen are admitted fall, spring, and summer. There are deferred admissions and rolling admissions plans. Applications should be filed by July 21 for fall entry; December 6 for spring entry, along with a $30 fee. Applications are accepted online.

Transfer: 454 transfer students enrolled in a recent year. Applicants must have completed 30 semester or 45 quarter hours. If fewer than 15 semester hours have been completed, students are considered as entering freshmen and are required to submit appropriate paperwork. 30 of 125 credits required for the bachelor's degree must be completed at Augusta.

Visiting: There are regularly scheduled orientations for prospective students, campus tour, discussion of schedules and deadlines, registration. There are guides for informal visits and visitors may sit in on classes. To schedule a visit, contact the Admissions Office.

Financial Aid: The FAFSA is required. The deadline for filing freshman financial aid applications for fall entry is March 1.

International Students: There are 93 international students enrolled. They must take the TOEFL with a minimum score of 500 on the paper-based TOEFL (PBT). They must also take the SAT or ACT.

Computers: The entire campus and the residential village are wi-fi accessible; there are 13 labs on campus, 7 of which are walk-in labs and 2 are 24-hour accessible. Students may also check out laptop computers from the IT department. All students may access the system. There are no time limits and no fees.

Graduates: In a recent year, 656 bachelor's degrees were awarded. The most popular majors were elementary education (13%), communications (8%), and psychology (7%). 100 companies recruited on campus in a recent year.

Admissions Contact: Registrar and Director of Admissions. E-Mail: *admissions@aug.edu* Web: *www.aug.edu*

GEORGIA SOUTHERN UNIVERSITY D-3

Statesboro, GA 30458 (912) 478-5391; (912) 478-7240

Full-time: 7896 men, 7866 women
Part-time: 1062 men, 1080 women
Graduate: 902 men, 1711 women
Year: semesters, summer session
Application Deadline: May 1
Freshman Class: 10134 applied, 5759 accepted, 3583 enrolled
SAT CR/M/W: 550/550/520 **ACT:** 23

Faculty: 696; IIA, --$
Ph.D.s: 82%
Student/Faculty: 22 to 1
Tuition: $7066 ($19,648)
Room & Board: $9348

COMPETITIVE

We are a Carnegie Doctoral-Research university providing the classic residential campus experience. Georgia's largest and most comprehensive center of higher education south of Atlanta, 45 states including the District of Columbia and 89 nations are represented in the student body. The University's hallmark is student-centered education for undergraduate and graduate students alike. There are 7 undergraduate schools and one graduate school. In addition to regional accreditation, Georgia Southern has baccalaureate program accreditation with AACSB, ABET, ACCE, NASAD, NASM, NCATE, and NRPA. The library contains 641,076 volumes, 896,509 microform items, and 29,683 audio/video tapes/CDs/DVDs, and subscribes to 44,827 periodicals including electronic. Computerized library services include interlibrary loans, database searching, Internet access, and Wi-Fi capability. Special learning facilities include an art gallery, natural history museum, planetarium, radio station, Center for Art and Theatre, Bureau of Business Research & Economic Development, Center for Retail Studies, Child Development Center, Division of Continuing Education, Garden of the Coastal Plain, Georgia Southern University Museum, Performing Arts Center, Small Business Development Center, Sustainability, and Wildlife Education Center. The 900-acre campus is in a small town 1 hour from Savannah, 2 hours from Florida, and about 3 hours from metropolitan Atlanta. Including any residence halls, there are 204 buildings.

Student Life: 95% of undergraduates are from Georgia. Others are from 47 states, 73 foreign countries, and Canada. 63% are White; 26% African American. 93% claim no religious affiliation. The average age of freshmen is 18; all undergraduates, 21. 20% do not continue beyond their first year; 50% remain to graduate.

Housing: 4947 students can be accommodated in college housing, which includes coed dorms, on-campus apartments, and off-campus apartments. In addition, there are honors houses and special-interest houses. On-campus housing is guaranteed for the freshman year only, is available on a first-come, first-served basis, and is available on a lottery system for upperclassmen. 71% of students commute. All students may keep cars.

Activities: 12% of men belong to 34 national fraternities; 15% of women belong to 12 national sororities. There are 280 groups on campus, including art, band, cheerleading, choir, chorale, chorus, communications, computers, dance, drama, environmental, ethnic, film, gay, honors, international, jazz band, literary magazine, marching band, musical theater, newspaper, opera, orchestra, photography, political, professional, radio and TV, religious, social, social service, student government, and symphony. Popular campus events include Eagle Camp, Boro Browse and Eagle Rally.

Sports: There are 6 intercollegiate sports for men and 9 for women, and 18 intramural sports for men and 18 for women. Facilities include a baseball, football, and softball stadiums; volleyball and basketball field house, natorium, tennis courts, track/soccer stadium, golf practice facility and rifle shooting range.

Disabled Students: 97% of the campus is accessible. Facilities include wheelchair ramps, elevators, special parking, specially equipped restrooms, special class scheduling, lowered drinking fountains, lowered telephones, and special housing.

Services: Counseling and information services are available, as is tutoring in most subjects. There is a reader service for the blind, and remedial math, reading, and writing.

Campus Safety and Security: Measures include 24-hour foot and vehicle patrol, emergency notification system, self-defense education, and security escort services. There are shuttle buses, emergency telephones, lighted pathways/sidewalks, panic button alarms in all residence hall rooms.

Programs of Study: Georgia Southern confers B.A., B.B.A., B.F.A, B.G.S., B.M., B.S.A.T., B.S., B.S.B., B.S.C.E., B.S.Chem., B.S.Cons., B.S.Ed., B.S.E.E., B.S.GraphCom., B.S.H.S., B.S.I.T., B.S.J.S., B.S.K., B.S.Mat., B.S.M.E., B.S.N. and B.S.P. degrees. Master's and doctoral degrees are also awarded. Bachelor's degrees are awarded in BIOLOGICAL SCIENCE (biology/biological science, nutritional sciences, and physiology), BUSINESS (accounting, fashion merchandising, finance, logistics, management information systems, marketing/retailing/merchandising, and sports management), COMMUNICATIONS AND THE ARTS (art, English, graphic communications management, graphic design, modern language, multimedia, music, music composition, music performance, public relations, theatre arts, and writing), COMPUTER AND PHYSICAL SCIENCE (chemistry, chemistry / chemical biology, computer science, geology, mathematics, and physics), EDUCATION (athletic training, early childhood education, health education, journalism education, middle school education, music education, reading education, recreation education, and special education), ENGINEERING AND ENVIRONMENTAL DESIGN (civil engineering, construction management, electrical/ electronics engineering, interior design, and mechanical engineering), HEALTH PROFESSIONS (exercise science, health promotion, and nursing), SOCIAL SCIENCE (anthropology, economics, geography, history, international studies, philosophy, political science/government, and sociology). Family nurse practitioner, (online graduate programs in business, education, information technology, and nursing), geology, geography, chemistry, and undergraduate game design program. Biology, psychology and general studies have the largest enrollments.

Required: All students must complete a total of 126 semester credit hours, including at least 30 in the major, with a minimum GPA of 2.0. Students must complete specific courses in English, math, humanities, science, and social sciences, a healthful living class, 2 physical activity courses, orientation course, and interdisciplinary studies class.

Special: Accounting, finance, construction management, biology, geology, engineering technology (civil, electrical, and mechanical) information technology, industrial management, engineering (electrical, civil, and mechanical), and Logistis. A number of academic degree programs require internships as part of the program requirements and offer academic credit for internship experiences. Non-academic internships are offered for all majors through the Office of career Services. Washington Semester: Yes. Accelerated degree program is a state-funded program for public and private high school students that provide dual enrollment tuition assistance in Georgia. The program offers the opportunity to earn dual credit, satisfying high school and college core curriculum requirements. Joint Enrollment is not a state-funded program and does not guarantee satisfaction of the high school core curriculum. Admissions requirements for Accel of joint enrollment are 1. Have earned an academic GPA of 3.0. 2. Submit SAT scores of at least 1000 or 21 ACT. 3. Excel in the field in which the student plans to enroll. 4. Have written consent of parent and guardian. 5. Must be on track to complete College Preparatory Curriculum (CPC) requirements. Dual majors; Students may be granted a second baccalaureate degree if the following conditions are met: 1. If the first degree is earned at GSU, a student may seek a second degree if it is different from the first degree. 2. The student must satisfy all major requirements. 3. The student must complete the history and constitution requirements. 4. Take a minimum of 30 additional credit hours at GSU. 5. The student must earn at least 50% of the credits toward the major at GSU. 6. The student may work on two degrees at the same time. 3-2 engineering degree with (name of university): Georgia Institute of Technology Cross registration with Georgia Southern has cross-registration available with East Georgia and GOML (Georgia OnMyLine) programs. Study abroad in Argentina, Australia, Austria, Belgium, Botswana, Brazil, Bulgaria, Canada, Chile, China, Colombia, Costa Rica, Czech Republic, Denmark, Ecuador, Estonia, Finland, France, Germany, Ghana, India, Indonesia, Ireland, Italy, Japan, Korea, Latvia, Lithuania, Malawi, Malaysia, Mexico, Morocco, the Netherlands, Norway, Poland, Russia, South Africa, Spain, Sweden, Switzerland, Thailand, Turkey, United Arab Emirates, United Kingdom, Uruguay, and Vietnam. Work-study programs with (name of employer): Career Services assists students in relevant work experience through several different formats. Through our Experiential Education program, students can participate in job shadowing, nonacademic internships, and cooperative education assignments. The student's assignments vary based on their majors and interests. Some of the companies that students are currently participating with are The Southern Company, Bell South, BMW, the United States Army Corps, Target, and Coca-Cola. B.A. degrees include: Modern Languages, English, Writing and Linguistics, Biology, Philosophy, Chemistry, Geology, Physics, Anthropology, Economics, Geography, International Studies, Political Science, Theatre, Art, Music, and History B.S. degrees include: Journalism, Multimedia Communication, Public Relations and Organizational Communications, Computer Science, Nutrition and Food Science, Child and Family Development, Fashion Merchandising and Apparel Design, Communication Studies, Mathematics. Recreation, Sport Management, Geology, Psychology, Geography, Political Science, Sociology, Interior Design, and International Trade. Student Designed Majors: Yes. There are 17 national honor societies, a freshman honors program, and 24 departmental honors programs.

Faculty/Classroom: 51% of faculty are male; 49% are female. 90% teach undergraduates, 72% do research, and 62% do both. Graduate students teach 6% of introductory courses. The average class size in an introductory lecture is 27; in a laboratory is 25; and in a regular course is 35.

Admissions: 57% of the 2013-2014 applicants were accepted. The SAT scores for the 2013-2014 freshman class were: Critical Reading--14% below 500, 63% between 500 and 599, 21% between 600 and 699, and 2% between 700 and 800; Math--12% below 500, 64% between 500 and 599, 22% between 600 and 699, and 1% between 700 and 800; Writing--33% below 500, 53% between 500 and 599, 13% between 600 and 699, and 1% between 700 and 800. The ACT scores were 6% below 21, 55% between 21 and 23, 25% between 24 and 26, 8% between 27 and 28, and 6% above 28. 38% of the current freshmen were in the top fifth of their class; 65% were in the top two fifths.

Requirements: The SAT or ACT is required. Applicants must have a high school diploma or the equivalent is required. A minimum of 17 credits in college preparatory courses should include 4 each in English and math, 3 each in social studies, 4 in science, and 2 in a foreign language. A GPA of 2.0 is required. AP and CLEP credits are accepted.

Procedure: Freshmen are admitted fall, spring, and summer. Entrance exams should be taken during the junior year. There are deferred admissions and rolling admissions plans. Applications should be filed by May 1 for fall entry; December 1 for spring entry; and April 1 for summer entry, along with a $30 fee. Notification is sent on a rolling basis. Applications are accepted online.

Transfer: 1031 transfer students enrolled in 2012-2013. Applicants must have completed at least 30 semester credit hours of college courses with a minimum GPA of 2.0. Those with fewer than 30 hours must meet freshman requirements. Students transferring with an associate degree must have a minimum GPA of 2.0 in a school with a parallel curriculum. 30 of 126 credits required for the bachelor's degree must be completed at Georgia Southern.

Visiting: There are regularly scheduled orientations for prospective students. There are guides for informal visits and visitors may sit in on classes. To schedule a visit, contact Kathryn Lockwood at (912) 478-5851.

Financial Aid: In 2013-2014, 93% of all full-time freshmen and 89% of continuing full-time students received some form of financial aid. 58% of all full-time freshmen and 54% of continuing full-time students received need-based aid. The average freshman award was $9,407. Need-based scholarships or need-based grants averaged $6,624 ($29,276 maximum); need-based self-help aid (loans and jobs) averaged $4,155 ($29,400 maximum); non-need-based athletic scholarships averaged $7,435 ($20,173 maximum); and other non-need-based awards and non-need-based scholarships averaged $1,500 ($5,499 maximum). Average annual earnings from campus work are $2315. The average financial indebtedness of the 2013 graduate was $22,805. Georgia Southern is a member of CSS. The FAFSA is required. The priority date for freshman financial aid applications for fall entry is April 20.

International Students: There are 228 international students enrolled. The school actively recruits these students. They must take the TOEFL with a minimum score of 523 on the paper-based TOEFL (PBT) or 69 on the Internet-based version (iBT), IELTS. They must also take the SAT or ACT, scoring 1010. International students whose native language is not English, but whose secondary instruction was exclusively in English, must submit TOEFL or SAT/ACT.

Computers: All students may access the system 24 hours a day. There are no time limits. The fee is $100.

Graduates: From July 1, 2012 to June 30, 2013, 2912 bachelor's

degrees were awarded. The most popular majors were business/marketing (20%), education (8%), and liberal arts/general studies (8%). 120 companies recruited on campus in 2012-2013. In an average class, 1% graduate in 3 years or less, 26% graduate in 4 years or less, 45% graduate in 5 years or less, and 50% graduate in 6 years or less.

Admissions Contact: Amy Smith, Interim Director. E-Mail: *admissions@georgiasouthern.edu* Web: *www.georgiasouthern.edu*

GEORGIA SOUTHWESTERN STATE UNIVERSITY B-4

Americus, GA 31709 (912) 928-1273
(800) 338-0082; (912) 931-2983

Full-time: 600 men, 1000 women
Part-time: 170 men, 335 women
Graduate: 110 men, 560 women
Year: semesters, summer session
Application Deadline:
Freshman Class: n/av
SAT or ACT: required
Faculty: n/av; IIA, --$
Ph.D.s: 72%
Student/Faculty: n/av
Tuition: $12,218 ($24,140)
Room & Board: n/av

COMPETITIVE

Georgia Southwestern State University, founded in 1906, is a liberal arts, professional and teachers' college that is part of the public University System of Georgia. The figures in the above capsule and in this profile are approximate. There are 5 undergraduate schools and 4 graduate schools. In addition to regional accreditation, GSW has baccalaureate program accreditation with NCATE and NLN. The library contains 190,000 volumes, 618,842 microform items, and 1,849 audio/video tapes/CDs/DVDs, and subscribes to 825 periodicals including electronic. Computerized library services include interlibrary loans and database searching. Special learning facilities include an art gallery and TV station. The 225-acre campus is in a small town 38 miles north of Albany. Including any residence halls, there are 37 buildings.

Student Life: 95% of undergraduates are from Georgia. Others are from 18 states, 33 foreign countries, and Canada. 70% are from public schools. 72% are White; 25% African American. The average age of freshmen is 20; all undergraduates, 22. 27% do not continue beyond their first year; 25% remain to graduate.

Housing: 597 students can be accommodated in college housing, which includes single-sex dorms. In addition, there are special-interest houses, and independent fraternity and sorority houses. On-campus housing is guaranteed for all 4 years. 62% of students commute. All students may keep cars.

Activities: 13% of men belong to 7 national fraternities; 15% of women belong to 8 national sororities. There are 55 groups on campus, including and nursing., art, band, cheerleading, choir, chorale, chorus, computers, dance, drama, ethnic, forensics, Habitat for Humanity, honors, international, jazz band, literary magazine, musical theater, newspaper, orchestra, photography, political, radio and TV, religious, social, social service, and student government. Popular campus events include Convocation Series.

Sports: There are 3 intercollegiate sports for men and 4 for women, and 9 intramural sports for men and 9 for women. Facilities include 2 gyms, tennis courts, an indoor/outdoor pool, a lake for canoeing, and playing fields for baseball, softball, football, and soccer. The larger gym seats 3000; the smaller seats 500.

Disabled Students: 85% of the campus is accessible. Facilities include wheelchair ramps, elevators, special parking, specially equipped restrooms, special class scheduling, lowered drinking fountains, and accessible dorms.

Services: Counseling and information services are available, as is tutoring in most subjects. There is a reader service for the blind, and remedial math, reading, and writing.

Campus Safety and Security: Measures include 24-hour foot and vehicle patrol, self-defense education, and security escort services. There are emergency telephones and lighted pathways/sidewalks.

Programs of Study: GSW confers B.A., B.S., B.A.S., B.B.A., B.F.A., B.S.Ed. and B.S.N. degrees. Associate and master's degrees are also awarded. Bachelor's degrees are awarded in BIOLOGICAL SCIENCE (biology/biological science), BUSINESS (accounting, business administration and management, and marketing/retailing/merchandising), COMMUNICATIONS AND THE ARTS (English, fine arts, and music), COMPUTER AND PHYSICAL SCIENCE (chemistry, computer programming, computer science, geology, and mathematics), EDUCATION (art education, business education, early childhood education, elementary education, English education, foreign languages education, mathematics education, middle school education, music education, recreation education, science education, secondary education, social science education, and special education), ENGINEERING AND ENVIRONMENTAL DESIGN (computer technology), HEALTH PROFESSIONS (nursing), SOCIAL SCIENCE (history, political science/government, psychology, and sociology). Geology, preprofessional health and nursing, and education are the strongest academically. Business, education, and nursing have the largest enrollments.

Required: To graduate, students must complete 120 credit hours, including 18 in the major, with a minimum GPA of 2.0. The core curriculum consists of 12 hours each in English and the humanities, science, math, and social science. The student must also complete 4 courses in health and phys ed, including swimming, and pass tests in reading, writing, and geography.

Special: The college offers a 3-2 engineering degree with the Georgia Institute of Technology, cooperative programs with the South Georgia Technical School, a 2-2 degree program in nursing, internships through the Governor's Intern Program, study abroad, and credit for military phys ed and training. There are 15 national honor societies, a freshman honors program, and 1 departmental honors programs.

Faculty/Classroom: 56% of faculty are male; 44% are female. All teach undergraduates, and 25% do research. No introductory courses are taught by graduate students. The average class size in an introductory lecture is 22; in a laboratory is 19; and in a regular course is 18.

Requirements: The SAT or ACT is required. The SAT I is preferred. Those who do not meet the required score may gain acceptance through the Developmental Studies Program. Students must be graduates of an accredited secondary school or have a GED certificate. The college requires 16 academic credits and 21 Carnegie units, based on 4 years of English, 3 of science and 4 of math, 2 each of history and a foreign language, and 1 of social studies. An art portfolio and a music audition are recommended for appropriate majors. A GPA of 2.0 is required. AP and CLEP credits are accepted. Important factors in the admissions decision are advanced placement or honors courses, evidence of special talent, and geographical diversity.

Procedure: Freshmen are admitted to all sessions. Entrance exams should be taken before the end of the senior year. There is a rolling admissions plan. Check with the school for current application deadlines. The fall 2013 application fee was $20. applicants were on the 2013 waiting list; 8 were admitted. Applications are accepted online.

Transfer: Applicants should be in good standing at their former institutions. Those with fewer than 30 hours of transfer credit must meet freshman requirements. 30 of 120 credits required for the bachelor's degree must be completed at GSW.

Visiting: There are regularly scheduled orientations for prospective students. There are guides for informal visits, visitors may sit in on classes, and stay overnight. To schedule a visit, contact the Admissions Office.

Financial Aid: The FAFSA is required. Check with the school for current application deadlines.

International Students: The school actively recruits these students. They must take the TOEFL.

Computers: All students may access the system 8 a.m. to 12 midnight Monday through Friday and selected hours on weekends. There are no time limits and no fees.

Admissions Contact: Dean of Students and Admissions. Web: *www.gsw.edu*

GEORGIA STATE UNIVERSITY B-2

Atlanta, GA 30302-3965 (404) 413-2500; (404) 413-2002

Full-time: 5455 men, 8305 women
Part-time: 2020 men, 3195 women
Graduate: 2880 men, 4110 women
Year: semesters, summer session
Application Deadline: open
Freshman Class: n/av
SAT or ACT: required
Faculty: n/av; I, --$
Ph.D.s: 85%
Student/Faculty: n/av
Tuition: $5500 ($16,500)
Room & Board: $7000

VERY COMPETITIVE

Georgia State University, founded in 1913 and a part of the University System of Georgia, is a public residential university offering programs in liberal arts and sciences, business administration, education, law, health sciences, and public policy. Figures in the above capsule are approximate. There are 5 undergraduate schools and 6 graduate schools. In addition to regional accreditation, Georgia State has baccalaureate program accreditation with AACSB, ADA, APTA, CAHEA, CSWE, NASAD, NASM, NCATE, and NLN. The 2 libraries contain 1.4 million volumes, 1.7 million microform items, and 22,551 audio/video tapes/CDs/DVDs, and subscribe to 7,788 periodicals including electronic. Computerized library services include interlibrary loans, database searching, Internet access, and laptop Internet portals. Special learning facilities include a learning resource center, art gallery, radio station, TV station, digital arts lab, observatory, instructional technology center, and distance learning classrooms. The 33-acre campus is in an urban area in downtown Atlanta. Including any residence halls, there are 46 buildings.

Student Life: 92% of undergraduates are from Georgia. Others are from 48 states, 139 foreign countries, and Canada. 37% are white; 31% African American. The average age of freshmen is 20; all undergraduates, 24. 24% do not continue beyond their first year; 44% remain to graduate.

Housing: 2435 students can be accommodated in college housing, which includes coed on-campus apartments. In addition, there are honors houses and special-interest houses. On-campus housing is available on a first-come and first-served basis. 90% of students commute. All students may keep cars.

Activities: 3% of men belong to 10 national fraternities; 4% of women belong to 11 national sororities. There are 203 groups on campus, including art, band, cheerleading, chess, chorale, chorus, computers, dance, debate, drama, ethnic, film, gay, honors, international, jazz band, literary magazine, musical theater, newspaper, opera, orchestra, outdoor., pep band, photography, political, professional, radio and TV, religious, social, social service, and student government. Popular campus events include International Student Festival, Honors Day, and Greek Week.

Sports: There are 7 intercollegiate sports for men and 8 for women, and 30 intramural sports for men and 30 for women. Facilities include a phys ed complex with 3 gyms, a pool, a diving well, a weight room, indoor and outdoor tennis courts, a climbing wall, a jogging track, exercise rooms, a dance studio, and racquetball courts. In addition, the Indian Creek recreation area has a pool, 3 tennis courts, picnic facilities, regular and sand volleyball, basketball courts, and a rope challenge course. There are also athletic fields.

Disabled Students: All of the campus is accessible. Facilities include wheelchair ramps, elevators, special parking, specially equipped restrooms, special class scheduling, lowered drinking fountains, and lowered telephones.

Services: Counseling and information services are available, as is tutoring in most subjects. There is a reader service for the blind, and remedial math, reading, and writing. Programs are available in effective studying, reading comprehension, speed reading, test and note taking, test anxiety, fear of public speaking, and organization and planning.

Campus Safety and Security: Measures include 24-hour foot and vehicle patrol, self-defense education, and security escort services. There are shuttle buses, emergency telephones, lighted pathways/sidewalks, , 24-hour security at university housing, and a bicycle patrol.

Programs of Study: Georgia State confers B.A., B.S., B.B.A., B.F.A., B.I.S., B.M., B.S.Ed., and B.S.W. degrees. Master's and doctoral degrees are also awarded. Bachelor's degrees are awarded in BIOLOGICAL SCIENCE (biology/biological science and nutrition), BUSINESS (accounting, banking and finance, business administration and management, business economics, hospitality management services, insurance and risk management, management information systems, marketing/retailing/merchandising, office supervision and management, and real estate), COMMUNICATIONS AND THE ARTS (art, art history and appreciation, classics, English, film arts, fine arts, French, German, journalism, music, music business management, Spanish, speech/debate/rhetoric, and studio art), COMPUTER AND PHYSICAL SCIENCE (actuarial science, chemistry, computer science, geology, mathematics, physics, and statistics), EDUCATION (art education, early childhood education, and physical education), HEALTH PROFESSIONS (exercise science, nursing, and respiratory therapy), SOCIAL SCIENCE (African American studies, anthropology, criminal justice, economics, geography, history, interdisciplinary studies, philosophy, political science/government, psychology, religious education, social work, sociology, urban studies, and women's studies). Biological sciences, psychology, and management are the largest.

Required: Students must complete distribution requirements, including courses in English composition, humanities, natural science and math, social science, U.S. history, and political science. A minimum of 120 hours must be completed for graduation with a minimum GPA of 2.0.

Special: There is cross-registration with the Atlanta Regional Consortium for Higher Education (ARCHE). Internships with numerous employers and government agencies can be arranged. Study abroad is available in various countries. Work-study, an accelerated degree program in nursing, and dual majors are available. The Summer Scholar program allows high school seniors to take college-level course work. There is a freshman honors program.

Faculty/Classroom: 56% of faculty are male; 44% are female. No introductory courses are taught by graduate students.

Requirements: The SAT or ACT is required. The ACT Optional Writing test is also required. Applicants must graduate from a regionally accredited high school. A total of 16 academic credits is required. Students should prepare with 4 years each of English and math, 3 years each of science and social science, and 2 years of the same foreign language. They must have a minimum 2.80 high school GPA calculated on the 16 courses listed above. A GPA of 2.8 is required. AP and CLEP credits are accepted. Important factors in the admissions decision are evidence of special talent, advanced placement or honors courses, and extracurricular activities record.

Procedure: Freshmen are admitted fall, spring, and summer. Entrance exams should be taken during the first semester of the senior year. There is a rolling admissions plan. Check with the school for current application deadlines and fee. Applications are accepted online.

Transfer: 1962 transfer students enrolled in a recent year. Transfer applicants must submit official transcripts of all college-level work, have a minimum GPA of 2.5, have earned 30 semester hours, and be in good academic standing. Those with fewer than 30 semester hours earned must meet freshman requirements. 39 of 120 credits required for the bachelor's degree must be completed at Georgia State.

Visiting: There are guides for informal visits and visitors may sit in on classes. To schedule a visit, contact Admissions.

Financial Aid: The FAFSA is required. Check with the school for current application deadlines.

International Students: The school actively recruits these students. They must take the TOEFL and the college's own test, If the TOEFL is not taken they may take the GSTEP with a passing score of 6, or the SAT with a verbal score of 430 or the ACT with an English subtest score of 17. They must also take the SAT or ACT.

Computers: Wireless access is available. The Georgia State University Wireless Communication Infrastructure (CatChat) is designed and implemented as an adjunet to the existing wired data network. Georgia State's open access computer labs are available to all Georgia State faculty, staff, and students. Users are required to use their Novell user ID/password to gain access to the workstation and the campus network. There are open access PC labs in 6 buildings. Additionally, Georgia State maintains 15 classrooms with PC workstations. These rooms have between 27 to 54 PCs installed for student use during class. All students may access the system. 24 hours per day. There are no time limits and no fees. It is strongly recommended that all students have a personal computer. Students enrolled in Computer Information Systems (CIS) must have a personal computer.

Admissions Contact: Stephanie Buchanan. E-Mail: *admissions@.gsu.edu* Web: *www.gsu.edu*

KENNESAW STATE UNIVERSITY — B-2

Kennesaw, GA 30144 — **(770) 423-6300; (770) 420-4435**

Full-time: 2455 men, 3297 women	**Faculty:** 755; IIA, --$
Part-time: 6994 men, 9875 women	**Ph.D.s:** n/av
Graduate: 754 men, 1254 women	**Student/Faculty:** 21 to 1
Year: semesters, summer session	**Tuition:** $6807 ($19,390)
Application Deadline: May 8	**Room & Board:** $6210
Freshman Class: 10058 applied, 5572 accepted, 3146 enrolled	
SAT CR/M/W: 540/530/510	**ACT:** 22 **VERY COMPETITIVE**

Kennesaw State University (KSU) is the third-largest university in Georgia with more than 24,600 undergraduate and graduate students representing 121 countries. Accredited by the Southern Association of Colleges and Schools (SACS), KSU offers 80 bachelor's, master's and doctorate degree programs including undergraduate degrees in education, health, business, the humanities, the arts, science and math. The university's graduate degree programs include nursing, business, information systems, conflict management, public administration, education and professional writing. KSU's expanding doctoral programs currently offer doctorates in education, business and nursing, as well as KSU's first Ph.D program in International Conflict Management. There are 7 undergraduate schools and 6 graduate schools. In addition to regional accreditation, Kennesaw State has baccalaureate program accreditation with AACSB, ABET, CSWE, NASAD, NASM, NCATE, and NLN. The 2 libraries contain 614,198 volumes, 125,000 microform items, and 9,000 audio/video tapes/CDs/DVDs, and subscribe to 55,000 periodicals including electronic. Computerized library services include interlibrary loans, database searching, Internet access, and Wi-Fi capability. Special learning facilities include an art gallery, radio station, The Museum of History and Holocaust Education, The Civil War Center for Regional History & Culture Center for African and African Diaspora Studies Center for Hispanic Studies Confucius Institute at Kennesaw State University. The 384-acre campus is in a suburban area 25 miles north of Atlanta. Including any residence halls, there are 91 buildings.

Student Life: 97% of undergraduates are from Georgia. Others are from 48 states, 120 foreign countries, and Canada. 65% are White; 17% African American. The average age of freshmen is 18; all undergraduates, 24.

Housing: 3497 students can be accommodated in college housing, which includes coed on-campus apartments. On-campus housing is available on a first-come and first-served basis. 86% of students commute. Alcohol is not permitted. All students may keep cars.

Activities: 4% of men belong to 9 national fraternities; 5% of women belong to 10 national sororities. There are 180 groups on campus, including art, band, cheerleading, choir, chorale, chorus, computers, dance, drama, ethnic, gay, honors, international, jazz band, literary magazine, musical theater, newspaper, pep band, political, professional, radio and TV, religious, social, social service, student government, and symphony. Popular campus events include KSU College Colors Day, Black History Month, Country Study Program, Tricycle Derby, and Turkey Trot.

Sports: There are 6 intercollegiate sports for men and 9 for women, and 9 intramural sports for men and 9 for women. Facilities include Athletic Complex for Softball; A Stadium for Soccer, Lacrosee, and Football; Convocation Center for Men's & Women's Basketball and Volleyball; Indoor Golf Practice Facility; Outdoor Track and Field Facility; Rehabilitation Facility; Baseball Stadium; Strength and Conditioning Facility.

Disabled Students: All of the campus is accessible. Facilities include wheelchair ramps, elevators, special parking, specially equipped restrooms, special class scheduling, lowered drinking fountains, lowered telephones.

Services: Counseling and information services are available, as is tutoring

in some subjects, Math, Foreign Languages, and English. Academic Coaching for Writing/Research Skills. There is a reader service for the blind, and remedial math, reading, and writing.

Campus Safety and Security: Measures include 24-hour foot and vehicle patrol, emergency notification system, self-defense education, and security escort services. There are shuttle buses, emergency telephones, lighted pathways/sidewalks, Full-service police department, siren system with messages, pop-up computer notification on the KSU network, telephone emergency message system, email emergency notification, security badges, electronic access control, intrusion alarms and video surveillance.

Programs of Study: Kennesaw State confers B.A., B.S., B.B.A., B.F.A., B.M., B.S.N., and B.S.N.C. degrees. Master's and doctoral degrees are also awarded. Bachelor's degrees are awarded in BIOLOGICAL SCIENCE (biochemistry, biology/biological science, and biotechnology), BUSINESS (accounting, business administration and management, finance, international business management, management science, and marketing/retailing/merchandising), COMMUNICATIONS AND THE ARTS (art history, art, communications, dance, English, modern language, music, music performance, and theatre arts), COMPUTER AND PHYSICAL SCIENCE (chemistry, computer science, computer security and information assurance, information sciences and systems, and mathematics), EDUCATION (art education, (Education) Childhood Education, early childhood education, English education, health education, mathematics education, middle school education, music education, and physical education), HEALTH PROFESSIONS (exercise science and nursing), SOCIAL SCIENCE (African studies, anthropology, criminal justice, economics, geography, history, human services, interdisciplinary studies, international studies, philosophy, political science/government, psychology, and sociology). Business, nursing and biology are the strongest academically. Communication, nursing, and psychology have the largest enrollments.

Required: Requirements vary by degree program. Generally, all students must complete 123 semester hours, including 45 to 47 in core curriculum courses and 39 in upper-level courses, with a minimum GPA of 2.0 and grades of C or better in the major and in required English courses. Students must also successfully complete the University System of Georgia Regents' Testing Program and demonstrate (by course or exam) competency in the history and constitutions of the United States and Georgia. 3 hours of Fitness for Living are also required.

Special: Students may register for courses with any of the colleges in the University System of Georgia, study abroad in over 60 countries, and participate in work-study programs and internships, some with pass/fail options. Dual majors, student-designed majors, and nondegree programs also are offered. There are 21 national honor societies and a freshman honors program.

Faculty/Classroom: 42% of faculty are male; 58% are female. All teach and do research. No introductory courses are taught by graduate students. The average class size in an introductory lecture is 41; in a laboratory is 22; and in a regular course is 35.

Admissions: 55% of the 2013-2014 applicants were accepted. The SAT scores for the 2013-2014 freshman class were: Critical Reading--18% below 500, 60% between 500 and 599, 20% between 600 and 699, and 2% between 700 and 800; Math--26% below 500, 56% between 500 and 599, 17% between 600 and 699, and 1% between 700 and 800; Writing--39% below 500, 47% between 500 and 599, 13% between 600 and 699, and 1% between 700 and 800. The ACT scores were 22% below 21, 52% between 21 and 23, 21% between 24 and 26, 4% between 27 and 28, and 1% above 28.

Requirements: The SAT or ACT is required. For applicants graduating from high school prior to 2012, a minimum of 16 RHSC units (Carnegie units which equate to four years of completed high school study) are required in the following subject areas: English (4), Mathematics (4), Science (3), Social Science (3), Foreign Language (2), Applicants graduating from high school in 2012 or later must meet the above requirements with the following changes (17 units): Mathematics (4), Science (4). KSU's minimum requirements for admission as a regular first year freshman include the following: Graduation from a regionally accredited high school or a high school accredited by the Georgia Accreditation Commission (GAC), or from a public school under the authority of the state department of education. Completion of at least the 17 required units for graduates 2012 or later (16 units for graduates 2011 or earlier) in the University System's Required High School Curriculum. Have a combined Critical Reading and Math total of 950 on the SAT (20 ACT Composite), Freshman Index of at least 1940, with a SAT-Critical Reading/Verbal of at least 490 (ACT 20) and a SAT-Math of at least 460 (ACT 19), and an academic HSGPA of at least 2.5 in the Required High School Curriculum as calculated by KSU. (The SAT essay portion must be submitted, but will not be used in the decision.) A GPA of 2.5 is required. AP and CLEP credits are accepted.

Procedure: Freshmen are admitted fall, spring, and summer. Entrance exams should be taken before June 1. There is a rolling admissions plan. Applications should be filed by May 8 for fall entry; November 1 for spring entry; and April 4 for summer entry. The fall 2013 application fee was $40. Applications are accepted online.

Transfer: 2205 transfer students enrolled in 2012-2013. Applicants with fewer than 30 semester hours of acceptable transfer credit must meet the same admissions requirements identified earlier for freshmen admitted from high school. Freshman transfer applicants may be required to take the COMPASS in English and/or math depending upon SAT/ACT scores, and are held to appropriate standards based upon results. Transfer freshmen must be in good standing at previous institutions. Transfer applicants with sufficient transferable hours to be classified as a sophomore, junior or senior at KSU must have completed any and all learning support requirements prior to admission and have a cumulative GPA of at least 2.0 in the previous institutions attended. Students transferring from another institution in the University System of Georgia must have satisfied any and all learning support requirements before being admitted to KSU. Transferring students taking physical education hours at one institution will not be required to duplicate these hours at KSU. However, students taking an orientation course at another institution may be required to take the KSU 1101 orientation course. All admission application deadlines cited earlier apply to transfer applicants. All of the documents cited earlier and required for a complete application file apply to transfer applicants with the following exceptions: High school transcripts are not required for applicants with 30 or more earned semester hours of acceptable transfer credit. (All college and university transcripts are required, however); SAT I or ACT scores are not required for applicants with 30 or more earned semester hours of acceptable transfer credit; Freshman transfer applicants (less than 30 semester hours of transferable credit) may be required to take the COMPASS in English and/or math depending upon SAT/ACT scores. 30 of 123 credits required for the bachelor's degree must be completed at Kennesaw State.

Visiting: There are regularly scheduled orientations for prospective students, Mondays, Wednesdays and Fridays: 10 a.m. and 2 p.m. Information session followed by a student led walking tour of the academic areas of campus with a tour of University Housing and optional post-tour meal in The Commons. Tuesdays and Thursdays: 10 a. There are guides for informal visits. To schedule a visit, contact the Office of Undergraduate Admissions.

Financial Aid: In 2013-2014, 94% of all full-time freshmen and 44% of continuing full-time students received some form of financial aid. 96% of all full-time freshmen and 49% of continuing full-time students received need-based aid. The average freshman award was $7,990. Need-based scholarships or need-based grants averaged $4,242 ($6,626 maximum); need-based self-help aid (loans and jobs) averaged $2,494 ($2,884 maximum); non-need-based athletic scholarships averaged $4,055 ($7,565 maximum); and other non-need-based awards and non-need-based scholarships averaged $5,303 ($18,981 maximum). 4% of undergraduate students work part-time. Average annual earnings from campus work are $7924. The average financial indebtedness of the 2013 graduate was $22,407. Kennesaw State is a member of CSS. The FAFSA is required. The priority date for freshman financial aid applications for fall entry is April 1.

International Students: There are 971 international students enrolled. The school actively recruits these students. They must take the TOEFL with a minimum score of 527 on the paper-based TOEFL (PBT) or 75 on the Internet-based version (iBT), IELTS score of 6.0. They must also take the SAT or ACT, scoring SAT 950 combined. SAT scores a minimum of 950 points combined, minimum score of 430 in the verbal section and 400 in math.

Computers: All students may access the system 24 hours a day. There are no time limits and no fees.

Graduates: From July 1, 2012 to June 30, 2013, 3488 bachelor's degrees were awarded. The most popular majors were communication (8%), early childhood education (8%), and management (7%). In an average class, 15% graduate in 4 years or less, 35% graduate in 5 years or less, and 43% graduate in 6 years or less. Of the 2012 graduating class, 24% were enrolled in graduate school within 6 months of graduation, and 43% were employed.

Admissions Contact: Angela Evans, Director of Admissions. E-Mail: *ksuadmit@kennesaw.edu* Web: *http:/www.kennesaw.edu/*

LAGRANGE COLLEGE — A-3

LaGrange, GA 30240 — (706) 880-8217
(800) 593-2885; (706) 880-8010

Full-time: 380 men, 406 women	**Faculty:** 66
Part-time: 14 men, 56 women	**Ph.D.s:** 82%
Graduate: 17 men, 67 women	**Student/Faculty:** 12 to 1
Year: 4-1-4, summer session	**Tuition:** $25,630
Application Deadline:	**Room & Board:** $10,680

Freshman Class: 1648 applied, 962 accepted, 270 enrolled
SAT CR/M: 490/500 — **ACT:** 21 — **COMPETITIVE**

LaGrange College, founded in 1831, is a private liberal arts institution affiliated with the United Methodist Church. Major undergraduate programs include business, visual and performing arts, education, biology, psychology, and exercise science. There is one graduate school. In addition to regional accreditation, LaGrange has baccalaureate program accreditation with ACBSP and NLN. The library contains 402,389 volumes, 119,677 microform items, and 7,763 audio/video tapes/CDs/DVDs, and subscribes to 493 periodicals including electronic. Computerized library services include interlibrary loans, database searching, Internet access, and Wi-Fi capability. Special learning facilities include an art gallery, 2 music technology labs, an exercise science lab, and a performing arts theater and auditorium. The 120-acre campus is in a small town 70 miles southwest of Atlanta. Including any residence halls, there are 26 buildings.

Student Life: 91% of undergraduates are from Georgia. Others are from 14 states, and 8 foreign countries. 88% are from public schools. 70% are White; 23% African American. 57% are Protestant; 35% Unknown Religious affiliation. The average age of freshmen is 18. 39% do not continue beyond their first year; 38% remain to graduate.

Housing: 632 students can be accommodated in college housing, which includes single-sex and coed dorms and on-campus apartments. In addition, there are special-interest houses, fraternity houses, and sorority houses. On-campus housing is guaranteed for all 4 years. 62% of students live on campus; of those, 66% remain on campus on weekends. Alcohol is not permitted. All students may keep cars.

Activities: 24% of men belong to 3 national fraternities; 22% of women belong to 3 national sororities. There are 55 groups on campus, including art, cheerleading, choir, chorale, chorus, drama, environmental, ethnic, gay, honors, international, literary magazine, musical theater, newspaper, orchestra, pep band, political, professional, religious, social, social service, and student government. Popular campus events include Homecoming, Spirit and Traditions Kickoff, May Day, Family Weekend, Vegas on the Hill, Christmas on the Hill, and Halloween on the Hill.

Sports: There are 8 intercollegiate sports for men and 9 for women, and 8 intramural sports for men and 8 for women. Facilities include a fitness center, West Point Lake, an auditorium, indoor and outdoor pools, 2 gyms, 10 lighted tennis courts, lighted softball, baseball stadium, and soccer fields, a football practice field, and a football stadium.

Disabled Students: 80% of the campus is accessible. Facilities include wheelchair ramps, elevators, special parking, specially equipped rest rooms, special class scheduling, lowered drinking fountains, and special housing.

Services: Counseling and information services are available, as is tutoring in most subjects, including chemistry, French, religion, Spanish, nursing, political science, American experience, psychology, art history, statistics, problem solving, biology, economics, and history. There is remedial math and reading.

Campus Safety and Security: Measures include 24-hour foot and vehicle patrol, emergency notification system, and security escort services. There are lighted pathways/sidewalks and controlled access to dorms/residences.

Programs of Study: LaGrange confers B.A, B.S., B.S.N., B.B.A. and B.M. degrees. Master's degrees are also awarded. Bachelor's degrees are awarded in BIOLOGICAL SCIENCE (biochemistry and biology/biological science), BUSINESS (accounting and business administration and management), COMMUNICATIONS AND THE ARTS (art, English, music, Spanish, and theatre arts), COMPUTER AND PHYSICAL SCIENCE (chemistry, computer science, and mathematics), EDUCATION (early childhood education and education), HEALTH PROFESSIONS (exercise science and nursing), SOCIAL SCIENCE (history, interdisciplinary studies, political science/government, psychology, religion, and sociology). Nursing, exercise science, and education have the largest enrollments.

Required: To graduate, all students must complete 120 semester hours. The core curriculum includes First-Year Cornerstone, rhetoric and compostion, math, world languages and culture, laboratory science, problem solving, computer applications, humanities, fine arts, religion, and the American experience. All students must have a minimum GPA of 2.0.

Special: Students may participate in an international study tour progam currently offered through the Interim Program in January. A 3-2 engineering degree is offered with Georgia Institute of Technology and Auburn University. A self-designed B.A. in Interdisciplinary Studies is also available to qualifying students. Internships and work-study programs are offered in numerous disciplines. The CHIP program allows students to work and study in Washington, D.C. Cross-registration relationships have been established with postsecondary institutions in Japan. There are 13 national honor societies.

Faculty/Classroom: 54% of faculty are male; 46% are female. All teach undergraduates. No introductory courses are taught by graduate students.

Admissions: 58% of the 2013-2014 applicants were accepted. The SAT scores for the 2013-2014 freshman class were: Critical Reading--50% below 500, 39% between 500 and 599, 11% between 600 and 699; Math--52% below 500, 40% between 500 and 599, 7% between 600 and 699, and 1% between 700 and 800. The ACT scores were 44% below 21, 34% between 21 and 23, 15% between 24 and 26, 5% between 27 and 28, and 3% above 28. 36% of the current freshmen were in the top fifth of their class; 54% were in the top two fifths.

Requirements: The SAT or ACT is required. In addition, applicants should be graduates of accredited secondary schools or have a GED certificate. They should have completed a minimum of 4 units of English and math, 3 of social studies, 3 each of social studies and science, and 2 units of a foreign language is recommended. A GPA of 2.5 is required. AP and CLEP credits are accepted. Important factors in the admissions decision are personality/intangible qualities, recommendations by alumni, recommendations by school officials, parents or siblings attended the school, evidence of special talent, extracurricular activities record, and geographical diversity.

Procedure: Freshmen are admitted to all sessions. There are early admissions, deferred admissions, and rolling admissions plans. Application deadlines are open. Application fee is $30. Applications are accepted online. Application fees are waived if application is completed online.

Transfer: 75 transfer students enrolled in 2012-2013. Transfer students must have a minimum 2.5 College GPA and be in good standing with the previous college. Transfer students must also have a minimum high school GPA of 2.5 if less than 30 hours of college credit is transferred. 39 of 120 credits required for the bachelor's degree must be completed at LaGrange.

Visiting: There are regularly scheduled orientations for prospective students, consisting of welcome and introduction to the college, guided campus tour, showcase sessions (including major departments and financial aid). There are guides for informal visits, visitors may sit in on classes, and stay overnight. To schedule a visit, contact Michael Thomas at (760) 880-8005.

Financial Aid: In 2013-2014, 100% of all full-time freshmen and 99% of continuing full-time students received some form of financial aid. 89% of all full-time freshmen and 84% of continuing full-time students received need based aid. The average freshman award was $27,675. Need-based scholarships or need-based grants averaged $6,882 ($21,645 maximum); need-based self-help aid (loans and jobs) averaged $4,545 ($15,135 maximum); other non-need-based awards and non-need-based scholarships averaged $12,542 ($36,280 maximum); and $3,515 from other forms of aid. 37% of undergraduate students work part-time. Average annual earnings from campus work are $1690. The average financial indebtedness of the 2013 graduate was $32,343. The FAFSA and the college's own financial statement are required. The priority date for freshman financial aid applications for fall entry is March 1.

International Students: There are 6 international students enrolled. The school actively recruits these students. They must take the TOEFL with a minimum score of 500 on the paper-based TOEFL (PBT) or 61 on the Internet-based version (iBT). They must also take the SAT or ACT, scoring 450.

Computers: All students may access the system 24 hours a day. There are no time limits and no fees.

Graduates: From July 1, 2012 to June 30, 2013, 200 bachelor's degrees were awarded. The most popular majors were nursing (16%), biology (9%), and psychology (8%). 13 companies recruited on campus in 2012-2013. In an average class, 31% graduate in 4 years or less, 37% graduate in 5 years or less, and 38% graduate in 6 years or less. Of the 2012 graduating class, 17% were enrolled in graduate school within 6 months of graduation, and 67% were employed.

Admissions Contact: Michael Thomas, Director of Admission. E-Mail: *mthomas@lagrange.edu* Web: *www.lagrange.edu*

MERCER UNIVERSITY C-3

Macon, GA 31207 (478) 301-2650
(800) 840-8577; (478) 301-2828

Full-time: 1258 men, 1214 women	**Faculty:** n/av; IIA, -$
Part-time: 35 men, 31 women	**Ph.D.s:** 94%
Graduate: 1410 men, 2522 women	**Student/Faculty:** 12 to 1
Year: semesters, summer session	**Tuition:** $33,120
Application Deadline: April 1	**Room & Board:** $11,081

Freshman Class: 3864 applied, 2666 accepted, 727 enrolled
SAT CR/M/W: 580/590/560 **ACT:** 26 **VERY COMPETITIVE+**

Mercer University, founded in 1833, is a private institution of higher learning that seeks to achieve excellence and scholarly discipline in the fields of liberal learning and professional knowledge. The university offers degree programs in liberal arts, music, business and economics, education, engineering, nursing and professional studies. Mercer also offers a Great Books program as an alternative to the traditional core curriculum. There are 5 undergraduate schools and 11 graduate schools. In addition to regional accreditation, Mercer has baccalaureate program accreditation with AACSB, ABET, NASM, and NCATE. The 2 libraries contain 864,793 volumes, 3.4 million microform items, and 70,477 audio/video tapes/CDs/DVDs, and subscribe to 14,491 periodicals including electronic. Computerized library services include interlibrary loans, database searching, and Internet access. Special learning facilities include a radio station, TV station, music building. The 130-acre campus is in a suburban area 85 miles south of Atlanta.

Student Life: 83% of undergraduates are from Georgia. Others are from 37 states, 42 foreign countries, and Canada. 59% are White; 19% African American. 50% are Protestant; 23% claim no religious affiliation; 11%

Catholic. The average age of freshmen is 18; all undergraduates, 20. 18% do not continue beyond their first year; 61% remain to graduate.

Housing: 1647 students can be accommodated in college housing, which includes single-sex and coed dorms, on-campus apartments, off-campus apartments, and married student housing. In addition, there are special-interest houses and fraternity houses. On-campus housing is available on a first-come, first-served basis, and is available on a lottery system for upperclassmen. Priority is given to out-of-town students. 65% of students live on campus. Alcohol is not permitted. All students may keep cars.

Activities: 22% of men belong to 8 national fraternities; 24% of women belong to 7 national sororities. There are 115 groups on campus, including bagpipe, band, cheerleading, choir, chorale, chorus, computers, dance, debate, drama, environmental, ethnic, film, gay, honors, international, jazz band, literary magazine, marching band, musical theater, newspaper, opera, orchestra, pep band, photography, political, professional, radio and TV, religious, social, social service, student government, and symphony. Popular campus events include Bearstock (outdoor concert), Pilgrimage to Penfield, Homecoming and Mercer Madness.

Sports: There are 8 intercollegiate sports for men and 10 for women, and 10 intramural sports for men and 10 for women. Facilities include 2 gyms, 3 playing fields, a student center, a swimming pool, a lighted intramural complex, and tennis, volleyball, and racquetball courts.

Disabled Students: 85% of the campus is accessible. Facilities include wheelchair ramps, elevators, special parking, specially equipped restrooms, special class scheduling, lowered drinking fountains, lowered telephones, and assistance with registration.

Services: Counseling and information services are available, as is tutoring in most subjects. There is a reader service for the blind, and remedial math.

Campus Safety and Security: Measures include 24-hour foot and vehicle patrol, emergency notification system, self-defense education, and security escort services. There are shuttle buses, emergency telephones, lighted pathways/sidewalks, controlled access to dorms/residences, and external CCTV cameras monitored by the police department.

Programs of Study: Mercer confers B.A., B.S., B.B.A., B.M., B.M.E., B.S.E., B.S.E.D., B.S.M. and B.S.N. degrees. Master's and doctoral degrees are also awarded. Bachelor's degrees are awarded in AGRICULTURE (environmental studies), BIOLOGICAL SCIENCE (biochemistry, biology/biological science, and environmental biology), BUSINESS (accounting, business administration and management, finance, international business management, and marketing management), COMMUNICATIONS AND THE ARTS (art, communications, communication rhetoric/communication, creative writing, dramatic arts, English literature, French, German, journalism, Latin, media arts, music, Technical Communication, and Spanish), COMPUTER AND PHYSICAL SCIENCE (chemistry, computer science, earth science, information sciences and systems, mathematics, natural sciences, and physics), EDUCATION (early childhood education, education, elementary education, music education, secondary education, and special education), ENGINEERING AND ENVIRONMENTAL DESIGN (computational sciences, engineering, and industrial administration/management), HEALTH PROFESSIONS (predentistry, premedicine, and prepharmacy), SOCIAL SCIENCE (African studies, anthropology, area studies, Christian studies, criminal justice, economics, gender studies, history, philosophy, political science/government, prelaw, psychology, religion, social science, sociology, and women's studies). Engineering, business, and biology have the largest enrollments.

Required: To graduate, all students must complete at least 120 semester hours with a minimum GPA of 2.0.

Special: Mercer offers co-op programs in all majors, cross-registration with Wesleyan and Macon State Colleges, B.A.-B.S. degrees in various science and math fields, internships, student-designed majors, work-study programs, and satisfactory-unsatisfactory options for elective courses. Mercer offers a wide variety of study-abroad opportunities, including independent semester or year-long programs, faculty-led programs, or Mercer on Mission. There are 2 national honor societies, a freshman honors program, and 20 departmental honors programs.

Faculty/Classroom: 50% of faculty are male; 50% are female. No introductory courses are taught by graduate students. The average class size in a laboratory is 20 and in a regular course is 20.

Admissions: 69% of the 2013-2014 applicants were accepted. The SAT scores for the 2013-2014 freshman class were: Critical Reading--9% below 500, 47% between 500 and 599, 35% between 600 and 699, and 9% between 700 and 800; Math--7% below 500, 48% between 500 and 599, 37% between 600 and 699, and 8% between 700 and 800; Writing--19% below 500, 46% between 500 and 599, 29% between 600 and 699, and 6% between 700 and 800.

Requirements: The SAT or ACT is required. In addition, Applicants must be graduates of an accredited secondary school and have completed 16 academic units. Students should submit their transcript and class rank, a recommendation from a guidance counselor, and a list of extracurricular activities, including employment. A GPA of 3.0 is required. AP and CLEP credits are accepted.

Procedure: Freshmen are admitted fall, spring, and summer. Entrance exams should be taken in the spring of the junior year or fall of the senior year. There are deferred admissions and rolling admissions plans. Applications should be filed by April 1 for fall entry. The fall 2013 application fee was $50. Notification is sent on a rolling basis. Applications are accepted online.

Transfer: A minimum GPA of 2.0 is required for all transfer students. Applicants with fewer than 9 semester hours must meet freshman entrance requirements. Those with fewer than 20 semester hours must submit a high school transcript and SAT or ACT scores, and those with more than 20 semester hours must submit transcripts from all colleges attended and be in good academic standing at their present school, or present evidence of satisfactory work in a previously attended college. 30 of 120 credits required for the bachelor's degree must be completed at Mercer.

Visiting: There are regularly scheduled orientations for prospective students. There are guides for informal visits, visitors may sit in on classes, and stay overnight. To schedule a visit, contact the Office of Admissions at (478) 301-2650.

Financial Aid: In 2013-2014, 99% of all full-time freshmen and 97% of continuing full-time students received some form of financial aid. 81% of all full-time freshmen and 73% of continuing full-time students received need-based aid. The average financial indebtedness of the 2013 graduate was $29,101. The FAFSA and the college's own financial statement are required. The deadline for filing freshman financial aid applications for fall entry is April 1.

International Students: There are 103 international students enrolled. The school actively recruits these students. They must take the TOEFL, or Mercer's ELI exit examination. They must also take the SAT or ACT, scoring 1000.

Computers: All students may access the system. There are no time limits and no fees.

Graduates: From July 1, 2012 to June 30, 2013, 446 bachelor's degrees were awarded. The most popular majors were business (18%), biology (12%), and engineering (10%). In an average class, 45% graduate in 4 years or less, 59% graduate in 5 years or less, and 61% graduate in 6 years or less.

Admissions Contact: Alejandra Sosa, Director of Freshman Admissions. E-Mail: *admissions@mercer.edu* Web: *www.mercer.edu*

MOREHOUSE COLLEGE — B-2

Atlanta, GA 30314 — (404) 215-2632; (800) 851-1254; (404) 524-5635

Full-time: 2016 men	**Faculty:** 162; IIB, -$
Part-time: 167 men	**Ph.D.s:** 89%
Graduate: n/av	**Student/Faculty:** 12 to 1
Year: semesters, summer session	**Tuition:** $25,460
Application Deadline: February 15	**Room & Board:** $13,180
Freshman Class: 2689 applied, 1797 accepted, 485 enrolled	
SAT CR/M/W: 500/505/490 — **ACT:** 21	**COMPETITIVE**

Founded in 1867 and located in Atlanta, Georgia, Morehouse is an academic community dedicated to teaching, scholarship, service, and the continuing search for truth as a liberating force. The College offers undergardaute programs in three divisions - business and economics, humanities and social sciences, and science and mathematics as well as extracurriclar activities to develop well-rounded future leaders. In addition to regional accreditation, Morehouse has baccalaureate program accreditation with AACSB and NASM. The library contains 550,000 volumes, 15,000 microform items, and 8,000 audio/video tapes/CDs/DVDs, and subscribes to 110 periodicals including electronic. Computerized library services include interlibrary loans and database searching. The 61-acre campus is in an urban area 3 miles southwest of downtown Atlanta. Including any residence halls, there are 36 buildings.

Student Life: 71% of undergraduates are from out of state, mostly the South. Students are from 41 states, 15 foreign countries, and Canada. 80% are from public schools. 95% are African American. The average age of freshmen is 18; all undergraduates, 20. 15% do not continue beyond their first year; 55% remain to graduate.

Housing: 1500 students can be accommodated in college housing, which includes single-sex dorms and on-campus apartments. In addition, there are special-interest houses. On-campus housing is guaranteed for the freshman year only, is available on a first-come, first-served basis, and is available on a lottery system for upperclassmen. 63% of students live on campus; of those, 90% remain on campus on weekends. Alcohol is not permitted. Upperclassmen may keep cars.

Activities: 1% of men belong to 6 national fraternities. There are 60 groups on campus, including band, cheerleading, chess, choir, chorus, computers, dance, debate, drama, ethnic, gay, honors, international, jazz band, literary magazine, marching band, musical theater, newspaper, orchestra, political, professional, religious, social, social service, speech and glee club, student government, and yearbook. Popular campus events include Founders Day, Religious Emphasis Week and Parents Weekend.

Sports: There are 5 intercollegiate sports for men, and 10 intramural sports for men. Facilities include a comprehensive health and phys ed center, a 9000-seat football stadium, a track, and a 5700-seat basketball arena.

Disabled Students: 85% of the campus is accessible. Facilities include wheelchair ramps, elevators, special parking, specially equipped restrooms, lowered drinking fountains, and lowered telephones.

Services: Counseling and information services are available, as is tutoring in most subjects. There is remedial math, reading, and writing.

Campus Safety and Security: Measures include 24-hour foot and vehicle patrol and security escort services. There are shuttle buses, emergency telephones, and lighted pathways/sidewalks.

Programs of Study: Morehouse confers B.A. and B.S. degrees. Bachelor's degrees are awarded in BIOLOGICAL SCIENCE (biology/biological science), BUSINESS (business administration and management), COMMUNICATIONS AND THE ARTS (art, English, French, music, and Spanish), COMPUTER AND PHYSICAL SCIENCE (chemistry, computer science, mathematics, physics, and science), EDUCATION (drama education and education), ENGINEERING AND ENVIRONMENTAL DESIGN (engineering), HEALTH PROFESSIONS (health), SOCIAL SCIENCE (African American studies, economics, history, international studies, philosophy, political science/government, psychology, religion, sociology, and urban studies). Political science, biology, English, pre-engineering, and business administration are the strongest academically. Business administration, political science, biology, English, pre-engineering and psychology have the largest enrollments.

Required: Students must complete a minimum of 120 semester hours, including 53 hours in general studies, plus 8 noncredit hours in Freshman Orientation and College Assembly. A 2.0 GPA is required, with no grade below C in the major.

Special: Morehouse is a member of the Atlanta University Center; students may register for courses at 4 of the 5 member institutions. They may complete a major at Spellman College, one of the 5 member institutions. Atlanta Regional Consortium for Higher Education (ARCHE) enables students to take courses at Atlanta regional colleges. In addition, students may study abroad in Europe or Africa. A dual-degree program is offered in architecture with the University of Michigan and in engineering with Columbia, Dartmouth, Georgia Tech, Rensselaer, and other schools; students in these programs are offered summer internships. Work study is also available. There are 6 national honor societies, including Phi Beta Kappa, a freshman honors program, and 10 departmental honors programs.

Faculty/Classroom: 64% of faculty are male; 36% are female. All teach undergraduates, and 20% do research. No introductory courses are taught by graduate students. The average class size in an introductory lecture is 25; in a laboratory is 30; and in a regular course is 20.

Admissions: 67% of the 2013-2014 applicants were accepted. The SAT scores for the 2013-2014 freshman class were: Critical Reading--45% below 500, 42% between 500 and 599, 11% between 600 and 699, and 2% between 700 and 800; Math--49% below 500, 36% between 500 and 599, 14% between 600 and 699, and 1% between 700 and 800; Writing--57% below 500, 33% between 500 and 599, 9% between 600 and 699, and 1% between 700 and 800. The ACT scores were 46% below 21, 29% between 21 and 23, 15% between 24 and 26, 6% between 27 and 28, and 4% above 28. 37% of the current freshmen were in the top fifth of their class; 60% were in the top two fifths.

Requirements: The SAT or ACT is required. In addition, Applicants should be graduates of accredited secondary schools or have the GED. Secondary preparation should include 4 units in English, 3 in math, 2 each in natural and social sciences, and 5 in other disciplines. Applicants must write an essay and are urged to seek an interview. A GPA of 2.8 is required. AP and CLEP credits are accepted. Important factors in the admissions decision are advanced placement or honors courses, leadership record, and recommendations by school officials.

Procedure: Freshmen are admitted fall and spring. Entrance exams should be taken by the fall of the senior year. There are early decision, early admissions, and deferred admissions plans. Early decision applications should be filed by October 15; regular applications, by February 15 for fall entry; and October 15 for spring entry. The fall 2013 application fee was $45. 101 early decision candidates were accepted for the 2013-2014 class. Applications are accepted online.

Transfer: 67 transfer students enrolled in 2012-2013. Transfer applicants must have at least a 2.5 GPA and a minimum of 26 semester hours of credit. 64 of 120 credits required for the bachelor's degree must be completed at Morehouse.

Visiting: There are regularly scheduled orientations for prospective students. There are guides for informal visits and visitors may sit in on classes. To schedule a visit, contact Director of On-Campus Recruitment at (404) 653-7736.

Financial Aid: In 2013-2014, 93% of all full-time freshmen and 93% of continuing full-time students received some form of financial aid. 93% of all full-time freshmen and 93% of continuing full-time students received need-based aid. The average freshman award was $33,188. Need-based scholarships or need-based grants averaged $16,712 ($46,290 maximum); need-based self-help aid (loans and jobs) averaged $19,511 ($45,290 maximum); and non-need-based athletic scholarships averaged $10,073 ($31,675 maximum). 40% of undergraduate students work part-time. Average annual earnings from campus work are $2800. The average financial indebtedness of the 2013 graduate was $37,962. Morehouse is a member of CSS. The FAFSA and the college's own financial statement are required. The priority date for freshman financial aid applications for fall entry is Febuary 1.

International Students: There are 53 international students enrolled. The school actively recruits these students. They must take the TOEFL.

Computers: All students may access the system.

Graduates: From July 1, 2012 to June 30, 2013, 437 bachelor's degrees were awarded. The most popular majors were business administration (22%), poliical science (10%), and biology (9%). 60 companies recruited on campus in 2012-2013. In an average class, 39% graduate in 4 years or less, 50% graduate in 5 years or less, and 55% graduate in 6 years or less. Of the 2012 graduating class, 30% were enrolled in graduate school within 6 months of graduation, and 35% were employed.

Admissions Contact: Darryl Isom, Director of Admissions and Recruitment. Web: *http:/www.morehouse.edu/admissions*

NORTH GEORGIA COLLEGE & STATE UNIVERSITY C-1

Dahlonega, GA 30597 (706) 864-1754
(800) 498-9581; (706) 864-1478

Full-time: 1280 men, 1905 women	**Faculty:** n/av
Part-time: 245 men, 575 women	**Ph.D.s:** n/av
Graduate: 150 men, 450 women	**Student/Faculty:** n/av
Year: semesters, summer session	**Tuition:** $4500 ($13,500)
Application Deadline: open	**Room & Board:** $5000
Freshman Class: n/av	
SAT: required	

COMPETITIVE

North Georgia College and State University, founded in 1873 as a military college, is today a liberal arts college that is part of the public University System of Georgia. One of 4 colleges in the United States classified as military colleges by the Department of the Army, the school requires all male resident students to join its Corps of Cadets; other students are given an option to join. Figures in the above capsule and in this profile are approximate. There are 4 undergraduate schools and 1 graduate school. In addition to regional accreditation, NGCSU has baccalaureate program accreditation with ACBSP, APTA, NCATE, and NLN. The 2 libraries contain 142,807 volumes, 774,482 microform items, and 3,118 audio/video tapes/CDs/DVDs, and subscribe to 2,546 periodicals including electronic. Computerized library services include interlibrary loans, database searching, and Internet access. Special learning facilities include an art gallery, planetarium, a math lab, language lab, and writing center. The 665-acre campus is in a small town 60 miles north of Atlanta. Including any residence halls, there are 25 buildings.

Student Life: 95% of undergraduates are from Georgia. Others are from 33 states, 8 foreign countries, and Canada. 90% are from public schools. 93% are white. The average age of freshmen is 19; all undergraduates, 22.

Housing: 1200 students can be accommodated in college housing, which includes single-sex dorms and on-campus apartments. On-campus housing is available on a first-come and first-served basis. 69% of students commute. Alcohol is not permitted. All students may keep cars.

Activities: 13% of men belong to 2 local and 4 national fraternities; 10% of women belong to 4 national sororities. There are 52 groups on campus, including band, cheerleading, choir, chorale, chorus, drama, drill team, ethnic, honors, jazz band, literary magazine, marching band, newspaper, pep band, political, professional, religious, student government, symphony, and yearbook. Popular campus events include Spring Jam, frisbee golf, and military reviews.

Sports: There are 5 intercollegiate sports for men and 6 for women, and 7 intramural sports for men and 7 for women. Facilities include a swimming pool, a track, a fully equipped exercise room, a rappeling tower, a confidence course, a picnic area, a 2000-seat gym, and a 250-seat arena.

Disabled Students: 50% of the campus is accessible. Facilities include wheelchair ramps, elevators, special parking, specially equipped rest rooms, and lowered drinking fountains.

Services: Counseling and information services are available, as is tutoring in most subjects. There is a reader service for the blind, and remedial math, reading, and writing.

Campus Safety and Security: Measures include 24-hour foot and vehicle patrol and security escort services. There are emergency telephones and lighted pathways/sidewalks.

Programs of Study: NGCSU confers A.B., B.S., B.B.A., and B.S.N. degrees. Associates and master's degrees are also awarded. Bachelor's degrees are awarded in BIOLOGICAL SCIENCE (biology/biological science), BUSINESS (accounting, banking and finance, business administration and management, business economics, marketing/retailing/merchandising, and recreation and leisure services), COMMUNICATIONS

AND THE ARTS (art, arts administration/management, English, French, music, and Spanish), COMPUTER AND PHYSICAL SCIENCE (chemistry, computer science, mathematics, and physics), EDUCATION (art education, early childhood education, elementary education, foreign languages education, mathematics education, middle school education, music education, physical education, science education, secondary education, social science education, and special education), ENGINEERING AND ENVIRONMENTAL DESIGN (preengineering), HEALTH PROFESSIONS (nursing, predentistry, premedicine, prepharmacy, and preveterinary science), SOCIAL SCIENCE (criminal justice, history, political science/government, prelaw, psychology, social science, and sociology). Education and premedicine are the strongest academically. Business and teacher education have the largest enrollments.

Required: To graduate, students must complete 120 semester credit hours with a minimum GPA of 2.0. English, math, lab sciences, and social sciences are required.

Special: Special academic programs include a co-op program in business, internships, a 3-2 engineering degree with Georgia Institute of Technology, study abroad in Europe, South America, and Canada, dual majors, and credit for life, military, or work experience. There are 9 national honor societies, including Phi Beta Kappa, a freshman honors program, and 8 departmental honors programs.

Faculty/Classroom: 50% of faculty are male; 50% are female. All teach undergraduates. No introductory courses are taught by graduate students.

Requirements: The SAT or ACT is required. Students must have graduated from a secondary school with 4 years each of English and math, 3 each of science and social science, and 2 of a foreign language. The GED is accepted if granted at least 5 years later than expected high school graduation date. SAT II Subject Tests are required of home-schooled students. A GPA of 2.0 is required. AP and CLEP credits are accepted. Important factors in the admissions decision are leadership record, advanced placement or honors courses, and evidence of special talent.

Procedure: Freshmen are admitted fall, spring, and summer. Entrance exams should be taken in the junior year. There are deferred admissions and rolling admissions plans. Check with the school for current application deadlines and fee. Applications are accepted online. A waiting list is maintained.

Transfer: Transfer students must have maintained a C average and a clear conduct record, and be in good academic standing. Those who have not completed 90 quarter hours of transferable credit must have completed the approved precollege curriculum and must submit high school transcripts and the SAT or ACT results. 45 of 120 credits required for the bachelor's degree must be completed at NGCSU.

Visiting: There are regularly scheduled orientations for prospective students, including an admissions video, college overview, tour, and a meeting with an admissions counselor. There are guides for informal visits and visitors may stay overnight. To schedule a visit, contact the Admissions Office.

Financial Aid: The FAFSA and the college's own financial statement are required. Check with the school for current application deadlines.

International Students: They must take the TOEFL, IELTS, SAT, or ACT.

Computers: All students may access the system. There are no time limits and no fees.

Admissions Contact: Undergraduate Admissions and Recruiting. A campus DVD is available. E-Mail: *admissions@northgeorgia.edu* Web: *www.northgeorgia.edu*

OGLETHORPE UNIVERSITY — B-2

Atlanta, GA 30319 — (404) 364-8307; (800) 428-8491; (404) 364-8500

Full-time: 434 men, 558 women	**Faculty:** 59
Part-time: 30 men, 51 women	**Ph.D.s:** 98%
Graduate: 9 women	**Student/Faculty:** 17 to 1
Year: semesters, summer session	**Tuition:** $31,280
Application Deadline: open	**Room & Board:** $11,300
Freshman Class: 4404 applied, 2455 accepted, 282 enrolled	
SAT CR/M/W: 570/550/550 **ACT:** 24	**VERY COMPETITIVE**

Oglethorpe University, founded in 1835, is an independent institution offering programs in the liberal arts and science, business, and preprofessional studies. There are 2 undergraduate schools and one graduate school. The library contains 155,000 volumes, 4,189 microform items, and 6,786 audio/video tapes/CDs/DVDs, and subscribes to 775 periodicals including electronic. Computerized library services include interlibrary loans, database searching, Internet access, and Wi-Fi capability. Special learning facilities include an art gallery, radio station, an in-residence, professional theatre program, Georgia Shakespeare: a Center for Civic Engagement. The 102-acre campus is in a suburban area 10 miles northeast of downtown Atlanta. Including any residence halls, there are 25 buildings.

Student Life: 73% of undergraduates are from Georgia. Others are from 35 states, 29 foreign countries, and Canada. 74% are from public schools. 34% are White; 27% race unknown; 18% African American. The average age of freshmen is 18; all undergraduates, 21. 20% do not continue beyond their first year; 58% remain to graduate.

Housing: 803 students can be accommodated in college housing, which includes single-sex and coed dorms. In addition, there are fraternity houses and sorority houses. On-campus housing is guaranteed for the freshman year only, is available on a first-come, and first-served basis. Priority is given to out-of-town students. 65% of students live on campus; of those, 75% remain on campus on weekends. All students may keep cars.

Activities: 26% of men belong to 1 local and 2 national fraternities; 22% of women belong to 1 local and 4 national sororities. There are 51 groups on campus, including art, cheerleading, choir, chorale, chorus, computers, dance, drama, ethnic, gay, honors, international, literary magazine, newspaper, orchestra, pep band, photography, political, professional, radio and TV, religious, social, social service, student government, and yearbook. Popular campus events include Oglethorpe Day, and Liberal Arts Symposium.

Sports: There are 8 intercollegiate sports for men and 8 for women, and 6 intramural sports for men and 6 for women. Facilities include a field house and recreation center housing basketball and volleyball courts, a running track, handball courts, and a weight room. Outdoor facilities include 6 tennis courts, an all-weather track, a sand volleyball court, and soccer, baseball, and intramural fields.

Disabled Students: 80% of the campus is accessible. Facilities include wheelchair ramps, elevators, special parking, specially equipped restrooms, special class scheduling, lowered drinking fountains, and special housing.

Services: Counseling and information services are available, as is tutoring in most subjects, including all core (general education) courses, English, writing, accounting, and math.

Campus Safety and Security: Measures include 24-hour foot and vehicle patrol, emergency notification system, self-defense education, and security escort services. There are lighted pathways/sidewalks, entrance to residence halls is on an ID card-swipe system.

Programs of Study: Oglethorpe confers B.A., B.S., B.A.L.S. and B.B.A. degrees. Master's degrees are also awarded. Bachelor's degrees are awarded in BIOLOGICAL SCIENCE (biology/biological science), BUSINESS (accounting and business administration and management), COMMUNICATIONS AND THE ARTS (art, art history and appreciation, communications, English, French, and Spanish), COMPUTER AND PHYSICAL SCIENCE (chemistry, mathematics, and physics), SOCIAL SCIENCE (American studies, behavioral science, biopsychology, economics, history, international studies, philosophy, political science/government, psychology, social work, and sociology). Accounting, biology and English are the strongest academically. Business administration, biology, communications and rhetoric have the largest enrollments.

Required: To graduate with a B.A. or B.S., all students must complete at least 128 credit hours (120 for B.B.A. and B.A.L.S.). They must fulfill a major as well as complete the core curriculum and achieve a minimum GPA of 2.0. The core curriculum is a unique 4-year sequence of related interdisciplinary courses, 1 per semester. All freshman must complete the first-year experience program.

Special: Oglethorpe offers co-op programs in all majors, cross-registration through the Atlanta Regional Consortium for Higher Education, international exchange agreements with several universities in Europe, Asia, and South America, and other study-abroad options. Internships are available in all areas of study for up to 15 credit hours for upperclassmen with a minimum 2.8 GPA, and a Washington semester offers internships with Georgia senators and others. There is a 3-2 engineering program with Georgia Institute of Technology, the Universities of Florida and Southern California, and Auburn University. Accelerated degrees, dual majors, student-designed majors, federal work-study programs, and nondegree study are offered. There are 7 national honor societies, a freshman honors program, and 99 departmental honors programs.

Faculty/Classroom: 60% of faculty are male; 40% are female. 96% teach undergraduates. No introductory courses are taught by graduate students. The average class size in an introductory lecture is 20; in a laboratory is 18; and in a regular course is 15.

Admissions: 56% of the 2013-2014 applicants were accepted. The SAT scores for the 2013-2014 freshman class were: Critical Reading--12% below 500, 50% between 500 and 599, 28% between 600 and 699, and 10% between 700 and 800; Math--19% below 500, 48% between 500 and 599, 30% between 600 and 699, and 3% between 700 and 800; Writing--26% below 500, 44% between 500 and 599, 24% between 600 and 699, and 6% between 700 and 800. The ACT scores were 11% below 21, 30% between 21 and 23, 29% between 24 and 26, 14% between 27 and 28, and 16% above 28. 45% of the current freshmen were in the top fifth of their class; 78% were in the top two fifths.

Requirements: The SAT or ACT is required. Students should graduate from an accredited high school or have a GED certificate. They should have completed 4 courses in English, 3 each in science and social studies, and a math sequence of algebra I and II and geometry. A counselor's or teacher's recommendation is required, and an essay is required for a scholarship.

An interview is recommended. AP and CLEP credits are accepted. Important factors in the admissions decision are recommendations by school officials, extracurricular activities record, and advanced placement or honors courses.

Procedure: Freshmen are admitted to all sessions. Entrance exams should be taken late in the junior year or early in the senior year. There are early decision, early admissions, deferred admissions, and rolling admissions plans. Check with the school for current application deadlines. The application fee is $50. Notification is sent on a rolling basis. Applications are accepted online.

Transfer: 42 transfer students enrolled in 2012-2013. Applicants who have completed less than a full year of college work must take the SAT or ACT. All transfers must be in good academic standing with a minimum GPA of 2.5. An interview is recommended. 64 of 128 credits required for the bachelor's degree must be completed at Oglethorpe.

Visiting: There are regularly scheduled orientations for prospective students, including placement tests, class registration, an activities fair, and group activities. There are guides for informal visits, visitors may sit in on classes, and stay overnight. To schedule a visit, contact the Admissions Office.

Financial Aid: In 2013-2014, 76% of all full-time freshmen and 68% of continuing full-time students received some form of financial aid. 76% of all full-time freshmen and 68% of continuing full-time students received need-based aid. The average freshman award was $27,111. Need-based scholarships or need-based grants averaged $24,354; need-based self-help aid (loans and jobs) averaged $2,757; and other non-need-based awards and non-need-based scholarships averaged $15,459. The average financial indebtedness of the 2013 graduate was $27,650. Oglethorpe is a member of CSS. The FAFSA is required. Check with the school for current application deadlines.

International Students: There are 57 international students enrolled. The school actively recruits these students. They must take the TOEFL with a minimum score of 550 on the paper-based TOEFL (PBT), or demonstrate proficiency in English by other means. They must also take the SAT or ACT.

Computers: All students may access the system. There are no time limits and no fees.

Graduates: From July 1, 2012 to June 30, 2013, 192 bachelor's degrees were awarded. The most popular majors were English and communications (22%), business and accounting (17%), and social sciences (11%). In an average class, 1% graduate in 3 years or less, 42% graduate in 4 years or less, 53% graduate in 5 years or less, and 55% graduate in 6 years or less. Of the 2012 graduating class, 35% were enrolled in graduate school within 6 months of graduation, and 65% were employed.

Admissions Contact: Lucy Leusch, Vice President for Enrollment. E-Mail: *admission@oglethorpe.edu* Web: *www.oglethorpe.edu*

PAINE COLLEGE — D-2

Augusta, GA 30901 (706) 821-8320
(800) 476-7703; (706) 821-8691

Full-time: 293 men, 472 women	**Faculty:** 53
Part-time: 27 men, 45 women	**Ph.D.s:** 75%
Graduate: n/av	**Student/Faculty:** 13 to 1
Year: semesters, summer session	**Tuition:** $12,502
Application Deadline: July 1	**Room & Board:** $6092

Freshman Class: 2174 applied, 1683 accepted, 176 enrolled
SAT or ACT: required

LESS COMPETITIVE

Paine College, founded in 1882, is a largely African American private institution with residential, commuter, and off-site units affiliated with the Christian Methodist Episcopal Church and the United Methodist Church. It offers programs in liberal arts, business, and teacher preparation. There are 2 undergraduate schools. In addition to regional accreditation, Paine has baccalaureate program accreditation with ACBSP and NCATE. The library contains 75,090 volumes, 6,979 microform items, and 573 audio/video tapes/CDs/DVDs, and subscribes to 23,393 periodicals including electronic. Computerized library services include interlibrary loans, database searching, and Internet access. Special learning facilities include an art gallery, tutorial and enrichment center and mathematics support center. The 65-acre campus is in an urban area 150 miles east of Atlanta and 72 miles west of Columbia, South Carolina. Including any residence halls, there are 31 buildings.

Student Life: 74% of undergraduates are from Georgia. Others are from 28 states, and 5 foreign countries. 91% are African American. 54% claim no religious affiliation; 41% Protestant. The average age of freshmen is 19; all undergraduates, 22. 35% do not continue beyond their first year; 28% remain to graduate.

Housing: 589 students can be accommodated in college housing, which includes single-sex dorms and off-campus apartments. In addition, there are honors houses. On-campus housing is available on a first-come and first-served basis. 52% of students commute. Alcohol is not permitted. All students may keep cars.

Activities: 7% of men belong to 4 national fraternities; 4% of women belong to 4 national sororities. There are 34 groups on campus, including art, cheerleading, choir, chorus, computers, dance, drama, environmental, film, honors, international, literary magazine, NAACP, newspaper, professional, radio and TV, religious, social, social service, student government, and yearbook. Popular campus events include Painefest, Religious Emphasis Week and Black History Activities.

Sports: There are 5 intercollegiate sports for men and 5 for women, and 7 intramural sports for men and 7 for women. Facilities include a basketball arena, a track, a baseball field, intramural field, and outside basketball and volleyball courts.

Disabled Students: 80% of the campus is accessible. Facilities include wheelchair ramps, elevators, special parking, specially equipped restrooms, lowered drinking fountains, and special housing.

Services: Counseling and information services are available, as is tutoring in most subjects. There is remedial math, reading, and writing.

Campus Safety and Security: Measures include 24-hour foot and vehicle patrol, emergency notification system, and security escort services. There are emergency telephones, lighted pathways/sidewalks, controlled access to dorms/residences, security cameras.

Programs of Study: Paine confers B.A., and B.S. degrees. Bachelor's degrees are awarded in BIOLOGICAL SCIENCE (biology/biological science), BUSINESS (business administration and management), COMMUNICATIONS AND THE ARTS (communications and English), COMPUTER AND PHYSICAL SCIENCE (chemistry and mathematics), EDUCATION (early childhood education, middle school education, and secondary education), SOCIAL SCIENCE (history, philosophy and religion, psychology, and sociology). Education and business is the strongest academically. Business has the largest enrollment.

Required: Common curriculum requirements include 18 hours in world citizenship/society, 14 in science/technology, 9 to 11 in fundamentals, 9 in spiritual and social values, and 6 in the aesthetic heritage. From 42 to 84 hours are required in the major. A minimum GPA of 2.5 in the major is needed. To graduate, at least 124 credits must be completed. A thesis in most programs and comprehensive exams in some programs may also be required, as well as a national standardized test.

Special: Paine has cross-registration with Georgia Regents University (any department), internships for business administration and sociology majors, and study abroad as they become available and students apply. A 3-2 engineering degree is offered with Tuskegee University. There are 6 national honor societies and 4 departmental honors programs.

Faculty/Classroom: 58% of faculty are male; 42% are female. All teach undergraduates. No introductory courses are taught by graduate students. The average class size in an introductory lecture is 20 and in a regular course is 20.

Admissions: 77% of the 2013-2014 applicants were accepted. 13% of the current freshmen were in the top fifth of their class; 34% were in the top two fifths.

Requirements: The SAT or ACT is required. An SAT or ACT score must be submitted. Applicants should be graduates of an accredited secondary school or have a GED. A total of 16 academic credits is required, including 4 units of English, 3 each of math, social studies, and science. A GPA of 2.0 is required. AP and CLEP credits are accepted. Important factors in the admissions decision are recommendations by school officials, advanced placement or honors courses, and evidence of special talent.

Procedure: Freshmen are admitted to all sessions. Entrance exams should be taken The ACT or SAT must be taken before enrollment. There are early admissions, deferred admissions, and rolling admissions plans. Applications should be filed by July 1 for fall entry; December 1 for spring entry; and June 1 for summer entry, along with a $35 fee. Notification is sent on a rolling basis. Applications are accepted online.

Transfer: 60 transfer students enrolled in 2012-2013. A transfer student who has completed fewer than 28 semester credit hours of college work at another regionally accredited institution must meet the general admission criteria for a freshmen applicant.A minimum cumulative grade point average (CGPA) of 2.0 from previous college work (official transcript(s) must be submitted) is required. 31 of 124 credits required for the bachelor's degree must be completed at Paine.

Visiting: There are regularly scheduled orientations for prospective students, opportunity to become familiar with College rules and regulations and to become acquainted with the staff and facilities of the College. Social events and other activities are arranged to assist students in adjusting to their new environment. There are guides for informal visits, visitors may sit in on classes, and stay overnight. To schedule a visit, contact Marshall Rainey, Director of Admissions.

Financial Aid: In 2013-2014, 94% of all full-time freshmen and 90% of continuing full-time students received some form of financial aid. 91% of all full-time freshmen and 89% of continuing full-time students received need-based aid. The average freshman award was $10,173. Need-based scholarships or need-based grants averaged $7,098 ($18,595 maximum); need-based self-help aid (loans and jobs) averaged $3,828 ($9,500 maximum); and non-need-based athletic scholarships averaged $6,915

($18,595 maximum). 100% of undergraduate students work part-time. Average annual earnings from campus work are $3400. The average financial indebtedness of the 2013 graduate was $24,600. The FAFSA is required. The priority date for freshman financial aid applications for fall entry is March 1.

International Students: There are 13 international students enrolled. They must take the TOEFL with a minimum score of 500 on the paper-based TOEFL (PBT) or 76 on the Internet-based version (iBT), ESL (English as a Second Language) Placement Test. They must also take the SAT or ACT. if the test is not offered in the student's country they will be required to take the test during their first semester.

Computers: All students may access the system. There are no time limits. The fee is $131.

Graduates: From July 1, 2012 to June 30, 2013, 100 bachelor's degrees were awarded. The most popular majors were business administration (24%), sociology (18%), and media studies (14%). 40 companies recruited on campus in 2012-2013. In an average class, 10% graduate in 4 years or less, 21% graduate in 5 years or less, and 26% graduate in 6 years or less. Of the 2012 graduating class, 5% were enrolled in graduate school within 6 months of graduation, and 25% were employed.

Admissions Contact: Marshall Rainey, Director of Admissions. E-Mail: *mrainey@paine.edu* Web: *http:/www.paine.edu/admissions/*

PIEDMONT COLLEGE C-1

Demorest, GA 30535 (706) 778-3000, ext. 1188
(800) 277-7020; (706) 776-6635

Full-time: 380 men, 751 women	**Faculty:** n/av
Part-time: 45 men, 105 women	**Ph.D.s:** 70%
Graduate: 242 men, 845 women	**Student/Faculty:** 14 to 1
Year: semesters, summer session	**Tuition:** $20,730
Application Deadline:	**Room & Board:** $8530
Freshman Class: n/av	

COMPETITIVE

Piedmont College, founded in 1897, is a private, liberal arts institution affiliated with the National Association of Congregational Christian Churches and the United Church of Christ. There are 4 undergraduate schools and 2 graduate schools. In addition to regional accreditation, Piedmont has baccalaureate program accreditation with ACBSP and NLN. The 2 libraries contain 259,518 volumes, and 8,973 audio/video tapes/CDs/DVDs, and subscribe to 20,900 periodicals including electronic. Computerized library services include interlibrary loans, database searching, Internet access, and Wi-Fi capability. Special learning facilities include an art gallery, radio station, and TV station. The 186-acre campus is in a small town 75 miles northeast of Atlanta. Including any residence halls, there are 35 buildings.

Student Life: 92% of undergraduates are from Georgia. Others are from 18 states, 6 foreign countries, and Canada. 77% are White. The average age of freshmen is 19; all undergraduates, 24. 30% do not continue beyond their first year; 46% remain to graduate.

Housing: 587 students can be accommodated in college housing, which includes single-sex and coed dorms and on-campus apartments. On-campus housing is guaranteed for all 4 years, is available on a first-come, and first-served basis. 55% of students commute. Alcohol is not permitted. All students may keep cars.

Activities: There are no fraternities or sororities. There are 32 groups on campus, including art, cheerleading, choir, chorale, chorus, debate, drama, environmental, film, honors, jazz band, musical theater, newspaper, pep band, photography, professional, radio and TV, religious, social, social service, student government, and yearbook. Popular campus events include Piedmont hosts events at our Arrendale Amphitheatre: Festivals, Bands, Campus performing groups, and more. Athletic events, Music Recitals, and Art Museum Receptions also contribute to campus life.

Sports: There are 7 intercollegiate sports for men and 8 for women, and 5 intramural sports for men and 5 for women. Facilities include An athletic center, 8 tennis courts, beach volleyball courts, and regulation baseball, softball, and soccer fields, indoor training facilty for baseball and softball.

Disabled Students: 85% of the campus is accessible. Facilities include wheelchair ramps, elevators, special parking, specially equipped restrooms, special class scheduling, and special housing.

Services: Counseling and information services are available, as is tutoring in most subjects, The Learning Center offers academic support in all areas, including accounting, foreign languages, math, science, and writing.

Campus Safety and Security: Measures include 24-hour foot and vehicle patrol, emergency notification system, self-defense education, and security escort services. There are emergency telephones, lighted pathways/sidewalks, controlled access to dorms/residences, Campus also patrolled by the local police department; Student security hosts in each residence hall.

Programs of Study: Piedmont confers B.A., B.S., B.F.A. and B.S.N. degrees. Master's and doctoral degrees are also awarded. Bachelor's degrees are awarded in AGRICULTURE (environmental studies), BIOLOGICAL SCIENCE (biology/biological science), BUSINESS (business administration and management and sports management), COMMUNICATIONS AND THE ARTS (art, arts administration/management, communications, dramatic arts, English, fine arts, music, musical theater, Spanish, theatre arts, and theater design), COMPUTER AND PHYSICAL SCIENCE (applied mathematics, applied physics, chemistry, computer mathematics, mathematics, physics, and science), EDUCATION (art education, athletic training, early childhood education, education, English education, mathematics education, middle school education, music education, science education, social science education, and special education), ENGINEERING AND ENVIRONMENTAL DESIGN (environmental science), HEALTH PROFESSIONS (nursing), SOCIAL SCIENCE (criminal justice, history, interdisciplinary studies, philosophy, political science/government, psychology, religion, social science, and sociology). Social sciences, nursing, education, business, English and natural sciences are the strongest academically. Education, business administration, nursing and social sciences have the largest enrollments.

Required: To graduate, a minimum of 120 credit hours is required. Students must complete 24 to 56 credit hours in their major, 23 to 26 in humanities, 14 to 18 in math and natural science, 9 in social science, 3 in fine arts, and 3 in computer science.

Special: Piedmont College assists students with internships in business, psychology, education, art management, criminal justice, sociology, and political science and other academic majors. Study abroad and Interdisciplinary majors are available . There are 4 national honor societies and 1 departmental honors programs.

Faculty/Classroom: 43% of faculty are male; 57% are female. No introductory courses are taught by graduate students. The average class size in a regular course is 14.

Requirements: The SAT is required. Applicants must be graduates of an accredited secondary school or have a GED certificate. Students must have completed a minimum of 21 academic units. A portfolio is required for art scholarship applicants and an audition for music scholarship applicants. An interview is recommended for all students. AP and CLEP credits are accepted. Important factors in the admissions decision are leadership record, advanced placement or honors courses, and extracurricular activities record.

Procedure: Freshmen are admitted to all sessions. There are deferred admissions and rolling admissions plans. Application deadlines are open. Applications are accepted online.

Transfer: 99 transfer students enrolled in 2012-2013. Applicants must have a GPA of 2.0 at each institution attended. An interview is recommended. 30 of 120 credits required for the bachelor's degree must be completed at Piedmont.

Visiting: There are regularly scheduled orientations for prospective students, campus tour, introduction to student activities, academic overview, admissions counseling, resident orientation, and a financial aid presentation. There are guides for informal visits, visitors may sit in on classes, and stay overnight. To schedule a visit, contact the Undergraduate Office at ugrad@piedmont.edu.

Financial Aid: In 2013-2014, 100% of all full-time freshmen and 98% of continuing full-time students received some form of financial aid. 73% of all full-time freshmen and 75% of continuing full-time students received need-based aid. The average freshman award was $21,460. Need-based scholarships or need-based grants averaged $4,688 ($11,344 maximum); need-based self-help aid (loans and jobs) averaged $3,474 ($6,330 maximum); and other non-need-based awards and non-need-based scholarships averaged $12,960 ($22,630 maximum). 33% of undergraduate students work part-time. Average annual earnings from campus work are $2490. The average financial indebtedness of the 2013 graduate was $17,190. The FAFSA and the state aid form are required. Check with the school for current application deadlines.

International Students: There are 6 international students enrolled. They must take the TOEFL with a minimum score of 550 on the paper-based TOEFL (PBT) or 80 on the Internet-based version (iBT). They must also take the SAT or ACT.

Computers: All students may access the system. There are no time limits and no fees.

Graduates: From July 1, 2012 to June 30, 2013, 254 bachelor's degrees were awarded. The most popular majors were education/early childhood/middle grades (27%), business administration (24%), and social sciences (18%). In an average class, 39% graduate in 4 years or less, 45% graduate in 5 years or less, and 46% graduate in 6 years or less.

Admissions Contact: Brenda Boonstra, Director of Undergraduate Admissions. E-Mail: *bboonstra@piedmont.edu* Web: *www.piedmont.edu*

REINHARDT COLLEGE B-1

Waleska, GA 30183-2981 (770) 720-5526
1-87REINHARDT; (770) 720-5899

Full-time: 390 men, 575 women
Part-time: 65 men, 90 women
Graduate: n/av
Year: semesters, summer session
Application Deadline: open
Freshman Class: n/av
SAT or ACT: required
Faculty: n/av
Ph.D.s: n/av
Student/Faculty: n/av
Tuition: $15,000
Room & Board: $10,000

COMPETITIVE

Reinhardt College, founded in 1883, is a private institution affiliated with the Methodist Church and offering undergraduate degrees. The figures in the above capsule and in this profile are approximate. There are 4 undergraduate schools. The library contains 48,000 volumes, 1,983 microform items, and 3,598 audio/video tapes/CDs/DVDs, and subscribes to 315 periodicals including electronic. Computerized library services include interlibrary loans, database searching, and Internet access. Special learning facilities include an art gallery, natural history museum, radio station, and TV station. The 600-acre campus is in a small town 40 miles north of Atlanta. Including any residence halls, there are 31 buildings.

Student Life: 98% of undergraduates are from Georgia. Others are from 4 states, 6 foreign countries, and Canada. 90% are from public schools. 82% are white, 70% are Protestant, 23% claim no religious affiliation. The average age of freshmen is 18; all undergraduates, 23. 36%, do not continue beyond their first year; 50% remain to graduate.

Housing: 400 students can be accommodated in college housing, which includes single-sex dorms. On-campus housing is guaranteed for all 4 years. 64% of students commute. Alcohol is not permitted. All students may keep cars.

Activities: There are no fraternities or sororities. There are 14 groups on campus, including cheerleading, honors, newspaper, professional, radio and TV, religious, social, social service, student government, and yearbook. Popular campus events include Spring Day, Spring Formal, and Diversity Days.

Sports: There are 5 intercollegiate sports for men and 4 for women, and 4 intramural sports for men and 4 for women. Facilities include parks, jogging trails, outdoor volleyball, tennis, and basketball courts, soccer and softball fields, a pool, a weight room, a bowling alley, and racquetball courts.

Disabled Students: 90% of the campus is accessible. Facilities include wheelchair ramps, elevators, special parking, specially equipped rest rooms, special class scheduling, and lowered drinking fountains.

Services: Counseling and information services are available, as is tutoring in every subject.

Campus Safety and Security: Measures include 24-hour foot and vehicle patrol and self-defense education. There are lighted pathways/sidewalks.

Programs of Study: Reinhardt confers B.A., B.S., B.F.A., and B.S.B.A. degrees. Associates degrees are also awarded. Bachelor's degrees are awarded in BIOLOGICAL SCIENCE (biology/biological science), BUSINESS (business administration and management), COMMUNICATIONS AND THE ARTS (communications), SOCIAL SCIENCE (liberal arts/general studies). Business and liberal studies are the largest.

Required: To graduate, students must have a core curriculum in the humanities, math and science, social science, language, phys ed, and wellness. A total of 120 semester hours is required, including 65 in the major. A 2.0 GPA must be maintained.

Special: Internships, study abroad, and work-study programs are available. There is an accelerated degree program in organizational leadership. There is 1 national honor society and a freshman honors program.

Faculty/Classroom: 45% of faculty are male; 55% are female. All teach undergraduates.

Requirements: The SAT or ACT is required. The GED is accepted and a placement test may be required. A GPA of 2.0 is required. AP and CLEP credits are accepted. Important factors in the admissions decision are recommendations by alumni, recommendations by school officials, and parents or siblings attended your school.

Procedure: Freshmen are admitted to all sessions. Entrance exams should be taken before acceptance. There are early admissions and rolling admissions plans. Check with the school for current application deadlines and fee. Applications are accepted online.

Transfer: A GPA of 2.0 or better may be considered for transfer applicants. 40 of 120 credits required for the bachelor's degree must be completed at Reinhardt.

Visiting: There are regularly scheduled orientations for prospective students. There are guides for informal visits and visitors may sit in on classes.

Financial Aid: Reinhardt is a member of CSS. The FAFSA is required. Check with the school for current application deadlines.

International Students: They must take the TOEFL, SAT, or ACT.

Computers: All students may access the system. There are no time limits and no fees. It is strongly recommended that all students have a personal computer.

Admissions Contact: Admissions. E-Mail: *admissions@reinhardt.edu*
Web: *www.reinhardt.edu*

SAVANNAH COLLEGE OF ART AND DESIGN E-4

Savannah, GA 31401 (912) 525-5100
(800) 869-7223; (912) 525-5995

Full-time: 2718 men, 5021 women
Part-time: 599 men, 994 women
Graduate: 906 men, 1380 women
Year: quarters, summer session
Application Deadline: open
Freshman Class: n/av
Faculty: 520
Ph.D.s: 81%
Student/Faculty: 15 to 1
Tuition: $33,450
Room & Board: $13,374

SPECIAL

The Savannah College of Art and Design is a private, nonprofit, accredited institution conferring bachelor's and master's degrees at distinctive locations and online to prepare talented students for professional careers. SCAD offers degrees in more than 40 majors, as well as minors in more than 60 disciplines in Savannah and Atlanta, Georgia; in Hong Kong; in Lacoste, France; and online through SCAD eLearning. There are 8 undergraduate schools and 8 graduate schools. In addition to regional accreditation, SCAD has baccalaureate program accreditation with NAAB. The 4 libraries contain 265,407 volumes, 7,053 microform items, and 4,907 audio/video tapes/CDs/DVDs, and subscribe to 37,881 periodicals including electronic. Computerized library services include interlibrary loans, database searching, Internet access, and Wi-Fi capability. Special learning facilities include an art gallery, radio station, TV station, international student center, writing center, internet labs, and SCAD Museum of Art. The campus is in an urban area in Savannah, Georgia on the southeast coast of Georgia, midway between Charleston, SC and Jacksonville, FL. There are also locations in Atlanta, Georgia, Lacoste, France and Hong Kong. Including any residence halls, there are 70 buildings.

Student Life: 77% of undergraduates are from out of state, mostly the South. Students are from 49 states, 107 foreign countries, and Canada. 54% are White; 12% Foreign. The average age of freshmen is 19; all undergraduates, 21. 19% do not continue beyond their first year; 68% remain to graduate.

Housing: 4344 students can be accommodated in college housing, which includes coed dorms, on-campus apartments, and off-campus apartments. freshmen-only buildings. On-campus housing is available on a first-come and first-served basis. 59% of students commute. Alcohol is not permitted. All students may keep cars.

Activities: There are no fraternities or sororities. There are 107 groups on campus, including art, chorale, communications, computers, dance, drama, ethnic, film, gay, honors, international, Jewelry and Objects Student Association; American Institute of Architecture Students; Graphic Design Club; Contemporary Animation Society; Digital Media Club; MOME Love (motion media design); and Fibers Force, literary magazine, musical theater, newspaper, photography, professional, radio and TV, religious, social service, and student government. Popular campus events include Savannah Film Festival, Fashion Show, deFINE ART, SCAD Style, Sidewalk Arts Festival, Sand Arts Festival, Alumni Concert and the Game Developers Exchange.

Sports: There are 8 intercollegiate sports for men and 8 for women, and 12 intramural sports for men and 12 for women. Facilities include Club SCAD; Turner fitness center; Atlanta fitness center; Studio; Waranch Equestrian center and athletic fields.

Disabled Students: 85% of the campus is accessible. Facilities include wheelchair ramps, elevators, special parking, specially equipped restrooms, special class scheduling, lowered drinking fountains, lowered telephones. Facilities vary by building and location. Individual situations are accommodated.

Services: Counseling and information services are available, as is tutoring in most subjects. There is a sign language interpreter for hearing-impaired students, a coordinator of disability services; writing center, drawing center, and learning resource hive.

Campus Safety and Security: Measures include 24-hour foot and vehicle patrol, emergency notification system, self-defense education, and security escort services. There are shuttle buses, emergency telephones, lighted pathways/sidewalks, controlled access to dorms/residences, video surveillance cameras.

Programs of Study: SCAD confers B.A., and B.F.A. degrees. Master's degrees are also awarded. Bachelor's degrees are awarded in AGRICULTURE (equine science), BUSINESS (fashion merchandising), COMMUNICATIONS AND THE ARTS (advertising, animation, art, art history and appreciation, audio technology, broadcasting, communications, design, fiber/textiles/weaving, film arts, graphic design, historic preservation, illustration, industrial design, media arts, metal/jewelry, painting, performing arts, photography, printmaking, sculpture, visual effects, and writing), COMPUTER AND PHYSICAL SCIENCE (digital arts/technology), ENGINEERING AND ENVIRONMENTAL DESIGN (architectural history, architecture, computer graphics, furniture design, and interior design), SOCIAL SCIENCE (fashion design and technology). Animation, graphic design, illustration, photography, and fashion have the largest enrollments.

Required: All undergraduate programs of study require 25 to 45 credit hours of foundation studies (drawing/design) courses, 55 to 90 hours of liberal arts courses, 45 to 85 hours of coursework in the major discipline, and 10 to 20 hours of electives for a total of 180 quarter credit hours. In order to graduate, students must have a minimum overall GPA of 2.0 and a 3.0 GPA in the major discipline.

Special: The college offers study abroad in France and Hong Kong, cross-registration with Atlanta Regional Council of Higher Education, on-campus work-study programs, dual majors in all disciplines, sessions for credit in New York and other domestic locations, and internships with artists, designers, museums, agencies, and architectural firms in the United States and abroad. There are 2 national honor societies.

Faculty/Classroom: 58% of faculty are male; 42% are female. All teach undergraduates. No introductory courses are taught by graduate students.

Requirements: The SAT or ACT is required. Students must submit a completed application and high school transcript indicating successful completion. Preference is given to students with a 3.0 GPA or above and to students whose SAT or ACT scores are above the national average (B.F.A. Architecture candidates with math scores below 540 or 23, respectively, may be admitted to architecture on a conditional basis); 3 letters of recommendation and a statement of purpose are required. An interview is recommended, and a portfolio is encouraged. AP and CLEP credits are accepted. Important factors in the admissions decision are recommendations by school officials, evidence of special talent, and leadership record.

Procedure: Freshmen are admitted to all sessions. Entrance exams should be taken by January of the senior year. There are deferred admissions and rolling admissions plans. Application deadlines are open. Application fee is $35. Applications are accepted online.

Transfer: 678 transfer students enrolled in 2012-2013. Transfer students must submit a completed application and college transcripts. (High school transcripts may be required if the number of college credits is insufficient for evaluating performance.) An official report of SAT or ACT scores (architecture majors only) and 3 recommendations are required. A portfolio and an interview are encouraged but not required. 45 of 180 credits required for the bachelor's degree must be completed at SCAD.

Visiting: There are regularly scheduled orientations for prospective students, Tours, visits with faculty from areas of interest, portfolio reviews, financial aid counseling, admissions counseling, and workshops. There are guides for informal visits and visitors may sit in on classes. To schedule a visit, contact the Admission Office at (800) 869-7223.

Financial Aid: SCAD is a member of CSS. The FAFSA, the state aid form, and the college's own financial statement are required. The priority date for freshman financial aid applications for fall entry is April 1. The deadline for filing freshman financial aid applications for fall entry is September 1.

International Students: There are 1489 international students enrolled. The school actively recruits these students. They must take the TOEFL with a minimum score of 550 on the paper-based TOEFL (PBT) or 85 on the Internet-based version (iBT). They must also take the SAT or ACT.

Computers: All students may access the system. Some of the buildings in which the computer labs are housed have specific hours of operation. There are no fees.

Graduates: From July 1, 2012 to June 30, 2013, 1811 bachelor's degrees were awarded. The most popular majors were graphic design (9%), illustration (8%), and animation (8%). In an average class, 47% graduate in 4 years or less, 66% graduate in 5 years or less, and 68% graduate in 6 years or less.

Admissions Contact: Jenny Jaquillard, Exec Director of Admission, Recruitment . E-Mail: *admission@scad.edu* Web: *www.scad.edu*

SAVANNAH STATE UNIVERSITY E-4

Savannah, GA 31404 912-358-4338 (800) 788-0478; 912-358-3171

Full-time: 1727 men, 2077 women	**Faculty:** n/av
Part-time: 277 men, 332 women	**Ph.D.s:** n/av
Graduate: 38 men, 131 women	**Student/Faculty:** 23 to 1
Year: semesters, summer session	**Tuition:** $6192 ($18,096)
Application Deadline: July 15	**Room & Board:** $6964
Freshman Class: 3374 applied, 2134 accepted, 1104 enrolled	
SAT or ACT: required	

COMPETITIVE

Savannah State University, founded in 1890, is a liberal arts institution that is part of the University System of Georgia. Undergraduate and graduate degrees are offered through the colleges of business, liberal arts and social sciences, and sciences and technology. Preprofessional programs are available. There are 3 undergraduate schools and 5 graduate schools. In addition to regional accreditation, Savannah State has baccalaureate program accreditation with ABET, CSWE, and NCATE. The library contains 209,714 volumes, 586,633 microform items, and 3,725 audio/video tapes/CDs/DVDs, and subscribes to 360 periodicals including electronic. Computerized library services include interlibrary loans, database searching, and Internet access. Special learning facilities include a radio station, arts center, and marine science lab. The 165-acre campus is in a suburban area 265 miles southeast of Atlanta. Including any residence halls, there are 45 buildings.

Student Life: Students are from 38 states, 33 foreign countries, and Canada. 87% are African American. The average age of freshmen is 19; all undergraduates, 21. 28% do not continue beyond their first year; 32% remain to graduate.

Housing: 2745 students can be accommodated in college housing, which includes single-sex dorms, on-campus apartments, and married student housing. On-campus housing is available on a first-come and first-served basis. Alcohol is not permitted. All students may keep cars.

Activities: 2% of men belong to 7 national fraternities; 3% of women belong to 6 national sororities. Groups on campus include art, band, cheerleading, choir, chorale, computers, dance, debate, drama, drill team, ethnic, international, jazz band, literary magazine, marching band, newspaper, political, professional, radio and TV, religious, and student government. Popular campus events include Drama Presentations, a Fine Arts Festival, and Christmas and Spring Concerts.

Sports: There are 5 intercollegiate sports for men and 4 for women, and 1 intramural sports for men. Facilities include a student center, a gym complex, a swimming pool, a stadium, a field house, a tennis court, a track, and a field.

Disabled Students: Facilities include wheelchair ramps, elevators, special parking, specially equipped restrooms, lowered drinking fountains, and special housing.

Services: Counseling and information services are available, as is tutoring in every subject. There is remedial math, reading, and writing.

Campus Safety and Security: Measures include 24-hour foot and vehicle patrol and emergency notification system. There are shuttle buses, emergency telephones, lighted pathways/sidewalks, The campus police department is staffed with public safety officers, building attendants, security guards, safety inspectors, and telephone operators.

Programs of Study: Savannah State confers B.A., B.S., B.B.A. and B.S.W. degrees. Associate and master's degrees are also awarded. Bachelor's degrees are awarded in BIOLOGICAL SCIENCE (biology/biological science and marine biology), BUSINESS (accounting, business administration and management, management information systems, and marketing/retailing/merchandising), COMMUNICATIONS AND THE ARTS (communications, English, and visual and performing arts), COMPUTER AND PHYSICAL SCIENCE (chemistry, computer science, and mathematics), ENGINEERING AND ENVIRONMENTAL DESIGN (civil engineering, electrical/electronics engineering technology, and environmental science), SOCIAL SCIENCE (African studies, behavioral science, criminal justice, history, homeland security, political science/government, social work, and sociology). Marine science, social work, and computer information systems are the strongest academically. Biology, mass communications and management have the largest enrollments.

Required: To graduate, all students must complete a minimum of 120 credit hours with satisfactory completion of the core curriculum requirements. Students must maintain a minimum 2.0 GPA. Exit competency exams and other requirements may be required.

Special: The college offers co-op programs, cross-registration with Armstrong Atlantic State University, study abroad, a dual-degree program with Georgia Institute of Technology, the Georgia Legislative Internship Program, and a variety of other internship programs across the curriculum, on- and off-campus work-study programs, correspondence study, credit for military experience, and non-degree study. There are a freshman honors program.

Faculty/Classroom: 54% of faculty are male; 46% are female. No introductory courses are taught by graduate students.

Admissions: 63% of the 2013-2014 applicants were accepted.

Requirements: The SAT or ACT is required. A minimum composite score of 830 on the SAT, or 17 on the ACT is required. In addition, applicants must be graduates of an accredited secondary school. Students should have completed 4 units each of english, math and science, 3 units of social science, and 2 units of 1 foreign language. A GPA of 2.0 is required. AP and CLEP credits are accepted.

Procedure: Freshmen are admitted fall, spring, and summer. Entrance exams should be taken Early in the senior year. There are early admissions and deferred admissions plans. Applications should be filed by July 15 for fall entry; November 15 for spring entry; and May 1 for summer entry, along with a $20 fee. Notification is sent on a rolling basis. Applications are accepted online.

Transfer: Applicants with at least 45 quarter hours or 30 semester hours of core curriculum credit do not need to submit high school transcripts, but must have a 2.0 average. All transfers must submit college transcripts, standardized test scores, and proof of good standing at the previous institution. 30 of 120 credits required for the bachelor's degree must be completed at Savannah State.

Visiting: There are guides for informal visits and visitors may sit in on classes. To schedule a visit, contact The Office of Admissions at (912) 358-4338.

Financial Aid: The CSS/Profile, FAFSA, and the college's own financial statement, and Scholarship Application Form are required. The priority date for freshman financial aid applications for fall entry is July 15. The deadline for filing freshman financial aid applications for fall entry is July 15.

International Students: There are 50 international students enrolled. The school actively recruits these students. They must take the TOEFL with a minimum score of 530 on the paper-based TOEFL (PBT). They must also take the SAT or ACT, and the college's own entrance exam. or the Collegiate Placement Exams.

Computers: All students may access the system. There are no time limits and no fees.

Graduates: From July 1, 2012 to June 30, 2013, 395 bachelor's degrees were awarded. The most popular majors were mass communications (10%), business management (10%), and criminal justice (8%). In an average class, 32% graduate in 6 years or less.

Admissions Contact: Cynthia Stephens, Interim Director of Admissions. E-Mail: *admissions@savannahstate.edu* Web: *www.savannahstate.edu*

SHORTER UNIVERSITY A-2

Rome, GA 30165-4298 **(706) 233-7319**
(800) 868-6980; (706) 233-7224

Full-time: 694 men, 816 women	**Faculty:** 92; IIB, --$
Part-time: 64 men, 68 women	**Ph.D.s:** 70%
Graduate: 19 men, 35 women	**Student/Faculty:** 16 to 1
Year: semesters, summer session	**Tuition:** $17,870
Application Deadline: open	**Room & Board:** $8600

Freshman Class: 1944 applied, 1263 accepted, 405 enrolled
SAT CR/M/W: 475/490/460 **ACT:** 20 **COMPETITIVE**

Shorter College, founded in 1873, is a private institution affiliated with the Georgia Baptist Convention that offers undergraduate degree programs in communications, education, business, fine arts, humanities, social sciences, religion, and natural sciences. There are 6 undergraduate schools. In addition to regional accreditation, Shorter has baccalaureate program accreditation with NASM. The library contains 144,673 volumes, 8,320 microform items, and 65,397 audio/video tapes/CDs/DVDs, and subscribes to 92 periodicals including electronic. Computerized library services include interlibrary loans, database searching, and Internet access. Special learning facilities include a learning resource center, art gallery, natural history museum, radio station, college museum, and archives. The 150-acre campus is in a small town 70 miles northwest of Atlanta. Including any residence halls, there are 22 buildings.

Student Life: 88% of undergraduates are from Georgia. Others are from 35 states, 46 foreign countries, and Canada. 87% are from public schools. 69% are white; 17% African American. 88% are Protestant; 13% claim no religious affiliation. The average age of freshmen is 19; all undergraduates, 23. 30% do not continue beyond their first year; 51% remain to graduate.

Housing: 852 students can be accommodated in college housing, which includes single-sex dorms, on-campus apartments, and off-campus apartments. On-campus housing is guaranteed for the freshman year only, is available on a first-come, and first-served basis. 52% of students commute. Alcohol is not permitted. All students may keep cars.

Activities: 9% of men belong to 3 national fraternities; 23% of women belong to 1 local and 2 national sororities. There are 44 groups on campus, including art, band, cheerleading, choir, chorale, chorus, dance, drama, ethnic, honors, international, literary magazine, marching band, musical theater, newspaper, opera, pep band, political, professional, radio and TV, religious, social, social service, student government, and yearbook. Popular campus events include Sporting events, Midnight Breakfasts, and Celebrate Shorter.

Sports: There are 11 intercollegiate sports for men and 10 for women, and 10 intramural sports for men and 11 for women. Facilities include an 54,000-square foot activities complex that houses a basketball arena, dance and aerobics studios, racquetball courts, a weight room, and an indoor jogging track. In addition, there are tennis courts and a swimming pool.

Disabled Students: 50% of the campus is accessible. Facilities include wheelchair ramps, elevators, special parking, specially equipped restrooms, and lowered drinking fountains.

Services: Counseling and information services are available, as is tutoring in every subject. There is a reader service for the blind, and remedial math, reading, and writing. Computerized study skills assessment and training is offered.

Campus Safety and Security: Measures include 24-hour foot and vehicle patrol, emergency notification system, self-defense education, and security escort services. There are shuttle buses, lighted pathways/sidewalks, controlled access to dorms/residences, campus access is controlled via a gatehouse from 6 p.m. to 6 a.m., and during all weekends and vacations.

Programs of Study: Shorter confers B.A., B.S., B.B.A., B.C.M., B.F.A., B.M., B.M.Ed., B.S.N., and B.S.E. degrees. Associate and master's degrees are also awarded. Bachelor's degrees are awarded in BIOLOGICAL SCIENCE (biology/biological science), BUSINESS (accounting, business administration and management, recreational facilities management, and sports management), COMMUNICATIONS AND THE ARTS (art, communications, dramatic arts, English, French, music, musical theater, piano/organ, public relations, Spanish, and voice), COMPUTER AND PHYSICAL SCIENCE (chemistry, mathematics, and natural sciences), EDUCATION (early childhood education, mathematics education, middle school education, and music education), HEALTH PROFESSIONS (medical laboratory technology and nursing), SOCIAL SCIENCE (Christian studies, economics, history, parks and recreation management, psychology, religion, religious music, social science, and sociology). Music, education, and natural sciences are the strongest academically. Business, early childhood education, and music have the largest enrollments.

Required: To be eligible for graduation, students must maintain at least a 2.0 overall GPA, or 2.5 for education degrees, with grades of C or better in the 27 to 96 credits required for a major. The core curriculum requires 33 hours in english, speech, literature, religion, social science, science, math, phys ed, and the arts. Those seeking B.A. and B.S. degrees will have additional core requirements. In addition, students must complete 42 hours in upper-level courses and pass an English writing exam.

Special: Shorter offers internships in most programs, cross-registration with Berry College, and study abroad in 12 countries. Dual and student-designed majors and pass/fail options are available. There are 6 national honor societies, a freshman honors program, and 20 departmental honors programs.

Faculty/Classroom: 50% of faculty are male; 50% are female. All teach undergraduates. No introductory courses are taught by graduate students. The average class size in an introductory lecture is 22; in a laboratory is 19; and in a regular course is 17.

Admissions: 65% of the 2011-2012 applicants were accepted. The SAT scores for the 2011-2012 freshman class were: Critical Reading--56% below 500, 32% between 500 and 599, 11% between 600 and 700, and 1% above 700; Math--52% below 500, 34% between 500 and 599, 13% between 600 and 700, and 1% above 700; Writing--65% below 500, 26% between 500 and 599, and 9% between 600 and 700. The ACT scores were 51% below 21, 23% between 21 and 23, 15% between 24 and 26, 8% between 27 and 28, and 4% above 28. 37% of the current freshmen were in the top fifth of their class; 67% were in the top two fifths. 12 freshmen graduated first in their class.

Requirements: The SAT or ACT is required. Applicants should be graduates of accredited secondary schools or have a GED certificate. Secondary preparation should include 4 units in English, 3 each in history or social sciences, math, and natural sciences, and 2 in foreign language. Prospective music majors must audition and take a theory placement test, and prospective theater majors must audition as well. A GPA of 2.0 is required. AP and CLEP credits are accepted. Important factors in the admissions decision are advanced placement or honors courses, evidence of special talent, and extracurricular activities record.

Procedure: Freshmen are admitted to all sessions. Entrance exams should be taken by the fall of the senior year. There is a rolling admissions plan. Application deadlines are open. Application fee is $25. Applications are accepted online.

Transfer: 195 transfer students enrolled in 2010-2011. Applicants must submit transcripts, a character reference, and catalogs from any out-of-state colleges attended. A minimum 2.0 GPA based on transferable credit is required. 30 of 126 credits required for the bachelor's degree must be completed at Shorter.

Visiting: There are regularly scheduled orientations for prospective students, Visiting students can take advantage of financial aid workshops, a student-administration panel discussion, faculty consultations, admissions consultations, and campus/residence hall tours. There are guides for informal visits, visitors may sit in on classes, and stay overnight. To schedule a visit, contact the Admissions Office.

Financial Aid: In 2011-2012, 99% of all full-time freshmen and 91% of continuing full-time students received some form of financial aid. 79% of all full-time freshmen and 78% of continuing full-time students received need-based aid. The average freshman award was $21,834. Need-based scholarships or need-based grants averaged $12,505; need-based self-help aid (loans and jobs) averaged $3,376; non-need-based athletic scholarships averaged $12,523; and other non-need-based awards and non-need-based scholarships averaged $5,890. 59% of undergraduate students work part-time. Average annual earnings from campus work are $2000. The average financial indebtedness of the 2011 graduate was $25,441. The FAFSA, the state aid form, and the college's own financial statement are required. The priority date for freshman financial aid applications for fall entry is April 1.

International Students: There are 62 international students enrolled.

The school actively recruits these students. They must take the TOEFL or MELAB, the ELS English Proficiency Evaluation. They must also take the SAT or ACT.

Computers: Wireless access is available. All of the campus has wireless access. Students are encouraged to use password protected web interface for checking on course assignments and grades. All students may access the system. There are no time limits and no fees.

Graduates: From July 1, 2010 to June 30, 2011, 234 bachelor's degrees were awarded. The most popular majors were business (26%), education (17%), and visual and performing arts (12%). In an average class, 2% graduate in 3 years or less, 42% graduate in 4 years or less, 50% graduate in 5 years or less, and 51% graduate in 6 years or less.

Admissions Contact: Dr. John Head, Vice President for Enrollment Management. E-Mail: *admissions@shorter.edu* Web: *www.shorter.edu*

SOUTHERN POLYTECHNIC STATE UNIVERSITY B-2

Marietta, GA 30060 (678) 915-7778
(800) 635-3204; (678) 915-7496

Full-time: 3206 men, 657 women	**Faculty:** 209; II A, --$
Part-time: 1210 men, 329 women	**Ph.D.s:** 71%
Graduate: 483 men, 317 women	**Student/Faculty:** 18 to 1
Year: semesters, summer session	**Tuition:** $6678 ($20,126)
Application Deadline: July 1	**Room & Board:** $7280
Freshman Class: 1507 applied, 1189 accepted, 778 enrolled	
SAT CR/M/W: 550/590/520	**ACT:** 24 **VERY COMPETITIVE**

Southern Polytechnic State University, founded in 1948, is a member of the University System of Georgia. Through a fusion of technology with the liberal arts and sciences, SPSU creates a learning community that encourages thoughtful inquiry, diverse perspectives, and strong preparation of its graduates to be leaders in an increasingly technological world. The university offers degree programs in accounting, applied science, architecture, biology, business administration, chemistry, computer science, computer game design and development, construction management, education, English and professional communication, engineering, engineering technology, fashion design, information and instructional design, information design and communication, information technology, international studies, math, new media arts, physics, political science, psychology, quality assurance, surveying and mapping, and technical communication. There are 5 undergraduate schools and 5 graduate schools. In addition to regional accreditation, Southern Poly has baccalaureate program accreditation with ABET, ACBSP, ACCE, and NAAB. The library contains 126,779 volumes, 3,493 microform items, and 355 audio/video tapes/CDs/DVDs, and subscribes to 510 periodicals including electronic. Computerized library services include interlibrary loans, database searching, Internet access, and Wi-Fi capability. Special learning facilities include a radio station. The 198-acre campus is in a suburban area 15 miles northwest of Atlanta, GA. Including any residence halls, there are 64 buildings.

Student Life: 98% of undergraduates are from Georgia. Others are from 38 states, 51 foreign countries, and Canada. 96% are from public schools. 55% are White; 21% African American. The average age of freshmen is 20; all undergraduates, 25. 25% do not continue beyond their first year; 37% remain to graduate.

Housing: 1673 students can be accommodated in college housing, which includes single-sex and coed dorms and on-campus apartments. In addition, there are honors houses, special-interest houses, fraternity houses, and sorority houses. On-campus housing is guaranteed for the freshman year only, is available on a first-come, and first-served basis. 75% of students commute. All students may keep cars.

Activities: 7% of men belong to 10 national fraternities; 8% of women belong to 4 national sororities. There are 128 groups on campus, including cheerleading, computers, debate, drama, environmental, ethnic, forensics, gay, honors, international, newspaper, pep band, political, professional, religious, social, social service, and student government. Popular campus events include SPSU Live Fall Concert, Goat Night, Fall Carnival, Pumpkin Launch and Bathtub Race.

Sports: There are 3 intercollegiate sports for men and 1 for women, and 14 intramural sports for men and 14 for women. Facilities include a 1000-seat gym, a baseball field, softball fields, outdoor areas for basketball and volleyball, a multipurpose soccer field, an outdoor running track, an indoor health/wellness facility with a swimming pool, racquetball courts, exercise and weight training rooms, and basketball courts that are suitable for badminton and volleyball.

Disabled Students: All of the campus is accessible. Facilities include wheelchair ramps, elevators, special parking, specially equipped restrooms, special class scheduling, lowered drinking fountains, lowered telephones, and special housing.

Services: Counseling and information services are available, as is tutoring in some subjects, English, core math, physics, chemistry, computer science, and biology There is a reader service for the blind.

Campus Safety and Security: Measures include 24-hour foot and vehicle patrol, emergency notification system, self-defense education, and security escort services. There are emergency telephones, lighted pathways/sidewalks, controlled access to dorms/residences, audits of campus lighting and emergency call boxes are conducted monthly.

Programs of Study: Southern Poly confers B.A., B.S., B.A.R.C.H., B.A.S., B.A.T., B.S.A, B.S.C.E, B.S.C.G.D.D., B.S.C.V.E., B.S.E.E., B.S.I.T., B.S.M.E., B.S.P., B.S.P.S., B.S.S.E.N.G., B.S.S.W.E. and B.S.T.E.T. degrees. Associate and master's degrees are also awarded. Bachelor's degrees are awarded in BIOLOGICAL SCIENCE (biology/biological science), BUSINESS (accounting, apparel and textiles, and business administration and management), COMMUNICATIONS AND THE ARTS (information technology, media arts, English and Professional Communication, Technical Communication, and Telecommunications Engineering Technology), COMPUTER AND PHYSICAL SCIENCE (applied science, chemistry, Computer Engineering Technology, computer game design/development, computer science, mathematics, physics, and software engineering), EDUCATION (education), ENGINEERING AND ENVIRONMENTAL DESIGN (architecture, civil engineering, civil engineering technology, construction engineering, construction management, electrical/electronics engineering, electrical/electronics engineering technology, industrial engineering technology, mechanical engineering, mechanical engineering technology, Mechatronics Engineering, survey and mapping technology, and systems engineering), SOCIAL SCIENCE (international studies, political science/government, and psychology). Engineering, engineering technology, computer science and information technology, and architecture have the largest enrollments.

Required: SPSU's minimum requirements for admission as a regular freshman include the following: Graduation from a regionally accredited high school, or a high school accredited by the Georgia Accreditation Commission, or an approved University System of Georgia agency, or from a public school under the authority of the State Department of Education. Completion of the 17 required CPC units, plus 2 additional academic units. Have an academic high school GPA of at least a 2.5 and minimum scores on the ACT or SAT as follows: Minimum Score SAT I Critical Reading 500 SAT I Math 500 ACT-English 21 ACT-Math 21 Curriculum Framework for the Common Core A. Essential Skills (9-10 hours) English Composition I English Composition II College Algebra, Pre-Calculus or Calculus I, depending on major B. Institutional Options (4 hours) These courses address institution-wide general education outcomes chosen by the University. Examples include, but are not limited to, global issues, oral communication, information technology, critical thinking, wellness, geography, and foreign languages. At Southern Polytechnic State University, the Institutional Option courses are: Public Speaking (COMM 2400) Science, Technology and Society (STS 2400) C. Humanities/Fine Arts (6 hours) These are courses that address humanities/fine arts learning outcomes and which the undergraduate curriculum committee has approved. Interdisciplinary courses are acceptable. D. Science, Mathematics, and Technology (10-11 hours) These are courses approved by the undergraduate curriculum committee that address learning outcomes in the sciences, mathematics, and technology. These need not be sequential courses. Interdisciplinary courses are acceptable. Required are: Two four-hour laboratory science courses Three additional credit hours in mathematics, science, or technology E. Social Sciences (12 hours) These are courses approved by the undergraduate curriculum committee that address learning outcomes in the social sciences, including, but not limited to, history and American government. Interdisciplinary courses are acceptable. If credit course work is used to satisfy the U.S./Georgia history and constitution requirement, course(s) shall be part of this area. F. Courses Related to the Program of Study (18 hours) These are courses numbered below 3000 that are related to your program of study, and courses which are prerequisites to major courses at higher levels.

Special: Southern Polytechnic offers cross-registration through ARCHE cooperative programs, dual majors in all disciplines, internships, and co-ops. There are 4 national honor societies and a freshman honors program.

Faculty/Classroom: 66% of faculty are male; 34% are female. All teach undergraduates, 81% do research, and 81% do both. No introductory courses are taught by graduate students. The average class size in an introductory lecture is 23; in a laboratory is 18; and in a regular course is 20.

Admissions: 79% of the 2013-2014 applicants were accepted. The SAT scores for the 2013-2014 freshman class were: Critical Reading--20% below 500, 52% between 500 and 599, 24% between 600 and 699, and 4% between 700 and 800; Math--9% below 500, 45% between 500 and 599, 39% between 600 and 699, and 7% between 700 and 800; Writing--39% below 500, 46% between 500 and 599, 14% between 600 and 699, and 1% between 700 and 800. The ACT scores were 17% below 21, 29% between 21 and 23, 29% between 24 and 26, 12% between 27 and 28, and 13% above 28.

Requirements: The SAT or ACT is required. The ACT Optional Writing test is also required. Applicants must be graduates of an accredited secondary school. Students must have completed 19 CPC units in high school, including 4 years each of English, math, and science, 3 years of social studies, and 2 years of a foreign language, plus 2 additional units. A GPA of 2.5 is required. AP and CLEP credits are accepted.

Procedure: Freshmen are admitted fall, spring, and summer. Entrance

exams should be taken by the end of the junior year or early in the senior year. There is a rolling admissions plan. Applications should be filed by July 1 for fall entry; November 1 for spring entry; and April 1 for summer entry, along with a $40 fee. Notification is sent on a rolling basis. Applications are accepted online.

Transfer: 547 transfer students enrolled in 2012-2013. Transfer applicants must have a minimum cumulative college GPA of 2.0 and must submit all college transcripts. Transfer applicants must have completed and exited all required remedial courses at their previous institution. Transfer applicants with less than 30 transferable hours must meet Freshmen requirements and have completed and exited all required remedial courses at their previous institution.

Visiting: There are regularly scheduled orientations for prospective students, Orientations cover the following areas and more: Advising, Registration, Housing/Board, Financial Aid, Student Activities, Student Government, Payments, Library, Parent Sessions, Location of Faculty and Staff Offices, Classroom Locations. There are guides for informal visits and visitors may sit in on classes. To schedule a visit, contact Becca Tuck at (678) 915-3521.

Financial Aid: In 2013-2014, 91% of all full-time freshmen and 83% of continuing full-time students received some form of financial aid. 40% of all full-time freshmen and 44% of continuing full-time students received need-based aid. The average freshman award was $1,970. Need-based scholarships or need-based grants averaged $2,217 ($2,775 maximum); need-based self-help aid (loans and jobs) averaged $1,656 ($3,342 maximum); non-need-based athletic scholarships averaged $2,867 ($4,500 maximum); and other non-need-based awards and non-need-based scholarships averaged $2,006 ($7,070 maximum). 26% of undergraduate students work part-time. The average financial indebtedness of the 2013 graduate was $16,624. Southern Poly is a member of CSS. The FAFSA is required. The priority date for freshman financial aid applications for fall entry is April 1.

International Students: There are 195 international students enrolled. The school actively recruits these students. They must take the TOEFL with a minimum score of 550 on the paper-based TOEFL (PBT) or 79 on the Internet-based version (iBT), or Minimum overall band of 6.5 on the International English Language Testing System (IELTS). . They must also take the SAT or ACT.

Computers: All students may access the system. There are no time limits and no fees.

Graduates: From July 1, 2012 to June 30, 2013, 729 bachelor's degrees were awarded. The most popular majors were mechanical engineering technology (12%), construction management (10%), and business admisitration (9%). 176 companies recruited on campus in 2012-2013. In an average class, 7% graduate in 4 years or less, 26% graduate in 5 years or less, and 37% graduate in 6 years or less.

Admissions Contact: Gary Bush, Director of Admissions. E-Mail: *admiss@spsu.edu* Web: *http:/www.spsu.edu/*

SPELMAN COLLEGE — B-2

Atlanta, GA 30314 — **(404) 270-5193; (800) 982-2411**

Full-time: 2100 women	**Faculty:** n/av; IIB, -$
Part-time: 100 women	**Ph.D.s:** n/av
Graduate: n/av	**Student/Faculty:** n/av
Year: semesters	**Tuition:** $22,500
Application Deadline: February 1	**Room & Board:** $11,000

Freshman Class: 5100 applied, 2000 accepted, 500 enrolled
SAT or ACT: required

VERY COMPETITIVE

Spelman College, founded in 1881, is a private, nonsectarian, liberal arts college for black women. The figures in the above capsule and in this profile are approximate. In addition to regional accreditation, Spelman has baccalaureate program accreditation with NASM and NCATE. The library contains 500,000 volumes, and 385,500 microform items, and subscribes to 1,400 periodicals including electronic. Special learning facilities include a learning resource center, art gallery, a language lab, a media center, and music and art studios. The 39-acre campus is in an urban area 3 miles southwest of downtown Atlanta. Including any residence halls, there are 26 buildings.

Student Life: 71% of undergraduates are from out of state, mostly the South. Students are from 45 states, 9 foreign countries, and Canada. 86% are from public schools. 88% are African American. The average age of freshmen is 18; all undergraduates, 20. 10% do not continue beyond their first year; 72% remain to graduate.

Housing: 1169 students can be accommodated in college housing, which includes dorms. In addition, there are honors houses. On-campus housing is guaranteed for the freshman year only, is available on a first-come, first-served basis, and is available on a lottery system for upperclassmen. Priority is given to out-of-town students. 60% of students live on campus; of those, 67% remain on campus on weekends. Alcohol is not permitted. Upperclassmen may keep cars.

Activities: There are no fraternities; 8% of women belong to 4 local and 4 national sororities. There are 60 groups on campus, including art, band, cheerleading, choir, chorus, communications, dance, drama, gay, honors, international, jazz band, literary magazine, musical theater, newspaper, political, religious, social, student government, and yearbook. Popular campus events include Founders Day and Martin Luther King Jr.'s Birthday.

Sports: There are 4 intercollegiate sports for women, and 6 intramural sports for women. Facilities include a gym, tennis courts, a swimming pool, a weight room, dance studios, and bowling lanes.

Disabled Students: 25% of the campus is accessible. Facilities include wheelchair ramps, elevators, special parking, and specially equipped rest rooms.

Services: Counseling and information services are available, as is tutoring in every subject.

Campus Safety and Security: Measures include 24-hour foot and vehicle patrol, self-defense education, and security escort services. There are shuttle buses, emergency telephones, and lighted pathways/sidewalks.

Programs of Study: Spelman confers B.A. and B.S. degrees. Bachelor's degrees are awarded in BIOLOGICAL SCIENCE (biochemistry and biology/biological science), COMMUNICATIONS AND THE ARTS (art, dramatic arts, English, fine arts, French, music, and Spanish), COMPUTER AND PHYSICAL SCIENCE (chemistry, computer science, mathematics, natural sciences, and physics), EDUCATION (art education), ENGINEERING AND ENVIRONMENTAL DESIGN (engineering), SOCIAL SCIENCE (anthropology, child psychology/development, economics, history, philosophy, political science/government, psychology, religion, sociology, and women's studies). Biology and engineering are the strongest academically. Psychology, biology, and English have the largest enrollments.

Required: To graduate, students must complete 120 semester hours, including at least 30 or more in the major and maintain a GPA of 2.0. Core requirements include 8 credits of African studies, up to 8 of foreign language, 4 of international or women's studies, up to 4 each of English composition, computer literacy, and math, and 2 to 3 of phys ed, plus freshman orientation and sophomore assembly. Students also must complete 4 credits each of divisional requirements in social science, humanities, natural science, and fine arts. A reading course may be required, based on the placement test scores.

Special: Students may cross-register with Atlanta University Center member institutions. Spelman offers internships, study abroad in several countries, student-designed majors, work-study programs at the school, B.A.-B.S. degrees, and dual majors, as well as a 3-2 engineering degree with Georgia Tech, Rochester Institute of Technology, University of Alabama at Huntsville, Auburn and Boston Universities, and North Carolina Agricultural and Technical State University. The college grants credit for life experience and permits nondegree study. There are 9 national honor societies, including Phi Beta Kappa, and a freshman honors program.

Faculty/Classroom: 36% of faculty are male; 64% are female. No introductory courses are taught by graduate students.

Admissions: 37% of a recent year's applicants were accepted.

Requirements: The SAT or ACT is required. In addition, applicants should be high school graduates or have a GED certificate. It is recommended that students have 3 to 4 years each in English, history and social studies, foreign language, science, and math. AP and honors courses are considered more competitive. An essay is required. An audition or portfolio is recommended for art majors. A GPA of 2.0 is required. AP and CLEP credits are accepted. Important factors in the admissions decision are advanced placement or honors courses, leadership record, and recommendations by school officials.

Procedure: Freshmen are admitted fall. Entrance exams should be taken by December of the senior year. There are early decision, early action, early admissions, and deferred admissions plans. Early decision applications should be filed by November 1, regular applications by February 1 for fall entry, along with a $35 fee. Notifications of early decision are sent by December 15; regular decision, by April 1. A waiting list is maintained.

Transfer: A 3.0 GPA is recommended, with a minimum 2.0 required. Applicants must submit high school and college transcripts, as well as 2 recommendations from instructors at the last school attended. Students with fewer than 30 semester hours of credit must also submit SAT or ACT scores. 30 of 120 credits required for the bachelor's degree must be completed at Spelman.

Visiting: There are regularly scheduled orientations for prospective students, including a general information session and a campus tour. There are also high school senior days and junior days. There are guides for informal visits. To schedule a visit, contact the Admissions Office.

Financial Aid: Spelman is a member of CSS. The FAFSA and the college's own financial statement are required. Check with the school for current application deadlines.

International Students: The school actively recruits these students. They must take the TOEFL. They must also take the SAT or ACT.

Computers: All students may access the system 24 hours a day. There are no time limits. There is a fee. It is strongly recommended that all students have a personal computer.

Graduates: In a recent year, 471 bachelor's degrees were awarded.

Admissions Contact: Admissions. E-Mail: *admiss@spelman.edu* Web: *www.spelman.edu*

THOMAS UNIVERSITY B-5

Thomasville, GA 31792-7499 (229) 226-1621
(800) 538-9784; (229) 226-1653

Full-time: 170 men, 350 women
Part-time: 45 men, 135 women
Graduate: 35 men, 60 women
Year: semesters, summer session
Application Deadline: open
Freshman Class: n/av
SAT or ACT: recommended
Faculty: 38
Ph.D.s: 65%
Student/Faculty: 13 to 1
Tuition: $10,100
Room & Board: $2910

NON COMPETITIVE

Thomas University, founded in 1950, is a private institution offering 20 undergraduate degrees and master's programs in business administration and rehabilitation counseling. In addition to regional accreditation, has baccalaureate program accreditation with NLN. The library contains 54,209 volumes, and 823 audio/video tapes/CDs/DVDs, and subscribes to 413 periodicals including electronic. Computerized library services include interlibrary loans and database searching. Special learning facilities include a learning resource center. The 25-acre campus is in a rural area 28 miles north of Tallahassee. Including any residence halls, there are 20 buildings.

Student Life: 90% of undergraduates are from Georgia. Others are from 9 states, 11 foreign countries, and Canada. 99% are from public schools. 64% are white; 24% African American. The average age of freshmen is 24; all undergraduates, 27.

Housing: 64 students can be accommodated in college housing, which includes single-sex and coed dorms and off-campus apartments. 89% of students commute. Alcohol is not permitted. All students may keep cars.

Activities: There are no fraternities or sororities. There are 23 groups on campus, including chorus, jazz band, literary magazine, newspaper, religious, social, and student government.

Sports: There are 5 intercollegiate sports for men and 5 for women, and 3 intramural sports for men and 3 for women. The university contracts with the city of Thomasville and other groups to use existing public athletic facilities. On-campus facilities include a soccer field, a tennis court, a beach volleyball court, and an outdoor basketball court.

Disabled Students: 90% of the campus is accessible. Facilities include wheelchair ramps, special parking, specially equipped restrooms, and lowered telephones.

Services: Counseling and information services are available, as is tutoring in most subjects. There is a reader service for the blind, and remedial math, reading, and writing.

Campus Safety and Security: There are lighted pathways/sidewalks, an evening vehicle patrol, and sheriff's deputies on campus.

Programs of Study: Thomas confers B.A. and B.S. degrees. Associate and master's degrees are also awarded. Bachelor's degrees are awarded in BIOLOGICAL SCIENCE (biology/biological science), BUSINESS (business administration and management), COMMUNICATIONS AND THE ARTS (English), EDUCATION (early childhood education, middle school education, and secondary education), HEALTH PROFESSIONS (nursing and rehabilitation therapy), SOCIAL SCIENCE (criminal justice, humanities, liberal arts/general studies, psychology, social science, and social work). Early childhood education and criminal justice have the largest enrollments.

Required: To graduate, students must complete 120 semester hours, including 30 to 60 in the major, with a minimum GPA of 2.0 (2.5 for education majors). Core requirements include 48 to 49 semester hours in English composition, history, biology, math, political science, music or art, and computer science. All students must pass a posttest.

Special: There are 6 national honor societies, including Phi Beta Kappa, and 6 departmental honors programs.

Faculty/Classroom: All teach undergraduates. No introductory courses are taught by graduate students. The average class size in an introductory lecture is 16; in a laboratory is 14; and in a regular course is 12.

Requirements: The SAT or ACT is recommended. Students should be graduates of an accredited high school or its equivalent. AP and CLEP credits are accepted.

Procedure: Freshmen are admitted to all sessions. Entrance exams should be taken prior to enrollment. There is a rolling admissions plan. Application deadlines are open. Application fee is $25. Applications are accepted online.

Transfer: 74 transfer students enrolled in 2010-2011. Applicants should have a minimum college GPA of 2.0 and be in good standing at their current or previous institution. 30 of 120 credits required for the bachelor's degree must be completed at Thomas University.

Visiting: There are regularly scheduled orientations for prospective students. There are guides for informal visits. To schedule a visit, contact Admissions.

Financial Aid: In a recent year, 95% of all full-time freshmen and 96% of continuing full-time students received some form of financial aid. 50% of all full-time freshmen and 48% of continuing full-time students received need-based aid. The average freshman award was $5,500. 2% of undergraduate students work part-time. The FAFSA and the college's own financial statement are required. The priority date for freshman financial aid applications for fall entry is open.

International Students: There are 44 international students enrolled. The school actively recruits these students. They must take the TOEFL or the MAPS (Multiple Assessment Program/Services).

Computers: All students may access the system 8 a.m. to 9 p.m. Students are limited to 1 hour. There are no fees. It is strongly recommended that all students have a personal computer. A Gateway E-1000 is recommended.

Graduates: In a recent year, 117 bachelor's degrees were awarded. In an average class, 18% graduate in 4 years or less and 35% graduate in 5 years or less.

Admissions Contact: Director of Student Affairs. Web: *www.thomasu.edu*

TOCCOA FALLS COLLEGE C-1

Toccoa Falls, GA 30598 (706) 886-6831, ext. 5380
(888) 785-5624; (706) 282-6012

Full-time: 340 men, 420 women
Part-time: 30 men, 30 women
Graduate: n/av
Year: semesters, summer session
Application Deadline: see profile
Freshman Class: n/av
SAT or ACT: required
Faculty: 49; IIB, --$
Ph.D.s: 55%
Student/Faculty: n/av
Tuition: $16,910
Room & Board: $6300

COMPETITIVE

Toccoa Falls College is a private, interdenominational Christian college founded in 1907 that offers programs in Biblical studies, biology, business administration, counseling, Christian education, communication, education, history, theology, music, philosophy, science, youth ministries, and general studies. Some of the figures in the above capsule and in this profile are approximate. There are 3 undergraduate schools. In addition to regional accreditation, TFC has baccalaureate program accreditation with NASM. The library contains 151,427 volumes, 6,471 microform items, and 3,008 audio/video tapes/CDs/DVDs, and subscribes to 20,310 periodicals including electronic. Computerized library services include interlibrary loans, database searching, Internet access, and laptop Internet portals. Special learning facilities include a learning resource center and radio station. The 1100-acre campus is in a small town 90 miles northeast of Atlanta. Including any residence halls, there are 45 buildings.

Student Life: 55% of undergraduates are from Georgia. Others are from 42 states, 27 foreign countries, and Canada. 61% are from public schools. 85% are white. 100% are Protestant. The average age of freshmen is 18; all undergraduates, 22. 30% do not continue beyond their first year; 47% remain to graduate.

Housing: 616 students can be accommodated in college housing, which includes single-sex dorms, on-campus apartments, and married student housing. On-campus housing is guaranteed for all 4 years. 64% of students live on campus; of those, 50% remain on campus on weekends. Alcohol is not permitted. All students may keep cars.

Activities: There are no fraternities or sororities. There are more than 15 groups on campus, including band, choir, chorus, drama, ethnic, international, jazz band, newspaper, orchestra, outdoor club, photography, radio and TV, religious, social, social service, and student government. Popular campus events include Spiritual Emphasis Week, Lecture Series, and World Outreach Conference.

Sports: There are 5 intercollegiate sports for men and 5 for women, and 5 intramural sports for men and 5 for women. Facilities include a gymnatorium with racquetball courts and a weight room, tennis courts, and soccer and baseball fields.

Disabled Students: 70% of the campus is accessible. Facilities include wheelchair ramps, elevators, special parking, specially equipped restrooms, special class scheduling, lowered drinking fountains, and special housing.

Services: Counseling and information services are available, as is tutoring in most subjects.

Campus Safety and Security: Measures include 24-hour foot and vehicle patrol, emergency notification system, and security escort services. There are emergency telephones and lighted pathways/sidewalks. The campus is closed at night, with a guard at the entrance.

Programs of Study: TFC confers B.A., B.S., and B.M. degrees. Associate degrees are also awarded. Bachelor's degrees are awarded in BIOLOGICAL SCIENCE (biology/biological science), BUSINESS (business administration and management), COMMUNICATIONS AND THE ARTS (choral music, communications, English, music, and music performance), EDUCATION (early childhood education, middle school education, music education, recreation education, and science education), SOCIAL SCIENCE (biblical studies, Christian studies, counseling/psychology, cross-cultural studies, history, ministries, pastoral studies, philosophy, and youth ministry). Counseling/psychology, cross-cultural studies, and early childhood education are the strongest academically and have the largest enrollments.

Required: Students must successfully complete at least 126 semester hours, with an average of 42 hours in the major, maintaining a C- or better, to earn a bachelor's degree. All students must also complete a core curriculum of 69 hours, which includes 30 hours of Bible and doctrine. A GPA of at least 2.0 must be maintained. Additional requirements for graduation include 4 semesters of student ministry, and a senior oral comprehensive exam or a thesis in some majors.

Special: The college offers dual majors, and B.A.-B.S. degrees are available. An on-campus work-study program and internships for many majors are also provided. There are 2 national honor societies.

Faculty/Classroom: 75% of faculty are male; 25% are female. 94% teach undergraduates. No introductory courses are taught by graduate students. The average class size in an introductory lecture, 23, in a laboratory, 12, and in a regular course, 12.

Admissions: 55% of a recent year's applicants were accepted.

Requirements: The SAT or ACT is required. In addition, a high school education or GED certificate is required. A personal reference from the student's pastor and an essay submitted with the student's application are also required. Admission is based on an index found by multiplying high school GPA by the best total standardized test score. A GPA of 2.0 is required. AP and CLEP credits are accepted. Important factors in the admissions decision are personality/intangible qualities, extracurricular activities record, and leadership record.

Procedure: Freshmen are admitted to all sessions. Entrance exams should be taken early in the senior year. There are deferred admissions and rolling admissions plans. Check with the school for current application deadlines. Application fee is $25. Notification is sent on a rolling basis. Applications are accepted online.

Transfer: 66 transfer students enrolled in a recent year. Transfer students must have successfully completed 12 semester hours of college credit courses and have maintained a minimum GPA of 2.0. Students must also provide 3 references and write an essay.

Visiting: There are regularly scheduled orientations for prospective students, including visits to the admissions counselor, school directors, and the financial aid office arranged 2 weeks in advance. There are guides for informal visits; visitors may sit in on classes and stay overnight. To schedule a visit, contact the Office of Admissions.

Financial Aid: In a recent year, 99% of all full-time freshmen and 98% of continuing full-time students received some form of financial aid. 66% of all full-time freshmen and 67% of continuing full-time students received need-based aid. The average freshman award was $12,728. 31% of undergraduate students work part-time. The average financial indebtedness of a recent year's graduate was $17,341. The FAFSA, the state aid form, and the college's own financial statement are required. Check with the school for current application deadlines.

International Students: They must take the TOEFL. They must also take the SAT or ACT.

Computers: Wireless access is available. TFC provides network and Internet service to all students through in-room network connections, academic labs, library, and dial-in connections. A wireless network is available in several dorms and buildings on campus with more added on a regular basis. 60 computers for student use are available in the computer lab and in the library. All students may access the system. There are no time limits and no fees. It is strongly recommended that all students have a personal computer.

Graduates: In a recent year, 185 bachelor's degrees were awarded. The most popular majors were counseling psychology (18%), cross cultural studies (13%), and early childhood education (8%). 75 companies recruited on campus in a recent year. In an average class, 1% graduate in 3 years or less, 43% graduate in 4 years or less, 47% graduate in 5 years or less, and 47% graduate in 6 years or less.

Admissions Contact: Director of Enrollment. E-Mail: *admission@tfc.edu* Web: *www.tfc.edu*

UNIVERSITY OF GEORGIA C-2

Athens, GA 30602 **(706) 542-2112**

Full-time: 10528 men, 14228 women	**Faculty:** n/av; I, -$
Part-time: 792 men, 725 women	**Ph.D.s:** 88%
Graduate: 3453 men, 4766 women	**Student/Faculty:** n/av
Year: semesters, summer session	**Tuition:** $10,262 ($28,472)
Application Deadline: January 15	**Room & Board:** $9246

Freshman Class: 20340 applied, 11054 accepted, 5258 enrolled
SAT or ACT: required

VERY COMPETITIVE

The University of Georgia, chartered in 1785 and part of the University System of Georgia, offers degree programs in agricultural and environmental sciences, arts and sciences, business, ecology, education, engineering, environment and design, family and consumer sciences, forestry and natural resources, journalism and mass communication, law, pharmacy, public health, public and international affairs, social work and veterinary medicine. There are 17 undergraduate schools and one graduate school. In addition to regional accreditation, UGA has baccalaureate program accreditation with AACSB, ABET, ACEJMC, ACPE, ADA, ASLA, CSWE, NASAD, NASM, NCATE, NRPA, and SAF. The 3 libraries contain 4.9 million volumes. Computerized library services include interlibrary loans, database searching, Internet access, and Wi-Fi capability. Special learning facilities include an art gallery, natural history museum, radio station, TV station, Bioscience Learning Center, Rare Book and Manuscript Library, Performing Arts Center, broadcast newsroom, State Botanical Garden of Georgia, Peabody Awards Archives, Cox Institute for Newspaper Management Studies, and Georgia Museum of Art. The 759-acre campus is in a small town 70 miles northeast of Atlanta. Including any residence halls, there are 455 buildings.

Student Life: 90% of undergraduates are from Georgia. Others are from 50 states, 122 foreign countries, and Canada. 71% are White. 24% are Protestant. The average age of freshmen is 19; all undergraduates, 21. 6% do not continue beyond their first year; 84% remain to graduate.

Housing: 9804 students can be accommodated in college housing, which includes single-sex and coed dorms, on-campus apartments, and married student housing. In addition, there are honors houses, language houses, fraternity houses, sorority houses, learning communities within residence halls. On-campus housing is guaranteed for the freshman year only, is available on a first-come, and first-served basis. 7% of students commute. Alcohol is not permitted. All students may keep cars.

Activities: 22% of men belong to 36 national fraternities; 29% of women belong to 27 national sororities. There are 627 groups on campus, including art, band, cheerleading, chess, choir, chorale, chorus, computers, dance, debate, drama, drill team, environmental, ethnic, film, forensics, gay, honors, international, jazz band, literary magazine, marching band, musical theater, newspaper, orchestra, pep band, photography, political, professional, radio and TV, religious, social, social service, student government, symphony, and yearbook. Popular campus events include Dance Marathon, Relay for Life and Dawgs after Dark.

Sports: There are 8 intercollegiate sports for men and 11 for women, and 24 intramural sports for men and 24 for women. Facilities include a 92,746-seat stadium, a 12,000-seat basketball arena, a 4,500-seat tennis stadium, 4 indoor tennis courts, a 3,200-seat baseball field, complete football-training facilities, and a sports complex with a lake, a beach, playing fields, and trails. There is also the Ramsey Student Center with 5 gyms, 3 swimming pools, a strength/conditioning room, 10 racquetball courts, an indoor track, and a climbing wall. The Women's Athletic Complex hosts women's soccer and softball programs with 3,000-spectator capacity.

Disabled Students: 90% of the campus is accessible. Facilities include wheelchair ramps, elevators, special parking, specially equipped restrooms, special class scheduling, lowered drinking fountains, lowered telephones, special housing. wheelchair vans, auxiliary aides, residence hall accommodations, and an adaptive technology lab.

Services: Counseling and information services are available, as is tutoring in every subject. There is a reader service for the blind, and remedial math, reading, and writing. Alternate format textbooks and class materials, note takers, modifications for tests and assignments, and counseling and advisement from learning disability specialists are available. There are also sign language interpreters, text type machines, FM/assistive listening devices, and a pilot closed-captioning program.

Campus Safety and Security: Measures include 24-hour foot and vehicle patrol, emergency notification system, self-defense education, and security escort services. There are shuttle buses, emergency telephones, and lighted pathways/sidewalks.

Programs of Study: UGA confers A.B., A.B.J., B.B.A., B.F.A., B.L.A., B.Mus., B.S., B.S.A., B.S.A.B., B.S.A.E., B.S.Bch.E., B.S.B.E., B.S.C.E., B.S.Chem., B.S.C.S.E., B.S.Ed., B.S.Env.E., B.S.E.H., B.S.Env., B.S.E.S., B.S.F.C.S., B.S.F.R., B.S.H.P., B.S.M.E. and B.S.W. degrees. Master's and doctoral degrees are also awarded. Bachelor's degrees are awarded in AGRICULTURE (agricultural communications, agricultural economics, animal science, dairy science, fishing and fisheries, forestry and related sciences, horticulture, natural resource/environmental economics, natural resources, plant science, poultry science, soil science, and turfgrass and landscape management), BIOLOGICAL SCIENCE (biochemistry, bioinformatics, biology/biological science, biotechnology, ecology, entomology, genetics, marine science, microbiology, neurosciences, nutritional sciences, plant pathology, and toxicology), BUSINESS (accounting, accounting/CPA, business administration and management, business administration, mgmt, operations, fashion merchandising, finance, human resources, international business, management information systems, management science, marketing, nonprofit/public organization management, real estate, recreation and leisure services, and sports management), COMMUNICATIONS AND THE ARTS (advertising, Arabic, art history, art, art history and appreciation, broadcasting, Chinese, classical languages, communication studies, communication science, comparative literature, dance, English, French, German, Germanic languages and literature, Greek, historic preservation, Italian, Japanese, journalism,

Latin, linguistics, media arts, music, music composition, music performance, music theory and composition, public relations, romance languages and literature, Russian, Spanish, studio art, and theatre arts), COMPUTER AND PHYSICAL SCIENCE (astronomy and physics, chemistry, computer science, environmental chemistry, geology, mathematics, physics, and statistics), EDUCATION (agricultural education, art education, athletic training, early childhood education, education administration, elementary education, English education, health education, mathematics education, middle school education, music education, reading education, school psychology, science education, social studies education, special education, and teaching English as a second/foreign language (TESOL/TEFOL)), ENGINEERING AND ENVIRONMENTAL DESIGN (agricultural engineering, civil engineering, electrical/electronics engineering, engineering, environmental engineering, landscape architecture, and mechanical engineering), HEALTH PROFESSIONS (biology, biomedical science, environmental health science, exercise science, health promotion, kinesiology, music therapy, pharmaceutical science, pharmacy, public health, and veterinary science), SOCIAL SCIENCE (African American studies, anthropology, communication sciences & disorders, cognitive science, counseling/psychology, criminal justice, dietetics, economics, food production/management/services, food science, geography, history, home economics, human development, industrial and organizational psychology, interdisciplinary studies, Latin American studies, law, philosophy, political science/government, psychology, public administration, religion, social work, sociology, water resources, and women's studies). Psychology, biology, and finance have the largest enrollments.

Required: Students must have to a 2.0 GPA graduate, and must complete a minimum of 120 semester hours. A baccalaureate degree program must require at least 21 semester hours of upper division courses in the major field and at least 39 semester hours of upper division work overall. The core curriculum include 9 credit hours of Foundation courses, 7-8 hours of Sciences, 3-4 hours of Quantitative Reasoning, 12 hours of World Languages and Culture, Humanities and the Arts, 9 hours of Social Sciences, Required specific disciplines are grammar, composition, literature, math, biological sciences, history, American government, and environmental literacy. Specific courses include basic phys ed and English 1101 and 1102. UGA also requires all students to pass the Regents Exit Exam, as well as exams on the federal and state constitutions.

Special: UGA offers cross-registration with University Center institutions in urban Atlanta. With the Governor's Intern Program, students may serve a full-time 10-week internship in a state government agency; many other internships are available within the departments, as well as work-study programs within the university and with many area businesses. A Washington semester, an accelerated degree program in business, a general studies degree, student-designed majors, dual degrees and double majors, and non-degree study are also available. There are 25 national honor societies, including Phi Beta Kappa, and a freshman honors program.

Faculty/Classroom: 65% of faculty are male; 35% are female. No introductory courses are taught by graduate students.

Admissions: 54% of the 2013-2014 applicants were accepted. There were 40 National Merit finalists.

Requirements: The SAT or ACT is required. UGA admits freshmen primarily on the basis of high school curriculum, grades earned, and college admissions test scores. The university may consider qualitative information to determine a student's potential for success. Applicants should be high school graduates or present a GED certificate. Students should have taken 4 years of English, 4 each of math and science, 3 of social studies, and 2 of a foreign language. Satisfactory scores are required on the SAT or ACT. An audition is required for music majors. AP and CLEP credits are accepted.

Procedure: Freshmen are admitted fall, spring, and summer. Entrance exams should be taken by January of the senior year. There is a deferred admissions plan. Early decision applications should be filed by October 15; regular applications, by January 15 for fall entry; October 1 for spring entry; and January 15 for summer entry, along with a $60 fee. Notification of early decision is sent December 1; regular decision, April 1. Applications are accepted online.

Transfer: A transfer GPA of 3.2 is required of all sophomores (30-59 hrs) and 2.8 required with 60 hrs or more. These students are admitted based on space availability and there is no minimum GPA that guarantees admission. Students with fewer than 30 transferable hours are not eligible for transfer admission. 45 of 120 credits required for the bachelor's degree must be completed at UGA.

Visiting: There are regularly scheduled orientations for prospective students, including walking and driving tours of the campus and meetings with faculty, staff, and students. There are guides for informal visits, visitors may sit in on classes, and stay overnight. To schedule a visit, contact the Visitor Center at (706) 542-0842.

Financial Aid: UGA is a member of CSS. The FAFSA is required. The priority date for freshman financial aid applications for fall entry is March 1.

International Students: There are 1123 international students enrolled. They must take the TOEFL with a minimum score of 550 on the paper-based TOEFL (PBT) or 80 on the Internet-based version (iBT). They must also take the SAT or ACT.

Computers: All students may access the system. Open access in computer center/labs, residence hall, library and student center. There are no time limits and no fees.

Graduates: From July 1, 2012 to June 30, 2013, 7335 bachelor's degrees were awarded. The most popular majors were psychology (7%), biology (6%), and finance (5%). In an average class, 3% graduate in 3 years or less, 62% graduate in 4 years or less, 82% graduate in 5 years or less, and 83% graduate in 6 years or less. Of the 2012 graduating class, 20% were enrolled in graduate school within 6 months of graduation, and 67% were employed.

Admissions Contact: Nancy G. McDuff, VP of Admissions and Enrollment Management. E-Mail: *nmcduff@uga.edu* Web: *https:/www.admissions.uga.edu*

UNIVERSITY OF WEST GEORGIA — A-2

Carrollton, GA 30118	**(678) 839-5600; (678) 839-4747**
Full-time: 3090 men, 5279 women	**Faculty:** 427; IIA, --$
Part-time: 612 men, 978 women	**Ph.D.s:** 80%
Graduate: 552 men, 1418 women	**Student/Faculty:** 19 to 1
Year: semesters, summer session	**Tuition:** $6832 ($19,414)
Application Deadline: June 1	**Room & Board:** $8020
Freshman Class: 7266 applied, 3913 accepted, 2206 enrolled	
SAT CR/M/W: 485/476/470	**ACT:** 20 **LESS COMPETITIVE**

University of West Georgia, founded in 1906 as part of the University System of Georgia, is a public institution offering degree programs in liberal arts, business, nursing, and teacher preparation. There are 6 undergraduate schools and 6 graduate schools. In addition to regional accreditation, West Georgia has baccalaureate program accreditation with AACSB, ABET, NASAD, NASM, and NCATE. The library contains 671,683 volumes, 21,052 microform items, and 23,935 audio/video tapes/CDs/DVDs, and subscribes to 178,790 periodicals including electronic. Computerized library services include interlibrary loans, database searching, Internet access, and Wi-Fi capability. Special learning facilities include an art gallery, radio station, TV station, observatory, performing arts center, the Advanced Academy of Georgia, and the Waring Archaeology Laboratory. The 645-acre campus is in a rural area 50 miles southwest of Atlanta. Including any residence halls, there are 82 buildings.

Student Life: 97% of undergraduates are from Georgia. Others are from 40 states, 58 foreign countries, and Canada. 95% are from public schools. 53% are White; 34% African American. The average age of freshmen is 18; all undergraduates, 22. 30% do not continue beyond their first year; 42% remain to graduate.

Housing: 3077 students can be accommodated in college housing, which includes single-sex and coed dorms. In addition, there are special-interest houses, fraternity houses, sorority houses, and housing for the Advanced Academy of Georgia students. On-campus housing is guaranteed for the freshman year only, is available on a first-come, first-served basis, and is available on a lottery system for upperclassmen. Priority is given to out-of-town students. 69% of students commute. All students may keep cars.

Activities: 3% of men belong to 10 national fraternities; 4% of women belong to 11 national sororities. There are 160 groups on campus, including art, band, cheerleading, choir, chorus, communications, computers, dance, debate, drama, drill team, ethnic, gay, honors, international, jazz band, literary magazine, marching band, musical theater, newspaper, opera, pep band, political, professional, radio and TV, religious, social, social service, and student government. Popular campus events include Fine Arts Festival, Spring Fling and International Student Night.

Sports: There are 5 intercollegiate sports for men and 8 for women, and 8 intramural sports for men and 8 for women. Facilities include a university stadium, a soccer stadium, a softball field, a baseball stadium, a coliseum, an athletic complex, a weight room, an Olympic-size metric track, and various intramural and practice fields.

Disabled Students: 85% of the campus is accessible. Facilities include wheelchair ramps, elevators, special parking, specially equipped restrooms, special class scheduling, lowered drinking fountains, lowered telephones, and special housing.

Services: Counseling and information services are available, as is tutoring in some subjects, most core subjects There is a reader service for the blind. There is also braille equipment and a speech recognition computer.

Campus Safety and Security: Measures include 24-hour foot and vehicle patrol, emergency notification system, self-defense education, and security escort services. There are shuttle buses, emergency telephones, lighted pathways/sidewalks, and controlled access to dorms/residences.

Programs of Study: West Georgia confers B.A., B.S., B.B.A., B.F.A., B.M., B.S.Chem., B.S.Ed., B.S.N. and B.S.N.C. degrees. Master's and doctoral degrees are also awarded. Bachelor's degrees are awarded in AGRICULTURE (environmental studies), BIOLOGICAL SCIENCE (biology/biological science), BUSINESS (accounting, business administration and management, business economics, economics – statistics, finance, international economics, management information systems, marketing and distribution, real estate, and sports management), COMMUNICATIONS AND THE ARTS (art, English, journalism, music composition, music performance, and theatre arts), COMPUTER AND PHYSICAL SCIENCE (chemistry, computer science, earth science / adolescence education, geology, mathematics, and physics), EDUCATION (business education, early childhood education, foreign languages education, music education, physical education, secondary education, and special education), ENGINEERING AND ENVIRONMENTAL DESIGN (environmental science), HEALTH PROFESSIONS (nursing and speech pathology/audiology), SOCIAL SCIENCE (anthropology, criminology, economics, geography, history, philosophy, political science/government, psychology, and sociology). Geology/dual engineering, chemistry/dual engineering, and chemistry - pre-pharmacy are the strongest academically. Biology, mass communications, and criminology have the largest enrollments.

Required: To graduate, students must have earned 120 semester credit hours with a minimum GPA of 2.0. Distribution requirements include 39 hours in courses numbered 3000 and above.

Special: The university offers short-term internships and supervised work experience, usually for credit. The student may undertake an accelerated-degree program in any major, a dual major in physics/chemistry or geology/engineering, a 3-2 engineering degree program with Mercer University, Georgia Tech, University of Georgia, or Auburn University, nondegree study for teacher certification, and study abroad. There are 8 national honor societies, a freshman honors program, and 10 departmental honors programs.

Faculty/Classroom: 41% of faculty are male; 59% are female. 91% teach undergraduates, 70% do research, and 70% do both. No introductory courses are taught by graduate students. The average class size in an introductory lecture is 34; in a laboratory is 16; and in a regular course is 30.

Admissions: 54% of the 2013-2014 applicants were accepted. The SAT scores for the 2013-2014 freshman class were: Critical Reading--71% below 500, 25% between 500 and 599, and 4% between 600 and 699; Math--75% below 500, 21% between 500 and 599, and 4% between 600 and 699; Writing--75% below 500, 22% between 500 and 599, 3% between 600 and 699. The ACT scores were 62% below 21, 25% between 21 and 23, 9% between 24 and 26, 3% between 27 and 28, and 1% above 28.

Requirements: The SAT or ACT is required. All freshman applicants must satisfactorily complete the required subject units of the Required High School Curriculum (RHSC) or College Preparatory Curriculum (CPC)* and graduate with a RHSC/CPC diploma. All freshman applicants must satisfactorily complete the required subject units of the Required High School Curriculum (RHSC) or College Preparatory Curriculum (CPC)* and graduate with a RHSC/CPC diploma. *CPC course requirements only apply to students graduating prior to 2012. For a detailed list of Required High School Curriculum Courses impacting students graduating in 2012 or later, including acceptable math course sequences, please visit www.westga.edu/rhsc. Minimum requirements: SAT (UWG Code: 5900) ACT (UWG Code: 0878) 430 Critical Reading 17 English 410 Math 17 Math The Office of Admissions will always consider an applicant's best Critical Reading/English and best Math scores when evaluating an applicant for admission. Therefore, UWG encourages students to improve their test scores by taking the SAT and/or ACT more than once. Please note, however, that SAT scores and ACT scores cannot be "mixed" in determining admission eligibility. Students must have a minimum Freshman Index of 2120. Freshman Index Formula: SAT : Freshman Index = (500 x Academic High School GPA) + (Critical Reading SAT + Math SAT) ACT: Freshman Index = (500 x Academic High School GPA) + (ACT Composite x 42) + 88 *Requirements are subject to change based on Board of Regents and University directives. If you do not meet the Freshman Index requirements listed above, learn about our Summer Transition Program. A GPA of 3.1 is required. AP and CLEP credits are accepted.

Procedure: Freshmen are admitted fall, spring, and summer. Entrance exams should be taken by December of the senior year. There are deferred admissions and rolling admissions plans. Applications should be filed by June 1 for fall entry; November 15 for spring entry; and May 15 for summer entry, along with a $40 fee. Notification is sent on a Rolling basis. Applications are accepted online.

Transfer: 598 transfer students enrolled in 2012-2013. A transfer applicant must meet the following Admission criteria: Transfer applicants who have more than 30 semester hours/ 45 quarter hours of transferable credit must have: • Cumulative college GPA of 2.00 calculated on all attempted college credit courses that are transferable to UWG, at all colleges attended (this includes failed courses and repeated courses) • Completion of any required remedial college coursework • Completion of any required College Preparatory Curriculum (CPC) deficiency • Eligible to return to the last college attended Transfer applicants who have less than 30 semester hours/ 45 quarter hours of transferable credit must meet the above requirements in addition to the following : • SAT Critical Reading score of 430 or ACT English score of 17 and • SAT Math score of 410 or ACT Math score of 17 and • Complete college prep high school diploma requirements and all 16 required units of College Preparatory Curriculum (CPC) and • Freshman Index of 2050 ? The Freshman Index is calculated as follows: ? SAT: Freshman Index = (Academic High School GPA x 500) + total SAT ? ACT: Freshman Index = (Academic High School GPA x 500) + (ACT Composite x 42) + 88 *Requirements subject to change based on Board of Regents and University directives.* Admission to the University does not guarantee admission to a specific college or department. The College of Education, Richards College of Business, and certain programs in the College of Arts & Sciences have additional admission requirements which must be met before a student can begin taking upper division classes in their degree program. It is the student's responsibility to contact the appropriate academic department for additional admission requirements upon acceptance to the University granted by the Office of Admissions. 30 of 120 credits required for the bachelor's degree must be completed at West Georgia.

Visiting: There are regularly scheduled orientations for prospective students, Re-acquaint yourself with UWG services, policies, faculty, staff, and campus buildings, and meet new freshmen. There are guides for informal visits. To schedule a visit, contact the Admissions Office.

Financial Aid: In 2013-2014, 80% of all full-time freshmen and 76% of continuing full-time students received some form of financial aid. 55% of all full-time freshmen and 53% of continuing full-time students received need-based aid. The average freshman award was $6,450. Need-based scholarships or need-based grants averaged $4,685; need-based self-help aid (loans and jobs) averaged $3,536; non-need-based athletic scholarships averaged $3,851; other non-need-based awards and non-need-based scholarships averaged $2,188; and $4,685 from other forms of aid. Average annual earnings from campus work are $4350. The average financial indebtedness of the 2013 graduate was $21,328. West Georgia is a member of CSS. The FAFSA is required. The priority date for freshman financial aid applications for fall entry is April 1. The deadline for filing freshman financial aid applications for fall entry is July 1.

International Students: There are 116 international students enrolled. The school actively recruits these students. They must take the TOEFL with a minimum score of 523 on the paper-based TOEFL (PBT) or 69 on the Internet-based version (iBT). They must also take the SAT or ACT, scoring 840.

Computers: All students may access the system. There are no time limits and no fees.

Graduates: From July 1, 2012 to June 30, 2013, 1609 bachelor's degrees were awarded. The most popular majors were nursing (12%), early childhood education (11%), and biology (7%). 383 companies recruited on campus in 2012-2013. In an average class, 16% graduate in 4 years or less, 34% graduate in 5 years or less, and 42% graduate in 6 years or less.

Admissions Contact: Justin Barlow, Director of Admissions. E-Mail: *jbarlow@westga.edu* Web: *www.westga.edu*

UNIVERSITY SYSTEM OF GEORGIA

The University System of Georgia, established in 1932, is a public system in Georgia. It is governed by an 18-member board of regents, whose chief administrator is the chancellor. The primary goal of the system is teaching, research, and public service. The main priorities are to provide broad access to undergraduate education with a high level of excellence, to provide sound programs of graduate education and research, addressing state and national problems and advancing the frontiers of knowledge, and to work cooperatively with all levels and sectors of education to improve the social, cultural, and economic welfare of the state's citizens. The total student enrollment for all 35 campuses is usually 318,027, with 17,767 faculty members. Altogether there are 1,007 baccalaureate, 645 master's, and 214 doctoral programs offered in the University System of Georgia. Profiles of the 4-year campuses are included in this section.

VALDOSTA STATE UNIVERSITY — C-5

Valdosta, GA 31698 — (229) 333-5791; (800) 618-1878; (229) 333-5482

Full-time: 3739 men, 5280 women	**Faculty:** 416; IIA, --$
Part-time: 557 men, 792 women	**Ph.D.s:** 75%
Graduate: 518 men, 1545 women	**Student/Faculty:** 20 to 1
Year: semesters, summer session	**Tuition:** $5206 ($14,788)
Application Deadline: July 1	**Room & Board:** $6980
Freshman Class: 6703 applied, 4744 accepted, 2467 enrolled	
SAT CR/M/W: 503/492/482 **ACT:** 21	**COMPETITIVE**

Valdosta State University, founded in 1906 and a unit of the University System of Georgia, is a public liberal arts institution offering degrees in arts and sciences, education, business administration, nursing, fine arts, social work, and library There are 5 undergraduate schools and 1 graduate school. In addition to regional accreditation, VSU has baccalaureate program accreditation with AACSB, NASAD, NASM, and NCATE. The library contains 539,557 volumes, 1.1 million microform items, and

27,582 audio/video tapes/CDs/DVDs, and subscribes to 2,732 periodicals including electronic. Computerized library services include interlibrary loans, database searching, Internet access, and laptop Internet portals. Special learning facilities include a learning resource center, art gallery, planetarium, radio station, TV station, herbarium. The 172-acre campus is in a suburban area in southern Georgia, 3 1/2 hours from Atlanta and from Orlando, Florida. Including any residence halls, there are 94 buildings. The figures in the above capsule and in this profile are approximate.

Student Life: 96% of undergraduates are from Georgia. Others are from 45 states, 70 foreign countries, and Canada. 64% are white; 28% African American. The average age of freshmen is 18; all undergraduates, 22.

Housing: 2896 students can be accommodated in college housing, which includes coed dorms and on-campus apartments. In addition, there are honors houses, language houses, special-interest houses, honors, wellness, and many other living learning communities are available and 24-hour quiet wings in the dorms. On-campus housing is available on a first-come and first-served basis. 72% of students commute. All students may keep cars.

Activities: 9% of women belong to 9 national sororities. There are 163 groups on campus, including art, band, cheerleading, chess, chorale, chorus, computers, dance, debate, drama, drum and bugle corps, environmental, ethnic, film, gay, honors, international, jazz band, literary magazine, marching band, musical theater, newspaper, orchestra, outdoor/recreation, pep band, political, professional, radio and TV, religious, social, social service, student government, and symphony. Popular campus events include Family Day, and the Happening.

Sports: There are 6 intercollegiate sports for men and 5 for women, and 12 intramural sports for men and 12 for women. Facilities include a phys ed complex with a 5500-seat basketball arena, a health fitmess center, a weight traning room, and a human performance lab; and a gym with a weight room, training room, dance studio, auxiliary gym, outdoor pool, climbing wall, racketball courts, and a indoor track.

Disabled Students: All of the campus is accessible. Facilities include wheelchair ramps, elevators, special parking, specially equipped restrooms, special class scheduling, lowered drinking fountains, lowered telephones, special housing. Students registered with the Access Office are able to register for classes on the first day of registration regardless of classification. Also all campus transportation is accessible.

Services: Counseling and information services are available, as is tutoring in some subjects, biiology, chemistry, physics, math computer science, foreign languges, social science, and writing. There is a reader service for the blind.

Campus Safety and Security: Safety measures include a 24-hour foot and vehicle patrol, emergency notification system, self-defense education, and security escort services. There are shuttle buses, emergency telephones, lighted pathways/sidewalks, bicycle patrol, security cameras, and electronic key card access to residence halls.

Programs of Study: VSU confers B.A., B.S., B.B.A., B.G.S., B.M., B.S.Ed., B.S.E.P., and B.S.N. degrees. Associate degrees are also awarded. Bachelor's degrees are awarded in Biology, early childhood education, and nursing are the largest.

Required: To graduate, all students must complete a minimum of 120 semester hours, including 60 in the core curriculm and 21 in a major, with a GPA of 2.0. Reseasonable proficiency in written and spoken English is also required.

Special: Valdosta offers co-op programs, internships, study abrod, accelerated degree program in RN to BSN/MSN Nursing program and 3-2 engineering degree with Georgia Institute of Technoloigy. There are 28 national honor societies, including Phi Beta Kappa, and a freshman honors program.

Faculty/Classroom: 48% of faculty are male; 52% are female. 91% teach undergraduates. No introductory courses are taught by graduate students. The average class size in an introductory lecture is 30; in a laboratory is 23; and in a regular course is 18.

Admissions: In a recent year, 71% of applicants were accepted. The SAT scores for a recent freshman class were: Critical Reading--51% below 500, 40% between 500 and 599, 8% between 600 and 700; Math--58% below 500, 35% between 500 and 599, 7% between 600 and 700; Writing--59% below 500, 35% between 500 and 599, 6% between 600 and 700.

Requirements: The SAT or ACT is required. AP and CLEP credits are accepted.

Procedure: There are deferred admissions and rolling admissions plans. Applications should be filed by July 1 for fall entry; December 1 for spring entry; and May 1 for summer entry. Notification is sent on a rolling basis.

Transfer: In a recent year, 2094 transfer students enrolled. 30 of 120 credits required for the bachelor's degree must be completed at VSU.

Visiting: There are regularly scheduled orientations for prospective students, including a tour of the campus, information sessins, advising, meal plan selection, fee payment. There are guides for informal visits and visitors may sit in on classes. To schedule a visit, contact the Admissions Office.

Financial Aid: In a recent year, 89% of all full-time freshmen and 83% of continuing full-time students received some form of financial aid. 56% of all full-time freshmen and 53% of continuing full-time students received need-based aid. The average freshman award was $14,351. Need-based scholarships or need-based grants averaged $4,044 ($6,700 maximum); need-based self-help aid (loans and jobs) averaged $2,840 ($7,000 maximum); non-need-based athletic scholarships averaged $3,339 ($12,176 maximum); and other non-need-based awards and non-need-based scholarships averaged $9,895 ($26,226 maximum). 6% of undergraduate students work part-time. VSU is a member of CSS. The priority date for freshman financial aid applications for fall entry is May 1. The deadline for filing freshman financial aid applications for fall entry is June 1.

International Students: There are 200 international students enrolled. They must take the TOEFL with a minimum score of 523 on the paper-based TOEFL (PBT) or 69 on the Internet-based version (iBT). TOEFL can be subsituted with SAT.

Computers: Wireless access is available. There are 61 computer labs and classrooms, open during business days and evenings, housing 1225 PCs. Wireless connections are available in all academic buildings and residence halls. All students may access the system. There are no time limits and no fees.

Graduates: In a recent year, 1631 bachelor's degrees were awarded. The most popular majors were childhood education (11%), communication arts (6%), and nursing (6%). In an average class, 16% graduate in 4 years or less, 37% graduate in 5 years or less, and 43% graduate in 6 years or less.

Admissions Contact: Director of Admissions. A campus DVD is available. E-Mail: *admissions@valdosta.edu* Web. *www.valdosta.edu*

WESLEYAN COLLEGE — C-3

Macon, GA 31210 (912) 757-5206
(800) 447-6610; (912) 757-4030

Full-time: no men, 379 women	**Faculty:** 50; IIB, --$
Part-time: 3 men, 210 women	**Ph.D.s:** 94%
Graduate: 13 men, 86 women	**Student/Faculty:** 10 to 1
Year: semesters, summer session	**Tuition:** $16,500
Application Deadline: February 1	**Room & Board:** $7500
Freshman Class: 617 applied, 302 accepted, 135 enrolled	
SAT: required	**ACT:** 22 **COMPETITIVE+**

Wesleyan College, founded in 1836, is a private, liberal arts college for women, affiliated with the United Methodist Church. It is the world's first college chartered to grant degrees to women. In addition to regional accreditation, Wesleyan has baccalaureate program accreditation with NASM. The library contains 143,071 volumes, 33,438 microform items, and 4,267 audio/video tapes/CDs/DVDs, and subscribes to 615 periodicals including electronic. Computerized library services include interlibrary loans, database searching, and Internet access. Special learning facilities include an art gallery, a computerized teaching classroom, language and math labs, collaborative research science labs, and an arboretum. The 200-acre campus is in a suburban area 90 miles south of Atlanta. Including any residence halls, there are 19 buildings.

Student Life: 74% of undergraduates are from Georgia. Others are from 25 states, and 16 foreign countries. 90% are from public schools. 48% are White; 23% Foreign; 22% African American. 53% are Protestant; 34% claim no religious affiliation. The average age of freshmen is 18; all undergraduates, 22. 32% do not continue beyond their first year; 56% remain to graduate.

Housing: 600 students can be accommodated in college housing, which includes single-sex dorms and on-campus apartments. On-campus housing is guaranteed for all 4 years. 76% of students live on campus; of those, 60% remain on campus on weekends. Alcohol is not permitted. All students may keep cars.

Activities: There are no fraternities or sororities. There are 51 groups on campus, including art, choir, chorus, computers, dance, debate, drama, ethnic, forensics, gay, honors, international, literary magazine, musical theater, newspaper, photography, political, professional, recreation, religious, social, social service, and student government. Popular campus events include Casino Night, Benefit Ball, and STUNT.

Sports: There are 6 intercollegiate sports for women. Facilities include an equestrian arena, softball and soccer fields, an indoor pool, a gym, a dance studio, a weight room, a lake, a fitness trail, and a fitness center.

Disabled Students: 65% of the campus is accessible. Facilities include wheelchair ramps, elevators, special parking, specially equipped restrooms, special class scheduling, lowered drinking fountains, and lowered telephones.

Services: Counseling and information services are available, as is tutoring in some subjects. There is remedial math and reading. Free tutors are available upon request, and the Academic Center is available for all students.

Campus Safety and Security: Measures include 24-hour foot and vehicle patrol, self-defense education, and security escort services. There are emergency telephones, lighted pathways/sidewalks, dorm entrances are locked 24 hours a day, 7 days a week.

Programs of Study: Wesleyan confers A.B., and B.S.B.A. degrees. Master's degrees are also awarded. Bachelor's degrees are awarded in BIO-

LOGICAL SCIENCE (biology/biological science), BUSINESS (business administration and management and international business management), COMMUNICATIONS AND THE ARTS (advertising, art history and appreciation, communications, dramatic arts, English, French, music, Spanish, and studio art), COMPUTER AND PHYSICAL SCIENCE (chemistry, information sciences and systems, mathematics, physical sciences, and physics), EDUCATION (early childhood education and middle school education), ENGINEERING AND ENVIRONMENTAL DESIGN (environmental science), SOCIAL SCIENCE (American studies, economics, history, humanities, interdisciplinary studies, international relations, philosophy, political science/government, psychology, religion, and social science). Chemistry, biology, and philosophy are the strongest academically. Business, education, psychology, advertising and marketing have the largest enrollments.

Required: To graduate, students must complete 120 credit hours with a minimum GPA of 2.0. Requirements include proficiency in writing, math, and modern foreign language, 10 courses distributed with 2 but no more than 3 from fine arts, humanities, science and math, and social sciences. A first-year seminar, a speech-intensive course, cross-cultural and workplace experience, and integrative experience in the major are also required. All classes are seminar based.

Special: Wesleyan offers cross-registration with Mercer University and a 3-2 engineering degree with Georgia Institute of Technology and Auburn and Mercer Universities. More than 150 internships are available, as are interdisciplinary, student-designed, and dual majors, study abroad in 10 countries, a Washington semester, work-study programs, credit for life experience, nondegree study, and pass/fail options. There are 10 national honor societies and a freshman honors program.

Faculty/Classroom: 42% of faculty are male; 58% are female. All teach undergraduates, and 75% do both. No introductory courses are taught by graduate students. The average class size in an introductory lecture is 13; in a laboratory is 12; and in a regular course is 10.

Admissions: 49% of the 2013-2014 applicants were accepted. The ACT scores were 36% below 21, 27% between 21 and 23, 25% between 24 and 26, 7% between 27 and 28, and 7% above 28. 49% of the current freshmen were in the top fifth of their class; 72% were in the top two fifths. 3 freshmen graduated first in their class.

Requirements: The SAT or ACT is required. The ACT Optional Writing test is also required. In addition, Each applicant for admission is reviewed on the following: performance in and quality of a college preparatory curriculum, standardized test score, counselor and teacher recommendation, writing ability, and cocurricular involvement. A minimum of 15 Carnegie units is required, including 4 units of English, 3 each of math, natural sciences, and social sciences, and 2 of foreign language. Admitted students must graduate from an accredited secondary school or have a GED certificate. The admission staff does not require but welcomes the opportunity to interview prospective students. Students who wish to be considered for a performance arts scholarship must submit a portfolio or audition. AP and CLEP credits are accepted. Important factors in the admissions decision are advanced placement or honors courses, evidence of special talent, and leadership record.

Procedure: Freshmen are admitted fall and spring. Entrance exams should be taken by the fall of the senior year. There are early decision, early admissions, deferred admissions, and rolling admissions plans. Early decision applications should be filed by November 15; regular applications, by February 1 for fall entry; and December 1 for spring entry, along with a $30 fee. Notification of early decision is sent December 15; regular decision, 40 early decision candidates were accepted for the 2013-2014 class. Applications are accepted online.

Transfer: 5 transfer students enrolled in 2012-2013. Applicants with fewer than 24 transferable semester hours must submit a final high school transcript and record of standardized test scores in addition to their college transcripts. 30 of 120 credits required for the bachelor's degree must be completed at Wesleyan.

Visiting: There are regularly scheduled orientations for prospective students, including a campus tour, parent/student panels, class visits, admission and financial aid sessions, and meals in the dining hall. There are guides for informal visits, visitors may sit in on classes, and stay overnight. To schedule a visit, contact the Admissions Office.

Financial Aid: In 2013-2014, 99% of all full-time freshmen and 96% of continuing full-time students received some form of financial aid. 71% of all full-time freshmen and 58% of continuing full-time students received need-based aid. The average freshman award was $13,842. Need-based scholarships or need-based grants averaged $10,116; need-based self-help aid (loans and jobs) averaged $3,064; and other non-need-based awards and non-need-based scholarships averaged $12,230. 40% of undergraduate students work part-time. Average annual earnings from campus work are $1000. The average financial indebtedness of the 2013 graduate was $21,872. The FAFSA and the college's own financial statement are required. The priority date for freshman financial aid applications for fall entry is March 1. The deadline for filing freshman financial aid applications for fall entry is May 1.

International Students: There are 79 international students enrolled. The school actively recruits these students. They must take the TOEFL. They must also take the SAT or ACT.

Computers: All students may access the system. There are no time limits. The fee is $300.

Graduates: From July 1, 2012 to June 30, 2013, 92 bachelor's degrees were awarded. The most popular majors were business administration (28%), education (12%), and psychology (11%). In an average class, 41% graduate in 4 years or less, 44% graduate in 5 years or less, and 45% graduate in 6 years or less. Of the 2012 graduating class, 22% were enrolled in graduate school within 6 months of graduation, and 36% were employed.

Admissions Contact: Patricia M. Gibbs, Vice President of Enrollment Services and Student Affairs. E-Mail: *admission@wesleyancollege.edu*
Web: *www.wesleyancollege.edu*

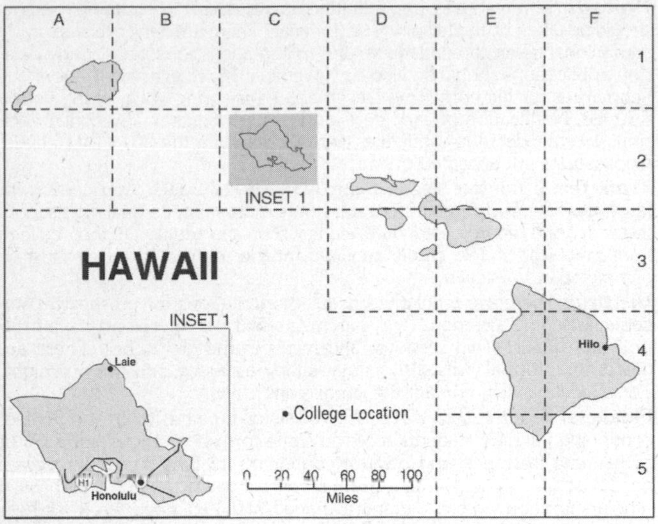

BRIGHAM YOUNG UNIVERSITY/HAWAII C-2

Laie, HI 96762 **(808) 675-3731; (808) 675-3741**

Full-time: 945 men, 1200 women	**Faculty:** 120
Part-time: 99 men, 153 women	**Ph.D.s:** 60%
Graduate: n/av	**Student/Faculty:** 18 to 1
Year: semesters, summer session	**Tuition:** $3750
Application Deadline: February 15	**Room & Board:** $5864
Freshman Class: 1265 applied, 603 accepted, 297 enrolled	
SAT: recommended **ACT:** 23	**VERY COMPETITIVE**

BYU-Hawaii is a private, comprehensive undergraduate institution that educates 2,400 students each year from 70 countries in Asia, the Pacific, the U.S., and other parts of the world. There are 4 undergraduate schools. In addition to regional accreditation, BYU - Hawai'i has baccalaureate program accreditation with NCATE. The library contains 21,004 volumes, 450,000 microform items, and 9,538 audio/video tapes/CDs/DVDs, and subscribes to 17,000 periodicals including electronic. Computerized library services include interlibrary loans, database searching, Internet access, and laptop Internet portals. Special learning facilities include a learning resource center, art gallery, natural history museum. The nearby Polynesian Cultural Center, which houses an art collection and an artifact collection, provides valuable research opportunities for students in related programs. The 200-acre campus is in a rural area 38 miles from Honolulu. Including any residence halls, there are 42 buildings. The figures in the above capsule and in this profile are approximate.

Student Life: 83% of undergraduates are from out of state, mostly the West. Students are from 41 states, 75 foreign countries, and Canada. 44% are foreign nationals; 29% white; 22% Asian American. The average age of freshmen is 21; all undergraduates, 23. 35% do not continue beyond their first year; 47% remain to graduate.

Housing: 1635 students can be accommodated in college housing, which includes single-sex dorms, on-campus apartments, and married student housing. On-campus housing is guaranteed for the freshman year only, is available on a first-come, and first-served basis. 62% of students live on campus. Alcohol is not permitted. All students may keep cars.

Activities: There are no fraternities or sororities. There are 41 groups on campus, including art, band, cheerleading, chess, choir, chorale, communications, computers, dance, drama, ethnic, film, honors, international, jazz band, literary magazine, musical theater, newspaper, pep band, political, professional, religious, social, social service, and student government. Popular campus events include International Food Fest, International Cultural Night, and Talent Show.

Sports: There are 5 intercollegiate sports for men and 6 for women, and 10 intramural sports for men and 10 for women. Facilities include 3 softball fields, 2 soccer fields, a rugby field, 10 tennis and 4 racquetball courts, a swimming pool, a weight room, a bowling alley, a dance studio, pool tables, and 2 gyms.

Disabled Students: 95% of the campus is accessible. Facilities include wheelchair ramps, elevators, special parking, specially equipped restrooms, lowered drinking fountains, and lowered telephones.

Services: Counseling and information services are available, as is tutoring in most subjects. There is remedial math, reading, and writing.

Campus Safety and Security: Measures include 24-hour foot and vehicle patrol and security escort services. There are emergency telephones and lighted pathways/sidewalks.

Programs of Study: BYU - Hawai'i confers B.A., B.S., B.F.A., and B.S.W. degrees. Bachelor's degrees are awarded in BIOLOGICAL SCIENCE (biology/biological science), BUSINESS (accounting, hospitality management services, international business management, and tourism), COMMUNICATIONS AND THE ARTS (art, English, fine arts, and music), COMPUTER AND PHYSICAL SCIENCE (computer science, information sciences and systems, and mathematics), EDUCATION (art education, business education, elementary education, English education, mathematics education, science education, social science education, special education, and teaching English as a second/foreign language (TESOL/TEFOL)), HEALTH PROFESSIONS (predentistry and premedicine), SOCIAL SCIENCE (Hawaiian studies, history, interdisciplinary studies, international studies, Pacific area studies, physical fitness/movement, political science/government, psychology, and social work). International business management, accounting, hospitality and tourism management have the largest enrollments.

Required: Students must complete the 31 to 43 credits in general education curriculum, as well as meet English proficiency, religious education, and exercise science requirements. A total of 120 credit hours, including 40 in the major, must be earned with a minimum GPA of 2.0 for graduation. A thesis is required in certain areas.

Special: BYUH offers work-study programs with the Polynesian Cultural Center, internships, cooperative programs in most majors, non-degree study, student-designed majors in interdisciplinary studies, and pass/fail options. There are 5 national honor societies and a freshman honors program.

Faculty/Classroom: 80% of faculty are male; 20% are female. All teach undergraduates. No introductory courses are taught by graduate students. The average class size in an introductory lecture is 21; in a laboratory is 17; and in a regular course is 19.

Admissions: In a recent year, 48% of the applicants were accepted. The ACT scores were 26% below 21, 22% between 21 and 23, 24% between 24 and 26, 16% between 27 and 28, and 12% above 28.

Requirements: The ACT is required. The SAT is recommended. Applicants should be high school graduates. Home-schooled and other nontraditional students should call for more information. A GPA of 2.0 is required. AP and CLEP credits are accepted. Important factors in the admissions decision are geographical diversity, recommendations by alumni, and personality/intangible qualities.

Procedure: Freshmen are admitted to all sessions. Entrance exams should be taken prior to the application deadline. There is a deferred admissions plan. Applications should be filed by February 15 for fall entry; October 1 for winter entry; February 15 for spring entry; and February 15 for summer entry, along with a $35 fee. Notifications are sent April 1. Applications are accepted online.

Transfer: In a recent year, 209 transfer students enrolled. Applicants must have 30 hours of college credit, with a minimum GPA of 2.5. 30 of 120 credits required for the bachelor's degree must be completed at BYU--Hawai'i.

Visiting: There are guides for informal visits. To schedule a visit, contact the University Advancement Office.

Financial Aid: The FAFSA is required. Check with the school for current application deadlines.

International Students: There are 942 international students enrolled. The school actively recruits these students. They must take the TOEFL with a minimum score of 500 on the paper-based TOEFL (PBT). They must also take the ACT.

Computers: Wireless access is available. All students may access the system. The system is available 24 hours a day via personally owned computers. The main computing labs are open until midnight. There are no time limits and no fees.

Graduates: In a recent year, 557 bachelor's degrees were awarded. The most popular majors were international business management (15%), information systems (8%), and social work (6%). In an average class, 47% graduate in 6 years or less. Of a recent graduating class, 44% were enrolled in graduate school within 6 months of graduation, and 61% were employed.

Admissions Contact: Dean of Admissions and Records. A campus DVD is available. E-Mail: *adm@byuh.edu* Web: *www.byuh.edu*

CHAMINADE UNIVERSITY OF HONOLULU C-2

Honolulu, HI 96816 (808) 735-4735
(800) 735-3733; (808) 739-4647

Full-time: 410 men, 876 women
Part-time: 16 men, 24 women
Graduate: 228 men, 508 women
Year: semesters, summer session
Application Deadline:
Freshman Class: n/av
Faculty: n/av; IIB, -$
Ph.D.s: n/av
Student/Faculty: 14 to 1
Tuition: $20,234
Room & Board: $11,430

COMPETITIVE

Chaminade University, a private Catholic college in Honolulu, Hawai'i, offers a rich educational environment with a dedicated, involved faculty, small class sizes, and a safe, beautiful campus. There are 5 undergraduate schools and 5 graduate schools. The library contains 68,256 volumes, 134,000 microform items, and 231 audio/video tapes/CDs/DVDs, and subscribes to 273 periodicals including electronic. Computerized library services include interlibrary loans, database searching, and Internet access. The 65-acre campus is in an urban area 4 miles east of downtown Honolulu. Including any residence halls, there are 16 buildings.

Student Life: 66% of undergraduates are from Hawaii. Others are from 40 states, 12 foreign countries, and Canada. 37% are Asian American; 18% two or more races; 16% White. 44% are Catholic; 12% claim no religious affiliation. The average age of freshmen is 18; all undergraduates, 21. 28% do not continue beyond their first year; 36% remain to graduate.

Housing: 397 students can be accommodated in college housing, which includes single-sex and coed dorms, on-campus apartments, and off-campus apartments. On-campus housing is available on a first-come and first-served basis. 73% of students commute. All students may keep cars.

Activities: There are no fraternities or sororities. There are 38 groups on campus, including art, cheerleading, chorale, computers, dance, drama, ethnic, forensics, honors, international, literary magazine, musical theater, newspaper, orchestra, political, professional, radio and TV, religious, social, social service, student government, and yearbook. Popular campus events include Spring Serendipity, International Extravaganza and Club Fest.

Sports: There are 4 intercollegiate sports for men and 7 for women. Facilities include volleyball, tennis, and basketball courts, fitness and weight-training facilities, and a student center.

Disabled Students: 95% of the campus is accessible. Facilities include wheelchair ramps, elevators, special parking, specially equipped restrooms, special class scheduling, lowered drinking fountains, lowered telephones, and special housing.

Services: Counseling and information services are available, as is tutoring in most subjects. There is remedial math, reading, and writing.

Campus Safety and Security: Measures include 24-hour foot and vehicle patrol, emergency notification system, self-defense education, and security escort services. There are emergency telephones and lighted pathways/sidewalks.

Programs of Study: Chaminade confers B.A., B.S., B.S.N. and B.F.A. degrees. Associate and master's degrees are also awarded. Bachelor's degrees are awarded in AGRICULTURE (environmental studies), BIOLOGICAL SCIENCE (biochemistry and biology/biological science), BUSINESS (accounting, business administration and management, management science, and marketing/retailing/merchandising), COMMUNICATIONS AND THE ARTS (communications and English), COMPUTER AND PHYSICAL SCIENCE (computer science and information sciences and systems), EDUCATION (early childhood education, elementary education, and secondary education), ENGINEERING AND ENVIRONMENTAL DESIGN (interior design), HEALTH PROFESSIONS (nursing), SOCIAL SCIENCE (behavioral science, criminal justice, forensic studies, history, humanities, international relations, liberal arts/general studies, psychology, religion, and social studies). Forsensic sciences, nursing, biology, and education are the strongest academically. Nursing, criminal justice, and psychology have the largest enrollments.

Required: To graduate, students must complete 120 credit hours, including 61 in general education courses and at least 24 in the major at the upper-division level. A 2.0 GPA is required in all majors except criminal justice (2.5), communications (2.5), and education (2.75). Students must complete courses in Art, English, History, Humanities, Mathematics, Philosophy, Sciences, Social Science, and Communications.

Special: Internships are available with local companies through the Career Development office. Students may design majors toward a B.A. in humanities. There is a sister university exchange program with the University of Dayton and St. Mary's University. There are 7 national honor societies.

Faculty/Classroom: 55% of faculty are male; 44% are female. All teach undergraduates. No introductory courses are taught by graduate students. The average class size in an introductory lecture is 18; in a laboratory is 15; and in a regular course is 18.

Admissions: 4% of the current freshmen were in the top fifth of their class; 15% were in the top two fifths.

Requirements: The SAT or ACT is required. General Requirements: minimum GPA 2.5, minimum SAT 920 or minimum ACT 19, and high school diploma or equivalent. Recommendations: four years of English, three years of Social Studies, three years of Mathematics, two years of Science, and four years of College Preparatory Electives. Nursing Requirements: minimum GPA of 2.75, minimum SAT 950 or minimum ACT 20, one year of high school chemistry or equivalent, completion of algebra II, a 1-page personal statement, and at least 2 letters of recommendation. A GPA of 2.5 is required. AP and CLEP credits are accepted. Important factors in the admissions decision are leadership record, personality/intangible qualities, and extracurricular activities record.

Procedure: Freshmen are admitted fall and spring. Entrance exams should be taken during the first semester of the senior year. There are deferred admissions and rolling admissions plans. Application deadlines are open. Application fee is $50. Notification is sent on a rolling basis. Applications are accepted online.

Transfer: 85 transfer students enrolled in 2012-2013. Applicants must have a minimum GPA of 2.00. If fewer than 24 college credits, applicants must meet requirements for first-year students. Nursing Applicants must have minimum GPA of 2.75 and meet same requirements of first-year nursing applicants. 30 of 120 credits required for the bachelor's degree must be completed at Chaminade.

Visiting: There are guides for informal visits and visitors may sit in on classes. To schedule a visit, contact the Admissions Office.

Financial Aid: In 2013-2014, 99% of all full-time freshmen and 98% of continuing full-time students received some form of financial aid. 72% of all full-time freshmen and 71% of continuing full-time students received need-based aid. The average freshman award was $14,534. Need-based scholarships or need-based grants averaged $4,877 ($10,650 maximum); need-based self-help aid (loans and jobs) averaged $4,149 ($8,500 maximum); non-need-based athletic scholarships averaged $8,901 ($40,122 maximum); and other non-need-based awards and non-need-based scholarships averaged $9,480 ($38,742 maximum). The average financial indebtedness of the 2013 graduate was $30,866. Chaminade is a member of CSS. The FAFSA is required. The priority date for freshman financial aid applications for fall entry is March 1.

International Students: There are 24 international students enrolled. They must take the TOEFL with a minimum score of 550 on the paper-based TOEFL (PBT) or 79 on the Internet-based version (iBT). They must also take the SAT or ACT.

Computers: All students may access the system. There are no time limits and no fees.

Graduates: From July 1, 2012 to June 30, 2013, 315 bachelor's degrees were awarded. The most popular majors were criminal justice (22%), psychology (16%), and forensic sciences (14%). 38 companies recruited on campus in 2012-2013. In an average class, 26% graduate in 5 years or less and 36% graduate in 6 years or less.

Admissions Contact: Shauna Pimental-Motooka, Director of Admissions. E-Mail: *admissions@chaminade.edu* Web: *www.chaminade.edu*

HAWAII PACIFIC UNIVERSITY C-2

Honolulu, HI 96813 808-543-8088
(866) 225-5478; (808) 543-8065

Full-time: 1566 men, 2378 women
Part-time: 1197 men, 1027 women
Graduate: 578 men, 717 women
Year: semesters, summer session
Application Deadline:
Freshman Class: 4129 applied, 2980 accepted, 492 enrolled
SAT CR/M/W: 480/490/470
Faculty: 235; IIB, av$
Ph.D.s: 64%
Student/Faculty: 17 to 1
Tuition: $20,080
Room & Board: $13,230
ACT: 21

COMPETITIVE

Hawaii Pacific University, founded in 1965, is a private institution offering undergraduate and graduate programs in liberal arts, business, natural sciences, nursing, international studies, and communication. There are no undergraduate schools. In addition to regional accreditation, HPU has baccalaureate program accreditation with CSWE and NLN. The 2 libraries contain 175,000 volumes, 415,000 microform items, and 6,300 audio/video tapes/CDs/DVDs, and subscribe to 45,000 periodicals including electronic. Computerized library services include interlibrary loans, database searching, Internet access, and Wi-Fi capability. Special learning facilities include an art gallery, A research vessel. The 135 acre campus is in an urban area in downtown Honolulu and suburban Kaneohe on the island of Oahu. Including any residence halls, there are 16 buildings.

Student Life: 64% of undergraduates are from Hawaii. Others are from 50 states, 78 foreign countries, and Canada. 67% are from public schools. 29% are White; 19% Asian American; 13% Hispanic; 13% Foreign. The average age of freshmen is 19; all undergraduates, 26. 34% do not continue beyond their first year; 39% remain to graduate.

Housing: 200 students can be accommodated in college housing, which includes single-sex and coed dorms and off-campus apartments, and a homestay program. The housing office assists students in finding apartments and other living arrangements in Honolulu. On-campus housing is available on a first-come and first-served basis. Priority is given to out-of-town students. 97% of students commute. Alcohol is not permitted. All students may keep cars.

Activities: There are no fraternities or sororities. There are 93 groups on campus, including art, band, cheerleading, chorale, computers, dance, debate, drama, environmental, ethnic, film, gay, honors, international, literary magazine, musical theater, newspaper, orchestra, pep band, political, professional, religious, social, social service, and student government. Popular campus events include Intercultural Day, Honors Banquet and Club Carnival.

Sports: There are 6 intercollegiate sports for men and 6 for women, and 6 intramural sports for men and 6 for women. Facilities include soccer and softball fields, tennis courts, and 2 regulation basketball courts.

Disabled Students: 75% of the campus is accessible. Facilities include wheelchair ramps, elevators, special parking, specially equipped restrooms, special class scheduling, lowered drinking fountains, and lowered telephones.

Services: Counseling and information services are available, as is tutoring in most subjects. There is remedial math, reading, and writing.

Campus Safety and Security: Measures include 24-hour foot and vehicle patrol, emergency notification system, and security escort services. There are shuttle buses, emergency telephones, and lighted pathways/sidewalks.

Programs of Study: HPU confers B.A., B.S., B.S.B.A., B.S.N., B.S.W., B.Ed. and B.S.H.S. degrees. Associate and master's degrees are also awarded. Bachelor's degrees are awarded in AGRICULTURE (environmental studies), BIOLOGICAL SCIENCE (biochemistry, biology/biological science, and marine science), BUSINESS (accounting, banking and finance, business administration and management, business economics, entrepreneurial studies, human resources, international business management, management science, marketing management, personnel management, small business management, and tourism), COMMUNICATIONS AND THE ARTS (advertising, communications, English, journalism, multimedia, and public relations), COMPUTER AND PHYSICAL SCIENCE (applied mathematics, chemistry, computer programming, computer science, mathematics, oceanography, and science), EDUCATION (elementary education and teaching English as a second/foreign language (TESOL/TEFOL)), ENGINEERING AND ENVIRONMENTAL DESIGN (environmental science and military science), HEALTH PROFESSIONS (nursing and premedicine), SOCIAL SCIENCE (anthropology, classical/ancient civilization, criminal justice, economics, history, human services, humanities, international relations, international studies, Pacific area studies, political science/government, psychology, public administration, social science, social work, and sociology). Marine biology, nursing and computer science are the strongest academically. Nursing, computer science and management have the largest enrollments.

Required: Seniors who have completed a minimum of 100 semester hours of credit toward their undergraduate degree program and have a cumulative GPA of at least 3.0 may enroll concurrently in certain graduate degree programs. Students enrolled in this program may earn a maximum of 12 semester hours of dual graduate and undergraduate credit while pursuing both degrees. (MA-TESL allows only 6 AL concurrent credits)

Special: Upperclassmen may participate in internships and work-study programs with numerous companies and study abroad in 16 countries. HPU also offers accelerated degree and co-op programs in all majors, B.A.-B.S. degrees in most majors, student-designed majors, dual majors in all business subjects, a 3-2 engineering degree with Washington University in St. Louis and the University of Southern California, credit for military experience, nondegree study, and pass/fail options. There are 18 national honor societies, a freshman honors program, and 7 departmental honors programs.

Faculty/Classroom: 54% of faculty are male; 46% are female. 91% teach undergraduates, and 42% do both. No introductory courses are taught by graduate students. The average class size in an introductory lecture is 18; in a laboratory is 10; and in a regular course is 18.

Admissions: 72% of the 2013-2014 applicants were accepted. The SAT scores for the 2013-2014 freshman class were: Critical Reading--57% below 500, 35% between 500 and 599, 8% between 600 and 699, and 1% between 700 and 800; Math--52% below 500, 38% between 500 and 599, 9% between 600 and 699, and 1% between 700 and 800; Writing--63% below 500, 32% between 500 and 599, and 5% between 600 and 699. The ACT scores were 47% below 21, 30% between 21 and 23, 14% between 24 and 26, 5% between 27 and 28, and 5% above 28. 44% of the current freshmen were in the top fifth of their class; 76% were in the top two fifths. 18 freshmen graduated first in their class.

Requirements: The SAT or ACT is required. The university prefers completion of 20 credits based on 4 years of English, 2 each of math and social studies, and 2 each of history and science. An essay and an interview are recommended. Certain programs, for example, marine science and nursing, have more specific admission requirements. A GPA of 2.5 is required. AP and CLEP credits are accepted. Important factors in the admissions decision are recommendations by school officials, extracurricular activities record, and evidence of special talent.

Procedure: Freshmen are admitted to all sessions. Entrance exams should be taken during the spring or summer of the junior year or the fall of the senior year. There are early admissions, deferred admissions, and rolling admissions plans. Application deadlines are open. Application fee is $50. Applications are accepted online.

Transfer: 890 transfer students enrolled in 2012-2013. Applicants must have a GPA of 2.0 in a minimum of 24 credit hours. The SAT or ACT and an interview are recommended. 30 of 124 credits required for the bachelor's degree must be completed at HPU.

Visiting: There are regularly scheduled orientations for prospective students, at 9 a.m. daily, with an appointment required. There are guides for informal visits and visitors may sit in on classes. To schedule a visit, contact the Admissions Office.

Financial Aid: 36% of all full-time freshmen received need-based aid. The FAFSA is required. The priority date for freshman financial aid applications for fall entry is March 1.

International Students: There are 632 international students enrolled. The school actively recruits these students. They must take the TOEFL with a minimum score of 550 on the paper-based TOEFL (PBT) or 80 on the Internet-based version (iBT) and the college's own test, or take the IELTS, scoring a minimum of 6, or the APIEL, scoring a minimum of 3.

Computers: All students may access the system 7 days a week during day and evening hours. There are no time limits. The fee is $50.

Graduates: From July 1, 2012 to June 30, 2013, 926 bachelor's degrees were awarded. The most popular majors were business administration (33%), nursing (28%), and psychology (7%). 133 companies recruited on campus in 2012-2013. In an average class, 4% graduate in 3 years or less, 23% graduate in 4 years or less, 36% graduate in 5 years or less, and 39% graduate in 6 years or less. Of the 2012 graduating class, 40% were enrolled in graduate school within 6 months of graduation, and 69% were employed.

Admissions Contact: Sara Sato, Asst. V.P. Enrollment Management. E-Mail: *admissions@hpu.edu* Web: *www.hpu.edu*

UNIVERSITY OF HAWAII SYSTEM

The University of Hawaii System, established in 1907, is a public system in Hawaii. It is governed by a board of regents, whose chief administrators are the president and the chancellor. The primary goal of the system is to provide all qualified people in Hawaii an equal opportunity for quality college and university education, to create knowledge and gain insights through research and scholarship, to preserve and contribute to the artistic and cultural heritage of the community, and to provide other public service through the dissemination of current and new ideas and techniques. The main priorities are serving the state of Hawaii, achieving program quality, establishing Pacific/Asian focus, and adapting to scientific change. The total student enrollment of all 10 campuses is usually 55,500, with 3500 faculty members. Altogether there are 130 baccalaureate, 89 master's, and 52 doctoral programs offered in University of Hawaii System. 4-year campuses are located in Hilo, Manoa. and West Oahu. Profiles of the 4-year campuses are included in this section.

UNIVERSITY OF HAWAII AT HILO — F-4

Hilo, HI 96720-4091 — (808) 974-7414; (800) 897-4456; (808) 933-0861

Full-time: 880 men, 1335 women	**Faculty:** 162; IIB, av$
Part-time: 235 men, 400 women	**Ph.D.s:** 80%
Graduate: 30 men, 75 women	**Student/Faculty:** 14 to 1
Year: semesters, summer session	**Tuition:** $2200 ($8000)
Application Deadline: open	**Room & Board:** $5340
Freshman Class: n/av	
SAT or ACT: required	
	COMPETITIVE

The University of Hawaii at Hilo, founded in 1970, is part of the public University of Hawaii and offers degree programs through its Colleges of Agriculture, Arts and Sciences, and Hawaiian language. It has a branch campus at Kealakekua, West Hawaii. Major programs include marine science, volcanology, and astronomy. There are 3 undergraduate schools and 2 graduate schools. In addition to regional accreditation, UH Hilo has baccalaureate program accreditation with NLN. The library contains 240,000 volumes, 11,000 microform items, and subscribes to 1,200 periodicals including electronic. Computerized library services include interlibrary loans and database searching. Special learning facilities include a learning resource center, art gallery, space science center and marine education center. The 115-acre campus is in a small town 200 miles southeast of Honolulu. Including any residence halls, there are 54 buildings. The figures in the above capsule and in this profile are approximate.

Student Life: 69% of undergraduates are from Hawaii. Others are from 46 states, 32 foreign countries, and Canada. 76% are from public schools. 31% are white; 27% Asian American; 18% Native American/Eskimo. The average age of all undergraduates is 27. 29% do not continue beyond their first year; 31% remain to graduate.

Housing: 800 students can be accommodated in college housing, which

includes coed dorms, on-campus apartments, off-campus apartments, and married student housing. In addition, there are honors houses, special-interest houses, is an educational/recreational enrichment hall. On-campus housing is available on a first-come and first-served basis. Priority is given to out-of-town students. 79% of students commute. Alcohol is not permitted. All students may keep cars.

Activities: There are no fraternities or sororities. There are 40 groups on campus, including art, band, cheerleading, chess, choir, chorale, chorus, computers, dance, drama, ethnic, gay, honors, international, jazz band, literary magazine, musical theater, newspaper, pep band, political, professional, religious, social, social service, and student government. Popular campus events include International Night, May Day, and Dances.

Sports: There are 5 intercollegiate sports for men and 4 for women, and 10 intramural sports for men and 10 for women. Facilities include a student activities center with billiards and a game room, an athletic complex with basketball courts and a weight room, 8 tennis courts, and baseball, softball, and soccer fields.

Disabled Students: 95% of the campus is accessible. Facilities include wheelchair ramps, elevators, special parking, specially equipped restrooms, special class scheduling, lowered drinking fountains, lowered telephones.

Services: Counseling and information services are available, as is tutoring in most subjects. There is remedial math, reading, and writing.

Campus Safety and Security: Measures include 24-hour foot and vehicle patrol and self-defense education. There are emergency telephones and lighted pathways/sidewalks.

Programs of Study: UH Hilo confers B.A., B.S., B.B.A., and B.S.N. degrees. Master's degrees are also awarded. Bachelor's degrees are awarded in AGRICULTURE (agriculture), BIOLOGICAL SCIENCE (biology/biological science and marine science), BUSINESS (business administration and management), COMMUNICATIONS AND THE ARTS (art, communications, English, linguistics, and music), COMPUTER AND PHYSICAL SCIENCE (astronomy, chemistry, computer science, geology, mathematics, natural sciences, and physics), HEALTH PROFESSIONS (nursing), SOCIAL SCIENCE (anthropology, criminal justice, economics, geography, Hawaiian studies, history, Japanese studies, liberal arts/general studies, philosophy, political science/government, psychology, and sociology). Business, computer science, biology are the strongest academically. Business, psychology, and marine science have the largest enrollments.

Required: To graduate, students must earn a minimum of 120 semester hours, including at least 30 in the college from which a degree is sought, with a 2.0 GPA overall and in the major. Students also must complete general education requirements, including 10 semester hours of natural sciences with 1 hour of lab, 9 each of humanitites and social sciences, 6 of world cultures, and 3 each of English composition and quantitative reasoning. 3 writing-intensive sourses and 1 Hawaiian/Asian/Pacific course are also required.

Special: UH Hilo offers cross-registration with Hawaii Community College, a political science legislative internship and other internships in business and psychology, and many work-study programs. Students may study abroad through a variety of programs and other internships in business and psychology. The school permits a student-designed liberal studies major, dual degrees, a 3-2 engineering degree with the University of Hawaii at Manoa, nondegree study, pass/fail options, and credit for military experience. There is a freshman honors program and 1 departmental honors program.

Faculty/Classroom: 60% of faculty are male; 40% are female. All teach and do research. No introductory courses are taught by graduate students. The average class size in an introductory lecture is 25; in a laboratory is 25; and in a regular course is 17.

Admissions: 4 freshmen graduated first in their class.

Requirements: The SAT or ACT is required. Applicants should be high school graduates or present a GED certificate. Students should have earned 22 academic credits, including 4 units of English, 3 of math, 3 of life and physical sciences, and 7 of electives. Applications are accepted online. A GPA of 2.5 is required. AP and CLEP credits are accepted. Important factors in the admissions decision are advanced placement or honors courses, recommendations by school officials, and evidence of special talent.

Procedure: Freshmen are admitted fall and spring. Entrance exams should be taken by November of the senior year. There are early admissions and rolling admissions plans. Applications should be filed by December 1 for spring entry, along with a $25 fee. Applications are accepted online.

Transfer: 577 transfer students enrolled in 2010-2011. Applicants must have a GPA of 2.0; those with fewer than 24 college credits must submit their high school transcript and SAT or ACT results. 30 of 120 credits required for the bachelor's degree must be completed at UH Hilo.

Visiting: There are regularly scheduled orientations for prospective students, including a campus tour and a meeting with an admissions counselor. There are guides for informal visits and visitors may sit in on classes. To schedule a visit, contact the Admissions Office.

Financial Aid: In a recent year, 55% of all full-time freshmen and 41% of continuing full-time students received some form of financial aid. The average freshman award was $3,853. 70% of undergraduate students work part-time. The average financial indebtedness in a recent year, was $10,698. UH Hilo is a member of CSS. The FAFSA and the college's own financial statement are required. The deadline for filing freshman financial aid applications for fall entry is March 1.

International Students: There are 311 international students enrolled. The school actively recruits these students. They must take the TOEFL and the college's own test. The SAT or ACT is not required, but is recommended.

Computers: All students may access the system at posted times in person and any time by modem. There are no time limits and no fees.

Graduates: In a recent year, 419 bachelor's degrees were awarded. The most popular majors were psychology (15%), business administration (11%), and marine science (8%). In an average class, 1% graduate in 3 years or less, 10% graduate in 4 years or less, 25% graduate in 5 years or less, and 31% graduate in 6 years or less.

Admissions Contact: Admissions Office A campus DVD is available. E-Mail: *uhhadm@hawaii.edu* Web: *www.uhh.hawaii.edu*

UNIVERSITY OF HAWAII AT MANOA C-2

Honolulu, HI 96822 (808) 956-8975
(800) 823-9771; (808) 956-4148

Full-time: 5388 men, 6246 women	**Faculty:** 1000; I, -$
Part-time: 1261 men, 1507 women	**Ph.D.s:** 85%
Graduate: 2473 men, 3554 women	**Student/Faculty:** 14 to 1
Year: semesters, summer session	**Tuition:** $9100 ($23,932)
Application Deadline: May 1	**Room & Board:** $10,279
Freshman Class: 6541 applied, 5130 accepted, 2010 enrolled	
SAT CR/M/W: 530/560/520 **ACT:** 23	**VERY COMPETITIVE**

The University of Hawaii at Manoa, founded in 1907, is a public research institution in the University of Hawaii system. The undergraduate programs offered include liberal arts and sciences, business, education, engineering, nursing, tropical agriculture, architecture, travel industry management, physical science, technology, Hawaiian, Asian-Pacific Studies, social work, and medicine. There are 14 undergraduate schools and 15 graduate schools. In addition to regional accreditation, UHM has baccalaureate program accreditation with AACSB, ABET, ADA, CSWE, NAAB, NASM, NCATE, and NLN. The 5 libraries contain 3.4 million volumes, 2.4 million microform items, and 73,000 audio/video tapes/CDs/DVDs, and subscribe to 59,000 periodicals including electronic. Computerized library services include interlibrary loans, database searching, Internet access, and laptop Internet portals. Special learning facilities include a learning resource center, art gallery, radio station, and TV station. The 304-acre campus is in a small town in Honolulu. Including any residence halls, there are 255 buildings. The figures in the above capsule and in this profile are approximate.

Student Life: 77% of undergraduates are from Hawaii. Others are from 50 states, 54 foreign countries, and Canada. 68% are from public schools. 41% are Asian American; 21% white. The average age of freshmen is 18; all undergraduates, 22. 23% do not continue beyond their first year; 55% remain to graduate.

Housing: 3696 students can be accommodated in college housing, which includes single-sex and coed dorms, on-campus apartments, and married student housing. In addition, there are honors houses, language houses, special-interest houses, substance free/wellness, first-year experience, technology, and 24-hour quiet halls. On-campus housing is guaranteed for the freshman year only and is available on a lottery system for upperclassmen. Priority is given to out-of-town students. 81% of students commute. All students may keep cars.

Activities: 1% of men belong to 1 local and 2 national fraternities; 1% of women belong to 1 local and 1 national sororities. There are 100 groups on campus, including art, band, cheerleading, chess, choir, chorale, chorus, dance, drama, drill team, ethnic, film, gay, honors, international, literary magazine, marching band, musical theater, newspaper, opera, pep band, photography, political, professional, radio and TV, religious, social, social service, student government, and symphony. Popular campus events include Live band at Bale, late night programming, movie nights, sustainable UH, and recreational sports events.

Sports: There are 9 intercollegiate sports for men and 13 for women, and 24 intramural sports for men and 21 for women. Facilities include a 10,300-seat arena that houses men and women's basketball, and mean and women's volleyball. In addition, the university has 2 gymnasiums, an over 10,000 square foot weight training and conditioning center, a 4312-seat baseball stadium, swimming facilities, 2 weight rooms, a turf field and rubberized track, 2 grass fields, 2 gyms, a softball field, and 12 tennis courts.

Disabled Students: 40% of the campus is accessible. Facilities include wheelchair ramps, elevators, special parking, specially equipped restrooms, special class scheduling, lowered drinking fountains, lowered telephones. disability access information is available on request, and auxiliary aids and program adjustments can be arranged on an individual basis.

Services: Counseling and information services are available, as is tutoring in some subjects. There is a reader service for the blind.

Campus Safety and Security: Measures include 24-hour foot and vehicle patrol, emergency notification system, and security escort services. There are shuttle buses, emergency telephones, lighted pathways/sidewalks, crime alerts via campuswide e-mail, and a campus security web site.

Programs of Study: UHM confers B.A., B.S., B.B.A., B.Ed., B.F.A., B.Mus., and B.S.W. degrees. Master's and doctoral degrees are also awarded. Bachelor's degrees are awarded in AGRICULTURE (animal science, natural resource management, plant protection (pest management), plant science, and soil science), BIOLOGICAL SCIENCE (biology/biological science, botany, marine biology, microbiology, and zoology), BUSINESS (accounting, banking and finance, business administration and management, human resources, international business management, management information systems, management science, marketing/retailing/merchandising, recreation and leisure services, and tourism), COMMUNICATIONS AND THE ARTS (apparel design, art, Chinese, classics, communications, dance, dramatic arts, English, English as a second/foreign language, French, German, Hawaiian, Japanese, journalism, Korean, linguistics, music, Russian, Spanish, and speech/debate/rhetoric), COMPUTER AND PHYSICAL SCIENCE (atmospheric sciences and meteorology, chemistry, computer science, geology, geophysics and seismology, information sciences and systems, mathematics, and physics), EDUCATION (elementary education, physical education, and secondary education), ENGINEERING AND ENVIRONMENTAL DESIGN (bioengineering, civil engineering, electrical/electronics engineering, environmental science, and mechanical engineering), HEALTH PROFESSIONS (dental hygiene, exercise science, medical laboratory technology, medical technology, nursing, and speech pathology/audiology), SOCIAL SCIENCE (American studies, anthropology, Asian/Oriental studies, economics, ethnic studies, family/consumer resource management, food science, geography, Hawaiian studies, history, interdisciplinary studies, Pacific area studies, peace studies, philosophy, political science/government, psychology, religion, social work, sociology, and women's studies). Biology, art, and business have the largest enrollments.

Required: In most disciplines, a minimum GPA of 2.0 and a total of 124 credit hours are required for graduation. The total number of hours required in the major varies according to discipline. All students must fulfill general education core requirements.

Special: Internships are available with a variety of employers, including the state legislature, and through 55 different offices as well as academic departments via career services. Co-op and work-study programs, and internships are also offered. Dual majors, non-degree study, and pass/fail options are available. The liberal studies program offers student-designed majors. Students may study abroad in any one of 20 countries for a summer, a semester, or a year. There are 9 national honor societies, including Phi Beta Kappa, a freshman honors program, and 45 departmental honors programs.

Faculty/Classroom: 56% of faculty are male; 44% are female. 81% teach undergraduates. Graduate students teach 20% of introductory courses. The average class size in an introductory lecture is 38; in a laboratory is 15; and in a regular course is 22.

Admissions: In a recent year, 78% of the applicants were accepted. The SAT scores for a recent freshman class were: Critical Reading--34% below 500, 46% between 500 and 599, 18% between 600 and 700, and 2% above 700; Math--24% below 500, 47% between 500 and 599, 25% between 600 and 700, and 4% above 700; Writing--36% below 500, 49% between 500 and 599, 14% between 600 and 700, and 1% above 700. The ACT scores were 25% below 21, 32% between 21 and 23, 26% between 24 and 26, 10% between 27 and 28, and 7% above 28. 60% of the current freshmen were in the top fifth of their class; 82% were in the top two fifths. 24 freshmen graduated first in their class.

Requirements: The SAT or ACT is required. The ACT Optional Writing test is also required. In addition, applicants must be graduates of an accredited secondary school, and have the minimum required score of 510 for each SAT section, or 22 on the ACT composite. The GED is also accepted. UHM requires 22 Carnegie units or 17 academic credits, including 4 units of English and 3 units each of math, science, and social studies, as well as 4 additional units of college preparatory courses and 5 electives. UHM requires applicants to be in the upper 40% of their class. A GPA of 2.8 is required. AP and CLEP credits are accepted. Important factors in the admissions decision are advanced placement or honors courses, recommendations by school officials, and leadership record.

Procedure: Freshmen are admitted fall and spring. Entrance exams should be taken by December of the senior year for fall admission. There is a rolling admissions plan. Applications should be filed by May 1 for fall entry; October 1 for spring entry, along with a $70 fee. Notification is sent on a rolling basis. Applications are accepted online.

Transfer: 1855 transfer students enrolled in 2010-2011. Applicants must have a total of 24 semester credits with a minimum GPA of 2.5. 30 of 124 credits required for the bachelor's degree must be completed at UHM.

Visiting: There are regularly scheduled orientations for prospective students, Visiting students can meet with an admissions representative and tour the campus with a current UH Manoa Student. To schedule a visit, contact School and College Services.

Financial Aid: In a recent year, 66% of all full-time freshmen and 59% of continuing full-time students received some form of financial aid. 38% of all full-time freshmen and 42% of continuing full-time students received need-based aid. Need-based scholarships or need-based grants averaged $9,133 ($14,050 maximum); need-based self-help aid (loans and jobs) averaged $3,246 ($7,700 maximum); non-need-based athletic scholarships averaged $10,460 ($16,900 maximum); and other non-need-based awards and non-need-based scholarships averaged $8,863 ($28,019 maximum). 27% of undergraduate students work part-time. Average annual earnings from campus work are $3211. The FAFSA and the college's own financial statement are required. The deadline for filing freshman financial aid applications for fall entry is March 1.

International Students: There are 628 international students enrolled. The school actively recruits these students. They must take the TOEFL with a minimum score of 500 on the paper-based TOEFL (PBT) or 100 on the Internet-based version (iBT). They must also take the SAT or ACT, scoring 510.

Computers: All areas on campus have access to wirless. Students need to use a log on username and password to access wireless. All students may access the system. There are no time limits and no fees. It is strongly recommended that all students have a personal computer. Students enrolled in architecture must have a personal computer.

Graduates: In a recent year, 2957 bachelor's degrees were awarded. The most popular majors were business/marketing (21%), social sciences (11%), and education (7%). In an average class, 15% graduate in 4 years or less, 40% graduate in 5 years or less, and 51% graduate in 6 years or less.

Admissions Contact: Director of Admissions and Records. E-Mail: *ar-info@hawaii.edu* Web: *www.manoa@hawaii.edu*

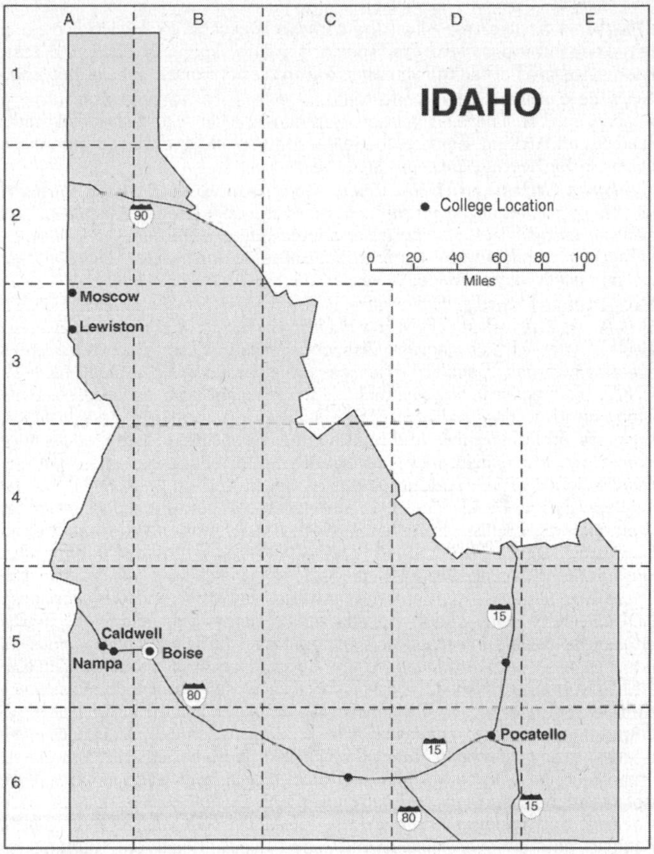

BOISE STATE UNIVERSITY B-5

Boise, ID 83725 (208) 426-1479
(800) 824-7017; (208) 426-3765

Full-time: 6245 men, 6538 women
Part-time: 2927 men, 3943 women
Graduate: 1157 men, 1864 women
Year: semesters, summer session
Application Deadline: May 15
Freshman Class: 9333 applied, 5485 accepted, 2266 enrolled
SAT: recommended
Faculty: 530; IIA, --$
Ph.D.s: 67%
Student/Faculty: 24 to 1
Tuition: $5566 ($15,966)
Room & Board: $7236

COMPETITIVE

Boise State University, founded in 1932, is a public, metropolitan research university offering an array of undergraduate and graduate degrees in the arts and sciences, business, education, engineering, health science, public affairs, and technology. There are 7 undergraduate schools and one graduate school. In addition to regional accreditation, Boise State has baccalaureate program accreditation with AACSB, ABET, ACCE, CAHEA, CSWE, NASAD, NASM, NCATE, and NLN. The library contains 713,000 volumes, 1.5 million microform items, and 107,000 audio/video tapes/CDs/DVDs, and subscribes to 4,797 periodicals including electronic. Computerized library services include interlibrary loans, database searching, Internet access, and Wi-Fi capability. Special learning facilities include an art gallery, radio station, technology center. The 266-acre campus is in an urban area in Boise. Including any residence halls, there are 60 buildings.

Student Life: 80% of undergraduates are from Idaho. Others are from 49 states, 73 foreign countries, and Canada. 77% are White. The average age of freshmen is 21; all undergraduates, 25. 28% do not continue beyond their first year; 30% remain to graduate.

Housing: 2456 students can be accommodated in college housing, which includes coed dorms, on-campus apartments, and married student housing. In addition, there are honors houses and special-interest houses. On-campus housing is available on a first-come and first-served basis. 90% of students commute. All students may keep cars.

Activities: 1% of men belong to 6 national fraternities; 1% of women belong to 4 national sororities. There are 170 groups on campus, including art, band, cheerleading, choir, chorale, communications, dance, debate, drama, drill team, environmental, ethnic, film, gay, honors, international, jazz band, literary magazine, marching band, newspaper, orchestra, pep band, political, professional, radio and TV, religious, social, social service, and student government. Popular campus events include Beat Coach Pete Scholarship Run/Walk, Bronco Welcome, Annual Seven Arrows Contest Pow Wow, Homecoming, Annual Spring Fling, Tunnel of Oppression, Undergraduate Research & Scholarship Conference.

Sports: There are 7 intercollegiate sports for men and 10 for women, and 20 intramural sports for men and 20 for women. Facilities include Student Recreation Center, a 37,000-seat stadium, a 12,000-seat indoor arena, aquatic complex, racquetball courts, indoor and outdoor tennis courts, indoor and outdoor tracks.

Disabled Students: 97% of the campus is accessible. Facilities include wheelchair ramps, elevators, special parking, specially equipped restrooms, special class scheduling, lowered drinking fountains, lowered telephones.

Services: Counseling and information services are available, as is tutoring in most subjects. There is a reader service for the blind, and remedial math, reading, and writing.

Campus Safety and Security: Measures include 24-hour foot and vehicle patrol and emergency notification system. There are shuttle buses, emergency telephones, and lighted pathways/sidewalks.

Programs of Study: Boise State confers B.A., B.A.S., B.G.S., B.B.A., B.F.A., B.S. and B.Mus. degrees. Associate, master's, and doctoral degrees are also awarded. Bachelor's degrees are awarded in AGRICULTURE (environmental studies), BIOLOGICAL SCIENCE (biology/biological science), BUSINESS (accounting, business administration and management, economics – statistics, finance, international business management, marketing/retailing/merchandising, and supply chain management), COMMUNICATIONS AND THE ARTS (art, communications, dramatic arts, English, English literature, English Writing, fine arts, French, German, music, Spanish, and theatre arts), COMPUTER AND PHYSICAL SCIENCE (chemistry, computer science, geology, geophysics and seismology, geoscience, information sciences and systems, mathematics, physics, and radiological technology), EDUCATION (art education, education, elementary education, English education, music education, physical education, secondary education, social science education, and special education), ENGINEERING AND ENVIRONMENTAL DESIGN (civil engineering, construction management, electrical/electronics engineering, materials science, and mechanical engineering), HEALTH PROFESSIONS (environmental health science, health science, nursing, predentistry, premedicine, prepharmacy, prephysical therapy, preveterinary science, and respiratory therapy), SOCIAL SCIENCE (anthropology, criminal justice, early childhood studies, economics, history, interdisciplinary studies, philosophy, political science/government, psychology, social science, social work, and sociology). Communicatin, psychology, biological sciences, criminal justice, health science studies and nursing have the largest enrollments.

Required: To graduate, students must complete the number of credits specified for their degree with a minimum GPA of 2.0. Requirements include 6 semester hours in English composition and 12 each in arts and humanities, social sciences, math, and natural sciences. A minimum grade of C is required in all major courses and courses used to meet the core requirements.

Special: Boise State offers internships, work-study programs, dual majors, a general studies degree, nondegree study, pass/fail options, and study abroad.

Faculty/Classroom: 49% of faculty are male; 51% are female. 89% teach undergraduates. Graduate students teach 13% of introductory courses. The average class size in an introductory lecture is 42 and in a laboratory is 20.

Admissions: 59% of the 2013-2014 applicants were accepted. 14% of the current freshmen were in the top fifth of their class; 36% were in the top two fifths.

Requirements: The SAT or ACT is recommended. Students must graduate from an accredited high school and have an appropriate GPA and ACT or SAT test score (as rated by the school's admission index). Students must have completed 4 years of English, 3 each of math (algebra I and higher) and natural science, 2 1/2 of social science, 1 of humanities or foreign language, and 1 1/2 in other college-preparatory classes. Students who have not completed all the above classes but meet the other admission requirements will be considered for provisional admission status. AP and CLEP credits are accepted.

Procedure: Freshmen are admitted fall, spring, and summer. There is a rolling admissions plan. Applications should be filed by May 15 for fall entry; November 15 for spring entry, along with a $50 fee. Notification is sent on a rolling basis. Applications are accepted online.

Transfer: 1119 transfer students enrolled in 2012-2013. A minimum GPA of 2.0 is required for students with at least 14 college credits. Those students with fewer credits must submit SAT or ACT scores and a high school transcript. 30 of 120 credits required for the bachelor's degree must be completed at Boise State.

Visiting: There are regularly scheduled orientations for prospective students, Information session, campus tour, workshops, housing and stadium tour. There are guides for informal visits and visitors may sit in on classes. To schedule a visit, contact the Admissions Office.

Financial Aid: In 2013-2014, 76% of all full-time freshmen and 78% of continuing full-time students received some form of financial aid. 60% of all full-time freshmen and 69% of continuing full-time students received need-based aid. The average freshman award was $12,006. Need-based scholarships or need-based grants averaged $4,469; need-based self-help aid (loans and jobs) averaged $3,420; non-need-based athletic scholarships averaged $8,629; and other non-need-based awards and non-need-based scholarships averaged $6,565. The average financial indebtedness of the 2013 graduate was $44,870. Boise State is a member of CSS. The FAFSA is required. The priority date for freshman financial aid applications for fall entry is February 15. The deadline for filing freshman financial aid applications for fall entry is May 15.

International Students: There are 581 international students enrolled. The school actively recruits these students. They must take the TOEFL with a minimum score of 587 on the paper-based TOEFL (PBT) or 95 on the Internet-based version (iBT). They must also take the SAT or ACT.

Computers: All students may access the system. There are no time limits and no fees.

Graduates: From July 1, 2012 to June 30, 2013, 2587 bachelor's degrees were awarded. The most popular majors were nursing (8%), management (8%), and communication (7%). 151 companies recruited on campus in 2012-2013. In an average class, 6% graduate in 4 years or less, 18% graduate in 5 years or less, and 25% graduate in 6 years or less. Of the 2012 graduating class, 25% were enrolled in graduate school within 6 months of graduation, and 92% were employed.

Admissions Contact: Ramon Silva, Interium Associate Director of Admission. E-Mail: *bsuinfo@boisestate.edu* Web: *http:/admissions.boisestate.edu/*

IDAHO STATE UNIVERSITY — D-6

Pocatello, ID 83209 — **(208) 282-2475; (208) 282-4511**

Full-time: 3657 men, 3784 women	**Faculty:** n/av
Part-time: 1928 men, 2774 women	**Ph.D.s:** n/av
Graduate: 906 men, 1160 women	**Student/Faculty:** 16 to 1
Year: semesters, summer session	**Tuition:** $6070 ($17,870)
Application Deadline: August 1	**Room & Board:** $5838
Freshman Class: 3184 applied, 2925 accepted, 1705 enrolled	
SAT CR/M/W: 528/530/515	**ACT:** 22 — **COMPETITIVE**

Idaho State University, founded in 1901, is a public institution offering programs in the liberal arts and sciences, business, education, engineering, and health professions. There are 10 undergraduate schools and one graduate school. In addition to regional accreditation, ISU has baccalaureate program accreditation with AACSB, ABET, ACPE, ADA, CSWE, NASM, and NCATE. The library contains 6.0 million volumes, 2.0 million microform items, and 6,170 audio/video tapes/CDs/DVDs, and subscribes to 113,787 periodicals including electronic. Computerized library services include interlibrary loans, database searching, Internet access, and Wi-Fi capability. Special learning facilities include an art gallery, natural history museum, radio station, TV station, accelerator center, performing arts building, multi-use building (housing, classrooms, food service, shopping, study space, computer lab), RISE building used for special research. The 1100-acre campus is in an urban area 150 miles north of Salt Lake City. Including any residence halls, there are 100 buildings.

Student Life: 90% of undergraduates are from Idaho. Others are from 48 states, 62 foreign countries, and Canada. 95% are from public schools. 77% are White. 53% claim no religious affiliation; 23% Latter-day Saints (Mormon). The average age of freshmen is 20; all undergraduates, 25.

Housing: 1214 students can be accommodated in college housing, which includes single-sex and coed dorms, on-campus apartments, and married student housing. In addition, there are special-interest houses, graduate students housing, and a new apartment/classroom/meeting place/food court complex. On-campus housing is available on a first-come and first-served basis. 92% of students commute. Alcohol is not permitted. All students may keep cars.

Activities: 1% of men belong to 3 local and 3 national fraternities; 1% of women belong to 2 local and 3 national sororities. There are 156 groups on campus, including and outdoor, band, cheerleading, chess, choir, chorale, chorus, computers, dance, debate, drama, drill team, ethnic, gay, honors, international, jazz band, marching band, musical theater, newspaper, opera, pep band, photography, political, professional, radio and TV, religious, social, student government, symphony, and yearbook. Popular campus events include International Festivals, Tribal Events, Rodeo and Concerts.

Sports: There are 5 intercollegiate sports for men and 8 for women, and 15 intramural sports for men and 14 for women. Facilities include playing fields, a field house, a gym, a recreation center, a swimming pool, tennis courts, an athletic arena, a fitness/wellness center, and facilities for bowling and billiards.

Disabled Students: All of the campus is accessible. Facilities include wheelchair ramps, elevators, special parking, specially equipped restrooms, lowered drinking fountains, lowered telephones, special housing.

Services: Counseling and information services are available, as is tutoring in every subject. There is a reader service for the blind, and remedial math, reading, and writing. Sign language interpreters and special equipment are available for hearing-impaired students.

Campus Safety and Security: Measures include 24-hour foot and vehicle patrol, emergency notification system, self-defense education, and security escort services. There are shuttle buses, emergency telephones, lighted pathways/sidewalks, controlled access to dorms/residences, and an e-mail bulletin alert service, Reverse 911 available in Pocatello.

Programs of Study: ISU confers B.A., B.S., B.A.G.S., B.A.S., B.A.T., B.B.A., B.F.A., B.M., B.M.E., B.U.S., H.B.A., H.B.B.A., H.B.F.A., B.S.H.S. and H.B.S. degrees. Associate, master's, and doctoral degrees are also awarded. Bachelor's degrees are awarded in BIOLOGICAL SCIENCE (biochemistry, biology/biological science, botany, ecology, microbiology, and zoology), BUSINESS (accounting, banking and finance, business administration and management, business data processing, human resources, insurance, management information systems, management science, and marketing/retailing/merchandising), COMMUNICATIONS AND THE ARTS (art, communications, communication science, dramatic arts, English, French, German, music, music performance, and Spanish), COMPUTER AND PHYSICAL SCIENCE (chemistry, computer programming, computer science, geology, geoscience, information sciences and systems, mathematics, physics, statistics, and web services), EDUCATION (early childhood education, elementary education, health education, health information management, music education, physical education, secondary education, and specific learning disabilities), ENGINEERING AND ENVIRONMENTAL DESIGN (aircraft mechanics, automotive technology, civil engineering, civil engineering technology, computer technology, construction technology, electrical/electronics engineering, electromechanical technology, energy management technology, environmental science, graphic arts technology, laser electro-optics technology, manufacturing technology, mechanical engineering, nuclear engineering, and welding engineering), HEALTH PROFESSIONS (dental hygiene, emergency medical technologies, health, health care administration, health science, medical laboratory science, medical technology, nursing, physical therapy assistant, radiological science, and speech pathology/audiology), SOCIAL SCIENCE (anthropology, culinary arts, dietetics, early childhood studies, economics, family/consumer studies, fire services administration, history, international studies, interpreter for the deaf, law enforcement and corrections, liberal arts/general studies, paralegal studies, philosophy, political science/government, psychology, social work, and sociology). Nursing, psychology and biology have the largest enrollments.

Required: Students must satisfy general education requirements in the areas of written and spoken English, math, biological and physical sciences, fine arts, literature, philosophy, U.S. and non-U.S. history, government/economics, foreign language, psychology, anthropology, and sociology. General education courses that fulfill specific goals must be taken. To graduate, students must complete 120 credit hours, including 24 to 50 in the major, with a minimum GPA of 2.0.

Special: ISU participates in the Idaho Dental Education Program and several other medical co-op programs. Students may cross-register through the Western Undergraduate Exchange. ISU also offers on- and off-campus work-study, study abroad in over 50 countries, dual and student-designed majors, internships, credit by challenge exam or for life/military/work experience, nondegree study, and a general studies degree. As many as 16 credits of correspondence study may be applied toward the bachelor's degree. ISU also offers 4 honor's bachelor's degrees, a teacher certification program, as well as a joint MS/BS degree in Chemistry. There are 10 national honor societies, a freshman honors program, and 4 departmental honors programs.

Faculty/Classroom: 53% of faculty are male; 47% are female. No introductory courses are taught by graduate students. The average class size in an introductory lecture is 19 and in a laboratory is 14.

Admissions: 92% of the 2013-2014 applicants were accepted. The SAT scores for the 2013-2014 freshman class were: Critical Reading--42% below 500, 32% between 500 and 599, 21% between 600 and 699, and 6% between 700 and 800; Math--36% below 500, 40% between 500 and 599, 21% between 600 and 699, and 3% between 700 and 800; Writing--40% below 500, 43% between 500 and 599, 14% between 600 and 699, and 3% between 700 and 800. The ACT scores were 44% below 21, 25% between 21 and 23, 18% between 24 and 26, 7% between 27 and 28, and 7% above 28. 23% of the current freshmen were in the top fifth of their class; 48% were in the top two fifths. 22 freshmen graduated first in their class.

Requirements: The ACT is required. The SAT is recommended. Both the SAT and ACT are accepted, but the ACT is preferred. Applicants must be graduates of an accredited secondary school or have a GED. They should prepare with 4 units of English, 3 each of math and science, 2.5 of social studies, 1.5 of health and humanities, and 1 of foreign language. A GPA of 2.3 is required. AP and CLEP credits are accepted.

Procedure: Freshmen are admitted fall, spring, and summer. Entrance exams should be taken mid junior year or early in the senior year. There are deferred admissions and rolling admissions plans. Applications should be filed by August 1 for fall entry; December 1 for spring entry, along with a $40 fee. Applications are accepted online.

Transfer: 500 transfer students enrolled in 2012-2013. Applicants must submit a final, official transcript from each college attended. At least 14 credit hours with a minimum GPA of 2.0 is required; students with fewer credit hours are subject to freshman admission requirements. Applicants with fewer than 25 credits must submit high school transcripts. 32 of 120 credits required for the bachelor's degree must be completed at ISU.

Visiting: There are regularly scheduled orientations for prospective students, including a meeting with an administration specialist and a campus tour. After the tour, students meet with a faculty member from their desired program of study. There are guides for informal visits, visitors may sit in on classes, and stay overnight. To schedule a visit, contact the Admissions Office.

Financial Aid: In 2013-2014, 64% of all full-time freshmen and 64% of continuing full-time students received some form of financial aid. 50% of all full-time freshmen and 48% of continuing full-time students received need-based aid. The average freshman award was $8,971. Need-based scholarships or need-based grants averaged $4,559 ; need-based self-help aid (loans and jobs) averaged $3,159; non-need-based athletic scholarships averaged $8,144; other non-need-based awards and non-need-based scholarships averaged $2,586; and $3,100 from other forms of aid. The average financial indebtedness of the 2013 graduate was $24,602. The FAFSA is required. The deadline for filing freshman financial aid applications for fall entry is February 20.

International Students: There are 499 international students enrolled. The school actively recruits these students. They must take the TOEFL with a minimum score of 500 on the paper-based TOEFL (PBT) or 61 on the Internet-based version (iBT), or take the IELTS. U.S. high school graduates with an A or B in English are exempted as are students who complete ELS level 112. Students from countries where English is the official language can be exempted depending on academic performance.

Computers: All students may access the system. There are no time limits. The fee is $35.

Graduates: From July 1, 2012 to June 30, 2013, 1118 bachelor's degrees were awarded. The most popular majors were nursing (11%), elementary education (5%), and human resources (5%). 144 companies recruited on campus in 2012-2013.

Admissions Contact: Matthew Kroeger, Director of Recruitment and Admissions. E-Mail: *admiss@isu.edu* Web: *www.isu.edu*

LEWIS-CLARK STATE COLLEGE — A-3

Lewiston, ID 83501-2698 — **(208) 792-2210**
(800) 933-LCSC; (208) 792-2876

Full-time: 960 men, 1315 women	**Faculty:** 134; IIB, --$
Part-time: 415 men, 805 women	**Ph.D.s:** 71%
Graduate: n/av	**Student/Faculty:** 17 to 1
Year: semesters, summer session	**Tuition:** $4592 ($11,882)
Application Deadline: open	**Room & Board:** $4360
Freshman Class: n/av	
SAT or ACT: required	

COMPETITIVE

Lewis-Clark State College, founded in 1893 and today part of the Idaho Higher Education System, offers programs in the arts and sciences, business, education, nursing, and preprofessional and technical training. It is named for the famed explorers, who once camped near what is now the campus. There are 8 undergraduate schools. In addition to regional accreditation, Lewis-Clark has baccalaureate program accreditation with AACSB, NASDTEC, NCATE, and NLN. The library contains 253,000 volumes, 53,000 microform items, and 7,000 audio/video tapes/CDs/DVDs, and subscribes to 4,000 periodicals including electronic. Computerized library services include interlibrary loans and database searching. Special learning facilities include a learning resource center, art gallery, planetarium, radio station, TV station, an educational technology center. The 44-acre campus is in an urban area 100 miles southeast of Spokane. Including any residence halls, there are 29 buildings. The figures in the above capsule and in this profile are approximate.

Student Life: 86% of undergraduates are from Idaho. Others are from 20 states, 30 foreign countries, and Canada. 82% are white. The average age of freshmen is 21; all undergraduates, 25. 46% do not continue beyond their first year; 28% remain to graduate.

Housing: 300 students can be accommodated in college housing, which includes single-sex and coed dorms, off-campus apartments, and married student housing. In addition, there are honors houses and language houses. On-campus housing is available on a first-come and first-served basis. 91% of students commute. Alcohol is not permitted. All students may keep cars.

Activities: There are no fraternities or sororities. There are 46 groups on campus, including and departmental., art, chess, choir, chorale, chorus, computers, dance, debate, drama, ethnic, honors, international, jazz band, literary magazine, musical theater, newspaper, orchestra, political, professional, radio and TV, religious, social, and student government. Popular campus events include Artists Series and Dogwood Festival.

Sports: There are 5 intercollegiate sports for men and 5 for women, and 8 intramural sports for men and 7 for women. Facilities include a gym, indoor tennis courts, and a baseball field.

Disabled Students: 99% of the campus is accessible. Facilities include wheelchair ramps, elevators, special parking, specially equipped restrooms, and special class scheduling.

Services: Counseling and information services are available, as is tutoring in every subject. There is a reader service for the blind, and remedial math, reading, and writing.

Campus Safety and Security: Measures include 24-hour foot and vehicle patrol, self-defense education, and security escort services. There are shuttle buses and lighted pathways/sidewalks.

Programs of Study: Lewis-Clark confers B.A., B.S., B. Applied Sc., B. Applied Tech., B.S.N., and B.S.W. degrees. Associate degrees are also awarded. Bachelor's degrees are awarded in BIOLOGICAL SCIENCE (biology/biological science), BUSINESS (business administration and management), COMMUNICATIONS AND THE ARTS (communications and English), COMPUTER AND PHYSICAL SCIENCE (chemistry, computer science, geoscience, mathematics, and natural sciences), EDUCATION (elementary education and secondary education), HEALTH PROFESSIONS (nursing), SOCIAL SCIENCE (criminal justice, history, liberal arts/general studies, physical fitness/movement, psychology, social science, and social work). Education, business, and nursing are the strongest academically and have the largest enrollments.

Required: Students must earn 128 credit hours, including 38 to 40 in the core curriculum and 48 in their major, with a minimum GPA of 2.0 to graduate.

Special: Lewis-Clark offers cooperative programs and cross-registration with 3 Idaho universities, on-campus internships, work-study programs, student-designed majors, nondegree study, and pass/fail options. The college grants credit for military experience. There are also between-semester and weekend academic programs, and flexible scheduling in a variety of programs. A 3-2 engineering degree is available at Boise or Idaho State Universities. There is 1 national honor society and a freshman honors program.

Faculty/Classroom: 58% of faculty are male; 42% are female. All teach undergraduates. No introductory courses are taught by graduate students. The average class size in an introductory lecture is 33 and in a laboratory is 25.

Admissions: 5 freshmen graduated first in their class.

Requirements: The SAT or ACT is required. Lewis-Clark has a liberal admissions policy, but students must be high school graduates or present a GED certificate. They must have fulfilled requirements in English, math, social and natural sciences, fine arts, and speech, with a minimum GPA of 2.0. A GPA of 2.0 is required. AP and CLEP credits are accepted.

Procedure: Freshmen are admitted to all sessions. Entrance exams should be taken before registration. There are early admissions, deferred admissions, and rolling admissions plans. Application deadlines are open. Application fee is $35. Applications are accepted online.

Transfer: In a recent year, 389 transfer students enrolled. Applicants who do not have a minimum GPA of 2.0 must submit standardized test scores. 32 of 128 credits required for the bachelor's degree must be completed at Lewis-Clark.

Visiting: There are regularly scheduled orientations for prospective students, including STAR (Student Advising and Registration), and Warrior Discovery Day. There are guides for informal visits, visitors may sit in on classes, and stay overnight. To schedule a visit, contact the Office of Recruitment and Retention.

Financial Aid: In a recent year, 68% of all full-time freshmen and 62% of continuing full-time students received some form of financial aid. 52% of all full-time freshmen and 50% of continuing full-time students received need-based aid. The average freshman award was $4,033. Need-based scholarships or need-based grants averaged $2,781 ($4,500 maximum); need-based self-help aid (loans and jobs) averaged $2,652 ($6,625 maximum); non-need-based athletic scholarships averaged $4,485 ($8,562 maximum); and other non-need-based awards and non-need-based scholarships averaged $2,873. 10% of undergraduate students work part-time. Average annual earnings from campus work are $1360. Lewis-Clark is a member of CSS. The FAFSA is required. The priority date for freshman financial aid applications for fall entry is March 1.

International Students: There are 94 international students enrolled. The school actively recruits these students. They must take the TOEFL.

Computers: All students may access the system 7 days a week. There are no time limits and no fees.

Graduates: In a recent year, 299 bachelor's degrees were awarded. The

most popular majors were business (25%), justice studies (15%), and nursing (14%). Of the 2010 graduating class, 8% were enrolled in graduate school within 6 months of graduation.

Admissions Contact: Director of Admission and Market Development. E-Mail: *admissions@lcsc.edu* Web: *www.lcsc.edu*

NORTHWEST NAZARENE UNIVERSITY A-5

Nampa, ID 83686 (208) 467-8950
(877) NNU-4-YOU; (208) 467-8645

Full-time: 471 men, 683 women **Faculty:** n/av
Part-time: 191 men, 132 women **Ph.D.s:** 72%
Graduate: 292 men, 463 women **Student/Faculty:** 14 to 1
Year: semesters, summer session **Tuition:** $24,275
Application Deadline: August 15 **Room & Board:** n/a
Freshman Class: 1099 applied, 1150 accepted, 271 enrolled
SAT CR/M/W: 510/540/510 **ACT:** 22 **NONCOMPETITIVE**

Northwest Nazarene University, a comprehensive Christian university, offers over 60 areas of study, 19 master's degrees in seven different disciplines and one doctoral degree. In addition to its 85-acre campus located in Nampa, Idaho, the University also offers programs online as well as in Boise, Idaho Falls, McCall, Twin Falls and in cooperation with programs in 10 countries. Founded in 1913, the University now serves over 2,000 undergraduate and graduate students, more than 6,000 continuing education students, and 2,300 high school students through the concurrent credit program. There are 6 undergraduate schools and 7 graduate schools. In addition to regional accreditation, NNU has baccalaureate program accreditation with ACBSP, CSWE, NASM, and NCATE. Computerized library services include interlibrary loans, database searching, Internet access, and Wi-Fi capability. Special learning facilities include an art gallery, an educational media center. The 85-acre campus is in a small town 20 miles west of Boise. Including any residence halls, there are 38 buildings.

Student Life: 57% of undergraduates are from Idaho. Others are from 30 states, 28 foreign countries, and Canada. 73% are White. 66% are Protestant; 12% claim no religious affiliation. The average age of freshmen is 19; all undergraduates, 22. 28% do not continue beyond their first year; 48% remain to graduate.

Housing: College-sponsored housing includes single-sex dorms, on-campus apartments, and married student housing. On-campus housing is guaranteed for all 4 years. 51% of students live on campus; of those, 80% remain on campus on weekends. Alcohol is not permitted. All students may keep cars.

Activities: There are no fraternities or sororities. There are 50 groups on campus, including American marketing association, art, band, cheerleading, choir, chorale, chorus, computers, debate, drama, environmental, ethnic, film, forensics, honors, international, jazz band, literary magazine, musical theater, newspaper, orchestra, pep band, photography, political, professional, radio and TV, religious, social, social service, student government, Students in free enterprise/enactus, symphony, and yearbook. Popular campus events include Welcome Week, Week One and Spiritual Emphasis Week.

Sports: There are 6 intercollegiate sports for men and 6 for women, and 7 intramural sports for men and 7 for women. Facilities include baseball field, 2 soccer fields, outdoor basketball, tennis, and sand volleyball courts, a track-and-field facility, a field house, a park, and a softball field.

Disabled Students: Facilities include wheelchair ramps, elevators, special parking, specially equipped restrooms, special class scheduling, lowered drinking fountains, lowered telephones, special housing, and alternate testing and evaluation methods.

Services: Counseling and information services are available, as is tutoring in every subject. There is remedial math, reading, and writing.

Campus Safety and Security: Measures include 24-hour foot and vehicle patrol, emergency notification system, and security escort services. There are emergency telephones, lighted pathways/sidewalks, a professional security company, student lock-up-unlock and walk-around-campus teams, and a city police substation.

Programs of Study: NNU confers B.A., and B.S. degrees. Master's degrees are also awarded. Bachelor's degrees are awarded in BIOLOGICAL SCIENCE (biochemistry, biology/biological science, cell biology, ecology, molecular biology, and neurosciences), BUSINESS (accounting, business administration and management, and recreation and leisure services), COMMUNICATIONS AND THE ARTS (art, ceramic art and design, communications, English, graphic design, journalism, music, painting, printmaking, Spanish, and speech/debate/rhetoric), COMPUTER AND PHYSICAL SCIENCE (chemistry, computer science, digital arts/technology, mathematics, and physics), EDUCATION (art education, Christian education, education of the exceptional child, elementary education, English education, health education, mathematics education, music education, physical education, recreation education, science education, secondary education, and social science education), ENGINEERING AND ENVIRONMENTAL DESIGN (engineering, engineering physics, and pre-engineering), HEALTH PROFESSIONS (nursing, preallied health, predentistry, premedicine, preoptometry, prepharmacy, prephysical therapy, and preveterinary science), SOCIAL SCIENCE (biblical languages, history, interdisciplinary studies, international studies, liberal arts/general studies, ministries, missions, pastoral studies, philosophy and religion, political science/government, prelaw, psychology, social work, and youth ministry). Nursing, engineering, biology, chemistry, business and graphic design are the strongest academically. Nursing, engineering, biology/chemistry and business have the largest enrollments.

Required: All students must complete 124 semester credits, of which 43 must be upper division. Students must show competency in communication and language skills, have a 2.0 GPA, demonstrate math proficiency, complete a major field of study, and take a comprehensive exam. In addition, each student must complete general education requirements, which are divided into three categories: abilities (17 credits of English, communications, kinesiology, math, and humanities courses), contextual disciplines (15 credits of bible, theology, philosophy, and history courses as well as a cross-cultural experience), and explorations (23 credits of upper-division bible literature or theology, humanities, science, and social sciences electives). The number of hours required varies per major, as do senior internships and projects.

Special: NNU offers cross-registration with other Nazarene schools and study abroad in 14 countries. The university also offers internships, which are required in many majors, a work-study program, a general studies degree, dual and student-designed majors, and credit for military experience (Army ROTC program). Adult and Professional programs are offered in business, education and religion. There are 4 national honor societies, a freshman honors program, and 3 departmental honors programs.

Faculty/Classroom: 57% of faculty are male; 43% are female. No introductory courses are taught by graduate students.

Admissions: The SAT scores for the 2013-2014 freshman class were: Critical Reading--36% below 500, 38% between 500 and 599, 21% between 600 and 699, and 5% between 700 and 800; Math--32% below 500, 46% between 500 and 599, 20% between 600 and 699, and 2% between 700 and 800; Writing--45% below 500, 35% between 500 and 599, 18% between 600 and 699, and 2% between 700 and 800. The ACT scores were 36% below 21, 26% between 21 and 23, 22% between 24 and 26, 9% between 27 and 28, and 7% above 28. There were 43 National Merit finalists. 10 freshmen graduated first in their class.

Requirements: The SAT or ACT is required. Applicants should be graduates of an accredited secondary school; the GED may also be accepted. For standard admission, students must fulfill 2 of the 3 following requirements: graduate with a 2.5 (or higher) GPA on a 4.0 scale, rank in the top 50% of their graduating class, or have an ACT composite score of 18 or a combined score of 870 on the Math and Critical Reasoning sections of the SAT. Provisional admission may be available for students who do not meet the above requirements. Applicants should prepare with 4 years of English, 3 each of math, science, and history or social science, and 2 of foreign language. NNU requires applicants to be in the upper 50% of their class. A GPA of 2.5 is required. AP and CLEP credits are accepted.

Procedure: Freshmen are admitted fall, spring, and summer. Entrance exams should be taken early in the senior year. There are early admissions and rolling admissions plans. Early decision applications should be filed by December 15; regular applications, by August 15 for fall entry; and December 15 for winter entry, along with a $25 fee. Notification is sent on a rolling basis. Applications are accepted online.

Transfer: 78 transfer students enrolled in 2012-2013. Students wishing to transfer to NNU must have completed 28 college or university semester credits and have a cumulative GPA of at least 2.0 and be in good academic standing at their previous institution. Students below the required GPA may be accepted provisionally at the discretion of the Admissions Committee. Students who have earned the equivalent of 12 semester credits may be admitted as transfer students. Official transcripts from all colleges previously attended must be submitted. 24 of 124 credits required for the bachelor's degree must be completed at NNU.

Visiting: There are regularly scheduled orientations for prospective students, including overnight stay in a dorm. campus tour, class attendance, financial and admission counseling, meetings with professor and coaches, and music and athletic try-outs. . There are guides for informal visits, visitors may sit in on classes, and stay overnight. To schedule a visit, contact the Campus Visit Coordinator at (208) 467-8000.

Financial Aid: In 2013-2014, 98% of all full-time freshmen received some form of financial aid. 70% of all full-time freshmen and % of continuing full-time students received need-based aid. The average freshman award was $17,934. Need-based scholarships or need-based grants averaged $3,990 ($8,100 maximum); need-based self-help aid (loans and jobs) averaged $3,872; and non-need-based athletic scholarships averaged $6,257 ($21,632 maximum). 66% of undergraduate students work part-time. Average annual earnings from campus work are $883. The average financial indebtedness of the 2013 graduate was $29,313. The FAFSA is required. The priority date for freshman financial aid applications for fall entry is March 1.

International Students: There are 28 international students enrolled.

The school actively recruits these students. They must take the TOEFL with a minimum score of 500 on the paper-based TOEFL (PBT) or 61 on the Internet-based version (iBT). They must also take the SAT or ACT, scoring 18.

Computers: All students may access the system. There are no time limits and no fees.

Graduates: From July 1, 2012 to June 30, 2013, 280 bachelor's degrees were awarded. The most popular majors were business (19%), nursing (16%), and applied studies (9%). 100 companies recruited on campus in 2012-2013. In an average class, 49% graduate in 6 years or less.

Admissions Contact: Mike Marston, Director of Admissions. E-Mail: *admissions@nnu.edu* Web: *www.nnu.edu*

THE COLLEGE OF IDAHO — A-5

Caldwell, ID 83605 — (208) 459-5305; (800) 224-3246; (208) 459-5757

Full-time: 418 men, 585 women	**Faculty:** 75
Part-time: 20 men, 19 women	**Ph.D.s:** 85%
Graduate: 2 men, 15 women	**Student/Faculty:** 12 to 1
Year: other	**Tuition:** $19,750
Application Deadline: July 15	**Room & Board:** $8252
Freshman Class: 1388 applied, 901 accepted, 292 enrolled	
SAT CR/M/W: 545/540/525	**ACT:** 24 **VERY COMPETITIVE**

The College of Idaho, founded in 1891, is a private institution offering degree programs in liberal arts education and the sciences. The college runs on a 13-4-13 calendar, with a 6-week intercession. There are no undergraduate schools. In addition to regional accreditation, C of I has baccalaureate program accreditation with NASDTEC. Computerized library services include interlibrary loans, database searching, Internet access, and Wi-Fi capability. Special learning facilities include an art gallery, natural history museum, planetarium, A rock and mineral collection and the Robert E. Smylie Archives. The 50-acre campus is in a small town 25 miles west of Boise. Including any residence halls, there are 21 buildings.

Student Life: 83% of undergraduates are from Idaho. Others are from 28 states, 53 foreign countries, and Canada. 55% are White; 14% Hispanic; 11% Foreign. The average age of freshmen is 18; all undergraduates, 20. 17% do not continue beyond their first year; 64% remain to graduate.

Housing: 668 students can be accommodated in college housing, which includes single-sex and coed dorms, on-campus apartments, and off-campus apartments. an honors residence hall and special lifestyle floors (substance free, etc). On-campus housing is guaranteed for the freshman year only, is available on a first-come, first-served basis, and is available on a lottery system for upperclassmen. 62% of students live on campus; of those, 65% remain on campus on weekends. All students may keep cars.

Activities: 15% of men belong to 3 national fraternities; 22% of women belong to 1 local and 3 national sororities. There are 33 groups on campus, including international indoor soccer, math club and men's lacrosse, art, band, cheerleading, chess, choir, chorale, chorus, Coyote cinemas, dance, debate, drama, environmental, ethnic, forensics, gay, honors, international, jazz band, literary magazine, musical theater, newspaper, pep band, political, professional, religious, social, social service, student government, and yearbook. Popular campus events include Spring Fling, Coyote Connection, Taste of Harvest and Winterfest.

Sports: There are 8 intercollegiate sports for men and 10 for women, and 7 intramural sports for men and 7 for women. Facilities include The J.A. Albertson Activities Center is the home of The College of Idaho athletics and the center for student recreation on campus. Built in 1991, it has been hailed as one of the finest small college gymnasiums in the United States. The Activities Center serves as the arena for all C of I's men's and women's basketball and volleyball home contests, and has been the host of numerous IDHSAA basketball tournaments. In addition to basketball and volleyball, the Activities Center has a full service weight room, athletic training facility, a 25-yard swimming pool, dance room, and a rock climbing wall. The College plays its home football and soccer games at 5,000 seat Simplot Stadium, two blocks from campus - a facility that is maintained by the City of Caldwell. The College has also partnered with the City of Caldwell on Wolfe Field, the only synthetic turf baseball field in Idaho. Home tennis matches are played on campus on the all-weather Laura Moore Cunningham Courts, while softball games are played at Symms Fields on the C of I campus.

Disabled Students: 95% of the campus is accessible. Facilities include wheelchair ramps, elevators, special parking, specially equipped restrooms, lowered drinking fountains, special housing.

Services: Counseling and information services are available, as is tutoring in most subjects.

Campus Safety and Security: Measures include 24-hour foot and vehicle patrol, emergency notification system, self-defense education, and security escort services. There are emergency telephones, lighted pathways/sidewalks, controlled access to dorms/residences, electronic identification cards to all dorms and certain buildings throughout the campus.

Programs of Study: C of I confers B.A., and B.S. degrees. Master's degrees are also awarded. Bachelor's degrees are awarded in AGRICULTURE (environmental studies), BIOLOGICAL SCIENCE (biology/biological science), BUSINESS (accounting, business administration and management, and international economics), COMMUNICATIONS AND THE ARTS (art, creative writing, literature, music, music theory and composition, Spanish, and theatre arts), COMPUTER AND PHYSICAL SCIENCE (chemistry and mathematics), EDUCATION (education, elementary education, and physical education), ENGINEERING AND ENVIRONMENTAL DESIGN (preengineering), HEALTH PROFESSIONS (clinical science, exercise science, health, nursing, pharmacy, and speech pathology/audiology), SOCIAL SCIENCE (anthropology, history, philosophy, political science/government, psychology, and religion). Biology, business, and psychology have the largest enrollments.

Required: In order to earn the BA or BS degree, students must complete 124 credits, to include at least one major and three minors, covering all four PEAKs: Humanities and Fine Arts, Natural Sciences and Mathematics, Social Sciences and History, Professional Studies and Enhancement. Beyond the majors and minors chosen from the four PEAKs above, students must complete the following: The First-Year Seminar- This requirement covers the essential elements of academic inquiry: analytical reading, critical thinking, and well-reasoned writing Pre-modern Civilization- This requirement provides students with exposure to pre-1800 historical developments that form the foundation of modern systems of thought and ideals of education, thus conveying essential knowledge of the basic dimensions of Western or World intellectual cultures Liberal Arts Expectations- students are expected to engage in each of the areas listed below as part of their academic program •Writing •History •Mathematics •Natural Science •Foreign Language •Social Science •Literature •Philosophy/Religion •Fine Arts •Cultural Diversity GPA Requirements- •A grade-point average of at least 2.00 (a) in The College of Idaho record and (b) in the entire undergraduate record. •A grade-point average of at least 2.00 in the major field (a) in The College of Idaho record and (b) in the entire undergraduate record. •A grade-point average of at least 2.00 in all minors.

Special: Co-op Programs: •Idaho State University Dual Degree Doctoral Program in Pharmacy (BS/Pharm.D.) •Idaho State University Dual Degree Program in Nursing (BS/BS) •Idaho State University Dual Degree in Medical Laboratory Science (BS/BS) •Idaho State University Speech-Language Pathology and Audiology (BS/BS) •University of Idaho Juris Doctor (BA or BS/JD) Study Abroad: In January 2013, faculty are leading month-long study courses in Australia, London, and Idaho's Sawtooth Mountains. The College of Idaho offers two types of off-campus study opportunities: •C of I study programs led by faculty for our students •Foreign study opportunities for individual students offered by partner institutions. During the past few years, C of I faculty have led study tours to such places as Australia, China, Florida, France, Greece, Italy, London, Mexico, and Peru. C of I students also can study for a semester or more in more than 57 countries through our partner institutions. Approved Partner Programs for Study Abroad: •Arcadia University-Center for Education Abroad •Brethren Colleges Abroad (BCA) •Council Study Centers (CIEE) •International Studies Abroad •Schiller International University •School for International Training (SIT) •University Studies Abroad Consortium •University of Idaho

Faculty/Classroom: 55% of faculty are male; 45% are female. All teach undergraduates. No introductory courses are taught by graduate students.

Admissions: 65% of the 2013-2014 applicants were accepted. The SAT scores for the 2013-2014 freshman class were: Critical Reading--33% below 500, 30% between 500 and 599, 23% between 600 and 699, and 13% between 700 and 800; Math--33% below 500, 38% between 500 and 599, 27% between 600 and 699, and 3% between 700 and 800; Writing--39% below 500, 35% between 500 and 599, 24% between 600 and 699, and 2% between 700 and 800. The ACT scores were 20% below 21, 23% between 21 and 23, 27% between 24 and 26, 14% between 27 and 28, and 16% above 28. 46% of the current freshmen were in the top fifth of their class; 80% were in the top two fifths.

Requirements: The SAT or ACT is required. The ACT Optional Writing test is also required. Freshmen applicants who have graduated from high school, presented acceptable GED scores in lieu of a high school record, or met the college's home school policy (see section on home school applicants), and transfer applicants whose college record is of sufficient quality, may be admitted to the college in clear standing. Students not meeting the minimum standard for regular or conditional admission may be admitted to the college on a probational basis. Students may begin the application process any time after the last semester of their junior year in high school. In order to be considered for admission, students should submit the following materials to the Admission Office, The College of Idaho, 2112 Cleveland Blvd., Caldwell, Idaho 83605: •An application for admission. •An official high school transcript •A transcript of any college work attempted. •If you are considered for the Boone Program, you will need an on-campus interview with the Dean of Students and Dean of Enrollment. •Official ACT or SAT test scores. While there is no required pattern of high school study necessary for admission, the following combination is strongly recommended: •English -- 4 years •Language -- 3 years •History and Social Science -- 4 years •Laboratory Science -- 3 years •Mathematics -- 4 years AP credits are accepted. Important factors in the admissions decision are leadership record, advanced placement or honors courses, evidence of special talent, recommendations by school officials, personality/intangible qualities, extracurricular activities record, recommendations by alumni, geographical diversity, ability to finance college education, and parents or siblings attended your school.

Procedure: Freshmen are admitted fall and spring. Entrance exams should be taken by the fall of the senior year. There are early admissions, deferred admissions, and rolling admissions plans. Early decision applications should be filed by November 15; regular applications, by July 15 for fall entry; December 1 for winter entry; and January 15 for spring entry. Notification of early decision is sent December 15; regular decision, March 15. Applications are accepted online.

Transfer: 52 transfer students enrolled in 2012-2013. Students who have already completed at least 28 semester credits or 42 quarter credits of continuous enrollment at accredited colleges or universities will be considered for admission on the basis of that academic record (rather than the secondary school record) provided they have a cumulative GPA of 2.0 or better. Transfer applicants should submit an application for admission and an official high school transcript, as well as official transcripts from all post-secondary institutions attended. A one to two page essay/personal statement and faculty evaluation is required. The transfer application deadline is August 1. Any applications submitted after this date will be considered by petition only. 30 of 124 credits required for the bachelor's degree must be completed at C of I.

Visiting: There are regularly scheduled orientations for prospective students, Student visits include an overnight stay with student hosts, class visitations, personal appointments with financial aid counselors, professors, and coaches, social events, and a campus tour. Individual tours can also be arranged. There are guides for informal visits, visitors may sit in on classes, and stay overnight. To schedule a visit, contact the Visit and Event Coordinator at visitcenter@collegeofidaho.com.

Financial Aid: In 2013-2014, 98% of all full-time freshmen and 96% of continuing full-time students received some form of financial aid. 76% of all full-time freshmen and 71% of continuing full-time students received need-based aid. The average freshman award was $24,707. Need-based scholarships or need-based grants averaged $7,630; need-based self-help aid (loans and jobs) averaged $3,969; non-need-based athletic scholarships averaged $3,676; and other non-need-based awards and non-need-based scholarships averaged $13,304. 40% of undergraduate students work part-time. Average annual earnings from campus work are $792. The average financial indebtedness of the 2013 graduate was $27,000. The FAFSA and the college's own financial statement are required. The priority date for freshman financial aid applications for fall entry is February 15.

International Students: There are 107 international students enrolled. The school actively recruits these students. They must take the TOEFL with a minimum score of 550 on the paper-based TOEFL (PBT) or 79 on the Internet-based version (iBT), IELTS language proficiency. They must also take the SAT or ACT.

Computers: All students may access the system at designated times in computer labs; 24 hours in residence halls. There are no time limits and no fees.

Graduates: From July 1, 2012 to June 30, 2013, 191 bachelor's degrees were awarded. The most popular majors were business (23%), biology (and related programs) (20%), and history (9%). 3 companies recruited on campus in 2012-2013. In an average class, 50% graduate in 4 years or less, 60% graduate in 5 years or less, and 64% graduate in 6 years or less.

Admissions Contact: Brian Bava, Dean of Enrollment Management. E-Mail: *admissions@collegeofidaho.edu* Web: *www.collegeofidaho.edu*

UNIVERSITY OF IDAHO — A-3

Moscow, ID 83844 — (208) 885-6326; (888) 884-3246; (208) 885-9119

Full-time: 4260 men, 3667 women	**Faculty:** n/av
Part-time: 717 men, 812 women	**Ph.D.s:** 74%
Graduate: 1349 men, 1029 women	**Student/Faculty:** n/av
Year: semesters, summer session	**Tuition:** $6524 ($20,662)
Application Deadline: August 1	**Room & Board:** $8034
Freshman Class: 5614 applied, 5172 accepted, 1630 enrolled	
SAT CR/M/W: 520/520/500	**ACT:** 22 — **COMPETITIVE**

The University of Idaho, founded in 1889 as a land-grant institution, offers programs in art, architecture, agriculture, business and economics, education, engineering, letters and science, and natural resources, forestry, wildlife, and range sciences. There are 8 undergraduate schools and one graduate school. In addition to regional accreditation, U Idaho has baccalaureate program accreditation with AACSB, ABET, ADA, ASLA, CSAB, FIDER, NAAB, NASAD, NASM, NCATE, NRPA, and SAF. The 2 libraries contain 1.4 million volumes, 2.6 million microform items, and 11,329 audio/video tapes/CDs/DVDs, and subscribe to 25,475 periodicals including electronic. Computerized library services include interlibrary loans, database searching, Internet access, and Wi-Fi capability. Special learning facilities include an art gallery, radio station, TV station, an electron microscopy center, an IQ-Station (virtual reality tool) a lab animal facility, research institutes for water resources, geospacial lab, microelectronics, and aquaculture, university farms, experimental forests, and an arboretum and botanical garden. The 1585-acre campus is in a small town 90 miles southeast of Spokane, Washington. Including any residence halls, there are 146 buildings.

Student Life: 74% of undergraduates are from Idaho. Others are from 47 states, 40 foreign countries, and Canada. 98% are from public schools. 79% are White. The average age of freshmen is 18; all undergraduates, 22. 21% do not continue beyond their first year; 54% remain to graduate.

Housing: 2246 students can be accommodated in college housing, which includes single-sex and coed dorms, on-campus apartments, and married student housing. In addition, there are honors houses, special-interest houses, fraternity houses, sorority houses, alcohol-free, smoke-free, and living-learning communities. On-campus housing is guaranteed for all 4 years. 61% of students commute. Alcohol is not permitted. All students may keep cars.

Activities: 20% of men belong to 17 national fraternities; 20% of women belong to 10 national sororities. There are 191 groups on campus, including art, band, cheerleading, choir, chorale, chorus, computers, dance, drama, drill team, environmental, ethnic, film, gay, honors, international, jazz band, literary magazine, marching band, musical theater, newspaper, opera, orchestra, pep band, photography, political, professional, radio and TV, religious, social, social service, student government, and symphony. Popular campus events include Lionel Hampton Jazz Festival, the Borah Symposium, and Palouse fest, Homecoming, Mom's Weekend and Dad's Weekend.

Sports: There are 6 intercollegiate sports for men and 8 for women, and 15 intramural sports for men and 16 for women. Facilities include an activity center, a 16,000-seat domed stadium for basketball and football games, indoor and outdoor tracks, a 2-pool swim center, 3 gyms, a 500-seat auditorium, an 18-hole championship golf course, tennis, racquetball, and handball courts, and a student recreation center with a 55-foot climbing wall.

Disabled Students: 87% of the campus is accessible. Facilities include wheelchair ramps, elevators, special parking, specially equipped restrooms, special class scheduling, lowered drinking fountains, lowered telephones, special housing.

Services: Counseling and information services are available, as is tutoring in most subjects. There is a reader service for the blind, and remedial math and writing. There are centers for academic advising and counseling and testing.

Campus Safety and Security: Measures include 24-hour foot and vehicle patrol, emergency notification system, and self-defense education. There are shuttle buses, emergency telephones, lighted pathways/sidewalks, controlled access to dorms/residences, the city police department has a campus division, and there is a violence prevention programs office.

Programs of Study: U Idaho confers B.A., B.F.A., B.G.S., B.I.D., B.Mus., B.S., B.S.A.L.S., B.S.A.V.S., B.S.Ag.Econ., B.S.Ag.Ed., B.S.Ag.L.S., B.S.Arch., B.S.Art.Ed., B.S.B.A.E., B.S.Biochem., B.S.Bus., B.S.C.E., B.S.C.S., B.S.Ch.E., B.S.Comp.E., B.S.Dan.,B.S.E.E., B.S.Ecol.Cons.Biol., B.S.Ed., B.S.Env.S., B.S.Erly.Chdhd.Dev.Ed., B.S.F.C.S., B.S.F.S. ,B.S.Fire.Ecol.Mgmt., B.S.Fish.Res., B.S.For.Prod., B.S.For.Res., B.S.I.S., B.S.L.A., B.S.M.B.B., B.S.M.E., B.S.M.S.E., B.S.Microbiol., B.S.P.E., B.S.Rangeland Ecol.-Mgt., B.S.Rec., B.S.Res.Rc.,B.S.Tech. and B.S.Wildl.Res. degrees. Master's and doctoral degrees are also awarded. Bachelor's degrees are awarded in AGRICULTURE (agricultural business management, agricultural communications, agricultural economics, agricultural mechanics, agricultural sciences, agriculture, animal science, conservation and regulation, dairy science, fishing and fisheries, forestry production and processing, forestry and related sciences, horticulture, natural resource management, plant science, range/farm management, soil science, and wildlife management), BIOLOGICAL SCIENCE (biochemistry, biology/biological science, botany, microbiology, and molecular biology), BUSINESS (accounting, business administration and management, business economics, human resources, management information systems, marketing management, marketing/retailing/merchandising, operations management, recreation and leisure services, and sports management), COMMUNICATIONS AND THE ARTS (advertising, animation, apparel design, applied art, applied music, art, broadcasting, creative writing, dance, design, digital communications, dramatic arts, English, English Writing, fine arts, French, journalism, music, music history and appreciation, music performance, music theory and composition, musical theater, public relations, Spanish, studio art, telecommunications, and theater management), COMPUTER AND PHYSICAL SCIENCE (applied mathematics, chemistry, computer science, digital arts/technology, geology, information sciences and systems, mathematics, and physics), EDUCATION (agricultural education, art education, athletic training, business education, education, education administration, elementary education, foreign languages education, general studies, industrial arts education, mathematics education, music education, physical education, recreation education, science education, secondary education, special education, and technical education), ENGINEERING AND ENVIRONMENTAL DESIGN (agricultural engineering, architecture, bioengineering, biomedical engineering, chemical engineering, civil engineering, computer engineering, electrical and computer engineering, electrical/electronics engineering, engineering, environmental engineering, environmental science, geological engineering, interior design, landscape architecture/design, materials engineering, and mechanical engineering), HEALTH PROFESSIONS (clinical science, exercise science, medical technology, movement science, and veterinary science), SOCIAL SCIENCE (American studies, anthropology, child care/child and family studies, counseling/psychology, criminal justice, economics, family/consumer studies, food science, geography, history, human development, interdisciplinary studies, international relations, international studies, Latin American studies, parks and recreation management, philosophy, political science/government, psychology, rural economics, sociology, and textiles and clothing). engineering, natural resources, and business are the strongest academically. Business, engineering, and psychology have the largest enrollments.

Required: To graduate, students must complete at least 120 credit hours (128 for some majors), including 36 in upper-division courses and 40 in the major, with a minimum GPA of 2.0. The core curriculum requires a total of 33 to 36 credits in the following categories: communication, natural and applied science, mathematics, statistics, or computer science, humanities/social sciences, and an international course.

Special: UI offers cooperative programs and cross-registration with Washington State and Idaho State Universities, internships, extensive study-abroad programs, work-study programs, B.A.-B.S. degrees, dual and student-designed majors, a general studies degree, credit for life and work experience, nondegree study, and pass/fail options. There are 11 national honor societies and a freshman honors program.

Faculty/Classroom: 65% of faculty are male; 35% are female. 90% teach undergraduates, 75% do research, and 95% do both. No introductory courses are taught by graduate students. The average class size in an introductory lecture is 30; in a laboratory is 17; and in a regular course is 24.

Admissions: 92% of the 2013-2014 applicants were accepted. The SAT scores for the 2013-2014 freshman class were: Critical Reading--40% below 500, 39% between 500 and 599, 17% between 600 and 699, and 4% between 700 and 800; Math--39% below 500, 36% between 500 and 599, 21% between 600 and 699, and 4% between 700 and 800; Writing--46% below 500, 39% between 500 and 599, 13% between 600 and 699, and 2% between 700 and 800. The ACT scores were 31% below 21, 27% between 21 and 23, 20% between 24 and 26, 11% between 27 and 28, and 12% above 28. 34% of the current freshmen were in the top fifth of their class; 61% were in the top two fifths. There were 25 National Merit finalists. 1 freshman graduated first in the class.

Requirements: Either SAT or ACT test are required. Students from accredited high schools must have graduated and completed at least 8 credits in English, 6 each in math and natural science, 5 in social science, 3 in electives, and 2 in humanities/language. Home-schooled students, students from nonaccredited high schools, and GED students will have their application for admission referred to a committee for a decision. A GPA of 2.5 is required. AP and CLEP credits are accepted.

Procedure: Freshmen are admitted to all sessions. Entrance exams should be taken during the junior or senior year of high school. There are deferred admissions and rolling admissions plans. Applications should be filed by August 1 for fall entry; December 15 for spring entry; and May 1 for summer entry, along with a $60 fee. Notification is sent on a rolling basis. Applications are accepted online.

Transfer: 665 transfer students enrolled in 2012-2013. Applicants must have completed at least 14 credit hours with a cumulative GPA of at least 2.0. Students transferring from out-of-state schools into the College of Engineering must have a minimum cumulative GPA of 2.8. 32 of 120 credits required for the bachelor's degree must be completed at U Idaho.

Visiting: There are regularly scheduled orientations for prospective students, including a visit with faculty and financial aid personnel, a tour of campus, and an overnight stay in the dorms or Greek houses and a visit to the Recreation Center. There are guides for informal visits, visitors may sit in on classes, and stay overnight. To schedule a visit, contact the Office of Admissions and Campus Visits.

Financial Aid: In 2013-2014, 66% of all full-time freshmen and 65% of continuing full-time students received some form of financial aid. 53% of all full-time freshmen and 49% of continuing full-time students received need-based aid. The average freshman award was $13,670. Need-based scholarships or need-based grants averaged $4,575; need-based self-help aid (loans and jobs) averaged $5,971; non-need-based athletic scholarships averaged $18,220; and other non-need-based awards and non-need-based scholarships averaged $3,033. 88% of undergraduate students work part-time. The average financial indebtedness of the 2013 graduate was $25,691. U Idaho is a member of CSS. The FAFSA is required. The deadline for filing freshman financial aid applications for fall entry is February 15.

International Students: There are 320 international students enrolled. The school actively recruits these students. They must take the TOEFL with a minimum score of 550 on the paper-based TOEFL (PBT) or 79 on the Internet-based version (iBT). They must also take the SAT or ACT.

Computers: All students may access the system 23 hours a day. There are no time limits and no fees.

Graduates: From July 1, 2012 to June 30, 2013, 1981 bachelor's degrees were awarded. The most popular majors were business/marketing (10%), education (10%), and psychology (9%). 250 companies recruited on campus in 2012-2013. In an average class, 1% graduate in 3 years or less, 29% graduate in 4 years or less, 52% graduate in 5 years or less, and 54% graduate in 6 years or less.

Admissions Contact: Cezar Mesquita, Director, Admissions . E-Mail: *admappl@uidaho.edu* Web: *www.uidaho.edu/admissions*

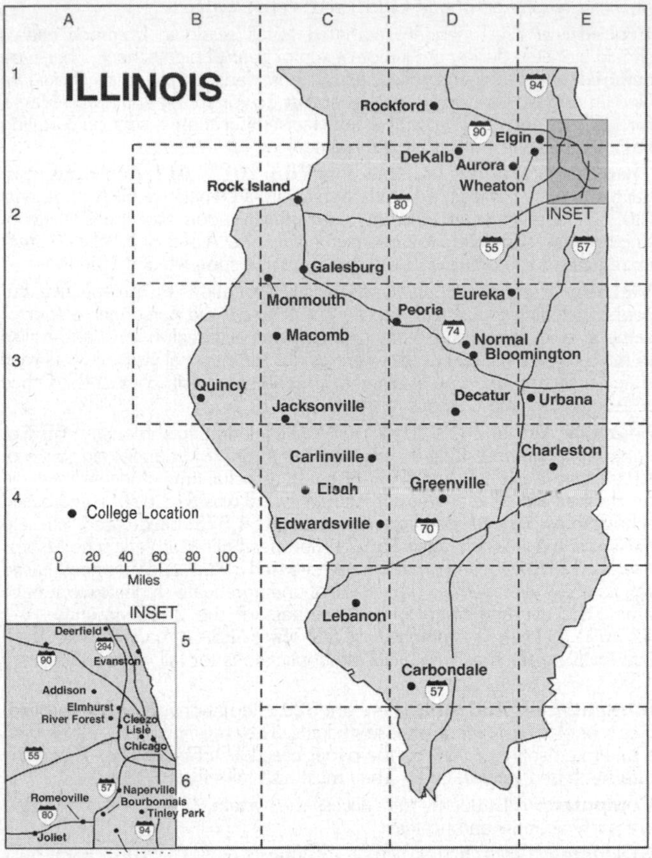

AUGUSTANA COLLEGE C-2

Rock Island, IL 61201 (309) 794-7341
(800) 798-8100; (309) 794-7422

Full-time: 1075 men, 1457 women
Part-time: 11 men, 8 women
Graduate: n/av
Year: quarters, summer session
Application Deadline: open
Faculty: 178; IIB, -$
Ph.D.s: 95%
Student/Faculty: 12 to 1
Tuition: $34,614
Room & Board: $8784
Freshman Class: 4230 applied, 2912 accepted, 656 enrolled
SAT: recommended **ACT:** 26 **HIGHLY COMPETITIVE**

Augustana College, founded in 1860, is a private liberal arts institution affiliated with the Evangelical Lutheran Church in America. In addition to regional accreditation, Augustana has baccalaureate program accreditation with NASM and NCATE. The 3 libraries contain 209,688 volumes, 78,666 microform items, and 2,748 audio/video tapes/CDs/DVDs, and subscribe to 3,067 periodicals including electronic. Computerized library services include interlibrary loans, database searching, Internet access, and Wi-Fi capability. Special learning facilities include an art gallery, natural history museum, radio station, a preschool, a center for communicative disorders, a geology museum, a planetarium/observatory, a U.S. Geological Survey map repository, a Swedish immigration research center, 3 outdoor environmental labs, and an educational technology building. The 115-acre campus is in a suburban area 165 miles west of Chicago. Including any residence halls, there are 47 buildings.

Student Life: 85% of undergraduates are from Illinois. Others are from 31 states, 24 foreign countries, and Canada. 79% are White. 34% are Protestant; 33% Catholic; 11% Unknown. The average age of freshmen is 18; all undergraduates, 20. 16% do not continue beyond their first year; 78% remain to graduate.

Housing: 1786 students can be accommodated in college housing, which includes single-sex and coed dorms, on-campus apartments, and off-campus apartments. In addition, there are special-interest houses. On-campus housing is guaranteed for all 4 years. 73% of students live on campus; of those, 75% remain on campus on weekends. Alcohol is not permitted. All students may keep cars.

Activities: 23% of men belong to 7 local fraternities; 34% of women belong to 7 local sororities. There are 110 groups on campus, including volunteer, alcohol responsibility, band, cheerleading, choir, chorale, chorus, computers, dance, debate, drama, environmental, ethnic, gay, honors, international, jazz band, literary magazine, musical theater, newspaper, opera, orchestra, pep band, political, professional, radio and TV, religious, social, social service, student government, and symphony. Popular campus events include Messiah performances, Greek Olympics and Humanities Festival.

Sports: There are 11 intercollegiate sports for men and 10 for women, and 19 intramural sports for men and 18 for women. Facilities include a recreational center with an indoor 200-meter track, courts for basketball, volleyball, racquetball, and tennis, a weight room, and physical conditioning equipment. A phys ed center has courts for basketball, volleyball, racquetball, and badminton, weight and physical conditioning rooms, wrestling facilities, and a swimming pool. There is a lighted field and an all-weather track for football, soccer, and track and field, with stadium seating for 3,500. Facilities also include a baseball field, 10 outdoor tennis courts, and a dance studio.

Disabled Students: 75% of the campus is accessible. Facilities include wheelchair ramps, elevators, special parking, specially equipped restrooms, lowered drinking fountains, lowered telephones, special housing, and automatic door openers.

Services: Counseling and information services are available, as is tutoring in every subject. There is a reader service for the blind.

Campus Safety and Security: Measures include 24-hour foot and vehicle patrol, emergency notification system, self-defense education, and security escort services. There are shuttle buses, lighted pathways/sidewalks, and controlled access to dorms/residences.

Programs of Study: Augustana confers B.A. degrees. Bachelor's degrees are awarded in BIOLOGICAL SCIENCE (biochemistry and biology/biological science), BUSINESS (accounting, business administration and management, and international business management), COMMUNICATIONS AND THE ARTS (art, art history and appreciation, classics, communications, dramatic arts, English, French, German, music, music performance, Scandinavian languages, Spanish, speech/debate/rhetoric, and studio art), COMPUTER AND PHYSICAL SCIENCE (chemistry, computer science, earth science, geology, mathematics, and physics), EDUCATION (art education, elementary education, music education, physical education, and secondary education), ENGINEERING AND ENVIRONMENTAL DESIGN (engineering physics, landscape architecture/design, and preengineering), HEALTH PROFESSIONS (occupational therapy, premedicine, and speech pathology/audiology), SOCIAL SCIENCE (anthropology, Asian/Oriental studies, economics, geography, history, philosophy, political science/government, psychology, public administration, religion, social work, sociology, and women's studies). Premedicine, business/accounting, and biology have the largest enrollments.

Required: A total of 123 credits with a minimum GPA of 2.0 is required to graduate. Courses in foreign language, religion, writing, phys ed, fine arts, humanities, literature, and the sciences must be completed.

Special: Cooperative degree programs are offered in engineering, environmental management, forestry, landscape architecture, and occupational therapy with Duke, Iowa State, Northwestern, Purdue, and Washington (St. Louis) Universities and the University of Illinois (Urbana-Champaign). Domestic and international internships are offered. Study abroad is possible in 17 countries, including China, Peru, Sweden, Germany, and France, as is fall term study in East Asia, Europe, and Latin America. Interdisciplinary majors are offered in earth science, teaching, Asian studies, and public administration. A B.A.-B.S. degree in occupational therapy is offered, as well as 3-2 engineering programs with the University of Illinois and Purdue, Washington (St. Louis), and Iowa State Universities. Work-study programs, double majors, phys ed credits, and pass/fail options are available. There are 13 national honor societies, including Phi Beta Kappa, a freshman honors program, and 12 departmental honors programs.

Faculty/Classroom: 52% of faculty are male; 48% are female. All teach undergraduates, and 60% do both. No introductory courses are taught by graduate students. The average class size in an introductory lecture is 21; in a laboratory is 17; and in a regular course is 20.

Admissions: 69% of the 2013-2014 applicants were accepted. The ACT scores were 8% below 21, 23% between 21 and 23, 28% between 24 and 26, 18% between 27 and 28, and 23% above 28. 58% of the current freshmen were in the top fifth of their class; 83% were in the top two fifths.

Requirements: The SAT or ACT is recommended. Applicants should be graduates of an accredited secondary school with 16 academic credits, including 4 in English, 3 in math, 2 each in science and social studies, 1 in foreign language, and other science and math courses for appropriate majors. An audition for music majors and an interview are recommended. The GED is accepted. Students who choose not to submit ACT or SAT scores must interview and submit a photocopy of a graded high school paper. AP credits are accepted. Important factors in the admissions decision are advanced placement or honors courses, evidence of special talent, and recommendations by school officials.

Procedure: Freshmen are admitted fall, winter, and spring. Entrance exams should be taken by fall of the senior year. There are early admissions, deferred admissions, and rolling admissions plans. Application deadlines are open. The fall 2013 application fee was $35. Notification is sent on a rolling basis. Applications are accepted online.

Transfer: 54 transfer students enrolled in 2012-2013. A minimum GPA of 2.0 is required. SAT or ACT scores and an interview are recommended. 60 of 123 credits required for the bachelor's degree must be completed at Augustana.

Visiting: There are regularly scheduled orientations for prospective students, including information sessions with speakers, exhibits, campus tours, meetings with faculty, counselors, and students, and social activities. There are guides for informal visits, visitors may sit in on classes, and stay overnight. To schedule a visit, contact Vice President of Enrollment.

Financial Aid: In 2013-2014, 80% of all full-time freshmen and 75% of continuing full-time students received some form of financial aid. 79% of all full-time freshmen and 75% of continuing full-time students received need-based aid. The average freshman award was $24,505. Need-based scholarships or need-based grants averaged $15,396; need-based self-help aid (loans and jobs) averaged $6,572; and other non-need-based awards and non-need-based scholarships averaged $6,025. 80% of undergraduate students work part-time. Average annual earnings from campus work are $900. The average financial indebtedness of the 2013 graduate was $15,705. Augustana is a member of CSS. The FAFSA and the college's own financial statement are required. The deadline for filing freshman financial aid applications for fall entry is April 5.

International Students: There are 44 international students enrolled. The school actively recruits these students. They must take the TOEFL with a minimum score of 550 on the paper-based TOEFL (PBT) or 79 on the Internet-based version (iBT).

Graduates: From July 1, 2012 to June 30, 2013, 521 bachelor's degrees were awarded. The most popular majors were business/marketing (21%), biological/life science (18%), and psychology (8%). 238 companies recruited on campus in 2012-2013. In an average class, 70% graduate in 4 years or less, 76% graduate in 5 years or less, and 78% graduate in 6 years or less. Of the 2012 graduating class, 47% were enrolled in graduate school within 6 months of graduation, and 50% were employed.

Admissions Contact: Kent Brands, Vice President of Enrollment. E-Mail: *admissions@augustana.edu* Web: *www.augustana.edu*

AURORA UNIVERSITY D-2

Aurora, IL 60506-4892 **(630) 844-5533**
(800) 742-5281; (630) 844-5535

Full-time: 716 men, 1350 women	**Faculty:** 113; IIA, --$
Part-time: 85 men, 240 women	**Ph.D.s:** 82%
Graduate: 528 men, 1436 women	**Student/Faculty:** 18 to 1
Year: semesters, summer session	**Tuition:** $19,700
Application Deadline: June 20	**Room & Board:** $8820
Freshman Class: 1872 applied, 1367 accepted, 501 enrolled	
SAT CR/M: 470/470	**ACT:** 22 **COMPETITIVE**

Aurora University, founded in 1893, is a private, independent institution that offers graduate and undergraduate degrees in arts and sciences, education, accounting, business, information technology, communication, criminal justice, nursing, health sciences, physical education, athletic training, recreation, special education, and social work. The figures in the above capsule and in this profile are approximate. There are 4 undergraduate schools and 4 graduate schools. In addition to regional accreditation, AU has baccalaureate program accreditation with CSWE, NCATE, and NRPA. The library contains 83,589 volumes, and 7,038 audio/video tapes/CDs/DVDs, and subscribes to 4,206 periodicals including electronic. Computerized library services include interlibrary loans, database searching, Internet access, and laptop Internet portals. Special learning facilities include a learning resource center, art gallery, A Native American museum and a lakefront campus in southeastern Wisconsin. The 35-acre campus is in a suburban area 40 miles west of Chicago. Including any residence halls, there are 28 buildings.

Student Life: 91% of undergraduates are from Illinois. Others are from 26 states. 90% are from public schools. 71% are white; 13% Hispanic. 69% claim no religious affiliation; 15% Catholic; 15% Protestant. The average age of freshmen is 18; all undergraduates, 24. 25% do not continue beyond their first year; 50% remain to graduate.

Housing: 583 students can be accommodated in college housing, which includes single-sex and coed dorms. On-campus housing is available on a first-come and first-served basis. 75% of students commute. Alcohol is not permitted. All students may keep cars.

Activities: 1% of men belong to 1 local and 1 national fraternities; 1% of women belong to 1 local and 1 national sororities. There are 46 groups on campus, including art, cheerleading, chorale, computers, dance, drama, ethnic, honors, jazz band, literary magazine, newspaper, pep band, photography, political, professional, radio and TV, religious, social, social service, and student government. Popular campus events include Spring Fling, Arts and Ideas Series.

Sports: There are 9 intercollegiate sports for men and 9 for women, and 10 intramural sports for men and 10 for women. Facilities include a fitness center, a weight room, a 2,000-seat gym, football and soccer fields, a racquetball court, and a climbing wall.

Disabled Students: 98% of the campus is accessible. Facilities include wheelchair ramps, elevators, special parking, specially equipped restrooms, special class scheduling, and lowered drinking fountains.

Services: Counseling and information services are available, as is tutoring in most subjects. There is remedial math, reading, and writing. There are professional and peer tutors, workshops, and computer based tutorials.

Campus Safety and Security: Measures include 24-hour foot and vehicle patrol, emergency notification system, self-defense education, and security escort services. There are emergency telephones and lighted pathways/sidewalks.

Programs of Study: AU confers B.A., B.S., B.S.N., and B.S.W. degrees. Master's and doctoral degrees are also awarded. Bachelor's degrees are awarded in BIOLOGICAL SCIENCE (biology/biological science), BUSINESS (accounting, business administration and management, management information systems, management science, marketing management, marketing/retailing/merchandising, organizational leadership and management, and recreation and leisure services), COMMUNICATIONS AND THE ARTS (art, communications, dramatic arts, English, and Spanish), COMPUTER AND PHYSICAL SCIENCE (actuarial science, computer science, and mathematics), EDUCATION (athletic training, elementary education, physical education, secondary education, and special education), HEALTH PROFESSIONS (health science and nursing), SOCIAL SCIENCE (criminal justice, history, parks and recreation management, philosophy, political science/government, psychology, religion, social work, and sociology). Nursing, education, business are the strongest academically.

Required: To graduate, students must complete a minimum of 120 semester hours with a GPA of at least 2.0 on a 4.0 scale, including at least 52 semester hours at a senior college. General education distribution requirements include completion of a minimum of 38 semester hours in Aurora University's core sequences of Composition; Ways of Knowing (24 semester hours minimum), which includes Observation of Ourselves and Others, Observation of the Natural World, Aesthetic and Philosophical Expression, Mathematical and Technological Application, and a senior capstone in the major or equivalent cumulative senior year experience; and Ways of Living (8 semester hours minimum). Completion at Aurora University of at least 30 semester hours, including the last 24 semester hours in the degree, and including at least 18 semester hours in the major. A minimum of 30 semester hours numbered 3000 or above of which 15 semester hours must lie within the major and 15 semester hours must be completed at AU. Completion of the major requirements (with no grades lower than "C") for an approved major, including the senior capstone. Completion of writing intensive courses which include IDS1600, IDS2000 and the Writing for Success 3000-level requirement with no grades lower than "C."

Special: AU offers cross-registration with North Central College and Benedictine University, field-related job experience, work-study programs, study abroad in a number of countries and travel programs during the May term. Internships, student-designed and dual majors, and dual-degree options such as B.A.-B.S. are available. There are 3 national honor societies, a freshman honors program, and 9 departmental honors programs.

Faculty/Classroom: 45% of faculty are male; 55% are female. 96% teach undergraduates. No introductory courses are taught by graduate students. The average class size in an introductory lecture is 24; in a laboratory is 16; and in a regular course is 22.

Admissions: 73% of the 2011-2012 applicants were accepted. The SAT scores for the 2011-2012 freshman class were: Critical Reading--69% below 500, 22% between 500 and 599, and 9% between 600 and 700; Math--69% below 500, 22% between 500 and 599, and 9% between 600 and 700. The ACT scores were 32% below 21, 37% between 21 and 23, 20% between 24 and 26, 7% between 27 and 28, and 4% above 28. 30% of the current freshmen were in the top fifth of their class; 65% were in the top two fifths.

Requirements: The ACT is required. The SAT is recommended. Applicants must be graduates of an accredited secondary school or have earned the GED. Secondary school academic units must include a minimum of 4 years of English and 3 years each of mathematics, social studies, science, and electives. An interview is recommended but not required. AU requires applicants to be in the upper 60% of their class. A GPA of 2.0 is required. AP and CLEP credits are accepted. Important factors in the admissions decision are advanced placement or honors courses, extracurricular activities record, and leadership record.

Procedure: Freshmen are admitted fall and spring. Entrance exams should be taken by late in the junior year or early in the senior year. There are deferred admissions and rolling admissions plans. Applications should be filed by June 20 for fall entry, along with a $25 fee. Notifications are sent September 1. Applications are accepted online.

Transfer: 462 transfer students enrolled in 2010-2011. Applicants are required to have a minimum GPA of 2.0 and must have completed at least 15 semester hours at the post-secondary level. 30 of 120 credits required for the bachelor's degree must be completed at AU.

Visiting: There are regularly scheduled orientations for prospective students, including meeting with an admission representative, a campus tour with students, and classroom visits if set up. There are guides for informal visits, visitors may sit in on classes, and stay overnight. To schedule a visit, contact the Office of Admission and Financial Aid.

Financial Aid: In a recent year, 99% of all full-time freshmen and 97% of continuing full-time students received some form of financial aid. 86% of all full-time freshmen and 86% of continuing full-time students received need-based aid. The average freshman award was $18,208. Need-based scholarships or need-based grants averaged $7,628 ($15,466 maximum); need-based self-help aid (loans and jobs) averaged $4,279 ($6,500 maximum); and other non-need-based awards and non-need-based scholarships averaged $9,138 ($11,500 maximum). 100% of undergraduate students work part-time. Average annual earnings from campus work are $4500. The average financial indebtedness of the recent graduate was $24,083. The FAFSA is required. The priority date for freshman financial aid applications for fall entry is April 15.

International Students: There is 1 international student enrolled. They must take the TOEFL with a minimum score of 550 on the paper-based TOEFL (PBT) or 79 on the Internet-based version (iBT).

Graduates: In a recent year, 551 bachelor's degrees were awarded. The most popular majors were education (22%), business (19%), and health professions and related services (18%). 41 companies recruited on campus in 2010-2011. In an average class, 42% graduate in 4 years or less, 11% graduate in 5 years or less, and 1% graduate in 6 years or less. Of the recent graduating class, 20% were enrolled in graduate school within 6 months of graduation, and 80% were employed.

Admissions Contact: Admissions Office. A campus DVD is available. E-Mail: *admission@aurora.edu* Web: *www.aurora.edu*

BENEDICTINE UNIVERSITY E-2

Lisle, IL 60532 **(630) 829-6300; (630) 829-6301**

Full-time: 1028 men, 1402 women	**Faculty:** n/av; IIA, --$
Part-time: 204 men, 326 women	**Ph.D.s:** 91%
Graduate: 701 men, 1707 women	**Student/Faculty:** 18 to 1
Year: semesters, summer session	**Tuition:** $26,940
Application Deadline:	**Room & Board:** $8280

Freshman Class: 2108 applied, 1465 accepted, 469 enrolled
ACT: 23

COMPETITIVE

Benedictine University, founded in 1887, is a private, Roman Catholic liberal arts and sciences institution. There are 4 undergraduate schools and 4 graduate schools. In addition to regional accreditation, Benedictine has baccalaureate program accreditation with ADA. The library contains 240,500 volumes, 23,011 microform items, and 3,317 audio/video tapes/CDs/DVDs, and subscribes to 64,586 periodicals including electronic. Computerized library services include interlibrary loans, database searching, Internet access, and Wi-Fi capability. Special learning facilities include an art gallery, natural history museum, and TV station. The 108-acre campus is in a suburban area 25 miles west of Chicago. Including any residence halls, there are 11 buildings.

Student Life: 74% of undergraduates are from Illinois. Others are from 50 states, 14 foreign countries, and Canada. 44% are White; 23% race unknown; 13% Asian American; 11% African American. The average age of freshmen is 18; all undergraduates, 25. 23% do not continue beyond their first year; 52% remain to graduate.

Housing: 756 students can be accommodated in college housing, which includes single-sex and coed dorms. On-campus housing is available on a first-come and first-served basis. All students may keep cars.

Activities: There are no fraternities or sororities. There are 46 groups on campus, including art, band, cheerleading, choir, chorus, computers, dance, debate, ethnic, honors, international, jazz band, literary magazine, musical theater, newspaper, pep band, political, professional, radio and TV, religious, social, social service, and student government. Popular campus events include Relay for Life, Quad Day, and Spring Ball.

Sports: There are 8 intercollegiate sports for men and 9 for women, and 11 intramural sports for men and 11 for women. Facilities include a recreation center housing a main arena, a weight room, and a dance room; racquetball and tennis courts; and a sports complex that includes a football/soccer/track stadium, a baseball stadium, and a softball stadium.

Disabled Students: All of the campus is accessible. Facilities include wheelchair ramps, elevators, special parking, specially equipped restrooms, and lowered drinking fountains.

Services: Counseling and information services are available, as is tutoring in most subjects. There is a reader service for the blind, and remedial math, reading, and writing.

Campus Safety and Security: Measures include 24-hour foot and vehicle patrol, self-defense education, and security escort services. There are emergency telephones and lighted pathways/sidewalks.

Programs of Study: Benedictine confers B.A., B.S., B.B.A. and B.S.N. degrees. Associate, master's, and doctoral degrees are also awarded. Bachelor's degrees are awarded in BIOLOGICAL SCIENCE (biochemistry, biology/biological science, molecular biology, and nutrition), BUSINESS (accounting, banking and finance, business administration and management, business economics, international business management, management information systems, marketing management, marketing/retailing/merchandising, and organizational behavior), COMMUNICATIONS AND THE ARTS (arts administration/management, communications, creative writing, fine arts, literature, music, publishing, Spanish, and studio art), COMPUTER AND PHYSICAL SCIENCE (chemistry, computer science, mathematics, and physics), EDUCATION (elementary education and special education), ENGINEERING AND ENVIRONMENTAL DESIGN (engineering and applied science and environmental science), HEALTH PROFESSIONS (clinical science, health care administration, health science, nuclear medical technology, nursing, and radiation therapy), SOCIAL SCIENCE (economics, history, international studies, philosophy, political science/government, psychology, social science, sociology, and theological studies). Management, health science, and psychology have the largest enrollments.

Required: To graduate, students must complete 120 semester hours, including 36 in their majors, and maintain a minimum GPA of 2.0. They must complete 12 hours in the arts and humanities, 9 each in social sciences, natural sciences, and cultural heritage, 6 in rhetoric, and 3 each in speech, math, and freshman seminar. A thesis, capstone course or project, or comprehensive exam is required in specific departments.

Special: There is cross-registration with North Central College, Aurora University, and the Illinois Institute of Technology. Benedictine offers study abroad in 9 countries, and exchange programs can be arranged through other colleges. There are 3-2 pre-engineering degrees with Marquette University and the Universities of Illinois, Detroit, and Notre Dame, and an engineering degree with the Illinois Institute of Technology. Preprofessional programs including pre-podiatry, pre-physical therapy, and pre-nursing are offered. Work-study programs with a number of surrounding firms, internships, an accelerated degree program in management, credit for work and life experience, and dual majors are also offered. There are 11 national honor societies and a freshman honors program.

Faculty/Classroom: 49% of faculty are male; 51% are female. All teach and do research. No introductory courses are taught by graduate students. The average class size in an introductory lecture is 21; in a laboratory is 17; and in a regular course is 19.

Admissions: 69% of the 2013-2014 applicants were accepted. The ACT scores were 26% below 21, 27% between 21 and 23, 25% between 24 and 26, 11% between 27 and 28, and 10% above 28. 39% of the current freshmen were in the top fifth of their class; 70% were in the top two fifths. 3 freshmen graduated first in their class.

Requirements: The ACT is required. To be admitted, students must complete 4 years of English, 3 each of social studies, math, and lab science, and 2 of foreign language. The GED is accepted. Benedictine requires applicants to be in the upper 50% of their class. AP and CLEP credits are accepted.

Procedure: Freshmen are admitted fall and spring. There is a rolling admissions plan. Application deadlines are open. Application fee is $40. Applications are accepted online.

Transfer: 449 transfer students enrolled in 2012-2013. Applicants must have a C average. A minimum GPA of 2.0 is necessary, and an interview is required in some cases. Students who have completed fewer than 20 semester hours must submit ACT or SAT scores. 30 of 120 credits required for the bachelor's degree must be completed at Benedictine.

Visiting: There are regularly scheduled orientations for prospective students, Student visits include a regularly scheduled Visit Day and open houses each semester. There are guides for informal visits, visitors may sit in on classes, and stay overnight. To schedule a visit, contact the Enrollment Center.

Financial Aid: The FAFSA is required. The priority date for freshman financial aid applications for fall entry is April 15.

International Students: There are 41 international students enrolled. The school actively recruits these students. They must take the TOEFL with a minimum score of 550 on the paper-based TOEFL (PBT) or 79 on the Internet-based version (iBT).

Graduates: From July 1, 2012 to June 30, 2013, 723 bachelor's degrees were awarded. The most popular majors were health science (12%), management (9%), and biology (9%).

Admissions Contact: Kari A. Gibbons, Director of Admissions. E-Mail: *admissions@ben.edu* Web: *www.ben.edu*

BLACKBURN COLLEGE C-4

Carlinville, IL 62626 (217) 854-3231
(800) 233-3550; (217) 854-3713

Full-time: 242 men, 363 women	**Faculty:** 38
Part-time: 9 men, 13 women	**Ph.D.s:** 87%
Graduate: n/av	**Student/Faculty:** 14 to 1
Year: semesters, summer session	**Tuition:** $16,796
Application Deadline: July 31	**Room & Board:** $5554

Freshman Class: 660 applied, 452 accepted, 142 enrolled
SAT: reccommended **ACT:** 21 **COMPETITIVE**

Blackburn College, founded in 1837, is a private liberal arts institution affiliated with the Presbyterian Church. The college is noted for its work program, which allows resident students to reduce their education costs and develop useful skills by managing and administering all essential campus jobs. The figures in the above capsule and in this profile are approximate. The library contains 65,500 volumes, 10,897 microform items, and 1,299 audio/video tapes/CDs/DVDs, and subscribes to 85 periodicals including electronic. Computerized library services include interlibrary loans, database searching, Internet access, and laptop Internet portals. Special learning facilities include a learning resource center and art gallery. The 80-acre campus is in a rural area 60 miles north of St. Louis, 45 miles south of Springfield, and 250 miles south of Chicago. Including any residence halls, there are 20 buildings.

Student Life: 91% of undergraduates are from Illinois. Others are from 16 states, and 1 foreign countries. 85% are from public schools. 85% are white. 55% claim no religious affiliation; 25% Protestant; 12% Catholic. The average age of freshmen is 18; all undergraduates, 21. 39% do not continue beyond their first year; 32% remain to graduate.

Housing: 480 students can be accommodated in college housing, which includes single-sex and coed dorms. In addition, there are language houses, special-interest houses, a quiet residence hall. On-campus housing is guaranteed for all 4 years. 66% of students live on campus; of those, 60% remain on campus on weekends. All students may keep cars.

Activities: There are no fraternities or sororities. There are 37 groups on campus, including art, band, cheerleading, chess, choir, chorale, chorus, dance, debate, drama, ethnic, gay, jazz band, literary magazine, musical theater, newspaper, political, religious, social, social service, student government, and yearbook. Popular campus events include Goodwill Games, residence hall events, and all college convocations.

Sports: There are 5 intercollegiate sports for men and 6 for women, and 15 intramural sports for men and 15 for women. Facilities include a gym, racquetball and tennis courts, weight rooms, an outdoor track, and playing fields for baseball, soccer, and softball.

Disabled Students: 50% of the campus is accessible. Facilities include wheelchair ramps, elevators, special parking, specially equipped restrooms, special class scheduling, lowered drinking fountains, and lowered telephones.

Services: Counseling and information services are available, as is tutoring in most subjects.

Campus Safety and Security: Measures include emergency notification system, self-defense education, and security escort services. There are lighted pathways/sidewalks, security service department through the work program.

Programs of Study: Blackburn confers B.A. degrees. Bachelor's degrees are awarded in BIOLOGICAL SCIENCE (biochemistry, biology/biological science, and environmental biology), BUSINESS (accounting, business administration and management, marketing/retailing/merchandising, organizational leadership and management, and sports management), COMMUNICATIONS AND THE ARTS (art, arts administration/management, communications, creative writing, English literature, graphic design, music performance, musical theater, performing arts, and Spanish), COMPUTER AND PHYSICAL SCIENCE (chemistry, computer science, and mathematics), EDUCATION (art education, elementary education, English education, mathematics education, physical education, science education, secondary education, and social science education), HEALTH PROFESSIONS (medical laboratory technology and premedicine), SOCIAL SCIENCE (counseling/psychology, criminal justice, experimental psychology, history, interdisciplinary studies, political science/government, prelaw, psychology, and public administration). Elementary education, biology, criminal justice are the strongest academically.

Required: To graduate, students must complete 122 semester hours with a minimum 2.0 GPA. Requirements include intercultural courses in foreign languages or English, and foundation courses in writing, literature, math, social sciences, philosophy or religion, analysis, fine arts, and phys ed. Work program participation is required of resident students. All students must complete their last year in residence.

Special: Blackburn offers supervised off-campus internships related to student majors, co-op programs, work-study programs, and a semester in Ecuador, Wales, or Washington, D.C. A 3-2 engineering degree with Washington University in St. Louis or at the University of Missouri-Kansas City is offered. Students may design their own majors. There is 1 national honor society.

Faculty/Classroom: 56% of faculty are male; 44% are female. All teach undergraduates, and 55% do research. No introductory courses are taught by graduate students. The average class size in an introductory lecture is 25; in a laboratory is 20; and in a regular course is 18.

Admissions: 68% of a recent year applicants were accepted. The ACT scores were 48% below 21, 30% between 21 and 23, 12% between 24 and 26, 7% between 27 and 28, and 3% above 28. 30% of the current freshmen were in the top fifth of their class; 57% were in the top two fifths. 4 freshmen graduated first in their class.

Requirements: The ACT is required. The SAT is recommended. Applicants should be graduates of an accredited secondary school or have a GED certificate. Blackburn recommends completion of 4 years of English, 2 to 4 of math, and 2 each of lab sciences, social sciences, and foreign language. A personal essay is required. Blackburn requires applicants to be in the upper 60% of their class. A GPA of 2.0 is required. AP and CLEP credits are accepted. Important factors in the admissions decision are leadership record, personality/intangible qualities, and recommendations by school officials.

Procedure: Freshmen are admitted fall, spring, and summer. Entrance exams should be taken in the junior year or early in the senior year. There is a rolling admissions plan. Applications should be filed by July 31 for fall entry; November 30 for spring entry, along with a $20 fee. Notification is sent on a rolling basis. Applications are accepted online.

Transfer: 51 transfer students enrolled in a recent year. Applicants must submit official transcripts of college-level work and be in good standing at the previous institution attended. Students from accredited colleges may receive credit for grades of C or better; those with associate degrees may transfer some D grades. Credit for work at unaccredited institutions may be accepted provisionally. 30 of 122 credits required for the bachelor's degree must be completed at Blackburn.

Visiting: There are regularly scheduled orientations for prospective students, including a campus tour and meetings with an admissions representative, the financial aid director, student life staff, a work program representative, and an academic faculty member. There are guides for informal visits, visitors may sit in on classes, and stay overnight. To schedule a visit, contact the Office of Admissions.

Financial Aid: In a recent year, 99% of all full-time freshmen and 98% of continuing full-time students received some form of financial aid. 97% of all full-time freshmen and 94% of continuing full-time students received need-based aid. The average freshman award was $15,401. Need-based scholarships or need-based grants averaged $7,414 ($22,650 maximum); need-based self-help aid (loans and jobs) averaged $4,181 ($6,140 maximum); and other non-need-based awards and non-need-based scholarships averaged $7,278 ($22,650 maximum). 108% of undergraduate students work part-time. Average annual earnings from campus work are $2738. The average financial indebtedness of the 2011 graduate was $16,456. Blackburn is a member of CSS. The FAFSA is required. The priority date for freshman financial aid applications for fall entry is March 1.

International Students: They must take the TOEFL with a minimum score of 550 on the paper-based TOEFL (PBT) or 80 on the Internet-based version (iBT). They must also take the SAT or ACT, scoring 17.

Admissions Contact: Kristi Nelma *kristi.nelms@blackburn.edu*

BRADLEY UNIVERSITY D-3

Peoria, IL 61625 (309) 677-1000
(800) 447-6460; (309) 677-2797

Full-time: 2200 men, 2600 women	**Faculty:** 345; IIA, av$
Part-time: 100 men, 150 women	**Ph.D.s:** 83%
Graduate: 370 men, 370 women	**Student/Faculty:** n/av
Year: semesters, summer session	**Tuition:** $26,900
Application Deadline: open	**Room & Board:** $8700

Freshman Class: n/av
SAT or ACT: required
VERY COMPETITIVE

Bradley University, founded in 1897, is an independent, privately endowed institution offering a full range of baccalaureate and graduate-level programs. Some figures in the above capsule and in this profile are approximate. There are 5 undergraduate schools and 1 graduate school. In addition to regional accreditation, Bradley has baccalaureate program accreditation with AACSB, ABET, ACCE, ADA, NASAD, NASM, NCATE, and NLN. The library contains 511,000 volumes, 86,504 microform items, and 13,774 audio/video tapes/CDs/DVDs, and subscribes to 41,689 periodicals including electronic. Computerized library services include interlibrary loans, database searching, Internet access, and laptop Internet portals. Special learning facilities include a learning resource center, art gallery, radio station, and TV station. The 85-acre campus is in an urban area 160 miles southwest of Chicago. Including any residence halls, there are 44 buildings.

Student Life: 88% of undergraduates are from Illinois. Others are from 39 states, 30 foreign countries, and Canada. 85% are from public schools. 80% are white. 42% are Protestant; 34% Catholic; 14% claim no religious affiliation. The average age of freshmen is 18; all undergraduates, 20. 13% do not continue beyond their first year; 78% remain to graduate.

Housing: 2200 students can be accommodated in college housing, which includes single-sex and coed dorms and on-campus apartments. In addition, there are fraternity houses and sorority houses. On-campus housing is guaranteed for all 4 years. 97% of students live on campus; of those, 99% remain on campus on weekends. Upperclassmen may keep cars.

Activities: 35% of men belong to 16 national fraternities; 27% of women belong to 12 national sororities. There are 250 groups on campus, including art, band, cheerleading, chess, choir, chorale, chorus, computers, dance, drama, environmental, ethnic, forensics, gay, honors, international, jazz band, literary magazine, musical theater, newspaper, orchestra, pep band, photography, political, professional, radio and TV, religious, social, social service, student government, and symphony. Popular campus events include Late Night BU, Founders Day, and Greek Week.

Sports: There are 6 intercollegiate sports for men and 7 for women, and 24 intramural sports for men and 24 for women. Facilities include tennis courts, a civic center, playing fields, a field house, outdoor lighted basketball courts, and a 130,000-square-foot student recreation center with a pool, an indoor track, weights, cardio machines, a spinning room, and a climbing wall.

Disabled Students: 80% of the campus is accessible. Facilities include wheelchair ramps, elevators, special parking, specially equipped restrooms, and lowered drinking fountains.

Services: Counseling and information services are available, as is tutoring in introductory subjects and selected higher-level classes. There is remedial math and writing.

Campus Safety and Security: Measures include 24-hour foot and vehicle patrol, emergency notification system, self-defense education, and security escort services. There are emergency telephones, lighted pathways/sidewalks, engravers for marking personal property, and a medical escort service.

Programs of Study: Bradley confers B.A., B.F.A., B.M., B.S., B.S.C., B.S.C.E., B.S.E.E., B.S.I.E., B.S.M.E., B.S.M.F.E., B.S.M.F.E.T., and B.S.N. degrees. Master's and doctoral degrees are also awarded. Bachelor's degrees are awarded in BIOLOGICAL SCIENCE (biochemistry, biology/biological science, and molecular biology), BUSINESS (accounting, banking and finance, business administration and management, entrepreneurial studies, international business management, management information systems, and marketing/retailing/merchandising), COMMUNICATIONS AND THE ARTS (art history and appreciation, communications, dramatic arts, English, French, German, graphic design, multimedia, music, music business management, music performance, music theory and composition, Spanish, and studio art), COMPUTER AND PHYSICAL SCIENCE (actuarial science, chemistry, computer science, information sciences and systems, mathematics, and physics), EDUCATION (art education, drama education, early childhood education, elementary education, music education, and special education), ENGINEERING AND ENVIRONMENTAL DESIGN (civil engineering, construction engineering, electrical/electronics engineering, engineering physics, environmental science, industrial engineering, manufacturing engineering, manufacturing technology, and mechanical engineering), HEALTH PROFESSIONS (health science, medical technology, and nursing), SOCIAL SCIENCE (criminal justice, dietetics, economics, family/consumer studies, history, international studies, liberal arts/general studies, philosophy, political science/government, psychology, religion, social work, and sociology). Business, engineering, and natural sciences are the strongest academically. Communication, elementary education, and psychology have the largest enrollments.

Required: To graduate, students must complete the school's basic skills and general education curriculum. Overall, the college requires 124 total credit hours, with 32 hours in the student's major and a minimum GPA of 2.0.

Special: Special academic programs include an honors program, co-op programs, internships, a Washington semester, work-study programs, study abroad in 30 countries, B.A.-B.S. degrees in most majors, dual and student-designed majors, and leadership fellowships. There are 31 national honor societies and a freshman honors program.

Faculty/Classroom: 62% of faculty are male; 38% are female. All teach and do research. No introductory courses are taught by graduate students. The average class size in a laboratory is 14 and in a regular course, 23.

Admissions: 74% of a recent year's applicants were accepted. 51% of a recent year's freshmen were in the top fifth of their class; 83% were in the top two fifths. There were 5 National Merit finalists. 41 freshmen graduated first in their class.

Requirements: The SAT or ACT is required. A GPA of 2.0 is required. AP and CLEP credits are accepted. Important factors in the admissions decision are advanced placement or honors courses, extracurricular activities record, and evidence of special talent.

Procedure: Freshmen are admitted to all sessions. Entrance exams should be taken in the spring of the junior year or the fall of the senior year. There is a rolling admissions plan. Application deadlines are open. There is no fee for online applications. Paper applications submitted after November 30 require a $35 fee; those submitted February 1 and after require a $50 fee. A waiting list is maintained.

Transfer: 303 transfer students enrolled in a recent year. Transfer students must have a minimum GPA of 2.0. Those with fewer than 15 hours of college credit must submit their ACT or SAT scores and a high school transcript. 30 of 124 credits required for the bachelor's degree must be completed at Bradley.

Visiting: There are regularly scheduled orientations for prospective students, including class visits, campus tours, admissions information, financial assistance seminars, lunch, and student and parent meetings. There are guides for informal visits, and visitors may sit in on classes and stay overnight. To schedule a visit, contact the Office of Undergraduate Admissions.

Financial Aid: In a recent year, 64% of all full-time freshmen and 57% of continuing full-time students received need-based aid. The average freshman award was $20,164, with $14,179 ($23,950 maximum) from need-based scholarships or need-based grants; $4,660 ($7,000 maximum) from need-based self-help aid (loans and jobs); $15,700 ($31,894 maximum) from non-need-based athletic scholarships; and $8,388 ($23,950 maximum) from other non-need-based awards and non-need-based scholarships. 22% of undergraduate students work part-time. Average annual earnings from campus work are $1142. Bradley is a member of CSS. The FAFSA is required. Check with the school for current application deadlines.

International Students: There were 40 international students enrolled in a recent year. The school actively recruits these students. They must take the TOEFL with a minimum score of 550 on the paper-based TOEFL (PBT) or 79 on the Internet-based version (iBT). The SAT or ACT is recommended.

Graduates: In a recent year, 1169 bachelor's degrees were awarded. The most popular majors were nursing (6%), psychology (5%), and health science (5%). 403 companies recruited on campus in a recent year. In an average class, 54% graduate in 4 years or less, 76% graduate in 5 years or less, and 78% graduate in 6 years or less. Of a recent year's graduating class, 16% were enrolled in graduate school within 6 months of graduation, and 94% were employed.

Admissions Contact: Associate Provost for Enrollment Management. A campus DVD is available. E-Mail: *admissions@bradley.edu* Web: *www.bradley.edu*

CHICAGO STATE UNIVERSITY E-2

Chicago, IL 60628 **(773) 995-2513**
(800) 278-3011; (773) 995-3820

Full-time: 917 men, 2092 women	**Faculty:** n/av
Part-time: 392 men, 1211 women	**Ph.D.s:** 62%
Graduate: 467 men, 1022 women	**Student/Faculty:** n/av
Year: other, summer session	**Tuition:** $5482 ($9712)
Application Deadline: July 15	**Room & Board:** n/app
Freshman Class: n/av	
ACT: required	

COMPETITIVE

Chicago State University, founded in 1867, is a public commuter and residential institution controlled by the State of Illinois. It offers day and evening undergraduate programs through the Colleges of Arts and Sciences, Health Sciences, Business Administration, Education, and non traditional programs. There are 5 undergraduate schools and 2 graduate schools. In addition to regional accreditation, Chicago State has baccalaureate program accreditation with AACSB, ACPE, ADA, CAHEA, NCATE, and NLN. The library contains 26,000 volumes, 388,028 microform items, and 0 audio/video tapes/CDs/DVDs, and subscribes to 1,734 periodicals including electronic. Computerized library services include interlibrary loans, database searching, and Internet access. Special learning facilities include an art gallery, radio station, and a TV studio. The 161-acre campus is in an urban area 12 miles south of downtown Chicago. Including any residence halls, there are 13 buildings.

Student Life: 98% of undergraduates are from Illinois. Others are from 24 states, 21 foreign countries, and Canada. 80% are African American. The average age of freshmen is 21; all undergraduates, 29.

Housing: 360 students can be accommodated in college housing, which includes coed dorms. On-campus housing is available on a first-come and first-served basis. 97% of students commute. Alcohol is not permitted. All students may keep cars.

Activities: 12% of men belong to 4 national fraternities. There are 72 groups on campus, including cheerleading, chess, choir, dance, honors, international, jazz band, literary magazine, newspaper, political, professional, radio and TV, religious, social, social service, and student government. Popular campus events include Welcome Week activities, Black Writers Conference and Hispanic Heritage Month.

Sports: There are 6 intercollegiate sports for men and 6 for women, and 4 intramural sports for men and 2 for women. Facilities include tennis courts, indoor/outdoor tracks, an Olympic-size swimming pool, weight rooms, basketball courts, a fitness center, dance studio, a baseball field, and Convocation Center with 6300 seating capacity.

Disabled Students: All of the campus is accessible. Facilities include

wheelchair ramps, elevators, special parking, specially equipped restrooms, lowered drinking fountains, and lowered telephones.

Services: Counseling and information services are available, as is tutoring in some subjects. There is remedial math, reading, and writing. math, science and accounting.

Campus Safety and Security: Measures include 24-hour foot and vehicle patrol and security escort services. There are emergency telephones and lighted pathways/sidewalks.

Programs of Study: Chicago State confers B.A., B.S., B.M.E. and B.S.Ed. degrees. Master's and doctoral degrees are also awarded. Bachelor's degrees are awarded in BIOLOGICAL SCIENCE (biochemistry and biology/biological science), BUSINESS (accounting, banking and finance, business administration and management, management science, marketing/retailing/merchandising, and recreation and leisure services), COMMUNICATIONS AND THE ARTS (art, broadcasting, English, music, Spanish, and speech/debate/rhetoric), COMPUTER AND PHYSICAL SCIENCE (chemistry, computer science, information sciences and systems, mathematics, and physics), EDUCATION (art education, bilingual/bicultural education, business education, early childhood education, elementary education, industrial arts education, music education, physical education, secondary education, and vocational education), HEALTH PROFESSIONS (health, health care administration, health science, nursing, predentistry, and premedicine), SOCIAL SCIENCE (African American studies, criminal justice, economics, geography, history, political science/government, prelaw, psychology, and sociology). Business administration and computer science are the strongest academically. Elementary education and nursing have the largest enrollments.

Required: All students must complete 120 credit hours, including 40 hours in the major, maintain a 2.0 GPA, and fulfill foreign language requirement. They must complete a 39-hour core curriculum as well as examinations in English, math, reading, and the U.S. Constitution.

Special: Chicago State offers a combined B.A.-B.S. degree, a board of governors degree program, a University Without Walls Program, and an individualized curriculum program. Study abroad in Liberia and life experience credits are also provided. There is a freshman honors program.

Faculty/Classroom: 99% teach undergraduates. No introductory courses are taught by graduate students. The average class size in an introductory lecture is 60; in a laboratory is 26; and in a regular course is 35.

Requirements: The ACT is required, but scores need not be submitted if the applicant is over 25 years of age. Graduation from an accredited secondary school is required; a GED will be accepted. Minimum credits submitted should include 4 units of English, 3 of math, 3 of science, and 3 of social sciences. A GPA of 2.5 is required. AP and CLEP credits are accepted.

Procedure: Freshmen are admitted to all sessions. There is a rolling admissions plan. Applications should be filed by July 15 for fall entry; November 15 for spring entry; and May 1 for summer entry, along with a $25 fee. Notification is sent on a rolling basis. Applications are accepted online.

Transfer: Transfer students must have a minimum GPA of 2.0, and those with fewer than 24 hours must also meet freshman admission requirements. 30 of 120 credits required for the bachelor's degree must be completed at Chicago State.

Visiting: There are regularly scheduled orientations for prospective students, including a tour of campus, admissions overview, and financial aid information. To schedule a visit, contact The Office of Admissions at (773) 995-2513.

Financial Aid: In 2013-2014, 97% of all full-time freshmen and 97% of continuing full-time students received some form of financial aid. 97% of all full-time freshmen and 97% of continuing full-time students received need-based aid. The average freshman award was $16,154. Need-based scholarships or need-based grants averaged $7,263 ($9,540 maximum); need-based self-help aid (loans and jobs) averaged $3,473 ($7,000 maximum); non-need-based athletic scholarships averaged $10,575 ($17,010 maximum); and other non-need-based awards and non-need-based scholarships averaged $6,898 ($19,522 maximum). 5% of undergraduate students work part-time. Average annual earnings from campus work are $1918. The average financial indebtedness of the 2013 graduate was $28,955. The FAFSA is required. The priority date for freshman financial aid applications for fall entry is February 1. The deadline for filing freshman financial aid applications for fall entry is April 15.

International Students: There are 26 international students enrolled. The school actively recruits these students. They must take the TOEFL with a minimum score of 525 on the paper-based TOEFL (PBT) or 69 on the Internet-based version (iBT) and the college's own test, Students have the option of taking the IETLS with a score of 7 and minimum. They must also take the SAT or ACT, scoring 16.

Graduates: From July 1, 2012 to June 30, 2013, 839 bachelor's degrees were awarded. The most popular majors were general studies (26%), business administration (13%), and criminal justice (6%). In an average class, 7% graduate in 4 years or less and 22% graduate in 6 years or less.

Admissions Contact: Matt Harrison, Director of Admissions. E-Mail: *ug-admissions@csu.edu* Web: *www.csu.edu*

COLUMBIA COLLEGE CHICAGO — E-2

Chicago, IL 60605 (312) 369-7130
(800) 838-1226; (312) 369-8024

Full-time: 5200 men, 5400 women	**Faculty:** 286
Part-time: 650 men, 640 women	**Ph.D.s:** 35%
Graduate: 200 men, 400 women	**Student/Faculty:** n/av
Year: semesters, summer session	**Tuition:** $20,094
Application Deadline: see profile	**Room & Board:** $13,120
Freshman Class: n/av	

LESS COMPETITIVE

Columbia College Chicago, founded in 1890, is a private liberal arts institution with special emphasis on educating students for creative occupations in the visual, performing, and media and communication arts. Some figures in the above capsule and in this profile are approximate. There are 3 undergraduate schools and 1 graduate school. The library contains 2054 volumes, 128,615 microform items, and 13,772 audio/video tapes/CDs/DVDs, and subscribes to 1204 periodicals including electronic. Computerized library services include interlibrary loans, database searching, Internet access, and laptop Internet portals. Special learning facilities include a learning resource center, art gallery, radio station, TV station, and contemporary photography museum. The campus is in an urban area in Chicago. Including any residence halls, there are 23 buildings.

Student Life: 66% of undergraduates are from Illinois. Others are from 49 states, 46 foreign countries, and Canada. 80% are from public schools. 63% are white; 14% African American. The average age of freshmen is 18; all undergraduates, 21.

Housing: 3000 students can be accommodated in college housing, which includes coed dorms. In addition, there are special-interest houses. On-campus housing is available on a first-come, first-served basis. Priority is given to out-of-town students. 78% of students commute. Alcohol is not permitted. All students may keep cars.

Activities: There are no fraternities or sororities. There are 85 groups on campus, including art, chorus, computers, dance, drama, ethnic, film, gay, international, jazz band, literary magazine, musical theater, photography, political, professional, radio and TV, religious, social service, student government, and yearbook. Popular campus events include African Heritage, Dr. Martin Luther King Jr.'s birthday, and Women in the Arts.

Disabled Students: 95% of the campus is accessible. Facilities include wheelchair ramps, elevators, specially equipped rest rooms, special class scheduling, and lowered telephones.

Services: Counseling and information services are available, as is tutoring in some subjects. There is a reader service for the blind, and remedial math, reading, and writing.

Campus Safety and Security: Measures include emergency notification system, self-defense education, and security escort services. There are emergency telephones and lighted pathways/sidewalks.

Programs of Study: Columbia confers B.A. and B.F.A. degrees. Master's degrees are also awarded. Bachelor's degrees are awarded in BUSINESS (marketing management), COMMUNICATIONS AND THE ARTS (advertising, art, audio technology, creative writing, dance, dramatic arts, film arts, journalism, multimedia, music, music business management, photography, and radio/television technology), EDUCATION (early childhood education), ENGINEERING AND ENVIRONMENTAL DESIGN (computer graphics), SOCIAL SCIENCE (crosscultural studies and interpreter for the deaf). Art, film/video, and management are the largest.

Required: To graduate, all students must complete 124 semester hours of study with a minimum 2.0 GPA. General studies distribution consists of 9 hours each of literature/humanities and science/math, 6 each of English, history, and social science, and 3 each of computer applications, oral communications, senior seminar, and electives; 1 intensive writing course also is required.

Special: Columbia offers study abroad in many countries, independent study, internships, work-study programs, student-designed majors, and a general studies degree.

Faculty/Classroom: 56% of faculty are male; 44% are female. All teach undergraduates. No introductory courses are taught by graduate students. The average class size in a regular course is 17.

Requirements: Applicants should be graduates of accredited secondary schools. The GED is also accepted. An interview is recommended. AP and CLEP credits are accepted.

Procedure: Freshmen are admitted to all sessions. There are deferred admissions and rolling admissions plans. Check with the school for current application deadlines. Application fee is $35. Applications are accepted online.

Transfer: Up to 88 credit hours are accepted with a grade of C or better; up to 62 credit hours from 2-year colleges with a grade of C or better are accepted. 36 of 124 credits required for the bachelor's degree must be completed at Columbia.

Visiting: There are regularly scheduled orientations for prospective students. There are guides for informal visits and visitors may sit in on classes. To schedule a visit, contact the Undergraduate Admissions Office.

Financial Aid: The FAFSA is required. Check with the school for current application deadlines.

International Students: There were 250 international students enrolled in a recent year. The school actively recruits these students. They must take the TOEFL.

Graduates: In a recent year, 1370 bachelor's degrees were awarded. The most popular majors were film/video (12%), marketing (9%), and art and design (9%).

Admissions Contact: Director of Admissions. E-Mail: *admissions@colum.edu* Web: *www.colum.edu*

CONCORDIA UNIVERSITY, RIVER FOREST E-2

River Forest, IL 60305-1402 (708) 209-3101
(866) GO-2-CURF; (708) 209-3473

Full-and part-time: 1500 men, and women
Graduate: 3700 men and women
Year: semesters, summer session
Application Deadline: open
Freshman Class: n/av
SAT or ACT: required
Faculty: n/av; IIB, --$
Ph.D.s: 65%
Student/Faculty: n/av
Tuition: $27,000
Room & Board: $8600

COMPETITIVE

Concordia University, founded in 1864, is a private liberal arts institution affiliated with the Lutheran Church, Missouri Synod. There are 3 undergraduate schools and 1 graduate school. In addition to regional accreditation, Concordia University has baccalaureate program accreditation with NCATE and NLN. The library contains 140,000 volumes, 480,000 microform items, and 2,250 audio/video tapes/CDs/DVDs, and subscribes to 235 periodicals including electronic. Computerized library services include interlibrary loans, database searching, Internet access, and laptop Internet portals. Special learning facilities include a learning resource center, art gallery, natural history museum, radio station, TV station, early childhood resource center, human performance lab, language lab, computer center, and weather station. The 40-acre campus is in a suburban area 10 miles west of downtown Chicago. Including any residence halls, there are 24 buildings.

Student Life: 65% of undergraduates are from Illinois. Others are from 30 states, 12 foreign countries, and Canada. 66% are from public schools. 51% are white. 59% are undeclared; 31% Protestant; 13% Catholic. The average age of freshmen is 18; all undergraduates, 22. 27% do not continue beyond their first year; 53% remain to graduate.

Housing: 775 students can be accommodated in college housing, which includes single-sex and coed dorms and married student housing. On-campus housing is guaranteed for all 4 years. 65% of students live on campus; of those, 75% remain on campus on weekends. Alcohol is not permitted. All students may keep cars.

Activities: There are no fraternities or sororities. There are 43 groups on campus, including band, cheerleading, choir, chorale, chorus, communications, dance, drama, ethnic, honors, jazz band, literary magazine, musical theater, newspaper, pep band, professional, religious, social, social service, student government, symphony, and yearbook. Popular campus events include Orientation Week, Campus Awareness Day, and Family Weekend.

Sports: There are 7 intercollegiate sports for men and 7 for women, and 12 intramural sports for men and 12 for women. Facilities include 2 gyms, an indoor swimming pool, weight training room, human performance lab, football and soccer fields, tennis courts, baseball and softball fields, track, first aid training room, table tennis, billiards, and table games.

Disabled Students: 74% of the campus is accessible. Facilities include wheelchair ramps, elevators, special parking, specially equipped restrooms, special class scheduling, lowered drinking fountains, and lowered telephones.

Services: Counseling and information services are available, as is tutoring in every subject. There is remedial math, reading, and writing.

Campus Safety and Security: Measures include 24-hour foot and vehicle patrol, self-defense education, and security escort services. There are shuttle buses, emergency telephones, and lighted pathways/sidewalks.

Programs of Study: Concordia University confers B.A., B.Mus., and B.Mus.Ed. degrees. Master's and doctoral degrees are also awarded. Bachelor's degrees are awarded in BIOLOGICAL SCIENCE (biology/biological science), BUSINESS (accounting and business administration and management), COMMUNICATIONS AND THE ARTS (art, communications, English, and music), COMPUTER AND PHYSICAL SCIENCE (chemistry, computer programming, computer science, mathematics, natural sciences, and physical sciences), EDUCATION (computer education, early childhood education, elementary education, middle school education, music education, physical education, science education, and secondary education), HEALTH PROFESSIONS (premedicine), SOCIAL SCIENCE (geography, history, physical fitness/movement, political science/government, prelaw, psychology, religion, social science, social work, sociology, and theological studies). Elementary education, exercise science, and theology are the strongest academically. Elementary education, business, and psychology have the largest enrollments.

Required: All students are required to take 2 years of liberal arts, including humanities, English, science, religion, and social science, and 5 quarter hours of phys ed. A 2.0 to 2.25 GPA and a total of 128 to 150 quarter hours are required. The number of hours required for the major varies by program.

Special: Cross-registration is possible with Dominican University and the Chicago Consortium of Colleges. Concordia also offers internships for liberal arts majors in the Chicago area, which provides numerous opportunities, study abroad in England, and pass/fail options. Work-study is possible, as is an accelerated degreee program in organizational management. There are 3 national honor societies, including Phi Beta Kappa, and a freshman honors program.

Faculty/Classroom: 50% of faculty are male; 50% are female. 82% teach undergraduates, and all teach and do research. No introductory courses are taught by graduate students. The average class size in an introductory lecture is 20; in a laboratory is 18; and in a regular course is 25.

Admissions: 92% of a recent year applicants were accepted. The ACT scores were 36% below 21, 23% between 21 and 23, 20% between 24 and 26, 9% between 27 and 28, and 12% above 28. 30% of the current freshmen were in the top fifth of their class; 41% were in the top two fifths.

Requirements: The ACT is required. Applicants should have 15 units of credit, with 11 units in college preparatory courses, including English, math, lab science, and social studies. A letter of recommendation is required, as is a minimum GPA of 2.0 in the college preparatory subjects and a ranking in the top half of their graduating class. Concordia University requires applicants to be in the upper 50% of their class. A GPA of 2.0 is required. AP and CLEP credits are accepted. Important factors in the admissions decision are advanced placement or honors courses, recommendations by school officials, and leadership record.

Procedure: Freshmen are admitted to all sessions. Entrance exams should be taken in the spring of the junior year or fall of the senior year. There is a rolling admissions plan. Application deadlines are open. Applications are accepted online.

Transfer: 90 transfer students enrolled in 2010-2011. A cumulative GPA of 2.0 or higher at all previous colleges plus a letter of recommendation are required. 48 of 128 credits required for the bachelor's degree must be completed at Concordia University.

Visiting: There are regularly scheduled orientations for prospective students, consisting of daily planned activities during orientation in the first week of the fall semester. There are guides for informal visits, visitors may sit in on classes, and stay overnight. To schedule a visit, contact the Office of Admission.

Financial Aid: In a recent year, all full-time freshmen and continuing full-time students received some form of financial aid. The average freshman award was $12,000. The FAFSA and the college's own financial statement, and student and parent 1040 U.S. tax forms are required. Check with the school for current application deadlines.

International Students: They must take the TOEFL or MELAB, or successfully complete Level 109 at an ELS language center.

Graduates: In a recent year, 216 bachelor's degrees were awarded. The most popular majors were education (34%), business (8%), and sociology/social work (4%). In an average class, 36% graduate in 4 years or less, 41% graduate in 5 years or less, and 41% graduate in 6 years or less. Of the 2010 graduating class, 23% were enrolled in graduate school within 6 months of graduation, and 98% were employed.

Admissions Contact: James P. Malley, Director of Admissions. E-Mail: *crfmalleyjp@curf.edu* Web: *www.curf.edu*

DEPAUL UNIVERSITY E-2

Chicago, IL 60604 (312) 362-8300
(800) 4-DEPAUL; (312) 362-5749

Full-time: 6364 men, 7230 women
Part-time: 1252 men, 1574 women
Graduate: 3781 men, 4213 women
Year: quarters, summer session
Application Deadline: February 1
Faculty: 798
Ph.D.s: 87%
Student/Faculty: 16 to 1
Tuition: $33,990
Room & Board: $12,130
Freshman Class: 19957 applied, 11648 accepted, 2425 enrolled
SAT CR/M: 581/569 **ACT:** 25 **VERY COMPETITIVE**

DePaul University is the nation's largest Catholic university, with over 24,000 students and about 300 degree programs. Its partnerships throughout Chicago enable DePaul to provide an exceptional educational experience that is vibrant, pragmatic and socially engaged. Classes are small and taught by knowledgeable and experienced faculty members who take full advantage of Chicago's resources. DePaul's mission to provide a quality education to students from a broad range of backgrounds has resulted in one of the nation's most diverse student bodies. With ten colleges and schools, DePaul has campuses in Chicago's Loop and Lincoln Park neighborhoods and three suburban locations. There are 9 undergraduate schools and 10 graduate schools. In addition to regional accreditation, DePaul has baccalaureate program accreditation with AACSB and NASM. The 6 libraries contain 1.1 million volumes, 239,340 microform items, and 35,031 audio/video tapes/CDs/DVDs, and subscribe to 69,010 periodicals including electronic. Computerized library services include interlibrary loans, database searching, Internet access, and Wi-Fi capability. Special learning facilities include an art gallery, radio station, LEED-certified environmental science & chemistry building with greenhouse & green roof, digital cinema laboratory with motion-capture system, green-screen studio, converged newsroom, 10 specialized computer research labs including artificial intelligence, biomedics informatics & mobile e-commerce, 1,300-seat theatre, art museum, and a fitness & recreational center with pool. DePaul University has campuses in Chicago's Loop and Lincoln Park neighborhoods and three suburban locations (Naperville, O'Hare, and Oak Forest). Including any residence halls, there are 48 buildings.

Student Life: 78% of undergraduates are from Illinois. Others are from 48 states, 84 foreign countries, and Canada. 77% are from public schools. 56% are White; 17% Hispanic. 37% are Catholic. The average age of freshmen is 18; all undergraduates, 23. 15% do not continue beyond their first year; 70% remain to graduate.

Housing: 2677 students can be accommodated in college housing, which includes coed dorms, on-campus apartments, and off-campus apartments. In addition, there are special-interest houses, private studios and apartments, and traditional residence-style units. On-campus housing is available on a first-come, first-served basis, and is available on a lottery system for upperclassmen. Priority is given to out-of-town students. 83% of students commute. All students may keep cars.

Activities: 6% of men belong to 10 national fraternities; 9% of women belong to 16 national sororities. There are 313 groups on campus, including art, cheerleading, chess, choir, chorale, chorus, communications, computers, dance, debate, drama, environmental, ethnic, film, gay, honors, international, literary magazine, newspaper, pep band, photography, political, professional, radio and TV, religious, social, social service, and student government. Popular campus events include FEST or University Festival, Homecoming and Welcome Week.

Sports: There are 6 intercollegiate sports for men and 7 for women, and 33 intramural sports for men and 33 for women. The Ray Meyer Fitness and Recreation Center is located on DePaul University's Lincoln Park Campus location. The 123,000 square foot facility provides the DePaul community with a wide variety of fitness and recreation opportunities including a diverse offering of facility spaces, equipment, programs, and services. This state-of-the art facility offers: - 12,000 square foot strength and conditioning area with more than 100 pieces of cardio equipment, selectorized equipment, and free weight area - 25-yard, six-lane swimming pool - Four-court gymnasium for basketball, volleyball, and badminton - Three racquetball courts - 1/8 mile banked jogging track - Locker rooms - Over 65 weekly Group Fitness classes, free to members - Instructional Classes including aquatics, yoga, dance, Pilates, marital arts, fitness training, and safety training. - Personal training - Massage therapy - Intramural sports and club sports for students, faculty, and staff - Outdoor equipment rentals - Outdoor Adventure trips for students, faculty, and staff - Team Challenge.

Disabled Students: Facilities include wheelchair ramps, elevators, special parking, specially equipped restrooms, special class scheduling, lowered drinking fountains, lowered telephones, special housing. The Center for Students with Disabilities coordinates DePaul University's provision of accommodations and other services to students with documented disabilities in accordance with the Americans with Disabilities Act and Section 504 of the Rehabilitation Act. All CSD programs and services are free of charge with the exception of a modest fee for students requesting weekly clinician services for academic support strategies. CSD works with the range of all documented disabilities, e.g., LD, AD/HD, medical conditions, chronic illness, psychiatric, physical/visual/hearing impaired, etc. Students may be full time, part-time, and undergraduate or graduate. CSD students are enrolled in university-wide colleges and schools such as Education, Business, Science and health, Cinema Digital Media (CDM), Communication, Law, Music, Theatre, Liberal Arts and social Sciences, and the School for New Learning (SNL) with declared majors across a wide spectrum of career tracks.

Services: . There is a reader service for the blind, and remedial reading and writing. The Center for Students with Disabilities offers clinician services which includes remediation of skills for time management, organizational skills, reading strategies and writing skills. The University provides free tutoring services across a range of departments and subjects area: University Writing Center, Quantitative Reasoning Lab, Math Department, College of Science/Health, computer software (Word, Excel, etc.), Computer Programming, and Accounting, amongst others.

Campus Safety and Security: Measures include 24-hour foot and vehicle patrol, emergency notification system, self-defense education, and security escort services. There are emergency telephones, lighted pathways/sidewalks, and controlled access to dorms/residences.

Programs of Study: DePaul confers B.A., B.S., B.F.A., B.M., B.S.B. and B.S.P.E. degrees. Master's and doctoral degrees are also awarded. Bachelor's degrees are awarded in BIOLOGICAL SCIENCE (biology/biological science), BUSINESS (accounting, banking and finance, business administration and management, business economics, finance, hospitality management services, human resources, management information systems, management science, marketing management, organizational behavior, and real estate), COMMUNICATIONS AND THE ARTS (animation, Arabic, art history, art, Chinese, communications, creative writing, dramatic arts, English, fine arts, French, German, graphic design, information technology, Italian, jazz, journalism, media arts, music, music business management, music performance, music theory and composition, performing arts, playwriting/screenwriting, public relations, Spanish, speech/debate/rhetoric, theatre arts, theater design, and theater management), COMPUTER AND PHYSICAL SCIENCE (applied mathematics, chemistry, computer programming, computer game design/development, computer science, computer security and information assurance, digital arts/technology, information sciences and systems, mathematics, physical sciences, and physics), EDUCATION (art education, early childhood education, education, education administration, elementary education, foreign languages education, health education, music education, physical education, secondary education, and special education), ENGINEERING AND ENVIRONMENTAL DESIGN (architectural history, computational sciences, computer graphics, computer technology, and environmental science), HEALTH PROFESSIONS (art therapy, clinical science, health science, and nursing), SOCIAL SCIENCE (African studies, American studies, anthropology, community services, East Asian studies, economics, geography, history, humanities, international studies, Islamic studies, Judaic studies, Latin American studies, peace studies, philosophy, political science/government, psychology, public administration, public affairs, religion, social science, social studies, sociology, urban studies, and women's studies).

Required: At DePaul, our core curriculum--the Liberal Studies Program--consists of two primary components: the Common Core and six distinct learning domains. All students (except School for New Learning) must complete general education requirements, including 4 courses in arts and literature, philisophical inquiry, religious dimensions, scientific inquiry self, society and the modern world, and understanding the past. These liberal studies vary by college. A total of 192 quarter hour credits, and a minimum GPA of 2.0 is required to graduate.

Special: DePaul University is known and respected for its nearly 300 graduate and undergraduate programs and concentrations. The Irwin W. Steans Center for Community-based service learning (CbSL) and community service studies provides opportunities and experiences for students to develop social agency through CbSL courses, community internships, research, scholarships, placements, and community-based student employment. The University Internship Program assists students in finding an internship that fits their course of study and career goals. With several locations and programs available, the study abroad office is available to students who are looking for a variety of study abroad opportunities and programs. DePaul also offers accelerated degree programs, dual majors, certificate programs, pass/fail options, and concentrations within the theater major, including acting, costume design, general theater studies, lighting design, playwriting, production theater management, and theater technology. The School for New Learning provides evening and weekend degree programs for adult learners, with credit given for life and work experience. There are 19 national honor societies and a freshman honors program.

Faculty/Classroom: 54% of faculty are male; 46% are female. 79% do both. Graduate students teach 2% of introductory courses. The average class size in an introductory lecture is 25; in a laboratory is 18; and in a regular course is 27.

Admissions: 58% of the 2013-2014 applicants were accepted. The SAT scores for the 2013-2014 freshman class were: Critical Reading--12% below 500, 48% between 500 and 599, 33% between 600 and 699, and 7% between 700 and 800; Math--14% below 500, 49% between 500 and 599, 33% between 600 and 699, and 5% between 700 and 800. The ACT scores were 8% below 21, 23% between 21 and 23, 32% between 24 and 26, 17% between 27 and 28, and 21% above 28. 48% of the current freshmen were in the top fifth of their class; 79% were in the top two fifths. 16 freshmen graduated first in their class.

Requirements: The SAT or ACT is recommended. Based on research and DePaul's student-centered approach to education, DePaul has adopted a test-optional alternative for freshman admission. Students applying for freshman admission can choose whether or not to submit ACT or SAT scores as part of the application. Students who do not submit test scores will be required to send responses to several short essay questions. Music School applicants and applicants for the Acting Program in the Theatre School are required to schedule an audition. An interview or portfolio review is required for Design, Technical, or Theatre Studies program applicants. Please visit our website for more information: http:/www.depaul.edu/admission-and-aid/types-of-admission/Pages/default.aspx. A GPA of 2.0 is required. AP and CLEP credits are accepted. Important factors in the admissions decision are advanced placement or honors courses, leadership record, and personality/intangible qualities.

Procedure: Freshmen are admitted to all sessions. Entrance exams should be taken Scores need to be submitted by 2/1. There are early admissions, deferred admissions, and rolling admissions plans. Early decision applications should be filed by November 15; regular applications, by February 1 for fall entry; November 1 for winter entry; March 1 for spring entry; and May 1 for summer entry, along with a $25 fee. Notification of early decision is sent January 15; regular decision, March 15. Applications are accepted online.

Transfer: 1698 transfer students enrolled in 2012-2013. A 2.0 GPA is required for most programs; a 2.5 for Driehaus College of Business, College of Education, and School of Music. Applicants with fewer than 30 semester hours or 44 quarter hours should submit high school transcripts and SAT or ACT scores. An audition is required for music and theater majors. 60 of 192 credits required for the bachelor's degree must be completed at DePaul.

Visiting: There are regularly scheduled orientations for prospective students, Freshmen orientation, DePaul Premiere, and Transfer and Adult student orientation, Transition DePaul, provide academic advising, assessment testing, and course registration, and information on social activities and residence life. There are guides for informal visits, visitors may sit in on classes, and stay overnight. To schedule a visit, contact Office of Admission.

Financial Aid: In 2013-2014, 71% of all full-time freshmen and 69% of continuing full-time students received some form of financial aid. 61% of all full-time freshmen and 59% of continuing full-time students received need-based aid. The average freshman award was $22,215. Need-based scholarships or need-based grants averaged $11,417; need-based self-help aid (loans and jobs) averaged $3,597; non-need-based athletic scholarships averaged $24,683; and other non-need-based awards and non-need-based scholarships averaged $10,011. 17% of undergraduate students work part-time. The average financial indebtedness of the 2013 graduate was $24,030. The FAFSA is required. The priority date for freshman financial aid applications for fall entry is January 1. The deadline for filing freshman financial aid applications for fall entry is March 1.

International Students: There are 420 international students enrolled. The school actively recruits these students. They must take the TOEFL with a minimum score of 550 on the paper-based TOEFL (PBT) or 80 on the Internet-based version (iBT).

Graduates: From July 1, 2012 to June 30, 2013, 3802 bachelor's degrees were awarded. The most popular majors were psychology (7%), accounting (7%), and finance (7%). 587 companies recruited on campus in 2012-2013. In an average class, 1% graduate in 3 years or less, 54% graduate in 4 years or less, 68% graduate in 5 years or less, and 70% graduate in 6 years or less.

Admissions Contact: Carlene Klaas-Kennelly, Dean of Undergraduate Admission. E-Mail: *admission@depaul.edu* Web: *http:/www.depaul.edu/admission-and-aid/types-of-admission/Pages/default.aspx*

DOMINICAN UNIVERSITY — E-2

River Forest, IL 60305 — (708) 524-6795; (800) 828-8475; (708) 524-6864

Full-time: 643 men, 1264 women	**Faculty:** 135
Part-time: 56 men, 106 women	**Ph.D.s:** 63%
Graduate: 344 men, 1057 women	**Student/Faculty:** 11 to 1
Year: semesters, summer session	**Tuition:** $28,810
Application Deadline: July 1	**Room & Board:** $8818
Freshman Class: 3502 applied, 2100 accepted, 497 enrolled	
SAT CR/M/W: 520/548/527	**ACT:** 22 — **COMPETITIVE**

Dominican University, founded in 1901, is an independent liberal arts institution affiliated with the Roman Catholic Church and sponsored by the Sinsinawa Dominicans. There are 3 undergraduate schools and 4 graduate schools. In addition to regional accreditation, Dominican University has baccalaureate program accreditation with ACBSP, ADA, CSWE, and NCATE. The library contains 250,000 volumes, 50,000 microform items, and 5,000 audio/video tapes/CDs/DVDs, and subscribes to 35,000 periodicals including electronic. Computerized library services include interlibrary loans, database searching, Internet access, and Wi-Fi capability. Special learning facilities include an art gallery, a language lab, and a writing center. The 37-acre campus is in a suburban area 10 miles west of Chicago. Including any residence halls, there are 13 buildings.

Student Life: 91% of undergraduates are from Illinois. Others are from 42 states, 17 foreign countries, and Canada. 66% are from public schools. 44% are White; 40% Hispanic. The average age of freshmen is 19; all undergraduates, 21. 63% remain to graduate.

Housing: 610 students can be accommodated in college housing, which includes single-sex and coed dorms, off-campus apartments, and married student housing. On-campus housing is available on a first-come and first-served basis. Priority is given to out-of-town students. 71% of students commute. All students may keep cars.

Activities: There are no fraternities or sororities. There are 31 groups on campus, including art, choir, communications, computers, dance, drama, environmental, ethnic, gay, honors, international, literary magazine, musical theater, newspaper, photography, political, professional, religious, social, social service, student government, and Students for Peace and Justice. Popular campus events include Caritas Veritas.

Sports: There are 7 intercollegiate sports for men and 6 for women, and 6 intramural sports for men and 6 for women. Facilities include a gym, an indoor running track, a weight room, a training room, a fitness center, a dance room, racquetball courts, and soccer fields.

Disabled Students: All of the campus is accessible. Facilities include wheelchair ramps, elevators, special parking, specially equipped restrooms, special class scheduling, lowered drinking fountains, and special housing.

Services: Counseling and information services are available, as is tutoring in most subjects. There is remedial math and writing.

Campus Safety and Security: Measures include 24-hour foot and vehicle patrol, emergency notification system, self-defense education, and security escort services. There are shuttle buses, emergency telephones, lighted pathways/sidewalks, controlled access to dorms/residences, door alarms.

Programs of Study: Dominican University confers B.A., B.S. and B.M.S. degrees. Master's and doctoral degrees are also awarded. Bachelor's degrees are awarded in BIOLOGICAL SCIENCE (biochemistry, biology/biological science, neurosciences, and nutrition), BUSINESS (accounting, apparel and accessories marketing, business administration and management, fashion merchandising, finance, international business management, and marketing management), COMMUNICATIONS AND THE ARTS (apparel design, art history, communications, dramatic arts, English, film arts, fine arts, French, graphic design, Italian, journalism, music, painting, performing arts, photography, Spanish, and theatre arts), COMPUTER AND PHYSICAL SCIENCE (chemistry, computer science, digital arts/technology, mathematics, and natural sciences), EDUCATION (early childhood education, education, elementary education, and secondary education), ENGINEERING AND ENVIRONMENTAL DESIGN (engineering and environmental science), HEALTH PROFESSIONS (nursing, predentistry, premedicine, and prepharmacy), SOCIAL SCIENCE (American studies, criminal justice, dietetics, economics, fashion design and technology, food production/management/services, food science, gender studies, history, international relations, legal studies, ministries, philosophy, political science/government, prelaw, psychology, religion, social science, sociology, theological studies, and women's studies). Business administration, health professions, and psychology are the strongest academically. Business administration, psychology, and biology have the largest enrollments.

Required: To graduate, students must complete 124 credit hours with a minimum GPA of 2.0. A total of 30 to 56 hours is required in the major. All students must demonstrate proficiency, through a placement exam or the completion of specified courses, in English composition, math, computer competency, and library skills. In addition, students must take 1 interdisciplinary seminar at each academic level and 1 course each in natural sciences, history, fine arts and literature, social sciences, theology, and philosophy. 1 course must meet the multicultural requirement.

Special: Co-op programs in nursing with Rush University, cross-registration with Concordia University, internships, study abroad in 11 countries, and a Washington semester are offered. Student-designed majors and interdisciplinary majors, including computer information systems, math and computer science, and environmental science, credit for prior learning, and pass/fail options are possible. There is an accelerated degree program in organizational leadership, a joint B.A.-B.S. in engineering with the Illinois Institute of Technology, and a dual admission program with Midwestern University for pharmacy. There are 11 national honor societies and a freshman honors program.

Faculty/Classroom: 41% of faculty are male; 59% are female. 75% teach undergraduates, and 25% do both. No introductory courses are taught by graduate students. The average class size in an introductory lecture is 19; in a laboratory is 15; and in a regular course is 17.

Admissions: 60% of the 2013-2014 applicants were accepted. The SAT scores for the 2013-2014 freshman class were: Critical Reading--38% below 500, 56% between 500 and 599, and 6% between 600 and 699; Math--38% below 500, 31% between 500 and 599, 25% between 600 and 699, and 6% between 700 and 800; Writing--31% below 500, 50% between 500 and 599, and 19% between 600 and 699. The ACT scores were 37% below 21, 34% between 21 and 23, 20% between 24 and 26, 4% between 27 and 28, and 5% above 28. 1 freshman graduated first in the class.

Requirements: The SAT or ACT is required. Graduation from an accredited secondary school or satisfactory scores on the GED are required for admission. The school requires 14 academic credits or 16 Carnegie units. High school courses should include English, math, foreign language, social science, and lab science. An essay is required and an interview is recommended. AP and CLEP credits are accepted. Important factors in the admissions decision are advanced placement or honors courses, recommendations by school officials, and leadership record.

Procedure: Freshmen are admitted fall and spring. Entrance exams should be taken in the junior year. There are deferred admissions and rolling admissions plans. Application deadlines are open. Application fee is $25. Notification is sent on a rolling basis. Applications are accepted online.

Transfer: 125 transfer students enrolled in 2012-2013. A college transcript is required. Applicants must have a minimum of 12 credit hours with a GPA of 2.5. An interview is recommended. The high school record will be evaluated if GPA is below 2.5 at the previous college. 34 of 124 credits required for the bachelor's degree must be completed at Dominican University.

Visiting: There are regularly scheduled orientations for prospective students, including visiting day and open house programs, which consist of faculty and student presentations, tours, and an academic and co-curricular fair. Special events are also held during the summer. There are guides for informal visits, visitors may sit in on classes, and stay overnight. To schedule a visit, contact Office of Undergraduate Admissions at (708) 524-6800.

Financial Aid: In 2013-2014, 95% of all full-time freshmen and 92% of continuing full-time students received some form of financial aid. 91% of all full-time freshmen and 87% of continuing full-time students received need-based aid. The average freshman award was $23,897. Need-based scholarships or need-based grants averaged $20,145; need-based self-help aid (loans and jobs) averaged $3,293; and other non-need-based awards and non-need-based scholarships averaged $6,222. 20% of undergraduate students work part-time. Average annual earnings from campus work are $2500. The average financial indebtedness of the 2013 graduate was $31,356. Dominican University is a member of CSS. The FAFSA is required. The priority date for freshman financial aid applications for fall entry is February 15.

International Students: There are 57 international students enrolled. They must take the TOEFL with a minimum score of 550 on the paper-based TOEFL (PBT) or 79 on the Internet-based version (iBT). They must also take the SAT or ACT.

Graduates: From July 1, 2012 to June 30, 2013, 444 bachelor's degrees were awarded. The most popular majors were business (23%), health professions (14%), and social sciences (12%). 30 companies recruited on campus in 2012-2013. In an average class, 48% graduate in 4 years or less, 61% graduate in 5 years or less, and 63% graduate in 6 years or less. Of the 2012 graduating class, 32% were enrolled in graduate school within 6 months of graduation, and 53% were employed.

Admissions Contact: Glenn Hamilton, Assistant Vice President for Enrollment . E-Mail: *domadmis@dom.edu* Web: *http:/www.dom.edu/admission/index.html*

EASTERN ILLINOIS UNIVERSITY E-4

Charleston, IL 61920 **(217) 581-2223; (217) 581-7060**

Full-time: 3002 men, 4325 women	**Faculty:** n/av; IIA, -$
Part-time: 366 men, 654 women	**Ph.D.s:** 70%
Graduate: 559 men, 869 women	**Student/Faculty:** n/av
Year: semesters, summer session	**Tuition:** $11,144 ($28,124)
Application Deadline: Rolling	**Room & Board:** $9358
Freshman Class: 7881 applied, 4879 accepted, 1254 enrolled	
ACT: 22	**SAT:** required **COMPETITIVE**

Eastern Illinois University is a public comprehensive university that offers superior, accessible undergraduate and graduate education. Students learn the methods and results of free and rigorous inquiry in the arts, humanities, sciences, and professions, guided by a faculty known for its excellence in teaching, research, creative activity, and service. The University community is committed to diversity and inclusion and fosters opportunities for student-faculty scholarship and applied learning experiences within a student-centered campus culture. Throughout their education, students refine their abilities to reason and to communicate clearly so as to become responsible citizens and leaders. There are 4 undergraduate schools and one graduate school. In addition to regional accreditation, EIU has baccalaureate program accreditation with AACSB, ACEJMC, ADA, NASAD, NASM, NCATE, and NRPA. The library contains 1.8 million volumes, 576,533 microform items, and 43,033 audio/video tapes/CDs/DVDs, and subscribes to 39,156 periodicals including electronic. Computerized library services include interlibrary loans, database searching, Internet access, and Wi-Fi capability. Special learning facilities include an art gallery, radio station, TV station, Obervatory, Scanning Electon Microscope (SEM) Laboratory, and Greenhouse. The 320-acre campus is in a small town 188 miles from Chicago, 127 miles from Indianapolis, and 139 miles from St. Louis, Missouri. Including any residence halls, there are 80 buildings.

Student Life: 97% of undergraduates are from Illinois. Others are from 30 states, 30 foreign countries, and Canada. 70% are White; 18% African American. The average age of freshmen is 18; all undergraduates, 22. 23% do not continue beyond their first year; 60% remain to graduate.

Housing: 5410 students can be accommodated in college housing, which includes single-sex and coed dorms, on-campus apartments, and married student housing. In addition, there are honors houses, fraternity houses, and sorority houses. On-campus housing is guaranteed for the freshman year only, is available on a first-come, and first-served basis. 63% of students commute. All students may keep cars.

Activities: 21% of men belong to 15 national fraternities; 18% of women belong to 12 national sororities. There are 214 groups on campus, including art, band, cheerleading, choir, chorale, chorus, communications, dance, drama, drill team, environmental, ethnic, film, gay, honors, international, jazz band, literary magazine, marching band, musical theater, newspaper, orchestra, pep band, political, professional, radio and TV, religious, social, social service, student government, symphony, and yearbook. Popular campus events include Celebration of the Arts, Homecoming and Family Weekend.

Sports: There are 10 intercollegiate sports for men and 11 for women, and 11 intramural sports for men and 11 for women. Facilities include a swimming pool, gym, student recreation center, track, tennis courts, racquetball courts, jogging trail, baseball field, softball field, football field, basketball court, soccer field, and a rugby field.

Disabled Students: 80% of the campus is accessible. Facilities include wheelchair ramps, elevators, special parking, specially equipped restrooms, special class scheduling, lowered drinking fountains, lowered telephones, and special housing.

Services: Counseling and information services are available, as is tutoring in most subjects, biology, business, chemistry, writing (all subjects), economics, foreign language, geology/geography, history, mathematics, physics, political science, psychology and sociology. There is remedial math, reading, and writing. Student success center for help on study skills, test-taking and time management.

Campus Safety and Security: Measures include 24-hour foot and vehicle patrol, emergency notification system, self-defense education, and security escort services. There are shuttle buses, emergency telephones, lighted pathways/sidewalks, and controlled access to dorms/residences.

Programs of Study: EIU confers B.A., B.F.A., B.M., B.S., B.S.Bus. and B.S.Ed. degrees. Master's degrees are also awarded. Bachelor's degrees are awarded in BIOLOGICAL SCIENCE (biology/biological science), BUSINESS (accounting, banking and finance, business administration and management, management information systems, marketing/retailing/merchandising, and organizational leadership and management), COMMUNICATIONS AND THE ARTS (art, communications, communication science, dramatic arts, English, journalism, languages, and music), COMPUTER AND PHYSICAL SCIENCE (chemistry, computer science, geology, mathematics, and physics), EDUCATION (athletic training, early childhood education, elementary education, middle school education, recreation education, science education, social science education, special education, sports studies, and technical education), ENGINEERING AND ENVIRONMENTAL DESIGN (engineering and industrial engineering technology), HEALTH PROFESSIONS (health, medical laboratory science, nursing, and speech pathology/audiology), SOCIAL SCIENCE (African studies, economics, family/consumer studies, geography, history, liberal arts/general studies, philosophy, political science/government, psychology, and sociology). Nursing is the strongest academically. Kinesiology and sports studies, biological sciences and general studies have the largest enrollments.

Required: A total of 120 credit hours, with a minimum of 40 hours in upper-division courses, must be completed for graduation. The minimum GPA required for graduation is 2.0 (2.65 in education). A core curriculum of 40 to 46 hours includes courses in language, humanities and fine arts, math, and social and behavioral science.

Special: EIU offers a co-op program in engineering with the University of Illinois at Champaign-Urbana or Southern Illinois University at Carbondale. Internships, study abroad,and double majors are available. Credit for life experience may be granted through the General Studies program and the Organizational and Professional Development program. There are 44 national honor societies, a freshman honors program, and 24 departmental honors programs.

Faculty/Classroom: 51% of faculty are male; 49% are female. No introductory courses are taught by graduate students. The average class size in a regular course is 17.

Admissions: 62% of the 2013-2014 applicants were accepted. The ACT scores were 40% below 21, 34% between 21 and 23, 16% between 24 and 26, 6% between 27 and 28, and 4% above 28. 24% of the current freshmen were in the top fifth of their class; 53% were in the top two fifths.

Requirements: The SAT or ACT is required. All applicants must submit ACT or SAT scores and meet one of the following: rank in the top quarter of their high school class based on 6 or more semesters or have a GPA of 3.0 and have an ACT composite of at least 18 (SAT 860); rank in the top one half of their high school class based on 6 or more semesters or have a GPA of 2.5 and have an ACT composite score of at least 19 (SAT 910); rank in the top three quarters of their high school class based on 6 or more semesters or have a GPA of 2.25 and an ACT composite score of at least 22 (SAT 1020). Applicants must be graduates of an accredited secondary school. The GED is accepted. 13 academic credits are required and should include 4 years of English and 3 years each of math, science, and social studies, including 1 year of U.S. history. EIU requires applicants to be in the upper 75% of their class. A GPA of 2.3 is required. AP and CLEP credits are accepted.

Procedure: Freshmen are admitted fall, spring, and summer. Entrance exams should be taken EIU does not require entrance exams. There are deferred admissions and rolling admissions plans. Application deadlines are open. Application fee is $30. Notification is sent on a Rolling basis. Applications are accepted online.

Transfer: 938 transfer students enrolled in 2012-2013. Applicants with 30 or more college-level semester hours must have a cumulative grade point average of 2.0 on a 4.0 grading scale based on all college-level work attempted and a 2.0 cumulative grade point average on a 4.0 scale from the last institution attended. Applicants with 24 or more college-level semester hours must have a cumulative grade point average of 2.5 on a 4.0 grading scale based on all college-level work attempted and a 2.0 cumulative grade point average on a 4.0 scale from the last institution attended. Applicants with fewer than the required number of hours of earned credit must have at least a 2.0 grade point average on a 4.0 scale based on all college-level work attempted, a 2.0 grade point average on a 4.0 scale from the last institution attended and meet the freshman admission criteria. 42 of 120 credits required for the bachelor's degree must be completed at EIU.

Visiting: There are regularly scheduled orientations for prospective students, tour of campus and residence halls, sessions on financial aid, housing, admission process, tips for academic success, steps to take after admission, transfer admission, academic & student services fair. There are guides for informal visits and visitors may sit in on classes. To schedule a visit, contact the Office of Admissions.

Financial Aid: In 2013-2014, 72% of all full-time freshmen and 68% of continuing full-time students received some form of financial aid. 49% of all full-time freshmen and 47% of continuing full-time students received need-based aid. The average freshman award was $11,079. Need-based scholarships or need-based grants averaged $3,617; need-based self-help aid (loans and jobs) averaged $3,021; non-need-based athletic scholarships averaged $7,255; and other non-need-based awards and non-need-based scholarships averaged $3,364. 27% of undergraduate students work part-time. Average annual earnings from campus work are $1559. The average financial indebtedness of the 2013 graduate was $29,837. The FAFSA is required. The priority date for freshman financial aid applications for fall entry is March 1. The deadline for filing freshman financial aid applications for fall entry is Rolling.

International Students: There are 69 international students enrolled. The school actively recruits these students. They must take the TOEFL with a minimum score of 500 on the paper-based TOEFL (PBT) or 61 on the Internet-based version (iBT) or take the MELAB, IELTS.

Graduates: From July 1, 2012 to June 30, 2013, 2238 bachelor's degrees were awarded. The most popular majors were general studies (10%), kinesiology and sports studies (9%), and elementary education (8%). 265 companies recruited on campus in 2012-2013. In an average class, 34% graduate in 4 years or less, 56% graduate in 5 years or less, and 60% graduate in 6 years or less.

Admissions Contact: Mary Herrington-Perry, Assistant VPAA/ Enrollment Management . E-Mail: *admissions@eiu.edu* Web: *http:/www.eiu.edu*

EAST-WEST UNIVERSITY — E-2

Chicago, IL 60605 — (312) 939-0111; (877) 398-9376; (312) 939-0083

Full-time: 380 men, 630 women	**Faculty:** n/av
Part-time: 10 men, 20 women	**Ph.D.s:** 8%
Graduate: n/av	**Student/Faculty:** n/av
Year: trimesters, summer session	**Tuition:** $16,695
Application Deadline: open	**Room & Board:** n/app
Freshman Class: n/av	
ACT: required	**COMPETITIVE**

East-West University, founded in 1978, is a private commuter institution offering undergraduate programs in the arts and sciences, business, computer science, and engineering. The figures in the above capsule and in this profile are approximate. The library contains 21,500 volumes, 8500 microform items, and subscribes to 95 periodicals including electronic. The campus is in an urban area in Chicago. There is 1 building.

Student Life: 85% of undergraduates are from Illinois. 97% are from public schools. 75% are African American; 13% Hispanic. The average age of freshmen is 19; all undergraduates, 20.

Housing: There are no residence halls. All students commute.

Activities: There are no fraternities or sororities. There are 3 groups on campus, including drama, international, and student government. Popular campus events include International Day, Mother's Day Banquet, and Black History Celebration.

Sports: There is no sports program at East-West.

Disabled Students: 50% of the campus is accessible. Facilities include elevators and specially equipped rest rooms.

Services: Counseling and information services are available, as is tutoring in most subjects. There is remedial math, reading, and writing.

Programs of Study: East-West confers B.A. and B.S. degrees. Associate degrees are also awarded. Bachelor's degrees are awarded in BUSINESS (business administration and management), COMMUNICATIONS AND THE ARTS (communications and English), COMPUTER AND PHYSICAL SCIENCE (computer science), ENGINEERING AND ENVIRONMENTAL DESIGN (electrical/electronics engineering technology), SOCIAL SCIENCE (behavioral science). Business administration has the largest enrollment.

Required: General education requirements vary according to the degree program. To graduate, students must complete at least 180 quarter hours, including 60 in a major field, with a minimum GPA of 2.0.

Special: East-West offers co-op programs in all majors.

Faculty/Classroom: All teach undergraduates. The average class size in an introductory lecture is 15; in a laboratory, 15; and in a regular course,15.

Requirements: The ACT is required. Applicants must be graduates of accredited secondary schools or have earned a GED. Placement exams are required in math and English. A GPA of 2.5 is required. AP and CLEP credits are accepted.

Procedure: Freshmen are admitted to all sessions. There is a rolling admissions plan. Application deadlines are open. Check with the school for the current application fee.

Transfer: East-West accepts only courses with grades of C or better. 48 of 180 credits required for the bachelor's degree must be completed at East-West.

Visiting: There are regularly scheduled orientations for prospective students. There are guides for informal visits and visitors may sit in on classes.

Financial Aid: The CSS/Profile is required. Check with the school for current application deadlines.

International Students: The school actively recruits these students. They must take the college's own test and are encouraged but not required to submit TOEFL scores.

Admissions Contact: Director of Admissions. E-Mail: *seeyou@eastwest.edu* Web: *www.eastwest.edu*

ELMHURST COLLEGE — E-2

Elmhurst, IL 60126 — (630) 617-3400; (800) 697-1871; (630) 617-5501

Full-time: 1083 men, 1653 women	**Faculty:** 136; IIB
Part-time: 77 men, 87 women	**Ph.D.s:** 81%
Graduate: 103 men, 207 women	**Student/Faculty:** 20 to 1
Year: 4-1-4, summer session	**Tuition:** $32,920
Application Deadline:	**Room & Board:** $9112
Freshman Class: 2730 applied, 1950 accepted, 506 enrolled	
SAT CR/M/W: 490/510/490 — **ACT:** 24	**COMPETITIVE+**

Elmhurst College is a premier, private, liberal arts college located in suburban Chicago. Among Elmhurst's specialties is its synergy of two indispensable elements of a quality college experience: professional preparation and liberal learning. For 142 years, Elmhurst College has sought to prepare students superbly, both for their first jobs and for fulfilling lives. On a classic campus, in an optimal location, Elmhurst offers students of many backgrounds purposeful learning for the whole of life. There is one graduate school. The library contains 237,539 volumes, 49,798 microform items, and 49,413 audio/video tapes/CDs/DVDs, and subscribes to 24,245 periodicals including electronic. Computerized library services include interlibrary loans, database searching, Internet access, and Wi-Fi capability. Special learning facilities include an art gallery, radio station, a recording studio that offers recording and control room spaces with grand piano and isolation booth and a digital 24-track hard drive Otari Radar system with automated status console; the SimBaby, a life-size, robotic model of an infant and SimMan, an adult patient simulator; an electron microscopy lab; an accelerator lab. The 48-acre campus is in a suburban area 15 miles west of Chicago. Including any residence halls, there are 23 buildings.

Student Life: 90% of undergraduates are from Illinois. Others are from 36 states, 35 foreign countries, and Canada. 89% are from public schools. 72% are White; 13% Hispanic. 38% are Catholic; 18% Protestant; 13% claim no religious affiliation. The average age of freshmen is 18; all undergraduates, 22. 22% do not continue beyond their first year; 74% remain to graduate.

Housing: 1132 students can be accommodated in college housing, which includes coed dorms, on-campus apartments, and off-campus apartments. 64% of students commute. Some may keep cars.

Activities: 9% of men belong to 3 national fraternities; 11% of women belong to 4 national sororities. There are 92 groups on campus, including art, band, cheerleading, chess, choir, chorale, chorus, communications, computers, dance, drama, environmental, ethnic, film, gay, honors, international, jazz band, literary magazine, musical theater, newspaper, orchestra, pep band, political, professional, radio and TV, religious, social, social service, student government, symphony, and yearbook. Popular campus events include Elmhurst College Jazz Festival, Lecture Series, Theater Performances, Summer Extravaganza, and the Performances by Elmhurst College Ensembles.

Sports: There are 10 intercollegiate sports for men and 9 for women, and

7 intramural sports for men and 7 for women. Facilities include a phys ed center, weight rooms, and courts for tennis, racquetball, and handball. Langhorst Athletic Field is home to the College's football, soccer, track and field teams.

Disabled Students: 95% of the campus is accessible. Facilities include wheelchair ramps, elevators, special parking, specially equipped restrooms, lowered drinking fountains, and lowered telephones.

Services: Counseling and information services are available, as is tutoring in most subjects. There is remedial math, reading, and writing.

Campus Safety and Security: Measures include 24-hour foot and vehicle patrol, emergency notification system, and security escort services. There are shuttle buses, emergency telephones, lighted pathways/sidewalks, and controlled access to dorms/residences.

Programs of Study: Elmhurst confers B.A., B.F.A, B.S., B.L.S. and B.Mus. degrees. Master's degrees are also awarded. Bachelor's degrees are awarded in BIOLOGICAL SCIENCE (biology/biological science and (Biological) Pre-Health Studies), BUSINESS (accounting, business administration and management, finance, international business management, management science, marketing/retailing/merchandising, and supply chain management), COMMUNICATIONS AND THE ARTS (art, arts administration/management, communications, communication science, English, French, German, graphic design, information technology, jazz, music, music business management, music theory and composition, Spanish, and theatre arts), COMPUTER AND PHYSICAL SCIENCE (chemistry, computer game design/development, computer science, information sciences and systems, mathematics, and physics), EDUCATION (art education, early childhood education, elementary education, mathematics education, music education, physical education, secondary education, and special education), ENGINEERING AND ENVIRONMENTAL DESIGN (environmental science and preengineering), HEALTH PROFESSIONS (exercise science, nursing, Pre-Health Studies, premedicine, prephysical therapy, preveterinary science, and speech pathology/audiology), SOCIAL SCIENCE (American studies, criminal justice, economics, geography, history, liberal arts/general studies, philosophy, political science/government, psychology, religion, sociology, theological studies, and urban studies). Biology, English, nursing and education are the strongest academically. Business, psychology, nursing and education-related programs have the largest enrollments.

Required: Complete all aspects of the Integrated Curriculum or General Education program; Complete all the requirements for a major; Earn a minimum of 32.00 course credits; Complete at least 10.00 course credits at the 300/400 level at a four-year institution; Achieve a minimum combined and institutional GPA of 2.0 (some majors require a higher GPA); Earn one's final 8.00 course credits at Elmhurst College (residency requirement)

Special: There are cooperative programs in all majors. In keeping with the hallmarks of the Elmhurst Experience, self-formation and early professional preparation, Career Education starts early-on in most students' academic experience. The Center for Professional Excellence provides experiential opportunities for career exploration to majors in 23 academic departments, e.g., internships, informational interviews, career shadowing, and connections to professional mentors. Internships varying from 1 month to one term are available in approximately 20 major fields. Students may study abroad in over 40 countries. Elmhurst also offers a Washington and Chicago Semester and a 3-2 engineering degree with the Illinois Institute of Technology, Washington University, and the Universities of Illinois and Southern California. There are accelerated degree programs in business administration, organizational leadership & communication, information technology, and pre-clinical psychology. Credit for life, military, and work experience, nondegree study and pass/fail options are possible. There are 23 national honor societies, a freshman honors program, and 25 departmental honors programs.

Faculty/Classroom: 45% of faculty are male; 55% are female. All teach and do research. No introductory courses are taught by graduate students. The average class size in an introductory lecture is 19; in a laboratory is 15; and in a regular course is 16.

Admissions: 71% of the 2013-2014 applicants were accepted. The SAT scores for the 2013-2014 freshman class were: Critical Reading--59% below 500, 27% between 500 and 599, and 15% between 600 and 699; Math--44% below 500, 39% between 500 and 599, 15% between 600 and 699, and 2% between 700 and 800; Writing--51% below 500, 37% between 500 and 599, and 12% between 600 and 699. The ACT scores were 21% below 21, 29% between 21 and 23, 25% between 24 and 26, 12% between 27 and 28, and 13% above 28. 40% of the current freshmen were in the top fifth of their class; 65% were in the top two fifths. 4 freshmen graduated first in their class.

Requirements: The ACT or SAT is required, with the ACT preferred. Candidates for admission must have completed 16 academic units of credit including at least 3 in English and 2 each of math, social science, and natural science lab courses. 2 years of a foreign language are recommended. AP and CLEP credits are accepted. Important factors in the admissions decision are advanced placement or honors courses, leadership record, and extracurricular activities record.

Procedure: Freshmen are admitted fall and spring. Entrance exams should be taken by the spring of the senior year. There are early admissions, deferred admissions, and rolling admissions plans. Applications should be filed by January 15 for spring entry. Notification is sent on a rolling basis. Applications are accepted online.

Transfer: 309 transfer students enrolled in 2012-2013. Qualified applicants should show evidence of their ability to successfully complete college-level work, based on their good standing at the last college or university attended. 32 of 128 credits required for the bachelor's degree must be completed at Elmhurst.

Visiting: There are regularly scheduled orientations for prospective students, including an admissions interview, a campus tour, and faculty meetings if desired. There are guides for informal visits, visitors may sit in on classes, and stay overnight. To schedule a visit, contact Francesca Garza at (630) 617-3400.

Financial Aid: The FAFSA and the college's own financial statement are required. The priority date for freshman financial aid applications for fall entry is March 1.

International Students: There are 78 international students enrolled. The school actively recruits these students. They must take the TOEFL with a minimum score of 550 on the paper-based TOEFL (PBT) or 79 on the Internet-based version (iBT) or take the MELAB.

Graduates: From July 1, 2012 to June 30, 2013, 772 bachelor's degrees were awarded. The most popular majors were business (20%), health sciences (13%), and education (12%). 30 companies recruited on campus in 2012-2013. In an average class, 59% graduate in 4 years or less, 72% graduate in 5 years or less, and 74% graduate in 6 years or less. Of the 2012 graduating class, 33% were enrolled in graduate school within 6 months of graduation, and 78% were employed.

Admissions Contact: Stephanie Levenson, Director of Admissions. E-Mail: *admit@elmhurst.edu* Web: *www.elmhurst.edu*

EUREKA COLLEGE — D-3

Eureka, IL 61530 — (309) 467-6350; (888) 4-EUREKA; (309) 467-6576

Full-time: 550 men and women	**Faculty:** n/av; IIB, --$
Part-time: 15 men and women	**Ph.D.s:** 85%
Graduate: n/av	**Student/Faculty:** n/av
Year: semesters, summer session	**Tuition:** $18,750
Application Deadline: see profile	**Room & Board:** $8000
Freshman Class: n/av	
SAT or ACT: required	

COMPETITIVE

Eureka College, founded in 1855, is a small, private, liberal arts college affiliated with the Christian Church (Disciples of Christ). In addition to regional accreditation, E.C. has baccalaureate program accreditation with NCATE. The library contains 85,000 volumes, 4989 microform items, and 977 audio/video tapes/CDs/DVDs, and subscribes to 343 periodicals including electronic. Computerized library services include interlibrary loans, database searching, and Internet access. Special learning facilities include a learning resource center, art gallery, and the Ronald Reagan Museum. The 112-acre campus is in a small town 20 minutes east of Peoria, 20 minutes west of Bloomington, and 2 hours south of Chicago. Including any residence halls, there are 23 buildings.

Student Life: 90% of undergraduates are from Illinois. Others are from 17 states and 3 foreign countries. 80% are from public schools. 87% are white. 37% claim no religious affiliation; 31% Protestant; 28% Catholic. The average age of freshmen is 18; all undergraduates, 21. 25% do not continue beyond their first year; 65% remain to graduate.

Housing: 550 students can be accommodated in college housing, which includes single-sex and coed dorms. In addition, there are fraternity houses and sorority houses. On-campus housing is guaranteed for all 4 years. 80% of students live on campus; of those, 70% remain on campus on weekends. All students may keep cars.

Activities: 35% of men belong to 3 national fraternities; 35% of women belong to 1 local sorority and 2 national sororities. There are 41 groups on campus, including art, band, cheerleading, choir, chorale, chorus, communications, computers, dance, drama, ethnic, honors, international, literary magazine, musical theater, newspaper, pep band, photography, political, professional, religious, social, social service, student government, and yearbook. Popular campus events include Pride Day, Tree Lighting Ceremony, and Ivy Ceremony.

Sports: There are 8 intercollegiate sports for men and 8 for women, and 6 intramural sports for men and 6 for women. Facilities include a gym, a pool, a weight room, tennis courts, football, softball, and baseball fields, and a wellness center.

Disabled Students: 50% of the campus is accessible. Facilities include wheelchair ramps, elevators, special parking, and specially equipped rest rooms.

Services: Counseling and information services are available, as is tutoring in most subjects. There is remedial reading and writing. There is a writing center and math lab located within the Learning Center.

Campus Safety and Security: There are lighted pathways/sidewalks.

A city police officer provides campus security in the evenings and on weekends.

Programs of Study: E.C. confers B.A. and B.S. degrees. Bachelor's degrees are awarded in BIOLOGICAL SCIENCE (biology/biological science), BUSINESS (accounting, business administration and management, business economics, and management information systems), COMMUNICATIONS AND THE ARTS (communications, dramatic arts, English, fine arts, and music), COMPUTER AND PHYSICAL SCIENCE (chemistry, computer science, mathematics, and physical sciences), EDUCATION (athletic training, education, elementary education, music education, physical education, science education, and secondary education), HEALTH PROFESSIONS (medical laboratory technology), SOCIAL SCIENCE (child care/child and family studies, history, liberal arts/general studies, philosophy, physical fitness/movement, political science/government, psychology, religion, social science, and sociology). Chemistry, biology, and business administration are the strongest academically. Business administration, education, and psychology have the largest enrollments.

Required: All students must take English composition, biological and physical sciences, general studies, math, phys ed, Western civilization, 3 humanities courses, 3 social science courses, and a global awareness component. A total of at least 124 hours is required for graduation, including 32 hours in the major. A minimum GPA of 2.0 is required.

Special: Cooperative programs include a 3-2 engineering degree with Washington University in St. Louis and Illinois Institute of Technology, a 2-2 B.S.N. with Mennonite College of Nursing or St. Francis College of Nursing, and a 3-1 clinical lab science degree with St. Francis or St. John's School of Clinical Laboratory Science. Students may study abroad in most countries. Professional programs in arts management, art therapy, communications, prelaw, premedicine, preministry, and teacher education are offered. An interdisciplinary major in arts and letters combines visual, performing, and literary arts. Internships and student-designed and dual majors are offered in various areas. A Washington semester is available. There are 7 national honor societies and a freshman honors program. All departments have honors programs.

Faculty/Classroom: 64% of faculty are male; 36% are female. All teach undergraduates. The average class size in an introductory lecture is 15; in a laboratory, 10; and in a regular course, 15.

Requirements: The SAT or ACT is required. Applicants should be graduates of accredited secondary schools or have the GED. E.C. requires applicants to be in the upper 50% of their class. A GPA of 2.3 is required. AP and CLEP credits are accepted. Important factors in the admissions decision are recommendations by school officials, extracurricular activities record, and leadership record.

Procedure: Freshmen are admitted to all sessions. Entrance exams should be taken by December of the senior year. There are deferred admissions and rolling admissions plans. Check with the school for current application deadlines and fee. Notification is sent on a rolling basis. Applications are accepted online.

Transfer: Applicants must have at least a 2.0 GPA in previous college work. Those with fewer than 30 hours of transferable credit must submit high school transcripts and ACT scores. Courses with grades below C are not accepted. 30 of 124 credits required for the bachelor's degree must be completed at E.C.

Visiting: There are regularly scheduled orientations for prospective students, including visits with admissions and financial aid advisers, observing student panels, meetings with faculty and coaches, and campus tours. There are guides for informal visits, and visitors may sit in on classes and stay overnight. To schedule a visit, contact the Office of Admissions.

Financial Aid: E.C. is a member of CSS. The FAFSA is required. Check with the school for current application deadlines.

International Students: The school actively recruits these students. They must take the TOEFL.

Admissions Contact: Dean of Admissions and Financial Aid. A campus DVD is available. E-Mail: *admissions@eureka.edu* Web: *www.eureka.edu*

GREENVILLE COLLEGE D-4

Greenville, IL 62246-0159 **(618) 664-7100**
(800) 345-4440; (618) 664-9841

Full-time: 610 men, 730 women	**Faculty:** 63; IIB, --$
Part-time: 20 men, 30 women	**Ph.D.s:** 66%
Graduate: 50 men, 140 women	**Student/Faculty:** n/av
Year: semesters, summer session	**Tuition:** $22,198
Application Deadline: see profile	**Room & Board:** $7338
Freshman Class: n/av	
SAT or ACT: required	

COMPETITIVE

Greenville College, founded in 1892, is a private liberal arts institution affiliated with the Free Methodist Church. Greenville College seeks to transform students for lives of character and service through a Christ-centered education in the liberal arts and sciences. The figures in the above capsule and in this profile are approximate. There are 3 undergraduate schools. The library contains 135,210 volumes, 17,384 microform items, and 3873 audio/video tapes/CDs/DVDs, and subscribes to 8543 periodicals including electronic. Computerized library services include interlibrary loans, database searching, and Internet access. Special learning facilities include a learning resource center, art gallery, radio station, and the Bock Museum. The 25-acre campus is in a small town 50 miles east of St. Louis. Including any residence halls, there are 48 buildings.

Student Life: 72% of undergraduates are from Illinois. Others are from 42 states, 12 foreign countries, and Canada. 87% are white. 72% are Protestant; 21% claim no religious affiliation. The average age of freshmen is 18; all undergraduates, 24. 27% do not continue beyond their first year; 48% remain to graduate.

Housing: 792 students can be accommodated in college housing, which includes single-sex dorms and on-campus apartments. On-campus housing is guaranteed for all 4 years. 54% of students live on campus; of those, 60% remain on campus on weekends. Alcohol is not permitted. All students may keep cars.

Activities: There are no fraternities or sororities. There are 20 groups on campus, including radio, art, band, cheerleading, choir, chorale, chorus, drama, ethnic, honors, jazz band, musical theater, newspaper, orchestra, pep band, professional, religious, social, social service, and student government. Popular campus events include Agape Music Festival, All College Hike, and Back to School Bash.

Sports: There are 7 intercollegiate sports for men and 7 for women, and 6 intramural sports for men and 6 for women. Facilities include a gym, a sports training annex, a recreational center, 6 tennis courts, a fitness pool, an all-weather track, and softball, baseball, football, soccer, and practice fields.

Disabled Students: 25% of the campus is accessible. Facilities include wheelchair ramps, elevators, special parking, specially equipped restrooms, special class scheduling, and lowered drinking fountains.

Services: Counseling and information services are available, as is tutoring in lower-division general education courses. There is remedial math, reading, and writing, and a program for at-risk freshmen.

Campus Safety and Security: Measures include self-defense education and security escort services. There are emergency telephones, lighted pathways/sidewalks, controlled access to dorms/residences, and alarm systems in some buildings.

Programs of Study: Greenville confers B.A., B.Mus.Ed., and B.S. degrees. Master's degrees are also awarded. Bachelor's degrees are awarded in BIOLOGICAL SCIENCE (biology/biological science and environmental biology), BUSINESS (accounting, business administration and management, management information systems, marketing/retailing/merchandising, organizational leadership and management, and recreation and leisure services), COMMUNICATIONS AND THE ARTS (art, communications, contemporary Christian music, dramatic arts, English, media arts, music, music business management, public relations, recording industry, Spanish, and speech/debate/rhetoric), COMPUTER AND PHYSICAL SCIENCE (chemistry, computer science, digital arts/technology, mathematics, and physics), EDUCATION (early childhood education, elementary education, English education, mathematics education, music education, physical education, science education, and special education), SOCIAL SCIENCE (criminal justice, history, international studies, liberal arts/general studies, ministries, pastoral studies, philosophy, psychology, religion, social work, sociology, and youth ministry). Biology, chemistry, and physics are the strongest academically. Education, music, and biology have the largest enrollments.

Required: A minimum of 126 credits and a 2.0 GPA are required for graduation. All students must successfully complete the core requirements in addition to specific courses in communication, English, history, phys ed, and foreign language (B.A. only). Other degree requirements are fulfilled by in-depth study in biblical studies, cross-cultural experience, physical fitness activities, lab science, math, literature, philosophy, fine arts, psychology or sociology, and a writing-intensive course.

Special: The college provides opportunities for dual majors in such areas as psychology/religion, B.A.-B.S. degrees, student-designed programs in work-study programs, study abroad, credit by exam, internships, a general studies degree, pass/fail options, and nondegree study. A 3-2 engineering degree with the University of Illinois and Washington University, a 2-2 degree with St. John's College of Nursing, a 3-3 degree with Logan College of Chiropractic, an early acceptance program with Kirksville College of Osteopathic Medicine of A.T. Still University, and an American Studies program in Washington, D.C. are also available. Cross-registration is offered within the Wesleyan Urban Coalition, the Christian College Consortium, and the Council of Christian Colleges and Universities. There are 6 national honor societies and a freshman honors program.

Faculty/Classroom: 67% of faculty are male; 33% are female. 95% teach undergraduates. No introductory courses are taught by graduate students. The average class size in an introductory lecture is 20; in a laboratory, 16; and in a regular course, 19.

Admissions: 78% of a recent year's applicants were accepted. 33% of a recent year's freshmen were in the top fifth of their class; 62% were in the top two fifths. 7 freshmen graduated first in their class.

Requirements: The SAT or ACT is required. In addition, the college recommends that applicants have 4 years of English, 2 years of foreign language, and 1 year each of algebra and geometry, laboratory science, and American history. Personal and academic references may also be considered in the application process. An essay is required. A GED certificate will be accepted. Greenville requires applicants to be in the upper 50% of their class. A GPA of 2.0 is required. AP and CLEP credits are accepted. Important factors in the admissions decision are leadership record, advanced placement or honors courses, and personality/intangible qualities.

Procedure: Freshmen are admitted to all sessions. Entrance exams should be taken in the spring of the junior year. There is a rolling admissions plan. Check with the school for current application deadlines and fee. Notification is sent on a rolling basis. Applications are accepted online.

Transfer: 170 transfer students enrolled in a recent year. A minimum average grade of C or better is required. An associate degree will be accepted for transfer. 40 of 126 credits required for the bachelor's degree must be completed at Greenville.

Visiting: There are regularly scheduled orientations for prospective students, including campus visits during scheduled preview days. There are guides for informal visits, and visitors may sit in on classes and stay overnight. To schedule a visit, contact the Admissions Office.

Financial Aid: In a recent year, 92% of all full-time freshmen and 95% of continuing full-time students received some form of financial aid. 87% of all full-time freshmen and 66% of continuing full-time students received need-based aid. The average freshman award was $18,738. 30% of undergraduate students work part-time. Average annual earnings from campus work are $996. The average financial indebtedness of a recent year's graduate was $25,000. Greenville is a member of CSS. The FAFSA is required. Check with the school for current application deadlines.

International Students: There were 26 international students enrolled in a recent year. The school actively recruits these students. They must take the TOEFL with a minimum score of 500 on the paper-based TOEFL (PBT).

Graduates: In a recent year, 357 bachelor's degrees were awarded. The most popular majors were education (19%), biology (7%), and music (6%). In an average class, 1% graduate in 3 years or less, 39% graduate in 4 years or less, 49% graduate in 5 years or less, and 50% graduate in 6 years or less.

Admissions Contact: Assistant VP for Enrollment. E-Mail: *admissions@greenville.edu* Web: *www.greenville.edu*

ILLINOIS COLLEGE C-3

Jacksonville, IL 62650 — **(217) 245-3030; (866) 464-5265; (217) 245-3034**

Full-time: 487 men, 474 women	**Faculty:** 71; IIB, -$
Part-time: 5 men, 4 women	**Ph.D.s:** 80%
Graduate: 1 men, 16 women	**Student/Faculty:** 14 to 1
Year: semesters	**Tuition:** $18,800
Application Deadline: August 15	**Room & Board:** $6970

Freshman Class: 2357 applied, 1370 accepted, 285 enrolled
SAT or ACT: required

VERY COMPETITIVE

Illinois College, founded in 1829, is a private liberal arts institution with historical ties to the Presbyterian Church and the United Church of Christ. The figures in the above capsule and in this profile are approximate. The library contains 183,172 volumes, 8,049 microform items, and 4,041 audio/video tapes/CDs/DVDs, and subscribes to 631 periodicals including electronic. Computerized library services include interlibrary loans, database searching, Internet access, and Wi-Fi capability. Special learning facilities include an art gallery, theater, and observatory. The 62-acre campus is in a small town 30 miles west of Springfield. Including any residence halls, there are 36 buildings.

Student Life: 89% of undergraduates are from Illinois. Others are from 22 states, and 15 foreign countries. 91% are White. 62% are Protestant; 25% Catholic; 12% claim no religious affiliation. The average age of freshmen is 18; all undergraduates, 20. 20% do not continue beyond their first year; 60% remain to graduate.

Housing: 742 students can be accommodated in college housing, which includes single-sex and coed dorms and on-campus apartments. In addition, there are honors houses, language houses, and special-interest houses. On-campus housing is guaranteed for all 4 years. 67% of students live on campus; of those, 65% remain on campus on weekends. All students may keep cars.

Activities: There are no fraternities or sororities. There are 72 groups on campus, including art, band, cheerleading, chess, choir, chorale, communications, computers, dance, debate, drama, ethnic, forensics, gay, honors, international, literary magazine, music ensembles, newspaper, photography, political, professional, radio and TV, religious, social, social service, student government, and symphony. Popular campus events include Osage Orange Picnic, Honors Retreat and McGaw Fine Arts Series.

Sports: There are 10 intercollegiate sports for men and 10 for women, and 7 intramural sports for men and 7 for women. Facilities include a fitness center with an olympic sized swimming pool, whirl pool and sauna, several gyms, and expansive weight and exercise room, and aerobics room, 7 basketball courts, volleyball courts, an indoor track, an outdoor track, and playing fields for soccer and football that have an artifical turf surface, a baseball field, an all-weather track, and 6 tennis courts.

Disabled Students: 35% of the campus is accessible. Facilities include wheelchair ramps, elevators, special parking, specially equipped restrooms, special class scheduling, lowered drinking fountains, lowered telephones, and special housing.

Services: Counseling and information services are available, as is tutoring in every subject. There is a reader service for the blind. Note takers, scribes, and test readers are also available.

Campus Safety and Security: Measures include 24-hour foot and vehicle patrol, self-defense education, and security escort services. There are shuttle buses, emergency telephones, and lighted pathways/sidewalks.

Programs of Study: IC confers B.A., and B.S. degrees. Bachelor's degrees are awarded in BIOLOGICAL SCIENCE (biochemistry and biology/biological science), BUSINESS (accounting and business administration and management), COMMUNICATIONS AND THE ARTS (communications, dramatic arts, English, fine arts, French, German, music, Spanish, and speech/debate/rhetoric), COMPUTER AND PHYSICAL SCIENCE (chemistry, computer science, information sciences and systems, mathematics, and physics), EDUCATION (elementary education, foreign languages education, science education, and secondary education), ENGINEERING AND ENVIRONMENTAL DESIGN (environmental science), HEALTH PROFESSIONS (exercise science and medical laboratory technology), SOCIAL SCIENCE (American studies, economics, history, international relations, philosophy, political science/government, prelaw, psychology, religion, and sociology). Life sciences is the strongest academically. Business management, education, and biology have the largest enrollments.

Required: To graduate, all students must fulfill general graduation and convocation requirements and complete at least 120 semester hours, including 24 hours of electives outside of the major discipline. Other requirements include 1 unit in public speaking, 1 unit in writing, 1 unit of library research methods, and a first-year seminar. To meet the Convocation requirement, students must attend 30 cultural, artistic, or public affairs events. A 2.0 GPA is required.

Special: The college offers study abroad in various countries, on- and off-campus work-study programs, and internships through the departments of communication, computer science and information systems, economics and business administration, English, and political science, and sociology. Also available are student-designed and dual majors, B.A.-B.S. degrees, a 3-2 engineering degree with the University of Illinois, Washington University, or Southern Illinois University-Edwardsville, and a 3-2 occupational therapy program with Washington University. A 3-1 cytotechnology program with Mayo School of Health-related Sciences, a 3-1 program in Medical Technology with St. John's Hospital in Springfield, an Intercultural Exchange Program with Ritsumeikan University in Kyoto, Japan, Model United Nations simulations, and the Urban Studies Program of Associated Colleges of the Midwest in Chicago are offered. The College also offers opportunities for collaborative student/faculty research. There are 12 national honor societies, including Phi Beta Kappa, and 12 departmental honors programs.

Faculty/Classroom: 57% of faculty are male; 43% are female. All teach undergraduates. No introductory courses are taught by graduate students. The average class size in an introductory lecture is 40; in a laboratory is 20; and in a regular course is 16.

Admissions: 58% of the 2013-2014 applicants were accepted. 13 freshmen graduated first in their class.

Requirements: The SAT or ACT is required. The ACT Optional Writing test is also required. Applicants must be graduates of an accredited secondary school or have a GED certificate. Students should have completed at least 15 academic credits, including 3 in English and 7 from the following: English, foreign language, history, lab science, math, and social studies. 1 recommendation and 1 essay or 2 letters recommendations are required. A GPA of 2.5 is required. AP and CLEP credits are accepted. Important factors in the admissions decision are advanced placement or honors courses, evidence of special talent, and ability to finance college education.

Procedure: Freshmen are admitted to all sessions. Entrance exams should be taken in the spring of the junior year or fall of the senior year of high school. There is a rolling admissions plan. Application deadlines are open. Notification is sent on a rolling basis. Applications are accepted online.

Transfer: 44 transfer students enrolled in 2012-2013. Transfer students must have graduated from an accredited four year high school. A minimum of 2.0 for their most recent full-time semester of college level work and a minimum cumulative 2.0 GPA for all college work attempted. If 24 credits have not been completed, these student's high school record will be reviewed. 36 of 120 credits required for the bachelor's degree must be completed at IC.

Visiting: There are regularly scheduled orientations for prospective stu-

dents, including general information sessions with a member of the admissions staff, meeting with faculty, a campus tour, and lunch. There are guides for informal visits and visitors may sit in on classes. To schedule a visit, contact the Admissions Office.

Financial Aid: In 2013-2014, 99% of all full-time freshmen and 98% of continuing full-time students received some form of financial aid. 73% of all full-time freshmen and 67% of continuing full-time students received need-based aid. 55% of undergraduate students work part-time. Average annual earnings from campus work are $999. The average financial indebtedness of the 2013 graduate was $23,156. The FAFSA is required. The priority date for freshman financial aid applications for fall entry is March 1. The deadline for filing freshman financial aid applications for fall entry is May 1.

International Students: There are 24 international students enrolled. They must take the TOEFL.

Graduates: From July 1, 2012 to June 30, 2013, 168 bachelor's degrees were awarded. The most popular majors were biological/life sciences (18%), intersidciplinary studies (16%), and education (13%). 6 companies recruited on campus in 2012-2013. In an average class, 1% graduate in 3 years or less, 50% graduate in 4 years or less, 62% graduate in 5 years or less, and 62% graduate in 6 years or less. Of the 2012 graduating class, 20% were enrolled in graduate school within 6 months of graduation, and 80% were employed.

Admissions Contact: Barbara J. Lundberg, Vice President for Enrollment. E-Mail: *Barb.Lundberg@ic.edu* Web: *www.ic.edu/apply*

ILLINOIS INSTITUTE OF TECHNOLOGY E-2

Chicago, IL 60616 (312) 567-3000
(800) 448-2329; (312) 567-6939

Full-time: 1793 men, 817 women	**Faculty:** 250; I, av$
Part-time: 147 men, 44 women	**Ph.D.s:** 88%
Graduate: 2899 men, 1984 women	**Student/Faculty:** 9 to 1
Year: semesters, summer session	**Tuition:** $38,512
Application Deadline: open	**Room & Board:** n/a
Freshman Class: 2597 applied, 1427 accepted, 408 enrolled	
SAT CR/M/W: 600/660/590	**ACT:** 28 **HIGHLY COMPETITIVE+**

Founded in 1890, IIT is a Ph.D.-granting university with more than 7,300 students in engineering, sciences, architecture, psychology, design, humanities, business and law. IIT's interprofessional, technology-focused curriculum is designed to advance knowledge through research and scholarship, to cultivate invention improving the human condition, and to prepare students from throughout the world for a life of professional achievement, service to society, and individual fulfillment. There are 6 undergraduate schools and 8 graduate schools. In addition to regional accreditation, IIT has baccalaureate program accreditation with ABET and NAAB. The 3 libraries contain 1.3 million volumes, 0 microform items, and 4,256 audio/video tapes/CDs/DVDs, and subscribe to 24,596 periodicals including electronic. Computerized library services include interlibrary loans, database searching, Internet access, and Wi-Fi capability. Special learning facilities include an art gallery and radio station. The 120-acre campus is in an urban area 3 miles south of downtown Chicago. Including any residence halls, there are 33 buildings.

Student Life: 57% of undergraduates are from Illinois. Others are from 47 states, 83 foreign countries, and Canada. 83% are from public schools. 50% are White; 16% Foreign; 14% Asian American. The average age of freshmen is 18; all undergraduates, 22. 15% do not continue beyond their first year; 85% remain to graduate.

Housing: 1184 students can be accommodated in college housing, which includes single-sex and coed dorms, on-campus apartments, and married student housing. In addition, there are fraternity houses and sorority houses. On-campus housing is guaranteed for all 4 years. 53% of students live on campus. All students may keep cars.

Activities: 13% of men belong to 7 national fraternities; 15% of women belong to 2 local and 1 national sororities. There are 100 groups on campus, including and union, art, chess, choir, chorus, commuter, computers, dance, drama, environmental, ethnic, film, gay, honors, international, jazz band, musical theater, newspaper, photography, professional, radio and TV, religious, social, social service, student government, and yearbook. Popular campus events include International Fest, Greek Week and Spring Formal.

Sports: There are 5 intercollegiate sports for men and 5 for women, and 10 intramural sports for men and 10 for women. Facilities include tennis, basketball, volleyball, racquetball, and squash courts, soccer and softball fields, a swimming pool, an exercise room, a weight room, a bowling alley, and a game room.

Disabled Students: 90% of the campus is accessible. Facilities include wheelchair ramps, elevators, special parking, specially equipped restrooms, lowered drinking fountains, special housing.

Services: Counseling and information services are available, as is tutoring in some subjects, math, electrical and computer engineering, chemistry, biology, mechanical, materials and aerospace engineering, physics, computer science and writing courses. There is a reader service for the blind.

Campus Safety and Security: Measures include 24-hour foot and vehicle patrol, emergency notification system, and security escort services. There are shuttle buses, emergency telephones, lighted pathways/sidewalks, and controlled access to dorms/residences.

Programs of Study: IIT confers B.A., and B.S. degrees. Master's and doctoral degrees are also awarded. Bachelor's degrees are awarded in BIOLOGICAL SCIENCE (biochemistry, biology/biological science, biophysics, and molecular biology), COMMUNICATIONS AND THE ARTS (technical and business writing), COMPUTER AND PHYSICAL SCIENCE (applied mathematics, chemistry, computer science, information sciences and systems, physics, and web technology), ENGINEERING AND ENVIRONMENTAL DESIGN (aeronautical engineering, architectural engineering, architecture, chemical engineering, civil engineering, computer engineering, electrical/electronics engineering, engineering management, industrial administration/management, manufacturing technology, materials science, mechanical engineering, and metallurgical engineering), SOCIAL SCIENCE (humanities, political science/government, and psychology). architecture, engineering, and science and letters have the largest enrollments.

Required: To graduate, all degree-seeking undergraduate students must complete: departmental curriculum, credit hour requirements as appropriate to the various curricula (a minimum of 126 hours total, a minimum of 45 hours taken at IIT), general education requirements and a minimum cumulative GPA of and a minimum major GPA of 2.00. General education requirements include 5 credit hours of mathematics, 2 credit hours in computer science, 21 credit hours in humanities and social or behavioral sciences, 11 credit hours in natural science or engineering, 2 credit hours of Introduction to the Profession and 6 credit hours of Interprofessional Projects (IPRO).

Special: Co-op programs and internships are available to all majors. All countries are eligible for study abroad. Dual majors may include a variety of majors. Cross-registration available. There are 3 national honor societies.

Faculty/Classroom: 78% of faculty are male; 22% are female. No introductory courses are taught by graduate students. The average class size in an introductory lecture is 24; in a laboratory is 22; and in a regular course is 15.

Admissions: 55% of the 2013-2014 applicants were accepted. The SAT scores for the 2013-2014 freshman class were: Critical Reading--14% below 500, 31% between 500 and 599, 44% between 600 and 699, and 11% between 700 and 800; Math--1% below 500, 17% between 500 and 599, 54% between 600 and 699, and 28% between 700 and 800; Writing--15% below 500, 40% between 500 and 599, 37% between 600 and 699, and 8% between 700 and 800. The ACT scores were 2% below 21, 10% between 21 and 23, 24% between 24 and 26, 24% between 27 and 28, and 40% above 28. 61% of the current freshmen were in the top fifth of their class; 87% were in the top two fifths. 2 freshmen graduated first in their class.

Requirements: Graduation from an accredited secondary school is required for admission. 17 academic credits are required for admission: 4 units of English; 4 units of math: 3 units of science, of these, 2 units must be laboratory science; 2 units of social studies and 2 units of history. In addition, 2 units of foreign language and 1 unit of computer science are recommended. AP credits are accepted. Important factors in the admissions decision are recommendations by school officials, leadership record, and advanced placement or honors courses.

Procedure: Freshmen are admitted fall, spring, and summer. There are deferred admissions and rolling admissions plans. Application deadlines are open. Notification is sent on a rolling basis. Applications are accepted online.

Transfer: 277 transfer students enrolled in 2012-2013. Good academic standing at previous postsecondary institution, and a minimum 3.0 cumulative GPA 45 of 126 credits required for the bachelor's degree must be completed at IIT.

Visiting: There are regularly scheduled orientations for prospective students, including special events and open houses. Open houses include a brief welcome, tours of Main Campus, academic exploration sessions with faculty members, discussion panels with current students, and staff from numerous student service departments on hand to answer questions. There are guides for informal visits, visitors may sit in on classes, and stay overnight. To schedule a visit, contact the Office of Undergraduate Admission.

Financial Aid: In 2013-2014, 100% of all full-time freshmen and 98% of continuing full-time students received some form of financial aid. 70% of all full-time freshmen and 58% of continuing full-time students received need-based aid. IIT is a member of CSS. The FAFSA is required. The priority date for freshman financial aid applications for fall entry is April 15.

International Students: There are 388 international students enrolled. The school actively recruits these students. They must take the TOEFL with a minimum score of 550 on the paper-based TOEFL (PBT) or 80 on the Internet-based version (iBT).

Graduates: From July 1, 2012 to June 30, 2013, 518 bachelor's degrees were awarded. The most popular majors were engineering (49%), natural resources and conservation (20%), and computer and information sciences (9%). In an average class, 3% graduate in 3 years or less, 38% graduate in 4 years or less, 62% graduate in 5 years or less, and 67% graduate in 6 years or less.

Admissions Contact: Gerald Doyle, Associate Vice President, Undergraduate Admissions. E-Mail: *admission@iit.edu* Web: *www.iit.edu*

ILLINOIS STATE UNIVERSITY D-3

Normal, IL 61761 (309) 438-2181
(800) 366-2478; (309) 438-3932

Full-time: 7447 men, 9236 women	**Faculty:** 886; I, --$
Part time: 509 men, 527 women	**Ph.D.s:** 83%
Graduate: 892 men, 1631 women	**Student/Faculty:** 17 to 1
Year: semesters, summer session	**Tuition:** $13,010 ($20,450)
Application Deadline: March 1	**Room & Board:** $9624

Freshman Class: 15354 applied, 10582 accepted, 2981 enrolled
ACT: 24

VERY COMPETITIVE

Illinois State University, founded in 1857, is a public institution offering instruction through schools of applied science and technology, arts and sciences, business, education, fine arts, and nursing. There are 6 undergraduate schools and one graduate school. In addition to regional accreditation, ISU has baccalaureate program accreditation with AACSB, ABET, ACCE, CSWE, NASAD, NASM, NCATE, and NRPA. The library contains 1.6 million volumes, 84,824 microform items, and 41,690 audio/video tapes/CDs/DVDs, and subscribes to 83,375 periodicals including electronic. Computerized library services include interlibrary loans, database searching, Internet access, and Wi-Fi capability. Special learning facilities include an art gallery, planetarium, radio station, TV station, a distance-learning classrooms, a farm and japanese gardens. The 1000-acre campus is in an urban area 125 miles south of Chicago and 180 miles north of St. Louis. Including any residence halls, there are 163 buildings.

Student Life: 97% of undergraduates are from Illinois. Others are from 41 states, 67 foreign countries, and Canada. 79% are White. The average age of freshmen is 18; all undergraduates, 20. 19% do not continue beyond their first year; 72% remain to graduate.

Housing: 6004 students can be accommodated in college housing, which includes single-sex and coed dorms, on-campus apartments, and married student housing. In addition, there are honors houses and special-interest houses. On-campus housing is available on a first-come and first-served basis. 69% of students commute. Alcohol is not permitted. All students may keep cars.

Activities: 8% of men belong to 18 national fraternities; 11% of women belong to 14 national sororities. There are 309 groups on campus, including art, band, cheerleading, chess, choir, chorale, chorus, computers, dance, debate, drama, drill team, ethnic, film, forensics, gay, honors, international, jazz band, literary magazine, marching band, musical theater, newspaper, opera, orchestra, pep band, photography, political, professional, radio and TV, religious, social, social service, student government, and symphony. Popular campus events include Festival ISU, International Fair and Madrigal Dinners.

Sports: There are 7 intercollegiate sports for men and 10 for women, and 28 intramural sports for men and 28 for women. Facilities include a student recreational building, a basketball arena, a football stadium, a field house, baseball diamonds, tennis courts, olympic-size pools, an 18-hole golf course, a soccer and softball field, 18 acre field area that is devoted to intramurals and sport clubs, and a bowling and billiards center.

Disabled Students: All of the campus is accessible. Facilities include wheelchair ramps, elevators, special parking, specially equipped restrooms, special class scheduling, lowered drinking fountains, lowered telephones.

Services: Counseling and information services are available, as is tutoring in most subjects. There is a reader service for the blind. tutoring available for most 100 level courses. course materials are provided in an alternate format

Campus Safety and Security: Measures include 24-hour foot and vehicle patrol, emergency notification system, self-defense education, and security escort services. There are shuttle buses, emergency telephones, lighted pathways/sidewalks, and controlled access to dorms/residences.

Programs of Study: ISU confers B.S., B.A., B.S. Ed., B.S.W., B.S./M.P.A., B.F.A, B.M.E., B.M. and B.S.N. degrees. Master's and doctoral degrees are also awarded. Bachelor's degrees are awarded in AGRICULTURE (agricultural business management and agriculture), BIOLOGICAL SCIENCE (biochemistry and biology/biological science), BUSINESS (accounting, banking and finance, business administration and management, insurance, international business management, management science, and marketing/retailing/merchandising), COMMUNICATIONS AND THE ARTS (art, communications, dramatic arts, English, French, German, journalism, media arts, music, music performance, public relations, Spanish, speech/debate/rhetoric, and telecommunications), COMPUTER AND PHYSICAL SCIENCE (chemistry, computer science, digital arts/technology, geology, information sciences and systems, mathematics, and physics), EDUCATION (athletic training, business education, early childhood education, elementary education, health education, middle school education, music education, physical education, social science education, special education, and technical education), ENGINEERING AND ENVIRONMENTAL DESIGN (construction management, energy management technology, and industrial engineering technology), HEALTH PROFESSIONS (environmental health science, exercise science, health care administration, medical laboratory technology, nursing, and speech pathology/audiology), SOCIAL SCIENCE (anthropology, criminal justice, economics, family/consumer studies, fashion design and technology, geography, history, home economics, interdisciplinary studies, parks and recreation management, philosophy, political science/government, psychology, safety management, social science, social work, and sociology). Elementary education, special education and business administration have the largest enrollments.

Required: Students must complete 45 hours of General Education and a total of 120 credit hours with a minimum GPA of 2.0. In addition, they must the senior college hours must total at least 42 hours. Every student must have successfully completed a course designated as a course in the cultures and traditions of societies or peoples from Asia, the Middle East, Africa, Latin America, or Indigenous Peoples of the World.

Special: There are numerous cooperative programs and internships, dual majors, student-designed majors, and work-study programs both on campus and with nonprofit organizations. There is also a general studies degree, a 3-2 engineering program with the University of Illinois, a BS/MPA, and study abroad in 16 countries. Pass/fail options are available and credit is given for military experience. ISU is part of the National Student Exchange, enabling qualifying juniors and seniors to study for up to 1 year at one of several hundred colleges around the country. There are 22 national honor societies, a freshman honors program, and 1 departmental honors programs.

Faculty/Classroom: 48% of faculty are male; 52% are female. All teach undergraduates. Graduate students teach 40% of introductory courses. The average class size in an introductory lecture is 45 and in a laboratory is 26.

Admissions: 69% of the 2013-2014 applicants were accepted. The ACT scores were 11% below 21, 35% between 21 and 23, 36% between 24 and 26, 11% between 27 and 28, and 8% above 28.

Requirements: The ACT is required. Admission is based on a combination of factors including rigor of secondary school record, academic GPA, Standardized test scores and application essay. AP and CLEP credits are accepted.

Procedure: Freshmen are admitted fall, spring, and summer. Entrance exams should be taken in the spring of the junior year. There are deferred admissions and rolling admissions plans. Applications should be filed by March 1 for fall entry, along with a $40 fee. 844 applicants were on the 2013 waiting list; 781 were admitted. Applications are accepted online.

Transfer: 1856 transfer students enrolled in 2012-2013. Graduates of Illinois community colleges holding associate degrees are admitted pending receipt of transcripts. Other students must meet the requirements for beginning freshmen with a minimum 2.0 GPA. 30 of 120 credits required for the bachelor's degree must be completed at ISU.

Visiting: There are regularly scheduled orientations for prospective students, While attending Preview, students will have the opportunity to meet with their academic advisor, register for classes, meet current Illinois State students and their future classmates, interact with faculty and staff from various academic departments. There are guides for informal visits, visitors may sit in on classes, and stay overnight. To schedule a visit, contact the Admissions Office at (800) 366-2478.

Financial Aid: The FAFSA and CCS/Profile, or FAFSA, or FFS, or SFS are required. The deadline for filing freshman financial aid applications for fall entry is March 1.

International Students: There are 125 international students enrolled. The school actively recruits these students. They must take the TOEFL with a minimum score of 550 on the paper-based TOEFL (PBT) or 79 on the Internet-based version (iBT). They must also take the SAT or ACT.

Graduates: From July 1, 2012 to June 30, 2013, 4438 bachelor's degrees were awarded. The most popular majors were elemetery education (5%), marketing (5%), and English (4%). 636 companies recruited on campus in 2012-2013. In an average class, 46% graduate in 4 years or less, 68% graduate in 5 years or less, and 71% graduate in 6 years or less.

Admissions Contact: Stacy Ramsey, Acting Director of Admissions. E-Mail: *admissions@ilstu.edu* Web: *http:/admissions.illinoisstate.edu/*

ILLINOIS WESLEYAN UNIVERSITY D-3

Bloomington, IL 61702 (309) 556-3031; (800) 332-2498

Full-time: 882 men, 1119 women
Part-time: 4 men, 4 women
Graduate: none
Year: other
Application Deadline: March 1
Freshman Class: 3556 applied, 2076 accepted, 529 enrolled
SAT CR/M: 571/648
Faculty: n/av; IIB, av$
Ph.D.s: 92%
Student/Faculty: 11 to 1
Tuition: $39,316
Room & Board: $9136
ACT: 27 **VERY COMPETITIVE+**

Illinois Wesleyan University, founded in 1850, is a private institution offering major programs in liberal arts, fine arts, and nursing. There are 5 undergraduate schools. In addition to regional accreditation, Illinois Wesleyan has baccalaureate program accreditation with NASM. The library contains 328,368 volumes, 443 microform items, and 14,653 audio/video tapes/CDs/DVDs, and subscribes to 33,435 periodicals including electronic. Computerized library services include interlibrary loans, database searching, Internet access, and Wi-Fi capability. Special learning facilities include an art gallery, radio station, TV station, an observatory, a multicultural center, Action Research Center, Center for Human Rights, Peace Garden and a 20-acre tract of virgin timberland. The 80-acre campus is in a suburban area 130 miles from Chicago and 160 miles from St. Louis, Missouri. Including any residence halls, there are 54 buildings.

Student Life: 88% of undergraduates are from Illinois. Others are from 33 states, 23 foreign countries, and Canada. 80% are from public schools. 71% are White. The average age of freshmen is 18; all undergraduates, 20. 78% remain to graduate.

Housing: 1709 students can be accommodated in college housing, which includes coed dorms and on-campus apartments. In addition, there are honors houses, language houses, special-interest houses, fraternity houses, sorority houses, internationalism, environmentalism, art and interfaith learning housing areas. 72% of students live on campus; of those, 75% remain on campus on weekends. All students may keep cars.

Activities: 32% of men belong to 6 national fraternities; 30% of women belong to 1 local and 4 national sororities. There are 185 groups on campus, including art, band, cheerleading, choir, chorale, chorus, computers, dance, drama, ethnic, film, gay, honors, international, jazz band, literary magazine, musical theater, newspaper, opera, orchestra, pep band, political, professional, radio and TV, religious, social, social service, student government, symphony, and yearbook. Popular campus events include Family Days, Comedy Clubs and International Festivals.

Sports: There are 9 intercollegiate sports for men and 9 for women, and 15 intramural sports for men and 13 for women. Facilities include a fitness center with weight/exercise equipment and racquetball courts; a swimming pool with 1- and 3-meter diving boards; an activity center with a 200-meter, 6-lane indoor track and courts for tennis, recreational basketball, and volleyball; a separate gym for intercollegiate and other activities; an outdoor track; and softball, baseball, and soccer fields.

Disabled Students: 90% of the campus is accessible. Facilities include wheelchair ramps, elevators, special parking, specially equipped restrooms, special class scheduling, lowered drinking fountains, lowered telephones, and special housing.

Services: Counseling and information services are available, as is tutoring in every subject. There is a reader service for the blind. Assistance in writing and study skills is also available but not at the remedial level.

Campus Safety and Security: Measures include 24-hour foot and vehicle patrol, emergency notification system, self-defense education, and security escort services. There are shuttle buses, emergency telephones, lighted pathways/sidewalks, controlled access to dorms/residences, an emergency response team of key executives and staff members has developed policies and procedures for natural disasters and other crises.

Programs of Study: Illinois Wesleyan confers B.A., B.S., B.F.A., B.Mus., B.Mus.Ed. and B.S.N. degrees. Bachelor's degrees are awarded in AGRICULTURE (environmental studies), BIOLOGICAL SCIENCE (biology/biological science), BUSINESS (accounting, business administration and management, insurance and risk management, and international business management), COMMUNICATIONS AND THE ARTS (art, classics, English, French, German, guitar, music, music performance, music theory and composition, musical theater, performing arts, piano/organ, theater design, theater management, and voice), COMPUTER AND PHYSICAL SCIENCE (chemistry, computer science, and physics), EDUCATION (education and music education), HEALTH PROFESSIONS (nursing), SOCIAL SCIENCE (American studies, anthropology, economics, history, interdisciplinary studies, international studies, philosophy, political science/government, psychology, religion, sociology, and women & gender studies). Business administration/accounting, biology, and psychology have the largest enrollments.

Required: For B.A., B.S., B.S.N., and B.F.A. degrees, a total of 32 course units (128 semester hours) is required for the bachelor's degree with a 2.0 GPA. General education requirements include 2 course units in natural sciences and 1 each in literature, English, intellectual traditions, formal reasoning, cultural and historical change, contemporary social institutions, the arts, history, humanities, math, and social science, analysis of values, and Gateway Colloquium, plus demonstrated proficiency in a foreign language. 2 additional writing-intensive courses are required, as is coursework focusing on U.S. and global diversity issues. 2 degree programs (B.M.Ed.and B.M.) require more than 32 course units due to additional requirements in the major. Phys ed is a noncredit graduation requirement.

Special: There are several combined degree programs, including a 3-2 degree in forestry and environmental studies with Duke University and a 2-2 engineering degree with the University of Illinois. Students may study abroad in many locations throughout the world through the Institute for the International Education of Students (IES), Pembroke College, Keio University, University of Oxford, Arcadia University Center for Study Abroad, and other programs. Illinois Wesleyan also offers its own semester-long programs in London and Barcelona. The university also offers on-campus work-study, both credit and noncredit internships, Washington and United Nations semesters, B.A.-B.S. degrees, dual and student-designed majors, pass/fail options, and an honors research program for upperclass students. There are 25 national honor societies, including Phi Beta Kappa, and 44 departmental honors programs.

Faculty/Classroom: 55% of faculty are male; 45% are female. All teach and do research. No introductory courses are taught by graduate students. The average class size in a laboratory is 13 and in a regular course is 17.

Admissions: 58% of the 2013-2014 applicants were accepted. The SAT scores for the 2013-2014 freshman class were: Critical Reading--4% below 500, 35% between 500 and 599, 36% between 600 and 699, and 25% between 700 and 800; Math--5% below 500, 25% between 500 and 599, 44% between 600 and 699, and 25% between 700 and 800. There were 5 National Merit finalists.

Requirements: The SAT or ACT is required. Applicants should graduate from an accredited secondary school; a GED may be accepted. 15 academic credits are required. It is strongly recommended that these units include 4 units of English, 3 each of natural science, math, and a foreign language, and 2 of social studies. An audition is required for theater and music majors and a portfolio for art majors. Illinois Wesleyan requires applicants to be in the upper 65% of their class. A GPA of 3.0 is required. AP credits are accepted. Important factors in the admissions decision are advanced placement or honors courses, evidence of special talent, and personality/intangible qualities.

Procedure: Freshmen are admitted fall and spring. Entrance exams should be taken in the spring of the junior year. There are early admissions, deferred admissions, and rolling admissions plans. Early decision applications should be filed by November 1; regular applications, by March 1 for fall entry; and November 1 for spring entry. Notification is sent on a rolling basis. 149 applicants were on the 2013 waiting list; 2 were admitted. Applications are accepted online.

Transfer: 32 transfer students enrolled in 2012-2013. Applicants must submit all high school and college transcripts. A GPA of at least 2.5 is required. An essay or personal statement is required. 16 of 32 credits required for the bachelor's degree must be completed at Illinois Wesleyan.

Visiting: There are regularly scheduled orientations for prospective students, including a 1 to 1-1/2 hour guided tour in small groups, and with advance scheduling, interviews with an admissions counselor and faculty members in the fields of the student interest. Accepted applicants may visit classes or stay overnight. There are guides for informal visits, visitors may sit in on classes, and stay overnight. To schedule a visit, contact the Admissions Office.

Financial Aid: In 2013-2014, 71% of all full-time freshmen and 67% of continuing full-time students received some form of financial aid. 71% of all full-time freshmen and 67% of continuing full-time students received need-based aid. The average freshman award was $30,443. Need-based scholarships or need-based grants averaged $24,699; need-based self-help aid (loans and jobs) averaged $6,174; other non-need-based awards and non-need-based scholarships averaged $17,763; and $4,422 from other forms of aid. The average financial indebtedness of the 2013 graduate was $31,343. Illinois Wesleyan is a member of CSS. The FAFSA and the college's own financial statement are required. The deadline for filing freshman financial aid applications for fall entry is March 1.

International Students: There are 105 international students enrolled. The school actively recruits these students. They must take the TOEFL. They must also take the SAT or ACT.

Graduates: From July 1, 2012 to June 30, 2013, 482 bachelor's degrees were awarded. The most popular majors were business/marketing (21%), visual and performing arts (11%), and psychology (9%). 49 companies recruited on campus in 2012-2013. In an average class, 72% graduate in 4 years or less, 77% graduate in 5 years or less, and 78% graduate in 6 years or less.

Admissions Contact: Tony Bankston, Dean of Admissions. E-Mail: *iwuadmit@iwu.edu* Web: *www.iwu.edu*

JUDSON UNIVERSITY E-1

Elgin, IL 60123-1498 (847) 628-2500
(800) 879-5376; (847) 695-0216

Full-time: 394 men, 521 women **Faculty:** 54; IIB, -$
Part-time: 106 men, 174 women **Ph.D.s:** 65%
Graduate: 27 men, 23 women **Student/Faculty:** 17 to 1
Year: semesters **Tuition:** $20,500
Application Deadline: open **Room & Board:** $7750
Freshman Class: 626 applied, 484 accepted, 221 enrolled
SAT or ACT: required
COMPETITIVE

Judson College is an evangelical Christian college of the liberal arts, sciences, and professions. Some information in this capsule and profile are approximate. There is 1 graduate school. In addition to regional accreditation, Judson has baccalaureate program accreditation with NAAB. The library contains 92,000 volumes, 27,000 microform items, and 17,000 audio/video tapes/CDs/DVDs, and subscribes to 470 periodicals including electronic. Computerized library services include interlibrary loans, database searching, and Internet access. Special learning facilities include a learning resource center, art gallery, and radio station. The 90-acre campus is in a suburban area 40 miles west of Chicago. Including any residence halls, there are 16 buildings.

Student Life: 65% of undergraduates are from Illinois. Others are from 21 states, 25 foreign countries, and Canada. 71% are white. 80% are Protestant. The average age of freshmen is 18; all undergraduates, 20. 22% do not continue beyond their first year; 50% remain to graduate.

Housing: 670 students can be accommodated in college housing, which includes single-sex dorms, on-campus apartments, and married student housing. On-campus housing is guaranteed for all 4 years. 65% of students live on campus. Alcohol is not permitted. All students may keep cars.

Activities: There are no fraternities or sororities. There are 23 groups on campus, including art, band, business, cheerleading, choir, chorale, chorus, computers, drama, ethnic, honors, international, literary magazine, newspaper, orchestra, photography, political, radio and TV, religious, social, social service, and student government. Popular campus events include Spiritual Enrichment Week, Fall Orientation, and Christmas by Candlelight.

Sports: There are 3 intercollegiate sports for men and 4 for women, and 9 intramural sports for men and 8 for women. Facilities include a fitness center, a 1500-seat gym, a soccer field, lighted baseball and softball diamonds, lighted tennis courts, racquetball and handball courts, indoor and outdoor running tracks, and a Nautilus and free-weight room.

Disabled Students: 80% of the campus is accessible. Facilities include wheelchair ramps, elevators, special parking, specially equipped restrooms, special class scheduling, lowered drinking fountains, lowered telephones, and special housing.

Services: Counseling and information services are available, as is tutoring in some subjects. There is remedial math, reading, and writing.

Campus Safety and Security: Measures include 24-hour foot and vehicle patrol and security escort services. There are emergency telephones and lighted pathways/sidewalks.

Programs of Study: Judson confers B.A. degrees. Master's degrees are also awarded. Bachelor's degrees are awarded in BIOLOGICAL SCIENCE (biology/biological science), BUSINESS (accounting, business administration and management, international business management, and sports management), COMMUNICATIONS AND THE ARTS (communications, dramatic arts, English, fine arts, media arts, and music), COMPUTER AND PHYSICAL SCIENCE (chemistry, computer science, and mathematics), EDUCATION (early childhood education, elementary education, English education, mathematics education, music education, physical education, science education, and secondary education), ENGINEERING AND ENVIRONMENTAL DESIGN (preengineering), HEALTH PROFESSIONS (medical laboratory technology, nursing, predentistry, and premedicine), SOCIAL SCIENCE (anthropology, history, political science/government, prelaw, psychology, sociology, and youth ministry). Architecture, visual communications/graphic design, and education are the strongest academically. Business, youth ministry, worship arts, and psychology have the largest enrollments.

Required: Most students must have a GPA of 2.0; education majors must have a 2.5. Students must complete at least 126 credit hours, including 45 to 66 in the major, and take the college's core courses of Bible study, writing, speech, literature, math, science, history, fine arts, human relations, and phys ed, as well as a course in either psychology or sociology.

Special: The college has co-op programs with North Park College, Rush University, and the Mennonite College of Nursing, cross-registration with the Christian College Coalition, and work-study programs with many businesses. Students may serve internships in art and business, take a Washington semester, a film studies semester in Hollywood, an ecology studies semester at Sable Institute in Michigan, or study abroad in numerous external programs recognized by Judson College. The college allows dual majors, student-designed majors, and accelerated degrees in business leadership and management, human services, human resource management, and criminal justice management. There is 1 national honor society, a freshman honors program, and 2 departmental honors programs.

Faculty/Classroom: 66% of faculty are male; 34% are female. 80% teach undergraduates. No introductory courses are taught by graduate students. The average class size in an introductory lecture is 28; in a laboratory is 9; and in a regular course is 16.

Admissions: 77% of the 2011-2012 applicants were accepted.

Requirements: The SAT or ACT is required with a minimum ACT score of 18 or SAT score of 840. Judson requires applicants to be in the upper 50% of their class. A GPA of 2.0 is required. AP and CLEP credits are accepted.

Procedure: Freshmen are admitted to all sessions. Entrance exams should be taken in the spring of the junior year or the fall of the senior year. There are deferred admissions and rolling admissions plans. Application deadlines are open. Application fee is $35. Notification is sent on a rolling basis. Applications are accepted online.

Transfer: 86 transfer students enrolled in a recent year. Students with fewer than 28 hours of college credit must submit high school transcripts showing a GPA of at least 2.0, as well as ACT results with a composite score of at least 18 or 840 on the SAT. Transfer students with more than 28 hours must have a GPA of at least 2.0. 30 of 126 credits required for the bachelor's degree must be completed at Judson.

Visiting: There are regularly scheduled orientations for prospective students, including a tour, class visits, individual meetings with professors, coaches, choir and or band director, and other select campus administrators if requested. In addition, lunch or dinner in the cafeteria and the opportunity to meet with current students and the opportunity to stay a night in the dorms. There are guides for informal visits, visitors may sit in on classes, and stay overnight. To schedule a visit, contact the Enrollment Services Office.

Financial Aid: In a recent year, 90% of all full-time freshmen and 90% of continuing full-time students received some form of financial aid. 90% of all full-time freshmen and 90% of continuing full-time students received need-based aid. The average freshman award was $9,486. Need-based scholarships or need-based grants averaged $7,212 ; need-based self-help aid (loans and jobs) averaged $8,568; and non-need-based athletic scholarships averaged $8,999. The average financial indebtedness of the 2011 graduate was $19,216. The FAFSA and the college's own financial statement are required. Check with the school for current application deadlines.

International Students: There are 44 international students enrolled. The school actively recruits these students. They must take the TOEFL or MELAB. They must also take the SAT or ACT.

Admissions Contact: Director of Admissions *skiser@judson.edu*

KENDALL COLLEGE E-2

Chicago, IL 60642 (312) 752-2240
(877) 588-8860; (312) 752-2241

Full-time: 498 men, 982 women **Faculty:** 41
Part-time: 162 men, 903 women **Ph.D.s:** 11%
Graduate: n/av **Student/Faculty:** 35 to 1
Year: quarters, summer session **Tuition:** $22,625
Application Deadline: rolling **Room & Board:** $10,985
Freshman Class: 361 applied, 353 accepted, 163 enrolled
NONCOMPETITIVE

Kendall College, part of Laureate Internationl Universities, was founded in 1934 and is a private institution committed to cultivating extraordinary talent for the global business, hospitality, culinary, and education fields. Kendall offers 4 schools of study: Culinary Arts, Business, Hospitality Management, and Education. There are 4 undergraduate schools. The figures in the abokve capsule and in this profile are approximate. The library contains 36,293 volumes, and 453 audio/video tapes/CDs/DVDs, and subscribes to 187 periodicals including electronic. Computerized library services include interlibrary loans, database searching, and Internet access. Special learning facilities include a learning resource center. The Culinary Curiosity Exhibition is a permanent display of nearly 300 cooking antiques. The campus is in an urban area in Chicago. Including any residence halls, there is 1 building.

Student Life: 73% of undergraduates are from Illinois. Others are from 35 states, 62 foreign countries, and Canada. 51% are white; 20% African American; 12% Hispanic. The average age of freshmen is 21; all undergraduates, 31. 46% do not continue beyond their first year; 37% remain to graduate.

Housing: 180 students can be accommodated in college housing, which includes single-sex and coed off-campus apartments. On-campus housing is available on a first-come and first-served basis. 89% of students commute. Alcohol is not permitted. No one may keep cars.

Activities: There are no fraternities or sororities. There are 10 groups on campus, including chorus, computers, dance, environmental, ethnic, gay, honors, international, professional, social, social service, and student government. Popular campus events include Fright Fest, African American History Community Dinner, and monthly birthday celebrations.

Sports: There is no sports program at Kendall.

Disabled Students: All of the campus is accessible. Facilities include wheelchair ramps, elevators, special parking, specially equipped restrooms, special class scheduling, lowered drinking fountains, and lowered telephones.

Services: Counseling and information services are available, as is tutoring in every subject. There is remedial math, reading, and writing. Other services, if needed.

Campus Safety and Security: Measures include 24-hour foot and vehicle patrol and emergency notification system. There are lighted pathways/sidewalks and controlled access to dorms/residences.

Programs of Study: Kendall confers B.A. degrees. Associate degrees are also awarded. Bachelor's degrees are awarded in BUSINESS (business administration and management, hospitality management services, and hotel/motel and restaurant management), EDUCATION (early childhood education), SOCIAL SCIENCE (culinary arts). Culinary arts and education are the largest.

Required: Students must complete 180 credit hours and meet all major requirements as well as the residency requirement. A 2.0 GPA is required to graduate.

Special: All majors require internships. Study abroad in 8 countries and work-study programs are available. An accelerated degree in culinary arts and B.A.-B.S. degrees are also possible. There are 2 national honor societies.

Faculty/Classroom: 50% of faculty are male; 50% are female. 91% teach undergraduates. No introductory courses are taught by graduate students. The average class size in an introductory lecture is 25; in a laboratory is 18; and in a regular course is 20.

Requirements: Applicants need to submit a high school transcript with a minimum 2.0 GPA or a GED, and a personal statement. ACT or SAT scores are required for all applicants who have graduated within 5 years of intended start date and have a GPA below 2.5. An interview with an Enrollment Advisor is required and a campus tour is recommended. A GPA of 2.0 is required. AP and CLEP credits are accepted.

Procedure: Freshmen are admitted to all sessions. There are deferred admissions and rolling admissions plans. Application deadlines are open. Application fee is $50. Applications are accepted online.

Transfer: 217 transfer students enrolled in 2010-2011. Students must submit an official college transcript with at least 12 earned semester credits (or 18 quarter credits) with a cumulative GPA of at least 2.0. An interview and a personal statement are required. A campus tour is recommended. 45 of 180 credits required for the bachelor's degree must be completed at Kendall.

Visiting: There are regularly scheduled orientations for prospective students, including program overviews, financial aid information and campus tours. There are guides for informal visits and visitors may sit in on classes. To schedule a visit, contact the Admissions Office.

Financial Aid: In a recent year, 84% of all full-time freshmen and 73% of continuing full-time students received some form of financial aid. 71% of all full-time freshmen and 64% of continuing full-time students received need-based aid. The average freshman award was $6,659. Need-based scholarships or need-based grants averaged $1,136 ($10,990 maximum); need-based self-help aid (loans and jobs) averaged $1,927 ($4,000 maximum); and other non-need-based awards and non-need-based scholarships averaged $3,596 ($32,000 maximum). 8% of undergraduate students work part-time. Average annual earnings from campus work are $3825. The average financial indebtedness of the recent graduate was $11,801. The FAFSA and the college's own financial statement are required. Check with the school for current application deadlines.

International Students: There are 180 international students enrolled. The school actively recruits these students. They must take the TOEFL with a minimum score of 525 on the paper-based TOEFL (PBT) or 71 on the Internet-based version (iBT).

Admissions Contact: Amber Cerda *acerda@kendall.edu*

KNOX COLLEGE C-2

Galesburg, IL 61401 (309) 341-7100
(800) 678-KNOX; (309) 341-7070

Full-time: 599 men, 800 women	**Faculty:** 125; IIB, -$
Part-time: 15 men, 10 women	**Ph.D.s:** 91%
Graduate: n/av	**Student/Faculty:** 11 to 1
Year: trimesters	**Tuition:** n/av
Application Deadline: February 1	**Room & Board:** n/app

Freshman Class: 2660 applied, 1994 accepted, 381 enrolled
VERY COMPETITIVE

Knox College, founded in 1837, is an independent liberal arts college. 2 libraries contain 340,357 volumes, 98,733 microform items, and 13,960 audio/video tapes/CDs/DVDs, and subscribe to 14,613 periodicals including electronic. Computerized library services include interlibrary loans, database searching, and Internet access. Special learning facilities include a radio station. 760–acre biological field station--is both a research and recreation area. Green Oaks Biological Field Station consists of forest, grassland, aquatic habitats and is the second site in the nation with a tallgrass prairie restoration. 30" x 60" high tunnel like a greenhouse, the high tunnel is used to extend the growing season but with crops sewn directly into the ground. The high tunnel will be used in various academic courses, including Urban Agriculture. The 82-acre campus is in a small town 180 miles southwest of Chicago. Including any residence halls, there are 58 buildings.

Student Life: 58% of undergraduates are from Illinois. Others are from 42 states, and 35 foreign countries. 75% are from public schools. 66% are White; 12% Hispanic; 11% Foreign. The average age of freshmen is 18; all undergraduates, 20. 12% do not continue beyond their first year; 79% remain to graduate.

Housing: 1191 students can be accommodated in college housing, which includes single-sex and coed dorms and on-campus apartments. In addition, there are special-interest houses, fraternity houses, Cultural Centers (International House, Casa Latina, ABLE (Allied Blacks for Liberty and Equality) House. On-campus housing is guaranteed for all 4 years and is available on a lottery system for upperclassmen. 86% of students live on campus; of those, 75% remain on campus on weekends. All students may keep cars.

Activities: 26% of men belong to 1 local and 5 national fraternities; 16% of women belong to 4 national sororities. There are 95 groups on campus, including art, band, chess, choir, communications, computers, dance, drama, environmental, ethnic, film, gay, honors, international, jazz band, literary magazine, newspaper, photography, political, professional, radio and TV, religious, social, social service, student government, and symphony. Popular campus events include International Fair (January), Rootabaga Jazz Festival (March) Lincoln Fest (Local Band All Day Festival).

Sports: There are 11 intercollegiate sports for men and 10 for women, and 3 intramural sports for men and 3 for women. Knox has a fitness center that includes cardio and selectorized equipment, fitness studio, and free weight area. Fieldhouse that includes an enclosed six-lane track and court space for various activities. Additionally Knox has a gymnasium, natatorium, football field, softball field, baseball field, outdoor track, tennis courts, and a soccer field.

Disabled Students: 40% of the campus is accessible. Facilities include wheelchair ramps, elevators, special parking, specially equipped restrooms, and special housing.

Services: Counseling and information services are available, as is tutoring in most subjects. There is a reader service for the blind. The Center for Teaching and Learning provides academic support to students in most subjects, particularly development of writing skills.

Campus Safety and Security: Measures include 24-hour foot and vehicle patrol, emergency notification system, self-defense education, and security escort services. There are emergency telephones, lighted pathways/sidewalks, and controlled access to dorms/residences.

Programs of Study: Knox confers B.A. degrees. Bachelor's degrees are awarded in BIOLOGICAL SCIENCE (biochemistry, biology/biological science, and neurosciences), COMMUNICATIONS AND THE ARTS (art history and appreciation, classics, creative writing, dramatic arts, English literature, French, German, Greek (classical), Latin, modern language, music, Spanish, and studio art), COMPUTER AND PHYSICAL SCIENCE (chemistry, computer science, mathematics, and physics), EDUCATION (elementary education, secondary education, and social science education), ENGINEERING AND ENVIRONMENTAL DESIGN (environmental science), SOCIAL SCIENCE (African American studies, American studies, anthropology, Asian/Oriental studies, economics, history, international relations, philosophy, political science/government, psychology, sociology, and women's studies). Creative writing, computer science, psychology, theatre, pre-health, pre-law, biology, and educational studies are the strongest academically. Creative writing, educational studies and psychology have the largest enrollments.

Required: Students must take a 1-term interdisciplinary preceptorial emphasizing writing and discussion skills. In addition to this, 2 writing intensive courses and 1 course emphasizing oral presentation are required. Two courses focusing on diversity are also required, as well as documentation of a significant experiential learning project outside the classroom. Breadth requirements include 1 course each in the 4 areas of arts, humanities, math and natural science, and social sciences. An additional minor or major, not in the department of the first major, is required. A 2.0 GPA is required, overall and in each major and minor.

Special: The normal academic load is 3 courses per term, with 3 terms per year. Cooperative programs are offered with Washington University in St. Louis in architecture and engineering; Columbia University in engineering and law; University of Illinois at Urbana-Champaign and Rensselaer Polytechnic Institute in engineering; Rush University in nursing and medical technology; Duke University in forestry and environmental management; and University of Chicago in law and social work. Study abroad is available in 30 countries. Other programs include a Washington semester, an urban studies semester, science and library research programs, work-study programs, and numerous internships. Dual majors, student-designed majors, and pass/fail options are available. Early admission to George Washington University Medical School is possible. Nondegree study is possible. Knox College participates in the Kemper Scholars Program. There are 8 national honor societies, including Phi Beta Kappa, and 39 departmental honors programs.

Faculty/Classroom: 57% of faculty are male; 43% are female. All teach and do research. No introductory courses are taught by graduate students. The average class size in an introductory lecture is 22; in a laboratory is 14; and in a regular course is 18.

Admissions: 75% of the 2013-2014 applicants were accepted. The SAT scores for the 2013-2014 freshman class were: Critical Reading--13% below 500, 21% between 500 and 599, 42% between 600 and 699, and 24% between 700 and 800; Math--11% below 500, 32% between 500 and 599, 41% between 600 and 699, and 16% between 700 and 800; Writing--15% below 500, 30% between 500 and 599, 47% between 600 and 699, and 8% between 700 and 800. The ACT scores were 4% below 21, 13% between 21 and 23, 20% between 24 and 26, 22% between 27 and 28, and 41% above 28. 51% of the current freshmen were in the top fifth of their class; 83% were in the top two fifths. There were 3 National Merit finalists. 4 freshmen graduated first in their class.

Requirements: Successful applicants have excelled in a challenging college preparatory course of study, including at least 4 years of English; 3-4 years each of mathematics, science, and social studies; and 2-3 years of a second language. An essay is required and interview strongly recommended. Submission of ACT or SAT scores is optional for most applicants; scores will be considered if submitted. Auditions or portfolio presentations are required for scholarship consideration only. AP credits are accepted. Important factors in the admissions decision are advanced placement or honors courses, recommendations by school officials, and personality/intangible qualities.

Procedure: Freshmen are admitted in the fall. Entrance exams should be taken by December 14. There are early admissions and deferred admissions plans. Applications should be filed by February 1 for fall entry; November 1 for winter entry; and January 15 for spring entry, along with a $40 fee. Notifications are sent March 31. 25 applicants were on the 2013 waiting list; 1 were admitted. Applications are accepted online.

Transfer: 24 transfer students enrolled in 2012-2013. A 3.0 GPA is expected. An interview is recommended. 45 of 120 credits required for the bachelor's degree must be completed at Knox.

Visiting: There are regularly scheduled orientations for prospective students, Open houses for prospective students are offered in July, October, November, and January, and offer campus tours, class visits, lunch with students and professors, and informational sessions. Interviews are available on request. There are guides for informal visits, visitors may sit in on classes, and stay overnight. To schedule a visit, contact Beth Jonsberg at (800) 678-KNOX.

Financial Aid: In 2013-2014, 99% of all full-time freshmen and 95% of continuing full-time students received some form of financial aid. 81% of all full-time freshmen and 75% of continuing full-time students received need-based aid. The average freshman award was $33,030. Need-based scholarships or need-based grants averaged $27,850; and need-based self-help aid (loans and jobs) averaged $5,180. 44% of undergraduate students work part-time. Average annual earnings from campus work are $1500. The average financial indebtedness of the 2013 graduate was $28,300. The FAFSA and the college's own financial statement are required. The priority date for freshman financial aid applications for fall entry is February 1.

International Students: There are 162 international students enrolled. The school actively recruits these students. They must take the TOEFL with a minimum score of 550 on the paper-based TOEFL (PBT) or 80 on the Internet-based version (iBT), IELTS.

Graduates: From July 1, 2012 to June 30, 2013, 316 bachelor's degrees were awarded. The most popular majors were creative writing (10%), psychology (9%), and economics (6%). 78 companies recruited on campus in 2012-2013. In an average class, 71% graduate in 4 years or less, 79% graduate in 5 years or less, and 79% graduate in 6 years or less. Of the 2012 graduating class, 15% were enrolled in graduate school within 6 months of graduation, and 60% were employed.

Admissions Contact: Paul Steenis, Dean of Admission. E-Mail: *admission@knox.edu* Web: *www.knox.edu*

LAKE FOREST COLLEGE — E-1

Lake Forest, IL 60045 — (847) 735-5000; (800) 828-4751; (847) 735-6271

Full-time: 643 men, 891 women	**Faculty:** 100; IIB, +$
Part-time: 8 men, 10 women	**Ph.D.s:** 98%
Graduate: 6 men, 12 women	**Student/Faculty:** 15 to 1
Year: semesters, summer session	**Tuition:** $36,920
Application Deadline: February 15	**Room & Board:** $8660

Freshman Class: 3479 applied, 1981 accepted, 416 enrolled

VERY COMPETITIVE

Founded in 1857, Lake Forest College is a private liberal arts institution located 30 miles north of Chicago and offers an innovative and challenging curriculum with abundant internship and research opportunities. The library contains 292,523 volumes, 108,774 microform items, and 9,035 audio/video tapes/CDs/DVDs, and subscribes to 3,289 periodicals including electronic. Computerized library services include interlibrary loans, database searching, Internet access, and Wi-Fi capability. Special learning facilities include an art gallery, radio station, a multimedia language lab, an electronic music studio with practice rooms, a technology resource center equipped with high-end computing hardware and software, a rhetoric and production room. The 110-acre campus is in a suburban area 30 miles north of Chicago. Including any residence halls, there are 43 buildings.

Student Life: 50% of undergraduates are from out of state, mostly the Mid-West. Students are from 47 states, 79 foreign countries, and Canada. 69% are from public schools. 60% are White; 13% Hispanic; 11% Foreign. The average age of freshmen is 18; all undergraduates, 20. 17% do not continue beyond their first year; 70% remain to graduate.

Housing: 1133 students can be accommodated in college housing, which includes single-sex and coed dorms and on-campus apartments. In addition, there are special-interest houses, options for 24-hour quiet floors. On-campus housing is guaranteed for the freshman year only and is available on a lottery system for upperclassmen. Priority is given to out-of-town students. 72% of students live on campus; of those, 80% remain on campus on weekends. Upperclassmen may keep cars.

Activities: 7% of men belong to 2 national fraternities; 11% of women belong to 5 national sororities. There are 51 groups on campus, including art, band, cheerleading, chess, choir, chorus, computers, dance, debate, drama, environmental, ethnic, film, gay, honors, international, jazz band, literary magazine, musical theater, newspaper, orchestra, pep band, photography, political, professional, radio and TV, religious, social, social service, and student government. Popular campus events include Homecoming, Global Fest, Gates Day of Service and Spring Concert.

Sports: There are 8 intercollegiate sports for men and 9 for women, and 16 intramural sports for men and 16 for women. The Sports and Recreation Center houses a gymnasium, 1,200-square-foot training room, 9,600-square-foot weight room, 2,500 square-foot cardio suite, dance studio, basketball courts, racquetball and handball courts, three playing surfaces (wood court, tartan-surface, and artificial turf), batting/golf cages, suspended track, a pool, separate varsity locker rooms, and a cafe. Adjacent is an indoor hockey rink, outdoor sand volleyball courts, tennis courts, baseball, football, soccer, and intramural fields.

Disabled Students: 80% of the campus is accessible. Facilities include wheelchair ramps, elevators, special parking, specially equipped restrooms, special class scheduling, lowered drinking fountains, lowered telephones, and special housing.

Services: Counseling and information services are available, as is tutoring in every subject.

Campus Safety and Security: Measures include 24-hour foot and vehicle patrol, emergency notification system, self-defense education, and security escort services. There are shuttle buses, emergency telephones, lighted pathways/sidewalks, and controlled access to dorms/residences.

Programs of Study: Lake Forest confers B.A. degrees. Master's degrees are also awarded. Bachelor's degrees are awarded in BIOLOGICAL SCIENCE (biology/biological science and neurosciences), BUSINESS (business economics and finance), COMMUNICATIONS AND THE ARTS (art, communications, English, French, music, Spanish, and theatre arts), COMPUTER AND PHYSICAL SCIENCE (chemistry, computer science, mathematics, and physics), EDUCATION (education and music education), ENGINEERING AND ENVIRONMENTAL DESIGN (environmental science), SOCIAL SCIENCE (American studies, anthropology, area studies, Asian/Oriental studies, economics, history, international relations, Latin American studies, philosophy, political science/government, psychology, religion, and sociology). Business, communication and biology have the largest enrollments.

Required: All students are required to complete 32 courses with a minimum GPA of 2.0. General education requirements include 2 courses in natural science or math, 2 cultural diversity courses, and 1 course each in freshman studies, freshman writing, humanities, social science, and senior studies.

Special: Lake Forest offers cross-registration with Associated Colleges of the Midwest, an extensive internship program, a student-designed Independent Scholar major, extensive off-campus study opportunities in 15 + countries with international internships available. Lake Forest has a number of accelerated and dual-degree programs including a 3-3 program in cooperation with a number of law schools whereby a student can earn a BA and JD in six years instead of seven. Students at Lake Forest can choose to earn a BA degree in communication or philosophy in just three years. The College also offers accelerated and dual degree programs in engineering, international studies, pharmacy, and nursing.

Faculty/Classroom: 50% of faculty are male; 50% are female. All teach and do research. No introductory courses are taught by graduate students. The average class size in an introductory lecture is 42; in a laboratory is 16; and in a regular course is 21.

Admissions: 57% of the 2013-2014 applicants were accepted. 52% of the current freshmen were in the top fifth of their class; 76% were in the top two fifths.

Requirements: Applicants are advised to complete a minimum of 16 academic credits, including 4 in English, 3 in math, 2 to 4 each in social and natural sciences, and study in 1 or more foreign languages. A GED is accepted. An interview is encouraged. AP credits are accepted. Important factors in the admissions decision are personality/intangible qualities, advanced placement or honors courses, and extracurricular activities record.

Procedure: Freshmen are admitted fall and spring. Entrance exams should be taken in the junior or senior year. There are early decision and deferred admissions plans. Early decision applications should be filed by December 1; regular applications, by February 15 for fall entry; and December 1 for spring entry. Notification of early decision is sent December 20; regular decision, March 20. 45 early decision candidates were accepted for the 2013-2014 class. 30 applicants were on the 2013 waiting list; 15 were admitted. Applications are accepted online.

Transfer: 68 transfer students enrolled in 2012-2013. Transfer applicants should have a minimum C average in all college work and should be in good standing with their previous institution. High school and college transcripts and a letter of recommendation from the academic dean or a teacher at the most recent college attended are required. 16 of 32 credits required for the bachelor's degree must be completed at Lake Forest.

Visiting: There are regularly scheduled orientations for prospective students. Visits include class visitation, panel presentations, tours and individual appointments with faculty, coaches, and/or admission officers. There are guides for informal visits, visitors may sit in on classes, and stay overnight. To schedule a visit, contact the Admissions Office at (800) 828-4751.

Financial Aid: In 2013-2014, 94% of all full-time freshmen and 91% of continuing full-time students received some form of financial aid. 80% of all full-time freshmen and 85% of continuing full-time students received need-based aid. The average freshman award was $30,300. Need-based scholarships or need-based grants averaged $27,875 ($49,000 maximum); need-based self-help aid (loans and jobs) averaged $4,700 ($10,000 maximum); and other non-need-based awards and non-need-based scholarships averaged $17,325 ($25,000 maximum). 140% of undergraduate students work part-time. Average annual earnings from campus work are $2000. The average financial indebtedness of the 2013 graduate was $26,899. Lake Forest is a member of CSS. The FAFSA is required. The priority date for freshman financial aid applications for fall entry is February 15. The deadline for filing freshman financial aid applications for fall entry is May 1.

International Students: There are 171 international students enrolled. The school actively recruits these students. They must take the TOEFL with a minimum score of 550 on the paper-based TOEFL (PBT) or 83 on the Internet-based version (iBT). They must also take the SAT or ACT.

Graduates: From July 1, 2012 to June 30, 2013, 320 bachelor's degrees were awarded. The most popular majors were communication (12%), economics (12%), and politics (10%). 694 companies recruited on campus in 2012-2013. In an average class, 62% graduate in 4 years or less, 70% graduate in 5 years or less, and 70% graduate in 6 years or less. Of the 2012 graduating class, 21% were enrolled in graduate school within 6 months of graduation, and 71% were employed.

Admissions Contact: William G. Motzer, Vice President for Admissions and Career Services. E-Mail: *admissions@lakeforest.edu* Web: *www.lakeforest.edu*

LEWIS UNIVERSITY E-2

Romeoville, IL 60446 **(815) 838-0500, ext. 5250 (800) 897-9000; (815) 836-5002**

Full-time: 1030 men, 1250 women	**Faculty:** n/av; IIA, av$
Part-time: 330 men, 660 women	**Ph.D.s:** 57%
Graduate: 480 men, 800 women	**Student/Faculty:** n/av
Year: semesters, summer session	**Tuition:** $24,770
Application Deadline: see profile	**Room & Board:** $8900
Freshman Class: n/av	
SAT or ACT: required	

COMPETITIVE

Lewis University, founded in 1932, is a private institution affiliated with the Roman Catholic Church and sponsored by the De La Salle Christian Brothers. A comprehensive liberal arts university, Lewis offers classes at its main campus and at more than 20 satellite locations in the Chicago metropolitan area. The figures in the above capsule and in this profile are approximate. There are 4 undergraduate schools and 11 graduate schools. In addition to regional accreditation, Lewis has baccalaureate program accreditation with NCATE and NLN. The library contains 180,000 volumes, 13,100 microform items, and 2300 audio/video tapes/CDs/DVDs, and subscribes to 800 periodicals including electronic. Computerized library services include interlibrary loans, database searching, and Internet access. Special learning facilities include a learning resource center, art gallery, radio station, TV station, and aviation building and airport. The 350-acre campus is in a suburban area 30 miles southwest of downtown Chicago. Including any residence halls, there are 21 buildings.

Student Life: 97% of undergraduates are from Illinois. Others are from 24 states, 30 foreign countries, and Canada. 75% are from public schools. 71% are white; 14% African American. 60% are Catholic. The average age of freshmen is 19; all undergraduates, 28. 19% do not continue beyond their first year.

Housing: 900 students can be accommodated in college housing, which includes single-sex and coed dorms. On-campus housing is available on a first-come, first-served basis, and is available on a lottery system for upperclassmen. Priority is given to out-of-town students. 73% of students commute. All students may keep cars.

Activities: 3% of men belong to 4 local and 5 national fraternities; 2% of women belong to 3 national sororities. There are 27 groups on campus, including band, cheerleading, choir, chorale, chorus, dance, debate, drama, ethnic, flight team, forensics, honors, international, jazz band, literary magazine, musical theater, newspaper, orchestra, pep band, photography, political, professional, radio and TV, religious, social, social service, student government, symphony, and yearbook. Popular campus events include Fall and Spring Formals, Greek Stock, and International Student Food Festival.

Sports: There are 9 intercollegiate sports for men and 9 for women, and 10 intramural sports for men and 10 for women. Facilities include a recreation center containing a field house with 4 multipurpose courts, a fitness center, an aerobics studio, an 8-lane pool, and an indoor track; a tennis complex, an outdoor track, and baseball, softball, and soccer fields.

Disabled Students: 95% of the campus is accessible. Facilities include wheelchair ramps, elevators, special parking, specially equipped rest rooms, special class scheduling, lowered drinking fountains, and lowered telephones.

Services: Counseling and information services are available, as is tutoring in most subjects. There is remedial math, reading, and writing. The University Success Program provides assistance to those students who do not meet the outright scholastic requirements.

Campus Safety and Security: Measures include 24-hour foot and vehicle patrol and security escort services. There are emergency telephones and lighted pathways/sidewalks.

Programs of Study: Lewis confers B.A., B.S., B.E.S., and B.S.N. degrees. Associate and master's degrees are also awarded. Bachelor's degrees are awarded in BIOLOGICAL SCIENCE (biochemistry and biology/biological science), BUSINESS (accounting, banking and finance, business administration and management, human resources, management information systems, marketing/retailing/merchandising, and sports management), COMMUNICATIONS AND THE ARTS (broadcasting, communications, communications technology, dramatic arts, drawing, English, illustration, journalism, multimedia, music, music business management, painting, public relations, radio/television technology, and studio art), COMPUTER AND PHYSICAL SCIENCE (atmospheric sciences and meteorology, chemistry, computer science, mathematics, and physics), EDUCATION (athletic training, elementary education, secondary education, special education, and speech correction), ENGINEERING AND ENVIRONMENTAL DESIGN (aircraft mechanics, airline piloting and navigation, aviation administration/management, computer graphics, environmental science, and preengineering), HEALTH PROFESSIONS (community health work, health care administration, nursing, physical therapy, predentistry, premedicine, preoptometry, prepharmacy, and preveterinary science), SOCIAL SCIENCE (Christian studies, criminal justice, economics, history, liberal arts/general studies, philosophy, political science/government, prelaw, psychology, public administration, religion, safety and security technology, social work, and sociology). Aviation, criminal social justice, and nursing education are the strongest academically and have the largest enrollments.

Required: All students must earn 128 credit hours in courses acceptable for graduation, with one third of these courses in the core curriculum. Students must maintain a minimum GPA of 2.0. At least 4 upper-division courses must be taken in the major. Students must complete the Introduction to the College Experience course and pass a writing proficiency exam.

Special: Lewis offers a general education degree, co-op programs with Chicago College of Pharmacy and Logan Chiropractic College, student-designed majors, B.A.-B.S. degrees in nursing, pass/fail options, dual majors, work-study programs, and nondegree study. Internships are required for some majors and are optional for all others. There are accelerated-degree programs in business administration, computer network administration, health care leadership, RN-BSN, social and community studies, and nursing. The aviation program permits graduates to qualify for the FAA Airframe and Powerplant certificate. There are 10 national honor societies, a freshman honors program, and 10 departmental honors programs.

Faculty/Classroom: 57% of faculty are male; 43% are female. All teach undergraduates. No introductory courses are taught by graduate students. The average class size in an introductory lecture is 14; in a laboratory, 11; and in a regular course, 13.

Requirements: The SAT or ACT is required, with a minimum composite score of 20 on the ACT; the ACT is preferred. In addition, applicants should be graduates of an accredited secondary school. The GED is accepted. Students should have 18 units, consisting of 3 in English and 15 in other college preparatory subjects. A GPA of 2.0 is required. AP and CLEP credits are accepted. Important factors in the admissions decision are advanced placement or honors courses, leadership record, and extracurricular activities record.

Procedure: Freshmen are admitted to all sessions. Entrance exams should be taken prior to enrollment. There is a rolling admissions plan. The freshman early response deadline is December 1, the priority deadline for freshman scholarship consideration is February 1, and the regular admission deadline is April 15. Application fee is $40. Notification is sent on a rolling basis. Applications are accepted online.

Transfer: Applicants must have a 2.0 GPA in transferable course work of at least 12 semester hours, submit official transcripts from all colleges attended, and be in good standing at the previous institution. 32 of 128 credits required for the bachelor's degree must be completed at Lewis.

Visiting: There are regularly scheduled orientations for prospective students, consisting of 1- or 2-day sessions (overnight optional) and parent orientation followed by a welcome weekend before the first class day in the fall. There are guides for informal visits; visitors may sit in on classes and stay overnight. To schedule a visit, contact the Admissions Office.

Financial Aid: Lewis is a member of CSS. The FAFSA is required. Check with the school for current application deadlines.

International Students: The school actively recruits these students. They must take the TOEFL. They must also take the SAT or ACT.

Admissions Contact: Ryan Cockerill, Director of Admission. E-Mail: *admissions@lewisu.edu* Web: *www.lewisu.edu*

LOYOLA UNIVERSITY CHICAGO — E-2

Chicago, IL 60660 — (773) 508-3075; (800) 262-2373; (773) 508-8926

Full-time: 3345 men, 5994 women	**Faculty:** n/av; I, av$
Part-time: 343 men, 486 women	**Ph.D.s:** 93%
Graduate: 2083 men, 3706 women	**Student/Faculty:** 12 to 1
Year: semesters, summer session	**Tuition:** $36,660
Application Deadline: April 1	**Room & Board:** $12,900
Freshman Class: 14355 applied, 13121 accepted, 2512 enrolled	
SAT CR/M/W: 590/580/580	**ACT:** 27 **VERY COMPETITIVE+**

Loyola University of Chicago, founded in 1870, is a private Roman Catholic (Jesuit) university offering undergraduate curricula in the arts and sciences, business, nursing, social work, and education. There are 8 undergraduate schools and 7 graduate schools. In addition to regional accreditation, Loyola has baccalaureate program accreditation with AACSB, CSWE, and NCATE. The 7 libraries contain 1.8 million volumes, 1.6 million microform items, and 13,249 audio/video tapes/CDs/DVDs, and subscribe to 55,664 periodicals including electronic. Computerized library services include interlibrary loans, database searching, Internet access, and Wi-Fi capability. Special learning facilities include an art gallery, radio station, theaters, art museums, digital media labs, convergence media studio, language learning resource center, neuroscience labs, clean energy lab, mock trial room, performance and specialized fine arts rooms, clinical simulation nursing laboratory, histology lab, geothermal system, ecodome greenhouse, aquaponics system showcase, artificial stream research facility, retreat and ecology campus The 105-acre campus is in an urban area in Chicago. Including any residence halls, there are 76 buildings.

Student Life: 65% of undergraduates are from Illinois. Others are from 48 states, 80 foreign countries, and Canada. 68% are from public schools. 61% are White; 13% Hispanic; 11% Asian American. 61% are Catholic; 21% Orthodox Hindu, Buddhist and Islam; 16% Protestant. The average age of freshmen is 18; all undergraduates, 21. 15% do not continue beyond their first year; 71% remain to graduate.

Housing: 4465 students can be accommodated in college housing, which includes single-sex and coed dorms and on-campus apartments. In addition, there are honors houses, fraternity houses, sorority houses, and living-learning community floors. On-campus housing is available on a lottery system for upperclassmen. 57% of students commute. All students may keep cars.

Activities: 9% of men belong to 7 national fraternities; 12% of women belong to 10 national sororities. There are 247 groups on campus, including fencing, ice hockey, lacrosse, quidditch, rugby, running club, soccer, softball, swim club, tennis, ultimate frisbee, volleyball, art, band, chess, choir, chorus, dance, debate, drama, environmental, ethnic, film, gay, honors, international, jazz band, literary magazine, newspaper, photography, political, professional, radio and TV, religious, social, social service, student government, and waterpolo. Popular campus events include New Year's Festival, President's Ball and Department of Programming Concert/Mainstage Events.

Sports: There are 7 intercollegiate sports for men and 8 for women, and 20 intramural sports for men and 20 for women. Facilities include Loyola Soccer park with new seating capacity of 500 and state-of-the-art press box. Norville Center - The new three-story athletics complex includes a student-athlete academic center, a sports medicine facility, modern and fully furnished locker rooms, state-of-the-art strength and conditioning equipment, a Loyola athletics Wall of Fame, and other facilities that will transform the on-campus experience of all our students and help take Loyola's athletics to the next level. Gentile Arena - In 2011, Joseph J. Gentile Arena underwent a major renovation as the facility was upgraded to one of the top venues not only in the Horizon League, but also in the Midwest. The renovations to Gentile Arena resulted in more of a stadium atmosphere with chairback seating added to enhance the fan experience. A concourse was constructed, and the Arena l features brand new concession stands, restrooms, locker rooms, hospitality rooms and storage areas. Furthermore, the main playing floor, which previously ran north/south, now runs east/west. Loyola Soccer/Softball Park - Recently, the soccer field underwent a major renovation as FieldTurf was installed, replacing a natural grass surface. The park, which also received a facelift with new lights includes bleacher seating, a public address system, scoreboard and free parking. Construction of the Stevens Field House includes a locker room facility, a concession stand and a storage area. Situated in a residential area of Rogers Park, Loyola Softball Park features permanent home and visitor dugouts, bleacher seating, a public address system, electronic scoreboard, concession stand, locker rooms, restrooms and lights.

Disabled Students: 90% of the campus is accessible. Facilities include wheelchair ramps, elevators, specially equipped restrooms, special class scheduling, lowered drinking fountains, lowered telephones. Selected dorms are wheelchair accessible.

Services: Counseling and information services are available, as is tutoring in some subjects, general education courses. A writing center is also available for student use; small group tutoring; tutor-led study halls; academic skills workshop.

Campus Safety and Security: Measures include 24-hour foot and vehicle patrol, emergency notification system, self-defense education, and security escort services. There are shuttle buses, emergency telephones, lighted pathways/sidewalks, hot spot tours, and bicycle safety U-lock program.

Programs of Study: Loyola confers B.A., B.S., B.A.Classics., B.B.A., B.F.A., B.G., B.S.Ed., B.S.N and B.S.W. degrees. Master's and doctoral degrees are also awarded. Bachelor's degrees are awarded in BIOLOGICAL SCIENCE (biochemistry, bioinformatics, biology/biological science, and biophysics), BUSINESS (accounting, business administration and management, business economics, entrepreneurial studies, finance, human resources, international business management, management information systems, marketing/retailing/merchandising, organizational leadership and management, and sports management), COMMUNICATIONS AND THE ARTS (advertising, art history, communications, dance, English, fine arts, French, Greek, Italian, journalism, Latin, media arts, music, Spanish, studio art, theatre arts, and visual design), COMPUTER AND PHYSICAL SCIENCE (chemistry, computer science, computer security and information assurance, information sciences and systems, mathematics, mathematics/computational, physics, software engineering, and statistics), EDUCATION (bilingual/bicultural education, early childhood education, elementary education, health information management, mathematics education, science education, secondary education, and special education), ENGINEERING AND ENVIRONMENTAL DESIGN (environmental science), HEALTH PROFESSIONS (clinical science, exercise science, and nursing), SOCIAL SCIENCE (African studies, anthropology, applied psychology, classical/ancient civilization, criminal justice, economics, forensic studies, history, human services, international studies, pastoral studies, philosophy, political science/government, psychology, religious education, social work, sociology, theological studies, and women's studies). Biology, psychology and nursing have the largest enrollments.

Required: To graduate, students must have a total of 120 credit hours with a minimum GPA of 2.0. There is a core requirement. The Core includes a total of 15 courses (45 credit hours of coursework), primarily from the arts and sciences, which develop important college-level skills and integrate an understanding of values through 10 required areas of knowledge. Important skills on which the Core focuses are communication, critical thinking, ethical awareness, information literacy, quantitativeand qualitative analysis, research methods, and technological literacy. The 10 required areas of knowledge include a college writing seminar, artistic knowledge and experience, historical knowledge, literary knowledge, quantitative analysis, scientific literacy, societal and cultural knowledge, philosophical knowledge, theological and religious studies, and ethics For the core requirement, all students must take 9 hours each of theology, philosophy, and social sciences and 6 hours each of English composition and humanities.

Special: There are study abroad service learning opportunities in Vietnam, Peru, El Salvador, South Africa, Chile, Spain, and India. Dual majors in math education/secondary education and physics/engineering, nondegree study, and pass/fail options are available. The school also offers a B.A.-B.S. degree in chemistry and a 3-2 engineering degree with Columbia and Washington Universities. There are 5-year programs and combination bachelor's/master's available. There are 8 national honor societies, including Phi Beta Kappa, and a freshman honors program.

Faculty/Classroom: 50% of faculty are male; 50% are female. 92% teach undergraduates, and all do research. No introductory courses are taught by graduate students.

Admissions: 91% of the 2013-2014 applicants were accepted. The SAT scores for the 2013-2014 freshman class were: Critical Reading--10% below 500, 43% between 500 and 599, 39% between 600 and 699, and 8% between 700 and 800; Math--9% below 500, 47% between 500 and 599, 37% between 600 and 699, and 7% between 700 and 800; Writing--9% below 500, 46% between 500 and 599, 36% between 600 and 699, and 9% between 700 and 800. The ACT scores were 2% below 21, 15% between 21 and 23, 31% between 24 and 26, 22% between 27 and 28, and 31% above 28. 59% of the current freshmen were in the top fifth of their class; 84% were in the top two fifths. There were 10 National Merit finalists. 22 freshmen graduated first in their class.

Requirements: The SAT or ACT is required. Graduation from an accredited secondary school or satisfactory scores on the GED are required for admission. 15 academic credits are required. Secondary school courses should include 4 credits of English and 3 each of math, science, and social studies. AP and CLEP credits are accepted. Important factors in the admissions decision are advanced placement or honors courses, leadership record, and extracurricular activities record.

Procedure: Freshmen are admitted to all sessions. Entrance exams should be taken as early as possible, normally in the spring of the junior year. There is a rolling admissions plan. Applications should be filed by April 1 for fall entry. Applications are accepted online.

Transfer: 597 transfer students enrolled in 2012-2013. Transfer students must have 20 transferable semester hours of credit, with a minimum GPA of 2.0 for the schools of arts and sciences and education. A minimum GPA of 2.5 is required for the schools of nursing and business administration. If transfers have fewer then 20 hours, students must meet the same requirements as entering freshmen. 45 of 120 credits required for the bachelor's degree must be completed at Loyola.

Visiting: There are regularly scheduled orientations for prospective students, including interviews and tours; students may attend classes if previous arrangements have been made. There are guides for informal visits and visitors may stay overnight. To schedule a visit, contact the Undergraduate Admissions Office.

Financial Aid: In 2013-2014, 96% of all full-time freshmen and 93% of continuing full-time students received some form of financial aid. 93% of all full-time freshmen and 66% of continuing full-time students received need-based aid. The average freshman award was $30,750. Need-based scholarships or need-based grants averaged $19,482 ($57,347 maximum); need-based self-help aid (loans and jobs) averaged $12,810 ($37,000 maximum); non-need-based athletic scholarships averaged $25,991 ($50,400 maximum); and other non-need-based awards and non-need-based scholarships averaged $12,765 ($40,580 maximum). 27% of undergraduate students work part-time. Average annual earnings from campus work are $2404. The average financial indebtedness of the 2013 graduate was $34,404. The FAFSA is required. The deadline for filing freshman financial aid applications for fall entry is March 1.

International Students: There are 274 international students enrolled. The school actively recruits these students. They must take the TOEFL with a minimum score of 550 on the paper-based TOEFL (PBT) or 79 on the Internet-based version (iBT). They must also take the SAT or ACT.

Graduates: From July 1, 2012 to June 30, 2013, 2220 bachelor's degrees were awarded. The most popular majors were biology (13%), psychology (10%), and Nursing (10%). 447 companies recruited on campus in 2012-2013. In an average class, 1% graduate in 3 years or less, 64% graduate in 4 years or less, 70% graduate in 5 years or less, and 71% graduate in 6 years or less.

Admissions Contact: Lori Greene, Director for Undergraduate Admissions. E-Mail: *admission@luc.edu* Web: *www.luc.edu*

MACMURRAY COLLEGE C-3

Jacksonville, IL 62650 (217) 479-7056
(800) 252-7485; (217) 291-0702

Full-time: 270 men, 380 women	**Faculty:** n/av
Part-time: 20 men, 45 women	**Ph.D.s:** 62%
Graduate: n/av	**Student/Faculty:** n/av
Year: semesters, summer session	**Tuition:** $20,900
Application Deadline: see profile	**Room & Board:** $8150
Freshman Class: n/av	
SAT or ACT: required	

COMPETITIVE

MacMurray College, founded in 1846, is a private liberal arts institution affiliated with the United Methodist Church. The figures in the above capsule and in this profile are approximate. In addition to regional accreditation, MacMurray has baccalaureate program accreditation with CSWE. The library contains 1.8 million volumes, 28,093 microform items, and 1085 audio/video tapes/CDs/DVDs, and subscribes to 130 periodicals including electronic. Computerized library services include interlibrary loans, database searching, Internet access, and laptop Internet portals. Special learning facilities include a learning resource center and art gallery. The 60-acre campus is in a small town 30 miles west of Springfield. Including any residence halls, there are 17 buildings.

Student Life: 88% of undergraduates are from Illinois. Others are from 17 states, 3 foreign countries, and Canada. 90% are from public schools. 79% are white; 11% African American. 78% are Protestant; 18% Catholic. The average age of freshmen is 19; all undergraduates, 22. 40% do not continue beyond their first year; 56% remain to graduate.

Housing: 725 students can be accommodated in college housing, which includes single-sex and coed dorms. On-campus housing is guaranteed for all 4 years. 54% of students live on campus; of those, 70% remain on campus on weekends. All students may keep cars.

Activities: 9% of men belong to 1 local fraternity and 2 national fraternities; 15% of women belong to 3 local sororities. There are 31 groups on campus, including art, bagpipe, band, cheerleading, choir, chorale, chorus, dance, drama, ethnic, gay, international, literary magazine, musical theater, newspaper, orchestra, pep band, photography, professional, religious, social, social service, student government, and yearbook. Popular campus events include spring formal, Sigma Tau Gamma Day, and midnight breakfasts.

Sports: There are 9 intercollegiate sports for men and 8 for women, and 15 intramural sports for men and 15 for women. Facilities include a gym, 3 basketball courts, tennis and outdoor basketball courts, a competition-size swimming pool, a weight room, a wrestling room, dance studios, a game room, and a TV lounge.

Disabled Students: 90% of the campus is accessible. Facilities include wheelchair ramps, elevators, special parking, specially equipped rest rooms, special class scheduling, and special housing.

Services: Counseling and information services are available, as is tutoring in every subject. There is remedial math, reading, and writing. The college provides services to visually and hearing impaired students through interpreters, readers, and note takers.

Campus Safety and Security: Measures include security escort services. There are emergency telephones, lighted pathways/sidewalks, evening patrols, and evening sign-in at dorms.

Programs of Study: MacMurray confers B.A., B.S., B.S.N., and B.S.W. degrees. Associate degrees are also awarded. Bachelor's degrees are awarded in BIOLOGICAL SCIENCE (biology/biological science), BUSINESS (accounting, business administration and management, management information systems, marketing/retailing/merchandising, and sports management), COMMUNICATIONS AND THE ARTS (art, dramatic arts, English, music, and Spanish), COMPUTER AND PHYSICAL SCIENCE (chemistry, computer science, mathematics, and physics), EDUCATION (education of the deaf and hearing impaired, elementary education, music education, physical education, science education, secondary education, and special education), ENGINEERING AND ENVIRONMENTAL DESIGN (preengineering), HEALTH PROFESSIONS (nursing, predentistry, premedicine, and preveterinary science), SOCIAL SCIENCE (criminal justice, history, interpreter for the deaf, liberal arts/general studies, philosophy, political science/government, prelaw, psychology, religion, social work, and youth ministry). Education of the hearing impaired and nursing are the strongest academically. Business, education, and criminal justice have the largest enrollments.

Required: To graduate, students must complete 120 semester hours with a minimum GPA of 2.0. All students must take 3 courses in rhetorical skills, a 3-course sequence on major ideas in Western civilization, and a course in Diversity and the American Experience and satisfy the requirements of the breadth component, a 16-hour distribution of nonmajor courses. They also must pass a proficiency exam in writing, given when students attain junior standing.

Special: The school has co-op programs in modern languages and international studies and cross-registration with 5 colleges through the West Central Illinois Foreign Language Consortium. A 3-2 engineering degree with Washington and Columbia Universities, a Washington semester, internships in all majors, work-study programs, dual majors, and pass/fail options are available. Students may study abroad in England, Germany, Japan, or Russia. There are 4 national honor societies, a freshman honors program, and 5 departmental honors programs.

Faculty/Classroom: 42% of faculty are male; 58% are female. All teach undergraduates. The average class size in an introductory lecture is 41; in a laboratory, 14; and in a regular course, 17.

Admissions: 57% of a recent year's applicants were accepted. 28% of a recent year's freshmen were in the top fifth of their class; 50% were in the top two fifths. 3 freshmen graduated first in their class.

Requirements: The SAT or ACT is required. Applicants must be graduates of an accredited secondary school. The GED is accepted. Secondary school courses should include 4 years of English, 3 of math, and 2 each of science, foreign language, and social studies. MacMurray requires applicants to be in the upper 50% of their class. A GPA of 2.5 is required. AP and CLEP credits are accepted. Important factors in the admissions decision are advanced placement or honors courses, extracurricular activities record, and leadership record.

Procedure: Freshmen are admitted to all sessions. Entrance exams

should be taken in the spring of the junior year. There are deferred admissions and rolling admissions plans. Application deadlines are open. MacMurray does not require an application fee. Notification is sent on a rolling basis. Applications are accepted online.

Transfer: 101 transfer students enrolled in a recent year. Transfer students must have a minimum GPA of 2.0 in at least 28 transferable semester credits. Nursing applicants must have a GPA of 2.75 and a minimum score of 20 on the ACT. 30 of 120 credits required for the bachelor's degree must be completed at MacMurray.

Visiting: There are regularly scheduled orientations for prospective students, including a financial aid conference, a tour, and faculty appointments. There are guides for informal visits, and visitors may sit in on classes and stay overnight. To schedule a visit, contact the Office of Admissions.

Financial Aid: In a recent year, 99% of all full-time students received some form of financial aid. 92% of all full-time freshmen and 80% of continuing full-time students received need-based aid. The average freshman award was $16,385, with $5512 ($15,000 maximum) from need-based scholarships or need-based grants; $4607 ($5500 maximum) from need-based self-help aid (loans and jobs); and $11,279 ($15,300 maximum) from other non-need-based awards and non-need-based scholarships. 55% of undergraduate students work part-time. Average annual earnings from campus work are $1134. The average financial indebtedness of a recent year's graduate was $13,926. MacMurray is a member of CSS. The FAFSA is required. The deadline for filing freshman financial aid applications for fall entry is open.

International Students: There were 8 international students enrolled in a recent year. They must take the TOEFL. Some may be required to take the SAT or ACT with a minimum score of 950 (SAT) or 20 (ACT).

Admissions Contact: James Malley, Vice President for Admissions. A campus DVD is available. E-Mail: *admissions@mac.edu* Web: *www.mac.edu*

MCKENDREE UNIVERSITY

C-5

Lebanon, IL 62254

(618) 537-6833
(800) BEARCAT; (618) 537-6496

Full-time: 706 men, 823 women	**Faculty:** 94
Part-time: 289 men, 376 women	**Ph.D.s:** 90%
Graduate: 259 men, 754 women	**Student/Faculty:** 16 to 1
Year: semesters, summer session	**Tuition:** $22,050
Application Deadline:	**Room & Board:** $8350

Freshman Class: 1097 applied, 778 accepted, 304 enrolled
ACT: 24

COMPETITIVE+

McKendree University, founded in 1828, is the oldest college in Illinois. It is a private liberal arts institution affiliated with the United Methodist Church. The figures in the above capsule and in this profile are approximate. There are 4 undergraduate schools and 4 graduate schools. In addition to regional accreditation, McKendree has baccalaureate program accreditation with NCATE and NLN. The library contains 140,000 volumes, 40,000 microform items, and 30,000 audio/video tapes/CDs/DVDs, and subscribes to 9,000 periodicals including electronic. Computerized library services include interlibrary loans, database searching, Internet access, and laptop Internet portals. Special learning facilities include a learning resource center, greenhouse, and archives. The 115-acre campus is in a suburban area 23 miles east of St. Louis. Including any residence halls, there are 34 buildings.

Student Life: 66% of undergraduates are from Illinois. Others are from 11 states, 13 foreign countries, and Canada. 92% are from public schools. 76% are white; 13% African American. 25% are Protestant; 23% Catholic. The average age of freshmen is 18; all undergraduates, 27. 22% do not continue beyond their first year; 70% remain to graduate.

Housing: 692 students can be accommodated in college housing, which includes coed dorms and on-campus apartments. On-campus housing is guaranteed for all 4 years. 50% of students commute. Alcohol is not permitted. All students may keep cars.

Activities: 1% of men belong to 2 local and 3 national fraternities; 1% of women belong to 3 local sororities. There are 75 groups on campus, including art, band, cheerleading, choir, chorale, chorus, computers, dance, debate, drama, ethnic, film, forensics, gay, honors, international, jazz band, literary magazine, marching band, musical theater, newspaper, pep band, photography, political, professional, religious, social, social service, and student government. Popular campus events include Model United Nations, Family Festival, and Midnight Breakfast.

Sports: There are 10 intercollegiate sports for men and 10 for women, and 13 intramural sports for men and 13 for women. Facilities include a 1600-seat gym, an intramural gym, a fitness center, tennis courts, a student center with table tennis and billiards, an all-weather track, a 3000-seat football stadium, and playing fields for baseball, softball, and intramurals.

Disabled Students: 80% of the campus is accessible. Facilities include wheelchair ramps, elevators, special parking, specially equipped rest rooms, special class scheduling, and lowered drinking fountains.

Services: Counseling and information services are available, as is tutoring in every subject. There is a reader service for the blind, and remedial reading and writing.

Campus Safety and Security: Measures include 24-hour foot and vehicle patrol, emergency notification system, and security escort services. There are shuttle buses, emergency telephones, and lighted pathways/sidewalks.

Programs of Study: McKendree confers B.A., B.S., B.B.A., B.F.A., B.S.Ed., and B.S.N. degrees. Master's degrees are also awarded. Bachelor's degrees are awarded in BIOLOGICAL SCIENCE (biology/biological science), BUSINESS (accounting, banking and finance, business administration and management, and marketing/retailing/merchandising), COMMUNICATIONS AND THE ARTS (art, dramatic arts, English, music, music business management, music history and appreciation, public relations, and speech/debate/rhetoric), COMPUTER AND PHYSICAL SCIENCE (chemistry, computer science, information sciences and systems, and mathematics), EDUCATION (art education, athletic training, business education, elementary education, music education, and physical education), HEALTH PROFESSIONS (health, medical laboratory technology, and nursing), SOCIAL SCIENCE (criminal justice, economics, gerontology, history, international relations, philosophy, political science/government, psychology, religion, religious music, social science, social work, and sociology). Business, math, and computer science are the strongest academically. Business, education, and nursing have the largest enrollments.

Required: To graduate, students must complete 128 semester hours, with a minimum GPA of 2.0. The 51-credit-hour core curriculum includes 9 credits of social science, 7 of science, 6 of freshman English, 3 each of speech, math, ethics, philosophy or religion, history, cross-cultural studies, literature, fine or performing arts, and computer competency, and 1 to 2 of phys ed. In addition, 2 writing-intensive courses and a writing proficiency exam must be taken. A thesis is required for biology majors seeking a B.S. degree.

Special: McKendree offers internships, work-study programs, study abroad in 11 countries, a Washington semester, dual and student-designed majors, and nondegree study, as well as a 3-2 program in occupational therapy with Washington University in St. Louis. There are 12 national honor societies, a freshman honors program, and 1 departmental honors program.

Faculty/Classroom: 48% of faculty are male; 52% are female. All teach and do research. No introductory courses are taught by graduate students. The average class size in an introductory lecture is 20; in a laboratory, 15; and in a regular course, 12.

Admissions: 71% of a recent year's applicants were accepted. 40% of a recent year's freshmen were in the top fifth of their class; 70% were in the top two fifths. There were 96 National Merit finalists. 97 freshmen graduated first in their class.

Requirements: The SAT or ACT is required. In addition, students must be high school graduates or submit the GED certificate. Completion of at least 15 units of high school work is recommended. A recommendation from the secondary school counselor is required. McKendree requires applicants to be in the upper 50% of their class. A GPA of 2.5 is required. AP and CLEP credits are accepted. Important factors in the admissions decision are advanced placement or honors courses, leadership record, and evidence of special talent.

Procedure: Freshmen are admitted to all sessions. Entrance exams should be taken in the junior year. There is a rolling admissions plan. Application deadlines are open. Application fee is $40. Applications are accepted online.

Transfer: 217 transfer students enrolled in a recent year. Applicants must have a minimum 2.25 GPA from all colleges previously attended. 64 of 128 credits required for the bachelor's degree must be completed at McKendree.

Visiting: There are regularly scheduled orientations for prospective students, consisting of Preview Days, where faculty members and personnel from several departments answer questions. Student-led tours of the campus and various other events are also available. There are guides for informal visits; visitors may sit in on classes and stay overnight.

Financial Aid: In a recent year, all full-time freshmen and 96% of continuing full-time students received some form of financial aid. 94% of all full-time freshmen and 89% of continuing full-time students received need-based aid. The average freshman award was $20,472, with $17,039 ($29,920 maximum) from need-based scholarships or need-based grants; $4093 ($11,500 maximum) from need-based self-help aid (loans and jobs); and $7956 ($29,920 maximum) from non-need-based athletic scholarships. 22% of undergraduate students work part-time. Average annual earnings from campus work are $972. The average financial indebtedness of a recent year's graduate was $17,839. The FAFSA is required. Check with the school for current application deadlines.

International Students: There were 30 international students enrolled in a recent year. The school actively recruits these students. They must take the TOEFL with a minimum score of 520 on the paper-based TOEFL (PBT) or 70 on the Internet-based version (iBT). They must also take the SAT or ACT, scoring 20 on the ACT.

Graduates: In a recent year, 516 bachelor's degrees were awarded. The

most popular majors were business (37%), education (20%), and nursing (20%). 150 companies recruited on campus in a recent year. In an average class, 48% graduate in 4 years or less, 66% graduate in 5 years or less, and 70% graduate in 6 years or less. Of a recent year's class, 29% were enrolled in graduate school within 6 months of graduation, and 90% were employed.

Admissions Contact: Chris Hall, Vice President for Admission and Financial Aid. A campus DVD is available. E-Mail: *chall@mckendree.edu* Web: *www.mckendree.edu*

MILLIKIN UNIVERSITY — D-3

Decatur, IL 62522 — (217) 424-6210; (800) 373-7733; (217) 425-4669

Full-time: 845 men, 1199 women	**Faculty:** 149; IIB, --$
Part-time: 36 men, 74 women	**Ph.D.s:** 83%
Graduate: 53 men, 55 women	**Student/Faculty:** 14 to 1
Year: semesters, summer session	**Tuition:** $28,512
Application Deadline:	**Room & Board:** $8950
Freshman Class: 3906 applied, 2153 accepted, 451 enrolled	
SAT CR/M/W: 542/513/510 **ACT:** 23	**COMPETITIVE**

Millikin is an independent, four-year university in Decatur, Ill. with approximately 2,300 students in traditional and non-traditional undergraduate and Masters degree programs. The signature of a Millikin University education is a unique experience we like to call Performance Learning. When James Millikin founded the university more than 110 years ago, he did so based upon the idea of combining theory and practice. While this was a radical idea at the time, today, we know that practice is not enough. Today's students must perform their knowledge in order to be truly prepared for life after college. Internships. Co-teaching. Student-run Businesses. Presentations. Market Research. You name it; our students are finding new ways to live out their learning and reap the rewards of their hard work. The result -- Millikin students graduate with experience and the confidence to succeed. Millikin offers undergraduate programs in arts and sciences, fine arts, professional studies and business, graduate studies in business administration and nursing, and accelerated adult learning programs. There are 4 undergraduate schools and 2 graduate schools. In addition to regional accreditation, Millikin has baccalaureate program accreditation with ACBSP, NASM, and NCATE. The library contains 221,922 volumes, 21,000 microform items, and 13,934 audio/video tapes/CDs/DVDs, and subscribes to 1,600 periodicals including electronic. Computerized library services include interlibrary loans, database searching, Internet access, and Wi-Fi capability. Special learning facilities include an art gallery, radio station, 32-track recording studio, computer imaging center, art museum and galleries, observatory with 20" reflecting telescope, 280-seat proscenium theater, 90-seat experimental space for student-directed productions, 3D arts building; student-owned and operated art gallery (Blue Connection), business incubator (The Hub), printing press (Carriage House Press), record label (First Step Records), publishing company (Bronze Man Books), and theatre company (Pipe Dreams Studio Theatre). The 75-acre campus is in a suburban area 180 miles southwest of Chicago and 130 miles northeast of St. Louis. Including any residence halls, there are 33 buildings.

Student Life: 89% of undergraduates are from Illinois. Others are from 33 states, and 17 foreign countries. 90% are from public schools. 75% are White; 12% African American. The average age of freshmen is 18; all undergraduates, 22. 24% do not continue beyond their first year; 76% remain to graduate.

Housing: 1386 students can be accommodated in college housing, which includes single-sex and coed dorms, on-campus apartments, and married student housing. In addition, there are special-interest houses, fraternity houses, sorority houses, living-learning communities. On-campus housing is available on a first-come, first-served basis, and is available on a lottery system for upperclassmen. 64% of students live on campus; of those, 75% remain on campus on weekends. Upperclassmen may keep cars.

Activities: 16% of men belong to 5 national fraternities; 18% of women belong to 6 national sororities. There are 90 groups on campus, including art, band, cheerleading, chess, choir, chorale, chorus, computers, dance, debate, drama, drill team, environmental, ethnic, film, gay, honors, international, jazz band, literary magazine, musical theater, newspaper, opera, orchestra, pep band, photography, political, professional, radio and TV, religious, social, social service, student government, and symphony. Popular campus events include Homecoming, Fall Family Weekend, Millipalooza, University Event.

Sports: There are 8 intercollegiate sports for men and 9 for women, and 5 intramural sports for men and 5 for women. Facilities include an 87,000-square feet indoor sports center with a 4-lane, 200-meter competitive-grade track, indoor soccer, 5 basketball/volleyball courts, batting cages, golf practice area, a climbing wall, aerobic and dance areas, and a fitness/wellness center; phys ed center with a 6-lane, 25-yard pool; a 3000-seat field house with 3 regulation-sized basketball courts; a 4000-seat football field encircled by 8-lane all-weather track; 2 outdoor soccer fields; additional practice fields; and tennis courts.

Disabled Students: 66% of the campus is accessible. Facilities include wheelchair ramps, elevators, special parking, specially equipped restrooms, special class scheduling, lowered drinking fountains, and special housing.

Services: Counseling and information services are available, as is tutoring in most subjects. There is a reader service for the blind. Math and writing centers, workshops on various topics are available.

Campus Safety and Security: Measures include 24-hour foot and vehicle patrol, emergency notification system, and security escort services. There are shuttle buses, emergency telephones, lighted pathways/sidewalks, and controlled access to dorms/residences.

Programs of Study: Millikin confers B.A., B.S., B.F.A., B.M. and B.S.N. degrees. Master's and doctoral degrees are also awarded. Bachelor's degrees are awarded in BIOLOGICAL SCIENCE (biochemistry, biology/adolescence education, biology/biological science, and molecular biology), BUSINESS (accounting, business administration and management, entrepreneurial studies, finance, international business management, management science, marketing/retailing/merchandising, organizational leadership and management, recreational facilities management, and sports management), COMMUNICATIONS AND THE ARTS (acting, art, communication, dramatic arts, English, journalism, music, music business management, music performance, musical theater, piano/organ, public relations, Spanish, studio art, theater design, visual and performing arts, and voice), COMPUTER AND PHYSICAL SCIENCE (actuarial science, chemistry, chemistry/adolescence education, information sciences and systems, mathematics, and physics), EDUCATION (art education, athletic training, early childhood education, education, elementary education, English education, mathematics education, music education, physical education, secondary education, and social science education), ENGINEERING AND ENVIRONMENTAL DESIGN (commercial art, computer graphics, and preengineering), HEALTH PROFESSIONS (allied health, art therapy, health and physical activity, nursing, predentistry, premedicine, preoptometry, prepharmacy, prephysical therapy, and preveterinary science), SOCIAL SCIENCE (ethics, politics, and social policy, history, human services, interdisciplinary studies, philosophy, political science/government, prelaw, psychology, and sociology). Music and theater is the strongest academically. Nursing, music, and biology have the largest enrollments.

Required: Requirements for graduation include courses in writing, math, fine arts, natural sciences, and oral communication. Sequential interdisciplinary requirements include first-year seminar, critical writing, reading, and research 1 and 2, U.S. culture studies, U.S. social structures, and global issues. Nonsequential requirements include quantitative reasoning, natural science with a lab, oral communication, and 2 courses in international cultures and structures. The minimum GPA is 2.0 (higher for some programs); additional requirements for specific programs must be met. Students must complete a minimum of 121 credits (or more for some programs) with a minimum of 39 credits earned in courses numbered 300 or above; at least 12 credits must be in the major department or area.

Special: Millikin offers internships, a Washington semester through American University, study abroad in 28 countries, student-designed majors, a 3-2 engineering degree with Washington University, B.A.-B.S. degrees, credit by exam, and pass/fail options. Students may study multiple majors of their choice; Millikin also offers dual degree programs. There are preprofessional programs in engineering, law, optometry, dentistry, medicine, veterinary science, occupational therapy, medical technology, physical therapy, chiropractic, physician's assistant, and pharmacy. Students are also offered a United Nations semester at Drew University and can benefit from affiliate agreements with programs such as the Institute for the International Education of Students (IES), Ecole Superieure de Gestion et Commerce International (ESGCI), International Teacher-Scholars Program (ITSP), Tunghai University and the Chicago Center for Urban Life and Culture semester. There are 11 national honor societies, a freshman honors program, and 10 departmental honors programs.

Faculty/Classroom: 44% of faculty are male; 56% are female. All teach undergraduates. No introductory courses are taught by graduate students. The average class size in an introductory lecture is 22; in a laboratory is 13; and in a regular course is 18.

Admissions: 55% of the 2013-2014 applicants were accepted. The SAT scores for the 2013-2014 freshman class were: Critical Reading--29% below 500, 52% between 500 and 599, 15% between 600 and 699, and 4% between 700 and 800; Math--48% below 500, 33% between 500 and 599, and 19% between 600 and 699; Writing--43% below 500, 38% between 500 and 599, and 19% between 600 and 699. The ACT scores were 22% below 21, 29% between 21 and 23, 26% between 24 and 26, 12% between 27 and 28, and 10% above 28. 34% of the current freshmen were in the top fifth of their class; 60% were in the top two fifths. 10 freshmen graduated first in their class.

Requirements: The SAT or ACT is required. Applicants should be graduates of an accredited secondary school or have a GED. They should prepare with 4 units of English, 3 each of math and science, and 2 each of foreign language, social studies, and history. An audition is required for music-theater, music, or theater majors. A portfolio is required for art majors. Millikin requires applicants to be in the upper 50% of their class.

A GPA of 2.5 is required. AP and CLEP credits are accepted. Important factors in the admissions decision are recommendations by school officials, advanced placement or honors courses, and leadership record.

Procedure: Freshmen are admitted fall, spring, and summer. Entrance exams should be taken by May 1. There are deferred admissions and rolling admissions plans. Application deadlines are open. Notification is sent on a rolling basis. Applications are accepted online.

Transfer: 100 transfer students enrolled in 2012-2013. Applicants are required to provide official transcripts from previous institutions and may submit ACT/SAT scores. Applicants who are in good standing at the previous institution and who have earned at least a C average in all college study previously attempted will be favorably considered for admission (additional requirements for specific programs). 33 of 124 credits required for the bachelor's degree must be completed at Millikin.

Visiting: There are regularly scheduled orientations for prospective students, consisting of meetings with students, faculty, coaches, and staff, a tour of the campus facilities, and curriculum, honors, housing, and financial aid presentations. There is also an opportunity for students to audition or have portfolios reviewed. There are guides for informal visits, visitors may sit in on classes, and stay overnight. To schedule a visit, contact the Admission Office.

Financial Aid: In 2013-2014, 100% of all full-time freshmen and 98% of continuing full-time students received some form of financial aid. 86% of all full-time freshmen and 81% of continuing full-time students received need-based aid. The average freshman award was $23,447. Need-based scholarships or need-based grants averaged $8,899 ; need-based self-help aid (loans and jobs) averaged $3,823; and other non-need-based awards and non-need-based scholarships averaged $13,148. 43% of undergraduate students work part-time. Average annual earnings from campus work are $797. The average financial indebtedness of the 2013 graduate was $31,833. The FAFSA is required. The priority date for freshman financial aid applications for fall entry is March 1. The deadline for filing freshman financial aid applications for fall entry is May 1.

International Students: There are 31 international students enrolled. The school actively recruits these students. They must take the TOEFL with a minimum score of 550 on the paper-based TOEFL (PBT) or 79 on the Internet-based version (iBT).

Graduates: From July 1, 2012 to June 30, 2013, 480 bachelor's degrees were awarded. The most popular majors were visual and performing arts (22%), business/marketing (18%), and education (14%). 37 companies recruited on campus in 2012-2013. In an average class, 48% graduate in 4 years or less, 59% graduate in 5 years or less, and 60% graduate in 6 years or less. Of the 2012 graduating class, 24% were enrolled in graduate school within 6 months of graduation, and 72% were employed.

Admissions Contact: Kevin Brinkman, Associate Director Admission. E-Mail: *admis@millikin.edu* Web: *www.millikin.edu*

MONMOUTH COLLEGE

C-2

Monmouth, IL 61462

309-457-2143
1-800-747-2687; 309-457-2141

Full-time: 563 men, 675 women	**Faculty:** 91; IIB, -$
Part-time: 4 men, 6 women	**Ph.D.s:** 90%
Graduate: n/av	**Student/Faculty:** 12 to 1
Year: semesters	**Tuition:** $31,690
Application Deadline:	**Room & Board:** $7600
Freshman Class: 2973 applied, 1912 accepted, 392 enrolled	
SAT: required **ACT:** 23	**COMPETITIVE**

Monmouth College, founded in 1853, is a selective, residential, private liberal arts and sciences college. The library contains 199,087 volumes, 266,956 microform items, 12,019 audio/video tapes/CDs/DVDs, and subscribes to 3,053 periodicals including electronic. Computerized library services include interlibrary loans, database searching, Internet access, and Wi-Fi capability. Special learning facilities include an art gallery, planetarium, radio station, TV station. Monmouth College has a prairie-habitat biology field station, Spring Grove Prairie, one of the finest virgin prairie plots in Illinois, a freshwater pond for field research on amphibians and reptiles, an educational garden (and a farm under development), the 16.5-acre Le Suer Nature Preserve, the James Christie Shields Collection of Art and Antiquities collection housed in the Len G. Everett Galleries, the Lewis L. Gould U.S. First Ladies letter collection, and the region's largest collection of Western Illinois Native American artifacts and archeology lab. Hewes Library is a federal government documents repository. The 112-acre campus is in a small town in west-central Illinois, 20 miles east of the Mississippi River, and 45 miles south of Rock Island and Moline. Including any residence halls, there are 39 buildings.

Student Life: 92% of undergraduates are from Illinois. Others are from 19 states, 17 foreign countries, and Canada. 90% are from public schools. 70% are White; 13% African American. 70% claim no religious affiliation; 21% Catholic. The average age of freshmen is 18; all undergraduates, 20. 25% do not continue beyond their first year; 58% remain to graduate.

Housing: 1435 students can be accommodated in college housing, which includes single-sex and coed dorms and on-campus apartments. In addition, there are honors houses, special-interest houses, fraternity houses, and sorority houses. On-campus housing is guaranteed for all 4 years. 92% of students live on campus; of those, 75% remain on campus on weekends. All students may keep cars.

Activities: 24% of men belong to 5 national fraternities; 25% of women belong to 3 national sororities. There are 69 groups on campus, including art, bagpipe, band, cheerleading, chess, choir, chorale, chorus, computers, dance, debate, drama, environmental, ethnic, film, forensics, gay, honors, international, jazz band, literary magazine, marching band, musical theater, newspaper, orchestra, pep band, photography, political, professional, radio and TV, religious, social, social service, and student government. Popular campus events include Homecoming, Scots Day (Founders Day) and Parents Weekend.

Sports: There are 11 intercollegiate sports for men and 11 for women, and 14 intramural sports for men and 14 for women. The Huff Athletic Center includes gym, indoor and outdoor track, all-purpose indoor courts, indoor batting cages, natatorium, 6-court tennis stadium, weight room, fitness/wellness center, dance studio, football, baseball, soccer, and softball fields, sand volleyball court, climbing wall, sauna, and steam room.

Disabled Students: 98% of the campus is accessible. Facilities include wheelchair ramps, elevators, special parking, specially equipped restrooms, special class scheduling, lowered drinking fountains, lowered telephones, and special housing.

Services: Counseling and information services are available, as is tutoring in most subjects, Accounting, biology, chemistry, education, math/statistics, Spanish, French, business/economics, psychology, sociolgy/anthropology There is a reader service for the blind, and remedial math, reading, and writing. There is also individualized academic-support services to students who seek assistance, including one-on-one tutoring and small-group.

Campus Safety and Security: Measures include 24-hour foot and vehicle patrol, emergency notification system, self-defense education, and security escort services. There are shuttle buses, emergency telephones, lighted pathways/sidewalks, controlled access to dorms/residences, 24-hour foot and vehicle patrols, and key cards are required for entrance to all residence halls.

Programs of Study: MC confers B.A. degrees. Bachelor's degrees are awarded in BIOLOGICAL SCIENCE (biochemistry and biology/biological science), BUSINESS (accounting, business administration and management, and international business management), COMMUNICATIONS AND THE ARTS (art, classics, communications, dramatic arts, English, French, Greek, Latin, music, and Spanish), COMPUTER AND PHYSICAL SCIENCE (chemistry, computer programming, computer science, mathematics, and physics), EDUCATION (elementary education, physical education, and secondary education), ENGINEERING AND ENVIRONMENTAL DESIGN (environmental science), HEALTH PROFESSIONS (exercise science), SOCIAL SCIENCE (anthropology, biopsychology, economics, history, international studies, philosophy, political science/government, psychology, religion, and sociology). English, classics (Greek and Latin), history, chemistry & biochemistry, physics and psychology are the strongest academically. Business, communications, sociology, psychology and education have the largest enrollments.

Required: To graduate, all students must complete 32 course credits (equivalent to 128 credit hours) with a minimum GPA of 2.0. A major program must be completed with a minimum of C in all courses. Students must also fulfill 9 courses within the general education program, including an art course, science course and language course(s) (to competency at the 102 level). Students must successfully complete the integrated studies curriculum (one course per year)within this general education program. A topical major (of the student's design) is also possible.

Special: Monmouth has agreements with Rush University, Chicago, for nursing, occupational therapy, and medical technology; and 5- and 6-year coordinated degree partnerships (Masters) with Case Western Reserve (engineering), the University of Southern California (engineering) and Creighton University (atmospheric science). Students have the opportunity to study in more than 25 countries in Europe, Asia, Central and South America and Africa, as well as in programs within the United States. All Associated Colleges of the Midwest (ACM) programs, as well as internships, a Washington semester, and duel and student-designed majors are available. There are 13 national honor societies, a freshman honors program, and 20 departmental honors programs.

Faculty/Classroom: 53% of faculty are male; 47% are female. All teach undergraduates, 65% do research, and 65% do both. No introductory courses are taught by graduate students. The average class size in an introductory lecture is 22; in a laboratory is 12; and in a regular course is 15.

Admissions: 64% of the 2013-2014 applicants were accepted. The ACT scores were 30% below 21, 35% between 21 and 23, 21% between 24 and 26, 8% between 27 and 28, and 6% above 28. 35% of the current freshmen were in the top fifth of their class; 62% were in the top two fifths.

Requirements: The SAT or ACT is required. A score of at least 22 on the ACT is highly recommended. Applicants must be graduates of accredited high schools with a GPA of 2.5. We strongly recommend that applicants have completed 4 years of English, 2 each of math, social studies, and science, including 1 of lab, 2 years of foreign language, and at least 1 of history. We accept the GED. A GPA of 2.5 is required. AP credits are accepted. Important factors in the admissions decision are advanced placement or honors courses, evidence of special talent, and extracurricular activities record.

Procedure: Freshmen are admitted fall and spring. Entrance exams should be taken by the spring of the junior year. There are early admissions, deferred admissions, and rolling admissions plans. Application deadlines are open. Notification is sent on a rolling basis. Applications are accepted online.

Transfer: Students must have a minimum GPA of 2.5. A satisfactory score of at least 19 on the ACT is recommended. 64 of 128 credits required for the bachelor's degree must be completed at MC.

Visiting: There are regularly scheduled orientations for prospective students, including tours, admissions and financial aid discussions, faculty appointments, lunch and entertainment, and a talk with the president. There are guides for informal visits, visitors may sit in on classes, and stay overnight. To schedule a visit, contact Angela Reimolds at admissions@monmouthcollege.edu.

Financial Aid: In 2013-2014, 100% of all full-time freshmen and 99% of continuing full-time students received some form of financial aid. 88% of all full-time freshmen and 88% of continuing full-time students received need-based aid. The average freshman award was $29,665. Need-based scholarships or need-based grants averaged $24,370; and need-based self-help aid (loans and jobs) averaged $5,147. 51% of undergraduate students work part-time. Average annual earnings from campus work are $1400. The average financial indebtedness of the 2013 graduate was $25,048. The FAFSA is required. The priority date for freshman financial aid applications for fall entry is March 1. The deadline for filing freshman financial aid applications for fall entry is May 1.

International Students: There are 18 international students enrolled. The school actively recruits these students. They must take the TOEFL with a minimum score of 550 on the paper-based TOEFL (PBT) or 79 on the Internet-based version (iBT), IELTS or ELS certificate of completion for academic English program (SAT/ACT may substitute for proficiency test). They must also take the SAT or ACT.

Graduates: From July 1, 2012 to June 30, 2013, 284 bachelor's degrees were awarded. The most popular majors were business management (20%), education (15%), and communication/journalism (14%). 7 companies recruited on campus in 2012-2013. In an average class, 47% graduate in 4 years or less, 58% graduate in 5 years or less, and 59% graduate in 6 years or less. Of the 2012 graduating class, 26% were enrolled in graduate school within 6 months of graduation, and 74% were employed.

Admissions Contact: Phil Betz, Director of Admissions. E-Mail: *admissions@monmouthcollege.edu* Web: *www.monmouthcollege.edu*

NATIONAL LOUIS UNIVERSITY — E-2

Chicago, IL 60603 — **(312) 621-9650; (888) NLU TODAY**

Full-time: 433 men, 1137 women
Part-time: 83 men, 431 women
Graduate: 1098 men, 3637 women
Year: trimesters, summer session
Application Deadline: open
Freshman Class: n/av
SAT or ACT: required

Faculty: 100
Ph.D.s: n/av
Student/Faculty: 16 to 1
Tuition: $18,500
Room & Board: n/app

LESS COMPETITIVE

National Louis University, founded in 1886, is an independent institution offering programs in education, liberal arts, health science, business, and human services for the traditional and the adult student. 4 Chicago-area campuses, in Evanston, Wheaton, Wheeling, and the Chicago Loop, accommodate commuters, and academic centers in Elgin, Illinois, Virginia, Missouri, Georgia, Florida, Wisconsin, and Germany offer selected programs for working adults. The figures in the above capsule and in this profile are approximate. There are 3 undergraduate schools and 3 graduate schools. In addition to regional accreditation, NLU has baccalaureate program accreditation with CAHEA and NCATE. The library contains 137,620 volumes, 1 million microform items, and 7,130 audio/video tapes/CDs/DVDs, and subscribes to 2,872 periodicals including electronic. Computerized library services include interlibrary loans, database searching, and Internet access. Special learning facilities include a learning resource center and a pre-K through 8 elementary demonstration school. The 12-acre campus is in a suburban area 12 miles north of Chicago. Including any residence halls, there are 3 buildings.

Student Life: 99% of undergraduates are from Illinois. Others are from 30 states and 4 foreign countries. 39% are white; 15% African American. The average age of freshmen is 25; all undergraduates, 33. 39% do not continue beyond their first year.

Housing: 160 students can be accommodated in college housing, which includes coed dorms. On-campus housing is available on a first-come, first-served basis. Priority is given to out-of-town students. 99% of students commute. Alcohol is not permitted. Upperclassmen may keep cars.

Activities: There are no fraternities or sororities. There are 30 groups on campus, including chorus, drama, ethnic, honors, musical theater, newspaper, professional, religious, and student government. Popular campus events include cultural clubs and celebrating various holidays (e.g. Chinese New Year).

Sports: There is no sports program at NLU. Facilities include a 300-seat gym, a 700-seat auditorium, and a swimming pool.

Disabled Students: 90% of the campus is accessible. Facilities include wheelchair ramps, elevators, and special parking.

Services: Counseling and information services are available, as is tutoring in most subjects. There is remedial math, reading, and writing. A center for academic development provides services to academically at-risk students.

Campus Safety and Security: Measures include security escort services. There are emergency telephones, lighted pathways/sidewalks, and security guards when campus buildings are open.

Programs of Study: NLU confers B.A. and B.S. degrees. Master's and doctoral degrees are also awarded. Bachelor's degrees are awarded in BIOLOGICAL SCIENCE (biology/biological science), BUSINESS (business administration and management and management science), COMMUNICATIONS AND THE ARTS (English and fine arts), COMPUTER AND PHYSICAL SCIENCE (information sciences and systems, mathematics, and science), EDUCATION (early childhood education and elementary education), HEALTH PROFESSIONS (health care administration and medical laboratory technology), SOCIAL SCIENCE (anthropology, crosscultural studies, human development, human services, psychology, and social science). Education and business are the strongest academically. Management and education have the largest enrollments.

Required: Students must take courses in humanities, natural sciences, and behavioral sciences, for a minimum of 50 hours in general education requirements. Other course requirements vary by program. All students must pass an English competency writing exam. A minimum 2.0 GPA and 180 quarter hours, including 45 in the major, are required to graduate. There is a 45 quarter-hour residency requirement.

Special: NLU offers credit by exam and for experiential learning, internships in teaching and human services, and limited nondegree and pass/fail options. There are special completion programs for adults in management, applied behavioral science, and health care leadership. In addition, NLU offers several programs in the field as well as customized programs for working adults. There is 1 national honor society, Phi Beta Kappa.

Faculty/Classroom: 33% of faculty are male; 67% are female. No introductory courses are taught by graduate students. The average class size in an introductory lecture is 16 and in a regular course, 16.

Requirements: The SAT or ACT is required for first-time freshman under 21 years of age. A satisfactory score on the SAT or 19 on the ACT is required. Applicants should graduate from an accredited secondary school with 15 academic credits, including 4 in English, 3 in social studies, and 2 each in math and science. The GED is accepted. 2 letters of recommendation, with 1 from the high school counselor, are required; an interview is strongly encouraged. NLU requires applicants to be in the upper 50% of their class. AP and CLEP credits are accepted. Important factors in the admissions decision are recommendations by school officials, leadership record, and evidence of special talent.

Procedure: Freshmen are admitted fall, winter, and spring. Entrance exams should be taken the winter before application. There are deferred admissions and rolling admissions plans. Application deadlines are open. Application fee is $40.

Transfer: A minimum GPA of 2.0 is required. Applicants must be in good standing at the college previously attended. Official transcripts from previously attended colleges and letters of recommendation are required. Personal interviews are strongly encouraged. 45 of 180 credits required for the bachelor's degree must be completed at NLU.

Visiting: There are regularly scheduled orientations for prospective students, including campus tours, meetings with students and key administrators, attending typical campus entertainment, and visiting classes. There are guides for informal visits and visitors may sit in on classes. To schedule a visit, contact the Undergraduate Enrollment Office.

Financial Aid: NLU is a member of CSS. The FAFSA is required. Check with the school for current application deadlines.

International Students: They must take the college's own test.

Admissions Contact: Admissions Director. E-Mail: *nluinfo@nl.edu* Web: *www.nl.edu*

NORTH CENTRAL COLLEGE E-2

Naperville, IL 60540 (630) 637-5800
(800) 411-1861; (630) 637-5819

Full-time: 1091 men, 1469 women	**Faculty:** 130; IIA, -$
Part-time: 90 men, 105 women	**Ph.D.s:** 89%
Graduate: 140 men, 147 women	**Student/Faculty:** 20 to 1
Year: quarters, summer session	**Tuition:** $29,733
Application Deadline:	**Room & Board:** $8610

Freshman Class: 3987 applied, 2401 accepted, 552 enrolled
ACT: 24

VERY COMPETITIVE

North Central College, founded in 1861, is a private comprehensive liberal arts institution affiliated with the United Methodist Church. The college is highly selective, primarily residential, and primarily full-time undergraduate. There is one undergraduate school and one graduate school. The library contains 138,968 volumes, 105,494 microform items, and 4,405 audio/video tapes/CDs/DVDs, and subscribes to 11,821 periodicals including electronic. Computerized library services include interlibrary loans, database searching, and Internet access. Special learning facilities include an art gallery, radio station, a foreign language lab, academic support services center, and a writing center. The 64-acre campus is in a suburban area 30 miles west of Chicago. Including any residence halls, there are 42 buildings.

Student Life: 93% of undergraduates are from Illinois. Others are from 30 states, 22 foreign countries, and Canada. 90% are from public schools. 79% are White. 56% are Protestant; 34% Catholic. The average age of freshmen is 18; all undergraduates, 21. 20% do not continue beyond their first year; 66% remain to graduate.

Housing: 1537 students can be accommodated in college housing, which includes single-sex and coed dorms, on-campus apartments, and off-campus apartments. and substance free housing. On-campus housing is available on a lottery system for upperclassmen. 54% of students live on campus; of those, 90% remain on campus on weekends. All students may keep cars.

Activities: There are no fraternities or sororities. There are 60 groups on campus, including art, band, cheerleading, choir, chorale, chorus, dance, drama, environmental, ethnic, forensics, gay, honors, international, jazz band, literary magazine, musical theater, newspaper, pep band, photography, political, professional, radio and TV, religious, social, social service, and student government. Popular campus events include Springfest, Winter Comedy Series and Honors Day.

Sports: There are 10 intercollegiate sports for men and 10 for women, and 12 intramural sports for men and 12 for women. Facilities include a indoor and outdoor tracks, a recreation center, a weight room, football and baseball stadiums, soccer fields, a swimming pool, tennis courts, an athletic training facility, and a human performance lab.

Disabled Students: 90% of the campus is accessible. Facilities include wheelchair ramps, elevators, special parking, specially equipped restrooms, special class scheduling, lowered drinking fountains, lowered telephones, and special housing.

Services: Counseling and information services are available, as is tutoring in most subjects. There is a reader service for the blind, and remedial math. limited technology for students with disabilities

Campus Safety and Security: Measures include 24-hour foot and vehicle patrol, emergency notification system, self-defense education, and security escort services. There are emergency telephones, lighted pathways/sidewalks, and controlled access to dorms/residences.

Programs of Study: North Central confers B.A., and B.S. degrees. Master's degrees are also awarded. Bachelor's degrees are awarded in BIOLOGICAL SCIENCE (biochemistry and biology/biological science), BUSINESS (accounting, business administration and management, finance, human resources, international business management, marketing/retailing/merchandising, and sports management), COMMUNICATIONS AND THE ARTS (art history, art, broadcasting, Chinese, communications, English, English literature, English Writing, French, German, Japanese, jazz, journalism, music, Spanish, speech/debate/rhetoric, studio art, and theatre arts), COMPUTER AND PHYSICAL SCIENCE (actuarial science, applied mathematics, chemistry, computer science, mathematics, and physics), EDUCATION (art education, athletic training, elementary education, music education, and secondary education), ENGINEERING AND ENVIRONMENTAL DESIGN (graphic arts technology and preengineering), HEALTH PROFESSIONS (exercise science, nuclear medical technology, predentistry, premedicine, preveterinary science, and radiation therapy), SOCIAL SCIENCE (anthropology, classical/ancient civilization, East Asian studies, economics, history, philosophy, political science/government, prelaw, psychology, religion, social science, and sociology). Business and education have the largest enrollments.

Required: All students must complete a general education core, including 9 hours in humanities and fine arts, 9 hours in social sciences, 6.5 hours in life and physical sciences, 3 to 6 hours in composition, and 3 hours each in speech communication and math. All freshman must complete an interdisciplinary course. In addition, all students take an intercultural seminar, a leadership, ethics, and values seminar, and a course in religion and ethics. A GPA of 2.0 and a total of 120 credit hours are required for graduation, with 27 to 51 credits taken in the major. Students in the College Scholars program must complete an Honor Thesis.

Special: North Central offers co-op programs in radiation therapy, nuclear medicine technology, and chemical microscopy; cross-registration with Benedictine University and Aurora University; a Washington semester; and study abroad. Internships in most subject areas, a 3-2 engineering degree with the Universities of Minnesota and Illinios at Urbana-Champaign, experiential credit, and nondegree study are available. Dual majors, student-designed majors, and 5-year integrated Bachelor's/Master's degree programs are available. There are 18 national honor societies, a freshman honors program, and 14 departmental honors programs.

Faculty/Classroom: 53% of faculty are male; 47% are female. All teach undergraduates. No introductory courses are taught by graduate students. The average class size in an introductory lecture is 24; in a laboratory is 20; and in a regular course is 22.

Admissions: 60% of the 2013-2014 applicants were accepted. The ACT scores were 11% below 21, 30% between 21 and 23, 31% between 24 and 26, 15% between 27 and 28, and 13% above 28. 47% of the current freshmen were in the top fifth of their class; 78% were in the top two fifths. 5 freshmen graduated first in their class.

Requirements: The ACT is required, with a minimum of 20 on the ACT or 940 on the SAT. Minimum requirements also include a GPA of at least 2.5 and involvement in school and/or community. An admission essay and/or admission interview may be recommended. The GED is accepted. The recommended secondary school courses are 4 years of English and 3 years each of math, science, social science, and foreign language. A GPA of 2.5 is required. AP and CLEP credits are accepted.

Procedure: Freshmen are admitted to all sessions. Entrance exams should be taken in the spring of the junior year or the fall of the senior year. There are deferred admissions and rolling admissions plans. Application deadlines are open. Application fee is $25. Applications are accepted online.

Transfer: 360 transfer students enrolled in 2012-2013. Applicants need a minimum 2.5 transferrable GPA or better and 27 transferrable semester hours. If they have not earned 27 transferrable hours, their high school transcripts and ACT/SAT scores are also considered. Students can be considered for admission with a college grade point average of 2.25 or above. 30 of 120 credits required for the bachelor's degree must be completed at North Central.

Visiting: There are regularly scheduled orientations for prospective students, including the opportunity to hear a presentation about academic programs, student life, admission guidelines, and financial aid. Campus tours, faculty presentations, and coaches are also available. There are guides for informal visits, visitors may sit in on classes, and stay overnight. To schedule a visit, contact the Office of Admissions at admissions@noctrl.edu.

Financial Aid: In 2013-2014, 99% of all full-time freshmen and 98% of continuing full-time students received some form of financial aid. 80% of all full-time freshmen and 76% of continuing full-time students received need-based aid. The average freshman award was $28,066. Need-based scholarships or need-based grants averaged $6,140; need-based self-help aid (loans and jobs) averaged $2,418; other non-need-based awards and non-need-based scholarships averaged $12,966; and $6,542 from other forms of aid. The average financial indebtedness of the 2013 graduate was $25,644. The FAFSA and the college's own financial statement are required. Check with the school for current application deadlines.

International Students: There are 28 international students enrolled. The school actively recruits these students. They must take the TOEFL with a minimum score of 520 on the paper-based TOEFL (PBT) or 68 on the Internet-based version (iBT), IELTS.

Computers: All students may access the system 7 a.m. to midnight in the computer center or at any time from residence hall or wireless access points. There are no time limits and no fees.

Graduates: From July 1, 2012 to June 30, 2013, 582 bachelor's degrees were awarded. The most popular majors were psychology (7%), marketing (6%), and elementary education (6%). In an average class, 1% graduate in 3 years or less, 57% graduate in 4 years or less, 66% graduate in 5 years or less, and 68% graduate in 6 years or less.

Admissions Contact: Marty Sauer, Dean of Admission and Financial Aid. E-Mail: *admissions@noctrl.edu* Web: *www.northcentralcollege.edu*

NORTH PARK UNIVERSITY E-2

Chicago, IL 60625 **(773) 244-5500; (800) 888-6728**

Full-time: 699 men, 1070 women
Part-time: 158 men, 297 women
Graduate: 322 men, 683 women
Year: semesters, summer session
Application Deadline: April 1
Freshman Class: 1864 applied, 1618 accepted, 425 enrolled
SAT CR/M: 530/500
Faculty: 108; IIA, --$
Ph.D.s: 90%
Student/Faculty: 18 to 1
Tuition: $21,990
Room & Board: $8040
ACT: 22
COMPETITIVE

North Park University, founded in 1891, is a private comprehensive university affiliated with the Evangelical Covenant Church offering undergraduate and graduate education liberal arts and professional and theological programs. There are 6 undergraduate schools and 5 graduate schools. In addition to regional accreditation, North Park has baccalaureate program accreditation with NLN. The library contains 225,000 volumes, 93,000 microform items, and 6,500 audio/video tapes/CDs/DVDs, and subscribes to 995 periodicals including electronic. Computerized library services include interlibrary loans, database searching, Internet access, and Wi-Fi capability. Special learning facilities include an art gallery. The 30-acre campus is in an urban area 10 miles northwest of downtown Chicago. Including any residence halls, there are 30 buildings.

Student Life: 66% of undergraduates are from Illinois. Others are from 40 states, 28 foreign countries, and Canada. 58% are White; 11% Hispanic. 33% are Protestant; 20% Catholic; 20% claim no religious affiliation. The average age of freshmen is 18; all undergraduates, 21. 23% do not continue beyond their first year; 58% remain to graduate.

Housing: 1130 students can be accommodated in college housing, which includes single-sex dorms, on-campus apartments, and off-campus apartments. In addition, there are special-interest houses. On-campus housing is guaranteed for all 4 years. Priority is given to out-of-town students. 50% of students commute. Alcohol is not permitted. Upperclassmen may keep cars.

Activities: There are no fraternities or sororities. There are 25 groups on campus, including art, band, cheerleading, choir, chorale, chorus, communications, computers, drama, environmental, ethnic, honors, international, jazz band, literary magazine, musical theater, newspaper, opera, orchestra, pep band, photography, political, professional, religious, social, social service, student government, symphony, and yearbook. Popular campus events include Dances, Concerts and Film Festivals.

Sports: There are 7 intercollegiate sports for men and 8 for women, and 5 intramural sports for men and 5 for women. Facilities include football, baseball, track, and soccer fields, tennis courts, a weight room, a gym, and a fitness center.

Disabled Students: 90% of the campus is accessible. Facilities include wheelchair ramps, elevators, special parking, specially equipped restrooms, lowered drinking fountains, lowered telephones, and special housing.

Services: Counseling and information services are available, as is tutoring in every subject. There is a reader service for the blind, and remedial math, reading, and writing. An extended orientation program is available.

Campus Safety and Security: Measures include 24-hour foot and vehicle patrol, emergency notification system, self-defense education, and security escort services. There are emergency telephones, lighted pathways/sidewalks, and controlled access to dorms/residences.

Programs of Study: North Park confers B.A., B.S., B.Mus., B.S.N., B.G.S. and B.M.E. degrees. Master's and doctoral degrees are also awarded. Bachelor's degrees are awarded in BIOLOGICAL SCIENCE (biology/biological science), BUSINESS (accounting, banking and finance, business administration and management, international business management, and marketing/retailing/merchandising), COMMUNICATIONS AND THE ARTS (advertising, communications, English, French, music, music theory and composition, Scandinavian languages, and Spanish), COMPUTER AND PHYSICAL SCIENCE (chemistry, mathematics, and physics), EDUCATION (athletic training, early childhood education, elementary education, and secondary education), ENGINEERING AND ENVIRONMENTAL DESIGN (environmental science), HEALTH PROFESSIONS (exercise science, medical laboratory technology, nursing, physical therapy, predentistry, and premedicine), SOCIAL SCIENCE (African studies, anthropology, biblical studies, criminal justice, economics, French studies, history, international relations, philosophy, political science/government, prelaw, psychology, sociology, and youth ministry). Sciences, nursing, education, and liberal arts are the strongest academically. Business has the largest enrollments.

Required: Students must successfully complete 120 semester hours with a minimum 2.0 GPA. The required number of hours in the major varies. Students must meet a general education requirement of 46 semester hours.

Special: Opportunities are provided for a co-op program in occupational therapy, internships, work-study, a Washington semester, 3-2 engineering degrees, accelerated degree programs in organization management and nursing, credit by examination, dual majors, student-designed majors, B.A.-B.S. degrees, pass/fail options, and study abroad. There are 6 national honor societies, a freshman honors program, and 5 departmental honors programs.

Faculty/Classroom: 47% of faculty are male; 53% are female. All teach undergraduates. No introductory courses are taught by graduate students. The average class size in an introductory lecture is 25; in a laboratory is 25; and in a regular course is 18.

Admissions: 87% of the 2013-2014 applicants were accepted. The SAT scores for the 2013-2014 freshman class were: Critical Reading--33% below 500, 49% between 500 and 599, 17% between 600 and 699, and 1% between 700 and 800; Math--40% below 500, 43% between 500 and 599, 14% between 600 and 699, and 3% between 700 and 800. The ACT scores were 41% below 21, 25% between 21 and 23, 16% between 24 and 26, 9% between 27 and 28, and 9% above 28. 32% of the current freshmen were in the top fifth of their class; 61% were in the top two fifths.

Requirements: The SAT or ACT and ACT Writing Test are recommended. Graduation from an accredited secondary school is required; a GED will be accepted. Students should have completed course work in a foreign language, 4 years of English, and 3 years each of math, science, and social studies. A recommendations from a teacher is required. An essay is required. An interview is recommended and sometimes required. A GPA of 2.8 is required. AP and CLEP credits are accepted. Important factors in the admissions decision are evidence of special talent, personality/intangible qualities, and extracurricular activities record.

Procedure: Freshmen are admitted fall and winter. Entrance exams should be taken during spring of the junior year or fall of the senior year. There is a rolling admissions plan. Applications should be filed by April 1 for fall entry; December 15 for winter entry, along with a $40 fee. Applications are accepted online.

Transfer: 300 transfer students enrolled in 2012-2013. To be eligible for transfer admission, students must submit 1 letter of recommendation and official transcripts from the previous college and must have maintained a minimum GPA of 2.5. An interview is also recommended. 30 of 120 credits required for the bachelor's degree must be completed at North Park.

Visiting: There are regularly scheduled orientations for prospective students. There are guides for informal visits, visitors may sit in on classes, and stay overnight. To schedule a visit, contact the Campus Visit Counselor at (773) 244-5511.

Financial Aid: In 2013-2014, 98% of all full-time freshmen and 95% of continuing full-time students received some form of financial aid. 79% of all full-time freshmen received need-based aid. 20% of undergraduate students work part-time. Average annual earnings from campus work are $2000. The average financial indebtedness of the 2013 graduate was $28,467. The FAFSA is required. The priority date for freshman financial aid applications for fall entry is March 1. The deadline for filing freshman financial aid applications for fall entry is August 15.

International Students: There are 100 international students enrolled. The school actively recruits these students. They must take the TOEFL with a minimum score of 550 on the paper-based TOEFL (PBT) or 80 on the Internet-based version (iBT) and the college's own test.

Graduates: From July 1, 2012 to June 30, 2013, 481 bachelor's degrees were awarded. The most popular majors were business and marketing (23%), health and related programs (22%), and communication (8%). In an average class, 39% graduate in 4 years or less, 52% graduate in 5 years or less, and 58% graduate in 6 years or less.

Admissions Contact: Mark Olson, Acting Director Undergraduate Admission. E-Mail: *molson@northpark.edu* Web: *www.northpark.edu*

NORTHEASTERN ILLINOIS UNIVERSITY E-2

Chicago, IL 60625 **(773) 442-4044; (773) 442-4020**

Full-time: 2493 men, 2971 women
Part-time: 1550 men, 2126 women
Graduate: 729 men, 1280 women
Year: semesters, summer session
Application Deadline: July 1
Freshman Class: 5400 applied, 3375 accepted, 1040 enrolled
ACT: 19
Faculty: n/av; IIA, --$
Ph.D.s: 70%
Student/Faculty: n/av
Tuition: n/av
Room & Board: n/app
COMPETITIVE

Northeastern Illinois University, founded in 1867, is a public liberal arts institution offering degree programs in Arts and Sciences, Business Management, and Education, as well as Non-Traditional programs There are 3 undergraduate schools and one graduate school. In addition to regional accreditation, Northeastern has baccalaureate program accreditation with CSWE, NASAD, NASM, and NCATE. The library contains 697,087 volumes, 359,250 microform items, and 10,637 audio/video tapes/CDs/DVDs, and subscribes to 76,900 periodicals including electronic. Computerized library services include interlibrary loans and database searching. Special learning facilities include an art gallery and radio station. The 67-acre campus is in an urban area eight miles northwest of downtown Chicago. Including any residence halls, there are 18 buildings.

Student Life: 98% of undergraduates are from Illinois. Others are from 15 states, 104 foreign countries, and Canada. 43% are from public schools. 38% are White; 34% Hispanic. The average age of freshmen is 19; all undergraduates, 24. 38% do not continue beyond their first year; 21% remain to graduate.

Housing: Alcohol is not permitted. All students commute. All students may keep cars.

Activities: 1% of men belong to 4 national fraternities; 2% of women belong to 2 local and 6 national sororities. There are 92 groups on campus, including art, band, cheerleading, chess, computers, dance, drama, environmental, ethnic, film, gay, honors, international, jazz band, literary magazine, musical theater, newspaper, opera, orchestra, photography, political, professional, radio and TV, religious, social, social service, and student government. Popular campus events include International Day, Visiting Lecture Series and Music Performance Series.

Sports: There are 10 intramural sports for men and 10 for women. Facilities include basketball, tennis, and racquetball courts, indoor and outdoor tracks, a pool, a weight room, and baseball and softball fields.

Disabled Students: 95% of the campus is accessible. Facilities include wheelchair ramps, elevators, special parking, specially equipped restrooms, special class scheduling, lowered drinking fountains, lowered telephones, and an Accessibility Center that allows priority registration.

Services: Counseling and information services are available, as is tutoring in most subjects. There is a reader service for the blind, and remedial math, reading, and writing.

Campus Safety and Security: Measures include 24-hour foot and vehicle patrol, emergency notification system, and security escort services. There are emergency telephones and lighted pathways/sidewalks.

Programs of Study: Northeastern confers B.A., and B.S. degrees. Master's degrees are also awarded. Bachelor's degrees are awarded in AGRICULTURE (environmental studies), BIOLOGICAL SCIENCE (biology/biological science), BUSINESS (accounting, banking and finance, business administration and management, human resources, management science, and marketing/retailing/merchandising), COMMUNICATIONS AND THE ARTS (art history, art, communications, dance, English, English literature, French, Italian, Korean, linguistics, media arts, music, Spanish, and theatre arts), COMPUTER AND PHYSICAL SCIENCE (chemistry, computer science, earth science, geoenvironmental studies, mathematics, and physics), EDUCATION (bilingual/bicultural education, early childhood education, elementary education, English education, health education, music education, physical education, recreation education, secondary education, special education, and teaching English as a second/foreign language (TESOL/TEFOL)), HEALTH PROFESSIONS (health and public health), SOCIAL SCIENCE (African American studies, anthropology, criminal justice, economics, French studies, gender studies, geography, gerontology, Hispanic American studies, history, interdisciplinary studies, philosophy, political science/government, psychology, social work, sociology, urban studies, and women's studies). Elementary education, accounting and psychology are the strongest academically. Interdisciplinary, elementary education and justice studies have the largest enrollments.

Required: All students are required to take at least 120 semester hours, including 39 hours of general education and 30 to 60 hours in the major. General education includes 12 hours in social sciences, 9 hours in natural sciences (1 lab), 9 hours in humanities, and 6 hours in fine arts, one college level math. A 2.0 overall GPA is required for graduation. An overall GPA and college major GPA of 2.5 are required within the College of Business Management and the College of Education.

Special: Alternative degree and nondegree programs are available, as are opportunities for cooperative education, study abroad, and teacher certification. Dual and student-designed majors are possible. There are 12 national honor societies, a freshman honors program, and 18 departmental honors programs.

Faculty/Classroom: 49% of faculty are male; 51% are female. No introductory courses are taught by graduate students. The average class size in a laboratory is 20 and in a regular course is 17.

Admissions: 63% of the 2013-2014 applicants were accepted. The ACT scores were 69% below 21, 20% between 21 and 23, 9% between 24 and 26, 2% between 27 and 28, and 1% above 28. 23% of the current freshmen were in the top fifth of their class; 59% were in the top two fifths.

Requirements: The ACT is required. In addition, for freshmen under 21 years of age. Students must be in the top half of their high school class or present satisfactory scores on the ACT. Applicants must have graduated from a regionally accredited high school or passed the GED. High school preparation should total at least 15 credits, including 4 years in English, 3 each in math, sciences, and social studies, and 2 in foreign language, music, art, or vocational education (only 1 vocational course is accepted). Northeastern requires applicants to be in the upper 50% of their class. AP and CLEP credits are accepted. Important factors in the admissions decision are evidence of special talent.

Procedure: Freshmen are admitted to all sessions. Entrance exams should be taken No entrance exam required. There are deferred admissions and rolling admissions plans. Applications should be filed by July 1 for fall entry; November 1 for spring entry; and April 1 for summer entry, along with a $30 fee. Notification is sent on a rolling basis. Applications are accepted online.

Transfer: 2230 transfer students enrolled in 2012-2013. Applicants are considered if they have completed at least 24 semester hours of study with a C average. Those with fewer than 24 hours of credit must meet freshman admissions requirements. 30 of 120 credits required for the bachelor's degree must be completed at Northeastern.

Visiting: There are guides for informal visits and visitors may sit in on classes. To schedule a visit, contact Patricia Johnson at (773) 442-4011.

Financial Aid: In 2013-2014, 80% of all full-time freshmen and 84% of continuing full-time students received some form of financial aid. 18% of all full-time freshmen and 36% of continuing full-time students received need-based aid. The average freshman award was $5,245. Need-based scholarships or need-based grants averaged $3,030 ($10,500 maximum); need-based self-help aid (loans and jobs) averaged $3,235 ($10,500 maximum); and other non-need-based awards and non-need-based scholarships averaged $795 ($8,500 maximum). 4% of undergraduate students work part-time. Average annual earnings from campus work are $2398. The average financial indebtedness of the 2013 graduate was $12,100. The FAFSA is required. The priority date for freshman financial aid applications for fall entry is February 28. The deadline for filing freshman financial aid applications for fall entry is July 1.

International Students: There are 114 international students enrolled. They must take the TOEFL with a minimum score of 500 on the paper-based TOEFL (PBT) or 61 on the Internet-based version (iBT).

Graduates: From July 1, 2012 to June 30, 2013, 1741 bachelor's degrees were awarded. The most popular majors were interdisciplinary studies (10%), elementary education (8%), and justice studies (7%). In an average class, 5% graduate in 4 years or less, 15% graduate in 5 years or less, and 23% graduate in 6 years or less. Of the 2012 graduating class, 60% were employed within 6 months of graduation.

Admissions Contact: Claudia Mercado, Director of Admissions. E-Mail: *admrec@neiu.edu* Web: *www.neiu.edu*

NORTHERN ILLINOIS UNIVERSITY D-2

DeKalb, IL 60115 **(815) 753-0446**
(800) 892-3050; (815) 753-8312

Full-time: 8050 men, 8300 women	**Faculty:** 922; I, --$
Part-time: 900 men, 1025 women	**Ph.D.s:** 83%
Graduate: 2635 men, 3500 women	**Student/Faculty:** n/av
Year: semesters, summer session	**Tuition:** $11,728 ($20,648)
Application Deadline: August 1	**Room & Board:** $9346
Freshman Class: n/av	
SAT or ACT: required	

COMPETITIVE

Northern Illinois University, founded in 1895, is a publicly funded institution offering undergraduate and graduate programs in a comprehensive range of disciplines. Some figures in the above capsule and in this profile are approximate. There are 6 undergraduate schools and 2 graduate schools. In addition to regional accreditation, NIU has baccalaureate program accreditation with AACSB, ABET, ACEJMC, APTA, ASLA, CAHEA, NASAD, NASM, NCATE, and NLN. The 4 libraries contain 2.2 million volumes, 3.6 million microform items, audio/video tapes/CDs/DVDs, and subscribe to 32,722 periodicals including electronic. Computerized library services include interlibrary loans and database searching. Special learning facilities include an art gallery, radio station, TV station, and anthropology museum. The 755-acre campus is in a small town 65 miles west of Chicago. Including any residence halls, there are 55 buildings.

Student Life: 95% of undergraduates are from Illinois. Others are from 49 states, 95 foreign countries, and Canada. 84% are from public schools. 73% are white; 13% African American. The average age of freshmen is 18; all undergraduates, 22. 22% do not continue beyond their first year; 78% remain to graduate.

Housing: 5800 students can be accommodated in college housing, which includes single-sex and coed dorms, on-campus apartments, and married student housing. In addition, there are honors houses, language houses, special-interest houses, and houses for law, computer science, music, political science, and health professions. On-campus housing is guaranteed for the freshman year only and is available on a first-come, first-served basis. 67% of students live on campus; of those, 60% remain on campus on weekends. All students may keep cars.

Activities: 15% of men belong to 22 national fraternities; 11% of women belong to 15 national sororities. There are 200 groups on campus, including art, band, cheerleading, chess, choir, chorale, chorus, computers, dance, drama, drill team, ethnic, film, gay, honors, international, jazz band, literary magazine, marching band, musical theater, newspaper, orchestra, pep band, photography, political, professional, radio and TV, religious, social, social service, student government, and symphony. Popular campus events include Unity in Diversity Week, Greek Week, and Springfest.

Sports: There are 8 intercollegiate sports for men and 8 for women, and 15 intramural sports for men and 15 for women. Facilities include a sports stadium, a recreation center and field house with facilities for basketball, volleyball, badminton, table tennis, tennis, racquetball/handball, and weight training, and 2 swimming pools.

Disabled Students: 85% of the campus is accessible. Facilities include

wheelchair ramps, elevators, special parking, specially equipped restrooms, special class scheduling, lowered drinking fountains, lowered telephones, special housing, and transportation.

Services: Formal tutoring is provided for eligible students.

Campus Safety and Security: Measures include 24-hour foot and vehicle patrol, self-defense education, and security escort services. There are shuttle buses, emergency telephones, lighted pathways/sidewalks, and a bicycle patrol.

Programs of Study: NIU confers B.A., B.S., B.F.A., B.G.S., B.M., and B.S.Ed. degrees. Master's and doctoral degrees are also awarded. Bachelor's degrees are awarded in BIOLOGICAL SCIENCE (biology/biological science and nutrition), BUSINESS (accounting, banking and finance, business administration and management, and marketing/retailing/merchandising), COMMUNICATIONS AND THE ARTS (art, art history and appreciation, communications, dramatic arts, English, French, German, journalism, music, Russian, Spanish, and studio art), COMPUTER AND PHYSICAL SCIENCE (atmospheric sciences and meteorology, chemistry, computer science, geology, geoscience, information sciences and systems, mathematics, and physics), EDUCATION (art education, early childhood education, elementary education, health education, music education, physical education, and special education), ENGINEERING AND ENVIRONMENTAL DESIGN (electrical/electronics engineering, industrial engineering, mechanical engineering, and technological management), HEALTH PROFESSIONS (clinical science, community health work, health science, nursing, and speech pathology/audiology), SOCIAL SCIENCE (anthropology, child care/child and family studies, dietetics, early childhood studies, economics, geography, history, liberal arts/general studies, philosophy, physical fitness/movement, political science/government, psychology, sociology, and textiles and clothing). Business, engineering, and sciences are the strongest academically. Business, education, and communications have the largest enrollments.

Required: To graduate, students must have a minimum of 124 credit hours and a minimum GPA of 2.0. All students must take English 103 and 104 and Communication Studies 100. In addition, they must take Math 101 or obtain at least a C in Math 155, 201, 206, 210, 211, or 229. The school also requires that students complete 29 hours in distributive studies areas, consisting of 9 to 12 hours in the humanities and arts, 7 to 11 hours in science and math, 6 to 9 hours in social science, and 3 to 6 hours in interdisciplinary studies.

Special: NIU offers internships in several areas. Students may study abroad in 30 countries. A physics/engineering degree is offered in cooperation with the University of Illinois. Either a B.A. or a B.S. may be obtained in the social science programs. Work-study programs, a general studies degree, co-op programs, pass/fail options, and student-designed majors are available. There are 5 national honor societies, a freshman honors program, and 18 departmental honors programs.

Faculty/Classroom: 54% of faculty are male; 46% are female. Graduate students teach 20% of introductory courses. The average class size in an introductory lecture is 37; in a laboratory, 17; and in a regular course, 30.

Admissions: 59% of a recent year's applicants were accepted. 23% of a recent year's freshmen were in the top fifth of their class; 54% were in the top two fifths.

Requirements: The SAT or ACT is required. Students must have a minimum score of 19 on the ACT and be in the top half of their class, or have an ACT score of 23 and be in the upper two thirds of their class. Graduation from an accredited secondary school or satisfactory scores on the GED are required for admission. Secondary school courses must include 4 years of English and 2 to 3 years each of math, science, and social studies. In addition, students must have completed 1 to 2 years of art, film, foreign language, music, or theater. AP and CLEP credits are accepted.

Procedure: Freshmen are admitted to all sessions. Entrance exams should be taken during the junior year. There is a rolling admissions plan. Applications should be filed by August 1 for fall entry. Application fee is $40. Applications are accepted online. A waiting list is maintained.

Transfer: Transfer students with 24 or more credit hours must have a minimum GPA of 2.0. The core competency requirement in English, math, and speech must be satisfied by all transfer students. 30 of 124 credits required for the bachelor's degree must be completed at NIU.

Visiting: There are regularly scheduled orientations for prospective students, including open house programs, bus tours, faculty meetings, residence hall tours, and department receptions. There are guides for informal visits; visitors may sit in on classes and stay overnight. To schedule a visit, contact the Office of Orientation and Student Assistance.

Financial Aid: In a recent year, 85% of all full-time freshmen and 75% of continuing full-time students received some form of financial aid. 67% of all full-time freshmen and 58% of continuing full-time students received need-based aid. The average financial indebtedness of a recent year's graduate was $16,838. The FAFSA and the college's own financial statement are required. Check with the school for current application dates.

International Students: International students must take the TOEFL with a minimum score of 527 on the paper-based TOEFL (PBT) or 71 on the Internet-based version (iBT).

Graduates: In a recent year, 4027 bachelor's degrees were awarded. The most popular majors were teacher education (7%), communication studies (6%), and accountancy (6%). 800 companies recruited on campus in a recent year. In an average class, 47% graduate in 5 years or less and 48% graduate in 6 years or less. Of a recent year's graduating class, 19% were enrolled in graduate school within 6 months of graduation.

Admissions Contact: Director of Admissions. E-mail: *admissions-info@niu.edu* Web: *www.niu.edu*

NORTHWESTERN UNIVERSITY — E-2

Evanston, IL 60208 — **(847) 491-7271**

Full-time: 3700 men, 4110 women	**Faculty:** 900; I, ++$
Part-time: 90 men, 120 women	**Ph.D.s:** 100%
Graduate: 4000 men, 2890 women	**Student/Faculty:** 9 to 1
Year: trimesters, summer session	**Tuition:** $29,000
Application Deadline:	**Room & Board:** $8970
Freshman Class: n/av	
SAT or ACT: required	

MOST COMPETITIVE

Northwestern University, founded in 1851, is an independent, nonprofit liberal arts institution offering undergraduate study in the arts and sciences, education and social policy, journalism, music, communication, and engineering and applied science. The figures in the above capsule and in this profile are approximate. There are 6 undergraduate schools and 7 graduate schools. In addition to regional accreditation, Northwestern has baccalaureate program accreditation with AACSB, ABET, ACEJMC, APTA, and NASM. The 3 libraries contain 4.3 million volumes, 4.2 million microform items, 75,358 audio/video tapes/CDs/DVDs, and subscribes to 39,310 periodicals including electronic. Computerized library services include interlibrary loans, database searching, and Internet access. Special learning facilities include an art gallery, radio station, TV station, an observatory. The 231-acre campus is in a suburban area 12 miles north of Chicago on the shores of Lake Michigan. Including any residence halls, there are 180 buildings.

Student Life: 75% of undergraduates are from out of state, mostly the Mid-West. Students are from 50 states, 51 foreign countries, and Canada. 73% are from public schools. 60% are White; 17% Asian American. 33% are Protestant; 25% claim no religious affiliation; 23% Catholic; 16% Jewish. The average age of freshmen is 19; all undergraduates, 20. 3% do not continue beyond their first year; 93% remain to graduate.

Housing: 4250 students can be accommodated in college housing, which includes single-sex and coed dorms. In addition, there are special-interest houses, fraternity houses, and sorority houses. On-campus housing is guaranteed for the freshman year only. 65% of students live on campus; of those, 95% remain on campus on weekends. Upperclassmen may keep cars.

Activities: 30% of men belong to 22 national fraternities; 39% of women belong to 19 national sororities. There are 415 groups on campus, including art, band, cheerleading, chess, choir, chorale, chorus, communications, dance, debate, drama, ethnic, film, gay, honors, international, jazz band, literary magazine, marching band, musical theater, newspaper, opera, orchestra, pep band, photography, political, professional, radio and TV, religious, social, social service, student government, symphony, and yearbook. Popular campus events include Waa-Mu Variety Show, Armadillo Day, and Dance Marathon.

Sports: There are 9 intercollegiate sports for men and 12 for women, and 21 intramural sports for men and 19 for women. Facilities include a stadium, an arena, a gym, lakefront playing fields for soccer, field hockey, and Frisbee, a boat house, and recreation and sports centers housing basketball, volleyball, tennis, racquetball, swimming, badminton, weight training, jogging, squash, fitness facilities, and a golf center.

Disabled Students: All of the campus is accessible. Facilities include wheelchair ramps, elevators, special parking, specially equipped restrooms, special class scheduling, lowered drinking fountains, lowered telephones, and special housing.

Services: There is a reader service for the blind. one-on-one compensation, remediation, ADHD coaching, note taking, and real-time captioning.

Campus Safety and Security: Measures include 24-hour foot and vehicle patrol, self-defense education, and security escort services. There are shuttle buses, emergency telephones, lighted pathways/sidewalks, a security keycard system in residence halls.

Programs of Study: Northwestern confers B.A., B.S., B.A.C.M.N., B.A.Mus., B.M.E., B.Mus., B.Ph., B.P.H.C., B.S.A.M., B.S.B.M., B.S.C.H., B.S.C.I., B.S.C.M.N., B.S.C.O., B.S.C.S., B.S.Ed., B.S.E.E., B.S.E.N., B.S.E.S., B.S.G.E., B.S.G.S., B.S.I.E., B.S.J., B.S.M., B.S.M.D., B.S.M.E., B.S.M.F., B.S.M.T., B.S.S.E. and B.S.S.P. degrees. Master's and doctoral degrees are also awarded. Bachelor's degrees are awarded in BIOLOGICAL SCIENCE (biology/biological science, ecology, molecular biology, and neurosciences), BUSINESS (organizational behavior), COMMUNICATIONS AND THE ARTS (art, art history and appreciation, classics, communications, communications technology, comparative literature, dance, dramatic arts, English, fine arts, French, German, Italian, jazz, journalism, linguistics, music, music performance, music technology, music theory and composition, percussion, performing arts, piano/organ, radio/television technology, Slavic languages, Spanish, strings, voice, and winds), COMPUTER AND PHYSICAL SCIENCE (applied mathematics, astronomy, chemistry, computer science, geology, information sciences and systems, mathematics, physics, and statistics), EDUCATION (education, mathematics education, music education, and secondary education), ENGINEERING AND ENVIRONMENTAL DESIGN (biomedical engineering, chemical engineering, civil engineering, computer engineering, electrical/electronics engineering, engineering, environmental engineering, environmental science, industrial engineering, manufacturing engineering, materials engineering, materials science, and mechanical engineering), HEALTH PROFESSIONS (premedicine and speech pathology/audiology), SOCIAL SCIENCE (African American studies, American studies, anthropology, cognitive science, economics, ethics, politics, and social policy, European studies, gender studies, geography, history, human development, international studies, philosophy, political science/government, psychology, religion, science and society, sociology, and urban studies). Journalism, communications, and physical and life sciences are the strongest academically. Economics, political science, and engineering have the largest enrollments.

Required: Requirements for graduation vary by school and degree program. Students must maintain a minimum 2.0 GPA and complete a total of 45 to 48 quarter units (courses).

Special: The university offers cooperative engineering programs throughout the country, many off-campus field studies and research opportunities, internships in the arts, journalism, and teaching, study abroad in 46 countries around the world, a Washington semester, and numerous work-study programs both on and off campus. There is an accelerated degree program in medical education, and B.A.-B.S. degrees in liberal arts and engineering, liberal arts and music, and music and engineering. An integrated science program, an interdisciplinary study in mathematical methods in social sciences and numerous other interdisciplinary majors, a variety of dual and student-designed majors, pass/fail options, and a teaching media program are also available. There are 23 national honor societies, including Phi Beta Kappa, a freshman honors program, and 40 departmental honors programs.

Faculty/Classroom: 71% of faculty are male; 29% are female. All teach and do research. Graduate students teach 3% of introductory courses. The average class size in an introductory lecture is 35; in a laboratory is 14; and in a regular course is 22.

Admissions: 187 freshmen graduated first in their class.

Requirements: The SAT or ACT is required. Applicants must be graduates of an accredited secondary school or have a GED certificate, and have completed a minimum of 16 units, including 4 units of English, 3 of math, 2 or 3 each of a foreign language and history, and 2 of lab sciences. SAT II: Subject tests are required for the accelerated honors program in medical education and the integrated science program. Auditions are required for applicants to the School of Music. AP credits are accepted. Important factors in the admissions decision are advanced placement or honors courses, recommendations by school officials, and extracurricular activities record.

Procedure: Freshmen are admitted to all sessions. Entrance exams should be taken by December of the senior year. There are early decision and deferred admissions plans. Early decision applications should be filed by November 1; regular applications, by November 1 for winter entry; February 1 for spring entry; and May 1 for summer entry, along with a $65 fee. Notification of early decision is sent December 15; regular decision, April 15. 451 early decision candidates were accepted for the 2013-2014 class. 330 applicants were on the 2013 waiting list; 102 were admitted. Applications are accepted online.

Transfer: 129 transfer students enrolled in 2012-2013. Transfer students need a minimum 3.0 GPA, SAT I or ACT scores, high school record, 1 essay, and the dean's reference form. Applicants are required to have a minimum of 1 year of completed college work to apply to Northwestern. 23 of 45 credits required for the bachelor's degree must be completed at Northwestern.

Visiting: There are regularly scheduled orientations for prospective students, including daily information sessions Monday through Friday. There are guides for informal visits, visitors may sit in on classes, and stay overnight. To schedule a visit, contact the Admission Office.

Financial Aid: In 2013-2014, 55% of all full-time freshmen and 60% of continuing full-time students received some form of financial aid. 45% of all full-time freshmen and 50% of continuing full-time students received need-based aid. The average freshman award was $23,587. 32% of undergraduate students work part-time. Average annual earnings from campus work are $1842. The average financial indebtedness of the 2013 graduate was $15,136. Northwestern is a member of CSS. The CSS/Profile and FAFSA, and tax returns under certain conditions are required. The deadline for filing freshman financial aid applications for fall entry is February 1.

International Students: There are 415 international students enrolled. The school actively recruits these students. They must take the TOEFL. They must also take the SAT or ACT.

Graduates: From July 1, 2012 to June 30, 2013, 2022 bachelor's degrees were awarded. The most popular majors were engineering (15%), economics (11%), and journalism (7%). 350 companies recruited on campus in 2012-2013. In an average class, 84% graduate in 4 years or less, 92% graduate in 5 years or less, and 93% graduate in 6 years or less.

Admissions Contact: Christopher Watson, Dean of Undergraduate Admission. Web: *www.northwestern.edu*

OLIVET NAZARENE UNIVERSITY E-2

Bourbonnais, IL 60914 (815) 939-5203
(800) 648-1463; (815) 935-5069

Full-time: 1000 men, 1500 women	**Faculty:** n/av
Part-time: 130 men, 440 women	**Ph.D.s:** 74%
Graduate: 450 men, 1050 women	**Student/Faculty:** n/av
Year: semesters, summer session	**Tuition:** $28,090
Application Deadline: May 1	**Room & Board:** $6900
Freshman Class: n/av	
SAT or ACT: required	

COMPETITIVE

Olivet Nazarene University, established in 1907, is a private, Christian, liberal arts institution affiliated with the Church of the Nazarene. Its undergraduate and graduate programs emphasize the liberal arts, business, communication, health science, art and fine arts, engineering, music, Bible and religious studies, and teacher preparation in an atmosphere of Christian culture. The figures in the above capsule and in this profile are approximate. There are 4 undergraduate schools and 1 graduate school. In addition to regional accreditation, Olivet has baccalaureate program accreditation with ABET, ADA, CSWE, NASM, and NCATE. The library contains 529,092 volumes, 312,729 microform items, 7703 audio/video tapes/CDs/DVDs, and subscribes to 12,100 periodicals including electronic. Computerized library services include interlibrary loans, database searching, Internet access, and laptop Internet portals. Special learning facilities include a learning resource center, art gallery, radio station, TV station, smart board classrooms, a greenhouse, a solar telescope, a planetarium, and observation rooms. The 250-acre campus is in a suburban area 50 miles south of Chicago. Including any residence halls, there are 53 buildings.

Student Life: 64% of undergraduates are from Illinois. Others are from 45 states, 10 foreign countries, and Canada. 83% are white. 76% are Protestant; 14% Catholic. The average age of freshmen is 18; all undergraduates, 20. 27% do not continue beyond their first year; 55% remain to graduate.

Housing: 2131 students can be accommodated in college housing, which includes single-sex dorms, on-campus apartments, and married student housing. In addition, there are honors houses. On-campus housing is guaranteed for all 4 years. 93% of students live on campus; of those, 80% remain on campus on weekends. Alcohol is not permitted. All students may keep cars.

Activities: There are no fraternities or sororities. There are 79 groups on campus, including art, band, cheerleading, choir, chorale, chorus, computers, drama, ethnic, FCA, film, honors, international, jazz band, literary magazine, marching band, musical theater, newspaper, orchestra, pep band, photography, political, professional, radio and TV, religious, social, social service, student government, and yearbook. Popular campus events include Revival Services, Tiger Championship Wrestling, and Ollies Follies.

Sports: There are 9 intercollegiate sports for men and 9 for women, and 19 intramural sports for men and 19 for women. Facilities include a 2,400-seat arena with basketball, volleyball, and racquetball courts; a separate gymnasium; a fitness center and a weight-lifting room; and an indoor track. There is a football field and an athletic park with softball, baseball, and soccer fields, a jogging track, track and field facilities, and tennis courts.

Disabled Students: 95% of the campus is accessible. Facilities include wheelchair ramps, elevators, special parking, specially equipped rest rooms, special class scheduling, lowered drinking fountains, lowered telephones, and special housing.

Services: Counseling and information services are available, as is tutoring in every subject. There is remedial math, reading, and writing, as well as assistive technology.

Campus Safety and Security: Measures include 24-hour foot and vehicle patrol, emergency notification system, self-defense education, and security escort services. There are emergency telephones and lighted pathways/sidewalks.

Programs of Study: Olivet confers B.A., B.B.A., B.M., B.S., B.S.N., and B.S.W. degrees. Associate, master's, and doctoral degrees are also awarded. Bachelor's degrees are awarded in BIOLOGICAL SCIENCE (biology/biological science and zoology), BUSINESS (accounting, business administration and management, business communications, fashion merchandising, international business management, marketing/retailing/merchandising, recreation and leisure services, and sports management), COMMUNICATIONS AND THE ARTS (art, communications, digital communications, dramatic arts, drawing, English, journalism, media arts, music, music performance, music theory and composition, and Spanish),

COMPUTER AND PHYSICAL SCIENCE (actuarial science, chemistry, computer science, digital arts/technology, geoscience, information sciences and systems, mathematics, and physical sciences), EDUCATION (art education, athletic training, Christian education, early childhood education, elementary education, English education, mathematics education, music education, physical education, science education, and social science education), ENGINEERING AND ENVIRONMENTAL DESIGN (computer engineering, engineering, environmental design, environmental science, and geological engineering), HEALTH PROFESSIONS (exercise science and nursing), SOCIAL SCIENCE (biblical studies, child psychology/development, criminal justice, crosscultural studies, dietetics, economics, family/consumer studies, geography, history, ministries, missions, pastoral studies, philosophy, political science/government, psychology, public affairs, religion, religious music, social science, social work, sociology, Spanish studies, and youth ministry). Engineering and physical science are the strongest academically. Business administration and education have the largest enrollments.

Required: To graduate, students must complete 128 semester hours of credit, with 32 to 70 in a major and a minimum of 40 hours of credit in upper-division courses, and maintain a minimum GPA of 2.0. The required general education studies, 50 to 61 hours, include 12 credit hours of Christianity, 9 to 10 of communication, 9 of natural science and math, 6 to 8 of international culture, 6 of social sciences, 6 of literature and the arts, and 3 of wellness/nutrition.

Special: Special academic programs include a work-study program, which can be arranged with other institutions, and a general studies degree. A 4-year engineering program (ABET) is available. There are 6 national honor societies, a freshman honors program, and 5 departmental honors programs.

Faculty/Classroom: 57% of faculty are male; 43% are female. No introductory courses are taught by graduate students.

Admissions: 81% of a recent year's applicants were accepted. 44% of a recent year's freshmen were in the top fifth of their class; 67% were in the top two fifths.

Requirements: The SAT or ACT is required. The minimum ACT score required is 18. Olivet requires graduation from an accredited secondary school. Olivet does not have any specific high school course requirements, but there are some suggestions for high school courses. College preparatory courses completed with a C or above are recommended. In general, you should have 3 years of English and 2 years each of math, foreign language, and natural or social science. To enroll in the nursing program, you need a year of biology and a year of chemistry. In choosing high school courses, you should also take into consideration the career/major you intend to pursue. The GED is accepted. A GPA of 2.0 is required. AP and CLEP credits are accepted.

Procedure: Freshmen are admitted to all sessions. Entrance exams should be taken during the spring of the junior year or the fall of the senior year. There are deferred admissions and rolling admissions plans. Applications should be filed by May 1 for fall entry. Check with the school for the current application fee. Applications are accepted online.

Transfer: 268 transfer students enrolled in a recent year. Transcripts of all college work must be submitted. 30 of 128 credits required for the bachelor's degree must be completed at Olivet.

Visiting: There are regularly scheduled orientations for prospective students, including class visits, financial aid appointments, an information tour, lunch, and personal professor meetings. There are guides for informal visits, and visitors may sit in on classes and stay overnight. To schedule a visit, contact the Campus Visit Coordinator, Office of Admissions.

Financial Aid: In a recent year, 99% of all full-time students received some form of financial aid. 83% of all full-time freshmen and 74% of continuing full-time students received need-based aid. The average freshmen award was $24,742, with $10,732 ($30,490 maximum) from need-based scholarships or need-based grants; $2794 ($6500 maximum) from need-based self-help aid (loans and jobs); $4510 ($16,000 maximum) from non-need-based athletic scholarships; and $14,016 ($30,490 maximum) from other non-need-based awards and non-need-based scholarships. 36% of undergraduate students work part-time. Average annual earnings from campus work are $1319. The average financial indebtedness of a recent year's graduate was $23,366. The FAFSA is required. Check with the school for current application deadlines.

International Students: There were 19 international students enrolled in a recent year. They must take the TOEFL with a minimum score of 500 on the paper-based TOEFL (PBT) or 61 on the Internet-based version (iBT). They must also take the ACT, scoring 18.

Graduates: In a recent year, 647 bachelor's degrees were awarded. The most popular majors were elementary education (11%), business/marketing (8%), and nursing (5%). 65 companies recruited on campus in a recent year. In an average class, 1% graduate in 3 years or less, 44% graduate in 4 years or less, 56% graduate in 5 years or less, and 57% graduate in 6 years or less.

Admissions Contact: Director of Admissions. E-Mail: *admissions@olivet.edu* Web: *www.olivet.edu*

PRINCIPIA COLLEGE — C-4

Elsah, IL 62028 — (618) 374-5181; (800) 277-4648; (618) 374-4000

Full-time: 221 men, 265 women	**Faculty:** n/av
Part-time: 2 men, 3 women	**Ph.D.s:** 45%
Graduate: n/av	**Student/Faculty:** 7 to 1
Year: semesters	**Tuition:** $25,640
Application Deadline: March 1	**Room & Board:** $9500
Freshman Class: 228 applied, 213 accepted, 152 enrolled	
SAT CR/M/W: 549/525/537 **ACT:** 24	**COMPETITIVE+**

Principia College, founded in 1910, is a private liberal arts and sciences college for Christian Scientists. It is the only college in the world strictly for Christian Scientists. In addition to regional accreditation, Prin has baccalaureate program accreditation with NCATE. The library contains 217,257 volumes, 115,665 microform items, 4,847 audio/video tapes/CDs/DVDs, and subscribes to 12,813 periodicals including electronic. Computerized library services include interlibrary loans, database searching, and Internet access. Special learning facilities include an art gallery, planetarium, radio station, and TV station. The 2600-acre campus is in a rural area 30 miles northeast of St. Louis. Including any residence halls, there are 33 buildings.

Student Life: 90% of undergraduates are from out of state, mostly the Mid-West. Students are from 42 states, 23 foreign countries, and Canada. 61% are from public schools. 81% are White; 15% Foreign. The average age of freshmen is 18; all undergraduates, 20. 12% do not continue beyond their first year; 75% remain to graduate.

Housing: 625 students can be accommodated in college housing, which includes single-sex and coed dorms, on-campus apartments, and married student housing. In addition, there are special-interest houses. On-campus housing is guaranteed for all 4 years. 99% of students live on campus; of those, 100% remain on campus on weekends. Alcohol is not permitted. All students may keep cars.

Activities: There are no fraternities or sororities. There are 34 groups on campus, including art, cheerleading, choir, chorus, computers, dance, drama, ethnic, honors, international, jazz band, literary magazine, musical theater, newspaper, orchestra, photography, political, radio and TV, religious, social, social service, and student government. Popular campus events include Athletic Events, Dances, and Drama and Dance Performances.

Sports: There are 7 intercollegiate sports for men and 8 for women, and 3 intramural sports for men and 3 for women. Facilities include 2 gyms, a pool, indoor and outdoor tennis courts, a racquetball court, basketball/volleyball courts, a dance studio, a weight room, baseball, football, soccer, and practice fields, and a 6-lane track.

Disabled Students: 85% of the campus is accessible. Facilities include wheelchair ramps, elevators, special parking, specially equipped restrooms, and lowered drinking fountains.

Services: Counseling and information services are available, as is tutoring in most subjects. There is remedial reading and writing. Assistance in study skills is available.

Campus Safety and Security: Measures include 24-hour foot and vehicle patrol and emergency notification system. There are emergency telephones, lighted pathways/sidewalks, and controlled access to dorms/residences.

Programs of Study: Prin confers B.A., and B.S. degrees. Bachelor's degrees are awarded in BIOLOGICAL SCIENCE (biology/biological science), BUSINESS (business administration and management and sports management), COMMUNICATIONS AND THE ARTS (communications, dramatic arts, English, fine arts, French, languages, music, Spanish, and studio art), COMPUTER AND PHYSICAL SCIENCE (chemistry, computer science, mathematics, and physics), EDUCATION (elementary education), ENGINEERING AND ENVIRONMENTAL DESIGN (environmental science), SOCIAL SCIENCE (economics, history, international relations, philosophy, political science/government, religion, and sociology). Education, studio art, and biology are the strongest academically. Business administration, studio art, and education have the largest enrollments.

Required: All students must complete a minimum of 180 quarter hours, with 45 to 93 quarter hours in the major (10 to 15 courses) and at least a 2.0 overall GPA. Courses in foreign language, literature, arts, religion and philosophy, history, social science, math, and natural sciences are required. In addition, students must be certified as proficient in written English, pass a moral reasoning seminar, and earn 4 credits in individual and team phys ed activities.

Special: Students may design their own majors, study abroad, or pursue a B.A.-B.S. degree. Internships, student-planned with a professor, independent study, work-study, and an interdisciplinary major, global studies, are available. A 3-2 engineering program with Washington University in St. Louis, Southern Illinois University at Carbondale, the University of Southern California, or another university with approval is also possible. There are 1 national honor societies, a freshman honors program, and 3 departmental honors programs.

Faculty/Classroom: 45% of faculty are male; 55% are female. All teach undergraduates, and 60% do research. No introductory courses are taught by graduate students. The average class size in an introductory lecture is 13; in a laboratory is 12; and in a regular course is 10.

Admissions: 93% of the 2013-2014 applicants were accepted. The SAT scores for the 2013-2014 freshman class were: Critical Reading--31% below 500, 37% between 500 and 599, 21% between 600 and 699, and 11% between 700 and 800; Math--40% below 500, 35% between 500 and 599, 18% between 600 and 699, and 7% between 700 and 800; Writing--39% below 500, 36% between 500 and 599, 15% between 600 and 699, and 10% between 700 and 800. The ACT scores were 12% below 21, 45% between 21 and 23, 15% between 24 and 26, 16% between 27 and 28, and 12% above 28. 28% of the current freshmen were in the top fifth of their class; 59% were in the top two fifths. There were 1 National Merit finalists. 2 freshmen graduated first in their class.

Requirements: The SAT or ACT is required. An essay is required. SAT Subject Tests in foreign language and math are recommended. High school preparation should include 4 years of English, 3 of math (including algebra II), 2 to 3 of a foreign language, 2 to 3 of natural sciences, history or social sciences, and electives. A GPA of 2.3 is required. AP and CLEP credits are accepted. Important factors in the admissions decision are advanced placement or honors courses, recommendations by school officials, and recommendations by alumni.

Procedure: Freshmen are admitted fall and spring. Entrance exams should be taken in the spring of the junior year and again in the fall of the senior year. There are deferred admissions and rolling admissions plans. Applications should be filed by March 1 for fall entry; November 1 for winter entry. Notification of early decision is sent December 1; regular decision, March 15. Applications are accepted online.

Transfer: 23 transfer students enrolled in 2012-2013. Applicants must be in good standing at their previous college or university and have a 2.3 GPA. 45 of 180 credits required for the bachelor's degree must be completed at Prin.

Visiting: There are regularly scheduled orientations for prospective students, including a visit to classes, meeting professors, living in a dorm, and meeting students (3-day weekend). There are guides for informal visits, visitors may sit in on classes, and stay overnight. To schedule a visit, contact Amber McCartt at (618) 374-5175.

Financial Aid: In 2013-2014, 95% of all full-time freshmen and 92% of continuing full-time students received some form of financial aid. 74% of all full-time freshmen and 76% of continuing full-time students received need-based aid. The average freshman award was $21,888. Need-based scholarships or need-based grants averaged $23,091 ($33,500 maximum); need-based self-help aid (loans and jobs) averaged $5,502 ($6,000 maximum); and other non-need-based awards and non-need-based scholarships averaged $20,642 ($25,500 maximum). 52% of undergraduate students work part-time. Average annual earnings from campus work are $1368. The average financial indebtedness of the 2013 graduate was $15,784. Prin is a member of CSS. The CSS/Profile is required. The priority date for freshman financial aid applications for fall entry is March 1. The deadline for filing freshman financial aid applications for fall entry is March 1.

International Students: There are 95 international students enrolled. The school actively recruits these students. They must take the TOEFL. They must also take the SAT or ACT, scoring 1380.

Computers: All students may access the system. 24 hours a day.

Graduates: From July 1, 2012 to June 30, 2013, 134 bachelor's degrees were awarded. The most popular majors were business administration (17%), studio art (13%), and mass communication (7%). 20 companies recruited on campus in 2012-2013. In an average class, 74% graduate in 4 years or less, 72% graduate in 5 years or less, and 78% graduate in 6 years or less.

Admissions Contact: Brian McCauley, Dean of Enrollment Management. E-Mail: *brian.mccauley@principia.edu* Web: *www.principiacollege.edu*

QUINCY UNIVERSITY B-3

Quincy, IL 62301 **(217) 228-5210**
(800) 688-4295; (217) 228-5479

Full-time: 486 men, 608 women	**Faculty:** 50; IIB, --$
Part-time: 61 men, 86 women	**Ph.D.s:** 77%
Graduate: 185 men, 419 women	**Student/Faculty:** 19 to 1
Year: semesters, summer session	**Tuition:** $25,180
Application Deadline:	**Room & Board:** $9800

Freshman Class: 986 applied, 892 accepted, 249 enrolled
SAT CR/M: 450/460 **ACT:** 21 **LESS COMPETITIVE**

Founded in 1860 by Franciscan friars, Quincy University is a Catholic, residential university offering undergraduate, graduate, and adult education programs that integrate liberal arts, active learning, practical experience, and Franciscan values. There are 3 undergraduate schools and 3 graduate schools. The library contains 212,930 volumes, 193,810 microform items, 9,334 audio/video tapes/CDs/DVDs, and subscribes to 324 periodicals including electronic. Computerized library services include interlibrary loans, database searching, Internet access, and Wi-Fi capability. Special learning facilities include an art gallery, TV station, a 200-seat theater, Center for Music, multimedia and graphic design labs, an environmental studies institute, a temperature-controlled rare books library archive, a hospital simulation lab, an aviation facility, and University Chapel and a nondenominational praise/worship chapel. The 70-acre campus is in a small town 120 miles from St. Louis, 250 miles from Kansas City, 275 miles from Indianapolis. Including any residence halls, there are 55 buildings.

Student Life: 75% of undergraduates are from Illinois. Others are from 25 states, 4 foreign countries, and Canada. 48% are from public schools. 75% are White. 46% are Catholic; 28% Protestant; 21% claim no religious affiliation. The average age of freshmen is 19; all undergraduates, 23. 31% do not continue beyond their first year; 42% remain to graduate.

Housing: 690 students can be accommodated in college housing, which includes single-sex and coed dorms, on-campus apartments, and married student housing. In addition, there are honors houses, special-interest houses, fraternity houses, and sorority houses. On-campus housing is guaranteed for all 4 years. 58% of students live on campus; of those, 85% remain on campus on weekends. All students may keep cars.

Activities: 3% of men belong to 1 national fraternity; 13% of women belong to 2 national sororities. There are 40 groups on campus, including band, cheerleading, choir, chorale, chorus, communications, computers, dance, drama, environmental, ethnic, honors, international, jazz band, literary magazine, musical theater, newspaper, opera, orchestra, pep band, political, professional, radio and TV, religious, social, social service, student government, and symphony. Popular campus events include Hawk Wild Weekend, Hawk Back Weekend and Family Weekend.

Sports: There are 7 intercollegiate sports for men and 6 for women, and 18 intramural sports for men and 17 for women. Facilities include the Health & Fitness Center, which features 3 multipurpose gym courts, a 3,600-square-foot fitness room, 17 cardio machines, an aerobics room, an indoor walking/running track, 2 racquetball courts, and a 6-lane intercollegiate pool with whirlpool. QU also has a 2,000-seat basketball/volleyball arena, a large campus recreation field, as well as a softball complex, a football/baseball stadium, and a 3-field soccer complex with support building.

Disabled Students: 95% of the campus is accessible. Facilities include wheelchair ramps, elevators, special parking, specially equipped restrooms, special class scheduling, and lowered drinking fountains.

Services: Counseling and information services are available, as is tutoring in every subject. There is a reader service for the blind, and remedial math and writing. Academic Success workshops and courses are available.

Campus Safety and Security: Measures include 24-hour foot and vehicle patrol, emergency notification system, self-defense education, and security escort services. There are shuttle buses, emergency telephones, lighted pathways/sidewalks, and controlled access to dorms/residences.

Programs of Study: QU confers B.A., B.F.A., B.S. and B.S.N. degrees. Associate and master's degrees are also awarded. Bachelor's degrees are awarded in BIOLOGICAL SCIENCE (biology/biological science), BUSINESS (accounting, banking and finance, business administration and management, marketing/retailing/merchandising, and sports management), COMMUNICATIONS AND THE ARTS (communications, English, graphic design, and music), COMPUTER AND PHYSICAL SCIENCE (chemistry, computer science, information sciences and systems, and mathematics), EDUCATION (education, elementary education, music education, physical education, and special education), ENGINEERING AND ENVIRONMENTAL DESIGN (aviation administration/management), HEALTH PROFESSIONS (clinical science, exercise science, and nursing), SOCIAL SCIENCE (criminal justice, history, human services, humanities, interpreter for the deaf, political science/government, psychology, social work, and theological studies). Business, education and science are the strongest academically. Elementary education, nursing and management have the largest enrollments.

Required: Each student is required to complete a minimum of 124 credit hours, with at least 33 in the major and a minimum of 39 in upper-level courses. In addition, students must complete required courses in rhetoric, science, math, social sciences, humanities, fine arts, theology, and phys ed; complete a senior comprehensive seminar or practicum; maintain a minimum GPA of 2.0; earn at least 30 semester hours in residency at QU, including 21 hours in the major; and earn a minimum of 56 semester hours from a 4-year college/university.

Special: Dual majors, study abroad in 31 countries, credit by exam, and upper-class and early exploratory internships are available. Pass/fail options, credit for life experience, student-designed majors, adult accelerated degree programs, and a 3-2 degree with Washington University in St. Louis are also offered. An interdisciplinary major in communication and music production is available. Study abroad in Assisi, London, Rome or other programs in 29 countries. There are 8 national honor societies, a freshman honors program, and 1 departmental honors programs.

Faculty/Classroom: 46% of faculty are male; 54% are female. 94%

teach undergraduates. No introductory courses are taught by graduate students. The average class size in an introductory lecture is 35; in a laboratory is 20; and in a regular course is 20.

Admissions: 90% of the 2013-2014 applicants were accepted. The SAT scores for the 2013-2014 freshman class were: Critical Reading--79% below 500, and 21% between 500 and 599; Math--53% below 500, 32% between 500 and 599, 10% between 600 and 699, and 5% between 700 and 800. The ACT scores were 44% below 21, 30% between 21 and 23, 15% between 24 and 26, 8% between 27 and 28, and 3% above 28. 27% of the current freshmen were in the top fifth of their class; 55% were in the top two fifths. 3 freshmen graduated first in their class.

Requirements: The SAT or ACT is required. The GED is accepted. The recommended high school curriculum includes 4 years of English and 3 each in math, sciences, and social studies. Courses in another language, computers, and the arts are helpful. Art students must submit a portfolio, and music students must audition. QU requires applicants to be in the upper 50% of their class. A GPA of 2.0 is required. AP and CLEP credits are accepted. Important factors in the admissions decision are leadership record, evidence of special talent, and recommendations by school officials.

Procedure: Freshmen are admitted fall and spring. Entrance exams should be taken in October of the senior year. There are deferred admissions and rolling admissions plans. Application deadlines are open. Application fee is $25. Notification is sent on a rolling basis. Applications are accepted online.

Transfer: 200 transfer students enrolled in 2012-2013. Applicants must have a minimum GPA of 2.0. Grades of C or better in college-level courses normally transfer for credit. 30 of 124 credits required for the bachelor's degree must be completed at QU.

Visiting: There are regularly scheduled orientations for prospective students, including advising and registration programs throughout the summer. There are guides for informal visits, visitors may sit in on classes, and stay overnight. To schedule a visit, contact the Admissions Office at admissions@quincy.edu.

Financial Aid: In 2013-2014, 99% of all full-time freshmen and 91% of continuing full-time students received some form of financial aid. 76% of all full-time freshmen and 71% of continuing full-time students received need-based aid. The average freshman award was $26,877. Need-based scholarships or need-based grants averaged $10,727 ($22,331 maximum); need-based self-help aid (loans and jobs) averaged $3,907 ($4,500 maximum); non-need-based athletic scholarships averaged $10,800 ($30,410 maximum); and other non-need-based awards and non-need-based scholarships averaged $11,281 ($29,900 maximum). 26% of undergraduate students work part-time. Average annual earnings from campus work are $2000. The average financial indebtedness of the 2013 graduate was $19,935. QU is a member of CSS. The FAFSA is required. The priority date for freshman financial aid applications for fall entry is March 1.

International Students: There are 7 international students enrolled. The school actively recruits these students. They must take the TOEFL with a minimum score of 500 on the paper-based TOEFL (PBT) or 61 on the Internet-based version (iBT). They must also take the SAT or ACT.

Computers: All students may access the system. There are no time limits and no fees.

Graduates: From July 1, 2012 to June 30, 2013, 208 bachelor's degrees were awarded. The most popular majors were nursing (12%), elementary education (9%), and marketing (9%). 43 companies recruited on campus in 2012-2013. In an average class, 31% graduate in 4 years or less, 41% graduate in 5 years or less, and 42% graduate in 6 years or less. Of the 2012 graduating class, 23% were enrolled in graduate school within 6 months of graduation, and 59% were employed.

Admissions Contact: Syndi Peck, Director of Admissions. E-Mail: *pecksy@quincy.edu* Web: *www.quincy.edu*

ROCKFORD COLLEGE D-1

Rockford, IL 61108

(815) 226-3383
(800) 892-2984; (815) 226-2822

Full-time: 299 men, 454 women	**Faculty:** 69
Part-time: 46 men, 70 women	**Ph.D.s:** 71%
Graduate: 176 men, 295 women	**Student/Faculty:** 11 to 1
Year: semesters, summer session	**Tuition:** $25,500
Application Deadline: August 15	**Room & Board:** $7150
Freshman Class: n/av	
ACT: 22	

COMPETITIVE

Rockford College, founded in 1847, is a private coeducational institution offering undergraduate and graduate instruction in liberal arts and professional programs. There is 1 undergraduate school and 2 graduate schools. The figures in the above capsule and in this profile are approximate. In addition to regional accreditation, Rockford College has baccalaureate program accreditation with NLN. The library contains 146,829 volumes, 8,430 microform items, 2,819 audio/video tapes/CDs/DVDs, and subscribes to 389 periodicals including electronic. Computerized library services include interlibrary loans, database searching, and Internet access. Special learning facilities include a learning resource center, art gallery, and radio station. The 135-acre campus is in a suburban area 90 miles west of Chicago. Including any residence halls, there are 27 buildings.

Student Life: 91% of undergraduates are from Illinois. Others are from 26 states, and 2 foreign countries. 73% are white. The average age of freshmen is 18; all undergraduates, 24.

Housing: 356 students can be accommodated in college housing, which includes single-sex and coed dorms. In addition, there are special-interest houses, first-year student housing, substance-free, and 24- hour quiet hours housing and health and science major housing. On-campus housing is guaranteed for all 4 years. 65% of students commute. All students may keep cars.

Activities: There are no fraternities or sororities. There are 21 groups on campus, including senior club, Anime, Black Student Union, bowling, Gamers Assn, Mulicultural, Nursing, poker, RAGE, Rockford Paranormal Society, Alpha Helix, art, band, cheerleading, chess, choir, chorale, dance, drama, environmental, ethnic, gay, honors, international, literary magazine, musical theater, opera, orchestra, pep band, political, professional, religious, social, social service, and student government. Popular campus events include Snowball Dance, International Food Fair, and Black History month events.

Sports: There are 9 intercollegiate sports for men and 8 for women, and 7 intramural sports for men and 7 for women. Facilities include a swimming pool, athletic fields, tennis courts, and a fitness center.

Disabled Students: All of the campus is accessible. Facilities include wheelchair ramps, elevators, special parking, specially equipped restrooms, special class scheduling, lowered drinking fountains, lowered telephones, and special housing.

Services: Counseling and information services are available, as is tutoring in most subjects. There is a reader service for the blind, and remedial math and reading. Diagnostic testing is available.

Campus Safety and Security: Measures include 24-hour foot and vehicle patrol, emergency notification system, and security escort services. There are emergency telephones and lighted pathways/sidewalks.

Programs of Study: Rockford College confers B.A., B.S., B.F.A., and B.S.N. degrees. Master's degrees are also awarded. Bachelor's degrees are awarded in BIOLOGICAL SCIENCE (biochemistry and biology/biological science), BUSINESS (accounting, business administration and management, and management information systems), COMMUNICATIONS AND THE ARTS (art, art history and appreciation, classics, dramatic arts, English, French, German, Latin, music, music performance, romance languages and literature, and Spanish), COMPUTER AND PHYSICAL SCIENCE (chemistry, computer science, mathematics, and science), EDUCATION (elementary education, physical education, and special education), HEALTH PROFESSIONS (nursing), SOCIAL SCIENCE (anthropology, economics, history, humanities, international studies, philosophy, political science/government, psychology, social science, and sociology). Business, education, nursing, and psychology have the largest enrollments.

Required: To graduate, students must have a total of at least 124 credit hours and a minimum GPA of 2.0 (nursing 2.75). The required hours for each major varies. Students are required to take 12 hours of social sciences, 8 to 12 of science, mathematics, and computer science, 8 of language and literature, 11 of rhetoric, 6 of art, and 2 hours each of physical education. All students must complete a senior seminar or project.

Special: Rockford College offers a variety of special academic opportunities including community-based learning, liberal arts honors program, internships, study abroad, and Washington semester. In addition to our traditional undergraduate programs, we offer English as a second language and an accelerated bachelor's degree in management studies. There are 6 national honor societies.

Faculty/Classroom: 56% of faculty are male; 44% are female. All teach undergraduates. No introductory courses are taught by graduate students. The average class size in an introductory lecture is 18; in a laboratory is 11; and in a regular course is 15.

Admissions: The ACT scores were 43% below 21, 26% between 21 and 23, 24% between 24 and 26, and 3% between 27 and 28. 28% of the current freshmen were in the top fifth of their class; 55% were in the top two fifths.

Requirements: The ACT is required. In addition, admission to Rockford College is based primarily on high school GPA and test scores (GED also accepted). Prospective students are expected to have completed a college preparatory program of 15 units including 4 years of English; 3 years of mathematics (introductory through advanced algebra, geometry and trigonometry); 3 years of social sciences (emphasizing history and government); 3 years of laboratory science; and 2 years of electives chosen from music, art and/or foreign language at an accredited secondary school. Home schooled students also should meet the unit requirements. Auditions are required for performing arts students. Rockford College requires applicants to be in the upper 50% of their class. A GPA of 2.7 is required. AP and CLEP credits are accepted.

Procedure: Freshmen are admitted to all sessions. There are early admissions, deferred admissions, and rolling admissions plans. Application deadlines are open. Application fee is $35. Notifications are sent September 15. Applications are accepted online.

Transfer: 164 transfer students enrolled in a recent year. In order to be considered for transfer admission, prospective students must have completed at least 12 credit hours of college-level work (at the 100-level or higher). Students transferring from other colleges must be in good academic standing in order to be considered for standard admission. High school transcripts and standardized test scores (ACT/SAT) also may be requested. 30 of 124 credits required for the bachelor's degree must be completed at Rockford College.

Visiting: There are regularly scheduled orientations for prospective students, consisting of an academic fair, opportunity to meet with social/athletic programs, and administrative offices, admission presentation, meal, tour, and meet with current students. There are guides for informal visits, visitors may sit in on classes, and stay overnight. To schedule a visit, contact the Admissions Office.

Financial Aid: In a recent year, 100% of all full-time freshmen and 100% of continuing full-time students received some form of financial aid. 81% of all full-time freshmen and 95% of continuing full-time students received need-based aid. The average freshman award was $24,895. Need-based scholarships or need-based grants averaged $8,332 ($13,468 maximum); need-based self-help aid (loans and jobs) averaged $3,768 ($11,600 maximum); and other non-need-based awards and non-need-based scholarships averaged $14,970 ($35,660 maximum). 24% of undergraduate students work part-time. Average annual earnings from campus work are $1355. The average financial indebtedness of the recent graduate was $26,000. The FAFSA is required. The priority date for freshman financial aid applications for fall entry is March 15.

International Students: There are 4 international students enrolled. The school actively recruits these students. They must take the TOEFL with a minimum score of 550 on the paper-based TOEFL (PBT) or 79 on the Internet-based version (iBT). Rockford College will also accept the IELTS test. They must also take the SAT or ACT.

Computers: Wireless access is available. All students may access the system. There are no time limits and no fees. It is strongly recommended that all students have a personal computer.

Admissions Contact: Emmalee Wilson *wilson2@rockford.edu*

ROOSEVELT UNIVERSITY E-2

Chicago, IL 60605 (312) 341-2101
(877) APPLYRU; (847) 619-8636

Full-time: 685 men, 1185 women	**Faculty:** n/av; IIA, av$
Part-time: 750 men, 1700 women	**Ph.D.s:** 85%
Graduate: 1040 men, 2210 women	**Student/Faculty:** n/av
Year: semesters, summer session	**Tuition:** $26,750
Application Deadline: see profile	**Room & Board:** $11,500
Freshman Class: n/av	
SAT or ACT: required	

VERY COMPETITIVE

Roosevelt University, founded in 1945, is an independent, comprehensive university. Some figures in the above capsule and in this profile are approximate. There are 5 undergraduate schools and 5 graduate schools. In addition to regional accreditation, Roosevelt has baccalaureate program accreditation with AACSB, NASM, and NCATE. The 2 libraries contain 405,022 volumes, 130,233 microform items, 10,000 audio/video tapes/CDs/DVDs, and subscribe to 1601 periodicals including electronic. Computerized library services include interlibrary loans and database searching. Special learning facilities include a learning resource center and radio station. The campus is in an urban area in downtown Chicago. Including any residence halls, there are 2 buildings.

Student Life: 90% of undergraduates are from Illinois. Others are from 24 states, 70 foreign countries, and Canada. 44% are white; 27% African American; 12% Hispanic. The average age of freshmen is 21; all undergraduates, 27.

Housing: 300 students can be accommodated in college housing, which includes coed dorms. On-campus housing is available on a first-come, first-served basis. 94% of students commute.

Activities: 1% of men belong to 1 local fraternity; 1% of women belong to 1 local sorority. There are 45 groups on campus, including band, choir, chorale, chorus, computers, cultural, drama, ethnic, honors, international, jazz band, literary magazine, model United Nations, musical theater, newspaper, opera, orchestra, political, professional, radio and TV, religious, social service, student government, and symphony.

Sports: There is 1 intramural sport for men and 1 for women. Facilities include a fitness center and a recreational gym for basketball, volleyball, soccer, and intramural activities.

Disabled Students: All of the campus is accessible. Facilities include wheelchair ramps, elevators, specially equipped rest rooms, special class scheduling, and lowered telephones. For special needs, contact the Disabled Student Services Office.

Services: Counseling and information services are available, as is tutoring in most subjects. There is remedial math, reading, and writing, arranged counseling, and testing. Emphasis is placed on individual program planning.

Campus Safety and Security: There are shuttle buses and lighted pathways/sidewalks.

Programs of Study: Roosevelt confers B.A., B.S., B.A.Comp.Sci., B.A.Ed., B.F.A.Mus.Theater, B.G.S., B.M., B.S.B.A., B.S. in Hospitality Mgt., and B.S.Telecomm. degrees. Master's and doctoral degrees are also awarded. Bachelor's degrees are awarded in BIOLOGICAL SCIENCE (biology/biological science), BUSINESS (accounting, banking and finance, business administration and management, hotel/motel and restaurant management, insurance, insurance and risk management, management science, marketing/retailing/merchandising, and personnel management), COMMUNICATIONS AND THE ARTS (advertising, art history and appreciation, broadcasting, communications, dramatic arts, English, French, guitar, jazz, journalism, languages, literature, media arts, music, music history and appreciation, music performance, music theory and composition, musical theater, percussion, performing arts, piano/organ, public relations, Spanish, strings, telecommunications, theater design, theater management, voice, and winds), COMPUTER AND PHYSICAL SCIENCE (actuarial science, chemistry, computer science, information sciences and systems, mathematics, and statistics), EDUCATION (early childhood education, elementary education, music education, and secondary education), ENGINEERING AND ENVIRONMENTAL DESIGN (electrical/electronics engineering technology and environmental science), HEALTH PROFESSIONS (allied health, medical technology, nuclear medical technology, predentistry, premedicine, prepharmacy, and preveterinary science), SOCIAL SCIENCE (African American studies, American studies, economics, history, international studies, liberal arts/general studies, philosophy, political science/government, prelaw, psychology, public administration, social science, sociology, urban studies, and women's studies). Journalism, accounting, and psychology are the strongest academically.

Required: For graduation, students must complete 120 credit hours, including 54 in the major, with a minimum GPA of 2.0, or 2.5 in the College of Education. The core curriculum consists of courses in the social sciences, natural sciences, and humanities, including English 101 and 102. The last 54 hours must be from a 4-year school.

Special: Roosevelt offers internships in approximately 20 subject areas, on-campus work-study, study abroad in 4 countries, dual and student-designed majors, pass/fail options, and noncredit courses. Adults older than 25 years of age may earn a Bachelor of General Studies through an accelerated degree program. Credit for life, military, and work experience is available in some majors through continuing education. The Roosevelt Scholars Program is offered. There are 4 national honor societies, a freshman honors program, and 20 departmental honors programs.

Faculty/Classroom: All teach undergraduates. No introductory courses are taught by graduate students.

Requirements: The SAT or ACT is required. Students must have completed 15 academic units, including 4 of English, 3 of math, 2 each of science, social studies, and foreign language, and 1 each of history and electives. An interview is recommended for all applicants, and an audition is required for music and theater candidates. A GPA of 2.3 is required. AP and CLEP credits are accepted. Important factors in the admissions decision are advanced placement or honors courses, evidence of special talent, and extracurricular activities record.

Procedure: Freshmen are admitted to all sessions. There are early decision, early admissions, deferred admissions, and rolling admissions plans. Application deadlines are open. Application fee is $25. Notifications are sent ongoing. Applications are accepted online.

Transfer: Applicants must have earned a minimum GPA of 2.0 in all accredited college course work. Official transcripts must be received from each college where course work was attempted. 30 of 120 credits required for the bachelor's degree must be completed at Roosevelt.

Visiting: There are regularly scheduled orientations for prospective students, including open houses and Transfer Days. There are guides for informal visits and visitors may sit in on classes. To schedule a visit, contact the Undergraduate Admissions Office.

Financial Aid: The FAFSA and the college's own financial statement are required. Check with the school for current application deadlines.

International Students: The school actively recruits these students. They must take the college's own test.

Computers: All students may access the system 1 hour when demand is great. There are no fees.

Admissions Contact: Director of Admissions. E-Mail: *applyru@roosevelt.edu* Web: *www.roosevelt.edu*

SAINT XAVIER UNIVERSITY E-2

Chicago, IL 60655 (773) 298-3050
(800) 462-9288; (773) 298-3076

Full-time: 700 men, 1630 women
Part-time: 170 men, 560 women
Graduate: 510 men, 2000 women
Year: semesters, summer session
Application Deadline: see profile
Freshman Class: n/av
SAT or ACT: required
Faculty: n/av; IIA, av$
Ph.D.s: 86%
Student/Faculty: n/av
Tuition: $27,560
Room & Board: $9540

COMPETITIVE

Saint Xavier University is a private institution founded by the Sisters of Mercy in 1846 and affiliated with the Roman Catholic Church. The figures in the above capsule and in this profile are approximate. There are 4 undergraduate schools and 4 graduate schools. In addition to regional accreditation, SXU has baccalaureate program accreditation with NASM and NLN. The library contains 172,104 volumes, 10,519 microform items, 2282 audio/video tapes/CDs/DVDs, and subscribes to 798 periodicals including electronic. Computerized library services include interlibrary loans, database searching, and Internet access. Special learning facilities include a learning resource center, art gallery, and radio station. The 70-acre campus is in an urban area 15 miles southwest of Chicago's loop. Including any residence halls, there are 16 buildings.

Student Life: 96% of undergraduates are from Illinois. Others are from 21 states and 4 foreign countries. 50% are from public schools. 63% are white; 18% African American; 11% Hispanic. 80% are Catholic; 16% Protestant. The average age of freshmen is 18; all undergraduates, 23. 24% do not continue beyond their first year.

Housing: 630 students can be accommodated in college housing, which includes single-sex and coed dorms. On-campus housing is guaranteed for all 4 years. 81% of students commute. Alcohol is not permitted. All students may keep cars.

Activities: There are no fraternities or sororities. There are 37 groups on campus, including art, band, cheerleading, choir, chorus, computers, drama, ethnic, honors, international, jazz band, literary magazine, marching band, musical theater, newspaper, pep band, political, professional, radio and TV, religious, social service, student government, and yearbook. Popular campus events include Xavierfest, Boat Bash, and Octoberfest.

Sports: There are 4 intercollegiate sports for men and 5 for women, and 4 intramural sports for men and 4 for women. Facilities include baseball and softball diamonds, an outdoor sports facility, and a football field. The convocation and athletic center seats 2200 in the main arena with 4 additional competition courts. It also has racquetball courts, an indoor running track, training rooms, and a health and fitness center.

Disabled Students: 98% of the campus is accessible. Facilities include wheelchair ramps, elevators, special parking, specially equipped restrooms, special class scheduling, lowered drinking fountains, and lowered telephones.

Services: Counseling and information services are available, as is tutoring in every subject. There are reading and language clinics and a center for learning disabilities.

Campus Safety and Security: Measures include 24-hour foot and vehicle patrol, self-defense education, and security escort services. There are shuttle buses, emergency telephones, and lighted pathways/sidewalks.

Programs of Study: SXU confers B.A., B.S., and B.M. degrees. Master's degrees are also awarded. Bachelor's degrees are awarded in BIOLOGICAL SCIENCE (biology/biological science), BUSINESS (accounting, banking and finance, business administration and management, international business management, and marketing/retailing/merchandising), COMMUNICATIONS AND THE ARTS (communications, English, French, music, and Spanish), COMPUTER AND PHYSICAL SCIENCE (chemistry, computer science, and mathematics), EDUCATION (art education, early childhood education, elementary education, foreign languages education, middle school education, music education, science education, and secondary education), HEALTH PROFESSIONS (nursing, predentistry, premedicine, prepharmacy, and speech pathology/audiology), SOCIAL SCIENCE (criminal justice, history, philosophy, political science/government, prelaw, psychology, religion, social science, and sociology). Business, nursing, and education are the strongest programs academically and have the largest enrollments.

Required: To graduate, students must complete 120 credit hours, including the school's 57-semester-hour core curriculum, and earn a GPA of 2.0. The credit hours required in the student's major vary by subject.

Special: The university offers internships and study abroad in England, Ireland, and Italy. There is a freshman honors program.

Faculty/Classroom: 44% of faculty are male; 56% are female. All teach undergraduates. No introductory courses are taught by graduate students. The average class size in an introductory lecture is 20; in a laboratory, 15; and in a regular course, 16.

Requirements: The SAT or ACT is required. Students must be graduates of an accredited secondary school and have earned 16 specific academic credits, including 4 years each of English and the natural and social sciences, 3 each of math and academic electives, and 2 years of a foreign language. The GED is accepted. AP and CLEP credits are accepted.

Procedure: Freshmen are admitted fall and spring. Entrance exams should be taken during the spring of the junior year. There are deferred admissions and rolling admissions plans. Check with the school for current application deadlines. Application fee is $25, unless applying online, which requires no application fee. Notification is sent on a rolling basis. Applications are accepted online.

Transfer: Applicants must have completed 12 semester hours with a GPA of 2.25. An interview is recommended. 30 of 120 credits required for the bachelor's degree must be completed at SXU.

Visiting: There are regularly scheduled orientations for prospective students. There are guides for informal visits, and visitors may sit in on classes and stay overnight. To schedule a visit, contact the Director of Admissions.

Financial Aid: The FAFSA is required. Check with the school for current application deadlines.

International Students: The school actively recruits these students. They must take the TOEFL.

Computers: All students may access the system. There are no time limits and no fees.

Admissions Contact: Director of Enrollment Services. E-mail: *admissions@sxu.edu* Web: *www.sxu.edu*

SCHOOL OF THE ART INSTITUTE OF CHICAGO E-2

Chicago, IL 60603 (312) 629-6100; (800) 232-7242

Full-time: 700 men, 1225 women
Part-time: 40 men, 100 women
Graduate: 200 men, 400 women
Year: semesters, summer session
Application Deadline: see profile
Freshman Class: n/av
SAT or ACT: required
Faculty: n/av
Ph.D.s: 87%
Student/Faculty: n/av
Tuition: $35,500
Room & Board: $10,500

SPECIAL

The School of the Art Institute of Chicago, founded in 1866, offers a comprehensive college education centered in the visual and related arts. Figures in the above capsule and in this profile are approximate. In addition to regional accreditation, SAIC has baccalaureate program accreditation with NASAD. The library contains 7100 volumes, 157 microform items, 4000 audio/video tapes/CDs/DVDs, and subscribes to 350 periodicals including electronic. Computerized library services include interlibrary loans and database searching. Special learning facilities include a learning resource center, an art gallery, a TV station, the Gene Siskel Film Center, a video data bank, the Fashion Resource Center, student galleries, a poetry center, Free Radio SAIC, the Roger Brown Study Collection, the Joan Flasch Artists Book Collection, and the Collection of the Art Institute of Chicago. The campus is in an urban area in downtown Chicago. Including any residence halls, there are 5 buildings.

Student Life: 77% of undergraduates are from out of state, mostly the mideast. Students are from 47 states, 28 foreign countries, and Canada. 59% are white; 16% foreign nationals. The average age of freshmen is 19; all undergraduates, 22. 23% do not continue beyond their first year.

Housing: 706 students can be accommodated in college housing, which includes coed dorms. On-campus housing is available on a first-come, first-served basis and is available on a lottery system for upperclassmen. 64% of students commute. Alcohol is not permitted. All students may keep cars.

Activities: There are no fraternities or sororities. There are 28 groups on campus, including art, dance, ethnic, film, gay, international, literary magazine, newspaper, performance, political, professional, radio and TV, religious, social, social service, and student government. Popular campus events include film center screenings, visiting artist lectures, and holiday and spring art sales.

Sports: There is no sports program at SAIC.

Disabled Students: 98% of the campus is accessible. Facilities include wheelchair ramps, elevators, special parking, specially equipped restrooms, special class scheduling, lowered drinking fountains, and lowered telephones. Assistance in other areas is available on an individual basis.

Services: Counseling and information services are available, as is tutoring in every subject. There is remedial reading and writing. Tutoring for students with learning disabilities is provided through the learning center.

Campus Safety and Security: Measures include 24-hour foot and vehicle patrol, self-defense education, and security escort services. There are emergency telephones and lighted pathways/sidewalks.

Programs of Study: SAIC confers B.A., B.F.A., and B.I.A. degrees. Master's degrees are also awarded. Bachelor's degrees are awarded in COMMUNICATIONS AND THE ARTS (art history and appreciation, audio technology, ceramic art and design, creative writing, design, drawing, fiber/textiles/weaving, film arts, painting, photography, printmaking, sculpture, video, and visual and performing arts), COMPUTER AND PHYSICAL SCIENCE (digital arts/technology), EDUCATION (art education), ENGINEERING AND ENVIRONMENTAL DESIGN (drafting and design technology and interior design), SOCIAL SCIENCE (fashion design and technology).

Required: All students are required to take 72 credit hours of studio courses, 30 hours of liberal arts, 18 hours of art history, and 12 hours of electives. A total of 132 credit hours must be completed to graduate. All students are required to take English literature and composition, natural science, social science, and humanities courses as well as course work in the first-year experience.

Special: The school offers internships, student-designed majors, a credit/no-credit grading system, visual arts co-op programs, cross-registration with Roosevelt University, and many cooperative work-study opportunities. Dual and student-designed majors, 6 undergraduate degrees, and study abroad in 20 countries with active exchange programs are possible.

Faculty/Classroom: 55% of faculty are male; 45% are female. No introductory courses are taught by graduate students.

Requirements: The SAT or ACT is required. Applicants must be graduates of an accredited secondary school. The GED is accepted. All students must submit a portfolio and an essay. An interview is recommended. AP and CLEP credits are accepted. Important factors in the admissions decision are evidence of special talent, recommendations by school officials, and personality/intangible qualities.

Procedure: Freshmen are admitted fall and spring. There are early admissions, deferred admissions, and rolling admissions plans. Check with the school for current application deadlines. The application fee is $65. Notification is sent on a rolling basis.

Transfer: Transfer students must take the SAT or ACT. A minimum score of 500 is required on the verbal section of the SAT and a minimum English score of 20 is required on the ACT. Students must submit a portfolio. 36 of 132 credits required for the bachelor's degree must be completed at SAIC.

Visiting: There are regularly scheduled orientations for prospective students, including tours and meetings with faculty counselors Monday through Friday. There are guides for informal visits. To schedule a visit, contact the Office of Admissions.

Financial Aid: The FAFSA is required. Check with the school for current application deadlines.

International Students: The school actively recruits these students. They must take the TOEFL and the college's own test.

Computers: Wireless access is available. All students may access the system. There are no time limits and no fees.

Admissions Contact: Director of Admissions. E-Mail: *admiss@saic.edu* Web: *www.saic.edu*

SHIMER COLLEGE C-1

Chicago, IL 60616 — **312-235-3504; (312) 235-3501**

Full-time: 54 men, 51 women	**Faculty:** 11
Part-time: 11 men, 11 women	**Ph.D.s:** 100%
Graduate: n/av	**Student/Faculty:** 10 to 1
Year: semesters, summer session	**Tuition:** $24,875
Application Deadline:	**Room & Board:** $8000
Freshman Class: n/av	

VERY COMPETITIVE

Shimer College, the Great Books College of Chicago, is a private liberal arts institution that shares space on the campus of the Illinois Institute of Technology. Founded in 1853 the College offers a curriculum based on original sources and a Socratic teaching method in discussion classes of 12 or fewer students. There is one undergraduate school. The 3 libraries contain 20,500 volumes, 100 microform items. Computerized library services include interlibrary loans, database searching, and Internet access. Special learning facilities include a radio station. The 120-acre campus is in an urban area Chicago. Including any residence halls, there are 40 buildings.

Student Life: 52% of undergraduates are from out of state. 77% are White. The average age of freshmen is 19; all undergraduates, 23. 16% do not continue beyond their first year; 63% remain to graduate.

Housing: 76 students can be accommodated in college housing, which includes single-sex and coed dorms, on-campus apartments, and married student housing. On-campus housing is guaranteed for all 4 years. 95% of students commute. All students may keep cars.

Activities: There are no fraternities or sororities. There are 62 groups on campus, including art, chess, computers, drama, ethnic, film, gay, international, literary magazine, newspaper, photography, political, radio and TV, religious, social, social service, and student government. Popular campus events include Community Lunch, Poetry Readings and a Talent Show.

Sports: There is no sports program at Shimer. Students have use of a full service athletic facility and access to intramural sports.

Disabled Students: All of the campus is accessible. Facilities include wheelchair ramps, elevators, special parking, specially equipped restrooms, and special housing.

Services: Counseling and information services are available, as is tutoring in every subject.

Campus Safety and Security: Measures include 24-hour foot and vehicle patrol, emergency notification system, and security escort services. There are shuttle buses, emergency telephones, lighted pathways/sidewalks, and controlled access to dorms/residences.

Programs of Study: Shimer confers B.A., and B.S. degrees. Bachelor's degrees are awarded in COMPUTER AND PHYSICAL SCIENCE (natural sciences), SOCIAL SCIENCE (humanities, liberal arts/general studies, and social science). Humanities and social science is the strongest academically. Humanities is the largest.

Required: To graduate, students must earn 125 credit hours with a GPA of at least 2.0, complete 2 comprehensive exams, and submit a thesis. The school requires 60 credit hours in the major for the B.S. degree, 40 for the B.A.; 65 in the core curriculum for the B.S., 85 for the B.A.

Special: Shimer offers internships in all areas of study and study abroad at Oxford in England. There is an accelerated degree program, a B.A.-B.S. degree, dual majors in all areas, and a general studies degree. Nondegree study and pass/fail options are possible.

Faculty/Classroom: 67% of faculty are male; 33% are female. All teach undergraduates. No introductory courses are taught by graduate students. The average class size in a regular course is 9.

Admissions: The SAT scores for the 2013-2014 freshman class were: Critical Reading--66% between 600 and 699, and 33% between 700 and 800; Math--33% below 500; Writing--33% between 500 and 599, 66% between 600 and 699. The ACT scores were 50% between 24 and 26, 50% between 27 and 28.

Requirements: Applicants must submit essays, letters of recommendation, and an interview. The SAT or ACT required only of students who are applying for our Early Entrance program, a 55 year old program that offers full admission to high school age students - those who would be enrolling in their junior or senior years of high school, but prefer to matriculate early. Important factors in the admissions decision are evidence of special talent, personality/intangible qualities, and recommendations by school officials.

Procedure: Freshmen are admitted fall and spring. There are deferred admissions and rolling admissions plans. Application deadlines are open. Application fee is $25. Applications are accepted online.

Transfer: 15 transfer students enrolled in 2012-2013. Same as for all other applicants plus all post-secondary transcripts. 65 of 125 credits required for the bachelor's degree must be completed at Shimer.

Visiting: There are regularly scheduled orientations for prospective students, consisting of class visits, lunch, a tour, and an admission interview. There are guides for informal visits and visitors may sit in on classes.

Financial Aid: In 2013-2014, 74% of all full-time freshmen and 84% of continuing full-time students received some form of financial aid. 74% of all full-time freshmen and 84% of continuing full-time students received need-based aid. The average freshman award was $17,741. Need-based scholarships or need-based grants averaged $9,399; need-based self-help aid (loans and jobs) averaged $3,854; and other non-need-based awards and non-need-based scholarships averaged $3,500. 52% of undergraduate students work part-time. Average annual earnings from campus work are $1800. The average financial indebtedness of the 2013 graduate was $30,000. Shimer is a member of CSS. The FAFSA and the college's own financial statement are required. The priority date for freshman financial aid applications for fall entry is April 15. The deadline for filing freshman financial aid applications for fall entry is July 30.

International Students: The school actively recruits these students. They must take the TOEFL with a minimum score of 590 on the paper-based TOEFL (PBT) or 97 on the Internet-based version (iBT).

Computers: All students may access the system 24 hours a day. There are no time limits and no fees.

Graduates: From July 1, 2012 to June 30, 2013, 18 bachelor's degrees were awarded. The most popular majors were humanities (67%), liberal arts (17%), and social sciences (11%). In an average class, 7% graduate in 3 years or less, 50% graduate in 4 years or less, 53% graduate in 5 years or less, and 58% graduate in 6 years or less. Of the 2012 graduating class, 20% were enrolled in graduate school within 6 months of graduation, and 70% were employed.

Admissions Contact: Elaine Vincent, Director of Admissions. E-Mail: *admission@shimer.edu* Web: *www.shimer.edu*

SOUTHERN ILLINOIS UNIVERSITY SYSTEM

The Southern Illinois University System, established in 1965, is a public system in Illinois. It is governed by a board of trustees, whose chief administrator is the president. The primary goal of the system is to create and sustain the internal and external conditions that enable the campuses to fulfill their missions with excellence. The main priorities are to achieve and maintain excellence in teaching, research, and service; to achieve and maintain cultural diversity; and to provide educational opportunity to the disadvantaged. The total student enrollment is usually 35,500 with 2500 faculty members. Altogether there are approximately 128 baccalaureate, 112 master's, and 43 doctoral programs offered in the Southern Illinois University System. Profiles of the 4-year campuses are included in this section.

SOUTHERN ILLINOIS UNIVERSITY CARBONDALE D-5

Carbondale, IL 62901 (618) 453-2987; (618) 453-4609

Full-time: 6419 men, 5425 women	**Faculty:** 869; I, --$
Part-time: 880 men, 627 women	**Ph.D.s:** 73%
Graduate: 2345 men, 2268 women	**Student/Faculty:** 15 to 1
Year: semesters, summer session	**Tuition:** $11,528 ($22,844)
Application Deadline: May 1	**Room & Board:** $9126

Freshman Class: 11573 applied, 9176 accepted, 2612 enrolled

SAT CR/M: 520/545 **ACT:** 22 **COMPETITIVE**

Southern Illinois University Carbondale, founded in 1869, is a public institution that is part of the Southern Illinois University system. The multicampus university offers undergraduate programs in the Colleges of Applied Sciences and Arts, Agricultural Sciences, Business, College of Education and Human Services, Engineering, Liberal Arts, Mass Communication and Media Arts, and Science. There is also a Graduate school and schools of Law and Medicine. There are 8 undergraduate schools and 3 graduate schools. In addition to regional accreditation, Southern has baccalaureate program accreditation with AACSB, ABET, ABFSE, ACEJMC, ADA, APTA, CAHEA, CSWE, FIDER, NAAB, NASAD, NCATE, NRPA, and SAF. The 2 libraries contain 2.9 million volumes, and subscribes to 43,161 periodicals including electronic. Computerized library services include interlibrary loans, database searching, Internet access, and Wi-Fi capability. Special learning facilities include a natural history museum, radio station, TV station, student-run newspaper, farms and timberlands, greenhouses, livestock facilities, archeological center, aviation program, crime study center, wildlife lab, international programs and services, broadcasting division that operates public television and radio stations, a dental lab,a child development lab, craft shop and museum. The 1136-acre campus is in a rural area 100 miles from St. Louis, MO. Including any residence halls, there are 242 buildings.

Student Life: 87% of undergraduates are from Illinois. Others are from 47 states, 45 foreign countries, and Canada. 64% are White; 22% African American. The average age of freshmen is 19; all undergraduates, 23. 39% do not continue beyond their first year; 50% remain to graduate.

Housing: 4622 students can be accommodated in college housing, which includes single-sex and coed dorms, on-campus apartments, and married student housing. In addition, there are honors houses, special-interest houses, family housing, Junior/Senior residence halls, and residence halls that stay open during breaks. On-campus housing is guaranteed for the freshman year only, is available on a first-come, and first-served basis. 71% of students commute. All students may keep cars.

Activities: 4% of men belong to 21 national fraternities; 4% of women belong to 9 national sororities. There are 450 groups on campus, including band, cheerleading, chess, choir, chorale, computers, dance, drama, drill team, environmental, ethnic, film, forensics, gay, honors, international, jazz band, literary magazine, marching band, musical theater, newspaper, opera, pep band, photography, political, professional, radio and TV, religious, social, social service, student government, symphony, and yearbook. Popular campus events include Cardboard Boat Regatta, International Festival and Hispanic Month.

Sports: There are 10 intercollegiate sports for men and 10 for women, and 27 intramural sports for men and 27 for women. Facilities include a 17,324-seat stadium, a 10,014-seat arena, a skate park, 3 softball fields, a baseball field, 4 flag football fields, 2 rugby fields, 4 soccer fields, a lake and beach with boat docks, tennis courts, track and field complex, ultimate frisbee fields, Saluki stadium, and a cross-country course. The 214,000-square-foot student recreation center houses an Olympic-size pool, indoor tracks, racquetball, squash, and tennis courts, aerobics equipment, a weight room, a nautilus room, and numerous exercise stations. The center also offers volleyball, basketball, badminton, handball, indoor soccer, a climbing wall, a dance studio, a boxing practice room, and a martial arts practice room.

Disabled Students: 99% of the campus is accessible. Facilities include wheelchair ramps, elevators, special parking, specially equipped restrooms, special class scheduling, lowered drinking fountains, lowered telephones, special housing.

Services: Counseling and information services are available, as is tutoring in most subjects. There is a reader service for the blind. There is new student orientation, a mentoring program, a writing skills lab, premajor advisement, student development programs, and career counseling. Students often are required to pay for tutorial assistance. SIUC also has an Achieve Program.

Campus Safety and Security: Measures include 24-hour foot and vehicle patrol, emergency notification system, self-defense education, and security escort services. There are shuttle buses, emergency telephones, lighted pathways/sidewalks, controlled access to dorms/residences, a student patrol program.

Programs of Study: Southern confers B.A., B.S., B.F.A. and B.Mus. degrees. Associate, master's, and doctoral degrees are also awarded. Bachelor's degrees are awarded in AGRICULTURE (agricultural economics, agriculture, animal science, forestry and related sciences, and plant science), BIOLOGICAL SCIENCE (avian sciences, biology/biological science, botany, microbiology, physiology, and zoology), BUSINESS (accounting, banking and finance, business administration and management, business economics, fashion merchandising, funeral home services, management science, marketing/retailing/merchandising, and recreation and leisure services), COMMUNICATIONS AND THE ARTS (art, broadcasting, classics, design, dramatic arts, English, English literature, film arts, fine arts, French, German, journalism, linguistics, music, photography, radio/television technology, Russian, Spanish, and speech/debate/rhetoric), COMPUTER AND PHYSICAL SCIENCE (chemistry, computer science, geology, information sciences and systems, mathematics, physics, and radiological technology), EDUCATION (early childhood education, elementary education, health education, physical education, special education, and vocational education), ENGINEERING AND ENVIRONMENTAL DESIGN (architecture, automotive technology, aviation administration/management, aviation computer technology, civil engineering, computer engineering, electrical/electronics engineering, electrical/electronics engineering technology, engineering technology, industrial engineering technology, interior design, mechanical engineering, and mining and mineral engineering), HEALTH PROFESSIONS (dental hygiene, dental laboratory technology, health care administration, physician's assistant, rehabilitation therapy, respiratory therapy, and speech pathology/audiology), SOCIAL SCIENCE (anthropology, clothing and textiles management/production/services, criminal justice, economics, family/consumer resource management, fire protection, food science, geography, German area studies, history, law, liberal arts/general studies, paralegal studies, philosophy, political science/government, psychology, social science, social work, and sociology). Workforce education and development, biological sciences, psychology, criminology, and healthcare management has the largest enrollments.

Special: There are 10 national honor societies, a freshman honors program, and 5 departmental honors programs.

Faculty/Classroom: 63% of faculty are male; 37% are female. 85% teach undergraduates, 40% do research, and 40% do both. Graduate students teach 30% of introductory courses. The average class size in an introductory lecture is 130.

Admissions: 79% of the 2013-2014 applicants were accepted. The SAT scores for the 2013-2014 freshman class were: Critical Reading--39% below 500, 35% between 500 and 599, 21% between 600 and 699, and 4% between 700 and 800; Math--33% below 500, 35% between 500 and 599, 26% between 600 and 699, and 5% between 700 and 800. The ACT scores were 14% below 21, 50% between 21 and 23, 30% between 24 and 26, and 6% above 28. 21% of the current freshmen were in the top fifth of their class; 44% were in the top two fifths. 13 freshmen graduated first in their class.

Requirements: The SAT or ACT is required. AP and CLEP credits are accepted.

Procedure: Freshmen are admitted fall, spring, and summer. Entrance exams should be taken during spring of the junior year. There is a deferred admissions plan. Applications should be filed by May 1 for fall entry, along with a $30 fee. Applications are accepted online.

Transfer: 1616 transfer students enrolled in 2012-2013. All transfer students must have a minimum 2.0 GPA. Students are required to meet freshman admission requirements if they are under 21 years old and have fewer than 26 credit hours of acceptable transfer work. Some academic programs have higher admission requirements. 26 of 120 credits required for the bachelor's degree must be completed at Southern.

Visiting: There are regularly scheduled orientations for prospective students, including admission counseling, academic program exhibits, student organization exhibits, workshops on financial aid and housing, and tours of the campus, academic departments, and residence halls. There are guides for informal visits, visitors may sit in on classes, and stay overnight. To schedule a visit, contact the Undergraduate Admissions.

Financial Aid: In 2013-2014, 68% of all full-time freshmen students received some form of financial aid. 68% of all full-time freshmen students received need-based aid. The average freshman award was $13,707. Need-based scholarships or need-based grants averaged $7,784; need-based self-help aid (loans and jobs) averaged $6,173; non-need-based athletic scholarships averaged $16,691; other non-need-based awards and non-need-based scholarships averaged $5,699; and $4,441 from other forms of aid. The average financial indebtedness of the 2013 graduate was $36,172. The FAFSA is required. The deadline for filing freshman financial aid applications for fall entry is April 1.

International Students: There are 396 international students enrolled. The school actively recruits these students. They must take the TOEFL with a minimum score of 520 on the paper-based TOEFL (PBT) or 68 on the Internet-based version (iBT). They must also take the SAT or ACT, and their own country's standardized college entrance exam.

Computers: All students may access the system all the time, all year. There are no time limits and no fees.

Graduates: From July 1, 2012 to June 30, 2013, 3864 bachelor's degrees were awarded. The most popular majors were education (17%), business/marketing (9%), and health professions and related programs (8%). 178 companies recruited on campus in 2012-2013. In an average class, 26% graduate in 4 years or less and 50% graduate in 6 years or less. Of the 2012 graduating class, 55% were enrolled in graduate school within 6 months of graduation, and 75% were employed.

Admissions Contact: Katharine Suski, Director/Undergraduate Admissions. E-Mail: *ksuski@siu.edu* Web: *http:/admissions.siu.edu/*

SOUTHERN ILLINOIS UNIVERSITY EDWARDSVILLE C-4

Edwardsville, IL 62026 **(618) 650-3705**
(800) 447-SIUE; (618) 650-5013

Full-time: 4496 men, 5152 women	**Faculty:** 556; IIA, -$
Part-time: 810 men, 883 women	**Ph.D.s:** 79%
Graduate: 1089 men, 1625 women	**Student/Faculty:** 15 to 1
Year: semesters, summer session	**Tuition:** $9251 ($19,673)
Application Deadline: May 1	**Room & Board:** $8281

Freshman Class: 7660 applied, 6272 accepted, 2075 enrolled
ACT: 23

COMPETITIVE

Southern Illinois University Edwardsville, founded in 1957, is part of the Southern Illinois University system and offers undergraduate programs in business, education, engineering, arts and sciences, and nursing. Graduate programs also are offered in 34 subject areas, including professional programs in pharmacy and dental medicine. There are 5 undergraduate schools and one graduate school. In addition to regional accreditation, SIUE has baccalaureate program accreditation with AACSB, ABET, ACCE, ACEJMC, CSWE, NASM, and NCATE. The library contains 810,537 volumes, 1.7 million microform items, 33,438 audio/video tapes/CDs/DVDs, and subscribes to 32,858 periodicals including electronic. Computerized library services include interlibrary loans, database searching, and Internet access. Special learning facilities include an art gallery, radio station, TV station, a recording studio, engineering labs, an anthropology museum, a greenhouse, an arboretum, and a nursing psychomotor skills lab. The 2660-acre campus is in a suburban area 18 miles northeast of downtown St. Louis, Missouri. Including any residence halls, there are 25 buildings.

Student Life: 90% of undergraduates are from Illinois. Others are from 36 states, 40 foreign countries, and Canada. 74% are White; 13% African American. The average age of all undergraduates is 21. 27% do not continue beyond their first year; 52% remain to graduate.

Housing: 3524 students can be accommodated in college housing, which includes coed dorms, on-campus apartments, and married student housing. In addition, there are fraternity houses, honors wings and special-interest wings. On-campus housing is available on a first-come and first-served basis. Priority is given to out-of-town students. 71% of students commute. All students may keep cars.

Activities: 7% of men belong to 9 national fraternities; 5% of women belong to 7 national sororities. There are 170 groups on campus, including academic and recreational, art, band, cheerleading, choir, chorale, chorus, dance, drama, environmental, ethnic, gay, honors, international, jazz band, literary magazine, musical theater, newspaper, opera, orchestra, pep band, photography, political, professional, radio and TV, religious, social, social service, student government, and symphony. Popular campus events include Welcome Week, Arts and Issues Series, International Week and Homecoming.

Sports: There are 9 intercollegiate sports for men and 9 for women, and 17 intramural sports for men and 17 for women. Facilities include the Vadalabene Center and Student Fitness Center, which offer racquetball, basketball, aquatics, volleyball, indoor track, exercise, and weight training; the University Center, which features restaurants, a recreation center, billiards, and a bowling alley; an outdoor swimming pool; a lake for canoeing and sailing; an outdoor track-and-field and soccer stadium; baseball, softball, and soccer fields; extensive walking and biking trails; and a Frisbee course.

Disabled Students: All of the campus is accessible. Facilities include wheelchair ramps, elevators, special parking, specially equipped restrooms, special class scheduling, lowered drinking fountains, lowered telephones, a Visualtek large-screen TV, Kurzweil readers, test-taking facilities, accessible weight-training equipment, and a swimming pool.

Services: Counseling and information services are available, as is tutoring in most subjects. There is a reader service for the blind, and remedial math, reading, and writing.

Campus Safety and Security: Measures include 24-hour foot and vehicle patrol, emergency notification system, self-defense education, and security escort services. There are shuttle buses, emergency telephones, lighted pathways/sidewalks, and emergency blue lights located throughout campus.

Programs of Study: SIUE confers B.A., B.S., B.F.A., B.L.S., B.M., B.S.A. and B.S.W. degrees. Master's degrees are also awarded. Bachelor's degrees are awarded in BIOLOGICAL SCIENCE (biochemistry, biology/biological science, ecology, and genetics), BUSINESS (accounting, business administration and management, business economics, entrepreneurial studies, human resources, international business management, management information systems, and marketing and distribution), COMMUNICATIONS AND THE ARTS (American literature, art, art history and appreciation, communications, dance, dramatic arts, English, French, German, journalism, languages, media arts, music, music business management, music history and appreciation, music performance, music theory and composition, musical theater, public relations, radio/television technology, Spanish, speech/debate/rhetoric, studio art, and theater design), COMPUTER AND PHYSICAL SCIENCE (actuarial science, applied mathematics, chemistry, computer management, computer science, earth science, mathematics, physics, and statistics), EDUCATION (art education, early childhood education, elementary education, health education, health information management, mathematics education, music education, physical education, science education, social science education, and special education), ENGINEERING AND ENVIRONMENTAL DESIGN (civil engineering, computer engineering, construction management, electrical/electronics engineering, industrial engineering, manufacturing engineering, and mechanical engineering), HEALTH PROFESSIONS (community health work, exercise science, medical technology, medical science, nursing, and speech pathology/audiology), SOCIAL SCIENCE (anthropology, criminal justice, economics, forensic studies, geography, gerontology, history, liberal arts/general studies, philosophy, political science/government, psychology, social work, and sociology). Nursing, biological sciences, and business administration have the largest enrollments.

Required: To graduate, students must complete a total of 124 semester hours with a minimum GPA of 2.0. Students must fulfill general education requirements, including 9 hours of math/science, and complete a senior project.

Special: SIUE offers cross-registration with the University of Missouri at St. Louis, co-op programs, internships, which are required by several majors, including mass communications and sociology, work-study programs, dual majors, B.A.-B.S. degrees, student-designed majors (available to specific honors students only), study abroad in 5 countries (England, France, Germany, the Netherlands, and Mexico), a liberal studies degree, and a 5-year (3+2) program in dental medicine. There are 20 national honor societies, a freshman honors program, and 15 departmental honors programs.

Faculty/Classroom: 51% of faculty are male; 49% are female. 84% teach undergraduates. Graduate students teach 4% of introductory courses.

Admissions: 82% of the 2013-2014 applicants were accepted. The ACT scores were 31% below 21, 30% between 21 and 23, 22% between 24 and 26, 9% between 27 and 28, and 8% above 28. 33% of the current freshmen were in the top fifth of their class; 64% were in the top two fifths.

Requirements: The ACT is required. Applicants must be graduates of an accredited secondary school or have a GED certificate. They must have completed 15 academic credits, based on 4 years of English, 3 each of math and lab science, 2 years of any combination of art, foreign language, music, and vocational education, at least 2 years of government and/or history, plus 1 more year of social studies. A GPA of 2.5 is required. AP and CLEP credits are accepted.

Procedure: Freshmen are admitted to all sessions. Entrance exams should be taken before high school graduation. There is a rolling admissions plan. Applications should be filed by May 1 for fall entry; December 15 for spring entry; and May 3 for summer entry, along with a $30 fee. Notification is sent on a rolling basis. Applications are accepted online.

Transfer: 1242 transfer students enrolled in 2012-2013. Applicants must have a minimum 2.0 GPA in at least 30 semester hours earned. 30 of 124 credits required for the bachelor's degree must be completed at SIUE.

Visiting: There are regularly scheduled orientations for prospective students, including visits before the semester starts. There are guides for informal visits and visitors may sit in on classes. To schedule a visit, contact the Office of Admissions.

Financial Aid: In 2013-2014, 75% of all full-time freshmen and 65% of continuing full-time students received some form of financial aid. 70% of all full-time freshmen and 65% of continuing full-time students received need-based aid. The average freshman award was $11,620. Need-based scholarships or need-based grants averaged $8,827; need-based self-help aid (loans and jobs) averaged $8,130; and non-need-based athletic scholarships averaged $10,660. 27% of undergraduate students work part-time. Average annual earnings from campus work are $7800. The average financial indebtedness of the 2013 graduate was $25,998. The FAFSA is required. The deadline for filing freshman financial aid applications for fall entry is March 1.

International Students: There are 320 international students enrolled. The school actively recruits these students. They must take the TOEFL with a minimum score of 550 on the paper-based TOEFL (PBT) or 80 on the Internet-based version (iBT).

Computers: All students may access the system daily at designated hours with some labs open 24 hours. There are no time limits and no fees.

Graduates: From July 1, 2012 to June 30, 2013, 2223 bachelor's

degrees were awarded. The most popular majors were business administration (20%), education (19%), and engineering (10%). 550 companies recruited on campus in 2012-2013. In an average class, 1% graduate in 3 years or less, 28% graduate in 4 years or less, 45% graduate in 5 years or less, and 50% graduate in 6 years or less.

Admissions Contact: Office of Admissions E-Mail: *admissions@siue.edu* Web: *www.siue.edu*

TRINITY CHRISTIAN COLLEGE — E-2

Palos Heights, IL 60463 — (708) 597-3000; (866) TRIN-4-ME; (708) 385-5665

Full-time: 370 men, 720 women
Part-time: 110 men, 260 women
Graduate: n/av
Year: semesters, summer session
Application Deadline: see profile
Freshman Class: n/av
SAT or ACT: required
Faculty: 79; IIB, -$
Ph.D.s: 67%
Student/Faculty: n/av
Tuition: $22,572
Room & Board: $8202

COMPETITIVE

Trinity Christian College, founded in 1959, is a private college offering programs in arts and sciences, business, health science, liberal arts, music, religion, and teacher preparation. The figures in the above capsule and in this profile are approximate. In addition to regional accreditation, Trinity has baccalaureate program accreditation with AACSB and CSWE. The library contains 75,298 volumes, 54,158 microform items, 1841 audio/video tapes/CDs/DVDs, and subscribes to 16,711 periodicals including electronic. Computerized library services include interlibrary loans, database searching, Internet access, and laptop Internet portals. Special learning facilities include a learning resource center, art gallery, and Dutch heritage collection. The 59-acre campus is in a suburban area 20 miles southwest of the Chicago Loop. Including any residence halls, there are 22 buildings.

Student Life: 71% of undergraduates are from Illinois. Others are from 34 states, 3 foreign countries, and Canada. 52% are from public schools. 80% are white. 86% are Protestant; 14% Catholic. The average age of freshmen is 18; all undergraduates, 21. 27% do not continue beyond their first year; 58% remain to graduate.

Housing: 726 students can be accommodated in college housing, which includes coed dorms and off-campus apartments. On-campus housing is guaranteed for all 4 years. 61% of students live on campus; of those, 45% remain on campus on weekends. Alcohol is not permitted. All students may keep cars.

Activities: There are no fraternities or sororities. There are 18 groups on campus, including art, band, cheerleading, choir, chorale, chorus, dance, drama, ethnic, honors, jazz band, literary magazine, newspaper, pep band, photography, political, professional, religious, social, social service, student government, and yearbook. Popular campus events include the Opus fine arts festival and the Trollstock Concert.

Sports: There are 6 intercollegiate sports for men and 6 for women, and 7 intramural sports for men and 7 for women. Facilities include a gym, a track, a stadium, a baseball diamond, and softball and soccer fields.

Disabled Students: 95% of the campus is accessible. Facilities include wheelchair ramps, elevators, special parking, specially equipped rest rooms, and lowered drinking fountains.

Services: Counseling and information services are available, as is tutoring in every subject.

Campus Safety and Security: Measures include 24-hour foot and vehicle patrol, self-defense education, and security escort services. There are emergency telephones and lighted pathways/sidewalks.

Programs of Study: Trinity confers B.A. B.S., B.S.N., and B.S.W. degrees. Bachelor's degrees are awarded in BIOLOGICAL SCIENCE (biology/biological science), BUSINESS (accounting and business administration and management), COMMUNICATIONS AND THE ARTS (applied music, art, communications, English, music, music performance, Spanish, and studio art), COMPUTER AND PHYSICAL SCIENCE (chemistry, computer science, information sciences and systems, and mathematics), EDUCATION (art education, education, elementary education, music education, special education, and sports studies), HEALTH PROFESSIONS (nursing, predentistry, premedicine, and preoptometry), SOCIAL SCIENCE (biblical studies, criminal justice, history, ministries, philosophy, prelaw, psychology, social work, sociology, and theological studies). Business, education, and nursing are the strongest academically and have the largest enrollments.

Required: All students must take 9 credits in English, 6 each in philosophy, history, and theology, as well as distribution requirements in cross-cultural studies, natural sciences, social sciences, fine arts, math, and phys ed. Students must complete 125 credit hours and maintain a minimum GPA of 2.0 to graduate.

Special: Students may have various part-time or full-time internships in their major field. There are study-abroad programs in Spain, Nicaragua, Ecuador, and South Korea. Pass/fail options exist. Dual majors are offered. There is 1 national honor society and a freshman honors program.

Faculty/Classroom: 60% of faculty are male; 40% are female. All teach and do research. The average class size in an introductory lecture is 25; in a laboratory, 18; and in a regular course, 18.

Admissions: 86% of a recent year's applicants were accepted. 36% of a recent year's freshmen were in the top fifth of their class; 60% were in the top two fifths. 3 freshmen graduated first in their class.

Requirements: The SAT or ACT is required. Applicants should graduate from an accredited high school or have a GED. They should prepare with 3 or 4 years of high school English, 3 years of math, science, and social studies, or 2 years each of a combination of 2 subject areas chosen among foreign language, math, science, or social studies. An interview is required. A GPA of 2.0 is required. AP and CLEP credits are accepted. Important factors in the admissions decision are advanced placement or honors courses, leadership record, and recommendations by school officials.

Procedure: Freshmen are admitted fall and spring. Entrance exams should be taken during the last semester of the junior year. There is a rolling admissions plan. Application fee is $20. Notification is sent on a rolling basis.

Transfer: 218 transfer students enrolled in a recent year. Applicants must have 24 hours of acceptable credits and a minimum 2.3 GPA. Associate degrees are recognized for transfer. 45 of 125 credits required for the bachelor's degree must be completed at Trinity.

Visiting: There are regularly scheduled orientations for prospective students, including a tour, an interview, a seminar, and class visits. There are guides for informal visits, and visitors may sit in on classes and stay overnight. To schedule a visit, contact the Admissions Office.

Financial Aid: In a recent year, 96% of all full-time freshmen and 93% of continuing full-time students received some form of financial aid. 76% of all full-time freshmen and 71% of continuing full-time students received need-based aid. The average freshmen award was $15,134. Need-based scholarships or need-based grants averaged $4287 ($17,696 maximum); need-based self-help aid (loans and jobs) averaged $3698 ($9000 maximum); and non-need-based athletic scholarships averaged $3710 ($11,000 maximum). Average annual earnings from campus work are $1600. The FAFSA is required. Check with the school for current application deadlines.

International Students: There were 36 international students enrolled in a recent year. They must take the TOEFL. They must also take the SAT or ACT; the ACT is recommended.

Computers: Wireless access is available. All students may access the system. There are no time limits and no fees. It is strongly recommended that all students have a personal computer.

Graduates: In a recent year, 303 bachelor's degrees were awarded. The most popular majors were elementary education (38%), business (17%), and nursing (13%). 10 companies recruited on campus in a recent year. In an average class, 54% graduate in 4 years or less, 58% graduate in 5 years or less, and 59% graduate in 6 years or less. Of a recent graduating class, 10% were enrolled in graduate school within 6 months of graduation and 82% were employed.

Admissions Contact: Director of Admissions. E-Mail: *admissions@trnty.edu* Web: *www.trnty.edu*

TRINITY COLLEGE OF NURSING & HEALTH SCIENCES — C-2

Rock Island, IL 61201 — (309) 779-7812; (309) 779-7748

Full-time: n/av
Part-time: n/av
Graduate: n/av
Year: semesters, summer session
Application Deadline: November 1
Freshman Class: 99 applied, 45 accepted, 30 enrolled
Faculty: 16
Ph.D.s: 19%
Student/Faculty: 9 to 1
Tuition: $40,792
Room & Board: $12,346

SPECIAL

Trinity College is a private, institution. The College offers Associate Degrees in Nursing, Radiography and Respiratory Care, as well as a Bachelor and Accelerated Bachelor of Science Degree in Nursing. There is one undergraduate school. In addition to regional accreditation, Trinity College has baccalaureate program accreditation with NLN. The library contains 8,500 volumes, and subscribes to 791 periodicals including electronic. Computerized library services include interlibrary loans, database searching, Internet access, and Wi-Fi capability. The 2-acre campus is in an urban area 2 hours west of Chicago, in Rock Island Illinois, part of the Quad Cities. Including any residence halls, there is 1 building.

Student Life: 52% of undergraduates are from Illinois. Others are from 7 states. 84% are White. The average age of all undergraduates is 28. 14% do not continue beyond their first year; 86% remain to graduate.

Housing: College-sponsored housing includes single-sex and coed Alcohol is not permitted. All students commute. All students may keep cars.

Activities: There are no fraternities or sororities. There are 3 groups on campus, including honors, professional, and student government. Popular campus events include Homecoming.

Sports: There is no sports program at Trinity College.

Disabled Students: All of the campus is accessible. Facilities include

wheelchair ramps, special parking, specially equipped restrooms, special class scheduling, lowered drinking fountains, and lowered telephones.

Services: Counseling and information services are available, as is tutoring in every subject. Faculty will meet with students on an individual basis.

Campus Safety and Security: Measures include 24-hour foot and vehicle patrol and emergency notification system. There are emergency telephones and lighted pathways/sidewalks. There is a safety and security overview during orientation.

Programs of Study: Trinity College confers B.S.N. degrees. Associate degrees are also awarded. Bachelor's degrees are awarded in HEALTH PROFESSIONS (nursing).

Required: Requirements for graduation for degree programs include: * Successful completion of general education courses and specific major courses required by the appropriate curriculum plan * Compliance with all special requirements listed by the individual program * Achievement of a satisfactory cumulative grade point average (2.0 on a 4.0 scale * Satisfaction of all financial obligations

Special: Accelerated BSN Program, Study abroad in Nicaragua, Clinical Internships in the Radiography Program There are 2 national honor societies, a freshman honors program, and 3 departmental honors programs.

Faculty/Classroom: 4% of faculty are male; 96% are female. All teach undergraduates. No introductory courses are taught by graduate students.

Admissions: 45% of the 2013-2014 applicants were accepted.

Requirements: Admissions requirements vary by program. AP and CLEP credits are accepted. Important factors in the admissions decision are advanced placement or honors courses, ability to finance college education, and leadership record.

Procedure: Freshmen are admitted fall, spring, and summer. There are early decision, early admissions, and rolling admissions plans. Early decision applications should be filed by November 1; regular applications, by November 1 for fall entry; November 1 for spring entry; and November 1 for summer entry, along with a $50 fee. Notification of early decision is sent December 15; regular decision, February 1. 26 early decision candidates were accepted for the 2013-2014 class. 28 applicants were on the 2013 waiting list; 12 were admitted. Applications are accepted online.

Transfer: 81 transfer students enrolled in 2012-2013. Applicants must submit a completed application, application fee, completed Clinical Performance Standards form showing that they have the physical ability to provide safe and effective client care, official transcripts from all high schools and postsecondary institutions attended, ACT or SAT scores, if applicable, confirmation of fluency in the English language, and proof of licensure, if applicable. Students must complete the last 19 hours in nursing at the college for the R.N.-B.S.N. completion option. The R.N.-B.S.N. program requires completion of at least 52 hours and the accelerated B.S.N. option requires completion of at least 121 hours. 19 of 122 credits required for the bachelor's degree must be completed at Trinity College.

Visiting: There are guides for informal visits and visitors may sit in on classes. To schedule a visit, contact the Admissions Representatives at (309) 779-7700.

Financial Aid: In 2013-2014, 87% of all full-time freshmen and 82% of continuing full-time students received some form of financial aid. 87% of all full time freshmen and 82% of continuing full-time students received need-based aid. The average freshman award was $5,548. Need-based scholarships or need-based grants averaged $3,191 ($5,550 maximum); and need-based self-help aid (loans and jobs) averaged $1,884 ($5,500 maximum). The average financial indebtedness of the 2013 graduate was $20,000. The FAFSA and the college's own financial statement are required. The priority date for freshman financial aid applications for fall entry is May 1. The deadline for filing freshman financial aid applications for fall entry is July 1.

Graduates: From July 1, 2012 to June 30, 2013, 26 bachelor's degrees were awarded. The most popular majors were nursing (66%), radiography (20%), and repiratory care (13%). 1 company recruited on campus in 2012-2013.

Admissions Contact: Lori Perez, Admissions Representative. E-Mail: *perezlj@ihs.org* Web: *www.trinitycollegeqc.edu*

TRINITY INTERNATIONAL UNIVERSITY E-2

Deerfield, IL 60015 **(847) 317-7000**
(800) 822-3225; (847) 317-7081

Full-time: 445 men, 590 women
Part-time: 45 men, 185 women
Graduate: 1080 men, 550 women
Year: semesters, summer session
Application Deadline: open
Freshman Class: n/av
SAT or ACT: required

Faculty: n/av; IIA, av$
Ph.D.s: 85%
Student/Faculty: n/av
Tuition: $23,870
Room & Board: $8200

COMPETITIVE

Trinity International University, established in 1897 by the Evangelical Free Church, is a Christian liberal arts institution offering undergraduate, graduate, and doctoral programs. The figures in the above capsule and in this profile are approximate. There are 8 undergraduate schools and 3 graduate schools. The library contains 247,650 volumes, 110,503 microform items, 6741 audio/video tapes/CDs/DVDs, and subscribes to 1091 periodicals including electronic. Computerized library services include interlibrary loans, database searching, and Internet access. Special learning facilities include a learning resource center. The 111-acre campus is in a suburban area 25 miles north of Chicago. Including any residence halls, there are 34 buildings.

Student Life: 52% of undergraduates are from Illinois. Others are from 40 states, 45 foreign countries, and Canada. 69% are from public schools. 77% are white. 96% are Protestant. The average age of freshmen is 18; all undergraduates, 21. 22% do not continue beyond their first year; 47% remain to graduate.

Housing: 700 students can be accommodated in college housing, which includes single-sex dorms, on-campus apartments, and married student housing. On-campus housing is guaranteed for all 4 years. 58% of students live on campus; of those, 75% remain on campus on weekends. Alcohol is not permitted. Upperclassmen may keep cars.

Activities: There are no fraternities or sororities. There are 36 groups on campus, including art, band, cheerleading, choir, chorale, computers, debate, drama, ethnic, handbell choir and gospel choir, honors, international, jazz band, literary magazine, newspaper, orchestra, pep band, political, religious, social service, student government, and symphony. Popular campus events include Santa Lucia Festival, Fine Arts Series, and Day of Prayer.

Sports: There are 4 intercollegiate sports for men and 4 for women, and 6 intramural sports for men and 6 for women. Facilities include a student center, a sports complex, and football and soccer fields. Students have access to a nearby indoor tennis and racquetball club.

Disabled Students: 75% of the campus is accessible. Facilities include wheelchair ramps, elevators, special parking, specially equipped rest rooms, and special class scheduling.

Services: Counseling and information services are available, as is tutoring in every subject. There is a reader service for the blind and remedial math, reading, and writing.

Campus Safety and Security: Measures include 24-hour foot and vehicle patrol, self-defense education, and security escort services. There are emergency telephones and lighted pathways/sidewalks.

Programs of Study: Trinity confers B.A. degrees. Master's and doctoral degrees are also awarded. Bachelor's degrees are awarded in BIOLOGICAL SCIENCE (biology/biological science), BUSINESS (accounting, business administration and management, human resources, international business management, marketing/retailing/merchandising, and sports management), COMMUNICATIONS AND THE ARTS (communications, English, and music), COMPUTER AND PHYSICAL SCIENCE (chemistry and mathematics), EDUCATION (athletic training, elementary education, physical education, and secondary education), HEALTH PROFESSIONS (physical therapy, premedicine, and sports medicine), SOCIAL SCIENCE (biblical studies, Christian studies, history, humanities, liberal arts/general studies, philosophy, psychology, social science, and youth ministry). Music, education, and biblical studies are the strongest academically. Business, Christian ministries, and education have the largest enrollments.

Required: To graduate, all students must complete 126 semester hours, including 58 general education hours and a variable 36 to 54 hours in the major. A GPA of 2.0 is required. Chapel attendance, Christian service, Bible study, and science are also required.

Special: Students can cross-register with the Christian College Consortium and at Trinity Evangelical Divinity School. Trinity offers 3 levels of internships, study abroad in 7 countries, and an opportunity through the American Studies Program to spend a semester in Washington. Dual majors, a general studies degree, and nondegree study are offered. There are 2 national honor societies, a freshman honors program, and 15 departmental honors programs.

Faculty/Classroom: 68% of faculty are male; 32% are female. 56% teach undergraduates. No introductory courses are taught by graduate students. The average class size in an introductory lecture is 40; in a laboratory, 20; and in a regular course, 15.

Requirements: The SAT or ACT is required; the ACT is preferred. Applicants should be graduates of an accredited high school and have completed 15 academic credits in English, math, science, social studies, art, a foreign language, and music. A GED is accepted. A recommendation from a pastor must be submitted. A GPA of 2.5 is required. AP and CLEP credits are accepted. Important factors in the admissions decision are personality/intangible qualities, leadership record, and advanced placement or honors courses.

Procedure: Freshmen are admitted fall and spring. Entrance exams should be taken during spring of the junior year or fall of the senior year. There is a rolling admissions plan. Application deadlines are open. Application fee is $25; the fee is waived for students who apply online before November 1. Applications are accepted online.

Transfer: Applicants must submit college transcripts and have a cumulative college GPA of 2.0 or higher. 30 of 126 credits required for the bachelor's degree must be completed at Trinity.

Visiting: There are regularly scheduled orientations for prospective students, including class visits, meetings with professors and admission counselors, and a dorm visit. There are guides for informal visits, and visitors may sit in on classes and stay overnight. To schedule a visit, contact the Campus Visit Coordinator.

Financial Aid: Trinity is a member of CSS. The FAFSA is required. Check with the school for current application deadlines.

International Students: They must take the TOEFL with a minimum score of 580 on the paper-based TOEFL (PBT). They must also take the SAT or ACT, scoring 19 on the ACT.

Admissions Contact: Director of Undergraduate Admissions. E-Mail: *tcadmissions@tiu.edu* Web: *www.tiu.edu*

UNIVERSITY OF CHICAGO — E-2

Chicago, IL 60637 — **(773) 702-8650; (773) 702-4199**

Full-time: 2921 men, 2610 women	**Faculty:** 1261; I, ++$
Part-time: 31 men, 28 women	**Ph.D.s:** 100%
Graduate: 4301 men, 2617 women	**Student/Faculty:** 6 to 1
Year: quarters, summer session	**Tuition:** $42,783
Application Deadline: January 2	**Room & Board:** $12,633

Freshman Class: 25273 applied, 3345 accepted, 1527 enrolled

SAT CR/M: 744/742 — **ACT:** 33 — **MOST COMPETITIVE**

The University of Chicago, founded in 1890, is a private liberal arts institution offering undergraduate and graduate programs with emphases on the biological and physical sciences, the humanities, and the social sciences. There are 11 graduate schools. In addition to regional accreditation, Chicago has baccalaureate program accreditation with NCATE. The 5 libraries contain 11.3 million volumes, 98,000 audio/video tapes/CDs/DVDs, and subscribe to 122,000 periodicals including electronic. Computerized library services include interlibrary loans, database searching, Internet access, and Wi-Fi capability. Special learning facilities include an art gallery, radio station, film studies center, language labs, museum of Near Eastern antiquities, and Renaissance Society (contemporary art). The 215-acre campus is in an urban area in Chicago. Including any residence halls, there are 249 buildings.

Student Life: 81% of undergraduates are from out of state, mostly the Mid-West. Students are from 50 states, 103 foreign countries, and Canada. 46% are White; 18% Asian American. The average age of freshmen is 18; all undergraduates, 19. 1% do not continue beyond their first year; 92% remain to graduate.

Housing: 2992 students can be accommodated in college housing, which includes single-sex and coed dorms and on-campus apartments and an international house. On-campus housing is guaranteed for all 4 years. 55% of students live on campus. Upperclassmen may keep cars.

Activities: There are 400 groups on campus, including college bowl, improv groups, art, bagpipe, band, cheerleading, chess, choir, chorale, chorus, computers, dance, debate, drama, ethnic, film, gay, honors, international, jazz band, literary magazine, Model UN, musical theater, newspaper, orchestra, pep band, photography, political, professional, radio and TV, religious, social, social service, student government, and symphony. Popular campus events include Scavenger Hunt, Summer Breeze Festival, Kuviasungnerk Winter Festival and Festival of the Arts.

Sports: There are 10 intercollegiate sports for men and 9 for women, and 32 intramural sports for men and 32 for women. The athletic facilities include a field house, a 1,500-seat stadium, outdoor 400m track, baseball and softball fields, a 1,500-seat arena, indoor basketball and squash courts, an indoor 200m track, weight and wrestling rooms, aerobic machines, and an indoor Olympic-sized pool. The University of Chicago also has a student activities center housing a movie theater, TV and pool rooms, and a pub.

Disabled Students: Facilities include wheelchair ramps, elevators, special parking, specially equipped restrooms, special class scheduling, lowered drinking fountains, lowered telephones, and special housing.

Services: Counseling and information services are available, as is tutoring in some subjects, including math, physics, chemistry, writing and biology There is also a reader service for the blind.

Campus Safety and Security: Measures include 24-hour foot and vehicle patrol, emergency notification system, self-defense education, and security escort services. There are shuttle buses, emergency telephones, lighted pathways/sidewalks, and controlled access to dorms/residences.

Programs of Study: Chicago confers B.A., and B.S. degrees. Master's and doctoral degrees are also awarded. Bachelor's degrees are awarded in BIOLOGICAL SCIENCE (biochemistry and biology/biological science), COMMUNICATIONS AND THE ARTS (art history and appreciation, classics, comparative literature, East Asian languages and literature, English, film arts, German, linguistics, media arts, music, romance languages and literature, Russian, Slavic languages, and visual and performing arts), COMPUTER AND PHYSICAL SCIENCE (applied mathematics, chemistry, computer science, geoscience, mathematics, physics, and statistics), ENGINEERING AND ENVIRONMENTAL DESIGN (environmental science), HEALTH PROFESSIONS (medical science), SOCIAL SCIENCE (African American studies, anthropology, classical/ancient civilization, economics, gender studies, geography, history, human development, humanities, interdisciplinary studies, international studies, Judaic studies, Latin American studies, law, medieval studies, Near Eastern studies, philosophy, political science/government, psychology, public affairs, religion, social science, sociology, South Asian studies, and theological studies). Social sciences, biological and biomedical science have the largest enrollments.

Required: To graduate, students must complete 42 quarter courses, including 9 to 13 courses in the major, with an overall GPA of at least 1.75 and at least 2.0 in the major. The core curriculum includes sequences in humanities, social sciences, biological and physical sciences, civilization studies, and foreign languages. Also required are 2 quarters of math and 1 of art, music, or drama.

Special: Special academic programs include cross-registration through the Committee on Institutional Cooperation, summer internship in Washington, and study abroad programs in 18 countries. B.A.-B.S. and general studies degrees are offered, as are student-designed majors. Bachelors-Masters joint programs are offered in many fields. Professional options in Public Policy Studies, Social Service Administration, and early admission to the University of Chicago Pritzker School of Medicine are available. Non-degree study and pass/fail options are possible. There is 1 national honor society.

Faculty/Classroom: 68% of faculty are male; 32% are female. No introductory courses are taught by graduate students. The average class size in an introductory lecture is 22; in a laboratory is 14; and in a regular course is 25.

Admissions: 13% of the 2013-2014 applicants were accepted. The SAT scores for the 2013-2014 freshman class were: Critical Reading--16% between 600 and 699, and 84% between 700 and 800; Math--1% between 500 and 599, 18% between 600 and 699, and 81% between 700 and 800; Writing--1% between 500 and 599, 21% between 600 and 699, and 78% between 700 and 800. 99% of the current freshmen were in the top fifth of their class.

Requirements: The SAT or ACT is required. Other admissions criteria include a recommended secondary school curriculum of 4 years each of English, Mathematics, and Science, 3 years of foreign language, and 2 years each of history and social studies. The GED is accepted. An essay must be submitted, and an interview is recommended. AP credits are accepted. Important factors in the admissions decision are advanced placement or honors courses, personality/intangible qualities, and extracurricular activities record.

Procedure: Freshmen are admitted fall. Entrance exams should be taken during the junior or senior year. There are early admissions and deferred admissions plans. Early decision applications should be filed by November 1; regular applications, by January 2 for fall entry, along with a $75 fee. Notification of early decision is sent December 17; regular decision, April 1. applicants were on the 2013 waiting list; were admitted. Applications are accepted online.

Transfer: 16 transfer students enrolled in 2012-2013. Proven ability and interest in liberal arts education is considered. Essay, broad course work, and solid performance at the home institution is considered critical. A recommendation is required from a secondary school, instructors, and dean of previous institution. A 2-year residency is a requirement. 105 of 140 credits required for the bachelor's degree must be completed at Chicago.

Visiting: There are regularly scheduled orientations for prospective students, including meeting with an admissions counselor and students, sitting in on classes, visiting faculty, and staying in a residence hall. There are guides for informal visits, visitors may sit in on classes, and stay overnight. To schedule a visit, contact the College Admissions.

Financial Aid: In 2013-2014, 63% of all full-time freshmen and 56% of continuing full-time students received some form of financial aid. 45% of all full-time freshmen and 45% of continuing full-time students received need-based aid. The average freshman award was $42,128. Need-based scholarships or need-based grants averaged $39,904; need-based self-help aid (loans and jobs) averaged $3,476; and other non-need-based awards and non-need-based scholarships averaged $11,707. The average financial indebtedness of the 2013 graduate was $23,930. Chicago is a member of CSS. The CSS/Profile, FAFSA, and the college's own financial statement are required. The deadline for filing freshman financial aid applications for fall entry is February 1.

International Students: There are 522 international students enrolled. The school actively recruits these students. They must take the TOEFL with a minimum score of 104 on the Internet-based version (iBT), or take the IELTS, with a minimum overall score of 7. They must also take the SAT or ACT.

Computers: All students may access the system any time. There are no time limits and no fees.

Graduates: From July 1, 2012 to June 30, 2013, 1242 bachelor's degrees were awarded. The most popular majors were economics (18%), biological sciences (10%), and political science (9%).

Admissions Contact: James Nondorf, Vice President and Dean, College Admissions and Financial Ai. E-Mail: *jnondorf@uchicago.edu* Web: *www.uchicago.edu*

UNIVERSITY OF ILLINOIS SYSTEM

The University of Illinois System, established in 1867, is a public system in Illinois. It is governed by a board of trustees, whose chief administrator is the president. The primary goal of the system is to provide undergraduate, graduate and professional education, conduct research, public service and to promote economic development in the state. The main priorities are develop University of Illinois Urbana-Champaign (UIUC) into the nation's preeminent public research university, develop University of Illinois – Chicago (UIC) into the nation's premier urban public research university, position the University of Illinois Medical Center and health sciences colleges for the next quarter century, and develop University of Springfield (UIS) into one of the nation's top five small, public, liberal arts universities. The total student enrollment in a recent year for all 3 campuses was 76,886, there were 5654 faculty members. Altogether there are 224 baccalaureates, 220 masters, and 150 doctoral programs offered in the University of Illinois System. Profiles of the 4-year campuses are included in this section.

UNIVERSITY OF ILLINOIS AT CHICAGO E-2

Chicago, IL 60680 312-996-4366; 312-413-7628

Full-time: 7391 men, 8141 women	**Faculty:** n/av; I, av$
Part-time: 676 men, 717 women	**Ph.D.s:** 83%
Graduate: 4508 men, 6658 women	**Student/Faculty:** n/av
Year: semesters, summer session	**Tuition:** $12,771 ($25,064)
Application Deadline: January 15	**Room & Board:** $10,194
Freshman Class: 14889 applied, 9411 accepted, 3204 enrolled	
SAT: required **ACT:** 24	**VERY COMPETITIVE**

The University of Illinois at Chicago, founded in 1946, is a public institution with undergraduate and graduate programs in the liberal arts, art and fine arts, business, engineering, architecture, health sciences, music, teacher preparation, social work, and professional training in dentistry, medicine, and pharmacy. There are 8 undergraduate schools and 1 graduate school. In addition to regional accreditation, UIC has baccalaureate program accreditation with AACSB, ABET, ACPE, CSWE, NAAB, and NASAD. The 3 libraries contain 3.5 million volumes, 4.2 million microform items, and 15,953 audio/video tapes/CDs/DVDs, and subscribe to 54,977 periodicals including electronic. Computerized library services include interlibrary loans, database searching, Internet access, and laptop Internet portals. Special learning facilities include a learning resource center, art gallery, radio station, Jane Addams Hull House, which is a restored settlement house, and the James Woodworth Prairie Reserve. The 240-acre campus is in an urban area just west of downtown Chicago. Including any residence halls, there are 117 buildings.

Student Life: 99% of undergraduates are from Illinois. Others are from 44 states, 49 foreign countries, and Canada. 90% are from public schools. 44% are white; 21% Asian American; 20% Hispanic. The average age of freshmen is 18; all undergraduates, 21. 18% do not continue beyond their first year; 53% remain to graduate.

Housing: 3800 students can be accommodated in college housing, which includes coed dorms and on-campus apartments. In addition, there are honors houses, special-interest houses, the President's Award House, and special-interest floors. On-campus housing is available on a first-come and first-served basis. 81% of students commute. All students may keep cars.

Activities: 3% of men belong to 15 national fraternities; 4% of women belong to 14 national sororities. There are 400 groups on campus, including art, band, cheerleading, chess, choir, chorus, computers, dance, drama, ethnic, gay, honors, international, jazz band, literary magazine, musical theater, newspaper, political, professional, religious, social, social service, and student government. Popular campus events include Fun Fair, UIC Fashion Show, and New Student Convocation.

Sports: There are 8 intercollegiate sports for men and 8 for women, and 50 intramural sports for men and 50 for women. Facilities include a 12,000-seat sports pavilion, 2 sports and fitness centers, a recreation center, a 1000-seat gym, 3 pools, racquetball and tennis courts, baseball, softball, and soccer fields, a bowling alley, indoor and outdoor tracks, and weight rooms.

Disabled Students: 80% of the campus is accessible. Facilities include wheelchair ramps, elevators, special parking, specially equipped restrooms, special class scheduling, lowered drinking fountains, and lowered telephones.

Services: Counseling and information services are available, as is tutoring in most subjects. There is a reader service for the blind, and remedial math, reading, and writing. a writing center, and academic skills classes.

Campus Safety and Security: Measures include 24-hour foot and vehicle patrol, emergency notification system, self-defense education, and security escort services. There are shuttle buses, emergency telephones, lighted pathways/sidewalks, emergency call buttons across campus.

Programs of Study: UIC confers B.A., B.S., and B.F.A. degrees. Master's and doctoral degrees are also awarded. Bachelor's degrees are awarded in BIOLOGICAL SCIENCE (biochemistry, biology/biological science, neurosciences, and nutrition), BUSINESS (accounting, banking and finance, business administration and management, electronic business, entrepreneurial studies, management science, and marketing/retailing/merchandising), COMMUNICATIONS AND THE ARTS (art history and appreciation, communications, dramatic arts, English, film arts, French, German, graphic design, industrial design, Italian, music, photography, Polish, Russian, Spanish, and studio art), COMPUTER AND PHYSICAL SCIENCE (chemistry, computer mathematics, computer science, earth science, information sciences and systems, mathematics, physics, and statistics), EDUCATION (art education, elementary education, and health education), ENGINEERING AND ENVIRONMENTAL DESIGN (architecture, bioengineering, chemical engineering, civil engineering, computer engineering, electrical/electronics engineering, engineering management, engineering physics, industrial engineering technology, and mechanical engineering), HEALTH PROFESSIONS (dental hygiene and nursing), SOCIAL SCIENCE (African American studies, anthropology, classical/ancient civilization, criminal justice, criminology, economics, gender studies, German area studies, history, Latin American studies, philosophy, physical fitness/movement, political science/government, psychology, public affairs, sociology, urban studies, and women's studies). Math, health professions, and business are the strongest academically. Psychology, biological science, and accounting are the largest.

Required: Students must demonstrate proficiency in written English through either course work or testing and complete 24 hours of general education, including at least 1 course in each of the general education categories: Analyzing the Natural World, Understanding the Individual and Society, Understanding the Past, Understanding the Creative Arts, Exploring the World Cultures, and Understanding U.S. Society. A minimum overall GPA of 2.0 is required. Total number of hours to graduate varies by major but is always at least 120.

Special: Special academic programs include a wide variety of co-op and program internships, work-study with some 70 on- and off-campus employers, and study abroad opportunities at accredited foreign universities, as well as special programs in France, Italy, Canada, Austria, Spain, and Mexico. Interdisciplinary majors are offered in architectural studies, communications and theater, math and computer science, bioengineering, and information and decision sciences. Up to 4 semester hours of credit may be granted for military experience. Dual and student-designed majors, nondegree study, and pass/fail options are available. There are 10 national honor societies, including Phi Beta Kappa, a freshman honors program, and 90 departmental honors programs.

Faculty/Classroom: 53% of faculty are male; 47% are female. No introductory courses are taught by graduate students. The average class size in an introductory lecture is 67; in a laboratory is 18; and in a regular course is 25.

Admissions: 63% of the 2011-2012 applicants were accepted. The SAT scores for the 2011-2012 freshman class were: Critical Reading--37% below 500, 34% between 500 and 599, 22% between 600 and 700, and 7% above 700; Math--21% below 500, 34% between 500 and 599, 33% between 600 and 700, and 12% above 700; Writing--31% below 500, 36% between 500 and 599, 26% between 600 and 700, and 8% above 700. The ACT scores were 19% below 21, 32% between 21 and 23, 29% between 24 and 26, 11% between 27 and 28, and 10% above 28. 48% of the current freshmen were in the top fifth of their class; 82% were in the top two fifths.

Requirements: The SAT or ACT is required. In addition, applicants should be graduates of an accredited secondary school; the GED is accepted. The recommended secondary school curriculum varies according to the college program chosen, but 15 high school credits are required as follows: English: 4; math: 3; science: 3; foreign language: 2; social studies. AP and CLEP credits are accepted.

Procedure: Freshmen are admitted fall. Entrance exams should be taken in the spring of the junior year or the fall of the senior year. There is a rolling admissions plan. Applications should be filed by January 15 for fall entry, along with a $40 fee. Notification is sent on a rolling basis. Applications are accepted online.

Transfer: 1656 transfer students enrolled in 2010-2011. Transferable hours and minimum GPA vary according to program. 30 of 120 credits required for the bachelor's degree must be completed at UIC.

Visiting: There are regularly scheduled orientations for prospective students, consisting of a general meeting, a college meeting, and campus tours. There are guides for informal visits and visitors may sit in on classes. To schedule a visit, contact the Office of Undergraduate Admissions.

Financial Aid: In 2011-2012, 73% of all full-time freshmen and 70% of continuing full-time students received some form of financial aid. 60% of all full-time freshmen and 57% of continuing full-time students received need-based aid. The average freshman award was $15,472. Need-based scholarships or need-based grants averaged $1,656; need-based self-help aid (loans and jobs) averaged $4,597; and non-need-based athletic scholarships averaged $17,248. 18% of undergraduate students work part-time. Average annual earnings from campus work are $3738. The average financial indebtedness of the 2011 graduate was $16,937. UIC is a member of CSS. The FAFSA is required. The priority date for freshman financial aid applications for fall entry is March 1.

International Students: There are 241 international students enrolled.

They must take the TOEFL with a minimum score of 550 on the paper-based TOEFL (PBT) or 80 on the Internet-based version (iBT). They must also take the SAT or ACT. Minimum required scores depend on the specific college.

Computers: Wireless access is available. The Academic Computing and Communications Center (ACCC) supports the educational and research needs of the UIC community by providing a variety of computing and communications resources. Student have ready access to both Unix systems and personal PCs. Through 1333 workstations, ACCC provides Internet connections in residence halls, libraries, and student centers. A wireless network in public areas on campus is also available. All students may access the system 24 hours daily. There are no time limits and no fees. It is strongly recommended that all students have a personal computer.

Admissions Contact: Edward Valentine *eav@uillinois.edu*

UNIVERSITY OF ILLINOIS AT URBANA-CHAMPAIGN E-3

Urbana, IL 61820 (213) 333-0302; (217) 244-4614

Full-time: 15,970 men, 14,240 women	**Faculty:** n/av; I, av$
Part-time: 420 men, 280 women	**Ph.D.s:** 92%
Graduate: 5920 men, 5520 women	**Student/Faculty:** n/av
Year: semesters, summer session	**Tuition:** $15,500 ($31,000)
Application Deadline: see profile	**Room & Board:** $10,580
Freshman Class: n/av	
SAT or ACT: required	

HIGHLY COMPETITIVE

The University of Illinois at Urbana-Champaign, founded in 1867, is the oldest and largest campus in the University of Illinois system, offering some 150 undergraduate and more than 100 graduate degree programs. The figures in the above capsule and in this profile are approximate. There are 18 undergraduate schools. In addition to regional accreditation, Illinois has baccalaureate program accreditation with AACSB, AALE, ABET, ACEJMC, ADA, ASLA, CSAB, CSWE, NAAB, NASAD, NASM, NCATE, NRPA, and SAF. The 27 libraries contain 11 million volumes and 1 million audio/video tapes/CDs/DVDs. Computerized library services include interlibrary loans, database searching, Internet access, and laptop Internet portals. Special learning facilities include a learning resource center, art gallery, natural history museum, planetarium, radio station, TV station, language learning lab, performing arts center, graphic technologies lab, world history and cultural museum, rehabilitation-education center, center for American music, Japan House and gardens, and rare books and special collections libraries. The 4938-acre campus is in a small town 140 miles south of Chicago, 125 miles west of Indianapolis, and 180 miles northeast of St. Louis. Including any residence halls, there are 705 buildings.

Student Life: 87% of undergraduates are from Illinois. Others are from 49 states, 71 foreign countries, and Canada. 66% are white; 13% Asian American. The average age of freshmen is 18; all undergraduates, 20. 7% do not continue beyond their first year; 83% remain to graduate.

Housing: 11,034 students can be accommodated in college housing, which includes single-sex and coed dorms, on-campus apartments, and married student housing. In addition, there are language houses, special-interest houses, privately owned university-approved residence halls, and fraternity and sorority houses. On-campus housing is guaranteed for all 4 years. 50% of students commute. All students may keep cars.

Activities: 22% of men belong to 3 local and 59 national fraternities; 23% of women belong to 2 local and 34 national sororities. There are 900 groups on campus, including art, band, cheerleading, chess, choir, chorale, chorus, computers, dance, debate, drama, drill team, environmental, ethnic, film, forensics, gay, honors, international, jazz band, literary magazine, marching band, musical theater, newspaper, opera, orchestra, pep band, photography, political, professional, radio and TV, religious, social, social service, student government, symphony, and yearbook. Popular campus events include Quad Day to introduce campus organizations, Dad's Weekend, and Mom's Weekend.

Sports: There are 10 intercollegiate sports for men and 12 for women, and 21 intramural sports for men and 21 for women. Facilities include a 470,000-square-foot state-of-the-art indoor recreation space, along with 42 acres of outdoor recreation space for students' fitness and wellness needs, all major varsity sport facilities, and numerous student union facilities from bowling to exercise facilities.

Disabled Students: All of the campus is accessible. Facilities include wheelchair ramps, elevators, special parking, specially equipped rest rooms, special class scheduling, lowered drinking fountains, lowered telephones, special housing, adjustable tables and labs, textbook and supply services, and fitness equipment for all students with disabilities, including wheelchair sports such as basketball, track and sport camps, and housing and bus service.

Services: Counseling and information services are available, as is tutoring in every subject. There is a reader service for the blind, and remedial math, reading, and writing. Transportation and rehabilitation services are offered, as well as interpreters, note taking, taped lectures, and priority registration.

Campus Safety and Security: Measures include 24-hour foot and vehicle patrol, emergency notification system, self-defense education, and security escort services. There are shuttle buses, emergency telephones, lighted pathways/sidewalks, controlled access to dorms/residences, a Saferides program, safety presentations, and evaluations by campus police.

Programs of Study: Illinois confers A.B., B.S., B.A.U.P., B.F.A., B.Land.Arch., B.Mus., B.S.Ed., B.S.J., B.S.W., and B.V.M. degrees. Master's and doctoral degrees are also awarded. Bachelor's degrees are awarded in AGRICULTURE (agricultural business management, agricultural communications, agricultural economics, agricultural mechanics, agronomy, animal science, forestry and related sciences, horticulture, natural resource management, range/farm management, and wildlife management), BIOLOGICAL SCIENCE (biology/biological science, biophysics, biotechnology, botany, cell biology, entomology, microbiology, molecular biology, nutrition, physiology, plant physiology, and wildlife biology), BUSINESS (accounting, banking and finance, entrepreneurial studies, hospitality management services, human resources, insurance, labor studies, logistics, management information systems, management science, marketing and distribution, marketing management, marketing/retailing/merchandising, operations research, organizational behavior, personnel management, purchasing/inventory management, real estate, and recreation and leisure services), COMMUNICATIONS AND THE ARTS (advertising, art history and appreciation, broadcasting, classics, communications, comparative literature, crafts, dance, dramatic arts, East Asian languages and literature, English, English literature, film arts, fine arts, French, Germanic languages and literature, graphic design, Hebrew, industrial design, Italian, journalism, linguistics, media arts, music, music history and appreciation, music performance, music theory and composition, painting, photography, Portuguese, Russian languages and literature, sculpture, Spanish, speech/debate/rhetoric, and voice), COMPUTER AND PHYSICAL SCIENCE (actuarial science, astronomy, chemistry, computer management, computer mathematics, computer programming, geology, mathematics, physics, and statistics), EDUCATION (agricultural education, art education, athletic training, computer education, early childhood education, education, education of the multiply handicapped, elementary education, English education, foreign languages education, mathematics education, music education, physical education, science education, secondary education, and vocational education), ENGINEERING AND ENVIRONMENTAL DESIGN (aeronautical engineering, agricultural engineering, airline piloting and navigation, architectural engineering, architecture, aviation administration/management, bioengineering, ceramic engineering, chemical engineering, city/community/regional planning, civil engineering, computational sciences, computer engineering, computer technology, electrical/electronics engineering, engineering, engineering mechanics, engineering physics, geological engineering, industrial administration/management, industrial engineering, landscape architecture/design, materials engineering, materials science, mechanical engineering, metallurgical engineering, nuclear engineering, and plastics engineering), HEALTH PROFESSIONS (biomedical science, community health work, exercise science, health care administration, preveterinary science, public health, and rehabilitation therapy), SOCIAL SCIENCE (anthropology, child psychology/development, dietetics, East Asian studies, economics, family/consumer studies, food production/management/services, food science, geography, history, human development, humanities, international studies, Latin American studies, liberal arts/general studies, parks and recreation management, philosophy, political science/government, prelaw, psychology, religion, Russian and Slavic studies, sociology, textiles and clothing, and women's studies). Engineering, computer science, and business are the strongest academically. Psychology, biology, and electrical and computer engineering have the largest enrollments.

Required: All students must demonstrate satisfactory proficiency in the use of the English language and 6 hours each in approved composition classes, Western/non-Western cultural studies, arts and humanities, social sciences/behavior, natural sciences/technology, and quantitative reasoning. Successful completion of either the third or fourth year (depending on college) of a language other than the student's primary language is required. Students must maintain a minimum GPA of 2.0 while completing 120 to 132 credit hours (depending on the major) to graduate.

Special: Illinois offers cooperative engineering programs with many Midwestern liberal arts colleges and summer, semester, and full-year programs abroad and numerous exchange opportunities. Unusual opportunities include a leisure studies semester in Scotland and a summer parliamentary internship in London. Dual degrees are offered, as well as student-designed majors and a 3-2 engineering program with numerous universities. Work-study and pass/fail options are possible. There are 89 national honor societies, including Phi Beta Kappa, a freshman honors program, and 99 departmental honors programs.

Faculty/Classroom: 70% of faculty are male; 30% are female. 95% teach undergraduates, all do research. Graduate students teach 38% of introductory courses. The average class size in an introductory lecture is 19; in a laboratory, 22; and in a regular course, 29.

Requirements: The SAT or ACT is required. The ACT Optional Writing test is also required. In addition, applicants should be graduates of accredited secondary schools or have the GED. High school preparation must include 4 years of English, 3 or more of math, 2 each of lab science and social studies, 2 of the same foreign language, and 2 of flexible academic units. A personal and professional essay is required. Visual arts applicants must submit a portfolio; performing arts applicants are required to audition. AP credits are accepted. Important factors in the admissions decision are advanced placement or honors courses, evidence of special talent, and geographical diversity.

Procedure: Freshmen are admitted fall. There are early decision, early admissions, and deferred admissions plans. Check with the school for current application deadlines. Application fee is $50. Applications are accepted online.

Transfer: Transfer application requirements differ by degree program. Generally, students transferring should have junior standing of 60 hours. Admission is also subject to the number of places available. 30 of 132 credits required for the bachelor's degree must be completed at Illinois.

Visiting: There are regularly scheduled orientations for prospective students, consisting of a university overview and admission presentation followed by student-led campus tour. There are guides for informal visits and visitors may sit in on classes. To schedule a visit, contact the Campus Visitors Center.

Financial Aid: The FAFSA is required. Check with the school for current application deadlines.

International Students: The school actively recruits these students. They must take the TOEFL with a minimum score of 550 on the paper-based TOEFL (PBT) or 79 on the Internet-based version (iBT), or take the IELTS. They must also take the SAT and ACT if the student has attended a U.S. institution for 2 or more years.

Computers: Wireless access is available. All students may use the college network in residence halls, classrooms, computer labs, or public spaces on campus. There are 3507 general access computers in on-campus computer labs, residence hall labs, and libraries. There are approximately another 1000 computers accessible in various departmental labs. There are also e-mail kiosks scattered over the campus, as well as wireless access to all buildings across campus. All students may access the system 24 hours a day. Students are limited to 20 hours per week on dial-in access only, unlimited for DCL or wireless. There are no fees. It is strongly recommended that all students have a personal computer. Students enrolled in law school must have a personal computer.

Admissions Contact: Stacey Kostell, Director of Undergraduate Admissions. A campus DVD is available. E-Mail: *admissions@illinois.edu* Web: *www.illinois.edu*

UNIVERSITY OF ST. FRANCIS — E-2

Joliet, IL 60435 (815) 740-3400
(800) 735-7500; (815) 740-5032

Full-time: 475 men, 889 women	**Faculty:** 80; IIA, -$
Part-time: 19 men, 39 women	**Ph.D.s:** 69%
Graduate: 194 men, 782 women	**Student/Faculty:** 14 to 1
Year: semesters, summer session	**Tuition:** $27,970
Application Deadline: August 1	**Room & Board:** $8520

Freshman Class: 1706 applied, 887 accepted, 237 enrolled
ACT: 23

COMPETITIVE

The University of St. Francis, founded as a college in 1920, is a private liberal arts and professional institution affiliated with the Roman Catholic Church. There are 4 undergraduate schools and 4 graduate schools. In addition to regional accreditation, USF has baccalaureate program accreditation with ACBSP, CSWE, NCATE, and NRPA. The library contains 142,761 volumes, 1,767 microform items, 8,718 audio/video tapes/CDs/DVDs, and subscribes to 20,585 periodicals including electronic. Computerized library services include interlibrary loans, database searching, Internet access, and Wi-Fi capability. Special learning facilities include an art gallery, radio station, TV station, Greenhouse, wireless education classroom, SimLab for nursing students, multimedia classrooms, Mock Trail courtroom in the Mode Building, and the Rialto Square Theater. The 24-acre campus is in a suburban area 35 miles southwest of Chicago. Including any residence halls, there are 7 buildings.

Student Life: 95% of undergraduates are from Illinois. Others are from 17 states. 90% are from public schools. 71% are White; 15% Hispanic. 55% are Catholic; 28% Protestant. The average age of freshmen is 18; all undergraduates, 22. 21% do not continue beyond their first year; 57% remain to graduate.

Housing: 402 students can be accommodated in college housing, which includes coed dorms and on-campus apartments. In addition, there are honors houses. On-campus housing is guaranteed for the freshman year only, is available on a first-come, first-served basis, and is available on a lottery system for upperclassmen. 74% of students commute. All students may keep cars.

Activities: There are no fraternities or sororities. There are 57 groups on campus, including and saints ambassador corps, business, nursing, art, cheerleading, choir, chorale, chorus, communications, computers, dance, drama, education, environmental, ethnic, gay, honors, international, literary magazine, musical theater, newspaper, opera, orchestra, pep band, political, professional, radio and TV, religious, social, social service, student government, and symphony. Popular campus events include Exchanging Cultures, Coming Out Week, Francis and Claire Week, Spring Fling, Homecoming, Sibs Weekend, Black History Month.

Sports: There are 9 intercollegiate sports for men and 9 for women, and 10 intramural sports for men and 10 for women. Facilities include A 10,000-seat football/soccer stadium with a Mondo-surface track around the turfed field and a 5,000-seat minor league baseball stadium are among the many off-campus facilities, as well as a six-field, lighted softball complex, three golf courses, two soccer fields and an indoor/outdoor tennis complex. On campus, a recreation center houses a 1,200-seat gymnasium, two racquetball courts, a golf hitting studio, and a state-of-the-art fitness center.

Disabled Students: All of the campus is accessible. Facilities include wheelchair ramps, elevators, special parking, specially equipped restrooms, special class scheduling, lowered drinking fountains, and special housing.

Services: Counseling and information services are available, as is tutoring in most subjects.

Campus Safety and Security: Measures include 24-hour foot and vehicle patrol, emergency notification system, and security escort services. There are shuttle buses, emergency telephones, lighted pathways/sidewalks, controlled access to dorms/residences, routine fire inspection.

Programs of Study: USF confers B.A., B.S., B.B.A., B.S.N and B.S.W. degrees. Master's and doctoral degrees are also awarded. Bachelor's degrees are awarded in BIOLOGICAL SCIENCE (biology/biological science), BUSINESS (accounting, banking and finance, business administration and management, entrepreneurial studies, international business management, logistics, management science, marketing/retailing/merchandising, organizational leadership and management, and recreational facilities management), COMMUNICATIONS AND THE ARTS (communications, English, journalism, music, and visual and performing arts), COMPUTER AND PHYSICAL SCIENCE (computer programming, computer science, information sciences and systems, mathematics, and web technology), EDUCATION (art education, elementary education, secondary education, and special education), ENGINEERING AND ENVIRONMENTAL DESIGN (computer technology and environmental science), HEALTH PROFESSIONS (allied health, health administration and policy, health care administration, medical technology, nuclear medical technology, nursing, predentistry, premedicine, preoptometry, prepharmacy, prephysical therapy, preveterinary science, radiation therapy, and radiograph medical technology), SOCIAL SCIENCE (counseling/psychology, criminal justice, history, liberal arts/general studies, political science/government, psychology, social work, and theological studies). Biology, education, and nursing are the strongest academically. Business, nursing, and biology have the largest enrollments.

Required: Undergraduate Graduation Requirements Candidates for the bachelor's degree must complete the following: -complete the Application for Graduation available in the Registrar's Office or through the MyUSF portal (Consult the Academic Calendar for specific deadlines) -earn a minimum of 128 semester hours of college credit -complete the residency requirement of a minimum of 32 semester hours of approved undergraduate credit at USF. All students must complete a minimum of fifteen (15) hours of upper division (300-400) course work, in the major, in residence at USF. In addition, thirty (30) of the last thirty-six (36) hours taken before graduation must be USF courses. (Note: individual colleges may have additional residency requirements) -complete all requirements with respect to the major program, support courses, liberal education, and electives -complete the writing intensive (WI) course requirements as listed below -achieve a cumulative grade point average of 2.0 or higher at USF -earn grades of "C" or higher in all courses required by the major and any minor programs -satisfy all financial requirements with the Business and Financial Aid Offices It is the responsibility of the student to see that all graduation requirements are met. If a student withdraws for more than one semester, the catalog and regulations in effect at the time of their return will apply. Students completing a double major must select which degree they wish to receive since the University only awards one degree at graduation (however, the second major will appear on the transcript). If a student returns to complete a second major, they may apply for a second degree only if the new major leads to a different degree and they have met the current general education requirements in place at the time of awarding.

Special: Internships, on- and off-campus, paid and unpaid, are available in most majors. Dual and interdisciplinary majors, a pass/fail option, a Washington semester, study abroad, cross-registration with OCICU (Online Consortium of Independent Colleges and Universities), and credit for life, military, and work experience are available. There are 16 national honor societies and a freshman honors program.

Faculty/Classroom: 41% of faculty are male; 59% are female. 77% teach undergraduates. No introductory courses are taught by graduate stu-

dents. The average class size in an introductory lecture is 20 and in a laboratory is 20.

Admissions: 52% of the 2013-2014 applicants were accepted. The SAT scores for the 2013-2014 freshman class were: Critical Reading--22% below 500, 56% between 500 and 599, and 22% between 600 and 699; Math--45% below 500, 33% between 500 and 599, and 22% between 600 and 699; Writing--45% below 500, 33% between 500 and 599, and 22% between 600 and 699. The ACT scores were 23% below 21, 33% between 21 and 23, 30% between 24 and 26, 9% between 27 and 28, and 5% above 28. 37% of the current freshmen were in the top fifth of their class; 72% were in the top two fifths.

Requirements: The ACT is required. In addition, applicants must take 4 years of English, 3 of either art, music, foreign language, or computer science, and 3 math, including geometry, 2 science (1 lab), 2 social studies and 3 electives. USF requires applicants to be in the upper 50% of their class. A GPA of 2.5 is required. AP and CLEP credits are accepted. Important factors in the admissions decision are leadership record, advanced placement or honors courses, and personality/intangible qualities.

Procedure: Freshmen are admitted fall and spring. Entrance exams should be taken in the spring of the junior year or the fall of the senior year. There are deferred admissions and rolling admissions plans. Applications should be filed by August 1 for fall entry, along with a $30 fee. Notifications are sent September 15. Applications are accepted online.

Transfer: 190 transfer students enrolled in 2012-2013. Transfer students must have a GPA of 2.5 and must submit transcripts from colleges previously attended. Applicants with fewer than 30 semester hours must also submit high school transcripts. Applicants must have taken English at the college level, and math at the intermediate algebra level. 32 of 128 credits required for the bachelor's degree must be completed at USF.

Visiting: There are regularly scheduled orientations for prospective students, Visiting students can participate in an orientation, meet faculty, a tour, and student presentations. There are guides for informal visits, visitors may sit in on classes, and stay overnight. To schedule a visit, contact the Welcome Center at (815) 740-2270.

Financial Aid: In 2013-2014, 100% of all full-time freshmen and 99% of continuing full-time students received some form of financial aid. 59% of all full-time freshmen and 64% of continuing full-time students received need-based aid. The average freshman award was $24,654. Need-based scholarships or need-based grants averaged $8,914; need-based self-help aid (loans and jobs) averaged $5,422; non-need-based athletic scholarships averaged $9,434; and other non-need-based awards and non-need-based scholarships averaged $13,321. Average annual earnings from campus work are $1340. The average financial indebtedness of the 2013 graduate was $24,941. The FAFSA and the college's own financial statement are required. The priority date for freshman financial aid applications for fall entry is Febraury 15.

International Students: There are 19 international students enrolled. They must take the TOEFL with a minimum score of 550 on the paper-based TOEFL (PBT) or 79 on the Internet-based version (iBT). They must also take the SAT or ACT, scoring 20.

Computers: All students may access the system. 24 hours a day. There are no time limits. There is a fee.

Graduates: From July 1, 2012 to June 30, 2013, 343 bachelor's degrees were awarded. The most popular majors were nursing (27%), business (14%), and education (1%). 42 companies recruited on campus in 2012-2013. In an average class, 32% graduate in 4 years or less, 54% graduate in 5 years or less, and 57% graduate in 6 years or less.

Admissions Contact: Cynthia Lambert, Director of Undergraduate Admissions. E-Mail: *admissions@stfrancis.edu* Web: *www.stfrancis.edu*

VANDERCOOK COLLEGE OF MUSIC — E-2

Chicago, IL 60616-3731 (312) 225-6288
(800) 448-2655; (312) 225-5211

Full-time: 50 men, 35 women	**Faculty:** n/av
Part-time: 1 man, 4 women	**Ph.D.s:** 70%
Graduate: 35 men, 40 women	**Student/Faculty:** n/av
Year: semesters	**Tuition:** $23,690
Application Deadline: see profile	**Room & Board:** $10,400
Freshman Class: n/av	
SAT or ACT: required	**SPECIAL**

VanderCook College of Music, founded in 1909, is devoted solely to the preparation of music educators. The figures in the above capsule and in this profile are approximate. There is 1 graduate school. In addition to regional accreditation, VCM has baccalaureate program accreditation with NASM. The 2 libraries contain 20,000 volumes, 2000 microform items, and 5000 audio/video tapes/CDs/DVDs, and subscribe to 80 periodicals including electronic. Computerized library services include interlibrary loans and database searching. Special learning facilities include a learning resource center. The 1-acre campus is in an urban area 3 miles from the center of Chicago.

Student Life: 60% of undergraduates are from Illinois. Others are from 11 states, 1 foreign country, and Canada. 80% are from public schools. 63% are white; 32% African American. The average age of freshmen is 19; all undergraduates, 21. 8% do not continue beyond their first year; 80% remain to graduate.

Housing: 100 students can be accommodated in college housing, which includes single-sex and coed dorms, on-campus apartments, and married student housing. In addition, there are fraternity houses. On-campus housing is guaranteed for all 4 years. 60% of students live on campus; of those, 90% remain on campus on weekends. Alcohol is not permitted. All students may keep cars.

Activities: 50% of men belong to 2 local fraternities and 1 national fraternity; 20% of women belong to 2 local sororities and 1 national sorority. There are 10 groups on campus, including band, choir, chorale, chorus, jazz band, musical theater, orchestra, pep band, religious, and student government.

Sports: There is no sports program at VCM. Facilities include a swimming pool, a gym, and tennis courts.

Disabled Students: Facilities include special parking and special class scheduling.

Campus Safety and Security: Measures include 24-hour foot and vehicle patrol, self-defense education, and security escort services. There are shuttle buses, emergency telephones, and lighted pathways/sidewalks.

Programs of Study: VCM confers B.M.Ed degrees. Master's degrees are also awarded. Bachelor's degrees are awarded in EDUCATION (music education).

Required: To graduate, students must complete a total of 134 semester hours distributed in the 5 major categories of general education, professional education, applied music performance, fundamentals and theory, and music education. They must also pass performance proficiency exams on 17 instruments and a vocal proficiency exam.

Faculty/Classroom: 44% of faculty are male; 56% are female. All teach undergraduates. No introductory courses are taught by graduate students. The average class size in an introductory lecture is 15; in a laboratory, 15; and in a regular course, 15.

Requirements: The SAT or ACT is required. Graduation from an accredited secondary school or a satisfactory score on the GED is required for admission. Secondary school courses must include 3 units each of English and science, 2 each of math, social studies, music, and a foreign language, and 1 each of history and art. An audition and an interview are required. VCM requires applicants to be in the upper 75% of their class. A GPA of 2.0 is required. AP and CLEP credits are accepted. Important factors in the admissions decision are evidence of special talent, recommendations by alumni, and extracurricular activities record.

Procedure: Freshmen are admitted fall and spring. Entrance exams should be taken during the junior year. There are early decision, early admissions, deferred admissions, and rolling admissions plans. Check with the school for current application deadlines. Application fee is $35.

Transfer: Transfer students must have a minimum GPA of 2.5. An audition and an interview are required. Courses taken at other institutions in performance, theory, and history must be validated.

Visiting: There are regularly scheduled orientations for prospective students, including the opportunity to observe a class, meet students and faculty, and tour the campus. There are guides for informal visits, and visitors may sit in on classes and stay overnight. To schedule a visit, contact the Director of Admission.

Financial Aid: The FAFSA is required. Check with the school for current application deadlines.

International Students: They must take the TOEFL. They must also take the SAT or ACT.

Computers: All students may access the system. There are no time limits and no fees.

Admissions Contact: Director of Admissions. E-mail: *admissions@vandercook.edu* Web: *www.vandercook.edu*

WESTERN ILLINOIS UNIVERSITY — C-3

Macomb, IL 61455 (309) 298-3157
(877) PICK WIU; (309) 298-3111

Full-time: 4531 men, 4274 women	**Faculty:** 589; IIA, -$	
Part-time: 522 men, 546 women	**Ph.D.s:** 73%	
Graduate: 745 men, 1089 women	**Student/Faculty:** 15 to 1	
Year: semesters, summer session	**Tuition:** $10,940 ($15,143)	
Application Deadline: May 15	**Room & Board:** $9190	
Freshman Class: 10544 applied, 6260 accepted, 1652 enrolled		
SAT: required	**ACT:** 23	**COMPETITIVE**

WIU-Macomb, a traditional, residential four-year campus, opened its doors in September 1902. WIU-Quad Cities, a metropolitan, non-residential campus and the only public university in the Quad Cities, has been providing educational opportunities to the region for more than 50 years. There are 5 undergraduate schools and one graduate school. In addition to regional accreditation, WIU has baccalaureate program accreditation with

AACSB, ABET, ADA, ASLA, CAHEA, CSWE, NASAD, NASM, NCATE, and NRPA. The 5 libraries contain 994,880 volumes, 107,614 microform items, 21,908 audio/video tapes/CDs/DVDs, and subscribes to 7,098 periodicals including electronic. Computerized library services include interlibrary loans, database searching, Internet access, and Wi-Fi capability. Special learning facilities include an art gallery, natural history museum, radio station, TV station, international studies center. The 1050-acre campus is in a rural area 76 miles from Peoria and 151 miles from St. Louis, Missouri. Including any residence halls, there are 64 buildings.

Student Life: 86% of undergraduates are from Illinois. Others are from 38 states, 49 foreign countries, and Canada. 81% are from public schools. 70% are White; 16% African American. The average age of freshmen is 18; all undergraduates, 22. 37% do not continue beyond their first year; 56% remain to graduate.

Housing: 4400 students can be accommodated in college housing, which includes single-sex and coed dorms, on-campus apartments, and married student housing. In addition, there are honors houses, special-interest houses, academic majors, honors, and wellness floors in residence halls. On-campus housing is guaranteed for all 4 years. 58% of students commute. Alcohol is not permitted. All students may keep cars.

Activities: 6% of men belong to 19 national fraternities; 6% of women belong to 10 national sororities. There are 254 groups on campus, including art, band, cheerleading, chess, choir, chorale, chorus, computers, dance, drama, drill team, environmental, ethnic, gay, honors, international, jazz band, literary magazine, marching band, musical theater, newspaper, opera, orchestra, pep band, photography, political, professional, radio and TV, religious, social, social service, student government, and symphony. Popular campus events include Family Weekend, Homecoming Weekend, and International Bazaar.

Sports: There are 10 intercollegiate sports for men and 10 for women, and 40 intramural sports for men and 40 for women. Facilities include an 18 hole golf course, tennis courts, a basketball court, a swimming pool, a recreation center, and softball, soccer, and football fields.

Disabled Students: 95% of the campus is accessible. Facilities include wheelchair ramps, elevators, special parking, specially equipped restrooms, special class scheduling, lowered drinking fountains, and lowered telephones.

Services: Counseling and information services are available, as is tutoring in some subjects, business, art, English, math, computer science, science, social sciences, and humanities There is a reader service for the blind, and remedial math and writing.

Campus Safety and Security: Measures include 24-hour foot and vehicle patrol, emergency notification system, self-defense education, and security escort services. There are shuttle buses, emergency telephones, lighted pathways/sidewalks, a beacon/call box system, student patrols.

Programs of Study: WIU confers B.A., B.B., B.F.A, B.M., B.S., B.S.Ed. and B.S.W degrees. Master's and doctoral degrees are also awarded. Bachelor's degrees are awarded in AGRICULTURE (agriculture), BIOLOGICAL SCIENCE (biology/biological science), BUSINESS (accounting, banking and finance, business administration and management, finance, management information systems, marketing/retailing/merchandising, personnel management, and supply chain management), COMMUNICATIONS AND THE ARTS (art, broadcasting, communications, dramatic arts, English, French, journalism, music, musical theater, and Spanish), COMPUTER AND PHYSICAL SCIENCE (chemistry, computer science, geology, mathematics, and physics), EDUCATION (athletic training, bilingual/bicultural education, elementary education, general studies, industrial arts education, physical education, and special education), ENGINEERING AND ENVIRONMENTAL DESIGN (construction management, engineering, fire protection science, industrial engineering technology, and manufacturing technology), HEALTH PROFESSIONS (exercise science, health science, kinesiology, medical technology, nursing, and speech pathology/audiology), SOCIAL SCIENCE (African American studies, anthropology, economics, family/consumer studies, geography, history, interdisciplinary studies, law enforcement and corrections, liberal arts/general studies, parks and recreation management, philosophy, political science/government, psychology, religion, social work, sociology, and women's studies). Accounting, chemistry, and human resource management are the strongest academically. Law enforcement and justice administration and elementary education has the largest enrollments.

Required: To graduate, all students must complete at least 120 credit hours with at least 32 hours in the major and have a minimum 2.0 GPA. Students must take 43 hours in the fields of basic skills, well-being, natural science and math, historical and social foundations, and humanities.

Special: WIU offers internships in business, law enforcement, and physical training to name a few; study abroad group and exchange programs; and dual programs in engineering and clinical laboratory science. Student-designed majors and independent study are available through the Experimental Studies, General Studies, and Interdisciplinary Studies programs. The General Studies degree program offers credit for work experience. Also available are a field campus and a life science station on the Mississippi River. There are 30 national honor societies, a freshman honors program, and 34 departmental honors programs.

Faculty/Classroom: 55% of faculty are male; 45% are female. 99% teach undergraduates, 90% do research, and 90% do both. Graduate students teach 3% of introductory courses. The average class size in an introductory lecture is 28; in a laboratory is 21; and in a regular course is 20.

Admissions: 59% of the 2013-2014 applicants were accepted. The ACT scores were 50% below 21, 27% between 21 and 23, 12% between 24 and 26, 5% between 27 and 28, and 5% above 28. 19% of the current freshmen were in the top fifth of their class; 44% were in the top two fifths.

Requirements: The SAT or ACT is required. Students must have 4 years of English, 3 years each of math, science, and social studies, and 2 electives in art, film, foreign language, music, speech, theater, journalism, religion, philosophy, or vocational education. Academic Services is a program for selected students who do not meet regular admission requirements. A GPA of 2.2 is required. AP and CLEP credits are accepted.

Procedure: Freshmen are admitted fall, spring, and summer. Entrance exams should be taken by April of the senior year. There are deferred admissions and rolling admissions plans. Applications should be filed by May 15 for fall entry, along with a $30 fee. Applications are accepted online.

Transfer: 1243 transfer students enrolled in 2012-2013. Students transferring fewer than 24 semester credits or 36 quarter credits must meet freshman admissions standards, have a combined C average for all hours attempted, and be in good standing at their previous college. 30 of 120 credits required for the bachelor's degree must be completed at WIU.

Visiting: There are regularly scheduled orientations for prospective students, Registration, Continental Breakfast, University Fair, Program & Q/A, Tours, Meet w/ an Advisor, Lunch & Residence Hall tour, Financial Aid session. There are guides for informal visits, visitors may sit in on classes, and stay overnight. To schedule a visit, contact the Admissions Office.

Financial Aid: In 2013-2014, 88% of all full-time freshmen and 88% of continuing full-time students received some form of financial aid. 71% of all full-time freshmen and 67% of continuing full-time students received need-based aid. The average freshman award was $13,775. Need-based scholarships or need-based grants averaged $5,588; need-based self-help aid (loans and jobs) averaged $2,848; non-need-based athletic scholarships averaged $269; other non-need-based awards and non-need-based scholarships averaged $1,060; and $4,010 from other forms of aid. 18% of undergraduate students work part-time. Average annual earnings from campus work are $2080. The average financial indebtedness of the 2013 graduate was $25,187. The priority date for freshman financial aid applications for fall entry is February 15. The deadline for filing freshman financial aid applications for fall entry is open.

International Students: There are 159 international students enrolled. The school actively recruits these students. They must take the TOEFL with a minimum score of 550 on the paper-based TOEFL (PBT) or 79 on the Internet-based version (iBT), or successfully complete WIU's ESL program.

Computers: All students may access the system any time. There are no time limits and no fees.

Graduates: From July 1, 2012 to June 30, 2013, 2353 bachelor's degrees were awarded. The most popular majors were law enforcement and justice (16%), bachelor of general studies (10%), and elementary education (6%). 105 companies recruited on campus in 2012-2013. In an average class, 31% graduate in 4 years or less, 50% graduate in 5 years or less, and 54% graduate in 6 years or less.

Admissions Contact: Office of Admissions E-Mail: *admissions@wiu.edu* Web: *http:/www.wiu.edu/student_services/undergraduate_admissions/*

WHEATON COLLEGE E-2

Wheaton, IL 60187 (630) 752-5005
(800) 222-2419; (630) 752-5285

Full-time: 1152 men, 1226 women	**Faculty:** n/av; IIB, av$
Part-time: 38 men, 28 women	**Ph.D.s:** 96%
Graduate: 222 men, 327 women	**Student/Faculty:** n/av
Year: semesters, summer session	**Tuition:** n/av
Application Deadline: January 10	**Room & Board:** $8770
Freshman Class: 1941 applied, 1364 accepted, 597 enrolled	
SAT CR/M/W: 660/650/660 **ACT:** 30	**HIGHLY COMPETITIVE+**

Wheaton College, founded in 1860, is a private nondenominational institution committed to providing students with a Christian education. A liberal arts school, it offers undergraduate programs in the sciences, business, the arts and fine arts, music, teacher preparation, and religious and Biblical studies. There is one undergraduate school and one graduate school. In addition to regional accreditation, Wheaton has baccalaureate program accreditation with NASM and NCATE. The library contains 489,856 volumes, 202,133 microform items, 36,668 audio/video tapes/CDs/DVDs, and subscribes to 6,325 periodicals including electronic. Computerized library services include interlibrary loans, database searching, Internet access, and Wi-Fi capability. Special learning facilities include an art gallery, radio station, TV station, a communications resource center with TV and audio studios, a special collection of British authors' books and papers, an evangelical museum with document archives, and the Center for Applied Christian Ethics. The Science Building includes A unique, interactive atrium museum featuring the Perry Mastodon, a geology exhibit, a natural history exhibit, a Foucault pendulum, and additional exhibits. The 80-acre campus is in a suburban area 25 miles west of Chicago. Including any residence halls, there are 54 buildings.

Student Life: 74% of undergraduates are from out of state, mostly the Mid-West. Students are from 50 states, 36 foreign countries, and Canada. 54% are from public schools. 78% are White. 99% are Protestant. The average age of freshmen is 18; all undergraduates, 20. 5% do not continue beyond their first year; 87% remain to graduate.

Housing: 2156 students can be accommodated in college housing, which includes single-sex and coed dorms, on-campus apartments, off-campus apartments, and married student housing. In addition, the college owns and rents houses to groups of students. On-campus housing is guaranteed for all 4 years, is available on a first-come, first-served basis, and is available on a lottery system for upperclassmen. 90% of students live on campus; of those, 95% remain on campus on weekends. Alcohol is not permitted. Upperclassmen may keep cars.

Activities: There are no fraternities or sororities. There are 92 groups on campus, including art, band, cheerleading, chess, choir, chorale, chorus, dance, debate, drama, environmental, ethnic, film, international, jazz band, literary magazine, musical theater, newspaper, opera, orchestra, pep band, political, professional, radio and TV, religious, social, social service, student government, symphony, and yearbook. Popular campus events include New Student Orientation, College Union Concerts and Talent Show.

Sports: There are 11 intercollegiate sports for men and 10 for women, and 11 intramural sports for men and 9 for women. Facilities include A sports and recreation complex that features an 8,000-square-foot weight room, 3 student recreational gyms, an elevated jogging track, a climbing wall, recreation center, natatorium, and the King Arena.

Disabled Students: 97% of the campus is accessible. Facilities include wheelchair ramps, elevators, special parking, specially equipped restrooms, lowered drinking fountains, lowered telephones. including housing for disabled students is provided as needed.

Services: Counseling and information services are available, as is tutoring in most subjects. There is a reader service for the blind. and a writing center. Other services are provided as needed.

Campus Safety and Security: Measures include 24-hour foot and vehicle patrol, emergency notification system, self-defense education, and security escort services. There are shuttle buses, emergency telephones, lighted pathways/sidewalks, and controlled access to dorms/residences.

Programs of Study: Wheaton confers B.A., B.S., B.M. and B.M.E. degrees. Master's and doctoral degrees are also awarded. Bachelor's degrees are awarded in BIOLOGICAL SCIENCE (biology/biological science), BUSINESS (business economics), COMMUNICATIONS AND THE ARTS (art, classical languages, communications, English, French, German, music, and Spanish), COMPUTER AND PHYSICAL SCIENCE (chemistry, computer science, geology, mathematics, and physics), EDUCATION (Christian education, elementary education, music education, and secondary education), ENGINEERING AND ENVIRONMENTAL DESIGN (engineering and environmental science), HEALTH PROFESSIONS (health science and nursing), SOCIAL SCIENCE (anthropology, archeology, biblical studies, economics, history, interdisciplinary studies, international relations, philosophy, political science/government, psychology, social science, sociology, and urban studies). Business economics, English and biology have the largest enrollments.

Required: To graduate, students must complete 124 semester hours, with 36 in upper-division courses and a minimum of 32 in a major, and maintain at least a 2.0 GPA. Students must satisfactorily meet all general education requirements in the areas of competency, Applied Health Science, and five learning clusters that include Studies in Faith and Reason, Nature, Society, Diversity, and Literature and the Arts; as well as a senior capstone course in the major.

Special: There are 12 national honor societies and 15 departmental honors programs.

Faculty/Classroom: 64% of faculty are male; 36% are female. All teach and do research. No introductory courses are taught by graduate students. The average class size in an introductory lecture is 31; in a laboratory is 16; and in a regular course is 21.

Admissions: 70% of the 2013-2014 applicants were accepted. The SAT scores for the 2013-2014 freshman class were: Critical Reading--2% below 500, 22% between 500 and 599, 44% between 600 and 699, and 32% between 700 and 800; Math--2% below 500, 24% between 500 and 599, 47% between 600 and 699, and 27% between 700 and 800; Writing--2% below 500, 18% between 500 and 599, 53% between 600 and 699, and 27% between 700 and 800. 78% of the current freshmen were in the top fifth of their class; 93% were in the top two fifths. There were 20 National Merit finalists.

Requirements: The SAT or ACT is required. The ACT Optional Writing test is also required. A high school diploma is required and the GED is accepted. Wheaton requires a general college preparatory program of 18 units, including 4 of English, 3 to 4 of math, science, and social studies, and 2 to 3 of a foreign language. AP credits are accepted. Important factors in the admissions decision are recommendations by school officials, advanced placement or honors courses, and personality/intangible qualities.

Procedure: Freshmen are admitted fall. Entrance exams should be taken in October of senior year (early action) and December. There are early admissions and deferred admissions plans. Applications should be filed by January 10 for fall entry, along with a $50 fee. Notifications are sent April 1. 126 applicants were on the 2013 waiting list; 45 were admitted. Applications are accepted online.

Transfer: 75 transfer students enrolled in 2012-2013. Applicants must have completed 15 semester hours with a 3.0 average and present a high school transcript, college transcript, and an essay or personal statement. 48 of 124 credits required for the bachelor's degree must be completed at Wheaton.

Visiting: There are regularly scheduled orientations for prospective students, consisting of presentations by faculty, administrators, students, and financial aid, and admissions staff, as well as social activities. There are guides for informal visits, visitors may sit in on classes, and stay overnight. To schedule a visit, contact the Admissions Office.

Financial Aid: In 2013-2014, 72% of all full-time freshmen and 71% of continuing full-time students received some form of financial aid. 54% of all full-time freshmen and 51% of continuing full-time students received need-based aid. The average freshman award was $22,638. Need-based scholarships or need-based grants averaged $20,336 ($42,390 maximum); need-based self-help aid (loans and jobs) averaged $4,991 ($7,500 maximum); and other non-need-based awards and non-need-based scholarships averaged $6,950 ($43,929 maximum). 41% of undergraduate students work part-time. Average annual earnings from campus work are $1181. The average financial indebtedness of the 2013 graduate was $25,413. Wheaton is a member of CSS. The FAFSA and the college's own financial statement are required. The priority date for freshman financial aid applications for fall entry is February 15.

International Students: There are 45 international students enrolled. The school actively recruits these students. They must take the TOEFL with a minimum score of 587 on the paper-based TOEFL (PBT) or 95 on the Internet-based version (iBT), and also take the TSE and TWE. They must also take the SAT or ACT.

Computers: All students may access the system 24 hours a day. There are no time limits and no fees.

Graduates: From July 1, 2012 to June 30, 2013, 652 bachelor's degrees were awarded. The most popular majors were business economics (9%), English (8%), and biology (6%). In an average class, 78% graduate in 4 years or less, 86% graduate in 5 years or less, and 87% graduate in 6 years or less. Of the 2012 graduating class, 25% were enrolled in graduate school within 6 months of graduation, and 77% were employed.

Admissions Contact: Shawn Leftwich, Director of Admissions. E-Mail: *admissions@wheaton.edu* Web: *www.wheaton.edu*

INDIANA

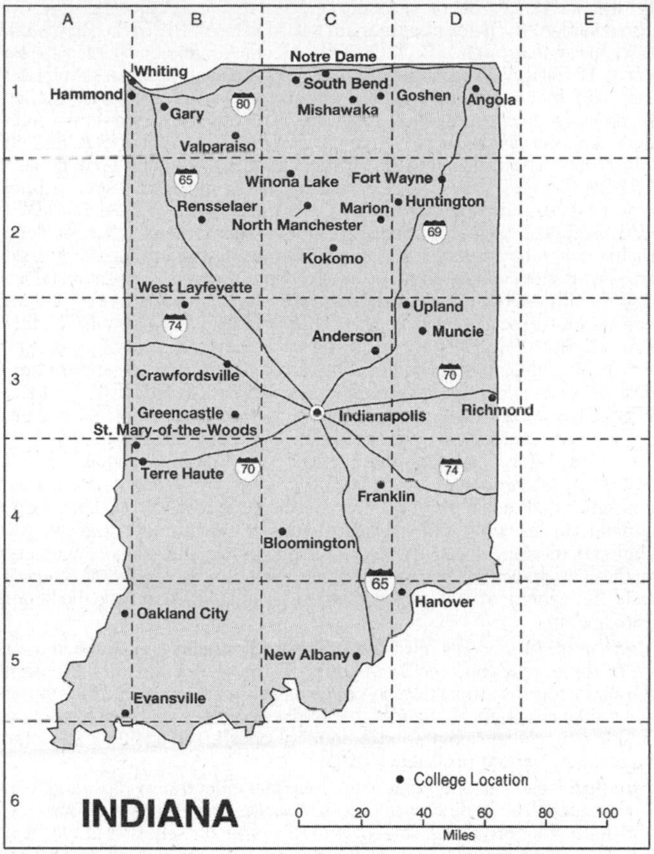

ANDERSON UNIVERSITY — C-3

Anderson, IN 46012 (765) 641-4080
(800) 428-6414; (765) 641-4091

Full-time: 703 men, 1034 women	**Faculty:** 132; IIB, --$
Part-time: 102 men, 177 women	**Ph.D.s:** 70%
Graduate: 255 men, 171 women	**Student/Faculty:** 11 to 1
Year: semesters, summer session	**Tuition:** $26,200
Application Deadline: open	**Room & Board:** $9110

Freshman Class: 2734 applied, 1516 accepted, 444 enrolled
SAT CR/M: 515/527 **ACT:** 23 **COMPETITIVE**

Anderson University, founded in 1917, is a private liberal arts institution affiliated with the Church of God. The university offers programs in theoretical and applied science, social and professional studies, the arts, culture, and religion. There are 5 undergraduate schools and 4 graduate schools. In addition to regional accreditation, Anderson has baccalaureate program accreditation with ACBSP, CSWE, NASM, NCATE, and NLN. The library contains 263,058 volumes, 54,767 microform items, 8,280 audio/video tapes/CDs/DVDs, and subscribes to 457 periodicals including electronic. Computerized library services include interlibrary loans and database searching. Special learning facilities include an art gallery, radio station, and the Museum of the Bible and the Ancient Near East. The 163-acre campus is in a suburban area 40 miles northeast of Indianapolis. Including any residence halls, there are 36 buildings.

Student Life: 72% of undergraduates are from Indiana. Others are from 42 states, 18 foreign countries, and Canada. 97% are from public schools. 80% are White. 48% are Protestant; 42% claim no religious affiliation. The average age of freshmen is 19; all undergraduates, 22. 27% do not continue beyond their first year; 57% remain to graduate.

Housing: 1271 students can be accommodated in college housing, which includes single-sex dorms, on-campus apartments, off-campus apartments, and married student housing. On-campus housing is guaranteed for all 4 years. 64% of students live on campus; of those, 50% remain on campus on weekends. Alcohol is not permitted. All students may keep cars.

Activities: There are no fraternities or sororities. There are 41 groups on campus, including art, band, cheerleading, choir, chorale, dance, debate, drama, ethnic, film, honors, international, jazz band, literary magazine, musical theater, newspaper, opera, orchestra, photography, political, professional, radio and TV, religious, social, social service, student government, and symphony. Popular campus events include Heritage Week, Spiritual Emphasis Week, Candles and Carols Christmas Performance.

Sports: There are 8 intercollegiate sports for men and 8 for women, and 7 intramural sports for men and 7 for women. Facilities include 2 gyms, football, baseball/softball, and soccer fields, an 8-lane all-weather track, tennis courts, a bowling alley, and a game room. The campus stadium seats 4200 and the indoor gym seats 2400.

Disabled Students: 97% of the campus is accessible. Facilities include wheelchair ramps, elevators, special parking, specially equipped restrooms, special class scheduling, lowered drinking fountains, and lowered telephones.

Services: Counseling and information services are available, as is tutoring in most subjects. There is a reader service for the blind, and remedial math, reading, and writing.

Campus Safety and Security: Measures include 24-hour foot and vehicle patrol, emergency notification system, self defense education, and security escort services. There are emergency telephones, lighted pathways/sidewalks, and Indiana State police academy graduates are security officers.

Programs of Study: Anderson confers B.A., B.S., B.Mus., B.S.N. and B.S.E. degrees. Associate, master's, and doctoral degrees are also awarded. Bachelor's degrees are awarded in BIOLOGICAL SCIENCE (biology/biological science), BUSINESS (accounting, banking and finance, business administration and management, management science, marketing/retailing/merchandising, and sports management), COMMUNICATIONS AND THE ARTS (communications, dramatic arts, English, fine arts, French, graphic design, music business management, music performance, and Spanish), COMPUTER AND PHYSICAL SCIENCE (chemistry, computer science, mathematics, and physics), EDUCATION (art education, Christian education, elementary education, foreign languages education, health education, music education, physical education, science education, and social studies education), HEALTH PROFESSIONS (medical laboratory technology and nursing), SOCIAL SCIENCE (criminal justice, economics, family/consumer studies, history, philosophy, political science/government, psychology, religion, social work, and sociology). Physical sciences is the strongest academically. Business, education and nursing have the largest enrollments.

Required: Requirements for graduation include 124 credit hours with 40 to 58 hours in the general education core and at least 36 hours in the major. A minimum 2.0 GPA overall and in the major is required. All students must complete a liberal arts seminar. The last 24 credit hours must be taken in residence.

Special: Anderson offers co-op programs with Purdue University, internships, study abroad in 25 countries through the International Studies Program, and a Washington semester. Also available are credit for military experience and pass/fail options. Courses in electronic engineering may be taken through the Purdue Anderson campus. Preprofessional programs are offered in medical, podiatry, dentistry, law, engineering, seminary, and several allied health fields. There are 16 national honor societies, a freshman honors program, and 10 departmental honors programs.

Faculty/Classroom: 60% of faculty are male; 40% are female. 94% teach undergraduates. No introductory courses are taught by graduate students. The average class size in an introductory lecture is 22; in a laboratory is 18; and in a regular course is 17.

Admissions: 55% of the 2013-2014 applicants were accepted. The SAT scores for the 2013-2014 freshman class were: Critical Reading--43% below 500, 43% between 500 and 599, 13% between 600 and 699, and 1% between 700 and 800; Math--34% below 500, 46% between 500 and 599, 17% between 600 and 699, and 3% between 700 and 800. The ACT scores were 23% below 21, 32% between 21 and 23, 27% between 24 and 26, 9% between 27 and 28, and 9% above 28. 45% of the current freshmen were in the top fifth of their class; 71% were in the top two fifths. 10 freshmen graduated first in their class.

Requirements: The SAT or ACT is required. Applicants must be graduates of an accredited secondary school or have a GED certificate and submit a photograph, references, and a health form. A GPA of 2.0 is required. AP and CLEP credits are accepted. Important factors in the admissions decision are leadership record, recommendations by alumni, and personality/intangible qualities.

Procedure: Freshmen are admitted fall and spring. Entrance exams should be taken in the fall of the junior year. There is a rolling admissions plan. Application deadlines are open. Application fee is $25. Applications are accepted online.

Transfer: 98 transfer students enrolled in 2012-2013. Applicants must have a minimum 2.0 GPA, satisfactory SAT or ACT scores, and transcripts for all previously attended colleges. 24 of 124 credits required for the bachelor's degree must be completed at Anderson.

Visiting: There are regularly scheduled orientations for prospective stu-

dents, including a campus tour, an academic overview, a financial aid and athletics overview, and appointments with professors and departmental chairs. There are guides for informal visits, visitors may sit in on classes, and stay overnight. To schedule a visit, contact the Admissions Office at (765) 641-4082.

Financial Aid: Anderson is a member of CSS. The FAFSA is required. Check with the school for current application deadlines.

International Students: There are 63 international students enrolled. They must take the TOEFL with a minimum score of 547 on the paper-based TOEFL (PBT). They must also take the SAT, scoring 880.

Graduates: From July 1, 2012 to June 30, 2013, 426 bachelor's degrees were awarded. The most popular majors were business/marketing (24%), education (13%), and health professions and related programs (10%). 35 companies recruited on campus in 2012-2013. In an average class, 46% graduate in 4 years or less, 56% graduate in 5 years or less, and 57% graduate in 6 years or less.

Admissions Contact: Admissions Counselor E-Mail: *info@anderson.edu* Web: *www.anderson.edu*

BALL STATE UNIVERSITY D-3

Muncie, IN 47306 (765) 285-8300
(800) 482-4BSU; (765) 285-1632

Full-time: 6711 men, 8886 women	**Faculty:** 949; I, --$
Part-time: 447 men, 608 women	**Ph.D.s:** 73%
Graduate: 1409 men, 2992 women	**Student/Faculty:** 16 to 1
Year: semesters, summer session	**Tuition:** $8980 ($23,650)
Application Deadline: May 1	**Room & Board:** $8870
Freshman Class: 14302 applied, 9659 accepted, 3844 enrolled	
SAT CR/M/W: 530/530/510	**ACT:** 22 **COMPETITIVE**

Ball State University, founded in 1918, is a public university offering undergraduate and graduate programs through 7 academic colleges in applied sciences and technology, architecture and planning, business, communication, information, and media, fine arts, sciences and humanities, and teacher education. There are 7 undergraduate schools and 1 graduate school. In addition to regional accreditation, Ball State has baccalaureate program accreditation with AACSB, ABET, ACBSP, ACEJMC, ADA, AHEA, ASLA, CAHEA, CSAB, CSWE, NAAB, NASAD, NASM, NCATE, NLN, and TEAC. The 3 libraries contain 1.1 million volumes, 1.1 million microform items, and 433,494 audio/video tapes/CDs/DVDs, and subscribe to 2,944 periodicals including electronic. Computerized library services include interlibrary loans, database searching, Internet access, and Wi-Fi capability. Special learning facilities include an art gallery, planetarium, radio station, TV station, research centers in solar energy, human performance, and international programs. The 1140-acre campus is in a suburban area 56 miles northwest of Indianapolis. Including any residence halls, there are 106 buildings.

Student Life: 90% of undergraduates are from Indiana. Others are from 50 states, 44 foreign countries, and Canada. 91% are from public schools. 85% are White. The average age of freshmen is 18; all undergraduates, 20.

Housing: 6906 students can be accommodated in college housing, which includes single-sex and coed dorms, on-campus apartments, and married student housing. In addition, there are honors houses, special-interest houses, living learning communities, wellness housing. On-campus housing is guaranteed for the freshman year only. 58% of students commute. Alcohol is not permitted. All students may keep cars.

Activities: 10% of men belong to 15 national fraternities; 11% of women belong to 1 local and 16 national sororities. There are 369 groups on campus, including art, band, cheerleading, chess, choir, chorale, chorus, computers, dance, debate, drama, drill team, ethnic, film, forensics, gay, honors, international, jazz band, literary magazine, marching band, musical theater, newspaper, opera, orchestra, pep band, photography, political, professional, radio and TV, religious, social, social service, student government, and symphony. Popular campus events include Late Night Carnival, Unity Week and Family Weekend.

Sports: Facilities include the student recreation/wellness facility, which holds a 13,000-sq-ft fitness center with elevated jogging track, a 5-court basketball/volleyball gym, a 33-ft climbing wall, indoor turf field including 2 batting cages, an auxiliary gym, a game room, 9 racquetball/handball and 2 wallyball courts, a 6-lane, 25-yd competitive pool, and a field sports building. There is also a fitness center, an 11,500-seat arena and a 22,500-seat stadium.

Disabled Students: 95% of the campus is accessible. Facilities include wheelchair ramps, elevators, special parking, specially equipped restrooms, special class scheduling, lowered drinking fountains, lowered telephones, special housing, A special resource guide, an accessibility map (including tactile), and text telephones (TDD) in all key offices are also available.

Services: Counseling and information services are available, as is tutoring in most subjects. There is a reader service for the blind.

Campus Safety and Security: Measures include 24-hour foot and vehicle patrol, emergency notification system, self-defense education, and security escort services. There are shuttle buses, emergency telephones, lighted pathways/sidewalks, and controlled access to dorms/residences.

Programs of Study: Ball State confers B.A., B.S., B.F.A., B.G.S., B.Mus. and B.S.W. degrees. Associate, master's, and doctoral degrees are also awarded. Bachelor's degrees are awarded in AGRICULTURE (natural resource management), BIOLOGICAL SCIENCE (biology/biological science), BUSINESS (accounting, banking and finance, business administration and management, business economics, entrepreneurial studies, human resources, marketing/retailing/merchandising, operations management, and personnel management), COMMUNICATIONS AND THE ARTS (art, classical languages, classics, dance, dramatic arts, English, French, German, Japanese, journalism, music, radio/television technology, Spanish, and speech/debate/rhetoric), COMPUTER AND PHYSICAL SCIENCE (actuarial science, chemistry, computer science, geology, mathematics, and physics), EDUCATION (business education, early childhood education, education of the multiply handicapped, elementary education, health education, industrial arts education, library science, physical education, and science education), ENGINEERING AND ENVIRONMENTAL DESIGN (architecture, engineering, environmental design, graphic arts technology, industrial engineering technology, landscape architecture/design, preengineering, and urban planning technology), HEALTH PROFESSIONS (medical laboratory technology, medical technology, nursing, predentistry, premedicine, preoptometry, prepharmacy, preveterinary science, respiratory therapy, and speech pathology/audiology), SOCIAL SCIENCE (anthropology, criminal justice, dietetics, economics, family/consumer studies, geography, history, Latin American studies, liberal arts/general studies, philosophy, political science/government, prelaw, psychology, religion, social work, sociology, urban studies, and women's studies). Architecture, business and education are the strongest academically. Elementary education, business, radio and television have the largest enrollments.

Required: All students must take at least 120 credits and maintain a 2.0 GPA for graduation; required hours in the major vary by program. Required courses are in English composition, math, speech, history, personal finance, physical sciences, social or behavioral sciences, humanities or fine arts, global studies, and 2 hours of phys ed. In addition, all juniors must pass a writing proficiency exam.

Special: Nearly all undergraduate disciplines offer internships, and work study is available. Study abroad is possible at the university's London center and in 20 other programs; students may also spend a semester in Washington, D.C. Most disciplines offer dual majors, and accelerated degrees are available. There is a B.A.-B.S. degree in elementary/special education, 3-2 program in engineering, an award-winning program in entrepreneurship, a general studies degree, nondegree study, and pass/fail options. There are 33 national honor societies and a freshman honors program.

Faculty/Classroom: 53% of faculty are male; 47% are female. No introductory courses are taught by graduate students.

Admissions: 68% of the 2013-2014 applicants were accepted. The SAT scores for the 2013-2014 freshman class were: Critical Reading--34% below 500, 47% between 500 and 599, 17% between 600 and 699, and 2% between 700 and 800; Math--33% below 500, 47% between 500 and 599, 19% between 600 and 699, and 1% between 700 and 800; Writing--41% below 500, 46% between 500 and 599, 12% between 600 and 699, and 1% between 700 and 800.

Requirements: Admission is a holistic review based on strength of applicants' curriculum, grades in English, math, lab scienes, social sciences, and foreign language, curricula patterns and grade trends, and the SAT or ACT scores. AP and CLEP credits are accepted.

Procedure: Freshmen are admitted fall, spring, and summer. Entrance exams should be taken during the spring of the junior year or early in the senior year. There are deferred admissions and rolling admissions plans. Applications should be filed by May 1 for fall entry; December 1 for spring entry; and April 1 for summer entry, along with a $55 fee. Notification is sent on a rolling basis. Applications are accepted online.

Transfer: 684 transfer students enrolled in 2012-2013. Transfer applicants should have earned a 2.0 GPA on a 4.0 scale (as computed by Ball State) to be considered for admission. An official high school transcript or GED score report and official transcripts from each post-secondary institution are required. 60 of 126 credits required for the bachelor's degree must be completed at Ball State.

Visiting: There are regularly scheduled orientations for prospective students, consisting of twice-a-day presentations and tours. There are guides for informal visits and visitors may sit in on classes. To schedule a visit, contact the Visitors Desk at (765) 285-5683.

Financial Aid: In 2013-2014, 76% of all full-time freshmen and 78% of continuing full-time students received some form of financial aid. 48% of all full-time freshmen and 47% of continuing full-time students received need-based aid. The average freshman award was $10,271. Need-based scholarships or need-based grants averaged $5,638; need-based self-help aid (loans and jobs) averaged $3,703; non-need-based athletic scholarships averaged $18,410; and other non-need-based awards and non-need-based scholarships averaged $7,514. The average financial indebtedness of the

2013 graduate was $27,373. Ball State is a member of CSS. The FAFSA is required. The priority date for freshman financial aid applications for fall entry is March 1.

International Students: There are 369 international students enrolled. The school actively recruits these students. They must take the TOEFL with a minimum score of 550 on the paper-based TOEFL (PBT) or 79 on the Internet-based version (iBT). The SAT or ACT is recommended.

Graduates: From July 1, 2012 to June 30, 2013, 3299 bachelor's degrees were awarded. The most popular majors were general studies (12%), telecommunications (8%), and elementary education (6%).

Admissions Contact: Chris Munchel, Director of Admissions. E-Mail: *askus@.bsu.edu* Web: *www.bsu.edu/admissions*

BETHEL COLLEGE C-1

Mishawaka, IN 46545 (574) 807-7600
(800) 422-4101; (574) 807-7650

Full-time: 499 men, 916 women	**Faculty:** 82; IIB, --$
Part-time: 95 men, 291 women	**Ph.D.s:** 61%
Graduate: 78 men, 84 women	**Student/Faculty:** 17 to 1
Year: semesters, summer session	**Tuition:** n/av
Application Deadline:	**Room & Board:** $7280
Freshman Class: 721 applied, 702 accepted, 225 enrolled	
SAT CR/M/W: 510/510/490 **ACT:** 23	**COMPETITIVE**

Bethel College, founded in 1947, is a private institution affiliated with the Missionary Church, offering a liberal arts education with a Christian perspective. There are 4 graduate schools. In addition to regional accreditation, Bethel has baccalaureate program accreditation with NASM, NCATE, and NLN. The library contains 146,563 volumes, 4,577 microform items, 3,252 audio/video tapes/CDs/DVDs, and subscribes to 2,678 periodicals including electronic. Computerized library services include interlibrary loans, database searching, Internet access, and Wi-Fi capability. Special learning facilities include an art gallery and radio station. The 80-acre campus is in a suburban area Northern Indiana, adjacent to South Bend, 90 miles east of Chicago. Including any residence halls, there are 52 buildings.

Student Life: 76% of undergraduates are from Indiana. Others are from 31 states, 15 foreign countries, and Canada. 81% are from public schools. 79% are White; 12% African American. 74% are Protestant; 18% claim no religious affiliation. The average age of freshmen is 19; all undergraduates, 27. 25% do not continue beyond their first year; 60% remain to graduate.

Housing: 863 students can be accommodated in college housing, which includes single-sex dorms, on-campus apartments, off-campus apartments, and married student housing. In addition, there are special-interest houses, a cultural awareness house, missions house, and urban ministries house. On-campus housing is guaranteed for all 4 years. 55% of students commute. Alcohol is not permitted. Upperclassmen may keep cars.

Activities: There are no fraternities or sororities. There are 18 groups on campus, including art, band, cheerleading, choir, chorale, chorus, computers, drama, Fellowship of Christian Athletes, honors, international, jazz band, literary magazine, musical theater, newspaper, pep band, political, professional, radio and TV, religious, social, social service, student government, and yearbook. Popular campus events include Christmas Banquet, Junior-Senior Banquet, and Spiritual Emphasis Week and Midnight Breakfast.

Sports: There are 8 intercollegiate sports for men and 9 for women, and 10 intramural sports for men and 8 for women. Facilities include two gyms; two weight rooms; two exercise rooms; indoor baseball training facilities; baseball, softball, and soccer fields; tennis courts; a practice track.

Disabled Students: 80% of the campus is accessible. Facilities include wheelchair ramps, elevators, special parking, specially equipped restrooms, lowered drinking fountains, and special housing.

Services: Counseling and information services are available, as is tutoring in every subject. There is remedial math, reading, and writing.

Campus Safety and Security: Measures include 24-hour foot and vehicle patrol, emergency notification system, self-defense education, and security escort services. There are emergency telephones, lighted pathways/sidewalks, and controlled access to dorms/residences.

Programs of Study: Bethel confers B.A., B.S. and B.S.N. degrees. Associate and master's degrees are also awarded. Bachelor's degrees are awarded in BIOLOGICAL SCIENCE (biology/biological science, cell biology, environmental biology, and (Biological) Pre-Health Studies), BUSINESS (accounting, business administration and management, business economics, international business management, and sports management), COMMUNICATIONS AND THE ARTS (American Sign Language, art, communications, creative writing, dramatic arts, English, English Writing, graphic design, journalism, music performance, performing arts, Spanish, studio art, and theatre arts), COMPUTER AND PHYSICAL SCIENCE (chemistry, digital arts/technology, mathematics, and physical sciences), EDUCATION (art education, (Education) Childhood Education, early childhood education, education, elementary education, English education, mathematics education, music education, physical education, science education, secondary education, social studies education, and sports studies), ENGINEERING AND ENVIRONMENTAL DESIGN (chemical engineering, civil engineering, electrical/electronics engineering, engineering, engineering physics, environmental design, environmental science, mechanical engineering, and preengineering), HEALTH PROFESSIONS (art therapy, exercise science, nursing, Pre-Health Studies, predentistry, premedicine, preoptometry, and prephysical therapy), SOCIAL SCIENCE (biblical studies, Christian studies, criminal justice, economics, history, human services, interdisciplinary studies, international studies, interpreter for the deaf, liberal arts/general studies, ministries, missions, pastoral studies, philosophy, philosophy and religion, prelaw, psychology, religion, social science, sociology, and youth ministry). Psychology, Religion/philosophy and nursing are the strongest academically. Nursing, business, and elementary education have the largest enrollments.

Required: To graduate, students must complete 124 credits, including 24 to 52 in the major, with a minimum 2.0 GPA. Also required are 2 semesters of phys ed, 9 credits in Bible and religion, courses in communication skills, social science and history, fine arts and humanities, and natural sciences and math, and a Fitness/Wellness course.

Special: Students may cross-register for courses at various local colleges including Northern Indiana Consortium for Education (NICE). Also available are a 3-2 engineering degree with the University of Notre Dame and Trine University (Angola), a liberal arts degree, degree programs for nontraditional students, and an online degree program in business. Bethel also offers a pass/fail option, student teaching, internships, and study abroad in 12 countries. There are 2 national honor societies, a freshman honors program, and 2 departmental honors programs.

Faculty/Classroom: 55% of faculty are male; 45% are female. All teach undergraduates. No introductory courses are taught by graduate students. The average class size in an introductory lecture is 30; in a laboratory is 10; and in a regular course is 17.

Admissions: 97% of the 2013-2014 applicants were accepted. The SAT scores for the 2013-2014 freshman class were: Critical Reading--41% below 500, 39% between 500 and 599, 18% between 600 and 699, and 2% between 700 and 800; Math--40% below 500, 36% between 500 and 599, 22% between 600 and 699, and 2% between 700 and 800; Writing--52% below 500, 35% between 500 and 599, 12% between 600 and 699, and 1% between 700 and 800. The ACT scores were 31% below 21, 20% between 21 and 23, 25% between 24 and 26, 10% between 27 and 28, and 14% above 28. 42% of the current freshmen were in the top fifth of their class; 74% were in the top two fifths. There was 1 National Merit finalist. 8 freshmen graduated first in their class.

Requirements: The SAT or ACT is required. Applicants should be graduates of a secondary school program or have the GED. Required secondary school credits include 8 units in English, 6 each in math, lab science, and social science, and 4 in a foreign language. Chemistry is required for nursing majors. An audition is required of music program applicants. A GPA of 2.0 is required. AP and CLEP credits are accepted.

Procedure: Freshmen are admitted to all sessions. Entrance exams should be taken as early as possible in the junior or senior year. There are early admissions, deferred admissions, and rolling admissions plans. Application deadlines are open. Application fee is $25. Applications are accepted online.

Transfer: 237 transfer students enrolled in 2012-2013. Grades of C or better are eligible for transfer; students without a minimum GPA of 2.0 may be admitted on probation. Other admission requirements are the same as for entering freshmen. 30 of 124 credits required for the bachelor's degree must be completed at Bethel.

Visiting: There are regularly scheduled orientations for prospective students, including an interview, chapel visit, tour, lunch, and a class or professor visit as requested. There are guides for informal visits, visitors may sit in on classes, and stay overnight. To schedule a visit, contact the Office of Admission at (574) 807-7361.

Financial Aid: In 2013-2014, 88% of all full-time freshmen and 87% of continuing full-time students received some form of financial aid. 78% of all full-time freshmen and 71% of continuing full-time students received need-based aid. The average freshman award was $20,242. Need-based scholarships or need-based grants averaged $8,680; need-based self-help aid (loans and jobs) averaged $3,626; non-need-based athletic scholarships averaged $7,630; and other non-need-based awards and non-need-based scholarships averaged $8,338. 30% of undergraduate students work part-time. Average annual earnings from campus work are $1000. The average financial indebtedness of the 2013 graduate was $24,207. Bethel is a member of CSS. The FAFSA and the college's own financial statement are required. The priority date for freshman financial aid applications for fall entry is March 1. The deadline for filing freshman financial aid applications for fall entry is March 10.

International Students: There are 35 international students enrolled. They must take the TOEFL with a minimum score of 540 on the paper-based TOEFL (PBT) or 76 on the Internet-based version (iBT), IELTS.

Graduates: From July 1, 2012 to June 30, 2013, 397 bachelor's degrees

were awarded. The most popular majors were business areas (39%), nursing (12%), and liberal studies (12%). 40 companies recruited on campus in 2012-2013. In an average class, 2% graduate in 3 years or less, 54% graduate in 4 years or less, 61% graduate in 5 years or less, and 62% graduate in 6 years or less. Of the 2012 graduating class, 11% were enrolled in graduate school within 6 months of graduation.

Admissions Contact: Andrea Helmuth, Director of Admission. E-Mail: *Andrea.Helmuth@BethelCollege.edu* Web: *www.bethelcollege.edu*

BUTLER UNIVERSITY C-3

Indianapolis, IN 46208 (317) 940-8100
(888) 940-8100; (317) 940-8150

Full-time: 1570 men, 2479 women	**Faculty:** n/av; IIA, -$
Part-time: 46 men, 31 women	**Ph.D.s:** 79%
Graduate: 340 men, 436 women	**Student/Faculty:** 11 to 1
Year: semesters, summer session	**Tuition:** $34,368
Application Deadline: 2 1	**Room & Board:** $11,530
Freshman Class: 9357 applied, 6185 accepted, 1014 enrolled	
SAT CR/M/W: 580/590/570	**ACT:** 27 **VERY COMPETITIVE+**

Butler University, founded in 1855, is an independent, private institution offering programs in liberal arts and sciences, business administration, fine arts, pharmacy, health sciences, and education. There are 6 undergraduate schools and 5 graduate schools. In addition to regional accreditation, Butler has baccalaureate program accreditation with AACSB, ACPE, NASAD, NASM, and NCATE. The 2 libraries contain 254,432 volumes, 32,261 microform items, 15,345 audio/video tapes/CDs/DVDs, and subscribe to 35,834 periodicals including electronic. Computerized library services include interlibrary loans, database searching, Internet access, and Wi-Fi capability. Special learning facilities include a planetarium, TV station, an observatory. The 290-acre campus is in a suburban area 5 miles from downtown Indianapolis. Including any residence halls, there are 40 buildings.

Student Life: 56% of undergraduates are from out of state, mostly the Mid-West. Students are from 44 states, 51 foreign countries, and Canada. 82% are White. 43% are Catholic; 30% Protestant. The average age of freshmen is 18; all undergraduates, 20. 10% do not continue beyond their first year; 74% remain to graduate.

Housing: 2064 students can be accommodated in college housing, which includes single-sex and coed dorms and on-campus apartments. In addition, there are special-interest houses, and special-interest units available in the residence halls. 67% of students live on campus. Alcohol is not permitted. All students may keep cars.

Activities: 29% of men belong to 6 national fraternities; 33% of women belong to 9 national sororities. There are 153 groups on campus, including art, band, cheerleading, chess, choir, chorale, chorus, computers, dance, debate, drama, environmental, ethnic, gay, honors, international, jazz band, literary magazine, marching band, newspaper, opera, orchestra, pep band, photography, political, professional, radio and TV, religious, social, social service, student government, symphony, and yearbook. Popular campus events include Homecoming, Dance Marathon, Spring Sing and Spring Sports Spectacular.

Sports: There are 9 intercollegiate sports for men and 10 for women, and 23 intramural sports for men and 23 for women. Butler University is host to a 10,000-seat field house, a 20,000-seat football stadium, tennis courts, indoor and outdoor tracks, a weight-training room, an aerobics/exercise room, intramural fields, and baseball, softball, and soccer fields. Butler University's HRC offers many new services to students, faculty and staff, while expanding others presently available. In addition to being the main stomping ground for Butler's department of recreation, the HRC also houses Counseling and Consultation Services, Health Education and Health Services, making it a true wellness center on campus.

Disabled Students: All of the campus is accessible. Facilities include wheelchair ramps, elevators, special parking, specially equipped restrooms, special class scheduling, and lowered drinking fountains.

Services: Counseling and information services are available, as is tutoring in every subject. There is a reader service for the blind. A writer's studio offers assistance in all areas of the writing process.

Campus Safety and Security: Measures include 24-hour foot and vehicle patrol, emergency notification system, self-defense education, and security escort services. There are shuttle buses, emergency telephones, lighted pathways/sidewalks, and controlled access to dorms/residences.

Programs of Study: Butler confers B.A., B.S., B.F.A., B.M., B.S.H.S. and B.S.E. degrees. Associate and master's degrees are also awarded. Bachelor's degrees are awarded in BIOLOGICAL SCIENCE (biology/biological science), BUSINESS (accounting, banking and finance, international business management, management information systems, and marketing/retailing/merchandising), COMMUNICATIONS AND THE ARTS (advertising, art, arts administration/management, communications, dance, dramatic arts, English, French, German, Greek (classical), journalism, Latin, media arts, music, music performance, music theory and composition, performing arts, public relations, Spanish, speech/debate/rhetoric, theatre arts, and voice), COMPUTER AND PHYSICAL SCIENCE (actuarial science, chemistry, computer science, mathematics, physics, and software engineering), EDUCATION (elementary education, middle school education, music education, secondary education, and special education), ENGINEERING AND ENVIRONMENTAL DESIGN (biomedical engineering and engineering), HEALTH PROFESSIONS (health science, pharmacy, and speech pathology/audiology), SOCIAL SCIENCE (anthropology, criminal justice, economics, gender studies, history, international studies, philosophy, political science/government, psychology, religion, science and society, and sociology). Physician assistant, dance, and business are the strongest academically. Pharmacy, biology, and marketing have the largest enrollments.

Required: Our Core Curriculum is divided into two parts - a relatively structured set of common Core elements and a more varied set of general Core elements in which students have a broader choice of course within areas defined by specific learning objectives. In all of our Core elements, we are committed to courses structured by learning objectives rather than disciplines. We seek to have Core courses taught by the whole University community. We espouse Butler's mission that claims our students' learning ought to proceed by creating and fostering a stimulating intellectual community built upon interactive dialogue and inquiry among faculty, staff and students.

Special: Butler offers cross-registration with the 4 other members of the Consortium for Urban Education, co-op programs in business administration, and internships in pharmacy, arts administration, and business programs. A 3-2 degree program in engineering with Indiana University-Purdue University in Indianapolis, extensive study-abroad programs, and work-study programs are available. There are dual majors including French, German, and Spanish combined with business studies, student-designed majors, a general studies degree, pass/fail options, and nondegree study. There are 5 national honor societies, including Phi Beta Kappa, and a freshman honors program.

Faculty/Classroom: 53% of faculty are male; 47% are female. No introductory courses are taught by graduate students. The average class size in an introductory lecture is 23; in a laboratory is 18; and in a regular course is 22.

Admissions: 66% of the 2013-2014 applicants were accepted. The SAT scores for the 2013-2014 freshman class were: Critical Reading--14% below 500, 44% between 500 and 599, 37% between 600 and 699, and 5% between 700 and 800; Math--12% below 500, 40% between 500 and 599, 42% between 600 and 699, and 7% between 700 and 800; Writing--16% below 500, 45% between 500 and 599, 33% between 600 and 699, and 6% between 700 and 800. The ACT scores were 2% below 21, 11% between 21 and 23, 28% between 24 and 26, 21% between 27 and 28, and 38% above 28. 73% of the current freshmen were in the top fifth of their class; 94% were in the top two fifths. There were 5 National Merit finalists. 53 freshmen graduated first in their class.

Requirements: The SAT or ACT is required. In addition, applicants should be graduates of an accredited secondary school, but Butler will consider talented or gifted students without a diploma. Students should have earned at least 17 academic units, based on 4 years of English, 3 each of math and lab science, 2 each of a foreign language and history/social science, and the rest of electives. An audition is required for dance, music, and theater majors, and an interview is required for radio/TV majors. Butler requires applicants to be in the upper 50% of their class. A GPA of 2.0 is required. AP and CLEP credits are accepted. Important factors in the admissions decision are advanced placement or honors courses, evidence of special talent, and leadership record.

Procedure: Freshmen are admitted to all sessions. Entrance exams should be taken during the junior year. There are early admissions and deferred admissions plans. Applications should be filed by 2 1 for fall entry, along with a $35 fee. Notifications are sent 2 15. 165 applicants were on the 2013 waiting list; 6 were admitted. Applications are accepted online.

Transfer: 83 transfer students enrolled in 2012-2013. Applicants who have completed more than 12 hours of college work must present transcripts from all previous college attended, indicating good standing and a minimum GPA of 2.0, and an official high school transcript showing a posted date of graduation. Those students with fewer than 12 hours must also,submit SAT or ACT scores. Students wishing to transfer into pharmacy must apply through PharmCAS; Students applying to the professional phase of physician assistant program must apply through CASPA. No credits transfer for classes taken online. 45 of 126 credits required for the bachelor's degree must be completed at Butler.

Visiting: There are regularly scheduled orientations for prospective students, including a campus tour, faculty visit, and financial aid interview. There are guides for informal visits, visitors may sit in on classes, and stay overnight. To schedule a visit, contact the Office of Admission.

Financial Aid: 25% of undergraduate students work part-time. Average annual earnings from campus work are $1200. Butler is a member of CSS. The FAFSA and the college's own financial statement are required. The deadline for filing freshman financial aid applications for fall entry is March 1.

International Students: There are 121 international students enrolled.

The school actively recruits these students. They must take the TOEFL with a minimum score of 550 on the paper-based TOEFL (PBT) or 79 on the Internet-based version (iBT), or complete level 5 at the American Language Academy on Butler's campus.

Graduates: From July 1, 2012 to June 30, 2013, 1041 bachelor's degrees were awarded. The most popular majors were marketing (6%), finance (5%), and health sciences (5%). In an average class, 63% graduate in 4 years or less, 72% graduate in 5 years or less, and 72% graduate in 6 years or less. Of the 2012 graduating class, 19% were enrolled in graduate school within 6 months of graduation, and 71% were employed.

Admissions Contact: Scott Ham, Director of Admissions. E-Mail: *admission@butler.edu* Web: *www.butler.edu*

CALUMET COLLEGE OF ST. JOSEPH — B-1

Whiting, IN 46394 (219) 473-4739
(877) 700-9100; (219) 473-4259

Full-time: 160 men, 310 women
Part-time: 345 men, 385 women
Graduate: 100 men, 40 women
Year: semesters, summer session
Application Deadline: open
Freshman Class: n/av
SAT or ACT: recommended
Faculty: n/av; IIB, --$
Ph.D.s: 50%
Student/Faculty: n/av
Tuition: $15,500
Room & Board: n/app

LESS COMPETITIVE

Calumet College of St. Joseph, founded in 1951, is a private Catholic institution offering commuting students a liberal arts education in a Christian environment. The figures in the above capsule and in this profile are approximate. The library contains 93,055 volumes, 3,035 microform items, 6,412 audio/video tapes/CDs/DVDs, and subscribes to 354 periodicals including electronic. Computerized library services include interlibrary loans and database searching. Special learning facilities include a learning resource center and art gallery. The 256-acre campus is in a small town 15 miles southeast of Chicago in northwest Indiana. Including any residence halls, there is 1 building.

Student Life: 70% of undergraduates are from Indiana. Others are from 2 states. 65% are from public schools. 46% are white; 33% African American; 19% Hispanic. 45% are Catholic. The average age of freshmen is 21; all undergraduates, 35. 42% do not continue beyond their first year; 58% remain to graduate.

Housing: There are no residence halls. All students commute.

Activities: There are no fraternities or sororities. There are 15 groups on campus, including cheerleading, drama, ethnic, literary magazine, musical theater, newspaper, photography, professional, religious, social, social service, and student government. Popular campus events include Thanksgiving Ethnicfest and Student Appreciation Week.

Sports: 1 intramural sports for men.

Disabled Students: All of the campus is accessible. Facilities include wheelchair ramps, elevators, special parking, and specially equipped restrooms.

Services: Counseling and information services are available, as is tutoring in most subjects. There is remedial math, reading, and writing.

Campus Safety and Security: There are emergency telephones and lighted pathways/sidewalks.

Programs of Study: CCSJ confers B.A., B.S., B.S.Ed., and B.S.M.T. degrees. Associate and master's degrees are also awarded. Bachelor's degrees are awarded in BUSINESS (accounting, business administration and management, and institutional management), COMMUNICATIONS AND THE ARTS (English and media arts), COMPUTER AND PHYSICAL SCIENCE (information sciences and systems), EDUCATION (elementary education and secondary education), HEALTH PROFESSIONS (health care administration), SOCIAL SCIENCE (criminal justice, human services, law enforcement and corrections, liberal arts/general studies, paralegal studies, psychology, religion, theological studies, and urban studies). Management, accounting, and criminal justice are the strongest academically. Management, human services, and education have the largest enrollments.

Required: All students must complete 42 semester hours of general education courses, including English composition, economics, speech, theology, philosophy, communication and fine arts, science and math, and social and behavioral science. A total of 124 semester hours with a minimum GPA of 2.0 is required to graduate.

Special: The college offers a cooperative 3-1 baccalaureate degree in medical technology with the schools of St. Margaret-Mercy Hospital in Indiana, where students complete their study and a clinical internship. Accelerated degree programs in organizational management, health-care management, and law enforcement management are possible. The LEAP program offers credit for life experience. Study abroad, internships, work-study programs, a general studies degree, pass/fail options, and nondegree study are possible.

Faculty/Classroom: 75% of faculty are male; 25% are female. All teach undergraduates. No introductory courses are taught by graduate students. The average class size in an introductory lecture is 25; in a laboratory is 20; and in a regular course is 20.

Requirements: The SAT or ACT is recommended. Applicants should have completed 4 years of high school English, 3 to 4 of math, 2 to 3 of science, and 2 of social studies. The GED is accepted. An essay and an interview are recommended. The Vocabulary and Reading Assessment Test is required. A GPA of 2.0 is required. AP and CLEP credits are accepted. Important factors in the admissions decision are extracurricular activities record, leadership record, and evidence of special talent.

Procedure: Freshmen are admitted to all sessions. There are deferred admissions and rolling admissions plans. Application deadlines are open. Applications are accepted online.

Transfer: A 2.0 GPA is required. An interview is recommended. The Vocabulary and Reading Assessment Test is required. 30 of 124 credits required for the bachelor's degree must be completed at CCSJ.

Visiting: There are regularly scheduled orientations for prospective students. There are guides for informal visits and visitors may sit in on classes. To schedule a visit, contact Director of Admissions.

Financial Aid: CCSJ is a member of CSS. The FAFSA and the college's own financial statement are required. Check with the school for current application deadlines.

International Students: They must take the TOEFL.

Admissions Contact: Director of Admissions and Financial Aid. Web: *www.ccsj.edu*

DEPAUW UNIVERSITY — B-3

Greencastle, IN 46135 (765) 658-4006
(800) 447-2495; (765) 658-4007

Full-time: 1035 men, 1296 women
Part-time: 10 men, 11 women
Graduate: n/av
Year: semesters
Application Deadline: March 1
Freshman Class: 4347 applied, 2950 accepted, 584 enrolled
SAT CR/M/W: 580/600/580
Faculty: 224; IIB, +$
Ph.D.s: 91%
Student/Faculty: 10 to 1
Tuition: $36,970
Room & Board: $9730
ACT: 27

VERY COMPETITIVE+

DePauw University, founded in 1837, is a private institution affiliated with the United Methodist Church offering programs in the fields of liberal arts and music. The figures in the above capsule and in this profile are approximate. There are 2 undergraduate schools. In addition to regional accreditation, DePauw has baccalaureate program accreditation with NASM and NCATE. The 3 libraries contain 818,618 volumes, 381,066 microform items, 34,325 audio/video tapes/CDs/DVDs, and subscribe to 29,188 periodicals including electronic. Computerized library services include interlibrary loans, database searching, and Internet access. Special learning facilities include a learning resource center, art gallery, natural history museum, radio station, TV station, an observatory, an arboretum, a digital video studio, and a digital media lab. The 175-acre campus is in a small town 45 miles west of Indianapolis. Including any residence halls, there are 81 buildings.

Student Life: 59% of undergraduates are from out of state. Students are from 41 states, and 19 foreign countries. 88% are from public schools. 75% are white. 45% are Protestant; 20% Catholic. The average age of freshmen is 19; all undergraduates, 20. 10% do not continue beyond their first year; 83% remain to graduate.

Housing: 1490 students can be accommodated in college housing, which includes coed dorms, on-campus apartments, and off-campus apartments. In addition, there are special-interest houses, fraternity houses, sorority houses, international student housing. On-campus housing is guaranteed for all 4 years. 99% of students live on campus. All students may keep cars.

Activities: 78% of men belong to 12 national fraternities; 64% of women belong to 10 national sororities. There are 80 groups on campus, including art, band, cheerleading, chess, choir, chorale, chorus, computers, dance, debate, drama, ethnic, film, forensics, gay, honors, international, jazz band, literary magazine, musical theater, newspaper, opera, orchestra, political, professional, radio and TV, religious, social, social service, student government, and symphony. Popular campus events include Little 5 track meet, Monon Bell football game, and Old Gold Day.

Sports: There are 17 intercollegiate sports for men and 16 for women, and 14 intramural sports for men and 12 for women. Facilities include a recreation center, a 4000-seat stadium, baseball, soccer, and field hockey fields, 3 basketball courts, indoor/outdoor tennis courts and tracks, a pool, a fitness center, volleyball and badminton courts, and a 3200-seat indoor gym.

Disabled Students: 85% of the campus is accessible. Facilities include wheelchair ramps, elevators, special parking, specially equipped restrooms, special class scheduling, lowered drinking fountains, and lowered telephones.

Services: Counseling and information services are available, as is tutoring in most subjects. There is a reader service for the blind.

Campus Safety and Security: Measures include 24-hour foot and vehicle patrol, emergency notification system, self-defense education, and security escort services. There are shuttle buses, emergency telephones, and lighted pathways/sidewalks.

Programs of Study: DePauw confers B.A., B.M.A., B.M.E., and B.Mu.

degrees. Bachelor's degrees are awarded in AGRICULTURE (natural resource management), BIOLOGICAL SCIENCE (biochemistry and biology/biological science), COMMUNICATIONS AND THE ARTS (art history and appreciation, classical languages, communications, English, English literature, French, German, Greek, Latin, linguistics, literature, music, music business management, music performance, music theory and composition, romance languages and literature, Spanish, and studio art), COMPUTER AND PHYSICAL SCIENCE (chemistry, computer science, earth science, geology, mathematics, and physics), EDUCATION (elementary education, foreign languages education, and music education), ENGINEERING AND ENVIRONMENTAL DESIGN (environmental science and preengineering), HEALTH PROFESSIONS (health), SOCIAL SCIENCE (African American studies, anthropology, classical/ancient civilization, East Asian studies, economics, gender studies, geography, history, interdisciplinary studies, peace studies, philosophy, physical fitness/movement, political science/government, psychology, religion, Russian and Slavic studies, sociology, and women's studies). English, economics, and communications have the largest enrollments.

Required: Students must demonstrate competence in oral communications, quantitative reasoning, and writing. Successful completion of 124 semester hours, including 32 to 40 in the major, is required for graduation. In addition, students must fulfill distribution requirements in natural sciences, social and behavioral sciences, literature and the arts, historical and philosophical understanding, foreign language, and self-expression. A comprehensive exam, thesis, or seminar is required for each major.

Special: DePauw offers dual majors in any 2 disciplines, student-designed majors, internships for honors programs and winter-term projects, unlimited study-abroad options through cooperative arrangements with other universities, a Washington semester, pass/fail options, and credit by departmental examination. Also available are 3-2 engineering degrees with Case Western Reserve, Columbia, and Washington Universities and a 3-2 nursing program with Rush University Hospital in Chicago. The Media Fellows, Management Fellows, and Science Research Fellows programs offer majors in any discipline, plus a semester-long internship. There are 13 national honor societies, including Phi Beta Kappa, a freshman honors program, and 12 departmental honors programs.

Faculty/Classroom: 55% of faculty are male; 45% are female. All teach undergraduates, and 82% do research. No introductory courses are taught by graduate students. The average class size in an introductory lecture is 20; in a laboratory is 14; and in a regular course is 18.

Admissions: 68% of the 2011-2012 applicants were accepted. The SAT scores for the 2011-2012 freshman class were: Critical Reading--14% below 500, 40% between 500 and 599, 35% between 600 and 700, and 10% above 700; Math--8% below 500, 36% between 500 and 599, 41% between 600 and 700, and 14% above 700; Writing--13% below 500, 42% between 500 and 599, 37% between 600 and 700, and 7% above 700.

Requirements: The SAT or ACT is required. Graduation from an accredited secondary school or a GED is required for admission. Course distribution should include 4 each in English and math, 3 to 4 each in social studies, and science (2 or more with lab), and 2 to 4 in a foreign language. An essay is required, and an interview is strongly recommended. Applicants for the School of Music must audition. AP credits are accepted. Important factors in the admissions decision are advanced placement or honors courses, recommendations by school officials, and personality/intangible qualities.

Procedure: Freshmen are admitted fall and spring. Entrance exams should be taken as early as possible. There are early decision, early admissions, and deferred admissions plans. Early decision applications should be filed by November 1; regular applications, by March 1 for fall entry; and December 1 for spring entry, along with a $40 fee. Notification of early decision is sent January 1; regular decision, April 1. 50 early decision candidates were accepted for the 2011-2012 class. 216 applicants were on the 2011 waiting list; 112 were admitted. Applications are accepted online.

Transfer: 20 transfer students enrolled in a recent year. Applicants must submit either SAT or ACT scores. High school and college transcripts are required, and a minimum GPA on previous college work of 3.0 is preferred. 60 of 124 credits required for the bachelor's degree must be completed at DePauw.

Visiting: There are regularly scheduled orientations for prospective students, consisting of day-long student/parent programs that include campus tours, faculty viewpoints, conversations with students, admissions information, financial aid and career planning sessions, and a meal in a residence hall. There are guides for informal visits, visitors may sit in on classes, and stay overnight. To schedule a visit, contact Admission Program and Visit Coordinator.

Financial Aid: DePauw is a member of CSS. The CSS/Profile, FAFSA, and the college's own financial statement are required. The priority date for freshman financial aid applications for fall entry is February 15.

International Students: There are 185 international students enrolled. The school actively recruits these students. They must take the TOEFL with a minimum score of 560 on the paper-based TOEFL (PBT) or 83 on the Internet-based version (iBT), or IELTS. They must also take the SAT or ACT.

Graduates: In a recent year, 507 bachelor's degrees were awarded. The most popular majors were social sciences (21%), communication/journalism (13%), and English (11%). In an average class, 79% graduate in 4 years or less and 81% graduate in 5 years or less.

Admissions Contact: Admission Officer A campus DVD is available. E-Mail: *admission@depauw.edu* Web: *www.depauw.edu*

EARLHAM COLLEGE D-3

Richmond, IN 47374 **(765) 983-1600**
(800) 327-5426; (765) 983-1560

Full-time: 458 men, 573 women	**Faculty:** 102; IIB, av$
Part-time: 16 men, 17 women	**Ph.D.s:** 92%
Graduate: 40 men, 60 women	**Student/Faculty:** 10 to 1
Year: semesters	**Tuition:** $41,450
Application Deadline: February 15	**Room & Board:** $8260

Freshman Class: 1890 applied, 1204 accepted, 254 enrolled
SAT CR/M: 640/600 **ACT:** 28 **VERY COMPETITIVE+**

At Earlham, we believe learning is a pathway to a life of consequence. We expect our students to be fully present: to think rigorously, value directness and genuineness, and actively seek insights from differing perspectives The values that we model and practice at Earlham are rooted in centuries of Quaker tradition. But they also constitute the ideal toolkit for contemporary success. Earlham graduates are astute and adept at building consensus. They're able to discern the signal from the noise. They exemplify transparency and accountability. They're ready for working environments where progress hinges on people from diverse backgrounds "rowing together" whether it's in medicine, business, education, or fields and careers that have yet to be invented. Nowhere is the world closer than it is here at Earlham. We are consistently ranked among the top liberal arts colleges for enrolling the highest percentage of international students. Our students represent more than 75 countries. It is impossible to come to our campus and not leave with a wider perspective and an intellectual framework that is rich in global content. There is one undergraduate school and 2 graduate schools. The 2 libraries contain 378,895 volumes, 191,754 microform items, 9,387 audio/video tapes/CDs/DVDs, and subscribe to 54,838 periodicals including electronic. Computerized library services include interlibrary loans, database searching, Internet access, and Wi-Fi capability. Special learning facilities include an art gallery, natural history museum, planetarium, radio station, an observatory, herbarium, and greenhouse. The 800-acre campus is in a small town 70 miles east of Indianapolis and 40 miles west of Dayton. Including any residence halls, there are 63 buildings.

Student Life: 81% of undergraduates are from out of state, mostly the Mid-West. Students are from 43 states, 76 foreign countries, and Canada. 65% are from public schools. 54% are White; 18% Foreign; 14% African American. 47% claim no religious affiliation; 22% Protestant. The average age of freshmen is 18; all undergraduates, 20. 16% do not continue beyond their first year; 72% remain to graduate.

Housing: 976 students can be accommodated in college housing, which includes single-sex and coed dorms. In addition, there are language houses, special-interest houses, service learning house, Jewish cultural center, an African American cultural center, International Cultural Center, LBGTQA. On-campus housing is guaranteed for all 4 years. 96% of students live on campus; of those, 84% remain on campus on weekends. All students may keep cars.

Activities: There are no fraternities or sororities. There are 70 groups on campus, including art, cheerleading, choir, chorale, chorus, computers, dance, drama, environmental, ethnic, film, gay, honors, international, jazz band, literary magazine, newspaper, orchestra, photography, political, professional, radio and TV, religious, social, social service, student government, and symphony. Popular campus events include Research Conference and International Festival.

Sports: There are 7 intercollegiate sports for men and 7 for women, and 6 intramural sports for men and 5 for women. Facilities include a fitness center with cardiovascular equipment and weights, group fitness and dance rooms, a field house with 4 indoor courts for tennis, volleyball, and basketball, 2 racquetball courts, an indoor climbing wall, an indoor running track, a 25-meter pool, a performance gym, and a massage therapist. Outdoor facilities include a natural grass football field, 10 all-weather tennis courts, basketball courts, a trail for cross-country running and skiing, and baseball, softball, soccer, lacrosse, and field hockey fields.

Disabled Students: 80% of the campus is accessible. Facilities include wheelchair ramps, elevators, special parking, specially equipped restrooms, lowered drinking fountains, lowered telephones, and special housing.

Services: Counseling and information services are available, as is tutoring in most subjects, as requested for most 100 and 200 level courses and some 300 level courses. A writing center is available. There is a reader service for the blind.

Campus Safety and Security: Measures include 24-hour foot and

vehicle patrol, emergency notification system, self-defense education, and security escort services. There are shuttle buses, emergency telephones, lighted pathways/sidewalks, and controlled access to dorms/residences.

Programs of Study: Earlham confers B.A. degrees. Master's degrees are also awarded. Bachelor's degrees are awarded in AGRICULTURE (environmental studies), BIOLOGICAL SCIENCE (biochemistry, biology/biological science, and neurosciences), BUSINESS (business administration and management), COMMUNICATIONS AND THE ARTS (art, dramatic arts, English, French, German, languages, linguistics, music, and Spanish), COMPUTER AND PHYSICAL SCIENCE (chemistry, computer science, geology, mathematics, and physics), ENGINEERING AND ENVIRONMENTAL DESIGN (environmental science), HEALTH PROFESSIONS (premedicine), SOCIAL SCIENCE (African American studies, anthropology, classical/ancient civilization, economics, history, human development, international studies, Japanese studies, Latin American studies, peace studies, philosophy, political science/government, psychology, religion, sociology, and women's studies). Biology, interdisciplinary studies, and social sciences have the largest enrollments.

Required: To graduate, all students must complete the general education curriculum (scientific inquiry, analytical reasoning, the arts, domestic diversity, international diversity, wellness). Students must also maintain a minimum GPA of 2.0 and complete a total of 122 semester hours, including 32 semester hours in the major and at least 36-upper level semester hours and 40 outside the major division. A senior capstone experience is required.

Special: Collaboration is the key to research and scholarly practice at Earlham. Students develop working relationships with faculty in the classroom, laboratory and in the field through Ford/Knight projects and many other types of research opportunities. Independent Study, self-directed learning, internships and May Term intensive courses can be important aspects of an Earlham education as well. Earlham's Center for Integrated Learning is a key feature for all Earlham students in developing what we call "the 10-Year Mindset." Your education is much more than the four years of coursework in your chosen major. It did not begin at Earlham nor will it end upon graduation. The 10-Year Mindset is our guiding principle that helps you build a comprehensive and long-term plan of action. Features of this program include immersion experiences, career discernment, community based learning and learning in action. There are 2 national honor societies including Phi Beta Kappa.

Faculty/Classroom: 46% of faculty are male; 54% are female. All teach undergraduates. No introductory courses are taught by graduate students. The average class size in an introductory lecture is 45; in a laboratory is 18; and in a regular course is 14.

Admissions: 64% of the 2013-2014 applicants were accepted. The SAT scores for the 2013-2014 freshman class were: Critical Reading--17% below 500, 33% between 500 and 599, 32% between 600 and 699, and 18% between 700 and 800; Math 15% below 500, 29% between 500 and 599, 42% between 600 and 699, and 14% between 700 and 800; Writing--16% below 500, 37% between 500 and 599, 36% between 600 and 699, and 11% between 700 and 800.

Requirements: In most cases, graduation from an accredited secondary school is required; a GED will be accepted. Home-schooled students are not required to take the GED or have a high school diploma. Students must have completed at least 15 academic credits, including 4 years of English, 3 of math, and 2 each of science, history or social studies, and a foreign language. Students are required to submit an essay and letters of recommendation from a teacher and guidance counselor. An interview is recommended. A GPA of 2.5 is required. AP credits are accepted. Important factors in the admissions decision are advanced placement or honors courses, evidence of special talent, and extracurricular activities record.

Procedure: Freshmen are admitted fall and spring. Entrance exams should be taken during the spring of the junior year or early fall of the senior year. There are early decision, early admissions, and deferred admissions plans. Early decision applications should be filed by November 1; regular applications, by February 15 for fall entry; November 15 for winter entry; and November 15 for spring entry. Notification of early decision is sent December 15; regular decision, February 15. 13 early decision candidates were accepted for the 2013-2014 class. 190 applicants were on the 2013 waiting list; 54 were admitted. Applications are accepted online.

Transfer: 14 transfer students enrolled in 2012-2013. Applicants must have a minimum GPA of 2.5 in college course work. An interview is recommended. High school and college transcripts, an essay, and a statement of good standing from the prior institution are required. 62 of 122 credits required for the bachelor's degree must be completed at Earlham.

Visiting: There are regularly scheduled orientations for prospective students, including class visitation, an admissions interview, a tour, and special appointments with faculty. There are guides for informal visits, visitors may sit in on classes, and stay overnight. To schedule a visit, contact the Admissions Office.

Financial Aid: In 2013-2014, 94% of all full-time freshmen and 94% of continuing full-time students received some form of financial aid. 62% of all full-time freshmen and 63% of continuing full-time students received need-based aid. The average freshman award was $22,882. Need-based scholarships or need-based grants averaged $22,882 ($43,000 maximum); need-based self-help aid (loans and jobs) averaged $5,550 ($9,320 maximum); and other non-need-based awards and non-need-based scholarships averaged $9,214 ($10,383 maximum). Average annual earnings from campus work are $1856. The average financial indebtedness of the 2013 graduate was $14,594. Earlham is a member of CSS. The FAFSA is required. The priority date for freshman financial aid applications for fall entry is March 1. The deadline for filing freshman financial aid applications for fall entry is March 1.

International Students: There are 182 international students enrolled. The school actively recruits these students. They must take the TOEFL with a minimum score of 550 on the paper-based TOEFL (PBT) or 80 on the Internet-based version (iBT).

Graduates: From July 1, 2012 to June 30, 2013, 218 bachelor's degrees were awarded. The most popular majors were biology/life sciences (16%), interdisciplinary studies (15%), and social sciences (11%). In an average class, 61% graduate in 4 years or less, 70% graduate in 5 years or less, and 71% graduate in 6 years or less.

Admissions Contact: Jonathan Stroud, VP for Enrollment and Communications. E-Mail: *admission@earlham.edu* Web: *www.earlham.edu*

FRANKLIN COLLEGE C-4

Franklin, IN 46131 (317) 738-8758
(800) 852-0232; (317) 738-8274

Full-time: 471 men, 481 women	**Faculty:** n/av; IIB, --$
Part-time: 31 men, 31 women	**Ph.D.s:** 83%
Graduate: n/av	**Student/Faculty:** n/av
Year: 4-1-4, summer session	**Tuition:** $27,695
Application Deadline: open	**Room & Board:** $8190

Freshman Class: 1684 applied, 1333 accepted, 272 enrolled
SAT CR/M/W: 500/510/480 **ACT:** 22 **COMPETITIVE**

Franklin College, founded in 1834, is a private liberal arts college affiliated with the American Baptist Church. There is one undergraduate school. In addition to regional accreditation, Franklin College has baccalaureate program accreditation with NCATE. The library contains 132,248 volumes, 310,676 microform items, 7,815 audio/video tapes/CDs/DVDs, and subscribes to 12,520 periodicals including electronic. Computerized library services include interlibrary loans, database searching, and Wi-Fi capability. Special learning facilities include a radio station and TV station. The 207-acre campus is in a small town 20 miles south of Indianapolis. Including any residence halls, there are 23 buildings.

Student Life: 98% of undergraduates are from Indiana. Others are from 19 states, and 12 foreign countries. 84% are White. 50% are Protestant; 27% claim no religious affiliation; 14% Catholic. The average age of freshmen is 19; all undergraduates, 22.

Housing: 724 students can be accommodated in college housing, which includes single-sex and coed dorms. In addition, there are special-interest houses, fraternity houses, a substance/alcohol-free residence hall living area. On-campus housing is available on a first-come, first-served basis, and is available on a lottery system for upperclassmen. 77% of students live on campus. All students may keep cars.

Activities: 49% of men belong to 5 national fraternities; 52% of women belong to 3 national sororities. There are 66 groups on campus, including art, band, cheerleading, choir, chorus, drama, environmental, ethnic, film, gay, honors, international, literary magazine, marching band, musical theater, newspaper, pep band, photography, political, professional, radio and TV, religious, social, social service, and student government. Popular campus events include Grizzly Grand Prix, Annual Kite Carnival, and Greek Week.

Sports: There are 11 intercollegiate sports for men and 10 for women, and 6 intramural sports for men and 6 for women. Facilities include athletic and soccer fields, tennis courts, a phys ed center, and a fitness center.

Disabled Students: All of the campus is accessible. Facilities include wheelchair ramps, elevators, special parking, specially equipped restrooms, special class scheduling, lowered drinking fountains, and special housing.

Services: Counseling and information services are available, as is tutoring in most subjects. There is a reader service for the blind, and remedial math, reading, and writing.

Campus Safety and Security: Measures include 24-hour foot and vehicle patrol, emergency notification system, and security escort services. There are emergency telephones and lighted pathways/sidewalks.

Programs of Study: Franklin College confers B.A. degrees. Bachelor's degrees are awarded in BIOLOGICAL SCIENCE (biology/biological science and life science secondary school education), BUSINESS (accounting, business (dual major program), and recreation and leisure services), COMMUNICATIONS AND THE ARTS (art history, art, English, French, journalism, music, public relations, Spanish, and theatre arts), COMPUTER AND PHYSICAL SCIENCE (chemistry, computer information technology, computer science, information sciences and systems, and mathematics),

EDUCATION (athletic training, elementary education, English education, mathematics education, physical education, science education, secondary education, and social studies education), HEALTH PROFESSIONS (exercise science), SOCIAL SCIENCE (American studies, Canadian studies, economics, history, philosophy, political science/government, psychology, religion, and sociology). Biology, chemistry, journalism, public relations, business and education are the strongest academically. Journalism, education, biology and business have the largest enrollments.

Required: Requirements for graduation include 80 hours outside the major, including general education, a minimum of 40 hours in the major, and 120 total credit hours. Each student must maintain a minimum GPA of 2.0 and must pass the Senior Competency Test, which is administered by the department in which the student completes a major.

Special: Cooperative programs engineering are available, as are fall, winter, spring, and summer internships. Study abroad in various countries and cross-registration with 7 Indiana universities and college. A 3-2 engineering degree with Indiana University-Purdue University in Indianapolis is possible. There are 10 national honor societies including Phi Beta Kappa.

Faculty/Classroom: 55% of faculty are male; 45% are female. All teach undergraduates. No introductory courses are taught by graduate students. The average class size in an introductory lecture is 18; in a laboratory is 15; and in a regular course is 16.

Admissions: 79% of the 2013-2014 applicants were accepted. The SAT scores for the 2013-2014 freshman class were: Critical Reading--46% below 500, 42% between 500 and 599, and 11% between 600 and 699; Math--41% below 500, 43% between 500 and 599, and 15% between 600 and 699; Writing--55% below 500, and 36% between 500 and 599. The ACT scores were 12% below 21, 33% between 21 and 23, and 16% between 24 and 26. 36% of the current freshmen were in the top fifth of their class; 81% were in the top two fifths.

Requirements: The SAT or ACT is required. The ACT Optional Writing test is also required. Candidates for admission should have completed 4 years of English, 3 to 4 of math, 2 to 3 of science, 2 each of art and music, social studies, and a foreign language, and typing and basic computing skill courses. The GED is accepted and an essay is required. A GPA of 2.0 is required. AP and CLEP credits are accepted. Important factors in the admissions decision are leadership record, recommendations by school officials, and advanced placement or honors courses.

Procedure: Freshmen are admitted to all sessions. Entrance exams should be taken in spring of the junior year or fall of the senior year. There is a rolling admissions plan. Application deadlines are open. Application fee is $30. Notification is sent on a rolling basis. Applications are accepted online.

Transfer: 26 transfer students enrolled in 2012-2013. Transfer students must have at least a 2.0 cumulative GPA and submit official transcripts from previously attended colleges. 40 of 120 credits required for the bachelor's degree must be completed at Franklin College.

Visiting: There are regularly scheduled orientations for prospective students, including academic presentations, admissions and financial presentations, a student life presentation, campus tours, lunch, and opportunities to talk to professors. There are guides for informal visits, visitors may sit in on classes, and stay overnight. To schedule a visit, contact the Admissions Office.

Financial Aid: In 2013-2014, 100% of all full-time freshmen and 100% of continuing full-time students received some form of financial aid. 87% of all full-time freshmen and 84% of continuing full-time students received need-based aid. The average freshman award was $22,973. Need-based scholarships or need-based grants averaged $17,999 ($35,185 maximum); and need-based self-help aid (loans and jobs) averaged $5,486 ($16,500 maximum). 37% of undergraduate students work part-time. Average annual earnings from campus work are $629. The average financial indebtedness of the 2013 graduate was $33,566. The FAFSA and the college's own financial statement are required. The priority date for freshman financial aid applications for fall entry is March 10.

International Students: There are 6 international students enrolled. They must take the TOEFL with a minimum score of 550 on the paper-based TOEFL (PBT), Completion of level 109 in an English language service (ELS) center is necessary. They must also take the SAT or ACT.

Graduates: From July 1, 2012 to June 30, 2013, 213 bachelor's degrees were awarded. The most popular majors were journalism (15%), elementary education (14%), and biology (9%). Of the 2012 graduating class, 18% were enrolled in graduate school within 6 months of graduation.

Admissions Contact: Jennifer Bostrom, Director of Admissions. E-Mail: *admissions@franklincollege.edu* Web: *www.franklincollege.edu*

GOSHEN COLLEGE — C-1

Goshen, IN 46526 — (574) 535-7535, (800) 348-7422; (574) 535-7609

Full-time: 328 men, 443 women
Part-time: 27 men, 81 women
Graduate: 10 men, 34 women
Year: 4-1-4, summer session
Application Deadline:
Freshman Class: n/av
SAT or ACT: required

Faculty: 76; IIB, --$
Ph.D.s: 64%
Student/Faculty: 12 to 1
Tuition: $26,900
Room & Board: $9000

VERY COMPETITIVE

Goshen College, founded in 1894, is a private, Christian, liberal arts institution affiliated with the Mennonite Church offering bachelor's and master's degrees in a variety of fields. In addition to regional accreditation, Goshen College has baccalaureate program accreditation with CSWE and NCATE. The library contains 120,000 volumes, 140,000 microform items, 1,500 audio/video tapes/CDs/DVDs, and subscribes to 900 periodicals including electronic. Computerized library services include interlibrary loans, database searching, and Internet access. Special learning facilities include an art gallery, radio station, and TV station. The 135-acre campus is in a small town. Goshen is approximately 120 miles east of Chicago, and 30 miles southeast of South Bend, IN. Including any residence halls, there are 25 buildings.

Student Life: 53% of undergraduates are from out of state, mostly the Mid-West. Students are from 33 states, 38 foreign countries, and Canada. 82% are White; 12% Hispanic. 87% are Protestant. The average age of freshmen is 18; all undergraduates, 21. 15% do not continue beyond their first year; 69% remain to graduate.

Housing: 700 students can be accommodated in college housing, which includes single-sex and coed dorms, on-campus apartments, off-campus apartments, and married student housing. In addition, there are special-interest houses. On-campus housing is guaranteed for all 4 years. 70% of students live on campus; of those, 85% remain on campus on weekends. Alcohol is not permitted. All students may keep cars.

Activities: There are no fraternities or sororities. There are 24 groups on campus, including art, choir, chorale, chorus, drama, environmental, ethnic, international, jazz band, literary magazine, musical theater, newspaper, opera, orchestra, photography, professional, radio and TV, religious, social, social service, student government, and yearbook. Popular campus events include Kick Off (student talent show), Martin Luther King Jr Day and Homecoming.

Sports: There are 8 intercollegiate sports for men and 8 for women, and 3 intramural sports for men and 3 for women. Facilities include a fitness center with an indoor track, weight room, 3 basketball courts, 3 racquetball courts, and workout equipment. Athletic facilities include a soccer field, tennis courts, a sand volleyball court, a 400-meter all-weather track, and baseball and softball diamonds.

Disabled Students: All of the campus is accessible. Facilities include wheelchair ramps, elevators, special parking, specially equipped restrooms, special class scheduling, lowered drinking fountains, and lowered telephones.

Services: Counseling and information services are available, as is tutoring in every subject. There is a reader service for the blind, and remedial math, reading, and writing.

Campus Safety and Security: Measures include 24-hour foot and vehicle patrol, emergency notification system, and security escort services. There are lighted pathways/sidewalks and controlled access to dorms/residences.

Programs of Study: Goshen College confers B.A., B.S. and B.S.N. degrees. Master's degrees are also awarded. Bachelor's degrees are awarded in AGRICULTURE (environmental studies), BIOLOGICAL SCIENCE (biochemistry, biology/biological science, ecology, and molecular biology), BUSINESS (accounting, business administration and management, and institutional management), COMMUNICATIONS AND THE ARTS (American Sign Language, art, broadcasting, communications, creative writing, dramatic arts, English, English Writing, graphic design, journalism, music, Spanish, and theatre arts), COMPUTER AND PHYSICAL SCIENCE (chemistry, computer programming, information sciences and systems, mathematics, and physics), EDUCATION (art education, business education, early childhood education, elementary education, English education, environmental education, foreign languages education, health education, mathematics education, middle school education, music education, physical education, science education, secondary education, and teaching English as a second/foreign language (TESOL/TEFOL)), ENGINEERING AND ENVIRONMENTAL DESIGN (environmental science and preengineering), HEALTH PROFESSIONS (nursing, predentistry, premedicine, prepharmacy, and preveterinary science), SOCIAL SCIENCE (biblical studies, economics, history, interdisciplinary studies, peace studies, psychology, religion, social work, sociology, and youth ministry). Nursing, elementary education, and biology have the largest enrollments.

Required: All students must complete the general education program,

including courses in literature and communication, fine arts, Bible, religion, philosophy, natural science, math, social science, and history, and 12 hours of international education in the Study Service Term and 1 hour of phys ed. A total of 120 credit hours with a minimum GPA of 2.0 is required to graduate.
Special: A semester-abroad in the required Study Service Term is possible in Cambodia, Morocco, Peru, Tanzania, Nicaragua, China & Senegal.
Faculty/Classroom: 50% of faculty are male; 50% are female. All teach undergraduates. No introductory courses are taught by graduate students. The average class size in an introductory lecture is 28; in a laboratory is 12; and in a regular course is 20.
Requirements: The SAT or ACT is required. Applicants should be graduates of an accredited secondary school or have a GED equivalent, with 4 years of high school English, 2 to 4 years of math, and 2 years each of foreign language, science, history, and social studies. AP and CLEP credits are accepted. Important factors in the admissions decision are advanced placement or honors courses, leadership record, and recommendations by school officials.
Procedure: Freshmen are admitted to all sessions. Entrance exams should be taken by fall of the senior year. There are deferred admissions and rolling admissions plans. Application deadlines are open. Application fee is $25. Notification is sent on a rolling basis. Applications are accepted online.
Transfer: A GPA of 2.0 or higher is required on previous college work.
Visiting: There are regularly scheduled orientations for prospective students, campus tour, a parents session, talks with professors, a financial aid session, visiting classes, an overnight stay in residence halls, a student panel, and a campus interview. There are guides for informal visits, visitors may sit in on classes, and stay overnight. To schedule a visit, contact the Admission Office at (800) 348.7422.
Financial Aid: Goshen College is a member of CSS. The FAFSA is required. Check with the school for current application deadlines.
International Students: There are 82 international students enrolled. The school actively recruits these students. They must take the TOEFL. They must also take the SAT or ACT.
Graduates: From July 1, 2012 to June 30, 2013, 221 bachelor's degrees were awarded. The most popular majors were nursing (19%), interdisciplinary (8%), and biology (6%). In an average class, 56% graduate in 4 years or less and 70% graduate in 6 years or less.
Admissions Contact: Dan Koop Liechty, Director of Admissions. E-Mail: *admission@goshen.edu* Web: *www.goshen.edu*

GRACE COLLEGE AND THEOLOGICAL SEMINARY C-2

Winona Lake, IN 46590 (574) 372-5100, ext. 6004
(800) 54-GRACE; (574) 372-5120

Full-time: 300 men, 470 women	**Faculty:** n/av
Part-time: 50men, 65 women	**Ph.D.s:** 63%
Graduate: 20 men, 35 women	**Student/Faculty:** n/av
Year: semesters, summer session	**Tuition:** $23,046
Application Deadline: see profile	**Room & Board:** $7714
Freshman Class: n/av	
SAT or ACT: recommended	

COMPETITIVE

Grace College, founded in 1948, is a Christian liberal arts institution affiliated with the Fellowship of Grace Brethren Churches. The figures in the above capsule and in this profile are approximate. There is 1 graduate school. In addition to regional accreditation, Grace has baccalaureate program accreditation with CSWE, NASM, and NCATE. The library contains 150,843 volumes, 26,000 microform items, 3714 audio/video tapes/CDs/DVDs, and subscribes to 19,360 periodicals including electronic. Computerized library services include interlibrary loans, database searching, Internet access, and laptop Internet portals. Special learning facilities include a learning resource center and art gallery. The 150-acre campus is in a small town 40 miles west of Fort Wayne. Including any residence halls, there are 15 buildings.
Student Life: 58% of undergraduates are from Indiana. Others are from 27 states, 5 foreign countries, and Canada. 74% are from public schools. 91% are white. 99% are Protestant. The average age of freshmen is 18; all undergraduates, 23. 17% do not continue beyond their first year; 58% remain to graduate.
Housing: 684 students can be accommodated in college housing, which includes single-sex dorms and on-campus apartments. On-campus housing is available on a first-come, first-served basis and is available on a lottery system for upperclassmen. Priority is given to out-of-town students. 75% of students live on campus; of those, 80% remain on campus on weekends. Alcohol is not permitted. All students may keep cars.
Activities: There are no fraternities or sororities. There are 14 groups on campus, including band, cheerleading, choir, chorale, drama, honors, international, musical theater, newspaper, orchestra, pep band, religious, social, student government, and yearbook. Popular campus events include Fall Fest, Heart of the Holidays, and VIP Days.
Sports: There are 8 intercollegiate sports for men and 8 for women, and 3 intramural sports for men and 3 for women. Facilities include a gym, soccer fields, tennis courts, softball and baseball diamonds, and a recreation center with basketball courts, indoor track, and weight and exercise rooms.
Disabled Students: 80% of the campus is accessible. Facilities include wheelchair ramps, elevators, special parking, and specially equipped restrooms.
Services: Counseling and information services are available, as is tutoring in most subjects. There is remedial math, reading, and writing.
Campus Safety and Security: Measures include 24-hour foot and vehicle patrol and security escort services. There are lighted pathways/sidewalks.
Programs of Study: Grace confers B.A., B.S., B.M., and B.S.W. degrees. Associate and master's degrees are also awarded. Bachelor's degrees are awarded in BIOLOGICAL SCIENCE (biology/biological science), BUSINESS (accounting, business administration and management, and management information systems), COMMUNICATIONS AND THE ARTS (art, communications, English, French, German, graphic design, journalism, music, and Spanish), COMPUTER AND PHYSICAL SCIENCE (mathematics and science), EDUCATION (art education, business education, elementary education, English education, foreign languages education, journalism education, mathematics education, music education, physical education, science education, and special education), HEALTH PROFESSIONS (predentistry and premedicine), SOCIAL SCIENCE (biblical studies, counseling/psychology, criminal justice, prelaw, psychology, religion, social work, sociology, and youth ministry). Biology, psychology, and business are the strongest academically. Psychology, elementary education, and biblical studies have the largest enrollments.
Required: To graduate, students must complete 124 hours, including 36 to 54 in the major, and have a minimum GPA of 2.0. The required core curriculum of 56 hours consists of languages/literature, humanities, religion/philosophy, education, social sciences, and natural sciences.
Special: Students may study abroad in 5 countries. A B.A.-B.S. degree is available in all majors except languages, English, and biblical studies. Dual majors are offered in psychology, sociology, communication, business, accounting, youth ministries, and management information technology. There is 1 national honor society and a freshman honors program.
Faculty/Classroom: 72% of faculty are male; 23% are female. All teach undergraduates. No introductory courses are taught by graduate students. The average class size in an introductory lecture is 48; in a laboratory, 14; and in a regular course, 17.
Requirements: The SAT or ACT is recommended. Applicants must have completed 15 Carnegie units, including 4 of English, 3 each of math and science, 2 each of a foreign language and social studies, and 1 of history. A GED is accepted. Grace requires applicants to be in the upper 50% of their class. A GPA of 2.3 is required. AP and CLEP credits are accepted. Important factors in the admissions decision are advanced placement or honors courses, leadership record, and personality/intangible qualities.
Procedure: Freshmen are admitted to all sessions. Entrance exams should be taken in October, December, or February. There are deferred admissions and rolling admissions plans. Check with the school for current application deadlines. The application fee is $30. Notification is sent on a rolling basis. Applications are accepted online.
Transfer: Transfer applicants should have a minimum 2.0 GPA in addition to fulfilling freshman entrance requirements. 60 of 124 credits required for the bachelor's degree must be completed at Grace.
Visiting: There are regularly scheduled orientations for prospective students, including tours, class visits, and meetings with professors. There are guides for informal visits, and visitors may sit in on classes, and stay overnight. To schedule a visit, contact the Visitors Center.
Financial Aid: The FAFSA is required. Check with the school for current application deadlines.
International Students: They must take the TOEFL. They must also take the SAT or ACT.
Admissions Contact: Admissions Counselor. E-Mail: *enroll@grace.edu* Web: *www.grace.edu*

HANOVER COLLEGE D-5

Hanover, IN 47243 (812) 866-7022
(800) 213-2178; (812) 866-7098

Full-time: 497 men, 661 women	**Faculty:** 101; IIB, av$
Part-time: 2 men, 3 women	**Ph.D.s:** 98%
Graduate: n/av	**Student/Faculty:** 12 to 1
Year: 4-1-4	**Tuition:** $31,760
Application Deadline:	**Room & Board:** $9690
Freshman Class: n/av	

VERY COMPETITIVE

Hanover College, founded in 1827 and the oldest private college in Indiana, is a liberal arts school affiliated with the United Presbyterian Church. In addition to regional accreditation, Hanover has baccalaureate program accreditation with NCATE. The library contains 299,841 volumes, 53,006 microform items, 7,501 audio/video tapes/CDs/DVDs, and subscribes to 45,968 periodicals including electronic. Computerized library services include interlibrary loans, database searching, Internet access, and Wi-Fi capability. Special learning facilities include an art gallery, planetarium, radio station, TV station, a geology museum. The 650-acre campus is in a rural area 45 miles northeast of Louisville, Kentucky, 70 miles southwest of Cincinnati, and 90 miles south of Indianapolis. Including any residence halls, there are 36 buildings.

Student Life: 69% of undergraduates are from Indiana. Others are from 24 states, and 19 foreign countries. 80% are from public schools. 82% are White. The average age of freshmen is 18; all undergraduates, 19. 19% do not continue beyond their first year; 72% remain to graduate.

Housing: 1100 students can be accommodated in college housing, which includes single-sex and coed dorms and on-campus apartments. In addition, there are honors houses, special-interest houses, fraternity houses, sorority houses, and a multicultural center. On-campus housing is guaranteed for all 4 years. 95% of students live on campus. All students may keep cars.

Activities: 44% of men belong to 5 national fraternities; 29% of women belong to 4 national sororities. There are 60 groups on campus, including art, band, cheerleading, choir, chorus, computers, dance, debate, drama, environmental, ethnic, film, gay, honors, international, jazz band, literary magazine, marching band, musical theater, newspaper, orchestra, pep band, photography, political, professional, radio and TV, religious, social, social service, student government, and yearbook. Popular campus events include Community Artist Series, Wiffleball Tournament, MLK Marade.

Sports: There are 9 intercollegiate sports for men and 9 for women, and 10 intramural sports for men and 10 for women. Facilities include a health and recreation center consisting of a 2000-seat performance gym, a multisports forum, a suspended running track, racquetball and squash courts, a weight room, a training room, and a physiology lab. There also is an outdoor athletic complex consisting of a new 5000-seat football/track stadium, baseball, softball and soccer fields, new tennis courts, and a lacrosse field.

Disabled Students: 75% of the campus is accessible. Facilities include wheelchair ramps, elevators, special parking, specially equipped restrooms, special class scheduling, lowered drinking fountains, lowered telephones, and special housing.

Services: Counseling and information services are available, as is tutoring in most subjects. There is remedial writing.

Campus Safety and Security: Measures include 24-hour foot and vehicle patrol, emergency notification system, self-defense education, and security escort services. There are shuttle buses, emergency telephones, lighted pathways/sidewalks, and controlled access to dorms/residences.

Programs of Study: Hanover confers B.A. degrees. Bachelor's degrees are awarded in BIOLOGICAL SCIENCE (biochemistry, biology/biological science, and environmental biology), COMMUNICATIONS AND THE ARTS (art, art history and appreciation, classics, communications, dramatic arts, English, French, German, music, and Spanish), COMPUTER AND PHYSICAL SCIENCE (chemistry, computer science, environmental geology, geology, mathematics, and physics), EDUCATION (elementary education), ENGINEERING AND ENVIRONMENTAL DESIGN (environmental science), HEALTH PROFESSIONS (health and physical activity and kinesiology), SOCIAL SCIENCE (anthropology, economics, gender studies, history, international studies, medieval studies, philosophy, political science/government, psychology, sociology, and theological studies). Arts and sciences and interdisciplinary studies is the strongest academically. Psychology, biology, and communication have the largest enrollments.

Required: To graduate, students must complete 36 units of credit, including 8 to 12 in the major, LADRs (12 to 13 units of general degree requirements), maintain a GPA of 2.0 overall and in the major, pass a comprehensive exam, and participate in a culminating experience in the major.

Special: Internships, study abroad in Australia, Belgium, France, Turkey, City Semesters programs in Philadelphia, Washington, D.C., and Chicago, and self-designed majors including 2 or more disciplines, are offered. The Business Scholars Program provides preparation for a career in business, built on a liberal arts foundation, where everyone in the program completes an internship. There are 8 national honor societies and 8 departmental honors programs.

Faculty/Classroom: 59% of faculty are male; 41% are female. All teach undergraduates. No introductory courses are taught by graduate students. The average class size in an introductory lecture is 14; in a laboratory is 15; and in a regular course is 14.

Admissions: 53% of the current freshmen were in the top fifth of their class; 86% were in the top two fifths. 8 freshmen graduated first in their class.

Requirements: The SAT or ACT is required. In addition, admission is competitive, based on the applicant pool. The college requires 18 academic credits, including 4 years of English and 2 each of a foreign language, math, science, and either history or social studies. The GED is accepted. The college also requires a foreign language achievement test for those who wish to meet their world language requirement in the language they studied in high school, as well as an essay; an interview is recommended. AP credits are accepted. Important factors in the admissions decision are recommendations by school officials, advanced placement or honors courses, and extracurricular activities record.

Procedure: Freshmen are admitted fall and winter. Entrance exams should be taken late in the spring of the junior year. There are deferred admissions and rolling admissions plans. Check with the school for current application deadlines. The application fee is $40. Applications are accepted online. Application fees are waived if application is completed online.

Transfer: 10 transfer students enrolled in 2012-2013. Transfer students must submit transcripts from all colleges attended and must have performed successfully. SAT or ACT scores and high school record may also be taken into consideration. 17 of 36 credits required for the bachelor's degree must be completed at Hanover.

Visiting: There are regularly scheduled orientations for prospective students. There are guides for informal visits, visitors may sit in on classes, and stay overnight. To schedule a visit, contact Lyn Lyon at (800) 213-2178.

Financial Aid: In 2013-2014, 99% of all full-time freshmen and 97% of continuing full-time students received some form of financial aid. 85% of all full time freshmen and 83% of continuing full-time students received need-based aid. The average freshman award was $24,172. Hanover is a member of CSS. The FAFSA is required. Check with the school for current application deadlines.

International Students: There are 53 international students enrolled. The school actively recruits these students. They must take the TOEFL with a minimum score of 550 on the paper-based TOEFL (PBT) or 80 on the Internet-based version (iBT). They must also take the SAT or ACT.

Graduates: From July 1, 2012 to June 30, 2013, 221 bachelor's degrees were awarded. The most popular majors were psychology (10%), elementary education (9%), and biology (8%). 24 companies recruited on campus in 2012-2013. In an average class, 68% graduate in 4 years or less, 71% graduate in 5 years or less, and 72% graduate in 6 years or less. Of the 2012 graduating class, 24% were enrolled in graduate school within 6 months of graduation, and 60% were employed.

Admissions Contact: Chris Gage, Dean of Admission. E-Mail: *admission@hanover.edu* Web: *www.hanover.edu*

HUNTINGTON UNIVERSITY — D-2

Huntington, IN 46750 — (260) 358-4000; (800) 642-6493; (260) 358-3699

Full-time: 406 men, 555 women	**Faculty:** 53; IIB, --$
Part-time: 42 men, 50 women	**Ph.D.s:** 87%
Graduate: 32 men, 49 women	**Student/Faculty:** 13 to 1
Year: 4-1-4, summer session	**Tuition:** $24,040
Application Deadline:	**Room & Board:** $8180
Freshman Class: 780 applied, 759 accepted, 226 enrolled	
SAT CR/M/W: 509/503/486 — **ACT:** 24	**COMPETITIVE**

Huntington University is a comprehensive Christian college of the liberal arts offering graduate and undergraduate programs in more than 70 academic concentrations. Founded in 1897 by the Church of the United Brethren in Christ, Huntington University is located on a contemporary, lakeside campus in northeast Indiana. The university is a member of the Council for Christian Colleges and Universities (CCCU). There is one graduate school. In addition to regional accreditation, Huntington has baccalaureate program accreditation with CSWE, NASM, and NCATE. The library contains 236,659 volumes, 11,803 microform items, 7,718 audio/video tapes/CDs/DVDs, and subscribes to 52,798 periodicals including electronic. Computerized library services include interlibrary loans, database searching, Internet access, and Wi-Fi capability. Special learning facilities include an art gallery, radio station, TV station, a writing center and an Enterprise Resource Center which helps students with internships, resumes, job training and practicum; herbarium, nature preserve (Thornhill Nature Preserve), arboretum, greenhouse, studio theatre, exercise science training facilities (including a BODPOD), historical archives (United Brethren Historical Center). The 170-acre campus is in a small town 20 miles southwest of Fort Wayne. Including any residence halls, there are 25 buildings.

Student Life: 64% of undergraduates are from Indiana. Others are from 31 states, 20 foreign countries, and Canada. 88% are White. 57% are Protestant; 38% Non-denominational. The average age of freshmen is 18; all undergraduates, 20. 21% do not continue beyond their first year; 59% remain to graduate.

Housing: 831 students can be accommodated in college housing, which includes single-sex dorms, off-campus apartments, and married student housing. On-campus housing is guaranteed for all 4 years. 74% of students live on campus; of those, 50% remain on campus on weekends. Alcohol is not permitted. All students may keep cars.

Activities: There are no fraternities or sororities. There are 35 groups on campus, including a service organization where students, faculty and staff volunteer more than 11, 000 hours each year, art, band, cheerleading, choir, chorale, chorus, communications, computers, dance, drama, environmental, ethnic, film, Friesen Center for Volunteer Service, honors, international, jazz band, literary magazine, musical theater, newspaper, orchestra, pep band, political, professional, radio and TV, religious, social, social service, student government, and symphony. Popular campus events include Olympiad, Forester Night, Chapel series and Hoe Down.

Sports: There are 8 intercollegiate sports for men and 8 for women, and 9 intramural sports for men and 9 for women. Facilities include a fieldhouse with an indoor running track, 3 basketball courts, one outdoor basketball court, indoor and outdoor tennis courts, softball and baseball diamonds, an outdoor track, soccer and intramural fields, weight room and aerobic facility, and a gym.

Disabled Students: 64% of the campus is accessible. Facilities include wheelchair ramps, elevators, special parking, specially equipped restrooms, lowered drinking fountains, and special housing.

Services: Counseling and information services are available, as is tutoring in some subjects, English, math, and others There is a reader service for the blind, and remedial math and writing.

Campus Safety and Security: Measures include emergency notification system and security escort services. There are emergency telephones, lighted pathways/sidewalks, controlled access to dorms/residences, and security on duty from 6 p.m. to 6 a.m.

Programs of Study: Huntington confers B.A., B.S., B.Mus., B.S.Sc. and B.S.N. degrees. Associate, master's, and doctoral degrees are also awarded. Bachelor's degrees are awarded in BIOLOGICAL SCIENCE (biology/biological science), BUSINESS (accounting, business administration and management, entrepreneurial studies, marketing management, nonprofit/public organization management, organizational behavior, small business management, and sports management), COMMUNICATIONS AND THE ARTS (animation, art, broadcasting, communications, creative writing, dramatic arts, English, English as a second/foreign language, English literature, film arts, fine arts, graphic design, journalism, media arts, music business management, music performance, music theory and composition, performing arts, public relations, studio art, theatre arts, and theater design), COMPUTER AND PHYSICAL SCIENCE (chemistry, computer science, information sciences and systems, mathematics, and physics), EDUCATION (art education, education, elementary education, English education, mathematics education, music education, physical education, science education, secondary education, social studies education, sports studies, and teaching English as a second/foreign language (TESOL/TEFOL)), HEALTH PROFESSIONS (exercise science, nursing, premedicine, prepharmacy, prephysical therapy, and recreation therapy), SOCIAL SCIENCE (area studies, biblical studies, counseling/psychology, criminal justice, economics, history, ministries, parks and recreation management, philosophy, prelaw, psychology, religion, religious music, social work, sociology, and youth ministry). Film, animation, exercise science, psychology, business and nursing are the strongest academically. Film and animation, exercise science and nursing have the largest enrollments.

Required: Students must complete a minimum of 128 credit hours including 36 in the major, and maintain a GPA of 2.0 overall and a major GPA of at least 2.0 (higher for some programs). Students must complete a program in general education, and take 36 hours in upper-division courses numbered 300 or above, 3 hours of math or computer science and religion courses are required.

Special: Companies in the area offer a number of internships to students in concentrations such as business, sociology, social work, ministry and missions, education, graphic design, digital media arts, music business, and sport and recreation management. Students may study abroad in a number of countries. A Washington semester, a Hollywood semester, dual majors, correspondence courses with other schools, and an accelerated degree program in organizational management, business administration, accounting, nursing, marketing, human resource management, and organizational management are available. There are 11 national honor societies, a freshman honors program, and 6 departmental honors programs.

Faculty/Classroom: 52% of faculty are male; 48% are female. 88% teach undergraduates. No introductory courses are taught by graduate students. The average class size in an introductory lecture is 25; in a laboratory is 19; and in a regular course is 19.

Admissions: 97% of the 2013-2014 applicants were accepted. The SAT scores for the 2013-2014 freshman class were: Critical Reading--43% below 500, 42% between 500 and 599, 12% between 600 and 699, and 3% between 700 and 800; Math--49% below 500, 36% between 500 and 599, 12% between 600 and 699, and 3% between 700 and 800; Writing--56% below 500, 33% between 500 and 599, 10% between 600 and 699, and 1% between 700 and 800. The ACT scores were 7% below 21, 42% between 21 and 23, 44% between 24 and 26, 30% between 27 and 28, and 8% above 28. 53% of the current freshmen were in the top fifth of their class; 79% were in the top two fifths.

Requirements: The SAT or ACT is required. Applicants must have 4 years of English, 2 of college-preparatory math, and 3 of social studies. A GPA of 2.3 is required. AP and CLEP credits are accepted. Important factors in the admissions decision are recommendations by school officials, recommendations by alumni, and personality/intangible qualities.

Procedure: Freshmen are admitted to all sessions. Entrance exams should be taken before or during the fall semester of the senior year. There are deferred admissions and rolling admissions plans. Application deadlines are open. Application fee is $20. Applications are accepted online.

Transfer: 39 transfer students enrolled in 2012-2013. Transfer applicants should be in good standing at the college previously attended and have maintained a GPA of 2.0. Courses with a grade of C or better transfer. All transcripts and an essay are required. 90 of 128 credits required for the bachelor's degree must be completed at Huntington.

Visiting: There are regularly scheduled orientations for prospective students, available on 3 days notice. There are guides for informal visits, visitors may sit in on classes, and stay overnight. To schedule a visit, contact Carlene Peters at (260) 359-4020.

Financial Aid: In 2013-2014, 90% of all full-time freshmen and 90% of continuing full-time students received some form of financial aid. The average freshman award was $19,659. Need-based scholarships or need-based grants averaged $17,218 ; need-based self-help aid (loans and jobs) averaged $4,455; non-need-based athletic scholarships averaged $7,266; and other non-need-based awards and non-need-based scholarships averaged $12,362. 25% of undergraduate students work part-time. Average annual earnings from campus work are $3450. The average financial indebtedness of the 2013 graduate was $34,662. The FAFSA and the college's own financial statement are required. The priority date for freshman financial aid applications for fall entry is March 10.

International Students: There are 38 international students enrolled. The school actively recruits these students. They must take the TOEFL with a minimum score of 525 on the paper-based TOEFL (PBT) or 65 on the Internet-based version (iBT).

Graduates: From July 1, 2012 to June 30, 2013, 252 bachelor's degrees were awarded. The most popular majors were business (19%), education (15%), and theology and religious vocations (13%). In an average class, 59% graduate in 6 years or less.

Admissions Contact: Jeff Berggren, Vice President for Enrollment Management & Marketing. E-Mail: *admissions@huntington.edu* Web: *www.huntington.edu*

INDIANA INSTITUTE OF TECHNOLOGY D-2

Fort Wayne, IN 46803 **(260) 422-5561, ext. 2121**
(800) 937-2448; (260) 422-7696

Full-time: 1415 men, 2291 women	**Faculty:** n/av
Part-time: 739 men, 1252 women	**Ph.D.s:** n/av
Graduate: 292 men, 294 women	**Student/Faculty:** n/av
Year: semesters, summer session	**Tuition:** $24,860
Application Deadline: open	**Room & Board:** $9380
Freshman Class: 2320 applied, 1674 accepted, 360 enrolled	
SAT CR/M/W: 447/468/430 **ACT:** 20	**LESS COMPETITIVE**

The Indiana Institute of Technology, established in 1930, is a private, nonprofit, comprehensive university offering undergraduate and graduate degrees primarily in business, engineering, and computer science. We also offer a PhD in Global Leadership and a Law school that started August 2013. There are 3 undergraduate schools and 3 graduate schools. In addition to regional accreditation, Indiana Tech has baccalaureate program accreditation with ABET. The library contains 20,536 volumes, 286 audio/video tapes/CDs/DVDs, and subscribes to 50,000 periodicals including electronic. Computerized library services include interlibrary loans and database searching. Special learning facilities include a The 40-acre campus is in an urban area 150 miles east of Chicago, 120 miles north of Indianapolis, and 160 miles southwest of Detroit, Michigan. Including any residence halls, there are 18 buildings.

Student Life: 82% of undergraduates are from Indiana. Others are from 44 states, 20 foreign countries, and Canada. 43% are White; 34% African American; 15% race unknown. The average age of freshmen is 24; all undergraduates, 33. 55% do not continue beyond their first year.

Housing: 615 students can be accommodated in college housing, which includes coed dorms and on-campus apartments. In addition, there are sorority houses. On-campus housing is guaranteed for all 4 years, is available on a first-come, and first-served basis. Priority is given to out-of-town students. 55% of students commute. Alcohol is not permitted. All students may keep cars.

Activities: There are 28 groups on campus, including cheerleading, choir, computers, environmental, film, honors, international, newspaper, pep band, professional, religious, social, and social service.

Sports: There are 11 intercollegiate sports for men and 10 for women, and 6 intramural sports for men and 5 for women. Facilities include basketball court, volleyball courts, baseball field, soccer and lacrosse field, indoor track.

Disabled Students: 95% of the campus is accessible. Facilities include wheelchair ramps, elevators, special parking, specially equipped restrooms, lowered drinking fountains, lowered telephones, and special housing.

Services: Counseling and information services are available, as is tutoring in most subjects. There is remedial math, reading, and writing.

Campus Safety and Security: Measures include 24-hour foot and vehicle patrol, self-defense education, and security escort services. There are emergency telephones, lighted pathways/sidewalks, and controlled access to dorms/residences.

Programs of Study: Indiana Tech confers B.A., and B.S. degrees. Associate, master's, and doctoral degrees are also awarded. Bachelor's degrees are awarded in BUSINESS (accounting, business administration and management, fashion merchandising, recreation and leisure services, and sports management), COMMUNICATIONS AND THE ARTS (communications and digital communications), COMPUTER AND PHYSICAL SCIENCE (computer game design/development, computer science, information sciences and systems, software engineering, and web services), EDUCATION (elementary education, health information management, and physical education), ENGINEERING AND ENVIRONMENTAL DESIGN (biomedical engineering, computer engineering, electrical/electronics engineering, engineering, environmental engineering technology, industrial engineering, and mechanical engineering), HEALTH PROFESSIONS (recreation therapy), SOCIAL SCIENCE (criminal justice, criminology, human services, law, law enforcement and corrections, parks and recreation management, prelaw, and psychology). Software Engineering and Pre-Law are the strongest academically. Business Administration has the largest enrollments.

Required: To graduate, students must complete a minimum of 120 credit hours, including at least 35 in the major, with a 2.0 minimum GPA. General education requirements include at least 18 hours in social science/humanities and 9 in English.

Special: The school offers internships, work-study programs, and accelerated degree programs in evening and online formats through the College of Professional Studies (CPS). Credit for life experience is offered through the CPS. Dual majors and nondegree studies are available. Undergraduate to Graduate 4+1 program is also available. There is 1 national honor society.

Faculty/Classroom: No introductory courses are taught by graduate students.

Admissions: 72% of the 2013-2014 applicants were accepted. The SAT scores for the 2013-2014 freshman class were: Critical Reading--69% below 500, 27% between 500 and 599, and 4% between 600 and 699; Math--59% below 500, 32% between 500 and 599, 8% between 600 and 699, and 1% between 700 and 800; Writing--81% below 500, 18% between 500 and 599, and 1% between 600 and 699. The ACT scores were 53% below 21, 27% between 21 and 23, 16% between 24 and 26, 2% between 27 and 28, and 2% above 28. 19% of the current freshmen were in the top fifth of their class; 47% were in the top two fifths.

Requirements: The SAT or ACT is required. Applicants must be graduates of an accredited secondary school, or obtained a GED. Students applying as freshmen are required to submit ACT or SAT test scores and official high school transcript. Transfer applicants are required to submit official high school transcript and ACT or SAT test scores, unless a college degree has already been earned and official college transcript(s). Applicants with a GED are not required to submit ACT or SAT test scores. The minimum GPA for acceptance is 2.0. A GPA of 2.0 is required. AP and CLEP credits are accepted. Important factors in the admissions decision are advanced placement or honors courses, ability to finance college education, leadership record, parents or siblings attended your school, evidence of special talent, personality/intangible qualities, extracurricular activities record, recommendations by alumni, and geographical diversity.

Procedure: Freshmen are admitted to all sessions. Entrance exams should be taken by January of the senior year. There is a rolling admissions plan. Application deadlines are open. Application fee is $50. Applications are accepted online.

Transfer: 71 transfer students enrolled in 2012-2013. Applicants must be in good standing and have a minimum GPA of 2.0. 30 of 124 credits required for the bachelor's degree must be completed at Indiana Tech.

Visiting: There are regularly scheduled orientations for prospective students, Students tour campus with a student tour guide, attend sessions on financial aid and the admissions process, eat lunch, and have the opportunity to meet with faculty and coaches. . There are guides for informal visits, visitors may sit in on classes, and stay overnight. To schedule a visit, contact the Admissions Office.

Financial Aid: The FAFSA and the college's own financial statement are required. The priority date for freshman financial aid applications for fall entry is March 10.

International Students: There are 38 international students enrolled. The school actively recruits these students. They must take the TOEFL with a minimum score of 523 on the paper-based TOEFL (PBT) or 70 on the Internet-based version (iBT), IELTS, and PTE. They must also take the SAT or ACT, scoring 860. SAT is required for international athletes for athletic eligiblity purposes.

Graduates: From July 1, 2012 to June 30, 2013, 568 bachelor's degrees were awarded. The most popular majors were business administration - general (48%), accounting (10%), and organizational leadership (10%).

Admissions Contact: Steven A Herendeen, Vice President for Enrollment Management. E-Mail: *SAHerendeen@indianatech.edu* Web: *www.indianatech.edu*

INDIANA STATE UNIVERSITY — B-4

Terre Haute, IN 47809 — (812) 237-2121; (800) GO-2-ISU; (812) 237-8023

Full-time: 3700 men, 3625 women	**Faculty:** n/av; I, --$
Part-time: 520 men, 720 women	**Ph.D.s:** 80%
Graduate: 835 men, 1235 women	**Student/Faculty:** n/av
Year: semesters, summer session	**Tuition:** $8500 ($17,500)
Application Deadline: open	**Room & Board:** $8000
Freshman Class: n/av	
SAT or ACT: required	

COMPETITIVE

Indiana State University, founded in 1865, is a publicly supported institution offering undergraduate and graduate study in liberal arts and sciences, business, health, phys ed and recreation, education, nursing, and technology. The figures in the above capsule and in this profile are approximate. There are 6 undergraduate schools and 1 graduate school. In addition to regional accreditation, ISU has baccalaureate program accreditation with AACSB, ADA, AHEA, CAHEA, CSWE, FIDER, NASAD, NASM, NCATE, NLN, and NRPA. The library contains 1.3 million volumes, 961,984 microform items, 37,474 audio/video tapes/CDs/DVDs, and subscribes to 43,707 periodicals including electronic. Computerized library services include interlibrary loans, database searching, and Internet access. Special learning facilities include a learning resource center, art gallery, planetarium, radio station, an African American cultural center. The 235-acre campus is in an urban area 75 miles west of Indianapolis. Including any residence halls, there are 55 buildings.

Student Life: 86% of undergraduates are from Indiana. Others are from 50 states, 65 foreign countries, and Canada. 81% are white; 12% African American. The average age of freshmen is 19; all undergraduates, 23. 31% do not continue beyond their first year; 45% remain to graduate.

Housing: 3284 students can be accommodated in college housing, which includes single-sex and coed dorms and married student housing. In addition, there are honors houses, special-interest houses, and special freshman dorms. On-campus housing is guaranteed for all 4 years. 64% of students commute. Alcohol is not permitted. All students may keep cars.

Activities: 10% of men belong to 19 national fraternities; 9% of women belong to 13 national sororities. There are 180 groups on campus, including art, band, cheerleading, choir, chorale, chorus, computers, dance, drama, drill team, ethnic, film, gay, honors, international, jazz band, literary magazine, marching band, musical theater, newspaper, orchestra, pep band, political, professional, radio and TV, religious, social, social service, student government, symphony, and yearbook. Popular campus events include a contemporary music festival, theaterfest, and black history month.

Sports: There are 6 intercollegiate sports for men and 8 for women, and 29 intramural sports for men and 29 for women. Facilities include a 20,000-seat football stadium, a 10,000-seat basketball arena, 2 softball diamonds, a baseball field, a soccer field, 2 indoor and outdoor tracks, 2 pools, indoor and outdoor basketball and tennis courts, racquetball, sand volleyball, and volleyball courts, a physical fitness center with weight-training facilities, a climbing wall, and fitness/wellness facilities located in 2 residence halls and the student union.

Disabled Students: 98% of the campus is accessible. Facilities include wheelchair ramps, elevators, special parking, specially equipped restrooms, special class scheduling, lowered drinking fountains, lowered telephones, special housing, and special dining hall facilities.

Services: Counseling and information services are available, as is tutoring in most subjects. There is a reader service for the blind. A learning skills center, an academic advisement center, a counseling center, student support services, a math lab, and a writing lab are available.

Campus Safety and Security: Measures include 24-hour foot and vehicle patrol, emergency notification system, self-defense education, and security escort services. There are emergency telephones, lighted pathways/sidewalks, in-room safes, and bicycle and car registration.

Programs of Study: ISU confers B.A., B.S., B.F.A., B.M., B.M.E., and B.S.W. degrees. Associate, master's, and doctoral degrees are also awarded. Bachelor's degrees are awarded in BIOLOGICAL SCIENCE (biology/biological science), BUSINESS (accounting, banking and finance, business administration and management, insurance, management information systems, marketing and distribution, marketing/retailing/merchandising, recreation and leisure services, and sports management), COMMUNICATIONS AND THE ARTS (art history and appreciation, communications, dramatic arts, English, fine arts, French, German, journalism, music, Spanish, and studio art), COMPUTER AND PHYSICAL SCIENCE (chemistry, computer science, geology, mathematics, and physics), EDUCATION (art education, business education, early childhood education, elementary education, foreign languages education, health education, home economics education, industrial arts education, middle school education, music education, physical education, science education, secondary education, social studies education, and special education), ENGINEERING AND ENVIRONMENTAL DESIGN (aeronautical technology, airline piloting and navigation, computer technology, construction technology, electrical/electronics engineering technology, industrial engineering technology, interior design, manufacturing technology, and mechanical engineering technology), HEALTH PROFESSIONS (environmental health science, medical laboratory technology, nursing, and speech pathology/audiology), SOCIAL SCIENCE (African American studies, anthropology, child care/child and family studies, criminology, dietetics, economics, food science, geography, history, home economics, interdisciplinary studies, liberal arts/general studies, parks and recreation management, philosophy, political science/government, psychology, safety management, social work, sociology, and textiles and clothing). Financial services, teacher education, and aerospace technology are the strongest academically. Criminology, nursing, and elementary education have the largest enrollments.

Required: All students must complete the general education program, as well as a minimum of 50 hours of upper-division course work. Specific courses required include phys ed, English, speech, math, foreign language, and computer science. A minimum GPA of 2.0 (2.5 for education majors) and a total of 124 credit hours are required for graduation. The number of hours required in the major varies.

Special: There is a freshman honors program.

Faculty/Classroom: 56% of faculty are male; 44% are female. 86% teach undergraduates, 44% do research, and 39% do both. Graduate students teach 11% of introductory courses. The average class size in an introductory lecture is 31; in a laboratory is 22; and in a regular course is 25.

Admissions: 18 freshmen graduated first in their class.

Requirements: The SAT or ACT is required. In addition, the applicant must be a graduate of an accredited secondary school. The GED is accepted. An essay is not required. Applicants are reviewed based on a combination of class rank, GPA, strength of curriculum, academic progress, and standardized test scores. Those students who rank in the top 50% of their class are routinely admitted, whereas those in the bottom 50% of their class are reviewed on an individual basis. Routine admission does not guarantee admission to specific majors. A GPA of 2.5 is required. AP and CLEP credits are accepted. Important factors in the admissions decision are advanced placement or honors courses, leadership record, and extracurricular activities record.

Procedure: Freshmen are admitted fall, spring, and summer. Entrance exams should be taken before January 1. There are deferred admissions and rolling admissions plans. Check with the school for current application deadlines. The application fee is $25. Applications are accepted online.

Transfer: 629 transfer students enrolled in 2010-2011. Transfer students must have a minimum GPA of 2.0. 30 of 124 credits required for the bachelor's degree must be completed at ISU.

Visiting: There are regularly scheduled orientations for prospective students, consisting of Sycamore Preview Days, which include campus tours, opportunities to meet with academic advisers in the majors students are considering, and formal sessions with representatives from financial aid and the career center. There are guides for informal visits, visitors may sit in on classes, and stay overnight. To schedule a visit, contact the Admissions Office.

Financial Aid: In a recent year, 68% of all full-time freshmen and 61% of continuing full-time students received some form of financial aid. 40% of all full-time freshmen and 39% of continuing full-time students received need-based aid. The average freshman award was $7,721. Need-based scholarships or need-based grants averaged $5,398; need-based self-help aid (loans and jobs) averaged $2,560; non-need-based athletic scholarships averaged $8,891; other non-need-based awards and non-need-based scholarships averaged $3,504; and $2,508 from other forms of aid. The average financial indebtedness of the recent graduate was $20,868. The FAFSA is required. Check with the school for current application deadlines.

International Students: There are 136 international students enrolled. The school actively recruits these students. They must take the TOEFL with a minimum score of 500 on the paper-based TOEFL (PBT) or 61 on the Internet based version (iBT). They must also take the SAT or ACT.

Graduates: In a recent year, 1415 bachelor's degrees were awarded. The most popular majors were criminology (8%), elementary education (5%), and psychology (4%). 250 companies recruited on campus in a recent year. In an average class, 3% graduate in 3 years or less, 21% graduate in 4 years or less, 37% graduate in 5 years or less, and 42% graduate in 6 years or less.

Admissions Contact: Richard Toomey, Director. E-Mail: *admissions@indstate.edu* Web: *www.indiana.edu*

INDIANA UNIVERSITY SYSTEM

The Indiana University System, established in 1820, is a public system in Indiana. It is governed by a board of trustees, whose chief administrator is the president. The primary goal of the system is research, teaching, and service. The main priorities are undergraduate education, research, graduate education, economical growth, and access to education. The total student enrollment is usually about 95,000 with 3800 faculty members. Altogether there are 313 baccalaureate, 207 master's, and 108 doctoral programs offered in Indiana University System. Profiles of the 4-year campuses are included in this section.

INDIANA UNIVERSITY BLOOMINGTON C-4

Bloomington, IN 47405 **(812) 855-0661; (812) 855-5102**

Full-time: 15417 men, 15633 women	**Faculty:** n/av; I, av$
Part-time: 2510 men, 3302 women	**Ph.D.s:** 78%
Graduate: 5214 men, 4741 women	**Student/Faculty:** 18 to 1
Year: semesters, summer session	**Tuition:** $10,209 ($32,350)
Application Deadline: February 1	**Room & Board:** $9149

Freshman Class: 37826 applied, 27300 accepted, 7604 enrolled

SAT CR/M/W: 575/600/565 **ACT:** 27 **HIGHLY COMPETITIVE**

Founded in 1820, IU Bloomington is the flagship campus of Indiana University's eight campuses statewide. Innovation, creativity, and academic freedom are hallmarks of IU Bloomington and its world-class contributions in research and the arts. Our school traditions include the world-famous Little 500 bicycle race, which furthur recognizes our commitment to emerging technologies. We nurture bright minds with an exceptional support network and breadth of programs. For technology infrastructure and support, our campus was named "most wired" among public universities by PC Magazine in 2006. There are 15 undergraduate schools. In addition to regional accreditation, IU has baccalaureate program accreditation with AACSB, ACBSP, ACEJMC, ADA, APTA, ASLA, CAHEA, CSWE, FIDER, NASAD, NASM, NCATE, and NLN. The 20 libraries contain 9.5 million volumes, 3.6 million microform items, and 0 audio/video tapes/CDs/DVDs, and subscribe to 72,093 periodicals including electronic. Computerized library services include interlibrary loans, database searching, Internet access, and Wi-Fi capability. Special learning facilities include an art gallery, natural history museum, radio station, TV station, an observatory, arboretum, museum of world cultures, garden and nature center, musical arts center, and more than 70 research centers. The 1928-acre campus is in a small town 50 miles southwest of Indianapolis. Including any residence halls, there are 556 buildings.

Student Life: 67% of undergraduates are from Indiana. Others are from 50 states, 138 foreign countries, and Canada. 70% are White; 14% Foreign. The average age of freshmen is 18; all undergraduates, 20.

Housing: 12871 students can be accommodated in college housing, which includes single-sex and coed dorms, on-campus apartments, off-campus apartments, and married student housing. In addition, there are honors houses, language houses, special-interest houses, living-learning centers, an international center, a center for women, a wellness center, freshman interest groups (FIGs), and thematic communities. On-campus housing is guaranteed for the freshman year only, is available on a first-come, and first-served basis. 72% of students commute. Alcohol is not permitted. All students may keep cars.

Activities: There are 650 groups on campus, including art, band, cheerleading, chess, choir, chorale, chorus, communications, computers, dance, debate, drama, drill team, environmental, ethnic, film, gay, honors, international, jazz band, literary magazine, marching band, musical theater, newspaper, opera, orchestra, photography, political, professional, radio and TV, religious, social, social service, student government, and symphony. Popular campus events include Little 500, Founder's Day, Homecoming Parade and IU Dance Marathon.

Sports: There are 10 intercollegiate sports for men and 12 for women, and 27 intramural sports for men and 27 for women. The 204,000 square foot Student Recreational Sports Center (SRSC) features three multi-sport gyms, a spacious Strength & Conditioning area with more than 400 pieces of cardiovascular and weight-training equipment, the Counsilman/Billingsley Aquatic Center, an elevated running track, and much more. The historic, newly renovated Wildermuth Intramural Center (WIC) features 10 basketball/volleyball courts, a brand new track, squash courts, new Strength & Conditioning areas, and Royer Pool (home training ground of legendary Olympian Mark Spitz). Facilities also include Woodlawn Field (perfect for soccer, flag football, and more) and numerous tennis courts. IUB also has the Harry Gladstein Fieldhouse for track & field, the Andy Mohr softball field, the Bart Kaufman baseball complex with indoor and outdoor hitting cages, Bill Armstrong Stadium for soccer, the Memorial Stadium for football, Assembly Hall for basketball, the IU Field Hockey Complex, the IU Championship Golf Course, a cross-country course and the Dale England rowing center.

Disabled Students: 95% of the campus is accessible. Facilities include wheelchair ramps, elevators, special parking, specially equipped restrooms, special class scheduling, lowered drinking fountains, lowered telephones. scheduled transportation.

Services: Counseling and information services are available, as is tutoring in most subjects. There is a reader service for the blind, and remedial math, reading, and writing. Skills workshops are also offered.

Campus Safety and Security: Measures include 24-hour foot and

vehicle patrol, emergency notification system, self-defense education, and security escort services. There are shuttle buses, emergency telephones, lighted pathways/sidewalks, controlled access to dorms/residences, Safety awareness education.

Programs of Study: IU confers B.A., B.F.A., B.G.S., B.M., B.M.Ed., B.S., B.S.Ed., B.S.N., B.S.P.A., B.S.P.H. and B.S.W. degrees. Master's and doctoral degrees are also awarded. Bachelor's degrees are awarded in AGRICULTURE (environmental studies), BIOLOGICAL SCIENCE (biochemistry, biotechnology, human biology, health, and society, microbiology, and neurosciences), BUSINESS (accounting, apparel and accessories marketing, business administration and management, entrepreneurial studies, finance, international business, labor studies, marketing, nonprofit/public organization management, policy analysis and management, real estate, recreation and leisure services, sports management, sports marketing, supply chain management, and tourism), COMMUNICATIONS AND THE ARTS (art history, arts administration/management, ballet, communication, communication studies, communication studies, composition, comparative literature, dance, East Asian languages and literature, English, fine arts, folklore and mythology, French, German, german studies, Germanic languages and literature, Greek (classical), guitar, Italian, jazz, journalism, languages, Latin, linquistics, music, music performance, music theatre accompanying , musical theater, percussion, piano/organ, Portuguese, Scandinavian languages, sculpture, Slavic languages, Spanish, studio art, telecommunications, theatre arts, theatre studies, visual and performing arts, and voice), COMPUTER AND PHYSICAL SCIENCE (applied science, astronomy, astrophysics, chemistry, computer science, earth science, geology, informatics and computer science, mathematics, physics, and statistics), EDUCATION (art education, athletic training, early childhood education, education, elementary education, general studies, health education, music education, physical education, secondary education, social studies education, and special education), ENGINEERING AND ENVIRONMENTAL DESIGN (environmental science, interior design, and operations research and engineering), HEALTH PROFESSIONS (biology, exercise science, health administration and policy, health care administration, health science, kinesiology, kinesiology, nursing, nutrition and dietetics, optometry, public health, recreation therapy, and speech pathology/audiology), SOCIAL SCIENCE (African studies, African American studies, American studies, anthropology, asian studies, classical/ancient civilization, cognitive science, criminal justice, dietetics, East Asian studies, Eastern European studies, economics, fashion design and technology, gender studies, geography, history, interdisciplinary studies, international studies, Judaic studies, legal studies, Near Eastern studies, philosophy, political science/government, psychology, public affairs, religious studies, Russian and Slavic studies, safety science, social work, and sociology). Business, biology and biomedical sciences, parks recreation and fitness studies have the largest enrollments.

Required: The general requirements for graduation include courses in English and writing, math, foreign language, arts and humanities, social and behavioral sciences, natural sciences, and culture studies. Students must complete 120 credit hours, with approximately 36 hours in the major. Many degrees have intensive writing requirements, and the minimum GPA requirement varies by department. Liberal arts requirements are common throughout all degree programs.

Special: IU offers cooperative programs with universities in many countries, a variety of internships, and study abroad in more than 57 countries. A Washington semester, work-study programs, B.A.-B.S. degrees in the sciences and liberal arts, dual majors, online degrees and the general studies degree are available. Student-designed majors through the Individualized Major Program, credit for military experience, nondegree study and pass/fail options are also available. There are 10 national honor societies, including Phi Beta Kappa, and a freshman honors program.

Faculty/Classroom: 59% of faculty are male; 41% are female. No introductory courses are taught by graduate students.

Admissions: 72% of the 2013-2014 applicants were accepted. The SAT scores for the 2013-2014 freshman class were: Critical Reading--18% below 500, 44% between 500 and 599, 30% between 600 and 699, and 8% between 700 and 800; Math--10% below 500, 39% between 500 and 599, 37% between 600 and 699, and 15% between 700 and 800; Writing--19% below 500, 45% between 500 and 599, 29% between 600 and 699, and 7% between 700 and 800.

Requirements: The SAT or ACT is required. Applicants must be graduates of an accredited secondary high school or have a GED certificate. Indiana residents must be on track to complete Core 40 curriculum, Core 40 academic curriculum, or the equivalent as a condition of offered admission. SAT: Subject tests are recommended for credit and placement. Auditions for music majors are required. An interview is recommended for information purposes. AP and CLEP credits are accepted. Important factors in the admissions decision are advanced placement or honors courses, parents or siblings attended your school, and recommendations by school officials.

Procedure: Freshmen are admitted to all sessions. Entrance exams should be taken Late in the junior year or early in the senior year. There are deferred admissions and rolling admissions plans. Applications should be filed by February 1 for fall entry; November 1 for spring entry; and February 1 for summer entry, along with a $60 fee. Applications are accepted online.

Transfer: 950 transfer students enrolled in 2012-2013. Admission for transfers is selective. Decisions based on high school background, college curriculum, grade trends, choice of major, overall performance. If transferring with fewer than 26 credit hours, must also meet freshman guidelines. 2.3 GPA required for residents; 2.5 GPA for non-residents for consideration. 30 of 120 credits required for the bachelor's degree must be completed at IU.

Visiting: There are regularly scheduled orientations for prospective students, admissions counseling and answers to students' questions about the school. There are guides for informal visits, visitors may sit in on classes, and stay overnight. To schedule a visit, contact the Office of Admissions at (812) 855-0661.

Financial Aid: In 2013-2014, 72% of all full-time freshmen and 70% of continuing full-time students received some form of financial aid. 45% of all full-time freshmen and 43% of continuing full-time students received need-based aid. The average freshman award was $12,941. Need-based scholarships or need-based grants averaged $11,393 ($45,292 maximum); need-based self-help aid (loans and jobs) averaged $3,191 ($6,500 maximum); non-need-based athletic scholarships averaged $22,376 ($49,259 maximum); and other non need based awards and non-need-based scholarships averaged $3,323 ($49,579 maximum). 19% of undergraduate students work part-time. Average annual earnings from campus work are $1747. IU is a member of CSS. The FAFSA is required. The priority date for freshman financial aid applications for fall entry is March 1. The deadline for filing freshman financial aid applications for fall entry is March 10.

International Students: There are 3347 international students enrolled. The school actively recruits these students. They must take the TOEFL with a minimum score of 550 on the paper-based TOEFL (PBT) or 79 on the Internet-based version (iBT). They must also take the SAT or ACT.

Graduates: From July 1, 2012 to June 30, 2013, 7309 bachelor's degrees were awarded. The most popular majors were business, management and marketing (19%), education (9%), and biological and biomedical sciences (8%).

Admissions Contact: Mary Ellen Anderson, Director of Admissions. E-Mail: *iuadmit@indiana.edu* Web: *www.iub.edu*

INDIANA UNIVERSITY EAST D-3

Richmond, IN 47374 **(765) 973-8208**
(800) 959-4485; (765) 973-8209

Full-time: 686 men, 1262 women	**Faculty:** n/av; IIB, --$
Part-time: 847 men, 1531 women	**Ph.D.s:** 57%
Graduate: 30 men, 100 women	**Student/Faculty:** 15 to 1
Year: semesters, summer session	**Tuition:** $6639 ($17,778)
Application Deadline: open	**Room & Board:** n/app
Freshman Class: 1219 applied, 656 accepted, 404 enrolled	
SAT CR/M/W: 465/460/445	**ACT:** 21 **LESS COMPETITIVE**

Indiana University East, a regional campus of Indiana University, offers residents of eastern Indiana, western Ohio and beyond a broad range of bachelor's degrees and selected master's degrees and certificates through its traditional main campus in Richmond, off-campus sites, and online program options. Indiana University East challenges students to grow intellectually and personally in a supportive and scholarly environment where faculty teaching skills and participation in the creation and dissemination of new knowledge and artistic work enhance learning opportunities for all. Indiana University East values a diversity of backgrounds, experiences, and intellectual perspectives among its faculty, staff, and students and in its contributions to the cultural and economic development of the communities it serves. There are 8 undergraduate schools. In addition to regional accreditation, IU East has baccalaureate program accreditation with ACBSP, CSWE, and NCATE. The library contains 82,500 volumes. Computerized library services include interlibrary loans, database searching, Internet access, and Wi-Fi capability. Special learning facilities include an art gallery. The 182-acre campus is in a small town 45 miles west of Dayton, Ohio. Including any residence halls, there are 8 buildings.

Student Life: 76% of undergraduates are from Indiana. Others are from 38 states, 32 foreign countries, and Canada. 89% are White. The average age of freshmen is 19; all undergraduates, 28.

Housing: College-sponsored housing includes Alcohol is not permitted. All students commute. All students may keep cars.

Activities: There are 30 groups on campus, including art, cheerleading, computers, dance, drama, environmental, ethnic, gay, honors, newspaper, pep band, political, professional, radio and TV, religious, social, social service, and student government. Popular campus events include Homecoming, and Spirit of Philanthropy.

Sports: There are 5 intercollegiate sports for men and 6 for women. Facilities include Graf Recreation/Fitness Center, a softball field, tennis and sand volleyball courts, and a field house.

Disabled Students: 98% of the campus is accessible. Facilities include

wheelchair ramps, elevators, special parking, lowered drinking fountains, lowered telephones. special testing accommodations and note taking.
Services: Counseling and information services are available, as is tutoring in some subjects, for several freshman-level courses. There is a reader service for the blind, and remedial math, reading, and writing.
Campus Safety and Security: Measures include emergency notification system and security escort services. There are emergency telephones, lighted pathways/sidewalks, a 14-hour foot and vehicle patrol.
Programs of Study: IU East confers B.A., B.S., B.G.S., B.S.Ed., B.S.N and B.S.W. degrees. Associate and master's degrees are also awarded. Bachelor's degrees are awarded in BIOLOGICAL SCIENCE (biochemistry, biotechnology, and life science), BUSINESS (business administration and management, finance, management information systems, and marketing), COMMUNICATIONS AND THE ARTS (communication studies, English, fine arts, and information technology), COMPUTER AND PHYSICAL SCIENCE (mathematics and natural sciences/mathematics), EDUCATION (elementary education, general studies, and secondary education), HEALTH PROFESSIONS (biology and nursing), SOCIAL SCIENCE (criminal justice, history, humanities, political science/government, psychology, social work, and sociology). Business, nursing, and general studies have the largest enrollments.
Required: To graduate, students must satisfactorily complete the General Education Curriculum (30 credit hours)applies to all IU East students admitted effective Summer 2013: Written Communication Competency (6 cr. hrs.); Speaking and Listening Competency(3 cr. hrs.); Quantitative Reasoning Competency (3 cr. hrs.); Natural Sciences Competency (5-6 cr. hrs.) -must include at least one course with laboratory; Humanistic Artistic Competency (6 cr. hrs.)- must include at least two different disciplines; Social-Behavioral Competency (6 cr. hrs.)- must include at least two different disciplines. Students must complete a minimum of 120 semester hours (30 hours taken at IU East) with a GPA of at least 2.0.
Special: IU East offers a cooperative program in criminal justice with Indiana University-Purdue University and an organizational leadership program through Purdue's Statewide Technology program. IU East also offers online degrees, cross-registration with Earlham College, dual majors, independent study, an internship in social work, pass/fail options, study abroad through Indiana University Bloomington, and credit for life experience. Nondegree study is possible. There are 3 national honor societies and a freshman honors program.
Faculty/Classroom: 40% of faculty are male; 60% are female. No introductory courses are taught by graduate students.
Admissions: 54% of the 2013-2014 applicants were accepted. The SAT scores for the 2013-2014 freshman class were: Critical Reading--67% below 500, 28% between 500 and 599, and 5% between 600 and 699; Math--68% below 500, 24% between 500 and 599, and 7% between 600 and 699; Writing--78% below 500, 19% between 500 and 599, and 4% between 600 and 699.
Requirements: The SAT is required. The ACT is recommended. Recent high school graduates from Indiana are expected to complete the Core 40 curriculum. Out-of-state students are expected to complete a minimum of 28 semester hours of college prep courses listed above. The four units of academic electives include additional Math, Lab Science, Social Science, Computer Science, Foreign Language, or other college-prep courses. Recent high school graduates should rank in the upper half of their graduating class. AP and CLEP credits are accepted.
Procedure: Freshmen are admitted to all sessions. Entrance exams should be taken during the junior or senior year. There are early admissions, deferred admissions, and rolling admissions plans. Application deadlines are open. Application fee is $35. Applications are accepted online.
Transfer: 471 transfer students enrolled in 2012-2013. Completion of 12 or more semester hours at an accredited university or college (including junior and community colleges), with a GPA of 2.0 (2.5 for out-of-state transfer applicants) and submit college transcripts. Grades of C or better transfer for credit. 30 of 120 credits required for the bachelor's degree must be completed at IU East.
Visiting: There are regularly scheduled orientations for prospective students. Visits include tours, counseling, registration, and financial aid sessions. There are guides for informal visits and visitors may sit in on classes. To schedule a visit, contact the Admissions Office.
Financial Aid: In 2013-2014, 93% of all full-time freshmen and 90% of continuing full-time students received some form of financial aid. 82% of all full-time freshmen and 80% of continuing full-time students received need-based aid. The average freshman award was $8,974. Need-based scholarships or need-based grants averaged $7,211 ($18,238 maximum); need-based self-help aid (loans and jobs) averaged $3,026 ($6,546 maximum); non-need-based athletic scholarships averaged $2,107 ($8,000 maximum); and other non-need-based awards and non-need-based scholarships averaged $905 ($13,790 maximum). 7% of undergraduate students work part-time. Average annual earnings from campus work are $2096. The FAFSA and the college's own financial statement are required. The priority date for freshman financial aid applications for fall entry is March 1. The deadline for filing freshman financial aid applications for fall entry is March 10.
International Students: There are 5 international students enrolled. They must take the TOEFL with a minimum score of 550 on the paper-based TOEFL (PBT) or 79 on the Internet-based version (iBT).
Graduates: From July 1, 2012 to June 30, 2013, 563 bachelor's degrees were awarded. The most popular majors were business, management, marketing (29%), health professions and related programs (18%), liberal arts and sciences, and general studies and humanities (15%).
Admissions Contact: Molly Vanderpool, Director of Admissions. E-Mail: *applynow@iue.edu* Web: *www.iue.edu/admissions*

INDIANA UNIVERSITY KOKOMO C-2

Kokomo, IN 46904 (765) 455-9217
(888) 875-4485; (765) 455-9537

Full-time: 692 men, 1320 women	**Faculty:** n/av; IIB, --$
Part-time: 727 men, 1242 women	**Ph.D.s:** 61%
Graduate: 84 men, 113 women	**Student/Faculty:** 16 to 1
Year: semesters, summer session	**Tuition:** $6674 ($17,778)
Application Deadline: August 5	**Room & Board:** n/a
Freshman Class: 1066 applied, 784 accepted, 508 enrolled	
SAT CR/M/W: 475/470/460 **ACT:** 20	**LESS COMPETITIVE**

Indiana University Kokomo is a small, friendly campus where you can earn a well-respected degree from Indiana University. Choose from a wide variety of academic majors, attend classes on campus as well as online, and utilize services that empower you to achieve your educational and personal goals. It is the mission of IU Kokomo is to enhance the lives of the residents of north central Indiana through our academic programs, through our activities and organizations, and through our community engagement. At Indiana University Kokomo, the faculty care enough to learn your name and value your input. Flexible class schedules help you to schedule your classes according to your needs, and online class offerings help bring some of the classes to you. Use the latest computer technology while on campus, and take advantage of the modern library, classroom, and laboratory facilities. Scholarships, grants, loans, and work-study programs offered through the Office of Financial Aid make your education affordable as well as convenient. There are 7 undergraduate schools. In addition to regional accreditation, IUK has baccalaureate program accreditation with AACSB, NCATE, and NLN. The library contains 140,805 volumes. Computerized library services include interlibrary loans, database searching, and Internet access. Special learning facilities include an art gallery, radio station, an observatory. The 51-acre campus is in a small town 53 miles north of Indianapolis. Including any residence halls, there are 12 buildings.
Student Life: 100% of undergraduates are from Indiana. Others are from 10 states, 24 foreign countries, and Canada. 83% are White. The average age of freshmen is 20; all undergraduates, 26.
Housing: 100% of students commute. Alcohol is not permitted. All students commute. All students may keep cars.
Activities: There are 30 groups on campus, including chorale, computers, drama, ethnic, honors, international, literary magazine, newspaper, political, professional, radio and TV, religious, social, social service, and student government. Popular campus events include Campus Fall Kick-off BBQ, Campus Beautification Day, Dance-a-Thon and Take Back the Night.
Sports: There are 2 intercollegiate sports for men and 3 for women.
Disabled Students: All of the campus is accessible. Facilities include wheelchair ramps, elevators, special parking, specially equipped restrooms, special class scheduling, lowered drinking fountains, and lowered telephones.
Services: Counseling and information services are available, as is tutoring in most subjects. There is remedial math, reading, and writing. Students who do not meet regular admissions standards can be admitted under the Guided Study Program, which includes courses in basic skills as needed, counseling and tutoring, and a seminar on studying.
Campus Safety and Security: Measures include emergency notification system and security escort services. There are emergency telephones, lighted pathways/sidewalks, campus police are on duty from 7 a.m. to 10 p.m.
Programs of Study: IUK confers B.A., B.S., B.F.A., B.G.S., B.S.B., B.S.Ed. and B.S.N. degrees. Associate and master's degrees are also awarded. Bachelor's degrees are awarded in BIOLOGICAL SCIENCE (biochemistry and biology/biological science), BUSINESS (accounting, business administration and management, finance, hospitality management services, international business, labor studies, marketing, marketing management, and tourism), COMMUNICATIONS AND THE ARTS (communication studies, communications, English, fine arts, and information technology), COMPUTER AND PHYSICAL SCIENCE (chemistry, mathematics, and physical sciences), EDUCATION (early childhood education, elementary education, general studies, and secondary education), HEALTH PROFESSIONS (biology, health administration and policy, health science, medical imaging, medical imaging, nursing, occupational therapy, predentistry, premedicine, prepharmacy, and prephysical therapy), SOCIAL SCIENCE (criminal justice, economics, history, human ser-

vices, humanities, political science/government, prelaw, psychology, public administration, and sociology). Nursing, business, and criminal justice have the largest enrollments.

Required: All students must maintain a minimum GPA of 2.0 while taking 120 credit hours. The following general education curriculum is required of each student who is granted a baccalaureate degree at the Indiana University Kokomo campus. Total credit hours will typically number 42 or 44. Each course must be completed with a passing grade, and students must obtain a minimum GPA of 2.0 in the General Education curriculum. If a student takes more than the required number of courses within a section, the course(s) with the highest grade(s) will be used in the GPA calculation. Additional departments and/or schools may have specific general education requirements rather than the general ones listed here. Students should consult with their advisor for more information. General education curriculum: Communication Skills Requirement – three required courses (total of 9 hours); Information Literacy; Quantitative Literacy (total of 4 – 8 hours); Critical Thinking (total of 3 hours); Cultural Diversity (total of 3 hours); Ethics and Civic Engagement (total of 3 hours); Social and Behavioral Sciences - two 3 credit hour courses, each from a different area (total of 6 hours); Humanities and Arts - two 3 credit hour courses, each from a different area (total of 6 hours); Physical and Life Sciences - one 5 credit hour course with a lab and one 3 credit hour course from a different area (total of 8 hours). All students must complete course work in English, computer, and math.

Special: Student-designed majors, a general studies degree, internships, study abroad, joint programs with other Indiana University campuses and with Purdue University, pass/fail options, nondegree study, credit for military experience and by exam are available and online degrees. There is 1 national honor society and a freshman honors program.

Faculty/Classroom: 40% of faculty are male; 60% are female. No introductory courses are taught by graduate students.

Admissions: 74% of the 2013-2014 applicants were accepted. The SAT scores for the 2013-2014 freshman class were: Critical Reading--64% below 500, 30% between 500 and 599, 6% between 600 and 699, and 1% between 700 and 800; Math--59% below 500, 32% between 500 and 599, 8% between 600 and 699, and 1% between 700 and 800; Writing--69% below 500, 26% between 500 and 599, and 5% between 600 and 699.

Requirements: The SAT or ACT is required. If you have not earned an Academic Honors or Core 40 high school diploma, your high school preparation should include a minimum of at least the 40 college preparatory courses listed above. The academic electives include foreign language, additional mathematics, laboratory science, social science, computer science or other college preparatory courses. AP and CLEP credits are accepted. Important factors in the admissions decision are recommendations by school officials and advanced placement or honors courses.

Procedure: Freshmen are admitted to all sessions. Entrance exams should be taken prior to registration. There are deferred admissions and rolling admissions plans. Applications should be filed by August 5 for fall entry; December 20 for spring entry; and April 30 for summer entry, along with a $35 fee. Applications are accepted online.

Transfer: 310 transfer students enrolled in 2012-2013. Transfer applicants must have at least 13 credits with a minimum GPA of 2.0 and clear records of conduct from previously attended colleges. Transcripts are required. Transfers are considered on a case-by-case basis. 30 of 120 credits required for the bachelor's degree must be completed at IUK.

Visiting: There are regularly scheduled orientations for prospective students. There are guides for informal visits and visitors may sit in on classes. To schedule a visit, contact the Admissions Office at 765 455-9217.

Financial Aid: In 2013-2014, 90% of all full-time freshmen and 87% of continuing full-time students received some form of financial aid. 71% of all full-time freshmen and 74% of continuing full-time students received need-based aid. The average freshman award was $7,606. Need-based scholarships or need-based grants averaged $6,353 ($14,573 maximum); need-based self-help aid (loans and jobs) averaged $3,009 ($5,793 maximum); and other non-need-based awards and non-need-based scholarships averaged $998 ($17,792 maximum). 9% of undergraduate students work part-time. Average annual earnings from campus work are $1629. The FAFSA is required. The priority date for freshman financial aid applications for fall entry is March 1. The deadline for filing freshman financial aid applications for fall entry is March 10.

International Students: There are 9 international students enrolled. They must take the TOEFL with a minimum score of 530 on the paper-based TOEFL (PBT) or 61 on the Internet-based version (iBT).

Graduates: From July 1, 2012 to June 30, 2013, 507 bachelor's degrees were awarded. The most popular majors were health professions (37%), education (14%), liberal arts and sciences, and general studies and humanities (13%).

Admissions Contact: Angie Siders, Director of Admissions. E-Mail: *iuadmis@iuk.edu* Web: *http:/www.iuk.edu/admissions/*

INDIANA UNIVERSITY NORTHWEST — B-1

Gary, IN 46408 — **(219) 980-6991; (219) 981-4219**

Full-time: 1077 men, 2144 women	**Faculty:** n/av; IIA, --$
Part-time: 907 men, 1776 women	**Ph.D.s:** 71%
Graduate: 140 men, 343 women	**Student/Faculty:** 16 to 1
Year: semesters, summer session	**Tuition:** $6738 ($17,778)
Application Deadline: July 1	**Room & Board:** n/a

Freshman Class: 1773 applied, 1352 accepted, 830 enrolled

SAT CR/M/W: 450/450/445 **ACT:** 20 **LESS COMPETITIVE**

The mission of Indiana University Northwest, a regional campus of Indiana University, is to provide a high-quality and relevant education to the citizens of Northwest Indiana, the most diverse and industrialized area of the state. The institution strives to create a community dedicated to the pursuit of knowledge and intellectual development, leading to undergraduate and selected graduate degrees in the liberal arts, sciences and professional disciplines. The campus is strongly dedicated to the value of education, lifelong learning, diversity, celebration of cultures and opportunity for all, as well as to participating in the sustainable economic development of the region and of the state. Indiana University Northwest is committed to the health and well-being of the communities it serves. There are 4 undergraduate schools. In addition to regional accreditation, IUN has baccalaureate program accreditation with AACSB, CSWE, and NCATE. The library contains 227,500 volumes. Computerized library services include interlibrary loans, database searching, Internet access, and Wi-Fi capability. Special learning facilities include an art gallery and radio station. The 38-acre campus is in an urban area 35 miles southeast of Chicago. Including any residence halls, there are 26 buildings.

Student Life: 99% of undergraduates are from Indiana. Others are from 17 states, 37 foreign countries, and Canada. 53% are White; 19% African American; 16% Hispanic. The average age of freshmen is 20; all undergraduates, 26.

Housing: College-sponsored housing includes 100% of students commute. Alcohol is not permitted. All students commute. All students may keep cars.

Activities: There are 30 groups on campus, including art, cheerleading, chess, chorale, computers, dance, drama, environmental, ethnic, film, gay, honors, international, literary magazine, musical theater, newspaper, political, professional, radio and TV, religious, social, social service, and student government. Popular campus events include Back2School Week, Table Tennis Tournament, Communications Week, and Health Fair.

Sports: There are 2 intercollegiate sports for men and 3 for women, and 3 intramural sports for men and 3 for women. Facilities include The Savannah Fitness and Recreation Center is open to students, staff, faculty, and the public. The center has a full work-out room with Cybex equipment. A suspended 1/12th mile walking/running track and a 3-court gymnasium where the IU Northwest RedHawk Basketball and Volleyball teams play in NAIA competitions.

Disabled Students: 90% of the campus is accessible. Facilities include wheelchair ramps, elevators, special parking, specially equipped restrooms, special class scheduling, lowered drinking fountains, and lowered telephones.

Services: Counseling and information services are available, as is tutoring in some subjects. There is a reader service for the blind, and remedial math, reading, and writing.

Campus Safety and Security: Measures include 24-hour foot and vehicle patrol, emergency notification system, and security escort services. There are emergency telephones and lighted pathways/sidewalks.

Programs of Study: IUN confers B.A., B.S., B.G.S., B.S.Ed., B.S.N and B.S.W. degrees. Associate and master's degrees are also awarded. Bachelor's degrees are awarded in BIOLOGICAL SCIENCE (biology/adolescence education), BUSINESS (business administration and management and labor studies), COMMUNICATIONS AND THE ARTS (communication, English, fine arts, French, information technology, Spanish, spanish / adolescence education, and theatre studies), COMPUTER AND PHYSICAL SCIENCE (actuarial science, chemistry, chemistry/adolescence education, computer information systems, geology, and mathematics), EDUCATION (elementary education, English education, general studies, health information management, mathematics education, secondary education, and social studies education), ENGINEERING AND ENVIRONMENTAL DESIGN (computer graphics), HEALTH PROFESSIONS (biology, dental hygiene, health administration and policy, health care administration, health services technology, nursing, and radiological science), SOCIAL SCIENCE (African American studies, anthropology, criminal justice, economics, history, philosophy, political science/government, psychology, public affairs, social work, and sociology). Nursing, general studies, and business have the largest enrollments.

Required: Each division sets its own degree requirements. All students must maintain a minimum GPA of 2.0 and complete at least 120 credit hours to graduate. Students must fulfill general education requirements for graduation. The courses required to fulfill the general education requirements vary depending upon the specific major that the student chooses.

Each academic division has incorporated specific general education courses into the degree requirements to insure that the following five principles and their learning outcomes are achieved. Principle 1: Foundations for Effective Learning and Communication - Fluency in reading, writing, and oral communication; mastery of the basic principles of logical, mathematical, and scientific reasoning; and literacy in information resources and learning technologies. Principle 2: Breadth of Learning - Mastery of the core concepts, principles, and methods in arts and humanities, cultural and historical studies, the social and behavioral sciences, and the mathematical, physical, and life sciences. Principle 3: Critical Thinking, Integration, and Application of Knowledge Logical analysis and synthesis of information and ideas from multiple perspectives; critical acquisition, integration, and application of knowledge in students' intellectual, personal, professional, and community lives. Principle 4: Diversity - Valuing the diversity of human experience, as exemplified in race, ethnicity, social class, language, religion, gender, sexual orientation, age, or disabilities; understanding how these categories are often used to create injustice; recognizing our common human heritage and the interconnectedness of communities in the region, the nation, and the world. Principle 5: Ethics and Citizenship - The application of the principles of ethics and governance to the larger society, one's immediate community, and to individual conduct on campus and in society.

Special: IUN offers cross-registration with Purdue University, work-study, dual majors, independent study, internships, study abroad, credit for life, military, work experience, nondegree study, accelerated degree programs, student-designed majors, pass/fail options and online degrees. There are 5 national honor societies.

Faculty/Classroom: 40% of faculty are male; 60% are female. No introductory courses are taught by graduate students.

Admissions: 76% of the 2013-2014 applicants were accepted. The SAT scores for the 2013-2014 freshman class were: Critical Reading--70% below 500, 25% between 500 and 599, 4% between 600 and 699, and 1% between 700 and 800; Math--70% below 500, 223% between 500 and 599, and 6% between 600 and 699; Writing--74% below 500, 20% between 500 and 599, and 4% between 600 and 699.

Requirements: The SAT or ACT is required. In addition, Freshman applicants should be on track to graduate, or should have graduated, from a commissioned Indiana high school, comparable out-of-state institution or an approved homeschool, successfully completing a college prep curriculum. The Indiana Core 40 Diploma is a minimum requirement for admission. Students not achieving a Core 40 should apply to Ivy Tech Community College and complete 12 general education credit hours (100 level or higher) then apply to transfer to IU Northwest. In addition, applicants should: Have a minimum cumulative grade point average of 2.0 on a 4.0 scale; Rank in the upper half of the high school graduating class; Score above the median established by northwest Indiana students on the SAT or ACT. (If you have been out of school for more than one year, these scores are not required.); GED recipients must have a total score that is above the average for Indiana residents. IU Northwest may accept students who are deficient in the standards listed above after additional testing. AP and CLEP credits are accepted. Important factors in the admissions decision are advanced placement or honors courses, leadership record, and recommendations by school officials.

Procedure: Freshmen are admitted to all sessions. Entrance exams should be taken as early as possible. There are deferred admissions and rolling admissions plans. Applications should be filed by July 1 for fall entry; December 1 for spring entry; and April 1 for summer entry, along with a $35 fee. Notification is sent on a rolling basis. Applications are accepted online.

Transfer: 383 transfer students enrolled in 2012-2013. Transfer Students requirements are; an official high school transcript (unless 26 semester hours of 100 level or above work has been completed at the time of the application); an official college or university transcript showing average or above average achievement (at least a 2.0 on a 4.0 scale). A IU Intercampus Transfer Application if transferring from another IU campus, and a criminal activity disclosure policy, if applicable. A list of courses that will transfer among all Indiana public college and university campuses can be found at Indiana Core Transfer Library. A grade of "C" or better is required for credit. 30 of 120 credits required for the bachelor's degree must be completed at IUN.

Visiting: There are regularly scheduled orientations for prospective students. There are guides for informal visits and visitors may sit in on classes. To schedule a visit, contact the Admissions Office at (219) 980-6991.

Financial Aid: In 2013-2014, 87% of all full-time freshmen and 86% of continuing full-time students received some form of financial aid. 73% of all full-time freshmen and 75% of continuing full-time students received need-based aid. The average freshman award was $8,350. Need-based scholarships or need-based grants averaged $6,123 ($21,394 maximum); need-based self-help aid (loans and jobs) averaged $3,141 ($4,858 maximum); non-need-based athletic scholarships averaged $650 ($1,000 maximum); and other non-need-based awards and non-need-based scholarships averaged $928 ($14,711 maximum). 7% of undergraduate students work part-time. Average annual earnings from campus work are $2276. The FAFSA is required. The priority date for freshman financial aid applications for fall entry is March 1. The deadline for filing freshman financial aid applications for fall entry is March 10.

International Students: There are 2 international students enrolled.

Graduates: From July 1, 2012 to June 30, 2013, 507 bachelor's degrees were awarded. The most popular majors were health professions (22%), liberal arts and sciences, general studies and humanities (14%), business, management, and marketing (13%).

Admissions Contact: Linda Templeton, Director of Admissions. E-Mail: *admit@iun.edu* Web: *http:/www.iun.edu/admissions/*

INDIANA UNIVERSITY SOUTH BEND — C-1

South Bend, IN 46634 — (574) 520-4839; (877) GO-2-IUSB; (574) 520-4834

Full-time: 1529 men, 2455 women	**Faculty:** n/av; IIA, --$
Part-time: 1416 men, 2112 women	**Ph.D.s:** 65%
Graduate: 193 men, 368 women	**Student/Faculty:** 13 to 1
Year: semesters, summer session	**Tuition:** $6815 ($17,778)
Application Deadline: July 31	**Room & Board:** $8478
Freshman Class: 2456 applied, 1720 accepted, 921 enrolled	
SAT CR/M/W: 480/480/450 **ACT:** 21	**COMPETITIVE**

Indiana University South Bend is the only comprehensive public university in North Central Indiana and the third largest campus in the Indiana University system. We're a university grounded in academic excellence that also offers the full collegiate experience including student housing, more than 100 degree programs, men's and women's NAIA basketball and a full complement of activities to enhance your college career. There are 7 undergraduate schools. In addition to regional accreditation, IUSB has baccalaureate program accreditation with AACSB, NASM, and NCATE. The library contains 328,284 volumes. Computerized library services include interlibrary loans, database searching, Internet access, and Wi-Fi capability. Special learning facilities include an art gallery, science labs, studios for fine and performing arts, instructional media services, and an academic resource center. The 102-acre campus is in a suburban area 95 miles east of Chicago. Including any residence halls, there are 29 buildings.

Student Life: 96% of undergraduates are from Indiana. Others are from 19 states, 75 foreign countries, and Canada. 78% are White. The average age of freshmen is 19; all undergraduates, 25.

Housing: 388 students can be accommodated in college housing, which includes single-sex and coed on-campus apartments and off-campus apartments. special housing for international students. On-campus housing is available on a first-come and first-served basis. 94% of students commute. Alcohol is not permitted. All students may keep cars.

Activities: There are 90 groups on campus, including art, cheerleading, chess, chorus, debate, drama, ethnic, film, forensics, gay, honors, international, jazz band, literary magazine, musical theater, newspaper, opera, orchestra, pep band, photography, political, professional, religious, social, social service, student government, and symphony. Popular campus events include Titan Fest, Red & White Dance, Mini University Welcome Week and Alternative Spring Break Trips.

Sports: There are 1 intercollegiate sports for men and 2 for women, and 7 intramural sports for men and 7 for women. Facilities include Student Activities Center features: Courtside Café, Competition Basketball / Volleyball Courts (3), Racquetball / Wallyball Courts (3), Indoor Running Track (1/8 mile), Group Exercise / Aerobic Room, Table Tennis / Billiards Tables, Locker Rooms, Athletic Offices and a Wellness Center. The state-of- the-art fitness center features Life Fitness(plate-loaded) equipment and Hampton Strength free-weight equipment, along with 23 pieces of cardiovascular machines and weight training machines.

Disabled Students: 95% of the campus is accessible. Facilities include wheelchair ramps, elevators, special parking, specially equipped restrooms, special class scheduling, lowered drinking fountains, and lowered telephones.

Services: Counseling and information services are available, as is tutoring in most subjects. There is remedial math, reading, and writing. Taped texts, note takers, and interpreters or transcription services are available.

Campus Safety and Security: Measures include 24-hour foot and vehicle patrol, emergency notification system, and security escort services. There are emergency telephones and lighted pathways/sidewalks.

Programs of Study: IUSB confers B.A., B.S., B.F.A, B.G.S., B.M., B.S.Ed., B.S.N. and B.S.W. degrees. Associate and master's degrees are also awarded. Bachelor's degrees are awarded in BIOLOGICAL SCIENCE (biochemistry and biology/biological science), BUSINESS (accounting, banking and finance, business administration and management, finance, human resources/organizational mgmt, international business, labor studies, management information systems, and small business management), COMMUNICATIONS AND THE ARTS (advertising, communication, drawing, English, fine arts, French, German, graphic design, information technology, instrumental performance, journalism, music, music composition, organ performance, painting, photography, piano performance, printmaking, public relations, sculpture, Spanish, theatre studies, and voice), COMPUTER AND PHYSICAL SCIENCE (actuarial science, applied mathematics, chemistry, computer science, mathematics, and physics), EDUCATION (elementary education, English education, mathematics education, music education, secondary education, social studies education, and special education), HEALTH PROFESSIONS (biology, dental education, dental hygiene, health care administration, medical imaging, nursing, and speech pathology/audiology), SOCIAL SCIENCE (anthropology, criminal justice, economics, history, history, philosophy, political science/government, psychology, social work, sociology, and women & gender studies). business, nursing, elementary education, have the largest enrollments.

Required: All students must complete the campus-wide general education curriculum which is composed of three elements and requires a total of between 33 and 39 credit hours of course work. I.Fundamental Literacies Courses (13-19 cr.) -Writing, Critical Thinking, Oral Communication, Visual Literacy, Quantitative Reasoning, Information Literacy and Computer Literacy II.Common Core Courses (12 cr.) -The Natural World, Human Behavior and Social Institutions, Literary and Intellectual Traditions, Art, Aesthetics, and Creativity III.Contemporary Social Values Courses (8 cr.) -Non-Western Cultures, Diversity in U.S. Society, Health and Wellness. A total of 120 semester hours, with a minimum GPA of 2.0, is required to graduate.

Special: Cross-registration with Northern Indiana Consortium for education (NICE), internships, study abroad, accelerated degree programs, online degrees and dual majors are possible. There are 2 national honor societies and a freshman honors program.

Faculty/Classroom: 48% of faculty are male; 52% are female. No introductory courses are taught by graduate students.

Admissions: 70% of the 2013-2014 applicants were accepted. The SAT scores for the 2013-2014 freshman class were: Critical Reading--61% below 500, 32% between 500 and 599, 6% between 600 and 699, and 1% between 700 and 800; Math--62% below 500, 31% between 500 and 599, 7% between 600 and 699, and 1% between 700 and 800; Writing--72% below 500, 24% between 500 and 599, and 4% between 600 and 699.

Requirements: The SAT or ACT is required. Indiana high school graduates are expected to complete the Core 40 curriculum and are strongly encouraged to earn the Academic Honors Diploma. Out-of-state students are expected to complete a comparable college-prep curriculum. CLEP credits are accepted. Important factors in the admissions decision are advanced placement or honors courses, extracurricular activities record, and leadership record.

Procedure: Freshmen are admitted to all sessions. Entrance exams should be taken 1 year to 6 months before entering the university. There are deferred admissions and rolling admissions plans. Application deadlines are open. Application fee is $35. Applications are accepted online.

Transfer: 407 transfer students enrolled in 2012-2013. A 2.0 GPA is required. College transcripts must be submitted. 30 of 120 credits required for the bachelor's degree must be completed at IUSB.

Visiting: There are regularly scheduled orientations for prospective students, including a visit to the admissions office, a campus tour, professor meetings, and information on financial aid. There are guides for informal visits, visitors may sit in on classes, and stay overnight. To schedule a visit, contact the Admissions Office.

Financial Aid: In 2013-2014, 989% of all full-time freshmen and 87% of continuing full-time students received some form of financial aid. 78% of all full-time freshmen and 77% of continuing full-time students received need-based aid. The average freshman award was $8,185. Need-based scholarships or need-based grants averaged $6,189 ($18,600 maximum); need-based self-help aid (loans and jobs) averaged $3,015 ($7,992 maximum); non-need-based athletic scholarships averaged $490 ($500 maximum); and other non-need-based awards and non-need-based scholarships averaged $973 ($21,014 maximum). 9% of undergraduate students work part-time. Average annual earnings from campus work are $1877. The FAFSA is required. The priority date for freshman financial aid applications for fall entry is March 1. The deadline for filing freshman financial aid applications for fall entry is March 10.

International Students: There are 89 international students enrolled. The school actively recruits these students. They must take the TOEFL with a minimum score of 530 on the paper-based TOEFL (PBT) or 71 on the Internet-based version (iBT).

Graduates: From July 1, 2012 to June 30, 2013, 822 bachelor's degrees were awarded. The most popular majors were business, management, marketing (19%), health professions (17%), liberal arts and sciences, and general studies and humanities (15%).

Admissions Contact: Connie Peterson-Miller, Director of Admissions. E-Mail: *admissions@iusb.edu* Web: *https:/www.iusb.edu/admissions*

INDIANA UNIVERSITY SOUTHEAST C-5

New Albany, IN 47150 **(812) 941-2212; (812) 941-2595**

Full-time: 1510 men, 2155 women
Part-time: 1063 men, 1420 women
Graduate: 209 men, 376 women
Year: semesters, summer session
Application Deadline: August 17
Freshman Class: 2097 applied, 1666 accepted, 1026 enrolled
SAT CR/M/W: 475/475/460 **ACT:** 20 **LESS COMPETITIVE**
Faculty: n/av; IIA, --$
Ph.D.s: 67%
Student/Faculty: 15 to 1
Tuition: $6699 ($17,778)
Room & Board: $9108

Indiana University Southeast is the regional campus of Indiana University that serves Southern Indiana and the Greater Louisville metropolitan area. As a public comprehensive university, its mission is to provide high-quality educational programs and services that promote student learning and prepare students for productive citizenship in a diverse society, and to contribute to the intellectual, cultural, and economic development of the region. Its academic programs include a comprehensive array of baccalaureate degrees, a limited number of associate degrees, and a selected set of master's programs. The campus is committed to offering educational programs and services which promote and support diversity in all its aspects. The faculty engage in research and creative activities which strengthen teaching and learning through inquiry into both the content and the pedagogy of the disciplines and create opportunities for students to engage in applied learning. Finally, members of the campus community are committed to using their professional and personal expertise to address the intellectual, cultural, and economic development needs of the campus's service region. There are 7 undergraduate schools. In addition to regional accreditation, IUS has baccalaureate program accreditation with AACSB and NCATE. The library contains 374,981 volumes, computerized library services include interlibrary loans, database searching, Internet access, and Wi-Fi capability. Special learning facilities include an art gallery. The 177-acre campus is in a suburban area 10 miles northwest of Louisville, Kentucky, and 114 miles south of Indianapolis. Including any residence halls, there are 50 buildings.

Student Life: 71% of undergraduates are from Indiana. Others are from 13 states, 48 foreign countries, and Canada. 86% are White. The average age of freshmen is 19; all undergraduates, 25.

Housing: 399 students can be accommodated in college housing, which includes single-sex on-campus apartments. On-campus housing is available on a first-come and first-served basis. 94% of students commute. Alcohol is not permitted. All students may keep cars.

Activities: There are 90 groups on campus, including art, band, cheerleading, choir, chorus, computers, dance, debate, drama, environmental, ethnic, film, gay, honors, international, literary magazine, newspaper, orchestra, pep band, political, professional, religious, social, social service, and student government. Popular campus events include International Festival, Wares of the World, Common Experience, and Hunger Banquet.

Sports: There are 3 intercollegiate sports for men and 4 for women, and 9 intramural sports for men and 9 for women. Facilities include The campus Fitness Center, housed inside of the Activities Building, has strength machines, a free weight area, plus a variety of cardiovascular exercise equipment that includes, Treadmills, Bikes, Elliptical, Stairmaster and Crosstrainers. In addition, SE has a basketball court, facilities for jogging, badminton, volleyball, gymnastics, 6 tennis courts, baseball and softball fields and playing fields.

Disabled Students: All of the campus is accessible. Facilities include wheelchair ramps, elevators, special parking, specially equipped restrooms, lowered drinking fountains, lowered telephones, and special accommodations as needed.

Services: Counseling and information services are available, as is tutoring in most subjects. There is a reader service for the blind, and remedial math, reading, and writing. The coordinator for services to students with disabilities provides information and coordination of needed services.

Campus Safety and Security: Measures include 24-hour foot and vehicle patrol, emergency notification system, and self-defense education. There are emergency telephones and lighted pathways/sidewalks.

Programs of Study: IUS confers B.A., B.F.A., B.G.S., B.S., B.S.Ed. and B.S.N. degrees. Associate and master's degrees are also awarded. Bachelor's degrees are awarded in BIOLOGICAL SCIENCE (biochemistry and biology/adolescence education), BUSINESS (accounting, business administration and management, finance, human resources/organizational mgmt, international business, international business, and supply chain management), COMMUNICATIONS AND THE ARTS (ceramic art and design, communication, drawing, English, fine arts, French, German, graphic design, information technology, journalism, music, music business management, music composition, music performance, music technology, painting, printmaking, and Spanish), COMPUTER AND PHYSICAL SCIENCE (chemistry, clinical laboratory science, computer science, geoscience, and mathematics), EDUCATION (elementary education, English education, general studies, health information management, mathematics education, secondary education, social studies education, and special education), HEALTH PROFESSIONS (biology, health care administration, and nursing), SOCIAL SCIENCE (criminal justice, criminology, economics, German area studies, history, international studies, philosophy, political science/government, psychology, and sociology). Business, nursing and general studies have the largest enrollments.

Required: Students must complete 120 credit hours, with 30 in upper-level courses and at least 25 in the major, and must maintain a minimum cumulative GPA of 2.0. All students must complete the following general education requirements: Written Communication - Students are required to take ENG-W 131 Elementary Composition. (Honors program students may take HON-H 103 to meet this requirement.) Students are also required to take one course, selected on the basis of their major, from the list of second-level approved courses. Students should consult with their advisor to determine which second course is appropriate for their intended major. Oral Communication - Students are required to take SPCH-S 121 Public Speaking. (Honors program students may take HON-H 104 to meet this requirement.) Quantitative Reasoning - Students are required to choose one course from the list of approved courses. http:/www.ius.edu/generaleducation/approved.cfm Reasoning about Ethical Questions or Diversity - Students are required to choose one course from the list of approved courses. http:/www.ius.edu/generaleducation/approved.cfm Information Literacy/FYS- Students are required to choose one course from the list of approved courses. http:/www.ius.edu/generaleducation/approved.cfm Critical Thinking - a.Students are required to take one course in either the Humanities or the Arts from the list of approved courses in those disciplines. b.Students are required to take 5 credit hours from the list of approved courses in the Natural Sciences. The five hours are generally met by completing a course with a built in laboratory component (i.e. BIOL-L 100) OR by enrolling in a combination of lecture and laboratory courses (i.e. CHEM-C 100 and CHEM-C 121). c.Students are required to take one course from different disciplines from the list of approved courses in the Social and Behavioral Sciences. d.Students must choose one additional course from either Arts, Humanities, or Social/Behavioral Sciences. The course chosen cannot be from the same discipline as any of the courses chosen to meet the aforementioned Arts & Humanities or Social/Behavioral Science requirement.

Special: Cross-registration with Metroversity is possible, and opportunities are provided for study abroad, internships, work-study programs, dual majors, a general studies degree, credit by exam, nondegree study, online degree, accelerated degree programs, and pass/fail options. There are 18 national honor societies.

Faculty/Classroom: 43% of faculty are male; 47% are female. No introductory courses are taught by graduate students.

Admissions: 79% of the 2013-2014 applicants were accepted. The SAT scores for the 2013-2014 freshman class were: Critical Reading--61% below 500, 31% between 500 and 599, 8% between 600 and 699, and 1% between 700 and 800; Math--61% below 500, 33% between 500 and 599, and 6% between 600 and 699; Writing--67% below 500, 28% between 500 and 599,and 4% between 600 and 699.

Requirements: The SAT or ACT is required. High school graduates from Indiana are expected to complete the Core 40 curriculum. Out-of-state students are expected to complete a minimum of 28 semester hours of college preparatory courses. Scores from either the SAT or ACT are required for those applicants who graduated from high school within the past two years - or who completed a GED and are 19 years of age or younger. Students who have been out of high school for over two years and do not meet the minimum requirements listed for traditional students may be asked to arrange for an interview with an admissions counselor to demonstrate intention through maturity and experience. AP and CLEP credits are accepted.

Procedure: Freshmen are admitted to all sessions. Entrance exams should be taken late junior, early senior year. There are early admissions, deferred admissions, and rolling admissions plans. Applications should be filed by August 17 for fall entry; December 31 for spring entry, along with a $35 fee. Notification is sent on a rolling basis. Applications are accepted online.

Transfer: 510 transfer students enrolled in 2012-2013. A GPA of 2.0 is required for Indiana residents, 2.5 for out-of-state applicants. If the student has earned less than 26 hours of college transfer credit, high school transcripts or GED test scores are required as well as SAT or ACT scores if you have been out of high school less than 2 years. Transfer students are required to submit official transcripts from all previously attended colleges. 30 of 120 credits required for the bachelor's degree must be completed at IUS.

Visiting: There are regularly scheduled orientations for prospective students, including an opportunity for students to apply for admission, financial aid, and scholarships, a faculty perspective, a student perspective, and a campus tour. There are guides for informal visits and visitors may sit in on classes. To schedule a visit, contact the Office of Admissions at 812) 941-2212.

Financial Aid: In 2013-2014, 85% of all full-time freshmen and 82% of continuing full-time students received some form of financial aid. 70% of all full-time freshmen and 66% of continuing full-time students received need-based aid. The average freshman award was $7,820. Need-based scholarships or need-based grants averaged $6,284 ($17,056 maximum); need-based self-help aid (loans and jobs) averaged $3,114 ($7,787 maximum); non-need-based athletic scholarships averaged $983 ($1,500 maximum); and other non-need-based awards and non-need-based scholarships averaged $980 ($17,944 maximum). 9% of undergraduate students work part-time. Average annual earnings from campus work are $1818. The FAFSA is required. The priority date for freshman financial aid applications for fall entry is March 1. The deadline for filing freshman financial aid applications for fall entry is March 10.

International Students: There are 16 international students enrolled. They must take the TOEFL with a minimum score of 530 on the paper-based TOEFL (PBT) or 75 on the Internet-based version (iBT). special tests as directed.

Graduates: From July 1, 2012 to June 30, 2013, 832 bachelor's degrees were awarded. The most popular majors were business, management, marketing (18%), education (16%), liberal arts and sciences, and general studies and humanities (16%).

Admissions Contact: Chris Crews, Interim Director of Admissions. E-Mail: *admissions@ius.edu* Web: *http:/www.ius.edu/admissions/*

INDIANA UNIVERSITY-PURDUE UNIVERSITY FORT WAYNE — D-2

Fort Wayne, IN 46805 — (260) 481-6812; (866) 597-0010; (260) 481-5450

Full-time: 3431 men, 3987 women	**Faculty:** 408; IIA, -$
Part-time: 2396 men, 3114 women	**Ph.D.s:** 85%
Graduate: 215 men, 316 women	**Student/Faculty:** 17 to 1
Year: semesters, summer session	**Tuition:** $7793 ($18,718)
Application Deadline: August 1	**Room & Board:** $7632
Freshman Class: 3702 applied, 3076 accepted, 1660 enrolled	
SAT CR/M/W: 495/505/478 **ACT:** 22	**COMPETITIVE**

Indiana University at Fort Wayne, founded in 1917, joined Purdue University at Fort Wayne, founded in 1944. The combined school, a state-controlled institution, offers programs in liberal arts, science, business, education, health sciences, engineering, technology, public affairs, and visual and performing arts. There are 8 undergraduate schools and 5 graduate schools. In addition to regional accreditation, IPFW has baccalaureate program accreditation with AACSB, ABET, ADA, NASM, NCATE, and NLN. The library contains 366,918 volumes, 481,548 microform items, 4,634 audio/video tapes/CDs/DVDs, and subscribes to 29,848 periodicals including electronic. Computerized library services include interlibrary loans, database searching, and Internet access. Special learning facilities include an art gallery and TV station. The 683-acre campus is in a suburban area 113 miles north of Indianapolis. Including any residence halls, there are 51 buildings.

Student Life: 97% of undergraduates are from Indiana. Others are from 39 states, 46 foreign countries, and Canada. 80% are from public schools. 82% are White. The average age of freshmen is 19; all undergraduates, 22. 33% do not continue beyond their first year; 22% remain to graduate.

Housing: 1204 students can be accommodated in college housing, which includes coed on-campus apartments. On-campus housing is available on a first-come and first-served basis. 93% of students commute. Alcohol is not permitted. All students may keep cars.

Activities: There are 127 groups on campus, including art, band, cheerleading, chess, choir, chorus, dance, debate, drama, ethnic, film, forensics, gay, honors, international, jazz band, literary magazine, musical theater, newspaper, opera, orchestra, pep band, political, professional, radio and TV, religious, social, social service, student government, and symphony. Popular campus events include Mastodon Roast, and Freshmen Fest.

Sports: There are 7 intercollegiate sports for men and 8 for women, and 16 intramural sports for men and 16 for women. Facilities include a physical fitness center with a gym, 3 basketball courts, an indoor track, a weight room, 4 racquetball courts, 1 wallyball court, a fencing and dance room, baseball and soccer fields, and an indoor soccer facility.

Disabled Students: All of the campus is accessible. Facilities include wheelchair ramps, elevators, special parking, specially equipped restrooms, special class scheduling, lowered drinking fountains, lowered telephones, and special housing.

Services: Counseling and information services are available, as is tutoring in most subjects. There is a reader service for the blind, and remedial math, reading, and writing.

Campus Safety and Security: Measures include 24-hour foot and vehicle patrol, emergency notification system, self-defense education, and security escort services. There are shuttle buses, emergency telephones, lighted pathways/sidewalks, and controlled access to dorms/residences.

Programs of Study: IPFW confers B.A., B.S., B.F.A., B.G.S, B.Mus., B.Mus.Ed., B.S.B., B.S.C., B.S.C.E., B.S.Cp.E., B.S.Ed., B.S.E.E., B.S.G., B.S.M.E., B.S.P.A., B.S.L.S. and B.S.M.T. degrees. Associate and master's degrees are also awarded. Bachelor's degrees are awarded in BIOLOGICAL SCIENCE (biochemistry and biology/biological science), BUSINESS (accounting, banking and finance, business administration and management, business economics, hospitality management services, labor studies, management science, marketing/retailing/merchandising, and organizational leadership and management), COMMUNICATIONS AND THE ARTS (communications, crafts, dramatic arts, drawing, English, English literature, fine arts, French, German, graphic design, music, music performance, painting, percussion, photography, piano/organ, printmaking, sculpture, Spanish, speech/debate/rhetoric, strings, technical and business writing, telecommunications, visual design, and voice), COMPUTER AND PHYSICAL SCIENCE (actuarial science, chemistry, computer programming, computer science, earth science, geology, information sciences and systems, mathematics, physical sciences, physics, and statistics), EDUCATION (art education, computer education, early childhood education, elementary education, English education, foreign languages education, mathematics education, middle school education, music education, science education, and secondary education), ENGINEERING AND ENVIRONMENTAL DESIGN (civil engineering, computer engineering, computer graphics, electrical/electronics engineering, electrical/electronics engineering technology, engineering, engineering technology, industrial engineering technology, interior design, mechanical engineering, and mechanical engineering technology), HEALTH PROFESSIONS (health care administration, medical technology, music therapy, nursing, predentistry, premedicine, preoptometry, prepharmacy, preveterinary science, and speech pathology/audiology), SOCIAL SCIENCE (anthropology, criminal justice, economics, history, human services, liberal arts/general studies, philosophy, political science/government, prelaw, psychology, public administration, public affairs, social science, sociology, and women's studies). Engineering and biology is the strongest academically. Business, education and engineering have the largest enrollments.

Required: All bachelor's degree students must complete 120 credits, including 33 general education hours, with a GPA of 2.0, and take English composition, speech communication, and math to graduate. Students must take 32 credit hours at the 200 level or above (including 15 credit hours at the 300 level or above) in their major.

Special: There are continuing education, co-op, and work-study programs, as well as study abroad in 5 countries. An accelerated general studies degree, cross-registration with other Fort Wayne colleges, B.A.-B.S. degrees, dual majors, a Washington semester for public affairs students, internships, and credit for military experience are available. Nondegree study and pass/fail options are possible. An accelerated MBA degree is also offered. There are 16 national honor societies and a freshman honors program.

Faculty/Classroom: 56% of faculty are male; 44% are female. All teach undergraduates, and 92% do research. Graduate students teach 3% of introductory courses. The average class size in an introductory lecture is 20; in a laboratory is 19; and in a regular course is 20.

Admissions: 83% of the 2013-2014 applicants were accepted. The SAT scores for the 2013-2014 freshman class were: Critical Reading--54% below 500, 36% between 500 and 599, 9% between 600 and 699, and 1% between 700 and 800; Math--50% below 500, 35% between 500 and 599, 13% between 600 and 699, and 2% between 700 and 800; Writing--64% below 500, 28% between 500 and 599, 7% between 600 and 699, and 1% between 700 and 800. The ACT scores were 41% below 21, 28% between 21 and 23, 14% between 24 and 26, 7% between 27 and 28, and 9% above 28. 29% of the current freshmen were in the top fifth of their class; 64% were in the top two fifths. 10 freshmen graduated first in their class.

Requirements: The SAT or ACT is required, with a minimum composite score of 1420 on the SAT or a minimum composite score of 20 on the ACT. Indiana Core 40, Academic Honors, or Technical Honors Diploma. Out-of-state students must complete a college prep curriculum IPFW requires applicants to be in the upper 50% of their class. A GPA of 2.8 is required. AP and CLEP credits are accepted. Important factors in the admissions decision are recommendations by school officials, evidence of special talent, and advanced placement or honors courses.

Procedure: Freshmen are admitted fall, spring, and summer. Entrance exams should be taken in the senior year of high school. There are deferred admissions and rolling admissions plans. Applications should be filed by August 1 for fall entry; December 15 for spring entry; and May 1 for summer entry, along with a $50 fee. Notification is sent on a rolling basis. Applications are accepted online.

Transfer: 536 transfer students enrolled in 2012-2013. Transfer applicants must have a minimum GPA of 2.0. Grades of C or better transfer for credit. 32 of 120 credits required for the bachelor's degree must be completed at IPFW.

Visiting: There are regularly scheduled orientations for prospective students. There are guides for informal visits and visitors may sit in on classes. To schedule a visit, contact the Admissions Office.

Financial Aid: In 2013-2014, 74% of all full-time freshmen students received some form of financial aid. 51% of all full-time freshmen students received need-based aid. The average freshman award was $9,274. Need-based scholarships or need-based grants averaged $5,601 ($13,021 maximum); need-based self-help aid (loans and jobs) averaged $3,176 ($26,398 maximum); non-need-based athletic scholarships averaged $12,779 ($39,791 maximum); and other non-need-based awards and non-need-based scholarships averaged $4,001 ($24,867 maximum). 1% of undergraduate students work part-time. Average annual earnings from campus work are $2000. The average financial indebtedness of the 2013 graduate was $28,930. IPFW is a member of CSS. The FAFSA is required. The priority date for freshman financial aid applications for fall entry is March 10.

International Students: There are 182 international students enrolled. The school actively recruits these students. They must take the TOEFL with a minimum score of 550 on the paper-based TOEFL (PBT) or 79 on the Internet-based version (iBT), or pass level 112 of an ESL program. They may also take the ACT or SAT.

Graduates: From July 1, 2012 to June 30, 2013, 1370 bachelor's degrees were awarded. The most popular majors were business (18%), general studies (14%), and health and education (11%). 181 companies recruited on campus in 2012-2013. In an average class, 4% graduate in 4 years or less, 15% graduate in 5 years or less, and 22% graduate in 6 years or less.

Admissions Contact: Frank Guzik, Interim Director of Admissions. E-Mail: *ASK@ipfw.edu* Web: *www.ipfw.edu/admissions*

INDIANA UNIVERSITY-PURDUE UNIVERSITY INDIANAPOLIS — C-3

Indianapolis, IN 46202	**(317) 274-4591; (317) 278-1862**
Full-time: 7303 men, 9457 women	**Faculty:** n/av; IIA, av$
Part-time: 2444 men, 3205 women	**Ph.D.s:** 83%
Graduate: 3526 men, 4554 women	**Student/Faculty:** 18 to 1
Year: semesters, summer session	**Tuition:** $8756 ($29,571)
Application Deadline: May 1	**Room & Board:** $8534
Freshman Class: 12230 applied, 8510 accepted, 3796 enrolled	
SAT CR/M/W: 495/510/485 **ACT:** 22	**COMPETITIVE**

Indiana University-Purdue University Indianapolis, ranked third in "up and coming" American universities home of nationally-ranked programs in nursing, public and environmental affairs, law, and health; and a campus renowned for service learning and civic engagement. IUPUI is Indiana's premier urban university, with 19 schools and academic units which grant degrees in more than 200 programs from both Indiana University and Purdue University. Its location within blocks of downtown Indianapolis facilitates advancement of research and teaching, and presents unique opportunities for internships, partnerships, community engagement, and more. IUPUI enrolls more than 30,000 students representing all 50 states and 122 countries. Join us, and see how IUPUI offers what matters, where it matters. There are 19 undergraduate schools. In addition to regional accreditation, IUPUI has baccalaureate program accreditation with AACSB, ABET, CSWE, NASAD, and NLN. The 5 libraries contain 1.9 million volumes. Computerized library services include interlibrary loans, database searching, Internet access, and Wi-Fi capability. Special learning facilities include an art gallery, an 85-acre medical center, 100 research centers, 27 signature centers, the IU Research and Technology Corporation. The 507-acre campus is in an urban area near downtown Indianapolis. Including any residence halls, there are 134 buildings.

Student Life: 94% of undergraduates are from Indiana. Others are from 49 states, 145 foreign countries, and Canada. 71% are White. The average age of freshmen is 19; all undergraduates, 24.

Housing: 1947 students can be accommodated in college housing, which includes coed dorms, on-campus apartments, off-campus apartments, and married student housing. In addition, there are honors houses, special-interest houses, international house, women in science house, sustainability house. On-campus housing is available on a first-come and first-served basis. 91% of students commute. Alcohol is not permitted. All students may keep cars.

Activities: 1% of men belong to 10 national fraternities; 2% of women belong to 10 national sororities. There are 300 groups on campus, including art, band, cheerleading, chess, computers, dance, debate, drama, environmental, ethnic, film, forensics, gay, honors, international, jazz band, literary magazine, newspaper, pep band, photography, political, professional, radio and TV, religious, social, social service, and student government. Popular campus events include Weeks of Welcome, Spring Dance, InternationalFest, Jag-A-Palooza, Cultural Heritage Months, IUPUI Regatta and FountainFest.

Sports: There are 7 intercollegiate sports for men and 9 for women, and 11 intramural sports for men and 11 for women. IUPUI Gymnasium (The Jungle) -features basketball and volleyball courts, Kuntz Memorial Soccer Stadium - features two FIFA regulated game fields, Natatorium - a competition pool, instructional pool and diving well, IUPUI Softball Complex -3 fields, Michael A. Carroll Stadium -12,000-seat track and field stadium, and the National Institute for Fitness and Sport -a 117,000-square foot facility with a 200-meter indoor track, free weights, Cybex and cardio equipment, pilates studio, indoor batting nets, half size basketball courts.

Disabled Students: All of the campus is accessible. Facilities include wheelchair ramps, elevators, special parking, specially equipped restrooms, special class scheduling, lowered drinking fountains, lowered telephones. classroom aids and sign language interpreters.

Services: Counseling and information services are available, as is tutoring in most subjects. There is a reader service for the blind, and remedial math, reading, and writing.

Campus Safety and Security: Measures include 24-hour foot and vehicle patrol, emergency notification system, self-defense education, and security escort services. There are shuttle buses, emergency telephones, and lighted pathways/sidewalks.

Programs of Study: IUPUI confers B.A., B.S., B.S.B., B.A.E.D., B.F.A., B.G.S., B.S.B., B.S.C.E., B.S.E.D., B.S.E.E., B.S.H.S.M., B.S.M.E., B.S.P.A., B.S.P.E., B.S.P.H. and B.S.W. degrees. Associate, master's, and doctoral degrees are also awarded. Bachelor's degrees are awarded in BIOLOGICAL SCIENCE (biology/adolescence education, biotechnology, forensic science, and neurosciences), BUSINESS (accounting, business administration and management, finance, labor studies, marketing, organizational leadership and management, sports management, supply chain management, sustainable management, and tourism), COMMUNICATIONS AND THE ARTS (American Sign Language, art history, ceramic art and design, communication studies, English, fine arts, French, German, information technology, journalism, media arts, Technical Communication, music technology, painting, printmaking, public relations, sculpture, Spanish, and spanish / adolescence education), COMPUTER AND PHYSICAL SCIENCE (actuarial science, chemistry, chemistry/ adolescence education, clinical laboratory science, Computer Engineering Technology, computer information technology, earth science / adolescence education, energy science, geology, mathematics, and physics), EDUCATION (art education, elementary education, English education, English education, general studies, health education, health information management, mathematics education, and social studies education), ENGINEERING AND ENVIRONMENTAL DESIGN (bioengineering, biomedical engineering, computer engineering, computer graphics, computer technology, electrical and computer engineering, electrical/electronics engineering, environmental science, furniture design, interior design, mechanical engineering technology, and nuclear medicine technology), HEALTH PROFESSIONS (biology, cytotechnology, dental hygiene, exercise science, health, health administration and policy, health science, medical imaging, kinesiology, mental health/human services, nursing, premedicine, prepharmacy, preveterinary science, public health, radiation therapy, and respiratory therapy), SOCIAL SCIENCE (africana studies, anthropology, criminal justice, economics, geography, history, human services, interdisciplinary studies, philosophy, political science/government, psychology, public affairs, religious studies, safety management, social work, and sociology). Nursing, business, and general studies have the largest enrollments.

Required: All students must complete 120 to 126 credits required for the bachelor's degree. Most schools also require grades of C or higher in major courses. Beginning in fall 2013, all beginning first-year students at Indiana University–Purdue University Indianapolis (IUPUI) will complete 30 hours of general education course work (the IUPUI General Education Core) prior to graduation with either an associate degree a baccalaureate degree. Course work is divided into the broad domains of Foundational Intellectual Skills (Core Communication, Analytical Reasoning, and Cultural Understanding) and course work that promotes Intellectual Breadth and Adaptiveness (Life and Physical Sciences; and Arts, Humanities, and Social Sciences).

Special: There is a metropolitan studies program for career work in the city and cross-registration with the Consortium for Urban Education. IUPUI also offers study abroad, combined B.A.-B.S. degree programs, internships, work-study programs, dual and student-designed majors, online degrees, nondegree study, nontraditional programs for adult learners, and interdisciplinary majors such as business economics and public policy, health occupations education, and interdisciplinary engineering. There are 10 national honor societies and a freshman honors program.

Faculty/Classroom: 55% of faculty are male; 45% are female. No introductory courses are taught by graduate students.

Admissions: 70% of the 2013-2014 applicants were accepted. The SAT scores for the 2013-2014 freshman class were: Critical Reading--51% below 500, 36% between 500 and 599, 12% between 600 and 699, and 1% between 700 and 800; Math--45% below 500, 38% between 500 and 599, 15% between 600 and 699, and 2% between 700 and 800; Writing--57% below 500, 33% between 500 and 599, 9% between 600 and 699, and 1% between 700 and 800.

Requirements: The SAT or ACT is required. Indiana high school graduates are expected to complete the Core 40 curriculum, and are strongly encouraged to earn the Academic Honors Diploma. Out-of-state students are expected to complete the required core of classes listed above to be considered for admission. The units of academic electives can be a combination of additional mathematics, laboratory science, social science, computer science, foreign language, or other courses of college preparatory nature. Some IUPUI schools require additional courses. Rank in upper half of high school class or show above average on the GED. SAT or ACT scores for Indiana residents should be at or above the Indiana median. Student who have been out of high school for more than 1 year are nor required to submit. AP and CLEP credits are accepted.

Procedure: Freshmen are admitted to all sessions. Entrance exams should be taken by the end of junior year or fall of senior year. There are deferred admissions and rolling admissions plans. Application deadlines are open. Application fee is $50. Notification is sent on a rolling basis. Applications are accepted online.

Transfer: 1796 transfer students enrolled in 2012-2013. Transfers who are Indiana residents must present a minimum GPA of 2.0 in all previous college work; out-of-state residents need a minimum 2.5. All applicants must be in good standing at their former schools. 30 of 120 credits required for the bachelor's degree must be completed at IUPUI.

Visiting: There are regularly scheduled orientations for prospective students, consisting of a campus tour and talks with students. There are guides for informal visits and visitors may sit in on classes. To schedule a visit, contact the Office of Admissions.

Financial Aid: In 2013-2014, 89% of all full-time freshmen and 85% of continuing full-time students received some form of financial aid. 70% of all full-time freshmen and 70% of continuing full-time students received need-based aid. The average freshman award was $10,752. Need-based scholarships or need-based grants averaged $8,114 ($32,550 maximum); need-based self-help aid (loans and jobs) averaged $3,598 ($8,851 maximum); non-need-based athletic scholarships averaged $9,902 ($42,798 maximum); and other non-need-based awards and non-need-based scholarships averaged $2,267 ($42,798 maximum). 10% of undergraduate students work part-time. Average annual earnings from campus work are $2467. The FAFSA is required. The priority date for freshman financial aid applications for fall entry is March 1. The deadline for filing freshman financial aid applications for fall entry is March 10.

International Students: There are 686 international students enrolled. The school actively recruits these students. They must take the TOEFL with a minimum score of 550 on the paper-based TOEFL (PBT) or 80 on the Internet-based version (iBT).

Graduates: From July 1, 2012 to June 30, 2013, 3783 bachelor's degrees were awarded. The most popular majors were health professions (16%), business, management and marketing (16%), liberal arts and sciences, and general studies and humanities (12%).

Admissions Contact: Chris J. Foley, Director of Undergraduate Admissions. E-Mail: *apply@iupui.edu* Web: *http:/enroll.iupui.edu/admissions/*

INDIANA WESLEYAN UNIVERSITY — C-2

Marion, IN 46953 — **765-677-1677**
1-866-GO-TO-IWU; 765-677-2333

Full-time: 957 men, 1804 women	**Faculty:** 160; IIB, -$
Part-time: 60 men, 112 women	**Ph.D.s:** 67%
Graduate: 45 men, 40 women	**Student/Faculty:** 14 to 1
Year: semesters, summer session	**Tuition:** $24,102
Application Deadline:	**Room & Board:** $7713
Freshman Class: 2606 applied, 2521 accepted, 718 enrolled	
SAT CR/M/W: 525/535/515	**ACT:** 24 **VERY COMPETITIVE**

Indiana Wesleyan University, founded in 1920, is a private, evangelical Christian, liberal arts university located in Marion, Indiana. The University mission states: "Indiana Wesleyan University is a Christ-centered academic community committed to changing the world by developing students in character, scholarship, and leadership." There are 6 undergraduate schools and 3 graduate schools. In addition to regional accreditation, IWU has baccalaureate program accreditation with CSWE, NASM, and NCATE. The library contains 276,070 volumes, 315,162 microform items, 11,479 audio/video tapes/CDs/DVDs, and subscribes to 106,118 periodicals including electronic. Computerized library services include interlibrary loans, database searching, Internet access, and Wi-Fi capability. Special learning facilities include an art gallery, radio station, TV station, a globe theatre, and the daily planet. The 345-acre campus is in a small town located in north-central Indiana, 70 miles north of Indianapolis, 50 miles south of Fort Wayne. Including any residence halls, there are 64 buildings.

Student Life: 53% of undergraduates are from Indiana. Others are from 46 states, 7 foreign countries, and Canada. 91% are White. 92% are Protestant. The average age of freshmen is 18; all undergraduates, 20. 26% do not continue beyond their first year; 70% remain to graduate.

Housing: 2801 students can be accommodated in college housing, which includes single-sex dorms, on-campus apartments, and married student housing. In addition, there are special-interest houses. On-campus housing is guaranteed for all 4 years, is available on a first-come, and first-served basis. 82% of students live on campus; of those, 75% remain on campus on weekends. Alcohol is not permitted. All students may keep cars.

Activities: There are no fraternities or sororities. There are 35 groups on campus, including art, band, cheerleading, choir, chorale, chorus, computers, drama, environmental, ethnic, film, honors, international, jazz band, literary magazine, musical theater, newspaper, opera, orchestra, pep band, photography, political, professional, radio and TV, religious, social, social service, student government, symphony, and yearbook. Popular campus events include Spotted Cow Music Festival, Friday Night Live and Taste of Marion.

Sports: There are 9 intercollegiate sports for men and 9 for women, and

21 intramural sports for men and 21 for women. Facilities include Recreation and Wellness Center: fitness rooms, weight rooms, swimming pool, athletic training center, indoor track, practice/intramural gym, basketball gymnasium, locker rooms. Outdoor fields: soccer, baseball, softball, track and field, tennis courts. Indoor Sports Complex: long/triple jump pits, pole vault area, indoor weight throw, 8 lane 200 meter track.

Disabled Students: 95% of the campus is accessible. Facilities include wheelchair ramps, elevators, special parking, specially equipped restrooms, special class scheduling, lowered drinking fountains, lowered telephones, special housing.

Services: Counseling and information services are available, as is tutoring in most subjects. There is a reader service for the blind, and remedial math, reading, and writing. External testing, a note-taker service, and advocacy are available.

Campus Safety and Security: Measures include 24-hour foot and vehicle patrol, emergency notification system, and security escort services. There are emergency telephones, lighted pathways/sidewalks, and controlled access to dorms/residences.

Programs of Study: IWU confers A.B., B.A., B.S.N., B.S.M. and M.A. degrees. Associate, master's, and doctoral degrees are also awarded. Bachelor's degrees are awarded in BIOLOGICAL SCIENCE (biology/biological science), BUSINESS (accounting, banking and finance, business administration and management, management science, marketing/retailing/merchandising, and recreational facilities management), COMMUNICATIONS AND THE ARTS (applied music, art, ceramic art and design, communications, creative writing, English, illustration, music, music theory and composition, painting, photography, printmaking, Spanish, and studio art), COMPUTER AND PHYSICAL SCIENCE (chemistry, computer science, information sciences and systems, mathematics, and science), EDUCATION (art education, athletic training, elementary education, English education, mathematics education, music education, nursing education, physical education, science education, secondary education, social studies education, and special education), ENGINEERING AND ENVIRONMENTAL DESIGN (computer graphics and interior design), HEALTH PROFESSIONS (health, medical laboratory technology, nursing, and premedicine), SOCIAL SCIENCE (addiction studies, biblical studies, criminal justice, economics, history, law enforcement and corrections, liberal arts/general studies, ministries, political science/government, prelaw, psychology, religion, religious education, religious music, social studies, social work, and sociology). Nursing, education, pre-medicine, religion are the strongest academically. Nursing, education, business, psychology, pre-medicine, religion have the largest enrollments.

Required: A 52-credit general education core includes 12 credit hours of humanities, 10 of math and science, 9 each of English and history or social studies, 6 of biblical literature, and 3 each of intercultural experience and phys ed. Foreign language courses are required for the B.A., computer literacy courses for the B.S. To graduate, students must complete at least 124 semester hours, including 40 to 60 in a major field of study, with a minimum GPA of 2.0 overall and 2.25 in the major. A thesis is required for the honors college.

Special: Students may study abroad in 20 countries. IWU also offers business, pastoral, nursing, and social work internships, cross-registration with CCCU, a Washington semester, work-study programs with the Economic Growth Council, pass/fail options, and nondegree study. Accelerated degree programs are available in accounting, business administration, business information, management, and nursing. Students may earn a B.A.-B.S. degree in management, business, and education. Dual majors and student-designed majors are available. Adult learners may earn credit for life experience toward bachelor's degrees in business. There are 6 national honor societies, a freshman honors program, and 12 departmental honors programs.

Faculty/Classroom: 60% of faculty are male; 40% are female. 98% teach undergraduates, 20% do research, and 20% do both. No introductory courses are taught by graduate students. The average class size in an introductory lecture is 50; in a laboratory is 15; and in a regular course is 18.

Admissions: 97% of the 2013-2014 applicants were accepted. The SAT scores for the 2013-2014 freshman class were: Critical Reading--33% below 500, 45% between 500 and 599, 19% between 600 and 699, and 3% between 700 and 800; Math--32% below 500, 44% between 500 and 599, 22% between 600 and 699, and 2% between 700 and 800; Writing--43% below 500, 40% between 500 and 599, 15% between 600 and 699, and 2% between 700 and 800. The ACT scores were 5% below 21, 38% between 21 and 23, 47% between 24 and 26, and 10% above 28. 57% of the current freshmen were in the top fifth of their class; 85% were in the top two fifths. There were 10 National Merit finalists. 28 freshmen graduated first in their class.

Requirements: The SAT or ACT is required. In addition, The completed application, high school transcript, test scores including an essay (SAT or ACT), recommendation, and a community values contract are necessary for an admission decision. A tuition deposit is required before registration and is fully refundable until May 1. The admission decision may be made with a high school transcript at the end of the junior year. It is to be followed later by the full four-year record and certification of graduation. A student should have a minimum of each of the following: 8 credits in language arts (equivalent to 4 years); 6-8 credits in mathematics (equivalent to 3-4 years); 6 credits in science (equivalent to 3 years); 6 credits in social studies (equivalent to 3 years); 4 credits in foreign language (equivalent to 2 years); 2 credits in health, physical education, safety (equivalent to 1 year); and 4-6 credits from other courses offered (equivalent to 2-3 years). Regular admission requires that applicants have at least a 2.6 cumulative high school GPA on a 4.0 scale and a 880 SAT (Math and Critical Reading) or 18 ACT score. Applicants who do not meet the requirements for regular admission may request special consideration. A GPA of 2.6 is required. AP and CLEP credits are accepted. Important factors in the admissions decision are ability to finance college education, advanced placement or honors courses, parents or siblings attended your school, evidence of special talent, personality/intangible qualities, extracurricular activities record, recommendations by alumni, recommendations by school officials, leadership record, and geographical diversity.

Procedure: Freshmen are admitted to all sessions. Entrance exams should be taken Junior year, or early in their senior year. There are early decision, deferred admissions, and rolling admissions plans. Application deadlines are open. Application fee is $25. Applications are accepted online.

Transfer: 106 transfer students enrolled in 2012-2013. Addition to standard admissions requirements, transfers must submit transcripts of all previous college work and be in good standing at their former school. 30 of 124 credits required for the bachelor's degree must be completed at IWU.

Visiting: There are regularly scheduled orientations for prospective students, includes appointments with admissions counselors and professors, campus tours, classroom visits, and meals. There are guides for informal visits, visitors may sit in on classes, and stay overnight. To schedule a visit, contact the Admissions Office.

Financial Aid: In 2013-2014, 99% of all full-time freshmen and 94% of continuing full-time students received some form of financial aid. 73% of all full-time freshmen and 63% of continuing full-time students received need-based aid. The average freshman award was $21,377. Need-based scholarships or need-based grants averaged $13,847; need-based self-help aid (loans and jobs) averaged $7,446; non-need-based athletic scholarships averaged $6,994; and other non-need-based awards and non-need-based scholarships averaged $5,185. 51% of undergraduate students work part-time. Average annual earnings from campus work are $4100. The average financial indebtedness of the 2013 graduate was $31,482. The FAFSA and the college's own financial statement are required. The deadline for filing freshman financial aid applications for fall entry is March 1.

International Students: There are 111 international students enrolled. The school actively recruits these students. They must take the TOEFL with a minimum score of 550 on the paper-based TOEFL (PBT) or 79 on the Internet-based version (iBT). They must also take the SAT or ACT, scoring 18.

Graduates: From July 1, 2012 to June 30, 2013, 635 bachelor's degrees were awarded. The most popular majors were nursing (18%), elementary education (8%), and psychology (6%). In an average class, 56% graduate in 4 years or less, 68% graduate in 5 years or less, and 70% graduate in 6 years or less.

Admissions Contact: Tracy Curfman, Admissions Admistrative Assistant. E-Mail: *admissions@indwes.edu* Web: *http:/www.indwes.edu/Admissions/Undergraduate/*

MANCHESTER COLLEGE — C-2

North Manchester, IN 46962-0365 — **(260) 982-5055 (800) 852-3648; (260) 982-5239**

Full-time: 600 men, 600 women	**Faculty:** n/av; IIB, --$
Part-time: 5 men, 10 women	**Ph.D.s:** n/av
Graduate: n/av	**Student/Faculty:** n/av
Year: semesters, summer session	**Tuition:** $26,470
Application Deadline: open	**Room & Board:** $9600
Freshman Class: n/av	
SAT or ACT: required	

COMPETITIVE

Manchester College, established in 1889, is a private liberal arts college affiliated with the Church of the Brethren offering undergraduate programs in accounting, business and economics, premedicine, education, psychology, the social sciences, and the humanities. The figures in the above capsule and in this profile are approximate. In addition to regional accreditation, Manchester has baccalaureate program accreditation with CSWE and NCATE. The library contains 174,078 volumes, 23,014 microform items, and 5,258 audio/video tapes/CDs/DVDs, subscribes to 973 periodicals including electronic. Computerized library services include interlibrary loans, database searching, and Internet access. Special learning facilities include a learning resource center, art gallery, planetarium, radio station, a 100-acre nature preserve. The 124-acre campus is in a small town 35 miles west of Fort Wayne, IN. Including any residence halls, there are 44 buildings.

Student Life: 90% of undergraduates are from Indiana. Others are from 21 states, 20 foreign countries, and Canada. 99% are from public schools. 89% are white. 36% are Protestant; 15% Catholic. The average age of freshmen is 18; all undergraduates, 20. 30% do not continue beyond their first year; 55% remain to graduate.

Housing: 995 students can be accommodated in college housing, which includes single-sex and coed dorms, on-campus apartments, off-campus apartments, and married student housing. In addition, there are special-interest houses, The Intercultural Center is a special interest facility providing social, cultural, and educational opportunities to students. Theme units for students interested in science, health, and international issues are located within the residence hall system. On-campus housing is guaranteed for all 4 years. 79% of students live on campus; of those, 50% remain on campus on weekends. Alcohol is not permitted. All students may keep cars.

Activities: There are no fraternities or sororities. There are 53 groups on campus, including band, cheerleading, choir, chorale, chorus, computers, dance, drama, environmental, ethnic, gay, honors, international, jazz band, literary magazine, musical theater, newspaper, opera, orchestra, pep band, photography, political, professional, radio and TV, religious, social, social service, student government, symphony, and yearbook. Popular campus events include Parents Weekend, Sibling Weekend, International Fair, and May Day Weekend.

Sports: There are 9 intercollegiate sports for men and 8 for women, and 13 intramural sports for men and 12 for women. Facilities include an 1800-seat gym, racquetball courts, a fitness center, tennis courts, a cross-country and an all-weather track, and athletic fields for baseball, softball, soccer, and football.

Disabled Students: 50% of the campus is accessible. Facilities include wheelchair ramps, elevators, special parking, specially equipped restrooms, special class scheduling, lowered drinking fountains, lowered telephones, and special housing.

Services: Counseling and information services are available, as is tutoring in every subject. There is a reader service for the blind. There is also a learning center with an academic assistance program, a seminar to enhance study and learning skills, and time and project management.

Campus Safety and Security: Measures include 24-hour foot and vehicle patrol, emergency notification system, and security escort services. There are emergency telephones and lighted pathways/sidewalks.

Programs of Study: Manchester confers B.A. and B.S. degrees. Associate degrees are also awarded. Bachelor's degrees are awarded in AGRICULTURE (environmental studies), BIOLOGICAL SCIENCE (biochemistry and biology/biological science), BUSINESS (accounting, banking and finance, and business administration and management), COMMUNICATIONS AND THE ARTS (art, communications, English, French, German, music, and Spanish), COMPUTER AND PHYSICAL SCIENCE (chemistry, computer science, mathematics, and physics), EDUCATION (art education, elementary education, health education, middle school education, and secondary education), ENGINEERING AND ENVIRONMENTAL DESIGN (engineering), HEALTH PROFESSIONS (medical laboratory technology), SOCIAL SCIENCE (economics, history, interdisciplinary studies, peace studies, philosophy, political science/government, prelaw, psychology, religion, social work, and sociology). Education, accounting, and biology-chemistry are the strongest academically. Education, accounting, and communication studies have the largest enrollments.

Required: Students must complete a core curriculum, including requirements in humanities, social sciences, and natural sciences, as well as specific courses in English composition, public communication, Western civilization, and physical fitness. In order to graduate, students must complete a minimum of 128 semester hours, including 26 to 52 hours in a major field, with a GPA of at least 2.0 (2.5 for the education and athletic training majors). A comprehensive exam in the major is also required. A thesis for honors students is optional.

Special: The college offers cooperative programs in nursing and engineering science. The Brethren Colleges Abroad program allows study abroad in 13 countries, including Ecuador, China, England, France, Germany, Ireland, Japan, Mexico, and Spain. Manchester also offers B.A.-B.S. degrees, internships, work-study programs, dual majors, student-designed majors, a 3-2 engineering program, pass/fail options, and nondegree study. Other special academic features include independent study, required study in non-Western culture, and interdisciplinary programs in both peace studies and environmental studies. A January interterm permits internships, travel abroad, and concentrated classes on campus. There are 6 national honor societies, a freshman honors program, and 5 departmental honors programs.

Faculty/Classroom: 53% of faculty are male; 47% are female. All teach undergraduates, 20% do research, and 20% do both. No introductory courses are taught by graduate students. The average class size in an introductory lecture is 30; in a laboratory is 15; and in a regular course is 20.

Requirements: The SAT or ACT is required. Applicants must have a minimum SAT composite of 900, with 450 on each part, or an ACT composite of 18. Each application is reviewed on an individual basis. The GED is accepted. For high school students, the college recommends completion of 28 academic credits, based on 4 years each of English, math, and science, and 2 years each of foreign language, history, and social studies. A GPA of 2.3 is required. AP and CLEP credits are accepted. Important factors in the admissions decision are advanced placement or honors courses, leadership record, and recommendations by school officials.

Procedure: Freshmen are admitted to all sessions. Entrance exams should be taken by November of the senior year. There are deferred admissions and rolling admissions plans. Application deadlines are open. Application fee is $20. Notification is sent on a rolling basis. Applications are accepted online.

Transfer: 29 transfer students enrolled in 2010-2011. Transfer students must present a minimum GPA of 2.0 in all previous college work. 96 of 128 credits required for the bachelor's degree must be completed at Manchester.

Visiting: There are regularly scheduled orientations for prospective students, Student visits include meetings about financial aid, meetings with faculty and admissions, and campus tours. Visitors may also eat meals on campus, sit in on classes, and meet with current students. There are guides for informal visits, visitors may sit in on classes, and stay overnight. To schedule a visit, contact Campus Visit Coordinator.

Financial Aid: In 2011-2012, 100% of all full-time freshmen and 96% of continuing full-time students received some form of financial aid. 84% of continuing full-time students received need-based aid. The average freshman award was $18,110. 40% of undergraduate students work part-time. The average financial indebtedness of the 2011 graduate was $16,333. The FAFSA is required. The deadline for filing freshman financial aid applications for fall entry is rolling.

International Students: There are 41 international students enrolled. The school actively recruits these students. They must take the TOEFL with a minimum score of 550 on the paper-based TOEFL (PBT).

Admissions Contact: Adam Hohman, Associate Director of Admissions. E-Mail: *admitinfo@manchester.edu* Web: *www.manchester.edu*

MARIAN UNIVERSITY/INDIANAPOLIS C-3

Indianapolis, IN 46222 **(317) 955-6300**
(800) 772-7264; (317) 955-6401

Full-time: 663 men, 1018 women	**Faculty:** 110
Part-time: 164 men, 415 women	**Ph.D.s:** 64%
Graduate: 172 men, 283 women	**Student/Faculty:** 15 to 1
Year: semesters, summer session	**Tuition:** $28,400
Application Deadline: August 1	**Room & Board:** $8658
Freshman Class: 2064 applied, 1196 accepted, 338 enrolled	
SAT CR/M/W: 490/490/470	**ACT:** 22 **COMPETITIVE**

Marian University, is a private institution founded in 1851 by the Sisters of St. Francis and now affiliated with the Roman Catholic Church. The college offers undergraduate programs in the arts and sciences, business, education, fine arts, and the health professions. It also offers graduate programs in education as well as a doctorate in osteopathic medicine. In addition to regional accreditation, Marian has baccalaureate program accreditation with AHEA, NCATE, and NLN. The library contains 113,000 volumes, 150 microform items, 2,200 audio/video tapes/CDs/DVDs, and subscribes to 230,000 periodicals including electronic. Computerized library services include interlibrary loans, database searching, Internet access, and Wi-Fi capability. Special learning facilities include an art gallery, the 35-acre Wetlands Ecology Laboratory. The 114-acre campus is in a suburban area 6 miles from downtown Indianapolis. Including any residence halls, there are 23 buildings.

Student Life: 90% of undergraduates are from Indiana. Others are from 32 states, and 8 foreign countries. 84% are from public schools. 74% are White; 13% African American. 51% are unknown religion; 32% Catholic; 16% Protestant. The average age of freshmen is 19; all undergraduates, 24. 29% do not continue beyond their first year; 54% remain to graduate.

Housing: 792 students can be accommodated in college housing, which includes coed dorms and on-campus apartments. In addition, there are special-interest houses, The Dorothy Day House for Peace and Justice is a special-interest house for those interested in living in community working for peace and justice. Marian also has the Bishop Brute House of Formation on-campus, where men studying for the priesthood live in community within a specific dormitory. On-campus housing is guaranteed for all 4 years. 66% of students commute. Alcohol is not permitted. All students may keep cars.

Activities: There are no fraternities or sororities. There are 42 groups on campus, including and departmental, art, band, cheerleading, choir, chorale, chorus, computers, dance, debate, drama, drill team, ethnic, forensics, honors, international, jazz band, literary magazine, marching band, musical theater, newspaper, pep band, photography, political, professional, religious, social, social service, student government, and yearbook. Popular campus events include Global Speaker Series, Field Day and Knightly Music Awards.

Sports: There are 10 intercollegiate sports for men and 10 for women, and 4 intramural sports for men and 4 for women. Facilities include varsity and intramural gyms, stadium, Velodrome and cycling center,racquetball courts, a fitness center, a weight-training room, and a phys ed assessment lab.

Disabled Students: 95% of the campus is accessible. Facilities include wheelchair ramps, elevators, special parking, specially equipped restrooms, and special class scheduling.

Services: Counseling and information services are available, as is tutoring in most subjects. There is a reader service for the blind, and remedial math, reading, and writing. Study skills training and peer tutoring are available.

Campus Safety and Security: Measures include 24-hour foot and vehicle patrol, emergency notification system, self-defense education, and security escort services. There are shuttle buses, emergency telephones, lighted pathways/sidewalks, and controlled access to dorms/residences.

Programs of Study: Marian confers B.A., B.S. and B.S.N. degrees. Associate, master's, and doctoral degrees are also awarded. Bachelor's degrees are awarded in BIOLOGICAL SCIENCE (biology/biological science), BUSINESS (accounting, banking and finance, business administration and management, and sports management), COMMUNICATIONS AND THE ARTS (art history and appreciation, communications, English, French, graphic design, music, Spanish, and studio art), COMPUTER AND PHYSICAL SCIENCE (chemistry and mathematics), EDUCATION (elementary education, physical education, and special education), ENGINEERING AND ENVIRONMENTAL DESIGN (environmental science), HEALTH PROFESSIONS (nursing), SOCIAL SCIENCE (economics, history, pastoral studies, philosophy, political science/government, psychology, religious education, sociology, and theological studies). Accounting, nursing, and biology are the strongest academically. Business administration, nursing and education have the largest enrollments.

Required: To graduate, students must complete 128 semester hours, including 30 to 40 in the major, with a minimum GPA of 2.0 overall and in the major. General education requirements include 14 semester hours in cultural awareness, 10 to 12 in scientific and quantitative reasoning, 9 to 17 in written and oral communication and foreign language, and 9 each in moral reasoning and individual and social awareness.

Special: Co-op programs in accounting, finance, business administration, chemistry, management information systems, and sociology and cross-registration through the Consortium for Urban Education are offered. A dual degree program in math and computer science, a 3-2 engineering degree, and accelerated degrees in nursing and business administration are also offered. Internships, study abroad, work-study, independent study, dual and student-designed majors, and pass/fail options are available. There are 10 national honor societies, a freshman honors program, and 7 departmental honors programs.

Faculty/Classroom: 38% of faculty are male; 62% are female. 80% teach undergraduates. No introductory courses are taught by graduate students. The average class size in an introductory lecture is 22; in a laboratory is 18; and in a regular course is 16.

Admissions: 58% of the 2013-2014 applicants were accepted. The SAT scores for the 2013-2014 freshman class were: Critical Reading--50% below 500, 38% between 500 and 599, 10% between 600 and 699, and 2% between 700 and 800; Math--53% below 500, 32% between 500 and 599, 13% between 600 and 699, and 2% between 700 and 800; Writing--64% below 500, 28% between 500 and 599, and 7% between 600 and 699. The ACT scores were 36% below 21, 28% between 21 and 23, 21% between 24 and 26, 8% between 27 and 28, and 7% above 28. 33% of the current freshmen were in the top fifth of their class; 63% were in the top two fifths. 5 freshmen graduated first in their class.

Requirements: The SAT or ACT is required. The ACT Optional Writing test is also required. Applicants must be graduates of an accredited secondary school or have a GED. Marian requires 20 academic units, including 4 units in English, 2 each in a foreign language and math, of which algebra and geometry are recommended, and 2 each in a lab science and social studies. A GPA of 2.3 is required. AP and CLEP credits are accepted. Important factors in the admissions decision are recommendations by school officials, recommendations by alumni, and leadership record.

Procedure: Freshmen are admitted to all sessions. Entrance exams should be taken at the end of the junior year or the beginning of the senior year. There are deferred admissions and rolling admissions plans. Applications should be filed by August 1 for fall entry; December 10 for spring entry; and April 15 for summer entry, along with a $35 fee. Notification is sent on a rolling basis. Applications are accepted online. Application fees are waived if application is completed online.

Transfer: 345 transfer students enrolled in 2012-2013. In addition to meeting standard admissions requirements, applicants must submit transcripts of all college work and be in good standing at their former school. Students transferring must have a 2.0 GPA. 30 of 128 credits required for the bachelor's degree must be completed at Marian.

Visiting: There are regularly scheduled orientations for prospective students, including a campus tour, visits with faculty and coaches, and financial aid information. There are guides for informal visits, visitors may sit in on classes, and stay overnight. To schedule a visit, contact the Office of Admissions.

Financial Aid: In 2013-2014, 99% of all full-time freshmen and 72% of continuing full-time students received some form of financial aid. 96% of all full-time freshmen and % of continuing full-time students received need-based aid. 11% of undergraduate students work part-time. Average annual earnings from campus work are $1300. The average financial indebtedness of the 2013 graduate was $32,700. The FAFSA and the college's own financial statement are required. The priority date for freshman financial aid applications for fall entry is March 10.

International Students: There are 10 international students enrolled. The school actively recruits these students. They must take the TOEFL with a minimum score of 550 on the paper-based TOEFL (PBT) or 80 on the Internet-based version (iBT). They must also take the SAT or ACT.

Graduates: From July 1, 2012 to June 30, 2013, 636 bachelor's degrees were awarded. The most popular majors were nursing (42%), business/marketing (29%), and education (4%). In an average class, 35% graduate in 4 years or less, 52% graduate in 5 years or less, and 54% graduate in 6 years or less.

Admissions Contact: Luann Brames, Director of Enrollment. E-Mail: *admissions@marian.edu* Web: *www.marian.edu*

MARTIN UNIVERSITY C-3

Indianapolis, IN 46218 **(317) 543-3237; (317) 543-4790**

Full-time: 55 men, 210 women	**Faculty:** n/av
Part-time: 110 men, 265 women	**Ph.D.s:** 36%
Graduate: 35men, 55 women	**Student/Faculty:** n/av
Year: semesters, summer session	**Tuition:** $14,020
Application Deadline: open	**Room & Board:** n/app
Freshman Class: n/av	
SAT or ACT: not required	**SPECIAL**

Martin University, established in 1977, is a private liberal arts institution offering undergraduate programs primarily to low-income minority-group adults. The figures in the above capsule and in this profile are approximate. It also offers graduate degrees in urban community psychology and urban ministry studies. There are 2 graduate schools. Computerized library services include interlibrary loans and database searching. Special learning facilities include a learning resource center and English and math labs. The 8-acre campus is in an urban area in Indianapolis. There are 4 buildings.

Student Life: 90% of students are from public schools. 90% are African American. The average age of freshmen is 33; all undergraduates, 38.

Housing: There are no residence halls. All students commute.

Activities: There are no fraternities or sororities. Groups on campus include choir, civil rights, computers, drama, newspaper, opera, and social service. Popular campus events include internal and external conferences, St. Martin de Porres Feast Day, and Fine Arts Festival.

Sports: There is no sports program at Martin U.

Disabled Students: 90% of the campus is accessible. Facilities include wheelchair ramps, elevators, special parking, specially equipped restrooms, lowered drinking fountains, and lowered telephones.

Services: Counseling and information services are available, as is tutoring in most subjects. There is remedial math, reading, and writing and addiction services.

Campus Safety and Security: Measures include 24-hour foot and vehicle patrol and security escort services. There are lighted pathways/sidewalks.

Programs of Study: Martin U confers B.A. and B.S. degrees. Master's degrees are also awarded. Bachelor's degrees are awarded in BIOLOGICAL SCIENCE (biology/biological science), BUSINESS (accounting, business administration and management, insurance, and marketing/retailing/merchandising), COMMUNICATIONS AND THE ARTS (communications, fine arts, music, and Spanish), COMPUTER AND PHYSICAL SCIENCE (chemistry and mathematics), EDUCATION (early childhood education, education, and vocational education), ENGINEERING AND ENVIRONMENTAL DESIGN (computer technology and environmental science), SOCIAL SCIENCE (African American studies, community services, counseling/psychology, criminal justice, history, humanities, political science/government, psychology, religion, and sociology). Humanities and psychology are the strongest academically. Business has the largest enrollments.

Required: Students must successfully complete 134 credits, including 36 in the humanities, 12 in English, and 6 each in social science and math, with at least 36 in the major and a minimum GPA of 2.0. Other required courses include computer science and critical thinking, plus a foreign language for the B.A. Students must complete a final project in their major.

Special: Cross-registration is permitted with 7 schools in the Consortium of Urban Education in the area. Opportunities are provided for internships, student-designed majors, and credit based on assessment of prior learning. There is 1 departmental honors program.

Faculty/Classroom: 55% of faculty are male; 45% are female. All teach undergraduates, and 10% do research. No introductory courses are taught by graduate students. The average class size in an introductory lecture is 13 and in a laboratory is 8.

Requirements: Graduation from an accredited secondary school is required; a GED will be accepted. No specific number of academic credits is required. An essay, an interview, and diagnostic testing are required. CLEP credits are accepted.

Procedure: Freshmen are admitted to all sessions. Entrance exams should be taken at the time of admission. There is a rolling admissions plan. Application deadlines are open. The application fee is $25.

Transfer: Transfers are accepted from accredited regional schools. 34 of 134 credits required for the bachelor's degree must be completed at Martin U.

Visiting: There are regularly scheduled orientations for prospective students, consisting of 4 3-hour sessions. There are guides for informal visits and visitors may sit in on classes. To schedule a visit, contact the Recruitment Office.

Financial Aid: The FAFSA is required. Check with the school for current application deadlines.

International Students: They must take the TOEFL.

Admissions Contact: Brenda Shaheed, Vice President of Enrollment. E-Mail: *bshaheed@martin.edu* Web: *www.martin.edu*

OAKLAND CITY UNIVERSITY A-5

Oakland City, IN 47660 **(812) 749-1221; (812) 749-1233**

Full-time: 2100 men and women
Year: semesters, summer session
Application Deadline:
Freshman Class: n/av
SAT or ACT: required

Faculty: n/av
Ph.D.s: 71%
Student/Faculty: n/av
Tuition: $16,700
Room & Board: $7800

NONCOMPETITIVE

Oakland City University, founded in 1885, is a private liberal arts institution affiliated with the General Association of General Baptists. The figures in the above capsule and in this profile are approximate. There are 6 undergraduate schools and 2 graduate schools. In addition to regional accreditation, OCU has baccalaureate program accreditation with NCATE. The library contains 83,404 volumes, 100,318 microform items, and 2,576 audio/video tapes/CDs/DVDs, subscribes to 8,000 periodicals including electronic. Computerized library services include interlibrary loans, database searching, and Internet access. The 20-acre campus is in a small town 30 miles north of Evansville, Illinois. Including any residence halls, there are 15 buildings.

Student Life: 88% of undergraduates are from Indiana. Others are from 18 states, and 15 foreign countries. 90% are from public schools. 96% are White. 76% are Protestant; 30% claim no religious affiliation; 13% Catholic. The average age of freshmen is 19; all undergraduates, 24. 30% do not continue beyond their first year; 70% remain to graduate.

Housing: 246 students can be accommodated in college housing, which includes single-sex dorms and on-campus apartments. In addition, there are honors houses and special-interest houses. On-campus housing is available on a first-come and first-served basis. 57% of students commute. Alcohol is not permitted. All students may keep cars.

Activities: There are no fraternities or sororities. There are 19 groups on campus, including art, cheerleading, choir, chorus, computers, departmental, drama, honors, international, musical theater, newspaper, pep band, photography, professional, religious, social, social service, student government, and yearbook. Popular campus events include Fall Festival Week, Spring Fling, and Fine Arts Festival.

Sports: There are 6 intercollegiate sports for men and 7 for women, and 14 intramural sports for men and 14 for women. Facilities include a gym, a health and phys ed center with a 1600-seat gym, a soccer field, a baseball field, and a tennis complex.

Disabled Students: 99% of the campus is accessible. Facilities include wheelchair ramps, elevators, special parking, specially equipped restrooms, lowered drinking fountains, and special housing.

Services: Counseling and information services are available, as is tutoring in every subject. There is a reader service for the blind, and remedial math, reading, and writing.

Campus Safety and Security: Measures include self-defense education and security escort services. There are emergency telephones, lighted pathways/sidewalks, and security in the evenings.

Programs of Study: OCU confers B.A., and B.S. degrees. Associate and master's degrees are also awarded. Bachelor's degrees are awarded in BIOLOGICAL SCIENCE (biology/biological science), BUSINESS (accounting and business administration and management), COMMUNICATIONS AND THE ARTS (English, fine arts, and music), COMPUTER AND PHYSICAL SCIENCE (mathematics), EDUCATION (art education, business education, elementary education, middle school education, music education, science education, and secondary education), HEALTH PROFESSIONS (premedicine), SOCIAL SCIENCE (prelaw and religion). Education is the strongest academically.

Required: Liberal arts students must take a general studies core, including 1 computer science course and 2 hours of phys ed. A minimum GPA of 2.0 (2.5 in the major) and 120 total semester hours are needed to graduate.

Special: OCU offers campus work-study programs, an accelerated business degree program, business and networking internships, a B.A.-B.S. degree, dual majors, credit for significant work or service experience, nondegree study, pass/fail options, and a general studies degree. There are 3 national honor societies.

Faculty/Classroom: 58% of faculty are male; 42% are female. All teach and do research. No introductory courses are taught by graduate students. The average class size in an introductory lecture is 25; in a laboratory is 16; and in a regular course is 25.

Requirements: The SAT or ACT is required, with a satisfactory SAT score or ACT composite score of 18. Preparatory programs usually include 4 units of English, 2 each of social science and science, 2 to 4 of a foreign language, and 3 to 4 of math. An interview is recommended. The GED is accepted. AP and CLEP credits are accepted. Important factors in the admissions decision are personality/intangible qualities, evidence of special talent, and extracurricular activities record.

Procedure: Freshmen are admitted to all sessions. Entrance exams should be taken in the fall of the senior year. There are deferred admissions and rolling admissions plans. Application deadlines are open. The fall 2013 application fee was $35.

Transfer: Transfer applicants need a minimum GPA of 2.0 and a satisfactory score on the SAT or 18 on the ACT. An interview is recommended. 35 of 120 credits required for the bachelor's degree must be completed at OCU.

Visiting: There are regularly scheduled orientations for prospective students. There are guides for informal visits, visitors may sit in on classes, and stay overnight. To schedule a visit, contact the Admissions Office.

Financial Aid: OCU is a member of CSS. The FAFSA and the college's own financial statement are required. The deadline for filing freshman financial aid applications for fall entry is open.

International Students: The school actively recruits these students. They must take the TOEFL. They must also take the SAT or ACT.

Admissions Contact: Brian Baker, Director of Admissions. E-Mail: *bbaker@oak.edu* Web: *www.oak.edu*

PURDUE UNIVERSITY SYSTEM

The Purdue University System, established in 1869, is a land-grant system in Indiana. It is governed by a board of trustees, whose chief administrator is the president. The primary goal of the system is to provide quality education to the citizens of Indiana. The main priorities are teaching, research, and public service. The total student enrollment is usually 74,341, with 4500 faculty members. Altogether there are approximately 375 baccalaureate, 88 master's, and 58 doctoral programs offered in the Purdue University System. Profiles of the 4-year campuses are included in this section.

PURDUE UNIVERSITY/CALUMET B-1

Hammond, IN 46323 **(219) 989-2213**
(800) HI PURDUE; (219) 989-2775

Full-time: 2210 men, 2840 women
Part-time: 1975 men, 1380 women
Graduate: 350 men, 615 women
Year: semesters, summer session
Application Deadline:
Freshman Class: n/av
SAT or ACT: required

Faculty: n/av; IIA, -$
Ph.D.s: 90%
Student/Faculty: n/av
Tuition: $6821 ($14,798)
Room & Board: $7515

COMPETITIVE

Purdue University/Calumet, established in 1946, is a public commuter institution offering undergraduate degrees in general studies, liberal arts, and professional studies. There are 7 undergraduate schools and one graduate school. In addition to regional accreditation, Purdue Cal has baccalaureate program accreditation with ABET, NCATE, and NLN. The library contains 269,648 volumes, 764,621 microform items, 998 audio/video tapes/CDs/DVDs, and subscribes to 228 periodicals including electronic. Computerized library services include interlibrary loans, database searching, and Internet access. Special learning facilities include an art gallery, a computer education building, and an educational media laboratory. The 167-acre campus is in an urban area 25 miles southeast of Chicago. Including any residence halls, there are 21 buildings.

Student Life: 91% of undergraduates are from Indiana. Others are from 30 states, and 27 foreign countries. 72% are from public schools. 68% are White; 15% African American; 14% Hispanic. The average age of freshmen is 19; all undergraduates, 25. 64% do not continue beyond their first year; 24% remain to graduate.

Housing: 376 students can be accommodated in college housing, which includes coed On-campus housing is available on a first-come and first-served basis. 97% of students commute. Alcohol is not permitted. All students may keep cars.

Activities: There are 40 groups on campus, including art, cheerleading, chorus, computers, dance, drama, ethnic, film, gay, honors, international, literary magazine, musical theater, newspaper, political, professional, religious, social, social service, Special Interest and Student Organization Executive Board, and student government. Popular campus events include Orientation, Latin Culture Month, and Black History Month.

Sports: There are 2 intercollegiate sports for men and 2 for women, and 22 intramural sports for men and 22 for women. Facilities include a 1500-seat gym, racquetball courts, an outdoor volleyball court, a running track, a weight room, and a total fitness center.

Disabled Students: All of the campus is accessible. Facilities include wheelchair ramps, elevators, special parking, specially equipped restrooms, special class scheduling, lowered drinking fountains, lowered telephones. There are electric door openers on all but 1 student building.

Services: Counseling and information services are available, as is tutoring in most subjects. There is a reader service for the blind, and remedial math, reading, and writing.

Campus Safety and Security: Measures include 24-hour foot and vehicle patrol, self-defense education, and security escort services. There are emergency telephones, lighted pathways/sidewalks, and student patrols.

Programs of Study: Purdue Cal confers B.A., B.S., B.A.B., B.S.A., B.S.Chm., B.S.E. and B.S.I.M. degrees. Associate and master's degrees are also awarded. Bachelor's degrees are awarded in BIOLOGICAL SCIENCE (biology/biological science, biotechnology, and microbiology), BUSINESS (accounting, banking and finance, business economics, hotel/motel and restaurant management, and marketing/retailing/merchandising), COMMUNICATIONS AND THE ARTS (broadcasting, communications, English, English literature, French, German, public relations, and Spanish), COMPUTER AND PHYSICAL SCIENCE (chemistry, computer programming, computer science, information sciences and systems, mathematics, and physics), EDUCATION (early childhood education, elementary education, foreign languages education, science education, and secondary education), ENGINEERING AND ENVIRONMENTAL DESIGN (computer engineering, computer graphics, computer technology, construction technology, electrical/electronics engineering, electrical/electronics engineering technology, engineering, engineering technology, industrial engineering technology, mechanical engineering, and mechanical engineering technology), HEALTH PROFESSIONS (medical laboratory technology, nursing, optometry, and physical therapy), SOCIAL SCIENCE (criminal justice, history, philosophy, political science/government, psychology, and sociology). Education, nursing, and foreign language are the strongest academically. Management, behavioral sciences, and manufacturing have the largest enrollments.

Required: Graduation requirements vary depending on the program. The total number of credit hours required for a degree varies from 126 to 136, with 24 to 73 in the major. All students must take English composition and 36 hours of general education courses and maintain a C average.

Special: Some cooperative programs, internships, and work-study programs are available. Purdue Cal offers cross-registration in philosophy, study in Spain, and credit for military experience, as well as nondegree study and pass/fail options. There are 7 national honor societies, a freshman honors program, and 80 departmental honors programs.

Faculty/Classroom: 51% of faculty are male; 49% are female. No introductory courses are taught by graduate students. The average class size in an introductory lecture is 26; in a laboratory is 16; and in a regular course is 21.

Admissions: 3 freshmen graduated first in their class.

Requirements: The SAT or ACT is required. The ACT Optional Writing test is also required. The SAT Subject test in math is required. Applicants must be graduates of an accredited secondary school. The GED is accepted. 33 Carnegie units are required for admission. Required courses vary, depending on the curriculum, and include 3 or 4 years of English, 2 or 3 years of math, 2 years of foreign language, and 1 year of history or social studies. A GPA of 2.0 is required. AP and CLEP credits are accepted. Important factors in the admissions decision are recommendations by school officials, advanced placement or honors courses, and personality/intangible qualities.

Procedure: Freshmen are admitted to all sessions. SAT and ACT can be taken anytime during junior and senior year in high school. There are early admissions, deferred admissions, and rolling admissions plans. Check with the school for current application deadlines. Applications are accepted online.

Transfer: Applicants must have a minimum GPA of 2.0. for transfer credit. 32 of 126 credits required for the bachelor's degree must be completed at Purdue Cal.

Visiting: There are regularly scheduled orientations for prospective students. There are guides for informal visits and visitors may sit in on classes. To schedule a visit, contact The Office of Admissions and Recruitment.

Financial Aid: Purdue Cal is a member of CSS. The CSS/Profile is required. Check with the school for current application deadlines.

International Students: The school actively recruits these students. They must take the TOEFL or MELAB. International students can take the SAT in place of the TOEFL.

Admissions Contact: Paul McGuinness, Admissions Director. E-Mail: *adms.@calumet.purdue.edu* Web: *www.calumet.purdue.edu*

PURDUE UNIVERSITY/WEST LAFAYETTE — B-3

West Lafayette, IN 47907 — **(765) 494-1776; (765) 494-0544**

Full-time: 16146 men, 11996 women	**Faculty:** n/av
Part-time: 697 men, 601 women	**Ph.D.s:** 97%
Graduate: 5562 men, 3786 women	**Student/Faculty:** 14 to 1
Year: semesters, summer session	**Tuition:** $9900 ($28,702)
Application Deadline: March 1	**Room & Board:** $10,378

Freshman Class: 30955 applied, 18684 accepted, 6283 enrolled

SAT CR/M/W: 574/626/573 **ACT:** 27 **HIGHLY COMPETITIVE**

Purdue University, founded in 1869, is a publicly supported institution offering degree programs with an emphasis on engineering, business, communications, arts, social sciences, and technology. There are 12 undergraduate schools and one graduate school. In addition to regional accreditation, Purdue has baccalaureate program accreditation with AACSB, ABET, ACCE, ACPE, ADA, ASLA, FIDER, NASM, NCATE, NLN, and SAF. The 13 libraries contain 2.5 million volumes, 3.0 million microform items, 7,780 audio/video tapes/CDs/DVDs, and subscribe to 62,028 periodicals including electronic. Computerized library services include interlibrary loans, database searching, Internet access, and Wi-Fi capability. Special learning facilities include an art gallery and radio station. The 2602-acre campus is in a suburban area 65 miles northwest of Indianapolis. Including any residence halls, there are 376 buildings.

Student Life: 57% of undergraduates are from Indiana. Others are from 50 states, 126 foreign countries, and Canada. 62% are White; 22% Foreign. The average age of freshmen is 18; all undergraduates, 21. 9% do not continue beyond their first year; 71% remain to graduate.

Housing: 11104 students can be accommodated in college housing, which includes single-sex and coed dorms, on-campus apartments, and married student housing. In addition, there are fraternity houses, sorority houses, 3 floors in a women's hall for women in engineering or women in science; there are residences and floors for living and learning communities. On-campus housing is guaranteed for all 4 years. 65% of students commute. Alcohol is not permitted. Upperclassmen may keep cars.

Activities: 11% of men belong to 50 national fraternities; 7% of women belong to 31 national sororities. There are 948 groups on campus, including band, cheerleading, chess, choir, chorale, chorus, computers, dance, debate, drama, ethnic, gay, honors, international, jazz band, literary magazine, marching band, newspaper, orchestra, pep band, photography, political, professional, radio and TV, religious, social, social service, student government, and symphony. Popular campus events include Grand Prix Race, Old Masters, and Gala week.

Sports: There are 9 intercollegiate sports for men and 9 for women, and 29 intramural sports for men and 29 for women. Facilities include a 14,000-seat arena, a 62,000-seat stadium, an intercollegiate athletic facility, a recreational gym, a field house, an athletic center, intramural playing fields, 2 golf courses, and baseball, softball, track, and women's soccer fields.

Disabled Students: 90% of the campus is accessible. Facilities include wheelchair ramps, elevators, special parking, specially equipped restrooms, special class scheduling, lowered drinking fountains, lowered telephones, special housing, a lab with assistive technology and special computers.

Services: Counseling and information services are available, as is tutoring in every subject. There is a reader service for the blind, and remedial math, reading, and writing.

Campus Safety and Security: Measures include 24-hour foot and vehicle patrol, emergency notification system, self-defense education, and security escort services. There are shuttle buses, emergency telephones, lighted pathways/sidewalks, and public transportation routes throughout campus.

Programs of Study: Purdue confers B.A., B.S., B.S.A.A.E., B.S.A.B.E., B.S.B.M.E., B.S.C.E., B.S.Ch., B.S.Ch.E., B.S.C.M.P.E., B.S.C.N.E., B.S.E., B.S.E.E., B.S.E.H., B.S.F.O.R., B.S.I.E., B.S.I.M., B.S.L.A., B.S.L.S.G.E., B.S.M.E., B.S.M.S.E. and B.S.N.E. degrees. Associate, master's, and doctoral degrees are also awarded. Bachelor's degrees are awarded in AGRICULTURE (agricultural business management, agricultural communications, agricultural economics, agriculture, agronomy, animal science, fishing and fisheries, forestry and related sciences, horticulture, natural resource management, plant protection (pest management), plant science, soil science, and wood science), BIOLOGICAL SCIENCE (biochemistry, biology/biological science, cell biology, ecology, entomology, genetics, microbiology, molecular biology, nutrition, plant genetics, plant physiology, and wildlife biology), BUSINESS (accounting, banking and finance, entrepreneurial studies, fashion merchandising, hospitality management services, human resources, marketing management, marketing/retailing/merchandising, organizational leadership and management, retailing, and tourism), COMMUNICATIONS AND THE ARTS (advertising, apparel design, art history and appreciation, audio technology, broadcasting, classics, communications, comparative literature, creative writing, dramatic arts, English, film arts, fine arts, French, German, graphic design, industrial design, Japanese, journalism, Latin, Latin, linguistics, photography, public relations, Russian, Spanish, and visual and performing arts), COMPUTER AND PHYSICAL SCIENCE (actuarial science, applied mathematics, applied physics, atmospheric sciences and meteorology, chemistry, computer science, earth science, geology, information sciences and systems, mathematics, physics, radiological technology, science, software engineering, and statistics), EDUCATION (agricultural education, art education, athletic training, early childhood education, education, elementary education, English education, foreign languages education, health education, mathematics education, science education, secondary education, social studies education, special education, and technical education), ENGINEERING AND ENVIRONMENTAL DESIGN (aeronautical engineering, aeronautical technology, agricultural engineering, air traffic control, airline piloting and navigation, aviation administration/management, aviation computer technology, bioengineering, biomedical engineering, chemical engineering, chemical engineering technology, civil engineering, computational sciences, computer engineering, computer graphics, computer technology, construction engineering, construction management, construction technology, electrical/electronics engineering, electrical/electronics engineering technology, engineering management, environmental science, food services technology, industrial administration/management, industrial engineering, industrial engineering technology, interior design, landscape architecture/design, manufacturing engineering, manufacturing technology, materials science, mechanical engineering, mechanical engineering technology, nuclear engineering, occupational safety and health, and surveying engineering), HEALTH PROFESSIONS (clinical science, environmental health science, exercise science, health science, medical laboratory technology, nursing, pharmaceutical science, radiological science, and speech pathology/audiology), SOCIAL SCIENCE (African American studies, anthropology, Asian/American studies, Asian/Oriental studies, behavioral science, criminal justice, dietetics, economics, family and community services, family/consumer studies, fashion design and technology, food production/management/services, food science, French studies, history, Italian studies, Japanese studies, Judaic studies, liberal arts/general studies, medieval studies, philosophy, physical fitness/movement, political science/government, psychology, religion, Russian and Slavic studies, social studies, social work, sociology, Spanish studies, and women's studies). Engineering, actuarial science, and industrial management are the strongest academically. Management, preengineering, and mechanical engineering have the largest enrollments.

Required: To graduate, students must be enrolled for at least 2 semesters and complete 32 semester hours of course work, complete approximately 128 hours and earn a minimum GPA of 2.0. In most majors, students must take courses in English, math, science, computer science, and social sciences.

Special: Cooperative programs are available in engineering, technology, agriculture, science, and consumer and family sciences. Cross-registration with Purdue's regional campuses, numerous internships, study abroad in 44 countries, dual majors, student-designed majors, nondegree study, and pass/fail options are also offered. There are 33 national honor societies, including Phi Beta Kappa, a freshman honors program, and 10 departmental honors programs.

Faculty/Classroom: 66% of faculty are male; 34% are female. No introductory courses are taught by graduate students. The average class size in an introductory lecture is 50; in a laboratory is 22; and in a regular course is 30.

Admissions: 60% of the 2013-2014 applicants were accepted. The SAT scores for the 2013-2014 freshman class were: Critical Reading--17% below 500, 46% between 500 and 599, 29% between 600 and 699, and 8% between 700 and 800; Math--8% below 500, 30% between 500 and 599, 38% between 600 and 699, and 24% between 700 and 800; Writing--18% below 500, 43% between 500 and 599, 32% between 600 and 699, and 7% between 700 and 800. The ACT scores were 4% below 21, 14% between 21 and 23, 24% between 24 and 26, 19% between 27 and 28, and 39% above 28. 73% of the current freshmen were in the top fifth of their class; 94% were in the top two fifths. 99 freshmen graduated first in their class.

Requirements: The SAT or ACT is required. The ACT Optional Writing test is also required. Purdue recommends that most students have 15 semester credits including 4 years of English, 3 to 4 of math, and 2 to 4 of lab science, and 4 semesters of a foreign language. The GED is accepted. AP and CLEP credits are accepted. Important factors in the admissions decision are advanced placement or honors courses, extracurricular activities record, and geographical diversity.

Procedure: Freshmen are admitted to all sessions. Entrance exams should be taken at the end of the junior year. There is a rolling admissions plan. Applications should be filed by March 1 for fall entry, along with a $60 fee. Applications are accepted online.

Transfer: 614 transfer students enrolled in 2012-2013. Transfer students must file a regular application at least 30 days before the start of the semester and submit SAT/ACT results and high school and college transcripts. Students must be in good academic standing and meet the same subject-matter requirements as a beginning student. A minimum 2.2 GPA is required; many programs require a higher average, and some course and grade requirements. 32 of 128 credits required for the bachelor's degree must be completed at Purdue.

Visiting: There are regularly scheduled orientations for prospective students, including fall and spring preview days, which consist of admission, financial aid, housing, and school sessions, a campus tour, and dormitory visits. The Summer Visit Program consists of a counselors' orientation and campus and residence hall visits. There are guides for informal visits and visitors may sit in on classes. To schedule a visit, contact the Office of Admissions.

Financial Aid: In 2013-2014, 78% of all full-time freshmen and 74% of continuing full-time students received some form of financial aid. 70% of all full-time freshmen and 58% of continuing full-time students received need-based aid. The average freshman award was $12,719. Need-based scholarships or need-based grants averaged $3,903; need-based self-help aid (loans and jobs) averaged $4,677; non-need-based athletic scholarships averaged $424; and other non-need-based awards and non-need-based scholarships averaged $3,715. 27% of undergraduate students work part-time. Average annual earnings from campus work are $1912. The average financial indebtedness of the 2013 graduate was $29,121. The FAFSA is required. The deadline for filing freshman financial aid applications for fall entry is March 1.

International Students: There are 4868 international students enrolled. The school actively recruits these students. They must take the TOEFL with a minimum score of 570 on the paper-based TOEFL (PBT) or 88 on the Internet-based version (iBT).

Graduates: From July 1, 2012 to June 30, 2013, 6829 bachelor's degrees were awarded. The most popular majors were management (6%), mechanical engineering (4%), and accounting (3%). 980 companies recruited on campus in 2012-2013. In an average class, 1% graduate in 3 years or less, 39% graduate in 4 years or less, 65% graduate in 5 years or less, and 69% graduate in 6 years or less. Of the 2012 graduating class, 66% were employed within 6 months of graduation.

Admissions Contact: Pamela Horne, Dean of Admissions/Assistant VP for Enrollment. E-Mail: *admissions@purdue.edu* Web: *www.purdue.edu/*

ROSE-HULMAN INSTITUTE OF TECHNOLOGY B-4

Terre Haute, IN 47803 **(812) 877-1511**
(800) 248-7448; (812) 877-8941

Full-time: 1715 men, 471 women	**Faculty:** 170; IIB, +$
Part-time: 12 men, 7 women	**Ph.D.s:** 99%
Graduate: 76 men, 21 women	**Student/Faculty:** 13 to 1
Year: quarters, summer session	**Tuition:** $40,254
Application Deadline: March 1	**Room & Board:** $11,484
Freshman Class: 5046 applied, 2837 accepted, 559 enrolled	
SAT CR/M/W: 630/680/600 **ACT:** 30	**MOST COMPETITIVE**

Rose Hulman Institute of Technology, founded in 1874, is a private college emphasizing engineering, science, and math. In addition to regional accreditation, Rose-Hulman has baccalaureate program accreditation with ABET. The library contains 149,409 volumes, 556 audio/video tapes/CDs/DVDs, and subscribes to 9,114 periodicals including electronic. Computerized library services include interlibrary loans, database searching, and Internet access. Special learning facilities include an art gallery, planetarium, and radio station. The 200-acre campus is in a suburban area on the east side of Terre Haute. Including any residence halls, there are 37 buildings.

Student Life: 65% of undergraduates are from out of state, mostly the Mid-West. Students are from 47 states, 14 foreign countries, and Canada. 76% are White. The average age of freshmen is 18; all undergraduates, 20. 9% do not continue beyond their first year; 91% remain to graduate.

Housing: 1284 students can be accommodated in college housing, which includes single-sex and coed dorms and on-campus apartments. In addition, there are fraternity houses, sorority houses, and sophomore residence halls. On-campus housing is guaranteed for the freshman year only, is available on a first-come, first-served basis, and is available on a lottery system for upperclassmen. 61% of students live on campus; of those, 60% remain on campus on weekends. All students may keep cars.

Activities: 28% of men belong to 8 national fraternities; 26% of women belong to 3 national sororities. There are 111 groups on campus, including art, band, cheerleading, chess, chorale, chorus, computers, dance, debate, drama, drill team, ethnic, film, gay, honors, international, jazz band, literary magazine, musical theater, newspaper, pep band, photography, political, professional, radio and TV, religious, social, social service, and student government. Popular campus events include Art Shows, Concerts and Plays.

Sports: There are 11 intercollegiate sports for men and 11 for women, and 20 intramural sports for men and 20 for women. Facilities include a field house, a recreational center, swimming pool, tennis courts, and intramural fields.

Disabled Students: 95% of the campus is accessible. Facilities include wheelchair ramps, elevators, special parking, specially equipped restrooms, special class scheduling, and lowered drinking fountains.

Services: Counseling and information services are available, as is tutoring in most subjects.

Campus Safety and Security: Measures include 24-hour foot and vehicle patrol, emergency notification system, and security escort services. There are emergency telephones, lighted pathways/sidewalks, medical transports, and free traffic assistance.

Programs of Study: Rose-Hulman confers B.S. degrees. Master's degrees are also awarded. Bachelor's degrees are awarded in BIOLOGICAL SCIENCE (biochemistry and biology/biological science), COMPUTER AND PHYSICAL SCIENCE (chemistry, computer science, mathematics, physics, and software engineering), ENGINEERING AND ENVIRONMENTAL DESIGN (biomedical engineering, chemical engineering, civil engineering, computer engineering, electrical/electronics engineering, engineering physics, mechanical engineering, and optical engineering), SOCIAL SCIENCE (economics). Engineering, science, and mathematics are the strongest academically. Mechanical engineering, chemical engineering, and electrical engineering have the largest enrollments.

Required: All students must complete at least 192 to 195 quarter hours with a minimum GPA of 2.0 and 36 hours in the humanities and social sciences. Freshmen are required to take math, biology, chemistry, or physics. The total number of hours required in the major varies.

Special: The Institute offers co op programs, independent study, cross-registration with Indiana State University and Saint Mary-of-the-Woods College, summer industrial internships, study abroad in 8 countries, and dual majors. Pass/fail options also are available. There are 7 national honor societies and 3 departmental honors programs.

Faculty/Classroom: 79% of faculty are male; 21% are female. All teach undergraduates, and 20% do research. No introductory courses are taught by graduate students. The average class size in an introductory lecture is 20; in a laboratory is 22; and in a regular course is 20.

Admissions: 56% of the 2013-2014 applicants were accepted. The SAT scores for the 2013-2014 freshman class were: Critical Reading--4% below 500, 34% between 500 and 599, 46% between 600 and 699, and 17% between 700 and 800; Math--10% between 500 and 599, 58% between 600 and 699, and 32% between 700 and 800; Writing--12% below 500, 38% between 500 and 599, 42% between 600 and 699, and 8% between 700 and 800. The ACT scores were 6% between 21 and 23, 16% between 24 and 26, 15% between 27 and 28, and 62% above 28. 87% of the current freshmen were in the top fifth of their class; 98% were in the top two fifths. There were 12 National Merit finalists. 60 freshmen graduated first in their class.

Requirements: The SAT or ACT is required. Candidates should have at least 16 units of credit, including 4 in English, 2 in social sciences, and 1 each in math, chemistry, physics, and electives. An essay and interview are recommended. Rose-Hulman requires applicants to be in the upper 25% of their class. AP credits are accepted. Important factors in the admissions decision are advanced placement or honors courses, recommendations by school officials, and extracurricular activities record.

Procedure: Freshmen are admitted fall. Entrance exams should be taken in the fall of the senior year or spring of the junior year. There are deferred admissions and rolling admissions plans. Applications should be filed by March 1 for fall entry, along with a $40 fee. 420 applicants were on the 2013 waiting list; 55 were admitted. Applications are accepted online.

Transfer: 14 transfer students enrolled in 2012-2013. Applicants need 1 year each of calculus, physics, and chemistry and a minimum GPA of 3.0. An interview is recommended.

Visiting: There are regularly scheduled orientations for prospective students, including interviews, campus tours, and academic meetings. There are guides for informal visits, visitors may sit in on classes, and stay overnight. To schedule a visit, contact Nancy Apple at (800) 248-7448.

Financial Aid: In 2013-2014, 99% of all full-time freshmen and 97% of continuing full-time students received some form of financial aid. 68% of all full-time freshmen and 65% of continuing full-time students received need-based aid. The average freshman award was $27,044. Need-based scholarships or need-based grants averaged $24,478 ($56,268 maximum); need-based self-help aid (loans and jobs) averaged $7,011 ($44,000 maximum); and other non-need-based awards and non-need-based scholarships averaged $11,254 ($54,010 maximum). 45% of undergraduate students work part-time. Average annual earnings from campus work are $1331. The average financial indebtedness of the 2013 graduate was $42,689. Rose-Hulman is a member of CSS. The FAFSA is required. The priority date for freshman financial aid applications for fall entry is March 1.

International Students: There are 198 international students enrolled. The school actively recruits these students. They must take the TOEFL with a minimum score of 550 on the paper-based TOEFL (PBT) or 80 on the Internet-based version (iBT). They must also take the SAT or ACT, scoring 550.

Graduates: From July 1, 2012 to June 30, 2013, 402 bachelor's degrees were awarded. The most popular majors were mechanical engineering (28%), electrical engineering (13%), and chemical engineering (11%). 308 companies recruited on campus in 2012-2013. In an average class, 1% graduate in 3 years or less, 71% graduate in 4 years or less, 78% graduate in 5 years or less, and 78% graduate in 6 years or less. Of the 2012 graduating class, 21% were enrolled in graduate school within 6 months of graduation, and 74% were employed.

Admissions Contact: James Goecker, Vice President of Enrollment Management. E-Mail: *admissions@rose-hulman.edu* Web: *www.rose-hulman.edu*

SAINT JOSEPH'S COLLEGE B-2

Rensselaer, IN 47978 (219) 866-6170
(800) 447-8781; (219) 866-6122

Full-time: 438 men, 598 women	**Faculty:** 55; IIB, --$
Part-time: 34 men, 78 women	**Ph.D.s:** 69%
Graduate: 14 men, 8 women	**Student/Faculty:** 19 to 1
Year: semesters, summer session	**Tuition:** $27,350
Application Deadline: open	**Room & Board:** $8440
Freshman Class: 1639 applied, 1052 accepted, 273 enrolled	
SAT CR/M: 492/501	**ACT:** 22 **COMPETITIVE**

Saint Joseph's College, founded in 1889, is a private Catholic institution providing a liberal arts core curriculum with an interdisciplinary approach and practical, career-oriented experiences. There is one undergraduate school and one graduate school. In addition to regional accreditation, SJC has baccalaureate program accreditation with NCATE. The library contains 127,984 volumes, 67,760 microform items, 16,707 audio/video tapes/CDs/DVDs, and subscribes to 13,262 periodicals including electronic. Computerized library services include interlibrary loans, database searching, Internet access, and Wi-Fi capability. Special learning facilities include a radio station and TV station. The 180-acre campus is in a small town 80 miles south of Chicago and 90 miles north of Indianapolis. Including any residence halls, there are 26 buildings.

Student Life: 75% of undergraduates are from Indiana. Others are from 22 states, 5 foreign countries, and Canada. 84% are from public schools. 73% are White; 11% African American. 41% are Protestant; 36% Catholic; 23% claim no religious affiliation. The average age of freshmen is 19; all undergraduates, 22. 28% do not continue beyond their first year; 44% remain to graduate.

Housing: 852 students can be accommodated in college housing, which includes single-sex and coed dorms and on-campus apartments. housing for nontraditional or adult students and special-interest floors. On-campus housing is guaranteed for all 4 years. 69% of students live on campus; of those, 60% remain on campus on weekends. All students may keep cars.

Activities: There are no fraternities or sororities. There are 35 groups on campus, including art, band, cheerleading, chess, choir, chorale, chorus, computers, dance, debate, drama, environmental, ethnic, film, forensics, honors, jazz band, literary magazine, marching band, musical theater, newspaper, orchestra, pep band, photography, political, professional, radio and TV, religious, social, social service, and student government. Popular campus events include Little 500 Go-Kart Race, Little Siblings Weekend and Science Olympiad Regional Tournament.

Sports: There are 9 intercollegiate sports for men and 9 for women, and 8 intramural sports for men and 8 for women. Facilities include a field house, a 2500-seat gym, a recreation center, a baseball complex, a softball complex, a lighted soccer field, a football facility, an outdoor track and field facility, and a lake with a sand beach.

Disabled Students: 74% of the campus is accessible. Facilities include wheelchair ramps, elevators, special parking, specially equipped restrooms, special class scheduling, lowered drinking fountains, and lowered telephones.

Services: Counseling and information services are available, as is tutoring in every subject. There is a reader service for the blind, and remedial math, reading, and writing.

Campus Safety and Security: Measures include 24-hour foot and vehicle patrol, emergency notification system, and security escort services. There are lighted pathways/sidewalks and controlled access to dorms/residences.

Programs of Study: SJC confers B.A., B.S. and B.S.N. degrees. Associate and master's degrees are also awarded. Bachelor's degrees are awarded in BIOLOGICAL SCIENCE (biology/biological science), BUSINESS (accounting, business administration and management, and sports management), COMMUNICATIONS AND THE ARTS (art, communications, creative writing, dramatic arts, English, music, music business management, and theatre arts), COMPUTER AND PHYSICAL SCIENCE (chemistry, computer science, and mathematics), EDUCATION (athletic training, elementary education, middle school education, physical education, and secondary education), HEALTH PROFESSIONS (medical technology, nursing, predentistry, and premedicine), SOCIAL SCIENCE (criminal justice, economics, history, international studies, ministries, philosophy, political science/government, prelaw, psychology, religion, and sociology). Accounting, biology-chemistry, and education are the strongest academically. Business administration, biological sciences, and nursing have the largest enrollments.

Required: Students must complete 45 hours in the general education program and 36 hours in the major. A total of 120 credit hours with a minimum GPA of 2.0 is required to graduate.

Special: Cross-registration with Saint Elizabeth's School of Nursing is offered. Internships in all fields, a Washington semester, accelerated degree programs, and study abroad throughout Europe and Latin America are available. Dual majors are offered in biology/chemistry and music/business administration. Credit for life, military, and work experience, nondegree study, student-designed majors, and pass/fail options are offered. The Core program consists of lectures and discussions over a 4 year period. There are 4 national honor societies and a freshman honors program.

Faculty/Classroom: 54% of faculty are male; 46% are female. All teach undergraduates. No introductory courses are taught by graduate students. The average class size in an introductory lecture is 17; in a laboratory is 15; and in a regular course is 14.

Admissions: 64% of the 2013-2014 applicants were accepted. The SAT scores for the 2013-2014 freshman class were: Critical Reading--55% below 500, 32% between 500 and 599, 11% between 600 and 699, and 2% between 700 and 800; Math--48% below 500, 42% between 500 and 599, and 10% between 600 and 699. The ACT scores were 40% below 21, 32% between 21 and 23, 19% between 24 and 26, 4% between 27 and 28, and 5% above 28. 27% of the current freshmen were in the top fifth of their class; 56% were in the top two fifths. 4 freshmen graduated first in their class.

Requirements: The SAT or ACT is required. Applicants should be graduates of an accredited secondary school or have earned the GED. They should have completed 15 academic credits, 10 of which must be from the following academic fields: English, foreign language, social studies, math, and natural sciences. Acceptance is based on high school GPA and SAT or ACT scores. A GPA of 2.0 is required. AP and CLEP credits are accepted. Important factors in the admissions decision are advanced placement or honors courses, extracurricular activities record, and leadership record.

Procedure: Freshmen are admitted fall and spring. Entrance exams should be taken by January of the senior year. There are deferred admissions and rolling admissions plans. Application deadlines are open. Application fee is $25. Notifications are sent December 15. Applications are accepted online. Application fees are waived if application is completed online.

Transfer: 44 transfer students enrolled in 2012-2013. Applicants must have a GPA of 2.0. Grades of C or better transfer for credit. 30 of 120 credits required for the bachelor's degree must be completed at SJC.

Visiting: There are regularly scheduled orientations for prospective students, consisting of Discover Days, Special Interest Days, early registration, and Freshman Orientation. There are guides for informal visits, visitors may sit in on classes, and stay overnight. To schedule a visit, contact the Admissions Office.

Financial Aid: In 2013-2014, 100% of all full-time freshmen and 99% of continuing full-time students received some form of financial aid. 92% of all full-time freshmen and 85% of continuing full-time students received need-based aid. The average freshman award was $26,602. Need-based scholarships or need-based grants averaged $11,101 ($36,500 maximum); need-based self-help aid (loans and jobs) averaged $2,249 ($36,500 maximum); non-need-based athletic scholarships averaged $3,507 ($35,410 maximum); and other non-need-based awards and non-need-based scholarships averaged $9,869 ($36,500 maximum). 32% of undergraduate students work part-time. Average annual earnings from campus work are $1500. The average financial indebtedness of the 2013 graduate was $32,463. SJC is a member of CSS. The FAFSA, and the combined admission and financial aid application is required. The deadline for filing freshman financial aid applications for fall entry is March 1.

International Students: There are 5 international students enrolled. They must take the TOEFL with a minimum score of 550 on the paper-based TOEFL (PBT) or 80 on the Internet-based version (iBT).

Computers: All students may access the system at any time. There are no time limits and no fees.

Graduates: From July 1, 2012 to June 30, 2013, 212 bachelor's degrees were awarded. The most popular majors were nursing (33%), biological sciences (11%), and business administration (10%). 8 companies recruited on campus in 2012-2013. In an average class, 1% graduate in 3 years or less, 37% graduate in 4 years or less, 46% graduate in 5 years or less, and 46% graduate in 6 years or less. Of the 2012 graduating class, 27% were enrolled in graduate school within 6 months of graduation, and 46% were employed.

Admissions Contact: Mike Ramian, Director of Admissions. E-Mail: *admissions@saintjoe.edu* Web: *www.saintjoe.edu*

SAINT MARY-OF-THE-WOODS COLLEGE — B-4

St Mary of the Woods, IN 47876 — (812) 535-5101; (800) 926-SMWC; (812) 535-5010

Full-time: 10 men, 381 women	**Faculty:** n/av
Part-time: 21 men, 336 women	**Ph.D.s:** n/av
Graduate: 13 men, 169 women	**Student/Faculty:** n/av
Year: semesters, summer session	**Tuition:** $27,672
Application Deadline:	**Room & Board:** $10,050
Freshman Class: 325 applied, 317 accepted, 62 enrolled	
SAT CR/M/W: 460/440/450 **ACT:** 20	**LESS COMPETITIVE**

Saint Mary-of-the Woods, founded in 1840, is a private, liberal arts women's college affiliated with the Roman Catholic Church. The traditional undergraduate program admits only women; the distance education format and the graduate programs admit both women and men. There is one undergraduate school and 3 graduate schools. In addition to regional accreditation, The Woods has baccalaureate program accreditation with NASM and NCATE. The library contains 96,835 volumes, 754 audio/video tapes/CDs/DVDs, and subscribes to 62 periodicals including electronic. Computerized library services include interlibrary loans, database searching, Internet access, and Wi-Fi capability. Special learning facilities include an art gallery. The 67-acre campus is in a rural area 5 miles northwest of Terre Haute. Including any residence halls, there are 10 buildings.

Student Life: 76% of undergraduates are from Indiana. Others are from 35 states, and 6 foreign countries. 83% are White. The average age of freshmen is 19; all undergraduates, 30. 54% remain to graduate.

Housing: 345 students can be accommodated in college housing, which includes single-sex dorms. On-campus housing is guaranteed for all 4 years. Alcohol is not permitted. All students may keep cars.

Activities: There are no fraternities or sororities. There are 30 groups on campus, including band, choir, chorale, chorus, computers, dance, drama, environmental, ethnic, honors, international, jazz band, literary magazine, musical theater, newspaper, orchestra, professional, religious, social, social service, and student government. Popular campus events include Ring Day, Pops Concert and Play Series.

Sports: There are 6 intercollegiate sports for women. Facilities include an indoor riding arena, stables, athletic field, tennis and volleyball courts, a weight room, fitness course, and soccer fields.

Disabled Students: All of the campus is accessible. Facilities include wheelchair ramps, elevators, special parking, specially equipped restrooms, and special class scheduling.

Services: Counseling and information services are available, as is tutoring in most subjects. There is remedial math and writing.

Campus Safety and Security: Measures include 24-hour foot and vehicle patrol and emergency notification system. There are emergency telephones and lighted pathways/sidewalks.

Programs of Study: The Woods confers B.A., B.S. and B.S.N. degrees. Associate and master's degrees are also awarded. Bachelor's degrees are awarded in AGRICULTURE (equine science), BIOLOGICAL SCIENCE (biology/biological science), BUSINESS (accounting, business administration and management, human resources, and marketing/retailing/merchandising), COMMUNICATIONS AND THE ARTS (art, creative writing, English, journalism, literature, and music), COMPUTER AND PHYSICAL SCIENCE (computer science and mathematics), EDUCATION (art education, early childhood education, elementary education, mathematics education, science education, social science education, and special education), HEALTH PROFESSIONS (health care administration, medical technology, music therapy, nursing, predentistry, premedicine, and preveterinary science), SOCIAL SCIENCE (criminology, human services, humanities, paralegal studies, prelaw, psychology, and theological studies). Education, biology/preprofessional, and equine studies are the strongest academically.

Required: All students must complete a 39 credit hour general education curriculum, which includes a freshman course about the values and ideals of education and Saint Mary-of-the-Woods College, writing, speech, history, literature, philosophy, religion/spirituality, math, social science, fine arts, life science, foreign language/culture, and a senior capstone course. Completion of 125 credit hours with a minimum GPA of 2.0 is necessary for graduation. Some majors require a higher GPA.

Special: The college offers cross-registration with Indiana State University and Rose-Hulman Institute of Technology, student-designed majors, study abroad, internships, on-campus work-study, an accelerated degree program in education for students who already have a baccalaureate degree, and non-degree study. The Woods Online program, offering more than 20 majors, provides educational opportunities to students who study mostly through distance education. There is a freshman honors program.

Faculty/Classroom: No introductory courses are taught by graduate students.

Admissions: 98% of the 2013-2014 applicants were accepted. The SAT scores for the 2013-2014 freshman class were: Critical Reading--66% below 500, 30% between 500 and 599, 2% between 600 and 699, and

2% between 700 and 800; Math--68% below 500, 32% between 500 and 599; Writing--75% below 500, 16% between 500 and 599, 7% between 600 and 699. The ACT scores were 60% below 21, 20% between 21 and 23, 5% between 24 and 26, and 15% above 28.

Requirements: The SAT or ACT is required. Candidates should be graduates of an accredited secondary school. The GED is accepted. Documents needed for acceptance include an application for admission, letter of recommendation, and a high school transcript. Students should have completed 4 years of English, 3 years each of social sciences, lab science, and math (algebra 1, algebra 2, and geometry), and 2 years of a foreign language (foreign language recommended, but not required). AP and CLEP credits are accepted. Important factors in the admissions decision are recommendations by school officials, advanced placement or honors courses, and leadership record.

Procedure: Freshmen are admitted fall and spring. There is a rolling admissions plan. Application deadlines are open. The fall 2013 application fee was $30. Applications are accepted online. Application fees are waived if application is completed online.

Transfer: Transfer students should be in good academic standing at their most recent institution with a minimum GPA of 2.0. 30 of 125 credits required for the bachelor's degree must be completed at The Woods.

Visiting: There are regularly scheduled orientations for prospective students, Includes a campus tour, class visit, and meetings with faculty, financial aid, and admissions staff. There are guides for informal visits, visitors may sit in on classes, and stay overnight. To schedule a visit, contact the Office of Undergraduate Admission at (800) 926-7692.

Financial Aid: In 2013-2014, 100% of all full-time freshmen and 89% of continuing full-time students received some form of financial aid. 77% of all full-time freshmen and 70% of continuing full-time students received need-based aid. The average freshman award was $19,897. Need-based scholarships or need-based grants averaged $2,921 ($13,153 maximum); need-based self-help aid (loans and jobs) averaged $4,300 ($6,500 maximum); non-need-based athletic scholarships averaged $10,611 ($18,000 maximum); and other non-need-based awards and non-need-based scholarships averaged $6,813 ($27,672 maximum). The average financial indebtedness of the 2013 graduate was $21,000. The FAFSA is required. Check with the school for current application deadlines.

International Students: There are 14 international students enrolled. The school actively recruits these students. They must take the TOEFL with a minimum score of 500 on the paper-based TOEFL (PBT) or 62 on the Internet-based version (iBT). The SAT or the ACT is recommended if English is the student's first language.

Computers: All students may access the system. During posted lab hours, or access can be made by PCs at any time. There are no time limits and no fees.

Graduates: From July 1, 2012 to June 30, 2013, 256 bachelor's degrees were awarded. The most popular majors were education (29%), business (19%), and psychology (11%).

Admissions Contact: Karen Dyer, Interim VP for Enrollment Management. E-Mail: *smwcadms@smwc.edu* Web: *www.smwc.edu*

SAINT MARY'S COLLEGE C-1

Notre Dame, IN 46556 (574) 284-4587
(800) 551-7621; (574) 284-4716

Full-time: 1469 women	**Faculty:** 133; IIB, -$
Part-time: 10 women	**Ph.D.s:** 83%
Graduate: n/av	**Student/Faculty:** 11 to 1
Year: semesters, summer session	**Tuition:** $34,600
Application Deadline: February 15	**Room & Board:** $10,560
Freshman Class: 1529 applied, 1310 accepted, 437 enrolled	
SAT CR/M/W: 560/540/550 **ACT:** 25	**VERY COMPETITIVE**

Saint Mary's College, established in 1844, was founded and sponsored by the Congregation of the Sisters of the Holy Cross. It continues to be a Catholic comprehensive college for women in the liberal arts tradition. There is one undergraduate school. In addition to regional accreditation, Saint Mary's has baccalaureate program accreditation with CSWE, NASAD, NASM, and NCATE. The library contains 244,651 volumes, 18,729 microform items, 3,539 audio/video tapes/CDs/DVDs, and subscribes to 30,704 periodicals including electronic. Computerized library services include interlibrary loans, database searching, Internet access, and Wi-Fi capability. Special learning facilities include an art gallery and TV station. The 100-acre campus is in a suburban area in South Bend, IN and 90 miles east of Chicago. Including any residence halls, there are 20 buildings.

Student Life: 75% of undergraduates are from out of state, mostly the Mid-West. Students are from 40 states, 17 foreign countries, and Canada. 55% are from public schools. 77% are White; 12% Hispanic. 87% are Catholic; 11% Protestant. The average age of freshmen is 18; all undergraduates, 20. 13% do not continue beyond their first year; 71% remain to graduate.

Housing: 1350 students can be accommodated in college housing, which includes single-sex dorms and on-campus apartments. On-campus housing is guaranteed for all 4 years, is available on a first-come, and first-served basis. 91% of students live on campus; of those, 75% remain on campus on weekends. All students may keep cars.

Activities: There are no fraternities or sororities. There are 75 groups on campus, including art, band, cheerleading, choir, chorale, chorus, dance, drama, environmental, ethnic, gay, honors, international, literary magazine, marching band, musical theater, newspaper, opera, orchestra, pep band, photography, political, professional, radio and TV, religious, social, social service, student government, and yearbook. Popular campus events include Back to School Dance, School Formal and Dance Marathon.

Sports: There are 8 intercollegiate sports for women, and 8 intramural sports for women. Facilities include an athletic facility, outdoor tennis and volleyball courts, and soccer and softball fields.

Disabled Students: All of the campus is accessible. Facilities include wheelchair ramps, elevators, special parking, specially equipped restrooms, lowered drinking fountains, and special housing.

Services: Counseling and information services are available, as is tutoring in most subjects. writing center, math center and Student Success Program

Campus Safety and Security: Measures include 24-hour foot and vehicle patrol, emergency notification system, self-defense education, and security escort services. There are shuttle buses, emergency telephones, lighted pathways/sidewalks, controlled access to dorms/residences, key cards for controlled residence hall entry.

Programs of Study: Saint Mary's confers B.A., B.S., B.B.A., B.F.A. and B.Mus. degrees. Bachelor's degrees are awarded in BIOLOGICAL SCIENCE (biology/biological science), BUSINESS (accounting, business administration and management, and management information systems), COMMUNICATIONS AND THE ARTS (art, communications, creative writing, English literature, fine arts, French, Italian, music, Spanish, and visual and performing arts), COMPUTER AND PHYSICAL SCIENCE (chemistry, mathematics, and statistics), EDUCATION (elementary education), HEALTH PROFESSIONS (nursing and speech pathology/audiology), SOCIAL SCIENCE (economics, history, humanities, international studies, philosophy, political science/government, psychology, religion, social work, and sociology). Nursing, communication studies and psychology are the largest.

Required: Students must successfully complete 128 credits, with at least 24 in the major, and must maintain a minimum GPA of 2.0. Students must complete the Sophia Program, a learning outcomes based general education curriculum promoting integration with majors and minors. Advanced proficiency in composition within the student's major must also be demonstrated, and a comprehensive exam in the major area is required by the end of the senior year.

Special: Cross-registration is permitted with the University of Notre Dame and a consortium of 6 northern Indiana colleges. Opportunities are provided for internships, a Washington semester, dual and student-designed majors, a 3-2 engineering degree with the University of Notre Dame, non-degree study, pass/fail options, and study abroad in more than 20 countries. All students must complete a senior comprehensive project or exam and demonstrate proficiency in writing before graduating. There are 14 national honor societies.

Faculty/Classroom: 31% of faculty are male; 69% are female. All teach undergraduates, all do research, and all teach and do research. No introductory courses are taught by graduate students. The average class size in an introductory lecture is 20; in a laboratory is 15; and in a regular course is 15.

Admissions: 86% of the 2013-2014 applicants were accepted. The SAT scores for the 2013-2014 freshman class were: Critical Reading--23% below 500, 46% between 500 and 599, 26% between 600 and 699, and 6% between 700 and 800; Math--28% below 500, 46% between 500 and 599, 22% between 600 and 699, and 5% between 700 and 800; Writing--23% below 500, 49% between 500 and 599, 21% between 600 and 699, and 6% between 700 and 800. The ACT scores were 12% below 21, 21% between 21 and 23, 29% between 24 and 26, 18% between 27 and 28, and 20% above 28. 48% of the current freshmen were in the top fifth of their class; 82% were in the top two fifths. 6 freshmen graduated first in their class.

Requirements: The SAT or ACT is required. Graduation from an accredited secondary school is required; a GED will be accepted. Applicants must have completed 16 academic credits, including 4 in English, 3 in math, and 2 in a foreign language, history or social studies, and lab science with the remainder from college preparatory electives in the above areas. An essay is required. AP and CLEP credits are accepted. Important factors in the admissions decision are extracurricular activities record, advanced placement or honors courses, and recommendations by school officials.

Procedure: Freshmen are admitted fall and spring. Entrance exams should be taken between March of the junior year and December of senior year. There are early decision, deferred admissions, and rolling admissions plans. Early decision applications should be filed by November 15; regular applications, by February 15 for fall entry; and November 15 for spring entry. Notification of early decision is sent December 15; regular decision, January 15. 72 early decision candidates were accepted for the 2013-2014 class. Applications are accepted online.

Transfer: 18 transfer students enrolled in 2012-2013. Students must submit a transcript from high school and each previous college attended, along with an essay, a recommendation from a college adviser, and SAT or ACT test scores if the student has fewer than 30 semester hours of transferable credit. All transfer applicants must have maintained a minimum GPA of 3.0. An interview is recommended. Syllabi or course description required for credit evaluation. 60 of 128 credits required for the bachelor's degree must be completed at Saint Mary's.

Visiting: There are regularly scheduled orientations for prospective students, including campus tours and visits with admissions and financial aid counselors and faculty and athletic staff. There are guides for informal visits, visitors may sit in on classes, and stay overnight. To schedule a visit, contact Wanda Dudley at (800) 551-7621.

Financial Aid: In 2013-2014, 99% of all full-time freshmen and 97% of continuing full-time students received some form of financial aid. 69% of all full-time freshmen and 56% of continuing full-time students received need-based aid. The average freshman award was $29,550. Need-based scholarships or need-based grants averaged $24,872; need-based self-help aid (loans and jobs) averaged $4,457; and other non-need-based awards and non-need-based scholarships averaged $13,429. 83% of undergraduate students work part-time. Average annual earnings from campus work are $1800. The average financial indebtedness of the 2013 graduate was $31,986. Saint Mary's is a member of CSS. The CSS/Profile and FAFSA are required. The priority date for freshman financial aid applications for fall entry is March 1.

International Students: There are 31 international students enrolled. The school actively recruits these students. They must take the TOEFL with a minimum score of 500 on the paper-based TOEFL (PBT) or 80 on the Internet-based version (iBT), IELTS. They must also take the SAT or ACT.

Computers: All students may access the system 24 hours a day, 7 days a week. There are no time limits and no fees.

Graduates: From July 1, 2012 to June 30, 2013, 373 bachelor's degrees were awarded. The most popular majors were nursing (14%), elementary education (11%), and biology (9%). 30 companies recruited on campus in 2012-2013. In an average class, 68% graduate in 4 years or less, 70% graduate in 5 years or less, and 71% graduate in 6 years or less. Of the 2012 graduating class, 31% were enrolled in graduate school within 6 months of graduation, and 77% were employed.

Admissions Contact: Kristin McAndrew, Director of Admissions. E-Mail: *admission@saintmarys.edu* Web: *www.saintmarys.edu*

TAYLOR UNIVERSITY D-3

Upland, IN 46989 (765) 998-5134
(800) 882-3456; (765) 998-4925

Full-time: 841 men, 1011 women	**Faculty:** 125; IIB, --$
Part-time: 119 men, 175 women	**Ph.D.s:** 88%
Graduate: 40 men, 59 women	**Student/Faculty:** 14 to 1
Year: 4-1-4, summer session	**Tuition:** $28,753
Application Deadline: December 1	**Room & Board:** $7989

Freshman Class: 1637 applied, 1434 accepted, 459 enrolled
SAT CR/M/W: 590/580/560 **ACT:** 26 **VERY COMPETITIVE+**

Taylor University, founded in 1846, is a private Christian interdenominational liberal arts institution. There are 3 undergraduate schools and one graduate school. In addition to regional accreditation, Taylor has baccalaureate program accreditation with ABET, CSWE, NASM, and NCATE. The library contains 202,766 volumes, 14,661 microform items, 15,841 audio/video tapes/CDs/DVDs, and subscribes to 41,429 periodicals including electronic. Computerized library services include interlibrary loans, database searching, Internet access, and Wi-Fi capability. Special learning facilities include an art gallery, radio station, TV station, environmental study laboratory, NASA-approved clean room, particle accelerator, NASA project space research equipment, 65-acre arboretum, C. S. Lewis Collection, observatory room, 10 kW Photo-Voltaic Solar Array and two 50 kW Wind Turbines available for student data collection. The 952-acre campus is in a rural area 70 miles north of Indianapolis and 45 miles south of Fort Wayne. Including any residence halls, there are 43 buildings.

Student Life: 64% of undergraduates are from out of state, mostly the Mid-West. Students are from 41 states, 36 foreign countries, and Canada. 86% are White. 99% are Protestant; 67% Unkonwn. The average age of freshmen is 19; all undergraduates, 21. 11% do not continue beyond their first year; 74% remain to graduate.

Housing: 1692 students can be accommodated in college housing, which includes single-sex dorms, on-campus apartments, off-campus apartments, and married student housing. On-campus housing is guaranteed for all 4 years. 86% of students live on campus; of those, 83% remain on campus on weekends. Alcohol is not permitted. Upperclassmen may keep cars.

Activities: There are no fraternities or sororities. There are 67 groups on campus, including art, band, choir, chorale, chorus, computers, debate, drama, ethnic, film, honors, international, jazz band, literary magazine, musical theater, newspaper, opera, orchestra, pep band, photography, political, professional, radio and TV, religious, social, social service, student government, and symphony. Popular campus events include Taylathon, AirBand, Silent Night and Spiritual Renewal and Emphasis Weeks.

Sports: There are 8 intercollegiate sports for men and 8 for women, and 9 intramural sports for men and 9 for women. Facilities include Odle Arena and Kesler Student Activities Center house an indoor track, multi-purpose athletic courts and fitness center with swimming/lap pool. A field house, newly renovated Wheeler football stadium and practice fields with artificial turf, tennis and racquetball courts, outdoor track, multiple baseball and softball fields, soccer field and a lake for swimming and ice skating.

Disabled Students: 95% of the campus is accessible. Facilities include wheelchair ramps, elevators, special parking, specially equipped restrooms, special class scheduling, lowered drinking fountains, and lowered telephones.

Services: Counseling and information services are available, as is tutoring in most subjects. There is a reader service for the blind, and remedial math, reading, and writing.

Campus Safety and Security: Measures include 24-hour foot and vehicle patrol, emergency notification system, self-defense education, and security escort services. There are lighted pathways/sidewalks.

Programs of Study: Taylor confers B.A., B.B.A., B.Mus. and B.S. degrees. Associate and master's degrees are also awarded. Bachelor's degrees are awarded in AGRICULTURE (environmental studies), BIOLOGICAL SCIENCE (biology/adolescence education and biology/biological science), BUSINESS (accounting, banking and finance, business administration and management, finance, international business management, management information systems, management science, marketing management, and sports management), COMMUNICATIONS AND THE ARTS (art, communications, communications technology, dramatic arts, English, English literature, English Writing, film arts, film, television and digital media, fine arts, journalism, media arts, English and Professional Communication, music, music performance, music theory and composition, public relations, Spanish, technical and business writing, theatre arts, visual and performing arts, and writing), COMPUTER AND PHYSICAL SCIENCE (chemistry, Computer Engineering Technology, computer science, mathematics, natural sciences, physics, and web services), EDUCATION (art education, (Education) Childhood Education, Christian education, early childhood education, education, elementary education, English education, foreign languages education, health education, mathematics education, music education, physical education, science education, secondary education, social studies education, and teaching English as a second/foreign language (TESOL/TEFOL)), ENGINEERING AND ENVIRONMENTAL DESIGN (computer engineering, computer graphics, engineering physics, environmental engineering, environmental science, and systems engineering), HEALTH PROFESSIONS (exercise science, health science, premedicine, and public health), SOCIAL SCIENCE (biblical studies, development economics, economics, geography, history, humanities, interdisciplinary studies, international relations, international studies, liberal arts/general studies, ministries, philosophy, philosophy and religion, political science/government, psychology, social work, and sociology). Engineering physics, and biology are the strongest academically. Business and education have the largest enrollments.

Required: Students must complete at least 128 total hours of which at least 42 must be upper division (300/400). To graduate, students must have a minimum cumulative GPA of 2.0 and a 2.3 GPA (2.5 in social work) in all majors and minors and demonstrate proficiency in writing, math, science, and reading. Students must also complete a senior paper, exam, or project in their major(s). General education requirements include courses in spiritual formation, speech, expository writing, fine arts, computer science, literature, science, history, math, social science, and a course designated as cross-cultural. The B.A. degree requires the equivalency of 2 years of 1 foreign language. Most B.S. degrees must be combined with systems analysis curriculum.

Special: Opportunities are provided for internships, cooperative programs, a Washington semester, very active study abroad program in over 35 countries, work-study programs, dual majors, student-designed majors, and B.A.-B.S. degrees. There is cross-registration with the other members of the Council for Christian Colleges and Universities, and the Christian College Consortium. There are 7 national honor societies, including Phi Beta Kappa, a freshman honors program, and 23 departmental honors programs.

Faculty/Classroom: 71% of faculty are male; 29% are female. 96% teach undergraduates. No introductory courses are taught by graduate students. The average class size in an introductory lecture is 25; in a laboratory is 11; and in a regular course is 20.

Admissions: 88% of the 2013-2014 applicants were accepted. The SAT scores for the 2013-2014 freshman class were: Critical Reading--20% below 500, 33% between 500 and 599, 32% between 600 and 699, and 15% between 700 and 800; Math--20% below 500, 37% between 500 and 599, 37% between 600 and 699, and 8% between 700 and 800; Writing--25% below 500, 36% between 500 and 599, 32% between 600 and 699, and 7% between 700 and 800. The ACT scores were 11% below 21, 15% between 21 and 23, 22% between 24 and 26, 15% between 27 and 28, and 38% above 28. 60% of the current freshmen were in the top fifth of their class; 85% were in the top two fifths. 9 freshmen graduated first in their class.

Requirements: The SAT or ACT and ACT Writing Test are recommended. Graduation from an accredited secondary school is required; a GED will be accepted. It is recommended that applicants complete 4 years of English, 3 to 4 each of math and lab science, 2 each of social studies and a foreign language, and course work in computing, typing/keyboarding, and the arts. The applications includes 1 essay. Either ACT or SAT scores are required. High school transcripts and recommendation forms from a guidance counselor and pastor are also required. An interview is recommended for all students, and an audition is required for music majors. Taylor requires applicants to be in the upper 40% of their class. A GPA of 2.8 is required. AP and CLEP credits are accepted. Important factors in the admissions decision are recommendations by school officials, extracurricular activities record, and leadership record.

Procedure: Freshmen are admitted fall, winter, and spring. Entrance exams should be taken during the spring of the junior year or fall of the senior year. There are early admissions and deferred admissions plans. Early decision applications should be filed by November 1; regular applications, by December 1 for fall entry; February 1 for winter entry; and April 1 for spring entry, along with a $25 fee. Notification of early decision is sent November 20; regular decision, Applications are accepted online.

Transfer: 58 transfer students enrolled in 2012-2013. Applicants must have maintained a minimum GPA of 2.5 and have completed at least 12 credit hours at the previous college. An interview is recommended. 64 of 128 credits required for the bachelor's degree must be completed at Taylor.

Visiting: There are regularly scheduled orientations for prospective students, including a campus tour, lunch, class meetings, faculty meetings, a financial aid session, and an admissions interview. There are guides for informal visits, visitors may sit in on classes, and stay overnight. To schedule a visit, contact the Campus Visit Coordinator at (765) 998-5134.

Financial Aid: In 2013-2014, 98% of all full-time freshmen and 95% of continuing full-time students received some form of financial aid. 65% of all full-time freshmen and 60% of continuing full-time students received need-based aid. The average freshman award was $18,053. Need-based scholarships or need-based grants averaged $2,752 ($14,000 maximum); need-based self-help aid (loans and jobs) averaged $3,309 ($7,400 maximum); non-need-based athletic scholarships averaged $1,040 ($28,514 maximum); and other non-need-based awards and non-need-based scholarships averaged $10,952 ($28,514 maximum). 60% of undergraduate students work part-time. Average annual earnings from campus work are $1165. The average financial indebtedness of the 2013 graduate was $26,367. Taylor is a member of CSS. The FAFSA is required. The priority date for freshman financial aid applications for fall entry is March 10.

International Students: There are 96 international students enrolled. The school actively recruits these students. They must take the TOEFL with a minimum score of 550 on the paper-based TOEFL (PBT) or 84 on the Internet-based version (iBT). They must also take the SAT or ACT. The school will accept the TOEFL in lieu of the SAT or the ACT.

Computers: All students may access the system. There are no time limits and no fees.

Graduates: From July 1, 2012 to June 30, 2013, 433 bachelor's degrees were awarded. The most popular majors were business (11%), elementary education (11%), and communication (8%). 100 companies recruited on campus in 2012-2013. In an average class, 3% graduate in 3 years or less, 65% graduate in 4 years or less, 74% graduate in 5 years or less, and 74% graduate in 6 years or less. Of the 2012 graduating class, 17% were enrolled in graduate school within 6 months of graduation, and 73% were employed.

Admissions Contact: Lisa Wallace E-Mail: *admissions@taylor.edu* Web: *www.taylor.edu*

TRINE UNIVERSITY
Tri-State University

D-1

Angola, IN 46703

(260) 665-4365
(800) 347-4878; (260) 665-4578

Full-time: 1023 men, 407 women	**Faculty:** 87; IIB, --$
Part-time: 192 men, 253 women	**Ph.D.s:** 61%
Graduate: 1 men	**Student/Faculty:** 15 to 1
Year: semesters, summer session	**Tuition:** $28,900
Application Deadline: August 1	**Room & Board:** $9500
Freshman Class: n/av	
SAT CR/M: 510/570	**ACT:** 24 **VERY COMPETITIVE**

Trine University, formerly Tri-State University, was founded in 1884 and is a private, independent university. There are 5 undergraduate schools and one graduate school. In addition to regional accreditation, has baccalaureate program accreditation with ABET, ACBSP, and NCATE. The library contains 115,719 volumes, 314 microform items, 1,945 audio/video tapes/CDs/DVDs, and subscribes to 31,993 periodicals including electronic. Computerized library services include interlibrary loans, database searching, Internet access, and Wi-Fi capability. Special learning facilities include a radio station. The 400-acre campus is in a small town 40 miles north of Ft. Wayne. Including any residence halls, there are 22 buildings.

Student Life: 64% of undergraduates are from Indiana. Others are from 29 states, 14 foreign countries, and Canada. 80% are from public schools. 85% are White. The average age of freshmen is 18; all undergraduates, 21. 31% do not continue beyond their first year; 45% remain to graduate.

Housing: 1067 students can be accommodated in college housing, which includes single-sex and coed dorms and on-campus apartments. In addition, there are honors houses. On-campus housing is guaranteed for all 4 years. 85% of students live on campus; of those, 65% remain on campus on weekends. Alcohol is not permitted. All students may keep cars.

Activities: 23% of men belong to 8 national fraternities; 24% of women belong to 6 local sororities. There are 35 groups on campus, including band, cheerleading, choir, chorus, computers, dance, drama, ethnic, honors, international, jazz band, marching band, newspaper, pep band, professional, radio and TV, religious, social service, student government, and yearbook. Popular campus events include Homecoming, Bingo for Bucks and Moonlight Breakfast.

Sports: There are 10 intercollegiate sports for men and 10 for women, and 6 intramural sports for men and 5 for women. Facilities include a gym, basketball and racquetball courts, an 18-hole golf course, a tennis court, a football stadium, and practice and playing fields for soccer, lacrosse, baseball, and softball.

Disabled Students: 98% of the campus is accessible. Facilities include wheelchair ramps, elevators, special parking, specially equipped restrooms, special class scheduling, lowered drinking fountains, lowered telephones, and special housing.

Services: Counseling and information services are available, as is tutoring in some subjects, math, business, engineering, accounting, science, and English. There is remedial math.

Campus Safety and Security: Measures include 24-hour foot and vehicle patrol, emergency notification system, self-defense education, and security escort services. There are emergency telephones and lighted pathways/sidewalks.

Programs of Study: confers B.A., and B.S. degrees. Associate and master's degrees are also awarded. Bachelor's degrees are awarded in BIOLOGICAL SCIENCE (biology/biological science), BUSINESS (accounting, banking and finance, business administration and management, management information systems, management science, marketing/retailing/merchandising, recreation and leisure services, recreational facilities management, and sports management), COMMUNICATIONS AND THE ARTS (communications), COMPUTER AND PHYSICAL SCIENCE (chemistry, computer science, information sciences and systems, mathematics, and physical sciences), EDUCATION (elementary education, English education, mathematics education, physical education, science education, secondary education, and social science education), ENGINEERING AND ENVIRONMENTAL DESIGN (chemical engineering, civil engineering, computer engineering, drafting and design technology, electrical/electronics engineering, engineering management, environmental science, industrial administration/management, and mechanical engineering), HEALTH PROFESSIONS (premedicine), SOCIAL SCIENCE (criminal justice, forensic studies, psychology, and social science). Engineering, math/computer science, and science are the strongest academically. Engineering, and business have the largest enrollments.

Required: Candidates for graduation must complete 120 to 132 semester hours, satisfying the general education program and major requirements and maintaining a minimum overall GPA of 2.0. Required courses vary by degree sought. All students must complete a general education curriculum including science, math, American studies, social science, global studies, English composition, humanistics, computer literacy, and oral communication course work. Some majors have senior design projects. The number of hours in the major varies from 40 to 60.

Special: Cooperative education programs are available in engineering, business, and computer science. Opportunities exist for internships and work-study programs with the university and many companies. Study abroad is offered in more than 31 countries. There are 12 national honor societies and a freshman honors program.

Faculty/Classroom: 68% of faculty are male; 32% are female. All teach undergraduates, and 10% do research. No introductory courses are taught by graduate students. The average class size in an introductory lecture is 30; in a laboratory is 16; and in a regular course is 18.

Admissions: The SAT scores for the 2013-2014 freshman class were: Critical Reading--42% below 500, 43% between 500 and 599, 15% between 600 and 699, and 2% between 700 and 800; Math--22% below 500, 43% between 500 and 599, 32% between 600 and 699, and 4% between 700 and 800. 41% of the current freshmen were in the top fifth of their class; 71% were in the top two fifths. 19 freshmen graduated first in their class.

Requirements: The SAT or ACT is required. In addition, Candidates for admission should be graduates of accredited secondary schools. The GED is accepted. Most students should have 4 years of English and 3 years each of science, social studies, and math. A GPA of 2.5 is required. AP and CLEP credits are accepted. Important factors in the admissions decision are advanced placement or honors courses, recommendations by school officials, and leadership record.

Procedure: Freshmen are admitted to all sessions. Entrance exams should be taken in the junior or senior year. There are deferred admissions and rolling admissions plans. Applications should be filed by August 1 for fall entry. Notifications are sent August 15. Applications are accepted online.

Transfer: 52 transfer students enrolled in 2012-2013. In addition to meeting the university's requirements for freshmen, applicants must have satisfactory records from previous institutions. 30 of 120 credits required for the bachelor's degree must be completed at Trine University.

Visiting: There are regularly scheduled orientations for prospective students, including meetings with faculty, administrators, financial aid personnel, and a coach (if the student is an athlete), and a campus tour. There are guides for informal visits, visitors may sit in on classes, and stay overnight. To schedule a visit, contact the Admissions Office.

Financial Aid: In 2013-2014, 84% of all full-time freshmen and 77% of continuing full-time students received some form of financial aid. 74% of all full-time freshmen and 55% of continuing full-time students received need-based aid. The average freshman award was $23,417. Need-based scholarships or need-based grants averaged $4,308 ($7,000 maximum); need-based self-help aid (loans and jobs) averaged $4,331 ($5,500 maximum); and other non-need-based awards and non-need-based scholarships averaged $12,050 ($17,000 maximum). 56% of undergraduate students work part-time. Average annual earnings from campus work are $774. The average financial indebtedness of the 2013 graduate was $32,662. The FAFSA is required. The priority date for freshman financial aid applications for fall entry is March 1.

International Students: There are 74 international students enrolled. The school actively recruits these students. They must take the TOEFL with a minimum score of 550 on the paper-based TOEFL (PBT) or 79 on the Internet-based version (iBT), Applicants not transferring credits in math or English must be tested in those subjects.

Computers: All students may access the system 24 hours a day, 7 days a week. There are no time limits and no fees.

Graduates: From July 1, 2012 to June 30, 2013, 295 bachelor's degrees were awarded. The most popular majors were engineering (33%), business (19%), and education (9%). 63 companies recruited on campus in 2012-2013. In an average class, 35% graduate in 4 years or less, 45% graduate in 5 years or less, and 55% graduate in 6 years or less. Of the 2012 graduating class, 13% were enrolled in graduate school within 6 months of graduation, and 92% were employed.

Admissions Contact: Dr. Stuart Jones, Dean of Admissions. E-Mail: *admit@trine.edu* Web: *www.trine.edu*

UNIVERSITY OF EVANSVILLE — A-5

Evansville, IN 47722 — **(812) 488-2468** — **(800) 423-8633; (812) 488-4076**

Full-time: 956 men, 1334 women	**Faculty:** 178; IIA, -$
Part-time: 81 men, 106 women	**Ph.D.s:** 87%
Graduate: 49 men, 104 women	**Student/Faculty:** 13 to 1
Year: semesters, summer session	**Tuition:** $30,596
Application Deadline: February 3	**Room & Board:** $10,460
Freshman Class: 2935 applied, 2468 accepted, 543 enrolled	
SAT CR/M/W: 550/570/540	**ACT:** 26 **VERY COMPETITIVE+**

The University of Evansville, founded in 1854, is a private institution affiliated with the United Methodist Church. The University offers undergraduate degree programs in arts and sciences, business administration, education and health sciences, and engineering and computer science. There are 4 undergraduate schools and 4 graduate schools. In addition to regional accreditation, UE has baccalaureate program accreditation with AACSB, ABET, APTA, NASM, NCATE, and NLN. The library contains 284,157 volumes, 474,391 microform items, 14,563 audio/video tapes/CDs/DVDs, and subscribes to 169 periodicals including electronic. Computerized library services include interlibrary loans, database searching, Internet access, and Wi-Fi capability. Special learning facilities include an art gallery and radio station. The 75-acre campus is in an urban area 180 miles southwest of Indianapolis, 170 miles east of St. Louis, and 120 miles west of Louisville. Including any residence halls, there are 54 buildings.

Student Life: 55% of undergraduates are from Indiana. Others are from 41 states, 53 foreign countries, and Canada. 77% are White. 60% are Protestant; 33% Catholic. The average age of freshmen is 18; all undergraduates, 20. 14% do not continue beyond their first year; 63% remain to graduate.

Housing: 1922 students can be accommodated in college housing, which includes single-sex and coed dorms and on-campus apartments. In addition, there are honors houses, fraternity houses, international connection, students in math and sciences. On-campus housing is guaranteed for the freshman year only, is available on a first-come, first-served basis, and is available on a lottery system for upperclassmen. Priority is given to out-of-town students. 65% of students live on campus; of those, 85% remain on campus on weekends. Alcohol is not permitted. All students may keep cars.

Activities: 30% of men belong to 6 national fraternities; 28% of women belong to 1 local and 4 national sororities. There are 142 groups on campus, including art, band, cheerleading, choir, chorale, chorus, computers, dance, drama, environmental, ethnic, film, gay, honors, international, jazz band, literary magazine, musical theater, newspaper, opera, orchestra, pep band, photography, political, professional, radio and TV, religious, social, social service, student government, symphony, and yearbook. Popular campus events include Labor Day Picnic and Student Organization Fair, Bike Race and Sunset Concert.

Sports: There are 6 intercollegiate sports for men and 8 for women, and 18 intramural sports for men and 18 for women. Facilities include A 2500-seat soccer stadium, a 650-seat softball stadium, and a 1200-seat baseball stadium. The university fitness center includes a 25-yard pool, a conditioning room, an aerobics room, three free weight rooms, an indoor track, eight outdoor tennis courts, a 1/2-mile security lighted jogging trail, and basketball, racquetball, and volleyball courts.

Disabled Students: 87% of the campus is accessible. Facilities include wheelchair ramps, elevators, special parking, specially equipped restrooms, special class scheduling, lowered drinking fountains, and special housing.

Services: Counseling and information services are available, as is tutoring in some subjects, especially science, math, and foreign language; special requests in most subjects are accommodated There is remedial writing.

Campus Safety and Security: Measures include 24-hour foot and vehicle patrol, emergency notification system, self-defense education, and security escort services. There are emergency telephones and lighted pathways/sidewalks.

Programs of Study: UE confers B.A., B.S., B.F.A. and B.M. degrees. Associate, master's, and doctoral degrees are also awarded. Bachelor's degrees are awarded in AGRICULTURE (environmental studies), BIOLOGICAL SCIENCE (biochemistry, biology/biological science, and neurosciences), BUSINESS (accounting, business administration and management, finance, international business, management information systems, marketing, and sports management), COMMUNICATIONS AND THE ARTS (art history, art, communications, creative writing, dramatic arts, French, German, graphic design, literature, music, music business management, music performance, Spanish, and theater management), COMPUTER AND PHYSICAL SCIENCE (chemistry, clinical laboratory science, computer science, mathematics, and physics), EDUCATION (art education, athletic training, drama education, elementary education, English education, foreign languages education, mathematics education, music education, science education, social studies education, and special education), ENGINEERING AND ENVIRONMENTAL DESIGN (civil engineering, computer engineering, electrical/electronics engineering, environmental science, and mechanical engineering), HEALTH PROFESSIONS (exercise science, health care administration, music therapy, nursing, predentistry, premedicine, preoptometry, prepharmacy, preveterinary science, and public health), SOCIAL SCIENCE (archeology, biblical studies, classical/ancient civilization, cognitive science, criminal justice, economics, history, interdisciplinary studies, international studies, liberal arts/general studies, philosophy, political science/government, prelaw, psychology, sociology, and theological studies). Theater, engineering and doctorate in physical therapy are the strongest academically. Exercise science, nursing and theatre have the largest enrollments.

Required: To graduate, students must complete at least 120 semester hours with a minimum GPA of 2.0 cumulative and in their major. All students must complete a 41-hour general education program. A demonstration of writing proficiency, a capstone course in the major, and a demonstration of foreign language proficiency are required for graduation. Students must complete at least 39 credit hours in courses numbered 300 or above, at least 48 credit hours in residence at UE, and at least 51 percent of course work in their major at UE.

Special: Students may study abroad at the University of Evansville British campus, Harlaxton College, and many places throughout the world. There is also an Israeli archeological excavation program, an accelerated bachelor of science in global leadership degree, combined bachelor's/graduate degrees, cooperative education (business administration, chemistry, engineering, environmental studies), dual enrollment of high school students, ESL, and teacher certification, as well as honors, independent study programs, internships, and student-designed majors. There are 15 national honor societies and a freshman honors program.

Faculty/Classroom: 56% of faculty are male; 44% are female. All teach undergraduates. No introductory courses are taught by graduate students.

Admissions: 84% of the 2013-2014 applicants were accepted. The SAT scores for the 2013-2014 freshman class were: Critical Reading--25% below 500, 47% between 500 and 599, 23% between 600 and 699, and 5% between 700 and 800; Math--24% below 500, 39% between 500 and

599, 33% between 600 and 699, and 4% between 700 and 800; Writing--31% below 500, 41% between 500 and 599, 24% between 600 and 699, and 4% between 700 and 800. The ACT scores were 12% below 21, 18% between 21 and 23, 26% between 24 and 26, 17% between 27 and 28, and 27% above 28. 56% of the current freshmen were in the top fifth of their class; 85% were in the top two fifths. There were 2 National Merit finalists. 28 freshmen graduated first in their class.

Requirements: The SAT or ACT is required. The ACT Optional Writing test is also required. To be competitive for admission, students should submit a minimum SAT composite score of 1500 (math, critical reading, and writing) or ACT composite of 21. Applicants must be graduates of accredited secondary schools; applicants who have been homeschooled are also considered. The University requires completion of 4 years of college preparatory English, 3 years of math, 3 years of science, and 3 years of social studies. Two years of a foreign language are recommended. An interview is recommended but not required. UE requires applicants to be in the upper 50% of their class. A GPA of 2.8 is required. AP and CLEP credits are accepted. Important factors in the admissions decision are extracurricular activities record, personality/intangible qualities, and recommendations by school officials.

Procedure: Freshmen are admitted fall and spring. Entrance exams should be taken by fall of senior year. There is a deferred admissions plan. Early decision applications should be filed by December 2; regular applications, by February 3 for fall entry. Notification of early decision is sent December 16; regular decision, February 17. Applications are accepted online.

Transfer: 80 transfer students enrolled in 2012-2013. Applicants must submit official transcripts from each college from which they earned credit and must have a minimum GPA of 2.0 in all previous college work. High school transcripts, standardized test scores, and comments from the Dean of Students Recommendation Form are optional but considered if submitted with the application. 48 of 120 credits required for the bachelor's degree must be completed at UE.

Visiting: There are regularly scheduled orientations for prospective students, including a campus tour, faculty academic sessions, financial aid and admission appointments, and study abroad and honors program sessions. There are guides for informal visits, visitors may sit in on classes, and stay overnight. To schedule a visit, contact Office of Admission.

Financial Aid: In 2013-2014, 96% of all full-time freshmen and 96% of continuing full-time students received some form of financial aid. 70% of all full-time freshmen and 69% of continuing full-time students received need-based aid. The average freshman award was $27,504. Need-based scholarships or need-based grants averaged $24,280 ($26,600 maximum); need-based self-help aid (loans and jobs) averaged $4,535 ($11,025 maximum); and non-need-based athletic scholarships averaged $25,722 ($41,856 maximum). 16% of undergraduate students work part-time. Average annual earnings from campus work are $1525. The average financial indebtedness of the 2013 graduate was $25,708. UE is a member of CSS. The FAFSA is required. The deadline for filing freshman financial aid applications for fall entry is March 10.

International Students: There are 202 international students enrolled. The school actively recruits these students. They must take the TOEFL with a minimum score of 61 on the Internet-based version (iBT).

Computers: All students may access the system at any time. There are no time limits and no fees.

Graduates: From July 1, 2012 to June 30, 2013, 583 bachelor's degrees were awarded. The most popular majors were business/marketing (12%), visual and performing arts (12%), and health professions and related programs (10%). 212 companies recruited on campus in 2012-2013. In an average class, 53% graduate in 4 years or less, 62% graduate in 5 years or less, and 63% graduate in 6 years or less. Of the 2012 graduating class, 20% were enrolled in graduate school within 6 months of graduation, and 65% were employed.

Admissions Contact: Scott Henne, Dean of Admission. E-Mail: *admission@evansville.edu* Web: *www.evansville.edu*

UNIVERSITY OF INDIANAPOLIS C-3

Indianapolis, IN 46227 (317) 788-3216
(800) 232-8634; (317) 788-3300

Full-time: 1089 men, 1947 women
Part-time: 270 men, 899 women
Graduate: 326 men, 886 women
Year: semesters, summer session
Application Deadline: open
Faculty: n/av; IIA, --$
Ph.D.s: 76%
Student/Faculty: 15 to 1
Tuition: $23,010
Room & Board: $8730
Freshman Class: 5396 applied, 4245 accepted, 797 enrolled
SAT or ACT: required

LESS COMPETITIVE

The University of Indianapolis, established in 1902, is a private liberal arts school affiliated with the United Methodist Church. It provides undergraduate and graduate studies with an emphasis on education, business, nursing, and arts and sciences. There are 7 undergraduate schools and 6 graduate schools. In addition to regional accreditation, UIndy has baccalaureate program accreditation with ACBSP, ACEJMC, CSWE, NASAD, NASM, NCATE, and NLN. The library contains 202,699 volumes, 21,183 microform items, 9,820 audio/video tapes/CDs/DVDs, and subscribes to 972 periodicals including electronic. Computerized library services include interlibrary loans, database searching, Internet access, and Wi-Fi capability. Special learning facilities include an art gallery, planetarium, radio station, TV station, an archeology lab. The 65-acre campus is in a small town on the south side of Indianapolis. Including any residence halls, there are 31 buildings.

Student Life: 93% of undergraduates are from Indiana. Others are from states, 45 foreign countries, and Canada. 73% are White. 38% are Protestant; 35% claim no religious affiliation; 15% Catholic. The average age of freshmen is 18; all undergraduates, 24. 23% do not continue beyond their first year; 50% remain to graduate.

Housing: 1600 students can be accommodated in college housing, which includes single-sex and coed dorms, on-campus apartments, off-campus apartments, and married student housing. In addition, there are honors houses. On-campus housing is guaranteed for all 4 years. 64% of students commute. Alcohol is not permitted. All students may keep cars.

Activities: There are no fraternities or sororities. There are 45 groups on campus, including academic, art, cheerleading, chess, choir, chorale, chorus, computers, dance, debate, drama, ethnic, forensics, gay, honors, international, jazz band, literary magazine, musical theater, newspaper, orchestra, pep band, photography, political, professional, radio and TV, religious, social, social service, and student government. Popular campus events include Winter and Spring Formals, Ceremony of Flags, and Midnight Breakfast.

Sports: There are 11 intercollegiate sports for men and 10 for women, and 7 intramural sports for men and 6 for women. Facilities include a health and fitness center including a 3500-seat gym, an Olympic-size swimming pool, racquetball courts, a weight room, and a dance studio.

Disabled Students: 95% of the campus is accessible. Facilities include wheelchair ramps, elevators, special parking, specially equipped restrooms, special class scheduling, lowered drinking fountains, and lowered telephones.

Services: Counseling and information services are available, as is tutoring in every subject. There is remedial math and writing. There is a special learning disabled program (BUILD).

Campus Safety and Security: Measures include 24-hour foot and vehicle patrol, emergency notification system, self-defense education, and security escort services. There are emergency telephones and lighted pathways/sidewalks.

Programs of Study: UIndy confers B.A., B.S., B.F.A., B.L.S., B.M., B.S.N. and B.S.W. degrees. Associate, master's, and doctoral degrees are also awarded. Bachelor's degrees are awarded in BIOLOGICAL SCIENCE (biology/biological science), BUSINESS (accounting, banking and finance, business administration and management, business communications, business economics, entrepreneurial studies, international business management, management information systems, marketing/retailing/merchandising, and sports management), COMMUNICATIONS AND THE ARTS (art, broadcasting, communications, dramatic arts, English, French, German, journalism, music, music performance, musical theater, public relations, Spanish, speech/debate/rhetoric, and studio art), COMPUTER AND PHYSICAL SCIENCE (chemistry, computer science, earth science, mathematics, and physics), EDUCATION (art education, athletic training, business education, drama education, elementary education, English education, foreign languages education, mathematics education, middle school education, music education, physical education, science education, secondary education, and social studies education), ENGINEERING AND ENVIRONMENTAL DESIGN (commercial art, electrical/electronics engineering, environmental science, and mechanical engineering), HEALTH PROFESSIONS (art therapy, exercise science, medical laboratory technology, nursing, and respiratory therapy), SOCIAL SCIENCE (anthropology, archeology, corrections, economics, history, international relations, law enforcement and corrections, philosophy, political science/government, psychology, religion, social science, social work, sociology, and youth ministry). Education, nursing, and science (biology/chemistry) are the strongest academically. Business has the largest enrollment.

Required: All undergraduates must complete at least 124 hours, including 24 hours or more in the major with a GPA of 2.0 or better. Requirements include a core curriculum in which 8 learning goals must be met. Students must also take a health and phys ed course and 1 spring term, and attend lecture/performance events. Specific courses include math, social inquiry, history, and cross-cultural understanding and global awareness.

Special: Cross-registration is offered in conjunction with 6 area colleges. Cooperative programs, internships, various work-study programs, study abroad, dual and student-designed majors, accelerated programs in liberal studies and organizational leadership, pass/fail options, and a 3-2 engineering degree with Indiana University-Purdue University Indianapolis are available. A fleximester, which is a 3-week spring term, is also offered. There are 14 national honor societies and a freshman honors program.

Faculty/Classroom: 43% of faculty are male; 57% are female. No

introductory courses are taught by graduate students. The average class size in a regular course is 18.

Admissions: 79% of the 2013-2014 applicants were accepted.

Requirements: The SAT or ACT is required. Each applicant should complete a college preparatory curriculum with 15 to 20 academic credits from English/language arts, social studies, science, math, and world languages. The GED is accepted. An interview is recommended. AP and CLEP credits are accepted. Important factors in the admissions decision are recommendations by school officials, extracurricular activities record, and recommendations by alumni.

Procedure: Freshmen are admitted to all sessions. There are deferred admissions and rolling admissions plans. Application deadlines are open. Application fee is $25. 801 applicants were on the 2013 waiting list; 12 were admitted. Applications are accepted online.

Transfer: 222 transfer students enrolled in 2012-2013. No ACT or SAT is needed if applicants have a GPA of C and 20 semester hours of credit. 30 of 124 credits required for the bachelor's degree must be completed at UIndy.

Visiting: There are regularly scheduled orientations for prospective students, including campus visits and tours. There are guides for informal visits, visitors may sit in on classes, and stay overnight. To schedule a visit, contact the Admissions Office.

Financial Aid: UIndy is a member of CSS. The FAFSA and the college's own financial statement, and parent and student tax returns are required. The deadline for filing freshman financial aid applications for fall entry is March 10.

International Students: The school actively recruits these students. They must take the TOEFL with a minimum score of 500 on the paper-based TOEFL (PBT) or 61 on the Internet-based version (iBT) or take the MELAB, or Cambridge Examinations (IELTS, CPE, CAE). They must also take the SAT or ACT.

Computers: All students may access the system 7 days per week. There are no time limits and no fees.

Graduates: From July 1, 2012 to June 30, 2013, 619 bachelor's degrees were awarded. 180 companies recruited on campus in 2012-2013. In an average class, 37% graduate in 4 years or less, 48% graduate in 5 years or less, and 49% graduate in 6 years or less.

Admissions Contact: Ron Wilks, Director of Admissions. E-Mail: *admissions@uindy.edu* Web: *www.uindy.edu*

UNIVERSITY OF NOTRE DAME C-1

Notre Dame, IN 46556 **(574) 631-7505; (574) 631-8865**

Full-time: 4452 men, 4007 women	**Faculty:** n/av; I, +$
Part-time: 13 men, 5 women	**Ph.D.s:** 90%
Graduate: 2185 men, 1462 women	**Student/Faculty:** 11 to 1
Year: semesters, summer session	**Tuition:** $44,605
Application Deadline: January 1	**Room & Board:** $12,512

Freshman Class: 17647 applied, 3936 accepted, 2070 enrolled

SAT CR/M/W: 710/720/700 **ACT:** 33 **MOST COMPETITIVE**

The University of Notre Dame, founded in 1842, is a comprehensive Catholic research university. Programs are offered through the Colleges of Arts and Letters, Mendoza College of Business, Engineering, Science and the School of Architecture. Its 1,250-acre campus is located adjacent to South Bend, Ind., the center of a metropolitan area with a population of more than 315,000. There are 5 undergraduate schools and 6 graduate schools. In addition to regional accreditation, Notre Dame has baccalaureate program accreditation with AACSB, ABET, and NAAB. The 10 libraries contain 3.5 million volumes, 4.2 million microform items, 290,052 audio/video tapes/CDs/DVDs, and subscribe to 7,687 periodicals including electronic. Computerized library services include interlibrary loans, database searching, Internet access, and Wi-Fi capability. Special learning facilities include an art gallery, radio station, art museum and performing arts center. The campus is in a suburban area 90 miles east of Chicago. Including any residence halls, there are 159 buildings.

Student Life: 92% of undergraduates are from out of state, mostly the Mid-West. Students are from 50 states, 87 foreign countries, and Canada. 42% are from public schools. 71% are White. The average age of freshmen is 18; all undergraduates, 20. 1% do not continue beyond their first year; 99% remain to graduate.

Housing: 7121 students can be accommodated in college housing, which includes single-sex dorms. On-campus housing is guaranteed for the freshman year only, is available on a first-come, and first-served basis. 80% of students live on campus; of those, 95% remain on campus on weekends. Upperclassmen may keep cars.

Activities: There are no fraternities or sororities. There are 400 groups on campus, including art, bagpipe, band, cheerleading, chess, choir, chorale, chorus, computers, dance, debate, drama, drill team, ethnic, film, forensics, honors, international, jazz band, literary magazine, marching band, musical theater, newspaper, orchestra, pep band, photography, political, professional, radio, religious, social, social service, student government, symphony, and yearbook. Popular campus events include Spring Festival, Home Football Weekends and Collegiate Jazz Festival.

Sports: There are 13 intercollegiate sports for men and 13 for women, and 16 intramural sports for men and 13 for women. Facilities include (1) indoor and outdoor tennis; (2) two swimming pools; (3) two golf courses; (4) several outdoor general use recreational fields; (5) indoor, 100-yard general use facility with track; (6) two full-service fitness and rec centers; (7) lake/beach; (8) boat house on river; (9) varsity softball/baseball stadiums; (10) football stadium; (11) basketball/volleyball arena; (12) track; (13) soccer stadium, (14) lacrosse stadium; (15) hockey arena; (16) fencing gym; (17) Volleyball practice area; (18) varsity rowing erg gym; (19) varsity football practice fields.

Disabled Students: 95% of the campus is accessible. Facilities include wheelchair ramps, elevators, special parking, specially equipped restrooms, special class scheduling, lowered drinking fountains, lowered telephones, and special housing.

Services: There is a reader service for the blind.

Campus Safety and Security: Measures include 24-hour foot and vehicle patrol, emergency notification system, self-defense education, and security escort services. There are shuttle buses, emergency telephones, lighted pathways/sidewalks, controlled access to dorms/residences, Vehicle access is controlled, pedestrian access is not; property registration; lost and found; monthly electronic safety newsletter.

Programs of Study: Notre Dame confers B.A., B.S., B.Arch., B.B.A. and B.F.A. degrees. Master's and doctoral degrees are also awarded. Bachelor's degrees are awarded in BIOLOGICAL SCIENCE (biochemistry and biology/biological science), BUSINESS (accounting, banking and finance, management information systems, management science, and marketing/retailing/merchandising), COMMUNICATIONS AND THE ARTS (Arabic, art history and appreciation, Chinese, design, English, film arts, French, German, Greek, Italian, Japanese, music, romance languages and literature, Russian, Spanish, and studio art), COMPUTER AND PHYSICAL SCIENCE (applied physics, chemistry, computer science, geoenvironmental studies, mathematics, medical physics, and physics), EDUCATION (science education), ENGINEERING AND ENVIRONMENTAL DESIGN (aeronautical engineering, architecture, chemical engineering, civil engineering, computer engineering, electrical/electronics engineering, environmental science, and mechanical engineering), HEALTH PROFESSIONS (predentistry and premedicine), SOCIAL SCIENCE (African studies, American studies, anthropology, classical/ancient civilization, economics, history, liberal arts/general studies, medieval studies, philosophy, philosophy and religion, political science/government, psychology, sociology, and theological studies). Engineering, theology and business are the strongest academically. finance, psychology, and economics have the largest enrollments.

Required: All students must complete courses in English, philosophy, science, history, theology, math, social science, and phys ed. A total of 125 semester hours with a minimum GPA of 2.0 is required to graduate.

Special: Cross-registration is offered with Saint Mary's College. Study abroad is possible in 20 countries. A 5-year arts and letters/engineering B.A.-B.S. degree is offered. There is a program of liberal studies, centered on the discussion of great books. Internships, an accelerated degree program, a Washington semester, dual majors, 3-2 engineering degrees, and pass/fail options are available. There are 16 national honor societies, including Phi Beta Kappa, and 24 departmental honors programs.

Faculty/Classroom: 69% of faculty are male; 31% are female. No introductory courses are taught by graduate students. The average class size in an introductory lecture is 38; in a laboratory is 21; and in a regular course is 30.

Admissions: 22% of the 2013-2014 applicants were accepted. The SAT scores for the 2013-2014 freshman class were: Critical Reading--1% below 500, 8% between 500 and 599, 33% between 600 and 699, and 58% between 700 and 800; Math--4% between 500 and 599, 27% between 600 and 699, and 69% between 700 and 800; Writing--2% below 500, 9% between 500 and 599, 37% between 600 and 699, and 52% between 700 and 800. The ACT scores were 10% between 27 and 28, and 90% above 28.

Requirements: The SAT or ACT is required. Applicants should be graduates of an accredited secondary school with 16 Carnegie credits completed, including 4 years of English, 3 of math, and 2 each of science, foreign language, and history. The SAT subject test in a foreign language is recommended. An essay is required. An audition or a portfolio is recommended for some majors. AP credits are accepted.

Procedure: Freshmen are admitted fall. Entrance exams should be taken by fall of the senior year. There is a deferred admissions plan. Applications should be filed by January 1 for fall entry, along with a $75 fee. Notification of early decision is sent December 21; regular decision, April 10. 1521 applicants were on the 2013 waiting list. Applications are accepted online.

Transfer: 127 transfer students enrolled in 2012-2013. Applicants should have completed at least 27 semester hours of transferable credit and maintained a 3.3 GPA in all courses. Admission depends on openings in each undergraduate college. 60 of 125 credits required for the bachelor's degree must be completed at Notre Dame.

Visiting: There are regularly scheduled orientations for prospective stu-

dents, including small group sessions for students, larger sessions for parents, and tours for all. Visitors may sit in on classes and stay overnight. To schedule a visit, contact the Admissions Office.

Financial Aid: In 2013-2014, 73% of all full-time freshmen and 82% of continuing full-time students received some form of financial aid. 95% of all full-time freshmen and 95% of continuing full-time students received need-based aid. The average freshman award was $38,664. Need-based scholarships or need-based grants averaged $30,722; need-based self-help aid (loans and jobs) averaged $5,483; non-need-based athletic scholarships averaged $31,019; and other non-need-based awards and non-need-based scholarships averaged $14,793. 27% of undergraduate students work part-time. Average annual earnings from campus work are $1948. The average financial indebtedness of the 2013 graduate was $29,480. Notre Dame is a member of CSS. The CSS/Profile and FAFSA, and Federal Tax form(s), W-2 forms are required. The priority date for freshman financial aid applications for fall entry is February 15. The deadline for filing freshman financial aid applications for fall entry is February 15.

International Students: There are 354 international students enrolled. The school actively recruits these students. They must take the TOEFL with a minimum score of 560 on the paper-based TOEFL (PBT) or 100 on the Internet-based version (iBT). They must also take the SAT or ACT.

Computers: All students may access the system 24 hours a day. There are no time limits and no fees.

Graduates: From July 1, 2012 to June 30, 2013, 2173 bachelor's degrees were awarded. The most popular majors were finance (11%), accountancy (8%), and political science (7%). 576 companies recruited on campus in 2012-2013. In an average class, 89% graduate in 4 years or less, 94% graduate in 5 years or less, and 95% graduate in 6 years or less. Of the 2012 graduating class, 29% were enrolled in graduate school within 6 months of graduation, and 55% were employed.

Admissions Contact: Donald Bishop, AVP for Undergraduate Enrollment. E-Mail: *admissions@nd.edu* Web: *www.nd.edu*

UNIVERSITY OF SAINT FRANCIS D-2

Fort Wayne, IN 46808 **(260) 399-8000; (800) 729-4732**

Full-time: 500 men, 1000 women	**Faculty:** n/av
Part-time: 100 men, 300 women	**Ph.D.s:** 46%
Graduate: 100 men, 200 women	**Student/Faculty:** n/av
Year: semesters, summer session	**Tuition:** $24,500
Application Deadline: open	**Room & Board:** $8500
Freshman Class: n/av	
SAT or ACT: required	
	COMPETITIVE

University of Saint Francis is a private Roman Catholic liberal arts college founded in 1890 by the Sisters of Saint Francis. The figures in the above capsule and in this profile are approximate. There are 5 undergraduate schools and 1 graduate school. In addition to regional accreditation, USF has baccalaureate program accreditation with CAHEA, CSWE, NCATE, and NLN. The 2 libraries contain 85,500 volumes, 618,800 microform items, 1490 audio/video tapes/CDs/DVDs, and subscribe to 500 periodicals including electronic. Computerized library services include interlibrary loans, database searching, and Internet access. Special learning facilities include a learning resource center, art gallery, and planetarium. The 108-acre campus is in a suburban area on the west side of Fort Wayne. Including any residence halls, there are 22 buildings.

Student Life: 91% of undergraduates are from Indiana. Others are from 13 states and 2 foreign countries. 75% are white. 40% are Protestant; 30% claim no religious affiliation; 28% Catholic. The average age of freshmen is 24; all undergraduates, 25. 33% do not continue beyond their first year; 54% remain to graduate.

Housing: 400 students can be accommodated in college housing, which includes coed dorms and on-campus apartments. On-campus housing is guaranteed for the freshman year only, and is available on a first-come, first-served basis. 80% of students commute. Alcohol is not permitted. All students may keep cars.

Activities: There are no fraternities or sororities. There are 30 groups on campus, including art, cheerleading, choir, dance, drama, ethnic, film, honors, jazz band, musical theater, newspaper, pep band, photography, professional, radio and TV, religious, social, social service, and student government. Popular campus events include Little Regatta and Spring Fling.

Sports: There are 7 intercollegiate sports for men and 8 for women, and 4 intramural sports for men and 4 for women. Facilities include a gym with 2 basketball courts or 3 volleyball courts, a weight room, a baseball diamond, a beach volleyball pit, a football stadium, and soccer, baseball, and softball fields.

Disabled Students: 95% of the campus is accessible. Facilities include wheelchair ramps, elevators, special parking, specially equipped restrooms, and lowered drinking fountains.

Services: Counseling and information services are available, as is tutoring in most subjects. There is remedial math, reading, and writing, help for the learning disabled, individual counseling, and peer tutoring.

Campus Safety and Security: Measures include 24-hour foot and vehicle patrol and security escort services. There are emergency telephones and lighted pathways/sidewalks.

Programs of Study: USF confers B.A., B.S., B.B.A., B.L.S., B.S.Ed., B.S.N., and B.S.W. degrees. Associates and master's degrees are also awarded. Bachelor's degrees are awarded in BIOLOGICAL SCIENCE (biology/biological science), BUSINESS (accounting and business administration and management), COMMUNICATIONS AND THE ARTS (communications, English, fine arts, music technology, and studio art), COMPUTER AND PHYSICAL SCIENCE (chemistry, mathematics, and science), EDUCATION (art education, business education, elementary education, English education, health education, mathematics education, science education, secondary education, social studies education, and special education), ENGINEERING AND ENVIRONMENTAL DESIGN (environmental science), HEALTH PROFESSIONS (exercise science, medical laboratory technology, nursing, predentistry, and premedicine), SOCIAL SCIENCE (American studies, history, liberal arts/general studies, ministries, philosophy, psychology, religion, social work, and sociology). Nursing, education, and history are the strongest academically. Business, art, and nursing have the largest enrollments.

Required: All students must complete courses in humanities, social and behavioral science, religious studies, life and physical sciences, oral and written communication, phys ed, computer science, and math. 128 semester hours with a minimum GPA of 2.0 and at least 30 hours in the major are required to graduate. A comprehensive exam is required in biology and business administration, and a thesis is required in history.

Special: Internships in art, business, and communication are available, as well as nondegree study. Students also can receive credit for life experience. Cross-registration with the Fort Wayne Higher Education Consortium is available, as well as dual and student-designed majors. There is 1 national honor society, a freshman honors program, and 1 departmental honors program.

Faculty/Classroom: 40% of faculty are male; 60% are female. 94% teach undergraduates. No introductory courses are taught by graduate students.

Requirements: The SAT or ACT is required. A GPA of 2.3 is required. AP and CLEP credits are accepted. Important factors in the admissions decision are recommendations by school officials, advanced placement or honors courses, and extracurricular activities record.

Procedure: Freshmen are admitted to all sessions. Entrance exams should be taken in the spring of the junior year or fall of the senior year. There are deferred admissions and rolling admissions plans. Application deadlines are open. The application fee is $20. Notification is sent on a rolling basis.

Transfer: Applicants need a minimum cumulative GPA of 2.3 and must submit all college transcripts. 32 of 128 credits required for the bachelor's degree must be completed at USF.

Visiting: There are regularly scheduled orientations for prospective students, including meetings with faculty and staff and student tours. There are guides for informal visits; visitors may sit in on classes and stay overnight. To schedule a visit, contact the Admissions Office.

Financial Aid: USF is a member of CSS. The FAFSA is required. Check with the school for current application deadlines.

International Students: They must take the TOEFL.

Computers: All students may access the system 7 days a week.

Admissions Contact: Admissions. E-mail: *admis@sf.edu* Web: *www.sf.edu*

UNIVERSITY OF SOUTHERN INDIANA A-5

Evansville, IN 47712 **(812) 464-1765 (800) 467-1965; (812) 465-7154**

Full-time: 3079 men, 4296 women	**Faculty:** n/av; IIA, --$
Part-time: 558 men, 980 women	**Ph.D.s:** 70%
Graduate: 187 men, 802 women	**Student/Faculty:** 16 to 1
Year: semesters, summer session	**Tuition:** $6977 ($16,317)
Application Deadline: August 15	**Room & Board:** $7680
Freshman Class: 6204 applied, 4302 accepted, 1709 enrolled	
SAT CR/M/W: 499/508/478 **ACT:** 22	**COMPETITIVE**

The University of Southern Indiana, founded in 1965, is a public institution offering undergraduate programs in business, liberal arts, nursing and health professions, and science, engineering, and education. There are 4 undergraduate schools and one graduate school. In addition to regional accreditation, USI has baccalaureate program accreditation with AACSB, ABET, ACEJMC, ADA, CSWE, and NCATE. The library contains 361,072 volumes, 541,116 microform items, 3,618 audio/video tapes/CDs/DVDs, and subscribes to 60,575 periodicals including electronic. Computerized library services include interlibrary loans, database searching, Internet access, and Wi-Fi capability. Special learning facilities include an art gallery, radio station, and TV station. The 330-acre campus is in a suburban area 150 miles south of Indianapolis. Including any residence halls, there are 85 buildings.

Student Life: 84% of undergraduates are from Indiana. Others are from

39 states, 45 foreign countries, and Canada. 86% are White. The average age of freshmen is 18; all undergraduates, 23. 31% do not continue beyond their first year; 37% remain to graduate.

Housing: 2808 students can be accommodated in college housing, which includes coed dorms, on-campus apartments, off-campus apartments, and married student housing. In addition, there are honors houses, special-interest houses, fraternity houses, and sorority houses. On-campus housing is available on a first-come and first-served basis. Priority is given to out-of-town students. 73% of students commute. Alcohol is not permitted. All students may keep cars.

Activities: 7% of men belong to 7 national fraternities; 8% of women belong to 4 national sororities. There are 143 groups on campus, including art, cheerleading, chess, choir, chorus, computers, dance, drama, environmental, ethnic, film, gay, honors, international, jazz band, literary magazine, musical theater, newspaper, pep band, photography, political, professional, radio and TV, religious, social, social service, and student government. Popular campus events include Welcome Week, Welcome Fun Fest, Midnight Madness and International Food Festival.

Sports: There are 7 intercollegiate sports for men and 8 for women, and 16 intramural sports for men and 16 for women. Facilities include a physical activities center with a swimming pool, a weight room, 6 tennis courts, and a 3000-seat multipurpose area and a recreation and fitness center with weights, cardiovascular equipment, climbing center, and exercise programs.

Disabled Students: 95% of the campus is accessible. Facilities include wheelchair ramps, elevators, special parking, specially equipped restrooms, special class scheduling, lowered drinking fountains, lowered telephones, and student assistance through the counseling center.

Services: Counseling and information services are available, as is tutoring in most subjects. There is a reader service for the blind, and remedial math, reading, and writing.

Campus Safety and Security: Measures include 24-hour foot and vehicle patrol, emergency notification system, self-defense education, and security escort services. There are shuttle buses, emergency telephones, and lighted pathways/sidewalks.

Programs of Study: USI confers B.A., B.S., B.G.S., B.S.E., B.S.N. and B.S.W. degrees. Associate, master's, and doctoral degrees are also awarded. Bachelor's degrees are awarded in BIOLOGICAL SCIENCE (biology/biological science, biophysics, and nutrition), BUSINESS (accounting, business administration and management, business communications, electronic business, finance, management information systems, marketing/retailing/merchandising, and sports management), COMMUNICATIONS AND THE ARTS (advertising, art, broadcasting, communications, English, French, German, journalism, performing arts, public relations, radio/television technology, Spanish, speech/debate/rhetoric, and theatre arts), COMPUTER AND PHYSICAL SCIENCE (chemistry, computer science, geology, and mathematics), EDUCATION (art education, business education, early childhood education, elementary education, English education, mathematics education, middle school education, physical education, science education, secondary education, social science education, and special education), ENGINEERING AND ENVIRONMENTAL DESIGN (engineering, environmental science, industrial administration/management, and manufacturing technology), HEALTH PROFESSIONS (dental hygiene, exercise science, health care administration, nursing, occupational therapy, and radiological science), SOCIAL SCIENCE (anthropology, criminal justice, economics, history, international studies, philosophy, political science/government, psychology, social work, and sociology). Nursing is the strongest academically. Nursing, business administration, and biology have the largest enrollments.

Required: The university core curriculum's goals focus on four areas: The Mind (enhancement of cognitive abilities), The Self (enhancement of individual development), The World (enhancement of cultural and natural awareness), and The Synthesis (the integration and application of knowledge). These are then subdivided into 13 objectives concerned with critical thinking, oral and written communication, math, information processing, ethics, the arts, health and lifestyle, history, individual development and social behavior, science, Western culture, global communities, and interdisciplinary studies. A total of 50 credit hours is distributed among the objectives with a total of 120 credit hours needed to graduate. A minimum cumulative 2.0 GPA is required.

Special: Students may participate in cooperative programs, internships in business and communications, and work-study programs. Study abroad, dual majors, pass/fail options, and B.A.-B.S. degrees are possible. There are 5 national honor societies and a freshman honors program.

Faculty/Classroom: 43% of faculty are male; 57% are female. All teach undergraduates. No introductory courses are taught by graduate students. The average class size in an introductory lecture is 52; in a laboratory is 24; and in a regular course is 24.

Admissions: 69% of the 2013-2014 applicants were accepted. The SAT scores for the 2013-2014 freshman class were: Critical Reading--49% below 500, 39% between 500 and 599, 11% between 600 and 699, and 1% between 700 and 800; Math--44% below 500, 42% between 500 and 599, 13% between 600 and 699, and 1% between 700 and 800; Writing--58% below 500, 33% between 500 and 599, 8% between 600 and 699, and 1% between 700 and 800. The ACT scores were 39% below 21, 32% between 21 and 23, 18% between 24 and 26, 7% between 27 and 28, and 4% above 28. 28% of the current freshmen were in the top fifth of their class; 58% were in the top two fifths. 14 freshmen graduated first in their class.

Requirements: The SAT or ACT is required. Applicants must be graduates of an accredited secondary school, with a minimum GPA of 2.0. The GED is accepted. An interview is recommended if the student is below admissions standards. A GPA of 2.0 is required. AP and CLEP credits are accepted. Important factors in the admissions decision are advanced placement or honors courses, evidence of special talent, and leadership record.

Procedure: Freshmen are admitted fall, spring, and summer. Entrance exams should be taken in the spring term of the junior year. There is a rolling admissions plan. Applications should be filed by August 15 for fall entry, along with a $40 fee. Applications are accepted online.

Transfer: 570 transfer students enrolled in 2012-2013. Grades of C- and above will transfer for credit. 30 of 120 credits required for the bachelor's degree must be completed at USI.

Visiting: There are regularly scheduled orientations for prospective students, including meetings with counselors and faculty and campus tours. There are guides for informal visits, visitors may sit in on classes, and stay overnight. To schedule a visit, contact the Office of Admission.

Financial Aid: In 2013-2014, 67% of all full-time freshmen and 64% of continuing full-time students received some form of financial aid. 90% of all full-time freshmen and 91% of continuing full-time students received need-based aid. The average freshman award was $4,818. Need-based scholarships or need-based grants averaged $7,274 ($18,252 maximum); need-based self-help aid (loans and jobs) averaged $3,266 ($17,223 maximum); non-need-based athletic scholarships averaged $4,039 ($14,117 maximum); and other non-need-based awards and non-need-based scholarships averaged $2,655 ($16,050 maximum). 10% of undergraduate students work part-time. Average annual earnings from campus work are $1117. The average financial indebtedness of the 2013 graduate was $24,685. The FAFSA and the college's own financial statement are required. The deadline for filing freshman financial aid applications for fall entry is March 1.

International Students: There are 234 international students enrolled. The school actively recruits these students. They must take the TOEFL with a minimum score of 525 on the paper-based TOEFL (PBT) or 71 on the Internet-based version (iBT). They must also take the SAT or ACT.

Computers: All students may access the system. There are no time limits and no fees.

Graduates: From July 1, 2012 to June 30, 2013, 1653 bachelor's degrees were awarded. The most popular majors were health services (11%), nursing (10%), and elementary education (9%). 239 companies recruited on campus in 2012-2013. In an average class, 15% graduate in 4 years or less, 33% graduate in 5 years or less, and 37% graduate in 6 years or less. Of the 2012 graduating class, 21% were enrolled in graduate school within 6 months of graduation, and 75% were employed.

Admissions Contact: Mark Rusk, Interim Director of Admissions. E-Mail: *mrusk@usi.edu* Web: *www.usi.edu*

VALPARAISO UNIVERSITY — B-1

Valparaiso, IN 46383 — **(219) 464-5011**
(888) GO-VALPO; (219) 464-6898

Full-time: 1522 men, 1614 women	**Faculty:** 236; IIA, -$
Part-time: 44 men, 71 women	**Ph.D.s:** 92%
Graduate: 578 men, 679 women	**Student/Faculty:** 13 to 1
Year: semesters, summer session	**Tuition:** $33,480
Application Deadline: rolling	**Room & Board:** $9560
Freshman Class: n/av	

VERY COMPETITIVE+

Valparaiso University, founded in 1859, is an independent institution affiliated with the Lutheran Church and offering degree programs in arts and sciences, business, engineering, nursing and health professions, and law. There are 5 undergraduate schools and 4 graduate schools. In addition to regional accreditation, Valpo has baccalaureate program accreditation with AACSB, ABET, CSWE, NASM, and NCATE. The 2 libraries contain 565,651 volumes, 1.9 million microform items, and 10,020 audio/video tapes/CDs/DVDs, and subscribe to 48,302 periodicals including electronic. Computerized library services include interlibrary loans, database searching, Internet access, and Wi-Fi capability. Special learning facilities include an art gallery, planetarium, radio station, observatory, weather station, center for visual and performing arts, virtual nursing learning center, solar energy research facility, and scientific visualization laboratory. The 320-acre campus is in a small town 55 miles southeast of Chicago. Including any residence halls, there are 60 buildings.

Student Life: 59% of undergraduates are from out of state, mostly the Mid-West. Students are from 45 states, 44 foreign countries, and Canada.

74% are White. 57% are Protestant; 25% Catholic. The average age of freshmen is 18; all undergraduates, 21. 16% do not continue beyond their first year; 72% remain to graduate.

Housing: 2026 students can be accommodated in college housing, which includes single-sex and coed dorms and off-campus apartments. In addition, there are language houses and fraternity houses. On-campus housing is guaranteed for all 4 years. 67% of students live on campus. Alcohol is not permitted. Upperclassmen may keep cars.

Activities: 20% of men belong to 8 national fraternities; 20% of women belong to 6 national sororities. There are 94 groups on campus, including art, band, cheerleading, choir, chorale, chorus, dance, debate, drama, environmental, ethnic, film, gay, honors, international, jazz band, literary magazine, musical theater, newspaper, orchestra, pep band, photography, political, professional, radio and TV, religious, social, social service, student government, symphony, and yearbook. Popular campus events include Christmas Concert, Martin Luther King Day Celebration and Jazz Festival.

Sports: There are 9 intercollegiate sports for men and 10 for women, and 20 intramural sports for men and 20 for women. Facilities include a 5,100-seat arena, swimming pool, 7 additional playing floors, a nine-lap-per-mile track, racquetball/handball courts, a fitness center, a football stadium, a tennis complex, soccer, softball, and baseball fields, and indoor batting facilities.

Disabled Students: 57% of the campus is accessible. Facilities include wheelchair ramps, elevators, special parking, specially equipped restrooms, and lowered drinking fountains.

Services: Counseling and information services are available, as is tutoring in most subjects. There is a reader service for the blind. A writing center provides assistance. The Academic Success Center coordinates all academic support services and resources, including tutoring, advising, and support groups.

Campus Safety and Security: Measures include 24-hour foot and vehicle patrol, emergency notification system, and security escort services. There are shuttle buses, emergency telephones, lighted pathways/sidewalks, and controlled access to dorms/residences.

Programs of Study: Valpo confers B.A., B.L.P.S., B.Mus., B.Mus.Ed., B.S., B.S.Acc., B.S.Bus.Adm., B.S.C.E., B.S.Comp.Eng., B.S.Ed., B.S.E.E., B.S.H.C.L., B.S.M.E., B.S.N., B.S.P.E. and B.S.W. degrees. Associate, master's, and doctoral degrees are also awarded. Bachelor's degrees are awarded in BIOLOGICAL SCIENCE (biochemistry and biology/biological science), BUSINESS (accounting, banking and finance, business administration and management, finance, international economics, management science, marketing/retailing/merchandising, and sports management), COMMUNICATIONS AND THE ARTS (art, classics, communications, creative writing, digital communications, dramatic arts, English, English Writing, French, German, music, music performance, music theory and composition, Spanish, technical and business writing, theatre arts, and voice), COMPUTER AND PHYSICAL SCIENCE (actuarial science, astronomy, atmospheric sciences and meteorology, chemistry, computer science, geology, mathematics, and physics), EDUCATION (art education, elementary education, English education, foreign languages education, mathematics education, music education, physical education, psychology education, science education, secondary education, social science education, and social studies education), ENGINEERING AND ENVIRONMENTAL DESIGN (civil engineering, computer engineering, computer technology, electrical/electronics engineering, environmental science, and mechanical engineering), HEALTH PROFESSIONS (exercise science, health care administration, nursing, Pre-Health Studies, and premedicine), SOCIAL SCIENCE (American studies, criminology, East Asian studies, economics, geography, history, humanities, interdisciplinary studies, international public service, international relations, ministries, philosophy, political science/government, prelaw, psychology, religion, religious music, social science, social work, sociology, and theological studies). Nursing, business, and engineering have the largest enrollments.

Required: General education requirements include the 10-credit Valpo core plus 2 courses in theology, courses in natural sciences, humanities, cultural diversity, and social sciences, 1 course in quantitative analysis, and 1 credit hour in physical education. Requirements may vary by degree program, particularly in the professional colleges. To graduate, students must complete at least 124 credit hours, including a minimum of 27 in the major, with GPA of at least 2.0.

Special: There is cross-registration with Indiana University Northwest at the undergraduate level in geology. Off-campus study programs in the United States include 2 Washington semester programs, a United Nations semester, a Chicago urban semester, a Chicago arts semester, and a Chicago Business, Entrepreneurship, and Society program. Students may also study abroad in 16 countries including Greece, England, Spain, China, Japan, Namibia, France, Germany, Mexico, India, Thailand, Costa Rica, Chile, Israel, Ireland, and Italy. Co-op programs, internships, the B.A.-B.S. degree, work-study programs, dual and student-designed majors, an accelerated degree program in numerous majors, pass/fail options, and nondegree study are also available. Other special academic features include Christ College, which is the honors college. There are 8 national honor societies, including Phi Beta Kappa, a freshman honors program, and 26 departmental honors programs.

Faculty/Classroom: 55% of faculty are male; 45% are female. 86% teach undergraduates. No introductory courses are taught by graduate students. The average class size in an introductory lecture is 27; in a laboratory is 23; and in a regular course is 21.

Admissions: 61% of the current freshmen were in the top fifth of their class; 88% were in the top two fifths. There were 6 National Merit finalists. 17 freshmen graduated first in their class.

Requirements: The SAT or ACT is required. Valparaiso University requires completion of 4 years of English, 3 to 4 years of math, 2 to 3 years of lab science, 2 years each of history and foreign language, and 3 years of additional academic courses. An application essay is required and an interview is recommended for all applicants; an audition is required for music majors. AP and CLEP credits are accepted. Important factors in the admissions decision are advanced placement or honors courses, extracurricular activities record, and evidence of special talent.

Procedure: Freshmen are admitted fall, spring, and summer. Entrance exams should be taken prior to the senior year. There are deferred admissions and rolling admissions plans. Application deadlines are open. Notifications are sent October 1. Applications are accepted online.

Transfer: 173 transfer students enrolled in 2012-2013. Applicants must submit official transcripts from all colleges attended. To be considered for admission, a minimum 2.0 cumulative grade point average in college coursework is required for most programs. However, some programs require a minimum 3.0 grade point average for transfer students. If the applicant has completed fewer than 24 credit hours, entrance exam scores and a high school transcript are required. A completed transfer evaluation form from the Dean of Students of the current institution must also be submitted. An interview is recommended. 30 of 124 credits required for the bachelor's degree must be completed at Valpo.

Visiting: There are regularly scheduled orientations for prospective students, includes a campus tour conducted by a current student, an interview with a counselor, the option to meet with professors, attend a class, and meet with a coach. There are guides for informal visits, visitors may sit in on classes, and stay overnight. To schedule a visit, contact the Office of Admission.

Financial Aid: In 2013-2014, 95% of all full-time freshmen and 96% of continuing full-time students received some form of financial aid. 77% of all full-time freshmen and 76% of continuing full-time students received need-based aid. The average freshman award was $26,773. Need-based scholarships or need-based grants averaged $22,837; need-based self-help aid (loans and jobs) averaged $4,837; non-need-based athletic scholarships averaged $15,036; and other non-need-based awards and non-need-based scholarships averaged $14,418. 35% of undergraduate students work part-time. Average annual earnings from campus work are $1700. The average financial indebtedness of the 2013 graduate was $31,891. The FAFSA is required. The priority date for freshman financial aid applications for fall entry is March 1.

International Students: There are 273 international students enrolled. The school actively recruits these students. They must take the TOEFL with a minimum score of 550 on the paper-based TOEFL (PBT) or 80 on the Internet-based version (iBT), IELTS, GCE, or GCSE English Exam, IB Higher Level English Exam, or SAT or ACT exams. They must also take the SAT or ACT.

Computers: All students may access the system 7 days a week. There are no time limits and no fees.

Graduates: From July 1, 2012 to June 30, 2013, 618 bachelor's degrees were awarded. The most popular majors were nursing (19%), English (5%), and biology (5%). 135 companies recruited on campus in 2012-2013. In an average class, 1% graduate in 3 years or less, 59% graduate in 4 years or less, 69% graduate in 5 years or less, and 72% graduate in 6 years or less. Of the 2012 graduating class, 20% were enrolled in graduate school within 6 months of graduation, and 76% were employed.

Admissions Contact: David Fevig, Asst. Vice President, Enrollment Mgt.. E-Mail: *undergrad.admission@valpo.edu* Web: *www.valpo.edu*

WABASH COLLEGE B-3

Crawfordsville, IN 47933 **(765) 361-6253**
(800) 345-5385; (765) 361-6437

Full-time: 902 men	**Faculty:** 81; IIB, av$
Part-time: n/av	**Ph.D.s:** 99%
Graduate: n/av	**Student/Faculty:** 11 to 1
Year: semesters	**Tuition:** $35,650
Application Deadline: December 1	**Room & Board:** $8510
Freshman Class: 1129 applied, 786 accepted, 241 enrolled	
SAT CR/M/W: 550/570/520	**ACT:** 25 **VERY COMPETITIVE**

Wabash College, founded in 1832, is a private liberal arts college that educates men to think critically, act responsibly, lead effectively, and live humanely. There is one undergraduate school. In addition to regional accreditation, Wabash has baccalaureate program accreditation with NCATE. The library contains 276,184 volumes, 18,418 microform items, 17,064 audio/video tapes/CDs/DVDs, and subscribes to 19,782 periodicals including electronic. Computerized library services include interlibrary loans, database searching, Internet access, and Wi-Fi capability. Special learning facilities include an art gallery, radio station, an archival center; research centers for the study of theology and religion and inquiry in the liberal arts; two biological field stations. The 60-acre campus is in a small town 45 miles northwest of Indianapolis. Including any residence halls, there are 66 buildings.

Student Life: 75% of undergraduates are from Indiana. Others are from 35 states, and 12 foreign countries. 93% are from public schools. 75% are White. The average age of freshmen is 19; all undergraduates, 20. 15% do not continue beyond their first year; 72% remain to graduate.

Housing: 893 students can be accommodated in college housing, which includes single-sex dorms and on-campus apartments. In addition, there are fraternity houses. On-campus housing is guaranteed for the freshman year only, is available on a first-come, and first-served basis. 89% of students live on campus. All students may keep cars.

Activities: 60% of men belong to 9 national fraternities. There are 75 groups on campus, including art, band, cheerleading, chess, choir, chorale, chorus, communications, computers, dance, debate, drama, environmental, ethnic, film, forensics, gay, honors, international, jazz band, literary magazine, musical theater, newspaper, orchestra, pep band, photography, political, professional, radio and TV, religious, social, social service, student government, symphony, and yearbook. Popular campus events include Homecoming, Pan-Hel Weekend, Monon Bell, Scholars Weekend, and Chapel Sing.

Sports: There are 11 intercollegiate sports for men, and 20 intramural sports for men. Facilities include a 4500-seat stadium with FieldTurf Duraspine Pro surface; indoor and outdoor tennis courts; baseball stadium; soccer stadium; swimming pool; indoor track; all-weather outdoor track; wrestling room; fitness center/weight room; racquetball and handball courts; aerobics room; 1800-seat basketball arena; wellness center.

Disabled Students: 60% of the campus is accessible. Facilities include wheelchair ramps, elevators, special parking, specially equipped restrooms, special class scheduling, lowered drinking fountains, special housing. Braille signage in some buildings. Theater equipped for hearing-impared patrons. Some laboratory rooms with lowered work stations.

Services: Counseling and information services are available, as is tutoring in some subjects, Economics, math, physics, biology, chemistry, and Spanish There is a reader service for the blind. There is a quantitative skills center as well as a writing center where, under professional supervision, students help each other.

Campus Safety and Security: Measures include 24-hour foot and vehicle patrol, emergency notification system, and security escort services. There are emergency telephones and lighted pathways/sidewalks.

Programs of Study: Wabash confers A.B. degrees. Bachelor's degrees are awarded in BIOLOGICAL SCIENCE (biochemistry and biology/biological science), COMMUNICATIONS AND THE ARTS (art, classics, dramatic arts, English, French, German, Greek, Latin, music, Spanish, and speech/debate/rhetoric), COMPUTER AND PHYSICAL SCIENCE (chemistry, mathematics, and physics), SOCIAL SCIENCE (economics, history, philosophy, political science/government, psychology, and religion). Economics, chemistry, and biology are the strongest academically. History, economics, and psychology are the largest.

Required: All students must complete at least 3 courses each in literature/fine arts, behavioral science, and natural science/math, 2 in history, philosophy, or religion, and 1 in quantitative skills. To graduate, students must maintain a minimum 2.0 GPA for 136 credit hours (34 courses), which include a freshman tutorial and the all-freshmen course Enduring Questions. The student must pass a written comprehensive exam in the major as well as a senior oral exam and must demonstrate proficiency in English and proficiency in a foreign language at a level equivalent to 2 college courses.

Special: Wabash offers internships with off-campus organizations, study abroad in an unlimited number of countries, a Washington semester with American University, dual majors, a B.A.-B.S. degree in engineering, and a 3-2 engineering program with Purdue University, Columbia University and Washington University in St. Louis. A tuition-free Ninth Semester Teacher Education Program is also available. Wabash also has a 4-1 program with the Indiana University Kelley School of Business that leads to a BA-MS (in accounting). There are 9 national honor societies including Phi Beta Kappa.

Faculty/Classroom: 66% of faculty are male; 34% are female. All teach undergraduates. No introductory courses are taught by graduate students. The average class size in an introductory lecture is 20; in a laboratory is 15; and in a regular course is 13.

Admissions: 70% of the 2013-2014 applicants were accepted. The SAT scores for the 2013-2014 freshman class were: Critical Reading--25% below 500, 44% between 500 and 599, 25% between 600 and 699, and 6% between 700 and 800; Math--11% below 500, 52% between 500 and 599, 30% between 600 and 699, and 7% between 700 and 800; Writing--39% below 500, 40% between 500 and 599, 18% between 600 and 699, and 3% between 700 and 800. The ACT scores were 13% below 21, 24% between 21 and 23, 28% between 24 and 26, 15% between 27 and 28, and 20% above 28. 58% of the current freshmen were in the top fifth of their class; 87% were in the top two fifths. 8 freshmen graduated first in their class.

Requirements: The SAT or ACT is required. The ACT Optional Writing test is also required. Wabash recommends applicants to have 4 high school courses in English, 3 to 4 in math, and 2 each in foreign language, lab science, and social studies. An essay is required, and an interview is recommended. AP and CLEP credits are accepted. Important factors in the admissions decision are advanced placement or honors courses, leadership record, and extracurricular activities record.

Procedure: Freshmen are admitted fall and spring. Entrance exams should be taken by the Spring of the junior year or Fall of the senior year. There are early decision, deferred admissions, and rolling admissions plans. Early decision applications should be filed by November 15; regular applications, by December 1 for fall entry; and December 1 for spring entry, along with a $40 fee. Notification of early decision is sent December 1; regular decision, on a rolling basis. 53 early decision candidates were accepted for the 2013-2014 class. 36 applicants were on the 2013 waiting list; 3 were admitted. Applications are accepted online.

Transfer: 4 transfer students enrolled in 2012-2013. Applicants must submit official transcripts of all college courses attended. Wabash strongly considers the overall high school and college background of applicants.Courses must be liberal arts in nature with a minimum GPA of 2.0 to transfer. Recommendations from the college adviser and dean of students at the previous college attended and a personal written statement are required, with an interview strongly recommended. 24 of 34 credits required for the bachelor's degree must be completed at Wabash.

Visiting: There are regularly scheduled orientations for prospective students, Consisting of a tour, lunch, opportunity to meet faculty, coaches, and alumni, and panel discussions on academics, extracurricular activities, and financial aid. There are guides for informal visits, visitors may sit in on classes, and stay overnight. To schedule a visit, contact Mary Towell at (800) 345-5385.

Financial Aid: In 2013-2014, 83% of all full-time freshmen and 78% of continuing full-time students received some form of financial aid. 80% of all full-time freshmen and 78% of continuing full-time students received need-based aid. The average freshman award was $36,017. Need-based scholarships or need-based grants averaged $22,633; need-based self-help aid (loans and jobs) averaged $9,405; and other non-need-based awards and non-need-based scholarships averaged $16,260. 76% of undergraduate students work part-time. Average annual earnings from campus work are $2600. The average financial indebtedness of the 2013 graduate was $30,118. Wabash is a member of CSS. The CSS/Profile and FAFSA, and Federal tax form with W-2 statements are required. The priority date for freshman financial aid applications for fall entry is February 15. The deadline for filing freshman financial aid applications for fall entry is March 1.

International Students: There are 55 international students enrolled. The school actively recruits these students. They must take the TOEFL with a minimum score of 550 on the paper-based TOEFL (PBT) or 80 on the Internet-based version (iBT) or take the MELAB. They must also take the SAT or ACT.

Computers: All students may access the system 24 hours per day or at designated times for specific computers. There are no time limits and no fees.

Graduates: From July 1, 2012 to June 30, 2013, 189 bachelor's degrees were awarded. The most popular majors were history (12%), English (11%), and economics (11%). 45 companies recruited on campus in 2012-2013. In an average class, 1% graduate in 3 years or less, 64% graduate in 4 years or less, 69% graduate in 5 years or less, and 69% graduate in 6 years or less. Of the 2012 graduating class, 23% were enrolled in graduate school within 6 months of graduation, and 69% were employed.

Admissions Contact: Steve Klein, Dean of Admissions and Financial Aid. E-Mail: *admissions@wabash.edu* Web: *www.wabash.edu*

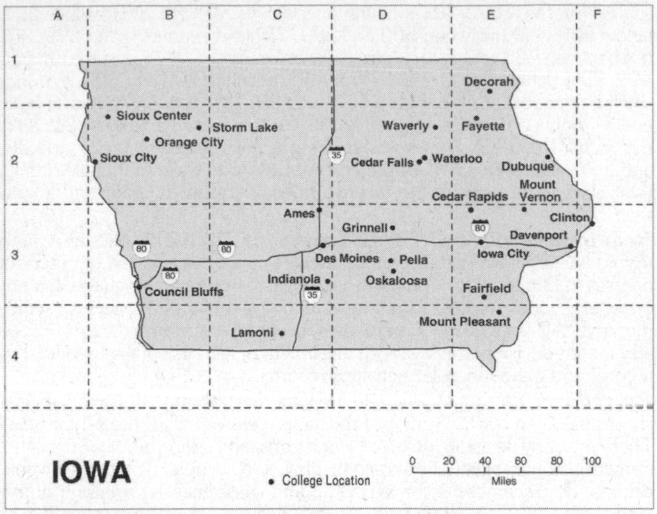

ALLEN COLLEGE D-2

Waterloo, IA 50703 319-226-2001; (319) 226-2010

Full-time: 20 men, 237 women	**Faculty:** 23
Part-time: 6 men, 134 women	**Ph.D.s:** 36%
Graduate: 13 men, 165 women	**Student/Faculty:** n/av
Year: semesters, summer session	**Tuition:** $18,829
Application Deadline: February 1	**Room & Board:** $7281
Freshman Class: n/av	
ACT: required	**SPECIAL**

Allen College, founded in 1989, is a private institution offering a baccalaureate program in nursing and is part of the Iowa Health System. There are 2 undergraduate schools and one graduate school. In addition to regional accreditation, has baccalaureate program accreditation with NLN. The library contains 4,600 volumes, and 905 audio/video tapes/CDs/DVDs, and subscribes to 240 periodicals including electronic. Computerized library services include interlibrary loans, database searching, Internet access, and Wi-Fi capability. The 20-acre campus is in a suburban area in Waterloo. Including any residence halls, there are 4 buildings.

Student Life: 95% of undergraduates are from Iowa. Others are from 7 states, and 2 foreign countries. 96% are White. The average age of freshmen is 18; all undergraduates, 26.7. 100% remain to graduate.

Housing: 24 students can be accommodated in college housing, which includes coed on-campus apartments. Living facilities are available at cooperative colleges. On-campus housing is available on a first-come and first-served basis. 96% of students commute. Alcohol is not permitted. All students may keep cars.

Activities: There are no fraternities or sororities. There are 6 groups on campus, including chorus and student government.

Disabled Students: All of the campus is accessible. Facilities include wheelchair ramps, elevators, special parking, specially equipped restrooms, and lowered drinking fountains.

Services: Counseling and information services are available, as is tutoring in some subjects, lower division major courses.

Campus Safety and Security: Measures include emergency notification system. There are emergency telephones, lighted pathways/sidewalks, and controlled access to dorms/residences.

Programs of Study: confers B.S.N., and B.H.S. degrees. Associate, master's, and doctoral degrees are also awarded. Bachelor's degrees are awarded in COMPUTER AND PHYSICAL SCIENCE (radiological technology), EDUCATION (nursing education), HEALTH PROFESSIONS (medical laboratory science, nuclear medical technology, nursing, and public health). Nursing is the largest.

Required: To graduate, all students must complete general education courses in humanities, social science, natural science, electives and major courses and maintain a 2.5 GPA or higher. 124 credits are required.

Special: There are 2 departmental honors programs.

Faculty/Classroom: 2% of faculty are male; 98% are female. 73% teach undergraduates. No introductory courses are taught by graduate students. The average class size in an introductory lecture is 40; in a laboratory is 8; and in a regular course is 30.

Requirements: The ACT is required. A GPA of 3.0 is required. AP and CLEP credits are accepted. Important factors in the admissions decision are leadership record, evidence of special talent, extracurricular activities record, advanced placement or honors courses, parents or siblings attended your school, personality/intangible qualities, recommendations by alumni, geographical diversity, recommendations by school officials, and ability to finance college education.

Procedure: Freshmen are admitted summer. Applications should be filed by February 1 for fall entry; June 1 for spring entry; and June 1 for summer entry, along with a $50 fee. Applications are accepted online.

Transfer: 130 transfer students enrolled in 2012-2013. Students must have a minimum college GPA of 2.7 and complete all admission requirements. Admission is competitive. 30 of 124 credits required for the bachelor's degree must be completed at Allen.

Visiting: There are regularly scheduled orientations for prospective students, General overview of admissions requirements, financial aid and a tour. There are guides for informal visits and visitors may sit in on classes. To schedule a visit, contact Andrea Schupbach at (319) 226-2014.

Financial Aid: In 2013-2014, 100% of all full-time freshmen and 92% of continuing full-time students received some form of financial aid. 100% of all full-time freshmen and 86% of continuing full-time students received need-based aid. The average freshman award was $18,293. Need-based scholarships or need-based grants averaged $9,393 ($12,500 maximum); need-based self-help aid (loans and jobs) averaged $1,900 ($11,500 maximum); and $7,000 from other forms of aid. 8% of undergraduate students work part-time. Average annual earnings from campus work are $3000. The average financial indebtedness of the 2013 graduate was $27,358. The FAFSA and the college's own financial statement are required. The priority date for freshman financial aid applications for fall entry is July 1.

International Students: There are 2 international students enrolled. They must take the TOEFL with a minimum score of 580 on the paper-based TOEFL (PBT) or 92 on the Internet-based version (iBT) or take the MELAB, the Comprehensive English Language Test, and the college's own test. They must also take the SAT or ACT, scoring 20.

Graduates: From July 1, 2012 to June 30, 2013, 212 bachelor's degrees were awarded. The most popular majors were nursing (87%) and health sciences (13%). In an average class, 65% graduate in 4 years or less, 67% graduate in 5 years or less, and 67% graduate in 6 years or less.

Admissions Contact: Molly Quinn, Admissions Counselor. E-Mail: *Admissions@AllenCollege.edu* Web: *www.allencollege.edu*

ASHFORD UNIVERSITY F-3

Clinton, IA 52733-2967 (563) 243-6102
(800) 242-4153; (563) 242-2003

Full-time: 2210 men, 7525women	**Faculty:** n/av
Part-time: 25men, 45women	**Ph.D.s:** n/av
Graduate: 210 men, 410 women	**Student/Faculty:** n/av
Year: semesters, summer session	**Tuition:** $16,500
Application Deadline: see profile	**Room & Board:** $6500
Freshman Class: n/av	
SAT or ACT: required	
	COMPETITIVE

Ashford University is a private liberal arts college founded in 1918. Figures in the above capsule and in this profile are approximate. The library contains 80,759 volumes, 73,405 microform items, and 2,458 audio/video tapes/CDs/DVDs, and subscribes to 645 periodicals including electronic. Computerized library services include interlibrary loans, database searching, Internet access, and laptop Internet portals. Special learning facilities include a learning resource center, art gallery, and a living lab adjacent to the campus. The 25-acre campus is in a small town 135 miles west of Chicago, Illinois. Including any residence halls, there are 6 buildings.

Student Life: 55% of undergraduates are from Iowa. Others are from 49 states, 8 foreign countries, and Canada. 62% are white; 23% African American. The average age of freshmen is 33; all undergraduates, 34.

Housing: 242 students can be accommodated in college housing, which includes single-sex and coed dorms. On-campus housing is guaranteed for all 4 years. 68% of students commute. Alcohol is not permitted. All students may keep cars.

Activities: There are no fraternities or sororities. There are 20 groups on campus, including band, choir, computers, drama, ethnic, gay, honors, international, musical theater, newspaper, professional, religious, SISEA (Iowa State Education Association), social, social service, and student government. Popular campus events include Family Weekend, Matriculation Ceremony, and Earth Day.

Sports: There are 6 intercollegiate sports for men and 6 for women, and 6 intramural sports for men and 6 for women. Facilities include an arena with 2 regulation-size basketball courts, a fitness center, a 4-lane perimeter track, and 2 locker rooms, plus 2 additional rooms and a training room. There is also a gym and a soccer field.

Disabled Students: 95% of the campus is accessible. Facilities include wheelchair ramps, elevators, special parking, specially equipped rest rooms, lowered drinking fountains, and special doors for the disabled.
Services: Counseling and information services are available, as is tutoring in most subjects. There is a reader service for the blind, and remedial math, reading, and writing. There is also voice-activated computer software, proctoring exams, and prep courses for the GRE and MCAT.
Campus Safety and Security: Measures include self defense education and security escort services. There are emergency telephones and lighted pathways/sidewalks. The campus has 24-hour security through the Clinton Police Department. On-campus security is available Sunday to Wednesday 4 p.m. to 12 a.m. and Thursday to Saturday 6 p.m. to 2 a.m.
Programs of Study: AU confers B.A., B.S., B.A.S., and B.G.S degrees. Associate and master's degrees are also awarded. Bachelor's degrees are awarded in BIOLOGICAL SCIENCE (biology/biological science), BUSINESS (accounting, business administration and management, management information systems, and sports management), COMMUNICATIONS AND THE ARTS (English, public relations, and visual and performing arts), COMPUTER AND PHYSICAL SCIENCE (computer mathematics, computer science, and natural sciences), EDUCATION (business education, elementary education, physical education, and science education), ENGINEERING AND ENVIRONMENTAL DESIGN (computer graphics), HEALTH PROFESSIONS (clinical science, cytotechnology, health care administration, health science, and nuclear medical technology), SOCIAL SCIENCE (criminal justice, environmental studies, history, psychology, social science, and sociology). Accounting, business administration, and elementary education are the strongest academically. Liberal arts, elementary education, and business administration have the largest enrollments.
Required: Students must complete 120 semester hours, including 34 semester hours of general education requirements, 12 hours of competencies (computer/writing/math), and 30 hours in a major, with a minimum 2.0 GPA; a higher GPA is required for some programs. A final exam, report, or project is required in every course.
Special: Special academic programs include a dual major in accounting and business. There are 2 national honor societies, a freshman honors program, and 1 departmental honors program.
Faculty/Classroom: All teach undergraduates. No introductory courses are taught by graduate students.
Requirements: The ACT is required and preferred, but the SAT is accepted. Applicants must be graduates of an accredited secondary school, have completed secondary-level home schooling as defined by state law, or have earned a GED. In addition, they must meet 2 of the following requirements: a GPA of 2.0 in college preparatory or regular high school courses, rank in the upper half of the graduating class, or a minimum ACT or SAT score. AP and CLEP credits are accepted.
Procedure: Freshmen are admitted to all sessions. Entrance exams should be taken before enrolling. There are deferred admissions and rolling admissions plans. Check with the school for current application deadlines and fees. Applications are accepted online.
Transfer: Applicants may have up to 99 semester hours maximum. 21 of 120 credits required for the bachelor's degree must be completed at AU.
Visiting: There are regularly scheduled orientations for prospective students, including 2-day orientation sessions held prior to the first week of classes for students and parents. There are guides for informal visits, visitors may sit in on classes, and stay overnight. To schedule a visit, contact the Admissions Office.
Financial Aid: AU is a member of CSS. The FAFSA and parents' and student's income tax forms are required. Check with the school for current deadlines.
International Students: The school actively recruits these students. They must take the TOEFL.
Admissions Contact: Director of Enrollment and Admissions. A campus DVD is available. E-mail: *admissions@ashford.edu* Web: *www.ashford.edu*

BRIAR CLIFF UNIVERSITY B-2

Sioux City, IA 51104 (712) 279-5200
(800) 662-3303; (712) 279-1632

Full-time: 417 men, 476 women	**Faculty:** 61; IIB, --$
Part-time: 54 men, 132 women	**Ph.D.s:** 75%
Graduate: 13 men, 66 women	**Student/Faculty:** 13 to 1
Year: trimesters, summer session	**Tuition:** $22,536
Application Deadline: open	**Room & Board:** $6978

Freshman Class: 1774 applied, 1035 accepted, 237 enrolled
ACT: 21

COMPETITIVE

Briar Cliff University, founded in 1930, is a private Roman Catholic-Franciscan liberal arts institution. There are 2 undergraduate schools and 1 graduate school. In addition to regional accreditation, Briar Cliff University has baccalaureate program accreditation with AACSB, CSWE, and NLN. The library contains 82,007 volumes, 21,664 microform items, and 1,244 audio/video tapes/CDs/DVDs. Computerized library services include interlibrary loans, database searching, Internet access, and Wi-Fi capability. Special learning facilities include an art gallery, radio station, TV station, an integrated multimedia center, a nursing simulation lab, a human anatomy/cadaver lab, and an entrepreneurship lab. The 70-acre campus is in a suburban area minutes from downtown Sioux City. Including any residence halls, there are 13 buildings.
Student Life: 65% of undergraduates are from Iowa. Others are from 26 states, 2 foreign countries, and Canada. 82% are from public schools. 82% are White. 55% are Catholic; 26% claim no religious affiliation; 23% Protestant. The average age of freshmen is 18; all undergraduates, 23. 34% do not continue beyond their first year; 41% remain to graduate.
Housing: 577 students can be accommodated in college housing, which includes coed dorms. In addition, there are special-interest houses. On-campus housing is guaranteed for the freshman year only. 63% of students live on campus. All students may keep cars.
Activities: There are no fraternities or sororities. There are 44 groups on campus, including art, cheerleading, choir, chorale, chorus, computers, dance, drama, ethnic, film, honors, jazz band, literary magazine, musical theater, newspaper, pep band, photography, professional, radio and TV, religious, social, social service, and student government. Popular campus events include Texas Hold 'em Tournaments, Welcome Week, and Theater Productions.
Sports: There are 9 intercollegiate sports for men and 10 for women, and 9 intramural sports for men and 9 for women. Facilities include baseball, softball, and soccer fields, and a recreation center with 2 racquetball courts, a running track, tennis courts, 2 basketball/volleyball courts, and weightlifting facilities.
Disabled Students: 90% of the campus is accessible. Facilities include wheelchair ramps, elevators, special parking, specially equipped restrooms, lowered drinking fountains, and lowered telephones.
Services: Counseling and information services are available, as is tutoring in most subjects. There is remedial math, reading, and writing.
Campus Safety and Security: Measures include 24-hour foot and vehicle patrol, emergency notification system, and security escort services. There are emergency telephones, lighted pathways/sidewalks, and controlled access to dorms/residences.
Programs of Study: Briar Cliff University confers B.A., B.S., B.S.N. and B.S.W. degrees. Associate and master's degrees are also awarded. Bachelor's degrees are awarded in BIOLOGICAL SCIENCE (biology/biological science), BUSINESS (accounting, business administration and management, and human resources), COMMUNICATIONS AND THE ARTS (art, communications, dramatic arts, English, graphic design, journalism, media arts, music, and Spanish), COMPUTER AND PHYSICAL SCIENCE (chemistry, computer science, information sciences and systems, mathematics, and radiological technology), EDUCATION (elementary education, health education, and secondary education), ENGINEERING AND ENVIRONMENTAL DESIGN (environmental science), HEALTH PROFESSIONS (medical technology, nursing, and sports medicine), SOCIAL SCIENCE (criminal justice, history, political science/government, psychology, social work, sociology, and theological studies). Biology, business administration, and education are the strongest academically. Nursing has the largest enrollment.
Required: To graduate, students must complete a minimum of 124 semester hours, maintain a GPA of 2.0 with no more than 1 D in the major, complete the three components of Briar Cliff's general educational program, and complete a major field of concentration.
Special: Internships, study abroad, dual majors, work-study programs, accelerated degree programs in business administration, human resource management, and professional studies, student-designed interdisciplinary majors, and pass/fail options are available. Students may earn a 3-2 engineering degree with Iowa State University. There are 4 national honor societies, a freshman honors program, and 3 departmental honors programs.
Faculty/Classroom: 48% of faculty are male; 52% are female. All teach undergraduates. No introductory courses are taught by graduate students. The average class size in an introductory lecture is 20; in a laboratory is 18; and in a regular course is 20.
Admissions: 58% of the 2013-2014 applicants were accepted. The ACT scores were 40% below 21, 28% between 21 and 23, 20% between 24 and 26, 9% between 27 and 28, and 3% above 28. 25% of the current freshmen were in the top fifth of their class; 50% were in the top two fifths. 2 freshmen graduated first in their class.
Requirements: The ACT is required. SAT is accepted but the ACT is preferred, and a score of 18 qualifies for automatic acceptance review. Applicants need not be graduates of an accredited secondary school. The GED is accepted. Admission to freshman standing requires 4 years each of English and math, 3 of science, 2 of history, and 1 of social studies. Two years of foreign language is recommended A GPA of 2.0 is required. AP and CLEP credits are accepted. Important factors in the admissions decision are leadership record, extracurricular activities record, and advanced placement or honors courses.

Procedure: Freshmen are admitted to all sessions. Entrance exams should be taken by October for scholarship consideration, and by April for admission. There is a rolling admissions plan. Application deadlines are open. Application fee is $20. Notification is sent on a rolling basis. Applications are accepted online.

Transfer: 37 transfer students enrolled in 2012-2013. Applicants must have a minimum GPA of 2.0 with at least 10 credit hours earned and satisfactory dismissal from the previous institution. Grades of D or better transfer for credit. 31 of 124 credits required for the bachelor's degree must be completed at Briar Cliff University.

Visiting: There are regularly scheduled orientations for prospective students, including a presidential welcome, a meeting with faculty and student panels, a luncheon, campus tours, a slide show, and financial aid information. There are guides for informal visits, visitors may sit in on classes, and stay overnight. To schedule a visit, contact the Admissions Office.

Financial Aid: In 2013-2014, 100% of all full-time freshmen and 98% of continuing full-time students received some form of financial aid. 73% of all full-time freshmen and 64% of continuing full-time students received need-based aid. The average freshman award was $12,250. Need-based scholarships or need-based grants averaged $3,900; need-based self-help aid (loans and jobs) averaged $7,255, and non need-based athletic scholarships averaged $5,109. 23% of undergraduate students work part-time. Average annual earnings from campus work are $750. The average financial indebtedness of the 2013 graduate was $30,100. The FAFSA is required. The priority date for freshman financial aid applications for fall entry is March 1.

International Students: There are 6 international students enrolled. They must take the TOEFL or MELAB. Students may be required to have a telephone interview with an ESL advisor.

Graduates: From July 1, 2012 to June 30, 2013, 204 bachelor's degrees were awarded. The most popular majors were business/ marketing (33%), health professions and related sciences (11%), and biological/ life sciences (8%). 46 companies recruited on campus in 2012-2013. In an average class, 43% graduate in 4 years or less, 53% graduate in 5 years or less, and 55% graduate in 6 years or less. Of the 2012 graduating class, 37% were enrolled in graduate school within 6 months of graduation.

Admissions Contact: Sharisue Wilcoxon, Vice President/Enrollment Management. E-Mail: *Sharisue.Wilcoxon@briarcliff.edu* Web: *www.briarcliff.edu*

BUENA VISTA UNIVERSITY B-2

Storm Lake, IA 50588 **(712) 749-2235**
(800) 383-9600; (712) 749-2035

Full-time: 429 men, 470 women	**Faculty:** 84; IIB, -$
Part-time: 18 men, 3 women	**Ph.D.s:** 83%
Graduate: 11 men, 64 women	**Student/Faculty:** 11 to 1
Year: 4-1-4, summer session	**Tuition:** $29,448
Application Deadline: open	**Room & Board:** $8506

Freshman Class: 1409 applied, 980 accepted, 269 enrolled
ACT: 23

COMPETITIVE

Buena Vista University, founded in 1891, is a private institution affiliated with the Presbyterian Church. The university offers undergraduate degree programs in business, education, communication and arts, science, social science, philosophy, and religion, and an accredited master's program in education. Programs emphasize career education with a liberal arts foundation. There are 5 undergraduate schools and 1 graduate school. In addition to regional accreditation, Buena Vista has baccalaureate program accreditation with CSWE. The library contains 5,000 volumes, 41,372 microform items, and 6,000 audio/video tapes/CDs/DVDs, and subscribes to 639 periodicals including electronic. Computerized library services include interlibrary loans, database searching, Internet access, and Wi-Fi capability. Special learning facilities include an art gallery, radio station, TV station, a student newspaper desktop production lab. The 60-acre campus is in a small town 65 miles east of Sioux City. Including any residence halls, there are 16 buildings.

Student Life: 80% of undergraduates are from Iowa. Others are from 26 states, and 11 foreign countries. 92% are from public schools. 75% are White. 43% are Protestant; 29% Catholic; 18% claim no religious affiliation. The average age of freshmen is 18; all undergraduates, 20. 28% do not continue beyond their first year.

Housing: 1012 students can be accommodated in college housing, which includes single-sex and coed dorms. In addition, there are honors houses and special-interest houses. On-campus housing is guaranteed for all 4 years. 87% of students live on campus; of those, 60% remain on campus on weekends. All students may keep cars.

Activities: There are no fraternities or sororities. There are 60 groups on campus, including art, band, cheerleading, choir, chorale, chorus, communications, computers, dance, debate, drama, drill team, environmental, ethnic, gay, gender, honors, international, jazz band, musical theater, newspaper, pep band, photography, political, professional, radio and TV, religious, social, social service, and student government. Popular campus events include Academic and Cultural Events Series, Buenafication Day, American Heritage Lecture Series, and Scholars Day.

Sports: There are 9 intercollegiate sports for men and 8 for women, and 10 intramural sports for men and 10 for women. Facilities include a 380-seat auditorium, a 1000-seat auditorium, a 4000-seat stadium, a field house with a 4000-seat gym, basketball, volleyball, racquetball, and tennis courts, football, softball, and baseball fields, a track, facilities for weight training and other recreational activities, an Olympic-size indoor pool, and a game room.

Services: Counseling and information services are available, as is tutoring in most subjects. There is a reader service for the blind, and remedial math, reading, and writing.

Campus Safety and Security: Measures include 24-hour foot and vehicle patrol, emergency notification system, self-defense education, and security escort services. There are shuttle buses, emergency telephones, lighted pathways/sidewalks, controlled access to dorms/residences, and an enhanced 911 system on campus.

Programs of Study: Buena Vista confers B.A., B.S. and B.A.S degrees. Master's degrees are also awarded. Bachelor's degrees are awarded in BIOLOGICAL SCIENCE (biology/biological science), BUSINESS (accounting, banking and finance, business administration and management, business economics, international business management, marketing/retailing/merchandising, and sports management), COMMUNICATIONS AND THE ARTS (art, arts administration/management, communications, English, graphic design, music, Spanish, and speech/debate/rhetoric), COMPUTER AND PHYSICAL SCIENCE (chemistry, computer science, mathematics, physics, and science), EDUCATION (art education, business education, elementary education, music education, science education, secondary education, and special education), ENGINEERING AND ENVIRONMENTAL DESIGN (environmental science), SOCIAL SCIENCE (criminal justice, economics, history, philosophy, physical fitness/movement, political science/government, psychology, public administration, religion, social science, and social work). Biology, mathematics, business are the strongest academically. Biology, education, management have the largest enrollments.

Required: All students must complete 9 semester hours each of natural sciences, humanities, social sciences, and 3 semester hours of fine arts. In addition, students must successfully complete requirements in intellectual foundation courses in mathematics, communication and technology skills. Students must also participate in the Academic and Cultural Events Series, through which they attend lectures and performances by national and world leaders. The bachelor's degree requires a minimum of 128 semester hours, including 32 to 64 hours in the major, with a GPA of at least 2.0, or higher for some majors.

Special: Special academic offerings include 3-2 engineering degree program with Washington University in St. Louis. Students may study abroad in Japan, Taiwan, Australia, and Europe. Buena Vista offers dual and student-designed majors, credit for life experience, and pass/fail options in courses outside the major field. Nondegree study is possible. Internships are required in many majors and encouraged in most. The J. Leslie Rollins Fellowship allows 1 or 2 students each year to design an internship anywhere in the world. There are 5 national honor societies and a freshman honors program.

Faculty/Classroom: 46% of faculty are male; 54% are female. All teach undergraduates. No introductory courses are taught by graduate students. The average class size in an introductory lecture is 25; in a laboratory is 20; and in a regular course is 14.

Admissions: 70% of the 2013-2014 applicants were accepted. The ACT scores were 35% below 21, 29% between 21 and 23, 21% between 24 and 26, 7% between 27 and 28, and 8% above 28. 33% of the current freshmen were in the top fifth of their class; 58% were in the top two fifths. 11 freshmen graduated first in their class.

Requirements: The ACT is required. SAT scores may be submitted instead. Applicants must be graduates of an accredited secondary school or have earned a GED. The college requires 13 academic credits, including 4 of English and 3 each of math, social studies, and science. Campus visits and an interview are recommended. AP and CLEP credits are accepted. Important factors in the admissions decision are advanced placement or honors courses, leadership record, and recommendations by school officials.

Procedure: Freshmen are admitted fall, winter, and spring. Entrance exams should be taken during the spring of the junior year or October of the senior year. There are deferred admissions and rolling admissions plans. Application deadlines are open. Notification is sent on a rolling basis. Applications are accepted online.

Transfer: 75 transfer students enrolled in 2012-2013. A high school diploma and a minimum GPA of 2.5 from the applicant's college are required. 30 of 128 credits required for the bachelor's degree must be completed at Buena Vista.

Visiting: There are regularly scheduled orientations for prospective students, including a campus tour and meetings with an admissions counselor, faculty representatives, coaches, and activity representatives in the student's areas of interest. There are guides for informal visits, visitors may sit in on classes, and stay overnight. To schedule a visit, contact Bridget Kurkowski at (712) 749-2078.

Financial Aid: In 2013-2014, 99% of all full-time freshmen and 98% of continuing full-time students received some form of financial aid. The FAFSA and the college's own financial statement are required. The deadline for filing freshman financial aid applications for fall entry is June 1.

International Students: There are 51 international students enrolled. The school actively recruits these students. They must take the TOEFL with a minimum score of 500 on the paper-based TOEFL (PBT) or 59 on the Internet-based version (iBT) and the college's own test,.

Graduates: From July 1, 2012 to June 30, 2013, 199 bachelor's degrees were awarded. The most popular majors were biology (15%), elementary education (10%), and management (9%). 40 companies recruited on campus in 2012-2013.

Admissions Contact: Bridget Kurkowski, Director of Admissions. E-Mail: *admissions@bvu.edu* Web: *www.bvu.edu*

CENTRAL COLLEGE D-3

Pella, IA 50219 (641) 628-7637
(877) 462-3687; (641) 628-5316

Full-time: 721 men, 846 women	**Faculty:** 88; IIB, --$
Part-time: 19 men, 18 women	**Ph.D.s:** 88%
Graduate: n/av	**Student/Faculty:** 17 to 1
Year: semesters, summer session	**Tuition:** $28,344
Application Deadline: March 1	**Room & Board:** $9636
Freshman Class: 2633 applied, 1926 accepted, 412 enrolled	
SAT: required	**ACT:** 24 **VERY COMPETITIVE**

Central College, founded in 1853, is a private, residential, liberal arts institution affiliated with the Reformed Church in America. The college offers undergraduate degree programs in applied arts, behavioral sciences, cross-cultural studies, fine arts, humanities, and natural sciences. There is 1 undergraduate school. In addition to regional accreditation, Central Dutch has baccalaureate program accreditation with NASM and NCATE. The 3 libraries contain 197,672 volumes, 51,906 microform items, and 10,986 audio/video tapes/CDs/DVDs, and subscribe to 11,206 periodicals including electronic. Computerized library services include interlibrary loans, database searching, Internet access, and laptop Internet portals. Special learning facilities include a learning resource center and art gallery. The 169-acre campus is in a small town 45 miles southeast of Des Moines, Iowa. Including any residence halls, there are 50 buildings. The figures in the above capsule and in this profile are approximate.

Student Life: 83% of undergraduates are from Iowa. Others are from 32 states, 14 foreign countries, and Canada. 96% are from public schools. 88% are white. 56% are Protestant; 26% Unknown; 15% Catholic. The average age of freshmen is 18; all undergraduates, 20. 21% do not continue beyond their first year; 63% remain to graduate.

Housing: 1408 students can be accommodated in college housing, which includes single-sex and coed dorms and on-campus apartments. In addition, there are language houses, special-interest houses, fraternity houses, and sorority houses. On-campus housing is guaranteed for all 4 years. 93% of students live on campus; of those, 70% remain on campus on weekends. Alcohol is not permitted. All students may keep cars.

Activities: 3% of men belong to 5 local fraternities; 3% of women belong to 3 local sororities. There are 80 groups on campus, including art, band, cheerleading, choir, chorus, drama, drill team, environmental, ethnic, gay, honors, international, jazz band, literary magazine, musical theater, newspaper, orchestra, pep band, photography, political, professional, religious, social, social service, student government, and students concerned about the environment (Habitat for Humanity). Popular campus events include Charity Ball, Lemming Race, and Service Day.

Sports: There are 10 intercollegiate sports for men and 9 for women, and 11 intramural sports for men and 11 for women. Facilities include A field-house with indoor track, tennis, and basketball court surface, state-of-the-art fitness center, a football/track stadium, a competition soccer field, a golf range, a cross country course, and a gym.

Disabled Students: 90% of the campus is accessible. Facilities include wheelchair ramps, elevators, special parking, specially equipped restrooms, special class scheduling, lowered drinking fountains, lowered telephones, and special housing.

Services: Counseling and information services are available, as is tutoring in every subject.

Campus Safety and Security: Measures include 24-hour foot and vehicle patrol, emergency notification system, self-defense education, and security escort services. There are emergency telephones, lighted pathways/sidewalks, and controlled access to dorms/residences.

Programs of Study: Central Dutch confers B.A. degrees. Bachelor's degrees are awarded in BIOLOGICAL SCIENCE (biochemistry and biology/biological science), BUSINESS (accounting, business administration and management, and international business management), COMMUNICATIONS AND THE ARTS (art, communications, dramatic arts, English, French, German, linguistics, music, and Spanish), COMPUTER AND PHYSICAL SCIENCE (actuarial science, chemistry, computer science, mathematics, natural sciences, and physics), EDUCATION (athletic training, elementary education, and music education), ENGINEERING AND ENVIRONMENTAL DESIGN (environmental science), HEALTH PROFESSIONS (exercise science), SOCIAL SCIENCE (anthropology, economics, history, international studies, philosophy, political science/government, psychology, religion, and sociology). Exercise science, business management, and biology have the largest enrollments.

Required: Students are required to complete 120 semester hours, including at least 20 hours of 300-level or above, with a minimum 2.0 cumulative and major GPA. Core requirements include courses in integrative studies, disciplinary studies, global sustainability, global perspective, and writing intensive.

Special: Nearly half the students participate in study abroad programs in London, Paris, Vienna, Mexico, Spain, Wales, China and the Netherlands. Central also offers a Washington, D.C. semester, a Chicago program, and numerous internship opportunities. General studies and individualized interdisciplinary majors are also available. There is a freshman honors program.

Faculty/Classroom: 56% of faculty are male; 44% are female. All teach and do research. No introductory courses are taught by graduate students. The average class size in an introductory lecture is 18; in a laboratory is 17; and in a regular course is 18.

Admissions: 73% of the 2011-2012 applicants were accepted. The ACT scores were 18% below 21, 34% between 21 and 23, 25% between 24 and 26, 11% between 27 and 28, and 12% above 28. 53% of the current freshmen were in the top fifth of their class; 85% were in the top two fifths. 25 freshmen graduated first in their class.

Requirements: The SAT or ACT is required. All applicants must be graduates of an accredited secondary school or have earned a GED. Candidates who have an ACT composite score of 20 or above (940-970 SAT critical reading and mathematics combined), have a 2.70 cumulative high school GPA, rank in the top half of their secondary school graduating class and have met the recommended college-preparatory curriculum are typically admitted. Central requires applicants to be in the upper 50% of their class. A GPA of 2.7 is required. AP and CLEP credits are accepted. Important factors in the admissions decision are advanced placement or honors courses, extracurricular activities record, and parents or siblings attended your school.

Procedure: Freshmen are admitted fall, spring, and summer. Entrance exams should be taken Spring junior year of high school. There are deferred admissions and rolling admissions plans. Applications should be filed by March 1 for fall entry; November 1 for spring entry; and May 1 for summer entry, along with a $25 fee. Notification is sent on a rolling basis. Applications are accepted online.

Transfer: 86 transfer students enrolled in 2010-2011. Each transfer student is considered individually. Interviews are encouraged. 45 of 120 credits required for the bachelor's degree must be completed at Central.

Visiting: There are regularly scheduled orientations for prospective students, A registration session with academic an advisor, and presentations by the academic dean, student life dean, financial aid director, registrar and admissions staff. There are guides for informal visits, visitors may sit in on classes, and stay overnight. To schedule a visit, contact the Admissions Office.

Financial Aid: In 2011-2012, 89% of all full-time freshmen and 82% of continuing full-time students received some form of financial aid. 89% of all full-time freshmen and 82% of continuing full-time students received need-based aid. The average freshman award was $23,302. Need-based scholarships or need-based grants averaged $17,824; need-based self-help aid (loans and jobs) averaged $5,273; and other non-need-based awards and non-need-based scholarships averaged $12,169. 63% of undergraduate students work part-time. Average annual earnings from campus work are $722. The average financial indebtedness of the 2011 graduate was $15,811. Central is a member of CSS. The FAFSA is required. The priority date for freshman financial aid applications for fall entry is March 15.

International Students: There are 17 international students enrolled. They must take the TOEFL with a minimum score of 530 on the paper-based TOEFL (PBT) or 71 on the Internet-based version (iBT). They must also take the SAT or ACT.

Graduates: From July 1, 2010 to June 30, 2011, 344 bachelor's degrees were awarded. The most popular majors were business management (17%), exercise science (13%), and biology (8%). 12 companies recruited on campus in 2010-2011. In an average class, 58% graduate in 4 years or less, 63% graduate in 5 years or less, and 63% graduate in 6 years or less. Of the 2010 graduating class, 24% were enrolled in graduate school within 6 months of graduation, and 63% were employed.

Admissions Contact: Chevy Frieburger, Director of Admissions. E-Mail: *admissions@central.edu* Web: *www.central.edu*

CLARKE UNIVERSITY E-2

Dubuque, IA 52001 (563) 588-6436
(800) 383-2345; (563) 588-6789

Full-time: 274 men, 555 women	**Faculty:** 84
Part-time: 50 men, 88 women	**Ph.D.s:** 69%
Graduate: 61 men, 163 women	**Student/Faculty:** 11 to 1
Year: semesters, summer session	**Tuition:** $28,000
Application Deadline: open	**Room & Board:** $8400
Freshman Class: 1249 applied, 969 accepted, 176 enrolled	
SAT CR/M: 473/506 **ACT:** 23	**COMPETITIVE**

Clarke University, established in 1843, is a private Catholic institution. A strong liberal arts core is integrated into all majors and pre-professional programs. In addition to regional accreditation, Clarke has baccalaureate program accreditation with APTA, CSWE, NASM, NCATE, and NLN. The library contains 102,000 volumes, 7,800 microform items, and 1,700 audio/video tapes/CDs/DVDs, and subscribes to 48,152 periodicals including electronic. Computerized library services include interlibrary loans, database searching, Internet access, and Wi-Fi capability. Special learning facilities include an art gallery, planetarium, an art slide library, electronic music studio, and several computer-integrated specialized departmental labs. The 55-acre campus is in a small town 150 miles west of Chicago. Including any residence halls, there are 14 buildings.

Student Life: 62% of undergraduates are from Iowa. Others are from 28 states, and 9 foreign countries. 80% are from public schools. 88% are White. 51% are Catholic; 30% claim no religious affiliation; 12% Protestant. The average age of freshmen is 18; all undergraduates, 24. 24% do not continue beyond their first year; 70% remain to graduate.

Housing: 577 students can be accommodated in college housing, which includes single-sex and coed dorms and on-campus apartments. a residence hall reserved for upperclassmen, and an apartment residence building reserved for juniors and seniors. On-campus housing is guaranteed for all 4 years. 60% of students live on campus; of those, 33% remain on campus on weekends. All students may keep cars.

Activities: There are no fraternities or sororities. There are 50 groups on campus, including art, cheerleading, choir, chorus, computers, drama, environmental, ethnic, gay, honors, international, jazz band, literary magazine, newspaper, pep band, photography, political, professional, religious, social, social service, and student government. Popular campus events include Family Weekend, New Year's Dance and Midnight Pancake Breakfast.

Sports: There are 8 intercollegiate sports for men and 8 for women, and 15 intramural sports for men and 13 for women. Facilities include a 1000-seat gym, a 700-seat arena, an indoor track, a soccer field, basketball, volleyball, tennis, and racquetball courts, a fitness trail, weight and aerobics rooms, and an indoor batting cage/pitching mound area. There are baseball/softball fields and 2 alpine ski courses nearby, plus a municipal golf course adjacent to the campus.

Disabled Students: 90% of the campus is accessible. Facilities include wheelchair ramps, elevators, special parking, specially equipped restrooms, special class scheduling, lowered drinking fountains, and lowered telephones.

Services: Counseling and information services are available, as is tutoring in most subjects. There is remedial math, reading, and writing.

Campus Safety and Security: Measures include 24-hour foot and vehicle patrol, emergency notification system, and security escort services. There are emergency telephones, lighted pathways/sidewalks, and controlled access to dorms/residences.

Programs of Study: Clarke confers B.A., B.S., B.A.S., B.F.A. and B.S.N. degrees. Associate, master's, and doctoral degrees are also awarded. Bachelor's degrees are awarded in BIOLOGICAL SCIENCE (biochemistry, bioinformatics, and biology/biological science), BUSINESS (accounting, business administration and management, marketing management, and sports management), COMMUNICATIONS AND THE ARTS (advertising, art, art history and appreciation, communications, dramatic arts, English, music, musical theater, Spanish, and studio art), COMPUTER AND PHYSICAL SCIENCE (chemistry, computer science, computer security and information assurance, information sciences and systems, and mathematics), EDUCATION (art education, athletic training, elementary education, music education, secondary education, and special education), HEALTH PROFESSIONS (nursing and physical therapy), SOCIAL SCIENCE (criminology, history, liberal arts/general studies, philosophy, physical fitness/movement, political science/government, psychology, religion, social work, and sociology). Physical therapy, biology, chemistry and math are the strongest academically. Business administration, nursing and education have the largest enrollments.

Required: To graduate, all students must complete 124 semester hours, with 30 to 70 in the major, and maintain a GPA of 2.0 (2.5 for education majors or 3.25 for physical therapy majors). Students must complete Cornerstone I and II, a Capstone course, and 6 hours each in religious studies, philosophy, fine arts, humanities, math, natural sciences, and social sciences

Special: There are 4 national honor societies, a freshman honors program, and 3 departmental honors programs.

Faculty/Classroom: 34% of faculty are male; 66% are female. All teach and do research. No introductory courses are taught by graduate students. The average class size in an introductory lecture is 24; in a laboratory is 11; and in a regular course is 14.

Admissions: 78% of the 2013-2014 applicants were accepted. The SAT scores for the 2013-2014 freshman class were: Critical Reading--75% below 500; Math--37% below 500, 63% between 500 and 599. The ACT scores were 24% below 21, 23% between 21 and 23, 23% between 24 and 26, 10% between 27 and 28, and 8% above 28. 34% of the current freshmen were in the top fifth of their class; 71% were in the top two fifths.

Requirements: The SAT or ACT is required. The high school transcript should include 4 years of English, 3 each of math, history/social science, and science (4 for human biology and physical therapy majors), 2 of the same foreign language, and 5 of electives. A GPA of 2.0 is required. AP and CLEP credits are accepted. Important factors in the admissions decision are advanced placement or honors courses.

Procedure: Freshmen are admitted to all sessions. Entrance exams should be taken in the spring of the junior year or the fall of the senior year. There are deferred admissions and rolling admissions plans. Application deadlines are open. Application fee is $25. Applications are accepted online.

Transfer: 106 transfer students enrolled in 2012-2013. Applicants must submit a transcript and a recommendation from the dean of students for each college attended. Students with fewer than 24 completed semester hours must also submit a high school transcript and SAT or ACT scores. 30 of 124 credits required for the bachelor's degree must be completed at Clarke.

Visiting: There are guides for informal visits, visitors may sit in on classes, and stay overnight. To schedule a visit, contact the Admissions Office.

Financial Aid: In 2013-2014, 87% of all full-time freshmen and 67% of continuing full-time students received some form of financial aid. 87% of all full-time freshmen and 67% of continuing full-time students received need-based aid. The average freshman award was $23,314. Need-based scholarships or need-based grants averaged $13,168; need-based self-help aid (loans and jobs) averaged $5,220; non-need-based athletic scholarships averaged $6,833; and other non-need-based awards and non-need-based scholarships averaged $15,913. 25% of undergraduate students work part-time. Average annual earnings from campus work are $919. The average financial indebtedness of the 2013 graduate was $30,793. The FAFSA is required. The priority date for freshman financial aid applications for fall entry is April 15. The deadline for filing freshman financial aid applications for fall entry is rolling.

International Students: There are 7 international students enrolled. The school actively recruits these students. They must take the TOEFL with a minimum score of 527 on the paper-based TOEFL (PBT) or 71 on the Internet-based version (iBT). They must also take the SAT or ACT, scoring 1000.

Graduates: From July 1, 2012 to June 30, 2013, 218 bachelor's degrees were awarded. The most popular majors were nursing (24%), business administration (13%), and education (11%). 50 companies recruited on campus in 2012-2013. In an average class, 48% graduate in 4 years or less, 66% graduate in 5 years or less, and 70% graduate in 6 years or less. Of the 2012 graduating class, 22% were enrolled in graduate school within 6 months of graduation, and 68% were employed.

Admissions Contact: Emily Kruse, Assistant Director of Admissions. E-Mail: *Emily.kruse@clarke.edu* Web: *www.clarke.edu*

COE COLLEGE E-3

Cedar Rapids, IA 52402 (319) 399-8046
(877) CALL-COE; (319) 399-8816

Full-time: 620 men, 731 women	**Faculty:** 93; IIB, -$
Part-time: 31 men, 38 women	**Ph.D.s:** 89%
Graduate: n/av	**Student/Faculty:** 11 to 1
Year: semesters, summer session	**Tuition:** $35,730
Application Deadline: March 1	**Room & Board:** $7860
Freshman Class: 2972 applied, 1834 accepted, 389 enrolled	
SAT CR/M/W: 597/583/560 **ACT:** 25	**VERY COMPETITIVE**

Coe College offers superb academics and exciting social opportunities in a thriving urban setting that allows students to grow and succeed. With a residential campus established in 1851, Coe has a distinctive reputation for quality. In addition to regional accreditation, Coe has baccalaureate program accreditation with NASM. The library contains 46,339 volumes, 5,979 microform items, and 11,566 audio/video tapes/CDs/DVDs, and subscribes to 3,479 periodicals including electronic. Computerized library services include interlibrary loans, database searching, and Internet access. Special learning facilities include an art gallery, radio station, an ornithological wing. The 53-acre campus is in an urban area In the heart of the Cedar Rapids community, miles away from major interstate and regional airport, 225 miles west of Chicago and other major midwest cities. Including any residence halls, there are 32 buildings.

Student Life: 51% of undergraduates are from Iowa. Others are from 40

states, 21 foreign countries, and Canada. 76% are White. The average age of freshmen is 18; all undergraduates, 20. 21% do not continue beyond their first year; 67% remain to graduate.

Housing: 1150 students can be accommodated in college housing, which includes single-sex and coed dorms and on-campus apartments. In addition, there are special-interest houses, a substance-free facility. On-campus housing is guaranteed for all 4 years. 84% of students live on campus; of those, 75% remain on campus on weekends. All students may keep cars.

Activities: 12% of men belong to 5 national fraternities; 13% of women belong to 3 national sororities. There are 80 groups on campus, including Student Activities Committee, Student Alumni Association, Student-Athletic Advisory Committee, art, band, cheerleading, choir, chorale, chorus, communications, computers, dance, drama, environmental, ethnic, film, gay, honors, international, jazz band, literary magazine, musical theater, newspaper, orchestra, pep band, photography, political, professional, radio and TV, religious, social, social service, student government, Student Senate, symphony, and yearbook. Popular campus events include Coe Olympics, International Student Banquet and Cultural Show, Flunk Day, and Prez Ball.

Sports: There are 11 intercollegiate sports for men and 10 for women. Facilities include a racquet center with 4 indoor and 6 outdoor tennis courts, 4 racquetball courts, 2 squash courts, and a 200-meter indoor track and a field house with an indoor natatorium, a wrestling room, a fitness center, a rock-climbing wall, courts for basketball and volleyball, and batting cages for baseball and softball. There also are a 400-meter outdoor track, softball diamond, and 2000-seat football/soccer stadium, baseball field and soccer practice field.

Disabled Students: 80% of the campus is accessible. Facilities include wheelchair ramps, elevators, special parking, specially equipped restrooms, special class scheduling, lowered drinking fountains, lowered telephones, and special housing.

Services: Counseling and information services are available, as is tutoring in most subjects. There is a reader service for the blind, and remedial math and reading. A writing center and an academic achievement program are available.

Campus Safety and Security: Measures include 24-hour foot and vehicle patrol, emergency notification system, and security escort services. There are emergency telephones, lighted pathways/sidewalks, and controlled access to dorms/residences.

Programs of Study: Coe confers B.A., B.M. and B.S.N. degrees. Bachelor's degrees are awarded in AGRICULTURE (environmental studies), BIOLOGICAL SCIENCE (biochemistry, biology/biological science, molecular biology, and neurosciences), BUSINESS (accounting, business administration and management, and organizational behavior), COMMUNICATIONS AND THE ARTS (art, art history and appreciation, communications, creative writing, English, film arts, French, German, literature, music, public relations, Spanish, theatre arts, and writing), COMPUTER AND PHYSICAL SCIENCE (chemistry, computer science, mathematics, physics, and science), EDUCATION (athletic training, elementary education, music education, physical education, and secondary education), ENGINEERING AND ENVIRONMENTAL DESIGN (environmental science and preengineering), HEALTH PROFESSIONS (nursing, physical therapy, predentistry, premedicine, prephysical therapy, and preveterinary science), SOCIAL SCIENCE (African American studies, American studies, Asian/Oriental studies, economics, French studies, gender studies, German area studies, history, human services, industrial and organizational psychology, interdisciplinary studies, philosophy, political science/government, prelaw, psychology, religion, sociology, Spanish studies, and women's studies). Chemistry, physics, and psychology are the strongest academically. Business administration and biology have the largest enrollments.

Required: All students must take 5 writing-emphasis courses, a first-year seminar, and a distribution of courses in fine arts, humanities, natural sciences and mathematics, social sciences, and diverse cultural perspectives. A minimum of 32 course credits, including 9 to 12 in the major, and a 2.0 GPA are required for graduation. All students are required to do a practicum experience including an internship, independent research project, or off-campus study program. Students in the honors program must submit a thesis.

Special: Coe offers cross-registration with nearby Mount Mercy College and the University of Iowa. 31 Off-campus programs are offered; 8 domestic and 23 international in 19 countries. Nondegree study, dual majors and student-designed majors also are possible. Practicum experience is required for graduation. Core course instructors serve as students' academic advisors. There are 8 national honor societies, including Phi Beta Kappa, and a freshman honors program.

Faculty/Classroom: 60% of faculty are male; 40% are female. All teach undergraduates, and 95% do both. No introductory courses are taught by graduate students. The average class size in an introductory lecture is 13; in a laboratory is 14; and in a regular course is 16.

Admissions: 62% of the 2013-2014 applicants were accepted. The SAT scores for the 2013-2014 freshman class were: Critical Reading--21% below 500, 30% between 500 and 599, 27% between 600 and 699, and 24% between 700 and 800; Math--27% below 500, 27% between 500 and 599, 33% between 600 and 699, and 12% between 700 and 800; Writing--42% below 500, 16% between 500 and 599, 26% between 600 and 699, and 16% between 700 and 800. The ACT scores were 17% below 21, 18% between 21 and 23, 29% between 24 and 26, 16% between 27 and 28, and 20% above 28. 49% of the current freshmen were in the top fifth of their class; 82% were in the top two fifths. 23 freshmen graduated first in their class.

Requirements: The SAT or ACT is required. Coe recommends that applicants have 4 years in English, 3 each in math, history, science, and social studies, and 2 in foreign language. All students must submit an essay. Coe requires ACT or SAT scores for admittance. The GED is accepted. A GPA of 3.0 is required. AP and CLEP credits are accepted. Important factors in the admissions decision are advanced placement or honors courses, recommendations by school officials, and extracurricular activities record.

Procedure: Freshmen are admitted fall and spring. Entrance exams should be taken in the spring of the junior year or the fall of the senior year. There are deferred admissions and rolling admissions plans. Applications should be filed by March 1 for fall entry, along with a $30 fee. Notification is sent on a rolling basis. Applications are accepted online.

Transfer: 29 transfer students enrolled in 2012-2013. Applicants must be high school graduates, have a minimum GPA of 2.5, and submit either SAT or ACT scores. An associate degree and an interview also are recommended. 8 of 32 credits required for the bachelor's degree must be completed at Coe.

Visiting: There are regularly scheduled orientations for prospective students, consisting of tours, a luncheon, and informational sessions on admission, financial aid, and student life. There are guides for informal visits, visitors may sit in on classes, and stay overnight. To schedule a visit, contact Sharon Fair at (319) 399-8500.

Financial Aid: In 2013-2014, 98% of all full-time freshmen and 99% of continuing full-time students received some form of financial aid. 87% of all full-time freshmen and 81% of continuing full-time students received need-based aid. The average freshman award was $32,350. 46% of undergraduate students work part-time. Average annual earnings from campus work are $1132. The average financial indebtedness of the 2013 graduate was $31,084. The FAFSA is required. The priority date for freshman financial aid applications for fall entry is March 1.

International Students: There are 35 international students enrolled. The school actively recruits these students. They must take the TOEFL with a minimum score of 520 on the paper-based TOEFL (PBT) or 68 on the Internet-based version (iBT), IELTS. They must also take the SAT or ACT, scoring 20 or 940 MV.

Graduates: From July 1, 2012 to June 30, 2013, 298 bachelor's degrees were awarded. The most popular majors were business administration (22%), psychology (12%), and health professions (9%). In an average class, 61% graduate in 4 years or less, 69% graduate in 5 years or less, and 70% graduate in 6 years or less. Of the 2012 graduating class, 28% were enrolled in graduate school within 6 months of graduation, and 70% were employed.

Admissions Contact: Julie Staker, Dean of Admission. E-Mail: *jstaker@coe.edu* Web: *www.coe.edu*

CORNELL COLLEGE — E-4

Mount Vernon, IA 52314 — (319) 895-4215; (800) 747-1112; (319) 895-4451

Full-time: 502 men, 612 women	**Faculty:** 89; IIB, -$
Part-time: 3 men, 5 women	**Ph.D.s:** 96%
Graduate: n/av	**Student/Faculty:** 13 to 1
Year: other, summer session	**Tuition:** $36,430
Application Deadline: March 1	**Room & Board:** $8500
Freshman Class: 2498 applied, 1471 accepted, 270 enrolled	
SAT CR/M/W: 610/570/580 **ACT:** 26	**HIGHLY COMPETITIVE**

Cornell College, founded in 1853, is private institution affiliated with the United Methodist Church. Its emphases are on the liberal arts and on student service and leadership. Cornell has a one-course-at-a-time calendar in which the year is divided into eight 3 1/2 week terms. The library contains 232,914 volumes, 69,348 microform items, and 9,467 audio/video tapes/CDs/DVDs, and subscribes to 491 periodicals including electronic. Computerized library services include interlibrary loans, database searching, Internet access, and Wi-Fi capability. Special learning facilities include an art gallery, natural history museum, and radio station. The 129-acre campus is in a small town 15 miles east of Cedar Rapids and 3 hours west of Chicago. Including any residence halls, there are 44 buildings.

Student Life: 83% of undergraduates are from out of state, mostly the Mid-West. Students are from 46 states, and 17 foreign countries. 68% are from public schools. 65% are White; 13% Hispanic. The average age of freshmen is 18; all undergraduates, 20. 17% do not continue beyond their first year; 66% remain to graduate.

Housing: 1124 students can be accommodated in college housing, which

includes single-sex and coed dorms and on-campus apartments. In addition, there are special-interest houses, living and learning communities and connect floors. On-campus housing is guaranteed for all 4 years, is available on a first-come, first-served basis, and is available on a lottery system for upperclassmen. 91% of students live on campus; of those, 66% remain on campus on weekends. All students may keep cars.

Activities: 16% of men belong to 8 local fraternities; 22% of women belong to 8 local sororities. There are 175 groups on campus, including mock trial, performing arts, steel drum band., art, band, cheerleading, chess, choir, chorale, chorus, communications, computers, dance, debate, drama, environmental, ethnic, gay, honors, international, jazz band, leadership development, literary magazine, musical theater, newspaper, opera, orchestra, pep band, photography, political, professional, radio and TV, religious, social, social service, student government, and yearbook. Popular campus events include Knock Your Block Off and Music Mondays.

Sports: There are 8 intercollegiate sports for men and 7 for women, and 12 intramural sports for men and 12 for women. Facilities include a multisport center, including a 2000-seat basketball and volleyball arena, sports fitness and training facilities, 200 meter indoor track, a wrestling room, 4 multipurpose courts for tennis, basketball, and volleyball, batting cages, golf hitting nets; a 2500-seat football and track stadium; and baseball, soccer, softball, and football practice fields and 6 outdoor tennis courts.

Disabled Students: 50% of the campus is accessible. Facilities include wheelchair ramps, elevators, special parking, specially equipped restrooms, special class scheduling, lowered drinking fountains, and lowered telephones.

Services: Counseling and information services are available, as is tutoring in most subjects.

Campus Safety and Security: Measures include 24-hour foot and vehicle patrol, emergency notification system, self-defense education, and security escort services. There are emergency telephones and lighted pathways/sidewalks.

Programs of Study: Cornell confers B.A., B.Mus. and B.S.S. degrees. Bachelor's degrees are awarded in BIOLOGICAL SCIENCE (biochemistry and biology/biological science), BUSINESS (business economics), COMMUNICATIONS AND THE ARTS (art history and appreciation, dramatic arts, English, fine arts, French, German, languages, music, Russian, Spanish, and studio art), COMPUTER AND PHYSICAL SCIENCE (chemistry, computer science, geology, mathematics, and physics), EDUCATION (art education, elementary education, foreign languages education, music education, science education, and secondary education), ENGINEERING AND ENVIRONMENTAL DESIGN (environmental science), SOCIAL SCIENCE (archeology, classical/ancient civilization, economics, ethnic studies, history, international relations, Latin American studies, medieval studies, philosophy, political science/government, psychology, religion, Russian and Slavic studies, sociology, and women's studies). Art, English, and theatre are the strongest academically. Psychology, economics and business, biochemistry, and molecular biology have the largest enrollments.

Required: Students choosing the BA degree must complete 31 course credits (124 semester hours), with at least a 2.0 cumulative GPA. B.A. candidates must complete the requirements of a faculty approved major usually 8 to 15 courses in the major and distribution requirements including: a first year seminar, a first year writing course, 2 courses in humanities, 1 courses in the natural sciences, 1 course in social sciences, 1 course each in fine arts and math, 1 interdisciplinary thinking experience, and 1 to 4 courses in a foreign language.

Special: Special academic programs include study abroad in 25 to 30 countries, internships including a Washington semester, double majors, student-designed majors, and interdisciplinary majors in biochemistry and molecular biology, environmental studies, classical studies, ethnic studies, Latin American studies, Russian studies, anthropolgy and sociology, international relations, and women's studies. A cooperative degree program in Medical Technology with St. Luke's Methodist Hospital, a degree program in Nursing and Allied Health Science with Rush University, a 3-2 engineering program with the University of Minnesota, and a 3-4 architecture program with Washington University, and a 3-2 forestry or environmental management program with Duke University are also available. There are 16 national honor societies including Phi Beta Kappa.

Faculty/Classroom: 56% of faculty are male; 54% are female. All teach undergraduates, 80% do research, and 80% do both. No introductory courses are taught by graduate students. The average class size in an introductory lecture is 18; in a laboratory is 18; and in a regular course is 16.

Admissions: 59% of the 2013-2014 applicants were accepted. The SAT scores for the 2013-2014 freshman class were: Critical Reading--13% below 500, 33% between 500 and 599, 35% between 600 and 699, and 19% between 700 and 800; Math--19% below 500, 37% between 500 and 599, 34% between 600 and 699, and 10% between 700 and 800; Writing--18% below 500, 42% between 500 and 599, 33% between 600 and 699, and 7% between 700 and 800. The ACT scores were 5% below 21, 17% between 21 and 23, 29% between 24 and 26, 17% between 27 and 28, and 32% above 28. 62% of the current freshmen were in the top fifth of their class; 84% were in the top two fifths. 13 freshmen graduated first in their class.

Requirements: The SAT or ACT is required. Applicants should be graduates of an accredited secondary school, with a recommended 4 years each of English, 3 or more years of math and science, and social studies, 2 or more years of a foreign language. An essay and a secondary school report are required, and an interview is advised. The GED is accepted. AP credits are accepted. Important factors in the admissions decision are advanced placement or honors courses, evidence of special talent, and leadership record.

Procedure: Freshmen are admitted fall. There are early decision, early admissions, and deferred admissions plans. Early decision applications should be filed by November 1; regular applications, by March 1 for fall entry, along with a $30 fee. Notification of early decision is sent December 15; regular decision, April 1. 7 early decision candidates were accepted for the 2013-2014 class. 81 applicants were on the 2013 waiting list; 33 were admitted. Applications are accepted online.

Transfer: 45 transfer students enrolled in 2012-2013. Applicants must provide all items required of traditional students; in addition, they must submit official college transcripts from all other institutions they have attended. 15 of 31 credits required for the bachelor's degree must be completed at Cornell.

Visiting: There are regularly scheduled orientations for prospective students, including campus tours and meetings with an informational panel, a student panel, financial aid staff, and faculty and coaches as requested. There are guides for informal visits, visitors may sit in on classes, and stay overnight. To schedule a visit, contact the Visit Coordinator at (800) 747-1112.

Financial Aid: In 2013-2014, 99% of all full-time freshmen and 97% of continuing full-time students received some form of financial aid. 80% of all full-time freshmen and 77% of continuing full-time students received need-based aid. The average freshman award was $33,552. Need-based scholarships or need-based grants averaged $10,000 ($41,219 maximum); need-based self-help aid (loans and jobs) averaged $250 ($8,500 maximum); and other non-need-based awards and non-need-based scholarships averaged $6,000 ($30,000 maximum). 63% of undergraduate students work part-time. Average annual earnings from campus work are $1900. The average financial indebtedness of the 2013 graduate was $27,342. Cornell is a member of CSS. The FAFSA is required. The priority date for freshman financial aid applications for fall entry is March 1. The deadline for filing freshman financial aid applications for fall entry is March 1.

International Students: There are 64 international students enrolled. The school actively recruits these students. They must take the TOEFL with a minimum score of 550 on the paper-based TOEFL (PBT) or 79 on the Internet-based version (iBT), IELTS or STEP or SAT or ACT exams may also be submitted.

Graduates: From July 1, 2012 to June 30, 2013, 275 bachelor's degrees were awarded. The most popular majors were psychology (14%), biochemistry and molecular biology (13%), and art/art history (10%). 15 companies recruited on campus in 2012-2013. In an average class, 1% graduate in 3 years or less, 64% graduate in 4 years or less, 66% graduate in 5 years or less, and 68% graduate in 6 years or less.

Admissions Contact: Colleen Murphy, Vice President of Enrollment.
E-Mail: *admissions@cornellcollege.edu* Web: *www.cornellcollege.edu*

DORDT COLLEGE — B-2

Sioux Center, IA 51250 — **(712) 722-6080**
(800) 34-DORDT; (712) 722-1967

Full-time: 728 men, 658 women	**Faculty:** 80; IIB, --$
Part-time: 44 men, 41 women	**Ph.D.s:** 85%
Graduate: 25 men, 29 women	**Student/Faculty:** 15 to 1
Year: semesters	**Tuition:** $26,540
Application Deadline: August 1	**Room & Board:** $7620
Freshman Class: 1355 applied, 1022 accepted, 381 enrolled	
ACT: 25	**SAT:** required **VERY COMPETITIVE**

Dordt College, founded in 1955, is a private institution affiliated with the Christian Reformed Church. The curriculum, which is designed to reflect the principles of the Christian faith, leads to degrees in liberal arts, agriculture, art, music, business, engineering, and teaching preparation. In addition to regional accreditation, Dordt has baccalaureate program accreditation with ABET and CSWE. The library contains 185,000 volumes, 14,819 microform items, and 5,000 audio/video tapes/CDs/DVDs, and subscribes to 700 periodicals including electronic. Computerized library services include interlibrary loans. Special learning facilities include a planetarium, radio station, and 2 observatories, as well as a 160-acre agriculture stewardship center just north of the campus. The 120-acre campus is in a rural area 42 miles north of Sioux City. Including any residence halls, there are 25 buildings.

Student Life: 60% of undergraduates are from out of state, mostly the Mid-West. Students are from 34 states, 26 foreign countries, and Canada. 40% are from public schools. 88% are White. 99% are Protestant. The average age of freshmen is 18; all undergraduates, 21. 15% do not continue beyond their first year; 68% remain to graduate.

Housing: 1300 students can be accommodated in college housing, which includes single-sex dorms, on-campus apartments, and off-campus apartments. On-campus housing is guaranteed for all 4 years. 90% of students live on campus; of those, 80% remain on campus on weekends. Alcohol is not permitted. All students may keep cars.

Activities: There are no fraternities or sororities. There are 25 groups on campus, including band, choir, chorale, chorus, computers, dance, debate, drama, drill team, environmental, film, forensics, international, jazz band, literary magazine, newspaper, opera, orchestra, pep band, photography, PLIA (Putting Love into Action), political, professional, radio and TV, religious, social, social service, student government, symphony, and yearbook. Popular campus events include Parents Day in October.

Sports: There are 7 intercollegiate sports for men and 7 for women, and 10 intramural sports for men and 10 for women. Facilities include a 2500-seat gym with 2 courts; an 85,000-square-foot recreation center, which includes a 200-meter indoor track, 3 courts adaptable for basketball, volleyball, and tennis, 3 racquetball courts, weight-lifting and exercise equipment rooms, and a golf simulation room; an outdoor track; tennis courts; soccer, softball, and baseball fields; and an indoor pool and ice arena adjacent to the campus.

Disabled Students: All of the campus is accessible. Facilities include wheelchair ramps, elevators, special parking, specially equipped restrooms, special class scheduling, lowered drinking fountains, lowered telephones, and special housing.

Services: Counseling and information services are available, as is tutoring in every subject. There is a reader service for the blind, and remedial math, reading, and writing.

Campus Safety and Security: Measures include 24-hour foot and vehicle patrol. There are lighted pathways/sidewalks.

Programs of Study: Dordt confers B.A., B.S., B.S.N. and B.S.W. degrees. Associate and master's degrees are also awarded. Bachelor's degrees are awarded in AGRICULTURE (agricultural business management, agriculture, and animal science), BIOLOGICAL SCIENCE (biology/biological science), BUSINESS (accounting, banking and finance, business administration and management, business economics, management information systems, marketing management, recreational facilities management, secretarial studies/office management, and sports management), COMMUNICATIONS AND THE ARTS (advertising, art history, art, broadcasting, church music, communication, communications, dramatic arts, Dutch, English, English as a second/foreign language, film, television and digital media, fine arts, German, graphic design, journalism, languages, literature, music, music performance, music theory and composition, Spanish, speech/debate/rhetoric, theatre acting, theatre arts, visual and performing arts, and vocal music education), COMPUTER AND PHYSICAL SCIENCE (actuarial science, chemistry, computer programming, computer science, information sciences and systems, mathematics, physical sciences, and physics), EDUCATION (agricultural education, art education, athletic training, business education, (Education) Childhood Education, early childhood education, education, elementary education, English education, foreign languages education, mathematics education, middle school education, music education, physical education, physical science secondary school education, science education, secondary education, social science education, and special education), ENGINEERING AND ENVIRONMENTAL DESIGN (architectural engineering, bioengineering, chemical engineering, civil engineering, computer engineering, construction management, electrical/electronics engineering, engineering, environmental science, and mechanical engineering), HEALTH PROFESSIONS (exercise science, health science, medical laboratory technology, nursing, predentistry, premedicine, preoptometry, prepharmacy, prephysical therapy, and preveterinary science), SOCIAL SCIENCE (criminal justice, economics, history, ministries, missions, philosophy, philosophy and religion, political science/government, prelaw, psychology, public administration, religion, religious studies, social science, social work, sociology, and youth ministry). Engineering, business administration, and social work are the strongest academically. Education has the largest enrollment.

Required: All students must complete a college introductory course and a distribution of 14 other courses in the various academic disciplines, including General Education 300. Proficiency requirements must be met in English, math, and phys ed. To graduate, students must complete a minimum of 126 credits with a 2.0 GPA.

Special: Students may study abroad in 10 countries. Dordt also offers a Washington semester, a Chicago Metro semester, a joint nursing degree program with St. Luke's School of Nursing, a B.S.N. with Briar Cliff University, B.A.-B.S. degrees in engineering and agriculture, and numerous internships in all majors. Dual majors, student-designed majors, and pass/fail options are available. There is a freshman honors program.

Faculty/Classroom: 85% of faculty are male; 15% are female. All teach undergraduates. No introductory courses are taught by graduate students. The average class size in an introductory lecture is 30; in a laboratory is 20; and in a regular course is 25.

Admissions: 75% of the 2013-2014 applicants were accepted. The SAT scores for the 2013-2014 freshman class were: Critical Reading--47% below 500, 29% between 500 and 599, 21% between 600 and 699, and 3% between 700 and 800; Math--22% below 500, 45% between 500 and 599, 30% between 600 and 699, and 3% between 700 and 800; Writing--43% below 500, 40% between 500 and 599, and 17% between 600 and 699. The ACT scores were 15% below 21, 25% between 21 and 23, 36% between 24 and 26, 20% between 27 and 28, and 15% above 28. 62% of the current freshmen were in the top fifth of their class; 75% were in the top two fifths.

Requirements: The SAT or ACT is required. Applicants must be graduates of accredited secondary schools or have earned a GED. The college requires 18 academic credits, including 4 in English and 2 each in foreign language, math, science, and social studies. A GPA of 2.3 is required. AP and CLEP credits are accepted. Important factors in the admissions decision are advanced placement or honors courses, evidence of special talent, and leadership record.

Procedure: Freshmen are admitted fall and spring. Entrance exams should be taken by October of the senior year and no later than April. There is a rolling admissions plan. Applications should be filed by August 1 for fall entry; December 1 for spring entry. Applications are accepted online.

Transfer: 60 transfer students enrolled in 2012-2013. Transfer students must have a GPA of 2.0. 62 of 126 credits required for the bachelor's degree must be completed at Dordt.

Visiting: There are regularly scheduled orientations for prospective students, including tours, class visits, personal visits with professors and coaches, and a financial aid session. There are guides for informal visits, visitors may sit in on classes, and stay overnight. To schedule a visit, contact the Admissions Office.

Financial Aid: In 2013-2014, 98% of all full-time freshmen and 95% of continuing full-time students received some form of financial aid. 85% of all full-time freshmen and 85% of continuing full-time students received need-based aid. The average freshman award was $21,900. Need-based scholarships or need-based grants averaged $4,000 ($6,000 maximum); need-based self-help aid (loans and jobs) averaged $8,000 ($12,000 maximum); non-need-based athletic scholarships averaged $6,000 ($9,000 maximum); and other non-need-based awards and non-need-based scholarships averaged $7,000 ($12,500 maximum). 70% of undergraduate students work part-time. Average annual earnings from campus work are $1500. The average financial indebtedness of the 2013 graduate was $22,400. Dordt is a member of CSS. The FAFSA and the college's own financial statement are required. Check with the school for current application deadlines.

International Students: There are 60 international students enrolled. The school actively recruits these students. They must take the TOEFL with a minimum score of 72 on the Internet-based version (iBT), . They must also take the SAT or ACT, scoring 19.

Graduates: From July 1, 2012 to June 30, 2013, 290 bachelor's degrees were awarded. The most popular majors were business, education, and engineering. 40 companies recruited on campus in 2012-2013. In an average class, 68% graduate in 4 years or less. Of the 2012 graduating class, 15% were enrolled in graduate school within 6 months of graduation, and 96% were employed.

Admissions Contact: Quentin Van Essen, Executive Director of Admissions. E-Mail: *admissions@dordt.edu* Web: *www.dordt.edu*

DRAKE UNIVERSITY C-3

Des Moines, IA 50311 (515) 271-3181
(800) 44-DRAKE; (515) 271-2831

Full-time: 1368 men, 1817 women	**Faculty:** 246; IIA, av$
Part-time: 107 men, 91 women	**Ph.D.s:** 91%
Graduate: 668 men, 1088 women	**Student/Faculty:** 11 to 1
Year: semesters, summer session	**Tuition:** $30,980
Application Deadline:	**Room & Board:** $9000
Freshman Class: 5930 applied, 3911 accepted, 850 enrolled	
SAT: required **ACT:** 27	**VERY COMPETITIVE+**

Drake University, founded in 1881, is a private institution offering undergraduate and graduate programs in arts and sciences, business and public administration, pharmacy and health sciences, journalism and mass communication, education, fine arts, and law. There are 5 undergraduate schools and 1 graduate school. In addition to regional accreditation, Drake has baccalaureate program accreditation with AACSB, ACEJMC, ACPE, NASAD, and NASM. The 2 libraries contain 1.2 million volumes, 936,702 microform items, and 2,969 audio/video tapes/CDs/DVDs, and subscribe to 93,729 periodicals including electronic. Computerized library services include interlibrary loans, database searching, and Internet access. Special learning facilities include an art gallery, radio station, TV station, an observatory, and the Henry G. Harmon Fine Arts Center. The 120-acre campus is in an urban area in Des Moines. Including any residence halls, there are 49 buildings.

Student Life: 53% of undergraduates are from out of state, mostly the

Mid-West. Students are from 42 states, 42 foreign countries, and Canada. 89% are from public schools. 82% are White. The average age of freshmen is 18; all undergraduates, 21. 12% do not continue beyond their first year; 73% remain to graduate.

Housing: 1787 students can be accommodated in college housing, which includes coed dorms, on-campus apartments, off-campus apartments, and married student housing. On-campus housing is guaranteed for the freshman year only, is available on a first-come, first-served basis, and is available on a lottery system for upperclassmen. 75% of students live on campus; of those, 80% remain on campus on weekends. All students may keep cars.

Activities: 34% of men belong to 9 national fraternities; 28% of women belong to 5 national sororities. There are 160 groups on campus, including art, band, cheerleading, chess, choir, chorale, chorus, computers, dance, drama, drill team, ethnic, film, gay, honors, international, jazz band, literary magazine, marching band, musical theater, newspaper, opera, orchestra, pep band, photography, political, professional, radio and TV, religious, social, social service, student government, and symphony. Popular campus events include Drake Relays, Supreme Court Days and Iowa Caucuses.

Sports: There are 8 intercollegiate sports for men and 10 for women, and 24 intramural sports for men and 24 for women. Facilities include a football stadium, an indoor swimming pool, an aerobics room, 2 weight rooms, basketball, volleyball, and badminton courts, 2 indoor tracks and 1 outdoor track, 4 racquetball courts, and 6 indoor and 6 outdoor tennis courts. A recreation and sports facility seats 7000.

Disabled Students: 90% of the campus is accessible. Facilities include wheelchair ramps, elevators, special parking, specially equipped restrooms, special class scheduling, lowered drinking fountains, lowered telephones. an IBM-compatible computer and scanner that includes a voice and screen enlargement program, closed-caption television, and TDD at multiple locations.

Services: There is a reader service for the blind. The Student Disability Service works with Recordings for the Blind dyslexic students.

Campus Safety and Security: Measures include 24-hour foot and vehicle patrol, emergency notification system, self-defense education, and security escort services. There are shuttle buses, emergency telephones, and lighted pathways/sidewalks.

Programs of Study: Drake confers B.A., B.S., B.A.Journ. and Mass Comm., B.F.A., B.Mus., B.Mus.Ed., B.S.B.A. and B.S.Ed. degrees. Master's and doctoral degrees are also awarded. Bachelor's degrees are awarded in BIOLOGICAL SCIENCE (biology/biological science and neurosciences), BUSINESS (accounting, banking and finance, business administration and management, international business management, management science, and marketing management), COMMUNICATIONS AND THE ARTS (advertising, art history and appreciation, broadcasting, communications, dramatic arts, English, graphic design, journalism, music, music business management, music performance, printmaking, public relations, speech/debate/rhetoric, and studio art), COMPUTER AND PHYSICAL SCIENCE (actuarial science, chemistry, computer science, information sciences and systems, mathematics, and physics), EDUCATION (elementary education, mathematics education, music education, and secondary education), ENGINEERING AND ENVIRONMENTAL DESIGN (environmental science), HEALTH PROFESSIONS (pharmacy), SOCIAL SCIENCE (economics, ethics, politics, and social policy, history, international relations, philosophy, political science/government, psychology, religion, and sociology). Actuarial science, pharmacy, and physics/astronomy are the strongest academically. Pharmacy, marketing, and actuarial science have the largest enrollments.

Required: Undergraduates must take a first-year seminar and general education courses and satisfy 11 areas of inquiry requirements that include writing, critical thinking, artistic experience, historical consciousness, information and technical literacy, multicultural experience, scientific and quantitative literacy, values and ethics, and the engaged citizen. A capstone demonstration is required. For graduation, 124 credit hours are required with 27 to 36 hours in the major. The minimum GPA is 2.0.

Special: Study abroad is available in 60 countries and at sea. The university offers cross-registration with Des Moines area colleges, including Grand View, internships, a Washington semester, cooperative programs in computer science, and work-study programs. Dual majors, B.A.-B.S. degrees, a 3-2 engineering degree with Washington University, student-designed majors, credit for military experience, and nondegree study are possible. Students may take a maximum of 12 hours of course work on a credit/no credit basis. There are 25 national honor societies, including Phi Beta Kappa, a freshman honors program, and 19 departmental honors programs.

Faculty/Classroom: 56% of faculty are male; 64% are female. 84% teach undergraduates. No introductory courses are taught by graduate students. The average class size in an introductory lecture is 29; in a laboratory is 14; and in a regular course is 27.

Admissions: 66% of the 2013-2014 applicants were accepted. The SAT scores for the 2013-2014 freshman class were: Critical Reading--14% below 500, 42% between 500 and 599, 31% between 600 and 699, and 13% between 700 and 800; Math--10% below 500, 36% between 500 and 599, 36% between 600 and 699, and 19% between 700 and 800. The ACT scores were: 16% between 24 and 26, 57% between 27 and 28, and 26% above 28.

Requirements: The SAT or ACT is required. Applicants must be graduates of an accredited secondary school. The GED is accepted. Students should have completed 4 years of English, 3 years of math, and 9 other units to be selected from English, foreign languages, social studies, math, lab sciences, and others. A portfolio is required for art majors and for those seeking scholarship consideration. An audition is necessary for admission to the music and theatre programs. Tapes are accepted. A GPA of 3.3 is required. AP and CLEP credits are accepted. Important factors in the admissions decision are advanced placement or honors courses, recommendations by school officials, and extracurricular activities record.

Procedure: Freshmen are admitted to all sessions. Entrance exams should be taken during the spring of the junior year or early fall of the senior year. There are deferred admissions and rolling admissions plans. Check with the school for current application deadlines. The application fee is $25. Applications are accepted online. Application fees are waived if application is completed online.

Transfer: Applicants must have a minimum GPA of 2.0 and have completed 24 credit hours for evaluation. Grades of C or better transfer for credit. There is no assurance that all courses transferred will apply toward the major requirement. The final 30 hours must be completed in residence. Transfer students are admitted in the fall, spring, and summer. 30 of 124 credits required for the bachelor's degree must be completed at Drake.

Visiting: There are regularly scheduled orientations for prospective students, including an opportunity for students and parents to confer with professors, meet with current students, and attend information sessions on academic programs, financial aid, housing, and the Drake campus. Also included are a walking tour and lunch. There are guides for informal visits, visitors may sit in on classes, and stay overnight. To schedule a visit, contact the Office of Admission.

Financial Aid: 76% of all full-time freshmen and 76% of continuing full-time students received need-based aid. The average freshman award was $22,999. Need-based scholarships or need-based grants averaged $17,454; need-based self-help aid (loans and jobs) averaged $4,733; and non-need-based athletic scholarships averaged $18,692. The average financial indebtedness of the 2013 graduate was $25,633. Drake is a member of CSS. The FAFSA is required. Check with the school for current application deadlines.

International Students: There are 265 international students enrolled. The school actively recruits these students. They must take the TOEFL with a minimum score of 550 on the paper-based TOEFL (PBT) or 79 on the Internet-based version (iBT). They must also take the SAT or ACT.

Graduates: From July 1, 2012 to June 30, 2013, 938 bachelor's degrees were awarded. The most popular majors were business/marketing (36%), communication/journalism (12%), and social sciences (7%). In an average class, 66% graduate in 4 years or less, 72% graduate in 5 years or less, and 73% graduate in 6 years or less.

Admissions Contact: Laura Linn, Director of Admissions. E-Mail: *admission@drake.edu* Web: *www.drake.edu*

GRACELAND UNIVERSITY — C-4

Lamoni, IA 50140 — (641) 784-5119
(866) 893-6882; (641) 784-5480

Full-time: 575 men, 775 women	**Faculty:** n/av
Part-time: 135 men, 560 women	**Ph.D.s:** 47%
Graduate: 75 men, 265 women	**Student/Faculty:** n/av
Year: semesters, summer session	**Tuition:** $22,000
Application Deadline: open	**Room & Board:** $8000
Freshman Class: n/av	
SAT or ACT: required	

COMPETITIVE

Graceland University, established in 1895, is a private liberal arts college sponsored by the Community of Christ. Graceland also maintains a campus in Independence, Missouri. The figures in the above capsule and in this profile are approximate. There are 4 undergraduate schools and 4 graduate schools. In addition to regional accreditation, Graceland has baccalaureate program accreditation with NCATE and NLN. The library contains 199,447 volumes, 914 microform items, and 3,658 audio/video tapes/CDs/DVDs, and subscribes to 624 periodicals including electronic. Computerized library services include interlibrary loans, database searching, and Internet access. Special learning facilities include a learning resource center, art gallery, a center for the study of the Korean War. The 167-acre campus is in a small town 80 miles south of Des Moines. Including any residence halls, there are 28 buildings.

Student Life: 60% of undergraduates are from out of state, mostly the Mid-West. Students are from 49 states, 35 foreign countries, and Canada. 64% are white. 16% are Protestant. The average age of freshmen is 18; all undergraduates, 20. 30% do not continue beyond their first year; 47% remain to graduate.

Housing: 715 students can be accommodated in college housing, which

includes single-sex dorms and married student housing. On-campus housing is guaranteed for all 4 years. 64% of students live on campus; of those, 68% remain on campus on weekends. Alcohol is not permitted. All students may keep cars.

Activities: There are no fraternities or sororities. There are 54 groups on campus, including environmental, art, band, cheerleading, chess, choir, chorale, chorus, computers, dance, drama, drill team, entrepreneurial, ethnic, gay, honors, international, jazz band, musical theater, newspaper, orchestra, pep band, political, professional, radio and TV, religious, social, social service, student government, symphony, and yearbook. Popular campus events include Renaissance Week, Multicultural Week, and New Year's in November.

Sports: There are 9 intercollegiate sports for men and 8 for women, and 17 intramural sports for men and 17 for women. Facilities include a sports complex with an all-weather track and lighted soccer and football fields; a phys ed center with an indoor junior Olympic-size pool, a 5-court gym, an indoor track, a weight room, and courts for racquetball, basketball, volleyball, and tennis; an intramural sports complex; 8 lighted tennis courts; an 18-hole disc golf course; and 2 small lakes.

Disabled Students: 86% of the campus is accessible. Facilities include wheelchair ramps, elevators, special parking, specially equipped restrooms, special class scheduling, lowered drinking fountains, lowered telephones.

Services: Counseling and information services are available, as is tutoring in most subjects. There is a reader service for the blind, and remedial math, reading, and writing.

Campus Safety and Security: Measures include 24-hour foot and vehicle patrol and security escort services. There are emergency telephones, lighted pathways/sidewalks, night security personnel.

Programs of Study: Graceland confers B.A., B.S., and B.S.N. degrees. Master's degrees are also awarded. Bachelor's degrees are awarded in BIOLOGICAL SCIENCE (biology/biological science), BUSINESS (accounting, business administration and management, international business management, recreation and leisure services, and recreational facilities management), COMMUNICATIONS AND THE ARTS (communications, dramatic arts, English, German, graphic design, literature, modern language, music, Spanish, speech/debate/rhetoric, and studio art), COMPUTER AND PHYSICAL SCIENCE (chemistry, computer science, information sciences and systems, mathematics, and science), EDUCATION (athletic training, elementary education, music education, and physical education), ENGINEERING AND ENVIRONMENTAL DESIGN (commercial art), HEALTH PROFESSIONS (health, medical laboratory technology, nursing, predentistry, premedicine, and preveterinary science), SOCIAL SCIENCE (addiction studies, criminal justice, economics, history, human services, international studies, liberal arts/general studies, philosophy, psychology, religion, social science, and sociology). Business administration, education, and nursing have the largest enrollments.

Required: To graduate, students must complete 128 credit hours, including 39 in upper-division courses and an average of 40 in the major, and maintain a minimum GPA of 2.0 overall and in the major. General education requirements include studies in humanities, social sciences, natural sciences, behavioral sciences, ethics, math, computer science, leadership, thinking skills, human diversity, and the arts.

Special: Internships are required in business, education, recreation, communications, and publication design. Graceland offers study abroad, cross-registration, B.A.-B.S. degrees, work-study, dual and student-designed majors, and a general studies degree. Credit for life, military, or work experience is possible. A pass/fail option is available for 2 courses each semester. The university also offers nondegree study, home study in addiction studies and nursing, a program for students with learning disabilities, an accelerated degree program in nursing, and a 3-2 engineering degree with the University of Iowa and the University of Missouri-Rolla. There are 3 national honor societies, a freshman honors program, and 6 departmental honors programs.

Faculty/Classroom: 47% of faculty are male; 53% are female. 93% teach undergraduates, and 10% do research. No introductory courses are taught by graduate students. The average class size in an introductory lecture is 24; in a laboratory is 24; and in a regular course is 11.

Requirements: The SAT or ACT is required. Graceland requires applicants to meet 2 of the following 3 criteria: rank in the upper 50% of their class, a GPA of 2.5, or a minimum score on the SAT or ACT. Applicants must be graduates of an accredited secondary school. The GED is accepted. An interview is recommended. A GPA of 2.5 is required. AP and CLEP credits are accepted. Important factors in the admissions decision are advanced placement or honors courses, evidence of special talent, and leadership record.

Procedure: Freshmen are admitted to all sessions. Entrance exams should be taken in the junior or senior year. There is a rolling admissions plan. Check with the school for current application deadlines. The application fee is $50. Applications are accepted online.

Transfer: Applicants must submit official transcripts from all colleges attended and from high school. The required GPA varies by the number of hours of college study completed. Transfer students are admitted every term. 32 of 128 credits required for the bachelor's degree must be completed at Graceland.

Visiting: There are regularly scheduled orientations for prospective students, including a campus tour and opportunities to meet students, faculty, and campus personnel. There are guides for informal visits, visitors may sit in on classes, and stay overnight.

Financial Aid: The FAFSA is required. Check with the school for current application deadlines.

International Students: The school actively recruits these students. They must take the TOEFL.

Admissions Contact: Admissions OfficeE-Mail: Web: *www.graceland.edu*

GRAND VIEW UNIVERSITY — C-3

Des Moines, IA 50316 — (515) 263-2810; (800) 444-6083; (515) 263-2974

Full-time: 766 men, 962 women	**Faculty:** 95
Part-time: 117 men, 251 women	**Ph.D.s:** 68%
Graduate: 11 men, 22 women	**Student/Faculty:** 18 to 1
Year: semesters, summer session	**Tuition:** $23,496
Application Deadline: open	**Room & Board:** $7554
Freshman Class: n/av	
SAT: recommended	

COMPETITIVE

Grand View University, formerly Grand View College, founded in 1896, is a private liberal arts college affiliated with the Evangelical Lutheran Church in America, that focuses on connecting liberal arts with career preparation. There is one graduate school. In addition to regional accreditation, Grand View has baccalaureate program accreditation with NLN. The library contains 135,448 volumes, 11,334 microform items, 3,801 audio/video tapes/CDs/DVDs, and subscribes to 27,077 periodicals including electronic. Computerized library services include interlibrary loans, database searching, and Internet access. Special learning facilities include an art gallery, radio and TV station. The 25-acre campus is in an urban area in a residential area of Des Moines. Including any residence halls, there are 27 buildings.

Student Life: 87% of undergraduates are from Iowa. Others are from 34 states, 16 foreign countries, and Canada. 80% are White. 15% are Catholic; 13% Protestant. The average age of freshmen is 18; all undergraduates, 22. 31% do not continue beyond their first year; 49% remain to graduate.

Housing: 900 students can be accommodated in college housing, which includes coed dorms and on-campus apartments. In addition, there are special-interest houses. On-campus housing is available on a first-come, first-served basis, and is available on a lottery system for upperclassmen. Priority is given to out-of-town students. 63% of students commute. All students may keep cars.

Activities: There are no fraternities or sororities. There are 43 groups on campus, including art, band, cheerleading, choir, chorale, chorus, computers, dance, departmental, drama, drill team, ethnic, gay, honors, international, jazz band, literary magazine, newspaper, pep band, political, professional, radio and TV, religious, social service, student government, and yearbook.

Sports: There are 12 intercollegiate sports for men and 12 for women, and 8 intramural sports for men and 8 for women. Facilities include a 1200-seat wellness with facilities for varsity athletics and recreation programs and an athletic field.

Disabled Students: 90% of the campus is accessible. Facilities include wheelchair ramps, elevators, special parking, specially equipped restrooms, special class scheduling, lowered drinking fountains, lowered telephones. support services for the disabled.

Services: Counseling and information services are available, as is tutoring in every subject. There is a reader service for the blind.

Campus Safety and Security: Measures include 24-hour foot and vehicle patrol, emergency notification system, and security escort services. There are emergency telephones, lighted pathways/sidewalks, and controlled access to dorms/residences.

Programs of Study: Grand View confers B.A., and B.S.N. degrees. Master's degrees are also awarded. Bachelor's degrees are awarded in BIOLOGICAL SCIENCE (biochemistry, biology/biological science, and biotechnology), BUSINESS (accounting, business administration and management, management information systems, and sports management), COMMUNICATIONS AND THE ARTS (broadcasting, communications, English, graphic design, journalism, music, and visual and performing arts), COMPUTER AND PHYSICAL SCIENCE (computer science and mathematics), EDUCATION (art education, elementary education, music education, physical education, and secondary education), HEALTH PROFESSIONS (nursing), SOCIAL SCIENCE (criminal justice, human services, political science/government, and psychology). Art, nursing and education are the strongest academically. Business, nursing, biology and education have the largest enrollments.

Required: Students must complete core requirements, including courses in English, public speaking, liberal arts, integrating seminar, other culture encounter, religion or philosophy, history or other humanities, lab science, and social science. Students must complete at least 124 hours of work, including 60 hours in courses other than the major and 24 hours in the major. Students must maintain an overall GPA of 2.0 and a 2.2 GPA in the major. Students must also demonstrate computer proficiency.

Special: Co-op programs, cross-registration with Drake University and Des Moines Area Community College, student-designed majors, study abroad, and internships for most majors are available. Dual majors, a B.A.-B.S. degree, a Washington semester, work-study programs, and an accelerated degree program in business administration are offered. Nondegree study, a liberal arts degree, a certificate in art therapy, and pass/fail options are possible. There are 10 national honor societies, a freshman honors program, and 1 departmental honors program.

Faculty/Classroom: 39% of faculty are male; 61% are female. All teach undergraduates. No introductory courses are taught by graduate students. The average class size in an introductory lecture is 20; in a laboratory is 10; and in a regular course is 15.

Admissions: 8 freshmen graduated first in their class.

Requirements: The ACT is required. The SAT and ACT Writing Test are recommended. In addition, with a minimum recommended score of 18 on the ACT or the equivalent on the SAT. Students must be graduates of an accredited secondary school. The GED is also accepted. Grand View recommends that students should have completed 4 courses in English, 3 courses each in math, science, and social science, and 2 courses in a foreign language. A GPA of 2.0 is required. AP and CLEP credits are accepted.

Procedure: Freshmen are admitted fall, spring, and summer. Entrance exams should be taken during the second semester of the junior year. There are deferred admissions and rolling admissions plans. Application deadlines are open. Applications are accepted online.

Transfer: 303 transfer students enrolled in 2012-2013. Applicants must submit transcripts from each college attended. Students who are not transferring in with an associate or bachelor's degree must submit a high school transcript. Those with less than 24 college credits must also submit ACT or SAT test results. 30 of 124 credits required for the bachelor's degree must be completed at Grand View.

Visiting: There are regularly scheduled orientations for prospective students, including placement tests, a financial aid session, lunch, advisor meetings, and a registration session. There are guides for informal visits, visitors may sit in on classes, and stay overnight. To schedule a visit, contact the Admissions Office.

Financial Aid: In 2013-2014, 99% of all full-time freshmen and 98% of continuing full-time students received some form of financial aid. 90% of all full-time freshmen and 86% of continuing full-time students received need-based aid. Average annual earnings from campus work are $1500. The average financial indebtedness of the 2013 graduate was $36,794. The FAFSA is required. The deadline for filing freshman financial aid applications for fall entry is April 15.

International Students: There are 35 international students enrolled. They must take the TOEFL with a minimum score of 550 on the paper-based TOEFL (PBT) or 77 on the Internet-based version (iBT). They must also take the SAT or ACT, scoring 18.

Graduates: From July 1, 2012 to June 30, 2013, 460 bachelor's degrees were awarded. The most popular majors were business administration (23%), nursing (14%), and education (10%). 70 companies recruited on campus in 2012-2013. In an average class, 39% graduate in 4 years or less, 47% graduate in 5 years or less, and 49% graduate in 6 years or less. Of the 2012 graduating class, 8% were enrolled in graduate school within 6 months of graduation, and 90% were employed.

Admissions Contact: Diane Schafer Johnson, Director of Admissions. E-Mail: *djohnson@grandview.edu* Web: *www.admissions.grandview.edu*

GRINNELL COLLEGE
D-3

Grinnell, IA 50112

(641) 269-3600
(800) 247-0113; (641) 269-4800

Full-time: 751 men, 913 women	**Faculty:** 160; IIB, +$
Part-time: 40 men, 17 women	**Ph.D.s:** 100%
Graduate: n/av	**Student/Faculty:** 10 to 1
Year: semesters	**Tuition:** $43,656
Application Deadline: April 1	**Room & Board:** $9998

Freshman Class: 3979 applied, 1395 accepted, 423 enrolled
SAT or ACT: required

HIGHLY COMPETITIVE

Grinnell College, founded in 1846, is a private institution that offers undergraduate degree programs in the arts and sciences. The 3 libraries contain 649,916 volumes, 416,593 microform items, and 34,144 audio/video tapes/CDs/DVDs, and subscribe to 22,059 periodicals including electronic. Computerized library services include interlibrary loans, database searching, Internet access, and Wi-Fi capability. Special learning facilities include an art gallery, radio station, an observatory, physics museum, and print and drawing gallery. The 120-acre campus is in a small town 55 miles east of Des Moines. Including any residence halls, there are 64 buildings.

Student Life: 88% of undergraduates are from out of state, mostly the Mid-West. Students are from 50 states, 51 foreign countries, and Canada. 70% are from public schools. 57% are White; 12% Foreign. 41% claim no religious affiliation; 21% Protestant; 18% includes Muslim, Hindu and Buddhist; 14% Catholic. The average age of freshmen is 18; all undergraduates, 20. 7% do not continue beyond their first year; 86% remain to graduate.

Housing: 1340 students can be accommodated in college housing, which includes single-sex and coed dorms and on-campus apartments. In addition, there are language houses and special-interest houses. On-campus housing is guaranteed for all 4 years. 88% of students live on campus; of those, 95% remain on campus on weekends. All students may keep cars.

Activities: There are no fraternities or sororities. There are 250 groups on campus, including art, chess, choir, chorale, chorus, computers, dance, debate, drama, environmental, ethnic, film, forensics, gay, honors, international, jazz band, literary magazine, musical theater, newspaper, orchestra, photography, political, radio and TV, religious, social, social service, student government, and yearbook. Popular campus events include Titular Head Student Film Festival and Grinnell Relays.

Sports: There are 10 intercollegiate sports for men and 10 for women, and 16 intramural sports for men and 16 for women. Facilities include a phys ed complex, a gym, a fitness center, 5 sports fields, a track, a pool, and 3 intramural fields.

Disabled Students: 80% of the campus is accessible. Facilities include wheelchair ramps, elevators, special parking, specially equipped restrooms, special class scheduling, lowered drinking fountains, lowered telephones, and special housing.

Services: Counseling and information services are available, as is tutoring in every subject. There is a reader service for the blind. There are reading, writing, math, and science labs.

Campus Safety and Security: Measures include 24-hour foot and vehicle patrol, emergency notification system, self-defense education, and security escort services. There are emergency telephones, lighted pathways/sidewalks, controlled access to dorms/residences, fire drills, and a committee on personal safety education.

Programs of Study: Grinnell confers B.A. degrees. Bachelor's degrees are awarded in BIOLOGICAL SCIENCE (biochemistry and biology/biological science), COMMUNICATIONS AND THE ARTS (art, Chinese, classics, dramatic arts, English, French, German, music, Russian, and Spanish), COMPUTER AND PHYSICAL SCIENCE (chemistry, computer science, mathematics, physics, and science), SOCIAL SCIENCE (anthropology, economics, history, philosophy, political science/government, psychology, religion, sociology, and women's studies). Economics, psychology and political science have the largest enrollments.

Required: All students are required to take a tutorial in the first semester focusing on writing. All students must also complete a major field, which includes between 32 and 48 credits in most departments. Of the total 124 credits needed for the bachelor's degree, no more than 48 may be earned in any one department or 92 in any one division, and a minimum 2.0 GPA must be maintained.

Special: Students may participate in 63 study-abroad programs in 33 countries or in off-campus study at selected locations in the United States. Grinnell offers cooperative programs in architecture with Washington University in St. Louis and a 3-2 engineering program with California Institute of Technology, Columbia University, Washington University, and Rensselaer Polytechnic Institute. There is also an extensive internship program, a Washington semester, a general studies degree in science, student-designed majors, and S/D/F grading options in selected courses. Grinnell's special "plus-2" option permits students to add 2 credits to a regular course through independent study. Students may pursue one of 11 interdisciplinary concentrations in addition to their major. Accelerated degree programs of 6 to 7 semesters may be approved on an individual basis. There are 2 national honor societies including Phi Beta Kappa.

Faculty/Classroom: 54% of faculty are male; 46% are female. All teach and do research. No introductory courses are taught by graduate students. The average class size in an introductory lecture is 20; in a laboratory is 13; and in a regular course is 17.

Admissions: 35% of the 2013-2014 applicants were accepted. The SAT scores for the 2013-2014 freshman class were: Critical Reading--1% below 500, 17% between 500 and 599, 46% between 600 and 699, and 36% between 700 and 800; Math--1% below 500, 13% between 500 and 599, 37% between 600 and 699, and 49% between 700 and 800. 70% of the current freshmen were in the top fifth of their class; 92% were in the top two fifths.

Requirements: The SAT or ACT is required. Applicants must be graduates of accredited secondary schools. The college recommends 20 Carnegie units, 4 each in English and math and 3 to 4 each in lab science, social studies or history, and a foreign language. An essay is required and an interview is recommended. AP credits are accepted. Important factors in the admissions decision are advanced placement or honors courses, extracurricular activities record, and leadership record.

Procedure: Freshmen are admitted fall. Entrance exams should be taken during the second semester of the junior year or early in the fall semester of the senior year. There are early decision, early admissions, and deferred admissions plans. Early decision applications should be filed by November 15; regular applications, by April 1 for fall entry; and November 1 for spring entry, along with a $30 fee. Notification of early decision is sent December 15; regular decision, May 15. 137 early decision candidates were accepted for the 2013-2014 class. 1266 applicants were on the 2013 waiting list; 8 were admitted. Applications are accepted online.

Transfer: 14 transfer students enrolled in 2012-2013. Students must have a 3.0 GPA and submit all high school transcripts, college transcripts, an essay or personal statement, standardized test scores, and a statement of good standing from prior institutions. 62 of 124 credits required for the bachelor's degree must be completed at Grinnell.

Visiting: There are regularly scheduled orientations for prospective students, including a campus tour, an interview with a member of the admissions staff, an opportunity to attend classes, presentations/discussions with students and faculty from a number of academic departments, and complimentary meals. There are guides for informal visits, visitors may sit in on classes, and stay overnight. To schedule a visit, contact the Admissions Office.

Financial Aid: In 2013-2014, 89% of all full-time freshmen and 87% of continuing full-time students received some form of financial aid. 73% of all full-time freshmen and 71% of continuing full-time students received need-based aid. The average freshman award was $42,392. Need-based scholarships or need-based grants averaged $36,762; need-based self-help aid (loans and jobs) averaged $4,974; and other non-need-based awards and non-need-based scholarships averaged $656. The average financial indebtedness of the 2013 graduate was $16,570. Grinnell is a member of CSS. The CSS/Profile and FAFSA, and a noncustodial profile are required. The priority date for freshman financial aid applications for fall entry is February 1. The deadline for filing freshman financial aid applications for fall entry is February 1.

International Students: There are 210 international students enrolled. The school actively recruits these students. They must take the TOEFL with a minimum score of 550 on the paper-based TOEFL (PBT) or 80 on the Internet-based version (iBT). They must also take the SAT or ACT.

Computers: All students may access the system 24 hours a day. There are no time limits and no fees.

Graduates: From July 1, 2012 to June 30, 2013, 334 bachelor's degrees were awarded. The most popular majors were economics (9%), political science (8%), and history (8%). 19 companies recruited on campus in 2012-2013. In an average class, 81% graduate in 4 years or less, 86% graduate in 5 years or less, and 86% graduate in 6 years or less. Of the 2012 graduating class, 33% were enrolled in graduate school within 6 months of graduation, and 50% were employed.

Admissions Contact: Joseph P. Bagnoli Jr., Vice President for Enrollment, Dean of A. E-Mail: *askgrin@grinnell.edu* Web: *www.grinnell.edu*

HAMILTON COLLEGE
(See Kaplan University)

IOWA BOARD OF REGENTS

The Iowa Board of Regents, established in 1905, is a public system in Iowa. It is governed by the Iowa State board of regents, whose chief administrator is the executive director. The primary goal of the system is teaching, research, and public service. The total student enrollment is usually about 67,500 with 4500 faculty members. Altogether there are 276 baccalaureate, 290 master's, and 183 doctoral programs offered in the Iowa Board of Regents. Profiles of the 4-year campuses are included in this section.

IOWA STATE UNIVERSITY C-3

Ames, IA 50011-2011 (515) 294-5836
(800) 262-3810; (515) 294-2592

Full-time: 11,100 men, 9500 women
Part-time: 775 men, 610 women
Graduate: 2825 men, 2240 women
Year: semesters, summer session
Application Deadline: open
Freshman Class: n/av
SAT or ACT: required
Faculty: n/av; I, -$
Ph.D.s: 88%
Student/Faculty: n/av
Tuition: $9008 ($20,724)
Room & Board: $8395

COMPETITIVE

Iowa State University, established in 1858, is a public land-grant institution offering undergraduate and graduate programs in agriculture, business, design, engineering, human sciences, liberal arts and sciences, and veterinary medicine. The figures in the above capsule and in this profile are approximate. There are 7 undergraduate schools and 1 graduate school. In addition to regional accreditation, Iowa State has baccalaureate program accreditation with AACSB, ABET, ACEJMC, ADA, AHEA, ASLA, CSAB, FIDER, NAAB, NASM, and SAF. The library contains 2.4 million volumes, 3.4 million microform items, and 64,524 audio/video tapes/CDs/DVDs, and subscribes to 29,850 periodicals including electronic. Computerized library services include interlibrary loans and database searching. Special learning facilities include a learning resource center, art gallery, natural history museum, planetarium, radio station, and TV station. The 1788-acre campus is in an urban area 30 miles north of Des Moines. Including any residence halls, there are 284 buildings.

Student Life: 77% of undergraduates are from Iowa. Others are from 50 states, 115 foreign countries, and Canada. 94% are from public schools. 84% are white. The average age of freshmen is 18; all undergraduates, 21. 14% do not continue beyond their first year; 68% remain to graduate.

Housing: 10,000 students can be accommodated in college housing, which includes single-sex and coed dorms, on-campus apartments, and married student housing. In addition, there are honors houses, special-interest houses, fraternity houses, sorority houses, nonalcoholic houses, cross-cultural houses, nonsmoking houses, quiet houses, academic learning communities, and adult undergraduate housing. On-campus housing is guaranteed for all 4 years. 52% of students live on campus. All students may keep cars.

Activities: 13% of men belong to 1 local and 29 national fraternities; 12% of women belong to 1 local and 17 national sororities. There are 687 groups on campus, including and special interest., recreation/sports, art, band, cheerleading, chess, choir, chorale, chorus, computers, dance, debate, drama, drum and bugle corps, ethnic, film, forensics, gay, honoraries, honors, international, jazz band, literary magazine, marching band, musical theater, newspaper, opera, orchestra, pep band, photography, political, professional, radio and TV, religious, social, social service, student government, and symphony. Popular campus events include VEISHEA, spring festival, and Honors Week.

Sports: There are 7 intercollegiate sports for men and 12 for women, and 43 intramural sports for men and 43 for women. Facilities include a coliseum, a stadium/field, a baseball and softball complex, a track complex, a tennis complex, multipurpose gyms, swimming pools, an ice center, a phys ed building, recreation centers, multipurpose intramural-recreation fields, and a competitive soccer site.

Disabled Students: 95% of the campus is accessible. Facilities include wheelchair ramps, elevators, special parking, specially equipped restrooms, special class scheduling, lowered drinking fountains, lowered telephones.

Services: Counseling and information services are available, as is tutoring in most subjects. There is a reader service for the blind, and remedial math and writing. A Kurzweil Reader, an Arkanstone Reader, enlargement services, talking and braille text from the Iowa Commission for the Blind, a braille printer, loaner computers, steno-captioning service, a TTY telecommunications device, FM listeners, and sign interpreters are also available.

Campus Safety and Security: Measures include 24-hour foot and vehicle patrol, self-defense education, and security escort services. There are shuttle buses, emergency telephones, lighted pathways/sidewalks, and a Help Van for motorists.

Programs of Study: Iowa State confers B.A, B.S., B.Arch., B.B.A., B.F.A., B.L.A., B.L.S., and B.Mus. degrees. Master's and doctoral degrees are also awarded. Bachelor's degrees are awarded in AGRICULTURE (agricultural business management, agriculture, agronomy, animal science, dairy science, forestry and related sciences, horticulture, international agriculture, plant protection (pest management), and plant science), BIOLOGICAL SCIENCE (biochemistry, biology/biological science, biophysics, entomology, genetics, microbiology, nutrition, and plant pathology), BUSINESS (accounting, banking and finance, business administration and management, fashion merchandising, hotel/motel and restaurant management, international business management, management science, marketing/retailing/merchandising, and transportation management), COMMUNICATIONS AND THE ARTS (advertising, communications, design, English, fine arts, French, German, graphic design, journalism, linguistics, music, Russian, Spanish, and speech/debate/rhetoric), COMPUTER AND PHYSICAL SCIENCE (atmospheric sciences and meteorology, chemistry, computer science, earth science, geology, mathematics, physics, and statistics), EDUCATION (agricultural education, early childhood education, elementary education, health education, industrial arts education, music education, physical education, and secondary education), ENGINEERING AND ENVIRONMENTAL DESIGN (aeronautical engineering, agricultural engineering, architecture, chemical engineering, city/community/regional planning, civil engineering, computer engineering, construction engineering, electrical/electronics engineering, engineering, engineering technology, environmental science, industrial engineering technology, interior design, landscape architecture/design, materials engineering, and mechanical engineering), SOCIAL SCIENCE (anthropology, child care/child and family studies, child psychology/development, dietetics, economics, family/consumer resource management, family/consumer studies, fashion design and technology, food science, history, international relations, liberal arts/general studies, philosophy, political science/

government, psychology, religion, sociology, and textiles and clothing). Engineering, agriculture, and statistics are the strongest academically. Engineering, business, and agriculture have the largest enrollments.

Required: A minimum of 120 1/2 to 169 1/2 credit hours, depending on the major, and a GPA of 2.0 are required for graduation. The total number of credits required in the major varies. All students must take freshman English, library instruction, 3 credits in U.S. diversity, and 3 credits in internationalization.

Special: Iowa State offers cooperative programs in engineering, forestry, agronomy, chemistry, computer science, economics, agricultural systems technology, business administration, industrial technology, and performing arts and cross-registration with the Universities of Iowa and Northern Iowa. Internships, study abroad in 38 countries, dual majors, the B.A.-B.S. degree, student-designed majors, and accelerated degree programs are available. Interdisciplinary studies include agricultural biochemistry, agricultural systems technology, animal ecology, public service and administration in agriculture, and engineering operations. There are work-study programs, a Washington semester, nondegree study, and pass/no pass options. There are 16 national honor societies, including Phi Beta Kappa, and a freshman honors program.

Faculty/Classroom: 66% of faculty are male; 34% are female. 85% teach undergraduates, 95% do research, and 98% do both. Graduate students teach 15% of introductory courses. The average class size in a laboratory is 18 and in a regular course is 31.

Requirements: The SAT or ACT is required. Applicants must graduate from an accredited secondary school. The GED is accepted. For admission to freshman standing, students must have completed 4 years of English, 3 each of math and science, and 2 to 3 of social studies. For the College of Liberal Arts and Sciences, 2 years of a single foreign language are also required. Iowa State requires applicants to be in the upper 50% of their class. AP and CLEP credits are accepted.

Procedure: Freshmen are admitted to all sessions. Entrance exams should be taken during the spring of the junior year or the fall of the senior year. There are deferred admissions and rolling admissions plans. Check with the school for current application deadlines. The fall 2011 application fee was $30. Applications are accepted online.

Transfer: Applicants must have a minimum GPA of 2.0 and at least 24 semester credits of acceptable transfer course work. They must also submit standardized test scores and provide a statement of good standing from prior institutions. 32 of 125 credits required for the bachelor's degree must be completed at Iowa State.

Visiting: There are regularly scheduled orientations for prospective students, including presentations on academics, admissions, residence hall living, fraternity and sorority life, and financial aid. There is also a group session with an adviser and a tour of the campus. There are guides for informal visits, visitors may sit in on classes, and stay overnight.

Financial Aid: The FAFSA is required. Check with the school for current application deadlines.

International Students: The school actively recruits these students. They must take the TOEFL and the college's own test.

Computers: Wireless access is available. All students may access the system at any time. There are no time limits and no fees.

Admissions Contact: Phil Caffrey, Associate Director of Admissions. E-Mail: *admissions@iastate.edu* Web: *www.iastate.edu*

IOWA WESLEYAN COLLEGE — E-4

Mount Pleasant, IA 52641 — (319) 385-6231; (800) 582-2383; (319) 385-6240

Full-time: n/av	**Faculty:** n/av
Part-time: n/av	**Ph.D.s:** 57%
Graduate: n/av	**Student/Faculty:** n/av
Year: trimesters, summer session	**Tuition:** $23,660
Application Deadline: open	**Room & Board:** $7690
Freshman Class: n/av	
SAT or ACT: required	

LESS COMPETITIVE

Iowa Wesleyan College, founded in 1842, is a private institution affiliated with the United Methodist Church. The college offers undergraduate degree programs in business, education, fine arts, human studies, language and literature, nursing, and science. The figures in the above capsule and in this profile are approximate. In addition to regional accreditation, IWC has baccalaureate program accreditation with NLN. The library contains 83,244 volumes, 25,305 microform items, and 27,259 audio/video tapes/CDs/DVDs, and subscribes to 11,460 periodicals including electronic. Computerized library services include interlibrary loans, database searching, and Internet access. Special learning facilities include a learning resource center, art gallery, and radio station. The 60-acre campus is in a small town 45 miles south of Iowa City. Including any residence halls, there are 16 buildings.

Student Life: 53% of undergraduates are from Iowa. Others are from 22 states, 22 foreign countries, and Canada. 65% are white; 19% African American. 46% claim no religious affiliation. The average age of freshmen is 19; all undergraduates, 28. 47% do not continue beyond their first year; 38% remain to graduate.

Housing: 493 students can be accommodated in college housing, which includes single-sex and coed dorms. In addition, there are honors houses. On-campus housing is guaranteed for all 4 years. 60% of students live on campus. All students may keep cars.

Activities: 8% of men belong to 1 national fraternity; 12% of women belong to 1 national sorority. There are 35 groups on campus, including art, band, cheerleading, choir, chorus, dance, drama, ethnic, film, honors, international, jazz band, literary magazine, newspaper, orchestra, pep band, photography, political, professional, radio and TV, religious, social, social service, student government, symphony, and yearbook. Popular campus events include Forum, Winterfest, and Spring Thing.

Sports: There are 6 intercollegiate sports for men and 6 for women, and 11 intramural sports for men and 11 for women. Facilities include a 32-acre complex with baseball, softball, and football fields and an all-weather quarter-mile track. There is also a 35,000-square-foot, 2-story structure with basketball/volleyball courts, an athletic training room, bleacher seating for 800 people, a walking/jogging track, and a fitness/wellness center.

Disabled Students: 77% of the campus is accessible. Facilities include wheelchair ramps, elevators, special parking, and special class scheduling.

Services: Counseling and information services are available, as is tutoring in every subject. There is remedial math, reading, and writing.

Campus Safety and Security: Measures include 24-hour foot and vehicle patrol, self-defense education, and security escort services. There are emergency telephones and lighted pathways/sidewalks.

Programs of Study: IWC confers B.A., B.S., B.G.S., B.M.E., and B.S.N. degrees. Bachelor's degrees are awarded in BIOLOGICAL SCIENCE (biology/biological science and life science), BUSINESS (accounting, business administration and management, and sports management), COMMUNICATIONS AND THE ARTS (communications, English, fine arts, and music), COMPUTER AND PHYSICAL SCIENCE (chemistry, computer science, and mathematics), EDUCATION (art education, early childhood education, elementary education, music education, physical education, science education, and secondary education), ENGINEERING AND ENVIRONMENTAL DESIGN (preengineering), HEALTH PROFESSIONS (environmental health science, nursing, predentistry, premedicine, preoptometry, and preveterinary science), SOCIAL SCIENCE (criminal justice, history, prelaw, psychology, religion, and sociology). English, communications, and art are the strongest academically. Business, elementary education, and nursing have the largest enrollments.

Required: General education requirements of 35 to 40 hours include 6 of English, 4 of science, and 3 each of computer science, math, communication, civic issues, fine arts, religion, English literature, and global issues. Students must complete English 102 with a minimum of C-, satisfy a safety and survival requirement, and complete 6 semester hours of service learning and 6 to 14 semester hours of a field experience in the major. A minimum of 124 semester hours is required for the bachelor's degree; 28 or more must be in the major.

Special: There are internships in every major, a study-abroad program in Japan, China, and Mexico, a selective studies option, a general studies degree, credit in nursing through challenge exam, and satisfactory/unsatisfactory grade options. Work-study programs on campus and a Washington semester are also available. Cross-registration is available with Southeastern, Muscatine, and Indian Hills Community Colleges. There are 5 national honor societies and 2 departmental honors programs.

Faculty/Classroom: 59% of faculty are male; 41% are female. All teach undergraduates. No introductory courses are taught by graduate students. The average class size in an introductory lecture is 22; in a laboratory is 24; and in a regular course is 14.

Requirements: The SAT or ACT is required. Applicants must be graduates of accredited secondary schools or have earned a GED. A GPA of 2.5 is required. AP and CLEP credits are accepted. Important factors in the admissions decision are geographical diversity, extracurricular activities record, and evidence of special talent.

Procedure: Freshmen are admitted fall and spring. Entrance exams should be taken in April of the junior year or in June, October, or December of the senior year. There are deferred admissions and rolling admissions plans. Application deadlines are open. Applications are accepted online.

Transfer: A minimum cumulative college GPA of 2.0 is required. 30 of 124 credits required for the bachelor's degree must be completed at IWC.

Visiting: There are regularly scheduled orientations for prospective students, including meetings with admissions, financial aid, and academic staff, as well as social activities. There are guides for informal visits, visitors may sit in on classes, and stay overnight. To schedule a visit, contact the Admissions Office.

Financial Aid: IWC is a member of CSS. The FAFSA and the college's own financial statement are required. The deadline for filing freshman financial aid applications for fall entry is open.

International Students: The school actively recruits these students.

They must take the TOEFL with a minimum score of 500 on the paper-based TOEFL (PBT).

Computers: All students may access the system 8 a.m. to 12 a.m. There are no time limits and no fees.

Admissions Contact: Dean of Admissions. E-Mail: *admit@iwc.edu* Web: *www.iwc.edu*

KAPLAN UNIVERSITY E-3

Davenport, IA 52807 **(563) 355-3500**

Full-time: 106 men, 339 women
Part-time: 36 men, 76 women
Graduate: n/av
Year: trimesters, summer session
Application Deadline: open
Freshman Class: 256 applied, 256 accepted, 144 enrolled
Faculty: n/av
Ph.D.s: 17%
Student/Faculty: n/av
Tuition: $14,025
Room & Board: n/a

NONCOMPETITIVE

Kaplan University, founded in 1900, is a private university. Figures in the above capsule and this profile are approximate. Computerized library services include interlibrary loans, database searching, and Internet access. Special learning facilities include a learning resource center. The 1-acre campus is in an urban area 160 miles from Des Moines and 180 miles from Chicago, Illinois.

Student Life: 29% of undergraduates are from out of state, mostly the Midwest. 80% are white; 14% African American.

Housing: There are no residence halls. All students commute.

Activities: There are no fraternities or sororities. Groups on campus include newspaper and student government.

Sports: There is no sports program at Kaplan.

Disabled Students: Facilities include wheelchair ramps and special parking.

Services: Counseling and information services are available, as is tutoring in most subjects.

Programs of Study: Kaplan confers B.S. degrees. Associate degrees are also awarded. Bachelor's degrees are awarded in BUSINESS (business administration and management), COMMUNICATIONS AND THE ARTS (communications), COMPUTER AND PHYSICAL SCIENCE (information sciences and systems), SOCIAL SCIENCE (criminal justice, law, and paralegal studies).

Required: To graduate, students must have a GPA of 2.0.

Faculty/Classroom: 31% of faculty are male; 69% are female. The average class size in a regular course is 19.

Requirements: Students are required to have an interview on campus with an admissions representative. An essay or personal statement is required. A high school diploma or GED and entrance test are required in most programs. Specific test scores are required for MA and CJ programs. CLEP credits are accepted.

Procedure: Freshmen are admitted to all sessions. There are deferred admissions and rolling admissions plans. Application deadlines are open.

Transfer: Requirements include a high school transcript, college transcript(s), and an interview.

Visiting: To schedule a visit, contact an Admissions Representative.

Financial Aid: Check with the school for current application deadlines.

International Students: They must take the TOEFL with a minimum score of 525 on the paper-based TOEFL (PBT) or 71 on the Internet-based version (iBT).

Computers: There are computers in the library, computer center, and student center. All students may access the system. There are no time limits and no fees.

Admissions Contact: Director of Admissions. Web: *www.davenport.kaplanuniversity.edu*

LORAS COLLEGE E-2

Dubuque, IA 52004-0178 **(563) 588-7236**
(800) 245-6727; (563) 588-7119

Full-time: 765 men, 705 women
Part-time: 25 men, 40 women
Graduate: 30 men, 75 women
Year: semesters, summer session
Application Deadline: open
Freshman Class: n/av
SAT or ACT: required
Faculty: n/av; IIB, --$
Ph.D.s: 89%
Student/Faculty: n/av
Tuition: $30,408
Room & Board: $8024

VERY COMPETITIVE

Loras College, founded in 1839, is a private Roman Catholic liberal arts institution offering degree programs in humanities, social and behavioral studies, natural sciences, philosophy and religious studies, and professional studies. The figures in the above capsule and in this profile are approximate. In addition to regional accreditation, Loras has baccalaureate program accreditation with NCATE. The library contains 374,740 volumes, 10,322 microform items, and 2,175 audio/video tapes/CDs/DVDs, and subscribes to 16,169 periodicals including electronic. Computerized library services include interlibrary loans, database searching, Internet access, and laptop Internet portals. Special learning facilities include a learning resource center, art gallery, planetarium, radio station, TV station, the Center for Dubuque History. The 60-acre campus is in a small town 180 miles west of Chicago and 250 miles south of Minneapolis. Including any residence halls, there are 18 buildings.

Student Life: 54% of undergraduates are from Iowa. Others are from 21 states, and 7 foreign countries. 61% are from public schools. 93% are white. 64% are Catholic; 24% claim no religious affiliation. The average age of freshmen is 18; all undergraduates, 20. 21% do not continue beyond their first year; 65% remain to graduate.

Housing: 1027 students can be accommodated in college housing, which includes single-sex and coed dorms, on-campus apartments, and off-campus apartments. In addition, there are honors houses. On-campus housing is guaranteed for all 4 years and is available on a lottery system for upperclassmen. 66% of students live on campus; of those, 65% remain on campus on weekends. All students may keep cars.

Activities: There are no fraternities; 3% of women belong to 1 national sorority. There are 150 groups on campus, including band, cheerleading, choir, chorus, computers, dance, debate, drama, ethnic, film, forensics, gay, honors, international, jazz band, literary magazine, musical theater, newspaper, photography, political, professional, programming board, radio and TV, religious, social, social service, student government, and yearbook. Popular campus events include Family Weekend, Tri-College Free Day, and Awareness Week.

Sports: There are 11 intercollegiate sports for men and 10 for women, and 75 intramural sports for men and 72 for women. Facilities include a 74,000-square-foot athletic wellness facility, a sports center with 3 gym floors, a swimming pool, 4 racquetball courts, and an 8-lane Olympic indoor/outdoor track. There are also 5 outdoor tennis courts, a field house for basketball games, a football field, a soccer field, and a softball field. The campus stadium seats 3500.

Disabled Students: 65% of the campus is accessible. Facilities include wheelchair ramps, elevators, special parking, specially equipped restrooms, special class scheduling, lowered drinking fountains, lowered telephones, special housing. An LD program is designed for helping physically disabled students.

Services: Counseling and information services are available, as is tutoring in every subject. There is a reader service for the blind, and remedial math and writing.

Campus Safety and Security: Measures include 24-hour foot and vehicle patrol and security escort services. There are lighted pathways/sidewalks.

Programs of Study: Loras confers B.A., B.S., and B.M. degrees. Associate and master's degrees are also awarded. Bachelor's degrees are awarded in BIOLOGICAL SCIENCE (biochemistry and biology/biological science), BUSINESS (banking and finance, business administration and management, management information systems, and marketing/retailing/merchandising), COMMUNICATIONS AND THE ARTS (broadcasting, creative writing, English literature, journalism, media arts, music, public relations, Spanish, studio art, and visual and performing arts), COMPUTER AND PHYSICAL SCIENCE (chemistry, computer science, mathematics, and science), EDUCATION (athletic training, early childhood education, education, elementary education, physical education, and special education), ENGINEERING AND ENVIRONMENTAL DESIGN (electrical/electronics engineering), HEALTH PROFESSIONS (exercise science), SOCIAL SCIENCE (criminal justice, economics, history, international studies, philosophy, political science/government, psychology, religion, social work, and sociology). Accounting and business, education, and social sciences have the largest enrollments.

Required: To earn any degree students must complete a total of 120 hours with a minimum GPA of 2.0 and 36 to 37 hours of general education. There are additional requirements for a bachelor of music degree. All students must complete and present 2 1-credit student portfolios for review. A thesis and/or comprehensive exam is required for some majors.

Special: The college offers cross-registration with Clarke College and the University of Dubuque and study abroad in 10 countries. Also available are various internships, on-campus work-study programs, a 3-2 engineering degree, a Washington semester, pass/fail options, combined liberal arts and preprofessional programs, dual and student-designed majors, and adult degree programs offering a B.A.-B.S. degree. There are 3 national honor societies and a freshman honors program.

Faculty/Classroom: 56% of faculty are male; 44% are female. All teach undergraduates. No introductory courses are taught by graduate students. The average class size in an introductory lecture is 18; in a laboratory is 15; and in a regular course is 17.

Admissions: 46 freshmen graduated first in their class.

Requirements: The SAT or ACT is required. Applicants must be graduates of an accredited secondary school or have a GED certificate and have completed 4 units of English and 3 each of math, science, social studies, and history. An essay and an interview are recommended. A GPA of 2.5

is required. AP and CLEP credits are accepted. Important factors in the admissions decision are evidence of special talent, advanced placement or honors courses, and leadership record.

Procedure: Freshmen are admitted fall and spring. Entrance exams should be taken in April or June before the senior year or October of the senior year. There is a rolling admissions plan. Application deadlines are open. Application fee is $25. Notification is sent on a rolling basis. Applications are accepted online.

Transfer: Transfer students must have a minimum 2.0 GPA and submit transcripts of previous college work. Other requirements apply. 30 of 120 credits required for the bachelor's degree must be completed at Loras.

Visiting: There are regularly scheduled orientations for prospective students, consisting of 5 fall visitation days for all students and 7 programs for specific geographic locations. There are guides for informal visits, visitors may sit in on classes, and stay overnight. To schedule a visit, contact the Office of Admissions.

Financial Aid: The FAFSA is required. Check with the school for current application deadlines.

International Students: The school actively recruits these students. They must take the TOEFL.

Computers: Wireless access is available. PCs are available throughout the campus to connect to the wireless system. All students may access the system. All computer equipment is available for student use on all school days. There are no time limits and no fees. All students are required to have a personal computer. An IBM ThinkPad is recommended.

Admissions Contact: Director of Admissions. A campus DVD is available. E-Mail: *adms@loras.edu* Web: *www.loras.edu*

LUTHER COLLEGE — E-1

Decorah, IA 52101 — (563) 387-1287; (800) 458-8437; (563) 387-2159

Full-time: 1040 men, 1373 women	**Faculty:** 180; IIB, av$
Part-time: 26 men, 27 women	**Ph.D.s:** 93%
Graduate: n/av	**Student/Faculty:** 13 to 1
Year: 4-1-4, summer session	**Tuition:** $37,530
Application Deadline:	**Room & Board:** $6850
Freshman Class: 3490 applied, 2517 accepted, 628 enrolled	
SAT CR/M/W: 525/550/530 **ACT:** 26	**VERY COMPETITIVE+**

Founded in 1861, Luther College is a residential, liberal arts institution affiliated with the Evangelical Lutheran Church. One of the outstanding undergraduate institutions in the Midwest, Luther offers more than 60 majors, minors, pre-professional and special programs leading to the bachelor of arts degree. A Phi Beta Kappa chapter attests the academic excellence of the college. Forty states and 56 countries are represented in the 2,500-member student body. In addition to regional accreditation, Luther has baccalaureate program accreditation with CSWE, NASM, NCATE, and NLN. The library contains 339,055 volumes, 24,839 microform items, and 11,454 audio/video tapes/CDs/DVDs, and subscribes to 30,000 periodicals including electronic. Computerized library services include interlibrary loans, database searching, and Internet access. Special learning facilities include an art gallery, natural history museum, planetarium, and radio station. The 200-acre campus is in a small town in Northeast Iowa at the intersection of State Highway 9 and U.S. Route 52, and is 70 miles southeast of Rochester, Minnesota, and 56 miles southwest of La Crosse, WI. Including any residence halls, there are 35 buildings.

Student Life: 70% of undergraduates are from out of state, mostly the Mid-West. Students are from 40 states, 56 foreign countries, and Canada. 90% are from public schools. 85% are White. 58% are Protestant; 17% Catholic. The average age of freshmen is 18; all undergraduates, 20. 13% do not continue beyond their first year; 77% remain to graduate.

Housing: 2134 students can be accommodated in college housing, which includes coed dorms, on-campus apartments, off-campus apartments, and married student housing. In addition, there are special-interest houses, sustainability house, dialogue floors, and wellness floors. On-campus housing is guaranteed for all 4 years. 84% of students live on campus; of those, 90% remain on campus on weekends. All students may keep cars.

Activities: 1% of men belong to 41 local fraternities; 2% of women belong to 43 local sororities. There are 84 groups on campus, including art, band, cheerleading, choir, chorale, chorus, communications, computers, dance, drama, drill team, environmental, ethnic, forensics, gay, honors, international, jazz band, literary magazine, musical theater, newspaper, opera, orchestra, pep band, photography, political, professional, radio and TV, religious, social, social service, student government, symphony, and yearbook. Popular campus events include Christmas at Luther, Ethnic Arts Fair and Parents Weekend.

Sports: There are 10 intercollegiate sports for men and 9 for women, and 45 intramural sports for men and 45 for women. Facilities include 5 hardwood basketball courts, a new 25-yard, six-lane pool with a seating capacity of 600, 4 batting cages, a fitness center, a climbing wall, 3 soccer fields, a golf driving range, a dance studio, a 4000-seat stadium and 3500-seat gym, 6 indoor tennis courts, 3 racquetball courts, an indoor 6-lane 200-meter track, an outdoor 8-lane polyurethane 400-meter track, and 12 outdoor tennis courts.

Disabled Students: 95% of the campus is accessible. Facilities include wheelchair ramps, elevators, special parking, specially equipped restrooms, lowered drinking fountains, lowered telephones, and special housing.

Services: Counseling and information services are available, as is tutoring in every subject. There is a reader service for the blind, and remedial reading and writing. Reading machines, tape recorders, note taking, and a learning center are available.

Campus Safety and Security: Measures include 24-hour foot and vehicle patrol, emergency notification system, self-defense education, and security escort services. There are emergency telephones, lighted pathways/sidewalks, and controlled access to dorms/residences.

Programs of Study: Luther confers B.A. degrees. Bachelor's degrees are awarded in AGRICULTURE (environmental studies), BIOLOGICAL SCIENCE (biology/biological science), BUSINESS (accounting and management science), COMMUNICATIONS AND THE ARTS (art, classical languages, communications, dance, dramatic arts, English, French, German, music, Russian, Spanish, and theatre arts), COMPUTER AND PHYSICAL SCIENCE (chemistry, computer science, mathematics, physics, and statistics), EDUCATION (athletic training, elementary education, and physical education), HEALTH PROFESSIONS (health and nursing), SOCIAL SCIENCE (African American studies, anthropology, biblical languages, economics, history, international studies, philosophy, political science/government, psychology, religion, Scandinavian studies, social work, sociology, and women's studies). Biology, music and English are the strongest academically. Biology, music, and management have the largest enrollments.

Required: Students must complete 128 credit hours for a B.A. with a cumulative grade-point average of 2.0 (C) or higher. The 128 hours must include the following: 30 fall/spring full courses or their equivalents. A full course is equivalent to 4 credit hours; other courses offered are equivalent to 2 credit hours or 1 credit hour. 2 January terms. These 2 month-long terms must include a first-year seminar, and one of the following types of experiences: study away, directed readings, student-initiated project. At least 20 course equivalents outside the student's major discipline. 64 credit hours completed in residence. All-college requirements: Common ground; Fields of inquiry; Integrative understanding; Perspectives and skills.

Special: Internships in most disciplines, study away opportunities both domestically and in many countries, a Washington semester, student-designed and dual majors, and 3-2 engineering degrees with Washington University in St. Louis and the University of Minnesota are available, work-study programs. There are 13 national honor societies, including Phi Beta Kappa, and a freshman honors program.

Faculty/Classroom: 49% of faculty are male; 51% are female. All teach undergraduates. No introductory courses are taught by graduate students. The average class size in an introductory lecture is 25; in a laboratory is 11; and in a regular course is 19.

Admissions: 72% of the 2013-2014 applicants were accepted. The SAT scores for the 2013-2014 freshman class were: Critical Reading--37% below 500, 31% between 500 and 599, 26% between 600 and 699, and 6% between 700 and 800; Math--22% below 500, 40% between 500 and 599, 26% between 600 and 699, and 12% between 700 and 800; Writing--34% below 500, 45% between 500 and 599, 16% between 600 and 699, and 5% between 700 and 800. The ACT scores were 8% below 21, 21% between 21 and 23, 28% between 24 and 26, 17% between 27 and 28, and 26% above 28. 50% of the current freshmen were in the top fifth of their class; 75% were in the top two fifths. 24 freshmen graduated first in their class.

Requirements: The SAT or ACT is required. In order to be considered for admission, the applicant should be within 2 semesters of graduation from an accredited high school and should complete the following college preparatory coursework: 4 years of English, which may include 1 year of speech, communications, or journalism; 3 years of math; 3 years of social science; 2 years of natural science, including 1 year of lab science; and 2 years of a foreign language study are recommended. Applicants who do not meet these standards will be considered for admission if they submit above-average ACT or SAT scores. A GPA of 2.5 is required. AP and CLEP credits are accepted. Important factors in the admissions decision are advanced placement or honors courses, evidence of special talent, and extracurricular activities record.

Procedure: Freshmen are admitted fall, winter, and spring. Entrance exams should be taken by the fall of the senior year. There are deferred admissions and rolling admissions plans. Application deadlines are open. Notifications are sent November 1. Applications are accepted online. Application fees are waived if application is completed online.

Transfer: 39 transfer students enrolled in 2012-2013. Applicants must meet the same high school standards and the SAT or ACT requirements as entering freshmen, with a minimum GPA of 2.5 in parallel college course work. 64 of 128 credits required for the bachelor's degree must be completed at Luther.

Visiting: There are regularly scheduled orientations for prospective stu-

dents. There are guides for informal visits, visitors may sit in on classes, and stay overnight. To schedule a visit, contact the Admissions Office at (563) 387-1287.

Financial Aid: In 2013-2014, 100% of all full-time freshmen and 100% of continuing full-time students received some form of financial aid. 73% of all full-time freshmen and 70% of continuing full-time students received need-based aid. The average freshman award was $31,153. Need-based scholarships or need-based grants averaged $23,827; and need-based self-help aid (loans and jobs) averaged $6,360. 77% of undergraduate students work part-time. Average annual earnings from campus work are $1208. The average financial indebtedness of the 2013 graduate was $26,179. Luther is a member of CSS. The FAFSA and the college's own financial statement, and a family tax return are required. The priority date for freshman financial aid applications for fall entry is March 1.

International Students: There are 142 international students enrolled. The school actively recruits these students. They must take the TOEFL with a minimum score of 550 on the paper-based TOEFL (PBT) or 80 on the Internet-based version (iBT), or the IELTS.

Computers: All students may access the system anytime. There are no time limits and no fees.

Graduates: From July 1, 2012 to June 30, 2013, 549 bachelor's degrees were awarded. The most popular majors were biology (16%), music (13%), and management (10%). 203 companies recruited on campus in 2012-2013. In an average class, 67% graduate in 4 years or less, 75% graduate in 5 years or less, and 76% graduate in 6 years or less. Of the 2012 graduating class, 18% were enrolled in graduate school within 6 months of graduation, and 62% were employed.

Admissions Contact: Scot Schaeffer, Vice President for Enrollment Management. E-Mail: *admissions@luther.edu* Web: *https:/www.luther.edu/admissions/*

MAHARISHI UNIVERSITY OF MANAGEMENT E-3

Fairfield, IA 52557 (641) 472-1110
(800) 369-6480; (641) 472-1179

Full-time: 120 men, 80 women	**Faculty:** n/av
Part-time: 10 men, 10 women	**Ph.D.s:** 100%
Graduate: 610 men, 145 women	**Student/Faculty:** n/av
Year: semesters	**Tuition:** $25,500
Application Deadline: open	**Room & Board:** $6500
Freshman Class: n/av	
	VERY COMPETITIVE

Maharishi University of Management, established in 1971, is a private institution offering undergraduate and graduate programs in a broad range of disciplines. The University provides consciousness-based education and incorporates the group practice of the Maharishi Transcendental Meditation technique into a traditional academic program. The figures in the above capsule and in this profile are approximate. There are 5 undergraduate schools and 5 graduate schools. The library contains 150,294 volumes, 59,851 microform items, and 21,291 audio/video tapes/CDs/DVDs, and subscribes to 23,345 periodicals including electronic. Computerized library services include interlibrary loans, database searching, and Internet access. Special learning facilities include a learning resource center, art gallery, radio station, psychophysiology, electronic engineering, visual technology, and physics labs, a scanning electron microscope, and domes for practicing the Transcendental Meditation Sidhi program. The 272-acre campus is in a small town 114 miles southeast of Des Moines and 60 miles southwest of Iowa City. Including any residence halls, there are 50 buildings.

Student Life: 61% of undergraduates are from out of state, mostly the Mid-West. Students are from 21 states, 29 foreign countries, and Canada. 74% are white; 17% foreign nationals. 39% do not continue beyond their first year; 46% remain to graduate.

Housing: 350 students can be accommodated in college housing, which includes single-sex dorms, on-campus apartments, and married student housing. In addition, there are special-interest houses, privately owned, on-campus family housing for students with families. On-campus housing is guaranteed for all 4 years. 70% of students live on campus; of those, 90% remain on campus on weekends. Alcohol is not permitted. All students may keep cars.

Activities: There are no fraternities or sororities. There are 15 groups on campus, including entrepreneurial, international, permaculture, art, chess, chorale, chorus, dance, drama, ecology, environmental, ethnic, international, musical theater, newspaper, photography, political, professional, radio and TV, religious, social, social service, student government, and yearbook. Popular campus events include sports festivals, seasonal celebrations, and International Cultural Exchange Festival.

Sports: There are 2 intercollegiate sports for men and 1 for women, and 5 intramural sports for men and 5 for women. Facilities include outdoor and indoor tennis, basketball, and volleyball courts, a gym, a weight-training room, a field house, a swimming pool, a table tennis room, batting and golf driving cages, a golf putting range, an indoor 4-lane jogging track, a dance studio, and a rock-climbing wall.

Disabled Students: 95% of the campus is accessible. Facilities include wheelchair ramps, special parking, specially equipped restrooms, and lowered telephones.

Services: Counseling and information services are available, as is tutoring in every subject. There is remedial math, reading, and writing.

Campus Safety and Security: Measures include 24-hour foot and vehicle patrol and security escort services. There are emergency telephones and lighted pathways/sidewalks.

Programs of Study: confers B.A., B.S., and B.F.A. degrees. Master's and doctoral degrees are also awarded. Bachelor's degrees are awarded in BUSINESS (management science), COMMUNICATIONS AND THE ARTS (dramatic arts, fine arts, and literature), COMPUTER AND PHYSICAL SCIENCE (computer science and mathematics), EDUCATION (education). Sustainable living, Maharishi Vedic science, and business are the largest.

Required: Students must complete 166 credit units with a minimum of 60 credits in the major and must also complete the core curriculum of 18 units as well as 20 units in a distribution of academic fields. All students must maintain a minimum GPA of 2.0. Requirements include health and fitness courses, the Science of Creative Intelligence course with its applied aspect, the Transcendental Meditation program, and courses in math and writing. The 42-week school year and block scheduling system allow students to take 1 course at a time.

Special: Opportunities are provided for internships, study abroad, and nondegree study. Systematic programs are offered in the Science of Creative Intelligence, by which students apply knowledge to practical professional values. There are several 1-month blocks a year during which students may study, for example, art in Italy, literature in Switzerland, or business in China. There is a freshman honors program.

Faculty/Classroom: 80% of faculty are male; 20% are female. All teach undergraduates, 20% do research, and 20% do both. No introductory courses are taught by graduate students. The average class size in an introductory lecture is 35 and in a regular course is 10.

Admissions: There is 1 National Merit finalist.

Requirements: Applicants must graduate from an accredited secondary school or have a GED. An essay and 2 personal recommendations are required. An interview is recommended. A GPA of 2.5 is required. AP and CLEP credits are accepted. Important factors in the admissions decision are personality/intangible qualities, recommendations by school officials, and leadership record.

Procedure: Freshmen are admitted fall and spring. Entrance exams should be taken in the fall of the senior year or spring of the junior year. There are early admissions, deferred admissions, and rolling admissions plans. Application deadlines are open. Application fee is $15. Applications are accepted online.

Transfer: Students must have a 2.5 GPA and acceptable recommendations as well as meet all standards set by the university. 66 of 166 credits required for the bachelor's degree must be completed at MUOM.

Visiting: There are regularly scheduled orientations for prospective students, including campus tours, visits to classes, interviews, student panels, and informal dinners. There are guides for informal visits, visitors may sit in on classes, and stay overnight. To schedule a visit, contact Admissions.

Financial Aid: The FAFSA is required. Check with the school for current application deadlines.

International Students: The school actively recruits these students. They must take the TOEFL and the college's own test.

Computers: All students may access the system daytime and evenings. There are no time limits and no fees. It is strongly recommended that all students have a personal computer.

Admissions Contact: Associate Dean of Admissions. A campus DVD is available. E-Mail: *admissions@mum.edu* Web: *www.mum.edu*

MERCY COLLEGE OF HEALTH SCIENCES C-3

Des Moines, IA 50309 (515) 643-6604
(800) 637-2994; (515) 643-6698

Full-time: 55 men, 335 women	**Faculty:** 51
Part-time: 46 men, 410 women	**Ph.D.s:** 22%
Graduate: n/av	**Student/Faculty:** 7 to 1
Year: semesters, summer session	**Tuition:** $14,460
Application Deadline: June 15	**Room & Board:** n/av
Freshman Class: 111 applied, 93 accepted, 43 enrolled	
ACT: required	**SPECIAL**

Mercy College of Health Sciences was founded in 1995 and is a private school affiliated with the Religious Sisters of Mercy (RSM), a religious order of Roman Catholic women. There are 3 undergraduate schools. The 5 libraries contain 12,188 volumes, and 796 audio/video tapes/CDs/DVDs, and subscribe to 7,000 periodicals including electronic. Computerized library services include interlibrary loans, database searching, Internet access, and Wi-Fi capability. The 5-acre campus is in an urban area downtown Des Moines, Iowa. Including any residence halls, there are 5 buildings.

Student Life: 98% of undergraduates are from Iowa. Others are from 13 states. 85% are White. The average age of freshmen is 26; all undergraduates, 26.

Housing: Alcohol is not permitted. All students may keep cars.

Activities: There are no fraternities or sororities. Groups on campus include association of nursing students, alpha beta kappa national honor society, Sigma Theta Tau International Honor Society of Nursing, honors, professional, science club, and student government. Popular campus events include Cultural Fair, and Community Service Opportunities.

Sports: There is no sports program at Mercy College.

Disabled Students: All of the campus is accessible. Facilities include wheelchair ramps, elevators, special parking, specially equipped restrooms, and lowered drinking fountains.

Services: Counseling and information services are available, as is tutoring in most subjects.

Campus Safety and Security: Measures include security escort services. There are shuttle buses and lighted pathways/sidewalks.

Programs of Study: Mercy College confers B.S. degrees. Associate degrees are also awarded. Bachelor's degrees are awarded in HEALTH PROFESSIONS (health care administration, health science, nursing, and premedicine). Nursing, nuclear medicine, radiologic technology and surgical technology are the strongest academically. Nursing has the largest enrollment.

Required: Graduation requirements: service learning, critical thinking, communication. Critical thinking and caring courses, and a minimum GPA is also required.

Special: Clinical experience is an integral component for most academic programs. Bachelor of Science degrees in Nursing, Health Care Administration, Health Sciences (Pre-Medicine). There are 2 national honor societies and 2 departmental honors programs.

Faculty/Classroom: 17% of faculty are male; 83% are female. All teach undergraduates. No introductory courses are taught by graduate students.

Admissions: 84% of the 2013-2014 applicants were accepted.

Requirements: The ACT is required. A GPA of 2.3 is required. AP and CLEP credits are accepted.

Procedure: Freshmen are admitted fall, spring, and summer. There is a rolling admissions plan. Applications should be filed by June 15 for fall entry; October 15 for spring entry; and March 15 for summer entry. Applications are accepted online.

Transfer: Requirements vary by program. 30 credits required for the bachelor's degree must be completed at Mercy College.

Visiting: There are regularly scheduled orientations for prospective students. There are guides for informal visits. To schedule a visit, contact the Admissions Office.

Financial Aid: In 2013-2014, 91% of all full-time freshmen and 92% of continuing full-time students received some form of financial aid. 88% of all full-time freshmen and 89% of continuing full-time students received need-based aid. The average freshman award was $8,291. Need-based scholarships or need-based grants averaged $5,739 ($16,413 maximum); and need-based self-help aid (loans and jobs) averaged $6,869 ($20,886 maximum). 1% of undergraduate students work part-time. Average annual earnings from campus work are $2125. The average financial indebtedness of the 2013 graduate was $29,111. The FAFSA is required. The priority date for freshman financial aid applications for fall entry is April 1. The deadline for filing freshman financial aid applications for fall entry is July 1.

Computers: All students may access the system. There are no time limits and no fees.

Graduates: From July 1, 2012 to June 30, 2013, 70 bachelor's degrees were awarded. The most popular majors were Associate of science in nursing (49%), Bachelors of science in nursing (17%), and Associate of science radiologic technology (4%).

Admissions Contact: Kara Donovan, Director of Admissions. E-Mail: *admissions@mchs.edu* Web: *www.mchs.edu*

MORNINGSIDE COLLEGE

B-2

Sioux City, IA 51106

(712) 274-5111
(800) 831-0806; (712) 274-5101

Full-time: 598 men, 671 women	**Faculty:** 77; IIB, --$
Part-time: 20 men, 31 women	**Ph.D.s:** 71%
Graduate: 154 men, 573 women	**Student/Faculty:** 17 to 1
Year: semesters, summer session	**Tuition:** $24,050
Application Deadline: open	**Room & Board:** $7320

Freshman Class: 2798 applied, 1792 accepted, 377 enrolled
ACT: 23

COMPETITIVE

Morningside College, founded in 1894, is a private college affiliated with the United Methodist Church. Its curriculum includes the liberal arts and pre-professional and professional programs of study. There is 1 undergraduate school and 1 graduate school. In addition to regional accreditation, Morningside has baccalaureate program accreditation with NASM, NCATE, and NLN. The library contains 74,445 volumes, 288,382 microform items, and 1,927 audio/video tapes/CDs/DVDs, and subscribes to 207 periodicals including electronic. Computerized library services include interlibrary loans, database searching, and Internet access. Special learning facilities include a learning resource center, art gallery, radio station, TV station, a theater. The 69-acre campus is in a suburban area 100 miles north of Omaha at the convergence of the states of South Dakota, Iowa, and Nebraska. Including any residence halls, there are 23 buildings.

Student Life: 64% of undergraduates are from Iowa. Others are from 20 states, and 10 foreign countries. 86% are white. 54% are Protestant; 21% claim no religious affiliation; 18% Catholic. The average age of freshmen is 18; all undergraduates, 20. 25% do not continue beyond their first year; 48% remain to graduate.

Housing: 880 students can be accommodated in college housing, which includes coed dorms, on-campus apartments, and married student housing. In addition, there are fraternity houses, sorority houses, freshman halls, upperclassman leadership-themed, and apartment-style residence hall. On-campus housing is guaranteed for all 4 years. 65% of students live on campus; of those, 65% remain on campus on weekends. All students may keep cars.

Activities: 4% of men belong to 2 national fraternities; 2% of women belong to 1 national sorority. There are 41 groups on campus, including art, band, cheerleading, choir, chorale, chorus, computers, dance, drama, drill team, environmental, ethnic, honors, international, jazz band, literary magazine, newspaper, orchestra, pep band, photography, political, professional, radio and TV, religious, social, and student government. Popular campus events include Friday is Writing Day, Campus Event Series, and Christmas at Morningside.

Sports: There are 11 intercollegiate sports for men and 10 for women, and 13 intramural sports for men and 13 for women. Facilities include an 8000-seat stadium, a football field, a campus recreation center with basketball, volleyball, and racquetball/handball courts, an elevated track, a weight room, and a 6-lane, 25-yard pool.

Disabled Students: 80% of the campus is accessible. Facilities include wheelchair ramps, elevators, special parking, specially equipped restrooms, special class scheduling, lowered drinking fountains, and lowered telephones.

Services: Counseling and information services are available, as is tutoring in most subjects. There is a reader service for the blind, and remedial math, reading, and writing.

Campus Safety and Security: Measures include emergency notification system, self-defense education, and security escort services. There are emergency telephones, lighted pathways/sidewalks, and controlled access to dorms/residences.

Programs of Study: Morningside confers B.A., B.S., B.Mus., B.Mus.Ed., and B.S.N. degrees. Master's degrees are also awarded. Bachelor's degrees are awarded in BIOLOGICAL SCIENCE (biology/biological science), BUSINESS (business administration and management and management information systems), COMMUNICATIONS AND THE ARTS (advertising, art, communications, dramatic arts, English, graphic design, music, photography, and Spanish), COMPUTER AND PHYSICAL SCIENCE (chemistry, computer science, mathematics, and physics), EDUCATION (art education, education, elementary education, English education, mathematics education, music education, science education, social studies education, and special education), HEALTH PROFESSIONS (medical technology and nursing), SOCIAL SCIENCE (history, international relations, philosophy, political science/government, psychology, and religion). Biology, business administration, and education are the largest.

Required: The total number of credit hours required for graduation is 124 with 44 hours of core curriculum in liberal arts and 30 hours minimum in the major. Students must have a minimum GPA of 2.0 to graduate.

Special: There is a co-op program in medical technology. Internships are available in all departments. Study abroad in 11 countries, a Washington semester, work-study programs, both on campus and with 20 nonprofit agencies, and student-designed majors are available. There are 15 national honor societies and a freshman honors program.

Faculty/Classroom: 56% of faculty are male; 44% are female. All teach undergraduates. No introductory courses are taught by graduate students. The average class size in an introductory lecture is 27; in a laboratory is 17; and in a regular course is 21.

Admissions: 64% of the 2011-2012 applicants were accepted. The ACT scores were 21% below 21, 34% between 21 and 23, 27% between 24 and 26, 10% between 27 and 28, and 8% above 28. 37% of the current freshmen were in the top fifth of their class; 66% were in the top two fifths. 14 freshmen graduated first in their class.

Requirements: The ACT is required. In addition, applicants must be graduates of an accredited secondary school. The GED is accepted. A portfolio is required for all studio art majors and an audition for performing music majors. Applicants graduating from high school 5 years or more prior to entering college are exempted from submitting the ACT scores. Those entering from a home-schooled environment must submit a completed Home School Credit Evaluation form, which may be obtained in the

Office of Admissions. Morningside requires applicants to be in the upper 50% of their class. A GPA of 2.5 is required. AP and CLEP credits are accepted. Important factors in the admissions decision are recommendations by school officials, evidence of special talent, and advanced placement or honors courses.

Procedure: Freshmen are admitted to all sessions. Entrance exams should be taken in the junior year. There is a rolling admissions plan. Application deadlines are open. Applications are accepted online.

Transfer: 80 transfer students enrolled in 2010-2011. Transfer applicants must take the ACT and have an interview. They must have 24 semester hours with a 2.25 or above cumulative GPA. They must present official transcripts of previous collegiate records. 30 of 124 credits required for the bachelor's degree must be completed at Morningside.

Visiting: There are regularly scheduled orientations for prospective students, consists of a campus tour, appointments with faculty and financial aid, and an interview with an admissions counselor. There are guides for informal visits, visitors may sit in on classes, and stay overnight. To schedule a visit, contact Office of Admissions.

Financial Aid: In 2011-2012, 100% of all full-time freshmen and 100% of continuing full-time students received some form of financial aid. 80% of all full-time freshmen and 84% of continuing full-time students received need-based aid. The average freshman award was $25,417. Need-based scholarships or need-based grants averaged $12,800 ($17,225 maximum); need-based self-help aid (loans and jobs) averaged $1,660 ($6,700 maximum); non-need-based athletic scholarships averaged $2,900 ($9,000 maximum); other non-need-based awards and non-need-based scholarships averaged $2,000 ($24,500 maximum); and $1,500 from other forms of aid. 58% of undergraduate students work part-time. Average annual earnings from campus work are $1651. The average financial indebtedness of the 2011 graduate was $36,309. The FAFSA is required. The priority date for freshman financial aid applications for fall entry is March 1.

International Students: There are 15 international students enrolled. The school actively recruits these students. They must take the TOEFL with a minimum score of 500 on the paper-based TOEFL (PBT) or 61 on the Internet-based version (iBT). They must also take the ACT.

Computers: Wireless access is available. Wired access is available in dorm rooms, and wireless access is available across campus in common areas and classrooms. Each full-time student has a college-issued notebook PC. All students may access the system. There are no time limits and no fees. All students are required to have a personal computer. A Dell or Apple is recommended.

Graduates: From July 1, 2010 to June 30, 2011, 252 bachelor's degrees were awarded. The most popular majors were business (28%), education (13%), and biology (13%). 19 companies recruited on campus in 2010-2011. In an average class, 2% graduate in 3 years or less, 48% graduate in 4 years or less, 58% graduate in 5 years or less, and 57% graduate in 6 years or less. Of the 2010 graduating class, 15% were enrolled in graduate school within 6 months of graduation, and 98% were employed.

Admissions Contact: Terri Curry, VP Admissions. E-Mail: *mscadm@morningside.edu* Web: *www.morningside.edu*

MOUNT MERCY UNIVERSITY — E-3
Mount Mercy College

Cedar Rapids, IA 52402 — (319) 368-6460; (800) 248-4504; (319) 363-5270

Full-time: 273 men, 609 women	**Faculty:** 77
Part-time: 181 men, 413 women	**Ph.D.s:** 65%
Graduate: 88 men, 197 women	**Student/Faculty:** 14 to 1
Year: 4-1-4, summer session	**Tuition:** $26,310
Application Deadline:	**Room & Board:** $8075
Freshman Class: 542 applied, 371 accepted, 154 enrolled	
SAT: recommended	**ACT:** 21 — **COMPETITIVE**

The men and women who make up our student body come from all over Iowa and the world. They choose Mount Mercy for our small, hands-on classes, meaningful faculty interaction, vibrant student life and our commitment to leadership and compassionate service. There are 4 graduate schools. In addition to regional accreditation, Mount Mercy has baccalaureate program accreditation with CSWE and NLN. The library contains 130,508 volumes, 54,904 microform items, and 5,586 audio/video tapes/CDs/DVDs, and subscribes to 3,511 periodicals including electronic. Computerized library services include interlibrary loans, database searching, Internet access, and Wi-Fi capability. Special learning facilities include an art gallery, all of the classrooms are "smart" technology classrooms. The 40-acre campus is in an urban area in Cedar Rapids in eastern Iowa. Including any residence halls, there are 19 buildings.

Student Life: 91% of undergraduates are from Iowa. Others are from 20 states, 27 foreign countries, and Canada. 86% are White. 25% are Catholic; 25% Protestant; 25% claim no religious affiliation. The average age of freshmen is 18; all undergraduates, 26. 18% do not continue beyond their first year; 73% remain to graduate.

Housing: 480 students can be accommodated in college housing, which includes single-sex and coed dorms and on-campus apartments. In addition, there are special-interest houses, Themed Living Learning Communities. On-campus housing is guaranteed for all 4 years. 63% of students commute. All students may keep cars.

Activities: There are no fraternities or sororities. There are 34 groups on campus, including academic, art, cheerleading, choir, chorale, chorus, computers, dance, drama, drill team, environmental, film, honors, international, jazz band, literary magazine, musical theater, newspaper, political, professional, religious, social, social service, and student government. Popular campus events include Octoberfest, Bingo Nights, and Vegas Night.

Sports: There are 7 intercollegiate sports for men and 8 for women, and 17 intramural sports for men and 17 for women. Facilities include Hennessey Recreation Facility is a 32,000 sq ft facility, built in 1985 and named in honor of Sr Mary Agnes Hennessey,and is home court for Mount Mercy athletics. Built into a hill on the northeast corner of campus, the recreation center offers practice facilities, a weight room, fully-equipped training room, and separate locker rooms for general use and those designated for the student-athletes in men's and women's sports. At the heart of the Hennessey Recreation Center is the gymnasium with seating for 2,000 fans. In addition, Hennessey has a regulation-sized racquetball court, lounge and reception areas, a classroom/conference room, and the athletic department offices. The Lundy Fitness Center offers a cardio and weight area, plus a large group exercise rooms where classes are offered each semester. The Center offers equipment and spaces for a variety of cardiovascular and muscle-building workout routines.

Disabled Students: 95% of the campus is accessible. Facilities include wheelchair ramps, elevators, special parking, specially equipped restrooms, and lowered drinking fountains.

Services: Counseling and information services are available, as is tutoring in most subjects, all communication skills. There is a reader service for the blind, and remedial math, reading, and writing.

Campus Safety and Security: Measures include 24-hour foot and vehicle patrol, emergency notification system, self-defense education, and security escort services. There are emergency telephones, lighted pathways/sidewalks, controlled access to dorms/residences, Safety personnel who are on duty 24-hours-a-day, 365-days-a-year, with regularly scheduled patrols, extensive video monitoring of building entrances building exits, and most parking facilities. Surveillance is monitored and recorded. After hours, use of residence elevators and entry to student room corridors require a resident-only passkey.

Programs of Study: Mount Mercy confers B.A., B.A.A., B.A.S., B.B.A., B.S. and B.S.N. degrees. Master's degrees are also awarded. Bachelor's degrees are awarded in AGRICULTURE (conservation and regulation), BIOLOGICAL SCIENCE (biology/biological science), BUSINESS (accounting, business administration and management, finance, human resources, management information systems, and marketing/retailing/merchandising), COMMUNICATIONS AND THE ARTS (art, communications, English, graphic design, journalism, music, and speech/debate/rhetoric), COMPUTER AND PHYSICAL SCIENCE (computer science and mathematics), EDUCATION (early childhood education, elementary education, middle school education, and secondary education), HEALTH PROFESSIONS (health care administration, medical laboratory technology, and nursing), SOCIAL SCIENCE (criminal justice, history, humanities, international studies, philosophy, political science/government, psychology, religion, social work, and sociology). Business, nursing, education, and criminal justice have the largest enrollments.

Required: To graduate, students must complete 123 semester hours; have a minimum cumulative GPA of at least 2.00; a minimum cumulative GPA in all credits taken at MMU; completion of the core curriculum requirements; completions of a major program of study; at least 12 semester hours, above course number 200, completed in the major at MMU; a minimum of 30 semester hours completed at MMU; a minimum of 30 consecutive semester hours completed at MMU immediately preceding graduation.

Special: Mount Mercy offers internships in most majors, study abroad opportunities, work-study programs on campus, several adult accelerated business majors, an accelerated degree completion program for RNs, and student-designed, interdisciplinary majors. Credit for prior experiential learning may be granted, and pass/fail options are available. There are 3 national honor societies, a freshman honors program, and 10 departmental honors programs.

Faculty/Classroom: 36% of faculty are male; 64% are female. 93% teach undergraduates. No introductory courses are taught by graduate students. The average class size in an introductory lecture is 25; in a laboratory is 14; and in a regular course is 25.

Admissions: 68% of the 2013-2014 applicants were accepted. The ACT scores were 36% below 21, 45% between 21 and 23, 14% between 24 and 26, 2% between 27 and 28, and 3% above 28. 28% of the current freshmen were in the top fifth of their class; 62% were in the top two fifths. 1 freshman graduated first in the class.

Requirements: The SAT or ACT is recommended. In addition, The Admissions Committee evaluates all applications on an individual basis.

Strong consideration will be given to applicants with the following: Cumulative grade point average of 2.75 (on a 4.0 scale) Composite ACT score of 20 (940 SAT) with sub-scores of 17 or higher Class rank in the top half of their graduating class. While specific courses are not required for admission, students applying to Mount Mercy are encouraged to complete the following high school coursework: four years of English three years of mathematics three years of social studies three years of science A GPA of 2.5 is required. AP and CLEP credits are accepted. Important factors in the admissions decision are leadership record, extracurricular activities record, and geographical diversity.

Procedure: Freshmen are admitted to all sessions. Entrance exams should be taken in the junior year or the fall of the senior year. There are deferred admissions and rolling admissions plans. Check with the school for current application deadlines. Notification is sent on a rolling basis. Applications are accepted online. Application fees are waived if application is completed online.

Transfer: 190 transfer students enrolled in 2012-2013. Mount Mercy evaluates all files on an individual basis. While specific courses are not required for admission, the transcripts will be evaluated to ensure that strong college curriculum has been successfully completed. Strong consideration will be given to applicants who have the following: Cumulative transfer grade point average of 2.50 (on a 4.0 scale). Application by students looking to transfer with two semesters or less will be reviewed by the Admission Committee. A complete admission file includes: application for admission, official high school transcripts. For applicants who have not earned an associates degree or higher from an accredited college or university official transcripts from all previous colleges attended. Updated copies of college transcripts will need to be sent prior to enrollment for students who apply for admission while enrolled at another college. 30 of 123 credits required for the bachelor's degree must be completed at Mount Mercy.

Visiting: There are regularly scheduled orientations for prospective students, consisting of a presidential welcome, campus tour, student panel, faculty academic fair, presentations on college selection and admission requirements, and student evaluation. There are guides for informal visits, visitors may sit in on classes, and stay overnight. To schedule a visit, contact the Admissions Office at admission@mtmercy.edu.

Financial Aid: In 2013-2014, 100% of all full-time freshmen and 97% of continuing full-time students received some form of financial aid. 90% of all full-time freshmen and 80% of continuing full-time students received need-based aid. The average freshman award was $27,966. 46% of undergraduate students work part-time. Average annual earnings from campus work are $1268. The average financial indebtedness of the 2013 graduate was $27,400. The FAFSA is required. Check with the school for current application deadlines.

International Students: There are 51 international students enrolled. The school actively recruits these students. They must take the TOEFL with a minimum score of 550 on the paper-based TOEFL (PBT) or 79 on the Internet-based version (iBT), ICHS 6.5; Step EIKEN Grade 1; IELTS (6.5); ACT (20); SAT (940). They must also take the SAT or ACT, scoring 20.

Computers: All students may access the system 24 hours a day. There are no time limits and no fees.

Graduates: From July 1, 2012 to June 30, 2013, 401 bachelor's degrees were awarded. The most popular majors were nursing (22%), business (12%), and accounting (9%). 47 companies recruited on campus in 2012-2013. In an average class, 1% graduate in 3 years or less, 65% graduate in 4 years or less, 72% graduate in 5 years or less, and 73% graduate in 6 years or less. Of the 2012 graduating class, 9% were enrolled in graduate school within 6 months of graduation, and 95% were employed.

Admissions Contact: Terri Crumley, Dean of Admissions. E-Mail: *admission@.mtmercy.edu* Web: *www.mtmercy.edu*

NORTHWESTERN COLLEGE OF IOWA — B-2

Orange City, IA 51041 (712) 707-7130
(800) 747-4757; (712) 707-7164

Full-time: 500 men, 633 women	**Faculty:** 84; IIB, --$
Part-time: 32 men, 68 women	**Ph.D.s:** 82%
Graduate: n/av	**Student/Faculty:** 13 to 1
Year: semesters, summer session	**Tuition:** $26,764
Application Deadline: open	**Room & Board:** $8084
Freshman Class: 1221 applied, 929 accepted, 284 enrolled	
SAT CR/M/W: 550/540/500 **ACT:** 25	**COMPETITIVE+**

Northwestern College is a Christian college engaging students in courageous and faithful learning and living that empowers them to follow Christ and pursue God's redeeming work in the world. In addition to regional accreditation, Northwestern has baccalaureate program accreditation with CSWE and NCATE. The library contains 120,000 volumes, 110,000 microform items, and 6,000 audio/video tapes/CDs/DVDs, and subscribes to 840 periodicals including electronic. Computerized library services include interlibrary loans, database searching, Internet access, and Wi-Fi capability. Special learning facilities include an art gallery. The 100-acre campus is in a small town 40 miles northeast of Sioux City, and 75 miles southeast of Sioux Falls, South Dakota. Including any residence halls, there are 30 buildings.

Student Life: 51% of undergraduates are from Iowa. Others are from 36 states, 24 foreign countries, and Canada. 76% are from public schools. 84% are White. 80% are Protestant; 11% claim no religious affiliation. The average age of freshmen is 18; all undergraduates, 20. 21% do not continue beyond their first year; 63% remain to graduate.

Housing: 1141 students can be accommodated in college housing, which includes single-sex dorms, on-campus apartments, and married student housing. In addition, there are language houses and special-interest houses. On-campus housing is guaranteed for all 4 years. 89% of students live on campus; of those, 80% remain on campus on weekends. Alcohol is not permitted. All students may keep cars.

Activities: There are no fraternities or sororities. There are 35 groups on campus, including art, band, cheerleading, choir, chorus, computers, dance, drama, drill team, environmental, ethnic, film, honors, international, jazz band, literary magazine, musical theater, newspaper, orchestra, photography, political, professional, radio and TV, religious, social, social service, student government, symphony, and yearbook. Popular campus events include Clash of the Classes, Airband, Coly Christmas Bash, Homecoming, NC/DC Singing Competition, RUSH Student Dance Exhibition, and Winter Formal.

Sports: There are 8 intercollegiate sports for men and 8 for women, and 19 intramural sports for men and 19 for women. Facilities include A wood-floored gymnasium for basketball and volleyball that seats 2200, a turf football field surrounded by an eight-lane polyurethane track with 2200-seat stadium seating, 2 full-sized practice football fields, 2 soccer fields, a football/track locker room , a one-tenth-mile/six-lane indoor track, 3 handball/racquetball courts, 4 basketball and volleyball courts for recreational use, 2 indoor tennis courts, gymnastics/wrestling rooms, athletes' weight room and training room, student and community fitness center with free weights and fitness equipment.

Disabled Students: 90% of the campus is accessible. Facilities include wheelchair ramps, elevators, special parking, specially equipped restrooms, lowered drinking fountains, and special housing.

Services: Counseling and information services are available, as is tutoring in most subjects. There is remedial math, reading, and writing.

Campus Safety and Security: Measures include emergency notification system. There are emergency telephones, lighted pathways/sidewalks, and controlled access to dorms/residences.

Programs of Study: Northwestern confers B.A., B.A.A.T. and B.S.N. degrees. Bachelor's degrees are awarded in AGRICULTURE (agricultural business management), BIOLOGICAL SCIENCE (biology/biological science), BUSINESS (accounting, business administration and management, and business economics), COMMUNICATIONS AND THE ARTS (dramatic arts, graphic design, journalism, literature, music, public relations, and Spanish), COMPUTER AND PHYSICAL SCIENCE (actuarial science, chemistry, computer science, information sciences and systems, and mathematics), EDUCATION (art education, athletic training, business education, Christian education, early childhood education, elementary education, foreign languages education, middle school education, music education, physical education, science education, secondary education, and special education), HEALTH PROFESSIONS (medical laboratory technology, nursing, predentistry, and premedicine), SOCIAL SCIENCE (economics, history, philosophy, physical fitness/movement, political science/government, prelaw, psychology, religion, religious music, social work, sociology, and youth ministry). Biology, education, and religion are the strongest academically. Business, biology, and education have the largest enrollments.

Required: All students are required to take an integrated general education core curriculum, including a first-year seminar, eight credits of Christian story and tradition courses, between 31 and 44 credits in a variety of disciplines, and a senior seminar. Students must maintain a 2.0 GPA for 124 total credits and pass both writing and math competency levels.

Special: Northwestern offers cross-registration with Dordt College, student-designed majors, numerous internships, semester programs in Chicago, Washington, D.C., and Denver, and study abroad in over 20 countries, including China, Oman, Romania, Egypt, Spain, France, and the Netherlands. There are 2 national honor societies, a freshman honors program, and 23 departmental honors programs.

Faculty/Classroom: 62% of faculty are male; 38% are female. All teach undergraduates, 75% do research, and 75% do both. No introductory courses are taught by graduate students. The average class size in an introductory lecture is 24; in a laboratory is 12; and in a regular course is 16.

Admissions: 76% of the 2013-2014 applicants were accepted. The SAT scores for the 2013-2014 freshman class were: Critical Reading--39% below 500, 36% between 500 and 599, 13% between 600 and 699, and 13% between 700 and 800; Math--34% below 500, 49% between 500 and 599, 15% between 600 and 699, and 2% between 700 and 800; Writing--52% below 500, 32% between 500 and 599, 8% between 600 and 699, and 8% between 700 and 800. The ACT scores were 16% below 21, 29% between 21 and 23, 23% between 24 and 26, 20% between 27 and 28, and 12% above 28. 37% of the current freshmen were in the top fifth of their class; 66% were in the top two fifths. 10 freshmen graduated first in their class.

Requirements: The ACT is required. Applicants with a minimum ACT composite of 19, in the top half of their high school class, and with a 2.4 GPA are generally accepted. Applicants should be graduates of an accredited secondary school. The suggested distribution of high school courses is 4 years of English, 3 years each of math, foreign language, and social studies, and 2 of natural science. The GED is accepted. Northwestern requires applicants to be in the upper 50% of their class. A GPA of 2.0 is required. AP and CLEP credits are accepted. Important factors in the admissions decision are personality/intangible qualities, leadership record, and evidence of special talent.

Procedure: Freshmen are admitted to all sessions. Entrance exams should be taken Spring semester of the junior year of high school. There is a rolling admissions plan. Application deadlines are open. Notifications are sent November 1. Applications are accepted online. Application fees are waived if application is completed online.

Transfer: 52 transfer students enrolled in 2012-2013. Transfer applicants must submit a transcript and letter of recommendation. A minimum college GPA of 2.0 is required. 30 of 124 credits required for the bachelor's degree must be completed at Northwestern.

Visiting: There are regularly scheduled orientations for prospective students, Campus tour, meeting with financial aid and admissions personnel, attending chapel, meeting a faculty member and attending a class in the student's area of interest. There are guides for informal visits, visitors may sit in on classes, and stay overnight. To schedule a visit, contact Laura De Boer at (712) 707-7142.

Financial Aid: In 2013-2014, 100% of all full-time freshmen and 99% of continuing full-time students received some form of financial aid. 93% of all full-time freshmen and 92% of continuing full-time students received need-based aid. The average freshman award was $25,800. Need-based scholarships or need-based grants averaged $7,139 ($31,784 maximum); need-based self-help aid (loans and jobs) averaged $4,243 ($10,574 maximum); non-need-based athletic scholarships averaged $4,957 ($18,000 maximum); and other non-need-based awards and non-need-based scholarships averaged $13,243 ($37,850 maximum). 59% of undergraduate students work part-time. Average annual earnings from campus work are $1466. The average financial indebtedness of the 2013 graduate was $29,325. The FAFSA is required. The priority date for freshman financial aid applications for fall entry is April 1. The deadline for filing freshman financial aid applications for fall entry is June 30.

International Students: There are 33 international students enrolled. The school actively recruits these students. They must take the TOEFL with a minimum score of 475 on the paper-based TOEFL (PBT) or 53 on the Internet-based version (iBT).

Computers: All students may access the system 24 hours a day in residence halls; 7 a.m. to midnight in academic buildings. There are no time limits and no fees.

Graduates: From July 1, 2012 to June 30, 2013, 253 bachelor's degrees were awarded. The most popular majors were business administration (16%), elementary education (13%), and nursing (9%). In an average class, 2% graduate in 3 years or less, 53% graduate in 4 years or less, 62% graduate in 5 years or less, and 63% graduate in 6 years or less. Of the 2012 graduating class, 14% were enrolled in graduate school within 6 months of graduation, and 75% were employed.

Admissions Contact: Kenton Pauls, Dean of Enrollment Management. E-Mail: *admissions@nwciowa.edu* Web: *www.nwciowa.edu*

SIMPSON COLLEGE C-3

Indianola, IA 50125 **(515) 961-1624**
(800) 362-2454, ext. 1624; (515) 961-1870

Full-time: 618 men, 777 women	**Faculty:** 98
Part-time: 187 men, 235 women	**Ph.D.s:** 84%
Graduate: 19 men, 30 women	**Student/Faculty:** 15 to 1
Year: semesters, summer session	**Tuition:** $28,623
Application Deadline: open	**Room & Board:** $8463
Freshman Class: 1343 applied, 1145 accepted, 332 enrolled	
SAT: required **ACT:** 24	**VERY COMPETITIVE**

Founded in 1860, Simpson College is a private liberal arts college affiliated with the United Methodist Church. Simpson is building on the traditions of 150 years of academic excellence and the campus is undergoing several multi-million dollar projects. The figures in the bove capsule and in this profile are approximate. With the completion of the expansion and renovation to Blank Performing Arts Center, further improvement of athletic facilities and construction of the new Kent Campus Center, Simpson continues to blend the beauty of the historic tree-lined campus with cutting edge amenities. The library contains 160,044 volumes, 9,894 microform items, and 4,422 audio/video tapes/CDs/DVDs, and subscribes to 26,749 periodicals including electronic. Special learning facilities include a learning resource center, art gallery, radio station, Avery O. Craven antebellum period collection, the George Washington Carver papers, the Iowa History Center, the John C. Culver Center for Public Policy Studies, an education lab, and a cadaver lab. The 80-acre campus is in a small town 12 miles south of Des Moines, Iowa's capital city. Including any residence halls, there are 45 buildings.

Student Life: 89% of undergraduates are from Iowa. Others are from 24 states, and 7 foreign countries. 98% are from public schools. 88% are white. 32% are unknown, Buddhist, or no preference; 29% Protestant; 18% Catholic. The average age of freshmen is 18; all undergraduates, 23. 23% do not continue beyond their first year; 70% remain to graduate.

Housing: 1268 students can be accommodated in college housing, which includes single-sex and coed dorms and on-campus apartments. In addition, there are special-interest houses, fraternity houses, sorority houses, theme houses. On-campus housing is guaranteed for all 4 years. 83% of students live on campus; of those, 80% remain on campus on weekends. All students may keep cars.

Activities: 18% of men belong to 1 local and 3 national fraternities; 20% of women belong to 3 national sororities. There are 75 groups on campus, including art, band, Campus Activities Board, cheerleading, choir, chorale, computers, drama, drill team, environmental, ethnic, gay, honors, international, jazz band, literary magazine, musical theater, newspaper, opera, pep band, political, professional, radio and TV, religious, social, social service, student government, and yearbook. Popular campus events include Back to School Stand-Around, Homecoming Yell Like Hell Pep Rally, and Lessons and Carols Christmas Concert.

Sports: There are 10 intercollegiate sports for men and 9 for women, and 50 intramural sports for men and 50 for women. Facilities include an athletic center with a gym, a wrestling practice room, a weight room/workout facility, a training facility, 2 racquetball courts, a 25-meter swimming pool, a sauna, and classrooms; a field house for volleyball, basketball, and wrestling; a football and soccer stadium with artificial turf and an 8-lane all-weather track; a tennis center with 6 all-weather courts; a baseball field and a softball complex; practice and intramural fields; and outdoor basketball and sand volleyball courts.

Disabled Students: All of the campus is accessible. Facilities include wheelchair ramps, elevators, special parking, specially equipped restrooms, special class scheduling, lowered drinking fountains, and special housing.

Services: Counseling and information services are available, as is tutoring in every subject. There is a reader service for the blind.

Campus Safety and Security: Measures include 24-hour foot and vehicle patrol, emergency notification system, and security escort services. There are emergency telephones, lighted pathways/sidewalks, and controlled access to dorms/residences.

Programs of Study: Simpson confers B.A., and B.Mus. degrees. Master's degrees are also awarded. Bachelor's degrees are awarded in BIOLOGICAL SCIENCE (biochemistry and biology/biological science), BUSINESS (accounting, business administration and management, international business management, marketing management, and sports management), COMMUNICATIONS AND THE ARTS (art, communications, dramatic arts, English, French, German, graphic design, journalism, multimedia, music, music performance, and Spanish), COMPUTER AND PHYSICAL SCIENCE (actuarial science, chemistry, computer science, information sciences and systems, mathematics, and physics), EDUCATION (athletic training, elementary education, music education, physical education, and secondary education), ENGINEERING AND ENVIRONMENTAL DESIGN (environmental science and preengineering), HEALTH PROFESSIONS (exercise science, predentistry, premedicine, preoptometry, prepharmacy, prephysical therapy, and preveterinary science), SOCIAL SCIENCE (criminal justice, economics, forensic studies, history, interdisciplinary studies, international relations, philosophy, political science/government, prelaw, psychology, religion, and sociology). Management, communication studies, and marketing have the largest enrollments.

Required: Students must satisfactorily complete the Engaged Citizenship curriculum, and including a first-year colloquium; a senior capstone course; complete two May term courses; and complete a major course load.

Special: Internships, study abroad, a Washington semester, and work-study are all available. Dual and student-designed majors are possible. There is a preprofessional program in ministry, and 3-2 engineering degrees are offered with Washington University at St. Louis, Iowa State University, and Institute of Technology (University of Minnesota). There are 10 national honor societies, a freshman honors program, and 8 departmental honors programs.

Faculty/Classroom: 56% of faculty are male; 44% are female. All teach undergraduates. No introductory courses are taught by graduate students. The average class size in an introductory lecture is 26; in a laboratory is 22; and in a regular course is 22.

Admissions: 85% of the 2011-2012 applicants were accepted. The ACT scores were 20% below 21, 33% between 21 and 23, 22% between 24 and 26, 14% between 27 and 28, and 11% above 28. 42% of the current freshmen were in the top fifth of their class; 75% were in the top two fifths. 18 freshmen graduated first in their class.

Requirements: The SAT or ACT is required. Applicants must be graduates of an accredited secondary school; however, the GED is accepted. ACT or SAT test scores, counselor recommendations, GPA, college prep course grades, and class rank are all considered in a selective admissions process. The college strongly recommends that applicants complete 4 years of English and 3 each of math, lab science, social science, and a foreign language. A visit to campus to speak with an admissions representative is also recommended. AP and CLEP credits are accepted. Important factors in the admissions decision are recommendations by school officials, advanced placement or honors courses, and extracurricular activities record.

Procedure: Freshmen are admitted to all sessions. Entrance exams should be taken during the junior or senior year. There are deferred admissions and rolling admissions plans. Application deadlines are open. Notification is sent on a rolling basis. Applications are accepted online.

Transfer: 79 transfer students enrolled in 2010-2011. In addition to freshman requirements, transfer applicants are considered on the basis of college work taken and grades received. It is recommended that applicants take either the SAT or ACT. The recommended GPA is 2.5, and grades of 2.0 and above transfer for credit. 32 of 128 credits required for the bachelor's degree must be completed at Simpson.

Visiting: There are regularly scheduled orientations for prospective students, Orientation is scheduled 4 times throughout the summer to allow incoming students to meet with an academic advisor, register for classes, and participate in activity information sessions. Parents are encouraged to attend. There are guides for informal visits, visitors may sit in on classes, and stay overnight. To schedule a visit, contact the Visit Coordinator.

Financial Aid: In a recent year, 100% of all full-time freshmen and 99% of continuing full-time students received some form of financial aid. 88% of all full-time freshmen and 86% of continuing full-time students received need-based aid. The average freshman award was $30,412. Need-based scholarships or need-based grants averaged $8,227; need-based self-help aid (loans and jobs) averaged $3,458; and other non-need-based awards and non-need-based scholarships averaged $18,727. 44% of undergraduate students work part-time. Average annual earnings from campus work are $1000. The average financial indebtedness of a recent graduate was $34,055. The FAFSA is required. The priority date for freshman financial aid applications for fall entry is April 1. The deadline for filing freshman financial aid applications for fall entry is July 1.

International Students: There are 13 international students enrolled. The school actively recruits these students. They must take the TOEFL with a minimum score of 550 on the paper-based TOEFL (PBT) or 79 on the Internet-based version (iBT). SAT or ACT scores are also required.

Computers: The campus is equipped with 362 computers in various computer labs in almost every building on campus (including residence halls) offering high-speed Internet access. The campus is completely wireless. Students are provided with required anti-virus software. All students may access the system 24 hours a day. There are no time limits. Check with the school for current fees.

Graduates: In a recent year, 431 bachelor's degrees were awarded. The most popular majors were management (12%), communication studies (9%), and marketing (8%). In an average class, 57% graduate in 4 years or less, 66% graduate in 5 years or less, and 68% graduate in 6 years or less. Of the 2010 graduating class, 15% were enrolled in graduate school within 6 months of graduation, and 78% were employed.

Admissions Contact: Admissions and Enrollment. A campus DVD is available. E-Mail: *admiss@simpson.edu* Web: *www.simpson.edu*

ST. AMBROSE UNIVERSITY — E-3

Davenport, IA 52803 — (563) 333-6300, (800) 383-2627; (563) 333-6038

Full-time: 995 men, 1419 women	**Faculty:** 163; IIB, -$
Part-time: 140 men, 333 women	**Ph.D.s:** 74%
Graduate: 287 men, 555 women	**Student/Faculty:** 11 to 1
Year: semesters, summer session	**Tuition:** $24,000
Application Deadline: open	**Room & Board:** $9200
Freshman Class: 2075 applied, 1702 accepted, 577 enrolled	
ACT: 23	
	COMPETITIVE

St. Ambrose University, a private institution founded in 1882 in affiliation with the Roman Catholic Church, offers degree programs through the colleges of arts and sciences, business, education, health sciences, and professional studies. There also is a college-level seminary. There are 4 undergraduate schools and 15 graduate schools. In addition to regional accreditation, St. Ambrose has baccalaureate program accreditation with ABET, ACBSP, and CSWE. The library contains 156,303 volumes, 7,066 microform items, and 3,606 audio/video tapes/CDs/DVDs, and subscribes to 15,552 periodicals including electronic. Computerized library services include interlibrary loans, database searching, Internet access, and laptop Internet portals. Special learning facilities include a learning resource center, art gallery, radio station, TV station, an observatory. The 123-acre campus is in an urban area 180 miles west of Chicago. Including any residence halls, there are 29 buildings. The figures in the above capsule and in this profile are approximate.

Student Life: 56% of undergraduates are from out of state, mostly the Mid-West. Students are from 26 states, 12 foreign countries, and Canada. 70% are from public schools. 81% are white. 64% are Catholic; 36% Protestant. The average age of freshmen is 18; all undergraduates, 23. 26% do not continue beyond their first year; 65% remain to graduate.

Housing: 1507 students can be accommodated in college housing, which includes single-sex and coed dorms, on-campus apartments, and off-campus apartments. townhouse residences for upper-division students. On-campus housing is guaranteed for all 4 years. 52% of students live on campus; of those, 60% remain on campus on weekends. All students may keep cars.

Activities: There are no fraternities or sororities. There are 45 groups on campus, including art, band, cheerleading, choir, chorale, chorus, computers, dance, debate, drama, ethnic, gay, honors, international, jazz band, literary magazine, musical theater, newspaper, opera, orchestra, pep band, photography, political, professional, radio and TV, religious, social, social service, student government, and symphony. Popular campus events include Multicultural Weeks and Brother/Sister Weekend.

Sports: There are 11 intercollegiate sports for men and 11 for women, and 63 intramural sports for men and 63 for women. Facilities include tennis, handball/racquetball, and volleyball courts, a golf room, an archery range, a gym, a weight-lifting room, and a jogging track.

Disabled Students: 96% of the campus is accessible. Facilities include wheelchair ramps, elevators, special parking, specially equipped restrooms, special class scheduling, lowered drinking fountains, and special housing.

Services: Counseling and information services are available, as is tutoring in most subjects. There is a reader service for the blind, and remedial math, reading, and writing.

Campus Safety and Security: Measures include 24-hour foot and vehicle patrol, emergency notification system, self-defense education, and security escort services. There are emergency telephones, lighted pathways/sidewalks, and controlled access to residence halls from 7 p.m. to 7 a.m.

Programs of Study: St. Ambrose confers B.A., B.S., B.A.M.T., B.B.A., B.B.A.A., B.E.D., B.E.S., B.M.E., B.S.I.E., B.S.N., and B.S.S. degrees. Master's and doctoral degrees are also awarded. Bachelor's degrees are awarded in BIOLOGICAL SCIENCE (biology/biological science), BUSINESS (accounting, business administration and management, business economics, international business management, management science, marketing/retailing/merchandising, and sports management), COMMUNICATIONS AND THE ARTS (communications, English, fine arts, French, German, graphic design, music, Spanish, and speech/debate/rhetoric), COMPUTER AND PHYSICAL SCIENCE (chemistry, computer science, mathematics, and physics), EDUCATION (art education, early childhood education, elementary education, music education, physical education, and secondary education), ENGINEERING AND ENVIRONMENTAL DESIGN (engineering physics and industrial engineering), HEALTH PROFESSIONS (health science), SOCIAL SCIENCE (criminal justice, criminology, economics, forensic studies, history, philosophy, political science/government, psychology, public administration, sociology, and theological studies). Biology, chemistry, and engineering physics are the strongest academically. Business, psychology, and elementary education have the largest enrollments.

Required: To graduate, all students must complete at least 120 credit hours, including 45 outside the major and 30 in upper-level courses. A minimum GPA of 2.0 is required. Students must also demonstrate proficiency in English composition, math, public speaking, and library skills, among other requirements. Selections of courses must include those that provide an opportunity to develop specific skills, content knowledge, and exposure to attitude and value development.

Special: The university offers co-op and work-study programs, study abroad in England, Ireland, Ecuador, Italy, Spain, Austria, and Germany, internships, a 3-2 engineering degree with the University of Iowa and Iowa State University, accelerated degree programs, and student-designed majors. Credit for life, military, and work experience, nondegree study, and pass/fail options also are available. There are 12 national honor societies and 7 departmental honors programs.

Faculty/Classroom: 52% of faculty are male; 48% are female. 88% teach undergraduates. No introductory courses are taught by graduate students. The average class size in an introductory lecture is 17; in a laboratory is 14; and in a regular course is 17.

Admissions: 82% of the 2011-2012 applicants were accepted. The ACT scores were 28% below 21, 35% between 21 and 23, 19% between 24 and 26, 9% between 27 and 28, and 9% above 28. 28% of the current freshmen were in the top fifth of their class; 54% were in the top two fifths. 36 freshmen graduated first in their class.

Requirements: The ACT is required. The ACT Optional Writing test is also required. The SAT with a satisfactory score, may be substituted. Applicants must be graduates of an accredited secondary school; the GED is accepted. An interview is recommended. St. Ambrose requires applicants to be in the upper 50% of their class. A GPA of 2.5 is required. AP and CLEP credits are accepted. Important factors in the admissions decision are recommendations by school officials, leadership record, and parents or siblings attended the school.

Procedure: Freshmen are admitted to all sessions. Entrance exams should be taken in the spring of the junior year. There is a rolling admissions plan. Application deadlines are open. Application fee is $25. Applications are accepted online.

Transfer: 284 transfer students enrolled in a recent year. Applicants must have a college GPA of 2.0. 30 of 120 credits required for the bachelor's degree must be completed at St. Ambrose.

Visiting: There are regularly scheduled orientations for prospective students, including breakfast, welcome, testing, panel given by current students, student and parent meeting with faculty mentor, and evening meeting and activity; on the next day, there is advising and registration. Parents follow their own agenda (with panels and tours). There are guides for informal visits, visitors may sit in on classes, and stay overnight. To schedule a visit, contact the Admissions Office.

Financial Aid: In a recent year, 99% of all full-time freshmen and 98% of continuing full-time students received some form of financial aid. 75% of all full-time freshmen and 72% of continuing full-time students received need-based aid. The average freshman award was $21,901. Need-based scholarships or need-based grants averaged $5,997 ($13,350 maximum); need-based self-help aid (loans and jobs) averaged $4,254 ($8,048 maximum); non-need-based athletic scholarships averaged $4,689 ($17,500 maximum); and other non-need-based awards and non-need-based scholarships averaged $8,472 ($22,590 maximum). 100% of undergraduate students work part-time. Average annual earnings from campus work are $1392. The average financial indebtedness of a recent graduate was $30,013. St. Ambrose is a member of CSS. The FAFSA is required. The priority date for freshman financial aid applications for fall entry is March 15.

International Students: There are 14 international students enrolled. They must take the TOEFL with a minimum score of 500 on the paper-based TOEFL (PBT) or 61 on the Internet-based version (iBT). They must also take the SAT or ACT.

Computers: Wireless access is available. The student union has wireless access for anyone that is in the building. All of the rooms in our residence halls are wired for access to the Internet. There are computer labs that have 200 PCs that can be used by the students. The library is also set up to work with student laptops. All students may access the system 24 hours a day. There are no time limits and no fees.

Graduates: In a recent year, 647 bachelor's degrees were awarded. The most popular majors were business (28%), education (11%), and nursing (10%). 130 companies recruited on campus in a recent year. In an average class, 2% graduate in 3 years or less, 53% graduate in 4 years or less, 64% graduate in 5 years or less, and 65% graduate in 6 years or less. Of the 2010 graduating class, 18% were enrolled in graduate school within 6 months of graduation, and 98% were employed.

Admissions Contact: Director of Admissions. Web: *www.sau.edu*

UNIVERSITY OF DUBUQUE E-2

Dubuque, IA 52001

(563) 589-3214
(800) 722-5583; (563) 589-3690

Full-time: 710 men, 410 women	**Faculty:** n/av
Part-time: 30 men, 35 women	**Ph.D.s:** 80%
Graduate: 170 men, 110 women	**Student/Faculty:** n/av
Year: semesters, summer session	**Tuition:** $23,120
Application Deadline: open	**Room & Board:** $8080
Freshman Class: n/av	
SAT or ACT: required	

COMPETITIVE

The University of Dubuque, established in 1852, is a private, liberal arts institution affiliated with the Presbyterian Church. Strengths in the undergraduate curriculum include environmental science, business, aviation, education, and computer graphics/interactive media. The figures in the above capsule and in this profile are approximate. There are 3 undergraduate schools and 2 graduate schools. The library contains 164,859 volumes, 20,739 microform items, and 2,180 audio/video tapes/CDs/DVDs, and subscribes to 801 periodicals including electronic. Computerized library services include interlibrary loans, database searching, and Internet access. Special learning facilities include a learning resource center, art gallery, and planetarium. The 56-acre campus is in a suburban area 180 miles northwest of Chicago. Including any residence halls, there are 24 buildings.

Student Life: 60% of undergraduates are from out of state, mostly the Mid-West. Students are from 35 states, and 21 foreign countries. 90% are from public schools. 79% are white; 12% African American. 50% are Catholic; 40% Protestant; 35% claim no religious affiliation. The average age of freshmen is 18; all undergraduates, 22. 12% do not continue beyond their first year; 59% remain to graduate.

Housing: 600 students can be accommodated in college housing, which includes coed dorms, on-campus apartments, and married student housing. In addition, there are special-interest houses. On-campus housing is guaranteed for all 4 years. 30% of students commute. Alcohol is not permitted. All students may keep cars.

Activities: 11% of men belong to 5 local fraternities; 10% of women belong to 3 local sororities. There are 50 groups on campus, including art, cheerleading, choir, chorale, chorus, computers, dance, drama, ecology, ethnic, honors, international, musical theater, newspaper, pep band, political, professional, religious, social, social service, and student government. Popular campus events include Founder's Day Ball, Annual Gala, and Family Weekend.

Sports: There are 10 intercollegiate sports for men and 9 for women, and 13 intramural sports for men and 13 for women. Facilities include a sports center with basketball and volleyball courts, 2 racquetball courts, a wrestling room, and an athletic training room; a football field and track; baseball and softball fields; and a practice football/intramural field; and a cardiovascular workout center.

Disabled Students: 50% of the campus is accessible. Facilities include wheelchair ramps, elevators, special parking, specially equipped restrooms, special class scheduling, and lowered drinking fountains.

Services: Counseling and information services are available, as is tutoring in some subjects, English, math, economics, accounting, and computer literacy There is remedial math, reading, and writing.

Campus Safety and Security: Measures include 24-hour foot and vehicle patrol, self-defense education, and security escort services. There are shuttle buses, emergency telephones, lighted pathways/sidewalks, and security-locked residence halls.

Programs of Study: UD confers B.A., B.S., and B.B.A. degrees. Associate, master's, and doctoral degrees are also awarded. Bachelor's degrees are awarded in BIOLOGICAL SCIENCE (biology/biological science), BUSINESS (accounting and business administration and management), COMMUNICATIONS AND THE ARTS (English and speech/debate/rhetoric), COMPUTER AND PHYSICAL SCIENCE (computer science), EDUCATION (education and physical education), ENGINEERING AND ENVIRONMENTAL DESIGN (aviation administration/management, computer graphics, and environmental science), HEALTH PROFESSIONS (nursing), SOCIAL SCIENCE (philosophy, psychology, religion, and sociology). Nursing, computer graphics, and business are the strongest academically. Business, aviation management/flight operations, and computer graphics have the largest enrollments.

Required: As part of our mission, the University aims to prepare students for successful, professional careers and fulfilling lives by providing them with an education that encourages their growth as whole persons. A total of 120 credits must be earned, with a minimum GPA of 2.0 (2.5 for education majors) for graduation. At UD, we combine professional preparation and the liberal arts to create programs that serve our students.

Special: UD offers cross-registration with Loras and Clarke Colleges, internships, study abroad through the Maastricht Center for Transatlantic Studies, work-study programs, accelerated degree programs, B.A.-B.S. degrees, dual and student-designed majors, credit for life, military, and work experience, nondegree study, and pass/fail options. B.A.-M.A. programs are offered in conjunction with the university's theological seminary. Adult degree programs and an environmental field trip to Colorado and New Mexico are available. There are 8 national honor societies and 2 departmental honors programs.

Faculty/Classroom: 55% of faculty are male; 45% are female. All teach undergraduates. No introductory courses are taught by graduate students. The average class size in an introductory lecture is 25; in a laboratory is 16; and in a regular course is 17.

Admissions: 10 freshmen graduated first in their class.

Requirements: The SAT or ACT is required. Applicants must graduate from an accredited secondary school with a minimum of 4 years in English and 3 each in math, social sciences, and natural sciences. Other academic areas, such as foreign languages, business courses, computer programming, and the fine and performing arts, are also considered. The GED is accepted. Essays and recommendations are required. Auditions are required for music scholarship candidates. A GPA of 2.5 is required. AP and CLEP credits are accepted. Important factors in the admissions decision are leadership record, recommendations by school officials, and extracurricular activities record.

Procedure: Freshmen are admitted fall and spring. Entrance exams should be taken before the senior year. There are deferred admissions and rolling admissions plans. Check with the school for current application deadlines. The fall 2011 application fee was $25. Applications are accepted online.

Transfer: A minimum GPA of 2.0 is required. The applicant must be in good standing at all previously attended institutions. 30 of 120 credits required for the bachelor's degree must be completed at UD.

Visiting: There are regularly scheduled orientations for prospective students, including a campus tour and visits with coaches, faculty, admissions, and financial aid advisers. There are guides for informal visits, visitors may sit in on classes, and stay overnight.

Financial Aid: The FAFSA is required. Check with the school for current application deadlines.

International Students: The school actively recruits these students. They must take the TOEFL and the college's own test.

Computers: All resident halls are wired with fiber-optic. There are many PC labs across campus. All students may access the system 24 hours a day, 7 days a week. There are no time limits and no fees.

Admissions Contact: Jesse L. James, Admission Director. E-Mail: *jjames@dbq.edu* Web: *www.dbq.edu*

UNIVERSITY OF IOWA E-3

Iowa City, IA 52242 **(319) 335-3847; (319) 335-1535**

Full-time: 9390 men, 10132 women	**Faculty:** 1521; I, av$
Part-time: 1160 men, 1292 women	**Ph.D.s:** 97%
Graduate: 4588 men, 4503 women	**Student/Faculty:** 16 to 1
Year: semesters, summer session	**Tuition:** $8079 ($27,409)
Application Deadline: April 1	**Room & Board:** $9420
Freshman Class: 21644 applied, 17363 accepted, 4460 enrolled	
SAT CR/M: 545/611	**ACT:** 25 **VERY COMPETITIVE**

Home to more than 30,000 students and some of the nation's top scholars and researchers, the University of Iowa offers more than 200 areas of study on a vibrant and diverse campus. The University delivers the energy and opportunity of a leading university, but remains one of the smallest and most affordable universities among its peer institutions. There are 6 undergraduate schools and 10 graduate schools. In addition to regional accreditation, Iowa has baccalaureate program accreditation with AACSB, ABET, ACEJMC, ACPE, ADA, AHEA, APTA, CAHEA, CSWE, NASM, and NLN. The 8 libraries contain 6.9 million volumes. Computerized library services include interlibrary loans, database searching, Internet access, and Wi-Fi capability. Special learning facilities include an art gallery, natural history museum, radio station, TV station, UI hospitals and clinics, the Iowa Center for the Arts, Oakdale Research Center, Macbride Raptor Project, Iowa Lakeside lab, and a driving simulator. The 1700-acre campus is in a small town 110 miles east of Des Moines and 220 miles west of Chicago. Including any residence halls, there are 264 buildings.

Student Life: 55% of undergraduates are from Iowa. Others are from 50 states, 40 foreign countries, and Canada. 92% are from public schools. 71% are White. The average age of freshmen is 18; all undergraduates, 21. 14% do not continue beyond their first year; 70% remain to graduate.

Housing: 5546 students can be accommodated in college housing, which includes coed dorms, on-campus apartments, off-campus apartments, and married student housing. In addition, there are honors houses, special-interest houses, Living-Learning Communities: Arts, Business, Education, Global Village, healthy Living, Honors, Chemistry, journalism, Leadership, Engineering, Pre-Med, Sustainability, Iowa Writers. On-campus housing is available on a first-come and first-served basis. 75% of students commute. Alcohol is not permitted. All students may keep cars.

Activities: 12% of men belong to 25 national fraternities; 17% of women belong to 22 national sororities. There are 487 groups on campus, including art, bagpipe, band, cheerleading, chess, choir, chorale, chorus, computers, dance, debate, drama, drill team, environmental, ethnic, film, forensics, gay, honors, international, jazz band, literary magazine, marching band, musical theater, newspaper, opera, orchestra, pep band, photography, political, professional, radio and TV, religious, social, social service, student government, and symphony. Popular campus events include Dance Marathon, Riverfest, RiverRun and Cultural Diversity Festival.

Sports: There are 10 intercollegiate sports for men and 12 for women, and 36 intramural sports for men and 32 for women. Facilities include Campus Recreation & Wellness Center which includes: a climbing wall, competive swimming pool, Lazy River, deep diving well, leisure pool, jogging track, two basketball/vollgyball courts, a multi-activity Gym, a cafe, locker rooms, and fitness rooms. Iowa has a 70,397-seat stadium for Hawkeye football, a 15,500-seat arena, softball and baseball stadiums, an 18-hole golf course, a pool, basketball, racquetball, and handball courts, outdoor and indoor tennis courts and running tracks, weight and fitness rooms, a 1000-seat field hockey stadium, a field campus for hiking (Lake Macbride), cross-country skiing, canoeing, and a soccer field.

Disabled Students: 98% of the campus is accessible. Facilities include wheelchair ramps, elevators, special parking, specially equipped restrooms, special class scheduling, lowered drinking fountains, lowered telephones, special housing, a transportation service.

Services: Counseling and information services are available, as is tutoring in most subjects. There is a reader service for the blind, and remedial math, reading, and writing.

Campus Safety and Security: Measures include 24-hour foot and vehicle patrol, emergency notification system, self-defense education, and security escort services. There are shuttle buses, emergency telephones, lighted pathways/sidewalks, controlled access to dorms/residences, Code Blue Phones; defense courses, and WhistleSAFE Program.

Programs of Study: Iowa confers B.A., B.S., B.A.S., B.B.A., B.F.A., B.L.S., B.M., B.S.E. and B.S.N. degrees. Master's and doctoral degrees are also awarded. Bachelor's degrees are awarded in BIOLOGICAL SCIENCE (biochemistry, biology/biological science, and microbiology), BUSINESS (accounting, banking and finance, business administration and management, business economics, management science, marketing management, recreation and leisure services, and recreational facilities management), COMMUNICATIONS AND THE ARTS (Arabic, art, art history and appreciation, ceramic art and design, Chinese, classics, communications, comparative literature, dance, dramatic arts, drawing, English, film arts, fine arts, French, German, graphic design, Greek, Italian, Japanese, jazz, journalism, Latin, linguistics, metal/jewelry, music, painting, percussion, performing arts, photography, piano/organ, Portuguese, printmaking, Russian, sculpture, Spanish, speech/debate/rhetoric, strings, theatre arts, and voice), COMPUTER AND PHYSICAL SCIENCE (actuarial science, applied physics, astronomy, chemistry, computer science, geology, information sciences and systems, mathematics, physics, and statistics), EDUCATION (art education, athletic training, elementary education, foreign languages education, health education, mathematics education, middle school education, music education, science education, secondary education, and sports studies), ENGINEERING AND ENVIRONMENTAL DESIGN (biomedical engineering, chemical engineering, civil engineering, electrical/electronics engineering, engineering, environmental science, industrial administration/management, industrial engineering, and mechanical engineering), HEALTH PROFESSIONS (medical laboratory science, medical laboratory technology, music therapy, nuclear medical technology, nursing, pharmacy, predentistry, premedicine, preoptometry, prepharmacy, prephysical therapy, prepodiatry, preveterinary science, radiological science, recreation therapy, and speech pathology/audiology), SOCIAL SCIENCE (African American studies, American studies, anthropology, Asian/Oriental studies, classical/ancient civilization, economics, gender studies, geography, history, international studies, liberal arts/general studies, parks and recreation management, philosophy, political science/government, prelaw, psychology, religion, Russian and Slavic studies, Sanskrit and Indian studies, social science, social work, sociology, and women's studies). Business, engineering, English, communication studies are the strongest academically. Business, engineering, nursing, premedicine, pharmacy, and psychology have the largest enrollments.

Required: To graduate, students must complete at least 120 semester hours, with a GPA of 2.0. The general education program includes rhetoric, historical perspectives, world language, quantitative and formal reasoning, international & global issues, values, society and diversity, and natural and social sciences.

Special: The University of Iowa offers cooperative education programs and internships in more than 70 academic departments, 6 joint-degree programs in computer science, engineering, German, linguistics, nursing, and urban and regional planning, and study abroad in 60 countries. Student-designed majors, B.A.-B.S. degrees, certificate programs including Aging Studies, Writing, Native American studies, global studies, international business, and nonprofit management. Credit for military experience, and pass/nonpass options are also available. There are 18 national honor societies, including Phi Beta Kappa, a freshman honors program, and 52 departmental honors programs.

Faculty/Classroom: 67% of faculty are male; 33% are female. Graduate students teach 20% of introductory courses. The average class size in an introductory lecture is 103; in a laboratory is 17; and in a regular course is 18.

Admissions: 80% of the 2013-2014 applicants were accepted. The SAT scores for the 2013-2014 freshman class were: Critical Reading--36% below 500, 29% between 500 and 599, 24% between 600 and 699, and 11% between 700 and 800; Math--14% below 500, 28% between 500 and 599, 37% between 600 and 699, and 21% between 700 and 800. The ACT scores were 9% below 21, 25% between 21 and 23, 29% between 24 and 26, 17% between 27 and 28, and 20% above 28. 48% of the current freshmen were in the top fifth of their class; 81% were in the top two fifths. There were 21 National Merit finalists. 122 freshmen graduated first in their class.

Requirements: The SAT or ACT is required. All applicants must have completed 4 years of high school English, 3 each of social studies, science, and math (including 2 years of algebra and 1 of geometry), and 2 years of a single world language. Music and dance students must audition. AP and CLEP credits are accepted.

Procedure: Freshmen are admitted to all sessions. Entrance exams should be taken in the junior year. There are deferred admissions and rolling admissions plans. Applications should be filed by April 1 for fall entry; November 15 for spring entry; and April 1 for summer entry, along with a $40 fee. Notification is sent on a rolling basis. applicants were on the 2013 waiting list; were admitted. Applications are accepted online.

Transfer: 1141 transfer students enrolled in 2012-2013. For the College of Liberal Arts, a GPA of at least 2.5 is required for applicants with 24 or more semester hours of credit. Those with fewer credits are considered on the same criteria as freshmen. Other colleges have different requirements. 30 of 120 credits required for the bachelor's degree must be completed at Iowa.

Visiting: There are regularly scheduled orientations for prospective students, including information sessions, campus tours, lunch, and visits to departments and residence halls. There are guides for informal visits and visitors may sit in on classes. To schedule a visit, contact the Admission Visitors Center at (319) 335-1569.

Financial Aid: In 2013-2014, 80% of all full-time freshmen and 80% of

continuing full-time students received some form of financial aid. 46% of all full-time freshmen and 46% of continuing full-time students received need-based aid. The average freshman award was $12,603. Need-based scholarships or need-based grants averaged $6,824 ($17,000 maximum); need-based self-help aid (loans and jobs) averaged $5,857 ($12,000 maximum); non-need-based athletic scholarships averaged $20,455 ($26,000 maximum); and other non-need-based awards and non-need-based scholarships averaged $1,800 ($12,500 maximum). 80% of undergraduate students work part-time. Average annual earnings from campus work are $5220. The average financial indebtedness of the 2013 graduate was $26,296. The FAFSA and the college's own financial statement are required. Check with the school for current application deadlines.

International Students: There are 2128 international students enrolled. The school actively recruits these students. They must take the TOEFL with a minimum score of 530 on the paper-based TOEFL (PBT) or 80 on the Internet-based version (iBT), International students must submit TOEFL for admission purposes and may be asked to take a proficiency exam after arriving on campus.

Computers: All students may access the system 24 hours a day, 7 days a week. There are no time limits and no fees.

Graduates: From July 1, 2012 to June 30, 2013, 5192 bachelor's degrees were awarded. The most popular majors were business (20%), engineering (6%), and Interdepartmental Studies (5%). 679 companies recruited on campus in 2012-2013. In an average class, 1% graduate in 3 years or less, 47% graduate in 4 years or less, 68% graduate in 5 years or less, and 70% graduate in 6 years or less.

Admissions Contact: E-Mail: *admissions@uiowa.edu* Web: *www.uiowa.edu*

UNIVERSITY OF NORTHERN IOWA D-2

Cedar Falls, IA 50614-0018 **(319) 273-2281**
(800) 772-2037; (319) 273-2885

Full-time: 4342 men, 5867 women	**Faculty:** 501; IIA, -$
Part-time: 636 men, 563 women	**Ph.D.s:** 73%
Graduate: 523 men, 1237 women	**Student/Faculty:** 16 to 1
Year: semesters, summer session	**Tuition:** $7350 ($16,106)
Application Deadline: August 15	**Room & Board:** $7426

Freshman Class: 4666 applied, 3607 accepted, 1937 enrolled
ACT: 23

COMPETITIVE

The University of Northern Iowa, established in 1876, is a public institution offering degree programs in business administration, education, humanities and fine arts, natural science, and social and behavioral sciences. There are 4 undergraduate schools and 1 graduate school. The figures in the above capsule and in this profile are approximate. In addition to regional accreditation, UNI has baccalaureate program accreditation with AACSB, ADA, ASLA, CSWE, NASAD, NASM, and NRPA. The library contains 973,231 volumes, 1.1 million microform items, and 29,302 audio/video tapes/CDs/DVDs, and subscribes to 54,529 periodicals including electronic. Computerized library services include interlibrary loans, database searching, Internet access, and laptop Internet portals. Special learning facilities include a learning resource center, art gallery, natural history museum, planetarium, radio station, The university sponsors a lab school, the Native Roadside Vegetation Center, the Iowa Center for Immigrant Leadership and Integration, a waste reduction center, a performing arts center, and several research institutes. The 910-acre campus is in a small town about 100 miles north of Des Moines. Including any residence halls, there are 64 buildings.

Student Life: 92% of undergraduates are from Iowa. Others are from 44 states, 54 foreign countries, and Canada. 87% are white. The average age of freshmen is 19; all undergraduates, 21. 18% do not continue beyond their first year; 66% remain to graduate.

Housing: 4929 students can be accommodated in college housing, which includes single-sex and coed dorms, on-campus apartments, and married student housing. In addition, there are honors houses and special-interest houses. On-campus housing is guaranteed for all 4 years. 62% of students commute. All students may keep cars.

Activities: 3% of men belong to 4 national fraternities; 3% of women belong to 4 national sororities. There are 318 groups on campus, including and nontraditional students, art, band, cheerleading, chess, choir, chorale, chorus, computers, dance, debate, drama, drill team, environmental, ethnic, film, forensics, gay, honors, international, jazz band, literary magazine, marching band, musical theater, newspaper, opera, orchestra, pep band, political, professional, radio and TV, religious, social, social service, student government, and symphony. Popular campus events include Celebrate the Seasons, Welcome Week, Diversity Week, Homecoming, and Thursdaze.

Sports: There are 7 intercollegiate sports for men and 10 for women, and 23 intramural sports for men and 25 for women. Facilities include a domed stadium, a field house, a basketball facility, and a wellness and recreation center with an 8-lane swimming pool, 6 handball/racquetball courts, a climbing wall, weight rooms, and basketball courts.

Disabled Students: 95% of the campus is accessible. Facilities include wheelchair ramps, elevators, special parking, specially equipped restrooms, special class scheduling, lowered drinking fountains, lowered telephones, and special housing.

Services: Counseling and information services are available, as is tutoring in some subjects. There is a reader service for the blind, and remedial math, reading, and writing.

Campus Safety and Security: Measures include 24-hour foot and vehicle patrol, emergency notification system, self-defense education, and security escort services. There are shuttle buses, emergency telephones, lighted pathways/sidewalks, and controlled access to dorms/residences.

Programs of Study: UNI confers B.A., B.S., B.A.T., B.F.A., B.L.S., and B.Mus. degrees. Master's and doctoral degrees are also awarded. Bachelor's degrees are awarded in BIOLOGICAL SCIENCE (biochemistry, bioinformatics, biology/biological science, biotechnology, microbiology, and nutrition), BUSINESS (accounting, banking and finance, management information systems, management science, marketing/retailing/merchandising, real estate, and recreation and leisure services), COMMUNICATIONS AND THE ARTS (art history and appreciation, broadcasting, communications, dramatic arts, English, fine arts, French, German, graphic design, music, music performance, music theory and composition, public relations, Spanish, speech/debate/rhetoric, studio art, and theater design), COMPUTER AND PHYSICAL SCIENCE (chemistry, computer management, computer science, earth science, geology, information sciences and systems, mathematics, physics, and science), EDUCATION (art education, athletic training, business education, early childhood education, elementary education, foreign languages education, health education, middle school education, music education, physical education, science education, special education, teaching English as a second/foreign language (TESOL/TEFOL), and technical education), ENGINEERING AND ENVIRONMENTAL DESIGN (computer technology, construction management, electromechanical technology, energy management technology, industrial engineering technology, and manufacturing technology), HEALTH PROFESSIONS (speech pathology/audiology), SOCIAL SCIENCE (anthropology, clothing and textiles management/production/services, criminology, economics, family and community services, geography, gerontology, history, humanities, Latin American studies, liberal arts/general studies, philosophy, political science/government, psychology, public administration, religion, Russian and Slavic studies, social science, social work, and sociology). Accounting, management, and education are the strongest academically. Elementary education, accounting, and management have the largest enrollments.

Required: Degree requirements include completion of 120 to 130 credits, with 30 to 60 in the major. Liberal arts majors must maintain a minimum GPA of 2.0 (2.5 for business, communication, and education majors). Liberal arts core requirements include 11 hours of civilizations and cultures, 9 each of natural science/technology, social science, and communication, 6 of arts/literature/philosophy/religion, and 3 of personal wellness. Students must meet requirements in foreign language and complete a capstone course. Education students must complete a 32-credit professional sequence.

Special: Internships and co-op programs are offered through all colleges of the university. Students may study abroad in 28 countries and may participate in a Washington semester. Interdisciplinary majors include safety education, chemistry/marketing, design/human environment, and natural history interpretation. Cross-registration, work-study programs, a general studies degree, dual and student-designed majors, nondegree study, and pass/fail options are also available. There are 25 national honor societies and a freshman honors program.

Faculty/Classroom: 53% of faculty are male; 47% are female. 95% do both. Graduate students teach 4% of introductory courses. The average class size in an introductory lecture is 34; in a laboratory is 23; and in a regular course is 27.

Admissions: 77% of a recent year applicants were accepted. The ACT scores were 33% below 21, 23% between 21 and 23, 23% between 24 and 26, 11% between 27 and 28, and 8% above 28. 37% of the current freshmen were in the top fifth of their class; 71% were in the top two fifths. 63 freshmen graduated first in their class.

Requirements: The ACT is required. In addition, a Regents Admissions Index (RAI) score of 245 guarantees admission. High school requirements include 4 years of English, 3 each of math, social studies, and science, and 2 or more of electives, which may include foreign language and fine arts. The GED, with a minimum standard score average of 57, and no single score below 500, is accepted. AP and CLEP credits are accepted. Important factors in the admissions decision are advanced placement or honors courses, evidence of special talent, and recommendations by school officials.

Procedure: Freshmen are admitted to all sessions. Entrance exams should be taken by October of the senior year. There is a rolling admissions plan. Applications should be filed by August 15 for fall entry; December 31 for spring entry; and May 15 for summer entry, along with a $40 fee. Applications are accepted online.

Transfer: 1138 transfer students enrolled in 2010-2011. Applicants

must have a minimum GPA of 2.0 to 2.5, depending on the number of credits they wish to transfer. A small number of applicants may be admitted on academic probation. 32 of 120 credits required for the bachelor's degree must be completed at UNI.

Visiting: There are regularly scheduled orientations for prospective students, including a student panel, lunch, a campus tour, and presentations by admissions, financial aid, housing, and academic departments. There are guides for informal visits, visitors may sit in on classes, and stay overnight. To schedule a visit, contact the Admissions Office.

Financial Aid: In a recent year, 87% of all full-time freshmen and 81% of continuing full-time students received some form of financial aid. 61% of all full-time freshmen and 58% of continuing full-time students received need-based aid. The average freshman award was $18,400. Need-based scholarships or need-based grants averaged $4,715 ($16,648 maximum); need-based self-help aid (loans and jobs) averaged $3,424 ($10,772 maximum); non-need-based athletic scholarships averaged $11,049 ($24,058 maximum); and other non-need-based awards and non-need-based scholarships averaged $2,928 ($18,252 maximum). 31% of undergraduate students work part-time. Average annual earnings from campus work are $2090. The average financial indebtedness of a recent year graduate was $25,523. The FAFSA is required. The deadline for filing freshman financial aid applications for fall entry is open.

International Students: There are 488 international students enrolled. The school actively recruits these students. They must take the TOEFL with a minimum score of 550 on the paper-based TOEFL (PBT) or 79 on the Internet-based version (iBT).

Computers: Wireless access is available. The network is available to students through approximately 500 PCs located in 15 public access labs and approximately 1500 PCs in college labs. Nearly all buildings have wireless access. All students may have accounts on the system and Internet privileges. Residence halls have wired and wirless access. All students may access the system 24 hours a day. There are no time limits and no fees.

Graduates: In a recent year, 2198 bachelor's degrees were awarded. The most popular majors were elementary education (10%), management (6%), and psychology (5%). 387 companies recruited on campus in a recent year. In an average class, 35% graduate in 4 years or less, 63% graduate in 5 years or less, and 67% graduate in 6 years or less. Of a recent year graduating class, 16% were enrolled in graduate school within 6 months of graduation, and 66% were employed.

Admissions Contact: Director of Admissions. E-Mail: *admissions@uni.edu* Web: *www.uni.edu*

UPPER IOWA UNIVERSITY — E-2

Fayette, IA 52142-1857 — **(563) 425-5281**
(800) 553-4150; (563) 425-5323

Full-time: 410 men, 275 women
Part-time: 15 men, 20 women
Graduate: n/av
Year: semesters
Application Deadline: open
Freshman Class: n/av
SAT or ACT: required
Faculty: n/av; IIB, --$
Ph.D.s: n/av
Student/Faculty: n/av
Tuition: $23,856
Room & Board: $7070

NONCOMPETITIVE

Upper Iowa University, founded in 1857, is a private institution with a liberal arts focus. The figures in the above capsule and in this profile are approximate. There is 1 graduate school. The library contains 132,175 volumes, 8,895 microform items, and 2,040 audio/video tapes/CDs/DVDs, and subscribes to 287 periodicals including electronic. Computerized library services include interlibrary loans and database searching. Special learning facilities include a learning resource center and art gallery. The 100-acre campus is in a rural area 65 miles north of Cedar Rapids. Including any residence halls, there are 14 buildings.

Student Life: 60% of undergraduates are from Iowa. Others are from 14 states, 5 foreign countries, and Canada. 90% are from public schools. 75% are white; 13% African American. The average age of freshmen is 19; all undergraduates, 22. 32% do not continue beyond their first year; 68% remain to graduate.

Housing: 515 students can be accommodated in college housing, which includes single-sex dorms and on-campus apartments. On-campus housing is guaranteed for all 4 years. 70% of students live on campus; of those, 50% remain on campus on weekends. All students may keep cars.

Activities: 19% of men belong to 5 local and 1 national fraternities; 40% of women belong to 5 local sororities. There are 31 groups on campus, including and outdoor pursuits, art, cheerleading, computers, drama, environmental, international, newspaper, political, religious, social, social service, student government, and yearbook. Popular campus events include Winterfest, Greek Week, and Springfest.

Sports: There are 9 intercollegiate sports for men and 8 for women, and 4 intramural sports for men and 4 for women. Facilities include a recreation center, a golf course, an indoor swimming pool, a rock climbing wall, a weight room, and nearby cross-country skiing areas.

Disabled Students: 70% of the campus is accessible. Facilities include wheelchair ramps, elevators, special parking, specially equipped restrooms, special class scheduling, lowered drinking fountains, lowered telephones. The school will make accommodations when necessary.

Services: Counseling and information services are available, as is tutoring in most subjects. There is remedial math, reading, and writing.

Campus Safety and Security: Measures include security escort services. There are emergency telephones, lighted pathways/sidewalks, and a security officer living in each residence hall.

Programs of Study: Upper Iowa confers B.A. and B.S. degrees. Associate and master's degrees are also awarded. Bachelor's degrees are awarded in AGRICULTURE (conservation and regulation), BIOLOGICAL SCIENCE (biology/biological science), BUSINESS (accounting, banking and finance, business administration and management, management information systems, management science, marketing/retailing/merchandising, and recreation and leisure services), COMMUNICATIONS AND THE ARTS (art, arts administration/management, communications, English, fine arts, and graphic design), COMPUTER AND PHYSICAL SCIENCE (chemistry, mathematics, and science), EDUCATION (athletic training, elementary education, and physical education), HEALTH PROFESSIONS (health and health care administration), SOCIAL SCIENCE (American studies, criminology, human services, physical fitness/movement, psychology, social science, and sociology). Business, education, and preprofessional science are the strongest academically. Conservation management, education, and management information systems have the largest enrollments.

Required: All students must complete at least 120 semester hours with a GPA of 2.0 overall and 2.5 in the major. Distribution requirements include 9 hours each in English and speech, 6 each in arts and humanities, natural sciences, and social science, and 3 each in math, computer skills, and cultures.

Special: Internships, a work-study program, study abroad, a 3-year B.A. degree in any major except education, and student-designed majors are available. There are 3 national honor societies and a freshman honors program.

Faculty/Classroom: 55% of faculty are male; 45% are female. All teach undergraduates, 20% do research, and 20% do both. No introductory courses are taught by graduate students. The average class size in an introductory lecture is 30; in a laboratory is 10; and in a regular course is 15.

Requirements: The SAT or ACT is required. Recommendations from counselors and extracurricular activities in school, church, and community are considered in the admissions process. A GPA of 2.0 is required. AP and CLEP credits are accepted.

Procedure: Freshmen are admitted to all sessions. Entrance exams should be taken in the spring of junior year. There is a rolling admissions plan. Application deadlines are open. Application fee is $15. Notification is sent on a rolling basis.

Transfer: The prime consideration for transfer students is continued good standing in an accredited institution. Credit is generally given for all lecture and lab courses. 30 of 120 credits required for the bachelor's degree must be completed at Upper Iowa.

Visiting: There are regularly scheduled orientations for prospective students, including campus tours, meals, and visits with faculty and admissions counselors. There are guides for informal visits, visitors may sit in on classes, and stay overnight. To schedule a visit, contact Admissions Administrative Assistant/Office Manager.

Financial Aid: The FAFSA and the college's own financial statement are required. The deadline for filing freshman financial aid applications for fall entry is rolling.

International Students: The school actively recruits these students. They must take the TOEFL.

Computers: All students may access the system. There are no time limits and no fees.

Admissions Contact: Director of Admissions. E-Mail: *admissions@uiu.edu* Web: *www.uiu.edu*

WARTBURG COLLEGE — D-2

Waverly, IA 50677 — **(319) 352-8264**
(800) 772-2085; (319) 352-8579

Full-time: 788 men, 885 women
Part-time: 34 men, 40 women
Graduate: n/av
Year: other, summer session
Application Deadline:
Freshman Class: n/av
SAT or ACT: required
Faculty: n/av; IIB, --$
Ph.D.s: 83%
Student/Faculty: 11 to 1
Tuition: $32,740
Room & Board: $8315

VERY COMPETITIVE

Wartburg College is a selective liberal arts college of the ELCA, internationally recognized for community engagement. Wartburg is dedicated to challenging and nurturing students for lives of leadership and service as a spirited expression of their faith and learning. Opportunities for service-learning, leadership, undergraduate research, global and multicultural studies, and participation in co-curricular activities enrich the academic experience. Wartburg helps students discover their life's purpose through meaning and vocal discernment. In addition to regional accreditation, Wartburg has baccalaureate program accreditation with CSWE, NASM, and NCATE. The library contains 367,895 volumes, 8,611 microform items, and 5,983 audio/video tapes/CDs/DVDs, and subscribes to 83,318 periodicals including electronic. Computerized library services include interlibrary loans, database searching, Internet access, and Wi-Fi capability. Special learning facilities include an art gallery, radio station, TV station, a business center, classroom technology center, fine arts center, journalism lab, symbolic computation lab, music computer lab, Center for Community Engagement, Institute for Leadership Education, 6 acres of native grasses and prairie plants, and more than 100 acres of native timber used for field trips and research. The 118-acre campus is in a small town 15 miles north of Waterloo/Cedar Falls, Iowa. Including any residence halls, there are 37 buildings.

Student Life: 68% of undergraduates are from Iowa. Others are from 29 states, 53 foreign countries, and Canada. 84% are White. 70% are Protestant; 22% Catholic. The average age of freshmen is 18; all undergraduates, 20. 24% do not continue beyond their first year; 65% remain to graduate.

Housing: 1443 students can be accommodated in college housing, which includes single-sex and coed dorms and on-campus apartments. In addition, there are honors houses, language houses, and special-interest houses. On-campus housing is guaranteed for all 4 years. 83% of students live on campus; of those, 75% remain on campus on weekends. All students may keep cars.

Activities: There are no fraternities or sororities. There are 100 groups on campus, including art, band, cheerleading, chess, choir, chorale, chorus, communications, computers, dance, debate, drama, drum and bugle corps, environmental, ethnic, forensics, gay, honors, international, jazz band, literary magazine, musical theater, newspaper, opera, orchestra, pep band, political, professional, radio and TV, religious, social, social service, student government, and symphony. Popular campus events include Artist Series, Convocations, Family Weekend, Homecoming, Culture Week, Martin Luther King Week and Outfly.

Sports: There are 10 intercollegiate sports for men and 9 for women, and 8 intramural sports for men and 8 for women. Facilities include a 200,000 square-foot sports and wellness center that includes an indoor pool, 200-meter track, racquetball courts, batting cages, golf hitting area, tennis/badminton/volleyball courts, weight rooms, a fitness area, and an aerobics and wrestling room; a 5000-seat stadium with a football field and all-weather track; a 2000-seat gym; a lighted baseball park; football, soccer, and softball fields; and outdoor tennis courts.

Disabled Students: 85% of the campus is accessible. Facilities include wheelchair ramps, elevators, special parking, specially equipped restrooms, special class scheduling, lowered drinking fountains, lowered telephones, and special housing.

Services: Counseling and information services are available, as is tutoring in most subjects. There is remedial math. There is a comprehensive academic support center, a supplemental instruction program, and assistance with mathematics, and speech writing and delivery. A writing and reading center is also available. Academic support services are also delivered in the residence halls.

Campus Safety and Security: Measures include 24-hour foot and vehicle patrol, emergency notification system, and security escort services. There are emergency telephones, lighted pathways/sidewalks, controlled access to dorms/residences, 24-hour patrol, and student escort service.

Programs of Study: Wartburg confers B.A., B.A.A., B.A.S., B.M. and B.M.E. degrees. Bachelor's degrees are awarded in BIOLOGICAL SCIENCE (biochemistry and biology/biological science), BUSINESS (accounting, banking and finance, business administration and management, international business management, marketing/retailing/merchandising, and recreation and leisure services), COMMUNICATIONS AND THE ARTS (applied music, art, arts administration/management, broadcasting, communications, creative writing, dramatic arts, English, French, German, graphic design, journalism, music, music performance, music theory and composition, public relations, and Spanish), COMPUTER AND PHYSICAL SCIENCE (chemistry, computer science, information sciences and systems, mathematics, and physics), EDUCATION (art education, elementary education, English education, foreign languages education, journalism education, mathematics education, music education, physical education, science education, secondary education, and social studies education), ENGINEERING AND ENVIRONMENTAL DESIGN (engineering and applied science), HEALTH PROFESSIONS (medical laboratory technology, music therapy, and occupational therapy), SOCIAL SCIENCE (economics, French studies, German area studies, history, international relations, peace studies, philosophy, political science/government, psychology, religion, religious music, social work, and sociology). Biology, music, mathematics, chemistry, biochemistry, and engineering are the strongest academically. Business, biology and communication arts have the largest enrollments.

Required: Degree requirements include a minimum cumulative and major GPA of 2.0 and completion of 36 course credits (128 semester hours), including 4 May term course credits. All students must complete the Wartburg Plan of Essential Education, an integrative and interdisciplinary program of study, based on course work in thinking strategies, reasoning skills, faith and reflection, health and wellness, and literacy in writing, diversity, and a foreign lanaguage. Students must also demonstrate proficiency in information systems and in oral communication and must complete a Capstone course. Inquiry Studies 101/201 are required of all students.

Special: Special academic programs at Wartburg include those in leadership education and global and multicultural studies. Internships are available in all majors and there are internship programs in Denver, Washington, D.C., and abroad. Study abroad in 65 countries, on and off campus work-study, dual majors in any combination, and individualized majors are possible. 3-1 degrees are possible in clinical laboratory science and occupational therapy, as well as 3-1 and 2-2 degrees in nursing. A deferred admit program with the University of Iowa College of Dentistry is offered, as is an array of experiential learning opportunities. There are 11 national honor societies and a freshman honors program.

Faculty/Classroom: 52% of faculty are male; 48% are female. All teach undergraduates, and 42% do research. No introductory courses are taught by graduate students. The average class size in a laboratory is 20 and in a regular course is 20.

Admissions: There was 1 National Merit finalist. 32 freshmen graduated first in their class.

Requirements: The SAT or ACT is required, with a minimum score of 910 on the SAT or 19 on the ACT expected. Candidates for admission must be graduates of an accredited secondary school, having completed 4 years of English, 3 each of math and science, 2 each of social studies and foreign language, and 1 of introduction to computers. The GED is accepted, with an average of 50 or above. A GPA of 2.2 is required. AP and CLEP credits are accepted. Important factors in the admissions decision are advanced placement or honors courses, recommendations by school officials, and leadership record.

Procedure: Freshmen are admitted fall and winter. Entrance exams should be taken before the senior year. There are early admissions and rolling admissions plans. Check with the school for current application deadlines. Notification is sent on a rolling basis. Applications are accepted online.

Transfer: Applicants must have earned an associate degree or have maintained a minimum GPA of 2.0 in previous college work for 1 year. The ACT or the SAT must be taken; the minimum acceptable ACT score is 19. Students must submit official transcripts from all colleges attended. 7 of 36 credits required for the bachelor's degree must be completed at Wartburg.

Visiting: There are regularly scheduled orientations for prospective students, including an introduction to academic and student life conducted by administrators, faculty, and students. There are guides for informal visits, visitors may sit in on classes, and stay overnight. To schedule a visit, contact the Admissions Office.

Financial Aid: In 2013-2014, 99% of all full-time freshmen and 99% of continuing full-time students received some form of financial aid. 91% of all full-time freshmen and 88% of continuing full-time students received need-based aid. The average freshman award was $28,965. Need-based scholarships or need-based grants averaged $9,527 ($29,050 maximum); need-based self-help aid (loans and jobs) averaged $5,442 ($8,000 maximum); and other non-need-based awards and non-need-based scholarships averaged $20,676 ($43,707 maximum). 60% of undergraduate students work part-time. Average annual earnings from campus work are $2500. The average financial indebtedness of the 2013 graduate was $36,567. The FAFSA is required. The priority date for freshman financial aid applications for fall entry is March 1.

International Students: There are 141 international students enrolled. The school actively recruits these students. They must take the TOEFL with a minimum score of 480 on the paper-based TOEFL (PBT) or 55 on the Internet-based version (iBT). SAT or ACT scores are not required but are useful in admissions decisions and for placement.

Computers: All students may access the system. There are no time limits and no fees.

Graduates: From July 1, 2012 to June 30, 2013, 402 bachelor's degrees were awarded. The most popular majors were biology (15%), business administration (13%), and communication arts (9%). In an average class, 3% graduate in 3 years or less, 64% graduate in 4 years or less, 65% graduate in 5 years or less, and 65% graduate in 6 years or less. Of the 2012 graduating class, 24% were enrolled in graduate school within 6 months of graduation, and 64% were employed.

Admissions Contact: Todd Coleman, Assistant Vice President for Admissions . E-Mail: *admissions@wartburg.edu* Web: *www.wartburg.edu*

WILLIAM PENN UNIVERSITY D-3

Oskaloosa, IA 52577 (641) 673-1012
(800) 779-7366; (641) 673-2113

Full-time: 900 men, 750 women
Part-time: 70 men, 115 women
Graduate: 40 men, 45 women
Year: varies, summer session
Application Deadline: open
Freshman Class: n/av
ACT: required

Faculty: n/av
Ph.D.s: n/av
Student/Faculty: n/av
Tuition: $20,500
Room & Board: $6500

COMPETITIVE

William Penn University, founded in 1873, is a private liberal arts institution affiliated with the Society of Friends (Quakers). The figures in the above capsule and in this profile are approximate. There are 2 undergraduate schools and 1 graduate school. In addition to regional accreditation, William Penn has baccalaureate program accreditation with NCATE. The library contains 64,974 volumes, and 1,733 audio/video tapes/CDs/DVDs, and subscribes to 31,974 periodicals including electronic. Computerized library services include interlibrary loans, database searching, Internet access, and Wi-Fi capability. Special learning facilities include an art gallery, radio station, and Mideast collection. The 53-acre campus is in a rural area 58 miles southeast of Des Moines. Including any residence halls, there are 13 buildings.

Student Life: 73% of undergraduates are from Iowa. Others are from 41 states, 10 foreign countries, and Canada. 90% are from public schools. 83% are White. 44% are Protestant; 39% claim no religious affiliation; 13% Catholic. The average age of freshmen is 19; all undergraduates, 25. 35% do not continue beyond their first year; 35% remain to graduate.

Housing: 500 students can be accommodated in college housing, which includes single-sex and coed dorms, on-campus apartments, and married student housing. On-campus housing is guaranteed for all 4 years. 55% of students commute. Alcohol is not permitted. All students may keep cars.

Activities: 5% of men belong to 2 local fraternities; 5% of women belong to 2 local and 1 national sororities. There are 25 groups on campus, including art, band, cheerleading, choir, chorale, chorus, computers, dance, drama, drum and bugle corps, ethnic, honors, international, jazz band, literary magazine, marching band, musical theater, newspaper, pep band, photography, political, professional, radio and TV, religious, social, social service, student government, and yearbook. Popular campus events include Multicultural Day and Campus Beautification Day.

Sports: There are 8 intercollegiate sports for men and 7 for women, and 6 intramural sports for men and 6 for women. Facilities include include a gym with 2 regulation-size basketball courts and wrestling and weight training rooms, baseball and softball fields, 3 tennis courts, and football and soccer practice fields. Pen Activity Center houses a 300 meter walking/jogging track, 2 full-sized basketball/volleyball courts, an aerobic fitness area, and 40 yards of artificial turf.

Disabled Students: 70% of the campus is accessible. Facilities include wheelchair ramps, elevators, special parking, specially equipped restrooms, special class scheduling, and lowered drinking fountains.

Services: Counseling and information services are available, as is tutoring in most subjects. There is remedial math, reading, and writing.

Campus Safety and Security: Measures include 24-hour foot and vehicle patrol, emergency notification system, and self-defense education. There are emergency telephones, lighted pathways/sidewalks, and controlled access to dorms/residences.

Programs of Study: William Penn confers B.A., B.S., and B.S.N. degrees. Associate and master's degrees are also awarded. Bachelor's degrees are awarded in BIOLOGICAL SCIENCE (biology/biological science and biotechnology), BUSINESS (accounting, business administration and management, recreation and leisure services, and sports management), COMMUNICATIONS AND THE ARTS (communications, digital communications, English, fine arts, journalism, and public relations), COMPUTER AND PHYSICAL SCIENCE (computer science), EDUCATION (elementary education, health education, physical education, science education, secondary education, and special education), ENGINEERING AND ENVIRONMENTAL DESIGN (environmental science, industrial administration/management, and industrial engineering technology), SOCIAL SCIENCE (criminology, history, human services, political science/government, psychology, and sociology). Elementary and secondary education, industrial technology, and business are the strongest academically. Education and business have the largest enrollments.

Required: To graduate, students must complete 124 hours, with 30 to 75 hours in the major. A GPA of 2.0 overall and in major and minor courses is required. Leadership core requirements total 47 hours in English/communications, math, natural science, social science, religion, fine arts, and philosophy.

Special: William Penn offers internships, work-study programs with local businesses, dual majors, nondegree study, pass/fail options, and 3-2 engineering degree programs with Iowa State and Washington Universities. Preprofessional studies, driver and safety education, and endorsements in numerous secondary education subjects are also offered. There are 2 national honor societies, including Phi Beta Kappa.

Faculty/Classroom: 57% of faculty are male; 43% are female. All teach undergraduates. No introductory courses are taught by graduate students. The average class size in an introductory lecture is 25.

Admissions: 2 freshmen graduated first in their class.

Requirements: The ACT is required. In addition, Applicants must be graduates of an accredited secondary and should have completed 15 high school units. The GED is accepted. ACT is required of traditional undergraduates only. Our college for working adults does not require ACT scores. A GPA of 2.0 is required. AP and CLEP credits are accepted. Important factors in the admissions decision are evidence of special talent, extracurricular activities record, and leadership record.

Procedure: Freshmen are admitted to all sessions. Entrance exams should be taken late in the junior year or early in the senior year. There are early admissions, deferred admissions, and rolling admissions plans. Application deadlines are open. Application fee is $20. Applications are accepted online.

Transfer: 189 transfer students enrolled in 2012-2013. Applicants must be in good standing at their previous institution and submit official transcripts from previously attended schools. 30 of 124 credits required for the bachelor's degree must be completed at William Penn.

Visiting: There are regularly scheduled orientations for prospective students, including a 1-day visit comprised of meetings with faculty, student services, financial aid, personnel, and people who share students' interests. There are guides for informal visits, visitors may sit in on classes, and stay overnight. To schedule a visit, contact the Visitor Coordinater.

Financial Aid: In 2013-2014, 99% of all full-time freshmen and 99% of continuing full-time students received some form of financial aid. 96% of all full-time freshmen and 96% of continuing full-time students received need-based aid. The average freshman award was $18,373.. 70% of undergraduate students work part-time. Average annual earnings from campus work are $1600. The average financial indebtedness of the 2013 graduate was $18,600. The FAFSA is required. Check with the school for current application deadlines.

International Students: There are 20 international students enrolled. The school actively recruits these students. They must take the TOEFL with a minimum score of 500 on the paper-based TOEFL (PBT).

Computers: All students may access the system. There are no time limits and no fees.

Graduates: From July 1, 2012 to June 30, 2013, 220 bachelor's degrees were awarded. The most popular majors were business management (61%), elementary education (9%), and psychology (5%). 160 companies recruited on campus in 2012-2013. In an average class, 56% graduate in 4 years or less, 90% graduate in 5 years or less, and 98% graduate in 6 years or less. Of the 2012 graduating class, 15% were enrolled in graduate school within 6 months of graduation, and 75% were employed.

Admissions Contact: Director of Admissions. E-Mail: *admissions@wmpenn.edu* Web: *www.wmpenn.edu*

KANSAS

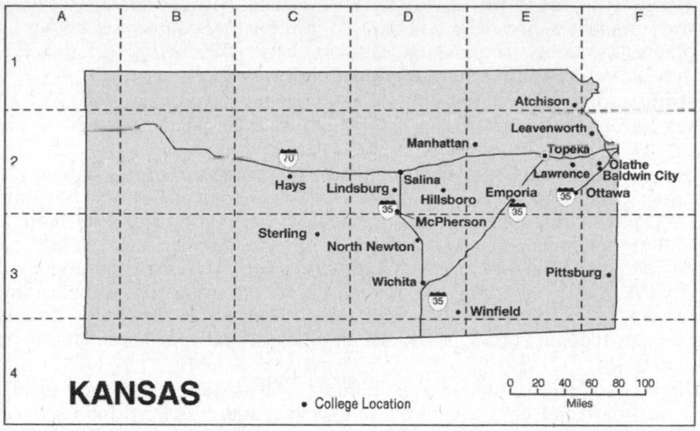

BAKER UNIVERSITY F-2

Baldwin City, KS 66006 (785) 594-8359
(800) 873-4282; (785) 594-8353

Full-time: 422 men, 378 women	**Faculty:** 56; IIB, --$
Part-time: 41 men, 101 women	**Ph.D.s:** 82%
Graduate: n/av	**Student/Faculty:** 14 to 1
Year: 4-1-4, summer session	**Tuition:** $25,500
Application Deadline: open	**Room & Board:** $7850
Freshman Class: 870 applied, 756 accepted, 235 enrolled	
SAT: required **ACT:** 24	**COMPETITIVE+**

Baker University, founded in 1858, is a private liberal arts institution affiliated with the United Methodist Church. There are 4 undergraduate schools and 2 graduate schools. In addition to regional accreditation, Baker has baccalaureate program accreditation with ACBSP, NASM, and NCATE. The library contains 106,549 volumes, 160,000 microform items, and 6,366 audio/video tapes/CDs/DVDs, and subscribes to 160 periodicals including electronic. Computerized library services include interlibrary loans, database searching, and Internet access. Special learning facilities include an art gallery, natural history museum, radio station, TV station, a greenhouse, and wetlands. The 26-acre campus is in a rural area 50 miles southwest of Kansas City and 15 miles south of Lawrence. Including any residence halls, there are 26 buildings.

Student Life: 74% of undergraduates are from Kansas. Others are from 24 states, 8 foreign countries, and Canada. 95% are from public schools. 76% are White. The average age of freshmen is 19; all undergraduates, 20. 24% do not continue beyond their first year; 58% remain to graduate.

Housing: 588 students can be accommodated in college housing, which includes single-sex and coed dorms and on-campus apartments. In addition, there are fraternity houses and sorority houses. On-campus housing is guaranteed for all 4 years. 74% of students live on campus; of those, 50% remain on campus on weekends. Alcohol is not permitted. All students may keep cars.

Activities: 27% of men belong to 1 local and 4 national fraternities; 42% of women belong to 3 national sororities. There are 55 groups on campus, including art, band, cheerleading, choir, chorale, chorus, communications, computers, dance, drama, drill team, environmental, ethnic, gay, honors, international, jazz band, literary magazine, newspaper, orchestra, pep band, photography, professional, radio and TV, religious, social, social service, and student government. Popular campus events include Maple Leaf Festival, International Education Week and Springfest Week.

Sports: There are 10 intercollegiate sports for men and 10 for women, and 5 intramural sports for men and 5 for women. Facilities include a 3,500-seat football/track stadium, a 2,500-seat gym, a 500-seat baseball stadium, practice and varsity fields for football, track, soccer, softball and baseball, 2 basketball courts, 4 racquetball courts, 4 tennis courts, a jogging track, a wellness facility, and a weight room.

Disabled Students: 90% of the campus is accessible. Facilities include wheelchair ramps, elevators, special parking, specially equipped restrooms, special class scheduling, lowered drinking fountains, lowered telephones, and special housing.

Services: Counseling and information services are available, as is tutoring in most subjects. There is a reader service for the blind, and remedial math, reading, and writing.

Campus Safety and Security: Measures include 24-hour foot and vehicle patrol, emergency notification system, and security escort services. There are lighted pathways/sidewalks.

Programs of Study: Baker confers B.A., B.M.E. and B.S. degrees. Bachelor's degrees are awarded in BIOLOGICAL SCIENCE (biology/biological science), BUSINESS (accounting, business administration and management, international business management, and sports management), COMMUNICATIONS AND THE ARTS (art history and appreciation, communications, dramatic arts, English, French, German, media arts, music, Spanish, and studio art), COMPUTER AND PHYSICAL SCIENCE (chemistry, computer science, mathematics, and physics), EDUCATION (art education, elementary education, English education, mathematics education, music education, physical education, science education, and secondary education), HEALTH PROFESSIONS (exercise science and nursing), SOCIAL SCIENCE (economics, history, international studies, philosophy, psychology, religion, and sociology). Business, exercise science, and elementary education have the largest enrollments.

Required: To graduate, all students must complete 128 credit hours, including 24 to 36 hours in the major, a cornerstone liberal arts core,6 core liberal studies courses and 4 linked courses in disciplines, and a minimal level of proficiency in written and oral communication and math. A minimum GPA of 2.0 is required.

Special: Internships are encouraged for students in most majors. Baker also offers study abroad, work-study, B.A.-B.S. degrees, accelerated degrees, and dual and student-designed majors. A 3-2 engineering degree may be earned in conjunction with Washington University in St. Louis, the University of Kansas, and University of Missouri in Kansas City. Interdisciplinary majors are offered in international studies. There are 21 national honor societies, a freshman honors program, and 1 departmental honors programs.

Faculty/Classroom: 51% of faculty are male; 49% are female. All teach undergraduates. No introductory courses are taught by graduate students. The average class size in an introductory lecture is 25; in a laboratory is 15; and in a regular course is 16.

Admissions: 87% of the 2013-2014 applicants were accepted. The ACT scores were 24% below 21, 26% between 21 and 23, 31% between 24 and 26, 9% between 27 and 28, and 11% above 28. 29% of the current freshmen were in the top fifth of their class; 64% were in the top two fifths. 8 freshmen graduated first in their class.

Requirements: The SAT or ACT is required. Candidates for admission must graduate from an accredited secondary school or earn a GED. High school course work in English, a foreign language, social studies, math, and natural science is recommended. Applications of students not meeting these requirements will be reviewed, and students may be invited for an on-campus interview, as necessary. AP and CLEP credits are accepted.

Procedure: Freshmen are admitted to all sessions. Entrance exams should be taken in the fall of the senior year. There is a rolling admissions plan. Application deadlines are open. Applications are accepted online.

Transfer: 67 transfer students enrolled in 2012-2013. Transfer applicants must supply a recommendation form, available from the Baker Admissions Office. The ACT or the SAT score, official high school transcript, and official transcripts of all college courses are required. The minimum GPA is 2.3. 31 of 132 credits required for the bachelor's degree must be completed at Baker.

Visiting: There are regularly scheduled orientations for prospective students, including Preview Days scheduled for both freshman and transfers in spring and fall. Individual visits are scheduled daily. There are guides for informal visits, visitors may sit in on classes, and stay overnight. To schedule a visit, contact the Admissions Office.

Financial Aid: The FAFSA and the college's own financial statement are required. The priority date for freshman financial aid applications for fall entry is March 1. The deadline for filing freshman financial aid applications for fall entry is rolling.

International Students: There are 12 international students enrolled. The school actively recruits these students. They must take the TOEFL with a minimum score of 525 on the paper-based TOEFL (PBT) or 69 on the Internet-based version (iBT). They must also take the SAT or ACT.

Computers: All students may access the system. There are no time limits and no fees.

Graduates: From July 1, 2012 to June 30, 2013, 185 bachelor's degrees were awarded. The most popular majors were business (16%), exercise science (9%), and elementary education (8%). In an average class, 2% graduate in 3 years or less, 40% graduate in 4 years or less, 56% graduate in 5 years or less, and 58% graduate in 6 years or less.

Admissions Contact: Kevin Kropf, Director of Enrollemtn Management.
E-Mail: *admissions@bakeru.edu* Web: *www.bakeru.edu*

BENEDICTINE COLLEGE E-1

Atchison, KS 66002 (913) 367-5340
(800) 467-5340; (913) 367-6102

Full-time: 766 men, 899 women
Part-time: 158 men, 170 women
Graduate: 33 men, 44 women
Year: semesters, summer session
Application Deadline:
Freshman Class: 3538 applied, 2081 accepted, 470 enrolled
ACT: required
Faculty: 95
Ph.D.s: 76%
Student/Faculty: 14 to 1
Tuition: $21,975
Room & Board: $8205

VERY COMPETITIVE

Benedictine College, established in 1971 by a merger of St. Benedict's College and Mount Saint Scholastics College, is a liberal arts, Catholic, Benedictine institution. There are one undergraduate school and 2 graduate schools. In addition to regional accreditation, Benedictine has baccalaureate program accreditation with NASM and NCATE. The library contains 231,796 volumes, 10,803 microform items, and 737 audio/video tapes/CDs/DVDs, and subscribes to 425 periodicals including electronic. Computerized library services include interlibrary loans, database searching, and Internet access. Special learning facilities include a learning resource center. The 225-acre campus is in a small town 45 miles north of Kansas City. Including any residence halls, there are 27 buildings.

Student Life: 60% of undergraduates are from out of state, mostly the Mid-West. Students are from 44 states, 12 foreign countries, and Canada. 55% are from public schools. 84% are White. 76% are Catholic. The average age of freshmen is 18; all undergraduates, 20. 20% do not continue beyond their first year; 55% remain to graduate.

Housing: 1240 students can be accommodated in college housing, which includes single-sex and coed dorms. On-campus housing is guaranteed for all 4 years. 77% of students live on campus; of those, 70% remain on campus on weekends. All students may keep cars.

Activities: There are no fraternities or sororities. There are 35 groups on campus, including band, cheerleading, choir, chorale, computers, dance, drama, drill team, ethnic, honors, international, jazz band, literary magazine, musical theater, newspaper, orchestra, pep band, photography, political, professional, religious, social, social service, student government, and symphony. Popular campus events include Discovery Week, Parents Weekend, and All School Mass.

Sports: There are 7 intercollegiate sports for men and 8 for women, and 7 intramural sports for men and 7 for women. Facilities include a gym, weight rooms, a football and track stadium, baseball, softball, and track fields, and an isometrics training room.

Disabled Students: 80% of the campus is accessible. Facilities include wheelchair ramps, elevators, special parking, specially equipped restrooms, special class scheduling, and lowered drinking fountains.

Services: Counseling and information services are available, as is tutoring in most subjects. There is remedial math, reading, and writing.

Campus Safety and Security: Measures include 24-hour foot and vehicle patrol, emergency notification system, and security escort services. There are lighted pathways/sidewalks and controlled access to dorms/residences.

Programs of Study: Benedictine confers B.A., B.S. and B.Mus.Ed degrees. Associate and master's degrees are also awarded. Bachelor's degrees are awarded in BIOLOGICAL SCIENCE (biochemistry and biology/biological science), BUSINESS (accounting and business administration and management), COMMUNICATIONS AND THE ARTS (art, dramatic arts, English, French, journalism, music, Spanish, and theater management), COMPUTER AND PHYSICAL SCIENCE (astronomy, chemistry, computer science, mathematics, natural sciences, and physics), EDUCATION (athletic training, elementary education, music education, physical education, secondary education, and special education), ENGINEERING AND ENVIRONMENTAL DESIGN (engineering), HEALTH PROFESSIONS (nursing), SOCIAL SCIENCE (economics, history, liberal arts/general studies, philosophy, political science/government, psychology, religion, social science, sociology, and youth ministry). Biology, engineering, and education are the strongest academically. Business, and theology have the largest enrollments.

Required: To graduate, students must complete 128 semester hours, pass a comprehensive exam in their major, and earn a minimum GPA of 2.0 overall and in the major. Curriculum requirements include 9 hours each in philosophy and religious studies, 8 hours each in English, natural science, and foreign language, 6 each in Western civilization and social science, 4 in math, 3 in fine arts, and 2 each in speech communication and phys. ed. A dean's colloquium and a comprehensive exam are also required.

Special: Benedictine offers cross-registration with the 14 other members of the Kansas City Regional Council for Higher Education and study abroad in several countries. The school also offers a 3-2 occupational therapy program with Washington University of St. Louis and a 3-2 engineering degree. Internships, work-study programs, dual majors, B.A.-B.S. degrees in chemistry and biology, an interdisciplinary music marketing major, student-designed majors, pass/fail options, and nondegree study are also available. There are 4 national honor societies, a freshman honors program, and 4 departmental honors programs.

Faculty/Classroom: 66% of faculty are male; 34% are female. All teach undergraduates, and 40% do both. No introductory courses are taught by graduate students. The average class size in an introductory lecture is 25; in a laboratory is 20; and in a regular course is 20.

Admissions: 59% of the 2013-2014 applicants were accepted. 47% of the current freshmen were in the top fifth of their class; 70% were in the top two fifths.

Requirements: The ACT is required. Applicants should graduate in the upper 50% of their class at an accredited secondary school. Students should have 16 academic units, including 4 in English, 3 to 4 in math, 2 to 4 in foreign language and science, 2 in social science, and 1 in history. An interview is recommended. Counselor recommendations are required. A GPA of 2.0 is required. AP and CLEP credits are accepted. Important factors in the admissions decision are advanced placement or honors courses, recommendations by school officials, and recommendations by alumni.

Procedure: Freshmen are admitted to all sessions. Entrance exams should be taken before the July following graduation from high school. There are deferred admissions and rolling admissions plans. Application deadlines are open. Application fee is $25. Notification is sent on a rolling basis. Applications are accepted online.

Transfer: 78 transfer students enrolled in 2012-2013. Applicants must submit transcripts from all colleges attended, a statement of courses in progress, and, if transferring with less than 60 hours, a high school transcript and ACT score. A minimum GPA of 2.0 is required. 30 of 128 credits required for the bachelor's degree must be completed at Benedictine.

Visiting: There are regularly scheduled orientations for prospective students, consisting of an advanced placement exam, preregistration, meetings with the dean, student affairs, and business office and financial aid representatives, and campus tours. The orientations are scheduled for April, June, and July. There are guides for informal visits, visitors may sit in on classes, and stay overnight. To schedule a visit, contact the Admissions Office.

Financial Aid: In 2013-2014, 100% of all full-time freshmen and 99% of continuing full-time students received some form of financial aid. 64% of all full-time freshmen and 64% of continuing full-time students received need-based aid. The average freshman award was $21,132. Need-based scholarships or need-based grants averaged $4,015 ($8,550 maximum); need-based self-help aid (loans and jobs) averaged $3,880 ($5,234 maximum); non-need-based athletic scholarships averaged $14,444 ($28,900 maximum); other non-need-based awards and non-need-based scholarships averaged $12,426 ($20,000 maximum); and $2,828 from other forms of aid. 28% of undergraduate students work part-time. Average annual earnings from campus work are $778. The average financial indebtedness of the 2013 graduate was $27,303. Benedictine is a member of CSS. The FAFSA and the college's own financial statement are required. The priority date for freshman financial aid applications for fall entry is April 1. The deadline for filing freshman financial aid applications for fall entry is August 1.

International Students: There are 21 international students enrolled. The school actively recruits these students. They must take the TOEFL with a minimum score of 533 on the paper-based TOEFL (PBT) or 72 on the Internet-based version (iBT) or take the MELAB. They must also take the SAT or ACT, scoring 18.

Computers: All students may access the system 24 hours a day in residence halls, and 7:45 a.m. to 11 p.m. weekdays, with shorter hours on weekends. There are no time limits and no fees.

Graduates: From July 1, 2012 to June 30, 2013, 336 bachelor's degrees were awarded. The most popular majors were business (20%), education (10%), and theology/youth ministry (6%). 26 companies recruited on campus in 2012-2013. In an average class, 42% graduate in 4 years or less, 46% graduate in 5 years or less, and 53% graduate in 6 years or less. Of the 2012 graduating class, 15% were enrolled in graduate school within 6 months of graduation, and 75% were employed.

Admissions Contact: Pete Helgesen, Dean of Enrollment Management. E-Mail: *phelgesen@benedictine.edu* Web: *www.benedictine.edu*

BETHANY COLLEGE D-2

Lindsborg, KS 67456 (785) 227-3311
(800) 826-2281; (785) 227-2004

Full-time: 360 men, 243 women
Part-time: 36 men, 26 women
Graduate: n/av
Year: 4-1-4, summer session
Application Deadline:
Freshman Class: 506 applied, 486 accepted, 180 enrolled
SAT or ACT: required
Faculty: 39
Ph.D.s: n/av
Student/Faculty: n/av
Tuition: $23,305
Room & Board: $7300

NONCOMPETITIVE

Bethany College, founded in 1881, is a small private liberal arts institution affiliated with the Evangelical Lutheran Church. There is one undergraduate school. In addition to regional accreditation, Bethany has baccalaureate program accreditation with NASM and NCATE. The library contains 103,646 volumes, 51,442 microform items, and 2,366 audio/video tapes/CDs/DVDs, and subscribes to 57 periodicals including electronic. Computerized library services include interlibrary loans, database searching, and Internet access. Special learning facilities include an art gallery, archives. The 80-acre campus is in a small town 65 miles north of Wichita and 20 miles south of Salina. Including any residence halls, there are 17 buildings.

Student Life: 51% of undergraduates are from out of state, mostly the Mid-West. Students are from 32 states, 19 foreign countries, and Canada. 95% are from public schools. 71% are White; 12% African American; 11% Hispanic. 41% claim no religious affiliation; 40% Protestant; 18% Catholic. The average age of freshmen is 18; all undergraduates, 20. 36% do not continue beyond their first year; 33% remain to graduate.

Housing: 455 students can be accommodated in college housing, which includes single-sex and coed dorms and on-campus apartments. On-campus housing is guaranteed for the freshman year only, is available on a first-come, and first-served basis. 75% of students live on campus; of those, 65% remain on campus on weekends. Alcohol is not permitted. All students may keep cars.

Activities: 6% of men belong to 3 local fraternities; 16% of women belong to 4 local sororities. There are 34 groups on campus, including art, band, cheerleading, choir, chorale, chorus, dance, drama, drill team, environmental, honors, international, jazz band, musical theater, newspaper, orchestra, pep band, professional, religious, social, social service, student government, symphony, and yearbook. Popular campus events include Messiah Festival of Art, Music Holy Week Festival, and Hyllingsfest.

Sports: There are 8 intercollegiate sports for men and 7 for women, and 15 intramural sports for men and 15 for women. Facilities include a 1500-seat gym, a 4000-seat stadium, tennis courts, track and field facilities, handball/racquetball courts, a weight training area, 2 softball and 1 baseball diamond, and a soccer field.

Disabled Students: 98% of the campus is accessible. Facilities include wheelchair ramps, elevators, special parking, specially equipped restrooms, special class scheduling, and special housing.

Services: Counseling and information services are available, as is tutoring in most subjects. There is remedial math and writing.

Campus Safety and Security: Measures include emergency notification system, self-defense education, and security escort services. There are lighted pathways/sidewalks, controlled access to dorms/residences, and a campus patrol at night. There is a 24-hour on-call number.

Programs of Study: Bethany confers B.A., B.M., B.M.E. and B.S.W. degrees. Bachelor's degrees are awarded in BIOLOGICAL SCIENCE (biology/biological science and forensic science), BUSINESS (accounting, business administration and management, business economics, finance, marketing management, and sports management), COMMUNICATIONS AND THE ARTS (art, arts administration/management, communications, English, music, and theatre arts), COMPUTER AND PHYSICAL SCIENCE (chemistry and mathematics), EDUCATION (art education, athletic training, business education, Christian education, elementary education, English education, health education, mathematics education, middle school education, music education, physical education, science education, and secondary education), HEALTH PROFESSIONS (art therapy), SOCIAL SCIENCE (addiction studies, criminal justice, history, psychology, and social science). Education, and biology are the strongest academically. Business, education, criminal justice and biology have the largest enrollments.

Required: All students must complete 31-34 credits in the General Education Program including the courses Thinking and Writing and Christianity in the Global Context or New Testament Literature and Thought. The Core Experience (11-14 hrs) consists of four interdisciplinary courses. All students will complete a portfolio that documents their mastery of the core competencies. A total of 124 credit hours with a minimum GPA of 2.0 is required for graduation.

Special: Bethany offers co-op programs and cross-registration through the Associated Colleges of Central Kansas and a 3-2 engineering degree with Wichita State University. Internships, a Chicago semester, a Washington semester, work-study programs, accelerated degree programs in economics/business and pre-engineering, dual majors, student-designed majors are also available. There are 6 national honor societies and a freshman honors program.

Faculty/Classroom: 60% of faculty are male; 40% are female. All teach undergraduates. No introductory courses are taught by graduate students.

Admissions: 96% of the 2013-2014 applicants were accepted. 31% of the current freshmen were in the top fifth of their class; 51% were in the top two fifths. 6 freshmen graduated first in their class.

Requirements: The SAT or ACT is required. Applicants should be graduates of an accredited secondary school, with 4 years of English, 3 each of social studies, math, and science, and 1 of foreign language. Bethany requires applicants to be in the upper 50% of their class. A GPA of 2.5 is required. AP and CLEP credits are accepted.

Procedure: Freshmen are admitted to all sessions. There is a rolling admissions plan. Application deadlines are open. Applications are accepted online.

Transfer: 84 transfer students enrolled in 2012-2013. A GPA of 2.3 in 24 credit hours is required. 32 of 124 credits required for the bachelor's degree must be completed at Bethany.

Visiting: There are regularly scheduled orientations for prospective students, including a campus tours a class visit, a financial aid visit, and lunch in the cafeteria. There are guides for informal visits, visitors may sit in on classes, and stay overnight. To schedule a visit, contact the Office of Admissions.

Financial Aid: In 2013-2014, 99% of all full-time freshmen and 98% of continuing full-time students received some form of financial aid. 83% of all full-time freshmen and 83% of continuing full-time students received need-based aid. The average freshman award was $20,726. Need-based scholarships or need-based grants averaged $7,838 ($11,103 maximum); need-based self-help aid (loans and jobs) averaged $5,495 ($8,000 maximum); and other non-need-based awards and non-need-based scholarships averaged $4,394 ($15,250 maximum). 64% of undergraduate students work part-time. Average annual earnings from campus work are $1500. The average financial indebtedness of the 2013 graduate was $17,800. The priority date for freshman financial aid applications for fall entry is March 15. The deadline for filing freshman financial aid applications for fall entry is August 1.

International Students: There are 26 international students enrolled. The school actively recruits these students. They must take the TOEFL with a minimum score of 525 on the paper-based TOEFL (PBT) or 70 on the Internet-based version (iBT). They must also take the SAT or ACT.

Computers: All students may access the system 24 hours a day. There are no time limits and no fees.

Graduates: From July 1, 2012 to June 30, 2013, 95 bachelor's degrees were awarded. The most popular majors were education (27%), economics and business (19%), and criminal justice and biology (11%). In an average class, 34% graduate in 4 years or less.

Admissions Contact: Director of Admissions E-Mail: *admissions@bethanylb.edu* Web: *www.bethanylb.edu*

BETHEL COLLEGE D-3

North Newton, KS 67117
(316) 284-5230
(800) 522-1887, ext. 230;
(316) 284-5870

Full-time: 232 men, 232 women	**Faculty:** 36
Part-time: 5 men, 13 women	**Ph.D.s:** 46%
Graduate: n/av	**Student/Faculty:** 12 to 1
Year: 4-1-4, summer session	**Tuition:** $21,700
Application Deadline:	**Room & Board:** $7400
Freshman Class: n/av	
SAT CR/M/W: 455/500/445	**ACT:** 23 **COMPETITIVE**

Bethel College, established in 1887, is a private liberal arts institution affiliated with the Mennonite Church. There is one undergraduate school. In addition to regional accreditation, Bethel has baccalaureate program accreditation with CSWE and NCATE. The 2 libraries contain 147,965 volumes, 14,377 microform items, and 7,113 audio/video tapes/CDs/DVDs, and subscribe to 32,765 periodicals including electronic. Computerized library services include interlibrary loans, database searching, Internet access, and Wi-Fi capability. Special learning facilities include an art gallery, natural history museum, radio station, TV station, an observatory. The 90-acre campus is in a suburban area 25 miles north of Wichita. Including any residence halls, there are 21 buildings.

Student Life: 93% of undergraduates are from Kansas. Others are from 24 states, and 10 foreign countries. 73% are White; 13% African American; 11% Hispanic. 28% are Protestant; 20% claim no religious affiliation. The average age of freshmen is 18; all undergraduates, 21. 23% do not continue beyond their first year; 52% remain to graduate.

Housing: 434 students can be accommodated in college housing, which includes coed dorms, off-campus apartments, and married student housing. Coed dorms, and pecial housing for disabled students. On-campus housing is guaranteed for all 4 years. 72% of students live on campus; of those, 93% remain on campus on weekends. Alcohol is not permitted. All students may keep cars.

Activities: There are no fraternities or sororities. There are 30 groups on campus, including choral groups, theater and music ensembles, art, band, campus ministries, cheerleading, chess, choir, chorale, chorus, computers, debate, drama, environmental, ethnic, forensics, gay, international, jazz band, literary magazine, newspaper, orchestra, political, professional, radio and TV, religious, social, social service, student government, and yearbook. Popular campus events include Fall Festival, Christmas Gala and Spring Fling.

Sports: There are 7 intercollegiate sports for men and 7 for women, and 18 intramural sports for men and 18 for women. Facilities include 2 indoor gyms, 2 weight rooms, a cardio-exercise room, 8 tennis courts, 2 soccer practice fields, an all-weather track, an outdoor stadium complex for football, soccer, and track with an 8-lane track and artificial field turf, a football practice field, an outdoor basketball court, and an outdoor sand volleyball court.

Disabled Students: 75% of the campus is accessible. Facilities include wheelchair ramps, elevators, special parking, specially equipped restrooms, special class scheduling, lowered drinking fountains, and special housing.

Services: Counseling and information services are available, as is tutoring in most subjects. There is a reader service for the blind, and remedial math, reading, and writing.

Campus Safety and Security: There are emergency telephones and lighted pathways/sidewalks.

Programs of Study: Bethel confers B.A., B.S., B.S.N. and B.S.S.W. degrees. Bachelor's degrees are awarded in BIOLOGICAL SCIENCE (biology/biological science), BUSINESS (business administration and management), COMMUNICATIONS AND THE ARTS (art, communications, English, and music), COMPUTER AND PHYSICAL SCIENCE (chemistry, mathematics, and natural sciences), EDUCATION (athletic training, elementary education, and health education), HEALTH PROFESSIONS (nursing), SOCIAL SCIENCE (history, psychology, religion, and social work). English, biology, and psychology are the strongest academically. Nursing, and elementary education have the largest enrollments.

Required: To graduate, students must earn a total of 124 credits, including 24 to 50 in the major, 12 to 50 of those in upper-level courses, with a GPA of 2.0. Students must also meet general education requirements that include demonstrating competency in writing, math, speech, and foreign language. Additional core requirements include convocation, religious studies, cross-cultural learning, and peace, justice, and conflict studies. Distribution requirements include at least six hours in each division: arts and humanities, science and mathematics, and social sciences.

Special: Students may cross-register with Associated Colleges of Central Kansas (ACCK) institutions and Hesston College. Internships are required in many majors. Work-study programs, study abroad, dual majors, and a Washington semester are available. The college offers a 3-2 engineering degree with University of Kansas, Kansas State University, and Wichita State University.

Faculty/Classroom: 46% of faculty are male; 54% are female. All teach undergraduates, 50% do research, and 50% do both. No introductory courses are taught by graduate students. The average class size in an introductory lecture is 21; in a laboratory is 11; and in a regular course is 18.

Admissions: 64% of the 2013-2014 applicants were accepted. The SAT scores for the 2013-2014 freshman class were: Critical Reading--73% below 500, 14% between 500 and 599, 10% between 600 and 699, and 3% between 700 and 800; Math--48% below 500, 38% between 500 and 599, 7% between 600 and 699, and 7% between 700 and 800; Writing--72% below 500, 21% between 500 and 599, 7% between 600 and 699. The ACT scores were 4% below 21, 56% between 21 and 23, 30% between 24 and 26, and 10% above 28.

Requirements: The SAT or ACT is required. Applicants should present a satisfactory score for SAT and ACT, with a minimum GPA of 2.5 for automatic admission. The GED is accepted. Auditions are required of candidates applying for some scholarships, and interviews are recommended for all applicants. Specific departmental requirements may vary. CLEP, AP, and International Baccalaureate credit may be awarded. A GPA of 2.0 is required. AP and CLEP credits are accepted. Important factors in the admissions decision are evidence of special talent, recommendations by alumni, and parents or siblings attended your school.

Procedure: Freshmen are admitted to all sessions. Entrance exams should be taken by the fall of the senior year. There is a rolling admissions plan. Application deadlines are open. Application fee is $20. Notification is sent on a rolling basis. Applications are accepted online.

Transfer: 74 transfer students enrolled in 2012-2013. A high school transcript (or GED), or official college transcript (minimum 2.0 GPA), ACT or SAT scores (waived if the student has more than 24 hours accepted in transfer to Bethel College), and a transfer recommendation are required. Automatic admission requires a cumulative GPA of 2.0 and satisfactory ACT or SAT scores. 30 of 30 credits required for the bachelor's degree must be completed at Bethel.

Visiting: There are regularly scheduled orientations for prospective students, including a campus tour, classroom observations, visits with faculty, an interview with an admissions counselor, and lunch, and overnight residence hall lodging. There are guides for informal visits, visitors may sit in on classes, and stay overnight. To schedule a visit, contact the Admissions Office at (800) 522-1887 ext 230.

Financial Aid: In 2013-2014, 100% of all full-time freshmen and 78% of continuing full-time students received some form of financial aid. 87% of all full-time freshmen and 78% of continuing full-time students received need-based aid. The average freshman award was $23,689. Need-based scholarships or need-based grants averaged $5,190; need-based self-help aid (loans and jobs) averaged $9,607; other non-need-based awards and non-need-based scholarships averaged $8,784; and $8,989 from other forms of aid. 42% of undergraduate students work part-time. Average annual earnings from campus work are $1384. The average financial indebtedness of the 2013 graduate was $25,616. The FAFSA is required. The priority date for freshman financial aid applications for fall entry is August 15.

International Students: There are 11 international students enrolled. They must take the TOEFL with a minimum score of 540 on the paper-based TOEFL (PBT) or 76 on the Internet-based version (iBT). They must also take the SAT or ACT.

Computers: All students may access the system 18 hours a day. There are no time limits and no fees.

Graduates: From July 1, 2012 to June 30, 2013, 106 bachelor's degrees were awarded. The most popular majors were health professions/related programs (22%), business/marketing (11%), and visual and performing arts (10%). In an average class, 35% graduate in 4 years or less and 15% graduate in 5 years or less.

Admissions Contact: Todd H. Moore, Vice President for Amisssions.
E-Mail: *admissions@bethelks.edu* Web: *www.bethel-college.edu*

EMPORIA STATE UNIVERSITY — E-2

Emporia, KS 66801 — (620) 341-5465
(877) GO-TO-ESU; (620) 341-5599

Full-time: 1353 men, 2092 women — **Faculty:** 250; IIA, --$
Part-time: 179 men, 249 women — **Ph.D.s:** 78%
Graduate: 703 men, 1457 women — **Student/Faculty:** 17 to 1
Year: semesters, summer session — **Tuition:** $5614 ($17,388)
Application Deadline: open — **Room & Board:** $7283
Freshman Class: 2452 applied, 1488 accepted, 696 enrolled
ACT: 22

COMPETITIVE

Emporia State University will be a premier comprehensive university focused on academic excellence, student success, leadership, and community and global engagement. Emporia State University is a dynamic and progressive student-centered learning community that fosters student success through engagement in academic excellence, community and global involvement, and the pursuit of personal and professional fulfillment. There are 3 undergraduate schools and one graduate school. In addition to regional accreditation, ESU has baccalaureate program accreditation with AACSB, NASAD, NASM, NCATE, and NLN. The library contains 826,379 volumes, 60,262 microform items, and 2,998 audio/video tapes/CDs/DVDs, and subscribes to 41,417 periodicals including electronic. Computerized library services include interlibrary loans, database searching, Internet access, and Wi-Fi capability. Special learning facilities include an art gallery, natural history museum, planetarium, theaters, geology museum, and Great Plains study center. The 207-acre campus is in a small town 110 miles from Kansas City. Including any residence halls, there are 20 buildings.

Student Life: 92% of undergraduates are from Kansas. Others are from 46 states, and 45 foreign countries. 74% are White. The average age of freshmen is 18; all undergraduates, 22. 27% do not continue beyond their first year; 42% remain to graduate.

Housing: 792 students can be accommodated in college housing, which includes single-sex and coed dorms and on-campus apartments. In addition, there are honors houses, special-interest houses, fraternity houses, and sorority houses. On-campus housing is guaranteed for the freshman year only, is available on a first-come, and first-served basis. Priority is given to out-of-town students. 74% of students commute. All students may keep cars.

Activities: 16% of men belong to 8 national fraternities; 12% of women belong to 6 national sororities. There are 130 groups on campus, including art, band, cheerleading, choir, chorale, chorus, computers, debate, drama, drill team, environmental, ethnic, film, gay, honors, international, jazz band, literary magazine, marching band, musical theater, newspaper, opera, orchestra, pep band, political, professional, religious, social, social service, student government, symphony, and yearbook. Popular campus events include Family Day, International Student Festival, and Homecoming.

Sports: There are 7 intercollegiate sports for men and 8 for women, and 12 intramural sports for men and 12 for women. Facilities include a 7000-seat stadium, a student recreation center, an Olympic-size pool, 5 gyms, 6 handball courts, exercise, physical therapy, and dance rooms, a sports complex with 3 softball fields and 1 baseball diamond, an all-weather 8-lane track, and 3 additional softball fields separate from the sports complex.

Disabled Students: All of the campus is accessible. Facilities include wheelchair ramps, elevators, special parking, specially equipped restrooms, special class scheduling, lowered drinking fountains, lowered telephones, and special housing.

Services: There is a reader service for the blind, and remedial math, reading, and writing.

Campus Safety and Security: Measures include 24-hour foot and vehicle patrol, emergency notification system, self-defense education, and

security escort services. There are emergency telephones, lighted pathways/sidewalks, motorist-assist programs, safety and self-awareness programs for students and parents, 24-hour residence hall monitoring, and smoke detectors in residence halls.

Programs of Study: ESU confers B.A., B.S., B.F.A., B.I.S., B Mus., B.Mus.Ed., B.S.Bus., B.S.Ed. and B.S.N. degrees. Master's and doctoral degrees are also awarded. Bachelor's degrees are awarded in BIOLOGICAL SCIENCE (biochemistry and biology/biological science), BUSINESS (accounting, business administration and management, marketing/retailing/merchandising, and recreation and leisure services), COMMUNICATIONS AND THE ARTS (art, communications, dramatic arts, English, modern language, music, and theatre arts), COMPUTER AND PHYSICAL SCIENCE (chemistry, computer science, earth science, information sciences and systems, mathematics, physical sciences, and physics), EDUCATION (art education, athletic training, business education, elementary education, foreign languages education, health education, music education, physical education, and secondary education), HEALTH PROFESSIONS (health care administration, health science, nursing, and rehabilitation therapy), SOCIAL SCIENCE (criminal justice, economics, history, liberal arts/general studies, political science/government, psychology, social science, and sociology). Teacher education, both elementary and secondary are the strongest academically. Elementary education, business administration, and biology have the largest enrollments.

Required: To graduate, all students must complete at least 124 credit hours, including 40 in upper-division courses, with a minimum GPA of 2.0. Students must also pass competency exams in reading, math, and writing and complete the general education program for their field of study, which includes courses in math, physical and applied science, humanities, history, speech, cultural diversity, and fitness and phys ed.

Special: ESU offers internships in many majors, study abroad in 34 countries, work-study programs, on-campus and online general studies degrees, B.A.-B.S. degrees, dual and student-designed majors, 3-2 engineering degrees with Kansas State University, Wichita State University, and the University of Kansas, credit for military experience, non-degree study, independent study, evening and Saturday classes, and pass/no credit options. There are 22 national honor societies and a freshman honors program.

Faculty/Classroom: 53% of faculty are male; 47% are female. All teach undergraduates. Graduate students teach 9% of introductory courses. The average class size in an introductory lecture is 20; in a laboratory is 10; and in a regular course is 23.

Admissions: 61% of the 2013-2014 applicants were accepted. The ACT scores were 35% below 21, 31% between 21 and 23, 19% between 24 and 26, 9% between 27 and 28, and 8% above 28. 2% of the current freshmen were in the top fifth of their class. 31 freshmen graduated first in their class.

Requirements: The ACT is required. In addition, Applicants must meet 1 of these 3 criteria: an ACT score of 21 or above, class rank in the top third, or a 2.0 GPA in the Kansas core curriculum in-state and a 2.5 for out-of-state applicants. Students should have completed 4 units of English, 3 each of natural science, math, and social science, and 1 of computer technology. Applicants may also be admitted through an exceptions window and are encouraged to apply. A GPA of 2.0 is required. AP and CLEP credits are accepted.

Procedure: Freshmen are admitted to all sessions. Entrance exams should be taken during October or December of the senior year. There are deferred admissions and rolling admissions plans. Application deadlines are open. Application fee is $30. applicants were on the 2013 waiting list; were admitted. Applications are accepted online.

Transfer: 387 transfer students enrolled in 2012-2013. Applicants must submit official transcripts of all previous college work. The minimum GPA depends on the number of semester hours earned. Physical activity requirements must be met. 30 of 124 credits required for the bachelor's degree must be completed at ESU.

Visiting: There are regularly scheduled orientations for prospective students, Visits include campus and residence hall tours, meetings with admissions and financial aid personnel, and appointments with academic and extracurricular personnel. There are guides for informal visits, visitors may sit in on classes, and stay overnight. To schedule a visit, contact Lyndel Landgren at (877) 468-6378.

Financial Aid: In 2013-2014, 95% of all full-time freshmen and 88% of continuing full-time students received some form of financial aid. 67% of all full-time freshmen and 66% of continuing full-time students received need-based aid. The average freshman award was $11,730. Need-based scholarships or need-based grants averaged $5,696 ($27,136 maximum); need-based self-help aid (loans and jobs) averaged $5,464 ($12,216 maximum); non-need-based athletic scholarships averaged $2,719 ($23,287 maximum); and other non-need-based awards and non-need-based scholarships averaged $7,743 ($19,271 maximum). 15% of undergraduate students work part-time. Average annual earnings from campus work are $3300. The average financial indebtedness of the 2013 graduate was $23,538. The FAFSA and the state aid form are required. The priority date for freshman financial aid applications for fall entry is February 2.

International Students: There are 519 international students enrolled. The school actively recruits these students. They must take the TOEFL with a minimum score of 520 on the paper-based TOEFL (PBT) or 68 on the Internet-based version (iBT). They must also take the ACT.

Computers: All students may access the system 24/7. There are no time limits and no fees.

Graduates: From July 1, 2012 to June 30, 2013, 713 bachelor's degrees were awarded. The most popular majors were education (22%), business administration (15%), and health fields (10%). 185 companies recruited on campus in 2012-2013. In an average class, 20% graduate in 4 years or less, 35% graduate in 5 years or less, and 41% graduate in 6 years or less. Of the 2012 graduating class, 20% were enrolled in graduate school within 6 months of graduation, and 22% were employed.

Admissions Contact: Laura Eddy, Director of Admissions. E-Mail: *go2esu@emporia.edu* Web: *www.emporia.edu*

FORT HAYS STATE UNIVERSITY C-2

Hays, KS 67601 (785) 628-5666
(800) 628-FHSU; (785) 628-4014

Full-time: 2010 men, 2310 women	**Faculty:** n/av; IIA, --$
Part-time: 1550 men, 2000 women	**Ph.D.s:** 77%
Graduate: 510 men, 870 women	**Student/Faculty:** n/av
Year: semesters, summer session	**Tuition:** $4354 ($15,320)
Application Deadline: open	**Room & Board:** $7000
Freshman Class: n/av	
ACT: recommended	

COMPETITIVE

Fort Hays State University, established in 1902, is a public liberal arts institution offering programs in arts and sciences, business and entrepreneurship, education, health and life sciences, and pre-professional study. The figures in the above capsule and in this profile are approximate. There are 4 undergraduate schools and one graduate school. In addition to regional accreditation, FHSU has baccalaureate program accreditation with AACSB, NASM, NCATE, and NLN. The library contains 300,000 volumes, 500,000 microform items, and 1,480 audio/video tapes/CDs/DVDs, and subscribes to 3,100 periodicals including electronic. Computerized library services include interlibrary loans, database searching, Internet access, and Wi-Fi capability. Special learning facilities include an art gallery, radio station, TV station, an English lab. The 200-acre campus is in a small town 180 miles northwest of Wichita. Including any residence halls, there are 44 buildings.

Student Life: 93% of undergraduates are from Kansas. Others are from 36 states, 32 foreign countries, and Canada. 95% are from public schools. 87% are White. The average age of freshmen is 18; all undergraduates, 23. 61% do not continue beyond their first year; 40% remain to graduate.

Housing: 1000 students can be accommodated in college housing, which includes single-sex and coed dorms, on-campus apartments, and married student housing. In addition, there are fraternity houses, sorority houses, apartments for students with families, and apartments for nontraditional-age students. 82% of students commute. All students may keep cars.

Activities: 1% of men belong to 3 national fraternities; 1% of women belong to 3 national sororities. There are 85 groups on campus, including art, band, cheerleading, choir, chorale, chorus, computers, dance, debate, drama, drill team, ethnic, film, gay, honors, international, jazz band, literary magazine, marching band, musical theater, newspaper, opera, orchestra, pep band, photography, political, professional, radio and TV, religious, social, social service, student government, symphony, and yearbook. Popular campus events include Octoberfest and Parents Day.

Sports: There are 8 intercollegiate sports for men and 7 for women, and 40 intramural sports for men and 40 for women. Facilities include a 6300-seat stadium, tennis courts, and a coliseum containing a 6800-seat basketball arena, a track, and wrestling and training rooms.

Disabled Students: 95% of the campus is accessible. Facilities include wheelchair ramps, elevators, special parking, specially equipped restrooms, special class scheduling, lowered drinking fountains, lowered telephones.

Services: Counseling and information services are available, as is tutoring in most subjects. There is remedial math and reading.

Campus Safety and Security: Measures include 24-hour foot and vehicle patrol and security escort services. There are emergency telephones and lighted pathways/sidewalks.

Programs of Study: FHSU confers B.A., B.S., B.B.A., B.F.A., B.G.S., B.M. and B.S.W. degrees. Associate and master's degrees are also awarded. Bachelor's degrees are awarded in AGRICULTURE (agricultural business management and agriculture), BIOLOGICAL SCIENCE (biology/biological science), BUSINESS (accounting, banking and finance, business administration and management, management information systems, marketing/retailing/merchandising, and office supervision and management), COMMUNICATIONS AND THE ARTS (art, communications, English, fine arts, French, German, modern language, music, music performance, music theory and composition, Spanish, and telecommunications),

COMPUTER AND PHYSICAL SCIENCE (chemistry, computer science, geology, information sciences and systems, mathematics, physical sciences, physics, radiological technology, and science), EDUCATION (art education, elementary education, music education, physical education, and technical education), HEALTH PROFESSIONS (nursing and speech pathology/audiology), SOCIAL SCIENCE (criminal justice, economics, history, liberal arts/general studies, philosophy, political science/government, psychology, social work, and sociology). Speech pathology is the strongest academically. Interdisciplinary studies, teacher education, and business administration have the largest enrollments.

Required: To graduate, students must earn an overall minimum GPA of 2.0 or higher in some departments for 124 credit hours, including 40 hours in upper-level study, and 30 hours minimum in the major. The 55-hour liberal arts general education curriculum includes courses addressing personal wellness, analysis and communication, international studies, humanities, math, and natural, social, and behavioral sciences.

Special: Students may, with approval, earn their degrees through a cooperative program with FHSU and another accredited institution, or a correspondence or extension school. Cross-registration with several community colleges, internships, study abroad, work-study programs, a 3-2 engineering degree with Kansas State University, B.A.-B.S. degrees, a general studies degree, and pass/fail options are available. There are 21 national honor societies and a freshman honors program.

Faculty/Classroom: 59% of faculty are male; 41% are female. All teach undergraduates. No introductory courses are taught by graduate students. The average class size in an introductory lecture is 17; in a laboratory is 17; and in a regular course is 18.

Requirements: The ACT is recommended. A GPA of 2.0 is required. AP and CLEP credits are accepted.

Procedure: Freshmen are admitted fall, spring, and summer. Entrance exams should be taken in the senior year. There is a rolling admissions plan. Application deadlines are open. Application fee is $30. Applications are accepted online.

Transfer: Applicants must have a minimum college GPA of 2.0 and submit official college transcripts from all institutions previously attended. 30 of 124 credits required for the bachelor's degree must be completed at FHSU.

Visiting: There are regularly scheduled orientations for prospective students. There are guides for informal visits, visitors may sit in on classes, and stay overnight. To schedule a visit, contact Tina Schiel at tlschiel@fhsu.edu.

Financial Aid: The FFS and the college's own financial statement are required. Check with the school for current application deadlines.

International Students: The school actively recruits these students. They must take the TOEFL.

Computers: All students may access the system. The modem pool may be used 24 hours a day, the labs until 11 p.m. There are no time limits and no fees.

Admissions Contact: Roger Schieferecke, Director of Admissions. E-Mail: *tigers@fhsu.edu* Web: *www.fhsu.edu*

FRIENDS UNIVERSITY — D-3

Wichita, KS 67213 — (316) 295-5000; (800) 794-6945; (316) 295-5101

Full-time: 640 men, 788 women	**Faculty:** n/av; IIA, --$
Part-time: 142 men, 199 women	**Ph.D.s:** n/av
Graduate: 257 men, 476 women	**Student/Faculty:** n/av
Year: semesters, summer session	**Tuition:** $22,500
Application Deadline: open	**Room & Board:** $6600
Freshman Class: 786 applied, 456 accepted, 196 enrolled	

COMPETITIVE

Friends University, established in 1898, is a nondenominational, independent Christian University that incorporates liberal arts instruction and professional studies into a high-quality undergraduate and graduate education. There are 2 undergraduate schools and one graduate school. In addition to regional accreditation, Friends has baccalaureate program accreditation with NASM and NCATE. Computerized library services include interlibrary loans, database searching, and Internet access. Special learning facilities include an art gallery, Observatory. The 54-acre campus is in an urban area In the heart of Wichita, Kansas adjacent to highway 54, approximately 200 miles southwest of Kansas City. Including any residence halls, there are 19 buildings.

Student Life: 81% of undergraduates are from Kansas. Others are from 18 states, 11 foreign countries, and Canada. 81% are from public schools. 70% are White; 11% African American; 11% Hispanic. 66% are Protestant; 37% claim no religious affiliation; 13% Catholic. The average age of freshmen is 18; all undergraduates, 21. 40% do not continue beyond their first year; 60% remain to graduate.

Housing: 423 students can be accommodated in college housing, which includes coed dorms, on-campus apartments, and off-campus apartments. a limited number of university-owned houses are available. On-campus housing is available on a first-come and first-served basis. 56% of students commute. Alcohol is not permitted. All students may keep cars.

Activities: There are no fraternities or sororities. There are 24 groups on campus, including psychology club, Spanish club, zoo science, art, band, cheerleading, choir, chorale, chorus, communications, computers, dance, drama, ethnic, honors, international, jazz band, literary magazine, musical theater, newspaper, orchestra, pep band, photography, political, professional, religious, singing Quakers, social, social service, student government, symphony, and yearbook. Popular campus events include Homecoming Week, Cherry Carnival and Chili Cookoff.

Sports: There are 9 intercollegiate sports for men and 8 for women, and 8 intramural sports for men and 8 for women. Friends University is home to Adair-Austin Stadium, a 2600-seat stadium with Sportexe Momentum 46 brand turf for football and soccer, "Eurotan S" Sandwich Track surface system, Forrest C. Lattner Tennis Courts, and Garvey PE Center with 2,300 capcity gymnasium for basketball and volleyball games. The center also includes an auxillary indoor practic facility for baseball, softball, and track programs as well as spacious lockers rooms, racquetball courts, two weight rooms, and the athletic training and sports medicine facilities.

Disabled Students: 95% of the campus is accessible. Facilities include wheelchair ramps, elevators, special parking, specially equipped restrooms, special class scheduling, lowered drinking fountains, and lowered telephones.

Services: Counseling and information services are available, as is tutoring in most subjects. There is a reader service for the blind. Please contact ADA coordinator on campus for all available services

Campus Safety and Security: Measures include 24-hour foot and vehicle patrol, emergency notification system, and security escort services. There are lighted pathways/sidewalks and controlled access to dorms/residences.

Programs of Study: Friends confers B.A., B.S., B.B.A., B.F.A. and B.Mus. degrees. Associate and master's degrees are also awarded. Bachelor's degrees are awarded in BIOLOGICAL SCIENCE (biology/biological science, wildlife biology, and zoology), BUSINESS (accounting, banking and finance, business administration and management, business economics, human resources, international business management, and management information systems), COMMUNICATIONS AND THE ARTS (art, ballet, communications, English, fine arts, music, music performance, musical theater, performing arts, and Spanish), COMPUTER AND PHYSICAL SCIENCE (chemistry, computer science, information sciences and systems, mathematics, and radiological technology), EDUCATION (art education, business education, drama education, education, elementary education, English education, foreign languages education, health education, music education, recreation education, science education, secondary education, and social science education), ENGINEERING AND ENVIRONMENTAL DESIGN (environmental science), HEALTH PROFESSIONS (health science, premedicine, and radiological science), SOCIAL SCIENCE (Christian studies, counseling/psychology, criminal justice, forensic studies, history, human services, liberal arts/general studies, philosophy and religion, political science/government, psychology, and religion). Science is the strongest academically. Business and education have the largest enrollments.

Required: To graduate, students must complete 124 credit hours, including 33 to 54 in general education (varies by degree sought) and 24 to 45 in the major, with a minimum GPA of 2.0. Distribution requirements include course work in humanities, fine arts, religion and philosophy, behavioral science, and natural science.

Special: Students may cross-register with Newman University at no additional charge. Oportunity to participate in a long-standing study-abroad program is available in Cancun, Mexico; several other study-abroad programs of both shorter and longer duration have occurred in London, Paris, Italy, Cuba, Germany, Scotland,to name a few. Friends University offers several accelerated degree completion programs for the adult student in the College of Adult and Professional Studies. Friends also offers credit for life, military, and work experience. There is 1 national honor society, a freshman honors program, and 1 departmental honors programs.

Faculty/Classroom: 92% teach undergraduates. No introductory courses are taught by graduate students. The average class size in an introductory lecture is 35; in a laboratory is 18; and in a regular course is 25.

Admissions: 58% of the 2013-2014 applicants were accepted. The SAT scores for the 2013-2014 freshman class were: Critical Reading--67% below 500, 21% between 500 and 599, and 12% between 600 and 699; Math--63% below 500, 25% between 500 and 599, and 12% between 600 and 699.

Requirements: Candidates for admission must graduate from an accredited secondary school or earn a GED, having completed 4 courses in English, 2 each in history and math, and 1 each in science and social studies. The composite ACT score or converted SAT score is multiplied by the high school GPA. A result of 45 is the minimum for full admission; students scoring lower may be admitted provisionally. Transfer students with at least 15 transferrable hours and adult students aged 23 or older are not required to submit test scores. A GPA of 2.0 is required. AP and CLEP credits are accepted.

Procedure: Freshmen are admitted fall and spring. Entrance exams

should be taken in the spring of the junior year or fall of the senior year. There is a rolling admissions plan. Application deadlines are open. Application fee is $35. Notification is sent on a rolling basis.

Transfer: Applicants with fewer than 15 semester hours must submit ACT or SAT I scores and high school and college transcripts. 30 of 124 credits required for the bachelor's degree must be completed at Friends.

Visiting: There are regularly scheduled orientations for prospective students, including half-day classroom visits, individual instructor visits, discussion with current students, a tour, lunch, and a financial aid session. There are guides for informal visits, visitors may sit in on classes, and stay overnight. To schedule a visit, contact the Admissions Office.

Financial Aid: The FAFSA is required. Check with the school for current application deadlines.

International Students: The school actively recruits these students. They must take the TOEFL, unless they are either native speakers of English or non-native speakers who attended an English-speaking high school. SAT or ACT scores may be submited in place of TOEFL scores.

Computers: All students may access the system. There are no time limits and no fees.

Admissions Contact: Tony Myers, Director of Admissions. Web: *www.friends.edu*

KANSAS STATE UNIVERSITY — E-2

Manhattan, KS 66506 — **(785) 532-6250; (785) 532-6393**

Full-time: 9496 men, 8614 women	**Faculty:** n/av; I, --$
Part-time: 1007 men, 1052 women	**Ph.D.s:** 82%
Graduate: 1956 men, 2456 women	**Student/Faculty:** n/av
Year: semesters, summer session	**Tuition:** $8585 ($21,530)
Application Deadline: open	**Room & Board:** $7710

Freshman Class: 9839 applied, 9437 accepted, 3821 enrolled

ACT: 24

VERY COMPETITIVE

Kansas State University, established in 1863, is a land-grant institution offering degree programs in agriculture, arts and sciences, business, engineering, human ecology, architecture, education, veterinary medicine, technology and aviation. There are 9 undergraduate schools and one graduate school. In addition to regional accreditation, K-State has baccalaureate program accreditation with AACSB, ABET, ACCE, ACEJMC, AHEA, CSWE, FIDER, NAAB, NASAD, NASM, NCATE, and NRPA. The 5 libraries contain 3.0 million volumes, 1.6 million microform items, and 148,382 audio/video tapes/CDs/DVDs, and subscribe to 81,942 periodicals including electronic. Computerized library services include interlibrary loans, database searching, and Internet access. Special learning facilities include an art gallery, planetarium, radio station, TV station, a nuclear reactor, laser center, a cancer research center, and telecommunications satellite teaching. The 668-acre campus is in a suburban area 125 miles west of Kansas City. Including any residence halls, there are 96 buildings.

Student Life: 78% of undergraduates are from Kansas. Others are from 50 states, 112 foreign countries, and Canada. 76% are White. The average age of freshmen is 18; all undergraduates, 20. 18% do not continue beyond their first year; 60% remain to graduate.

Housing: 4580 students can be accommodated in college housing, which includes single-sex and coed dorms, on-campus apartments, off-campus apartments, and married student housing. In addition, there are honors houses, special-interest houses, fraternity houses, and sorority houses. On-campus housing is available on a first-come and first-served basis. 75% of students commute. All students may keep cars.

Activities: 14% of men belong to 28 national fraternities; 20% of women belong to 18 national sororities. There are 478 groups on campus, including band, cheerleading, chess, choir, chorale, chorus, computers, dance, debate, drama, drill team, ethnic, film, gay, honors, international, jazz band, literary magazine, marching band, musical theater, newspaper, orchestra, pep band, photography, political, professional, radio and TV, religious, social, social service, student government, symphony, and yearbook. Popular campus events include Family Weekend and K-State Open House.

Sports: There are 6 intercollegiate sports for men and 8 for women, and 49 intramural sports for men and 49 for women. Facilities include indoor and outdoor tracks, baseball fields, tennis courts, basketball courts, swimming pools, a football stadium, and an indoor practice field. A multipurpose recreation facility is open 16 hours a day.

Disabled Students: 90% of the campus is accessible. Facilities include wheelchair ramps, elevators, special parking, specially equipped restrooms, special class scheduling, lowered drinking fountains, lowered telephones, a campus shuttle service.

Services: Counseling and information services are available, as is tutoring in every subject. There is a reader service for the blind, and remedial math, reading, and writing.

Campus Safety and Security: Measures include 24-hour foot and vehicle patrol, emergency notification system, self-defense education, and security escort services. There are shuttle buses, emergency telephones, lighted pathways/sidewalks, , televised monitors in parking lots, CPR classes, and vehicle assistance devices.

Programs of Study: K-State confers B.A., B.S., B.F.A., B.M. and B.M.E. degrees. Associate, master's, and doctoral degrees are also awarded. Bachelor's degrees are awarded in AGRICULTURE (agricultural business management, agricultural communications, agricultural economics, agronomy, animal science, animal feed science, bakery science, fish and game management, horticulture, milling science, and wildlife management), BIOLOGICAL SCIENCE (biochemistry, biology/biological science, life science, microbiology, nutrition, and wildlife biology), BUSINESS (accounting, apparel and accessories marketing, banking and finance, business administration and management, entrepreneurial studies, hotel/motel and restaurant management, management information systems, marketing/retailing/merchandising, and personal financial planning), COMMUNICATIONS AND THE ARTS (apparel design, applied music, art, communications, dramatic arts, English, journalism, modern language, and music), COMPUTER AND PHYSICAL SCIENCE (chemistry, computer science, geology, information sciences and systems, mathematics, physical sciences, physics, and statistics), EDUCATION (agricultural education, art education, athletic training, early childhood education, elementary education, music education, and secondary education), ENGINEERING AND ENVIRONMENTAL DESIGN (aeronautical technology, agricultural engineering, agricultural engineering technology, airline piloting and navigation, architectural engineering, architecture, chemical engineering, civil engineering, computer engineering, construction management, electrical/electronics engineering, electrical/electronics engineering technology, engineering management, engineering technology, industrial engineering, interior design, landscape architecture/design, manufacturing engineering, and mechanical engineering), HEALTH PROFESSIONS (exercise science, medical technology, preveterinary science, and speech pathology/audiology), SOCIAL SCIENCE (anthropology, child care/child and family studies, dietetics, economics, ethnic studies, family and community services, family/consumer studies, food science, geography, history, human ecology, humanities, parks and recreation management, philosophy, physical fitness/movement, political science/government, psychology, social science, social work, sociology, textiles and clothing, and women's studies). Architecture, engineering, and accounting are the strongest academically. Business administration, mechanical engineering and animal sciences have the largest enrollments.

Required: Bachelor's degree programs require a minimum of 120 or more semester credit hours for completion. All undergraduates must complete 6 credit hours of expository writing and 2 credit hours of public speaking. Other requirements vary by college and program.

Special: K-State offers co-op programs, internships, and dual degrees and majors through most of its colleges. Study abroad is available in more than 100 countries. Concurrent bachelor's/master's degree programs are available in 11 major areas. There are 78 national honor societies, including Phi Beta Kappa, a freshman honors program, and 7 departmental honors programs.

Faculty/Classroom: 61% of faculty are male; 39% are female. No introductory courses are taught by graduate students. The average class size in a regular course is 30.

Admissions: 96% of the 2013-2014 applicants were accepted. The ACT scores were 17% below 21, 27% between 21 and 23, 26% between 24 and 26, 12% between 27 and 28, and 18% above 28.

Requirements: In addition, Applicants must meet 1 of these 3 criteria: an ACT score of 21 or above, class rank in the top third, or a 2.0 GPA in the Kansas core curriculum. It is recommended that students complete 4 units of English, 3 each of natural science, math, and social studies, and 1 of computer technology. The GED is accepted. AP and CLEP credits are accepted.

Procedure: Freshmen are admitted to all sessions. Entrance exams should be taken in the junior and senior years. There is a rolling admissions plan. Application deadlines are open. The fall 2013 application fee was $30. Notification is sent on a rolling basis. Applications are accepted online.

Transfer: 1509 transfer students enrolled in 2012-2013. Applicants must have a minimum of 24 transfer credit hours and a college GPA of 2.0 or otherwise must meet freshman requirements. Students must submit official transcripts from previous colleges attended. 30 of 120 credits required for the bachelor's degree must be completed at K-State.

Visiting: There are regularly scheduled orientations for prospective students, including campus tours and visits with academic advisers and admissions representatives. There are guides for informal visits, visitors may sit in on classes, and stay overnight. To schedule a visit, contact the Office of Admissions.

Financial Aid: In 2013-2014, 83% of all full-time freshmen and 70% of continuing full-time students received some form of financial aid. 43% of all full-time freshmen and 45% of continuing full-time students received need-based aid. The average freshman award was $12,619. Need-based scholarships or need-based grants averaged $4,140; need-based self-help aid (loans and jobs) averaged $3,855; non-need-based athletic scholarships averaged $12,762; and other non-need-based awards and non-need-based scholarships averaged $6,568. K-State is a member of CSS. The FAFSA is required. The priority date for freshman financial aid applications for fall entry is March 1.

International Students: There are 1376 international students enrolled. The school actively recruits these students. They must take the TOEFL with a minimum score of 550 on the paper-based TOEFL (PBT) or 79 on the Internet-based version (iBT), or present acceptable scores on the SAT or the ACT. an English proficiency test given at the university.

Computers: All students may access the system 24 hours a day. There are no time limits and no fees.

Graduates: From July 1, 2012 to June 30, 2013, 3677 bachelor's degrees were awarded. The most popular majors were business administration (11%), animal sciences (5%), and family studies and human services (5%). In an average class, 26% graduate in 4 years or less, 53% graduate in 5 years or less, and 60% graduate in 6 years or less. Of the 2012 graduating class, 21% were enrolled in graduate school within 6 months of graduation, and 71% were employed.

Admissions Contact: Larry Moeder, Asst VP for Student Life/Dir Adm & FA. E-Mail: *k-state@k-state.edu* Web: *www.k-state.edu*

KANSAS WESLEYAN UNIVERSITY — D-2

Salina, KS 67401-6196 — **(785) 827-5541, ext. 1285; (800) 874-1154; (785) 827-0927**

Full-time: 310 men, 380 women	**Faculty:** n/av; IIB, --$
Part-time: 40 men, 70 women	**Ph.D.s:** n/av
Graduate: 45 men, 30 women	**Student/Faculty:** n/av
Year: semesters, summer session	**Tuition:** $25,000
Application Deadline: open	**Room & Board:** $7000
Freshman Class: n/av	
SAT or ACT: required	

COMPETITIVE

Kansas Wesleyan, founded in 1886, is affiliated with the United Methodist Church. The college offers undergraduate programs in the arts and sciences, business, and education. The figures in the above capsule and in this profile are approximate. There is 1 graduate school. In addition to regional accreditation, Kansas Wesleyan has baccalaureate program accreditation with NCATE and NLN. The library contains 82,000 volumes, 33,505 microform items, and 984 audio/video tapes/CDs/DVDs, and subscribes to 421 periodicals including electronic. Computerized library services include interlibrary loans, database searching, and Internet access. Special learning facilities include a learning resource center, art gallery, planetarium, and TV station. The 25-acre campus is in an urban area 85 miles north of Wichita. Including any residence halls, there are 12 buildings.

Student Life: 75% of undergraduates are from Kansas. Others are from 14 states, 12 foreign countries, and Canada. 92% are from public schools. 85% are white. 48% are Protestant; 39% claim no religious affiliation; 13% Catholic. The average age of freshmen is 20; all undergraduates, 24. 33% do not continue beyond their first year.

Housing: 450 students can be accommodated in college housing, which includes single-sex dorms, on-campus apartments, and married student housing. On-campus housing is guaranteed for all 4 years. 55% of students live on campus; of those, 45% remain on campus on weekends. Alcohol is not permitted. All students may keep cars.

Activities: There are no fraternities or sororities. There are 38 groups on campus, including art, band, cheerleading, choir, chorale, chorus, computers, dance, departmental, drama, ethnic, film, honors, international, literary magazine, musical theater, newspaper, pep band, photography, professional, radio and TV, religious, social, social service, student government, and yearbook. Popular campus events include Lilac Fete, Sweetheart Dance, and Family Weekend.

Sports: There are 7 intercollegiate sports for men and 7 for women, and 8 intramural sports for men and 6 for women. Facilities include a student activities center, a gym, a sand volleyball court, football practice and game fields, a multipurpose courtyard, a track and a weight room.

Disabled Students: 90% of the campus is accessible. Facilities include wheelchair ramps, elevators, special parking, specially equipped restrooms, special class scheduling, lowered drinking fountains, and lowered telephones.

Services: Counseling and information services are available, as is tutoring in most subjects. There is remedial reading and writing.

Campus Safety and Security: Measures include self-defense education and security escort services. There are lighted pathways/sidewalks, random security checks and private service security guards.

Programs of Study: Kansas Wesleyan confers B.A., B.S., and B.S.N. degrees. Associate and master's degrees are also awarded. Bachelor's degrees are awarded in BIOLOGICAL SCIENCE (biology/biological science), BUSINESS (accounting and business economics), COMMUNICATIONS AND THE ARTS (communications, dramatic arts, English, music, Spanish, speech/debate/rhetoric, and studio art), COMPUTER AND PHYSICAL SCIENCE (chemistry, computer science, mathematics, and physics), EDUCATION (art education, music education, physical education, secondary education, and special education), HEALTH PROFESSIONS (nursing), SOCIAL SCIENCE (addiction studies, criminal justice, history, prelaw, psychology, religion, religious education, and sociology). Premedicine, nursing, and preengineering are the strongest academically. Education, nursing, and business have the largest enrollments.

Required: Students must demonstrate proficiency in English and math and must fulfill distribution requirements in 15 liberal arts components, including environmental awareness, biblical heritage, and lifetime recreation. Courses in phys ed and computers are required. To graduate, students must complete at least 126 credit hours, including 30 to 40 in a major field of study, with a minimum GPA of 2.0.

Special: Cross-registration is available with other members of the Associated Colleges of Central Kansas and the Salina College Consortium. Cooperative degree programs are offered in agriculture, cytotechnology, engineering, environmental studies, and medical technology. Kansas Wesleyan also offers January interterm study trips throughout the United States and abroad, Washington, D.C., and UN semesters, internships, dual majors, student designed majors, credit for life experience, and nondegree study. A 3-2 engineering degree is offered with Columbia University and Washington University at St. Louis. There are 4 national honor societies and a freshman honors program.

Faculty/Classroom: All teach undergraduates. No introductory courses are taught by graduate students. The average class size in an introductory lecture is 24; in a laboratory is 7; and in a regular course is 13.

Requirements: The SAT or ACT is required. Applicants must be graduates of accredited secondary schools or have earned a GED. An interview is recommended. A GPA of 2.5 is required. AP and CLEP credits are accepted.

Procedure: Freshmen are admitted to all sessions. Entrance exams should be taken as early as possible. There are deferred admissions and rolling admissions plans. Application deadlines are open. Check with the school for current application fee. Notification is sent on a rolling basis.

Transfer: Transfers must submit transcripts from all colleges previously attended. Those students transferring fewer than 15 credit hours must submit ACT scores and a high school transcript. A minimum GPA of 2.0 is recommended. 63 of 126 credits required for the bachelor's degree must be completed at Kansas Wesleyan.

Visiting: There are regularly scheduled orientations for prospective students. There are guides for informal visits, visitors may sit in on classes, and stay overnight. To schedule a visit, contact the Admissions Office.

Financial Aid: The FAFSA, and tax forms is required. Check with the school for current application deadlines.

International Students: The school actively recruits these students. They must take the TOEFL.

Computers: All students may access the system at any time. There are no time limits and no fees.

Admissions Contact: Admissions Office E-Mail: *admissions@kwu.edu* Web: *www.kwu.edu*

MCPHERSON COLLEGE — D-2

McPherson, KS 67460 — **(620) 241-0731; (800) 365-7402; (620) 241-8443**

Full-time: 365 men, 234 women	**Faculty:** n/av
Part-time: 18 men, 15 women	**Ph.D.s:** 72%
Graduate: 5 men, 7 women	**Student/Faculty:** 15 to 1
Year: 4-1-4, summer session	**Tuition:** $21,100
Application Deadline:	**Room & Board:** $8035
Freshman Class: n/av	
SAT or ACT: required	

COMPETITIVE

McPherson College, founded in 1887 and affiliated with the Church of the Brethren, is a private, institution offering undergraduate programs in the arts and sciences, business, and education. The figures in the above capsule and in this profile are approximate. There is one undergraduate school and one graduate school. In addition to regional accreditation, McPherson has baccalaureate program accreditation with NCATE. The library contains 98,214 volumes, 60,799 microform items, and 4,626 audio/video tapes/CDs/DVDs, and subscribes to 26,828 periodicals including electronic. Computerized library services include interlibrary loans, database searching, Internet access, and Wi-Fi capability. Special learning facilities include an art gallery, natural history museum, an automobile restoration center. The 23-acre campus is in a small town 60 miles north of Wichita. Including any residence halls, there are 16 buildings.

Student Life: 53% of undergraduates are from Kansas. Others are from 29 states, and 2 foreign countries. 99% are from public schools. 80% are White; 13% African American. 43% claim no religious affiliation; 13% Catholic. The average age of freshmen is 18; all undergraduates, 21.

Housing: 392 students can be accommodated in college housing, which includes single-sex and coed dorms and on-campus apartments. On-campus housing is guaranteed for all 4 years. 79% of students live on campus; of those, 65% remain on campus on weekends. Alcohol is not permitted. All students may keep cars.

Activities: There are no fraternities or sororities. There are 18 groups on campus, including art, band, cheerleading, choir, chorus, computers, drama, ethnic, gay, honors, international, musical theater, newspaper, orchestra, pep band, professional, religious, social service, and student government. Popular campus events include Family Weekend.

Sports: There are 5 intercollegiate sports for men and 6 for women, and 6 intramural sports for men and 6 for women. Facilities include a sports center with 2 full-size basketball/volleyball courts, a racquetball court, and a fitness center with an open weight-training room, football/track stadium, practice fields, tennis courts.

Disabled Students: 95% of the campus is accessible. Facilities include wheelchair ramps, elevators, special parking, specially equipped restrooms, special class scheduling, lowered drinking fountains, and special housing.

Services: Counseling and information services are available, as is tutoring in most subjects. There is remedial reading and writing.

Campus Safety and Security: Measures include emergency notification system. There are emergency telephones and lighted pathways/sidewalks.

Programs of Study: McPherson confers B.A., and B.S. degrees. Master's degrees are also awarded. Bachelor's degrees are awarded in BIOLOGICAL SCIENCE (biology/biological science), BUSINESS (business administration and management), COMMUNICATIONS AND THE ARTS (art, communications, dramatic arts, English, music, Spanish, and speech/debate/rhetoric), COMPUTER AND PHYSICAL SCIENCE (chemistry and mathematics), EDUCATION (elementary education, physical education, secondary education, and special education), SOCIAL SCIENCE (history, philosophy, psychology, religion, and sociology). Business, education and technology are the largest.

Required: To graduate, students must complete 124 credits, including 32 in the major, with a GPA of 2.0. All students must fulfill general education requirements in the following areas: written and oral communication, aesthetics, history, society, natural sciences, technology and culture, and religion/beliefs/values. Students must also participate in an integrative seminar and a service experience, and must complete a global/intercultural experience, which may include intercultural studies courses or modern language courses.

Special: Cross-registration with other colleges is available through the Associated Colleges of Central Kansas. McPherson also offers internships, study abroad in 10 countries, co-op programs, credit by exam, a general studies degree, student-designed majors, and pass/fail options. There are preprofessional programs in health, engineering, law, forestry, veterinary medicine, nursing and medicine, optometry, and dentistry. There are 3 national honor societies, including Phi Beta Kappa, and 3 departmental honors programs.

Faculty/Classroom: 72% of faculty are male; 28% are female. All teach undergraduates. No introductory courses are taught by graduate students. The average class size in an introductory lecture is 30; in a laboratory is 12; and in a regular course is 15.

Requirements: The SAT or ACT is required. In addition, The GED is accepted. A GPA of 2.0 is required. AP and CLEP credits are accepted. Important factors in the admissions decision are recommendations by school officials, evidence of special talent, and parents or siblings attended your school.

Procedure: Freshmen are admitted fall, winter, and spring. Entrance exams should be taken in the junior year of high school. There are deferred admissions and rolling admissions plans. Application deadlines are open. Application fee is $25. Notification is sent on a rolling basis. Applications are accepted online.

Transfer: 288 transfer students enrolled in 2012-2013. Applicants must have satisfactorily completed 12 credit hours of college course work covering 3 academic areas with a 2.0 GPA. 32 of 124 credits required for the bachelor's degree must be completed at McPherson.

Visiting: There are regularly scheduled orientations for prospective students, consisting of campus tours, meetings with admissions personnel, and class attendance. There are guides for informal visits, visitors may sit in on classes, and stay overnight. To schedule a visit, contact the Admissions Office.

Financial Aid: The FAFSA is required. Check with the school for current application deadlines.

International Students: There are 12 international students enrolled. They must take the TOEFL. They must also take the ACT, scoring 18.

Computers: All students may access the system. There are no time limits and no fees.

Graduates: From July 1, 2012 to June 30, 2013, 105 bachelor's degrees were awarded.

Admissions Contact: Carol Williams, Director of Admissions and Financial Aid. E-Mail: *admiss@mcpherson.edu* Web: *www.mcpherson.edu*

MIDAMERICA NAZARENE UNIVERSITY F-2

Olathe, KS 66062 (913) 791-3380
(800) 800-8887; (913) 791-3487

Full-time: 550 men, 620 women
Part-time: 45 men, 105 women
Graduate: 120 men, 325 women
Year: semesters, summer session
Application Deadline:
Freshman Class: n/av
SAT or ACT: required
Faculty: n/av
Ph.D.s: n/av
Student/Faculty: n/av
Tuition: $21,250
Room & Board: $6750

COMPETITIVE

MidAmerica Nazarene University was founded in 1966 as a private liberal arts institution affiliated with the Church of the Nazarene. The figures in the above capsule and in this profile are approximate. There are 4 graduate schools. In addition to regional accreditation, MNU has baccalaureate program accreditation with ACBSP, NASM, and NLN. The library contains 120,520 volumes, 354,309 microform items, and 4,640 audio/video tapes/CDs/DVDs, and subscribes to 225 periodicals including electronic. Computerized library services include interlibrary loans, database searching, Internet access, and Wi-Fi capability. Special learning facilities include a radio station and TV station. The 105-acre campus is in a suburban area 19 miles southwest of downtown Kansas City, Missouri. Including any residence halls, there are 22 buildings.

Student Life: 66% of undergraduates are from Kansas. Others are from 38 states, and 10 foreign countries. 88% are from public schools. 81% are White. 74% are Protestant; 15% claim no religious affiliation. The average age of freshmen is 18; all undergraduates, 24. 33% do not continue beyond their first year; 55% remain to graduate.

Housing: 699 students can be accommodated in college housing, which includes single-sex dorms, on-campus apartments, and off-campus apartments. On-campus housing is guaranteed for all 4 years. 55% of students live on campus; of those, 75% remain on campus on weekends. Alcohol is not permitted. All students may keep cars.

Activities: There are no fraternities or sororities. There are 43 groups on campus, including and psychology, writers, agriculture, cheerleading, choir, chorus, computers, drama, ethnic, honors, international, jazz band, newspaper, orchestra, pep band, political, professional, radio and TV, religious, student government, and yearbook. Popular campus events include Mr. MNU and Welcome Week.

Sports: There are 6 intercollegiate sports for men and 6 for women, and 6 intramural sports for men and 6 for women. Facilities include a weight room, a football stadium, basketball/volleyball arena, a gym, a track, tennis and sand volleyball courts, and softball, baseball, and soccer fields.

Disabled Students: 90% of the campus is accessible. Facilities include wheelchair ramps, elevators, special parking, specially equipped restrooms, special class scheduling, and lowered drinking fountains.

Services: Counseling and information services are available, as is tutoring in most subjects. There is a reader service for the blind, and remedial math, reading, and writing. There are also test-taking accommodations, interpreters for the hearing impaired, and note takers for the blind, hearing impaired, and learning disabled.

Campus Safety and Security: Measures include 24-hour foot and vehicle patrol, self-defense education, and security escort services. There are emergency telephones and lighted pathways/sidewalks.

Programs of Study: MNU confers B.A., B.M.Ed. and B.S.N. degrees. Associate and master's degrees are also awarded. Bachelor's degrees are awarded in AGRICULTURE (international agriculture), BIOLOGICAL SCIENCE (biology/biological science), BUSINESS (accounting, business administration and management, international business management, marketing/retailing/merchandising, and sports management), COMMUNICATIONS AND THE ARTS (communications, dramatic arts, English, graphic design, modern language, music, music performance, and Spanish), COMPUTER AND PHYSICAL SCIENCE (chemistry, computer science, mathematics, and physics), EDUCATION (athletic training, business education, Christian education, elementary education, English education, health education, mathematics education, music education, physical education, science education, social studies education, and speech correction), HEALTH PROFESSIONS (nursing), SOCIAL SCIENCE (criminal justice, history, ministries, missions, psychology, sociology, urban studies, and youth ministry). Management and human relations, nursing, and elementary education have the largest enrollments.

Required: All students must meet core curriculum requirements in humanities-communications, natural sciences-math, social sciences, religion-philosophy, and phys ed. Students must maintain a minimum GPA of 2.0 and complete 126 semester hours to graduate.

Special: MNU offers nondegree study, cross-registration with the Christian College Coalition, study abroad in 4 countries, internships, and a Washington semester. There are accelerated degree programs in management and human relations and in nursing. There are 1 national honor societies and 4 departmental honors programs.

Faculty/Classroom: 64% of faculty are male; 36% are female. All teach

undergraduates. No introductory courses are taught by graduate students. The average class size in an introductory lecture is 15; in a laboratory is 33; and in a regular course is 17.

Admissions: 15 freshmen graduated first in their class.

Requirements: The SAT or ACT is required. In addition, recommended composite score of 18 on the ACT or a satisfactory score on the SAT. Candidates for admission should be graduates of an accredited secondary school. The GED is accepted. Students should have completed 15 units of study, including 4 units of English and 3 each of natural science, social studies, and math. An essay is optional. AP and CLEP credits are accepted.

Procedure: Freshmen are admitted to all sessions. Entrance exams should be taken during the senior year. There is a rolling admissions plan. Check with the school for current application deadlines. The application fee is $25.

Transfer: 116 transfer students enrolled in 2012-2013. Transfer applicants should have earned 24 or more hours at an accredited institution and not be on academic or disciplinary probation. ACT or SAT scores are required. 30 of 126 credits required for the bachelor's degree must be completed at MNU.

Visiting: There are regularly scheduled orientations for prospective students, including an academic fair, advising, class visitation, informational meetings, social activities, and experiencing residential life. There are guides for informal visits, visitors may sit in on classes, and stay overnight. To schedule a visit, contact the Office of Admissions.

Financial Aid: The FAFSA and the college's own financial statement are required. Check with the school for current application deadlines.

International Students: They must take the TOEFL, ACT and/or SAT if from a world area where English is the official first language. They must also take the SAT or ACT. and placement tests for incoming freshmen.

Computers: All students may access the system 7:30 a.m. to 11 p.m. Monday to Thursday and to 5 p.m. Friday. There are no time limits. The fee is $200.

Admissions Contact: Brigit Mattox, Associate Director. E-Mail: *admissions@mnu.edu* Web: *www.mnu.edu*

NEWMAN UNIVERSITY D-3

Wichita, KS 67213 **(316) 942-4291, ext. 2144**
(877) NEWMANU; (316) 942-4483

Full-time: 394 men, 727 women	**Faculty:** 74; IIB, --$
Part-time: 668 men, 1006 women	**Ph.D.s:** 61%
Graduate: 219 men, 722 women	**Student/Faculty:** 17 to 1
Year: semesters, summer session	**Tuition:** $23,580
Application Deadline: open	**Room & Board:** $6800
Freshman Class: n/av	

COMPETITIVE+

Newman University established in 1933, is a private, liberal arts institution affiliated with the Roman Catholic Church, named for John Henry Cardinal Newman and founded by the Adorers of the Blood of Christ for the purpose of empowering graduates to transform society. There are 3 undergraduate schools and 3 graduate schools. In addition to regional accreditation, NU has baccalaureate program accreditation with CSWE and NCATE. The library contains 90,129 volumes, 143,723 microform items, and 2,300 audio/video tapes/CDs/DVDs, and subscribes to 7,015 periodicals including electronic. Computerized library services include interlibrary loans, database searching, Internet access, and Wi-Fi capability. Special learning facilities include an art gallery, allied health and nursing labs, and ITV studio facilities. The 61-acre campus is in an urban area in Wichita west of downtown. Including any residence halls, there are 12 buildings.

Student Life: 91% of undergraduates are from Kansas. Others are from 28 states, 30 foreign countries, and Canada. 54% are from public schools. 74% are White. 59% are Catholic. The average age of freshmen is 18; all undergraduates, 21. 24% do not continue beyond their first year; 52% remain to graduate.

Housing: 406 students can be accommodated in college housing, which includes single-sex and coed dorms, on-campus apartments, and married student housing. In addition, there are special-interest houses. On-campus housing is guaranteed for the freshman year only, is available on a first-come, and first-served basis. 75% of students commute. Alcohol is not permitted. All students may keep cars.

Activities: There are no fraternities or sororities. There are 26 groups on campus, including art, cheerleading, choir, chorale, chorus, communications, computers, dance, drama, environmental, ethnic, honors, international, literary magazine, musical theater, newspaper, pep band, photography, political, professional, religious, social, social service, and student government. Popular campus events include Family Weekend, Newman Week, Homecoming, Weeks of Welcome/Welcome Back Bash and Gerber Institute Activities.

Sports: There are 8 intercollegiate sports for men and 9 for women, and 10 intramural sports for men and 9 for women. Facilities include baseball and softball fields, soccer fields, and a gym with 1 main basketball court, 2 side-by-side courts, 6 locker rooms, weight room, aerobics room, and wrestling room.

Disabled Students: All of the campus is accessible. Facilities include wheelchair ramps, elevators, special parking, specially equipped restrooms, special class scheduling, and lowered drinking fountains.

Services: Counseling and information services are available, as is tutoring in most subjects. There is a reader service for the blind, and remedial math and writing.

Campus Safety and Security: Measures include 24-hour foot and vehicle patrol, emergency notification system, self-defense education, and security escort services. There are emergency telephones, lighted pathways/sidewalks, and controlled access to dorms/residences.

Programs of Study: NU confers B.A., B.B.A., B.S. and B.S.N. degrees. Associate and master's degrees are also awarded. Bachelor's degrees are awarded in BIOLOGICAL SCIENCE (biochemistry and biology/biological science), BUSINESS (accounting, business administration and management, and management information systems), COMMUNICATIONS AND THE ARTS (art, communications, English, and sports media), COMPUTER AND PHYSICAL SCIENCE (chemistry, information sciences and systems, and mathematics), EDUCATION (early childhood education, elementary education, and secondary education), HEALTH PROFESSIONS (health science, nursing, and ultrasound technology), SOCIAL SCIENCE (counseling/psychology, criminal justice, forensic studies, history, interdisciplinary studies, liberal arts/general studies, pastoral studies, philosophy, psychology, sociology, and theological studies). Nursing, allied health and pre-med, biology, and chemistry are the strongest academically. Nursing, biology and education have the largest enrollments.

Required: Degree requirements include completion of 124 credit hours, 40 of which must be upper division and 30 resident. The number of credits required in the major varies. A minimum GPA of 2.0 is required for graduation, and students must fulfill the university's Newman Studies Program requirements which include skills, general education and core courses.

Special: Newman University offers co-op placements in most majors, internships, dual majors, and study abroad in England, Europe, and Latin America. Majors in counseling, business studies, education, RN to BSN, and interdisciplinary studies can be satisfied through evening, weekend and online classes. There are 11 national honor societies and a freshman honors program.

Faculty/Classroom: 33% of faculty are male; 67% are female. 94% teach undergraduates, 25% do research, and 25% do both. No introductory courses are taught by graduate students. The average class size in an introductory lecture is 22; in a laboratory is 16; and in a regular course is 19.

Admissions: 45% of the current freshmen were in the top fifth of their class; 68% were in the top two fifths. 10 freshmen graduated first in their class.

Requirements: Criteria: cumulative grade point average of at least 2.0 on a 4.0 scale or an average GED score of 450 with no individual score below 410, ACT composite score of 18 or a combined verbal, math and writing SAT score of 1290. The recommended high school curriculum is 4 units English, 3 unit math, 3 units science and 3 units social science. A GPA of 2.0 is required. AP and CLEP credits are accepted. Important factors in the admissions decision are leadership record, advanced placement or honors courses, evidence of special talent, personality/intangible qualities, recommendations by alumni, recommendations by school officials, ability to finance college education, parents or siblings attended your school, extracurricular activities record, and geographical diversity.

Procedure: Freshmen are admitted fall, spring, and summer. Entrance exams should be taken during the spring of the junior year or fall of the senior year. There are deferred admissions and rolling admissions plans. Application deadlines are open. Application fee is $20. Notification is sent on a rolling basis. Applications are accepted online. Application fees are waived if application is completed online.

Transfer: 309 transfer students enrolled in 2012-2013. A minimum GPA of 2.0 is required. 30 of 124 credits required for the bachelor's degree must be completed at NU.

Visiting: There are regularly scheduled orientations for prospective students, include meetings with faculty, athletic coaches, co-curricular sponsors, financial aid counselors, admissions counselors, and a campus tour. There are guides for informal visits, visitors may sit in on classes, and stay overnight. To schedule a visit, contact Jann Reusser at (316) 942-4291 ext. 2144.

Financial Aid: In 2013-2014, 99% of all full-time freshmen and 94% of continuing full-time students received some form of financial aid. 68% of all full-time freshmen and 68% of continuing full-time students received need-based aid. The average freshman award was $11,344. Need-based scholarships or need-based grants averaged $2,777 ($6,448 maximum); need-based self-help aid (loans and jobs) averaged $1,574 ($2,750 maximum); non-need-based athletic scholarships averaged $3,870 ($10,714 maximum); and other non-need-based awards and non-need-based scholarships averaged $9,641 ($17,863 maximum). 10% of undergraduate students work part-time. Average annual earnings from campus work are

$1748. The average financial indebtedness of the 2013 graduate was $25,936. The FAFSA is required. The priority date for freshman financial aid applications for fall entry is March 1.

International Students: There are 73 international students enrolled. They must take the TOEFL with a minimum score of 530 on the paper-based TOEFL (PBT) or 74 on the Internet-based version (iBT).

Computers: All students may access the system. There are no time limits and no fees.

Graduates: From July 1, 2012 to June 30, 2013, 266 bachelor's degrees were awarded. The most popular majors were nursing (18%), education (14%), and biology (11%). 48 companies recruited on campus in 2012-2013. In an average class, 36% graduate in 4 years or less and 52% graduate in 6 years or less. Of the 2012 graduating class, 17% were enrolled in graduate school within 6 months of graduation, and 76% were employed.

Admissions Contact: Jann Reusser, Admissions Secretary/Receptionist. E-Mail: *admissions@newmanu.edu* Web: *www.newmanu.edu*

OTTAWA UNIVERSITY E-2

Ottawa, KS 66067-3399 (785) 242-5200, ext. 5555 (800) 755-5200,; (785) 229-1008

Full-time: 350 men, 200 women
Part-time: 15 men, 20 women
Graduate: n/av
Year: semesters, summer session
Application Deadline: open
Freshman Class: n/av
ACT: required
Faculty: n/av; IIB, --$
Ph.D.s: n/av
Student/Faculty: n/av
Tuition: $15,500
Room & Board: n/av

VERY COMPETITIVE

Ottawa University, founded in 1865 and affiliated with the American Baptist Churches, is a private institution offering programs through the divisions of arts and humanities, natural sciences, and social and behavioral sciences. The figures in the above capsule and in this profile are approximate. The library contains 90,000 volumes, and subscribes to 400 periodicals including electronic. Computerized library services include interlibrary loans and database searching. Special learning facilities include a learning resource center, art gallery, and radio station. The 64-acre campus is in a small town 45 miles southwest of Kansas City. Including any residence halls, there are 15 buildings.

Student Life: 55% of undergraduates are from Kansas. Others are from 18 states, 5 foreign countries, and Canada. 99% are from public schools. 77% are white; 11% African American. 64% are Protestant; 20% claim no religious affiliation; 13% Catholic. The average age of freshmen is 19; all undergraduates, 22. 25% do not continue beyond their first year; 30% remain to graduate.

Housing: 428 students can be accommodated in college housing, which includes single-sex dorms, on-campus apartments, and married student housing. On-campus housing is guaranteed for all 4 years. 58% of students live on campus; of those, 65% remain on campus on weekends. Alcohol is not permitted. All students may keep cars.

Activities: There are no fraternities or sororities. There are 35 groups on campus, including cheerleading, choir, chorale, chorus, computers, dance, debate, drama, ethnic, forensics, honors, international, jazz band, musical theater, newspaper, orchestra, pep band, photography, professional, radio and TV, religious, social, social service, student government, and yearbook. Popular campus events include Family Day, Charter Day, and Christmas Feast.

Sports: There are 7 intercollegiate sports for men and 7 for women, and 12 intramural sports for men and 12 for women. Facilities include a field, a sports complex, an athletic center, and a gym with a wellness center.

Disabled Students: 50% of the campus is accessible. Facilities include wheelchair ramps, elevators, special parking, specially equipped restrooms, and special class scheduling.

Services: Counseling and information services are available, as is tutoring in most subjects. There is remedial math, reading, and writing.

Campus Safety and Security: Measures include self-defense education and security escort services. There are lighted pathways/sidewalks, and a night security guard. In addition, students are issued individual residence hall security and room keys.

Programs of Study: OU confers B.A. degrees. Bachelor's degrees are awarded in BIOLOGICAL SCIENCE (biology/biological science), BUSINESS (accounting, business administration and management, and management information systems), COMMUNICATIONS AND THE ARTS (art, communications, dramatic arts, English, and music), COMPUTER AND PHYSICAL SCIENCE (chemistry, information sciences and systems, and mathematics), EDUCATION (elementary education and physical education), SOCIAL SCIENCE (history, human services, political science/government, psychology, religion, and sociology). English, business, and math are the strongest academically. Business, teacher education, and human services have the largest enrollments.

Required: To graduate, students must complete 9 courses in 8 academic areas with a minimum GPA of 2.0. The university requires students to complete 124 semester hours, with 24 to 40 in the major. Three interdisciplinary general education seminars must be completed. In addition, students must attend 10 University Program events each semester for 6 semesters.

Special: Internships are available, especially in business, human services, and teacher education. Student-designed majors are an option. 3/2 engineering degrees with Kansas state and the University of Kansas, 3 +1 degree in medical technology, and preprofessional programs in premedicine, predentistry, prelaw, and preministry are available. Work-study programs are also offered. There are 2 national honor societies.

Faculty/Classroom: 60% of faculty are male; 40% are female. All teach undergraduates. No introductory courses are taught by graduate students. The average class size in a laboratory is 12.

Requirements: The ACT is required. The GED is accepted. There are no specific high school courses required, but a sound college preparatory curriculum is highly recommended. A GPA of 2.5 is required. AP and CLEP credits are accepted. Important factors in the admissions decision are parents or siblings attended your school, recommendations by alumni, and recommendations by school officials.

Procedure: Freshmen are admitted to all sessions. Entrance exams should be taken as early as possible. There is a rolling admissions plan. Application deadlines are open. Check with the school for the currant application fee.

Transfer: Transfer applicants must submit transcripts from all colleges attended and must have a 2.0 GPA and 12 hours of college credit, or else they must meet freshman requirements. 30 of 124 credits required for the bachelor's degree must be completed at OU.

Visiting: There are regularly scheduled orientations for prospective students, including Discovery Day in the early spring, which gives prospective students a chance to meet faculty, students, and staff and to learn more about Ottawa University, the admissions process, and financial aid. There are guides for informal visits, visitors may sit in on classes, and stay overnight. To schedule a visit, contact the Admissions Office.

Financial Aid: The FAFSA and the college's own financial statement are required. Check with the school for current application deadlines.

International Students: The school actively recruits these students. They must take the TOEFL or MELAB.

Computers: All students may access the system. There are no time limits and no fees.

Admissions Contact: Director of Admissions. A campus DVD is available. E-Mail: *admiss@ottawa.edu* Web: *www.ottawa.edu*

PITTSBURG STATE UNIVERSITY F-3

Pittsburg, KS 66762 (620) 235-4251 (800) 854-PITT; (620) 235-6003

Full-time: 3005 men, 2729 women
Part-time: 214 men, 218 women
Graduate: 426 men, 697 women
Year: semesters, summer session
Application Deadline: open
Freshman Class: 2876 applied, 2280 accepted, 1116 enrolled
ACT: 22
Faculty: 316; IIA, --$
Ph.D.s: 77%
Student/Faculty: 19 to 1
Tuition: $5494 ($15,050)
Room & Board: $6538

COMPETITIVE

Pittsburg State University, founded in 1903, is a state-supported institution offering programs in arts and sciences, business, education, and technology. There are 4 undergraduate schools and one graduate school. In addition to regional accreditation, Pitt State has baccalaureate program accreditation with AACSB, ABET, CSWE, NASM, NCATE, and NRPA. The 2 libraries contain 712,681 volumes, 100,614 microform items, and 10,151 audio/video tapes/CDs/DVDs, and subscribe to 35,360 periodicals including electronic. Computerized library services include interlibrary loans, database searching, Internet access, and Wi-Fi capability. Special learning facilities include an art gallery, planetarium, radio station, TV station, a dedicated channel on local cable TV, a nature reach, an herbarium, an observatory, a field biology reserve, a technology center, a mammal collection, a greenhouse, a polymer research lab, a broadcasting lab, and a cadaver lab. The 630-acre campus is in a small town 120 miles south of Kansas City. Including any residence halls, there are 54 buildings.

Student Life: 74% of undergraduates are from Kansas. Others are from 39 states, and 41 foreign countries. 82% are White. The average age of freshmen is 19; all undergraduates, 22. 27% do not continue beyond their first year; 47% remain to graduate.

Housing: 1192 students can be accommodated in college housing, which includes coed dorms and married student housing. substance free, and academic excellence floors. On-campus housing is available on a first-come and first-served basis. 80% of students commute. Alcohol is not permitted. All students may keep cars.

Activities: 7% of men belong to 6 national fraternities; 8% of women belong to 3 national sororities. There are 150 groups on campus, including recreational and special interest, art, band, cheerleading, chess, choir, chorale, chorus, computers, dance, debate, drama, drill team, environmental, ethnic, film, forensics, gay, honors, housing, international, jazz band, literary magazine, marching band, newspaper, opera, orchestra, pep band, photography, political, professional, radio and TV, religious, social, social service, student government, symphony, and yearbook. Popular campus events include Greek Week, Multicultural Month, Homecoming and Apple Day.

Sports: There are 7 intercollegiate sports for men and 6 for women, and 24 intramural sports for men and 24 for women. Facilities include a football stadium, indoor and outdoor tracks, a basketball arena, softball diamonds, a baseball field, a weight room, an Olympic-size pool, volleyball, racquetball, and badminton courts, indoor and outdoor tennis courts, outdoor basketball courts and sand volleyball courts, a 50,000-square-foot recreation center, 4 gyms, a cardio and strength fitness center with a 1/10-mile track, and a dance studio.

Disabled Students: 70% of the campus is accessible. Facilities include wheelchair ramps, elevators, special parking, specially equipped restrooms, special class scheduling, lowered drinking fountains, and lowered telephones.

Services: Counseling and information services are available, as is tutoring in most subjects, accounting, biology, chemistry, elementary education, English, modern language/Spanish, math, music, computers, physics, psychology, reading/study, art, sociology, and writing. There is a reader service for the blind. There are also counseling services, a center for student accommodations, and a writing center.

Campus Safety and Security: Measures include 24-hour foot and vehicle patrol, emergency notification system, self-defense education, and security escort services. There are emergency telephones, lighted pathways/sidewalks, controlled access to dorms/residences, crime prevention programs, an engraving program for valuables, a crisis management plan and procedures, and e-mail, text, and phone alerts.

Programs of Study: Pitt State confers B.B.A., B.F.A., B.A.S., B.S.T., B.A., B.M.T., B.S., B.S.E., B.S.E.T., B.M., B.M.E., B.S.N. and B.S.V.T.E., B.I.S. and B.G.S. degrees. Associate and master's degrees are also awarded. Bachelor's degrees are awarded in AGRICULTURE (environmental studies, plant science, and wood science), BIOLOGICAL SCIENCE (biochemistry, biology/biological science, cell biology, environmental biology, molecular biology, plant physiology, and wildlife biology), BUSINESS (accounting, banking and finance, business administration and management, business economics, fashion merchandising, international business management, marketing management, recreation and leisure services, and recreational facilities management), COMMUNICATIONS AND THE ARTS (advertising, art, broadcasting, ceramic art and design, communications, creative writing, dramatic arts, English, French, journalism, literature, metal/jewelry, music, music performance, painting, public relations, Spanish, and technical and business writing), COMPUTER AND PHYSICAL SCIENCE (actuarial science, chemistry, computer security and information assurance, environmental chemistry, information sciences and systems, mathematics, physics, and polymer science), EDUCATION (art education, early childhood education, education, elementary education, English education, home economics education, mathematics education, music education, physical education, psychology education, secondary education, social studies education, technical education, and vocational education), ENGINEERING AND ENVIRONMENTAL DESIGN (automotive technology, commercial art, construction management, construction technology, electrical/electronics engineering technology, graphic arts technology, graphic and printing production, interior design, manufacturing technology, mechanical engineering technology, plastics technology, preengineering, technological management, and woodworking), HEALTH PROFESSIONS (medical technology, nursing, pharmaceutical chemistry, predentistry, premedicine, preoptometry, prepharmacy, prephysical therapy, preveterinary science, and recreation therapy), SOCIAL SCIENCE (counseling/psychology, criminal justice, early childhood studies, family/consumer resource management, family/consumer studies, geography, history, international studies, liberal arts/general studies, political science/government, prelaw, psychology, safety management, social work, and sociology). Education, nursing, business, and technology have the largest enrollments.

Required: To graduate, students must complete at least 124 semester hours, including 36 to 60 hours in the major, with a minimum GPA of 2.0. General education requirements total 46 to 54 hours (up to 54 for education majors) and include courses in English, speech, math, humanities, social and behavioral sciences, natural and physical sciences, producing and consuming, nutrition, and health/well-being.

Special: Co-op and work-study programs by arrangement, internships in psychology, technology, social work, and by arrangement elsewhere, a general studies degree, B.A.-B.S. degrees, dual majors, credit by exam, non-degree study, student-designed majors, and pass/fail options are available. Pitt State has student exchange programs with 20 countries. There are 9 national honor societies, a freshman honors program, and 26 departmental honors programs.

Faculty/Classroom: 54% of faculty are male; 46% are female. 94% teach undergraduates. Graduate students teach 10% of introductory courses. The average class size in an introductory lecture is 33; in a laboratory is 21; and in a regular course is 22.

Admissions: 79% of the 2013-2014 applicants were accepted. The ACT scores were 40% below 21, 32% between 21 and 23, 16% between 24 and 26, 6% between 27 and 28, and 6% above 28. 28% of the current freshmen were in the top fifth of their class; 55% were in the top two fifths. 53 freshmen graduated first in their class.

Requirements: The ACT is required. Applicants must meet 1 of these 4 criteria: an ACT score of 21 or above, class rank in the top third, a 2.0 GPA in the Kansas core curriculum (2.5 GPA for out-of-state students), or have 24 or more transferable college credit hours with at least a 2.0 GPA. Candidates may also be accepted through an exceptions window. The GED is accepted. Pitt State requires applicants to be in the upper 33% of their class. A GPA of 2.0 is required. AP and CLEP credits are accepted.

Procedure: Freshmen are admitted to all sessions. Entrance exams should be taken before the first semester of the freshman year of college. There is a rolling admissions plan. Application deadlines are open. Application fee is $30. Applications are accepted online.

Transfer: 530 transfer students enrolled in 2012-2013. Applicants must have 24 credit hours and a college GPA of 2.0 or else meet freshman admissions requirements. 30 of 124 credits required for the bachelor's degree must be completed at Pitt State.

Visiting: There are regularly scheduled orientations for prospective students. Meet with current students, other offices on campus, tours. There are guides for informal visits and visitors may sit in on classes. To schedule a visit, contact the Admission Office.

Financial Aid: The FAFSA is required. The priority date for freshman financial aid applications for fall entry is March 1.

International Students: There are 289 international students enrolled. The school actively recruits these students. They must take the TOEFL with a minimum score of 520 on the paper-based TOEFL (PBT) or 68 on the Internet-based version (iBT), the IELTS.

Computers: All students may access the system anytime. There are no time limits and no fees.

Graduates: From July 1, 2012 to June 30, 2013, 1131 bachelor's degrees were awarded. The most popular majors were engineering technology (17%), business/marketing (15%), and education (13%). 423 companies recruited on campus in 2012-2013. In an average class, 4% graduate in 3 years or less, 26% graduate in 4 years or less, 48% graduate in 5 years or less, and 50% graduate in 6 years or less. Of the 2012 graduating class, 76% were employed within 6 months of graduation.

Admissions Contact: Melinda Roelfs, Director of Admission. E-Mail: *psuadmit@pittstate.edu* Web: *www.pittstate.edu*

SOUTHWESTERN COLLEGE — D-3

Winfield, KS 67156 — (620) 229-6364
(800) 846-1543 x6236; (620) 229-6344

Full-time: 247 men, 256 women	**Faculty:** 45; IIB, --$
Part-time: 13 men, 6 women	**Ph.D.s:** 71%
Graduate: 25 men, 35 women	**Student/Faculty:** 12 to 1
Year: semesters, summer session	**Tuition:** $22,756
Application Deadline: August 1	**Room & Board:** $6514
Freshman Class: 339 applied, 298 accepted, 148 enrolled	
SAT CR/M/W: 455/486/433 **ACT:** 22	**COMPETITIVE**

Southwestern College, established in 1885, is a private institution affiliated with the Kansas West Conference of the United Methodist Church. In addition to regional accreditation, Southwestern has baccalaureate program accreditation with CSWE, NASM, and NCATE. The library contains 68,081 volumes, 192 microform items, and 9,758 audio/video tapes/CDs/DVDs, and subscribes to 26,372 periodicals including electronic. Computerized library services include interlibrary loans, database searching, Internet access, and Wi-Fi capability. Special learning facilities include an art gallery, radio station, TV station, a biological field station. The 82-acre campus is in a small town 45 miles southeast of Wichita. Including any residence halls, there are 20 buildings.

Student Life: 59% of undergraduates are from Kansas. Others are from 20 states, and 9 foreign countries. 66% are White. 36% claim no religious affiliation; 31% Protestant; 11% Catholic. The average age of freshmen is 19; all undergraduates, 21. 40% do not continue beyond their first year; 51% remain to graduate.

Housing: 625 students can be accommodated in college housing, which includes single-sex and coed dorms, on-campus apartments, and married student housing. In addition, there are honors houses. On-campus housing is guaranteed for the freshman year only, is available on a first-come, and first-served basis. 71% of students live on campus; of those, 42% remain on campus on weekends. Alcohol is not permitted. All students may keep cars.

Activities: There are 33 groups on campus, including and discipleship, green team, band, cheerleading, choir, chorus, computers, dance, drama, environmental, ethnic, film, honors, international, jazz band, leadership, literary magazine, musical theater, newspaper, orchestra, pep band, photography, political, professional, radio and TV, religious, social, student government, symphony, and yearbook. Popular campus events include Movie Nights, Spring Formal and Stau Bau.

Sports: There are 7 intercollegiate sports for men and 8 for women, and 4 intramural sports for men and 4 for women. Facilities include a 2400-seat stadium, tennis and basketball courts, playing floors, exercise rooms, a gym, an indoor swimming pool, a running track, a soccer field, a weight room, and a Frisbee golf course.

Disabled Students: 80% of the campus is accessible. Facilities include wheelchair ramps, elevators, special parking, specially equipped restrooms, special class scheduling, lowered drinking fountains, and lowered telephones.

Services: Counseling and information services are available, as is tutoring in every subject. There is remedial math, reading, and writing. A reader service is available for dyslexic students.

Campus Safety and Security: Measures include 24-hour foot and vehicle patrol, emergency notification system, self-defense education, and security escort services. There are lighted pathways/sidewalks and controlled access to dorms/residences.

Programs of Study: Southwestern confers B.A., B.S., B.G.S., B.Mus. and B.Ph. degrees. Master's and doctoral degrees are also awarded. Bachelor's degrees are awarded in BIOLOGICAL SCIENCE (biochemistry, biology/biological science, and marine biology), BUSINESS (accounting, business administration and management, business communications, and sports management), COMMUNICATIONS AND THE ARTS (communications, dramatic arts, English, music, and music performance), COMPUTER AND PHYSICAL SCIENCE (chemistry, computer science, digital arts/technology, and mathematics), EDUCATION (athletic training, drama education, early childhood education, elementary education, mathematics education, music education, physical education, and sports and wellness studies), SOCIAL SCIENCE (history, interdisciplinary studies, liberal arts/general studies, philosophy and religion, and psychology). Biology, business administration, and education have the largest enrollments.

Required: To graduate, students must earn 124 credits, fulfill all requirements of the major, and maintain a GPA of 2.0. Students must complete the general education requirements.

Special: Southwestern offers internships in industry and social and civic agencies and a Washington semester through The Institute for Experiential Learning. Exchange programs are available. Combinations or degrees are possible with approval from the Academic Affairs Committee. Work-study programs, nondegree study, and pass/fail options are also available. There are 3 national honor societies, a freshman honors program, and 2 departmental honors programs.

Faculty/Classroom: 51% of faculty are male; 49% are female. All teach undergraduates. No introductory courses are taught by graduate students. The average class size in an introductory lecture is 16; in a laboratory is 10; and in a regular course is 7.

Admissions: 88% of the 2013-2014 applicants were accepted. The SAT scores for the 2013-2014 freshman class were: Critical Reading--69% below 500, 25% between 500 and 599, 3% between 600 and 699, and 3% between 700 and 800; Math--61% below 500, 29% between 500 and 599, 7% between 600 and 699, and 3% between 700 and 800; Writing--75% below 500, 22% between 500 and 599, 3% between 600 and 699. The ACT scores were 31% below 21, 29% between 21 and 23, 27% between 24 and 26, 9% between 27 and 28, and 4% above 28. 34% of the current freshmen were in the top fifth of their class; 70% were in the top two fifths. 8 freshmen graduated first in their class.

Requirements: The ACT is required. The SAT is recommended. All candidates for admission must graduate from an accredited secondary school with a specified college-bound curriculum. The GED is accepted and an essay is required. Interviews are recommended. A GPA of 2.5 is required. AP and CLEP credits are accepted.

Procedure: Freshmen are admitted fall, spring, and summer. There is a rolling admissions plan. Applications should be filed by August 1 for fall entry; January 1 for spring entry, along with a $25 fee. Applications are accepted online.

Transfer: 79 transfer students enrolled in 2012-2013. Applicants must have a college GPA of 2.0 and must submit an essay. 30 of 124 credits required for the bachelor's degree must be completed at Southwestern.

Visiting: There are regularly scheduled orientations for prospective students, including 4 Explore More events. There are guides for informal visits, visitors may sit in on classes, and stay overnight. To schedule a visit, contact the Admissions Office.

Financial Aid: In 2013-2014, 100% of all full-time freshmen and 98% of continuing full-time students received some form of financial aid. 74% of all full-time freshmen and 75% of continuing full-time students received need-based aid. The average freshman award was $25,059. Need-based scholarships or need-based grants averaged $5,809 ($9,550 maximum); need-based self-help aid (loans and jobs) averaged $4,894 ($9,000 maximum); non-need-based athletic scholarships averaged $4,000 ($4,000 maximum); and other non-need-based awards and non-need-based scholarships averaged $8,124 ($13,500 maximum). Average annual earnings from campus work are $1400. The average financial indebtedness of the 2013 graduate was $34,056. The FAFSA and the college's own financial statement are required. Check with the school for current application deadlines.

International Students: There are 31 international students enrolled. The school actively recruits these students. They must take the TOEFL with a minimum score of 550 on the paper-based TOEFL (PBT) or 80 on the Internet-based version (iBT).

Computers: All students may access the system 24 hours a day, 7 days a week. There are no time limits and no fees.

Graduates: From July 1, 2012 to June 30, 2013, 137 bachelor's degrees were awarded. The most popular majors were nursing (10%), biology (8%), and psychology (7%). In an average class, 1% graduate in 3 years or less, 41% graduate in 4 years or less, 50% graduate in 5 years or less, and 51% graduate in 6 years or less. Of the 2012 graduating class, 39% were enrolled in graduate school within 6 months of graduation, and 39% were employed.

Admissions Contact: Marla Sexson, Vice President for Enrollment Management. E-Mail: *marla.sexson@sckans.edu* Web: *http:/www.sckans.edu/admissions/*

STERLING COLLEGE — C-3

Sterling, KS 67579 (620) 278-4275
(800) 346-1017; (620) 278-4416

Full-time: 327 men, 310 women	**Faculty:** 38; IIB, --$
Part-time: 40 men, 59 women	**Ph.D.s:** 53%
Graduate: n/av	**Student/Faculty:** 14 to 1
Year: semesters, summer session	**Tuition:** $20,550
Application Deadline: open	**Room & Board:** $7166
Freshman Class: 821 applied, 414 accepted, 149 enrolled	
SAT CR/M/W: 460/470/460 **ACT:** 21	**COMPETITIVE**

Sterling College, established in 1887, is a private liberal arts institution affiliated with the Presbyterian Church, offering undergraduate curricula in 17 majors plus teacher preparation. In addition to regional accreditation, Sterling has baccalaureate program accreditation with NCATE. The library contains 61,430 volumes, 2,120 microform items, and 2,125 audio/video tapes/CDs/DVDs, and subscribes to 846 periodicals including electronic. Computerized library services include interlibrary loans, database searching, and Internet access. Special learning facilities include a learning resource center, art gallery, radio station, a museum, and a theater. The 43-acre campus is in a rural area 70 miles northwest of Wichita. Including any residence halls, there are 19 buildings. The figures in the above capsule and in this profile are approximate.

Student Life: 51% of undergraduates are from Kansas. Others are from 32 states, and 6 foreign countries. 85% are from public schools. 79% are white. 54% are Protestant; 31% claim no religious affiliation; 15% Catholic. The average age of freshmen is 18; all undergraduates, 20. 35% do not continue beyond their first year; 46% remain to graduate.

Housing: 589 students can be accommodated in college housing, which includes single-sex dorms. On-campus housing is guaranteed for all 4 years. 73% of students live on campus; of those, 70% remain on campus on weekends. Alcohol is not permitted. All students may keep cars.

Activities: There are no fraternities or sororities. There are 23 groups on campus, including art, band, cheerleading, choir, chorale, dance, debate, drama, ethnic, forensics, honors, jazz band, literary magazine, musical theater, newspaper, photography, political, professional, radio and TV, religious, social, social service, student government, and yearbook. Popular campus events include Mission trips, Last Blast (end of year party), and fall musical and other theater productions.

Sports: There are 6 intercollegiate sports for men and 6 for women, and 6 intramural sports for men and 6 for women. Facilities include a weight-training facility, exercise deck, swimming pool, track, football field and stadium, baseball diamond, soccer field, practice fields, basketball and tennis courts, sand volleyball, outdoor basketball, and horseshoe pits.

Disabled Students: 88% of the campus is accessible. Facilities include wheelchair ramps, elevators, special parking, specially equipped restrooms, and special class scheduling.

Services: Counseling and information services are available, as is tutoring in most subjects. There is remedial writing. Special accommodations are provided on an as-needed basis.

Campus Safety and Security: Measures include emergency notification system. There are lighted pathways/sidewalks, controlled access to dorms/residences, and evening and nighttime foot and vehicle patrol.

Programs of Study: Sterling confers B.A., and B.S. degrees. Bachelor's degrees are awarded in BIOLOGICAL SCIENCE (biology/biological science), BUSINESS (business administration and management and sports management), COMMUNICATIONS AND THE ARTS (art, communications, dramatic arts, English, and music), COMPUTER AND PHYSICAL SCIENCE (chemistry and mathematics), EDUCATION (athletic training, elementary education, and music education), HEALTH PROFESSIONS (exercise science), SOCIAL SCIENCE (behavioral science, history, religious education, and theological studies). Business administration, education, exercise science, and sports management have the largest enrollments.

Required: To graduate, students must complete 52 to 57 credits in a general education curriculum, including writing, math, science, social science, philosophy,fine arts, and religion. They must have an overall GPA of 2.0, with 2.5 in the major. A total of 124 credits must be earned, with 45 to 60 in the major. Chapel/convocation requirements must also be met.

Special: Sterling offers cross-registration with the Associated Colleges of Central Kansas and the Council of Christian Colleges and Universities. Internships are available in most majors, as is study abroad in 7 countries. A Washington semester and work-study programs are offered. Student-designed majors and a dual degree program in biology and medical technology with Wichita State University are possible. There are 3 national honor societies.

Faculty/Classroom: 71% of faculty are male; 29% are female. All teach undergraduates. No introductory courses are taught by graduate students. The average class size in an introductory lecture is 40; in a laboratory is 25; and in a regular course is 20.

Admissions: 50% of a recent year, applicants were accepted. The SAT scores for the 2011-2012 freshman class were: Critical Reading--73% below 500, 23% between 500 and 599, and 4% between 600 and 700; Math--65% below 500, 31% between 500 and 599, and 4% between 600 and 700; Writing--77% below 500, 15% between 500 and 599, and 8% between 600 and 700. The ACT scores were 37% below 21, 31% between 21 and 23, 20% between 24 and 26, 5% between 27 and 28, and 7% above 28. 19% of the current freshmen were in the top fifth of their class; 49% were in the top two fifths. 4 freshmen graduated first in their class.

Requirements: The SAT or ACT is required. Applicants must graduate from an accredited secondary school or have a GED. An interview is recommended. A GPA of 2.2 is required. AP and CLEP credits are accepted. Important factors in the admissions decision are personality/intangible qualities, extracurricular activities record, and leadership record.

Procedure: Freshmen are admitted fall and spring. Entrance exams should be taken in the spring of the junior year. There are early admissions, deferred admissions, and rolling admissions plans. Application deadlines are open. Application fee is $25. Notification is sent on a rolling basis. Applications are accepted online.

Transfer: 77 transfer students enrolled in a recent year. Transfer students must have a minimum composite ACT score of 18 or a satisfactory SAT score if they have fewer than 12 hours of college credit; and a 2.2 GPA. 24 of 124 credits required for the bachelor's degree must be completed at Sterling.

Visiting: There are regularly scheduled orientations for prospective students, including visits with admissions, financial aid, current students, and faculty and campus and housing tours. There are guides for informal visits, visitors may sit in on classes, and stay overnight. To schedule a visit, contact the Admissions Office.

Financial Aid: Average annual earnings from campus work are $1200. The FAFSA is required. The deadline for filing freshman financial aid applications for fall entry is April 1.

International Students: There are 6 international students enrolled. They must take the TOEFL with a minimum score of 525 on the paper-based TOEFL (PBT) or 70 on the Internet-based version (iBT). They must also take the SAT or ACT.

Computers: Wireless access is available. Students can use the network and/or wireless system anywhere on campus. There are PCs available for students' use in the library, classrooms, residence halls and student union, or the system can be accessed through the student's own computer. All students may access the system anytime in residence hall or anytime academic buildings are open. There are no time limits and no fees.

Graduates: In an recent year, 42% graduate in 4 years or less, 48% graduate in 5 years or less, and 49% graduate in 6 years or less.

Admissions Contact: Admissions and Enrollment Services. A campus DVD is available. E-Mail: *admissions@sterling.edu* Web: *www.sterling.edu*

TABOR COLLEGE D-2

Hillsboro, KS 67063 **(620) 947-3121**
(800) TABOR-99; (620) 947-6276

Full-time: 350 men, 250 women	**Faculty:** n/av; IIB, --$
Part-time: 40 men, 100 women	**Ph.D.s:** n/av
Graduate: 5 men, 10 women	**Student/Faculty:** n/av
Year: semesters	**Tuition:** $22,060
Application Deadline: open	**Room & Board:** $7950
Freshman Class: n/av	
ACT: required	

LESS COMPETITIVE

Tabor College, established in 1908, is a private liberal arts facility affiliated with the Mennonite Brethren Church. The figures in the above capsule and in this profile are approximate. There are 2 undergraduate schools. In addition to regional accreditation, Tabor has baccalaureate program accreditation with CSWE and NASM. The library contains 80,099 volumes, 435 microform items, and 1,640 audio/video tapes/CDs/DVDs, and subscribes to 265 periodicals including electronic. Computerized library services include interlibrary loans, database searching, and Internet access. Special learning facilities include a learning resource center, a writing center. The 26-acre campus is in a rural area 50 miles north of Wichita. Including any residence halls, there are 28 buildings.

Student Life: 68% of undergraduates are from Kansas. Others are from 23 states, 5 foreign countries, and Canada. 90% are from public schools. 89% are white. 89% are Protestant. The average age of freshmen is 18; all undergraduates, 20. 10% do not continue beyond their first year; 87% remain to graduate.

Housing: 210 students can be accommodated in college housing, which includes single-sex dorms and off-campus apartments. On-campus housing is guaranteed for all 4 years. 78% of students live on campus; of those, 85% remain on campus on weekends. Alcohol is not permitted. All students may keep cars.

Activities: There are no fraternities or sororities. There are 18 groups on campus, including art, band, cheerleading, choir, chorale, chorus, computers, drama, drill team, ethnic, honors, international, jazz band, musical theater, newspaper, pep band, photography, political, religious, social service, student government, and yearbook. Popular campus events include Service Emphasis Week and Mission Emphasis Week.

Sports: There are 8 intercollegiate sports for men and 8 for women, and 10 intramural sports for men and 10 for women. Facilities include 4 lighted tennis courts, 2 racquetball courts, lighted football and baseball fields, several practice fields, a soccer field, a curbed metric all-weather track, a gym with 2 playing floors, a practice/intramural gym, an indoor soccer court, and aerobic exercise, athletic training, and weight rooms.

Disabled Students: 75% of the campus is accessible. Facilities include wheelchair ramps, elevators, special parking, specially equipped restrooms, special class scheduling, lowered drinking fountains, and lowered telephones.

Services: Counseling and information services are available, as is tutoring in most subjects. Tutoring is available for most learning disabled students and for those on academic probation.

Campus Safety and Security: There are lighted pathways/sidewalks.

Programs of Study: Tabor confers B.A. and B.S. degrees. Associate degrees are also awarded. Bachelor's degrees are awarded in BIOLOGICAL SCIENCE (biology/biological science), BUSINESS (accounting, business administration and management, marketing/retailing/merchandising, and office supervision and management), COMMUNICATIONS AND THE ARTS (applied art, communications, English, graphic design, and music), COMPUTER AND PHYSICAL SCIENCE (chemistry, computer science, mathematics, and natural sciences), EDUCATION (athletic training, business education, elementary education, health education, middle school education, music education, physical education, science education, secondary education, and special education), SOCIAL SCIENCE (biblical studies, history, humanities, international studies, ministries, philosophy, psychology, religion, social science, and sociology). The sciences are the strongest academically. Business and education have the largest enrollments.

Required: All students must complete 47 to 59 hours of general education courses including biblical and religious studies, history of diverse cultures, creative expression, natural and mathematical systems, values, social sciences, language, communication, computer literacy, physical fitness, and a college success seminar. A total of 124 credits, 16 of which must be in the major, with a minimum GPA of 2.0, are required in order to graduate.

Special: Cross-registration is offered with the Association of Colleges of Central Kansas. Study abroad in 5 countries is possible. Dual majors, student-designed majors, internships, a Washington semester for juniors or seniors, and pass/fail options are available, as is a 3-2 engineering degree with Wichita State University. An accelerated degree program in management organizational development and preprofessional curricula in allied health, law, and medicine are also offered. There is a freshman honors program and 1 departmental honors program.

Faculty/Classroom: 65% of faculty are male; 35% are female. All teach undergraduates. No introductory courses are taught by graduate students. The average class size in an introductory lecture is 32; in a laboratory is 12; and in a regular course is 20.

Requirements: The ACT is required. In addition, an essay is required and an interview is recommended. A GPA of 2.0 is required. AP and CLEP credits are accepted.

Procedure: Freshmen are admitted to all sessions. Entrance exams should be taken in October of the senior year. There is a rolling admissions plan. Check with the school for current application deadlines. Applications are accepted online.

Transfer: A minimum 2.0 GPA is required and an interview is recommended. 33 of 124 credits required for the bachelor's degree must be completed at Tabor.

Visiting: There are regularly scheduled orientations for prospective students, including a tour, admissions interview, and faculty, class, and financial aid visits. If requested, an audition or tryout will be scheduled. There are guides for informal visits, visitors may sit in on classes, and stay overnight. To schedule a visit, contact Admissions Counselors.

Financial Aid: The FAFSA, and a federal income tax form, and W-2 forms. is required. Check with the school for current application deadlines.
International Students: They must take the TOEFL. They must also take the SAT or ACT.
Computers: All students may access the system. There are no time limits and no fees.
Admissions Contact: Director of Admissions. E-Mail: *admissions@tabor.edu* Web: *www.tabor.edu*

UNIVERSITY OF KANSAS E-2

Lawrence, KS 66045 **(785) 864-3911; (785) 864-5017**

Full-time: 8611 men, 8582 women	**Faculty:** 1297; I, -$
Part-time: 1028 men, 996 women	**Ph.D.s:** 91%
Graduate: 3498 men, 4253 women	**Student/Faculty:** 18 to 1
Year: semesters, summer session	**Tuition:** $9278 ($22,757)
Application Deadline: April 1	**Room & Board:** $7702
Freshman Class: 13256 applied, 11715 accepted, 4000 enrolled	
SAT: required **ACT:** 25	**COMPETITIVE+**

The University of Kansas, founded in 1866, is a public, comprehensive research institution. Its undergraduate and graduate programs emphasize the liberal arts, business, fine arts, music, teacher preparation, journalism, engineering, architecture, social welfare, law, and health science, including pharmacy. Its medical center campus is located in Kansas City. There are 11 undergraduate schools and 3 graduate schools. In addition to regional accreditation, KU has baccalaureate program accreditation with AACSB, ABET, ACEJMC, ACPE, APTA, CSWE, NAAB, NASAD, NASM, and NCATE. The 12 libraries contain 4.5 million volumes. Computerized library services include interlibrary loans, database searching, Internet access, and Wi-Fi capability. Special learning facilities include a natural history museum, radio station, TV station, film studio, space technology center, state-of-the-art performing arts center, art museum, classics museum, entomology museum, invertebrate paleontology museum, organ recital hall, Robert J.Dole Institute of Politics, and Hall Center for the Humanities. The 1000-acre campus is in a suburban area 30 miles west of Kansas City. Including any residence halls, there are 220 buildings.
Student Life: 71% of undergraduates are from Kansas. Others are from 49 states, 71 foreign countries, and Canada. 74% are White. The average age of freshmen is 18; all undergraduates, 21. 20% do not continue beyond their first year; 62% remain to graduate.
Housing: 5235 students can be accommodated in college housing, which includes single-sex and coed dorms, on-campus apartments, and married student housing. In addition, there are honors houses, special-interest floors, and 1 residence hall with a fine arts emphasis. On-campus housing is available on a first-come and first-served basis. 76% of students commute. Alcohol is not permitted. All students may keep cars.
Activities: 14% of men belong to 28 national fraternities; 20% of women belong to 16 national sororities. There are 574 groups on campus, including art, band, cheerleading, chess, choir, chorale, chorus, communications, computers, dance, debate, drama, environmental, ethnic, film, gay, honors, international, jazz band, literary magazine, marching band, musical theater, newspaper, opera, orchestra, pep band, photography, political, professional, radio and TV, religious, social, social service, student government, and symphony. Popular campus events include Late Night in the Phog (basketball season kickoff), Homecoming and Rock Chalk Revue.
Sports: There are 7 intercollegiate sports for men and 11 for women, and 21 intramural sports for men and 21 for women. Facilities include a 16,300-seat basketball arena; a 50,100-seat football stadium with an outdoor track; a sports pavilion with an indoor football field and indoor track; a health and phys ed center with 2 indoor pools, handball and racquetball courts, and gyms; lacrosse, Ultimate, cricket, and rugby fields; tennis courts; a bowling alley; a student recreation center containing an indoor climbing wall, a gym, a suspended jogging track, 4 racquetball courts, a free weight/cardiovascular gym area, aerobic and martial arts rooms, multipurpose courts, squash court, and golf simulator; a rowing boathouse; an athletic center with volleyball and basketball courts; a football complex; a softball park; a baseball park with clubhouse; a soccer complex; a strength center; a golf training center; and an outdoor education center/challenge course.
Disabled Students: 95% of the campus is accessible. Facilities include wheelchair ramps, elevators, special parking, specially equipped restrooms, special class scheduling, lowered drinking fountains, and lowered telephones.
Services: Counseling and information services are available, as is tutoring in most subjects, including how-to sessions on study and organizational skills and a workshop. There is a reader service for the blind, and remedial math. A writing center is available to students.
Campus Safety and Security: Measures include 24-hour foot and vehicle patrol, emergency notification system, and security escort services. There are shuttle buses, emergency telephones, lighted pathways/sidewalks, and controlled access to dorms/residences.
Programs of Study: KU confers B.A., B.S., B.A.E., B.B.A., B.F.A., B.G.S., B.M., B.M.E., B.S.B., B.S.E., B.S.J., B.S.N. and B.S.W. degrees. Master's and doctoral degrees are also awarded. Bachelor's degrees are awarded in AGRICULTURE (environmental studies), BIOLOGICAL SCIENCE (biochemistry, biology/biological science, microbiology, and molecular biology), BUSINESS (accounting, business administration and management, finance, management information systems, marketing/retailing/merchandising, sports management, and supply chain management), COMMUNICATIONS AND THE ARTS (art, art history and appreciation, ceramic art and design, choral music, classical languages, dance, design, dramatic arts, East Asian languages and literature, English, fiber/textiles/weaving, film arts, fine arts, French, German, Germanic languages and literature, graphic design, illustration, industrial design, information technology, journalism, linguistics, metal/jewelry, music, music history and appreciation, music performance, music theory and composition, musicology/ethnomusicology, painting, percussion, piano/organ, printmaking, sculpture, Slavic languages, Spanish, speech/debate/rhetoric, strings, theater design, voice, and winds), COMPUTER AND PHYSICAL SCIENCE (astronomy, atmospheric sciences and meteorology, chemistry, computer science, geology, information sciences and systems, mathematics, and physics), EDUCATION (art education, athletic training, early childhood education, elementary education, health education, health information management, middle school education, music education, physical education, and secondary education), ENGINEERING AND ENVIRONMENTAL DESIGN (aeronautical engineering, architectural engineering, architectural history, architecture, chemical engineering, civil engineering, computer engineering, electrical/electronics engineering, engineering physics, interior design, mechanical engineering, and petroleum/natural gas engineering), HEALTH PROFESSIONS (community health work, cytotechnology, medical laboratory technology, music therapy, nursing, occupational therapy, pharmacy, respiratory therapy, and sports medicine), SOCIAL SCIENCE (African studies, African American studies, American studies, anthropology, archeology, behavioral science, classical/ancient civilization, developmental psychology, economics, European studies, geography, history, humanities, international studies, Latin American studies, liberal arts/general studies, philosophy, political science/government, psychology, public administration, religion, Russian and Slavic studies, social work, sociology, and women's studies). Pharmacy and engineering are the strongest academically. Engineering, biological sciences, and business have the largest enrollments.
Required: To graduate with a B.A., B.S., or B.G.S. degree, all students must complete at least 120 credit hours, including 30 to 50 credit hours in the major, and maintain a GPA of at least 2.0. These, as well as curricula and distribution requirements, vary according to the school and the major.
Special: Special academic programs include Honors program, internships, study abroad in over 70 countries, a Washington semester, and work-study programs with the university. A cooperative program in engineering is offered, as are B.A.-B.S. degrees in many combinations, interdisciplinary majors, and dual majors in any approved combination. General studies degrees are available in many areas, and student-designed majors are possible. Nondegree study and pass/fail options are offered. There are 17 national honor societies, including Phi Beta Kappa, and a freshman honors program.
Faculty/Classroom: 58% of faculty are male; 42% are female. 98% teach undergraduates, all do research, and 98% do both. Graduate students teach 20% of introductory courses. The average class size in a laboratory is 15 and in a regular course is 21.
Admissions: 88% of the 2013-2014 applicants were accepted. The ACT scores were 12% below 21, 22% between 21 and 23, 28% between 24 and 26, 15% between 27 and 28, and 23% above 28. There were 37 National Merit finalists.
Requirements: The SAT or ACT is required. Kansas resident applicants must have a minimum 2.0 GPA in the qualified admissions college preparatory curriculum; or have an ACT composite score of 21 or SAT combined score (math and critical reading) of 980; or rank in the top third of their high school class. College preparatory curriculum includes 4 units of English, 3 of college preparatory math, 3 of natural science (1 must be chemistry or physics), and 3 of social sciences (includes history). Two units of foreign language are recommended. Nonresidents have the same curriculum requirements, but they must have a minimum GPA of 2.5; or an ACT composite score of 24 or SAT combined score of 1090; or be in the top third of their high school class. A GPA of 2.0 is required. AP and CLEP credits are accepted.
Procedure: Freshmen are admitted to all sessions. Entrance exams should be taken by the end of the junior year. There is a rolling admissions plan. Applications should be filed by April 1 for fall entry; December 1 for spring entry; and February 1 for summer entry, along with a $30 fee. Applications are accepted online.
Transfer: 1294 transfer students enrolled in 2012-2013. For entrance to the College of Liberal Arts and Sciences, transfer students must have at least 24 credit hours with a minimum GPA of 2.0 in state or 2.5 out of state. The criteria vary widely within the other KU schools, some of which may also consider the ACT score and course work. 30 of 120 credits required for the bachelor's degree must be completed at KU.
Visiting: There are regularly scheduled orientations for prospective stu-

dents, consisting of a summer orientation program that includes a 1-day campus visit. There are guides for informal visits, visitors may sit in on classes, and stay overnight. To schedule a visit, contact the KU Visitor Center at (785) 864-3911.

Financial Aid: In 2013-2014, 69% of all full-time freshmen and 56% of continuing full-time students received some form of financial aid. 32% of all full-time freshmen and 31% of continuing full-time students received need-based aid. The average freshman award was $8,716. Need-based scholarships or need-based grants averaged $5,678; need-based self-help aid (loans and jobs) averaged $3,384; non-need-based athletic scholarships averaged $19,309; and other non-need-based awards and non-need-based scholarships averaged $3,235. 15% of undergraduate students work part-time. Average annual earnings from campus work are $4800. The average financial indebtedness of the 2013 graduate was $27,219. The FAFSA is required. The deadline for filing freshman financial aid applications for fall entry is March 1.

International Students: There are 1098 international students enrolled. The school actively recruits these students. They must take the TOEFL, IELTS.

Computers: All students may access the system 24 hours a day, 7 days a week. There are no time limits and no fees.

Graduates: From July 1, 2012 to June 30, 2013, 4265 bachelor's degrees were awarded. The most popular majors were business (13%), social sciences (7%), and engineering (7%). 500 companies recruited on campus in 2012-2013. In an average class, 1% graduate in 3 years or less, 37% graduate in 4 years or less, 56% graduate in 5 years or less, and 62% graduate in 6 years or less. Of the 2012 graduating class, 26% were enrolled in graduate school within 6 months of graduation, and 70% were employed.

Admissions Contact: Lisa Pinamonti Kress, Director of Admissions. E-Mail: *adm@ku.edu* Web: *admissions.ku.edu*

UNIVERSITY OF SAINT MARY — F-2

Leavenworth, KS 66048 — (913) 682-5151; (800) 752-7043; (913) 758-6140

Full-time: 250 men, 300 women
Part-time: 60 men, 215 women
Graduate: 95 men, 220 women
Year: semesters, summer session
Application Deadline: open
Freshman Class: n/av
SAT or ACT: required
Faculty: n/av
Ph.D.s: n/av
Student/Faculty: n/av
Tuition: $21,250
Room & Board: $8150

COMPETITIVE+

The University of Saint Mary, formerly Saint Mary College, founded in 1923, is a private liberal arts institution affiliated with the Roman Catholic Church and sponsored by the Sisters of Charity of Leavenworth. The figures in the above capsule and in this profile are approximate. There is 1 undergraduate school and 1 graduate school. In addition to regional accreditation, USM has baccalaureate program accreditation with NCATE. The library contains 120,000 volumes and 1,675 microform items, and subscribes to 301 periodicals including electronic. Computerized library services include interlibrary loans, database searching, and Internet access. Special learning facilities include a learning resource center, art gallery, several special library collections. The 240-acre campus is in a small town 25 miles northwest of Kansas City, Missouri. Including any residence halls, there are 10 buildings.

Student Life: 65% of undergraduates are from Kansas. Others are from 39 states, and 4 foreign countries. 74% are white. 34% are Catholic; 34% claim no religious affiliation; 32% Protestant. The average age of freshmen is 18; all undergraduates, 26. 40% do not continue beyond their first year; 44% remain to graduate.

Housing: 333 students can be accommodated in college housing, which includes single-sex and coed dorms. On-campus housing is guaranteed for all 4 years. 56% of students commute. All students may keep cars.

Activities: There are no fraternities or sororities. There are 25 groups on campus, including art, cheerleading, choir, chorale, chorus, computers, dance, drama, honors, literary magazine, musical theater, newspaper, opera, political, professional, religious, social, social service, and student government. Popular campus events include Fall Convocation, Founders Day, and Family Weekend.

Sports: There are 4 intercollegiate sports for men and 4 for women, and 8 intramural sports for men and 8 for women. Facilities include a 500-seat sports center, soccer and softball fields, a multipurpose field, 3 tennis courts, a sandlot volleyball court, 2 racquetball courts, a weight and exercise room, a swimming pool, a dance and aerobics space, a walking trail, and an indoor jogging track.

Disabled Students: 90% of the campus is accessible. Facilities include wheelchair ramps, elevators, special parking, and specially equipped restrooms.

Services: Counseling and information services are available, as is tutoring in most subjects.

Campus Safety and Security: Measures include self-defense education. There are lighted pathways/sidewalks, 14-hour foot and vehicle patrols, and controlled access to residence halls.

Programs of Study: USM confers B.A. and B.S. degrees. Associate and master's degrees are also awarded. Bachelor's degrees are awarded in BIOLOGICAL SCIENCE (biology/biological science), BUSINESS (accounting, business administration and management, and sports management), COMMUNICATIONS AND THE ARTS (art, dramatic arts, and English), COMPUTER AND PHYSICAL SCIENCE (chemistry, information sciences and systems, and mathematics), EDUCATION (elementary education), HEALTH PROFESSIONS (biomedical science, clinical science, and nursing), SOCIAL SCIENCE (applied psychology, child psychology/development, criminology, history, interdisciplinary studies, international studies, liberal arts/general studies, pastoral studies, political science/government, psychology, sociology, and theological studies). Elementry education, business administration, psychology, and information are the strongest academically.

Required: To graduate, students must complete all general education requirements and earn at least 128 credits, including 30 to 60 in the major, with a minimum GPA of 2.0. The core curriculum includes freshman humanities and a senior integration project. Distribution requirements include courses in English, math, natural science, social and behavioral sciences, philosophy, history, and foreign language, plus an additional literature course, a fine arts course, and 2 courses in theology. Students must also fulfill cultural literacy and lifetime physical wellness requirements.

Special: The university offers study abroad at various locations in Europe, Latin America, or Australia. CLEP and credit for life experience, internships in most major programs, evening and weekend study programs, pass/fail option, and dual majors are also available. There are 2 national honor societies.

Faculty/Classroom: 43% of faculty are male; 57% are female. All teach undergraduates. No introductory courses are taught by graduate students. The average class size in an introductory lecture is 25 and in a laboratory is 12.

Requirements: The SAT or ACT is required. Applicants should be graduates of an accredited secondary school. The GED is accepted. A GPA of 2.5 is required. AP and CLEP credits are accepted. Important factors in the admissions decision are parents or siblings attended your school, recommendations by alumni, and recommendations by school officials.

Procedure: Freshmen are admitted fall and spring. Entrance exams should be taken in the spring of the junior year and fall of the senior year. There are early decision, early admissions, and rolling admissions plans. Application deadlines are open. Application fee is $25. Notification is sent on a rolling basis.

Transfer: A college GPA of 2.0 is required. 30 of 128 credits required for the bachelor's degree must be completed at USM.

Visiting: There are regularly scheduled orientations for prospective students, Visits include interviews with faculty and financial aid representatives, and touring the campus. There are guides for informal visits and visitors may sit in on classes. To schedule a visit, contact the Admissions Office.

Financial Aid: USM is a member of CSS. The FAFSA is required. Check with the school for current application deadlines.

International Students: The school actively recruits these students. They must take the TOEFL with a minimum score of 500 on the paper-based TOEFL (PBT) or 61 on the Internet-based version (iBT).

Computers: All students may access the system. There are no time limits and no fees. It is strongly recommended that all students have a personal computer.

Admissions Contact: Director of Admissions. A campus DVD is available. E-Mail: *admissions@stmary.edu* Web: *www.stmary.edu*

WASHBURN UNIVERSITY — E-2

Topeka, KS 66621 — (785) 670-1030; 1-877-281-2637; (785) 670-1113

Full-time: 1671 men, 2401 women
Part-time: 847 men, 1260 women
Graduate: 331 men, 463 women
Year: semesters, summer session
Application Deadline: August 1
Faculty: 245; IIA, -$
Ph.D.s: 87%
Student/Faculty: 15 to 1
Tuition: $5774 ($12,926)
Room & Board: $6391
Freshman Class: 2079 applied, 2041 accepted, 851 enrolled
ACT: 22

NONCOMPETITIVE

Washburn is a publicly funded, independently governed, state-coordinated university. Established in 1865, the school offers more than 200 programs leading to certification, associate, bachelor, master, and juris doctor degrees through the College of Arts and Sciences and the Schools of Law, Business, Nursing, and Applied Studies. There are 4 undergraduate schools and 5 graduate schools. In addition to regional accreditation, Washburn has baccalaureate program accreditation with AACSB, CAHEA, CSWE, NASAD, NASM, and NCATE. The 2 libraries contain 467,524 volumes, 92,066 microform items, and 4,342 audio/video tapes/CDs/DVDs, and subscribe to 42,657 periodicals including electronic. Computerized library services include interlibrary loans, database searching, Internet access, and Wi-Fi capability. Special learning facilities include an art gallery, planetarium, and TV station. The 160-acre campus is in an urban area 60 miles west of Kansas City. Including any residence halls, there are 29 buildings.

Student Life: 91% of undergraduates are from Kansas. Others are from 43 states, 37 foreign countries, and Canada. 92% are from public schools. The average age of freshmen is 19; all undergraduates, 25. 35% do not continue beyond their first year; 34% remain to graduate.

Housing: 674 students can be accommodated in college housing, which includes coed dorms and on-campus apartments. In addition, there are special-interest houses, fraternity houses, and sorority houses. On-campus housing is available on a first-come and first-served basis. Priority is given to out-of-town students. 85% of students commute. Alcohol is not permitted. All students may keep cars.

Activities: 7% of men belong to 1 local and 4 national fraternities; 7% of women belong to 4 national sororities. There are 122 groups on campus, including and peer educators., art, band, campus activities board, cheerleading, chess, choir, chorus, computers, dance, debate, drama, drill team, drum and bugle corps, environmental, ethnic, forensics, gay, honors, international, jazz band, literary magazine, marching band, musical theater, newspaper, orchestra, pep band, political, professional, radio and TV, religious, social, social service, student government, symphony, and yearbook. Popular campus events include Greek Week, Student Activities Fair and the Annual Music Festival.

Sports: There are 5 intercollegiate sports for men and 5 for women, and 20 intramural sports for men and 20 for women. Facilities include a recreation and wellness center with rock-climbing wall, indoor track, gym, cardiovascular and resistance training area, and wellness suite; a 2,700-seat field house for indoor sports; a 7,200-seat stadium for intercollegiate football; and a health center with a 6-lane swimming pool.

Disabled Students: 95% of the campus is accessible. Facilities include wheelchair ramps, elevators, special parking, specially equipped restrooms, special class scheduling, lowered drinking fountains, lowered telephones, special housing. note takers, readers, library assistance, recorders, reading machines, videotaped classes, oral tests, learning center, tutors, and extended time for tests are also available.

Services: Counseling and information services are available, as is tutoring in most subjects. There is a reader service for the blind, and remedial math and writing.

Campus Safety and Security: Measures include 24-hour foot and vehicle patrol, emergency notification system, self-defense education, and security escort services. There are emergency telephones, lighted pathways/sidewalks, , whistle campaign, operation ID, textbook ID program, bicycle patrol, and fire safety programs for residential living facilities.

Programs of Study: Washburn confers B.A., B.A.S., B.B.A., B.Ed., B.F.A., B.H.S., B.I.S., B.L.S., B.M., B.P.A., B.S., B.S.C.J., B.S.N. and B.S.W. degrees. Associate, master's, and doctoral degrees are also awarded. Bachelor's degrees are awarded in BIOLOGICAL SCIENCE (biochemistry and biology/biological science), BUSINESS (accounting, banking and finance, business administration and management, business economics, and marketing/retailing/merchandising), COMMUNICATIONS AND THE ARTS (art, art history and appreciation, communications, dramatic arts, English, French, German, media arts, music, music performance, Spanish, speech/debate/rhetoric, and theater design), COMPUTER AND PHYSICAL SCIENCE (chemistry, computer science, mathematics, physics, and science), EDUCATION (art education, athletic training, early childhood education, education, elementary education, music education, physical education, and secondary education), ENGINEERING AND ENVIRONMENTAL DESIGN (technological management), HEALTH PROFESSIONS (clinical science, health care administration, nursing, and ultrasound technology), SOCIAL SCIENCE (anthropology, corrections, criminal justice, economics, forensic studies, history, human services, interdisciplinary studies, law enforcement and corrections, liberal arts/general studies, paralegal studies, philosophy, political science/government, psychology, public administration, religion, social work, and sociology). Natural sciences, art, and music are the strongest academically. Business administration, criminal justice, and nursing have the largest enrollments.

Special: Washburn offers a co-op program in computer information science, engineering, social/behavioral science, education, and health professions; internships in numerous departments; and study abroad in 20 countries. Dual and student-designed majors, B.A.-B.S. degrees, an integrated studies degree, credit by examination, nondegree study, and pass/fail options are also available. A 3-2 engineering degree is possible in conjunction with the University of Kansas and Kansas State University. There are 11 national honor societies and a freshman honors program.

Faculty/Classroom: 46% of faculty are male; 54% are female. 92% teach undergraduates. No introductory courses are taught by graduate students. The average class size in an introductory lecture is 25; in a laboratory is 17; and in a regular course is 20.

Admissions: 98% of the 2013-2014 applicants were accepted. The ACT scores were 35% below 21, 30% between 21 and 23, 20% between 24 and 26, 8% between 27 and 28, and 7% above 28. 30 freshmen graduated first in their class.

Requirements: The ACT is required. Applicants should be graduates of an accredited secondary school or have the GED. AP and CLEP credits are accepted.

Procedure: Freshmen are admitted to all sessions. Entrance exams should be taken during the junior year. There is a rolling admissions plan. Applications should be filed by August 1 for fall entry; January 2 for spring entry; and May 14 for summer entry. The fall 2013 application fee was $20. Applications are accepted online.

Transfer: 494 transfer students enrolled in 2012-2013. Applicants must meet the same requirements as incoming freshmen. 30 of 120 credits required for the bachelor's degree must be completed at Washburn.

Visiting: There are regularly scheduled orientations for prospective students, consisting of a campus visit program Monday through Friday at 9:00 a.m. and 2:00 p.m. that includes a tour, visits with faculty, financial aid information, and the opportunity to have all questions answered. There are guides for informal visits, visitors may sit in on classes, and stay overnight. To schedule a visit, contact The Admissions Office.

Financial Aid: In 2013-2014, 63% of all full-time freshmen and 64% of continuing full-time students received some form of financial aid. 40% of all full-time freshmen and 41% of continuing full-time students received need-based aid. The average freshman award was $9,288. Need-based scholarships or need-based grants averaged $5,022; need-based self-help aid (loans and jobs) averaged $3,849; non-need-based athletic scholarships averaged $5,357; and other non-need-based awards and non-need-based scholarships averaged $2,589. 12% of undergraduate students work part-time. Average annual earnings from campus work are $2019. The average financial indebtedness of the 2013 graduate was $17,995. Washburn is a member of CSS. The FAFSA, and admission/scholarship application is required. The priority date for freshman financial aid applications for fall entry is February 15.

International Students: There are 195 international students enrolled. The school actively recruits these students. They must take the TOEFL with a minimum score of 523 on the paper-based TOEFL (PBT) or 72 on the Internet-based version (iBT).

Computers: All students may access the system. There are no time limits and no fees.

Graduates: From July 1, 2012 to June 30, 2013, 830 bachelor's degrees were awarded. The most popular majors were nursing/health professions (30%), business (14%), and education (8%). 172 companies recruited on campus in 2012-2013. In an average class, 34% graduate in 6 years or less. Of the 2012 graduating class, 45% were enrolled in graduate school within 6 months of graduation, and 84% were employed.

Admissions Contact: Kris Klima, Director of Admissions. E-Mail: *admissions@washburn.edu* Web: *http:/www.washburn.edu/admissions/*

WICHITA STATE UNIVERSITY — D-3

Wichita, KS 67260 (316) 978-3085
(800) 362-2594; (316) 978-3174

Full-time: 4016 men, 4513 women	**Faculty:** 445; I, --$
Part-time: 1666 men, 2048 women	**Ph.D.s:** 80%
Graduate: 1273 men, 1584 women	**Student/Faculty:** 20 to 1
Year: semesters, summer session	**Tuition:** $6689 ($14,224)
Application Deadline: open	**Room & Board:** $6950

Freshman Class: 3304 applied, 3102 accepted, 1365 enrolled

SAT CR/M: 460/530 **ACT:** 23 **COMPETITIVE**

Wichita State University, established in 1895, is a public institution offering programs in the liberal arts and sciences, business, engineering, education, and health professions. There are 6 undergraduate schools and 1 graduate school. In addition to regional accreditation, WSU has baccalaureate program accreditation with AACSB, ABET, ADA, APTA, CAHEA, CSWE, NASM, NCATE, and NLN. The library contains 1.8 million volumes, 1.2 million microform items, and 198,724 audio/video tapes/CDs/DVDs, and subscribes to 61,010 periodicals including electronic. Computerized library services include interlibrary loans, database searching, Internet access, and laptop Internet portals. Special learning facilities include a learning resource center, art gallery, natural history museum, radio station, TV station, electronic classroom, telecourses, the National Institute for Aviation Research, museum of art, and public observatory. The 330-acre campus is in an urban area in the metropolitan Wichita area. Including any residence halls, there are 61 buildings. The figures in the above capsule and in this profile are approximate.

Student Life: 96% of undergraduates are from Kansas. Others are from 49 states, 88 foreign countries, and Canada. 64% are white. 19% are unknown. The average age of freshmen is 19; all undergraduates, 23. 27% do not continue beyond their first year; 43% remain to graduate.

Housing: 1453 students can be accommodated in college housing, which includes coed dorms, on-campus apartments, and married student housing. In addition, there are honors houses, fraternity houses, and sorority houses. On-campus housing is available on a first-come and first-served basis. 92% of students commute. All students may keep cars.

Activities: 4% of men belong to 10 national fraternities; 5% of women belong to 8 national sororities. There are 200 groups on campus, including art, band, cheerleading, chess, choir, chorus, computers, dance, debate, drama, environmental, ethnic, film, gay, honors, international, jazz band, literary magazine, musical theater, newspaper, opera, orchestra, pep band, photography, political, professional, radio and TV, religious, social, social service, student government, and symphony. Popular campus events include Hippodrome, International Week, and ShocktoberFest.

Sports: There are 14 intercollegiate sports for men and 12 for women, and 30 intramural sports for men and 30 for women. Facilities include a 10,656-seat arena, 2 stadiums, an 18-hole golf course, a baseball field, a tennis complex, and a recreation and sports center.

Disabled Students: 98% of the campus is accessible. Facilities include wheelchair ramps, elevators, special parking, specially equipped restrooms, special class scheduling, lowered drinking fountains, lowered telephones. wheelchairs, and braille typewriters. Interpreters for the hearing impaired, note taking, and typing services are also offered.

Services: Counseling and information services are available, as is tutoring in most subjects. There is a reader service for the blind, and remedial math, reading, and writing. Group and individual psychological services are available for students and their families.

Campus Safety and Security: Measures include 24-hour foot and vehicle patrol, self-defense education, and security escort services. There are shuttle buses, emergency telephones, lighted pathways/sidewalks, and a bicycle patrol.

Programs of Study: WSU confers A.A.,B.A., B.A.Ed., BAES., BASM., B.B.A, B.F.A., B.G.S., B.M., B.M.E., B.S., BSASE., B.S.CPE., B.S.E.E., B.S.H.S., B.S.I.E., B.S.M.E., B.S.M.F.E., B.S.N. degrees. Associate, master's, and doctoral degrees are also awarded. Bachelor's degrees are awarded in BIOLOGICAL SCIENCE (biology/biological science), BUSINESS (accounting, banking and finance, business administration and management, entrepreneurial studies, human resources, international business management, management science, marketing/retailing/merchandising, and sports management), COMMUNICATIONS AND THE ARTS (art, art history and appreciation, communications, English, French, graphic design, Latin, music, Spanish, studio art, and visual and performing arts), COMPUTER AND PHYSICAL SCIENCE (chemistry, computer science, geology, mathematics, and physics), EDUCATION (art education, elementary education, music education, physical education, secondary education, and special education), ENGINEERING AND ENVIRONMENTAL DESIGN (aeronautical engineering, computer engineering, electrical/electronics engineering, industrial engineering, manufacturing engineering, and mechanical engineering), HEALTH PROFESSIONS (health care administration, medical laboratory technology, nursing, physician's assistant, and speech pathology/audiology), SOCIAL SCIENCE (anthropology, criminal justice, economics, ethnic studies, gerontology, history, liberal arts/general studies, philosophy, political science/government, psychology, social work, sociology, and women's studies). Engineering programs, physics, chemistry are the strongest academically. Psychology, nursing, elementary education and business administration have the largest enrollments.

Required: To graduate, students need at least 124 credit hours, with a GPA of 2.0 to 2.5, depending on the major. Specific distribution requirements, as well as department requirements, must also be met. The core curriculum consists of 14 courses (42 hours) in general education. Students must have a minimum of 45 credit hours in courses numbered 300 or above.

Special: WSU offers co-op programs, internships, study abroad, work-study programs, and a Washington semester. Dual and student-designed majors, a general studies degree, credit by exam, nondegree study, and pass/fail options are also available. There are 14 national honor societies and a freshman honors program.

Faculty/Classroom: 58% of faculty are male; 42% are female. Graduate students teach 23% of introductory courses. The average class size in an introductory lecture is 23; in a laboratory is 20; and in a regular course is 15.

Admissions: 94% of a recent year applicants were accepted. The SAT scores for the recent freshman class were: Critical Reading--45% below 500, 30% between 500 and 599, 18% between 600 and 700, and 7% above 700; Math--44% below 500, 26% between 500 and 599, 16% between 600 and 700, and 6% above 700. The ACT scores were 28% below 21, 32% between 21 and 23, 23% between 24 and 26, 10% between 27 and 28, and 7% above 28. 36% of the current freshmen were in the top fifth of their class; 65% were in the top two fifths.

Requirements: The SAT or ACT is required. Applicants must submit a minimum composite ACT score of 21 or a satisfactory SAT score, rank in the top one third of their high school graduating class, and have a 2.0 GPA (non-residents 2.5). Requirements include 4 years of English, 3 each of math, natural and social sciences, and 1 of computer technology. AP and CLEP credits are accepted.

Procedure: Freshmen are admitted to all sessions. There are deferred admissions and rolling admissions plans. Application deadlines are open. Check with the school for the current application fee. Applications are accepted online.

Transfer: 1471 transfer students enrolled in 2010-2011. Applicants must have a minimum GPA of 2.0 to 2.5, depending on the WSU college they wish to enter. 30 of 124 credits required for the bachelor's degree must be completed at WSU.

Visiting: There are regularly scheduled orientations for prospective students, Students may schedule their visit online through the school's web site. There are guides for informal visits, visitors may sit in on classes, and stay overnight. To schedule a visit, contact the Admissions Office.

Financial Aid: In a recent year, 72% of all full-time freshmen and 73% of continuing full-time students received some form of financial aid. 37% of all full-time freshmen and 34% of continuing full-time students received need-based aid. The average freshman award was $3,090. Need-based scholarships or need-based grants averaged $3,224; need-based self-help aid (loans and jobs) averaged $3,802; and non-need-based athletic scholarships averaged $6,008. 7% of undergraduate students work part-time. Average annual earnings from campus work are $3640. The FAFSA is required. The deadline for filing freshman financial aid applications for fall entry is March 15.

International Students: There are 713 international students enrolled. The school actively recruits these students. They must take the TOEFL with a minimum score of 530 on the paper-based TOEFL (PBT) or 72 on the Internet-based version (iBT).

Computers: Wireless access is available. All students may access the system 24 hours a day. There are no fees.

Graduates: In a recent year, 1959 bachelor's degrees were awarded. The most popular majors were elementary education (6%), nursing (6%), and Business Administration (4%). 75 companies recruited on campus in 2010-2011. In an average class, 17% graduate in 4 years or less, 36% graduate in 5 years or less, and 41% graduate in 6 years or less.

Admissions Contact: Director of Admissions. A campus DVD is available. E-Mail: *admissions@wichita.edu* Web: *www.wichita.edu*

KENTUCKY

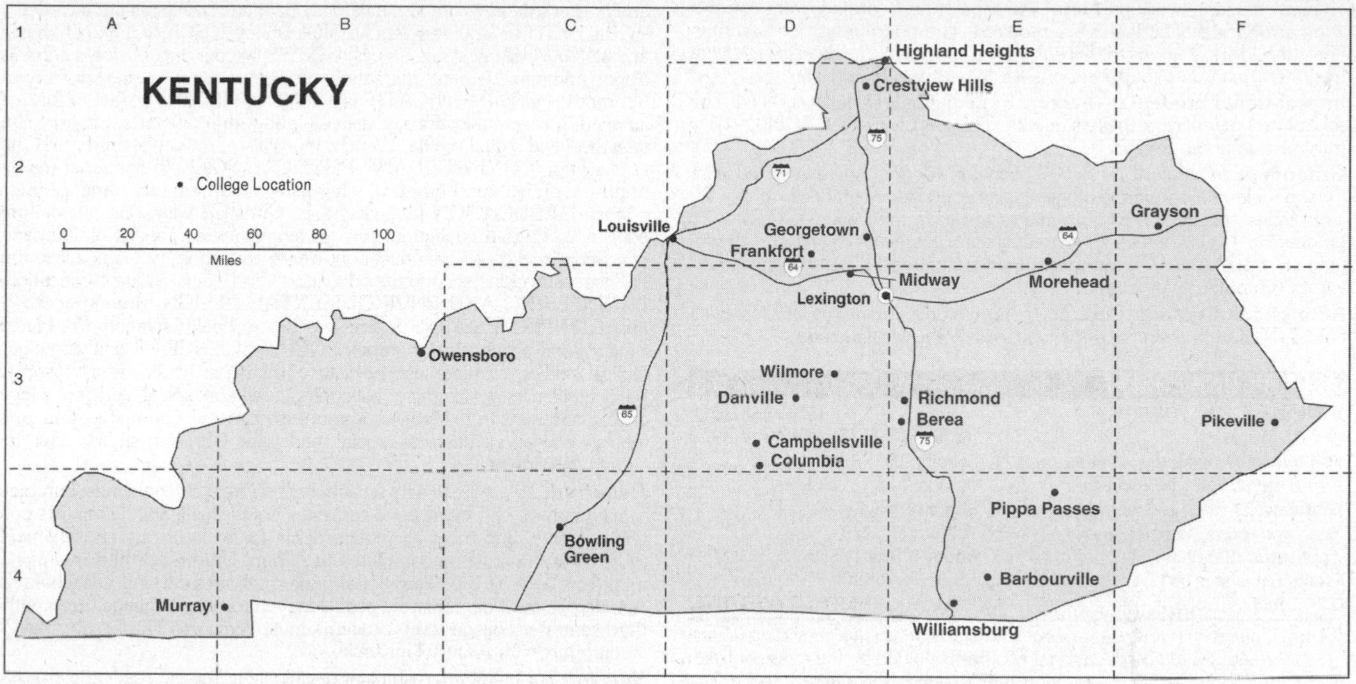

ALICE LLOYD COLLEGE E-4

Pippa Passes, KY 41844 (606) 368-2101
(888) 280-4252; (606) 368-6215

Full-time: 281 men, 308 women
Part-time: 11 men, 12 women
Graduate: n/av
Year: semesters
Application Deadline: open
Freshman Class: n/av
SAT: required
Faculty: 27
Ph.D.s: 65%
Student/Faculty: 22 to 1
Tuition: $2,700 ($8700)
Room & Board: $4700
ACT: 20 **COMPETITIVE**

Alice Lloyd College, founded in 1923, is a private liberal arts facility emphasizing Christian values and serving the Appalachian community. In addition to regional accreditation, ALC has baccalaureate program accreditation with NCATE. The library contains 62,000 volumes, 1,500 microform items, and 300 audio/video tapes/CDs/DVDs, and subscribes to 300 periodicals including electronic. Computerized library services include interlibrary loans, database searching, and Internet access. Special learning facilities include a learning resource center, art gallery, radio station, TV station, a performing arts center. The 225-acre campus is in a rural area. Including any residence halls, there are 38 buildings.

Student Life: 85% of undergraduates are from Kentucky. Others are from 7 states, and 2 foreign countries. 90% are from public schools. 97% are white. The average age of freshmen is 18; all undergraduates, 20. 37% do not continue beyond their first year.

Housing: 451 students can be accommodated in college housing, which includes single-sex dorms. a Caney Cottage scholarship program, which provides housing for students to continue their education after the undergraduate level. On-campus housing is guaranteed for all 4 years. 78% of students live on campus; of those, 35% remain on campus on weekends. Alcohol is not permitted. All students may keep cars.

Activities: There are no fraternities or sororities. There are 16 groups on campus, including art, cheerleading, choir, chorus, computers, drama, honors, newspaper, pep band, photography, professional, radio and TV, religious, social, student government, and yearbook. Popular campus events include Religious Emphasis Week, Alcohol Awareness Week, and Appalachia Day.

Sports: There are 5 intercollegiate sports for men and 5 for women, and 11 intramural sports for men and 11 for women. Facilities include an indoor pool, weight rooms, a 1500-seat gym, recreation areas, 2 tennis courts, a baseball/athletic field, and 2 racquetball courts.

Disabled Students: 95% of the campus is accessible. Facilities include wheelchair ramps, elevators, special parking, specially equipped restrooms, and special class scheduling.

Services: Counseling and information services are available, as is tutoring in every subject. There is remedial math, reading, and writing.

Campus Safety and Security: Measures include 24-hour foot and vehicle patrol, self-defense education, and security escort services. There are emergency telephones and lighted pathways/sidewalks.

Programs of Study: ALC confers B.A. and B.S. degrees. Bachelor's degrees are awarded in BIOLOGICAL SCIENCE (biology/biological science), BUSINESS (business administration and management), COMMUNICATIONS AND THE ARTS (English), EDUCATION (elementary education, middle school education, physical education, secondary education, and social studies education), ENGINEERING AND ENVIRONMENTAL DESIGN (preengineering), HEALTH PROFESSIONS (prepharmacy), SOCIAL SCIENCE (history). Biology, education, and business administration are the strongest academically. Biology has the largest enrollment.

Required: To graduate, students must complete a work-study requirement extending through each semester and a 49-semester-hour general education requirement, including phys ed, health, composition, philosophy, and speech. 128 credit hours are required. Students must maintain a 2.0 GPA (2.5 for education majors) to graduate. The number of hours required in the major varies.

Special: Special arrangements include a 2-2 engineering degree with the Universities of Kentucky, Louisville, and West Virginia. Credit by exam is possible. There is 1 national honor society.

Faculty/Classroom: 74% of faculty are male; 26% are female. All teach undergraduates, and 10% do research. No introductory courses are taught by graduate students. The average class size in an introductory lecture is 25; in a laboratory is 12; and in a regular course is 17.

Admissions: The ACT scores were 48% below 21, 35% between 21 and 23, 13% between 24 and 26, 3% between 27 and 28, and 1% above 28. 50% of the current freshmen were in the top fifth of their class; 82% were in the top two fifths. 6 freshmen graduated first in their class.

Requirements: The SAT or ACT is required. Applicants must graduate from an accredited secondary school or have a GED, having successfully completed 12 academic credits, including 4 in English, 3 each in math and science, and 2 in social studies. A GPA of 2.3 is required. AP and CLEP credits are accepted. Admissions decision are based on leadership record, recommendations by alumni and school officials.

Procedure: Freshmen are admitted fall and spring. Entrance exams should be taken in the fall of the senior year. There is a rolling admissions plan. Application deadlines are open. In a recent year, 31 applicants were on the waiting list; 22 admitted. Applications are accepted online.

Transfer: 35 transfer students enrolled in a recent year. Applicants must have a minimum 2.0 GPA, 2.5 for some majors, be in good standing at their previous school, and have a minimum ACT score of 17. 30 of 128 credits required for the bachelor's degree must be completed at ALC.

Visiting: There are regularly scheduled orientations for prospective students, consisting of summer and fall orientations. There are guides for informal visits, visitors may sit in on classes, and stay overnight. To schedule a visit, contact the Admissions Assistant.

Financial Aid: In a recent year, 100% of all full-time freshmen and 100%

of continuing full-time students received some form of financial aid. 52% of all full-time freshmen and 4% of continuing full-time students received need-based aid. The average freshman award was $7,783. 100% of undergraduate students work part-time. Average annual earnings from campus work are $1648. The FAFSA is required. The priority date for freshman financial aid applications for fall entry is February 15. The deadline for filing freshman financial aid applications for fall entry is March 15.

International Students: There are 3 international students enrolled. The school actively recruits these students. They must take the TOEFL. They must also take the SAT or ACT.

Graduates: In a recent year, 107 bachelor's degrees were awarded. The most popular majors were biology, business, and elementary education. 30 companies recruited on campus in a recent year. In an average class, 20% graduate in 4 years or less, 21% graduate in 5 years or less, and 22% graduate in 6 years or less. Of the recent graduating class, 96% were employed within 6 months of graduation.

Admissions Contact: Director of Admissions. A campus DVD is available. E-Mail: *admissions@alicelloyd.edu* Web: *www.alc.edu*

ASBURY UNIVERSITY D-3

Wilmore, KY 40390 (859) 858-3511
(800) 888-1818; (859) 858-3921

Full-time: 517 men, 809 women	**Faculty:** 87; IIB, --$
Part-time: 90 men, 116 women	**Ph.D.s:** 74%
Graduate: 54 men, 196 women	**Student/Faculty:** 12 to 1
Year: semesters, summer session	**Tuition:** $26,076
Application Deadline:	**Room & Board:** $5962
Freshman Class: 1211 applied, 796 accepted, 322 enrolled	
SAT CR/M: 568/558	**ACT:** 24 **VERY COMPETITIVE**

Asbury University is an independent liberal arts university, providing undergraduate and graduate educational programs guided by the classical tradition of orthodox Christian thought. On this foundation, we seek to provide an excellent integrated educational experience that appreciates truth in all areas of life and develops whole persons for achievement and service. There are 3 undergraduate schools and 3 graduate schools. In addition to regional accreditation, Asbury has baccalaureate program accreditation with CSWE, NASM, and NCATE. The library contains 184,084 volumes, 13,238 microform items, and 7,188 audio/video tapes/CDs/DVDs, and subscribes to 299 periodicals including electronic. Computerized library services include interlibrary loans, database searching, Internet access, and Wi-Fi capability. Special learning facilities include an art gallery, radio station, TV station, Miller Center for Communication Arts features a 6,050 square foot television studio, and a 5,122 square foot blackbox theatre. Equine Center houses classrooms, stables, and riding arena. The 65-acre campus is in a small town 20 minutes south of Lexington, KY. Including any residence halls, there are 30 buildings.

Student Life: 51% of undergraduates are from out of state, mostly the South. Students are from 42 states, 17 foreign countries, and Canada. 67% are from public schools. 87% are White. 83% are Protestant; 15% denomination not identified. The average age of freshmen is 18; all undergraduates, 20. 17% do not continue beyond their first year; 68% remain to graduate.

Housing: 1168 students can be accommodated in college housing, which includes single-sex dorms, on-campus apartments, off-campus apartments, and married student housing. In addition, there are language houses. On-campus housing is guaranteed for all 4 years. 85% of students live on campus; of those, 70% remain on campus on weekends. Alcohol is not permitted. Upperclassmen may keep cars.

Activities: There are no fraternities or sororities. There are 45 groups on campus, including art, band, cheerleading, choir, chorale, chorus, computers, debate, drama, ethnic, film, forensics, honors, international, jazz band, literary magazine, missionary, musical theater, newspaper, opera, orchestra, photography, political, professional, radio and TV, religious, social service, student government, and yearbook. Popular campus events include High Bridge Film Festival, Homecoming, Fall Revival, and Missions Conference.

Sports: There are 8 intercollegiate sports for men and 9 for women; 7 intramural sports for men and 7 for women. Facilities include a 1,500-seat gym, athletic fields, tennis courts, indoor swimming pool, indoor/outdoor basketball courts, indoor horseback riding arena, and student center.

Disabled Students: 80% of the campus is accessible. Facilities include wheelchair ramps, elevators, special parking, specially equipped restrooms, special class scheduling, lowered drinking fountains, and lowered telephones.

Services: Counseling and information services are available, as is tutoring in most subjects. There is remedial writing. For students on academic probation, there are special classes and mentors who provide help in such areas as time management and test-taking skills. There is some help available for the visually impaired, such as tapes and agencies that offer aid.

Campus Safety and Security: Measures include 24-hour foot and vehicle patrol, emergency notification system, and security escort services. There are lighted pathways/sidewalks, There are planning forums and a student parking and safety committee.

Programs of Study: Asbury confers B.A., and B.S. degrees. Associate and master's degrees are also awarded. Bachelor's degrees are awarded in AGRICULTURE (equine science), BIOLOGICAL SCIENCE (biochemistry and biology/biological science), BUSINESS (accounting, business administration and management, recreation and leisure services, and sports management), COMMUNICATIONS AND THE ARTS (art, classical languages, communications, creative writing, dramatic arts, English, film, television and digital media, French, journalism, music, Spanish, and theatre acting), COMPUTER AND PHYSICAL SCIENCE (actuarial mathematics, applied mathematics, chemistry, mathematics, and physical sciences), EDUCATION (art education, Christian education, elementary education, English education, foreign languages education, mathematics education, middle school education, music education, physical education, science education, secondary education, and social studies education), ENGINEERING AND ENVIRONMENTAL DESIGN (preengineering), HEALTH PROFESSIONS (exercise science, health science, Pre-Health Studies, and prephysical therapy), SOCIAL SCIENCE (biblical languages, biblical studies, criminal justice, history, ministries, missions, philosophy, political science/government, psychology, religion, social work, sociology, and youth ministry). Media communications and communication arts, teacher education, business, social work, and Christian studies have the largest enrollments.

Required: To graduate with a bachelor's degree, students must complete a minimum of 124 cumulative semester hours, fulfill any liberal arts core requirements, and meet all requirements for at least one chosen major (50% of which must be completed at Asbury University), plus maintain a minimum GPA of 2.0. Traditional undergraduates earning a Bachelor of Arts degree must demonstrate proficiency in foreign language through the third semester college level. Students must complete 12 of their final 21 credit hours with Asbury University.

Special: For-credit internships are available in several academic areas as are opportunities for study abroad in 14 countries. 3-2 engineering degrees are offered with the University of Kentucky. There are 6 national honor societies.

Faculty/Classroom: 51% of faculty are male; 49% are female. 94% teach undergraduates, and 1% do both teaching and research. No introductory courses are taught by graduate students. The average class size in an introductory lecture is 20; in a laboratory is 16; and in a regular course is 18.

Admissions: 66% of the 2013-2014 applicants were accepted. The SAT scores for the 2013-2014 freshman class were: Critical Reading--21% below 500, 41% between 500 and 599, 33% between 600 and 699, and 5% between 700 and 800; Math--24% below 500, 40% between 500 and 599, 32% between 600 and 699, and 4% between 700 and 800. The ACT scores were 17% below 21, 27% between 21 and 23, 26% between 24 and 26, 11% between 27 and 28, and 19% above 28. 47% of the current freshmen were in the top fifth of their class; 75% were in the top two fifths. 9 freshmen graduated first in their class.

Requirements: The SAT or ACT is required. An official high school transcript or the GED is required for all new students and for transfer students with fewer than 30 college credit hours. Applicants should have completed 15 high school academic credits, including 4 units of English, 3 of math, and 2 each of lab science, social studies, and a foreign language. A GPA of 2.5 is required. AP and CLEP credits are accepted.

Procedure: Freshmen are admitted to all sessions. Entrance exams should be taken in the junior year or in the first semester of the senior year. There are early admissions, deferred admissions, and rolling admissions plans. Application deadlines are open. Notification is sent on a rolling basis. applicants were on the 2013 waiting list; were admitted. Applications are accepted online.

Transfer: 52 transfer students enrolled in 2012-2013. Applicants with 18 quarter hours or 12 semester hours of college are considered transfers, and must have an overall minimum GPA of 2.5 and be in good standing at previous institution attended. Transfers with fewer than 30 semester hours of college work must submit a high school transcript. 49 of 124 credits required for the bachelor's degree must be completed at Asbury.

Visiting: There are regularly scheduled orientations for prospective students, including visits, scheduled individually or during planned visitation weekends, in which students stay overnight in dorms, visit classes, attend departmental open houses and financial aid sessions, and participate in chapel and campus events. There are guides for informal visits, visitors may sit in on classes, and stay overnight. To schedule a visit, contact the Admissions Visit Coordinators at visit@asbury.edu.

Financial Aid: In 2013-2014, 79% of all full-time freshmen and 79% of continuing full-time students received some form of financial aid. 79% of all full-time freshmen and 77% of continuing full-time students received need-based aid. The average freshman award was $19,835. Need-based scholarships or need-based grants averaged $14,781; need-based self-help aid (loans and jobs) averaged $4,117; non-need-based athletic scholarships averaged $5,261; and other non-need-based awards and non-need-based scholarships averaged $13,764. The average financial indebtedness of the 2013 graduate was $27,916. The FAFSA and the college's own financial statement are required. The priority date for freshman financial aid applications for fall entry is March 1. The deadline for filing freshman financial aid applications for fall entry is May 1.

International Students: There are 25 international students enrolled. They must take the TOEFL with a minimum score of 550 on the paper-based TOEFL (PBT) or 80 on the Internet-based version (iBT).

Graduates: From July 1, 2012 to June 30, 2013, 323 bachelor's degrees were awarded. The most popular majors were media communication (16%), education (13%), and business management (9%). In an average class, 2% graduate in 3 years or less, 56% graduate in 4 years or less, 63% graduate in 5 years or less, and 64% graduate in 6 years or less.

Admissions Contact: Lisa Harper, Director of Admissions . E-Mail: *admissions@asbury.edu* Web: *http:/www.asbury.edu/admissions/undergraduate*

BELLARMINE UNIVERSITY D-2

Louisville, KY 40205 (502) 272-8131
(800) 274-4723; (502) 272-8002

Full-time: 824 men, 1465 women	**Faculty:** 129; IIA, -$
Part-time: 77 men, 274 women	**Ph.D.s:** 82%
Graduate: 272 men, 520 women	**Student/Faculty:** 17 to 1
Year: semesters, summer session	**Tuition:** $32,140
Application Deadline: February 1	**Room & Board:** $9560
Freshman Class: 6816 applied, 3507 accepted, 577 enrolled	
SAT CR/M: 546/551	**ACT:** 24 **VERY COMPETITIVE**

Bellarmine University, founded in 1950, is an independent Catholic university offering undergraduate and graduate programs in the liberal arts and professional studies. There are 6 undergraduate schools and 6 graduate schools. In addition to regional accreditation, Bellarmine has baccalaureate program accreditation with AACSB and NCATE. The library contains 135,303 volumes, 335,294 microform items, and 5,547 audio/video tapes/CDs/DVDs, and subscribes to 514 periodicals including electronic. Computerized library services include interlibrary loans, database searching, Internet access, and laptop Internet portals. Special learning facilities include a learning resource center, art gallery, radio station, The Thomas Merton Center is the official repository of the collection of materials by and about Thomas Merton (1915-1968 writer and Trappist Monk at Our Lady of Gethsemani Abbey in Kentucky). The 144-acre campus is in a suburban area of Louisville. Including any residence halls, there are 42 buildings.

Student Life: 68% of undergraduates are from Kentucky. Others are from 29 states, 20 foreign countries, and Canada. 63% are from public schools. 81% are white. 49% are Catholic; 25% Protestant. The average age of freshmen is 18; all undergraduates, 21. 22% do not continue beyond their first year; 63% remain to graduate.

Housing: 966 students can be accommodated in college housing, which includes single-sex and coed dorms. In addition, there are honors houses and special-interest houses. On-campus housing is available on a first-come, first-served basis, and is available on a lottery system for upperclassmen. Priority is given to out-of-town students. 53% of students commute. Alcohol is not permitted. All students may keep cars.

Activities: 1% of men belong to 3 national fraternities; 1% of women belong to 1 national sorority. There are 50 groups on campus, including wind ensemble, art, band, cheerleading, chess, choir, chorale, chorus, computers, dance, debate, drama, ethnic, gay, honors, international, jazz band, literary magazine, mock trial team, musical theater, newspaper, opera, pep band, photography, political, professional, radio and TV, religious, social, social service, and student government. Popular campus events include Hillside Concerts, Midnight Breakfast, and Ball on the Belle (Halloween Cruise).

Sports: There are 9 intercollegiate sports for men and 10 for women, and 8 intramural sports for men and 8 for women. Facilities include a 3000-seat basketball and volleyball arena and a fully lit, 2000-seat soccer, field hockey, lacrosse, and track stadium with an artificial turf field and an 8-lane dual-durometer polyurethane poured surface.

Disabled Students: 85% of the campus is accessible. Facilities include wheelchair ramps, elevators, special parking, specially equipped restrooms, special class scheduling, lowered drinking fountains, lowered telephones, and special housing.

Services: Counseling and information services are available, as is tutoring in every subject. The Academic Resource Center provides one-on-one or group tutoring for all 100- and 200-level courses. Disability Services provides note takers, distraction-reduced testing environments, extended time, books on tape, and scribe services.

Campus Safety and Security: Measures include 24-hour foot and vehicle patrol, self-defense education, and security escort services. There are shuttle buses, emergency telephones, lighted pathways/sidewalks, controlled access to dorms/residences, security alert bulletins, CPR-certified security, and security cameras in residence halls and in the parking lot.

Programs of Study: Bellarmine confers B.A., B.S., B.S.H.S., and B.S.N. degrees. Master's and doctoral degrees are also awarded. Bachelor's degrees are awarded in BIOLOGICAL SCIENCE (biochemistry, biology/biological science, biophysics, and molecular biology), BUSINESS (accounting, banking and finance, and business administration and management), COMMUNICATIONS AND THE ARTS (arts administration/management, communications, English, fine arts, languages, music, music technology, Spanish, speech/debate/rhetoric, and studio art), COMPUTER AND PHYSICAL SCIENCE (actuarial science, chemistry, computer science, mathematics, and physics), EDUCATION (elementary education, middle school education, and special education), ENGINEERING AND ENVIRONMENTAL DESIGN (computer engineering, computer technology, and preengineering), HEALTH PROFESSIONS (clinical science, exercise science, medical technology, nursing, predentistry, premedicine, prephysical therapy, preveterinary science, and respiratory therapy), SOCIAL SCIENCE (criminal justice, economics, history, interdisciplinary studies, international studies, liberal arts/general studies, philosophy, political science/government, psychology, sociology, and theological studies). Preprofessional programs, nursing, and accounting are the strongest academically.

Required: In order to graduate, students must complete a minimum of 126 credit hours with a minimum GPA of 2.0. Between 24 and 52 hours are required in the major. All students must fulfill 49 credit hours of core requirements, including English, philosophy, theology, math, social sciences, natural sciences, fine arts, and Western civilization. Required freshman, sophomore, junior, and senior seminars focus on the American experience, transcultural experience, and Catholic social justice. Students in the honors program must complete a senior honors thesis.

Special: Cross-registration may be arranged through Kentuckiana Metroversity, a consortium of colleges in Kentucky and southern Indiana. Bellarmine also offers study abroad in more than 50 countries, internships in most majors, a Washington semester, liberal studies degree, dual majors, accelerated degree programs, credit for life experience, pass/fail options during the junior and senior years, and a marine biology program in the Bahamas. There is also an honors program and the Brown Leadership Program. There are 5 national honor societies and a freshman honors program.

Faculty/Classroom: 52% of faculty are male; 48% are female. 85% teach undergraduates. No introductory courses are taught by graduate students. The average class size in an introductory lecture is 21; in a laboratory is 17; and in a regular course is 21.

Admissions: 51% of a recent year applicants were accepted. The SAT scores for a recent freshman class were: Critical Reading--28% below 500, 46% between 500 and 599, 25% between 600 and 700, and 1% above 700; Math--24% below 500, 48% between 500 and 599, 24% between 600 and 700, and 4% above 700. The ACT scores were 12% below 21, 33% between 21 and 23, 30% between 24 and 26, 12% between 27 and 28, and 11% above 28. 50% of the current freshmen were in the top fifth of their class; 80% were in the top two fifths. 10 freshmen graduated first in their class.

Requirements: The SAT or ACT is required. In addition, high school courses should include 4 years of English, 3 years of math, and 2 years each of science and social studies. 2 years of foreign language is recommended. The GED is accepted. An essay may be requested. A GPA of 2.5 is required. AP and CLEP credits are accepted. Important factors in the admissions decision are recommendations by school officials, advanced placement or honors courses, and extracurricular activities record.

Procedure: Freshmen are admitted fall, spring, and summer. Entrance exams should be taken by December of the senior year. There is a deferred admissions plan. Applications should be filed by February 1 for fall entry, along with a $25 fee. Applications are accepted online.

Transfer: 72 transfer students enrolled in a recent year. Applicants should have a minimum college GPA of 2.0 and submit transcripts from all postsecondary schools attended. 36 of 126 credits required for the bachelor's degree must be completed at Bellarmine.

Visiting: There are regularly scheduled orientations for prospective students, including an admissions and financial aid session, a campus tour, interviews with faculty, and participation in a student panel. There are guides for informal visits, visitors may sit in on classes, and stay overnight. To schedule a visit, contact the Office of Admission.

Financial Aid: In a recent year, 100% of all full-time freshmen and 97% of continuing full-time students received some form of financial aid. 77% of all full-time freshmen and 71% of continuing full-time students received need-based aid. The average freshman award was $26,601. Need-based scholarships or need-based grants averaged $17,560; need-based self-help aid (loans and jobs) averaged $6,538; non-need-based athletic scholarships averaged $7,604; and other non-need-based awards and non-need-based scholarships averaged $17,935. 65% of undergraduate students work part-time. Average annual earnings from campus work are $1000. The average financial indebtedness of the 2011 graduate was $23,925. The FAFSA is required. The priority date for freshman financial aid applications for fall entry is March 1. The deadline for filing freshman financial aid applications for fall entry is May 1.

International Students: There are 51 international students enrolled.

The school actively recruits these students. They must take the TOEFL with a minimum score of 550 on the paper-based TOEFL (PBT) or 80 on the Internet-based version (iBT) or take the MELAB. The SAT or ACT may be used in lieu of the TOEFL.

Graduates: In a recent year, 422 bachelor's degrees were awarded. Most popular majors were nursing (22%), psychology (9%), and business administration (9%). In an average class, 1% graduate in 3 years or less, 51% graduate in 4 years or less, 65% graduate in 5 years or less, and 66% graduate in 6 years or less. Of the recent graduating class, 23% were enrolled in graduate school within 6 months of graduation, and 90% were employed.

Admissions Contact: Dean of Admissions. E-Mail: *admissions@bellarmine.edu* Web: *www.bellarmine.edu*

BEREA COLLEGE E-3

Berea, KY 40404 **(859) 985-3500**
(800) 326-5948; (859) 985-3512

Full-time: 685 men, 916 women **Faculty:** 133; IIB, -$
Part-time: 28 men, 29 women **Ph.D.s:** 89%
Graduate: none **Student/Faculty:** 11 to 1
Year: semesters, summer session **Tuition:** $1070
Application Deadline: **Room & Board:** $6150
Freshman Class: 1620 applied, 551 accepted, 397 enrolled
SAT CR/M/W: 550/550/550 **ACT:** 24 **HIGHLY COMPETITIVE**

Berea College, founded in 1855, is a private liberal arts institution. Berea combines college, federal, and state grants, as well as outside scholarships earned by students, to provide every admitted student with a 4-year, full-tuition scholarship. The college provides a laptop for every student. As part of these scholarship agreements, each student is required to work on campus at least 10 hours weekly while carrying a normal academic load. There is one undergraduate school. In addition to regional accreditation, Berea has baccalaureate program accreditation with NCATE. The library contains 377,794 volumes, 149,004 microform items, and 13,728 audio/video tapes/CDs/DVDs, and subscribes to 1,430 periodicals including electronic. Computerized library services include interlibrary loans, database searching, Internet access, and Wi-Fi capability. Special learning facilities include an art gallery, planetarium, a geology museum. The 140-acre campus is in a suburban area 40 miles south of Lexington, KY. Including any residence halls, there are 46 buildings.

Student Life: 56% of undergraduates are from out of state, mostly the South. Students are from 46 states, and 55 foreign countries. 66% are White; 18% African American. The average age of freshmen is 18; all undergraduates, 21. 18% do not continue beyond their first year; 67% remain to graduate.

Housing: 1389 students can be accommodated in college housing, which includes single-sex dorms, on-campus apartments, and married student housing. In addition, there are special-interest houses, and an Ecovillage. On-campus housing is guaranteed for all 4 years. 84% of students live on campus. Alcohol is not permitted. Some may keep cars.

Activities: There are no fraternities or sororities. There are 75 groups on campus, including art, band, cheerleading, chess, choir, chorus, communications, dance, debate, drama, environmental, ethnic, gay, honors, international, jazz band, literary magazine, newspaper, orchestra, pep band, photography, political, professional, religious, social, social service, and student government. Popular campus events include Mountain Day and Labor Day.

Sports: There are 9 intercollegiate sports for men and 9 for women, and 4 intramural sports for men and 4 for women. Facilities include an indoor swimming pool, 5 racquetball courts, 15 tennis courts, playing fields, a dance studio, a 3-lane indoor walking track, an 8-lane all-weather track, and weight training and cardiovascular exercise rooms.

Disabled Students: 53% of the campus is accessible. Facilities include wheelchair ramps, elevators, special parking, specially equipped restrooms, special class scheduling, lowered drinking fountains, lowered telephones. electronic doors, and a lift chair for the indoor pool.

Services: Counseling and information services are available, as is tutoring in some subjects. There is a reader service for the blind, and remedial math, reading, and writing. The Learning Center supports research, writing, and public speaking across the curriculum, valuing writing in all disciplines including the spoken and written word.

Campus Safety and Security: Measures include 24-hour foot and vehicle patrol, emergency notification system, self-defense education, and security escort services. There are emergency telephones, lighted pathways/sidewalks, ongoing programs on campus safety, theft prevention, assault and rape prevention, fire prevention, defensive driving, and occupational safety including work with hazardous materials.

Programs of Study: Berea confers B.A., and B.S. degrees. Bachelor's degrees are awarded in AGRICULTURE (agriculture), BIOLOGICAL SCIENCE (biology/biological science), BUSINESS (business administration and management), COMMUNICATIONS AND THE ARTS (art, communications, dramatic arts, English, French, German, music, Spanish, and theatre arts), COMPUTER AND PHYSICAL SCIENCE (applied mathematics, chemistry, computer science, mathematics, and physics), EDUCATION (education, elementary education, and physical education), ENGINEERING AND ENVIRONMENTAL DESIGN (industrial engineering technology), HEALTH PROFESSIONS (nursing), SOCIAL SCIENCE (African studies, African American studies, Asian/Oriental studies, child care/child and family studies, economics, history, philosophy, political science/government, psychology, religion, sociology, and women's studies). Business administration, technology and applied design, child and family studies have the largest enrollments.

Required: Berea's curriculum offers the advantage of interdisciplinary general study coupled with intensive study in 31 major fields (some of which have multiple concentrations) and 32 minor fields of study. In all academic disciplines, students acquire knowledge and deepen their understanding of the subject area, while gaining competency in applying the content and methods of inquiry to daily life. A degree is conferred upon the completion of both the General Education curriculum and the curriculum of a selected major, provided the student has earned the minimum number of credits (including 20 outside the major), and has earned a cumulative grade point average (GPA) of 2.00 or higher in all courses, as well as in the major course work. (Please be aware that some academic programs require a GPA higher than the College requirement of 2.00.) To calculate the minimum GPA requirement for a major, the College combines all grades earned in both the discipline (requirements and electives in the major rubric and concentration, if any) and in collateral courses, unless otherwise indicated by a particular program for its major requirements. A minimum of 32 earned course credits (typically 34 in Nursing) is required for graduation, with at least 20 courses taken outside the major discipline.

Special: Students may study abroad in many countries. They can also participate in internships, independent and team-initiated studies. Student-designed majors are available. A 3-2 engineering degree is offered with Washington University (St. Louis)and the University of Kentucky. All students must participate in an on-campus work program 10 to 15 hours per week. There are 19 national honor societies.

Faculty/Classroom: 55% of faculty are male; 45% are female. All teach undergraduates. No introductory courses are taught by graduate students. The average class size in a laboratory is 20 and in a regular course is 20.

Admissions: 34% of the 2013-2014 applicants were accepted. The SAT scores for the 2013-2014 freshman class were: Critical Reading--21% below 500, 43% between 500 and 599, 33% between 600 and 699, and 3% between 700 and 800; Math--16% below 500, 48% between 500 and 599, 31% between 600 and 699, and 5% between 700 and 800; Writing--29% below 500, 43% between 500 and 599, 26% between 600 and 699, and 2% between 700 and 800. The ACT scores were 13% below 21, 26% between 21 and 23, 36% between 24 and 26, 13% between 27 and 28, and 11% above 28. 59% of the current freshmen were in the top fifth of their class; 89% were in the top two fifths. 16 freshmen graduated first in their class.

Requirements: Either the ACT or SAT is required. Applicants should be graduates of an accredited secondary school. The GED is accepted. Home-schooled students are also encouraged to apply. Financial need is a requirement for admission. Berea recommends 4 units in English, 3 in math, and 2 each in foreign language, science, and social studies. AP and CLEP credits are accepted. Important factors in the admissions decision are ability to finance college education, geographical diversity, and advanced placement or honors courses.

Procedure: Freshmen are admitted fall. Entrance exams should be taken during the junior year or early in the senior year. There is a rolling admissions plan. Application deadlines are open. Applications are accepted online.

Transfer: 47 transfer students enrolled in 2012-2013. Applicants must be in good standing at the last college attended, and have a minimum GPA of 2.0. 8 of 33 credits required for the bachelor's degree must be completed at Berea.

Visiting: There are regularly scheduled orientations for prospective students, Student visits consist of an introductory session and a tour of campus and residence halls. For applicants, the visit includes a private interview and/or conversation with an admissions representative. There are guides for informal visits, visitors may sit in on classes, and stay overnight. To schedule a visit, contact the Campus Visit Reservation Center at (800) 326-5948 or (859) 985-3500.

Financial Aid: In 2013-2014, 100% of all full-time freshmen and 100% of continuing full-time students received some form of financial aid. 100% of all full-time freshmen and 100% of continuing full-time students received need-based aid. The average freshman award was $30,465. Need-based scholarships or need-based grants averaged $28,206; and need-based self-help aid (loans and jobs) averaged $1,646. 100% of undergraduate students work part-time. Average annual earnings from campus work are $2248. The average financial indebtedness of the 2013 graduate was $7,403. The FAFSA is required. The priority date for freshman financial aid applications for fall entry is January 31. The deadline for filing freshman financial aid applications for fall entry is March 1.

International Students: There are 120 international students enrolled.

They must take the TOEFL with a minimum score of 500 on the paper-based TOEFL (PBT) or 61 on the Internet-based version (iBT), IELTS, scoring 5 overall and 5 in each exam area; SAT, scoring 1210 (430 Critical Reading); or ACT, scoring 17.

Graduates: From July 1, 2012 to June 30, 2013, 284 bachelor's degrees were awarded. The most popular majors were English (8%), child and family (7%), and business administration (6%). 110 companies recruited on campus in 2012-2013. In an average class, 44% graduate in 4 years or less, 62% graduate in 5 years or less, and 62% graduate in 6 years or less.

Admissions Contact: Luke Hodson, Director of Admissions . E-Mail: *hodsonl@berea.edu* Web: *www.berea.edu*

BRESCIA UNIVERSITY B-3

Owensboro, KY 42301 (270) 685-3131; (877) BRESCIA

Full-time: 199 men, 443 women	**Faculty:** 38
Part-time: 23 men, 136 women	**Ph.D.s:** 70%
Graduate: 6 men, 11 women	**Student/Faculty:** 13 to 1
Year: semesters, summer session	**Tuition:** $18,140
Application Deadline: open	**Room & Board:** $8000

Freshman Class: 5798 applied, 1189 accepted, 163 enrolled
SAT or ACT: required

VERY COMPETITIVE+

Brescia University, founded in 1925 as a women's junior college, became a 4-year, coeducational liberal arts institution in 1950. It is a private school affiliated with the Roman Catholic Church. The university offers certificates, associate, baccalaureate, and master's degrees through on-ground and online classes. There are 6 undergraduate schools and 2 graduate schools. In addition to regional accreditation, Brescia has baccalaureate program accreditation with CSWE and NCATE. The library contains 156,380 volumes, 55,283 microform items, 3,709 audio/video tapes/CDs/DVDs, and subscribes to 27,527 periodicals including electronic. Computerized library services include interlibrary loans and database searching. Special learning facilities include an art gallery. The 6-acre campus is in an urban area 32 miles southeast of Evansville, Indiana, and 125 miles from both Louisville and Nashville. Including any residence halls, there are 19 buildings.

Student Life: 78% of undergraduates are from Kentucky. Others are from 42 states, 8 foreign countries, and Canada. 89% are White. 39% are Catholic; 32% Protestant; 27% claim no religious affiliation. The average age of freshmen is 19; all undergraduates, 26. 33% do not continue beyond their first year.

Housing: 224 students can be accommodated in college housing, which includes single-sex and coed dorms and on-campus apartments. In addition, there are special-interest houses, Honors housing will be made available Fall 2013. On-campus housing is available on a first-come, first-served basis, and is available on a lottery system for upperclassmen. 60% of students commute. Alcohol is not permitted. All students may keep cars.

Activities: There are no fraternities or sororities. There are 25 groups on campus, including philosophy, art, choir, chorus, communications, computers, creative writing, drama, honors, international, literary magazine, musical theater, newspaper, pep band, political, professional, religious, social, social service, and student government. Popular campus events include Homecoming, Opening Year Mass, Founders Convocation and Inaugural Ball.

Sports: There are 7 intercollegiate sports for men and 8 for women, and 5 intramural sports for men and 5 for women. Facilities include a gym, two tennis courts, a weight room, a game room, a cardiovascular workout room, a racquetball court, a batting cage, a baseball field and soccer field.

Disabled Students: 95% of the campus is accessible. Facilities include wheelchair ramps, elevators, special parking, specially equipped restrooms, lowered drinking fountains, and lowered telephones.

Services: Counseling and information services are available, as is tutoring in most subjects. There is remedial math, reading, and writing.

Campus Safety and Security: Measures include emergency notification system and security escort services. There are emergency telephones, lighted pathways/sidewalks, night security.

Programs of Study: Brescia confers B.A., B.S., and B.S.W. degrees. Associate and master's degrees are also awarded. Bachelor's degrees are awarded in BIOLOGICAL SCIENCE (biochemistry and biology/biological science), BUSINESS (accounting, banking and finance, business administration and management, business economics, and human resources), COMMUNICATIONS AND THE ARTS (art, English, graphic design, Spanish, and theatre arts), COMPUTER AND PHYSICAL SCIENCE (chemistry, computer science, mathematics, and physical sciences), EDUCATION (art education, early childhood education, education of the mentally handicapped, elementary education, and special education), HEALTH PROFESSIONS (medical laboratory technology, medical technology, and speech pathology/audiology), SOCIAL SCIENCE (addiction studies, history, liberal arts/general studies, pastoral studies, psychology, religion, social studies, and social work). Education, business, and English are the strongest academically. Business, social work, and education have the largest enrollments.

Required: All students must earn 128 credit hours, including 42 upper-division hours, and 30 or more hours in the major, while maintaining an overall GPA of 2.0 and 2.5 in the major. Distribution requirements include 18 hours in aesthetics, language, and literature, 12 in social science, 9 each in fine arts, science, and math, 6 in religious studies, and 3 in philosophy. Students must also demonstrate computer competency.

Special: Brescia offers a combined engineering degree with the University of Kentucky and the University of Louisville. Work-study programs, student-designed majors, nondegree study, dual majors, study abroad in Mexico, an internship in professional writing, pass/fail options and cross-registration with Kentucky Wesleyan are available. The Weekend College offers four 9-week modules of study. There are 2 national honor societies and a freshman honors program.

Faculty/Classroom: 47% of faculty are male; 53% are female. All teach undergraduates. No introductory courses are taught by graduate students. The average class size in an introductory lecture is 14; in a laboratory is 10; and in a regular course is 12.

Admissions: 21% of the 2013-2014 applicants were accepted. The ACT scores were 20% below 21, 45% between 21 and 23, 17% between 24 and 26, 15% between 27 and 28, and 3% above 28.

Requirements: The SAT or ACT is required. Essays and recommendations are helpful. High school units should include 4 of English, 3 of math, and 2 each in social studies, science, foreign language, fine arts, and computer science. Applications are accepted online at the university's web site. A GPA of 2.5 is required. AP and CLEP credits are accepted. Important factors in the admissions decision are advanced placement or honors courses and recommendations by school officials.

Procedure: Freshmen are admitted to all sessions. Entrance exams should be taken at the end of the junior year. There is a rolling admissions plan. Application deadlines are open. The fall 2013 application fee was $25. Applications are accepted online.

Transfer: 120 transfer students enrolled in 2012-2013. Transfer students must have a minimum GPA of 2.0. 42 of 128 credits required for the bachelor's degree must be completed at Brescia.

Visiting: There are regularly scheduled orientations for prospective students, including spring and fall open houses for freshmen and a spring transfer open house. There are guides for informal visits, visitors may sit in on classes, and stay overnight. To schedule a visit, contact The Office of Admissions.

Financial Aid: 100% of undergraduate students work part-time. Brescia is a member of CSS. The FAFSA is required. The deadline for filing freshman financial aid applications for fall entry is March 1.

International Students: The school actively recruits these students. They must take the TOEFL. They must also take the SAT or ACT.

Graduates: From July 1, 2012 to June 30, 2013, 87 bachelor's degrees were awarded. The most popular majors were social work (25%), business (16%), and communication sciences and disorders (10%). In an average class, 17% graduate in 4 years or less, 26% graduate in 5 years or less, and 32% graduate in 6 years or less.

Admissions Contact: Christy Rohner, Director of Admissions. E-Mail: *admissions@brescia.edu* Web: *www.brescia.edu*

CAMPBELLSVILLE UNIVERSITY D-3

Campbellsville, KY 42718 (270) 789-5220
(800) 264-6014; (270) 789-5071

Full-time: 875 men, 954 women	**Faculty:** 146
Part-time: 392 men, 757 women	**Ph.D.s:** 67%
Graduate: 182 men, 271 women	**Student/Faculty:** 14 to 1
Year: semesters, summer session	**Tuition:** $21,600
Application Deadline:	**Room & Board:** $7120

Freshman Class: 2477 applied, 1651 accepted, 579 enrolled
SAT: recommended **ACT:** 21 **COMPETITIVE**

Campbellsville University, founded in 1906, is a private, comprehensive institution affiliated with the Kentucky Baptist Convention. There are 7 undergraduate schools and 8 graduate schools. In addition to regional accreditation, Campbellsville has baccalaureate program accreditation with NASM. The 2 libraries contain 108,000 volumes, 24,000 microform items, and 8,000 audio/video tapes/CDs/DVDs, and subscribe to 360 periodicals including electronic. Computerized library services include interlibrary loans, database searching, and Internet access. Special learning facilities include an art gallery, radio station, TV station, a teacher resource center, the Kentuckiana Collection, Clay Hill Memorial Forest, and the American Civil War Institute. The 90-acre campus is in a small town 85 miles southwest of Lexington and 85 miles southeast of Louisville. Including any residence halls, there are 56 buildings.

Student Life: 84% of undergraduates are from Kentucky. Others are from 33 states, 36 foreign countries, and Canada. 95% are from public schools. 80% are White; 11% African American. 60% are Protestant; 12% claim no religious affiliation. The average age of freshmen is 19; all undergraduates, 25. 30% do not continue beyond their first year; 42% remain to graduate.

Housing: 1044 students can be accommodated in college housing, which

includes single-sex dorms, on-campus apartments, and married student housing. In addition, there are honors houses and special-interest houses. On-campus housing is guaranteed for all 4 years. 64% of students commute. Alcohol is not permitted. All students may keep cars.

Activities: There are no fraternities or sororities. There are 45 groups on campus, including art, band, cheerleading, choir, chorale, chorus, computers, dance, drama, environmental, ethnic, honors, international, jazz band, literary magazine, marching band, musical theater, newspaper, opera, orchestra, pep band, photography, political, professional, radio and TV, religious, social, social service, student government, and symphony. Popular campus events include Valentine Banquet, a Christmas Celebration, and Heritage Day.

Sports: There are 9 intercollegiate sports for men and 9 for women, and 10 intramural sports for men and 10 for women. Facilities include a swimming pool, a 1700-seat gym, a football stadium, a baseball field, an intramural activities center with skating facilities and large game rooms, and softball and soccer fields, and an indoor practice field.

Disabled Students: 85% of the campus is accessible. Facilities include wheelchair ramps, elevators, special parking, specially equipped restrooms, special class scheduling, lowered drinking fountains, lowered telephones, and widened doorways.

Services: Counseling and information services are available, as is tutoring in most subjects. There is remedial math, reading, and writing. There is also an AIDS education program and a study skills program.

Campus Safety and Security: Measures include 24-hour foot and vehicle patrol, emergency notification system, self-defense education, and security escort services. There are emergency telephones, lighted pathways/sidewalks, and controlled access to dorms/residences.

Programs of Study: Campbellsville confers B.A., B.S., B.M., B.S.B.A., B.S.Med.Tech. and B.S.W. degrees. Associate and master's degrees are also awarded. Bachelor's degrees are awarded in BIOLOGICAL SCIENCE (biology/biological science), BUSINESS (accounting, business administration and management, business economics, marketing management, office supervision and management, and sports management), COMMUNICATIONS AND THE ARTS (art, communications, English, music, music performance, theatre arts, and voice), COMPUTER AND PHYSICAL SCIENCE (chemistry, computer science, information sciences and systems, and mathematics), EDUCATION (athletic training, early childhood education, elementary education, health education, middle school education, music education, physical education, recreation education, social science education, and teaching English as a second/foreign language (TESOL/TEFOL)), ENGINEERING AND ENVIRONMENTAL DESIGN (preengineering), HEALTH PROFESSIONS (exercise science, medical laboratory technology, nursing, predentistry, premedicine, prepharmacy, and sports medicine), SOCIAL SCIENCE (biblical studies, Christian studies, criminal justice, economics, history, political science/government, prelaw, psychology, religious education, religious music, social work, sociology, and youth ministry). Biology, chemistry and music are the strongest academically. Elementary education, business administration and social work have the largest enrollments.

Required: All candidates must be of good moral character. All students must complete a minimum of 128 semester hours, including 30 in the major, 21 in the minor, and 51 in general education courses. The minimum GPA is 2.5 for education majors, 2.1 for all others. All students must fulfill an English composition requirement.

Special: Legislative and public administration internships, a Washington semester, and federal work-study programs are available. The university also offers a semester in London program, a 3-2 engineering degree with the University of Kentucky, dual majors, credit by exam, credit for life, military, and work experience, non-degree study, and pass/fail options. There is a freshman honors program.

Faculty/Classroom: 51% of faculty are male; 49% are female. All teach undergraduates. No introductory courses are taught by graduate students. The average class size in an introductory lecture is 24; in a laboratory is 12; and in a regular course is 17.

Admissions: 67% of the 2013-2014 applicants were accepted. The ACT scores were 46% below 21, 27% between 21 and 23, 15% between 24 and 26, 6% between 27 and 28, and 6% above 28. 46% of the current freshmen were in the top fifth of their class; 74% were in the top two fifths.

Requirements: The SAT may be substituted for the ACT. Applicants must be graduates of an accredited secondary school with a GPA of 2.0. The GED is accepted. An interview is recommended. A GPA of 2.0 is required. AP and CLEP credits are accepted. Important factors in the admissions decision are evidence of special talent, leadership record, and advanced placement or honors courses.

Procedure: Freshmen are admitted to all sessions. Entrance exams should be taken no later than February of the senior year. There are deferred admissions and rolling admissions plans. Check with the school for current application deadlines. The fall 2013 application fee was $20. Applications are accepted online.

Transfer: 239 transfer students enrolled in 2012-2013. Of the 128 credits needed to graduate, all students must complete one third of the credits required for the major and the minor at the university. The last year must be completed in residence. 30 of 120 credits required for the bachelor's degree must be completed at Campbellsville.

Visiting: There are regularly scheduled orientations for prospective students, consisting of visitation days held in October, February and April. There are guides for informal visits, visitors may sit in on classes, and stay overnight. To schedule a visit, contact the Admissions Office.

Financial Aid: In 2013-2014, 95% of all full-time freshmen and 94% of continuing full-time students received some form of financial aid. 87% of all full-time freshmen and 83% of continuing full-time students received need-based aid. 44% of undergraduate students work part-time. Average annual earnings from campus work are $1700. The average financial indebtedness of the 2013 graduate was $18,132. The FAFSA is required. The priority date for freshman financial aid applications for fall entry is February 20. The deadline for filing freshman financial aid applications for fall entry is July 31.

International Students: There are 159 international students enrolled. The school actively recruits these students. They must take the TOEFL. They must also take the SAT or ACT, scoring 19.

Graduates: From July 1, 2012 to June 30, 2013, 325 bachelor's degrees were awarded. The most popular majors were education (18%), business (16%), and religion (16%). In an average class, 42% graduate in 6 years or less.

Admissions Contact: David Walters, Vice President for Admissions. E-Mail: *admissions@campbellsville.edu* Web: *www.campbellsville.edu*

CENTRE COLLEGE — D-3

Danville, KY 40422 (859) 238-5350
(800) 423-6236; (859) 238-5373

Full-time: 539 men, 647 women	**Faculty:** 102; IIB, av$
Part-time: 1 men, 2 women	**Ph.D.s:** 98%
Graduate: n/av	**Student/Faculty:** 12 to 1
Year: semesters	**Tuition:** $28,500
Application Deadline: February 1	**Room & Board:** $7500
Freshman Class: 2159 applied, 1312 accepted, 316 enrolled	
SAT CR/M: 625/615	**ACT:** 28 **HIGHLY COMPETITIVE+**

Centre College, founded in 1819 by the Presbyterian Church, is a private liberal arts and sciences institution. The library contains 361,512 volumes, 56,755 microform items, and 4,357 audio/video tapes/CDs/DVDs, and subscribes to 19,397 periodicals including electronic. Computerized library services include interlibrary loans, database searching, Internet access, and laptop Internet portals. Special learning facilities include a learning resource center, art gallery, natural history museum, radio station, TV station, a performing arts center. The 150-acre campus is in a small town 35 miles southwest of Lexington, KY and 80 miles southeast of Louisville, KY. Including any residence halls, there are 67 buildings.

Student Life: 56% of undergraduates are from Kentucky. Others are from 40 states, 11 foreign countries, and Canada. 64% are from public schools. 90% are white. 52% are Protestant; 23% Catholic; 23% claim no religious affiliation. The average age of freshmen is 18; all undergraduates, 20. 5% do not continue beyond their first year; 80% remain to graduate.

Housing: 1050 students can be accommodated in college housing, which includes single-sex and coed dorms and on-campus apartments. In addition, there are special-interest houses, fraternity houses, sorority houses, an International Student house. On-campus housing is guaranteed for all 4 years. 95% of students live on campus; of those, 90% remain on campus on weekends. All students may keep cars.

Activities: 46% of men belong to 4 national fraternities; 52% of women belong to 4 national sororities. There are 105 groups on campus, including art, band, cheerleading, choir, chorale, chorus, computers, dance, debate, drama, environmental, ethnic, film, forensics, gay, honors, international, jazz band, literary magazine, musical theater, newspaper, orchestra, pep band, photography, political, professional, radio and TV, religious, social, social service, student government, and yearbook. Popular campus events include Carnival, Honors Convocation, and Honor Walk.

Sports: There are 9 intercollegiate sports for men and 10 for women, and 8 intramural sports for men and 8 for women. Facilities include a complex with a 1500-seat gym, 3 basketball courts, 2 volleyball courts, training room, game room, sauna, weight room, fitness center, and racquetball/handball courts. There is also a 2500-seat stadium, tennis courts, and playing fields for football, track, baseball, softball, soccer, field hockey, and other sports. The natatorium has a 25-yard, 6-lane swimming pool. Golf teams compete at the local country club.

Disabled Students: 70% of the campus is accessible. Facilities include wheelchair ramps, elevators, special parking, specially equipped restrooms, special class scheduling, lowered drinking fountains, lowered telephones, special housing, and electronic doors.

Services: Counseling and information services are available, as is tutoring in most subjects. There is a reader service for the blind.

Campus Safety and Security: Measures include 24-hour foot and vehicle patrol, emergency notification system, self-defense education, and

security escort services. There are emergency telephones, lighted pathways/sidewalks, controlled access to dorms/residences, and a working relationship with outside agencies.

Programs of Study: Centre confers B.A. and B.S. degrees. Bachelor's degrees are awarded in BIOLOGICAL SCIENCE (biochemistry, biology/biological science, and molecular biology), COMMUNICATIONS AND THE ARTS (art history and appreciation, dramatic arts, English, fine arts, French, German, music, and Spanish), COMPUTER AND PHYSICAL SCIENCE (chemical physics, chemistry, computer science, mathematics, physical chemistry, and physics), EDUCATION (elementary education), SOCIAL SCIENCE (anthropology, classical/ancient civilization, economics, history, international relations, philosophy, political science/government, psychobiology, psychology, religion, and sociology). Biology, history, and psychology are the strongest academically and have the largest enrollments.

Required: All students must earn an overall GPA of 2.0 and complete a minimum of 111 credit hours. Students also must demonstrate competency in writing, foreign language, and math plus 1 course beyond basic skills in math, foreign language, or computer science. A freshman humanities program and a freshman seminar must be completed. Core curriculum, requirements include 2 courses each in the humanities or art from the aesthetic context, the scientific/technological context; the social context; and the fundamental questions context. 2 phys ed courses must be completed by the end of sophomore year.

Special: Centre offers internships, study abroad in 12 countries, a Washington semester through American University, work-study, and a 3-2 engineering degree with Vanderbilt University, Washington University at St. Louis, Columbia University, and the University of Kentucky. Student-designed majors, interdisciplinary majors including chemical physics, secondary education certification, and pre-law, pre-business, and pre-medicine programs are available. Pass/fail options also are available. There are 8 national honor societies, including Phi Beta Kappa.

Faculty/Classroom: 64% of faculty are male; 37% are female. All teach and do research. No introductory courses are taught by graduate students. The average class size in an introductory lecture is 25; in a laboratory is 15; and in a regular course is 19.

Admissions: In a recent year, 61% of applicants were accepted. The SAT scores for a recent freshman class were: Critical Reading--6% below 500, 31% between 500 and 599, 38% between 600 and 700, and 25% above 700; Math--6% below 500, 28% between 500 and 599, 56% between 600 and 700, and 10% above 700. The ACT scores were 2% below 21, 6% between 21 and 23, 25% between 24 and 26, 22% between 27 and 28, and 45% above 28. 79% of the current freshmen were in the top fifth of their class; 95% were in the top two fifths. There were 8 National Merit finalists. 29 freshmen graduated first in their class.

Requirements: The SAT or ACT and ACT Writing Test are recommended. Students should have completed a minimum of 15 academic credits, including 4 years each in English and math, 3 years each in science and social studies, 2 years in foreign language, and 1 year in an art- or music-related course. An essay is required, and an interview is strongly recommended. AP credits are accepted. Important factors in the admissions decision are advanced placement or honors courses, extracurricular activities record, and recommendations by school officials.

Procedure: Freshmen are admitted fall. Entrance exams should be taken by February of the senior year. There is a deferred admissions plan. Applications should be filed by February 1 for fall entry. The fall application fee was $40. Notification of early decision is sent January 15; regular decision, March 15. 186 applicants were on the waiting list; 19 were admitted. Applications are accepted online.

Transfer: 6 transfer students enrolled in a recent year. Applicants for transfer must have all previous college transcripts on file and a recommendation from the dean of the most recent college attended. If the student has completed fewer than 2 years of college work, high school records must also be submitted. 45 of 111 credits required for the bachelor's degree must be completed at Centre.

Visiting: There are regularly scheduled orientations for prospective students, including a campus tour, an interview, pre-tour, and faculty appointments. There are guides for informal visits, visitors may sit in on classes, and stay overnight. To schedule a visit, contact the Office of Admission.

Financial Aid: In a recent year, 95% of all full-time freshmen and 96% of continuing full-time students received some form of financial aid. 58% of all full-time freshmen and 56% of continuing full-time students received need-based aid. The average freshman award was $22,193. Need-based scholarships or need-based grants averaged $19,673 ($28,000 maximum); and need-based self-help aid (loans and jobs) averaged $4,599 ($5,300 maximum). 24% of undergraduate students work part-time. Average annual earnings from campus work are $1750. The average financial indebtedness of the 2011 graduate was $15,700. Centre is a member of CSS. The FAFSA and the college's own financial statement are required. The priority date for freshman financial aid applications for fall entry is February 15. The deadline for filing freshman financial aid applications for fall entry is March 1.

International Students: There are 25 international students enrolled. They must take the TOEFL, or may submit SAT or ACT scores.

Graduates: In a recent year, 270 bachelor's degrees were awarded. The most popular majors were English (13%), anthropology/sociology (13%), and Spanish (12%). 21 companies recruited on campus in a recent year. In an average class, 80% graduate in 4 years or less, 80% graduate in 5 years or less, and 80% graduate in 6 years or less. Of a recent graduating class, 30% were enrolled in graduate school within 6 months of graduation, and 63% were employed.

Admissions Contact: Director of Admissions. A campus DVD is available. E-Mail: *admission@centre.edu* Web: *www.centre.edu*

EASTERN KENTUCKY UNIVERSITY — E-3

Richmond, KY 40475 — (859) 622-2106; (800) 465-9191; (859) 622-3024

Full-time: 4653 men, 6345 women	**Faculty:** 584; IIA, -$
Part-time: 898 men, 1763 women	**Ph.D.s:** 66%
Graduate: 691 men, 1489 women	**Student/Faculty:** 19 to 1
Year: semesters, summer session	**Tuition:** $6,700 ($17,700)
Application Deadline: August 1	**Room & Board:** $6400
Freshman Class: n/av	
ACT: required	

COMPETITIVE

Eastern Kentucky University, established in 1906, is a public, state-supported institution offering degree programs in the arts and sciences, business, environmental studies, health fields, education, and public service occupations. There are 5 undergraduate schools and 1 graduate school. In addition to regional accreditation, EKU has baccalaureate program accreditation with AACSB, ADA, AHEA, CSWE, FIDER, NASM, NCATE, NLN, and NRPA. The 3 libraries contain 764,662 volumes, 1.3 million microform items, and 12,209 audio/video tapes/CDs/DVDs, and subscribe to 19,033 periodicals including electronic. Computerized library services include interlibrary loans, database searching, and Internet access. Special learning facilities include a learning resource center, art gallery, natural history museum, planetarium, radio station, TV station, a law enforcement complex that includes a training tank for underwater rescue and recovery. The 628-acre campus is in a small town 20 miles south of Lexington, KY. Including any residence halls, there are 98 buildings.

Student Life: 87% of undergraduates are from Kentucky. Others are from 43 states, 32 foreign countries, and Canada. 90% are from public schools. 91% are white. The average age of freshmen is 19; all undergraduates, 23. 35% do not continue beyond their first year; 37% remain to graduate.

Housing: 5260 students can be accommodated in college housing, which includes single-sex and coed dorms, on-campus apartments, and married student housing. In addition, there are honors houses, special-interest houses, and special accommodations for senior home economics students. On-campus housing is guaranteed for all 4 years. 71% of students commute. Alcohol is not permitted. All students may keep cars.

Activities: There are 140 groups on campus, including art, band, cheerleading, choir, chorale, chorus, computers, dance, debate, drama, drill team, ethnic, film, gay, honors, international, jazz band, marching band, musical theater, newspaper, orchestra, pep band, photography, political, professional, radio and TV, religious, social service, student government, and symphony. Popular campus events include Hanging of the Greens at Christmas, International Month, and fraternity/sorority competitions.

Sports: There are 8 intercollegiate sports for men and 8 for women, and 12 intramural sports for men and 12 for women. Facilities include a dance studio, 5 gyms, 1 outdoor and 2 indoor swimming pools, 19 outdoor hard-court and 4 indoor tennis courts, handball and racquetball courts, training rooms, a martial arts room, a wellness center, a 7000-seat basketball arena, a 20,000-seat stadium, an 8-lane outdoor track, a field hockey area, an 18-hole golf course, fields for baseball, softball, soccer, weight facilities, and a conditioning center.

Disabled Students: 85% of the campus is accessible. Facilities include wheelchair ramps, elevators, special parking, specially equipped restrooms, special class scheduling, lowered drinking fountains, and lowered telephones.

Services: Counseling and information services are available, as is tutoring in some subjects, math, English, and reading There is a reader service for the blind, and remedial math, reading, and writing. Tutoring is available in other fields upon request.

Campus Safety and Security: Measures include 24-hour foot and vehicle patrol, emergency notification system, self-defense education, and security escort services. There are shuttle buses, emergency telephones, lighted pathways/sidewalks, 16 crime-prevention programs.

Programs of Study: EKU confers B.A., B.S., B.B.A., B.F.A., B.I.S., B.M., B.M.Ed., B.S.N., and B.S.W. degrees. Associate and master's degrees are also awarded. Bachelor's degrees are awarded in AGRICULTURE (agriculture, horticulture, and wildlife management), BIOLOGICAL SCIENCE (biology/biological science and microbiology), BUSINESS (accounting, banking and finance, business administration and management, and marketing/retailing/merchandising), COMMUNICATIONS AND THE ARTS (art, broadcasting, dramatic arts, English, French, journalism, music, performing arts, public relations, Spanish, and speech/

debate/rhetoric), COMPUTER AND PHYSICAL SCIENCE (chemistry, computer programming, computer science, geology, mathematics, and statistics), EDUCATION (art education, business education, education of the deaf and hearing impaired, elementary education, foreign languages education, health education, home economics education, industrial arts education, middle school education, music education, physical education, secondary education, special education, and technical education), ENGINEERING AND ENVIRONMENTAL DESIGN (airline piloting and navigation, construction technology, environmental science, interior design, and manufacturing technology), HEALTH PROFESSIONS (environmental health science, health care administration, nursing, and occupational therapy), SOCIAL SCIENCE (anthropology, child care/child and family studies, corrections, dietetics, economics, fire protection, forensic studies, geography, history, paralegal studies, philosophy, political science/government, psychology, social work, and sociology). Occupational therapy, psychology, and nursing are the strongest academically. Education, nursing, and law enforcement have the largest enrollments.

Required: All students must complete 51 credit hours of general education requirements, including courses in phys ed, health, English, natural science, social science, math, and the humanities. Students must complete a total of 128 credit hours, including 45 to 60 credits in the major, with a minimum GPA of 2.0.

Special: EKU offers cooperative programs with all academic colleges, internships, study abroad in various European countries, and a 3-2 engineering degree with The University of Kentucky or Auburn University. Students may opt for credit by exam, non-degree study, pass/fail options, student-designed and dual majors, and a general studies degree. There are 23 national honor societies, including Phi Beta Kappa, a freshman honors program, and 1 departmental honors program.

Faculty/Classroom: 49% of faculty are male; 51% are female. 98% teach undergraduates. No introductory courses are taught by graduate students. The average class size in an introductory lecture is 30; in a laboratory is 15; and in a regular course is 25.

Requirements: The ACT is required. A GPA of 2.0 is required. AP and CLEP credits are accepted. Important factors in the admissions decision are evidence of special talent, extracurricular activities record, and leadership record.

Procedure: Freshmen are admitted to all sessions. Entrance exams should be taken prior to enrollment. There is a rolling admissions plan. Applications should be filed by August 1 for fall entry, along with a $30 fee. Applications are accepted online.

Transfer: 952 transfer students enrolled in 2010-2011. Applicants must have a 2.0 cumulative GPA from all accredited institutions previously attended and must not have been dismissed. 30 of 128 credits required for the bachelor's degree must be completed at EKU.

Visiting: There are regularly scheduled orientations for prospective students, consisting of a 1-day program during the summer prior to fall enrollment. There are guides for informal visits, visitors may sit in on classes, and stay overnight. To schedule a visit, contact the Admissions Office.

Financial Aid: EKU is a member of CSS. The CSS/Profile and the college's own financial statement are required. The deadline for filing freshman financial aid applications for fall entry is April 15.

International Students: There are 159 international students enrolled. The school actively recruits these students. They must take the TOEFL. They must also take the ACT, scoring 21, or the SAT for those applicants from states where the SAT is dominant.

Graduates: From July 1, 2010 to June 30, 2011, 1979 bachelor's degrees were awarded. The most popular majors were criminal justice and police studies (9%), nursing (9%), and curriculum and instruction (9%).

Admissions Contact: Stephen A. Byrn, Director of Admissions. E-Mail: *admissions@eku.edu* Web: *www.eku.edu*

GEORGETOWN COLLEGE D-2

Georgetown, KY 40324

(502) 863-8009
(800) 788-9985; (502) 868-7733

Full-time: 494 men, 593 women	**Faculty:** 110; IIB, --$
Part-time: 14 men, 15 women	**Ph.D.s:** 94%
Graduate: 97 men, 330 women	**Student/Faculty:** 9 to 1
Year: semesters, summer session	**Tuition:** $30,770
Application Deadline: August 1	**Room & Board:** $7920

Freshman Class: 1735 applied, 1426 accepted, 237 enrolled

SAT CR/M: 515/521 **ACT:** 23 **COMPETITIVE**

Georgetown College, dating back to 1787 and chartered in 1829, is a small residential liberal arts college distinguished by a combination of respected, rigorous undergraduate and graduate programs, an array of opportunities for involvement and leadership, a commitment to Christian values and its distinctive heritage. There is one graduate school. In addition to regional accreditation, Georgetown has baccalaureate program accreditation with NCATE. The library contains 185,592 volumes, 189,600 microform items, and 10,465 audio/video tapes/CDs/DVDs, and subscribes to 42,015 periodicals including electronic. Computerized library services include interlibrary loans, database searching, Internet access, and Wi-Fi capability. Special learning facilities include an art gallery, planetarium, and radio station. The 104-acre campus is in a suburban area 12 miles north of Lexington. Including any residence halls, there are 40 buildings.

Student Life: 78% of undergraduates are from Kentucky. Others are from 25 states, and 12 foreign countries. 85% are from public schools. 83% are White. 75% are Protestant; 12% Catholic; 12% claim no religious affiliation. The average age of freshmen is 18; all undergraduates, 20. 25% do not continue beyond their first year; 60% remain to graduate.

Housing: 1331 students can be accommodated in college housing, which includes single-sex dorms, on-campus apartments, and married student housing. In addition, there are fraternity houses and sorority houses. On-campus housing is guaranteed for all 4 years. 91% of students live on campus; of those, 50% remain on campus on weekends. Alcohol is not permitted. All students may keep cars.

Activities: 52% of men belong to 1 local and 4 national fraternities; 44% of women belong to 4 national sororities. There are 101 groups on campus, including art, band, cheerleading, choir, chorale, chorus, computers, dance, drama, environmental, ethnic, forensics, honors, international, jazz band, literary magazine, musical theater, newspaper, opera, pep band, photography, political, professional, radio and TV, religious, social, social service, and student government. Popular campus events include Festival of Song, Parents Day, and Hanging of the Green.

Sports: There are 8 intercollegiate sports for men and 9 for women, and 11 intramural sports for men and 11 for women. Facilities include a 3000-seat stadium, 8 tennis courts, soccer, baseball, football, softball and intramural fields, a 1550-seat gym, racquetball courts, a training room, and a fitness center housing a Nautilus area, a weight lifting area, basketball courts, recreation room, and dressing rooms.

Disabled Students: 70% of the campus is accessible. Facilities include wheelchair ramps, elevators, special parking, specially equipped restrooms, special class scheduling, and lowered drinking fountains.

Services: Counseling and information services are available, as is tutoring in every subject.

Campus Safety and Security: Measures include 24-hour foot and vehicle patrol, emergency notification system, self-defense education, and security escort services. There are shuttle buses, emergency telephones, lighted pathways/sidewalks, and controlled access to dorms/residences.

Programs of Study: Georgetown confers B.A., B.S., B.M. and B.M.E. degrees. Master's degrees are also awarded. Bachelor's degrees are awarded in BIOLOGICAL SCIENCE (biology/biological science), BUSINESS (accounting, banking and finance, business administration and management, business economics, international business management, management information systems, and marketing/retailing/merchandising), COMMUNICATIONS AND THE ARTS (art, communications, dramatic arts, English, French, German, music, performing arts, and Spanish), COMPUTER AND PHYSICAL SCIENCE (chemistry, computer science, mathematics, and physics), EDUCATION (athletic training, elementary education, foreign languages education, middle school education, and music education), ENGINEERING AND ENVIRONMENTAL DESIGN (environmental science), HEALTH PROFESSIONS (exercise science), SOCIAL SCIENCE (American studies, European studies, history, interdisciplinary studies, liberal arts/general studies, philosophy, political science/government, psychology, religion, religious music, safety and security technology, and sociology). Biology and English are the strongest academically. Kinesiology, business administration and communications have the largest enrollments.

Required: All students are required to complete the Foundations and Core curriculum, a general education program including courses from several disciplines across campus emphasizing writing, quantitative skills, world languages, wellness, science and inquiry, religion, and culture. A minimum of 120 semester hours, including 33 to 72 in the major, with a minimum GPA of 2.0, is required to graduate, as is successful completion of a comprehensive exam in the major.

Special: Georgetown offers cross-registration with the University of Kentucky Air Force ROTC for aerospace studies. A 3-2 engineering degree is available with the University of Kentucky. Internships, co-op programs in math and computer science, study abroad in 28 countries, work-study programs, dual and student-designed majors, and pass/fail options are available. Interdisciplinary majors include business administration/communication arts and business administration/ethics. A dual degree is offered in engineering and nursing. There are 20 national honor societies and a freshman honors program.

Faculty/Classroom: 54% of faculty are male; 46% are female. 92% teach undergraduates. No introductory courses are taught by graduate students. The average class size in an introductory lecture is 16 and in a regular course is 14.

Admissions: 82% of the 2013-2014 applicants were accepted. The SAT scores for the 2013-2014 freshman class were: Critical Reading--39% below 500, 27% between 500 and 599, 28% between 600 and 699, and 6% between 700 and 800; Math--44% below 500, 27% between 500 and 599, 6% between 600 and 699, and 6% between 700 and 800. The ACT scores were 23% below 21, 32% between 21 and 23, 24% between 24 and 26, 6% between 27 and 28, and 8% above 28. 40% of the current freshmen were in the top fifth of their class; 69% were in the top two fifths. 13 freshmen graduated first in their class.

Requirements: The SAT or ACT is required. Applicants should have completed 4 high school credits in English, 3 each in math and science, 2 in a foreign language, and 1 each in social studies and history, with additional credits in electives strongly encouraged. A student essay is required; Kentucky high school applicants may substitute a writing portfolio entry. A GPA of 2.0 is required. AP and CLEP credits are accepted. Important factors in the admissions decision are advanced placement or honors courses, evidence of special talent, and leadership record.

Procedure: Freshmen are admitted to all sessions. Entrance exams should be taken from December of the junior year through October of the senior year. There are early decision, early admissions, deferred admissions, and rolling admissions plans. Early decision applications should be filed by October 15; regular applications, by August 1 for fall entry, along with a $30 fee. Notification is sent on a rolling basis. Applications are accepted online.

Transfer: 45 transfer students enrolled in 2012-2013. Applicants must be in good standing at the school most recently attended and must submit official college and high school transcripts.

Visiting: There are regularly scheduled orientations for prospective students, consisting of campus tours and information on admissions, financial assistance, student life, academic programs, and meetings with faculty. There are guides for informal visits, visitors may sit in on classes, and stay overnight. To schedule a visit, contact Bethany Roll Farley at (800) 788-9985.

Financial Aid: In 2013-2014, 100% of all full-time freshmen and 100% of continuing full-time students received some form of financial aid. 86% of all full-time freshmen and 85% of continuing full-time students received need-based aid. The average freshman award was $30,405. Need-based scholarships or need based grants averaged $21,767 ($39,690 maximum); need-based self-help aid (loans and jobs) averaged $4,375 ($8,500 maximum); non-need-based athletic scholarships averaged $7,089 ($29,147 maximum); and other non-need-based awards and non-need-based scholarships averaged $17,169 ($38,690 maximum). 61% of undergraduate students work part-time. Average annual earnings from campus work are $937. The average financial indebtedness of the 2013 graduate was $26,730. The FAFSA is required. The priority date for freshman financial aid applications for fall entry is February 1. The deadline for filing freshman financial aid applications for fall entry is March 1.

International Students: There are 25 international students enrolled. The school actively recruits these students. They must take the TOEFL with a minimum score of 520 on the paper-based TOEFL (PBT) or 68 on the Internet-based version (iBT).

Computers: All students may access the system. There are no time limits and no fees.

Graduates: From July 1, 2012 to June 30, 2013, 219 bachelor's degrees were awarded. The most popular majors were biology (10%), education (9%), and kinesiology (9%). 80 companies recruited on campus in 2012-2013. In an average class, 51% graduate in 4 years or less, 60% graduate in 5 years or less, and 60% graduate in 6 years or less.

Admissions Contact: Michelle Lynch, V.P. for Enrollment Management. E-Mail: *admissions@georgetowncollege.edu* Web: *http:/www.georgetowncollege.edu/admissions/*

KENTUCKY CHRISTIAN UNIVERSITY F-2

Grayson, KY 41143 606-474-3186
(800) 522-3181; (606) 474-3155

Full-time: 277 men, 274 women	**Faculty:** 34; IIB, --$
Part-time: 8 men, 11 women	**Ph.D.s:** 74%
Graduate: 16 men, 3 women	**Student/Faculty:** 16 to 1
Year: semesters, summer session	**Tuition:** $16,000
Application Deadline: open	**Room & Board:** $7000
Freshman Class: 443 applied, 292 accepted, 176 enrolled	
SAT CR/M: 450/460 **ACT:** 19	**LESS COMPETITIVE**

Kentucky Christian University was established in 1919, and is a private Christian college affiliated with the Independent Christian Church/Church of Christ, offering undergraduate programs in Christian ministry, psychology, social work, business administration, teacher education, music, history, and intercultural studies. There are 7 undergraduate schools and 1 graduate school. In addition to regional accreditation, KCU has baccalaureate program accreditation with CSWE. The library contains 96,000 volumes, 8,640 microform items, and 2,657 audio/video tapes/CDs/DVDs, and subscribes to 13,000 periodicals including electronic. Computerized library services include interlibrary loans, database searching, Internet access, and laptop Internet portals. Special learning facilities include a learning resource center. The 121-acre campus is in a small town 20 miles from Ashland and 90 miles east of Lexington. Including any residence halls, there are 25 buildings.

Student Life: 55% of undergraduates are from out of state, mostly the Mid-West. Students are from 27 states, and 6 foreign countries. 87% are white. 98% are Protestant. The average age of freshmen is 18; all undergraduates, 22. 32% do not continue beyond their first year; 43% remain to graduate.

Housing: 520 students can be accommodated in college housing, which includes single-sex dorms, on-campus apartments, and married student housing. On-campus housing is guaranteed for all 4 years. 81% of students live on campus. Alcohol is not permitted. All students may keep cars.

Activities: There are no fraternities or sororities. There are 114 groups on campus, including band, choir, chorale, drama, jazz band, musical theater, professional, religious, social service, student government, and yearbook. Popular campus events include Feast of Christmas, Days of Future Knights, and Summer in the Son.

Sports: There are 4 intercollegiate sports for men and 4 for women, and 16 intramural sports for men and 16 for women. Facilities include a gym, soccer recreational fields, a student life recreational center, racquetball and tennis courts, and an athletic field house.

Disabled Students: 95% of the campus is accessible. Facilities include wheelchair ramps, elevators, special parking, specially equipped restrooms, lowered drinking fountains, lowered telephones, special housing.

Services: Counseling and information services are available, as is tutoring in most subjects, The Academic Resource Center provides tutoring for various subjects as needed. There is a reader service for the blind, and remedial math, reading, and writing.

Campus Safety and Security: Measures include emergency notification system and security escort services. There are emergency telephones, lighted pathways/sidewalks, controlled access to dorms/residences, and an overnight security guard (7:00 p.m. to 7:00 a.m.).

Programs of Study: KCU confers B.A., B.S., B.B.A., and B.S.N. degrees. Master's degrees are also awarded. Bachelor's degrees are awarded in BUSINESS (business administration and management), COMMUNICATIONS AND THE ARTS (music, music business management, and music performance), EDUCATION (elementary education, English education, middle school education, music education, and social studies education), HEALTH PROFESSIONS (nursing), SOCIAL SCIENCE (biblical studies, counseling/psychology, crosscultural studies, history, humanities, liberal arts/general studies, ministries, pastoral studies, religious music, social work, and youth ministry). Bible/ministry, teacher education, and nursing have the largest enrollments.

Required: To graduate, students must complete 121 semester hours with at least 30 hours in the major and a minimum GPA of 2.0. Candidates for the B.A. degree must fulfill a 12-hour language requirement. All students major in Bible in addition to their selected field of study.

Special: Internships, work-study programs, B.A.-B.S. degrees, and dual majors are offered. Internships are required in business, teacher, education, counseling psychology, ministry, and social work. Study abroad in 5 countries in association with the Council for Christian Colleges and Universities is available. Students have the opportunity to participate in the American studies program in Washington, D.C., the Contemporary Music Program in Nashville, and the Los Angeles Film Studies Center in Los Angeles.

Faculty/Classroom: 62% of faculty are male; 38% are female. All teach undergraduates. No introductory courses are taught by graduate students. The average class size in an introductory lecture is 30; in a laboratory is 15; and in a regular course is 17.

Admissions: 66% of the 2011-2012 applicants were accepted. The SAT scores for the 2011-2012 freshman class were: Critical Reading--73% below 500, 20% between 500 and 599, 7% between 600 and 700; Math--53% below 500, 40% between 500 and 599, 7% between 600 and 700. The ACT scores were 62% below 21, 22% between 21 and 23, 10% between 24 and 26, 3% between 27 and 28, and 2% above 28. 19% of the current freshmen were in the top fifth of their class; 39% were in the top two fifths. 3 freshmen graduated first in their class.

Requirements: The ACT is required. A GPA of 2.0 is required. AP and CLEP credits are accepted.

Procedure: Freshmen are admitted to all sessions. There are deferred admissions and rolling admissions plans. Application deadlines are open. The fall application fee was $30. Applications are accepted online.

Transfer: 36 transfer students enrolled in a recent ear. Applicants must have a cumulative GPA of 2.0. They must submit transcripts from all previous institutions and must be in good standing at the last college attended. 32 of 121 credits required for the bachelor's degree must be completed at KCU.

Visiting: There are regularly scheduled orientations for prospective students, consisting of an interview, a campus tour, lunch, and attending classes. There are guides for informal visits, visitors may sit in on classes, and stay overnight. To schedule a visit, contact the Director of Admissions.

Financial Aid: In a recent yrar, 100% of all full-time freshmen and 100% of continuing full-time students received some form of financial aid. 80% of all full-time freshmen and 83% of continuing full-time students received need-based aid. The average freshman award was $10,455. 47% of undergraduate students work part-time. Average annual earnings from campus work are $1922. The average financial indebtedness of a recent graduate was $22,538. The FAFSA is required. The deadline for filing freshman financial aid applications for fall entry is August 1.

International Students: There are 19 international students enrolled. They must take the TOEFL with a minimum score of 500 on the paper-based TOEFL (PBT). They must also take the SAT or ACT.

Computers: All students may access the system.

Graduates: In a recent year, 84 bachelor's degrees were awarded. The most popular majors were teacher education (19%), nursing (17%), and ministry (13%). In an average class, 31% graduate in 4 years or less, 42% graduate in 5 years or less, and 44% graduate in 6 years or less.

Admissions Contact: Director of Admission. Web: *www.kcu.edu*

KENTUCKY STATE UNIVERSITY D-2

Frankfort, KY 40601 (502) 597-6322
(800) 325-1716; (502) 597-5814

Full-time: 700 men, 900 women	**Faculty:** 152
Part-time: 300 men, 400 women	**Ph.D.s:** n/av
Graduate: 70 men, 70 women	**Student/Faculty:** n/av
Year: semesters, summer session	**Tuition:** $7,000 ($15,000)
Application Deadline: open	**Room & Board:** $7700
Freshman Class: n/av	
SAT: required	**ACT:** 17 LESS COMPETITIVE

Kentucky State University, founded in 1886, is a public liberal arts institution that emphasizes student involvement in seminars and course planning. There are 4 undergraduate schools and one graduate school. In addition to regional accreditation, KSU has baccalaureate program accreditation with AACSB, ADA, AHEA, CSWE, NASM, NCATE, and NLN. The library contains 438,355 volumes, 323,864 microform items, and 3,453 audio/video tapes/CDs/DVDs, and subscribes to 1,160 periodicals including electronic. Computerized library services include interlibrary loans, database searching, and Internet access. Special learning facilities include a learning resource center, art gallery, a 167-acre agricultural research farm. The 308-acre campus is in a small town 25 miles west of Lexington, KY. Including any residence halls, there are 34 buildings.

Student Life: 62% of undergraduates are from Kentucky. Others are from 34 states, 29 foreign countries, and Canada. 99% are from public schools. 60% are African American; 34% white. The average age of freshmen is 21; all undergraduates, 25. 44% do not continue beyond their first year; 35% remain to graduate.

Housing: 849 students can be accommodated in college housing, which includes single-sex dorms and on-campus apartments. In addition, there are special-interest houses. On-campus housing is guaranteed for the freshman year only, is available on a first-come, and first-served basis. 67% of students commute. Alcohol is not permitted. All students may keep cars.

Activities: 3% of men belong to 6 national fraternities; 4% of women belong to 5 national sororities. There are 70 groups on campus, including art, band, cheerleading, choir, chorale, computers, dance, drama, drill team, honors, international, jazz band, literary magazine, marching band, musical theater, newspaper, opera, orchestra, political, professional, religious, social, social service, student government, and symphony. Popular campus events include plays, concerts, and talent shows.

Sports: There are 7 intercollegiate sports for men and 6 for women. Facilities include a 6500-seat football stadium, an indoor swimming pool, tennis courts, a bowling alley, training and weight rooms, a field house, and baseball, track, and field complexes.

Disabled Students: All of the campus is accessible. Facilities include wheelchair ramps, elevators, special parking, specially equipped restrooms, lowered drinking fountains, lowered telephones.

Services: Counseling and information services are available, as is tutoring in every subject. There is a reader service for the blind, and remedial math, reading, and writing.

Campus Safety and Security: Measures include 24-hour foot and vehicle patrol and self-defense education. There are lighted pathways/sidewalks.

Programs of Study: KSU confers B.A. and B.S. degrees. Associate and master's degrees are also awarded. Bachelor's degrees are awarded in BIOLOGICAL SCIENCE (biology/biological science), BUSINESS (apparel and accessories marketing and business administration and management), COMMUNICATIONS AND THE ARTS (art, English, fine arts, music performance, and studio art), COMPUTER AND PHYSICAL SCIENCE (applied mathematics, chemistry, computer science, and mathematics), EDUCATION (art education, early childhood education, elementary education, mathematics education, music education, physical education, secondary education, and social studies education), HEALTH PROFESSIONS (nursing), SOCIAL SCIENCE (criminal justice, history, liberal arts/general studies, political science/government, psychology, public administration, social work, and sociology).

Required: A total of 128 credits is required to graduate with 64 in the major and a minimum 2.0 GPA. An assessment may include, but is not limited to, a portfolio, written examination, presentation, recital, and/or capstone course.

Special: There is 1 national honor society, a freshman honors program, and 10 departmental honors programs.

Faculty/Classroom: 95% teach undergraduates. No introductory courses are taught by graduate students.

Requirements: The SAT or ACT is required. Applicants are required to have 4 years in English, 3 in math, 2 each in science and history, and 9 additional pre-college curriculum classes. The GED is accepted. A GPA of 2.0 is required. AP and CLEP credits are accepted.

Procedure: Freshmen are admitted to all sessions. Entrance exams should be taken from October to April. There are early admissions, deferred admissions, and rolling admissions plans. Application deadlines are open. The fall application fee was $22. Applications are accepted online.

Transfer: 109 transfer students enrolled in a recent year. Transfer applicants must have a 2.0 minimum GPA at previous colleges. Only C grades or higher transfer. If fewer than 30 semester credits are transferable, applicants must meet freshman criteria. 45 of 128 credits required for the bachelor's degree must be completed at KSU.

Visiting: There are regularly scheduled orientations for prospective students, including tours and meetings with faculty and financial aid officers. There are guides for informal visits and visitors may sit in on classes. To schedule a visit, contact Admissions.

Financial Aid: In 2011-2012, 80% of all full-time freshmen and 85% of continuing full-time students received some form of financial aid. 65% of all full-time freshmen and 60% of continuing full-time students received need-based aid. The average freshman award was $6,500. Need-based scholarships or need-based grants averaged $500 ($800 maximum); need-based self-help aid (loans and jobs) averaged $3,040 ($5,500 maximum); non-need-based athletic scholarships averaged $7,426 ($14,500 maximum); and other non-need-based awards and non-need-based scholarships averaged $1,950 ($14,500 maximum). 55% of undergraduate students work part-time. Average annual earnings from campus work are $1000. The average financial indebtedness of the 2011 graduate was $12,000. KSU is a member of CSS. The FAFSA and the college's own financial statement are required. The priority date for freshman financial aid applications for fall entry is April 15.

International Students: They must take the TOEFL. They must also take the SAT or ACT.

Computers: All students may access the system 13 hours a day. There are no time limits and no fees. All students must have a personal computer.

Graduates: From July 1, 2010 to June 30, 2011, 330 bachelor's degrees were awarded. The most popular majors were business (15%), computer science (7%), and criminal justice (7%).

Admissions Contact: James Burrell, Director of Admissions. A campus DVD is available. E-Mail: *James.Burrell@kysu.edu* Web: *www.kysu.edu.*

KENTUCKY WESLEYAN COLLEGE B-3

Owensboro, KY 42301 (270) 852-3120
(800) 999-0592; (270) 852-3133

Full-time: 326 men, 315 women	**Faculty:** 48; IIB, --$
Part-time: 19 men, 18 women	**Ph.D.s:** 84%
Graduate: n/av	**Student/Faculty:** 12 to 1
Year: semesters, summer session	**Tuition:** $20,240
Application Deadline: open	**Room & Board:** $7200
Freshman Class: 910 applied, 193 accepted, 158 enrolled	
SAT CR/M/W: 470/490/460	**ACT:** 22 VERY COMPETITIVE+

Kentucky Wesleyan College, founded in 1858, is a private liberal arts institution affiliated with the United Methodist Church. KWC offers undergraduate programs in natural sciences, humanities and fine arts, and social sciences. The library contains 99,795 volumes, 144,661 microform items, and 2,027 audio/video tapes/CDs/DVDs, and subscribes to 145 periodicals including electronic. Computerized library services include interlibrary loans, database searching, Internet access, and Wi-Fi capability. Special learning facilities include an art gallery and radio station. The 52-acre campus is in a suburban area 95 miles southwest of Louisville and 120 miles north of Nashville. Including any residence halls, there are 15 buildings.

Student Life: 72% of undergraduates are from Kentucky. Others are from 22 states, 6 foreign countries, and Canada. 90% are from public schools. 74% are White. 60% are Protestant; 25% claim no religious affiliation; 12% Catholic. The average age of freshmen is 18; all undergraduates, 22. 30% do not continue beyond their first year; 44% remain to graduate.

Housing: 520 students can be accommodated in college housing, which includes single-sex and coed dorms, on-campus apartments, and off-campus apartments. On-campus housing is guaranteed for all 4 years. 55% of students commute. Alcohol is not permitted. All students may keep cars.

Activities: 11% of men belong to 3 national fraternities; 11% of women belong to 2 national sororities. There are 48 groups on campus, including art, band, cheerleading, choir, chorale, chorus, computers, dance, drama, ethnic, literary magazine, marching band, musical theater, newspaper, pep band, photography, political, professional, radio and TV, religious, social, social service, student government, symphony, and yearbook. Popular campus events include Family Weekend, Theater Productions and Lessons in Carols.

Sports: There are 6 intercollegiate sports for men and 7 for women, and 7 intramural sports for men and 7 for women. Facilities include a health and recreation center, which houses an 800-seat gym, a fully equipped weight training center, racquetball courts, indoor batting and pitching facilities for softball and baseball, and a multipurpose auxiliary gym. Outdoor facilities include a baseball park, a softball park, a soccer field, a football field, and additional practice fields for football and soccer. Varsity basketball games are played in the 5,000-seat Owensboro Sports Center.

Disabled Students: 95% of the campus is accessible. Facilities include wheelchair ramps, elevators, special parking, specially equipped restrooms, special class scheduling, and lowered drinking fountains.

Services: Counseling and information services are available, as is tutoring in most subjects. There is a reader service for the blind, and remedial math, reading, and writing.

Campus Safety and Security: Measures include 24-hour foot and vehicle patrol, emergency notification system, and security escort services. There are lighted pathways/sidewalks and controlled access to dorms/residences.

Programs of Study: KWC confers B.A., B.S., B.M. and B.M.E. degrees. Bachelor's degrees are awarded in BIOLOGICAL SCIENCE (biology/biological science and zoology), BUSINESS (accounting, business administration and management, business economics, human resources, and sports management), COMMUNICATIONS AND THE ARTS (art, communications, English, fine arts, music, music business management, and Spanish), COMPUTER AND PHYSICAL SCIENCE (chemistry, computer science, and physics), EDUCATION (art education, elementary education, middle school education, music education, physical education, and secondary education), ENGINEERING AND ENVIRONMENTAL DESIGN (pre-engineering), HEALTH PROFESSIONS (health, predentistry, and premedicine), SOCIAL SCIENCE (criminal justice, history, political science/government, prelaw, psychology, and sociology). Natural sciences, education and business are the strongest academically. Business administration, biology and education have the largest enrollments.

Required: All students are required to complete the following general education program of skills and content requirements: 9 hours each in humanities, 6 hours each in aesthetics and social sciences, 3 hours each in math, religion, multicultural studies, and communication skills, 7 in natural science. Students must demonstrate proficiency in math, computing, and oral and written communication. To graduate, students must complete a total of 128 credit hours, including 36 in the major, with a 2.0 GPA.

Special: Internships, dual majors, and student-designed majors are available in many programs and are established on an individual basis. A 3-2 degree in engineering is offered with Auburn University and the University of Kentucky. A Washington semester and study abroad in 5 countries are also available. There are 8 national honor societies and 7 departmental honors programs.

Faculty/Classroom: 50% of faculty are male; 50% are female. All teach undergraduates. No introductory courses are taught by graduate students. The average class size in an introductory lecture is 20; in a laboratory is 15; and in a regular course is 15.

Admissions: 21% of the 2013-2014 applicants were accepted. The SAT scores for the 2013-2014 freshman class were: Critical Reading--58% below 500, 36% between 500 and 599, 6% between 600 and 699; Math--55% below 500, 36% between 500 and 599, 9% between 600 and 699; Writing--61% below 500, 36% between 500 and 599, 3% between 600 and 699. The ACT scores were 38% below 21, 29% between 21 and 23, 16% between 24 and 26, 7% between 27 and 28, and 10% above 28. 1 freshman graduated first in the class.

Requirements: The SAT or ACT is required. Applicants should have completed 13 high school units in college preparatory English, math, science, social studies, and a foreign language, or the GED equivalent. Applicants are considered individually. AP and CLEP credits are accepted.

Procedure: Freshmen are admitted to all sessions. Entrance exams should be taken during the spring of the junior year or the fall of the senior year. There are deferred admissions and rolling admissions plans. Application deadlines are open. Notification is sent on a rolling basis. Applications are accepted online.

Transfer: 95 transfer students enrolled in 2012-2013. Transfer applicants should have a minimum GPA of 2.0 in all course work and be in good standing at the previously attended institution. 30 of 120 credits required for the bachelor's degree must be completed at KWC.

Visiting: There are regularly scheduled orientations for prospective students, including a campus tour, faculty and student meetings, and campus dining. There are guides for informal visits, sitting in on classes, and stay overnight. To schedule a visit, contact the Admissions Office.

Financial Aid: In 2013-2014, 100% of all full-time freshmen and 95% of continuing full-time students received some form of financial aid. 100% of all full-time freshmen and 95% of continuing full-time students received need-based aid. 50% of undergraduate students work part-time. The FAFSA is required. The priority date for freshman financial aid applications for fall entry is March 15. The deadline for filing freshman financial aid applications for fall entry is August 1.

International Students: 10 international students are enrolled. The school actively recruits these students. They must take the TOEFL with a minimum score of 500 on the paper-based TOEFL (PBT) or 70 on the Internet-based version (iBT). SAT or ACT scores are required of international students who do not have a TOEFL score or who want to play NCAA sports.

Computers: All students may access the system. There are no time limits and no fees.

Graduates: From July 1, 2012 to June 30, 2013, 155 bachelor's degrees were awarded. The most popular majors were business (22%), education (12%), and biology (9%). 20 companies recruited on campus in 2012-2013. In an average class, 30% graduate in 4 years or less, 40% graduate in 5 years or less, and 44% graduate in 6 years or less. Of the 2012 graduating class, 21% were enrolled in graduate school within 6 months of graduation, and 21% were employed.

Admissions Contact: Rahad Smith, Director of Admissions. E-Mail: *rsmith@kwc.edu* Web: *www.kwc.edu*

LINDSEY WILSON COLLEGE D-3

Columbia, KY 42728 (270) 384-8100
(800) 264-0138; (270) 384-8591

Full-time: 873 men, 1228 women	**Faculty:** 65
Part-time: 30 men, 69 women	**Ph.D.s:** 72%
Graduate: 106 men, 338 women	**Student/Faculty:** 27 to 1
Year: semesters, summer session	**Tuition:** $22,070
Application Deadline: open	**Room & Board:** $8400
Freshman Class: n/av	
ACT: required	

VERY COMPETITIVE

Lindsey Wilson College, founded in 1903, is a private liberal arts college affiliated with the United Methodist Church, offering undergraduate programs in arts and sciences, business administration, education, human services, and pre-health. There is one graduate school. In addition to regional accreditation, Lindsey has baccalaureate program accreditation with NCATE. The library contains 105,000 volumes, 16,000 microform items, and 5,250 audio/video tapes/CDs/DVDs, and subscribes to 16,000 periodicals including electronic. Computerized library services include interlibrary loans, database searching, and Internet access. Special learning facilities include an art gallery. The 45-acre campus is in a small town 100 miles southeast of Louisville. Including any residence halls, there are 44 buildings.

Student Life: 81% of undergraduates are from Kentucky. Others are from 30 states, 28 foreign countries, and Canada. 57% are White. 67% are Protestant. 42% do not continue beyond their first year; 31% remain to graduate.

Housing: 1150 students can be accommodated in college housing, which includes single-sex dorms and on-campus apartments. In addition, there are honors houses. On-campus housing is guaranteed for all 4 years, is available on a first-come, first-served basis, and is available on a lottery system for upperclassmen. 52% of students live on campus; of those, 50% remain on campus on weekends. Alcohol is not permitted. All students may keep cars.

Activities: There are no fraternities or sororities. There are 40 groups on campus, including art, band, cheerleading, choir, chorale, chorus, computers, dance, drama, environmental, film, honors, international, jazz band, literary magazine, marching band, musical theater, newspaper, pep band, photography, political, professional, religious, social, social service, and student government. Popular campus events include Founders Day and Malvina Farkle Day (community service).

Sports: There are 10 intercollegiate sports for men and 13 for women, and 10 intramural sports for men and 10 for women. Facilities include a sports center with a 1000-seat gym and a 72000 sq ft health and wellness center with a weight-training room, competition swimming pool and many other amenities, a sand volleyball court, and the student union building.

Disabled Students: 95% of the campus is accessible. Facilities include wheelchair ramps, elevators, special parking, specially equipped restrooms, special class scheduling, lowered drinking fountains, and special housing.

Services: Counseling and information services are available, as is tutoring in every subject. There is remedial math, reading, and writing.

Campus Safety and Security: Measures include 24-hour foot and vehicle patrol, emergency notification system, and security escort services. There are lighted pathways/sidewalks and controlled access to dorms/residences.

Programs of Study: Lindsey confers B.A., and B.S. degrees. Associate and master's degrees are also awarded. Bachelor's degrees are awarded in BIOLOGICAL SCIENCE (biology/biological science), BUSINESS (accounting, business administration and management, and recreation and leisure services), COMMUNICATIONS AND THE ARTS (art, communications, English, media arts, and theatre studies), COMPUTER AND PHYSICAL SCIENCE (mathematics), EDUCATION (art education, elementary education, music education, and secondary education), HEALTH PRO-

FESSIONS (nursing), SOCIAL SCIENCE (American studies, criminal justice, history, human services, liberal arts/general studies, ministries, psychobiology, psychology, and social science). Human services and biology are the strongest academically. Human services, business, and education have the largest enrollments.

Required: All students must complete 45 hours of general education core requirements, including courses in communication of ideas, math, natural science, religion, humanities, fine arts, social behavioral science, and phys ed, as well as a 1-hour personal development career seminar. A total of 120 semester hours, with a minimum GPA of 2.0, is required to graduate.

Special: Human services majors are offered a social services practicum in their field of study. Internships, work-study programs, a Washington semester, a general studies degree, student-designed majors, and pass/fail options in some courses are available. Study abroad is possible through Lindsey in London and the Northern Ireland Exchange. There are 3 national honor societies and a freshman honors program.

Faculty/Classroom: 47% of faculty are male; 53% are female. All teach undergraduates. No introductory courses are taught by graduate students. The average class size in an introductory lecture is 20; in a laboratory is 20; and in a regular course is 20.

Admissions: The ACT scores were 42% below 21, 8% between 21 and 23, 26% between 24 and 26, 14% between 27 and 28, and 9% above 28. 37 freshmen graduated first in their class.

Requirements: The ACT is required. Applicants should have completed 20 academic high school credits or the GED equivalent. A GPA of 2.5 is required. AP and CLEP credits are accepted. Important factors in the admissions decision are geographical diversity, recommendations by alumni, and recommendations by school officials.

Procedure: Freshmen are admitted to all sessions. Entrance exams should be taken during the junior year. There is a rolling admissions plan. Application deadlines are open. Applications are accepted online.

Transfer: 96 transfer students enrolled in 2012-2013. Transfer applicants are required to submit an official transcript from schools previously attended. An interview is recommended. 120 credits required for the bachelor's degree must be completed at Lindsey.

Visiting: There are regularly scheduled orientations for prospective students. There are guides for informal visits, visitors may sit in on classes, and stay overnight. To schedule a visit, contact the Admissions Office at admissions@lindsey.edu.

Financial Aid: In 2013-2014, 95% of all full-time freshmen students received some form of financial aid. 95% of all full-time freshmen students received need-based aid. 31% of undergraduate students work part-time. Average annual earnings from campus work are $1200. The average financial indebtedness of the 2013 graduate was $12,400. Lindsey is a member of CSS. The FAFSA is required. The priority date for freshman financial aid applications for fall entry is February 1.

International Students: There are 156 international students enrolled. The school actively recruits these students. They must take the TOEFL with a minimum score of 450 on the paper-based TOEFL (PBT) or 45 on the Internet-based version (iBT). They must also take the SAT or ACT.

Computers: All students may access the system. There are no time limits and no fees.

Graduates: From July 1, 2012 to June 30, 2013, 523 bachelor's degrees were awarded. In an average class, 1% graduate in 3 years or less, 15% graduate in 4 years or less, 26% graduate in 5 years or less, and 28% graduate in 6 years or less. Of the 2012 graduating class, 8% were enrolled in graduate school within 6 months of graduation.

Admissions Contact: Charity Fergurson, Director of Admissions. E-Mail: *fergusonc@lindsey.edu* Web: *www.lindsey.edu*

MIDWAY COLLEGE D-3

Midway, KY 40347 (859) 846-4421
(800) 755-0031; (859) 846-5822

Full-time: 103 men, 672 women	**Faculty:** 50
Part-time: 83 men, 311 women	**Ph.D.s:** 22%
Graduate: 55 men, 82 women	**Student/Faculty:** 18 to 1
Year: semesters, summer session	**Tuition:** $13,950 ($15,750)
Application Deadline:	**Room & Board:** $6200
Freshman Class: 423 applied, 319 accepted, 159 enrolled	
SAT: required	**ACT:** 20 **COMPETITIVE**

Midway College, founded in 1847, is a private institution affiliated with the Disciples of Christ. The day college is for women only and the evening program is an accelerated coed program. The library contains 52,000 volumes, 57,000 microform items, 8,900 audio/video tapes/CDs/DVDs, and subscribes to 450 periodicals including electronic. Computerized library services include interlibrary loans and database searching. The 105-acre campus is in a rural area 15 minutes from Lexington. Including any residence halls, there are 10 buildings.

Student Life: 88% of undergraduates are from Kentucky. Others are from 31 states, 5 foreign countries, and Canada. 87% are White. The average age of freshmen is 23; all undergraduates, 27.

Housing: 225 students can be accommodated in college housing, which includes single-sex dorms. On-campus housing is guaranteed for the freshman year only, is available on a first-come, and first-served basis. 87% of students commute. Alcohol is not permitted. All students may keep cars.

Activities: There are no fraternities or sororities. There are 15 groups on campus, including art, chorale, honors, newspaper, professional, religious, social, social service, student government, and yearbook.

Sports: There are 4 intercollegiate sports for women. Facilities include a full service gym, a weight room, tennis courts, soccer and softball fields, and an equine arena.

Disabled Students: 65% of the campus is accessible. Facilities include wheelchair ramps, elevators, special parking, specially equipped restrooms, special class scheduling, lowered drinking fountains, and lowered telephones.

Services: Counseling and information services are available, as is tutoring in most subjects. There are writing and math labs.

Campus Safety and Security: Measures include 24-hour foot and vehicle patrol. There are emergency telephones and lighted pathways/sidewalks.

Programs of Study: confers B.A., and B.S. degrees. Associate and master's degrees are also awarded. Bachelor's degrees are awarded in AGRICULTURE (equine science), BIOLOGICAL SCIENCE (biology/biological science), BUSINESS (business administration and management, human resources, and sports management), COMMUNICATIONS AND THE ARTS (English), COMPUTER AND PHYSICAL SCIENCE (chemistry and mathematics), EDUCATION (education), ENGINEERING AND ENVIRONMENTAL DESIGN (environmental science), HEALTH PROFESSIONS (nursing), SOCIAL SCIENCE (liberal arts/general studies and psychology). Biology, nursing, and equine science education are the strongest academically. Nursing, equine science, and business education have the largest enrollments.

Required: All students must complete 130 credits, including 82 to 91 major and elective credits and 38 to 48 general education credits. Core requirements include courses in math, computing, science, communication, and composition. A 2.0 GPA must be maintained.

Special: A cooperative program in teacher education and an accelerated degree program in management and education degrees are offered. There are 2 national honor societies, including Phi Beta Kappa, and a freshman honors program.

Faculty/Classroom: 37% of faculty are male; 63% are female. All teach undergraduates, and all do research. No introductory courses are taught by graduate students. The average class size in an introductory lecture is 16; in a laboratory is 9; and in a regular course is 13.

Admissions: 75% of the 2013-2014 applicants were accepted. The ACT scores were 62% below 21, 21% between 21 and 23, 10% between 24 and 26, 3% between 27 and 28, and 4% above 28. 2 freshmen graduated first in their class.

Requirements: The SAT or ACT is required. A score of 50 or better on the GED is required for acceptance. A GPA of 2.2 is required. AP and CLEP credits are accepted. Important factors in the admissions decision are leadership record, extracurricular activities record, and recommendations by school officials.

Procedure: Freshmen are admitted fall, spring, and summer. SAT or ACT scores must be received by the school by August 1. There is a rolling admissions plan. Application deadlines are open. The fall 2013 application fee was $25.

Transfer: 249 transfer students enrolled in 2012-2013. Applicants must have a minimum college GPA of 2.0. 39 of 130 credits required for the bachelor's degree must be completed at Midway.

Visiting: There are regularly scheduled orientations for prospective students, including campus tours, faculty and student conferences, and the president's address. There are guides for informal visits and visitors may sit in on classes.

Financial Aid: In 2013-2014, 81% of all full-time freshmen and 80% of continuing full-time students received some form of financial aid. 81% of all full-time freshmen and 69% of continuing full-time students received need-based aid. The average freshman award was $12,678. Need-based scholarships or need-based grants averaged $6,530; need-based self-help aid (loans and jobs) averaged $2,860; non-need-based athletic scholarships averaged $1,250; and other non-need-based awards and non-need-based scholarships averaged $2,594. 9% of undergraduate students work part-time. Average annual earnings from campus work are $1372. The average financial indebtedness of the 2013 graduate was $15,407. Midway is a member of CSS. The FAFSA is required. The deadline for filing freshman financial aid applications for fall entry is April 15.

International Students: There are 9 international students enrolled. They must take the TOEFL. They must also take the SAT or ACT.

Computers: All students may access the system. There are no time limits and no fees.

Graduates: From July 1, 2012 to June 30, 2013, 218 bachelor's degrees were awarded. The most popular majors were business/organizational management (38%), teacher education (34%), and nursing (12%). 8 companies recruited on campus in 2012-2013. In an average class, 20% graduate in 4 years or less.

Admissions Contact: Emily Coleman, Director of Student Affairs. E-Mail: *ecoleman@midway.edu* Web: *www.midway.edu*

MOREHEAD STATE UNIVERSITY E-2

Morehead, KY 40351 (606) 783-2000
(800) 585-6781; (606) 783-5038

Full-time: 2565 men, 3644 women	**Faculty:** n/av; IIA, --$
Part-time: 1400 men, 2467 women	**Ph.D.s:** 68%
Graduate: 482 men, 800 women	**Student/Faculty:** n/av
Year: semesters, summer session	**Tuition:** $5280 ($13,340)
Application Deadline: open	**Room & Board:** $5620
Freshman Class: 5241 applied, 4364 accepted, 1685 enrolled	
SAT: required **ACT:** 22	**COMPETITIVE**

Morehead State University, founded in 1887, is a public institution offering degree programs in applied science and technology, humanities, educational and behavioral sciences, and business. There are 4 undergraduate schools and 1 graduate school. In addition to regional accreditation, MSU has baccalaureate program accreditation with AACSB, ACBSP, CSWE, NASM, NCATE, and NLN. The library contains 522,673 volumes, 819,736 microform items, and 22,194 audio/video tapes/CDs/DVDs, and subscribes to 3,046 periodicals including electronic. Computerized library services include interlibrary loans, database searching, Internet access, and Wi-Fi capability. Special learning facilities include an art gallery, planetarium, radio station, TV station, a 320-acre farm complex, space science center, and robotics lab. The 1016-acre campus is located 60 miles east of Lexington. Including residence halls, there are 140 buildings.

Student Life: 86% of undergraduates are from Kentucky. Others are from 37 states, 22 foreign countries, and Canada. 95% are from public schools. 96% are White. The average age of freshmen is 18; all undergraduates, 23. 39% do not continue beyond their first year.

Housing: 3250 students can be accommodated in college housing, which includes coed dorms, on-campus apartments, and married student housing. In addition, there are honors houses, language houses, fraternity houses, sorority houses, a cross-cultural house, and housing for farm students, handicapped housing, some private rooms available. On-campus housing is guaranteed for all 4 years. 70% of students commute. Alcohol is not permitted. All students may keep cars.

Activities: 27% of men and 20 of women belong to 12 national fraternities; 21% of women belong to 9 national sororities. There are 95 groups on campus, including art, band, cheerleading, choir, chorale, chorus, computers, dance, drama, drill team, drum and bugle corps, environmental, ethnic, gay, honors, international, jazz band, marching band, musical theater, newspaper, orchestra, pep band, photography, political, professional, radio and TV, religious, social, social service, student government, symphony, and yearbook. Popular campus events include Greek Week, Black History Month, and Welcome Week.

Sports: There are 9 intercollegiate sports for men and 9 for women, and 24 intramural sports for men and 24 for women. Facilities include an athletic complex, a 6500-seat gym, a 10000-seat stadium, a pool, bowling lanes, and a wellness/fitness center.

Disabled Students: 85% of the campus is accessible. Facilities include wheelchair ramps, elevators, special parking, specially equipped restrooms, special class scheduling, lowered drinking fountains, lowered telephones, and special housing.

Services: Counseling and information services are available, as is tutoring in most subjects. There is a reader service for the blind, and remedial math, reading, and writing.

Campus Safety and Security: Measures include 24-hour foot and vehicle patrol, emergency notification system, self-defense education, and security escort services. There are shuttle buses, emergency telephones, and lighted pathways/sidewalks.

Programs of Study: MSU confers A.B., B.S., B.B.A., B.M., B.M.Ed., B.S.N., B.S.W. and B.U.S. degrees. Associate, master's, and doctoral degrees are also awarded. Bachelor's degrees are awarded in AGRICULTURE (agriculture), BIOLOGICAL SCIENCE (biology/biological science and ecology), BUSINESS (accounting, banking and finance, business economics, management information systems, management science, marketing management, and real estate), COMMUNICATIONS AND THE ARTS (communications, dramatic arts, English, music, and speech/debate/rhetoric), COMPUTER AND PHYSICAL SCIENCE (chemistry, computer science, earth science, geology, mathematics, and physics), EDUCATION (agricultural education, business education, elementary education, health education, industrial arts education, middle school education, physical education, and special education), ENGINEERING AND ENVIRONMENTAL DESIGN (industrial engineering technology), HEALTH PROFESSIONS (medical technology and nursing), SOCIAL SCIENCE (geography, history, liberal arts/general studies, paralegal studies, philosophy, political science/government, psychology, social science, social work, and sociology). Biology, music, and nursing are the strongest academically. Elementary education has the largest enrollment.

Required: All students must complete 42 semester hours (45 for teacher certification) of general education courses, including 15 hours in communications and humanities, 12 in natural and mathematical sciences, 12 in social and behavioral sciences, and 3 in health or phys ed. A total of 128 semester hours, with a minimum GPA of 2.0, is required to graduate.

Special: Cross-registration is offered with the University of Kentucky. Students may earn specialist certification in education, co-op programs, internships, study abroad in 3 countries, a Washington semester, a 3-2 engineering degree, dual and student-designed majors, a general studies degree, credit for life experience, pass/fail options, and non-degree study. There are 12 national honor societies and a freshman honors program.

Faculty/Classroom: 55% of faculty are male; 45% are female. All teach undergraduates. No introductory courses are taught by graduate students. The average class size in a regular course is 19.

Admissions: 83% of the 2013-2014 applicants were accepted. The ACT scores were 10% below 21, 55% between 21 and 23. 33% of the current freshmen were in the top fifth of their class; 58% were in the top two fifths.

Requirements: The SAT or ACT is required. In addition, applicants should have completed the Kentucky Pre-College Curriculum requirement. An interview is recommended. A GPA of 2.0 is required. AP and CLEP credits are accepted.

Procedure: Freshmen are admitted fall, spring, and summer. Entrance exams should be taken in the spring of the junior year. There is a rolling admissions plan. Application deadlines are open. Application fee is $30. Notification is sent on a rolling basis. Applications are accepted online.

Transfer: 501 transfer students enrolled in 2012-2013. Applicants should have a minimum GPA of 2.0 with at least 12 credit hours earned and be in good standing at their previous institution. They must have completed a pre-college curriculum or meet any deficiencies. 32 of 128 credits required for the bachelor's degree must be completed at MSU.

Visiting: There are regularly scheduled orientations for prospective students, consisting of registration for classes, advisement, and an overview of MSU. There are guides for informal visits and visitors may sit in on classes. To schedule a visit, contact the Enrollment Services.

Financial Aid: In 2013-2014, 98% of all full-time freshmen students received some form of financial aid. 60% of all full-time freshmen students received need-based aid. The average freshman award was $7,778. Need-based scholarships or need-based grants averaged $2,174 ($4,050 maximum); need-based self-help aid (loans and jobs) averaged $1,985 ($2,625 maximum); non-need-based athletic scholarships averaged $3,645 ($9,688 maximum); and other non-need-based awards and non-need-based scholarships averaged $2,095 ($6,000 maximum). 16% of undergraduate students work part-time. Average annual earnings from campus work are $1496. The average financial indebtedness of the 2013 graduate was $16,431. The FAFSA and the college's own financial statement are required. The deadline for filing freshman financial aid applications for fall entry is April 1.

International Students: There are 44 international students enrolled. The school actively recruits these students. They must take the TOEFL with a minimum score of 500 on the paper-based TOEFL (PBT) or 61 on the Internet-based version (iBT). They must also take the SAT or ACT. with the ACT preferred.

Computers: All students may access the system 24 hours a day, 7 days a week. There are no time limits and no fees.

Graduates: From July 1, 2012 to June 30, 2013, 1116 bachelor's degrees were awarded. The most popular majors were education (13%), liberal arts/general studies and business/marketing (12%), and health professions and related programs (9%). 70 companies recruited on campus in 2012-2013. In an average class, 40% graduate in 6 years or less.

Admissions Contact: Erin Wright, Director of Institutional Research. E-Mail: *admissions@moreheadstate.edu* Web: *www.moreheadstate.edu*

MURRAY STATE UNIVERSITY B-4

Murray, KY 42071 (270) 809-2896
(800) 272-4678; (270) 809-3780

Full-time: 3044 men, 4109 women	**Faculty:** 420; IIA, --$
Part-time: 766 men, 1253 women	**Ph.D.s:** 79%
Graduate: 654 men, 1117 women	**Student/Faculty:** 16 to 1
Year: semesters, summer session	**Tuition:** $7044 ($10,390)
Application Deadline: August 1	**Room & Board:** $7900
Freshman Class: 4956 applied, 4068 accepted, 1581 enrolled	
ACT: 23	**COMPETITIVE**

Murray State University, founded in 1922, is a public institution offering degree programs in business, education, health sciences and human services, humanities and fine arts, engineering, technology and science, nursing, and agriculture. There are 7 undergraduate schools and 7 graduate schools. In addition to regional accreditation, MSU has baccalaureate program accreditation with AACSB, ABET, ACEJMC, CSWE, NASAD, NASM, and NCATE. The 2 libraries contain 401,618 volumes, 210,000 microform items, and 35,600 audio/video tapes/CDs/DVDs, and subscribe to 1,273 periodicals including electronic. Computerized library services include interlibrary loans, database searching, Internet access, and Wi-Fi capability. Special learning facilities include an art gallery, natural history museum, radio station, TV station, arboretum, biological station. The 253-acre campus is in a small town 120 miles northwest of Nashville in Murray, Kentucky. Including any residence halls, there are 75 buildings.

Student Life: 70% of undergraduates are from Kentucky. Others are from 43 states, 59 foreign countries, and Canada. 88% are from public schools. 82% are White. The average age of freshmen is 19; all undergraduates, 23. 27% do not continue beyond their first year; 53% remain to graduate.

Housing: 3200 students can be accommodated in college housing, which includes single-sex and coed dorms, on-campus apartments, and married student housing. On-campus housing is guaranteed for all 4 years, is available on a first-come, and first-served basis. 67% of students commute. Alcohol is not permitted. All students may keep cars.

Activities: 14% of men belong to 13 national fraternities; 15% of women belong to 8 national sororities. There are 210 groups on campus, including art, band, cheerleading, chess, choir, chorale, chorus, communications, computers, dance, debate, drama, drill team, environmental, ethnic, film, forensics, gay, honors, international, jazz band, literary magazine, marching band, musical theater, newspaper, opera, orchestra, pop band, photography, political, professional, radio and TV, religious, social, social service, student government, and symphony. Popular campus events include Mr. MSU and Miss MSU, Campus Lights, and All Campus Sing.

Sports: There are 9 intercollegiate sports for men and 13 for women, and 10 intramural sports for men and 10 for women. Facilities include a 73,00-square-foot recreation and wellness center, a 16,500-seat stadium, 2 gyms seating 6000 and 8,500, gymnastics and weight rooms, an indoor jogging track, racquetball courts, a swimming pool, outdoor tennis, basketball, and volleyball courts, a golf course, a physical fitness trail, and the 8500-seat Regional Special Events Center. A physical fitness center includes 2 pools, 3 gyms, racquetball courts, jogging and walking tracks, cardio and weight areas, an Internet lounge, aerobic studios, and a fitness assessment center.

Disabled Students: 98% of the campus is accessible. Facilities include wheelchair ramps, elevators, special parking, specially equipped restrooms, special class scheduling, lowered drinking fountains, lowered telephones, and special housing.

Services: Counseling and information services are available, as is tutoring in most subjects. There is a reader service for the blind, and remedial math, reading, and writing.

Campus Safety and Security: Measures include 24-hour foot and vehicle patrol, emergency notification system, self-defense education, and security escort services. There are shuttle buses, emergency telephones, lighted pathways/sidewalks, and controlled access to dorms/residences.

Programs of Study: MSU confers B.A., B.S., B.A.B., B.S.B., B.F.A., B.I.S., B.M., B.M.E., B.S.A., B.S.N., B.S.E and B.S.W. degrees. Associate, master's, and doctoral degrees are also awarded. Bachelor's degrees are awarded in AGRICULTURE (agriculture, fishing and fisheries, horticulture, and wildlife management), BIOLOGICAL SCIENCE (biology/biological science and nutrition), BUSINESS (accounting, banking and finance, business administration and management, business economics, international business management, management science, marketing and distribution, marketing management, marketing/retailing/merchandising, and recreation and leisure services), COMMUNICATIONS AND THE ARTS (advertising, broadcasting, communications, creative writing, dramatic arts, English, fine arts, French, German, graphic communications management, Japanese, journalism, literature, music, public relations, Spanish, speech/debate/rhetoric, studio art, and telecommunications), COMPUTER AND PHYSICAL SCIENCE (chemistry, Computer Engineering Technology, computer management, computer programming, computer science, earth science, geoscience, information sciences and systems, mathematics, and physics), EDUCATION (agricultural education, art education, athletic training, early childhood education, elementary education, foreign languages education, health education, industrial arts education, music education, secondary education, social studies secondary school education, special education, teaching English as a second/foreign language (TESOL/TEFOL), and technical education), ENGINEERING AND ENVIRONMENTAL DESIGN (civil engineering technology, computer engineering, computer graphics, computer technology, electromechanical technology, engineering physics, manufacturing technology, occupational safety and health, and technological management), HEALTH PROFESSIONS (exercise science, nursing, preventive/wellness health care, speech pathology/audiology, and veterinary science), SOCIAL SCIENCE (criminal justice, economics, history, liberal arts/general studies, parks and recreation management, philosophy, political science/government, psychology, public administration, social work, and sociology). Premedicine, engineering and physics, and management of information systems are the strongest academically. Health professions, business and marketing, and liberal arts have the largest enrollments.

Required: All students must complete University Studies Program requirements, including courses in communications and basic skills, lab sciences and math, humanities and fine arts, social sciences, and for the B.A. degree, foreign language. A total of 120 semester hours with a minimum of 40 hours earned in residence with Murray State University. 42 of the 120 hours must be earned in 300 level or above courses. Refer to the catalog for further information on specific major requirements.

Special: MSU offers cooperative programs in most majors, cross-registration through the National Student Exchange, internships, study abroad in 25 countries, work-study, dual majors, B.A.-B.S. degrees, and a 3-2 engineering degrees with the University of Louisville and the University of Kentucky. Credit for life experience and a degree in integrated studies are also offered. Non-degree study is available. There are 7 national honor societies, including Phi Beta Kappa, a freshman honors program, and 15 departmental honors programs.

Faculty/Classroom: 54% of faculty are male; 46% are female, and teach undergraduates. Introductory courses are not taught by graduate students. Average class size in an introductory lecture is 30; laboratory, 20.

Admissions: 82% of the 2013-2014 applicants were accepted. The ACT scores were 33% below 21, 28% between 21 and 23, 23% between 24 and 26, 8% between 27 and 28, and 8% above 28. 36% of the current freshmen were in the top fifth of their class; 64% were in the top two fifths. 42 freshmen graduated first in their class.

Requirements: The ACT is required. Students must have a minimum composite score of 18 on the ACT. Applicants must rank in the top half of their class or have a 3.0 GPA. Applicants should have successfully completed 22 high school academic credits, which includes 4 units in English, 3 in math, 3 in science with at least 1 lab science and 3 in social studies, 2 years in a foreign language, 1 in visual/performing arts and 5 in electives; in addition, MSU strongly recommends a fourth year of math, 1 in art appreciation. Social Sciences must include U. S. history and world civilization. Math must include 3 algebra I and above courses. Sciences must include biology and chemistry or physics. A portfolio or audition is required for art and music majors. MSU requires applicants to be in the upper 50% of their class. A GPA of 3.0 is required. AP and CLEP credits are accepted.

Procedure: Freshmen are admitted to all sessions. Entrance exams should be taken before January of the enrollment year. There are early admissions and rolling admissions plans. Applications should be filed by August 1 for fall entry; December 1 for spring entry; and May 1 for summer entry, along with a $40 fee. Applications are accepted online.

Transfer: 692 transfer students enrolled in 2012-2013. Students having 24 semester hours or more of transferable degree credits and minimum of a 2.00 (C) cumulative grade point average on all previous courses, are eligible for admission. Applicants must be in good standing academically and financially at all previous schools attended. Students who have a minimum of 2.0 grade point average, but less than 24 hours of credit, must present official copies of high school transcript and either the ACT or SAT. 40 of 120 credits required for the bachelor's degree must be completed at MSU.

Visiting: There are regularly scheduled orientations for prospective students, Students are invited to attend sessions planned before all academic terms for which they are first enrolling. These sessions contain both academic and social orientation. There are guides for informal visits and visitors may sit in on classes. To schedule a visit, contact Shawn Smee at ssmee@murraystate.edu.

Financial Aid: In 2013-2014, 88% of all full-time freshmen and 87% of continuing full-time students received some form of financial aid. 63% of all full-time freshmen and 63% of continuing full-time students received need-based aid. The average freshman award was $12,541. Need-based scholarships or need-based grants averaged $5,932 ($22,439 maximum); need-based self-help aid (loans and jobs) averaged $6,226 ($23,597 maximum); non-need-based athletic scholarships averaged $10,110 ($28,852 maximum); and other non-need-based awards and non-need-based scholarships averaged $7,693 ($39,233 maximum). 21% of undergraduate students work part-time. Average annual earnings from campus work are $2193. The average financial indebtedness of the 2013 graduate was $21,526. The FAFSA and the college's own financial statement, and International Student's Certification of Finances are required. The priority date for freshman financial aid applications for fall entry is April 1. The deadline for filing freshman financial aid applications for fall entry is April 1.

International Students: There are 456 international students enrolled. The school actively recruits these students. They must take the TOEFL with a minimum score of 71 on the Internet-based version (iBT), Minimum score of 71 on TOEFL Internet-based Test (IBT). They must also take the SAT or ACT, scoring 18. ACT or SAT considered if submitted.

Computers: All students may access the system. There are no time limits and no fees.

Graduates: From July 1, 2012 to June 30, 2013, 1399 bachelor's degrees were awarded. The most popular majors were health professions and related programs (15%), education (13%), and business/marketing (11%). 715 companies recruited on campus in 2012-2013. In an average class, 28% graduate in 4 years or less, 48% graduate in 5 years or less, and 53% graduate in 6 years or less.

Admissions Contact: Shawn Smee, Director of Recruitment. E-Mail: *ssmee@Murraystate.edu* Web: *www.murraystate.edu*

NORTHERN KENTUCKY UNIVERSITY D-1

Highland Heights, KY 41099 (859) 572-5220, ext. 5744
(800) 637-9948; (859) 572-6665

Full-time: 4478 men, 5258 women
Part-time: 1334 men, 1724 women
Graduate: 901 men, 1568 women
Year: semesters, summer session
Application Deadline: August 1
Freshman Class: 2225 enrolled
SAT or ACT: required
Faculty: n/av
Ph.D.s: 72%
Student/Faculty: 19 to 1
Tuition: $7872 ($15,744)
Room & Board: $7430

LESS COMPETITIVE

Northern Kentucky University, founded in 1968, is a publicly controlled institution offering undergraduate and graduate programs in arts and sciences, business, health professions, informatics, and education and human services. There are 5 undergraduate schools and 6 graduate schools. In addition to regional accreditation, NKU has baccalaureate program accreditation with AACSB, ABET, ACCE, CSWE, NASM, NCATE, and NLN. Computerized library services include interlibrary loans, database searching, Internet access, and Wi-Fi capability. Special learning facilities include an art gallery, planetarium, radio station, TV station, digitorium, herbarium, and the anthropology museum. The 424-acre campus is in a suburban area 7 miles southeast of Cincinnati, Ohio. The campus is located in Highland Heights, Kentucky. Including any residence halls, there are 41 buildings.

Student Life: 68% of undergraduates are from Kentucky. Others are from 43 states, 52 foreign countries, and Canada. 82% are White. The average age of freshmen is 19; all undergraduates, 24. 33% do not continue beyond their first year.

Housing: 1822 students can be accommodated in college housing, which includes single-sex and coed dorms and on-campus apartments. On-campus housing is available on a first-come and first-served basis. Priority is given to out-of-town students. 87% of students commute. Alcohol is not permitted. All students may keep cars.

Activities: 5% of men belong to 7 national fraternities; 9% of women belong to 7 national sororities. There are 221 groups on campus, including and mock trial, leadership, recreational, special interest, art, cheerleading, choir, chorale, chorus, computers, cultural, dance, drama, drill team, environmental, ethnic, film, gay, honors, international, jazz band, literary magazine, musical theater, newspaper, pep band, photography, political, professional, radio and TV, religious, social, social service, and student government. Popular campus events include Welcome Week, Freshfusion, Pumpkin Bust, Feast4Finals and Homecoming.

Sports: There are 8 intercollegiate sports for men and 9 for women, and 12 intramural sports for men and 13 for women. Facilities include a 2000-seat gym, baseball and soccer fields, tennis and racquetball courts, a track, weight room, and swimming pool.

Disabled Students: All of the campus is accessible. Facilities include wheelchair ramps, elevators, special parking, specially equipped restrooms, special class scheduling, lowered drinking fountains, lowered telephones, and special housing.

Services: Counseling and information services are available, as is tutoring in most subjects. There is a reader service for the blind, and remedial math, reading, and writing. there are also developmental education courses.

Campus Safety and Security: Measures include 24-hour foot and vehicle patrol, emergency notification system, and security escort services. There are shuttle buses, emergency telephones, lighted pathways/sidewalks, controlled access to dorms/residences, and ALICE training.

Programs of Study: NKU confers B.A., B.S., B.M., B.S.N., B.F.A , B.H.S. and B.S.W. degrees. Associate, master's, and doctoral degrees are also awarded. Bachelor's degrees are awarded in BIOLOGICAL SCIENCE (biology/biological science), BUSINESS (accounting, business administration and management, business economics, finance, human resources, information & communication technology, labor studies, management information systems, management science, marketing and distribution, marketing/retailing/merchandising, organizational behavior, and sports management), COMMUNICATIONS AND THE ARTS (art, art history and appreciation, communications, dramatic arts, English, fine arts, French, German, graphic design, journalism, music, performing arts, radio/television technology, Spanish, speech/debate/rhetoric, and studio art), COMPUTER AND PHYSICAL SCIENCE (chemistry, Computer Engineering Technology, computer science, geology, information sciences and systems, mathematics, mathematics/computational, mathematics – economics, physics, and statistics), EDUCATION (art education, athletic training, business education, early childhood education, elementary education, health information management, industrial arts education, middle school education, physical education, science education, secondary education, special education, and trade and industrial education), ENGINEERING AND ENVIRONMENTAL DESIGN (architectural engineering, commercial art, construction management, construction technology, electrical/electronics engineering technology, environmental science, industrial engineering technology, manufacturing engineering, manufacturing technology, and preengineering), HEALTH PROFESSIONS (mental health/human services, nursing, predentistry, premedicine, prepharmacy, and preveterinary science), SOCIAL SCIENCE (anthropology, criminal justice, economics, forensic studies, French studies, geography, history, international relations, international studies, liberal arts/general studies, philosophy, philosophy and religion, physical fitness/movement, political science/government, prelaw, psychology, public administration, public history/archives, social science, social work, sociology, and urban studies). Organizational leadership, computer information technology and nursing have the largest enrollments.

Required: All students must complete 37 semester hours of general studies, including communication--written and oral, mathematics/statistics, natural sciences, culture, self & society, and global viewpoints, along with major and minor requirements. A total of 120 semester hours, with a minimum GPA of 2.0, is required to graduate.

Special: A 3-2 engineering degree is offered with the University of Kentucky. Cross-registration is possible through the Greater Cincinnati Area Consortium of colleges and universities. Study abroad in 34 countries, a Washington semester, on-campus work-study programs, an accelerated degree program, an interdisciplinary honors program, B.A.-B.S. degrees, dual majors, and pass/fail options are offered. There are co-op programs in most majors. Student-designed majors and credit for work experience are available. Non-degree study is possible. There are 14 national honor societies, a freshman honors program, and 9 departmental honors programs.

Faculty/Classroom: 54% of faculty are male; 46% are female. No introductory courses are taught by graduate students.

Admissions: The SAT scores for the 2013-2014 freshman class were: Critical Reading--46% below 500, 38% between 500 and 599, 13% between 600 and 699, and 2% between 700 and 800; Math--55% below 500, 31% between 500 and 599, 12% between 600 and 699, and 2% between 700 and 800. The ACT scores were 37% below 21, 29% between 21 and 23, 20% between 24 and 26, 7% between 27 and 28, and 7% above 28.

Requirements: The SAT or ACT is required. A GPA of 2.0 is required. AP and CLEP credits are accepted.

Procedure: Freshmen are admitted fall, spring, and summer. Entrance exams should be taken prior to enrollment. There are deferred admissions and rolling admissions plans. Early decision applications should be filed by February 1; regular applications, by August 1 for fall entry; December 1 for winter entry; December 1 for spring entry; and May 1 for summer entry, along with a $40 fee. Applications are accepted online.

Transfer: 694 transfer students enrolled in 2012-2013. Students must be eligible to return to their previous institution. College transcripts from previous institutions are required. 30 of 120 credits required for the bachelor's degree must be completed at NKU.

Visiting: There are regularly scheduled orientations for prospective students, consisting of a 1-day program with sessions on student services and financial aid, activities, a campus tour, and academic information, advising, and registration. There are guides for informal visits, visitors may sit in on classes, and stay overnight. To schedule a visit, contact the Office of Admissions.

Financial Aid: 60% of all full-time freshmen and 53% of continuing full-time students received need-based aid. The FAFSA and the college's own financial statement are required. The priority date for freshman financial aid applications for fall entry is March 1. The deadline for filing freshman financial aid applications for fall entry is April 1.

International Students: 483 international students enrolled. The school actively recruits these students, who must take the TOEFL or MELAB.

Computers: All students may access the system 7 days a week. There are no time limits and no fees.

Graduates: From July 1, 2012 to June 30, 2013, 1980 bachelor's degrees were awarded. The most popular majors were business/marketing (27%), communication/journalism (9%), and education (8%). 225 companies recruited on campus in 2012-2013. In an average class, 13% graduate in 4 years or less, 30% graduate in 5 years or less, and 37% graduate in 6 years or less.

Admissions Contact: Melissa Gorbrandt, Director of Admissions. E-Mail: *gorbrandt@nku.edu* Web: *www.nku.edu*

SPALDING UNIVERSITY D-2

Louisville, KY 40203 (502) 873-4178
(800) 896-8941, ext. 2111; (502) 992-2418

Full-time: 274 men, 680 women
Part-time: 141 men, 276 women
Graduate: 216 men, 780 women
Year: other, summer session
Application Deadline:
Freshman Class: 1094 applied, 887 accepted, 196 enrolled
Faculty: n/av
Ph.D.s: n/av
Student/Faculty: n/av
Tuition: $21,450
Room & Board: $10,400

LESS COMPETITIVE

Spalding University, established in 1814, is a private institution affiliated with the Roman Catholic Church. Today this urban, co-educational institution offers over two dozen degree programs at the bachelor's, master's and doctoral level, providing quality, real-world learning in liberal and professional studies to over 2,400 students. There are 3 undergraduate schools and 3 graduate schools. In addition to regional accreditation, Spalding has baccalaureate program accreditation with CSWE, NCATE, and NLN. The library contains 104,623 volumes, 2,330 audio/video tapes/CDs/DVDs, and subscribes to 17,600 periodicals including electronic. Computerized library services include interlibrary loans, database searching, and Internet access. Special learning facilities include an art gallery, radio station, a writing center and mathematics lab. The 6-acre campus is in an urban area Downtown Louisville, KY. Including any residence halls, there are 11 buildings.

Student Life: 89% of undergraduates are from Kentucky. Others are from 15 states, 6 foreign countries, and Canada. 60% are White; 22% African American. The average age of freshmen is 19; all undergraduates, 26. 27% do not continue beyond their first year.

Housing: 442 students can be accommodated in college housing, which includes coed dorms. On-campus housing is guaranteed for all 4 years, is available on a first-come, and first-served basis. Alcohol is not permitted. All students may keep cars.

Activities: There are no fraternities or sororities. There are 31 groups on campus, including environmental, ethnic, gay, honors, international, political, professional, radio and TV, recreational, religious, social, social service, and student government. Popular campus events include Annual Running of the Rodents, Scholarship and Learning Day.

Sports: There are 6 intercollegiate sports for men and 8 for women. Facilities include a gym and an exercise room.

Disabled Students: 85% of the campus is accessible. Facilities include wheelchair ramps, elevators, special parking, specially equipped restrooms, special class scheduling, lowered drinking fountains.

Services: Counseling and information services are available, as is tutoring in every subject. There is remedial math and reading.

Campus Safety and Security: Measures include 24-hour foot and vehicle patrol, emergency notification system, and security escort services. There are emergency telephones, lighted pathways/sidewalks, controlled access to dorms/residences, emergency call boxes, camera surveillance, in campus buildings and parking lots, and direct access to campus security from campus phones.

Programs of Study: Spalding confers B.A., B.S., B.S.B.A., B.F.A., B.S.N., B.S.S.W., B.S.A. and B.S./M.S.O.T. degrees. Associate, master's, and doctoral degrees are also awarded. Bachelor's degrees are awarded in BIOLOGICAL SCIENCE (biology/biological science), BUSINESS (accounting and business administration and management), COMMUNICATIONS AND THE ARTS (creative writing and media arts), EDUCATION (education and elementary education), HEALTH PROFESSIONS (nursing and occupational therapy), SOCIAL SCIENCE (humanities and social science, liberal arts/general studies, psychology, and social work). Education, and psychology have the largest enrollments.

Required: To graduate, students must earn 120 credits and a minimum overall GPA of 2.0. All students must complete a university studies requirement (average 51 credits) in humanities, social sciences, communication, natural sciences and math, credits in religious studies, and one general introduction course to the college.

Special: Internships, study abroad, B.A. - B.S. degrees, dual majors, work-study programs, and accelerated degree programs in business, psychology, and nursing are available. The Adult Accelerated Program enables students to earn a bachelor's degree by attending classes on weekends and evenings. Credit is given for military experience and pass/fail options are available. Cross-registration is offered with the Kentuckiana Metroversity Consortium. There are 8 national honor societies.

Faculty/Classroom: No introductory courses are taught by graduate students.

Admissions: 81% of the 2013-2014 applicants were accepted.

Requirements: The SAT or ACT is required. In addition, applicants must be graduates of an accredited secondary school and should have completed 4 years of high school English and 2 years each of a foreign language, math, science, and social studies. A GED may be substituted for the high school degree. A GPA of 2.5 is required. AP and CLEP credits are accepted. Important factors in the admissions decision are advanced placement or honors courses, recommendations by school officials, and evidence of special talent.

Procedure: Freshmen are admitted to all sessions. There are deferred admissions and rolling admissions plans. Application deadlines are open. Application fee is $20. Notification is sent on a rolling basis. Applications are accepted online.

Transfer: 129 transfer students enrolled in 2012-2013. It is preferred that applicants have a 2.5 GPA.

Visiting: There are regularly scheduled orientations for prospective students, New Student Orientation, AAP Orientation, Graduate Program Specific Orientation. There are guides for informal visits, visitors may sit in on classes, and stay overnight. To schedule a visit, contact the Office of Admission at (502) 585-7111.

Financial Aid: The FAFSA is required. The deadline for filing freshman financial aid applications for fall entry is March 15.

International Students: There are 10 international students enrolled. The school actively recruits these students. They must take the TOEFL with a minimum score of 535 on the paper-based TOEFL (PBT) or 75 on the Internet-based version (iBT). They must also take the SAT or ACT, scoring 20.

Computers: All students may access the system. There are no time limits and no fees.

Graduates: From July 1, 2012 to June 30, 2013, 220 bachelor's degrees were awarded. The most popular majors were nursing (33%), business (16%), and psychology (16%).

Admissions Contact: Patty Goodman, Director of Admissions. E-Mail: *admissions@spalding.edu* Web: *www.spalding.edu*

THOMAS MORE COLLEGE — D-2

Crestview Hills, KY 41017 — (859) 344-3514; (800) 825-4557; (859) 344-3444

Full-time: 579 men, 561 women	**Faculty:** 72
Part-time: 223 men, 139 women	**Ph.D.s:** 75%
Graduate: 56 men, 42 women	**Student/Faculty:** 16 to 1
Year: semesters, summer session	**Tuition:** $27,220
Application Deadline: August 1	**Room & Board:** $7540
Freshman Class: n/av	
SAT CR/M: 480/490	**ACT:** 22 — **COMPETITIVE**

Thomas More College, founded in 1921 as Villa Madonna College, is a private Catholic institution offering undergraduate programs in liberal arts and sciences, plus graduate degrees in business administration and education. There is 1 undergraduate school and 2 graduate schools. In addition to regional accreditation, Thomas More has baccalaureate program accreditation with NLN. The library contains 114,230 volumes, 28,429 microform items, and 2,386 audio/video tapes/CDs/DVDs, and subscribes to 368 periodicals including electronic. Computerized library services include interlibrary loans, database searching, and Internet access. Special learning facilities include an art gallery, observatory on campus and biology field station on the Ohio River. The 100-acre campus is in a suburban area 8 miles south of Cincinnati. Including any residence halls, there are 10 buildings.

Student Life: 53% of undergraduates are from out of state, mostly the Mid-West. Students are from 17 states, and 3 foreign countries. 65% are from public schools. 78% are White. 46% claim no religious affiliation; 28% Catholic; 22% Protestant. The average age of freshmen is 18; all undergraduates, 23. 39% do not continue beyond their first year; 50% remain to graduate.

Housing: 400 students can be accommodated in college housing, which includes single-sex and coed dorms. On-campus housing is available on a first-come and first-served basis. Priority is given to out-of-town students. 68% of students commute. All students may keep cars.

Activities: 2% of men belong to 1 national fraternity; 2% of women belong to 1 national sorority. There are 35 groups on campus, including art, cheerleading, chorus, computers, drama, environmental, ethnic, honors, international, literary magazine, marching band, political, professional, religious, social, social service, student government, and yearbook. Popular campus events include Spring Pig Roast, Welcome Carnival, and Presidential Inauguration Ball.

Sports: There are 8 intercollegiate sports for men and 8 for women, and 5 intramural sports for men and 5 for women. Facilities include an athletic/convocation center with a 1500-seat indoor gym, a football/soccer complex plus baseball and softball fields, 16 tennis courts (8 indoor), 4 racquetball courts, an indoor pool, a track, and weight and exercise rooms.

Disabled Students: 90% of the campus is accessible. Facilities include wheelchair ramps, elevators, special parking, and specially equipped restrooms.

Services: Counseling and information services are available, as is tutoring in every subject. There is a reader service for the blind, and remedial math, reading, and writing. Signing for the hearing impaired is available.

Campus Safety and Security: Measures include 24-hour foot and vehicle patrol, emergency notification system, self-defense education, and security escort services. There are lighted pathways/sidewalks and controlled access to dorms/residences.

Programs of Study: Thomas More confers B.A., B.S., B.B.A., B.E.S. and B.S.N. degrees. Associate and master's degrees are also awarded. Bachelor's degrees are awarded in BIOLOGICAL SCIENCE (biology/biological science), BUSINESS (accounting, business administration and management, and sports marketing), COMMUNICATIONS AND THE ARTS (art, communications, dramatic arts, English, and Spanish), COMPUTER AND PHYSICAL SCIENCE (chemistry, computer science, mathematics, and physics), EDUCATION (art education, business education, elementary education, middle school education, secondary education, and social studies education), ENGINEERING AND ENVIRONMENTAL DESIGN (environmental science), HEALTH PROFESSIONS (health care administration, medical laboratory technology, and nursing), SOCIAL SCIENCE (criminal justice, economics, forensic studies, history, humanities, international studies, liberal arts/general studies, philosophy, political science/government, psychology, sociology, and theological studies). Business, biology and nursing have the largest enrollments.

Required: All students must complete 56 to 61 hours of core requirements, including 9 credits in theology, 6 each in English, social sciences, global history, fine arts, foreign language, philosophy, and natural sciences, and 3 each in communication and math. A total of 128 credit hours, including 36 to 76 in the major, with a minimum GPA of 2.0 is required to graduate.

Special: There are co-op programs in all majors except nursing. The 3-2 engineering degree is available from the accredited engineering school of the student's choice. Cross-registration is possible through the Greater Cincinnati Consortium. There are also internships, study abroad in many countries, many B.A. & B.S. degrees, student-designed majors, work-study programs, credit for life experience, and pass/fail options. The Bachelor of Elected Studies and Bachelor of Arts-Student Initiated degrees provide students with an individualized program. Nondegree study is possible. There are 9 national honor societies and 9 departmental honors programs.

Faculty/Classroom: 59% of faculty are male; 41% are female. All teach undergraduates. No introductory courses are taught by graduate students. The average class size in an introductory lecture is 14; in a laboratory is 11; and in a regular course is 14.

Admissions: The SAT scores for the 2013-2014 freshman class were: Critical Reading--55% below 500, 36% between 500 and 599, and 9% between 600 and 699; Math--51% below 500, 31% between 500 and 599, 13% between 600 and 699, and 5% between 700 and 800. The ACT scores were 28% below 21, 35% between 21 and 23, 24% between 24 and 26, 5% between 27 and 28, and 8% above 28. 23% of the current freshmen were in the top fifth of their class; 52% were in the top two fifths.

Requirements: The SAT or ACT is required, with a minimum composite score of 20 on the ACT (20 on the English section) or 1010 on the SAT (480 on the verbal section). Applicants should have completed 17 high school academic units, including 4 of English, 3 each of math, science, and social studies, 2 of non-native language, and 1 each of arts appreciation and computer literacy. Thomas More requires applicants to be in the upper 50% of their class. A GPA of 2.0 is required. AP and CLEP credits are accepted. Important factors in the admissions decision are advanced placement or honors courses, leadership record, and personality/intangible qualities.

Procedure: Freshmen are admitted to all sessions. Entrance exams should be taken in the spring of the junior year or in the fall of the senior year. There are deferred admissions and rolling admissions plans. Applications should be filed by August 1 for fall entry; January 2 for spring entry, along with a $25 fee. Applications are accepted online.

Transfer: 65 transfer students enrolled in 2012-2013. Applicants should be in good academic standing and have a minimum GPA of 2.0 in 24 semester hours earned. 38 of 128 credits required for the bachelor's degree must be completed at Thomas More.

Visiting: Regularly scheduled orientations for prospective students, including a campus tour and meetings with an admissions counselor, a professor in one's major field (if decided), and financial aid staff. There are guides for informal visits, visitors may sit in on classes, and stay overnight. To schedule a visit, contact the Admissions Office at (859) 344-3332.

Financial Aid: In 2013-2014, 100% of all full-time freshmen and 86% of continuing full-time students received some form of financial aid. 82% of all full-time freshmen and 63% of continuing full-time students received need-based aid. The average freshman award was $21,063. Need-based scholarships or need-based grants averaged $16,356; need-based self-help aid (loans and jobs) averaged $4,458; and other non-need-based awards and non-need-based scholarships averaged $15,861. Average annual earnings from campus work are $2100. The average financial indebtedness of the 2013 graduate was $32,601. Thomas More is a member of CSS. The FAFSA and the college's own financial statement are required. The deadline for filing freshman financial aid applications for fall entry is January 15.

International Students: There are 8 international students enrolled. The school actively recruits these students. They must take the TOEFL with a minimum score of 515 on the paper-based TOEFL (PBT) or 66 on the Internet-based version (iBT). They must also take the SAT or ACT, scoring 20.

Computers: All students may access the system any time. There are no time limits and no fees.

Graduates: From July 1, 2012 to June 30, 2013, 254 bachelor's degrees were awarded. The most popular majors were business (42%), nursing (10%), and education (8%). 46 companies recruited on campus in 2012-2013. In an average class, 35% graduate in 4 years or less, 46% graduate in 5 years or less, and 49% graduate in 6 years or less. Of the 2012 graduating class, 27% were enrolled in graduate school within 6 months of graduation, and 95% were employed.

Admissions Contact: Kristi Lehmer, Executive Dir. of Enrollment Management. E-Mail: *lehmerk@thomasmore.edu* Web: *www.thomasmore.edu*

TRANSYLVANIA UNIVERSITY D-3

Lexington, KY 40508 (859) 233-8242
(800) 872-6798; (859) 233-8797

Full-time: 453 men, 613 women | **Faculty:** 96; IIB, av$
Part-time: 9 men, 6 women | **Ph.D.s:** 100%
Graduate: none | **Student/Faculty:** 11 to 1
Year: 4-1-4, summer session | **Tuition:** $31,560
Application Deadline: February 1 | **Room & Board:** $8750
Freshman Class: 1540 applied, 1275 accepted, 295 enrolled
SAT CR/M: 590/560 | **ACT:** 27 | **VERY COMPETITIVE+**

Transylvania University, founded in 1780, is an independent liberal arts institution affiliated with the Christian Church (Disciples of Christ). Through an engagement with the liberal arts, Transylvania prepares its students for a humane and fulfilling personal and public life by cultivating independent thinking, open-mindedness, creative expression, and commitment to lifelong learning and social responsibility in a diverse world. There is one undergraduate school. In addition to regional accreditation, Transy has baccalaureate program accreditation with NCATE. The library contains 276,000 volumes, 60 microform items, and 4,483 audio/video tapes/CDs/DVDs, and subscribes to 19,000 periodicals including electronic. Computerized library services include interlibrary loans, database searching, Internet access, and Wi-Fi capability. Special learning facilities include an art gallery, natural history museum, and radio station. The 48-acre campus is in an urban area of historic district of downtown Lexington. Including any residence halls, there are 24 buildings.

Student Life: 77% of undergraduates are from Kentucky. Others are from 28 states, 8 foreign countries, and Canada. 85% are from public schools. 82% are White. 35% are Protestant; 28% Mormon, Muslim, Orthodox and Buddhist; 18% Catholic; 18% claim no religious affiliation. The average age of freshmen is 18; all undergraduates, 20. 12% do not continue beyond their first year; 74% remain to graduate.

Housing: 900 students can be accommodated in college housing, which includes single-sex and coed dorms and on-campus apartments. In addition, there are language houses. On-campus housing is guaranteed for all 4 years. 76% of students live on campus; of those, 80% remain on campus on weekends. All students may keep cars.

Activities: 45% of men belong to 4 national fraternities; 60% of women belong to 4 national sororities. There are 65 groups on campus, including art, band, cheerleading, choir, chorale, chorus, computers, dance, debate, drama, environmental, ethnic, forensics, gay, honors, international, jazz band, literary magazine, musical theater, newspaper, opera, orchestra, pep band, political, professional, radio and TV, religious, social, social service, student government, and yearbook.

Sports: There are 7 intercollegiate sports for men and 9 for women, and 10 intramural sports for men and 10 for women. Facilities include a 1300-seat performance gym, a fitness center with an indoor jogging track, a swimming pool, basketball and racquetball/handball courts, 6 tennis courts, and 3 athletic fields (baseball, men's soccer/field hockey, and women's soccer/softball).

Disabled Students: 90% of the campus is accessible. Facilities include wheelchair ramps, elevators, special parking, specially equipped restrooms, special class scheduling, lowered drinking fountains. Arrangements are made according to individual needs.

Services: Counseling and information services are available, as is tutoring in every subject.

Campus Safety and Security: Measures include 24-hour foot and vehicle patrol, emergency notification system, self-defense education, and security escort services. There are shuttle buses, emergency telephones, and lighted pathways/sidewalks.

Programs of Study: Transy confers B.A. degrees. Bachelor's degrees are awarded in BIOLOGICAL SCIENCE (biochemistry, biology/biological science, and neurosciences), BUSINESS (accounting and business administration and management), COMMUNICATIONS AND THE ARTS (art history, art, classics, dramatic arts, English, French, Germanic languages and literature, music, Spanish, studio art, and theatre arts), COMPUTER AND PHYSICAL SCIENCE (chemistry, computer science, mathematics, and physics), EDUCATION (education, elementary education, and middle school education), HEALTH PROFESSIONS (exercise science), SOCIAL SCIENCE (anthropology, economics, history, philosophy, political science/government, psychology, religion, and sociology). Business, biology, and psychology have the largest enrollments.

Required: The college believes that all students, no matter what career or vocation they choose, benefit from liberal education; and so the college encourages the free search for knowledge and understanding drawn from the natural and social sciences, the humanities, and the arts. By so doing, the college strives to empower students to develop lifelong habits of learning and intelligent, respectful discussion. Therefore, students must fulfill requirements in five general areas: Area I Introduction to Critical Skills Area II Approaches to Learning Area III Cultural Traditions Area IV Upper-level Liberal Arts (2+2) and Area V Writing Intensive Courses.

Special: 3-2 engineering degrees with the University of Kentucky and

Vanderbilt University are offered. Cross-registration with May Term Consortium schools, internships, study abroad in 17 countries, work-study programs, a Washington semester, dual majors, and student-designed majors are available. There are 9 national honor societies.

Faculty/Classroom: 58% of faculty are male; 42% are female. All teach undergraduates. No introductory courses are taught by graduate students. The average class size in an introductory lecture is 21; in a laboratory is 14; and in a regular course is 18.

Admissions: 83% of the 2013-2014 applicants were accepted. The SAT scores for the 2013-2014 freshman class were: Critical Reading--14% below 500, 36% between 500 and 599, 41% between 600 and 699, and 9% between 700 and 800; Math--14% below 500, 52% between 500 and 599, 24% between 600 and 699, and 10% between 700 and 800. The ACT scores were 5% below 21, 13% between 21 and 23, 26% between 24 and 26, 19% between 27 and 28, and 37% above 28. 61% of the current freshmen were in the top fifth of their class; 89% were in the top two fifths. There were 4 National Merit finalists.

Requirements: The SAT or ACT is required. One essay and 2 recommendations are required. An interview is strongly recommended. Transy requires applicants to be in the upper 50% of their class. A GPA of 3.0 is required. AP credits are accepted. Important factors in the admissions decision are advanced placement or honors courses, recommendations by school officials, and extracurricular activities record.

Procedure: Freshmen are admitted fall and winter. Entrance exams should be taken during the junior year and no later than December of the senior year for scholarship consideration or February for general admission. There is a deferred admissions plan. Early decision applications should be filed by December 1; regular applications, by February 1 for fall entry; and December 5 for winter entry. Notification of early decision is sent January 15; regular decision, March 15. Applications are accepted online.

Transfer: 12 transfer students enrolled in 2012-2013. Applicants must have a minimum college GPA of 2.75 and should submit official copies of all college transcripts, 2 recommendations, and 1 essay. A high school transcript or GED is required. 18 of 36 credits required for the bachelor's degree must be completed at Transy.

Visiting: There are regularly scheduled orientations for prospective students, consisting of campus open houses in fall and winter for high school juniors and seniors, including a welcome program, an academic information fair, campus tours, a luncheon, a financial aid session, and a faculty session. There are guides for informal visits, visitors may sit in on classes, and stay overnight. To schedule a visit, contact Office of Admissions.

Financial Aid: In 2013-2014, 99% of all full-time freshmen and 98% of continuing full-time students received some form of financial aid. 66% of all full-time freshmen and 68% of continuing full-time students received need-based aid. The average freshman award was $22,143. Need-based scholarships or need-based grants averaged $22,779 ($40,310 maximum); need-based self-help aid (loans and jobs) averaged $5,028 ($7,825 maximum); and other non-need-based awards and non-need-based scholarships averaged $14,057 ($40,310 maximum). 40% of undergraduate students work part-time. Average annual earnings from campus work are $1265. The average financial indebtedness of the 2013 graduate was $28,026. Transy is a member of CSS. The FAFSA is required. The deadline for filing freshman financial aid applications for fall entry is March 1.

International Students: There are 23 international students enrolled. The school actively recruits these students. They must take the TOEFL. They must also take the SAT or ACT, scoring 1030.

Computers: All students may access the system 24 hours a day. There are no time limits and no fees.

Graduates: From July 1, 2012 to June 30, 2013, 248 bachelor's degrees were awarded. The most popular majors were business administration (12%), biology (12%), and psychology (9%). 13 companies recruited on campus in 2012-2013. In an average class, 1% graduate in 3 years or less, 68% graduate in 4 years or less, 71% graduate in 5 years or less, and 72% graduate in 6 years or less. Of the 2012 graduating class, 40% were enrolled in graduate school within 6 months of graduation, and 41% were employed.

Admissions Contact: Brad Goan, VP for Enrollment and Dean of Admissions. E-Mail: *admissions@transy.edu* Web: *www.transy.edu*

UNION COLLEGE E-4

Barbourville, KY 40906	**(606) 546-1709** **(800) 489-8646; (606) 546-1667**
Full-time: 385 men, 344 women	**Faculty:** 53; IIB, --$
Part-time: 30 men, 59 women	**Ph.D.s:** 77%
Graduate: 131 men, 215 women	**Student/Faculty:** 14 to 1
Year: semesters, summer session	**Tuition:** $22,075
Application Deadline: open	**Room & Board:** $6700
Freshman Class: 1390 applied, 1038 accepted, 241 enrolled	
SAT CR/M: 469/506 **ACT:** 22	**COMPETITIVE**

Union College, founded in 1879, is a private liberal arts institution affiliated with the United Methodist Church. There is one graduate school. The library contains 230,938 volumes, 453,787 microform items, and 4,686 audio/video tapes/CDs/DVDs, and subscribes to 114,865 periodicals including electronic. Computerized library services include interlibrary loans, database searching, Internet access, and Wi-Fi capability. The 100-acre campus is in a small town 95 miles south of Lexington, Kentucky and 85 miles north of Knoxville, Tennessee. Including any residence halls, there are 20 buildings.

Student Life: 72% of undergraduates are from Kentucky. Others are from 30 states, 73 foreign countries, and Canada. 79% are White. 38% are Baptist, Pentecostal, Church of Christ, and unknown; 34% claim no religious affiliation; 20% Protestant. The average age of freshmen is 19; all undergraduates, 22. 44% do not continue beyond their first year; 34% remain to graduate.

Housing: 408 students can be accommodated in college housing, which includes single-sex dorms, on-campus apartments, off-campus apartments, and married student housing. On-campus housing is guaranteed for all 4 years, is available on a first-come, and first-served basis. 55% of students commute. Alcohol is not permitted. All students may keep cars.

Activities: There are no fraternities or sororities. There are 31 groups on campus, including cheerleading, choir, chorale, chorus, computers, drama, ethnic, gay, honors, international, literary magazine, pep band, professional, radio and TV, religious, social, social service, student government, and yearbook. Popular campus events include Springfest, Student Holiday Dinner, and CIRCLES Ceremony.

Sports: There are 12 intercollegiate sports for men and 13 for women, and 5 intramural sports for men and 3 for women. Facilities include a 3,000-seat campus stadium, an 1,800-seat gym, an indoor pool with bleachers for 300, 6 tennis courts, a weight-training center, an athletic training center, a 500-seat baseball stadium with 3 batting cages and a practice infield, a soccer field with stands for 250, a softball field with stands for 150, and practice fields for football and soccer.

Disabled Students: 85% of the campus is accessible. Facilities include wheelchair ramps, elevators, special parking, specially equipped restrooms, special class scheduling, and lowered drinking fountains.

Services: Counseling and information services are available, as is tutoring in most subjects, There is a tutoring lab with computer support. There is a reader service for the blind, and remedial math, reading, and writing.

Campus Safety and Security: Measures include 24-hour foot and vehicle patrol, emergency notification system, self-defense education, and security escort services. There are emergency telephones, lighted pathways/sidewalks, controlled access to dorms/residences, The campus web site has a notification system (alert system) that provides information about recent crimes on campus.

Programs of Study: Union confers B.A., and B.S. degrees. Master's degrees are also awarded. Bachelor's degrees are awarded in BIOLOGICAL SCIENCE (biology/biological science), BUSINESS (accounting, business administration and management, international business management, marketing management, organizational leadership and management, recreational facilities management, and sports management), COMMUNICATIONS AND THE ARTS (communications, dramatic arts, English, and fine arts), COMPUTER AND PHYSICAL SCIENCE (chemistry and mathematics), EDUCATION (athletic training, education, elementary education, middle school education, physical education, science education, secondary education, social studies education, and special education), ENGINEERING AND ENVIRONMENTAL DESIGN (computer technology), HEALTH PROFESSIONS (exercise science, health, and nursing), SOCIAL SCIENCE (criminal justice, history, Latin American studies, ministries, psychology, religion, social work, and sociology). Education, business, and psychology are the strongest academically.

Required: All students are required to complete 43 credits in a liberal education core, including 21 hours in humanities, 7 to 8 of general science, 6 of social science, and 3 each of wellness, math, and cultural studies.

Special: A 3-2 enginering degree is offered with the University of Kentucky and Auburn University. Work-study programs, study abroad in 7 countries, an accelerated business degree completion program, and internships in business, sociology, psychology, recreational management, and mass communications are available. There are 2 national honor societies and a freshman honors program.

Faculty/Classroom: 59% of faculty are male; 41% are female. 84% teach undergraduates. No introductory courses are taught by graduate students. The average class size in an introductory lecture is 25 and in a regular course is 20.

Admissions: 75% of the 2013-2014 applicants were accepted. The SAT scores for the 2013-2014 freshman class were: Critical Reading--58% below 500, 38% between 500 and 599, and 4% between 600 and 699; Math--54% below 500, 38% between 500 and 599, and 8% between 600 and 699. The ACT scores were 41% below 21, 25% between 21 and 23, 26% between 24 and 26, 5% between 27 and 28, and 3% above 28.

Requirements: The SAT or ACT is required. In addition, Standardized text scores are not required for students 25 of older. All first-year students should have completed a pre-college high school curriculum that includes

4 units of English, 3 of math, 2 each of lab science and social science, and the study of a foreign language. An official, sealed high school transcript or an official GED score report is also required. A GPA of 2.0 is required. AP and CLEP credits are accepted. Important factors in the admissions decision are evidence of special talent, geographical diversity, and advanced placement or honors courses.

Procedure: Freshmen are admitted to all sessions. Entrance exams should be taken by January of the senior year. There are deferred admissions and rolling admissions plans. Application deadlines are open. Application fee is $10. Notification is sent on a rolling basis. Applications are accepted online.

Transfer: 72 transfer students enrolled in 2012-2013. Applicants should have a minimum GPA of 2.0. 32 of 120 credits required for the bachelor's degree must be completed at Union.

Visiting: There are regularly scheduled orientations for prospective students, consisting of advising and registration, parent sessions, and breakout sessions. There are guides for informal visits, visitors may sit in on classes, and stay overnight. To schedule a visit, contact Summer Jackson at sjackson@unionky.edu.

Financial Aid: In 2013-2014, 87% of all full-time freshmen and 92% of continuing full-time students received some form of financial aid. 87% of all full-time freshmen and 92% of continuing full-time students received need-based aid. The average freshman award was $21,242. Need-based scholarships or need-based grants averaged $18,212; need-based self-help aid (loans and jobs) averaged $3,481; and other non-need-based awards and non-need-based scholarships averaged $14,779. Union is a member of CSS. The CSS/Profile and FAFSA are required. The deadline for filing freshman financial aid applications for fall entry is March 15.

International Students: There are 29 international students enrolled. The school actively recruits these students. They must take the TOEFL with a minimum score of 550 on the paper-based TOEFL (PBT) and the college's own test, , and also complete an ELS program at level 109. They must also take the SAT or ACT.

Computers: All students may access the system. There are no time limits and no fees.

Graduates: From July 1, 2012 to June 30, 2013, 112 bachelor's degrees were awarded. The most popular majors were education (19%), business/marketing (14%), and health professions/related programs (12%). In an average class, 16% graduate in 4 years or less, 32% graduate in 5 years or less, and 34% graduate in 6 years or less.

Admissions Contact: Summet Jackson, Director: Undergraduate Enrollment. E-Mail: *enrollme@unionky.edu* Web: *www.unionky.edu*

UNIVERSITY OF KENTUCKY D-3

Lexington, KY 40506 **(859) 257-2000; (859) 257-3823**

Full-time: 9445 men, 9733 women	**Faculty:** 1207; I, --$
Part-time: 878 men, 771 women	**Ph.D.s:** 93%
Graduate: 3152 men, 4055 women	**Student/Faculty:** n/av
Year: semesters, summer session	**Tuition:** $9676 ($19,864)
Application Deadline:	**Room & Board:** $10,192
Freshman Class: n/av	
SAT or ACT: required	

COMPETITIVE

The University of Kentucky, founded in 1865, is a public land-grant institution offering undergraduate and graduate programs in a variety of areas. There are 13 undergraduate schools and 1 graduate school. In addition to regional accreditation, UK has baccalaureate program accreditation with AACSB, ABET, ACEJMC, ACPE, ADA, AHEA, APTA, ASLA, CAHEA, CSWE, FIDER, NAAB, NASAD, NASM, NCATE, NLN, NRPA, and SAF. The 13 libraries contain 2.8 million volumes, 5.9 million microform items, and 73,600 audio/video tapes/CDs/DVDs, and subscribe to 26,539 periodicals including electronic. Computerized library services include database searching. Special learning facilities include an art gallery, natural history museum, radio station, and TV station. The 764-acre campus is in a suburban area 75 miles south of Cincinnati. Including any residence halls, there are 335 buildings.

Student Life: 79% of undergraduates are from Kentucky. Others are from 49 states, 114 foreign countries, and Canada. 79% are White. The average age of freshmen is 18; all undergraduates, 21. 19% do not continue beyond their first year; 58% remain to graduate.

Housing: 6166 students can be accommodated in college housing, which includes single-sex and coed dorms, on-campus apartments, and married student housing. In addition, there are honors houses, language houses, special-interest houses, fraternity houses, and sorority houses. On-campus housing is available on a first-come and first-served basis. 74% of students commute. Alcohol is not permitted. All students may keep cars.

Activities: 16% of men belong to 24 national fraternities; 25% of women belong to 19 national sororities. There are 272 groups on campus, including band, cheerleading, chess, choir, chorale, chorus, computers, dance, debate, drama, drill team, environmental, ethnic, gay, honors, international, jazz band, literary magazine, marching band, musical theater, newspaper, orchestra, pep band, photography, political, professional, radio and TV, religious, social, social service, student government, symphony, and yearbook. Popular campus events include Little Kentucky Derby, Cultural Diversity Week, and Spotlight Jazz Series.

Sports: There are 11 intercollegiate sports for men and 12 for women, and 22 intramural sports for men and 22 for women. Facilities include a 67600-seat football stadium, a 24500-seat arena for basketball and other activities, an aquatic center and swimming pool, baseball fields, a training center, indoor tennis courts, and a field house.

Disabled Students: 90% of the campus is accessible. Facilities include wheelchair ramps, elevators, special parking, specially equipped restrooms, special class scheduling, lowered drinking fountains, and lowered telephones.

Services: There is a reader service for the blind, and remedial math.

Campus Safety and Security: Measures include 24-hour foot and vehicle patrol, emergency notification system, self-defense education, and security escort services. There are shuttle buses, emergency telephones, lighted pathways/sidewalks, and controlled access to dorms/residences.

Programs of Study: UK confers B.A., B.S., B.Arch., B.B.A., B.F.A., B.H.S. and B.M. degrees. Master's and doctoral degrees are also awarded. Bachelor's degrees are awarded in AGRICULTURE (agricultural economics, agriculture, animal science, and forestry and related sciences), BIOLOGICAL SCIENCE (biology/biological science, botany, and zoology), BUSINESS (accounting, banking and finance, business economics, hotel/motel and restaurant management, and marketing/retailing/merchandising), COMMUNICATIONS AND THE ARTS (advertising, art history and appreciation, arts administration/management, communications, dramatic arts, English, French, German, Italian, journalism, linguistics, music, music performance, Russian, Spanish, and telecommunications), COMPUTER AND PHYSICAL SCIENCE (chemistry, computer science, geology, mathematics, and physics), EDUCATION (agricultural education, art education, business education, early childhood education, elementary education, foreign languages education, health education, mathematics education, middle school education, music education, physical education, science education, secondary education, social studies education, and special education), ENGINEERING AND ENVIRONMENTAL DESIGN (chemical engineering, civil engineering, electrical/electronics engineering, landscape architecture/design, materials engineering, mechanical engineering, and mining and mineral engineering), HEALTH PROFESSIONS (nursing, physical therapy, and physician's assistant), SOCIAL SCIENCE (anthropology, economics, food science, geography, history, Latin American studies, philosophy, political science/government, psychology, social work, sociology, and textiles and clothing). Pharmacy, architecture, and allied health are the strongest academically. Finance, accounting, and marketing have the largest enrollments.

Required: All students must maintain a minimum 2.0 GPA and complete at least 120 credit hours. Students must demonstrate competency in math, foreign language, writing, and oral communications. Required studies include courses in basic skills, inference, and communicative skills, along with disciplinary and cross-disciplinary studies.

Special: Co-op programs are offered in engineering, business, computer science, math, and agriculture. The Academic Common Market allows students in 14 southern states to study outside the university. Internships in a variety of fields, study abroad in 36 countries, work-study programs with the university and local businesses, and credit for life experience are also available. An accelerated degree program, B.A.-B.S. degrees, dual and double majors, a general studies degree, student-designed majors, a 3-2 engineering degree with several smaller schools in Kentucky, non-degree study, and pass/fail options are also offered. There are 12 national honor societies, including Phi Beta Kappa, and a freshman honors program.

Faculty/Classroom: 64% of faculty are male; 36% are female. No introductory courses are taught by graduate students.

Requirements: The SAT or ACT is required. Minimum scores vary with the GPA. Applicants must complete 20 Carnegie units, including 4 years of English, 3 of math, and 2 each of science and social studies. A fourth year of math, 2 years of foreign language, and 1 year of fine arts also are recommended. A portfolio is required for art studio courses, and an audition is required for music performance. A GPA of 2.0 is required. AP and CLEP credits are accepted.

Procedure: Freshmen are admitted to all sessions. Entrance exams should be taken before Christmas of the senior year. There is a rolling admissions plan. Applications should be filed by October 15 for spring entry; April 15 for summer entry, along with a $20 fee.

Transfer: 1443 transfer students enrolled in 2012-2013. Transfer students need a minimum GPA of 2.0. If they have fewer than 24 credit hours, they must meet freshmen admission standards. With 24 credits or more, the SAT I or ACT is not required. 30 of 120 credits required for the bachelor's degree must be completed at UK.

Visiting: There are regularly scheduled orientations for prospective students, including a campus tour and information on admissions, housing, financial aid, and campus activities. There are guides for informal visits and visitors may sit in on classes.

Financial Aid: 32% of all full-time freshmen and 34% of continuing full-time students received need-based aid. The average freshman award was $6,007. UK is a member of CSS. The FAFSA is required. The deadline for filing freshman financial aid applications for fall entry is February 15.

International Students: There are 366 international students enrolled. The school actively recruits these students. They must take the TOEFL.

Computers: All students may access the system. 24 hours daily in the computing center, and various hours in labs. There are no time limits and no fees.

Graduates: From July 1, 2012 to June 30, 2013, 3285 bachelor's degrees were awarded. The most popular majors were business (20%), engineering (10%), and health professions (9%). In an average class, 21% graduate in 4 years or less, 43% graduate in 5 years or less, and 51% graduate in 6 years or less.

Admissions Contact: Randy Mills, Associate Director for Recruitment. E-Mail: *admissions@uky.edu* Web: *www.uky.edu*

UNIVERSITY OF LOUISVILLE D-2

Louisville, KY 40292 **(502) 852-6531**
(800) 334-8635; (502) 852-4476

Full-time: 5975 men, 6451 women	**Faculty:** n/av; I, --$
Part-time: 1795 men, 1736 women	**Ph.D.s:** 86%
Graduate: 2570 men, 2920 women	**Student/Faculty:** 18 to 1
Year: semesters, summer session	**Tuition:** $9750 ($23,638)
Application Deadline: August 19	**Room & Board:** $7710
Freshman Class: 9142 applied, 6496 accepted, 2855 enrolled	
SAT CR/M: 540/570	**ACT:** 24 **VERY COMPETITIVE**

The University of Louisville, founded in 1798, is a public institution offering a wide range of undergraduate and graduate academic programs. There are 9 undergraduate schools and 12 graduate schools. In addition to regional accreditation, U of L has baccalaureate program accreditation with AACSB, ABET, ADA, CSAB, CSWE, FIDER, NASM, and NCATE. The 6 libraries contain 2.3 million volumes, 2.2 million microform items, and 56,077 audio/video tapes/CDs/DVDs, and subscribe to 73,000 periodicals including electronic. Computerized library services include interlibrary loans, database searching, Internet access, and Wi-Fi capability. Special learning facilities include an art gallery, planetarium, and radio station. The 604-acre campus is in an urban area in Louisville, KY. Including any residence halls, there are 173 buildings.

Student Life: 84% of undergraduates are from Kentucky. Others are from 50 states, 54 foreign countries, and Canada. 75% are White. The average age of freshmen is 18; all undergraduates, 24. 22% do not continue beyond their first year; 54% remain to graduate.

Housing: 4772 students can be accommodated in college housing, which includes coed dorms, on-campus apartments, off-campus apartments, and married student housing. In addition, there are honors houses, special-interest houses, fraternity houses, and sorority houses. On-campus housing is available on a first-come and first-served basis. Priority is given to out-of-town students. 79% of students commute. All students may keep cars.

Activities: 28% of men belong to 18 national fraternities; 17% of women belong to 13 national sororities. There are 324 groups on campus, including art, band, cheerleading, chess, choir, chorale, chorus, computers, dance, ethnic, gay, honors, international, jazz band, literary magazine, marching band, newspaper, opera, orchestra, pep band, photography, political, professional, radio and TV, religious, social, social service, student government, and symphony. Popular campus events include Homecoming, Block Party, Welcome Week, International Fashion Show and Fryberger Greek Sing.

Sports: There are 9 intercollegiate sports for men and 12 for women, and 37 intramural sports for men and 37 for women. Facilities include 22,000-seat downtown multi-purpose arena, 55,000-seat football stadium, tennis center, golf course, track, soccer field, baseball stadium, field hockey, lacross, softball, volleyball courts, and natatorium, 128-000 square foot student recreation center that includes exercise and weight facility, six basketball courts, a multi-activity court, jogging track, aerobics studio, fitness labs, a gaming area and classrooms.

Disabled Students: 90% of the campus is accessible. Facilities include wheelchair ramps, elevators, special parking, specially equipped restrooms, special class scheduling, lowered drinking fountains, lowered telephones, and special housing.

Services: Counseling and information services are available, as is tutoring in most subjects. There is a reader service for the blind.

Campus Safety and Security: Measures include 24-hour foot and vehicle patrol, emergency notification system, and security escort services. There are shuttle buses, emergency telephones, lighted pathways/sidewalks, and controlled access to dorms/residental.

Programs of Study: U of L confers B.A., B.B.E., B.C.C., B.C.E., B.C.H., B.E.E., B.F.A., B.I.E., B.M., B.M.C., B.M.E., B.S., B.S.B.A., B.S.E., B.S.N., B.S.R. and B.S.W. degrees. Associate, master's, and doctoral degrees are also awarded. Bachelor's degrees are awarded in AGRICULTURE (equine science), BIOLOGICAL SCIENCE (biology/biological science), BUSINESS (accounting, banking and finance, business administration and management, business economics, management science, marketing/retailing/merchandising, and sports management), COMMUNICATIONS AND THE ARTS (American Sign Language, art history, art, art history and appreciation, communications, dramatic arts, English, French, linguistics, music, and Spanish), COMPUTER AND PHYSICAL SCIENCE (atmospheric sciences and meteorology, chemistry, computer science, information sciences and systems, mathematics, and physics), EDUCATION (art education, business education, early childhood education, elementary education, foreign languages education, middle school education, music education, physical education, science education, secondary education, and teaching English as a second/foreign language (TESOL/TEFOL)), ENGINEERING AND ENVIRONMENTAL DESIGN (bioengineering, chemical engineering, civil engineering, computer engineering, electrical/electronics engineering, engineering, engineering management, industrial engineering, and mechanical engineering), HEALTH PROFESSIONS (dental hygiene, health, medical laboratory technology, medical science, music therapy, and nursing), SOCIAL SCIENCE (administration of justice, anthropology, criminal justice, geography, history, humanities, liberal arts/general studies, paralegal studies, philosophy, political science/government, psychology, social work, sociology, and women's studies). Engineering, health professional, and business management are the strongest academically. The arts and sciences, business, and education have the largest enrollments.

Required: Distribution requirements include at least 6 hours each in social sciences, natural sciences, the history of world civilizations, and humanities. Freshmen are required to take college writing or advanced composition and 2 phys ed courses. A total of 123 semester hours, including 46 to 60 hours in the major, with a minimum GPA of 2.5 (2.0 in education, 2.75 in engineering) is required to graduate.

Special: Cross-registration with other schools, study abroad in 5 countries (China, Panama, Portugal, Trinidad, Canada), work-study programs, and B.A.-B.S. degrees are offered. A general studies degree, nondegree study, and pass/fail options are available. Co-op programs in engineering and business and internships are also possible. There are 16 national honor societies, a freshman honors program, and 1 departmental honors programs.

Faculty/Classroom: 58% of faculty are male; 42% are female. No introductory courses are taught by graduate students.

Admissions: 71% of the 2013-2014 applicants were accepted. The SAT scores for the 2013-2014 freshman class were: Critical Reading--24% below 500, 41% between 500 and 599, 24% between 600 and 699, and 11% between 700 and 800; Math--20% below 500, 40% between 500 and 599, 32% between 600 and 699, and 8% between 700 and 800. The ACT scores were 85% below 21, 5% between 21 and 23, 5% between 24 and 26, 3% between 27 and 28, and 2% above 28. There were 22 National Merit finalists.

Requirements: The SAT or ACT is required. Applicants must be graduates from an accredited high school or have received a GED, must have completed a precollege curriculum with a GPA of 2.5, and must have at least 1 of the following: a composite ACT score of 20 or a satisfactory SAT score; completion of the U of L enhanced precollege curriculum (PCC) with a minimum GPA of 2.5; or a rank in the top 15% of the high school graduating class. A GPA of 2.5 is required. AP and CLEP credits are accepted.

Procedure: Freshmen are admitted fall, spring, and summer. Entrance exams should be taken in the spring or the summer of the junior year. There are early admissions, deferred admissions, and rolling admissions plans. Applications should be filed by August 19 for fall entry, along with a $50 fee. Applications are accepted online.

Transfer: 1142 transfer students enrolled in 2012-2013. Transfer students must have a minimum GPA of 2.0. 30 of 123 credits required for the bachelor's degree must be completed at U of L.

Visiting: There are regularly scheduled orientations for prospective students. There are guides for informal visits and visitors may sit in on classes. To schedule a visit, contact the Admissions Office.

Financial Aid: In 2013-2014, 91% of all full-time freshmen students received some form of financial aid. 46% of all full-time freshmen students received need-based aid. The average freshman award was $6,600. Need-based scholarships or need-based grants averaged $1,463 ($6,972 maximum); need-based self-help aid (loans and jobs) averaged $1,598 ($2,750 maximum); non-need-based athletic scholarships averaged $2,257 ($13,697 maximum); other non-need-based awards and non-need-based scholarships averaged $1,849 ($11,819 maximum); and $2,370 from other forms of aid. The average financial indebtedness of the 2013 graduate was $24,858. The FAFSA is required. The priority date for freshman financial aid applications for fall entry is February 15.

International Students: There are 419 international students enrolled. They must take the TOEFL with a minimum score of 550 on the paper-based TOEFL (PBT) or 79 on the Internet-based version (iBT). They must also take the ACT, scoring 20.

Computers: All students may access the system. There are no time limits and no fees.

Graduates: From July 1, 2012 to June 30, 2013, 2731 bachelor's

degrees were awarded. The most popular majors were engineering (13%), biology (8%), and psychology (6%). In an average class, 25% graduate in 4 years or less, 47% graduate in 5 years or less, and 54% graduate in 6 years or less.

Admissions Contact: Jenny Sawyer, Executive Director of Admissions. E-Mail: *admitme@louisville.edu* Web: *www.louisville.edu*

UNIVERSITY OF PIKEVILLE F-3

Pikeville, KY 41501 (606) 218-5251
(866) 232-7700; (606) 218-5255

Full-time: 647 men, 635 women
Faculty: 69; IIB, --$
Part-time: 165 men, 290 women
Ph.D.s: 64%
Graduate: 247 men, 220 women
Student/Faculty: 19 to 1
Year: semesters, summer session
Tuition: n/av
Application Deadline: August 16
Room & Board: $7000
Freshman Class: 1804 applied, 1804 accepted, 386 enrolled
ACT: 19

NONCOMPETITIVE

The University of Pikeville, founded in 1889 by the Presbyterian Church, is a private institution that offers a broad liberal arts and sciences education. UPike offers associate, baccalaureate, and graduate degree programs that prepare students for a variety of professions or careers. There are 2 undergraduate schools and 2 graduate schools. In addition to regional accreditation, UPIKE has baccalaureate program accreditation with CSWE. The 2 libraries contain 86,637 volumes, 44,680 microform items, and 2,893 audio/video tapes/CDs/DVDs, and subscribe to 117,412 periodicals including electronic. Computerized library services include interlibrary loans, database searching, and Internet access. Special learning facilities include an art gallery and TV station. The 25-acre campus is in a small town 20 miles from the Virginia border, in the eastern Kentucky hills. Including any residence halls, there are 19 buildings.

Student Life: 81% of undergraduates are from Kentucky. Others are from 32 states, 17 foreign countries, and Canada. 99% are from public schools. 82% are White; 13% African American. 77% are Protestant. The average age of freshmen is 18; all undergraduates, 21. 48% do not continue beyond their first year; 28% remain to graduate.

Housing: 785 students can be accommodated in college housing, which includes single-sex and coed dorms. In addition, there are special-interest houses. On-campus housing is available on a first-come and first-served basis. 60% of students live on campus; of those, 25% remain on campus on weekends. Alcohol is not permitted. All students may keep cars.

Activities: There are no fraternities or sororities. There are 30 groups on campus, including art, cheerleading, choir, chorus, dance, honors, newspaper, pep band, political, professional, radio and TV, religious, social service, and student government. Popular campus events include Homecoming.

Sports: There are 9 intercollegiate sports for men and 9 for women, and 4 intramural sports for men and 4 for women. Facilities include East Kentucky Expo Center, Hoops training facility, gymnasium, basketball and volleyball courts, softball and baseball fields, and a football stadium.

Disabled Students: 97% of the campus is accessible. Facilities include wheelchair ramps, elevators, special parking, specially equipped restrooms, and lowered drinking fountains.

Services: Counseling and information services are available, as is tutoring in most subjects, math, English, biology, all physical sciences, computers, accounting, social sciences and Spanish There is a reader service for the blind, and remedial math, reading, and writing.

Campus Safety and Security: Measures include 24-hour foot and vehicle patrol, emergency notification system, and self-defense education. There are shuttle buses, emergency telephones, lighted pathways/sidewalks, and controlled access to dorms/residences.

Programs of Study: UPIKE confers B.A., B.S. and B.B.A. degrees. Associate, master's, and doctoral degrees are also awarded. Bachelor's degrees are awarded in BIOLOGICAL SCIENCE (biology/biological science), BUSINESS (business administration and management), COMMUNICATIONS AND THE ARTS (art, communications, English, film, television and digital media, and Spanish), COMPUTER AND PHYSICAL SCIENCE (chemistry, computer science, and mathematics), EDUCATION (elementary education, middle school education, and secondary education), HEALTH PROFESSIONS (nursing), SOCIAL SCIENCE (criminal justice, history, interdisciplinary studies, political science/government, psychology, religion, social work, and sociology). Biology, English, and religion are the strongest academically. Business, biology, and nursing have the largest enrollments.

Required: All students must complete core courses in humanities, English, social sciences, natural sciences, and math, as well as 2 courses each in religion, phys ed, and history and 1 course in computer science. Additional requirements include 6 hours in a foreign language for the B.A. degree and 2 lab science courses for the B.S. degree. An overall GPA of 2.0 is required. To graduate, students must complete 120 semester hours, with 30 to 60 hours in the major.

Special: Our faculty at the University of Pikeville is committed to student engagement and learning outside the classroom. We have a constantly evolving global studies initiative on campus. Our undergraduate programs continue to send students to professional conferences, immerse them in fieldwork, and place them in internships. There are 6 national honor societies and 6 departmental honors programs.

Faculty/Classroom: 49% of faculty are male; 51% are female. All teach undergraduates. No introductory courses are taught by graduate students. The average class size in an introductory lecture is 21; in a laboratory is 12; and in a regular course is 16.

Admissions: 100% of the 2013-2014 applicants were accepted. The SAT scores for the 2013-2014 freshman class were: Math--67% below 500, 19% between 500 and 599, and 14% between 600 and 699; Writing--71% below 500, 24% between 500 and 599, and 5% between 600 and 699. The ACT scores were 62% below 21, 22% between 21 and 23, 11% between 24 and 26, 3% between 27 and 28, and 2% above 28. 31% of the current freshmen were in the top fifth of their class; 54% were in the top two fifths. 16 freshmen graduated first in their class.

Requirements: The ACT is required. In addition, Applicants must graduate from an accredited secondary school or have a GED. AP and CLEP credits are accepted.

Procedure: Freshmen are admitted fall, spring, and summer. There are deferred admissions and rolling admissions plans. Applications should be filed by August 16 for fall entry; January 10 for spring entry; and June 4 for summer entry. Notification is sent on a rolling basis. Applications are accepted online.

Transfer: 113 transfer students enrolled in 2012-2013. Transfer students are required to submit official transcripts from all colleges previously attended by the designated document deadline. Admission to the University will be based on the overall grade point average achieved. Applicants with a cumulative 2.0 grade point average or higher (on 0 4 quality point scale) will be admitted in good standing. Transfer applicants with less than a 2.0 grade point average will be reviewed for admission to the University. 30 of 120 credits required for the bachelor's degree must be completed at UPIKE.

Visiting: There are guides for informal visits, visitors may sit in on classes, and stay overnight. To schedule a visit, contact Amber Collins at (606) 218-5251.

Financial Aid: In 2013-2014, 100% of all full-time freshmen and 99% of continuing full-time students received some form of financial aid. 100% of all full-time freshmen and 99% of continuing full-time students received need-based aid. The average freshman award was $23,537. Need-based scholarships or need-based grants averaged $17,314; and need-based self-help aid (loans and jobs) averaged $6,550. 15% of undergraduate students work part-time. Average annual earnings from campus work are $1736. The average financial indebtedness of the 2013 graduate was $20,743. The FAFSA is required. The priority date for freshman financial aid applications for fall entry is February 15. The deadline for filing freshman financial aid applications for fall entry is May 1.

International Students: There are 33 international students enrolled. The school actively recruits these students. They must take the TOEFL with a minimum score of 68 on the Internet-based version (iBT). They must also take the ACT.

Computers: All students may access the system. There are no time limits and no fees.

Graduates: From July 1, 2012 to June 30, 2013, 145 bachelor's degrees were awarded. The most popular majors were business (23%), criminal justice (12%), and social sciences (12%). In an average class, 16% graduate in 4 years or less, 26% graduate in 5 years or less, and 28% graduate in 6 years or less. Of the 2012 graduating class, 46% were enrolled in graduate school within 6 months of graduation, and 69% were employed.

Admissions Contact: Amber Collins, Director of Admissions. E-Mail: *wewantyou@upike.edu* Web: *www.upike.edu*

UNIVERSITY OF THE CUMBERLANDS E-4

Williamsburg, KY 40769 (606) 539-4241
(800) 343-1609; (606) 539-4303

Full-time: 795 men, 719 women
Faculty: 97
Part-time: 256 men, 326 women
Ph.D.s: 75%
Graduate: 763 men, 2065 women
Student/Faculty: 15 to 1
Year: semesters, summer session
Tuition: $20,000
Application Deadline: open
Room & Board: $7500
Freshman Class: 1937 applied, 1803 accepted, 488 enrolled
SAT CR/M: 488/494 **ACT:** 22 **LESS COMPETITIVE**

University of the Cumberlands, founded in 1888, is a private liberal arts institution affiliated with the Kentucky Baptist Convention. There is 1 undergraduate school and 7 graduate schools. The library contains 137,158 volumes, 823,805 microform items, and 4,946 audio/video tapes/CDs/DVDs, and subscribes to 56,112 periodicals including electronic. Computerized library services include interlibrary loans, database searching, Internet access, and Wi-Fi capability. Special learning facilities include an art gallery, natural history museum, radio station, TV station, a distance learning lab. The 100-acre campus is in a small town 100 miles south of Lexington and 65 miles north of Knoxville. Including any residence halls, there are 38 buildings.

Student Life: 69% of undergraduates are from Kentucky. Others are from 35 states, 30 foreign countries, and Canada. 95% are from public schools. 81% are White. 34% are Protestant; 13% claim no religious affiliation. The average age of freshmen is 18; all undergraduates, 21. 39% do not continue beyond their first year; 40% remain to graduate.

Housing: 1213 students can be accommodated in college housing, which includes single-sex dorms. On-campus housing is guaranteed for all 4 years. 74% of students live on campus; of those, 45% remain on campus on weekends. Alcohol is not permitted. All students may keep cars.

Activities: There are no fraternities or sororities. There are 49 groups on campus, including art, band, cheerleading, choir, chorale, chorus, dance, debate, drama, drill team, environmental, forensics, honors, international, jazz band, literary magazine, marching band, musical theater, newspaper, Outdoor Adventure Club, pep band, political, professional, radio and TV, religious, social, social service, and student government. Popular campus events include Madrigal Dinner, Hanging of the Greens, and Valentine's Dance.

Sports: There are 11 intercollegiate sports for men and 11 for women, and 8 intramural sports for men and 8 for women. Facilities include a gym for intramurals and recreation; an athletic complex with facilities for men's and women's basketball and volleyball, a weight room, and a swimming pool; a game room; tennis courts; baseball and softball fields; a practice football field, a football field, a soccer practice field, a soccer field, and a wrestling gym.

Disabled Students: 75% of the campus is accessible. Facilities include wheelchair ramps, elevators, special parking, specially equipped restrooms, special class scheduling, lowered drinking fountains, and lowered telephones.

Services: Counseling and information services are available, as is tutoring in every subject.

Campus Safety and Security: Measures include 24-hour foot and vehicle patrol, emergency notification system, self-defense education, and security escort services. There are lighted pathways/sidewalks and controlled access to dorms/residences.

Programs of Study: Patriots confers B.A., B.S., B.G.S. and B.M. degrees. Master's degrees are also awarded. Bachelor's degrees are awarded in BIOLOGICAL SCIENCE (biology/biological science), BUSINESS (accounting, business administration and management, and office supervision and management), COMMUNICATIONS AND THE ARTS (art, communications, dramatic arts, English, and music), COMPUTER AND PHYSICAL SCIENCE (chemistry, information sciences and systems, mathematics, and physics), EDUCATION (art education, business education, elementary education, English education, health education, mathematics education, middle school education, music education, physical education, science education, social studies education, and special education), HEALTH PROFESSIONS (health, medical laboratory technology, and public health), SOCIAL SCIENCE (history, political science/government, psychology, religion, religious music, and social work). Biology, business, and chemistry are the strongest academically. Biology has the largest enrollment.

Required: All students must complete 128 semester hours, including 40 hours of liberal arts courses and an average of 36 hours in a major, while maintaining an overall GPA of 2.0 (2.5 for those seeking teacher certification). General education requirements include courses from the areas of art, music, theater, speech, religion, English composition, literature, history, math, natural and social sciences, community service, and fine arts or philosophy. A comprehensive exam may be required. Programs presented for graduation must include 2 majors, 1 major and 1 minor, 1 major with 15 hours of restricted electives, or 3 minors, or 1 concentration.

Special: Internships, study abroad in England, China, Spain, France, and Thailand, and work-study programs with the university, local businesses, and other educational institutions are available. The university offers B.A.-B.S. degrees in all majors except music, dual majors in all major fields, a general studies degree, nondegree study, and a 3-2 engineering degree with University of Kentucky. There are 13 national honor societies, a freshman honors program, and 13 departmental honors programs.

Faculty/Classroom: 58% of faculty are male; 42% are female. 75% teach undergraduates. No introductory courses are taught by graduate students. The average class size in an introductory lecture is 36; in a laboratory is 10; and in a regular course is 14.

Admissions: 93% of the 2013-2014 applicants were accepted. The SAT scores for the 2013-2014 freshman class were: Critical Reading--63% below 500, 24% between 500 and 599, 10% between 600 and 699, and 3% between 700 and 800; Math--55% below 500, 32% between 500 and 599, and 13% between 600 and 699. The ACT scores were 44% below 21, 24% between 21 and 23, 15% between 24 and 26, 8% between 27 and 28, and 9% above 28. 30% of the current freshmen were in the top fifth of their class; 60% were in the top two fifths. 5 freshmen graduated first in their class.

Requirements: The SAT or ACT is required. In addition, with composite scores of better than 17 for the ACT or 780 for the SAT required. Consideration is given to those with ACT scores of 16 and 17, provided the high school GPA is 2.5 or above in college prep classes. Although each application is considered individually, students must have fulfilled general high school requirements of 4 years of English, 3 each of math and science, and 2 of social studies. A GPA of 2.0 is required. AP and CLEP credits are accepted. Important factors in the admissions decision are leadership record, advanced placement or honors courses, and extracurricular activities record.

Procedure: Freshmen are admitted to all sessions. Entrance exams should be taken prior to admission consideration. There is a rolling admissions plan. Application deadlines are open. Application fee is $30. Applications are accepted online. Application fees are waived if application is completed online.

Transfer: 89 transfer students enrolled in 2012-2013. Applicants must have verification from their previous school that they are eligible to return. Students with fewer than 30 semester or 45 quarter hours must meet freshman admissions requirements. 30 of 128 credits required for the bachelor's degree must be completed at Patriots.

Visiting: There are regularly scheduled orientations for prospective students, consisting of a tour, a departmental conference, an advising session, adjustment information, general information, and first college class. There are guides for informal visits, visitors may sit in on classes, and stay overnight. To schedule a visit, contact Shelleigh Moses at shelleigh.moses@ucumberlands.edu.

Financial Aid: In 2013-2014, 100% of all full-time freshmen and 85% of continuing full-time students received some form of financial aid. 78% of all full-time freshmen and 65% of continuing full-time students received need-based aid. The average freshman award was $24,095. Need-based scholarships or need-based grants averaged $6,627 ($27,113 maximum); need-based self-help aid (loans and jobs) averaged $3,691 ($11,500 maximum); non-need-based athletic scholarships averaged $2,156 ($27,500 maximum); other non-need-based awards and non-need-based scholarships averaged $8,873 ($27,500 maximum); and $2,748 from other forms of aid. 66% of undergraduate students work part-time. Average annual earnings from campus work are $1703. The average financial indebtedness of the 2013 graduate was $15,958. The FAFSA is required. The priority date for freshman financial aid applications for fall entry is February 1.

International Students: There are 102 international students enrolled. The school actively recruits these students. They must take the college's own test.

Computers: All students may access the system 24 hours a day, 7 days a week. There are no time limits. The fee is $260 per year.

Graduates: From July 1, 2012 to June 30, 2013, 256 bachelor's degrees were awarded. The most popular majors were business (20%), biology, and life sciences (15%), and education (14%). 30 companies recruited on campus in 2012-2013. In an average class, 1% graduate in 3 years or less, 21% graduate in 4 years or less, 36% graduate in 5 years or less, and 40% graduate in 6 years or less. Of the 2012 graduating class, 20% were enrolled in graduate school within 6 months of graduation, and 75% were employed.

Admissions Contact: Erica Harris, Director of Admissions. E-Mail: *admiss@ucumberlands.edu* Web: *www.ucumberlands.edu*

WESTERN KENTUCKY UNIVERSITY C-4

Bowling Green, KY 42101-3576 (270) 745-2551
(800) 495-8463; (270) 745-6133

Full-time: 6000 men, 7000 women	**Faculty:** 621; IIA, --$
Part-time: 1000 men, 2000 women	**Ph.D.s:** 74%
Graduate: 800 men, 1900 women	**Student/Faculty:** n/av
Year: semesters, summer session	**Tuition:** $8,000 ($18,500)
Application Deadline: August 1	**Room & Board:** $6800
Freshman Class: n/av	
SAT: required	**ACT:** 20 LESS COMPETITIVE

Western Kentucky University, founded in 1906, is a public institution which provides students with rigorous academic programs in the liberal arts and sciences, and traditional and emerging professional programs, with emphasis at the baccalaureate level, complemented by relevant associate and graduate-level programs. There are 6 undergraduate schools and 1 graduate school. In addition to regional accreditation, Western has baccalaureate program accreditation with AACSB, ABET, ACEJMC, ADA, CSAB, CSWE, NASAD, NASM, NCATE, NLN, and NRPA. The 3 libraries contain 656,517 volumes, 2.0 million microform items, and 19,805 audio/video tapes/CDs/DVDs, and subscribe to 13,912 periodicals including electronic. Computerized library services include interlibrary loans, database searching, Internet access, and laptop Internet portals. Special learning facilities include a learning resource center, art gallery, planetarium, radio station, TV station, Kentucky Museum. The 200-acre campus is in a suburban area 65 miles north of Nashville, Tennessee and 110 miles south of Louisville. Including any residence halls, there are 66 buildings.

Student Life: 83% of undergraduates are from Kentucky. Others are from

46 states, 55 foreign countries, and Canada. 85% are white. The average age of freshmen is 19; all undergraduates, 23. 27% do not continue beyond their first year; 41% remain to graduate.

Housing: 4662 students can be accommodated in college housing, which includes single-sex and coed dorms. In addition, there are honors houses and special-interest houses. On-campus housing is available on a first-come and first-served basis. 68% of students commute. Alcohol is not permitted. All students may keep cars.

Activities: 9% of men belong to 16 national fraternities; 7% of women belong to 12 national sororities. There are 251 groups on campus, including art, band, cheerleading, chess, choir, chorale, chorus, communications, computers, dance, debate, drama, drill team, ethnic, film, forensics, forensics, gay, honors, international, jazz band, literary magazine, marching band, musical theater, newspaper, opera, orchestra, pep band, photography, political, professional, radio and TV, religious, social, social service, student government, symphony, and yearbook. Popular campus events include Step Show, Concerts, and Cultural Enhancement Series.

Sports: There are 11 intercollegiate sports for men and 10 for women, and 17 intramural sports for men and 16 for women. There are 11 intercollegiate sports for men and 10 for women, and 17 intramural sports for men and 16 for women. Facilities include a 17,500-seat football stadium, a basketball arena, baseball fields, softball fields, a soccer complex, and tennis courts. The Preston Center adds a weight room, a fitness room, a gym, a dance studio, racquetball courts, a swimming pool, a pro shop, an outdoor recreation and adventure center, and a health and fitness lab.

Disabled Students: 75% of the campus is accessible. Facilities include wheelchair ramps, elevators, special parking, specially equipped restrooms, special class scheduling, lowered telephones.

Services: Counseling and information services are available, as is tutoring in some subjects, with both departmental and freelance tutoring offered. The Student Support Services program offers tutoring in general education courses. There is a reader service for the blind, and remedial math, reading, and writing.

Campus Safety and Security: Measures include 24-hour foot and vehicle patrol and security escort services. There are shuttle buses, emergency telephones, and lighted pathways/sidewalks.

Programs of Study: Western confers A.B., B.S., B.F.A., B.G.S., B.M., and B.S.N. degrees. Associate and master's degrees are also awarded. Bachelor's degrees are awarded in AGRICULTURE (agriculture), BIOLOGICAL SCIENCE (biochemistry, biology/biological science, and genetics), BUSINESS (accounting, banking and finance, business economics, hospitality management services, management engineering, management information systems, management science, marketing and distribution, and recreation and leisure services), COMMUNICATIONS AND THE ARTS (advertising, broadcasting, communications, design, dramatic arts, English, French, German, journalism, language arts, music, performing arts, public relations, Spanish, and visual and performing arts), COMPUTER AND PHYSICAL SCIENCE (chemistry, computer science, geology, mathematics, and physics), EDUCATION (art education, business education, early childhood education, education of the exceptional child, elementary education, home economics education, marketing and distribution education, middle school education, physical education, technical education, and vocational education), ENGINEERING AND ENVIRONMENTAL DESIGN (civil engineering, construction management, electrical/electronics engineering, electromechanical technology, industrial engineering technology, mechanical engineering, and technology and public affairs), HEALTH PROFESSIONS (dental hygiene, environmental health science, health care administration, medical technology, nursing, public health, and speech pathology/audiology), SOCIAL SCIENCE (anthropology, economics, geography, history, liberal arts/general studies, philosophy, political science/government, psychology, religion, social studies, social work, sociology, and textiles and clothing). Elementary education, psychology, and nursing are the strongest academically.

Required: To graduate, all students must complete at least 128 semester hours, with a varying number of hours in the major, and maintain a minimum GPA of 2.0. Curricula must include 44 semester hours of general education requirements and 42 semester hours in upper-division courses, and includes 6 semester hours of English composition and 3 semester hours each of Western civilization, foreign language, speech, and literature.

Special: Internships in many areas, study abroad in 34 countries, work-study programs, and cooperative programs with the Universities of Louisville and Kentucky and Eastern Kentucky University are offered. Accelerated degree programs are available in some majors. Dual majors include math and physical science, and physics and engineering. A general studies degree, student-designed majors, a Washington semester, and a 3-2 engineering degree are offered. Credit for life, military, or work experience may be granted, and nondegree study is possible. There are 36 national honor societies and a freshman honors program.

Faculty/Classroom: 56% of faculty are male; 44% are female. No introductory courses are taught by graduate students.

Admissions: The ACT scores were 52% below 21, 24% between 21 and 23, 14% between 24 and 26, 6% between 27 and 28, and 4% above 28. 30% of the current freshmen were in the top fifth of their class; 55% were in the top two fifths. 76 freshmen graduated first in their class.

Requirements: The SAT or ACT is required. Other admissions requirements include graduation from an accredited secondary school and a minimum college preparatory curriculum that includes 4 years of English, 3 years each of math, social studies, and science, 2 years of a foreign language, and one-half year each of health, phys ed, and visual or performing arts. The GED is accepted. A GPA of 2.5 is required. AP and CLEP credits are accepted.

Procedure: Freshmen are admitted to all sessions. Entrance exams should be taken by fall of the senior year. There are early admissions, deferred admissions, and rolling admissions plans. Applications should be filed by August 1 for fall entry; January 1 for spring entry; and May 1 for summer entry, along with a $35 fee. Notification is sent on a rolling basis. Applications are accepted online.

Transfer: 865 transfer students enrolled in 2010-2011. Transfer students must have a minimum GPA 2.0 for the last semester or term of full-time work, a cumulative GPA of 2.0, and be in good standing at the institution from which they are transferring. Students with fewer that 24 hours earned are required to have completed the pre-college curriculum. 32 of 128 credits required for the bachelor's degree must be completed at Western.

Visiting: There are regularly scheduled orientations for prospective students, campus tours, informational sessions, presentations, departmental visits, residence hall visits, and a video. There are guides for informal visits, visitors may sit in on classes, and stay overnight. To schedule a visit, contact the Office of Admissions.

Financial Aid: In a recent year, 57% of all full-time freshmen and 54% of continuing full-time students received some form of financial aid. 35% of all full-time freshmen and 35% of continuing full-time students received need-based aid. The average freshman award was $6,769. Need-based scholarships or need-based grants averaged $3,650; need-based self-help aid (loans and jobs) averaged $2,492; non-need-based athletic scholarships averaged $7,387; and other non-need-based awards and non-need-based scholarships averaged $2,296. 8% of undergraduate students work part-time. Average annual earnings from campus work are $2098. The average financial indebtedness of the 2011 graduate was $12,250. Western is a member of CSS. The FAFSA is required. The deadline for filing freshman financial aid applications for fall entry is April 1.

International Students: There are 201 international students enrolled. They must take the TOEFL or MELAB. They must also take the SAT or ACT, scoring 20.

Computers: Wireless access is available. WKU provides open computer labs for all students at locations across the university. In addition to 6 labs on the main campus, there is one at each extended campus location, and another at the South Campus (Community College). Labs are equipped with hardware, software, scanners, and free laser printing. One location, in the Mass Media and Technology Hall, is open 24 hours a day, 7 days a week while classes are in session. All students may access the system.

Graduates: In a recent year, 2166 bachelor's degrees were awarded. The most popular majors were education (19%), business (16%), and communications/journalism (11%). In an average class, 27% graduate in 4 years or less, 14% graduate in 5 years or less, and 4% graduate in 6 years or less.

Admissions Contact: Dr. Dean R. Kahler, Admissions and Academic Services Director. A campus DVD is available. E-Mail: *admission@wku.edu* Web: *www.wku.edu*

LOUISIANA

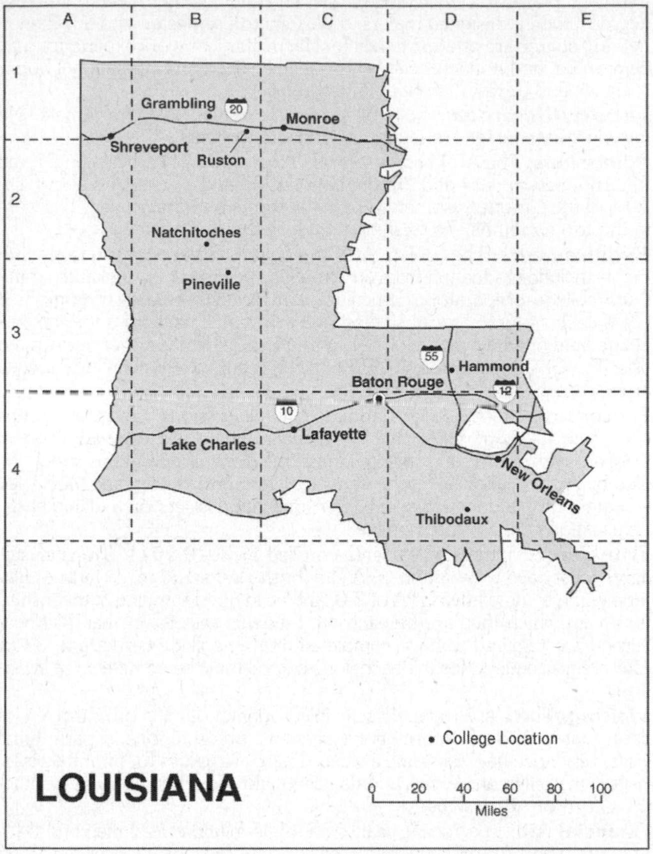

CENTENARY COLLEGE OF LOUISIANA — A-1

Shreveport, LA 71134 (318) 869-5131
(800) 234-4448; (318) 869-5005

Full-time: 294 men, 379 women — **Faculty:** 72; IIB, -$
Part-time: 11 men, 14 women — **Ph.D.s:** 94%
Graduate: 34 men, 44 women — **Student/Faculty:** n/av
Year: semesters, summer session — **Tuition:** $29,750
Application Deadline: August 1 — **Room & Board:** $9320
Freshman Class: 933 applied, 598 accepted, 158 enrolled
SAT: required — **ACT:**25 — **COMPETITIVE+**

Centenary College of Louisiana is a private, four-year arts and sciences college affiliated with the United Methodist Church. Founded in 1825, it is the oldest chartered liberal arts college west of the Mississippi River and is accredited by the Southern Association of Colleges and Schools. There are 2 graduate schools. In addition to regional accreditation, Centenary College has baccalaureate program accreditation with NASM. The 2 libraries contain 180,000 volumes, 310,671 microform items, and 425 audio/video tapes/CDs/DVDs, and subscribe to 942 periodicals including electronic. Computerized library services include interlibrary loans, database searching, and Internet access. Special learning facilities include an art gallery, radio station, a theater, and an art museum. The 65-acre campus is in an urban area of Shreveport/Bossier City located in the northwest corner of Louisiana near the Texas and Arkansas borders. Including any residence halls, there are 23 buildings.

Student Life: 62% of undergraduates are from Louisiana. Others are from 31 states, 13 foreign countries, and Canada. 83% are White. 60% are Protestant; 20% Catholic; 14% claim no religious affiliation. The average age of freshmen is 18; all undergraduates, 20. 26% do not continue beyond their first year; 55% remain to graduate.

Housing: 616 students can be accommodated in college housing, which includes single-sex and coed dorms. In addition, there are fraternity houses, sorority houses, theme housing. On-campus housing is guaranteed for all 4 years, is available on a first-come, and first-served basis. 77% of students live on campus; of those, 36% remain on campus on weekends. Alcohol is not permitted. All students may keep cars.

Activities: 23% of men belong to 4 national fraternities; 26% of women belong to 2 national sororities. There are 61 groups on campus, including cheerleading, choir, chorale, communications, dance, drama, environmental club, film, gay, honors, international, jazz band, musical theater, newspaper, opera, orchestra, photography, political, professional, radio and TV, religious, social, social service, student government, symphony, and yearbook. Popular campus events include Spring Fling, President's Convocation and Freak Week.

Sports: There are 7 intercollegiate sports for men and 9 for women, and 16 intramural sports for men and 16 for women. Facilities include a 3000-seat gym, 2 weight rooms, basketball, racquetball, volleyball, and tennis courts, baseball, soccer, and softball fields; a fitness center with aerobic exercise and strengthening equipment, and a natatorium.

Disabled Students: 90% of the campus is accessible. Facilities include wheelchair ramps, elevators, special parking, specially equipped restrooms, special class scheduling, lowered drinking fountains, lowered telephones, and lowered security phones.

Services: Counseling and information services are available, as is tutoring in most subjects.

Campus Safety and Security: Measures include 24-hour foot and vehicle patrol and security escort services. There are emergency telephones and lighted pathways/sidewalks.

Programs of Study: B.A., B.S. and B.M. degrees. Master's degrees are also awarded. Bachelor's degrees are awarded in BIOLOGICAL SCIENCE (biochemistry, biology/biological science, biophysics, and neurosciences), BUSINESS (accounting, banking and finance, business administration and management, business economics, and finance), COMMUNICATIONS AND THE ARTS (art, communications, dance, dramatic arts, English, French, German, Latin, music, music performance, Spanish, and studio art), COMPUTER AND PHYSICAL SCIENCE (chemistry, geology, mathematics, and physics), EDUCATION (elementary education, foreign languages education, music education, physical education, and social studies education), ENGINEERING AND ENVIRONMENTAL DESIGN (environmental science), HEALTH PROFESSIONS (exercise science), SOCIAL SCIENCE (economics, history, interdisciplinary studies, liberal arts/general studies, philosophy, political science/government, psychology, religion, religious music, and sociology). Physical sciences, life sciences and political science are the strongest academically. Business, biology and psychology have the largest enrollments.

Required: To graduate, all students must complete 124 semester hours, with a maximum of 45 in a non-interdisciplinary major and a minimum of 30 at the upper-division level, including a writing and speaking class in the major at the junior level, and maintain a minimum GPA of 2.0. There are 48 to 52 hours of distribution requirements. Core curriculum requirements include courses in the humanities, social sciences, hard sciences, and math. In addition, freshmen must take a liberal arts orientation course. All students must complete a community service project, participate in cultural perspective events, study or live in a different culture, or study abroad, and fulfill career explorations.

Special: Centenary offers study abroad in 7 countries, cross-registration with Associated Colleges of the South, internships in all majors, a Washington semester, and a work-study program within the college. A 3-1 communications disorders degree with Louisiana State University Medical Center is possible, as is a 3-2 engineering degree with Washington University in St. Louis, University of Southern California, and Columbia University, Texas A&M University, Louisiana Tech, and Case Western Reserve Universities. A 3-2 applied science pre-professional degree combines with health administration or medical school. Pre-veterinary studies, general studies and interdisciplinary degrees, and student-designed majors are available. There are 7 national honor societies and 15 departmental honors programs.

Faculty/Classroom: 93% teach undergraduates. No introductory courses are taught by graduate students. The average class size in an introductory lecture is 25; in a laboratory is 24; and in a regular course is 20.

Admissions: 64% of the 2013-2014 applicants were accepted. The ACT scores were 13% below 21, 23% between 21 and 23, 31% between 24 and 26, 14% between 27 and 28, and 1% above 28. 61% of the current freshmen were in the top fifth of their class; 85% were in the top two fifths. 20 freshmen graduated first in their class.

Requirements: The SAT or ACT is required. Applicants should be high school graduates with a minimum composite score of 950 on the SAT or 20 on the ACT, although accepted students average 1145 and 26 respectively. Secondary school preparation should include 15 academic credits, including 4 of English, 3 each of math and science, 2 each of a foreign language and history, 1 of social studies, and electives. Music students must audition; art students are advised to present a portfolio. A GPA of 2.0 is required. AP credits are accepted. Important factors in the admissions decision are advanced placement or honors courses, extracurricular activities record, and personality/intangible qualities.

Procedure: Freshmen are admitted fall, spring, and summer. Entrance

exams should be taken by the fall of the senior year. There are early decision, early admissions, and rolling admissions plans. Early decision applications should be filed by February 15; regular applications, by August 1 for fall entry, along with a $30 fee. Notifications are sent September 1. 33 early decision candidates were accepted for the 2013-2014 class. Applications are accepted online.

Transfer: 26 transfer students enrolled in 2012-2013. Transfer applicants must have a minimum GPA of 2.0 and demonstrate good performance in a liberal arts curriculum. 45 credits required for the bachelor's degree must be completed at Centenary College.

Visiting: There are regularly scheduled orientations for prospective students, consisting of information sessions with a counselor, a tour of the campus, a visit to a class or with faculty, and lunch. There are guides for informal visits, visitors may sit in on classes, and stay overnight.

Financial Aid: The FAFSA and the college's own financial statement are required. The priority date for freshman financial aid applications for fall entry is February 15.

International Students: There are 21 international students enrolled. The school actively recruits these students. They must take the TOEFL.

Graduates: From July 1, 2012 to June 30, 2013, 153 bachelor's degrees were awarded. The most popular majors were business/marketing (14%), visual and performing arts (13%), and biological/life sciences (12%). In an average class, 1% graduate in 3 years or less, 42% graduate in 4 years or less, 54% graduate in 5 years or less, and 55% graduate in 6 years or less.

Admissions Contact: Tim Crowley, Director of Admissions. E-Mail: *tcrowley@centenary.edu* Web: *www.centenary.edu*

DILLARD UNIVERSITY — D-4

New Orleans, LA 70122 — **(504) 816-4670; (800) 216-6637**

Full-time: n/av	**Faculty:** 82
Part-time: n/av	**Ph.D.s:** 56%
Graduate: n/av	**Student/Faculty:** n/av
Year: semesters, summer session	**Tuition:** $15,250
Application Deadline:	**Room & Board:** $5690
Freshman Class: n/av	
SAT or ACT: recommended	

VERY COMPETITIVE

Dillard University, established in 1869, is an independent, nonsectarian, liberal arts institution, affiliated with the United Church of Christ and the United Methodist Church. It offers undergraduate programs 19 baccalaureate degrees in the colleges of arts of sciences, professional studies, and general studies. There are 3 undergraduate schools. In addition to regional accreditation, Dillard has baccalaureate program accreditation with NLN. The library contains 104,615 volumes, 21,638 microform items, and 426 audio/video tapes/CDs/DVDs, and subscribes to 295 periodicals including electronic. Computerized library services include interlibrary loans and database searching. Special learning facilities include an art gallery and radio station. The 55-acre campus is in an urban area in New Orleans. Including any residence halls, there are 21 buildings.

Student Life: 67% of undergraduates are from Louisiana. Others are from 29 states, 12 foreign countries, and Canada. 98% are African American. 28% do not continue beyond their first year.

Housing: College-sponsored housing includes single-sex dorms, on-campus apartments, and off-campus apartments. On-campus housing is guaranteed for the freshman year only, is available on a first-come, first-served basis, and is available on a lottery system for upperclassmen. Priority is given to out-of-town students. 30% of students commute. Alcohol is not permitted. All students may keep cars.

Activities: 4% of men belong to 4 national fraternities; 11% of women belong to 4 national sororities. There are 64 groups on campus, including art, cheerleading, chess, choir, chorus, dance, drama, ethnic, honors, professional, religious, social service, student government, and yearbook. Popular campus events include Coronation, Avenue of the Oaks Gala, and Founder's Day.

Sports: There are 3 intercollegiate sports for men and 3 for women. Facilities include a gym, swimming pool, Nautilus room, tennis courts, dance facility, and game room.

Disabled Students: 70% of the campus is accessible. Facilities include wheelchair ramps, elevators, special parking, specially equipped restrooms, and special class scheduling.

Services: Counseling and information services are available, as is tutoring in every subject. There is remedial math, reading, and writing.

Campus Safety and Security: Measures include 24-hour foot and vehicle patrol. There are shuttle buses and lighted pathways/sidewalks.

Programs of Study: Dillard confers B.A., B.S. and B.S.N. degrees. Bachelor's degrees are awarded in BIOLOGICAL SCIENCE (biology/biological science), BUSINESS (accounting and business administration and management), COMMUNICATIONS AND THE ARTS (art, communications, English, music, music business management, and music performance), COMPUTER AND PHYSICAL SCIENCE (chemistry, computer science, and physics), HEALTH PROFESSIONS (nursing and public health), SOCIAL SCIENCE (economics, history, political science/government, psychology, sociology, and urban studies). Biological sciences has the largest enrollment.

Required: Students must successfully complete 125 semester hours and maintain a minimum overall GPA of 2.0 and a GPA of 2.0 or better in all courses in the major. In addition, all students must complete 35 semester hours in the core curriculum, which includes courses in English composition, world literature, English literature, math, natural sciences, world history, political science, economics, university assembly, phys ed, and academic orientation. Additionally, each student must engage in a minimum of 120 clock hours of volunteer service in the community.

Special: Opportunities are provided for internships, work-study programs, credit by exam, nondegree study, and pass/fail options. All social science majors are encouraged to pursue a double major. There is a 4-year co-op degree in music therapy with Loyola University, a clinical public health curriculum with Howard University, a 5-year joint degree in urban studies with Columbia University, and preengineering dual degree programs with the Georgia Institute of Technology and Auburn and Columbia Universities. There are 3 national honor societies.

Faculty/Classroom: 43% of faculty are male; 57% are female. All teach undergraduates. No introductory courses are taught by graduate students. The average class size in an introductory lecture is 30.

Requirements: The SAT or ACT is recommended. Graduation from an accredited secondary school is required; a GED will be accepted. Applicants must submit an academic record of 20 units, distributed as follows: 4 units in English, 3 each in math and natural sciences, 2 in social studies, and 8 in other academic electives. Recommendations from a high school teacher and the principal or a student counselor are required. A GPA of 2.2 is required. AP credits are accepted. Important factors in the admissions decision are recommendations by school officials, leadership record, and personality/intangible qualities.

Procedure: Freshmen are admitted spring. Entrance exams should be taken between April of the junior year and December of the senior year. There are early admissions, deferred admissions, and rolling admissions plans. Applications should be filed by December 1 for spring entry, along with a $30 fee. Notification is sent on a rolling basis. Applications are accepted online.

Transfer: 46 transfer students enrolled in 2012-2013. Applicants for transfer must submit a secondary school record or equivalent, transcripts from previous colleges showing an average grade of C, and personal recommendations. No more than 60 semester hours may be submitted for transfer credit. 65 of 125 credits required for the bachelor's degree must be completed at Dillard.

Visiting: There are regularly scheduled orientations for prospective students, scheduled on individual basis. There are guides for informal visits, visitors may sit in on classes, and stay overnight. To schedule a visit, contact Coordinator of Campus Tours and Special Events at (504) 816-4670.

Financial Aid: In 2013-2014, 99% of all full-time freshmen students received some form of financial aid. 93% of all full-time freshmen students received need-based aid. 25% of undergraduate students work part-time. Average annual earnings from campus work are $2000. The average financial indebtedness of the 2013 graduate was $26,250. Dillard is a member of CSS. The FAFSA and the college's own financial statement are required. The deadline for filing freshman financial aid applications for fall entry is March 1.

International Students: There are 12 international students enrolled. They must take the TOEFL with a minimum score of 550 on the paper-based TOEFL (PBT). They must also take the SAT or ACT, scoring 18.

Graduates: From July 1, 2012 to June 30, 2013, 278 bachelor's degrees were awarded. The most popular majors were public health (16%), biology (13%), and mass communications (9%). Of the 2012 graduating class, 45% were enrolled in graduate school within 6 months of graduation, and 45% were employed.

Admissions Contact: Alecia Cyprian E-Mail: *acyprian@dillard.edu* Web: *www.dillard.edu*

GRAMBLING STATE UNIVERSITY — B-1

Grambling, LA 71245 — **(318) 274-6423** **(888) 863-3655; (318) 274-3292**

Full-time: 1657 men, 2430 women	**Faculty:** n/av
Part-time: 113 men, 235 women	**Ph.D.s:** 59%
Graduate: 240 men, 602 women	**Student/Faculty:** n/av
Year: semesters, summer session	**Tuition:** $4886 ($8643)
Application Deadline: June 1	**Room & Board:** $8498
Freshman Class: 5154 applied, 2170 accepted, 756 enrolled	
SAT CR/M: 430/430	**ACT:** 17

LESS COMPETITIVE

Founded in 1901, Grambling State University, a constituent member of the University of Louisiana System, is a historically and predominantly black comprehensive university, offering degrees ranging from associate to doctorate. There are 4 undergraduate schools and 1 graduate school. In addition to regional accreditation, GSU has baccalaureate program accreditation with AACSB, ABET, ACEJMC, CSAB, CSWE, NASAD, NASM, NCATE, NLN, and NRPA. The library contains 363,216 volumes, 122,298 microform items, and 6,394 audio/video tapes/CDs/DVDs, and subscribes to 109,517 periodicals including electronic. Computerized library services include interlibrary loans, database searching, and Internet access. Special learning facilities include an art gallery, radio station, TV station, student technology labs. The 433-acre campus is in a small town 60 miles from Shreveport. Including any residence halls, there are 101 buildings.

Student Life: 63% of undergraduates are from Louisiana. Others are from 40 states, 29 foreign countries, and Canada. 86% are African American. The average age of freshmen is 19; all undergraduates, 22.

Housing: 2586 students can be accommodated in college housing, which includes single-sex and coed On-campus housing is guaranteed for all 4 years. 87% of students live on campus. Alcohol is not permitted. All students may keep cars.

Activities: There are 62 groups on campus, including art, band, cheerleading, choir, communications, computers, dance, drama, honors, international, jazz band, marching band, newspaper, orchestra, political, professional, radio and TV, religious, social, social service, student government, symphony, and yearbook. Popular campus events include Candlelight and Pinning Ceremony, Founder's Day/Week, Black History Month and Springfest.

Sports: There are 5 intercollegiate sports for men and 8 for women, and 4 intramural sports for men and 4 for women. Facilities include Men's Memorial Gymnasium, Eddie G. Robinson Stadium, Frederick C. Hobdy Assembly Center, stadium, and tennis courts.

Disabled Students: Facilities include wheelchair ramps, elevators, special parking, specially equipped restrooms, special class scheduling, lowered drinking fountains, and lowered telephones.

Services: Counseling and information services are available, as is tutoring in biology, English, chemistry, history, math and physics There is remedial math, reading, and writing.

Campus Safety and Security: Measures include 24-hour foot and vehicle patrol and emergency notification system. There are shuttle buses, emergency telephones, and lighted pathways/sidewalks.

Programs of Study: GSU confers B.A., B.S., B.S.W., B.P.A. and B.S.N. degrees. Associate, master's, and doctoral degrees are also awarded. Bachelor's degrees are awarded in BIOLOGICAL SCIENCE (biology/biological science), BUSINESS (accounting, business administration and management, business economics, hotel/motel and restaurant management, marketing/retailing/merchandising, and recreation and leisure services), COMMUNICATIONS AND THE ARTS (communications, English, music, and visual and performing arts), COMPUTER AND PHYSICAL SCIENCE (chemistry, computer science, information sciences and systems, mathematics, and physics), EDUCATION (early childhood education, elementary education, English education, mathematics education, physical education, secondary education, social studies education, and special education), ENGINEERING AND ENVIRONMENTAL DESIGN (engineering technology), HEALTH PROFESSIONS (nursing), SOCIAL SCIENCE (criminal justice, economics, history, political science/government, psychology, public administration, social work, and sociology). Criminal justice, nursing, and business management are the strongest academically. Nursing, and criminal justice have the largest enrollments.

Required: In order to graduate and be awarded a bachelor's degree from Grambling State University, students must: complete all course requirements in an academic major, with no grades lower than C; complete all academic requirements in the General Education Program; complete at least 125 credit hours of course work; pass examinations required for the chosen major; pass the Rising Junior Examination; have a minimum grade point average of 2.0; and earn at least 25 percent of the required credit hours for graduation in residence.

Special: Special training programs available in the Department of Biological Sciences are designed to: encourage and assist biology majors interested in medicine, dentistry or allied health professions to apply for summer programs conducted by medical/dental schools at major universities throughout the nation; prepare students for graduate schools to earn Ph.D. or MD/Ph.D. degrees and pursue research careers in biomedical sciences; and increase the number and quality of students earning baccalaureate and doctoral degrees in the areas of science, engineering, and mathematics. The College of Business faculty members have partnered with various organizations and/or economic programs to provide students with economic development activities. Industry-based internships are available in accounting and finance, housekeeping, recreation, banquet/catering, front office, restaurants, culinary and pastry arts, human resources, and sales. Through an agreement with Southern University at Shreveport their students are enabled to engage in a military science curriculum at Grambling State University. The university-wide Honors College provides unique intellectual and educational experiences for academically talented students to extend their academic, personal, and social development while completing requirements in their chosen majors. There are 5 national honor societies and a freshman honors program.

Faculty/Classroom: 52% of faculty are male; 48% are female. No introductory courses are taught by graduate students.

Admissions: 42% of the 2013-2014 applicants were accepted. The SAT scores for the 2013-2014 freshman class were: Critical Reading--82% below 500, 16% between 500 and 599, 2% between 600 and 699; Math--80% below 500, 18% between 500 and 599, 1% between 600 and 699. The ACT scores were 85% below 21, 12% between 21 and 23, 3% between 24 and 26, 1% between 27 and 28. 18% of the current freshmen were in the top fifth of their class; 43% were in the top two fifths.

Requirements: The SAT or ACT is required. All applicants must submit the general admissions documents, complete 19 units from Core 4 Curriculum, have a minimum 2.00 overall GPA (on 4.0 scale), need no more than one developmental course, and, either a minimum 2.00 GPA on Core 4 Curriculum or ACT Composite 20 or SAT 940 (Reading & Math combined). Admission to the university is conditional until evidence of graduation from high school and completion of required core units are received. Applicants with Certificate of Achievement diplomas and General Equivalency Diplomas (GED) are not eligible for admission to Grambling; however, assistance is provided with a referral to the BPCC at GSU Program where requirements for admission to Grambling State University can be completed. A GPA of 2.0 is required. AP and CLEP credits are accepted.

Procedure: Freshmen are admitted fall, spring, and summer. There is a rolling admissions plan. Applications should be filed by June 1 for fall entry; December 1 for spring entry, and May 1 for summer entry, along with a $20 fee. Notifications are sent in Daily. Applications are accepted online.

Transfer: 281 transfer students enrolled in 2012-2013. Transfer applicants must submit an application fee of $20; submit proof of immunization; submit official transcript from EACH regionally, accredited institution attended, regardless if credits appear on another transcript; have earned at least 18 semester hours of college-level course work (excluding developmental courses)-Students must have completed a college-level English and math course designed to fulfill general education requirement; have earned a cumulative GPA of at least 2.0 on college-level courses; and be in good standing and eligible to return to the last college or university of attendance. 30 of 120 credits required for the bachelor's degree must be completed at GSU.

Visiting: There are guides for informal visits. To schedule a visit, contact the Office of Admissions and Recruitment.

Financial Aid: In 2013-2014, 94% of all full-time freshmen students received some form of financial aid. 82% of all full-time freshmen students received need-based aid. The average freshman award was $6,201. The FAFSA and the college's own financial statement are required. The deadline for filing freshman financial aid applications for fall entry is June 1.

International Students: There are 263 international students enrolled. The school actively recruits these students. They must take the TOEFL with a minimum score of 500 on the paper-based TOEFL (PBT) or 62 on the Internet-based version (iBT). They must also take the SAT or ACT, scoring 24.

Graduates: From July 1, 2012 to June 30, 2013, 686 bachelor's degrees were awarded. The most popular majors were criminal justice (16%), nursing (15%), and business management (10%). In an average class, 28% graduate in 6 years or less.

Admissions Contact: Annie Moss, Director of Admissions/Recruitment. E-Mail: *mossa@gram.edu* Web: *http:/www.gram.edu/admissions/*

LOUISIANA COLLEGE B-3

Pineville, LA 71359 (318) 487-7259
(800) 487-1906; (318) 487-7550

Full-time: 436 men, 420 women	**Faculty:** 60; IIB, --$
Part-time: 67 men, 133 women	**Ph.D.s:** 60%
Graduate: n/av	**Student/Faculty:** 14 to 1
Year: semesters, summer session	**Tuition:** $11,490
Application Deadline: open	**Room & Board:** $4256
Freshman Class: 549 applied, 429 accepted, 246 enrolled	
SAT: required **ACT:** 22	**COMPETITIVE**

Louisiana College, founded in 1906, is a private liberal arts college affiliated with the Southern Baptist Churches of Louisiana. In addition to regional accreditation, LC has baccalaureate program accreditation with AACSB, ACBSP, CSWE, NASM, and NLN. The library contains 138,985 volumes, 126,266 microform items, and 2,500 audio/video tapes/CDs/DVDs, and subscribes to 19,993 periodicals including electronic. The figures in the above capsule and in this profile are approximate. Computerized library services include interlibrary loans, database searching, and Internet access. Special learning facilities include a learning resource center, art gallery, radio station, a performing arts center. The 81-acre campus is in a small town. Including any residence halls, there are 16 buildings.

Student Life: 92% of undergraduates are from Louisiana. Others are from 16 states, 5 foreign countries, and Canada. 88% are white. 66% are Protestant; 18% claim no religious affiliation; 13% Catholic. The average age of freshmen is 18; all undergraduates, 22. 36% do not continue beyond their first year; 43% remain to graduate.

Housing: 726 students can be accommodated in college housing, which

includes single-sex dorms, on-campus apartments, and married student housing. On-campus housing is guaranteed for all 4 years. 54% of students live on campus. Alcohol is not permitted. All students may keep cars.

Activities: 5% of men belong to 4 local fraternities; 15% of women belong to 4 local sororities. There are 57 groups on campus, including Union Board (campus programming), art, band, Breaking All Barriers (Diversity), cheerleading, choir, chorale, chorus, communications, debate, drama, honors, international, jazz band, literary magazine, marching band, musical theater, newspaper, opera, pep band, political, professional, radio and TV, religious, social, social service, student government, symphony, and yearbook. Popular campus events include Gala Christmas, Sanders Lecture Series, and Miss LC Pageant.

Sports: There are 5 intercollegiate sports for men and 5 for women, and 11 intramural sports for men and 11 for women. Facilities include a field house for basketball, a baseball field, a fitness/wellness center, a jogging trail, tennis courts, an intramural/soccer/football field, an outdoor beach volleyball court, softball field, and a practice football field.

Disabled Students: 95% of the campus is accessible. Facilities include wheelchair ramps, elevators, special parking, specially equipped restrooms, and lowered telephones.

Services: Counseling and information services are available, as is tutoring in most subjects. There is a reader service for the blind, and remedial math and writing. PASS (Program to Assist Student Success) offers services for students with documented learning disabilities.

Campus Safety and Security: Measures include 24-hour foot and vehicle patrol, self-defense education, and security escort services. There are lighted pathways/sidewalks.

Programs of Study: LC confers B.A., B.S., B.G.S., B.M., B.S.N., and B.S.W. degrees. Associate degrees are also awarded. Bachelor's degrees are awarded in BIOLOGICAL SCIENCE (biology/biological science), BUSINESS (business administration and management), COMMUNICATIONS AND THE ARTS (communications, dramatic arts, English, French, graphic design, journalism, languages, multimedia, music, speech/debate/rhetoric, and studio art), COMPUTER AND PHYSICAL SCIENCE (chemistry and mathematics), EDUCATION (art education, athletic training, business education, elementary education, English education, health education, mathematics education, music education, science education, secondary education, social studies education, and special education), HEALTH PROFESSIONS (exercise science, medical laboratory technology, music therapy, nursing, predentistry, premedicine, preoptometry, and preveterinary science), SOCIAL SCIENCE (criminal justice, economics, history, philosophy, prelaw, psychology, public administration, religion, religious education, religious music, social work, and sociology). Education, biology, and business have the largest enrollments.

Required: To graduate, students must complete 127 total credit hours, 42 of which must be junior-senior level, including a central core of 56 hours in all degree programs, and maintain a minimum GPA of 2.0, 2.25 in the major. They must also complete Cultural/Intellectual and Spiritual Enrichment requirements and earn at least 25% of credit applied toward degree through instruction offered by LC. They must complete the last 30 hours of course work at LC, and take 3 hours each of phys ed and computer applications.

Special: Study abroad in London and Hong Kong, interdisciplinary studies, work-study programs, non-degree study, internships, dual majors, and pass/fail options are offered. There are 13 national honor societies and a freshman honors program.

Faculty/Classroom: 57% of faculty are male; 43% are female. All teach undergraduates. No introductory courses are taught by graduate students. The average class size in an introductory lecture is 30; in a laboratory is 20; and in a regular course is 18.

Admissions: 78% of a recent year, applicants were accepted. The ACT scores were 38% below 21, 29% between 21 and 23, 16% between 24 and 26, 9% between 27 and 28, and 8% above 28.

Requirements: The SAT or ACT is required. Candidates for admission must have completed 17 units, which must include 4 of English, 3 of math (algebra I, II, and geometry), 3 of social studies, and 3 of science (2 with lab). Graduates of accredited high school's must meet one of the following requirements for unconditional admission: (1) Score at least 20 composite on ACT or satisfactorily on the SAT and possess a GPA of 2.0 on a 4.0 scale; or (2) Possess an academic GPA of 2.0 on a 4.0 scale and rank in the upper 50% of their graduating class with an acceptable ACT or SAT score. A GPA of 2.0 is required. AP and CLEP credits are accepted. Important factors in the admissions decision are extracurricular activities record, leadership record, and advanced placement or honors courses.

Procedure: Freshmen are admitted fall, spring, and summer. Entrance exams should be taken during the junior or senior year. There is a rolling admissions plan. Application deadlines are open. Application fee is $25. Notification is sent on a rolling basis. Applications are accepted online.

Transfer: Applicants must have an overall minimum GPA of 2.0 and finish all remedial course work prior to transfer. 30 of 127 credits required for the bachelor's degree must be completed at LC.

Visiting: There are regularly scheduled orientations for prospective students, consisting of spring and fall campus preview days and a 2-day orientation and pre-registration in June. There are guides for informal visits, visitors may sit in on classes, and stay overnight. To schedule a visit, contact the Office of Admissions.

Financial Aid: 19% of undergraduate students work part-time. The FAFSA, FFS, and the college's own financial statement are required. The priority date for freshman financial aid applications for fall entry is March 15. The deadline for filing freshman financial aid applications for fall entry is October 1.

International Students: The TOEFL is waived for students taking the SAT who earn 480 on the verbal section. They must also take the SAT or ACT.

Graduates: In a recent year, 159 bachelor's degrees were awarded. The most popular majors were nursing (9%), biology (9%), and social work (8%). 65 companies recruited on campus in a recent year. In an average class, 24% graduate in 4 years or less, 41% graduate in 5 years or less, and 45% graduate in 6 years or less.

Admissions Contact: Director of Admissions E-Mail: *admissions@lacollege.edu* Web: *www.lacollege.edu*

LOUISIANA STATE UNIVERSITY SYSTEM

The Louisiana State University System, established in 1860, is a public system in Louisiana. It is governed by a board of supervisors, whose chief administrator is the president. The primary goal of the system is to foster excellence in teaching, research, and public service. The main priorities are undergraduate education, graduate education, and economic development. The total student enrollment is usually about 56,000, with 3500 faculty members. Altogether there are approximately 228 baccalaureate, 220 master's, and 86 doctoral programs offered in the Louisiana State University System. Profiles of the 4-year campuses are included in this section.

LOUISIANA STATE UNIVERSITY C-4

Baton Rouge, LA 70803 **(225) 578-1175; (225) 578-4433**

Full-time: 10979 men, 11832 women	**Faculty:** 1053
Part-time: 1101 men, 1011 women	**Ph.D.s:** 89%
Graduate: 2713 men, 2842 women	**Student/Faculty:** 22 to 1
Year: semesters, summer session	**Tuition:** $7873 ($25,790)
Application Deadline: April 15	**Room & Board:** $10,804
Freshman Class: 16005 applied, 12002 accepted, 5501 enrolled	
SAT CR/M: 559/577	**ACT:** 26 **VERY COMPETITIVE+**

Louisiana State University in Baton Rouge, a public institution founded in 1860, and part of the Louisiana State University System, offers programs in the colleges of agriculture, humanities and social sciences, business administration, coast and environment, art and design, human sciences and education, engineering, music and dramatic arts, mass communication, and science. There are 11 undergraduate schools and 2 graduate schools. In addition to regional accreditation, LSU has baccalaureate program accreditation with AACSB, ABET, ACCE, ACEJMC, ASLA, CSWE, FIDER, NAAB, NASAD, NASM, NCATE, and SAF. The 5 libraries contain 3.8 million volumes, 2.3 million microform items, and 26,938 audio/video tapes/CDs/DVDs, and subscribe to 337,837 periodicals including electronic. Computerized library services include interlibrary loans, database searching, Internet access, and Wi-Fi capability. Special learning facilities include an art gallery, natural history museum, radio station, TV station, 3 herbaria, and museums of natural science, natural history, geoscience, rural life, and art. The 2000-acre campus is in an urban area in Baton Rouge, Louisiana. Including any residence halls, there are 250 buildings.

Student Life: 80% of undergraduates are from Louisiana. Others are from 49 states, 81 foreign countries, and Canada. 52% are from public schools. 76% are White; 11% African American. 40% are Catholic; 33% Protestant; 23% claim no religious affiliation. The average age of freshmen is 19; all undergraduates, 21. 18% do not continue beyond their first year; 69% remain to graduate.

Housing: 7450 students can be accommodated in college housing, which includes single-sex and coed dorms, on-campus apartments, and married student housing. In addition, there are honors houses, special-interest houses, fraternity houses, and sorority houses. 75% of students commute. All students may keep cars.

Activities: 17% of men belong to 23 national fraternities; 26% of women belong to 16 national sororities. There are 300 groups on campus, including art, band, cheerleading, choir, chorus, communications, computers, dance, debate, drama, environmental, ethnic, film, gay, honors, international, jazz band, literary magazine, marching band, musical theater, newspaper, opera, orchestra, pep band, political, professional, radio and TV, religious, social, social service, student government, symphony, and yearbook. Popular campus events include Fall Fest, Home Football Games, and Groovin on the Grounds.

Sports: There are 9 intercollegiate sports for men and 11 for women, and

23 intramural sports for men and 23 for women. Facilities include a 92,300-seat football stadium, a 13,500-seat domed sports center, a 9,200-seat baseball stadium, a 400-meter track with seating for 5,600, a natatorium with an 8-lane Olympic pool and diving well, an indoor track, and courts for handball, badminton, volleyball, and tennis. The campus recreation facility provides a multifaceted program that includes aquatics, sports clubs, informal recreation, fitness classes, instructional sports, personal training, intramural sports, outdoor recreation, challenge course, climbing wall, and special-events activities. There is also an indoor practice facility for football, a soccer field that seats 1,200, and a softball stadium that seats 1,200.

Disabled Students: 85% of the campus is accessible. Facilities include wheelchair ramps, elevators, special parking, specially equipped restrooms, special class scheduling, lowered drinking fountains, lowered telephones, special housing.

Services: Counseling and information services are available, as is tutoring in some subjects, including English, math, foreign languages, and sciences. There is remedial reading and writing.

Campus Safety and Security: Measures include 24-hour foot and vehicle patrol, emergency notification system, self-defense education, and security escort services. There are shuttle buses, emergency telephones, lighted pathways/sidewalks, controlled access to dorms/residences, and specialized crime prevention programs.

Programs of Study: LSU confers B.A., B.S., B.A.M.C., B.Arch., B.F.A., B.I.S., B.I.D., B.L.A., B.M., B.M.Ed., B.S.B.E., B.S.C.E., B.S.Ch.E., B.S.E.E., B.S.Env.E., B.S.C.M., B.S.F., B.S.I.E., B.S. in Coastal Environmental Science, B.S. in Geol., B.S.M.E. and B.S.P.E. degrees. Master's and doctoral degrees are also awarded. Bachelor's degrees are awarded in AGRICULTURE (agricultural business management, animal science, environmental studies, forestry and related sciences, natural resource management, and plant science), BIOLOGICAL SCIENCE (biochemistry, biology/biological science, microbiology, and nutrition), BUSINESS (accounting, banking and finance, business administration and management, human resources, international economics, management science, marketing/retailing/merchandising, and sports management), COMMUNICATIONS AND THE ARTS (communications, dramatic arts, English, French, journalism, music, Spanish, and studio art), COMPUTER AND PHYSICAL SCIENCE (chemistry, computer science, geology, information sciences and systems, mathematics, and physics), EDUCATION (agricultural education, athletic training, early childhood education, elementary education, music education, and special education), ENGINEERING AND ENVIRONMENTAL DESIGN (architecture, bioengineering, chemical engineering, civil engineering, computer engineering, construction management, electrical/electronics engineering, environmental engineering, environmental science, industrial engineering, interior design, landscape architecture/design, mechanical engineering, and petroleum/natural gas engineering), HEALTH PROFESSIONS (speech pathology/audiology), SOCIAL SCIENCE (anthropology, child care/child and family studies, economics, geography, history, interdisciplinary studies, international studies, liberal arts/general studies, philosophy, physical fitness/movement, political science/government, psychology, sociology, and textiles and clothing). Biological sciences, chemistry, civil and environmental engineering, English and French studies are the strongest academically. Biological sciences, mass communication and kinesiology have the largest enrollments.

Required: To graduate, all students must have a minimum overall 2.0 GPA in 120 to 162 credit hours. They must complete a general education component of 39 semester hours in approved courses in 6 major areas, including humanities, natural sciences, English composition, analytical reasoning, social sciences, and the arts. Students must earn at least 25% of required hours for their degree at LSU and meet college residency requirements.

Special: Co-op programs in all areas of engineering and landscape architecture, cross-registration with Southern University and Baton Rouge Community College, study abroad, and work-study programs are offered. B.A.-B.S. degrees, dual majors, a general studies degree, non-degree study, an evening school, a program of study for adult learners, and pass/fail options are available. There are 23 national honor societies, including Phi Beta Kappa, and a freshman honors program.

Faculty/Classroom: 64% of faculty are male; 36% are female. 89% teach undergraduates, 75% do research, and 73% do both. Graduate students teach 17% of introductory courses. The average class size in an introductory lecture is 52; in a laboratory is 25; and in a regular course is 38.

Admissions: 75% of the 2013-2014 applicants were accepted. The SAT scores for the 2013-2014 freshman class were: Critical Reading--22% below 500, 51% between 500 and 599, 24% between 600 and 699, and 4% between 700 and 800; Math--15% below 500, 44% between 500 and 599, 35% between 600 and 699, and 6% between 700 and 800. The ACT scores were 5% below 21, 27% between 21 and 23, 31% between 24 and 26, 17% between 27 and 28, and 21% above 28. 44% of the current freshmen were in the top fifth of their class; 73% were in the top two fifths. There were 43 National Merit finalists. 355 freshmen graduated first in their class.

Requirements: The SAT or ACT is required. In addition, applicants must be graduates of an accredited secondary school. GED certificates may be accepted in unusual circumstances. Students must have completed 19 units, including 4 credits in English, 4 each in specific math, science, and social studies courses, 2 credits in a foreign language, and one additional credit from certain courses in the visual and performing arts. A GPA of 3.0 is required. AP and CLEP credits are accepted. Important factors in the admissions decision are advanced placement or honors courses, extracurricular activities record, and evidence of special talent.

Procedure: Freshmen are admitted to all sessions. Entrance exams should be taken in spring of the junior year or fall of the senior year. There are early admissions, deferred admissions, and rolling admissions plans. Applications should be filed by April 15 for fall entry; December 1 for spring entry; and April 15 for summer entry, along with a $40 fee. Notification is sent on a rolling basis. Applications are accepted online.

Transfer: 866 transfer students enrolled in 2012-2013. Transfer students must submit an official transcript from each previously attended school. Requirements are 30 or more semester hours with a minimum 2.5 GPA, and college level English and math courses. 30 of 120 credits required for the bachelor's degree must be completed at LSU.

Visiting: There are regularly scheduled orientations for prospective students, including an information session and a tour of campus. Department appointments can be arranged. There are guides for informal visits. To schedule a visit, contact the Office of Enrollment Management at (225) 578-6908.

Financial Aid: In 2013-2014, 93% of all full-time freshmen and 84% of continuing full-time students received some form of financial aid. 38% of all full-time freshmen and 35% of continuing full-time students received need-based aid. The average freshman award was $12,800. Need-based scholarships or need-based grants averaged $7,300; need-based self-help aid (loans and jobs) averaged $3,400; non-need-based athletic scholarships averaged $19,500; and other non-need-based awards and non-need-based scholarships averaged $6,600. 27% of undergraduate students work part-time. Average annual earnings from campus work are $2500. The average financial indebtedness of the 2013 graduate was $21,613. The FAFSA and the college's own financial statement are required. The priority date for freshman financial aid applications for fall entry is April 1.

International Students: There are 442 international students enrolled. The school actively recruits these students. They must take the TOEFL with a minimum score of 550 on the paper-based TOEFL (PBT) or 79 on the Internet-based version (iBT), IELTS (minimum score of 6.5). They must also take the SAT or ACT.

Graduates: From July 1, 2012 to June 30, 2013, 4529 bachelor's degrees were awarded. The most popular majors were biological sciences (7%), kinesiology (6%), and mass communication (6%). 527 companies recruited on campus in 2012-2013. In an average class, 40% graduate in 4 years or less, 65% graduate in 5 years or less, and 69% graduate in 6 years or less. Of the 2012 graduating class, 22% were enrolled in graduate school within 6 months of graduation, and 58% were employed.

Admissions Contact: David Kurpius, Associate VC Enrollment Management. E-Mail: *admissions@lsu.edu* Web: *www.lsu.edu*

LOUISIANA STATE UNIVERSITY IN SHREVEPORT A-1

Shreveport, LA 71115	**(318) 797-5061; (318) 797-5286**
Full-time: 776 men, 1084 women	**Faculty:** 127
Part-time: 719 men, 1076 women	**Ph.D.s:** 79%
Graduate: 551 men, 774 women	**Student/Faculty:** 20 to 1
Year: semesters, summer session	**Tuition:** $5606 ($15,020)
Application Deadline: July 15	**Room & Board:** n/app
Freshman Class: 695 applied, 621 accepted, 345 enrolled	
SAT CR/M: 500/530	**ACT:** 22 **COMPETITIVE**

Louisiana State University in Shreveport, established in 1965, is a state-supported, primarily commuter institution offering undergraduate and graduate programs through the colleges of liberal arts, business, education, and sciences. There are 4 undergraduate schools and 4 graduate schools. In addition to regional accreditation, LSUS has baccalaureate program accreditation with AACSB, ABET, and NCATE. The library contains 915,751 volumes, 396,114 microform items, and 4,508 audio/video tapes/CDs/DVDs, and subscribes to 2,000 periodicals including electronic. Computerized library services include interlibrary loans, database searching, and Internet access. Special learning facilities include an art gallery, natural history museum, radio station, a pioneer heritage center, and a museum of life sciences. The 258-acre campus is in an urban area 7 miles south of downtown Shreveport. Including any residence halls, there are 18 buildings.

Student Life: 92% of undergraduates are from Louisiana. Others are from 40 states, 25 foreign countries, and Canada. 95% are from public schools. 63% are White; 20% African American. The average age of freshmen is 18; all undergraduates, 23. 35% do not continue beyond their first year; 30% remain to graduate.

Housing: 480 students can be accommodated in college housing, which includes single-sex and coed on-campus apartments. On-campus housing is guaranteed for all 4 years, is available on a first-come, and first-served basis. All students may keep cars.

Activities: 5% of men belong to 6 national fraternities; 2% of women belong to 4 national sororities. There are 70 groups on campus, including cheerleading, computers, dance, debate, drama, ethnic, film, forensics, honors, international, literary magazine, photography, political, professional, religious, social, social service, student activities board, student government, and yearbook. Popular campus events include Fall Fest, Spring Fling and Welcome Back Bash.

Sports: There are 3 intercollegiate sports for men and 3 for women. Facilities include tennis and racquetball courts, sand or volleyball courts, a swimming pool, gym, weight room, dance studio, football fields, softball diamonds, and a soccer field.

Disabled Students: All of the campus is accessible. Facilities include wheelchair ramps, elevators, special parking, specially equipped restrooms, special class scheduling, lowered drinking fountains, lowered telephones, special housing.

Services: Counseling and information services are available, as is tutoring in some subjects, math and English There is remedial math and writing.

Campus Safety and Security: Measures include 24-hour foot and vehicle patrol, self-defense education, and security escort services. There are emergency telephones, lighted pathways/sidewalks, and commissioned University police officers.

Programs of Study: LSUS confers B.A., B.S., B.C.J. and B.G.S. degrees. Master's degrees are also awarded. Bachelor's degrees are awarded in BIOLOGICAL SCIENCE (biochemistry and biology/biological science), BUSINESS (accounting, banking and finance, business administration and management, management science, and marketing/retailing/merchandising), COMMUNICATIONS AND THE ARTS (communications, English, and fine arts), COMPUTER AND PHYSICAL SCIENCE (chemistry, computer science, mathematics, and physics), EDUCATION (elementary education and secondary education), HEALTH PROFESSIONS (community health work), SOCIAL SCIENCE (history, liberal arts/general studies, psychology, and sociology). Biology, computer science, chemistry, and business administration, are the strongest academically. Psychology, and biology have the largest enrollments.

Required: A minimum of 120 semester hours, with a minimum GPA of 2.0, is required for the bachelor's degree.

Special: Opportunities are provided internships, a Washington semester, a general studies degree, credit for military service schools, non-degree study, and pass/fail options. There are 12 national honor societies and a freshman honors program.

Faculty/Classroom: 59% of faculty are male; 41% are female. 80% teach undergraduates, 70% do research, and 70% do both. No introductory courses are taught by graduates. The average class size in an introductory lecture is 30; in a laboratory is 18; and in a regular course is 19.

Admissions: 89% of the 2013-2014 applicants were accepted. The SAT scores for the 2013-2014 freshman class were: Critical Reading--40% below 500, and 60% between 500 and 599; Math--17% below 500, and 83% between 500 and 599. The ACT scores were 30% below 21, 32% between 21 and 23, 24% between 24 and 26, 6% between 27 and 28, and 5% above 28.

Requirements: The ACT is required. Students must have a minimum composite score of 20. Graduation from an accredited secondary school is required with the 19 State approved core courses. A GPA of 2.0 is required. AP and CLEP credits are accepted.

Procedure: Freshmen are admitted to all sessions. Entrance exams should be taken at least 2 months before start of the current semester. There is a rolling admissions plan. Applications should be filed by July 15 for fall entry; December 1 for spring entry; and May 1 for summer entry, along with a $10 fee. Notification is sent on a rolling basis.

Transfer: Transfers must be in good academic standing, with 18 transferable hours and a GPA of 2.0. They must be eligible to continue at the last institution attended. 30 of 120 credits required for the bachelor's degree must be completed at LSUS.

Visiting: There are regularly scheduled orientations for prospective students, including a preview program during the spring semester for high school juniors and seniors, students may stay overnight for this scheduled visit. There are guides for informal visits. To schedule a visit, contact Kimberly Thornton at kimberly.thornton@lsus.edu.

Financial Aid: 90% of undergraduate students work part-time. Average annual earnings from campus work are $3200. The FAFSA is required. The deadline for filing freshman financial aid applications for fall entry is June 1.

International Students: There are 43 international students enrolled. They must take the TOEFL with a minimum score of 173 on the paper-based TOEFL (PBT) or 61 on the Internet-based version (iBT). They must also take the SAT or ACT, scoring 20.

Graduates: From July 1, 2012 to June 30, 2013, 639 bachelor's degrees were awarded. The most popular majors were business/marketing (23%), general studies (14%), and biology (11%). In an average class, 30% graduate in 6 years or less.

Admissions Contact: Kimberly.thornton@lsus.edu, Director of Admissions. E-Mail: *kimberly.thornton@lsus.edu* Web: *www.lsus.edu*

LOUISIANA TECH UNIVERSITY — B-1

Ruston, LA 71272 — **(318) 257-3036**
(800) LATECH-1; (318) 257-2499

Full-time: 854 men, 681 women	**Faculty:** 397; IIA, -$
Part-time: 56 men, 9 women	**Ph.D.s:** 80%
Graduate: 521 men, 522 women	**Student/Faculty:** 21 to 1
Year: trimesters, summer session	**Tuition:** $4000 ($8000)
Application Deadline: January 3	**Room & Board:** $4000
Freshman Class: n/av	
ACT: required	

COMPETITIVE

Louisiana Tech University, founded in 1894, is a public institution offering programs in arts and sciences, business, agriculture, engineering, health science, education, fine and liberal arts, and human ecology. There are 5 undergraduate schools and 5 graduate schools. In addition to regional accreditation, Tech has baccalaureate program accreditation with AACSB, ABET, ADA, AHEA, ASLA, CAHEA, FIDER, NAAB, NASAD, NASM, NCATE, NLN, and SAF. The library contains 1.1 million volumes, 2.1 million microform items, and 511 audio/video tapes/CDs/DVDs, and subscribes to 2,932 periodicals including electronic. Computerized library services include interlibrary loans and database searching. Special learning facilities include a learning resource center, art gallery, natural history museum, planetarium, and radio station. The 260-acre campus is in a small town 30 miles west of Monroe and 90 miles east of Shreveport, Louisiana. Including any residence halls, there are 146 buildings. The figures in the above capsule and in this profile are approximate.

Student Life: 85% of undergraduates are from Louisiana. Others are from 48 states, 70 foreign countries, and Canada. 70% are white; 16% African American. 51% are Protestant; 12% Catholic. The average age of freshmen is 19; all undergraduates, 20. 22% do not continue beyond their first year; 49% remain to graduate.

Housing: 3067 students can be accommodated in college housing, which includes single-sex and coed dorms and married student housing. In addition, there are honors houses. On-campus housing is guaranteed for all 4 years. 74% of students commute. Alcohol is not permitted. All students may keep cars.

Activities: 7% of men belong to 9 national fraternities; 11% of women belong to 5 national sororities. There are 121 groups on campus, including art, band, cheerleading, choir, chorale, chorus, computers, dance, debate, drama, drill team, drum and bugle corps, ethnic, film, honors, international, jazz band, marching band, musical theater, newspaper, opera, orchestra, pep band, photography, political, professional, radio and TV, religious, social, social service, student government, symphony, and yearbook. Popular campus events include International Student Festival, Spring Fling, and Little Theater concerts.

Sports: There are 5 intercollegiate sports for men and 5 for women, and 10 intramural sports for men and 10 for women. Facilities include a football stadium, a coliseum, an intramural complex, a natatorium, a 9-hole golf course, and 10 lighted tennis courts.

Disabled Students: 95% of the campus is accessible. Facilities include wheelchair ramps, elevators, special parking, specially equipped restrooms, lowered drinking fountains, and lowered telephones.

Services: Counseling and information services are available, as is tutoring in some subjects. There is a reader service for the blind, and remedial math, reading, and writing.

Campus Safety and Security: Measures include 24-hour foot and vehicle patrol, self-defense education, and security escort services. There are emergency telephones and lighted pathways/sidewalks.

Programs of Study: Tech confers B.A., B.S., B. Arch., B.F.A., and B.G.S. degrees. Associate, master's, and doctoral degrees are also awarded. Bachelor's degrees are awarded in AGRICULTURE (agricultural business management, animal science, forestry and related sciences, and wildlife management), BIOLOGICAL SCIENCE (biology/biological science), BUSINESS (accounting, banking and finance, business administration and management, business economics, business systems analysis, management science, marketing/retailing/merchandising, and personnel management), COMMUNICATIONS AND THE ARTS (English, fine arts, French, journalism, music, music performance, Spanish, and speech/debate/rhetoric), COMPUTER AND PHYSICAL SCIENCE (chemistry, computer science, geology, mathematics, and physics), EDUCATION (art education, early childhood education, elementary education, foreign languages education, music education, physical education, secondary education, and special education), ENGINEERING AND ENVIRONMENTAL DESIGN (airline piloting and navigation, architecture, aviation administration/management, biomedical engineering, chemical engineering, civil engineering, construction engineering, electrical/electronics engineering technology, environmental science, industrial engineering, and mechanical engineering), HEALTH PROFESSIONS (medical laboratory technology, medical records administration/services, and speech pathology/audiology), SOCIAL SCIENCE (dietetics, geography, history, liberal arts/general studies, political science/government, psychology, and sociology). Business and engineering are the strongest academically and have the largest enrollments.

Required: All students must complete 45 quarter hours of general education courses, including 12 hours in humanities, 9 each in natural and social sciences, 6 each in English and math, and 3 in arts or computer literacy. A total of 120 to 142 quarter hours, with a minimum GPA of 2.0, is required to graduate.

Special: Co-op programs are available in engineering and applied and natural sciences, and cross-registration with Grambling State University is offered. Internships in agriculture, engineering, dietetics, and human ecology are offered. Study abroad, work-study programs, dual majors, a general studies degree, non-degree study, and pass/fail options are available.

Faculty/Classroom: 65% of faculty are male; 35% are female. 95% teach undergraduates. Graduate students teach 2% of introductory courses. The average class size in an introductory lecture is 40; in a laboratory is 20; and in a regular course is 26.

Admissions: There were 5 National Merit finalists.

Requirements: The ACT is required. Applicants must be graduates of an accredited secondary school or have a GED. Students must have graduated in the upper half of their class. A GPA of 2.3 is required. AP credits are accepted.

Procedure: Freshmen are admitted to all sessions. There is a rolling admissions plan. Applications should be filed by October 21 for winter entry; January 30 for spring entry; and May 9 for summer entry. The fall 2011 application fee was $20.

Transfer: 526 transfer students enrolled in in a recent year. Transfer applicants should have a 2.0 GPA and be eligible to enroll in the school from which they are transferring. 30 of 120 credits required for the bachelor's degree must be completed at LTech.

Visiting: There are regularly scheduled orientations for prospective students. There are guides for informal visits and visitors may stay overnight. To schedule a visit, contact the Admissions Office.

Financial Aid: 27% of undergraduate students work part-time. The FAFSA is required. The deadline for filing freshman financial aid applications for fall entry is July 16.

International Students: There are 139 international students enrolled. The school actively recruits these students. They must take the TOEFL. but a minimum 2.5 GPA is required.

Graduates: In a recent year, 1401 bachelor's degrees were awarded. The most popular majors were business (22%), engineering (17%), and education (11%). 632 companies recruited on campus in 2010-2011. In an average class, 29% graduate in 4 years or less, 49% graduate in 5 years or less, and 55% graduate in 6 years or less.

Admissions Contact: Admissions Office. A campus DVD is available. E-Mail: *bulldog@latech.edu* Web: *www.latech.edu*

LOYOLA UNIVERSITY NEW ORLEANS — D-4

New Orleans, LA 70118 — **(504) 865-3240**
(800) 4-LOYOLA; (504) 865-3383

Full-time: 1242 men, 1744 women	**Faculty:** 266; IIA, av$
Part-time: 91 men, 123 women	**Ph.D.s:** 75%
Graduate: 597 men, 1136 women	**Student/Faculty:** 10 to 1
Year: semesters, summer session	**Tuition:** $34,592
Application Deadline:	**Room & Board:** $11,629

Freshman Class: 6486 applied, 4257 accepted, 877 enrolled
SAT or ACT: required

VERY COMPETITIVE

Loyola University New Orleans, founded in 1912, is a private institution operated by the Society of Jesus and affiliated with the Roman Catholic Church. There are 4 undergraduate schools and 6 graduate schools. In addition to regional accreditation, Loyola has baccalaureate program accreditation with AACSB, NASM, and NLN. The 2 libraries contain 584,939 volumes, 1.4 million microform items, and 17,352 audio/video tapes/CDs/DVDs, and subscribe to 169,032 periodicals including electronic. Computerized library services include interlibrary loans, database searching, and Internet access. Special learning facilities include an art gallery, radio station, TV station, art gallery, humanities lab with Perseus Project and TLG TV, multimedia classrooms graphic lab, visual arts lab,ad club communications lab, business computer lab, multimedia training center, and center for non-profit communication. The 26-acre campus is in a suburban area 5 miles from downtown New Orleans. Including any residence halls, there are 29 buildings.

Student Life: 58% of undergraduates are from out of state, mostly the South. Students are from 53 states, 48 foreign countries, and Canada. 47% are from public schools. 52% are White; 15% African American; 15% Hispanic. 41% are Catholic; 17% Protestant. The average age of freshmen is 18; all undergraduates, 20. 33% do not continue beyond their first year; 67% remain to graduate.

Housing: 1350 students can be accommodated in college housing, which includes single-sex and coed dorms and on-campus apartments. In addition, there are special-interest houses, honors floor. On-campus housing is available on a first-come and first-served basis. Priority is given to out-of-town students. 65% of students live on campus; of those, 75% remain on campus on weekends. Upperclassmen may keep cars.

Activities: 6% of women belong to 4 national sororities. There are 85 groups on campus, including art, band, cheerleading, choir, chorale, chorus, computers, dance, drama, environmental, ethnic, film, forensics, gay, honors, international, jazz band, literary magazine, musical theater, newspaper, opera, orchestra, photography, political, professional, radio and TV, religious, social, social service, student government, symphony, and yearbook. Popular campus events include Loyola Week, Wolves on the Prowl Community Service Day, and Loyolapalooza Spring Music Festival.

Sports: There are 6 intercollegiate sports for men and 7 for women, and 7 intramural sports for men and 7 for women. Facilities include a sports complex with an arena, 6 multipurpose courts for basketball, tennis, volleyball, badminton, and floor hockey, 2 racquetball courts, an Olympic-style natatorium, a jogging track, and a weight-lifting and conditioning area.

Disabled Students: 99% of the campus is accessible. Facilities include wheelchair ramps, elevators, special parking, specially equipped restrooms, lowered drinking fountains, lowered telephones, special housing. special class relocation to provide accessibility.

Services: Counseling and information services are available, as is tutoring in most subjects. There is remedial math and writing. Peer tutoring is available in all introductory common curriculum courses. A reader service for the blind is provided for all exams and for course work if books on tape are not sufficient.

Campus Safety and Security: Measures include 24-hour foot and vehicle patrol, emergency notification system, self-defense education, and security escort services. There are shuttle buses, emergency telephones, lighted pathways/sidewalks, controlled access to dorms/residences, CCTV coverage, card access control, intrusion alarm monitoring, first aid medical assistance, motor vehicle assistance, bicycle registration, fingerprinting services, and crime prevention services.

Programs of Study: Loyola confers B.A., B.S., B.Acc., B.B.A., B.C.J., B.F.A., B.L.S., B.Mus., B.Mus.Ed., B.Mus. Therapy, B.S.N., B.A. Music, B.S. Mus. Industry, and B.A.Mus. degrees. Master's and doctoral degrees are also awarded. Bachelor's degrees are awarded in AGRICULTURE (environmental studies), BIOLOGICAL SCIENCE (biology/biological science), BUSINESS (accounting, banking and finance, business administration and management, international business management, management science, and marketing/retailing/merchandising), COMMUNICATIONS AND THE ARTS (communications, creative writing, dramatic arts, English literature, fine arts, French, graphic design, guitar, jazz, music, music business management, music performance, music theory and composition, piano/organ, Spanish, studio art, visual and performing arts, and voice), COMPUTER AND PHYSICAL SCIENCE (chemistry, mathematics, and physics), EDUCATION (music education), ENGINEERING AND ENVIRONMENTAL DESIGN (preengineering), HEALTH PROFESSIONS (music therapy, nursing, predentistry, premedicine, and preveterinary science), SOCIAL SCIENCE (anthropology, classical/ancient civilization, criminal justice, economics, forensic studies, history, Latin American studies, liberal arts/general studies, philosophy, political science/government, psychology, religion, religious education, social science, and sociology). Mass communication, psychology, and marketing (business) have the largest enrollments.

Required: All students must complete a core curriculum that includes courses in English composition and literature, math, philosophy, science, world civilization, social science and religious studies; the number of credit hours varies by college. At least 120 credit hours, with at least 30 in the major, and a minimum GPA of 2.0 are required to graduate.

Special: Cross-registration is available with, our Lady of Holy Cross, Xavier University, Notre Dame Seminary, the University of New Orleans, Tulane University, and Southern University of New Orleans. Internships with the New Orleans business community are also available. Study abroad in 8 countries, dual and student-designed majors, nondegree studies, an accelerated R.N. to M.S.N. program, and a general studies degree are offered. A Washington semester through American University and a 3-2 engineering degree with Tulane University and the University of New Orleans is also available. There are 7 national honor societies, a freshman honors program, and 8 departmental honors programs.

Faculty/Classroom: 55% of faculty are male; 45% are female. 84% teach undergraduates, and 90% do research. No introductory courses are taught by graduate students. The average class size in an introductory lecture is 26; in a laboratory is 26; and in a regular course is 18.

Admissions: 66% of the 2013-2014 applicants were accepted.

Requirements: The SAT or ACT is required. Candidates for admission must be graduates of an accredited secondary school or have a GED. They should have completed 4 units in high school English and 3 each in math, science, and social sciences, along with 4 academic electives; 2 units in a foreign language are recommended. A portfolio is required for fine arts students; an audition for music majors. An interview is recommended for scholarship consideration. AP and CLEP credits are accepted. Important factors in the admissions decision are advanced placement or honors courses, evidence of special talent, extracurricular activities record, recommendations by school officials, parents or siblings attended your school, personality/intangible qualities, recommendations by alumni, and geographical diversity.

Procedure: Freshmen are admitted to all sessions. Entrance exams should be taken during the junior or senior year. There is a rolling admissions plan. Application deadlines are open. Application fee is $20. Applications are accepted online.

Transfer: 150 transfer students enrolled in 2012-2013. Applicants must have a minimum 2.25 GPA on all attempted college-level work; 12 credit hours are needed for consideration. 30 of 120 credits required for the bachelor's degree must be completed at Loyola.

Visiting: There are regularly scheduled orientations for prospective students, including class and department visits, a student panel, a tour, a financial aid session, a campus support panel, and meetings with faculty members. There are guides for informal visits, visitors may sit in on classes, and stay overnight. To schedule a visit, contact the Admissions Office at (504) 865-3240.

Financial Aid: In 2013-2014, 86% of all full-time freshmen and 88% of continuing full-time students received some form of financial aid. 86% of all full-time freshmen and 88% of continuing full-time students received need-based aid. The average freshman award was $30,148. Need-based scholarships or need-based grants averaged $26,199; need-based self-help aid (loans and jobs) averaged $4,682; non-need-based athletic scholarships averaged $11,094; and other non-need-based awards and non-need-based scholarships averaged $14,633. 33% of undergraduate students work part-time. Average annual earnings from campus work are $1920. The average financial indebtedness of the 2013 graduate was $23,178. The FAFSA is required. The priority date for freshman financial aid applications for fall entry is March 1. The deadline for filing freshman financial aid applications for fall entry is May 1.

International Students: There are 123 international students enrolled. The school actively recruits these students. They must take the TOEFL with a minimum score of 550 on the paper-based TOEFL (PBT) or 79 on the Internet-based version (iBT) and the college's own test, Scores are minimum score for a student to be admitted through the LIEP Pilot Program. They must also take the SAT or ACT.

Graduates: From July 1, 2012 to June 30, 2013, 546 bachelor's degrees were awarded. The most popular majors were psychology (10%), communications (10%), and music business (7%). 320 companies recruited on campus in 2012-2013. In an average class, 47% graduate in 4 years or less, 58% graduate in 5 years or less, and 58% graduate in 6 years or less.

Admissions Contact: Salvadore A. Liberto, VP for Enrollment Managementent. E-Mail: *admit@loyno.edu* Web: *www.loyno.edu*

MCNEESE STATE UNIVERSITY B-4

Lake Charles, LA 70609 (337) 475-5504
(800) 622-3352; (337) 475-5151

Full-time: 2300 men, 3659 women
Part-time: 582 men, 960 women
Graduate: 270 men, 578 women
Year: semesters, summer session
Application Deadline:
Freshman Class: n/av

Faculty: n/av; IIA, --$
Ph.D.s: 66%
Student/Faculty: 21 to 1
Tuition: n/av
Room & Board: n/av

COMPETITIVE

McNeese State University, founded in 1939, and part of the University of Louisiana System, is a public institution offering programs in business, engineering, education, science, liberal arts, and nursing. There are 7 undergraduate schools and 1 graduate school. In addition to regional accreditation, MSU has baccalaureate program accreditation with AACSB, ABET, ADA, CAHEA, CSAB, NASAD, NASM, NCATE, and NLN. Computerized library services include interlibrary loans, database searching, Internet access, and Wi-Fi capability. Special learning facilities include an art gallery, planetarium, radio station, a farm, a vertebrate museum,a community health care clinic, meat processing plant, Southwest Louisiana Entrepreneurial and Economic Development Center. The 121-acre campus is in a suburban area 130 miles west of Baton Rouge and 150 miles east of Houston, Texas. Including any residence halls, there are 88 buildings.

Student Life: 90% of undergraduates are from Louisiana. Others are from 38 states, 49 foreign countries, and Canada. 73% are White; 18% African American. The average age of freshmen is 20; all undergraduates, 23. 31% do not continue beyond their first year.

Housing: 975 students can be accommodated in college housing, which includes coed dorms and on-campus apartments. On-campus housing is guaranteed for all 4 years, is available on a first-come, and first-served basis. Alcohol is not permitted. All students may keep cars.

Activities: Groups on campus include art, band, cheerleading, choir, chorale, chorus, computers, dance, debate, drama, drill team, ethnic, honors, international, jazz band, marching band, musical theater, newspaper, orchestra, pep band, political, professional, religious, social, social service, student government, symphony, and yearbook. Popular campus events include Homecoming, Spring Fling.

Sports: Facilities include a football stadium, softball and intramural fields, an indoor/outdoor track, a 50-meter pool, baseball complex, outdoor tennis courts, weight room, racquetball courts, and 3 regulation basketball courts.

Disabled Students: Facilities include wheelchair ramps, elevators, special parking, specially equipped restrooms, lowered drinking fountains, academic planning and registration assistance, and classroom and testing accommodations.

Services: Counseling and information services are available, as is tutoring in some subjects.

Campus Safety and Security: Measures include 24-hour foot and vehicle patrol, emergency notification system, and security escort services. There are emergency telephones and lighted pathways/sidewalks.

Programs of Study: MSU confers B.A., B.S., B.S.N. and B.G.S. degrees. Associate and master's degrees are also awarded. Bachelor's degrees are awarded in AGRICULTURE (agriculture and natural resource management), BIOLOGICAL SCIENCE (biology/biological science and nutritional sciences), BUSINESS (accounting, business administration and management, marketing, and organizational leadership and management), COMMUNICATIONS AND THE ARTS (art, communication, English, languages, and music), COMPUTER AND PHYSICAL SCIENCE (chemistry, computer science, mathematics, and radiological technology), EDUCATION (athletic training, early childhood education, elementary education, and health education), ENGINEERING AND ENVIRONMENTAL DESIGN (engineering and engineering technology), HEALTH PROFESSIONS (clinical science and nursing), SOCIAL SCIENCE (criminal justice, gender studies, history, liberal arts/general studies, political science/government, psychology, and sociology). Nursing, engineering, and education have the largest enrollments.

Required: McNeese State University's general education curriculum consists of coursework from six, broad disciplinary areas: Writing (6 hours), Mathematics (6 hours), Natural Sciences (9 hours), Humanities (9 hours), Social and Behavioral Sciences (6 hours), and Fine Arts (3 hours). The mission of this core curriculum is to provide students with a foundation of knowledge, skills, and methods of inquiry that support advanced study in their chosen degree program and constitute the characteristics of an informed, college-educated citizen.

Special: MSU offers co-op programs in engineering, internships in clinical lab sciences, radiologic science, business and education, dual majors, a general studies degree, nondegree study, and credit for military experience. Innovation program available. There are a freshman honors program.

Faculty/Classroom: 48% of faculty are male; 52% are female. No introductory courses are taught by graduate students.

Admissions: The ACT scores were 36% below 21, 37% between 21 and 23, 17% between 24 and 26, 5% between 27 and 28, and 5% above 28.

Requirements: First-time freshmen who are graduates of state-approved Louisiana high schools must meet the following admission criteria: completion of the Regents' High School Core 4 Curriculum; need no developmental courses; and have a minimum high school overall GPA of 2.35; and ONE of the following: minimum high school core GPA of 2.0 on a 4.0 scale as reported by the Department of Education OR ACT composite score of 20 or greater (SAT combined mathematics and critical reading score of 940). AP and CLEP credits are accepted.

Procedure: Freshmen are admitted to all sessions. There are early admissions and rolling admissions plans. Application deadlines are open. Application fee is $20. Applications are accepted online.

Transfer: Transfer students who have earned 18 or more college-level academic credit hours must either have earned a transferable associate degree or higher from a regionally accredited institution OR meet the following admission standards: Cumulative GPA of at least 2.0 on all college-level academic courses; Be eligible to return to the institution from which they are transferring; AND Have completed a college-level English and mathematics course designed to fulfill general education requirements. Transfer students who have a cumulative GPA of at least 2.0 on all college-level academic courses, but who have earned less than 18 college-level academic hours, must meet first-time freshman admission standards. 30 of 120 credits required for the bachelor's degree must be completed at MSU.

Visiting: There are regularly scheduled orientations for prospective students. There are guides for informal visits, visitors may sit in on classes, and stay overnight.

Financial Aid: The FAFSA, FFS, and the college's own financial statement are required. Check with the school for current application deadlines.

International Students: There are 292 international students enrolled. The school actively recruits these students. They must take the TOEFL with a minimum score of 500 on the paper-based TOEFL (PBT) or 173 on the Internet-based version (iBT). They must also take the SAT or ACT.

Graduates: From July 1, 2012 to June 30, 2013, 1177 bachelor's degrees were awarded. The most popular majors were general studies (15%), nursing (14%), and engineering (6%).

Admissions Contact: Kara Smith, Director of Admissions and Recruiting. E-Mail: *admissions@mcneese.edu* Web: *www.mcneese.edu*

NICHOLLS STATE UNIVERSITY D-4

Thibodaux, LA 70310 (985) 448-4507
(877) 642-4655; (985) 448-4929

Full-time: 2000 men, 3000 women
Part-time: 390 men, 840 women
Graduate: 150 men, 540 women
Year: semesters, summer session
Application Deadline: August 15
Freshman Class: n/av
ACT: required
Faculty: 283
Ph.D.s: 56%
Student/Faculty: 18 to 1
Tuition: $5,000 ($11,500)
Room & Board: $6000
COMPETITIVE

Nicholls State University, established in 1948, and part of the University of Louisiana System, is a public liberal arts institution offering instruction in health sciences, fine arts, business, teacher preparation, and agricultural and technical disciplines. There are 6 undergraduate schools and 4 graduate schools. In addition to regional accreditation, Nicholls has baccalaureate program accreditation with AACSB, ACEJMC, ADA, CSAB, NASAD, NASM, NCATE, and NLN. Computerized library services include interlibrary loans, database searching, and Internet access. Special learning facilities include a learning resource center, art gallery, radio station, TV station, a culinary institute, a rural development institute, and centers for the study of dyslexia, women and government, and economic education. The 210-acre campus is in a small town 50 miles southwest of New Orleans and 60 miles southeast of Baton Rouge. Including any residence halls, there are 48 buildings.

Student Life: 96% of undergraduates are from Louisiana. Others are from 32 states, 45 foreign countries, and Canada. 69% are from public schools. 75% are white; 18% African American. 37% are Catholic; 18% Protestant. The average age of freshmen is 20; all undergraduates, 23. 34% do not continue beyond their first year; 26% remain to graduate.

Housing: 1503 students can be accommodated in college housing, which includes single-sex and coed dorms, on-campus apartments, and married student housing. On-campus housing is guaranteed for the freshman year only, is available on a first-come, and first-served basis. 83% of students commute. Alcohol is not permitted. All students may keep cars.

Activities: 10% of men belong to 7 national fraternities; 5% of women belong to 7 national sororities. Groups on campus include art, band, cheerleading, choir, chorale, chorus, computers, dance, debate, drama, drill team, ethnic, gay, honors, international, jazz band, literary magazine, marching band, musical theater, newspaper, pep band, photography, political, professional, radio and TV, religious, social, social service, student government, symphony, and yearbook. Popular campus events include Midterm Exam Week Breakfast, Family Day, and Crawfish Boil.

Sports: There are 6 intercollegiate sports for men and 8 for women, and 4 intramural sports for men and 4 for women. Facilities include a stadium, 2 gyms, tennis and racquetball courts, a soccer field, a swimming pool, baseball and softball fields, and a weight room.

Disabled Students: All of the campus is accessible. Facilities include wheelchair ramps, elevators, special parking, specially equipped restrooms, special class scheduling, lowered drinking fountains, and lowered telephones.

Services: Counseling and information services are available, as is tutoring in most subjects. There is a reader service for the blind, and remedial math and writing. Tutoring is available in math, English, computer science, biology, chemistry, physics, and foreign languages.

Campus Safety and Security: Measures include 24-hour foot and vehicle patrol, emergency notification system, self-defense education, and security escort services. There are emergency telephones and lighted pathways/sidewalks.

Programs of Study: Nicholls confers B.A., B.S., B.G.S., B.M.E., and B.S.N. degrees. Associate and master's degrees are also awarded. Bachelor's degrees are awarded in AGRICULTURE (agricultural business management), BIOLOGICAL SCIENCE (biology/biological science), BUSINESS (accounting, banking and finance, business administration and management, marketing/retailing/merchandising, and personnel management), COMMUNICATIONS AND THE ARTS (art, communications, English, French, journalism, and music), COMPUTER AND PHYSICAL SCIENCE (chemistry, computer science, information sciences and systems, and mathematics), EDUCATION (business education, elementary education, music education, secondary education, and special education), ENGINEERING AND ENVIRONMENTAL DESIGN (manufacturing technology and petroleum/natural gas engineering), HEALTH PROFESSIONS (health science, nursing, and speech pathology/audiology), SOCIAL SCIENCE (dietetics, family/consumer studies, food production/management/services, history, political science/government, psychology, and sociology). Languages, literature, biological sciences, accounting, and business law are the strongest academically. Nursing, general studies, and teacher education have the largest enrollments.

Required: All students must complete general education requirements, including 9 hours each in English, natural sciences, and humanities, 6 hours each in social sciences and math, 3 hours in the arts, and student development, freshman and computer science course. At least 120 total credit hours, plus a minimum of 24 hours in the major, with a minimum GPA of 2.0, are required to graduate. Students also take a general education competency test before graduation.

Special: Internships are offered in business areas, government, home economics, computer science, and psychology. A Washington semester congressional internship and dual majors in education are available. Cross-registration with Fletcher Community College and River Parishes Community College and study abroad in 5 countries are offered. There are 12 national honor societies, a freshman honors program, and 1 departmental honors program.

Faculty/Classroom: 51% of faculty are male; 49% are female. Graduate students teach 1% of introductory courses.

Admissions: In a recent year, 84% applicants were accepted.

Requirements: The ACT is recommended. In addition, applicants must be graduates of an accredited secondary school or have the GED. Institutional placement tests are given for English, math, and reading. Nicholls requires applicants to be in the upper 50% of their class. A GPA of 2.0 is required. AP and CLEP credits are accepted.

Procedure: Freshmen are admitted to all sessions. Entrance exams should be taken as early as possible. There are deferred admissions and rolling admissions plans. Application deadlines are open. Check with the school for current application fee. Notification is sent on a rolling basis. Applications are accepted online.

Transfer: In a recent year, 240 transfer students enrolled. Transfer applicants must be eligible to return to the institution from which they are transferring, must have earned a minimum of 12 college-level hours, have a GPA of 2.0 on college-level courses, and require not more than 1 developmental course. 30 of 120 credits required for the bachelor's degree must be completed at Nicholls.

Visiting: There are regularly scheduled orientations for prospective students, consisting of general information, advising, and registration. There are guides for informal visits, visitors may sit in on classes, and stay overnight. To schedule a visit, contact Admissions.

Financial Aid: The FAFSA is required. The priority date for freshman financial aid applications for fall entry is April 15. Check with the school for deadlines, and fall entry.

International Students: In a recent year, there were 42 international students enrolled. The school actively recruits these students. They must take the TOEFL.

Admissions Contact: Director of Admissions. E-Mail: *nicholls@nicholls.edu* Web: *www.nicholls.edu*

NORTHWESTERN STATE UNIVERSITY OF LOUISIANA B-2

Natchitoches, LA 71497 (318) 357-4503
(800) 327-1903; (318) 357-5567

Full-time: 1767 men, 6579 women
Part-time: 746 men, 2077 women
Graduate: 236 men, 872 women
Year: semesters, summer session
Application Deadline: July 6
Freshman Class: 4127 applied, 2371 accepted, 1169 enrolled
SAT CR/M: 480/500
Faculty: 248; IIA, --$
Ph.D.s: 61%
Student/Faculty: 20 to 1
Tuition: $6246 ($16,366)
Room & Board: $8122
ACT: 21
COMPETITIVE

Northwestern State University is a responsive, student-oriented institution that is committted to the creation, dissemination, and acquisition of knowledge through teaching, research, and service. The University maintains as its highest priority excellence in teaching in graduate and undergraduate programs. Northwestern State University will prepare its students to become productive members of society and will promote economic development and improvements in the quality of life of the citizens in its region. There are 4 undergraduate schools and 1 graduate school. In addition to regional accreditation, NSU has baccalaureate program accreditation with AACSB, ABET, CSWE, NASAD, NASM, NCATE, and NLN. The library contains 331,637 volumes, 632,689 microform items, and 5,514 audio/video tapes/CDs/DVDs, and subscribes to 700 periodicals including electronic. Computerized library services include interlibrary loans, database searching, Internet access, and Wi-Fi capability. Special learning facilities include an art gallery, natural history museum, radio station, TV station, Cammie G. Henry Research Center (collection of Louisiana books, rare books and documents). Creole Heritage Center (center related to the promotion, fostering, and engagement of activities and endeavors related to Louisiana Creoles and their culture). The 916-acre campus is in a small town in central Louisiana, 60 miles south of Shreveport. Including any residence halls, there are 56 buildings.

Student Life: 87% of undergraduates are from Louisiana. Others are from 46 states, 34 foreign countries, and Canada. 59% are White; 26% African American. The average age of freshmen is 19; all undergraduates, 24. 27% do not continue beyond their first year; 40% remain to graduate.

Housing: 1517 students can be accommodated in college housing, which includes coed dorms and on-campus apartments. In addition, there are honors houses and special-interest houses. On-campus housing is available on a first-come and first-served basis. 81% of students commute. Alcohol is not permitted. All students may keep cars.

Activities: 10% of men belong to 7 national fraternities; 6% of women belong to 8 national sororities. There are 103 groups on campus, including art, band, cheerleading, choir, chorale, chorus, communications, computers, dance, debate, drama, drill team, ethnic, gay, honors, international, jazz band, literary magazine, marching band, musical theater, newspaper, opera, orchestra, pep band, photography, political, professional, radio and TV, religious, social, social service, student government, symphony, and yearbook. Popular campus events include Spring Fling Weeks, Greek Week and Welcome Week.

Sports: There are 5 intercollegiate sports for men and 5 for women, and 18 intramural sports for men and 18 for women. Facilities include a 16,000-seat football stadium, a 5000-seat indoor gym, sports training and basketball centers, a track, and a coliseum. The largest auditorium/arena seats 1500. NSU also has a wellness, recreation, and activity center that contains 2 gyms with 4 basketball courts, a 3000-square foot free weights area, a 2800-square foot strength machine weight area, a 2800-square foot cardio-equipment area, a group exercise studio, a spin cycle class studio, a fitness assessment lab, 2 game rooms, 3 racquetball courts, men's and women's locker areas, steam rooms, a massage room, an equipment service center, a student café, meeting rooms, and an indoor track.

Disabled Students: 96% of the campus is accessible. Facilities include wheelchair ramps, elevators, special parking, specially equipped restrooms, special class scheduling, lowered drinking fountains, lowered telephones, and special housing.

Services: Counseling and information services are available, as is tutoring in most subjects. There is a reader service for the blind, and remedial math.

Campus Safety and Security: Measures include 24-hour foot and vehicle patrol, emergency notification system, self-defense education, and security escort services. There are shuttle buses, emergency telephones, and lighted pathways/sidewalks.

Programs of Study: NSU confers B.A., B.A.S, B.S., B.F.A., B.G.S., B.M., B.M.Ed., B.S.N. and B.S.W. degrees. Associate, master's, and doctoral degrees are also awarded. Bachelor's degrees are awarded in BIOLOGICAL SCIENCE (biology/biological science), BUSINESS (accounting, business administration and management, hospitality management services, and organizational leadership and management), COMMUNICATIONS AND THE ARTS (communications, dramatic arts, English, fine arts, foreign language, music, music business management, and musical theater), COMPUTER AND PHYSICAL SCIENCE (information sciences and systems, mathematics, and physical sciences), EDUCATION (early childhood education, elementary education, health education, music education, and secondary education), ENGINEERING AND ENVIRONMENTAL DESIGN (electrical/electronics engineering technology, industrial engineering, and industrial engineering technology), HEALTH PROFESSIONS (allied health, biology, exercise science, nursing, and radiological science), SOCIAL SCIENCE (addiction studies, criminal justice, family/consumer studies, geography, history, humanities, humanities and social science, international relations, liberal arts/general studies, psychology, public administration, and social work). Liberal arts (Scholars' College), creative and performing arts, and computer information systems are the strongest academically. Nursing, liberal arts/general studies, business administration, education/teaching and learning have the largest enrollments.

Required: To graduate, all students must complete their senior year in residence, plus an approved 39-hour core curriculum, the university education requirement, and a minimum of 120 semester hours, with at least 30 semester hours in the major field. Distribution requirements include 9 credits each of humanities and natural sciences; 6 each of english, mathematics, and social/behavioral sciences; as well as 3 of fine arts. A minimum 2.0 GPA is needed for all hours taken at NSU.

Special: NSU offers cooperative programs with local businesses, internships, an exchange program in education with South Korea, and work-study programs. A general studies degree, credit for experience, nondegree study, dual majors, and pass/fail options are available. There are 9 national honor societies, a freshman honors program, and 5 departmental honors programs.

Faculty/Classroom: 41% of faculty are male; 59% are female. 90% teach undergraduates. Graduate students teach 1% of introductory courses. The average class size in an introductory lecture is 30; in a laboratory is 19; and in a regular course is 29.

Admissions: 57% of the 2013-2014 applicants were accepted. The SAT scores for the 2013-2014 freshman class were: Critical Reading--68% below 500, 28% between 500 and 599, 3% between 600 and 699, and 1% between 700 and 800; Math--51% below 500, 40% between 500 and 599, 7% between 600 and 699, and 1% between 700 and 800. The ACT scores were 42% below 21, 30% between 21 and 23, 17% between 24 and 26, 7% between 27 and 28, and 4% above 28. 35% of the current freshmen were in the top fifth of their class; 64% were in the top two fifths. 45 freshmen graduated first in their class.

Requirements: The ACT is required. Applicants must complete 4 units of English, math, science, and social studies, 2 units of foreign language, and 1 unit of fine arts. Students must have a score of 21 on the ACT (or SAT equivalent)or have a 2.35 high school GPA in the above classes and they must need no more than 1 development course. A minimum 2.0 high school GPA is required. Different admission standards apply for students who are out of state, home schooled, over 24, or foreign. Certain GED students can be admitted. Developmental needs can be met by taking the COMPASS. Exceptions are available for some students. The Louisiana Scholars' College has more stringent admission criteria. A GPA of 2.0 is required. AP and CLEP credits are accepted.

Procedure: Freshmen are admitted fall, spring, and summer. Entrance exams should be taken before the semester begins. There are deferred admissions and rolling admissions plans. Applications should be filed by July 6 for fall entry; November 2 for spring entry; and April 5 for summer entry, along with a $20 fee. Applications are accepted online.

Transfer: 606 transfer students enrolled in 2012-2013. Transfer students must be eligible for readmission to their former university or college in order to enter NSU, and they must submit college transcripts and a statement of good standing. Students also must have completed a college-level english and a college-level math and must have a 2.0 nondevelopmental college GPA. Students with less than 18 hours of nondevelopmental classes must also meet the freshman admission standards. 30 of 120 credits required for the bachelor's degree must be completed at NSU.

Visiting: There are regularly scheduled orientations for prospective students, consisting of a campus tour, with special focus on financial aid, housing and board, academic requirements, selecting a major, registration, campus organizations, and adapting to the college. There are guides for informal visits and visitors may sit in on classes. To schedule a visit, contact Jana Lucky at (318) 357-4503.

Financial Aid: In 2013-2014, 93% of all full-time freshmen and 86% of continuing full-time students received some form of financial aid. 68% of all full-time freshmen and 65% of continuing full time students received need-based aid. The average freshman award was $9,142. Need-based scholarships or need-based grants averaged $4,518 ($6,550 maximum); need-based self-help aid (loans and jobs) averaged $5,254 ($15,613 maximum); non-need-based athletic scholarships averaged $8,021 ($19,820 maximum); other non-need-based awards and non-need-based scholarships averaged $3,453 ($17,792 maximum); and $959 from other forms of aid. 5% of undergraduate students work part-time. The average financial indebtedness of the 2013 graduate was $23,710. The FAFSA and the college's own financial statement are required. The priority date for freshman financial aid applications for fall entry is May 1.

International Students: There are 59 international students enrolled. The school actively recruits these students. They must take the TOEFL with a minimum score of 500 on the paper-based TOEFL (PBT) or 61 on the Internet-based version (iBT). They must also take the SAT or ACT, scoring 21.

Graduates: From July 1, 2012 to June 30, 2013, 1119 bachelor's degrees were awarded. The most popular majors were nursing/health professions (21%), general studies/liberal arts (12%), and business administration (8%). 271 companies recruited on campus in 2012-2013. In an average class, 1% graduate in 3 years or less, 21% graduate in 4 years or less, 37% graduate in 5 years or less, and 42% graduate in 6 years or less.

Admissions Contact: Jana Lucky, Director of University Recruiting. E-Mail: *recruiting@nsula.edu* Web: *www.nsula.edu*

OUR LADY OF HOLY CROSS COLLEGE D-4

New Orleans, LA 70131-7399 **(504) 394-7744; (504) 391-2421**

Full-time: 1001 men and women	**Faculty:** n/av
Part-time: n/av	**Ph.D.s:** n/av
Graduate: 296 men and women	**Student/Faculty:** n/av
Year: semesters, summer session	**Tuition:** $9,000
Application Deadline: July 20	**Room & Board:** n/av
Freshman Class: n/av	
ACT: required	

LESS COMPETITIVE

Our Lady of Holy Cross College, founded in 1916, is a private commuter college affiliated with the Roman Catholic Church. In addition to regional accreditation, OLHCC has baccalaureate program accreditation with NLN. The figures in the above capsule and in this profile are approximate. The library contains 56,700 volumes, 136,015 microform items, and 13,598 audio/video tapes/CDs/DVDs, and subscribes to 601 periodicals including electronic. Computerized library services include interlibrary loans and database searching. The 15-acre campus is in an urban area in New Orleans. Including any residence halls, there are 2 buildings.

Student Life: 99% of undergraduates are from Louisiana. Others are from 4 states. 39% are from public schools. 74% are white; 15% African American. 74% are Catholic; 14% Protestant. The average age of freshmen is 18; all undergraduates, 25. 10% do not continue beyond their first year; 70% remain to graduate.

Housing: There are no residence halls. All students commute.

Activities: There are no fraternities or sororities. There are 11 groups

on campus, including choir, chorus, computers, drama, ethnic, honors, international, literary magazine, professional, social, social service, and student government. Popular campus events include Fall Fest, Crawfish Boil, and Christmas dances.

Sports: There are 5 intramural sports for men and 4 for women.

Disabled Students: All of the campus is accessible. Facilities include wheelchair ramps, elevators, special parking, specially equipped restrooms, lowered drinking fountains, and lowered telephones.

Services: There is remedial math, reading, and writing.

Campus Safety and Security: Measures include self-defense education and security escort services. There are emergency telephones, lighted pathways/sidewalks, There is a foot patrol inside and outside of the building from 7:30 a.m. to 10 p.m.

Programs of Study: OLHCC confers B.A. and B.S. degrees. Associate and master's degrees are also awarded. Bachelor's degrees are awarded in BIOLOGICAL SCIENCE (biology/biological science), BUSINESS (accounting, business administration and management, and marketing and distribution), COMMUNICATIONS AND THE ARTS (English), EDUCATION (elementary education and secondary education), HEALTH PROFESSIONS (health science and nursing), SOCIAL SCIENCE (behavioral science, history, liberal arts/general studies, social psychology, and social science). Nursing is the strongest academically. Nursing, business, and education have the largest enrollments.

Required: A total of 128 credit hours, with 33 to 36 hours in the major, and a minimum GPA of 2.0 are required to graduate. All students must take courses in theology, philosophy, literature, English composition, math, natural sciences, library orientation, social sciences, speech, fine arts, and computer science.

Special: Co-op programs in business, internships with the Navy Civilian Personnel Office, study abroad in France, and credit for life, military, and work experience are offered

Faculty/Classroom: 20% of faculty are male; 80% are female. 98% teach undergraduates, and 2% do research. No introductory courses are taught by graduate students. The average class size in an introductory lecture is 25; in a laboratory is 24; and in a regular course is 20.

Admissions: In a recent year, 92% applicants were accepted.

Requirements: The ACT is required. The GED is accepted. A GPA of 2.0 is required. AP and CLEP credits are accepted. Important factors in the admissions decision are leadership record, recommendations by school officials, and recommendations by alumni.

Procedure: Freshmen are admitted to all sessions. Entrance exams should be taken a week before registration. Applications should be filed by July 20 for fall entry; December 20 for spring entry; and May 1 for summer entry. The fall 2011 application fee was $15.

Transfer: Transfer applicants must have an overall 2.0 GPA for unconditional admission. 30 of 128 credits required for the bachelor's degree must be completed at OLHCC.

Visiting: There are regularly scheduled orientations for prospective students. There are guides for informal visits and visitors may sit in on classes. To schedule a visit, contact the Office of Enrollment Services.

Financial Aid: 3% of undergraduate students work part-time. Average annual earnings from campus work are $1000. The FAFSA and the college's own financial statement are required. The deadline for filing freshman financial aid applications for fall entry is April 15.

International Students: They must take the TOEFL.

Admissions Contact: Kristine H. Kopecky, VP for Student Affairs. A campus DVD is available. E-Mail: *kkopecky@olhcc.edu* Web: *www.olhcc.edu*

SOUTHEASTERN LOUISIANA UNIVERSITY D-3

Hammond, LA 70402 (985) 549-5910
(800) 222-7358; (985) 549-5632

Full-time: 3934 men, 6065 women
Part-time: 1552 men, 2193 women
Graduate: 270 men, 935 women
Year: semesters, summer session
Application Deadline: July 15
Faculty: 510; IIA, --$
Ph.D.s: 65%
Student/Faculty: 23 to 1
Tuition: $5715 ($17,734)
Room & Board: $7610
Freshman Class: 3665 applied, 3263 accepted, 2438 enrolled
ACT: 21

COMPETITIVE

Southeastern Louisiana University, founded in 1925, is a public university offering more than 70 undergraduate and graduate degree programs There are 5 undergraduate schools. In addition to regional accreditation, Southeastern has baccalaureate program accreditation with AACSB, ABET, CSWE, NASAD, NASM, and NCATE. The library contains 494,881 volumes, 513,432 microform items, and 35,208 audio/video tapes/CDs/DVDs, and subscribes to 1,539 periodicals including electronic. Computerized library services include interlibrary loans, database searching, Internet access, and Wi-Fi capability. Special learning facilities include an art gallery, radio station, and TV station. The 365-acre campus is in a small town 60 miles northwest of New Orleans and 50 miles east of Baton Rouge. Including any residence halls, there are 102 buildings.

Student Life: 95% of undergraduates are from Louisiana. Others are from 39 states, 40 foreign countries, and Canada. 67% are White; 15% African American. The average age of freshmen is 18.2; all undergraduates, 21.7. 32% do not continue beyond their first year; 33% remain to graduate.

Housing: 2387 students can be accommodated in college housing, which includes single-sex and coed dorms and on-campus apartments. In addition, there are honors houses, fraternity houses, and sorority houses. On-campus housing is guaranteed for the freshman year only, is available on a first-come, and first-served basis. Priority is given to out-of-town students. 83% of students commute. All students may keep cars.

Activities: 5% of men belong to 13 local and 13 national fraternities; 5% of women belong to 8 local and 8 national sororities. There are 131 groups on campus, including art, band, cheerleading, choir, computers, dance, environmental, ethnic, film, gay, honors, international, jazz band, marching band, musical theater, newspaper, orchestra, photography, political, professional, radio and TV, religious, social, social service, student government, and yearbook. Popular campus events include Fanfare (cultural events month), Strawberry Jubilee, and Gumbo Ya Ya.

Sports: There are 7 intercollegiate sports for men and 8 for women. Facilities include a weight, fitness, and aerobics rooms, an indoor elevated track, basketball, volleyball, badminton, tennis, and racquetball courts, multipurpose fields, a pool, gym, a football stadium, and baseball and soccer fields.

Disabled Students: 90% of the campus is accessible. Facilities include wheelchair ramps, elevators, special parking, specially equipped restrooms, special class scheduling, special housing.

Services: Counseling and information services are available, as is tutoring in some subjects, math, English, biology, physics, chemistry, foreign languages, accounting, economics, and computer science. There is remedial math and reading.

Campus Safety and Security: Measures include 24-hour foot and vehicle patrol, emergency notification system, self-defense education, and security escort services. There are shuttle buses, emergency telephones, lighted pathways/sidewalks, controlled access to dorms/residences, community policing, bicycle patrols, and video cameras.

Programs of Study: Southeastern confers B.A., B.S., B.B.A., B.G.S. and B.M. degrees. Associate, master's, and doctoral degrees are also awarded. Bachelor's degrees are awarded in BIOLOGICAL SCIENCE (biology/biological science), BUSINESS (accounting, business administration and management, marketing/retailing/merchandising, sports management, and supply chain management), COMMUNICATIONS AND THE ARTS (art, communications, English, music, and Spanish), COMPUTER AND PHYSICAL SCIENCE (chemistry, computer science, mathematics, and physics), EDUCATION (athletic training, early childhood education, elementary education, English education, health education, middle school education, physical education, social science education, and special education), ENGINEERING AND ENVIRONMENTAL DESIGN (engineering technology, industrial engineering technology, and occupational safety and health), HEALTH PROFESSIONS (health and nursing), SOCIAL SCIENCE (criminal justice, family/consumer studies, history, liberal arts/general studies, political science/government, psychology, social work, and sociology). Nursing, general studies, and biological sciences have the largest enrollments.

Required: To graduate, students must complete one of the curricula, including demonstrated proficiency in English and math and have a cumulative degree GPA of 2.0 (2.5 in some majors).

Special: Through a special adult learning initiative known as CALL (Center for Adult Learning in Louisiana), Southeastern is now offering registered nurses who are graduates of associate or diploma programs the opportunity to earn their bachelor of science degree in nursing completely online. The Turtle Cove Environmental Research Station is the environmental research, education, outreach, and restoration facility for Southeastern Louisiana University. The Institute for Biodiversity and Interdisciplinary Studies (IBIS)- The mission of IBIS is to increase our understanding of the ecosystems of the Gulf Coast and the Lake Pontchartrain drainage basin in particular with an emphasis on fostering interdisciplinary understanding for students and other participants that will allow a generation to address environmental and biodiversity issues in a more comprehensive and inclusive manner. The University also offers summer abroad programs. There are 16 national honor societies, a freshman honors program, and 20 departmental honors programs.

Faculty/Classroom: 45% of faculty are male; 55% are female. 97% teach undergraduates. Graduate students teach 1% of introductory courses. The average class size in an introductory lecture is 37; in a laboratory is 20; and in a regular course is 29.

Admissions: 89% of the 2013-2014 applicants were accepted. The ACT scores were 35% below 21, 37% between 21 and 23, 18% between 24 and 26, 6% between 27 and 28, and 4% above 28. 17% of the current freshmen were in the top fifth of their class; 32% were in the top two fifths. 57 freshmen graduated first in their class.

Requirements: The ACT is required. Applicants should have completed the Louisiana Regents High School core curriculum, no developmental course requirement, have a minimum high school GPA of 2.0. and ACT 21. A GPA of 2.0 is required. AP and CLEP credits are accepted.

Procedure: Freshmen are admitted fall, spring, and summer. Entrance exams should be taken prior to registering for classes. There are deferred admissions and rolling admissions plans. Applications should be filed by July 15 for fall entry; December 1 for spring entry; and May 1 for summer entry, along with a $20 fee. Applications are accepted online.

Transfer: 599 transfer students enrolled in 2012-2013. Option 1 - Transferrable associates degree or higher from regionally accredited institution & cumulative GPA of 2.0 or higher. Option 2 - Cumulative GPA of 2.0 or higher on all college work, college-level English and Math credits earned, must be eligible to return to last institution attended. 30 of 120 credits required for the bachelor's degree must be completed at Southeastern.

Visiting: There are regularly scheduled orientations for prospective students, Includes a 2-day program of credit exams, academic advising, class registration, social programs, and session presentations. There are guides for informal visits, visitors may sit in on classes, and stay overnight. To schedule a visit, contact Mr. Richard Beaugh at *admission@selu.edu*.

Financial Aid: The average financial indebtedness of the 2013 graduate was $20,044. Southeastern is a member of CSS. The FAFSA is required. The priority date for freshman financial aid applications for fall entry is May 1.

International Students: There are 181 international students enrolled. They must take the TOEFL with a minimum score of 500 on the paper-based TOEFL (PBT) or 61 on the Internet-based version (iBT). They must also take the ACT, scoring 21.

Graduates: From July 1, 2012 to June 30, 2013, 1967 bachelor's degrees were awarded. The most popular majors were general studies (12%), management (10%), and nursing (8%). In an average class, 12% graduate in 4 years or less, 27% graduate in 5 years or less, and 33% graduate in 6 years or less.

Admissions Contact: Richard Beaugh, Director of Admissions. E-Mail: *admissions@selu.edu* Web: *http:/www.southeastern.edu/admin/admissions/index.html*

SOUTHERN UNIVERSITY SYSTEM

The Southern University System, established in 1975, is a public system in Louisiana. It is governed by the Southern University board of supervisors and the Louisiana Board of Regents, whose chief administrator is the president. The primary goal of the system is teaching. The main priorities are teaching, public service, and research. The total student enrollment is usually about 14,000 with 650 faculty members. Altogether there are 144 baccalaureate, 42 master's, and 1 doctoral program offered by the Southern University System. Profiles of the 4-year campuses are included in this section.

SOUTHERN UNIVERSITY AND A&M COLLEGE C-4

Baton Rouge, LA 70813 **(504) 771-2430**
(800) 256-1531; (504) 772-2500

Full-time: 2372 men, 3501 women	**Faculty:** 352; IIA, --$
Part-time: 264 men, 354 women	**Ph.D.s:** 65%
Graduate: 326 men, 810 women	**Student/Faculty:** 17 to 1
Year: semesters, summer session	**Tuition:** $5000 (10,500)
Application Deadline: July 1	**Room & Board:** $6500
Freshman Class: n/app	
ACT: required	

COMPETITIVE+

Southern University and A&M College, founded in 1880, is a publicly supported, nonsectarian, land-grant institution offering degree programs in agriculture, family and consumer science, arts and humanities, architecture, business, education, engineering, nursing, public policy and urban affairs, and the sciences. The figures in the above capsule and in this profile are approximate. There are 11 undergraduate schools and 1 graduate school. In addition to regional accreditation, SUBR has baccalaureate program accreditation with AACSB, ABET, ACEJMC, ADA, CSAB, CSWE, NAAB, NASM, NCATE, and NLN. The 2 libraries contain 695,768 volumes, 745,555 microform items, and 22,101 audio/video tapes/CDs/DVDs, and subscribe to 6,605 periodicals including electronic. Computerized library services include interlibrary loans and database searching. Special learning facilities include a learning resource center, art gallery, a Black Heritage Collection, and museum of art. The 884-acre campus is in an urban area of Baton Rouge. Including any residence halls, there are 180 buildings.

Student Life: 82% of undergraduates are from Louisiana. Others are from 42 states, 24 foreign countries, and Canada. 86% are African American. The average age of freshmen is 19; all undergraduates, 23. 28% do not continue beyond their first year; 30% remain to graduate.

Housing: 2702 students can be accommodated in college housing, which includes single-sex dorms. 65% of students commute. Alcohol is not permitted. Upperclassmen may keep cars.

Activities: 2% of men belong to 5 national fraternities; 1% of women belong to 4 national sororities. There are 80 groups on campus, including art, band, cheerleading, chess, choir, chorale, computers, drama, ethnic, honors, international, jazz band, marching band, newspaper, political, professional, religious, social, and student government. Popular campus events include Founders Day and Bayou Classic football game at the New Orleans Super Dome.

Sports: There are 6 intercollegiate sports for men and 8 for women, and 2 intramural sports for men and 2 for women. Facilities include a center around the main activity complex, which accommodates theater, convocations, and athletic contests.

Disabled Students: All of the campus is accessible. Facilities include wheelchair ramps, elevators, special parking, specially equipped restrooms, special class scheduling, and special housing.

Services: Counseling and information services are available, as is tutoring in every subject. There is a reader service for the blind, and remedial math, reading, and writing.

Campus Safety and Security: Measures include 24-hour foot and vehicle patrol and emergency notification system. There are emergency telephones and lighted pathways/sidewalks.

Programs of Study: SUBR confers B.A., B.A.R., B.M.E., B.S., B.S.C.E., B.S.E.E., B.S.M.E., and B.S.N. degrees. Master's and doctoral degrees are also awarded. Bachelor's degrees are awarded in AGRICULTURE (agricultural economics, agriculture, and forestry and related sciences), BIOLOGICAL SCIENCE (biology/biological science), BUSINESS (accounting, banking and finance, business administration and management, business economics, electronic business, and marketing/retailing/merchandising), COMMUNICATIONS AND THE ARTS (communications, dramatic arts, English, fine arts, French, music, and Spanish), COMPUTER AND PHYSICAL SCIENCE (chemistry, computer science, mathematics, and physics), EDUCATION (agricultural education, art education, early childhood education, elementary education, English education, mathematics education, middle school education, music education, secondary education, social studies education, and special education), ENGINEERING AND ENVIRONMENTAL DESIGN (architecture, civil engineering, electrical/electronics engineering, engineering technology, and mechanical engineering), HEALTH PROFESSIONS (nursing, recreation therapy, rehabilitation therapy, speech pathology/audiology, and speech therapy), SOCIAL SCIENCE (criminal justice, family/consumer studies, history, political science/government, psychology, social work, and sociology). Nursing, engineering, and chemistry are the strongest academically. Nursing, business management, and biology have the largest enrollments.

Required: Courses in English composition and literature, math, natural sciences, arts, humanities, social sciences, health, and phys ed are required, as well as 60 hours of community service and 3 hours of African-American studies. All students also must take a writing proficiency test. To graduate, they must complete 124 semester hours (at least 31 in the major) with a minimum GPA of 2.0 on a 4.0 scale.

Special: Cross-registration, co-op education, study abroad, work-study, and dual majors in chemistry/chemical engineering with Louisiana State University are available. There are 33 national honor societies, a freshman honors program, and 1 departmental honors program.

Faculty/Classroom: 53% of faculty are male; 47% are female. 87% teach undergraduates. No introductory courses are taught by graduate students. The average class size in an introductory lecture is 28; in a laboratory is 19; and in a regular course is 30.

Admissions: 39% of a recent year applicants were accepted. The SAT scores for the recent year freshman class were: Critical Reading--81% below 500, 16% between 500 and 599, 2% between 600 and 700; Math--77% below 500, 19% between 500 and 599, 3% between 600 and 700, and 1% above 700. The ACT scores were 76% below 21, 17% between 21 and 23, 2% between 24 and 26, 1% between 27 and 28, and 1% above 28. 8% of the current freshmen were in the top fifth of their class; 24% were in the top two fifths. 16 freshmen graduated first in their class.

Requirements: The ACT is required. Southern requires the following core courses: English (4), math (3), science (3), foreign languages (2), social studies (2), history (1), fine arts (1), and computer literacy (1). Also required are a high school GPA of 2.0, an ACT score of 20 or better, or a rank in the top 50% of graduating class with no more than 1 remedial class required. SUBR requires applicants to be in the upper 50% of their class. A GPA of 2.0 is required. AP and CLEP credits are accepted.

Procedure: Freshmen are admitted to all sessions. Entrance exams should be taken during the junior year. There is a rolling admissions plan. Applications should be filed by July 1 for fall entry; December 1 for spring entry; and April 1 for summer entry. The fall 2011 application fee was $20. Notification is sent on a rolling basis. Applications are accepted online.

Transfer: 274 transfer students enrolled in 2010-2011. Students with fewer than 24 hours must meet regular admission requirements. If applicants have 24 or more hours they must have a 2.0 GPA based on 4.0 scale. 31 of 124 credits required for the bachelor's degree must be completed at SUBR.

Visiting: There are regularly scheduled orientations for prospective students, consisting of summer and fall orientation programs. There are guides for informal visits. To schedule a visit, contact the Office of Admissions.

Financial Aid: In a recent year, 90% of all full-time freshmen and 90% of continuing full-time students received some form of financial aid. 90% of all full-time freshmen and 90% of continuing full-time students received need-based aid. The average freshman award was $6,868. Need-based scholarships or need-based grants averaged $4000 ($5,200 maximum); need-based self-help aid (loans and jobs) averaged $2,625 ($2,625 maximum); non-need-based athletic scholarships averaged $3,740 ($3,740 maximum); and other non-need-based awards and non-need-based scholarships averaged $2,625 ($2,625 maximum). 12% of undergraduate students work part-time. The average financial indebtedness of the 2011 graduate was $23,000. The FAFSA is required. The deadline for filing freshman financial aid applications for fall entry is May 31.

International Students: There are 45 international students enrolled. The school actively recruits these students. They must take the TOEFL with a minimum score of 500 on the paper-based TOEFL (PBT) or 61 on the Internet-based version (iBT). They must also take the SAT or ACT.

Graduates: In a recent year, 896 bachelor's degrees were awarded. The most popular majors were nursing (10%), psychology (9%), and business management (8%). 160 companies recruited on campus in 2010-2011. In an average class, 6% graduate in 4 years or less, 20% graduate in 5 years or less, and 30% graduate in 6 years or less. Of the 2010 graduating class, 9% were enrolled in graduate school within 6 months of graduation, and 27% were employed.

Admissions Contact: Director of Admissions. Web: *www.subr.edu*

SOUTHERN UNIVERSITY AT NEW ORLEANS — D-4

New Orleans, LA 70126 (504) 286-5314

Full- and part-time: 3188 men and women
Year: n/av
Application Deadline: open
Faculty: n/av
Ph.D.s: n/av
Student/Faculty: n/av
Tuition: $3,688 ($4,238)
Room & Board: $5,800 ($9,970)
Freshman Class: n/av
ACT: required
NONCOMPETITIVE

Southern University at New Orleans, established in 1956, is a public commuter institution offering programs in liberal arts and sciences, business, education, and the technologies. The figures given in the above capsule are approximate. In addition to regional accreditation, SUNO has baccalaureate program accreditation with CSWE. The library contains 300,000 volumes. The 22-acre campus is in a suburban area. Including any residence halls, there are 10 buildings.

Activities: There are no fraternities or sororities.

Sports: Men's and women's basketball, track, and field.

Disabled Students: All of the campus is accessible.

Programs of Study: Bachelor's degrees are awarded in BIOLOGICAL SCIENCE (biology/biological science), BUSINESS (accounting, business administration and management, secretarial studies/office management, and transportation management), COMMUNICATIONS AND THE ARTS (English, fine arts, journalism, Spanish, and speech/debate/rhetoric), COMPUTER AND PHYSICAL SCIENCE (chemistry, computer science, mathematics, and physics), EDUCATION (art education, business education, education of the deaf and hearing impaired, elementary education, English education, foreign languages education, mathematics education, music education, physical education, recreation education, science education, secondary education, and social studies education), ENGINEERING AND ENVIRONMENTAL DESIGN (technological management), HEALTH PROFESSIONS (health care administration), SOCIAL SCIENCE (addiction studies, criminal justice, economics, history, political science/government, psychology, social work, and sociology).

Faculty/Classroom: No introductory courses are taught by graduate students.

Requirements: The ACT is required.

Procedure: There is a rolling admissions plan. Applications should be filed by December 1 for spring entry; May 1 for summer entry. Check with the school for current fee.

Financial Aid: Check with the school for filing freshman current financial aid applications.

International Students: They must take the TOEFL. In many cases the ACT may also be required.

Admissions Contact: Director of Admissions and Registrar Web: *www.suno.edu*

TULANE UNIVERSITY — D-4

New Orleans, LA 70118 (504) 865-5731
(800) 873-9283; (504) 862-8715

Full-time: 2740 men, 3747 women
Part-time: 760 men, 1105 women
Graduate: 2392 men, 2718 women
Year: semesters, summer session
Application Deadline: January 15
Faculty: n/av; I, -$
Ph.D.s: 93%
Student/Faculty: 9 to 1
Tuition: $46,930
Room & Board: $12,012
Freshman Class: 30122 applied, 7961 accepted, 1609 enrolled
SAT CR/M/W: 656/660/669 **ACT:** 30 **MOST COMPETITIVE**

Tulane University, founded in 1834, is a private institution offering degree programs in liberal arts and sciences, business, architecture, science and engineering, and social work. There are 6 undergraduate schools and 8 graduate schools. In addition to regional accreditation, Tulane University has baccalaureate program accreditation with AACSB, ABET, CSAB, CSWE, and NAAB. The 8 libraries contain 4.4 million volumes, 2.5 million microform items, 150,475 audio/video tapes/CDs/DVDs, and subscribe to 131,224 periodicals including electronic. Computerized library services include interlibrary loans, database searching, Internet access, and Wi-Fi capability. Special learning facilities include an art gallery, natural history museum, radio station, TV station, an observatory, Middle American Research Institute, Amistad Research Center, Tulane Jazz Archives, Latin American Library, and Tulane Center for Research on Women. The 110-acre campus is in an urban area New Orleans (Uptown). Including any residence halls, there are 71 buildings.

Student Life: 73% of undergraduates are from out of state, mostly the Northeast. Students are from 50 states, 100 foreign countries, and Canada. 74% are White. The average age of freshmen is 18; all undergraduates, 22.

Housing: 3800 students can be accommodated in college housing, which includes single-sex and coed dorms, on-campus apartments, and married student housing. In addition, there are honors houses, and special-interest floors. On-campus housing is available on a lottery system for upperclassmen. 57% of students commute. Upperclassmen may keep cars.

Activities: 26% of men belong to 12 national fraternities; 43% of women belong to 10 national sororities. There are 344 groups on campus, including art, band, cheerleading, chess, choir, chorale, chorus, communications, computers, dance, debate, drama, drill team, drum and bugle corps, environmental, ethnic, film, gay, honors, international, jazz band, literary magazine, marching band, musical theater, newspaper, orchestra, pep band, photography, political, professional, radio and TV, religious, social, social service, student government, symphony, and yearbook. Popular campus events include Crawfest, Wave Good-Bye, and Technology Expo, and Homecoming.

Sports: There are 6 intercollegiate sports for men and 7 for women, and 24 intramural sports for men and 24 for women. Facilities include a baseball diamond, a track complex, a tennis facility, and a recreation center with indoor and outdoor pools, an indoor track, squash and racquetball courts, a gymnastics area, a weight room, and exercise rooms and equipment, and basketball and volleyball facilities.

Disabled Students: 60% of the campus is accessible. Facilities include wheelchair ramps, elevators, special parking, specially equipped restrooms, lowered drinking fountains, lowered telephones, and special housing.

Services: Counseling and information services are available, as is tutoring in some subjects, high-demand math and science classes and some languages. There is a reader service for the blind.

Campus Safety and Security: Measures include 24-hour foot and vehicle patrol, emergency notification system, self-defense education, and security escort services. There are shuttle buses, emergency telephones, lighted pathways/sidewalks, controlled access to dorms/residences, trained student patrols, and programs about living safely off campus. Victim resources include academic assistance, legal counseling, emergency housing, and security review of home and personal security habits. In addition, there are bike patrols, limited dorm access, smoke detectors in dorms, and surveillance cameras.

Programs of Study: Tulane University confers B.A., B.S., B.A.R., B.B.S., B.F.A., B.P.H., B.S.E., B.S.M. and M. Arch degrees. Associate, master's, and doctoral degrees are also awarded. Bachelor's degrees are awarded in BIOLOGICAL SCIENCE (biochemistry, cell biology, ecology, environmental biology, evolutionary biology, molecular biology, and neurosciences), BUSINESS (accounting, banking and finance, business administration and management, entrepreneurial studies, management science, and marketing management), COMMUNICATIONS AND THE ARTS (art history and appreciation, classics, communications, dance, dramatic arts, English, film arts, French, German, Greek (modern), Italian, jazz, journalism, linguistics, media arts, music, Portuguese, Russian, Spanish, studio art, and theater design), COMPUTER AND PHYSICAL SCIENCE (chemistry, earth science, geology, information sciences and systems, mathematics, physics, and science), EDUCATION (early childhood education and psychology education), ENGINEERING AND ENVI-

RONMENTAL DESIGN (architecture, biomedical engineering, chemical engineering, engineering physics, and environmental science), HEALTH PROFESSIONS (public health), SOCIAL SCIENCE (African studies, American studies, anthropology, Asian/Oriental studies, cognitive science, economics, gender studies, history, humanities, Judaic studies, Latin American studies, liberal arts/general studies, medieval studies, paralegal studies, philosophy, political science/government, psychology, religion, Russian and Slavic studies, social science, social studies, sociology, and women's studies). Environmental sciences, political economy, and preprofessional programs. are the strongest academically. Liberal arts, business, science and engineering have the largest enrollments.

Required: All students in the liberal arts and sciences must meet proficiency requirements in english, foreign language, and math. They must take a distribution component including courses in humanities and fine arts, social sciences, and sciences and math. A total of 120 credits, including at least 24 in the major, with a minimum cumulative GPA of 2.0, is required to graduate.

Special: Students may pursue cross-registration with Loyola and Xavier Universities, numerous internships, study abroad in 23 countries, work-study programs, a Washington semester, and B.A.-B.S. degrees in liberal arts, engineering, and architecture. Tulane also offers accelerated joint degrees with its schools of medicine, law, business, and public health; student-designed, dual, and interdisciplinary majors, including art and biology, Greek and Latin, mathematical economics, political economy, and cognitive studies; a 3-2 engineering degree with Xavier University of Louisiana, joint graduate/professional programs, and 4+1 programs. There are 38 national honor societies, including Phi Beta Kappa, and a freshman honors program.

Faculty/Classroom: 61% of faculty are male; 39% are female. No introductory courses are taught by graduate students.

Admissions: 26% of the 2013-2014 applicants were accepted. The SAT scores for the 2013-2014 freshman class were: Critical Reading--2% below 500, 15% between 500 and 599, 54% between 600 and 699, and 29% between 700 and 800; Math--1% below 500, 14% between 500 and 599, 59% between 600 and 699, and 27% between 700 and 800; Writing--2% below 500, 10% between 500 and 599, 54% between 600 and 699, and 34% between 700 and 800.

Requirements: The SAT or ACT is required. A GPA of 3.5 is required. AP credits are accepted. Important factors in the admissions decision are advanced placement or honors courses, recommendations by school officials, and extracurricular activities record.

Procedure: Freshmen are admitted fall and spring. Entrance exams should be taken during spring of the junior year or fall of the senior year. There is a deferred admissions plan. Applications should be filed by January 15 for fall entry; November 1 for spring entry. Notifications are sent April 1. 2774 applicants were on the 2013 waiting list; 327 were admitted. Applications are accepted online.

Transfer: 90 transfer students enrolled in 2012-2013. Applicants must submit SAT or ACT scores, high school transcripts, proof of good standing at previously attended institutions, and transcripts (with course descriptions) from all colleges or universities attended. A minimum 3.0 GPA is recommended. 60 of 120 credits required for the bachelor's degree must be completed at Tulane University.

Visiting: There are regularly scheduled orientations for prospective students, including 3 on-campus Saturday programs in the fall, daily information sessions, and tours Monday through Friday and Saturday mornings during the academic year. Also, selected classes are open to visitors. In the spring semester, more structured programs are available daily. There are guides for informal visits, visitors may sit in on classes, and stay overnight. To schedule a visit, contact the Office of Undergraduate Admissions.

Financial Aid: In 2013-2014, 43% of all full-time freshmen students received some form of financial aid. 43% of all full-time freshmen students received need-based aid. The average freshman award was $31,890. Need-based scholarships or need-based grants averaged $26,439; need-based self-help aid (loans and jobs) averaged $9,122; non-need-based athletic scholarships averaged $33,361; and other non-need-based awards and non-need-based scholarships averaged $7,523. Average annual earnings from campus work are $2500. Tulane University is a member of CSS. The CSS/Profile and FAFSA, and the Noncustodial Profile and the Business/Farm Supplement (as applicable). are required. The priority date for freshman financial aid applications for fall entry is February 15.

International Students: There are 251 international students enrolled. The school actively recruits these students. They must take the TOEFL with a minimum score of 550 on the paper-based TOEFL (PBT) or 88 on the Internet-based version (iBT). They must also take the SAT or ACT.

Graduates: From July 1, 2012 to June 30, 2013, 2129 bachelor's degrees were awarded. The most popular majors were business (22%), social science (18%), and biological/life science (9%). 141 companies recruited on campus in 2012-2013.

Admissions Contact: Earl Retif, VP for Enrollment Management.
E-Mail: *undergrad.admission@tulane.edu* Web: *www.tulane.edu*

UNIVERSITY OF LOUISIANA AT LAFAYETTE C-4

Lafayette, LA 70504 **(337) 482-6473; (337) 482-6195**

Full- and part-time: 16,885 men and women
Graduate: 1,200
Year: semesters, summer session
Application Deadline: open
Freshman Class: n/av
SAT or ACT: required

Faculty: 666; I, --$
Ph.D.s: 79%
Student/Faculty: 18 to 1
Tuition: $4600 ($13,100)
Room & Board: $5100

COMPETITIVE

The University of Louisiana at Lafayette founded in 1898, is a public institution offering degree programs in liberal arts, fine arts, business, agriculture, technical disciplines, health science, engineering, and teacher preparation. The figures in the above capsule and in this profile are approximate. There are 9 undergraduate schools and 1 graduate school. In addition to regional accreditation, UL Lafayette has baccalaureate program accreditation with AACSB, ABET, ACEJMC, ADA, AHEA, ASLA, CAHEA, CSAB, FIDER, NAAB, NASM, NCATE, and NLN. The library contains 873,173 volumes, 1.8 million microform items, and 255,992 audio/video tapes/CDs/DVDs, and subscribes to 4,965 periodicals including electronic. Computerized library services include interlibrary loans and database searching. Special learning facilities include a learning resource center, art gallery, radio station, numerous research centers for environmental, business, science, computer, and business studies. The 1375-acre campus is in an urban area 129 miles west of New Orleans. Including any residence halls, there are 239 buildings.

Student Life: 95% of undergraduates are from Louisiana. Others are from 48 states, 102 foreign countries, and Canada. 74% are white; 17% African American. 50% are Catholic; 31% claim no religious affiliation; 12% Protestant. The average age of freshmen is 19; all undergraduates, 24. 28% do not continue beyond their first year; 30% remain to graduate.

Housing: 1860 students can be accommodated in college housing, which includes single-sex dorms, on-campus apartments, and married student housing. and residence halls for athletes and for Pan-Hellenic groups. On-campus housing is guaranteed for all 4 years. 89% of students commute. All students may keep cars.

Activities: 3% of men belong to 14 national fraternities; 5% of women belong to 8 national sororities. There are 200 groups on campus, including band, cheerleading, choir, chorus, computers, dance, debate, drama, drum and bugle corps, ethnic, forensics, gay, honors, international, jazz band, marching band, musical theater, newspaper, opera, orchestra, photography, political, professional, radio and TV, religious, social, social service, student government, and yearbook. Popular campus events include Rajun Roar, Black Expo Week, and Entertainment Week.

Sports: There are 8 intercollegiate sports for men and 7 for women, and 16 intramural sports for men and 16 for women. Facilities include a 31,000-seat stadium, a 12,000-seat basketball arena, a gym, a track, a softball park, tennis courts, various playing fields, and a health and phys ed complex.

Disabled Students: 90% of the campus is accessible. Facilities include wheelchair ramps, elevators, special parking, specially equipped restrooms, special class scheduling.

Services: Counseling and information services are available, as is tutoring in most subjects. There is remedial math, reading, and writing. An entering freshman can only be in 1 remedial course.

Campus Safety and Security: Measures include 24-hour foot and vehicle patrol and security escort services. There are shuttle buses, emergency telephones, and lighted pathways/sidewalks.

Programs of Study: UL Lafayette confers B.A., B.S., B.A.M., B.F.A., B.G.S., B.M.E., B.M.P., B.M.P.P., B.S.A., B.S.A.E., B.S.B.A., B.S.C.E., B.S.C.I.E., B.S.E.E., B.S.I.T., B.S.M.E., B.S.N., and B.S.P.E. degrees. Master's and doctoral degrees are also awarded. Bachelor's degrees are awarded in BUSINESS (accounting, banking and finance, business administration and management, fashion merchandising, hotel/motel and restaurant management, management science, marketing/retailing/merchandising, and personnel management), COMMUNICATIONS AND THE ARTS (advertising, broadcasting, communications, dance, dramatic arts, English, fine arts, French, music, public relations, Spanish, and telecommunications), COMPUTER AND PHYSICAL SCIENCE (chemistry, computer science, geology, mathematics, physics, and statistics), EDUCATION (agricultural education, art education, elementary education, English education, foreign languages education, health education, home economics education, industrial arts education, mathematics education, music education, science education, secondary education, social studies education, and special education), ENGINEERING AND ENVIRONMENTAL DESIGN (chemical engineering, civil engineering, computer engineering, electrical/electronics engineering, industrial engineering, interior design, land use management and reclamation, mechanical engineering, and petroleum/natural gas engineering), HEALTH PROFESSIONS (nursing and speech pathology/audiology), SOCIAL SCIENCE (anthropology, criminal justice, dietetics, economics, history, philosophy, political science/government, psychology, and sociology). Computer science, engineering, and math/statistics/physical sciences are the strongest academically. Nursing, elementary education, and business administration have the largest enrollments.

Required: Students are required to complete 42 semester hours of general education courses in the arts, literature, history, math, sciences, behavioral sciences, and composition. Phys ed is required in all but engineering and nursing programs. A minimum of 124 semester hours, with at least 33 in the major, is required for graduation. A minimum GPA of 2.0 is needed; some majors require higher GPAs.

Special: Various internships are available, including a Washington semester. Students may study in France, Canada, Belgium, Japan, and Mexico. UL Lafayette also offers an accelerated degree program in nursing, B.A.-B.S. degrees, and dual majors. There are 6 national honor societies and a freshman honors program.

Faculty/Classroom: 59% of faculty are male; 41% are female. No introductory courses are taught by graduate students.

Requirements: The SAT or ACT is required. In addition, admissions criteria are based on a sliding scale of standardized test scores and GPA. Students should be graduates of accredited secondary schools or have the GED. UL Lafayette requires that students have at least 4 units in English, 3 each in math, science, and social studies, and 4 1/2 in electives, recommended to include 2 in foreign language, 1 each in fine arts and speech, and 1/2 in computer studies. A GPA of 2.0 is required. AP and CLEP credits are accepted.

Procedure: Freshmen are admitted to all sessions. There are early admissions, deferred admissions, and rolling admissions plans. Application deadlines are open. Application fee is $20.

Transfer: 740 transfer students enrolled in a recent year. A cumulative GPA of 2.0 is required. 30 of 124 credits required for the bachelor's degree must be completed at UL Lafayette.

Visiting: There are regularly scheduled orientations for prospective students, including campus tours. There are guides for informal visits. To schedule a visit, contact the Secretary of High School Relations.

Financial Aid: 30% of undergraduate students work part-time. Average annual earnings from campus work are $1250. UL Lafayette is a member of CSS. The FAFSA is required. The deadline for filing freshman financial aid applications for fall entry is March 1.

International Students: There are 259 international students enrolled. The school actively recruits these students. They must take the TOEFL. They must also take the SAT or ACT.

Graduates: In a recent year, 2025 bachelor's degrees were awarded. The most popular majors were business (20%), general studies (14%), and education (14%). 114 companies recruited on campus in 2010-2011. In an average class, 7% graduate in 4 years or less, 21% graduate in 5 years or less, and 29% graduate in 6 years or less.

Admissions Contact: Director of Admissions. A campus DVD is available. E-Mail: *admissions@louisiana.edu* Web: *www.louisiana.edu*

UNIVERSITY OF LOUISIANA AT MONROE — C-1

Monroe, LA 71209 — **(318) 342-5430; (318) 342-1915**

Full-time: 1785 men, 3109 women	**Faculty:** n/av
Part-time: 942 men, 1440 women	**Ph.D.s:** 50%
Graduate: 481 men, 888 women	**Student/Faculty:** n/av
Year: semesters, summer session	**Tuition:** $6318 ($16,890)
Application Deadline: open	**Room & Board:** $6680
Freshman Class: 3454 applied, 2668 accepted, 1325 enrolled	
SAT CR/M: 500/540	**ACT:** 22 **COMPETITIVE**

The University of Louisiana at Monroe, founded in 1931, is a public institution offering programs in business, education, liberal arts, pharmacy and health sciences, and pure and applied science. There are 5 undergraduate schools and 1 graduate school. In addition to regional accreditation, ULM has baccalaureate program accreditation with AACSB, ABET, ACCE, ACEJMC, ACPE, ADA, CSWE, NASM, and NCATE. The library contains 1.2 million volumes, 579,146 microform items, and 87 audio/video tapes/CDs/DVDs, and subscribes to 579,146 periodicals including electronic. Computerized library services include interlibrary loans, database searching, Internet access, and Wi-Fi capability. Special learning facilities include an art gallery, natural history museum, planetarium, radio station, a herbarium, state poison control center, and state tumor registry. The 238-acre campus is in an urban area in Northeast Louisiana, 90 miles east of Shreveport on I-20. Including any residence halls, there are 75 buildings.

Student Life: 91% of undergraduates are from Louisiana. Others are from 45 states, 64 foreign countries, and Canada. 64% are White; 24% African American. The average age of freshmen is 18.1; all undergraduates, 21.2.

Housing: 1862 students can be accommodated in college housing, which includes single-sex and coed dorms and on-campus apartments and a scholastic residence hall. On-campus housing is available on a first-come and first-served basis. 76% of students commute. Alcohol is not permitted. All students may keep cars.

Activities: 4% of men belong to 1 local and 6 national fraternities; 4% of women belong to 7 national sororities. There are 118 groups on campus, including art, band, cheerleading, choir, chorale, chorus, computers, dance, debate, drama, drill team, drum and bugle corps, ethnic, film, honors, international, jazz band, literary magazine, marching band, musical theater, newspaper, opera, orchestra, pep band, political, professional, radio and TV, religious, social, social service, student government, symphony, and yearbook. Popular campus events include Week of Welcome, Lyceum Series, Spring Fever, Athletics Events, and Casino Night.

Sports: There are 7 intercollegiate sports for men and 9 for women, and 44 intramural sports for men and 31 for women. Facilities include a coliseum, 2 stadiums, a natatorium, tennis courts, a softball complex, an activity center, a baseball complex, outdoor volleyball courts, and a bayou.

Disabled Students: 98% of the campus is accessible. Facilities include wheelchair ramps, elevators, special parking, specially equipped restrooms, special class scheduling, lowered drinking fountains. specially equipped dorm rooms.

Services: Counseling and information services are available, as is tutoring in most subjects. There is remedial math, reading, and writing.

Campus Safety and Security: Measures include 24-hour foot and vehicle patrol, emergency notification system, self-defense education, and security escort services. There are emergency telephones, lighted pathways/sidewalks, and controlled access to dorms/residences.

Programs of Study: ULM confers B.A., B.S., B.B.A., B.F.A., B.G.S., B.M. and B.M.E. degrees. Associate, master's, and doctoral degrees are also awarded. Bachelor's degrees are awarded in AGRICULTURE (agricultural business management), BIOLOGICAL SCIENCE (biology/biological science, forensic psychology, and toxicology), BUSINESS (accounting, business administration and management, finance, insurance, insurance and risk management, management information systems, management science, marketing, marketing/retailing/merchandising, organizational leadership and management, and professional program in accounting), COMMUNICATIONS AND THE ARTS (art, communication, communication studies, communications, English, foreign language, French, modern language, music, and Spanish), COMPUTER AND PHYSICAL SCIENCE (atmospheric sciences and meteorology, computer information systems, computer science, information sciences and systems, mathematics, and radiological technology), EDUCATION (childhood education: 1-6, education administration, elementary education, English education, foreign languages education, health education, mathematics education, middle school education, music education, secondary education, social studies education, and special education), ENGINEERING AND ENVIRONMENTAL DESIGN (aviation administration/management, construction, and construction management), HEALTH PROFESSIONS (biology, clinical science, dental hygiene, dental laboratory technology, exercise science, health, medical imaging, kinesiology, medical laboratory science, nursing, nursing home administration, occupational therapy, pharmaceutical science, pharmacology, pharmacy, and speech pathology/audiology), SOCIAL SCIENCE (clinical psychology, communication sciences & disorders, counseling/psychology, criminal justice, economics, experimental psychology, gerontology, history, liberal arts/general studies, political science/government, psychology, social work, and sociology). Pharmacy, health sciences, business, and education. are the strongest academically. Pharmacy, nursing, and general studies have the largest enrollments.

Required: Students are required to take the freshmen year seminar, 9 hours each of natural/physical sciences and humanities, 6 each of English, social sciences, and math, and 3 of the arts. An overall minimum GPA of 2.0 is required for graduation along with a total number of credits that varies by degree.

Special: ULM offers cross-registration with Grambling State University and Louisiana Tech University. Internships are available in accounting, information sciences, pharmacy, nursing, clinical laboratory science, radiological technology, dental hygiene, occupational therapy, and communication disorders are available. In addition, students may participate in the accelerated degree programs in speech language and nursing. There are 22 national honor societies, a freshman honors program, and 2 departmental honors programs.

Faculty/Classroom: 45% of faculty are male; 55% are female. No introductory courses are taught by graduate students. The average class size in an introductory lecture is 24; in a laboratory is 5; and in a regular course is 24.

Admissions: 77% of the 2013-2014 applicants were accepted. The SAT scores for the 2013-2014 freshman class were: Critical Reading--45% below 500, 32% between 500 and 599, 22% between 600 and 699, and 1% between 700 and 800; Math--37% below 500, 37% between 500 and 599, 22% between 600 and 699, and 4% between 700 and 800. The ACT scores were 34% below 21, 30% between 21 and 23, 22% between 24 and 26, 6% between 27 and 28, and 7% above 28.

Requirements: The ACT is required. Applicants must be graduates of an accredited high school or have a GED. A GPA of 2.0 is required. CLEP credits are accepted.

Procedure: Freshmen are admitted to all sessions. Entrance exams should be taken by April 1. There is a rolling admissions plan. Application deadlines are open. The fall 2013 application fee was $20. Applications are accepted online.

Transfer: Applicants must have a minimum overall GPA of 2.0 from a regionally accredited institution and at least 12 semester hours of college-level credit above the remedial level, including a math and an English course. Students who have completed fewer than 12 semester hours of college credit must meet ULM freshman admission requirements. 30 credits required for the bachelor's degree must be completed at ULM.

Visiting: There are regularly scheduled orientations for prospective students. Visiting students may participate in the mandatory PREP program, which includes campus tours, meetings with deans/advisers, class registration, and placement examinations. There are guides for informal visits and visitors may sit in on classes. To schedule a visit, contact the Office of Recruitment and Admissions.

Financial Aid: The FAFSA is required. Check with the school for current application deadlines.

International Students: There are 153 international students enrolled. The school actively recruits these students. They must take the TOEFL with a minimum score of 500 on the paper-based TOEFL (PBT). Only athletes are required to submit ACT/SAT scores due to NCAA requirements.

Graduates: From July 1, 2012 to June 30, 2013, 1025 bachelor's degrees were awarded. The most popular majors were general studies (10%), nursing (5%), and psychology (5%).

Admissions Contact: Mary Schmeer, Associate Director of Admissions. E-Mail: *schmeer@ulm.edu* Web: *www.ulm.edu*

UNIVERSITY OF NEW ORLEANS D-4

New Orleans, LA 70148 **(504) 280-6595; (504) 280-5522**

Full- and part-time: 8,300 men and women	**Faculty:** 526
Graduate: 2,700	**Ph.D.s:** 80%
Year: semesters, summer session	**Student/Faculty:** 19 to 1
Application Deadline: July 1	**Tuition:** $5000 ($13,000)
Freshman Class: n/av	**Room & Board:** $7100
SAT or ACT: required	

VERY COMPETITIVE

University of New Orleans, founded in 1958, is a public liberal arts institution. There are 6 undergraduate schools. The figures in the above capsule and in this profile are approximate. In addition to regional accreditation, UNO has baccalaureate program accreditation with AACSB, ABET, CACREP, NASM, NAST, and NCATE. The library contains 896,000 volumes, 12.4 million microform items, and 22,775 audio/video tapes/CDs/DVDs, and subscribes to 4950 periodicals including electronic. Computerized library services include interlibrary loans, database searching, and Internet access. Special learning facilities include a learning resource center, art gallery, and radio station. The 395-acre campus is in an urban area in a residential area of New Orleans. Including any residence halls, there are 34 buildings.

Student Life: 70% of undergraduates are from Louisiana. Others are from 50 states, 85 foreign countries, and Canada. 62% are from public schools. 60% are white; 19% African American. 67% claim no religious affiliation; 19% Catholic. The average age of freshmen is 19; all undergraduates, 24. 31% do not continue beyond their first year.

Housing: 1426 students can be accommodated in college housing, which includes coed dorms and married student housing. On-campus housing is available on a first-come, first-served basis. 95% of students commute. All students may keep cars.

Activities: 1% of men belong to 8 national fraternities; 1% of women belong to 8 national sororities. There are 108 groups on campus, including art, band, choir, chorale, chorus, computers, dance, drama, ethnic, film, gay, honors, international, jazz band, literary magazine, newspaper, opera, orchestra, pep band, political, professional, radio and TV, religious, social, social service, and student government. Popular campus events include International Night, Cultural Tea Hour, and Swamp Ball.

Sports: There are 3 intercollegiate sports for men and 3 for women, and 10 intramural sports for men and 10 for women. Facilities include the UNO Lakefront Arena, Privateer Park, a 1/10-mile indoor jogging/walking track, various group exercise classes such as indoor cycling, yoga, and step aerobics, 2 dry saunas, 2 racquetball courts, 3 basketball courts, a snack bar, an outdoor deck adjacent to the pool, and a natatorium for water group exercise and lap/recreational swimming.

Disabled Students: 80% of the campus is accessible. Facilities include wheelchair ramps, elevators, special parking, specially equipped restrooms, lowered drinking fountains, lowered telephones, and special housing.

Services: Counseling and information services are available, as is tutoring in most subjects. There is a reader service for the blind, and remedial math, reading, and writing.

Campus Safety and Security: Measures include 24-hour foot and vehicle patrol, emergency notification system, self-defense education, and security escort services. There are emergency telephones, lighted pathways/sidewalks, and monitored parking.

Programs of Study: UNO confers B.A., B.S., and B.G.S. degrees. Master's and doctoral degrees are also awarded. Bachelor's degrees are awarded in BIOLOGICAL SCIENCE (biology/biological science), BUSINESS (accounting, banking and finance, business administration and management, hotel/motel and restaurant management, marketing/retailing/merchandising, and tourism), COMMUNICATIONS AND THE ARTS (art, art history and appreciation, communications, dramatic arts, English, fine arts, French, music, Spanish, and studio art), COMPUTER AND PHYSICAL SCIENCE (chemistry, computer science, earth science, geology, geophysics and seismology, mathematics, and physics), EDUCATION (early childhood education, elementary education, English education, foreign languages education, mathematics education, music education, physical education, and secondary education), ENGINEERING AND ENVIRONMENTAL DESIGN (civil engineering, electrical/electronics engineering, environmental science, marine engineering, mechanical engineering, and naval architecture and marine engineering), HEALTH PROFESSIONS (health, medical technology, premedicine, and preveterinary science), SOCIAL SCIENCE (anthropology, economics, geography, history, international studies, philosophy, political science/government, psychology, sociology, and urban studies). Business administration, general studies, and film, theater, and communication arts have the largest enrollments.

Required: Requirements for graduation include completion of courses in English, literature, math, humanities and art, science, social science, and computer literacy. Students must complete 120 hours with a minimum GPA of 2.0.

Special: Students may participate in co-op programs and may cross-register with Southern University in New Orleans, Elaine P. Nunez Community College, and Delgado Community College. Internships are available, and work-study programs are available with various federal agencies and private companies. Students may study abroad in 14 countries or participate in a Washington semester. UNO also offers dual majors, B.A.-B.S. degrees, preprofessional programs in cardiopulmonary science, dental hygiene, dentistry, medical technology, medicine, nursing, occupational therapy, ophthalmic medical technology, pharmacy, physical therapy, physician's assistant, rehabilitation counseling, and veterinary medicine. 3-2 engineering degrees with Xavier University, Southern University in New Orleans, Loyola University New Orleans, and Dillard University are offered. There are 12 national honor societies, a freshman honors program, and 29 departmental honors programs.

Faculty/Classroom: 59% of faculty are male; 41% are female. No introductory courses are taught by graduate students.

Admissions: 81% of a recent year's applicants were accepted.

Requirements: The SAT or ACT is required. In addition, students who graduate from state-approved high schools must complete the Louisiana Board of Regents Core Curriculum and require no more than 1 developmental/remedial course (ACT of 19 or higher or equivalent SAT score of 460 or higher in Mathematics and ACT of 18 or higher or equivalent SAT score of 450 or higher in Critical Reading is nonremedial) AND 1 of the following: ACT composite score of 23 or greater (SAT 1060, Critical Reading and Math) OR high school cumulative GPA of 2.5 or greater and nonremedial in English and Math subscores OR high school graduation rank in top 25% of class. UNO requires applicants to be in the upper 25% of their class. A GPA of 2.5 is required. AP and CLEP credits are accepted. Important factors in the admissions decision are advanced placement or honors courses, recommendations by school officials, and evidence of special talent.

Procedure: Freshmen are admitted to all sessions. Entrance exams should be taken at least 6 months prior to enrollment. There are early admissions, deferred admissions, and rolling admissions plans. The priority application date for fall entry is July 1. Application fee is $40. Applications are accepted online.

Transfer: A student must have completed at least 18 hours of nonremedial course work, have a 2.25 GPA from an accredited college or university, and have completed all developmental course work before transferring. Students who have not earned st least 18 hours of nonremedial course work are required to submit an official high school transcript and official ACT or SAT scores. 30 of 120 credits required for the bachelor's degree must be completed at UNO.

Visiting: There are guides for informal visits. To schedule a visit, contact the Office of Admissions.

Financial Aid: In a recent year, 71% of all full-time freshmen and 67% of continuing full-time students received some form of financial aid. 46% of all full-time freshmen and 45% of continuing full-time students received need-based aid. The average freshmen award was $6830. UNO is a member of CSS. The FAFSA is required. Check with the school for current application deadlines.

International Students: There were 267 international students enrolled in a recent year. The school actively recruits these students. They must take the TOEFL with a minimum score of 525 on the paper-based TOEFL (PBT) or 71 on the Internet-based version (iBT). If they do not have the TOEFL, they must submit the ACT or SAT.

Graduates: In a recent year, 1368 bachelor's degrees were awarded. The

most popular majors were business (16%), psychology (5%), and film, theater, and communication arts (5%). 284 companies recruited on campus in a recent year.

Admissions Contact: Office of Admissions. E-mail: *admissions@uno.edu* Web: *http:/www.uno.edu*

XAVIER UNIVERSITY OF LOUISIANA D-4

New Orleans, LA 70125 (504) 520-7388
877-XAVIERU; (504) 520-7941

Full-time: 751 men, 1884 women	**Faculty:** 161
Part-time: 39 men, 76 women	**Ph.D.s:** 84%
Graduate: 185 men, 464 women	**Student/Faculty:** 13 to 1
Year: semesters, summer session	**Tuition:** $17,900
Application Deadline: July 1	**Room & Board:** $7400
Freshman Class: 4463 applied, 2860 accepted, 786 enrolled	
SAT CR/M/W: 480/480/470	**ACT:** 22 **COMPETITIVE**

Xavier University of Louisiana, founded in 1925, is a private, historically black liberal arts university affiliated with the Roman Catholic Church. There is one undergraduate school and one graduate school. In addition to regional accreditation, Xavier has baccalaureate program accreditation with ACPE, NASM, and NCATE. The library contains 261,000 volumes, 779,654 microform items, and 6,074 audio/video tapes/CDs/DVDs, and subscribes to 1,624 periodicals including electronic. Computerized library services include interlibrary loans and database searching. Special learning facilities include a TV station, electronic classrooms. The 29-acre campus is in an urban area 2 miles from downtown New Orleans. Including any residence halls, there are 65 buildings.

Student Life: 58% of undergraduates are from Louisiana. Others are from 34 states, and 5 foreign countries. 20% are from public schools. 75% are African American; 11% Asian American. 26% are Catholic; 24% Baptist. The average age of freshmen is 18; all undergraduates, 20. 30% do not continue beyond their first year; 46% remain to graduate.

Housing: 1433 students can be accommodated in college housing, which includes single-sex and coed dorms and on-campus apartments. In addition, there are honors houses. On-campus housing is available on a first-come and first-served basis. Priority is given to out-of-town students. 53% of students commute. Alcohol is not permitted. All students may keep cars.

Activities: 5% of men belong to 4 national fraternities; 1% of women belong to 4 national sororities. There are 80 groups on campus, including art, band, cheerleading, chess, choir, chorus, computers, dance, drill team, ethnic, honors, international, jazz band, literary magazine, newspaper, opera, pep band, political, professional, radio and TV, religious, social, social service, student government, and symphony. Popular campus events include Wellness Week, Octoberfest, and Culturefest.

Sports: There are 4 intercollegiate sports for men and 3 for women, and 12 intramural sports for men and 12 for women. Facilities include a recreation room.

Disabled Students: 99% of the campus is accessible. Facilities include wheelchair ramps, elevators, special parking, specially equipped restrooms, special class scheduling, lowered drinking fountains, lowered telephones, and special housing.

Services: Counseling and information services are available, as is tutoring in every subject. There is a reader service for the blind, and remedial math, reading, and writing.

Campus Safety and Security: Measures include 24-hour foot and vehicle patrol and security escort services. There are shuttle buses, emergency telephones, and lighted pathways/sidewalks.

Programs of Study: Xavier confers B.A., B.S. and B.M. degrees. Master's and doctoral degrees are also awarded. Bachelor's degrees are awarded in BIOLOGICAL SCIENCE (biochemistry and biology/biological science), BUSINESS (accounting, business administration and management, and business economics), COMMUNICATIONS AND THE ARTS (communications, English, fine arts, French, languages, music, music performance, and Spanish), COMPUTER AND PHYSICAL SCIENCE (chemistry, computer science, mathematics, physics, and statistics), EDUCATION (art education, elementary education, English education, mathematics education, middle school education, music education, science education, and social studies education), HEALTH PROFESSIONS (premedicine and speech pathology/audiology), SOCIAL SCIENCE (history, philosophy, political science/government, psychology, sociology, and theological studies). Science, education, and English are the strongest academically. Pharmacy, biology, and business have the largest enrollments.

Required: Requirements for graduation include 9 semester hours in English, 6 each in history, social science, language, theology, philosophy, and natural sciences, 3 each in speech, math, and the arts, and 1 in health and phys ed. Students must complete 128 to 132 total credit hours, including 24 to 54 total hours in the major. Students must maintain a minimum GPA of 2.0, take Introduction to African American History/Culture, pass a comprehensive exam, and by the beginning of the junior year declare a minor in an academic discipline other than the major.

Special: The university offers cooperative programs in any major and 3-2 engineering degrees with Tulane, Louisiana State, Morgan State, and Southern Universities as well as the Universities of Wisconsin, Maryland, New Orleans, and Detroit, and Georgia Institute of Technology. In addition, students may cross-register at colleges of the New Orleans Consortium. Internships are available in legal, political, and pharmaceutical areas. Students may earn an accelerated degree in biology, chemistry, psychology, or political science, pursue dual majors in engineering and biostatistics, opt for non-degree study, and earn a B.A.-B.S. degree in almost any combination. Students may study abroad in 6 countries or participate in an exchange program with Notre Dame University. There are 7 national honor societies, a freshman honors program, and 7 departmental honors programs.

Faculty/Classroom: 50% of faculty are male; 50% are female. No introductory courses are taught by graduate students. The average class size in an introductory lecture is 25; in a laboratory is 21; and in a regular course is 21.

Admissions: 64% of the 2013-2014 applicants were accepted. The SAT scores for the 2013-2014 freshman class were: Critical Reading--55% below 500, 35% between 500 and 599, 9% between 600 and 699, and 1% between 700 and 800; Math--57% below 500, 32% between 500 and 599, and 11% between 600 and 699; Writing--63% below 500, 31% between 500 and 599, and 6% between 600 and 699. The ACT scores were 14% below 21, 56% between 21 and 23, 29% between 24 and 26, 29% between 27 and 28, and 1% above 28. 29% of the current freshmen were in the top fifth of their class; 55% were in the top two fifths.

Requirements: The SAT or ACT is required. Applicants must have earned a high school diploma or the GED. Candidates must also have completed 4 units of English, 2 of math, 1 each of science and social studies, and 8 of academic electives. A GPA of 2.0 is required. AP and CLEP credits are accepted. Important factors in the admissions decision are advanced placement or honors courses, recommendations by school officials, and evidence of special talent.

Procedure: Freshmen are admitted fall, spring, and summer. Entrance exams should be taken in the spring of the junior year or the fall of the senior year. Early decision applications should be filed by March 1; regular applications, by July 1 for fall entry, along with a $25 fee. Notification of early decision is sent October 15; regular decision, April 15. Applications are accepted online.

Transfer: 122 transfer students enrolled in 2012-2013. Applicants must submit college transcripts. High school transcripts are required of applicants with fewer than 30 transferable credits. 30 of 128 credits required for the bachelor's degree must be completed at Xavier.

Visiting: There are guides for informal visits, visitors may sit in on classes, and stay overnight. To schedule a visit, contact the Admissions Office.

Financial Aid: In 2013-2014, 93% of all full-time freshmen and 90% of continuing full-time students received some form of financial aid. 86% of all full-time freshmen and 82% of continuing full-time students received need-based aid. The average freshman award was $17,144. Need-based scholarships or need-based grants averaged $5,701; need-based self-help aid (loans and jobs) averaged $5,222; and non-need-based athletic scholarships averaged $16,360. The average financial indebtedness of the 2013 graduate was $26,106. Xavier is a member of CSS. The FAFSA is required. The priority date for freshman financial aid applications for fall entry is January 1. The deadline for filing freshman financial aid applications for fall entry is rolling.

International Students: There are 33 international students enrolled. They must take the TOEFL. They must also take the SAT or ACT.

Graduates: From July 1, 2012 to June 30, 2013, 280 bachelor's degrees were awarded. The most popular majors were biological/life sciences (38%), physical sciences (17%), and psychology (10%). 25 companies recruited on campus in 2012-2013. In an average class, 29% graduate in 4 years or less, 40% graduate in 5 years or less, and 42% graduate in 6 years or less. Of the 2012 graduating class, 31% were enrolled in graduate school within 6 months of graduation, and 14% were employed.

Admissions Contact: Winston D. Brown, Dean of Admissions. E-Mail: *apply@xula.edu* Web: *www.xula.edu*

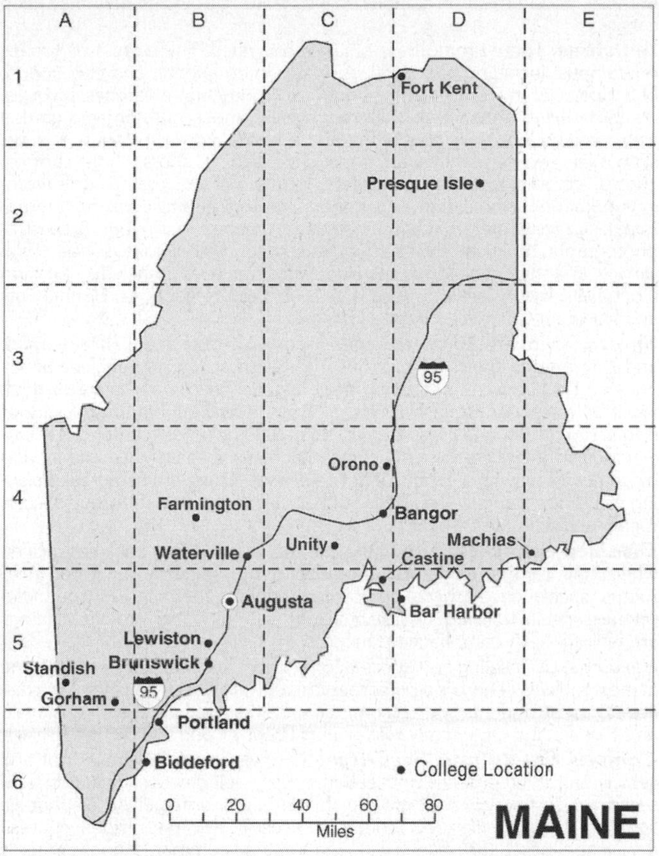

BATES COLLEGE B-5

Lewiston, ME 04240 (207) 786-6000
1-855-228-3755; (207) 786-6025

Full-time: 890 men, 901 women	**Faculty:** 155; IIB, +$
Part-time: n/av	**Ph.D.s:** 90%
Graduate: n/av	**Student/Faculty:** 10 to 1
Year: other	**Tuition:** $45,650
Application Deadline: January 1	**Room & Board:** $13,300

Freshman Class: 5243 applied, 1267 accepted, 500 enrolled
SAT CR/M/W: 680/680/680 **ACT:** 31 **MOST COMPETITIVE**

Founded in 1855, Bates College is a private, highly selective residential college devoted to undergraduate study in the traditional disciplines of the liberal arts and sciences as well as in emerging interdisciplinary programs. Located in Lewiston Maine, Bates offers the B.A. or B.S. to an enrollment of approximately 1,775 students, from 45 states, districts, and territories, and 60 countries. With a student-faculty ratio of 10-to-1 and a commitment to supporting scholar-teachers of highest distinction, the educational community challenges and supports students as they reach toward their full intellectual potential. There is one undergraduate school. The library contains 600,000 volumes, 183,300 microform items, and 38,000 audio/video tapes/CDs/DVDs, and subscribes to 67,500 periodicals including electronic. Computerized library services include interlibrary loans, database searching, Internet access, and Wi-Fi capability. Special learning facilities include an art gallery, planetarium, radio station, TV station, Bates College has a learning research center, art gallery, planetarium, radio station, television studio, a 654-acre mountain conservation area, an observatory, a language resource center, and the Edmund S. Muskie archives. The 109-acre campus in a small town is located 35 miles north of Portland. With residence halls, there are 78 buildings.

Student Life: 90% of undergraduates are from out of state, mostly the Northeast. Students are from 44 states, 55 foreign countries, and Canada. 55% are from public schools. 72% are White. The average age of freshmen is 19; all undergraduates, 20. 8% do not continue beyond their first year; 93% remain to graduate.

Housing: 1650 students can be accommodated in college housing, which includes single-sex and coed dorms. In addition, there are special-interest houses, Bates College offers chemical-free housing, quiet/study housing, and themed-based housing (by application; ex. sustainability, arts). On-campus housing is guaranteed for all 4 years. 93% of students live on campus; of those, 95% remain on campus on weekends. All students may keep cars.

Activities: There are no fraternities or sororities. There are 110 groups on campus, including art, chess, choir, chorale, chorus, computers, dance, debate, drama, environmental, ethnic, film, gay, honors, international, jazz band, literary magazine, musical theater, newspaper, orchestra, pep band, photography, political, professional, radio and TV, religious, social, social service, student government, symphony, and yearbook. Popular campus events include Parents and Family Weekend, Homecoming, Mount David Summit, Winter Carnival, Reunion Weekend, International Dinners, and Ocean Clambakes.

Sports: There are 16 intercollegiate sports for men and 17 for women, and 12 intramural sports for men and 12 for women. Facilities include Bates offers a pool, a field house, indoor and outdoor tracks, indoor and outdoor tennis courts, 3 basketball courts, 3 volleyball courts, dance and fencing space, squash and racquetball courts, training rooms, a rock-climbing wall, a boat house, a winter sports arena, a weight room and football, soccer, baseball, softball, and lacrosse fields.

Disabled Students: 80% of the campus is accessible. Facilities include wheelchair ramps, elevators, special parking, specially equipped restrooms, special class scheduling, lowered drinking fountains, and lowered telephones.

Services: Counseling and information services are available, as is tutoring in every subject. There is a reader service for the blind, and remedial math and writing.

Campus Safety and Security: Measures include 24-hour foot and vehicle patrol, emergency notification system, self-defense education, and security escort services. There are shuttle buses, emergency telephones, lighted pathways/sidewalks, controlled access to dorms/residences, Bates College offers electronic access control in residence halls and all major buildings on campus, automated 911 telephone system and emergency public address system.

Programs of Study: Bates confers B.A., and B.S. degrees. Bachelor's degrees are awarded in AGRICULTURE (environmental studies), BIOLOGICAL SCIENCE (biochemistry, biology/biological science, and neurosciences), COMMUNICATIONS AND THE ARTS (art/visual culture, Chinese, English, french and francophone studies, German, Japanese, music, Russian, Spanish, speech/debate/rhetoric, and theatre acting), COMPUTER AND PHYSICAL SCIENCE (chemistry, geology, mathematics, and physics), SOCIAL SCIENCE (African American studies, American studies, anthropology, asian studies, classical/ancient civilization, East Asian studies, economics, European studies, history, interdisciplinary studies, Latin American studies, medieval studies, philosophy, political science/government, psychology, religious studies, sociology, and women & gender studies). Psychology, economics, and history have the largest enrollments.

Required: Requirements for graduation include one major plus two general education concentrations (which are comprised of four courses and may alternatively be satisfied by another major(s) or minor(s) or a combination thereof); three writing attentive courses; and three courses focused on scientific reasoning, laboratory experience, and quantitative literacy. The total number of hours in the major varies by department, but students should take at least 32 courses, plus 2 short terms, and maintain a minimum GPA of 2.0. All majors require a senior thesis or capstone project.

Special: Bates College offers Co-op programs in engineering, internships, research apprenticeships, work-study programs, study abroad, and a Washington semester. Student-designed, and interdisciplinary majors, and a dual-degree 3-2 engineering degree with Columbia University, Dartmouth College, Case Western Reserve University, Rensselaer Polytechnic Institute, and Washington University in St. Louis are available. Students in any major may graduate in 3 years. Students may also participate in the Williams-Mystic Seaport program in marine biology and maritime history, and exchanges with Spelman College, Morehouse College, Washington and Lee University, and McGill University are possible. There are 2 national honor societies, including Phi Beta Kappa, and 32 departmental honors programs.

Faculty/Classroom: 50% of faculty are male; 50% are female. All teach and do research. No introductory courses are taught by graduate students. The average class size in an introductory lecture is 26; in a laboratory is 24; and in a regular course is 24.

Admissions: 24% of the 2013-2014 applicants were accepted. The SAT scores for the 2013-2014 freshman class were: Critical Reading--1% below 500, 8% between 500 and 599, 49% between 600 and 699, and 42% between 700 and 800; Math--9% between 500 and 599, 59% between 600 and 699, and 32% between 700 and 800; Writing--1% below 500, 8% between 500 and 599, 52% between 600 and 699, and 39% between 700 and 800. The ACT scores were 5% between 24 and

26, 11% between 27 and 28, and 84% above 28. 81% of the current freshmen were in the top fifth of their class.

Requirements: Candidates for admission should have completed at least 4 years of English, 3 each of math, social science, and a foreign language, and 2 of lab science. Essays are required and an interview on or off campus is strongly recommended. The submission of test scores is optional. AP credits are accepted. Important factors in the admissions decision are advanced placement or honors courses, evidence of special talent, and leadership record.

Procedure: Freshmen are admitted fall and winter. There are early decision and deferred admissions plans. Early decision applications should be filed by November 15; regular applications, by January 1 for fall entry; and November 1 for winter entry, along with a $60 fee. Notification of early decision is sent December 20; regular decision, March 31. 242 early decision candidates were accepted for the 2013-2014 class. applicants were on the 2013 waiting list; were admitted. Applications are accepted online.

Transfer: 21 transfer students enrolled in 2012-2013. More weight is given to the student's college record than to high school credentials. Applicants must submit official college and final high school transcripts, a statement of good standing, 3 letters of recommendation, and an essay. An interview is strongly recommended. 16 of 32 credits required for the bachelor's degree must be completed at Bates.

Visiting: There are guides for informal visits, visitors may sit in on classes, and stay overnight. To schedule a visit, contact the Office of Admission.

Financial Aid: In 2013-2014, 47% of all full-time freshmen and 46% of continuing full-time students received some form of financial aid. 47% of all full-time freshmen and 45% of continuing full-time students received need-based aid. The average freshman award was $41,833. 50% of undergraduate students work part-time. Average annual earnings from campus work are $1338. The average financial indebtedness of the 2013 graduate was $22,534. Bates is a member of CSS. The CSS/Profile and FAFSA, and the CSS/Profile, FAFSA, and parent and student tax returns and W-2 forms are required. The deadline for filing freshman financial aid applications for fall entry is February 15.

International Students: There are 117 international students enrolled. The school actively recruits these students. They must take the TOEFL, The TOEFL is preferred.

Graduates: From July 1, 2012 to June 30, 2013, 436 bachelor's degrees were awarded. The most popular majors were psychology (13%), economics (11%), and history (9%). In an average class, 83% graduate in 4 years or less, 88% graduate in 5 years or less, and 93% graduate in 6 years or less.

Admissions Contact: Leigh Weisenburger, Dean of Admission and Financial Aid. E-Mail: *admission@bates.edu* Web: *www.bates.edu*

BOWDOIN COLLEGE B-5

Brunswick, ME 04011	**(207) 725-3100; (207) 725-3101**
Full-time: 901 men, 890 women	**Faculty:** 183; IIB, +$
Part-time: 1 men, 3 women	**Ph.D.s:** 99%
Graduate: n/av	**Student/Faculty:** 9 to 1
Year: semesters	**Tuition:** $45,446
Application Deadline: January 1	**Room & Board:** $12,388
Freshman Class: 7052 applied, 1054 accepted, 497 enrolled	
SAT CR/M/W: 720/720/730	**ACT:** 32 **MOST COMPETITIVE**

Bowdoin College, established in 1794, is a private liberal arts institution. The 5 libraries contain 1.0 million volumes, 108,310 microform items, and 28,876 audio/video tapes/CDs/DVDs, and subscribe to 49,212 periodicals including electronic. Computerized library services include interlibrary loans, database searching, Internet access, and Wi-Fi capability. Special learning facilities include an art gallery, radio station, TV station, a museum of art, arctic museum, language media center, women's resource center, electronic classroom, coastal studies center, African American center, crafts center, ceramics studio, photography darkroom, printmaking studio, woodworking studio, digital media lab, sculpture studio, dance studio, scientific station located in the Bay of Fundy, educational research and development program, theaters, music halls, recording studio, community service resource center, environmental studies center, and visual arts center. The 205-acre campus is in a small town 25 miles northeast of Portland. Including any residence halls, there are 119 buildings.

Student Life: 89% of undergraduates are from out of state, mostly the Northeast. Students are from 47 states, 34 foreign countries, and Canada. 54% are from public schools. 64% are White; 12% Hispanic. 39% claim no religious affiliation; 25% Protestant; 22% Catholic. The average age of freshmen is 18; all undergraduates, 20. 3% do not continue beyond their first year; 93% remain to graduate.

Housing: 1742 students can be accommodated in college housing, which includes coed dorms, on-campus apartments, and off-campus apartments. All first-year students participate in the College House System; their residence floor is affiliated with 1 of 8 College Houses. All upperclass students are also eligible to participate. Housing is guaranteed for first-year and sophomore students; historically we have also accommodated any junior or senior who desired on-campus housing. On-campus housing is available on a lottery system for upperclassmen. 92% of students live on campus; of those, 95% remain on campus on weekends. Upperclassmen may keep cars.

Activities: There are no fraternities or sororities. There are 110 groups on campus, including alpine ski, Amnesty International, and club sports, bird club, cultural clubs, curling club, environmental awareness groups, equestrian club, fencing club, literary society, mock trial, organic garden club, outing club, peer counseling and advising, robocup, science clubs, slam poets, women's clubs, art, band, cheerleading, chess, choir, chorale, chorus, communications, computers, dance, debate, drama, drill team, environmental, ethnic, film, gay, honors, Improvisational comedy, international, jazz band, literary magazine, musical theater, newspaper, orchestra, photography, political, professional, radio and TV, religious, social, social service, and student government. Popular campus events include Common Good Day, Ivies Weekend, Asia Week, Museum Receptions, Spring Gala and Bowdoin-Colby Ice Hockey Games.

Sports: There are 16 intercollegiate sports for men and 17 for women, and 7 intramural sports for men and 7 for women. Facilities include an ice arena, a field house, a swimming pool, 2 gyms, indoor and outdoor track facilities, tennis and squash courts, a climbing wall, a boathouse, outdoor leadership center, and cross-country ski trails. The fitness center offers cardiovascular fitness equipment, weight machines, free weights, and rowing machines along with a variety of fitness classes. There are 60 acres of playing fields for football, baseball, softball, lacrosse, field hockey, soccer, rugby, and ultimate frisbee.

Disabled Students: 72% of the campus is accessible. Facilities include wheelchair ramps, elevators, special parking, specially equipped restrooms, special class scheduling, lowered drinking fountains, lowered telephones, special housing. all new buildings and renovations to old buildings are built to ADA compliance standards.

Services: Counseling and information services are available, as is tutoring in most subjects. There is a reader service for the blind. A counselor is available to assist students with accommodations as needed. Tutoring is available through the Quantitative Reasoning Program and the Writing Project.

Campus Safety and Security: Measures include 24-hour foot and vehicle patrol, emergency notification system, self-defense education, and security escort services. There are shuttle buses, emergency telephones, lighted pathways/sidewalks, controlled access to dorms/residences, residences are locked 24 hours a day, and a staffed communications center is available around the clock.

Programs of Study: Bowdoin confers A.B. degrees. Bachelor's degrees are awarded in AGRICULTURE (environmental studies), BIOLOGICAL SCIENCE (biochemistry, biology/biological science, and neurosciences), COMMUNICATIONS AND THE ARTS (art history, classics, English, French, German, music, romance languages and literature, Russian, Spanish, studio art, and theatre arts), COMPUTER AND PHYSICAL SCIENCE (chemical physics, chemistry, computer mathematics, computer science, earth science, mathematics, mathematics – economics, oceanography, and physics), EDUCATION (mathematics education), SOCIAL SCIENCE (africana studies, anthropology, asian studies, classical/ancient civilization, Eastern European studies, economics, gender studies, history, interdisciplinary studies, Latin American studies, philosophy, political science/government, psychology, religion, sociology, and women's studies). Biology, economics, and government and legal studies are the strongest academically. Government and legal studies, economics, and mathematics have the largest enrollments.

Required: To qualify for the bachelor of arts degree, a student must have: successfully passed thirty-two full-credit courses (or the equivalent); completed a first-year seminar; completed at least one full-credit course (or the equivalent) in each of the following five distribution areas mathematical, computational, or statistical reasoning; inquiry in the natural sciences; exploring social differences; international perspectives; and visual and performing arts; completed at least one full-credit course (or the equivalent) in natural sciences and mathematics, social and behavioral sciences, and humanities (in addition to the required course in the visual and performing arts); and completed an approved major.

Special: A.B. degrees in 42 majors (including 9 interdisciplinary majors), with single, coordinate, double and self-designed major options. Plus (+) and minus (-) grading system, with credit/D/fail option. Dean's list, Latin Honors and departmental honors awarded. First-year seminars, intermediate and advanced independent study, student research and close work with faculty advisors strongly emphasized. Study abroad during the junior year encouraged. Washington semester. Academic support programs include the Baldwin Program for Academic Development, Quantitative Reasoning Program, Writing Project, Office of Student Fellowships and Research, Health Professions Advising. Dual-degree programs offered in Engineering (3-2 with California Inst of Tech, Columbia University, Dartmouth College,and University of Maine, Orono) and Law (3-3 with Columbia University). Teacher Certification program. There is 1 national honor societies including Phi Beta Kappa.

Faculty/Classroom: 52% of faculty are male; 48% are female. All teach

and do research. No introductory courses are taught by graduate students. The average class size in an introductory lecture is 28; in a laboratory is 14; and in a regular course is 16.

Admissions: 15% of the 2013-2014 applicants were accepted. The SAT scores for the 2013-2014 freshman class were: Critical Reading--3% between 500 and 599, 30% between 600 and 699, and 67% between 700 and 800, Math--3% between 500 and 599, 31% between 600 and 699, and 66% between 700 and 800; Writing--3% between 500 and 599, 29% between 600 and 699, and 68% between 700 and 800. The ACT scores were 1% between 24 and 26, 5% between 27 and 28, and 94% above 28. 92% of the current freshmen were in the top fifth of their class; 99% were in the top two fifths. There were 36 National Merit finalists. 32 freshmen graduated first in their class.

Requirements: Typical applicants for admission will have had 4 years each of English, social studies, foreign language, and math; 3 to 4 years of laboratory sciences; and one course each in art, music, and history. A high school record, 2 teacher recommendations, an advisor's estimate of the applicant's character and accomplishments, and an essay are required. Applicants must submit the Common Application as well as the Bowdoin Supplement to be considered for admission. AP credits are accepted. Important factors in the admissions decision are advanced placement or honors courses, recommendations by school officials, and extracurricular activities record.

Procedure: Freshmen are admitted fall. Entrance exams should be taken by the late summer before the freshman year. There are early decision and deferred admissions plans. Early decision applications should be filed by November 15; regular applications, by January 1 for fall entry, along with a $60 fee. Notification of early decision is sent December 15; regular decision, April 5. 224 early decision candidates were accepted for the 2013-2014 class. Applications are accepted online.

Transfer: 1 transfer students enrolled in 2012-2013. College grades of B or better are required to transfer. Applicants should submit high school and college transcripts, a dean's or advisor's statement from the most recent college attended, and 2 recommendations from recent professors. Transfer applicants must submit the Common Application, transfer essay and Bowdoin Supplement to be considered for admission. 16 of 32 credits required for the bachelor's degree must be completed at Bowdoin.

Visiting: There are regularly scheduled orientations for prospective students, the Admissions Office offers student-led campus tours, one-hour information sessions with an Admissions representative, and personal interviews. There are guides for informal visits, visitors may sit in on classes, and stay overnight. To schedule a visit, contact the Admissions Office.

Financial Aid: In 2013-2014, 50% of all full-time freshmen and 48% of continuing full-time students received some form of financial aid. 48% of all full-time freshmen and 43% of continuing full-time students received need-based aid. The average freshman award was $40,879. Need-based scholarships or need-based grants averaged $39,205 ($64,400 maximum); need-based self-help aid (loans and jobs) averaged $1,550 ($1,900 maximum); and other non-need-based awards and non-need-based scholarships averaged $1,000 ($1,000 maximum). 60% of undergraduate students work part-time. Average annual earnings from campus work are $1435. The average financial indebtedness of the 2013 graduate was $21,292. Bowdoin is a member of CSS. The CSS/Profile and FAFSA, and Noncustodial PROFILE and Business/Farm Supplement are required. The deadline for filing freshman financial aid applications for fall entry is February 15.

International Students: There are 90 international students enrolled. The school actively recruits these students. They must take the TOEFL with a minimum score of 600 on the paper-based TOEFL (PBT) or 100 on the Internet-based version (iBT). SAT scores are not required for admission but must be submitted at matriculation for counseling and placement.

Graduates: From July 1, 2012 to June 30, 2013, 458 bachelor's degrees were awarded. The most popular majors were government and legal studies (18%), economics (17%), and mathematics (9%). 120 companies recruited on campus in 2012-2013. In an average class, 88% graduate in 4 years or less, 92% graduate in 5 years or less, and 93% graduate in 6 years or less. Of the 2012 graduating class, 15% were enrolled in graduate school within 6 months of graduation, and 71% were employed.

Admissions Contact: Scott A. Meiklejohn, Dean of Admissions and Financial Aid. E-Mail: *admissions@bowdoin.edu* Web: *www.bowdoin.edu/admissions/*

COLBY COLLEGE — B-4

Waterville, ME 04901 (207) 859-4818
(800) 723-3032; (207) 859-4828

Full-time: 874 men, 946 women	**Faculty:** 173; IIB, +$
Part-time: n/av	**Ph.D.s:** 98%
Graduate: n/av	**Student/Faculty:** 10 to 1
Year: 4-1-4	**Tuition:** $45,760
Application Deadline: January 1	**Room & Board:** $11,750
Freshman Class: 5407 applied, 1408 accepted, 483 enrolled	
SAT CR/M/W: 660/680/670 **ACT:** 30	**MOST COMPETITIVE**

Colby College, founded in 1813, is a private liberal arts college. There is one undergraduate school. The 3 libraries contain 1.6 million volumes, 300,500 microform items, and 26,052 audio/video tapes/CDs/DVDs, and subscribe to 19,877 periodicals including electronic. Computerized library services include interlibrary loans, database searching, Internet access, and Wi-Fi capability. Special learning facilities include an art gallery, radio station, an astronomy observatory and classroom, 128-acre arboretum, electronic-research classroom, MIDI studio/electronic-music lab, Language Resource Center, proscenium-style theater, research greenhouses, world-class collection in Maine's largest art museum. The 714-acre campus is in a small town 75 miles north of Portland. Including any residence halls, there are 60 buildings.

Student Life: 88% of undergraduates are from out of state, mostly the Northeast. Students are from 42 states, 76 foreign countries, and Canada. 51% are from public schools. 60% are White; 11% race unknown. The average age of freshmen is 18; all undergraduates, 20. 7% do not continue beyond their first year; 90% remain to graduate.

Housing: 1779 students can be accommodated in college housing, which includes coed dorms and on-campus apartments. In addition, there are special-interest houses, substance-free halls, quiet residence halls and apartments for seniors. On-campus housing is guaranteed for all 4 years. 96% of students live on campus; of those, 95% remain on campus on weekends. All students may keep cars.

Activities: There are no fraternities or sororities. There are 107 groups on campus, including outdoor, women's and coed woodsmen's team, art, band, choir, chorale, chorus, communications, computers, dance, debate, drama, environmental, ethnic, film, gay, honors, human rights, international, jazz band, literary magazine, musical theater, newspaper, orchestra, photography, political, professional, radio and TV, religious, social, social service, student government, symphony, and yearbook. Popular campus events include Winter Carnival, Foss Arts Festival and International Extravaganza.

Sports: There are 16 intercollegiate sports for men and 17 for women, and 8 intramural sports for men and 8 for women. Facilities include an athletic center with fitness, weight training, yoga and exercise areas; a gym with badminton, volleyball, and basketball courts; a hockey and skating rink; a field house for track and field, climbing wall, soccer, baseball, softball, tennis, lacrosse, and golf; a swimming pool and saunas; physical therapy and athletic training center, and squash and handball courts. Outdoor playing fields including two artificial-turf fields, tennis courts, an all-weather track, cross-country skiing and running trails, and an FIS-certified Nordic ski race course adjacent to campus. Woodsmen's area for lumberjack events and competition.

Disabled Students: 93% of the campus is accessible. Facilities include wheelchair ramps, elevators, special parking, specially equipped restrooms, special class scheduling, lowered drinking fountains, and lowered telephones.

Services: Counseling and information services are available, as is tutoring in every subject. There is a reader service for the blind. There is also a writing center and a support program for learning-disabled students.

Campus Safety and Security: Measures include 24-hour foot and vehicle patrol, emergency notification system, self-defense education, and security escort services. There are shuttle buses, emergency telephones, lighted pathways/sidewalks, controlled access to dorms/residences, radical attack defense classes for women, fire safety with drills and inspections, ID program for bikes, computers, party checks and alcohol education.

Programs of Study: Colby confers B.A. degrees. Bachelor's degrees are awarded in AGRICULTURE (environmental studies), BIOLOGICAL SCIENCE (biochemistry, biology/biological science, environmental biology, and neurosciences), COMMUNICATIONS AND THE ARTS (art history, classics, creative writing, English, Germanic languages and literature, music, Russian languages and literature, Spanish, studio art, and theatre arts), COMPUTER AND PHYSICAL SCIENCE (applied mathematics, chemistry, computer science, geology, geoscience, mathematics, physics, and science technology), SOCIAL SCIENCE (African American studies, American studies, anthropology, classical/ancient civilization, East Asian studies, economics, French studies, (Social Science) Global Studies, history, Latin American studies, philosophy, political science/government, psychology, religion, sociology, and women's studies). Economics, biology and global studies have the largest enrollments.

Required: To graduate, all students must take English composition and fulfill a three-semester foreign language requirement. They must also take 2 courses in the natural sciences and 1 course each in the arts, historical studies, literature, quantitative reasoning, the social sciences, and human or cultural diversity, and meet Colby's wellness requirement by attending 8 lectures. Students must complete a total of 128 credit hours, including 3 January term courses, and maintain a GPA of 2.0.

Special: Colby incorporates research in majors across the curriculum and showcases research results at its annual Colby Liberal Arts Symposium. Study abroad is accessible through more than 200 programs in more than 60 countries, and two thirds of students participate during their time at Colby. Colby offers opportunities to study or intern in Washington, D.C, on-campus work-study, exchange programs with the Claremont Colleges and Howard University, 3-2 engineering degree programs with Dartmouth College and Columbia University, and a semester-in-residence program working with research scientists at the Bigelow Laboratory for Ocean Sciences. Students, with approval, may pursue independent majors. Colby offers combined and interdisciplinary majors including four that combine interdisciplinary computation with biology, environmental studies, music, and theater and dance. The Jan Plan, pioneered by Colby in 1962, offers a month-long term for internships or focused study on or off campus. There are 9 national honor societies, including Phi Beta Kappa, and 26 departmental honors programs.

Faculty/Classroom: 58% of faculty are male; 42% are female. All teach undergraduates, and all teach and do research. No introductory courses are taught by graduate students. The average class size in an introductory lecture is 27; in a laboratory is 16; and in a regular course is 16.

Admissions: 26% of the 2013-2014 applicants were accepted. The SAT scores for the 2013-2014 freshman class were: Critical Reading--2% below 500, 15% between 500 and 599, 51% between 600 and 699, and 31% between 700 and 800; Math--12% between 500 and 599, 49% between 600 and 699, and 39% between 700 and 800; Writing--1% below 500, 14% between 500 and 599, 48% between 600 and 699, and 36% between 700 and 800. The ACT scores were 1% between 21 and 23, 8% between 24 and 26, 16% between 27 and 28, and 74% above 28. 84% of the current freshmen were in the top fifth of their class; 98% were in the top two fifths. There were 2 National Merit finalists. 4 freshmen graduated first in their class.

Requirements: The SAT or ACT is required. Must submit either SAT, ACT, or three SAT Subject Tests. Candidates should be high school graduates with a recommended academic program of 4 years of English, 3 each of foreign language and math, and 2 each of science (including lab work), social studies/history, and other college-preparatory courses. AP credits are accepted. Important factors in the admissions decision are recommendations by school officials, extracurricular activities record, and personality/intangible qualities.

Procedure: Freshmen are admitted fall and spring. Entrance exams should be taken by January of the senior year. There are early decision and deferred admissions plans. Early decision applications should be filed by November 15; regular applications, by January 1 for fall entry; and January 1 for winter entry. Notification of early decision is sent December 15; regular decision, April 1. 259 early decision candidates were accepted for the 2013-2014 class. 637 applicants were on the 2013 waiting list; 3 were admitted. Applications are accepted online. Application fees are waived if application is completed online.

Transfer: 9 transfer students enrolled in 2012-2013. Applicants must have a minimum GPA of 3.0 and, as a rule, have earned enough credit hours to qualify for at least sophomore standing. They must be in good academic and social standing and should submit references from a faculty member and a dean of their current school. If the SAT or ACT has been taken, the results may be submitted as well. 64 of 128 credits required for the bachelor's degree must be completed at Colby.

Visiting: There are regularly scheduled orientations for prospective students, including panel discussions, tours, class visits, complimentary meals, interviews, and information sessions. There are guides for informal visits, visitors may sit in on classes, and stay overnight. To schedule a visit, contact the Admissions Office.

Financial Aid: In 2013-2014, 48% of all full-time freshmen and 49% of continuing full-time students received some form of financial aid. 42% of all full-time freshmen and 42% of continuing full-time students received need-based aid. The average freshman award was $40,541. Need-based scholarships or need-based grants averaged $43,302 ($60,190 maximum); need-based self-help aid (loans and jobs) averaged $1,635 ($1,800 maximum); and other non-need-based awards and non-need-based scholarships averaged $4,085 ($21,345 maximum). 67% of undergraduate students work part-time. Average annual earnings from campus work are $1325. Colby is a member of CSS. The CSS/Profile, FAFSA, and the college's own financial statement, and Tax returns to finalize awards are required. The deadline for filing freshman financial aid applications for fall entry is February 1.

International Students: There are 153 international students enrolled. The school actively recruits these students. They must take the TOEFL, or IELTS if English is neither your first language nor your current language of instruction. SAT or ACT or three SAT Subject Tests of your choice, sent by the testing agency.

Graduates: From July 1, 2012 to June 30, 2013, 510 bachelor's degrees were awarded. The most popular majors were economics (15%), biology (12%), and global studies (10%). 46 companies recruited on campus in 2012-2013. In an average class, 86% graduate in 4 years or less, 90% graduate in 5 years or less, and 90% graduate in 6 years or less. Of the 2012 graduating class, 24% were enrolled in graduate school within 6 months of graduation, and 87% were employed.

Admissions Contact: Steve Thomas, Director of Admissions. E-Mail: *admissions@colby.edu* Web: *www.colby.edu/admissions*

COLLEGE OF THE ATLANTIC — D-5

Bar Harbor, ME 04609 — (207) 288-5015, (800) 528-0025; (207) 288-4126

Full-time: 112 men, 232 women	**Faculty:** 29
Part-time: 2 men, 10 women	**Ph.D.s:** 90%
Graduate: 1 men, 7 women	**Student/Faculty:** 10 to 1
Year: trimesters	**Tuition:** $38,952
Application Deadline: February 15	**Room & Board:** $9258
Freshman Class: 455 applied, 333 accepted, 104 enrolled	
SAT CR/M/W: 640/610/610	**ACT:** 28 **HIGHLY COMPETITIVE+**

College of the Atlantic was founded in 1969 on the premise that education should go beyond understanding the world as it is, to enabling students to actively shape its future. There is one undergraduate school and one graduate school. The library contains 60,000 volumes, 37,000 microform items, and 3,300 audio/video tapes/CDs/DVDs, and subscribes to 30,000 periodicals including electronic. Computerized library services include interlibrary loans, database searching, Internet access, and Wi-Fi capability. Special learning facilities include an art gallery, natural history museum, writing center, taxidermy lab, sculpture, painting, animation and ceramics studios, marine mammal research center, 2 greenhouses, community garden on campus, 2 organic farms (a few miles off campus), sustainable enterprise hatchery, ocean-going vessels and 2 offshore island research centers. The 35-acre campus is in a small town 45 miles southeast of Bangor, along the Atlantic Ocean shoreline. Including any residence halls, there are 20 buildings.

Student Life: 82% of undergraduates are from out of state, mostly the Northeast. Students are from 38 states, 36 foreign countries, and Canada. 73% are from public schools. 70% are White; 16% Foreign. The average age of freshmen is 19; all undergraduates, 21. 19% do not continue beyond their first year; 69% remain to graduate.

Housing: 153 students can be accommodated in college housing, which includes coed dorms. substance-free houses. On-campus housing is guaranteed for the freshman year only, is available on a first-come, first-served basis, and is available on a lottery system for upperclassmen. Priority is given to out-of-town students. 58% of students commute. Alcohol is not permitted. All students may keep cars.

Activities: There are no fraternities or sororities. There are 20 groups on campus, including botany club, fiber club, international student club, taxidermy club and gentleman's club, art, campus committee on sustainability, chess, chorus, computers, dance, drama, environmental, film, gay, international, jazz band, literary magazine, newspaper, orchestra, photography, political, social, social service, student government, and yearbook. Popular campus events include Bar Island Swim, Fandango Talent Show, Earth Day, Aurora Ball-ealis (winter dance), Spanish Festival, Human Ecology Forums, Fall Community Show.

Sports: There is no sports program at COA. All students are members of the local YMCA and may use its pool, Nautilus equipment, and volleyball and basketball facilities, as well as nearby tennis courts. Acadia National Park offers seasonal outdoor activities - hiking, biking, cross-country skiing especially. The college has an active outdoor program, with camping and outdoor equipment and canoes, sea kayaks, and sailboats for student use; it also offers a sailing class, sea kayaking class, and wilderness first responder class. There are yoga and martial arts classes on campus, as well as a bouldering wall and an ice-skating rink in winter. SCUBA instruction is offered using the Y facilities. Dance instruction is also available.

Disabled Students: 80% of the campus is accessible. Facilities include wheelchair ramps, elevators, special parking, specially equipped restrooms, lowered drinking fountains, lowered telephones.

Services: Counseling and information services are available, as is tutoring in some subjects, including writing, math, language, photography and computer use There is remedial math and writing.

Campus Safety and Security: Measures include 24-hour foot and vehicle patrol and security escort services. There are shuttle buses, emergency telephones, and lighted pathways/sidewalks.

Programs of Study: COA confers B.A. degrees. Master's degrees are also awarded. Bachelor's degrees are awarded in SOCIAL SCIENCE (human ecology). Human ecology is the strongest academically and has the largest enrollment.

Required: All students major in human ecology, which serves as a focus for a self-designed pathway to understanding the relationships between humans and our environment. Students complete a total of 36 COA credits, including an interdisciplinary core course, two courses each in environmental science, human studies, and arts and design, along with a history, writing, and quantitative reasoning course. Also required are a 3-credit internship (taking students off-campus either for a term, or during the summer), a human ecology essay, community service and a culminating 3-credit senior, or capstone, project, which can be accomplished either in one term, or spread out throughout the senior year.

Special: Students may cross-register with the University of Maine; Eco League exchanges are available with Alaska Pacific University, and Green Mountain, Northland, and Prescott colleges. COA offers study abroad programs in Mexico, Guatemala, and France, and supports other study abroad programs as well as independent residencies abroad. A 10-week internship is a requirement of graduationl; students are assisted in finding internships in the US and abroad in an area of interest. All students design their own path to completion of their B.A. in human ecology.

Faculty/Classroom: 56% of faculty are male; 44% are female. All teach undergraduates and 80% do research. No introductory courses are taught by graduate students. The average class size in an introductory lecture is 12; in a laboratory is 12; and in a regular course is 12.

Admissions: 73% of the 2013-2014 applicants were accepted. The SAT scores for the 2013-2014 freshman class were: Critical Reading--2% below 500, 23% between 500 and 599, 54% between 600 and 699, and 21% between 700 and 800; Math--5% below 500, 42% between 500 and 599, and 53% between 600 and 699; Writing--7% below 500, 33% between 500 and 599, 58% between 600 and 699, and 2% between 700 and 800. The ACT scores were 50% between 21 and 23, 30% between 24 and 26, 20% between 27 and 28, and 50% above 28. 69% of the current freshmen were in the top fifth of their class.

Requirements: Candidates for admission must be high school graduates who have completed 4 years of English, 3-4 years of math, 2-3 years of science, 2 years of a foreign language, and 1 year of history. AP credits are accepted. Important factors in the admissions decision are personality/intangible qualities, extracurricular activities record, and recommendations by school officials.

Procedure: Freshmen are admitted fall, winter, and spring. Entrance exams should be taken in the junior or senior year. There are early decision and deferred admissions plans. Early decision applications should be filed by December 1; regular applications, by February 15 for fall entry; November 15 for winter entry; and February 15 for spring entry, along with a $50 fee. Notification of early decision is sent December 15; regular decision, April 1. 37 early decision candidates were accepted for the 2013-2014 class. Applications are accepted online.

Transfer: 43 transfer students enrolled in 2012-2013. Only coursework for which the student has received a grade of "C" (2.0) or better will be accepted for transfer credit. Students need to apply and send a transcript. COA credits refer to one COA course (one trimester course). 18 of 36 credits required for the bachelor's degree must be completed at COA.

Visiting: There are regularly scheduled orientations for prospective students, there is an annual fall tour for high school seniors on Columbus day. Students attend classes, stay in student housing, and are invited to join outings at Acadia National Park. There is also a weekend for transfer students. . There are guides for informal visits, visitors may sit in on classes, and stay overnight. To schedule a visit, call (207) 288-5015.

Financial Aid: In 2013-2014, 97% of all full-time freshmen and 93% of continuing full-time students received some form of financial aid. 90% of all full-time freshmen and 81% of continuing full-time students received need-based aid. The average freshman award was $38,035. Need-based scholarships or need-based grants averaged $35,233 ($49,890 maximum); need-based self-help aid (loans and jobs) averaged $5,767 ($8,000 maximum); and other non-need-based awards and non-need-based scholarships averaged $9,213 ($10,000 maximum). 74% of undergraduate students work part-time. Average annual earnings from campus work are $2500. The average financial indebtedness of the 2013 graduate was $19,285. COA is a member of CSS. The FAFSA and the college's own financial statement are required. The deadline for filing freshman financial aid applications for fall entry is February 15.

International Students: There are 56 international students enrolled. The school actively recruits these students. They must take the TOEFL, or submit SAT scores or the IB English exam score.

Graduates: From July 1, 2012 to June 30, 2013, 75 bachelor's degrees were awarded. The most popular majors were human ecology (100%). 15 companies recruited on campus in 2012-2013. In an average class, 59% graduate in 4 years or less, 68% graduate in 5 years or less, and 69% graduate in 6 years or less. Of a recent class, 3% were enrolled in graduate school within 6 months of graduation, and 80% were employed.

Admissions Contact: Heather Albert-Knopp, Dean. E-Mail: *inquiry@coa.edu* Web: *www.coa.edu*

HUSSON UNIVERSITY C-4

Bangor, ME 04401 (207) 941-7067
(800) 448-7766; (207) 941-7935

Full-time: 783 men, 1086 women
Part-time: 175 men, 309 women
Graduate: 261 men, 438 women
Year: semesters, summer session
Application Deadline: August 15
Freshman Class: 1581 applied, 1263 accepted, 463 enrolled
SAT CR/M/W: 475/471/485 **ACT:** 20 **LESS COMPETITIVE**

Faculty: 81
Ph.D.s: 66%
Student/Faculty: 23 to 1
Tuition: $15,130
Room & Board: $8256

Husson University, previously known as Husson College, was founded in 1898 and is a private institution offering BS and graduate degrees in business and health careers, a doctorate in pharmacy, masters in counseling, as well a bachelor's degree in teaching, English, biology, chemistry, criminal justice, environmental and forensic sciences, psychology and health care studies. There are 10 undergraduate schools and 7 graduate schools. The library contains 42,326 volumes, 14,947 microform items, and 475 audio/video tapes/CDs/DVDs, and subscribes to 49,800 periodicals including electronic. Computerized library services include interlibrary loans, database searching, Internet access, and Wi-Fi capability. Special learning facilities include an art gallery and radio station. The 208-acre campus is in a suburban area in the city of Bangor. Including any residence halls, there are 10 buildings.

Student Life: 84% of undergraduates are from Maine. Others are from 36 states, 14 foreign countries, and Canada. 87% are from public schools. 86% are White. The average age of freshmen is 18; all undergraduates, 23. 29% do not continue beyond their first year; 44% remain to graduate.

Housing: 1075 students can be accommodated in college housing, which includes coed dorms. upper level undergraduates and graduate student suite housing. On-campus housing is guaranteed for all 4 years, is available on a first-come, and first-served basis. 66% of students commute. All students may keep cars.

Activities: 8% of men belong to 1 local and 1 national fraternities; 12% of women belong to 3 local sororities. There are 47 groups on campus, including cheerleading, choir, chorus, computers, dance, drama, environmental, ethnic, international, literary magazine, musical theater, newspaper, pep band, political, professional, radio and TV, religious, social, social service, and student government. Popular campus events include Spring Fling, Winter Carnival, and Greek Alumni Weekend.

Sports: There are 8 intercollegiate sports for men and 10 for women, and 9 intramural sports for men and 9 for women. Facilities include a gym, an Olympic-size swimming pool, weight training and mat rooms, a health and fitness center, basketball and tennis courts, a baseball complex, and a turf soccer field.

Disabled Students: All of the campus is accessible. Facilities include wheelchair ramps, elevators, special parking and equipped restrooms, lowered water fountains, lowered telephones, special housing.

Services: Counseling and information services are available, as is tutoring in most subjects. There is remedial math and writing.

Campus Safety and Security: Measures include 24-hour foot and vehicle patrol, emergency notification system, self-defense education, and security escort services. There are lighted pathways/sidewalks and controlled access to dorms/residences.

Programs of Study: Husson confers B.S. degrees. Associate, master's, and doctoral degrees are also awarded. Bachelor's degrees are awarded in BIOLOGICAL SCIENCE (biology/biological science), BUSINESS (accounting, banking and finance, business administration and management, business systems analysis, hospitality management services, marketing/retailing/merchandising, and sports management), COMMUNICATIONS AND THE ARTS (English), COMPUTER AND PHYSICAL SCIENCE (chemistry and computer programming), EDUCATION (elementary education, English education, physical education, and science education), ENGINEERING AND ENVIRONMENTAL DESIGN (environmental science), HEALTH PROFESSIONS (health, health care administration, nursing, occupational therapy, pharmacy, physical therapy, and prepharmacy), SOCIAL SCIENCE (counseling/psychology, criminal justice, forensic studies, paralegal studies, and psychology). physical therapy, pharmacy, nursing, accounting are the strongest academically. Business administration has the largest enrollment.

Required: Requirements for graduation vary by program. The minimum requirement is a total of 120 credit hours with a GPA of 2.0 or higher.

Special: Experiential learning is part of the core curriculum in all majors. Internships are incorporated in accounting, sports management, hospitality management, nursing, physical therapy, occupational therapy, international business, and family business. Co-op programs, externships, and clinicals are included in the curriculum in all other majors. Students can go a fifth year and obtain a master's in business in accounting, business administration, or CIS, and in phys ed with a concentration in sports management. An accelerated degree program, dual majors, and student-designed majors are also available.

Faculty/Classroom: 50% of faculty are male; 50% are female. 76%

teach undergraduates, and 25% do both. No introductory courses are taught by graduate students. The average class size in an introductory lecture is 22; in a laboratory is 17; and in a regular course is 20.

Admissions: 80% of the 2013-2014 applicants were accepted. The SAT scores for the 2013-2014 freshman class were: Critical Reading--62% below 500, 34% between 500 and 599, 2% between 600 and 699, and 1% between 700 and 800; Math--55% below 500, 37% between 500 and 599, 7% between 600 and 699, and 1% between 700 and 800; Writing--63% below 500, 32% between 500 and 599, 5% between 600 and 699. The ACT scores were 70% below 21, 16% between 21 and 23, 9% between 24 and 26, 4% between 27 and 28, and 1% above 28. 51% of the current freshmen were in the top fifth of their class; 74% were in the top two fifths.

Requirements: The SAT is required. The ACT and ACT Writing Test are recommended. Applicants must be graduates of an accredited secondary school or have earned a GED. A recommendation from a high school counselor is required. A GPA of 2.0 is required. AP and CLEP credits are accepted. Important factors in the admissions decision are advanced placement or honors courses, recommendations by school officials, and leadership record.

Procedure: Freshmen are admitted to all sessions. Entrance exams should be taken prior to enrollment. There are deferred admissions and rolling admissions plans. Applications should be filed by August 15 for fall entry, along with a $40 fee. Notification is sent on a rolling basis. Applications are accepted online.

Transfer: 280 transfer students enrolled in 2012-2013. Applicants must have a 2.0 GPA. Courses with a C grade or better transfer. 30 of 120 credits required for the bachelor's degree must be completed at Husson.

Visiting: There are regularly scheduled orientations for prospective students, including an interview and campus tour. There are guides for informal visits, visitors may sit in on classes, and stay overnight. To schedule a visit, contact the Admissions Office.

Financial Aid: In 2013-2014, 82% of all full-time freshmen and 80% of continuing full-time students received some form of financial aid. 81% of all full-time freshmen and 76% of continuing full-time students received need-based aid. The average freshman award was $14,612. Need-based scholarships or need-based grants averaged $10,765 ($14,760 maximum); need-based self-help aid (loans and jobs) averaged $4,249 ($7,200 maximum); and other non-need-based awards and non-need-based scholarships averaged $3,930 ($8,000 maximum). 50% of undergraduate students work part-time. Average annual earnings from campus work are $1560. The average financial indebtedness of the 2013 graduate was $31,000. Husson is a member of CSS. The FAFSA is required. The deadline for filing freshman financial aid applications for fall entry is open.

International Students: There are 34 international students enrolled. The school actively recruits these students. They must take the TOEFL with a minimum score of 500 on the paper-based TOEFL (PBT) or 80 on the Internet-based version (iBT). They must also take the SAT or ACT. Students who score unsatisfactorily on the TOEFL may be accepted conditionally.

Graduates: From July 1, 2012 to June 30, 2013, 396 bachelor's degrees were awarded. The most popular majors were business administration (22%), health professions (22%), and criminal justice (14%). 75 companies recruited on campus in 2012-2013. In an average class, 25% graduate in 4 years or less, 39% graduate in 5 years or less, and 44% graduate in 6 years or less. Of the 2012 graduating class, 31% were enrolled in graduate school within 6 months of graduation, and 55% were employed.

Admissions Contact: Carlena Bean, Director E-Mail: *admit@husson.edu* Web: *www.husson.edu*

MAINE COLLEGE OF ART — B-6

Portland, ME 04101 — (207) 775-5157, ext. 254; (800) 639-4808; (207) 772-5069

Full-time: 100 men, 220 women	**Faculty:** n/av
Part-time: 20 men, 30 women	**Ph.D.s:** n/av
Graduate: 20 men, 20 women	**Student/Faculty:** n/av
Year: semesters	**Tuition:** $28,280
Application Deadline: open	**Room & Board:** $9676
Freshman Class: n/av	
SAT or ACT: required	**SPECIAL**

Maine College of Art, established in 1882, is a private, independent visual art college. There is 1 graduate school. The figures in the above capsule and in this profile are approximate. In addition to regional accreditation, MECA has baccalaureate program accreditation with NASAD. The library contains 18,500 volumes and 150 audio/video tapes/CDs/DVDs, and subscribes to 100 periodicals including electronic. Computerized library services include interlibrary loans and database searching. Special learning facilities include an art gallery. The campus is in an urban area 100 miles north of Boston in downtown Portland. Including any residence halls, there are 6 buildings.

Student Life: 65% of undergraduates are from out of state, mostly the Northeast. Students are from 29 states and 6 foreign countries. 94% are white. The average age of freshmen is 20; all undergraduates, 22. 30% do not continue beyond their first year.

Housing: 100 students can be accommodated in college housing, which includes coed dorms and on-campus apartments. On-campus housing is available on a first-come, first-served basis. 75% of students commute. Alcohol is not permitted. All students may keep cars.

Activities: There are no fraternities or sororities. There are 10 groups on campus, including art, computers, dance, drama, gay, international, newspaper, photography, social, and student government. Popular campus events include an annual art sale, and Earth Day celebration.

Sports: There is no sports program at MECA.

Disabled Students: 65% of the campus is accessible. Facilities include wheelchair ramps, elevators, specially equipped restrooms, and lowered drinking fountains.

Services: Counseling and information services are available, as is tutoring in every subject. There is remedial math, reading, and writing. Academic support for writing papers, study skills, and time management is available, as is help for students with learning disabilities.

Campus Safety and Security: Measures include self-defense education. There are emergency telephones and safety training by local police.

Programs of Study: MECA confers B.F.A. degrees. Master's degrees are also awarded. Bachelor's degrees are awarded in COMMUNICATIONS AND THE ARTS (graphic design, media arts, metal/jewelry, painting, photography, printmaking, and sculpture), ENGINEERING AND ENVIRONMENTAL DESIGN (ceramic science). Painting, photography, and ceramics are the largest.

Required: All students must take 2 years of studio foundation courses and 2 years in the studio major, as well as 5 semesters of art history, 3 of humanities or social science, 2 each of English composition, natural science, and Western civilization, and 1 of critical issues. 129 total credit hours are necessary, with 36 in the major. Students must maintain a minimum GPA of 2.0. A senior thesis is required.

Special: Cross-registration with Bowdoin College, the Greater Portland Alliance of Colleges and Universities, and AICAD Mobility is available, as are internships utilizing professional artists and design and photography studios. There are also Art in Service internships. The continuing studies program provides for nondegree study. Minors in art history, drawing, and illustration are also offered, as are dual and student-designed majors.

Faculty/Classroom: 50% of faculty are male; 50% are female. All teach undergraduates. No introductory courses are taught by graduate students. The average class size in an introductory lecture is 136; in a laboratory, 18; and in a regular course, 20.

Requirements: The SAT or ACT is required. It is recommended that candidates for admission complete 4 years of English, 3 years each of art and math, and 2 years each of foreign language, science, and social studies. AP credits are accepted. Important factors in the admissions decision are personality/intangible qualities, advanced placement or honors courses, and evidence of special talent.

Procedure: Freshmen are admitted fall and spring. Entrance exams should be taken in the fall of the senior year. There are deferred admissions and rolling admissions plans. Application deadlines are open. Application fee is $40.

Transfer: Transfers must submit an official copy of their college transcripts. 65 of 129 credits required for the bachelor's degree must be completed at MECA.

Visiting: There are regularly scheduled orientations for prospective students, including a tour, a portfolio review, a faculty-student panel, and opportunities to observe classes and meet with an admissions counselor or other staff. There are guides for informal visits, and visitors may sit in on classes. To schedule a visit, contact the Admissions Office.

Financial Aid: MECA is a member of CSS. The FAFSA is required. Check with the school for current application deadlines.

International Students: The school actively recruits these students. They must take the TOEFL. They must also take the SAT or ACT.

Admissions Contact: Dean of Admissions. A campus DVD is available. E-mail: *admissions@meca.edu* Web: *www.meca.edu*

MAINE MARITIME ACADEMY — C-5

Castine, ME 04420 — (207) 326-2215; (800) 227-8465; (207) 326-2515

Full-time: 750 men, 175 women	**Faculty:** n/av
Part-time: 5 men, 5 women	**Ph.D.s:** n/av
Graduate: 10 men, 10 women	**Student/Faculty:** n/av
Year: semesters	**Tuition:** $11,525 ($21,525)
Application Deadline: May 1	**Room & Board:** $9548
Freshman Class: n/av	
SAT or ACT: required	**COMPETITIVE**

Maine Maritime Academy, founded in 1941, is a public institution offering degree programs in ocean and marine-oriented studies with emphasis on engineering, transportation, business management, and ocean sciences, to prepare graduates for private and public sector careers and the uniformed services of the United States. There are 4 undergraduate schools and one graduate school. In addition to regional accreditation, MMA has baccalaureate program accreditation with ABET. The library contains 88,490 volumes, 5,000 microform items, and 808 audio/video tapes/CDs/DVDs, and subscribes to 1,311 periodicals including electronic. Computerized library services include interlibrary loans, database searching, Internet access, and Wi-Fi capability. Special learning facilities include a natural history museum, planetarium, More than 60 vessels, bridge simulator, radar sims, power plant sims, and cargo system simulators; multiple sophisticated training vessels. See the world. The 50-acre campus is in a small town 38 miles south of Bangor on the east coast of Penobscot Bay. Including any residence halls, there are 14 buildings.

Student Life: 69% of undergraduates are from Maine. Others are from 40 states, 7 foreign countries, and Canada. 90% are from public schools. 98% are White. The average age of freshmen is 19; all undergraduates, 24. 12% do not continue beyond their first year; 75% remain to graduate.

Housing: 625 students can be accommodated in college housing, which includes single-sex and coed dorms and on-campus apartments. graduate housing. On-campus housing is guaranteed for all 4 years. 85% of students live on campus; of those, 40% remain on campus on weekends. Alcohol is not permitted. All students may keep cars.

Activities: 10% of men belong to 1 national fraternity. There are no sororities. There are 30 groups on campus, including billiards, chess, engineering, hockey, marshal arts, outing, rugby, sailing, scuba, social, amateur radio, bagpipe, band, chess, chorale, drama, drill team, drum and bugle corps, environmental, ethnic, international, newspaper, pep band, photography, professional, social, social service, student government, and yearbook. Popular campus events include GSA Weekend, BSA Klondike Derby and Veterans Day.

Sports: There are 6 intercollegiate sports for men and 6 for women, and 10 intramural sports for men and 10 for women. Facilities include Olympic pool, two weight rooms, field house with 3 climbing walls, gym, racquetball/squash courts, aerobics room, weight/workout room on training ship, and synthetic multi sport athletic field.

Disabled Students: All of the campus is accessible. Facilities include wheelchair ramps, elevators, special parking, specially equipped restrooms, and special housing.

Services: Counseling and information services are available, as is tutoring in most subjects. There is a reader service for the blind, and remedial math, reading, and writing.

Campus Safety and Security: Measures include 24-hour foot and vehicle patrol and self-defense education. There are emergency telephones, lighted pathways/sidewalks, controlled access to dorms/residences, on-campus medical and counseling services, and locked dorm.

Programs of Study: MMA confers B.S. degrees. Associate and master's degrees are also awarded. Bachelor's degrees are awarded in BUSINESS (international business management), COMPUTER AND PHYSICAL SCIENCE (oceanography), ENGINEERING AND ENVIRONMENTAL DESIGN (engineering, engineering technology, marine engineering, maritime science, and transportation technology). Marine systems engineering is the strongest academically. Marine transportation and marine engineering degree programs has the largest enrollments.

Required: A minimum GPA of 2.0 in an average of 140 total credit hours is required for graduation. GPA in the major must be at least 2.25. A senior thesis is required for some majors and a comprehensive exam is required for USCG license candidates.

Special: The 2-month freshman and junior year training cruises give students practical experience aboard the academy's 500-foot ship. Cadet shipping co-ops on assigned merchant ships for 65 to 90 days. Co-op programs and internships for all programs are offered, as is study abroad through special agreements with other maritime colleges worldwide. Dual and student-designed majors are possible.

Faculty/Classroom: 75% of faculty are male; 25% are female. All teach undergraduates. No introductory courses are taught by graduate students. The average class size in an introductory lecture is 30; in a laboratory is 15; and in a regular course is 25.

Requirements: The SAT or ACT is required. Candidates for admission must have completed 4 years of English, 3 years of math, and 2 years of lab science. Courses must include algebra I, algebra II, trigonometry, geometry, and either chemistry or physics with a lab. A GPA of 2.0 is required. AP and CLEP credits are accepted. Important factors in the admissions decision are advanced placement or honors courses, evidence of special talent, and leadership record.

Procedure: Freshmen are admitted fall and spring. Entrance exams should be taken as early as possible in the senior year. There are early decision, deferred admissions, and rolling admissions plans. Early decision applications should be filed by December 31; regular applications, by May 1 for fall entry; and November 1 for spring entry. The fall 2013 application fee was $15. Applications are accepted online.

Transfer: 16 transfer students enrolled in 2012-2013. Applicants must have a minimum 2.0 GPA in previous college work and meet the same prerequisites as entering freshmen.

Visiting: There are regularly scheduled orientations for prospective students, consisting of 3 open houses per year; campus visits are available weekdays throughout the year. Visitors may sit in on classes and stay overnight. To schedule a visit, contact the Admissions Office.

Financial Aid: The FAFSA, and student and parent tax returns, and a verification worksheet is required. Check with the school for current application deadlines.

International Students: They must take the TOEFL.

Graduates: From July 1, 2012 to June 30, 2013, 160 bachelor's degrees were awarded. The most popular majors were marine engineering (30%), marine transportation (30%), and power engineering (15%).

Admissions Contact: Jeff Wright, Director of Admissions. E-Mail: *jeff.wright@mma.edu* Web: *www.mainemaritime.edu*

SAINT JOSEPH'S COLLEGE OF MAINE — A-5

Standish, ME 04084-5263 — (207) 893-7746; (800) 338-7057; (207) 893-7862

Full-time: 300 men, 600 women	**Faculty:** 63
Part-time: 9 men, 21 women	**Ph.D.s:** 98%
Graduate: n/av	**Student/Faculty:** 15 to 1
Year: semesters, summer session	**Tuition:** $27,000
Application Deadline: open	**Room & Board:** $10,700
Freshman Class: n/av	
SAT: required	**ACT:** 21 — **COMPETITIVE**

Saint Joseph's College of Maine, founded in 1912, is a private, Roman Catholic institution offering liberal arts and preprofessional programs. The figures in the above capsule and in this profile are approximate. The library contains 98,626 volumes, 29,010 microform items, and 1000 audio/video tapes/CDs/DVDs, and subscribes to 11,461 periodicals including electronic. Computerized library services include interlibrary loans, database searching, and Internet access. Special learning facilities include a learning resource center, radio station, and telescope observatory. The 350-acre campus is in a rural area 18 miles west of Portland. Including any residence halls, there are 20 buildings.

Student Life: 60% of undergraduates are from Maine. Others are from 15 states, 3 foreign countries, and Canada. 82% are white. The average age of freshmen is 18; all undergraduates, 20. 18% do not continue beyond their first year; 59% remain to graduate.

Housing: 829 students can be accommodated in college housing, which includes single-sex and coed dorms and substance-free housing. On-campus housing is guaranteed for all 4 years. 83% of students live on campus; of those, 65% remain on campus on weekends. All students may keep cars.

Activities: There are no fraternities or sororities. There are 28 groups on campus, including campus activities board, campus ministry, cheerleading, choir, chorale, computers, dance, drama, ethnic, Habitat for Humanity, high adventure club, honors, international, literary magazine, musical theater, newspaper, pep band, photography, political, professional, radio and TV, religious, social, social service, student government, and yearbook. Popular campus events include Family Weekend, Christmas Benefit Concert, and Spring Fling.

Sports: There are 5 intercollegiate sports for men and 6 for women, and 12 intramural sports for men and 12 for women. Facilities include a multipurpose facility housing a gym, a workout room with free weights, Nautilus and other weight-training equipment, a cardiovascular workout room, dance aerobics rooms, a climbing wall, a 25-meter pool, saunas, and an elevated jogging track. There are also soccer and field hockey fields, a private beach on a lake, lighted athletic fields for baseball and softball, cross-country running and ski trails, and a low ropes course.

Disabled Students: 75% of the campus is accessible. Facilities include wheelchair ramps, elevators, special parking, specially equipped restrooms, special class scheduling, and lowered drinking fountains.

Services: Counseling and information services are available, as is tutoring in every subject. There is a reader service for the blind.

Campus Safety and Security: Measures include 24-hour foot and vehicle patrol, self-defense education, and security escort services. There are emergency telephones, lighted pathways/sidewalks, and round-the-clock security officers.

Programs of Study: Saint Joseph's College of Maine confers B.A., B.S., B.S.B.A., and B.S.N. degrees. Associate degrees are also awarded. Bachelor's degrees are awarded in BIOLOGICAL SCIENCE (biology/biological science), BUSINESS (business administration and management), COMMUNICATIONS AND THE ARTS (communications and English), COMPUTER AND PHYSICAL SCIENCE (chemistry and mathematics), EDUCATION (elementary education and physical education), ENGINEERING AND ENVIRONMENTAL DESIGN (environmental science), HEALTH PROFESSIONS (nursing and prepharmacy), SOCIAL SCIENCE (criminal justice, history, philosophy, psychology, sociology, and theological studies). Business, nursing, and biology are the strongest academically. Elementary education, business, and nursing have the largest enrollments.

Required: To graduate, students must complete 128 credit hours with a minimum GPA of 2.0, including 8 hours of English, history, theology, and a foreign language, 4 each of science and math, and 8 of electives.

Special: Saint Joseph's offers internships, cross-registration with 4 southern Maine colleges, study abroad in 5 countries, a semester at sea, dual majors, work-study programs, and non-degree study. There are 2 national honor societies, a freshman honors program, and 6 departmental honors programs.

Faculty/Classroom: 48% of faculty are male; 52% are female. The average class size in an introductory lecture is 25; in a laboratory, 12; and in a regular course, 18.

Requirements: The SAT or ACT is required. Candidates for admission must be high school graduates who have completed a college preparatory curriculum with a recommended 4 units in English, 3 to 4 in math, 2 in foreign language, and 1 to 3 each in history, science, and social studies. A GPA of 2.0 is required. AP and CLEP credits are accepted. Important factors in the admissions decision are advanced placement or honors courses, recommendations by school officials, and extracurricular activities record.

Procedure: Freshmen are admitted fall and spring. Entrance exams should be taken by January of the senior year. There are early admissions, deferred admissions, and rolling admissions plans. Application deadlines are open. Check with the school for current application deadlines and fee. Applications are accepted online.

Transfer: Transfer students should have a minimum GPA of 2.0. 32 of 128 credits required for the bachelor's degree must be completed at Saint Joseph's College of Maine.

Visiting: There are regularly scheduled orientations for prospective students, including Application and Acceptance Day programs, visits on 5 fall Saturdays, and summer visits. There are guides for informal visits, and visitors may sit in on classes and stay overnight. To schedule a visit, contact the Office of Admission.

Financial Aid: Saint Joseph's College of Maine is a member of CSS. The FAFSA and the college's own financial statement are required. Check with the school for current application deadlines.

International Students: For non-English speaking students, the TOEFL is required. English-speaking international students must take the SAT or ACT.

Admissions Contact: Dean of Admissions. E-mail: *admission@sjcme.edu* Web: *www.sjcme.edu*

THOMAS COLLEGE — B-4

Waterville, ME 04901 — **(207) 877-0101; (207) 877-0114**

Full-time: 415 men, 365 women	**Faculty:** 31
Part-time: 225 men, 334 women	**Ph.D.s:** 55%
Graduate: 67 men, 117 women	**Student/Faculty:** 25 to 1
Year: semesters, summer session	**Tuition:** $19,210
Application Deadline: open	**Room & Board:** $8060
Freshman Class: 1129 applied, 829 accepted, 298 enrolled	
SAT CR/M/W: 445/453/435	**ACT:** 18 — **LESS COMPETITIVE**

Thomas College, founded in 1894, is a private institution offering undergraduate programs in business and practical liberal arts. There is one graduate school. The library contains 17,702 volumes, and 770 audio/video tapes/CDs/DVDs. Computerized library services include interlibrary loans, database searching, Internet access, and Wi-Fi capability. Special learning facilities include an art gallery. The 120-acre campus is in a rural area 75 miles north of Portland. Including any residence halls, there are 16 buildings.

Student Life: 80% of undergraduates are from Maine. Others are from 22 states, and 8 foreign countries. 85% are from public schools. 92% are White. The average age of freshmen is 18; all undergraduates, 21. 35% do not continue beyond their first year; 42% remain to graduate.

Housing: 573 students can be accommodated in college housing, which includes coed dorms. On-campus housing is guaranteed for the freshman year only, is available on a first-come, first-served basis, and is available on a lottery system for upperclassmen. 65% of students live on campus; of those, 65% remain on campus on weekends. All students may keep cars.

Activities: 2% of men belong to 1 national fraternity. There are no sororities. There are 20 groups on campus, including chorale, computers, dance, drama, environmental, gay, honors, international, professional, religious, social, social service, student government, and yearbook. Popular campus events include Winter Carnival, Welcome Week, Thanksgiving Convocation and Student Appreciation Day.

Sports: There are 6 intercollegiate sports for men and 7 for women, and 6 intramural sports for men and 6 for women. Facilities include a gym, basketball court, a weight, fitness, and aerobics room, soccer and softball fields, a training area, a baseball field, field hockey field, an intramural field, and cross-country skiing and snowshoe trails. Facilities for swimming, indoor tennis, racquetball, and hockey are available locally. Additionally, two state of the art turf field complex is home for soccer, field hockey and lacrosse teams.

Disabled Students: 80% of the campus is accessible. Facilities include wheelchair ramps, elevators, special parking, specially equipped restrooms, special class scheduling, and lowered drinking fountains.

Services: Counseling and information services are available, as is tutoring in most subjects. There is remedial math, reading, and writing.

Campus Safety and Security: Measures include 24-hour foot and vehicle patrol, emergency notification system, self-defense education, and security escort services. There are emergency telephones, lighted pathways/sidewalks, controlled access to dorms/residences, including emergency blue lights.

Programs of Study: Thomas confers A.S., A.A., B.S., B.A., M.B.A., and M.S.Ed. degrees. Associate and master's degrees are also awarded. Bachelor's degrees are awarded in BUSINESS (accounting, business administration and management, business economics, finance, human resources, management information systems, management science, marketing management, and sports management), COMMUNICATIONS AND THE ARTS (communications and English), COMPUTER AND PHYSICAL SCIENCE (computer information technology, computer science, computer security and information assurance, and information sciences and systems), EDUCATION (business education, early childhood education, and elementary education), SOCIAL SCIENCE (criminal justice, international studies, and psychology). Accounting and management information systems are the strongest academically. Business administration, criminal justice, and sport management have the largest enrollments.

Required: To graduate, students must achieve a minimum GPA of 2.0, fulfill all course requirements, and complete a minimum of 120 total credit hours of study including 30 hours in the major.

Special: Students may cross-register with Colby College and Unity College. There are co-op programs and internships available in most majors. 5-year degrees are offered in most majors where a B.S. is available. Accelerated 3+1 programs are available. Dual enrollment programs are available with local high schools. There are 2 national honor societies.

Faculty/Classroom: 60% of faculty are male; 40% are female. 96% teach undergraduates. No introductory courses are taught by graduate students. The average class size in an introductory lecture is 22 and in a regular course is 18.

Admissions: 73% of the 2013-2014 applicants were accepted. The SAT scores for the 2013-2014 freshman class were: Critical Reading--70% below 500, 26% between 500 and 599, 3% between 600 and 699, and 1% between 700 and 800; Math--66% below 500, 27% between 500 and 599, and 7% between 600 and 699; Writing--77% below 500, 19% between 500 and 599, and 4% between 600 and 699. The ACT scores were 50% below 21, 40% between 21 and 23, and 10% between 24 and 26. 24% of the current freshmen were in the top fifth of their class; 56% were in the top two fifths.

Requirements: The SAT or ACT is required. Candidates for admission must be high school graduates with an academic program that includes 4 years of English, 3 of math, 3 of sciences, 2 of social studies, 2 of foreign language, and 2 other. A letter of recommendation from a secondary school counselor is required. An interview is highly recommended. Thomas requires applicants to be in the upper 46% of their class. A GPA of 2.0 is required. AP and CLEP credits are accepted. Important factors in the admissions decision are advanced placement or honors courses, recommendations by school officials, and personality/intangible qualities.

Procedure: Freshmen are admitted to all sessions. Entrance exams should be taken by the fall of the senior year. There are deferred admissions and rolling admissions plans. Application deadlines are open. Application fee is $40. Applications are accepted online.

Transfer: 36 transfer students enrolled in 2012-2013. Applicants should have a minimum college GPA of 2.0. The school recommends an interview. Official transcripts from all previously attended post-secondary institutions are required. 60 of 120 credits required for the bachelor's degree must be completed at Thomas.

Visiting: There are regularly scheduled orientations for prospective students, includes open house events, Saturday Visit Days, and 1 new student orientation/pre-registration. There are guides for informal visits and visitors may sit in on classes. To schedule a visit, contact Jessica Rodrigue at admissions@thomas.edu.

Financial Aid: In 2013-2014, 98% of all full-time freshmen and 91% of continuing full-time students received some form of financial aid. 90% of all full-time freshmen and 84% of continuing full-time students received need-based aid. The average freshman award was $20,748. Need-based scholarships or need-based grants averaged $16,032 ($19,050 maximum); need-based self-help aid (loans and jobs) averaged $4,583 ($11,600 maximum); and other non-need-based awards and non-need-based scholarships averaged $8,948 ($12,000 maximum). 100% of undergraduate students work part-time. Average annual earnings from campus work are $1591. The average financial indebtedness of the 2013 graduate was $36,061. The FAFSA is required. The priority date for freshman financial aid applications for fall entry is October 15.

International Students: There are 30 international students enrolled. The school actively recruits these students. They must take the TOEFL with a minimum score of 72 on the Internet-based version (iBT), IELTS. They must also take the SAT or ACT.

Graduates: From July 1, 2012 to June 30, 2013, 143 bachelor's degrees were awarded. The most popular majors were criminal justice (17%), business management/marketing (16%), and sport management (13%). 60 companies recruited on campus in 2012-2013. In an average class, 48% graduate in 5 years or less and 51% graduate in 6 years or less. Of the 2012 graduating class, 11% were enrolled in graduate school within 6 months of graduation, and 91% were employed.

Admissions Contact: Wendy Martin, Dean of Admissions. E-Mail: *admiss@thomas.edu* Web: *www.thomas.edu*

UNITY COLLEGE C-4

Unity, ME 04988 800-624-1024
800-624-1024; 207-948-9205

Full-time: 267 men, 279 women	**Faculty:** 38
Part-time: 6 men, 2 women	**Ph.D.s:** 80%
Graduate: n/av	**Student/Faculty:** 12 to 1
Year: semesters	**Tuition:** $25,000
Application Deadline: February 15	**Room & Board:** $9054
Freshman Class: 407 applied, 350 accepted, 120 enrolled	
SAT or ACT: recommended	**COMPETITIVE**

Unity College is a small, private college in rural Maine that provides dedicated, engaged students with a liberal arts education that emphasizes the environment and natural resources. Unity College graduates are prepared to be environmental stewards, effective leaders, and responsible citizens through active learning experiences within a supportive community. There is one undergraduate school. The library contains 52,467 volumes, and 2,625 audio/video tapes/CDs/DVDs, and subscribes to 1,748 periodicals including electronic. Computerized library services include interlibrary loans, database searching, Internet access, and Wi-Fi capability. The 225-acre campus is in a small town in mid-coast Maine. Including any residence halls, there are 30 buildings.

Student Life: 74% of undergraduates are from out of state, mostly the Northeast. Students are from 40 states, and 1 foreign countries. 97% are from public schools. 92% are White. The average age of freshmen is 18; all undergraduates, 20. 23% do not continue beyond their first year; 53% remain to graduate.

Housing: 360 students can be accommodated in college housing, which includes single-sex and coed dorms and on-campus apartments. On-campus housing is guaranteed for all 4 years and is available on a lottery system for upperclassmen. 71% of students live on campus; of those, 89% remain on campus on weekends. All students may keep cars.

Activities: There are no fraternities or sororities. There are 36 groups on campus, including art, band, chorus, drama, environmental, gay, honors, literary magazine, outdoor and environmental clubs, photography, and student government. Popular campus events include Regional Woodsman's Meet in October, Empty Bowls Community Service and Earth Day Activities.

Sports: There are 3 intercollegiate sports for men and 4 for women, and 10 intramural sports for men and 10 for women. Facilities include a gym, a weight training room, playing fields, a nature trail, and game rooms.

Disabled Students: Facilities include wheelchair ramps, special parking, specially equipped restrooms, and special housing.

Services: Counseling and information services are available, as is tutoring in most subjects. There is a reader service for the blind, and remedial math, reading, and writing. A learning disability specialist is on staff.

Campus Safety and Security: Measures include 24-hour foot and vehicle patrol and emergency notification system. There are emergency telephones, lighted pathways/sidewalks, and controlled access to dorms/residences.

Programs of Study: Unity confers B.A., and B.S. degrees. Associate degrees are also awarded. Bachelor's degrees are awarded in AGRICULTURE (agriculture, animal science, conservation and regulation, environmental studies, natural resource management, range/farm management, and wildlife management), BIOLOGICAL SCIENCE (biology/biological science, ecology, marine biology, and wildlife biology), BUSINESS (recreation and leisure services), COMMUNICATIONS AND THE ARTS (art and English), COMPUTER AND PHYSICAL SCIENCE (geology and natural sciences), EDUCATION (education and secondary education), ENGINEERING AND ENVIRONMENTAL DESIGN (environmental science and land use management and reclamation), HEALTH PROFESSIONS (recreation therapy), SOCIAL SCIENCE (ethics, politics, and social policy, law enforcement and corrections, and parks and recreation management). Biology, earth and environmental science, and sustainable agriculture are the strongest academically. Conservation law enforcement, captive wildlife care and education, and wildlife biology have the largest enrollments.

Required: General education requirements include 38 credits. Included are Composition and Communication, math, computer science proficiency, life science, physical science, humanities, art, Community-based learning, and Environmental Studies. Students must complete 120 credit hours with a minimum GPA of 2.0. An capstone course is required in all bachelor's degree programs. A minimum of 30 credits must be taken at the junior and senior level.

Special: The college offers credit-bearing internships, study abroad, a Washington semester, work-study programs, accelerated degree programs, dual majors, and an honors program. There is a freshman honors program.

Faculty/Classroom: 54% of faculty are male; 46% are female. All teach undergraduates, and all teach and do research. No introductory courses are taught by graduate students. The average class size in an introductory lecture is 19; in a laboratory is 14; and in a regular course is 18.

Admissions: 86% of the 2013-2014 applicants were accepted. 20% of the current freshmen were in the top fifth of their class; 55% were in the top two fifths.

Requirements: The SAT or ACT and ACT Writing Test are recommended. Applicants must be graduates of an accredited secondary school with a minimum GPA of 2.3. The GED is accepted. SAT or ACT scores, though not required, should be submitted, if available, for placement purposes. Five short answer essays are required and an interview is recommended. A GPA of 2.3 is required. AP and CLEP credits are accepted. Important factors in the admissions decision are extracurricular activities record, advanced placement or honors courses, and leadership record.

Procedure: Freshmen are admitted fall and spring. Entrance exams should be taken in the junior or senior year. There are early decision, early admissions, and deferred admissions plans. Early decision applications should be filed by December 15; regular applications, by February 15 for fall entry; and November 1 for spring entry, along with a $25 fee. Notification of early decision is sent January 2; regular decision, March 1. Applications are accepted online.

Transfer: 34 transfer students enrolled in 2012-2013. Applicants must present a minimum college GPA of 2.4 and are encouraged to submit SAT scores. 30 of 120 credits required for the bachelor's degree must be completed at Unity.

Visiting: There are regularly scheduled orientations for prospective students. There are guides for informal visits, visitors may sit in on classes, and stay overnight. To schedule a visit, contact the Admissions Office.

Financial Aid: In 2013-2014, 99% of all full-time freshmen and 97% of continuing full-time students received some form of financial aid. 91% of all full-time freshmen and 86% of continuing full-time students received need-based aid. The average freshman award was $27,943. Need-based scholarships or need-based grants averaged $15,799 ($24,405 maximum); need-based self-help aid (loans and jobs) averaged $5,390 ($6,700 maximum); and other non-need-based awards and non-need-based scholarships averaged $6,754 ($22,659 maximum). 59% of undergraduate students work part-time. Average annual earnings from campus work are $1062. The average financial indebtedness of the 2013 graduate was $40,320. The FAFSA is required. The priority date for freshman financial aid applications for fall entry is March.

International Students: The school actively recruits these students. They must take the TOEFL.

Graduates: From July 1, 2012 to June 30, 2013, 138 bachelor's degrees were awarded. The most popular majors were conservation law enforcement (20%), captive wildlife care and education (17%), and wildlife biology/management (16%). 76 companies recruited on campus in 2012-2013. In an average class, 10% graduate in 3 years or less, 45% graduate in 4 years or less, 53% graduate in 5 years or less, and 53% graduate in 6 years or less. Of the 2012 graduating class, 13% were enrolled in graduate school within 6 months of graduation, and 90% were employed.

Admissions Contact: Joe Saltalamachia, Director of Admission. E-Mail: *admissions@unity.edu* Web: *www.unity.edu*

UNIVERSITY OF MAINE SYSTEM

The University of Maine System, established in 1968, is a private system in Maine. It is governed by a board of trustees, whose chief administrator is the chancellor. The primary goal of the system is teaching, research, and public service. The main priorities are to strengthen human services through programs in education, health, and social services; to provide international exchange and foreign language programs; and to conduct science and technology education and basic and applied research. Profiles of the 4-year campuses are included in this section.

UNIVERSITY OF MAINE C-4

Orono, ME 04473 (207) 581-1598
(877) 486-2364; (207) 581-1213

Full-time: 4165 men, 3757 women	**Faculty:** 378
Part-time: 604 men, 656 women	**Ph.D.s:** 84%
Graduate: 706 men, 1359 women	**Student/Faculty:** 16 to 1
Year: semesters, summer session	**Tuition:** $10,600 ($37,970)
Application Deadline: open	**Room & Board:** $9112
Freshman Class: 9336 applied, 7789 accepted, 2166 enrolled	
SAT CR/M/W: 530/540/510	**ACT:** 24 **COMPETITIVE+**

The University of Maine, established in 1865, is a publicly funded land-grant institution in the University of Maine system. The university offers degree programs in the arts and sciences, business, public policy, health fields, engineering, education, forestry, and agriculture. There are 6 undergraduate schools and one graduate school. In addition to regional accreditation, UMaine has baccalaureate program accreditation with AACSB, ABET, ADA, AHEA, CSAB, CSWE, NASM, NCATE, NLN, and SAF. The library contains 1.4 million volumes, 2.4 million microform items, and 18,713 audio/video tapes/CDs/DVDs, and subscribes to 92,000 periodicals including electronic. Computerized library services include interlibrary loans, database searching, Internet access, and Wi-Fi capability. Special learning facilities include an art gallery, natural history museum, planetarium, radio station, a concert hall and other music facilities, two theaters, a digital media lab, an anthropology museum, and a laboratory for surface science and technology. The 3300-acre campus is in a small town 8 miles north of Bangor. Including any residence halls, there are 202 buildings.

Student Life: 78% of undergraduates are from Maine. Others are from 49 states, 65 foreign countries, and Canada. 79% are White. The average age of freshmen is 18; all undergraduates, 21. 19% do not continue beyond their first year.

Housing: 3517 students can be accommodated in college housing, which includes coed dorms, on campus apartments, off-campus apartments, and married student housing. In addition, there are honors houses, language houses, special-interest houses, substance-free housing, quiet sections, graduate family, and first-year residential experience. On-campus housing is guaranteed for the freshman year only, is available on a first-come, and first-served basis. 60% of students commute. All students may keep cars.

Activities: There are 207 groups on campus, including art, band, cheerleading, chess, choir, chorale, chorus, computers, dance, debate, drama, drill team, environmental, ethnic, film, forensics, gay, honors, international, jazz band, literary magazine, marching band, musical theater, newspaper, opera, orchestra, pep band, photography, political, professional, radio and TV, religious, social, social service, student government, symphony, and yearbook. Popular campus events include Maine Day, Family and Friends Weekend, and International Week.

Sports: There are 8 intercollegiate sports for men and 9 for women, and 26 intramural sports for men and 26 for women. Facilities include on- and off-campus sports arenas for hockey and basketball, a field house, swimming and diving center, an indoor climbing center, a student recreation center, a recreation swimming pool, a weight room, an indoor track, a dance studio, basketball, volleyball, badminton, squash, tennis, and racquetball courts, and baseball, softball, soccer, field hockey, and football fields, sports dome, and a year-round maintained forest trail system.

Disabled Students: 90% of the campus is accessible. Facilities include wheelchair ramps, elevators, special parking, specially equipped restrooms, special class scheduling, lowered drinking fountains, lowered telephones, a transport van.

Services: Counseling and information services are available, as is tutoring in some subjects. There is a reader service for the blind. Developmental courses are offered in remedial math, reading and writing.

Campus Safety and Security: Measures include 24-hour foot and vehicle patrol, emergency notification system, self-defense education, and security escort services. There are emergency telephones, lighted pathways/sidewalks, text and email emergency communication system.

Programs of Study: UMaine confers B.A., B.S., B.F.A., B.M.E. and B.U.S. degrees. Master's and doctoral degrees are also awarded. Bachelor's degrees are awarded in AGRICULTURE (agriculture, animal science, fishing and fisheries, forest engineering, forestry and related sciences, horticulture, natural resource management, wildlife management, and wood science), BIOLOGICAL SCIENCE (biochemistry, biology/biological science, biotechnology, botany, cell biology, marine biology, marine science, microbiology, molecular biology, nutrition, and zoology), BUSINESS (accounting, business administration and management, and business economics), COMMUNICATIONS AND THE ARTS (art history, art, communication, communications, dramatic arts, English, French, German, journalism, Latin, media arts, modern language, music, music performance, romance languages and literature, Spanish, speech/debate/rhetoric, and studio art), COMPUTER AND PHYSICAL SCIENCE (chemistry, computer science, earth science, mathematics, and physics), EDUCATION (art education, athletic training, elementary education, health education, music education, physical education, recreation education, secondary education, and university studies), ENGINEERING AND ENVIRONMENTAL DESIGN (bioengineering, chemical engineering, civil engineering, computer engineering, construction technology, electrical/electronics engineering, electrical/electronics engineering technology, engineering physics, environmental science, landscape architecture, landscape architecture/design, mechanical engineering, mechanical engineering technology, paper and pulp science, and surveying engineering), HEALTH PROFESSIONS (clinical science, kinesiology, medical laboratory technology, nursing, and speech pathology/audiology), SOCIAL SCIENCE (anthropology, child care/child and family studies, economics, food science, history, interdisciplinary studies, international studies, parks and recreation management, philosophy, political science/government, psychology, public administration, social work, sociology, and women's studies). Psychology, engineering, and biological science are the largest.

Required: To graduate, students must complete a minimum of 120 credit hours, including at least 48 in the major, with a GPA of 2.0 or higher. 40 credits in approved courses must be taken. General education requirements include 18 credits in human values and social context, 6 credits in math/statistics/computer science, 2 courses in science, and at least 1 course in ethics. English composition is required. Students must demonstrate writing competency and complete a capstone.

Special: Cross-registration at other University of Maine campuses, internships at the upper level, a Washington semester, work-study programs both on- and off-campus, dual majors, a general studies degree, and pass/fail options are available. Students may study abroad in more than 40 countries. Cooperative programs are available in most majors, and accelerated degrees may be arranged. There are 43 national honor societies, including Phi Beta Kappa, and a freshman honors program.

Faculty/Classroom: 56% of faculty are male; 44% are female. 76% teach undergraduates. Graduate students teach 14% of introductory courses. The average class size in an introductory lecture is 50; in a laboratory is 18; and in a regular course is 41.

Admissions: 83% of the 2013-2014 applicants were accepted. The SAT scores for the 2013-2014 freshman class were: Critical Reading--34% below 500, 45% between 500 and 599, 17% between 600 and 699, and 4% between 700 and 800; Math--31% below 500, 43% between 500 and 599, 22% between 600 and 699, and 4% between 700 and 800; Writing--40% below 500, 43% between 500 and 599, 16% between 600 and 699, and 1% between 700 and 800. The ACT scores were 21% below 21, 27% between 21 and 23, 25% between 24 and 26, 16% between 27 and 28, and 12% above 28. 38% of the current freshmen were in the top fifth of their class; 67% were in the top two fifths. There were 2 National Merit finalists. 33 freshmen graduated first in their class.

Requirements: The SAT or ACT is required. In addition, The GED is accepted. The number of academic or Carnegie credits required varies according to the program. The required secondary school courses also vary with each program but should include 4 credits of English, 3 of math, 2 of lab science, 2 of social studies, 2 in a foreign language, and 3 of electives. Guidance counselor recommendation is required for high school students. An essay is required. An audition is required for music majors. A GPA of 2.0 is required. AP and CLEP credits are accepted. Important factors in the admissions decision are advanced placement or honors courses, recommendations by school officials, and evidence of special talent.

Procedure: Freshmen are admitted fall and spring. Entrance exams should be taken by January of the senior year. There are deferred admissions and rolling admissions plans. Application deadlines are open. The fall 2013 application fee was $40. Notifications are sent February 1. Applications are accepted online.

Transfer: 490 transfer students enrolled in 2012-2013. Applicants must submit transcripts of all college and high school records. A minimum GPA of 2.0 is required. Some majors specify a higher cumulative GPA. 30 of 120 credits required for the bachelor's degree must be completed at UMaine.

Visiting: There are regularly scheduled orientations for prospective students, Includes an opening welcome, campus tours, registration, department tours, a student panel, admissions, financial aid and student life sessions, a performing arts presentation, and music auditions. There are guides for informal visits and visitors may sit in on classes. To schedule a visit, contact Elizabeth A Downing at edowning@maine.edu.

Financial Aid: In 2013-2014, 95% of all full-time freshmen and 87% of continuing full-time students received some form of financial aid. 78% of all full-time freshmen and 75% of continuing full-time students received need-based aid. The average freshman award was $17,276. Need-based scholarships or need-based grants averaged $7,389; need-based self-help aid (loans and jobs) averaged $5,300; non-need-based athletic scholarships averaged $219; and other non-need-based awards and non-need-based scholarships averaged $4,376. 34% of undergraduate students work part-time. Average annual earnings from campus work are $2075. The average financial indebtedness of the 2013 graduate was $34,389. The FAFSA is required. The priority date for freshman financial aid applications for fall entry is March 1.

International Students: There are 237 international students enrolled. The school actively recruits these students. They must take the TOEFL with a minimum score of 530 on the paper-based TOEFL (PBT) or 71 on the Internet-based version (iBT). They must also take the SAT or ACT.

Graduates: From July 1, 2012 to June 30, 2013, 1588 bachelor's degrees were awarded. The most popular majors were education (12%), engineering (12%), and business/marketing (10%). 242 companies recruited on campus in 2012-2013. In an average class, 36% graduate in 4 years or less, 51% graduate in 5 years or less, and 56% graduate in 6 years or less.

Admissions Contact: Brian M. Manter, Director of Recruitment. E-Mail: *um-admit@maine.edu* Web: *www.umaine.edu*

UNIVERSITY OF MAINE AT AUGUSTA B-5

Augusta, ME 04430 **(207) 621-3465; (207) 621-3333**

Full-time: 639 men, 1260 women
Part-time: 772 men, 2319 women
Graduate: n/av
Year: semesters, summer session
Application Deadline: June 15
Freshman Class: 875 applied, 817 accepted, 512 enrolled
Faculty: 104; IIB, -$
Ph.D.s: 54%
Student/Faculty: 15 to 1
Tuition: $6855 ($15,375)
Room & Board: n/app

COMPETITIVE

The University of Maine at Augusta, founded in 1965, offers both associate and baccalaureate degrees and is part of the University of Maine System. There are 3 undergraduate schools. In addition to regional accreditation, UMA has baccalaureate program accreditation with ADA and NLN. The 2 libraries contain 93,897 volumes, 4,676 microform items, and 4,783 audio/video tapes/CDs/DVDs, and subscribe to 493 periodicals including electronic. Computerized library services include interlibrary loans, database searching, Internet access, and Wi-Fi capability. Special learning facilities include an art gallery, an interactive television system. The 159-acre campus is in a small town 50 miles north of Portland. Including any residence halls, there are 15 buildings.

Student Life: 97% of undergraduates are from Maine. Others are from 35 states, 3 foreign countries, and Canada. 99% are from public schools. 73% are White. The average age of freshmen is 27; all undergraduates, 32. 46% do not continue beyond their first year; 30% remain to graduate.

Housing: Alcohol is not permitted. All students commute. All students may keep cars.

Activities: There are no fraternities or sororities. There are 17 groups on campus, including and music ensembles, art, drama, gay, honors, international, jazz band, literary magazine, newspaper, pep band, professional, religious, social, social service, student government, and theater. Popular campus events include Mile of Art, Jazz Week and Plunkett Poetry Festival.

Sports: There are 2 intercollegiate sports for men and 3 for women, and 4 intramural sports for men and 4 for women. Facilities include the UMA Community Outdoor Leisure Center, which is also open to the public. Facilities provide for seasonal activities and feature a running and cross-country skiing trail, tennis courts, a soccer field, and a softball field. Indoor facilities include a small gym, a racquetball court, and a small fitness center.

Disabled Students: 95% of the campus is accessible. Facilities include wheelchair ramps, elevators, special parking, specially equipped restrooms, special class scheduling, lowered drinking fountains, and lowered telephones.

Services: Counseling and information services are available, as is tutoring in some subjects, developmental and introductory level courses There is remedial math and writing. There are workshops on a variety of student success skills, such as effective learning and reducing test anxiety

Campus Safety and Security: Measures include emergency notification system and security escort services. There are emergency telephones and lighted pathways/sidewalks.

Programs of Study: UMA confers B.A., B.A.S., B. Mus. and B.S. degrees. Associate degrees are also awarded. Bachelor's degrees are awarded in BIOLOGICAL SCIENCE (biology/biological science), BUSINESS (accounting and business administration and management), COMMUNICATIONS AND THE ARTS (art, English, and jazz), COMPUTER AND PHYSICAL SCIENCE (applied science and information sciences and systems), EDUCATION (library science), ENGINEERING AND ENVIRONMENTAL DESIGN (architecture), HEALTH PROFESSIONS (dental hygiene, mental health/human services, and nursing), SOCIAL SCIENCE (interdisciplinary studies, law enforcement and corrections, liberal arts/general studies, public administration, and social science). Mental health and human services have the largest enrollments.

Required: All students must complete at least 120 hours, including 30 to 40 in the major, with a minimum GPA of 2.0. All degree programs require courses in communications, humanities, college writing, and fine arts. 6 credits of writing-intensive course work is required.

Special: Work-study and internship programs with local employers, study abroad in Germany, and a student-designed interdisciplinary studies major are available. Cross-registration is offered with University of Maine System campuses. There is 1 national honor society.

Faculty/Classroom: 43% of faculty are male; 47% are female. All teach undergraduates. No introductory courses are taught by graduate students. The average class size in an introductory lecture is 20; in a laboratory is 16; and in a regular course is 18.

Admissions: 93% of the 2013-2014 applicants were accepted. 12% of the current freshmen were in the top fifth of their class; 63% were in the top two fifths.

Requirements: Students are encouraged to submit SAT scores for placement only. Applicants should have a high school diploma or the GED. Recommended secondary preparation varies according to the degree program. Applicants for the B.M. program must audition. UMA requires applicants to be in the upper 25% of their class. A GPA of 2.0 is required. AP and CLEP credits are accepted.

Procedure: Freshmen are admitted fall, spring, and summer. There are deferred admissions and rolling admissions plans. Applications should be filed by June 15 for fall entry; October 15 for spring entry, along with a $40 fee. Notification is sent on a rolling basis.

Transfer: 625 transfer students enrolled in 2012-2013. High school/college transcripts and a statement of good standing from prior institutions are required. Standardized test scores are required for some students, and an interview is recommended. 30 of 120 credits required for the bachelor's degree must be completed at UMA.

Visiting: There are regularly scheduled orientations for prospective students, during the month before the beginning of a semester. There are guides for informal visits and visitors may sit in on classes.

Financial Aid: In 2013-2014, 90% of all full-time freshmen and 99% of continuing full-time students received some form of financial aid. 84% of all full-time freshmen and 90% of continuing full-time students received need-based aid. The average freshman award was $8,026. Need-based scholarships or need-based grants averaged $5,816 ($6,640 maximum); need-based self-help aid (loans and jobs) averaged $6,164 ($7,500 maximum); non-need-based athletic scholarships averaged $2,850; and other non-need-based awards and non-need-based scholarships averaged $6,156 ($2,600 maximum). 5% of undergraduate students work part-time. Average annual earnings from campus work are $1757. The average financial indebtedness of the 2013 graduate was $24,353. The FAFSA is required. The priority date for freshman financial aid applications for fall entry is March 1.

International Students: There are 42 international students enrolled. They must take the TOEFL with a minimum score of 500 on the paper-based TOEFL (PBT).

Graduates: From July 1, 2012 to June 30, 2013, 362 bachelor's degrees were awarded. The most popular majors were health professions (29%), liberal arts/general studies (20%), and business/marketing (17%). 10 companies recruited on campus in 2012-2013.

Admissions Contact: Jonathan Henry, Dean of Enrollment Services. E-Mail: *jhenry@maine.edu* Web: *www.uma.edu*

UNIVERSITY OF MAINE AT FARMINGTON B-4

Farmington, ME 04938 **(207) 778-7086; (207) 778-8182**

Full-time: 609 men, 1175 women
Part-time: 31 men, 86 women
Graduate: 33 men, 127 women
Year: semesters, summer session
Application Deadline: rolling
Freshman Class: 1638 applied, 1371 accepted, 439 enrolled
SAT CR/M/W: 520/500/500
Faculty: 116; IIB, --$
Ph.D.s: 92%
Student/Faculty: 15 to 1
Tuition: $9167 ($18,255)
Room & Board: $8674

COMPETITIVE

The University of Maine at Farmington, founded in 1863 and part of the University of Maine System, is a public liberal arts institution offering programs in arts and sciences, teacher education, and human services. There is one undergraduate school and one graduate school. In addition to regional accreditation, UMF has baccalaureate program accreditation with NCATE. The 2 libraries contain 97,556 volumes, 97,678 microform items, and 3,311 audio/video tapes/CDs/DVDs, and subscribe to 38,502 periodicals including electronic. Computerized library services include interlibrary loans, database searching, Internet access, and Wi-Fi capability. Special learning facilities include an art gallery, radio station, an astronomy observatory, Alice James books poetry journal, assistive learning center, and on-site nursery school and day care as a teaching environment. The 55-acre campus is in a small town 38 miles northwest of Augusta, 80 miles north of Portland. Including any residence halls, there are 43 buildings.

Student Life: 85% of undergraduates are from Maine. Others are from 22 states, and 5 foreign countries. 90% are from public schools. 84% are White. The average age of freshmen is 18; all undergraduates, 21. 29% do not continue beyond their first year; 60% remain to graduate.

Housing: 1008 students can be accommodated in college housing, which includes single-sex and coed dorms. In addition, there are special-interest houses, interest-based themes floors available in residence halls. On-campus housing is guaranteed for all 4 years. 53% of students commute. All students may keep cars.

Activities: There are no fraternities or sororities. There are 53 groups on campus, including and club sports, commuter council, improvisation, student senate, art, band, choir, chorus, communications, computers, dance, drama, environmental, environmental sustainability, film, gay, honors, international, literary magazine, musical theater, newspaper, orchestra, political, professional, radio and TV, religious, social, social service, and student government. Popular campus events include Parents and Alumni weekends, adventures and excursions to Boston and other destinations, Outdoor Recreation Excursions, Spring Fling and Michael D. Wilson Symposium Day.

Sports: There are 11 intercollegiate sports for men and 11 for women, and 10 intramural sports for men and 10 for women. Facilities include a 500-seat gymnasium, with comprehensive training room; a historic community baseball field with grandstand seating, a skinned softball field with dugouts, practice and game field hockey, lacrosse and soccer fields as well as a rugby pitch, ultimate Frisbee and intramural field; a field house with an indoor jogging track, 4 multipurpose courts (one of which is split for use as a group fitness area and a cardio and strength area, plus a free weight area and a 25 yard swimming pool.

Disabled Students: 95% of the campus is accessible. Facilities include wheelchair ramps, elevators, special parking, specially equipped restrooms, special class scheduling, lowered drinking fountains, special housing, a swimming pool, and TDD.

Services: Counseling and information services are available, as is tutoring in most subjects. There is a reader service for the blind, and remedial math, reading, and writing.

Campus Safety and Security: Measures include 24-hour foot and vehicle patrol, emergency notification system, self-defense education, and security escort services. There are shuttle buses, emergency telephones, lighted pathways/sidewalks, controlled access to dorms/residences, safety whistles.

Programs of Study: UMF confers B.A., B.S., B.F.A. and B.G.S. degrees. Master's degrees are also awarded. Bachelor's degrees are awarded in AGRICULTURE (environmental studies), BIOLOGICAL SCIENCE (biology/biological science), BUSINESS (business administration and management and business economics), COMMUNICATIONS AND THE ARTS (art, creative writing, English, media arts, and visual and performing arts), COMPUTER AND PHYSICAL SCIENCE (actuarial science, computer science, geology, and mathematics), EDUCATION (early childhood education, elementary education, health education, health information management, secondary education, and special education), ENGINEERING AND ENVIRONMENTAL DESIGN (environmental science), HEALTH PROFESSIONS (community health work and rehabilitation therapy), SOCIAL SCIENCE (geography, history, interdisciplinary studies, international studies, liberal arts/general studies, philosophy and religion, political science/government, psychology, and sociology). Creative writing, English, psychology, history, special education, early childhood education, secondary education, and elementary education are the strongest academically. Elementary education, secondary education, and psychology have the largest enrollments.

Required: All students must maintain a minimum GPA of 2.0 while earning 128 semester hours, including 40 or more credits in their majors. Core requirements include First-Year Seminar, English composition, mathematics, natural sciences, social sciences, humanities, fine arts and a physical activity requirement.

Special: Many opportunities for travel courses to countries such as Costa Rica, Italy, St. Johns, Ireland, Argentina, Spain and more. Semester-long study abroad programs in China or France are available, as well as numerous other countries through co-operative arrangements with other universities. Also opportunities to participate in the National Student Exchange program. Student teaching is required of all education majors. Internships are required in rehabilitation and health and are also available in other disciplines under the sponsorship of the Partnership for Civic Advancement. There are multiple opportunities for student employment, including positions funded by the President's Work Initiative which aren available to all students. Individualized student-designed majors are available and encouraged. There are 2 national honor societies, a freshman honors program, and 9 departmental honors programs.

Faculty/Classroom: 40% of faculty are male; 60% are female. All teach undergraduates, 80% do research, and 80% do both. No introductory courses are taught by graduate students. The average class size in an introductory lecture is 39; in a laboratory is 17; and in a regular course is 17.

Admissions: 84% of the 2013-2014 applicants were accepted. The SAT scores for the 2013-2014 freshman class were: Critical Reading--44% below 500, 34% between 500 and 599, 19% between 600 and 699, and 3% between 700 and 800; Math--50% below 500, 37% between 500 and 599, 12% between 600 and 699, and 1% between 700 and 800; Writing--50% below 500, 34% between 500 and 599, 15% between 600 and 699, and 1% between 700 and 800. 33% of the current freshmen were in the top fifth of their class; 65% were in the top two fifths. 3 freshmen graduated first in their class.

Requirements: Applicants are required to have 4 credits in English, 3 in math, 3 sciences (2 that are labs), and 3 in social sciences. An essay and a counselor recommendation are required, and an interview is recommended for some. The GED is accepted for highly motivated students. AP credits are accepted. Important factors in the admissions decision are advanced placement or honors courses, recommendations by school officials, and extracurricular activities record.

Procedure: Freshmen are admitted fall and spring. There are early admissions, deferred admissions, and rolling admissions plans. Application deadlines are open. Application fee is $40. Notification of early decision is sent December 15; regular decision, on a rolling basis. Applications are accepted online.

Transfer: 169 transfer students enrolled in 2012-2013. Applicants must have a minimum GPA of 2.0 (2.5 for some majors). Submission of passing Praxis I, or Praxis Core, scores are required of all students seeking transfer into teacher education programs leading to certification. 32 of 128 credits required for the bachelor's degree must be completed at UMF.

Visiting: There are regularly scheduled orientations for prospective students, sessions on financial aid, majors, student life, the admissions process, and special opportunities such as study abroad, and tours of the campus. There are guides for informal visits and visitors may sit in on classes. To schedule a visit, contact Jamie Marcus at (207) 778-7086.

Financial Aid: In 2013-2014, 97% of all full-time freshmen and 93% of continuing full-time students received some form of financial aid. 89% of all full-time freshmen and 83% of continuing full-time students received need-based aid. The average freshman award was $14,869. Need-based scholarships or need-based grants averaged $6,713; need-based self-help aid (loans and jobs) averaged $4,054; other non-need-based awards and non-need-based scholarships averaged $2,959; and $1,143 from other forms of aid. 38% of undergraduate students work part-time. Average annual earnings from campus work are $1868. The average financial indebtedness of the 2013 graduate was $28,156. The FAFSA is required. The priority date for freshman financial aid applications for fall entry is March 1. The deadline for filing freshman financial aid applications for fall entry is May 1.

International Students: There are 12 international students enrolled. The school actively recruits these students. They must take the TOEFL with a minimum score of 550 on the paper-based TOEFL (PBT) or 79 on the Internet-based version (iBT), IELTS. The SAT is optional for admittance, but recommended for placement of matriculating first-year students.

Graduates: From July 1, 2012 to June 30, 2013, 422 bachelor's degrees were awarded. The most popular majors were education (37%), rehabilitation/health services (14%), and creative writing/English (9%). 41 companies recruited on campus in 2012-2013. In an average class, 41% graduate in 4 years or less, 56% graduate in 5 years or less, and 58% graduate in 6 years or less.

Admissions Contact: Jamie Marcus, Director of Admissions. E-Mail: *umfadmit@maine.edu* Web: *www.umf.maine.edu*

UNIVERSITY OF MAINE AT FORT KENT D-1

Fort Kent, ME 04743	**(207) 834-7600 ext. 7602** **(888) TRY-UMFK; (207) 834-7609**
Full-time: 222 men, 388 women	**Faculty:** 36; IIB, --$
Part-time: 213 men, 346 women	**Ph.D.s:** 80%
Graduate: n/av	**Student/Faculty:** 25 to 1
Year: semesters, summer session	**Tuition:** $7575 ($17,535)
Application Deadline: open	**Room & Board:** $7400
Freshman Class: 561 applied, 318 accepted, 181 enrolled	
SAT CR/M/W: 450/450/440 **ACT:** 18	**LESS COMPETITIVE**

The University of Maine at Fort Kent, founded in 1878, is a publicly funded liberal arts institution within the University of Maine system. There are 7 undergraduate schools and 2 graduate schools. The library contains 49,000 volumes, and 2,300 audio/video tapes/CDs/DVDs, and subscribes to 43,600 periodicals including electronic. Computerized library services include interlibrary loans, database searching, and Internet access. Special learning facilities include a The 52-acre campus is in a small town 200 miles north of Bangor. Including any residence halls, there are 16 buildings.

Student Life: 87% of undergraduates are from Maine. Others are from 23 states, 11 foreign countries, and Canada. 98% are from public schools. 76% are White. The average age of freshmen is 22; all undergraduates, 26. 34% do not continue beyond their first year; 42% remain to graduate.

Housing: 225 students can be accommodated in college housing, which includes coed dorms. On-campus housing is guaranteed for all 4 years. 80% of students commute. All students may keep cars.

Activities: 1% of men belong to 1 national fraternity; 2% of women belong to 1 national sorority. There are 15 groups on campus, including cheerleading, computers, drama, environmental, international, literary magazine, musical theater, newspaper, Nontraditional Students, professional, religious, and student government. Popular campus events include French Heritage Festival, Spring Meltdown and Winter Carnival.

Sports: There are 2 intercollegiate sports for men and 2 for women, and 4 intramural sports for men and 4 for women. Facilities include an 11,500-square-foot gym, racquetball courts, soccer field, weight room, cardiovascular room, intramural fields, and game rooms in the residence halls.

Disabled Students: 90% of the campus is accessible. Facilities include wheelchair ramps, elevators, special parking, specially equipped restrooms, special class scheduling, and special housing.

Services: Counseling and information services are available, as is tutoring in every subject. There is a reader service for the blind, and remedial math, reading, and writing.

Campus Safety and Security: There are lighted pathways/sidewalks, and night watchmen 11 p.m. to 7 a.m.

Programs of Study: UMFK confers B.A., B.S., B.S.E.S, B.S.N. and B.U.S. degrees. Associate degrees are also awarded. Bachelor's degrees are awarded in AGRICULTURE (forestry and related sciences), BIOLOGI-

CAL SCIENCE (biology/biological science), BUSINESS (business administration and management), COMMUNICATIONS AND THE ARTS (English and French), COMPUTER AND PHYSICAL SCIENCE (computer science), EDUCATION (elementary education and secondary education), ENGINEERING AND ENVIRONMENTAL DESIGN (environmental science), HEALTH PROFESSIONS (nursing), SOCIAL SCIENCE (behavioral science, criminal justice, liberal arts/general studies, and social science). Environmental studies, nursing and biology are the strongest academically. Nursing and business management have the largest enrollments.

Required: A minimum GPA of 2.0 and a total of 120 credit hours (2.5 GPA and 127 credit hours for nursing, 128 credit hours for business management) are required for graduation. Curricula and distribution requirements vary by major.

Special: Internships are required for business majors, nursing (clinicals), social sciences, public safety administration, and education (student teaching). A general studies degree, a B.A.-B.S. degree in bilingual-bicultural studies, credit for life experience, nondegree study, and an accelerated nursing program are available. Students may cross-register with the College Universitaire St. Louis Maillet in New Brunswick. Study abroad may be arranged in Canada, France, and Mexico through the University of Maine at Farmington. Interactive TV courses broadcast from other universities are available on campus. There is a freshman honors program.

Faculty/Classroom: 53% of faculty are male; 47% are female. 85% teach undergraduates, and 15% do both. No introductory courses are taught by graduate students. The average class size in an introductory lecture is 20; in a laboratory is 13; and in a regular course is 18.

Admissions: 57% of the 2013-2014 applicants were accepted. The SAT scores for the 2013-2014 freshman class were: Critical Reading--73% below 500, 25% between 500 and 599, 2% between 600 and 699; Math--75% below 500, 23% between 500 and 599, 2% between 600 and 699; Writing--78% below 500, 19% between 500 and 599, 3% between 600 and 699. The ACT scores were 64% below 21, 27% between 21 and 23, 9% between 24 and 26. 20% of the current freshmen were in the top fifth of their class; 54% were in the top two fifths.

Requirements: The SAT is recommended. Applicants should be graduates of an accredited secondary school. The GED is accepted. Required secondary school courses include 4 years of English and 2 each of social studies, math, and lab science. A foreign language is suggested. An essay and an interview are recommended. A GPA of 2.0 is required. AP and CLEP credits are accepted. Important factors in the admissions decision are recommendations by school officials, advanced placement or honors courses, and evidence of special talent.

Procedure: Freshmen are admitted fall and spring. Entrance exams should be taken before March of the senior year. There is a rolling admissions plan. Application deadlines are open. Application fee is $40. Notification is sent on a rolling basis. Applications are accepted online.

Transfer: 130 transfer students enrolled in 2012-2013. Applicants must submit transcripts from each college and secondary school attended. The SAT and an interview are recommended. 30 of 120 credits required for the bachelor's degree must be completed at UMFK.

Visiting: There are regularly scheduled orientations for prospective students, including placement testing, meetings with advisers, campus tours, and get-aquainted activities. There are guides for informal visits and visitors may sit in on classes. To schedule a visit, contact Brenda Plourde at (207) 834-7866.

Financial Aid: In 2013-2014, 88% of all full-time freshmen and 53% of continuing full-time students received some form of financial aid. 82% of all full-time freshmen and 80% of continuing full-time students received need-based aid. 75% of undergraduate students work part-time. Average annual earnings from campus work are $1500. The FAFSA, and and income tax forms is required. The deadline for filing freshman financial aid applications for fall entry is March 1.

International Students: There are 66 international students enrolled. The school actively recruits these students. They must take the TOEFL with a minimum score of 500 on the paper-based TOEFL (PBT). The SAT scores may be submitted in place of the TOEFL.

Computers: All students may access the system from 8 a.m. to 11 p.m. in the library and computer centers, and 24 hours a day in the dorms. There are no time limits. The fee is $5.

Graduates: From July 1, 2012 to June 30, 2013, 212 bachelor's degrees were awarded. The most popular majors were nursing (47%), education (15%), and business (10%). 7 companies recruited on campus in 2012-2013. In an average class, 20% graduate in 4 years or less, 18% graduate in 5 years or less, and 3% graduate in 6 years or less. Of the 2012 graduating class, 3% were enrolled in graduate school within 6 months of graduation, and 90% were employed.

Admissions Contact: Jill Cairns, Director of Admissions. E-Mail: *jillb@maine.edu* Web: *www.umfk.maine.edu*

UNIVERSITY OF MAINE AT MACHIAS — E-4

Machias, ME 04654 (207) 255-1318
(888) 468-6866; (207) 255-1363

Full-time: 200 men, 300 women	**Faculty:** 31; IIB, --$
Part-time: 145 men, 542 women	**Ph.D.s:** 71%
Graduate: n/av	**Student/Faculty:** 15 to 1
Year: semesters, summer session	**Tuition:** $8000 ($19,000)
Application Deadline: open	**Room & Board:** $8000
Freshman Class: 374 applied, 312 accepted, 120 enrolled	
SAT: required **ACT:** 22	**COMPETITIVE**

The University of Maine at Machias, founded in 1909, is a publicly funded liberal arts institution in the University of Maine system. In addition to regional accreditation, UMM has baccalaureate program accreditation with NRPA. The library contains 82,000 volumes, 5,000 microform items, and 3,000 audio/video tapes/CDs/DVDs, and subscribes to 320 periodicals including electronic. Computerized library services include interlibrary loans, database searching, and Internet access. Special learning facilities include an art gallery, radio station, aquariums for marine and aquaculture studies. The 42-acre campus is in a rural area 85 miles east of Bangor. Including any residence halls, there are 8 buildings.

Student Life: 82% of undergraduates are from Maine. Others are from 26 states, 16 foreign countries, and Canada. 98% are from public schools. 90% are White. The average age of freshmen is 20; all undergraduates, 29. 28% do not continue beyond their first year; 45% remain to graduate.

Housing: 353 students can be accommodated in college housing, which includes single-sex and coed dorms. On-campus housing is guaranteed for all 4 years. 76% of students commute. All students may keep cars.

Activities: 7% of men belong to 2 local and 2 national fraternities; 3% of women belong to 1 local and 3 national sororities. There are 34 groups on campus, including pop band, art, cheerleading, chorale, chorus, communications, computers, dance, drama, gay, honors, international, literary magazine, musical theater, outing club, pep band, photography, professional, radio and TV, religious, social service, and student government. Popular campus events include Winter Carnival, Spring Weekend, and Family Weekend.

Sports: There are 3 intercollegiate sports for men and 4 for women, and 10 intramural sports for men and 10 for women. Facilities include 2 gyms, weight/exercise rooms, handball/raquetball courts, a pool, and a 64-acre recreational center with a lodge and cabins on the lake.

Disabled Students: 85% of the campus is accessible. Facilities include wheelchair ramps, elevators, special parking, specially equipped restrooms, lowered drinking fountains, and automatic doors.

Services: Counseling and information services are available, as is tutoring in every subject. There is remedial math, reading, and writing. The Student Resource Coordinator provides one-on-one services, including learning strategies, study skills, and assistance with papers and learning styles.

Campus Safety and Security: Measures include self-defense education and security escort services. There are lighted pathways/sidewalks, a keyless entry system for residence halls, and security patrol from 5 p.m. to 5 a.m. daily.

Programs of Study: UMM confers B.A., B.S. and B.C.S. degrees. Bachelor's degrees are awarded in BIOLOGICAL SCIENCE (biology/biological science and marine biology), BUSINESS (accounting, business administration and management, marketing/retailing/merchandising, and recreation and leisure services), COMMUNICATIONS AND THE ARTS (English and fine arts), EDUCATION (business education and elementary education), ENGINEERING AND ENVIRONMENTAL DESIGN (environmental science), SOCIAL SCIENCE (behavioral science, history, human services, and liberal arts/general studies). Elementary education, marine biology, and environmental studies are the strongest academically. Elementary education, business administration, and behavioral science are the largest.

Required: To graduate, students must complete a minimum of 120 credit hours with a GPA of 2.0. The core curriculum consists of 40-43 hours in the areas of communication skills, science and math, humans in social context, fine arts, historical and cultural perspectives, and lifetime fitness.

Special: Co-op programs in all majors except education, cross-registration, internships, work-study programs, a B.A.-B.S. degree, study abroad in England and Wales, and a student designed concentration in environmental science are available. UMM also offers a Bachelor of College Studies program, credit for prior learning, nondegree study, and a pass/fail option in certain courses. There is a freshman honors program.

Faculty/Classroom: 54% of faculty are male; 46% are female. All teach undergraduates. No introductory courses are taught by graduate students. The average class size in an introductory lecture is 21; in a laboratory is 16; and in a regular course is 17.

Admissions: 83% of the 2013-2014 applicants were accepted. The ACT scores were 43% below 21, 14% between 21 and 23, 29% between 24 and 26, 7% between 27 and 28, and 7% above 28. 23% of the current freshmen were in the top fifth of their class; 53% were in the top two fifths.

Requirements: The SAT or ACT is required. All candidates must be graduates of an accredited secondary school, although the GED is accepted. UMM recommends that students place in the top half of their graduating class and that composite SAT scores be satisfactory. UMM also recommends completion of 4 units of English, 3 of math, 2 each of lab science, social science/history, and fine arts or foreign language, and 3 of electives. An essay is required and an interview is strongly recommended. UMM requires applicants to be in the upper 50% of their class. A GPA of 2.0 is required. AP and CLEP credits are accepted. Important factors in the admissions decision are extracurricular activities record, leadership record, and recommendations by school officials.

Procedure: Freshmen are admitted fall, spring, and summer. There are early admissions, deferred admissions, and rolling admissions plans. Application deadlines are open. Application fee is $40. Notification is sent on a rolling basis. Applications are accepted online.

Transfer: 36 transfer students enrolled in 2012-2013. A minimum college GPA of 2.0 and evidence of good standing are required of transfer applicants. 30 of 120 credits required for the bachelor's degree must be completed at UMM.

Visiting: There are regularly scheduled orientations for prospective students, consisting of traditional orientations prior to the fall and spring semesters, which include programming to guide students in all aspects of starting college—academic, student services and activities, and administrative. UMM also offers two summer student orientations, which include aspects of the fall orientations plus a parent orientation. There are guides for informal visits and visitors may sit in on classes.

Financial Aid: In 2013-2014, 88% of all full-time freshmen and 80% of continuing full-time students received some form of financial aid. 78% of all full-time freshmen and 82% of continuing full-time students received need-based aid. The average freshman award was $8,488. Need-based scholarships or need-based grants averaged $5,884 ; need-based self-help aid (loans and jobs) averaged $3,439; and other non-need-based awards and non-need-based scholarships averaged $6,420. The FAFSA is required. The deadline for filing freshman financial aid applications for fall entry is March 1.

International Students: There are 50 international students enrolled. The school actively recruits these students. They must take the TOEFL. They must also take the SAT or ACT.

Graduates: From July 1, 2012 to June 30, 2013, 100 bachelor's degrees were awarded. The most popular majors were behavioral science (15%), business administration (13%), and recreation management (13%). 10 companies recruited on campus in 2012-2013. In an average class, 19% graduate in 4 years or less, 42% graduate in 5 years or less, and 46% graduate in 6 years or less.

Admissions Contact: Sarah Guancial, Admissions Counselor. E-Mail: *ummadmissions@maine.edu* Web: *www.umm.maine.edu*

UNIVERSITY OF MAINE AT PRESQUE ISLE — D-2

Presque Isle, ME 04769 — **(207) 768-9453; (207) 768-9777**

Full-time: 400 men, 700 women	**Faculty:** 54; IIB, --$
Part-time: 119 men, 317 women	**Ph.D.s:** 56%
Graduate: n/av	**Student/Faculty:** 21 to 1
Year: semesters, summer session	**Tuition:** $7435 ($17,395)
Application Deadline:	**Room & Board:** $7576

Freshman Class: 483 applied, 417 accepted, 212 enrolled

LESS COMPETITIVE

The University of Maine at Presque Isle, founded in 1903, is a public institution within the University of Maine system offering liberal arts, teacher education, and professional programs leading to post-secondary certificates, associate and bachelor's degrees. There are 3 undergraduate schools. In addition to regional accreditation, UMPI has baccalaureate program accreditation with CSWE. The library contains 75,000 volumes, 750,000 microform items, and 1,400 audio/video tapes/CDs/DVDs, and subscribes to 2,000 periodicals including electronic. Computerized library services include interlibrary loans, database searching, and Internet access. Special learning facilities include an art gallery, natural history museum, radio station, a theater. The 150-acre campus is in a rural area 150 miles north of Bangor. Including any residence halls, there are 15 buildings.

Student Life: 73% of undergraduates are from Maine. Others are from 14 states, 5 foreign countries, and Canada. 67% are White. The average age of freshmen is 20; all undergraduates, 26. 45% do not continue beyond their first year; 28% remain to graduate.

Housing: 359 students can be accommodated in college housing, which includes coed dorms, off-campus apartments, and married student housing. On-campus housing is guaranteed for all 4 years. 78% of students commute. All students may keep cars.

Activities: 2% of men belong to 1 national fraternity; 1% of women belong to 1 national sorority. There are 25 groups on campus, including activities board, and diversity club., non-traditional students club, A Cappella group, art, band, chess, communications, drama, environmental, ethnic, gay, honors, international, literary magazine, newspaper, professional, radio and TV, religious, social, social service, and student government. Popular campus events include Spring Ball, Winter Blast, and Spring Fest.

Sports: There are 6 intercollegiate sports for men and 6 for women, and 15 intramural sports for men and 15 for women. Facilities include a facility that houses a swimming pool, gymnasium, track, fitness room and climbing wall. Another a multifunctional structure that houses a gym, a weight room, phys ed labs, a sports medicine facility, Athletic Hall of Fame, and an auditorium. A large playing field contains baseball, soccer, and tennis courts. There are also hiking trails, a bike path, and a ropes course. The campus also hosts a club ice hockey team.

Disabled Students: All of the campus is accessible. Facilities include wheelchair ramps, elevators, special parking, specially equipped restrooms, special class scheduling, lowered drinking fountains, and lowered telephones.

Services: Counseling and information services are available, as is tutoring in most subjects. There is remedial math, reading, and writing.

Campus Safety and Security: Measures include security escort services. There are lighted pathways/sidewalks.

Programs of Study: UMPI confers B.A., B.S., B.A.A.E., B.F.A., B.L.S. and B.S.W. degrees. Associate degrees are also awarded. Bachelor's degrees are awarded in BIOLOGICAL SCIENCE (biology/biological science), BUSINESS (accounting, business administration and management, and recreation and leisure services), COMMUNICATIONS AND THE ARTS (applied art, art, and English), EDUCATION (art education, athletic training, elementary education, health education, physical education, and secondary education), ENGINEERING AND ENVIRONMENTAL DESIGN (environmental science), SOCIAL SCIENCE (criminal justice, international studies, liberal arts/general studies, and social work). Education, social work, and criminal justice have the largest enrollments.

Required: Core requirements for the B.A. degrees include 18 credits in humanities, 12 in social science, 11 in math/science, and 4 in phys ed/health. The student must complete a minimum number of credits, which varies according to major, with a cumulative GPA of 2.0 in 120 to 128 credit hours. Requirements for the B.S. and other degrees vary considerably with each major.

Special: The university participates in transfer programs in agriculture, nutrition science, animal and veterinary science. There is a nursing program with the University of Maine at Fort Kent. There are study-abroad programs in France, Ireland, Canada (other countries are available), and internships in many majors. UM-Presque Isle offers work-study programs, dual and student-designed majors, a B.A.-B.S. degree, and nondegree study. Students can apply for credit by exam and credit for life, military, and work experience. A credit/no credit option is available. There is 1 national honor society, a freshman honors program, and 5 departmental honors programs.

Faculty/Classroom: 56% of faculty are male; 44% are female. All teach undergraduates. No introductory courses are taught by graduate students. The average class size in an introductory lecture is 20; in a laboratory is 12; and in a regular course is 15.

Admissions: 86% of the 2013-2014 applicants were accepted. 16% of the current freshmen were in the top fifth of their class; 38% were in the top two fifths.

Requirements: Applicants should have completed 16 academic credits at an accredited secondary school, including 4 in English, 3 each in math, and social studies, and 2 each in science with a lab, foreign language, and electives. A GED certificate may be substituted. The university recommends an essay and an interview for all candidates. Art majors must submit a portfolio. AP and CLEP credits are accepted. Important factors in the admissions decision are advanced placement or honors courses, recommendations by school officials, and extracurricular activities record.

Procedure: Freshmen are admitted fall, spring, and summer. Entrance exams should be taken by January 1. There are early decision, deferred admissions, and rolling admissions plans. Application deadlines are open. The fall 2013 application fee was $40. Applications are accepted online.

Transfer: 203 transfer students enrolled in 2012-2013. Applicants must have a 2.0 GPA from a regionally accredited two or four year college. Applicants must submit official transcripts from all colleges attended, along with an official ranscript from the high school from which they graduated. 30 of 120 credits required for the bachelor's degree must be completed at UMPI.

Visiting: There are regularly scheduled orientations for prospective students, including advisement, a campus tour, and meetings with faculty and coaches. There are guides for informal visits, visitors may sit in on classes, and stay overnight.

Financial Aid: In 2013-2014, 74% of all full-time freshmen and 79% of continuing full-time students received some form of financial aid. 89% of all full-time freshmen and 89% of continuing full-time students received need-based aid. The average freshman award was $6,790. Need-based scholarships or need-based grants averaged $5,287; need-based self-help aid (loans and jobs) averaged $3,095; and $4,389 from other forms of aid. The average financial indebtedness of the 2013 graduate was $5,193. The FAFSA is required. The deadline for filing freshman financial aid applications for fall entry is April 1.

International Students: There are 368 international students enrolled. The school actively recruits these students. They must take the TOEFL.

Graduates: From July 1, 2012 to June 30, 2013, 300 bachelor's degrees were awarded. The most popular majors were liberal arts/general studies (45%), education (18%), and business management and administrative (8%). 35 companies recruited on campus in 2012-2013. In an average class, 7% graduate in 4 years or less, 21% graduate in 5 years or less, and 28% graduate in 6 years or less. Of the 2012 graduating class, 7% were enrolled in graduate school within 6 months of graduation.

Admissions Contact: Erin V. Benson, Director of Enrollment Management and University Relations. E-Mail: *adventure@umpi.maine.edu* Web: *www.umpi.maine.edu*

UNIVERSITY OF NEW ENGLAND B-6

Biddeford, ME 04005 **1-800-477-4863**
(800) 477-4863; 207-602-4900

Full-time: 632 men, 1522 women	**Faculty:** n/av
Part-time: 10 men, 15 women	**Ph.D.s:** n/av
Graduate: 902 men, 2448 women	**Student/Faculty:** n/av
Year: semesters, summer session	**Tuition:** $33,145
Application Deadline: February 15	**Room & Board:** $13,000

Freshman Class: 4231 applied, 3632 accepted, 633 enrolled
SAT CR/M: 522/536 **ACT:** 24 **COMPETITIVE+**

The University of New England (UNE) is an innovative health sciences university grounded in the liberal arts, with two distinctive coastal Maine campuses and unique study abroad opportunities. UNE has internationally recognized scholars in the sciences, health, medicine and humanities; offers more than 40 undergraduate, graduate and professional degree programs; and is home to Maine's only medical school. It is one of a handful of private universities with a comprehensive health education mission including medicine, pharmacy, dental medicine, nursing and an array of allied health professions. UNE's interprofessional education initiatives prepare future healthcare professionals to practice comprehensive and collaborative team-based care. Both graduate and undergraduate students engage in research and scholarship alongside dedicated faculty who are committed to their academic and professional success. There are 2 undergraduate schools and 6 graduate schools. In addition to regional accreditation, UNE has baccalaureate program accreditation with ACBSP, ADA, APTA, CSWE, and NLN. The 2 libraries contain 135,000 volumes. Computerized library services include interlibrary loans, database searching, Internet access, and Wi-Fi capability. Special learning facilities include an art gallery, Marine Science Education Center. The main 623-acre campus is in a small town on the banks of the Saco River and the shore of the Atlantic Ocean in Biddeford, ME. Including any residence halls, there are 51 buildings.

Student Life: 66% of undergraduates are from out of state, mostly the Northeast. Students are from 38 states, 8 foreign countries, and Canada. 70% are White; 17% race unknown. The average age of freshmen is 18; all undergraduates, 20. 26% do not continue beyond their first year; 74% remain to graduate.

Housing: 1619 students can be accommodated in college housing, which includes single-sex and coed dorms. On-campus housing is guaranteed for the freshman year only. 65% of students live on campus. All students may keep cars.

Activities: There are no fraternities or sororities. There are 73 groups on campus, including art, communications, dance, drama, environmental, ethnic, gay, honors, international, literary magazine, musical theater, newspaper, pep band, professional, religious, sailing, social, social service, student government, and yearbook. Popular campus events include Welcome Week, Family and Friends Weekend and Full Leadership Retreat.

Sports: There are 6 intercollegiate sports for men and 9 for women, and 10 intramural sports for men and 10 for women. Facilities include The Harold Alfond Forum is a 106,500-square foot state-of-the-art facility that includes an ice hockey arena, a performance court, and a multi-purpose indoor. Additionally, there is a fitness center, team/locker rooms, two athletic training rooms, administrators/coaches' offices, academic offices, classroom space, meeting space, and a dining area. The Big Blue Turf is a synthetic turf field, which includes bleacher seating for 550 spectators, competition lighting, a press box, and state-of-the-art scoreboard. The Campus Center houses a gym, indoor track, fitness center, six-lane pool, lockers rooms, hot tub, saunas, campus bookstore, a racquetball court, The Hang (snack shop), and three multi-purpose rooms.

Disabled Students: 85% of the campus is accessible. Facilities include wheelchair ramps, elevators, special parking, specially equipped restrooms, special class scheduling, lowered drinking fountains, lowered telephones, special housing.

Services: Counseling and information services are available, as is tutoring in most subjects. There is a reader service for the blind, and remedial math, reading, and writing.

Campus Safety and Security: Measures include 24-hour foot and vehicle patrol, emergency notification system, self-defense education, and security escort services. There are shuttle buses, emergency telephones, lighted pathways/sidewalks, controlled access to dorms/residences, a safe-ride program provides drivers for students.

Programs of Study: UNE confers B.A., B.S. and B.S.N. degrees. Master's and doctoral degrees are also awarded. Bachelor's degrees are awarded in AGRICULTURE (animal science and environmental studies), BIOLOGICAL SCIENCE (biochemistry, biology/biological science, marine biology, and marine science), BUSINESS (business administration and management and sports management), COMMUNICATIONS AND THE ARTS (communications and English), COMPUTER AND PHYSICAL SCIENCE (chemistry and mathematics), EDUCATION (art education, athletic training, education, elementary education, and secondary education), ENGINEERING AND ENVIRONMENTAL DESIGN (environmental science), HEALTH PROFESSIONS (biomedical science, dental hygiene, exercise science, health care administration, health science, nursing, occupational therapy, premedicine, prepharmacy, and preventive/wellness health care), SOCIAL SCIENCE (history, liberal arts/general studies, philosophy, political science/government, psychobiology, psychology, social science, and sociology). Medical biology, nursing and marine science have the largest enrollments.

Required: A total of at least 120 credits with a minimum GPA of 2.0 is required for graduation. Some programs require more than 120 credits. Students must take 43 credits in a liberal arts core curriculum of humanities, sciences, and social sciences. Most majors require 1-semester internships. Courses in English composition, human traditions,environmental studies, lab science, creative arts, and math are required.

Special: UNE offers cross-registration with the Greater Portland Alliance of Colleges and Universities, internships in all majors, work-study programs, study abroad, dual majors in all departments, a 3-4 medical program, and a 3-2 pre-physician assistant program. There are 2 national honor societies.

Faculty/Classroom: 42% of faculty are male; 58% are female. 46% teach undergraduates. No introductory courses are taught by graduate students. The average class size in an introductory lecture is 24 and in a laboratory is 21.

Admissions: 86% of the 2013-2014 applicants were accepted. The SAT scores for the 2013-2014 freshman class were: Critical Reading--37% below 500, 49% between 500 and 599, 13% between 600 and 699, and 1% between 700 and 800; Math--30% below 500, 51% between 500 and 599, 17% between 600 and 699, and 1% between 700 and 800. The ACT scores were 17% below 21, 35% between 21 and 23, 31% between 24 and 26, 13% between 27 and 28, and 7% above 28.

Requirements: The SAT or ACT is required. Applicants should be high school graduates with 4 years of English, 3 years each of math and science, and 2 years each of history and social studies. The GED is accepted. SAT OR ACT scores are required (students do not need to submit scores from both exams.) AP and CLEP credits are accepted. Important factors in the admissions decision are advanced placement or honors courses, recommendations by school officials, and leadership record.

Procedure: Freshmen are admitted fall and spring. Entrance exams should be taken in the spring of the junior year or the fall of the senior year. There are early decision and deferred admissions plans. Early decision applications should be filed by December 1; regular applications, by February 15 for fall entry; and December 1 for spring entry, along with a $40 fee. Notification is sent on a rolling basis. Applications are accepted online.

Transfer: 122 transfer students enrolled in 2012-2013. Transfer applicants should present a GPA of at least 2.5 in prior college work. 30 of 120 credits required for the bachelor's degree must be completed at UNE.

Visiting: There are regularly scheduled orientations for prospective students, includes a tour and information session. There are guides for informal visits and visitors may sit in on classes. To schedule a visit, contact the Office of Undergraduate Admissions.

Financial Aid: In 2013-2014, 100% of all full-time freshmen and 70% of continuing full-time students received some form of financial aid. 88% of all full-time freshmen and 60% of continuing full-time students received need-based aid. The FAFSA is required. The deadline for filing freshman financial aid applications for fall entry is May 1.

International Students: There are 14 international students enrolled. They must take the TOEFL with a minimum score of 550 on the paper-based TOEFL (PBT) or 79 on the Internet-based version (iBT).

Graduates: From July 1, 2012 to June 30, 2013, 459 bachelor's degrees were awarded. The most popular majors were medical biology (13%), applied exercise science (11%), and health science/occupational studies (9%). In an average class, 49% graduate in 4 years or less, 57% graduate in 5 years or less, and 58% graduate in 6 years or less.

Admissions Contact: Cynthia Forrest, Vice President of Student Affairs. E-Mail: *admissions@une.edu* Web: *www.une.edu*

UNIVERSITY OF SOUTHERN MAINE A-5

Gorham, ME 04038-1088 (207) 780-5670
(800) 800-4876; (207) 780-5640

Full-time: 2200 men, 2700 women	**Faculty:** n/av
Part-time: 1200 men, 1700 women	**Ph.D.s:** 74%
Graduate: 700 men, 1500 women	**Student/Faculty:** n/av
Year: semesters, summer session	**Tuition:** $8500
Application Deadline: February 15	**Room & Board:** $9500
Freshman Class: n/av	
SAT or ACT: required	

COMPETITIVE

The University of Southern Maine, founded in 1878, is a publicly funded, multi-campus, comprehensive, residential, liberal arts institution serving the University of Maine system. The figures in the above capsule and in this profile are approximate. There are 5 undergraduate schools and 8 graduate schools. In addition to regional accreditation, USM has baccalaureate program accreditation with AACSB, ABET, CSAB, CSWE, NASM, NCATE, NLN, and NRPA. The 3 libraries contain 455,129 volumes, 731,755 microform items, and 5,288 audio/video tapes/CDs/DVDs, and subscribe to 3,219 periodicals including electronic. Computerized library services include interlibrary loans and database searching. Special learning facilities include a learning resource center, art gallery, planetarium, radio station, TV station, and cartography collections. The 144-acre campus is in an urban area 110 miles north of Boston, MA. Including any residence halls, there are 66 buildings.

Student Life: 90% of undergraduates are from Maine. Students are from 35 states, 27 foreign countries, and Canada. 97% are white. The average age of freshmen is 19; all undergraduates, 25.

Housing: 1835 students can be accommodated in college housing, which includes coed dorms, on-campus apartments, and married student housing. In addition, there are honors houses, special-interest houses, a fine arts house. On-campus housing is guaranteed for all 4 years. 81% of students commute. All students may keep cars.

Activities: 2% of men belong to 1 local and 3 national fraternities; 2% of women belong to 2 local and 2 national sororities. There are 100 groups on campus, including ski, commuter, environmental, art, band, cheerleading, chess, choir, chorale, chorus, computers, dance, drama, ethnic, gay, honors, international, jazz band, literary magazine, musical theater, opera, orchestra, outing, photography, political, professional, religious, social, social service, and student government. Popular campus events include Winter Weekend, Spring Fling, and comedy nights.

Sports: There are 12 intercollegiate sports for men and 13 for women, and 14 intramural sports for men and 14 for women. Facilities include gyms, tennis courts, athletic fields, racquetball and squash courts, cross-country ski trails, two weight-training and fitness facilities, an ice arena, a field house, and an indoor track.

Disabled Students: All of the campus is accessible. Facilities include wheelchair ramps, elevators, special parking, specially equipped restrooms, special class scheduling, lowered drinking fountains, and lowered telephones.

Services: Counseling and information services are available, as is tutoring in most subjects. There is a reader service for the blind, and remedial math, reading, and writing.

Campus Safety and Security: Measures include 24-hour foot and vehicle patrol, self-defense education, and security escort services. There are shuttle buses, emergency telephones, lighted pathways/sidewalks, and preventive programs within residence halls.

Programs of Study: USM confers B.A., B.S., B.F.A., and B.M. degrees. Associate, master's, and doctoral degrees are also awarded. Bachelor's degrees are awarded in BIOLOGICAL SCIENCE (biology/biological science), BUSINESS (accounting and business administration and management), COMMUNICATIONS AND THE ARTS (communications, dramatic arts, English, fine arts, French, music, and music performance), COMPUTER AND PHYSICAL SCIENCE (chemistry, computer science, geology, geoscience, mathematics, and physics), EDUCATION (music education and technical education), ENGINEERING AND ENVIRONMENTAL DESIGN (electrical/electronics engineering, environmental science, and industrial engineering technology), HEALTH PROFESSIONS (environmental health science, health science, nursing, recreation therapy, and sports medicine), SOCIAL SCIENCE (anthropology, economics, geography, history, philosophy, political science/government, psychology, social work, sociology, and women's studies). Electrical engineering, computer science, and nursing are the strongest academically. Business administration, nursing, and psychology have the largest enrollments.

Required: A total of 120 hours, of which 36 to 94 are in the major, and a minimum GPA of 2.0 are required for graduation. All students must fulfill the distribution requirements of the 3-part core curriculum: basic competence, methods of inquiry/ways of knowing, and interdisciplinary studies.

Special: Cross-registration within the University of Maine system and 4 Greater Portland colleges, a Washington semester, and study abroad in more than 12 countries are offered. Internships, co-op and work-study programs, a B.A.-B.S. degree, dual and student-designed majors, a 2-2 engineering program with the University of Maine, credit for life experience, nondegree study, and pass/fail options are also available. There is a January intersession. There are 2 national honor societies, a freshman honors program, and 1 departmental honors program.

Faculty/Classroom: 53% of faculty are male; 47% are female. 80% teach undergraduates, all do research, and 80% do both. No introductory courses are taught by graduate students. The average class size in an introductory lecture is 50; in a laboratory is 20; and in a regular course is 22.

Requirements: The SAT or ACT is required. Applicants must be graduates of an accredited secondary school. The GED is accepted. Either 41 academic credits or 20 1/2 Carnegie units are required. Secondary school courses should include 4 years of English, 3 of math, 2 each of a foreign language and lab science, and 1 each of history and social studies. An essay is required, as are auditions for music applicants and interviews for applicants to the School of Applied Science. Guidance counselor recommendations are required for those students applying during their senior year. A GPA of 2.0 is required. AP and CLEP credits are accepted. Important factors in the admissions decision are advanced placement or honors courses, recommendations by school officials, and extracurricular activities record.

Procedure: Freshmen are admitted fall and spring. Entrance exams should be taken by May of the junior year or January of the senior year. There are deferred admissions and rolling admissions plans. February 15 for fall entry. Applications are accepted online. Check with the school for application deadlines.

Transfer: 848 transfer students enrolled in a recent year. Applicants must have a minimum GPA of 2.0 or 2.75 for those from non-regionally accredited institutions. Students who have been out of high school for less than 3 years must submit SAT scores. 30 of 120 credits required for the bachelor's degree must be completed at USM.

Visiting: There are regularly scheduled orientations for prospective students, including regularly scheduled campus tours and group information sessions, as well as special events such as fall open houses. Interviews are also available on request. There are guides for informal visits and visitors may sit in on classes. To schedule a visit, contact the Office of Admission.

Financial Aid: The FAFSA is required. Check with the school for application deadlines.

International Students: They must take the TOEFL.

Graduates: In a recent year, 1101 bachelor's degrees were awarded. The most popular majors were health professions (20%), social sciences (19%), and business (13%).

Admissions Contact: Dean of Undergraduate Admission. E-Mail: *usmadm@maine.maine.edu* Web: *www.usm.maine.edu*

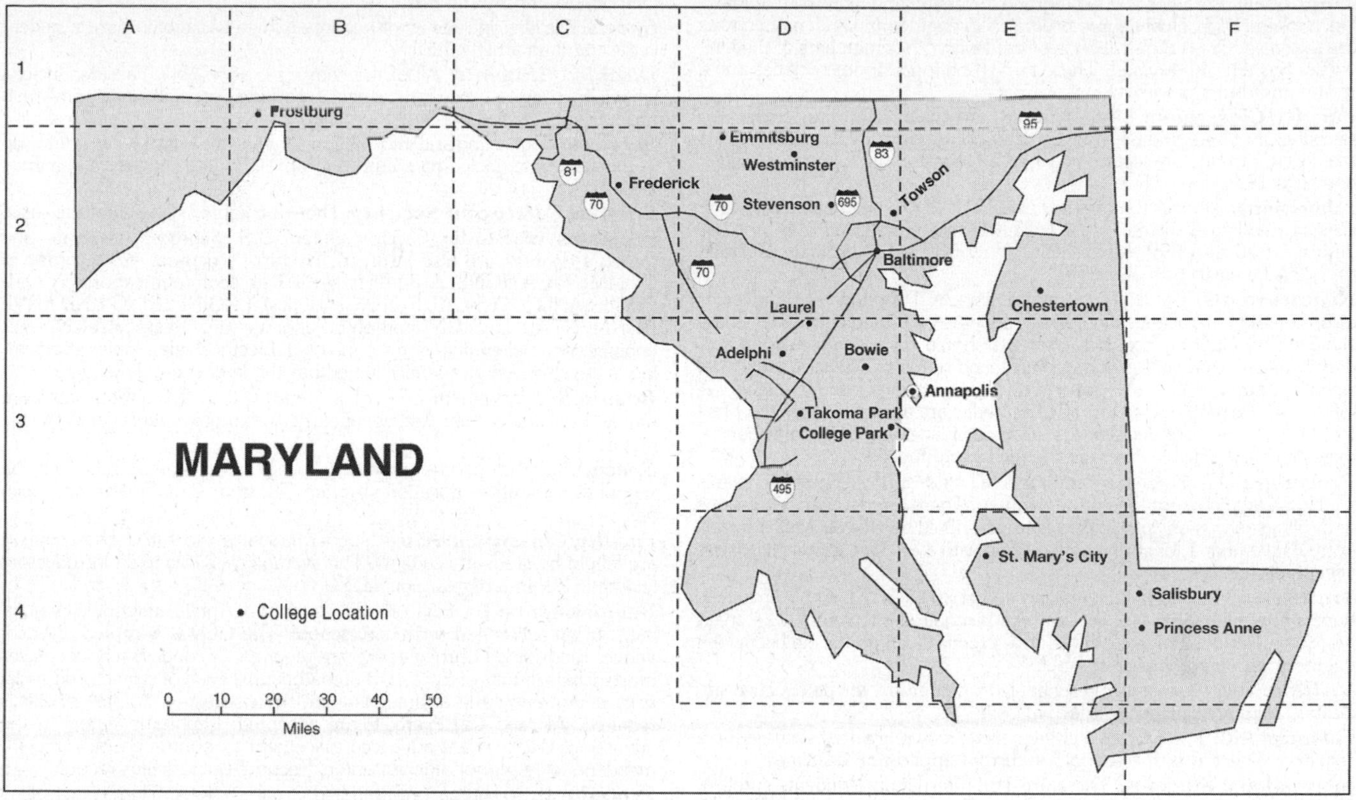

BOWIE STATE UNIVERSITY D-3

Bowie, MD 20715 **(301) 860-3427; (301)860-3438**

Full-time: 1356 men, 2165 women
Part-time: 301 men, 536 women
Graduate: 369 men, 834 women
Year: semesters, summer session
Application Deadline: April 1
Freshman Class: n/av
SAT CR/M/W: 410/400/390
Faculty: 154; IIA, --$
Ph.D.s: 80%
Student/Faculty: 16 to 1
Tuition: $6971 ($17,538)
Room & Board: $10,048

LESS COMPETITIVE

Bowie State University, founded in 1865, is a historically black, publicly supported comprehensive liberal arts institution within the University System of Maryland. There are 4 undergraduate schools and 1 graduate school. In addition to regional accreditation, BSU has baccalaureate program accreditation with ABET, ACBSP, CSAB, NCATE, and NLN. The library contains 245,336 volumes, 428,296 microform items, 6,164 audio/video tapes/CDs/DVDs, and subscribes to 748 periodicals including electronic. Computerized library services include interlibrary loans, database searching, Internet access, and Wi-Fi capability. Special learning facilities include an art gallery, radio station, TV station, media center, and satellite operations and control center. The 295-acre campus is in a suburban area 18 miles north of Washington, D.C. Including any residence halls, there are 26 buildings.

Student Life: 89% of undergraduates are from Maryland. Others are from 27 states, 19 foreign countries, and Canada. 96% are from public schools. 85% are African American. The average age of freshmen is 18; all undergraduates, 24. 20% do not continue beyond their first year; 72% remain to graduate.

Housing: 1400 students can be accommodated in college housing, which includes single-sex and coed dorms and off-campus apartments. In addition, there are honors houses. On-campus housing is available on a first-come and first-served basis. 75% of students commute. Alcohol is not permitted. Upperclassmen may keep cars.

Activities: 3% of men belong to 5 national fraternities; 1% of women belong to 4 national sororities. There are 50 groups on campus, including NAACP and urban league, art, band, cheerleading, choir, chorale, communications, commuter club, computers, dance, drama, drill team, honors, international, jazz band, literary magazine, marching band, musical theater, newspaper, pep band, political, professional, radio and TV, religious, social, social service, student government, and yearbook. Popular campus events include Black History Month Convocation, Parents/Founders Day and Honors Convocation.

Sports: There are 5 intercollegiate sports for men and 8 for women, and 10 intramural sports for men and 10 for women. Facilities include an athletic complex with a basketball arena, an olympic-size pool, 8 handball/racquetball courts, a wrestling room, weight training rooms, a dance studio, a gymnastics room, a 4500-seat football/soccer stadium, a baseball diamond, 6 outdoor tennis courts, 4 outdoor basketball courts, and a track-and-field facility with a walking/jogging lane, and a practice football field.

Disabled Students: All of the campus is accessible. Facilities include wheelchair ramps, elevators, special parking, specially equipped restrooms, lowered drinking fountains, lowered telephones, special housing.

Services: Counseling and information services are available, as is tutoring in most subjects. There is a reader service for the blind, remedial math, reading, and writing.

Campus Safety and Security: Measures include 24-hour foot and vehicle patrol, emergency notification system, self-defense education, and security escort services. There are shuttle buses, emergency telephones, lighted pathways/sidewalks, BEES---Bowie State University Electronic Emergency System---designed as a volunteer service that communicates campus disruptions (in real time) to multiple electronic devices provided by the student. Such events (like inclement weather) are also communicated through land based devices, and the university switch board.

Programs of Study: BSU confers B.A., and B.S. degrees. Master's and doctoral degrees are also awarded. Bachelor's degrees are awarded in BIOLOGICAL SCIENCE (biology/biological science), BUSINESS (business administration and management), COMMUNICATIONS AND THE ARTS (English and fine arts), COMPUTER AND PHYSICAL SCIENCE (computer science and mathematics), EDUCATION (early childhood education, elementary education, and science education), ENGINEERING AND ENVIRONMENTAL DESIGN (computer technology), HEALTH PROFESSIONS (nursing), SOCIAL SCIENCE (criminal justice, history, interdisciplinary studies, psychology, social work, and sociology). Business administration, organizational communication, school counseling, nursing and public administration have the largest enrollments.

Required: A total of 120 credit hours with a minimum GPA of 2.0 is required for graduation. The number of hours that must be taken in a student's major varies. General education requirements include 12 credits in social science, 9 in arts and humanities, 7 to 8 in sciences, 6 in English compositions and 3 each in math, computer literacy, health and wellness, and freshman seminar.

Special: BSU offers cooperative programs, internships in communications and practice teaching, work-study programs, B.A.-B.S. degrees, dual majors, credit for life experience, and a 3-2 engineering degree with Morgan State University, Howard University, University of Maryland Baltimore County, the George Washington University, and University of Maryland College Park. Dual-degree programs in engineering and mathematics are available. Cross-registration is offered with other members of the University System of Maryland. There are 16 national honor societies and a freshman honors program.

Faculty/Classroom: 54% of faculty are male; 46% are female. No introductory courses are taught by graduate students. The average class size in an introductory lecture is 50; in a laboratory is 7; and in a regular course is 19.

Admissions: The SAT scores for the 2013-2014 freshman class were: Critical Reading--77% below 500, 21% between 500 and 599, and 2% between 600 and 699; Math--82% below 500, 16% between 500 and 599, 2% between 600 and 699.

Requirements: The SAT is required. The ACT Optional Writing test is also required. Applicants should be graduates of an accredited secondary school. The GED is accepted. Students should have completed 15 academic units, including 4 min English, 3 each of math, sciences, and social science/history, and 2 of a foreign language or advanced technology. A GPA of 2.0 is required. AP and CLEP credits are accepted. Important factors in the admissions decision are advanced placement or honors courses, extracurricular activities record, and leadership record.

Procedure: Freshmen are admitted fall and spring. Entrance exams should be taken before the end of January. There are deferred admissions and rolling admissions plans. Applications should be filed by April 1 for fall entry; November 1 for spring entry, along with a $40 fee. Applications are accepted online.

Transfer: 434 transfer students enrolled in 2012-2013. Applicants must have a minimum GPA of 2.0. The SAT is required if fewer than 24 credit hours are being transferred. 30 of 120 credits required for the bachelor's degree must be completed at BSU.

Visiting: There are regularly scheduled orientations for prospective students. There are guides for informal visits.

Financial Aid: The FAFSA and the college's own financial statement are required. Check with the school for current application deadlines.

International Students: There are 192 international students enrolled. The school actively recruits these students. They must take the TOEFL with a minimum score of 500 on the paper-based TOEFL (PBT). They must also take the SAT or ACT, and the college's own entrance exam.

Computers: All students may access the system 24 hours a day. There are no time limits. The fee is $75.

Graduates: From July 1, 2012 to June 30, 2013, 621 bachelor's degrees were awarded. The most popular majors were business administration (18%), communication media (13%), and sociology (12%). 255 companies recruited on campus in 2012-2013. In an average class, 38% graduate in 6 years or less.

Admissions Contact: Lonnie Morris, Director of Admissions. E-Mail: *dkiah@bowiestate.edu* Web: *www.bowiestate.edu*

CAPITOL COLLEGE D-3

Laurel, MD 20708 (301) 369-2800
(800) 950-1992; (301) 953-1442

Full-time: 110 men, 45 women	**Faculty:** n/av
Part-time: 140 men, 35 women	**Ph.D.s:** n/av
Graduate: 350 men,135 women	**Student/Faculty:** n/av
Year: semesters, summer session	**Tuition:** $20,900
Application Deadline: open	**Room & Board:** $4700
Freshman Class: n/av	
SAT or ACT: required	

COMPETITIVE

Capitol College was founded in 1927 as the Capitol Radio Engineering Institute, a correspondence school. Today it is a private college offering undergraduate programs in engineering and computer technology, as well as graduate programs in management and electronic commerce. The figures in the above capsule and in this profile are approximate. There is 1 graduate school. In addition to regional accreditation, Capitol has baccalaureate program accreditation with ABET. The library contains 10,000 volumes and subscribes to 100 periodicals including electronic. Computerized library services include interlibrary loans and database searching. Special learning facilities include a learning resource center and state-of-the-art labs. The 52-acre campus is in a rural area 19 miles north of Washington, D.C. Including any residence halls, there are 9 buildings.

Student Life: 72% of undergraduates are from Maryland. Others are from 16 states and 21 foreign countries. 43% are white; 39% African American. The average age of freshmen is 23; all undergraduates, 28. 41% do not continue beyond their first year.

Housing: 100 students can be accommodated in college housing, which includes coed on-campus apartments. On-campus housing is available on a first-come, first-served basis. Priority is given to out-of-town students. 87% of students commute. All students may keep cars.

Activities: There are no fraternities or sororities. There are 17 groups on campus, including chess, computers, literary magazine, newspaper, professional, and student government. Popular campus events include Octoberfest and Spring Bash.

Sports: Facilities include an off-campus gym, a basketball court, a student center, and an athletic field.

Disabled Students: All of the campus is accessible. Facilities include wheelchair ramps, elevators, special parking, specially equipped restrooms, and lowered drinking fountains.

Services: Counseling and information services are available, as is tutoring in most subjects, including math, electronics, English, and developmental English.

Campus Safety and Security: There are lighted pathways/sidewalks.

Programs of Study: Capitol confers B.S. degrees. Associate and master's degrees are also awarded. Bachelor's degrees are awarded in COMMUNICATIONS AND THE ARTS (telecommunications), COMPUTER AND PHYSICAL SCIENCE (optics), ENGINEERING AND ENVIRONMENTAL DESIGN (computer engineering, electrical/electronics engineering, and engineering technology). Electrical/electronics engineering is the strongest academically and has the largest enrollments.

Required: A minimum GPA of 2.0 and 130 to 137 credit hours are required for graduation. Additional curriculum requirements vary with the major.

Special: Internships and work-study programs are offered through the school's cooperative education program. There are 2 national honor societies.

Faculty/Classroom: All teach undergraduates. No introductory courses are taught by graduate students. The average class size in an introductory lecture is 20; in a regular course, 22.

Requirements: The SAT or ACT is required. Applicants should be graduates of an accredited secondary school. The GED is accepted. 20 academic credits or 20 Carnegie units are required. Secondary school courses must include 4 units of English, 3 of math, and 2 each of science and social studies. An essay and an interview are recommended. A GPA of 2.8 is required. AP and CLEP credits are accepted. Important factors in the admissions decision are advanced placement or honors courses, recommendations by school officials, and extracurricular activities record.

Procedure: Freshmen are admitted to all sessions. There is a rolling admissions plan. Application deadlines are open. Application fee is $25. Applications are accepted online.

Transfer: Transfer students must have earned 15 college credits and a minimum GPA of 2.0. 40 of 130 credits required for the bachelor's degree must be completed at Capitol.

Visiting: There are regularly scheduled orientations for prospective students. There are guides for informal visits, and visitors may sit in on classes and stay overnight. To schedule a visit, contact the Admissions Office.

Financial Aid: Capitol is a member of CSS. The CSS/Profile is required. Check with the school for current application deadlines.

International Students: The school actively recruits these students. They must take the TOEFL.

Computers: All students may access the system. There are no time limits and no fees.

Admissions Contact: Director of Admissions. E-mail: *admissions@capitol-college.edu* Web: *www.capitol-college.edu*

COPPIN STATE UNIVERSITY D-2

Baltimore, MD 21216 (410) 951-3600
(800) 635-3674; (410) 523-7351

Full-time: 554 men, 1935 women	**Faculty:** 143; IIA, --$
Part-time: 137 men, 616 women	**Ph.D.s:** 55%
Graduate: 174 men, 516 women	**Student/Faculty:** 17 to 1
Year: semesters, summer session	**Tuition:** $6252 ($11,186)
Application Deadline: June 15	**Room & Board:** $8653
Freshman Class: 5593 applied, 1988 accepted, 632 enrolled	
SAT or ACT: required	

VERY COMPETITIVE

Coppin State University, founded in 1900 and part of the University System of Maryland, offers undergraduate programs in liberal arts, teacher education, and nursing. There are 5 undergraduate schools and 1 graduate school. In addition to regional accreditation, Coppin has baccalaureate program accreditation with NCATE and NLN. The library contains 200,000 volumes, 233,000 microform items, and subscribes to 715 periodicals including electronic. Computerized library services include interlibrary loans, database searching, and Internet access. Special learning facilities include an art gallery. The 65-acre campus is in an urban area in Baltimore. Including any residence halls, there are 13 buildings.

Student Life: 90% of undergraduates are from Maryland. Others are from 10 states, 5 foreign countries, and Canada. 90% are from public schools. 86% are African American. The average age of freshmen is 19; all undergraduates, 23.

Housing: 600 students can be accommodated in college housing, which

includes coed dorms. The housing office maintains lists of community housing available. On-campus housing is available on a first-come and first-served basis. 79% of students commute. Alcohol is not permitted. Upperclassmen may keep cars.

Activities: 20% of men belong to 5 national fraternities; 27% of women belong to 4 national sororities. There are 35 groups on campus, including art, cheerleading, choir, chorus, computers, dance, drama, ethnic, film, honors, international, marching band, musical theater, newspaper, political, professional, religious, social, social service, and student government. Popular campus events include the Lyceum Series, the Honors Program, and Black History Month.

Sports: There are 7 intercollegiate sports for men and 7 for women, and 5 intramural sports for men and 5 for women. Facilities include a 4,000-seat gym, an Olympic-size indoor swimming pool, handball and racquetball courts, a soccer field, a dance studio, a weight room, an outdoor track, a softball field, and tennis courts.

Disabled Students: 95% of the campus is accessible. Facilities include wheelchair ramps, elevators, special parking, specially equipped restrooms, lowered drinking fountains, lowered telephones, and individual attention for students requiring specialized materials, equipment, or instructional style accommodation.

Services: Counseling and information services are available, as is tutoring in every subject. There is remedial math, reading, and writing.

Campus Safety and Security: Measures include 24-hour foot and vehicle patrol, emergency notification system, and security escort services. There are shuttle buses, emergency telephones, lighted pathways/sidewalks, and controlled access to dorms/residences.

Programs of Study: Coppin confers B.A., B.S. and B.S.N. degrees. Master's degrees are also awarded. Bachelor's degrees are awarded in BIOLOGICAL SCIENCE (biology/biological science), BUSINESS (accounting, business administration and management, management science, and sports management), COMMUNICATIONS AND THE ARTS (English and visual and performing arts), COMPUTER AND PHYSICAL SCIENCE (chemistry, computer science, and mathematics), EDUCATION (elementary education, health information management, and special education), HEALTH PROFESSIONS (health, nursing, and rehabilitation therapy), SOCIAL SCIENCE (applied psychology, criminal justice, history, interdisciplinary studies, international studies, liberal arts/general studies, political science/government, psychology, social science, social work, and urban studies). Management science, education, and nursing are the strongest academically and have the largest enrollments.

Required: To graduate, all students must have a minimum 2.0 GPA and complete a minimum of 120 credit hours (varies by program of study), with 36 to 40 hours in the major. Students must complete about 50 hours of liberal arts courses in English, math, speech, history, health, physical education, natural and social sciences, and philosophy. All seniors must take a standardized exit exam relevant to their major.

Special: Internships are available in management science, as are B.A.-B.S. degrees in all majors. Student-designed majors are possible with approval. There are 3 national honor societies, including Phi Beta Kappa, and a freshman honors program.

Faculty/Classroom: 55% of faculty are male; 45% are female. No introductory courses are taught by graduate students. The average class size in a regular course is 25.

Admissions: 36% of the 2013-2014 applicants were accepted.

Requirements: The SAT or ACT is required. Applicants must be graduates of an accredited secondary school with a minimum GPA of 2.0 or have a GED certificate. Students must have completed 4 courses in English, 2 courses each in history, math, science, and social studies, and 1 course in foreign language. Up to 15% of a freshman class may be admitted conditionally without these requirements, and those students who graduated high school more than 5 years ago will be reviewed individually. A GPA of 2.5 is required. AP and CLEP credits are accepted. Important factors in the admissions decision are advanced placement or honors courses, extracurricular activities record, and evidence of special talent.

Procedure: Freshmen are admitted to all sessions. There is a rolling admissions plan. Applications should be filed by June 15 for fall entry; December 15 for spring entry. The fall 2013 application fee was $50. Applications are accepted online.

Transfer: Transfer students must have a minimum 2.0 GPA and be in good academic standing at their former institutions. Applicants with fewer than 25 credits must meet freshman requirements. 30 of 120 credits required for the bachelor's degree must be completed at Coppin.

Visiting: There are regularly scheduled orientations for prospective students, consisting of open houses. There are guides for informal visits and visitors may sit in on classes. To schedule a visit, contact the Office of Admissions at admissions@coppin.edu.

Financial Aid: Coppin is a member of CSS. The FAFSA and the college's own financial statement are required. The priority date for freshman financial aid applications for fall entry is March 1.

International Students: They must take the TOEFL with a minimum score of 500 on the paper-based TOEFL (PBT). They must also take the SAT or ACT.

Computers: All students may access the system. There are no time limits and no fees.

Graduates: From July 1, 2012 to June 30, 2013, 484 bachelor's degrees were awarded. The most popular majors were nursing (16%), criminal justice (12%), and applied psychology (10%).

Admissions Contact: Michelle Gross, Director of Admissions. E-Mail: *admissions@coppin.edu* Web: *www.coppin.edu/*

FROSTBURG STATE UNIVERSITY B-1

Frostburg, MD 21532 **(301) 687-4201; (301) 687-7074**

Full-time: 2220 men, 1972 women	**Faculty:** 252; IIA, --$
Part-time: 181 men, 331 women	**Ph.D.s:** 82%
Graduate: 304 men, 466 women	**Student/Faculty:** 17 to 1
Year: semesters, summer session	**Tuition:** $7728 ($18,376)
Application Deadline: open	**Room & Board:** $7536
Freshman Class: 3872 applied, 2302 accepted, 897 enrolled	
SAT CR/M/W: 488/492/469 **ACT:** 20	**LESS COMPETITIVE**

Frostburg State University, founded in 1898, is a part of the University System of Maryland. The university offers programs through the colleges of liberal arts and sciences, business, and education. There are 3 undergraduate schools and 3 graduate schools. In addition to regional accreditation, FSU has baccalaureate program accreditation with AACSB, ABET, CSWE, and NCATE. The library contains 356,200 volumes, 300,203 microform items, 71,985 audio/video tapes/CDs/DVDs, and subscribes to 3,390 periodicals including electronic. Computerized library services include interlibrary loans, database searching, Internet access, and Wi-Fi capability. Special learning facilities include an art gallery, planetarium, radio station, TV station, sustainable energy research facility, environmental lab, science discovery center, cotton top tamarin colony, distance education labs. The 260-acre campus is in a small town about 150 miles west of Baltimore and northwest of Washington, D.C. Including any residence halls, there are 32 buildings.

Student Life: 92% of undergraduates are from Maryland. Others are from 20 states, 40 foreign countries, and Canada. 63% are White; 24% African American. The average age of freshmen is 18; all undergraduates, 22. 23% do not continue beyond their first year; 47% remain to graduate.

Housing: 1700 students can be accommodated in college housing, which includes single-sex and coed dorms. In addition, there are honors houses, special-interest houses, international housing, honors housing, wellness halls, and STEM hall. On-campus housing is guaranteed for all 4 years. 68% of students commute. All students may keep cars.

Activities: 10% of men belong to 5 national fraternities; 10% of women belong to 5 national sororities. There are 150 groups on campus, including art, band, cheerleading, choir, chorale, chorus, communications, computers, dance, drama, drill team, environmental, ethnic, film, gay, honors, international, jazz band, literary magazine, marching band, musical theater, newspaper, orchestra, pep band, photography, political, professional, radio and TV, religious, social, social service, student government, and symphony. Popular campus events include Family Weekend, Cultural Events Series, Late at Lane, Spring Fest, Homecoming and Appalachian Festival.

Sports: There are 9 intercollegiate sports for men and 10 for women, and 5 intramural sports for men and 4 for women. Facilities include a fitness center and game room, 3,600-seat main arena, practice gym, 5 athletic fields, 2 intramural fields, indoor swimming pool, dance studio, 6 lighted tennis courts, weight rooms, dance lab with sprung floor, football stadium, 8-lane 400-meter track, training rooms, team rooms, indoor baseball room, racquetball and squash courts; bike trails, whitewater rafting, hiking skiing and snowboarding nearby.

Disabled Students: All of the campus is accessible. Facilities include wheelchair ramps, elevators, special parking, specially equipped restrooms, special class scheduling, lowered drinking fountains, lowered telephones, and special housing.

Services: Counseling and information services are available, as is tutoring in every subject. There is a reader service for the blind, and remedial math, reading, and writing.

Campus Safety and Security: Measures include 24-hour foot and vehicle patrol, emergency notification system, self-defense education, and security escort services. There are shuttle buses, emergency telephones, lighted pathways/sidewalks, controlled access to dorms/residences, bicycle patrol.

Programs of Study: FSU confers B.A., B.S., B.F.A., B.U.R., and B.S.N. degrees. Master's and doctoral degrees are also awarded. Bachelor's degrees are awarded in AGRICULTURE (fish and game management and wildlife management), BIOLOGICAL SCIENCE (biology/biological science), BUSINESS (accounting, business administration and management, and recreation and leisure services), COMMUNICATIONS AND THE ARTS (communications, dramatic arts, English, languages, and music), COMPUTER AND PHYSICAL SCIENCE (chemistry, computer science, computer security and information assurance, information sciences and systems, mathematics, and physics), EDUCATION (early childhood education, elementary education, middle school education, and physical education), ENGINEERING AND ENVIRONMENTAL DESIGN (environmental science), HEALTH PROFESSIONS (exercise science and nursing), SOCIAL SCIENCE (criminal justice, economics, geography, history, international studies, law enforcement and corrections, liberal arts/general studies, philosophy, political science/government, psychology, social science, social work, and sociology). Business, education, and the natural sciences are the strongest academically. Education, business, and psychology have the largest enrollments.

Required: A minimum GPA of 2.0 and 120 credit hours are required to graduate. All students must complete 7 to 14 credits in natural science, 6 to 9 credits in humanities and social sciences, and 3 to 6 credits in creative and performing arts. Courses in computer science, speech and composition, personalized health fitness, and math are also required.

Special: FSU offers co-op programs in applied physics (with UMBC), electrical engineering, and mechanical engineering (with University of Maryland, College Park); internships through individual departments; study abroad opportunities in China, Denmark, Ireland, United Kingdom, Australia, Latin America, Belize and over 140 locations worldwide; work-study and accelerated degree programs; B.A.-B.S. degrees in all majors; a dual major in engineering. The 3-2 engineering degree is coordinated with the University of Maryland at College Park. Cross-registration, non-degree study, and pass/fail options are also available. Distance learning and an advanced degree program are available. There are 18 national honor societies, a freshman honors program, and 15 departmental honors programs.

Faculty/Classroom: 55% of faculty are male; 45% are female. All teach undergraduates. No introductory courses are taught by graduate students. The average class size in an introductory lecture is 25; in a laboratory is 15; and in a regular course is 20.

Admissions: 59% of the 2013-2014 applicants were accepted. The SAT scores for the 2013-2014 freshman class were: Critical Reading--59% below 500, 33% between 500 and 599, 6% between 600 and 699, and 1% between 700 and 800; Math--58% below 500, 34% between 500 and 599, 8% between 600 and 699, and 1% between 700 and 800; Writing--66% below 500, 27% between 500 and 599, 6% between 600 and 699, and 1% between 700 and 800. 25% of the current freshmen were in the top fifth of their class; 56% were in the top two fifths.

Requirements: The SAT or ACT is required. Applicants must be graduates of an accredited secondary school or have the GED. Secondary preparation should include 4 units of English, 3 each of math and social studies, and 2 of a foreign language and science. An interview is recommended. A GPA of 2.0 is required. AP and CLEP credits are accepted. Important factors in the admissions decision are recommendations by school officials, extracurricular activities record, and advanced placement or honors courses.

Procedure: Freshmen are admitted to all sessions. Entrance exams should be taken in the junior or senior year. There are early decision and rolling admissions plans. Application deadlines are open. Application fee is $30. Applications are accepted online.

Transfer: 507 transfer students enrolled in 2012-2013. Transfer students with 12 to 23 credits must have a minimum GPA of 2.5 and provide an official high school transcript and SAT scores. Students with 24 or more credits must have a minimum GPA of 2.0. 30 of 120 credits required for the bachelor's degree must be completed at FSU.

Visiting: There are regularly scheduled orientations for prospective students, including tours Monday through Friday at 11 a.m. and 12 noon. There are guides for informal visits and visitors may sit in on classes. To schedule a visit, contact the Office of Admissions.

Financial Aid: In 2013-2014, 72% of all full-time freshmen and 65% of continuing full-time students received some form of financial aid. 49% of all full-time freshmen and 47% of continuing full-time students received need-based aid. The average freshman award was $8,699. Need-based scholarships or need-based grants averaged $4,441 ($9,400 maximum); need-based self-help aid (loans and jobs) averaged $2,379 ($2,625 maximum); and other non-need-based awards and non-need-based scholarships averaged $5,884 ($20,259 maximum). 13% of undergraduate students work part-time. Average annual earnings from campus work are $484. The average financial indebtedness of the 2013 graduate was $15,678. The FAFSA and the college's own financial statement are required. The deadline for filing freshman financial aid applications for fall entry is March 1.

International Students: There are 86 international students enrolled. The school actively recruits these students. They must take the TOEFL with a minimum score of 550 on the paper-based TOEFL (PBT) or 79 on the Internet-based version (iBT). They must also take the SAT or ACT.

Computers: All students may access the system 8 a.m. to 10 p.m. for most labs. One lab is available 24 / 7. There are no time limits and no fees.

Graduates: From July 1, 2012 to June 30, 2013, 969 bachelor's degrees were awarded. The most popular majors were business administration (10%), psychology (8%), and early childhood elementary education (6%). 61 companies recruited on campus in 2012-2013. In an average class, 25% graduate in 4 years or less, 43% graduate in 5 years or less, and 47% graduate in 6 years or less.

Admissions Contact: Trisha Gregory, Director of Admissions. E-Mail: *fsuadmissions@frostburg.edu* Web: *www.frostburg.edu*

GOUCHER COLLEGE — D-2

Baltimore, MD 21204 — (410) 337-6100; (800) 468-2437; (410) 337-6354

Full-time: 473 men, 951 women	**Faculty:** 138; IIB, av$
Part-time: 15 men, 10 women	**Ph.D.s:** 89%
Graduate: 156 men, 506 women	**Student/Faculty:** 9 to 1
Year: semesters	**Tuition:** $35,084
Application Deadline: February 1	**Room & Board:** $11,168
Freshman Class: 3466 applied, 2505 accepted, 401 enrolled	
SAT CR/M/W: 590/570/560 **ACT:** 26	**VERY COMPETITIVE+**

Since 1885, Goucher has been a small college with a big view of the world. In 2006, it became the first college in the nation to require that 100 percent of its undergraduates study abroad. Located just north of downtown Baltimore and 45 minutes from the nation's capital, Goucher enrolls 1,500 undergraduate students from 45 states and 28 countries. The college offers 33 majors and six interdisciplinary areas for undergraduates. With an average class size of 17, Goucher professors know their students by name. Goucher students learn not only how to relate to different cultures but also how to function effectively within them through three-week, semester, or yearlong study abroad experiences. With 60-plus programs in more than 30 countries, the possibilities are boundless. Goucher's campus is also within easy striking distance of the major cultural, political, and economic centers of the East Coast. And our students use this location to their advantage to find internships during their studies and jobs after they graduate. Goucher students put their education into action through collaborative research in the natural sciences, service-learning programs that support local communities, and leadership opportunities on its unusually active campus. Goucher helps students become nimble, creative, confident, and capable of carving their own successes, which is one reason it's one of only 40 colleges to be included in the well-known guide Colleges That Change Lives. Through their language proficiency, international exposure, and internship experience (most students complete at least one), Goucher graduates offer employers distinct advantages in a quickly changing, increasingly global economy. That's why 92 percent of Goucher graduates are employed or enrolled in graduate education within a year or less of graduation. There is one undergraduate school and one graduate school. The library contains 365,751 volumes, 22,268 microform items, 69,638 audio/video tapes/CDs/DVDs, and subscribes to 32,638 periodicals including electronic. Computerized library services include interlibrary loans, database searching, Internet access, and Wi-Fi capability. Special learning facilities include an art gallery, radio station, the Athenaeum is the flagship building of campus, weaving together the various threads of life at Goucher under one roof. The 103,000 square foot building, open 24 hours a day during the semester, features a technologically superior library; a forum for public events; classrooms; a café; an art gallery; a center for community service programming; and spaces for exercise, conversation, and relaxation. The Academic Center for Excellence offers study-skills workshops, peer-led supplemental instruction, and yoga, meditation, and Reiki sessions. Goucher also has a TV studio, three multi-purpose performance spaces ranging in size from a few hundred to 1,000 seats, a robotics lab, a rooftop observatory providing public observing, advanced teaching labs for physics and computer science, research labs for math, physics, and psychology, a technology/learning center, international technology and media center, and centers for writing, math, and politics. The 287-acre campus is in a suburban area 8 miles north of downtown Baltimore. Including any residence halls, there are 20 buildings.

Student Life: 74% of undergraduates are from out of state, mostly the Middle Atlantic. Students are from 45 states, 27 foreign countries, and Canada. 66% are from public schools. 68% are White. The average age of freshmen is 18; all undergraduates, 21. 14% do not continue beyond their first year; 86% remain to graduate.

Housing: 1210 students can be accommodated in college housing, which includes single-sex and coed dorms and on-campus apartments. In addition, there are language houses, special-interest houses, quiet houses, and healthy living. On-campus housing is available on a first-come, first-served basis, and is available on a lottery system for upperclassmen. 84% of students live on campus; of those, 78% remain on campus on weekends. All students may keep cars.

Activities: There are no fraternities or sororities. There are 60 groups on campus, including and martial arts, art, chorale, chorus, communications, computers, dance, debate, drama, environmental, ethnic, film, gay, honors, international, jazz band, literary magazine, musical theater, newspaper, opera, orchestra, political, professional, radio and TV, religious, social, social service, student government, symphony, and yearbook. Popular campus events include Get into Goucher Day, Spring Gala, and Blind Date Ball.

Sports: There are 8 intercollegiate sports for men and 11 for women, and

6 intramural sports for men and 6 for women. Facilities include 2 gyms, an indoor swimming pool, a weight room, a training room, a cardio fitness center, racquetball, squash, and tennis courts, indoor outdoor equestrian facilities, an outdoor track, an outdoor volleyball court, an outdoor basketball court, and a disc golf course.

Disabled Students: All of the campus is accessible. Facilities include wheelchair ramps, elevators, special parking, specially equipped restrooms, special class scheduling, special housing, and an auditorium loop for the hearing impaired.

Services: Many academic support options are available through the college's Academic Center for Excellence (ACE).

Campus Safety and Security: Measures include 24-hour foot and vehicle patrol, emergency notification system, self-defense education, and security escort services. There are shuttle buses, emergency telephones, lighted pathways/sidewalks, controlled access to dorms/residences, an officer-manned gatehouse during evening and overnight hours.

Programs of Study: Goucher confers B.A. degrees. Master's degrees are also awarded. Bachelor's degrees are awarded in AGRICULTURE (environmental studies), BIOLOGICAL SCIENCE (biochemistry and biology/biological science), BUSINESS (business administration and management), COMMUNICATIONS AND THE ARTS (art history, art, communications, dance, English, French, music, Russian, Spanish, and theatre arts), COMPUTER AND PHYSICAL SCIENCE (chemistry, computer science, mathematics, and physics), EDUCATION (education and special education), SOCIAL SCIENCE (American studies, anthropology, economics, history, interdisciplinary studies, international relations, peace studies, philosophy, political science/government, psychology, religion, sociology, and women's studies). Biology, chemistry, and history are the strongest academically. Psychology, communication, and biological sciences have the largest enrollments.

Required: To graduate, all students must complete 120 credit hours, with a minimum GPA of 2.00. The number of required hours for each major varies by major. Requirements include; 1 lab-related course in the natural sciences; 1 course each in Social Sciences, Mathematical Reasoning, Artistic/Creative Expression, Textual Analysis/Critical Perspectives, Understanding Diverse Perspectives, Environmental Sustainability, and a Physical Education activity course. Students are also required to demonstrate proficiency in college writing and a foreign language. Other requirements include a study abroad experience, for which students receive a voucher of $1000. First year students attending college full-time for the first time must also complete a transitions course and a Frontiers course.

Special: Goucher offers internships in Baltimore and Washington D.C., study abroad in 28 countries, and other off-campus experiences. The college also collaborates with many of the 14 other colleges in the Baltimore Collegetown Network. Students may cross-register with Johns Hopkins, Towson University, Peabody Institute, Stevenson University, Coppin State College, University of Maryland Baltimore, University of Maryland Baltimore County, Loyola College, and Maryland Institute College of Art. 3-2 engineering degrees with Johns Hopkins University and Columbia University are offered. Dual majors and student-designed, interdisciplinary majors are an option. There is 1 national honor society including Phi Beta Kappa.

Faculty/Classroom: 39% of faculty are male; 61% are female. All teach undergraduates. No introductory courses are taught by graduate students. The average class size in an introductory lecture is 17.

Admissions: 72% of the 2013-2014 applicants were accepted. The SAT scores for the 2013-2014 freshman class were: Critical Reading--18% below 500, 33% between 500 and 599, 33% between 600 and 699, and 14% between 700 and 800; Math--22% below 500, 42% between 500 and 599, 29% between 600 and 699, and 6% between 700 and 800; Writing--22% below 500, 34% between 500 and 599, 32% between 600 and 699, and 10% between 700 and 800. The ACT scores were 14% below 21, 17% between 21 and 23, 21% between 24 and 26, 24% between 27 and 28, and 24% above 28. 47% of the current freshmen were in the top fifth of their class; 79% were in the top two fifths.

Requirements: Applicants should be graduates of an accredited high school or have earned the GED. A personal essay is required, and an interview is recommended. Prospective performing or visual arts majors are urged to seek an audition or submit a portfolio. AP credits are accepted. Important factors in the admissions decision are extracurricular activities record, recommendations by school officials, and advanced placement or honors courses.

Procedure: Freshmen are admitted fall and spring. Entrance exams should be taken in spring of the junior year or fall of the senior year. There are early decision, early admissions, and deferred admissions plans. Early decision applications should be filed by November 15; regular applications, by February 1 for fall entry; and December 1 for spring entry, along with a $55 fee. Notification of early decision is sent December 15; regular decision, April 1. 44 early decision candidates were accepted for the 2013-2014 class. 38 applicants were on the 2013 waiting list; 2 were admitted. Applications are accepted online.

Transfer: 36 transfer students enrolled in 2012-2013. An interview, a personal essay, and recommendations from college teachers or counselors are also required, as is a graded paper. 60 of 120 credits required for the bachelor's degree must be completed at Goucher.

Visiting: There are regularly scheduled orientations for prospective students, A multi-day experience introducing students to Goucher, academic life, the campus community, and the Baltimore area. There are guides for informal visits, visitors may sit in on classes, and stay overnight. To schedule a visit, contact the Office of Admissions.

Financial Aid: In 2013-2014, 88% of all full-time freshmen and 91% of continuing full-time students received some form of financial aid. 84% of all full-time freshmen and 86% of continuing full-time students received need-based aid. The average freshman award was $29,709. Need-based scholarships or need-based grants averaged $26,020; need-based self-help aid (loans and jobs) averaged $4,416; and other non-need-based awards and non-need-based scholarships averaged $14,439. 63% of undergraduate students work part-time. Average annual earnings from campus work are $2100. The average financial indebtedness of the 2013 graduate was $27,921. Goucher is a member of CSS. The CSS/Profile, FAFSA, and the college's own financial statement are required. The priority date for freshman financial aid applications for fall entry is February 1. The deadline for filing freshman financial aid applications for fall entry is April 1.

International Students: There are 30 international students enrolled. The school actively recruits these students. They must take the TOEFL with a minimum score of 550 on the paper-based TOEFL (PBT) or 79 on the Internet-based version (iBT).

Computers: All students may access the system 24 hours a day, 7 days a week. There are no time limits and no fees.

Graduates: From July 1, 2012 to June 30, 2013, 311 bachelor's degrees were awarded. The most popular majors were psychology (15%), social sciences (13%), and visual and performing arts (12%). 35 companies recruited on campus in 2012-2013. In an average class, 1% graduate in 3 years or less, 58% graduate in 4 years or less, 66% graduate in 5 years or less, and 67% graduate in 6 years or less.

Admissions Contact: Carlton E. Surbeck, Director of Admissions. E-Mail: *admissions@goucher.edu* Web: *www.goucher.edu*

HOOD COLLEGE — C-2

Frederick, MD 21701 — (301) 696-3400; (800) 922-1599; (301) 696-3819

Full-time: 442 men, 823 women	**Faculty:** 81; IIA, --$
Part-time: 36 men, 86 women	**Ph.D.s:** 96%
Graduate: 347 men, 659 women	**Student/Faculty:** 12 to 1
Year: semesters, summer session	**Tuition:** $33,280
Application Deadline: June 15	**Room & Board:** $11,350
Freshman Class: 1686 applied, 1366 accepted, 281 enrolled	
SAT CR/M/W: 520/530/510 **ACT:** 21	**COMPETITIVE**

Hood College, founded in 1893, is an independent, comprehensive college that offers an integration of the liberal arts and professional preparation, as well as undergraduate majors in the natural sciences. There is one graduate school. In addition to regional accreditation, Hood has baccalaureate program accreditation with AACSB, CSWE, and NCATE. The library contains 214,180 volumes, 734,910 microform items, 7,726 audio/video tapes/CDs/DVDs, and subscribes to 24,926 periodicals including electronic. Computerized library services include interlibrary loans, database searching, Internet access, and Wi-Fi capability. Special learning facilities include an art gallery, radio station, aquatic center, a child development lab, an observatory, and information technology center. The 50-acre campus is in a suburban area 45 miles northwest of Washington, D.C. and 45 miles west of Baltimore. Including any residence halls, there are 34 buildings.

Student Life: 76% of undergraduates are from Maryland. Others are from 30 states, 20 foreign countries, and Canada. 82% are from public schools. 65% are White; 12% African American. 53% claim no religious affiliation; 30% Protestant. The average age of freshmen is 18; all undergraduates, 22. 22% do not continue beyond their first year; 68% remain to graduate.

Housing: 828 students can be accommodated in college housing, which includes single-sex and coed dorms and off-campus apartments. In addition, there are honors houses, language houses, special-interest floors in the residence halls include living/learning communities and a community service floor. On-campus housing is guaranteed for all 4 years, is available on a first-come, first-served basis, and is available on a lottery system for upperclassmen. 56% of students live on campus; of those, 65% remain on campus on weekends. All students may keep cars.

Activities: There are no fraternities or sororities. There are 79 groups on campus, including art, band, cheerleading, choir, chorale, chorus, computers, dance, drama, environmental, ethnic, film, gay, honors, international, jazz band, literary magazine, musical theater, newspaper, orchestra, political, professional, radio and TV, religious, social, social service, and student government. Popular campus events include Ring Formal, Liberation of the Black Mind Weekend, and Crab Fest.

Sports: There are 8 intercollegiate sports for men and 10 for women, and 4 intramural sports for men and 5 for women. Facilities include Athletic

Center for intercollegiate, recreational and intramural activites, including men's and women's basketball and volleyball, with two-level fitness center and cardio room, full-service athletic training room, and locker rooms 1600 seating capacity, swimming pool, multiuse turf fields (field hockey, soccer, and lacrosse).

Disabled Students: 50% of the campus is accessible. Facilities include wheelchair ramps, elevators, special parking, specially equipped restrooms, special class scheduling, and special housing.

Services: Counseling and information services are available, as is tutoring in some subjects, readers for the blind and interpreters for the hearing impaired. There is a reader service for the blind, and remedial math and writing. There are also services for students with learning disabilities, a language lab, and courses in time management and study skills.

Campus Safety and Security: Measures include 24-hour foot and vehicle patrol, emergency notification system, self-defense education, and security escort services. There are emergency telephones, lighted pathways/sidewalks, and controlled access to dorms/residences.

Programs of Study: Hood confers B.A., B.S. and B.S.N degrees. Master's degrees are also awarded. Bachelor's degrees are awarded in BIOLOGICAL SCIENCE (biochemistry and biology/biological science), BUSINESS (business administration and management, management science, and marketing), COMMUNICATIONS AND THE ARTS (art, communications, English, French, German, music, and Spanish), COMPUTER AND PHYSICAL SCIENCE (chemistry, computer science, and mathematics), EDUCATION (early childhood education, elementary education, English education, foreign languages education, mathematics education, science education, secondary education, and special education), ENGINEERING AND ENVIRONMENTAL DESIGN (computational sciences and environmental science), HEALTH PROFESSIONS (nursing), SOCIAL SCIENCE (archeology, economics, history, Latin American studies, law, Middle Eastern studies, philosophy, political science/government, psychology, religion, social work, and sociology). Chemistry, social work and psychology are the strongest academically. Management, psychology, and biology have the largest enrollments.

Required: To graduate, students must complete a total of 124 credit hours, with a minimum GPA of 2.0, and a 2.0 GPA in the major. 24 to 52 credits are required in a student's major. All students must complete 42 to 48 credits in the core curriculum, which includes English, math, and language courses, courses in methods of inquiry, and interdisciplinary courses in Western civilization, non-Western civilization and society, science, and technology. Phys ed courses are also required. Enrollment in the final 30 credits must be on the Hood Campus as a degree candidate.

Special: The college offers a Washington semester with American University, dual majors, student-designed majors, a B.A.-B.S. degree in engineering/math, credit for life experience, nondegree study, pass/fail options, and cross-registration with area colleges and the Duke University Marine Sciences Education Consortium. Internships of up to 15 credits are available in all majors at more than 100 sites throughout the United States and abroad. Students may study abroad in the Dominican Republic, Japan, Spain, France, and other countries. There is a 4-year honors program featuring 1 interdisciplinary course per semester and special co-curricular activities. There are 16 national honor societies, a freshman honors program, and 8 departmental honors programs.

Faculty/Classroom: 43% of faculty are male; 57% are female. All teach and do research. No introductory courses are taught by graduate students. The average class size in an introductory lecture is 16; in a laboratory is 13; and in a regular course is 14.

Admissions: 81% of the 2013-2014 applicants were accepted. The SAT scores for the 2013-2014 freshman class were: Critical Reading--39% below 500, 40% between 500 and 599, 19% between 600 and 699, and 2% between 700 and 800; Math--38% below 500, 40% between 500 and 599, 21% between 600 and 699, and 2% between 700 and 800; Writing--43% below 500, 43% between 500 and 599, 13% between 600 and 699, and 1% between 700 and 800. The ACT scores were 48% below 21, 19% between 21 and 23, 22% between 24 and 26, 7% between 27 and 28, and 4% above 28. 35% of the current freshmen were in the top fifth of their class; 66% were in the top two fifths. 1 freshman graduated first in the class.

Requirements: The SAT or ACT is required. Applicants should be graduates of an accredited secondary school. The GED is accepted. Hood recommends the completion of at least 16 academic credits in high school, including courses in English, social sciences, natural sciences, foreign languages, and math. Hood College is SAT Optional for students with a high school GPA of 3.25 or higher on a 4.0 scale. A GPA of 2.5 is required. AP and CLEP credits are accepted. Important factors in the admissions decision are advanced placement or honors courses, leadership record, and extracurricular activities record.

Procedure: Freshmen are admitted fall and spring. Entrance exams should be taken in spring of the junior year or fall of the senior year. There are early decision, early admissions, deferred admissions, and rolling admissions plans. Early decision applications should be filed by November 1; regular applications, by June 15 for fall entry; and December 31 for spring entry, along with a $35 fee. Notification of early decision is sent November 15; regular decision, March 1. 15 early decision candidates were accepted for the 2013-2014 class. Applications are accepted online. Application fees are waived if application is completed online.

Transfer: 119 transfer students enrolled in 2012-2013. Applicants must have at least 12 college credits and a minimum GPA of 2.5. A total of 70 credits may be transferred. 30 of 124 credits required for the bachelor's degree must be completed at Hood.

Visiting: There are regularly scheduled orientations for prospective students, including tours and meetings with faculty, students, and administrators; and admissions interviews. There are guides for informal visits, visitors may sit in on classes, and stay overnight. To schedule a visit, contact Lisa Troth at admission@hood.edu.

Financial Aid: In 2013-2014, 99% of all full-time freshmen and 98% of continuing full-time students received some form of financial aid. 85% of all full-time freshmen and 85% of continuing full-time students received need-based aid. The average freshman award was $26,703. Need-based scholarships or need-based grants averaged $23,480; need-based self-help aid (loans and jobs) averaged $6,202; and other non-need-based awards and non-need-based scholarships averaged $18,539. 24% of undergraduate students work part-time. Average annual earnings from campus work are $2000. The average financial indebtedness of the 2013 graduate was $26,890. Hood is a member of CSS. The FAFSA is required. The priority date for freshman financial aid applications for fall entry is February 15.

International Students: There are 36 international students enrolled. The school actively recruits these students. They must take the TOEFL with a minimum score of 550 on the paper-based TOEFL (PBT) or 79 on the Internet-based version (iBT). They must also take the SAT or ACT. SAT scores may be substituted for the TOEFL.

Computers: All students may access the system 24 hours per day, 7 days a week. There are no time limits and no fees.

Graduates: From July 1, 2012 to June 30, 2013, 317 bachelor's degrees were awarded. The most popular majors were education (14%), psychology (13%), and biology (10%). 110 companies recruited on campus in 2012-2013. In an average class, 2% graduate in 3 years or less, 54% graduate in 4 years or less, 66% graduate in 5 years or less, and 68% graduate in 6 years or less. Of the 2012 graduating class, 45% were enrolled in graduate school within 6 months of graduation, and 84% were employed.

Admissions Contact: Terry Whittum, Vice President for Enrollment Management. E-Mail: *admission@hood.edu* Web: *www.hood.edu/admission*

JOHNS HOPKINS UNIVERSITY D-2

Baltimore, MD 21218 **(410) 516-8341; (410) 516-6025**

Full-time: 2410 men, 2210 women	**Faculty:** n/av
Part-time: 30 men,10 women	**Ph.D.s:** 92%
Graduate: 1010 men, 610 women	**Student/Faculty:** n/av
Year: semesters, summer session	**Tuition:** $42,780
Application Deadline: see profile	**Room & Board:** $13,462
Freshman Class: n/av	
SAT or ACT: required	

MOST COMPETITIVE

The Johns Hopkins University, founded in 1876, is a private multicampus institution offering undergraduate degrees at the Homewood campus through the Zanvyl Krieger School of Arts and Sciences, the Whiting School of Engineering, and the Peabody Institute (music). The figures in the above capsule and in this profile are approximate. There are 5 undergraduate schools and 8 graduate schools. In addition to regional accreditation, Johns Hopkins has baccalaureate program accreditation with ABET. The 4 libraries contain 2.6 million volumes, 4.1 million microform items, 9707 audio/video tapes/CDs/DVDs, and subscribe to 30,120 periodicals including electronic. Computerized library services include interlibrary loans, database searching, Internet access, and laptop Internet portals. Special learning facilities include an art gallery, radio station, and Space Telescope Science Institute. The 140-acre campus is in a suburban area in a residential setting in northern Baltimore. Including any residence halls, there are 40 buildings.

Student Life: 85% of undergraduates are from out of state, mostly the Middle Atlantic. Students are from 50 states, 49 foreign countries, and Canada. 60% are from public schools. 46% are white; 24% Asian American. The average age of freshmen is 18; all undergraduates, 20. 3% do not continue beyond their first year; 93% remain to graduate.

Housing: 2700 students can be accommodated in college housing, which includes single-sex and coed dorms, on-campus apartments, and off-campus apartments. In addition, there are special-interest houses and non-university-sponsored fraternity and sorority houses. On-campus housing is available on a lottery system for upperclassmen. 61% of students live on campus. Upperclassmen may keep cars.

Activities: 24% of men belong to 11 national fraternities; 23% of women belong to 7 national sororities. There are 250 groups on campus, including art, band, cheerleading, chess, choir, chorale, chorus, computers, dance, debate, drama, ethnic, film, forensics, gay, honors, international, jazz band, literary magazine, marching band, musical theater, newspaper, opera, orchestra, pep band, photography, political, professional, radio and TV, religious, social, social service, student government, symphony, and volunteer organizations. Popular campus events include Culturefest, Fall Fest, and Spring Fair.

Sports: There are 14 intercollegiate sports for men and 12 for women, and 20 intramural sports for men and 20 for women. Facilities include a recreation center with a swimming pool and diving pool, wrestling and fencing rooms, a varsity weight room, a fitness center, saunas, a climbing wall, an indoor jogging track, and courts for basketball, badminton, squash, volleyball, and handball. There is also a 4000-seat stadium, outdoor playing fields, and tennis courts.

Disabled Students: Facilities include wheelchair ramps, elevators, special parking, specially equipped restrooms, special class scheduling, lowered drinking fountains, and lowered telephones. JHU works with all individuals to ensure access to all programs. Also, existing housing is accommodated as needed.

Services: Counseling and information services are available, as is tutoring in most subjects. There is a reader service for the blind.

Campus Safety and Security: Measures include 24-hour foot and vehicle patrol, emergency notification system, self-defense education, and security escort services. There are shuttle buses, emergency telephones, and lighted pathways/sidewalks.

Programs of Study: Johns Hopkins confers B.A. and B.S. degrees. Master's and doctoral degrees are also awarded. Bachelor's degrees are awarded in BIOLOGICAL SCIENCE (biology/biological science, biophysics, cell biology, molecular biology, and neurosciences), COMMUNICATIONS AND THE ARTS (art history and appreciation, classics, creative writing, English, French, German, Italian, media arts, romance languages and literature, and Spanish), COMPUTER AND PHYSICAL SCIENCE (applied mathematics, chemistry, computer science, earth science, mathematics, natural sciences, and physics), ENGINEERING AND ENVIRONMENTAL DESIGN (biomedical engineering, chemical engineering, civil engineering, computer engineering, electrical/electronics engineering, engineering, engineering mechanics, environmental engineering, environmental science, materials engineering, materials science, and mechanical engineering), SOCIAL SCIENCE (African studies, anthropology, cognitive science, East Asian studies, economics, history, history of science, humanities, interdisciplinary studies, international studies, Latin American studies, Near Eastern studies, philosophy, political science/government, psychology, social science, and sociology). International studies, public health studies, and biomedical engineering have the largest enrollments.

Required: Although there is no required core curriculum, all students must take 40 hours in the major and 30 hours outside their major field. The B.A. requires a total of 120 hours; the B.S. in engineering requires 120 to 128 hours, depending on the major. A GPA of at least 2.0 is required for graduation. All students must take at least 4 courses (2 for engineers) with a writing-intensive component to graduate.

Special: Internships, dual majors in music and arts and sciences/engineering, cross-registration with Baltimore-area colleges and Johns Hopkins divisions, a cooperative double degree with Peabody Conservatory of Music, a student-designed semester at the Johns Hopkins School of International Studies in Washington, D.C., and various multidisciplinary programs are offered. Students may enroll at Johns Hopkins in Bologna, Italy, or Nanjing, China, or arrange programs in Europe, South America, the Far East, or Australia. Students may earn combined B.A.-B.S. degrees in physics, computer science, applied math, and statistics. There are 4 national honor societies, including Phi Beta Kappa, and 25 departmental honors programs.

Faculty/Classroom: 72% of faculty are male; 28% are female. No introductory courses are taught by graduate students.

Requirements: The SAT or ACT with Writing is required. For those submitting SAT scores, Johns Hopkins recommends that applicants also submit 3 SAT Subject Tests. In addition, applicants should be graduates of an accredited secondary school or have the GED. The university recommends that secondary preparation include 4 years each of English and math, 2 (prefer 3) of social science or history and lab science, and 3 to 4 of a foreign language (2 for engineering majors). 2 personal essays are required, and an interview is recommended. AP credits are accepted. Important factors in the admissions decision are advanced placement or honors courses, extracurricular activities record, and personality/intangible qualities.

Procedure: Freshmen are admitted fall. Entrance exams should be taken by December for regular decision, or November for early decision. There are early decision and deferred admissions plans. Check with the school for application deadlines. Applications are accepted online. There is a $70.00 fee.

Transfer: Applicants should have sophomore or junior standing and at least a B average in previous college work. Applications must include a written essay and at least 1 letter of recommendation. High school records are also required. 60 of 120 credits required for the bachelor's degree must be completed at Johns Hopkins.

Visiting: There are regularly scheduled orientations for prospective students, including scheduled open house programs, campus tours and group information sessions offered weekday mornings and afternoons, and individual day visits with a current student. There are guides for informal visits, and visitors may sit in on classes and stay overnight. To schedule a visit, contact the Office of Undergraduate Admissions.

Financial Aid: Johns Hopkins is a member of CSS. The CSS/Profile and FAFSA are required. Check with the school for current application deadlines.

International Students: The school actively recruits these students. They must take the TOEFL with a minimum score of 600 on the paper-based TOEFL (PBT). They must also take the SAT or ACT.

Computers: Wireless access is available. All students may access the system 24 hours a day, 7 days a week. There are no time limits and no fees.

Admissions Contact: Director of Undergraduate Admissions. E-mail: *gotojhu@jhu.edu* Web: *www.jhu.edu*

LOYOLA UNIVERSITY MARYLAND D-2

Baltimore, MD 21210	**(410) 617-5012; (800) 221-9107**
Full-time: 1523 men, 2352 women	**Faculty:** 350; IIA, +$
Part-time: 19 men, 23 women	**Ph.D.s:** 95%
Graduate: 707 men, 1354 women	**Student/Faculty:** 12 to 1
Year: semesters, summer session	**Tuition:** n/av
Application Deadline: January 15	**Room & Board:** n/app
Freshman Class: 12066 applied, 8187 accepted, 1072 enrolled	
SAT CR/M: 586/591	**ACT:** 26 **VERY COMPETITIVE**

A Catholic, Jesuit comprehensive university in Baltimore, Loyola University Maryland is committed to the ideals of liberal education and the development of the whole person, a university dedicated to inspiring its students to learn, lead and serve in a diverse and changing world. This mission is embraced through an undergraduate curriculum, rooted in the Jesuit tradition of the liberal arts, which prepares students for success in wide-ranging professional pursuits and graduate studies. Loyola's undergraduate experience is complemented by its graduate programs, the region's leaders in professional education. The Loyola University Maryland education also promotes in all students a sense of their responsibility to others in their community and throughout the world. This ideal is underscored by a thriving program of community service that takes Loyola students into the greater Baltimore community and beyond to serve individuals who are materially disadvantaged, creating a synergy of mind, body and spirit that transforms lives. There are 3 undergraduate schools and 3 graduate schools. In addition to regional accreditation, has baccalaureate program accreditation with AACSB, ABET, CSAB, NASDTEC, and NCATE. The library contains 1.1 million volumes, 691 microform items, 19,086 audio/video tapes/CDs/DVDs, and subscribes to 56,888 periodicals including electronic. Computerized library services include interlibrary loans, database searching, and Internet access. Special learning facilities include an art gallery, radio station, and TV station. The 89-acre campus is in an urban area 3 miles from downtown Baltimore. Including any residence halls, there are 51 buildings.

Student Life: 82% of undergraduates are from out of state, mostly the Middle Atlantic. Students are from 38 states, 61 foreign countries, and Canada. 51% are from public schools. 80% are White. 73% are Catholic. The average age of freshmen is 18; all undergraduates, 20. 12% do not continue beyond their first year; 84% remain to graduate.

Housing: 3291 students can be accommodated in college housing, which includes single-sex and coed dorms and on-campus apartments. In addition, there are honors houses and special-interest houses. On-campus housing is guaranteed for the freshman year only, is available on a first-come, first-served basis, and is available on a lottery system for upperclassmen. 82% of students live on campus. Upperclassmen may keep cars.

Activities: There are no fraternities or sororities. There are 194 groups on campus, including art, band, cheerleading, chess, choir, chorale, chorus, computers, dance, drama, ethnic, film, gay, honors, international, jazz band, literary magazine, musical theater, newspaper, orchestra, pep band, photography, political, professional, radio and TV, religious, social, social service, student government, symphony, and yearbook. Popular campus events include Modern Masters Series, Humanities Symposium, Loyolapalooza, International Festival, Evergreen Players, ChordBusters, Luna Fest, Poisened Cup Players, Bull and Oyster Roast.

Sports: There are 8 intercollegiate sports for men and 9 for women, and 8 intramural sports for men and 8 for women. Facilities include The Ridley Athletic Complex is home of Loyola's NCAA Division I men's and women's lacrosse and soccer teams. It features a 6,000-seat grandstand; Sportexe Momentum synthetic turf competition field; video scoreboard; practice field; training facilities; locker rooms for home teams, visitors, coaches and officials; athletics staff offices; press, presidential, and VIP boxes; concession areas; and event space. The FAC's signature natatorium, the Mangione Aquatic Center, is bathed in sunshine from skylights that span the ceiling several stories above the pool's surface. The pool stretches eight lanes across its 25-yard length and 75-foot width. Movalbe bulkheads seperate the diving area from the swimming area. Seats for 500 spectators bank upward from the pool deck, which is also home to a whilpool and saunas. Other FAC highlights include a 30-foot indoor climbing wall, a 6,000-square foot fitness center with more than 70 pieces of fitness machinery, an elevated indoor track, four racquetball and two squash courts, two areobic/martial arts studios, a three-court gymnasium and a multi-activity court with rounded corners and plexi-glass walls for indoor soccer and floor hockey.

Disabled Students: 99% of the campus is accessible. Facilities include wheelchair ramps, elevators, special parking, specially equipped restrooms, special class scheduling, lowered drinking fountains, and lowered telephones.

Services: Counseling and information services are available, as is tutoring in most subjects. There is a reader service for the blind, and remedial math.

Campus Safety and Security: Measures include 24-hour foot and vehicle patrol, emergency notification system, self-defense education, and security escort services. There are shuttle buses, emergency telephones, lighted pathways/sidewalks, and controlled access to dorms/residences.

Programs of Study: confers B.A., B.S., B.B.A. and B.S.E. degrees. Master's and doctoral degrees are also awarded. Bachelor's degrees are awarded in BIOLOGICAL SCIENCE (biology/biological science), BUSINESS (accounting and business administration and management), COMMUNICATIONS AND THE ARTS (communications, creative writing, English, fine arts, French, German, Latin, and Spanish), COMPUTER AND PHYSICAL SCIENCE (chemistry, computer science, mathematics, and physics), EDUCATION (elementary education), ENGINEERING AND ENVIRONMENTAL DESIGN (engineering), HEALTH PROFESSIONS (speech pathology/audiology), SOCIAL SCIENCE (classical/ancient civilization, economics, history, philosophy, political science/government, psychology, sociology, and theological studies). General Business, Communication and Social Sciences have the largest enrollments.

Required: All students must complete 120 hours, including 36 in the major, with at least a 2.0 GPA. The required core curriculum includes 2 courses each in history, language (at the second-year level), literature, philosophy, social sciences, and theology; 1 course each in composition, ethics, fine arts, math, humanities, and natural sciences; and 1 additional course in math, natural science, or computer science.

Special: Loyola offers cross-registration with Johns Hopkins, Towson, and Morgan State Universities, Goucher College, the College of Notre Dame, Maryland Art Institute, and Peabody Conservatory. Credit-bearing internships are available in most majors and study abroad is possible in 27 countries. Work-study programs and dual majors are also offered. There are 28 national honor societies, including Phi Beta Kappa, a freshman honors program, and 1 departmental honors programs.

Faculty/Classroom: 92% of faculty are male; 8% are female. All teach undergraduates. No introductory courses are taught by graduate students.

Admissions: 68% of the 2013-2014 applicants were accepted. The SAT scores for the 2013-2014 freshman class were: Critical Reading--10% below 500, 47% between 500 and 599, 38% between 600 and 699, and 5% between 700 and 800; Math--12% below 500, 37% between 500 and 599, 46% between 600 and 699, and 5% between 700 and 800. The ACT scores were 4% below 21, 12% between 21 and 23, 39% between 24 and 26, 19% between 27 and 28, and 26% above 28.

Requirements: Loyola University is Test Optional. SAT and ACT are considered if submitted. All applicants should have graduated from an accredited secondary school or have earned the GED. Secondary preparation should include 4 years of English, 4 each of math, foreign language, natural science, and classical or modern foreign language, and 2 to 3 of history. AP and CLEP credits are accepted. Important factors in the admissions decision are advanced placement or honors courses, recommendations by school officials, and extracurricular activities record.

Procedure: Freshmen are admitted fall, spring, and summer. Entrance exams should be taken by December of the senior year. There are early admissions, deferred admissions, and rolling admissions plans. Early decision applications should be filed by November 1; regular applications, by January 15 for fall entry, along with a $50 fee. Notification of early decision is sent January 15; regular decision, March 15. 1692 applicants were on the 2013 waiting list; 177 were admitted. Applications are accepted online.

Transfer: 63 transfer students enrolled in 2012-2013. 60 of 120 credits required for the bachelor's degree must be completed at Loyola.

Visiting: There are regularly scheduled orientations for prospective students, We offer daily visits on most weekdays, Monday through Friday. Reservations are required. The visit lasts approximately 2.5 to 3 hours and includes a group information session, a campus tour, and an interview (optional). If senior and transfer studen. There are guides for informal visits and visitors may sit in on classes. To schedule a visit, contact the Admission Office.

Financial Aid: is a member of CSS. The CSS/Profile and FAFSA, and if applicable, a noncustodial parent's profile are required. The priority date for freshman financial aid applications for fall entry is February 15. The deadline for filing freshman financial aid applications for fall entry is February 15.

International Students: There are 22 international students enrolled. The school actively recruits these students. They must take the TOEFL with a minimum score of 550 on the paper-based TOEFL (PBT) or 79 on the Internet-based version (iBT).

Computers: All students may access the system. There are no time limits and no fees.

Graduates: From July 1, 2012 to June 30, 2013, 903 bachelor's degrees were awarded. The most popular majors were business/marketing (32%), communications/journalism (12%), and psychology (9%). 94 companies recruited on campus in 2012-2013. In an average class, 79% graduate in 4 years or less, 5% graduate in 5 years or less, and 84% graduate in 6 years or less. Of the 2012 graduating class, 25% were enrolled in graduate school within 6 months of graduation, and 26% were employed.

Admissions Contact: Office of Admission E-Mail: *admission@loyola.edu* Web: *www.loyola.edu*

MARYLAND INSTITUTE COLLEGE OF ART — D-2

Baltimore, MD 21217 — **(410) 225-2222; (410) 225-2337**

Full-time: 5605 men, 1110 women	**Faculty:** n/av
Part-time: 15 men, 15 women	**Ph.D.s:** 82%
Graduate: 85 men, 165 women	**Student/Faculty:** n/av
Year: semesters, summer session	**Tuition:** $36,870
Application Deadline: see profile	**Room & Board:** $9500
Freshman Class: n/av	
SAT: required	**SPECIAL**

Maryland Institute College of Art, founded in 1826, is a private accredited institution offering undergraduate and graduate degrees in the fine arts. The figures in the above capsule and this profile are approximate. There are 9 graduate schools. In addition to regional accreditation, MICA has baccalaureate program accreditation with NASAD. The library contains 83,564 volumes, 5600 audio/video tapes/CDs/DVDs, and subscribes to 402 periodicals including electronic. Computerized library services include interlibrary loans, database searching, Internet access, and laptop Internet portals. Special learning facilities include a learning resource center, an art gallery, 12 large art galleries, open to the public year-round and featuring work by MICA faculty, students, and nationally and internationally known artists, a slide library containing 220,000 slides, and 8 other galleries for undergraduate and graduate exhibitions. The 13-acre campus is in an urban area. Including any residence halls, there are 25 buildings.

Student Life: 80% of undergraduates are from out of state, mostly the Northeast. Students are from 47 states, 44 foreign countries, and Canada. 76% are from public schools. 67% are white. The average age of freshmen is 18; all undergraduates, 20. 15% do not continue beyond their first year; 76% remain to graduate.

Housing: 657 students can be accommodated in college housing, which includes coed dorms, on-campus apartments, and off-campus apartments. Residence halls include project rooms where students can do artwork 24 hours a day. On-campus housing is guaranteed for the freshman year only, is available on a first-come, first-served basis, and is available on a lottery system for upperclassmen. 88% of students live on campus; of those, 95% remain on campus on weekends. Alcohol is not permitted. All students may keep cars.

Activities: There are no fraternities or sororities. There are 50 groups on campus, including animation, art, ballet, belly dance, bowling, choir, chorale, comic, dance, drama, environmental, ethnic, film, gaming, gay, humor magazine, international, knitting, literary magazine, orchestra, outdoor, photography, pirate, playwriting, political, professional, radio, religious, running, social, social service, student government, ultimate frisbee, vampire, and Viking. Popular campus events include International Education Week, Fashion Show, and Caribbean Carnival.

Sports: There are 4 intramural sports for men and 4 for women. Facilities include an outdoor volleyball court and fitness center for weight lifting and aerobics on campus. The fitness center also includes a fitness studio where students take classes like yoga, meditation, aerobics, belly dancing, ballet, ballroom dancing, and break dancing. There is also a recreation center 5 blocks from campus with a basketball court and other fitness equipment.

Disabled Students: 85% of the campus is accessible. Facilities include wheelchair ramps, elevators, special parking, specially equipped restrooms, special class scheduling, lowered drinking fountains, lowered telephones, and lowered fire extinguishers.

Services: Counseling and information services are available, as is tutoring in some subjects, including writing and study skills. There is remedial writing.

Campus Safety and Security: Measures include 24-hour foot and vehicle patrol, self-defense education, and security escort services. There are shuttle buses, emergency telephones, lighted pathways/sidewalks, building monitors in most buildings, and periodic discussions and seminars on safety.

Programs of Study: MICA confers B.F.A. degrees. Master's degrees are also awarded. Bachelor's degrees are awarded in COMMUNICATIONS AND THE ARTS (animation, art history and appreciation, ceramic art and design, drawing, fiber/textiles/weaving, fine arts, graphic design, illustration, media arts, painting, photography, printmaking, sculpture, and video), ENGINEERING AND ENVIRONMENTAL DESIGN (environmental design). Painting, illustration, and general fine arts have the largest enrollments.

Required: All students complete a foundation program in their first year, including courses in painting, drawing, two- and three-dimensional design, liberal arts, and electronic arts. Of a total 126 credits, students must take one-third of the courses in liberal arts and two-thirds in studio arts, with 60 credits in the major and a minimum 2.0 GPA. Seniors must complete a focused, professionally oriented body of work.

Special: Exchange programs are offered with Goucher College, Loyola and Notre Dame Colleges, Johns Hopkins University, the Peabody Conservatory of Music, the University of Baltimore, University of Maryland Baltimore County, Towson University, Morgan State University, and Baltimore Hebrew College. Cross-registration is possible with any member schools in the Alliance of Independent Colleges of Art and the East Coast Art Schools Consortium. A New York studio semester is available as well as a semester of study with any member schools in the Association of Independent Colleges of Art and Design. Study abroad is possible in the junior year in any of 45 schools in 24 countries.

Faculty/Classroom: 50% of faculty are male; 50% are female. 87% teach undergraduates. No introductory courses are taught by graduate students. The average class size in an introductory lecture is 24 and in a regular course is 17.

Requirements: The SAT is required. Admission is based on a comprehensive set of criteria with the most emphasis placed on artistic ability as demonstrated in the portfolio and on academic achievement as demonstrated in test scores, GPA, and level of course work. Essays, recommendations, interview, and extracurricular activities are also considered. AP credits are accepted. Important factors in the admissions decision are evidence of special talent, advanced placement or honors courses, and extracurricular activities record.

Procedure: Freshmen are admitted fall and spring. Entrance exams should be taken in the spring of the junior year. There are early decisions, early admissions and deferred admissions plans. Check with the school for current application deadlines and fees. A waiting list is maintained.

Transfer: Transfer applicants must submit high school and college transcripts, a personal essay, a portfolio of artwork, letters of recommendation, and course descriptions. 63 of 126 credits required for the bachelor's degree must be completed at MICA.

Visiting: There are regularly scheduled orientations for prospective students, including campus tours and presentations about curriculum, student life, admission, and financial aid. There are guides for informal visits and visitors may sit in on classes. To schedule a visit, contact the Office of Undergraduate Admission.

Financial Aid: MICA is a member of CSS. The FAFSA and the college's own financial statement are required. Check with the school for current application deadlines.

International Students: The school actively recruits these students. They must take the TOEFL, with a minimum score of 550 on the paper-based TOEFL (PBT) or 80 on the Internet-based version (iBT), the Comprehensive English Language Test, the SAT, or the IELTS.

Computers: Wireless access is available. More than 350 PCs are available in more than 30 classrooms, labs, and public areas. 60% of the campus has wireless access. Students can use the student portal, Web galleries, student blogs, e-mail, and blackboard e-learning. All students may access the system 24 hours a day. There are no time limits and no fees. It is strongly recommended that all students have a personal computer.

Admissions Contact: Dean of Admission. E-Mail: *admissions@mica.edu* Web: *www.mica.edu*

MCDANIEL COLLEGE D-2

Westminster, MD 21157 **(410) 857-2230**
(800) 638-5005; 410857-2757

Full-time: 777 men, 881 women	**Faculty:** 107; IIB, av$
Part-time: 16 men, 18 women	**Ph.D.s:** 99%
Graduate: 373 men, 1191 women	**Student/Faculty:** 11 to 1
Year: 4-1-4, summer session	**Tuition:** $36,960
Application Deadline: February 15	**Room & Board:** $8640

Freshman Class: 2942 applied, 2232 accepted, 453 enrolled
SAT CR/M: 550/555 **ACT:** 24 **VERY COMPETITIVE**

McDaniel College, founded in 1867, is a four-year private college of the liberal arts and sciences offering more than 70 undergraduate programs of study, including dual and student-designed majors, plus highly regarded graduate and professional studies programs. A diverse student-centered community of 1,600 undergraduates and 1,560 part-time graduate students, McDaniel is centrally located between Baltimore, Washington, D.C., the Chesapeake Bay, and the Blue Ridge Mountains, and is the only American university with a European campus in Budapest, Hungary. The figures in the above capsule and in this profile are approximate. There is one undergraduate school and one graduate school. In addition to regional accreditation, McDaniel has baccalaureate program accreditation with CSWE and NCATE. The library contains 222,268 volumes, 1.4 million microform items, 24,477 audio/video tapes/CDs/DVDs, and subscribes to 717 periodicals including electronic. Computerized library services include interlibrary loans, database searching, Internet access, and Wi-Fi capability. Special learning facilities include an art gallery, radio station, TV station, Observatory, Human Performance Lab, Video Production Lab, Photography Studio, Graphics Lab, and student research science labs. The 160-acre campus is in a suburban area 30 miles from Baltimore's Inner Harbor and 60 miles from Washington, D.C. Including any residence halls, there are 73 buildings.

Student Life: 64% of undergraduates are from Maryland. Others are from 39 states, 25 foreign countries, and Canada. 80% are from public schools. 74% are White; 13% African American. The average age of freshmen is 18; all undergraduates, 20. 16% do not continue beyond their first year; 72% remain to graduate.

Housing: 1398 students can be accommodated in college housing, which includes single-sex and coed dorms and on-campus apartments. In addition, there are honors houses, language houses, special-interest houses, fraternity houses, sorority houses, fraternity and sorority floors, academic clusters, living-learning communities, substance-free floors, coed dorms, special housing for disabled students and theme housing. On-campus housing is guaranteed for all 4 years. 83% of students live on campus; of those, 60% remain on campus on weekends. Upperclassmen may keep cars.

Activities: 17% of men belong to 1 local and 3 national fraternities; 18% of women belong to 1 local and 5 national sororities. There are 100 groups on campus, including Green Terror Productions, Heroes Helping Hopkins, Outdoors Club, Ultimate Frisbee, various ethnic and cultural student organizations, art, band, Canine Companions for Independence, cheerleading, choir, chorale, chorus, computers, dance, drama, environmental, ethnic, film, forensics, gay, honors, international, jazz band, literary magazine, musical theater, newspaper, opera, orchestra, pep band, photography, political, professional, radio and TV, religious, social, social service, student government, symphony, and yearbook. Popular campus events include Homecoming, Late Night Carnival, Fall Fest, Midnight Madness, Cultural dinners, Spring Fling, Relay for Life, and Improv performances.

Sports: There are 12 intercollegiate sports for men and 12 for women, and 12 intramural sports for men and 12 for women. Facilities include The Kenneth R. Gill Stadium for football, field hockey, lacrosse, and track includes a synthetic turf field, an eight lane competition track, team rooms and a sports medicine room. The Gill Center includes the Merritt Fitness Center with an aerobic conditioning area, a selectorized machine area, and a power / free weight room. The facility also includes one 2000 seat competition wood court for basketball and volleyball, four multi-purpose synthetic courts, a wrestling room, locker rooms, exercise science labs, classrooms and meeting rooms, a sports medicine center, an equipment and laundry facilities. Outdoor athletics and intramural spaces include Preston Field (baseball), a softball competition and training facility, a soccer complex, and two practice/intramural field venues and a track throwing area. In addition, the college student center contains the Harlow pool for men's and women's swimming and a squash/racquetball court. Finally, the college has a 9-hole golf course and training facility on campus along with the Warfield Tennis Complex for men's and women's golf and tennis teams respectively.

Disabled Students: 85% of the campus is accessible. Facilities include wheelchair ramps, elevators, special parking, specially equipped restrooms, special class scheduling, lowered drinking fountains, lowered telephones, special housing.

Services: Counseling and information services are available, as is tutoring in most subjects. There is a reader service for the blind, and remedial math, reading, and writing.

Campus Safety and Security: Measures include 24-hour foot and vehicle patrol, emergency notification system, and security escort services. There are shuttle buses, emergency telephones, and lighted pathways/sidewalks.

Programs of Study: McDaniel confers B.A. degrees. Master's degrees are also awarded. Bachelor's degrees are awarded in BIOLOGICAL SCIENCE (biology/biological science), BUSINESS (business administration and management), COMMUNICATIONS AND THE ARTS (art history and appreciation, communications, dramatic arts, English, fine arts, French, German, music, and Spanish), COMPUTER AND PHYSICAL SCIENCE (chemistry, computer science, mathematics, and physics), EDUCATION (physical education), ENGINEERING AND ENVIRONMENTAL DESIGN (environmental science), SOCIAL SCIENCE (asian studies, economics, history, Middle Eastern studies, philosophy, political science/government, psychology, religion, social work, and sociology). Psychology, health and physical education/fitness, business administration, and biology have the largest enrollments.

Required: All students are required to complete the McDaniel Plan, which provides a liberal arts education combining a comprehensive program of general education and a rigorous program in the major, complemented by electives and a range of special opportunities. For the B.A.

degree, students must complete at least 128 credit hours distributed among the requirements of the McDaniel Plan, including a First Year Seminar, introduction to college writing, Sophomore Interdisciplinary Studies course, Global Citizenship, second language study, departmental writing, critical inquiries in the liberal arts, at least one January Term course, four physical activity and wellness courses, up to 50 credit hours of required coursework in the major, and electives. The minimum GPA for graduation is 2.0.

Special: The Center for Experience and Opportunity (CEO) provides students with experiential learning opportunities including community outreach, service learning, internships, work/study, undergraduate research, post-graduate fellowships, pre-professional studies, and learning communities. Global Initiatives offers programming and activities for members of the Global Fellows program in addition to innovative approaches to travel learning, such as study abroad either around the world or at McDaniel's campus in Budapest, Hungary, and global experiential and civic engagement opportunities. There is a Washington semester in conjunction with American University. The college offers dual and student-designed majors, credit by exam (in foreign languages), and pass/fail options. McDaniel College has 5-year B.A./M.S. programs and offers certification in elementary and secondary education. The college also offers advanced standing for international baccalaureate recipients. There are 20 national honor societies, including Phi Beta Kappa, a freshman honors program, and 24 departmental honors programs.

Faculty/Classroom: 44% of faculty are male; 56% are female. All teach undergraduates, and 50% do both. No introductory courses are taught by graduate students. The average class size in an introductory lecture is 18; in a laboratory is 17; and in a regular course is 15.

Admissions: 76% of the 2013-2014 applicants were accepted. The SAT scores for the 2013-2014 freshman class were: Critical Reading--25% below 500, 48% between 500 and 599, 22% between 600 and 699, and 5% between 700 and 800; Math--25% below 500, 44% between 500 and 599, 28% between 600 and 699, and 3% between 700 and 800. The ACT scores were 3% below 21, 38% between 21 and 23, and 13% above 28. There were 1 National Merit finalists. 18 freshmen graduated first in their class.

Requirements: The SAT or ACT is required. Applicants must be graduates of an accredited secondary school or have a GED. A minimum of 16 academic credits are required, including 4 years of English, 3 each of foreign language, math, and social studies, and 3 of a lab science. SAT Subject Tests and an interview are recommended. An essay and academic recommendations are required. McDaniel requires applicants to be in the upper 50% of their class. A GPA of 2.5 is required. AP and CLEP credits are accepted. Important factors in the admissions decision are advanced placement or honors courses, leadership record, and evidence of special talent.

Procedure: Freshmen are admitted fall and spring. Entrance exams should be taken at the end of the junior year. There are early admissions and deferred admissions plans. February 15 for fall entry, along with a $50 fee. 49 applicants were on the 2013 waiting list; 10 were admitted. Applications are accepted online.

Transfer: 50 transfer students enrolled in 2012-2013. A minimum college GPA of 2.5 is required. 32 of 128 credits required for the bachelor's degree must be completed at McDaniel.

Visiting: There are regularly scheduled orientations for prospective students, including an information session conducted by a counselor and/or the Director or Dean of Admissions and a student-led tour of campus. Individual visits and fall visit days include a class visit and lunch on campus. There are guides for informal visits and visitors may sit in on classes. To schedule a visit, contact Dawn Gold at (800) 638-5005.

Financial Aid: In 2013-2014, 76% of all full-time freshmen and 73% of continuing full-time students received some form of financial aid. 76% of all full-time freshmen and 72% of continuing full-time students received need-based aid. The average freshman award was $30,159. Need-based scholarships or need-based grants averaged $26,171; need-based self-help aid (loans and jobs) averaged $4,209; other non-need-based awards and non-need-based scholarships averaged $17,064; and $3,351 from other forms of aid. 18% of undergraduate students work part-time. Average annual earnings from campus work are $768. The average financial indebtedness of the 2013 graduate was $29,554. The FAFSA and the college's own financial statement are required. The priority date for freshman financial aid applications for fall entry is March 1.

International Students: There are 23 international students enrolled. The school actively recruits these students. They must take the TOEFL. They must also take the SAT.

Computers: All students may access the system. One lab is open 24 hours per day; other labs are open 8:30 a.m. to midnight daily. There are no time limits and no fees.

Graduates: From July 1, 2012 to June 30, 2013, 371 bachelor's degrees were awarded. The most popular majors were social sciences (16%), parks and recreation (10%), and communication/journalism/interdisciplinary studies/psychology (9%). 49 companies recruited on campus in 2012-2013. In an average class, 68% graduate in 4 years or less, 73% graduate in 5 years or less, and 74% graduate in 6 years or less. Of the 2012 graduating class, 36% were enrolled in graduate school within 6 months of graduation, and 88% were employed.

Admissions Contact: Florence W. Hines, VP,Dean of Admissions. E-Mail: *admissions@mcdaniel.edu* Web: *www.mcdaniel.edu/undergraduate*

MORGAN STATE UNIVERSITY D-2

Baltimore, MD 21251 (443) 885-3000
(800) 332-6674; (443) 319-3684

Full-time: 2522 men, 3272 women
Part-time: 341 men, 456 women
Graduate: 516 men, 845 women
Year: semesters, summer session
Application Deadline:
Faculty: n/av; I, --$
Ph.D.s: 80%
Student/Faculty: n/av
Tuition: $6500 ($14,500)
Room & Board: $8000
Freshman Class: 5644 applied, 3252 accepted, 1037 enrolled
SAT or ACT: required
VERY COMPETITIVE

Morgan State University, founded in 1867, is a comprehensive public institution offering undergraduate and graduate programs leading to liberal arts, preprofessional, and professional degrees. There are 6 undergraduate schools and 4 graduate schools. In addition to regional accreditation, Morgan State has baccalaureate program accreditation with AACSB, ABET, ADA, ASLA, CSWE, NAAB, NASAD, NASM, and NCATE. The library contains 389,516 volumes, 738,311 microform items, 45,855 audio/video tapes/CDs/DVDs, and subscribes to 3,011 periodicals including electronic. Computerized library services include interlibrary loans and database searching. Special learning facilities include an art gallery, radio station, and TV station. The 140-acre campus is in a suburban area in the northeast corner of Baltimore. Including any residence halls, there are 41 buildings.

Student Life: 60% of undergraduates are from Maryland. Others are from 40 states, 20 foreign countries, and Canada. 91% are from public schools. 92% are African American. The average age of freshmen is 18; all undergraduates, 21. 24% do not continue beyond their first year; 45% remain to graduate.

Housing: 1800 students can be accommodated in college housing, which includes single-sex dorms and on-campus apartments. In addition, there are honors houses. On-campus housing is guaranteed for the freshman year only, is available on a first-come, and first-served basis. 70% of students commute. Alcohol is not permitted. All students may keep cars.

Activities: 4% of men belong to 2 local and 4 national fraternities; 3% of women belong to 3 local and 4 national sororities. There are 150 groups on campus, including art, band, cheerleading, chess, choir, chorale, chorus, computers, dance, debate, drama, drill team, drum and bugle corps, ethnic, film, forensics, gay, honors, international, jazz band, literary magazine, marching band, musical theater, newspaper, opera, orchestra, pep band, photography, political, professional, radio and TV, religious, social, social service, student government, symphony, and yearbook. Popular campus events include Kwanzaa and I Love Morgan Day.

Sports: There are 6 intercollegiate sports for men and 6 for women, and 17 intramural sports for men and 16 for women. Facilities include a field house, a gym, a weight room, a swimming pool, tennis and racquetball courts, and various playing fields.

Disabled Students: 90% of the campus is accessible. Facilities include wheelchair ramps, elevators, special parking, specially equipped restrooms, special class scheduling, and lowered drinking fountains.

Services: Counseling and information services are available, as is tutoring in every subject. There is a reader service for the blind, and remedial math, reading, and writing. There are also note takers and sign language interpreters for disabled students.

Campus Safety and Security: Measures include 24-hour foot and vehicle patrol, self-defense education, and security escort services. There are shuttle buses, emergency telephones, and lighted pathways/sidewalks.

Programs of Study: Morgan State confers B.A., B.S., A.B. and B.S.Ed. degrees. Master's and doctoral degrees are also awarded. Bachelor's degrees are awarded in BIOLOGICAL SCIENCE (biology/biological science), BUSINESS (accounting, business administration and management, hospitality management services, and marketing/retailing/merchandising), COMMUNICATIONS AND THE ARTS (dramatic arts, English, fine arts, music, speech/debate/rhetoric, and telecommunications), COMPUTER AND PHYSICAL SCIENCE (chemistry, computer science, information sciences and systems, mathematics, and physics), EDUCATION (elementary education, health education, and physical education), ENGINEERING AND ENVIRONMENTAL DESIGN (civil engineering, electrical/electronics engineering, engineering physics, and industrial engineering technology), HEALTH PROFESSIONS (medical laboratory technology and mental health/human services), SOCIAL SCIENCE (African American studies, economics, history, home economics, philosophy, political science/government, psychology, religion, social work, and sociology). Engineering, chemistry and social work are the strongest academically. Business administration, accounting and electrical engineering have the largest enrollments.

Required: To graduate, students must complete at least 120 credit hours, including 74 in the major, with a 2.0 GPA. All students must pass speech and writing proficiency exams prior to their senior year. The 46-credit general education requirement includes courses in English, humanities, logic, history, behavioral science, science, math, African American history, and health and phys ed. Seniors must pass a proficiency exam in their major.
Special: Co-op programs in public and private institutions may be arranged for pharmacy honors, predentistry, premedicine, and special education students. The university also offers internships for juniors and seniors, study abroad in 3 countries, work-study programs, and preprofessional physical therapy and prelaw programs. Dual majors may be pursued but do not lead to a dual degree. There are 28 national honor societies and a freshman honors program.
Faculty/Classroom: 60% of faculty are male; 40% are female. All teach undergraduates, 76% do research, and 76% do both. No introductory courses are taught by graduate students. The average class size in an introductory lecture is 25; in a laboratory is 26; and in a regular course is 21.
Admissions: 58% of the 2013-2014 applicants were accepted.
Requirements: The SAT or ACT is required, with a satisfactory score on the SAT. Applicants should be high school graduates or have earned the GED, and are encouraged to have 4 years of English, 3 of math, 2 each of science, social studies, and history, and 1 of a foreign language. A personal essay is recommended and, when appropriate, an audition. A GPA of 2.5 is required. AP and CLEP credits are accepted. Important factors in the admissions decision are recommendations by school officials, evidence of special talent, and parents or siblings attended your school.
Procedure: Freshmen are admitted fall and spring. Entrance exams should be taken during the fall semester of the junior or senior year. There is a rolling admissions plan. Check with the school for current application deadlines. The application fee is $45.
Transfer: 482 transfer students enrolled in 2012-2013. Applicants with fewer than 24 credits must submit high school transcripts; those with fewer than 12 credits must also submit SAT scores. Applicants are expected to have at least a 2.0 GPA in all college work attempted and be in good standing at the last institution attended. 30 of 120 credits required for the bachelor's degree must be completed at Morgan State.
Visiting: There are regularly scheduled orientations for prospective students, including placement testing and academic advising. There are guides for informal visits, visitors may sit in on classes, and stay overnight.
Financial Aid: Morgan State is a member of CSS. The FAFSA and the college's own financial statement are required. Check with the school for current application deadlines.
International Students: They must take the TOEFL, or ALIGU. They must also take the SAT or ACT. Students who have not attended any school during the preceding 3 years are not required to submit standardized test scores.
Computers: All students may access the system. There are no time limits and no fees.
Graduates: From July 1, 2012 to June 30, 2013, 899 bachelor's degrees were awarded. The most popular majors were business/marketing (23%), communication/journalism (12%), and engineering (10%). 79 companies recruited on campus in 2012-2013. In an average class, 12% graduate in 4 years or less, 34% graduate in 5 years or less, and 41% graduate in 6 years or less. Of the 2012 graduating class, 47% were enrolled in graduate school within 6 months of graduation, and 89% were employed.
Admissions Contact: Edwin T. Johnson, Director of Admission and Recruitment. E-Mail: *Admissions@morgan.edu* Web: *www.morgan.edu*

MOUNT SAINT MARY'S UNIVERSITY D-2

Emmitsburg, MD 21727 (301) 447-5214
(800) 448-4347; (301) 447-5860

Full-time: 737 men, 913 women	**Faculty:** 106; IIA, --$
Part-time: 40 men, 51 women	**Ph.D.s:** 91%
Graduate: 299 men, 200 women	**Student/Faculty:** 13 to 1
Year: semesters, summer session	**Tuition:** $34,644
Application Deadline: March 1	**Room & Board:** $11,514
Freshman Class: 4942 applied, 3332 accepted, 429 enrolled	
SAT CR/M/W: 550/530/530 **ACT:** 21	**COMPETITIVE**

Mount St. Mary's University, founded in 1808, is a private liberal arts institution affiliated with the Roman Catholic Church. There are 4 undergraduate schools and 4 graduate schools. In addition to regional accreditation, The Mount has baccalaureate program accreditation with NASDTEC and NCATE. The library contains 175,842 volumes, 2,056 audio/video tapes/CDs/DVDs, and subscribes to 50,567 periodicals including electronic. Computerized library services include interlibrary loans, database searching, Internet access, and Wi-Fi capability. Special learning facilities include an art gallery, radio station, TV station, archives. The 1400-acre campus is in a rural area 60 miles northwest of Washington, D.C., and 50 miles west of Baltimore. Including any residence halls, there are 29 buildings.
Student Life: 51% of undergraduates are from Maryland. Others are from 38 states, 14 foreign countries, and Canada. 58% are from public schools. 73% are White. 76% are Catholic; 15% Protestant. The average age of freshmen is 18; all undergraduates, 20. 22% do not continue beyond their first year; 69% remain to graduate.
Housing: 1410 students can be accommodated in college housing, which includes coed dorms and on-campus apartments. In addition, there are special-interest houses, wellness floors, and quiet floors. On-campus housing is guaranteed for all 4 years. 82% of students live on campus; of those, 80% remain on campus on weekends. All students may keep cars.
Activities: There are no fraternities or sororities. There are 70 groups on campus, including art, band, cheerleading, chess, choir, chorale, computers, dance, debate, drama, environmental, ethnic, honors, international, literary magazine, musical theater, newspaper, pep band, political, professional, radio and TV, religious, social, social service, student government, and yearbook. Popular campus events include Acoustic Battle, Christmas Dance, Crab Feast, Homecoming and Special Olympics.
Sports: There are 7 intercollegiate sports for men and 9 for women, and 19 intramural sports for men and 16 for women. Facilities include multipurpose indoor courts, a track, a pool, aerobics facilities, a sauna, a weight room, a basketball arena, lighted tennis courts, and playing fields.
Disabled Students: 85% of the campus is accessible. Facilities include wheelchair ramps, elevators, special parking, specially equipped restrooms, special class scheduling, lowered drinking fountains, and lowered telephones.
Services: Counseling and information services are available, as is tutoring in every subject. There is a reader service for the blind, and remedial math. There is a study skills and language lab, and a writing center. Closed-caption TV and software for sight-impaired students are also available.
Campus Safety and Security: Measures include 24-hour foot and vehicle patrol, emergency notification system, and security escort services. There are emergency telephones, lighted pathways/sidewalks, and controlled access to dorms/residences.
Programs of Study: The Mount confers B.A., and B.S. degrees. Master's degrees are also awarded. Bachelor's degrees are awarded in BIOLOGICAL SCIENCE (biochemistry and biology/biological science), BUSINESS (accounting, business administration and management, and sports management), COMMUNICATIONS AND THE ARTS (communications, English, fine arts, French, German, and Spanish), COMPUTER AND PHYSICAL SCIENCE (chemistry, computer science, information sciences and systems, and mathematics), EDUCATION (elementary education), ENGINEERING AND ENVIRONMENTAL DESIGN (environmental science), SOCIAL SCIENCE (criminal justice, economics, history, interdisciplinary studies, international studies, philosophy, political science/government, psychology, social studies, sociology, and theological studies). Business, elementary education, and criminal justice have the largest enrollments.
Required: Students are required to take a 4-year, 33 credit core curriculum in liberal arts (with an additional 24 credits in domain areas, some of which overlap in the major area). The common educational experience includes a liberal arts symposium, a Western civilization sequence including art and literature, and courses in philosophy, theology, foreign language, math, American culture, and ethics. Graduation requirements include 120 credits, with most majors requiring 36 credits (30 to 36 in the major) and a minimum GPA of 2.0.
Special: Mount Saint Mary's offers cross-registration with an area community college, study abroad in the U.K., Europe, and South America, and secondary teacher certification in English, foreign languages, math, and social studies. Dual majors, interdisciplinary majors in biopsychology, American culture, and classical studies, a general studies degree, 3 dual degree programs, and nondegree and accelerated study are possible. A number of independently designed internships, work-study programs, and pass/fail options are available. The Veritas Program is a common 4 year curriculum integrated with every academic major. It includes leadership development and cultural components. There are 20 national honor societies and a freshman honors program.
Faculty/Classroom: 59% of faculty are male; 41% are female. 86% teach undergraduates, 48% do research, and 48% do both. No introductory courses are taught by graduate students. The average class size in an introductory lecture is 22; in a laboratory is 16; and in a regular course is 20.
Admissions: 67% of the 2013-2014 applicants were accepted. The SAT scores for the 2013-2014 freshman class were: Critical Reading--23% below 500, 52% between 500 and 599, 22% between 600 and 699, and 3% between 700 and 800; Math--28% below 500, 50% between 500 and 599, 21% between 600 and 699, and 1% between 700 and 800; Writing--31% below 500, 46% between 500 and 599, 21% between 600 and 699, and 2% between 700 and 800. The ACT scores were 49% below 21, 26% between 21 and 23, 20% between 24 and 26, 3% between 27 and 28, and 2% above 28. 28% of the current freshmen were in the top fifth of their class; 52% were in the top two fifths. 2 freshmen graduated first in their class.
Requirements: The SAT is required. Applicants should be graduates of

an accredited secondary school or hold the GED. Secondary preparation should include 4 years of English, 3 each of math, history, natural science, and social sciences, and 2 of a foreign language. An interview is recommended. AP and CLEP credits are accepted. Important factors in the admissions decision are recommendations by school officials, advanced placement or honors courses, and extracurricular activities record.

Procedure: Freshmen are admitted fall and spring. Entrance exams should be taken by January of the senior year. There are early admissions, deferred admissions, and rolling admissions plans. Application deadlines are open. Application fee is $45. Applications are accepted online.

Transfer: 48 transfer students enrolled in 2012-2013. Transfer applicants should have at least a 2.0 GPA in previous college work, be in good academic and disciplinary standing, and account for all time elapsed since graduation from high school. 30 of 120 credits required for the bachelor's degree must be completed at The Mount.

Visiting: There are regularly scheduled orientations for prospective students, including campus tours and information sessions on academic programs, community life, admissions, and financial aid. There are guides for informal visits, visitors may sit in on classes, and stay overnight. To schedule a visit, contact the Admissions Office.

Financial Aid: In 2013-2014, 99% of all full-time freshmen and 98% of continuing full-time students received some form of financial aid. 75% of all full-time freshmen and 70% of continuing full-time students received need-based aid. The average freshman award was $25,957. Need-based scholarships or need-based grants averaged $3,300 ($16,837 maximum); need-based self-help aid (loans and jobs) averaged $5,585 ($7,030 maximum); non-need-based athletic scholarships averaged $11,938 ($46,158 maximum); and other non-need-based awards and non-need-based scholarships averaged $16,200 ($33,674 maximum). 36% of undergraduate students work part-time. Average annual earnings from campus work are $1300. The average financial indebtedness of the 2013 graduate was $37,599. The FAFSA and the college's own financial statement are required. The deadline for filing freshman financial aid applications for fall entry is March 1.

International Students: There are 18 international students enrolled. They must take the TOEFL with a minimum score of 550 on the paper-based TOEFL (PBT) or 83 on the Internet-based version (iBT). They must also take the SAT or ACT.

Computers: All students may access the system 24 hours per day. There are no time limits and no fees.

Graduates: From July 1, 2012 to June 30, 2013, 413 bachelor's degrees were awarded. The most popular majors were business (20%), criminal justice (10%), and biology (8%). 26 companies recruited on campus in 2012-2013. In an average class, 62% graduate in 4 years or less, 65% graduate in 5 years or less, and 66% graduate in 6 years or less. Of the 2012 graduating class, 40% were enrolled in graduate school within 6 months of graduation, and 94% were employed.

Admissions Contact: Michael Post, Dean of Admissions and Enrollment Management. E-Mail: *admissions@msmary.edu* Web: *www.msmary.edu*

NOTRE DAME OF MARYLAND UNIVERSITY — D-2

Baltimore, MD 21210 — (410) 532-5330; (800) 435-0200; (410) 532-6287

Full-time: 670 women	**Faculty:** n/av; IIB, av$
Part-time: 105 men, 905 women	**Ph.D.s:** n/av
Graduate: 305 men, 1210 women	**Student/Faculty:** n/av
Year: semesters, summer session	**Tuition:** $28,750
Application Deadline: open	**Room & Board:** $9900
Freshman Class: n/av	
SAT or ACT: required	

COMPETITIVE

The College of Notre Dame of Maryland, founded in 1873, is a private liberal arts institution primarily for women and affiliated with the Catholic Church. The figures in the above capsule and in this profile are approximate. There is 1 graduate school. In addition to regional accreditation, Notre Dame has baccalaureate program accreditation with NLN. The library contains 290,000 volumes, 378,138 microform items, 24,000 audio/video tapes/CDs/DVDs, and subscribes to 2000 periodicals including electronic. Computerized library services include database searching. Special learning facilities include a learning resource center, art gallery, planetarium, radio station, TV station, graphic arts studio, roof-top greenhouse, and cultural center. The 58-acre campus is in a suburban area 10 miles north of Baltimore. Including any residence halls, there are 11 buildings.

Student Life: 70% of undergraduates are from Maryland. Others are from 21 states.

Housing: 450 students can be accommodated in college housing, which includes single-sex dorms. On-campus housing is guaranteed for all 4 years. 65% of students live on campus; of those, 60% remain on campus on weekends. Alcohol is not permitted. All students may keep cars.

Activities: There are no fraternities or sororities. There are 24 groups on campus, including art, choir, dance, drama, ethnic, honors, international, literary magazine, newspaper, political, professional, radio and TV, religious, social, social service, student government, and yearbook. Popular campus events include Honors Convocation, Antostal Day, and Multicultural Awareness Week.

Sports: Facilities include a sports/activities complex that houses racquetball courts, a dance studio, a fitness center, an indoor walking track, a game room, an activities resource center, and a basketball court.

Disabled Students: 98% of the campus is accessible. Facilities include wheelchair ramps, elevators, special parking, specially equipped restrooms, and lowered drinking fountains.

Services: Counseling and information services are available, as is tutoring in most subjects.

Campus Safety and Security: Measures include 24-hour foot and vehicle patrol, self-defense education, and security escort services. There are lighted pathways/sidewalks.

Programs of Study: Notre Dame confers B.A. and B.S. degrees. Master's degrees are also awarded. Bachelor's degrees are awarded in BIOLOGICAL SCIENCE (biology/biological science), BUSINESS (accounting, banking and finance, business administration and management, international business management, and marketing/retailing/merchandising), COMMUNICATIONS AND THE ARTS (art history and appreciation, classics, communications, English, graphic design, modern language, music, photography, and studio art), COMPUTER AND PHYSICAL SCIENCE (chemistry, computer science, information sciences and systems, mathematics, and physics), EDUCATION (art education, early childhood education, elementary education, foreign languages education, music education, science education, secondary education, and special education), ENGINEERING AND ENVIRONMENTAL DESIGN (preengineering), HEALTH PROFESSIONS (nursing, predentistry, premedicine, and prepharmacy), SOCIAL SCIENCE (economics, history, interdisciplinary studies, international relations, liberal arts/general studies, political science/government, prelaw, psychology, and religion). Business, education, and communication arts have the strongest academically.

Required: To graduate, students must complete a total of 128 credit hours with a minimum GPA of 2.0 (2.5 in many majors). All students must fulfill the distribution requirements in the general education core, the major, and electives, and must demonstrate proficiency in writing, public speaking, computer literacy, and library research. In most majors, a minimum of 42 hours is required. All students must take a speech course and 2 courses in phys ed, and some majors require senior practicums.

Special: The college offers cross-registration with Johns Hopkins, Towson State, and Morgan State Universities; Coppin State, Goucher, and Loyola Colleges; and the Maryland Institute College of Art. Study abroad, internships, dual bachelor's degrees in nursing and engineering, 3-2 engineering degrees with Johns Hopkins University and the University of Maryland, and pass/fail options are available. Notre Dame's Weekend College offers bachelor's degree programs for employed adults. There are 8 national honor societies, a freshman honors program, and 4 departmental honors programs.

Faculty/Classroom: 30% of faculty are male; 70% are female. All teach undergraduates. No introductory courses are taught by graduate students. The average class size in an introductory lecture is 30; in a laboratory, 20; and in a regular course, 20.

Requirements: The SAT or ACT is required. Applicants should be graduates of an accredited secondary school. 18 academic credits are required, including 4 units of English, 3 each of math and a foreign language, and 2 each of history and science, plus 4 electives. An essay is required, and an interview is recommended. A GPA of 2.5 is required. AP credits are accepted. Important factors in the admissions decision are recommendations by school officials, advanced placement or honors courses, and leadership record.

Procedure: Freshmen are admitted fall and spring. Entrance exams should be taken no later than January of the senior year. There are early decision, early admissions, deferred admissions, and rolling admissions plans. Application deadlines are open. Notification is sent on a rolling basis. Applications are accepted online.

Transfer: Notre Dame requires a minimum GPA of 2.5 for transfer students but recommends a GPA of 3.0. Students must also submit a letter of recommendation and an essay. 60 of 128 credits required for the bachelor's degree must be completed at Notre Dame.

Visiting: There are regularly scheduled orientations for prospective students, consisting of programs in June and January, each of which includes a stay in the dorm, registration, and advisement. There are guides for informal visits, and visitors may sit in on classes. To schedule a visit, contact the Office of Admissions.

Financial Aid: Notre Dame is a member of CSS. The CSS/Profile and FAFSA are required. Check with the school for current application deadlines.

International Students: The school actively recruits these students. They must take the TOEFL.

Computers: All students may access the system 7 days a week. There are no time limits and no fees.

Admissions Contact: Director of Admissions. E-mail: *admiss@ndm.edu*
Web: *www.ndm.edu*

SALISBURY UNIVERSITY F-4

Salisbury, MD 21801 **(410) 543-6161; (410) 546-6016**

Full-time: 3190 men, 4215 women	**Faculty:** 410
Part-time: 289 men, 310 women	**Ph.D.s:** 83%
Graduate: 168 men, 471 women	**Student/Faculty:** 18 to 1
Year: 4-1-4, summer session	**Tuition:** $8128 ($16,474)
Application Deadline: January 15	**Room & Board:** $10,240
Freshman Class: 8905 applied, 4895 accepted, 1246 enrolled	
SAT CR/M/W: 575/580/570	**ACT:** 24 **VERY COMPETITIVE**

Salisbury University, founded in 1925, is a public comprehensive university providing undergraduate programs in the liberal arts, sciences, preprofessional and professional programs, and select, mostly applied, graduate programs in business, education, nursing, psychology, English, and history. There are 4 undergraduate schools and one graduate school. In addition to regional accreditation, SU has baccalaureate program accreditation with AACSB, CSWE, NASM, and NCATE. The 2 libraries contain 287,318 volumes, 756,650 microform items, 1,798 audio/video tapes/CDs/ DVDs, and subscribe to 1,035 periodicals including electronic. Computerized library services include interlibrary loans, database searching, and Internet access. Special learning facilities include an art gallery, radio station, TV station, Nabb Research Center for Delmarva History and Culture, Scarborough Student Leadership Center, Center for Conflict Resolution, Richard A Henson Medical Simulation Center. The 182-acre campus is in a rural area 30 miles from Ocean City, 120 miles from Baltimore and 120 miles from Washington, D.C. Including any residence halls, there are 66 buildings.

Student Life: 85% of undergraduates are from Maryland. Others are from 29 states, 69 foreign countries, and Canada. 80% are from public schools. 74% are White; 12% African American. The average age of freshmen is 18; all undergraduates, 21. 19% do not continue beyond their first year; 67% remain to graduate.

Housing: 2264 students can be accommodated in college housing, which includes coed dorms, on-campus apartments, and off-campus apartments. Theme, Wellness, Disabled, International, Living/Learning. On-campus housing is available on a first-come and first-served basis. 72% of students commute. All students may keep cars.

Activities: 6% of men belong to 10 national fraternities; 4% of women belong to 5 national sororities. There are 132 groups on campus, including art, cheerleading, choir, chorale, chorus, computers, dance, debate, drama, ethnic, film, gay, honors, international, jazz band, literary magazine, musical theater, newspaper, opera, orchestra, pep band, photography, political, professional, radio and TV, religious, social, social service, student government, and symphony. Popular campus events include Oktoberfest, Gullfest, Homecoming Week, Big Event (Community Service), Relay for Life, Multicultural Festival.

Sports: There are 10 intercollegiate sports for men and 11 for women, and 17 intramural sports for men and 17 for women. Facilities include 3000-seat stadium, 2000-seat gym, multipurpose gym, 25-meter 6-lane swimming pool, indoor climbing walls, dance studio, racquetball and indoor and outdoor tennis courts, baseball diamond, varsity and practice fields, all-weather track, fitness center, 2 strength rooms, lighted intramural fields, outdoor sand volleyball courts.

Disabled Students: 95% of the campus is accessible. Facilities include wheelchair ramps, elevators, special parking, specially equipped restrooms, special class scheduling, lowered drinking fountains, lowered telephones, and special housing.

Services: Counseling and information services are available, as is tutoring in most subjects. There is a reader service for the blind, and remedial math and reading.

Campus Safety and Security: Measures include 24-hour foot and vehicle patrol, emergency notification system, self-defense education, and security escort services. There are shuttle buses, emergency telephones, lighted pathways/sidewalks, controlled access to dorms/residences, 24-hour University Police protection, Informal meetings/discussions, Student patrols, Phamplets/posters/fliers.

Programs of Study: SU confers B.A., B.S., B.A.S.W. and B.F.A. degrees. Master's and doctoral degrees are also awarded. Bachelor's degrees are awarded in AGRICULTURE (environmental studies), BIOLOGICAL SCIENCE (biology/biological science), BUSINESS (accounting, banking and finance, business administration and management, management information systems, and marketing/retailing/merchandising), COMMUNICATIONS AND THE ARTS (art, communications, English, English as a second/foreign language, fine arts, French, music, Spanish, and theater management), COMPUTER AND PHYSICAL SCIENCE (chemistry, computer science, earth science, information sciences and systems, mathematics, physical sciences, and physics), EDUCATION (athletic training, early childhood education, education, education administration, elementary education, health education, mathematics education, physical education, reading education, and teaching English as a second/foreign language (TESOL/TEFOL)), HEALTH PROFESSIONS (environmental health science, exercise science, health care administration, medical technology, nursing, and respiratory therapy), SOCIAL SCIENCE (economics, geography, history, interdisciplinary studies, international studies, peace studies, philosophy, political science/government, psychology, social science, social work, and sociology). Nursing, education, and business are the strongest academically. Biology, nursing, and elementary education have the largest enrollments.

Required: Students must successfully complete at least 120 credit hours of coursework with a cumulative GPA of 2.0 or higher. Students must take 30 of the last 37 credit hours at SU (special cooperative programs are exempt). Students completing their course requirements through an approved study abroad program are exempt from this policy. Complete at least 30 credit hours at SU by direct classroom instruction and/or lab experience and not through credit by examination. Complete at least 30 credit hours at the 300/400 level with grades of C or better. Transfer students must complete at least 15 hours of their 30 upper-level credits at SU (note: other than field-based courses in the Seidel School of Education and Professional Studies, courses taken on a PS/F basis do not satisfy this requirement). Satisfy the General Education requirements. Satisfy the requirements in at least one major program of study including the major's required GPA. Earn grades of C or better in English 101, 102 or 103.

Special: Cross registration with schools in the University System of Maryland and study abroad in numerous countries are offered. SU also offers an Annapolis semester, a Washington semester, internships, work-study programs, accelerated degree programs in dentistry, optometry, podiatric medicine, and pharmacy, dual majors in biology/environmental marine science, social work/sociology, and physical engineering, interdisciplinary and student-designed majors including physics/microelectronics, a 3-2 engineering degree with the University of Maryland at College Park, Old Dominion University, and Widener University, a co-op program in electrical engineering, and pass/fail options. There are 22 national honor societies and a freshman honors program.

Faculty/Classroom: 43% of faculty are male; 57% are female. All teach undergraduates, 6% do research, and 6% do both. Graduate students teach 4% of introductory courses. The average class size in an introductory lecture is 29; in a laboratory is 21; and in a regular course is 25.

Admissions: 55% of the 2013-2014 applicants were accepted. The SAT scores for the 2013-2014 freshman class were: Critical Reading--6% below 500, 62% between 500 and 599, 29% between 600 and 699, and 3% between 700 and 800; Math--4% below 500, 54% between 500 and 599, 39% between 600 and 699, and 3% between 700 and 800; Writing--7% below 500, 60% between 500 and 599, 31% between 600 and 699, and 2% between 700 and 800. The ACT scores were 3% below 21, 43% between 21 and 23, % between 24 and 26, 53% between 27 and 28, and 1% above 28. 59% of the current freshmen were in the top fifth of their class; 93% were in the top two fifths. There were 3 National Merit finalists. 2 freshmen graduated first in their class.

Requirements: Applicants must be graduates of accredited secondary schools or have earned a GED. The university requires 15 academic credits, including 4 in English, 3 each in math and social studies, 3 in science (2 with labs), and 2 in foreign language. Auditions are required for admission into the music and B.F.A. programs once admission to the university is granted. Essays are recommended but not required. A campus visit is recommended for all students. The SAT is not required for any enrolling student with a 3.5 or greater GPA. A GPA of 2.0 is required. AP and CLEP credits are accepted. Important factors in the admissions decision are advanced placement or honors courses, leadership record, and extracurricular activities record.

Procedure: Freshmen are admitted to all sessions. Entrance exams should be taken by December of Senior year. There are early decision and early admissions plans. Applications should be filed by January 15 for fall entry, along with a $50 fee. Notifications are sent March 15. Applications are accepted online.

Transfer: 915 transfer students enrolled in 2012-2013. Applicants must present a minimum GPA of 2.0 with at least 24 transferable credit hours earned from a regionally accredited community college or 4-year college or university. Contractural admission is extended to individuals who have complete 12 credit hours of transferable coursework and present a minimum GPA of 2.5 Students with fewer than 24 credit hours must be eligible for freshman admission in addition to maintaining at least a 2.0 GPA in college courses. 30 of 120 credits required for the bachelor's degree must be completed at SU.

Visiting: There are regularly scheduled orientations for prospective students, Presentations, tours, meets with faculty and staff. Saturday open house programs. There are guides for informal visits and visitors may sit in on classes. To schedule a visit, contact the Admissions Office.

Financial Aid: In 2013-2014, 88% of all full-time freshmen and 75% of continuing full-time students received some form of financial aid. 61% of all full-time freshmen and 66% of continuing full-time students received need-based aid. The average freshman award was $10,768. Need based scholarships or need-based grants averaged $5,460; need-based self-help aid (loans and jobs) averaged $3,118; and other non-need-based awards and non-need-based scholarships averaged $2,698. 18% of undergraduate students work part-time. Average annual earnings from campus work are $3000. The average financial indebtedness of the 2013 graduate was $23,545. SU is a member of CSS. The FAFSA is required. The priority date for freshman financial aid applications for fall entry is March 1. The deadline for filing freshman financial aid applications for fall entry is December 31.

International Students: There are 86 international students enrolled. They must take the TOEFL with a minimum score of 550 on the paper-based TOEFL (PBT) or 77 on the Internet-based version (iBT), Proof of VISA, Admissions application with financial declaration, Professional evaluation of foreign academic transcript. They must also take the SAT or ACT.

Computers: All students may access the system 24 hours daily via modem or in residence halls. There are no time limits. The fee is $104.

Graduates: From July 1, 2012 to June 30, 2013, 1872 bachelor's degrees were awarded. The most popular majors were business administration (13%), education (12%), and communication arts (10%). 275 companies recruited on campus in 2012-2013. In an average class, 2% graduate in 3 years or less, 49% graduate in 4 years or less, 64% graduate in 5 years or less, and 67% graduate in 6 years or less. Of the 2012 graduating class, 17% were enrolled in graduate school within 6 months of graduation, and 13% were employed.

Admissions Contact: Elizabeth Skoglund, Director of Admissions. E-Mail: *easkoglund@salisbury.edu* Web: *www.salisbury.edu*

SOJOURNER-DOUGLASS COLLEGE D-2

Baltimore, MD 21202 (410) 276-0306
(800) 732-2630; (410) 675-1810

Full-time: 40 men, 150 women
Part-time: 20 men, 40 women
Graduate: n/av
Year: varies
Application Deadline: open
Freshman Class: n/av
Faculty: n/av
Ph.D.s: 18%
Student/Faculty: n/av
Tuition: $9160
Room & Board: n/app
LESS COMPETITIVE

Sojourner-Douglass College, established in 1980, is a private institution offering undergraduate programs in administration, human and social resources, and human growth and development to a predominantly black student body. The figures in the above capsule and this profile are approximate. The library contains 20,000 volumes. Special learning facilities include a learning resource center. The campus is in an urban area in Baltimore.

Student Life: All undergraduates are from Maryland.

Housing: There are no residence halls. All students commute.

Activities: There are no fraternities or sororities. There are 5 groups on campus, including student government and yearbook.

Sports: There is no sports program at Sojourner-Douglass.

Disabled Students: Facilities include wheelchair ramps, elevators, and special parking.

Services: Counseling and information services are available, as is tutoring in some subjects, including reading, writing, math, and study skills.

Programs of Study: Sojourner-Douglass confers B.A. degrees. Bachelor's degrees are awarded in BUSINESS (business administration and management and tourism), COMMUNICATIONS AND THE ARTS (broadcasting), EDUCATION (early childhood education), HEALTH PROFESSIONS (health care administration), SOCIAL SCIENCE (criminal justice, gerontology, psychology, public administration, and social work).

Required: To graduate, students must earn 63 to 66 general education credits, with 15 credits in English literature and composition; 15 credits in political science, history, economics, sociology, geography, psychology, and anthropology; 12 credits in the humanities; 9 credits in natural science and math; and 3 credits each in career planning and personal development, psychology of the black family in America, and psychology of racism. 12 credits must be earned in a project that demonstrates competence in the major. 6 credits must be earned in the sociology of work. There is also a 3-credit education seminar requirement. A total of 132 credits is needed to graduate, with 54 to 69 in the major.

Special: Credit may be granted for life, military, and work experience. Faculty-supervised independent study is possible for adult students.

Requirements: The SAT or ACT is not required. Applicants must be graduates of an accredited secondary school or have a GED certificate. They must have completed 4 years of English and 2 years each of math, history, and social studies. Autobiographical essays, resumes, and interviews are required.

Procedure: Freshmen are admitted to all sessions. There is a rolling admissions plan. Application deadlines are open.

Transfer: Transfer criteria are the same as for entering freshmen; however, transfers are not accepted to all classes.

Visiting: There are regularly scheduled orientations for prospective students. To schedule a visit, contact the Office of Admissions.

Financial Aid: The CCS/Profile, FAFSA, FFS, or SFS and federal income tax form is required. Check with the school for current application deadlines.

Computers: There are no time limits and no fees.

Admissions Contact: Admissions Office. Web: *www.sdc.edu*

ST. JOHN'S COLLEGE-ANNAPOLIS E-3

Annapolis, MD 21404 (410) 626-2522
(800) 727-9238; (410) 269-7916

Full-time: 247 men, 215 women
Part-time: 1 men
Graduate: 46 men, 29 women
Year: semesters
Application Deadline: open
Freshman Class: 357 applied, 289 accepted, 136 enrolled
SAT CR/M: 640/570
Faculty: 73
Ph.D.s: 78%
Student/Faculty: 8 to 1
Tuition: $43,256
Room & Board: $10,334
ACT: 27 **HIGHLY COMPETITIVE**

St. John's College, founded as King William's School in 1696 and chartered as St. John's in 1784, is a private institution that offers a single all-required curriculum sometimes called the Great Books Program. Students and faculty work together in small discussion classes without lecture courses, written finals, or emphasis on grades. The program is a rigorous interdisciplinary curriculum based on the great works of literature, math, philosophy, theology, sciences, political theory, music, history, and economics. There is also a campus in Santa Fe, New Mexico. The figures in the above capsule and in this profile are approximate. There is 1 undergraduate school and 1 graduate school. The 2 libraries contain 133,000 volumes, 2,000 microform items, 5,000 audio/video tapes/CDs/DVDs, and subscribe to 240 periodicals including electronic. Computerized library services include interlibrary loans, database searching, Internet access, and laptop Internet portals. Special learning facilities include an art gallery and planetarium. The 36-acre campus is in a small town 35 miles east of Washington, D.C., and 32 miles south of Baltimore. Including any residence halls, there are 18 buildings.

Student Life: 83% of undergraduates are from out of state, mostly the South. Students are from 43 states, 12 foreign countries, and Canada. 60% are from public schools. 90% are white. 58% claim no religious affiliation; 22% Protestant. The average age of freshmen is 19; all undergraduates, 20. 20% do not continue beyond their first year; 76% remain to graduate.

Housing: 375 students can be accommodated in college housing, which includes single-sex and coed dorms. On-campus housing is guaranteed for the freshman year only and is available on a lottery system for upperclassmen. 75% of students live on campus; of those, 95% remain on campus on weekends. Upperclassmen may keep cars.

Activities: There are no fraternities or sororities. There are 49 groups on campus, including Christian fellowship, community garden, fencing and Jewish fellowship, vegetarian, waltz and swing, woodshop, chorus, dance, drama, film, international, literary magazine, newspaper, orchestra, photography, poetry, and student government. Popular campus events include Reality Weekend, Senior Prank, and College Navy Croquet Match.

Sports: There are 4 intercollegiate sports for men and 4 for women, and 19 intramural sports for men and 19 for women. Facilities include a gym with a weight room, cardio room, and indoor running track, tennis courts, a boathouse for sailing and crew, a pier with floating docks, and playing fields.

Disabled Students: 70% of the campus is accessible. Facilities include wheelchair ramps, elevators, special parking, specially equipped restrooms, special class scheduling, lowered drinking fountains, lowered telephones, and special housing.

Services: Counseling and information services are available, as is tutoring in some subjects, Greek, French, math, and writing There is remedial math and writing.

Campus Safety and Security: Measures include 24-hour foot and vehicle patrol, emergency notification system, self-defense education, and security escort services. There are emergency telephones, lighted pathways/sidewalks, and controlled access to dorms/residences.

Programs of Study: St. John's confers B.A. degrees. Master's degrees are also awarded. Bachelor's degrees are awarded in SOCIAL SCIENCE (liberal arts/general studies, Western European studies, and Western civilization/culture).

Required: The common curriculum, equivalent to 132 credits, covers a range of classic to modern works. Students attend small seminars; 9-week preceptorials on specific works or topics; language, music, and math tutorials; and a 3-year natural sciences lab. Active learning occurs through discussion, translations, writing, experiment, mathematical demonstration, and musical analysis. Students take oral exams each semester and submit annual essays. Sophomores also take a math exam and seniors an oral exam that admits them to degree candidacy. Seniors also present a final essay to the faculty and take a 1-hour public oral exam.

Special: St. John's offers summer internships and an informal study-abroad program.

Faculty/Classroom: 73% of faculty are male; 27% are female. All teach

undergraduates. No introductory courses are taught by graduate students. The average class size in a laboratory is 15 and in a regular course is 15.

Admissions: 81% of the 2011-2012 applicants were accepted. The SAT scores for the 2011-2012 freshman class were: Critical Reading--2% below 500, 10% between 500 and 599, 40% between 600 and 700, and 48% above 700; Math--4% below 500, 29% between 500 and 599, 44% between 600 and 700, and 23% above 700. The ACT scores were 12% between 24 and 26, 46% between 27 and 28, and 42% above 28. There were 4 National Merit finalists.

Requirements: Applicants need not be high school graduates; some students are admitted before they complete high school. Test scores may be submitted but are not required. Secondary preparation should include 4 years of English, 3 years of math, and 2 years each of foreign language, science, and history. Applicants must submit written essays, which are critical to the admissions decision, and are strongly urged to visit. Important factors in the admissions decision are recommendations by school officials, advanced placement or honors courses, and personality/intangible qualities.

Procedure: Freshmen are admitted in the fall. There are early admissions, deferred admissions, and rolling admissions plans. Application deadlines are open. Notification is sent on a rolling basis. Applications are accepted online.

Transfer: 16 transfer students enrolled in a recent year. Transfer students may enter only as freshmen and must complete the entire program at St. John's. The admissions criteria are the same as for regular students. Students in good academic standing may transfer to the Santa Fe campus at the beginning of any academic year. 132 of 132 credits required for the bachelor's degree must be completed at St. John's.

Visiting: There are regularly scheduled orientations for prospective students, consisting of an overnight stay on campus, class visits, and a tour. There are guides for informal visits, visitors may sit in on classes, and stay overnight. To schedule a visit, contact the Admission Office.

Financial Aid: In a recent year, 61% of all full-time freshmen and 68% of continuing full-time students received some form of financial aid. 57% of all full-time freshmen and 65% of continuing full-time students received need-based aid. The average freshman award was $30,545. Need-based scholarships or need-based grants averaged $23,445; and need-based self-help aid (loans and jobs) averaged $7,100. 75% of undergraduate students work part-time. Average annual earnings from campus work are $2700. The average financial indebtedness of a recent graduate was $23,760. St. John's is a member of CSS. The CSS/Profile and FAFSA, and parent and student federal tax returns are required. Check with the school for current application deadlines.

International Students: There are 12 international students enrolled. The school actively recruits these students. They must take the TOEFL. They must also take the SAT.

Computers: Wireless access is available. PCs located in student computer labs and library. Wireless access in some dorms and public areas. All students may access the system 24 hours a day. There are no time limits and no fees.

Graduates: In a recent year, 104 bachelor's degrees were awarded. The most popular majors were liberal arts (100%). In an average class, 63% graduate in 4 years or less, 71% graduate in 5 years or less, and 76% graduate in 6 years or less. Of the recent graduating class, 13% were enrolled in graduate school within 6 months of graduation, and 60% were employed.

Admissions Contact: Director of Admissions. A campus DVD is available. E-Mail: *admissions@sjca.edu* Web: *www.stjohnscollege.edu*

ST. MARY'S COLLEGE OF MARYLAND E-4

St. Marys City, MD 20686 **(240) 895-5000**
(800) 492-7181; (240) 895-5001

Full-time: 720 men, 1042 women	**Faculty:** 142; IIB, -$
Part-time: 24 men, 30 women	**Ph.D.s:** 97%
Graduate: 7 men, 32 women	**Student/Faculty:** 12 to 1
Year: semesters, summer session	**Tuition:** $14,864 ($28,664)
Application Deadline: January 1	**Room & Board:** $11,835

Freshman Class: 2321 applied, 1704 accepted, 383 enrolled
SAT CR/M/W: 600/590/590 **ACT:** 27 **HIGHLY COMPETITIVE**

St. Mary's College of Maryland, founded in 1840, is a small public liberal arts college designated by law as a Maryland honors college in 1992. There is one graduate school. The library contains 219,234 volumes, 18,821 microform items, 16,250 audio/video tapes/CDs/DVDs, and subscribes to 20,212 periodicals including electronic. Computerized library services include interlibrary loans, database searching, Internet access, and Wi-Fi capability. Special learning facilities include an art gallery, radio station, TV station, historic archeological site, and estuarine research facilities. The 319-acre campus is in a rural area 70 miles southeast of Washington, D.C. Including any residence halls, there are 58 buildings.

Student Life: 89% of undergraduates are from Maryland. Others are from 29 states, 23 foreign countries, and Canada. 75% are from public schools. 74% are White. The average age of freshmen is 18; all undergraduates, 20. 10% do not continue beyond their first year; 79% remain to graduate.

Housing: 1571 students can be accommodated in college housing, which includes single-sex and coed dorms and on-campus apartments. In addition, there are language houses and special-interest houses. On-campus housing is guaranteed for all 4 years. 83% of students live on campus; of those, 80% remain on campus on weekends. All students may keep cars.

Activities: There are no fraternities or sororities. There are 117 groups on campus, including academic, and sports, art, cheerleading, choir, chorale, chorus, computers, dance, debate, drama, drum and bugle corps, environmental, ethnic, forensics, gay, honors, international, jazz band, literary magazine, musical theater, newspaper, orchestra, outdoors, political, professional, radio and TV, religious, social, social service, student government, symphony, and yearbook. Popular campus events include World Carnival, River Concert Series, the Great Cardboard-Boat Race, Dance Club Shows, Burlesque Club Shows, Acapella Group Shows.

Sports: There are 8 intercollegiate sports for men and 9 for women, and 10 intramural sports for men and 10 for women. Facilities include an Olympic-size 50 meter pool, a 25-yard swimming pool, a 1,200-seat basketball and volleyball arena, an expanded health and fitness center, weight room, training room, exercise room, 2 gymnasiums, and locker and team rooms. Physical education, athletics, and recreation facilities also include 5 varsity practice fields, a track, 6 lighted tennis courts, an outdoor stadium, rowing center, and baseball facilities.

Disabled Students: 95% of the campus is accessible. Facilities include wheelchair ramps, elevators, special parking, specially equipped restrooms, special class scheduling, lowered drinking fountains, lowered telephones, special housing. living suites that meet ADA standards are also available.

Services: Counseling and information services are available, as is tutoring in some subjects, anthropology, biology, chemistry, computer science, economics, English, foreign languages, history, mathematics, physics, psychology, sociology, and writing. There is a reader service for the blind.

Campus Safety and Security: Measures include 24-hour foot and vehicle patrol, emergency notification system, self-defense education, and security escort services. There are emergency telephones, lighted pathways/sidewalks, controlled access to dorms/residences, student security-assistant foot patrols, and nighthawk program from 8 p.m. until midnight.

Programs of Study: SMCM confers B.A. degrees. Master's degrees are also awarded. Bachelor's degrees are awarded in BIOLOGICAL SCIENCE (biochemistry and biology/biological science), COMMUNICATIONS AND THE ARTS (art, art history and appreciation, dramatic arts, English, film arts, languages, music, and visual and performing arts), COMPUTER AND PHYSICAL SCIENCE (chemistry, computer science, mathematics, natural sciences, and physics), SOCIAL SCIENCE (anthropology, Asian/Oriental studies, economics, history, philosophy, political science/government, psychology, public affairs, religion, and sociology). Biology, psychology, and economics have the largest enrollments.

Required: Students must complete complete core curriculum requirements, six breadth categories, and experiencing liberal arts in the world. There is also a St. Mary's Project or a senior experience. Students must meet additional requirements in their major fields and complete at least 128 semester hours with at least a 2.0 GPA.

Special: St. Mary's offers internships, study abroad, national and international exchange programs, and work-study. Dual and student-designed majors and a 3-2 engineering degree with the University of Maryland, College Park, also are offered. Non-degree study and pass/fail options are possible. There are 8 national honor societies, including Phi Beta Kappa, and a freshman honors program.

Faculty/Classroom: 56% of faculty are male; 44% are female. All teach and do research. No introductory courses are taught by graduate students.

Admissions: 73% of the 2013-2014 applicants were accepted. The SAT scores for the 2013-2014 freshman class were: Critical Reading--11% below 500, 35% between 500 and 599, 38% between 600 and 699, and 16% between 700 and 800; Math--12% below 500, 39% between 500 and 599, 40% between 600 and 699, and 7% between 700 and 800; Writing--11% below 500, 40% between 500 and 599, 40% between 600 and 699, and 9% between 700 and 800. The ACT scores were 6% below 21, 14% between 21 and 23, 25% between 24 and 26, 23% between 27 and 28, and 32% above 28. 54% of the current freshmen were in the top fifth of their class; 81% were in the top two fifths. There were 1 National Merit finalists. 4 freshmen graduated first in their class.

Requirements: The SAT or ACT is required. The St. Mary's College of Maryland admissions committee takes pride in reviewing applications holistically, and we consider many facets of a student's application when making admissions decisions. A student's high school record is most important to us, with careful attention paid to co-curricular activities (including work and family responsibilities), essays, letters of recommendation, and standardized test scores (either SAT Reasoning or ACT required). A competitive candidate pursues a rigorous high school curriculum which includes four years of English, three years of social science, three years of mathematics, three years of science, and a range of academic electives. Study of a foreign language is strongly recommended. Advanced Placement, International Baccalaureate, and honors courses are highly valued. First-year applicants must possess an earned high school diploma or a satisfactory score on the General Education Development (GED) examination. AP credits are accepted. Important factors in the admissions decision are leadership record, advanced placement or honors courses, and recommendations by school officials.

Procedure: Freshmen are admitted fall and spring. Entrance exams should be taken by January of the senior year. There are early decision and deferred admissions plans. Early decision applications should be filed by November 1; regular applications, by January 1 for fall entry; and November 1 for spring entry, along with a $50 fee. Notification of early decision is sent December 15; regular decision, February 15. 113 early decision candidates were accepted for the 2013-2014 class. 246 applicants were on the 2013 waiting list; 43 were admitted. Applications are accepted online.

Transfer: 101 transfer students enrolled in 2012-2013. The St. Mary's College of Maryland admissions committee takes pride in reviewing applications holistically, and we consider many facets of a student's application when making admissions decisions. A student's success at their prior institution is most important to us, with careful attention paid to co-curricular activities (including work and family responsibilities), writing, and recommendations. A competitive candidate has completed at least 12 hours of credit with a minimum grade point average of 2.75 in all college courses and has earned a high school diploma or satisfactory score on the General Education Development (GED) examination. 38 of 128 credits required for the bachelor's degree must be completed at SMCM.

Visiting: There are regularly scheduled orientations for prospective students, Student visits include personal interviews, group presentations, open house programs, meetings with faculty and students, and campus tours. There are guides for informal visits and visitors may sit in on classes. To schedule a visit, contact Lindsey Siferd at (800) 492-7181.

Financial Aid: In 2013-2014, 74% of all full-time freshmen and 72% of continuing full-time students received some form of financial aid. 30% of all full-time freshmen and 30% of continuing full-time students received need-based aid. The average freshman award was $7,380. Need-based scholarships or need-based grants averaged $6,909 ($22,353 maximum); need-based self-help aid (loans and jobs) averaged $5,123 ($10,700 maximum); and other non-need-based awards and non-need-based scholarships averaged $4,969 ($22,105 maximum). 55% of undergraduate students work part-time. Average annual earnings from campus work are $1593. The average financial indebtedness of the 2013 graduate was $20,439. SMCM is a member of CSS. The FAFSA is required. The priority date for freshman financial aid applications for fall entry is February 15. The deadline for filing freshman financial aid applications for fall entry is March 1.

International Students: There are 55 international students enrolled. The school actively recruits these students. They must take the TOEFL with a minimum score of 550 on the paper-based TOEFL (PBT) or 90 on the Internet-based version (iBT). They must also take the SAT or ACT.

Computers: All students may access the system during all lab hours. There are no time limits and no fees.

Graduates: From July 1, 2012 to June 30, 2013, 450 bachelor's degrees were awarded. The most popular majors were psychology (13%), political science (11%), and biology/English (10%). 32 companies recruited on campus in 2012-2013. In an average class, 72% graduate in 4 years or less and 81% graduate in 6 years or less.

Admissions Contact: Gary Sherman, Vice President of Enrollment Management . E-Mail: *admissions@smcm.edu* Web: *www.smcm.edu*

STEVENSON UNIVERSITY — D-2

Stevenson, MD 21153 — 410-486-7001; 1-877-468-6852; 443-352-4440

Full-time: 1237 men, 2063 women	**Faculty:** 112; IIB, av$
Part-time: 116 men, 410 women	**Ph.D.s:** 70%
Graduate: 111 men, 332 women	**Student/Faculty:** 22 to 1
Year: semesters, summer session	**Tuition:** $27,082
Application Deadline:	**Room & Board:** $12,490
Freshman Class: n/av	
SAT or ACT: required	

COMPETITIVE

Stevenson University, founded as Villa Julie College in 1947, is the third-largest independent university in Maryland and offers more than 25 undergraduate degree programs, BS to MS degrees, and master's degrees. Stevenson is committed to providing career-focused programs based in theory, practice, and mentoring whereby students develop a deep knowledge coupled with practical application and mastery in their major areas. There are 5 undergraduate schools and one graduate school. In addition to regional accreditation, Stevenson has baccalaureate programs accreditation with NCATE and NLN. The 2 libraries contain 91,080 volumes, 199,324 microform items, 4,812 audio/video tapes/CDs/DVDs, and subscribe to 73,510 periodicals including electronic. Computerized library services include interlibrary loans, database searching, Internet access, and Wi-Fi capability. Special learning facilities include an art gallery, radio station, a theater, video studio. The 168-acre campus is in a suburban area 10 miles northwest of Baltimore. Including any residence halls, there are 31 buildings.

Student Life: 83% of undergraduates are from Maryland. Others are from 37 states, 15 foreign countries, and Canada. 75% are from public schools. 59% are White; 28% African American. The average age of freshmen is 19; all undergraduates, 23. 25% do not continue beyond their first year; 64% remain to graduate.

Housing: 1845 students can be accommodated in college housing, which includes single-sex and coed dorms and on-campus apartments. In addition, there are special-interest houses. On-campus housing is available on a first-come, first-served basis, and is available on a lottery system for upperclassmen. 52% of students commute. All students may keep cars.

Activities: There are no fraternities; 3% of women belong to 2 national sororities. There are 45 groups on campus, including art, band, cheerleading, chess, choir, computers, dance, drama, environmental, ethnic, film, forensics, gay, honors, international, jazz band, literary magazine, marching band, musical theater, Mustang Activities and Programming Board, newspaper, orchestra, pep band, photography, political, professional, radio and TV, religious, social, social service, and student government. Popular campus events include Welcome Picnic, Founder's Day and Homecoming, LOL Stevenson Comedy.

Sports: There are 11 intercollegiate sports for men and 12 for women, and 7 intramural sports for men and 7 for women. Facilities include Mustang stadium state-of-the-art 3,000+ seat stadium; Owings Mills gymnasium, 38,000 sf facility; Park stadium; Greenspring tennis courts; Weinberg-fine stadium (softball); and the Piney Branch Golf Club; Welcome.

Disabled Students: All of the campus is accessible. Facilities include wheelchair ramps, elevators, special parking, specially equipped restrooms, special class scheduling, lowered drinking fountains, lowered telephones, and special housing.

Services: Counseling and information services are available, as is tutoring in most subjects. There is remedial math, reading, and writing. Free individual tutoring as well as study groups led by a tutor, peer tutoring, paraprofessional tutoring, and faculty tutoring is available. Academic Link at both campuses.

Campus Safety and Security: Measures include 24-hour foot and vehicle patrol, emergency notification system, self-defense education, and security escort services. There are shuttle buses, emergency telephones, lighted pathways/sidewalks, and controlled access to dorms/residences.

Programs of Study: confers B.A., and B.S. degrees. Master's degrees are also awarded. Bachelor's degrees are awarded in BIOLOGICAL SCIENCE (biology/biological science and biotechnology), BUSINESS (accounting, business administration and management, business communications, business systems analysis, fashion merchandising, and marketing management), COMMUNICATIONS AND THE ARTS (art, dramatic arts, English literature, film arts, video, and visual design), COMPUTER AND PHYSICAL SCIENCE (applied mathematics, chemistry, computer security and information assurance, information sciences and systems, and mathematics), EDUCATION (early childhood education, elementary education, and middle school education), HEALTH PROFESSIONS (medical laboratory technology and nursing), SOCIAL SCIENCE (fashion design and technology, history, human services, interdisciplinary studies, paralegal studies, psychology, and public affairs). Sciences and education is the strongest academically. Nursing and business has the largest enrollments.

Required: The core curriculum includes courses in writing, communication, fine arts, social sciences, math, natural science, humanities, and phys ed. Courses in computer information systems are also required. Students must complete a minimum of 120 hours, including 45 hours in upper-level courses, with at least a 2.0 overall GPA. The number of hours required per major varies. Many majors require a capstone course or an internship.

Special: Co-op programs and internships are available. In addition, study abroad, service learning, field placements, independent study and research, and other experiential learning opportunities are offered as part of classes. Cross-registration, work study, accelerated degree programs, and student-designed majors are possible. There are 10 national honor societies, a freshman honors program, and 1 departmental honors programs.

Faculty/Classroom: 46% of faculty are male; 54% are female. 99% teach undergraduates, and 1% do both. No introductory courses are taught by graduate students. The average class size in an introductory lecture is 20 and in a regular course is 18.

Admissions: The SAT scores for the 2013-2014 freshman class were: Critical Reading--48% below 500, 44% between 500 and 599, 8% between 600 and 699; Math--48% below 500, 41% between 500 and 599, 11% between 600 and 699; Writing--51% below 500, 40% between 500 and 599, 9% between 600 and 699. 43% of the current freshmen were in the top fifth of their class; 65% were in the top two fifths.

Requirements: The SAT or ACT is required. Applicants must be graduates of an accredited secondary school. Although a secondary transcript is required, particular secondary preparation is not stipulated for all programs. Some degree programs do require specific high school courses, however. An essay is required and an interview is recommended. AP and CLEP credits are accepted.

Procedure: Freshmen are admitted fall, spring, and summer. Entrance exams should be taken between September and November of the senior year. There are deferred admissions and rolling admissions plans. Application deadlines are open. The fall 2013 application fee was $40. Applications are accepted online.

Transfer: 225 transfer students enrolled in 2012-2013. Transfer applicants must provide both college and high school transcripts and have a minimum 2.5 GPA. Transfer students with a 2.0 cumulative GPA and other accomplishments or experience may be granted conditional admission to the college. 30 of 120 credits required for the bachelor's degree must be completed at SU.

Visiting: There are regularly scheduled orientations for prospective students, including a general overview, information on how to apply and how to finance a college education, special academic presentations, tours, meetings with faculty and students, and lunch. There are guides for informal visits, visitors may sit in on classes, and stay overnight. To schedule a visit, contact the Admissions Office.

Financial Aid: In 2013-2014, 99% of all full-time freshmen and 92% of continuing full-time students received some form of financial aid. 93% of all full-time freshmen and 63% of continuing full-time students received need-based aid. The average freshman award was $13,840. Stevenson is a member of CSS. The FAFSA is required. The priority date for freshman financial aid applications for fall entry is February 15.

International Students: There are 20 international students enrolled. They must take the TOEFL with a minimum score of 550 on the paper-based TOEFL (PBT) or 80 on the Internet-based version (iBT).

Computers: All students may access the system at all times. There are no time limits and no fees.

Graduates: From July 1, 2012 to June 30, 2013, 760 bachelor's degrees were awarded. The most popular majors were business/marketing (21%), health professions and related programn (20%), and computer and information sciences (10%). 80 companies recruited on campus in 2012-2013. In an average class, 49% graduate in 4 years or less, 63% graduate in 5 years or less, and 64% graduate in 6 years or less. Of the 2012 graduating class, 17% were enrolled in graduate school within 6 months of graduation, and 75% were employed.

Admissions Contact: Mark J. Hergan, Vice President for Enrollment Management. E-Mail: *admissions@stevenson.edu* Web: *http:/www.stevenson.edu/admissions/default.asp*

TOWSON UNIVERSITY — D-2

Towson, MD 21252-0001 — (410) 704-2113; (888) 4-TOWSON; (410) 704-3030

Full-time: 5550 men, 8650 women	**Faculty:** n/av; IIA, -$
Part-time: 9405 men, 1110 women	**Ph.D.s:** 52%
Graduate: 900 men, 2660 women	**Student/Faculty:** n/av
Year: semesters, summer session	**Tuition:** $10,479 ($19,000)
Application Deadline: see profile	**Room & Board:** $10,740
Freshman Class: n/av	
SAT or ACT: required	

VERY COMPETITIVE

Towson University, founded in 1866, is part of the University System of Maryland and offers undergraduate and graduate programs in liberal arts and sciences, allied health sciences, education, fine arts, communication, and business and economics. The figures in the above capsule and this profile are approximate. There are 7 undergraduate schools and 1 graduate school. In addition to regional accreditation, Towson has baccalaureate program accreditation with AACSB, CAHEA, NASDTEC, NASM, NCATE, and NLN. The library contains 364,468 volumes, 830,286 microform items, 14,174 audio/video tapes/CDs/DVDs, and subscribes to 2164 periodicals including electronic. Computerized library services include interlibrary loans, database searching, and Internet access. Special learning facilities include a learning resource center, art gallery, planetarium, radio station, TV station, curriculum center, herbarium, animal museum, observatory, and greenhouse. The 328-acre campus is in a suburban area 2 miles north of Baltimore. Including any residence halls, there are 44 buildings.

Student Life: 80% of undergraduates are from Maryland. 69% are white; 12% African American. The average age of freshmen is 19; all undergraduates, 22.

Housing: 3518 students can be accommodated in college housing, which includes coed dorms and on-campus apartments. In addition, there are honors houses, special-interest houses, separate floors that are alcohol-free, smoke-free, and substance-free, leadership and quiet floors, and an international house. On-campus housing is available on a first-come, first-served basis and is available on a lottery system for upperclassmen. Priority is given to out-of-town students. 78% of students commute. Upperclassmen may keep cars.

Activities: 8% of men belong to 13 national fraternities; 6% of women belong to 11 national sororities. Groups on campus include art, band, cheerleading, choir, chorale, chorus, computers, dance, drama, drill team, environmental, ethnic, forensics, gay, honors, international, jazz band, literary magazine, marching band, musical theater, orchestra, pep band, photography, political, professional, religious, social, social service, student government, and symphony. Popular campus events include fraternity and sorority dances, Ethics Forum, and Tiger Fest.

Sports: There are 7 intercollegiate sports for men and 12 for women. Facilities include an athletic center, a stadium, baseball and softball fields, tennis courts, a pool, a soccer field, and 3 practice fields. Recreation facilities include 3 gyms, a weight room, a pool, lighted playing fields, and an indoor climbing wall.

Disabled Students: 85% of the campus is accessible. Facilities include wheelchair ramps, elevators, special parking, specially equipped restrooms, special class scheduling, lowered drinking fountains, lowered telephones, special housing, automatic doors, assistive listening devices in theaters and concert halls, and interior and exterior signage.

Services: Counseling and information services are available, as is tutoring in most subjects. There is a reader service for the blind and remedial math, reading, and writing. There are also note takers, English language and tuto rial services centers, a writing lab, and signers for the hearing impaired.

Campus Safety and Security: Measures include 24-hour foot and vehicle patrol, emergency notification system, self-defense education, and security escort services. There are shuttle buses, emergency telephones, lighted pathways/sidewalks, controlled access to dorms/residences, Operation ID, and a police dog on campus.

Programs of Study: Towson confers B.A., B.S., B.F.A., and B.M. degrees. Master's and doctoral degrees are also awarded. Bachelor's degrees are awarded in BIOLOGICAL SCIENCE (biology/biological science and molecular biology), BUSINESS (accounting, business administration and management, and sports management), COMMUNICATIONS AND THE ARTS (art, communications, dance, English, French, German, media arts, music, Spanish, and theater design), COMPUTER AND PHYSICAL SCIENCE (chemistry, computer science, earth science, geology, geoscience, information sciences and systems, mathematics, and physics), EDUCATION (art education, athletic training, dance education, early childhood education, education, education of the deaf and hearing impaired, elementary education, music education, physical education, and special education), ENGINEERING AND ENVIRONMENTAL DESIGN (environmental science), HEALTH PROFESSIONS (exercise science, health care administration, health science, medical laboratory technology, nursing, occupational therapy, speech pathology/audiology, and sports medicine), SOCIAL SCIENCE (anthropology, crosscultural studies, economics, family/consumer studies, geography, gerontology, history, interdisciplinary studies, international studies, law, philosophy, political science/government, psychology, religion, social science, sociology, and women's studies). Fine arts, business, and education are the strongest academically. Business disciplines, mass communications, and psychology have the largest enrollments.

Required: Students must complete course work in the arts, English, humanities, math, biological or physical science, social science, information technology, and global awareness.

Special: Towson University offers cooperative programs with other institutions in the University System of Maryland and at Loyola College, the College of Notre Dame, and Johns Hopkins University, cross-registration at more than 80 colleges through the National Student Exchange, and study abroad. Students may pursue a dual major in physics and engineering, an interdisciplinary studies degree, which allows them to design their own majors, a 3-2 engineering program with the University of Maryland at College Park and Penn State, or nondegree study. There are pass/fail options, extensive evening offerings, and opportunities to earn credits between semesters. Internships are available in most majors, and work-study programs are offered both on and off campus. There are 20 national honor societies, a freshman honors program, and 12 departmental honors programs.

Faculty/Classroom: 50% of faculty are male; 50% are female. No introductory courses are taught by graduate students. The average class size in an introductory lecture is 25; in a laboratory, 24; and in a regular course, 25.

Requirements: The SAT or ACT is required. The ACT Optional Writing test is also required. In addition, applicants should have graduated from an accredited secondary school or earned the GED. Secondary preparation should include 4 years of English, 3 each of math, lab science, and social studies, and 2 of foreign language. Prospective music and dance majors must audition. A GPA of 3.1 is required. AP and CLEP credits are accepted. Important factors in the admissions decision are advanced placement or honors courses, recommendations by school officials, and leadership record.

Procedure: Freshmen are admitted fall and spring. Entrance exams

should be taken in the junior or senior year. There are deferred admissions and rolling admissions plans. Check with the school for current application deadlines. Notification is sent on a rolling basis. Applications are accepted online. A waiting list is maintained.

Transfer: Transfer applicants should have earned at least 30 academic credits. For those with fewer than 30 attempted, freshmen requirements must be met. Minimum GPA requirements range from 2.0 to 2.5, depending on the number of credits completed. Transcripts are required. 30 of 120 credits required for the bachelor's degree must be completed at Towson.

Visiting: There are regularly scheduled orientations for prospective students, including campus tours, a session for parents, a session on the admissions process for transfers and freshmen, and a roundtable discussion. There are guides for informal visits. To schedule a visit, contact the Admissions Office.

Financial Aid: The FAFSA is required. Check with the school for current application deadlines.

International Students: The school actively recruits these students. They must take the TOEFL and the college's own test. The TOEFL is required at preadmission; a college test is required at postadmission. They must also take the SAT or ACT; the school accepts the TOEFL as a substitute for the verbal SAT.

Computers: Wireless access is available. All students may access the system. Systems are accessible 24 hours daily except 5 p.m. to 9 p.m. Fridays. There are no time limits and no fees.

Admissions Contact: Director of Admissions. A campus DVD is available. E-mail: *admissions@towson.edu* Web: *www.towson.edu*

UNITED STATES NAVAL ACADEMY E-3

Annapolis, MD 21402 (410) 293-4361
(888) 249-7707; (410) 293-1815

Full-time: 3550 men, 976 women	**Faculty:** 519; IIB, ++$
Part-time: n/av	**Ph.D.s:** 65%
Graduate: n/av	**Student/Faculty:** 8 to 1
Year: semesters	**Tuition:** see profile
Application Deadline: January 31	**Room & Board:** see profile
Freshman Class: 1408 accepted, 1200 enrolled	
SAT CR/M: 656/676	**ACT:** required **MOST COMPETITIVE**

The United States Naval Academy, founded in 1845, is a national military service college offering undergraduate degree programs and professional training in aviation, surface ships, submarines, and various military, maritime, and technical fields. The U.S. Navy pays tuition, room and board, medical and dental care, and a monthly stipend to all Naval Academy students. Graduates earn a Bachelor of Science degree and a commission in the United States Navy or the United States Marine Corps and have a five year obligation of active military service. There is one undergraduate school. In addition to regional accreditation, Annapolis has baccalaureate program accreditation with ABET and CSAB. The library contains 1.1 million volumes, 190,078 microform items, 7,689 audio/video tapes/CDs/DVDs, and subscribes to 75,186 periodicals including electronic. Computerized library services include interlibrary loans, database searching, Internet access, and Wi-Fi capability. Special learning facilities include a planetarium, radio station, propulsion lab, wind tunnels - both subsonic and supersonic, an oceanographic research vessel, field laboratory, and weather station, towing tanks, a flight simulator, a naval history museum, chamber facilities, environmental chamber facilities, 16-inch Cassegrain reflector telescope, 12-meter satellite earth station. The 338-acre campus is in a small town On the Chesapeake Bay 30 miles southeast of Baltimore and 32 miles east of Washington, D.C. Including any residence halls, there are 75 buildings.

Student Life: 96% of undergraduates are from out of state. Students are from 50 states, and 30 foreign countries. 65% are White; 11% Hispanic. The average age of freshmen is 18; all undergraduates, 20. 6% do not continue beyond their first year; 89% remain to graduate.

Housing: 4700 students can be accommodated in college housing, which includes coed dorms. On-campus housing is guaranteed for all 4 years. 100% of students live on campus; of those, 50% remain on campus on weekends. Some may keep cars.

Activities: There are no fraternities or sororities. There are 109 groups on campus, including bagpipe, cheerleading, chess, choir, chorus, computers, debate, drama, drill team, drum and bugle corps, ethnic, honors, international, jazz band, literary magazine, marching band, Military Professional, musical theater, orchestra, pep band, photography, professional, radio and TV, religious, social, social service, student government, and yearbook. Popular campus events include Commissioning Week, which includes the Plebe Recognition Ceremony, Ring Dance and Graduation.

Sports: There are 21 intercollegiate sports for men and 13 for women, and 23 intramural sports for men and 23 for women. Facilities include an 34,000-seat stadium, a 5700-seat basketball arena, Olympic pool with a diving well for 10-meter diving boards, wrestling arena, 200-meter indoor track, 400-meter outdoor track, indoor ice rink, 6 nautilus and weight rooms, facilities for gymnastics, boxing, volleyball, swimming, water polo, racquetball, basketball and personal conditioning, squash courts, climbing wall, baseball stadium, crew house, 18 hole golf course, soccer facility, a sailing center, indoor and outdoor tennis courts, and 2 athletic field houses.

Disabled Students: All of the campus is accessible. Facilities include wheelchair ramps, elevators, special parking, and specially equipped restrooms.

Services: Counseling and information services are available, as is tutoring in most subjects. There is remedial math, reading, and writing.

Campus Safety and Security: Measures include 24-hour foot and vehicle patrol, emergency notification system, and self-defense education. There are emergency telephones, lighted pathways/sidewalks, controlled access to dorms/residences, in-room safes, gate guards.

Programs of Study: Annapolis confers B.S. degrees. Bachelor's degrees are awarded in BUSINESS (operations research), COMMUNICATIONS AND THE ARTS (Arabic, Chinese, and English), COMPUTER AND PHYSICAL SCIENCE (chemistry, computer science, information sciences and systems, mathematics, oceanography, physics, and science), ENGINEERING AND ENVIRONMENTAL DESIGN (aeronautical engineering, computer engineering, electrical/electronics engineering technology, engineering, marine engineering, mechanical engineering, naval architecture and marine engineering, ocean engineering, and systems engineering), HEALTH PROFESSIONS (cytotechnology), SOCIAL SCIENCE (economics, history, and political science/government).

Required: Students must complete approximately 140 semester hours, including core requirements in mathematics, engineering, natural sciences, humanities, and social sciences. Professional Development courses and Physical Education are required during all 4 years. Physical readiness test must be passed semi-annually. During required summer training sessions, students train aboard U.S. Navy ships, submarines, and aircraft and with units of the U.S. Marine Corps. Graduates serve at least 5 years on active duty as commissioned officers of the Navy or Marine Corps.

Special: A voluntary graduate program is available for those midshipmen who complete academic graduation requirements by the end of their seventh semester and are selected to begin master's work at nearby universities. Midshipmen selected as Trident Scholars spend their senior year in independent research at the Naval Academy. Study abroad for one semester is available in countries around the world. Honors programs are available in selected majors. There are 10 national honor societies and 5 departmental honors programs.

Faculty/Classroom: 73% of faculty are male; 27% are female. All teach undergraduates, 80% do research, and 80% do both. No introductory courses are taught by graduate students. The average class size in an introductory lecture is 20; in a laboratory is 18; and in a regular course is 18.

Admissions: The SAT scores for the 2013-2014 freshman class were: Critical Reading--6% below 500, 30% between 500 and 599, 46% between 600 and 699, and 18% between 700 and 800; Math--1% below 500, 19% between 500 and 599, 51% between 600 and 699, and 29% between 700 and 800. 74% of the current freshmen were in the top fifth of their class; 91% were in the top two fifths.

Requirements: The SAT or ACT is required. Candidates must be unmarried with no dependents, U.S. citizens of good moral character, and between 17 and 22 years of age. Candidates should have a solid secondary school background, including 4 years each of English and math, 2 years of a foreign language, and 1 year each of U.S. history, world or European history, chemistry, physics, and computer literacy. Candidates must obtain an official nomination from congressional or military sources. An interview is conducted, and medical and physical aptitude exams must be passed to qualify for admission. AP credits are accepted.

Procedure: Freshmen are admitted summer. Entrance exams should be taken durning December of the junior year in high school. There are early admissions and rolling admissions plans. Applications should be filed by January 31 for fall entry. Notifications are sent April 15. 182 applicants were on the 2013 waiting list; 33 were admitted. Applications are accepted online.

Transfer: All students enter as freshmen/plebes. 140 of 140 credits required for the bachelor's degree must be completed at Annapolis.

Visiting: There are regularly scheduled orientations for prospective students, Visitation weekends for highly competitive candidates for admission, and summer seminar weeks for rising high school seniors. There are guides for informal visits, visitors may sit in on classes, and stay overnight. To schedule a visit, contact USNA Admissions.

Financial Aid: Check with the school for current application deadlines.

International Students: There are 59 international students enrolled. The school actively recruits these students. They must take the TOEFL. They must also take the SAT or ACT.

Computers: All students may access the system. There are no time limits and no fees.

Graduates: From July 1, 2012 to June 30, 2013, 1058 bachelor's degrees were awarded. The most popular majors were political science (13%), history (9%), and systems engineering (9%). 2 companies recruited on campus in 2012-2013. In an average class, 86% graduate in 4 years or less. Of the 2012 graduating class, 6% were enrolled in graduate school within 6 months of graduation, and 100% were employed.

Admissions Contact: Candidate Guidance Office E-Mail: *webmail@usna.edu* Web: *www.usna.edu*

UNIVERSITY OF MARYLAND/COLLEGE PARK D-3

College Park, MD 20742 (301) 314-8385
(800) 422-5867; (301) 314-9693

Full-time: 12873 men, 11575 women **Faculty:** 1677; I, av$
Part-time: 1130 men, 909 women **Ph.D.s:** 63%
Graduate: 5647 men, 5063 women **Student/Faculty:** 15 to 1
Year: semesters, summer session **Tuition:** $8908 ($27,287)
Application Deadline: January 20 **Room & Board:** $9893
Freshman Class: 25255 applied, 11825 accepted, 3903 enrolled
SAT or ACT: required

HIGHLY COMPETITIVE

University of Maryland/College Park, founded in 1856, is a land-grant institution, the flagship campus of the state's university system, offering undergraduate and graduate degrees. There are 11 undergraduate schools and 13 graduate schools. In addition to regional accreditation, Maryland has baccalaureate program accreditation with AACSB, ABET, ACEJMC, ASLA, NASM, and NCATE. The 7 libraries contain 3.9 million volumes, 5.9 million microform items, 396,467 audio/video tapes/CDs/DVDs, and subscribe to 150,889 periodicals including electronic. Computerized library services include interlibrary loans, database searching, Internet access, and Wi-Fi capability. Special learning facilities include an art gallery, radio station, TV station, an observatory. The 1250-acre campus is in a suburban area 3 miles northeast of Washington, D.C., and 35 miles south of Baltimore. Including any residence halls, there are 273 buildings.

Student Life: 76% of undergraduates are from Maryland. Others are from 46 states, 96 foreign countries, and Canada. 55% are White; 15% Asian American; 12% African American. The average age of freshmen is 18; all undergraduates, 21. 7% do not continue beyond their first year; 82% remain to graduate.

Housing: 11894 students can be accommodated in college housing, which includes single-sex and coed dorms and on-campus apartments. In addition, there are honors houses, language houses, special-interest houses, fraternity houses, and sorority houses. On-campus housing is guaranteed for the freshman year only and is available on a lottery system for upperclassmen. 53% of students commute. All students may keep cars.

Activities: 15% of men belong to 31 national fraternities; 15% of women belong to 25 national sororities. There are 854 groups on campus, including art, band, cheerleading, chess, choir, chorale, chorus, computers, dance, debate, drama, drill team, environmental, ethnic, film, forensics, gay, honors, international, jazz band, literary magazine, marching band, musical theater, newspaper, opera, orchestra, pep band, photography, political, professional, radio and TV, religious, social, social service, student government, symphony, and yearbook. Popular campus events include Art Attack, Union All-Niter and Maryland Day.

Sports: There are 8 intercollegiate sports for men and 11 for women, and 17 intramural sports for men and 17 for women. Facilities include 2 indoor and 2 outdoor swimming pools, intramural fields, tennis, squash, racquetball, volleyball, and basketball courts, a fitness center including weight rooms, aerobic rooms, martial arts rooms, saunas, and an indoor track, a bowling alley, a golf course, and an outdoor artificial turf field. Athletic facilities include a 51,000-seat stadium, a 17,950-seat gym, and indoor and outdoor artificial turf practice fields.

Disabled Students: 95% of the campus is accessible. Facilities include wheelchair ramps, elevators, special parking, specially equipped restrooms, special class scheduling, lowered drinking fountains, lowered telephones, a special shuttle service, and electronic doors.

Services: Counseling and information services are available, as is tutoring in most subjects, including all 100- and 200-level courses There is a reader service for the blind, and remedial math.

Campus Safety and Security: Measures include 24-hour foot and vehicle patrol, emergency notification system, self-defense education, and security escort services. There are shuttle buses, emergency telephones, lighted pathways/sidewalks, controlled access to dorms/residences, video surveillance.

Programs of Study: Maryland confers B.A., B.S., B.L.A., B.M. and B.M.E. degrees. Master's and doctoral degrees are also awarded. Bachelor's degrees are awarded in AGRICULTURE (agricultural business management, agricultural economics, agriculture, animal science, natural resource management, and plant science), BIOLOGICAL SCIENCE (biochemistry, biology/biological science, microbiology, and nutrition), BUSINESS (accounting, banking and finance, business administration and management, international business management, logistics, management information systems, marketing management, operations management, and supply chain management), COMMUNICATIONS AND THE ARTS (Arabic, art history and appreciation, Chinese, classics, communications, dance, dramatic arts, English, English literature, film arts, French, Germanic languages and literature, Japanese, journalism, linguistics, music, music performance, music theory and composition, romance languages and literature, Russian, Spanish, studio art, and theatre arts), COMPUTER AND PHYSICAL SCIENCE (astronomy, atmospheric sciences and meteorology, chemistry, computer science, geology, information sciences and systems, mathematics, natural sciences, physical sciences, and physics), EDUCATION (art education, drama education, early childhood education, education, elementary education, middle school education, music education, physical education, secondary education, and special education), ENGINEERING AND ENVIRONMENTAL DESIGN (aeronautical engineering, architecture, bioresource engineering, chemical engineering, civil engineering, computer engineering, electrical/electronics engineering, engineering, environmental science, fire protection engineering, landscape architecture/design, materials engineering, and mechanical engineering), HEALTH PROFESSIONS (community health work, preveterinary science, speech pathology/audiology, and veterinary science), SOCIAL SCIENCE (African American studies, American studies, anthropology, criminal justice, criminology, early childhood studies, economics, family/consumer studies, geography, history, interdisciplinary studies, Italian studies, Judaic studies, philosophy, political science/government, psychology, Russian and Slavic studies, sociology, and women's studies). Engineering, computer science and business are the strongest academically. Economics, criminology and criminal justice, and government and politics have the largest enrollments.

Required: Most programs require a minimum of 120 credits for graduation; the number of hours required in the major varies. All students are required to complete a set of General Education courses.

Special: Each of the 11 undergraduate schools offers special programs, and there is a campus-wide co-op education program offering engineering and other majors. In addition, the university offers cross-registration with other colleges in the Consortium of Universities of the Washington Metropolitan Area, several living learning programs for undergraduates, the B.A./B.S. degree in most majors, dual and student-designed majors, nondegree study, an accelerated veterinary medicine program, varied study abroad opportunities, work-study programs with government and nonprofit organizations, and internship opportunities with federal and state legislators, the local media, and various federal agencies. There are 50 national honor societies, including Phi Beta Kappa, a freshman honors program, and 39 departmental honors programs.

Faculty/Classroom: 62% of faculty are male; 38% are female. 57% teach undergraduates, and 43% do research. Graduate students teach 11% of introductory courses. The average class size in an introductory lecture is 47; in a laboratory is 20; and in a regular course is 36.

Admissions: 47% of the 2013-2014 applicants were accepted. The SAT scores for the 2013-2014 freshman class were: Critical Reading--6% below 500, 26% between 500 and 599, 47% between 600 and 699, and 21% between 700 and 800; Math--4% below 500, 16% between 500 and 599, 43% between 600 and 699, and 37% between 700 and 800.

Requirements: The SAT or ACT is required. The ACT Optional Writing test is also required. The university evaluates exam scores along with GPA, curriculum, and other criteria. Applicants should be graduates of accredited secondary schools or have the GED. Secondary preparation should include 4 years of English, 3 of history or social sciences, 2 of algebra and 1 of plane geometry, and 2 of lab sciences. An essay and counselor recommendation are required. Music majors must also audition. Applicants who submit the ACT rather than the SAT must submit the ACT Writing Test. AP and CLEP credits are accepted. Important factors in the admissions decision are advanced placement or honors courses, recommendations by school officials, and evidence of special talent.

Procedure: Freshmen are admitted fall, spring, and summer. Entrance exams should be taken at the end of the junior year or the beginning of the senior year. There are deferred admissions and rolling admissions plans. Early decision applications should be filed by November 1; regular applications, by January 20 for fall entry; and December 1 for spring entry, along with a $65 fee. Notification of early decision is sent February 15; regular decision, April 1. Applications are accepted online.

Transfer: 1854 transfer students enrolled in 2012-2013. Transfer applicants from regionally accredited institutions should have attempted at least 12 credits and have earned at least a 2.5 GPA, although this requirement varies depending on space available. Applicants from Maryland community colleges may be given special consideration. 30 of 120 credits required for the bachelor's degree must be completed at Maryland.

Visiting: There are regularly scheduled orientations for prospective students, consisting of 3 fall and 4 spring open house programs for admitted students, as well as regularly scheduled information sessions followed by a campus tour. There are guides for informal visits, visitors may sit in on classes, and stay overnight. To schedule a visit, contact the Office of Undergraduate Admissions.

Financial Aid: In 2013-2014, 62% of all full-time freshmen and 55% of continuing full-time students received some form of financial aid. 44% of all full-time freshmen and 43% of continuing full-time students received need-based aid. The average freshman award was $11,370. Need based scholarships or need-based grants averaged $6,966; need-based self-help aid (loans and jobs) averaged $4,338; non-need-based athletic scholarships averaged $16,869; and other non-need-based awards and non-need-based scholarships averaged $6,395. 19% of undergraduate students work part-time. Average annual earnings from campus work are $5700. The FAFSA is required. The priority date for freshman financial aid applications for fall entry is February 15.

International Students: There are 799 international students enrolled. They must take the TOEFL, or take the IELTS. They must also take the SAT or ACT.

Computers: All students may access the system 24 hours a day, 7 days a week. There are no time limits and no fees.

Graduates: From July 1, 2012 to June 30, 2013, 7044 bachelor's degrees were awarded. The most popular majors were criminology and criminal justice (19%), business/marketing (14%), and engineering (10%). In an average class, 67% graduate in 4 years or less, 82% graduate in 5 years or less, and 82% graduate in 6 years or less.

Admissions Contact: Admissions Officer E-Mail: *um-admit@uga.umd.edu* Web: *www.umd.edu*

UNIVERSITY OF MARYLAND/BALTIMORE COUNTY D-2

Baltimore, MD 21250 **(410) 455-2291; (410) 455-1094**

Full-time: 4365 men, 3610 women	**Faculty:** n/av; I, -$
Part-time: 765 men, 750 women	**Ph.D.s:** 85%
Graduate: 1165 men, 1425 women	**Student/Faculty:** n/av
Year: semesters, summer session	**Tuition:** $9967 ($20,370)
Application Deadline: see profile	**Room & Board:** $10,521
Freshman Class: n/av	
SAT or ACT: required	**VERY COMPETITIVE**

UMBC, founded in 1966, is a public research university offering programs in liberal arts and sciences and engineering. There are 4 undergraduate schools and 3 graduate schools. The figures in the above capsule and this profile are approximate. In addition to regional accreditation, UMBC has baccalaureate program accreditation with ABET, CSWE, and NCATE. The library contains 1.0 million volumes, 1.1 million microform items, 1.9 million audio/video tapes/CDs/DVDs, and subscribes to 4138 periodicals including electronic. Computerized library services include interlibrary loans, database searching, and Internet access. Special learning facilities include a learning resource center, an art gallery, a radio station, the Imaging Research Center, the Howard Hughes Medical Institute, and a telescope. The 530-acre campus is in a suburban area 5 miles southwest of Baltimore and 35 miles north of Washington, D.C. Including any residence halls, there are 50 buildings.

Student Life: 89% of undergraduates are from Maryland. Others are from 43 states, 95 foreign countries, and Canada. 52% are white; 18% Asian American; 15% African American. The average age of freshmen is 18; all undergraduates, 22. 15% do not continue beyond their first year; 56% remain to graduate.

Housing: 3850 students can be accommodated in college housing, which includes single-sex and coed dorms and on-campus apartments. In addition, there are honors houses, language houses, special-interest houses, wellness and quiet-study floors, and same-sex floors. On-campus housing is guaranteed for the freshman year only and is available on a first-come, first-served basis. 66% of students commute. Alcohol is not permitted. All students may keep cars.

Activities: 4% of men belong to 11 national fraternities; 4% of women belong to 8 national sororities. There are 180 groups on campus, including art, band, cheerleading, chess, choir, chorus, computers, Council of Majors, dance, debate, drama, ethnic, film, gay, honors, Intellectual Sports Council, international, jazz band, literary magazine, Model United Nations, musical threater, newspaper, opera, orchestra, pep band, political, professional, radio and TV, religious, social, social service, student government, and symphony. Popular campus events include Quadmania, Welcome Week, and Family Weekend.

Sports: There are 8 intercollegiate sports for men and 9 for women, and 16 intramural sports for men and 16 for women. Facilities include a multipurpose arena, an aquatic center, a fitness center, tennis courts, a 4500-seat stadium, playing and practice fields, an indoor track, an outdoor cross-country course, a golf driving range, a track and field complex, and a soccer stadium.

Disabled Students: 95% of the campus is accessible. Facilities include wheelchair ramps, elevators, special parking, specially equipped rest rooms, special class scheduling, lowered drinking fountains, lowered telephones, a Braille writer, tape recorders, talking book machines, TTY, talking calculators, Optacon, and information on the talking computer.

Services: Counseling and information services are available, as is tutoring in most subjects. There is a reader service for the blind and remedial math, reading, and writing. Other services include notetakers, readers, mobility training, American Sign Language interpreters, and scribes for students who have a need based on a manual or learning disability.

Campus Safety and Security: Measures include self-defense education and security escort services. There are shuttle buses, emergency telephones, lighted pathways/sidewalks, a 24-hour police department, and a campus risk management department.

Programs of Study: UMBC confers B.A., B.S., B.F.A., and B.S.E. degrees. Master's and doctoral degrees are also awarded. Bachelor's degrees are awarded in AGRICULTURE (environmental studies), BIOLOGICAL SCIENCE (biochemistry, bioinformatics, and biology/biological science), COMMUNICATIONS AND THE ARTS (communications, dance, dramatic arts, English, fine arts, French, German, linguistics, modern language, music, Russian, Spanish, theater design, and visual and performing arts), COMPUTER AND PHYSICAL SCIENCE (chemistry, computer science, information sciences and systems, mathematics, physics, and statistics), ENGINEERING AND ENVIRONMENTAL DESIGN (chemical engineering, computer engineering, environmental science, and mechanical engineering), HEALTH PROFESSIONS (emergency medical technologies and health science), SOCIAL SCIENCE (African American studies, American studies, anthropology, classical/ancient civilization, economics, gender studies, geography, history, interdisciplinary studies, philosophy, political science/government, psychology, social work, sociology, and women's studies). Information systems, computer science, and biological sciences have the largest enrollments.

Required: To graduate, students are required to complete at least 120 credits, including 45 at the upper-division level, with a minimum GPA of 2.0. The core curriculum includes courses in arts and humanities, social sciences, math and natural sciences, phys ed, and modern or classical language and culture. Students must pass an English composition course with a C or better.

Special: Dual and student-designed majors, cooperative education programs in all majors, a Washington semester, the Sondheim Public Affairs Scholars Program, cross-registration with University of Maryland schools and Johns Hopkins University, internships, both paid and nonpaid, in public, private, and nonprofit organizations, study abroad in 19 countries, work-study programs, B.A.-B.S. degrees, pass/fail options, and nondegree study are available. UMBC also offers various opportunities in interdisciplinary studies and in such fields as artificial intelligence and optical communications. There are 15 national honor societies, including Phi Beta Kappa, a freshman honors program, and 17 departmental honors programs.

Faculty/Classroom: 61% of faculty are male; 39% are female. No introductory courses are taught by graduate students. The average class size in an introductory lecture is 41; in a laboratory, 28; and in a regular course, 30.

Requirements: The SAT or ACT is required. Minimum high school preparation should include 4 years of English, 3 years each of social science/history and math, including algebra I and II and geometry, 3 years of lab sciences and 2 of a foreign language. An essay is required of all freshman applicants. A GPA of 3.0 is required. AP and CLEP credits are accepted. Important factors in the admissions decision are advanced placement or honors courses, recommendations by school officials, and leadership record.

Procedure: Freshmen are admitted to all sessions. Entrance exams should be taken by fall of the senior year. There is an early admissions plan. Check with the school for current application deadlines and fees. Applications are accepted online. A waiting list is maintained.

Transfer: A 2.5 cumulative GPA for all previous college work is recommended. Applicants with fewer than 30 semester hours should submit SAT scores and the high school transcript; they must also meet freshman admission requirements. 30 of 120 credits required for the bachelor's degree must be completed at UMBC.

Visiting: There are regularly scheduled orientations for prospective students, including a group information session with an admissions counselor followed by a student-guided walking tour of campus. Saturday information sessions and 4 campus open houses are also scheduled each fall. Summer preview days are in July and August. There are 2 transfer open houses. There are guides for informal visits, and visitors may sit in on classes and stay overnight. To schedule a visit, contact Office of Undergraduate Admissions.

Financial Aid: The FAFSA is required. Check with the school for current application deadlines.

International Students: There were 316 international students enrolled in a recent year. They must take the TOEFL with a minimum score of 550 on the paper-based TOEFL (PBT) or 80 on the Internet-based version (iBT).

Computers: There is wireless access throughout most academic buildings. There are 800 open, wired network connections available to students in the library, 107 in classrooms, 800 in computer labs, and 6000 elsewhere in the university. All college-owned and affiliated housing units are wired for high-speed Internet access. All students may access the system. For modem dial-up access, there is a 200 hour per month limit. All other access is unlimited. There are no fees. It is strongly recommended that all students have a personal computer.

Admissions Contact: Director of Admissions. E-Mail: *admissions@umbc.edu* Web: *www.umbc.edu*

UNIVERSITY OF MARYLAND/EASTERN SHORE F-4

Princess Anne, MD 21853 (410) 651-6410; (410) 651-7922

Full-time: 1230 men, 1815 women
Part-time: 1230 men, 180 women
Graduate: 195 men, 260 women
Year: semesters, summer session
Application Deadline: see profile
Freshman Class: n/av
SAT: required
Faculty: n/av; IIA, --$
Ph.D.s: 80%
Student/Faculty: n/av
Tuition: $7131 ($14,262)
Room & Board: $7050

COMPETITIVE

The University of Maryland/Eastern Shore, founded in 1886, is a public university and part of the University of Maryland System offering undergraduate and graduate programs in the arts and sciences, professional studies, and agricultural sciences. The figures in the above capsule and this capsule are approximate. There are 3 undergraduate schools and 1 graduate school. The library contains 150,000 volumes. Computerized library services include interlibrary loans and database searching. Special learning facilities include a learning resource center, art gallery, and radio station. The 700-acre campus is in a rural area 15 miles south of Salisbury. Including any residence halls, there are 40 buildings.

Student Life: 71% of undergraduates are from Maryland. Others are from 32 states, 48 foreign countries, and Canada. 85% are from public schools. 76% are African American; 18% white. 90% are Protestant. The average age of freshmen is 18; all undergraduates, 24. 25% do not continue beyond their first year; 36% remain to graduate.

Housing: 1530 students can be accommodated in college housing, which includes single-sex dorms, on-campus apartments, and off-campus apartments. In addition, there are honors houses and a residential complex. On-campus housing is available on a first-come, first-served basis and is available on a lottery system for upperclassmen. 50% of students commute. All students may keep cars.

Activities: 20% of men belong to 4 national fraternities; 20% of women belong to 4 national sororities. There are 25 groups on campus, including art, band, cheerleading, choir, chorale, chorus, computers, dance, drama, drill team, ethnic, honors, international, jazz band, literary magazine, musical theater, newspaper, pep band, photography, political, professional, radio and TV, religious, social, social service, student government, and yearbook. Popular campus events include Parents Day, Spring Festival, and Ethnic Festival.

Sports: There are 5 intercollegiate sports for men and 5 for women, and 4 intramural sports for men and 4 for women. Facilities include an indoor swimming pool and a 3000-seat stadium.

Disabled Students: 20% of the campus is accessible. Facilities include wheelchair ramps, elevators, special parking, specially equipped restrooms, special class scheduling, lowered drinking fountains, and lowered telephones.

Services: Counseling and information services are available, as is tutoring in every subject. There is remedial math, reading, and writing.

Campus Safety and Security: Measures include 24-hour foot and vehicle patrol and security escort services. There are shuttle buses, emergency telephones, lighted pathways/sidewalks, and a student security team.

Programs of Study: UMES confers B.A., B.S., B.G.S., and B.M. degrees. Master's and doctoral degrees are also awarded. Bachelor's degrees are awarded in AGRICULTURE (agriculture and poultry science), BIOLOGICAL SCIENCE (biology/biological science), BUSINESS (accounting, business administration and management, and hotel/motel and restaurant management), COMMUNICATIONS AND THE ARTS (English), COMPUTER AND PHYSICAL SCIENCE (chemistry, computer science, and mathematics), EDUCATION (agricultural education, art education, business education, elementary education, health education, home economics education, industrial arts education, mathematics education, music education, physical education, science education, secondary education, and social science education), ENGINEERING AND ENVIRONMENTAL DESIGN (aeronautical science, construction technology, engineering technology, and environmental science), HEALTH PROFESSIONS (physical therapy and rehabilitation therapy), SOCIAL SCIENCE (criminal justice, history, home economics, liberal arts/general studies, and sociology). Physical therapy, engineering, and environmental science are the strongest academically. Business, hotel restaurant management, and biology have the largest enrollments.

Required: Students must complete 122 hours, including 36 hours in the major, 15 in communicative and quantitative skills, 9 in humanities, 7 in natural sciences, 6 in social sciences, and 4 in health and phys ed. A minimum 2.0 overall GPA is required.

Special: Students may cross-register at Salisbury State University. A cooperative education program, internships, a winter term, work-study programs, a general studies degree, and dual and student-designed majors are offered. Also available are an accelerated degree program and a 3-2 engineering degree with the University of Maryland/College Park. There are pass/fail options. There is 1 national honor society, a freshman honors program, and 10 departmental honors programs.

Faculty/Classroom: 45% of faculty are male; 55% are female. 85% teach undergraduates, and 15% do research. Graduate students teach 1% of introductory courses. The average class size in an introductory lecture is 75; in a laboratory, 18; and in a regular course, 30.

Requirements: The SAT is required. Applicants should be graduates of accredited secondary schools or have the GED. High school preparation should include 4 years of English, 3 each of social science or history and math, including 2 of algebra and 1 of geometry, and 2 of lab science. An essay and interview are recommended. UMES recommends that prospective art education majors submit a portfolio. A GPA of 2.5 is required. AP and CLEP credits are accepted. Important factors in the admissions decision are advanced placement or honors courses, leadership record, and recommendations by school officials.

Procedure: Freshmen are admitted to all sessions. Entrance exams should be taken in April. There are early decision, early admissions, deferred admissions, and rolling admissions plans. Check with the school for current application deadlines.

Transfer: Transfer applicants must have attempted at least 9 credits at another institution and have at least a cumulative GPA of 2.0 or have earned an associate degree or completed 56 hours of community college work. 75 of 122 credits required for the bachelor's degree must be completed at UMES.

Visiting: There are regularly scheduled orientations for prospective students, including 2 formal orientation sessions and 9 visitation/open house days. There are guides for informal visits and visitors may sit in on classes. To schedule a visit, contact the Office of Recruitment.

Financial Aid: UMES is a member of CSS. The college's own financial statement is required. Check with the school for current application deadlines.

International Students: They must take the TOEFL. They must also take the SAT.

Computers: There are no fees. It is strongly recommended that all students have a personal computer.

Admissions Contact: Cheryll Collier-Mills, Director of Admissions and Recruitment. E-Mail: *ccmills@umes.edu* Web: *www.umes.edu*

UNIVERSITY OF MARYLAND/UNIVERSITY COLLEGE D-3

Adelphi, MD 20783 (249) 684-2163
(800) 888-8682; (240) 684-2153

Full-time: 2598 men, 3055 women
Part-time: 10543 men, 11923 women
Graduate: 6456 men, 8138 women
Year: semesters, summer session
Application Deadline: open
Freshman Class: n/av
Faculty: 113
Ph.D.s: 85%
Student/Faculty: n/av
Tuition: $6168 ($12,288)
Room & Board: n/app

SPECIAL

University of Maryland University College, founded in 1947, serves the needs of the adult continuing education student, offering daytime, evening, weekend, and online programs in convenient locations in the Maryland, D.C. Metro, and Virginia areas. There is 1 undergraduate school and 1 graduate school. The library contains 1,337 volumes, 33 audio/video tapes/CDs/DVDs, and subscribes to 103,944 periodicals including electronic. Computerized library services include interlibrary loans, database searching, and Internet access. Special learning facilities include a learning resource center and art gallery. The campus is in an urban area.

Student Life: 59% of undergraduates are from Maryland. Others are from 50 states, 28 foreign countries, and Canada. 39% are white; 36% African American. The average age of freshmen is 31; all undergraduates, 34.

Housing: There are no residence halls. All students commute.

Activities: There are no fraternities or sororities.

Sports: There is no sports program at UMUC.

Disabled Students: Facilities include wheelchair ramps, elevators, special parking, specially equipped restrooms, special class scheduling, and lowered drinking fountains.

Services: Counseling and information services are available, as is tutoring in some subjects, math, writing, accounting, economics, introductory finance, and computing There is a reader service for the blind.

Campus Safety and Security: Measures include 24-hour foot and vehicle patrol, emergency notification system, and self-defense education. There are emergency telephones and lighted pathways/sidewalks.

Programs of Study: UMUC confers B.A. and B.S. degrees. Master's and doctoral degrees are also awarded. Bachelor's degrees are awarded in BIOLOGICAL SCIENCE (biotechnology), BUSINESS (accounting, business administration and management, human resources, management information systems, management science, and marketing management), COMMUNICATIONS AND THE ARTS (communications, English, and Spanish), COMPUTER AND PHYSICAL SCIENCE (computer science, computer security and information assurance, digital arts/technology, and information sciences and systems), ENGINEERING AND ENVIRONMENTAL DESIGN (computer technology, emergency/disaster science, and environmental science), SOCIAL SCIENCE (Asian/Oriental studies, criminal justice, fire science, gerontology, history, humanities, liberal arts/general studies, paralegal studies, political science/government, psychology, and social science).

Required: A general education requirement of 41 credit hours includes courses in communications, humanities, social sciences, biological and social science, math/science, and interdisciplinary studies.

Special: UMUC offers cooperative programs in several career programs. There are work-study programs with local employers. Credit by exam, credit for prior learning, 6 nondegree study, and pass/fail options are available. Through UMUC's open learning program, a number of independent learning courses are available. There are 64 national honor societies.

Faculty/Classroom: 58% of faculty are male; 42% are female. 70% teach undergraduates. No introductory courses are taught by graduate students.

Requirements: Students should be graduates of an accredited secondary school or have a GED equivalent. AP and CLEP credits are accepted.

Procedure: Freshmen are admitted to all sessions. There is a rolling admissions plan. Application deadlines are open. Check with the school for current fee. Applications are accepted online.

Transfer: 30 of 120 credits required for the bachelor's degree must be completed at UMUC.

Financial Aid: The FAFSA, and SAR (for Pell grants) is required. Check with the school for current application deadlines.

International Students: There are 54 international students enrolled. They must take the TOEFL with a minimum score of 550 on the paper-based TOEFL (PBT) or 79 on the Internet-based version (iBT) and the college's own test.

Computers: Wireless access is available. All students may access the system. There are no time limits and no fees.

Graduates: In a recent year, 3837 bachelor's degrees were awarded. The most popular majors were business/marketing (40%), computer and information sciences (20%), and psychology (8%).

Admissions Contact: Director of Admissions. E-Mail: *enroll@umuc.edu* Web: *www.umuc.edu*

UNIVERSITY SYSTEM OF MARYLAND

The University System of Maryland, established in 1856, is a public system in Maryland. It is governed by a board of regents, whose chief administrator is chancellor. The primary goal of the system is research, teaching, and public service. The total student enrollment for all eleven campuses is usually 105,000 with 8,000 faculty members. Altogether there are 347 baccalaureate, 212 master's and 115 doctoral programs offered in the University System of Maryland. Profiles of the 4-year campuses are included in this section.

WASHINGTON ADVENTIST UNIVERSITY D-3

Takoma Park, MD 20912 **(301) 891-4080**
(800) 835-4212; (301) 891-4230

Full-time: 275 men, 435 women	**Faculty:** n/av
Part-time: 115 men, 200 women	**Ph.D.s:** 48%
Graduate: 35 men, 55 women	**Student/Faculty:** n/av
Year: semesters, summer session	**Tuition:** $20,000
Application Deadline: see profile	**Room & Board:** $7500
Freshman Class: n/av	
SAT or ACT: required	

COMPETITIVE+

Washington Adventist University, founded in 1904, is a Christ-centered institution offering degree programs in liberal arts, sciences, and selected professional fields. Some figures in the above capsule and in this profile are approximate. There is 1 graduate school. In addition to regional accreditation, WAU has baccalaureate program accreditation with CAHEA and NLN. The library contains 142,903 volumes and 7500 audio/video tapes/CDs/DVDs, and subscribes to 9000 periodicals including electronic. Computerized library services include interlibrary loans, database searching, and Internet access. Special learning facilities include a learning resource center and radio station. The 19-acre campus is in a suburban area 7 miles north of Washington, D.C. Including any residence halls, there are 17 buildings.

Student Life: 61% of undergraduates are from Maryland. Others are from 37 states, 22 foreign countries, and Canada. 50% are African American; 14% white. The average age of freshmen is 19; all undergraduates, 27.

Housing: 440 students can be accommodated in college housing, which includes single-sex dorms and married student housing. On-campus housing is guaranteed for all 4 years. 60% of students live on campus; of those, 70% remain on campus on weekends. Alcohol is not permitted. All students may keep cars.

Activities: There are no fraternities or sororities. There are 22 groups on campus, including band, choir, chorale, chorus, debate, drill team, ethnic, fitness, honors, international, musical theater, newspaper, orchestra, political, radio and TV, religious, running, social, social service, student government, volleyball, and yearbook. Popular campus events include Student Missions Week, Spirit Week, and Service Day.

Sports: There are 5 intercollegiate sports for men and 5 for women, and 5 intramural sports for men and 4 for women. Facilities include a gym, racquetball and tennis courts, a sports field, a weight room, and a student lounge with ping-pong and pool/billiards tables and table games.

Disabled Students: 30% of the campus is accessible. Facilities include wheelchair ramps, elevators, special parking, specially equipped restrooms, and lowered telephones.

Services: Counseling and information services are available, as is tutoring in some subjects, including all English, math, accounting, chemistry, biology, psychology, Spanish, and history courses, and other courses as needed. There is a reader service for the blind, and remedial math and writing.

Campus Safety and Security: Measures include 24-hour foot and vehicle patrol, emergency notification system, and security escort services. There are lighted pathways/sidewalks.

Programs of Study: WAU confers B.A., B.S., and B.M. degrees. Associate and master's degrees are also awarded. Bachelor's degrees are awarded in BIOLOGICAL SCIENCE (biochemistry and biology/biological science), BUSINESS (accounting, business administration and management, and organizational leadership and management), COMMUNICATIONS AND THE ARTS (communications, English, journalism, music, and music performance), COMPUTER AND PHYSICAL SCIENCE (chemistry, computer science, information sciences and systems, and mathematics), EDUCATION (elementary education, English education, mathematics education, music education, and physical education), HEALTH PROFESSIONS (exercise science, health care administration, nursing, predentistry, and respiratory therapy), SOCIAL SCIENCE (counseling/psychology, history, liberal arts/general studies, philosophy and religion, political science/government, prelaw, psychology, religion, and theological studies). Nursing, health care administration, and business administration have the largest enrollments.

Required: To graduate, students must earn 120 to 128 credit hours, including 36 upper division, with a minimum GPA of 2.0 overall and 2.5 in the major. Students must take 12 hours of religion, 9 of social sciences, 8 of physical sciences, natural sciences, and math, 6 of humanities and practical and applied arts, and 3 of phys ed and health. Courses in English, communication, and computer science are also required.

Special: WAU offers co-op programs in business, communication, computer science, English, biochemistry, and math, internships in counseling psychology, history and political science, and through a Washington D.C. Experience, work-study programs, a general studies degree, credit for life experience, nondegree study, and pass/fail options. Dual majors are available in engineering/chemistry and math, and a 3-2 engineering degree is offered with the University of Maryland. The School of Graduate and Professional Studies provides evening degree completion and an external (correspondence) degree. There are 6 national honor societies and a freshman honors program.

Faculty/Classroom: 56% of faculty are male; 44% are female. All teach undergraduates, and 10% both teach and do research. No introductory courses are taught by graduate students.

Requirements: The SAT or ACT is required. Applicants must be graduates of an accredited secondary school. The GED is accepted. 21 Carnegie units are required, including 4 years of high school English and 2 years each of history, math, and lab science. An essay is recommended. A GPA of 2.5 is required. Applicants with a GPA of 2.0 to 2.5 can be enrolled in an enrichment program, given they have satisfactory scores on the ACT or SAT. Applicants with a GPA of 3.25 or higher can be enrolled without standardized test scores. AP and CLEP credits are accepted. Important factors in the admissions decision are advanced placement or honors courses, leadership record, and recommendations by school officials.

Procedure: Freshmen are admitted to all sessions. Entrance exams should be taken in the fall semester of the senior year. There are early admissions, deferred admissions, and rolling admissions plans. Check with the school for current application deadlines and fee. Applications are accepted online.

Transfer: Transfer students must have at least 12 hours of college credit and a minimum GPA of 2.0. 30 of 120 to 128 credits required for the bachelor's degree must be completed at WAU.

Visiting: There are regularly scheduled orientations for prospective students. There are guides for informal visits, and visitors may sit in on classes and stay overnight. To schedule a visit, contact the Office of Enrollment Services.

Financial Aid: The FAFSA is required. Check with the school for current application deadlines.

International Students: They must take the TOEFL or MELAB and also take the SAT or ACT.

Computers: Wireless access is available. All students may access the system. There are no time limits. The fee is $575. It is strongly recommended that all students have a personal computer.

Admissions Contact: Director of Admissions. E-mail: *enroll@wau.edu* Web: *www.wau.edu*

WASHINGTON COLLEGE E-2

Chestertown, MD 21620 (410) 778-7700
(800) 422-1782; (410) 778-7287

Full-time: 613 men, 856 women
Part-time: 19 men, 24 women
Graduate: 21 men, 24 women
Year: semesters
Application Deadline: February 15
Freshman Class: 4484 applied, 2976 accepted, 401 enrolled
SAT CR/M: 585/570
Faculty: 91; IIB, av$
Ph.D.s: 95%
Student/Faculty: 12 to 1
Tuition: $39,944
Room & Board: $8824

VERY COMPETITIVE

Washington College, founded in 1782, is an independent college offering programs in the liberal arts and sciences, business management, and teacher preparation. There is one graduate school. The library contains 219,461 volumes, 100,635 microform items, 8,701 audio/video tapes/CDs/DVDs, and subscribes to 28,222 periodicals including electronic. Computerized library services include interlibrary loans, database searching, Internet access, and Wi-Fi capability. Special learning facilities include an art gallery, The Center for the American Experience, the Center for Environment and Society, the Kohl Gallery, and the Rose O'Neill Literary House. The 112-acre campus is in a small town 75 miles from Baltimore. Including any residence halls, there are 71 buildings.

Student Life: 52% of undergraduates are from Maryland. Others are from 35 states, 30 foreign countries, and Canada. 68% are from public schools. 80% are White. The average age of freshmen is 18; all undergraduates, 20. 15% do not continue beyond their first year; 80% remain to graduate.

Housing: 1269 students can be accommodated in college housing, which includes single-sex and coed dorms and on-campus apartments. In addition, there are special-interest houses, fraternity houses, an international house, a science house, and substance-free housing, theme housing and wellness housing. On-campus housing is guaranteed for the freshman year only and is available on a lottery system for upperclassmen. 85% of students live on campus; of those, 65% remain on campus on weekends. All students may keep cars.

Activities: 8% of men belong to 3 national fraternities; 14% of women belong to 3 national sororities. There are 100 groups on campus, including and education and leadership, band, chorale, chorus, computers, dance, debate, drama, environmental, ethnic, gay, honors, international, jazz band, literary magazine, minority and human rights, newspaper, orchestra, photography, political, professional, radio and TV, religious, social, social service, student government, and yearbook. Popular campus events include Fall and Spring Convocations, George Washington Birthday Ball and May Day.

Sports: There are 8 intercollegiate sports for men and 10 for women, and 12 intramural sports for men and 11 for women. Facilities include a stadium, a swim center, a gym, a field house, squash and racquetball courts, a fitness center, playing and practice fields, and a boathouse. There are riding facilities nearby.

Disabled Students: 95% of the campus is accessible. Facilities include wheelchair ramps, elevators, special parking, specially equipped restrooms, special class scheduling, lowered drinking fountains, lowered telephones.

Services: Counseling and information services are available, as is tutoring in every subject. There is remedial math and writing. a writing center, a math lab, a study skills tutor, and peer tutors

Campus Safety and Security: Measures include 24-hour foot and vehicle patrol, emergency notification system, and security escort services. There are emergency telephones, lighted pathways/sidewalks, peer education through student groups.

Programs of Study: WC confers B.A., and B.S. degrees. Master's degrees are also awarded. Bachelor's degrees are awarded in AGRICULTURE (environmental studies), BIOLOGICAL SCIENCE (biology/biological science), BUSINESS (business administration and management), COMMUNICATIONS AND THE ARTS (art, dramatic arts, English, fine arts, French, German, music, and Spanish), COMPUTER AND PHYSICAL SCIENCE (chemistry, computer science, mathematics, and physics), SOCIAL SCIENCE (American studies, anthropology, economics, history, humanities, interdisciplinary studies, international studies, philosophy, political science/government, psychology, and sociology). biology. business management, psychology and English are the largest.

Required: All students are required to take a freshman Global Perspective seminar and courses distributed among the social sciences, natural sciences, humanities, quantitative studies, foreign languages, and a writing requirement. The Senior Capstone Experience consists of a comprehensive exam, thesis, or independent project. Students must complete 128 credit hours, including at least 32 in the major, to graduate. A minimum GPA of 2.0 is required.

Special: Internships are available in all majors. There is study abroad in 26 countries and a Washington semester. The college offers a 3-2 engineering degree with the University of Maryland at College Park as well as a 3-2 nursing program with Johns Hopkins University and student-designed majors. There are 7 national honor societies and including Phi Beta Kappa.

Faculty/Classroom: 54% of faculty are male; 46% are female. All teach undergraduates. No introductory courses are taught by graduate students. The average class size in an introductory lecture is 15; in a laboratory is 16; and in a regular course is 15.

Admissions: 66% of the 2013-2014 applicants were accepted. The SAT scores for the 2013-2014 freshman class were: Critical Reading--9% below 500, 48% between 500 and 599, 38% between 600 and 699, and 5% between 700 and 800; Math--12% below 500, 47% between 500 and 599, 37% between 600 and 699, and 4% between 700 and 800. 55% of the current freshmen were in the top fifth of their class; 82% were in the top two fifths. There were 3 National Merit finalists. 3 freshmen graduated first in their class.

Requirements: The SAT is required. Applicants must be graduates of an accredited secondary school or have a GED. 16 Carnegie units are required; 20 are recommended. Applicants should take high school courses in English, foreign language, history, math, science, and social studies. An essay is required, and an interview is recommended. A GPA of 2.4 is required. AP credits are accepted. Important factors in the admissions decision are advanced placement or honors courses, recommendations by school officials, and leadership record.

Procedure: Freshmen are admitted fall and spring. Entrance exams should be taken in the spring of the junior year or fall of the senior year. There are early decision, deferred admissions, and rolling admissions plans. Early decision applications should be filed by November 1; regular applications, by February 15 for fall entry; and December 1 for spring entry, along with a $50 fee. Notification is sent on a rolling basis. 51 early decision candidates were accepted for the 2013-2014 class. 426 applicants were on the 2013 waiting list; 22 were admitted. Applications are accepted online.

Transfer: 27 transfer students enrolled in 2012-2013. Requirements for students are a minimum GPA of 2.3, a high school transcript, college transcript(s)and essay or personal statement. An interview and standardized test scores are recommended. 56 of 128 credits required for the bachelor's degree must be completed at WC.

Visiting: There are regularly scheduled orientations for prospective students, consisting of weekday visits. There are guides for informal visits and visitors may sit in on classes. To schedule a visit, contact the Admissions Office at ADM_OFF@washcoll.edu.

Financial Aid: In 2013-2014, 92% of all full-time freshmen and 90% of continuing full-time students received some form of financial aid. 100% of all full-time freshmen and 98% of continuing full-time students received need-based aid. The average freshman award was $31,111. Need-based scholarships or need-based grants averaged $25,047; need-based self-help aid (loans and jobs) averaged $3,834; other non-need-based awards and non-need-based scholarships averaged $15,782; and $3,413 from other forms of aid. 40% of undergraduate students work part-time. Average annual earnings from campus work are $1000. The average financial indebtedness of the 2013 graduate was $34,208. WC is a member of CSS. The FAFSA and the college's own financial statement, and signed copies of the student's and parents' federal tax returns and W2s are required. The deadline for filing freshman financial aid applications for fall entry is February 15.

International Students: There are 73 international students enrolled. The school actively recruits these students. They must take the TOEFL with a minimum score of 550 on the paper-based TOEFL (PBT) or 79 on the Internet-based version (iBT). They must also take the SAT or ACT.

Computers: All students may access the system. There are no time limits and no fees.

Graduates: From July 1, 2012 to June 30, 2013, 325 bachelor's degrees were awarded. The most popular majors were social sciences (20%), business/marketing (15%), and biological/life sciences (11%). 75 companies recruited on campus in 2012-2013. In an average class, 2% graduate in 3 years or less, 75% graduate in 4 years or less, 77% graduate in 5 years or less, and 80% graduate in 6 years or less. Of the 2012 graduating class, 15% were enrolled in graduate school within 6 months of graduation, and 75% were employed.

Admissions Contact: Kevin Coveney, Vice President of Admissions. E-Mail: *wc_admissions@washcoll.edu* Web: *http:/www.washcoll.edu/admissions/*

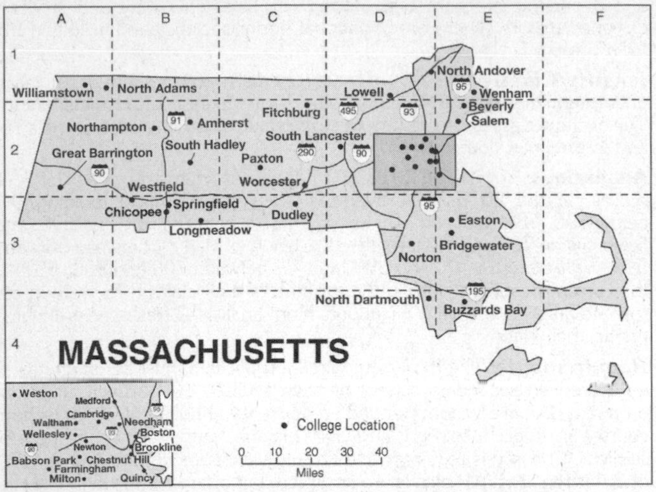

AMERICAN INTERNATIONAL COLLEGE B-3

Springfield, MA 01109 (413) 205-3201

(800) 242-3142; (413) 205-3051

Full-time: 700 men, 905 women
Part-time: 45 men, 110 women
Graduate: 365 men, 1310 women
Year: semesters, summer session
Application Deadline: open
Freshman Class: n/av
SAT or ACT: required
Faculty: n/av
Ph.D.s: 47%
Student/Faculty: n/av
Tuition: $28,402
Room & Board: $11,814

LESS COMPETITIVE

American International College, founded in 1885, is an independent institution offering programs in liberal arts, business, health science, and teacher preparation. The figures in the above capsule and in this profile are approximate. There are 4 undergraduate schools and 3 graduate schools. In addition to regional accreditation, AIC has baccalaureate program accreditation with APTA, NASDTEC, and NLN. The library contains 70,741 volumes, 293 microform items, 1,749 audio/video tapes/CDs/DVDs, and subscribes to 7,211 periodicals including electronic. Computerized library services include interlibrary loans, database searching, Internet access, and laptop Internet portals. Special learning facilities include a learning resource center, art gallery, radio station, and an anatomical lab for health sciences. The 58-acre campus is in an urban area 75 miles west of Boston. Including any residence halls, there are 22 buildings.

Student Life: 63% of undergraduates are from Massachusetts. Students are from 30 states, 15 foreign countries, and Canada. 85% are from public schools. 50% are white; 32% African American; 11% Hispanic. The average age of freshmen is 20; all undergraduates, 25. 32% do not continue beyond their first year; 60% remain to graduate.

Housing: 781 students can be accommodated in college housing, which includes single-sex and coed dorms and on-campus apartments. On-campus housing is guaranteed for all 4 years, is available on a first-come, first-served basis, and is available on a lottery system for upperclassmen. 50% of students commute. All students may keep cars.

Activities: 1% of men belong to 5 national fraternities; 1% of women belong to 2 national sororities. There are 40 groups on campus, including cheerleading, computers, dance, drama, ethnic, film, gay, honors, international, literary magazine, newspaper, pep band, photography, political, professional, radio and TV, religious, social, social service, student government, women's, and yearbook. Popular campus events include holiday semi-formals, international festival, and Caribbean and Asian-American Festival.

Sports: There are 12 intercollegiate sports for men and 10 for women, and 16 intramural sports for men and 12 for women. Facilities include a football stadium, tennis courts, playing fields, and a health and fitness center.

Disabled Students: 75% of the campus is accessible. Facilities include wheelchair ramps, elevators, special parking, specially equipped restrooms, special class scheduling, and lowered drinking fountains.

Services: Counseling and information services are available, as is tutoring in every subject. There is remedial math and writing.

Campus Safety and Security: Measures include 24-hour foot and vehicle patrol, emergency notification system, self-defense education, and security escort services. There are shuttle buses, emergency telephones, lighted pathways/sidewalks, and controlled access to dorms/residences.

Programs of Study: AIC confers B.A., B.S., B.B.A., B.S.B.A., B.S.N., and B.S.O.T. degrees. Associates, master's, and doctoral degrees are also awarded. Bachelor's degrees are awarded in BIOLOGICAL SCIENCE (biochemistry and biology/biological science), BUSINESS (accounting, business administration and management, business economics, entrepreneurial studies, human resources, international business management, and marketing/retailing/merchandising), COMMUNICATIONS AND THE ARTS (advertising, communications, English, and Spanish), COMPUTER AND PHYSICAL SCIENCE (chemistry, mathematics, and science), EDUCATION (early childhood education, elementary education, foreign languages education, middle school education, science education, secondary education, and special education), HEALTH PROFESSIONS (medical laboratory technology, nursing, occupational therapy, physical therapy, predentistry, and premedicine), SOCIAL SCIENCE (criminal justice, economics, history, international relations, liberal arts/general studies, philosophy, political science/government, prelaw, psychology, public administration, and sociology). Psychology, preprofessional, and health sciences are the strongest academically. Criminal justice, physical therapy, and nursing have the largest enrollments.

Required: Distribution requirements include 12 credits of social sciences, 9 of English, 8 of lab science, 6 of humanities, and 3 each of math and computer-oriented courses. A total of 120 credit hours is required for graduation, with 30 to 36 hours in the major. A minimum 2.0 GPA is required for graduation.

Special: Cross-registration with the Cooperative Colleges of Greater Springfield is permitted. Internships are available in all programs, for up to 6 credits in every major, and study abroad is offered, as is a Washington semester. There are 4 national honor societies, a freshman honors program, and 9 departmental honors programs.

Faculty/Classroom: 40% of faculty are male; 60% are female. All teach undergraduates, 15% do research, and 15% do both. No introductory courses are taught by graduate students. The average class size in an introductory lecture is 27; in a laboratory is 16; and in a regular course is 19.

Requirements: The SAT or ACT is required. Applicants must be graduates of an accredited secondary school or have a GED. They must have completed 16 academic credits of secondary school work with a minimum of 4 years of English, 2 each of history, math, and science, and 1 of social studies. An interview is recommended. A GPA of 2.0 is required. AP and CLEP credits are accepted.

Procedure: Freshmen are admitted to all sessions. Entrance exams should be taken by March of the senior year. There are deferred admissions and rolling admissions plans. Application deadlines are open. Application fee is $25. Notification is sent on a rolling basis. Applications are accepted online.

Transfer: 220 transfer students enrolled in a recent year. Transfer applicants must have at least a 2.0 GPA. 30 of 120 credits required for the bachelor's degree must be completed at AIC.

Visiting: There are regularly scheduled orientations for prospective students, open houses with faculty, a student life panel, departmental faculty presentations, a financial aid presentation, a tour, and brunch. There are guides for informal visits, visitors may sit in on classes, and stay overnight. To schedule a visit, contact the Admissions Office.

Financial Aid: In a recent year, 85% of all full-time freshmen and 88% of continuing full-time students received some form of financial aid. 85% of all full-time freshmen and 88% of continuing full-time students received need-based aid. The average freshmen award was $23,912. 17% of undergraduate students worked part-time. Average annual earnings from campus work were $1542. AIC is a member of CSS. The FAFSA is required. Check with the school for application deadlines.

International Students: There were 40 international students enrolled in a recent year. The school actively recruits these students. They must take the TOEFL with a minimum score of 550 on the paper-based TOEFL (PBT) or 80 on the Internet-based version (iBT). They must also take the SAT or ACT.

Admissions Contact: Admission Services. E-Mail: *inquiry@aic.edu* Web: *www.aic.edu*

AMHERST COLLEGE B-2

Amherst, MA 01002 **(413) 542-2321; (413) 542-2527**

Full-time: 900 men, 885 women
Part-time: n/av
Graduate: n/av
Year: semesters
Application Deadline: January 1
Freshman Class: n/av
SAT or ACT: required
Faculty: 220; IIB, ++$
Ph.D.s: 97%
Student/Faculty: 8 to 1
Tuition: $46,574
Room & Board: $12,170

MOST COMPETITIVE

Amherst College, founded in 1821, is a private liberal arts institution. The 5 libraries contain 1.5 million volumes, 544,991 microform items, and 59,039 audio/video tapes/CDs/DVDs, and subscribe to 15,780 periodicals including electronic. Computerized library services include interlibrary loans, database searching, Internet access, and Wi-Fi capability. Special learning facilities include an art gallery, natural history museum, planetarium, radio station, an observatory, the Emily Dickinson Museum, and the Amherst Center for Russian Culture. The 1015-acre campus is in a small town 90 miles west of Boston. Including any residence halls, there are 75 buildings.

Student Life: 88% of undergraduates are from out of state, mostly the Middle Atlantic. Students are from 46 states, 31 foreign countries, and Canada. 59% are from public schools. 42% are White; 13% Asian American; 13% Hispanic; 11% African American. The average age of freshmen is 18; all undergraduates, 20. 2% do not continue beyond their first year; 96% remain to graduate.

Housing: College-sponsored housing includes coed dorms. In addition, there are language houses, special-interest houses, and 1 cooperative house. On-campus housing is guaranteed for all 4 years. 99% of students live on campus; of those, 95% remain on campus on weekends. Upperclassmen may keep cars.

Activities: There are no fraternities or sororities. There are 110 groups on campus, including art, band, chess, choir, chorale, chorus, communications, computers, dance, debate, drama, environmental, ethnic, film, gay, honors, international, jazz band, literary magazine, musical theater, newspaper, opera, orchestra, photography, political, professional, radio and TV, religious, social, social service, student government, symphony, and yearbook. Popular campus events include Fall Festival, Harlem Renaissance, and Spring Weekend Concert.

Sports: There are 13 intercollegiate sports for men and 14 for women, and 6 intramural sports for men and 6 for women. Facilities include 2 gyms, a pool, a field house, a hockey rink, an outdoor track, a fitness center, 10 international squash courts, an indoor jogging track, 3 indoor and 30 outdoor tennis courts, baseball and softball diamonds, a 9-hole golf course, and playing fields.

Disabled Students: Facilities include wheelchair ramps, elevators, special parking, specially equipped restrooms, special class scheduling, lowered drinking fountains, and lowered telephones.

Services: Counseling and information services are available, as is tutoring in every subject. There is a reader service for the blind. A quantitative skills center and a writing center are also available.

Campus Safety and Security: Measures include 24-hour foot and vehicle patrol, emergency notification system, self-defense education, and security escort services. There are emergency telephones, lighted pathways/sidewalks, controlled access to dorms/residences, ACEMS (Amherst College Emergency Medical Service).

Programs of Study: Amherst confers B.A. degrees. Bachelor's degrees are awarded in AGRICULTURE (environmental studies), BIOLOGICAL SCIENCE (biochemistry, biology/biological science, biophysics, and neurosciences), COMMUNICATIONS AND THE ARTS (art history, classics, dance, English, film, television and digital media, fine arts, French, German, music, Russian, Spanish, and theatre studies), COMPUTER AND PHYSICAL SCIENCE (astronomy, chemistry, computer science, geology, mathematics, and physics), SOCIAL SCIENCE (African American studies, American studies, anthropology, architectural studies, asian studies, economics, European studies, history, interdisciplinary studies, law, philosophy, political science/government, psychology, religion, sociology, and women & gender studies). Economics, political science, and history have the largest enrollments.

Required: To earn the B.A., all students must complete 32 courses, equivalent to 128 credits, 8 to 14 of which are in the major, with at least a C average. Other than a 1-semester freshman seminar in liberal studies, there are no specific course requirements. A thesis or comparable work is required for honors candidates.

Special: Students may cross-register through the Five College Consortium, the other members of which are all within 10 miles of Amherst, or through the Twelve College Exchange Program. A number of Interterm and summer internships are available, as is study-abroad in 40 countries. Dual majors, triple majors, student-designed interdisciplinary majors based on independent study as of junior or senior year, and work-study programs are possible. There are limited pass/fail options. There are 2 national honor societies, including Phi Beta Kappa, and 37 departmental honors programs.

Faculty/Classroom: 53% of faculty are male; 47% are female. All teach and do research. No introductory courses are taught by graduate students. The average class size in a regular course is 16.

Admissions: 100% were in the top two fifths.

Requirements: The SAT or ACT is required. In addition, plus 2 SAT: Subject tests are required for admission. Amherst strongly recommends that applicants take 4 years of English, math through calculus, 3 or 4 years of a foreign language, 2 years of history and social science, and at least 2 years of natural science, including a lab science. 2 essays are required. Important factors in the admissions decision are advanced placement or honors courses, recommendations by school officials, and evidence of special talent.

Procedure: Freshmen are admitted fall. Entrance exams should be taken no later than December of the senior year. There are early decision and deferred admissions plans. Early decision applications should be filed by November 15; regular applications, by January 1 for fall entry, along with a $60 fee. Notification of early decision is sent December 15; regular decision, April 1. 182 early decision candidates were accepted for the 2013-2014 class. applicants were on the 2013 waiting list; were admitted. Applications are accepted online.

Transfer: 13 transfer students enrolled in 2012-2013. Applicants must have full sophomore standing prior to applying and a minimum 3.0 GPA in previous college work. Transfers are accepted for the sophomore and junior classes only, and Amherst recommends that they submit SAT or ACT scores, plus high school and college transcripts, and seek a personal interview. 64 of 128 credits required for the bachelor's degree must be completed at Amherst.

Visiting: There are regularly scheduled orientations for prospective students, dean-led information sessions and student-led tours. There are guides for informal visits, visitors may sit in on classes, and stay overnight. To schedule a visit, contact the Admission Office.

Financial Aid: In 2013-2014, 58% of all full-time freshmen and 61% of continuing full-time students received some form of financial aid. 57% of all full-time freshmen and 61% of continuing full-time students received need-based aid. The average freshman award was $48,528. Need-based scholarships or need-based grants averaged $47,553; and need-based self-help aid (loans and jobs) averaged $1,697. 60% of undergraduate students work part-time. Average annual earnings from campus work are $1250. The CSS/Profile and FAFSA are required. The deadline for filing freshman financial aid applications for fall entry is February 15.

International Students: There are 171 international students enrolled. The school actively recruits these students. They must take the TOEFL with a minimum score of 600 on the paper-based TOEFL (PBT) or 100 on the Internet-based version (iBT) or take the MELAB, or the SAT: ELAP if English is not the applicant's first language. They must also take the SAT or ACT.

Graduates: From July 1, 2012 to June 30, 2013, 464 bachelor's degrees were awarded. The most popular majors were economics (15%), political science (14%), and history (11%). 46 companies recruited on campus in 2012-2013. In an average class, 89% graduate in 4 years or less, 95% graduate in 5 years or less, and 96% graduate in 6 years or less. Of the 2012 graduating class, 16% were enrolled in graduate school within 6 months of graduation, and 69% were employed.

Admissions Contact: Peter Rooney, Director of Public Affairs. E-Mail: *prooney@amherst.edu* Web: *www.amherst.edu*

ANNA MARIA COLLEGE C-2

Paxton, MA 01612-1198 **(508) 849-3360**
(800) 344-4586; (508) 849-3362

Full-time: 315 men, 405 women
Part-time: 105 men, 125 women
Graduate: 130 men, 215 women
Year: semesters, summer session
Application Deadline: open
Freshman Class: n/av
SAT or ACT: required
Faculty: n/av
Ph.D.s: 50%
Student/Faculty: n/av
Tuition: $27,644
Room & Board: $11,304

LESS COMPETITIVE

Anna Maria College, founded in 1946, is a small, comprehensive Catholic college offering career-oriented programs in liberal and fine arts, business, and teacher preparation. The figures in the above capsule and this profile are approximate. There are 5 undergraduate schools and 1 graduate school. In addition to regional accreditation, AMC has baccalaureate program accreditation with CSWE and NLN. The library contains 75,789 volumes, 1702 microform items, 6095 audio/video tapes/CDs/DVDs, and subscribes to 291 periodicals including electronic. Computerized library services include interlibrary loans, database searching, and Internet access. Special learning facilities include a learning resource center, art gallery, audiovisual center, and nature trail. The 180-acre campus is in a rural area 8 miles northwest of Worcester. Including any residence halls, there are 13 buildings.

Student Life: 84% of undergraduates are from Massachusetts. Others are from 14 states, 2 foreign countries, and Canada. 78% are white. The average age of freshmen is 19; all undergraduates, 20. 36% do not continue beyond their first year; 49% remain to graduate.

Housing: 459 students can be accommodated in college housing, which includes coed dorms. In addition, there is substance-free housing. On-campus housing is guaranteed for the freshman year only, is available on a first-come, first-served basis, and is available on a lottery system for upperclassmen. Priority is given to out-of-town students. 54% of students commute. All students may keep cars.

Activities: There are no fraternities or sororities. There are 25 groups on campus, including art, cheerleading, choir, chorus, computers, dance, drama, ethnic, gay, honors, international, jazz band, musical theater, newspaper, political, professional, religious, social, social service, student government, and yearbook. Popular campus events include Harvest Weekend, Mr. AMC, and Trick or Treating for Children.

Sports: There are 5 intercollegiate sports for men and 5 for women, and 3 intramural sports for men and 2 for women. Facilities include an activities center with a basketball court, locker rooms, and weight and fitness equipment, soccer, baseball, and softball fields, an outdoor basketball court, and a fitness trail.

Disabled Students: 80% of the campus is accessible. Facilities include wheelchair ramps, elevators, special parking, specially equipped restrooms, special class scheduling, lowered drinking fountains, and special housing.

Services: Counseling and information services are available, as is tutoring in every subject through a tutoring lab There is a reader service for the blind and remedial math, reading, and writing.

Campus Safety and Security: Measures include 24-hour foot and vehicle patrol and security escort services. There are shuttle buses, emergency telephones, and lighted pathways/sidewalks.

Programs of Study: AMC confers B.A., B.S., B.M., and B.S.N. degrees. Associate and master's degrees are also awarded. Bachelor's degrees are awarded in BUSINESS (business administration and management and sports management), COMMUNICATIONS AND THE ARTS (art, English, graphic design, media arts, modern language, music, music performance, studio art, and visual and performing arts), COMPUTER AND PHYSICAL SCIENCE (computer science), EDUCATION (early childhood education, elementary education, and music education), ENGINEERING AND ENVIRONMENTAL DESIGN (environmental science), HEALTH PROFESSIONS (art therapy, music therapy, and nursing), SOCIAL SCIENCE (criminal justice, fire science, history, human development, humanities, liberal arts/general studies, paralegal studies, political science/government, psychology, religion, social science, social work, and sociology). Criminal justice, fire science, and business have the largest enrollments.

Required: The 60-credit core curriculum consists of classes in English, literature, math, computers, natural science, foreign language, fine arts, history, philosophy, social/behavioral sciences, and religious studies. A total of 120 credits is required for graduation, with a minimum of 30 in the major and a 2.0 GPA.

Special: Cross-registration with the Colleges of the Worcester Consortium and internships in all majors are available. The college offers study abroad, a Washington semester, student-designed majors, accelerated degree programs, a general studies degree, credit by exam, work-study programs, and 5-year advanced degree programs in business, counseling psychology, criminal justice, education, visual art, and fire science. There are 6 national honor societies.

Faculty/Classroom: 53% of faculty are male; 47% are female. All teach undergraduates. No introductory courses are taught by graduate students. The average class size in an introductory lecture is 20; in a laboratory, 20; and in a regular course, 13.

Requirements: The SAT or ACT is required. A GED is accepted. 16 academic units are recommended, including 4 years of English, 2 years each of foreign language, history, math, and sciences, and 1 year of social studies. An interview is recommended. When applicable, an audition and portfolio are required. Students who have been out of high school for 3 or more years, or transfer students with 10 or more college-level courses, do not need to submit standardized test scores. An essay is required. A GPA of 2.0 is required. AP and CLEP credits are accepted. Important factors in the admissions decision are advanced placement or honors courses, extracurricular activities record, and leadership record.

Procedure: Freshmen are admitted fall and spring. Entrance exams should be taken in spring of the junior year or fall of the senior year. There are deferred admissions and rolling admissions plans. Application deadlines are open. Check with the school for application fees. Notification is sent on a rolling basis. Applications are accepted online.

Transfer: Transfers with a minimum GPA of 2.0 are accepted for upper-division work. High school and college transcripts are required. An essay or personal statement and a statement of good standing from prior institutions are also required. 60 of 120 credits required for the bachelor's degree must be completed at AMC.

Visiting: There are regularly scheduled orientations for prospective students, including on-campus interviews, campus tours, day visitation program by appointment, and a fall open house. There are guides for informal visits, and visitors may sit in on classes and stay overnight. To schedule a visit, contact the Undergraduate Admission Office.

Financial Aid: The FAFSA and the state aid form are required. Check with the school for current application deadlines.

International Students: The school actively recruits these students. They must take the TOEFL with a minimum score of 470 on the paper-based TOEFL (PBT). They must also take the SAT or ACT.

Admissions Contact: Director of Admission. E-mail: *admission@annamaria.edu* Web: *www.annamaria.edu*

ART INSTITUTE OF BOSTON AT LESLEY UNIVERSITY E-2

Boston, MA 02215 (617) 585-6710
(800) 773-0494, ext. 6706; (617) 585-6720

Full-time: 301 men, 903 women	**Faculty:** n/av
Part-time: 18 men, 45 women	**Ph.D.s:** 43%
Graduate: n/av	**Student/Faculty:** n/av
Year: semesters, summer session	**Tuition:** $27,330
Application Deadline: February 15	**Room & Board:** $12,400
Freshman Class: 2523 applied, 1639 accepted, 328 enrolled	
	SPECIAL

The Art Institute of Boston at Lesley University, founded in 1912, is a private institution offering undergraduate visual art programs leading to baccalaureate degrees, 3-year diplomas, and advanced professional certificates, as well as continuing and professional education, intensive workshops, and precollege courses. There are 2 undergraduate schools and 1 graduate school. In addition to regional accreditation, AIB has baccalaureate program accreditation with NASAD. The 2 libraries contain 124,022 volumes, 878,938 microform items, 42,680 audio/video tapes/CDs/DVDs, and subscribe to 3,935 periodicals including electronic. Computerized library services include interlibrary loans, database searching, Internet access, and Wi-Fi capability. Special learning facilities include an art gallery, computer labs, state-of-the-art animation lab, print-making studio, clay studio, wood-working studio, photo lab, and digital-printing lab. The 2-acre campus is in an urban area in the Kenmore Square area of Boston. Including any residence halls, there are 53 buildings.

Student Life: 56% of undergraduates are from Massachusetts. Others are from 34 states, 10 foreign countries, and Canada. 83% are from public schools. 63% are White. The average age of freshmen is 18; all undergraduates, 20. 33% do not continue beyond their first year; 63% remain to graduate.

Housing: 650 students can be accommodated in college housing, which includes single-sex and coed dorms. On-campus housing is available on a first-come and first-served basis. 50% of students commute. All students may keep cars.

Activities: There are no fraternities or sororities. There are 25 groups on campus, including art, chorale, chorus, drama, ethnic, gay, international, literary magazine, musical theater, religious, social service, and student government. Popular campus events include Student Lunches, Student and Faculty Coffee Hours, and Edible Art.

Sports: There are 7 intercollegiate sports for men and 7 for women, and 3 intramural sports for men and 5 for women. Facilities include an outdoor tennis court, a fitness center with Nautilus circuit, free weights, and cardiovascular equipment on the main campus. In addition, students may use an Olympic-size swimming pool, playing field facilities, basketball and racquetball courts, a rowing tank, a softball court, an indoor track, and a lighted outdoor soccer field at a nearby school.

Disabled Students: 85% of the campus is accessible. Facilities include wheelchair ramps, elevators, specially equipped restrooms, special class scheduling, and lowered drinking fountains.

Services: Counseling and information services are available, as is tutoring in some subjects. There is a reader service for the blind, and remedial math and writing.

Campus Safety and Security: Measures include 24-hour foot and vehicle patrol, self-defense education, and security escort services. There are shuttle buses, emergency telephones, lighted pathways/sidewalks, alarms, and electronically operated entrances in some buildings.

Programs of Study: AIB confers B.F.A. degrees. Master's degrees are also awarded. Bachelor's degrees are awarded in COMMUNICATIONS AND THE ARTS (design, fine arts, illustration, and photography). Design and photography is the strongest academically. Illustration/animation has the largest enrollments.

Required: All students must complete 123 to 128 credits, including 31 credits in the foundation program and 82 or more in the major. Senior juries are required.

Special: There is cross-registration with Lesley University. Internships are required for design majors and encouraged for all other majors. Accelerated degree programs in all majors, study abroad in 6 countries and dual majors in fine art/illustration, design/illustration, illustration/animation, and art education are offered. There are a freshman honors program and 2 departmental honors programs.

Faculty/Classroom: 44% of faculty are male; 56% are female. All teach undergraduates. No introductory courses are taught by graduate students. The average class size in an introductory lecture is 20; in a laboratory is 14; and in a regular course is 14.

Admissions: 65% of the 2013-2014 applicants were accepted. The SAT scores for the 2013-2014 freshman class were: Critical Reading--27% below 500, 47% between 500 and 599, 24% between 600 and 699, and 2% between 700 and 800; Math--41% below 500, 46% between 500 and 599, 12% between 600 and 699, and 1% between 700 and 800; Writing--27% below 500, 50% between 500 and 599, 20% between 600 and 699, and 3% between 700 and 800. The ACT scores were 9% below 21, 50% between 21 and 23, 13% between 24 and 26, 24% between 27 and 28, and 4% above 28. 38% of the current freshmen were in the top fifth of their class; 70% were in the top two fifths.

Requirements: Applicants must submit an official high school transcript, an essay, and do a portfolio review. Letters of recommendation and a campus tour are encouraged. AP and CLEP credits are accepted. Important factors in the admissions decision are evidence of special talent, personality/intangible qualities, and advanced placement or honors courses.

Procedure: Freshmen are admitted fall and spring. Entrance exams should be taken by February 15. There is a deferred admissions plan. Applications should be filed by February 15 for fall entry; November 15 for spring entry. The fall 2013 application fee was $40. Applications are accepted online.

Transfer: High school and college transcripts, a portfolio review, an essay, and SAT or ACT scores (if graduated since 1995) are required. 45 of 123 credits required for the bachelor's degree must be completed at AIB.

Visiting: There are regularly scheduled orientations for prospective students, meeting with faculty and students. There are guides for informal visits and visitors may sit in on classes. To schedule a visit, contact the Office of Admissions.

Financial Aid: In 2013-2014, 72% of all full-time freshmen students received some form of financial aid. 72% of all full-time freshmen students received need-based aid. The average freshman award was $20,328. Need-based scholarships or need-based grants averaged $12,625; and need-based self-help aid (loans and jobs) averaged $9,044. 18% of undergraduate students work part-time. Average annual earnings from campus work are $2000. The average financial indebtedness of the 2013 graduate was $14,000. The FAFSA and the college's own financial statement are required. The priority date for freshman financial aid applications for fall entry is February 15.

International Students: There are 44 international students enrolled. The school actively recruits these students. They must take the TOEFL with a minimum score of 500 on the paper-based TOEFL (PBT) or 61 on the Internet-based version (iBT).

Graduates: From July 1, 2012 to June 30, 2013, 390 bachelor's degrees were awarded. The most popular majors were illustration (33%), design (24%), and photography (21%). In an average class, 36% graduate in 4 years or less, 53% graduate in 5 years or less, and 63% graduate in 6 years or less. Of the 2012 graduating class, 11% were enrolled in graduate school within 6 months of graduation, and 75% were employed.

Admissions Contact: Bob Gielow, Director of Admissions. E-Mail: *admissions@aiboston.edu* Web: *www.aiboston.edu*

ASSUMPTION COLLEGE C-2

Worcester, MA 01609 (508) 767-7285
(866) 477-7776; (508) 799-4412

Full-time: 794 men, 1204 women	**Faculty:** 146; IIB, -$
Part-time: 1 men, 3 women	**Ph.D.s:** 94%
Graduate: 142 men, 367 women	**Student/Faculty:** 12 to 1
Year: semesters, summer session	**Tuition:** $34,975
Application Deadline: February 15	**Room & Board:** $10,746
Freshman Class: 4659 applied, 3458 accepted, 502 enrolled	
SAT CR/M: 550/570 **ACT:** 25	**VERY COMPETITIVE**

Assumption College, founded in 1904 by Augustinians of the Assumption, offers a Catholic, liberal arts and sciences education to undergraduates, along with programs for graduate and continuing education students. There is one undergraduate school and one graduate school. The library contains 219,558 volumes, 24,166 microform items, 3,751 audio/video tapes/CDs/DVDs, and subscribes to 3,550 periodicals including electronic. Computerized library services include interlibrary loans, database searching, Internet access, and Wi-Fi capability. Special learning facilities include a TV station. The 180-acre campus is in a suburban area 45 miles west of Boston in New England's 2nd largest city, Worcester, MA. Including any residence halls, there are 48 buildings.

Student Life: 64% of undergraduates are from Massachusetts. Others are from 25 states, 36 foreign countries, and Canada. 68% are from public schools. 74% are White. The average age of freshmen is 18; all undergraduates, 20. 17% do not continue beyond their first year; 73% remain to graduate.

Housing: 1925 students can be accommodated in college housing, which includes single-sex dorms and on-campus apartments. In addition, there are special-interest houses, freshman dorms, substance-free dorms, first-year experience dorm, and a living/learning center. On-campus housing is guaranteed for all 4 years. 87% of students live on campus; of those, 80% remain on campus on weekends. Upperclassmen may keep cars.

Activities: There are no fraternities or sororities. There are 60 groups on campus, including art, band, cheerleading, choir, chorale, chorus, computers, dance, drama, environmental, ethnic, film, honors, international, jazz band, literary magazine, musical theater, newspaper, orchestra, pep band, photography, political, professional, radio and TV, religious, social, social service, and student government. Popular campus events include Midnight Madness Baketball Kickoff, Campus Concert and Duck Day.

Sports: There are 10 intercollegiate sports for men and 11 for women. Facilities include a 1,200-seat multisports stadium, a 3,000-seat gym, baseball and softball diamonds, a field hockey area, a soccer field, and tennis courts. A recreation center houses a 6-lane swimming pool, a jogging/walking track, 2 racquetball courts, an aerobics/dance studio, a multi-purpose room with TRX equipment, fully equipped Bodymaster and free-weight rooms, a fitness center, a varsity weight room, and a field house with 3 multipurpose courts for basketball, volleyball, and floor hockey.

Disabled Students: 71% of the campus is accessible. Facilities include wheelchair ramps, elevators, special parking, specially equipped restrooms, special class scheduling, lowered drinking fountains, lowered telephones, and special housing.

Services: Counseling and information services are available, as is tutoring in most subjects. There is a reader service for the blind. signing for the deaf, and technology services for the disabled.

Campus Safety and Security: Measures include 24-hour foot and vehicle patrol, emergency notification system, self-defense education, and security escort services. There are shuttle buses, emergency telephones, lighted pathways/sidewalks, and controlled access to dorms/residences.

Programs of Study: Assumption confers B.A. degrees. Master's degrees are also awarded. Bachelor's degrees are awarded in BIOLOGICAL SCIENCE (biology/biological science, biotechnology, and molecular biology), BUSINESS (accounting, business administration and management, international business management, marketing management, and organizational behavior), COMMUNICATIONS AND THE ARTS (art history, classics, English, French, graphic design, languages, music, Spanish, and studio art), COMPUTER AND PHYSICAL SCIENCE (chemistry, computer science, and mathematics), ENGINEERING AND ENVIRONMENTAL DESIGN (environmental science), HEALTH PROFESSIONS (rehabilitation therapy), SOCIAL SCIENCE (economics, history, human services, international studies, Italian studies, Latin American studies, philosophy, political science/government, psychology, sociology, and theological studies). Natural sciences; psychology; business studies is the strongest academically. Business studies; natural sciences; human services and rehabilitation studies have the largest enrollments.

Required: Students must complete a core curriculum of 3 courses from different disciplines in social science: 2 courses in 1 and 1 course in another of the 3 areas of math, natural science, and foreign languages; 2 courses each of English composition, philosophy, and theology; 1 each of literature, history, and either art, music, or theater arts, and 1 additional course in 2 of the 3 areas of philosophy and theology, literature, and history. A minimum of 120 semester credit hours, with a minimum of 38 semester courses, must be completed; 8 to 14 courses must be in the upper division of the major. A minimum 2.0 GPA is required.

Special: Co-op program in marine studies. Cross-registration with the Colleges of Worcester Consortium is offered. The college has its own study abroad campus in Rome, and study abroad is available through other providers as well. The college offers internships, a Washington semester, student-designed and dual majors, credit by exam, and credit for military experience. The college offers 6-in-5 programs in accounting (BA/MBA), special education(BA/MA), school counseling (BA/MA), and rehabilitation counseling (BA/MA); a 3/-2 program in engineering with the University of Notre Dame; and multiple combined degree programs with other institutions; see undergraduate catalog for details. There are 11 national honor societies and a freshman honors program.

Faculty/Classroom: 55% of faculty are male; 45% are female. All teach undergraduates. No introductory courses are taught by graduate students. The average class size in a laboratory is 17 and in a regular course is 21.

Admissions: 74% of the 2013-2014 applicants were accepted. The SAT scores for the 2013-2014 freshman class were: Critical Reading--18% below 500, 57% between 500 and 599, 22% between 600 and 699, and 5% between 700 and 800; Math--15% below 500, 50% between 500 and 599, 32% between 600 and 699, and 2% between 700 and 800. The ACT scores were 11% below 21, 20% between 21 and 23, 42% between 24 and 26, 16% between 27 and 28, and 11% above 28. 30% of the current freshmen were in the top fifth of their class; 62% were in the top two fifths.

Requirements: Applicants must graduate from an accredited secondary school or have a GED. 18 academic units are required, including 4 years of English, 3 of math, and 2 each of history, science, and foreign language.

An essay and an interview are recommended. AP and CLEP credits are accepted. Important factors in the admissions decision are advanced placement or honors courses, leadership record, and recommendations by school officials.

Procedure: Freshmen are admitted fall and spring. Entrance exams should be taken in May of the junior year or November of the senior year. There are early admissions and deferred admissions plans. Applications should be filed by February 15 for fall entry; December 21 for spring entry, along with a $50 fee. Notifications are sent March 15. 111 applicants were on the 2013 waiting list; 38 were admitted. Applications are accepted online.

Transfer: 55 transfer students enrolled in 2012-2013. Transfer students must have maintained a minimum 2.5 GPA at their previous college. SAT scores and high school and college transcripts are required. 60 of 120 credits required for the bachelor's degree must be completed at Assumption.

Visiting: There are regularly scheduled orientations for prospective students, consisting of new student orientation, meetings with future classmates, choosing roommates, registration, testing, conferences with academic advisers, and discussions of aspects of college life. There are guides for informal visits and visitors may sit in on classes. To schedule a visit, contact the Office of Admissions at (866) 477-7776.

Financial Aid: In 2013-2014, 94% of all full-time freshmen and 97% of continuing full-time students received some form of financial aid. 83% of all full-time freshmen and 78% of continuing full-time students received need-based aid. The average freshman award was $25,676. Need-based scholarships or need-based grants averaged $21,068 ($48,545 maximum); need-based self-help aid (loans and jobs) averaged $4,380 ($10,500 maximum); non-need-based athletic scholarships averaged $13,840 ($47,204 maximum); and other non-need-based awards and non-need-based scholarships averaged $13,672 ($26,000 maximum). The average financial indebtedness of the 2013 graduate was $33,481. The FAFSA is required. The deadline for filing freshman financial aid applications for fall entry is February 15.

International Students: There are 60 international students enrolled. The school actively recruits these students. They must take the TOEFL with a minimum score of 550 on the paper-based TOEFL (PBT) or 80 on the Internet-based version (iBT).

Graduates: From July 1, 2012 to June 30, 2013, 435 bachelor's degrees were awarded. The most popular majors were English (12%), psychology (11%), and human services and rehabilitation studies (11%). 416 companies recruited on campus in 2012-2013. In an average class, 70% graduate in 4 years or less, 73% graduate in 5 years or less, and 73% graduate in 6 years or less. Of the 2012 graduating class, 25% were enrolled in graduate school within 6 months of graduation, and 67% were employed.

Admissions Contact: Evan E. Lipp, Vice President for Enrollment Management. E-Mail: *admiss@assumption.edu* Web: *www.assumption.edu/admissions/undergraduate/*

ATLANTIC UNION COLLEGE — D-2

South Lancaster, MA 01561 — (978) 368-2239; (800) 282-2030; (978) 368-2517

Full-time: 155 men, 255 women	**Faculty:** n/av
Part-time: 25 men, 35 women	**Ph.D.s:** 42%
Graduate: 10 men, 15 women	**Student/Faculty:** n/av
Year: semesters, summer session	**Tuition:** $18,500
Application Deadline: see profile	**Room & Board:** $9000
Freshman Class: n/av	
SAT or ACT: required	

LESS COMPETITIVE

Atlantic Union College, established in 1882, is a private liberal arts institution associated with the Seventh-Day Adventist church and offers professional and preprofessional programs. The figures in the above capsule and this profile are approximate. In addition to regional accreditation, AUC has baccalaureate program accreditation with CSWE, NASM, and NLN. The library contains 139,000 volumes, 17,336 microform items, 4754 audio/video tapes/CDs/DVDs, and subscribes to 469 periodicals including electronic. Computerized library services include interlibrary loans, database searching, and Internet access. Special learning facilities include a learning resource center, art gallery, model elementary and secondary schools, and music conservatory. The 135-acre campus is in a small town 50 miles west of Boston. Including any residence halls, there are 54 buildings.

Student Life: 55% of undergraduates are from out of state, mostly the Northeast. Students are from 14 states, 21 foreign countries, and Canada. 53% are African American; 22% Hispanic; 20% white; 15% foreign nationals. The average age of freshmen is 21; all undergraduates, 23. 27% do not continue beyond their first year.

Housing: 469 students can be accommodated in college housing, which includes single-sex dorms, on-campus apartments, and married student housing. On-campus housing is guaranteed for all 4 years. 56% of students live on campus; of those, 85% remain on campus on weekends. Alcohol is not permitted. All students may keep cars.

Activities: There are no fraternities or sororities. There are 13 groups on campus, including art, band, choir, chorale, drama, ethnic, honors, newspaper, orchestra, religious, social, student government, and yearbook. Popular campus events include fall picnic, Cultural Heritage Weeks, and Fine Arts Week.

Sports: There are 7 intramural sports for men and 7 for women. Facilities include a gym and field house with a weight room and tennis/volleyball/badminton, racquetball/handball, and basketball courts, a swimming pool, and athletic fields for flag football, soccer, softball, and baseball.

Disabled Students: 73% of the campus is accessible. Facilities include wheelchair ramps, elevators, special parking, specially equipped restrooms, special class scheduling, and lowered drinking fountains.

Services: Counseling and information services are available, as is tutoring in most subjects. There is remedial math, reading, and writing. Additional services are provided upon request.

Campus Safety and Security: Measures include self-defense education and security escort services. There are lighted pathways/sidewalks.

Programs of Study: AUC confers B.A., B.S., and B.M. degrees. Associate and master's degrees are also awarded. Bachelor's degrees are awarded in BIOLOGICAL SCIENCE (biology/biological science and life science), BUSINESS (accounting and business administration and management), COMMUNICATIONS AND THE ARTS (art, English, and music), COMPUTER AND PHYSICAL SCIENCE (computer science, information sciences and systems, and mathematics), EDUCATION (early childhood education, elementary education, and music education), HEALTH PROFESSIONS (nursing), SOCIAL SCIENCE (culinary arts, history, liberal arts/general studies, ministries, psychology, religion, social work, and theological studies). Nursing, business, and psychology are the strongest academically. Nursing, business, and education have the largest enrollments.

Required: Students must complete 9 hours each in humanities, science, and social science and 12 hours in religion/ethics. Foreign language proficiency, a phys ed requirement, 40 hours of community service, and a course in college writing must also be completed. AUC requires 128 to 143 credit hours for the bachelor's degree, with 30 to 60 in the major, and a 2.0 GPA.

Special: There is cross-registration with Mount Wachusett Community College and the Colleges of Worcester Consortium. Students may study abroad in 6 countries. AUC also offers newspaper and biology research internships, cooperative programs in several majors, pass/fail options, and nondegree study. The Summer Advantage in New England program offers precollege credit to high school honor students. There is also an adult degree program, in which most study is done at home and in which student-designed majors are permited. Dual majors, an accelerated degree in management and professional studies, a 1-3 engineering degree with Walla Walla College, and preprofessional curricula in dentistry, dental hygiene, medicine, respiratory therapy, radiologic technology, and veterinary medicine in conjunction with Loma Linda University are offered. There are 3 national honor societies, a freshman honors program, and 4 departmental honors programs.

Faculty/Classroom: 45% of faculty are male; 55% are female. All teach undergraduates, and 10% both teach and do research. No introductory courses are taught by graduate students. The average class size in an introductory lecture is 18; in a laboratory, 30; and in a regular course, 16.

Requirements: The SAT or ACT is required. Applicants should be graduates of an accredited secondary school. The GED is accepted with a minimum score of 250. Required academic credits include 4 years of high school English and 2 years each of a foreign language, math, history, and science. A GPA of 2.2 is required. AP and CLEP credits are accepted. Important factors in the admissions decision are recommendations by school officials, recommendations by alumni, and personality/intangible qualities.

Procedure: Freshmen are admitted fall and spring. Entrance exams should be taken during the senior year of high school. There is a rolling admissions plan. Check with the school for current application deadlines and fees. Notification is sent on a rolling basis. Applications are accepted online.

Transfer: Applicants who have completed at least 24 semester hours are not required to submit SAT or ACT scores. Applicants from junior colleges may receive credit for up to 72 semester hours. Only a grade of C or better transfers for credit. 30 of 128 credits required for the bachelor's degree must be completed at AUC.

Visiting: There are regularly scheduled orientations for prospective students, including campus tours, class visits, and financial aid and admissions information sessions. There are guides for informal visits, and visitors may sit in on classes and stay overnight. To schedule a visit, contact Admissions.

Financial Aid: AUC is a member of CSS. The FAFSA is required. Check with the school for current application deadlines.

International Students: The school actively recruits these students. They must take the TOEFL. They must also take the ACT.

Admissions Contact: Director of Admissions. A campus DVD is available. E-mail: *enroll@atlanticuc.edu* Web: *www.atlanticuc.edu*

BABSON COLLEGE D-2

Babson Park, MA 02457 (781) 239-5522
(800) 488-3696; (781) 239-4135

Full-time: 1075 men, 735 women
Part-time: n/av
Graduate: 1205 men, 445 women
Year: semesters, summer session
Application Deadline: see profile
Freshman Class: n/av
SAT or ACT: required
Faculty: n/av
Ph.D.s: 72%
Student/Faculty: n/av
Tuition: $40,900
Room & Board: $13,830

HIGHLY COMPETITIVE

Babson College, founded in 1919, is a private business school. All students start their own businesses during their freshman year with money loaned by the college. The figures in the above capsule and this capsule are approximate. There is 1 graduate school. In addition to regional accreditation, Babson has baccalaureate program accreditation with AACSB. The library contains 132,024 volumes, 346,941 microform items, 4645 audio/video tapes/CDs/DVDs, and subscribes to 511 periodicals including electronic. Computerized library services include interlibrary loans, database searching, and Internet access. Special learning facilities include a learning resource center, art gallery, radio station, performing arts theater, and centers for entrepreneurial studies, management, language and culture, writing, math, visual arts, executive education, and women's leadership. The 370-acre campus is in a suburban area 14 miles west of Boston. Including any residence halls, there are 53 buildings.

Student Life: 70% of undergraduates are from out of state, mostly the Northeast. Students are from 47 states, 60 foreign countries, and Canada. 50% are from public schools. 44% are white; 18% foreign nationals; 11% Asian American. The average age of freshmen is 18; all undergraduates, 20. 5% do not continue beyond their first year; 85% remain to graduate.

Housing: 1441 students can be accommodated in college housing, which includes single-sex and coed dorms, on campus apartments, and married student housing. In addition, there are special-interest houses, substance-free living, fraternity and sorority towers, and a cultural house. On-campus housing is guaranteed for all 4 years. 85% of students live on campus; of those, 80% remain on campus on weekends. All students may keep cars.

Activities: 10% of men belong to 7 national fraternities; 12% of women belong to 3 national sororities. There are 60 groups on campus, including art, band, cappella, cheerleading, choir, chorus, dance, drama, ethnic, gay, honors, international, jazz band, literary magazine, musical theater, newspaper, photography, political, professional, radio and TV, religious, social, social service, student government, and yearbook. Popular campus events include Multicultural Week.

Sports: There are 11 intercollegiate sports for men and 11 for women, and 11 intramural sports for men and 11 for women. Facilities include a sports complex with an indoor pool, a 200-meter, 6-lane indoor track, a 1500-square-foot field house, a 600-seat gym with 3 basketball courts, 5 squash and 2 racquetball courts, a fitness center, a dance aerobics studio, locker rooms with saunas, and a sports medicine facility.

Disabled Students: 75% of the campus is accessible. Facilities include wheelchair ramps, elevators, special parking, specially equipped restrooms, special class scheduling, lowered drinking fountains, and special housing.

Services: Counseling and information services are available, as is tutoring in most subjects. There are writing/speech skills and math/science skills centers.

Campus Safety and Security: Measures include 24-hour foot and vehicle patrol, self-defense education, and security escort services. There are shuttle buses, emergency telephones, lighted pathways/sidewalks, a motorist assist program, a transportation service for the cross-registration program, vans available to students for school activities, and crime prevention programs.

Programs of Study: Babson confers B.S.M. degrees. Master's degrees are also awarded. Bachelor's degrees are awarded in BUSINESS (business administration and management).

Required: Students must complete a curriculum of general management and liberal arts, with 50% in management and 50% in liberal arts. A total of 128 semester hours is required for graduation. A minimum GPA of 2.0 is required.

Special: There is cross-registration with Brandeis University, Wellesley College, and F.W. Olin College of Engineering. Internships and study abroad in 27 countries are available. There is a freshman honors program and 10 departmental honors programs.

Faculty/Classroom: 69% of faculty are male; 31% are female. No introductory courses are taught by graduate students. The average class size in an introductory lecture is 34; in a laboratory, 20; and in a regular course, 27.

Requirements: The SAT or ACT is required. Applicants must be graduates of an accredited secondary school or have a GED. 16 academic courses are required, including 4 credits of English, 3 of math, 2 of social studies, and 1 of science. A fourth year of math is strongly recommended. Essays are required. SAT Subject tests in math are recommended. AP credits are accepted. Important factors in the admissions decision are advanced placement or honors courses, evidence of special talent, and leadership record.

Procedure: Freshmen are admitted in the fall. Entrance exams should be taken prior to application (SAT or ACT). There are early decision, early admissions and deferred admissions plans. Check with the school for current application deadlinesand fees. Applications are accepted online. A waiting list is maintained.

Transfer: Transfer applicants are expected to demonstrate solid academic performance at their prior institution and must submit 1 essay and 1 recommendation from a college teacher or administrator, in addition to a high school transcript and SAT scores. They must also submit course descriptions and syllabi for any courses they have taken. 64 of 128 credits required for the bachelor's degree must be completed at Babson.

Visiting: There are regularly scheduled orientations for prospective students, including an open house each year, personal interviews, campus tours, group information sessions and Fall Preview Days (select Saturdays). There are guides for informal visits. To schedule a visit, contact the Admission Office.

Financial Aid: The CSS/Profile, the FAFSA, and tax returns are required. Check with the school for current application deadlines.

International Students: The school actively recruits these students. They must take the TOEFL with a minimum score of 600, or take the English Language Proficiency Test. They must also take the SAT or ACT.

Admissions Contact: Dean of Undergraduate Admission. A campus DVD is available. E-mail: *ugradadmission@babson.edu* Web: *www.babson.edu*

BARD COLLEGE AT SIMON'S ROCK A-2

Great Barrington, MA 01230 (800) 235-7186; (413) 541-0081

Full-time: 141 men, 200 women
Part-time: 6 men, 3 women
Graduate: n/av
Year: semesters
Application Deadline: May 1
Faculty: 48
Ph.D.s: 89%
Student/Faculty: 6 to 1
Tuition: $46,703
Room & Board: $12,690
Freshman Class: 218 applied, 201 accepted, 145 enrolled
SAT CR/M/W: 690/650/640 **ACT:** 27 **HIGHLY COMPETITIVE+**

Bard College at Simon's Rock is the world's only four-year college of the liberal arts and sciences specifically designed for bright, highly motivated students ready to begin college after the tenth or eleventh grade. Students are taught exclusively in small seminars by a supportive, highly-trained faculty. Degrees are granted in over 40 areas of study. Most graduates proceed to earn graduate and professional degrees at highly selective universities. Simon's Rock was founded in 1964 and joined the Bard College network in 1979. There is one undergraduate school. The library contains 83,690 volumes, 3,896 microform items, 5,817 audio/video tapes/CDs/DVDs, and subscribes to 978 periodicals including electronic. Computerized library services include interlibrary loans, database searching, Internet access, and Wi-Fi capability. Special learning facilities include an art gallery. The 210-acre campus is in a small town in the Berkshire Hills of Western MA, approximately 2 hours from New York City and Boston. Including any residence halls, there are 47 buildings.

Student Life: 86% of undergraduates are from out of state, mostly the Middle Atlantic. Students are from 35 states, and 18 foreign countries. 72% are from public schools. 57% are White. The average age of freshmen is 16; all undergraduates, 17. 30% do not continue beyond their first year; 73% remain to graduate.

Housing: 347 students can be accommodated in college housing, which includes single-sex and coed dorms and on-campus apartments. On-campus housing is guaranteed for all 4 years. 94% of students live on campus; of those, 94% remain on campus on weekends. Alcohol is not permitted. Upperclassmen may keep cars.

Activities: There are no fraternities or sororities. There are 20 groups on campus, including QueerSA, student action service learning, USO, art, black student union, chess, choir, chorus, computers, dance, debate, drama, environmental, ethnic, film, gay, international, jazz band, literary magazine, musical theater, newspaper, opera, orchestra, photography, political, professional, religious, social, social service, student government, and yearbook. Popular campus events include May Fest, Prom and Dance Concert.

Sports: There are 3 intercollegiate sports for men and 3 for women, and 6 intramural sports for men and 6 for women. Facilities include an 8-lane swimming pool, a multicourt gym, 3 racquetball courts, an elevated running track, a fitness and weight-training center, a rock-climbing wall, a soccer field, 4 tennis courts, and hiking trails.

Disabled Students: 75% of the campus is accessible. Facilities include wheelchair ramps, elevators, special parking, specially equipped restrooms, special class scheduling, lowered drinking fountains, lowered telephones, and special housing.

Services: Counseling and information services are available, as is tutoring

in every subject. There is a reader service for the blind. Study skills instruction is available.

Campus Safety and Security: Measures include 24-hour foot and vehicle patrol, emergency notification system, self-defense education, and security escort services. There are shuttle buses, lighted pathways/sidewalks, and controlled access to dorms/residences.

Programs of Study: Simon's Rock confers B.A. degrees. Associate degrees are also awarded. Bachelor's degrees are awarded in AGRICULTURE (environmental studies), BIOLOGICAL SCIENCE (biology/biological science and ecology), COMMUNICATIONS AND THE ARTS (art/art studies, art history and appreciation, ceramic art and design, creative writing, dance, dramatic arts, drawing, intermedia/multimedia, linguistics, literature, music, painting, and photography), COMPUTER AND PHYSICAL SCIENCE (chemistry, computer science, mathematics, natural sciences, physics, and quantitative methods), ENGINEERING AND ENVIRONMENTAL DESIGN (preengineering), HEALTH PROFESSIONS (premedicine), SOCIAL SCIENCE (African American studies, American studies, Asian/Oriental studies, crosscultural studies, cultural studies/critical theory & analysis, French studies, gender studies, geography, German area studies, history, philosophy, political science/government, psychology, Russian and Slavic studies, and Spanish studies). Preengineering, theater, and psychology have the largest enrollments.

Required: Writing and Thinking Workshop/Book One Program, General Education Seminars I, II and III, Cultural Perspectives course, Arts course, Mathematics course, Natural Science course, one year of Foreign Language coursework. Students in the BA program must complete at least one BA Concentration and a Senior Thesis.

Special: 3-2 BA/BS engineering degree programs with Columbia University and Dartmouth University 3-2 BA/MS program in environmental science with Bard College's Center for Environmental Policy Articulated junior-year study abroad agreements with two colleges at Oxford University (Lincoln College and St. Catherine's College), the University of Manchester's Center for New Writing, Qingdao University in China, the University of Glasgow in Scotland, the London Dramatic Academy in London, and Eastern Carolina University's Italy Intensives abroad. There are also domestic study away opportunities with the Bard Globalization and International Affairs (BGIA) program in NYC, the Eugene O'Neil Theater in CT, the Washington Center in Washington DC, and the International Center of Photography in NYC. Internships may be completed for course credit through the Extended Campus Project program, and students are encouraged to work with the Director of Career Services to develop internships for credit or personal development that connect with their academic and career interests. Most Simon's Rock BA graduates complete more than one of the College's BA concentrations and students have the option of creating a self-designed 2nd concentration. Work-study opportunities are available on campus, as well as with several nonprofit organizations and schools in the community.

Faculty/Classroom: 45% of faculty are male; 54% are female. All teach and do research. No introductory courses are taught by graduate students. The average class size in an introductory lecture is 14; in a laboratory is 10; and in a regular course is 12.

Admissions: 92% of the 2013-2014 applicants were accepted. The SAT scores for the 2013-2014 freshman class were: Critical Reading--9% below 500, 9% between 500 and 599, 27% between 600 and 699, and 55% between 700 and 800; Math--9% below 500, 18% between 500 and 599, 46% between 600 and 699, and 27% between 700 and 800; Writing--9% between 500 and 599, 45% between 600 and 699, and 46% between 700 and 800. The ACT scores were 10% below 21, 10% between 21 and 23, 30% between 24 and 26, 30% between 27 and 28, and 20% above 28. 61% of the current freshmen were in the top fifth of their class; 81% were in the top two fifths.

Requirements: Applicants are required to submit application form, parent statement, 3 letters of recommendation, personal interview, high school transcript and school report, and application essays. Test scores are optional, but will be considered if submitted. Important factors in the admissions decision are personality/intangible qualities, recommendations by school officials, advanced placement or honors courses, evidence of special talent, recommendations by alumni, ability to finance college education, leadership record, parents or siblings attended your school, extracurricular activities record, and geographical diversity.

Procedure: Freshmen are admitted fall and spring. There is a rolling admissions plan. Applications should be filed by May 1 for fall entry; December 1 for spring entry, along with a $50 fee. Notification is sent on a Rolling basis. Applications are accepted online.

Transfer: 1 transfer students enrolled in 2012-2013. Transfer students must be evaluated by the Dean of Academic Affairs and Registrar. 60 of 120 credits required for the bachelor's degree must be completed at Simon's Rock.

Visiting: There are regularly scheduled orientations for prospective students, Includes a sample class, a campus tour, and an interview. There are guides for informal visits and visitors may sit in on classes. To schedule a visit, contact the Office of Admission at admit@simons-rock.edu.

Financial Aid: In 2013-2014, 87% of all full-time freshmen and 76% of continuing full-time students received some form of financial aid. 82% of all full-time freshmen and 72% of continuing full-time students received need-based aid. The average freshman award was $37,292. Need-based scholarships or need-based grants averaged $34,864; need-based self-help aid (loans and jobs) averaged $5,207; and other non-need-based awards and non-need-based scholarships averaged $21,108. The average financial indebtedness of the 2013 graduate was $28,175. Simon's Rock is a member of CSS. The CSS/Profile and FAFSA are required. The priority date for freshman financial aid applications for fall entry is February 1. The deadline for filing freshman financial aid applications for fall entry is May 1.

International Students: There are 34 international students enrolled. The school actively recruits these students. They must take the TOEFL with a minimum score of 600 on the paper-based TOEFL (PBT) or 100 on the Internet-based version (iBT).

Graduates: From July 1, 2012 to June 30, 2013, 50 bachelor's degrees were awarded. The most popular majors were visual and performing arts (18%), interdisciplinary studies (16%), and social sciences (11%). In an average class, 3% graduate in 3 years or less, 75% graduate in 4 years or less, 19% graduate in 5 years or less, and 3% graduate in 6 years or less.

Admissions Contact: Office of Admission E-Mail: *admit@simons-rock.edu* Web: *www.simons-rock.edu*

BAY PATH COLLEGE — B-3

Longmeadow, MA 01106 — (413) 565-1331; (800) 782-7284; (413) 565-1105

Full-time: 1105 women	**Faculty:** 36
Part-time: 240 women	**Ph.D.s:** 54%
Graduate: 30 men, 100 women	**Student/Faculty:** 31 to 1
Year: semesters	**Tuition:** $25,030
Application Deadline: open	**Room & Board:** $13,830
Freshman Class: n/av	
SAT or ACT: required	
	COMPETITIVE

Bay Path College, founded in 1897, is a comprehensive, private college offering innovative undergraduate programs for women only and graduate programs for men and women. The figures in the above capsule and this profile are approximate. There is 1 graduate school. The library contains 47,415 volumes, 4326 microform items, 3632 audio/video tapes/CDs/DVDs, and subscribes to 156 periodicals including electronic. Computerized library services include interlibrary loans, database searching, and Internet access. Special learning facilities include a learning resource center, radio station, and TV station. The 48-acre campus is in a suburban area 3 miles south of Springfield. Including any residence halls, there are 17 buildings.

Student Life: 59% of undergraduates are from Massachusetts. Others are from 15 states and 6 foreign countries. 93% are from public schools. 79% are white; 11% African American. The average age of freshmen is 18; all undergraduates, 35.

Housing: 376 students can be accommodated in college housing, which includes single-sex dorms. On-campus housing is guaranteed for all 4 years. 66% of students live on campus; of those, 60% remain on campus on weekends. Alcohol is not permitted. All students may keep cars.

Activities: There are no fraternities or sororities. There are 39 groups on campus, including cheerleading, choir, chorale, computers, dance, drama, ethnic, forensics, gay, Habitat for Humanity, honors, international, literary magazine, musical theater, newspaper, political, political awareness, professional, radio and TV, religious, social, social service, student government, Winter Guard, and yearbook. Popular campus events include father/daughter and mother/daughter banquets, Karaoke Unplugged, and Dinner with the President.

Sports: There are 5 intercollegiate sports for women. Facilities include a fitness center that houses a weight-training room, a dance studio, and an aerobics room and a nearby 12-acre playing field with soccer and softball fields, a walking/jogging track, and a field house.

Disabled Students: 50% of the campus is accessible. Facilities include wheelchair ramps, elevators, special parking, and specially equipped rest rooms.

Services: Counseling and information services are available, as is tutoring in every subject.

Campus Safety and Security: Measures include 24-hour foot and vehicle patrol, self-defense education, and security escort services. There are emergency telephones, lighted pathways/sidewalks, and fire, vehicle, and driving safety education programs.

Programs of Study: Bay Path confers B.A. and B.S. degrees. Associate and master's degrees are also awarded. Bachelor's degrees are awarded in BIOLOGICAL SCIENCE (biology/biological science), BUSINESS (business administration and management, international business management, and marketing/retailing/merchandising), COMMUNICATIONS AND THE ARTS (communications), EDUCATION (early childhood education and elementary education), ENGINEERING AND ENVIRONMENTAL

DESIGN (interior design), HEALTH PROFESSIONS (occupational therapy), SOCIAL SCIENCE (child psychology/development, criminal justice, forensic studies, law, liberal arts/general studies, and psychology).

Required: To graduate, students must complete at least 120 credits with a minimum GPA of 2.0. The 46-hour core curriculum includes course work in communication, science, social science, math, and fine and performing arts.

Special: Cross-registration is possible with other member schools of the Cooperating Colleges of Greater Springfield Consortium. Bay Path's capital of the world program allows students to visit a different world center during each spring break.

Faculty/Classroom: 40% of faculty are male; 60% are female. All teach undergraduates. No introductory courses are taught by graduate students.

Requirements: The SAT or ACT is required. Applicants should have completed at least 4 academic courses each year, including 4 years of English, 3 of math, at least 2 each of social studies and lab sciences, and 2 of a foreign language. An essay is required, as are letters of recommendation from a guidance counselor and a teacher. An interview is strongly recommended. A GPA of 2.0 is required. AP and CLEP credits are accepted.

Procedure: Freshmen are admitted fall and spring. Entrance exams should be taken in the spring of the junior year or by December of the senior year. There are deferred admissions and rolling admissions plans. Application deadlines are open. Applications are accepted online.

Transfer: Applicants must be in good standing at their previous school and are encouraged to arrange for an interview at Bay Path. Students who have earned fewer than 12 credits must submit SAT or ACT scores. 30 of 120 credits required for the bachelor's degree must be completed at Bay Path.

Visiting: There are regularly scheduled orientations for prospective students. There are guides for informal visits, and visitors may sit in on classes and stay overnight. To schedule a visit, contact Admissions.

Financial Aid: Bay Path is a member of CSS. The FAFSA, the college's own financial statement, and parent and student income tax forms are required. Check with the school for current application deadlines.

International Students: The school actively recruits these students. They must take the TOEFL. They must also take the SAT or ACT.

Admissions Contact: Director of Admissions. E-mail: *admiss@baypath.edu* Web: *www.baypath.edu*

BECKER COLLEGE C-2

Worcester, MA 01609 508-373-9400 1.877.523.2537; (508) 890-1500

Full-time: 670 men, 733 women	**Faculty:** 193
Part-time: 98 men, 325 women	**Ph.D.s:** 61%
Graduate: n/av	**Student/Faculty:** n/av
Year: semesters, summer session	**Tuition:** $30,340
Application Deadline: open	**Room & Board:** $11,080
Freshman Class: 3350 applied, 2088 accepted, 381 enrolled	

LESS COMPETITIVE

Becker College, founded in 1784, baccalaureate degree programs are offered on the College's two distinctive campuses, located in Worcester and Leicester, Massachusetts. Both undergraduate and adult learning programs make Becker a place where students gain the experience they need to contribute to a global society and rise to the top of their chosen professions. There are 4 undergraduate schools. In addition to regional accreditation, has baccalaureate program accreditation with NLN. Computerized library services include interlibrary loans, database searching, Internet access, and Wi-Fi capability. The campus is in an urban area about 40 miles west of Boston in Worcester. Including any residence halls, there are 49 buildings.

Student Life: 69% of undergraduates are from Massachusetts. Others are from 33 states, and 13 foreign countries. 67% are from public schools. 76% are White. The average age of freshmen is 18; all undergraduates, 24. 35% do not continue beyond their first year; 30% remain to graduate.

Housing: 700 students can be accommodated in college housing, which includes single-sex and coed dorms. In addition, there are special-interest houses, Living learning communities. On-campus housing is available on a first-come and first-served basis. 61% of students commute. All students may keep cars.

Activities: There are no fraternities or sororities. There are 22 groups on campus, including art, cheerleading, chorale, chorus, communications, dance, drama, ethnic, gay, honors, international, musical theater, newspaper, professional, religious, social, social service, student government, and yearbook.

Sports: There are 8 intercollegiate sports for men and 8 for women, and 5 intramural sports for men and 5 for women.

Disabled Students: Facilities include wheelchair ramps, elevators, special parking, specially equipped restrooms, lowered drinking fountains, lowered telephones, special housing. All classes are accessible.

Services: Counseling and information services are available, as is tutoring in most subjects. There is remedial math and writing. There is also an academic support center for students.

Campus Safety and Security: Measures include 24 hour foot and vehicle patrol, self-defense education, and security escort services. There are shuttle buses, emergency telephones, and lighted pathways/sidewalks.

Programs of Study: confers B.A., and B.S. degrees. Associate degrees are also awarded. Bachelor's degrees are awarded in AGRICULTURE (animal science), BIOLOGICAL SCIENCE (biology/biological science), BUSINESS (business administration and management, marketing and distribution, and sports management), COMMUNICATIONS AND THE ARTS (communications, design, and graphic design), COMPUTER AND PHYSICAL SCIENCE (computer game design/development), EDUCATION (early childhood education and elementary education), HEALTH PROFESSIONS (exercise science, nursing, preveterinary science, and veterinary science), SOCIAL SCIENCE (criminal justice, early childhood studies, forensic studies, liberal arts/general studies, and psychology). Interactive media (game design), veterinary science (pre-vet) are the strongest academically. Interactive media (game design) has the largest enrollments.

Required: To graduate, baccalaureate students must complete at least 122 semester hours and maintain a 2.0 minimum GPA. Distribution requirements vary with the program of study.

Special: Cross-registration is offered through the Worcester Consortium of Higher Education. There are co-op programs, internships, study abroad, work-study programs. There are 3 national honor societies and a freshman honors program.

Faculty/Classroom: 40% of faculty are male; 60% are female. 77% teach undergraduates, and 23% do both. No introductory courses are taught by graduate students. The average class size in an introductory lecture is 17; in a laboratory is 12; and in a regular course is 17.

Admissions: 62% of the 2013-2014 applicants were accepted. 17% of the current freshmen were in the top fifth of their class; 48% were in the top two fifths.

Requirements: The SAT or ACT is required. A high school transcript is required. A GPA of 2.0 is required. AP and CLEP credits are accepted.

Procedure: Freshmen are admitted fall and spring. Entrance exams should be taken before submitting the application. There are early admissions, deferred admissions, and rolling admissions plans. Application deadlines are open. Notifications are sent November 15. Applications are accepted online.

Transfer: 207 transfer students enrolled in 2012-2013. Requirements for transfer students depend on the program. Must have at least a 2.0 GPA from prior institution. 30 of 15 credits required for the bachelor's degree must be completed at Becker.

Visiting: There are regularly scheduled orientations for prospective students, fall and spring on campus events. There are guides for informal visits, visitors may sit in on classes, and stay overnight. To schedule a visit, contact the Admissions Receptionist at admissions@becker.edu.

Financial Aid: In 2013-2014, 100% of all full-time freshmen and 93% of continuing full-time students received some form of financial aid. 57% of all full-time freshmen and 61% of continuing full-time students received need-based aid. Average annual earnings from campus work are $993. The average financial indebtedness of the 2013 graduate was $41,666. The FAFSA, the state aid form, and the college's own financial statement are required. The priority date for freshman financial aid applications for fall entry is March 15.

International Students: There are 11 international students enrolled. The school actively recruits these students. They must take the TOEFL with a minimum score of 550 on the paper-based TOEFL (PBT) or 80 on the Internet-based version (iBT). They must also take the SAT or ACT.

Graduates: From July 1, 2012 to June 30, 2013, 347 bachelor's degrees were awarded. The most popular majors were business (28%), animal studies (including pre-veterinary science) (26%), and nursing (17%). In an average class, 31% graduate in 6 years or less. Of the 2012 graduating class, 15% were enrolled in graduate school within 6 months of graduation, and 79% were employed.

Admissions Contact: Debbie Gallo, Associate Director of Admissions. E-Mail: *admissions@becker.edu* Web: *www.becker.edu*

BENJAMIN FRANKLIN INSTITUTE OF TECHNOLOGY E-2

Boston, MA 02116 (617) 423-4630; (617) 482-3706

Full and part-time: 564 men and women	**Faculty:** n/av
Graduate: n/av	**Ph.D.s:** 3%
Year: semesters, summer session	**Student/Faculty:** 11 to 1
Application Deadline: open	**Tuition:** $17,690
	Room & Board: $10,500
Freshman Class: n/av	

SPECIAL

Benjamin Franklin Institute of Technology, founded in 1908, is a private technical college offering degree programs in industrial and engineering technologies. A bachelor's degree is offered in several majors, including automotive technology. The figures in the above capsule are approximate. In addition to regional accreditation, BFIT has baccalaureate program accreditation with ABET. The library contains 10,000 volumes, and subscribes to 70 periodicals including electronic. Computerized library services include interlibrary loans, database searching, and Internet access. Special learning facilities include a learning resource center. The 3-acre campus is in an urban area. Including any residence halls, there are 3 buildings.

Student Life: 95% of undergraduates are from Massachusetts. Others are from 7 states and 7 foreign countries. 35% are white; 35% African American; 14% Hispanic; 12% Asian American. The average age of freshmen is 22; all undergraduates, 22.

Housing: 20 students can be accommodated in college housing, which includes single-sex dorms. On-campus housing is available on a first-come, first-served basis. Priority is given to out-of-town students. Alcohol is not permitted. No one may keep cars.

Activities: There are no fraternities or sororities. There are 2 groups on campus, including student government and women's. Popular campus events include Technology Olympics and International Culture Day.

Sports: There are 2 intercollegiate sports for men and 2 intramural sports for men.

Disabled Students: 50% of the campus is accessible. Facilities include elevators and specially equipped restrooms.

Services: Counseling and information services are available, as is tutoring in every subject. There is remedial math, reading, and writing.

Programs of Study: BFIT confers B.S. degrees. Associate degrees are also awarded. Bachelor's degrees are awarded in Engineering and Enviromental Design (automotive technology).

Required: To graduate, students must earn a minimum cumulative GPA of 2.0. 2 college English courses are required.

Special: If qualified, 2-year BFIT graduates may transfer to Northeastern University. Automotive technology management students have access to Northeastern's facilities and resources.

Faculty/Classroom: 74% of faculty are male; 26% are female. All teach undergraduates. The average class size in an introductory lecture is 30; in a laboratory, 12; and in a regular course, 25.

Requirements: Applicants should be high school graduates or have the GED. A GPA of 2.0 is required.

Procedure: Freshmen are admitted fall and spring. There is a rolling admissions plan. Check with the school for current application deadlines and fee.

Visiting: Visitors may sit in on classes. To schedule a visit, contact the Office of Admission.

Financial Aid: BFIT is a member of CSS. The FAFSA and federal tax returns are required. Check with the school for current application deadlines.

International Students: They must take the TOEFL and the college's own test, or satisfactorily complete Franklin's or another recognized ESL program.

Admissions Contact: Dean of Enrollment Services. E-Mail: *admissions@bfit.edu* Web: *www.bfit.edu*

BENTLEY UNIVERSITY — D-2

Waltham, MA 02452 — (781) 891-2244; (800) 523-2354; (781) 891-3414

Full-time: 2482 men, 1660 women	**Faculty:** 219; IIA, +$
Part-time: 69 men, 38 women	**Ph.D.s:** 79%
Graduate: 706 men, 705 women	**Student/Faculty:** 14 to 1
Year: semesters, summer session	**Tuition:** $41,110
Application Deadline: January 7	**Room & Board:** $13,445
Freshman Class: 7493 applied, 3281 accepted, 974 enrolled	
SAT CR/M/W: 590/650/600	**ACT:** 28 **HIGHLY COMPETITIVE+**

Bentley University is an internationally recognized business university, dedicated to preparing the next generation of smart, nimble and compassionate leaders. Located on a classic New England campus minutes from Boston, Bentley combines an advanced business curriculum with the best of the arts and sciences, taught using the latest technology by a faculty that collaborates across disciplines. Bentley offers a wide variety of majors and minors, as well as optional Liberal Studies and Business Studies majors designed to create a modern intersection of the arts and sciences and business that's unique in higher education. Bentley students are highly sought after by today's leading organizations because of their professionalism, exposure to state-of-the-art research tools, and diverse, real-world experience. There is one graduate school. In addition to regional accreditation, Bentley has baccalaureate program accreditation with AACSB. The library contains 180,943 volumes, 8,303 microform items, 22,353 audio/video tapes/CDs/DVDs, and subscribes to 66,408 periodicals including electronic. Computerized library services include interlibrary loans, database searching, Internet access, and Wi-Fi capability. Special learning facilities include an art gallery, radio station, TV station, Academic Technology Center; Winer Accounting Center for Electronic Learning and Business Measurement (ACELAB); The Bentley Library; The Center for Languages and International Collaboration (CLIC); The Center for Marketing Technology (CMT); The Computer Information Systems (CIS) Sandbox; The Design and Usability Center (DUC); Media and Culture Labs and Studio; Trading Room (Hughey Center for Financial Services); Center for Arts and Sciences (Valente Center); Center for Business Ethics (CBE); Service-Learning Center; Center for Women in Business; The Center for Quantitative Analysis; Center for International Students and Scholars; The Multicultural Center; The Writing Center; Spiritual Life Center; The Cronin Office of International Education; Bentley Global Cyberlaw Center (BGCC); Center for Integration of Science and Industry. The 163-acre campus is in a suburban area Waltham, Massachusetts. Including any residence halls, there are 44 buildings.

Student Life: 54% of undergraduates are from out of state, mostly the Northeast. Students are from 40 states, 82 foreign countries, and Canada. 64% are from public schools. 61% are White; 16% Foreign. The average age of freshmen is 18; all undergraduates, 20. 6% do not continue beyond their first year; 87% remain to graduate.

Housing: College-sponsored housing includes coed dorms, on-campus apartments, and off-campus apartments. In addition, there are special-interest houses, suites, global living floors with a focus on connecting international and US students, and a women's leadership floor offering 21 incoming female students an experience that includes off-campus trips, presentations by high-profile corporate sponors, and numerous connections within the Bentley community. On-campus housing is guaranteed for all 4 years. 80% of students live on campus; of those, 85% remain on campus on weekends. Upperclassmen may keep cars.

Activities: 11% of men belong to 1 local and 7 national fraternities; 11% of women belong to 4 national sororities. There are 104 groups on campus, including art, band, cheerleading, chess, choir, chorus, computers, dance, debate, drama, environmental, ethnic, film, gay, honors, international, jazz band, literary magazine, musical theater, newspaper, orchestra, pep band, photography, political, professional, radio and TV, religious, social, social service, student government, and yearbook. Popular campus events include Groove Boston, Halloween Party, Culture Fest, Festival of Colors, Spring Day and Fashion Shows.

Sports: There are 12 intercollegiate sports for men and 11 for women, and 7 intramural sports for men and 7 for women. Facilities include The Dana Center, a 118,000-square foot multipurpose facility, features a field house, two-story fitness center, fitness center for varsity athletes, general locker rooms, a competition-sized swimming pool, athletic training room and rehabilitation area, athletic team and general locker rooms, and 24 athletic offices.

Disabled Students: 70% of the campus is accessible. Facilities include wheelchair ramps, elevators, special parking, specially equipped restrooms, special class scheduling, lowered drinking fountains, lowered telephones, and special housing.

Services: Counseling and information services are available, as is tutoring in most subjects. There is a reader service for the blind, and remedial math, reading, and writing. There is a Natural Reader, and additional assistive programs available upon request.

Campus Safety and Security: Measures include 24-hour foot and vehicle patrol, emergency notification system, self-defense education, and security escort services. There are shuttle buses, emergency telephones, lighted pathways/sidewalks, and controlled access to dorms/residences.

Programs of Study: Bentley confers B.A., and B.S. degrees. Master's and doctoral degrees are also awarded. Bachelor's degrees are awarded in BUSINESS (accounting, business administration and management, business (dual major program), business communications, business economics, finance, management information systems, and marketing/retailing/merchandising), COMMUNICATIONS AND THE ARTS (media arts), COMPUTER AND PHYSICAL SCIENCE (actuarial science, information sciences and systems, and mathematics), ENGINEERING AND ENVIRONMENTAL DESIGN (environmental science), SOCIAL SCIENCE (economics, history, interdisciplinary studies, international studies, liberal arts/general studies, philosophy, public administration, and Spanish studies). Accounting, management, finance, and marketing are the strongest academically. Accounting, economics and finance have the largest enrollments.

Required: All undergraduate students complete general education courses in areas such as IT, writing and literature, mathematics, economics, history and social science. Students in B.S. programs take a common core of nine courses covering areas such as business ethics, accounting, finance, business statistics, and strategic management. All students take elective courses that fulfill diversity, international and communication-intensive requirements. A total of 122 credit hours for students beginning as freshmen, 121 for transfer students with a minimum GPA of 2.0 overall and 2.0 in the major are required for graduation. All first year students must take a first-year seminar.

Special: Bentley offers a cross registration with Brandeis University and Regis College. Many students have been offered permanent, professional positions as a result of the participation in the internship program. Both for-credit and not-for-credit internships are available to students looking for valuable career-related work experience. Study abroad programs are offered in 39 countries as well as Semester at Sea. Work-study is offered through various departments throughout campus. Students can access available openings through an on-campus employment website. B.S. available in Accountancy; Actuarial Science; Computer Information Systems; Corporate Finance and Accounting; Economics-Finance; Finance; Information Design and Corporate Communication; Information Systems Audit and Control; Management; Managerial Economics; Marketing; Mathematical Sciences; B.A. available in Global Studies; History; Liberal Arts (single or interdisciplinary); Media and Culture; Philosophy; Public Policy; Spanish Studies; Sustainability Sciences. The optional Liberal Studies double major allows business majors to make meaningful connections across and within disciplines, and to develop valuable skills in critical thinking, creative analysis and communication---skills that are vital to succeed both professionally and personally. In addition, Bentley offers several 5-year programs through which students earn a bachelor's and master's degree. There are 5 national honor societies, a freshman honors program, and 17 departmental honors programs.

Faculty/Classroom: 61% of faculty are male; 39% are female. 83% teach undergraduates, and 68% do research. No introductory courses are taught by graduate students. The average class size in an introductory lecture is 28; in a laboratory is 18; and in a regular course is 28.

Admissions: 44% of the 2013-2014 applicants were accepted. The SAT scores for the 2013-2014 freshman class were: Critical Reading--10% below 500, 45% between 500 and 599, 40% between 600 and 699, and 6% between 700 and 800; Math--2% below 500, 21% between 500 and 599, 55% between 600 and 699, and 22% between 700 and 800; Writing--9% below 500, 38% between 500 and 599, 46% between 600 and 699, and 7% between 700 and 800. The ACT scores were 1% below 21, 8% between 21 and 23, 27% between 24 and 26, 27% between 27 and 28, and 38% above 28. 67% of the current freshmen were in the top fifth of their class; 95% were in the top two fifths. 6 freshmen graduated first in their class.

Requirements: The SAT or ACT is required. The ACT Optional Writing test is also required. The SAT or ACT with writing component is required. Applicants must be graduates of an accredited high school or have a GED. Recommended high school preparation is 4 units each in English and math, geometry, and a senior-year math course; 3 units science; 3 units in a foreign language; 3 units in history; and 2 additional units in English, math, social science or lab science, foreign language, or speech. AP and CLEP credits are accepted. Important factors in the admissions decision are advanced placement or honors courses, extracurricular activities record, and recommendations by school officials.

Procedure: Freshmen are admitted fall and spring. Entrance exams should be taken scores must be received by January 7. There are early decision, early admissions, and deferred admissions plans. Early decision applications should be filed by November 1; regular applications, by January 7 for fall entry, along with a $50 fee. Notification of early decision is sent December 21; regular decision, March 31. 102 early decision candidates were accepted for the 2013-2014 class. 500 applicants were on the 2013 waiting list; 88 were admitted. Applications are accepted online.

Transfer: 148 transfer students enrolled in 2012-2013. Transfer application, personal statement, mid-year progress report and two letters of recommendation 60 of 122 credits required for the bachelor's degree must be completed at Bentley.

Visiting: There are regularly scheduled orientations for prospective students, Fall, spring, and summer open house programs; Interviews are arranged by appointment; Campus tours and group information sessions take place regularly throughout the year; visits are available during the week and some selected Saturdays. There are guides for informal visits. To schedule a visit, contact the Office of Undergraduate Admission.

Financial Aid: In 2013-2014, 79% of all full-time freshmen and 72% of continuing full-time students received some form of financial aid. 49% of all full-time freshmen and 44% of continuing full-time students received need-based aid. The average freshman award was $32,877. Need-based scholarships or need-based grants averaged $28,589 ($49,000 maximum); need-based self-help aid (loans and jobs) averaged $5,091 ($7,500 maximum); non-need-based athletic scholarships averaged $26,757 ($55,620 maximum); and other non-need-based awards and non-need-based scholarships averaged $16,208 ($38,000 maximum). 29% of undergraduate students work part-time. Average annual earnings from campus work are $1400. The average financial indebtedness of the 2013 graduate was $31,208. Bentley is a member of CSS. The CSS/Profile and FAFSA, and Federal tax returns, including all schedules for parents and student, and business form supplement are required. The deadline for filing freshman financial aid applications for fall entry is February 1.

International Students: There are 650 international students enrolled. The school actively recruits these students. They must take the TOEFL with a minimum score of 577 on the paper-based TOEFL (PBT) or 90 on the Internet-based version (iBT), Pearson's. They must also take the SAT or ACT.

Graduates: From July 1, 2012 to June 30, 2013, 1073 bachelor's degrees were awarded. The most popular majors were marketing (15%), finance (15%), and accountancy (15%). 360 companies recruited on campus in 2012-2013. In an average class, 83% graduate in 4 years or less, 87% graduate in 5 years or less, and 87% graduate in 6 years or less.

Admissions Contact: Erik Vardaro, Director of Undergraduate Admission. E-Mail: *ugadmission@bentley.edu* Web: *www.bentley.edu*

BERKLEE COLLEGE OF MUSIC — E-2

Boston, MA 02215-3693 — **(617) 266-1400, ext. 2222; (800) BERKLEE; (617) 747-2047**

Full-time: 3740 men and women	**Faculty:** n/av
Part-time: 355 men and women	**Ph.D.s:** 12%
Graduate: n/av	**Student/Faculty:** n/av
Year: semesters, summer session	**Tuition:** $33,200
Application Deadline: see profile	**Room & Board:** $17,400
Freshman Class: n/av	
SAT or ACT: required	

SPECIAL

Berklee College of Music, founded in 1945, is a private institution offering programs in music production and engineering, film scoring, music business/management, composition, music synthesis, music education, music therapy, performance, contemporary writing and production, jazz composition, songwriting, and professional music. The figures in the above capsule and this profile are approximate. The library contains 47,993 volumes, 36,214 audio/video tapes/CDs/DVDs, and subscribes to 1232 periodicals including electronic. Computerized library services include interlibrary loans, database searching, Internet access, and laptop Internet portals. Special learning facilities include a learning resource center, a radio station, 12 recording studios, 5 performance venues, and film scoring, music synthesis, and songwriting labs. The campus is in an urban area in the Fenway Cultural District, Back Bay, Boston. Including any residence halls, there are 20 buildings.

Student Life: 79% of undergraduates are from out of state, mostly the Northeast. Students are from 50 states, 106 foreign countries, and Canada. 66% are white; 45% Asian American; 25% foreign nationals. The average age of freshmen is 20; all undergraduates, 22. 16% do not continue beyond their first year; 49% remain to graduate.

Housing: 840 students can be accommodated in college housing, which includes coed dorms. On-campus housing is available on a first-come, first-served basis and is available on a lottery system for upperclassmen. 88% of students commute. Alcohol is not permitted. No one may keep cars.

Activities: There are no fraternities or sororities. There are 62 groups on campus, including art, band, choir, chorale, chorus, computers, dance, ethnic, gay, international, jazz band, marching band, musical theater, newspaper, orchestra, pep band, political, professional, radio and TV, religious, social, social service, and student government. Popular campus events include International Night, daily recitals and concerts, and Singer Showcase.

Sports: There are 4 intramural sports for men and 4 for women. Discount memberships at the YMCA, a student rate at the Massachusetts College of Art fitness room, and membership at the Sheraton Fitness Center and the Tennis and Racquet Club of Boston are available.

Disabled Students: All of the campus is accessible. Facilities include wheelchair ramps, elevators, special class scheduling, lowered drinking fountains, and lowered telephones.

Services: Counseling and information services are available, as is tutoring in every subject. There is a reader service for the blind. Tape recorders, untimed testing, and learning center resources are available.

Campus Safety and Security: Measures include 24-hour foot and vehicle patrol and security escort services. There are emergency telephones and lighted pathways/sidewalks.

Programs of Study: Berklee confers B.M. degrees. Master's degrees are also awarded. Bachelor's degrees are awarded in COMMUNICATIONS AND THE ARTS (film arts, jazz, music, music business management, music performance, music technology, and music theory and composition), EDUCATION (music education), HEALTH PROFESSIONS (music therapy). Performance, professional music, music production, and engineering have the largest enrollments.

Required: Students working toward a degree must take general education courses in English composition/literature, history, physical science, and social sciences. Music course programs vary by specialization. A total of 120 credits must be completed with a minimum GPA of 2.0.

Special: Berklee offers cross-registration with the Pro-Arts Consortium, study abroad in the Netherlands, internships in music education, music therapy, and music production and engineering, 5-year dual majors, and a 4-year professional (nondegree) diploma program. Work-study programs, an accelerated degree program, student-designed majors, and credit by exam are available.

Faculty/Classroom: 74% of faculty are male; 26% are female. All teach undergraduates. The average class size in an introductory lecture is 14; in a laboratory, 7; and in a regular course, 6.

Requirements: The SAT or ACT is required. The ACT Optional Writing test is also required. Applicants must be graduates of an accredited secondary school that has a college preparatory program or have their GED. An audition and interview are recommended. Applicants must also submit a detailed reference letter regarding their training and experience in music and a letter from a private instructor, school music director, or professional musician. A GPA of 2.0 is required. AP credits are accepted. Important factors in the admissions decision are evidence of special talent, extracurricular activities record, and recommendations by alumni.

Procedure: Freshmen are admitted to all sessions. Entrance exams should be taken in the fall of the senior year of high school. There are early decision, deferred admissions and rolling admissions plans. Check with the school for current application deadlines. Check with the school for current application fee. Applications are accepted online. A waiting list is maintained.

Transfer: Applicants must go through the same application procedures as entering freshmen, as well as submit all previous college records. 60 of 120 credits required for the bachelor's degree must be completed at Berklee.

Visiting: There are regularly scheduled orientations for prospective students, consisting of 2 tours scheduled daily during semesters, with a morning tour followed by an information session given by an admissions counselor. There are guides for informal visits. To schedule a visit, contact the Admissions Office.

Financial Aid: In a recent year, 57% of all full-time freshmen and 38% of continuing full-time students received some form of financial aid. 26% of undergraduate students work part-time. Average annual earnings from campus work are $1880. Berklee is a member of CSS. The CSS/Profile, the FFS, and the college's own financial statement are required. Check with the school for current application deadlines.

International Students: There were 912 international students enrolled in a recent year. The school actively recruits these students. They must take the TOEFL and the college's own test. They must also take the SAT or ACT.

Graduates: In a recent year, the most popular majors were professional music (22%), music business/management (19%), and music production and engineering (11%).

Admissions Contact: Director of Admissions. A campus DVD is available. E-mail: *admissions@berklee.edu* Web: *www.berklee.edu*

BOSTON ARCHITECTURAL COLLEGE — E-2
Boston Architectural Center

Boston, MA 02115 — (617) 585-0200; (617) 585-0121

Full-time: 275 men, 121 women	**Faculty:** 1
Part-time: 8 men, 3 women	**Ph.D.s:** 80%
Graduate: 234 men, 225 women	**Student/Faculty:** n/av
Year: semesters, summer session	**Tuition:** $18,622
Application Deadline: open	**Room & Board:** n/app
Freshman Class: 32 applied, 32 accepted, 17 enrolled	**SPECIAL**

Boston Architectural College, founded in 1889 as the Boston Architectural Club, is an independent commuter institution offering professional programs in architecture and interior design. Students work in architectural and interior design offices during the day and attend classes at night. The BAC also offers a bachelor of design studies degree. A first professional degree in landscape architecture is offered at the undergraduate level. There are 4 undergraduate schools and 3 graduate schools. In addition to regional accreditation, The BAC has baccalaureate program accreditation with ASLA, FIDER, and NAAB. The library contains 50,000 volumes, 2,218 microform items, 357 audio/video tapes/CDs/DVDs, and subscribes to 120 periodicals including electronic. Computerized library services include database searching, Internet access, and Wi-Fi capability. Special learning facilities include an art gallery, Woodshop, Laser cutter lab, 3D printing, and CNC Router. The campus is in an urban area in Boston. Including any residence halls, there are 4 buildings.

Student Life: 75% of undergraduates are from Massachusetts. Others are from 20 states, 6 foreign countries, and Canada. 58% are White; 17% Hispanic. The average age of freshmen is 22; all undergraduates, 26. 36% do not continue beyond their first year.

Housing: College-sponsored housing includes assistance in finding housing is provided through the Roommate Network. Alcohol is not permitted. All students commute. No one may keep cars.

Activities: There are no fraternities or sororities. There are 9 groups on campus, including Atelier (Student Goverment) SASLA (Student ASLA Chapter), BAC Interior Design Society (ASID and IIDA) Veterans Community Collective, Design Studies Group, NOMAS, StudioQ (GLBTIQA), Sustainability Club, AIAS (American Institute of Architecture Students), art, environmental, ethnic, gay, international, professional, social, social service, and student government. Popular campus events include Food For Finals, Midnight Madness, NOMAS- Black History Month.

Sports: There is no sports program at The BAC.

Disabled Students: All of the campus is accessible. Facilities include wheelchair ramps, elevators, special parking, specially equipped restrooms, special class scheduling, and lowered drinking fountains.

Services: Counseling and information services are available, as is tutoring in every subject. The writing center provides one-on-one writing assistance and special services for ESL students.

Campus Safety and Security: Measures include 24-hour foot and vehicle patrol, emergency notification system, and security escort services. There are emergency telephones, lighted pathways/sidewalks, and full-time building security during operating hours.

Programs of Study: Master's degrees are also awarded. Bachelor's degrees are awarded in COMMUNICATIONS AND THE ARTS (design), ENGINEERING AND ENVIRONMENTAL DESIGN (architecture, interior design, and landscape architecture/design). Architecture has the largest enrollment.

Required: To graduate, students must complete a maximum of 150 academic credits, 75 of which are in professional subjects and 75 in general education courses. Students must also earn 5000 hours by working in architectural firms, design offices, or related fields. Academic study is divided into 3 segments, the final segment being the capstone year, which consists of 2 semesters of student-designed study under the guidance of a faculty adviser. A minimum 2.5 GPA is required.

Special: The BAC offers study abroad, and cross-registration with schools in the Professional Arts Consortium in Boston. The participating cross-registration schools are the BAC, Berklee College of Music, Boston Conservatory, Emerson College, Massachusetts College of Art, and School of the MFA.

Faculty/Classroom: 56% of faculty are male; 44% are female. 83% teach undergraduates. No introductory courses are taught by graduate students. The average class size in an introductory lecture is 33; in a laboratory is 8; and in a regular course is 13.

Admissions: 100% of the 2013-2014 applicants were accepted. 20% of the current freshmen were in the top fifth of their class; 36% were in the top two fifths. 1 freshman graduated first in the class.

Requirements: All applicants who have graduated from high school or have a college degree are admitted on a first-come, first-served basis. Official transcripts from previously attended secondary schools and colleges must be submitted to determine qualification for admission and advanced placement. AP and CLEP credits are accepted.

Procedure: Freshmen are admitted fall and spring. There are deferred admissions and rolling admissions plans. Application deadlines are open. Application fee is $50. Notification is sent on a rolling basis. Applications are accepted online.

Transfer: 44 transfer students enrolled in 2012-2013. Applicants for transfer must have a 2.0 GPA to receive transfer credit in most courses; 3.0 in math. 75 of 150 credits required for the bachelor's degree must be completed at The BAC.

Visiting: There are regularly scheduled orientations for prospective students, consisting of monthly presentations. There are guides for informal visits and visitors may sit in on classes. To schedule a visit, contact the Admissions Office at Admissions@the-bac.edu.

Financial Aid: The BAC is a member of CSS. The FAFSA is required. The priority date for freshman financial aid applications for fall entry is April 15.

International Students: There are 5 international students enrolled. They must take the TOEFL with a minimum score of 550 on the paper-based TOEFL (PBT) or 79 on the Internet-based version (iBT), IELTS exam.

Graduates: From July 1, 2012 to June 30, 2013, 34 bachelor's degrees were awarded. The most popular majors were architecture (58%), design studies (39%), and interior design (3%).

Admissions Contact: Mike Rivas, Director of Admissions. E-Mail: *admissions@the-bac.edu* Web: *www.the-bac.edu*

BOSTON COLLEGE — E-2

Chestnut Hill, MA 02467 — (617) 552-3100; (800) 360-2522; (617) 552-0798

Full-time: 4171 men, 4878 women	**Faculty:** n/av; I, +$
Part-time: n/av	**Ph.D.s:** 95%
Graduate: 1916 men, 2560 women	**Student/Faculty:** n/av
Year: semesters, summer session	**Tuition:** $45,622
Application Deadline: January 1	**Room & Board:** $12,884
Freshman Class: 24538 applied, 7905 accepted, 2215 enrolled	**MOST COMPETITIVE**

Boston College, founded in 1863, is an independent institution affiliated with the Roman Catholic Church and the Jesuit Order. It offers undergraduate programs in the arts and sciences, business, nursing, and education, and graduate and professional programs. There are 4 undergraduate schools and 7 graduate schools. In addition to regional accreditation, BC has baccalaureate program accreditation with AACSB, CSWE, NCATE, and NLN. The 8 libraries contain 2.8 million volumes, 4.3 million microform items, 2,099 audio/video tapes/CDs/DVDs, and subscribe to 42,089 periodicals including electronic. Computerized library services include interlibrary loans, database searching, and Internet access. Special learning facilities include an art gallery, radio station, and TV station. The 338-acre campus is in a suburban area 6 miles west of Boston. Including any residence halls, there are 146 buildings.

Student Life: 78% of undergraduates are from out of state, mostly the

Northeast. Students are from 49 states, 59 foreign countries, and Canada. 48% are from public schools. 60% are White; 11% Hispanic. The average age of freshmen is 18; all undergraduates, 21. 5% do not continue beyond their first year; 91% remain to graduate.

Housing: 7403 students can be accommodated in college housing, which includes single-sex and coed dorms and on-campus apartments. In addition, there are honors houses, special-interest houses, community and multicultural housing, quiet residences, single-sex freshman halls, perspectives academic program housing, and a substance-free residence. On-campus housing is guaranteed for the freshman year only and is available on a lottery system for upperclassmen. 85% of students live on campus; of those, 90% remain on campus on weekends. Upperclassmen may keep cars.

Activities: There are no fraternities or sororities. There are 225 groups on campus, including art, band, cheerleading, chess, choir, chorale, chorus, communications, computers, dance, debate, drama, environmental, ethnic, film, gay, honors, international, jazz band, literary magazine, marching band, musical theater, newspaper, orchestra, pep band, photography, political, professional, radio and TV, religious, social, social service, student government, symphony, and yearbook. Popular campus events include Middlemarch Ball, Christmas Chorale and Senior Week.

Sports: There are 12 intercollegiate sports for men and 15 for women, and 38 intramural sports for men and 30 for women. Facilities include BC has a 44,500-seat stadium, a forum that seats 8500 for basketball and 7600 for ice hockey, soccer fields, baseball fields, and a track. BC also has a student recreation complex with: equipment for cardio/weight/strength training, dozens of group exercise class options including spinning/yoga/pilates, an indoor pool diving/swimming, and dedicated indoor courts for basketball/racquetball/squash/tennis/volleyball.

Disabled Students: 95% of the campus is accessible. Facilities include wheelchair ramps, elevators, special parking, specially equipped restrooms, special class scheduling, lowered drinking fountains, lowered telephones, and special housing.

Services: Counseling and information services are available, as is tutoring in most subjects. There is a reader service for the blind. and an academic development center that serves all students.

Campus Safety and Security: Measures include 24-hour foot and vehicle patrol, emergency notification system, self-defense education, and security escort services. There are shuttle buses, emergency telephones, lighted pathways/sidewalks, controlled access to dorms/residences, safety seminars and safety walking tours are offered for incoming students during orientation. A fire safety awareness week is held every year with a mock dorm room burning demonstration, distribution of fire safety education materials, and drills. Students and faculty/staff members can also opt into an emergency alert system that can send emergency messages from the university to cell phones.

Programs of Study: BC confers B.A., and B.S. degrees. Master's and doctoral degrees are also awarded. Bachelor's degrees are awarded in BIOLOGICAL SCIENCE (biochemistry and biology/biological science), BUSINESS (accounting, banking and finance, business administration and management, business economics, human resources, management science, marketing/retailing/merchandising, and operations research), COMMUNICATIONS AND THE ARTS (art history and appreciation, classics, communications, dramatic arts, English, film arts, French, Italian, linguistics, music, romance languages and literature, and studio art), COMPUTER AND PHYSICAL SCIENCE (chemistry, computer science, geology, geophysics and seismology, information sciences and systems, mathematics, and physics), EDUCATION (early childhood education, elementary education, secondary education, and special education), ENGINEERING AND ENVIRONMENTAL DESIGN (environmental science), HEALTH PROFESSIONS (nursing), SOCIAL SCIENCE (applied psychology, classical/ancient civilization, economics, German area studies, Hispanic American studies, history, human development, philosophy, political science/government, psychology, Russian and Slavic studies, sociology, and theological studies). Finance, economics, chemistry and biology are the strongest academically. Communications, finance and economics have the largest enrollments.

Required: Core requirements include 2 courses each in natural science, social science, history, philosophy, and theology; 1 course each in literature, writing, math, and cultural diversity; and proficiency in a foreign language for College of Arts and Science students. To graduate, students must complete 120 credits (or 117 for nursing majors) including at least 30 in the major with a minimum 1.667 GPA (1.5 in management). Computer science is required for management majors, and a freshman writing seminar for all students except honors and AP students. Students in the honors program may elect to take courses in lieu of a thesis. Scholars of the college must complete a scholar's project before graduation.

Special: There are internship programs in management and in arts and sciences. Students may cross-register with Boston University, Brandeis University, Hebrew College, Pine Manor College, Regis College, and Tufts University. BC also offers a Washington semester in cooperation with American University, work-study programs with nonprofit agencies, study abroad, and dual and student-designed majors. Students may pursue a 3-2 engineering program with Boston University and accelerated 5-year programs in social work and education. There are 12 national honor societies, including Phi Beta Kappa, a freshman honors program, and 4 departmental honors programs.

Faculty/Classroom: 53% of faculty are male; 47% are female. All teach and do research. Graduate students teach 14% of introductory courses. The average class size in a laboratory is 15 and in a regular course is 30.

Admissions: 32% of the 2013-2014 applicants were accepted. The SAT scores for the 2013-2014 freshman class were: Critical Reading--2% below 500, 14% between 500 and 599, 51% between 600 and 699, and 33% between 700 and 800; Math--2% below 500, 9% between 500 and 599, 43% between 600 and 699, and 46% between 700 and 800; Writing--2% below 500, 9% between 500 and 599, 46% between 600 and 699, and 43% between 700 and 800. The ACT scores were 72% above 28. 96% of the current freshmen were in the top fifth of their class; 99% were in the top two fifths.

Requirements: The SAT or ACT is required. The ACT Optional Writing test is also required. Students may take either the SAT test with Writing and 2 subject tests of their choice or the ACT test with Writing. Applicants must be graduates of an accredited high school completing 4 units each of English, foreign language, science, and math. Those students applying to the school of nursing must complete at least 2 years of a lab science including 1 unit of chemistry. Applicants to the school of management are strongly encouraged to take 4 years of college preparatory math. An essay is required. AP credits are accepted.

Procedure: Freshmen are admitted fall and spring. Entrance exams should be taken no later than January of the senior year. There are early decision, early admissions, and deferred admissions plans. Early decision applications should be filed by November 1; regular applications, by January 1 for fall entry; and November 1 for spring entry, along with a $70 fee. Notification of early decision is sent December 25; regular decision, April 15. 2738 applicants were on the 2013 waiting list; 71 were admitted. Applications are accepted online.

Transfer: 91 transfer students enrolled in 2012-2013. Applicants must have a current GPA of at least 3.0 and must have earned a minimum of 9 semester hours. High school transcripts, letters of recommendation, and SAT or ACT scores are required. 60 of 120 credits required for the bachelor's degree must be completed at BC.

Visiting: There are regularly scheduled orientations for prospective students, group information sessions and campus tours Monday through Friday. There are guides for informal visits and visitors may sit in on classes. To schedule a visit, contact the Office of Undergraduate Admission.

Financial Aid: 43% of all full-time freshmen and 44% of continuing full-time students received need-based aid. The average freshman award was $34,871. Need-based scholarships or need-based grants averaged $31,019; need-based self-help aid (loans and jobs) averaged $6,158; non-need-based athletic scholarships averaged $47,338; and other non-need-based awards and non-need-based scholarships averaged $17,288. 26% of undergraduate students work part-time. Average annual earnings from campus work are $1700. The average financial indebtedness of the 2013 graduate was $20,601. BC is a member of CSS. The CSS/Profile and FAFSA, and the federal IRS income tax form, W-2s, Divorced/Separated Statement (when applicable) are required. The deadline for filing freshman financial aid applications for fall entry is February 1.

International Students: There are 579 international students enrolled. The school actively recruits these students. They must take the TOEFL with a minimum score of 600 on the paper-based TOEFL (PBT) or 100 on the Internet-based version (iBT). They must also take the SAT or ACT. Either SAT with 2 SAT Subject Tests or ACT with writing is accepted.

Graduates: From July 1, 2012 to June 30, 2013, 2238 bachelor's degrees were awarded. The most popular majors were communications (10%), finance (9%), and economics (8%). 300 companies recruited on campus in 2012-2013. In an average class, 89% graduate in 4 years or less and 92% graduate in 6 years or less. Of the 2012 graduating class, 21% were enrolled in graduate school within 6 months of graduation, and 70% were employed.

Admissions Contact: John L. Mahoney Jr., Director Undergraduate Admission. Web: *www.bc.edu*

BOSTON CONSERVATORY E-2

Boston, MA 02215 **(617) 912-9153**

Full-time: 217 men, 286 women	**Faculty:** n/av
Part-time: 2 men, 7 women	**Ph.D.s:** n/av
Graduate: 100 men, 107 women	**Student/Faculty:** 5 to 1
Year: semesters	**Tuition:** $37,300
Application Deadline: December 1	**Room & Board:** $17,080
Freshman Class: n/av	

SPECIAL

Boston Conservatory, founded in 1867, is a private college providing degree programs in music, musical theater, and dance. Figures in this profile are approximate. There are 3 graduate schools. In addition to regional accreditation, has baccalaureate program accreditation with NASM. The library contains 40,000 volumes, and subscribes to 120 periodicals including electronic. Computerized library services include interlibrary loans and database searching. Special learning facilities include a The campus is in an urban area in Boston's Back Bay. Including any residence halls, there are 9 buildings.

Student Life: 80% of undergraduates are from out of state, mostly the Northeast. Students are from 40 states, 24 foreign countries, and Canada. The average age of freshmen is 18. 19% do not continue beyond their first year.

Housing: 182 students can be accommodated in college housing, which includes coed dorms. On-campus housing is guaranteed for the freshman year only and is available on a lottery system for upperclassmen. 72% of students commute. Alcohol is not permitted. No one may keep cars.

Activities: There are 19 groups on campus, including band, choir, chorale, chorus, dance, drama, gay, international, musical theater, newspaper, opera, orchestra, political, professional, religious, social service, student government, and yearbook. Popular campus events include Parents Weekend, Off the Block Program, Drag Show, Thanksgiving Dinner.

Sports: There is no sports program at Boston.

Disabled Students: 20% of the campus is accessible. Facilities include elevators.

Services: Counseling and information services are available, as is tutoring in some subjects. writing, music theory, music history

Campus Safety and Security: Measures include 24-hour foot and vehicle patrol. There are emergency telephones and controlled access to dorms/residences.

Programs of Study: confers B.F.A., and B.M. degrees. Master's degrees are also awarded. Bachelor's degrees are awarded in COMMUNICATIONS AND THE ARTS (dance, guitar, music, music performance, music theory and composition, musical theater, opera, and piano/organ), EDUCATION (music education). Music is the largest.

Special: There are 3 national honor societies and 1 departmental honors programs.

Faculty/Classroom: All teach undergraduates. No introductory courses are taught by graduate students. The average class size in an introductory lecture is 15; in a laboratory is 5; and in a regular course is 15.

Requirements: Either the SAT or the ACT is required for undergraduate admission. An audition is the most important factor for acceptance and merit scholarship. GPA and standardized test scores are considered in concert with each other to determine ability to undertake the academic, liberal arts component of the undergraduate degree. A GPA of 2.7 is required. AP and CLEP credits are accepted. Important factors in the admissions decision are evidence of special talent, extracurricular activities record, and personality/intangible qualities.

Procedure: Freshmen are admitted fall. Entrance exams should be taken as early as possible. There is a deferred admissions plan. Applications should be filed by December 1 for fall entry, along with a $110 fee. Notifications are sent April 1. 30 applicants were on the 2013 waiting list. Applications are accepted online.

Transfer: 15 transfer students enrolled in 2012-2013. A successful audition and a 3.0 GPA are required. Transfer credits are determined through transcript review conducted by the dean and Registrar. The high school transcript is required if fewer than 2 semesters worth of college-level work have been undertaken/earned.

Visiting: Visitors may sit in on classes. To schedule a visit, contact the Admissions Office.

Financial Aid: The FAFSA is required. Check with the school for current application deadlines.

International Students: There are 62 international students enrolled. The school actively recruits these students. They must take the TOEFL or MELAB. They must also take the SAT or ACT. An audition also is required.

Graduates: From July 1, 2012 to June 30, 2013, 117 bachelor's degrees were awarded. The most popular majors were musical theater (46%), music (40%), and dance (14%).

Admissions Contact: Meghan Cadwallader, Director of Admissions. Web: *www.bostonconservatory.edu*

BOSTON UNIVERSITY E-2

Boston, MA 02215 **(617) 353-2300; (617) 353-9695**

Full-time: 6997 men, 10269 women
Part-time: 704 men, 744 women
Graduate: 6336 men, 7677 women
Year: semesters, summer session
Application Deadline: January 1
Faculty: n/av; I, +$
Ph.D.s: 85%
Student/Faculty: 13 to 1
Tuition: $41,920
Room & Board: $13,210
Freshman Class: 38275 applied, 22187 accepted, 4409 enrolled
SAT CR/M/W: 630/650/640 **ACT:** 28 **HIGHLY COMPETITIVE+**

Boston University is a private teaching and research university committed to excellence in undergraduate education. Students study with world-renowned faculty that include Fulbright Scholars, Pulitzer Prize winners, MacArthur Fellows, Nobel Prize winners, and a former Poet Laureate. In nine undergraduate schools and colleges, BU offers students more than 250 programs of study, internships in the US and abroad, one of the nations's most extensive study abroad programs, and cutting-edge research with faculty mentors. Housing is guaranteed for four years in a variety of on-campus residences including high-rise buildings and historic brownstones. BU students engage with their campus community through nearly 500 student organizations, club and intramural sports, and 23 NCAA Division-I varsity sports teams. Students experience the city of Boston as an extension of the campus for study, internships, employment, and cultural and recreational activities. There are 9 undergraduate schools and 15 graduate schools. In addition to regional accreditation, BU has baccalaureate program accreditation with AACSB, ABET, and NASM. The 23 libraries contain 3.0 million volumes, 4.8 million microform items, 69,901 audio/video tapes/CDs/DVDs, and subscribe to 65,037 periodicals including electronic. Computerized library services include interlibrary loans and database searching. Special learning facilities include a learning resource center, art gallery, planetarium, radio station, TV station, BU has over 2,000 research laboratories on campus, 3 supercomputers that are available for student use, and four specialized high-performance computer labs on campus. BU also has an astronomy observatory, 20th-century archives, a theater company in residence, the Geddes language lab, a speech, language, and hearing clinic, a performance center, a multi-media center, the Life Sciences and Engineering building, and the Photonics Center with houses state-of-the-art laboratories for developing new light-based technologies. The 133-acre campus is in a small town on the Charles River in Boston's Back Bay. Including any residence halls, there are 321 buildings.

Student Life: 77% of undergraduates are from out of state, mostly the Middle Atlantic. Students are from 50 states, 135 foreign countries, and Canada. 75% are from public schools. 57% are white; 13% Asian American. 34% are Catholic; 23% Protestant; 20% claim no religious affiliation; 13% Jewish. The average age of freshmen is 19; all undergraduates, 21. 9% do not continue beyond their first year; 77% remain to graduate.

Housing: 10616 students can be accommodated in college housing, which includes single-sex and coed dorms, on-campus apartments, off-campus apartments, and married student housing. In addition, there are honors houses, language houses, special-interest houses, international floors and houses and student residences. On-campus housing is guaranteed for all 4 years. 66% of students live on campus; of those, 80% remain on campus on weekends. All students may keep cars.

Activities: 3% of men belong to 1 local and 8 national fraternities; 5% of women belong to 9 national sororities. There are 525 groups on campus, including multicultural and sports, art, band, cheerleading, chess, choir, chorale, chorus, computers, dance, drama, ethnic, film, gay, honors, international, jazz band, literary magazine, marching band, musical theater, newspaper, opera, orchestra, pep band, photography, political, professional, radio and TV, religious, social, social service, student government, symphony, and yearbook. Popular campus events include Fall Welcome (Splash), World Fair and Culture Fest, and Head of the Charles River Regatta.

Sports: There are 12 intercollegiate sports for men and 14 for women, and 23 intramural sports for men and 23 for women. Facilities include 2 gyms, an ice-skating rink, saunas, a pool, a dance studio, a crew tank, a weight room, indoor and outdoor tracks, tennis and volleyball courts, multipurpose playing fields, and a boathouse.

Disabled Students: 90% of the campus is accessible. Facilities include wheelchair ramps, elevators, special parking, specially equipped restrooms, special class scheduling, lowered drinking fountains, lowered telephones, special housing. on-campus transportation, relocation of classes/events for access, tactile and access maps, visual fire alarms for the deaf, adaptive computers, and readers, notetakers and ASL interpreters.

Services: Counseling and information services are available, as is tutoring in most subjects, liberal arts, science, engineering, and management There is a reader service for the blind. Comprehensive learning strategy for learning disabled is available.

Campus Safety and Security: Measures include 24-hour foot and vehicle patrol, self-defense education, and security escort services. There are shuttle buses, emergency telephones, lighted pathways/sidewalksand a mountain bicycle patrol system. There is a uniformed safety/security assistant on duty 24 hours a day in large residence halls and there are 60 academy-trained officers in the university police department.

Programs of Study: BU confers B.A., B.S., B.F.A., B.L.S., B.Mus., and B.S.B.A. degrees. Master's and doctoral degrees are also awarded. Bachelor's degrees are awarded in AGRICULTURE (environmental studies), BIOLOGICAL SCIENCE (biochemistry, biology/biological science, ecology, environmental biology, neurosciences, nutrition, and physiology), BUSINESS (accounting, banking and finance, business administration and management, entrepreneurial studies, hotel/motel and restaurant management, international business management, management information systems, management science, marketing/retailing/merchandising, operations research, and organizational behavior), COMMUNICATIONS AND THE ARTS (apparel design, classics, communications, dramatic arts, East Asian languages and literature, English, film arts, French, German, Germanic languages and literature, graphic design, Greek (classical), Greek (modern), Italian, journalism, Latin, linguistics, music, music history and appreciation, music performance, music theory and composition, painting, performing arts, public relations, sculpture, Spanish, theater design, and theater management), COMPUTER AND PHYSICAL SCIENCE (astronomy, astrophysics, chemistry, computer science, earth science, geophysics and seismology, mathematics, physics, and planetary and space science), EDUCATION (art education, athletic training, bilingual/bicultural education, drama education, early childhood education, education, education of the deaf and hearing impaired, elementary education, English education, foreign languages education, mathematics education, music education, physical education, science education, social studies education, and special education), ENGINEERING AND ENVIRONMENTAL DESIGN (aeronautical engineering, biomedical engineering, computer engineering, electrical/electronics engineering, engineering, environmental science, manufacturing engineering, and mechanical engineering), HEALTH PROFESSIONS (exercise science, health, health science, physical therapy, rehabilitation therapy, and speech pathology/audiology), SOCIAL SCIENCE (American studies, anthropology, archeology, Asian/Oriental studies, classical/ancient civilization, East Asian studies, Eastern European studies, economics, French studies, geography, Hispanic American studies, history, interdisciplinary studies, international relations, Italian studies, Japanese studies, Latin American studies, philosophy, physical fitness/movement, political science/government, psychology, religion, sociology, and urban studies). The University Professors Program, accelerated medical and dental programs, and the management honors program are the strongest academically. Communications, business, and marketing have the largest enrollments.

Required: Most students are required to complete 128 credit hours to qualify for graduation from Boston University. The individual schools and colleges with BU have specific academic requirements and standards fro determining satisfactory completion of a program of study such as grades, concentrations, and divisional studies.

Special: Boston University offers many opportunities for students to excel, including: Kilachand Honors College--a university-wide honors program, the School of Management Honors Program designed specifically for management students, BU's Seven-Year Accelerated Medical and Dental Programs, with allow hight motivated students to complete their bachelor's degree and medical or dental doctorate in seven years, and the MMEDIC/ENGMEDIC integrated curriculums where students begin their medical studies as undergraduates. BU's Dual Degree program enables students to earn two degrees simultaneously. Combined bachelors and masters programs are also available in many disciplines. Students conduct research with faculty or independently though our Undergraduate Research Opportunities Progam and Work for Distinction. Students have many opportunities to intern in the US and abroad, and participate in more than 70 BU study abroad programs around the world. There are 16 national honor societies, a freshman honors program, and 6 departmental honors programs.

Faculty/Classroom: 69% of faculty are male; 31% are female. 56% teach undergraduates. No introductory courses are taught by graduate students. The average class size in an introductory lecture is 58; in a laboratory is 16; and in a regular course is 19.

Admissions: 58% of a recent year applicants were accepted. The SAT scores for a recent freshman class were: Critical Reading--1% below 500, 27% between 500 and 599, 59% between 600 and 700, and 13% above 700; Math--1% below 500, 22% between 500 and 599, 59% between 600 and 700, and 19% above 700; Writing--1% below 500, 22% between 500 and 599, 60% between 600 and 700, and 17% above 700. The ACT scores were 1% below 21, 5% between 21 and 23, 26% between 24 and 26, 25% between 27 and 28, and 44% above 28. 82% of the current freshmen were in the top fifth of their class; 97% were in the top two fifths. 80 freshmen graduated first in their class.

Requirements: The SAT or ACT is required. The ACT Optional Writing test is also required. Applicants are evaluated on an individual basis. For most BU programs, the recommended curriculum includes four years of English, three to four years of math (pre-calculus/calculus recommended), three to four years of lab sciences, three to four years of history/social science, and two to four years of a foreign language. Students taking the SAT are also required to submit two SAT Subject Tests in subject areas of their choice. Students may submit the ACT (with writing) in place of the SAT and SAT Subject Tests. Students applying to the Accelerated Medical or Dental Programs are required to submit Subject Tests in chemistry, math (level 2), and a foreign language (recommended). Candidates for the College of Fine Arts must present a portfolio or participate in an audition. AP and CLEP credits are accepted. Important factors in the admissions decision are advanced placement or honors courses.

Procedure: Freshmen are admitted fall and spring. Entrance exams should be taken in the junior year or early in the senior year. There are early decision, early admissions, and deferred admissions plans. Early decision applications should be filed by November 1; regular applications, by January 1 for fall entry. The fall 2011 application fee is $80. Notification of early decision is sent December 1; regular decision, April 1. Applications are accepted online.

Transfer: 224 transfer students enrolled in a recent year. College transcripts, SAT (with writing test) or ACT scores, and a complete high school transcript (or GED) should be submitted. Recommendations and an essay are also recommended.

Visiting: There are regularly scheduled orientations for prospective students, The Admissions Reception Center is open Monday through Friday and some Saturdays during the academic year. Appointments can be made for class visits or lunch with current students. Campus tours and information sessions are also offered. There are guides for informal visits, visitors may sit in on classes, and stay overnight. To schedule a visit, contact the Admissions Reception Center.

Financial Aid: In a recent year, 69% of all full-time freshmen and 64% of continuing full-time students received some form of financial aid. 54% of all full-time freshmen and 50% of continuing full-time students received need-based aid. The average freshman award was $25,842. Need-based scholarships or need-based grants averaged $23,413 ($53,000 maximum); need-based self-help aid (loans and jobs) averaged $7,180 ($8,500 maximum); non-need-based athletic scholarships averaged $40,659 ($55,395 maximum); and other non-need-based awards and non-need-based scholarships averaged $19,620 ($39,864 maximum). BU is a member of CSS. The CSS/Profile and FAFSA are required. The deadline for filing freshman financial aid applications for fall entry is February 15.

International Students: There are 1562 international students enrolled. The school actively recruits these students. They must take the TOEFL with a minimum score of 96 on the Internet-based version (iBT). They must also take the SAT or ACT.

Graduates: In a recent year, 4159 bachelor's degrees were awarded. The most popular majors were management (19%), communications (15%), and engineering (6%). In an average class, 81% graduate in 4 years or less and 84% graduate in 6 years or less. Of a recent graduating class, 20% were enrolled in graduate school within 6 months of graduation.

Admissions Contact: Director of Undergraduate Admissions. E-Mail: *admissions@bu.edu*, Web: *www.bu.edu*

BRANDEIS UNIVERSITY — D-2

Waltham, MA 02454 — **(781) 736-3500**
(800) 622-0622; (781) 736-3536

Full-time: 1562 men, 2037 women	**Faculty:** 318; I, av$
Part-time: 6 men, 9 women	**Ph.D.s:** 95%
Graduate: 1090 men, 1121 women	**Student/Faculty:** 10 to 1
Year: semesters, summer session	**Tuition:** $46,106
Application Deadline: January 1	**Room & Board:** $12,714

Freshman Class: 9496 applied, 3517 accepted, 833 enrolled
SAT or ACT: required

HIGHLY COMPETITIVE

Founded in 1948, Brandeis University is a private research university with a liberal arts focus located in Waltham, Massachusetts. The residential campus is a dynamic and diverse learning community known for its vibrant, free thinking intellectual atmosphere and offers easy access to Boston and its many attractions. The University is named for the late Louis Dembitz Brandeis, the distinguished associate justice of the United States Supreme Court, and reflects the values of academic excellence, commitment to social justice, respect for creativity and diversity, and concern for the world that he personified. There is one undergraduate school and 4 graduate schools. The 2 libraries contain 1.7 million volumes, 960,389 microform items, 43,766 audio/video tapes/CDs/DVDs, and subscribe to 104,329 periodicals including electronic. Computerized library services include interlibrary loans, database searching, Internet access, and Wi-Fi capability. Special learning facilities include an art gallery, radio station, TV station, a spatial orientation laboratory, an astronomical observatory, an emotion laboratory, a cultural center, a treasure hall, an art museum, and an audiovisual center. The 235-acre campus is in a suburban area 10 miles west of Boston. Including any residence halls, there are 97 buildings.

Student Life: 73% of undergraduates are from out of state, mostly the Northeast. Students are from 48 states, 65 foreign countries, and Canada. 50% are White; 15% Foreign; 12% Asian American. The average age of freshmen is 18; all undergraduates, 20. 7% do not continue beyond their first year; 90% remain to graduate.

Housing: College-sponsored housing includes coed dorms, on-campus apartments, and off-campus apartments. In addition, there are special-interest houses. On-campus housing is guaranteed for the freshman year only, is available on a first-come, first-served basis, and is available on a lottery system for upperclassmen. 76% of students live on campus. Upperclassmen may keep cars.

Activities: There are no fraternities or sororities. Groups on campus include art, cheerleading, chess, choir, chorale, chorus, computers, dance, debate, drama, environmental, ethnic, film, gay, honors, international, jazz band, literary magazine, musical theater, newspaper, orchestra, pep band, photography, political, professional, radio and TV, religious, social, social service, student government, symphony, and yearbook. Popular campus events include International Club Dances, Culture X and Spring Fest.

Sports: There are 8 intercollegiate sports for men and 9 for women, and 15 intramural sports for men and 15 for women. Facilities include a

70,000 square foot field house including a 1800 seat basketball arena, 3 indoor tennis courts, 3 indoor basketball courts, 7 squash courts, a 6 lane indoor track, several multipurpose rooms for aerobics, dance, group fitness, sauna in men's and women's lockerrooms, fencing room, weight room, turf soccer field, grass club field, baseball and softball diamonds, 12 outdoor tennis courts, 6 lane indoor pool, 8 lane outdoor track.

Disabled Students: Facilities include wheelchair ramps, elevators, special parking, specially equipped restrooms, special class scheduling, lowered drinking fountains, lowered telephones. Libraries, student centers, several other buildings, sports facilities, and the majority of residence halls are fully accessible.

Services: Counseling and information services are available, as is tutoring in most subjects.

Campus Safety and Security: Measures include 24-hour foot and vehicle patrol, emergency notification system, self-defense education, and security escort services. There are shuttle buses, emergency telephones, lighted pathways/sidewalks, controlled access to dorms/residences, Extensive Closed Circuit Television system on campus, a student EMT division that responds to medical calls during the academic year, and a Personal Safety Committee with student involvement.

Programs of Study: Brandeis confers B.A., and B.S. degrees. Master's and doctoral degrees are also awarded. Bachelor's degrees are awarded in AGRICULTURE (environmental studies), BIOLOGICAL SCIENCE (biochemistry, biology/biological science, biophysics, and neurosciences), BUSINESS (business administration and management), COMMUNICATIONS AND THE ARTS (art history and appreciation, classics, comparative literature, creative writing, English, film arts, French, German, linguistics, music, Russian languages and literature, Spanish, studio art, and theatre arts), COMPUTER AND PHYSICAL SCIENCE (chemistry, computer science, mathematics, and physics), HEALTH PROFESSIONS (health science), SOCIAL SCIENCE (African American studies, American studies, anthropology, East Asian studies, economics, European studies, history, interdisciplinary studies, international studies, Islamic studies, Judaic studies, Latin American studies, Middle Eastern studies, Near Eastern studies, philosophy, political science/government, psychology, sociology, and women's studies). Economics, psychology, and biology have the largest enrollments.

Required: All candidates for a bachelor's degree must satisfactorily complete a major, a writing requirement, a foreign language requirement, a group of courses designed to provide a strong foundation in general education, and the phys ed requirement. Oral communication, quantitative reasoning, and non-Western and comparative studies requirements also must be met. No courses used to fulfill any general university requirement may be taken on the pass/fail grading option.

Special: Students may pursue interdepartmental programs in 18 different fields. Students may cross-register with Boston, Wellesley, Babson, Bentley and Olin Colleges and Boston and Tufts Universities. Beginning Fall 2013 eligible upperclassmen may also enroll in one online consortium class through Semester Online. Study abroad is possible in 69 countries. Internships are available in virtually every field, and work-study is also available. Dual and student-designed majors can be arranged. The university also offers credit by exam, nondegree study, and pass/fail options. Opportunities for early acceptance to area medical schools are offered to Brandeis students. There are 3 national honor societies and including Phi Beta Kappa.

Faculty/Classroom: 58% of faculty are male; 42% are female. All teach and do research. No introductory courses are taught by graduate students.

Admissions: 37% of the 2013-2014 applicants were accepted. The SAT scores for the 2013-2014 freshman class were: Critical Reading--1% below 500, 14% between 500 and 599, 49% between 600 and 699, and 35% between 700 and 800; Math--2% below 500, 13% between 500 and 599, 48% between 600 and 699, and 37% between 700 and 800; Writing--2% below 500, 13% between 500 and 599, 45% between 600 and 699, and 40% between 700 and 800. The ACT scores were 1% between 21 and 23, 8% between 24 and 26, 18% between 27 and 28, and 72% above 28. 84% of the current freshmen were in the top fifth of their class; 97% were in the top two fifths. 25 freshmen graduated first in their class.

Requirements: The SAT or ACT is required. The ACT Optional Writing test is also required. In addition, Brandeis has a test-flexible policy and no longer requires that domestic applicants submit SAT or ACT scores for the purposes of admission. Eligible applicants can choose one of the following three submission options: Option 1: Submit SAT with writing or ACT with writing Option 2: Submit a combination of three SAT Subject Tests and/or AP tests (or IB exams) Option 3: Submit an academic portfolio through the Common Application including: One graded analytical paper from 11th or 12th grade and a second academic Teacher Evaluation *Home-schooled applicants and candidates applying from secondary schools that provide written evaluations rather than grades are required to submit the SAT or the ACT test with the writing section. *All international applicants must submit either the SAT or the ACT test with the writing section. AP credits are accepted.

Procedure: Freshmen are admitted fall and spring. Entrance exams should be taken by January of the senior year. There are early decision and deferred admissions plans. Early decision applications should be filed by November 1; regular applications, by January 1 for fall entry; and November 1 for spring entry, along with a $75 fee. Notification of early decision is sent December 15; regular decision, April 1. 245 early decision candidates were accepted for the 2013-2014 class. 1405 applicants were on the 2013 waiting list; 40 were admitted. Applications are accepted online.

Transfer: 69 transfer students enrolled in 2012-2013. Major consideration is given to the quality of college-level work completed, the secondary school record, professors' and deans' evaluations as well as the students fit for our institution. Because there is a 2-year residence requirement, students should apply before entering their junior year. 64 of 128 credits required for the bachelor's degree must be completed at Brandeis.

Visiting: There are regularly scheduled orientations for prospective students, Most weekdays we offer morning and afternoon information sessions led by admissions counselors and followed by student-led tours. Information sessions are typically held Mon-Fri at 10:15 a.m., 2:15 p.m.; tours at 9am, 11am, 1pm and 3pm. There are guides for informal visits and visitors may sit in on classes. To schedule a visit, contact the Office of Admissions at admissions@brandeis.edu.

Financial Aid: In 2013-2014, 67% of all full-time freshmen and 64% of continuing full-time students received some form of financial aid. 52% of all full-time freshmen and 50% of continuing full-time students received need-based aid. The average freshman award was $28,184. Need-based scholarships or need-based grants averaged $28,143 ($63,062 maximum); need-based self-help aid (loans and jobs) averaged $4,584 ($9,500 maximum); and other non-need-based awards and non-need-based scholarships averaged $5,457 ($52,970 maximum). 60% of undergraduate students work part-time. Average annual earnings from campus work are $2114. The average financial indebtedness of the 2013 graduate was $28,137. Brandeis is a member of CSS. The CSS/Profile and FAFSA, and copies of student and parent income tax returns for matriculating students. are required. The deadline for filing freshman financial aid applications for fall entry is February 1.

International Students: The school actively recruits these students. They must take the TOEFL with a minimum score of 100 on the Internet-based version (iBT). They must also take the SAT or ACT. Non-native English speakers must submit TOEFL or IELTS scores.

Graduates: From July 1, 2012 to June 30, 2013, 831 bachelor's degrees were awarded. The most popular majors were economics (11%), psychology (11%), and biology (9%). 513 companies recruited on campus in 2012-2013. In an average class, 86% graduate in 4 years or less, 88% graduate in 5 years or less, and 90% graduate in 6 years or less. Of the 2012 graduating class, 36% were enrolled in graduate school within 6 months of graduation, and 58% were employed.

Admissions Contact: Jennifer Walker, Executive Director of Admissions. E-Mail: *admissions@brandeis.edu* Web: *www.brandeis.edu*

BRIDGEWATER STATE UNIVERSITY — E-3

Bridgewater, MA 02325 — **(508) 531-1237; (508) 531-1746**

Full-time: 3337 men, 4695 women	**Faculty:** 321
Part-time: 712 men, 940 women	**Ph.D.s:** 92%
Graduate: 474 men, 1259 women	**Student/Faculty:** 25 to 1
Year: semesters, summer session	**Tuition:** $8052 ($14,192)
Application Deadline: February 15	**Room & Board:** $10,700
Freshman Class: 6170 applied, 4525 accepted, 1454 enrolled	
SAT CR/M: 499/511 **ACT:** 21	**COMPETITIVE**

As the comprehensive public university of Southeastern Massachusetts, Bridgewater State University has a responsibility to educate the residents of Southeastern Massachusetts and the commonwealth, and to use its intellectual, scientific and technological resources to support and advance the economic and cultural life of the region and the state. Bridgewater's growing number of innovative academic programs helps to ensure that Bridgewater State University students are prepared to think critically, communicate effectively and act responsibly within a context of personal and professional ethics. For example, BSU's Academic Achievement Center, and particularly its first-year advising program, is often cited as a model for other institutions to follow. At the same time, the Adrian Tinsley Program for Undergraduate Research represents an unparalleled opportunity for students to work closely with faculty mentors and to present research and creative work at regional and national conferences. While maintaining its historic focus on the preparation of teachers, Bridgewater State University provides a broad range of baccalaureate degree programs through its College of Humanities and Social Sciences, Bartlett College of Science and Mathematics, College of Education and Allied Studies and its Ricciardi College of Business. Bridgewater State University offers 32 undergraduate academic programs with 90 different areas of concentration as well as internships, research programs, study abroad and honors programs. Bridgewater is a leader in the adoption of technology for instruction and administration. Through its extensive information technology resources, the college makes technology an integral component of teaching and learning and serves as a regional resource on technology in higher education, K-12, and government and business settings. In addition to enjoying a fully wireless campus, our students and faculty benefit from having cutting edge educational technology in all classrooms, and from extensive computer support services. Bridgewater State University competes in NCAA Division III athletics in both men's and women's varsity sports with state-of-the-art athletic facilities. Bridgewater State University has over 90 clubs and organizations. There are three sororities, four fraternities and one co-educational fraternity offered at BSU. Bridgewater State's Student Government Association (SGA) is an organization of students which represent the Bridgewater State community. Through SGA, the student body can express their academic and social wants and needs. There are 5 undergraduate schools and 1 graduate school. In addition to regional accreditation, BSU has baccalaureate program accreditation with CSWE, NASAD, NASDTEC, NASM, and NCATE. The library contains 352,584 volumes, 715,736 microform items, 7,613 audio/video tapes/CDs/DVDs, and subscribes to 55,658 periodicals including electronic. Computerized library services include interlibrary loans, database searching, and Internet access. Special learning facilities include an art gallery, radio station, Observatory, and a Greenhouse. The 278-acre campus is in a suburban area 28 miles from Boston. Including any residence halls, there are 38 buildings.

Student Life: 96% of undergraduates are from Massachusetts. Others are from 27 states, 22 foreign countries, and Canada. 83% are White. The average age of freshmen is 18; all undergraduates, 22. 19% do not continue beyond their first year; 54% remain to graduate.

Housing: 2781 students can be accommodated in college housing, which includes coed dorms and on-campus apartments. There is also break housing for athletes, student teachers, visiting lecturers, international students and special housing for disabled students. On-campus housing is available on a first-come and first-served basis. 65% of students commute. Alcohol is not permitted. Upperclassmen may keep cars.

Activities: 7% of men belong to 4 national fraternities; 6% of women belong to 3 national sororities. There are 90 groups on campus, including art, band, chorale, communications, computers, dance, drama, environmental, ethnic, forensics, gay, honors, international, jazz band, musical theater, newspaper, political, professional, religious, social, social service, student government, and yearbook. Popular campus events include Homecoming, Springfest and Campus Movie Fest.

Sports: There are 9 intercollegiate sports for men and 10 for women, and 15 intramural sports for men and 16 for women. Facilities include Bridgewater State University has many athletic facilities including the Adrian Tinsley Center which has a Competition Court with NCAA regulation basketball and volleyball venue that seats 1000 spectators. This center also has Synthetic Multipurpose Courts which are lined for basketball, volleyball, badminton, and tennis. The Adrian Tinsley Center also houses a Walking/Jogging Track which is a 1/8 mile three lane track that encircles the 32,000 square foot gymnasium area. This center also houses the 9,000 square foot Thornburg Fitness Center which is equipped with some of the most current equipment on the market including cardiovascular machines, selectorized weight machines, plate-loaded equipment, free-weights, and Olympic lifting platforms. BSU also has the John J. Kelly Gymnasium which houses a large and small gym, the Dr. Mary Jo Moriarty Pool, weight room, classrooms and offices. Bridgewater State University also has the Edward C. Swenson Athletic Complex where the BSU Bears compete in football and soccer, Alumni Park where our baseball and softball players compete, and Dr. Henry Rosen Memorial Tennis Courts.

Disabled Students: All of the campus is accessible. Facilities include wheelchair ramps, elevators, special parking, specially equipped restrooms, special class scheduling, lowered drinking fountains, lowered telephones, special housing.

Services: Counseling and information services are available, as is tutoring in most subjects. There is a reader service for the blind, and remedial math, reading, and writing. There are recorded texts, classroom interpreters, scribes and note takers, testing accommodations, and a speech/hearing/language center.

Campus Safety and Security: Measures include 24-hour foot and vehicle patrol, emergency notification system, and security escort services. There are shuttle buses, emergency telephones, lighted pathways/sidewalks, controlled access to dorms/residences, Bridgewater State University Police Department, University-operated transit system that runs from 7:15 a.m. to 8:00 p.m., Monday through Friday, and a safety-escort van that runs from 7 p.m. to 3 a.m, 7 days a week.

Programs of Study: BSU confers B.A., B.S. and B.S.Ed. degrees. Master's degrees are also awarded. Bachelor's degrees are awarded in BIOLOGICAL SCIENCE (biology/biological science), BUSINESS (accounting, finance, and management science), COMMUNICATIONS AND THE ARTS (art, art history and appreciation, English, fine arts, music, Spanish, and speech/debate/rhetoric), COMPUTER AND PHYSICAL SCIENCE (chemistry, computer science, earth science, geochemistry, mathematics, and physics), EDUCATION (art education, athletic training, dance education, drama education, early childhood education, elementary education, health education, music education, physical education, and special education), ENGINEERING AND ENVIRONMENTAL DESIGN (aeronautical science), SOCIAL SCIENCE (anthropology, criminal justice, economics, geography, philosophy, political science/government, psychology, social work, and sociology). Geography, anthropology, and political science are the strongest academically. Education, business/management, and psychology have the largest enrollments.

Required: Students are required to complete a minimum of 120 semester hours, with 30 to 36 hours in the major and 52 to 55 hours in core curriculum courses. Students must maintain a minimum GPA of 2.0.

Special: Opportunities are provided for cross-registration with other Massachusetts Colleges and Universities, Internships available in most majors, double majors, joint/dual degree in B.S. & M.S. in Criminal Justice and B.S.Ed. in Elementary Education & M.Ed. in Special Education, core curriculum requirements, non-degree study, and study abroad programs. Bridgewater State University participates in The Washington Center Internship Program, National Student Exchange, Southeastern Association for Cooperation in Higher Education, and the College Academic Program Sharing. There are 13 national honor societies, including Phi Beta Kappa, a freshman honors program, and 28 departmental honors programs.

Faculty/Classroom: 50% of faculty are male; 50% are female. All teach undergraduates, and 6% do both. No introductory courses are taught by graduate students. The average class size in an introductory lecture is 23; in a laboratory is 17; and in a regular course is 19.

Admissions: 73% of the 2013-2014 applicants were accepted. The SAT scores for the 2013-2014 freshman class were: Critical Reading--48% below 500, 41% between 500 and 599, 10% between 600 and 699, and 1% between 700 and 800; Math--40% below 500, 47% between 500 and 599, 12% between 600 and 699, and 1% between 700 and 800. The ACT scores were 46% below 21, 43% between 21 and 23, 7% between 24 and 26, 2% between 27 and 28, and 2% above 28.

Requirements: The SAT or ACT is required. Graduation from an accredited secondary school is required; SAT or ACT scores required, a GED will be accepted. Applicants must have successfully completed 16 Carnegie units, including 4 units of English, 3 units of Mathematics, 3 units of Science with 2 lab units, 2 units of a foreign language, 2 units of Social Studies, and 2 in other college preparatory electives. An essay is recommended. A GPA of 2.0 is required. AP and CLEP credits are accepted. Important factors in the admissions decision are advanced placement or honors courses, leadership record, parents or siblings attended your school, evidence of special talent, extracurricular activities record, recommendations by alumni, recommendations by school officials, ability to finance college education, personality/intangible qualities, and geographical diversity.

Procedure: Freshmen are admitted fall and spring. There is early admissions and deferred admissions plans. Applications should be filed by February 15 for fall entry; November 1 for spring entry, along with a $40 fee. Notifications are sent April 15. 445 applicants were on the 2013 waiting list; 126 were admitted. Applications are accepted online.

Transfer: 1044 transfer students enrolled in 2012-2013. Transfer students must have maintained a minimum GPA of 2.5 from 12 to 24 credits or 2.0 from more than 24 credits at a previous institution. College transcripts and an essay are required of all transfer students; some students must submit high school transcripts and standardized test scores. 30 of 120 credits required for the bachelor's degree must be completed at BSU.

Visiting: There are regularly scheduled orientations for prospective students, Campus tours for prospective students Monday through Thursday at 11 a.m. and 3 p.m. when college is in session and 10 a.m. and 2 p.m. during summer months. There are guides for informal visits and visitors may sit in on classes. To schedule a visit, contact the Admissions Office.

Financial Aid: 13% of undergraduate students work part-time. Average annual earnings from campus work are $3570. The average financial indebtedness of the 2013 graduate was $30,189. The FAFSA is required. The deadline for filing freshman financial aid applications for fall entry is March 1.

International Students: There are 53 international students enrolled. They must take the TOEFL with a minimum score of 500 on the paper-based TOEFL (PBT) or 61 on the Internet-based version (iBT), IELTS-International English Lanuage Testing System. They must also take the SAT or ACT.

Graduates: From July 1, 2012 to June 30, 2013, 1747 bachelor's degrees were awarded. The most popular majors were education (19%), business/marketing (17%), and psychology (13%). 21 companies recruited on campus in 2012-2013. In an average class, 1% graduate in 3 years or less, 28% graduate in 4 years or less, 50% graduate in 5 years or less, and 54% graduate in 6 years or less. Of the 2012 graduating class, 17% were enrolled in graduate school within 6 months of graduation, and 79% were employed.

Admissions Contact: Gregg A. Meyer, Dean of University Admissions. E-Mail: *admissions@bridgew.edu* Web: *www2.bridgew.edu/content/admissions-aid*

CAMBRIDGE COLLEGE D-2

Cambridge, MA 02138 (617) 868-1000
800-877-4723; (617) 349-3561

Full-time: 74 men, 160 women	**Faculty:** 9; IIA, -$
Part-time: 283 men, 531 women	**Ph.D.s:** 73%
Graduate: 518 men, 1546 women	**Student/Faculty:** 13 to 1
Year: trimesters, summer session	**Tuition:** $13,392
Application Deadline:	**Room & Board:** n/app

Freshman Class: 282 applied, 231 accepted, 156 enrolled
NONCOMPETITIVE

Founded in 1971, Cambridge College is a private, institution dedicated to providing educational opportunities for working adults and underserved learners. The college has three graduate schools-the School of Education, the School of Management and the School of Psychology and Counseling-as well as undergraduate programs. Cambridge College is approved and accredited to offer programs through its main campus and 7 regional centers in Springfield and Lawrence, MA; Chesapeake, VA; Augusta, GA; San Juan, PR; Inland Empire, CA; and Memphis, TN. There is 1 undergraduate school and 3 graduate schools. Computerized library services include interlibrary loans, database searching, Internet access, and Wi-Fi capability. The campus is in an urban area Cambridge, MA. Including any residence halls, there are 3 buildings.

Student Life: 91% of undergraduates are from Massachusetts. Others are from 31 states, 69 foreign countries, and Canada. 32% are White; 30% African American; 16% Hispanic; 13% race unknown. The average age of freshmen is 36; all undergraduates, 37.

Housing: Alcohol is not permitted. All students commute.

Activities: There are no fraternities or sororities.

Sports: There is no sports program at Cambridge.

Disabled Students: All of the campus is accessible. Facilities include elevators, special parking, specially equipped restrooms, special class scheduling, lowered drinking fountains, and lowered telephones.

Services: Counseling and information services are available, as is tutoring in most subjects. There is remedial math, reading, and writing.

Campus Safety and Security: Measures include emergency notification system. There are emergency telephones and lighted pathways/sidewalks.

Programs of Study: confers B.A., and B.S. degrees. Master's and doctoral degrees are also awarded. Bachelor's degrees are awarded in BUSINESS (management science), SOCIAL SCIENCE (human services, interdisciplinary studies, and psychology). Management and Psychology has the largest enrollmenrs.

Required: Students must complete 120 credit hours, including 60 in general education requirements and 30 to 39 in the major to graduate. Students also must complete a final capstone project near the end of their program.

Special: There are 1 national honor society and 1 departmental honors program.

Faculty/Classroom: 38% of faculty are male; 62% are female. 23% teach undergraduates, and 12% do both. No introductory courses are taught by graduate students. The average class size in an introductory lecture is 14.

Admissions: 82% of the 2013-2014 applicants were accepted.

Requirements: CLEP credits are accepted.

Procedure: Freshmen are admitted to all sessions. There are deferred admissions and rolling admissions plans. Application deadlines are open. The fall 2013 application fee was $30. Applications are accepted online.

Transfer: 88 transfer students enrolled in 2012-2013. High school and college transcripts are required; an interview and a statement of good standing from the previous institution is recommended. 30 of 120 credits required for the bachelor's degree must be completed at Cambridge.

Visiting: There are regularly scheduled orientations for prospective students. There are guides for informal visits and visitors may sit in on classes. To schedule a visit, contact Carol Lombardi at carol.lombardi@cambridgecollege.edu.

Financial Aid: In 2013-2014, 61% of all full-time freshmen and 72% of continuing full-time students received some form of financial aid. 61% of all full-time freshmen and 72% of continuing full-time students received need-based aid. The average freshman award was $7,196. Need-based scholarships or need-based grants averaged $5,517 ($7,331 maximum); and need-based self-help aid (loans and jobs) averaged $3,500 ($3,500 maximum). Average annual earnings from campus work are $4722. The average financial indebtedness of the 2013 graduate was $27,813. The FAFSA and the college's own financial statement are required. The priority date for freshman financial aid applications for fall entry is August 1. The deadline for filing freshman financial aid applications for fall entry is August 1.

International Students: There are 245 international students enrolled. They must take the TOEFL with a minimum score of 550 on the paper-based TOEFL (PBT) or 79 on the Internet-based version (iBT).

Graduates: From July 1, 2012 to June 30, 2013, 253 bachelor's degrees were awarded. The most popular majors were multidisciplinary studies (46%), management studies (31%), and psychology (23%). In an average class, 31% graduate in 6 years or less.

Admissions Contact: Carol Lombardi, Director of Admissions. E-Mail: *carol.lombardi@cambridgecollege.edu* Web: *www.cambridgecollege.edu*

CLARK UNIVERSITY C-2

Worcester, MA 01610 (508) 793-7431
(800) 462-5275; (508) 793-8821

Full-time: 949 men, 1321 women	**Faculty:** 197; IIA, +$
Part-time: 48 men, 62 women	**Ph.D.s:** 96%
Graduate: 511 men, 660 women	**Student/Faculty:** 9 to 1
Year: semesters, summer session	**Tuition:** $39,550
Application Deadline: January 15	**Room & Board:** $7470

Freshman Class: 5551 applied, 3416 accepted, 621 enrolled
SAT CR/M/W: 620/600/620 **ACT:** 28 **HIGHLY COMPETITIVE+**

Clark University, founded in 1887, is an independent liberal arts and research institution. There are 2 undergraduate schools and 3 graduate schools. In addition to regional accreditation, Clark has baccalaureate program accreditation with AACSB and NASDTEC. The 6 libraries contain 650,601 volumes, 61,262 microform items, 2,390 audio/video tapes/CDs/DVDs, and subscribe to 2,133 periodicals including electronic. Computerized library services include interlibrary loans, database searching, Internet access, and Wi-Fi capability. Special learning facilities include an art gallery, radio station, a TV studio, campus cable network, center for music with 2 studios for electronic music, 2 theaters, and magnetic resonance imaging facility. The 50-acre campus is in an urban area 50 miles west of Boston. Including any residence halls, there are 69 buildings.

Student Life: 63% of undergraduates are from out of state, mostly the Northeast. Students are from 41 states, 62 foreign countries, and Canada. 75% are from public schools. 61% are White; 12% Foreign. 42% claim no religious affiliation; 18% Protestant; 15% Catholic; 12% Jewish. The average age of freshmen is 19; all undergraduates, 20. 10% do not continue beyond their first year; 81% remain to graduate.

Housing: 1745 students can be accommodated in college housing, which includes single-sex and coed dorms, on-campus apartments, and off-campus apartments. In addition, there are special-interest houses, wellness and quiet houses. On-campus housing is guaranteed for the freshman year only and is available on a lottery system for upperclassmen. 70% of students live on campus. All students may keep cars.

Activities: There are no fraternities or sororities. There are 120 groups on campus, including art, band, chess, choir, chorale, chorus, computers, dance, debate, drama, environmental, ethnic, film, gay, honors, international, jazz band, literary magazine, musical theater, newspaper, orchestra, pep band, photography, political, professional, radio and TV, religious, social, social service, student government, symphony, and yearbook. Popular campus events include Gryphon and Pleiades Honor Society Variety Show, International Gala, and Speaker's Forum.

Sports: There are 8 intercollegiate sports for men and 9 for women, and 14 intramural sports for men and 14 for women. Facilities include an athletic center with a 2000-seat gym, a pool, a fitness center, tennis courts, outdoor fields, and baseball and softball diamonds.

Disabled Students: 95% of the campus is accessible. Facilities include wheelchair ramps, elevators, special parking, specially equipped restrooms, special class scheduling, lowered drinking fountains, lowered telephones, and special housing.

Services: Counseling and information services are available, as is tutoring in some subjects, math, biology, chemistry, economics, and psychology. For learning-disabled students, the university provides early orientation, alternative test-taking accommodations, and a learning specialist.

Campus Safety and Security: Measures include 24-hour foot and vehicle patrol, emergency notification system, self-defense education, and security escort services. There are shuttle buses, emergency telephones, lighted pathways/sidewalks, and controlled access to dorms/residences.

Programs of Study: Clark confers B.A., and B.S. degrees. Master's and doctoral degrees are also awarded. Bachelor's degrees are awarded in BIOLOGICAL SCIENCE (biochemistry and biology/biological science), BUSINESS (business administration and management), COMMUNICATIONS AND THE ARTS (art history and appreciation, communications, comparative literature, dramatic arts, English, film arts, fine arts, French, languages, music, romance languages and literature, Spanish, studio art, and visual and performing arts), COMPUTER AND PHYSICAL SCIENCE (chemistry, computer science, mathematics, and physics), ENGINEERING AND ENVIRONMENTAL DESIGN (environmental science), HEALTH PROFESSIONS (predentistry and premedicine), SOCIAL SCIENCE (Asian/Oriental studies, classical/ancient civilization, economics, geography, history, international relations, international studies, philosophy, political science/government, prelaw, psychology, sociology, and women's studies). Psychology, political science, and biology/biochemistry have the largest enrollments.

Required: Each student is required to complete 2 critical thinking courses in 2 categories of verbal expression and formal analysis, and 6 perspectives courses, representing the categories of aesthetics, comparative, historical, language and culture, science, and values. A student must receive passing grades in a minimum of 32 full courses, with a C- or better in at least 24 of these courses, and maintain a minimum 2.0 GPA to graduate.

Special: For-credit internships are available in all disciplines with private corporations and small businesses, medical centers, and government agencies. There is cross-registration with members of the Worcester Consortium, including 9 other colleges and universities. Clark also offers study abroad in 16 countries, a Washington semester with American University, work-study programs, accelerated degree programs, dual and student-designed majors, pass/no record options, and a 3-2 engineering degree with Columbia University. A gerontology certificate is offered with the Worcester Consortium for Higher Education. There are 10 national honor societies, including Phi Beta Kappa, and 21 departmental honors programs.

Faculty/Classroom: 56% of faculty are male; 44% are female. All teach and do research. No introductory courses are taught by graduate students. The average class size in an introductory lecture is 25; in a laboratory is 17; and in a regular course is 21.

Admissions: 62% of the 2013-2014 applicants were accepted. The SAT scores for the 2013-2014 freshman class were: Critical Reading--6% below 500, 28% between 500 and 599, 47% between 600 and 699, and 19% between 700 and 800; Math--7% below 500, 42% between 500 and 599, 43% between 600 and 699, and 8% between 700 and 800; Writing--6% below 500, 31% between 500 and 599, 46% between 600 and 699, and 17% between 700 and 800. The ACT scores were 7% between 21 and 23, 25% between 24 and 26, 24% between 27 and 28, and 44% above 28. 65% of the current freshmen were in the top fifth of their class; 93% were in the top two fifths. 8 freshmen graduated first in their class.

Requirements: Clark is SAT/ACT optional. Applicants must graduate from an accredited secondary school or have a GED. 16 Carnegie units are required, including 4 years of English, 3 each of math and science, and 2 each of foreign languages and social studies, including history. AP credits are accepted.

Procedure: Freshmen are admitted fall and spring. Entrance exams should be taken by November of the senior year. There are early admissions and deferred admissions plans. Applications should be filed by January 15 for fall entry; November 15 for spring entry, along with a $55 fee. Notifications are sent April 1. 226 applicants were on the 2013 waiting list; 6 were admitted. Applications are accepted online.

Transfer: 42 transfer students enrolled in 2012-2013. Applicants should have a minimum GPA of about 2.8. At least one full semester of college course work is required. High school and college transcripts, recent SAT or ACT test scores, a statement of good standing from previous institutions attended, and a transfer statement are required. Grades of C or better in comparable course work transfer for credit. 16 of 32 credits required for the bachelor's degree must be completed at Clark.

Visiting: There are regularly scheduled orientations for prospective students, consisting of open houses during fall and spring semesters, which include tours, information sessions, and talks with faculty, administration, and coaches. There are guides for informal visits and visitors may sit in on classes. To schedule a visit, contact the Admissions Office at admissions@clarku.edu.

Financial Aid: In 2013-2014, 92% of all full-time freshmen and 92% of continuing full-time students received some form of financial aid. 62% of all full-time freshmen and 62% of continuing full-time students received need-based aid. The average freshman award was $28,417. Need-based scholarships or need-based grants averaged $26,375; and need-based self-help aid (loans and jobs) averaged $4,993. 75% of undergraduate students work part-time. Average annual earnings from campus work are $2000. The average financial indebtedness of the 2013 graduate was $24,990. Clark is a member of CSS. The CSS/Profile and FAFSA are required. The deadline for filing freshman financial aid applications for fall entry is February 1.

International Students: There are 280 international students enrolled. The school actively recruits these students. They must take the TOEFL with a minimum score of 550 on the paper-based TOEFL (PBT) or 80 on the Internet-based version (iBT), or take the IELTS, scoring 6.5.

Graduates: From July 1, 2012 to June 30, 2013, 519 bachelor's degrees were awarded. The most popular majors were psychology (17%), political science (9%), and biology and biochemistry (8%). 80 companies recruited on campus in 2012-2013. In an average class, 1% graduate in 3 years or less, 77% graduate in 4 years or less, 80% graduate in 5 years or less, and 81% graduate in 6 years or less. Of the 2012 graduating class, 40% were enrolled in graduate school within 6 months of graduation.

Admissions Contact: Donald Honeman, Dean of Admissions. E-Mail: *admissions@clarku.edu* Web: *www.clarku.edu*

COLLEGE OF THE HOLY CROSS — C-2

Worcester, MA 01610 (508) 793-2443
(800) 442-2421; (508) 793-3888

Full-time: 1438 men, 1439 women	**Faculty:** 279; IIB, +$
Part-time: 12 men, 23 women	**Ph.D.s:** 96%
Graduate: n/av	**Student/Faculty:** 10 to 1
Year: semesters	**Tuition:** $44,272
Application Deadline: January 15	**Room & Board:** $11,960
Freshman Class: 7115 applied, 2346 accepted, 722 enrolled	
SAT CR/M/W: 649/657/653	**ACT:** 29 **MOST COMPETITIVE**

The College of the Holy Cross is the only liberal arts college that embraces a Catholic, Jesuit identity. 28 Jesuit colleges and universities in the United States, Holy Cross stands alone in its exclusive commitment to undergraduate education. Students enjoy a full array of athletic facilities, a state-of-the-art fitness center, and outstanding arts spaces. There is one undergraduate school. The 7 libraries contain 637,559 volumes, 16,572 microform items, 36,362 audio/video tapes/CDs/DVDs, and subscribe to 957 periodicals including electronic. Computerized library services include interlibrary loans, database searching, Internet access, and Wi-Fi capability. Special learning facilities include an art gallery, radio station, including greenhouses; a research-level laboratories and equipment; and multimedia resource center. The 174-acre campus is in a suburban area 45 miles west of Boston. Including any residence halls, there are 35 buildings.

Student Life: 63% of undergraduates are from out of state, mostly the Northeast. Students are from 47 states, 20 foreign countries, and Canada. 50% are from public schools. 68% are White; 11% Hispanic. 75% are Catholic; 11% claim no religious affiliation. The average age of freshmen is 18; all undergraduates, 20. 5% do not continue beyond their first year; 91% remain to graduate.

Housing: 2503 students can be accommodated in college housing, which includes coed dorms and on-campus apartments. In addition, there are special-interest houses, substance-free housing, and first-year living and learning housing. On-campus housing is guaranteed for all 4 years. 92% of students live on campus; of those, 90% remain on campus on weekends. Upperclassmen may keep cars.

Activities: There are no fraternities or sororities. There are 100 groups on campus, including art, band, cheerleading, choir, chorale, chorus, computers, dance, debate, drama, drill team, environmental, ethnic, film, gay, honors, international, investing club, jazz band, literary magazine, marching band, musical theater, newspaper, orchestra, pep band, photography, political, professional, religious, social, social service, student government, and yearbook. Popular campus events include Spring Weekend, Family Weekend, and Winter Weekend.

Sports: There are 13 intercollegiate sports for men and 14 for women, and 11 intramural sports for men and 10 for women. Facilities include Baseball, football, soccer fields and stadiums; indoor and outdoor running tracks; swimming pool; ice rink; indoor crew tanks; basketball arena; weight and exercise rooms; wellness centers; tennis, squash, and racquetball courts.

Disabled Students: 85% of the campus is accessible. Facilities include wheelchair ramps, elevators, special parking, specially equipped restrooms, special class scheduling, lowered drinking fountains, lowered telephones, special housing.

Services: Counseling and information services are available, as is tutoring in some subjects, calculus, biology, chemistry, physics, economics, accounting, classics, Spanish, writing and psychology statistics.

Campus Safety and Security: Measures include 24-hour foot and vehicle patrol, emergency notification system, self-defense education, and security escort services. There are shuttle buses, emergency telephones, lighted pathways/sidewalks, and a card access control system.

Programs of Study: Holy Cross confers A.B. degrees. Bachelor's degrees are awarded in AGRICULTURE (environmental studies), BIOLOGICAL SCIENCE (biology/biological science), BUSINESS (accounting), COMMUNICATIONS AND THE ARTS (art history and appreciation, Chinese, classics, dramatic arts, English, French, German, Italian, literature, music, Russian, Spanish, and studio art), COMPUTER AND PHYSICAL SCIENCE (chemistry, computer science, mathematics, and physics), ENGINEERING AND ENVIRONMENTAL DESIGN (architecture), SOCIAL SCIENCE (anthropology, Asian/Oriental studies, economics, German area studies, history, Italian studies, medieval studies, philosophy, political science/government, psychology, religion, Russian and Slavic studies, and sociology). Psychology, economics, political science have the largest enrollments.

Required: Distribution requirements include social science, natural and mathematical science, cross-cultural studies, religious and philosophical studies, historical studies and the arts, and literature. In addition, students must demonstrate competence in a classical or modern language or American sign language. A total of 32 courses worth at least 1 unit each is required for graduation, with 10 to 14 courses in the major. The minimum GPA for graduation is 2.0.

Special: Academic internships are available through the Center for Interdisciplinary and Special Studies. Student-designed majors, dual majors including economics-accounting major, a Washington semester, and study abroad in approximately 15 countries are possible. The College also offers several 4- to 6-week programs in locations such as Jerusalem, London, Moscow, Paris and Rome. There is a 3-2 engineering program with Columbia University, internships, and an accelerated degree program. Students may cross-register with other universities in the Colleges of Worcester Consortium. There are 2 national honor societies, including Phi Beta Kappa, and 5 departmental honors programs.

Faculty/Classroom: 54% of faculty are male; 46% are female. All teach and do research. No introductory courses are taught by graduate students. The average class size in an introductory lecture is 23; in a laboratory is 16; and in a regular course is 19.

Admissions: 33% of the 2013-2014 applicants were accepted. The SAT scores for the 2013-2014 freshman class were: Critical Reading--1% below 500, 20% between 500 and 599, 56% between 600 and 699, and 23% between 700 and 800; Math--1% below 500, 14% between 500 and 599, 58% between 600 and 699, and 27% between 700 and 800; Writing--2% below 500, 16% between 500 and 599, 56% between 600 and 699, and 26% between 700 and 800. There were 1 National Merit finalists. 13 freshmen graduated first in their class.

Requirements: Applicants should be graduates of an accredited secondary school or hold the GED. Recommended preparatory courses include English, foreign language, history, math, and science. An essay is required. Students have the option to submit standardized test scores if they believe the results represent a fuller picture of their achievements and potential; students who opt not to submit scores will not be at any disadvantage in admissions decisions. An interview is recommended. AP credits are accepted. Important factors in the admissions decision are recommendations by school officials, advanced placement or honors courses, and extracurricular activities record.

Procedure: Freshmen are admitted fall. Entrance exams should be taken no later than January 15th of the senior year. There are early decision and deferred admissions plans. Early decision applications should be filed by December 15; regular applications, by January 15 for fall entry, along with a $60 fee. Notification of early decision is sent January 15; regular decision, April 1. 351 early decision candidates were accepted for the 2013-2014 class. 299 applicants were on the 2013 waiting list; 33 were admitted. Applications are accepted online.

Transfer: 21 transfer students enrolled in 2012-2013. Standardized test scores are not required but applicants must provide transcripts and 2 professor recommendations. Personal interviews are highly recommended. 64 of 128 credits required for the bachelor's degree must be completed at Holy Cross.

Visiting: There are regularly scheduled orientations for prospective students, including fall open houses in October and November consisting of informational panels on academics, admissions, financial aid, and student life, as well as tours of the facilities. There are guides for informal visits, visitors may sit in on classes, and stay overnight. To schedule a visit, contact the Admissions Office.

Financial Aid: In 2013-2014, 59% of all full-time freshmen and 61% of continuing full-time students received some form of financial aid. 49% of all full-time freshmen and 50% of continuing full-time students received need-based aid. The average freshman award was $35,735. Need-based scholarships or need-based grants averaged $28,684 ($49,300 maximum); need-based self-help aid (loans and jobs) averaged $7,628 ($7,700 maximum); non-need-based athletic scholarships averaged $56,842 ($57,000 maximum); and other non-need-based awards and non-need-based scholarships averaged $39,545 ($56,232 maximum). 45% of undergraduate students work part-time. Average annual earnings from campus work are $1800. The average financial indebtedness of the 2013 graduate was $30,880. Holy Cross is a member of CSS. The CSS/Profile and FAFSA, and student and parent federal tax returns are required. The deadline for filing freshman financial aid applications for fall entry is February 1.

International Students: There are 26 international students enrolled. The school actively recruits these students. They must take the TOEFL with a minimum score of 550 on the paper-based TOEFL (PBT) or 79 on the Internet-based version (iBT).

Graduates: From July 1, 2012 to June 30, 2013, 704 bachelor's degrees were awarded. The most popular majors were psychology (14%), economics (14%), and political science (12%). 85 companies recruited on campus in 2012-2013. In an average class, 89% graduate in 4 years or less, 91% graduate in 5 years or less, and 91% graduate in 6 years or less. Of the 2012 graduating class, 17% were enrolled in graduate school within 6 months of graduation, and 59% were employed.

Admissions Contact: Ann McDermott, Director. E-Mail: *admissions@holycross.edu* Web: *www.holycross.edu*

CURRY COLLEGE E-2

Milton, MA 02186 (617) 333-2210
(800) 669-0686; (617) 333-2114

Full-time: 871 men, 1124 women
Part-time: 172 men, 602 women
Graduate: 103 men, 168 women
Year: semesters, summer session
Application Deadline: April 1
Faculty: 125
Ph.D.s: 60%
Student/Faculty: 16 to 1
Tuition: $34,415
Room & Board: $13,130
Freshman Class: 5494 applied, 4621 accepted, 585 enrolled
SAT CR/M/W: 460/460/455 **ACT:** 19 **LESS COMPETITIVE**

Curry College, founded in 1879, is a private liberal arts institution. There is one graduate school. In addition to regional accreditation, Curry has baccalaureate program accreditation with NLN. The library contains 154,000 volumes, 4,000 audio/video tapes/CDs/DVDs, and subscribes to 48,000 periodicals including electronic. Computerized library services include interlibrary loans, database searching, Internet access, and Wi-Fi capability. Special learning facilities include a radio station and TV station. The 135-acre campus is in a suburban area 7 miles southwest of Boston. Including any residence halls, there are 43 buildings.

Student Life: 79% of undergraduates are from Massachusetts. Others are from 32 states, 7 foreign countries, and Canada. 66% are White; 17% race unknown. The average age of freshmen is 18; all undergraduates, 25. 31% do not continue beyond their first year; 43% remain to graduate.

Housing: 1385 students can be accommodated in college housing, which includes single-sex and coed dorms. In addition, there are honors houses and special-interest houses. On-campus housing is available on a first-come, first-served basis, and is available on a lottery system for upperclassmen. 70% of students live on campus. Upperclassmen may keep cars.

Activities: There are no fraternities or sororities. There are 33 groups on campus, including art, cheerleading, chorale, dance, drama, ethnic, film, gay, honors, international, literary magazine, musical theater, newspaper, photography, political, professional, radio and TV, religious, social, social service, and student government. Popular campus events include Formal Dances, Concert Series and Curry Connections Fair.

Sports: There are 7 intercollegiate sports for men and 7 for women, and 5 intramural sports for men and 5 for women. Facilities include a 500-seat gym, a dance studio, 13 outdoor tennis courts, an outdoor pool, 5 athletic fields, a 2,000-seat stadium, a 500-seat auditorium, and a 5,000-meter cross-country trail.

Disabled Students: Facilities include wheelchair ramps, elevators, special parking, specially equipped restrooms, and special class scheduling.

Services: Counseling and information services are available, as is tutoring in most subjects. There is a reader service for the blind, and remedial math, reading, and writing. General development courses in writing, reading, and math are designed to develop the student's basic skills.

Campus Safety and Security: Measures include 24-hour foot and vehicle patrol, emergency notification system, self-defense education, and security escort services. There are shuttle buses, emergency telephones, lighted pathways/sidewalks, a campus safety office offers security services.

Programs of Study: Curry confers B.A., B.S. and B.S.N. degrees. Master's degrees are also awarded. Bachelor's degrees are awarded in BIOLOGICAL SCIENCE (biology/biological science), BUSINESS (business administration and management), COMMUNICATIONS AND THE ARTS (communications, English, graphic design, and visual and performing arts), COMPUTER AND PHYSICAL SCIENCE (chemistry, information sciences and systems, and physics), EDUCATION (early childhood education, elementary education, health education, and special education), ENGINEERING AND ENVIRONMENTAL DESIGN (environmental science), HEALTH PROFESSIONS (nursing), SOCIAL SCIENCE (criminal justice, history, philosophy, political science/government, psychology, and sociology). Nursing is the strongest academically. Nusing, business, communications and criminal justice. have the largest enrollments.

Required: Successful completion of the liberal arts core curriculum and a total of 120 semester hours (121 for nursing), completion of a major, and a minimum 2.0 GPA, are required for graduation. Nursing students must pass a comprehensive exam. Transfer students have modified liberal arts requirements.

Special: Curry offers internships in all majors, study abroad, work-study programs, dual and student-designed majors, credit by exam and for life, work, and military experience, non-degree study, and pass/fail options. There are a freshman honors program.

Faculty/Classroom: No introductory courses are taught by graduate students. The average class size in an introductory lecture is 20; in a laboratory is 12; and in a regular course is 20.

Admissions: 84% of the 2013-2014 applicants were accepted. The SAT scores for the 2013-2014 freshman class were: Critical Reading--73% below 500, 24% between 500 and 599, and 3% between 600 and 699; Math--70% below 500, 27% between 500 and 599, and 3% between 600 and 699; Writing--71% below 500, 25% between 500 and 599, and 4% between 600 and 699.

Requirements: TOEFL for international applicants. The College's Program for the Advancement of Learning does not require nor does it consider SAT or ACT scores during the admissions process. A GPA of 2.0 is required. AP and CLEP credits are accepted. Important factors in the admissions decision are recommendations by school officials, extracurricular activities record, and evidence of special talent.

Procedure: Freshmen are admitted fall and spring. Entrance exams should be taken during the junior year or in November of the senior year. There are early admissions, deferred admissions, and rolling admissions plans. Early decision applications should be filed by December 1; regular applications, by April 1 for fall entry; and November 1 for spring entry, along with a $50 fee. Notification is sent on a rolling basis. Applications are accepted online.

Transfer: 67 transfer students enrolled in 2012-2013. Transfer applicants must be in good academic standing at their previous colleges, with a minimum GPA of 2.0. An interview is recommended. 30 of 120 credits required for the bachelor's degree must be completed at Curry.

Visiting: There are regularly scheduled orientations for prospective students, Student visits consist of interviews with an admissions counselor and tours with a student. There are guides for informal visits, visitors may sit in on classes, and stay overnight. To schedule a visit, contact the Admissions Office.

Financial Aid: In 2013-2014, 92% of all full-time freshmen and 85% of continuing full-time students received some form of financial aid. 79% of all full-time freshmen and 75% of continuing full-time students received need-based aid. The average freshman award was $23,406. Need-based scholarships or need-based grants averaged $13,856; need-based self-help aid (loans and jobs) averaged $5,508; and other non-need-based awards and non-need-based scholarships averaged $5,607. Curry is a member of CSS. The FAFSA is required. The priority date for freshman financial aid applications for fall entry is March 1.

International Students: There are 24 international students enrolled. They must take the TOEFL with a minimum score of 525 on the paper-based TOEFL (PBT) or 71 on the Internet-based version (iBT). They must also take the SAT or ACT.

Graduates: From July 1, 2012 to June 30, 2013, 632 bachelor's degrees were awarded. The most popular majors were nursing (35%), business (16%), and communicaiton (12%). In an average class, 36% graduate in 4 years or less, 42% graduate in 5 years or less, and 43% graduate in 6 years or less.

Admissions Contact: Jane Fidler, Dean of Admissions. E-Mail: *curryadm@curry.edu* Web: *www.curry.edu*

EASTERN NAZARENE COLLEGE E-2

Quincy, MA 02170 (617) 745-3711
(800) 883-6288; (617) 745-3980

Full-time: 250 men, 360 women	**Faculty:** n/av
Part-time: 20 men, 23 women	**Ph.D.s:** 57%
Graduate: 35 men, 145 women	**Student/Faculty:** n/av
Year: semesters, summer session	**Tuition:** $24,860
Application Deadline: see profile	**Room & Board:** $8600
Freshman Class: n/av	
SAT or ACT: required	

COMPETITIVE

Eastern Nazarene College, founded in 1918, is a private college affiliated with the Church of the Nazarene and offers a program in the liberal arts. The figures in the above capsule and this profile are approximate. There is one graduate school. In addition to regional accreditation, ENC has baccalaureate program accreditation with CSWE. The library contains 115,000 volumes and subscribes to 600 periodicals including electronic. Computerized library services include interlibrary loans and database searching. Special learning facilities include a learning resource center and radio station. The 15-acre campus is in a suburban area 6 miles south of Boston. Including any residence halls, there are 16 buildings.

Student Life: 55% of undergraduates are from out of state, mostly the Northeast. Students are from 27 states, 24 foreign countries, and Canada. 88% are white. 88% are Protestant. The average age of freshmen is 18; all undergraduates, 20. 25% do not continue beyond their first year; 60% remain to graduate.

Housing: 638 students can be accommodated in college housing, which includes single-sex dorms and married student housing. On-campus housing is guaranteed for all 4 years. 75% of students live on campus; of those, 75% remain on campus on weekends. Alcohol is not permitted. All students may keep cars.

Activities: There are no fraternities or sororities. There are 34 groups on campus, including band, cheerleading, choir, chorale, chorus, drama, jazz band, literary magazine, musical theater, newspaper, pep band, photography, professional, radio and TV, religious, social service, student government, and yearbook. Popular campus events include Freshmen Breakout, All-School Outing, and Junior/Senior Banquet.

Sports: There are 5 intercollegiate sports for men and 5 for women, and 4 intramural sports for men and 5 for women. Facilities include a phys ed center equipped with a basketball area, batting cage, and playing courts.

Disabled Students: 65% of the campus is accessible. Facilities include wheelchair ramps, elevators, special parking, and specially equipped restrooms.

Services: Counseling and information services are available, as is tutoring in most subjects. There is remedial math, reading, and writing.

Campus Safety and Security: Measures include 24-hour foot and vehicle patrol, self-defense education, and security escort services. There are emergency telephones and lighted pathways/sidewalks.

Programs of Study: ENC confers B.A. and B.S. degrees. Associate and master's degrees are also awarded. Bachelor's degrees are awarded in BIOLOGICAL SCIENCE (biology/biological science and marine biology), BUSINESS (accounting and business administration and management), COMMUNICATIONS AND THE ARTS (advertising, broadcasting, communications, dramatic arts, English, French, journalism, literature, music, music performance, Spanish, and speech/debate/rhetoric), COMPUTER AND PHYSICAL SCIENCE (chemistry, computer science, mathematics, physics, and science), EDUCATION (athletic training, education, elementary education, music education, science education, and social science education), ENGINEERING AND ENVIRONMENTAL DESIGN (computer engineering, engineering physics, and environmental science), HEALTH PROFESSIONS (sports medicine), SOCIAL SCIENCE (child psychology/development, Christian studies, clinical psychology, history, ministries, physical fitness/movement, psychology, religion, religious music, social studies, social work, and sociology). Chemistry, physics, and history are the strongest academically. Education, business, and psychology have the largest enrollments.

Required: All students must complete the core curriculum of writing and rhetoric, biblical history, social science, science or math, symbolic systems and intercultural awareness, philosophy and religion, and phys ed. A total of 130 credits is required for the B.A. or B.S., with 32 to 40 in the major. Minimum GPA for graduation is 2.0.

Special: Internships are available in the metropolitan Boston area. Study abroad in Costa Rica, a Washington semester, a 3-2 engineering degree with Boston University, and a cooperative program with the Massachusetts College of Pharmacy are offered. Work-study programs, dual majors, credit for life, military, and work experience, and pass/fail options are available. An off-campus degree-completion program for adults in business administration is offered. There is 1 national honor society.

Faculty/Classroom: 72% of faculty are male; 28% are female. 83% teach undergraduates. No introductory courses are taught by graduate students. The average class size in an introductory lecture is 75; in a laboratory, 20; and in a regular course, 22.

Requirements: The SAT or ACT is required. Applicants must be graduates of an accredited secondary school or have a GED. They must have a minimum of 16 academic credits, including 4 of English, 2 to 4 each of math and foreign language, 1 to 4 of science, and 1 to 2 each of history and social studies. Music students must audition. An essay and interview are recommended. A GPA of 2.3 is required. AP and CLEP credits are accepted. Important factors in the admissions decision are advanced placement or honors courses, recommendations by school officials, and leadership record.

Procedure: Freshmen are admitted to all sessions. Entrance exams should be taken in the spring of the junior year. There are deferred admissions and rolling admissions plans. Check with the school for current application deadlines and fee.

Transfer: A minimum 2.0 GPA is required. An interview is recommended. 60 of 130 credits required for the bachelor's degree must be completed at ENC.

Visiting: There are regularly scheduled orientations for prospective students. There are guides for informal visits, and visitors may sit in on classes and stay overnight. To schedule a visit, contact the Office of Admissions.

Financial Aid: ENC is a member of CSS. The FAFSA and the college's own financial statement are required. Check with the school for current application deadlines.

International Students: They must take the TOEFL.

Admissions Contact: Director of Admissions. E-Mail: *admission@enc .edu* Web: *www.enc.edu*

ELMS COLLEGE B-3

Chicopee, MA 01013 (413) 592-3189
(800) 255-ELMS; (413) 594-2781

Full-time: 70 men, 365 women	**Faculty:** n/av
Part-time: 30 men, 195 women	**Ph.D.s:** 76%
Graduate: 25 men, 85 women	**Student/Faculty:** n/av
Year: semesters	**Tuition:** $26,812
Application Deadline: open	**Room & Board:** $10,202
Freshman Class: n/av	
SAT or ACT: required	

VERY COMPETITIVE

Elms College, founded in 1928 as College of Our Lady of the Elms, is a Roman Catholic institution offering undergraduate degrees in liberal arts and sciences and graduate degrees in liberal arts, education, and theology. The figures in the above capsule and this profile are approximate. In addition to regional accreditation, Elms has baccalaureate program accreditation with CSWE and NLN. The library contains 103,136 volumes, 77,784 microform items, 2208 audio/video tapes/CDs/DVDs, and subscribes to 695 periodicals including electronic. Computerized library services include interlibrary loans and database searching. Special learning facilities include a learning resource center, art gallery, radio station, TV station, and rare books collection. The 32-acre campus is in a suburban area 2 miles north of Springfield and 90 miles west of Boston. Including any residence halls, there are 11 buildings.

Student Life: 85% of undergraduates are from Massachusetts. Others are from 9 states and 10 foreign countries. 74% are from public schools. 80% are white. 60% are Catholic. The average age of freshmen is 20; all undergraduates, 22. 11% do not continue beyond their first year.

Housing: 315 students can be accommodated in college housing, which includes single-sex and coed dorms. On-campus housing is guaranteed for all 4 years. 60% of students commute. All students may keep cars.

Activities: There are no fraternities or sororities. There are 41 groups on campus, including art, choir, chorale, chorus, computers, dance, drama, ethnic, honors, international, literary magazine, musical theater, newspaper, photography, professional, radio and TV, religious, social, social service, student government, and yearbook. Popular campus events include Soph Show, Cap and Gown, and Ring Ceremony.

Sports: There are 6 intercollegiate sports for men and 9 for women, and 6 intramural sports for men and 6 for women. Facilities include fitness and athletic center housing a suspended indoor track, a 25-meter, 6-lane pool, a weight and aerobics room, a multipurpose arena, a basketball court, and a volleyball court.

Disabled Students: 40% of the campus is accessible. Facilities include wheelchair ramps, elevators, special parking, specially equipped restrooms, special class scheduling, lowered drinking fountains, lowered telephones, and automated doors.

Services: Counseling and information services are available, as is tutoring in every subject. There is a reader service for the blind and remedial math, reading, and writing. There also is an academic advising and resource center, a counseling service office, career services, wellness services, a campus ministry office, and resident advisers.

Campus Safety and Security: Measures include 24-hour foot and vehicle patrol, self-defense education, and security escort services. There are emergency telephones and lighted pathways/sidewalks. A safety and security manual is published each year, and there is a safety and security committee of administrators, students, faculty, and staff.

Programs of Study: Elms confers B.A. and B.S. degrees. Associate and master's degrees are also awarded. Bachelor's degrees are awarded in BIOLOGICAL SCIENCE (biology/biological science), BUSINESS (accounting, business administration and management, international business management, and marketing/retailing/merchandising), COMMUNICATIONS AND THE ARTS (English, fine arts, and Spanish), COMPUTER AND PHYSICAL SCIENCE (chemistry, computer science, mathematics, and natural sciences), EDUCATION (bilingual/bicultural education, early childhood education, elementary education, foreign languages education, middle school education, science education, secondary education, special education, and teaching English as a second/foreign language (TESOL/TEFOL)), HEALTH PROFESSIONS (health science, medical laboratory technology, nursing, predentistry, premedicine, and speech pathology/audiology), SOCIAL SCIENCE (American studies, international studies, paralegal studies, prelaw, psychology, religion, social work, and sociology). Nursing, education, and biology are the strongest academically. Education, business, and nursing have the largest enrollments.

Required: To graduate, all students must complete 120 hours with a 2.0 GPA. 54 hours are required in courses in rhetoric, computer science, history, religion, phys ed, philosophy, sociology, fine arts, humanities, foreign language, math, senior seminar, and service learning experience.

Special: Students may cross-register at any of the Cooperating Colleges of Greater Springfield or Consortium of Sisters of St. Joseph Colleges. Internships are available with local hospitals, businesses, and schools. Study abroad, student-designed interdepartmental majors, accelerated degree programs, work-study, dual majors, nondegree study, and pass/fail options are offered. There are 5 national honor societies, including Phi Beta Kappa, and a freshman honors program.

Faculty/Classroom: 35% of faculty are male; 65% are female. 90% teach undergraduates, 93% do research, and 92% do both. No introductory courses are taught by graduate students. The average class size in an introductory lecture is 13; in a laboratory, 8; and in a regular course, 11.

Requirements: The SAT or ACT is required. Applicants should be graduates of accredited high schools or have earned the GED. Secondary preparation should include 4 units of English, 3 each of math and science, and 2 each of foreign language, history, and social studies. A personal essay is required; an interview is recommended. A GPA of 2.5 is required. AP and CLEP credits are accepted. Important factors in the admissions decision are advanced placement or honors courses, recommendations by school officials, and extracurricular activities record.

Procedure: Freshmen are admitted fall and spring. Entrance exams should be taken no later than November of the senior year. There are early admissions, deferred admissions, and rolling admissions plans. Application deadlines are open. Check with the school for current application fee. Applications are accepted online.

Transfer: Applicants must have a minimum 2.0 GPA. 45 of 120 credits required for the bachelor's degree must be completed at Elms.

Visiting: There are regularly scheduled orientations for prospective students, including tours and interviews scheduled weekdays between 9 a.m. and 4 p.m. as well as 2 open houses in the fall and 1 in the spring. There are guides for informal visits,and visitors may sit in on classes and stay overnight. To schedule a visit, contact the Admission Office.

Financial Aid: Elms is a member of CSS. The FAFSA and the college's own financial statement are required. Check with the school for current application deadlines.

International Students: The school actively recruits these students.

Admissions Contact: Director of Admission. E-mail: *admissions@elms.edu* Web: *www.elms.edu*

EMERSON COLLEGE E-2

Boston, MA 02116	**(617) 824-8600; (617) 824-8609**
Full-time: 1376 men, 2291 women	**Faculty:** 193; IIA, +$
Part-time: 26 men, 37 women	**Ph.D.s:** 138%
Graduate: 199 men, 610 women	**Student/Faculty:** 13 to 1
Year: semesters, summer session	**Tuition:** $35,730
Application Deadline: January 5	**Room & Board:** $14,516
Freshman Class: 8198 applied, 3933 accepted, 863 enrolled	
SAT CR/M/W: 640/590/630 **ACT:** 27	**HIGHLY COMPETITIVE**

Founded in 1880, Emerson is the premier college in the United States for the study of communication and the arts. There are 2 undergraduate schools and 2 graduate schools. The library contains 164,083 volumes, 9,392 microform items, 12,590 audio/video tapes/CDs/DVDs, and subscribes to 50,310 periodicals including electronic. Computerized library services include interlibrary loans, database searching, Internet access, and Wi-Fi capability. Special learning facilities include an art gallery, radio station, TV station, sound-treated television studios, film production facilities and digital production labs, speech-language-hearing clinics, several theaters, 2 radio stations, marketing research suite, and digital newsroom. The 8-acre campus is in an urban area on Boston Common in the Theater District. Including any residence halls, there are 10 buildings.

Student Life: 79% of undergraduates are from out of state, mostly the Middle Atlantic. Students are from 42 states, 21 foreign countries, and Canada. 75% are from public schools. 70% are White. The average age of freshmen is 18; all undergraduates, 20. 12% do not continue beyond their first year; 82% remain to graduate.

Housing: 2086 students can be accommodated in college housing, which includes coed dorms. living and learning communities such as a writers' block and digital culture floors. On-campus housing is guaranteed for the freshman year only, is available on a first-come, first-served basis, and is available on a lottery system for upperclassmen. 55% of students live on campus; of those, 75% remain on campus on weekends. No one may keep cars.

Activities: 3% of men belong to 2 local and 1 national fraternities; 3% of women belong to 2 local and 1 national sororities. There are 80 groups on campus, including digital media, marketing/PR clubs., radio stations, chorale, computers, dance, debate, drama, environmental, ethnic, film, forensics, gay, honors, international, literary magazine, musical theater, newspaper, photography, political, professional, radio and TV, religious, social, social service, student government, theatre troupes, and yearbook. Popular campus events include Evvy's Award Show, and Emerson Recognition and Achievement Awards.

Sports: There are 7 intercollegiate sports for men and 8 for women. Facilities include a gymnasium, 10,000-square-foot fitness center, and lighted athletic field.

Disabled Students: 85% of the campus is accessible. Facilities include wheelchair ramps, elevators, specially equipped restrooms, special class scheduling, and special housing.

Services: Counseling and information services are available, as is tutoring in most subjects. There is remedial math, reading, and writing.

Campus Safety and Security: Measures include 24-hour foot and vehicle patrol, emergency notification system, self-defense education, and security escort services. There are shuttle buses, emergency telephones, lighted pathways/sidewalks, and controlled access to dorms/residences.

Programs of Study: Emerson confers B.A., B.S. and B.F.A. degrees. Master's and doctoral degrees are also awarded. Bachelor's degrees are awarded in BUSINESS (marketing management), COMMUNICATIONS AND THE ARTS (advertising, broadcasting, communications, creative writing, dramatic arts, film arts, journalism, media arts, musical theater, performing arts, public relations, publishing, radio/television technology, speech/debate/rhetoric, theater design, and theater management), HEALTH PROFESSIONS (speech pathology/audiology), SOCIAL SCI-

ENCE (interdisciplinary studies). Visual and media arts, writing, and literature and publishing are the strongest academically. Visual and media arts, performing arts, and communication have the largest enrollments.

Required: All students must complete 128 credit hours, with 40 to 64 in their major and a minimum GPA of 2.0. The general education curriculum consists of 4 foundations courses (oral and written communication and quantitative reasoning), 7 perspectives courses (liberal arts humanities), and 2 global/U.S. diversity courses.

Special: Student-designed, interdisciplinary, and dual majors are available. Cross-registration is offered with the 6-member Boston ProArts consortium. Nearly 800 internships are possible, 600 in Boston and 200 in Los Angeles. Internships bear credit and are graded. Emerson has nondegree study as well as study abroad in the Netherlands, China, and a summer film program in Prague. There is 1 national honor society and a freshman honors program.

Faculty/Classroom: 52% of faculty are male; 48% are female. All teach undergraduates. Graduate students teach 4% of introductory courses. The average class size in an introductory lecture is 35; in a laboratory is 18; and in a regular course is 24.

Admissions: 48% of the 2013-2014 applicants were accepted. The SAT scores for the 2013-2014 freshman class were: Critical Reading--2% below 500, 24% between 500 and 599, 55% between 600 and 699, and 19% between 700 and 800; Math--6% below 500, 44% between 500 and 599, 42% between 600 and 699, and 8% between 700 and 800; Writing--2% below 500, 27% between 500 and 599, 54% between 600 and 699, and 16% between 700 and 800. The ACT scores were 2% below 21, 8% between 21 and 23, 27% between 24 and 26, 24% between 27 and 28, and 38% above 28. 58% of the current freshmen were in the top fifth of their class; 89% were in the top two fifths. 5 freshmen graduated first in their class.

Requirements: The SAT or ACT is required. The ACT Optional Writing test is also required. Emerson is a member of the Common Application and requires an Application Supplement. Candidates must have graduated from high school (or have a GED) and present 4 years of English and 3 years each in science, social studies, foreign language, and math. Candidates for performing arts programs are required to submit a theatre-related resume and either audition or interview, or submit a portfolio or an essay. Candidates for film are required to submit either a 5-8 minute video sample and statement, or a 5-10 page script. AP and CLEP credits are accepted. Important factors in the admissions decision are advanced placement or honors courses, evidence of special talent, and recommendations by school officials.

Procedure: Freshmen are admitted fall and spring. Entrance exams should be taken before December of the senior year. There are early decision and deferred admissions plans. Early decision applications should be filed by November 1; regular applications, by January 5 for fall entry; and November 1 for spring entry, along with a $65 fee. Notification of early decision is sent December 15; regular decision, April 1. 1190 applicants were on the 2013 waiting list; 25 were admitted. Applications are accepted online.

Transfer: 188 transfer students enrolled in 2012-2013. Requirements for transfer students are the same as for all students. Note that BFA Performance degrees do not accept transfer applicants. 48 of 128 credits required for the bachelor's degree must be completed at Emerson.

Visiting: There are regularly scheduled orientations for prospective students, including an information session with an admission representative and a tour lead by a current student. There are guides for informal visits and visitors may sit in on classes.

Financial Aid: In 2013-2014, 81% of all full-time freshmen and 71% of continuing full-time students received some form of financial aid. 56% of all full-time freshmen and 57% of continuing full-time students received need-based aid. The average freshman award was $26,916. Need-based scholarships or need-based grants averaged $19,272 ($43,167 maximum); need-based self-help aid (loans and jobs) averaged $4,576 ($9,000 maximum); and other non-need-based awards and non-need-based scholarships averaged $13,194 ($55,862 maximum). 52% of undergraduate students work part-time. Average annual earnings from campus work are $1906. The average financial indebtedness of the 2013 graduate was $15,262. The CSS/Profile and FAFSA are required. The priority date for freshman financial aid applications for fall entry is March 1.

International Students: There are 173 international students enrolled. The school actively recruits these students. They must take the TOEFL with a minimum score of 550 on the paper-based TOEFL (PBT) or 80 on the Internet-based version (iBT), or take the IELTS. They must also take the SAT or ACT.

Graduates: From July 1, 2012 to June 30, 2013, 854 bachelor's degrees were awarded. The most popular majors were visual and performing arts (22%), communication/journalism (22%), and business/marketing (12%). In an average class, 81% graduate in 6 years or less. Of the 2012 graduating class, 8% were enrolled in graduate school within 6 months of graduation, and 81% were employed.

Admissions Contact: Sara Brookshire Cummings, Director of Undergraduate Admission. E-Mail: *admission@emerson.edu* Web: *www.emerson.edu*

EMMANUEL COLLEGE — E-2

Boston, MA 02115 — **(617) 735-9715; (617) 735-9801**

Full-time: 533 men, 1324 women	**Faculty:** 97; IIB, av$
Part-time: 47 men, 272 women	**Ph.D.s:** 82%
Graduate: 50 men, 210 women	**Student/Faculty:** 14 to 1
Year: semesters, summer session	**Tuition:** $34,670
Application Deadline: February 15	**Room & Board:** $13,315

Freshman Class: 6623 applied, 4006 accepted, 515 enrolled

SAT CR/M/W: 550/540/550 **ACT:** 23 **VERY COMPETITIVE**

Emmanuel College, founded by the Sisters of Notre Dame de Namur in 1919, is a coed, residential, Catholic liberal arts and sciences college located in the city of Boston. The College's beautiful 17-acre campus is neighbored by a world-class medical center, two major art museums and Fenway Park. Its unique location gives students the opportunity to explore real-world experiences through internships, research and strategic partnerships within the Longwood Medical and Academic Area and the city of Boston. There is one graduate school. The library contains 185,400 volumes, 1,883 audio/video tapes/CDs/DVDs, and subscribes to 2,100 periodicals including electronic. Computerized library services include interlibrary loans, database searching, Internet access, and Wi Fi capability. Special learning facilities include an art gallery and radio station. The 17-acre campus is in an urban area in Boston. Including any residence halls, there are 10 buildings.

Student Life: 58% of undergraduates are from Massachusetts. Others are from 29 states, 44 foreign countries, and Canada. 71% are White; 11% race unknown. The average age of freshmen is 18; all undergraduates, 20. 19% do not continue beyond their first year; 58% remain to graduate.

Housing: 1290 students can be accommodated in college housing, which includes coed dorms. In addition, there are special-interest houses. On-campus housing is guaranteed for all 4 years. 72% of students live on campus; of those, 75% remain on campus on weekends. Alcohol is not permitted. Upperclassmen may keep cars.

Activities: There are no fraternities or sororities. There are 48 groups on campus, including art, band, cheerleading, chess, choir, chorus, dance, debate, drama, ethnic, gay, honors, international, jazz band, literary magazine, musical theater, newspaper, orchestra, pep band, photography, political, professional, radio and TV, religious, social, social service, student government, and yearbook. Popular campus events include Moonlight Breakfast, Student Leadership Reception, Latin Explosion, Midnight Madness, and Family Weekend.

Sports: There are 8 intercollegiate sports for men and 8 for women, and 19 intramural sports for men and 19 for women. Facilities include The Jean Yawkey Center's gymnasium includes one NCAA regulation court or two full-size practice courts for volleyball and basketball with bleacher seating for 1200-1400. The Yawkey Center also includes a fitness center, locker rooms, a training room and Athletics Department offices. Additionally, a fitness center is housed in St. Joseph Hall. Roberto Clemente Field serves as the home field for the College's softball, men's and women's soccer and women's lacrosse teams, as well as the practice facility for men's and women's track and field.

Disabled Students: 90% of the campus is accessible. Facilities include wheelchair ramps, elevators, special parking, specially equipped restrooms, special class scheduling, lowered drinking fountains, lowered telephones, and special housing.

Services: Counseling and information services are available, as is tutoring in every subject. There is a reader service for the blind, and remedial math and writing.

Campus Safety and Security: Measures include 24-hour foot and vehicle patrol, emergency notification system, self-defense education, and security escort services. There are shuttle buses, emergency telephones, lighted pathways/sidewalks, controlled access to dorms/residences, 24-hour staffed residence hall desks and security office, closed-circuit surveillance in public areas, off-campus escorts, bike patrol, first responders program, a Rape Aggression Defense program, and a mass notification system.

Programs of Study: confers B.A., B.F.A. and B.S. degrees. Master's degrees are also awarded. Bachelor's degrees are awarded in AGRICULTURE (environmental studies), BIOLOGICAL SCIENCE (biochemistry, biology/biological science, biomathematics, and neurosciences), BUSINESS (accounting, business administration and management, and sports management), COMMUNICATIONS AND THE ARTS (communications, English, English literature, Spanish, and studio art), COMPUTER AND PHYSICAL SCIENCE (chemistry and mathematics), EDUCATION (elementary education and secondary education), ENGINEERING AND ENVIRONMENTAL DESIGN (graphic arts technology), HEALTH PROFESSIONS (art therapy and nursing), SOCIAL SCIENCE (American studies, counseling/psychology, developmental psychology, forensic studies, history, interdisciplinary studies, international studies, liberal arts/

general studies, philosophy, political science/government, psychology, religion, and sociology). English and communication, management, psychology, and the sciences have the largest enrollments.

Required: Students must complete a total of 128 credit hours with 40 to 48 in the major and a 2.0 GPA to graduate. Distribution requirements include 15 general ed courses, 10 to 17 courses for the major, and 5 to 7 elective or minor courses. A capstone experience and first-year seminar is required.

Special: There is cross-registration with Wheelock College, Simmons College, Massachusetts College of Art, Massachusetts College of Pharmacy, and Wentworth Institute of Technology. The college offers internships, study abroad, a Washington semester, work-study programs on campus and in Boston-area organizations, an accelerated degree program in business administration for nontraditional students, dual and student-designed majors, and prelaw/prehealth preparation. There are 14 national honor societies, a freshman honors program, and 100 departmental honors programs.

Faculty/Classroom: 40% of faculty are male; 60% are female. All teach undergraduates. No introductory courses are taught by graduate students. The average class size in an introductory lecture is 22; in a laboratory is 18; and in a regular course is 20.

Admissions: 60% of the 2013-2014 applicants were accepted. The SAT scores for the 2013-2014 freshman class were: Critical Reading--20% below 500, 57% between 500 and 599, 21% between 600 and 699, and 2% between 700 and 800; Math--24% below 500, 54% between 500 and 599, 20% between 600 and 699, and 2% between 700 and 800; Writing--19% below 500, 55% between 500 and 599, 24% between 600 and 699, and 2% between 700 and 800. The ACT scores were 10% below 21, 43% between 21 and 23, 26% between 24 and 26, 12% between 27 and 28, and 9% above 28. 43% of the current freshmen were in the top fifth of their class; 75% were in the top two fifths.

Requirements: The SAT or ACT is required. Applicants must be graduates of an accredited secondary school or have a GED. 16 academic credits are required, including 4 years of English, 3 years of math and social studies, 2 years of the same foreign language, and 2 years of lab science. An essay and an interview are encouraged but not required. AP credits are accepted. Important factors in the admissions decision are advanced placement or honors courses, recommendations by school officials, leadership record, parents or siblings attended your school, evidence of special talent, personality/intangible qualities, extracurricular activities record, recommendations by alumni, geographical diversity, and ability to finance college education.

Procedure: Freshmen are admitted fall and spring. Entrance exams should be taken by November of the senior year. There are early admissions and deferred admissions plans. Applications should be filed by February 15 for fall entry, along with a $60 fee. Notification is sent on a rolling basis. applicants were on the 2013 waiting list; were admitted. Applications are accepted online. Application fees are waived if application is completed online.

Transfer: 45 transfer students enrolled in 2012-2013. Students must submit essays, college and high school transcripts, and 2 letters of recommendation. They must be financially and academically eligible to return to the previously attended institution. 64 of 128 credits required for the bachelor's degree must be completed at Emmanuel College.

Visiting: There are regularly scheduled orientations for prospective students, consisting of 2 open houses and weekday and weekend information sessions. There are guides for informal visits, visitors may sit in on classes, and stay overnight. To schedule a visit, contact the Office of Admissions.

Financial Aid: In 2013-2014, 99% of all full-time freshmen and 95% of continuing full-time students received some form of financial aid. 84% of all full-time freshmen and 80% of continuing full-time students received need-based aid. The average freshman award was $26,601. 38% of undergraduate students work part-time. Average annual earnings from campus work are $1800. The average financial indebtedness of the 2013 graduate was $33,452. The FAFSA and the college's own financial statement are required. The priority date for freshman financial aid applications for fall entry is February 15.

International Students: There are 26 international students enrolled. The school actively recruits these students. They must take the TOEFL with a minimum score of 550 on the paper-based TOEFL (PBT) or 79 on the Internet-based version (iBT), or take ELS level 109 or the equivalent. They must also take the SAT or ACT.

Graduates: From July 1, 2012 to June 30, 2013, 421 bachelor's degrees were awarded. The most popular majors were management (21%), English (with communication studies) (17%), and biology (10%). 124 companies recruited on campus in 2012-2013. In an average class, 57% graduate in 5 years or less and 58% graduate in 6 years or less.

Admissions Contact: Sandra Robbins, Dean of Enrollment. E-Mail: *enroll@emmanuel.edu* Web: *www.emmanuel.edu*

ENDICOTT COLLEGE E-2

Beverly, MA 01915 **(978) 921-1000**
(800) 325-1114; (978) 232-2520

Full-time: 1015 men, 1516 women	**Faculty:** 93; IIB, av$
Part-time: 120 men, 169 women	**Ph.D.s:** 67%
Graduate: 426 men, 1258 women	**Student/Faculty:** 26 to 1
Year: 4-1-4, summer session	**Tuition:** $28,926
Application Deadline: February 15	**Room & Board:** $13,464
Freshman Class: 3675 applied, 2633 accepted, 629 enrolled	
SAT CR/M/W: 528/541/531 **ACT:** 23	**COMPETITIVE**

Located in Beverly, Massachusetts on 235 acres of oceanfront property, Endicott College offers doctorate, Master's and Bachelor degree programs in the professional and liberal arts. Founded in 1939, Endicott provides an education built upon a combination of theory and practice, which is tested through internships and work experience. The figures in the above capsule and in this profile are approximate. There are 8 undergraduate schools and one graduate school. In addition to regional accreditation, Endicott has baccalaureate program accreditation with NASAD, NCATE, and NLN. The library contains 120,285 volumes, 6,987 microform items, 2,160 audio/video tapes/CDs/DVDs, and subscribes to 80,725 periodicals including electronic. Computerized library services include interlibrary loans, database searching, Internet access, and Wi-Fi capability. Special learning facilities include an art gallery, radio station, TV station, State-of-the-Art Nursing Labs, Science Labs, Several Fine Art Studios (interior design, graphic design, photography, painting, ceramics, etc.) Recital Hall, Black Box Theater, Nature Trails, Private Beaches and Marshland, Student-Run Restaurant, Archives Museum. The 235-acre campus is in a suburban area 20 miles north of Boston. Including any residence halls, there are 53 buildings.

Student Life: 52% of undergraduates are from out of state, mostly the Northeast. Students are from 30 states, and 32 foreign countries. 80% are from public schools. 84% are White. The average age of freshmen is 18; all undergraduates, 20. 18% do not continue beyond their first year; 71% remain to graduate.

Housing: 1960 students can be accommodated in college housing, which includes single-sex and coed dorms, on-campus apartments, and off-campus apartments. In addition, there are honors houses, special-interest houses, single-parent, international, academic themed, and healthy living housing available. On-campus housing is guaranteed for the freshman year only, is available on a first-come, first-served basis, and is available on a lottery system for upperclassmen. 82% of students live on campus; of those, 81% remain on campus on weekends. Upperclassmen may keep cars.

Activities: There are no fraternities or sororities. There are 60 groups on campus, including Crew, Outdoor Adventure and Fitness, art, band, cheerleading, chorale, chorus, computers, dance, debate, drama, environmental, ethnic, film, gay, honors, international, jazz band, literary magazine, musical theater, newspaper, pep band, photography, political, professional, radio and TV, religious, Sailing, social, social service, student government, and yearbook. Popular campus events include Family/Homecoming Weekend, Annual Regatta, Festival of Lights, Performing Arts Events and Ice Skating on campus ponds.

Sports: There are 10 intercollegiate sports for men and 9 for women, and 9 intramural sports for men and 9 for women. Facilities include Outdoor facilities include a 2,200-seat multi-purpose turf stadium with an athletic support building, a new turf baseball/soccer field, 6 outdoor tennis courts, a separate softball stadium, and sailing/kayaking based out of Winter Island, Salem, MA, and cross country courses (5k and 8k). Indoor facilities include a 1400-seat gym with a racquetball, indoor tennis, and basketball courts, weight, fitness, and group fitness rooms, indoor track, rock climbing wall, and a field house.

Disabled Students: 95% of the campus is accessible. Facilities include wheelchair ramps, elevators, special parking, specially equipped restrooms, special class scheduling, and lowered drinking fountains.

Services: Counseling and information services are available, as is tutoring in every subject. There is a reader service for the blind.

Campus Safety and Security: Measures include 24-hour foot and vehicle patrol, emergency notification system, self-defense education, and security escort services. There are shuttle buses, emergency telephones, lighted pathways/sidewalks, controlled access to dorms/residences, License plate reecognition system, security cameras, property identification, crime prevention workshops, and alcohol safety programs.

Programs of Study: Endicott confers B.A., B.S. and B.F.A. degrees. Associate, master's, and doctoral degrees are also awarded. Bachelor's degrees are awarded in BIOLOGICAL SCIENCE (biotechnology), BUSINESS (accounting, business administration and management, finance, hospitality management services, hotel/motel and restaurant management, international business management, marketing management, and sports management), COMMUNICATIONS AND THE ARTS (communications, digital communications, English, fine arts, graphic design, photography, and studio art), COMPUTER AND PHYSICAL SCIENCE (applied mathematics, computer science, and mathematics), EDUCATION (athletic training, education, and physical education), ENGINEERING AND ENVIRONMENTAL DESIGN (bioengineering, environmental science, and interior design), HEALTH PROFESSIONS (art therapy and nursing), SOCIAL SCIENCE (criminal justice, history, international studies, liberal arts/general studies, political science/government, and psychology). Business management, hospitality management, and sport management have the largest enrollments.

Required: Undergraduate students must complete core requirements in the areas of writing, academic inquiry, and college transition. General education requirements include completing at least 3 credits in each of the College's eight thematic categories. A senior thesis and multiple internships are required of all undergraduates.

Special: Three internships are required of most undergraduates. Students may study abroad. There are accelerated degree programs in Business Administration, Hospitality Management, Liberal Studies, Liberal Studies/Education, Nursing and Psychology. Cross-registration available through NECCUM. Five-year bachelor/master's programs available. There are 12 national honor societies, a freshman honors program, and 1 departmental honors program.

Faculty/Classroom: 43% of faculty are male; 57% are female. 64% teach undergraduates. No introductory courses are taught by graduate students. The average class size in an introductory lecture is 18; in a laboratory is 9; and in a regular course is 18.

Admissions: 72% of the 2013-2014 applicants were accepted. The SAT scores for the 2013-2014 freshman class were: Critical Reading--32% below 500, 52% between 500 and 599, 15% between 600 and 699, and 1% between 700 and 800; Math--25% below 500, 53% between 500 and 599, 21% between 600 and 699, and 1% between 700 and 800; Writing--30% below 500, 52% between 500 and 599, 17% between 600 and 699, and 1% between 700 and 800.

Requirements: The SAT or ACT is recommended. Essays and two science and math recommendations are required for Nursing (including chemistry) and Athletic Training majors. AP and CLEP credits are accepted.

Procedure: Freshmen are admitted fall and spring. Entrance exams should be taken in fall of the senior year. Applications should be filed by February 15 for fall entry; December 15 for spring entry, along with a $50 fee. 40 applicants were on the 2013 waiting list. Applications are accepted online.

Transfer: 57 transfer students enrolled in 2012-2013. Official high school and college transcripts and a letter of recommendation are required. 24 of 124 credits required for the bachelor's degree must be completed at Endicott.

Visiting: There are regularly scheduled orientations for prospective students, Orientation includes testing, preregistration, and an introduction to general student life. There are guides for informal visits, visitors may sit in on classes, and stay overnight. To schedule a visit, contact Jamie Zietler at (978) 921-1000.

Financial Aid: In 2013-2014, 91% of all full-time freshmen and 88% of continuing full-time students received some form of financial aid. 64% of all full-time freshmen and 63% of continuing full-time students received need-based aid. 36% of undergraduate students work part-time. Average annual earnings from campus work are $1500. The average financial indebtedness of the 2013 graduate was $40,090. Endicott is a member of CSS. The FAFSA and the college's own financial statement are required. The priority date for freshman financial aid applications for fall entry is March 15.

International Students: There are 49 international students enrolled. The school actively recruits these students. They must take the TOEFL with a minimum score of 550 on the paper-based TOEFL (PBT) or 79 on the Internet-based version (iBT). They must also take the SAT or ACT.

Graduates: From July 1, 2012 to June 30, 2013, 541 bachelor's degrees were awarded. The most popular majors were business administration (17%), sport management (10%), and psychology (10%). 93 companies recruited on campus in 2012-2013. In an average class, 66% graduate in 4 years or less, 70% graduate in 5 years or less, and 71% graduate in 6 years or less. Of the 2012 graduating class, 20% were enrolled in graduate school within 6 months of graduation, and 80% were employed.

Admissions Contact: Thomas J. Redman, Vice President Admissions. E-Mail: *admissio@endicott.edu* Web: *www.endicott.edu*

FITCHBURG STATE UNIVERSITY C-2

Fitchburg, MA 01420 (978) 665-3140
(800) 705-9692; (978) 665-4540

Full-time: 1529 men, 1909 women	**Faculty:** 194
Part-time: 372 men, 429 women	**Ph.D.s:** 91%
Graduate: 578 men, 1846 women	**Student/Faculty:** 15 to 1
Year: semesters	**Tuition:** $8985 ($15,065)
Application Deadline: March 1	**Room & Board:** $8256

Freshman Class: 3819 applied, 2835 accepted, 801 enrolled
SAT CR/M/W: 490/450/480 **ACT:** 21 **COMPETITIVE**

Fitchburg State University, founded in 1894, is a comprehensive public university offering undergraduate, graduate and continuing education programs. In addition to regional accreditation, Fitchburg State has baccalaureate program accreditation with ABET and NCATE. The library contains 208,450 volumes, 125,344 microform items, 2,774 audio/video tapes/CDs/DVDs, and subscribes to 757 periodicals including electronic. Computerized library services include interlibrary loans, database searching, Internet access, and Wi-Fi capability. Special learning facilities include an art gallery and radio station. The 78-acre campus is in a suburban area 45 miles west of Boston. Including any residence halls, there are 35 buildings.

Student Life: 92% of undergraduates are from Massachusetts. Others are from 26 states, and 4 foreign countries. 80% are from public schools. 85% are White. The average age of freshmen is 18; all undergraduates, 22. 27% do not continue beyond their first year; 50% remain to graduate.

Housing: 1623 students can be accommodated in college housing, which includes coed dorms and on-campus apartments. In addition, there are special-interest houses. 59% of students commute. All students may keep cars.

Activities: 1% of men belong to 2 national fraternities; 3% of women belong to 3 national sororities. There are 60 groups on campus, including band, cheerleading, choir, chorus, computers, dance, drama, environmental, ethnic, film, gay, honors, international, jazz band, literary magazine, newspaper, photography, political, professional, radio and TV, religious, social, social service, and student government. Popular campus events include Falcon Fest, Rock the Block, and Center Stage Performing Arts Series.

Sports: There are 8 intercollegiate sports for men and 8 for women, and 10 intramural sports for men and 10 for women. Facilities include A 1,000-seat gym, an indoor/outdoor track, a weight room, varsity and intramural fields, a student union, volleyball, basketball, and racquetball courts, a swimming pool, and a dance studio.

Disabled Students: 80% of the campus is accessible. Facilities include wheelchair ramps, elevators, special parking, specially equipped restrooms, special class scheduling, lowered drinking fountains, lowered telephones, special housing, and an adaptive computer lab.

Services: Counseling and information services are available, as is tutoring in most subjects. There is a reader service for the blind, and remedial math, reading, and writing.

Campus Safety and Security: Measures include 24-hour foot and vehicle patrol, emergency notification system, self-defense education, and security escort services. There are shuttle buses, emergency telephones, lighted pathways/sidewalks, and controlled access to dorms/residences.

Programs of Study: Fitchburg State confers B.A., B.S. and B.S.Ed. degrees. Master's degrees are also awarded. Bachelor's degrees are awarded in BIOLOGICAL SCIENCE (biology/biological science, biotechnology, environmental biology, and neurosciences), BUSINESS (accounting, business administration and management, international business management, international economics, management science, and marketing management), COMMUNICATIONS AND THE ARTS (communications, dramatic arts, English, graphic design, literature, photography, theater management, and video), COMPUTER AND PHYSICAL SCIENCE (applied mathematics, computer science, earth science, and mathematics), EDUCATION (early childhood education, education, elementary education, industrial arts education, middle school education, secondary education, special education, technical education, and vocational education), ENGINEERING AND ENVIRONMENTAL DESIGN (architectural technology, construction technology, electrical/electronics engineering technology, energy management technology, industrial engineering technology, and manufacturing technology), HEALTH PROFESSIONS (exercise science, health science, and nursing), SOCIAL SCIENCE (cognitive science, criminal justice, developmental psychology, economics, geography, history, human services, industrial and organizational psychology, interdisciplinary studies, political science/government, prelaw, psychology, and sociology). Business administration, and nursing have the largest enrollments.

Required: All students must complete a minimum of 120 credit hours with a GPA of at least 2.0 overall and in the major (some majors require a higher GPA). Core coursework is required in the arts, science/math and technology, citizenship and the world, and global diversity. Also required are 2 introductory semesters of writing.

Special: Students may cross-register at any other Massachusetts state universities. Internships in a variety of fields, study abroad in 9 countries, B.A. B.S. degrees, dual majors, and a student-designed interdisciplinary studies major are offered. There are 13 national honor societies, a freshman honors program, and 9 departmental honors programs.

Faculty/Classroom: 52% of faculty are male; 48% are female. All teach undergraduates. No introductory courses are taught by graduate students. The average class size in an introductory lecture is 27; in a laboratory is 15; and in a regular course is 24.

Admissions: 74% of the 2013-2014 applicants were accepted. The SAT scores for the 2013-2014 freshman class were: Critical Reading--48% below 500, 40% between 500 and 599, 11% between 600 and 699, and 1% between 700 and 800; Math--40% below 500, 46% between 500 and 599, 14% between 600 and 699, and 1% between 700 and 800; Writing-

-51% below 500, 39% between 500 and 599, 9% between 600 and 699, and 1% between 700 and 800. The ACT scores were 41% below 21, 37% between 21 and 23, 11% between 24 and 26, 7% between 27 and 28, and 4% above 28.

Requirements: The SAT or ACT is required. Applicants should be graduates of accredited high schools or have the GED. Secondary preparation should include 4 years of English, 3 years each of math and liberal arts or phys ed, and 2 years each of a foreign language, social studies, including U.S. history, and science. A GPA of 2.0 is required. AP and CLEP credits are accepted. Important factors in the admissions decision are advanced placement or honors courses, leadership record, and extracurricular activities record.

Procedure: Freshmen are admitted fall and spring. Entrance exams should be taken in the junior or senior year. There are deferred admissions and rolling admissions plans. Applications should be filed by March 1 for fall entry; December 1 for spring entry, along with a $25 fee. Notification is sent on a rolling basis. Applications are accepted online.

Transfer: 355 transfer students enrolled in 2012-2013. Applicants should have a minimum GPA of 2.0 in at least 12 credits of transferable college work. 45 of 120 credits required for the bachelor's degree must be completed at Fitchburg State.

Visiting: There are regularly scheduled orientations for prospective students, tours of the campus and residence halls, admissions/financial aid information, and academic program advising. There are guides for informal visits and visitors may sit in on classes. To schedule a visit, contact the Admissions Office.

Financial Aid: The FAFSA is required. The deadline for filing freshman financial aid applications for fall entry is March 1.

International Students: There are 13 international students enrolled. The school actively recruits these students. They must take the TOEFL with a minimum score of 550 on the paper-based TOEFL (PBT) or 79 on the Internet-based version (iBT). They must also take the SAT or ACT.

Graduates: From July 1, 2012 to June 30, 2013, 818 bachelor's degrees were awarded. The most popular majors were communications (14%) and business administration (14%). In an average class, 24% graduate in 4 years or less, 43% graduate in 5 years or less, and 50% graduate in 6 years or less. Of the 2012 graduating class, 10% were enrolled in graduate school within 6 months of graduation.

Admissions Contact: Elaine Lapomardo, Director of Admissions. E-Mail: *admissions@fitchburgstate.edu* Web: *www.fitchburgstate.edu/admissions*

FRAMINGHAM STATE UNIVERSITY D-2

Framingham, MA 01701 **(508) 626-4500; (508) 626-4017**

Full-time: 1388 men, 2416 women	**Faculty:** 176; IIA, -$
Part-time: 291 men, 395 women	**Ph.D.s:** 87%
Graduate: 397 men, 1619 women	**Student/Faculty:** 16 to 1
Year: semesters, summer session	**Tuition:** $7580 ($13,660)
Application Deadline: February 15	**Room & Board:** $9170
Freshman Class: 5433 applied, 2807 accepted, 826 enrolled	
SAT CR/M/W: 518/526/510 **ACT:** 22	**COMPETITIVE**

Framingham State University, founded in 1839, is a comprehensive public institution offering degree programs based on a liberal arts foundation that includes unique career programs. The figures in the above capsule and in this profile are approximate. There is one graduate school. In addition to regional accreditation, FSU has baccalaureate program accreditation with ADA and NLN. The library contains 216,902 volumes, 4,288 audio/video tapes/CDs/DVDs, and subscribes to 163 periodicals including electronic. Computerized library services include interlibrary loans, database searching, Internet access, and Wi-Fi capability. Special learning facilities include an art gallery, planetarium, radio station, Greenhouse, TV studio, Early Childhood Demonstration Lab, Curriculum Library, and the McAuliffe Challenger Learning Center. The 73-acre campus is in a suburban area 20 miles west of Boston. Including any residence halls, there are 22 buildings.

Student Life: 95% of undergraduates are from Massachusetts. Others are from states, 21 foreign countries, and Canada. 75% are White. The average age of freshmen is 18; all undergraduates, 22.

Housing: 1931 students can be accommodated in college housing, which includes single-sex and coed dorms. On-campus housing is available on a first-come and first-served basis. 52% of students live on campus; of those, 67% remain on campus on weekends. Alcohol is not permitted. Upperclassmen may keep cars.

Activities: There are no fraternities or sororities. There are 50 groups on campus, including art, cheerleading, chorale, chorus, computers, dance, drama, ethnic, gay, honors, international, literary magazine, musical theater, newspaper, political, professional, radio and TV, religious, social, social service, and student government. Popular campus events include Sandbox Festival, Super Weekends and Semi-Formal Dance.

Sports: There are 6 intercollegiate sports for men and 7 for women, and 9 intramural sports for men and 9 for women. Facilities include Athletic and Recreation Center, Gym, and a Student Center. In addition, there is an all-weather turf field for soccer, football, field hockey, and intramural sports available on lower campus fields.

Disabled Students: 95% of the campus is accessible. Facilities include wheelchair ramps, elevators, special parking, specially equipped restrooms, special class scheduling, lowered drinking fountains, and lowered telephones.

Services: Counseling and information services are available, as is tutoring in most subjects. There is a reader service for the blind, and remedial math, reading, and writing. The Center for Academic Support and Advising (CASA) offers free tutoring in writing, math, and reading. Subject tutoring may be arranged for an hourly fee. FSU also offers Supplemental Instruction attached to a variety of courses.

Campus Safety and Security: Measures include 24-hour foot and vehicle patrol, emergency notification system, self-defense education, and security escort services. There are shuttle buses, emergency telephones, lighted pathways/sidewalks, , security cameras, residence hall security and card access.

Programs of Study: FSU confers B.A., B.S. and B.S.Ed. degrees. Master's degrees are also awarded. Bachelor's degrees are awarded in BIOLOGICAL SCIENCE (biology/biological science and nutrition), BUSINESS (business administration and management and fashion merchandising), COMMUNICATIONS AND THE ARTS (art history and appreciation, communications, English, modern language, and studio art), COMPUTER AND PHYSICAL SCIENCE (chemistry, computer science, and mathematics), EDUCATION (business education, early childhood education, and elementary education), ENGINEERING AND ENVIRONMENTAL DESIGN (environmental science), HEALTH PROFESSIONS (nursing), SOCIAL SCIENCE (criminology, economics, family/consumer studies, fashion design and technology, food science, geography, history, interdisciplinary studies, political science/government, psychology, sociology, and textiles and clothing). Business administration, communication arts, and psychology have the largest enrollments.

Required: The university's goal-based general education model includes writing, math, language, literature or philosophy, visual or performing arts, physical science, life science, historical studies, social and behavioral sciences, forces in the United States, study of Constitutions, gender, class, and race; and non-Western studies. Every student must take 12 general education courses and fulfill all required goals. A total of 128 credits (32 courses), including 40 to 68 credits in the major, and a 2.0 GPA are required to graduate.

Special: The university offers a 2-3 preengineering program in cooperation with the University of Massachusetts at Amherst, Lowell, and Dartmouth. Study abroad in 8 countries, a Washington semester, and various internships are available. Pass/fail options are limited to 2 courses. There are 11 national honor societies, a freshman honors program, and 8 departmental honors programs.

Faculty/Classroom: 42% of faculty are male; 58% are female. All teach undergraduates. No introductory courses are taught by graduate students. The average class size in a regular course is 23.

Admissions: 52% of the 2013-2014 applicants were accepted. The SAT scores for the 2013-2014 freshman class were: Critical Reading--40% below 500, 47% between 500 and 599, 12% between 600 and 699, and 1% between 700 and 800; Math--33% below 500, 52% between 500 and 599, 14% between 600 and 699, and 1% between 700 and 800; Writing--41% below 500, 48% between 500 and 599, and 11% between 600 and 699.

Requirements: The SAT is required. Applicants must have a high school diploma or the GED. Secondary preparation must total 16 college-preparatory credits, including 4 years of English, 3 each of math and science (2 with lab), and 2 each of foreign language and social science. The required 2 years of electives may include additional academic subjects or art, music, or computer courses. Prospective studio art majors must submit a portfolio. A GPA of 3.0 is required. AP and CLEP credits are accepted. Important factors in the admissions decision are advanced placement or honors courses, leadership record, and recommendations by school officials.

Procedure: Freshmen are admitted fall and spring. Entrance exams should be taken In the spring of the junior year or fall of the senior year. There are early admissions, deferred admissions, and rolling admissions plans. Applications should be filed by February 15 for fall entry; December 1 for spring entry, along with a $45 fee. Notification is sent on a rolling basis. Applications are accepted online.

Transfer: 475 transfer students enrolled in 2012-2013. Applicants with more than 24 college credits must present a college GPA of at least 2.5; those with fewer than 24 credits must also meet freshman admission requirements. Official transcripts must be submitted from all colleges previously attended at the time of application. 32 of 128 credits required for the bachelor's degree must be completed at FSU.

Visiting: There are regularly scheduled orientations for prospective students, Orientations include campus tours, advising, and information sessions (majors, computing, campus life and resources). There are guides for informal visits and visitors may sit in on classes. To schedule a visit, contact The Office of Undergraduate Admissions.

Financial Aid: In 2013-2014, 84% of all full-time freshmen and 67% of continuing full-time students received some form of financial aid. 53% of all full-time freshmen and 47% of continuing full-time students received need-based aid. The average freshman award was $6,800. Need-based scholarships or need-based grants averaged $2,005; need-based self-help aid (loans and jobs) averaged $4,020; and other non-need-based awards and non-need-based scholarships averaged $2,208. 60% of undergraduate students work part-time. Average annual earnings from campus work are $1050. The average financial indebtedness of the 2013 graduate was $19,300. FSU is a member of CSS. The FAFSA is required. The priority date for freshman financial aid applications for fall entry is March 1.

International Students: They must take the TOEFL with a minimum score of 550 on the paper-based TOEFL (PBT) or 79 on the Internet-based version (iBT). They must also take the SAT or ACT.

Graduates: From July 1, 2012 to June 30, 2013, 703 bachelor's degrees were awarded. The most popular majors were business and management (16%), family and consumer sciences (13%), and social sciences (12%). 150 companies recruited on campus in 2012-2013. Of the 2012 graduating class, 20% were enrolled in graduate school within 6 months of graduation, and 93% were employed.

Admissions Contact: Shayna Eddy, Director of Undergraduate Admissions. E-Mail: *admissions@framingham.edu* Web: *www.framingham.edu*

FRANKLIN W. OLIN COLLEGE OF ENGINEERING D-2

Needham, MA 02492-1200 **781-292-2222; 781-292-2210**

Full-time: 177 men, 178 women
Part-time: n/av
Graduate: n/av
Year: semesters
Application Deadline: January 1
Freshman Class: 785 applied, 130 accepted, 82 enrolled
SAT CR/M/W: 730/770/710 **ACT:** 34 **SPECIAL**

Faculty: 38
Ph.D.s: 100%
Student/Faculty: 9 to 1
Tuition: $42,500
Room & Board: $15,000

Olin College is an undergraduate engineering institution that has been exploring innovative approaches to engineering education since its founding in 1997. Olin's dual mission is to offer an innovative engineering program to talented undergraduate students, and to play a leading role in the transformation of engineering education in the U.S. and abroad. Olin is increasingly recognized as a leader in engineering education reform for its interdisciplinary, hands-on curriculum and distinctive learning culture. There is one undergraduate school. In addition to regional accreditation, Olin College of Engineering has baccalaureate program accreditation with ABET. The library contains 15,798 volumes, 10 microform items, and 1,496 audio/video tapes/CDs/DVDs. Computerized library services include interlibrary loans, database searching, Internet access, and Wi-Fi capability. The 75-acre campus is in a suburban area 12 miles west of Boston. Including any residence halls, there are 10 buildings.

Student Life: 85% of undergraduates are from out of state, mostly the West. Students are from 39 states, 18 foreign countries, and Canada. 52% are White; 17% Asian American; 11% race unknown. The average age of freshmen is 18; all undergraduates, 20. 4% do not continue beyond their first year; 99% remain to graduate.

Housing: 352 students can be accommodated in college housing, which includes coed dorms. On-campus housing is guaranteed for all 4 years. All students may keep cars.

Activities: There are no fraternities or sororities. There are 50 groups on campus, including art, band, chess, chorus, computers, dance, drama, environmental, film, gay, jazz band, literary magazine, orchestra, photography, political, professional, religious, social, social service, student government, and yearbook. Popular campus events include Candidates' Weekend, Family Weekend, SAC Carnival, and EXPO.

Sports: There is no sports program at Olin College of Engineering.

Disabled Students: All of the campus is accessible. Facilities include wheelchair ramps, elevators, special parking, specially equipped restrooms, special class scheduling, lowered drinking fountains, lowered telephones, and special housing.

Services: Counseling and information services are available, as is tutoring in every subject.

Campus Safety and Security: Measures include 24-hour foot and vehicle patrol and emergency notification system. There are shuttle buses, emergency telephones, lighted pathways/sidewalks, and controlled access to dorms/residences.

Programs of Study: Olin College of Engineering confers B.S. degrees. Bachelor's degrees are awarded in ENGINEERING AND ENVIRONMENTAL DESIGN (electrical and computer engineering, engineering, and mechanical engineering).

Required: All students must complete a minimum of 120 credits, and must maintain a minimum cumulative GPA of 2.0 in order to graduate from Olin. Students must complete their program specific graduation requirements, as well as general requirements including 46 credits in Engineering, 30 credits in Math and Science, and 28 credits in Arts, Humanities, Social Sciences, and Entrepreneurship.

Special: Students may cross-register for courses at Babson College, Brandeis University, and Wellesley College. Many students choose to study away from Olin in an array of programs inside and outside of the US. All students complete an ambitious year-long culminating capstone that engages interdisciplinary student teams in significant design problems with realistic constraints for an external partner and prepares students for work in their chosen careers.

Faculty/Classroom: 58% of faculty are male; 42% are female. All teach undergraduates. No introductory courses are taught by graduate students. The average class size in an introductory lecture is 20; in a laboratory is 15; and in a regular course is 20.

Admissions: 17% of the 2013-2014 applicants were accepted. The SAT scores for the 2013-2014 freshman class were: Critical Reading--5% between 500 and 599, 24% between 600 and 699, and 71% between 700 and 800; Math--9% between 600 and 699, and 91% between 700 and 800; Writing--1% between 500 and 599, 41% between 600 and 699, and 58% between 700 and 800. The ACT scores were 8% between 27 and 28, and 92% above 28.

Requirements: The SAT or ACT is required. The ACT Optional Writing test is also required. The SAT with Subject tests in math and science, or the ACT with Writing are required. In addition, a high school profile with a counselor's letter of recommendation and letters of recommendation from a core math or science teacher and one other teacher, as well as two essays (of 300 and 500 words in length) are required. All finalists for admission must have an on-campus interview.

Procedure: Freshmen are admitted fall. Entrance exams should be taken by December of the senior year. There is a deferred admissions plan. Applications should be filed by January 1 for fall entry. The fall 2013 application fee was $80. Notifications are sent March 21. 41 applicants were on the 2013 waiting list; 11 were admitted. Applications are accepted online.

Transfer: Transfer students are subject to the same requirements and application process as first-time students.

Visiting: There are guides for informal visits, visitors may sit in on classes, and stay overnight.

Financial Aid: In 2013-2014, 100% of all full-time freshmen and 100% of continuing full-time students received some form of financial aid. 71% of all full-time freshmen and 44% of continuing full-time students received need-based aid. The average freshman award was $31,193. Need-based scholarships or need-based grants averaged $20,539 ($32,770 maximum); need-based self-help aid (loans and jobs) averaged $2,906 ($3,500 maximum); and other non-need-based awards and non-need-based scholarships averaged $21,000 ($22,000 maximum). The average financial indebtedness of the 2013 graduate was $16,092. The FAFSA is required. The priority date for freshman financial aid applications for fall entry is February 15.

International Students: There are 23 international students enrolled. They must also take the SAT or ACT.

Graduates: From July 1, 2012 to June 30, 2013, 76 bachelor's degrees were awarded. The most popular majors were engineering (47%), mechanical engineering (37%), and electrical and computer engineering (37%). 50 companies recruited on campus in 2012-2013. In an average class, 93% graduate in 4 years or less, 97% graduate in 5 years or less, and 99% graduate in 6 years or less. Of the 2012 graduating class, 11% were enrolled in graduate school within 6 months of graduation, and 82% were employed.

Admissions Contact: Charles Nolan, Dean of Admission. E-Mail: *info@olin.edu* Web: *www.olin.edu*

GORDON COLLEGE E-1

Wenham, MA 01984 **(978) 867-4221**
(866) 464-6736; (978) 867-4682

Full-time: 635 men, 1034 women
Part-time: 16 men, 22 women
Graduate: 74 men, 328 women
Year: semesters, summer session
Application Deadline: August 1
Freshman Class: n/av
SAT CR/M/W: 582/570/575 **ACT:** 26 **VERY COMPETITIVE+**

Faculty: 93; IIB, av$
Ph.D.s: 83%
Student/Faculty: 14 to 1
Tuition: $33,230
Room & Board: $9430

Gordon College is a distinctive blend---a multidenominational Christian liberal arts institution with a strong residential community and a splendid location, near the intellectual hub of Boston and the shoreline of Cape Ann. It has a strong heritage of community service and a long tradition of international education. The College offers 38 majors and 42 concentrations in the arts and sciences, with graduate programs in education and music education. Its overarching mission is to graduate men and women distinguished by intellectual maturity and Christian character, committed to lives of service and prepared for leadership worldwide. As a Christian institution whose students, faculty and staff represent over 40 denominations, Gordon retains a commitment to integrating faith and learning, a heritage once embraced by many esteemed New England institutions. This commitment is exemplified by Gordon's Center for Faith and Inquiry. Gordon also remains committed to the power of a liberal arts education to hone qualities most sought by employers---the ability to think holistically, reason analytically, communicate persuasively and---even more importantly---to act morally. Consistent with its founding vision, Gordon's identity and reach are worldwide. Through its own and affiliated programs, Gordon offers study options around the world, from an urban programs in nearby Boston and Lynn to Italy, Romania, France and China. The College also has a long history of humanitarian service both domestically and abroad, which is evident in high student participation in spring, summer and winter break service trips, and in service-learning and internship programs. Many of these opportunities have led to careers that blend compassion with the high-level business and professional skills. Along with its affiliations with the Christian College Consortium, the Council for Christian Colleges and Universities, and the Council of Independent Colleges, Gordon is actively involved with the Annapolis Group, an alliance of 130 of the nation's leading independent liberal arts colleges including Cornell, Wellesley, Williams, Pomona, Claremont and Scripps. Gordon's president and provost regularly join other presidents and chief academic officers to share best practices, seek higher levels of excellence, and advance the cause of liberal arts education. Gordon's location just north of Boston allows faculty ready access to vibrant intellectual and research communities. For instance, biology professor Craig Story has been involved with colleagues at M.I.T. in groundbreaking microengraving research, social work professor Judith Oleson is a respected player in a movement to promote peace and reconciliation studies. Biblical studies professor Marvin Wilson's public leadership and books on interfaith understanding have been recognized internationally; biology professor Dorothy Boorse is a frequent contributor to forums on environmental issues, such as Climate Week NYC, and has testified before Congress. These connections, in which Gordon faculty are valued contributors to major cultural conversations and research have paved the way for excellent internship, graduate school, and career opportunities for Gordon students. About 68 percent of current Gordon students aim to pursue graduate studies. Within five years of graduation, 50 percent of them will have either earned graduate degrees or be enrolled in graduate programs, and within two years 87 percent of will have entered full- or part-time work in their fields. Currently, Gordon graduates are pursuing or have received advanced degrees from institutions including Harvard Medical School, M.I.T., Yale, Tufts, Columbia, Princeton and the University of Notre Dame. There is 1 undergraduate school and 2 graduate schools. In addition to regional accreditation, Gordon has baccalaureate program accreditation with CSWE, NASDTEC, and NASM. The library contains 155,737 volumes, 32,076 microform items, 6,005 audio/video tapes/CDs/DVDs, and subscribes to 1,450 periodicals including electronic. Computerized library services include interlibrary loans, database searching, Internet access, and Wi-Fi capability. Special learning facilities include an art gallery and radio station. The 454-acre campus is in a suburban area 25 miles north of Boston. Including any residence halls, there are 38 buildings.

Student Life: 67% of undergraduates are from out of state, mostly the Northeast. Students are from 43 states, 41 foreign countries, and Canada. 77% are White. 96% are Protestant. The average age of freshmen is 18; all undergraduates, 20. 17% do not continue beyond their first year; 71% remain to graduate.

Housing: 1440 students can be accommodated in college housing, which includes single-sex dorms, on-campus apartments, and married student housing. In addition, there are special-interest houses. On-campus housing is guaranteed for all 4 years. 89% of students live on campus; of those, 70% remain on campus on weekends. Alcohol is not permitted. All students may keep cars.

Activities: There are no fraternities or sororities. There are 120 groups on campus, including art, band, cheerleading, choir, chorale, dance, debate, drama, environmental, ethnic, Extensive options for student outreaches and off-campus ministries, film, honors, international, jazz band, literary magazine, musical theater, newspaper, opera, orchestra, photography, political, professional, radio and TV, religious, social, social service, student government, symphony, and yearbook. Popular campus events include Golden Goose, Gordon Globes, Midnight Madness, 255 Grapevine, Senior Formal, Gordon Has Talent, and Christmas at Gordon.

Sports: There are 9 intercollegiate sports for men and 11 for women, and 15 intramural sports for men and 15 for women. Facilities include a gym, weight rooms, tennis courts, athletic fields, a training room, indoor swimming pool, climbing wall, racquetball courts, aerobics room, ski/running trails, outdoor ropes course, sauna, indoor walking track, outdoor track and field facilities.

Disabled Students: 80% of the campus is accessible. Facilities include wheelchair ramps, elevators, special parking, specially equipped restrooms, special class scheduling, lowered drinking fountains, lowered telephones, special housing.

Services: Counseling and information services are available, as is tutoring in most subjects, Math, writing, and core science. There is a reader service for the blind, and remedial math, reading, and writing. Writing and academic support centers. Student tutors in many subjects.

Campus Safety and Security: Measures include 24-hour foot and vehicle patrol, emergency notification system, self-defense education, and security escort services. There are shuttle buses, emergency telephones, lighted pathways/sidewalks, controlled access to dorms/residences, Gated entrance.

Programs of Study: Gordon confers B.A., B.S. and B.Mu. degrees. Master's degrees are also awarded. Bachelor's degrees are awarded in BIOLOGICAL SCIENCE (biology/biological science), BUSINESS (accounting, banking and finance, business administration and management, finance, and recreation and leisure services), COMMUNICATIONS AND THE ARTS (art, communications, dramatic arts, English, French, German, languages, linguistics, music, music performance, and Spanish), COMPUTER AND PHYSICAL SCIENCE (chemistry, computer science, mathematics, and physics), EDUCATION (early childhood education, elementary education, middle school education, music education, secondary education, and special education), HEALTH PROFESSIONS (physical therapy), SOCIAL SCIENCE (biblical studies, economics, history, international studies, philosophy, political science/government, psychology, social work, sociology, and youth ministry). Biology, physics, Christian Ministries, education, economics, music are the strongest academically. Psychology, business administration, and English have the largest enrollments.

Required: All students must demonstrate competency in writing, speech, and foreign language. The core curriculum consists of 8 credits in biblical studies, 8 in social and behavioral sciences, 8 in natural sciences, math, and computer science, 6 in humanities, and 4 each in fine arts and freshman seminar. A total of 124 credits is required for graduation, with 18 or more in the major and a minimum GPA of 2.0.

Special: Gordon offers cooperative education, internships, and cross-registration with other institutions in the Northeast Consortium of Colleges and Universities in Massachusetts. There is a 3-2 engineering program with the University of Southern California. B.A.-B.S. degrees, dual majors, student-designed majors, nondegree study, and pass/fail options are available. Off-campus study opportunities include a Washington semester, the Christian College Consortium Visitor Program, the LaVida Wilderness Expedition, and study abroad in Europe, the Middle East, and China. There are 7 national honor societies, a freshman honors program, and 13 departmental honors programs.

Faculty/Classroom: 54% of faculty are male; 46% are female. All teach and do research. No introductory courses are taught by graduate students.

Admissions: The SAT scores for the 2013-2014 freshman class were: Critical Reading--14% below 500, 43% between 500 and 599, 34% between 600 and 699, and 9% between 700 and 800; Math--20% below 500, 43% between 500 and 599, 29% between 600 and 699, and 8% between 700 and 800; Writing--18% below 500, 41% between 500 and 599, 32% between 600 and 699, and 9% between 700 and 800. The ACT scores were 15% above 28.

Requirements: The SAT or ACT is required. Applicants must graduate from an accredited secondary school or have a GED. A minimum of 17 Carnegie units is required, including 4 English courses and 2 courses each in math, science, and social studies. Foreign language is a recommended elective. A personal statement, a personal reference, and an interview are required. Music majors must audition. Art majors must submit a portfolio for acceptance to the program. AP credits are accepted. Important factors in the admissions decision are advanced placement or honors courses, leadership record, and personality/intangible qualities.

Procedure: Freshmen are admitted fall and spring. Entrance exams should be taken in the spring of the junior year and the fall of the senior year. There are early decision, early admissions, deferred admissions, and rolling admissions plans. Early decision applications should be filed by November 1; regular applications, by August 1 for fall entry; and November 1 for spring entry, along with a $50 fee. Notification of early decision is sent December 1; regular decision, January 1. 13 early decision candidates were accepted for the 2013-2014 class. 56 applicants were on the 2013 waiting list; 35 were admitted. Applications are accepted online.

Transfer: 60 transfer students enrolled in 2012-2013. Applicants must have a minimum GPA of 2.00. College transcripts, high school transcripts, and SAT or ACT scores if the applicant has completed less than 1 year of full-time study, an interview, and personal and academic references are required. 32 of 124 credits required for the bachelor's degree must be completed at Gordon.

Visiting: There are regularly scheduled orientations for prospective students, Consisting of numerous open house programs throughout the fall, winter, and spring. There are guides for informal visits, visitors may sit in on classes, and stay overnight. To schedule a visit, contact Alyssa Myhren at (866) 464-6736.

Financial Aid: In 2013-2014, 97% of all full-time freshmen and 96% of continuing full-time students received some form of financial aid. 74% of all full-time freshmen and 72% of continuing full-time students received need-based aid. The average freshman award was $21,586. Need-based scholarships or need-based grants averaged $17,449; need-based self-help aid (loans and jobs) averaged $4,992; and other non-need-based awards and non-need-based scholarships averaged $12,964. 79% of undergraduate students work part-time. Average annual earnings from campus work are $803. The average financial indebtedness of the 2013 graduate was $37,662. Gordon is a member of CSS. The FAFSA is required. The priority date for freshman financial aid applications for fall entry is March 1. The deadline for filing freshman financial aid applications for fall entry is March 1.

International Students: There are 83 international students enrolled. The school actively recruits these students. They must take the TOEFL with a minimum score of 85 on the Internet-based version (iBT), or take the SAT or ACT. They must also take the SAT or ACT.

Graduates: From July 1, 2012 to June 30, 2013, 402 bachelor's degrees were awarded. The most popular majors were education (11%), psychology (10%), and social sciences (9%). In an average class, 59% graduate in 4 years or less and 71% graduate in 6 years or less. Of the 2012 graduating class, 14% were enrolled in graduate school within 6 months of graduation, and 79% were employed.

Admissions Contact: Britt Carlson, Executive Director of Admissions. E-Mail: *admissions@gordon.edu* Web: *www.gordon.edu/admissions*

HAMPSHIRE COLLEGE B-2

Amherst, MA 01002 **(413) 559-5471; (413) 559-5631**

Full-time: 645 men, 846 women	**Faculty:** 121; IIB, +$
Part-time: n/av	**Ph.D.s:** 93%
Graduate: n/av	**Student/Faculty:** 12 to 1
Year: 4-1-4	**Tuition:** $46,290
Application Deadline:	**Room & Board:** $12,030
Freshman Class: n/av	

MOST COMPETITIVE

Hampshire College, founded in 1965, is a private institution offering a liberal arts education with an emphasis on independent research, creative work, and multidisciplinary study. The library contains 124,710 volumes, 4,534 microform items, 8,727 audio/video tapes/CDs/DVDs, and subscribes to 731 periodicals including electronic. Computerized library services include interlibrary loans, database searching, Internet access, and Wi-Fi capability. Special learning facilities include an art gallery, radio station, multimedia center, farm center, music and dance studios, optics lab, electronics shop, integrated greenhouse and aquaculture facility, fabrication shop, and performing arts center. The 800-acre campus is in a rural area in Amherst, Massachusetts. Including any residence halls, there are 28 buildings.

Student Life: 80% of undergraduates are from out of state, mostly the Northeast. Students are from 46 states, and Canada. 65% are from public schools. 66% are White. The average age of freshmen is 18; all undergraduates, 20. 19% do not continue beyond their first year; 66% remain to graduate.

Housing: 1400 students can be accommodated in college housing, which includes single-sex and coed dorms and on-campus apartments. In addition, there are special-interest houses, We have 3 living and learning communities plus various themed housing options. On-campus housing is guaranteed for all 4 years. All students may keep cars.

Activities: There are no fraternities or sororities. There are 80 groups on campus, including art, chorus, computers, dance, drama, environmental, ethnic, film, gay, international, literary magazine, musical theater, newspaper, orchestra, photography, political, radio and TV, religious, social, social service, and student government. Popular campus events include Hampshire Halloween, and Spring Jam,.

Sports: There are 3 intercollegiate sports for men and 3 for women, and 18 intramural sports for men and 18 for women. Facilities include 2 multipurpose sports centers housing a glass-enclosed swimming pool, a 12,000-square-foot playing floor, a 30-foot climbing wall, a weight-lifting area, 4 indoor tennis courts, and a jogging track. Other facilities include soccer fields, 10 outdoor tennis courts, 2 softball diamonds, and a 2-mile nature trail.

Disabled Students: 90% of the campus is accessible. Facilities include wheelchair ramps, elevators, special parking, specially equipped restrooms, special class scheduling, lowered drinking fountains, lowered telephones. The college provides a variety of support services to meet individual special needs.

Services: Counseling and information services are available, as is tutoring in most subjects. There is a reader service for the blind. Including an advising center, a writing and reading program, and a lab quantitative skills program.

Campus Safety and Security: Measures include 24-hour foot and vehicle patrol and security escort services. There are lighted pathways/sidewalks, an EMT on-call program, and dorm doors accessible by students only.

Programs of Study: Hampshire confers B.A. degrees. Bachelor's degrees are awarded in AGRICULTURE (agriculture and animal science), BIOLOGICAL SCIENCE (biology/biological science, botany, ecology, marine biology, nutrition, and physiology), COMMUNICATIONS AND THE ARTS (art history and appreciation, communications, comparative literature, creative writing, dance, dramatic arts, film arts, fine arts, journalism, linguistics, literature, media arts, music, performing arts, photography, and video), COMPUTER AND PHYSICAL SCIENCE (chemistry, computer science, geology, mathematics, physics, and science), EDUCATION (education), ENGINEERING AND ENVIRONMENTAL DESIGN (architecture, environmental design, and environmental science), HEALTH PROFESSIONS (health science and premedicine), SOCIAL SCIENCE (African studies, African American studies, American studies, anthropology, Asian/Oriental studies, cognitive science, crosscultural studies, economics, family/consumer studies, geography, history, humanities, international relations, international studies, Judaic studies, Latin American studies, law, Middle Eastern studies, peace studies, philosophy, political science/government, psychology, religion, sociology, urban studies, and women's studies). Film/photography/video is the strongest academically. Social sciences has the largest enrollment.

Required: All students must complete 3 divisions of study. In Division I: Basic Studies, students complete courses in cognitive science, humanities, arts and cultural studies, natural science, interdisciplinary arts, and social science and must complete 2 courses or the Division I exam project. In Division II: Concentration, students explore their field or fields of emphasis through individually designed internships or field studies. In Division III: Advanced Studies, students complete a major independent study project centered on a specific topic, question, or idea. Students must also partcipate in service to the college or the surrounding community and consider some aspect of their work from a non-Western perspective.

Special: Cross-registration is possible with other members of the Five College Consortium (Amherst College, the University of Massachusetts, Smith College, and Mount Holyoke). Internships, multidisciplinary dual majors, and study abroad (in the ISEP program, Tibetan Center, or a Costa Rica semester) are offered. All majors are student-designed. Students may complete their programs in fewer than 4 years.

Faculty/Classroom: 46% of faculty are male; 54% are female. All teach undergraduates. No introductory courses are taught by graduate students. The average class size in a regular course is 14.

Admissions: The SAT scores for the 2013-2014 freshman class were: Critical Reading--5% below 500, 20% between 500 and 599, 47% between 600 and 699, and 27% between 700 and 800; Math--14% below 500, 35% between 500 and 599, 41% between 600 and 699, and 10% between 700 and 800; Writing--8% below 500, 27% between 500 and 599, 46% between 600 and 699, and 19% between 700 and 800.

Requirements: Applicants must submit all transcripts from 9th grade on or GED/state equivalency exam results. Students are required to submit a personal statement and an analytic essay or academic paper. An interview is recommended. AP credits are accepted. Important factors in the admissions decision are personality/intangible qualities, evidence of special talent, and extracurricular activities record.

Procedure: Freshmen are admitted fall and spring. There are early decision, early admissions, and deferred admissions plans. Check with the school for current application deadlines. The fall 2013 application fee was $55. Applications are accepted online.

Transfer: 62 transfer students enrolled in 2012-2013. A proposed program of study, high school and college transcripts, and 1 recommendation must be submitted.

Visiting: There are regularly scheduled orientations for prospective students, including interviews, information sessions, campus tours, Discover Hampshire Days, Campus Visitation Days, and an overnight program. There are guides for informal visits, visitors may sit in on classes, and stay overnight. To schedule a visit, contact the Admissions Office.

Financial Aid: In 2013-2014, 61% of all full-time freshmen students received some form of financial aid. 61% of all full-time freshmen students received need-based aid. The average freshman award was $35,100. Need-based scholarships or need-based grants averaged $30,700; need-based self-help aid (loans and jobs) averaged $4,700; and other non-need-based awards and non-need-based scholarships averaged $12,400. The average financial indebtedness of the 2013 graduate was $20,085. Hampshire is a member of CSS. The CSS/Profile, FAFSA, and the college's own financial statement, and noncustodial parent statement are required. Check with the school for current application deadlines.

International Students: The school actively recruits these students. They must take the TOEFL.

Admissions Contact: Barbara L. Maryak, Acting Dean of Admissions. E-Mail: *admissions@hampshire.edu* Web: *www.hampshire.edu*

HARVARD UNIVERSITY/HARVARD COLLEGE D-2

Cambridge, MA 02138 **(617) 495-1551; (617) 495-8821**

Full-time: 3515 men, 3145 women	**Faculty:** n/av; I, ++$
Part-time: 15 men, 15 women	**Ph.D.s:** n/av
Graduate: 5570 men, 5370 women	**Student/Faculty:** n/av
Year: semesters, summer session	**Tuition:** $38,500
Application Deadline: see profile	**Room & Board:** $14,870
Freshman Class: n/av	
SAT or ACT: required	

MOST COMPETITIVE

Harvard College is the undergraduate college of Harvard University. Harvard College was founded in 1636. Harvard University also has 10 graduate schools. The figures in the above capsule and this profile are approximate. In addition to regional accreditation, Harvard has baccalaureate program accreditation with ABET. The 97 libraries contain 15.0 million volumes and subscribe to 100,000 periodicals including electronic. Computerized library services include interlibrary loans and database searching. Special learning facilities include a learning resource center, art gallery, natural history museum, planetarium, and radio station. The 380-acre campus is in an urban area across the Charles River from Boston. Including any residence halls, there are 400 buildings.

Student Life: 81% of undergraduates are from out of state, mostly the Middle Atlantic. Students are from 50 states, 118 foreign countries, and Canada. 67% are from public schools. 43% are white; 17% Asian American. The average age of freshmen is 18; all undergraduates, 20. 96% remain to graduate.

Housing: 6325 students can be accommodated in college housing, which includes coed dorms and on-campus apartments. On-campus housing is guaranteed for all 4 years. 97% of students live on campus. All students may keep cars.

Activities: There are no fraternities or sororities. There are 250 groups on campus, including art, band, cheerleading, chess, choir, chorale, chorus, computers, dance, debate, drama, ethnic, film, gay, honors, international, jazz band, literary magazine, marching band, musical theater, newspaper, opera, orchestra, pep band, photography, political, professional, radio and TV, religious, social, social service, student government, symphony, and yearbook. Popular campus events include Harvard/Yale football, Head of the Charles crew regatta, and Cultural Rhythms Festival.

Sports: There are 21 intercollegiate sports for men and 20 for women, and 16 intramural sports for men and 16 for women. Facilities include several gyms and athletic centers, pools, a track, boat houses, a sailing center, a hockey rink, and various courts and playing fields.

Disabled Students: Facilities include wheelchair ramps, elevators, special parking, specially equipped restrooms, special class scheduling, lowered drinking fountains, and lowered telephones.

Services: Counseling and information services are available, as is tutoring in every subject. There is a reader service for the blind.

Campus Safety and Security: Measures include 24-hour foot and vehicle patrol, self-defense education, and security escort services. There are shuttle buses, emergency telephones, and lighted pathways/sidewalks.

Programs of Study: Harvard confers A.B. and S.B. degrees. Master's and doctoral degrees are also awarded. Bachelor's degrees are awarded in BIOLOGICAL SCIENCE (biochemistry, biology/biological science, and biophysics), COMMUNICATIONS AND THE ARTS (art history and appreciation, Chinese, classics, creative writing, English, fine arts, folklore and mythology, French, German, Greek, Hebrew, Italian, Japanese, Latin, linguistics, literature, music, Portuguese, Russian, and Spanish), COMPUTER AND PHYSICAL SCIENCE (applied mathematics, astronomy, chemistry, computer science, geology, geophysics and seismology, mathematics, physical sciences, physics, and statistics), ENGINEERING AND ENVIRONMENTAL DESIGN (engineering, environmental design, environmental science, and preengineering), SOCIAL SCIENCE (African American studies, American studies, anthropology, Asian/Oriental studies, economics, European studies, history, humanities, Middle Eastern studies, philosophy, political science/government, psychology, religion, Russian and Slavic studies, Sanskrit and Indian studies, social science, social studies, sociology, and women's studies). Economics, government, and biology have the largest enrollments.

Required: In 8 semesters, students must pass a minimum of 32 1-semester courses. The average course load is 4 courses per semester, but the course rate may be varied for special reasons. A typical balanced program devotes about one-fourth of its courses to core curriculum requirements, one-half to the concentration (or major field), and the remaining one-fourth to electives.

Special: Students may cross-register with MIT and with other schools within the university and may design their own concentrations or enroll for nondegree study. Internships and study abroad may be arranged. Accelerated degree programs, dual majors, a 3-2 engineering degree, and a combined A.B.-S.B. in engineering are offered. There are pass/fail options. There is a Phi Beta Kappa honors program.

Faculty/Classroom: 98% teach undergraduates, 97% do research, and 95% do both. No introductory courses are taught by graduate students. The average class size in a regular course is 25.

Requirements: The SAT or ACT is required, as well as 3 SAT subject tests. Applicants need not be high school graduates but are expected to be well prepared academically. An essay and an interview are required, in addition to a transcript, a counselor report, and 2 teacher recommendations from academic disciplines. AP credits are accepted. Important factors in the admissions decision are evidence of special talent, personality/intangible qualities, and recommendations by school officials.

Procedure: Freshmen are admitted fall. Entrance exams should be taken by January of the senior year. There is a deferred admissions plan. Check with the school for current application deadlines and current fee. Applications are accepted online. A waiting list is maintained.

Transfer: Transfer applicants must have completed at least 1 full year of daytime study in a degree-granting program at 1 institution. Students are required to submit the SAT or ACT, 2 letters of recommendation, high school and college transcripts with a dean's report, and several essays. 16 of 32 credits required for the bachelor's degree must be completed at Harvard.

Visiting: There are regularly scheduled orientations for prospective students, consisting of group information sessions and tours. There are guides for informal visits, visitors may sit in on classes, and stay overnight. To schedule a visit, contact the Undergraduate Admissions Office.

Financial Aid: Harvard is a member of CSS. The CSS/Profile, FAFSA, the college's own financial statement, and federal tax forms are required. Check with the school for current application deadlines.

International Students: The school actively recruits these students. They must also take the SAT or ACT.

Admissions Contact: Director of Admissions. A campus DVD is available. E-Mail: *college@harvard.edu* Web: *www.college.harvard.edu*

HELLENIC COLLEGE/HOLY CROSS GREEK ORTHODOX SCHOOL OF THEOLOGY D-2

Brookline, MA 02445 **(617) 850-1285**
866-424-2338; (617) 850-1460

Full-time: 61 men, 38 women	**Faculty:** 13
Part-time: n/av	**Ph.D.s:** 90%
Graduate: 125 men, 16 women	**Student/Faculty:** 9 to 1
Year: semesters	**Tuition:** $2545
Application Deadline: May 1	**Room & Board:** $13,240
Freshman Class: 64 applied, 52 accepted, 38 enrolled	
SAT CR/M/W: 550/450/460 **ACT:** 22	**VERY COMPETITIVE**

Hellenic College, founded in 1968, is a private college affiliated with the Greek Orthodox Church. It offers programs in the classics, elementary education, religious studies, human development, management and leadership, and literature and history. There is 1 undergraduate school and 1 graduate school. In addition to regional accreditation, HCHC has baccalaureate program accreditation with NASDTEC. The library contains 63,374 volumes, 883 microform items, 3,015 audio/video tapes/CDs/DVDs, and subscribes to 720 periodicals including electronic. Computerized library services include interlibrary loans, database searching, and Internet access. Special learning facilities include a The 59-acre campus is in an urban area 4 miles southwest of Boston. Including any residence halls, there are 7 buildings.

Student Life: 90% of undergraduates are from out of state, mostly the Mid-West. Students are from 25 states, 9 foreign countries, and Canada. 90% are from public schools. 95% are white; 13% foreign nationals. 95% are Greek or Eastern Orthodox. The average age of freshmen is 20; all undergraduates, 22. 5% do not continue beyond their first year; 95% remain to graduate.

Housing: 220 students can be accommodated in college housing, which includes coed dorms, on-campus apartments, and married student housing. On-campus housing is available on a first-come and first-served basis. 90% of students live on campus; of those, 90% remain on campus on weekends. Alcohol is not permitted. All students may keep cars.

Activities: There are no fraternities or sororities. Groups on campus include choir, ethnic, religious, social, social service, and student government. Popular campus events include Feast of the Holy Cross, Matriculation Day, and Campus Christmas Party.

Sports: There are 4 intramural sports for men and 3 for women. Facilities include a gym, tennis, basketball, and racquetball courts, and a soccer field.

Disabled Students: 10% of the campus is accessible. Facilities include wheelchair ramps, elevators, special parking, specially equipped restrooms, and lowered drinking fountains.

Services: Counseling and information services are available, as is tutoring in some subjects, Greek and music writing and composition. There is remedial math, reading, and writing.

Campus Safety and Security: There are shuttle buses, lighted pathways/sidewalks, and a 16-hour security patrol.

Programs of Study: HCHC confers B.A. degrees. Master's degrees are also awarded. Bachelor's degrees are awarded in BUSINESS (business administration and management), COMMUNICATIONS AND THE ARTS (classics and literature), EDUCATION (elementary education), SOCIAL SCIENCE (history, human development, and religion). Religious studies and elementary education are the strongest academically. Religious studies and human development are the largest.

Required: To graduate, students must complete 129 credits, with 39 in the major, and maintain a minimum overall GPA of 2.0. General education requirements include 72 credits, with courses in English language and literature, music, history, science, philosophy, and social science.

Special: The college offers cross-registration with Boston Theological Institute, Newbury College, and Boston College, credit by examination, and study abroad in Greece. There is a freshman honors program.

Faculty/Classroom: 70% of faculty are male; 30% are female. No

introductory courses are taught by graduate students. The average class size in an introductory lecture is 20; in a laboratory is 20; and in a regular course is 15.

Admissions: 81% of a recent year applicants were accepted. The SAT scores for the 2011-2012 freshman class were: Critical Reading--30% below 500, 35% between 500 and 599, 30% between 600 and 700, and 5% above 700; Math--55% below 500, 35% between 500 and 599, 5% between 600 and 700, and 5% above 700; Writing--45% below 500, 35% between 500 and 599, 20% between 600 and 700. The ACT scores were 20% below 21, 60% between 21 and 23, 20% between 24 and 26.

Requirements: The SAT or ACT is required. Applicants should graduate from an accredited secondary school or have a GED. 15 academic credits are required, including 4 units of English, 2 each of math, foreign language, and social studies, and 1 of science. An essay is required. A GPA of 2.5 is required. AP and CLEP credits are accepted. Important factors in the admissions decision are recommendations by school officials, advanced placement or honors courses, and recommendations by alumni.

Procedure: Freshmen are admitted fall and spring. There are deferred admissions and rolling admissions plans. Early decision applications should be filed by December 1; regular applications, by May 1 for fall entry; and December 1 for spring entry. The application fee was $50. Notification of early decision is sent February 1; regular decision, June 15.

Transfer: 11 transfer students enrolled in a recent year. An essay, college transcripts, recommendation letters, an interview, and a health certificate are required. SAT or ACT scores and high school transcripts are waived if the student has 24 or more college credit hours. 60 of 129 credits required for the bachelor's degree must be completed at HCHC.

Visiting: There are regularly scheduled orientations for prospective students, including observation of classroom and student life. There are guides for informal visits, visitors may sit in on classes, and stay overnight. To schedule a visit, contact the Office of Admissions.

Financial Aid: In a recent year, 95% of all full-time freshmen and 95% of continuing full-time students received some form of financial aid. 95% of all full-time freshmen and 95% of continuing full-time students received need-based aid. 36% of undergraduate students work part-time. Average annual earnings from campus work are $1600. The FAFSA and the college's own financial statement are required. Check with the school for current application deadlines.

International Students: There are 5 international students enrolled. They must take the TOEFL with a minimum score of 500 on the paper-based TOEFL (PBT) or 61 on the Internet-based version (iBT).

Graduates: In a recent year, 12 bachelor's degrees were awarded. The most popular majors were religious studies (50%), management and leadership (25%), and human development (25%). In an average class, 97% graduate in 4 years or less. Of the 2010 graduating class, 60% were enrolled in graduate school within 6 months of graduation, and 30% were employed.

Admissions Contact: Director for Admissions. A campus DVD is available. Web: *www.hchc.edu*

LASELL COLLEGE D-2

Newton, MA 02466 **(617) 243-2225**
(888) LASELL-4; (617) 243-2380

Full-time: 594 men, 1055 women	**Faculty:** 82; IIB, av$
Part-time: 14 men, 24 women	**Ph.D.s:** 77%
Graduate: 118 men, 276 women	**Student/Faculty:** 20 to 1
Year: semesters, summer session	**Tuition:** $30,000
Application Deadline:	**Room & Board:** $12,500
Freshman Class: 3584 applied, 2729 accepted, 485 enrolled	
SAT CR/M/W: 480/480/480	**ACT:** 20 **LESS COMPETITIVE**

An innovator in education for over 150 years, Lasell College today is a comprehensive coeducational college offering professionally oriented bachelor's and master's degree programs. We are known for helping students make the connection between classroom lessons and real life through hands-on activities such as internships, practicum, service learning, and meaningful projects. There is one undergraduate school and one graduate school. The library contains 52,466 volumes, 2,579 audio/video tapes/CDs/DVDs, and subscribes to 221 periodicals including electronic. Computerized library services include interlibrary loans, database searching, Internet access, and Wi-Fi capability. Special learning facilities include an art gallery, radio station, a special learning facilities includes our Academic Achievement Center, Lasell Village (retirement community), the Center for Community-Based Learning, the Center for Teaching and Learning, two child study centers, a cultural center, and a fashion collection. The 50-acre campus is in a suburban area 8 miles west of Boston. Including any residence halls, there are 48 buildings.

Student Life: 56% of undergraduates are from Massachusetts. Others are from 26 states, and 14 foreign countries. 80% are from public schools. 71% are White. The average age of freshmen is 18; all undergraduates, 20. 26% do not continue beyond their first year.

Housing: College-sponsored housing includes single-sex and coed dorms and on-campus apartments. In addition, there are special-interest houses. On-campus housing is guaranteed for all 4 years. 77% of students live on campus; of those, 55% remain on campus on weekends. Upperclassmen may keep cars.

Activities: There are no fraternities or sororities. There are 55 groups on campus, including art, cheerleading, chorale, chorus, dance, drama, environmental, ethnic, gay, honors, international, jazz band, literary magazine, newspaper, political, professional, radio and TV, religious, social, social service, student government, and yearbook. Popular campus events include River Day, Torchlight Parade and Awards Night.

Sports: There are 8 intercollegiate sports for men and 9 for women, and 5 intramural sports for men and 5 for women. Facilities include an athletic center with a basketball court, a volleyball court, an indoor track, a dance studio, and locker rooms, plus tennis courts, 2 exercise rooms, and 2 athletic fields. Lasell also has a number of club sports.

Disabled Students: Facilities include wheelchair ramps, elevators, special parking, specially equipped restrooms, special class scheduling, lowered drinking fountains, and lowered telephones.

Services: Counseling and information services are available, as is tutoring in most subjects. There is remedial math and writing. The Academic Achievement Center offers individual assistance in math, accounting, and many other subjects, as well as in techniques for writing, coaching on presentation skills, and improving reading comprehension, as well as providing special resources for students with documented learning disabilities.

Campus Safety and Security: Measures include 24-hour foot and vehicle patrol, emergency notification system, self-defense education, and security escort services. There are shuttle buses, emergency telephones, lighted pathways/sidewalks, and controlled access to dorms/residences.

Programs of Study: Lasell confers B.A., and B.S. degrees. Master's degrees are also awarded. Bachelor's degrees are awarded in AGRICULTURE (environmental studies), BUSINESS (accounting, banking and finance, business administration and management, entrepreneurial studies, fashion merchandising, hospitality management services, international business management, marketing/retailing/merchandising, sports management, and tourism), COMMUNICATIONS AND THE ARTS (advertising, communications, English, graphic design, journalism, media arts, multimedia, public relations, sports media, and video), COMPUTER AND PHYSICAL SCIENCE (applied mathematics and web technology), EDUCATION (athletic training, early childhood education, elementary education, secondary education, and sports studies), SOCIAL SCIENCE (child care/child and family studies, criminal justice, fashion design and technology, history, human services, humanities, interdisciplinary studies, law, liberal arts/general studies, paralegal studies, physical fitness/movement, psychology, and sociology). Communication, fashion and retail management, and sport management have the largest enrollments.

Required: A graduate of Lasell receives the degree of Bachelor of Arts or Bachelor of Science. Specific requirements of the various curricula are described under each major. In order to graduate, each student must earn a minimum of 120 credits of academic work; out of these 120 credits, students must complete a minimum of 42 credits in the arts and sciences. Most degree programs at the College require between 120 and 127 credits to graduate. In order to graduate, students are required to complete 50% of their credits at Lasell College (the College allows a maximum of 60 transferable credits), the final semester of which must be at Lasell College, attain a cumulative GPA (grade point average) of 2.0 or higher, complete a major degree program, and meet Lasell's Core Curriculum competencies. All degree programs have additional requirements described in the catalog.

Special: Internships are built into the curriculum, and student employment options are available on campus. Student-designed majors are possible, as is a 5th year master's degree option. Many students participate in a Washington semester, study abroad or International service learning. All programs feature connected learning, which is an ongoing practical application of classroom theory. There are a freshman honors program.

Faculty/Classroom: 39% of faculty are male; 61% are female. All teach undergraduates. No introductory courses are taught by graduate students. The average class size in a regular course is 17.

Admissions: 76% of the 2013-2014 applicants were accepted. The SAT scores for the 2013-2014 freshman class were: Critical Reading--58% below 500, 35% between 500 and 599, and 6% between 600 and 699; Math--58% below 500, 35% between 500 and 599, and 6% between 600 and 699; Writing--60% below 500, 35% between 500 and 599, and 5% between 600 and 699. The ACT scores were 60% below 21, 24% between 21 and 23, 5% between 24 and 26, 7% between 27 and 28.

Requirements: The SAT is required. Applicants should have completed 16 Carnegie units of high school study. The GED is accepted. Two letters of recommendation and a personal essay are required, and an interview is recommended. AP and CLEP credits are accepted. Important factors in the admissions decision are advanced placement or honors courses, personality/intangible qualities, and leadership record.

Procedure: Freshmen are admitted fall and spring. There are early admissions and rolling admissions plans. Application deadlines are open. Application fee is $40. Notification of early decision is sent December 1; regular decision, December 15. Applications are accepted online.

Transfer: 73 transfer students enrolled in 2012-2013. Applicants must submit an application, as well as final secondary school transcript (if <30 college credits), official college/university transcripts, official SAT/ACT scores (if <30 college credits), personal statement or essay, 2 recommendations (1 must be academic), and if English is not the native language, applicants must submit TOEFL or other English proficiency exam score. 60 of 120 credits required for the bachelor's degree must be completed at Lasell.

Visiting: There are regularly scheduled orientations for prospective students, consisting of the president's welcome, faculty presentations, tours, and student panels. There are guides for informal visits, visitors may sit in on classes, and stay overnight. To schedule a visit, contact the Office of Undergraduate Admission.

Financial Aid: In 2013-2014, 97% of all full-time freshmen and 94% of continuing full-time students received some form of financial aid. 90% of all full-time freshmen and 85% of continuing full-time students received need-based aid. 66% of undergraduate students work part-time. Lasell is a member of CSS. The FAFSA and the college's own financial statement are required. The priority date for freshman financial aid applications for fall entry is March 1.

International Students: There are 53 international students enrolled. The school actively recruits these students. They must take the TOEFL with a minimum score of 525 on the paper-based TOEFL (PBT) or 71 on the Internet-based version (iBT), IELTS. They must also take the SAT or ACT.

Computers: All students may access the system 24 hours a day, 7 days a week. There are no time limits and no fees.

Graduates: From July 1, 2012 to June 30, 2013, 325 bachelor's degrees were awarded. The most popular majors were fashion and retail merchandising (14%), communication (11%), and fashion design and production (8%). Of the 2012 graduating class, 9% were enrolled in graduate school within 6 months of graduation, and 86% were employed.

Admissions Contact: James M. Tweed, Dean of Admission. E-Mail: *info@lasell.edu* Web: *www.lasell.edu*

LESLEY UNIVERSITY — D-2

Cambridge, MA 02138 — (617) 349-8800; (800) 999-1959; (617) 349-8810

Full-time: 323 men, 1075 women	**Faculty:** n/av; IIA, -$
Part-time: 45 men, 155 women	**Ph.D.s:** 85%
Graduate: 481 men, 2766 women	**Student/Faculty:** 20 to 1
Year: semesters, summer session	**Tuition:** $32,250
Application Deadline:	**Room & Board:** $14,100
Freshman Class: n/av	
SAT or ACT: required	**COMPETITIVE**

Lesley University, founded in 1909, is a private undergraduate institution, offering degree programs in education, human services, and the arts. Expanded resources, course work, and opportunities are available to students through the larger coeducational Lesley University system, including cross-registration with the Lesley University College of Art and Design. Figures in the above capsule and in this profile are approximate. There are 2 undergraduate schools and 2 graduate schools. In addition to regional accreditation, Lesley has baccalaureate program accreditation with NASAD and TEAC. The 2 libraries contain 124,022 volumes, 878,938 microform items, 42,680 audio/video tapes/CDs/DVDs, and subscribe to 861 periodicals including electronic. Computerized library services include interlibrary loans, database searching, Internet access, and Wi-Fi capability. Special learning facilities include an art gallery, center for teaching resources, media production facility, and instructional computing and math achievement center. The 5-acre campus is in an urban area Outside of Harvard Square in Cambridge, MA. Including any residence halls, there are 53 buildings.

Student Life: 58% of undergraduates are from Massachusetts. Others are from 33 states, 24 foreign countries, and Canada. 84% are from public schools. 71% are White; 12% race unknown. The average age of freshmen is 18; all undergraduates, 20. 27% do not continue beyond their first year; 73% remain to graduate.

Housing: 803 students can be accommodated in college housing, which includes single-sex and coed dorms. In addition, there are special-interest houses, social interest and themed housing. On-campus housing is available on a first-come and first-served basis. All students may keep cars.

Activities: There are no fraternities or sororities. There are 25 groups on campus, including and Third Wave (a women's group), Student Athlete Advisory Committee, choir, chorus, dance, drama, ethnic, gay, international, literary magazine, musical theater, photography, political, professional, religious, Second Start, social, social service, and student government. Popular campus events include Family and Friends Weekend, Quad Fest, and World Fest.

Sports: There are 7 intercollegiate sports for men and 7 for women, and 3 intramural sports for men and 5 for women. Facilities include outdoor tennis courts, and a fitness center with Nautilus circuit, free weights, and cardiovascular equipment. Students may also use an Olympic-size swimming pool at a nearby school as well as the indoor and outdoor facilities at a nearby school, including two full size basketball courts, two racquetball courts, a rowing tank, a softball court, an indoor track and a lighted outdoor soccer field.

Disabled Students: 85% of the campus is accessible. Facilities include wheelchair ramps, elevators, special parking, specially equipped restrooms, special class scheduling, lowered drinking fountains. The Disability Services Office provides document review and arranges for reasonable accommodations for special needs students.

Services: Counseling and information services are available, as is tutoring in most subjects. There is a reader service for the blind, and remedial math.

Campus Safety and Security: Measures include 24-hour foot and vehicle patrol, self-defense education, and security escort services. There are shuttle buses, emergency telephones, lighted pathways/sidewalks, and watch tours.

Programs of Study: Lesley confers B.S., and B.F.A. degrees. Associate, master's, and doctoral degrees are also awarded. Bachelor's degrees are awarded in BUSINESS (management science), COMMUNICATIONS AND THE ARTS (visual and performing arts), COMPUTER AND PHYSICAL SCIENCE (natural sciences), EDUCATION (early childhood education, elementary education, middle school education, and special education), SOCIAL SCIENCE (human services, humanities, psychology, and social science). Education, counseling, photography and art therapy have the largest enrollments.

Required: Students must complete 45 hours of general education requirements, including 15 of humanities, 12 of natural science, 9 of social science, 6 of multicultural perspectives, and 3 of first-year seminar; emphasis is given to cross-curriculum components in writing, critical and quantitative reasoning, global perspectives, and leadership and ethics. Art Institute of Boston Students must also complete a Foundation year. To graduate, students need 128 total credit hours, including 30 to 33 in the liberal arts majors or 41 to 43 in professional majors.

Special: Study abroad in Cuba, England, and Sweden, and 6 others by arrangement, a Washington Justice semester, and on-campus work-study programs are offered. All students participate in at least 3 field placement experiences, beginning in their freshman year. There are combined accelerated degree programs in management, counseling, and education majors. Dual majors and student-designed majors are also available. Accelerated and weekend course programs as well as cross-registration with AIB are offered for Adult Baccalaureate College and School of Education. There are a freshman honors program and 2 departmental honors programs.

Faculty/Classroom: 44% of faculty are male; 56% are female. All teach and do research. No introductory courses are taught by graduate students. The average class size in an introductory lecture is 20; in a laboratory is 14; and in a regular course is 14.

Admissions: The SAT scores for the 2013-2014 freshman class were: Critical Reading--23% below 500, 48% between 500 and 599, 24% between 600 and 699, and 5% between 700 and 800; Math--40% below 500, 40% between 500 and 599, 19% between 600 and 699, and 1% between 700 and 800; Writing--28% below 500, 50% between 500 and 599, 21% between 600 and 699, and 1% between 700 and 800. The ACT scores were 3% below 21, 59% between 21 and 23, 16% between 24 and 26, 20% between 27 and 28, and 2% above 28. 40% of the current freshmen were in the top fifth of their class; 75% were in the top two fifths.

Requirements: The SAT or ACT is required. It is recommended that students complete 20 academic units in high school, including 4 in English, 3 in science, 3 in math, and 2 in U.S. history. SAT or ACT scores, a writing sample, and 2 recommendations are also required as part of the application; a personal interview is recommended. Applicants must have a high school diploma from an accredited secondary school or a GED. AP and CLEP credits are accepted. Important factors in the admissions decision are evidence of special talent, personality/intangible qualities, and advanced placement or honors courses.

Procedure: Freshmen are admitted fall and spring. Entrance exams should be taken by February 15. There are deferred admissions and rolling admissions plans. Early decision applications should be filed by December 1; regular applications, by November 15 for spring entry, along with a $50 fee. Notification of early decision is sent January 1; regular decision, on a rolling basis. 2 applicants were on the 2013 waiting list. Applications are accepted online.

Transfer: 108 transfer students enrolled in 2012-2013. Applicants must have a minimum 2.5 GPA. They must provide high school and college transcripts, complete an essay or personal statement, and have a statement of good standing from prior institution. An interview is recommended for all Lesley College students and required of all Art Institute of Boston Students. 45 of 124 credits required for the bachelor's degree must be completed at Lesley.

Visiting: There are regularly scheduled orientations for prospective students, includes personal interviews with professional staff, student campus tours, information sessions, class visits, and meetings with financial aid. There are guides for informal visits, visitors may sit in on classes, and stay overnight. To schedule a visit, contact Lesley College Admissions.

Financial Aid: In 2013-2014, 75% of all full-time freshmen and 70% of continuing full-time students received some form of financial aid. 79% of all full-time freshmen and 71% of continuing full-time students received need-based aid. The average freshman award was $15,652. Need-based scholarships or need-based grants averaged $14,331; need-based self-help aid (loans and jobs) averaged $5,938; and other non-need-based awards and non-need-based scholarships averaged $12,667. 25% of undergraduate students work part-time. Average annual earnings from campus work are $1400. The average financial indebtedness of the 2013 graduate was $18,000. The FAFSA and the college's own financial statement, and parent and student federal tax returns are required. The priority date for freshman financial aid applications for fall entry is March 1. The deadline for filing freshman financial aid applications for fall entry is February 15.

International Students: There are 32 international students enrolled. The school actively recruits these students. They must take the TOEFL with a minimum score of 500 on the paper-based TOEFL (PBT).

Computers: All students may access the system 24/7, except for some computer labs. There are no time limits and no fees.

Graduates: From July 1, 2012 to June 30, 2013, 426 bachelor's degrees were awarded. The most popular majors were liberal studies (18%), visual and performing arts (7%), and psychology (7%). 100 companies recruited on campus in 2012-2013. In an average class, 33% graduate in 4 years or less, 10% graduate in 5 years or less, and 3% graduate in 6 years or less.

Admissions Contact: Deb Kocar, Director of Admissions. E-Mail: *lcadmission@lesley.edu* Web: *www.hchc.edu*

MASSACHUSETTS BOARD OF HIGHER EDUCATION

The Massachusetts Board of Higher Education, established in 1980, is a public system in Massachusetts. It is governed by a 16-member Board of Regents appointed by the governor, whose chief administrator is the chancellor. The primary goal of the system is to govern the state's public higher education system. The total student enrollment is usually about 175,000. Profiles of the 4-year campuses are included in this section.

MASSACHUSETTS COLLEGE OF ART AND DESIGN E-2

Boston, MA 02115 **(617) 879-7221; (617) 879-7250**

Full-time: 538 men, 1049 women
Faculty: 101
Part-time: 53 men, 132 women
Ph.D.s: 78%
Graduate: 60 men, 100 women
Student/Faculty: 16 to 1
Year: semesters, summer session
Tuition: $11,000 ($28,600)
Application Deadline: February 1
Room & Board: $12,600
Freshman Class: 1631 applied, 837 accepted, 315 enrolled
SAT CR/M/W: 560/540/540

SPECIAL

Massachusetts College of Art and Design, founded in 1873, is a public institution offering undergraduate and graduate programs in art, design, and education. There is one undergraduate school. Addition to regional accreditation, MassArt has baccalaureate program accreditation with NASAD. The library contains 231,586 volumes, 8,700 microform items, and subscribes to 757 periodicals including electronic. Computerized library services include interlibrary loans, database searching, Internet access, and Wi-Fi capability. Special learning facilities include an art gallery, 7 art galleries, a foundry, glass furnaces, ceramic kilns, video and film studios, performance and studio spaces, and a Polaroid 20 x 24 camera. The 5-acre campus is in an urban area in Boston. Including any residence halls, there are 9 buildings.

Student Life: 70% of undergraduates are from Massachusetts. Others are from 40 states, 28 foreign countries, and Canada. 85% are from public schools. 79% are White. The average age of freshmen is 18; all undergraduates, 22. 12% do not continue beyond their first year; 64% remain to graduate.

Housing: 375 students can be accommodated in college housing, which includes coed dorms and on-campus apartments. there is a visual art college residence hall with ventilated workrooms, a visiting artist suite, and gallery space. On-campus housing is guaranteed for the freshman year only, is available on a first-come, first-served basis, and is available on a lottery system for upperclassmen. Priority is given to out-of-town students. 77% of students commute. Alcohol is not permitted. No one may keep cars.

Activities: There are no fraternities or sororities. There are 30 groups on campus, including art, computers, ethnic, film, gay, international, literary magazine, newspaper, photography, political, professional, radio and TV, social, social service, and student government. Popular campus events include Eventworks, Annual Iron Pour, and First Night Ice Sculpture.

Sports: There are 7 intercollegiate sports for men and 6 for women, and 8 intramural sports for men and 6 for women. Facilities include a gym, a fitness center, and courts for squash, volleyball, and basketball.

Disabled Students: 95% of the campus is accessible. Facilities include wheelchair ramps, elevators, special parking, specially equipped restrooms, special class scheduling, lowered drinking fountains, and lowered telephones.

Services: There is remedial reading and writing.

Campus Safety and Security: Measures include 24-hour foot and vehicle patrol, self-defense education, and security escort services. There are shuttle buses, emergency telephones, and lighted pathways/sidewalks.

Programs of Study: MassArt confers B.F.A. degrees. Master's degrees are also awarded. Bachelor's degrees are awarded in COMMUNICATIONS AND THE ARTS (animation, art history and appreciation, ceramic art and design, fiber/textiles/weaving, film arts, fine arts, glass, graphic design, illustration, industrial design, media arts, metal/jewelry, painting, photography, printmaking, sculpture, and studio art), EDUCATION (art education), ENGINEERING AND ENVIRONMENTAL DESIGN (architecture), SOCIAL SCIENCE (fashion design and technology). Painting, illustration, and graphic design have the largest enrollments.

Required: A total of 120 semester credits is required for graduation; the minimum GPA varies by major. Typically, students take 42 credits in liberal arts, 18 in studio foundations, 36 in the major, and 24 in electives. Beginning in the sophomore year, the student's work is reviewed by panels of faculty and visiting artists.

Special: MassArt offers cross-registration with several consortiums, internships for advanced students, on- and off-campus work-study programs, study abroad and foreign-exchange programs, an open major for exceptional students, and dual majors in most combinations of concentrations.

Faculty/Classroom: 55% of faculty are male; 45% are female. All teach undergraduates. No introductory courses are taught by graduate students. The average class size in an introductory lecture is 23; in a laboratory is 12; and in a regular course is 14.

Admissions: 51% of the 2013-2014 applicants were accepted. The SAT scores for the 2013-2014 freshman class were: Critical Reading--18% below 500, 47% between 500 and 599, 30% between 600 and 699, and 5% between 700 and 800; Math--26% below 500, 49% between 500 and 599, 22% between 600 and 699, and 3% between 700 and 800; Writing--23% below 500, 49% between 500 and 599, 24% between 600 and 699, and 3% between 700 and 800. 35% of the current freshmen were in the top fifth of their class; 72% were in the top two fifths.

Requirements: The SAT is required. Applicants should be graduates of an accredited secondary school or have earned the GED. College preparatory studies should include as a minimum 4 years of English, 2 each of social studies, math, and science, 2 academic electives (1 math or science and 1 art elective), and a foreign language. A personal essay and portfolio are required, and an interview and letters of reference are recommended. A GPA of 3.0 is required. AP and CLEP credits are accepted. Important factors in the admissions decision are evidence of special talent, recommendations by school officials, and personality/intangible qualities.

Procedure: Freshmen are admitted fall. Entrance exams should be taken in early fall of the senior year. There are early admissions, deferred admissions, and rolling admissions plans. Early decision applications should be filed by December 1; regular applications, by February 1 for fall entry; and October 15 for spring entry, along with a $50 fee. Notification of early decision is sent December 20; regular decision, April 1. 10 applicants were on the 2013 waiting list; were admitted. Applications are accepted online.

Transfer: 130 transfer students enrolled in 2012-2013. Applicants must submit secondary school and postsecondary school transcripts, a statement of purpose, and a portfolio of at least 15 pieces, preferably in slides. An interview is recommended. 60 of 120 credits required for the bachelor's degree must be completed at MassArt.

Visiting: There are regularly scheduled orientations for prospective students, including an information session and a campus tour. There are guides for informal visits and visitors may sit in on classes. To schedule a visit, contact the Admissions Office.

Financial Aid: In 2013-2014, 81% of all full-time freshmen and 76% of continuing full-time students received some form of financial aid. 60% of all full-time freshmen and 62% of continuing full-time students received need-based aid. The average freshman award was $8,508. Need-based scholarships or need-based grants averaged $6,572; need-based self-help aid (loans and jobs) averaged $4,398; and other non-need-based awards and non-need-based scholarships averaged $3,265. 84% of undergraduate students work part-time. Average annual earnings from campus work are $1000. The FAFSA is required. The priority date for freshman financial aid applications for fall entry is March 1.

International Students: There are 36 international students enrolled. The school actively recruits these students. They must take the TOEFL with a minimum score of 550 on the paper-based TOEFL (PBT) or 85 on the Internet-based version (iBT), IELTS. International students are required to take the TOEFL. They may take the SAT or ACT in lieu of the TOEFL.

Computers: All students may access the system. There are no time limits and no fees.

Graduates: From July 1, 2012 to June 30, 2013, 290 bachelor's degrees were awarded. The most popular majors were painting (11%), graphic design/studio (10%), and photography (10%). 8 companies recruited on campus in 2012-2013. In an average class, 1% graduate in 3 years or less, 42% graduate in 4 years or less, 58% graduate in 5 years or less, and 64% graduate in 6 years or less. Of the 2012 graduating class, 5% were enrolled in graduate school within 6 months of graduation, and 89% were employed.

Admissions Contact: Karen Townsend, Director of Admissions. E-Mail: *admissions@massart.edu* Web: *www.massart.edu*

MASSACHUSETTS COLLEGE OF LIBERAL ARTS A-1

North Adams, MA 01247 **(413) 662-5410; (413) 662-5179**

Full-time: 577 men, 831 women	**Faculty:** 86
Part-time: 73 men, 119 women	**Ph.D.s:** 82%
Graduate: 70 men, 129 women	**Student/Faculty:** 13 to 1
Year: semesters, summer session	**Tuition:** $8075 ($17,020)
Application Deadline: open	**Room & Board:** $8658
Freshman Class: n/av	

COMPETITIVE

Massachusetts College of Liberal Arts (MCLA) delivers a high-quality, affordable education that provides students with the critical thinking and communication skills of greatest value to their development, their community and their future employers. As the public liberal arts college of the Commonwealth, MCLA is committed to preparing students for success at work and in life. MCLA provides unmatched, hands-on growth opportunities early, and often, in an inspiring, creative community. Ranked by US News & World Report as a top ten public liberal arts college, MCLA's unique features include a low faculty-to-student ratio; collaborations with the region's cultural venues for our fine and performing arts, visual arts and arts management degree programs; our Berkshire Hills Internship Program (B-HIP), where students get hands-on experience as arts administrators; science programs including a 3+2 pre-engineering program, an environmental studies major and athletic training; numerous study-away experiences; community service learning; a strong teacher education program and the opportunity to work with faculty on undergraduate research. Construction of a new 65,000 square foot state of the art Center for Science and Innovation building is underway and transform teaching, learning and research at MCLA. Academic departments that will be housed in this new building will be Biology, Chemistry, Environmental Science, Math, Physics and Psychology. Along with the sciences and the arts, MCLA offers Bachelor's degrees in business, education, English Communications, sociology, liberal arts and psychology. Our newest major in Political Science and Public Policy offers an opportunity to integrate academic study with practical experiences like internships and the chance to make connections with policy-makers in government agencies and through other vocational experiences. Other features include diverse on-campus residence halls, more than 40 clubs and organizations, a TV studio and radio station where students produce their own shows; and a very active Student Government Association. Division III sports range from soccer to golf. Beyond the undergraduate experience, MCLA also offers a comprehensive Master's degree in education and a Professional Master in Business Administration. This welcoming, caring place helps students develop the confidence to make contributions to this world as lasting as the Berkshire hills that surround us, ensuring that students earn a powerful lifelong return on their educational investment. The library contains 170,000 volumes, 290,000 microform items, and 6,300 audio/video tapes/CDs/DVDs, and subscribes to 70 periodicals including electronic. Computerized library services include interlibrary loans, database searching, and Internet access. Special learning facilities include an art gallery, radio station, and TV station. The 80-acre campus is in a rural area 45 miles east of Albany, NY. Including any residence halls, there are 19 buildings.

Student Life: 77% of undergraduates are from Massachusetts. Others are from 18 states, and 1 foreign countries. 79% are White. The average age of freshmen is 18; all undergraduates, 22. 25% do not continue beyond their first year.

Housing: College-sponsored housing includes single-sex and coed dorms and on-campus apartments. On-campus housing is guaranteed for all 4 years. 63% of students live on campus. Upperclassmen may keep cars.

Activities: There are 50 groups on campus, including band, cheerleading, choir, chorale, chorus, computers, dance, drama, environmental, ethnic, gay, honors, international, jazz band, literary magazine, musical theater, newspaper, photography, political, professional, radio and TV, religious, social, social service, student government, and yearbook.

Sports: There are 6 intercollegiate sports for men and 6 for women. Facilities include A campus center with a swimming pool, weight rooms, a fitness center, and handball, squash, and racquetball courts. The campus also features an outdoor complex with tennis courts and soccer, baseball, and softball fields, a 1,750-seat gym, and a 5-mile cross-country running trail.

Disabled Students: 95% of the campus is accessible. Facilities include wheelchair ramps, elevators, special parking, specially equipped restrooms, and special class scheduling.

Services: Counseling and information services are available, as is tutoring in some subjects. There is remedial math, reading, and writing.

Campus Safety and Security: Measures include 24-hour foot and vehicle patrol, emergency notification system, self-defense education, and security escort services. There are emergency telephones and lighted pathways/sidewalks.

Programs of Study: MCLA confers B.A., and B.S. degrees. Master's degrees are also awarded. Bachelor's degrees are awarded in AGRICULTURE (environmental studies), BIOLOGICAL SCIENCE (biology/biological science), BUSINESS (accounting and business administration and management), COMMUNICATIONS AND THE ARTS (art, arts administration/management, communications, English, English literature, English Writing, fine arts, performing arts, and visual and performing arts), COMPUTER AND PHYSICAL SCIENCE (chemistry, computer science, mathematics, and physics), EDUCATION (athletic training, (Education) Childhood Education, education, mathematics education, middle school education, and secondary education), HEALTH PROFESSIONS (allied health, cytotechnology, and Pre-Health Studies), SOCIAL SCIENCE (history, interdisciplinary studies, liberal arts/general studies, philosophy, philosophy and religion, political science/government, psychology, public administration, and sociology).

Required: All students must complete at least 120 credits, including 40 in the core curriculum, and maintain a GPA of at least 2.0.

Special: There are 8 national honor societies, a freshman honors program, and 7 departmental honors programs.

Faculty/Classroom: 56% of faculty are male; 44% are female. No introductory courses are taught by graduate students.

Requirements: The SAT or ACT is required. MCLA's admission criteria can be described as moderately selective with a strong emphasis placed on a student's academic performance in high school. Successful candidates for admission should meet MCLA's sliding scale which correlates high school grade point average with SAT or ACT scores. Secondly, applicants should demonstrate completion of 16 Carnegie units, including 4 courses in English, 3 each in science and math, and 2 each in foreign language, history/social science, and electives. The GED is also accepted. A GPA of 2.0 is required. AP and CLEP credits are accepted.

Procedure: Freshmen are admitted fall and spring. Entrance exams should be taken by January of the senior year. There are early decision, early admissions, deferred admissions, and rolling admissions plans. Application deadlines are open. Application fee is $40. Notification is sent on a rolling basis. 323 early decision candidates were accepted for the 2013-2014 class. Applications are accepted online.

Transfer: 143 transfer students enrolled in 2012-2013. MCLA's transfer policy is highly dependent on a student's performance at their previous college(s). A minimum grade point average is expected to be a 2.5 to be considered for admission. Students applying without an earned Associate's degree must submit official high school transcript and standardized test scores as well 45 of 120 credits required for the bachelor's degree must be completed at MCLA.

Visiting: There are regularly scheduled orientations for prospective students. There are guides for informal visits and visitors may sit in on classes. To schedule a visit, contact the Admissions Office.

Financial Aid: In 2013-2014, 81% of all full-time freshmen and 74% of continuing full-time students received some form of financial aid. 70% of all full-time freshmen and 61% of continuing full-time students received need-based aid. The average freshman award was $14,397. Need-based scholarships or need-based grants averaged $6,832; and need-based self-help aid (loans and jobs) averaged $3,812. The average financial indebtedness of the 2013 graduate was $29,534. MCLA is a member of CSS. The FAFSA and the college's own financial statement are required. The priority date for freshman financial aid applications for fall entry is March 1.

International Students: There are 10 international students enrolled. The school actively recruits these students. They must take the TOEFL with a minimum score of 550 on the paper-based TOEFL (PBT). They must also take the SAT.

Computers: All students may access the system. There are no time limits and no fees.

Graduates: From July 1, 2012 to June 30, 2013, 354 bachelor's degrees were awarded. The most popular majors were business (19%), English (17%), and psychology (11%). In an average class, 31% graduate in 4 years or less, 44% graduate in 5 years or less, and 47% graduate in 6 years or less.

Admissions Contact: Annette Jeffes, Dean of Admission & Enrollment Managemen. E-Mail: *admissions@mcla.edu* Web: *www.mcla.edu*

MASSACHUSETTS COLLEGE OF PHARMACY AND HEALTH SCIENCES E-2

Boston, MA 02115 **(617) 732-2850 (800) 225-5506; (617) 732-2118**

Full-time: 900 men, 1825 women	**Faculty:** 202
Part-time: 30 men, 90 women	**Ph.D.s:** 86%
Graduate: 450 men, 930 women	**Student/Faculty:** n/av
Year: semesters, summer session	**Tuition:** $26,960
Application Deadline: see profile	**Room & Board:** $13,350
Freshman Class: n/av	
SAT or ACT: required	

SPECIAL

The Massachusetts College of Pharmacy and Health Sciences, established in 1823, is a private institution offering undergraduate programs in chemistry, the pharmaceutical sciences, and the health sciences. The figures in the above capsule and in this profile are approximate. There are 5 undergraduate schools and 1 graduate school. In addition to regional accreditation, MCPHS has baccalaureate program accreditation with ACPE and ADA. The library contains 54,800 volumes, microform items, and audio/video tapes/CDs/DVDs, and subscribes to 32,800 periodicals including electronic. Computerized library services include interlibrary loans, database searching, Internet access, and laptop Internet portals. Special learning facilities include a learning resource center, pharmacy labs, dental hygiene clinic, and nursing labs. The 2-acre campus is in an urban area 1 mile from the center of Boston. Including any residence halls, there are 3 buildings.

Student Life: 56% of undergraduates are from Massachusetts. Others are from 43 states, 32 foreign countries, and Canada. 54% are white; 26% Asian American. The average age of freshmen is 18; all undergraduates, 21. 17% do not continue beyond their first year; 69% remain to graduate.

Housing: 785 students can be accommodated in college housing, which includes single-sex and coed dorms and on-campus apartments. On-campus housing is guaranteed for the freshman year only, is available on a first-come, first-served basis, and is available on a lottery system for upperclassmen. 74% of students commute. Alcohol is not permitted. No one may keep cars.

Activities: There are 5 national fraternities. There are 66 groups on campus, including academic, art, band, choir, chorale, chorus, cultural, dance, drama, environmental, ethnic, gay, honors, international, musical theater, newspaper, orchestra, professional, religious, social service, and student government. Popular campus events include International Fair and Mission Hill Walk for Health.

Sports: There are 6 intramural sports for men and 6 for women. Facilities are shared with the Massachusetts College of Art and include a wellness center with weight training equipment and a gym with court space for basketball, volleyball, and badminton.

Disabled Students: All of the campus is accessible. Facilities include wheelchair ramps, elevators, special parking, specially equipped restrooms, lowered drinking fountains, lowered telephones, and special housing. All dorm rooms have elevator access and meet ADA requirements.

Services: Counseling and information services are available, as is tutoring in some subjects. Tutoring is free of charge and includes both group and individual peer tutoring.

Campus Safety and Security: Measures include emergency notification system, self-defense education, and security escort services. There are shuttle buses, lighted pathways/sidewalks, controlled access to dorms/residences, security guards at all entrances, and admission to all buildings by means of a security pass worn by all students, faculty, and staff.

Programs of Study: MCPHS confers B.S. and B.S.N. degrees. Master's and doctoral degrees are also awarded. Bachelor's degrees are awarded in COMPUTER AND PHYSICAL SCIENCE (chemistry and radiological technology), HEALTH PROFESSIONS (dental hygiene, health science, nuclear medical technology, nursing, pharmaceutical science, and premedicine). Pharmacy and nursing have the largest enrollments.

Required: Graduation requirements vary by program. Students must complete course work in expository writing, history and politics, psychology, sociology, interpersonal communications in the health professions, evolution of the health professions, biomedical ethics, and humanities. Students must maintain a minimum GPA of 2.0 overall and a professional GPA that varies by program.

Special: MCPHS offers cross-registration with the other colleges of the Fenway Consortium and cooperative programs with several schools. Accelerated degrees and dual majors are available in some programs. There are 2 national honor societies.

Faculty/Classroom: 35% of faculty are male; 65% are female. All teach and do research. No introductory courses are taught by graduate students.

Requirements: The SAT or ACT is required. Applicants must graduate from an accredited secondary school with 16 units, including 4 of English, 3 of math, 2 of lab science, 1 of history, and 6 of other college-preparatory subjects. The college also advises advanced chemistry or physics with lab and an extra unit of math. Interviews are recommended. Letters of reference from a guidance counselor and a science or math teacher and 2 student essays are required. AP and CLEP credits are accepted. Important factors in the admissions decision are evidence of special talent, recommendations by school officials, and advanced placement or honors courses.

Procedure: Freshmen are admitted in fall. Entrance exams should be taken by December of the senior year. There are early admissions and deferred admissions plans. The application fee was $70. Applications are accepted online. Check with the school for current deadlines.

Transfer: 224 transfer students enrolled in a recent year. Applicants must have a minimum GPA of 2.5. Those with 1 year or less of college credit must submit secondary school transcripts. 30 of 124 credits required for the bachelor's degree must be completed at MCPHS.

Visiting: There are regularly scheduled orientations for prospective students, including a campus tour and information sessions. There are guides for informal visits, and visitors may sit in on classes. To schedule a visit, contact the Admissions Office.

Financial Aid: In a recent year, the average freshman award was $14,986. 20% of undergraduate students worked part-time. Average annual earnings from campus work were $1200. MCPHS is a member of CSS. The FAFSA is required. Check with the school for current application deadlines.

International Students: There were 153 international students enrolled in a recent year. The school actively recruits these students. They must take the TOEFL with a minimum score of 550 on the paper-based TOEFL (PBT) or 79 on the Internet-based version (iBT) and the college's own test. They must also take the SAT or ACT.

Computers: Wireless access is available. MPCHS provides Internet access in dorms, computer labs, hallway kiosks, and the library. There are more than 500 computers available to students. All students may access the system. There are no time limits and no fees. It is strongly recommended that all students have a personal computer.

Graduates: In a recent year, 279 bachelor's degrees were awarded. The most popular majors were pharmacy (64%), nursing (8%), and dental hygiene (6%). In an average class, 19% graduate in 3 years or less, 60% graduate in 4 years or less, 66% graduate in 5 years or less, and 69% graduate in 6 years or less.

Admissions Contact: Executive Director of Admissions. A campus DVD is available. E-mail: *admissions@mcphs.edu* Web: *www.mcphs.edu*

MASSACHUSETTS INSTITUTE OF TECHNOLOGY D-2

Cambridge, MA 02139	**(617) 253-3400; (617) 258-8304**
Full-time: 2449 men, 2031 women	**Faculty:** 1011; I, ++$
Part-time: 16 men, 7 women	**Ph.D.s:** 98%
Graduate: 4602 men, 2084 women	**Student/Faculty:** 4 to 1
Year: 4-1-4, summer session	**Tuition:** $42,050
Application Deadline: January 1	**Room & Board:** $12,188
Freshman Class: 18109 applied, 1620 accepted, 1135 enrolled	
SAT CR/M/W: 730/780/740 **ACT:** 34	**MOST COMPETITIVE**

Massachusetts Institute of Technology, founded in 1861, is a private, independent, institution offering programs in architecture and planning, engineering, humanities, arts, and social sciences, management, science, and health sciences, and technology. There are 5 undergraduate schools and 5 graduate schools. In addition to regional accreditation, MIT has baccalaureate program accreditation with AACSB, ABET, and CSAB. The 5 libraries contain 3.6 million volumes, 2.4 million microform items, and 47,457 audio/video tapes/CDs/DVDs. Computerized library services include interlibrary loans, database searching, Internet access, and Wi-Fi capability. Special learning facilities include an art gallery, radio station, TV station, numerous labs and centers. The 168-acre campus is in an urban area 1 mile north of Boston. Including any residence halls, there are 151 buildings.

Student Life: 91% of undergraduates are from out of state, mostly the Middle Atlantic. Students are from 50 states, 92 foreign countries, and Canada. 37% are White; 24% Asian American; 15% Hispanic. The average age of freshmen is 19; all undergraduates, 20. 3% do not continue beyond their first year; 97% remain to graduate.

Housing: 3570 students can be accommodated in college housing, which includes single-sex and coed dorms, on-campus apartments, and married student housing. In addition, there are language houses, special-interest houses, fraternity houses, sorority houses, off-campus independent living groups, and non-Greek cooperative houses. On-campus housing is guaranteed for all 4 years. 75% of students live on campus. Some may keep cars.

Activities: 42% of men belong to 2 local and 25 national fraternities; 31% of women belong to 6 national sororities. Groups on campus include art, band, cheerleading, chess, choir, chorale, chorus, computers, dance, debate, drama, environmental, ethnic, film, gay, honors, international, jazz band, literary magazine, marching band, musical theater, newspaper, orchestra, over 400 recognized organizations on campus, photography, political, professional, radio and TV, religious, social, social service, student government, symphony, and yearbook. Popular campus events include Independent Activities Period and Spring Weekend.

Sports: There are 16 intercollegiate sports for men and 15 for women, and 20 intramural sports for men and 20 for women. Facilities include an athletic complex with 10 buildings and 26 acres of playing fields.

Disabled Students: Facilities include wheelchair ramps, elevators, special parking, specially equipped restrooms, special class scheduling, lowered drinking fountains, lowered telephones. wheelchair lifts, and automatic doors. An assistive technology lab and assistance with library services are available, upon determination of need.

Services: Counseling and information services are available, as is tutoring in most subjects. There is a reader service for the blind. Accommodations for students with documented disabilities are determined on an individual basis.

Campus Safety and Security: Measures include 24-hour foot and vehicle patrol, emergency notification system, self-defense education, and security escort services. There are shuttle buses, emergency telephones, lighted pathways/sidewalks, automated external defibrillators (AEDs) are stationed across campus.

Programs of Study: MIT confers B.S. degrees. Master's and doctoral degrees are also awarded. Bachelor's degrees are awarded in BIOLOGICAL SCIENCE (biology/biological science and neurosciences), BUSINESS (management science), COMMUNICATIONS AND THE ARTS (creative writing, digital communications, linguistics, literature, media arts, and music), COMPUTER AND PHYSICAL SCIENCE (chemistry, computer science, earth science, mathematics, physics, and science technology), ENGINEERING AND ENVIRONMENTAL DESIGN (aeronautical engineering, aerospace studies, architecture, bioengineering, biomedical engineering, chemical engineering, civil engineering, electrical/electronics engineering, engineering, environmental engineering, materials engineering, materials science, mechanical engineering, nuclear engineering, and ocean engineering), SOCIAL SCIENCE (anthropology, archeology, cognitive science, economics, history, humanities, interdisciplinary studies, philosophy, political science/government, and urban studies). Engineering, science, management and social science programs are the strongest academically. Engineering has the largest enrollment.

Required: To graduate, students must fulfill the General Institute Requirements, as well as communication and physical education requirements, and fulfill departmental program requirements. The General Institute Requirements consist of 6 courses in science, 1 in lab science, 2 in restricted science and technology electives, and 8 in humanities, arts, and social sciences for a total of 17 courses.

Special: MIT offers cross-registration with Harvard, Wellesley, the Massachusetts College of Art and Design, and the School of the Museum of Fine Arts. Internships are offered in a number of programs. Short and long-term study abroad options are offered. The Undergraduate Research Opportunities Program (UROP) cultivates and supports research partnerships between MIT undergraduates and faculty. There are 10 national honor societies and including Phi Beta Kappa.

Faculty/Classroom: 79% of faculty are male; 21% are female. All teach and do research. No introductory courses are taught by graduate students.

Admissions: 9% of the 2013-2014 applicants were accepted. The SAT scores for the 2013-2014 freshman class were: Critical Reading--4% between 500 and 599, 32% between 600 and 699, and 65% between 700 and 800; Math--10% between 600 and 699, and 90% between 700 and 800; Writing--3% between 500 and 599, 28% between 600 and 699, and 69% between 700 and 800. The ACT scores were 2% between 27 and 28, and 98% above 28. 100% of the current freshmen were in the top fifth of their class; 100% were in the top two fifths. 203 freshmen graduated first in their class.

Requirements: The SAT or ACT is required. The ACT Optional Writing test is also required. In addition, 2 SAT Subject Tests, including 1 of math and 1 of science, are required. 14 academic units are recommended, including 4 each of English, math, and science, 2 of social studies, and a foreign language. The GED is accepted. Essays, 2 teacher evaluations, an official transcript, and a guidance counselor report are required. An interview is strongly recommended. AP credits are accepted.

Procedure: Freshmen are admitted fall. Entrance exams should be taken by the January test date. There are early admissions and deferred admissions plans. Applications should be filed by January 1 for fall entry, along with a $75 fee. Notifications are sent March 20. 849 applicants were on the 2013 waiting list; were admitted. Applications are accepted online.

Transfer: 23 transfer students enrolled in 2012-2013. In order to apply, applicant must have minimum of 2 semesters of college, but not more than 5 semesters, at the time they would enroll. Transfer credit is assessed by each academic department on a course by course basis. Enrolling transfer students are required to complete at least 3 semesters at MIT to earn a bachelors degree. For entry in the Spring semester, only U.S. Citizens and Permanent Residents may apply. Applicants who are not US Citizens or Permanent Residents must apply for entry in the Fall semester.

Visiting: There are regularly scheduled orientations for prospective students, including daily tours (Monday through Friday) preceded by an information session with admissions staff. Visitors may sit in on classes and stay overnight. To schedule a visit, contact the Office of Admissions.

Financial Aid: In 2013-2014, 86% of all full-time freshmen and 74% of continuing full-time students received some form of financial aid. 62% of all full-time freshmen and 62% of continuing full-time students received need-based aid. The average freshman award was $32,749. Need-based scholarships or need-based grants averaged $36,162 ($61,889 maximum); and need-based self-help aid (loans and jobs) averaged $4,438 ($6,000 maximum). 63% of undergraduate students work part-time. Average annual earnings from campus work are $2971. The average financial indebtedness of the 2013 graduate was $20,794. MIT is a member of CSS. The CSS/Profile and FAFSA, and parent W-2s, 1040s, and the business tax form are required. The deadline for filing freshman financial aid applications for fall entry is February 15.

International Students: There are 468 international students enrolled. The school actively recruits these students. They must also take the SAT or ACT. Non-English speakers may substitute the TOEFL for the SAT or ACT.

Computers: All students may access the system at all times. There are no time limits and no fees.

Graduates: From July 1, 2012 to June 30, 2013, 1011 bachelor's degrees were awarded. The most popular majors were computer science and engineering (9%), engineering (mechanical engineering 2-A) (7%), and electrical engineering/computer science (7%). 307 companies recruited on campus in 2012-2013. In an average class, 84% graduate in 4 years or less, 91% graduate in 5 years or less, and 93% graduate in 6 years or less. Of the 2012 graduating class, 39% were enrolled in graduate school within 6 months of graduation, and 52% were employed.

Admissions Contact: Stuart Schmill, Dean of Admissions. E-Mail: *admissions@mit.edu* Web: *web.mit.edu*

MASSACHUSETTS MARITIME ACADEMY E-4

Buzzards Bay, MA 02532-1803 **(508) 830-5000**
(800) 544-3411; (508) 830-5077

Full-time: 825 men, 110 women
Part-time: 45 men, 15 women
Graduate: 45 men, 10 women
Year: semesters
Application Deadline: see profile
Freshman Class: n/av
SAT or ACT: required
Faculty: n/av
Ph.D.s: n/av
Student/Faculty: n/av
Tuition: $7210 ($21,107)
Room & Board: $10,200

COMPETITIVE

Massachusetts Maritime Academy, founded in 1891, is the oldest continuously operating maritime academy in the country. Cooperative educational learning and leadership training opportunities prepare graduates for professional positions within private industry or, if opted, military commissions. The figures in the above capsule and this profile are approximate. The library contains 40,171 volumes, 11,674 microform items, and 1113 audio/video tapes/CDs/DVDs, and subscribes to 505 periodicals including electronic. Computerized library services include interlibrary loans, database searching, Internet access, and laptop Internet portals. Special learning facilities include a learning resource center, planetarium, full bridge-training simulator, oil-spill management simulator, liquid cargo-handling simulator, and computer-aided design lab. The 55-acre campus is in a small town 60 miles south of Boston. Including any residence halls, there are 9 buildings.

Student Life: 70% of undergraduates are from Massachusetts. Others are from 26 states and 11 foreign countries. 73% are from public schools. 90% are white. The average age of freshmen is 18; all undergraduates, 21. 15% do not continue beyond their first year; 70% remain to graduate.

Housing: 800 students can be accommodated in college housing, which includes coed dorms. On-campus housing is guaranteed for all 4 years. 97% of students live on campus; of those, 35% remain on campus on weekends. Alcohol is not permitted. All students may keep cars.

Activities: There are no fraternities or sororities. There are 15 groups on campus, including band, choir, chorus, computers, drill team, jazz band, marching band, newspaper, photography, professional, religious, scuba, social service, student government, and yearbook. Popular campus events include Ring Dance, Emory Rice Day, and Recognition.

Sports: There are 8 intercollegiate sports for men and 6 for women, and 13 intramural sports for men and 5 for women. Facilities include football and baseball fields, a pistol range, outdoor tennis and basketball courts, a sailing center, an Olympic-size swimming pool, 2 weight rooms, 3 multipurpose handball courts, and wrestling courts and fitness rooms. An indoor gym/auditorium seats 2500.

Disabled Students: 90% of the campus is accessible. Facilities include wheelchair ramps, elevators, special parking, and specially equipped restrooms.

Services: Counseling and information services are available, as is tutoring in most subjects.

Campus Safety and Security: Measures include 24-hour foot and vehicle patrol. There are lighted pathways/sidewalks.

Programs of Study: MMA confers B.S. degrees. Master's degrees are also awarded. Bachelor's degrees are awarded in BUSINESS (international business management and transportation management), ENGINEERING AND ENVIRONMENTAL DESIGN (environmental engineering, industrial engineering, and marine engineering). Marine engineering is the strongest academically and has the largest enrollment.

Required: All students must complete 164 credit hours with a minimum of 60 hours in the major and a GPA of 2.0. Requirements include 4 courses in phys ed, 2 each in chemistry and naval science, and 1 each in algebra/trigonometry, introduction to computers, English composition, American literature, Western civilization, economics, analysis, American government, first aid, admiralty law, introduction to marine transportation, introduction to marine engineering, and calculus. All students must complete at least 1 sea term.

Special: MMA offers a junior-year internship in a commercial shipping program. Educational experience includes a minimum of 120 days aboard a training ship, with visits to foreign ports. There are cooperative programs in facilities and environmental engineering and in marine safety and environmental protection. A dual major is available in marine engineering and marine transportaton. A concentration is available in emergency management.

Faculty/Classroom: 96% of faculty are male; 4% are female. All teach undergraduates, and 3% do research. No introductory courses are taught by graduate students. The average class size in an introductory lecture is 25; in a laboratory, 12; and in a regular course, 22.
Requirements: The SAT or ACT is required. Applicants must have graduated from an accredited secondary school or hold a GED certificate. They should have completed 16 Carnegie units, including 4 in English, 3 in math, and 2 each in a foreign language, science, and social science. An essay is required, and an interview is strongly recommended. A GPA of 2.0 is required. AP and CLEP credits are accepted. Important factors in the admissions decision are advanced placement or honors courses, leadership record, and extracurricular activities record.
Procedure: Freshmen are admitted fall. There are early decision, deferred admissions and rolling admissions plans. Application deadlines are open. Applications are accepted online.
Transfer: Students must have a minimum GPA of 2.0. 30 of 164 credits required for the bachelor's degree must be completed at MMA.
Visiting: There are regularly scheduled orientations for prospective students, including a campus tour and an admissions interview. An optional overnight visit can be arranged. There are also open house programs and guides for informal visits. To schedule a visit, contact Admissions.
Financial Aid: MMA is a member of CSS. The CSS/Profile, the FAFSA, and the college's own financial statement are required. Check with the school for current application deadlines.
International Students: They must take the TOEFL. They must also take the SAT or ACT.
Computers: All students may access the system 8 a.m. to 11 p.m. There are no time limits and no fees. All students are required to have a personal computer.
Admissions Contact: Dean of Enrollment Services. A campus DVD is available. E-mail: *admissions@maritime.edu* Web: *www.maritime.edu*

MERRIMACK COLLEGE D-1

North Andover, MA 01845 **(978) 837-5100; (978) 837-5133**

Full-time: 1135 men, 1035 women	**Faculty:** n/av
Part-time: 76 men, 73 women	**Ph.D.s:** 84%
Graduate: 18 men, 116 women	**Student/Faculty:** n/av
Year: semesters, summer session	**Tuition:** $33,365
Application Deadline: February 15	**Room & Board:** $11,850

Freshman Class: 3869 applied, 3400 accepted, 610 enrolled

COMPETITIVE

Founded in 1947, by the Order of St. Augustine, Merrimack College is a private, selective college located just outside of Boston. The College offers over 40 undergraduate majors. Merrimack also offers graduate programs in education and part-time degree completion and certificate programs. There are 4 undergraduate schools and 1 graduate school. The figures in the above capsule and in this profile are approximate. In addition to regional accreditation, Merrimack has baccalaureate program accreditation with ABET. The library contains 176,908 volumes, 2,672 audio/video tapes/CDs/DVDs, and subscribes to 4,800 periodicals including electronic. Computerized library services include interlibrary loans, database searching, Internet access, and laptop Internet portals. Special learning facilities include a learning resource center, art gallery, planetarium, TV station, Astronomy dome and telescope; Rogers Center for the Arts; Diversity Education Center; Center for Augustinian Study & Legacy; Center for Biotechnology and Biomedical Sciences; Center for the Study of Jewish-Christian-Muslim Relations; RFID (Radio Frequency Identification) technology lab. The 220-acre campus is in a suburban area 25 miles north of Boston. Including any residence halls, there are 34 buildings.
Student Life: 74% of undergraduates are from Massachusetts. Others are from 20 states, 22 foreign countries, and Canada. 73% are white. The average age of freshmen is 18; all undergraduates, 20. 13% do not continue beyond their first year; 69% remain to graduate.
Housing: 1634 students can be accommodated in college housing, which includes single-sex and coed dorms and on-campus apartments. In addition, there are special-interest houses, international, wellness, and theme housing, including Austin Scholars housing. On-campus housing is guaranteed for all 4 years. 81% of students live on campus; of those, 81% remain on campus on weekends. Upperclassmen may keep cars.
Activities: 3% of men belong to 2 national fraternities; 9% of women belong to 3 national sororities. There are 57 groups on campus, including art, cheerleading, choir, chorale, chorus, communications, computers, dance, drama, environmental, ethnic, film, gay, honors, international, jazz band, literary magazine, musical theater, newspaper, pep band, photography, political, professional, radio and TV, religious, social, social service, student government, and yearbook. Popular campus events include Spring Weekend, Mr. Merrimack, Cram Jam, Merrimack Survivor, and Relay for Life.
Sports: There are 10 intercollegiate sports for men and 12 for women, and 6 intramural sports for men and 5 for women. Facilities include an athletic complex, including an ice rink, a basketball court, an aerobics studio, and a well-equipped exercise room, and outdoor facilities including 2 sets of tennis courts, baseball, football, softball, soccer, lacrosse, and field hockey fields, and a turf field.
Disabled Students: 95% of the campus is accessible. Facilities include wheelchair ramps, elevators, special parking, specially equipped restrooms, special class scheduling, lowered drinking fountains, lowered telephones, and special housing.
Services: Counseling and information services are available, as is tutoring in every subject. There is a reader service for the blind. Math and writing resource centers are available to all students.
Campus Safety and Security: Measures include 24-hour foot and vehicle patrol, emergency notification system, self-defense education, and security escort services. There are shuttle buses, emergency telephones, lighted pathways/sidewalks, controlled access to dorms/residences, and Rape Aggressive Defense is available through police services.
Programs of Study: Merrimack confers B.A., and B.S. degrees. Associate and master's degrees are also awarded. Bachelor's degrees are awarded in BIOLOGICAL SCIENCE (biochemistry and biology/biological science), BUSINESS (accounting, business administration and management, business economics, international business management, and marketing/retailing/merchandising), COMMUNICATIONS AND THE ARTS (communications, English, and modern language), COMPUTER AND PHYSICAL SCIENCE (chemistry, computer science, mathematics, and physics), EDUCATION (elementary education and secondary education), ENGINEERING AND ENVIRONMENTAL DESIGN (civil engineering, electrical/electronics engineering, and environmental science), HEALTH PROFESSIONS (allied health, predentistry, premedicine, and sports medicine), SOCIAL SCIENCE (economics, history, philosophy, political science/government, prelaw, psychology, religion, and sociology). Science, engineering, and business are the strongest academically. Biology, business administration, sports medicine have the largest enrollments.
Special: Merrimack offers cooperative programs in business, engineering, liberal arts, and computer science, cross-registration through the Northeast Consortium, internships in all arts and science programs, study abroad in 9 countries, and a Washington semester at American University. Work-study programs, a 5-year combined B.A.-B.S. degree in many major fields, and dual and self-designed majors are available. General studies, nondegree study, and pass/fail options are possible. There are 7 national honor societies and 3 departmental honors programs.
Faculty/Classroom: 53% of faculty are male; 47% are female. No introductory courses are taught by graduate students. The average class size in an introductory lecture is 25; in a laboratory is 15; and in a regular course is 15.
Admissions: 88% of a recent year applicants were accepted. 16% of the current freshmen were in the top fifth of their class; 44% were in the top two fifths. 1 freshman graduated first in the class.
Requirements: For business administration, humanities, and social science majors, Merrimack recommends that applicants complete 4 units of English, 3 math and 2 science, 3 of social studies, and 2 foreign language. For other majors, an additional math course and 1 additional course in science are needed. An essay is required, and an interview is recommended. Applicants should have completed 19 Carnegie units. AP and CLEP credits are accepted.
Procedure: Freshmen are admitted fall and spring. Entrance exams should be taken during the spring of the junior year and the fall of the senior year. There are early decision, early admissions, and deferred admissions plans. Early decision applications should be filed by November 15; regular applications, by February 15 for fall entry. Notification of early decision is sent January 1; regular decision, March 15.
Transfer: 72 transfer students enrolled in a recent year. Applicants must have maintained a minimum 2.5 GPA; some programs require a higher GPA. Transfer students must complete the transfer application and essay and must submit official college/university transcript (from each college/university attended), course descriptions of all courses completed from each college/university (needed for evaluation and determination of transfer credit), and a letter of recommendation. Student must not be under disciplinary censure and must be eligible to return to previous institution. A high school transcript is required if the student has less than 30 semester hours of college-level credit completed at the time of application. 48 of 124 credits required for the bachelor's degree must be completed at Merrimack.
Visiting: There are regularly scheduled orientations for prospective students, including campus open houses (total of 4) and several Saturday information sessions for prospective freshman candidates during the fall months. Transfer students have 2 fall semester open house/information session and 2 during the winter/spring mont. Visitors may sit in on classes. To schedule a visit, contact the Office of Admissions.
Financial Aid: Merrimack is a member of CSS. The FAFSA, and Noncustodial profile, Business/Farm Supplement, Sibling verification is required. The deadline for filing freshman financial aid applications for fall entry is February 1.
International Students: There are 55 international students enrolled. The school actively recruits these students. They must take the TOEFL with

a minimum score of 550 on the paper-based TOEFL (PBT) or 75 on the Internet-based version (iBT).

Computers: The campus center has computers available for commuter students, and the library has several computer labs available to all students. The campus is wireless. All students may access the system. There are no time limits and no fees. It is strongly recommended that all students have a personal computer.

Graduates: In a recent year, 402 bachelor's degrees were awarded. The most popular majors were business administration (11%), finance (8%), and marketing (8%). 100 companies recruited on campus in 2010-2011. In an average class, 51% graduate in 4 years or less, 62% graduate in 5 years or less, and 69% graduate in 6 years or less.

Admissions Contact: Dean of Undergraduate Admissions. E-Mail: *admissions@merrimack.edu* Web: *www.merrimack.edu*

MONTSERRAT COLLEGE OF ART E-2

Beverly, MA 01915 (978) 921-4242
(800) 836-0487; (978) 921-4241

Full-time: 105 men, 185 women	**Faculty:** n/av
Part-time: 15 men, 18 women	**Ph.D.s:** 16%
Graduate: n/av	**Student/Faculty:** n/av
Year: semesters	**Tuition:** $25,250
Application Deadline: open	**Room & Board:** $10,200
Freshman Class: n/av	
SAT or ACT: required	

SPECIAL

Montserrat College of Art, founded in 1970, is a private residential, professional institution offering degrees in painting and drawing, fine arts, printmaking, graphic design, illustration, photography, and sculpture, with a complementary program in art education. The figures in the above capsule and this profile are approximate. In addition to regional accreditation, Montserrat has baccalaureate program accreditation with ACBSP and NASAD. The library contains 11,484 volumes 677 audio/video tapes/CDs/DVDs, and subscribes to 79 periodicals including electronic. Computerized library services include interlibrary loans and database searching. Special learning facilities include a learning resource center and art gallery. The 10-acre campus is in a suburban area 26 miles north of Boston. Including any residence halls, there are 17 buildings.

Student Life: 50% of undergraduates are from out of state, mostly the Northeast. Students are from 19 states. 93% are white. The average age of freshmen is 19; all undergraduates, 23. 49% do not continue beyond their first year; 49% remain to graduate.

Housing: 162 students can be accommodated in college housing, which includes single-sex and coed on-campus apartments. In addition, there is quiet housing. All housing is smoke-free. On-campus housing is available on a first-come, first-served basis and is available on a lottery system for upperclassmen. 52% of students commute. Alcohol is not permitted. All students may keep cars.

Activities: There are no fraternities or sororities. There are 6 groups on campus, including art, international, literary magazine, newspaper, radio and TV, social, and student government. Popular campus events include Forum Days, Halloween and holiday parties, and gallery openings.

Sports: There are 2 intramural sports for men and 2 for women. Montserrat uses the facilities of the local YMCA.

Disabled Students: 50% of the campus is accessible. Facilities include wheelchair ramps, elevators, special parking, specially equipped restrooms, and special class scheduling.

Services: Counseling and information services are available, as is tutoring in some subjects, including art history. There is remedial writing and a reader service for students with dyslexia.

Campus Safety and Security: There are emergency telephones and lighted pathways/sidewalks. In addition, there is a security guard in the main building and resident assistants trained in first aid and CPR who patrol the buildings.

Programs of Study: Montserrat confers B.F.A. degrees. Bachelor's degrees are awarded in COMMUNICATIONS AND THE ARTS (fine arts, graphic design, illustration, painting, photography, printmaking, and sculpture), EDUCATION (art education).

Required: To graduate, all students are required to complete 120 credits, including 78 in studio courses and 42 in liberal arts courses, with a 2.0 GPA. Requirements include 12 credits in art history, 9 in humanitites, and 6 each in English composition and liberal arts. Distribution requirements include 33 credits freshman year, 30 sophomore and junior year, and 27 senior year. To enter the senior program, Montserrat students must have a portfolio. During semester-end evaluations, each student displays work from all courses and is evaluated by a faculty panel.

Special: Montserrat is a member of the Northeast Consortium of Colleges and Universities in Massachusetts, which allows students to take classes at any member college for the same cost. Credit study is available through the continuing education department. Montserrat also offers internships, summer study in New York City or Italy, dual and student-designed majors in fine arts and in art education, and a mobility program that allows students to spend a semester at another school within the Association of Independent Colleges of Art and Design.

Faculty/Classroom: 44% of faculty are male; 55% are female. All teach undergraduates. The average class size in a regular course is 15.

Requirements: The SAT or ACT is required. Students must submit an artist's statement, a portfolio, 2 letters of recommendation, and a high school transcript, although no specific program of study is required. A portfolio interview is strongly recommended. A GPA of 2.3 is required. AP and CLEP credits are accepted. Important factors in the admissions decision are evidence of special talent, advanced placement or honors courses, and personality/intangible qualities.

Procedure: Freshmen are admitted fall and spring. There are deferred admissions and rolling admissions plans. Application deadlines are open. The application fee is $50.

Transfer: Applicants are required to submit a portfolio, transcripts from previous colleges, and an artist's statement. An interview is recommended. 60 of 120 credits required for the bachelor's degree must be completed at Montserrat.

Visiting: There are regularly scheduled orientations for prospective students, including tours of college studios, observation of classes, and portfolio consultations. There are guides for informal visits and visitors may sit in on classes. To schedule a visit, contact the Admissions Coordinator.

Financial Aid: The FAFSA and the college's own financial statement are required. Check with the school for current application deadlines.

International Students: The school actively recruits these students. They must take the TOEFL.

Computers: Wireless access is available. The college offers computer labs for work in design, illustration, photography, and video as well as for research, writing, and communication. Computers are available in classroom and studio spaces across campus; "smart classrooms" give instructors interactive control over visuals from electronic media. Printing is available at several campus locations. Wireless access is available in the senior design and sculpture studios. All students may access the system 8 a.m. to 11 p.m. daily. There are no time limits and no fees.

Admissions Contact: Dean of Admissions and Enrollment Management. E-Mail: *admiss@montserrat.edu* Web: *www.montserrat.edu*

MOUNT HOLYOKE COLLEGE B-2

South Hadley, MA 01075 (413) 538-2023; (413) 538-2409

Full-time: 2151 women	**Faculty:** 207; IIB, +$
Part-time: 2 men, 30 women	**Ph.D.s:** 91%
Graduate: 10 men, 58 women	**Student/Faculty:** 10 to 1
Year: semesters	**Tuition:** $41,456
Application Deadline: January 15	**Room & Board:** $12,140
Freshman Class: 3732 applied, 1747 accepted, 527 enrolled	

HIGHLY COMPETITIVE+

Mount Holyoke College, founded in 1837, is an independent, liberal arts college and the oldest institution of higher learning for women in the United States. Figures in the above capsule and in this profile are approximate. The 2 libraries contain 1.3 million volumes, 24,405 microform items, 11,498 audio/video tapes/CDs/DVDs, and subscribe to 8,149 periodicals including electronic. Computerized library services include interlibrary loans, database searching, Internet access, and Wi-Fi capability. Special learning facilities include an art gallery, radio station, an observatory, a child study center, a botanical garden and greenhouse, an equestrian center, a conference center, and centers for global initiatives, leadership, and the environment. The 800-acre campus is in a small town 90 miles west of Boston and 160 miles north of New York City. Including any residence halls, there are 68 buildings.

Student Life: 77% of undergraduates are from out of state, mostly the Middle Atlantic. Students are from 46 states, 80 foreign countries, and Canada. 55% are from public schools. 47% are White; 25% Foreign. The average age of freshmen is 18; all undergraduates, 20. 11% do not continue beyond their first year; 82% remain to graduate.

Housing: 2196 students can be accommodated in college housing, which includes single-sex dorms and on-campus apartments. special accommodations are available by need. On-campus housing is guaranteed for all 4 years. 95% of students live on campus; of those, 70% remain on campus on weekends. All students may keep cars.

Activities: There are no fraternities or sororities. There are 99 groups on campus, including art, band, cheerleading, choir, chorale, chorus, computers, dance, debate, drama, environmental, ethnic, film, gay, honors, international, jazz band, literary magazine, newspaper, orchestra, photography, political, professional, radio and TV, religious, social, social service, student government, and symphony. Popular campus events include Glascock Intercollegiate Poetry Contest, Mountain Day, Pangynaskeia Day, and Founders Day Ceremony.

Sports: There are 14 intercollegiate sports for women. Facilities include The majority of Mount Holyoke's indoor athletic and recreational facilities are housed in the Kendall Sports & Dance Complex. Originally constructed in 1950, the facility has quadrupled in size to 115,399 square feet as a result of significant expansions in both 1984 and 2009. Inside the building, which was named named for College trustee Henry P. Kendall and his family, are the Mount Holyoke Fitness Center, the Mildred S. Howard Gymnasium, the Mount Holyoke Natatorium, the Mount Holyoke Field House and the Mount Holyoke Dance Studios. It is surrounded on the outside by the Mount Holyoke Turf & Track Complex, the Mount Holyoke Soccer Field, the Mount Holyoke Activity Field and the Mount Holyoke Tennis Courts. Also in close proximity are the College's Canoe House and a scenic one-mile loop around Upper Lake for running, walking or riding a horse. The Kendall Sports and Dance Complex is open over 100 hours per week during the academic year. Built in 1987, the Mount Holyoke College Equestrian Center is considered to be one of the finest facilities for educational and competitive riding available to students anywhere. Its stable provides over 69 spacious, airy, rubber-matted stalls, a large outdoor all-weather footing show arena, a permanent dressage arena, two indoor arenas, all-weather turnout paddocks, hunt field and a cross-country course through 120 acres of woods, fields, and streams.

Disabled Students: Facilities include wheelchair ramps, elevators, special parking, specially equipped restrooms, special class scheduling, lowered drinking fountains, and special housing.

Services: Counseling and information services are available, as is tutoring in every subject, The writing center is available to all students at all levels. There is a reader service for the blind. Special testing accommodations, diagnostic testing services, note-taking services, as well as readers and tutors, are available. There is also an adaptive technology lab.

Campus Safety and Security: Measures include 24-hour foot and vehicle patrol, emergency notification system, self-defense education, and security escort services. There are shuttle buses, emergency telephones, lighted pathways/sidewalks, and controlled access to dorms/residences.

Programs of Study: Mount Holyoke confers A.B. degrees. Master's degrees are also awarded. Bachelor's degrees are awarded in AGRICULTURE (environmental studies), BIOLOGICAL SCIENCE (biochemistry, biology/biological science, and neurosciences), COMMUNICATIONS AND THE ARTS (art history and appreciation, classics, dance, dramatic arts, English, film arts, French, Greek, Italian, Latin, music, romance languages and literature, Spanish, and studio art), COMPUTER AND PHYSICAL SCIENCE (astronomy, chemistry, computer science, geology, mathematics, physics, and statistics), EDUCATION (psychology education), ENGINEERING AND ENVIRONMENTAL DESIGN (architecture), SOCIAL SCIENCE (African American studies, anthropology, Asian/Oriental studies, classical/ancient civilization, East Asian studies, economics, gender studies, geography, German area studies, history, international relations, Latin American studies, medieval studies, Middle Eastern studies, philosophy, political science/government, psychology, religion, Russian and Slavic studies, sociology, and South Asian studies). Sciences, social sciences and international relations are the strongest academically. Psychology, international relations, and economics have the largest enrollments.

Required: Students must maintain a minimum GPA of 2.0 while taking 128 total credits, with 32 to 56 in the major. At least 68 credits must be earned from course work outside the major department. Students must complete 3 courses in the humanities, 2 courses each in science/math and social studies, a foreign language, a multicultural perspective course, and 6 credits in phys ed. A minor field of study is necessary for those not pursuing a double major, or an interdisciplinary major.

Special: Mount Holyoke offers students cross-registration through the Five-College Consortium. Other opportunities include the 12-College Exchange Program, science and international studies internships, study abroad in over 50 countries (semester or full-year), a Washington semester, work-study, student-designed majors, dual majors, accelerated degrees, nondegree study, and pass/fail options. A teacher licensure program is available. Mount Holyoke's Nexus: Curriculum to Career program enables students to meaningfully link their liberal arts education with their career goals through internships, research projects, and summer employment. There are 6 national honor societies and including Phi Beta Kappa.

Faculty/Classroom: 42% of faculty are male; 58% are female. All teach and do research. No introductory courses are taught by graduate students.

Admissions: 47% of the 2013-2014 applicants were accepted. 79% of the current freshmen were in the top fifth of their class; 94% were in the top two fifths. 17 freshmen graduated first in their class.

Requirements: The school recommends that applicants have 4 years each of English and foreign language, 3 each of math and science, and 2 of social studies. An essay is required and an interview is strongly recommended. AP credits are accepted. Important factors in the admissions decision are advanced placement or honors courses, leadership record, and recommendations by school officials.

Procedure: Freshmen are admitted fall and spring. Entrance exams should be taken before the application deadline. There are early decision and deferred admissions plans. Early decision applications should be filed by November 15; regular applications, by January 15 for fall entry, along with a $60 fee. Notification of early decision is sent January 1; regular decision, April 1. 166 early decision candidates were accepted for the 2013-2014 class. 445 applicants were on the 2013 waiting list; 36 were admitted. Applications are accepted online.

Transfer: 58 transfer students enrolled in 2012-2013. A statement of good standing, transcripts of secondary school or college-level work, and an essay are required of transfer applicants. An interview is recommended. SAT scores will be considered if submitted but are not required. 64 of 128 credits required for the bachelor's degree must be completed at Mount Holyoke.

Visiting: There are regularly scheduled orientations for prospective students, including tours, on-campus interviews, overnight stays, and meetings with professors and coaches. There are guides for informal visits, visitors may sit in on classes, and stay overnight. To schedule a visit, contact the Admission Office.

Financial Aid: In 2013-2014, 79% of all full-time freshmen and 81% of continuing full-time students received some form of financial aid. 69% of all full-time freshmen and 68% of continuing full-time students received need-based aid. The average freshman award was $33,966. Need-based scholarships or need-based grants averaged $29,355; need-based self-help aid (loans and jobs) averaged $5,577; and other non-need-based awards and non-need-based scholarships averaged $15,720. 62% of undergraduate students work part-time. Average annual earnings from campus work are $2100. Mount Holyoke is a member of CSS. The CSS/Profile and FAFSA, and parent and student tax returns and noncustodial parent form are required. The priority date for freshman financial aid applications for fall entry is February 12. The deadline for filing freshman financial aid applications for fall entry is March 1.

International Students: There are 544 international students enrolled. The school actively recruits these students. They must take the TOEFL with a minimum score of 100 on the Internet-based version (iBT), if English is not their first language.

Computers: All students may access the system. There are no time limits and no fees.

Graduates: From July 1, 2012 to June 30, 2013, 612 bachelor's degrees were awarded. The most popular majors were psychology (10%), English (10%), and biology (9%). 68 companies recruited on campus in 2012-2013. In an average class, 76% graduate in 4 years or less, 81% graduate in 5 years or less, and 82% graduate in 6 years or less.

Admissions Contact: Diane C. Anci, VP of Enrollment and Dean of Admissions. E-Mail: *admission@mtholyoke.edu* Web: *www.mtholyoke.edu*

MOUNT IDA COLLEGE D-2

Newton, MA 02459 **(617) 928-4553; (617) 928-4507**

Full-time: 405 men, 710 women	**Faculty:** n/av; IIB
Part-time: 15 men, 25 women	**Ph.D.s:** 61%
Graduate: n/av	**Student/Faculty:** n/av
Year: semesters, summer session	**Tuition:** $26,150
Application Deadline: open	**Room & Board:** $13,000
Freshman Class: n/av	
SAT or ACT: required	

LESS COMPETITIVE

Mount Ida College, founded in 1899, is a private institution that prepares students for professional careers through a career centered curriculum that is integrated with liberal studies. The figures in the above capsule and in this profile are approximate. Mount Ida is accredited with ABFSE, ADA, FIDER, and NASAD. The library contains 62,500 volumes, 68 micro-form items, 2,000 audio/video tapes/CDs/DVDs, and subscribes to 530 periodicals including electronic. Computerized library services include interlibrary loans, database searching, and Internet access. Special learning facilities include a learning resource center, art gallery, radio station, TV station, communication lab, darkroom, sewing rooms, blueprint-making facility, and dental labs. The 72-acre campus is in a suburban area, 8 miles west of downtown Boston. Including residence halls, there are 18 buildings.

Student Life: 54% of undergraduates are from Massachusetts. Students are from 23 states, 33 foreign countries, and Canada. 80% are from public schools. 63% are white; 16% African American. The average age of freshmen is 19; all undergraduates, 21.

Housing: 803 students can be accommodated in college housing, which includes single-sex and coed dorms. In addition, there are honors houses and housing for students over age 21. On-campus housing is guaranteed for all 4 years. 60% of students live on campus. Upperclassmen may keep cars.

Activities: There are no fraternities or sororities. There are 25 groups on campus, including AIGA, commuter, equestrian, travel, vet technology, art, cheerleading, chess, choir, dance, drama, ethnic, fashion, gay, honors, international, literary magazine, newspaper, photography, professional, radio and TV, religious, social, social service, student government, and yearbook. Popular campus events include Welcome Week, Spring Fling, and Senior Week.

Sports: There are 7 intercollegiate sports for men and 6 for women; and 8 intramural sports for men and 10 for women. Facilities include a gym, playing fields, a fitness center, tennis courts, an outdoor swimming pool, athletic fields, and an athletic center.

Disabled Students: 75% of the campus is accessible. Facilities include wheelchair ramps, elevators, special parking, specially equipped rest rooms, special class scheduling, lowered drinking fountains, lowered telephones, and special housing.

Services: Counseling and information services are available, as is tutoring in most subjects. There is remedial math, reading, and writing. There is a program for learning disabled students, for which a fee is charged. Studies skills courses are also available. The Learning Circle is another innovative campus wide initiative that provides a professional learning specialist to assist students and monitor their academic progress.

Campus Safety and Security: Measures include 24-hour foot and vehicle patrol, self-defense education, and security escort services. There are shuttle buses, emergency telephones, and lighted pathways/sidewalks.

Programs of Study: Mount Ida confers B.A., B.S., and B.L.S. degrees. Associates degrees are also awarded. Bachelor's degrees are awarded in AGRICULTURE (equine science), BUSINESS (business administration and management, fashion merchandising, funeral home services, hospitality management services, marketing/retailing/merchandising, retailing, and small business management), COMMUNICATIONS AND THE ARTS (communications, graphic design, journalism, media arts, and radio/television technology), EDUCATION (early childhood education), ENGINEERING AND ENVIRONMENTAL DESIGN (interior design), HEALTH PROFESSIONS (veterinary science), SOCIAL SCIENCE (child psychology/development, criminal justice, fashion design and technology, law, and liberal arts/general studies). Veterinary technology, dental hygiene, and funeral service are the strongest academically. Business and veterinary technology have the largest enrollments.

Required: Candidates for a bachelor's degree must earn 128 credits with a 2.0 GPA. The distribution requirement varies for each major. 1 phys ed course is required. The all-college curriculum includes these common experiences for all students: a college success course, a junior year interdisciplinary seminar, and a senior capstone project.

Special: Internships in the form of work experience are available in each department. Work-study is provided by the college, student-designed majors, study abroad in 14 countries, exchange program with Strasbourg, France, a general studies degree, an interdisciplinary major in legal studies, non-degree study, and an accelerated degree program in funeral service are also available. There are 4 national honor societies, a freshman honors program, and 4 departmental honors programs.

Faculty/Classroom: 46% of faculty are male; 54% are female. All teach undergraduates. No introductory courses are taught by graduate students. The average class size in an introductory lecture is 25; in a laboratory it is 16; and in a regular course it is 20.

Requirements: The SAT or ACT is required. In addition, applicants are required to have 4 units of English, 2 of social studies, and 3 each of math and science. A portfolio is recommended for certain programs, while an interview is recommended for all applicants. The GED is accepted. A GPA of 2.0 is required. AP and CLEP credits are accepted. Important factors in the admissions decision are advanced placement or honors courses, evidence of special talent, and recommendations by school officials.

Procedure: Freshmen are admitted fall and spring. Entrance exams should be taken as early as possible by the junior year. There are early admissions, deferred admissions, and rolling admissions plans. Application deadlines are open. Check with the school for current application. Applications are accepted online.

Transfer: 144 transfer students enrolled in a recent year. Applicants need a minimum GPA of C and must submit college and high school transcripts. 32 of 120 credits required for the bachelor's degree must be completed at Mount Ida.

Visiting: There are regularly scheduled orientations for prospective students, consisting of fall and spring open houses, Saturday sessions, and weekday appointments. There are guides for informal visits, visitors may sit in on classes, and stay overnight. To schedule a visit, contact the Admissions Office.

Financial Aid: In a recent year, 70% of undergraduate students worked part-time. Average annual earnings from campus work were $1500. Mount Ida is a member of CSS. The FAFSA is required. Check with the school for current application deadlines.

International Students: There were 93 international students enrolled in a recent year. The school actively recruits these students. They must take the TOEFL. They must also take the SAT or ACT.

Computers: All students may access the system there are no time limits and no fees. It is strongly recommended that all students have a personal computer. A Mac for graphic design majors is recommended.

Graduates: In a recent year, 128 bachelor's degrees were awarded. The most popular majors were criminal justice (16%), graphic design (13%), and management (11%).

Admissions Contact: Judith A. Kaufman. E-Mail: *admissions@mountida.edu* Web: *www.mountida.edu*

NEW ENGLAND CONSERVATORY OF MUSIC E-2

Boston, MA 02115 (617) 585-1101; (617) 585-1115

Full-time: 232 men, 174 women	**Faculty:** 97
Part-time: 17 men, 13 women	**Ph.D.s:** 31%
Graduate: 193 men, 185 women	**Student/Faculty:** 4 to 1
Year: semesters	**Tuition:** $39,955
Application Deadline: December 1	**Room & Board:** $12,595

Freshman Class: 1004 applied, 304 accepted, 107 enrolled

SPECIAL

The New England Conservatory of Music, founded in 1867, is the oldest private school of its kind in the United States. It combines classroom study of music with an emphasis on performance for talented young musicians. There is one undergraduate school and one graduate school. In addition to regional accreditation, NEC has baccalaureate program accreditation with NASM. The 3 libraries contain 86,400 volumes, 265 microform items, 60,000 audio/video tapes/CDs/DVDs, and subscribe to 295 periodicals including electronic. Computerized library services include interlibrary loans, database searching, Internet access, and Wi-Fi capability. Special learning facilities include a The 8-acre campus is in an urban area in the Back Bay neighborhood of Boston. Including any residence halls, there are 4 buildings.

Student Life: 91% of undergraduates are from out of state, mostly the Northeast. Students are from 45 states, 36 foreign countries, and Canada. 75% are from public schools. 40% are White; 37% Foreign. The average age of freshmen is 18; all undergraduates, 21. 5% do not continue beyond their first year; 76% remain to graduate.

Housing: 169 students can be accommodated in college housing, which includes coed dorms. On-campus housing is guaranteed for the freshman year only. 75% of students commute. Alcohol is not permitted. No one may keep cars.

Activities: There are no fraternities or sororities. There are 6 groups on campus, including band, choir, chorale, chorus, ethnic, gay, international, jazz band, literary magazine, newspaper, opera, orchestra, religious, social service, student government, and symphony. Popular campus events include visits of Guest Performers and 600 NEC Concerts.

Sports: There is no sports program at NEC.

Disabled Students: All of the campus is accessible. Facilities include elevators, special parking, specially equipped restrooms, and lowered drinking fountains.

Services: Counseling and information services are available, as is tutoring in most subjects. There is remedial writing.

Campus Safety and Security: Measures include emergency notification system and security escort services. There are emergency telephones, controlled access to dorms/residences, and 24-hour security at the residence hall.

Programs of Study: NEC confers B.Mus degrees. Master's and doctoral degrees are also awarded. Bachelor's degrees are awarded in COMMUNICATIONS AND THE ARTS (applied music, jazz, music, music history and appreciation, music performance, music theory and composition, and visual and performing arts). Music performance is the strongest academically. Classical performance, Jazz, and Contemporary Improvisation are the largest.

Required: Requirements for graduation include successful completion of all core music courses and an annual music promotional, participation in required ensembles, a minimum 2.0 GPA, an average of 120 total credits, and a senior recital.

Special: NEC offers cross-registration with Northeastern and Tufts Universities, as well as 5 year double degree programs with Tufts University and Harvard University.

Faculty/Classroom: 67% of faculty are male; 33% are female. All teach undergraduates. Graduate students teach 1% of introductory courses. The average class size in an introductory lecture is 25 and in a regular course is 15.

Admissions: 30% of the 2013-2014 applicants were accepted.

Requirements: The applicant must be a graduate of an accredited secondary school or have a GED. An artistic resume, repertoire list and essay is required, as is an audition after submitting the formal application. In some cases, taped auditions are accepted; these must be submitted with the admissions application. Applicants are expected to have reached an advanced level of musical accomplishment. A GPA of 2.8 is required. AP and CLEP credits are accepted. Important factors in the admissions decision are evidence of special talent, recommendations by school officials, and parents or siblings attended your school.

Procedure: Freshmen are admitted fall and spring. Entrance exams should be taken by March 1. There is a deferred admissions plan. Applications should be filed by December 1 for fall entry; November 1 for spring entry, along with a $100 fee. Notifications are sent April 1. 100 applicants were on the 2013 waiting list; 3 were admitted. Applications are accepted online.

Transfer: 23 transfer students enrolled in 2012-2013. Transfer students must audition and submit all college-level transcripts and a transfer statement. 60 of 120 credits required for the bachelor's degree must be completed at NEC.

Visiting: There are regularly scheduled orientations for prospective students, consisting of tours offered regularly during the week. Visitors may sit in on classes. To schedule a visit, contact the Admissions Office.

Financial Aid: In 2013-2014, 80% of all full-time freshmen and 98% of continuing full-time students received some form of financial aid. 61% of all full-time freshmen and 82% of continuing full-time students received need-based aid. The average freshman award was $26,055. Need-based scholarships or need-based grants averaged $11,029 ($23,510 maximum); need-based self-help aid (loans and jobs) averaged $7,069 ($11,500 maximum); and other non-need-based awards and non-need-based scholarships averaged $10,436 ($15,500 maximum). 28% of undergraduate students work part-time. Average annual earnings from campus work are $1242. The average financial indebtedness of the 2013 graduate was $29,113. NEC is a member of CSS. The FAFSA and the college's own financial statement are required. The deadline for filing freshman financial aid applications for fall entry is December 1.

International Students: There are 139 international students enrolled. The school actively recruits these students. They must take the TOEFL with a minimum score of 500 on the paper-based TOEFL (PBT) or 61 on the Internet-based version (iBT).

Computers: All students may access the system. There are no time limits. The fee is $125.

Graduates: From July 1, 2012 to June 30, 2013, 82 bachelor's degrees were awarded. The most popular majors were performance (94%) and composition (6%). 50 companies recruited on campus in 2012-2013. In an average class, 61% graduate in 4 years or less and 75% graduate in 6 years or less. Of the 2012 graduating class, 85% were enrolled in graduate school within 6 months of graduation.

Admissions Contact: Christina Daly, Acting Director of Admissions. E-Mail: *admissions@newenglandconservatory.edu* Web: *www.newenglandconservatory.edu*

NEWBURY COLLEGE D-2

Brookline, MA 02445 **(617) 730-7007**
(800) NEWBURY; (617) 731-9618

Full-time: 382 men, 469 women	**Faculty:** 35
Part-time: 44 men, 67 women	**Ph.D.s:** n/av
Graduate: n/av	**Student/Faculty:** 24 to 1
Year: semesters, summer session	**Tuition:** $28,950
Application Deadline:	**Room & Board:** $12,900

Freshman Class: 4895 applied, 2908 accepted, 305 enrolled
SAT CR/M/W: 430/430/430 **ACT:** 20 **COMPETITIVE**

Newbury College, founded in 1962, is a private institution offering career-relevant degree programs in business, graphic design, legal studies, computer science, interior design, communication, culinary arts, hotel and restaurant management, and psychology. There are 3 undergraduate schools. The library contains 61,529 volumes, 311 audio/video tapes/CDs/DVDs, and subscribes to 18,200 periodicals including electronic. Computerized library services include interlibrary loans, database searching, Internet access, and Wi-Fi capability. Special learning facilities include an art gallery, radio station, and TV station. The 10-acre campus is in a suburban area 3 miles west of Boston. Including any residence halls, there are 10 buildings.

Student Life: 66% of undergraduates are from Massachusetts. Others are from 27 states, and 17 foreign countries. 42% are White; 34% African American; 15% Hispanic. The average age of freshmen is 19; all undergraduates, 21. 42% do not continue beyond their first year; 40% remain to graduate.

Housing: 322 students can be accommodated in college housing, which includes single-sex and coed dorms. In addition, there are special-interest houses. On-campus housing is guaranteed for all 4 years, is available on a first-come, first-served basis, and is available on a lottery system for upperclassmen. Priority is given to out-of-town students. 60% of students commute. Alcohol is not permitted. Some may keep cars.

Activities: There are no fraternities or sororities. There are 20 groups on campus, including choir, chorus, dance, ethnic, gay, honors, international, professional, radio and TV, religious, social, social service, and student government. Popular campus events include Multicultural Week, Spring Fling and Fall Fest.

Sports: There are 6 intercollegiate sports for men and 6 for women, and 9 intramural sports for men and 9 for women. Facilities include an off-site gym and a cardiovascular/weight room.

Disabled Students: 80% of the campus is accessible. Facilities include wheelchair ramps, elevators, special parking, specially equipped restrooms, special class scheduling, and lowered drinking fountains.

Services: Counseling and information services are available, as is tutoring in every subject. There is a reader service for the blind, and remedial math, reading, and writing.

Campus Safety and Security: Measures include 24-hour foot and vehicle patrol, emergency notification system, and security escort services. There are shuttle buses and lighted pathways/sidewalks.

Programs of Study: Newbury confers B.S., and B.A. degrees. Associate degrees are also awarded. Bachelor's degrees are awarded in BUSINESS (accounting, business administration and management, fashion merchandising, hotel/motel and restaurant management, international business management, and sports management), COMMUNICATIONS AND THE ARTS (communications and graphic design), COMPUTER AND PHYSICAL SCIENCE (computer science), ENGINEERING AND ENVIRONMENTAL DESIGN (interior design), HEALTH PROFESSIONS (health care administration), SOCIAL SCIENCE (criminal justice, food production/management/services, paralegal studies, prelaw, and psychology). Psychology, and legal studies are the strongest academically. Psychology, criminal justice, business management and culinary management have the largest enrollments.

Required: Candidates for a bachelor's degree must earn 120 credits or 60 credits beyond the associate degree, with a 2.0 GPA. Distribution requirements include courses in math, lab science, literature, and social science, as well as 3 additional credits in arts and sciences.

Special: Internships are part of the bachelor degree program. Dual majors are available. Credits earned for associate degrees in professional areas can be applied toward the college's bachelor degree programs. There are 2 national honor societies and a freshman honors program.

Faculty/Classroom: 56% of faculty are male; 44% are female. All teach undergraduates. No introductory courses are taught by graduate students. The average class size in an introductory lecture is 25; in a laboratory is 12; and in a regular course is 25.

Admissions: 59% of the 2013-2014 applicants were accepted. The SAT scores for the 2013-2014 freshman class were: Critical Reading--88% below 500, 9% between 500 and 599, and 3% between 600 and 699; Math--83% below 500, 14% between 500 and 599, and 3% between 600 and 699; Writing--89% below 500, 8% between 500 and 599, and 3% between 600 and 699.

Requirements: The SAT or ACT is recommended. Applicants must submit an application, 2 letters of recommendation, high school transcripts, and an essay. A GPA of 2.0 is required. AP and CLEP credits are accepted. Important factors in the admissions decision are leadership record, recommendations by alumni, and extracurricular activities record.

Procedure: Freshmen are admitted fall and spring. Entrance exams should be taken following acceptance. There are deferred admissions and rolling admissions plans. Application deadlines are open. Application fee is $25. Notification is sent on a rolling basis. Applications are accepted online. Application fees are waived if application is completed online.

Transfer: 34 transfer students enrolled in 2012-2013. Transfer students must submit an application, 2 recommendations, high school and college transcripts, and an essay. 30 of 120 credits required for the bachelor's degree must be completed at Newbury.

Visiting: There are regularly scheduled orientations for prospective students, including fall and spring open houses, daily interviews, and campus tours. There are guides for informal visits and visitors may sit in on classes. To schedule a visit, contact the Office of Admission.

Financial Aid: In 2013-2014, 84% of all full-time freshmen and 85% of continuing full-time students received some form of financial aid. 98% of all full-time freshmen and 98% of continuing full-time students received need-based aid. The average freshman award was $28,446. Need-based scholarships or need-based grants averaged $12,696 ($13,759 maximum); need-based self-help aid (loans and jobs) averaged $3,460 ($5,500 maximum); and other non-need-based awards and non-need-based scholarships averaged $6,064 ($18,000 maximum). 58% of undergraduate students work part-time. Average annual earnings from campus work are $1472. The average financial indebtedness of the 2013 graduate was $30,802. Newbury is a member of CSS. The FAFSA is required. The priority date for freshman financial aid applications for fall entry is March 15. The deadline for filing freshman financial aid applications for fall entry is May 1.

International Students: There are 35 international students enrolled. The school actively recruits these students. They must take the TOEFL.

Computers: All students may access the system. There are no time limits and no fees.

Graduates: From July 1, 2012 to June 30, 2013, 131 bachelor's degrees were awarded. The most popular majors were business management (26%), hospitiality adminisration (24%), and design (17%). 60 companies recruited on campus in 2012-2013. In an average class, 24% graduate in 4 years or less, 30% graduate in 5 years or less, and 31% graduate in 6 years or less. Of the 2012 graduating class, 12% were enrolled in graduate school within 6 months of graduation, and 96% were employed.

Admissions Contact: Joseph Chillo, Executive Vice President. E-Mail: *admissions@newbury.edu* Web: *www.newbury.edu*

NICHOLS COLLEGE C-3

Dudley, MA 01571 (508) 213-2274
(800) 470-3379; (508) 943-9885

Full-time: 750 men, 430 women	**Faculty:** n/av
Part-time: 65 men, 120 women	**Ph.D.s:** 61%
Graduate: 110 men, 110 women	**Student/Faculty:** n/av
Year: semesters, summer session	**Tuition:** $30,900 ($35,500)
Application Deadline: open	**Room & Board:** $10,545
Freshman Class: n/av	
SAT or ACT: required	

LESS COMPETITIVE

Nichols College, founded in 1815, is a private institution emphasizing business and liberal arts. There are campuses in Dudley, Auburn, and Worcester. The figures in the above capsule and in this profile are approximate. There is one graduate school. The library contains 80,000 volumes, 2936 microform items, 905 audio/video tapes/CDs/DVDs, and subscribes to 152 periodicals including electronic. Computerized library services include interlibrary loans, database searching, Internet access, and laptop Internet portals. Special learning facilities include a learning resource center, radio station, and the Robert C. Fischer Policy and Cultural Institute. The 200-acre campus is in a suburban area 20 miles south of Worcester. Including any residence halls, there are 24 buildings.

Student Life: 61% of undergraduates are from Massachusetts. Others are from 25 states, 4 foreign countries, and Canada. 88% are white. The average age of freshmen is 18; all undergraduates, 22. 34% do not continue beyond their first year; 53% remain to graduate.

Housing: 975 students can be accommodated in college housing, which includes coed dorms and on-campus apartments, substance-free housing, quiet lifestyle housing, and academic living housing. On-campus housing is guaranteed for all 4 years and is available on a lottery system for upperclassmen. 84% of students live on campus. All students may keep cars.

Activities: There are no fraternities or sororities. There are 25 groups on campus, including cheerleading, chess, computers, departmental, drama, ethnic, gay, honors, international, literary magazine, newspaper, political, professional, radio and TV, religious, social, social service, and student government. Popular campus events include Spring Weekend and 100 Days Social.

Sports: There are 8 intercollegiate sports for men and 7 for women. Facilities include a field house with basketball courts, a sauna, aerobics and weight training rooms, and athletic training facilities. There is also an athletic complex with a gym, a suspended jogging track, 2 racquetball courts, a squash court, an indoor climbing wall, and 2 fitness rooms. Outdoor facilities include 6 tennis courts, a volleyball court, and a basketball court.

Disabled Students: 67% of the campus is accessible. Facilities include wheelchair ramps, elevators, special parking, specially equipped restrooms, special class scheduling, lowered drinking fountains, and special housing. The college makes every effort to accommodate students with special needs.

Services: Counseling and information services are available, as is tutoring in most subjects. There is remedial math and writing, and ESL assistance by appointment.

Campus Safety and Security: Measures include 24-hour foot and vehicle patrol, emergency notification system, self-defense education, and security escort services. There are emergency telephones, lighted pathways/sidewalks, and access controls for dorms/residences.

Programs of Study: Nichols confers B.A. and B.S.B.A. degrees. Associate and master's degrees are also awarded. Bachelor's degrees are awarded in BUSINESS (accounting, business administration and management, business communications, human resources, international business management, management information systems, marketing/retailing/merchandising, and sports management), COMMUNICATIONS AND THE ARTS (arts administration/management and English), COMPUTER AND PHYSICAL SCIENCE (mathematics), SOCIAL SCIENCE (criminal justice, economics, history, law, and psychology). Accounting is the strongest academically. Sports management and criminal justice have the largest enrollments.

Required: All students must complete a program of study within 10 semesters and maintain a GPA of 2.0 overall and in their major. Business students need 33 hours of business core classes out of the total 122 hours required of all students for graduation. Students must complete 2 writing-intensive upper-level courses, and they must attend 28 events within the Cultural Experience: The Arts, Sciences, and Public Policy Program.

Special: Nichols offers cross-registration with the Worcester Consortium of Colleges, internships designed with departmental approval, study abroad at Regents College in London and European University, a Washington semester, a general business degree, a teacher certification program, an accelerated degree program in business administration, and nondegree study. There are 5 national honor societies, a freshman honors program, and 8 departmental honors programs.

Faculty/Classroom: 63% of faculty are male; 37% are female. All teach undergraduates and do research. No introductory courses are taught by graduate students. The average class size in an introductory lecture is 22; in a laboratory, 16; and in a regular course, 23.

Requirements: The SAT or ACT is required. Applicants must have graduated from an accredited secondary school or have earned a GED. Recommended preparation includes 4 years of high school English, 3 of math, and 2 each of science and social studies. A GPA of 2.0 is required. AP and CLEP credits are accepted. Important factors in the admissions decision are advanced placement or honors courses, recommendations by school officials, and personality/intangible qualities.

Procedure: Freshmen are admitted fall and spring. Entrance exams should be taken by November of the senior year. Check with the school for current application fee. Notification is sent on a rolling basis. Applications are accepted online.

Transfer: Applicants need an average GPA of 2.6 in courses to be transferred and must submit official transcripts of all previous college study. 30 of 122 credits required for the bachelor's degree must be completed at Nichols.

Visiting: There are regularly scheduled orientations for prospective students, including meetings with faculty members and preregistration; separate orientation programs are tailored for transfers only. There are guides for informal visits, visitors may sit in on classes, and stay overnight. To schedule a visit, contact the Admissions Office.

Financial Aid. The FAFSA is required. Check with the school for current application deadlines.

International Students: There were 5 international students enrolled in a recent year. The school actively recruits these students. They must take the TOEFL with a minimum score of 550 on the paper-based TOEFL (PBT), or have acceptable scores on the SAT or ACT.

Computers: Wireless access is available. Nichols students have 65 PCs available in the library, 24 in a classroom, and 8 in the alumni snack bar. All students may access the system 24 hours a day. There are no time limits and no fees. It is strongly recommended that all students have a personal computer. Nichols College has a discount agreement with Lenovo.

Graduates: In a recent year, 175 bachelor's degrees were awarded. The most popular majors were general business (23%), sport management (19%), and accounting (12%). In an average class, 45% graduate in 4 years or less, 52% graduate in 5 years or less, and 53% graduate in 6 years or less. 3% were enrolled in graduate school within 6 months of graduation, and 95% were employed.

Admissions Contact: Associate Director of Admissions. E-mail: *admissions@nichols.edu* Web: *www.nichols.edu*

NORTHEASTERN UNIVERSITY E-2

Boston, MA 02115 (617) 373-2200; (617) 373-8780

Full-time: 8466 men, 8461 women	**Faculty:** n/av
Part-time: n/av	**Ph.D.s:** 95%
Graduate: 4128 men, 3510 women	**Student/Faculty:** 13 to 1
Year: semesters, summer session	**Tuition:** $41,686
Application Deadline: January 1	**Room & Board:** $13,610
Freshman Class: n/av	

MOST COMPETITIVE

Founded in 1898, Northeastern University is a private research university located in the heart of Boston. Northeastern is the leader in worldwide experiential learning, urban engagement, and interdisciplinary research that meets global and societal needs. Our broad mix of experience-based education programs our signature cooperative education program, as well as student research, service learning, and global learning build the connections that enable students to transform their lives. The University offers a comprehensive range of undergraduate and graduate programs leading to degrees through the doctorate in nine colleges and schools. There are 7 undergraduate schools and 8 graduate schools. In addition to regional accreditation, Northeastern has baccalaureate program accreditation with AACSB, ABET, ACPE, and NAAB. The 3 libraries contain 896,213 volumes, 1.3 million microform items, 18,210 audio/video tapes/CDs/DVDs, and subscribe to 128,027 periodicals including electronic. Computerized library services include interlibrary loans, database searching, Internet access, and Wi-Fi capability. Special learning facilities include an art gallery, radio station, architecture studio, TV production suite, and various research labs. The 73-acre campus is in an urban area Located in the heart of Boston, on Huntington Avenue, also known as the Avenue of the Arts. Including any residence halls, there are 88 buildings.

Student Life: 67% of undergraduates are from out of state, mostly the Northeast. Students are from 48 states, 119 foreign countries, and Canada. The average age of freshmen is 18; all undergraduates, 20.

Housing: 8354 students can be accommodated in college housing, which includes single-sex and coed dorms, on-campus apartments, and off-campus apartments. In addition, there are honors houses, special-interest houses, academic/college-based, innovation, global perspective, leadership, creative expression, green living, community service. On-campus housing is guaranteed for the freshman year only, is available on a first-come, first-served basis, and is available on a lottery system for upperclassmen. Upperclassmen may keep cars.

Activities: 8% of men belong to 18 national fraternities; 12% of women belong to 11 national sororities. There are 331 groups on campus, including art, band, cheerleading, chess, chorale, chorus, computers, dance, debate, drama, environmental, ethnic, film, gay, honors, international, jazz band, literary magazine, musical theater, newspaper, orchestra, pep band, political, professional, radio and TV, religious, Resident Student Association, social, social service, student government, symphony, and yearbook. Popular campus events include Springfest, Senior Week, Welcome Week and Carnevale.
Sports: There are 7 intercollegiate sports for men and 9 for women, and 31 intramural sports for men and 31 for women. Facilities include an outdoor and indoor tracks, a indoor hockey arena, swimming pool, indoor and outdoor tennis courts, racquetball, squash, volleyball, basketball courts and three fitness centers.
Disabled Students: 95% of the campus is accessible. Facilities include wheelchair ramps, elevators, special parking, specially equipped restrooms, special class scheduling, lowered drinking fountains, lowered telephones, special housing. specially equipped labs, and a tunnel system connecting the major administrative and academic buildings.
Services: Counseling and information services are available, as is tutoring in most subjects. There is remedial math, reading, and writing.
Campus Safety and Security: Measures include 24-hour foot and vehicle patrol, emergency notification system, self-defense education, and security escort services. There are shuttle buses, emergency telephones, lighted pathways/sidewalks, controlled access to dorms/residences, and in-room safes.
Programs of Study: Northeastern confers B.A., B.S., B.F.A. and B.L.A. degrees. Master's and doctoral degrees are also awarded. Bachelor's degrees are awarded in AGRICULTURE (environmental studies), BIOLOGICAL SCIENCE (biochemistry, biology/biological science, marine biology, and neurosciences), BUSINESS (accounting, business administration and management, international business management, and management information systems), COMMUNICATIONS AND THE ARTS (American Sign Language, art, communications, dramatic arts, English, film arts, graphic design, journalism, languages, linguistics, multimedia, music, music technology, studio art, and theatre arts), COMPUTER AND PHYSICAL SCIENCE (applied physics, chemistry, computer programming, computer science, digital arts/technology, earth science, information sciences and systems, mathematics, and physics), ENGINEERING AND ENVIRONMENTAL DESIGN (architecture, chemical engineering, civil engineering, computer engineering, electrical/electronics engineering, environmental science, industrial engineering, landscape architecture/design, and mechanical engineering), HEALTH PROFESSIONS (health science, nursing, pharmaceutical science, pharmacy, physical therapy, and speech pathology/audiology), SOCIAL SCIENCE (African American studies, anthropology, Asian/Oriental studies, criminal justice, economics, history, interdisciplinary studies, Judaic studies, philosophy, philosophy and religion, political science/government, psychology, religion, and sociology). Business administration, engineering, and sciences have the largest enrollments.
Required: Although each college has its own requirements, students must generally complete at least 128 semester hours with a minimum GPA of 2.0. Students must also fulfill the university-wide general education requirement.
Special: Northeastern offers a variety of experiential learning opportunities -- co-op, research, global experience, and service-learning -- in Boston, throughout the U.S., and around the world to integrate classroom instruction with professional experience. Northeastern takes a flexible student-centered approach to academics that allows you to create the education that best suits your goals and aspirations. We offer four- and five-year programs, combined degree programs, interdisciplinary study options, study abroad in dozens of countries, undergraduate research opportunities, an Honors Program, work-study through the university and in neighboring public and private agencies, and student-designed majors. There are 14 national honor societies and a freshman honors program.
Faculty/Classroom: 57% of faculty are male; 43% are female. No introductory courses are taught by graduate students.
Admissions: 86% of the current freshmen were in the top fifth of their class; 97% were in the top two fifths.
Requirements: The SAT or ACT is required. The ACT Optional Writing test is also required. Northeastern requires that applicants have 17 academic units, including 4 in English, 3 each in math, science, and social studies, and 2 each in foreign language and history. Recommended are 4 units in math and science, and a foreign language. An essay is required. SAT or ACT required. AP credits are accepted. Important factors in the admissions decision are advanced placement or honors courses, leadership record, evidence of special talent, extracurricular activities record, geographical diversity, and recommendations by school officials.
Procedure: Freshmen are admitted fall. Entrance exams should be taken from May of the junior year through December of the senior year. There are early admissions and deferred admissions plans. Early decision applications should be filed by November 1; regular applications, by January 1 for fall entry, along with a $75 fee. Notification of early decision is sent December 31; regular decision, April 1. Applications are accepted online.
Transfer: 683 transfer students enrolled in 2012-2013. The most successful transfer students have earned a cumulative GPA of 3.3. Students have also completed the introductory-level courses for their intended majors. Transfer students with less than 24 semester hours of college-level credit must also submit their high school transcripts and SAT or ACT scores.
Visiting: There are regularly scheduled orientations for prospective students. There are guides for informal visits. To schedule a visit, contact the Office of Undergraduate Admissions.
Financial Aid: The CSS/Profile and FAFSA are required. The priority date for freshman financial aid applications for fall entry is February 15.
International Students: There are 2881 international students enrolled. The school actively recruits these students. They must take the TOEFL with a minimum score of 92 on the Internet-based version (iBT).
Computers: All students may access the system 24 hours daily. There are no time limits and no fees.
Graduates: From July 1, 2012 to June 30, 2013, 3368 bachelor's degrees were awarded. The most popular majors were business (20%), health professions (13%), and engineering (12%). 500 companies recruited on campus in 2012-2013. In an average class, 82% graduate in 6 years or less.
Admissions Contact: Ronne Patrick Turner, Associate VP, Enrollment/Dean, Admission. E-Mail: *admissions@neu.edu* Web: *www.northeastern.edu/admissions*

PINE MANOR COLLEGE — E-2

Chestnut Hill, MA 02467 — (617) 731-7104; (800) 762-1357; (617) 731-7102

Full-time: 455 women	**Faculty:** n/av; IIB, --$
Part-time: 10 women	**Ph.D.s:** 77%
Graduate: n/av	**Student/Faculty:** n/av
Year: semesters, summer session	**Tuition:** $35,500
Application Deadline: open	**Room & Board:** $12,500
Freshman Class: n/av	
SAT or ACT: required	

LESS COMPETITIVE

Pine Manor College, established in 1911, is a private liberal arts college for women. The figures in the above capsule and in this profile are approximate. The library contains 65,632 volumes, 62,386 microform items, 1,944 audio/video tapes/CDs/DVDs, and subscribes to 272 periodicals including electronic. Computerized library services include interlibrary loans, database searching, and Internet access. Special learning facilities include a learning resource center, art gallery, radio station, TV station, a language lab. The 60-acre campus is in a suburban area 5 miles west of Boston. Including any residence halls, there are 28 buildings.
Student Life: 75% of undergraduates are from Massachusetts. Students are from 21 states, 15 foreign countries, and Canada. 39% are African American; 14% Hispanic; 13% white. The average age of freshmen is 18; all undergraduates, 20. 32% do not continue beyond their first year; 53% remain to graduate.
Housing: 481 students can be accommodated in college housing, which includes single-sex dorms. In addition, there are special-interest houses, nonsmoking dorms, and a wellness floor (no alcohol allowed). On-campus housing is guaranteed for all 4 years. 68% of students live on campus; of those, 80% remain on campus on weekends. All students may keep cars.
Activities: There are no fraternities or sororities. There are 25 groups on campus, including student health (SHAB), interior design (ASID), minority (ALANA), psychology, art, chorus, dance, diversity, drama, environmental, ethnic, gay, honors, international, literary magazine, musical theater, newspaper, political, professional, radio and TV, religious, social, social service, student government, and yearbook. Popular campus events include Late Night Breakfast during finals, Stressbusters, and Casino Night.
Sports: There are 7 intercollegiate sports for women. Facilities include a modern gym, softball and soccer fields, cross-country trails, tennis courts, a dance studio, and a weight room.
Disabled Students: 40% of the campus is accessible. Facilities include wheelchair ramps, elevators, special parking, specially equipped restrooms, special class scheduling, lowered drinking fountains, and special housing.
Services: Counseling and information services are available, as is tutoring in every subject. There is remedial math, reading, and writing. The learning resource center has professional and peer tutoring and workshops.
Campus Safety and Security: Measures include 24-hour foot and vehicle patrol, self-defense education, and security escort services. There are shuttle buses, emergency telephones, and lighted pathways/sidewalks.
Programs of Study: PMC confers B.A. degrees. Associates and master's degrees are also awarded. Bachelor's degrees are awarded in BIOLOGICAL SCIENCE (biology/biological science), BUSINESS (business administration and management), COMMUNICATIONS AND THE ARTS (art,

communications, and English), SOCIAL SCIENCE (ethics, politics, and social policy, history, and psychology). Psychology, visual arts, and biology have the largest enrollments.

Required: An outcomes-based general education program, with portfolio assessment, is a college requirement. A 4-year leadership program complements the portfolio program. This assists students in exploring inclusive and socially responsible leadership. In addition, students must maintain a minimum GPA of 2.0 and take a total of 132 semester hours.

Special: Pine Manor offers cross-registration with area colleges, internships at more than 1000 sites, and study abroad throughout the world, and at sea. A Washington semester, work-study programs, dual majors, student-designed majors, a B.A.-B.S. degree, non-degree study within continuing education, and pass/fail options for 1 course each semester also are available as is the English Language Institute for students whose native language is not English. There is 1 national honor society and a freshman honors program.

Faculty/Classroom: 26% of faculty are male; 74% are female. All teach undergraduates. No introductory courses are taught by graduate students. The average class size in an introductory lecture is 16; in a laboratory is 16; and in a regular course is 13.

Requirements: The SAT or ACT is required. Applicants are required to have taken 4 courses in English and 3 in math. Additional courses in foreign language, social science, natural science, and elective areas are recommended. An essay is also required. An interview is recommended. The GED is accepted. AP and CLEP credits are accepted. Important factors in the admissions decision are advanced placement or honors courses, leadership record, and recommendations by school officials.

Procedure: Freshmen are admitted fall and spring. There are deferred admissions and rolling admissions plans. Application deadlines are open. Notification is sent on a rolling basis. Applications are accepted online.

Transfer: 24 transfer students enrolled in a recent year. Pine Manor requires transfer students to submit 2 letters of recommendation (1 from a professor) and college transcripts and recommends high school transcripts. The SAT or ACT also is recommended. 32 of 132 credits required for the bachelor's degree must be completed at PMC.

Visiting: There are regularly scheduled orientations for prospective students, including a campus tour and interview. There are guides for informal visits, visitors may sit in on classes, and stay overnight. To schedule a visit, contact the Admissions Office.

Financial Aid: In a recent year, 95% of all full-time freshmen and of continuing full-time students received some form of financial aid. Average annual earnings from campus work were $1500. The FAFSA is required. Check with the school for current application deadlines and fee.

International Students: There were 39 international students enrolled in a recent year. The school actively recruits these students. They must take the TOEFL.

Computers: Wireless access is available. Pine Manor College enjoys high-speed computing network. Students have access to e-mail, the Internet, a campus PC network, and PCs located throughout the campus. Laptop connections are also available in some areas. Software for word processing, spreadsheets, databases, statistics, Web page development, graphic design, desktop and electronic publishing, digital media, and specialized course software is available for student use on college PCs in classrooms and labs. Students are provided with an e-mail account, network storage space for files, and 25MB of Web space on our community Web site. All students may access the system. There are no time limits and no fees.

Graduates: In a recent year, 89 bachelor's degrees were awarded. The most popular majors were psychology (25%), business administration (19%), and biology (18%). In an average class, 33% graduate in 4 years or less, 38% graduate in 5 years or less, and 40% graduate in 6 years or less.

Admissions Contact: Dean of Student Recruitment and Retention. E-Mail: *admissions@pmc.edu* Web: *www.pmc.edu*

REGIS COLLEGE D-2

Weston, MA 02493 **(781) 768-7100**
(866) 438-7344; (781) 768-7071

Full-time: 226 men, 676 women	**Faculty:** 54; IIB, --$
Part-time: 32 men, 215 women	**Ph.D.s:** 74%
Graduate: 106 men, 736 women	**Student/Faculty:** 13 to 1
Year: semesters, summer session	**Tuition:** $34,380
Application Deadline: June 1	**Room & Board:** $13,185
Freshman Class: n/av	

LESS COMPETITIVE

Regis College, through education in the arts, sciences, and professions, empowers women and men to challenge themselves academically, to serve and to lead. A Catholic college, Regis is a diverse and welcoming community guided by the values of the Sisters of St. Joseph of Boston. There are 2 undergraduate schools and one graduate school. In addition to regional accreditation, Regis has baccalaureate program accreditation with CSWE, NASDTEC, and NLN. The library contains 134,706 volumes, 10,826 microform items, 7,856 audio/video tapes/CDs/DVDs, and subscribes to 24,774 periodicals including electronic. Computerized library services include interlibrary loans, database searching, Internet access, and Wi-Fi capability. Special learning facilities include an art gallery, radio station, museum of stamps and postal history, and fine arts center. The 131-acre campus is in a suburban area 12 miles west of Boston. Including any residence halls, there are 15 buildings.

Student Life: 87% of undergraduates are from Massachusetts. Others are from 21 states, and 13 foreign countries. 71% are from public schools. 47% are White; 21% African American; 13% race unknown; 12% Hispanic. The average age of freshmen is 18; all undergraduates, 20. 23% do not continue beyond their first year; 60% remain to graduate.

Housing: 675 students can be accommodated in college housing, which includes single-sex and coed dorms. quiet housing floors. On-campus housing is guaranteed for all 4 years. 57% of students live on campus; of those, 60% remain on campus on weekends. Upperclassmen may keep cars.

Activities: There are no fraternities or sororities. There are 27 groups on campus, including choir, chorale, chorus, computers, dance, drama, ethnic, honors, international, literary magazine, musical theater, newspaper, photography, political, professional, radio and TV, religious, social, social service, student government, and yearbook.

Sports: There are 7 intercollegiate sports for men and 9 for women, and 4 intramural sports for men and 4 for women. Facilities include an athletic facility, a softball diamond, soccer field, 4 tennis courts, an aerobics and dance studio, squash courts, a pool, a sauna and Jacuzzi. The on campus fitness center provides a full range of cardiovascular machines as well as free weights and Nautilus equipment.

Disabled Students: 87% of the campus is accessible. Facilities include wheelchair ramps, elevators, special parking, specially equipped restrooms, special class scheduling, lowered drinking fountains, and special housing.

Services: Counseling and information services are available, as is tutoring in most subjects. There is a reader service for the blind, and remedial math, reading, and writing. There are academic support services for learning-disabled students.

Campus Safety and Security: Measures include 24-hour foot and vehicle patrol, self-defense education, and security escort services. There are shuttle buses, emergency telephones, lighted pathways/sidewalks, and controlled access to dorms/residences.

Programs of Study: Regis confers B.A., B.S.N. and B.S.W. degrees. Associate, master's, and doctoral degrees are also awarded. Bachelor's degrees are awarded in BIOLOGICAL SCIENCE (biochemistry and biology/biological science), BUSINESS (management science), COMMUNICATIONS AND THE ARTS (communications, English, and Spanish), COMPUTER AND PHYSICAL SCIENCE (chemistry and computer science), EDUCATION (mathematics education), HEALTH PROFESSIONS (nursing, public health, and radiological science), SOCIAL SCIENCE (history, international relations, law, liberal arts/general studies, political science/government, psychology, social work, and sociology). Nursing, communication, and management have the largest enrollments.

Required: The baccalaureate degree is conferred upon candidates who have satisfactorily completed a minimum of 120 semester credit hours, with a cumulative gradepoint average of at least 2.00 and who have completed the requirements for a major field, as well as the General Education Program requirements. Certain programs, such as nursing, nuclear medicine technology, social work, and elementary and secondary teaching licensure programs, require the student to earn a higher GPA.

Special: Regis offers cross-registration with Boston, Babson, and Bentley Colleges and through the Sisters of St. Joseph Consortium. Students may study abroad at Regis affiliates in London, Ireland, and in Kyoto, Japan, or through programs of other American colleges. Regis also offers internships, an accelerated degree program, a Washington semester at American University, dual and self-designed majors, work-study, nondegree study, and pass/fail options. Students have the option of pursuing a minor in addition to their major field of study. There are 10 national honor societies and a freshman honors program.

Faculty/Classroom: 28% of faculty are male; 72% are female. 72% teach undergraduates. No introductory courses are taught by graduate students. The average class size in an introductory lecture is 18; in a laboratory is 10; and in a regular course is 11.

Admissions: 27% of the current freshmen were in the top fifth of their class; 54% were in the top two fifths.

Requirements: Applicants should have 4 years of English, 3 or 4 electives, 3 years of math, and 2 years each of foreign language, social studies, and natural science, including a lab science. An essay and 2 letters of recommendation are required. An interview is strongly encouraged. The GED is accepted. Online applications must be accompanied by the transcript, letters of recommendation, and official SAT or ACT scores for some programs. Regis requires applicants to be in the upper 50% of their class. A GPA of 2.5 is required. AP and CLEP credits are accepted. Important factors in the admissions decision are recommendations by school officials, extracurricular activities record, and ability to finance college education.

Procedure: Freshmen are admitted fall and spring. Entrance exams

should be taken during the fall before enrollment. There are deferred admissions and rolling admissions plans. Applications should be filed by June 1 for fall entry, along with a $50 fee. Notifications are sent 12 20. Applications are accepted online.

Transfer: 47 transfer students enrolled in 2012-2013. Transfer students must complete an admission application and fee. In addition, an official high school transcript is required if the applicant has completed fewer than 9 college courses, an official college transcript, 1 letter of recommendation from a professor at the previous college attended, the academic catalog of the previous college, an essay, SAT or ACT scores if fewer than 16 courses have been completed, and health records. 64 of 120 credits required for the bachelor's degree must be completed at Regis.

Visiting: There are regularly scheduled orientations for prospective students, Visiting students can participate in a welcome tour, lunch, speaker panels, and overnight programs offering class participation. There are guides for informal visits, visitors may sit in on classes, and stay overnight. To schedule a visit, contact the Admissions Office.

Financial Aid: In 2013-2014, 91% of all full-time freshmen and 72% of continuing full-time students received some form of financial aid. 77% of all full-time freshmen and 82% of continuing full-time students received need-based aid. The average freshman award was $29,462. Need-based scholarships or need-based grants averaged $14,755; need-based self-help aid (loans and jobs) averaged $5,186; and other non-need-based awards and non-need-based scholarships averaged $17,321. Average annual earnings from campus work are $1500. Regis is a member of CSS. The FAFSA and the college's own financial statement are required. The priority date for freshman financial aid applications for fall entry is February 15.

International Students: There are 13 international students enrolled. The school actively recruits these students. They must take the TOEFL with a minimum score of 550 on the paper-based TOEFL (PBT) or 79 on the Internet-based version (iBT). They must also take the SAT or ACT.

Computers: All students may access the system. There are no time limits and no fees.

Graduates: From July 1, 2012 to June 30, 2013, 215 bachelor's degrees were awarded. The most popular majors were nursing (53%), biological/life sciences (8%), and business/marketing (7%). In an average class, 36% graduate in 4 years or less, 48% graduate in 5 years or less, and 53% graduate in 6 years or less.

Admissions Contact: Wanda Suriel, Director of Admission. E-Mail: *admission@regiscollege.edu* Web: *www.regiscollege.edu*

SALEM STATE COLLEGE — E-2

Salem, MA 01970 — **(978) 542-6200; (978) 542-6893**

Full-time: 2050 men, 3450 women	**Faculty:** 296
Part-time: 635 men, 1200 women	**Ph.D.s:** 77%
Graduate: 580 men, 2000 women	**Student/Faculty:** n/av
Year: semesters, summer session	**Tuition:** $8,170 ($14,310)
Application Deadline: open	**Room & Board:** $11,510
Freshman Class: n/av	
SAT or ACT: required	

LESS COMPETITIVE

Salem State College, founded in 1854, is a public institution offering programs in liberal arts, business, education, and nursing. The figures in the above capsule and in this profile are approximate. There are 5 undergraduate schools and 1 graduate school. In addition to regional accreditation, Salem State has baccalaureate program accreditation with CSWE, NASAD, NCATE, and NLN. The library contains 301,876 volumes, 566,592 microform items, and subscribes to 1,145 periodicals including electronic. Computerized library services include inter-library loans, database searching, and Internet access. Special learning facilities include a learning resource center, art gallery, radio station, TV station, and an observatory. The 62-acre campus is in an urban area 18 miles northeast of Boston. Including any residence halls, there are 19 buildings.

Student Life: 90% of undergraduates are from Massachusetts. Students are from 20 states, 40 foreign countries, and Canada. 98% are from public schools. 83% are white. The average age of freshmen is 19; all undergraduates, 24. 25% do not continue beyond their first year; 36% remain to graduate.

Housing: 1470 students can be accommodated in college housing, which includes single-sex and coed dorms and on-campus apartments. On-campus housing is available on a first-come and first-served basis. Priority is given to out-of-town students. 78% of students commute. Alcohol is not permitted. Upperclassmen may keep cars.

Activities: There are no fraternities or sororities. There are 44 groups on campus, including art, band, cheerleading, choir, chorale, chorus, communications, computers, dance, drama, ethnic, gay, honors, international, jazz band, literary magazine, musical theater, newspaper, photography, political, radio and TV, religious, social, social service, and student government. Popular campus events include Welcome Week, Arts Festival, and Senior Week.

Sports: There are 10 intercollegiate sports for men and 10 for women, and 15 intramural sports for men and 15 for women. Facilities include an athletic center with 27 facilities, including a 1600-seat gym, a 2800-seat ice rink, an 8-lane swimming pool, 4 tennis courts, a weight room, a dance studio, and a wellness fitness center.

Disabled Students: 90% of the campus is accessible. Facilities include wheelchair ramps, elevators, special parking, specially equipped rest rooms, lowered drinking fountains, and lowered telephones.

Services: Counseling and information services are available, as is tutoring in every subject. There is a reader service for the blind, and remedial math, reading, and writing.

Campus Safety and Security: Measures include 24-hour foot and vehicle patrol, self-defense education, and security escort services. There are shuttle buses, emergency telephones, and lighted pathways/sidewalks.

Programs of Study: Salem State confers B.A., B.S., B.F.A., B.G.S., B.S.B.A., B.S.Ed., B.S.N., and B.S.W. degrees. Master's degrees are also awarded. Bachelor's degrees are awarded in BIOLOGICAL SCIENCE (biology/biological science), BUSINESS (accounting, banking and finance, business administration and management, and marketing/retailing/merchandising), COMMUNICATIONS AND THE ARTS (advertising, communications, design, dramatic arts, English, fine arts, and photography), COMPUTER AND PHYSICAL SCIENCE (chemistry, computer programming, earth science, geology, and mathematics), EDUCATION (art education, business education, education, science education, and secondary education), ENGINEERING AND ENVIRONMENTAL DESIGN (cartography), HEALTH PROFESSIONS (medical laboratory technology and nursing), SOCIAL SCIENCE (criminal justice, economics, geography, history, psychology, social work, and sociology). Sciences is the strongest academically. Business administration has the largest enrollment.

Required: All students must demonstrate basic competence in reading, math, and computer literacy, and are required to take a distribution of classes that includes 36 to 38 credits in humanities, sciences, and social sciences. Specific courses required are English composition, speech, physical education, and the first-year seminar. All core and distribution requirements may be waived if the student passes a departmentally prescribed exemption exam. A minimum GPA of 2.0 and a total of 127 credits, with 36 in the major, are needed to graduate.

Special: Study abroad is available in 3 countries. Cross-registration through a consortium, internships, work-study programs, a Washington semester, student-designed and dual majors, B.A.-B.S. degrees, and a general studies degree are offered. Life experience credit, non-degree study, and pass/fail options also are possible. There are 13 national honor societies, a freshman honors program, and 9 departmental honors programs.

Faculty/Classroom: All teach undergraduates. No introductory courses are taught by graduate students. The average class size in an introductory lecture is 22; in a laboratory is 12; and in a regular course is 17.

Requirements: The SAT or ACT is required. Salem State requires that applicants earn 16 credits, including 4 years of English, 3 years each of math and science, and 2 years each of foreign language and history. Courses in music, art, drama, computer science, and psychology are suggested. Art majors must provide a portfolio. A GED is acceptable. Students with a GED, those out of school more than 3 years, and the learning disabled do not need the SAT. A GPA of 2.0 is required. AP and CLEP credits are accepted. Important factors in the admissions decision are advanced placement or honors courses, evidence of special talent, and recommendations by school officials.

Procedure: Freshmen are admitted fall. Entrance exams should be taken November and December of the senior year. There are deferred admissions and rolling admissions plans. Application deadlines are open. Check with the school for current application fee. Applications are accepted online.

Transfer: 809 transfer students enrolled in a recent year. Transfer students are required to have a minimum GPA of 2.0 with more than 24 credits; 2.5 with fewer than 24 credits. 30 of 127 credits required for the bachelor's degree must be completed at Salem State.

Visiting: There are regularly scheduled orientations for prospective students. There are guides for informal visits and visitors may sit in on classes. To schedule a visit, contact the Admissions Office.

Financial Aid: In a recent year, 86% of undergraduate students worked part-time. Average annual earnings from campus work were $1600. The FAFSA is required. Check with the school for current application deadlines and fee.

International Students: There were 258 international students enrolled in a recent year. The school actively recruits these students. They must take the TOEFL. They must also take the SAT or ACT.

Computers: Wireless access is available. All students may access the system 7 days a week. There are no time limits and no fees. All students are required to have a personal computer.

Graduates: In a recent year, 845 bachelor's degrees were awarded. The most popular majors were business marketing (20%), education (12%), and psychology (10%).

Admissions Contact: Director of Admissions. E-Mail: admissions@salem.mass.edu Web: www.salemstate.edu

SIMMONS COLLEGE E-2

Boston, MA 02115 (617) 521-2051
(800) 345-8468; (617) 521-3190

Full-time: 1647 women	**Faculty:** 188; IIA, +$
Part-time: 1 men, 144 women	**Ph.D.s:** 83%
Graduate: 402 men, 2636 women	**Student/Faculty:** 8 to 1
Year: semesters, summer session	**Tuition:** $34,350
Application Deadline: February 1	**Room & Board:** $13,400

Freshman Class: 4440 applied, 2145 accepted, 401 enrolled
SAT CR/M/W: 575/570/580 **ACT:** 26 **VERY COMPETITIVE**

Simmons College, founded in 1899, is a private institution with an undergraduate college for women that offers a comprehensive education combining the arts, sciences, and humanities with preprofessional training. All graduate programs are co-ed, with the exception of the women-only MBA program. There are 4 undergraduate schools and 5 graduate schools. In addition to regional accreditation, Simmons has baccalaureate program accreditation with ADA, APTA, CSWE, and NLN. The library contains 277,169 volumes, 13,580 microform items, 7,122 audio/video tapes/CDs/DVDs, and subscribes to 59,134 periodicals including electronic. Computerized library services include interlibrary loans, database searching, Internet access, and Wi-Fi capability. Special learning facilities include an art gallery, radio station, physical therapy motion lab, nursing lab, and library science technology center. The 12-acre campus is in an urban area in Boston. Including any residence halls, there are 21 buildings.

Student Life: 63% of undergraduates are from Massachusetts. Others are from 36 states, 53 foreign countries, and Canada. 74% are from public schools. 68% are White. The average age of freshmen is 19; all undergraduates, 22. 15% do not continue beyond their first year; 85% remain to graduate.

Housing: 1039 students can be accommodated in college housing, which includes single-sex and coed dorms and off-campus apartments. In addition, there are special-interest houses, Theme housing, and wellness housing. On-campus housing is guaranteed for the freshman year only, is available on a first-come, first-served basis, and is available on a lottery system for upperclassmen. 55% of students commute. No one may keep cars.

Activities: There are no fraternities or sororities. There are 79 groups on campus, including art, cheerleading, choir, chorale, chorus, communications, dance, debate, drama, ethnic, film, gay, honors, international, literary magazine, musical theater, newspaper, orchestra, political, professional, radio and TV, religious, social, social service, student government, and yearbook. Popular campus events include Honors Convocation, May Day Breakfast, and Culture Shock.

Sports: There are 10 intercollegiate sports for women, and 4 intramural sports for women. Facilities include an 8-lane pool, a spa and sauna, 1 racquetball and 2 squash courts, 2 rowing tanks, 3 fitness rooms, a dance studio, an indoor running area, 2 volleyball courts, and a basketball court.

Disabled Students: 95% of the campus is accessible. Facilities include wheelchair ramps, elevators, special parking, specially equipped restrooms, special class scheduling, and lowered drinking fountains.

Services: Counseling and information services are available, as is tutoring in most subjects, basic freshman courses, languages, biology, chemistry, psychology, and math. There is a reader service for the blind. One on one course content tutoring,study groups for a number of the major courses are provided, study skills tutoring is provided to assit students with time management, test anxiety, motivation, and goal setting, and a math advisor is available to help students prepare to take/ot retake the college required Math Competency Test.

Campus Safety and Security: Measures include 24-hour foot and vehicle patrol, emergency notification system, self-defense education, and security escort services. There are shuttle buses, emergency telephones, lighted pathways/sidewalks, closed-circuit TV, ID card access, and security training in first response and crisis intervention.

Programs of Study: Simmons confers B.A., and B.S. degrees. Master's and doctoral degrees are also awarded. Bachelor's degrees are awarded in AGRICULTURE (environmental studies), BIOLOGICAL SCIENCE (biochemistry, biology/biological science, and biometrics and biostatistics), BUSINESS (business administration and management, finance, management information systems, marketing and distribution, and retailing), COMMUNICATIONS AND THE ARTS (art, arts administration/management, communications, English, French, information technology, music, and Spanish), COMPUTER AND PHYSICAL SCIENCE (chemistry, computer science, mathematics, and physics), EDUCATION (early childhood education, education, elementary education, and secondary education), HEALTH PROFESSIONS (exercise science, nursing, physical therapy, and public health), SOCIAL SCIENCE (African American studies, Asian/Oriental studies, biopsychology, dietetics, economics, ethnic studies, food production/management/services, gender studies, history, interdisciplinary studies, international political science, philosophy, political science/government, psychobiology, psychology, sociology, and women's studies). Physical therapy, biology, and communication are the strongest academically. Nursing, communications, and psychology have the largest enrollments.

Required: To graduate, students must complete 128 semester hours, including 24 to 48 in the major, and maintain a minimum GPA of 2.0. Eight semester hours in a supervised independent learning experience or an internship are also required. Students must also fulfill foreign language, math competency, and technology competency requirements. In addition to completing the multidisciplinary core courses, students must complete 1 course from each of the following 6 modes of inquiry categories: creative and performing arts; language, literature, and culture; quantitative analysis and reasoning; scientific inquiry; social and historical perspectives; and psychological and ethical development. A thesis is optional.

Special: Cross-registration is available with the New England Conservatory of Music, Hebrew, Emmanuel, and Wheelock Colleges, Massachusetts College of Art, Massachusetts College of Pharmacy and Health Sciences, and Wentworth Institute of Technology. Simmons offers study abroad in Europe through the Institute of European studies. A Washington semester at American University, accelerated degree programs, profit and nonprofit internship programs, a B.A.-B.S. degree, dual majors, interdisciplinary majors, student-designed majors, work-study programs, and pass/fail options are also offered. There is a dual-degree program in chemistry, pharmacy, and physician's assistant with Massachusetts College of Pharmacy. There are 3 national honor societies, a freshman honors program, and 23 departmental honors programs.

Faculty/Classroom: 21% of faculty are male; 79% are female. All teach and do research. No introductory courses are taught by graduate students. The average class size in an introductory lecture is 24; in a laboratory is 13; and in a regular course is 18.

Admissions: 48% of the 2013-2014 applicants were accepted. The SAT scores for the 2013-2014 freshman class were: Critical Reading--18% below 500, 47% between 500 and 599, 29% between 600 and 699, and 6% between 700 and 800; Math--13% below 500, 53% between 500 and 599, 29% between 600 and 699, and 5% between 700 and 800; Writing--12% below 500, 46% between 500 and 599, 35% between 600 and 699, and 7% between 700 and 800. The ACT scores were 21% below 21, 30% between 21 and 23, 28% between 24 and 26, 16% between 27 and 28, and 6% above 28. 46% of the current freshmen were in the top fifth of their class; 78% were in the top two fifths.

Requirements: The SAT or ACT is required. Simmons recommends that applicants have 4 years of English, math, foreign language, and social studies, as well as 3 years of science and history. An essay is required, and an interview is strongly recommended. AP and CLEP credits are accepted. Important factors in the admissions decision are advanced placement or honors courses, parents or siblings attended your school, evidence of special talent, personality/intangible qualities, extracurricular activities record, recommendations by alumni, and geographical diversity.

Procedure: Freshmen are admitted fall and spring. Entrance exams should be taken by February 1 of the senior year. There are early admissions and deferred admissions plans. Early decision applications should be filed by December 1; regular applications, by February 1 for fall entry; and December 1 for spring entry, along with a $55 fee. Notification of early decision is sent January 15; regular decision, March 15. 143 applicants were on the 2013 waiting list; 17 were admitted. Applications are accepted online.

Transfer: 60 transfer students enrolled in 2012-2013. Applicants should have a GPA of 2.8, at least 17 college-level credit hours, official transcripts from all colleges attended, and a faculty recommendation and dean's report from the previous college attended. 48 of 128 credits required for the bachelor's degree must be completed at Simmons.

Visiting: There are regularly scheduled orientations for prospective students, including a campus tour, class attendance, an interview, and meetings with faculty and students. There are guides for informal visits, visitors may sit in on classes, and stay overnight. To schedule a visit, contact the Admission Office at (800) 345-8468.

Financial Aid: In 2013-2014, 78% of all full-time freshmen and 67% of continuing full-time students received some form of financial aid. 76% of all full-time freshmen and 65% of continuing full-time students received need-based aid. The average freshman award was $21,501. Need-based scholarships or need-based grants averaged $6,569 ($21,250 maximum); and need-based self-help aid (loans and jobs) averaged $4,804 ($10,000 maximum). 34% of undergraduate students work part-time. Average annual earnings from campus work are $2500. The average financial indebtedness of the 2013 graduate was $42,174. Simmons is a member of CSS. The FAFSA, and federal tax returns or W2 forms is required. The priority date for freshman financial aid applications for fall entry is March 1. The deadline for filing freshman financial aid applications for fall entry is March 1.

International Students: There are 59 international students enrolled. The school actively recruits these students. They must take the TOEFL with a minimum score of 560 on the paper-based TOEFL (PBT) or 83 on the Internet-based version (iBT). They must also take the SAT or ACT.

Computers: All students may access the system. There are no time limits and no fees.

Graduates: From July 1, 2012 to June 30, 2013, 625 bachelor's degrees were awarded. The most popular majors were nursing (29%), communications (9%), and psychology (6%). 83 companies recruited on campus in 2012-2013. In an average class, 60% graduate in 4 years or less, 66% graduate in 5 years or less, and 67% graduate in 6 years or less. Of the 2012 graduating class, 27% were enrolled in graduate school within 6 months of graduation, and 68% were employed.

Admissions Contact: Catherine Capolupo, AVP, Undergraduate Admission. E-Mail: *ugadm@simmons.edu* Web: *www.simmons.edu*

SMITH COLLEGE B-2

Northampton, MA 01063 **(413) 585-2500; (413) 585-2527**

Full-time: 2 men, 2583 women	**Faculty:** 275; IIB, ++$
Part-time: 21 women	**Ph.D.s:** 99%
Graduate: 66 men, 361 women	**Student/Faculty:** 9 to 1
Year: semesters	**Tuition:** $43,114
Application Deadline: January 15	**Room & Board:** $14,410
Freshman Class: 4403 applied, 1897 accepted, 643 enrolled	
SAT CR/M/W: 665/670/680 **ACT:** 30	**MOST COMPETITIVE**

Smith College, founded in 1871, is the largest independent women's college in the United States and offers a liberal arts education. There is one undergraduate school and one graduate school. In addition to regional accreditation, Smith has baccalaureate program accreditation with ABET. The 4 libraries contain 1.5 million volumes, 149,402 microform items, 76,662 audio/video tapes/CDs/DVDs, and subscribe to 60,916 periodicals including electronic. Computerized library services include interlibrary loans, database searching, Internet access, and Wi-Fi capability. Special learning facilities include an art gallery, radio station, TV station, astronomy observatories, center for foreign languages and culture, digital design studio, plant and horticultural labs, art studios with casting, printmaking, and darkroom facilities, and specialized libraries for science, music, and art, and the Quantitative Learning Center, and the Jacobson Center for Writing, Teaching and Learning. The 156-acre campus is in a small town 90 miles west of Boston. Including any residence halls, there are 118 buildings.

Student Life: 77% of undergraduates are from out of state, mostly the Northeast. Students are from 48 states, 72 foreign countries, and Canada. 64% are from public schools. 46% are White; 13% Asian American; 13% Foreign. 40% are Hindu, Buddhist, Muslim, Unitarian, and Christian Scientists; 20% Protestant; 18% claim no religious affiliation; 14% Catholic. The average age of freshmen is 18; all undergraduates, 20. 9% do not continue beyond their first year; 86% remain to graduate.

Housing: 2440 students can be accommodated in college housing, which includes single-sex dorms and on-campus apartments. In addition, there are language houses, special-interest houses, non-smoking houses, 2 cooperative houses, housing for non-traditional-age students, an apartment complex for a limited number of juniors and seniors, a senior house, a French-speaking house and a Non-trad students with dependents. On-campus housing is guaranteed for all 4 years. 91% of students live on campus; of those, 95% remain on campus on weekends. Upperclassmen may keep cars.

Activities: There are no fraternities or sororities. There are 127 groups on campus, including art, cheerleading, chess, chorus, computers, dance, debate, drama, environmental, ethnic, gay, honors, international, jazz band, literary magazine, musical theater, newspaper, orchestra, photography, political, professional, radio and TV, religious, social, social service, student government, symphony, and yearbook. Popular campus events include International Student Day, Spring and Winter Weekends and Rally Day.

Sports: There are 14 intercollegiate sports for women, and 4 intramural sports for women. Facilities include indoor and outdoor tracks and tennis courts, riding rings, 2 gyms, a climbing wall, an indoor swimming pool with 1- and 3-meter diving boards, 2 weight-training rooms, a dance studio, 2 athletic training rooms, a human performance lab, squash courts, and field hockey, soccer, lacrosse, and softball fields. There is a performing arts center and a concert hall.

Disabled Students: 85% of the campus is accessible. Facilities include wheelchair ramps, elevators, special parking, specially equipped restrooms, special class scheduling, lowered drinking fountains, lowered telephones.

Services: Counseling and information services are available, as is tutoring in every subject. There is a reader service for the blind. Numerous services are provided for learning-disabled students, including note taking, oral tests, readers, tutors, books on tape, reading software, voice recognition, tape recorders, extended-timed tests, and writing counselors.

Campus Safety and Security: Measures include 24-hour foot and vehicle patrol, emergency notification system, self-defense education, and security escort services. There are shuttle buses, emergency telephones, lighted pathways/sidewalks, First-year students are required to attend panel discussions on campus safety. Specialized personal safety presentations, including self defense and sexual assault information, are provided to various houses and organizations. There are crime prevention programs including bicycle registration.

Programs of Study: Smith confers A.B., and B.S.Eng. degrees. Master's and doctoral degrees are also awarded. Bachelor's degrees are awarded in BIOLOGICAL SCIENCE (biochemistry, biology/biological science, and neurosciences), COMMUNICATIONS AND THE ARTS (art history and appreciation, classics, comparative literature, creative writing, dance, dramatic arts, East Asian languages and literature, English, film arts, French, Germanic languages and literature, Greek, Italian, Latin, music, Russian, Spanish, and studio art), COMPUTER AND PHYSICAL SCIENCE (astronomy, chemistry, computer science, geology, mathematics, and physics), EDUCATION (early childhood education, education, and elementary education), ENGINEERING AND ENVIRONMENTAL DESIGN (architecture, engineering, and environmental science), HEALTH PROFESSIONS (exercise science), SOCIAL SCIENCE (African studies, African American studies, American studies, anthropology, classical/ancient civilization, cognitive science, economics, ethics, politics, and social policy, European studies, French studies, history, international relations, Japanese studies, Judaic studies, Latin American studies, Luso-Brazilian studies, medieval studies, Middle Eastern studies, philosophy, political science/government, psychology, religion, Russian and Slavic studies, sociology, urban studies, and women's studies). Art, economics, government and psychology have the largest enrollments.

Required: All students plan individual programs in consultation with faculty advisers and take 64 credits outside their major and 36 to 64 credits in the major. Students must maintain a minimum 2.0 GPA in all academic work and during the senior year. A total of 128 credits is needed to graduate. A writing-intensive course is required for first-year students. A thesis is required for departmental honors programs. Distribution requirements are necessary for Latin honors eligibility.

Special: Smith offers study abroad in more than 50 countries including the Smith College programs in Italy, France, Germany, and Switzerland, affiliated programs in India, Japan, Russia, China, South Africa, Peru, Brazil, and Spain, and many others. Other opportunities include cross-registration with 5 area colleges, a Washington semester, Smithsonian internships, exchanges with historically Black colleges and other liberal arts colleges, and at BioSphere2. A 3-2 engineering degree is offered with Dartmouth College. Support for nontraditional-age students and for international students is provided, and funding for a summer internship is available for every undergraduate. Accelerated degree programs, student-designed majors, dual majors, and non-degree study are offered. There are 3 national honor societies and including Phi Beta Kappa.

Faculty/Classroom: 45% of faculty are male; 55% are female. All teach and do research. No introductory courses are taught by graduate students. The average class size in an introductory lecture is 25; in a laboratory is 13; and in a regular course is 20.

Admissions: 43% of the 2013-2014 applicants were accepted. The SAT scores for the 2013-2014 freshman class were: Critical Reading--2% below 500, 15% between 500 and 599, 45% between 600 and 699, and 38% between 700 and 800; Math--1% below 500, 19% between 500 and 599, 44% between 600 and 699, and 36% between 700 and 800; Writing--2% below 500, 12% between 500 and 599, 45% between 600 and 699, and 42% between 700 and 800. The ACT scores were 6% between 24 and 26, 45% between 27 and 28, and 49% above 28.

Requirements: Smith highly recommends that applicants have 4 years of English, 3 years each of math, science, and a foreign language, and 2 years of history. SAT and ACT are considered but not required. Interviews are recommended. The GED is accepted. AP credits are accepted.

Procedure: Freshmen are admitted fall. Entrance exams should be taken before January of the senior year. There are early decision, early admissions, and deferred admissions plans. Early decision applications should be filed by November 15; regular applications, by January 15 for fall entry, along with a $60 fee. Notification of early decision is sent December 15; regular decision, April 1. 158 early decision candidates were accepted for the 2013-2014 class. 289 applicants were on the 2013 waiting list; 44 were admitted. Applications are accepted online.

Transfer: 45 transfer students enrolled in 2012-2013. Criteria for transfer students are similar to those for entering freshmen, with more emphasis on the college record.

Visiting: There are regularly scheduled orientations for prospective students, including student-guided tours available 4 times a day, Monday through Friday, when school is in full session and on Saturday mornings from September to January. Interviews may also be scheduled during these times. Information sessions are offered twice daily most of the year. There are guides for informal visits, visitors may sit in on classes, and stay overnight. To schedule a visit, contact the Office of Admissions.

Financial Aid: In 2013-2014, 67% of all full-time freshmen and 69% of continuing full-time students received some form of financial aid. 58% of all full-time freshmen and 63% of continuing full-time students received need-based aid. The average freshman award was $40,057. Need-based scholarships or need-based grants averaged $36,851; need-based self-help aid (loans and jobs) averaged $4,510; other non-need-based awards and non-need-based scholarships averaged $14,220; and $3,216 from other forms of aid. The average financial indebtedness of the 2013 graduate was $22,699. Smith is a member of CSS. The CSS/Profile, FAFSA, and the college's own financial statement are required. The deadline for filing freshman financial aid applications for fall entry is February 15.

International Students: The school actively recruits these students. They must take the TOEFL with a minimum score of 600 on the paper-based TOEFL (PBT) or 95 on the Internet-based version (iBT). They must also take the SAT or ACT. if the language of instruction is English.

Computers: All students may access the system. There are no time limits and no fees.

Graduates: From July 1, 2012 to June 30, 2013, 698 bachelor's degrees were awarded. The most popular majors were psychology (13%), government (11%), and economics (10%). 71 companies recruited on campus in 2012-2013. In an average class, 82% graduate in 4 years or less, 85% graduate in 5 years or less, and 86% graduate in 6 years or less.

Admissions Contact: Debra Shaver, Director of Admissions. E-Mail: *admission@smith.edu* Web: *www.smith.edu*

SPRINGFIELD COLLEGE B-3

Springfield, MA 01109 (413) 748-3136
(800) 343-1257; (413) 748-3694

Full-time: 2115 men and women	**Faculty:** n/av; IIA, --$
Part-time: 110 men and women	**Ph.D.s:** 62%
Graduate: 925 men and women	**Student/Faculty:** n/av
Year: semesters, summer session	**Tuition:** $25,500
Application Deadline: see profile	**Room & Board:** $10,500
Freshman Class: n/av	
SAT or ACT: required	
	COMPETITIVE

Springfield College, established in 1885, is a private liberal arts and sciences institution. The figures in the above capsule and in this profile are approximate. There are 3 undergraduate schools and 1 graduate school. In addition to regional accreditation, S.C. has baccalaureate program accreditation with APTA, CAHEA, and NRPA. The library contains 168,332 volumes, 736,056 microform items, 3,200 audio/video tapes/CDs/DVDs, and subscribes to 831 periodicals including electronic. Computerized library services include inter-library loans and database searching. Special learning facilities include an art gallery, radio station, and an outdoor center. The 160-acre campus is in a suburban area 26 miles north of Hartford, Connecticut. Including any residence halls, there are 38 buildings.

Student Life: Students are from 30 states, 12 foreign countries, and Canada. 83% are from public schools. 93% are white. The average age of freshmen is 18; all undergraduates, 21. 12% do not continue beyond their first year.

Housing: 1980 students can be accommodated in college housing, which includes single-sex and coed dorms, on-campus apartments, off-campus apartments, and married student housing. In addition, there are special-interest houses and a wellness dorm. On-campus housing is guaranteed for all 4 years. 85% of students live on campus; of those, 70% remain on campus on weekends. Alcohol is not permitted. Upperclassmen may keep cars.

Activities: There are no fraternities or sororities. There are 58 groups on campus, including art, band, cheerleading, choir, chorus, club sports, communications, computers, dance, drama, ethnic, film, gay, honors, international, jazz band, literary magazine, musical theater, newspaper, pep band, professional, radio and TV, religious, social, social service, student government, and yearbook. Popular campus events include Parents Weekend and Stepping Up Day.

Sports: There are 13 intercollegiate sports for men and 11 for women, and 10 intramural sports for men and 10 for women. Facilities include a 2000-seat stadium, a 2000-seat gym, a super turf football/soccer/lacrosse/field hockey field, 8 tennis courts, baseball and softball fields, and free weight and Nautilus rooms.

Disabled Students: 75% of the campus is accessible. Facilities include wheelchair ramps, elevators, special parking, specially equipped rest rooms, special class scheduling, and lowered drinking fountains.

Services: Counseling and information services are available, as is tutoring in every subject. There is remedial math and writing.

Campus Safety and Security: Measures include 24-hour foot and vehicle patrol, self-defense education, and security escort services. There are shuttle buses, emergency telephones, and lighted pathways/sidewalks.

Programs of Study: S.C. confers B.A. and B.S. degrees. Master's and doctoral degrees are also awarded. Bachelor's degrees are awarded in BIOLOGICAL SCIENCE (biochemistry, biology/biological science, and biotechnology), BUSINESS (business administration and management and sports management), COMMUNICATIONS AND THE ARTS (English and fine arts), COMPUTER AND PHYSICAL SCIENCE (chemistry, information sciences and systems, and mathematics), EDUCATION (early childhood education, elementary education, health education, middle school education, physical education, science education, and secondary education), ENGINEERING AND ENVIRONMENTAL DESIGN (computer graphics), HEALTH PROFESSIONS (art therapy, emergency medical technologies, environmental health science, health care administration, predentistry, premedicine, recreation therapy, and rehabilitation therapy), SOCIAL SCIENCE (gerontology, history, human services, parks and recreation management, physical fitness/movement, political science/government, prelaw, psychology, and sociology). Physical therapy and athletic training are the strongest academically. Physical education has the largest enrollments.

Required: To graduate, students must complete a total of 130 credits with a 2.0 GPA. Core requirements include 50 semester hours in English, social and natural sciences, health, religion, philosophy, and art, and 4 credits in phys ed.

Special: There is a co-op program and cross-registration with cooperating colleges in the greater Springfield area. Internships are required in most majors, and there is limited study abroad. There are 2 national honor societies.

Faculty/Classroom: 52% of faculty are male; 48% are female. No introductory courses are taught by graduate students. The average class size in an introductory lecture is 125; in a laboratory is 20; and in a regular course is 30.

Requirements: The SAT or ACT is required. Applicants must be graduates of an accredited secondary school and have completed 4 years of English and 3 years each of history, math, and science. The school accepts the GED. An essay is required and an interview is recommended. Applications are accepted online. AP and CLEP credits are accepted. Important factors in the admissions decision are advanced placement or honors courses, leadership record, and extracurricular activities record.

Procedure: Freshmen are admitted fall and spring. Entrance exams should be taken by November of the senior year. There are early decision, early admissions, deferred admissions, and rolling admissions plans. Applications are accepted online. A waiting list is maintained. Check with the school for current application deadlines.

Transfer: Grades of 2.0 transfer for credit. Transfer students are admitted in the fall and spring.

Visiting: There are guides for informal visits, visitors may sit in on classes, and stay overnight. To schedule a visit, contact the Admissions Office.

Financial Aid: The CSS/Profile and FAFSA, and tax returns for parents and the student are required. Check with the school for current application deadlines.

International Students: There were 20 international students enrolled in a recent year. The school actively recruits these students. They must take the TOEFL. They must also take the SAT or ACT.

Computers: All students may access the system. There are no time limits and no fees.

Admissions Contact: Director of Admissions. A campus DVD is available. E-Mail: admissions@spfldcol.edu Web:www.springfieldcollege.edu

STONEHILL COLLEGE E-3

Easton, MA 02357-0100 (508) 565-1373; (508) 565-1545

Full-time: 984 men, 1575 women	**Faculty:** 156; IIB, av$
Part-time: 9 men, 14 women	**Ph.D.s:** 85%
Graduate: n/av	**Student/Faculty:** 16 to 1
Year: semesters, summer session	**Tuition:** $34,420
Application Deadline: January 15	**Room & Board:** $13,360
Freshman Class: 7052 applied, 4500 accepted, 728 enrolled	
SAT CR/M: 590/600 **ACT:** 26	**VERY COMPETITIVE+**

Stonehill is a selective Catholic college with a welcoming community and beautiful campus. Dedicated, supportive faculty mentor students in 80+ academic programs in the liberal arts, sciences, and business. Nearly 90% of students participate in internships, study abroad, research, practicum, and field work. Our location offers easy access to jobs, museums, sports games, and more. Stonehill is a vibrant community where students learn to live lives that make a difference. The library contains 243,500 volumes, 150,431 microform items, 9,593 audio/video tapes/CDs/DVDs, and subscribes to 13,111 periodicals including electronic. Computerized library services include interlibrary loans, database searching, Internet access, and laptop Internet portals. Special learning facilities include a learning resource center, art gallery, radio station, an observatory, an institute for the study of law and society, and several archives and special collections. The 384-acre campus is in a suburban area 20 miles south of Boston. Including any residence halls, there are 65 buildings. The figures in the above capsule and in this profile are approximate.

Student Life: 53% of undergraduates are from Massachusetts. Others are from 29 states, and 10 foreign countries. 90% are white. 71% are Catholic; 13% claim no religious affiliation. The average age of freshmen is 18; all undergraduates, 19. 8% do not continue beyond their first year; 85% remain to graduate.

Housing: 2199 students can be accommodated in college housing, which includes single-sex and coed dorms. In addition, there are special-interest houses, substance-free/wellness housing, and community service housing. On-campus housing is guaranteed for all 4 years. 92% of students live on campus; of those, 85% remain on campus on weekends. Upperclassmen may keep cars.

Activities: There are no fraternities or sororities. There are 77 groups on campus, including art, band, cheerleading, choir, chorale, chorus, computers, dance, drama, environmental, ethnic, film, gay, honors, international, literary magazine, musical theater, newspaper, pep band, photography, political, professional, radio and TV, religious, social, social service, student government, and yearbook. Popular campus events include Skyhawk Weekend, Spring Weekend, and Halloween Mixer.

Sports: There are 9 intercollegiate sports for men and 11 for women, and 20 intramural sports for men and 20 for women. Facilities include a 2400-seat stadium for football, field hockey, soccer, and lacrosse, a 500-seat field for men's and women's soccer, a 2000-seat gym with basketball and volleyball courts, 5000 square feet of weight and cardiovascular fitness areas, a recreational and intramural sports complex, tennis courts, baseball, softball, and field hockey fields, a regulation beach volleyball court, and 3 recreational fields for intramural and club sports.

Disabled Students: All of the campus is accessible. Facilities include wheelchair ramps, elevators, special parking, specially equipped restrooms, special class scheduling, lowered drinking fountains, lowered telephones, special housing.

Services: Counseling and information services are available, as is tutoring in most subjects, a learning disabilities specialist and free diagnostic testing are also available as are auxiliary aids for hearing impaired students, note takers, and other resources based on need There is a reader service for the blind, and remedial writing.

Campus Safety and Security: Measures include 24-hour foot and vehicle patrol, emergency notification system, self-defense education, and security escort services. There are emergency telephones, lighted pathways/sidewalks, controlled access to dorms/residences, bicycle patrols, and a weekend guest sign-in policy.

Programs of Study: Stonehill confers B.A., B.S., and B.S.B.A. degrees. Bachelor's degrees are awarded in AGRICULTURE (environmental studies), BIOLOGICAL SCIENCE (biochemistry, biology/biological science, and neurosciences), BUSINESS (accounting, banking and finance, business administration and management, international business management, and marketing/retailing/merchandising), COMMUNICATIONS AND THE ARTS (art history and appreciation, communications, English, fine arts, French, music, and Spanish), COMPUTER AND PHYSICAL SCIENCE (chemistry, computer science, mathematics, and physics), EDUCATION (education), HEALTH PROFESSIONS (health care administration), SOCIAL SCIENCE (American studies, Christian studies, criminology, economics, gender studies, history, interdisciplinary studies, international studies, philosophy, political science/government, psychology, public administration, religion, and sociology). Business, biology, and psychology have the largest enrollments.

Required: All students must complete a cornerstone program, which consists of 4 common courses within history/literature and philosophy/religious studies; a learning community consisting of 2 linked courses and a 3rd integrated course; a moral inquiry course; and a senior capstone experience within the major. Distribution requirements include 2 semesters of a foreign language and 1 course each in in natural scientific inquiry, social scientific inquiry, and statistical reasoning. Students must complete 120 hours 40 3- to 4-credit courses while maintaining a minimum GPA of 2.0.

Special: There are 20 national honor societies and a freshman honors program.

Faculty/Classroom: 58% of faculty are male; 42% are female. All teach and do research. No introductory courses are taught by graduate students. The average class size in an introductory lecture is 21.

Admissions: 64% of a recent year applicants were accepted. The SAT scores for a recent freshman class were: Critical Reading--4% below 500, 43% between 500 and 599, 47% between 600 and 700, and 6% above 700; Math--4% below 500, 37% between 500 and 599, 52% between 600 and 700, and 7% above 700. The ACT scores were 1% below 21, 10% between 21 and 23, 32% between 24 and 26, 33% between 27 and 28, and 24% above 28. 65% of the current freshmen were in the top fifth of their class; 92% were in the top two fifths. 7 freshmen graduated first in their class.

Requirements: Applicants should be graduates of an accredited high school or have earned the GED. Secondary preparation should include 4 units of English, 3 units of foreign language, 3 units of science, 4 units of math, and 3 combined units of history, political science, and social sciences plus 3 elective subjects. An essay, school report, 2 teacher evaluations, and a completed common application sent with a Stonehill Supplemental Information Form are required. AP credits are accepted. Important factors in the admissions decision are advanced placement or honors courses, leadership record, and extracurricular activities record.

Procedure: Freshmen are admitted fall and spring. There are early decision, early admissions, and deferred admissions plans. Early decision applications should be filed by November 1; regular applications, by January 15 for fall entry; and November 1 for spring entry, along with a $60 fee. Notification of early decision is sent December 25; regular decision, March 15. 44 early decision candidates were accepted for a recent graduating class. 67 applicants were on the 2011 waiting list; 33 were admitted. Applications are accepted online.

Transfer: 26 transfer students enrolled in a recent year. Applicants must have a minimum GPA of 2.0. Official high school transcripts and college transcripts along with catalogs with course descriptions from all colleges attended are required. An essay and 2 recommendations are required, and an interview is recommended. 60 of 120 credits required for the bachelor's degree must be completed at Stonehill.

Visiting: There are regularly scheduled orientations for prospective students, consisting of group information sessions and guided campus tours available by appointment throughout the year. Visitors may sit in on classes. To schedule a visit, contact the Admissions Office.

Financial Aid: In a recent year, 97% of all full-time freshmen and 88% of continuing full-time students received some form of financial aid. 60% of all full-time freshmen and 57% of continuing full-time students received need-based aid. The average freshman award was $24,000. Need-based scholarships or need-based grants averaged $18,000 ($43,000 maximum); need-based self-help aid (loans and jobs) averaged $7,700 ($9,000 maximum); non-need-based athletic scholarships averaged $9,000 ($48,000 maximum); and other non-need-based awards and non-need-based scholarships averaged $9,000 ($34,000 maximum). 47% of undergraduate students work part-time. Average annual earnings from campus work are $2120. The average financial indebtedness of the 2011 graduate was $30,000. Stonehill is a member of CSS. The CSS/Profile and FAFSA, and noncustodial profile and business/farm supplement are required. The deadline for filing freshman financial aid applications for fall entry is February 1.

International Students: There are 12 international students enrolled. The school actively recruits these students. They must take the TOEFL.

Computers: Wireless access is available. Stonehill College provides students with state of the art wired and wireless computing facilities including 10 multimedia labs with over 300 computers for classroom and student use. The software available on these computers includes extensive instructional packages, web page development tools, programming languages and database tools. Each lab is also equipped with printers including color where required. All students may access the system 7 days a week, 24 hours a day. There are no time limits and no fees. It is strongly recommended that all students have a personal computer.

Graduates: In a recent year, 573 bachelor's degrees were awarded. The most popular majors were business (25%), psychology (8%), and English (7%). 356 companies recruited on campus in a recent year. In an average class, 80% graduate in 4 years or less, 84% graduate in 5 years or less, and 85% graduate in 6 years or less. Of the recent graduating class, 41% were enrolled in graduate school within 6 months of graduation, and 71% were employed.

Admissions Contact: Dean of Admissions. E-Mail: *admissions@stonehill.edu* Web: *www.stonehill.edu*

SUFFOLK UNIVERSITY E-2

Boston, MA 02108 **(617) 573-8460**
(800) 6SUFFOL; (617) 742-4291

Full-time: 2375 men, 2987 women	**Faculty:** 364; IIA, ++$
Part-time: 215 men, 208 women	**Ph.D.s:** 86%
Graduate: 1301 men, 1710 women	**Student/Faculty:** 11 to 1
Year: semesters, summer session	**Tuition:** $31,712
Application Deadline: March 1	**Room & Board:** $14,836

Freshman Class: 9275 applied, 7652 accepted, 1188 enrolled
SAT CR/M/W: 500/510/500 **ACT:** 22 **COMPETITIVE**

Suffolk University, founded in 1906, is a private institution offering undergraduate and graduate degrees in the arts and sciences, business, and law. There are 2 undergraduate schools and 3 graduate schools. In addition to regional accreditation, Suffolk has baccalaureate program accreditation with AACSB, ABET, FIDER, and NASAD. The 3 libraries contain 155,248 volumes, 144,091 microform items, 1,973 audio/video tapes/CDs/DVDs, and subscribe to 23,949 periodicals including electronic. Computerized library services include interlibrary loans, database searching, Internet access, and Wi-Fi capability. Special learning facilities include an art gallery, radio station, and TV station. The 2-acre campus is in an urban area in the heart of downtown Boston. Including any residence halls, there are 13 buildings.

Student Life: 67% of undergraduates are from Massachusetts. Others are from 44 states, 100 foreign countries, and Canada. 66% are from public schools. 40% are White; 19% Foreign; 15% race unknown; 11% Hispanic. The average age of freshmen is 18; all undergraduates, 21. 25% do not continue beyond their first year; 55% remain to graduate.

Housing: 1249 students can be accommodated in college housing, which includes coed dorms. On-campus housing is available on a first-come, first-served basis, and is available on a lottery system for upperclassmen. Alcohol is not permitted. No one may keep cars.

Activities: 1% of men belong to 1 national fraternity. There are 75 groups on campus, including art, choir, chorale, chorus, computers, dance, debate, drama, ethnic, film, forensics, gay, honors, international, jazz band, literary magazine, musical theater, newspaper, orientation, photography, political, professional, radio and TV, religious, social, social service, and student government. Popular campus events include Hispanic Fiesta, Fallfest Talent Show, and Temple Street Fair.

Sports: There are 7 intercollegiate sports for men and 6 for women, and 2 intramural sports for men and 2 for women. Facilities include a basketball, volleyball, and aerobics facility, intramurals, and indoor baseball/softball practice and a fully equipped fitness center.

Disabled Students: Facilities include wheelchair ramps, elevators, specially equipped restrooms, special class scheduling, lowered drinking fountains, and lowered telephones.

Services: Counseling and information services are available, as is tutoring in every subject. There is a reader service for the blind, and remedial math, reading, and writing.

Campus Safety and Security: Measures include 24-hour foot and vehicle patrol, emergency notification system, self-defense education, and security escort services. There are emergency telephones and lighted pathways/sidewalks.

Programs of Study: Suffolk confers B.A., B.S., B.F.A., B.S.B.A., B.S.G.S. and B.S.J. degrees. Associate, master's, and doctoral degrees are also awarded. Bachelor's degrees are awarded in AGRICULTURE (environmental studies), BIOLOGICAL SCIENCE (biochemistry, biology/biological science, biotechnology, life science, and marine science), BUSINESS (accounting, banking and finance, entrepreneurial studies, international business management, international economics, management science, and marketing/retailing/merchandising), COMMUNICATIONS AND THE ARTS (advertising, art history and appreciation, broadcasting, communications, creative writing, dramatic arts, English, film arts, fine arts, French, graphic design, journalism, media arts, music history and appreciation, performing arts, public relations, Spanish, and speech/debate/rhetoric), COMPUTER AND PHYSICAL SCIENCE (chemistry, computer programming, computer science, information sciences and systems, mathematics, and physics), EDUCATION (business education, English education, mathematics education, and science education), ENGINEERING AND ENVIRONMENTAL DESIGN (computer engineering, electrical/electronics engineering, environmental engineering, environmental science, and interior design), HEALTH PROFESSIONS (medical laboratory technology and radiological science), SOCIAL SCIENCE (African American studies, American studies, criminal justice, economics, European studies, German area studies, history, human development, human services, humanities, international relations, paralegal studies, philosophy, political science/government, psychology, social science, sociology, and women's studies). Business, sociology, and communications. are the strongest academically. Communications and journalism, management, and marketing have the largest enrollments.

Required: All students must complete their semester hours with at least a 2.0 GPA. Distribution requirements vary by degree program.

Special: There are 15 national honor societies, a freshman honors program, and 11 departmental honors programs.

Faculty/Classroom: 58% of faculty are male; 42% are female. All teach undergraduates, and 84% do research. No introductory courses are taught by graduate students. The average class size in an introductory lecture is 26 and in a laboratory is 20.

Admissions: 83% of the 2013-2014 applicants were accepted. The SAT scores for the 2013-2014 freshman class were: Critical Reading--48% below 500, 37% between 500 and 599, 12% between 600 and 699, and 3% between 700 and 800; Math--46% below 500, 40% between 500 and 599, 13% between 600 and 699, and 1% between 700 and 800; Writing--45% below 500, 41% between 500 and 599, 13% between 600 and 699, and 1% between 700 and 800. The ACT scores were 28% below 21, 36% between 21 and 23, 19% between 24 and 26, 10% between 27 and 28, and 7% above 28. 30% of the current freshmen were in the top fifth of their class; 66% were in the top two fifths. 4 freshmen graduated first in their class.

Requirements: The SAT or ACT is required. The ACT Optional Writing test is also required. Applicants should have a high school diploma or the GED. Recommended secondary preparation includes 4 years of English, 3 of math, 2 each of a foreign language and science, and 1 of American history. Exact requirements differ by degree program. A personal essay is required, and an interview is recommended. A GPA of 2.0 is required. AP and CLEP credits are accepted. Important factors in the admissions decision are advanced placement or honors courses, recommendations by school officials, and leadership record.

Procedure: Freshmen are admitted fall, spring, and summer. Entrance exams should be taken by December of the senior year. There are early admissions and deferred admissions plans. Early decision applications should be filed by November 15; regular applications, by March 1 for fall entry; and December 15 for spring entry, along with a $50 fee. Notification of early decision is sent December 20; regular decision, January 15. 710 applicants were on the 2013 waiting list; 181 were admitted. Applications are accepted online.

Transfer: 448 transfer students enrolled in 2012-2013. Applicants should have a minimum 2.5 GPA from an accredited college. Those with fewer than 15 college credits must submit a high school transcript. 30 of 120 credits required for the bachelor's degree must be completed at Suffolk.

Visiting: There are regularly scheduled orientations for prospective students, Students visits include a general presentation and an overview panel presentation of student life, career and co-op opportunities, learning center services, and athletics and academic department meetings, and campus tours. There are guides for informal visits and visitors may sit in on classes. To schedule a visit, contact the Admissions Office at admission@suffolk.edu.

Financial Aid: In 2013-2014, 81% of all full-time freshmen and 72% of continuing full-time students received some form of financial aid. 70% of all full-time freshmen and 60% of continuing full-time students received need-based aid. The average freshman award was $26,879. Need-based scholarships or need-based grants averaged $5,155 ($29,797 maximum); need-based self-help aid (loans and jobs) averaged $2,878 ($3,500 maximum); and other non-need-based awards and non-need-based scholarships averaged $6,367 ($42,000 maximum). 44% of undergraduate students work part-time. Average annual earnings from campus work are $1607. The average financial indebtedness of the 2013 graduate was $33,812. The FAFSA and the college's own financial statement, and verification of income are required. The deadline for filing freshman financial aid applications for fall entry is February 15.

International Students: There are 1029 international students enrolled. The school actively recruits these students. They must take the TOEFL with a minimum score of 550 on the paper-based TOEFL (PBT) or 80 on the Internet-based version (iBT). They must also take the SAT or ACT, and the college's own entrance exam.

Computers: All students may access the system. There are no time limits and no fees.

Graduates: From July 1, 2012 to June 30, 2013, 1290 bachelor's degrees were awarded. The most popular majors were business/marketing (40%), communications (16%), and sociology (15%). 121 companies recruited on campus in 2012-2013. In an average class, 1% graduate in 3 years or less, 51% graduate in 4 years or less, 52% graduate in 5 years or less, and 55% graduate in 6 years or less. Of the 2012 graduating class, 30% were enrolled in graduate school within 6 months of graduation, and 26% were employed.

Admissions Contact: John Hamel, Director of Undergraduate Admissions. E-Mail: *admission@suffolk.edu* Web: *www.suffolk.edu*

TUFTS UNIVERSITY D-2

Medford, MA 02155	**(617) 627-3170; (617) 627-3860**
Full-time: 2541 men, 2603 women	**Faculty:** 480; I, av$
Part-time: 36 men, 52 women	**Ph.D.s:** 93%
Graduate: 2368 men, 3283 women	**Student/Faculty:** 9 to 1
Year: semesters, summer session	**Tuition:** $46,598
Application Deadline: January 1	**Room & Board:** $12,182
Freshman Class: 16389 applied, 3503 accepted, 1309 enrolled	
SAT CR/M/W: 715/720/720	**ACT:** 32 **MOST COMPETITIVE**

Tufts University, founded in 1852, is a private institution offering undergraduate programs in liberal arts and sciences and engineering. The figures in the above capsule and in this profile are approximate and apply to the Medford/Somerville campus resources unless otherwise noted. There are 2 undergraduate schools and 8 graduate schools. In addition to regional accreditation, Tufts has baccalaureate program accreditation with ABET, ADA, and CAHEA. The 2 libraries contain 1.1 million volumes, 1.2 million microform items, and 62,320 audio/video tapes/CDs/DVDs, and subscribe to 63,462 periodicals including electronic. Computerized library services include interlibrary loans, database searching, Internet access, and Wi-Fi capability. Special learning facilities include an art gallery, radio station, TV station, a 300 seat recital hall, theater in the round, Center for Scientific Visualization (ultra high resolution display wall w/HD capability). The 150-acre campus is in a suburban area 5 miles northwest of Boston. Including any residence halls, there are 135 buildings.

Student Life: 77% of undergraduates are from out of state, mostly the Northeast. Students are from 50 states, 56 foreign countries, and Canada. 64% are from public schools. 56% are White; 11% Asian American. The average age of freshmen is 18; all undergraduates, 20. 3% do not continue beyond their first year; 92% remain to graduate.

Housing: 3372 students can be accommodated in college housing, which includes single-sex and coed dorms and on-campus apartments. In addition, there are language houses, special-interest houses, fraternity houses, cooperative houses. On-campus housing is available on a lottery system for upperclassmen. 63% of students live on campus. Upperclassmen may keep cars.

Activities: 14% of men belong to 1 local and 9 national fraternities; 11% of women belong to 4 national sororities. There are 285 groups on campus, including Leonard Carmichael Society (community service), art, band, cheerleading, chess, choir, chorale, chorus, communications, computers, dance, debate, drama, environmental, ethnic, film, forensics, gay, honors, international, jazz band, literary magazine, marching band, musical theater, newspaper, opera, orchestra, pep band, photography, political, professional, radio and TV, religious, social, social service, student government, symphony, Tufts Mountain Club (outdoors), and yearbook. Popular campus events include Tuftonia's Day, Fan the Fire Athletics Event, student and faculty directed arts performances, and EPIIC International Symposium.

Sports: There are 14 intercollegiate sports for men and 15 for women, and 17 intramural sports for men and 18 for women. Facilities include Steve Tisch Sports and Fitness Center, football stadium, 2 gyms, an 8-lane all-weather track, 9 tennis courts, a field house, an indoor cage, an indoor track, 7 squash courts, a swimming pool, a dance room, a weight room, spin studio, yoga studio, a sauna, a sailing center, an exercise center, film room, and baseball, softball, soccer, lacrosse, and playing fields.

Disabled Students: 90% of the campus is accessible. Facilities include wheelchair ramps, elevators, special parking, specially equipped restrooms, special class scheduling, lowered drinking fountains, lowered telephones.

Services: Counseling and information services are available, as is tutoring in every subject, as needed through the Academic Resources Center. There is a reader service for the blind. Services are also available through other campus offices, groups, classes, and offices.

Campus Safety and Security: Measures include 24-hour foot and vehicle patrol, emergency notification system, self-defense education, and security escort services. There are shuttle buses, emergency telephones, lighted pathways/sidewalks, and controlled access to dorms/residences.

Programs of Study: Tufts confers B.A., B.S., B.F.A., B.S.C.E., B.S.Ch.E., B.S. Comp. Eng., B.S.E., B.S.E.E., B.S.E.S., B.S. Environmental Eng., B.S.M.E., B.S.B.M.E. and B.S.C.S degrees. Master's and doctoral degrees are also awarded. Bachelor's degrees are awarded in BIOLOGICAL SCIENCE (biochemistry, biology/biological science, biophysics, and biotechnology), COMMUNICATIONS AND THE ARTS (Arabic, art history and appreciation, Chinese, classics, dramatic arts, English, French, German, Greek, Italian, Japanese, Latin, music, Russian, and Spanish), COMPUTER AND PHYSICAL SCIENCE (applied mathematics, applied physics, astrophysics, chemical physics, chemistry, computer science, geology, mathematics, and physics), ENGINEERING AND ENVIRONMENTAL DESIGN (architecture, biomedical engineering, chemical engineering, civil engineering, computer engineering, electrical/electronics engineering, engineering, engineering and applied science, engineering physics, environmental engineering, environmental science, and mechanical engineering), HEALTH PROFESSIONS (community health work), SOCIAL SCIENCE (African studies, American studies, anthropology, archeology, Asian/Oriental studies, biopsychology, child psychology/development, cognitive science, economics, German area studies, history, international relations, Judaic studies, Latin American studies, Middle Eastern studies, peace studies, philosophy, political science/government, psychology, religion, Russian and Slavic studies, sociology, urban studies, and women's studies). International relations, engineering, philosophy, biology, cognitive and brain science are the strongest academically. International relations, economics, and political science have the largest enrollments.

Required: Liberal arts students must complete 34 courses, 10 of them in the area of concentration. Requirements include foundation courses in writing, quantitative reasoning, and foreign language or culture and courses in humanities, arts, social sciences, math, and natural sciences. Requirements for engineering students include a total of 38 courses, 10 are engineering introduction courses, 8 are engineering foundation courses, 12 of them in the area of concentration, and distribution requirements in English, humanities, arts, and social sciences.

Special: The university offers cross-registration at Boston University, Boston College, and Brandeis University, a Washington semester, domestic exchanges with Swarthmore College or Spellman College, and study abroad in England, Spain, France, Chile, Japan, Ghana, China, Hong Kong, and Germany. Many internships are available. Double majors in the liberal arts are common; student-designed majors are possible. There is a 5-year B.A./M.A. or B.S./M.S. program in liberal arts or engineering, a B.A.-B.F.A. program with the Museum School of Fine Arts, and a B.A.-B.M. program with the New England Conservatory of Music. There are 4 national honor societies and including Phi Beta Kappa.

Faculty/Classroom: 58% of faculty are male; 42% are female. All teach and do research. No introductory courses are taught by graduate students. The average class size in a regular course is 20.

Admissions: 21% of the 2013-2014 applicants were accepted. The SAT scores for the 2013-2014 freshman class were: Critical Reading--6% between 500 and 599, 30% between 600 and 699, and 64% between 700 and 800; Math--3% between 500 and 599, 28% between 600 and 699, and 69% between 700 and 800; Writing--4% between 500 and 599, 32% between 600 and 699, and 64% between 700 and 800. 99% of the current freshmen were in the top fifth of their class; 100% were in the top two fifths. There were 76 National Merit finalists.

Requirements: The SAT or ACT is required. The ACT Optional Writing test is also required. The university accepts either the SAT Reasoning Test and the results of 2 SAT: Subject tests or the ACT with Writing Section. Liberal arts applicants should take the 2 SAT: Subject test of their choice; engineering applicants should take a math level I or II, and either physics or chemistry. In addition, all applicants should be high school graduates or hold the GED. Academic preparation is expected to include 4 years each of English, foreign language, social studies, math, and natural sciences. AP credits are accepted. Important factors in the admissions decision are advanced placement or honors courses, recommendations by school officials, and personality/intangible qualities.

Procedure: Freshmen are admitted fall. Entrance exams should be taken by January of the senior year. There are early decision and deferred admissions plans. Early decision applications should be filed by November 1; regular applications, by January 1 for fall entry, along with a $70 fee. Notification of early decision is sent December 15; regular decision, April 1. 546 early decision candidates were accepted for the 2013-2014 class. applicants were on the 2013 waiting list; were admitted. Applications are accepted online.

Transfer: 50 transfer students enrolled in 2012-2013. Admission is competitive. Primary consideration is given to college and secondary school achievement and record of personal involvement. Transfer students must submit the Common Application for Transfer Students, the Tufts Supplement, transcripts from both high school and college, a college official's report, letters of recommendation, as well as either the SAT or the ACT with Writing. 17 of 34 credits required for the bachelor's degree must be completed at Tufts.

Visiting: There are regularly scheduled orientations for prospective students. There are guides for informal visits and visitors may sit in on classes. To schedule a visit, contact the Admissions Office at (617) 627-3170.

Financial Aid: In 2013-2014, 38% of all full-time freshmen and 39% of continuing full-time students received some form of financial aid. 38% of all full-time freshmen and 39% of continuing full-time students received need-based aid. The average freshman award was $35,839. Need-based scholarships or need-based grants averaged $34,098; and need-based self-help aid (loans and jobs) averaged $3,909. The average financial indebtedness of the 2013 graduate was $18,019. Tufts is a member of CSS. The CSS/Profile and FAFSA, and parent and student federal income tax forms are required. The deadline for filing freshman financial aid applications for fall entry is February 15.

International Students: There are 334 international students enrolled. The school actively recruits these students. They must take the TOEFL with a minimum score of 650 on the paper-based TOEFL (PBT) or 100 on the Internet-based version (iBT), IELTS exam is also accepted. They must also take the SAT or ACT. The student must also take the ACT with Writing or the SAT Reasoning Test and 2 SAT subject tests.

Computers: All students may access the system 24 hours a day. There are no time limits and no fees.

Graduates: From July 1, 2012 to June 30, 2013, 1396 bachelor's degrees were awarded. The most popular majors were international relations (13%), economics (6%), and biology (6%). 150 companies recruited on campus in 2012-2013. In an average class, 87% graduate in 4 years or less and 92% graduate in 6 years or less. Of the 2012 graduating class, 18% were enrolled in graduate school within 6 months of graduation, and 58% were employed.

Admissions Contact: Lee A. Coffin, Dean of Admissions. E-Mail: *admissions.inquiry@ase.tufts.edu* Web: *www.tufts.edu*

UNIVERSITY OF MASSACHUSETTS AMHERST B-2

Amherst, MA 01003	**(413) 545-0222; (413) 545-4312**
Full-time: n/av	**Faculty:** n/av
Part-time: n/av	**Ph.D.s:** 95%
Graduate: n/av	**Student/Faculty:** n/av
Year: semesters, summer session	**Tuition:** $13,258 ($27,974)
Application Deadline: January 15	**Room & Board:** $10,439
Freshman Class: 35868 applied, 22556 accepted, 4621 enrolled	
SAT CR/M: 590/610	**ACT:** 27 **VERY COMPETITIVE+**

Established in 1863, University of Massachusetts Amherst is a public research, land-grant institution offering over 100 academic majors. There are 8 undergraduate schools and 8 graduate schools. In addition to regional accreditation, UMass Amherst has baccalaureate program accreditation with AACSB, ABET, ASLA, FIDER, NASM, NCATE, NLN, and SAF. The 2 libraries contain 4.3 million volumes, 2.6 million microform items, 44,853 audio/video tapes/CDs/DVDs, and subscribe to 214,303 periodicals including electronic. Computerized library services include interlibrary loans, database searching, Internet access, and Wi-Fi capability. Special learning facilities include an art gallery, radio station, TV station, including botanical gardens, a astronomical observatory, and learning commons.

The 1463-acre campus is in a small town 90 miles west of Boston and 60 miles north of Hartford, Connecticut. Including any residence halls, there are 319 buildings.

Student Life: 77% of undergraduates are from Massachusetts. Others are from 48 states, 97 foreign countries, and Canada. 66% are White; 13% race unknown. The average age of freshmen is 18; all undergraduates, 21. 11% do not continue beyond their first year; 73% remain to graduate.

Housing: 13318 students can be accommodated in college housing, which includes single-sex and coed dorms, on-campus apartments, and married student housing. In addition, there are honors houses, language houses, special-interest houses, fraternity houses, sorority houses, international housing, and first-year housing. On-campus housing is guaranteed for the freshman year only and is available on a lottery system for upperclassmen. All students may keep cars.

Activities: 7% of men belong to 1 local and 21 national fraternities; 6% of women belong to 2 local and 6 national sororities. There are 324 groups on campus, including art, band, cheerleading, chess, choir, chorale, chorus, communications, computers, dance, debate, drama, environmental, ethnic, film, gay, honors, international, jazz band, literary magazine, marching band, musical theater, newspaper, opera, orchestra, pep band, photography, political, professional, radio and TV, religious, social, social service, student government, student-owned businesses, and symphony. Popular campus events include First Week, and Something Every Friday Movies.

Sports: There are 9 intercollegiate sports for men and 10 for women, and 13 intramural sports for men and 13 for women. Facilities include 120 acres of multipurpose fields, softball and soccer fields, a 20,000-seat football stadium, a track, and 22 tennis courts. Indoor facilities include a 120,000-sq-ft recreation center with weight and fitness equipment, a 3-court gym, a wellness center, and an elevated jogging track. Other facilities include 3 pools, 3 handball/squash, racquetball courts, 2 gyms, a wrestling room, 2 dance studios, weight-training rooms, fitness centers, basketball/volleyball/badminton courts, and an indoor track. The indoor sports arena has 10,500 seats and 2 Olympic-sized ice sheets. Body shops are also available in residential areas.

Disabled Students: All of the campus is accessible. Facilities include wheelchair ramps, elevators, special parking, specially equipped restrooms, special class scheduling, lowered drinking fountains, lowered telephones, special housing. All programs are made accessible through accommodations.

Services: Counseling and information services are available, as is tutoring in most subjects. There is a reader service for the blind.

Campus Safety and Security: Measures include 24-hour foot and vehicle patrol, emergency notification system, self-defense education, and security escort services. There are shuttle buses, emergency telephones, lighted pathways/sidewalks, and controlled access to dorms/residences.

Programs of Study: UMass Amherst confers B.A., B.S., B.B.A., B.F.A., B.G.S., B.S.N. and B.Mus. degrees. Associate, master's, and doctoral degrees are also awarded. Bachelor's degrees are awarded in AGRICULTURE (agricultural economics, animal science, natural resource management, plant science, soil science, and wood science), BIOLOGICAL SCIENCE (biochemistry, biology/biological science, microbiology, and nutrition), BUSINESS (accounting, banking and finance, business administration and management, hospitality management services, marketing management, operations management, and sports management), COMMUNICATIONS AND THE ARTS (art history and appreciation, Chinese, classics, communications, comparative literature, dance, dramatic arts, English, Germanic languages and literature, Japanese, journalism, linguistics, music, music performance, Portuguese, Spanish, and studio art), COMPUTER AND PHYSICAL SCIENCE (astronomy, chemistry, computer science, earth science, geology, mathematics, physics, and science), EDUCATION (education), ENGINEERING AND ENVIRONMENTAL DESIGN (architecture, chemical engineering, civil engineering, computer engineering, construction technology, electrical/electronics engineering, environmental design, environmental science, industrial engineering, landscape architecture/design, and mechanical engineering), HEALTH PROFESSIONS (exercise science, nursing, predentistry, premedicine, preveterinary science, public health, and speech pathology/audiology), SOCIAL SCIENCE (African American studies, anthropology, economics, food science, French studies, gender studies, geography, history, interdisciplinary studies, Italian studies, Judaic studies, law, liberal arts/general studies, Middle Eastern studies, philosophy, political science/government, psychology, Russian and Slavic studies, sociology, and women's studies). Psychology, management, and biology have the largest enrollemnts.

Required: Students must complete 120 credit hours and maintain a minimum GPA of 2.0 overall and in the major. For the general education requirement, students must take 4 courses in Social World, 2 courses in Social and Cultural Diversity, 2 courses in Biological and Physical World, 2 courses in Writing, and 1 each in Basic Math Skills, Integrative Experience, and Analytic Reasoning. There is an Interdisciplinary option.

Special: Cross-registration is possible with Smith, Mount Holyoke, Hampshire, and Amherst Colleges. Co-op programs, internships in every major, study abroad in more than 40 countries, a Washington semester, work-study programs, dual majors, and B.A.-B.S. degrees are available. Accelerated degrees are currently offered in the School of Management and Economics and are being planned for other programs. The Bachelor's Degree with Individual Concentration (BDIC) is also available. The Commonwealth Honors College welcomes honor students who meet entrance requirements. There are also teacher certification, distance learning, independent study, and ESL programs. There are 45 national honor societies, including Phi Beta Kappa, a freshman honors program, and 75 departmental honors programs.

Faculty/Classroom: All teach and do research. No introductory courses are taught by graduate students.

Admissions: 63% of the 2013-2014 applicants were accepted. The SAT scores for the 2013-2014 freshman class were: Critical Reading--8% below 500, 46% between 500 and 599, 36% between 600 and 699, and 9% between 700 and 800; Math--4% below 500, 36% between 500 and 599, 47% between 600 and 699, and 13% between 700 and 800. The ACT scores were 4% below 21, 14% between 21 and 23, 32% between 24 and 26, 22% between 27 and 28, and 28% above 28. 57% of the current freshmen were in the top fifth of their class; 92% were in the top two fifths.

Requirements: The SAT is required. Applicants must be graduates of an accredited secondary school or have the GED. The university recommends that students complete 16 Carnegie units including 4 years of English, 3 years each of math, and science (including 2 years lab), and 2 years each of electives, foreign language, and social studies. 4 years of math are required for business, computer science, and engineering majors. Students must present a portfolio for admission to the art program and must audition for admission to music and dance. A GPA of 2.0 is required. AP and CLEP credits are accepted. Important factors in the admissions decision are advanced placement or honors courses, extracurricular activities record, and recommendations by school officials.

Procedure: Freshmen are admitted fall and spring. Entrance exams should be taken as soon as possible after admissions deadline. There are early admissions, deferred admissions, and rolling admissions plans. Early decision applications should be filed by November 1; regular applications, by January 15 for fall entry; and October 1 for spring entry, along with a $75 fee. Notifications are sent in March. Applications are accepted online.

Transfer: Transfer applicants must submit transcripts from all colleges or universities attended and an essay. Those with fewer than 27 credits must submit high school transcripts and SAT scores. Priority is given to students with an associate degree. Grades of C- or better in comparable coursework transfer for credit. 45 of 120 credits required for the bachelor's degree must be completed at UMass Amherst.

Visiting: There are regularly scheduled orientations for prospective students, including 3 guided tours daily weekdays, 2 tours daily on weekends and twice-daily information sessions. There are guides for informal visits and visitors may sit in on classes.

Financial Aid: In 2013-2014, 57% of all full-time freshmen and 60% of continuing full-time students received some form of financial aid. 51% of all full-time freshmen and 50% of continuing full-time students received need-based aid. UMass Amherst is a member of CSS. The FAFSA is required. The priority date for freshman financial aid applications for fall entry is March 1.

International Students: There are 526 international students enrolled. The school actively recruits these students. They must take the TOEFL with a minimum score of 550 on the paper-based TOEFL (PBT) or 80 on the Internet-based version (iBT). They must also take the SAT or ACT.

Computers: All students may access the system. There are no time limits and no fees.

Graduates: From July 1, 2012 to June 30, 2013, 5737 bachelor's degrees were awarded. The most popular majors were psychology (8%), communication (5%), and biology (4%). In an average class, 59% graduate in 4 years or less, 72% graduate in 5 years or less, and 73% graduate in 6 years or less.

Admissions Contact: Kevin Kelly, Director of Admissions. E-Mail: *mail@admissions.umass.edu* Web: *www.umass.edu*

UNIVERSITY OF MASSACHUSETTS BOSTON E-2

Boston, MA 02125	**(617) 287-6000; (617) 287-5999**
Full-time: 3926 men, 4833 women	**Faculty:** 602; I, --$
Part-time: 1512 men, 2095 women	**Ph.D.s:** 96%
Graduate: 1226 men, 2685 women	**Student/Faculty:** 15 to 1
Year: semesters, summer session	**Tuition:** $11,966 ($27,430)
Application Deadline: April 1	**Room & Board:** n/av

Freshman Class: 8170 applied, 5834 accepted, 1413 enrolled

SAT CR/M: 510/540 **ACT:** required **COMPETITIVE**

The University of Massachusetts Boston, established in 1964, is a public research institution offering undergraduate studies in arts and sciences and in preprofessional training. There are 8 undergraduate schools and 10 graduate schools. In addition to regional accreditation, UMass Boston has baccalaureate program accreditation with AACSB and ABET. The library contains 600,000 volumes, 803,000 microform items, and subscribes to 75,000 periodicals including electronic. Computerized library services include interlibrary loans, database searching, Internet access, and Wi-Fi capability. Special learning facilities include an art gallery, planetarium, radio station, tropical greenhouse, observatory, adaptive computer lab, languages lab, and applied language and math center. The 187-acre campus is in an urban area 5 miles south of downtown Boston. Including any residence halls, there are 7 buildings.

Student Life: 95% of undergraduates are from Massachusetts. Others are from 40 states, 151 foreign countries, and Canada. 45% are White; 13% African American. The average age of freshmen is 19; all undergraduates, 25. 21% do not continue beyond their first year; 38% remain to graduate.

Housing: Alcohol is not permitted. All students commute. All students may keep cars.

Activities: There are no fraternities or sororities. There are 100 groups on campus, including art, band, cheerleading, chess, choir, chorale, chorus, computers, dance, drama, ethnic, film, gay, honors, international, jazz band, literary magazine, musical theater, newspaper, orchestra, photography, political, professional, radio and TV, religious, social, social service, and student government. Popular campus events include Convocation Day, Seasonal Festivals and Lecture Series.

Sports: There are 8 intercollegiate sports for men and 8 for women, and 12 intramural sports for men and 12 for women. Facilities include an athletic center with a 3500-seat gym with 4 basketball and 2 volleyball courts, an ice rink that seats 1000, a Olympic-size swimming pool with high-dive area, a multipurpose weight room, a sports medicine area; an 8-lane, 400-meter track; 8 tennis courts; a softball diamond, 3 multipurpose fields primarily used for soccer and lacrosse, and other recreational fields; a boat house, dock, and fleet of sailboats and rowing dories; and a fitness center with strength-training equipment.

Disabled Students: All of the campus is accessible. Facilities include wheelchair ramps, elevators, special parking, specially equipped restrooms, special class scheduling, lowered drinking fountains, lowered telephones. amplified phones, powered doors, indoor-connected building access, an accessible shuttle bus, an adaptive computer lab, and a center for students with disabilities.

Services: Counseling and information services are available, as is tutoring in every subject. There is a reader service for the blind, and remedial math, reading, and writing. There are also reading study skills workshops and a math resource center available.

Campus Safety and Security: Measures include 24-hour foot and vehicle patrol, emergency notification system, self-defense education, and security escort services. There are shuttle buses, emergency telephones, lighted pathways/sidewalks, Operation ID, motorist assistance, and crime prevention programs.

Programs of Study: UMass Boston confers B.A., and B.S. degrees. Master's and doctoral degrees are also awarded. Bachelor's degrees are awarded in BIOLOGICAL SCIENCE (biochemistry and biology/biological science), BUSINESS (labor studies and management science), COMMUNICATIONS AND THE ARTS (art, classical languages, classics, communications, dramatic arts, English, French, information technology, Italian, music, and Spanish), COMPUTER AND PHYSICAL SCIENCE (chemistry, computer science, earth science, information sciences and systems, mathematics, and physics), EDUCATION (early childhood education), ENGINEERING AND ENVIRONMENTAL DESIGN (electrical and computer engineering, engineering, and engineering physics), HEALTH PROFESSIONS (exercise science, medical technology, and nursing), SOCIAL SCIENCE (African American studies, American studies, anthropology, asian studies, community services, criminal justice, economics, ethics, politics, and social policy, geography, gerontology, Hispanic American studies, history, human services, paralegal studies, philosophy, physical fitness/movement, political science/government, psychology, sociology, and women's studies). Management, nursing, and psychology have the largest enrollments.

Required: For graduation, students must complete 120 credit hours (123 hours in the College of Nursing) and maintain a minimum GPA of 2.0. Distribution requirements vary by college. All students must demonstrate writing proficiency.

Special: Students may cross-register with Boston Public Colleges, Massachusetts College of Art, Bunker Hill Community College, Roxbury Community College, and Hebrew College. UMass Boston also offers cooperative programs, internships, study abroad, work-study programs, student-designed majors, B.A.-B.S. degrees, nondegree study, pass/fail options, and dual and interdisciplinary majors, including anthropology/history, biology/medical technology, philosophy/public policy, and psychology/sociology. Also available are 3-1 and 2-2 engineering programs with various area institutions. The College of Public and Community Service provides social-oriented education, There are 3 national honor societies and a freshman honors program.

Faculty/Classroom: 51% of faculty are male; 49% are female. All teach undergraduates. No introductory courses are taught by graduate students. The average class size in an introductory lecture is 27; in a laboratory is 16; and in a regular course is 27.

Admissions: 71% of the 2013-2014 applicants were accepted. The SAT scores for the 2013-2014 freshman class were: Critical Reading--43% below 500, 42% between 500 and 599, 14% between 600 and 699, and 2% between 700 and 800; Math--27% below 500, 47% between 500 and 599, 22% between 600 and 699, and 3% between 700 and 800.

Requirements: The SAT or ACT is required. Applicants should be graduates of an accredited secondary school. The GED is accepted. The university requires the completion of 16 Carnegie units, including 4 years of English, 3 of college preparatory math and science, 2 each of a foreign language and social studies, and 2 electives in the above academic areas or in humanities, arts, or computer science. A GPA of 3.0 is required. AP and CLEP credits are accepted.

Procedure: Freshmen are admitted fall and spring. Entrance exams should be taken by the fall of the senior year. There are deferred admissions and rolling admissions plans. Applications should be filed by April 1 for fall entry, along with a $60 fee. Notification is sent on a rolling basis. Applications are accepted online.

Transfer: 1719 transfer students enrolled in 2012-2013. Applicants with fewer than 24 credits must meet freshman requirements. To transfer, students must have a minimum college GPA of 2.5. Grades of C- or better transfer for credit. 30 of 120 credits required for the bachelor's degree must be completed at UMass Boston.

Visiting: There are regularly scheduled orientations for prospective students, including general information sessions about the university and the admissions process and a tour of the campus. There are guides for informal visits and visitors may sit in on classes. To schedule a visit, contact the Enrollment Information Services at (617) 287-6000.

Financial Aid: The FAFSA is required. The priority date for freshman financial aid applications for fall entry is March 1.

International Students: The school actively recruits these students. They must take the TOEFL with a minimum score of 550 on the paper-based TOEFL (PBT) or 79 on the Internet-based version (iBT). They must also take the SAT or ACT. if the language of instruction is English.

Computers: All students may access the system 24 hours a day. There are no time limits and no fees.

Graduates: From July 1, 2012 to June 30, 2013, 2275 bachelor's degrees were awarded. The most popular majors were management (20%), health professions and related programs (18%), and psychology (12%). In an average class, 13% graduate in 4 years or less, 32% graduate in 5 years or less, and 38% graduate in 6 years or less.

Admissions Contact: John Drew, Director of Undergraduate Admissions. E-Mail: *enrollment.info@umb.edu* Web: *www.umb.edu*

UNIVERSITY OF MASSACHUSETTS DARTMOUTH D-4

North Dartmouth, MA 02747	(508) 999-8605; (508) 999-8755
Full-time: 3430 men, 2943 women	**Faculty:** 378; IIA, +$
Part-time: 455 men, 609 women	**Ph.D.s:** 89%
Graduate: 753 men, 863 women	**Student/Faculty:** 17 to 1
Year: semesters, summer session	**Tuition:** $11,681 ($24,156)
Application Deadline: open	**Room & Board:** $10,542
Freshman Class: 8119 applied, 6094 accepted, 1435 enrolled	
SAT CR/M/W: 510/530/510 **ACT:** 23	**COMPETITIVE**

University of Massachusetts Dartmouth, founded in 1895, is a public institution that provides undergraduate and graduate programs in the liberal and creative arts and sciences and in professional training. There are 5 undergraduate schools and 3 graduate schools. In addition to regional accreditation, UMass Dartmouth has baccalaureate program accreditation with AACSB, ABET, NASAD, and NASDTEC. The 2 libraries contain 438,887 volumes, 69,407 microform items, 7,913 audio/video tapes/CDs/DVDs, and subscribe to 2,783 periodicals including electronic. Computerized library services include interlibrary loans, database searching, Internet access, and Wi-Fi capability. Special learning facilities include an art gallery, radio station, an observatory, marine research vessels, and a number of cultural and research centers. The 710-acre campus is in a suburban area approximately 60 miles south of Boston and 28 miles east of Providence, Rhode Island. Including any residence halls, there are 35 buildings.

Student Life: 94% of undergraduates are from Massachusetts. Others are from 42 states, 55 foreign countries, and Canada. 88% are from public schools. 66% are White. The average age of freshmen is 19; all undergraduates, 23. 26% do not continue beyond their first year; 50% remain to graduate.

Housing: 4494 students can be accommodated in college housing, which includes coed dorms and on-campus apartments. In addition, there are honors houses, special-interest houses, quiet housing; substance awareness housing; apartments and townhouses for upperclassmen. On-campus housing is guaranteed for the freshman year only, is available on a first-come, first-served basis, and is available on a lottery system for upperclassmen. Priority is given to out-of-town students. 54% of students live on campus; of those, 35% remain on campus on weekends. All students may keep cars.

Activities: 1% of men belong to 5 local and 1 national fraternities; 1% of women belong to 3 local and 3 national sororities. There are 128 groups on campus, including art, band, cheerleading, choir, chorale, chorus, computers, dance, drama, ethnic, gay, honors, international, jazz band, literary magazine, musical theater, newspaper, orchestra, political, professional, radio and TV, religious, social, social service, student government, symphony, and yearbook. Popular campus events include Welcome Back Week, Homecoming Weekend and Family Fall Weekend.

Sports: There are 11 intercollegiate sports for men and 12 for women, and 10 intramural sports for men and 7 for women. Facilities include a 1650-seat gym, an 1250-seat football stadium, an aquatic sports center, 10 tennis courts, a 10,000-sq-ft fitness center, a running track, and soccer, softball, and intramural fields.

Disabled Students: 97% of the campus is accessible. Facilities include wheelchair ramps, elevators, special parking, specially equipped restrooms, special class scheduling, lowered drinking fountains, lowered telephones, special housing.

Services: Counseling and information services are available, as is tutoring in most subjects, through the writing/reading, science/engineering, math/business, and academic resource centers There is a reader service for the blind, and remedial math.

Campus Safety and Security: Measures include 24-hour foot and vehicle patrol, emergency notification system, self-defense education, and security escort services. There are shuttle buses, emergency telephones, lighted pathways/sidewalks, controlled access to dorms/residences, and a bicycle patrol.

Programs of Study: UMass Dartmouth confers B.A., B.S. and B.F.A. degrees. Master's and doctoral degrees are also awarded. Bachelor's degrees are awarded in BIOLOGICAL SCIENCE (biochemistry, biology/biological science, biotechnology, and marine biology), BUSINESS (accounting, business administration and management, finance, management information systems, marketing/retailing/merchandising, and operations management), COMMUNICATIONS AND THE ARTS (art history and appreciation, ceramic art and design, English, English literature, English Writing, fiber/textiles/weaving, French, graphic design, illustration, metal/jewelry, music, painting, photography, Portuguese, sculpture, Spanish, and visual design), COMPUTER AND PHYSICAL SCIENCE (astronomy and physics, chemistry, computer science, mathematics, physics, and software engineering), EDUCATION (art education), ENGINEERING AND ENVIRONMENTAL DESIGN (bioengineering, civil engineering, computer engineering, electrical/electronics engineering, manufacturing engineering, materials science, and mechanical engineering), HEALTH PROFESSIONS (clinical science, cytotechnology, health science, medical laboratory science, and nursing), SOCIAL SCIENCE (anthropology, criminal justice, economics, history, interdisciplinary studies, liberal arts/general studies, philosophy, political science/government, psychology, sociology, and women & gender studies). Engineering, physical/life sciences and design/fine arts are the strongest academically. Nursing, psychology and liberal arts have the largest enrollments.

Required: Each student must complete the requirements of the 5 clusters that comprise the University Studies curriculum: Cluster 1 Foundations for Engagement, Cluster 2 the Natural World, Cluster 3 the Cultural World, Cluster 4 the Social World and Cluster 5 the Educated and Engaged Citizen. A freshman English composition course is required. Colleges set some additional distribution course requirements. The B.A. requires foreign language study. To graduate, students must complete 120 to 132 credit hours and maintain a 2.0 GPA.

Special: The university permits cross-registration through the SACHEM Consortium of 9 schools in Massachusetts. Study abroad in 9 countries, an engineering or business co-op program, a Washington semester, internships, numerous work-study programs, dual majors, service learning opportunities and student-designed majors are available. Non degree study, pass/fail options, B.S. to M.S. degrees in chemistry, nursing, computer science, electrical engineering, civil engineering, computer engineering, and mechanical engineering, a B.A.-M.A. in psychology, a English B.A. to Professional Writing Master's, a BA - MAT in several fields, along with MPP-JD and MBA - JD programs. There are a freshman honors program.

Faculty/Classroom: 52% of faculty are male; 48% are female. All teach undergraduates, and 60% do both. Graduate students teach 1% of introductory courses. The average class size in an introductory lecture is 33; in a laboratory is 23; and in a regular course is 14.

Admissions: 75% of the 2013-2014 applicants were accepted. The SAT scores for the 2013-2014 freshman class were: Critical Reading--41% below 500, 41% between 500 and 599, 16% between 600 and 699, and 2% between 700 and 800; Math--30% below 500, 47% between 500 and 599, 21% between 600 and 699, and 2% between 700 and 800; Writing--45% below 500, 41% between 500 and 599, 13% between 600 and 699, and 2% between 700 and 800. The ACT scores were 25% below 21, 30% between 21 and 23, 25% between 24 and 26, 6% between 27 and 28, and 14% above 28. 36% of the current freshmen were in the top fifth of their class; 66% were in the top two fifths. 5 freshmen graduated first in their class.

Requirements: The SAT is required. Applicants should have 4 years of English, 3 each of science and math, 2 of the same foreign language, 1 each of social studies and U.S. history, and 2 of college-preparatory electives. The GED is accepted. An audition is necessary for music majors, and a portfolio is recommended for studio arts and design applicants. All applicants must submit an essay. A GPA of 3.0 is required. AP and CLEP credits are accepted. Important factors in the admissions decision are recommendations by school officials, advanced placement or honors courses, and evidence of special talent.

Procedure: Freshmen are admitted fall and spring. Entrance exams should be taken spring of the junior year or early fall of the senior year. There are deferred admissions and rolling admissions plans. Application deadlines are open. Application fee is $60. Notification of early decision is sent December 15; regular decision, on a rolling basis. Applications are accepted online.

Transfer: 475 transfer students enrolled in 2012-2013. Applicants must submit all official college transcripts and must take the SAT unless they graduated from high school more than 3 years prior to applying. Those with fewer than 24 transferable credits may need to submit high school records. 45 of 120 credits required for the bachelor's degree must be completed at UMass Dartmouth.

Visiting: There are regularly scheduled orientations for prospective students, including scheduled campus tours Monday through Friday and most Saturdays. There are guides for informal visits and visitors may sit in on classes.

Financial Aid: The FAFSA is required. The priority date for freshman financial aid applications for fall entry is March 1.

International Students: There are 100 international students enrolled. They must take the TOEFL with a minimum score of 520 on the paper-based TOEFL (PBT) or 68 on the Internet-based version (iBT). They must also take the SAT or ACT.

Computers: All students may access the system. during the day and evening as well as on weekends. There are no time limits and no fees.

Graduates: From July 1, 2012 to June 30, 2013, 1241 bachelor's degrees were awarded. The most popular majors were marketing (8%), nursing (8%), and accounting (8%).

Admissions Contact: Michael Lynch, Director of Admissions. E-Mail: *admissions@umassd.edu* Web: *www.umassd.edu/undergraduate*

UNIVERSITY OF MASSACHUSETTS LOWELL D-1

Lowell, MA 01854 **(978) 934-3931**
(800) 410-4607; (978) 934-3086

Full-time: 4555 men, 3010 women	**Faculty:** n/av; I, +$
Part-time: 1760 men, 1235 women	**Ph.D.s:** 48%
Graduate: 1630 men, 1430 women	**Student/Faculty:** n/av
Year: semesters, summer session	**Tuition:** $12427 ($27,500)
Application Deadline: open	**Room & Board:** $10,020
Freshman Class: n/av	
SAT or ACT: required	

COMPETITIVE

The University of Massachussetts Lowell, founded in 1895, is a public institution offering undergraduate programs through the schools of arts and sciences, engineering, health professions, management science, and music and graduate programs in education. The figures in the above capsule and in this profile are approximate. There are 5 undergraduate schools and 1 graduate school. In addition to regional accreditation, UMass Lowell has baccalaureate program accreditation with AACSB, ABET, APTA, CAHEA, CSAB, NASAD, NASM, NCATE, and NLN. The 3 libraries contain 382,599 volumes, 91,022 microform items, 14,353 audio/video tapes/CDs/DVDs, and subscribe to 32,744 periodicals including electronic. Computerized library services include interlibrary loans, database searching, Internet access, and laptop Internet portals. Special learning facilities include a learning resource center, art gallery, natural history museum, radio station, many experimental and investigative labs, and the Research Foundation, which includes a materials testing division and centers for atmospheric research and tropical disease. The 100-acre campus is in an urban area 30 miles northwest of Boston. Including any residence halls, there are 37 buildings.

Student Life: 85% of undergraduates are from Massachusetts. Others are from 43 states, 28 foreign countries, and Canada. 72% are white. The average age of freshmen is 18; all undergraduates, 23. 21% do not continue beyond their first year; 79% remain to graduate.

Housing: 3081 students can be accommodated in college housing, which includes single-sex and coed dorms, off-campus apartments, and married student housing. In addition, there are special-interest houses. On-campus housing is guaranteed for the freshman year only and is available on a first-come, first-served basis. 64% of students commute. All students may keep cars.

Activities: There are no fraternities or sororities. There are 100 groups

on campus, including art, band, cheerleading, computers, drama, ethnic, gay, honors, international, marching band, musical theater, newspaper, pep band, photography, political, professional, radio and TV, religious, social, social service, and student government.

Sports: There are 15 intercollegiate sports for men and 10 for women, and 34 intramural sports for men and 34 for women. Facilities include a 2000-seat gym, a pool, weight-training facilities, and areas for gymnastics, wrestling, and judo. There are also courts for handball, squash, and tennis and various playing fields.

Disabled Students: 70% of the campus is accessible. Facilities include wheelchair ramps, elevators, special parking, specially equipped restrooms, special class scheduling, lowered drinking fountains, and lowered telephones.

Services: Counseling and information services are available, as is tutoring in most subjects. There is a reader service for the blind and remedial writing.

Campus Safety and Security: Measures include 24-hour foot and vehicle patrol, self-defense education, and security escort services. There are shuttle buses, emergency telephones, and lighted pathways/sidewalks.

Programs of Study: UMass Lowell confers B.A., B.F.A., B.L.A., B.M., B.S., B.S.B.A., B.S.E., B.S.E.T., B.S.I.M., and B.S.I.T. degrees. Associate, master's, and doctoral degrees are also awarded. Bachelor's degrees are awarded in BIOLOGICAL SCIENCE (biology/biological science), BUSINESS (business administration and management), COMMUNICATIONS AND THE ARTS (English, fine arts, modern language, and music performance), COMPUTER AND PHYSICAL SCIENCE (applied mathematics, chemistry, computer science, information sciences and systems, mathematics, and physics), ENGINEERING AND ENVIRONMENTAL DESIGN (chemical engineering, civil engineering, electrical/electronics engineering, engineering technology, environmental science, industrial administration/management, industrial engineering technology, mechanical engineering, and plastics engineering), HEALTH PROFESSIONS (clinical science, community health work, exercise science, and nursing), SOCIAL SCIENCE (American studies, criminal justice, economics, history, liberal arts/general studies, philosophy, political science/government, psychology, and sociology). Engineering and management have the largest enrollments.

Required: All students must complete a minimum of 120 credits with a 2.0 GPA. Core requirements include 6 credits of English composition, 3 credits of human values, and an area distribution requirement of 27 to 29 credits outside the major in behavioral and social science, fine arts and the humanities, and math and the sciences.

Special: Cross-registration, co-op, and work-study programs are available, as are opportunities for study abroad. The university offers a combined B.A.-B.S. degree in engineering, dual majors, nondegree study, and pass/fail options. There are 2 national honor societies, a freshman honors program, and all departments have honors programs.

Faculty/Classroom: 61% of faculty are male; 39% are female. No introductory courses are taught by graduate students.

Requirements: The SAT or ACT is required; the SAT is preferred. Applicants should have a high school diploma or the GED. The university recommends that secondary preparation include 4 courses in English, 3 each in social science/history and math, 2 each in science and a foreign language, and 2 academic electives. Prospective music majors must audition, and an interview is recommended for all students. A GPA of 3.0 is required. AP and CLEP credits are accepted.

Procedure: Freshmen are admitted fall and spring. Entrance exams should be taken by January of the senior year. There are deferred admissions and rolling admissions plans. Application deadlines are open. Check with the school for the current application fee. Applications are accepted online.

Transfer: 935 transfer students enrolled in in a recent year. Transfer applicants must present at least a 2.0 GPA in previous college work. Those with fewer than 30 credits must meet freshman admission requirements. 30 of 120 credits required for the bachelor's degree must be completed at UMass Lowell.

Visiting: There are regularly scheduled orientations for prospective students. To schedule a visit, contact the Office of Student Services.

Financial Aid: In a recent year, 94% of all full-time freshmen received some form of financial aid, including need-based aid. The average freshman award was $12,705. Need-based scholarships or need-based grants averaged $6805; need-based self-help aid (loans and jobs) averaged $6593; non-need-based athletic scholarships averaged $4834; and other non-need-based awards and non-need-based scholarships averaged $2435. 16% of undergraduate students worked part-time. Average annual earnings from campus work were $3090. The FAFSA is required. Check with the school for current application deadlines.

International Students: There were 55 international students enrolled in a recent year. They must take the TOEFL with a minimum score of 550 on the paper-based TOEFL (PBT) or 79 on the Internet-based version (iBT). They must also take the SAT or ACT.

Computers: Wireless access is available. All students may access the system. There are no time limits and no fees.

Graduates: In a recent year, 1337 bachelor's degrees were awarded. The most popular majors were business administration (16%), engineering (11%), and criminal justice (7%). In an average class, 22% graduate in 4 years or less, 44% graduate in 5 years or less, and 46% graduate in 6 years or less.

Admissions Contact: Director, Admissions. E-mail: *admissions@uml.edu* Web: *www.uml.edu*

WELLESLEY COLLEGE — D-2

Wellesley, MA 02481 — **(781) 283-2270; (781) 283-3678**

Full-time: 2185 women	**Faculty:** 259; IIB, ++$
Part-time: 83 women	**Ph.D.s:** 293%
Graduate: n/av	**Student/Faculty:** 8 to 1
Year: semesters	**Tuition:** $38,062
Application Deadline: January 15	**Room & Board:** $11,786
Freshman Class: 4156 applied, 1463 accepted, 589 enrolled	
SAT CR/M/W: 689/683/693	**ACT:** 30 **MOST COMPETITIVE**

Wellesley College, established in 1870, is a small, private, diverse liberal arts and sciences college for women. The 5 libraries contain 94,346 volumes, 536,499 microform items, 36,439 audio/video tapes/CDs/DVDs, and subscribe to 1,945 periodicals including electronic. Computerized library services include interlibrary loans, database searching, and Internet access. Special learning facilities include an art gallery, radio station, a science center, a botanic greenhouse, an observatory, a center for developmental studies and services, centers for research on women and child study, and a media and technology center. The 500-acre campus is in a suburban area 12 miles west of Boston. Including any residence halls, there are 64 buildings.

Student Life: 86% of undergraduates are from out of state, mostly the Middle Atlantic. Students are from 50 states, 60 foreign countries, and Canada. 63% are from public schools. 41% are White; 25% Asian American. The average age of freshmen is 18; all undergraduates, 20. 6% do not continue beyond their first year; 943% remain to graduate.

Housing: 2188 students can be accommodated in college housing, which includes single-sex dorms. In addition, there are language houses, special-interest houses, language corridors, and co-ops. On-campus housing is guaranteed for all 4 years. 97% of students live on campus. Upperclassmen may keep cars.

Activities: There are no fraternities or sororities. There are 160 groups on campus, including art, choir, chorus, computers, dance, debate, drama, environmental, ethnic, film, gay, honors, international, jazz band, literary magazine, musical theater, newspaper, orchestra, photography, political, professional, radio and TV, religious, social, social service, student government, symphony, and yearbook. Popular campus events include Lake Day, Spring Weekend, and International Week.

Sports: There are 13 intercollegiate sports for women, and 21 intramural sports for women. Facilities include an indoor pool, dance studios, a weight room, an indoor track, a golf course, and courts for racquetball, squash, tennis, and volleyball.

Disabled Students: All of the campus is accessible. Facilities include wheelchair ramps, elevators, special parking, specially equipped restrooms, special class scheduling, lowered drinking fountains, lowered telephones, special housing, and signage in braille.

Services: Counseling and information services are available, as is tutoring in every subject. There is a reader service for the blind.

Campus Safety and Security: Measures include 24-hour foot and vehicle patrol, emergency notification system, self-defense education, and security escort services. There are shuttle buses, emergency telephones, and lighted pathways/sidewalks.

Programs of Study: Wellesley confers B.A. degrees. Bachelor's degrees are awarded in AGRICULTURE (environmental studies), BIOLOGICAL SCIENCE (biochemistry, biology/biological science, and neurosciences), COMMUNICATIONS AND THE ARTS (art history and appreciation, Chinese, comparative literature, dramatic arts, English, film arts, French, German, Greek, Japanese, Latin, music, Russian, Russian languages and literature, Spanish, and studio art), COMPUTER AND PHYSICAL SCIENCE (astronomy, astrophysics, chemistry, computer science, geology, mathematics, and physics), ENGINEERING AND ENVIRONMENTAL DESIGN (architecture), SOCIAL SCIENCE (African American studies, American studies, anthropology, archeology, Asian/Oriental studies, classical/ancient civilization, cognitive science, economics, French studies, German area studies, history, international relations, Italian studies, Japanese studies, Judaic studies, Latin American studies, medieval studies, Middle Eastern studies, peace studies, philosophy, political science/government, psychology, religion, sociology, and women's studies). Psychology, English, economics, political science, biological sciences have the largest enrollments.

Required: All students must complete 32 units, at least 8 of which are in the major field, with a minimum 2.0 GPA. Requirements include 3 courses each in humanities, social science, and natural science and math; 1 multicultural course; 1 semester of expository writing in any department;

and 8 credits in phys ed. Students must also possess proficiency in a modern or ancient foreign language. A thesis is required for departmental honors. A quantitative reasoning requirement must be satisfied by all students.

Special: Students may cross-register at MIT, Brandeis University, or Babson College. Exchange programs are available with Spelman College in Georgia and Mills College in California, with members of the Twelve College Exchange Program, with Williams College's maritime studies program, and with Connecticut College's National Theater Institute. Study abroad is possible through Wellesley-administered programs in France and Austria, exchange programs in Argentina, Japan, Korea, and the United Kingdom, and other programs in Italy, Japan, Spain, South Africa, and China. There are more than 150 approved study abroad programs available. There are summer internship programs in Boston and Washington, D.C. Dual majors, student-designed majors, nondegree study, and pass/fail options are possible. A 3-2 program with MIT, Dartmouth, and Columbia awards a B.A.-B.S. degree. There are 2 national honor societies, including Phi Beta Kappa, and 51 departmental honors programs.

Faculty/Classroom: 37% of faculty are male; 63% are female. All teach undergraduates. No introductory courses are taught by graduate students. The average class size in an introductory lecture is 30 and in a regular course is 19.

Admissions: 35% of the 2013-2014 applicants were accepted. The SAT scores for the 2013-2014 freshman class were: Critical Reading--10% between 500 and 599, 38% between 600 and 699, and 52% between 700 and 800; Math--11% between 500 and 599, 45% between 600 and 699, and 43% between 700 and 800; Writing--8% between 500 and 599, 41% between 600 and 699, and 51% between 700 and 800. The ACT scores were 69% above 28. 96% of the current freshmen were in the top fifth of their class; 100% were in the top two fifths. 78 freshmen graduated first in their class.

Requirements: The SAT or ACT is required. The SAT Reasoning Test and 2 SAT subject tests, or the ACT with Writing are required. Wellesley College does not require a fixed plan of secondary school course preparation. Entering students normally have completed 4 years of college preparatory studies in secondary school that include training in clear and coherent writing and interpreting literature; history; principles of math (typically 4 years); competence in at least 1 foreign language, ancient or modern (usually 4 years of study); and experience in at least 2 lab sciences. An essay is required, and an interview is recommended. AP credits are accepted. Important factors in the admissions decision are advanced placement or honors courses, extracurricular activities record, and recommendations by school officials.

Procedure: Freshmen are admitted fall. Entrance exams should be taken during the spring of the junior year or fall of the senior year. There are early decision and deferred admissions plans. Early decision applications should be filed by November 1; regular applications, by January 15 for fall entry. The fall 2013 application fee was $50. Notification of early decision is sent December 15; regular decision, April 1. 120 early decision candidates were accepted for the 2013-2014 class. 543 applicants were on the 2013 waiting list; 30 were admitted. Applications are accepted online.

Transfer: 27 transfer students enrolled in 2012-2013. Applicants must provide high school and college transcripts, SAT or ACT scores, a personal statement, and a statement of good standing from institutions previously attended. An interview is required. 16 of 32 credits required for the bachelor's degree must be completed at Wellesley.

Visiting: There are guides for informal visits, visitors may sit in on classes, and stay overnight. To schedule a visit, contact the Admissions Office.

Financial Aid: In 2013-2014, 56% of all full-time freshmen and 54% of continuing full-time students received some form of financial aid. 58% of all full-time freshmen and 58% of continuing full-time students received need-based aid. The average freshman award was $36,064. Need-based scholarships or need-based grants averaged $34,246; and need-based self-help aid (loans and jobs) averaged $2,874. Average annual earnings from campus work are $2000. The average financial indebtedness of the 2013 graduate was $13,324. Wellesley is a member of CSS. The CSS/Profile, FAFSA, and the college's own financial statement, and and the most recent income tax returns of parents and student. are required. The deadline for filing freshman financial aid applications for fall entry is January 15.

International Students: There are 211 international students enrolled. The school actively recruits these students. They must also take the SAT or ACT.

Computers: All students may access the system. There are no time limits and no fees.

Graduates: From July 1, 2012 to June 30, 2013, 594 bachelor's degrees were awarded. The most popular majors were economics (15%), political science (12%), and English (10%). In an average class, 86% graduate in 4 years or less, 89% graduate in 5 years or less, and 89% graduate in 6 years or less.

Admissions Contact: Board of Admission E-Mail: *admission@wellesley .edu* Web: *www.wellesley.edu*

WENTWORTH INSTITUTE OF TECHNOLOGY — E-2

Boston, MA 02115 — (617) 989-4000, (800) 556-0610; (617) 989-4010

Full-time: 2660 men, 690 women	**Faculty:** 135
Part-time: 345 men, 53 women	**Ph.D.s:** 50%
Graduate: n/av	**Student/Faculty:** n/av
Year: semesters, summer session	**Tuition:** $24,500
Application Deadline: see profile	**Room & Board:** $11,800
Freshman Class: n/av	
SAT or ACT: required	

SPECIAL

Wentworth Institute of Technology, founded in 1904, is a private college specializing in architecture, design, engineering, technology, and management. The figures in the above capsule and in this profile are approximate. In addition to regional accreditation, Wentworth has baccalaureate program accreditation with ABET, ACCE, FIDER, and NAAB. The library contains 77,000 volumes, 90 microform items, 750 audio/video tapes/CDs/DVDs, and subscribes to 500 periodicals including electronic. Computerized library services include interlibrary loans, database searching, and Internet access. Special learning facilities include a learning resource center, radio station, printed-circuit lab, CAD/CAM/CAE labs, design studios, and numerically controlled manufacturing systems. The 35-acre campus is in an urban area in Boston. Including any residence halls, there are 27 buildings.

Student Life: 60% of undergraduates are from Massachusetts. Students are from 39 states, 51 foreign countries, and Canada. 72% are white. The average age of freshmen is 19; all undergraduates, 22. 31% do not continue beyond their first year; 52% remain to graduate.

Housing: 1665 students can be accommodated in college housing, which includes coed dorms and on-campus apartments. On-campus housing is guaranteed for all 4 years and is guaranteed for the freshman year only. 60% of students live on campus. Alcohol is not permitted. Upperclassmen may keep cars.

Activities: There are no fraternities or sororities. There are 50 groups on campus, including communications, computers, dance, drama, ethnic, gay, honors, international, literary magazine, musical threater, newspaper, orchestra, professional, radio and TV, religious, social, social service, student government, and yearbook. Popular campus events include Design Lecture Series, Beaux Arts Ball, and Women's History Month.

Sports: There are 9 intercollegiate sports for men and 6 for women, and 5 intramural sports for men and 5 for women. Facilities include gyms, tennis courts, a riflery range, a fitness center, an outdoor basketball court, and softball, soccer, and lacrosse playing fields.

Disabled Students: 30% of the campus is accessible. Facilities include wheelchair ramps, elevators, special parking, specially equipped rest rooms, special class scheduling, lowered drinking fountains, and lowered telephones.

Services: Counseling and information services are available, as is tutoring in every subject. There is remedial math and writing. Free tutoring is available to all students through the learning center.

Campus Safety and Security: Measures include 24-hour foot and vehicle patrol, self-defense education, and security escort services. There are shuttle buses, emergency telephones, lighted pathways/sidewalks, and campus police officers have emergency medical training.

Programs of Study: Wentworth confers B.S. and B.Arch. degrees. Associates degrees are also awarded. Bachelor's degrees are awarded in COMMUNICATIONS AND THE ARTS (industrial design), COMPUTER AND PHYSICAL SCIENCE (computer science and information sciences and systems), ENGINEERING AND ENVIRONMENTAL DESIGN (architecture, biomedical engineering, civil engineering technology, computer technology, construction management, construction technology, electrical/electronics engineering technology, electromechanical technology, environmental science, industrial administration/management, interior design, mechanical engineering technology, and technological management). Architecture, computer science, and electronic engineering technology have the largest enrollments.

Required: For a bachelor's degree, students must complete a total of 136 to 176 hours, depending on the major, with a minimum GPA of 2.0 overall and 2.5 in the major. An introductory computer course is required of all students. All full-time bachelor's degree candidates must complete 2 semesters of co-op, beginning after the first 2 years of study. A writing competency assessment is required at the end of the sophomore year.

Special: Wentworth offers extensive cooperative programs, cross-registration with other members of the Colleges of the Fenway Consortium, study abroad, including study in France for third-year architecture students, interdisciplinary majors, including engineering technology and facilities planning and management, a dual major in technical management, and nondegree study. Most students at the bachelor's level attend school in the summer, as most cooperative work occurs during the academic year. There is 1 national honor society.

Faculty/Classroom: 76% of faculty are male; 24% are female. All teach

undergraduates. No introductory courses are taught by graduate students. The average class size in an introductory lecture is 25; in a laboratory is 25; and in a regular course is 21.

Requirements: The SAT or ACT is required. Applicants must be graduates of an accredited secondary school or have the GED. High school course requirements vary by major. AP and CLEP credits are accepted. Important factors in the admissions decision are advanced placement or honors courses, leadership record, and extracurricular activities record.

Procedure: Freshmen are admitted fall and spring. Entrance exams should be taken in the spring of the junior year or the fall of the senior year. There are deferred admissions and rolling admissions plans. Check with the school for current application deadlines. Notification is sent on a rolling basis. Applications are accepted online. A waiting list is maintained.

Transfer: 197 transfer students enrolled in a recent year. Requirements for transfer students vary by program. All applicants must submit official college and high school transcripts. Portfolios and faculty reviews are recommended of applicants to industrial design, interior design, and architecture programs. Grades of C or better transfer for credit. Transfer students must take 50% of the course work in their degree program at Wentworth to graduate.

Visiting: There are regularly scheduled orientations for prospective students, including daily tours and information programs, Monday to Friday. There are guides for informal visits and visitors may sit in on classes. To schedule a visit, contact the Admissions Office.

Financial Aid: In a recent year, 80% of all full-time freshmen and 80% of continuing full-time students received some form of financial aid. 60% of all full-time freshmen and 65% of continuing full-time students received need-based aid. 29% of undergraduate students worked part-time. The FAFSA is required. Check with the school for current application deadlines.

International Students: There were 120 international students enrolled in a recent year. The school actively recruits these students. They must also take the SAT or ACT.

Computers: Wireless access is available. All students are issued a laptop with the software needed for their majors. This is included in tuition. All students may access the system. There are no time limits and no fees. It is strongly recommended that all students have a personal computer.

Admissions Contact: Office of Admissions. E-Mail: *admissions@wit.edu* Web: *www.wit.edu*

WESTERN NEW ENGLAND UNIVERSITY B-3

Springfield, MA 01119 **(413) 782-1321**
(800) 325-1122 ext. 1321; (413) 782-1777

Full-time: 1514 men, 984 women	**Faculty:** n/av; IIA, +$
Part-time: 96 men, 73 women	**Ph.D.s:** n/av
Graduate: 504 men, 629 women	**Student/Faculty:** 13 to 1
Year: semesters, summer session	**Tuition:** $33,020
Application Deadline: open	**Room & Board:** $12,570
Freshman Class: 5988 applied, 4881 accepted, 697 enrolled	
SAT CR/M: 510/550 **ACT:** 24	**COMPETITIVE**

Western New England University, founded in 1919, is a private nonsectarian institution offering undergraduate programs in business, engineering and arts and sciences. There are 3 undergraduate schools and 5 graduate schools. In addition to regional accreditation, WNE has baccalaureate program accreditation with AACSB, ABET, and CSWE. The 2 libraries contain 138,379 volumes, 188,300 microform items, 5,751 audio/video tapes/CDs/DVDs, and subscribe to 47,939 periodicals including electronic. Computerized library services include interlibrary loans, database searching, Internet access, and Wi-Fi capability. Special learning facilities include an art gallery, radio station, TV station, a math, writing and science centers. The 215-acre campus is in a suburban area 90 miles west of Boston, Ma, 30 miles from Hartford, CT, and 150 miles from New York City. Including any residence halls, there are 26 buildings.

Student Life: 53% of undergraduates are from out of state, mostly the Northeast. Students are from 26 states, 25 foreign countries, and Canada. 77% are White. 97% claim no religious affiliation. The average age of freshmen is 18; all undergraduates, 20.

Housing: 2000 students can be accommodated in college housing, which includes coed dorms, on-campus apartments, and married student housing. Freshmen are grouped by academic interest areas or theme housing. On-campus housing is guaranteed for all 4 years. 65% of students live on campus. All students may keep cars.

Activities: There are no fraternities or sororities. There are 60 groups on campus, including art, band, cheerleading, chorus, computers, dance, drama, environmental, ethnic, film, forensics, gay, honors, international, jazz band, literary magazine, musical theater, newspaper, pep band, photography, political, professional, radio and TV, religious, social, social service, student government, and yearbook. Popular campus events include Spring Week, Family and Friends Weekend, Midnight Madness and Mr. University.

Sports: There are 10 intercollegiate sports for men and 9 for women, and 13 intramural sports for men and 13 for women. Facilities include a healthful living center equipped for basketball (2,000 seats), wrestling, racquetball, squash, aerobics, fitness, and volleyball, as well as a weight room, an 8-lane pool, and a track. The 1,200-seat Golden Bear Stadium serves multiple varsity sports including football, field hockey, and men's and women's lacrosse.Volvo Outdoor Tennis Courts and baseball and softball fields. Suprenant Field which is home to the Golden Bear men's and women's soccer teams.

Disabled Students: Facilities include wheelchair ramps, elevators, special parking, specially equipped restrooms, special class scheduling, lowered drinking fountains, lowered telephones, and special housing.

Services: Counseling and information services are available, as is tutoring in most subjects. There is a reader service for the blind.

Campus Safety and Security: Measures include 24-hour foot and vehicle patrol, emergency notification system, self-defense education, and security escort services. There are emergency telephones, lighted pathways/sidewalks, controlled access to dorms/residences, security cameras, medical response, fire response, and a comprehensive public safety awareness program.

Programs of Study: WNE confers B.A., B.S., B.B.A., B.A.L.S., B.S.B.A., B.S.B.E., B.S.C.J., B.S.E.E., B.S.H.S., B.S.I.E. ,B.S.M.E., B.S.W., B.S.B.M.E. and B.S.C.E. degrees. Associate, master's, and doctoral degrees are also awarded. Bachelor's degrees are awarded in BIOLOGICAL SCIENCE (biology/biological science and neurosciences), BUSINESS (accounting, business administration and management, finance, management science, marketing/retailing/merchandising, and sports management), COMMUNICATIONS AND THE ARTS (advertising, communications, creative writing, English, and public relations), COMPUTER AND PHYSICAL SCIENCE (chemistry, computer science, information sciences and systems, and mathematics), EDUCATION (elementary education and secondary education), ENGINEERING AND ENVIRONMENTAL DESIGN (bioengineering, biomedical engineering, civil engineering, computer engineering, electrical/electronics engineering, industrial engineering, mechanical engineering, and preengineering), HEALTH PROFESSIONS (health science), SOCIAL SCIENCE (criminal justice, economics, forensic studies, history, international studies, law, liberal arts/general studies, parks and recreation management, philosophy, political science/government, psychology, social work, and sociology). Engineering is the strongest academically. Criminal justice, sports management and mechanical engineering have the largest enrollments.

Required: To graduate, students must complete 122 credit hours, with a minimum GPA of 2.0. Requirements include 2 courses each in English, math, lab science, and phys ed, and 1 course each in history, culture, and computers. A first-year seminar is also required for freshmen. Other requirements vary according to the major.

Special: Students may cross-register with cooperating colleges of Greater Springfield. The college offers internships, study abroad, a Washington semester, work-study programs, B.A.-B.S. degrees, an accelerated degree program, and dual and student-designed majors. The 3+3 law program offers qualified students the opportunity to earn a J.D. in 6 years. There is also a 6-year biomedical engineering/law program, a 5-year Bachelor/M.B.A., and a 5-year accounting/M.S.A. There are 14 national honor societies and a freshman honors program.

Faculty/Classroom: No introductory courses are taught by graduate students. The average class size in an introductory lecture is 20; in a laboratory is 17; and in a regular course is 19.

Admissions: 82% of the 2013-2014 applicants were accepted. The SAT scores for the 2013-2014 freshman class were: Critical Reading--38% below 500, 45% between 500 and 599, 16% between 600 and 699, and 1% between 700 and 800; Math--26% below 500, 42% between 500 and 599, 29% between 600 and 699, and 3% between 700 and 800. The ACT scores were 17% below 21, 24% between 21 and 23, 38% between 24 and 26, 9% between 27 and 28, and 12% above 28. 36% of the current freshmen were in the top fifth of their class; 64% were in the top two fifths.

Requirements: The SAT is required. Applicants must be graduates of an approved secondary school and must have completed 4 years of high school English, 2 or more years of math, 1 or more years of science, and 1 year of history and social science. An interview is recommended. Act is accepted in lieu of SAT. AP and CLEP credits are accepted. Important factors in the admissions decision are advanced placement or honors courses, extracurricular activities record, and recommendations by school officials.

Procedure: Freshmen are admitted fall and spring. Entrance exams should be taken In the spring of the junior year or fall of the senior year. There are early admissions, deferred admissions, and rolling admissions plans. Application deadlines are open. Application fee is $40. Notification is sent on a rolling basis. Applications are accepted online.

Transfer: 88 transfer students enrolled in 2012-2013. Applicants must have a minimum GPA of 2.3. Grades of C or better transfer for credit. The university admits transfer students in the fall and spring. 30 of 122 credits required for the bachelor's degree must be completed at WNE.

Visiting: There are regularly scheduled orientations for prospective students, including multiple open houses. There are guides for informal visits, visitors may sit in on classes, and stay overnight. To schedule a visit, contact the Undergraduate Admissions Office at (800) 325-1122.

Financial Aid: In 2013-2014, 98% of all full-time freshmen and 96% of continuing full-time students received some form of financial aid. The average freshman award was $28,550. Need-based scholarships or need-based grants averaged $16,100; need-based self-help aid (loans and jobs) averaged $10,900; and other non-need-based awards and non-need-based scholarships averaged $1,550. The FAFSA, and federal tax returns and W-2s is required. The priority date for freshman financial aid applications for fall entry is rolling. The deadline for filing freshman financial aid applications for fall entry is rolling.

International Students: There are 32 international students enrolled. The school actively recruits these students. They must take the TOEFL with a minimum score of 550 on the paper-based TOEFL (PBT) or 79 on the Internet-based version (iBT). They must also take the SAT or ACT.

Computers: All students may access the system 24 hours a day from residence halls. There are no time limits and no fees.

Graduates: From July 1, 2012 to June 30, 2013, 549 bachelor's degrees were awarded. The most popular majors were psychology (8%), sports management (7%), and mechanical engineering (7%). 40 companies recruited on campus in 2012-2013. In an average class, 1% graduate in 3 years or less and 61% graduate in 6 years or less.

Admissions Contact: Dr. Charles R. Pollock, Vice President for Enrollment Management. E-Mail: *ugradmis@wne.edu* Web: *www.wne.edu*

WESTFIELD STATE UNIVERSITY B-3
Westfield State College

Westfield, MA 01086 **(413) 572-5218; (413) 572-0520**

Full-time: 2411 men, 2609 women	**Faculty:** 222; IIA, -$
Part-time: 358 men, 338 women	**Ph.D.s:** 86%
Graduate: 218 men, 461 women	**Student/Faculty:** 21 to 1
Year: semesters, summer session	**Tuition:** $8694 ($14,774)
Application Deadline: March 1	**Room & Board:** $9795
Freshman Class: 5137 applied, 3846 accepted, 1288 enrolled	
SAT CR/M/W: 500/520/500 **ACT:** 20	**COMPETITIVE**

Westfield State University, founded in 1838, is a public university with liberal arts and teacher preparation programs and professional training. There is one undergraduate school and one graduate school. In addition to regional accreditation, Westfield State has baccalaureate program accreditation with ABET, CSWE, NASM, and NCATE. The library contains 158,451 volumes, 481,151 microform items, 5,517 audio/video tapes/CDs/DVDs, and subscribes to 1,933 periodicals including electronic. Computerized library services include interlibrary loans, database searching, Internet access, and Wi-Fi capability. Special learning facilities include an art gallery, natural history museum, radio station, TV station, a geology museum, and a greenhouse. The 256-acre campus is in a suburban area in western Massachusetts, 15 miles west of Springfield, 100 miles west of Boston. Including any residence halls, there are 25 buildings.

Student Life: 92% of undergraduates are from Massachusetts. Others are from 24 states, 10 foreign countries, and Canada. 80% are White. The average age of freshmen is 18; all undergraduates, 21. 21% do not continue beyond their first year; 59% remain to graduate.

Housing: 3109 students can be accommodated in college housing, which includes coed dorms, on-campus apartments, and off-campus apartments. special housing for disabilities students, and special housing for international students. On-campus housing is guaranteed for all 4 years. 55% of students live on campus. Upperclassmen may keep cars.

Activities: There are no fraternities or sororities. There are 77 groups on campus, including art, band, cheerleading, chess, choir, chorale, chorus, communications, computers, dance, drama, environmental, ethnic, gay, honors, international, jazz band, literary magazine, musical theater, newspaper, orchestra, pep band, photography, political, professional, radio and TV, religious, social, social service, student government, and symphony. Popular campus events include Halloween Dance, Spring Weekend and Comedy Night.

Sports: There are 8 intercollegiate sports for men and 10 for women, and 8 intramural sports for men and 5 for women. Facilities include a track, baseball and softball fields, a 400-seat gym, and a 5,000-seat stadium.

Disabled Students: 75% of the campus is accessible. Facilities include wheelchair ramps, elevators, special parking, specially equipped restrooms, special class scheduling, lowered telephones, and special housing.

Services: Counseling and information services are available, as is tutoring in every subject. There is a reader service for the blind.

Campus Safety and Security: Measures include 24-hour foot and vehicle patrol, emergency notification system, and security escort services. There are shuttle buses, emergency telephones, and lighted pathways/sidewalks.

Programs of Study: Westfield State confers B.A., B.S., B.S.E., B.S.N. and B.S.W. degrees. Master's degrees are also awarded. Bachelor's degrees are awarded in BIOLOGICAL SCIENCE (biology/biological science), BUSINESS (business administration and management), COMMUNICATIONS AND THE ARTS (art, communications, dramatic arts, English, music, and Spanish), COMPUTER AND PHYSICAL SCIENCE (chemistry, computer science, information sciences and systems, mathematics, and science), EDUCATION (athletic training, early childhood education, elementary education, secondary education, and special education), ENGINEERING AND ENVIRONMENTAL DESIGN (city/community/regional planning and environmental science), HEALTH PROFESSIONS (nursing), SOCIAL SCIENCE (criminal justice, economics, ethnic studies, history, liberal arts/general studies, physical fitness/movement, political science/government, psychology, social work, and sociology). Criminal justice, education and business management have the largest enrollments.

Required: Students must complete a total of 120 credit hours, with 43 or more credits in 9 specified areas and 30 to 40 hours in the major. The college requires a 2.0 GPA overall and 2.0 in major courses. U.S. history or government and diversity awareness courses are required.

Special: Students may cross-register through College Academic Program Sharing, National Student Exchange, and Cooperating Colleges of Greater Springfield. Internships are for credit only in conjunction with all major programs. The University offers international exchange programs in China, Ireland and Poland and hundreds of study abroad programs in over 35 countries, a Washington semester for political science, criminal justice, and psychology majors, an internship program with Walt Disney World, dual majors, student-designed majors, some credit for military experience and has a multi-department Honors Program. There are 9 national honor societies and a freshman honors program.

Faculty/Classroom: 50% of faculty are male; 50% are female. All teach undergraduates. No introductory courses are taught by graduate students. The average class size in an introductory lecture is 26; in a laboratory is 16; and in a regular course is 26.

Admissions: 75% of the 2013-2014 applicants were accepted. The SAT scores for the 2013-2014 freshman class were: Critical Reading--45% below 500, 45% between 500 and 599, and 10% between 600 and 699; Math--38% below 500, 47% between 500 and 599, 14% between 600 and 699, and 1% between 700 and 800; Writing--48% below 500, 43% between 500 and 599, 8% between 600 and 699. The ACT scores were 54% below 21, 33% between 21 and 23, 13% between 24 and 26. 17% of the current freshmen were in the top fifth of their class; 45% were in the top two fifths.

Requirements: The SAT is required. Applicants must achieve a minimum 3.0 cumulative average in academic subjects. Students who have between a 2.0 and a 3.0 GPA may be accepted via a sliding scale, contingent upon the SAT scores. They must be graduates of an accredited secondary school and must have completed 4 years of college preparatory level English, 3 years of math (algebra I and II and geometry), 2 years of social sciences (including 1 year of U.S history), 3 years of sciences, including 2 with lab, 2 foreign language, and 2 years of electives. The GED is accepted. A portfolio is required for admission to the art program, and an audition is necessary for admission to the music program. A GPA of 3.0 is required. AP and CLEP credits are accepted.

Procedure: Freshmen are admitted fall and spring. Entrance exams should be taken in the spring of the junior year and fall of the senior year. There are deferred admissions and rolling admissions plans. Applications should be filed by March 1 for fall entry; December 1 for spring entry, along with a $50 fee. Notifications are sent March 15. Applications are accepted online.

Transfer: 480 transfer students enrolled in 2012-2013. Transfer students must have 24 transferable credits with a minimum cumulative GPA of 2.0 (higher for some majors). A grade of C- or better with a 2.0 GPA will transfer for credit. Transfer students are admitted in the fall and spring. For students transferring from a Massachusetts Community College, a D may be transferred for credit. 30 of 120 credits required for the bachelor's degree must be completed at Westfield State.

Visiting: There are regularly scheduled orientations for prospective students, including a campus tour, classroom observation, academic department presentations, lunch with faculty, staff, and students, and a question-and-answer session moderated by a panel of administrators. There are guides for informal visits. To schedule a visit, contact The Admissions Office.

Financial Aid: Westfield State is a member of CSS. The FAFSA is required. The deadline for filing freshman financial aid applications for fall entry is March 1.

International Students: There are 25 international students enrolled. They must take the TOEFL with a minimum score of 550 on the paper-based TOEFL (PBT) or 79 on the Internet-based version (iBT), IELTS. They must also take the SAT.

Computers: All students may access the system. There are no time limits and no fees.

Graduates: From July 1, 2012 to June 30, 2013, 1373 bachelor's degrees were awarded. The most popular majors were criminal justice (15%), liberal studies (15%), and business management (12%). 220 companies recruited on campus in 2012-2013. In an average class, 44% graduate in 4 years or less, 57% graduate in 5 years or less, and 59% graduate in 6 years or less.

Admissions Contact: Kelly Hart, Director of Admissions. E-Mail: *admissions@westfield.ma.edu* Web: *www.westfield.ma.edu*

WHEATON COLLEGE D-3

Norton, MA 02766 (508) 286-8251
(800) 394-6003; (508) 286-8271

Full-time: 591 men, 1030 women	**Faculty:** 139; IIB, +$
Part-time: n/av	**Ph.D.s:** 88%
Graduate: n/av	**Student/Faculty:** 11 to 1
Year: semesters	**Tuition:** $42,394
Application Deadline: January 15	**Room & Board:** $11,170
Freshman Class: 3448 applied, 2075 accepted, 437 enrolled	
SAT CR/M: 625/620	**ACT:** 29 **HIGHLY COMPETITIVE+**

Wheaton College, established in 1834, is an independent liberal arts institution. The library contains 364,628 volumes, 56,204 microform items, 17,605 audio/video tapes/CDs/DVDs, and subscribes to 18,496 periodicals including electronic. Computerized library services include interlibrary loans, database searching, Internet access, and laptop Internet portals. Special learning facilities include a learning resource center, art gallery, planetarium, radio station, a greenhouse, and an observatory. The 400-acre campus is in a suburban area 35 miles south of Boston and 15 miles north of Providence. Including any residence halls, there are 81 buildings.

Student Life: 67% of undergraduates are from out of state, mostly the Northeast. Students are from 39 states, 41 foreign countries, and Canada. 62% are from public schools. 74% are white. The average age of freshmen is 18; all undergraduates, 20. 14% do not continue beyond their first year; 77% remain to graduate.

Housing: 1525 students can be accommodated in college housing, which includes single-sex and coed dorms. In addition, there are language houses, special-interest houses, special-interest houses include, among others, house of living arts, women of color/social responsibility, global awareness, and outdoors education. On-campus housing is guaranteed for all 4 years and is available on a lottery system for upperclassmen. 95% of students live on campus; of those, 60% remain on campus on weekends. Some may keep cars.

Activities: There are no fraternities or sororities. There are 90 groups on campus, including and Zen Meditation Group, Habitat for Humanity, Voices United to Jam (gospel choir), art, BACCHUS, band, choir, chorale, chorus, dance, debate, drama, environmental, ethnic, film, gay, honors, international, jazz band, literary magazine, musical theater, newspaper, orchestra, pep band, photography, political, professional, radio and TV, religious, social, social service, student government, symphony, and yearbook. Popular campus events include Otis Social Justice Symposium and Award, Spring Weekend, and Season of Service.

Sports: There are 9 intercollegiate sports for men and 12 for women, and 9 intramural sports for men and 9 for women. Facilities include an 8-lane stretch pool, a field house with 5 tennis courts, 1 outdoor and 5 indoor basketball courts, a 200-meter track, a golf/archery range and batting cage, an 850-seat gym, 7 lighted outdoor tennis courts, a running course, a baseball stadium, 2 athletic fields, a softball field, an aerobics/dance studio, and a fitness center.

Disabled Students: 50% of the campus is accessible. Facilities include wheelchair ramps, elevators, special parking, specially equipped restrooms, special class scheduling, and lowered telephones.

Services: Counseling and information services are available, as is tutoring in most subjects. There is a reader service for the blind, and remedial writing. Peer tutoring and note takers for hearing-impaired students are available.

Campus Safety and Security: Measures include 24-hour foot and vehicle patrol, emergency notification system, self-defense education, and security escort services. There are emergency telephones, lighted pathways/sidewalks, and controlled access to dorms/residences.

Programs of Study: Wheaton confers A.B. degrees. Bachelor's degrees are awarded in BIOLOGICAL SCIENCE (biochemistry, bioinformatics, biology/biological science, and neurosciences), COMMUNICATIONS AND THE ARTS (art history and appreciation, classics, creative writing, dance, dramatic arts, English, film arts, fine arts, German, Greek, Latin, literature, music, Russian, and studio art), COMPUTER AND PHYSICAL SCIENCE (chemistry, computer mathematics, computer science, mathematics, mathematics – economics, and physics), ENGINEERING AND ENVIRONMENTAL DESIGN (environmental science), SOCIAL SCIENCE (African studies, African American studies, American studies, anthropology, Asian/Oriental studies, economics, French studies, Hispanic American studies, history, international relations, Italian studies, philosophy, political science/government, psychology, religion, Russian and Slavic studies, sociology, and women's studies). Arts and sciences is the strongest academically. Psychology, economics, and English have the largest enrollments.

Required: Among the requirements for graduation are 32 course credits (4 semester hours each), with a minimum of 10 courses in the major. The requirements for each major are determined by the department. The core classes consist of First-year Seminar, English, quantitative skills, foreign language, and non-Western history. Students must maintain a minimum GPA of 2.0 (C-) in all courses to remain in good academic standing.

Special: Students may cross-register with Brown University as well as with colleges in the Southeastern Association for Cooperation in Higher Education in Massachusetts and with schools participating in the 12 College Exchange Program. Wheaton offers study abroad in 90 countries, internship programs, nondegree study, dual majors, student-designed majors, a Washington semester at American University, and interdisciplinary majors, including math and economics, math and computer science, physics and astronomy, and theater and English dramatic literature. Dual-degree programs exist with the following institutions: Thayer School of Engineering, Dartmouth College (B.S. Engineering); Emerson College (M.A. Integrated Marketing Communication); Graduate School of Management, University of Rochester (M.B.A.); George Washington University (B.S. Engineering); School of the Museum of Fine Arts (B.F.A.); Andover-Newton Theological School (M.A. Religion); and New England School of Optometry (Doctor of Optometry). There are 8 national honor societies, including Phi Beta Kappa, a freshman honors program, and 100 departmental honors programs.

Faculty/Classroom: 49% of faculty are male; 51% are female. All teach and do research. No introductory courses are taught by graduate students. The average class size in an introductory lecture is 40; in a laboratory is 20; and in a regular course is 35.

Admissions: 60% of the 2011-2012 applicants were accepted. The SAT scores for the 2011-2012 freshman class were: Critical Reading--6% below 500, 26% between 500 and 599, 50% between 600 and 700, and 17% above 700; Math--6% below 500, 26% between 500 and 599, 52% between 600 and 700, and 16% above 700. The ACT scores were 27% between 24 and 26, 19% between 27 and 28, and 54% above 28. 62% of the current freshmen were in the top fifth of their class; 88% were in the top two fifths. 184 freshmen graduated first in their class.

Requirements: Applicants must be graduates of an accredited secondary school. Recommended courses include English with emphasis on composition skills, 4 years; foreign language and math, 4 years each; social studies, 3 years; and 3 years science, 2 of which lab. Wheaton requires an essay and strongly recommends an interview. AP credits are accepted. Important factors in the admissions decision are advanced placement or honors courses, extracurricular activities record, and personality/intangible qualities.

Procedure: Freshmen are admitted fall and spring. Entrance exams should be taken in October and/or November. There are early decision, early admissions, and deferred admissions plans. Early decision applications should be filed by November 15; regular applications, by January 15 for fall entry; and November 1 for spring entry, along with a $55 fee. Notification of early decision is sent December 15; regular decision, April 1. 108 early decision candidates were accepted for the 2011-2012 class. 198 applicants were on the 2011 waiting list; 38 were admitted. Applications are accepted online.

Transfer: 14 transfer students enrolled in 2010-2011. Transfer students are encouraged to present a strong B average in their college work to date. Preference will be given to college over high school work. The college transcript is evaluated. High school and college transcripts, an essay or personal statement, a statement of good standing, 2 instructor recommendations, and a midterm evaluation are required. 16 of 32 credits required for the bachelor's degree must be completed at Wheaton.

Visiting: There are regularly scheduled orientations for prospective students, including class visits, tours, panels on financial aid, student life, and athletics, lunch with faculty, and department open houses. There are guides for informal visits, visitors may sit in on classes, and stay overnight. To schedule a visit, contact the Admissions Office.

Financial Aid: In a recent year, 77% of all full-time freshmen and 70% of continuing full-time students received some form of financial aid. 63% of all full-time freshmen and 57% of continuing full-time students received need-based aid. The average freshman award was $29,617. Need-based scholarships or need-based grants averaged $29,205 ($46,800 maximum); need-based self-help aid (loans and jobs) averaged $5,428 ($7,000 maximum); and other non-need-based awards and non-need-based scholarships averaged $13,939 ($15,000 maximum). 29% of undergraduate students work part-time. Average annual earnings from campus work are $1200. Wheaton is a member of CSS. The CSS/Profile and FAFSA, and parents' and student's federal tax returns, and if applicable, noncustodial profile and business/farm supplement are required. The deadline for filing freshman financial aid applications for fall entry is February 1.

International Students: There are 125 international students enrolled. The school actively recruits these students. They must take the TOEFL with a minimum score of 580 on the paper-based TOEFL (PBT) or 90 on the Internet-based version (iBT).

Computers: The campus has both wireless and wired Internet access from every residence hall and college classroom. While nearly all students bring a computer with them to Wheaton, there are 289 computers available in public spaces, labs, and classrooms. Many faculty members use Moodle, a course management software system, to post documents such as syllabi and assignments, have electronic discussions, give quizzes, make announcements, and more. Services including registration and access to academic records and campus news and events are all available through the Internet. All students may access the system 24 hours a day, 7 days a week. There are no time limits. The fee is $135 a year. It is strongly recommended that all students have a personal computer.

Graduates: In a recent year, 428 bachelor's degrees were awarded. The most popular majors were psychology (15%), English (9%), and economics (8%). 17 companies recruited on campus in a recent year. In an average class, 73% graduate in 4 years or less, 76% graduate in 5 years or less, and 77% graduate in 6 years or less. Of the recent graduating class, 31% were enrolled in graduate school within 6 months of graduation, and 37% were employed.

Admissions Contact: Admissions Office, E-Mail: *admission@wheatoncollege.edu* Web: *wheatoncollege.edu*

WHEELOCK COLLEGE E-2

Boston, MA 02215-4176 (617) 879-2206
(800) 734-5212; (617) 879-2449

Full-time: 45 men, 605 women
Part-time: 5 men, 40 women
Graduate: 25 men, 335 women
Year: semesters
Application Deadline: see profile
Freshman Class: n/av
SAT: required
Faculty: n/av; IIA, av$
Ph.D.s: 89%
Student/Faculty: n/av
Tuition: $29,490
Room & Board: $12,870

COMPETITIVE

Wheelock College, established in 1888, is a private institution with programs in education, child life and family studies, social work, juvenile justice and youth advocacy, and human services. The figures in the above capsule and in this profile are approximate. There is 1 graduate school. In addition to regional accreditation, Wheelock has baccalaureate program accreditation with CSWE and NCATE. The library contains 83,573 volumes, 483,257 microform items, 3,633 audio/video tapes/CDs/DVDs, and subscribes to 12,629 periodicals including electronic. Computerized library services include interlibrary loans, database searching, Internet access, and laptop Internet portals. Special learning facilities include a learning resource center, art gallery, and the Wheelock Family Theater. The 7-acre campus is in an urban area in Boston. Including any residence halls, there are 12 buildings.

Student Life: 63% of undergraduates are from Massachusetts. Students are from 22 states, and 2 foreign countries. 90% are from public schools. 85% are white. The average age of freshmen is 18; all undergraduates, 20. 29% do not continue beyond their first year; 73% remain to graduate.

Housing: 500 students can be accommodated in college housing, which includes single-sex and coed dorms. a cooperative living house, nonsmoking floors, and a wellness floor. On-campus housing is guaranteed for all 4 years. 73% of students live on campus; of those, 50% remain on campus on weekends. Upperclassmen may keep cars.

Activities: There are no fraternities or sororities. There are 25 groups on campus, including Sign Choir, women's center, Best Buddies, choir, chorale, chorus, dance, drama, ethnic, gay, honors, international, professional, religious, social, social service, and student government. Popular campus events include Kids Day, Family Weekend, and COF Concerts.

Sports: There are 5 intercollegiate sports for women, and 9 intramural sports for men and 9 for women. Facilities include a sports complex at a neighboring college with a pool and diving board, racquetball courts, a weight room, an indoor track, a basketball court, crew tanks, and cardiovascular equipment.

Disabled Students: 67% of the campus is accessible. Facilities include wheelchair ramps, elevators, special parking, specially equipped rest rooms, special class scheduling, lowered drinking fountains, lowered telephones, and assistive technology available in the learning center.

Services: Counseling and information services are available, as is tutoring in every subject. There is a reader service for the blind, and remedial math, reading, and writing. Academic support services provide individualized assistance upon request.

Campus Safety and Security: Measures include 24-hour foot and vehicle patrol and security escort services. There are emergency telephones and lighted pathways/sidewalks.

Programs of Study: Wheelock confers B.A., B.S., and B.S.W. degrees. Associates and master's degrees are also awarded. Bachelor's degrees are awarded in EDUCATION (early childhood education, elementary education, and special education), SOCIAL SCIENCE (child care/child and family studies, human development, and social work). Teaching, social work, and child life are the strongest academically and have the largest enrollments.

Required: To graduate, students must complete between 134 and 140 credit hours, with a minimum GPA of 2.0. Wheelock requires at least a 32-credit major combined with a 36-credit professional studies program. Students must earn 26 credits in English composition, math, human growth and development, children and their environments, first-year seminar, visual and performing arts, and 1 course in first aid.

Special: Wheelock offers cross-registration with all colleges in the Colleges of the Fenway and internships that include student teaching and social work practice. Dual majors, study-abroad programs, and pass/fail options are available. Students may receive credit for life and work experience. Students begin practical fieldwork their freshman year and continue for all 4 years. There is 1 national honor society.

Faculty/Classroom: 13% of faculty are male; 87% are female. 70% teach undergraduates. No introductory courses are taught by graduate students. The average class size in an introductory lecture is 20; in a laboratory is 17; and in a regular course is 15.

Requirements: The SAT is required. Applicants must be graduates of an accredited secondary school and must have completed 4 years of English, 3 years of math, and 2 years each of science and history. The GED is accepted. The college requires a graded writing sample and recommends an interview. A GPA of 2.0 is required. AP and CLEP credits are accepted. Important factors in the admissions decision are advanced placement or honors courses, evidence of special talent, and personality/intangible qualities.

Procedure: Freshmen are admitted fall and spring. Entrance exams should be taken in the spring of the junior year and/or fall of the senior year. There are early decision, deferred admissions and rolling admissions plans. Notification of early decision is sent December 15; other notification is sent on a rolling basis. Applications are accepted online. Check with the school for current application deadlines and fee.

Transfer: 75 transfer students enrolled in a recent year. Transfer students must have a minimum GPA of 2.0 and must present 1 letter of recommendation. Grades of C- or better transfer for credit. Applicants must submit all official high school and college transcripts. 67 of 134 credits required for the bachelor's degree must be completed at Wheelock.

Visiting: There are regularly scheduled orientations for prospective students, and information sessions are held on select Saturdays in the fall and spring. Students hear a presentation from a counselor, have a tour, and may speak to a counselor individually. There are guides for informal visits, visitors may sit in on classes, and stay overnight. To schedule a visit, contact the Undergraduate Admissions Office.

Financial Aid: In a recent year, 94% of all full-time freshmen and 82% of continuing full-time students received some form of financial aid. 63% of all full-time freshmen and 70% of continuing full-time students received need-based aid. The average freshmen award was $23,709, with $6,821 ($19,200 maximum) from need-based scholarships or need-based grants; $4,425 ($8,425 maximum) from need-based self-help aid (loans and jobs); and $18,026 ($23,600 maximum) from other non-need-based awards and non-need-based scholarships. 33% of undergraduate students worked part-time. Average annual earnings from campus work were $1800. The FAFSA is required. Check with the school for current application deadlines.

International Students: There were 5 international students enrolled. They must take the TOEFL. They must also take the SAT or ACT. Applicants should submit SAT or ACT scores or TOEFL scores if English is not their official language.

Computers: All students may access the system 24 hours a day any time school is in session. There are no time limits and no fees.

Graduates: In a recent year, 81 bachelor's degrees were awarded. The most popular majors were teacher education (68%), child life (16%), and social work (16%). In an average class, 48% graduate in 4 years or less, 52% graduate in 5 years or less, and 53% graduate in 6 years or less. 22% were enrolled in graduate school within 6 months of graduation, and 95% were employed.

Admissions Contact: Dean of Admissions. E-Mail: *undergrad@wheelock.edu* Web: *www.wheelock.edu*

WILLIAMS COLLEGE A-1

Williamstown, MA 01267 (413) 597-2211

Full-time: 994 men, 1051 women
Part-time: 14 men, 18 women
Graduate: 28 men, 26 women
Year: 4-1-4
Application Deadline: January 1
Faculty: 263; IIB, ++$
Ph.D.s: 98%
Student/Faculty: 8 to 1
Tuition: $46,330
Room & Board: $12,300
Freshman Class: 6853 applied, 1200 accepted, 544 enrolled
SAT CR/M: 730/720 **ACT:** 33 **MOST COMPETITIVE**

Williams College, founded in 1793, is a private institution offering undergraduate degrees in liberal arts and graduate degrees in art history and development economics. There are 2 graduate schools. The 11 libraries contain 948,365 volumes, 492,374 microform items, and 39,133 audio/video tapes/CDs/DVDs, and subscribe to 13,493 periodicals including electronic. Computerized library services include interlibrary loans, database searching, Internet access, and Wi-Fi capability. Special learning facilities include an art gallery, planetarium, radio station, a 2500-acre experimental forest, an environmental studies center, a center for foreign languages, literatures, and cultures, a rare book library, a studio art center, and a 3 stage center for the performing arts. The 450-acre campus is in a small town 150 miles north of New York City and west of Boston. Including any residence halls, there are 97 buildings.

Student Life: 87% of undergraduates are from out of state, mostly the Northeast. Students are from 49 states, 64 foreign countries, and Canada. 56% are White; 12% Hispanic; 11% Asian American. The average age of freshmen is 19; all undergraduates, 20. 2% do not continue beyond their first year; 95% remain to graduate.

Housing: 1978 students can be accommodated in college housing, which includes coed dorms and on-campus apartments. cooperative housing, in which students prepare their own meals. On-campus housing is guaranteed for all 4 years. Upperclassmen may keep cars.

Activities: There are no fraternities or sororities. Groups on campus include and capella singing groups, handbell choir, art, band, chess, choir, chorale, chorus, comedy group, communications, computers, dance, debate, drama, environmental, ethnic, film, gay, honors, international, jazz band, literary magazine, marching band, musical theater, newspaper, orchestra, pep band, photography, political, radio and TV, religious, social service, student government, symphony, and yearbook. Popular campus events include Winter Carnival, Mountain Day, and Claiming Williams.

Sports: There are 16 intercollegiate sports for men and 15 for women, and 17 intramural sports for men and 17 for women. Facilities include 2 gyms, a 50-meter pool, a dance studio, a weight room, rowing tanks, a boathouse, a golf course, playing fields, artificial turf field, indoor and outdoor tracks, and courts for tennis, squash, and paddle tennis.

Disabled Students: Facilities include wheelchair ramps, elevators, special parking, specially equipped restrooms, special class scheduling, lowered drinking fountains, lowered telephones.

Services: Counseling and information services are available, as is tutoring in every subject. There is a reader service for the blind, and remedial math, reading, and writing. Services include a peer health program, rape and sexual assault hotline, and 10-1 counseling service.

Campus Safety and Security: Measures include 24-hour foot and vehicle patrol, emergency notification system, self-defense education, and security escort services. There are emergency telephones, lighted pathways/sidewalks, and controlled access to dorms/residences.

Programs of Study: Williams confers B.A. degrees. Master's degrees are also awarded. Bachelor's degrees are awarded in BIOLOGICAL SCIENCE (biology/biological science), COMMUNICATIONS AND THE ARTS (Arabic, art, art history and appreciation, classics, dramatic arts, English, fine arts, French, German, literature, music, Russian, and Spanish), COMPUTER AND PHYSICAL SCIENCE (astronomy, astrophysics, chemistry, computer science, geology, mathematics, and physics), SOCIAL SCIENCE (American studies, anthropology, Asian/Oriental studies, economics, history, philosophy, political science/government, psychology, religion, sociology, and women's studies).

Required: All students must complete 4 winter study courses and 32 courses regular semester courses, 9 of which are in the major field, with a C- or higher. Requirements include 3 semester-long courses in each of 3 academic divisions: languages and arts, social sciences, and science and math.

Special: Students may cross-register at Bennington or Massachusetts College of Liberal Arts and study abroad in Madrid, Oxford, Cairo, Beijing, and Kyoto, or any approved program with another college or university. Teaching and medical field experiences, dual and student-designed majors, internships, and a 3-2 engineering program with Columbia University is offered. There are pass/fail options during the winter term. Each department offers at least 1 Oxford-model tutorial every year. There are 2 national honor societies and including Phi Beta Kappa.

Faculty/Classroom: 57% of faculty are male; 43% are female. No introductory courses are taught by graduate students.

Admissions: 18% of the 2013-2014 applicants were accepted. The SAT scores for the 2013-2014 freshman class were: Critical Reading--1% below 500, 5% between 500 and 599, 27% between 600 and 699, and 67% between 700 and 800; Math--1% below 500, 6% between 500 and 599, 29% between 600 and 699, and 64% between 700 and 800; Writing--5% between 500 and 599, 24% between 600 and 699, and 71% between 700 and 800.

Requirements: The SAT or ACT is required. In addition, Williams requires the following standardized tests: - SAT or ACT with Writing - Two SAT Subject Tests Applicants to Williams should pursue the strongest program of study offered by their secondary schools. While there are no absolute requirements for admission, competitive candidates typically study English, math, natural science, foreign language and social studies in four-year sequences and present a distinguished record throughout their secondary school career. AP credits are accepted.

Procedure: Freshmen are admitted fall. There are early decision and deferred admissions plans. Early decision applications should be filed by November 10; regular applications, by January 1 for fall entry, along with a $65 fee. Notification of early decision is sent 12 15; regular decision, 249 early decision candidates were accepted for the 2013-2014 class. 342 applicants were on the 2013 waiting list; 44 were admitted. Applications are accepted online.

Transfer: Transfer applicants should present a 3.5 GPA in previous college work and must submit either SAT or ACT scores. 16 of 32 credits required for the bachelor's degree must be completed at Williams.

Visiting: There are regularly scheduled orientations for prospective students, panels, forums, class visits, and campus tours. There are guides for informal visits, visitors may sit in on classes, and stay overnight. To schedule a visit, contact the Admission Office.

Financial Aid: In 2013-2014, 49% of all full-time freshmen and 52% of continuing full-time students received some form of financial aid. 49% of all full-time freshmen and 52% of continuing full-time students received need-based aid. The average freshman award was $46,953. The average financial indebtedness of the 2013 graduate was $12,474. The CSS/Profile and FAFSA are required. The deadline for filing freshman financial aid applications for fall entry is February 1.

International Students: There are 137 international students enrolled. The school actively recruits these students. They must take the TOEFL, If English is not the applicant's first language. They must also take the SAT or ACT.

Computers: All students may access the system. There are no time limits and no fees.

Graduates: From July 1, 2012 to June 30, 2013, 526 bachelor's degrees were awarded. The most popular majors were history (13%), math (13%), and English (13%). In an average class, 90% graduate in 4 years or less, 94% graduate in 5 years or less, and 95% graduate in 6 years or less.

Admissions Contact: Richard Nesbitt, Director of Admissions. E-Mail: *admission@williams.edu* Web: *www.williams,edu*

WORCESTER POLYTECHNIC INSTITUTE C-2

Worcester, MA 01609	**(508) 831-5286; (508) 831-5875**
Full-time: 2545 men, 1185 women	**Faculty:** 302; IIA, ++$
Part-time: 85 men, 26 women	**Ph.D.s:** 91%
Graduate: 1471 men, 534 women	**Student/Faculty:** 14 to 1
Year: quarters, summer session	**Tuition:** $40,790
Application Deadline: February 1	**Room & Board:** $12,650
Freshman Class: 6284 applied, 3989 accepted, 928 enrolled	
SAT CR/M/W: 610/670/600 **ACT:** 28	**HIGHLY COMPETITIVE+**

Worcester Polytechnic Institute, founded in 1865, is a private technological university offering degrees in the sciences, engineering, computer science, business management, and the liberal arts. The academic program emphasizes professional-level project work. There is one graduate school. In addition to regional accreditation, WPI has baccalaureate program accreditation with AACSB and ABET. The library contains 563,590 volumes, 112,960 microform items, and 2,772 audio/video tapes/CDs/DVDs, and subscribes to 84,460 periodicals including electronic. Computerized library services include interlibrary loans, database searching, Internet access, and Wi-Fi capability. Special learning facilities include an art gallery, radio station, a robotics lab, a wind tunnel, and a greenhouse. The 80-acre campus is in a suburban area 40 miles west of Boston. Including any residence halls, there are 48 buildings.

Student Life: 54% of undergraduates are from out of state, mostly the Northeast. Students are from 48 states, 63 foreign countries, and Canada. 74% are from public schools. 68% are White; 12% Foreign. The average age of freshmen is 18; all undergraduates, 20. 4% do not continue beyond their first year; 84% remain to graduate.

Housing: 1591 students can be accommodated in college housing, which includes coed dorms, on-campus apartments, and off-campus apartments. In addition, there are special-interest houses, fraternity houses, and sorority houses. On-campus housing is guaranteed for the freshman year only and is available on a lottery system for upperclassmen. 60% of students live on campus; of those, 75% remain on campus on weekends. Upperclassmen may keep cars.

Activities: 30% of men belong to 14 national fraternities; 41% of women belong to 1 local and 4 national sororities. There are 204 groups on campus, including art, band, cheerleading, chess, choir, chorale, chorus, computers, dance, debate, drama, environmental, ethnic, forensics, gay, honors, international, jazz band, literary magazine, marching band, musical theater, newspaper, orchestra, pep band, photography, political, professional, radio and TV, religious, social, social service, student government, symphony, and yearbook. Popular campus events include Traditions Day, New Voices Festival, and Winter Carnival.

Sports: There are 10 intercollegiate sports for men and 10 for women, and 10 intramural sports for men and 10 for women. Facilities include New athletics facility in 2012; an aerobics area, softball fields, an 8-lane synthetic surface track, a fitness center, a crew center, a playing field with artificial turf, a pool, basketball, tennis, racquetball and squash courts, and a 2800-seat gym. The sports and recreation center holds a 4-court gym, an indoor track, 14,000-sq-ft of fitness space, a rowing tank, and a 25-meter competition pool.

Disabled Students: 96% of the campus is accessible. Facilities include

wheelchair ramps, elevators, special parking, specially equipped restrooms, special class scheduling, and lowered drinking fountains.

Services: Counseling and information services are available, as is tutoring in every subject.

Campus Safety and Security: Measures include 24-hour foot and vehicle patrol, emergency notification system, self-defense education, and security escort services. There are shuttle buses, emergency telephones, lighted pathways/sidewalks, and a student-run emergency medical service supervised by the campus police department.

Programs of Study: WPI confers B.A., and B.S. degrees. Master's and doctoral degrees are also awarded. Bachelor's degrees are awarded in AGRICULTURE (environmental studies), BIOLOGICAL SCIENCE (biochemistry and biotechnology), BUSINESS (business administration and management, management engineering, and management information systems), COMMUNICATIONS AND THE ARTS (technical and business writing), COMPUTER AND PHYSICAL SCIENCE (actuarial science, chemistry, computer science, digital arts/technology, mathematics, and physics), ENGINEERING AND ENVIRONMENTAL DESIGN (aeronautical engineering, architectural engineering, biomedical engineering, chemical engineering, civil engineering, computer graphics, electrical/electronics engineering, engineering physics, environmental engineering, industrial engineering, materials engineering, mechanical engineering, and technology and public affairs), SOCIAL SCIENCE (economics, fire protection, humanities, interdisciplinary studies, social science, and systems science). Engineering, biology, and computer science have the largest enrollments.

Required: For a B.S. degree, WPI requires that students in science and engineering complete an individual project in the humanities. Students must also complete 2 major team projects. Distribution requirements vary according to the major, and all students must take courses in social sciences and phys ed.

Special: Students may cross-register with 9 other colleges in the Colleges of Worcester Consortium. Co-op programs in all majors, internships, work-study programs, dual majors in every subject, student-designed majors, non-degree study, and pass/fail options are all available. There is an accelerated degree program in fire protection engineering and math. There are 30 special project centers in 18 countries. There are 21 national honor societies.

Faculty/Classroom: 74% of faculty are male; 26% are female. All teach undergraduates. No introductory courses are taught by graduate students. The average class size in an introductory lecture is 100; in a laboratory is 20; and in a regular course is 20.

Admissions: 63% of the 2013-2014 applicants were accepted. The SAT scores for the 2013-2014 freshman class were: Critical Reading--8% below 500, 35% between 500 and 599, 43% between 600 and 699, and 14% between 700 and 800; Math--12% between 500 and 599, 54% between 600 and 699, and 34% between 700 and 800; Writing--6% below 500, 28% between 500 and 599, 45% between 600 and 699, and 11% between 700 and 800. The ACT scores were 2% below 21, 9% between 21 and 23, 20% between 24 and 26, 25% between 27 and 28, and 44% above 28. 80% of the current freshmen were in the top fifth of their class; 96% were in the top two fifths. There were 6 National Merit finalists. 46 freshmen graduated first in their class.

Requirements: Applicants must have completed 4 years of math, including precalculus, 4 years of English, and 2 lab sciences. An essay is required and a letter of recommendation from either a math or science teacher and the guidance counselor. Those opting for Flex Path will submit academic work in place of the SAT or ACT. AP credits are accepted. Important factors in the admissions decision are advanced placement or honors courses, recommendations by school officials, and extracurricular activities record.

Procedure: Freshmen are admitted fall and spring. Entrance exams should be taken between April and January. There is a deferred admissions plan. Applications should be filed by February 1 for fall entry; November 15 for spring entry, along with a $60 fee. Notifications are sent April 1. 2033 applicants were on the 2013 waiting list; 73 were admitted. Applications are accepted online.

Transfer: 55 transfer students enrolled in 2012-2013. Grades of C or better transfer for credit. A high school transcript or GED is required. Students who have been out of school for a year or more must present a resume or personal biography, and 2 academic recommendations. Also they must have completed a calculus course and 2 lab sciences courses. 75 of 135 credits required for the bachelor's degree must be completed at WPI.

Visiting: There are regularly scheduled orientations for prospective students, consisting of meetings and presentations from various academic and extracurricular groups. There are guides for informal visits, visitors may sit in on classes, and stay overnight. To schedule a visit, contact the Admissions Office.

Financial Aid: In 2013-2014, 997% of all full-time freshmen and 96% of continuing full-time students received some form of financial aid. 73% of all full-time freshmen and 64% of continuing full-time students received need-based aid. The average freshman award was $31,426. Need-based scholarships or need-based grants averaged $20,547; and need-based self-help aid (loans and jobs) averaged $3,122. 19% of undergraduate students work part-time. Average annual earnings from campus work are $1322. WPI is a member of CSS. The CSS/Profile and FAFSA, and CSS Noncustodial Profile, and WPI Upper-Class Application are required. The deadline for filing freshman financial aid applications for fall entry is February 1.

International Students: There are 459 international students enrolled. The school actively recruits these students. They must take the TOEFL with a minimum score of 550 on the paper-based TOEFL (PBT) or 80 on the Internet-based version (iBT) or take the MELAB and the college's own test, or IELTS. They must also take the SAT or ACT. or a Flex Path Supplement.

Computers: All students may access the system 24 hours daily. There are no time limits and no fees.

Graduates: From July 1, 2012 to June 30, 2013, 615 bachelor's degrees were awarded. The most popular majors were mechanical engineering (25%), electrical and computer engineering (13%), and civil and environmental enginerring (9%). 204 companies recruited on campus in 2012-2013. In an average class, 74% graduate in 4 years or less, 82% graduate in 5 years or less, and 84% graduate in 6 years or less. Of the 2012 graduating class, 19% were enrolled in graduate school within 6 months of graduation, and 66% were employed.

Admissions Contact: Edward J. Connor, Dean of Admissions. E-Mail: *admissions@wpi.edu* Web. *www.wpi.edu*

WORCESTER STATE UNIVERSITY C-2

Worcester, MA 01602 (508) 929-8040
(866) 972-2255; (508) 929-8183

Full-time: 1675 men, 2440 women	**Faculty:** n/av
Part-time: 559 men, 882 women	**Ph.D.s:** 80%
Graduate: 218 men, 673 women	**Student/Faculty:** 18 to 1
Year: semesters, summer session	**Tuition:** $8157 ($14,237)
Application Deadline: May 1	**Room & Board:** $10,500
Freshman Class: 4149 applied, 2514 accepted, 780 enrolled	
SAT CR/M: 504/520 **ACT:** 22	**COMPETITIVE**

Worcester State University, established in 1874, is part of the Massachusetts public higher education system and offer undergraduate and graduate programs. A liberal arts core is emphasized, as are selected areas of science, the health professions, education, business and management. There are 2 undergraduate schools and one graduate school. In addition to regional accreditation, WSU has baccalaureate program accreditation with NLN. The library contains 204,971 volumes, 16,459 microform items, 4,267 audio/video tapes/CDs/DVDs, and subscribes to 496 periodicals including electronic. Computerized library services include interlibrary loans, database searching, Internet access, and Wi-Fi capability. Special learning facilities include a radio station, including photographic labs, a audiovisual center, multimedia classrooms with satellite connectivity, discipline-specific computer labs, and a speech, language, and hearing clinic. The 58-acre campus is in an urban area On the west side of Worcester, Massachusetts, 45 miles west of Boston. Including any residence halls, there are 11 buildings.

Student Life: 97% of undergraduates are from Massachusetts. Others are from 22 states, 25 foreign countries, and Canada. 72% are White. The average age of freshmen is 19; all undergraduates, 24. 49% remain to graduate.

Housing: 1177 students can be accommodated in college housing, which includes single-sex and coed dorms and on-campus apartments. On-campus housing is available on a first-come and first-served basis. Priority is given to out-of-town students. 78% of students commute. Alcohol is not permitted. All students may keep cars.

Activities: There are no fraternities or sororities. There are 33 groups on campus, including cheerleading, chorale, computers, dance, drama, environmental, ethnic, gay, honors, jazz band, newspaper, political, professional, radio and TV, religious, social, social service, student government, and yearbook. Popular campus events include Multicultural Festival, Homecoming, SGA Auction to Benefit Homeless and Lecture Series.

Sports: There are 8 intercollegiate sports for men and 9 for women, and 7 intramural sports for men and 6 for women. Facilities include an auditorium, a gym, a fitness center, tennis courts, a track, baseball and softball diamonds, and football, field hockey, and all-purpose fields.

Disabled Students: All of the campus is accessible. Facilities include wheelchair ramps, elevators, special parking, specially equipped restrooms, lowered drinking fountains, lowered telephones, and special housing.

Services: Counseling and information services are available, as is tutoring in most subjects. There is a reader service for the blind, and remedial math, reading, and writing.

Campus Safety and Security: Measures include 24-hour foot and vehicle patrol, emergency notification system, self-defense education, and security escort services. There are emergency telephones, lighted pathways/sidewalks, controlled access to dorms/residences, crime prevention programs offered throughout the year to both students and faculty/staff.

Programs of Study: WSU confers B.A., and B.S. degrees. Master's degrees are also awarded. Bachelor's degrees are awarded in BIOLOGICAL SCIENCE (biology/biological science and biotechnology), BUSINESS (business administration and management), COMMUNICATIONS AND THE ARTS (communications, English, Spanish, and visual and performing arts), COMPUTER AND PHYSICAL SCIENCE (chemistry, computer science, mathematics, and natural sciences), EDUCATION (early childhood education, elementary education, and health education), HEALTH PROFESSIONS (nursing, occupational therapy, and speech pathology/audiology), SOCIAL SCIENCE (criminal justice, economics, geography, history, psychology, sociology, and urban studies). Occupational therapy and nursing is the strongest academically. Business administration, psychology, and criminal justice have the largest enrollments.

Required: Candidates for a baccalaureate degree must complete 120 semester-hour credits with a 2.0 cumulative grade point average (GPA) and a minimum of 2.0 GPA or higher in the departmental and ancillary courses of the major field of concentration. To receive a baccalaureate degree from Worcester State University, a student myst complete 30 of the last 40 credits at Worcester State University, earn a majority of credits in the major at Worcester State University and earn a majority of credits in the minor (if elected) at the University.

Special: Cross-registration with the Worcester Consortium for Higher Education is available, as are internships, study abroad, a Washington semester, work-study, B.A.-B.S. degrees, dual majors, non-degree study, and a pass/fail option. There are 17 national honor societies and a freshman honors program.

Faculty/Classroom: 44% of faculty are male; 55% are female. No introductory courses are taught by graduate students.

Admissions: 61% of the 2013-2014 applicants were accepted. The SAT scores for the 2013-2014 freshman class were: Critical Reading--48% below 500, 43% between 500 and 599, 9% between 600 and 699, and 1% between 700 and 800; Math--36% below 500, 51% between 500 and 599, 12% between 600 and 699, and 1% between 700 and 800. The ACT scores were 31% below 21, 46% between 21 and 23, 17% between 24 and 26, 5% between 27 and 28, and 1% above 28.

Requirements: The SAT or ACT is required. In addition, for students with a GPA of 2.9 or above, a minimum SAT or ACT score may be required. For students whose GPA is below 2.9, a minimum SAT or ACT score is applied according to a scale established by WSC. Applicants must graduate from an accredited secondary school. They should have completed 4 years of English, 3 of math, 2 each of a foreign language, a lab science, and social studies, including 1 year of U.S. history and government, and 2 electives. The College Board Student Descriptive questionnaire must be submitted. A GPA of 2.0 is required. AP and CLEP credits are accepted. A GPA of 2.0 is required. AP and CLEP credits are accepted.

Procedure: Freshmen are admitted fall, spring, and summer. Entrance exams should be taken in spring of the junior year or fall of the senior year. There is a rolling admissions plan. Applications should be filed by May 1 for fall entry, along with a $40 fee. Notification is sent on a rolling basis. Applications are accepted online.

Transfer: 606 transfer students enrolled in 2012-2013. Transfer applicants must have earned a minimum of 12 college credits with a minimum 2.5 GPA or 13 to 23 credits with a minimum 2.0 GPA. Students with fewer than 24 transfer credits may be admitted under the same criteria as first-time freshmen. 30 of 120 credits required for the bachelor's degree must be completed at WSU.

Visiting: There are regularly scheduled orientations for prospective students, including a campus tour and review of campus life and organizations, success in college, special opportunities, and available services. Visitors may sit in on classes. To schedule a visit, contact the Admissions Office at (508) 929-8040.

Financial Aid: The average freshman award was $4,759.. WSU is a member of CSS. The FAFSA and the college's own financial statement are required. The priority date for freshman financial aid applications for fall entry is March 1. The deadline for filing freshman financial aid applications for fall entry is May 1.

International Students: There are 56 international students enrolled. They must take the TOEFL with a minimum score of 550 on the paper-based TOEFL (PBT) or 79 on the Internet-based version (iBT). They must also take the SAT or ACT.

Computers: All students may access the system. There are no time limits and no fees.

Graduates: From July 1, 2012 to June 30, 2013, 923 bachelor's degrees were awarded. The most popular majors were business/marketing (17%), health professions and related programs (12%), and psychology (11%).

Admissions Contact: Joseph DiCarlo, Director of Admissions. E-Mail: *admissions@worcester.edu* Web: *www.worcester.edu*

MICHIGAN

ADRIAN COLLEGE E-5

Adrian, MI 49221-2575 **(517) 265-5161, ext. 4326**
(800) 877-2246; (517) 264-3878

Full-time: 678 men, 602 women	**Faculty:** 74; IIB, -$
Part-time: 27 men, 19 women	**Ph.D.s:** 85%
Graduate: n/av	**Student/Faculty:** 17 to 1
Year: semesters, summer session	**Tuition:** $25,900
Application Deadline: March 30	**Room & Board:** $7900

Freshman Class: 4067 applied, 2568 accepted, 577 enrolled
SAT CR/M: 490/490 **ACT:** required **COMPETITIVE**

Adrian College, founded in 1859, is a private liberal arts institution affiliated with the United Methodist Church. The figures in the above capsule and in this profile are approximate. In addition to regional accreditation, Adrian has baccalaureate program accreditation with CSWE and NCATE. The library contains 153,151 volumes, 50,170 microform items, and 2,626 audio/video tapes/CDs/DVDs, and subscribes to 10,373 periodicals including electronic. Computerized library services include interlibrary loans, database searching, and Internet access. Special learning facilities include a learning resource center, art gallery, planetarium, radio station, a solar greenhouse, and an observatory. The 100-acre campus is in a small town 35 miles southwest of Ann Arbor. Including any residence halls, there are 41 buildings.

Student Life: 76% of undergraduates are from out of state, mostly the Mid-West. Students are from 29 states, 6 foreign countries, and Canada. 81% are white. 48% claim no religious affiliation; 23% Protestant; 18% Catholic. 46% remain to graduate.

Housing: 1600 students can be accommodated in college housing, which includes single-sex and coed dorms, on-campus apartments, and off-campus apartments. In addition, there are special-interest houses, fraternity houses, substance-free, smoke-free, extended quiet hours, upperclassmen only residence halls, theme housing. On-campus housing is guaranteed for all 4 years. All students may keep cars.

Activities: 10% of men belong to 4 national fraternities; 15% of women belong to 3 national sororities. There are 80 groups on campus, including and Exercise Groups, Equestrian Team, Gamers Council, Sports, Various Outdoors, art, band, cheerleading, choir, chorale, chorus, computers, dance, drama, environmental, ethnic, Feminist Empowerment Movement, gay, honors, international, jazz band, literary magazine, marching band, musical theater, newspaper, opera, orchestra, pep band, photography, political, professional, radio and TV, religious, social, social service, student government, symphony, and yearbook. Popular campus events include Greek Week, Family Weekend, International Week, Dance Marathon, One-Act Plays, Rake and Run, Sadie Hawkins Dance, Sibs 'n' Kids Weekend, Chapel Series, and Disability Awareness.

Sports: There are 11 intercollegiate sports for men and 13 for women, and 6 intramural sports for men and 6 for women. Facilities include a sport and fitness center featuring a multipurpose forum with 3 courts for basketball, volleyball, and tennis, and an indoor track, racquetball courts, a weight room, and a 1,350-seat performance gym; a 5,000-seat football stadium; baseball and softball fields; 2 soccer fields; 6 tennis courts; a 400-meter track; and numerous intramural fields. Most of these facilities are new or have been remodeled in the past five years.

Disabled Students: 56 of the campus is accessible. Facilities include wheelchair ramps, elevators, special parking, specially equipped restrooms, lowered drinking fountains, lowered telephones, special housing.

Services: Counseling and information services are available, as is tutoring in most subjects. There is a reader service for the blind, and remedial math, reading, and writing.

Campus Safety and Security: Measures include 24-hour foot and vehicle patrol, self-defense education, and security escort services. There are emergency telephones and lighted pathways/sidewalks.

Programs of Study: Adrian confers B.A., B.S., B.B.A., B.F.A., B.M., B.M.E., and B.S.W. degrees. Associate degrees are also awarded. Bachelor's degrees are awarded in AGRICULTURE (environmental studies), BIOLOGICAL SCIENCE (biology/biological science), BUSINESS (accounting, business administration and management, international business management, and marketing management), COMMUNICATIONS AND THE ARTS (arts administration/management, communications, dramatic arts, English, French, German, journalism, literature, music, music performance, musical theater, Spanish, and studio art), COMPUTER AND PHYSICAL SCIENCE (chemistry, earth science, mathematics, and physics), EDUCATION (elementary education, physical education, and secondary education), ENGINEERING AND ENVIRONMENTAL DESIGN (environmental science and interior design), HEALTH PROFESSIONS (exercise science), SOCIAL SCIENCE (criminal justice, economics, history, international studies, Japanese studies, philosophy, political science/government, psychology, religion, social work, and sociology). Accounting and business administration, exercise science, and English have the largest enrollments.

Required: To graduate, students must maintain a 2.0 average over 124 credit hours, 30 of which must be in upper-division courses. 22 hours of distribution requirements and 21 of basic educational proficiency are required, including 2 semesters of foreign language and 1 each of communication, English, fine arts, fitness, humanities, math, natural or physical science, religion or philosophy, and social science.

Special: Adrian offers preprofessional programs in architectture, engineering, health sciences, law, ministry, medical technology, and art therapy; study abroad in 16 countries and a Washington Semester; student-designed majors and internships in more than 450 locations, and a 3-2 engineering degree with Washington University in St. Louis and the University of Detroit Mercy. There are 13 national honor societies and a freshman honors program.

Faculty/Classroom: 41% of faculty are male; 59% are female. All teach undergraduates. No introductory courses are taught by graduate students. The average class size in an introductory lecture is 19; in a laboratory is 15; and in a regular course is 12.

Admissions: 63% of the 2011-2012 applicants were accepted. The SAT scores for the 2011-2012 freshman class were: Critical Reading--57% below 500, 37% between 500 and 599, 3% between 600 and 700, and 3% above 700; Math--52% below 500, 35% between 500 and 599, and 13% between 600 and 700. The ACT scores were 32% below 21, 31% between 21 and 23, 24% between 24 and 26, 7% between 27 and 28, and 6% above 28. 38% of the current freshmen were in the top fifth of their class; 69% were in the top two fifths. 11 freshmen graduated first in their class.

Requirements: The SAT or ACT is required. In addition, applicants must be graduates of an accredited secondary school. The GED is accepted. Each student is reviewed individually based on several criteria. An interview is recommended. Adrian requires applicants to be in the upper 50% of their class. A GPA of 3.0 is required. AP and CLEP credits are accepted. Important factors in the admissions decision are advanced placement or honors courses, leadership record, and extracurricular activities record.

Procedure: Freshmen are admitted fall. Entrance exams should be taken during the spring of the junior year or fall of the senior year. There are deferred admissions and rolling admissions plans. Applications should be filed by March 30 for fall entry. Applications are accepted online.

Transfer: 65 transfer students enrolled in a recent year. Applicants must have an above-average GPA and provide final high school transcripts. If the student has completed fewer than 24 semester hours, ACT or SAT test scores are also required. Grades of 2.0 and above transfer for credit. The college admits transfer students every semester. 34 of 124 credits required for the bachelor's degree must be completed at Adrian.

Visiting: There are regularly scheduled orientations for prospective students, including a student guided campus tour and visits with an admissions counselor, professors from the student's area of interest, and an athletics coach. Visitors may sit in on classes and stay overnight. To schedule a visit, contact the Admissions Office.

Financial Aid: In a recent year, 97% of all full-time freshmen and 99% of continuing full-time students received some form of financial aid. 66% of all full-time freshmen and 67% of continuing full-time students received need-based aid. The average freshman award was $19,055. Need-based scholarships or need-based grants averaged $6,300; and need-based self-help aid (loans and jobs) averaged $5,316. 66% of undergraduate students work part-time. Average annual earnings from campus work was $1800. The average financial indebtedness of a recent graduate was $17,160. Adrian is a member of CSS. The FAFSA is required. The priority date for freshman financial aid applications for fall entry is March 1.

International Students: There are 52 international students enrolled. The school actively recruits these students. They must take the TOEFL with a minimum score of 500 on the paper-based TOEFL (PBT) or 73 on the Internet-based version (iBT). They must also take the SAT or ACT.

Graduates: In a recent year, 157 bachelor's degrees were awarded. The most popular majors were health, physical ed., and recreation (8%), art (7%), and biology (6%). 22 companies recruited on campus in a recent year. In an average class, 58% graduate in 6 years or less.

Admissions Contact: Director of Admissions. E-Mail: *admissions@adrian.edu* Web: *www.adrian.edu*

ALBION COLLEGE D-5

Albion, MI 49224 **(517) 629-0321**
(800) 858-6770; (517) 629-0569

Full-time: 688 men, 665 women	**Faculty:** 105; IIB, -$
Part-time: 10 men, 19 women	**Ph.D.s:** 91%
Graduate: n/av	**Student/Faculty:** 11 to 1
Year: semesters, summer session	**Tuition:** $34,191
Application Deadline: open	**Room & Board:** $9690
Freshman Class: 2383 applied, 1673 accepted, 360 enrolled	
SAT CR/M/W: 540/550/540 **ACT:** 24	**VERY COMPETITIVE**

Albion College, established in 1835, is a private institution affiliated with the United Methodist Church and offering undergraduate degrees in liberal arts curricula. In addition to regional accreditation, Albion has baccalaureate program accreditation with NASM. The library contains 356,176 volumes, 49,107 microform items, and 12,851 audio/video tapes/CDs/DVDs, and subscribes to 88,631 periodicals including electronic. Computerized library services include interlibrary loans, database searching, and Internet access. Special learning facilities include an art gallery, planetarium, radio station, nature center a and equestrian center. The 574-acre campus is in a small town in south central Michigan, 65 miles from Detroit. Including any residence halls, there are 94 buildings.

Student Life: 91% of undergraduates are from Michigan. Others are from 22 states, 20 foreign countries, and Canada. 80% are White. 55% claim no religious affiliation; 23% Catholic; 19% Protestant. The average age of freshmen is 18; all undergraduates, 20. 27% do not continue beyond their first year; 72% remain to graduate.

Housing: 1774 students can be accommodated in college housing, which includes single-sex and coed dorms, on-campus apartments, off-campus apartments, and married student housing. In addition, there are language houses, special-interest houses, fraternity houses, and special interest annexes. On-campus housing is guaranteed for all 4 years. 90% of students live on campus; of those, 70% remain on campus on weekends. All students may keep cars.

Activities: 51% of men belong to 6 national fraternities; 43% of women belong to 7 national sororities. There are 110 groups on campus, including art, band, cheerleading, chess, choir, chorale, chorus, computers, dance, drama, environmental, ethnic, film, gay, honors, international, jazz band, literary magazine, marching band, musical theater, newspaper, opera, orchestra, pep band, photography, political, professional, radio and TV, religious, social, social service, student government, symphony, and yearbook. Popular campus events include Briton Bash, Day of Woden and Party on Perry.

Sports: There are 11 intercollegiate sports for men and 11 for women, and 10 intramural sports for men and 8 for women. Facilities include a stadium, an aquatic center, a gym, baseball, soccer, and football fields, tennis courts, an archery range, an equestrian center, a surfaced track, a field events area, practice fields, and a canoeing facility. There is also a recreation and wellness center with intramural basketball, volleyball, badminton, racquetball, and tennis courts, a track, a weight training room, a human performance lab, and a training/rehabilitation unit.

Disabled Students: 95% of the campus is accessible. Facilities include wheelchair ramps, elevators, special parking, specially equipped restrooms, special class scheduling, lowered drinking fountains, and lowered telephones.

Services: Counseling and information services are available, as is tutoring in most subjects, and assistance for the deaf. There is a reader service for the blind. A skills center offers individual assistance to students for study skills enhancement.

Campus Safety and Security: Measures include 24-hour foot and vehicle patrol, emergency notification system, self-defense education, and security escort services. There are shuttle buses, emergency telephones, lighted pathways/sidewalks, and controlled access to dorms/residences.

Programs of Study: Albion confers B.A., and B.F.A. degrees. Bachelor's degrees are awarded in BIOLOGICAL SCIENCE (biology/biological science), COMMUNICATIONS AND THE ARTS (art, art history and appreciation, English, French, German, music, Spanish, speech/debate/rhetoric, and visual and performing arts), COMPUTER AND PHYSICAL SCIENCE (chemistry, computer science, earth science, geoscience, mathematics, and physics), EDUCATION (athletic training and physical education), HEALTH PROFESSIONS (predentistry and premedicine), SOCIAL SCIENCE (American studies, anthropology, economics, ethnic studies, gender studies, history, international studies, philosophy, political science/government, psychology, public affairs, religion, sociology, and women's studies). Economics, biology, and psychology have the largest enrollments.

Required: GRADUATION REQUIREMENTS: 32 units (128 semester hours) – a minimum of the last 12 units must be taken at Albion College.

Special: Albion offers study abroad in 40 countries, and study/internship programs in New York City, Philadelphia, Washington, D.C., Oak Ridge, and Chicago. Students may earn a dual engineering degree in conjunction with Columbia, Case Western, or Michigan Technological universities, or the University of Michigan. Student-designed majors and interdisciplinary majors in fields including environmental science, ethnic studies, international studies, and women's and gender studies are available. There are 5 national honor societies, including Phi Beta Kappa, a freshman honors program, and 13 departmental honors programs.

Faculty/Classroom: 60% of faculty are male; 40% are female. All teach undergraduates, 89% do research, and 89% do both. No introductory courses are taught by graduate students. The average class size in an introductory lecture is 20; in a laboratory is 12; and in a regular course is 15.

Admissions: 70% of the 2013-2014 applicants were accepted. The SAT scores for the 2013-2014 freshman class were: Critical Reading--39% below 500, 29% between 500 and 599, 26% between 600 and 699, and 6% between 700 and 800; Math--29% below 500, 32% between 500 and 599, 23% between 600 and 699, and 16% between 700 and 800. The ACT scores were 16% below 21, 23% between 21 and 23, 26% between 24 and 26, 13% between 27 and 28, and 16% above 28.

Requirements: The SAT or ACT is required. Applicants must graduate from an accredited secondary school or earn a GED. Completion of 15 Carnegie credits is required. A strong background in English, math, and the lab and social sciences is recommended as the best preparation for academic success. The Admission Committee will consider courses taken, grades earned, the academic rigor of the program and SAT/ACT scores as corroborative evidence. Applications are accepted online at the Albion web site and through the Common App. A GPA of 3.0 is required. AP and CLEP credits are accepted. Important factors in the admissions decision are advanced placement or honors courses, extracurricular activities record, and personality/intangible qualities.

Procedure: Freshmen are admitted fall and spring. Entrance exams should be taken in April or June of the junior year. There are early admissions, deferred admissions, and rolling admissions plans. Application deadlines are open. The fall 2013 application fee was $40. Notification is sent on a rolling basis. Applications are accepted online.

Transfer: 36 transfer students enrolled in 2012-2013. Transfer applicants must submit official college transcripts. Grades of 2.0 or better are considered for transfer credit. Albion evaluates the applicant's course work before conferring transfer credit. 48 of 128 credits required for the bachelor's degree must be completed at Albion.

Visiting: There are regularly scheduled orientations for prospective students, consisting of 4 programs held in early June and 1 in August for students and parents. There are guides for informal visits, visitors may sit in on classes, and stay overnight. To schedule a visit, contact Marsha Whitehouse, Admissions Office.

Financial Aid: In 2013-2014, 98% of all full-time freshmen and 98% of continuing full-time students received some form of financial aid. 74% of all full-time freshmen and 69% of continuing full-time students received need-based aid. The average freshman award was $26,742. Need-based scholarships or need-based grants averaged $21,465 ($37,112 maximum); and need-based self-help aid (loans and jobs) averaged $5,277 ($8,200 maximum). 36% of undergraduate students work part-time. Average annual earnings from campus work are $1021. The average financial indebtedness of the 2013 graduate was $36,029. The FAFSA is required. The priority date for freshman financial aid applications for fall entry is March 1.

International Students: There are 54 international students enrolled. The school actively recruits these students. They must take the TOEFL with a minimum score of 550 on the paper-based TOEFL (PBT) or 79 on the Internet-based version (iBT). They must also take the SAT or ACT.

Graduates: From July 1, 2012 to June 30, 2013, 450 bachelor's degrees were awarded. The most popular majors were economics and management (19%), biology (15%), and psychology (10%). 46 companies recruited on campus in 2012-2013. In an average class, 62% graduate in 4 years or less, 70% graduate in 5 years or less, and 72% graduate in 6 years or less. Of the 2012 graduating class, 37% were enrolled in graduate school within 6 months of graduation, and 54% were employed.

Admissions Contact: Peter Littlefield, Director of Admissions. E-Mail: *admission@albion.edu* Web: *www.albion.edu*

ALMA COLLEGE D-4

Alma, MI 48801-1599 (989) 463-7139
(800) 321-ALMA; (989) 463-7057

Full-time: 625 men, 753 women	**Faculty:** 96; IIB, -$
Part-time: 17 men, 24 women	**Ph.D.s:** 85%
Graduate: n/av	**Student/Faculty:** 12 to 1
Year: other	**Tuition:** $33,135
Application Deadline: open	**Room & Board:** $9265
Freshman Class: 2554 applied, 1772 accepted, 366 enrolled	
SAT CR/M/W: 561/571/552 **ACT:** 24	**VERY COMPETITIVE**

Alma College, a selective, residential college located in the middle of Michigan's Lower Peninsula, offers a personalized education with multiple paths and experiences leading to success. Strong academic programs and a deep regard for students as individuals are fundamental to an Alma education, with small classes and many opportunities for one-on-one collaboration with dedicated faculty. In addition to regional accreditation, Alma has baccalaureate program accreditation with NASM. The library contains 278,000 volumes, 247,000 microform items, and 12,655 audio/video tapes/CDs/DVDs, and subscribes to 1,500 periodicals including electronic. Computerized library services include interlibrary loans, database searching, Internet access, and Wi-Fi capability. Special learning facilities include an art gallery, planetarium, radio station, a Writing lab, and Digital Media Commons. The 125-acre campus is in a small town 50 miles north of Lansing. Including any residence halls, there are 26 buildings.

Student Life: 91% of undergraduates are from Michigan. Others are from 30 states, 13 foreign countries, and Canada. 92% are from public schools. 86% are White. 43% are Protestant; 33% claim no religious affiliation; 22% Catholic. The average age of freshmen is 18; all undergraduates, 20. 15% do not continue beyond their first year.

Housing: 1250 students can be accommodated in college housing, which includes coed dorms and on-campus apartments. In addition, there are special-interest houses, fraternity houses, sorority houses, and an international house for students who live or have traveled overseas. On-campus housing is guaranteed for all 4 years. 90% of students live on campus; of those, 65% remain on campus on weekends. All students may keep cars.

Activities: 24% of men belong to 1 local and 5 national fraternities; 30% of women belong to 1 local and 4 national sororities. There are 80 groups on campus, including art, bagpipe, band, cheerleading, chess, choir, chorale, chorus, computers, dance, drama, environmental, ethnic, gay, honors, international, jazz band, literary magazine, marching band, newspaper, orchestra, political, professional, radio and TV, religious, social, social service, student government, symphony, and yearbook. Popular campus events include Song Fest, and Highland Festival.

Sports: There are 11 intercollegiate sports for men and 11 for women, and 6 intramural sports for men and 6 for women. Facilities include a recreation center with a climbing wall, fitness center, 4 courts, and suspended 3-lane track; an indoor gym and pool; an outdoor sports complex with an artificial turf playing field, an 8-lane track, baseball, soccer, and softball fields; a weight training room; and racquetball and tennis courts.

Disabled Students: 75% of the campus is accessible. Facilities include wheelchair ramps, elevators, special parking, specially equipped restrooms, special class scheduling, lowered drinking fountains. 2 residence halls with private baths, and several small housing units.

Services: Counseling and information services are available, as is tutoring in every subject. Both individual and group tutoring are available. There is a reader service for the blind.

Campus Safety and Security: Measures include emergency notification system and security escort services. There are emergency telephones, lighted pathways/sidewalks, controlled access to dorms/residences, a 24-hour foot patrol, and ID card access to residence halls.

Programs of Study: Alma confers B.A., B.S., B.M., and B.F.A. degrees. Bachelor's degrees are awarded in AGRICULTURE (environmental studies), BIOLOGICAL SCIENCE (biochemistry, biology/biological science, and biotechnology), BUSINESS (business administration and management and international business management), COMMUNICATIONS AND THE ARTS (art, communications, dramatic arts, English, French, German, music, and Spanish), COMPUTER AND PHYSICAL SCIENCE (chemistry, computer science, mathematics, and physics), EDUCATION (athletic training, elementary education, and secondary education), HEALTH PROFESSIONS (exercise science, health care administration, and health science), SOCIAL SCIENCE (anthropology, economics, history, philosophy, political science/government, psychology, religion, and sociology). Integrative physiology and health science, biology, business administration, education, and English are the strongest academically. Business, integrative physiology and health science, and education have the largest enrollments.

Required: Degree requirements include completion of a minimum of 136 credit hours; 148 hours are required for the B.F.A. degree, 136 to 156 for the B.M. degree. Students must attain a minimum GPA of 2.0, or 3.0 for fine arts majors. All students must demonstrate proficiency in English, second language/international awareness, communication, and computation, and they must complete distribution requirements, which include 12 fine arts and humanities credits and 12 each of social science and natural science credits. The total number of program credits is 36 for a departmental major, 56 for an interdepartmental major, and 56 to 68 for self-directed majors.

Special: Alma offers internships in many fields, study abroad in 18 countries, experiential learning program at the Philadelphia Center, and a Washington semester at American University. There are work-study programs, dual majors, B.A.-B.S. degrees, and student-designed majors in a wide variety of subjects. The college confers 3-2 engineering degrees in conjunction with the University of Michigan and Michigan Technological University. Nondegree study may be pursued, and students have a pass/fail grading option. A 4-week spring term provides intensive study in 1 course, often combined with travel. There are 3 national honor societies, including Phi Beta Kappa, a freshman honors program, and 17 departmental honors programs.

Faculty/Classroom: 61% of faculty are male; 39% are female. All teach undergraduates, and all do research. No introductory courses are taught by graduate students. The average class size in an introductory lecture is 18; in a laboratory is 16; and in a regular course is 18.

Admissions: 69% of the 2013-2014 applicants were accepted. The SAT scores for the 2013-2014 freshman class were: Critical Reading--36% below 500, 28% between 500 and 599, 20% between 600 and 699, and 16% between 700 and 800; Math--24% below 500, 40% between 500 and 599, 24% between 600 and 699, and 12% between 700 and 800; Writing--32% below 500, 40% between 500 and 599, 12% between 600 and 699, and 16% between 700 and 800. The ACT scores were 21% below 21, 20% between 21 and 23, 25% between 24 and 26, 24% between 27 and 28, and 9% above 28. 10 freshmen graduated first in their class.

Requirements: The SAT or ACT is required. The ACT is preferred. Applicants must have graduated from an accredited secondary school and have earned 16 Carnegie units, including 4 years of English and 3 each of math, science, and social studies, with 2 of a foreign language recommended. Alma prefers applicants in the upper 25% of their class. Portfolio and audition are required for performing arts scholarships. A GPA of 3.0 is required. AP credits are accepted. Important factors in the admissions decision are advanced placement or honors courses, leadership record, and recommendations by school officials.

Procedure: Freshmen are admitted fall, winter, and spring. Entrance exams should be taken in the spring of the junior year or as late as the winter of the senior year. There are deferred admissions and rolling admissions plans. Application deadlines are open. Application fee is $25. Notification is sent on a rolling basis. Applications are accepted online. Application fees are waived if application is completed online.

Transfer: 36 transfer students enrolled in 2012-2013. Students wishing to transfer to Alma must have a minimum GPA of 2.0 from other colleges attended. 34 of 136 credits required for the bachelor's degree must be completed at Alma.

Visiting: There are regularly scheduled orientations for prospective students, consisting of faculty talks, tours, a meal on campus, financial aid information, and admissions sessions. There are guides for informal visits, visitors may sit in on classes, and stay overnight. To schedule a visit, contact the Admissions Office.

Financial Aid: In 2013-2014, 99% of all full-time freshmen and 99% of continuing full-time students received some form of financial aid. 90% of all full-time freshmen and 90% of continuing full-time students received need-based aid. The average freshman award was $17,153. Need-based scholarships or need-based grants averaged $24,779; and need-based self-help aid (loans and jobs) averaged $21,225. 31% of undergraduate students work part-time. Average annual earnings from campus work are $1184. The FAFSA is required. The priority date for freshman financial aid applications for fall entry is March 1.

International Students: There are 14 international students enrolled.

The school actively recruits these students. They must take the TOEFL with a minimum score of 550 on the paper-based TOEFL (PBT) or 79 on the Internet-based version (iBT). The SAT or ACT is required if the TOEFL is not submitted.

Graduates: From July 1, 2012 to June 30, 2013, 269 bachelor's degrees were awarded. The most popular majors were business administration (19%), integrative physiology and health science (11%), and biology (8%). In an average class, 1% graduate in 3 years or less, 47% graduate in 4 years or less, 60% graduate in 5 years or less, and 61% graduate in 6 years or less. Of the 2012 graduating class, 32% were enrolled in graduate school within 6 months of graduation, and 53% were employed.

Admissions Contact: Amanda Slenski, Director of Admissions. E-Mail: *admissions@alma.edu* Web: *www.alma.edu*

ANDREWS UNIVERSITY — C-5

Berrien Springs, MI 49104-0150 — (616) 471-6343; (800) 253-2874; (616) 471-3228

Full-time: 785 men, 935 women	**Faculty:** 148
Part-time: 110 men, 145 women	**Ph.D.s:** 72%
Graduate: 1100 men, 530 women	**Student/Faculty:** n/av
Year: semesters, summer session	**Tuition:** $23,180
Application Deadline: open	**Room & Board:** $7474
Freshman Class: n/av	
SAT or ACT: required	**COMPETITIVE+**

Andrews University, established in 1874, is a private institution affiliated with the Seventh-day Adventist Church that offers undergraduate degrees in business, education, arts and sciences, architecture, and technology. The figures in the above capsule and in this profile are approximate. There are 5 undergraduate schools and 6 graduate schools. In addition to regional accreditation, Andrews has baccalaureate program accreditation with AACSB, ABET, ADA, AHEA, APTA, CAHEA, CSWE, IACBE, NAAB, NASM, NCATE, and NLN. The library contains 747,764 volumes, 83,520 microform items, and 48,447 audio/video tapes/CDs/DVDs, and subscribes to 2,874 periodicals including electronic. Computerized library services include interlibrary loans, database searching, and Internet access. Special learning facilities include an art gallery, natural history museum, radio station, and an archeological museum. The 1600-acre campus is in a rural area 10 miles south of Benton Harbor. Including any residence halls, there are 51 buildings.

Student Life: 56% of undergraduates are from out of state, mostly the Middle Atlantic. Students are from 46 states, 51 foreign countries, and Canada. 23% are from public schools. 42% are white; 25% African American; 12% foreign nationals. 89% are Protestant; 12% unknown. The average age of freshmen is 18; all undergraduates, 22. 21% do not continue beyond their first year; 58% remain to graduate.

Housing: 1500 students can be accommodated in college housing, which includes single-sex dorms, on-campus apartments, and married student housing. On-campus housing is available on a first-come, first-served basis. 54% of students live on campus. Alcohol is not permitted. All students may keep cars.

Activities: There is 1 national fraternity and 1 national sorority. There are 30 groups on campus, including band, choir, chorale, chorus, computers, drama, ethnic, honors, international, newspaper, professional, religious, social, social service, and student government. Popular campus events include Alumni Weekend and International Food Fair.

Sports: There are 6 intramural sports for men and 4 for women. Facilities include a gym, a pool, racquetball courts, and health clubs in 2 of 3 dorms.

Disabled Students: 50% of the campus is accessible. Facilities include wheelchair ramps, elevators, special parking, specially equipped rest rooms, special class scheduling, lowered drinking fountains, lowered telephones, and special housing. A special committee handles needs as they arise.

Services: Counseling and information services are available, as is tutoring in most subjects. There are math, writing, and reading, learning, and assessment centers.

Campus Safety and Security: Measures include 24-hour foot and vehicle patrol and security escort services. There are lighted pathways/sidewalks and CPR training.

Programs of Study: Andrews confers B.A., B.S., B.B.A., B.F.A., B.Mus., B.S.D., B.S.Educ., B.S.El.Ed., B.S.Eng., B.S.W., and B.T. degrees. Associate, master's, and doctoral degrees are also awarded. Bachelor's degrees are awarded in AGRICULTURE (agriculture, animal science, and horticulture), BIOLOGICAL SCIENCE (anatomy, biochemistry, biology/biological science, biophysics, botany, molecular biology, nutrition, and zoology), BUSINESS (accounting, banking and finance, business administration and management, business economics, management information systems, and marketing/retailing/merchandising), COMMUNICATIONS AND THE ARTS (art, ceramic art and design, communications, creative writing, design, English, French, graphic design, journalism, literature, music, music performance, painting, photography, public relations, Spanish, and visual and performing arts), COMPUTER AND PHYSICAL SCIENCE (applied mathematics, chemistry, computer science, information sciences and systems, mathematics, and physics), EDUCATION (art education, elementary education, English education, mathematics education, music education, science education, secondary education, social studies education, and teaching English as a second/foreign language (TESOL/TEFOL)), ENGINEERING AND ENVIRONMENTAL DESIGN (aeronautical technology, aircraft mechanics, architecture, aviation administration/management, aviation computer technology, biomedical equipment technology, computer graphics, computer technology, electrical/electronics engineering, engineering, environmental science, graphic arts technology, and landscape architecture/design), HEALTH PROFESSIONS (allied health, art therapy, biomedical science, medical laboratory technology, nursing, preveterinary science, public health, and speech pathology/audiology), SOCIAL SCIENCE (anthropology, behavioral science, crosscultural studies, dietetics, economics, family/consumer studies, history, human development, interdisciplinary studies, pastoral studies, political science/government, psychology, religion, religious education, social studies, social work, sociology, theological studies, and youth ministry). Health sciences, business, and architecture have the largest enrollments.

Required: Students must complete a minimum of 124 semester credits. Specific course requirements include religion, English, behavioral sciences, fine arts, and phys ed.

Special: Students may pursue a second major in business administration. Study abroad, student-designed majors, nondegree study, and pass/fail options are available. There is a freshman honors program.

Faculty/Classroom: 64% of faculty are male; 36% are female. No introductory courses are taught by graduate students. The average class size in a laboratory is 16; in a regular course, 18.

Requirements: The SAT or ACT is required. Candidates for admission must graduate from an accredited secondary school or earn a GED. 10 Carnegie units are required, and students must have completed 4 courses in English and 2 courses each in history, math, and science. Interviews are recommended for all applicants. A GPA of 2.3 is required. CLEP credits are accepted. Important factors in the admissions decision are advanced placement or honors courses, recommendations by school officials, and evidence of special talent.

Procedure: Freshmen are admitted fall, spring, and summer. Entrance exams should be taken as early as possible. There are deferred admissions and rolling admissions plans. Application deadlines are open. Application fee is $30.

Transfer: 131 transfer students enrolled in a recent year. Transfer applicants must submit a high school transcript and transcripts from all colleges attended. A maximum of 70 semester credits from a 2-year school or 90 semester credits from a 4-year school may be transferred toward a bachelor's degree. Credits should be relevant to the student's major at Andrews. The minimum GPA is 2.25, and the ACT is preferred. Students must meet freshman entrance requirements if they are transferring with less than sophomore standing from an accredited college. 30 of 124 credits required for the bachelor's degree must be completed at Andrews.

Visiting: There are regularly scheduled orientations for prospective students, including tours, meetings with faculty, and social activities. There are guides for informal visits, and visitors may sit in on classes and stay overnight. To schedule a visit, contact the Admissions Office.

Financial Aid: The FAFSA is required. The priority date for freshman financial aid applications for fall entry is open.

International Students: There were 230 international students enrolled in a recent year. The school actively recruits these students. They must take the TOEFL with a minimum score of 550 on the paper-based TOEFL (PBT). They must also take the SAT or ACT.

Graduates: In a recent year, 341 bachelor's degrees were awarded. The most popular majors were health professions (20%), business (10%), and biology/life science (8%). In an average class, 34% graduate in 4 years or less, 51% graduate in 5 years or less, and 58% graduate in 6 years or less.

Admissions Contact: Undergraduate Admissions Supervisor. E-mail: *undergraduate@andrews.edu* Web: *www.andrews.edu*

AQUINAS COLLEGE — D-4

Grand Rapids, MI 49506 — (616) 632-2860; (800) 678-9593; (616) 732-4469

Full-time: 667 men, 1029 women		**Faculty:** 88
Part-time: 101 men, 125 women		**Ph.D.s:** 80%
Graduate: 52 men, 119 women		**Student/Faculty:** 13 to 1
Year: semesters, summer session		**Tuition:** $25,250
Application Deadline: open		**Room & Board:** $7810
Freshman Class: n/av		
SAT: recommended	**ACT:** 23	**COMPETITIVE**

Aquinas College, established in 1866, is a private liberal arts institution affiliated with the Roman Catholic Church and offers undergraduate and graduate degrees through day and evening programs. There is 1 undergraduate school and 2 graduate schools. In addition to regional accreditation, Aquinas has baccalaureate program accreditation with TEAC. The library contains 100,014 volumes, 227,444 microform items, and 41,050 audio/video tapes/CDs/DVDs, and subscribes to 558 periodicals including electronic. Computerized library services include interlibrary loans, database searching, Internet access, and Wi-Fi capability. Special learning facilities include an art gallery, radio station, greenhouses, observatory, nature trails. The 107-acre campus is in a suburban area east of downtown Grand Rapids, MI. Including any residence halls, there are 30 buildings.

Student Life: 95% of undergraduates are from Michigan. Others are from 22 states, 5 foreign countries, and Canada. 86% are White. 53% are Catholic; 18% claim no religious affiliation; 15% Non-denominational and unknown; 14% Protestant. The average age of freshmen is 18; all undergraduates, 22. 23% do not continue beyond their first year; 61% remain to graduate.

Housing: 862 students can be accommodated in college housing, which includes single-sex and coed dorms and on-campus apartments. In addition, there are special-interest houses, and service learning houses. On-campus housing is guaranteed for the freshman year only, is available on a first-come, first served basis, and is available on a lottery system for upperclassmen. Priority is given to out-of-town students. 71% of students live on campus; of those, 68% remain on campus on weekends. All students may keep cars.

Activities: There are no fraternities or sororities. There are 55 groups on campus, including art, band, cheerleading, choir, chorale, chorus, computers, dance, drama, environmental, ethnic, honors, international, jazz band, literary magazine, musical theater, newspaper, pep band, photography, political, professional, radio and TV, religious, social, social service, and student government. Popular campus events include Spring Fling, Moose Cafe and a Jazz Festival.

Sports: There are 10 intercollegiate sports for men and 12 for women, and 4 intramural sports for men and 4 for women. Facilities include Health and fitness center with volleyball and basketball competition courts, classrooms, athletic training lab and state of the art work out equipment. Artificial turf soccer and lacrosse field.

Disabled Students: 95% of the campus is accessible. Facilities include wheelchair ramps, elevators, special parking, specially equipped restrooms, special class scheduling, lowered drinking fountains, and lowered telephones.

Services: Counseling and information services are available, as is tutoring in most subjects. There is a reader service for the blind, and remedial math, reading, and writing.

Campus Safety and Security: Measures include 24-hour foot and vehicle patrol, emergency notification system, self-defense education, and security escort services. There are emergency telephones, lighted pathways/sidewalks, and controlled access to dorms/residences.

Programs of Study: Aquinas confers B.A., B.S., B.A.G.E., B.F.A., B.S.B.A. and B.S.I.B. degrees. Associate and master's degrees are also awarded. Bachelor's degrees are awarded in AGRICULTURE (environmental studies), BIOLOGICAL SCIENCE (biology/biological science and environmental biology), BUSINESS (accounting, business administration and management, business communications, business economics, human resources, information & communication technology, international business management, management information systems, marketing and distribution, marketing management, nonprofit/public organization management, recreation and leisure services, recreational facilities management, and sports management), COMMUNICATIONS AND THE ARTS (art history, art, art history and appreciation, arts administration/management, ceramic art and design, communications, drawing, English, English literature, English Writing, fine arts, French, German, jazz, journalism, language arts, literature, modern language, music, music business management, music history and appreciation, music performance, music theory and composition, musical theater, painting, performing arts, photography, printmaking, sculpture, Spanish, theater management, and visual and performing arts), COMPUTER AND PHYSICAL SCIENCE (chemistry, information sciences and systems, mathematics, mathematics/computational, and mathematics/theoretical), EDUCATION (art education, athletic training, (Education) Childhood Education, early childhood education, education, education of the multiply handicapped, education of the physically handicapped, elementary education, English education, health education, mathematics education, music education, physical education, science education, secondary education, social science education, special education, specific learning disabilities, sports and wellness studies, and teaching English as a second/foreign language (TESOL/TEFOL)), ENGINEERING AND ENVIRONMENTAL DESIGN (environmental science and preengineering), HEALTH PROFESSIONS (health, premedicine, and sports medicine), SOCIAL SCIENCE (Christian studies, community services, economics, French studies, geography, (Social Science) Global Studies, history, human services, interdisciplinary studies, international relations, international studies, liberal arts/general studies, philosophy, political science/government, prelaw, psychology, public administration, religion, religious music, social science, social studies, sociology, and theological studies). Business administration, English and biology have the largest enrollments.

Required: To graduate, students must complete 124 semester hours, with 30 to 48 in the major, and maintain a minimum GPA of 2.0. The general education program consists of a core of 18 to 30 hours, which includes, from the first to the fourth year, foreign language and a yearlong integrated skills course, and courses in the humanities, religion, and global perspectives; and distribution requirements of 30 to 33 hours, which include courses in cultural diversity, mythology and spirituality, natural sciences, the fine arts, and quantitative reasoning and technology.

Special: Students may cross-register with the Dominican Consortium and may study abroad in Ireland, Germany, France, Spain, Costa Rica, Italy, or Japan. Co-op programs and internships are available in all majors, and work-study programs are also available. Students may pursue dual majors in business administration and accounting, sports management, communication arts, or art and B.A.-B.S. degrees in business, geography, or psychology. Student-designed majors can be arranged. Aquinas offers a general studies degree and may confer credit for life, military experience. A pass/fail grading option is available. Preengineering, prehealth, and teacher certification programs are all available in conjunction with majors offered at Aquinas. There are 5 national honor societies, a freshman honors program, and 5 departmental honors programs.

Faculty/Classroom: 54% of faculty are male; 46% are female. All teach undergraduates. No introductory courses are taught by graduate students. The average class size in an introductory lecture is 20; in a laboratory is 20; and in a regular course is 17.

Admissions: The ACT scores were 28% below 21, 25% between 21 and 23, 28% between 24 and 26, 14% between 27 and 28, and 5% above 28. 25% of the current freshmen were in the top fifth of their class; 78% were in the top two fifths.

Requirements: The ACT is required. The SAT and ACT Writing Test are recommended. Candidates for admission must graduate from an accredited secondary school. Students must have completed 15 Carnegie units and 4 years of English and social studies and 3 to 4 years each of math and science. A GPA of 2.5 is required. AP and CLEP credits are accepted. Important factors in the admissions decision are advanced placement or honors courses, leadership record, and extracurricular activities record.

Procedure: Freshmen are admitted fall and winter. Entrance exams should be taken during the spring of the junior year. There is a rolling admissions plan. Application deadlines are open. Applications are accepted online.

Transfer: 74 transfer students enrolled in 2012-2013. Transfer applicants must have earned at least 12 credits in academic course work from an accredited junior or 4-year college with a minimum GPA of 2.0. Interviews are recommended. 30 of 124 credits required for the bachelor's degree must be completed at Aquinas.

Visiting: There are regularly scheduled orientations for prospective students, consisting of a tour of the campus and presentations by financial aid personnel, program directors, coaches, and faculty. There are guides for informal visits, visitors may sit in on classes, and stay overnight. To schedule a visit, contact the Admissions Office.

Financial Aid: In 2013-2014, 98% of all full-time freshmen and 90% of continuing full-time students received some form of financial aid. 90% of all full-time freshmen and 88% of continuing full-time students received need-based aid. The average freshman award was $20,873. Need-based scholarships or need-based grants averaged $18,711; need-based self-help aid (loans and jobs) averaged $3,200; non-need-based athletic scholarships averaged $3,212; and other non-need-based awards and non-need-based scholarships averaged $12,033. 26% of undergraduate students work part-time. Average annual earnings from campus work are $1632. The average financial indebtedness of the 2013 graduate was $14,983. The FAFSA is required. The deadline for filing freshman financial aid applications for fall entry is June 1.

International Students: There are 5 international students enrolled. They must take the TOEFL with a minimum score of 550 on the paper-based TOEFL (PBT). They must also take the ACT.

Graduates: From July 1, 2012 to June 30, 2013, 381 bachelor's degrees were awarded. The most popular majors were business administration, education, and social science. 50 companies recruited on campus in 2012-2013. In an average class, 34% graduate in 4 years or less, 51% graduate in 5 years or less, and 52% graduate in 6 years or less. Of the 2012 graduating class, 22% were enrolled in graduate school within 6 months of graduation, and 73% were employed.

Admissions Contact: Angela Schlosser Bacon, Director of Admissions. E-Mail: *schloang@aquinas.edu* Web: *www.aquinas.edu*

BAKER COLLEGE OF FLINT E-4

Flint, MI 48507-5508 (810) 766-4000
(800) 822-2537; (810) 766-4049

Full-time: 810 men, 1610 women
Part-time: 610 men, 1405 women
Graduate: n/av
Year: trimesters, summer session
Application Deadline: open
Freshman Class: n/av
Faculty: 23
Ph.D.s: 13%
Student/Faculty: n/av
Tuition: $7,880
Room & Board: $5,900

NONCOMPETITIVE

Baker College, established in 1911, is an independent institution offering undergraduate degrees in business, health science, and technical curricula. The figures in the above capsule and in this profile are approximate. It is part of the Baker College System. There is 1 graduate school. In addition to regional accreditation, Baker has baccalaureate program accreditation with CAHEA. The library contains 60,000 volumes, 1,200 microform items, 475 audio/video tapes/CDs/DVDs, and subscribes to 190 periodicals including electronic. Computerized library services include interlibrary loans and database searching. Special learning facilities include a learning resource center. The 30-acre campus is in an urban area 60 miles northwest of Detroit. Including any residence halls, there are 6 buildings.

Student Life: 92% of undergraduates are from Michigan. Students are also from 4 foreign countries, including Canada. 72% are white; 22% African American. The average age of all undergraduates is 28.

Housing: 189 students can be accommodated in college housing, which includes single-sex and coed dorms, on-campus apartments, and off-campus apartments. On-campus housing is available on a first-come and first-served basis. Priority is given to out-of-town students. 98% of students commute. Alcohol is not permitted. All students may keep cars.

Activities: There are no fraternities or sororities. There are 15 groups on campus, including computers, literary magazine, professional, and social. Popular campus events include Baker College Spirit Day and Martin Luther King Jr. Day.

Sports: There is no sports program at Baker. Facilities include a gym and a weight room.

Disabled Students: All of the campus is accessible. Facilities include wheelchair ramps, elevators, special parking, specially equipped rest rooms, lowered drinking fountains, and lowered telephones.

Services: Counseling and information services are available, as is tutoring in most subjects.

Campus Safety and Security: Measures include 24-hour foot and vehicle patrol, self-defense education, and security escort services. There are lighted pathways/sidewalks, and high-traffic areas of the college are monitored by video camera.

Programs of Study: Baker confers B.B.A., B.B.L., and B.I.M. degrees. Associates degrees are also awarded. Bachelor's degrees are awarded in BUSINESS (accounting, business administration and management, marketing management, and office supervision and management), COMPUTER AND PHYSICAL SCIENCE (computer programming), ENGINEERING AND ENVIRONMENTAL DESIGN (aviation administration/management, drafting and design technology, electrical/electronics engineering technology, and interior design), HEALTH PROFESSIONS (health care administration and occupational therapy). Business administration and health information management have the largest enrollments.

Required: Degree requirements include completion of 180 to 208 quarter hours with a minimum GPA of 2.0. All students must complete math and computer courses and an employment course.

Special: Co-op programs, work study internships, and dual and interdisciplinary majors are available. An accelerated degree program is possible in business administration.

Faculty/Classroom: 46% of faculty are male; 54% are female. All teach undergraduates. No introductory courses are taught by graduate students.

Requirements: There are no entrance requirements to Baker College. Students without either a high school diploma or a GED may still be admitted on the basis of Baker College test results.

Procedure: Freshmen are admitted to all sessions. There is a rolling admissions plan. Application deadlines are open. Application fee is $20. Notification is sent on a rolling basis.

Transfer: 527 transfer students enrolled in a recent year. Transcripts from all previous colleges must be submitted. Grades of C or better are eligible for transfer credit. 48 of 180 credits required for the bachelor's degree must be completed at Baker.

Visiting: There are regularly scheduled orientations for prospective students, including orientation and testing. There are guides for informal visits and visitors may sit in on classes. To schedule a visit, students may contact the Admissions Office.

Financial Aid: In a recent year, 75% of continuing full-time students received some form of financial aid. 75% of continuing full-time students received need-based aid. The FAFSA and the college's own financial statement are required. Check with the school for current application deadlines.

Graduates: In a recent year, 227 bachelor's degrees were awarded. The most popular majors were business/marketing (63%), health (23%), and information science (6%).

Admissions Contact: Mark Heaton, Vice President of Admissions. E-Mail: *heaton_m@flint.baker.edu* Web: *www.baker.edu*

CALVIN COLLEGE D-4

Grand Rapids, MI 49546 (616) 526-6106
(800) 688-0122; (616) 526-6777

Full-time: 1715 men, 2099 women
Part-time: 73 men, 73 women
Graduate: 22 men, 53 women
Year: 4-1-4, summer session
Application Deadline: August 15
Faculty: 291
Ph.D.s: 85%
Student/Faculty: 12 to 1
Tuition: $28,250
Room & Board: $9335
Freshman Class: 4001 applied, 2792 accepted, 1006 enrolled
SAT CR/M: 575/595 **ACT:** 26 VERY COMPETITIVE+

Calvin College, established in 1876, is a private institution affiliated with the Christian Reformed Church, that offers undergraduate and graduate degrees in liberal arts and in some professional programs. Calvin is best known for the integration of intellect and Christian faith in every aspect of college learning, including athletics and the arts, campus life and community activities. There is 1 undergraduate school and 2 graduate schools. In addition to regional accreditation, Calvin has baccalaureate program accreditation with ABET, CSWE, NASM, and NCATE. The library contains 1.3 million volumes, 809,327 microform items, and 25,936 audio/video tapes/CDs/DVDs, and subscribes to 37,307 periodicals including electronic. Computerized library services include interlibrary loans, database searching, Internet access, and Wi-Fi capability. Special learning facilities include an art gallery, a TV studio, an ecosystem preserve, an interpretive center, an electron microscope lab, an observatory with a 16-inch telescope, a greenhouse, and an audiology and speech pathology clinic. The 390-acre campus is in a suburban area 7 miles southeast of downtown Grand Rapids. Including any residence halls, there are 40 buildings.

Student Life: 51% of undergraduates are from Michigan. Others are from 44 states, 52 foreign countries, and Canada. 45% are from public schools. 75% are White. 53% are Protestant. The average age of freshmen is 18; all undergraduates, 20. 13% do not continue beyond their first year; 73% remain to graduate.

Housing: 2400 students can be accommodated in college housing, which includes single-sex dorms, on-campus apartments, and off-campus apartments. In addition, there are language houses, special-interest houses, a residence hall wing with 3 living-learning floors that are focused on either honors living, environmentalism, or multicultural living. Also, there are 5 urban houses designated as residential living with a community/urban focus. On-campus housing is available on a lottery system for upperclassmen. 61% of students live on campus; of those, 90% remain on campus on weekends. Alcohol is not permitted. All students may keep cars.

Activities: There are no fraternities or sororities. There are 60 groups on campus, including art, band, chess, choir, chorale, chorus, computers, dance, drama, environmental, ethnic, film, honors, international, jazz band, literary magazine, musical theater, newspaper, orchestra, pep band, political, professional, radio and TV, religious, social, social service, student government, symphony, and yearbook. Popular campus events include Spring and Fall Music, Art Festivals and Dance Guild.

Sports: There are 9 intercollegiate sports for men and 10 for women, and 18 intramural sports for men and 14 for women. Facilities include a 5000-seat field house, a 10000-square-foot fitness center, a 40-foot climbing wall, an Olympic-size pool, an additional 3 full-size basketball courts, a dance studio, an indoor track and tennis center with a 200-meter track and 4 full-size tennis courts, a soccer facility, baseball and softball diamonds, an 8K cross-country course, an 8-lane, 400-meter polyurethane track, a weight-training/exercise room, a natatorium that contains a diving pool, 6 tennis courts, 2 sand beach volleyball courts, and a paved recreational trail around campus.

Disabled Students: 95% of the campus is accessible. Facilities include wheelchair ramps, elevators, special parking, specially equipped restrooms, special class scheduling, lowered drinking fountains, lowered telephones, special housing.

Services: Counseling and information services are available, as is tutoring in most subjects. There is a reader service for the blind, and remedial math, reading, and writing. There is a braille print service for the blind, books on tape, note taking, interpreting, diagnostic testing, special advising, and early registration.

Campus Safety and Security: Measures include 24-hour foot and vehicle patrol, emergency notification system, self-defense education, and security escort services. There are emergency telephones, lighted pathways/sidewalks, controlled access to dorms/residences, a crime alert bulletin, and reports in the school newspaper.

Programs of Study: Calvin confers B.A., B.S., B.A.S.P.A., B.C.S., B.F.A., B.M.E., B.S.A., B.S.E., B.S.N., B.S.P.A., B.S.R, and B.S.W. degrees. Master's degrees are also awarded. Bachelor's degrees are awarded in AGRICULTURE (environmental studies), BIOLOGICAL SCIENCE (biochemistry, biology/biological science, and biotechnology), BUSINESS (accounting, business administration and management, business communications, recreation and leisure services, and sports management), COMMUNICATIONS AND THE ARTS (art history, art, art history and appreciation, Chinese, classical languages, classics, communications, creative writing, digital communications, dramatic arts, Dutch, English, English literature, film arts, fine arts, French, German, graphic design, Greek, information technology, Japanese, language arts, Latin, linguistics, literature, media arts, music, music history and appreciation, music performance, music theory and composition, piano/organ, Spanish, strategic communication, theatre arts, video, voice, vocal music education, and writing), COMPUTER AND PHYSICAL SCIENCE (chemistry, computer programming, computer science, digital arts/technology, earth science, environmental geology, geology, information sciences and systems, mathematics, natural sciences, and physics), EDUCATION (art education, early childhood education, education, elementary education, English education, mathematics education, music education, physical education, science education, secondary education, and special education), ENGINEERING AND ENVIRONMENTAL DESIGN (chemical engineering, civil engineering, computer engineering, electrical/electronics engineering, engineering, environmental science, and mechanical engineering), HEALTH PROFESSIONS (exercise science, nursing, occupational therapy, predentistry, premedicine, preoptometry, prepharmacy, prephysical therapy, preveterinary science, public health, recreation therapy, and speech pathology/audiology), SOCIAL SCIENCE (area studies, Asian/Oriental studies, development economics, economics, geography, history, interdisciplinary studies, international relations, international studies, philosophy, political science/government, prelaw, psychology, public administration, religion, religious music, social work, sociology, theology, and theological studies). Biology, chemistry, physics, accounting, English, history and philosophy are the strongest academically. Education, business and engineering have the largest enrollmetns.

Required: Degree requirements include completion of 124 credit hours, with 28 credits in the major. All students must complete specific course work in English, religion, history, science, math, communication, fine arts, psychology or sociology, economics or political science, philosophy, kinesiology, research and information technology, foreign language, and cross-cultural engagement. A minimum GPA of 2.0 is required.

Special: Dual and student-designed majors are available, as well as a combined curriculum program in occupational therapy. Students may study off-campus in semester-long programs in China, Hungary, Britain, France, Ghana, Honduras, Peru, Spain, Washington, D.C. and New Mexico. In addition, Calvin's January Interim takes students to more than 30 countries. Cooperative programs include Los Angeles film studies, the Au Sable Institute, the Chicago program, Oregon extension, Latin American, Middle East, Chinese, and Russian studies, and in business. Internships, work-study programs, and cross-registration at Grand Valley State University in special education is also available. There are 6 national honor societies, a freshman honors program, and 25 departmental honors programs.

Faculty/Classroom: 57% of faculty are male; 43% are female. All teach undergraduates, all do research, and all teach and do research. No introductory courses are taught by graduate students. The average class size in an introductory lecture is 29; in a laboratory is 20; and in a regular course is 24.

Admissions: 70% of the 2013-2014 applicants were accepted. The SAT scores for the 2013-2014 freshman class were: Critical Reading--17% below 500, 40% between 500 and 599, 31% between 600 and 699, and 11% between 700 and 800; Math--16% below 500, 34% between 500 and 599, 37% between 600 and 699, and 13% between 700 and 800. The ACT scores were 9% below 21, 18% between 21 and 23, 25% between 24 and 26, 18% between 27 and 28, and 29% above 28. 47% of the current freshmen were in the top fifth of their class; 73% were in the top two fifths. There were 12 National Merit finalists. 30 freshmen graduated first in their class.

Requirements: The ACT is required. Selecting students for admission, Calvin College looks for evidence of Christian commitment and for the capacity and desire to learn. Students who are interested in the Christian perspective and curriculum of Calvin, and who show interest in its aims, are eligible for consideration. Although the prospect of academic success is of primary consideration, the aspirations of the applicant, the recommendation of a high school teacher, and the ability of Calvin to be of service, will also be considered. Of the students who apply each year, 75% are admitted. A GPA of 2.5 is required. AP and CLEP credits are accepted. Important factors in the admissions decision are recommendations by school officials, leadership record, and extracurricular activities record.

Procedure: Freshmen are admitted fall, spring, and summer. Entrance exams should be taken during the spring of the junior year or fall of the senior year. There are deferred admissions and rolling admissions plans. Applications should be filed by August 15 for fall entry; January 15 for spring entry, along with a $35 fee. Applications are accepted online.

Transfer: 101 transfer students enrolled in 2012-2013. Applicants from 4-year colleges are required to have a minimum GPA of 2.0; from 2-year colleges, 2.5. The SAT minimum requirements are 390 on the critical reading section and 420 on the math section. A minimum score of 20 is required on the ACT. 32 of 124 credits required for the bachelor's degree must be completed at Calvin.

Visiting: There are regularly scheduled orientations for prospective students and their families. There are guides for informal visits, and visitors may sit in on classes, and stay overnight. To schedule a visit, contact the Admissions Office.

Financial Aid: In 2013-2014, 98% of all full-time freshmen and 95% of continuing full-time students received some form of financial aid. 74% of all full-time freshmen and 64% of continuing full-time students received need-based aid. The average freshman award was $14,671. Need-based scholarships or need-based grants averaged $14,671 ($33,000 maximum); need-based self-help aid (loans and jobs) averaged $5,400 ($7,000 maximum); and other non-need-based awards and non-need-based scholarships averaged $5,000 ($18,000 maximum). 50% of undergraduate students work part-time. Average annual earnings from campus work are $2500. The average financial indebtedness of the 2013 graduate was $32,957. Calvin is a member of CSS. The FAFSA and the college's own financial statement are required. The priority date for freshman financial aid applications for fall entry is February 15. The deadline for filing freshman financial aid applications for fall entry is August 1.

International Students: There are 384 international students enrolled. The school actively recruits these students. They must take the TOEFL with a minimum score of 550 on the paper-based TOEFL (PBT) or 80 on the Internet-based version (iBT), or take the MELAB if they scored low on the TOEFL. They must also take the SAT or ACT, scoring 20. Exceptions are made for strong students without access to standardized exams.

Graduates: From July 1, 2012 to June 30, 2013, 798 bachelor's degrees were awarded. The most popular majors were business administration and general management(8%), engineering, (7%), and registered nursing (7%). 106 companies recruited on campus in 2012-2013. In an average class, 1% graduate in 3 years or less, 57% graduate in 4 years or less, 71% graduate in 5 years or less, and 73% graduate in 6 years or less. Of the 2012 graduating class, 26% were enrolled in graduate school within 6 months of graduation, and 71% were employed.

Admissions Contact: Ben Arendt, Director of Admissions. E-Mail: *admissions@calvin.edu* Web: *www.calvin.edu*

CENTRAL MICHIGAN UNIVERSITY — D-4

Mount Pleasant, MI 48859 — **(989) 774-3076**
(888) 292-5366; (989) 774-7267

Full-time: 8200 men, 10600 women	**Faculty:** n/av; I, --$
Part-time: 968 men, 1359 women	**Ph.D.s:** 81%
Graduate: 2349 men, 4317 women	**Student/Faculty:** n/av
Year: semesters, summer session	**Tuition:** $25,748
Application Deadline: open	**Room & Board:** $8,500
Freshman Class: n/av	

COMPETITIVE

Central Michigan University, founded in 1892, is a public university offering programs in liberal arts, business, and health, education, and human services. The figures in the above capsule and in this profile are approximate. There are 8 undergraduate schools and 1 graduate school. In addition to regional accreditation, CMU has baccalaureate program accreditation with AACSB, ACCE, ACEJMC, NASM, NCATE, and NRPA. The library contains 101,277 volumes, 1.3 million microform items, and 28,008 audio/video tapes/CDs/DVDs, and subscribes to 3,330 periodicals including electronic. Computerized library services include interlibrary loans, database searching, and Internet access. Special learning facilities include a learning resource center, art gallery, natural history museum, radio station, TV station, Museum of Cultural and Natural History, Clarke Historical Library, Gerald L. Poor School Museum, Brooks Astronomical Observatory, leadership institute, and a multicultural education center. The 854-acre campus is in a small town 70 miles north of Lansing, MI. Including any residence halls, there are 56 buildings.

Student Life: 97% of undergraduates are from Michigan. Students are from 48 states, 72 foreign countries, and Canada. 89% are from public schools. 74% are white; 11% African American. The average age of freshmen is 18; all undergraduates, 21. 24% do not continue beyond their first year; 60% remain to graduate.

Housing: 7529 students can be accommodated in college housing, which includes single-sex and coed dorms, on-campus apartments, and married student housing. In addition, there are honors houses, residential colleges for business, education, and human services, health professions, science and technology, and music. On-campus housing is guaranteed for all 4 years. 67% of students commute. Alcohol is not permitted. All students may keep cars.

Activities: 5% of men belong to 14 national fraternities; 7% of women belong to 14 national sororities. There are 286 groups on campus, including art, band, cheerleading, choir, chorus, computers, dance, drama, environmental, ethnic, forensics, gay, honors, international, jazz band, literary magazine, marching band, musical theater, orchestra, pep band, photography, political, professional, religious, social, social service, student government, and symphony. Popular campus events include Homecoming, Michigan Story Festival, and Native American Pow Wow.

Sports: There are 6 intercollegiate sports for men and 8 for women, and 21 intramural sports for men and 21 for women. Facilities include a football stadium, softball fields, field hockey complex, indoor athletic complex, indoor and outdoor track, soccer field, baseball stadium, arena, and student activity center.

Disabled Students: 95% of the campus is accessible. Facilities include wheelchair ramps, elevators, special parking, specially equipped restrooms, special class scheduling, lowered drinking fountains, lowered telephones, special housing, and a student disability services office.

Services: Counseling and information services are available, as is tutoring in most subjects. There is a reader service for the blind, and remedial math, reading, and writing.

Campus Safety and Security: Measures include emergency notification system and security escort services. There are shuttle buses, emergency telephones, lighted pathways/sidewalks, and blue light phone system.

Programs of Study: CMU confers B.A., B.S., B.A.A., B.F.A., B.Indiv.S., B.Mus., B.S.B.A., B.S.E., and B.S.E.T. degrees. Master's and doctoral degrees are also awarded. Bachelor's degrees are awarded in AGRICULTURE (environmental studies and natural resource management), BIOLOGICAL SCIENCE (biochemistry, biology/biological science, and neurosciences), BUSINESS (accounting, banking and finance, business administration and management, entrepreneurial studies, hospitality management services, human resources, international business management, logistics, management information systems, management science, marketing and distribution, marketing management, marketing/retailing/merchandising, purchasing/inventory management, real estate, recreational facilities management, and retailing), COMMUNICATIONS AND THE ARTS (apparel design, art, broadcasting, communications, design, dramatic arts, English, French, German, graphic design, journalism, language arts, music, music history and appreciation, music performance, music theory and composition, musical theater, photography, piano/organ, public relations, Spanish, speech/debate/rhetoric, theater design, visual and performing arts, and voice), COMPUTER AND PHYSICAL SCIENCE (actuarial science, chemistry, computer science, earth science, geology, information sciences and systems, mathematics, oceanography, physical sciences, physics, science, and statistics), EDUCATION (athletic training, business education, education, elementary education, foreign languages education, music education, and physical education), ENGINEERING AND ENVIRONMENTAL DESIGN (computer technology, electrical/electronics engineering, engineering technology, environmental science, industrial administration/management, interior design, manufacturing technology, mechanical engineering, and mechanical engineering technology), HEALTH PROFESSIONS (biomedical science, health, health care administration, public health, recreation therapy, rehabilitation therapy, speech pathology/audiology, and sports medicine), SOCIAL SCIENCE (anthropology, child psychology/development, cognitive science, community services, criminal justice, dietetics, early childhood studies, economics, European studies, family/consumer studies, food production/management/services, geography, history, interdisciplinary studies, law, parks and recreation management, philosophy, psychology, religion, social science, social studies, social work, sociology, and women's studies). Psychology, marketing, and accounting have the largest enrollments.

Required: Students must complete 124 credit hours, including 30 in the major, with a GPA of 2.0. They must fulfill the requirements in the University Program (27-30 semester hours of coursework in humanities, natural science, and social science, an integrative and area studies), and fulfill University competency requirements in written English (Freshmen and Advanced Composition), oral English, and math.

Special: CMU offers internships in business administration, study abroad in 43 countries, and dual majors in chemistry/physics and computer science/math. Student-designed majors are available for a bachelor of individualized studies, and there is credit for life, military, and work experience. Students may take up to 25 hours for pass/fail grades. CMU off-campus programs offers external degree programs in which students can get degrees without attending classes on campus. There are 13 national honor societies, a freshman honors program, and 21 departmental honors programs.

Faculty/Classroom: 56% of faculty are male; 44% are female. All teach undergraduates. Graduate students teach 2% of introductory courses. The average class size in an introductory lecture is 39 and in a laboratory is 22.

Requirements: The ACT is required. Applicants must be high school graduates or hold a GED. The university strongly recommends 4 years each of English and math, 3 each of science and social studies, and 2 of foreign language, as well as 1 course each in computer science and fine arts. AP and CLEP credits are accepted.

Procedure: Freshmen are admitted to all sessions. Entrance exams should be taken during the junior or senior year of high school. There are deferred admissions and rolling admissions plans. Application deadlines are open. Check with the school for the current application fee. Applications are accepted online. A waiting list is maintained.

Transfer: 1160 transfer students enrolled in a recent year. Transfer students must have a GPA of 2.0. 30 of 124 credits required for the bachelor's degree must be completed at CMU.

Visiting: There are guides for informal visits, visitors may sit in on classes, and stay overnight. To schedule a visit, contact Admissions.

Financial Aid: In a recent year, 68% of all full-time freshmen and 63% of continuing full time students received some form of financial aid. 49% of all full-time freshmen and 43% of continuing full-time students received need-based aid. 25% of undergraduate students worked part-time. Average annual earnings from campus work are $3500. Check with the school for current application deadlines.

International Students: There were 433 international students enrolled in a recent year. The school actively recruits these students. They must take the TOEFL with a minimum score of 550 on the paper-based TOEFL (PBT) or 79 on the Internet-based version (iBT).

Graduates: In a recent year, 3571 bachelor's degrees were awarded. The most popular majors were business/marketing (26%), education (17%), and parks and recreation (8%). In an average class, 1% graduate in 3 years or less, 18% graduate in 4 years or less, 45% graduate in 5 years or less, and 57% graduate in 6 years or less. 15% were enrolled in graduate school within 6 months of graduation, and 80% were employed.

Admissions Contact: Betty Wagner, Director of Admissions. E-Mail: *cmuadmit@cmich.edu* Web: *www.cmich.edu*

CLEARY UNIVERSITY — E-5

Ann Arbor, MI 48105 — **(517) 548-3670; (517) 548-2170**

Full-time: 210 men, 210 women	**Faculty:** n/av; III, --$
Part-time: 105 men, 210 women	**Ph.D.s:** 12%
Graduate: n/av	**Student/Faculty:** n/av
Year: trimesters, summer session	**Tuition:** $12,340
Application Deadline: open	**Room & Board:** n/av
Freshman Class: n/av	
ACT: recommended	

COMPETITIVE

Cleary College, founded in 1883, is a private institution that offers bachelor and associate degrees in business. The figures in the above capsule and in this profile are approximate. The college serves an entirely commuter student body. A second campus, similar in size and programs, is located in Howell, and there are extension sites throughout southeastern Michigan. The library contains 7,877 volumes, 175 audio/video tapes/CDs/DVDs, and subscribes to 30 periodicals including electronic. Computerized library services include interlibrary loans and database searching. Special learning facilities include a learning resource center. The 27-acre campus is in a suburban area 25 miles east of Lansing and 40 miles west of Detroit. Including any residence halls, there is one building.

Student Life: 99% of undergraduates are from Michigan. Students are from 2 states, 1 foreign country, and Canada. 90% are from public schools. 91% are white. The average age of all undergraduates is 36.

Housing: There are no residence halls. All students commute.

Activities: There are no fraternities or sororities. Popular campus events include picnics.

Sports: There is no sports program at Cleary.

Disabled Students: All of the campus is accessible. Facilities include wheelchair ramps, special parking, specially equipped rest rooms, lowered drinking fountains, and lowered telephones.

Services: Counseling and information services are available, as is tutoring in some subjects, English, math, and computers. There is remedial math and writing.

Campus Safety and Security: There are lighted pathways/sidewalks.

Programs of Study: Cleary confers B.B.A. degrees. Associates degrees are also awarded. Bachelor's degrees are awarded in BUSINESS (accounting, banking and finance, business administration and management, human resources, and marketing management), COMPUTER AND PHYSICAL SCIENCE (information sciences and systems), HEALTH PROFESSIONS (health care administration). Accounting is the strongest academically. Business administration has the largest enrollment.

Required: Core requirements include 90 quarter credits of business courses in economics, management, basic accounting, communication, and ethics. To graduate, students must complete a senior project and at least 180 quarter credit hours with a minimum GPA of 2.5

Special: Cleary offers internships, work study, and co-op programs in all majors, accelerated degree programs in accounting, marketing, finance, management information technology, quality management, human resource management, health services management, corporate and public accounting, and business management. Cleary also offers credit for prior learning experiences and opportunities for individualized study. Nondegree study is possible.

Faculty/Classroom: 45% of faculty are male; 55% are female. All teach

undergraduates. No introductory courses are taught by graduate students. The average class size in an introductory lecture is 15; in a laboratory is 12; and in a regular course is 12.

Requirements: The ACT is recommended. Applicants must be graduates of an accredited secondary school or have earned a GED and have a minimum GPA of 2.5. A GPA of 2.5 is required. AP and CLEP credits are accepted.

Procedure: Freshmen are admitted to all sessions. There are early decision, early admissions, deferred admissions, and rolling admissions plans. Application deadlines are open. Notification is sent on a rolling basis.

Transfer: Applicants must submit official transcripts from all institutions previously attended and have a minimum GPA of 2.5. 45 of 180 credits required for the bachelor's degree must be completed at Cleary.

Visiting: There are regularly scheduled orientations for prospective students. There are guides for informal visits and visitors may sit in on classes. To schedule a visit, contact Admissions.

Financial Aid: Cleary is a member of CSS. The FAFSA is required. Check with the school for current application deadlines.

International Students: They must take the TOEFL or MELAB.

Admissions Contact: Carrie Bonofiglio, Director of Admissions. Web: *www.cleary.edu*

COLLEGE FOR CREATIVE STUDIES E-5

Detroit, MI 48202 (313) 664-7425
(800) 952-ARTS; (313) 872-2739

Full-time: 568 men, 514 women	**Faculty:** 51
Part-time: 133 men, 148 women	**Ph.D.s:** 76%
Graduate: 38 men, 22 women	**Student/Faculty:** 11 to 1
Year: semesters, summer session	**Tuition:** $37,090
Application Deadline: August 1	**Room & Board:** $8250
Freshman Class: 1284 applied, 624 accepted, 242 enrolled	
SAT: required **ACT:** 22	**SPECIAL**

The College for Creative Studies, established in 1906, is a private, independent institution offering comprehensive 4-year B.F.A programs in animation and digital media, crafts, fine arts, communication design, industrial design, interior design, and photography, as well as teacher certification in art education. In addition to regional accreditation, CCS has baccalaureate program accreditation with NASAD. The library contains 21,000 volumes, and subscribes to 100 periodicals including electronic. Special learning facilities include an art gallery. The 11-acre campus is in an urban area 3 miles from downtown Detroit. Including any residence halls, there are 6 buildings.

Student Life: 83% of undergraduates are from Michigan. Others are from 35 states, 18 foreign countries, and Canada. 71% are White. The average age of freshmen is 22; all undergraduates, 22. 27% do not continue beyond their first year; 56% remain to graduate.

Housing: 263 students can be accommodated in college housing, which includes coed dorms. Coed dorms. On-campus housing is available on a first-come and first-served basis. Priority is given to out-of-town students. 72% of students commute. Alcohol is not permitted. All students may keep cars.

Activities: There are no fraternities or sororities. There are 6 groups on campus, including ethnic, professional, and student government. Popular campus events include Student Exhibition, Noel Night, and Detroit Festival of the Arts.

Sports: There is no sports program at CCS.

Disabled Students: All of the campus is accessible. Facilities include wheelchair ramps, elevators, special parking, specially equipped restrooms, and lowered telephones.

Services: Counseling and information services are available, as is tutoring in every subject. There is remedial reading and writing.

Campus Safety and Security: Measures include 24-hour foot and vehicle patrol and security escort services. There are lighted pathways/sidewalks.

Programs of Study: CCS confers B.F.A degrees. Bachelor's degrees are awarded in COMMUNICATIONS AND THE ARTS (advertising, animation, ceramic art and design, fine arts, glass, graphic design, illustration, industrial design, metal/jewelry, painting, photography, printmaking, and sculpture), COMPUTER AND PHYSICAL SCIENCE (digital arts/technology), EDUCATION (art education), ENGINEERING AND ENVIRONMENTAL DESIGN (interior design), SOCIAL SCIENCE (textiles and clothing). Industrial design and communication design are the strongest academically. Animation and digital media have the largest enrollments.

Required: Degree requirements include work in English, computer literacy, sciences, behavioral science, art, history, speech, philosophy, and art and design. Students must complete 42 credits in liberal arts. A minimum GPA of 2.0 is required, and students must complete 126 credits with 63 in the major, to graduate.

Special: Internships are available within the student's departmental major. Credit for internships and dual majors are available. Study abroad is possible.

Faculty/Classroom: 60% of faculty are male; 40% are female. All teach undergraduates. No introductory courses are taught by graduate students. The average class size in an introductory lecture is 20; in a laboratory is 15; and in a regular course is 18.

Admissions: 49% of the 2013-2014 applicants were accepted.

Requirements: The SAT or ACT is required. Applicants must graduate from an accredited secondary school or earn a GED. A portfolio of representative work and an essay are required. A general college preparatory program is recommended. A GPA of 2.5 is required. AP and CLEP credits are accepted. Important factors in the admissions decision are advanced placement or honors courses and evidence of special talent.

Procedure: Freshmen are admitted fall and winter. There are deferred admissions and rolling admissions plans. Applications should be filed by August 1 for fall entry, along with a $35 fee. Notifications are sent September 15. Applications are accepted online.

Transfer: 148 transfer students enrolled in 2012-2013. Transfer applicants should submit a portfolio that includes artwork done at the previous college. Transcripts and portfolio review will determine how many credits may transfer. The approval of the chairperson of the department to which the student is applying is required for transfer of studio credit. High school and college transcripts are required. 33 of 126 credits required for the bachelor's degree must be completed at CCS.

Visiting: There are regularly scheduled orientations for prospective students, including an introduction to the college by an admission professional, a digital presentation of student work, application/financial aid information, and a campus tour. The orientations are scheduled every other week from September through April. There are guides for informal visits and visitors may sit in on classes. To schedule a visit, contact the Admission Office.

Financial Aid: The average financial indebtedness of the 2013 graduate was $54,000. The FAFSA is required. The priority date for freshman financial aid applications for fall entry is July 1.

International Students: The school actively recruits these students. They must take the TOEFL. They must also take the SAT or ACT.

Graduates: From July 1, 2012 to June 30, 2013, 248 bachelor's degrees were awarded. The most popular majors were visual and performing arts (100%). 35 companies recruited on campus in 2012-2013.

Admissions Contact: Admissions Officer E-Mail: *admissions@collegeforcreativestudies.edu* Web: *www.collegeforcreativestudies.edu*

CONCORDIA UNIVERSITY, ANN ARBOR E-5

Ann Arbor, MI 48105 (734) 995-7311
(800) 253-0680; (734) 995-4610

Full-time: 200 men, 245 women	**Faculty:** 39
Part-time: 60 men, 45 women	**Ph.D.s:** 60%
Graduate: 160 men, 405 women	**Student/Faculty:** n/av
Year: semesters, summer session	**Tuition:** $22,100
Application Deadline: open	**Room & Board:** $8478
Freshman Class: n/av	
SAT or ACT: required	**VERY COMPETITIVE**

Concordia University, established in 1963, is a private institution affiliated with the Missouri Synod of the Lutheran Church, offering undergraduate and graduate degrees in the arts and sciences, business, education, and human services. The figures in the above capsule and in this profile are approximate. There are 4 undergraduate schools and 2 graduate schools. In addition to regional accreditation, Concordia has baccalaureate program accreditation with NCATE. The library contains 117,000 volumes, 300,000 microform items, 1,400 audio/video tapes/CDs/DVDs, and subscribes to 660 periodicals including electronic. Computerized library services include interlibrary loans, database searching, Internet access, and laptop Internet portals. Special learning facilities include a learning resource center and an art gallery. The 187-acre campus is in a suburban area 40 miles west of Detroit. Including any residence halls, there are 30 buildings.

Student Life: 83% of undergraduates are from Michigan. Students are from 20 states, 6 foreign countries, and Canada. 85% are white. 30% are Protestant. The average age of freshmen is 18; all undergraduates, 23. 31% do not continue beyond their first year; 47% remain to graduate.

Housing: 436 students can be accommodated in college housing, which includes single-sex dorms and married student housing. On-campus housing is guaranteed for all 4 years. 57% of students live on campus; of those, 60% remain on campus on weekends. Alcohol is not permitted. All students may keep cars.

Activities: There are no fraternities or sororities. There are 21 groups on campus, including band, choir, chorale, communications, computers, dance, debate, drama, ethnic, jazz band, musical theater newspaper, pep band, religious, social, social service, student government, and yearbook. Popular campus events include Boar's Head Festival, Servant Events, and a fall carnival.

Sports: There are 5 intercollegiate sports for men and 5 for women, and

10 intramural sports for men and 10 for women. Facilities include a soccer field, baseball and softball diamonds, sand volleyball courts, a phys ed building (gym), and an open field for intramurals.

Disabled Students: 90% of the campus is accessible. Facilities include wheelchair ramps, elevators, special parking, specially equipped rest rooms, and lowered drinking fountains.

Services: Counseling and information services are available, as is tutoring in every subject. There is remedial math. There is also a writing lab with consultants.

Campus Safety and Security: Measures include 24-hour foot and vehicle patrol and security escort services. There are lighted pathways/sidewalks and controlled access to dorms/residences.

Programs of Study: Concordia confers B.A. degrees. Associates and master's degrees are also awarded. Bachelor's degrees are awarded in BIOLOGICAL SCIENCE (biology/biological science), BUSINESS (business administration and management and hospitality management services), COMMUNICATIONS AND THE ARTS (art, communications, dramatic arts, English, Greek, journalism, language arts, music, and Spanish), COMPUTER AND PHYSICAL SCIENCE (chemistry, mathematics, physical sciences, physics, and science), EDUCATION (early childhood education, elementary education, health education, physical education, and secondary education), ENGINEERING AND ENVIRONMENTAL DESIGN (preengineering), HEALTH PROFESSIONS (predentistry and premedicine), SOCIAL SCIENCE (biblical languages, criminal justice, family/consumer studies, history, philosophy, psychology, religion, religious music, safety management, social studies, and sociology). Education, business, and family life are the strongest academically. Business administration, teacher education, and English have the largest enrollments.

Required: Degree requirements include completion of 128 credit hours, with at least 30 in the major, up to 49 credit hours of general studies, and a minimum GPA of 2.0. The student must also demonstrate proficiency in foreign language, writing, speech, and math. Required courses include upper-level general studies, writing-intensive courses, a freshman seminar, physical activities, computer applications, religion, humanities, social science, language/communication, and science. A senior project is required. Education students must take the Michigan Test for Teacher Certification.

Special: Internships are available in most academic majors. Cross-registration is available with Eastern Michigan and Kettering Universities, Schoolcraft College, Henry Ford Community College, Michigan State Police Training Division, and Michigan Academy of Emergency Services. Students may study abroad in 6 countries. Accelerated degree programs are available in business administration, criminal justice administration, communication, hospitality management, and public safety. The college confers credit for life, military, and work experience through the School of Adult and Continuing Education. Nondegree study, dual majors in many combinations, student-designed majors, a 3-2 engineering degree with Kettering University, and a pass/fail grading option are available.

Faculty/Classroom: 47% of faculty are male; 53% are female. All teach undergraduates. No introductory courses are taught by graduate students. The average class size in an introductory lecture is 24; in a laboratory is 12; and in a regular course is 11.

Requirements: The SAT or ACT is required. However, the ACT is preferred. Applicants must graduate from an accredited secondary school or have the GED. 20 Carnegie units are recommended, including 4 units in English, 3 in math, and 2 each in science, social studies, and foreign language. AP and CLEP credits are accepted. Important factors in the admissions decision are leadership record, advanced placement or honors courses, and evidence of special talent.

Procedure: Freshmen are admitted fall and spring. There are deferred admissions and rolling admissions plans. Application deadlines are open. Check with the school for the current application fee. Notification is sent on a rolling basis. Applications are accepted online.

Transfer: 91 transfer students enrolled in a recent year. A GPA of 2.0 is required for transfer students; a GPA of 2.5 is required for admittance to the teacher education program. Transfer students who have earned 12 or more credits are not required to take the ACT. Interviews are recommended. 30 of 128 credits required for the bachelor's degree must be completed at Concordia.

Visiting: There are regularly scheduled orientations for prospective students, including several preview days, Senior Day, Junior Day, Art Day, Music Day, and Theater Day. Individual tours are arranged by appointment. There are guides for informal visits, visitors may sit in on classes, and stay overnight. To schedule a visit, contact the Admissions Office.

Financial Aid: In a recent year, all full-time freshmen and all of continuing full-time students received some form of financial aid. 65% of all full-time freshmen and 69% of continuing full-time students received need-based aid. The average freshmen award was $18,392, with $5,047 ($13,505 maximum) from need-based scholarships or need-based grants; $7,766 ($9,000 maximum) from need-based self-help aid (loans and jobs); $8,274 ($17,500 maximum) from non-need-based athletic scholarships; and $6,500 ($19,700 maximum) from other non-need-based awards and non-need-based scholarships. 42% of undergraduate students worked part-time. Average annual earnings from campus work are $1781. The average financial indebtedness of the recent graduate was $25,000. Check with the school for current application deadlines.

International Students: There were 7 international students enrolled in a recent year. They must take the TOEFL with a minimum score of 520 on the paper-based TOEFL (PBT) or 68 on the Internet-based version (iBT) or take the MELAB. They must also take the SAT or ACT.

Graduates: In a recent year, 112 bachelor's degrees were awarded. The most popular majors were teacher education (21%), business (21%), and criminal justice (10%). In an average class, 1% graduate in 3 years or less, 19% graduate in 4 years or less, 35% graduate in 5 years or less, and 37% graduate in 6 years or less.

Admissions Contact: Amy Becher, Executive Director of Enrollment Services. A campus DVD is available. E-Mail: *bechea@cuaa.edu* Web: *www.cuaa.edu*

CORNERSTONE UNIVERSITY AND GRAND RAPIDS THEOLOGICAL SEMINARY — D-4

Grand Rapids, MI 49525 — **(616) 222-1426**
(800) 787-9778; (616) 222-1418

Full-time: 684 men, 1017 women	**Faculty:** 55
Part-time: 191 men, 286 women	**Ph.D.s:** 40%
Graduate: 304 men, 316 women	**Student/Faculty:** 21 to 1
Year: semesters, summer session	**Tuition:** $23,260
Application Deadline:	**Room & Board:** $7606
Freshman Class: 2021 applied, 1438 accepted, 372 enrolled	
SAT: required	**ACT:** 23 — **COMPETITIVE**

Cornerstone University and Grand Rapids Theological Seminary, founded in 1941, is a private liberal arts college and graduate seminary educating students from a Christian perspective. Major undergraduate programs include business, media studies, teacher education and religion. There are 3 undergraduate schools and 2 graduate schools. In addition to regional accreditation, Cornerstone University has baccalaureate program accreditation with CSWE and NASM. The library contains 375,000 volumes, 276,107 microform items, and 5,226 audio/video tapes/CDs/DVDs, and subscribes to 39,500 periodicals including electronic. Computerized library services include interlibrary loans, database searching, Internet access, and Wi-Fi capability. Special learning facilities include a radio station, The Center for Excellence in Teaching and Learning, and The Cornerstone University Learning Center. The 132-acre campus is in a suburban area on the northeast side of Grand Rapids, MI. Including any residence halls, there are 35 buildings.

Student Life: 85% of undergraduates are from Michigan. Others are from 34 states, 10 foreign countries, and Canada. 62% are from public schools. 84% are White. 66% are Protestant. The average age of freshmen is 18; all undergraduates, 24. 22% do not continue beyond their first year; 47% remain to graduate.

Housing: 880 students can be accommodated in college housing, which includes single-sex dorms, on-campus apartments, and married student housing. In addition, there are honors houses. On-campus housing is guaranteed for the freshman year only, is available on a first-come, and first-served basis. Priority is given to out-of-town students. 65% of students live on campus; of those, 50% remain on campus on weekends. Alcohol is not permitted. All students may keep cars.

Activities: There are no fraternities or sororities. There are 22 groups on campus, including band, cheerleading, choir, chorale, chorus, dance, drama, environmental, ethnic, film, honors, international, jazz band, musical theater, newspaper, orchestra, pep band, photography, political, professional, radio and TV, religious, social, social service, student government, and symphony. Popular campus events include Sibling Weekends, Friends Weekend and Variety Show.

Sports: There are 5 intercollegiate sports for men and 5 for women, and 4 intramural sports for men and 4 for women. Facilities include a 2,700-seat basketball/volleyball arena, a field house servicing tennis, volleyball, basketball, soccer, and softball, a baseball diamond, 2 soccer fields/intramural fields, a softball field, a sand volleyball court, a fitness center, human performance labs, 6 locker rooms, a training room, and racquetball courts.

Disabled Students: All of the campus is accessible. Facilities include wheelchair ramps, elevators, special parking, specially equipped restrooms, special class scheduling, special housing, large computer monitors for the visually impaired, and soundproof rooms for using tape recorders that read books-on-tape.

Services: Counseling and information services are available, as is tutoring in every subject, There is a Learning Center with a computer lab and special adaptive software that specialize in writing and math, tutoring by appointment in the residence halls, test-taking assistance, and readers and typists as needed. There is a reader service for the blind, and remedial math and writing.

Campus Safety and Security: Measures include 24-hour foot and vehicle patrol, emergency notification system, self-defense education, and

security escort services. There are emergency telephones, lighted pathways/sidewalks, and controlled access to dorms/residences.

Programs of Study: Cornerstone University confers B.A., B.Mus., B.S. and A.A. degrees. Associate and master's degrees are also awarded. Bachelor's degrees are awarded in BIOLOGICAL SCIENCE (biology/biological science), BUSINESS (accounting, business administration and management, international business management, international economics, marketing/retailing/merchandising, and sports management), COMMUNICATIONS AND THE ARTS (advertising, applied music, audio technology, communications, English, English Writing, fine arts, graphic design, literature, media arts, music, music performance, musical theater, speech/debate/rhetoric, and video), COMPUTER AND PHYSICAL SCIENCE (chemistry), EDUCATION (education, elementary education, English education, middle school education, music education, physical education, science education, and secondary education), HEALTH PROFESSIONS (exercise science, Pre-Health Studies, predentistry, premedicine, and preveterinary science), SOCIAL SCIENCE (biblical studies, Christian studies, family/consumer studies, history, humanities, interdisciplinary studies, liberal arts/general studies, philosophy, psychology, religion, religious education, social work, and youth ministry). English, music and education are the strongest academically. Education, business and youth ministry have the largest enrollments.

Required: To graduate, students must complete 120 to 129 credit hours depending on the degree, including 46 in the liberal arts core. The number of hours in the major varies. The student must have an overall GPA of 2.0, 2.5 in the major, 2.0 in the minor, and pass a comprehensive exam in his or her field.

Special: All students choose a student-ministries assignment each semester. Cornerstone requires internships in many areas of study. Study abroad programs, accelerated degrees in organizational leadership, management, business administration, ministry leadership, and education, and a Washington semester are available. There are 3 national honor societies, including Phi Beta Kappa, and a freshman honors program.

Faculty/Classroom: 67% of faculty are male; 33% are female. All teach undergraduates, 50% do research, and 50% do both. No introductory courses are taught by graduate students. The average class size in an introductory lecture is 60; in a laboratory is 24; and in a regular course is 21.

Admissions: 71% of the 2013-2014 applicants were accepted. The ACT scores were 29% below 21, 23% between 21 and 23, 20% between 24 and 26, 17% between 27 and 28, and 7% above 28. 34% of the current freshmen were in the top fifth of their class; 56% were in the top two fifths. 17 freshmen graduated first in their class.

Requirements: The SAT or ACT is required. The ACT Optional Writing test is also required. The college requires a high school transcript or GED certificate, and recommends 15 Carnegie units, including 4 years of English, 3 each of math and social sciences, 2 of science, as well as 10 semesters of electives. The college recommends that the student appear for an interview and requires auditions for music scholarships. A pastoral reference is required. A GPA of 2.5 is required. AP and CLEP credits are accepted. Important factors in the admissions decision are personality/intangible qualities, extracurricular activities record, and leadership record.

Procedure: Freshmen are admitted to all sessions. Entrance exams should be taken during the junior or senior year. There are deferred admissions and rolling admissions plans. Application deadlines are open. Application fee is $25. Applications are accepted online.

Transfer: 64 transfer students enrolled in 2012-2013. The college requires high school and college transcripts from students, as well as a pastor's reference. The applicant must have taken the ACT if under 25 years of age with fewer than 30 hours of college credit. 32 of 120 credits required for the bachelor's degree must be completed at Cornerstone University.

Visiting: There are regularly scheduled orientations for prospective students, including admissions and financial aid presentations, class visits, and course preregistration. There are guides for informal visits, visitors may sit in on classes, and stay overnight. To schedule a visit, contact the Admissions Office.

Financial Aid: In 2013-2014, 98% of all full-time freshmen and 97% of continuing full-time students received some form of financial aid. 78% of all full-time freshmen and 76% of continuing full-time students received need-based aid. 34% of undergraduate students work part-time. Average annual earnings from campus work are $1011. The average financial indebtedness of the 2013 graduate was $32,071. The FAFSA is required. The priority date for freshman financial aid applications for fall entry is March 1.

International Students: There are 32 international students enrolled. The school actively recruits these students. They must take the TOEFL with a minimum score of 500 on the paper-based TOEFL (PBT) or 61 on the Internet-based version (iBT). They must also take the SAT or ACT, scoring 900.

Graduates: From July 1, 2012 to June 30, 2013, 359 bachelor's degrees were awarded. The most popular majors were business (49%), education (12%), and theology (12%). 30 companies recruited on campus in 2012-2013. In an average class, 1% graduate in 3 years or less, 26% graduate in 4 years or less, 35% graduate in 5 years or less, and 39% graduate in 6 years or less. Of the 2012 graduating class, 8% were enrolled in graduate school within 6 months of graduation, and 91% were employed.

Admissions Contact: Lisa Link, Director of Admissions. E-Mail: *admissions@cornerstone.edu* Web: *www.cornerstone.edu*

DAVENPORT UNIVERSITY D-4

Grand Rapids, MI 49512 (616) 698-7111
(866) 925-3884; (616) 698-0333

Full-time: 1261 men, 1164 women
Part-time: 2056 men, 4401 women
Graduate: 1015 men, 1407 women
Year: semesters, summer session
Application Deadline:
Faculty: 155; IIB, -$
Ph.D.s: 26%
Student/Faculty: 17 to 1
Tuition: $12,922 ($12,933)
Room & Board: $8080
Freshman Class: 1440 applied, 1344 accepted, 700 enrolled
SAT or ACT: recommended

LESS COMPETITIVE

Davenport University, founded in 1866, is a private university specializing in business, technology and health professions. The university serves students through its main campus in Caledonia Township (Grand Rapids), other locations in Michigan and online and offers graduate and undergraduate degrees. There are 4 undergraduate schools and 3 graduate schools. In addition to regional accreditation, Davenport has baccalaureate program accreditation with NLN. The library contains 79,243 volumes, and 5,371 audio/video tapes/CDs/DVDs. Computerized library services include interlibrary loans, database searching, and Internet access. The 60-acre campus is in a suburban area in Grand Rapids. Including any residence halls, there are 6 buildings.

Student Life: 92% of undergraduates are from Michigan. Others are from 50 states, 32 foreign countries, and Canada. 67% are White; 23% African American. The average age of freshmen is 22; all undergraduates, 30.

Housing: 500 students can be accommodated in college housing, which includes coed dorms and on-campus apartments. On-campus housing is available on a first-come and first-served basis. 96% of students commute. Alcohol is not permitted. All students may keep cars.

Activities: There are no fraternities or sororities. There are 31 groups on campus, including cheerleading, computers, ethnic, international, literary magazine, newspaper, professional, social, social service, and student government. Popular campus events include Panther Prowl, Alternative Spring Break, Homecoming, Family Weekend, PantherPalooza, Panther Pack, Constitution Day, Fall Crawl, Sibs & Kids Weekend, Spring Fling, March Madness and Green Week and DU Days of Service.

Sports: There are 13 intercollegiate sports for men and 13 for women. Facilities include A 87,000-square-foot student recreation center and field, which includes an auxiliary gym, climbing tower, running track, table games, lounge areas, weight room and cafe. A new sports complex includes a 300 seat baseball stadium, 200 seat softball stadium, 8 tennis courts, locker room and pressbox building.

Disabled Students: All of the campus is accessible. Facilities include wheelchair ramps, elevators, special parking, specially equipped restrooms, special class scheduling, lowered drinking fountains, and lowered telephones.

Services: Counseling and information services are available, as is tutoring in most subjects. There is remedial math, reading, and writing.

Campus Safety and Security: Measures include 24-hour foot and vehicle patrol, emergency notification system, and security escort services. There are emergency telephones and lighted pathways/sidewalks.

Programs of Study: Davenport confers B.S., B.A.S. and B.B.A. degrees. Associate and master's degrees are also awarded. Bachelor's degrees are awarded in BUSINESS (accounting, banking and finance, business administration and management, electronic business, entrepreneurial studies, human resources, international business management, management science, and marketing management), COMMUNICATIONS AND THE ARTS (advertising), COMPUTER AND PHYSICAL SCIENCE (information sciences and systems and web technology), ENGINEERING AND ENVIRONMENTAL DESIGN (technological management), HEALTH PROFESSIONS (medical records administration/services and nursing), SOCIAL SCIENCE (paralegal studies, parks and recreation management, and safety and security technology). Accounting and management are the strongest academically. Network security has the largest enrollment.

Required: Davenport requires all students to complete 120 credit hours, 37 in the major, with a minimum GPA of 2.0 overall and in career courses. The general education core consists of 42 credits and the business core, 26 credits.

Special: Davenport offers co-op programs in marketing and paralegal studies. There are internships in most disciplines. Study abroad is available in 10 countries. There is a freshman honors program and 1 departmental honors program.

Faculty/Classroom: 44% of faculty are male; 56% are female. All teach undergraduates. No introductory courses are taught by graduate students.

The average class size in an introductory lecture is 15 and in a regular course is 15.

Admissions: 93% of the 2013-2014 applicants were accepted.

Requirements: The SAT or ACT is recommended. Applicants must submit a high school transcript indicating graduation date or GED test scores with a pass/fail date as well as qualifying ACT scores, SAT scores, or COMPASS assessment results. AP and CLEP credits are accepted.

Procedure: Freshmen are admitted to all sessions. There is a rolling admissions plan. Application deadlines are open. Application fee is $25. Applications are accepted online.

Transfer: C is the minimum grade accepted for transfer. There is a 75% maximum credit transfer for the bachelor's degree. 30 of 120 credits required for the bachelor's degree must be completed at Davenport.

Visiting: There are regularly scheduled orientations for prospective students. There are guides for informal visits and visitors may sit in on classes. To schedule a visit, contact the Admissions Office.

Financial Aid: The FAFSA is required. Check with the school for current application deadlines.

International Students: There are 100 international students enrolled. The school actively recruits these students. They must take the TOEFL, the Comprehensive English Language Test, and the college's own test.

Graduates: From July 1, 2012 to June 30, 2013, 1885 bachelor's degrees were awarded. The most popular majors were management (8%), business administration (8%), and nursing (4%).

Admissions Contact: Admissions E-Mail: *info@davenport.edu* Web: *www.davenport.edu*

EASTERN MICHIGAN UNIVERSITY D-5

Ypsilanti, MI 48197 (734) 487-3060
(800) GO TO EMU; (734) 487-6559

Full-time: 5625 men, 7707 women
Part-time: 2197 men, 3032 women
Graduate: 1496 men, 2737 women
Year: semesters, summer session
Application Deadline: August 30
Faculty: 751; IIA, av$
Ph.D.s: 81%
Student/Faculty: 18 to 1
Tuition: $9364 ($26,284)
Room & Board: $8597
Freshman Class: 12936 applied, 7901 accepted, 2904 enrolled
SAT CR/M/W: 512/521/493 **ACT:** 22 **COMPETITIVE**

Eastern Michigan University, founded in 1849, is a public institution offering programs in arts and sciences, business, education, health and human services, and technology. There are 6 undergraduate schools and 1 graduate school. In addition to regional accreditation, EMU has baccalaureate program accreditation with AACSB, ACCE, CSWE, NASM, and NCATE. The library contains 1.1 million volumes, 993,519 microform items, and 20,214 audio/video tapes/CDs/DVDs, and subscribes to 41,728 periodicals including electronic. Computerized library services include interlibrary loans, database searching, Internet access, and Wi-Fi capability. Special learning facilities include an art gallery, radio station, and TV station. The 460-acre campus is in a suburban area 8 miles east of Ann Arbor. Including any residence halls, there are 120 buildings.

Student Life: 92% of undergraduates are from Michigan. Others are from 49 states, 55 foreign countries, and Canada. 90% are from public schools. 65% are White; 21% African American. The average age of freshmen is 18; all undergraduates, 22. 27% do not continue beyond their first year; 42% remain to graduate.

Housing: 3688 students can be accommodated in college housing, which includes coed dorms, on-campus apartments, and married student housing. In addition, there are honors houses, special-interest houses, sorority houses, special housing known as community of scholars, upper-class halls, and a first-year center. On-campus housing is available on a first-come and first-served basis. 77% of students commute. All students may keep cars.

Activities: 4% of men belong to 1 local and 10 national fraternities; 4% of women belong to 1 local and 11 national sororities. There are 300 groups on campus, including art, band, cheerleading, chess, choir, chorale, chorus, computers, dance, debate, drama, drill team, environmental, ethnic, film, forensics, gay, honors, international, jazz band, literary magazine, marching band, musical theater, newspaper, opera, orchestra, pep band, photography, political, professional, radio and TV, religious, social, social service, student government, and symphony. Popular campus events include Martin Luther King Birthday Celebration and Family Weekend.

Sports: There are 12 intercollegiate sports for men and 15 for women, and 20 intramural sports for men and 20 for women. Facilities include a 30,000-seat stadium, outdoor playing fields, a field house, a student recreation and intramural center, and an outdoor park including a lake, amphitheater, lighted basketball courts, volleyball courts, and lake house. There are 2 pools, a whirlpool/sauna, softball and soccer fields, 4 weight rooms, an aerobic studio, and a pro shop.

Disabled Students: 93% of the campus is accessible. Facilities include wheelchair ramps, elevators, special parking, specially equipped restrooms, special class scheduling, lowered drinking fountains, lowered telephones, and special housing.

Services: Counseling and information services are available, as is tutoring in every subject. There is a reader service for the blind, and remedial math, reading, and writing. Notetakers and interpreters are provided for the handicapped.

Campus Safety and Security: Measures include 24-hour foot and vehicle patrol, emergency notification system, self-defense education, and security escort services. There are shuttle buses, emergency telephones, lighted pathways/sidewalks, controlled access to dorms/residences, bicycle patrols, a crime prevention officer, area police officers in dorms, an anonymous tip line, Operation Identification, vehicle glass etching, a bike lock lease program, and surveillance cameras.

Programs of Study: EMU confers B.A., B.S., B.A.E., B.A. in Language and World Business, B.B.A., B.B.E., B.F.A., B.M.E., B.M.T., B.M.U., B.S.N. and B.S.W. degrees. Master's and doctoral degrees are also awarded. Bachelor's degrees are awarded in BIOLOGICAL SCIENCE (biochemistry, biology/biological science, and nutrition), BUSINESS (accounting, apparel and accessories marketing, banking and finance, business administration and management, business data processing, business economics, business systems analysis, entrepreneurial studies, fashion merchandising, hospitality management services, hotel/motel and restaurant management, international business management, labor studies, management information systems, management science, marketing management, marketing/retailing/merchandising, office supervision and management, personnel management, supply chain management, tourism, and trade and industrial supervision and management), COMMUNICATIONS AND THE ARTS (advertising, American literature, animation, applied music, art, art history and appreciation, arts administration/management, classical languages, communications, communications technology, creative writing, dance, design, dramatic arts, English, English literature, film arts, fine arts, French, German, graphic design, historic preservation, Japanese, journalism, language arts, linguistics, literature, media arts, music, music performance, percussion, performing arts, piano/organ, public relations, Spanish, speech/debate/rhetoric, strings, technical and business writing, telecommunications, visual and performing arts, voice, and winds), COMPUTER AND PHYSICAL SCIENCE (actuarial science, applied mathematics, astronomy, chemistry, computer programming, computer science, computer security and information assurance, earth science, geology, hydrogeology, information sciences and systems, mathematics, physics, polymer science, science, and statistics), EDUCATION (art education, athletic training, bilingual/bicultural education, business education, computer education, drama education, early childhood education, education, education of the deaf and hearing impaired, education of the emotionally handicapped, education of the mentally handicapped, education of the multiply handicapped, education of the physically handicapped, education of the visually handicapped, educational media, elementary education, English education, foreign languages education, health education, industrial arts education, mathematics education, middle school education, music education, physical education, psychology education, reading education, school psychology, science education, secondary education, social foundations, social studies education, special education, technical education, and trade and industrial education), ENGINEERING AND ENVIRONMENTAL DESIGN (airline piloting and navigation, applied aviation, aviation administration/management, city/community/regional planning, computer engineering, computer graphics, computer technology, construction management, electrical/electronics engineering technology, engineering physics, engineering technology, interior design, land use management and reclamation, manufacturing engineering, manufacturing technology, mechanical engineering technology, military science, plastics technology, and urban planning technology), HEALTH PROFESSIONS (allied health, exercise science, health care administration, medical laboratory science, medical laboratory technology, music therapy, nursing, occupational therapy, recreation therapy, speech pathology/audiology, and sports medicine), SOCIAL SCIENCE (African studies, African American studies, anthropology, area studies, Asian/Oriental studies, child care/child and family studies, clothing and textiles management/production/services, counseling/psychology, criminal justice, dietetics, economics, gender studies, geography, gerontology, history, interdisciplinary studies, international relations, Latin American studies, Middle Eastern studies, paralegal studies, philosophy, political science/government, psychology, public administration, Russian and Slavic studies, social studies, social work, sociology, textiles and clothing, urban studies, and women's studies). Education, business, and health/nursing are the strongest academically. Elementary education, arts/sciences, and business have the largest enrollments.

Required: To graduate, students must have a GPA of 2.0, and complete a minimum of 124 semester hours, including usually 30 in the major, 20 in the minor (or 50 in a comprehensive major), and 40 in General Education. In addition to distribution requirements, students must have a course in global awareness, a course in U.S. diversity, and satisfy requirements for learning beyond the classroom.

Special: EMU offers internships, work-study programs, a Washington semester in public administration, and co-op programs and cross-registration with the University of Michigan at Ann Arbor, Concordia College, and Washtenaw Community College. Students may study abroad in more than 23 countries. EMU allows dual majors, nondegree study, B.A.-B.S. degrees in all majors, student-designed majors, and accelerated degree programs, and confers a general studies degree, as well as a B.A.-B.B.A. degree in language and world business. Students may receive credit for life, military, and work experience, and pass/fail options are open. There are 9 national honor societies, a freshman honors program, and 36 departmental honors programs.

Faculty/Classroom: 50% of faculty are male; 50% are female. 95% teach undergraduates. Graduate students teach 2% of introductory courses. The average class size in an introductory lecture is 29; in a laboratory is 12; and in a regular course is 20.

Admissions: 61% of the 2013-2014 applicants were accepted. The SAT scores for the 2013-2014 freshman class were: Critical Reading--48% below 500, 33% between 500 and 599, 17% between 600 and 699, and 2% between 700 and 800; Math--42% below 500, 38% between 500 and 599, 17% between 600 and 699, and 3% between 700 and 800; Writing--50% below 500, 39% between 500 and 599, 9% between 600 and 699, and 2% between 700 and 800. The ACT scores were 36% below 21, 29% between 21 and 23, 22% between 24 and 26, 7% between 27 and 28, and 5% above 28. 13 freshmen graduated first in their class.

Requirements: The SAT or ACT is required. A minimum composite of 17 on the ACT, or a satisfactory score on the SAT is required. Applicants should be high school graduates or hold a GED. The university recommends that students complete 21 academic credits in high school, consisting of 4 each in English, math, and science, 2 each in foreign language and social studies, 1 in history, and 4 in other traditional college-preparatory courses. A portfolio is required for applicants to the art program, and an audition is required for music students. A GPA of 2.0 is required. AP and CLEP credits are accepted.

Procedure: Freshmen are admitted to all sessions. Entrance exams should be taken by November of the senior year of high school. There are early admissions and rolling admissions plans. Applications should be filed by August 30 for fall entry; January 2 for winter entry; April 25 for spring entry; and June 21 for summer entry. The fall 2013 application fee was $35. Notification is sent on a rolling basis. Applications are accepted online.

Transfer: 1949 transfer students enrolled in 2012-2013. Transfer students must have at least 12 semester hours of college credit, with a GPA of 2.0. 30 of 124 credits required for the bachelor's degree must be completed at EMU.

Visiting: There are regularly scheduled orientations for prospective students, including tours scheduled every morning and afternoon, as well as Saturday morning, with trained student tour guides. There are guides for informal visits, visitors may sit in on classes, and stay overnight. To schedule a visit, contact the Admissions On-Campus Programs.

Financial Aid: In 2013-2014, 99% of all full-time freshmen and 85% of continuing full-time students received some form of financial aid. 67% of all full-time freshmen and 64% of continuing full-time students received need-based aid. The average freshman award was $13,019. Need-based scholarships or need-based grants averaged $4,591 ($10,000 maximum); need-based self-help aid (loans and jobs) averaged $3,323 ($5,446 maximum); non-need-based athletic scholarships averaged $14,223 ($17,479 maximum); and other non-need-based awards and non-need-based scholarships averaged $7,809 ($23,063 maximum). 16% of undergraduate students work part-time. Average annual earnings from campus work are $3400. The average financial indebtedness of the 2013 graduate was $24,189. The FAFSA is required. The priority date for freshman financial aid applications for fall entry is February 1. The deadline for filing freshman financial aid applications for fall entry is December 19.

International Students: There are 417 international students enrolled. The school actively recruits these students. They must take the TOEFL with a minimum score of 500 on the paper-based TOEFL (PBT) or 61 on the Internet-based version (iBT) or take the MELAB, IELTS.

Graduates: From July 1, 2012 to June 30, 2013, 3108 bachelor's degrees were awarded. The most popular majors were psychology (6%), social work (5%), and management (4%). 802 companies recruited on campus in 2012-2013. In an average class, 1% graduate in 3 years or less, 12% graduate in 4 years or less, 30% graduate in 5 years or less, and 38% graduate in 6 years or less.

Admissions Contact: Christopher LaRusso, Interim Director for Admissions. E-Mail: *undergraduate.admissions@emich.edu* Web: *www.emich.edu*

FERRIS STATE UNIVERSITY D-4

Big Rapids, MI 49307 (231) 591-2100; (231) 591-3944

Full-time: 4751 men, 4504 women
Faculty: n/av; IIA, av$
Part-time: 1732 men, 2482 women
Ph.D.s: 30%
Graduate: 534 men, 704 women
Student/Faculty: 16 to 1
Year: semesters, summer session
Tuition: $10,628 ($17,742)
Application Deadline: August 1
Room & Board: $9070
Freshman Class: 10708 applied, 8128 accepted, 2006 enrolled
SAT: required **ACT:** 22 **COMPETITIVE**

Ferris State University, established in 1884, is a public institution offering day and evening courses through its Schools of Arts and Sciences, Education & Human Services, Health Professions, Engineering Technology, Business, and Pharmacy, MI College of Optometry, and Kendall College of Art and Design. There are 6 undergraduate schools and 5 graduate schools. In addition to regional accreditation, Ferris State has baccalaureate program accreditation with ABET, ACBSP, ACCE, ACPE, ADA, CSWE, and NLN. The library contains 273,210 volumes, 3.7 million microform items, and 2,551 audio/video tapes/CDs/DVDs, and subscribes to 74,452 periodicals including electronic. Computerized library services include interlibrary loans, database searching, Internet access, and Wi-Fi capability. Special learning facilities include an art gallery, natural history museum, radio station, and TV station. The 941-acre campus is in a small town 55 miles north of Grand Rapids. Including any residence halls, there are 115 buildings.

Student Life: 95% of undergraduates are from Michigan. Others are from 48 states, 30 foreign countries, and Canada. 79% are White. The average age of freshmen is 19; all undergraduates, 22. 29% do not continue beyond their first year.

Housing: 3680 students can be accommodated in college housing, which includes single-sex and coed dorms, on-campus apartments, and married student housing. In addition, there are honors houses, language houses, special-interest houses, Honors, Substance Free, 1st year experience, quiet house, Graphic Design & Sophomore Leadership. On-campus housing is guaranteed for all 4 years. 72% of students commute. All students may keep cars.

Activities: 4% of men belong to 30 national fraternities; 2% of women belong to 8 national sororities. There are 227 groups on campus, including art, band, cheerleading, choir, chorus, communications, computers, dance, debate, drama, drill team, ethnic, film, forensics, gay, honors, international, jazz band, musical theater, newspaper, orchestra, pep band, photography, political, professional, radio and TV, religious, social, social service, student government, and symphony. Popular campus events include Ferris Fest and Autumn a LIVE Concert.

Sports: There are 7 intercollegiate sports for men and 8 for women, and 9 intramural sports for men and 9 for women. Facilities include a golf course, a racquetball and fitness club, an ice arena, a 10,000-seat stadium, a student recreation center with a pool, and tennis courts.

Disabled Students: 98% of the campus is accessible. Facilities include wheelchair ramps, elevators, special parking, specially equipped restrooms, special class scheduling, lowered drinking fountains, lowered telephones, and special housing.

Services: Counseling and information services are available, as is tutoring in most subjects. There is a reader service for the blind, and remedial math, reading, and writing.

Campus Safety and Security: Measures include 24-hour foot and vehicle patrol, emergency notification system, self-defense education, and security escort services. There are emergency telephones, lighted pathways/sidewalks, and controlled access to dorms/residences.

Programs of Study: Ferris State confers B.A., B.S., B.F.A., B.S.N., B.S.W., B.B. and B.I.S. degrees. Associate, master's, and doctoral degrees are also awarded. Bachelor's degrees are awarded in BIOLOGICAL SCIENCE (biochemistry, biology/biological science, and biotechnology), BUSINESS (accounting, banking and finance, business administration and management, finance, hospitality management services, human resources, insurance, international business management, marketing, marketing/retailing/merchandising, and small business management), COMMUNICATIONS AND THE ARTS (advertising, art history and appreciation, communication, communications, drawing, English, English literature, fine arts, graphic design, music industry, painting, photography, printmaking, public relations, and sculpture), COMPUTER AND PHYSICAL SCIENCE (actuarial mathematics, applied mathematics, chemistry, computer programming, and computer information systems), EDUCATION (art education, business education, early childhood education, elementary education, English education, mathematics education, social studies education, and technical education), ENGINEERING AND ENVIRONMENTAL DESIGN (automotive technology, construction management, electrical/electronics engineering technology, engineering technology, furniture design, interior design, manufacturing engineering, mechanical engineering technology, plastics engineering, surveying engineering, and welding engineering), HEALTH PROFESSIONS (allied health, dental hygiene, health care administration, medical records administration/services, medical technology, nuclear medical technology, nursing, optometry, and pharmacy), SOCIAL SCIENCE (criminal justice, history, political science/government, psychology, social work, and sociology). Pharmacy and optometry are the strongest academically. Pharmacy/prepharmacy, nursing and criminal justice have the largest enrollments.

Required: Degree requirements include a minimum 2.0 GPA. The total number of credit hours required varies. General education courses required include English, speech, math, humanities, social science, cultural enrichment, and natural science subjects.

Special: Ferris State offers co-op programs in automotive service technology, internships, study abroad, work-study programs, accelerated degrees, dual and student-designed majors, credit for life, military, and work experience. There are 11 national honor societies and a freshman honors program.

Faculty/Classroom: 55% of faculty are male; 45% are female. All teach undergraduates. No introductory courses are taught by graduate students. The average class size in an introductory lecture is 24; in a laboratory is 14; and in a regular course is 17.

Admissions: 76% of the 2013-2014 applicants were accepted. The ACT scores were 40% below 21, 28% between 21 and 23, 9% between 24 and 26, 6% between 27 and 28, and 7% above 28.

Requirements: The SAT or ACT is required. Applicants must graduate from an accredited secondary school or earn a GED. 4 years each of English and math. 3 years of science (2 lab) and 3 social studies. 2 years of foreign language, and 1 visual/performing arts are advised. A GPA of 2.5 is required. AP and CLEP credits are accepted. Important factors in the admissions decision are personality/intangible qualities, leadership record, and advanced placement or honors courses.

Procedure: Freshmen are admitted fall, spring, and summer. Entrance exams should be taken before course registration. There is a rolling admissions plan. Applications should be filed by August 1 for fall entry, along with a $30 fee. Applications are accepted online. Application fees are waived if application is completed online.

Transfer: 1381 transfer students enrolled in 2012-2013. A GPA of at least 2.0 is required, as are college transcripts, and a statement of good standing from previously attended institutions. Some students may need to submit high school transcripts and test scores. 30 of 120 credits required for the bachelor's degree must be completed at Ferris State.

Visiting: There are regularly scheduled orientations for prospective students, Admission's presentation/lunch/campus tour. There are guides for informal visits. To schedule a visit, contact the Admissions Office.

Financial Aid: In 2013-2014, 76% of all full-time freshmen and 73% of continuing full-time students received some form of financial aid. 54% of all full-time freshmen and 52% of continuing full-time students received need-based aid. The average freshman award was $11,870. Need-based scholarships or need-based grants averaged $4,770; need-based self-help aid (loans and jobs) averaged $3,740; non-need-based athletic scholarships averaged $8,420; and other non need-based awards and non-need-based scholarships averaged $5,025. 41% of undergraduate students work part-time. Average annual earnings from campus work are $2499. The average financial indebtedness of the 2013 graduate was $37,325. Ferris State is a member of CSS. The FAFSA is required. The priority date for freshman financial aid applications for fall entry is February 15. The deadline for filing freshman financial aid applications for fall entry is rolling.

International Students: There are 305 international students enrolled. The school actively recruits these students. They must take the TOEFL with a minimum score of 500 on the paper-based TOEFL (PBT) or 61 on the Internet-based version (iBT). They must also take the SAT or ACT, scoring 17. a supplemental math exam.

Graduates: From July 1, 2012 to June 30, 2013, 2351 bachelor's degrees were awarded. The most popular majors were criminal justice (12%), nursing (6%), and pharmacy (3%). 280 companies recruited on campus in 2012-2013. In an average class, 15% graduate in 3 years or less, 29% graduate in 4 years or less, 43% graduate in 5 years or less, and 49% graduate in 6 years or less.

Admissions Contact: Admissions Officer E-Mail: *admissions@ferris.edu* Web: *www.ferris.edu*

GRACE BIBLE COLLEGE D-4

Grand Rapids, MI 49509 **(616) 538-2330**
(800) 968-1887; (616) 538-2330

Full-time: 110 men, 85 women	**Faculty:** n/av
Part-time: 10 men,10 women	**Ph.D.s:** 43%
Graduate: n/av	**Student/Faculty:** n/av
Year: semesters	**Tuition:** $15,350
Application Deadline: open	**Room & Board:** $7500
Freshman Class: n/av	
SAT or ACT: required	

COMPETITIVE

Grace Bible College, founded in 1939, is a private institution affiliated with the Grace Gospel Fellowship. The figures in the above capsule and in this profile are approximate. Its mission is to provide a curriculum that integrates general education and biblical studies and prepares students for service in their career, church, and society. In addition to regional accreditation, GBC has baccalaureate program accreditation with AABC. The library contains 42,867 volumes, 53 microform items, and 2,582 audio/video tapes/CDs/DVDs, and subscribes to 54,292 periodicals including electronic. Computerized library services include interlibrary loans, database searching, Internet access, and laptop Internet portals. The 21-acre campus is in a suburban area on the southwest side of Grand Rapids. Including any residence halls, there are 12 buildings.

Student Life: 80% of undergraduates are from Michigan. Others are from 15 states and 2 foreign countries. 93% are white. 97% are Protestant. The average age of freshmen is 19; all undergraduates, 21. 21% do not continue beyond their first year; 75% remain to graduate.

Housing: 110 students can be accommodated in college housing, which includes single-sex dorms, on-campus apartments, off-campus apartments, and married student housing. On-campus housing is guaranteed for all 4 years. 52% of students live on campus; of those, 75% remain on campus on weekends. Alcohol is not permitted. All students may keep cars.

Activities: There are no fraternities or sororities. Groups on campus include cheerleading, choir, drama, jazz band, musical theater, religious, and student government. Popular campus events include Winter Formal, Missions Conference, and Campus Service Days.

Sports: There are 2 intercollegiate sports for men and 2 for women. Facilities include a 300-seat soccer field and an athletic center with a 500-seat gym for basketball and volleyball, a racquetball court, and an exercise and weight room.

Disabled Students: 85% of the campus is accessible. Facilities include wheelchair ramps, elevators, special parking, specially equipped rest rooms, and lowered drinking fountains.

Services: Counseling and information services are available, as is tutoring in most subjects. There is remedial writing.

Campus Safety and Security: There are lighted pathways/sidewalks and an evening and overnight foot patrol.

Programs of Study: GBC confers B.S., B.Mus., B.R.E., and B.Th. degrees. Associate degrees are also awarded. Bachelor's degrees are awarded in BUSINESS (business administration and management), COMMUNICATIONS AND THE ARTS (music), COMPUTER AND PHYSICAL SCIENCE (digital arts/technology), EDUCATION (elementary education and secondary education), SOCIAL SCIENCE (biblical studies, early childhood studies, human services, interdisciplinary studies, missions, pastoral studies, religious education, and youth ministry). Elementary/secondary education, youth ministry, and human services have the largest enrollments.

Required: To graduate, students must complete 126 to 158 credits, depending on the major, with a minimum GPA of 2.0, and must be considered worthy in character and conduct by the faculty. Course work is required in arts and sciences, ministry studies, Bible/theology, math/computer science, lab science, and phys ed. Attendance is expected at worship services twice a week.

Special: Cross-registration is available with Cornerstone and Davenport Universities. GBC offers 6-month internships for theology majors. Most 4-year degree programs require a semester practicum.

Faculty/Classroom: 72% of faculty are male; 28% are female. All teach undergraduates. The average class size in an introductory lecture is 60; in a regular course, 16.

Requirements: The SAT or ACT is required; the ACT is preferred. Applicants must be graduates of accredited secondary schools or have earned a GED. The application must show involvement in Christian activities and personal salvation through Jesus Christ. GBC requires applicants to be in the upper 50% of their class. A GPA of 2.5 is required. AP and CLEP credits are accepted.

Procedure: Freshmen are admitted fall and spring. There is a rolling admissions plan. Application deadlines are open.

Transfer: 20 transfer students enrolled in a recent year. Applicants must present a GPA of 2.0 and be in good standing at their previous school. Those with fewer than 24 college credit hours must submit high school records. 63 of 126 credits required for the bachelor's degree must be completed at GBC.

Visiting: There are regularly scheduled orientations for prospective students, consisting of 7 Friday programs a year that include workshops, class visits, and campus tours. There are guides for informal visits, and visitors may sit in on classes and stay overnight. To schedule a visit, the Director of Enrollment.

Financial Aid: In a recent year, 98% of all full-time freshmen and 97% of continuing full-time students received some form of financial aid. 74% of all full-time freshmen and 81% of continuing full-time students received need-based aid. The average freshman award was $7780. Need-based scholarships or need-based grants averaged $3383 ($5350 maximum); need-based self-help aid (loans and jobs) averaged $2063 ($3500 maximum); and other non-need-based awards and non-need-based scholarships averaged $3946 ($4500 maximum). 43% of undergraduate students worked part-time. Average annual earnings from campus work were $2300. The FAFSA is required. Check with the school for current application deadlines.

International Students: They must take the TOEFL.

Graduates: In a recent year, 31 bachelor's degrees were awarded. The most popular majors were education (33%), youth and pastoral ministries (17%), and visual performing arts and digital media (17%). In an average class, 20% graduate in 3 years or less, 46% graduate in 4 years or less, 62% graduate in 5 years or less, and 75% graduate in 6 years or less.

Admissions Contact: Director of Enrollment. E-mail: *enrollment@gbcol.edu* Web: *www.gbcol.edu*

GRAND VALLEY STATE UNIVERSITY D-4

Allendale, MI 49401 (616) 331-5000
(800) 748-0246; (616) 331-2000

Full-time: 7699 men, 10964 women	**Faculty:** 1069; IIA, av$
Part-time: 1136 men, 1432 women	**Ph.D.s:** 78%
Graduate: 1102 men, 2235 women	**Student/Faculty:** 17 to 1
Year: semesters, summer session	**Tuition:** $10,078 ($14,568)
Application Deadline: July 23	**Room & Board:** $7920

Freshman Class: 17880 applied, 14590 accepted, 3066 enrolled
SAT: required **ACT:** 24 **VERY COMPETITIVE**

Grand Valley State University, founded in 1960, is a comprehensive public institution offering graduate and undergraduate liberal arts and professional education. There are 8 undergraduate schools and 7 graduate schools. In addition to regional accreditation, GVSU has baccalaureate program accreditation with AACSB, ABET, APTA, CSWE, NASAD, NASM, NCATE, and NLN. The 2 libraries contain 708,000 volumes, 868,850 microform items, and 19,804 audio/video tapes/CDs/DVDs, and subscribe to 73,759 periodicals including electronic. Computerized library services include interlibrary loans, database searching, Internet access, and Wi-Fi capability. Special learning facilities include an art gallery, radio station, TV station, a cadaver lab, 2 Great Lakes research vessels, a performance auditorium, and dance studios. The 1342-acre campus is in a small town 12 miles west of Grand Rapids. Including any residence halls, there are 72 buildings.

Student Life: 95% of undergraduates are from Michigan. Others are from 40 states, 73 foreign countries, and Canada. 75% are from public schools. 91% are White. The average age of freshmen is 18; all undergraduates, 21. 18% do not continue beyond their first year; 56% remain to graduate.

Housing: 5820 students can be accommodated in college housing, which includes single-sex and coed dorms, on-campus apartments, off-campus apartments, and married student housing. In addition, there are honors houses, language houses, special-interest houses, fraternity houses, and sorority houses. On-campus housing is guaranteed for the freshman year only, is available on a first-come, first-served basis, and is available on a lottery system for upperclassmen. Priority is given to out-of-town students. 73% of students commute. Alcohol is not permitted. All students may keep cars.

Activities: 5% of women belong to 10 national sororities. There are 250 groups on campus, including art, band, cheerleading, chess, choir, chorale, chorus, computers, dance, drama, environmental, ethnic, film, gay, honors, international, jazz band, literary magazine, marching band, musical theater, newspaper, opera, orchestra, pep band, photography, political, professional, radio and TV, religious, social, social service, student government, and symphony. Popular campus events include Family Day, Hispanic Awareness Week and Black History Month.

Sports: There are 9 intercollegiate sports for men and 10 for women, and 26 intramural sports for men and 26 for women. Facilities include a football stadium, a baseball field, a basketball arena, swimming and diving pools, an indoor track, a weight room, a fitness building/intramural center, an outdoor cross-country track, and an outdoor soccer field.

Disabled Students: 98% of the campus is accessible. Facilities include wheelchair ramps, elevators, special parking, specially equipped restrooms, special class scheduling, lowered drinking fountains, and lowered telephones.

Services: Counseling and information services are available, as is tutoring in most subjects. There is a reader service for the blind, and remedial math, reading, and writing.

Campus Safety and Security: Measures include 24-hour foot and vehicle patrol, emergency notification system, self-defense education, and security escort services. There are shuttle buses, emergency telephones, and lighted pathways/sidewalks.

Programs of Study: GVSU confers B.A., B.S., B.B.A., B.F.A., B.M., B.M.E., B.S.E., B.S.N. and B.S.W. degrees. Master's and doctoral degrees are also awarded. Bachelor's degrees are awarded in AGRICULTURE (natural resource management), BIOLOGICAL SCIENCE (biology/biological science and cell biology), BUSINESS (accounting, banking and finance, business administration and management, business economics, hotel/motel and restaurant management, international business management, management science, marketing/retailing/merchandising, and personnel management), COMMUNICATIONS AND THE ARTS (advertising, art, art history and appreciation, broadcasting, Chinese, classics, communications, creative writing, dance, design, dramatic arts, English, film arts, fine arts, French, German, journalism, languages, music, photography, and Spanish), COMPUTER AND PHYSICAL SCIENCE (chemistry, computer science, earth science, geochemistry, geology, information sciences and systems, mathematics, physics, science, and statistics), EDUCATION (art education, athletic training, elementary education, foreign languages education, middle school education, music education, science education, secondary education, and special education), ENGINEERING AND ENVIRONMENTAL DESIGN (engineering, industrial engineering technology, and occupational safety and health), HEALTH PROFESSIONS (biomedical science, clinical science, exercise science, health science, medical laboratory technology, nursing, physical therapy, physician's assistant, predentistry, premedicine, and recreation therapy), SOCIAL SCIENCE (anthropology, behavioral science, biopsychology, criminal justice, economics, geography, history, international relations, law, liberal arts/general studies, philosophy, political science/government, prelaw, psychology, public administration, Russian and Slavic studies, social science, social work, and sociology). Health sciences, English, and psychology have the largest enrollments.

Required: To graduate, students must have earned 30 credits in general education, composed of 10 courses selected from specific groups, and have completed the university's required courses in English and math, as well as the upper-division writing course. A total of 120 credits, with 36 to 60 in the major, and a GPA of 2.0, are required to graduate.

Special: Many programs offer dual majors and internships, and most majors qualify for B.A.-B.S. degrees. There is an engineering cooperative program, a student-designed major in liberal studies, and many work-study programs. Outside opportunities include study abroad in 10 countries and a Washington semester. There are 14 national honor societies, a freshman honors program, and 12 departmental honors programs.

Faculty/Classroom: 51% of faculty are male; 49% are female. 97% teach undergraduates. No introductory courses are taught by graduate students. The average class size in an introductory lecture is 37; in a laboratory is 21; and in a regular course is 27.

Admissions: 82% of the 2013-2014 applicants were accepted. The ACT scores were 19% below 21, 31% between 21 and 23, 28% between 24 and 26, 12% between 27 and 28, and 10% above 28. 45% of the current freshmen were in the top fifth of their class; 80% were in the top two fifths. 18 freshmen graduated first in their class.

Requirements: The SAT or ACT is required. Michigan residents must submit ACT test scores, nonresidents either ACT or SAT scores. In addition, high school transcripts should indicate 4 years of English with 1 composition course, 3 each of math (including 2 years of algebra), science (including 1 lab), and social studies, and 2 of a foreign language. Applicants who graduated from high school more than 3 years ago need not show test results. The GED is accepted. A GPA of 3.0 is required. AP and CLEP credits are accepted. Important factors in the admissions decision are extracurricular activities record, recommendations by school officials, and advanced placement or honors courses.

Procedure: Freshmen are admitted to all sessions. Entrance exams should be taken during the junior year. There is a rolling admissions plan. Applications should be filed by July 23 for fall entry, along with a $30 fee. Notification is sent on a rolling basis. Applications are accepted online.

Transfer: 1800 transfer students enrolled in 2012-2013. Transfer students must have a minimum of 30 college credits with a 2.0 GPA. They must submit previous college transcripts and a statement of good standing from prior institutions. 30 of 120 credits required for the bachelor's degree must be completed at GVSU.

Visiting: There are regularly scheduled orientations for prospective students, including registration activities. There are guides for informal visits, visitors may sit in on classes, and stay overnight. To schedule a visit, contact the Admissions Office.

Financial Aid: In 2013-2014, 67% of all full-time freshmen and 65% of continuing full-time students received some form of financial aid. 60% of all full-time freshmen and 59% of continuing full-time students received need-based aid. The average freshman award was $10,949. Need-based scholarships or need-based grants averaged $7,469; and need-based self-help aid (loans and jobs) averaged $4,937. 12% of undergraduate students work part-time. Average annual earnings from campus work are $3330. The average financial indebtedness of the 2013 graduate was $24,876. GVSU is a member of CSS. The FAFSA is required. The deadline for filing freshman financial aid applications for fall entry is February 15.

International Students: There are 272 international students enrolled. The school actively recruits these students. They must take the TOEFL with a minimum score of 550 on the paper-based TOEFL (PBT) or 80 on the Internet-based version (iBT) or take the MELAB and the Comprehensive English Language Test. They must also take the SAT or ACT.

Graduates: From July 1, 2012 to June 30, 2013, 4301 bachelor's degrees were awarded. The most popular majors were business/marketing (16%), biological/life sciences (9%), and health sciences (8%). 192 companies recruited on campus in 2012-2013. In an average class, 30% graduate in 4 years or less, 56% graduate in 5 years or less, and 63% graduate in 6 years or less. Of the 2012 graduating class, 25% were enrolled in graduate school within 6 months of graduation, and 79% were employed.

Admissions Contact: Jodi Chycinski, Director of Admissions. E-Mail: *admissions@gvsu.edu* Web: *www.gvsu.edu*

HILLSDALE COLLEGE D-5

Hillsdale, MI 49242 (517) 607-2327; (517) 607-2223

Full-time: 676 men, 768 women	**Faculty:** 110
Part-time: 24 men, 18 women	**Ph.D.s:** 90%
Graduate: 10 men, 15 women	**Student/Faculty:** 12 to 1
Year: semesters, summer session	**Tuition:** $22,890
Application Deadline: February 15	**Room & Board:** $9000
Freshman Class: 1401 applied, 900 accepted, 358 enrolled	
SAT CR/M/W: 670/630/650	**ACT:** 28 **HIGHLY COMPETITIVE+**

Hillsdale College, founded in 1844, is a private liberal arts college that enrolls approximately 1400 students emphasizing classical liberal arts, preprofessional, business, education, science and humanities. There is one graduate school. The 3 libraries contain 983,000 volumes, 82,000 microform items, and 20,000 audio/video tapes/CDs/DVDs, and subscribe to 30,000 periodicals including electronic. Computerized library services include interlibrary loans, database searching, Internet access, and Wi-Fi capability. The 400-acre campus is in a small town 120 miles southwest of Detroit. Including any residence halls, there are 84 buildings.

Student Life: 61% of undergraduates are from out of state, mostly the Mid-West. Students are from 48 states, 11 foreign countries, and Canada. 40% are from public schools. 40% claim no religious affiliation; 35% Protestant; 20% Catholic. The average age of freshmen is 18; all undergraduates, 20. 4% do not continue beyond their first year; 82% remain to graduate.

Housing: 1100 students can be accommodated in college housing, which includes single-sex dorms and on-campus apartments. In addition, there are honors houses, special-interest houses, fraternity houses, and sorority houses. On-campus housing is guaranteed for all 4 years. 80% of students live on campus; of those, 88% remain on campus on weekends. Alcohol is not permitted. All students may keep cars.

Activities: 33% of men belong to 4 national fraternities; 44% of women belong to 3 national sororities. There are 60 groups on campus, including and young life, intervarsity, art, cheerleading, chess, choir, chorale, chorus, communications, computers, dance, debate, drama, drill team, environmental, equestrian, ethnic, forensics, honors, international, jazz band, literary magazine, musical theater, newspaper, orchestra, pep band, photography, political, professional, religious, social, social service, student government, symphony, and yearbook. Popular campus events include Parents Weekend, President's Ball, and Greek Week, Homecoming, Convocation, and Centralhallapalooza.

Sports: There are 7 intercollegiate sports for men and 8 for women, and 7 intramural sports for men and 7 for women. Facilities include an athletic complex with a ProGrass artificial turf football field, a swimming pool, a 200-meter Mondo indoor track and tennis facility, a basketball arena, a weight room, a Mondo outdoor Olympic track, an exercise/physiology room, and volleyball, handball, racquetball, wallyball courts. The campus stadium seats 8000; the gym 2000.

Disabled Students: 85% of the campus is accessible. Facilities include wheelchair ramps, elevators, special parking, specially equipped restrooms, and lowered drinking fountains.

Services: Counseling and information services are available, as is tutoring in every subject. A writing center on campus and a peer tutoring program are administered by current students.

Campus Safety and Security: Measures include 24-hour foot and vehicle patrol and emergency notification system. There are emergency telephones, lighted pathways/sidewalks, and controlled access to dorms/residences.

Programs of Study: Hillsdale confers B.A., and B.S. degrees. Master's and doctoral degrees are also awarded. Bachelor's degrees are awarded in BIOLOGICAL SCIENCE (biology/biological science), BUSINESS (accounting, banking and finance, business administration and management, international business management, and marketing/retailing/merchandising), COMMUNICATIONS AND THE ARTS (classics, comparative literature, dramatic arts, English, fine arts, French, German, music, Spanish, and speech/debate/rhetoric), COMPUTER AND PHYSICAL SCIENCE (chemistry, mathematics, and physics), EDUCATION (art education, early childhood education, elementary education, foreign languages education, middle school education, music education, physical education, science education, and secondary education), HEALTH PROFESSIONS (predentistry, premedicine, and preveterinary science), SOCIAL SCIENCE (American studies, Christian studies, economics, European studies, history, political science/government, prelaw, psychology, religion, social science, and sociology). History, economics, and classics are the strongest academically. English, history, and biology have the largest enrollments.

Required: To graduate, the student must complete 124 semester hours with a GPA of 2.0. Required courses include 1 year of English, 1 year of science, 1 semester of Western Heritage and 1 semester of American Heritage, 1 semester of political science, 15 hours of the humanities, 12 of the natural sciences and math, 12 of the social sciences, and 2 of phys ed. Students must also enroll in 2 seminars at the school's Center for Constructive Alternatives. 12 credit hours in a foreign language for a B.A. degree and 34 credit hours in math and science for a B.S. degree are also required.

Special: Special academic programs include the Washington Journalism Internship at the National Journalism Center and the Washington-Hillsdale Intern Program (WHIP), which places students in congressional or government offices. Students may study abroad in France, Germany, or Spain, and qualified students are chosen to attend Oxford University for a year. A business internship is offered in London at Regents College. The Thomas Professional Sales Intern program is also available. The college offers an accelerated degree; interdisciplinary majors, including political economy combining economics, history, and political science; 3-2 and 2-2 engineering degrees; and work-study programs at the city radio station WCSR and the city newspaper, the Hillsdale Daily News. There are 24 national honor societies, a freshman honors program, and 24 departmental honors programs.

Faculty/Classroom: 74% of faculty are male; 26% are female. All teach undergraduates, and 10% do both. No introductory courses are taught by graduate students. The average class size in an introductory lecture is 23; in a laboratory is 7; and in a regular course is 21.

Admissions: 48% of the 2013-2014 applicants were accepted. The SAT scores for the 2013-2014 freshman class were: Critical Reading--10% between 500 and 599, 47% between 600 and 699, and 43% between 700 and 800; Math--2% below 500, 25% between 500 and 599, 48% between 600 and 699, and 25% between 700 and 800; Writing--16% between 500 and 599, 44% between 600 and 699, and 40% between 700 and 800. The ACT scores were 3% between 21 and 23, 22% between 24 and 26, 21% between 27 and 28, and 54% above 28. 78% of the current freshmen were in the top fifth of their class; 93% were in the top two fifths. There were 17 National Merit finalists. 30 freshmen graduated first in their class.

Requirements: The SAT or ACT is required. In addition, The student must be a high school graduate or have earned a GED, and must have completed 4 years of English, 3 each of math and science, and 2 each of history, social studies, and foreign language. The college requires 2 letters of recommendation and an essay. An interview is also recommended. For music majors, an audition is required for a scholarship. The school recommends taking SAT: Subject tests. Hillsdale requires applicants to be in the upper 50% of their class. A GPA of 3.3 is required. AP and CLEP credits are accepted. Important factors in the admissions decision are advanced placement or honors courses, leadership record, and extracurricular activities record.

Procedure: Freshmen are admitted fall, spring, and summer. Entrance exams should be taken in the spring of the junior year and/or the fall of the senior year. There are early decision and deferred admissions plans. Early decision applications should be filed by November 15; regular applications, by February 15 for fall entry; December 15 for spring entry; and May 1 for summer entry, along with a $35 fee. Notification of early decision is sent November 15; regular decision, April 1. 70 early decision candidates were accepted for the 2013-2014 class. 40 applicants were on the 2013 waiting list; 5 were admitted. Applications are accepted online.

Transfer: 18 transfer students enrolled in 2012-2013. Transfer students must have a GPA of 3.35, and have a transfer evaluation form completed by the dean of students of their school. Hillsdale also requires high school and college transcripts. 24 of 124 credits required for the bachelor's degree must be completed at Hillsdale.

Visiting: There are regularly scheduled orientations for prospective students, including a fall orientation and a formal junior and senior visitation program. There are guides for informal visits, visitors may sit in on classes, and stay overnight. To schedule a visit, contact Margaret Braman at mbraman@hillsdale.edu.

Financial Aid: In 2013-2014, 85% of all full-time freshmen and 87% of continuing full-time students received some form of financial aid. 75% of all full-time freshmen and 83% of continuing full-time students received need-based aid. The average freshman award was $14,800. Need-based scholarships or need-based grants averaged $3,400; and need-based self-help aid (loans and jobs) averaged $5,300. 68% of undergraduate students work part-time. Average annual earnings from campus work are $1300. The average financial indebtedness of the 2013 graduate was $17,000. Hillsdale is a member of CSS. The the college's own financial statement is required. The priority date for freshman financial aid applications for fall entry is February 1. The deadline for filing freshman financial aid applications for fall entry is April 1.

International Students: There are 23 international students enrolled. The school actively recruits these students. They must take the TOEFL with a minimum score of 560 on the paper-based TOEFL (PBT) or 83 on the Internet-based version (iBT) and the Comprehensive English Language Test. Applicants can also complete ESL level 108, with a minimum score of 15 in the motivational and proficiency categories.

Graduates: From July 1, 2012 to June 30, 2013, 332 bachelor's degrees were awarded. The most popular majors were business (22%), history (13%), and biology (12%). 50 companies recruited on campus in 2012-2013. In an average class, 1% graduate in 3 years or less, 68% graduate in 4 years or less, 73% graduate in 5 years or less, and 74% graduate in 6 years or less. Of the 2012 graduating class, 25% were enrolled in graduate school within 6 months of graduation, and 71% were employed.

Admissions Contact: Jeffrey S. Lantis, Director of Admissions. E-Mail: *jeff.lantis@hillsdale.edu* Web: *www.hillsdale.edu*

HOPE COLLEGE C-4

Holland, MI 49422 (616) 395-7850
(800) 968-7850; (616) 395-7130

Full-time: 1274 men, 1931 women	**Faculty:** 226; IIB, av$
Part-time: 64 men, 74 women	**Ph.D.s:** 78%
Graduate: none	**Student/Faculty:** 12 to 1
Year: semesters, summer session	**Tuition:** $27,810
Application Deadline: open	**Room & Board:** $8510

Freshman Class: 3573 applied, 2939 accepted, 815 enrolled
SAT CR/M: 600/610 **ACT:** 26 **VERY COMPETITIVE+**

Hope College, founded by Dutch pioneers in 1866, is a private liberal arts institution affiliated with the Reformed Church in America. In addition to regional accreditation, Hope has baccalaureate program accreditation with ABET, CSWE, NASAD, NASM, and NCATE. The 2 libraries contain 375,564 volumes, 385,797 microform items, and 20,296 audio/video tapes/CDs/DVDs, and subscribe to 6,873 periodicals including electronic. Computerized library services include interlibrary loans, database searching, Internet access, and Wi-Fi capability. Special learning facilities include an art gallery, planetarium, radio station, TV station, an academic support center, and a modern and classical language lab. The 120-acre campus is in an urban area 26 miles southwest of Grand Rapids and 5 miles east of Lake Michigan. Including any residence halls, there are 130 buildings.

Student Life: 69% of undergraduates are from Michigan. Others are from 44 states, 35 foreign countries, and Canada. 88% are from public schools. 86% are White. 69% are Protestant; 17% Catholic. The average age of freshmen is 18; all undergraduates, 19. 10% do not continue beyond their first year; 77% remain to graduate.

Housing: 2474 students can be accommodated in college housing, which includes single-sex and coed dorms, on-campus apartments, and married student housing. In addition, there are language houses, special-interest houses, fraternity houses, sorority houses, and student cottages. On-campus housing is guaranteed for all 4 years. 81% of students live on campus; of those, 75% remain on campus on weekends. Alcohol is not permitted. All students may keep cars.

Activities: 10% of men belong to 6 local and 1 national fraternities; 12% of women belong to 6 local and 1 national sororities. There are 78 groups on campus, including art, band, cheerleading, chess, choir, chorale, chorus, computers, dance, drama, environmental, ethnic, honors, international, jazz band, literary magazine, musical theater, newspaper, orchestra, pep band, political, professional, radio and TV, religious, social, social service, student government, symphony, and yearbook. Popular campus events include The Pull, Spring Festival, and Nykerk Cup Competition.

Sports: There are 10 intercollegiate sports for men and 10 for women, and 18 intramural sports for men and 17 for women. Facilities include athletic fields include 4 full-size soccer fields, softball and baseball stadium, and an outdoor track and field area. The fieldhouse/arena seats 3200 and hosts basketball and volleyball. There is also a 6-court indoor tennis center, a health and phys ed center that contains 3 basketball/volleyball courts, a running track, a swimming and diving pool, exercise rooms, 3 dance studios, 3 racquetball courts, and weight training and cardiovascular equipment. The athletic arena also includes a 6000-square-foot weight room.

Disabled Students: 95% of the campus is accessible. Facilities include wheelchair ramps, elevators, special parking, specially equipped restrooms, special class scheduling, lowered drinking fountains, special housing.

Services: Counseling and information services are available, as is tutoring in most subjects. There is a reader service for the blind.

Campus Safety and Security: Measures include 24-hour foot and vehicle patrol and security escort services. There are shuttle buses, emergency telephones, and lighted pathways/sidewalks.

Programs of Study: Hope confers B.A., B.S., B.Mus. and B.S.N. degrees. Bachelor's degrees are awarded in BIOLOGICAL SCIENCE (biology/biological science), BUSINESS (accounting and business administration and management), COMMUNICATIONS AND THE ARTS (communications, dance, dramatic arts, English, fine arts, French, German, Latin, music, and Spanish), COMPUTER AND PHYSICAL SCIENCE (chemistry, computer science, geology, mathematics, and physics), EDUCATION (art education, elementary education, foreign languages education, music education, science education, secondary education, and special education), ENGINEERING AND ENVIRONMENTAL DESIGN (engineering), HEALTH PROFESSIONS (nursing), SOCIAL SCIENCE (economics, history, international studies, philosophy, physical fitness/movement, political science/government, psychology, religion, social work, and sociology). Chemistry, biological sciences and psychology are the strongest academically. Management, communications and psychology have the largest enrollments.

Required: To graduate with a B.A. or B.S. degree, students must complete 126 semester hours with a 2.0 GPA. All students must take 56 hours of the general education program, including a first-year seminar, 10 hours of math and natural science, 8 of cultural heritage, 6 each of social science, performing and fine arts, and religion, 4 each of a language and writing, 4 in a senior seminar, 4 credits of cultural diversity courses, and 2 hours of health dynamics.

Special: The college offers internships in all academic areas as well as on-campus work-study programs, student-designed majors, study abroad in more than 57 countries, and Washington, Chicago, New York, and Philadelphia semesters. Students may have dual majors. There are 20 national honor societies, including Phi Beta Kappa, and 1 departmental honors program.

Faculty/Classroom: 53% of faculty are male; 47% are female. All teach undergraduates. No introductory courses are taught by graduate students. The average class size in an introductory lecture is 21; in a laboratory is 15; and in a regular course is 20.

Admissions: 82% of the 2013-2014 applicants were accepted. The SAT scores for the 2013-2014 freshman class were: Critical Reading--15% below 500, 37% between 500 and 599, 31% between 600 and 699, and 17% between 700 and 800; Math--16% below 500, 28% between 500 and 599, 42% between 600 and 699, and 14% between 700 and 800. 40% of the current freshmen were in the top fifth of their class; 58% were in the top two fifths.

Requirements: The SAT or ACT is required. All applicants must submit either an ACT or SAT score. The college requires a high school transcript, which must include 4 years of English, 2 each of math, a foreign language, and social science, and 1 year of a lab science, as well as 5 other academic courses. The college requires submission of an essay and recommends an interview. A portfolio or audition is required for certain majors. The GED is considered. AP and CLEP credits are accepted. Important factors in the admissions decision are advanced placement or honors courses, evidence of special talent, and leadership record.

Procedure: Freshmen are admitted fall and spring. Entrance exams should be taken during spring of the junior year or fall of the senior year. There are deferred admissions and rolling admissions plans. Application deadlines are open. The fall 2013 application fee was $35. Applications are accepted online.

Transfer: 60 transfer students enrolled in 2012-2013. Transfer students must have a GPA of 2.0 in at least 1 year of liberal arts courses. 30 of 126 credits required for the bachelor's degree must be completed at Hope.

Visiting: There are regularly scheduled orientations for prospective students, including tours, classes, lunch with a current student, and appointments with professors. There are guides for informal visits, visitors may sit in on classes, and stay overnight. To schedule a visit, contact the Admissions Office.

Financial Aid: In 2013-2014, 92% of all full-time freshmen and 79% of continuing full-time students received some form of financial aid. 58% of all full-time freshmen and 53% of continuing full-time students received need-based aid. The average freshman award was $17,612. Need-based scholarships or need-based grants averaged $10,660; need-based self-help aid (loans and jobs) averaged $2,703; and other non-need-based awards and non-need-based scholarships averaged $4,249. 24% of undergraduate students work part-time. Average annual earnings from campus work are $994. The average financial indebtedness of the 2013 graduate was $24,056. Hope is a member of CSS. The FAFSA and the college's own financial statement are required. The priority date for freshman financial aid applications for fall entry is March 1.

International Students: There are 67 international students enrolled. The school actively recruits these students. They must take the TOEFL with a minimum score of 79 on the Internet-based version (iBT). They must also take the SAT or ACT.

Graduates: From July 1, 2012 to June 30, 2013, 729 bachelor's degrees were awarded. The most popular majors were psychology (11%), management (9%), and communications (6%). 29 companies recruited on campus in 2012-2013. In an average class, 1% graduate in 3 years or less, 67% graduate in 4 years or less, 76% graduate in 5 years or less, and 77% graduate in 6 years or less. Of the 2012 graduating class, 26% were enrolled in graduate school within 6 months of graduation, and 76% were employed.

Admissions Contact: William C. Vanderbilt, Vice President for Admissions. E-Mail: *admissions@hope.edu* Web: *www.hope.edu*

KALAMAZOO COLLEGE D-5

Kalamazoo, MI 49006 (269) 337-7000
(800) 253-3602; (269) 337-7390

Full-time: 631 men, 815 women	**Faculty:** 100; IIB, av$
Part-time: 4 men, 8 women	**Ph.D.s:** 91%
Graduate: n/av	**Student/Faculty:** 13 to 1
Year: quarters	**Tuition:** $39,027
Application Deadline: February 1	**Room & Board:** $8175
Freshman Class: 2528 applied, 1691 accepted, 454 enrolled	
SAT CR/M/W: 615/640/605	**ACT:** 28 **HIGHLY COMPETITIVE+**

As a highly selective, nationally renowned, and internationally oriented four-year college of arts and sciences, Kalamazoo College has developed a tradition of excellence in the fulfillment of this mission. It is located in Kalamazoo, Michigan, and enrolls 1,379 students from 38 states and 32 countries. Founded in 1833, "K" College is among the 100 oldest colleges and universities in the nation. The library contains 397,384 volumes, 15,025 microform items, and 7,523 audio/video tapes/CDs/DVDs, and subscribes to 1,364 periodicals including electronic. Computerized library services include interlibrary loans, database searching, Internet access, and Wi-Fi capability. Special learning facilities include an art gallery, radio station, and TV station. The 60-acre campus is in a suburban area 140 miles from the Detroit and Chicago area. Including any residence halls, there are 30 buildings.

Student Life: 64% of undergraduates are from Michigan. Others are from 38 states, and 33 foreign countries. 80% are from public schools. 61% are White. The average age of freshmen is 18; all undergraduates, 20.

Housing: 875 students can be accommodated in college housing, which includes single-sex and coed dorms. In addition, there are special-interest houses, and a wellness house. On-campus housing is available on a lottery system for upperclassmen. 70% of students live on campus; of those, 75% remain on campus on weekends. Upperclassmen may keep cars.

Activities: There are no fraternities or sororities. There are 70 groups on campus, including art, cheerleading, chess, choir, chorus, computers, dance, drama, environmental, ethnic, film, gay, honors, international, jazz band, literary magazine, musical theater, newspaper, orchestra, photography, political, professional, radio and TV, religious, social, social service, student government, and symphony. Popular campus events include Homecoming, casino night, and K-Fest.

Sports: There are 8 intercollegiate sports for men and 9 for women, and 8 intramural sports for men and 7 for women. Facilities include a field house that houses a 2000-seat gym, basketball and volleyball courts, weight-training rooms, and a dance studio; a 1500-seat, 11-court tennis stadium; a racquet center with 4 tennis courts and 3 racquetball courts; a natatorium, an athletic field complex and field house, turf football and soccer/lacrosse fields as well as natural turf baseball and softball fields. A intramural/recreation field was also installed. Each of the athletic fields have bleachers, scoreboards, and press boxes. A stadium services building houses the football press box, restrooms, and a concession stand. The Kalamazoo College Field House has five team locker rooms, common meeting areas, a state-of-the-art athletic training facility, and the Hornets Suite used for larger gatherings and meetings.

Disabled Students: 25% of the campus is accessible. Facilities include wheelchair ramps, elevators, special parking, specially equipped restrooms, special class scheduling, and special housing.

Services: Counseling and information services are available, as is tutoring in most subjects.

Campus Safety and Security: Measures include 24-hour foot and vehicle patrol, emergency notification system, self-defense education, and security escort services. There are emergency telephones, lighted pathways/sidewalks, and controlled access to dorms/residences.

Programs of Study: Kalamazoo confers B.A. degrees. Bachelor's degrees are awarded in BIOLOGICAL SCIENCE (biology/biological science), BUSINESS (business economics), COMMUNICATIONS AND THE ARTS (art, art history and appreciation, dramatic arts, English, French, German, music, and Spanish), COMPUTER AND PHYSICAL SCIENCE (chemistry, computer science, mathematics, and physics), HEALTH PROFESSIONS (health science), SOCIAL SCIENCE (anthropology, classical/ancient civilization, economics, history, human development, interdisciplinary studies, international studies, philosophy, political science/government, psychology, religion, and sociology). Foreign languages, international studies and commerce, and health sciences are the strongest academically. Economics, business, pyschology, and biology have the largest enrollments.

Required: To graduate, students must complete 36 academic units, including a minimum of 8 units in the major, with a minimum 2.0 GPA. The college requires sophomore and senior seminars and completion of a senior individualized project. The student must also take 5 noncredit courses in phys ed and show proficiency in writing as well as in a foreign language.

Special: Kalamazoo College through the Center for International Programs currently sends students to 59 programs in 25 countries on 6 continents. Over the past four years, the K-College graduate participation rate in our study abroad programs is 80% to 85% and the school allows dual and interdisciplinary majors, and has Inter-Institutional enrollment with Western Michigan University. A 3-2 engineering degree is offered with Washington University and the University of Michigan. There are 3 national honor societies including Phi Beta Kappa.

Faculty/Classroom: 45% of faculty are male; 55% are female. All teach undergraduates. No introductory courses are taught by graduate students. The average class size in an introductory lecture is 26; in a laboratory is 14; and in a regular course is 22.

Admissions: 67% of the 2013-2014 applicants were accepted. The SAT scores for the 2013-2014 freshman class were: Critical Reading--12% below 500, 34% between 500 and 599, 37% between 600 and 699, and 17% between 700 and 800; Math--7% below 500, 31% between 500 and 599, 39% between 600 and 699, and 22% between 700 and 800; Writing--12% below 500, 35% between 500 and 599, 43% between 600 and 699, and 11% between 700 and 800. The ACT scores were 3% below 21, 11% between 21 and 23, 26% between 24 and 26, 24% between 27 and 28, and 35% above 28. 64 freshmen graduated first in their class.

Requirements: The SAT or ACT is required. The ACT Optional Writing test is also required. The college requires a high school transcript, an essay, supplement and teacher and counselor recommendations; an interview is recommended. Applications are online only. The College is a Common Application exclusive member. AP credits are accepted. Important factors in the admissions decision are recommendations by school officials, leadership record, and advanced placement or honors courses.

Procedure: Freshmen are admitted fall. Entrance exams should be taken by December of the senior year. There are early decision, early admissions, and deferred admissions plans. Early decision applications should be filed by November 10; regular applications, by February 1 for fall entry, along with a $40 fee. Notification of early decision is sent November 15; regular decision, January 15. 54 early decision candidates were accepted for the 2013-2014 class. 294 applicants were on the 2013 waiting list; were admitted. Applications are accepted online.

Transfer: 22 transfer students enrolled in 2012-2013. In addition to the Transfer Application, we require the College Official's Report, Instructor Evaluation, official high school and college transcripts. While an interview is not required, it is strongly recommended. And most cases, successful transfer applicants present grades of a B average or better in their current courses. 18 of 36 credits required for the bachelor's degree must be completed at Kalamazoo.

Visiting: There are regularly scheduled orientations for prospective students, including interviews, tours, overnight and class visits as requested. Special preview events include formal presentation of the unique curriculum and financial aid seminars. There are guides for informal visits, visitors may sit in on classes, and stay overnight. To schedule a visit, contact the Visit Coordinator at (877) 557-9755.

Financial Aid: In 2013-2014, 98% of all full-time freshmen and 98% of continuing full-time students received some form of financial aid. The average freshman award was $32,931. Need-based scholarships or need-based grants averaged $25,717; need-based self-help aid (loans and jobs) averaged $6,084; other non-need-based awards and non-need-based scholarships averaged $3,991; and $16,483 from other forms of aid. The average financial indebtedness of the 2013 graduate was $27,845. The FAFSA and the college's own financial statement are required. The priority date for freshman financial aid applications for fall entry is February 15.

International Students: There are 88 international students enrolled. The school actively recruits these students. They must take the TOEFL with a minimum score of 550 on the paper-based TOEFL (PBT) or 80 on the Internet-based version (iBT). They must also take the SAT or ACT.

Graduates: From July 1, 2012 to June 30, 2013, 312 bachelor's degrees were awarded. The most popular majors were social sciences (17%), biological/life sciences (13%), and physical sciences (9%). In an average class, 74% graduate in 4 years or less, 79% graduate in 5 years or less, and 80% graduate in 6 years or less. Of the 2012 graduating class, 21% were enrolled in graduate school within 6 months of graduation, and 48% were employed.

Admissions Contact: Eric P. Staab, Dean of Admission. E-Mail: *admissions@kzoo.edu* Web: *www.kzoo.edu*

KENDALL COLLEGE OF ART AND DESIGN OF FERRIS STATE UNIVERSITY D-4

Grand Rapids, MI 49503-3002 (616) 451-2787
(800) 676-2787; (616) 831-9689

Full-time: n/av	**Faculty:** n/av
Part-time: n/av	**Ph.D.s:** n/av
Graduate: n/av	**Student/Faculty:** n/av
Year: semesters, summer session	**Tuition:** $15,460 ($25,092)
Application Deadline: open	**Room & Board:** $8,744
Freshman Class: n/av	
SAT or ACT: required	**SPECIAL**

The Kendall College of Art and Design of Ferris State University, founded in 1928, is a commuter institution specializing in design studies and visual arts. The figures in the above capsule and in this profile are approximate. There is one graduate school. In addition to regional accreditation, Kendall has baccalaureate program accreditation with FIDER and NASAD. The library contains 23,000 volumes, 1,000 microform items, 3,500 audio/video tapes/CDs/DVDs, and subscribes to 150 periodicals including electronic. Computerized library services include interlibrary loans, database searching, Internet access, and laptop Internet portals. Special learning facilities include a learning resource center, art gallery, a model and wood shop, a photography lab, a printmaking lab, fine art studios, and a student gallery. The 3-acre campus is in an urban area in downtown Grand Rapids. Including any residence halls, there are 2 buildings.

Student Life: 91% of undergraduates are from Michigan. 90% are from public schools. 73% are white; 16% African American. The average age of all undergraduates is 24.

Housing: 144 students can be accommodated in college housing, which includes off-campus apartments. Alcohol is not permitted. All students commute.

Activities: There are no fraternities or sororities. There are 20 groups on campus, including art, computers, environmental, ethnic, film, gay, international, literary magazine, newspaper, photography, professional, and religious. Popular campus events include Annual Student Exhibition, Career Day Events, and Connect to Kendall events.

Sports: There is no sports program at Kendall. Facilities include Grand Rapids Community College's pool, track, and sports facilities, which students may use upon payment of an annual fee.

Disabled Students: All of the campus is accessible. Facilities include wheelchair ramps, elevators, special parking, specially equipped rest rooms, lowered drinking fountains, and lowered telephones.

Services: Counseling and information services are available, as is tutoring in every subject. There is a reader service for the blind.

Campus Safety and Security: Measures include emergency notification system and security escort services. There are emergency telephones, lighted pathways/sidewalks, and controlled access to dorms/residences.

Programs of Study: Kendall confers B.S. and B.F.A. degrees. Master's degrees are also awarded. Bachelor's degrees are awarded in COMMUNICATIONS AND THE ARTS (art history and appreciation, drawing, fine arts, graphic design, illustration, industrial design, media arts, metal/jewelry, multimedia, painting, photography, printmaking, and sculpture), COMPUTER AND PHYSICAL SCIENCE (digital arts/technology), EDUCATION (art education), ENGINEERING AND ENVIRONMENTAL DESIGN (furniture design, interior design, and woodworking). Illustration, graphic design, and interior design are the largest.

Required: To graduate, students must complete 120 credit hours, including 45 to 69 in the major, 30 to 45 of liberal arts and sciences, 12 to 18 of a foundation studio core, 12 to 15 of art history, and 12 to 15 of studio electives. All students must complete a graduation portfolio. A minimum GPA of 2.0 is required, with a minimum GPA of 2.25 in the student's major core courses.

Special: Study abroad may be arranged by the student and approved by the college; trips to Perugia, Italy, and London, England, are offered each year. Dual majors are possible.

Faculty/Classroom: 56% of faculty are male; 44% are female. All teach undergraduates. No introductory courses are taught by graduate students. The average class size in an introductory lecture is 30; in a laboratory is 15; and in a regular course is 20.

Requirements: The SAT or ACT is required. ACT or SAT are not required of applicants who are older than 23 years. In addition, a high school transcript is required. The GED certificate is accepted. Students must submit an essay with their application, and most majors require a portfolio review. An interview is recommended. Prospective students are encouraged to take courses in drawing, painting, and design in high school. A GPA of 2.5 is required. AP and CLEP credits are accepted. Important factors in the admissions decision are leadership record, personality/intangible qualities, and evidence of special talent.

Procedure: Freshmen are admitted to all sessions. There are early decision and rolling admissions plans. Application deadlines are open. Check with the school for the application fee.

Transfer: Applicants must have a GPA of 2.50 and pass a portfolio review. An interview is recommended. 30 of 120 credits required for the bachelor's degree must be completed at Kendall.

Visiting: There are regularly scheduled orientations for prospective students, consisting of "Connect to Kendall" events several times a year, during which prospective students may see student work, visit studios and classrooms, and talk with staff, faculty, and students. There are guides for informal visits and visitors may sit in on classes. To schedule a visit, contact the Admissions Office.

Financial Aid: The FAFSA is required. Check with the school for current application deadlines.

International Students: There were 8 international students enrolled in a recent year. The school actively recruits these students. They must take the TOEFL with a minimum score of 500 on the paper-based TOEFL (PBT) or 61 on the Internet-based version (iBT). They must also take the SAT or ACT.

Admissions Contact: Director of Enrollment Management. *Web: www.kcad.edu*

KETTERING UNIVERSITY E-4

Flint, MI 48504-4898 (810) 762-7865
(800) 955-4464; (810) 762-9837

Full-time: 1875 men, 330 women	**Faculty:** n/av; IIB, +$
Part-time: n/av	**Ph.D.s:** 93%
Graduate: 355 men, 150 women	**Student/Faculty:** n/av
Year: semesters, summer session	**Tuition:** $30,060
Application Deadline: open	**Room & Board:** $9,244
Freshman Class: n/av	

HIGHLY COMPETITIVE

Kettering University is a private college founded in 1919. The figures in the above capsule and in this profile are approximate. In the 4.5-year undergraduate program, students alternate 11-week terms of full-time classes with 12-week terms of full-time paid professional cooperative education (co-op) work experience in industry. Students typically begin co-op during their freshman year and co-op in 43 states and several countries. There are 3 undergraduate schools and one graduate school. In addition to regional accreditation, Kettering has baccalaureate program accreditation with ABET and ACBSP. The library contains 133,210 volumes, 35,000 microform items, 800 audio/video tapes/CDs/DVDs, and subscribes to 400 periodicals including electronic. Computerized library services include interlibrary loans, database searching, and Internet access. Special learning facilities include a learning resource center, art gallery, radio station, Industrial History Archives. The 85-acre campus is in a suburban area 60 miles north of Detroit. Including any residence halls, there are 10 buildings.

Student Life: 66% of undergraduates are from Michigan. Students are from 49 states, 18 foreign countries, and Canada. 85% are from public schools. 75% are white. The average age of freshmen is 18; all undergraduates, 21. 86% do not continue beyond their first year; 64% remain to graduate.

Housing: 623 students can be accommodated in college housing, which includes single-sex and coed dorms and on-campus apartments. In addition, there are fraternity houses and sorority houses. On-campus housing is guaranteed for the freshman year only and is available on a lottery system for upperclassmen. Priority is given to out-of-town students. 79% of students commute. Alcohol is not permitted. All students may keep cars.

Activities: 37% of men belong to 13 national fraternities; 31% of women belong to 6 national sororities. There are 43 groups on campus, including art, band, computers, dance, drama, environmental, ethnic, gay, honors, international, literary magazine, newspaper, photography, political, professional, radio and TV, religious, social, social service, student government, and yearbook. Popular campus events include Greek Week, Diversity Week, and Student and Alumni Industry Speaker Series.

Sports: Facilities include a recreation center with 2 basketball/volleyball and 2 tennis/basketball/volleyball courts; 3 racquetball and squash courts; a one-eighth mile track; an Olympic-size pool, free weight, Nautilus, fitness room with comprehensive assortment of fitness machines and group exercise room. A 5 acre sports and recreation complex includes 4 softball and 2 multipurpose fields, a golf green, a 1 km outdoor track, 2 sand volleyball courts, and a picnic pavilion.

Disabled Students: All of the campus is accessible. Facilities include wheelchair ramps, elevators, special parking, specially equipped rest rooms, special class scheduling, lowered drinking fountains, and lowered telephones.

Services: Counseling and information services are available, as is tutoring in most subjects. Tutoring is routinely available for most subjects in the Academic Support Center, in the residence hall, and with faculty. Supplemental tutoring is coordinated through the Academic Services Department. Math and writing labs are available. A Strategies for Academic Success program is available.

Campus Safety and Security: Measures include 24-hour foot and vehicle patrol, self-defense education, and security escort services. There are emergency telephones, lighted pathways/sidewalks, controlled access to dorms/residences, and after-hours access (e.g., to the academic building) is secure via the tunnel from the residence hall and campus center.

Programs of Study: Kettering confers B.S. degrees. Master's degrees are also awarded. Bachelor's degrees are awarded in BIOLOGICAL SCIENCE (biochemistry), COMPUTER AND PHYSICAL SCIENCE (applied mathematics, applied physics, chemistry, and computer science), ENGINEERING AND ENVIRONMENTAL DESIGN (computer engineering, electrical/electronics engineering, engineering physics, industrial engineering, and mechanical engineering). Mechanical, electrical, and computer engineering have the largest enrollments.

Required: Degree requirements include completion of 160 credit hours, with 60 in the major. All students must take specific courses in math, chemistry, physics, written and oral communication, humanities, and economics, and complete at least 5 terms of co-op experience in industry plus 2 work terms designated for a senior thesis project. A minimum grade average of 80 on a scale of 100 is required for graduation. The GPA is determined by a formula combining the numerical grades achieved and the number of credits attempted. Students must complete a thesis.

Special: All undergraduate students participate in paid professional cooperative education work experience. Students may pursue a dual major in any degree combination. Accelerated degree programs in engineering are available in most majors, as is study abroad in 3 countries. There are 8 national honor societies.

Faculty/Classroom: 80% of faculty are male; 20% are female. All teach undergraduates, 16% do research, and 16% do both. No introductory courses are taught by graduate students. The average class size in an introductory lecture is 40; in a laboratory is 14; and in a regular course is 20.

Requirements: The SAT or ACT is required. Applicants must graduate from an accredited secondary school with a minimum of 16 academic credits. Applicants must have completed 3 years of English, 3 1/2 years of math, including trigonometry, and 2 years of lab science, 1 of which must be chemistry or physics (both are strongly recommended). AP credits are accepted. Important factors in the admissions decision are leadership record, advanced placement or honors courses, and extracurricular activities record.

Procedure: Freshmen are admitted fall, winter, and summer. Entrance exams should be taken during the spring of the junior year and fall of the senior year. There are deferred admissions and rolling admissions plans. Application deadlines are open. Check with the school for the current application fee. Applications are accepted online.

Transfer: 40 transfer students enrolled in a recent year. Transfer applicants must present the same minimum preparation as freshmen in math and science and must submit both high school and college transcripts and SAT or ACT scores. Required courses can be taken in high school or college. A minimum GPA of 3.0 in English, math, and science is expected. Transfers who present less than 30 credits of full-time study will be judged on both their college and high school record and test scores. 88 of 160 credits required for the bachelor's degree must be completed at Kettering.

Visiting: There are regularly scheduled orientations for prospective students, including 2 open house programs for prospective students. There are guides for informal visits, visitors may sit in on classes, and stay overnight. To schedule a visit, contact the Admissions Office.

Financial Aid: In a recent year, 89% of all full-time freshmen and 84% of continuing full-time students received some form of financial aid. 79% of all full-time freshmen and 67% of continuing full-time students received need-based aid. The average freshmen award was $18,078, with $3,672 ($4,700 maximum) from need-based self-help aid (loans and jobs). 18% of undergraduate students work part-time. Average annual earnings from campus work are $820. The FAFSA and the college's own financial statement are required. Check with the school for current application deadlines.

International Students: There were 33 international students enrolled in a recent year. The school actively recruits these students. They must take the TOEFL or MELAB.

Graduates: In a recent year, 395 bachelor's degrees were awarded. The most popular majors were mechanical engineering (57%), electrical engineering (17%), and computer engineering (8%). In an average class, 5% graduate in 4 years or less, 52% graduate in 5 years or less, and 61% graduate in 6 years or less. 40% were enrolled in graduate school within 6 months of graduation, and 96% were employed.

Admissions Contact: Director of Admissions. E-Mail: *admissions@kettering.edu* Web: *www.kettering.edu*

LAKE SUPERIOR STATE UNIVERSITY D-2

Sault Sainte Marie, MI 49783 **(906) 635-2693**
(888) 800-5778; (906) 635-6669

Full-time: 1082 men, 1022 women	**Faculty:** 114
Part-time: 180 men, 237 women	**Ph.D.s:** 60%
Graduate: 1 men, 7 women	**Student/Faculty:** 17 to 1
Year: semesters, summer session	**Tuition:** $9640 ($14,510)
Application Deadline: open	**Room & Board:** $8481
Freshman Class: 1425 applied, 1278 accepted, 429 enrolled	
ACT: 21	

COMPETITIVE

Lake Superior State University, founded in 1946, is a public university that provides a blend of liberal and technical studies, offering undergraduate degrees in 45 areas of study. There are 12 undergraduate schools and 1 graduate school. In addition to regional accreditation, Lake State has baccalaureate program accreditation with ABET and NLN. The library contains 106,618 volumes, and 810 audio/video tapes/CDs/DVDs, and subscribes to 950 periodicals including electronic. Computerized library services include interlibrary loans and database searching. Special learning facilities include a natural history museum, planetarium, radio station, fish hatchery and aquatics lab, and interactive television for distance education. The 115-acre campus is in a small town in Michigan's Upper Peninsula, 45 minutes north of the Mackinac Bridge. Including any residence halls, there are 37 buildings.

Student Life: 90% of undergraduates are from Michigan. Others are from states, and Canada. 79% are White. The average age of freshmen is 18; all undergraduates, 23. 30% do not continue beyond their first year; 70% remain to graduate.

Housing: 900 students can be accommodated in college housing, which includes single-sex and coed dorms, on-campus apartments, and married student housing. In addition, there are honors houses, fraternity houses, and sorority houses. On-campus housing is guaranteed for the freshman year only, is available on a first-come, first-served basis, and is available on a lottery system for upperclassmen. 66% of students commute. All students may keep cars.

Activities: There are 60 groups on campus, including band, cheerleading, chess, chorale, computers, dance, drama, ethnic, film, gay, honors, jazz band, newspaper, pep band, political, professional, radio and TV, religious, social, social service, and student government. Popular campus events include Winter Carnival, Spring Fling and Great Lake State Weekend.

Sports: There are 5 intercollegiate sports for men and 6 for women. Facilities include a 4000-seat ice arena, a 2500-seat gym with a new hardwood floor, swimming and diving pools, 4 handball/squash courts, a weight-training and isometric room, a dance studio, a training room, a firing range, and offices.

Disabled Students: Facilities include wheelchair ramps, elevators, special parking, specially equipped restrooms, special class scheduling, lowered drinking fountains, and lowered telephones.

Services: Counseling and information services are available, as is tutoring in most subjects, on request and free of charge. There is a reader service for the blind, and remedial math, reading, and writing. There are also math, reading, and writing labs.

Campus Safety and Security: Measures include 24-hour foot and vehicle patrol, self-defense education, and security escort services. There are lighted pathways/sidewalks.

Programs of Study: Lake State confers B.A., and B.S. degrees. Associate and master's degrees are also awarded. Bachelor's degrees are awarded in AGRICULTURE (fish and game management and wildlife management), BIOLOGICAL SCIENCE (biology/biological science), BUSINESS (accounting, banking and finance, business administration and management, international business management, and marketing/retailing/merchandising), COMMUNICATIONS AND THE ARTS (communications, English, fine arts, and Spanish), COMPUTER AND PHYSICAL SCIENCE (chemistry, computer management, computer science, geology, information sciences and systems, and mathematics), EDUCATION (athletic training, early childhood education, elementary education, and secondary education), ENGINEERING AND ENVIRONMENTAL DESIGN (computer engineering, electrical/electronics engineering, engineering, engineering management, engineering technology, environmental engineering technology, environmental science, manufacturing technology, and mechanical engineering), HEALTH PROFESSIONS (clinical science, environmental health science, exercise science, medical laboratory technology, nursing, predentistry, premedicine, and recreation therapy), SOCIAL SCIENCE (criminal justice, economics, fire science, forensic studies, French studies, history, human services, paralegal studies, parks and recreation management, political science/government, prelaw, psychology, social science, and sociology). Engineering technology, nursing, and natural sciences are the strongest academically. Business and criminal justice have the largest enrollments.

Required: To graduate, students must complete 124 semester hours with a GPA of 2.0. The core curriculum includes course work in computer literacy, English, oral communications, aesthetics, critical thinking, humanities, math, science, social science, ethics, and cultural diversity. At least 32 of the final credits, and 50% of all upper-level courses, must be taken in residence at Lake State. Math and English competency must be met.

Special: Lake State offers internships in criminal justice, medical technology, human services, legal assistance studies, and natural resources technology, work-study programs, co-op programs in engineering technology, and cross-registration with the Canadian Colleges of Sault and Algoma and Bridge International Consortium. Study abroad and student-designed majors are available, as are B.A.-B.S. degrees and dual majors. Distance learning and weekend college study formats are offered. There is a freshman honors program.

Faculty/Classroom: 43% of faculty are male; 47% are female. All teach undergraduates, and 20% do both. No introductory courses are taught by graduate students. The average class size in an introductory lecture is 25; in a laboratory is 15; and in a regular course is 30.

Admissions: 90% of the 2013-2014 applicants were accepted. The ACT scores were 35% below 21, 29% between 21 and 23, 21% between 24 and 26, 9% between 27 and 28, and 6% above 28.

Requirements: The ACT is required. Applicants should be high school graduates with 4 years of English, 3 each of math and science, 2 each of a foreign language and social studies, and 1 of history and should have a GPA of 2.0. The GED is accepted. AP and CLEP credits are accepted. Important factors in the admissions decision are advanced placement or honors courses, recommendations by school officials, and recommendations by alumni.

Procedure: Freshmen are admitted to all sessions. There are deferred admissions and rolling admissions plans. Application deadlines are open. The fall 2013 application fee was $35. Applications are accepted online.

Transfer: 186 transfer students enrolled in 2012-2013. Applicants must be eligible to return to the last institution attended and must have an overall college GPA of 2.0. High school transcripts, ACT scores, and/or GED scores are required if transferring with fewer than 19 semester hours of credit. 32 of 124 credits required for the bachelor's degree must be completed at Lake State.

Visiting: There are regularly scheduled orientations for prospective students. There are guides for informal visits and visitors may sit in on classes. To schedule a visit, contact the Admissions Office.

Financial Aid: In 2013-2014, 73% of all full-time freshmen and 69% of continuing full-time students received some form of financial aid. 61% of all full-time freshmen and 62% of continuing full-time students received need-based aid. The average freshman award was $10,306. Average annual earnings from campus work are $2500. The average financial indebtedness of the 2013 graduate was $22,896. The FAFSA and OSAP is required. The priority date for freshman financial aid applications for fall entry is February 21.

International Students: The school actively recruits these students. They must take the TOEFL.

Graduates: From July 1, 2012 to June 30, 2013, 427 bachelor's degrees were awarded. The most popular majors were protective services (18%), business (17%), and health professions (12%). In an average class, 40% graduate in 6 years or less.

Admissions Contact: Allan Case, Director of Admissions. E-Mail: *admissions@lssu.edu* Web: *www.lssu.edu*

LAWRENCE TECHNOLOGICAL UNIVERSITY E-5

Southfield, MI 48075 **(248) 204-3160**
(800) CALL-LTU; (248) 204-3188

Full-time: 1097 men, 439 women	**Faculty:** 119
Part-time: 1193 men, 304 women	**Ph.D.s:** 67%
Graduate: 661 men, 308 women	**Student/Faculty:** 11 to 1
Year: semesters, summer session	**Tuition:** $28,948
Application Deadline:	**Room & Board:** $8682
Freshman Class: 2076 applied, 1196 accepted, 365 enrolled	
SAT CR/M/W: 510/620/550 **ACT:** 25	**VERY COMPETITIVE**

Lawrence Technological University, founded in 1932 as Lawrence Institute of Technology, is a private institution housing colleges of engineering, management, arts and sciences, and architecture and design. There are 4 undergraduate schools and 4 graduate schools. In addition to regional accreditation, Lawrence Tech has baccalaureate program accreditation with ABET, ACBSP, FIDER, NAAB, and NASAD. The library contains 213,260 volumes, 30,260 microform items, 768 audio/video tapes/CDs/DVDs, and subscribes to 90,100 periodicals including electronic. Computerized library services include interlibrary loans, database searching, Internet access, and Wi-Fi capability. The 102-acre campus is in a suburban area 30 minutes north of downtown Detroit. Including any residence halls, there are 11 buildings.

Student Life: 97% of undergraduates are from Michigan. Others are from 23 states, 33 foreign countries, and Canada. 46% are White; 23% Asian American; 18% race unknown. The average age of freshmen is 19; all undergraduates, 22. 18% do not continue beyond their first year; 48% remain to graduate.

Housing: 616 students can be accommodated in college housing, which includes coed on-campus apartments and off-campus apartments. On-campus housing is available on a first-come and first-served basis. 80% of students commute. All students may keep cars.

Activities: 6% of men belong to 1 local and 6 national fraternities; 6% of women belong to 2 local and 2 national sororities. There are 49 groups on campus, including art, cheerleading, chess, computers, dance, ethnic, gay, honors, international, literary magazine, newspaper, political, professional, religious, Robotics, social, and student government. Popular campus events include Discovery Days, New Student Convocation, and Welcome Back Picnic.

Sports: There are 5 intercollegiate sports for men and 6 for women, and 13 intramural sports for men and 13 for women. Facilities include a field house with 4 racquetball courts, a weight room, a track, a sauna, and a gym.

Disabled Students: 97% of the campus is accessible. Facilities include wheelchair ramps, elevators, special parking, specially equipped restrooms, special class scheduling, lowered drinking fountains, lowered telephones, and special housing.

Services: Counseling and information services are available, as is tutoring in most subjects. There is a reader service for the blind, and remedial math, reading, and writing. There is also an Academic Achievement Center

Campus Safety and Security: Measures include 24-hour foot and vehicle patrol, emergency notification system, and security escort services. There are emergency telephones, lighted pathways/sidewalks, and closed-circuit camera monitoring.

Programs of Study: Lawrence Tech confers B.A., B.S., B.F.A. and B.F.M. degrees. Associate, master's, and doctoral degrees are also awarded. Bachelor's degrees are awarded in BIOLOGICAL SCIENCE (biochemistry, biotechnology, and molecular biology), BUSINESS (business administration and management and international business management), COMMUNICATIONS AND THE ARTS (animation, audio technology, communications, English, game design and development, illustration, industrial design, information technology, media arts, and technical and business writing), COMPUTER AND PHYSICAL SCIENCE (chemistry, computer science, environmental chemistry, information sciences and systems, mathematics, mathematics/computational, and physics), ENGINEERING AND ENVIRONMENTAL DESIGN (architectural engineering, architecture, biomedical engineering, civil engineering, computer engineering, computer graphics, construction management, electrical/electronics engineering, engineering, engineering technology, industrial administration/management, industrial engineering, interior architecture, interior design, mechanical engineering, technological management, and transportation engineering), SOCIAL SCIENCE (architectural studies, humanities, and psychology). Mathematics, computer science, and engineering are the strongest academically. Engineering and architecture have the largest enrollments.

Required: To graduate, students must have completed, depending on the major, 120 to 131 semester credit hours, with a GPA no lower than 2.0. Senior projects are required in most degree programs.

Special: There are co-op programs in a number of majors, internships, study abroad in 8 countries and dual majors available. There are 8 national honor societies and 6 departmental honors programs.

Faculty/Classroom: 70% of faculty are male; 30% are female. 90% teach undergraduates. No introductory courses are taught by graduate students. The average class size in an introductory lecture is 17; in a laboratory is 12; and in a regular course is 15.

Admissions: 58% of the 2013-2014 applicants were accepted. The SAT scores for the 2013-2014 freshman class were: Critical Reading--41% below 500, 20% between 500 and 599, 26% between 600 and 699, and 13% between 700 and 800; Math--21% below 500, 23% between 500 and 599, 38% between 600 and 699, and 18% between 700 and 800; Writing--37% below 500, 42% between 500 and 599, 18% between 600 and 699, and 3% between 700 and 800. The ACT scores were 19% below 21, 16% between 21 and 23, 25% between 24 and 26, 12% between 27 and 28, and 27% above 28. 43% of the current freshmen were in the top fifth of their class; 69% were in the top two fifths. 3 freshmen graduated first in their class.

Requirements: The ACT is required. The SAT is recommended. Students must have a high school diploma and a GPA of no lower than 2.5, at least 2.0 in each subject area pertaining to their major. Applicants should have taken 4 years each of math, science, and English, and 3 years of social science. The GED is accepted. An interview is recommended. A GPA of 2.5 is required. AP and CLEP credits are accepted. Important factors in the admissions decision are advanced placement or honors courses, personality/intangible qualities, and leadership record.

Procedure: Freshmen are admitted to all sessions. Entrance exams should be taken in the semester preceding entry. There are deferred admissions and rolling admissions plans. Application deadlines are open. Application fee is $30. Notification is sent on a rolling basis. Applications are accepted online.

Transfer: 220 transfer students enrolled in 2012-2013. Admission is based on the college GPA, which must be 2.0 or higher, with 30 or more semester hours. If less than 30 hours have been completed, admission is based on high school transcripts. 30 of 120 credits required for the bachelor's degree must be completed at Lawrence Tech.

Visiting: There are regularly scheduled orientations for prospective students. There are guides for informal visits, visitors may sit in on classes, and stay overnight. To schedule a visit, contact the Admissions Office.

Financial Aid: In 2013-2014, 90% of all full-time freshmen and 77% of continuing full-time students received some form of financial aid. 57% of all full-time freshmen and 58% of continuing full-time students received need-based aid. The average freshman award was $15,354. Need-based scholarships or need-based grants averaged $15,644 ($29,565 maximum); need-based self-help aid (loans and jobs) averaged $6,957 ($15,500 maximum); non-need-based athletic scholarships averaged $9,401 ($35,628 maximum); and other non-need-based awards and non-need-based scholarships averaged $13,955 ($35,628 maximum). 93% of undergraduate students work part-time. Average annual earnings from campus work are $2114. The average financial indebtedness of the 2013 graduate was $42,044. Lawrence Tech is a member of CSS. The FAFSA is required. The deadline for filing freshman financial aid applications for fall entry is April 1.

International Students: There are 141 international students enrolled. The school actively recruits these students. They must take the TOEFL with a minimum score of 550 on the paper-based TOEFL (PBT) or 79 on the Internet-based version (iBT) or take the MELAB and the Comprehensive English Language Test. Placement exams for incoming freshman only.

Graduates: From July 1, 2012 to June 30, 2013, 405 bachelor's degrees were awarded. The most popular majors were architecture (31%), engineering (30%), and computer science (14%). 300 companies recruited on campus in 2012-2013. In an average class, 32% graduate in 4 years or less, 38% graduate in 5 years or less, and 42% graduate in 6 years or less. Of the 2012 graduating class, 19% were enrolled in graduate school within 6 months of graduation, and 87% were employed.

Admissions Contact: Jane Rohrback, Admissions Director. E-Mail: *admissions@ltu.edu* Web: *www.ltu.edu*

MADONNA UNIVERSITY E-5

Livonia, MI 48150 (734) 432-5341
(800) 852-4951; (734) 432-5424

Full-time: 502 men, 1165 women	**Faculty:** 95; IIB, -$
Part-time: 600 men, 1101 women	**Ph.D.s:** 54%
Graduate: 235 men, 824 women	**Student/Faculty:** 15 to 1
Year: semesters, summer session	**Tuition:** $16,340
Application Deadline: open	**Room & Board:** $8200
Freshman Class: 1071 applied, 665 accepted, 208 enrolled	
SAT CR/M/W: 630/580/560 **ACT:** 23	**VERY COMPETITIVE**

Founded in 1947 by the Felician Sisters with the values of St. Francis of Assisi, Madonna University is an independent Catholic university where students receive a quality liberal arts education combined with a career preparation and community service. There are 7 undergraduate schools and 1 graduate school. In addition to regional accreditation, MU has baccalaureate program accreditation with CSWE and NCATE. The library contains 191,242 volumes, 453,260 microform items, and 938 audio/video tapes/CDs/DVDs, and subscribes to 64,451 periodicals including electronic. Computerized library services include interlibrary loans, database searching, Internet access, and Wi-Fi capability. Special learning facilities include an art gallery, radio station, TV station, a writing lab, the center for Personalized Instruction, sign language studies lab, Franciscan Center for Science & Media, and nursing simulation labs. The 82-acre campus is in a suburban area 25 miles west of Detroit. Including any residence halls, there are 5 buildings.

Student Life: 99% of undergraduates are from Michigan. Others are from 6 states, 7 foreign countries, and Canada. 76% are from public schools. 61% are White; 16% Foreign; 12% African American. 36% are Catholic; 34% Hindu, Muslim, or undeclared; 21% Protestant. The average age of freshmen is 19; all undergraduates, 27. 18% do not continue beyond their first year; 57% remain to graduate.

Housing: 272 students can be accommodated in college housing, which includes single-sex dorms. On-campus housing is guaranteed for all 4 years. 92% of students commute. Alcohol is not permitted. All students may keep cars.

Activities: There are no fraternities or sororities. There are 40 groups on campus, including Future Alumni Network, art, choir, chorale, computers, dance, environmental, ethnic, film, honors, international, literary magazine, musical theater, newspaper, Peace and Justice, photography, professional, radio and TV, religious, social, social service, and student government. Popular campus events include Peace and Justice Week.

Sports: There are 5 intercollegiate sports for men and 6 for women. Facilities include Madonna athletic facilities include the Livonia campus Activities Center, where basketball and volleyball are played, as well as Ilitch Ballpark (baseball) Madonna University Field (softball), and a new synthetic turf soccer field. In addition, the golf teams use several area golf courses, and cross-country calls Cass Benton Park home. The activities center includes a weight training room, and a 1500 700-seat gym.

Disabled Students: All of the campus is accessible. Facilities include wheelchair ramps, elevators, special parking, specially equipped restrooms, special class scheduling, lowered drinking fountains, lowered telephones. telecommunication devices and visible fire alarms for hearing-impaired students, talking books, tape recorders, diagnostic testing service, early syllabus, recorded exams, a Learning Center, oral exams, proofreading service, reading machine, take-home exams, software for vision impaired students, and adjustable computer monitors.

Services: Counseling and information services are available, as is tutoring in most subjects. There is a reader service for the blind, and remedial math, reading, and writing. Interpreters and note takers for hearing-impaired and visually impaired students, controlled dormitory access, and student patrols are available.

Campus Safety and Security: Measures include 24-hour foot and vehicle patrol, emergency notification system, and security escort services. There are emergency telephones, lighted pathways/sidewalks, controlled access to dorms/residences, an emergency car service.

Programs of Study: MU confers B.A., B.S., B.A.S., B.Mus, B.S.N., B.S.W., B.A.P.M. and B.A.P.T. degrees. Associate, master's, and doctoral degrees are also awarded. Bachelor's degrees are awarded in BIOLOGICAL SCIENCE (biochemistry, biology/biological science, and nutrition), BUSINESS (accounting, business administration and management, hospitality management services, international business management, management science, marketing/retailing/merchandising, and sports management), COMMUNICATIONS AND THE ARTS (art, broadcasting, communications, English, fine arts, graphic design, journalism, language arts, music, Spanish, speech/debate/rhetoric, technical and business writing, and video), COMPUTER AND PHYSICAL SCIENCE (applied science, chemistry, computer science, information sciences and systems, mathematics, natural sciences, and science), EDUCATION (art education, music education, and secondary education), ENGINEERING AND ENVIRONMENTAL DESIGN (commercial art, environmental science, and occupational safety and health), HEALTH PROFESSIONS (allied health, hospice care, medical laboratory technology, and nursing), SOCIAL SCIENCE (child psychology/development, criminal justice, dietetics, family/consumer studies, fire science, food science, gerontology, history, interpreter for the deaf, Japanese studies, liberal arts/general studies, pastoral studies, psychology, religion, religious music, safety and security technology, social science have the largest enrollments.

Required: To graduate, students must complete at least 120 semester hours with a 2.0 GPA; required hours in the major vary from 30 to 65, including a capstone senior seminar. A minimum of 52 hours of general education courses are required, including a writing assessment unless waived per ACT writing subscore. There is a residency requirement that the last 15 (associates) or 30 (baccalaureate) semester hours must be completed at Madonna.

Special: Madonna University participates in a Metro Detroit Catholic College Consortium with Marygrove College, Sacred Heart Seminary, and the University of Detroit Mercy. Students may pursue co-op programs in 30 majors, internships, and may receive prior learning for life, military, or work experience. Work-study positions are available at Madonna University. Study abroad in 17 countries is also possible. There are 11 national honor societies.

Faculty/Classroom: 42% of faculty are male; 58% are female. 99% teach undergraduates. No introductory courses are taught by graduate students. The average class size in an introductory lecture is 18; in a laboratory is 15; and in a regular course is 18.

Admissions: 62% of the 2013-2014 applicants were accepted. The SAT scores for the 2013-2014 freshman class were: Critical Reading--20% below 500, 60% between 600 and 699, and 20% between 700 and 800; Math--20% below 500, 40% between 500 and 599, 20% between 600 and 699, and 20% between 700 and 800; Writing--20% below 500, 60% between 500 and 599, and 20% between 700 and 800. The ACT scores were 27% below 21, 29% between 21 and 23, 25% between 24 and 26, 11% between 27 and 28, and 8% above 28. 36% of the current freshmen were in the top fifth of their class. 1 freshman graduated first in the class.

Requirements: The ACT is required. In addition, a student should have completed 4 years of English, 3 of math, 2 of science, and 1 of history. The school accepts the GED. An essay is required. For some majors, students are asked to submit a portfolio or to appear for an interview or audition. A GPA of 2.8 is required. AP and CLEP credits are accepted. Important factors in the admissions decision are advanced placement or honors courses, recommendations by school officials, and leadership record.

Procedure: Freshmen are admitted to all sessions. Entrance exams should be taken during either the junior or senior year. There is a rolling admissions plan. Application deadlines are open. Application fee is $25. Notification is sent on a rolling basis. Applications are accepted online.

Transfer: 504 transfer students enrolled in 2012-2013. Applicants must be in good academic and personal standing at their previous colleges and must submit official transcripts of college and high school work. Courses completed at an accredited institution with a grade of C or better will be considered for transfer credit. 30 of 120 credits required for the bachelor's degree must be completed at MU.

Visiting: There are regularly scheduled orientations for prospective students, Includes an interview and a tour of the campus. Provides an opportunity to learn about academic and support services, opportunities, and programs for a successful college experience. There are guides for informal visits, visitors may sit in on classes, and stay overnight. To schedule a visit, contact Office of Undergraduate Admissions at admissions@madonna .edu.

Financial Aid: 15% of undergraduate students work part-time. Average annual earnings from campus work are $1216. The average financial indebtedness of the 2013 graduate was $26,510. The FAFSA is required. The priority date for freshman financial aid applications for fall entry is March 1.

International Students: There are 93 international students enrolled. The school actively recruits these students.

Graduates: From July 1, 2012 to June 30, 2013, 710 bachelor's degrees were awarded. The most popular majors were nursing (19%), criminal justice (10%), and international business (4%). 22 companies recruited on campus in 2012-2013. In an average class, 21% graduate in 4 years or less, 46% graduate in 5 years or less, and 56% graduate in 6 years or less. Of the 2012 graduating class, 21% were enrolled in graduate school within 6 months of graduation, and 88% were employed.

Admissions Contact: Michael Quattro, Director of Undergraduate Admissions. E-Mail: *mquattro@madonna.edu* Web: *www.madonna.edu*

MARYGROVE COLLEGE E-5

Detroit, MI 48221 (313) 927-1240
(866) 313-1927; (313) 927-1345

Full-time: 119 men, 339 women
Part-time: 56 men, 274 women
Graduate: 410 men, 1558 women
Year: semesters, summer session
Application Deadline: August 15
Freshman Class: 802 applied, 353 accepted, 127 enrolled
ACT: 17
Faculty: 55; IIA, --$
Ph.D.s: 85%
Student/Faculty: 8 to 1
Tuition: $14,690
Room & Board: $6600

COMPETITIVE

Founded in 1927 and grounded in the liberal arts, Marygrove College is a private comprehensive institution affiliated with the Catholic Church. In addition to regional accreditation, has baccalaureate program accreditation with CSWE. The library contains 76,689 volumes, 68,750 microform items, and 2,834 audio/video tapes/CDs/DVDs, and subscribes to 447 periodicals including electronic. Computerized library services include interlibrary loans and database searching. Special learning facilities include an art gallery, a writing center, a learning clinic, and a theater. The 50-acre campus is in an urban area 11 miles from downtown Detroit. Including any residence halls, there are 4 buildings.

Student Life: 99% of undergraduates are from Michigan. Others 9 foreign countries. 63% are African American. The average age of freshmen is 20; all undergraduates, 30.

Housing: 110 students can be accommodated in college housing, which includes coed dorms. 86% of students commute. Alcohol is not permitted. All students may keep cars.

Activities: 1% of men belong to 4 local and 4 national fraternities; 10% of women belong to 2 local and 2 national sororities. There are 12 groups on campus, including art, choir, chorale, computers, dance, honors, religious, social service, and student government. Popular campus events include Spirit Week, and Martin Luther King Week, and Contemporary American Authors Lecture Series.

Sports: There is 1 intercollegiate sports for men and 1 for women. Facilities include a fitness center and a gym.

Disabled Students: 90% of the campus is accessible. Facilities include wheelchair ramps, elevators, special parking, specially equipped restrooms, lowered drinking fountains.

Services: Counseling and information services are available, as is tutoring in most subjects. There is remedial math, reading, and writing.

Campus Safety and Security: Measures include 24-hour foot and vehicle patrol, emergency notification system, self-defense education, and security escort services. There are emergency telephones and lighted pathways/sidewalks.

Programs of Study: confers B.A., B.S., B.A.S., B.B.A., B.F.A., B.M. and B.S.W. degrees. Associate and master's degrees are also awarded. Bachelor's degrees are awarded in BIOLOGICAL SCIENCE (biology/biological science), BUSINESS (business administration and management), COMMUNICATIONS AND THE ARTS (art, dance, English, language arts, and music), COMPUTER AND PHYSICAL SCIENCE (chemistry, computer science, mathematics, and science), EDUCATION (early childhood education, social studies education, and special education), ENGINEERING AND ENVIRONMENTAL DESIGN (environmental science), HEALTH PROFESSIONS (art therapy), SOCIAL SCIENCE (child psychology/development, criminal justice, forensic studies, history, political science/government, psychology, religion, social science, and social work). Business, English, and education are the strongest academically. Business, English, forensic science, and education have the largest enrollments.

Required: To graduate, students must complete 128 semester hours with a minimum GPA of 2.0. The required core program includes 28 credit hours with a minimum of one 3 to 4 hour course in the following nine areas: historical and cultural traditions, literature and languages, scientific inquiry (lab science), identity and reason, social environment, religious and philosophical traditions, creative expression, local and national perspectives, and global awareness. Common Experience requirements include: liberal arts seminar (for freshmen only), communication, writing-intensive course in major, and senior seminar. The required number of hours in the major varies.

Special: A consortium program is offered with the University of Detroit Mercy, Sacred Heart Seminary, and Madonna University. Also available are nondegree study, student-designed and dual majors, study abroad in 5 countries, internships, pass/fail options, and work-study programs. Students may acquire credit for life experience by documenting their achievements in a portfolio. There are 4 national honor societies and a freshman honors program.

Faculty/Classroom: 43% of faculty are male; 57% are female. All teach undergraduates. No introductory courses are taught by graduate students.

Admissions: 44% of the 2013-2014 applicants were accepted.

Requirements: The ACT is required. The applicant must be a graduate of an accredited high school. An interview is recommended. The student's average, class rank, recommendations, and special talents are important factors in admission. Entering students must take the College Placement Examinations. A GPA of 2.0 is required. AP and CLEP credits are accepted. Important factors in the admissions decision are recommendations by school officials, evidence of special talent, and advanced placement or honors courses.

Procedure: Freshmen are admitted to all sessions. There are deferred admissions and rolling admissions plans. Applications should be filed by August 15 for fall entry. The fall 2013 application fee was $25. Applications are accepted online.

Transfer: 103 transfer students enrolled in 2012-2013. Transfer students must have a minimum 2.0 GPA. An associate degree or 24 completed credit hours and an interview are recommended. 30 of 128 credits required for the bachelor's degree must be completed at Marygrove.

Visiting: There are regularly scheduled orientations for prospective students, including a tour of the campus followed by college workshops, first-year-student panels, and a college financial planning seminar. There are guides for informal visits and visitors may sit in on classes. To schedule a visit, contact the Admissions Office at info@marygrove.edu.

Financial Aid: In 2013-2014, 98% of continuing full-time students received some form of financial aid. 90% of all full-time freshmen and 98% of continuing full-time students received need-based aid. Marygrove is a member of CSS. The CSS/Profile, FAFSA, and the college's own financial statement are required. The deadline for filing freshman financial aid applications for fall entry is March 15.

International Students: There are 11 international students enrolled. They must take the college's own test.

Graduates: From July 1, 2012 to June 30, 2013, 116 bachelor's degrees were awarded. The most popular majors were social work (16%), business and management (14%), and child development (13%). In an average class, 29% graduate in 6 years or less.

Admissions Contact: John Ambrose, Director of Admissions. E-Mail: *jambrose@marygrove.edu* Web: *www.marygrove.edu*

MICHIGAN STATE UNIVERSITY D-4

East Lansing, MI 48824 (517) 355-8332; (517) 353-1647

Full-time: 14860 men, 17350 women
Part-time: 1710 men, 1775 women
Graduate: 4020 men, 5475 women
Year: semesters, summer session
Application Deadline: see profile
Freshman Class: n/av
SAT or ACT: required
Faculty: n/av; I, av$
Ph.D.s: 90%
Student/Faculty: n/av
Tuition: $12,782 ($32,192)
Room & Board: $8,204

VERY COMPETITIVE

Michigan State University, a pioneer land-grant institution, was founded in 1855. The figures in the above capsule and in this profile are approximate. Its 14 colleges and more than 100 departments offer 200 undergraduate and 250 graduate fields of study. The university's Honors College offers students an alternative education program. There are 12 undergraduate schools and 13 graduate schools. In addition to regional accreditation, MSU has baccalaureate program accreditation with AACSB, ABET, ACEJMC, ADA, ASLA, CAHEA, CSWE, FIDER, NASM, NCATE, NLN, and SAF. The 10 libraries contain 4.5 million volumes, 5.6 million microform items, 299,287 audio/video tapes/CDs/DVDs, and subscribe to 33,760 periodicals including electronic. Computerized library services include inter-library loans, database searching, and Internet access. Special learning facilities include a learning resource center, art gallery, natural history museum, planetarium, radio station, TV station, a botanical garden, a superconducting cyclotron lab, environmental toxicology center, pesticide research center, a center for computer-aided and engineering and manufacturing. The 5239-acre campus is in a suburban area 80 miles northwest of Detroit. Including any residence halls, there are 564 buildings.

Student Life: 89% of undergraduates are from Michigan. Students are from 50 states, 120 foreign countries, and Canada. 78% are white. The average age of freshmen is 18; all undergraduates, 20. 9% do not continue beyond their first year; 71% remain to graduate.

Housing: 17,000 students can be accommodated in college housing, which includes coed dorms, on-campus apartments, and married student housing. In addition, there are honors houses, special-interest houses, 2 residential colleges, an international hall, 9 living-learning communities, quiet floors, and substance-free environments. On-campus housing is guaranteed for all 4 years. 58% of students commute. Upperclassmen may keep cars.

Activities: There are 525 groups on campus, including art, band, cheerleading, chess, choir, chorale, chorus, computers, dance, debate, drama, ethnic, film, gay, honors, international, jazz band, marching band, musical theater, newspaper, opera, orchestra, pep band, photography, political, professional, radio and TV, religious, social, social service, student government, symphony, and yearbook. Popular campus events include home football games, Spartan basketball, and Welcome Days.

Sports: There are 12 intercollegiate sports for men and 13 for women, and 22 intramural sports for men and 22 for women. Facilities include a 76,000-seat stadium, a 4000-seat gym and field house, an ice arena, and a multipurpose 15,500-seat student events center. The university also has an indoor football practice facility, 3 intramural facilities, indoor and outdoor tennis courts, ball fields, a running track, 2 golf courses, and 4 swimming pools, including 1 Olympic-size outdoor pool.

Disabled Students: 75% of the campus is accessible. Facilities include wheelchair ramps, elevators, special parking, specially equipped rest rooms, special class scheduling, lowered drinking fountains, lowered telephones, tape recorders, videotaped classes, reading machines, readers, and note takers.

Services: Counseling and information services are available, as is tutoring in most subjects. There is a reader service for the blind, and remedial math and writing.

Campus Safety and Security: Measures include 24-hour foot and vehicle patrol, self-defense education, and security escort services. There are shuttle buses, emergency telephones, lighted pathways/sidewalks, regional/campus bus service.

Programs of Study: MSU confers B.A., B.S., B.F.A., B.Land.Arch., B.Mus., and B.S. in Nursing degrees. Master's and doctoral degrees are also awarded. Bachelor's degrees are awarded in AGRICULTURE (agriculture, animal science, environmental studies, fishing and fisheries, forestry and related sciences, horticulture, natural resource management, soil science, and wildlife management), BIOLOGICAL SCIENCE (biochemistry, bioinformatics, biology/biological science, biotechnology, botany, entomology, environmental biology, microbiology, nutrition, physiology, plant pathology, and zoology), BUSINESS (accounting, banking and finance, business administration and management, hospitality management services, human resources, marketing management, marketing/retailing/merchandising, personnel management, and tourism), COMMUNICATIONS AND THE ARTS (advertising, art history and appreciation, communications, dramatic arts, East Asian languages and literature, English, French, German, jazz, journalism, Latin, linguistics, music, music performance, music theory and composition, Russian, Spanish, studio art, and telecommunications), COMPUTER AND PHYSICAL SCIENCE (astrophysics, chemical physics, chemistry, computer science, earth science, geology, geophysics and seismology, geoscience, information sciences and systems, mathematics, physical sciences, physics, and statistics), EDUCATION (agricultural education, art education, education, music education, physical education, and special education), ENGINEERING AND ENVIRONMENTAL DESIGN (chemical engineering, city/community/regional planning, civil engineering, computational sciences, computer engineering, construction management, electrical/electronics engineering, engineering, engineering mechanics, interior design, landscape architecture/design, manufacturing engineering, materials engineering, mechanical engineering, textile technology, and urban planning technology), HEALTH PROFESSIONS (clinical science, medical laboratory technology, music therapy, nursing, speech pathology/audiology, and veterinary science), SOCIAL SCIENCE (American studies, anthropology, child psychology/development, classical/ancient civilization, criminal justice, dietetics, economics, family and community services, family/consumer resource management, family/consumer studies, food production/management/services, food science, geography, history, humanities, interdisciplinary studies, parks and recreation management, philosophy, political science/government, prelaw, psychology, public administration, religion, social science, social work, sociology, and women's studies). Engineering, education, and business are the strongest academically. Business, communications, and social science have the largest enrollments.

Required: To graduate, students must complete a freshman writing course and a writing course specified by the major and degree program. Students must complete the 26-credit University Integrative Studies requirement consisting of 8 credits of arts and humanities, 8 of social, behavioral, and economic sciences, 8 of general science, and 3 of a trans-collegiate course. Students must also complete a math requirement determined by each undergraduate college (minimum of college algebra plus trigonometry/finite math/statistics). A minimum 2.0 GPA and 120 semester hours are required.

Special: Special academic programs include an engineering co-op program with business and industry; internships in business, education, political science, agriculture, and communication arts; study abroad in more than 62 countries; on-campus work-study programs; and a sea semester. An accelerated degree program in all majors and student-designed majors are offered at the Honors College. Non-degree study, pass/fail options in some courses, and dual majors are possible. Educationally disadvantaged students may avail themselves of the College Achievement Admissions Program (CAAP). Cross-registration with the Committee on Institutional Cooperation schools is available. There are 48 national honor societies, including Phi Beta Kappa, and a freshman honors program.

Faculty/Classroom: 63% of faculty are male; 37% are female. No introductory courses are taught by graduate students. The average class size in an introductory lecture is 100; in a laboratory is 30; and in a regular course is 30.

Requirements: The SAT or ACT is required. Applicants must be graduates of an accredited secondary school and have completed 4 years of English, 3 years each of math and social studies, 2 years of science, and 2 years of a single foreign language. A personal statement is strongly recommended. The GED is accepted. Music majors must audition. AP and CLEP credits are accepted. Important factors in the admissions decision are advanced placement or honors courses, recommendations by school officials, and evidence of special talent.

Procedure: Freshmen are admitted fall, spring, and summer. Entrance exams should be taken during the junior year of high school. There are deferred admissions and rolling admissions plans. Check with the school for current application deadlines.

Transfer: 2150 transfer students enrolled in a recent year. To transfer, a minimum GPA of 2.0 is required, (prefer 3.0 overall GPA). MSU Integrative Studies requirement should be fulfilled (28 general graduation credits), and college algebra completed. 30 of 120 credits required for the bachelor's degree must be completed at MSU.

Visiting: There are regularly scheduled orientations for prospective students, including a presentation and a tour of the campus. There are guides for informal visits, visitors may sit in on classes, and stay overnight. To schedule a visit, contact the Admissions office.

Financial Aid: In a recent year, 93% of all full-time freshmen and 68% of continuing full-time students received some form of financial aid. 28% of all full-time freshmen and 22% of continuing full-time students received need-based aid. The average freshmen award was $7,148. The FAFSA is required. Check with the school for current application deadlines and fee.

International Students: There were 1046 international students enrolled in a recent year. The school actively recruits these students. They must take the TOEFL or MELAB and the college's own test.

Graduates: In a recent year, 7733 bachelor's degrees were awarded. The most popular majors were business (19%), communications (14%), and social science (10%). In an average class, 36% graduate in 4 years or less, 66% graduate in 5 years or less, and 71% graduate in 6 years or less.

Admissions Contact: Director of Admissions and Scholarships. A campus DVD is available. E-Mail: *admis@msu.edu* Web: *www.msu.edu*

MICHIGAN TECHNOLOGICAL UNIVERSITY — B-2

Houghton, MI 49931-1295	**(906) 487-1888; (888) MTU-1885**
Full-time: 3980 men, 1338 women	**Faculty:** 389; I, --$
Part-time: 296 men, 117 women	**Ph.D.s:** 87%
Graduate: 919 men, 384 women	**Student/Faculty:** 14 to 1
Year: semesters, summer session	**Tuition:** $13,957 ($27,052)
Application Deadline: open	**Room & Board:** $9148
Freshman Class: 4573 applied, 3441 accepted, 1161 enrolled	
SAT CR/M/W: 590/630/570 **ACT:** 25	**VERY COMPETITIVE**

Michigan Technological University, founded in 1885, is a state-supported institution offering degrees in engineering, liberal arts, sciences, forestry, business, and technology. There are 5 undergraduate schools and 1 graduate school. In addition to regional accreditation, Michigan Tech has baccalaureate program accreditation with AACSB, ABET, and SAF. The library contains 796,762 volumes, 546,199 microform items, and 7,056 audio/video tapes/CDs/DVDs, and subscribes to 2,891 periodicals including electronic. Computerized library services include interlibrary loans, database searching, Internet access, and laptop Internet portals. Special learning facilities include a learning resource center, radio station, the A.E. Seaman Mineral Museum, the Rozsa Center for the Performing Arts, the Ford Forestry Center and Researh Forest, cosmic ray observatory, x-ray fluorescence spectrometer, process simulation and control center, remote sensing institute, computer-aided engineering lab, microfabrication lab, and subsurface visualization lab. The 925-acre campus is in a small town 325 miles northwest of Milwaukee, Wisconsin. Including any residence halls, there are 32 buildings.

Student Life: 72% of undergraduates are from out of state, mostly the Mid-West. Students are from 46 states, 71 foreign countries, and Canada. 76% are white. The average age of freshmen is 19; all undergraduates, 21. 17% do not continue beyond their first year; 62% remain to graduate.

Housing: 3070 students can be accommodated in college housing, which includes coed dorms, on-campus apartments, and married student housing. and each dorm has smoke-free and chemical-free areas. There are separate rooms for international students, the first year experience program, the healthy living house, and the computer science learing center. On-campus housing is guaranteed for the freshman year only, is available on a first-come, and first-served basis. 60% of students commute. All students may keep cars.

Activities: 9% of men belong to 1 local and 11 national fraternities; 15%

of women belong to 4 local and 4 national sororities. There are 269 groups on campus, including art, band, cheerleading, chess, choir, chorale, chorus, computers, dance, drama, drill team, ethnic, film, gay, honors, international, jazz band, literary magazine, musical theater, newspaper, orchestra, pep band, photography, political, professional, radio and TV, religious, social, social service, student government, and symphony. Popular campus events include Winter Carnival, K-Day, and Spring Fling.

Sports: There are 7 intercollegiate sports for men and 7 for women. Facilities include a complex with a 4200-seat ice arena and a 3200-seat gym, a lakeside golf course, football and softball fields, a tennis center, Mont Ripley Ski Hill and a cross-country ski trail, a multipurpose room, a pool, a fitness center, racquetball/squash courts, a dance room, and a gymnastics room.

Disabled Students: 90% of the campus is accessible. Facilities include wheelchair ramps, elevators, special parking, specially equipped restrooms, special class scheduling, lowered drinking fountains, and special housing.

Services: Counseling and information services are available, as is tutoring in some subjects. There is a reader service for the blind, and remedial math, reading, and writing. Learning centers for English, math, chemistry, physics, biology, computer science, and engineering are available.

Campus Safety and Security: Measures include 24-hour foot and vehicle patrol, self-defense education, and security escort services. There are shuttle buses, emergency telephones, lighted pathways/sidewalks, and controlled access to dorms/residences.

Programs of Study: Michigan Tech confers B.A., and B.S. degrees. Associate, master's, and doctoral degrees are also awarded. Bachelor's degrees are awarded in AGRICULTURE (forestry and related sciences and wildlife management), BIOLOGICAL SCIENCE (biochemistry, bioinformatics, biology/biological science, and ecology), BUSINESS (accounting and business administration and management), COMMUNICATIONS AND THE ARTS (audio technology, communications, English, technical and business writing, and theater design), COMPUTER AND PHYSICAL SCIENCE (applied physics, chemistry, computer science, geology, geophysics and seismology, mathematics, physics, and software engineering), EDUCATION (secondary education), ENGINEERING AND ENVIRONMENTAL DESIGN (biomedical engineering, chemical engineering, civil engineering, computer engineering, construction management, electrical/electronics engineering, electrical/electronics engineering technology, engineering, environmental engineering, geological engineering, materials engineering, mechanical engineering, mechanical engineering technology, and surveying engineering), HEALTH PROFESSIONS (clinical science, exercise science, pharmaceutical chemistry, predentistry, premedicine, prepharmacy, and prephysical therapy), SOCIAL SCIENCE (anthropology, economics, history, humanities, liberal arts/general studies, psychology, and social science). Engineering, forestry, and physical science are the strongest academically. Mechanical, civil, and electrical engineering have the largest enrollments.

Required: To graduate, students must complete 120 to 145 credit hours, maintain a miminum GPA of 2.0, and fulfill basic general education requirements. The basic general education curriculum consists of 4 core courses to be taken by every baccalaureate student, A 15 credit distribution requirement, physical education, and a science/math requirement. In general, 30 of the last 36 credit hours and 30 hours of advanced-level courses must be completed at MTU.

Special: Michigan Tech offers co-op programs in almost all majors, internships in medical technology and secondary teacher education, work-study programs, study abroad in more than 100 countries,duel majors, and a B.A-B.S. degree in scientific and technical communication. There are interinstitutional programs with Northwestern Michigan,Gogebic Community, and Delta Colleges. A 3-2 engineering degree is possible in conjunction with the University of Wisconsin/Superior, the College of St. Scholastica, and Adrian, Albion, Augsburg, Northland, and Olivet Colleges. There are 16 national honor societies.

Faculty/Classroom: 74% of faculty are male; 26% are female. All teach undergraduates, 84% do research, and 84% do both. No introductory courses are taught by graduate students. The average class size in an introductory lecture is 76; in a laboratory is 23; and in a regular course is 30.

Admissions: 75% of the 2011-2012 applicants were accepted. The ACT scores were 6% below 21, 19% between 21 and 23, 28% between 24 and 26, 24% between 27 and 28, and 23% above 28. 44% of the current freshmen were in the top fifth of their class; 66% were in the top two fifths.

Requirements: The SAT or ACT is required. Admissions requirements include graduation from an accredited secondary school, with 15 academic credits. These must include 3 credits in English, 1 credit of chemistry or physics, and 3 credits in math for engineering and science curricula; credits in social studies and foreign language are recommended. The GED is accepted. AP and CLEP credits are accepted. Important factors in the admissions decision are advanced placement or honors courses, leadership record, and recommendations by school officials.

Procedure: Freshmen are admitted to all sessions. Entrance exams should be taken in the junior year or fall of their senior year. There are deferred admissions and rolling admissions plans. Application deadlines are open. Notification is sent on a rolling basis. Applications are accepted online.

Transfer: 198 transfer students enrolled in a recent year. Transfer students must have a minimum GPA of 2.5 on a 4.0 scale; grades of B or better are expected in math and science courses (some programs require a 2.75 or higher). 30 of 120 credits required for the bachelor's degree must be completed at Michigan Tech.

Visiting: There are regularly scheduled orientations for prospective students, including campus tours 10 a.m. and 2 p.m. Monday through Friday. Separate interviews are available with academic department advisors, admissions counselors, and financial aid department. There are guides for informal visits, visitors may sit in on classes, and stay overnight. To schedule a visit, contact The Admissions Office.

Financial Aid: Michigan Tech is a member of CSS. The FAFSA is required. Check with the school for current application deadlines.

International Students: There are 990 international students enrolled. The school actively recruits these students. They must take the TOEFL with a minimum score of 550 on the paper-based TOEFL (PBT) or 79 on the Internet-based version (iBT).

Graduates: In a recent year, 1026 bachelor's degrees were awarded. The most popular majors were mechanical engineering (15%), civil engineering (7%), and electrical engineering (5%). 183 companies recruited on campus in a recent year. Of a recent graduating class, 15% were enrolled in graduate school within 6 months of graduation, and 94% were employed.

Admissions Contact: Allison Carter E-Mail: *mtu4u@mtu.edu* Web: *www.mtu.edu*

NORTHERN MICHIGAN UNIVERSITY C-2

Marquette, MI 49855 (906) 227-2650
(800) 682-9797; (906) 227-1747

Full-time: 3720 men, 4080 women	**Faculty:** n/av; IIA, -$
Part-time: 335 men, 455 women	**Ph.D.s:** 80%
Graduate: 245 men, 440 women	**Student/Faculty:** n/av
Year: semesters, summer session	**Tuition:** $8350 ($13,078)
Application Deadline: open	**Room & Board:** $7970
Freshman Class: n/av	
ACT: required	

VERY COMPETITIVE

Northern Michigan University, founded in 1899, is a public institution offering undergraduate programs in the arts and sciences, business, education, health science, human services, nursing, and technology. The figures in the above capsule and in this profile are approximate. There are 4 undergraduate schools and 1 graduate school. In addition to regional accreditation, NMU has baccalaureate program accreditation with AACSB, ADA, CSWE, NASM, NCATE, and NLN. The library contains 631,244 volumes, 344,002 microform items, and 7,718 audio/video tapes/CDs/DVDs, and subscribes to 20,657 periodicals including electronic. Computerized library services include interlibrary loans, database searching, Internet access, and laptop Internet portals. Special learning facilities include a learning resource center, art gallery, radio station, TV station, and an observatory. The 359-acre campus is in an urban area on the southern shores of Lake Superior. Including any residence halls, there are 55 buildings.

Student Life: 80% of undergraduates are from Michigan. Others are from 45 states, 24 foreign countries, and Canada. 88% are white. The average age of freshmen is 18.3; all undergraduates, 22.7. 27% do not continue beyond their first year; 49% remain to graduate.

Housing: 3250 students can be accommodated in college housing, which includes coed dorms, on-campus apartments, and married student housing. In addition, there are honors houses, special-interest houses, and smoke-free and chemical-free houses. On-campus housing is guaranteed for all 4 years. 67% of students commute. All students may keep cars.

Activities: 1% of men belong to 2 national fraternities; 1% of women belong to 3 national sororities. There are 308 groups on campus, including art, band, cheerleading, chess, choir, chorale, chorus, computers, dance, drama, drill team, ethnic, film, gay, health, honors, international, international dance club, jazz band, literary magazine, marching band, musical theater, newspaper, orchestra, pep band, philosophy, photography, political, professional, radio and TV, religious, social, social service, student government, and symphony. Popular campus events include Winterfest, Be a Part from the Start, and U.P. 200 Dog Sled Race.

Sports: There are 15 intercollegiate sports for men and 18 for women, and 14 intramural sports for men and 14 for women. Facilities include indoor and outdoor playing fields, an aerobic and fitness training area, an ice rink, a swimming pool, a diving tank, a field house, an 8000-seat stadium, a 4000-seat basketball and hockey arena, a rock-climbing wall, racquetball courts, the neighboring forests and rivers, and Lake Superior.

Disabled Students: All of the campus is accessible. Facilities include wheelchair ramps, elevators, special parking, specially equipped restrooms, lowered drinking fountains, lowered telephones, and special housing.

Services: Counseling and information services are available, as is tutoring

in most subjects. There is a reader service for the blind, and remedial math, reading, and writing.

Campus Safety and Security: Measures include 24-hour foot and vehicle patrol, self-defense education, and security escort services. There are shuttle buses, emergency telephones, lighted pathways/sidewalks, and a crime prevention program with a full-time staff.

Programs of Study: NMU confers B.A., B.S., B.F.A., B.M.Ed., B.S.N., and B.S.W. degrees. Associate and master's degrees are also awarded. Bachelor's degrees are awarded in BIOLOGICAL SCIENCE (biochemistry, biology/biological science, botany, ecology, microbiology, physiology, and zoology), BUSINESS (accounting, banking and finance, business administration and management, entrepreneurial studies, and marketing/retailing/merchandising), COMMUNICATIONS AND THE ARTS (broadcasting, communications, design, dramatic arts, English, fine arts, French, language arts, music, public relations, Spanish, and speech/debate/rhetoric), COMPUTER AND PHYSICAL SCIENCE (chemistry, computer programming, computer science, earth science, information sciences and systems, mathematics, and physics), EDUCATION (art education, business education, computer education, education of the mentally handicapped, elementary education, health education, industrial arts education, music education, physical education, science education, and secondary education), ENGINEERING AND ENVIRONMENTAL DESIGN (architecture, construction management, electrical/electronics engineering technology, industrial engineering technology, and manufacturing technology), HEALTH PROFESSIONS (chiropractic, clinical science, cytotechnology, medical laboratory technology, nursing, physician's assistant, predentistry, premedicine, preveterinary science, and speech pathology/audiology), SOCIAL SCIENCE (criminal justice, economics, geography, history, international studies, parks and recreation management, philosophy, physical fitness/movement, political science/government, prelaw, psychology, public administration, social work, sociology, and water resources). Nursing, chemistry, and education are the strongest academically. Art and design, education, and nursing have the largest enrollments.

Required: Students must earn 40 semester credits in liberal studies, including courses in humanities, composition, natural sciences/math, social sciences, communications, and visual and performing arts. Graduation requirements vary by degree program; at the minimum, students must earn 124 semester credits, including 32 in a major field, with a GPA of 2.0. Courses in phys ed/health and world culture are also required.

Special: NMU offers internships, a co-op program in business, study abroad in a number of countries, a Washington semester, dual majors in computer information and accounting, and student-designed majors in individual studies and liberal arts. There are 8 national honor societies, a freshman honors program, and 1 departmental honors program.

Faculty/Classroom: 58% of faculty are male; 42% are female. All teach undergraduates. Graduate students teach 1% of introductory courses. The average class size in an introductory lecture, 30, in a laboratory, 18, and in a regular course, 23.

Requirements: The ACT is required, with a GPA of 2.25 and a satisfactory score for the SAT and 19 for the ACT. Applicants must be graduates of accredited secondary schools or have earned a GED. NMU requires 12 to 16 Carnegie units; recommended secondary school preparation includes 4 years of English, 3 each of math, history, social studies, foreign language, and science, 2 of fine arts or performing arts, and 1 of computer instruction. Students seeking art scholarships must submit a portfolio; those seeking music and theater scholarships must audition. A GPA of 2.3 is required. AP and CLEP credits are accepted. Important factors in the admissions decision are advanced placement or honors courses, evidence of special talent, and recommendations by school officials.

Procedure: Freshmen are admitted to all sessions. Application fee was $35. Notification is sent on a rolling basis. Applications are accepted online.

Transfer: 524 transfer students enrolled in a recent year. Applicants must present a minimum GPA of 2.0 in at least 12 semester credits of college-level work. 32 of 124 credits required for the bachelor's degree must be completed at NMU.

Visiting: There are regularly scheduled orientations for prospective students, including an admissions interview, a tour, and a faculty visit. Visitors may sit in on classes and stay overnight. To schedule a visit, contact the Campus Visit Office.

Financial Aid: In a recent year, 86% of all full-time freshmen and 85% of continuing full-time students received some form of financial aid. 40% of all full-time freshmen and 35% of continuing full-time students received need-based aid. Need-based scholarships or need-based grants averaged $3,940 ($17,434 maximum); need-based self-help aid (loans and jobs) averaged $3,190 ($9,250 maximum); non-need based athletic scholarships averaged $6,443 ($19,466 maximum); and other non-need based awards and non-need based scholarships averaged $3,160 ($21,586 maximum). 16% of undergraduate students work part-time. Average annual earnings from campus work are $2884. Check with the school for current application deadlines.

International Students: There were 74 international students enrolled in a recent year. The school actively recruits these students. They must take the TOEFL with a minimum score of 500 on the paper-based TOEFL (PBT) or 61 on the Internet-based version (iBT). Canadian students must take the SAT or ACT.

Graduates: In a recent year, 1223 bachelor's degrees were awarded. The most popular majors were nursing (7%), art and design (6%), and criminal justice (5%). In an average class, 2% graduate in 3 years or less, 18% graduate in 4 years or less, 28% graduate in 5 years or less, and 49% graduate in 6 years or less.

Admissions Contact: Director of Admissions. A campus DVD is available. E-Mail: *admiss@nmu.edu* Web: *www.nmu.edu*

NORTHWOOD UNIVERSITY — D-4

Midland, MI 48640 — (989) 837-4273; (800) 457-7878; (989) 837-4490

Full-time: 1090 men, 680 women
Part-time: 30 men, 35 women
Graduate: 280 men, 145 women
Year: quarters, summer session
Application Deadline: see profile
Freshman Class: n/av
SAT or ACT: required
Faculty: 45
Ph.D.s: 32%
Student/Faculty: n/app
Tuition: $20,040
Room & Board: $8770

LESS COMPETITIVE

Northwood University, founded in 1959, is a private college offering undergraduate and graduate programs in business management. The figures in the above capsule and in this capsule are approximate. Campuses are located in Florida, Michigan, and Texas. There is one graduate school. The library contains 35,176 volumes and 144 audio/video tapes/CDs/DVDs, and subscribes to 341 periodicals including electronic. Computerized library services include interlibrary loans, database searching, Internet access, and laptop Internet portals. Special learning facilities include a learning resource center, an art gallery, and the Alden B. Dow Creativity Center. The 434-acre campus is in a suburban area 135 miles north of Detroit. Including any residence halls, there are 29 buildings.

Student Life: 89% of undergraduates are from Michigan. Others are from 25 states, 27 foreign countries, and Canada. 70% are from public schools. 74% are white; 12% African American. The average age of freshmen is 18; all undergraduates, 20. 23% do not continue beyond their first year; 54% remain to graduate.

Housing: 868 students can be accommodated in college housing, which includes single-sex dorms and on-campus apartments. On-campus housing is guaranteed for the freshman year only and is available on a first-come, first-served basis. 62% of students commute. All students may keep cars.

Activities: 10% of men belong to 1 local and 6 national fraternities; 15% of women belong to 5 national sororities. There are 45 groups on campus, including academic, cheerleading, chorus, computers, debate, drama, forensics, honors, international, newspaper, pep band, political, professional, religious, social, social service, and student government. Popular campus events include Family Day, MLK celebration, and community service events.

Sports: There are 8 intercollegiate sports for men and 9 for women, and 10 intramural sports for men and 10 for women. Facilities include a 1500-seat indoor gym, a 3500-seat stadium, 3 multipurpose courts, a 4-lane track, and a fitness center.

Disabled Students: 95% of the campus is accessible. Facilities include wheelchair ramps, elevators, special parking, specially equipped rest rooms, special class scheduling, and lowered drinking fountains.

Services: Counseling and information services are available, as is tutoring in most subjects. There is remedial math, reading, and writing.

Campus Safety and Security: Measures include 24-hour foot and vehicle patrol, emergency notification system, and security escort services. There are emergency telephones, lighted pathways/sidewalks, controlled access to dorms/residences, and a professional security force.

Programs of Study: Northwood confers B.B.A. degrees. Associates and master's degrees are also awarded. Bachelor's degrees are awarded in BUSINESS (accounting, banking and finance, business administration and management, business economics, fashion merchandising, hotel/motel and restaurant management, international business management, management information systems, marketing management, sports management, and transportation and travel marketing), COMMUNICATIONS AND THE ARTS (advertising), COMPUTER AND PHYSICAL SCIENCE (computer management). Accounting is the strongest academically. Entertainment and sports management have the largest enrollments.

Required: To graduate, all students must complete a minimum of 123 semester credit hours, with 24 in the major. A minimum GPA of 2.0 must be maintained. There is general studies core curriculum.

Special: Northwood offers on- and off-campus work-study and a competitive study-abroad program in 15 countries. Dual majors with management are available in all majors. Accelerated degree programs are available. There is a freshman honors program.

Faculty/Classroom: 64% of faculty are male; 36% are female. 91%

teach undergraduates. No introductory courses are taught by graduate students. The average class size in an introductory lecture is 25, in a laboratory, 14, and in a regular course, 22.

Requirements: The SAT or ACT is required. Graduation from an accredited secondary school is required. The GED is accepted. A GPA of 2.0 is required. AP and CLEP credits are accepted. Important factors in the admissions decision are advanced placement or honors courses, evidence of special talent, and leadership record.

Procedure: Freshmen are admitted to all sessions. Entrance exams should be taken in the spring of the junior year. There are deferred admissions and rolling admissions plans. Applications are accepted online. Check with the school for current application deadlines and fee.

Transfer: 217 transfer students enrolled in a recent year. Various factors are taken into consideration for admission of transfer students: college GPA for 12 credits or more should be 2.0 or better; if the student has completed fewer than 12 credits, the high school GPA should be 2.0, with an ACT of 16 or better. Probationary acceptance may be allowed. If an associate's degree has not been received, final high school transcripts are required. 31 of 123 credits required for the bachelor's degree must be completed at Northwood.

Visiting: There are regularly scheduled orientations for prospective students, including academic and social seminars and presentations. There are guides for informal visits; visitors may sit in on classes and stay overnight. To schedule a visit, contact the Admissions Department.

Financial Aid: In a recent year, 75% of all full-time freshmen and 71% of continuing full-time students received some form of financial aid. 66% of all full-time freshmen and 61% of continuing full-time students received need-based aid. The average freshmen award was $15,667, with $6272 ($14,640 maximum) from need-based scholarships or need-based grants; $4361 ($5500 maximum) from need-based self-help aid (loans and jobs); $5879 ($20,889 maximum) from non-need-based athletic scholarships; and $5660 ($12,650 maximum) from other non-need-based awards and non-need-based scholarships. 12% of undergraduate students work part-time. Average annual earnings from campus work were $1378. The average financial indebtedness was $18,024. The FAFSA is required. The deadline for filing freshman financial aid applications for fall entry is rolling.

International Students: There were 161 international students enrolled in a recent year. The school actively recruits these students. They must take the TOEFL with a minimum score of 500 on the paper-based TOEFL (PBT) or 61 on the Internet-based version (iBT).

Graduates: In a recent year, 511 bachelor's degrees were awarded. The most popular majors were marketing/management (18%), management (13%), and accounting (10%). 16% graduate in 4 years or less, 15% graduate in 5 years or less, and 54% graduate in 6 years or less. 5% were enrolled in graduate school within 6 months of graduation and 90% were employed.

Admissions Contact: Director of Admissions. A campus DVD is available. E-Mail: *admissions@northwood.edu* Web: *www.northwood.edu*

OAKLAND UNIVERSITY — E-4

Rochester, MI 48309 — **(248) 370-3360; (800) OAK-UNIV**

Full-time: 4719 men, 7161 women	**Faculty:** n/av; I, --$
Part-time: 1741 men, 2569 women	**Ph.D.s:** n/av
Graduate: 1339 men, 2211 women	**Student/Faculty:** n/av
Year: semesters, summer session	**Tuition:** $11,183 ($25,598)
Application Deadline:	**Room & Board:** $8208
Freshman Class: 12152 applied, 7551 accepted, 2464 enrolled	
ACT: 22	**VERY COMPETITIVE**

Oakland University, established in 1957, is a comprehensive state-supported institution serving a primarily commuter student body. There are 7 undergraduate schools and 7 graduate schools. In addition to regional accreditation, Oakland has baccalaureate program accreditation with AACSB, ABET, CSWE, NASM, and TEAC. The 2 libraries contain 851,190 volumes, 1.2 million microform items, and 29,868 audio/video tapes/CDs/DVDs, and subscribe to 43,501 periodicals including electronic. Computerized library services include interlibrary loans, database searching, Internet access, and Wi-Fi capability. Special learning facilities include an art gallery, radio station, TV station, the Product Development and Manufacturing Center, the Historical House Museum, and the Lean-Learning Institute. The 1444-acre campus is in a suburban area 25 miles north of Detroit. Including any residence halls, there are 46 buildings.

Student Life: 77% are White. The average age of freshmen is 18; all undergraduates, 23.

Housing: College-sponsored housing includes single-sex and coed dorms, on-campus apartments, and married student housing. In addition, there are honors houses, special-interest houses, fraternity houses, sorority houses, living learning communities, international village, and eco Interest, pre-Business, Pre-Nursing, Scholars tower. On-campus housing is guaranteed for all 4 years. All students may keep cars.

Activities: 2% of men belong to 6 national fraternities; 2% of women belong to 6 national sororities. There are 190 groups on campus, including art, band, cheerleading, choir, chorale, chorus, computers, dance, drama, environmental, ethnic, film, forensics, gay, honors, international, jazz band, musical theater, newspaper, orchestra, pep band, political, professional, radio and TV, religious, social, social service, student government, and symphony. Popular campus events include Welcome Week, Hispanic Celebration, and Week of Champions at OU.

Sports: There are 7 intercollegiate sports for men and 9 for women, and 18 intramural sports for men and 18 for women. Facilities include a 250,000-square-foot student recreation and athletic center that includes softball and baseball diamonds, an indoor track, soccer and touch football fields, and facilities for swimming, basketball, weight training, dance, fencing, handball, squash, racquetball, and golf.

Disabled Students: 99% of the campus is accessible. Facilities include wheelchair ramps, elevators, special parking, specially equipped restrooms, special class scheduling, lowered drinking fountains, lowered telephones, special housing, and automatic door openers.

Services: Counseling and information services are available, as is tutoring in most subjects, 100 and 200 level classes There is a reader service for the blind, and remedial math, reading, and writing. There is a mentorship program.

Campus Safety and Security: Measures include 24-hour foot and vehicle patrol, emergency notification system, self-defense education, and security escort services. There are shuttle buses, emergency telephones, lighted pathways/sidewalks, controlled access to dorms/residences, text alart.

Programs of Study: Oakland confers B.A., B.S., B.F.A., B.I.S., B.Mus., B.S.E., B.S.N. and B.S.W. degrees. Master's and doctoral degrees are also awarded. Bachelor's degrees are awarded in BIOLOGICAL SCIENCE (biochemistry and biology/biological science), BUSINESS (accounting, banking and finance, business administration and management, business economics, human resources, management information systems, marketing/retailing/merchandising, operations management, and personnel management), COMMUNICATIONS AND THE ARTS (art history and appreciation, Chinese, communications, dance, dramatic arts, English, film arts, French, German, Japanese, journalism, linguistics, music, performing arts, Spanish, and studio art), COMPUTER AND PHYSICAL SCIENCE (chemistry, computer science, information sciences and systems, mathematics, medical physics, physics, and statistics), EDUCATION (elementary education and music education), ENGINEERING AND ENVIRONMENTAL DESIGN (computer engineering, electrical/electronics engineering, engineering chemistry, engineering physics, environmental science, industrial engineering, mechanical engineering, and occupational safety and health), HEALTH PROFESSIONS (allied health, health science, medical laboratory science, nursing, and preventive/wellness health care), SOCIAL SCIENCE (African American studies, anthropology, East Asian studies, economics, history, international relations, Latin American studies, liberal arts/general studies, philosophy, political science/government, psychology, public administration, Russian and Slavic studies, social work, sociology, South Asian studies, and women's studies). Arts and health science are the strongest academically. Health science, elementary education, and nursing have the largest enrollments.

Required: To graduate, students must complete 124 credit hours (153 to 161 for the B.Mus. or 128 for the B.S.Env.Health). All students must complete 40 credits of general education requirements, including at least 1 course (3 or more credits) from the list of approved courses in each of the 10 knowledge areas: writing, formal reasoning, arts, foreign language and culture, global perspective, literature, natural science and technology, social science, Western civilization, and knowledge application. A GPA of 2.0 is required.

Special: Special academic programs include internships, cooperative programs for most disciplines, and many work-study opportunities. There are organized programs for study abroad in 8 countries; independent programs can be arranged. Oakland also offers a B.A. or B.S. degree in biology and economics, a general studies program, dual majors, a student-designed major, cross-registration with Macomb Community College, and preprofessional studies in medicine, dentistry, optometry, and veterinary medicine. There are 12 national honor societies and a freshman honors program.

Faculty/Classroom: 54% of faculty are male; 46% are female. No introductory courses are taught by graduate students.

Admissions: 62% of the 2013-2014 applicants were accepted.

Requirements: The ACT is required. Admissions requirements include graduation from an accredited secondary school and high school level college preparatory work, including 4 years of English and 3 years each of math, science, and social studies. 2 years of foreign language is recommended as well. Music and dance majors must audition. A GPA of 2.5 is required. AP and CLEP credits are accepted.

Procedure: Freshmen are admitted to all sessions. Entrance exams should be taken during the spring of the junior year or early fall of the senior year. There are deferred admissions and rolling admissions plans. Check with the school for current application deadlines. Notification is sent on a rolling basis. Applications are accepted online.

Transfer: 1891 transfer students enrolled in 2012-2013. Applicants

must have at least a 2.5 GPA; a higher GPA is required in some majors. 32 of 124 credits required for the bachelor's degree must be completed at Oakland.

Visiting: There are regularly scheduled orientations for prospective students, including a review of services, academic advising, and course registration. There are guides for informal visits, visitors may sit in on classes, and stay overnight. To schedule a visit, contact the Admissions Office at visit@oakland.edu.

Financial Aid: The average freshman award was $12,885. Need-based scholarships or need-based grants averaged $5,645 ; need-based self-help aid (loans and jobs) averaged $3,173; and non-need-based athletic scholarships averaged $11,515. The FAFSA is required. The deadline for filing freshman financial aid applications for fall entry is April 1.

International Students: They must take the TOEFL with a minimum score of 550 on the paper-based TOEFL (PBT) or 79 on the Internet-based version (iBT) or take the MELAB. They must also take the ACT.

Graduates: From July 1, 2012 to June 30, 2013, 2345 bachelor's degrees were awarded. The most popular majors were nursing (14%), business (13%), and education (8%). 190 companies recruited on campus in 2012-2013.

Admissions Contact: Eleanor Reynolds, Assistant Vice President Student Affairs Admissions. E-Mail: *ouinfo@oakland.edu* Web: *www.oakland.edu*

OLIVET COLLEGE D-4

Olivet, MI 49076 **(269) 749-7635; (800) 456-7189**

Full-time: 500 men, 400 women
Part-time: 100 men and women
Graduate: 30 men and women
Year: semesters, summer session
Application Deadline: see profile
Freshman Class: n/av
SAT or ACT: required
Faculty: 55; IIB, --$
Ph.D.s: 36%
Student/Faculty: n/av
Tuition: $21,600
Room & Board: $7500

COMPETITIVE

Olivet College, founded in 1844, is a private liberal arts institution affiliated with both the United Church of Christ and the Congregational Christian Churches. The figures in the above capsule and in this profile are approximate. There is one graduate school. The library contains 85,000 volumes, 117 microform items, and subscribes to 450 periodicals including electronic. Computerized library services include inter-library loans, database searching, and Internet access. Special learning facilities include a learning resource center, art gallery, planetarium, radio station, an observatory, and a nature preserve. The 92-acre campus is in a small town 30 miles south of Lansing and 120 miles west of Detroit. Including any residence halls, there are 24 buildings.

Student Life: 82% of undergraduates are from Michigan. Students are from 15 states, 12 foreign countries, and Canada. 92% are from public schools. 72% are white; 16% African American. 21% are Catholic; 18% claim no religious affiliation. The average age of freshmen is 19; all undergraduates, 23. 35% do not continue beyond their first year; 40% remain to graduate.

Housing: 700 students can be accommodated in college housing, which includes single-sex and coed dorms. In addition, there are honors houses, special-interest houses, fraternity houses, sorority houses, a global cultural center, and an African American cultural center. On-campus housing is guaranteed for all 4 years, is guaranteed for the freshman year only, is available on a first-come, first-served basis, and is available on a lottery system for upperclassmen. Priority is given to out-of-town students. 72% of students live on campus; of those, 45% remain on campus on weekends. All students may keep cars.

Activities: 9% of men belong to 6 local fraternities; 7% of women belong to 4 local sororities. There are 27 groups on campus, including art, band, cheerleading, choir, chorale, chorus, communications, computers, drama, drill team, drum and bugle corps, ethnic, gay, honors, international, literary magazine, musical theater, newspaper, pep band, photography, professional, radio and TV, religious, social, social service, student government, and yearbook. Popular campus events include Diversity Week, Community Service Week, and Honors Convocation.

Sports: There are 9 intercollegiate sports for men and 9 for women, and 6 intramural sports for men and 6 for women. Facilities include an athletic center, football field, gym, fitness center, soccer fields, softball and baseball fields, tennis courts, a student center, and a pool.

Disabled Students: 25% of the campus is accessible. Facilities include wheelchair ramps, elevators, special parking, and specially equipped rest rooms.

Services: Counseling and information services are available, as is tutoring in most subjects. There is a reader service for the blind, and remedial math, reading, and writing.

Campus Safety and Security: Measures include 24-hour foot and vehicle patrol, self-defense education, and security escort services. There are emergency telephones and lighted pathways/sidewalks.

Programs of Study: Olivet confers B.A. degrees. Master's degrees are also awarded. Bachelor's degrees are awarded in BIOLOGICAL SCIENCE (biochemistry and biology/biological science), BUSINESS (accounting, business administration and management, insurance, international business management, and marketing management), COMMUNICATIONS AND THE ARTS (communications, design, English, fine arts, illustration, and journalism), COMPUTER AND PHYSICAL SCIENCE (chemistry, computer science, and mathematics), EDUCATION (athletic training, elementary education, physical education, and secondary education), ENGINEERING AND ENVIRONMENTAL DESIGN (environmental science), HEALTH PROFESSIONS (health, predentistry, premedicine, and preveterinary science), SOCIAL SCIENCE (anthropology, criminal justice, economics, history, prelaw, psychology, social studies, and sociology). Business administration, teacher education, and criminal justice are the strongest academically.

Required: To graduate, students must complete 120 semester hours, with 36 to 60 in the major. Their minimum GPA must be 2.0; those seeking certification must maintain a minimum 2.5 GPA in all education courses and in all courses in their major and minor fields. Students must demonstrate competency in 16 areas and complete a 33-hour general education program. In addition, a 40-hour service learning course and senior experience class are required. Distribution requirements include arts, exploration, creative experience, and math proficiency. Specific courses required include self and community, writing and rhetoric, civilization, liberal arts, and natural world.

Special: Olivet offers internships, cooperative education opportunities, and both student-designed and dual majors. There are 2 national honor societies, a freshman honors program, and 4 departmental honors programs.

Faculty/Classroom: 55% of faculty are male; 45% are female. All teach undergraduates. No introductory courses are taught by graduate students. The average class size in an introductory lecture is 20; in a laboratory is 14; and in a regular course is 16.

Admissions: 45% of a recent year's applicants were accepted. The ACT scores were 25% below 21, 40% between 21 and 23, 15% between 24 and 26, 15% between 27 and 28, and 5% above 28. 25% of recent freshmen were in the top fifth of their class; 50% were in the top two fifths. 6 freshmen graduated first in their class.

Requirements: The SAT or ACT is required. Students must be graduates of an accredited secondary school, with a scholastic GPA of at least 2.6 and completion of college-preparatory courses. The GED is accepted. Individual consideration is given to applicants not meeting these criteria but demonstrating other potential. A GPA of 2.6 is required. AP and CLEP credits are accepted. Important factors in the admissions decision are evidence of special talent, extracurricular activities record, and recommendations by school officials.

Procedure: Freshmen are admitted fall, spring, and summer. There are deferred admissions and rolling admissions plans. Application deadlines are open. Check with the school for the current fee. Notification is sent on a rolling basis. Applications are accepted online.

Transfer: 105 transfer students enrolled in a recent year. Transcripts of college work completed elsewhere must show a 2.0 GPA. Transfer applicants must be high school graduates or the equivalent. 30 of 120 credits required for the bachelor's degree must be completed at Olivet.

Visiting: There are regularly scheduled orientations for prospective students, consisting of a day and a half of orientation. There are guides for informal visits, visitors may sit in on classes, and stay overnight. To schedule a visit, contact the Admissions Office.

Financial Aid: In a recent year, 94% of all full-time freshmen and 95% of continuing full-time students received some form of financial aid. 88% of all full-time freshmen and 92% of continuing full-time students received need-based aid. The average freshmen award was $6,500. 45% of undergraduate students work part-time. Average annual earnings from campus work are $1200. The average financial indebtedness of recent graduates was $18,000. The FAFSA is required. Check with the school for current financial aid deadlines.

International Students: There were 42 international students enrolled in a recent year. The school actively recruits these students. They must take the TOEFL.

Graduates: 147 bachelor's degrees were awarded in a recent year. The most popular majors were business administration (17%), psychology (11%), and biology (11%). 9 companies recruited on campus in a recent year.

Admissions Contact: Admissions. E-Mail: *admissions@olivetcollege.edu* Web: *www.olivetcollege.edu*

ROCHESTER COLLEGE E-4

Rochester Hills, MI 48307 (248) 218-2190
(800) 521-6010; (248) 218-2035

Full-time: 275 men, 300 women
Part-time: 130 men, 220 women
Graduate: 10 men, 5 women
Year: semesters
Application Deadline: see profile
Freshman Class: n/av
Faculty: 37
Ph.D.s: 40%
Student/Faculty: n/av
Tuition: $16,768
Room & Board: $5000

COMPETITIVE

Rochester College, founded in 1959, is a private institution affiliated with the Churches of Christ. The figures in the above capsule and in this profile are approximate. It offers undergraduate programs in business, behavioral sciences, Christian studies, English, interdisciplinary studies, history, music, communication, and general science, as well as graduate studies in theology. There are 3 undergraduate schools and 1 graduate school. The library contains 80,000 volumes, 21,868 microform items, 1,654 audio/video tapes/CDs/DVDs, and subscribes to 233 periodicals including electronic. Computerized library services include inter-library loans, database searching, Internet access, and laptop Internet portals. Special learning facilities include a learning resource center. The 83-acre campus is in a suburban area 25 miles north of Detroit. Including any residence halls, there are 12 buildings.

Student Life: 86% of undergraduates are from Michigan. Students are from 25 states, 9 foreign countries, and Canada. 81% are white. 87% are Protestant; 13% Catholic. The average age of freshmen is 18; all undergraduates, 23. 40% do not continue beyond their first year; 34% remain to graduate.

Housing: 366 students can be accommodated in college housing, which includes single-sex dorms and married student housing. On-campus housing is available on a first-come and first-served basis. 50% of students commute. Alcohol is not permitted. All students may keep cars.

Activities: 10% of men belong to 3 local fraternities; 10% of women belong to 3 local sororities. There are 22 groups on campus, including band, cheerleading, chorale, chorus, dance, drama, jazz band, newspaper, professional, religious, social, social service, and student government. Popular campus events include Celebration.

Sports: There are 4 intercollegiate sports for men and 5 for women, and 16 intramural sports for men and 16 for women. Facilities include a gym, plus soccer and baseball fields.

Disabled Students: 65% of the campus is accessible. Facilities include wheelchair ramps, elevators, special parking, specially equipped rest rooms, special class scheduling, and special housing.

Services: Counseling and information services are available, as is tutoring in some subjects. There is remedial math, reading, and writing.

Campus Safety and Security: There are lighted pathways/sidewalks, evening security guards.

Programs of Study: RC confers B.S., B.B.A., and B.A. degrees. Associates and master's degrees are also awarded. Bachelor's degrees are awarded in BUSINESS (accounting, marketing management, and sports management), COMMUNICATIONS AND THE ARTS (communications, English, and music), COMPUTER AND PHYSICAL SCIENCE (computer management), EDUCATION (technical education), SOCIAL SCIENCE (behavioral science, biblical studies, counseling/psychology, early childhood studies, history, interdisciplinary studies, ministries, psychology, and youth ministry). Management, education and psychology have the largest enrollments.

Required: All students must follow a core curriculum that includes courses in religion, communication, humanities, phys ed, science, math, and social science. To graduate, students must complete 128 credits with a minimum GPA of 2.0.

Special: A co-op program in education is available. Cross-registration with Oakland University, Madonna University, Oakland Community College, Mott Community College, Specs Howard School of Broadcast Arts, and Macomb Community College is offered. Internships, which are required for many majors, study abroad, student-designed majors and work-study programs are also offered. There are 2 national honors societies and 1 departmental honor program.

Faculty/Classroom: 50% of faculty are male; 50% are female. All teach undergraduates, 25% do research, and 25% do both. No introductory courses are taught by graduate students. The average class size in an introductory lecture is 35; in a laboratory is 20; and in a regular course is 20.

Requirements: A GPA of 2.3 is required. AP and CLEP credits are accepted. Important factors in the admissions decision are leadership record, personality/intangible qualities, and extracurricular activities record.

Procedure: Freshmen are admitted to all sessions. Entrance exams should be taken as early as possible. There are early admissions, deferred admissions, and rolling admissions plans. Notification is sent on a rolling basis. Applications are accepted online. Check with the school for current application deadlines and fee.

Transfer: 51 transfer students enrolled in a recent year. A 2.0 college GPA is required. 32 of 128 credits required for the bachelor's degree must be completed at RC.

Visiting: There are regularly scheduled orientations for prospective students, including several College Life Preview Days in fall and winter and Celebration Saturday in March. There are guides for informal visits, visitors may sit in on classes, and stay overnight. To schedule a visit, contact Enrollment Services Office.

Financial Aid: In a recent year, the average freshmen award was $7,824, with $3,376 ($7,322 maximum) from need-based scholarships or need-based grants; $1,565 ($8,206 maximum) from need-based self-help aid (loans and jobs); $2,019 ($3,534 maximum) from non-need-based athletic scholarships; and $3,311 ($8,299 maximum) from other non-need-based awards and non-need-based scholarships. 28% of undergraduate students worked part-time. Average annual earnings from campus work were $1000. The average financial indebtedness of the 2009 graduate was $10,520. The FAFSA, CCS/Profile, FAFSA, FFS, or SFS, and the college's own financial statement are required. Check with the school for current application deadlines.

International Students: There were 13 international students enrolled in a recent year. The school actively recruits these students. They must take the TOEFL.

Computers: Wireless access is available. Students may use a total of 84 computers as well as wireless hot spots across the campus. All students may access the system. Schedules for computer use vary. There are no time limits and no fees.

Graduates: In a recent year, 278 bachelor's degrees were awarded. The most popular majors were business communication (20%), early childhood education (17%), and counseling/psychology (15%). In an average class, 13% graduate in 4 years or less, 14% graduate in 5 years or less, and 5% graduate in 6 years or less. 10% were enrolled in graduate school within 6 months of graduation, and 80% were employed.

Admissions Contact: Enrollment Service. E-Mail: *admissions@rc.edu* *Web: www.rc.edu*

SAGINAW VALLEY STATE UNIVERSITY D-4

University Center, MI 48710 (989) 964-4200
(800) 968-9500; (989) 790-0180

Full-time: 3249 men, 4345 women
Part-time: 637 men, 744 women
Graduate: 357 men, 913 women
Year: semesters, summer session
Application Deadline:
Freshman Class: 6010 applied, 4733 accepted, 1593 enrolled
ACT: 22
Faculty: 307
Ph.D.s: 77%
Student/Faculty: 25 to 1
Tuition: $8423 ($28,199)
Room & Board: $8446

COMPETITIVE

Saginaw Valley State University, founded in 1963, is a state-supported institution offering undergraduate and graduate degrees in arts and behavioral sciences, business and management, education, nursing and health sciences, and science, engineering, and technology. There are 5 undergraduate schools and 5 graduate schools. In addition to regional accreditation, SVSU has baccalaureate program accreditation with AACSB, ABET, CSWE, NASM, and NCATE. The library contains 364,160 volumes, 354,265 microform items, and 27,070 audio/video tapes/CDs/DVDs, and subscribes to 48,336 periodicals including electronic. Computerized library services include interlibrary loans, database searching, Internet access, and Wi-Fi capability. Special learning facilities include an art gallery, and an observatory. The 782-acre campus is in a suburban area 5 miles north of Saginaw. Including any residence halls, there are 89 buildings.

Student Life: 93% of undergraduates are from Michigan. Others are from 19 states, 32 foreign countries, and Canada. 95% are from public schools. 71% are White; 11% African American. The average age of freshmen is 18; all undergraduates, 22. 30% do not continue beyond their first year; 42% remain to graduate.

Housing: 2736 students can be accommodated in college housing, which includes coed dorms and on-campus apartments. including healthy lifestyle floors and buildings, and first-year suites. On-campus housing is available on a first-come and first-served basis. 69% of students commute. Alcohol is not permitted. All students may keep cars.

Activities: 3% of men belong to 7 national fraternities; 3% of women belong to 1 local and 3 national sororities. There are 165 groups on campus, including art, band, cheerleading, chess, choir, chorus, computers, dance, drama, environmental, ethnic, film, gay, honors, international, jazz band, literary magazine, marching band, musical theater, newspaper, orchestra, pep band, photography, political, professional, religious, social, social service, and student government. Popular campus events include Battle of the Valleys, Cards Party and International Food Festival.

Sports: There are 9 intercollegiate sports for men and 9 for women, and 11 intramural sports for men and 11 for women. Facilities include a health and phys ed complex with an Olympic-size pool, indoor track, basketball courts, badminton courts, volleyball courts, racquetball courts, and a fitness center; tennis courts; intramural, baseball, softball, and soccer fields; an archery range; a fitness trail; a football stadium; a golf driving range and putting green; and horse shoe pits.

Disabled Students: 99% of the campus is accessible. Facilities include wheelchair ramps, elevators, special parking, specially equipped restrooms, special class scheduling, lowered drinking fountains, lowered telephones, special housing. electronically opened doors, and special access to the library. All buildings are interconnected on the second floor.

Services: Counseling and information services are available, as is tutoring in most subjects. There is a reader service for the blind, and remedial math, reading, and writing.

Campus Safety and Security: Measures include 24-hour foot and vehicle patrol, emergency notification system, self-defense education, and security escort services. There are emergency telephones, lighted pathways/sidewalks, the SVSU public safety department has commissioned police officers providing police services.

Programs of Study: SVSU confers B.A., B.S., B.A.S., B.B.A., B.F.A., B.P.A., B.S.E.E., B.S.M.E., B.S.N. and B.S.W. degrees. Master's degrees are also awarded. Bachelor's degrees are awarded in BIOLOGICAL SCIENCE (biochemistry and biology/biological science), BUSINESS (accounting, banking and finance, business administration and management, business economics, finance, international business management, and marketing management), COMMUNICATIONS AND THE ARTS (art, communications, creative writing, design, dramatic arts, English, fine arts, French, music, Spanish, and technical and business writing), COMPUTER AND PHYSICAL SCIENCE (applied mathematics, applied science, chemical physics, chemistry, computer science, information sciences and systems, mathematics, optics, and physics), EDUCATION (art education, athletic training, drama education, elementary education, English education, foreign languages education, mathematics education, music education, physical education, science education, social studies education, and special education), ENGINEERING AND ENVIRONMENTAL DESIGN (electrical/electronics engineering, engineering technology, industrial administration/management, mechanical engineering, and preengineering), HEALTH PROFESSIONS (exercise science, health science, medical laboratory science, medical technology, nursing, predentistry, premedicine, and prephysical therapy), SOCIAL SCIENCE (criminal justice, economics, history, interdisciplinary studies, international studies, political science/government, prelaw, psychology, public administration, social work, and sociology). Nursing, elementary education, and criminal justice have the largest enrollments.

Required: Students must complete a minimum of 124 credits, satisfy basic skills and general education requirements, and maintain a minimum GPA of 2.0. The General Education Program consists of 35 credit hours in 10 categories.

Special: Study abroad in 50 countries, internships, and Michigan Work Study and Federal College Work Study job opportunities within several on-campus departments. There are 3 national honor societies.

Faculty/Classroom: All teach undergraduates. No introductory courses are taught by graduate students. The average class size in an introductory lecture is 25 and in a laboratory is 17.

Admissions: 79% of the 2013-2014 applicants were accepted. The ACT scores were 42% below 21, 26% between 21 and 23, 19% between 24 and 26, 7% between 27 and 28, and 6% above 28. 33% of the current freshmen were in the top fifth of their class; 60% were in the top two fifths. 53 freshmen graduated first in their class.

Requirements: The ACT is required. Applicants must submit a completed undergraduate application for admission, an official high school transcript or GED, and ACT results. SVSU recommends high school students take a rigorous college preparatory curriculum prior to enrolling at SVSU: four years of English, three years of math, three years of natural sciences, three years of social sciences, and two years of the same foreign language. A GPA of 2.5 is required. AP and CLEP credits are accepted.

Procedure: Freshmen are admitted to all sessions. There are deferred admissions and rolling admissions plans. Application deadlines are open. Application fee is $30. Applications are accepted online.

Transfer: 586 transfer students enrolled in 2012-2013. Transfer students with fewer than 24 credits from a previous college must submit high school and college transcripts. ACT or SAT scores must be submitted, also. A minimum GPA of 2.0 is needed. An interview may be required. 31 of 124 credits required for the bachelor's degree must be completed at SVSU.

Visiting: There are regularly scheduled orientations for prospective students, including tours, help with schedules, basic information and counseling. There are guides for informal visits. To schedule a visit, contact the Office of Admissions.

Financial Aid: In 2013-2014, 72% of all full-time freshmen and 71% of continuing full-time students received some form of financial aid. 64% of all full-time freshmen and 68% of continuing full-time students received need-based aid. Average annual earnings from campus work are $1500. The FAFSA is required. Check with the school for current application deadlines.

International Students: There are 467 international students enrolled. The school actively recruits these students. They must take the TOEFL with a minimum score of 500 on the paper-based TOEFL (PBT) or 61 on the Internet-based version (iBT).

Graduates: From July 1, 2012 to June 30, 2013, 1374 bachelor's degrees were awarded. The most popular majors were nursing (10%), criminal justice (7%), and elementary education (7%). 307 companies recruited on campus in 2012-2013. In an average class, 1% graduate in 3 years or less, 10% graduate in 4 years or less, 32% graduate in 5 years or less, and 42% graduate in 6 years or less. Of the 2012 graduating class, 17% were enrolled in graduate school within 6 months of graduation, and 90% were employed.

Admissions Contact: Director of Admissions. E-Mail: *admissions@svsu.edu* Web: *www.svsu.edu*

SIENA HEIGHTS UNIVERSITY — E-5

Adrian, MI 49221 — (517) 264-7183; (800) 521-0009; (517) 264-7745

Full-time: 310 men, 510 women	**Faculty:** n/av; IIB, -$
Part-time: 105 men, 205 women	**Ph.D.s:** 64%
Graduate: 55 men, 105 women	**Student/Faculty:** n/av
Year: semesters, summer session	**Tuition:** $20,434
Application Deadline: see profile	**Room & Board:** $8390
Freshman Class: n/av	
ACT: required	

LESS COMPETITIVE

Siena Heights University, founded in 1919, is a private liberal arts institution affiliated with the Roman Catholic Church. The above figures in the above capsule and in this profile are approximate. There is one graduate school. In addition to regional accreditation, Siena has baccalaureate program accreditation with NASAD. The library contains 112,049 volumes, 24,214 microform items, 4,730 audio/video tapes/CDs/DVDs, and subscribes to 451 periodicals including electronic. Computerized library services include inter-library loans and database searching. Special learning facilities include an art gallery. The 140-acre campus is in a small town 75 miles southwest of Detroit. Including any residence halls, there are 12 buildings.

Student Life: 80% are from public schools. 84% are white. The average age of freshmen is 18; all undergraduates, 25. 45% do not continue beyond their first year.

Housing: 450 students can be accommodated in college housing, which includes coed dorms. On-campus housing is available on a first-come, first-served basis, and is available on a lottery system for upperclassmen. Priority is given to out-of-town students. 69% of students commute. All students may keep cars.

Activities: 10% of men belong to 2 national fraternities; 10% of women belong to 2 national sororities. There are 30 groups on campus, including art, cheerleading, choir, chorale, chorus, computers, drama, ethnic, international, jazz band, literary magazine, musical theater, newspaper, professional, religious, social, social service, student government, and symphony. Popular campus events include Alumni/Family Weekend, International Dinner, and athletic banquets.

Sports: There are 6 intercollegiate sports for men and 6 for women, and 6 intramural sports for men and 6 for women. Facilities include a 57000-square-foot student activity center, which houses 5 basketball, 4 volleyball, and 2 tennis courts, a 200-meter, 4-lane track, a baseball batting cage, training and exercise rooms, ballrooms, and the Sage Union. The indoor gym seats 4000. There is also a soccer field and a sand volleyball pit.

Disabled Students: 70% of the campus is accessible. Facilities include wheelchair ramps, elevators, special parking, specially equipped rest rooms, and lowered drinking fountains.

Services: Counseling and information services are available, as is tutoring in most subjects. There is remedial math, reading, and writing.

Campus Safety and Security: Measures include 24-hour foot and vehicle patrol, self-defense education, and security escort services. There are lighted pathways/sidewalks.

Programs of Study: Siena confers B.A., B.S., B.A.S., and B.F.A. degrees. Associates and master's degrees are also awarded. Bachelor's degrees are awarded in BIOLOGICAL SCIENCE (biology/biological science), BUSINESS (accounting, business administration and management, hotel/motel and restaurant management, and retailing), COMMUNICATIONS AND THE ARTS (art history and appreciation, communications, English, fine arts, music, and Spanish), COMPUTER AND PHYSICAL SCIENCE (chemistry, information sciences and systems, mathematics, and natural sciences), EDUCATION (business education, elementary education, and music education), HEALTH PROFESSIONS (premedicine), SOCIAL SCIENCE (American studies, child psychology/development, criminal justice, history, human services, humanities, liberal arts/general studies, philosophy, psychology, public administration, religion, social science, and social work). Art, business, and biology are the strongest academically. Business, art, and education are the largest.

Required: To graduate, students must complete 120 semester hours, including 30 hours in the major, and maintain at least a 2.0 GPA. A core curriculum of 33 to 35 semester hours is required, including 2 courses in English composition and 1 each in literature, math, science, fine/performing arts, social science, history, philosophy, and religious studies. A seminar in education is also required.

Special: Special academic programs include 2-2 engineering co-op programs with the University of Detroit and the University of Michigan, a 2-2 business administration program at Lake Michigan College, internships in a student's major, study abroad in Mexico for various majors and Siena, Italy, for art students, and on-and off-campus work-study. Also offered are dual and inverted majors, B.A.-B.S. degrees, a general studies degree, and student-designed majors. 3-year bachelor's degrees may be earned, and a directed student-teaching program is available for education majors. Flexible learning formats include weekend and evening courses. There is 1 national honor society.

Faculty/Classroom: 52% of faculty are male; 48% are female. 95% teach undergraduates. No introductory courses are taught by graduate students. The average class size in a regular course is 15.

Requirements: The ACT is required. Applicants must have a minimum score of 17. Admissions requirements include graduation from an accredited secondary school. The GED is accepted. Applications are accepted online. A GPA of 2.3 is required. AP and CLEP credits are accepted. Important factors in the admissions decision are recommendations by school officials, parents or siblings attended the school, and recommendations by alumni.

Procedure: Freshmen are admitted to all sessions. Entrance exams should be taken and SAT or ACT scores should be available when the application is filed. There are deferred admissions and rolling admissions plans. Application deadlines are open. Check with the school for current applications fee.

Transfer: 70 transfer students enrolled in a recent year. Applicants must have a 2.0 GPA. High school and college transcripts must be submitted. 30 of 120 credits required for the bachelor's degree must be completed at Siena.

Visiting: There are regularly scheduled orientations for prospective students. There are guides for informal visits, visitors may sit in on classes, and stay overnight. To schedule a visit, contact the Admissions Office.

Financial Aid: In a recent year, 95% of all full-time freshmen and 92% of continuing full-time students received some form of financial aid. 66% of all full-time freshmen and 68% of continuing full-time students received need-based aid. 75% of undergraduate students worked part-time. Average annual earnings from campus work were $1300. Siena is a member of CSS. The FAFSA is required. Check with the school for current application deadlines.

International Students: The school actively recruits these students. They must take the TOEFL. They must also take the ACT, scoring 17.

Graduates: In a recent year, 171 bachelor's degrees were awarded. The most popular majors were business administration (17%), art (11%), and psychology (8%).

Admissions Contact: Admissions and Enrollment Services. E-Mail: *admissions@sienahts.edu Web: www.sienaheights.edu*

SPRING ARBOR UNIVERSITY D-5

Spring Arbor, MI 49283-9799 **(517) 750-6468**
(800) 968-0011; (517) 750-6620

Full-time: 560 men, 820 women	**Faculty:** n/av; IIA, --$
Part-time: 70 men, 125 women	**Ph.D.s:** 61%
Graduate: 300 men, 975women	**Student/Faculty:** n/av
Year: semesters, summer session	**Tuition:** $21,480
Application Deadline: open	**Room & Board:** $8000
Freshman Class: n/av	
ACT: recommended	

COMPETITIVE

Founded in 1873 by leaders of the Free Methodist Church, Spring Arbor University offers a Christ-centered, liberal arts education. The figures in the above capsule and this profile are approximate. There are 3 undergraduate schools and 7 graduate schools. In addition to regional accreditation, SAU has baccalaureate program accreditation with CSWE and NCATE. The library contains 112,811 volumes, 576,594 microform items, and 3943 audio/video tapes/CDs/DVDs, and subscribes to 587 periodicals including electronic. Computerized library services include interlibrary loans, database searching, and Internet access. Special learning facilities include a learning resource center, art gallery, radio station, and TV production facilities and equipment. The 123-acre campus is in a small town 8 miles south west of Jackson. Including any residence halls, there are 36 buildings.

Student Life: 85% of undergraduates are from Michigan. Others are from 30 states, 6 foreign countries, and Canada. 90% are white. 67% are Protestant; 20% independent/ nondenominations; 11% claim no religious affiliation. 28% do not continue beyond their first year; 59% remain to graduate.

Housing: 1060 students can be accommodated in college housing, which includes single-sex dorms, on-campus apartments, and married student housing. On-campus housing is guaranteed for all 4 years. 68% of students live on campus; of those, 60% remain on campus on weekends. Alcohol is not permitted. Upperclassmen may keep cars.

Activities: There are no fraternities or sororities. There are 41 groups on campus, including art, band, choir, chorale, drama, ethnic, film, honors, international, jazz band, literary magazine, musical theater, newspaper, pep band, radio and TV, religious, social, social service, student government, symphony, and yearbook. Popular campus events include Porchfest, Arbor Games, and Midnight Breakfast.

Sports: There are 7 intercollegiate sports for men and 7 for women, and 7 intramural sports for men and 6 for women. Facilities include a weight room, basketball courts and volleyball courts, a 4-lane indoor track, an Olympic-sized swimming pool with sauna, an exercise lab, varsity and general locker rooms, and a training room. Other facilities include 3 batting cages, a Cougar Clubhouse (professional style locker rooms with separate wings for baseball, softball, and men's and women's soccer, including laundry and shower facilities), a 500-seat baseball stadium, softball diamonds, a soccer field, an 8-lane outdoor track (with long jump pit, high jump area, steeplechase hurdle, and throwing area), and 8 tennis courts (2 lighted).

Disabled Students: 80% of the campus is accessible. Facilities include wheelchair ramps, elevators, special parking, specially equipped restrooms, lowered drinking fountains, lowered telephones, and special housing.

Services: Counseling and information services are available, as is tutoring in most subjects. There is a reader service for the blind and remedial math, reading, and writing. Religious counseling and health services are also available.

Campus Safety and Security: Measures include 24-hour foot and vehicle patrol, emergency notification system, self-defense education, and security escort services. There are lighted pathways/sidewalks and key card entry to some dorms.

Programs of Study: SAU confers B.A. and B.S.W. degrees. Associate and master's degrees are also awarded. Bachelor's degrees are awarded in BIOLOGICAL SCIENCE (biochemistry and biology/biological science), BUSINESS (accounting, business administration and management, and management information systems), COMMUNICATIONS AND THE ARTS (advertising, art, broadcasting, communications, English, film arts, language arts, music, Spanish, video, and visual and performing arts), COMPUTER AND PHYSICAL SCIENCE (chemistry, computer science, mathematics, and physics), EDUCATION (Christian education, music education, and special education), HEALTH PROFESSIONS (exercise science and nursing), SOCIAL SCIENCE (biblical studies, history, missions, philosophy, philosophy and religion, physical fitness/movement, psychology, social science, social studies, social work, sociology, theological studies, and youth ministry). Business, teacher education, and English are the strongest academically. Teacher education, business, and philosophy/religion have the largest enrollments.

Required: Students must complete 4 Christian perspective courses plus cross-cultural studies, writing skills, speech, and physical fitness. Liberal arts requirements are in fine arts, humanities, natural science/math, philosophy/religion, and social science. To graduate, at least 124 semester hours, with 40 hours in upper-division courses and including 30 to 60 in the major, are needed. A minimum GPA of 2.0 overall and 2.2 in the major is also required. Students must also complete the University CORE, which includes communication skills, physical fitness, and liberal arts requirements.

Special: Study abroad is available in more than 12 countries. A Washington semester is available through the American Studies Program. The university also offers cross-registration with Jackson Community College, work-study, a dual major in physics/math, student-designed majors, pass/fail options, and nondegree study. Alternative programs for adult learners provide field-based study and assign credit for life experience. An accelerated B.A. program for such students is offered. A 3-2 engineering degree is offered with the University of Michigan, Western Michigan University, and Tri-State University. There are 3 national honor societies and a freshman honors program.

Faculty/Classroom: 60% of faculty are male; 40% are female. 94% teach undergraduates. No introductory courses are taught by graduate students. The average class size in a regular course is 18.

Requirements: The ACT is recommended. Applicants must be graduates of accredited secondary schools or have a GED. ACT or SAT test scores are required. An interview is advised for those who do not meet the requirements. Home-schooled applicants must take the ACT or the SAT, provide transcripts of course work, and submit a 2- to 3-page paper. A GPA of 2.6 is required. AP and CLEP credits are accepted. Important factors in the admissions decision are personality/intangible qualities, parents or siblings attended your school, and leadership record.

Procedure: Freshmen are admitted to all sessions. Entrance exams should be taken in the spring of the junior year or fall of the senior year. There are deferred admissions and rolling admissions plans. Application deadlines are open. Check with the school for current application fee. Notification is sent on a rolling basis. Applications are accepted online.

Transfer: Applicants should have a minimum GPA of 2.0 and are encouraged to arrange an interview. A release of information form is required from the previous college attended. 30 of 124 credits required for the bachelor's degree must be completed at SAU.

Visiting: There are regularly scheduled orientations for prospective students, including a tour, class and chapel attendance, lunch, and a student panel discussion. There are guides for informal visits, and visitors may sit in on classes and stay overnight. To schedule a visit, contact the Admissions Office.

Financial Aid. The FAFSA is required. Check with the school for current application deadlines.

International Students: They must take the TOEFL with a minimum score of 525 on the paper-based TOEFL (PBT). The SAT or ACT may be required for some students.

Admissions Contact: Director of Admissions. A campus DVD is available. E-mail: *admissions@arbor.edu* Web: *www.arbor.edu*

UNIVERSITY OF DETROIT MERCY — E-5

Detroit, MI 48219-0900 — (313) 993-1245; (800) 635-5020; (313) 993-3317

Full-time: 810 men, 1110 women	**Faculty:** n/av
Part-time: 405 men, 1105 women	**Ph.D.s:** 85%
Graduate: 1110 men, 12000 women	**Student/Faculty:** n/av
Year: semesters, summer session	**Tuition:** $32,550
Application Deadline: see profile	**Room & Board:** $9590
Freshman Class: n/av	
SAT or ACT: required	

COMPETITIVE

University of Detroit Mercy, founded in 1877, is a private, independent institution affiliated with the Jesuits and Sisters of Mercy. It offers undergraduate programs in liberal arts, education and human services, business administration, engineering and science, architecture, and nursing and health sciences. The figures in the above capsule and this profile are approximate. There are 7 undergraduate schools and 5 graduate schools. In addition to regional accreditation, U of DM has baccalaureate program accreditation with AACSB, ABET, ADA, CSWE, NAAB, and NLN. The 3 libraries contain 733,000 volumes, 1.0 million microform items, and 33,153 audio/video tapes/CDs/DVDs, and subscribe to 4049 periodicals including electronic. Computerized library services include interlibrary loans, database searching, and Internet access. Special learning facilities include a learning resource center and radio station. The 70-acre campus is in an urban area 7 miles north of downtown Detroit.

Student Life: 93% of undergraduates are from Michigan. Others are from 27 states, 19 foreign countries, and Canada. 50% are white; 33% African American. 32% are Catholic; 32% a variety of denominations and religions; 26% claim no religious affiliation; 11% Protestant. The average age of freshmen is 18; all undergraduates, 29. 12% do not continue beyond their first year.

Housing: 955 students can be accommodated in college housing, which includes coed dorms and married student housing. In addition, there is a freshman residence program, honors floors, and a peace and justice floor. On-campus housing is guaranteed for all 4 years. 79% of students commute. All students may keep cars.

Activities: There are 3 national fraternities and 3 national sororities. There are 50 groups on campus, including cheerleading, chorale, computers, drama, ethnic, honors, international, literary magazine, newspaper, pep band, political, professional, radio and TV, religious, social, social service, and student government. Popular campus events include Engineering and Architecture Week, Ethics Bowl, and Alternative Spring Break.

Sports: There are 7 intercollegiate sports for men and 8 for women, and 7 intramural sports for men and 7 for women. Facilities include a fitness center, a gym, racquetball/handball courts, an indoor track, a game room in the Student Union, and soccer, softball, and baseball fields.

Disabled Students: 80% of the campus is accessible. Facilities include wheelchair ramps, elevators, special parking, and special class scheduling.

Services: Counseling and information services are available, as is tutoring in most subjects, including all freshman courses and many other courses. There is remedial math, reading, and writing.

Campus Safety and Security: Measures include 24-hour foot and vehicle patrol, self-defense education, and security escort services. There are emergency telephones and lighted pathways/sidewalks.

Programs of Study: U of DM confers B.A., B.S., B.Arch., B.B.A., B.C.E., B.E.E., B.En., B.F.A., B.M.E., B.S.C.S., B.S.Ed., B.S.N., and B.S.W. degrees. Associate, master's, and doctoral degrees are also awarded. Bachelor's degrees are awarded in BIOLOGICAL SCIENCE (biochemistry and biology/biological science), BUSINESS (accounting and business administration and management), COMMUNICATIONS AND THE ARTS (communications, dramatic arts, and English), COMPUTER AND PHYSICAL SCIENCE (chemistry, computer science, information sciences and systems, and mathematics), EDUCATION (early childhood education, elementary education, middle school education, secondary education, and special education), ENGINEERING AND ENVIRONMENTAL DESIGN (architecture, civil engineering, electrical/electronics engineering, engineering, manufacturing engineering, and mechanical engineering), HEALTH PROFESSIONS (dental hygiene, health care administration, nursing, predentistry, premedicine, and sports medicine), SOCIAL SCIENCE (addiction studies, criminal justice, economics, history, human services, liberal arts/general studies, paralegal studies, philosophy, political science/government, prelaw, psychology, religion, social work, and sociology). Engineering, nursing, and business administration are the strongest academically. Business administration, nursing, and mechanical engineering have the largest enrollments.

Required: Students must successfully complete at least 126 credit hours, including a core curriculum, and maintain a minimum GPA of 2.0. Required courses include English composition, religion, philosophy, speech fundamentals, math, and a computer course.

Special: Cooperative education is mandatory for engineering, architecture, and nursing majors and is optional for others. Cross-registration is available with a consortium of Catholic colleges in the Detroit area. There are internships, and a B.A.-B.S. degree is available for math, chemistry, and biology majors. An accelerated 6-year degree program in dentistry is offered. Study abroad is available in England, China, Canada, Mexico, Italy, Poland, Israel, and Greece. Academic exploration courses are provided to help students who are undecided about a future vocation. There are 3 national honor societies and a freshman honors program.

Faculty/Classroom: No introductory courses are taught by graduate students.

Requirements: The SAT or ACT is required. In addition, graduation from an accredited secondary school is required; a GED will be accepted. Students must submit 16 academic credits, which should include, as a minimum, 4 units of English, 3 of math, and 2 each of history or social studies and natural science, including a lab course. Remaining credits should be distributed in a foreign language, speech, music, art, and other college preparatory electives. An interview is recommended. A GPA of 2.5 is required. AP and CLEP credits are accepted. Important factors in the admissions decision are advanced placement or honors courses.

Procedure: Freshmen are admitted to all sessions. Entrance exams should be taken during the junior or senior year. There are early admissions and rolling admissions plans. Check with the school for current application deadlines. Applications are accepted online.

Transfer: Transfer applicants with fewer than 24 semester hours of credit at an accredited institution must submit SAT or ACT scores and must have maintained a minimum GPA of 2.0. If the student is older than 23 years of age, SAT or ACT scores need not be submitted. 32 of 126 credits required for the bachelor's degree must be completed at U of DM.

Visiting: There are regularly scheduled orientations for prospective students, including information on student life, testing and advising, and registration. There are guides for informal visits, and visitors may sit in on classes and stay overnight. To schedule a visit, contact the Admissions Office.

Financial Aid: U of DM is a member of CSS. The FAFSA is required. Check with the school for current application deadlines.

International Students: The school actively recruits these students. They must take the college's own test.

Admissions Contact: Admissions Counselor. E-Mail: *admissions@udmercy.edu* Web: *www.udmercy.edu*

UNIVERSITY OF MICHIGAN/ANN ARBOR — E-5

Ann Arbor, MI 48109 — (734) 764-7433; (734) 936-0740

Full-time: 13478 men, 13019 women	**Faculty:** 2174; I, +$
Part-time: 504 men, 365 women	**Ph.D.s:** 91%
Graduate: 8863 men, 6946 women	**Student/Faculty:** 12 to 1
Year: trimesters, summer session	**Tuition:** $12,634 ($37,782)
Application Deadline: February 1	**Room & Board:** $9468
Freshman Class: n/av	
SAT or ACT: required	

HIGHLY COMPETITIVE+

The University of Michigan/Ann Arbor, founded in 1817, is the main campus of the University of Michigan. The public institution offers undergraduate programs in the arts and sciences, architecture, business administration, education, engineering, fine arts, kinesiology, natural resources, nursing, and professional studies, as well as a wide range of graduate and professional programs. The figures in the above capsule and in this profile are approximate. There are 12 undergraduate schools and 18 graduate schools. In addition to regional accreditation, UM has baccalaureate program accreditation with AACSB, ABET, ACEJMC, ACPE, ADA, ASLA, CSWE, NAAB, NASAD, NASM, NCATE, NLN, and SAF. The 27 libraries contain 10.6 million volumes, 10.6 million microform items, and 126,011 audio/video tapes/CDs/DVDs, and subscribe to 83,062 periodicals including electronic. Computerized library services include interlibrary loans, database searching, Internet access, and laptop Internet portals. Special learning facilities include a learning resource center, art gallery, natural history museum, planetarium, radio station, TV station, archeology museum, botanical gardens, two historical museums, electronics music studio, and Digital Media Commons. The 3177-acre campus is in a suburban area 38 miles west of Detroit. Including any residence halls, there are 538 buildings.

Student Life: 64% of undergraduates are from Michigan. Others are from 50 states, 86 foreign countries, and Canada. 66% are white; 11% Asian American. The average age of freshmen is 18; all undergraduates, 20. 4% do not continue beyond their first year; 90% remain to graduate.

Housing: 11664 students can be accommodated in college housing, which includes single-sex and coed dorms, on-campus apartments, and married student housing. In addition, there are honors houses, language houses, special-interest houses, fraternity houses, sorority houses, substance-free dorm rooms, women-in-science housing, and cooperative housing. On-campus housing is guaranteed for the freshman year only, is available on a first-come, first-served basis, and is available on a lottery system for upperclassmen. 63% of students commute. All students may keep cars.

Activities: 16% of men belong to 40 national fraternities; 20% of women belong to 1 local and 27 national sororities. There are 1303 groups on campus, including art, band, cheerleading, chess, choir, chorale, chorus, computers, dance, debate, drama, environmental, ethnic, film, forensics, gay, honors, international, jazz band, literary magazine, marching band, musical theater, newspaper, opera, orchestra, pep band, photography, political, professional, radio and TV, religious, social, social service, student government, symphony, and yearbook. Popular campus events include Martin Luther King Day, Native American Powwow, and FestiFall.

Sports: There are 14 intercollegiate sports for men and 14 for women, and 23 intramural sports for men and 23 for women. Facilities include a 107,501-seat stadium, a 1000-seat gym, an indoor track and tennis complex, an indoor practice center, 3 recreational buildings, 2 golf courses, a natatorium and separate swimming pools, an ice arena, soccer and field hockey fields, and several other athletic arenas, the largest of which seats 13,000.

Disabled Students: 99% of the campus is accessible. Facilities include wheelchair ramps, elevators, special parking, specially equipped restrooms, special class scheduling, lowered drinking fountains, lowered telephones, special housing. para-transit service, specially equipped vans, talking calculators, telecommunication devices for the deaf, and an adaptive technology computing site that includes a high-speed scanner, voice input and voice output, braille display and large-print screens, and a braille printer.

Services: Counseling and information services are available, as is tutoring in some subjects, introductory English and math There is a reader service for the blind.

Campus Safety and Security: Measures include 24-hour foot and vehicle patrol, emergency notification system, self-defense education, and security escort services. There are shuttle buses, emergency telephones, lighted pathways/sidewalks, controlled access to dorms/residences, a nite-owl bus service, officer bicycle patrols, and a taxi service.

Programs of Study: UM confers B.A., B.S., A.B.Ed., B.B.A., B.D.A., B.F.A., B.G.S., B.Mus., B.Mus.A., B.S.Chem., B.S.E, B.S.Ed., and B.S.N. degrees. Master's and doctoral degrees are also awarded. Bachelor's degrees are awarded in AGRICULTURE (environmental studies), BIOLOGICAL SCIENCE (biochemistry, biology/biological science, biophysics, botany, cell biology, ecology, evolutionary biology, microbiology, molecular biology, and neurosciences), BUSINESS (business administration and management, organizational behavior, and sports management), COMMUNICATIONS AND THE ARTS (Arabic, art, art history and appreciation, audio technology, ceramic art and design, classical languages, classics, communications, comparative literature, creative writing, dance, design, dramatic arts, drawing, English, English literature, fiber/textiles/weaving, film arts, French, German, Germanic languages and literature, graphic design, Greek, Greek (modern), Hebrew, historic preservation, illustration, industrial design, Italian, jazz, Latin, linguistics, literature, metal/jewelry, music, music history and appreciation, music performance, music technology, music theory and composition, musical theater, painting, performing arts, photography, printmaking, Russian, Russian languages and literature, sculpture, Spanish, speech/debate/rhetoric, theater design, video, and winds), COMPUTER AND PHYSICAL SCIENCE (astronomy, astrophysics, atmospheric sciences and meteorology, chemistry, computer science, earth science, environmental geology, geology, geoscience, mathematics, oceanography, physics, and statistics), EDUCATION (athletic training, elementary education, music education, and physical education), ENGINEERING AND ENVIRONMENTAL DESIGN (aeronautical engineering, aerospace studies, architecture, biomedical engineering, chemical engineering, civil engineering, computer engineering, electrical/electronics engineering, engineering, engineering physics, environmental engineering, geological engineering, geophysical engineering, industrial engineering, materials engineering, materials science, mechanical engineering, naval architecture and marine engineering, and nuclear engineering), HEALTH PROFESSIONS (dental hygiene, exercise science, nursing, pharmaceutical chemistry, pharmaceutical science, pharmacy, and radiological science), SOCIAL SCIENCE (African studies, African American studies, American studies, anthropology, archeology, Asian/Oriental studies, behavioral science, biblical studies, Caribbean studies, classical/ancient civilization, cognitive science, Eastern European studies, economics, European studies, Hispanic American studies, history, humanities, interdisciplinary studies, international studies, Islamic studies, Judaic studies, Latin American studies, liberal arts/general studies, medieval studies, Mexican-American/Chicano studies, Middle Eastern studies, Near Eastern studies, philosophy, physical fitness/movement, political science/government, psychology, public affairs, Puerto Rican studies, religion, Russian and Slavic studies, social science, sociology, Western European studies, and women's studies). All programs are equally strong. Psychology, engineering, and business administration. have the largest enrollments.

Required: Academic requirements vary by program. For the College of Literature, Science, and the Arts, most students must fulfill requirements in English, race and ethnicity, and foreign language. Students must also complete 9 semester hours each of humanities, social science, and natural science/math. Students must meet the quantitative reasoning requirement, designed to ensure proficiency in using and analyzing quantitative information. To graduate, students must complete 120 to 128 semester hours, including 24 to 30 in a major field, with a minimum GPA of 2.0.

Special: There are 22 national honor societies, including Phi Beta Kappa, and a freshman honors program.

Faculty/Classroom: 60% of faculty are male; 40% are female. All teach and do research. No introductory courses are taught by graduate students. The average class size in an introductory lecture is 70; in a laboratory is 18; and in a regular course is 31.

Admissions: 51% of the 2011-2012 applicants were accepted. 95% of the current freshmen were in the top fifth of their class; 99% were in the top two fifths. There were 83 National Merit finalists.

Requirements: The SAT or ACT is required. Applicants must be graduates of accredited secondary schools or have earned a GED. The university requires 16 Carnegie units, including 4 in English, 3 in math (4 for engineering majors), 3 in history and social studies, 2 in foreign language, and 3 in science. The following are recommended electives: 1 unit of hands-on computer study and 2 units of fine or performing arts. An essay is required for all applicants. Students applying to the School of Art must submit a portfolio; those applying to the School of Music must present an audition. AP and CLEP credits are accepted. Important factors in the admissions decision are advanced placement or honors courses, evidence of special talent, and geographical diversity.

Procedure: Freshmen are admitted to all sessions. Entrance exams should be taken by the end of the junior year or the beginning of the senior. There are deferred admissions and rolling admissions plans. Applications should be filed by February 1 for fall entry; October 1 for winter entry; February 1 for spring entry; and February 1 for summer entry. The application fee was $65. 9409 applicants were on a recent year, waiting list; 3724 were admitted. Applications are accepted online.

Transfer: 1032 transfer students enrolled in a recent year. A minimum college GPA of 3.0 is required for junior-level transfers. 60 of 120 credits required for the bachelor's degree must be completed at UM.

Visiting: There are regularly scheduled orientations for prospective students. Students visits include placement testing, academic advising, course registration, social activities, and informational programs on student life, computing resources, campus safety, and career planning. There are guides for informal visits and visitors may sit in on classes. To schedule a visit, contact the Office of Undergraduate Admissions.

Financial Aid: In a recent year, 47% of all full-time freshmen and 48% of continuing full-time students received some form of financial aid. 48% of all full-time freshmen and 48% of continuing full-time students received need-based aid. The average freshman award was $10,660. Need-based scholarships or need-based grants averaged $11,656; need-based self-help aid (loans and jobs) averaged $7,640; non-need-based athletic scholarships averaged $29,281; and other non-need-based awards and non-need-based scholarships averaged $5,450. The average financial indebtedness of a recent graduate was $27,828. UM is a member of CSS. The FAFSA, and noncustodial profile and tax returns is required. The priority date for freshman financial aid applications for fall entry is April 29. The deadline for filing freshman financial aid applications for fall entry is May 30.

International Students: There are 1644 international students enrolled. They must take the TOEFL with a minimum score of 570 on the paper-based TOEFL (PBT) or 88 on the Internet-based version (iBT) or take the MELAB. They must also take the SAT or ACT.

Graduates: From July 1, 2010 to June 30, 2011, 6457 bachelor's degrees were awarded. The most popular majors were engineering (18%), psychology (10%), and economics (6%). In an average class, 70% graduate in 4 years or less, 86% graduate in 5 years or less, and 88% graduate in 6 years or less.

Admissions Contact: A campus DVD is available. Web: *www.admissions.umich.edu*

UNIVERSITY OF MICHIGAN/DEARBORN E-5

Dearborn, MI 48128 (313) 593-5100; (313) 436-9167

Full-time: 2441 men, 2428 women **Faculty:** n/av; IIA, +$
Part-time: 1168 men, 1291 women **Ph.D.s:** 80%
Graduate: 861 men, 600 women **Student/Faculty:** n/av
Year: semesters, summer session **Tuition:** $9885 ($21,862)
Application Deadline: open **Room & Board:** n/av
Freshman Class: 4807 applied, 2908 accepted, 880 enrolled
VERY COMPETITIVE

The University of Michigan/Dearborn, founded in 1959, is a public, comprehensive commuter institution that is part of the University of Michigan system. The emphasis of its degree programs is on the liberal arts, management, engineering, and education. There are 4 undergraduate schools and 4 graduate schools. In addition to regional accreditation, UM - Dearborn has baccalaureate program accreditation with AACSB, ABET, and NCATE. The library contains 382,065 volumes, 544,977 microform items, and 6,070 audio/video tapes/CDs/DVDs, and subscribes to 16,828 periodicals including electronic. Computerized library services include interlibrary loans, database searching, and Internet access. Special learning facilities include an art gallery, natural history museum, radio station, TV station, a nature preserve, an Armenian research center, Early Childhood Education Center, an engineering education and practice center, a National Historic Landmark, and an astronomy dome. The 196-acre campus is in a suburban area 10 miles from Detroit. Including any residence halls, there are 20 buildings.

Student Life: 95% of undergraduates are from Michigan. Others are from 33 states, 76 foreign countries, and Canada. 68% are White; 11% African American. The average age of freshmen is 18; all undergraduates, 25.

Housing: College-sponsored housing includes Alcohol is not permitted. All students commute. All students may keep cars.

Activities: 2% of men belong to 7 national fraternities; 2% of women belong to 4 national sororities. There are 129 groups on campus, including art, cheerleading, chess, chorale, computers, dance, debate, drama, environmental, ethnic, film, gay, honors, international, jazz band, literary magazine, newspaper, pep band, photography, political, professional, radio and TV, religious, social, social service, and student government. Popular campus events include Martin Luther King Diversity Celebration, Native American Pow Wow and Fall Fest.

Sports: There are 1 intercollegiate sports for men and 2 for women, and 21 intramural sports for men and 20 for women. Facilities include a 1200-seat gym, an ice rink, an indoor/outdoor track, a playing field, sand volleyball courts, weight and exercise rooms, outdoor tennis courts, and River Rouge Trail.

Disabled Students: All of the campus is accessible. Facilities include wheelchair ramps, elevators, special parking, specially equipped restrooms, lowered drinking fountains, and lowered telephones.

Services: Counseling and information services are available, as is tutoring in most subjects, science, computer classes, composition, and math There is a reader service for the blind, and remedial math, reading, and writing.

Campus Safety and Security: Measures include 24-hour foot and vehicle patrol, self-defense education, and security escort services. There are emergency telephones, lighted pathways/sidewalks, vehicle etching, crime prevention day, CPR training, and a rape awareness seminar.

Programs of Study: UM - Dearborn confers B.A., B.S., B.B.A., B.G.S., B.S.A. and B.S.E. degrees. Master's degrees are also awarded. Bachelor's degrees are awarded in AGRICULTURE (environmental studies), BIOLOGICAL SCIENCE (biochemistry, biology/biological science, and microbiology), BUSINESS (accounting, business administration and management, management information systems, management science, and marketing management), COMMUNICATIONS AND THE ARTS (art history and appreciation, arts administration/management, communications, English, French, language arts, and music history and appreciation), COMPUTER AND PHYSICAL SCIENCE (chemistry, computer science, geology, mathematics, physics, science, and software engineering), EDUCATION (early childhood education, education, elementary education, mathematics education, science education, secondary education, social studies education, and special education), ENGINEERING AND ENVIRONMENTAL DESIGN (computer engineering, electrical/electronics engineering technology, engineering, environmental science, industrial engineering technology, manufacturing engineering, and mechanical engineering), HEALTH PROFESSIONS (health), SOCIAL SCIENCE (American studies, anthropology, behavioral science, criminal justice, economics, Hispanic American studies, history, humanities, international studies, liberal arts/general studies, philosophy, political science/government, psychology, social studies, sociology, urban studies, and women's studies). Electrical engineering and business administration are the strongest academically. Mechanical engineering, prebusiness, and business administration have the largest enrollments.

Required: Each college within the university has its own requirements. To graduate, students must complete 120 to 128 credit hours.

Special: UM-Dearborn offers internships, study abroad, work-study and accelerated degree programs, a general studies degree, a dual major in engineering math, student-designed majors, and co-op programs in engineering, business administration, and arts and sciences. Non-degree study and pass/fail options are possible. There are 1 national honor societies, a freshman honors program, and 2 departmental honors programs.

Faculty/Classroom: No introductory courses are taught by graduate students. The average class size in a regular course is 29.

Admissions: 60% of the 2013 2014 applicants were accepted. The ACT scores were 29% between 21 and 23, 28% between 24 and 26, 13% between 27 and 28, and 12% above 28. 14 freshmen graduated first in their class.

Requirements: Admissions requirements normally include graduation from an accredited secondary school; recommended high school units include 4 years each in math, English, and history, 3 each in science and foreign language, and 1 each in art and information technology. The GED is accepted with a minimum score of 55. An essay and interview are recommended. A GPA of 3.0 is required. AP credits are accepted. Important factors in the admissions decision are advanced placement or honors courses, recommendations by school officials, and leadership record.

Procedure: Freshmen are admitted to all sessions. Entrance exams should be taken in the spring of the junior year or the fall of the senior year. There are deferred admissions and rolling admissions plans. Check with the school for current application deadlines. The fall 2013 application fee was $30. Notification is sent on a rolling basis. Applications are accepted online.

Transfer: 843 transfer students enrolled in 2012-2013. Applicants are required to have 25 to 30 transferable semester/credit hours; if they have fewer than 25, the SAT or ACT is mandatory. The required minimum GPA ranges from 2.5 to 3.0, depending on major. 60 of 128 credits required for the bachelor's degree must be completed at UM - Dearborn.

Visiting: There are regularly scheduled orientations for prospective students, consisting of a tour, a student panel, academic unit introduction, and campus life sessions. There are guides for informal visits and visitors may sit in on classes. To schedule a visit, contact the Admissions Office.

Financial Aid: The average freshman award was $10,662. Need-based scholarships or need-based grants averaged $5,644 ; need-based self-help aid (loans and jobs) averaged $4,199; and $3,368 from other forms of aid. The average financial indebtedness of the 2013 graduate was $23,437. The FAFSA is required. Check with the school for current application deadlines.

International Students: There are 75 international students enrolled. They must take the TOEFL with a minimum score of 550 on the paper-based TOEFL (PBT) or 80 on the Internet-based version (iBT) or take the MELAB, or the APIEL exam. They must also take the SAT or ACT, scoring 22.

Graduates: From July 1, 2012 to June 30, 2013, 1227 bachelor's degrees were awarded. The most popular majors were psychology (8%), business/marketing (7%), and communication/journalism (5%). In an average class, 14% graduate in 4 years or less, 41% graduate in 5 years or less, and 50% graduate in 6 years or less.

Admissions Contact: Deb Peffer, Director of Admissions and Orientation. E-Mail: *admissions@umd.umich.edu* Web: *www.umd.umich.edu*

UNIVERSITY OF MICHIGAN-FLINT E-4

Flint, MI 48502 (810) 762-3300; (810) 762-3272

Full-time: 1960 men, 2530 women **Faculty:** 287; IIA, -$
Part-time: 889 men, 1764 women **Ph.D.s:** 69%
Graduate: 556 men, 856 women **Student/Faculty:** 15 to 1
Year: semesters, summer session **Tuition:** $9844 ($18,796)
Application Deadline: August 20 **Room & Board:** $7703
Freshman Class: 3003 applied, 2345 accepted, 724 enrolled
SAT CR/M/W: 610/595/580 **ACT:** 21 **COMPETITIVE+**

The University of Michigan-Flint, established in 1956, is a public institution offering programs in the liberal arts and sciences, education, health professions, and business. There are 4 undergraduate schools and 6 graduate schools. In addition to regional accreditation, UM-Flint has baccalaureate program accreditation with AACSB, APTA, CSWE, NASM, NCATE, and NLN. The library contains 353,617 volumes, 600,610 microform items, and 10,581 audio/video tapes/CDs/DVDs, and subscribes to 559 periodicals including electronic. Computerized library services include interlibrary loans, database searching, and Internet access. Special learning facilities include an art gallery. The 73-acre campus is in an urban area 60 miles northwest of Detroit, 50 miles east of Lansing, and 55 miles north of Ann Arbor. Including any residence halls, there are 9 buildings.

Student Life: 92% of undergraduates are from Michigan. Others are from 37 states, 34 foreign countries, and Canada. 97% are from public schools. 68% are White; 11% African American. The average age of freshmen is 19; all undergraduates, 26. 20% do not continue beyond their first year; 40% remain to graduate.

Housing: 310 students can be accommodated in college housing, which includes coed dorms and off-campus apartments. On-campus housing is available on a first-come and first-served basis. 96% of students commute. Alcohol is not permitted. All students may keep cars.

Activities: 5% of men belong to 6 national fraternities; 4% of women belong to 7 national sororities. There are 103 groups on campus, including art, band, cheerleading, choir, chorale, chorus, computers, dance, debate, drama, ethnic, gay, honors, jazz band, literary magazine, musical theater, newspaper, political, professional, radio and TV, religious, social, social service, and student government. Popular campus events include Welcome Back Week, Winter Block Party and Presidents Ball.

Sports: There are 13 intramural sports for men and 12 for women. Facilities include a recreation building housing a multipurpose gym, racquetball courts, a weight training area, and a swimming pool.

Disabled Students: 97% of the campus is accessible. Facilities include wheelchair ramps, elevators, special parking, specially equipped restrooms, special class scheduling, lowered drinking fountains, lowered telephones, a telephone for the hearing impaired. Reasonable accommodations may be made for students with documented disabilities.

Services: Counseling and information services are available, as is tutoring in every subject. There is a reader service for the blind, and remedial math, reading, and writing. Sign language interpreters, note takers, and testing accommodations

Campus Safety and Security: Measures include 24-hour foot and vehicle patrol, emergency notification system, self-defense education, and security escort services. There are shuttle buses, emergency telephones, and lighted pathways/sidewalks.

Programs of Study: UM-Flint confers B.A., B.S., B.A.S., B.B.A., B.F.A., B.S.E., B.S.N., B.S.W., B.M., B.M.E. and B.I.S. degrees. Master's and doctoral degrees are also awarded. Bachelor's degrees are awarded in BIOLOGICAL SCIENCE (biology/biological science and ecology), BUSINESS (accounting, banking and finance, business administration and management, human resources, and marketing/retailing/merchandising), COMMUNICATIONS AND THE ARTS (art, communications, dramatic arts, English, French, music, and Spanish), COMPUTER AND PHYSICAL SCIENCE (applied science, chemistry, computer science, mathematics, physical sciences, physics, and science), EDUCATION (early childhood education, education, elementary education, foreign languages education, music education, and secondary education), ENGINEERING AND ENVIRONMENTAL DESIGN (engineering), HEALTH PROFESSIONS (environmental health science, health care administration, health science, medical laboratory technology, nursing, physical therapy, and radiation therapy), SOCIAL SCIENCE (anthropology, applied psychology, community psychology, criminal justice, economics, geography, history, philosophy, political science/government, psychology, public administration, social science, social work, sociology, and urban studies). Business and nursing are the strongest academically. Business, education, and health sciences have the largest enrollments.

Required: To graduate, all students must complete at least 120 credits, including 30 to 70 in the major along with satisfying all major requirements, and maintain a GPA of 2.0. Distribution requirements total 50 credits in English composition, humanities, fine arts, social science, and natural science.

Special: Special arrangements include co-op programs and dual majors, student-designed majors, cross-registration with Mott Community College, internships, study abroad, work-study, a 3-2 engineering program, an accelerated business degree, a general studies degree, nondegree study, and pass/fail options. There are 5 national honor societies, including Phi Beta Kappa, a freshman honors program, and 47 departmental honors programs.

Faculty/Classroom: 42% of faculty are male; 58% are female. All teach and do research. No introductory courses are taught by graduate students. The average class size in an introductory lecture is 24; in a laboratory is 17; and in a regular course is 20.

Admissions: 78% of the 2013-2014 applicants were accepted. The SAT scores for the 2013-2014 freshman class were: Critical Reading--30% below 500, 10% between 500 and 599, 40% between 600 and 699, and 20% between 700 and 800; Math--20% below 500, 30% between 500 and 599, 30% between 600 and 699, and 20% between 700 and 800; Writing--20% below 500, 50% between 500 and 599, and 30% between 700 and 800. The ACT scores were 45% below 21, 25% between 21 and 23, 16% between 24 and 26, 7% between 27 and 28, and 7% above 28. 34% of the current freshmen were in the top fifth of their class; 63% were in the top two fifths. 7 freshmen graduated first in their class.

Requirements: The SAT or ACT is required, with the ACT preferred. Graduation from secondary school is required, with 4 years of English, 3 each of math and social studies, and 2 of science. The GED is accepted. SAT: Subject tests and an interview are recommended. Applied music students must audition. A GPA of 2.7 is required. AP and CLEP credits are accepted. Important factors in the admissions decision are advanced placement or honors courses, evidence of special talent, and leadership record.

Procedure: Freshmen are admitted to all sessions. Entrance exams should be taken in the spring of the junior year or fall of the senior year. There are deferred admissions and rolling admissions plans. Applications should be filed by August 20 for fall entry; December 1 for winter entry. The fall 2013 application fee was $30. Notification is sent on a rolling basis. Applications are accepted online.

Transfer: 857 transfer students enrolled in 2012-2013. Applicants must have at least 12 college credits and a minimum GPA of 2.0 in transferable courses. An associate degree and an interview are recommended. 45 of 120 credits required for the bachelor's degree must be completed at UM-Flint.

Visiting: There are regularly scheduled orientations for prospective students. There are guides for informal visits and visitors may sit in on classes. To schedule a visit, contact the Admissions Office at (810) 762-3300.

Financial Aid: In 2013-2014, 61% of all full-time freshmen and 73% of continuing full-time students received some form of financial aid. 41% of all full-time freshmen and 54% of continuing full-time students received need-based aid. The average freshman award was $10,259. Need-based scholarships or need-based grants averaged $5,897; need-based self-help aid (loans and jobs) averaged $3,699; and other non-need-based awards and non-need-based scholarships averaged $4,246. Average annual earnings from campus work are $2398. The average financial indebtedness of the 2013 graduate was $27,336. The FAFSA, and Institution's own financial form spring / summer sessions only is required. The deadline for filing freshman financial aid applications for fall entry is March 1.

International Students: There are 425 international students enrolled. The school actively recruits these students. They must take the TOEFL with a minimum score of 500 on the paper-based TOEFL (PBT) or 61 on the Internet-based version (iBT) or take the MELAB. They must also take the SAT or ACT.

Graduates: From July 1, 2012 to June 30, 2013, 1102 bachelor's degrees were awarded. The most popular majors were registered nursing (18%), health care administration / management (7%), and business administration / management (5%). 179 companies recruited on campus in 2012-2013. In an average class, 11% graduate in 4 years or less, 31% graduate in 5 years or less, and 39% graduate in 6 years or less.

Admissions Contact: Jon Davidson, Director of Admissions. E-Mail: *admissions@list.umich.edu* Web: *www.umflint.edu*

WAYNE STATE UNIVERSITY E-5

Detroit, MI 48202 **(313) 577-3577; (313) 577-7536**

Full-time: 5442 men, 7029 women	**Faculty:** n/av; I, -$
Part-time: 2906 men, 3965 women	**Ph.D.s:** n/av
Graduate: 3939 men, 5657 women	**Student/Faculty:** n/av
Year: semesters, summer session	**Tuition:** $10,989 ($23,615)
Application Deadline: August 28	**Room & Board:** $8504

Freshman Class: 10249 applied, 8255 accepted, 2338 enrolled
ACT: 21

COMPETITIVE

Founded in 1868, Wayne State University is a nationally recognized research institution dedicated to preparing students to excel in an increasingly fast-paced and interconnected global society. As Michigan's only urban research university, WSU occupies a unique niche as a catalyst for investigating and helping to resolve the myriad issues facing residents of the contemporary urban environment. With nearly 29,000 students enrolled in 13 schools and colleges, WSU prides itself on providing world-class education in the real world on six campuses throughout metro Detroit. There are 9 undergraduate schools and 12 graduate schools. In addition to regional accreditation, Wayne State has baccalaureate program accreditation with AACSB, ABET, ABFSE, ACPE, CSWE, and NASM. The 6 libraries contain 4.0 million volumes, 3.9 million microform items, and 81,279 audio/video tapes/CDs/DVDs, and subscribe to 66,300 periodicals including electronic. Computerized library services include interlibrary loans, database searching, Internet access, and Wi-Fi capability. Special learning facilities include an art gallery, natural history museum, planetarium, radio station, and TV station. The 191-acre campus is in an urban area 2 miles north of downtown Detroit in the New Center area. Including any residence halls, there are 100 buildings.

Student Life: 98% of undergraduates are from Michigan. Others are from 40 states, 39 foreign countries, and Canada. 50% are White; 23% African American; 12% race unknown. The average age of freshmen is 18; all undergraduates, 24. 25% do not continue beyond their first year; 75% remain to graduate.

Housing: College-sponsored housing includes single-sex and coed dorms and on-campus apartments. In addition, there are fraternity houses and sorority houses. On-campus housing is available on a first-come and first-served basis. 89% of students commute. All students may keep cars.

Activities: 2% of men belong to 12 national fraternities; 2% of women belong to 1 local and 11 national sororities. There are 395 groups on campus, including art, band, cheerleading, chess, choir, chorale, chorus, communications, computers, dance, debate, drama, drill team, environmental, ethnic, film, forensics, gay, honors, international, jazz band, literary magazine, marching band, musical theater, newspaper, orchestra, pep band, photography, political, professional, radio and TV, religious, social,

social service, student government, and symphony. Popular campus events include Student Organization Day, International Fair, and Detroit Festival of the Arts.

Sports: There are 8 intercollegiate sports for men and 8 for women, and 10 intramural sports for men and 10 for women. Facilities include an athletic complex with 3 gyms, a weight room, racquetball and squash courts, swimming pool, an outdoor track, tennis courts, baseball fields, softball, and football fields and a football stadium, indoor basketball courts, track, climbing wall and ropes course.

Disabled Students: All of the campus is accessible. Facilities include wheelchair ramps, elevators, special parking, specially equipped restrooms, lowered drinking fountains, lowered telephones, and educational accessibility services.

Services: Counseling and information services are available, as is tutoring in every subject. There is a reader service for the blind, and remedial math, reading, and writing. Tutorial services are available through centralized counseling or academic departments.

Campus Safety and Security: Measures include 24-hour foot and vehicle patrol, emergency notification system, self-defense education, and security escort services. There are shuttle buses, emergency telephones, lighted pathways/sidewalks, and controlled access to dorms/residences.

Programs of Study: Master's and doctoral degrees are also awarded. Bachelor's degrees are awarded in BIOLOGICAL SCIENCE (biochemistry, biology/biological science, biophysics, and nutrition), BUSINESS (accounting, banking and finance, business administration and management, funeral home services, labor studies, management information systems, marketing/retailing/merchandising, organizational leadership and management, and supply chain management), COMMUNICATIONS AND THE ARTS (art, art history and appreciation, classics, communications, communication science, dance, design, dramatic arts, English, film arts, fine arts, German, information technology, journalism, language arts, linguistics, media arts, music, public relations, romance languages and literature, Russian, Slavic languages, and theatre arts), COMPUTER AND PHYSICAL SCIENCE (astronomy, chemistry, computer science, geology, information sciences and systems, mathematics, physics, and radiological technology), EDUCATION (art education, elementary education, English education, health education, mathematics education, physical education, recreation education, science education, social studies education, special education, and technical education), ENGINEERING AND ENVIRONMENTAL DESIGN (biomedical engineering, chemical engineering, civil engineering, computer technology, construction management, electrical/electronics engineering, electrical/electronics engineering technology, electromechanical technology, environmental science, industrial engineering, industrial engineering technology, manufacturing technology, mechanical engineering, and mechanical engineering technology), HEALTH PROFESSIONS (clinical science, exercise science, health science, nursing, public health, radiation therapy, and speech pathology/audiology), SOCIAL SCIENCE (African studies, anthropology, Asian/Oriental studies, criminal justice, dietetics, economics, food science, history, liberal arts/general studies, Near Eastern studies, philosophy, political science/government, psychology, public affairs, social work, sociology, urban studies, and women's studies). Psychology, management, and biology have the largest enrollments.

Required: To graduate, students must complete at least 120 credit hours and have a minimum GPA of 2.0. General education has 2 components. Students must complete competencies in critical thinking, written communication, math, oral communication, and computer literacy. In addition, students must complete group requirements in natural science, humanities, society and institutions.

Special: Special academic programs include internships in business, industry, or communications; study abroad; on-campus work-study programs; accelerated degree programs in liberal arts and science, engineering, and nursing; co-op programs; and nondegree study. There is 1 national honor society, including Phi Beta Kappa, a freshman honors program, and 70 departmental honors programs.

Faculty/Classroom: 52% of faculty are male; 48% are female. No introductory courses are taught by graduate students.

Admissions: 81% of the 2013-2014 applicants were accepted. The ACT scores were 39% below 21, 22% between 21 and 23, 18% between 24 and 26, 11% between 27 and 28, and 11% above 28. 45% of the current freshmen were in the top fifth of their class; 72% were in the top two fifths. There were 8 National Merit finalists. 37 freshmen graduated first in their class.

Requirements: The ACT is required. At Wayne State, we know that students come from different backgrounds and experiences, which are things that make our students so great! That's why we look at each individual applicant as that - an individual. The Office of Undergraduate Admissions will review your grade-point average, ACT or SAT score and any other supporting documentation you provide us or we request from you. AP and CLEP credits are accepted.

Procedure: Freshmen are admitted to all sessions. Entrance exams should be taken ACT should be taken in the junior year or the SAT in the senior year. There are deferred admissions and rolling admissions plans. Applications should be filed by August 28 for fall entry; January 6 for winter entry; May 5 for spring entry; and May 5 for summer entry. Applications are accepted online.

Transfer: 2165 transfer students enrolled in 2012-2013. You can be admitted to Wayne State as a transfer student if you have at least 24 transferable credits of previous college work and a minimum 2.5 cumulative grade-point average from all higher education institutions you've attended. Students who have completed an Associate Degree may be admitted with a grade point average of a 2.0 or better. 30 of 120 credits required for the bachelor's degree must be completed at Wayne State.

Visiting: There are regularly scheduled orientations for prospective students, including meeting with advisors, registering for classes, meeting upperclassmen , and touring the campus. There are guides for informal visits, visitors may sit in on classes, and stay overnight. To schedule a visit, contact the Office of Undergraduate Admissions.

Financial Aid: In 2013-2014, 90% of all full-time freshmen students received some form of financial aid. The average financial indebtedness of the 2013 graduate was $22,420. Wayne State is a member of CSS. The FAFSA, federal tax returns, and W-2s are required. The priority date for freshman financial aid applications for fall entry is February 15. The deadline for filing freshman financial aid applications for fall entry is April 1.

International Students: There are 384 international students enrolled. The school actively recruits these students. They must take the TOEFL with a minimum score of 550 on the paper-based TOEFL (PBT) or 79 on the Internet-based version (iBT) or take the MELAB. They must also take the SAT or ACT.

Graduates: From July 1, 2012 to June 30, 2013, 2634 bachelor's degrees were awarded. The most popular majors were business, management, marketing, and related support services (16%), psychology (12%), and education (9%). 4852 companies recruited on campus in 2012-2013. In an average class, 10% graduate in 4 years or less, 21% graduate in 5 years or less, and 28% graduate in 6 years or less.

Admissions Contact: Judy Tatum, Director of Undergraduate Admissions. E-Mail: *admissions@wayne.edu* Web: *www.admissions.wayne.edu*

WESTERN MICHIGAN UNIVERSITY — D-5

Kalamazoo, MI 49008 — **(269) 387-2000; (800) 400-4968; (269) 387-2096**

Full-time: 7927 men, 7952 women	**Faculty:** 728; I, --$
Part-time: 1649 men, 1670 women	**Ph.D.s:** 80%
Graduate: 2165 men, 2931 women	**Student/Faculty:** 23 to 1
Year: semesters, summer session	**Tuition:** $10,355 ($24,109)
Application Deadline: open	**Room & Board:** $8687

Freshman Class: 14621 applied, 12113 accepted, 3190 enrolled

ACT: 22

COMPETITIVE

Western Michigan University is a dynamic, globally engaged institution that combines the resources of a national research university with the support and personal attention often found at a small college. There are 7 undergraduate schools and 1 graduate school. In addition to regional accreditation, WMU has baccalaureate program accreditation with AACSB, ABET, ADA, CSWE, FIDER, NASAD, NASM, and NCATE. The 4 libraries contain 1.9 million volumes, 2.1 million microform items, and 27,331 audio/video tapes/CDs/DVDs, and subscribe to 59,893 periodicals including electronic. Computerized library services include interlibrary loans, database searching, Internet access, and Wi-Fi capability. Special learning facilities include an art gallery, radio station, aviation flight simulators, electron microscope, particle accelerator, a paper manufacturing and fiber recovery pilot plant, a business technology and research park, health education facility, and numerous specialized labs in the academic departments. The 1200-acre campus is in an urban area 140 miles west of Detroit and 140 miles east of Chicago. Including any residence halls, there are 143 buildings.

Student Life: 89% of undergraduates are from Michigan. Others are from 38 states, 64 foreign countries, and Canada. 72% are White. The average age of freshmen is 18; all undergraduates, 22. 26% do not continue beyond their first year; 55% remain to graduate.

Housing: 6045 students can be accommodated in college housing, which includes single-sex and coed dorms, on-campus apartments, off-campus apartments, and married student housing. In addition, there are honors houses, special-interest houses, fraternity houses, sorority houses, Second year experience, and transfer student communities. On-campus housing is guaranteed for all 4 years, is available on a first-come, and first-served basis. 72% of students commute. All students may keep cars.

Activities: 5% of men belong to 17 national fraternities; 6% of women belong to 10 national sororities. There are 360 groups on campus, including art, band, cheerleading, chess, choir, chorale, chorus, computers, dance, drama, environmental, ethnic, film, gay, honors, international, jazz band, literary magazine, marching band, musical theater, newspaper, orchestra, pep band, photography, political, professional, radio and TV, religious, social, social service, student government, and symphony. Popular campus events include Campus Classic, CommUniversity, Bronco Bash and Family Weekend.

Sports: There are 6 intercollegiate sports for men and 9 for women, and 16 intramural sports for men and 16 for women. Facilities include a 240,000 sq. ft. recreation center designed as a sports village, which includes a recreational swimming pool, a swirl pool, a weight and fitness room with more than 100 stations, facilities for basketball, floor hockey, and indoor soccer, a climbing wall, an elevated track for jogging, and facilities for aerobics, indoor cycling, badminton, tennis, and volleyball. The field house includes a 5800-seat arena for basketball and volleyball competition and facilities for gymnasts. There is also a 400- meter Olympic model Martin-surface track, a cross-country course, tennis courts, a 30,000-seat stadium, a competition swimming pool, and an ice arena.

Disabled Students: 85% of the campus is accessible. Facilities include wheelchair ramps, elevators, special parking, specially equipped restrooms, special class scheduling, lowered drinking fountains, lowered telephones, special housing. The University contracts with Metro to provide door-to-door services with a lift as requested, and adaptive computer equipment are also available.

Services: Counseling and information services are available, as is tutoring in most subjects. There is a reader service for the blind, and remedial math, reading, and writing.

Campus Safety and Security: Measures include 24-hour foot and vehicle patrol, emergency notification system, self-defense education, and security escort services. There are shuttle buses, emergency telephones, lighted pathways/sidewalks, controlled access to dorms/residences, There is also a student watch program, Operation Identification, an enhanced telephone system, and a residence hall security system.

Programs of Study: WMU confers B.A., B.S., B.B.A., B.F.A., B.Mus., B.S.E., B.S.N. and B.S.W. degrees. Master's and doctoral degrees are also awarded. Bachelor's degrees are awarded in AGRICULTURE (environmental studies), BIOLOGICAL SCIENCE (biochemistry and biology/biological science), BUSINESS (accounting, banking and finance, business administration and management, business economics, fashion merchandising, finance, human resources, management information systems, marketing/retailing/merchandising, recreation and leisure services, supply chain management, and tourism), COMMUNICATIONS AND THE ARTS (advertising, art history, art, broadcasting, communications, creative writing, dance, dramatic arts, English, French, German, graphic design, jazz, journalism, Latin, music, music performance, music theory and composition, musical theater, performing arts, public relations, Spanish, telecommunications, and theater design), COMPUTER AND PHYSICAL SCIENCE (applied mathematics, chemistry, computer science, earth science, geochemistry, geology, geophysics and seismology, hydrogeology, mathematics, physics, and statistics), EDUCATION (art education, athletic training, business education, early childhood education, education, education of the emotionally handicapped, education of the mentally handicapped, elementary education, foreign languages education, health education, middle school education, music education, physical education, secondary education, and special education), ENGINEERING AND ENVIRONMENTAL DESIGN (aeronautical engineering, aircraft mechanics, airline piloting and navigation, aviation administration/management, chemical engineering, city/community/regional planning, civil engineering, computer engineering, construction engineering, drafting and design technology, electrical/electronics engineering, engineering management, graphic and printing production, industrial engineering, industrial engineering technology, interior design, manufacturing engineering, manufacturing technology, mechanical engineering, paper and pulp science, and paper engineering), HEALTH PROFESSIONS (biomedical science, community health work, exercise science, music therapy, nursing, occupational therapy, and speech pathology/audiology), SOCIAL SCIENCE (African studies, anthropology, behavioral science, child care/child and family studies, clothing and textiles management/production/services, criminal justice, dietetics, economics, family/consumer studies, food production/management/services, gender studies, geography, history, interdisciplinary studies, international studies, philosophy, political science/government, psychology, religion, social work, sociology, textiles and clothing, and women's studies). Psychology, business, criminal justice, biomedical sciences, and accountancy have the largest enrollments.

Required: Students must complete 122 semester hours, including 37 of general education courses and a minimum of 24 in the major. A minimum GPA of 2.0 is required. Students must complete courses in fine arts, humanities, US culture, non-Western world, social science, natural science with lab, science and technology, and health and well-being. Comprehensive exams are required in some departments. All students must demonstrate computer literacy.

Special: Cross-registration is available through the Kalamazoo Consortium. Opportunities are provided for internships in occupational and music therapy, teaching, business, history, and engineering and an accelerated degree program in mechanical engineering. Also available are work-study programs, student-designed majors, pass/fail options, and credit by exam. WMU offers students study abroad programs in 32 countries, and access to foreign study opportunities in almost every country in the world through linkages with other universities and organizations. There are 12 national honor societies, including Phi Beta Kappa, a freshman honors program, and 32 departmental honors programs.

Faculty/Classroom: 51% of faculty are male; 49% are female. Graduate students teach 24% of introductory courses. The average class size in an introductory lecture is 102; in a laboratory is 23; and in a regular course is 33.

Admissions: 83% of the 2013-2014 applicants were accepted. The ACT scores were 35% below 21, 29% between 21 and 23, 21% between 24 and 26, 9% between 27 and 28, and 6% above 28. 28% of the current freshmen were in the top fifth of their class; 56% were in the top two fifths. There were 3 National Merit finalists. 35 freshmen graduated first in their class.

Requirements: The ACT is required. Applicants must submit an official high school transcript. An audition is required for music majors. An interview may be recommended. The College of Fine Arts requires an audition, portfolio, or interview of all applicants. A GPA of 2.5 is required. AP and CLEP credits are accepted. Important factors in the admissions decision are advanced placement or honors courses, extracurricular activities record, and recommendations by school officials.

Procedure: Freshmen are admitted to all sessions. Entrance exams should be taken During the junior year or early in the senior year. There is a rolling admissions plan. Application deadlines are open. Application fee is $35. Notification is sent on a rolling basis. Applications are accepted online.

Transfer: 2914 transfer students enrolled in 2012-2013. Minimum 60 hours from a 4-year accredited institution for a bachelors degree at WMU. While students may transfer in unlimited number of hours, 60 hours must be completed at a four year institution and at least 30 hours at WMU. 30 of 122 credits required for the bachelor's degree must be completed at WMU.

Visiting: There are regularly scheduled orientations for prospective students, Visiting students can participate in an admission presentation, departmental advising, lunch, and a campus tour. There are guides for informal visits and visitors may sit in on classes. To schedule a visit, contact the Campus Visit Center at (269) 387-2289.

Financial Aid: In 2013-2014, 67% of all full-time freshmen and 72% of continuing full-time students received some form of financial aid. 46% of all full-time freshmen and 50% of continuing full-time students received need-based aid. The average freshman award was $11,870. Need-based scholarships or need-based grants averaged $6,050 ($10,245 maximum); need-based self-help aid (loans and jobs) averaged $3,550 ($5,500 maximum); non-need-based athletic scholarships averaged $23,231 ($44,919 maximum); and other non-need-based awards and non-need-based scholarships averaged $4,290 ($31,870 maximum). 17% of undergraduate students work part-time. Average annual earnings from campus work are $4880. The average financial indebtedness of the 2013 graduate was $26,799. The FAFSA is required. The priority date for freshman financial aid applications for fall entry is March 1.

International Students: There are 580 international students enrolled. The school actively recruits these students. They must take the TOEFL with a minimum score of 550 on the paper-based TOEFL (PBT) or 80 on the Internet-based version (iBT). V2>**Graduates:** From July 1, 2012 to June 30, 2013, 3988 bachelor's degrees were awarded. The most popular majors were education (10%), marketing (5%), and health services (4%). 442 companies recruited on campus in 2012-2013. In an average class, 23% graduate in 4 years or less, 46% graduate in 5 years or less, and 55% graduate in 6 years or less.

Admissions Contact: Penny Bundy, Director of Admissions. E-Mail: *ask-wmu@wmich.edu* Web: *www.wmich.edu*

MINNESOTA

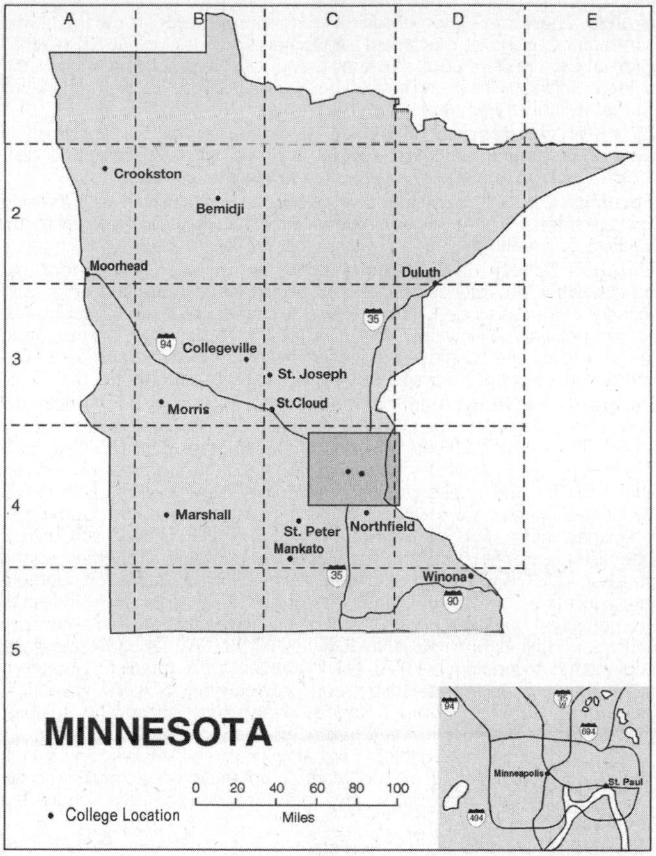

AUGSBURG COLLEGE C-4

Minneapolis, MN 55454 (612) 330-1001
(800) 788-5678; (612) 330-1581

Full-time: 1231 men, 1343 women
Part-time: 197 men, 353 women
Graduate: 286 men, 606 women
Year: varies, summer session
Application Deadline: May 1
Freshman Class: 2346 applied, 1217 accepted, 449 enrolled
SAT CR/M: 505/565

Faculty: 195; IIB, -$
Ph.D.s: 85%
Student/Faculty: 13 to 1
Tuition: $29,200
Room & Board: $8114
ACT: 22 **COMPETITIVE**

Augsburg College, established in 1869, is a private liberal arts institution affiliated with the Evangelical Lutheran Church in America. There is 1 undergraduate school and 1 graduate school. In addition to regional accreditation, Augsburg has baccalaureate program accreditation with CSWE, NASM, NCATE, and NLN. The library contains 182,289 volumes, 21,355 microform items, 3,477 audio/video tapes/CDs/DVDs, and subscribes to 686 periodicals including electronic. Computerized library services include interlibrary loans, database searching, Internet access, and laptop Internet portals. Special learning facilities include a learning resource center, art gallery, planetarium, and radio station. The 23-acre campus is in an urban area in Minneapolis. Including any residence halls, there are 26 buildings.

Student Life: 89% of undergraduates are from Minnesota. Others are from 41 states, 20 foreign countries, and Canada. 71% are white. 51% are Protestant; 30% claim no religious affiliation; 16% Catholic. The average age of freshmen is 19; all undergraduates, 26. 19% do not continue beyond their first year; 60% remain to graduate.

Housing: 1150 students can be accommodated in college housing, which includes coed dorms, on-campus apartments, and married student housing. In addition, there are special-interest houses. On-campus housing is guaranteed for the freshman year only, is available on a first-come, first-served basis, and is available on a lottery system for upperclassmen. Priority is given to out-of-town students. 54% of students live on campus; of those, 50% remain on campus on weekends. All students may keep cars.

Activities: There are no fraternities or sororities. There are 40 groups on campus, including art, band, cheerleading, choir, chorus, dance, drama, ethnic, gay, honors, international, jazz band, literary magazine, newspaper, orchestra, pep band, political, professional, radio and TV, religious, social, social service, and student government. Popular campus events include Days in May, Spring Affair, and Advent Vespers.

Sports: There are 9 intercollegiate sports for men and 7 for women, and 4 intramural sports for men and 4 for women. Facilities include a 1500-seat sports field, a 2800-seat gym, tennis courts, a double-rink ice arena, and a domed field facility for winter.

Disabled Students: 95% of the campus is accessible. Facilities include wheelchair ramps, elevators, special parking, specially equipped restrooms, special class scheduling, lowered drinking fountains, lowered telephones, and special housing.

Services: Counseling and information services are available, as is tutoring in every subject. There is a reader service for the blind, and remedial math and writing. Taped textbooks and adaptive computer technology, including a text scanner, speaking software, a touch tablet, and text magnification software are available.

Campus Safety and Security: Measures include 24-hour foot and vehicle patrol, self-defense education, and security escort services. There are emergency telephones, lighted pathways/sidewalks, and controlled access to dorms/residences.

Programs of Study: Augsburg confers B.A., B.S., B.M., and B.S.N. degrees. Master's degrees are also awarded. Bachelor's degrees are awarded in BIOLOGICAL SCIENCE (biology/biological science), BUSINESS (accounting, business administration and management, international business management, management information systems, and marketing/retailing/merchandising), COMMUNICATIONS AND THE ARTS (art history and appreciation, communications, dramatic arts, English, French, German, music, Scandinavian languages, Spanish, speech/debate/rhetoric, and studio art), COMPUTER AND PHYSICAL SCIENCE (chemistry, computer science, mathematics, and physics), EDUCATION (elementary education, health education, music education, physical education, and secondary education), HEALTH PROFESSIONS (music therapy), SOCIAL SCIENCE (East Asian studies, economics, history, international relations, philosophy, political science/government, psychology, religion, Russian and Slavic studies, Scandinavian studies, social work, sociology, urban studies, and women's studies). physics, chemistry, and English are the strongest academically. Business, communication, and education have the largest enrollments.

Required: To graduate, all students must have a minimum GPA of 2.0 and a total of 32 courses, with 10 to 15 in the major. They must complete 15 courses from 8 perspective areas and a first-year fall orientation and seminar. Students must also satisfy entry-level and graduation skills requirements in writing, critical thinking, math, quantitative reasoning, and speaking and demonstrate proficiency in 2 sports.

Special: Special academic programs include internships and co-op programs in business, government, and nonprofit and community-based organizations, a Washington semester, and study abroad in Europe, Latin America, and Africa. There are student-designed majors, cross-registration through the Associated Colleges of the Twin Cities (ACTC), dual and 3-2 engineering degrees with Washington University, Michigan Technological University, and the University of Minnesota, and preprofessional programs in dentistry, law, medicine, physical therapy, pharmacy, theology, and veterinary medicine. Credit for previous learning experience may be granted, and pass/fail options are possible. There is 1 national honor society, a freshman honors program, and 1 departmental honors program.

Faculty/Classroom: 49% of faculty are male; 51% are female. 99% teach undergraduates. No introductory courses are taught by graduate students. The average class size in an introductory lecture is 20; in a laboratory is 16; and in a regular course is 16.

Admissions: 52% of a recent year, applicants were accepted. The SAT scores for a recent freshman class were: Critical Reading--50% below 500, 25% between 500 and 599, 21% between 600 and 700, and 4% above 700; Math--21% below 500, 33% between 500 and 599, 38% between 600 and 700, and 8% above 700. The ACT scores were 38% below 21, 27% between 21 and 23, 23% between 24 and 26, 8% between 27 and 28, and 4% above 28. 28% of the current freshmen were in the top fifth of their class; 55% were in the top two fifths. 5 freshmen graduated first in their class.

Requirements: The ACT is required. The SAT is recommended with a minimum score of 22. Admissions requirements include graduation from an accredited secondary school with 4 years of English. The GED is also accepted. An essay is required, and an interview is recommended. AP and CLEP credits are accepted. Important factors in the admissions decision are advanced placement or honors courses, leadership record, and recommendations by school officials.

Procedure: Freshmen are admitted fall and spring. Entrance exams should be taken during the fall of the senior year in high school. There are deferred admissions and rolling admissions plans. Applications should be filed by May 1 for fall entry; December 1 for spring entry, along with a $25 fee. Notification is sent on a rolling basis. Applications are accepted online.

Transfer: 282 transfer students enrolled in a recent year. Applicants must have a minimum GPA of 2.2 in college course work. 9 of 32 credits required for the bachelor's degree must be completed at Augsburg.

Visiting: There are regularly scheduled orientations for prospective students, including admissions interviews and campus tours. Students may also arrange to meet with professors and coaches and to attend lectures. There are guides for informal visits, visitors may sit in on classes, and stay overnight. To schedule a visit, contact the Admissions Office.

Financial Aid: In a recent year, 97% of all full-time freshmen and 87% of continuing full-time students received some form of financial aid. 77% of all full-time freshmen and 64% of continuing full-time students received need-based aid. The average freshman award was $12,883. Need-based scholarships or need-based grants averaged $11,308 ($27,892 maximum); and $1,631 from other forms of aid. 44% of undergraduate students work part-time. Average annual earnings from campus work are $1710. The average financial indebtedness of a recent graduate was $27,000. The FAFSA and the college's own financial statement are required. The priority date for freshman financial aid applications for fall entry is April 15. The deadline for filing freshman financial aid applications for fall entry is August 1.

International Students: There are 44 international students enrolled. The school actively recruits these students. They must take the TOEFL with a minimum score of 550 on the paper-based TOEFL (PBT) or 80 on the Internet-based version (iBT). They must also take the SAT or ACT, scoring 22.

Computers: More than 282 PCs, Macs, and web kiosks are available for student use throughout the campus. Additionally, printers, scanners, and specialty software are accessible. Laptops may be checked out in the library by students, faculty, and staff. All students may access the system. There are no time limits and no fees. It is strongly recommended that all students have a personal computer.

Graduates: In a recent year, 539 bachelor's degrees were awarded. The most popular majors were business management (10%), accounting/public accounting (6%), and elementary education (6%). 66 companies recruited on campus in a recent year. In an average class, 7% graduate in 3 years or less, 38% graduate in 4 years or less, 53% graduate in 5 years or less, and 55% graduate in 6 years or less. Of a recent graduating class, 24% were enrolled in graduate school within 6 months of graduation, and 85% were employed.

Admissions Contact: Director of Admissions. E-Mail: *admissions@augsburg.edu* Web: *www.augsburg.edu*

BEMIDJI STATE UNIVERSITY B-2

Bemidji, MN 56601-2699 (218) 755-2040
(877) 236-4354; (218) 755-2074

Full-time: 1675 men, 1610 women	**Faculty:** n/av; IIB, av$
Part-time: 425 men, 730 women	**Ph.D.s:** 79%
Graduate: 210 men, 350 women	**Student/Faculty:** n/av
Year: semesters, summer session	**Tuition:** $8000
Application Deadline: open	**Room & Board:** $6676
Freshman Class: n/av	
ACT: required	

COMPETITIVE

Bemidji State University, founded in 1919, is a public liberal arts university. The figures in the above capsule and this profile are approximate. There are 3 undergraduate schools and 1 graduate school. In addition to regional accreditation, Bemidji has baccalaureate program accreditation with CSWE, NASM, and NLN. The library contains 190,000 volumes, 721,255 microform items, 2500 audio/video tapes/CDs/DVDs, and subscribes to 907 periodicals including electronic. Computerized library services include interlibrary loans and database searching. Special learning facilities include a learning resource center, art gallery, radio station, and TV station. The 89-acre campus is in a small town 220 miles northwest of Minneapolis. Including any residence halls, there are 21 buildings.

Student Life: 87% of undergraduates are from Minnesota. Others are from 46 states, 34 foreign countries, and Canada. 95% are from public schools. 89% are white. The average age of freshmen is 20; all undergraduates, 25. 28% do not continue beyond their first year; 44% remain to graduate.

Housing: 1700 students can be accommodated in college housing, which includes single-sex and coed dorms and on-campus apartments. In addition, there are special-interest houses, fraternity houses, and single-parent apartments. On-campus housing is available on a first-come, first-served basis. 68% of students commute. Alcohol is not permitted. All students may keep cars.

Activities: 1% of men belong to 2 national fraternities; 1% of women belong to 1 national sorority. There are 80 groups on campus, including art, band, cheerleading, choir, chorus, computers, dance, drama, environmental, ethnic, gay, honors, international, jazz band, literary magazine, musical theater, newspaper, opera, orchestra, pep band, political, professional, radio and TV, religious, social, social service, and student government. Popular campus events include Funtastic Dance Follies, madrigal music, and plays and concerts.

Sports: There are 7 intercollegiate sports for men and 7 for women, and 7 intramural sports for men and 4 for women. Facilities include a basketball gym, an Olympic-size pool, a hockey arena, a football stadium, indoor and outdoor tracks, baseball and softball fields, tennis, racquetball, and handball courts, weight rooms, and a dance studio.

Disabled Students: 95% of the campus is accessible. Facilities include wheelchair ramps, elevators, special parking, specially equipped restrooms, lowered drinking fountains, and lowered telephones.

Services: Counseling and information services are available, as is tutoring in every subject. There is a reader service for the blind and remedial math, reading, and writing.

Campus Safety and Security: Measures include 24-hour foot and vehicle patrol, emergency notification system, self-defense education, and security escort services. There are shuttle buses, emergency telephones, lighted pathways/sidewalks, controlled access to dorms/residences, and in-room safes. All buildings are locked overnight and there is controlled sportsman's weapons storage and a 24/7 campus security team.

Programs of Study: Bemidji confers B.A., B.S., and B.F.A. degrees. Associate and master's degrees are also awarded. Bachelor's degrees are awarded in AGRICULTURE (environmental studies), BIOLOGICAL SCIENCE (biology/biological science), BUSINESS (accounting and business administration and management), COMMUNICATIONS AND THE ARTS (broadcasting, communications, English, fine arts, German, journalism, languages, music, and Spanish), COMPUTER AND PHYSICAL SCIENCE (chemistry, computer science, earth science, geology, mathematics, and physics), EDUCATION (art education, early childhood education, elementary education, foreign languages education, health education, industrial arts education, middle school education, science education, and secondary education), ENGINEERING AND ENVIRONMENTAL DESIGN (industrial engineering technology), HEALTH PROFESSIONS (medical laboratory technology, nursing, predentistry, and premedicine), SOCIAL SCIENCE (community services, criminal justice, economics, geography, history, parks and recreation management, philosophy, political science/government, prelaw, psychology, social science, social work, and sociology). Nursing, accounting, and engineering are the strongest academically. Business administration, elementary and secondary education have the largest enrollments.

Required: All students must complete at least 128 semester hours, of which 42 are general education, including courses in freshman English, the humanities, social science, physical science, liberal education activities, and phys ed. Students must maintain a minimum GPA of 2.0; a 2.3 GPA is required in the major (2.5 for education majors).

Special: Students may attend other schools within the Minnesota State University system and study abroad in 10 countries. Paid internships and work-study programs are available in many fields. Students may receive credit for life, military, and work experience. Student-designed dual majors, nondegree study, and pass/fail options are offered. There are 2 national honor societies and a freshman honors program.

Faculty/Classroom: 59% of faculty are male; 41% are female. 99% teach undergraduates, and 15% do research. Graduate students teach 1% of introductory courses. The average class size in an introductory lecture is 35; in a laboratory, 20; and in a regular course, 23.

Requirements: The ACT is required. Applicants must have a minimum high school rank of 50% or a composite score of 21 on the ACT. They should have had 4 years of English and 3 years each of math, science, and social studies. A GPA of 2.0 is required. AP and CLEP credits are accepted. Important factors in the admissions decision are recommendations by school officials, advanced placement or honors courses, and extracurricular activities record.

Procedure: Freshmen are admitted to all sessions. Entrance exams should be taken during the junior year. There are deferred admissions and rolling admissions plans. Application deadlines are open. Applications are accepted online.

Transfer: Applicants must have a minimum GPA of 2.0. 32 of 128 credits required for the bachelor's degree must be completed at Bemidji.

Visiting: There are regularly scheduled orientations for prospective students, including an interview with an admissions counselor, a tour of the campus, and visits with faculty. There are guides for informal visits, and visitors may sit in on classes and stay overnight. To schedule a visit, contact the Admissions Office.

Financial Aid: The FAFSA and the college's own financial statement are required. Check with the school for current application deadlines.

International Students: The school actively recruits these students. They must take the TOEFL.

Computers: Wireless access is available. All academic and administrative buildings have wireless access. All students may access the system 24 hours a day on campus; 18 hours a day in other locations. There are no time limits.

Admissions Contact: Admissions. A campus DVD is available. E-mail: *admissions@bemidjistate.edu* Web: *www.bemidjistate.edu*

BETHEL UNIVERSITY C-4

St. Paul, MN 55112 (651) 638-6242
(800) 255-8706; (651) 635-1490

Full-time: 1135 men, 1625 women
Part-time: 200 men, 460 women
Graduate: 100 men, 1025 women
Year: semesters, summer session
Application Deadline: open
Freshman Class: n/av
SAT or ACT: required
Faculty: n/av; IIB, -$
Ph.D.s: 78%
Student/Faculty: n/av
Tuition: $29,820
Room & Board: $9130

VERY COMPETITIVE

Bethel University, established in 1871, is a private liberal arts university affiliated with the Converge Worldwide (Baptist General Conference). There are 2 undergraduate schools and 2 graduate schools. In addition to regional accreditation, Bethel has baccalaureate program accreditation with CSWE and TEAC. The library contains 194,196 volumes, 195,650 microform items, and 15,503 audio/video tapes/CDs/DVDs, and subscribes to 38,080 periodicals including electronic. Computerized library services include interlibrary loans, database searching, Internet access, and laptop Internet portals. Special learning facilities include a learning resource center, art gallery, and radio station. The 247-acre campus is in a suburban area 10 miles north of Minneapolis/St. Paul. Including any residence halls, there are 39 buildings.

Student Life: 78% of undergraduates are from Minnesota. Others are from 43 states, 22 foreign countries, and Canada. 80% are from public schools. 90% are white. 97% are Protestant. The average age of freshmen is 18; all undergraduates, 20. 15% do not continue beyond their first year; 75% remain to graduate.

Housing: 2076 students can be accommodated in college housing, which includes coed dorms, on-campus apartments, and off-campus apartments. On-campus housing is available on a first-come, first-served basis and is available on a lottery system for upperclassmen. 70% of students live on campus; of those, 60% remain on campus on weekends. Alcohol is not permitted. Upperclassmen may keep cars.

Activities: There are no fraternities or sororities. There are 74 groups on campus, including art, band, choir, chorale, chorus, dance, debate, drama, drill team, environmental, ethnic, film, forensics, honors, international, jazz band, literary magazine, musical theater, newspaper, orchestra, pep band, political, professional, radio and TV, religious, social, social service, student government, and symphony. Popular campus events include Nikdg and Gadkin (guy-ask-girl and girl-ask-guy events) and Festival of Christmas.

Sports: There are 9 intercollegiate sports for men and 9 for women, and 6 intramural sports for men and 6 for women. Facilities include a gym; an indoor recreation center, with 1/8-mile track and 4 multipurpose courts, weight room, and racquetball courts; soccer fields; tennis courts; and a football, baseball, and softball stadium.

Disabled Students: 99% of the campus is accessible. Facilities include wheelchair ramps, elevators, special parking, specially equipped rest rooms, special class scheduling, lowered drinking fountains, lowered telephones, and special housing.

Services: Counseling and information services are available, as is tutoring in every subject. There is a reader service for the blind. The Academic Enrichment and Support Center offers individual peer tutoring, student-led help sessions, a writing lab, and consultation on a variety of topics.

Campus Safety and Security: Measures include 24-hour foot and vehicle patrol, emergency notification system, self-defense education, and security escort services. There are shuttle buses, emergency telephones, lighted pathways/sidewalks, access controls for dorms/residences, and camera systems (parking lots and buildings).

Programs of Study: Bethel confers B.A., B.S., B.Mus., and B.Mus.Ed degrees. Associates, master's, and doctoral degrees are also awarded. Bachelor's degrees are awarded in AGRICULTURE (environmental studies), BIOLOGICAL SCIENCE (biochemistry, biology/biological science, and molecular biology), BUSINESS (accounting, banking and finance, and business administration and management), COMMUNICATIONS AND THE ARTS (art, communications, dramatic arts, English, English literature, French, journalism, multimedia, music, music performance, Spanish, and visual and performing arts), COMPUTER AND PHYSICAL SCIENCE (applied physics, chemistry, computer science, mathematics, and physics), EDUCATION (athletic training, business education, early childhood education, education, elementary education, English education, foreign languages education, health education, mathematics education, middle school education, music education, physical education, science education, secondary education, social studies education, and teaching English as a second/foreign language (TESOL/TEFOL)), ENGINEERING AND ENVIRONMENTAL DESIGN (engineering and applied science and environmental science), HEALTH PROFESSIONS (community health work, exercise science, and nursing), SOCIAL SCIENCE (biblical studies, economics, history, international relations, philosophy, political science/government, psychology, religious music, social studies, social work, theological studies, Third World studies, and youth ministry). Physics, chemistry, and nursing are the strongest academically. Business, education, and nursing have the largest enrollments.

Required: Students must complete a minimum of 122 semester credit hours, with 30 to 60 in the major and 51 to 52 in general education. Specific general education courses include Introduction to the Bible, Christianity and Western Culture, College Writing, Creativity in Fine Arts, and Physical Wellness. An overall GPA of 2.0 and a GPA of 2.25 in the major are needed.

Special: Cross-registration is available through the Council for Christian Colleges and Universities. Students may arrange internships and study abroad in various countries. Students may design their own major and earn a 3-2 engineering degree. An adult degree completion program is offered. There are 6 national honor societies, a freshman honors program, and 6 departmental honors programs.

Faculty/Classroom: 51% of faculty are male; 49% are female. All teach undergraduates. No introductory courses are taught by graduate students. The average class size in a laboratory is 20 and in a regular course is 22.

Requirements: The SAT or ACT is required. The PSAT is accepted. An interview is recommended. Requirements include a personal statement, contact information for an academic or spiritual reference, and an official transcript and class ranking from an accredited secondary school (GED is accepted). Bethel requires applicants to be in the upper 50% of their class. A GPA of 2.5 is required. AP and CLEP credits are accepted. Important factors in the admissions decision are advanced placement or honors courses, extracurricular activities record, and personality/intangible qualities.

Procedure: Freshmen are admitted fall and spring. Entrance exams should be taken spring of junior year. There is a rolling admissions plan. Application deadlines are open. Notification is sent on a rolling basis beginning October 1. Applications are accepted online.

Transfer: 164 transfer students enrolled in a recent year. Applicants must have a minimum GPA of 2.5 and must submit all college transcripts. 28 of the last 35 credits and half of the major must be completed at Bethel. 122 credits are required for the bachelor's degree.

Visiting: There are regularly scheduled orientations for prospective students, consisting of a campus tour, visits with advisers, faculty, and coaches, chapel and class visits, and meals in the dining center. There are guides for informal visits; visitors may sit in on classes and stay overnight. To schedule a visit, contact the Admissions Office.

Financial Aid: In a recent year, 99% of all full-time freshmen and 94% of continuing full-time students received some form of financial aid. 71% of all full-time freshmen and 68% of continuing full-time students received need-based aid. The average freshmen award was $19,129, with $7041 ($27,794 maximum) from need-based scholarships or need-based grants; $3753 ($8700 maximum) from need-based self-help aid (loans and jobs); and $8335 ($31,020 maximum) from other non-need-based awards and non-need-based scholarships. 56% of undergraduate students worked part-time. Bethel is a member of CSS. The FAFSA and the college's own financial statement are required. Check with school for current application deadlines.

International Students: There were 8 international students enrolled in a recent year. They must take the TOEFL with a minimum score of 525 on the paper-based TOEFL (PBT) or 70 on the Internet-based version (iBT).

Computers: Wireless access is available. In addition to many wired network ports throughout campus, wireless Internet is available in all academic buildings. More than 500 computers in labs, departments, and the library are available for student use. All students may access the system 24 hours a day. There are no time limits and no fees.

Graduates: In a recent year, 756 bachelor's degrees were awarded. The most popular majors were education (16%), business/marketing (14%), and health and related professions (11%). In an average class, 63% graduate in 4 years or less, 73% graduate in 5 years or less, and 75% graduate in 6 years or less. 22% were enrolled in graduate school within 6 months of graduation and 74% were employed.

Admissions Contact: Director of Admissions. E-Mail: *buadmissions-cas@bethel.edu* Web: *www.bethel.edu*

CARLETON COLLEGE C-4

Northfield, MN 55057 (507) 222-4190
(800) 995-CARL; (507) 222-4526

Full-time: 955 men, 1070 women
Part-time: 5 men, 15 women
Graduate: n/av
Year: trimesters
Application Deadline: January 15
Freshman Class: 7043 applied, 1475 accepted, 527 enrolled
SAT or ACT: required
Faculty: 247; IIB, +$
Ph.D.s: 95%
Student/Faculty: 9 to 1
Tuition: $46,167
Room & Board: $11,982

MOST COMPETITIVE

Carleton College, founded in 1866, is a private liberal arts college. The library contains 1.0 million volumes, 276,626 microform items, 24,059 audio/video tapes/CDs/DVDs, and subscribes to 43,234 periodicals including electronic. Computerized library services include interlibrary loans, database searching, Internet access, and Wi-Fi capability. Special learning facilities include an art gallery, radio station, an observatory, and an 880-acre arboretum, Weitz Center for Creativity. The 955-acre campus is in a small town 35 miles south of Minneapolis-St. Paul. Including any residence halls, there are 49 buildings.

Student Life: 81% of undergraduates are from out of state, mostly the Mid-West. Students are from 50 states, 41 foreign countries, and Canada. 60% are from public schools. 66% are White. 44% claim no religious affiliation; 23% Protestant; 12% Buddhist, Hindu and Muslim, Taoist, and Unitarian Universalist. The average age of freshmen is 18; all undergraduates, 20. 4% do not continue beyond their first year; 96% remain to graduate.

Housing: 1852 students can be accommodated in college housing, which includes single-sex and coed dorms, on-campus apartments, and off-campus apartments. In addition, there are language houses and special-interest houses. On-campus housing is guaranteed for all 4 years. 96% of students live on campus; of those, 97% remain on campus on weekends. No one may keep cars.

Activities: There are no fraternities or sororities. There are 132 groups on campus, including hobby, art, band, chess, choir, chorale, chorus, computers, dance, debate, drama, educational, environmental, ethnic, film, gay, honors, international, jazz band, literary magazine, musical theater, newspaper, orchestra, photography, political, professional, radio and TV, religious, social, social service, student government, symphony, and yearbook. Popular campus events include Mai Fete, Spring Concert, Mid-Winter Ball, Ebony, and Golden Shillers Film Festival.

Sports: There are 23 intercollegiate sports for men and 23 for women, and 8 intramural sports for men and 8 for women. Facilities include a gym with a 1220-seat arena, 6-lane swimming pool, and wrestling room, a recreation center with a gym, dance studio, indoor tennis court, sauna, and 5-lane swimming pool; a 7000-seat stadium complex with handball and racquetball courts, a 200-meter indoor track, a baseball batting cage, a weight room; and an additional recreation center with a 200-meter indoor track, sport courts, weight room, dance studio, and climbing wall. In addition, there are fields for baseball, softball, soccer, ultimate Frisbee, lacrosse, rugby, and field hockey; 12 outdoor tennis courts; and 16 miles of running, biking, hiking, and cross-country skiing trails in Carleton's 880-acre arboretum.

Disabled Students: 39% of the campus is accessible. Facilities include wheelchair ramps, elevators, special parking, specially equipped restrooms, special class scheduling, lowered drinking fountains, lowered telephones, and special housing.

Services: Counseling and information services are available, as is tutoring in every subject, There are also writing and math skills assistance centers. There is a reader service for the blind.

Campus Safety and Security: Measures include 24-hour foot and vehicle patrol, emergency notification system, self-defense education, and security escort services. There are emergency telephones, lighted pathways/sidewalks, controlled access to dorms/residences, and nighttime transport service.

Programs of Study: Carleton confers B.A. degrees. Bachelor's degrees are awarded in AGRICULTURE (environmental studies), BIOLOGICAL SCIENCE (biology/biological science), COMMUNICATIONS AND THE ARTS (art history and appreciation, classics, English, French, German, Greek, Latin, linguistics, media arts, music, romance languages and literature, Russian, Spanish, and studio art), COMPUTER AND PHYSICAL SCIENCE (chemistry, computer science, geology, mathematics, and physics), SOCIAL SCIENCE (African studies, African American studies, American studies, anthropology, Asian/Oriental studies, classical/ancient civilization, economics, history, international relations, Latin American studies, philosophy, political science/government, psychology, religion, sociology, and women's studies). Sciences, biological and physical sciences, History and psychology, English and languages, political science and economics are the strongest academically. Social sciences and history, physical sciences, biological/life science have the largest enrollments.

Required: To graduate, you must complete 210 credits and maintain a 2.0 cumulative GPA. A normal course load is 18 credits per term (there are 3 terms). Students also explore an integrated exercise in their major in the form of a comprehensive exam, an extensive research project, paper or public presentation. The goal is to demonstrate proficiency within your major. A first-year seminar and course work in Quantitative Reasoning and Global Citizenship are also required.

Special: Students may cross-register with Saint Olaf College and pursue a variety of internships. The college offers study abroad in over 50 countries. Dual majors in all areas and student-designed majors are available. Students may earn a 3-2 engineering degree with Washington or Columbia Universities. There are 3 national honor societies and including Phi Beta Kappa.

Faculty/Classroom: 52% of faculty are male; 48% are female. All teach and do research. No introductory courses are taught by graduate students. The average class size in an introductory lecture is 20; in a laboratory is 16; and in a regular course is 17.

Admissions: 21% of the 2013-2014 applicants were accepted. 95% of the current freshmen were in the top fifth of their class; 100% were in the top two fifths.

Requirements: The SAT or ACT is required. The ACT Optional Writing test is also required. There are no secondary school requirements, but it is recommended that applicants have completed 4 years of English, 3 years each of math and a foreign language, 2 years each of history and science, and 1 year of social studies. An essay and 2 teacher recommendations are required. AP credits are accepted. Important factors in the admissions decision are advanced placement or honors courses, personality/intangible qualities, and evidence of special talent.

Procedure: Freshmen are admitted fall. Entrance exams should be taken before February 15. There are early decision and deferred admissions plans. Early decision applications should be filed by November 15; regular applications, by January 15 for fall entry, along with a $30 fee. Notification of early decision is sent December 15; regular decision, April 15. 220 early decision candidates were accepted for the 2013-2014 class. 486 applicants were on the 2013 waiting list. Applications are accepted online. Application fees are waived if application is completed online.

Transfer: 7 transfer students enrolled in 2012-2013. Transfers are usually accepted for sophomore and junior classes. A 3.0 GPA is recommended. 108 of 210 credits required for the bachelor's degree must be completed at Carleton.

Visiting: There are regularly scheduled orientations for prospective students, Prospective students can attend an information session, take a tour, have an interview, sit in on classes have a meal in the dining halls or attend panels on particular topics pertinent to study abroad, financial aid or other topics. There are guides for informal visits, visitors may sit in on classes, and stay overnight. To schedule a visit, contact the Admissions Office.

Financial Aid: In 2013-2014, 76% of all full-time freshmen and 87% of continuing full-time students received some form of financial aid. 58% of all full-time freshmen and 55% of continuing full-time students received need-based aid. The average freshman award was $38,666. Need-based scholarships or need-based grants averaged $34,754; need-based self-help aid (loans and jobs) averaged $5,649; and other non-need-based awards and non-need-based scholarships averaged $2,000. 81% of undergraduate students work part-time. Average annual earnings from campus work are $1737. The average financial indebtedness of the 2013 graduate was $18,000. Carleton is a member of CSS. The CSS/Profile and FAFSA are required. The deadline for filing freshman financial aid applications for fall entry is February 15.

International Students: There are 172 international students enrolled. The school actively recruits these students. They must take the TOEFL with a minimum score of 600 on the paper-based TOEFL (PBT) or 100 on the Internet-based version (iBT). They must also take the SAT or ACT.

Computers: All students may access the system 24 hours a day. There are no time limits and no fees.

Graduates: From July 1, 2012 to June 30, 2013, 496 bachelor's degrees were awarded. The most popular majors were political science/international relations (13%), biology (12%), and economics (8%). In an average class, 90% graduate in 4 years or less, 92% graduate in 5 years or less, and 92% graduate in 6 years or less.

Admissions Contact: Paul Thiboutot, Dean of Admissions and Financial Aid. E-Mail: *admissions@carleton.edu* Web: *www.carleton.edu*

COLLEGE OF SAINT BENEDICT — C-3

St. Joseph, MN 56374 — **(320) 363-5055; (800) 544-1489; (320) 363-3206**

Full-time: 2015 women	**Faculty:** 153; IIB, av$
Part-time: 36 women	**Ph.D.s:** 82%
Graduate: n/av	**Student/Faculty:** 12 to 1
Year: semesters	**Tuition:** $37,926
Application Deadline: January 15	**Room & Board:** $9644

Freshman Class: 2077 applied, 1569 accepted, 538 enrolled

SAT or ACT: required

VERY COMPETITIVE

The College of Saint Benedict (CSB) and Saint John's University (SJU) are nationally-leading liberal arts colleges whose unique partnership offers students the educational choices of a large university and the individual attention of a premier small college. Students attend classes and activities together and have access to the resources of both campuses. Ranked nationally among the top baccalaureate institutions for the number of students who study abroad, CSB/SJU are committed to preparing students for leadership and service in a global society. The colleges enroll students from around the world and integrate global citizenship into the curriculum. A commitment to arts and culture creates a vibrant environment for creativity. The Benedicta Arts Center of the College of Saint Benedict is one of the finest performing arts center in the region. The Hill Museum and Manuscript Library at SJU is home to the Saint John's Bible and a remarkable collection of religious sculpture, paintings, prints, and artifacts. A compelling sense of place shapes the undergraduate experience. The learning experience is enlivened by Catholic and Benedictine traditions of hospitality, stewardship, service, and the lively engagement of faith and reason. The colleges' values have been shaped by a commitment to ecumenism and inter-faith dialogue. In addition to regional accreditation, Saint Ben's has baccalaureate program accreditation with ADA, NASM, and NCATE. The 2 libraries contain 637,419 volumes, 121,416 microform items, 40,564 audio/video tapes/CDs/DVDs, and subscribe to 81,268 periodicals including electronic. Computerized library services include interlibrary loans, database searching, Internet access, and Wi-Fi capability. Special learning facilities include an art gallery, radio station, TV station, a pottery studio and kiln, a labyrinth, dance studio, green house and Saint Benedict's Monastery Heritage Museum. At Saint John's University there is Saint John's Outdoor University, an observatory, a greenhouse, an herbarium, natural history museum, and the Hill Museum and Manuscript library. The 800-acre campus is in a small town 70 miles northwest of Minneapolis and 10 miles west of St. Cloud. Including any residence halls, there are 40 buildings.

Student Life: 78% of undergraduates are from Minnesota. Others are from 30 states, and 23 foreign countries. 76% are from public schools. 80% are White. 58% are Catholic; 24% Protestant; 16% claim no religious affiliation. The average age of freshmen is 18; all undergraduates, 20. 11% do not continue beyond their first year; 82% remain to graduate.

Housing: 1672 students can be accommodated in college housing, which includes single-sex dorms and on-campus apartments. In addition, there are special-interest houses, wellness floor, and sustainability houses. On-campus housing is guaranteed for the freshman year only, is available on a first-come, first-served basis, and is available on a lottery system for upperclassmen. 88% of students live on campus. All students may keep cars.

Activities: There are no fraternities or sororities. There are 95 groups on campus, including and academic clubs., art, band, choir, chorale, chorus, computers, dance, debate, drama, environmental, ethnic, gay, honors, international, jazz band, literary magazine, musical theater, newspaper, opera, orchestra, outdoor leadership center, pep band, political, professional, radio and TV, religious, social, social service, student government, and symphony. Popular campus events include Pines Spring Concert, Asian New Year, Festival of Culture, Community Barbecue, Club Involvement Fair and Johnnie Bennie Live fall Concert, Maple Syrup Festival, and Homecoming.

Sports: There are 11 intercollegiate sports for women. Facilities include a 1000-seat volleyball and basketball arena, racquetball and indoor and outdoor tennis courts, an indoor pool, a field house with an indoor running track, an aerobics studio, a fitness center with exercise and weight-training equipment, a softball diamond, and soccer fields. Students have access to St. John's University facilities as well, where they can also access lakes for canoeing, fishing, swimming, rowing, and kayaking and 20 miles of on-campus wooded hiking and jogging trails along with a climbing wall.

Disabled Students: 97% of the campus is accessible. Facilities include wheelchair ramps, elevators, special parking, specially equipped restrooms, special class scheduling, lowered drinking fountains, special housing. exterior power assist doors, and accessible busing options.

Services: Counseling and information services are available, as is tutoring in most subjects. a writing center, and a math skills center. The College of Saint Benedict and Saint John's University established a Disability Services Office. Accomodations are provided on a case by case basis for enrolled students who provide adequate documentation of a disability. Individual tutoring is available as needed. Academic and psychological counseling are available on an unlimited basis.

Campus Safety and Security: Measures include 24-hour foot and vehicle patrol, emergency notification system, self-defense education, and security escort services. There are shuttle buses, emergency telephones, lighted pathways/sidewalks, and controlled access to dorms/residences.

Programs of Study: Saint Ben's confers B.A., and B.S.N. degrees. Bachelor's degrees are awarded in AGRICULTURE (environmental studies), BIOLOGICAL SCIENCE (biochemistry, biology/biological science, and nutrition), BUSINESS (accounting and management science), COMMUNICATIONS AND THE ARTS (art, classics, communications, English, French, German, music, Spanish, and theatre arts), COMPUTER AND PHYSICAL SCIENCE (chemistry, computer science, mathematics, natural sciences, and physics), EDUCATION (elementary education), ENGINEERING AND ENVIRONMENTAL DESIGN (preengineering), HEALTH PROFESSIONS (nursing, occupational therapy, predentistry, premedicine, preoptometry, prepharmacy, prephysical therapy, and preveterinary science), SOCIAL SCIENCE (Asian/Oriental studies, economics, gender studies, Hispanic American studies, history, humanities, liberal arts/general studies, peace studies, philosophy, political science/government, prelaw, psychology, social science, sociology, and theological studies). Nursing, biology, and psychology are the largest.

Required: To graduate students must complete a first-year seminar and a junior-senior ethics seminar intended as a capstone for the liberal arts experience, and fulfill gender, intercultural, experiential learning, and fine arts requirements. Distribution requirements include 4 credits in fine arts, 2 courses each in humanities and theology, and 1 course each in math, natural science, and social science. All students must prove math and foreign language proficiency. A total of 124 credits must be earned, with a minimum GPA of 2.0. Attendance at 8 fine arts experiences is also required.

Special: Students may cross-register with St. Cloud State University. There are study-abroad programs in Australia, Austria, Chile, China, Coventry-England, France,Germany, Guatemala, Greece, Ireland (Cork and Galway), Italy,India, Japan,London-England, Northern Ireland, South Africa, and Spain. Many short term study abroad opportunities are also offered. Internships, dual and student-designed majors, preprofessional programs, and liberal studies degrees may be pursued. A 3-2 engineering program is offered through the University of Minnesota, as is a 3-1 program in dentistry. Nondegree study and a pass/fail grading option are also available. There are 4 national honor societies, including Phi Beta Kappa, and a freshman honors program.

Faculty/Classroom: 49% of faculty are male; 51% are female. All teach and do research. No introductory courses are taught by graduate students. The average class size in an introductory lecture is 21; in a laboratory is 13; and in a regular course is 17.

Admissions: 76% of the 2013-2014 applicants were accepted. The SAT scores for the 2013-2014 freshman class were: Critical Reading--37% below 500, 40% between 500 and 599, 15% between 600 and 699, and 8% between 700 and 800; Math--30% below 500, 38% between 500 and 599, and 32% between 600 and 699; Writing--37% below 500, 37% between 500 and 599, 18% between 600 and 699, and 8% between 700 and 800. The ACT scores were 12% below 21, 22% between 21 and 23, 34% between 24 and 26, 13% between 27 and 28, and 19% above 28. 61% of the current freshmen were in the top fifth of their class; 89% were in the top two fifths. There were 1 National Merit finalists.

Requirements: The SAT or ACT is required. In addition, students should be graduates of an accredited secondary school. Academic preparation should include 17 units, including 4 of English, 3 of math, 2 each of a lab science and social studies, and 4 electives. A foreign language is recommended. The GED is accepted. An essay is required. Home-schooled applicants are not required to have a high school diploma but are required to provide appropriate documentation of college preparatory curriculum. Saint Ben's requires applicants to be in the upper 50% of their class. A GPA of 3.0 is required. AP and CLEP credits are accepted. Important factors in the admissions decision are advanced placement or honors courses, leadership record, and extracurricular activities record.

Procedure: Freshmen are admitted fall and spring. Entrance exams should be taken during the spring of the junior year or fall of the senior year. There are early admissions and deferred admissions plans. Application deadlines are open. Notification of early decision is sent December 15; regular decision, April 1. Applications are accepted online.

Transfer: 22 transfer students enrolled in 2012-2013. Transfer applicants must have a minimum college GPA of 2.75. An essay or personal statement, high school and college transcripts, and a transfer student evaluation form are required. Standardized test scores may be required of some. 45 of 124 credits required for the bachelor's degree must be completed at Saint Ben's.

Visiting: There are regularly scheduled orientations for prospective students, Programs include Admissions and Financial Aid presentations, campus tours and student panels. There are guides for informal visits, visitors may sit in on classes, and stay overnight. To schedule a visit, contact the CSB/SJU Admissions Office at (320) 363-5055.

Financial Aid: In 2013-2014, 97% of all full-time freshmen and 95% of continuing full-time students received some form of financial aid. 75% of all full-time freshmen and 68% of continuing full-time students received need-based aid. The average freshman award was $31,950. Need-based scholarships or need-based grants averaged $26,018; need-based self-help aid (loans and jobs) averaged $6,435; and other non-need-based awards and non-need-based scholarships averaged $16,574. 60% of undergraduate students work part-time. Average annual earnings from campus work are $2830. The average financial indebtedness of the 2013 graduate was $40,034. Saint Ben's is a member of CSS. The FAFSA and the college's own financial statement are required. The priority date for freshman financial aid applications for fall entry is March 15.

International Students: There are 115 international students enrolled. The school actively recruits these students. They must take the TOEFL with a minimum score of 500 on the paper-based TOEFL (PBT) or 70 on the Internet-based version (iBT), IELTS also accepted. They must also take the SAT or ACT, scoring 21. In certain cases, the SAT or ACT may replace TOEFL.

Computers: All students may access the system 24 hours per day. There are no time limits. The fee is $256.

Graduates: From July 1, 2012 to June 30, 2013, 505 bachelor's degrees were awarded. The most popular majors were biology (11%), psychology (10%), and communication (10%). 133 companies recruited on campus in 2012-2013. In an average class, 1% graduate in 3 years or less, 74% graduate in 4 years or less, 81% graduate in 5 years or less, and 82% graduate in 6 years or less. Of the 2012 graduating class, 21% were enrolled in graduate school within 6 months of graduation, and 80% were employed.

Admissions Contact: Dr. Calvin Mosley, Vice President for Admission & Financial. E-Mail: *admissions@csbsju.edu* Web: *www.csbsju.edu*

COLLEGE OF SAINT SCHOLASTICA D-2

Duluth, MN 55811 (218) 723-6046
(800) 447-5444; (218) 723-5991

Full-time: 782 men, 1641 women
Part-time: 119 men, 394 women
Graduate: 306 men, 998 women
Year: semesters, summer session
Application Deadline:
Faculty: 156; IIB, -$
Ph.D.s: 56%
Student/Faculty: 13 to 1
Tuition: $31,612
Room & Board: $8348
Freshman Class: 1809 applied, 1315 accepted, 432 enrolled
SAT CR/M/W: 470/480/470 **ACT:** 24 **COMPETITIVE**

The College of St. Scholastica, founded in 1912, is an independent private college that provides intellectual and moral preparation for responsible living and meaningful work. Saint Scholastica has extended campuses in St. Paul, Brainerd, Rochester, and St. Cloud, MN. The college is guided by the Benedictine values of community, hospitality, respect, stewardship, and love of learning. There are 6 undergraduate schools and one graduate school. In addition to regional accreditation, Saints has baccalaureate program accreditation with APTA, CSWE, and TEAC. The library contains 111,192 volumes, 1,915 microform items, 14,932 audio/video tapes/CDs/DVDs, and subscribes to 55,088 periodicals including electronic. Computerized library services include interlibrary loans, database searching, Internet access, and Wi-Fi capability. Special learning facilities include a TV station, a music library. The 186-acre campus is in a suburban area 150 miles north of Minneapolis and St. Paul, MN. Including any residence halls, there are 18 buildings.

Student Life: 85% of undergraduates are from Minnesota. Others are from 49 states, 38 foreign countries, and Canada. 82% are White. 30% are Protestant; 29% Catholic; 25% claim no religious affiliation. The average age of freshmen is 18; all undergraduates, 23. 16% do not continue beyond their first year; 68% remain to graduate.

Housing: 1075 students can be accommodated in college housing, which includes single-sex and coed dorms and on-campus apartments. On-campus housing is available on a first-come, first-served basis, and is available on a lottery system for upperclassmen. 52% of students live on campus; of those, 75% remain on campus on weekends. All students may keep cars.

Activities: There are no fraternities or sororities. There are 68 groups on campus, including band, cheerleading, choir, chorale, chorus, computers, dance, drama, ethnic, gay, honors, international, jazz band, literary magazine, newspaper, pep band, photography, political, professional, radio and TV, religious, social, social service, and student government. Popular campus events include Mayfest Week, Fall Fest and International Week.

Sports: There are 9 intercollegiate sports for men and 9 for women, and 14 intramural sports for men and 14 for women. Facilities include A 63,000-square-foot wellness center, which includes a 6-lane 200 meter track, aerobic studio, free weight room, complete machine fitness space, athletic trainer's room, and climbing wall.

Disabled Students: 95% of the campus is accessible. Facilities include wheelchair ramps, elevators, special parking, specially equipped restrooms, special class scheduling, lowered drinking fountains, lowered telephones, and special housing.

Services: Counseling and information services are available, as is tutoring in most subjects. There is a reader service for the blind, and remedial writing. In addition, sign language interpreters, a note-taking service, tape recorders, voice input computers, and remedial study skills are also available.

Campus Safety and Security: Measures include 24-hour foot and vehicle patrol, emergency notification system, self-defense education, and security escort services. There are emergency telephones, lighted pathways/sidewalks, controlled access to dorms/residences, electronically operated dorm entrances and student door monitors in the evening and at night.

Programs of Study: Saints confers B.A. and B.S. degrees. Master's and doctoral degrees are also awarded. Bachelor's degrees are awarded in BIOLOGICAL SCIENCE (biochemistry and biology/biological science), BUSINESS (accounting, business administration and management, finance, management science, marketing management, and organizational behavior), COMMUNICATIONS AND THE ARTS (advertising, communications, English, journalism, languages, and music), COMPUTER AND PHYSICAL SCIENCE (chemistry, computer science, mathematics, and natural sciences), EDUCATION (education and social science education), HEALTH PROFESSIONS (exercise science, health care administration, health science, and nursing), SOCIAL SCIENCE (behavioral science, economics, history, humanities, Native American studies, peace studies, philosophy, psychology, religion, and social work). Nursing, management, and biological sciences have the largest enrollments.

Required: To graduate, students must complete 128 semester credits, with a 2.0 GPA. Approximately 52 credits of general education courses are required. The hours required in the major vary. Some majors require an internship for graduation. A senior project may be required.

Special: Students may cross-register with the University of Minnesota of Duluth and the University of Wisconsin of Superior. Self-designed majors, a Washington semester with American University, internships, study abroad in several countries, accelerated degrees, non-degree study, pass/fail options, and credit for life, military, or work experience are available. There is a 3-2 engineering degree with the Institute of Technology of the University of Minnesota. There are 2 national honor societies.

Faculty/Classroom: 37% of faculty are male; 63% are female. All teach undergraduates. No introductory courses are taught by graduate students. The average class size in an introductory lecture is 24; in a laboratory is 16; and in a regular course is 21.

Admissions: 73% of the 2013-2014 applicants were accepted. The SAT scores for the 2013-2014 freshman class were: Critical Reading--67% below 500, 20% between 500 and 599, 13% between 600 and 699; Math--67% below 500, 20% between 500 and 599, 13% between 600 and 699; Writing--60% below 500, 40% between 500 and 599. The ACT scores were 29% below 21, 22% between 21 and 23, 19% between 24 and 26, 17% between 27 and 28, and 13% above 28. 44% of the current freshmen were in the top fifth of their class; 76% were in the top two fifths. 11 freshmen graduated first in their class.

Requirements: The SAT or ACT is required. Students are also required to send official high school transcripts. AP and CLEP credits are accepted.

Procedure: Freshmen are admitted to all sessions. Entrance exams should be taken by January of the senior year of high school. There are deferred admissions and rolling admissions plans. Application deadlines are open. Notification is sent on a rolling basis. Applications are accepted online.

Transfer: 383 transfer students enrolled in 2012-2013. Applicants must have a GPA of 2.0. 32 of 128 credits required for the bachelor's degree must be completed at Saints.

Visiting: There are regularly scheduled orientations for prospective students, Visting students can participate in a class placement survey, peer and academic advisement, and registration. There are guides for informal visits, visitors may sit in on classes, and stay overnight. To schedule a visit, contact the Admissions Office.

Financial Aid: In 2013-2014, 83% of all full-time freshmen and 80% of continuing full-time students received some form of financial aid. 83% of all full-time freshmen and 80% of continuing full-time students received need-based aid. The average freshman award was $24,921. Need-based scholarships or need-based grants averaged $8,126; need-based self-help aid (loans and jobs) averaged $4,260; and other non-need-based awards and non-need-based scholarships averaged $14,622. 29% of undergraduate students work part-time. Average annual earnings from campus work are $1970. The average financial indebtedness of the 2013 graduate was $43,113. The FAFSA is required. The priority date for freshman financial aid applications for fall entry is March 1.

International Students: There are 117 international students enrolled. The school actively recruits these students. They must take the TOEFL with a minimum score of 550 on the paper-based TOEFL (PBT) or 79 on the Internet-based version (iBT).

Computers: All students may access the system. There are no time limits and no fees.

Graduates: From July 1, 2012 to June 30, 2013, 757 bachelor's degrees were awarded. The most popular majors were nursing (39%), management (19%), and biological sciences (13%). In an average class, 59% graduate in 4 years or less, 68% graduate in 5 years or less, and 68% graduate in 6 years or less. Of the 2012 graduating class, 29% were enrolled in graduate school within 6 months of graduation, and 63% were employed.

Admissions Contact: Eric Berg, Vice President for Enrollment Management. E-Mail: *eberg@css.edu* Web: *www.css.edu*

CONCORDIA COLLEGE, MOORHEAD A-2

Moorhead, MN 56562 (218) 299-3004
(800) 699-9897; (218) 299-4720

Full-time: 952 men, 1536 women
Part-time: 16 men, 27 women
Graduate: 4 men, 23 women
Year: semesters, summer session
Application Deadline: open
Faculty: 181; IIB, -$
Ph.D.s: 85%
Student/Faculty: 14 to 1
Tuition: $32,814
Room & Board: $7160
Freshman Class: 2493 applied, 1944 accepted, 684 enrolled
SAT CR/M: 570/550 **ACT:** 25 **COMPETITIVE+**

Concordia College, founded in 1891, is a private, liberal arts institution affiliated with the Evangelical Lutheran Church in America. There are 2 undergraduate schools and 1 graduate school. In addition to regional accreditation, Concordia has baccalaureate program accreditation with CSWE and NASM. The library contains 346,744 volumes, 44,055 microform items, 26,572 audio/video tapes/CDs/DVDs, and subscribes to 4,342 periodicals including electronic. Computerized library services include interlibrary loans, database searching, Internet access, and Wi-Fi capability. Special learning facilities include an art gallery, radio station, TV station, an observatory; a field biology research facility; a laser facility; a nursing simulation lab; a 2MeV hypervelocity dust particle accelerator. The

113-acre campus is in a suburban area 230 miles northwest of Minneapolis and St. Paul. Including any residence halls, there are 42 buildings.

Student Life: 67% of undergraduates are from Minnesota. Others are from 33 states, 31 foreign countries, and Canada. 94% are from public schools. 83% are White. 43% are Protestant; 36% unknown religion; 17% Catholic. The average age of freshmen is 18; all undergraduates, 20. 16% do not continue beyond their first year; 71% remain to graduate.

Housing: 1792 students can be accommodated in college housing, which includes single-sex and coed dorms and on-campus apartments. In addition, there are language houses, special-interest houses, townhouses. On-campus housing is guaranteed for the freshman year only, is available on a first-come, first-served basis, and is available on a lottery system for upperclassmen. 64% of students live on campus. Alcohol is not permitted. All students may keep cars.

Activities: There are no fraternities or sororities. There are 106 groups on campus, including art, band, cheerleading, choir, chorale, chorus, communications, dance, debate, drama, environmental, ethnic, forensics, gay, honors, international, jazz band, literary magazine, musical theater, newspaper, orchestra, pep band, photography, political, professional, radio and TV, religious, social, social service, student government, and symphony. Popular campus events include Christmas Concert, Martin Luther King Jr. Day, and National Book Award Celebration.

Sports: There are 11 intercollegiate sports for men and 11 for women, and 6 intramural sports for men and 5 for women. Facilities include a 200-meter indoor track with 4 multipurpose volleyball/basketball/tennis courts; an indoor swimming pool and sauna; a 7,000-seat stadium with an all-weather track; a field house with a 4,500-seat auditorium that features 2 basketball courts, an auxiliary gym, and a weight room; 6 outdoor tennis courts; softball and soccer competition fields; a baseball complex; a multi-sport locker room facility (under construction); and soccer practice fields.

Disabled Students: 95% of the campus is accessible. Facilities include wheelchair ramps, elevators, special parking, specially equipped restrooms, special class scheduling, lowered drinking fountains, special housing.

Services: Counseling and information services are available, as is tutoring in most subjects. There is a reader service for the blind. an interpreter service for the deaf

Campus Safety and Security: Measures include 24-hour foot and vehicle patrol, emergency notification system, and security escort services. There are emergency telephones, lighted pathways/sidewalks, and controlled access to dorms/residences.

Programs of Study: Concordia confers B.A., and B.M. degrees. Master's degrees are also awarded. Bachelor's degrees are awarded in BIOLOGICAL SCIENCE (biology/biological science and nutrition), BUSINESS (accounting, business administration and management, and international business management), COMMUNICATIONS AND THE ARTS (art, Chinese, classical languages, classics, communications, dramatic arts, English, French, German, journalism, Latin, music, music performance, music theory and composition, and Spanish), COMPUTER AND PHYSICAL SCIENCE (applied science, chemistry, mathematics, and physics), EDUCATION (art education, business education, elementary education, foreign languages education, health education, mathematics education, music education, physical education, secondary education, and social studies education), ENGINEERING AND ENVIRONMENTAL DESIGN (environmental science), HEALTH PROFESSIONS (clinical science, exercise science, health, and nursing), SOCIAL SCIENCE (history, humanities, international studies, philosophy, political science/government, psychology, religion, Scandinavian studies, social work, and sociology). Natural sciences is the strongest academically. Education, business, and biology have the largest enrollments.

Required: All students must maintain a minimum GPA of 2.0 while taking 126 semester hours, including at least 32 in the major. Required courses include written communication, oral communication, an introduction to liberal arts, and 2 courses each in physical education and religion. Exploration requirements include 7 courses taken from 6 areas: science and math, social science, world language, humanities and arts plus 2 Perspectives courses to include 1 U.S. Cultural Diversity course and 1 International and Global Perspectives course. The final course in the Core Curriculum is a writing-intensive capstone course.

Special: Co-op programs and internships are available in most majors, and dual majors are available in all majors. There is a Washington semester and an urban studies semester in Chicago. Study abroad in 26 countries, on- and off-campus work-study, a B.A.-B.M. degree in music, and a 3-2 engineering degree with the University of Minnesota are available. Nondegree study for special students and pass/fail options also are possible. Cross-registration is offered through the Tri-College University Consortium. There are 18 national honor societies, a freshman honors program, and 16 departmental honors programs.

Faculty/Classroom: 51% of faculty are male; 49% are female. All teach and do research. No introductory courses are taught by graduate students. The average class size in an introductory lecture is 23; in a laboratory is 17; and in a regular course is 19.

Admissions: 78% of the 2013-2014 applicants were accepted. The SAT scores for the 2013-2014 freshman class were: Critical Reading--23% below 500, 33% between 500 and 599, 35% between 600 and 699, and 10% between 700 and 800; Math--33% below 500, 29% between 500 and 599, 23% between 600 and 699, and 15% between 700 and 800; Writing--31% below 500, 37% between 500 and 599, 23% between 600 and 699, and 10% between 700 and 800. The ACT scores were 13% below 21, 22% between 21 and 23, 29% between 24 and 26, 16% between 27 and 28, and 20% above 28. 53% of the current freshmen were in the top fifth of their class; 81% were in the top two fifths. There were 4 National Merit finalists.

Requirements: The SAT or ACT is required. Two character references are required, and an interview is recommended. The GED is accepted. Academic performance and preparation, as evidenced in a high school transcript, are the most important factors in the admissions decision. ACT or SAT is required. AP and CLEP credits are accepted. Important factors in the admissions decision are advanced placement or honors courses, recommendations by school officials, and leadership record.

Procedure: Freshmen are admitted to all sessions. Entrance exams should be taken by the first semester of the senior year. There are early admissions, deferred admissions, and rolling admissions plans. Application deadlines are open. Application fee is $20. Notification is sent on a rolling basis. Applications are accepted online.

Transfer: 42 transfer students enrolled in 2012-2013. Transfer applicants must have a minimum 2.0 GPA and provide official transcripts from previously attended schools. 28 of 126 credits required for the bachelor's degree must be completed at Concordia.

Visiting: There are regularly scheduled orientations for prospective students, including an extensive campus tour and meetings with admissions counselors and faculty members. There are guides for informal visits, visitors may sit in on classes, and stay overnight. To schedule a visit, contact the Office of Admissions.

Financial Aid: In 2013-2014, 99% of all full-time freshmen and 97% of continuing full-time students received some form of financial aid. 77% of all full-time freshmen and 73% of continuing full-time students received need-based aid. The average freshman award was $27,769. Need-based scholarships or need-based grants averaged $21,188; and need-based self-help aid (loans and jobs) averaged $7,676. 52% of undergraduate students work part-time. Average annual earnings from campus work are $1405. Concordia is a member of CSS. The FAFSA is required. The deadline for filing freshman financial aid applications for fall entry is rolling.

International Students: There are 102 international students enrolled. The school actively recruits these students. They must take the TOEFL with a minimum score of 73 on the Internet-based version (iBT).

Computers: All students may access the system 24 hours per day. There are no time limits and no fees.

Graduates: From July 1, 2012 to June 30, 2013, 540 bachelor's degrees were awarded. The most popular majors were business (17%), education (15%), and biology (12%). In an average class, 65% graduate in 4 years or less, 71% graduate in 5 years or less, and 71% graduate in 6 years or less. Of the 2012 graduating class, 32% were enrolled in graduate school within 6 months of graduation, and 82% were employed.

Admissions Contact: Office of Admissions E-Mail: *admissions@cord.edu* Web: *www.concordiacollege.edu*

CONCORDIA UNIVERSITY SAINT PAUL C-4

St. Paul, MN 55104 **(651) 641-8230**
(800) 333-4705; (651) 603-6320

Full-time: 554 men, 663 women **Faculty:** 72
Part-time: 356 men, 598 women **Ph.D.s:** 77%
Graduate: 439 men, 1022 women **Student/Faculty:** 16 to 1
Year: semesters, summer session **Tuition:** $19,700
Application Deadline: August 1 **Room & Board:** $7500
Freshman Class: 1349 applied, 720 accepted, 278 enrolled
ACT: 21

COMPETITIVE

Concordia University, founded in 1893 and a member of the Concordia University System, is a private institution affiliated with the Lutheran Church Missouri Synod and offering programs in teacher education, business, church vocations, and the liberal arts. Master's programs and bachelor's degree completion programs for adult learners are also offered. There are 3 undergraduate schools and 1 graduate school. In addition to regional accreditation, CSP has baccalaureate program accreditation with ACBSP and NCATE. The library contains 165,968 volumes, 11,501 microform items, 3,828 audio/video tapes/CDs/DVDs, and subscribes to 346 periodicals including electronic. Computerized library services include interlibrary loans, database searching, Internet access, and Wi-Fi capability. Special learning facilities include an art gallery. The 37-acre campus is in an urban area in the Midway area of the Twin Cities, between Minneapolis and St. Paul. Including any residence halls, there are 26 buildings.

Student Life: 83% of undergraduates are from Minnesota. Others are from 45 states, 9 foreign countries, and Canada. 72% are White. 45% are

Protestant. The average age of freshmen is 18; all undergraduates, 26. 27% do not continue beyond their first year; 47% remain to graduate.

Housing: 514 students can be accommodated in college housing, which includes single-sex and coed dorms, on-campus apartments, and married student housing. On-campus housing is guaranteed for the freshman year only, is available on a first-come, and first-served basis. Priority is given to out-of-town students. 77% of students commute. All students may keep cars.

Activities: There are no fraternities or sororities. There are 40 groups on campus, including art, band, cheerleading, choir, drama, ethnic, honors, international, jazz band, musical theater, newspaper, pep band, political, professional, religious, social, social service, and student government. Popular campus events include Fine Arts Christmas Concert, and Spring Honors Convocation.

Sports: There are 6 intercollegiate sports for men and 7 for women, and 8 intramural sports for men and 8 for women. Facilities include a 1200-seat gym, a health and wellness center, a stadium for football, soccer, and track and field, and baseball and softball playing fields.

Disabled Students: 90% of the campus is accessible. Facilities include wheelchair ramps, elevators, special parking, specially equipped restrooms, special class scheduling, lowered drinking fountains, lowered telephones.

Services: Counseling and information services are available, as is tutoring in every subject. There is a reader service for the blind, and remedial math, reading, and writing.

Campus Safety and Security: Measures include 24-hour foot and vehicle patrol, emergency notification system, self-defense education, and security escort services. There are emergency telephones, lighted pathways/sidewalks, and controlled access to dorms/residences.

Programs of Study: CSP confers B.A., B.S. and B.B.A. degrees. Associate and master's degrees are also awarded. Bachelor's degrees are awarded in BIOLOGICAL SCIENCE (biology/biological science), BUSINESS (accounting, banking and finance, business administration and management, marketing management, organizational leadership and management, and sports management), COMMUNICATIONS AND THE ARTS (art, choral music, church music, communications, creative writing, design, dramatic arts, English, English Writing, graphic design, instrumental music education, music, music business management, strategic communication, studio art, theatre arts, and vocal music education), COMPUTER AND PHYSICAL SCIENCE (information sciences and systems and mathematics), EDUCATION (art education, childhood education: 1-6, Christian education, early childhood education, education of the emotionally handicapped, elementary education, English education, mathematics education, middle school education, music education, physical education, science education, secondary education, social studies education, social studies secondary school education, and special education), HEALTH PROFESSIONS (community health work and radiological science), SOCIAL SCIENCE (child care/child and family studies, criminal justice, food production/management/services, history, physical fitness/movement, psychology, religion, religious education, religious music, sociology, and theological studies). Business, teacher education, and church vocations have the largest enrollments.

Required: To graduate, students must complete 128 credit hours in the form of 1 major or 2 minors, GPA varies from 2.0 to 2.75, and required hours in the major vary from 32 to 44, depending on the program. The core curriculum consists of 48 hours of liberal arts courses.

Special: Concordia, St. Paul offers cross-registration with other members of the Concordia University System, internships in many programs, and study-abroad opportunities. Accelerated degree programs and interdisciplinary majors are also available. Credit for life experience, nondegree study, and pass/fail options are possible. Degree completion programs designed for working adults are offered in cohort-delivered format via face-to-face or online learning. There is 1 national honor society, and 1 departmental honors program.

Faculty/Classroom: 48% of faculty are male; 52% are female. 79% teach undergraduates. No introductory courses are taught by graduate students. The average class size in an introductory lecture is 14; in a laboratory is 19; and in a regular course is 14.

Admissions: 53% of the 2013-2014 applicants were accepted. The ACT scores were 49% below 21, 25% between 21 and 23, 20% between 24 and 26, 4% between 27 and 28, and 2% above 28. 18% of the current freshmen were in the top fifth of their class; 45% were in the top two fifths.

Requirements: The ACT is required. Applicants are normally expected to have 4 years of English, 2 each of math, science, fine arts, and history/social studies, and 1 of health or phys ed. An interview is recommended. 2 letters of recommendation are required. The GED is accepted. A GPA of 2.0 is required. AP and CLEP credits are accepted.

Procedure: Freshmen are admitted fall and spring. Entrance exams should be taken during the senior year. There are deferred admissions and rolling admissions plans. Applications should be filed by August 1 for fall entry; December 1 for spring entry, along with a $30 fee. Applications are accepted online.

Transfer: 650 transfer students enrolled in 2012-2013. Applicants must have a 2.0 GPA and submit 2 letters of recommendation. Students with fewer than 1 year of college credits must also submit ACT scores and an official high school transcript. 32 of 128 credits required for the bachelor's degree must be completed at CSP.

Visiting: There are regularly scheduled orientations for prospective students, including a campus tour, class visits, and a meeting with professors. There are guides for informal visits, visitors may sit in on classes, and stay overnight. To schedule a visit, contact the Office of Undergraduate Admission.

Financial Aid: In 2013-2014, 74% of all full-time freshmen and 79% of continuing full-time students received some form of financial aid. 74% of all full-time freshmen and 74% of continuing full-time students received need-based aid. The average freshman award was $15,690. Need-based scholarships or need-based grants averaged $11,157; need-based self-help aid (loans and jobs) averaged $4,985; non-need-based athletic scholarships averaged $3,328; and other non-need-based awards and non-need-based scholarships averaged $3,543. 14% of undergraduate students work part-time. Average annual earnings from campus work are $2227. The average financial indebtedness of the 2013 graduate was $31,629. The FAFSA and the college's own financial statement, and federal tax return are required. The priority date for freshman financial aid applications for fall entry is March 1.

International Students: There are 56 international students enrolled. The school actively recruits these students. They must take the TOEFL with a minimum score of 65 on the Internet-based version (iBT).

Computers: All students may access the system 24 hours a day. There are no time limits and no fees.

Graduates: From July 1, 2012 to June 30, 2013, 347 bachelor's degrees were awarded. The most popular majors were organizational leadership (14%), criminal justice (7%), and marketing (6%). 32 companies recruited on campus in 2012-2013. In an average class, 1% graduate in 3 years or less, 32% graduate in 4 years or less, 42% graduate in 5 years or less, and 46% graduate in 6 years or less.

Admissions Contact: Kristin Vogel, Director of Undergraduate Admission. E-Mail: *admissions@csp.edu* Web: *www.csp.edu*

GUSTAVUS ADOLPHUS COLLEGE — C-4

St. Peter, MN 56082 — (507) 933-7676; (800) GUSTAVU; (507) 933-6270

Full-time: 1117 men, 1306 women	**Faculty:** 201; IIB, -$
Part-time: 21 men, 11 women	**Ph.D.s:** 85%
Graduate: n/av	**Student/Faculty:** 12 to 1
Year: 4-1-4	**Tuition:** $39,120
Application Deadline: November 1	**Room & Board:** $9050
Freshman Class: 4804 applied, 3037 accepted, 610 enrolled	
ACT: 27	

HIGHLY COMPETITIVE

Gustavus Adolphus College, founded in 1862, is a private liberal arts college affiliated with the Evangelical Luteran Church in America. In addition to regional accreditation, Gustavus has baccalaureate program accreditation with NASM, NCATE, and NLN. The library contains 311,480 volumes, 43,075 microform items, 105,799 audio/video tapes/CDs/DVDs, and subscribes to 32,340 periodicals including electronic. Computerized library services include interlibrary loans, database searching, Internet access, and Wi-Fi capability. Special learning facilities include an art gallery, radio station, an arboretum, observatory, greenhouses,bronze-casting facility, geology museum, and many specialized laboratories. The 340-acre campus is in a small town 65 miles southwest of Minneapolis. Including any residence halls, there are 56 buildings.

Student Life: 81% of undergraduates are from Minnesota. Others are from 43 states, 15 foreign countries, and Canada. 94% are from public schools. 85% are White. 72% are Protestant; 21% Catholic. The average age of freshmen is 18; all undergraduates, 20. 9% do not continue beyond their first year; 80% remain to graduate.

Housing: 2103 students can be accommodated in college housing, which includes coed dorms and on-campus apartments. In addition, there are language houses and special-interest houses. On-campus housing is guaranteed for all 4 years and is available on a lottery system for upperclassmen. 85% of students live on campus; of those, 75% remain on campus on weekends. All students may keep cars.

Activities: 14% of men belong to 6 local and 1 national fraternities; 14% of women belong to 5 local and 1 national sororities. There are 125 groups on campus, including art, band, cheerleading, choir, chorus, computers, dance, debate, drama, environmental, ethnic, film, forensics, gay, honors, international, jazz band, literary magazine, musical theater, newspaper, orchestra, pep band, political, professional, radio and TV, religious, social, social service, student government, symphony, and yearbook. Popular campus events include Christmas in Christ Chapel, Earth Jam All-Day Music Festival, and Building Bridges Diversity Conference.

Sports: There are 12 intercollegiate sports for men and 13 for women, and 17 intramural sports for men and 10 for women. Facilities include an ice arena, an Olympic-size pool, a gymnastics area, an indoor tennis center, an arena, playing fields, artificial turf football field, racquetball and tennis courts, a weight room, an indoor and an outdoor running track, and varsity and intramural fields for soccer, softball, baseball, lacrosse, rugby, and ultimate Frisbee.

Disabled Students: All of the campus is accessible. Facilities include wheelchair ramps, elevators, special parking, specially equipped restrooms, special class scheduling, lowered drinking fountains, lowered telephones, and special housing.

Services: Counseling and information services are available, as is tutoring in most subjects. A writing lab is available; ESL services are available; disability services are also available.

Campus Safety and Security: Measures include 24-hour foot and vehicle patrol, emergency notification system, and security escort services. There are shuttle buses, emergency telephones, lighted pathways/sidewalks, and controlled access to dorms/residences.

Programs of Study: Gustavus confers B.A. degrees. Bachelor's degrees are awarded in AGRICULTURE (environmental studies), BIOLOGICAL SCIENCE (biochemistry and biology/biological science), BUSINESS (accounting, business administration and management, business economics, and international business management), COMMUNICATIONS AND THE ARTS (classics, communications, dance, dramatic arts, English, fine arts, French, music, Russian, Scandinavian languages, Spanish, and speech/debate/rhetoric), COMPUTER AND PHYSICAL SCIENCE (chemistry, computer science, geology, mathematics, and physics), EDUCATION (art education, business education, elementary education, foreign languages education, health education, middle school education, music education, science education, and secondary education), HEALTH PROFESSIONS (nursing, physical therapy, predentistry, and premedicine), SOCIAL SCIENCE (anthropology, economics, geography, history, philosophy, political science/government, prelaw, psychology, religion, social science, sociology, and women's studies). Physical science and social science are the strongest academically. Business, biology, and communication studies have the largest enrollments.

Required: All students are required to complete 32 courses plus 2 January interim courses and two-half courses in personal fitness and lifetime activity. Nine courses must be in the following areas (1 each): the arts, biblical, and theological studies, literary and rhetorical studies, historical and philosophical studies, mathematical and logical reasoning, natural science perspective, human behavior and social institutions, and non-western cultures. A minimum GPA of 2.0 is necessary for graduation. A total of 7 to 11 courses is required in the major.

Special: Co-op programs in nursing with St. Olaf College and cross-registration with Minnesota State University are available. The college offers internships, a Washington semester, study abroad in 22 countries, student-designed majors, nondegree study, work-study, and pass/fail options for some courses. A 3-2 engineering degree program with the University of Minnesota and Minnesota State University, Mankato is offered. The Curriculum II core offers a 12-course interdisciplinary program. There are 16 national honor societies, including Phi Beta Kappa, and 12 departmental honors programs.

Faculty/Classroom: 52% of faculty are male; 48% are female. All teach and do research. No introductory courses are taught by graduate students. The average class size in an introductory lecture is 25; in a laboratory is 15; and in a regular course is 15.

Admissions: 63% of the 2013-2014 applicants were accepted. The ACT scores were 2% below 21, 13% between 21 and 23, 31% between 24 and 26, 20% between 27 and 28, and 34% above 28. 56% of the current freshmen were in the top fifth of their class; 88% were in the top two fifths. There were 4 National Merit finalists. 23 freshmen graduated first in their class.

Requirements: Applicants must have completed 4 years of English, 3 each of math and science, and 2 each of a foreign language, history, and social studies. AP credits are accepted. Important factors in the admissions decision are advanced placement or honors courses and evidence of special talent.

Procedure: Freshmen are admitted fall, winter, and spring. Entrance exams should be taken in the fall of the senior year. There are deferred admissions and rolling admissions plans. Applications should be filed by November 1 for fall entry; December 1 for winter entry; and January 1 for spring entry. Notifications are sent in November. Applications are accepted online.

Transfer: 32 transfer students enrolled in 2012-2013. Transfer applicants must have earned a 2.4 GPA at their previous college. 72 of 140 credits required for the bachelor's degree must be completed at Gustavus.

Visiting: There are regularly scheduled orientations for prospective students, consisting of an interview, a tour, and meetings with faculty and students. There are guides for informal visits, visitors may sit in on classes, and stay overnight. To schedule a visit, contact the Admissions Office.

Financial Aid: In 2013-2014, 93% of all full-time freshmen and 92% of continuing full-time students received some form of financial aid. 69% of all full-time freshmen and 65% of continuing full-time students received need-based aid. The average freshman award was $31,279. Need-based scholarships or need-based grants averaged $26,732; and need-based self-help aid (loans and jobs) averaged $9,317. 71% of undergraduate students work part-time. Average annual earnings from campus work are $1600. The average financial indebtedness of the 2013 graduate was $33,523. Gustavus is a member of CSS. The CSS/Profile, FAFSA, and the college's own financial statement are required. The priority date for freshman financial aid applications for fall entry is January 1. The deadline for filing freshman financial aid applications for fall entry is April 15.

International Students: There are 58 international students enrolled. The school actively recruits these students. They must take the TOEFL.

Computers: All students may access the system. There are no time limits and no fees.

Graduates: From July 1, 2012 to June 30, 2013, 603 bachelor's degrees were awarded. The most popular majors were biology (9%), economics/management (6%), and psychology (5%). 40 companies recruited on campus in 2012-2013. In an average class, 2% graduate in 3 years or less, 80% graduate in 4 years or less, 82% graduate in 5 years or less, and 82% graduate in 6 years or less. Of the 2012 graduating class, 34% were enrolled in graduate school within 6 months of graduation, and 66% were employed.

Admissions Contact: Thomas Crady, Dean of Admissions. E-Mail: *admission@gustavus.edu* Web: *www.gustavus.edu*

HAMLINE UNIVERSITY C-4

St. Paul, MN 55104 (651) 523-2207
(800) 753-9753; (651) 523-2458

Full-time: 870 men, 1231 women	**Faculty:** n/av; IIA, -$
Part-time: 47 men, 63 women	**Ph.D.s:** n/av
Graduate: 833 men, 1537 women	**Student/Faculty:** 12 to 1
Year: 4-1-4, summer session	**Tuition:** $35,108
Application Deadline:	**Room & Board:** $9090
Freshman Class: 3727 applied, 2247 accepted, 536 enrolled	
SAT CR/M/W: 545/560/540	**ACT:** 24 **VERY COMPETITIVE**

Hamline University, founded in 1854, is a private liberal arts and sciences university affiliated with the United Methodist Church. There is 1 undergraduate school and 4 graduate schools. In addition to regional accreditation, Hamline has baccalaureate program accreditation with NASM and NCATE. The 2 libraries contain 368,313 volumes, 1.1 million microform items, 5,045 audio/video tapes/CDs/DVDs, and subscribe. Computerized library services include interlibrary loans, database searching, Internet access, and Wi-Fi capability. Special learning facilities include an art gallery, radio station, a center for Global and Environmental Education, center for Excellence in Urban Teaching, and a Writing center. The 60-acre campus is in an urban area between the downtowns of Minneapolis and St. Paul. Including any residence halls, there are 41 buildings.

Student Life: 80% of undergraduates are from Minnesota. Others are from 41 states, 33 foreign countries, and Canada. 72% are White. 19% are Catholic; 15% claim no religious affiliation. The average age of freshmen is 18; all undergraduates, 21. 19% do not continue beyond their first year; 66% remain to graduate.

Housing: 956 students can be accommodated in college housing, which includes coed dorms, on-campus apartments, and married student housing. In addition, there are language houses, special-interest houses, fraternity houses, PRIDE black student alliance house, Hmong student asociation house, and Amity Scholar house. On-campus housing is guaranteed for all 4 years. 60% of students commute. All students may keep cars.

Activities: There are 80 groups on campus, including art, band, cheerleading, chess, choir, chorale, chorus, computers, dance, drama, environmental, ethnic, film, forensics, gay, honors, international, jazz band, literary magazine, musical theater, newspaper, orchestra, pep band, photography, political, professional, radio and TV, religious, social, social service, student government, and symphony. Popular campus events include World Fest, Fall Organization Fair, and Women's Leadership Retreat.

Sports: There are 9 intercollegiate sports for men and 10 for women, and 7 intramural sports for men and 7 for women. Facilities include a stadium, a field house a swimming pool, a playing field, and an athletic center.

Disabled Students: Facilities include wheelchair ramps, elevators, special parking, specially equipped restrooms, special class scheduling, lowered drinking fountains, lowered telephones, and special housing.

Services: Counseling and information services are available, as is tutoring in every subject. There is a reader service for the blind, and remedial math, reading, and writing.

Campus Safety and Security: Measures include 24-hour foot and vehicle patrol, emergency notification system, self-defense education, and security escort services. There are emergency telephones, lighted pathways/sidewalks, and controlled access to dorms/residences.

Programs of Study: Hamline confers B.A., B.S., B.B.A. and B.F.A degrees. Master's and doctoral degrees are also awarded. Bachelor's degrees are awarded in AGRICULTURE (environmental studies), BIOLOGICAL SCIENCE (biochemistry and biology/biological science), BUSI-

NESS (accounting, business administration and management, global/general management, and international business management), COMMUNICATIONS AND THE ARTS (art history, art, communications, creative writing, dramatic arts, English, fine arts, French, German, music, music performance, Spanish, and theatre arts), COMPUTER AND PHYSICAL SCIENCE (chemistry, digital arts/technology, mathematics, and physics), EDUCATION (athletic training, education, elementary education, foreign languages education, music education, science education, and secondary education), HEALTH PROFESSIONS (exercise science and premedicine), SOCIAL SCIENCE (anthropology, criminal justice, East Asian studies, economics, forensic studies, history, Latin American studies, paralegal studies, peace studies, philosophy, political science/government, prelaw, psychology, religion, social science, social studies, sociology, urban studies, and women's studies). Social sciences, business, and psychology have the largest enrollments.

Required: To graduate, students must complete a minimum of 32 course credits within their field of concentration with a minimum overall GPA of 2.0. 63 course credits must be outside the major. In their first year, all students are required to take a freshman seminar and freshman English and demonstrate computer literacy. All students must also take a variety of general education courses to apply toward the "Hamline Plan." An independent study project and an internship are also required.

Special: Cross-registration with Augsburg, Macalester, Saint Catherine Colleges and the University of Saint Thomas is possible. Students may select cooperative programs, study abroad, a Washington semester with American University, dual majors, student-designed majors, and pass/fail options. Students may earn a 3-2 or 4-2 engineering degree at the University of Minnesota or Washington University. On-campus work-study is available, as are extensive internship opportunities on and off campus. There are including Phi Beta Kappa and a freshman honors program.

Faculty/Classroom: All teach undergraduates. No introductory courses are taught by graduate students.

Admissions: 60% of the 2013-2014 applicants were accepted. The SAT scores for the 2013-2014 freshman class were: Critical Reading--33% below 500, 31% between 500 and 599, 26% between 600 and 699, and 10% between 700 and 800; Math--22% below 500, 45% between 500 and 599, 31% between 600 and 699, and 2% between 700 and 800; Writing--29% below 500, 38% between 500 and 599, 29% between 600 and 699, and 3% between 700 and 800. The ACT scores were 18% below 21, 25% between 21 and 23, 27% between 24 and 26, 13% between 27 and 28, and 17% above 28. 11 freshmen graduated first in their class.

Requirements: The SAT or ACT is required. It is recommended that candidates for admission complete 4 years of English with 1 year of college preparatory writing, 4 years of social studies, 4 years of academic electives, 4 years each of math,3 years of lab science, 4 years of social science, and 2 years of a foreign language. The GED is accepted. AP and CLEP credits are accepted.

Procedure: Freshmen are admitted to all sessions. There are early decision, deferred admissions, and rolling admissions plans. Application deadlines are open. Notification of early decision is sent December 20; regular decision, 114 applicants were on the 2013 waiting list; 9 were admitted. Applications are accepted online.

Transfer: 142 transfer students enrolled in 2012-2013. Transfer applicants must submit the application form, transcript copies, teacher/advisor recommendation, and a secondary school transcript, if fewer than 32 semester hours have been competed. Applicants must submit an essay or personal statement. A minimum college GPA of 2.0 is required. 56 of 128 credits required for the bachelor's degree must be completed at Hamline.

Visiting: There are guides for informal visits, visitors may sit in on classes, and stay overnight. To schedule a visit, contact the Admissions Office.

Financial Aid: In 2013-2014, 100% of all full-time freshmen and 97% of continuing full-time students received some form of financial aid. 78% of all full-time freshmen and 80% of continuing full-time students received need-based aid. The average freshman award was $25,467. The average financial indebtedness of the 2013 graduate was $34,372. The FAFSA is required. The priority date for freshman financial aid applications for fall entry is March 15.

International Students: There are 47 international students enrolled. The school actively recruits these students. They must take the TOEFL with a minimum score of 550 on the paper-based TOEFL (PBT) or 80 on the Internet-based version (iBT). They must also take the SAT or ACT.

Computers: All students may access the system 24 hours a day, year-round. There are no time limits and no fees.

Graduates: From July 1, 2012 to June 30, 2013, 420 bachelor's degrees were awarded. The most popular majors were social sciences (17%), business (16%), and psychology (12%). 27 companies recruited on campus in 2012-2013. In an average class, 60% graduate in 4 years or less, 5% graduate in 5 years or less, and 66% graduate in 6 years or less.

Admissions Contact: Milyon Trulove, Director of Admission. E-Mail: *admission@.hamline.edu* Web: *www.hamline.edu*

MACALESTER COLLEGE C-4

St. Paul, MN 55105 (651) 696-6357
(800) 231-7974; (651) 696-6724

Full-time: 818 men, 1217 women	**Faculty:** 174; IIB, +$
Part-time: 17 men, 18 women	**Ph.D.s:** 94%
Graduate: n/av	**Student/Faculty:** 10 to 1
Year: semesters	**Tuition:** $43,693
Application Deadline: January 15	**Room & Board:** $9726

Freshman Class: 6030 applied, 2214 accepted, 534 enrolled
SAT CR/M/W: 700/680/680 **ACT:** 31 **MOST COMPETITIVE**

Macalester College, founded in 1874, is a nonsectarian liberal arts and sciences institution. In addition to regional accreditation, Macalester has baccalaureate program accreditation with NASM. The library contains 435,851 volumes, 87,004 microform items, 31,409 audio/video tapes/CDs/DVDs, and subscribes to 5,492 periodicals including electronic. Computerized library services include interlibrary loans, database searching, Internet access, and Wi-Fi capability. Special learning facilities include an art gallery, radio station, a 280-acre natural history study area 25 miles from campus. The 53-acre campus is in a small town midway between downtown St. Paul and Minneapolis. Including any residence halls, there are 53 buildings.

Student Life: 81% of undergraduates are from out of state, mostly the Mid-West. Students are from 50 states, 90 foreign countries, and Canada. 70% are from public schools. 66% are White; 13% Foreign. The average age of freshmen is 18; all undergraduates, 20. 6% do not continue beyond their first year; 90% remain to graduate.

Housing: 1296 students can be accommodated in college housing, which includes single-sex and coed dorms and on-campus apartments. In addition, there are language houses, special-interest houses, a vegetarian co-op, a cultural house, interfaith house, and gender neutral section. On-campus housing is available on a lottery system for upperclassmen. 66% of students live on campus; of those, 90% remain on campus on weekends. Upperclassmen may keep cars.

Activities: There are no fraternities or sororities. There are 108 groups on campus, including and cultural shows to annual events, art, bagpipe, band, chess, choir, chorale, chorus, computers, dance, debate, drama, environmental, ethnic, forensics, gay, honors, international, jazz band, literary magazine, newspaper, orchestra, photography, political, professional, radio and TV, religious, social, social service, student government, symphony, and winter ball. Popular campus events include Midnight Breakfast, Mac Idol, Spring Fest and Founders Day.

Sports: There are 10 intercollegiate sports for men and 11 for women, and 12 intramural sports for men and 12 for women. Facilities include a field house, a 1200-seat gym, 10-lane swimming pool, 4000-seat stadium for football, soccer, and outdoor track, 2 racquetball courts, 6 tennis courts, an indoor track and field facility, weight room, 2 racquetball/squash courts and baseball and softball diamonds.

Disabled Students: 80% of the campus is accessible. Facilities include wheelchair ramps, elevators, special parking, specially equipped restrooms, special class scheduling, lowered drinking fountains, lowered telephones, and special housing.

Services: Counseling and information services are available, as is tutoring in some subjects, math, chemistry, physics, and writing. There is a reader service for the blind.

Campus Safety and Security: Measures include 24-hour foot and vehicle patrol, emergency notification system, self-defense education, and security escort services. There are emergency telephones, lighted pathways/sidewalks, controlled access to dorms/residences, and a security site on the school's web site.

Programs of Study: Macalester confers B.A. degrees. Bachelor's degrees are awarded in AGRICULTURE (environmental studies), BIOLOGICAL SCIENCE (biology/biological science and neurosciences), COMMUNICATIONS AND THE ARTS (art, Chinese, classics, dramatic arts, English, French, Japanese, linguistics, media arts, music, Russian, and Spanish), COMPUTER AND PHYSICAL SCIENCE (chemistry, computer science, geology, mathematics, and physics), EDUCATION (education), SOCIAL SCIENCE (American studies, anthropology, Asian/Oriental studies, economics, geography, German area studies, history, humanities, international studies, Latin American studies, philosophy, political science/government, psychology, religion, sociology, and women's studies). International studies, economics, biology/chemistry, and political science are the strongest academically. Math and computer science, economics and English, social sciences, foreign languages and literature have the largest enrollments.

Required: All students are required to complete 128 semester hours, with 32 to 44 in the major, and an overall minimum GPA of 2.0. Required courses include 12 hours in humanities and fine arts, 8 hours in natural science and/or math, 8 hours in social science, 4 hours each in multiculturalism, internationalism and writing, 4 to 12 hours in quantitative reasoning, and a first-year course. Second language proficiency equivalent to 2 years of college-level language must be shown, and every major requires a capstone experience.

Special: Cross-registration at Minneapolis College of Art and Design is offered; in addition, the college belongs to several consortiums, including the Associated Colleges of the Twin Cities. There also are cooperative programs in liberal arts and architecture with Washington University in St. Louis, engineering with the same school and the University of Minnesota. Internships are available in government, financial services, law, medicine, research, the arts, and other fields. Students study abroad in more than 68 countries. Student-designed majors and pass/fail options for no more than 1 course per semester also are available. There are 13 national honor societies, including Phi Beta Kappa, and 30 departmental honors programs.

Faculty/Classroom: 52% of faculty are male; 48% are female. All teach undergraduates, and 90% do both. No introductory courses are taught by graduate students. The average class size in an introductory lecture is 20; in a laboratory is 16; and in a regular course is 16.

Admissions: 37% of the 2013-2014 applicants were accepted. The SAT scores for the 2013-2014 freshman class were: Critical Reading--7% between 500 and 599, 40% between 600 and 699, and 53% between 700 and 800; Math--9% between 500 and 599, 49% between 600 and 699, and 42% between 700 and 800; Writing--1% below 500, 10% between 500 and 599, 50% between 600 and 699, and 39% between 700 and 800. The ACT scores were 1% between 21 and 23, 12% between 24 and 26, 15% between 27 and 28, and 75% above 28. 89% of the current freshmen were in the top fifth of their class; 99% were in the top two fifths. There were 32 National Merit finalists. 43 freshmen graduated first in their class.

Requirements: The SAT or ACT is required. Applicants should have earned at least 16 academic credits, including 4 years of English and 3 each in math, laboratory science, foreign language, and social studies/history. The college also expects applicants to have taken honors, AP, or IB courses where available. An essay is required, and an interview is recommended. AP credits are accepted. Important factors in the admissions decision are advanced placement or honors courses, extracurricular activities record, and recommendations by school officials.

Procedure: Freshmen are admitted fall. Entrance exams should be taken in the fall of the senior year or before. There are early decision and deferred admissions plans. Early decision applications should be filed by November 15; regular applications, by January 15 for fall entry, along with a $40 fee. Notification of early decision is sent December 15; regular decision, March 30. 118 early decision candidates were accepted for the 2013-2014 class. 472 applicants were on the 2013 waiting list; 119 were admitted. Applications are accepted online.

Transfer: 25 transfer students enrolled in 2012-2013. Transfer students usually must present a GPA of 3.33 (B+), a secondary school transcript, and recommendations from 2 teachers and from the dean of students. In addition, the SAT or ACT is required, and an interview is recommended. Transferable grades are evaluated on the basis of the nature and quality of work. Generally, a grade of C or better is accepted. 64 of 128 credits required for the bachelor's degree must be completed at Macalester.

Visiting: There are regularly scheduled orientations for prospective students, including interviews, information sessions, a class visit, and a tour of campus. There are guides for informal visits, visitors may sit in on classes, and stay overnight. To schedule a visit, contact the Admissions Office.

Financial Aid: In 2013-2014, 78% of all full-time freshmen and 77% of continuing full-time students received some form of financial aid. 74% of all full-time freshmen and 72% of continuing full-time students received need-based aid. The average freshman award was $37,945. Need-based scholarships or need-based grants averaged $33,450; and need-based self-help aid (loans and jobs) averaged $4,495. 70% of undergraduate students work part-time. Average annual earnings from campus work are $1700. The average financial indebtedness of the 2013 graduate was $23,285. Macalester is a member of CSS. The CSS/Profile and FAFSA, and parent's W-2 and tax forms are required. The priority date for freshman financial aid applications for fall entry is February 8. The deadline for filing freshman financial aid applications for fall entry is March 1.

International Students: There are 259 international students enrolled. The school actively recruits these students. They must take the TOEFL with a minimum score of 600 on the paper-based TOEFL (PBT) or 100 on the Internet-based version (iBT), IELTS 7.0 minimum. They must also take the SAT or ACT.

Computers: All students may access the system 24 hours a day. There are no time limits and no fees.

Graduates: From July 1, 2012 to June 30, 2013, 438 bachelor's degrees were awarded. The most popular majors were biology (12%), economics (10%), and psychology (8%). 54 companies recruited on campus in 2012-2013. In an average class, 86% graduate in 4 years or less, 90% graduate in 5 years or less, and 90% graduate in 6 years or less. Of the 2012 graduating class, 16% were enrolled in graduate school within 6 months of graduation, and 60% were employed.

Admissions Contact: Lorne T. Robinson, Dean of Admissions and Financial Aid. E-Mail: *admissions@macalester.edu* Web: *www.macalester.edu*

METROPOLITAN STATE UNIVERSITY C-4

St. Paul, MN 55106 **(651) 793-1305; (651) 793-1310**

Full-time: 910 men, 1210 women	**Faculty:** n/av; IIA, av$
Part-time: 1460 men, 2430 women	**Ph.D.s:** 81%
Graduate: 235 men, 330 women	**Student/Faculty:** n/av
Year: quarters, summer session	**Tuition:** $6841 ($13,111)
Application Deadline: see profile	**Room & Board:** n/app
Freshman Class: n/av	
SAT or ACT: recommended	**SPECIAL**

Metropolitan State University, founded in 1971, is a public institution primarily serving working adults through a variety of majors and individually designed degree programs. The figures in the above capsule and this profile are approximate. There are 6 undergraduate schools and 2 graduate schools. In addition to regional accreditation, Metro State has baccalaureate program accreditation with NLN. The 2 libraries contain 33,655 volumes and 5112 audio/video tapes/CDs/DVDs, and subscribe to 242 periodicals including electronic. Computerized library services include interlibrary loans, database searching, Internet access, and laptop Internet portals. Special learning facilities include a learning resource center and art gallery. The campus is composed of several small dispersed sites throughout the Twin Cities Metro area. There are 7 buildings.

Student Life: 98% of undergraduates are from Minnesota. Others are from 21 states, 53 foreign countries, and Canada. 95% are from public schools. 72% are white; 12% African American. The average age of freshmen is 26; all undergraduates, 31.

Housing: There are no residence halls. All students commute.

Activities: There are no fraternities or sororities. There are 18 groups on campus, including drama, ethnic, gay, honors, international, literary magazine, newspaper, professional, religious, social, and student government.

Sports: There is no sports program at Metro State.

Disabled Students: All of the campus is accessible. Facilities include elevators, special parking, specially equipped restrooms, lowered drinking fountains, and lowered telephones.

Services: Counseling and information services are available, as is tutoring in some subjects, including accounting, finance, economics, writing, math, and ESL.

Campus Safety and Security: Measures include security escort services.

Programs of Study: Metro State confers B.A., B.S., B.A.S., and B.S.N. degrees. Master's degrees are also awarded. Bachelor's degrees are awarded in BIOLOGICAL SCIENCE (biology/biological science), BUSINESS (accounting, banking and finance, business administration and management, hospitality management services, human resources, international business management, management information systems, marketing and distribution, marketing management, operations management, and trade and industrial supervision and management), COMMUNICATIONS AND THE ARTS (advertising, communications, dramatic arts, English, playwriting/screenwriting, and technical and business writing), COMPUTER AND PHYSICAL SCIENCE (applied mathematics, computer science, computer security and information assurance, and information sciences and systems), EDUCATION (early childhood education), HEALTH PROFESSIONS (nursing), SOCIAL SCIENCE (addiction studies, child psychology/development, criminal justice, developmental psychology, early childhood studies, economics, ethnic studies, food production/management/services, history, human services, law enforcement and corrections, liberal arts/general studies, philosophy, psychology, public administration, social science, social work, and women's studies). Nursing is the strongest academically. Accounting and business administration have the largest enrollments.

Required: To graduate, all students must complete 120 to 124 semester credits, with a varying number of hours required in the major, 48 credits in a core curriculum, and a 2.0 GPA. Other requirements include natural/physical science, math/logic, global awareness, humanities, and fine arts.

Special: Internships, co-op programs in many areas, study abroad, dual majors, and student-designed programs are offered. There is departmental honors program.

Faculty/Classroom: 55% of faculty are male; 45% are female. All teach undergraduates. No introductory courses are taught by graduate students. The average class size in an introductory lecture is 24; in a laboratory, 24; and in a regular course, 19.

Requirements: The SAT or ACT is recommended. Metro State requires applicants to be in the upper 50% of their class or have ACT, PSAT, or SAT scores at or above the national median. Applicants not meeting these requirements will be considered in the alternative admissions process. The GED is accepted. AP and CLEP credits are accepted.

Procedure: Freshmen are admitted to all sessions. There is a deferred admissions plan. Check with the school for current application deadlines. Notification is sent on a rolling basis. Applications are accepted online.

Transfer: Applicants must have at least a C average. 30 of 120 credits required for the bachelor's degree must be completed at Metro State.

Visiting: There are regularly scheduled orientations for prospective stu-

dents, including a campus tour, meetings with a financial aid adviser, faculty, and students, and a general information session. To schedule a visit, contact the Admissions Office.
Financial Aid: Metro State is a member of CSS. The FAFSA is required. Check with the school for current application deadlines.
International Students: They must take the TOEFL or MELAB.
Computers: Wireless access is available. All students may access the system. There are no time limits.
Admissions Contact: Bruce Holzschuh, Admissions Counselor. E-Mail: *bruce.holzschul@metrostate.edu* Web: *www.metrostate.edu*

MINNEAPOLIS COLLEGE OF ART AND DESIGN C-4

Minneapolis, MN 55404 **(612) 874-3760**
(800) 874-6223; (612) 874-3701

Full-time: 330 men, 380 women	**Faculty:** n/av
Part-time: 25 men, 25 women	**Ph.D.s:** 67%
Graduate: 65 men, 65 women	**Student/Faculty:** n/av
Year: semesters, summer session	**Tuition:** $31,500
Application Deadline: see profile	**Room & Board:** $8500
Freshman Class: n/av	
SAT or ACT: required	**SPECIAL**

The Minneapolis College of Art and Design, founded in 1886, is a private nonprofit college of art offering 14 different majors in a bachelor of fine arts and 4 specializations in a bachelor of science for undergraduate study. The figures in the above capsule and this profile are approximate. There is 1 graduate school. In addition to regional accreditation, MCAD has baccalaureate program accreditation with NASAD. The library contains 62,500 volumes, 850 microform items, and 2100 audio/video tapes/CDs/DVDs, and subscribes to 180 periodicals including electronic. Computerized library services include interlibrary loans, database searching, and Internet access. Special learning facilities include a learning resource center, art gallery, and slide library of art. The 7-acre campus is in an urban area 1 mile south of downtown Minneapolis. Including any residence halls, there are 9 buildings.
Student Life: 64% of undergraduates are from Minnesota. Others are from 36 states, 21 foreign countries, and Canada. 78% are from public schools. 86% are white. The average age of freshmen is 19; all undergraduates, 22. 9% do not continue beyond their first year; 72% remain to graduate.
Housing: 285 students can be accommodated in college housing, which includes coed on-campus apartments. On-campus housing is guaranteed for the freshman year only, is available on a first-come, first-served basis, and is available on a lottery system for upperclassmen. Priority is given to out-of-town students. 53% of students commute. All students may keep cars.
Activities: There are no fraternities or sororities. There are 25 groups on campus, including art, computers, drama, environmental, ethnic, film, gay, photography, professional, radio and TV, social service, and student government. Popular campus events include Black and White Ball, Spa Day, and Artist Lectures.
Sports: There are 2 intramural sports for men and 2 for women. Facilities are off-campus.
Disabled Students: 95% of the campus is accessible. Facilities include wheelchair ramps, elevators, special parking, specially equipped restrooms, and special class scheduling.
Services: Counseling and information services are available, as is tutoring in most subjects. There is remedial reading and writing.
Campus Safety and Security: Measures include 24-hour foot and vehicle patrol, self-defense education, and security escort services. There are emergency telephones, lighted pathways/sidewalks, controlled access to dorms/residences, and an escort and taxi service.
Programs of Study: MCAD confers B.S. and B.F.A degrees. Master's degrees are also awarded. Bachelor's degrees are awarded in COMMUNICATIONS AND THE ARTS (advertising, animation, design, drawing, film arts, graphic design, illustration, painting, photography, printmaking, sculpture, studio art, and video), COMPUTER AND PHYSICAL SCIENCE (digital arts/technology), ENGINEERING AND ENVIRONMENTAL DESIGN (furniture design). Graphic design, illustration, and photography have the largest enrollments.
Required: All B.F.A. students must complete the first-year foundation studies program and matriculate through the 4-year core curriculum. They must satisfactorily complete 120 semester credits, including 27 to 42 in the major. A 2.0 minimum GPA must be maintained. A senior project and written senior thesis is required.
Special: MCAD offers cross-registration with Macalester College, internships, study abroad in 8 countries, and mobility programs with many other art and design colleges in the United States and Canada through the AICAD network. Work-study is possible, and internships are required of most majors. Dual majors are available in Fine Arts Studio. This allows students to juxtapose 2 fine art majors against a major from another division.
Faculty/Classroom: 55% of faculty are male; 45% are female. All teach undergraduates. No introductory courses are taught by graduate students. The average class size in an introductory lecture is 25; in a laboratory, 14; and in a regular course, 12.
Requirements: The SAT or ACT is required. Applicants must submit a personal statement of interest, an essay, a letter of recommendation, transcripts, and a portfolio (B.F.A.). An interview is strongly encouraged. The GED is accepted. A GPA of 2.5 is required. AP credits are accepted. Important factors in the admissions decision are evidence of special talent, personality/intangible qualities, and recommendations by school officials.
Procedure: Freshmen are admitted fall and spring. Entrance exams should be taken in the spring of the junior year in high school or early fall senior year. There are deferred admissions and rolling admissions plans. Check with the school for current application deadlines. Applications are accepted online. A waiting list is maintained.
Transfer: B.F.A. applicants must submit a portfolio for the transfer of studio credit and an official transcript from all postsecondary schools. 45 of 120 credits required for the bachelor's degree must be completed at MCAD.
Visiting: There are regularly scheduled orientations for prospective students, consisting of tours, a program about putting a portfolio together, and career and financial aid information. There are guides for informal visits and visitors may sit in on classes. To schedule a visit, contact the Admissions Office.
Financial Aid: MCAD is a member of CSS. The FAFSA and parent and student federal income tax forms are required. Check with the school for current application deadlines.
International Students: They must take the TOEFL.
Computers: Wireless access is available. All academic buildings and dorms have wireless access. 5 computer labs are available for student use. Students are required to purchase a Mac laptop their freshman year at reduced cost through MCAD. All students may access the system. There are no time limits and no fees.
Admissions Contact: Admissions Office. E-Mail: *admissions@mcad.edu* Web: *www.mcad.edu*

MINNESOTA STATE UNIVERSITY, MANKATO C-4

Mankato, MN 56001 **(507) 389-1822**
(800) 722-0544; (507) 389-1511

Full-time: 5791 men, 5677 women	**Faculty:** n/av; IIA, av$
Part-time: 735 men, 1082 women	**Ph.D.s:** 80%
Graduate: 726 men, 1184 women	**Student/Faculty:** n/av
Year: semesters, summer session	**Tuition:** $7532 ($15,010)
Application Deadline:	**Room & Board:** $7368
Freshman Class: 5605 applied, 5292 accepted, 2215 enrolled	
ACT: 21	**COMPETITIVE**

Minnesota State University, Mankato, founded in 1868 and a unit of Minnesota State Colleges and Universities, offers programs in the liberal arts and sciences, as well as business, education, engineering and technology, and nursing. There are 6 undergraduate schools and 1 graduate school. In addition to regional accreditation, Minnesota State or MSU has baccalaureate program accreditation with AACSB, ABET, ADA, CSWE, NASAD, NASM, NCATE, NLN, and NRPA. The library contains 1.2 million volumes, 253,560 microform items, and 30,686 audio/video tapes/CDs/DVDs, and subscribes to 3,126 periodicals including electronic. Computerized library services include interlibrary loans, database searching, Internet access, and Wi-Fi capability. Special learning facilities include an art gallery, radio station, 2 observatories. The 354-acre campus is in a rural area 85 miles southwest of Minneapolis-St. Paul. Including any residence halls, there are 25 buildings.
Student Life: 85% of undergraduates are from Minnesota. Others are from 47 states, 68 foreign countries, and Canada. 94% are from public schools. 82% are White. The average age of freshmen is 19; all undergraduates, 21. 22% do not continue beyond their first year; 49% remain to graduate.
Housing: 3100 students can be accommodated in college housing, which includes single-sex and coed dorms and on-campus apartments. special-interest floors including freshman quiet-study floors, upperclass floors, engineering floors, and computer science floors. On-campus housing is guaranteed for the freshman year only, is available on a first-come, and first-served basis. 78% of students commute. Alcohol is not permitted. All students may keep cars.
Activities: 4% of men belong to 7 national fraternities; 3% of women belong to 4 national sororities. There are 200 groups on campus, including art, band, cheerleading, choir, chorale, chorus, computers, dance, drama, ethnic, film, gay, honors, international, jazz band, literary magazine, musical theater, newspaper, opera, orchestra, pep band, photography, political, professional, radio and TV, religious, social, social service, and student government. Popular campus events include Greek Week and Multicultural Activities and Celebrations.
Sports: There are 11 intercollegiate sports for men and 11 for women,

and 55 intramural sports for men and 55 for women. Facilities include a 7000-seat stadium; a field house; a recreation center including an indoor swimming pool, racquetball courts, a walking/jogging track, multipurpose rooms, weights, and workout machines; 2 gyms; an indoor track; tennis courts; and a 5000-seat ice hockey arena (city owned).

Disabled Students: All of the campus is accessible. Facilities include wheelchair ramps, elevators, special parking, specially equipped restrooms, special class scheduling, lowered drinking fountains, lowered telephones, special housing, and assistive technology.

Services: Counseling and information services are available, as is tutoring in most subjects. There is a reader service for the blind, and remedial math, reading, and writing. Also available are alternative testing accommodations, note taking, sign language interpreting, and taped texts.

Campus Safety and Security: Measures include 24-hour foot and vehicle patrol, emergency notification system, self-defense education, and security escort services. There are shuttle buses, emergency telephones, lighted pathways/sidewalks, closed-circuit parking lot cameras, and motion-sensitive lights in low traffic areas.

Programs of Study: Minnesota State or MSU confers B.A., B.S., B.F.A., B.Mus., B.S.E.E. and B.S.M.E. degrees. Associate, master's, and doctoral degrees are also awarded. Bachelor's degrees are awarded in BIOLOGICAL SCIENCE (biochemistry, biology/biological science, biotechnology, and life science), BUSINESS (accounting, banking and finance, business administration and management, international business management, management science, and marketing/retailing/merchandising), COMMUNICATIONS AND THE ARTS (art, communications, dance, dramatic arts, English, French, German, journalism, music, music business management, Spanish, and speech/debate/rhetoric), COMPUTER AND PHYSICAL SCIENCE (astronomy, chemistry, computer security and information assurance, earth science, information sciences and systems, mathematics, and physics), EDUCATION (art education, athletic training, early childhood education, elementary education, foreign languages education, health education, music education, physical education, science education, and secondary education), ENGINEERING AND ENVIRONMENTAL DESIGN (automotive technology, aviation administration/management, civil engineering, computer engineering, computer technology, construction management, electrical/electronics engineering, electrical/electronics engineering technology, engineering technology, environmental science, interior design, manufacturing technology, mechanical engineering, and preengineering), HEALTH PROFESSIONS (clinical science, dental hygiene, health science, nursing, predentistry, premedicine, prepharmacy, preveterinary science, public health, and speech pathology/audiology), SOCIAL SCIENCE (anthropology, corrections, dietetics, economics, ethnic studies, family/consumer studies, food science, geography, history, human development, humanities, law enforcement and corrections, parks and recreation management, philosophy, political science/government, prelaw, psychology, Scandinavian studies, social studies, social work, sociology, urban studies, and women's studies). Engineering, nursing, and sciences are the strongest academically. Business, nursing, and education have the largest enrollments.

Required: To graduate, students must complete 128 semester hours of credit, with a minimum GPA of 2.0 and at least 45 hours in the major. Most programs require 44 hours of general education, including courses in English, speech, science, math, social/behavioral science, arts and humanities, cultural diversity, global perspective, ethnic/civic responsibility, and people and the environment.

Special: The university offers cross-registration within the Minnesota State University System and with Bethany Lutheran College and Gustavus Adolphus College. Students may serve internships, study abroad, or participate in an accelerated degree program. B.A.-B.S. degrees, dual and student-designed majors, nondegree study, and pass/fail options also are available. There are 25 national honor societies and a freshman honors program.

Faculty/Classroom: 51% of faculty are male; 49% are female. 96% teach undergraduates, and 51% do research. Graduate students teach 4% of introductory courses. The average class size in an introductory lecture is 43; in a laboratory is 11; and in a regular course is 21.

Admissions: 94% of the 2013-2014 applicants were accepted. The ACT scores were 9% below 21, 62% between 21 and 23, 16% between 24 and 26, 12% between 27 and 28, and 1% above 28. 20% of the current freshmen were in the top fifth of their class; 55% were in the top two fifths. 20 freshmen graduated first in their class.

Requirements: The ACT is required. Applicants must be graduates of an accredited secondary school and rank in the top 50% of their high school class or have an ACT composite score of 21 or higher along with a satisfactory class rank. AP and CLEP credits are accepted.

Procedure: Freshmen are admitted to all sessions. Entrance exams should be taken in the spring of the junior year or the fall of the senior year. There are deferred admissions and rolling admissions plans. Check with the school for current application deadlines. The application fee is $20. Notification is sent on a rolling basis. Applications are accepted online.

Transfer: 1014 transfer students enrolled in 2012-2013. Transfer applicants must have a minimum GPA of 2.0 and have completed at least 75% of all college-level courses attempted. 30 of 128 credits required for the bachelor's degree must be completed at Minnesota State or MSU.

Visiting: There are regularly scheduled orientations for prospective students, consisting of overview presentations, campus tours, and academic information fairs. There are guides for informal visits and visitors may sit in on classes. To schedule a visit, contact The Office of Admissions.

Financial Aid: In 2013-2014, 80% of all full-time freshmen and 80% of continuing full-time students received some form of financial aid. 80% of all full-time freshmen and 80% of continuing full-time students received need-based aid. The average freshman award was $6,134. Need-based scholarships or need-based grants averaged $5,290; need-based self-help aid (loans and jobs) averaged $4,409; non-need-based athletic scholarships averaged $5,827; and other non-need-based awards and non-need-based scholarships averaged $2,271. 21% of undergraduate students work part-time. Average annual earnings from campus work are $1960. The FAFSA is required. The priority date for freshman financial aid applications for fall entry is March 15.

International Students: There are 533 international students enrolled. The school actively recruits these students. They must take the TOEFL with a minimum score of 500 on the paper-based TOEFL (PBT) or 61 on the Internet-based version (iBT), an English placement test at matriculation.

Computers: All students may access the system. There are no time limits. The fee is $3.11 per semester credit.

Graduates: From July 1, 2012 to June 30, 2013, 2528 bachelor's degrees were awarded. The most popular majors were business, education, and social sciences. 238 companies recruited on campus in 2012-2013.

Admissions Contact: Director of Admissions. E-Mail: *admissions@mankato.msus.edu* Web: *www.mnsu.edu*

MINNESOTA STATE UNIVERSITY, MOORHEAD A-2

Moorhead, MN 56563	**(218) 477-2161; (218) 477-4374**
Full-time: 2526 men, 3304 women	**Faculty:** n/av; IIA, -$
Part-time: 484 men, 698 women	**Ph.D.s:** n/av
Graduate: 106 men, 379 women	**Student/Faculty:** n/av
Year: semesters, summer session	**Tuition:** $6924
Application Deadline: open	**Room & Board:** $6468
Freshman Class: 3393 applied, 2489 accepted, 2238 enrolled	
ACT: required	
	COMPETITIVE

Minnesota State University Moorhead, founded in 1887, is a public comprehensive institution. There are 4 undergraduate schools and 1 graduate school. In addition to regional accreditation, MSU Moorhead has baccalaureate program accreditation with ACCE, CSWE, NASAD, NASM, and NCATE. The library contains 656,104 volumes, 872,378 microform items, 25,290 audio/video tapes/CDs/DVDs, and subscribes to 2,245 periodicals including electronic. Computerized library services include interlibrary loans and database searching. Special learning facilities include an art gallery, planetarium, radio station, TV station, Regional Science Center. The 119-acre campus is in a suburban area 240 miles northwest of Minneapolis-St. Paul and across the river from Fargo, North Dakota. Including any residence halls, there are 28 buildings.

Student Life: 83% are white. The average age of freshmen is 19; all undergraduates, 23.

Housing: 1844 students can be accommodated in college housing, which includes single-sex and coed dorms and on-campus apartments. In addition, there are sorority houses, Living Learning Communities. On-campus housing is available on a first-come and first-served basis. 81% of students commute. Alcohol is not permitted. All students may keep cars.

Activities: 1% of women belong to 2 local and 2 national sororities. There are 150 groups on campus, including art, band, cheerleading, choir, chorus, computers, dance, drama, drill team, ethnic, film, gay, honors, international, jazz band, literary magazine, musical theater, newspaper, orchestra, pep band, photography, political, professional, radio and TV, religious, social, social service, and student government. Popular campus events include Celebrations of Nations, Straw Hat Summer Theatre, and Dragon Frost.

Sports: There are 5 intercollegiate sports for men and 9 for women, and 14 intramural sports for men and 14 for women. Facilities include The 40,000 square foot Dragon Wellness Center opened in 2009. Facility has 2 full basketball or volleyball courts, exercise room with cardio and strength training equipment, rock climing wall and an elevated indoor running track. Comstock Memorial Union provides meeting rooms, programming areas, TV lounges, and informal general lounges.

Disabled Students: All of the campus is accessible. Facilities include wheelchair ramps, elevators, special parking, specially equipped restrooms, lowered drinking fountains, and lowered telephones.

Services: Counseling and information services are available, as is tutoring in every subject. There is a reader service for the blind, and remedial math, reading, and writing.

Campus Safety and Security: Measures include 24-hour foot and

vehicle patrol, emergency notification system, self-defense education, and security escort services. There are emergency telephones, lighted pathways/sidewalks, and in-room safes.

Programs of Study: MSU Moorhead confers B.A., B.S., B.F.A., B.M., B.S.N., and B.S.W. degrees. Associate, master's, and doctoral degrees are also awarded. Bachelor's degrees are awarded in BIOLOGICAL SCIENCE (biology/biological science), BUSINESS (accounting, banking and finance, business administration and management, international business management, management science, marketing/retailing/merchandising, and operations management), COMMUNICATIONS AND THE ARTS (broadcasting, communications, dramatic arts, English, film arts, fine arts, journalism, music, music technology, public relations, Spanish, and speech/debate/rhetoric), COMPUTER AND PHYSICAL SCIENCE (chemistry, computer science, computer security and information assurance, earth science, geoscience, mathematics, and physics), EDUCATION (art education, athletic training, early childhood education, elementary education, English education, foreign languages education, health education, mathematics education, music education, physical education, science education, social studies education, and special education), ENGINEERING AND ENVIRONMENTAL DESIGN (construction management, graphic arts technology, and industrial engineering technology), HEALTH PROFESSIONS (community health work, exercise science, health care administration, medical laboratory technology, nursing, predentistry, premedicine, prepharmacy, preveterinary science, and speech pathology/audiology), SOCIAL SCIENCE (anthropology, criminal justice, East Asian studies, economics, gerontology, history, international studies, law, paralegal studies, philosophy, political science/government, prelaw, psychology, social work, sociology, Spanish studies, and women's studies).

Required: To graduate students must have a 2.0 GPA and complete 120 semester hours, including a liberal arts core of 45 credits and 43 semester hours in upper-division courses. Required courses include 2 in English, 6 credits each of natural science, social science, humanities, and communication systems, and 5 credits in cultural diversity. All students must complete an upper-level writing requirement.

Special: Internships are available in most disciplines. The university offers cross-registration with North Dakota State University and Concordia College and is a member of the National Student Exchange. Study abroad program allows students to study at any of 125 member universities. A variety of internships are available at local, state, and federal government agencies, service organizations and in the private sector. There are 7 national honor societies, a freshman honors program, and 1 departmental honors program.

Faculty/Classroom: 61% of faculty are male; 39% are female. No introductory courses are taught by graduate students.

Admissions: In a recent year, 73% of applicants were accepted.

Requirements: The ACT is required. In addition, a high school diploma is required, and the GED is accepted. A satisfactory score on the SAT or ACT is required for applicants whose high school rank is below the top half. MSU Moorhead requires applicants to be in the upper 50% of their class. AP and CLEP credits are accepted.

Procedure: Freshmen are admitted fall, spring, and summer. Entrance exams should be taken in the junior or senior year of high school. There is a rolling admissions plan. Check with the school for current application deadlines. Check with the school for the current application fee. Applications are accepted online.

Transfer: 659 transfer students enrolled in a recent year. Applicants must submit a high school transcript or GED score and all other transcripts for post-secondary schools attended. A minimum GPA of 2.0 (higher for entry in some departments) is necessary for transfer credit. 30 of 120 credits required for the bachelor's degree must be completed at MSU Moorhead.

Visiting: There are regularly scheduled orientations for prospective students, Including a campus tour, lunch, and meetings with faculty and an admissions officer. There are guides for informal visits. To schedule a visit, contact the Admissions Office.

Financial Aid: The FAFSA is required. Check with the school for current application deadlines.

International Students: There are 320 international students enrolled. The school actively recruits these students. They must take the TOEFL with a minimum score of 500 on the paper-based TOEFL (PBT) or 61 on the Internet-based version (iBT).

Computers: Wireless access is available. All students may access the system 24 hours a day, 7 days a week. There are no time limits. There is a fee.

Graduates: In a recent year, 1229 bachelor's degrees were awarded. The most popular majors were mass communication (8%), elementary education (5%), and social work (5%).

Admissions Contact: Jeremy Johnson, Interim Director of Admissions. E-Mail: *dragon@mnstate.edu* Web: *www.mnstate.edu*

NORTH CENTRAL UNIVERSITY C-4

Minneapolis, MN 55404 (612) 343-4460
(800) 289-6222; (612) 343-4146

Full-time: 485 men, 625 women	**Faculty:** 60
Part-time: 45 men, 60 women	**Ph.D.s:** 50%
Graduate: n/av	**Student/Faculty:** n/av
Year: semesters, summer session	**Tuition:** $17,000
Application Deadline: see profile	**Room & Board:** $6500
Freshman Class: n/av	
SAT or ACT: required	

COMPETITIVE

North Central University was founded in 1930 and is affiliated with the Assemblies of God. The figures in the above capsule and in this profile are approximate. The library contains 70,041 volumes, 29 microform items, 200 audio/video tapes/CDs/DVDs, and subscribes to 325 periodicals including electronic. Computerized library services include interlibrary loans, database searching, and Internet access. Special learning facilities include a learning resource center and radio station. The 9-acre campus is in an urban area in downtown Minneapolis. Including any residence halls, there are 24 buildings.

Student Life: 65% of undergraduates are from out of state, mostly the Midwest. Students are from 40 states, 11 foreign countries, and Canada. 88% are from public schools. 94% are white. 99% are Protestant. The average age of freshmen is 18; all undergraduates, 20. 25% do not continue beyond their first year; 40% remain to graduate.

Housing: 950 students can be accommodated in college housing, which includes single-sex dorms, on-campus apartments, and married student housing. On-campus housing is available on a first-come, first-served basis. 80% of students live on campus; of those, 80% remain on campus on weekends. Alcohol is not permitted. All students may keep cars.

Activities: There are no fraternities or sororities. There are 28 groups on campus, including art, band, cheerleading, choir, chorale, chorus, drama, jazz band, literary magazine, musical theater, newspaper, orchestra, photography, political, professional, radio and TV, religious, social, and student government. Popular campus events include All-College Picnic, Community Outreach Day, and Spring Banquet.

Sports: There are 6 intercollegiate sports for men and 6 for women, and 4 intramural sports for men and 4 for women. Facilities include Elliot Park, the Clark-Danielson College Life Center Gym, and the National Sports Complex.

Disabled Students: All of the campus is accessible. Facilities include wheelchair ramps, elevators, special parking, specially equipped restrooms, special class scheduling, lowered drinking fountains, and lowered telephones.

Services: Counseling and information services are available, as is tutoring in every subject.

Campus Safety and Security: Measures include 24-hour foot and vehicle patrol, emergency notification system, self-defense education, and security escort services. There are shuttle buses, lighted pathways/sidewalks, and controlled access to dorms/residences.

Programs of Study: NCU confers B.A. and B.S. degrees. Associates degrees are also awarded. Bachelor's degrees are awarded in COMMUNICATIONS AND THE ARTS (communications), EDUCATION (elementary education), SOCIAL SCIENCE (behavioral science, biblical languages, ministries, pastoral studies, religion, religious education, and religious music). Elementary education, English, and business are the strongest academically. Music, elementary education, and youth ministries have the largest enrollments.

Required: Students must complete 129 to 144 credits for the bachelor's degree. Each program has specific requirements, including general education and Biblical studies core classes. Internships are required for all programs. Students must take 60 or more total hours in their major, with a minimum overall GPA of 2.0 (2.2 for teacher education).

Special: Students may pursue co-op programs in nursing or secondary education, study abroad in 6 countries, and complete nondegree study. Credit for life, military, or work experience is possible. Work-study, dual majors, and student-designed majors are available. There is 1 national honor society and 1 departmental honors program.

Faculty/Classroom: 63% of faculty are male; 37% are female. All teach undergraduates. No introductory courses are taught by graduate students. The average class size in an introductory lecture is 80, in a laboratory, 15, and in a regular course, 25.

Requirements: The SAT or ACT is required. The college requires a minimum ACT score of 18, high school transcripts, and academic and pastoral references. A GPA of 2.2 is required. AP and CLEP credits are accepted.

Procedure: Freshmen are admitted fall and spring. Entrance exams should be taken during the junior or senior year of high school. There is a rolling admissions plan. Applications should be filed by June 1 for fall entry and December 31 for spring entry, along with a $25 fee. Notification is sent on a rolling basis. Check with the school for current application deadlines.

Transfer: Transfer applicants must submit a completed application, a pastor's reference, a high school transcript or the GED, and college transcripts. Applicants with less than a year of college credit must also submit ACT or SAT scores and academic references. 27 of 129 credits required for the bachelor's degree must be completed at North Central.

Visiting: There are regularly scheduled orientations for prospective students. There are guides for informal visits; visitors may sit in on classes and stay overnight. To schedule a visit, contact the Admissions Office.

Financial Aid: All undergraduate students work part-time. The FAFSA, FFS, and the college's own financial statement are required. Check with the school for current application deadlines.

International Students: They must take the TOEFL. They must also take the SAT and ACT, scoring 18 on the ACT.

Computers: All students may access the system. There are no time limits. The fee is $42.

Admissions Contact: Troy Pearson, Admissions Director. A campus DVD is available. E-Mail: *troy.pearson@northcentral.edu* Web: *www.northcentral.edu*

NORTHWESTERN COLLEGE C-4

St. Paul, MN 55113-1598 **(651) 631-5209**
(800) 827-6827; (651) 631-5680

Full-time: 770 men, 1040 women	**Faculty:** n/av; IIB, --$
Part-time: 25 men, 30 women	**Ph.D.s:** 61%
Graduate: 55 men, 40 women	**Student/Faculty:** n/av
Year: semesters, summer session	**Tuition:** $25,700
Application Deadline: see pofile	**Room & Board:** $8000
Freshman Class: n/av	
SAT or ACT: required	

COMPETITIVE

Northwestern College, founded in 1902, is a Christian college offering traditional undergraduate programs in liberal arts and professional studies with emphasis on a Biblical world view and providing nontraditional educational opportunities through its Graduate and Continuing Education Division. The figures in the above capsule and in this profile are approximate. In addition to regional accreditation, Northwestern has baccalaureate program accreditation with NASM. The library contains 124,574 volumes, 70,350 microform items, 5092 audio/video tapes/CDs/DVDs, and subscribes to 1263 periodicals including electronic. Computerized library services include interlibrary loans, database searching, Internet access, and laptop Internet portals. Special learning facilities include a learning resource center, art gallery, radio station, and TV station. The 107-acre campus is in a suburban area 3 miles from St. Paul and 5 miles from Minneapolis. Including any residence halls, there are 17 buildings.

Student Life: 68% of undergraduates are from Minnesota. Others are from 31 states and 25 foreign countries. 68% are from public schools. 90% are white. 99% are Protestant. The average age of freshmen is 18; all undergraduates, 20. 21% do not continue beyond their first year; 61% remain to graduate.

Housing: 1335 students can be accommodated in college housing, which includes single-sex dorms, on-campus apartments, and married student housing. In addition, there are special-interest houses. On-campus housing is guaranteed for the freshman year only, is available on a first-come, and first-served basis. Priority is given to out-of-town students. 67% of students live on campus; of those, 70% remain on campus on weekends. Alcohol is not permitted. Upperclassmen may keep cars.

Activities: There are no fraternities or sororities. There are 30 groups on campus, including band, cheerleading, chess, choir, chorale, chorus, computers, drama, ethnic, forensics, honors, international, jazz band, literary magazine, musical theater, newspaper, opera, orchestra, pep band, political, professional, radio and TV, religious, social, social service, student government, and yearbook. Popular campus events include Spring Variety Shows, Christmas at Northwestern, and Day of Prayer and Service.

Sports: There are 8 intercollegiate sports for men and 8 for women, and 8 intramural sports for men and 8 for women. Facilities include softball, baseball, soccer, and football fields, outdoor tennis courts, and a waterfront for aquatic sports in summer and broomball in winter. There is a health and physical education center, with a full basketball court, 2 racquetball courts, an elevated jogging surface, a fitness center, and an athletic training room. The student center and 1 apartment residence have small swimming pools.

Disabled Students: 70% of the campus is accessible. Facilities include wheelchair ramps, elevators, special parking, specially equipped restrooms, special class scheduling, lowered drinking fountains, and special housing.

Services: Counseling and information services are available, as is tutoring in some subjects, including writing, math, Spanish, Greek, science, accounting, and statistics for psychology. There is remedial math, reading, and writing.

Campus Safety and Security: Measures include 24-hour foot and vehicle patrol, emergency notification system, self-defense education, and security escort services. There are shuttle buses, emergency telephones, lighted pathways/sidewalks, and controlled access to dorms/residences. The campus has limited accessibility due to being surrounded on 3 sides by Lake Johanna, and the main entrance to the campus is gated.

Programs of Study: Northwestern confers B.A., B.S., B.M.E. (music education), and B.Mus. degrees. Associates degrees are also awarded. Bachelor's degrees are awarded in BIOLOGICAL SCIENCE (biochemistry and biology/biological science), BUSINESS (accounting, banking and finance, business administration and management, international business management, management information systems, and marketing management), COMMUNICATIONS AND THE ARTS (animation, broadcasting, communications, dramatic arts, English, English as a second/foreign language, graphic design, journalism, music, music performance, music theory and composition, piano/organ, public relations, Spanish, strings, studio art, and voice), COMPUTER AND PHYSICAL SCIENCE (mathematics), EDUCATION (art education, early childhood education, elementary education, English education, mathematics education, music education, physical education, and social studies education), HEALTH PROFESSIONS (exercise science), SOCIAL SCIENCE (biblical studies, criminal justice, crosscultural studies, history, interdisciplinary studies, ministries, pastoral studies, psychology, religious education, urban studies, and youth ministry). Education, music, and communication are the strongest academically. Education, business, and Christian ministries have the largest enrollments.

Required: To graduate, students must complete 125 to 166 semester credits (depends on specific major) with a 2.0 GPA. The number of credits required in the major varies from 36 to 100 (average of 58). A core curriculum of 64 to 68 credits is built around a biblical worldview theme, thoroughly integrating general education and biblical worldview studies.

Special: The college offers 8 study-abroad programs and 4 U.S. off-campus programs through the Council for Christian Colleges and Universities. International business majors are placed in overseas internships. A 3-2 engineering degree with the University of Minnesota-Twin Cities is offered. There are 6 national honor societies, a freshman honors program, and 11 departmental honors programs.

Faculty/Classroom: 56% of faculty are male; 44% are female. All teach undergraduates. No introductory courses are taught by graduate students. The average class size in an introductory lecture is 39; in a laboratory, 17; and in a regular course, 22.

Requirements: The ACT is preferred but the SAT is accepted. A high school diploma is required; the GED is accepted. The minimum high school GPA is 2.0, but a 3.0 or higher is recommended. Applicants are expected to have completed the following Carnegie units: 4 in English, 3 each in math, science, and social studies, and 2 others. 2 in foreign language are recommended. A statement of Christian faith and an assent to a lifestyle agreement are required. 2 letters of reference must be submitted, including 1 from the applicant's pastor. A personal interview is required for some students. Northwestern requires applicants to be in the upper 50% of their class. A GPA of 2.0 is required. AP and CLEP credits are accepted. Important factors in the admissions decision are personality/intangible qualities, recommendations by school officials, and leadership record.

Procedure: Freshmen are admitted to all sessions. Entrance exams should be taken during the fall of the senior year of high school. Notification is sent on a rolling basis. Applications are accepted online. Check with the school for current application deadlines and fee.

Transfer: 108 transfer students enrolled in a recent year. Applicants must have an average of C or better from an accredited institution. 30 of 125 credits required for the bachelor's degree must be completed at Northwestern.

Visiting: There are regularly scheduled orientations for prospective students. There are guides for informal visits; visitors may sit in on classes and stay overnight. To schedule a visit, contact the Admissions Office.

Financial Aid: In a recent year, 98% of all full-time freshmen and 94% of continuing full-time students received some form of financial aid. 80% of all full-time freshmen and 81% of continuing full-time students received need-based aid. The average freshmen award was $15,864. All undergraduate students worked part-time. Average annual earnings from campus work were $2516. The FAFSA and the college's own financial statement are required. Check with the school for current application deadlines.

International Students: In a recent year, there were 9 international students enrolled. They must take the TOEFL, scoring 530 on the paper-based version or 71 on the Internet version, or the MELAB. They must also take the SAT or ACT, scoring 18 on the ACT.

Computers: Wireless access is available. There is full wireless access in all academic buildings and all residence halls. Most dorms are also wired with Internet ports. All students may access the system any time. There are no time limits. The fee is $190. All students are required to have a personal computer. A laptop or notebook is recommended.

Graduates: In a recent year, 433 bachelor's degrees were awarded. The most popular majors were education (19%), Christian ministries/Biblical studies (19%), and business (15%). In an average class, 8% graduate in 3 years or less, 45% graduate in 4 years or less, 59% graduate in 5 years or less, and 61% graduate in 6 years or less. 6% were enrolled in graduate school within 6 months of graduation and 89% were employed.

Admissions Contact: Director of Admissions. A campus DVD is available. Web: *www.nwc.edu*

SAINT JOHN'S UNIVERSITY B-3

Collegeville, MN 56321 (320) 363-5055
(800) 544-1489; (320) 363-3206

Full-time: 1823 men
Part-time: 31 men
Graduate: 65 men, 64 women
Year: semesters
Application Deadline: January 15
Freshman Class: 1595 applied, 1193 accepted, 449 enrolled
SAT or ACT: required
Faculty: 133; IIB, av$
Ph.D.s: 85%
Student/Faculty: 12 to 1
Tuition: $37,162
Room & Board: $8984

COMPETITIVE

Saint John's University, founded in 1857, is a private Catholic Benedictine institution offering undergraduate liberal arts study for men in partnership with the College of Saint Benedict, a Catholic Benedictine institution for women. The coordinate institutions share an academic calendar, academic curriculum, and many combined extracurricular activities. There is one graduate school. In addition to regional accreditation, St. John's has baccalaureate program accreditation with ADA, NASM, and NCATE. The 2 libraries contain 647,908 volumes, 121,406 microform items, 40,623 audio/video tapes/CDs/DVDs, and subscribe to 43,129 periodicals including electronic. Computerized library services include interlibrary loans, database searching, Internet access, and Wi-Fi capability. Special learning facilities include an art gallery, natural history museum, radio station, TV station, a pottery studio and kiln, an arboretum, an observatory, a greenhouse, an herbarium, and the Hill Museum and Manuscript Library; a labyrinth, Saint Benedict's Monastery Heritage Museum and dance studio at the College of Saint Benedict. The 2500-acre campus is in a rural area 15 miles west of St. Cloud and 75 miles northwest of Minneapolis and St. Paul. Including any residence halls, there are 58 buildings.

Student Life: 76% of undergraduates are from Minnesota. Others are from 36 states, 26 foreign countries, and Canada. 71% are from public schools. 83% are White. 61% are Catholic; 22% Protestant; 16% claim no religious affiliation. The average age of freshmen is 18; all undergraduates, 20. 11% do not continue beyond their first year; 77% remain to graduate.

Housing: 1540 students can be accommodated in college housing, which includes single-sex dorms and on-campus apartments. On-campus housing is guaranteed for the freshman year only, is available on a first-come, first-served basis, and is available on a lottery system for upperclassmen. 84% of students live on campus. All students may keep cars.

Activities: There are no fraternities or sororities. There are 94 groups on campus, including and a outdoor leadership center, academic, art, band, choir, chorale, chorus, computers, dance, debate, drama, environmental, ethnic, gay, honors, international, jazz band, literary magazine, musical theater, newspaper, opera, orchestra, pep band, political, professional, radio and TV, religious, social, social service, student government, and symphony. Popular campus events include Pines, Asian New Year, Festival of Culture, Community Barbecue, Involvement Fair and Johnnie Bennie Live.

Sports: There are 12 intercollegiate sports for men. Facilities include an artificial turf football field (and 7,800-seat stadium), 3,000-seat basketball arena, hardwood racquetball courts, soccer, baseball, lacrosse, and rugby fields, indoor and outdoor tennis courts, indoor and outdoor tracks, a complete fitness center, a swimming pool, a climbing wall, a wrestling room, a training room, locker facilities for 12 intercollegiate teams, an outdoor intramural hockey rink, 5 lakes for canoeing, fishing, swimming, rowing, and kayaking, 20 miles of on-campus wooded hiking and jogging trails, and access to all athletic facilities at the College of Saint Benedict.

Disabled Students: 90% of the campus is accessible. Facilities include wheelchair ramps, elevators, special parking, specially equipped restrooms, special class scheduling, lowered drinking fountains, lowered telephones, special housing.

Services: Counseling and information services are available, as is tutoring in most subjects. a writing center and math skills center. The College of Saint Benedict and Saint John's University established a Disability Services Office. Accomodations are provided on a case by case basis for enrolled students who provide adequate documentation of a disability. Individual tutoring is available as needed. Academic and psychological counseling are available on an unlimited basis.

Campus Safety and Security: Measures include 24-hour foot and vehicle patrol, emergency notification system, self-defense education, and security escort services. There are shuttle buses, emergency telephones, and lighted pathways/sidewalks.

Programs of Study: St. John's confers B.A., and B.S.N. degrees. Master's degrees are also awarded. Bachelor's degrees are awarded in AGRICULTURE (environmental studies), BIOLOGICAL SCIENCE (biochemistry, biology/biological science, and nutrition), BUSINESS (accounting and management science), COMMUNICATIONS AND THE ARTS (art, classics, communications, English, French, German, music, Spanish, and theatre arts), COMPUTER AND PHYSICAL SCIENCE (chemistry, computer science, mathematics, natural sciences, and physics), EDUCATION (elementary education), ENGINEERING AND ENVIRONMENTAL DESIGN (preengineering), HEALTH PROFESSIONS (nursing, occupational therapy, predentistry, premedicine, preoptometry, prepharmacy, prephysical therapy, and preveterinary science), SOCIAL SCIENCE (Asian/Oriental studies, economics, gender studies, Hispanic American studies, history, humanities, liberal arts/general studies, peace studies, philosophy, political science/government, prelaw, psychology, social science, sociology, and theological studies).

Required: To graduate students must complete a first-year seminar and a junior-senior ethics seminar, and fulfill gender, intercultural, experiential learning, and fine arts experience requirements. Distribution requirements include 4 credits in fine arts, 2 courses each in humanities and theology, and 1 course each in math, natural science, and social science. All students must prove math and foreign language proficiency. A total of 124 credits must be earned, with a minimum GPA of 2.0.

Special: Students may cross-register with St. Cloud State University. There are study-abroad programs in Australia, Austria, Chile, China, Coventry-England, France, Germany, Guatemala, Greece, Ireland (Cork and Galway), Italy, India, Japan, London-England, Northern Ireland, South Africa, and Spain. Internships, dual and student-designed majors, preprofessional programs, and liberal studies degrees may be pursued. A 3-2 engineering program is offered through the University of Minnesota, as is a 3-1 program in dentistry. Nondegree study and a pass/fail grading option are also available. There are 4 national honor societies, including Phi Beta Kappa, and a freshman honors program.

Faculty/Classroom: 49% of faculty are male; 51% are female. All teach and do research. No introductory courses are taught by graduate students. The average class size in an introductory lecture is 21; in a laboratory is 14; and in a regular course is 21.

Admissions: 75% of the 2013-2014 applicants were accepted. The SAT scores for the 2013-2014 freshman class were: Critical Reading--33% below 500, 45% between 500 and 599, and 22% between 600 and 699; Math--32% below 500, 41% between 500 and 599, 21% between 600 and 699, and 6% between 700 and 800; Writing--38% below 500, 48% between 500 and 599, 13% between 600 and 699, and 2% between 700 and 800. The ACT scores were 9% below 21, 29% between 21 and 23, 29% between 24 and 26, 12% between 27 and 28, and 21% above 28. 43% of the current freshmen were in the top fifth of their class; 76% were in the top two fifths. There were 3 National Merit finalists.

Requirements: The SAT or ACT is required. Students should be graduates of an accredited secondary school. Academic preparation should include 17 units, including 4 of English, 3 of math, 2 each of a lab science and social studies, and 4 electives. A foreign language is recommended. The GED is accepted. An essay is required. Home-schooled applicants are not required to have a high school diploma but are required to provide appropriate documentation of college preparatory curriculum and standardized test scores. St. John's requires applicants to be in the upper 50% of their class. A GPA of 3.0 is required. AP and CLEP credits are accepted. Important factors in the admissions decision are advanced placement or honors courses, leadership record, and extracurricular activities record.

Procedure: Freshmen are admitted fall and spring. Entrance exams should be taken during the spring of the junior year or fall of the senior year. There are early admissions and deferred admissions plans. Application deadlines are open. Notification of early decision is sent December 15; regular decision, April 1. Applications are accepted online.

Transfer: 27 transfer students enrolled in 2012-2013. Transfer applicants must have a minimum college GPA of 2.75. An essay or personal statement, high school and college transcripts, and a transfer student evaluation form are required. Standardized test scores and an interview may be required of some. 45 of 124 credits required for the bachelor's degree must be completed at St. John's.

Visiting: There are regularly scheduled orientations for prospective students, Programs include Admissions and Financial Aid presentations, campus tours and student panels. There are guides for informal visits, visitors may sit in on classes, and stay overnight. To schedule a visit, contact the CSB/SJU Admissions Office.

Financial Aid: In 2013-2014, 94% of all full-time freshmen and 93% of continuing full-time students received some form of financial aid. 69% of all full-time freshmen and 64% of continuing full-time students received need-based aid. The average freshman award was $28,318. Need-based scholarships or need-based grants averaged $23,415; need-based self-help aid (loans and jobs) averaged $6,512; and other non-need-based awards and non-need-based scholarships averaged $14,539. 60% of undergraduate students work part-time. Average annual earnings from campus work are $2810. The average financial indebtedness of the 2013 graduate was $34,889. St. John's is a member of CSS. The FAFSA and the college's own financial statement are required. The priority date for freshman financial aid applications for fall entry is March 15.

International Students: There are 115 international students enrolled. The school actively recruits these students. They must take the TOEFL with a minimum score of 500 on the paper-based TOEFL (PBT) or 70 on the

Internet-based version (iBT), In certain cases, students may be allowed to substitute the SAT or ACT for the TOEFL. They must also take the SAT or ACT. In certain cases, students may be allowed to substitute the SAT or ACT for the TOEFL.

Computers: All students may access the system 24 hours a day. There are no time limits. The fee is $256.

Graduates: From July 1, 2012 to June 30, 2013, 417 bachelor's degrees were awarded. The most popular majors were business management (21%), accounting (12%), and biology (11%). 133 companies recruited on campus in 2012-2013. In an average class, 1% graduate in 3 years or less, 68% graduate in 4 years or less, 75% graduate in 5 years or less, and 77% graduate in 6 years or less. Of the 2012 graduating class, 13% were enrolled in graduate school within 6 months of graduation, and 78% were employed.

Admissions Contact: Cal Mosley, Vice President Admission and Financial Aid. E-Mail: *admissions@csbsju.edu* Web: *www.csbsju.edu*

SAINT MARY'S UNIVERSITY OF MINNESOTA D-5

Winona, MN 55987 (507) 457-1700
(800) 635-5987; (507) 457-1722

Full-time: 613 men, 694 women	**Faculty:** 86; IIA, --$
Part-time: 263 men, 362 women	**Ph.D.s:** 88%
Graduate: 1085 men, 2511 women	**Student/Faculty:** 14 to 1
Year: semesters	**Tuition:** $29,315
Application Deadline: May 1	**Room & Board:** $7700

Freshman Class: 1551 applied, 1161 accepted, 307 enrolled
SAT CR/M/W: 505/515/470 **ACT:** 23 **COMPETITIVE**

Founded in 1912, Saint Mary's is a private, Lasallian Catholic, comprehensive institution, guided by the De La Salle Christian Brothers since 1933. At the coeducational, residential Winona campus, the undergraduate college combines traditional liberal arts and sciences with career preparation in a student-centered environment. The Winona campus comprises 350 acres and 47 buildings, with excellent facilities for living, learning and recreation. The bachelor of arts program offers 60 majors. The Schools of Graduate and Professional Programs (SGPP) is one of the largest graduate schools in Minnesota. A pioneer in outreach education since 1984, SGPP offers certificate, bachelor completion, master's, specialist, and doctoral programs at the university's Twin Cities and Winona campuses, and centers in Rochester, Apple Valley, and Oakdale. Courses are also offered in greater Minnesota and Wisconsin, Kenya and Jamaica. There are 4 undergraduate schools and 4 graduate schools. In addition to regional accreditation, SMU has baccalaureate program accreditation with NASM. The library contains 209,807 volumes, 200,692 microform items, 9,789 audio/video tapes/CDs/DVDs, and subscribes to 40,015 periodicals including electronic. Computerized library services include interlibrary loans, database searching, Internet access, and Wi-Fi capability. Special learning facilities include an art gallery, radio station, an observatory. The 350-acre campus is in a small town 110 miles southeast of Twin Cities and 275 miles northwest of Chicago. Including any residence halls, there are 47 buildings.

Student Life: 60% of undergraduates are from Minnesota. Others are from 27 states, 18 foreign countries, and Canada. 70% are from public schools. 64% are White; 19% race unknown. 52% are Catholic; 15% Protestant. The average age of freshmen is 19; all undergraduates, 20. 21% do not continue beyond their first year; 55% remain to graduate.

Housing: 1216 students can be accommodated in college housing, which includes single-sex and coed dorms and on-campus apartments. In addition, there are special-interest houses, living learning communities, first-year residence halls, and substance-free residence halls. On-campus housing is guaranteed for all 4 years. 88% of students live on campus; of those, 75% remain on campus on weekends. All students may keep cars.

Activities: 4% of men belong to 2 national fraternities; 3% of women belong to 1 national sorority. There are 85 groups on campus, including art, band, cheerleading, choir, chorale, chorus, dance, drama, environmental, ethnic, gay, honors, international, jazz band, literary magazine, musical theater, newspaper, political, professional, radio and TV, religious, social, social service, student government, and yearbook. Popular campus events include Cardinal Days, Taylor Richmond Benefit Dance and Finals Breakfast.

Sports: There are 10 intercollegiate sports for men and 11 for women. Facilities include basketball, indoor tennis, and racquetball courts, an indoor ice arena, exercise and weight rooms, baseball, softball, and soccer fields, Nordic ski and running trails, an indoor track, an indoor swimming pool, a dance studio, a Frisbee disc course, an outdoor track, and a high ropes course.

Disabled Students: 93% of the campus is accessible. Facilities include wheelchair ramps, elevators, special parking, specially equipped restrooms, lowered drinking fountains, lowered telephones, special housing, and TDD phones.

Services: Counseling and information services are available, as is tutoring in most subjects. There is a reader service for the blind, and remedial math, reading, and writing.

Campus Safety and Security: Measures include 24-hour foot and vehicle patrol, emergency notification system, and security escort services. There are emergency telephones, lighted pathways/sidewalks, and controlled access to dorms/residences.

Programs of Study: SMU confers B.A., and B.S. degrees. Master's and doctoral degrees are also awarded. Bachelor's degrees are awarded in BIOLOGICAL SCIENCE (biochemistry, biology/biological science, biophysics, environmental biology, and life science secondary school education), BUSINESS (accounting, business administration and management, business intelligence and analytics, entrepreneurial studies, finance, international business, marketing, and sports management), COMMUNICATIONS AND THE ARTS (art, graphic design, journalism, literature, music, music industry, music performance, public relations, Spanish, studio art, and theatre arts), COMPUTER AND PHYSICAL SCIENCE (actuarial science, chemistry, chemistry/adolescence education, computer science, mathematics, and physics), EDUCATION ((Education) Childhood Education, elementary education, English education, foreign languages education, mathematics education, music education, secondary education, and social studies education), ENGINEERING AND ENVIRONMENTAL DESIGN (engineering physics and nuclear medicine technology), HEALTH PROFESSIONS (cardiac sonography, cytotechnology, medical laboratory science, and prephysical therapy), SOCIAL SCIENCE (criminal justice, (Social Science) Global Studies, history, human services, pastoral studies, philosophy, political science/government, psychology, religious education, social science, sociology, theology, and youth ministry). Biology, biochemistry, and theology are the strongest academically. marketing, biology, and accounting have the largest enrollments.

Required: Students must have a 2.0 cumulative major GPA and complete a minimum of 122 semester credits, including at least 45 at the upper-division level. Students must complete a major program and the general education program.

Special: Students may cross-register with Winona State University. Internships, co-op programs, student teaching and study abroad, work-study programs, and a Washington semester are available. The university also offers dual and student-designed majors, non-degree study, pass/fail options, credit for life, military, and work experience, and an honors program that also serves as an alternative general education program. There are 14 national honor societies.

Faculty/Classroom: 65% of faculty are male; 35% are female. All teach and do research. No introductory courses are taught by graduate students. The average class size in an introductory lecture is 16; in a laboratory is 14; and in a regular course is 15.

Admissions: 75% of the 2013-2014 applicants were accepted. The SAT scores for the 2013-2014 freshman class were: Critical Reading--50% below 500, 38% between 500 and 599, 6% between 600 and 699, and 6% between 700 and 800; Math--44% below 500, 39% between 500 and 599, 25% between 600 and 699; Writing--56% below 500, 13% between 500 and 599, 31% between 600 and 699. The ACT scores were 30% below 21, 26% between 21 and 23, 27% between 24 and 26, 10% between 27 and 28, and 7% above 28. 30% of the current freshmen were in the top fifth of their class; 54% were in the top two fifths. 1 freshman graduated first in the class.

Requirements: The SAT or ACT is required. Candidates for admission should have completed 4 units of English, 3 each of math and natural science, 2 of social studies, and 6 academic electives. Completion of 2 units of foreign language is recommended. A GPA of 2.5 is required. AP and CLEP credits are accepted. Important factors in the admissions decision are advanced placement or honors courses, leadership record, and extracurricular activities record.

Procedure: Freshmen are admitted fall and spring. Entrance exams should be taken by the fall of the senior year. There are early admissions, deferred admissions, and rolling admissions plans. Applications should be filed by May 1 for fall entry; December 1 for spring entry, along with a $25 fee. Notification is sent on a rolling basis. Applications are accepted online.

Transfer: 36 transfer students enrolled in 2012-2013. Applicants must have a 2.0 GPA with at least 12 credits. 60 of 122 credits required for the bachelor's degree must be completed at SMU.

Visiting: There are regularly scheduled orientations for prospective students, including an interview, a tour, class visits, and lunch. There are guides for informal visits, visitors may sit in on classes, and stay overnight. To schedule a visit, contact the Office of Admissions.

Financial Aid: In 2013-2014, 98% of all full-time freshmen and 96% of continuing full-time students received some form of financial aid. 78% of all full-time freshmen and 74% of continuing full-time students received need-based aid. The average freshman award was $22,144. 30% of undergraduate students work part-time. Average annual earnings from campus work are $1776. The average financial indebtedness of the 2013 graduate was $34,215. The FAFSA and the college's own financial statement are required. The priority date for freshman financial aid applications for fall entry is March 15. The deadline for filing freshman financial aid applications for fall entry is open.

International Students: There are 42 international students enrolled.

The school actively recruits these students. They must take the TOEFL with a minimum score of 550 on the paper-based TOEFL (PBT) or 79 on the Internet-based version (iBT).

Computers: All students may access the system any time. There are no time limits. The fee is $330.

Graduates: From July 1, 2012 to June 30, 2013, 258 bachelor's degrees were awarded. The most popular majors were marketing (8%), accounting (7%), and psychology (7%). 8 companies recruited on campus in 2012-2013. In an average class, 1% graduate in 3 years or less, 44% graduate in 4 years or less, 54% graduate in 5 years or less, and 55% graduate in 6 years or less.

Admissions Contact: Nathan Ament, Director of Admission. E-Mail: *admission@smumn.edu* Web: *www.smumn.edu*

SOUTHWEST MINNESOTA STATE UNIVERSITY B-4

Marshall, MN 56258 (507) 537-6286
(800) 642-0684; (507) 537-7154

Full-time: 1080 men, 1255 women	**Faculty:** n/av; IIB, av$
Part-time: 155 men, 240 women	**Ph.D.s:** 76%
Graduate: 160 men, 375 women	**Student/Faculty:** n/av
Year: semesters, summer session	**Tuition:** $9000
Application Deadline: see profile	**Room & Board:** $7500
Freshman Class: n/av	
SAT or ACT: required	
	COMPETITIVE

Southwest Minnesota State University, founded in 1963, is a public institution offering programs in liberal arts, technology, and preprofessional training. The figures in the above capsule and this profile are approximate. In addition to regional accreditation, SMSU has baccalaureate program accreditation with CSWE. The library contains 168,000 volumes, 228,000 microform items, 12,000 audio/video tapes/CDs/DVDs, and subscribes to 950 periodicals including electronic. Computerized library services include interlibrary loans, database searching, Internet access, and laptop Internet portals. Special learning facilities include a learning resource center, art gallery, natural history museum, planetarium, radio station, and TV station. The 216-acre campus is in a rural area 150 miles southwest of Minneapolis. Including any residence halls, there are 24 buildings.

Student Life: 75% of undergraduates are from Minnesota. Others are from 29 states, 33 foreign countries, and Canada. 95% are from public schools. 85% are white. The average age of freshmen is 19; all undergraduates, 22. 25% do not continue beyond their first year; 35% remain to graduate.

Housing: 1182 students can be accommodated in college housing, which includes single-sex and coed dorms and on-campus apartments. In addition, there are special-interest houses, a quiet house, a reduced quiet house, and a weekend programming house. On-campus housing is guaranteed for the freshman year only. Alcohol is not permitted. All students may keep cars.

Activities: There are no fraternities or sororities. There are 100 groups on campus, including art, band, cheerleading, chess, choir, chorus, computers, dance, debate, drama, ethnic, forensics, honors, international, jazz band, literary magazine, marching band, musical theater, newspaper, orchestra, pep band, political, professional, radio and TV, religious, social, social service, student government, and symphony. Popular campus events include Martin Luther King Celebration, Cinco de Mayo, and Dakota Indigenous Nations Studies Conference.

Sports: There are 5 intercollegiate sports for men and 6 for women, and 14 intramural sports for men and 13 for women. Facilities include a 2000-seat gym, a baseball complex, softball facilities, racquetball courts, a football stadium, wrestling rooms, a weight room, an Olympic-size pool, a 3800-seat mulitipurpose facility, a soccer field, and a fitness center.

Disabled Students: 98% of the campus is accessible. Facilities include wheelchair ramps, elevators, special parking, specially equipped restrooms, special class scheduling, lowered drinking fountains, lowered telephones, and special housing.

Services: Counseling and information services are available, as is tutoring in most subjects. There is a reader service for the blind and remedial math, reading, and writing.

Campus Safety and Security: Measures include 24-hour foot and vehicle patrol, self-defense education, and security escort services. There are emergency telephones and lighted pathways/sidewalks.

Programs of Study: SMSU confers B.A., B.S., and B.A.S. degrees. Associate and master's degrees are also awarded. Bachelor's degrees are awarded in AGRICULTURE (agricultural business management), BIOLOGICAL SCIENCE (biology/biological science), BUSINESS (accounting, business administration and management, hotel/motel and restaurant management, and marketing/retailing/merchandising), COMMUNICATIONS AND THE ARTS (art, communications, creative writing, dramatic arts, literature, music, and Spanish), COMPUTER AND PHYSICAL SCIENCE (applied science, chemistry, computer science, and mathematics), EDUCATION (art education, early childhood education, elementary education, foreign languages education, health education, mathematics education, music education, physical education, and science education), ENGINEERING AND ENVIRONMENTAL DESIGN (environmental science), HEALTH PROFESSIONS (dental laboratory technology and medical technology), SOCIAL SCIENCE (history, interdisciplinary studies, law enforcement and corrections, political science/government, psychology, public administration, social work, and sociology). Education, business administration, and psychology have the largest enrollments.

Required: To graduate, students must complete at least 128 semester credit hours, a minimum of 27 of which must be at the 300 or 400 level, and a liberal arts core curriculum, with a minimum GPA of 2.0.

Special: SMSU has cooperative programs with various local colleges, cross-registration with several state universities, and an accelerated degree. SMSU also offers internships in every discipline, work-study programs, student-designed and interdisciplinary majors including speech communication and theater arts, nondegree study, pass/fail options, and credit for life, military, and work experience. There are 2 national honor societies and a freshman honors program.

Faculty/Classroom: 56% of faculty are male; 44% are female. All teach undergraduates. No introductory courses are taught by graduate students. The average class size in an introductory lecture is 26; in a laboratory, 19; and in a regular course, 21.

Requirements: The ACT or SAT is required; the ACT is preferred. Admission is based on class rank or ACT/SAT composite. Students should be graduates of an accredited secondary school or have a GED certificate. An interview is recommended. SMSU requires applicants to be in the upper 50% of their class. AP and CLEP credits are accepted. Important factors in the admissions decision are recommendations by school officials, leadership record, and personality/intangible qualities.

Procedure: Freshmen are admitted to all sessions. Entrance exams should be taken during the junior or senior year. There are deferred admissions and rolling admissions plans. Check with the school for current application deadlines. Notification is sent on a rolling basis. Applications are accepted online.

Transfer: Applicants need a minimum GPA of 2.0 in previous college-level work at an accredited institution. High school transcripts are required if students are transferring with fewer than 24 semester credits. 48 of 128 credits required for the bachelor's degree must be completed at SMSU.

Visiting: There are regularly scheduled orientations for prospective students. There are guides for informal visits, and visitors may sit in on classes and stay overnight. To schedule a visit, contact the Admissions Office.

Financial Aid: The FAFSA and the college's own financial statement are required. Check with the school for current application deadlines.

International Students: The school actively recruits these students. They must take the TOEFL.

Computers: Wireless access is available. The library has 2 classroom/labs with computer workstations for each student and projection-ready instruction stations. All students may access the system 24 hours per day. There are no time limits.

Admissions Contact: Richard Shearer, Director of Enrollment. E-Mail: *shearerr@southwestmsu.edu* Web: *www.southwestmsu.edu*

ST. CATHERINE UNIVERSITY C-4

St. Paul, MN 55105 (651) 690-8850
(800) 656-KATE; (651) 690-8824

Full-time: 20 men, 2168 women		**Faculty:** 292
Part-time: 103 men, 1268 women		**Ph.D.s:** 55%
Graduate: 150 men, 1308 women		**Student/Faculty:** 12 to 1
Year: 4-1-4, summer session		**Tuition:** $29,780
Application Deadline: open		**Room & Board:** $8002
Freshman Class: 2375 applied, 1473 accepted, 682 enrolled		
SAT CR/M: 560/525	**ACT:** 24	**COMPETITIVE+**

A dynamic university educating students to lead and influence, St. Catherine prepares students to make a difference in their professions, their communities and the world. At the University's heart is the largest, most innovative college for women in the nation. St. Catherine also offers a range of graduate and associate programs for women and men. The figures in the above capsule and in this profile are approximate. There are 4 undergraduate schools and one graduate school. In addition to regional accreditation, SCU has baccalaureate program accreditation with ADA, APTA, CSWE, NASM, and NLN. The 2 libraries contain 250,865 volumes, 180,946 microform items, 7,844 audio/video tapes/CDs/DVDs, and subscribe to 2,763 periodicals including electronic. Computerized library services include interlibrary loans, database searching, Internet access, and Wi-Fi capability. Special learning facilities include an art gallery, radio station, an observatory, and anatomy lab. The 110-acre campus is in an urban area 6 miles southwest of downtown St. Paul, MN. Including any residence halls, there are 22 buildings.

Student Life: 89% of undergraduates are from Minnesota. Others are from 30 states, 34 foreign countries, and Canada. 86% are from public schools. 68% are White; 11% African American. 50% are Catholic; 20% Protestant. The average age of freshmen is 18; all undergraduates, 22. 16% do not continue beyond their first year; 67% remain to graduate.

Housing: 900 students can be accommodated in college housing, which includes single-sex dorms and on-campus apartments. apartments for student-parents, and theme housing. On-campus housing is available on a first-come, first-served basis, and is available on a lottery system for upperclassmen. 56% of students commute. All students may keep cars.

Activities: There are no fraternities or sororities. There are 42 groups on campus, including art, band, cheerleading, choir, chorale, chorus, dance, drama, ethnic, gay, honors, international, literary magazine, musical theater, newspaper, photography, political, professional, radio and TV, religious, social, social service, and student government. Popular campus events include Winter Charity Ball, Dew Drop Bop, and KatWalk Fashion Show.

Sports: There are 11 intercollegiate sports for women, and 8 intramural sports for women. Facilities include a fitness facility, a gym, a weight room, a swimming pool, an outdoor fitness course, tennis courts, a soccer field, and a softball field.

Disabled Students: 90% of the campus is accessible. Facilities include wheelchair ramps, elevators, special parking, specially equipped restrooms, special class scheduling, lowered drinking fountains, and lowered telephones.

Services: Counseling and information services are available, as is tutoring in most subjects. There is a reader service for the blind, and remedial math, reading, and writing.

Campus Safety and Security: Measures include 24-hour foot and vehicle patrol, emergency notification system, self-defense education, and security escort services. There are emergency telephones, lighted pathways/sidewalks, and controlled access to dorms/residences.

Programs of Study: SCU confers B.A., and B.S. degrees. Associate, master's, and doctoral degrees are also awarded. Bachelor's degrees are awarded in BIOLOGICAL SCIENCE (biochemistry, biology/biological science, and nutrition), BUSINESS (accounting, business administration and management, fashion merchandising, international business management, international economics, management information systems, and marketing/retailing/merchandising), COMMUNICATIONS AND THE ARTS (American Sign Language, art, classics, communications, dramatic arts, English, fine arts, French, Latin, media arts, music, musical theater, Spanish, and speech/debate/rhetoric), COMPUTER AND PHYSICAL SCIENCE (chemistry, information sciences and systems, and mathematics), EDUCATION (art education, early childhood education, elementary education, home economics education, music education, physical education, and secondary education), ENGINEERING AND ENVIRONMENTAL DESIGN (food services technology), HEALTH PROFESSIONS (exercise science, health care administration, medical records administration/services, nursing, occupational therapy, rehabilitation therapy, and respiratory therapy), SOCIAL SCIENCE (dietetics, economics, ethnic studies, family/consumer studies, fashion design and technology, history, international relations, interpreter for the deaf, philosophy, political science/government, psychology, social studies, social work, sociology, theological studies, and women's studies). Biology, chemistry, psychology are the strongest academically. Nursing, social work, and accounting have the largest enrollments.

Required: To graduate, students must complete 130 semester credits, including a liberal arts core with courses in history, foreign language, philosophy, math, fine arts, literature, and theology, and 80 credits outside the major. Required courses are the Reflective Woman and the Global Search for Justice. At least 36 hours are required in the major. Students must have a minimum 2.0 GPA and demonstrate proficiency in composition, math, and computer literacy.

Special: SCU offers co-op programs with Carondolet College, the University of Minnesota, and George Washington University, and cross-registration with the Associated Colleges of the Twin Cities and other colleges sponsored by the Sisters of St. Joseph. Students may arrange internships, a Washington semester, and study abroad. Dual majors are available in the sciences and engineering. Students may receive credit for life, military, or work experience. Student-designed majors, non-degree study, and pass/fail options are available. The Weekend College offers a B.A. degree. There are 24 national honor societies, including Phi Beta Kappa, and a freshman honors program.

Faculty/Classroom: 21% of faculty are male; 79% are female. All teach undergraduates. No introductory courses are taught by graduate students. The average class size in an introductory lecture is 19; in a laboratory is 14; and in a regular course is 13.

Admissions: 62% of the 2013-2014 applicants were accepted. The SAT scores for the 2013-2014 freshman class were: Critical Reading--27% below 500, 39% between 500 and 599, 17% between 600 and 699, and 17% between 700 and 800; Math--27% below 500, 56% between 500 and 599, 17% between 600 and 699. The ACT scores were 1% below 21, 48% between 24 and 26, 44% between 27 and 28, and 7% above 28. 53% of the current freshmen were in the top fifth of their class; 85% were in the top two fifths. 11 freshmen graduated first in their class.

Requirements: The SAT or ACT is required. Applicants must have completed a college preparatory program including 4 courses in English, 3 in math, and 2 each in a foreign language, science, and social studies. SCU requires applicants to be in the upper 50% of their class. A GPA of 2.5 is required. AP and CLEP credits are accepted. Important factors in the admissions decision are advanced placement or honors courses, recommendations by school officials, and extracurricular activities record.

Procedure: Freshmen are admitted fall and winter. Entrance exams should be taken during the senior year. There are deferred admissions and rolling admissions plans. Application deadlines are open. Notification is sent on a open basis. Applications are accepted online.

Transfer: 354 transfer students enrolled in 2012-2013. Transfer applicants must submit high school and college transcripts. 48 of 130 credits required for the bachelor's degree must be completed at SCU.

Visiting: There are regularly scheduled orientations for prospective students, including a tour, an admissions interview, and an appointment with a faculty member. There are guides for informal visits, visitors may sit in on classes, and stay overnight. To schedule a visit, contact the Admissions Office.

Financial Aid: In 2013-2014, 99% of all full-time freshmen and 91% of continuing full-time students received some form of financial aid. 63% of all full-time freshmen and 60% of continuing full-time students received need-based aid. The average freshman award was $30,592. Need-based scholarships or need-based grants averaged $10,581; need-based self-help aid (loans and jobs) averaged $5,504; other non-need-based awards and non-need-based scholarships averaged $11,278; and $5,215 from other forms of aid. 100% of undergraduate students work part-time. Average annual earnings from campus work are $3200. The average financial indebtedness of the 2013 graduate was $39,607. SCU is a member of CSS. The FAFSA and the college's own financial statement are required. The priority date for freshman financial aid applications for fall entry is April 15.

International Students: There are 48 international students enrolled. The school actively recruits these students. They must take the TOEFL with a minimum score of 500 on the paper-based TOEFL (PBT) or 61 on the Internet-based version (iBT) or take the MELAB and the college's own test. The SAT is required only if the student attended a U.S. high school, whether in this country or overseas.

Computers: All students may access the system 24 hours a day. There are no time limits and no fees.

Graduates: From July 1, 2012 to June 30, 2013, 534 bachelor's degrees were awarded. The most popular majors were health professions and related programs (32%), business/marketing (14%), and public administration and social service/education (7%). 13 companies recruited on campus in 2012-2013. In an average class, 45% graduate in 4 years or less, 63% graduate in 5 years or less, and 67% graduate in 6 years or less. Of the 2012 graduating class, 22% were enrolled in graduate school within 6 months of graduation, and 84% were employed.

Admissions Contact: Marlene Mohs, Associate Dean of Admissions. E-Mail: *admissions@stkate.edu* Web: *www.stkate.edu*

ST. CLOUD STATE UNIVERSITY C-3

St. Cloud, MN 56301-4498 **(320) 308-2244**
(800) 369-4260; (320) 308-2243

Full-time: 5410 men, 6255 women	**Faculty:** n/av; IIA, av$
Part-time: 1195 men, 1690 women	**Ph.D.s:** n/av
Graduate: 560 men, 930 women	**Student/Faculty:** n/av
Year: semesters, summer session	**Tuition:** $8500 ($14,500)
Application Deadline: open	**Room & Board:** $6500
Freshman Class: n/av	
ACT: required	

COMPETITIVE

Saint Cloud State University, founded in 1869, is a comprehensive university offering programs that include the liberal arts and career preparation with emphasis on diversity, hands-on learning, and service to the community. The figures in the above capsule and this capsule are approximate. There are 5 undergraduate schools and 5 graduate schools. In addition to regional accreditation, SCSU has baccalaureate program accreditation with AACSB, ABET, ACEJMC, ASLA, CSWE, NASAD, NASM, and NCATE. The library contains 887,462 volumes, 1.8 million microform items, 24,244 audio/video tapes/CDs/DVDs, and subscribes to 1762 periodicals including electronic. Computerized library services include interlibrary loans, database searching, and Internet access. Special learning facilities include a learning resource center, art gallery, natural history museum, planetarium, radio station, TV station, and National Hockey Center. The 922-acre campus is in a suburban area 60 miles northwest of Minneapolis. Including any residence halls, there are 35 buildings.

Student Life: 92% of undergraduates are from Minnesota. Others are from 50 states, 85 foreign countries, and Canada. 77% are white. The average age of freshmen is 19; all undergraduates, 22. 29% do not continue beyond their first year.

Housing: 3000 students can be accommodated in college housing, which

includes single-sex and coed dorms. In addition, there is special housing for international students. 82% of students commute. Alcohol is not permitted. All students may keep cars.

Activities: There are 5 national fraternities and 4 national sororities. There are 240 groups on campus, including art, band, cheerleading, chess, choir, chorale, chorus, computers, dance, drama, entrepreneurial, ethnic, film, gay, hobby, honors, international, jazz band, literary magazine, marching band, musical theater, opera, orchestra, pep band, photography, political, professional, radio and TV, religious, social, social service, sports, student government, symphony, travel, and yearbook. Popular campus events include Music Festival, Ethnic Awareness Week, and major speakers and workshops.

Disabled Students: 86% of the campus is accessible. Facilities include wheelchair ramps, elevators, special parking, specially equipped restrooms, special class scheduling, lowered drinking fountains, and lowered telephones.

Services: Counseling and information services are available, as is tutoring in every subject. There is a reader service for the blind and remedial math, reading, and writing.

Campus Safety and Security: Measures include 24-hour foot and vehicle patrol and security escort services. There are shuttle buses, emergency telephones, lighted pathways/sidewalks, and a required short safety course.

Programs of Study: SCSU confers B.A., B.S., B.E.S., B.F.A., and B.Mus. degrees. Associate, master's, and doctoral degrees are also awarded. Bachelor's degrees are awarded in BIOLOGICAL SCIENCE (biology/biological science), BUSINESS (accounting, banking and finance, business administration and management, business economics, international business management, marketing/retailing/merchandising, and personnel management), COMMUNICATIONS AND THE ARTS (advertising, broadcasting, communications, dramatic arts, English, fine arts, journalism, languages, music, and speech/debate/rhetoric), COMPUTER AND PHYSICAL SCIENCE (atmospheric sciences and meteorology, chemistry, computer science, earth science, geology, mathematics, physics, and statistics), EDUCATION (art education, early childhood education, elementary education, foreign languages education, guidance education, health education, industrial arts education, music education, science education, and secondary education), ENGINEERING AND ENVIRONMENTAL DESIGN (aviation administration/management, electrical/electronics engineering, engineering technology, and manufacturing engineering), HEALTH PROFESSIONS (predentistry, premedicine, public health, and speech pathology/audiology), SOCIAL SCIENCE (anthropology, criminal justice, economics, geography, history, international relations, philosophy, political science/government, prelaw, psychology, public administration, social science, social work, sociology, and urban studies). Mass communication, elementary education, and special education have the largest enrollments.

Required: Students must complete a minimum of 120 semester credit hours, including 40 hours of general education requirements and 60 to 180 hours in the major, and maintain at least a 2.0 GPA (higher for many majors). Students must complete English 191, English 192, Speech 192, 2 credits in phys ed, and 24 credits in philosophy/humanities/fine arts, natural science and math, social and behavioral science, and diversity courses.

Special: The university offers cross-registration, internships in almost all majors, work-study programs, and study abroad in 25 countries. Students may take dual majors, design their own majors for a Bachelor of Elective Studies degree, and earn a general degree or a B.A.-B.S. degree in all majors, including meteorology and photographic technology. The university gives credit for military experience and allows nondegree study and pass/fail options. There are 4 national honor societies and a freshman honors program.

Faculty/Classroom: 56% of faculty are male; 44% are female. All teach undergraduates. No introductory courses are taught by graduate students.

Requirements: The ACT is required. SCSU requires applicants to be in the upper 50% of their class. AP and CLEP credits are accepted.

Procedure: Freshmen are admitted fall, spring, and summer. Entrance exams should be taken in the junior or senior year. Application deadlines are open. Check with the school for the current application fee. Notification is sent on a rolling basis.

Transfer: Applicants must have a minimum 2.0 GPA from their previous college if they transfer with 12 or more credits. If they have fewer than 12 credits, they are treated as entering freshmen. 30 of 120 credits required for the bachelor's degree must be completed at SCSU.

Visiting: There are regularly scheduled orientations for prospective students. There are guides for informal visits and visitors may sit in on classes. To schedule a visit, contact the Admissions Office.

Financial Aid: The FAFSA and the college's own financial statement are required. Check with the school for current application deadlines.

International Students: The school actively recruits these students. They must take the TOEFL.

Computers: Wireless access is available. All students may access the system any time. There are no time limits and no fees.

Admissions Contact: Admissions. A campus DVD is available. E-mail: *scsu4u@stcloud.state.edu* Web: *www.stcloudstate.edu*

ST. OLAF COLLEGE — C-4

Northfield, MN 55057 — (507) 786-3025; (800) 800-3025; (507) 786-3832

Full-time: 1352 men, 1729 women	**Faculty:** 213; IIB, av$
Part-time: 18 men, 26 women	**Ph.D.s:** 95%
Graduate: n/av	**Student/Faculty:** 14 to 1
Year: 4-1-4, summer session	**Tuition:** $40,700
Application Deadline: January 15	**Room & Board:** $9260
Freshman Class: 4011 applied, 2312 accepted, 752 enrolled	
SAT CR/M/W: 660/650/650 — **ACT:** 29	**HIGHLY COMPETITIVE+**

St. Olaf College, founded in 1874, is a private liberal arts institution affiliated with the Evangelical Lutheran Church. There is one undergraduate school. In addition to regional accreditation, St. Olaf has baccalaureate program accreditation with CSWE, NASM, and NCATE. The 4 libraries contain 722,128 volumes, 14,567 microform items, 2.2 million audio/video tapes/CDs/DVDs, and subscribe to 70,420 periodicals including electronic. Computerized library services include interlibrary loans, database searching, Internet access, and Wi-Fi capability. Special learning facilities include an art gallery, radio station, TV station, and 700 acres of land dedicated to natural habitat, sustainable agriculture, and conventional agriculture. The 300-acre campus is in a small town 35 miles south of Minneapolis/St. Paul. Including any residence halls, there are 55 buildings.

Student Life: 50% of undergraduates are from out of state, mostly the Mid-West. Students are from 49 states, 68 foreign countries, and Canada. 75% are from public schools. 78% are White. 43% are Protestant; 17% Catholic; 12% Christian, 11% claim no religious affiliation. The average age of freshmen is 18; all undergraduates, 20. 6% do not continue beyond their first year; 87% remain to graduate.

Housing: 2790 students can be accommodated in college housing, which includes coed dorms. In addition, there are honors houses, language houses, and special-interest houses. On-campus housing is guaranteed for all 4 years. 92% of students live on campus; of those, 85% remain on campus on weekends. Alcohol is not permitted. Some may keep cars.

Activities: There are no fraternities or sororities. There are 252 groups on campus, including art, band, chess, choir, chorus, computers, dance, drama, drill team, ethnic, film, gay, honors, international, jazz band, literary magazine, musical theater, newspaper, opera, orchestra, pep band, photography, political, professional, radio and TV, religious, social, social service, student government, and symphony. Popular campus events include Christmas Festival, Wellstock, and President's Ball.

Sports: There are 22 intercollegiate sports for men and 19 for women, and 35 intramural sports for men and 32 for women. Facilities include 2 athletic complexes, a field house with batting cages, a long-jump pit, 5 indoor tennis courts, and a 6-lane indoor track, plus an upper level walking/running track, a fitness center, 45-foot climbing wall, a soccer pitch, baseball diamonds, 2 weight rooms, a football field, an 8-lane all-weather track and field, a 9-hole Frisbee golf course, and practice and recreation space.

Disabled Students: 76% of the campus is accessible. Facilities include wheelchair ramps, elevators, special parking, specially equipped restrooms, special class scheduling, lowered drinking fountains, lowered telephones, special housing. electric door openers, curb cuts, and a sling for swimming pool entry.

Services: Counseling and information services are available, as is tutoring in every subject. There is a reader service for the blind. Study sessions are available.

Campus Safety and Security: Measures include 24-hour foot and vehicle patrol, emergency notification system, self-defense education, and security escort services. There are emergency telephones, lighted pathways/sidewalks, and controlled access to dorms/residences.

Programs of Study: St. Olaf confers B.A., and B.Mus. degrees. Bachelor's degrees are awarded in AGRICULTURE (environmental studies), BIOLOGICAL SCIENCE (biology/biological science), COMMUNICATIONS AND THE ARTS (art history and appreciation, classics, dance, English, French, German, Greek, Latin, music, music performance, music theory and composition, Norwegian, Russian, Spanish, studio art, and theatre arts), COMPUTER AND PHYSICAL SCIENCE (chemistry, computer science, mathematics, and physics), EDUCATION (music education and social studies education), HEALTH PROFESSIONS (exercise science and nursing), SOCIAL SCIENCE (American studies, Asian/American studies, classical/ancient civilization, economics, ethnic studies, Hispanic American studies, history, interdisciplinary studies, medieval studies, philosophy, political science/government, psychology, religion, religious music, Russian and Slavic studies, social work, sociology, and women's studies). Biology, mathematics, and economics have the largest enrollments.

Required: In addition to the distribution requirements, students are required to demonstrate skills at an intermediate level in a foreign language, proficiency in English composition, to complete the phys ed requirement and to have taken a 1/4-credit oral communication course and a 1-credit mathematical reasoning course. A first-year writing course is also required. Distribution requirements include courses in history, literature, art, science, human behavior, Bible and theology, multicultural studies, and ethical issues. A minimum of 24 full-course credits out of 35 must be graded, 18 must be upper-division. A minimum of 8 full-credit courses in a disciplinary or interdisciplinary major are required. All majors include writing requirements. Students must complete 35 credits and maintain a minimum GPA of 2.0.

Special: St. Olaf offers cross-registration with Carleton College, study abroad in more than 50 countries, a dozen domestic off-campus programs, pre-professional programs, internships, and a 3-2 B.A.-B.S.E. degree in engineering with Washington University in St. Louis or the University of Minnesota. There are dual majors, non-degree study, on-campus work study, and pass/fail options. The Center for Integrative Studies allows students to design individual majors with an emphasis on tutorials and seminars. There are 22 national honor societies and including Phi Beta Kappa.

Faculty/Classroom: 54% of faculty are male; 46% are female. All teach and do research. No introductory courses are taught by graduate students. The average class size in an introductory lecture is 24; in a laboratory is 19; and in a regular course is 23.

Admissions: 58% of the 2013-2014 applicants were accepted. The SAT scores for the 2013-2014 freshman class were: Critical Reading--1% below 500, 14% between 500 and 599, 51% between 600 and 699, and 34% between 700 and 800; Math--4% below 500, 20% between 500 and 599, 43% between 600 and 699, and 29% between 700 and 800; Writing--5% below 500, 20% between 500 and 599, 46% between 600 and 699, and 29% between 700 and 800. The ACT scores were 1% below 21, 5% between 21 and 23, 17% between 24 and 26, 18% between 27 and 28, and 59% above 28. 73% of the current freshmen were in the top fifth of their class; 97% were in the top two fifths. There were 28 National Merit finalists. 47 freshmen graduated first in their class.

Requirements: The SAT or ACT is required. It is recommended that applicants completed 4 years of English, 4 of math and social studies/history, and 4 of science (2 labs) and 4 years of a foreign language. AP credits are accepted.

Procedure: Freshmen are admitted fall, winter, and spring. Entrance exams should be taken in the spring of the junior year or the fall of the senior year. There are early decision, early admissions, and deferred admissions plans. Early decision applications should be filed by November 15; regular applications, by January 15 for fall entry. Notification of early decision is sent December 15; regular decision, March 15. 186 early decision candidates were accepted for the 2013-2014 class. 694 applicants were on the 2013 waiting list; 68 were admitted. Applications are accepted online.

Transfer: 19 transfer students enrolled in 2012-2013. Applicants must have a 3.0 GPA at their previous institution. 17 of 35 credits required for the bachelor's degree must be completed at St. Olaf.

Visiting: There are regularly scheduled orientations for prospective students, offerings include: tours, class visits, information sessions, interviews and more. There are guides for informal visits, visitors may sit in on classes, and stay overnight.

Financial Aid: In 2013-2014, 89% of all full-time freshmen and 92% of continuing full-time students received some form of financial aid. 66% of all full-time freshmen and 65% of continuing full-time students received need-based aid. The average freshman award was $33,577. Need-based scholarships or need-based grants averaged $28,705; need-based self-help aid (loans and jobs) averaged $4,935; and other non-need-based awards and non-need-based scholarships averaged $13,319. 64% of undergraduate students work part-time. Average annual earnings from campus work are $1100. The average financial indebtedness of the 2013 graduate was $27,483. St. Olaf is a member of CSS. The CSS/Profile and FAFSA are required. The priority date for freshman financial aid applications for fall entry is February 1. The deadline for filing freshman financial aid applications for fall entry is February 1.

International Students: There are 186 international students enrolled. The school actively recruits these students. They must take the TOEFL with a minimum score of 90 on the Internet-based version (iBT), or Academic IELTS. They must also take the SAT or ACT.

Computers: All students may access the system. There are no time limits and no fees.

Graduates: From July 1, 2012 to June 30, 2013, 726 bachelor's degrees were awarded. The most popular majors were biology (12%), economics (8%), and pyschology (7%). 86 companies recruited on campus in 2012-2013. In an average class, 84% graduate in 4 years or less, 87% graduate in 5 years or less, and 87% graduate in 6 years or less.

Admissions Contact: Jeff McLaughlin, Dean of Admissions & Financial Aid. E-Mail: *admissions@stolaf.edu* Web: *wp.stolaf.edu*

UNIVERSITY OF MINNESOTA SYSTEM

The University of Minnesota System, established in 1851, is a public system in Minnesota. It is governed by a board of regents, whose chief administrator is the president. The primary goal of the system is teaching, research, and public service. The main priorities are undergraduate education, basic and applied research, and graduate education. The total student enrollment for all five campuses is usually 75,000 with 3500 faculty members. Altogether there are 236 baccalaureate, 191 master's, 123 doctoral programs offered in the University Minnesota System. Profiles of the 4-year campuses are included in this section.

UNIVERSITY OF MINNESOTA CROOKSTON A-2

Crookston, MN 56716 **(218) 281-8569**
(800) 232-6466; (218) 281-8575

Full-time: 724 men, 669 women	**Faculty:** 73; IIB, -$
Part-time: 590 men, 781 women	**Ph.D.s:** 40%
Graduate: n/av	**Student/Faculty:** 20 to 1
Year: semesters, summer session	**Tuition:** $11,456
Application Deadline:	**Room & Board:** $6378

Freshman Class: 670 applied, 472 accepted, 121 enrolled
SAT CR/M/W: 480/520/490 **ACT:** 22 **COMPETITIVE**

The University of Minnesota/Crookston, founded in 1965, is a public institution offering applied bachelor degree programs, including online opportunities, in agriculture, arts, humanities, and social sciences, business, math, science, technology and natural resources. There are 4 undergraduate schools. The library contains 244,686 volumes, 26,204 microform items, and 2,222 audio/video tapes/CDs/DVDs. Computerized library services include interlibrary loans, database searching, Internet access, and Wi-Fi capability. Special learning facilities include a The 108-acre campus is in a small town 290 miles northwest of Minneapolis, and 25 miles southeast of Grand Forks, North Dakota. Including any residence halls, there are 35 buildings.

Student Life: 67% of undergraduates are from Minnesota. Others are from 42 states, 16 foreign countries, and Canada. 76% are White. The average age of freshmen is 19; all undergraduates, 26. 24% do not continue beyond their first year; 51% remain to graduate.

Housing: 563 students can be accommodated in college housing, which includes coed dorms and on-campus apartments. On-campus housing is available on a first-come and first-served basis. Priority is given to out-of-town students. 20% of students commute. Alcohol is not permitted. All students may keep cars.

Activities: 1% of men belong to 1 national fraternity; 1% of women belong to 1 national sorority. There are 39 groups on campus, including cheerleading, chess, choir, chorale, chorus, computers, drama, environmental, ethnic, gay, honors, international, pep band, political, professional, religious, social, social service, and student government. Popular campus events include What's on Wednesday (WOW), Ag-Arama and Winter Wonderland.

Sports: There are 4 intercollegiate sports for men and 7 for women, and 10 intramural sports for men and 10 for women. Facilities include a 3200-seat gym; an indoor complex with basketball/volleyball and racquetball courts, a training room with a sauna, and a fitness center; a lit football field surrounded by an all-weather track; tennis courts; and soccer, baseball, and softball fields.

Disabled Students: 95% of the campus is accessible. Facilities include wheelchair ramps, elevators, special parking, specially equipped restrooms, special class scheduling, lowered drinking fountains, lowered telephones, and special housing.

Services: Counseling and information services are available, as is tutoring in most subjects. There is a reader service for the blind, and remedial math and writing. The Academic Assistance Center also provides help with study strategies and English as a second language, and federally funded Student Support Services are available to those who are eligible.

Campus Safety and Security: Measures include emergency notification system, self-defense education, and security escort services. There are shuttle buses, emergency telephones, and lighted pathways/sidewalks.

Programs of Study: UMC confers B.S., B.A.H. and B.M.M. degrees. Bachelor's degrees are awarded in AGRICULTURE (agricultural business management, agronomy, animal science, equine science, horticulture, and natural resource management), BIOLOGICAL SCIENCE (biology/biological science), BUSINESS (accounting, business administration and management, marketing management, organizational behavior, and sports management), COMMUNICATIONS AND THE ARTS (communications), COMPUTER AND PHYSICAL SCIENCE (information sciences and systems and software engineering), EDUCATION (early childhood education and elementary education), ENGINEERING AND ENVIRONMENTAL DESIGN (agricultural engineering technology, airline piloting and navigation, applied aviation, computer technology, environmental science, and industrial administration/management), HEALTH PROFESSIONS (health, health care administration, and health science), SOCIAL SCIENCE (criminal justice). Business management, natural resources, and equine science have the largest enrollments.

Required: To graduate, students must complete 120 credit hours, including 40 credits of liberal education and 40 upper-division credits, with a minimum GPA of 2.0. 3 credits of technology are required.

Special: UMC offers cross-registration with the University of North Dakota (Air Force ROTC). The internship or field experience requirement may be completed through on-the-job experience in the private sector, with a government agency, or through other appropriate work experience; a minimum of 450 hours of employment or volunteer assignments is usually required for satisfactory evaluation of the student's progress. Study abroad in more than 200 locations and student-designed majors are available. There are 1 national honor societies, a freshman honors program, and 1 departmental honors programs.

Faculty/Classroom: 558% of faculty are male; 48% are female. All teach undergraduates, 40% do research, and 40% do both. No introductory courses are taught by graduate students. The average class size in an introductory lecture is 25; in a laboratory is 18; and in a regular course is 25.

Admissions: 70% of the 2013-2014 applicants were accepted. The SAT scores for the 2013-2014 freshman class were: Critical Reading--53% below 500, 27% between 500 and 599, 13% between 600 and 699; Math--20% below 500, 53% between 500 and 599, 7% between 600 and 699, and 7% between 700 and 800; Writing--57% below 500, 43% between 500 and 599. The ACT scores were 41% below 21, 29% between 21 and 23, 19% between 24 and 26, 9% between 27 and 28, and 2% above 28. 37% of the current freshmen were in the top fifth of their class; 60% were in the top two fifths. 3 freshmen graduated first in their class.

Requirements: The ACT is recommended, with a minimum score of 21 on the ACT or 980 on the SAT. Applicants must have successfully completed a high school or college preparatory program; the GED is accepted. A minimum 2.0 GPA is required. The strength of the high school curriculum is considered. Students failing to meet minimum requirements of GPA and ACT or SAT scores will be referred to the Admissions Committee for an admission decision. AP and CLEP credits are accepted.

Procedure: Freshmen are admitted fall and spring. Entrance exams should be taken by May 1. There are deferred admissions and rolling admissions plans. Application deadlines are open. Application fee is $30. Notification is sent on a rolling basis. Applications are accepted online.

Transfer: 240 transfer students enrolled in 2012-2013. Transfer students with fewer than 24 earned college credits need to submit an official high school transcript, ACT or SAT scores, and official transcripts from previous colleges. Transfer students with 24 or more semester credits need to submit only official transcripts from previous colleges. A minimum 2.0 college GPA is required. 30 of 120 credits required for the bachelor's degree must be completed at UMC.

Visiting: There are regularly scheduled orientations for prospective students. There are guides for informal visits, visitors may sit in on classes, and stay overnight. To schedule a visit, contact the Admissions Office at umcinfo@umc.edu.

Financial Aid: In 2013-2014, 74% of all full-time freshmen and 70% of continuing full-time students received some form of financial aid. 71% of all full-time freshmen and 64% of continuing full-time students received need-based aid. The average freshman award was $13,370. Need-based scholarships or need-based grants averaged $9,574; need-based self-help aid (loans and jobs) averaged $4,780; and other non-need-based awards and non-need-based scholarships averaged $3,640. Average annual earnings from campus work are $1200. The average financial indebtedness of the 2013 graduate was $27,608. The FAFSA is required. The priority date for freshman financial aid applications for fall entry is March 1.

International Students: There are 145 international students enrolled. The school actively recruits these students. They must take the TOEFL with a minimum score of 520 on the paper-based TOEFL (PBT) or 68 on the Internet-based version (iBT) or take the MELAB, IELTS. Native English speaking students are not required to submit TOEFL scores but are required to submit ACT, SAT, or other standardized college entrance.

Computers: All students may access the system. There are no time limits.

Graduates: From July 1, 2012 to June 30, 2013, 314 bachelor's degrees were awarded. The most popular majors were business management (18%), natural resources (15%), and applied studies (7%). 30 companies recruited on campus in 2012-2013. In an average class, 11% graduate in 3 years or less, 36% graduate in 4 years or less, 42% graduate in 5 years or less, and 53% graduate in 6 years or less. Of the 2012 graduating class, 8% were enrolled in graduate school within 6 months of graduation, and 92% were employed.

Admissions Contact: Peter Phaiah, Vice Chancellor of Student Affairs.
E-Mail: *Info@UMCrookston.edu* Web: *www.umcrookston.edu*

UNIVERSITY OF MINNESOTA/DULUTH D-2

Duluth, MN 55812-2496 **(218) 726-7171**
(800) 232-1339; (218) 726-6394

Full-time: 5126 men, 4402 women	**Faculty:** 454; IIA, -$
Part-time: 566 men, 586 women	**Ph.D.s:** 63%
Graduate: 504 men, 622 women	**Student/Faculty:** 20 to 1
Year: semesters, summer session	**Tuition:** $12,850 ($15,360)
Application Deadline: February 1	**Room & Board:** $7114

Freshman Class: 7456 applied, 5694 accepted, 2105 enrolled
SAT CR/M/W: 510/540/530 **ACT:** 24 **COMPETITIVE+**

The University of Minnesota/Duluth, founded in 1947, is a liberal arts institution offering undergraduate and graduate programs as a campus of the University of Minnesota. There are 5 undergraduate schools and 1 graduate school. In addition to regional accreditation, UMD has baccalaureate program accreditation with AACSB, ABET, ACPE, ASLA, CSAB, CSWE, NASM, and NCATE. The library contains 738,103 volumes, 756,339 microform items, 19,443 audio/video tapes/CDs/DVDs, and subscribes to 65,521 periodicals including electronic. Computerized library services include interlibrary loans, database searching, Internet access, and laptop Internet portals. Special learning facilities include a learning resource center, art gallery, planetarium, radio station, Glensheen historic mansion, child care center, speech and hearing clinic, performing arts centers (theatre and music), and a visual imaging lab. The 250-acre campus is in a suburban area 150 miles north of Minneapolis and St. Paul. Including any residence halls, there are 58 buildings.

Student Life: 82% of undergraduates are from Minnesota. Others are from 28 states, 53 foreign countries, and Canada. 95% are from public schools. 90% are white. The average age of freshmen is 18; all undergraduates, 20. 19% do not continue beyond their first year; 53% remain to graduate.

Housing: 3081 students can be accommodated in college housing, which includes single-sex and coed dorms and on-campus apartments. In addition, there are honors houses. On-campus housing is available on a first-come, first-served basis, and is available on a lottery system for upperclassmen. 72% of students commute. Alcohol is not permitted. All students may keep cars.

Activities: 1% of men belong to 1 local and 3 national fraternities; 1% of women belong to 1 local and 2 national sororities. There are 231 groups on campus, including jazz choir, wind ensemble, art, band, chamber orchestra, cheerleading, chess, choir, chorale, chorus, computers, dance, drama, environmental, ethnic, film, gay, honors, international, jazz band, literary magazine, marching band, musical theater, newspaper, opera, orchestra, pep band, photography, political, professional, radio and TV, religious, social, social service, and student government. Popular campus events include Out Cold Winter Festival, Black History Month, and Hispanic Heritage Month.

Sports: There are 6 intercollegiate sports for men and 8 for women, and 26 intramural sports for men and 26 for women. Facilities include 2 rock-climbing walls, a multipurpose ice center, a football and track-and-field stadium, a baseball park, softball and soccer fields, a field house for track and tennis, a gym for basketball and volleyball, a nearby country club for cross-country and golf, and a cardio and weight facility.

Disabled Students: All of the campus is accessible. Facilities include wheelchair ramps, elevators, special parking, specially equipped restrooms, lowered drinking fountains, lowered telephones, and special housing.

Services: Counseling and information services are available, as is tutoring in some subjects, math, business, economics, sciences, accounting, computer science, accounting, physics, American Sign Language, and writing. There is a reader service for the blind, and remedial math and writing. Workshops and seminars are also offered on study skills, note taking, time management, test-taking strategies, and goal setting.

Campus Safety and Security: Measures include 24-hour foot and vehicle patrol, emergency notification system, self-defense education, and security escort services. There are emergency telephones and lighted pathways/sidewalks.

Programs of Study: UMD confers B.A., B.S., B.A.A., B.Acc., B.A.Sc., B.B.A., B.F.A., B.Mus., B.S.Ch.E., B.S.C.E., B.S.E.C.E., and B.S.M.E. degrees. Master's and doctoral degrees are also awarded. Bachelor's degrees are awarded in AGRICULTURE (environmental studies), BIOLOGICAL SCIENCE (biochemistry, biology/biological science, cell biology, and molecular biology), BUSINESS (accounting, business administration and management, management information systems, and organizational leadership and management), COMMUNICATIONS AND THE ARTS (art, art history and appreciation, communications, dramatic arts, English, graphic design, jazz, music, music performance, Spanish, and studio art), COMPUTER AND PHYSICAL SCIENCE (actuarial science, applied physics, chemistry, computer science, geology, information sciences and systems, mathematics, physics, and statistics), EDUCATION (art education, athletic training, elementary education, foreign languages education, health education, mathematics education, middle school education, music education, physical education, recreation education, science education, secondary education, and social studies education), ENGINEERING AND ENVIRONMENTAL DESIGN (chemical engineering, civil engineering, computer engineering, electrical/electronics engineering, environmental science, industrial engineering, and mechanical engineering), HEALTH PROFESSIONS (hospital administration), SOCIAL SCIENCE (anthropology, criminology, early childhood studies, economics, geography, German area studies, history, interdisciplinary studies, international studies, Native American studies, philosophy, political science/government, prelaw, psychology, sociology, urban studies, and women's studies). Business, sciences, and engineering are the strongest academically. Business administration, biology, and psychology have the largest enrollments.

Required: To graduate, students must complete 120 to 136 semester credits, including 2 courses in college writing, and a liberal education distribution of at least 35 credits in 10 academic areas. At least 4 credits of course work must emphasize cultural diversity, and 4 should emphasize an international perspective.

Special: Students may study abroad in England, Sweden, Finland, and Australia. UMD also offers cross-registration with the College of St. Scholastica and the University of Wisconsin/Superior, internships, work-study programs, a B.A.-B.S. degree in several fields, student-designed majors, and nondegree study. There is 1 national honor society, including Phi Beta Kappa, a freshman honors program, and 28 departmental honors programs.

Faculty/Classroom: 55% of faculty are male; 45% are female. All teach undergraduates. No introductory courses are taught by graduate students. The average class size in an introductory lecture is 60; in a laboratory is 20; and in a regular course is 30.

Admissions: In a recent year,76% of applicants were accepted. The SAT scores for a recent freshman class were: Critical Reading--40% below 500, 34% between 500 and 599, 23% between 600 and 700, and 3% above 700; Math--28% below 500, 46% between 500 and 599, 21% between 600 and 700, and 5% above 700; Writing--36% below 500, 41% between 500 and 599, 21% between 600 and 700, and 2% above 700. The ACT scores were 15% below 21, 33% between 21 and 23, 33% between 24 and 26, 11% between 27 and 28, and 8% above 28. 33% of the current freshmen were in the top fifth of their class; 71% were in the top two fifths.

Requirements: The ACT is required. The ACT Optional Writing test is also required. Applicants must have completed 4 years in English, 3 each in math and sciences, and 2 each in a single second language and social studies. Course work in the visual and performing arts and computer skills is recommended. Students with a GED certificate will be admitted selectively as space permits. AP and CLEP credits are accepted.

Procedure: Freshmen are admitted fall and spring. Entrance exams should be taken at the end of junior year or the beginning of senior year. There is a rolling admissions plan. Applications should be filed by February 1 for fall entry; November 15 for spring entry, along with a $35 fee. Notification is sent on a rolling basis. Applications are accepted online.

Transfer: 544 transfer students enrolled in a recent year. Applicants who have completed 26 or more semester credits must have a minimum 2.0 GPA and a 75% completion ratio; applicants who have attempted fewer than 26 semester credits must have a high school rank at or above the 50th percentile, a 1.8 GPA in their previous college work, and a 75% completion ratio.

Visiting: There are regularly scheduled orientations for prospective students, including an information session, a campus tour, and a chance to meet with admissions counselors, faculty, or coaches and representatives from the five collegiate units. There are guides for informal visits and visitors may sit in on classes. To schedule a visit, contact UMD Office of Admissions.

Financial Aid: In a recent year, 63% of all full-time freshmen and 61% of continuing full-time students received some form of financial aid. 63% of all full-time freshmen and 60% of continuing full-time students received need-based aid. The average freshman award was $10,478. Need-based scholarships or need-based grants averaged $7,658; need-based self-help aid (loans and jobs) averaged $3,740; and other non-need-based awards and non-need-based scholarships averaged $3,391. 14% of undergraduate students work part-time. The average financial indebtedness of a recent graduate was $18,214. The FAFSA is required. The priority date for freshman financial aid applications for fall entry is February 15.

International Students: There are 172 international students enrolled. The school actively recruits these students. They must take the TOEFL with a minimum score of 550 on the paper-based TOEFL (PBT) or 80 on the Internet-based version (iBT).

Computers: Wireless access to the Internet is provided throughout the entire campus. PCs are available at labs throughout campus. There are more than 350 PCs and 114 Macs for student use. All students may access the system 24 hours a day, 7 days a week. There are no time limits. The fee is $71.75. It is strongly recommended that all students have a personal computer. Students enrolled in Labovitz School of Business and Economics, the College of Education and Human Services must have a personal computer.

Graduates: In a recent year, 2168 bachelor's degrees were awarded. The most popular majors were psychology (7%), communication (5%), and finance (5%). In an average class, 1% graduate in 3 years or less, 28% graduate in 4 years or less, 49% graduate in 5 years or less, and 54% graduate in 6 years or less. Of the 2010 graduating class, 12% were enrolled in graduate school within 6 months of graduation, and 75% were employed.

Admissions Contact: Director of Admissions. E-Mail: *umdadmis@d.umn.edu* Web: *www.d.umn.edu*

UNIVERSITY OF MINNESOTA/MORRIS B-3

Morris, MN 56267-2199 **(320) 589-6035**
(888) UMM-EDUC; (320) 589-1673

Full-time: 730 men, 1130 women	**Faculty:** n/av; IIB, -$
Part-time: n/av	**Ph.D.s:** 97%
Graduate: n/av	**Student/Faculty:** n/av
Year: semesters, summer session	**Tuition:** $11,822
Application Deadline: see profile	**Room & Board:** $7620
Freshman Class: n/av	
SAT or ACT: required	

VERY COMPETITIVE

The University of Minnesota/Morris, founded in 1959, is a public liberal arts institution within the University of Minnesota system. The figures in the above capsule and this profile are approximate. In addition to regional accreditation, UMM has baccalaureate program accreditation with NCATE. The library contains 197,220 volumes, 221,216 microform items, 2140 audio/video tapes/CDs/DVDs, and subscribes to 885 periodicals including electronic. Computerized library services include interlibrary loans and database searching. Special learning facilities include a learning resource center, art gallery, radio station, TV station, language lab, observatory, and agricultural experiment station. The 130-acre campus is in a small town 150 miles northwest of Minneapolis. Including any residence halls, there are 36 buildings.

Student Life: 86% of undergraduates are from Minnesota. Others are from 27 states, 17 foreign countries, and Canada. 95% are from public schools. 79% are white. The average age of freshmen is 18; all undergraduates, 21. 18% do not continue beyond their first year; 60% remain to graduate.

Housing: 1032 students can be accommodated in college housing, which includes coed dorms and on-campus apartments. On-campus housing is guaranteed for all 4 years. 60% of students live on campus; of those, 80% remain on campus on weekends. Alcohol is not permitted. All students may keep cars.

Activities: There are no fraternities or sororities. There are 100 groups on campus, including art, band, campus activities, cheerleading, chess, choir, chorus, computers, dance, debate, drama, ethnic, forensics, gay, honors, international, jazz band, literary magazine, mentoring, musical theater, newspaper, orchestra, photography, political, professional, radio and TV, reading instruction, religious, riding, social, social service, student government, swing dancing, and yearbook. Popular campus events include Cultural Heritage Week, Diversity Jam, and Jazz Fest.

Sports: There are 6 intercollegiate sports for men and 10 for women, and 12 intramural sports for men and 12 for women. Facilities include a 4500-seat stadium, a phys ed center, 5 gyms, wrestling, exercise, and weight rooms, an Olympic-size pool, handball and racquetball courts, a track, fields for softball, baseball, soccer, and football, a diving well, a warm-water pool and slide, an indoor track, and a cardiovascular fitness room.

Disabled Students: 70% of the campus is accessible. Facilities include wheelchair ramps, elevators, special parking, specially equipped restrooms, special class scheduling, lowered drinking fountains, and a disability services coordinator. Special learning equipment and services are available through the academic assistance center.

Services: Counseling and information services are available, as is tutoring in every subject. There is a reader service for the blind and remedial math, reading, and writing.

Campus Safety and Security: Measures include 24-hour foot and vehicle patrol, self-defense education, and security escort services. There are shuttle buses, emergency telephones, and lighted pathways/sidewalks.

Programs of Study: UMM confers B.A. degrees. Bachelor's degrees are awarded in BIOLOGICAL SCIENCE (biology/biological science), BUSINESS (management science), COMMUNICATIONS AND THE ARTS (art history and appreciation, dramatic arts, English, French, German, music, Spanish, speech/debate/rhetoric, and studio art), COMPUTER AND PHYSICAL SCIENCE (chemistry, computer science, geology, mathematics, physics, and statistics), EDUCATION (elementary education and secondary education), HEALTH PROFESSIONS (premedicine), SOCIAL SCIENCE (anthropology, economics, European studies, history, Latin American studies, liberal arts/general studies, philosophy, political science/government, prelaw, psychology, social science, sociology, and women's studies). Psychology and sciences are the strongest academically. Education, English, and biology have the largest enrollments.

Required: In addition to 40 semester hours in the major, students are required to complete 60 credits of a general education curriculum, including courses in writing, computing, foreign language or equivalent, and advanced study, as well as courses focusing on the arts, the physical and abstract worlds, and the self and others. All first-year students participate in a freshman seminar, and the cumulative of their major work is presented in the senior seminar, which is a requirement for all seniors.

Special: UMM offers work-study programs, internships, study abroad, dual majors, student-designed majors, nondegree study, pass/fail options, and credit for life, military, and work experience. There is a 3-2 engineering degree with the University of Minnesota at Twin Cities. A competitive, merit-based program that pairs students and professors to undertake creative projects is available. There is a freshman honors program and 100 departmental honors programs.

Faculty/Classroom: 58% of faculty are male; 42% are female. All teach undergraduates, and 89% both teach and do research. The average class size in an introductory lecture is 16; in a laboratory, 16; and in a regular course, 16.

Requirements: The SAT or ACT is required. The ACT Optional Writing test is also required. Applicants should be graduates of an accredited secondary school or have a GED certificate. They must have completed 4 years of English, 3 each of math and science, 2 of a single foreign language, and 1 each of social studies and American history. A GPA of 3.0 is required. AP and CLEP credits are accepted. Important factors in the admissions decision are leadership record, extracurricular activities record, and advanced placement or honors courses.

Procedure: Freshmen are admitted fall and spring. Entrance exams should be taken before December 1 of the senior year. There are deferred admissions and rolling admissions plans. Check with the school for current application deadlines and fee. Applications are accepted online.

Transfer: Applicants must complete the application for admission, submit all college transcripts, and have maintained a minimum GPA of 2.5. 30 of 120 credits required for the bachelor's degree must be completed at UMM.

Visiting: There are regularly scheduled orientations for prospective students, including a campus tour, lunch with faculty, a session with admissions staff, and a student panel. There are guides for informal visits, and visitors may sit in on classes and stay overnight. To schedule a visit, contact the Admissions Office.

Financial Aid: The FAFSA is required. Check with the school for current application deadlines.

International Students: They must take either the SAT or the TOEFL.

Computers: All students may access the system 24 hours per day. There are no time limits and no fees.

Admissions Contact: Director of Admissions. E-Mail: *admissions@morris.umn.edu* Web: *www.morris.umn.edu*

UNIVERSITY OF MINNESOTA/TWIN CITIES C-4

Minneapolis, MN 55455 **(612) 625-2008**
(800) 752-1000; (612) 625-1693

Full-time: 14135 men, 14805 women	**Faculty:** n/av; 1, -$
Part-time: 2656 men, 2853 women	**Ph.D.s:** n/av
Graduate: 8259 men, 8818 women	**Student/Faculty:** n/av
Year: semesters, summer session	**Tuition:** n/av
Application Deadline:	**Room & Board:** n/av
Freshman Class: n/av	

HIGHLY COMPETITIVE

University of Minnesota/Twin Cities, founded in 1851, is a land-grant institution offering programs in liberal and fine arts, physical and biological sciences, health sciences, education, natural resources, human ecology, business, agriculture, and engineering and professional training in law, medicine, dentistry, pharmacy, and veterinary medicine. There are 11 undergraduate schools and 16 graduate schools. In addition to regional accreditation, The U has baccalaureate program accreditation with AACSB, ABET, ABFSE, ACEJMC, ADA, APTA, ASLA, CSWE, FIDER, NAAB, NASM, NCATE, NLN, and SAF. The 14 libraries contain 6.2 million volumes, 5.4 million microform items, 500,000 audio/video tapes/CDs/DVDs, and subscribe to 48,105 periodicals including electronic. Computerized library services include interlibrary loans, database searching, and Internet access. Special learning facilities include an art gallery, natural history museum, planetarium, radio station, and TV station. The 2000-acre campus is in an urban area within both Minneapolis and St. Paul. Including any residence halls, there are 205 buildings.

Student Life: 75% of undergraduates are from Minnesota. Others are from 50 states, 136 foreign countries, and Canada. 85% are from public schools. 67% are White; 12% Foreign. The average age of freshmen is 18; all undergraduates, 21. 10% do not continue beyond their first year; 75% remain to graduate.

Housing: 6930 students can be accommodated in college housing, which includes single-sex and coed dorms, on-campus apartments, off-campus apartments, and married student housing. In addition, there are honors houses, special-interest houses, fraternity houses, sorority houses, cooperative housing. On-campus housing is guaranteed for the freshman year only, is available on a first-come, first-served basis, and is available on a lottery system for upperclassmen. 77% of students commute. Alcohol is not permitted. All students may keep cars.

Activities: There are 600 groups on campus, including art, band, cheerleading, chess, choir, chorale, chorus, computers, dance, debate, drama, drill team, environmental, ethnic, film, gay, honors, international, jazz band, literary magazine, marching band, musical theater, newspaper, orchestra, pep band, photography, political, professional, radio and TV, religious, social, social service, student government, and symphony. Popular campus events include Homecoming.

Sports: There are 12 intercollegiate sports for men and 11 for women, and 16 intramural sports for men and 16 for women. Facilities include an outdoor stadium, 3 gyms, 2 field houses, a hockey rink, an Olympic-size aquatic center, and a student recreation center.

Disabled Students: Facilities include wheelchair ramps, elevators, special parking, specially equipped restrooms, special class scheduling, lowered drinking fountains, lowered telephones, special housing. listening devices, TTY and volume-control phones, print enlargers, and adaptive computers. In addition, support groups and counselors provide assistance with all areas of university life and career planning.

Services: Counseling and information services are available, as is tutoring in every subject. There is a reader service for the blind, and remedial math, reading, and writing. test proctoring, and sign language interpreters.

Campus Safety and Security: Measures include 24-hour foot and vehicle patrol, emergency notification system, self-defense education, and security escort services. There are shuttle buses, emergency telephones, lighted pathways/sidewalks, a 20-member university police force, and blue-light phone centers.

Programs of Study: The U confers B.A., B.S., B.A.E.M., B.C.E., B.S.Ch., B.Ch.E., B.Comp.Sci., B.E.E., B.F.A., B.G.E., B.I.S., B.Materials Sci.E., B.S. Mathematics, B.M.E., B.S.Bus., B.S.G., B.S. in Astrophysics, B.S. in Geophysics, B.S.N., B.S. Statistics., B.A.S., B.A.Sc., B.B.A.E., B.B.P.E., B.Bm.E., B.Comp.E., B.D.A., B.E.D., B.Mus. and B.S.Phys. degrees. Master's and doctoral degrees are also awarded. Bachelor's degrees are awarded in AGRICULTURE (agricultural business management, agricultural economics, animal science, fishing and fisheries, forestry production and processing, forestry and related sciences, and natural resource management), BIOLOGICAL SCIENCE (biochemistry, biology/biological science, botany, cell biology, ecology, evolutionary biology, genetics, microbiology, nutrition, physiology, and wildlife biology), BUSINESS (accounting, business administration and management, management science, marketing/retailing/merchandising, recreation and leisure services, recreational facilities management, and retailing), COMMUNICATIONS AND THE ARTS (apparel design, art, art history and appreciation, Chinese, classical languages, dance, English, film arts, French, German, Greek, Hebrew, Italian, Japanese, languages, Latin, linguistics, music, Russian, Scandinavian languages, Spanish, speech/debate/rhetoric, and studio art), COMPUTER AND PHYSICAL SCIENCE (actuarial science, astrophysics, chemistry, computer science, geology, geophysics and seismology, mathematics, physics, and statistics), EDUCATION (agricultural education, art education, bilingual/bicultural education, business education, early childhood education, elementary education, English education, home economics education, industrial arts education, mathematics education, music education, physical education, science education, social studies education, and teaching English as a second/foreign language (TESOL/TEFOL)), ENGINEERING AND ENVIRONMENTAL DESIGN (aerospace studies, architecture, bioengineering, chemical engineering, civil engineering, electrical/electronics engineering, environmental design, geological engineering, industrial engineering, interior design, landscape architecture/design, materials engineering, materials science, mechanical engineering, and metallurgical engineering), HEALTH PROFESSIONS (dental hygiene, medical laboratory technology, music therapy, nursing, occupational therapy, pharmacy, physical therapy, predentistry, premedicine, prepharmacy, preveterinary science, and speech pathology/audiology), SOCIAL SCIENCE (African studies, African American studies, American Indian studies, American studies, anthropology, Asian/Oriental studies, child psychology/development, East Asian studies, economics, food science, geography, history, humanities, international relations, Mexican-American/Chicano studies, Middle Eastern studies, philosophy, political science/government, prelaw, psychology, Russian and Slavic studies, sociology, South Asian studies, textiles and clothing, urban studies, and women's studies). Engineering, psychology, economics are the strongest academically and have the largest enrollments.

Required: To graduate, students must complete 120 to 130 semester credits, including 45 in the major, with a minimum GPA of 2.0. Distribution requirements include course work in the 4 areas of communication, language, and symbolic systems, physical and biological sciences, the individual and society, and artistic expression. Other requirements vary by program.

Special: The university offers cooperative programs, cross-registration with the Minnesota Community College system, internships, study abroad in 65 countries, work-study programs both on and off campus, a B.A.-B.S.

degree in all majors, a general studies degree, and dual and student-designed majors. Pass/fail options and credit for life, military, or work experience are available. There are 21 national honor societies, including Phi Beta Kappa, a freshman honors program, and 8 departmental honors programs.

Faculty/Classroom: 58% of faculty are male; 42% are female. All teach and do research. No introductory courses are taught by graduate students.

Admissions: 73% of the current freshmen were in the top fifth of their class; 98% were in the top two fifths.

Requirements: The SAT or ACT is required. The university uses a formula index in evaluating high school rank and ACT test scores. A portfolio is required for studio arts and architecture, an audition for music, and an interview for architecture and education. A high school diploma is required; the GED is accepted. AP and CLEP credits are accepted. Important factors in the admissions decision are advanced placement or honors courses, evidence of special talent, and leadership record.

Procedure: Freshmen are admitted to all sessions. Entrance exams should be taken by the end of the junior year or October/November/December of the senior year. There are early admissions, deferred admissions, and rolling admissions plans. Application deadlines are open. Application fee is $55. Notification is sent on a rolling basis. Applications are accepted online.

Transfer: Admission requirements vary by major/program, with a minimum 2.2 GPA needed for consideration. College transcripts are required. 30 of 120 credits required for the bachelor's degree must be completed at The U.

Visiting: There are regularly scheduled orientations for prospective students. There are guides for informal visits, visitors may sit in on classes, and stay overnight. To schedule a visit, contact the Visit Line at (612) 625-0000.

Financial Aid: In 2013-2014, 52% of all full-time freshmen students received some form of financial aid. The average freshman award was $13,574. Need-based scholarships or need-based grants averaged $9,875; and need-based self-help aid (loans and jobs) averaged $5,963. The FAFSA and the college's own financial statement are required. Check with the school for current application deadlines.

International Students: They must take the TOEFL or MELAB and the college's own test, Minnesota Battery and the Institutional TOEFL. They must also take the SAT or ACT. ACT for residents of Minnesota and neighboring states, SAT for residents of other states.

Computers: All students may access the system 24 hours a day, 7 days a week. 2 hours per session if there are others waiting or signed on. There is a fee.

Graduates: From July 1, 2012 to June 30, 2013, 7559 bachelor's degrees were awarded. The most popular majors were psychology (4%), journalism (3%), and communication studies (3%). In an average class, 5% graduate in 3 years or less, 59% graduate in 4 years or less, 76% graduate in 5 years or less, and 76% graduate in 6 years or less.

Admissions Contact: Director of Admissions. E-Mail: *admissions@tc.umn.edu*. Web: *www.umn.edu*

UNIVERSITY OF SAINT THOMAS C-4

St. Paul, MN 55105 (651) 962-6150
(800) 328-6819, ext. 2-6150; (651) 962-6160

Full-time: 3217 men, 2877 women	**Faculty:** n/av
Part-time: 137 men, 119 women	**Ph.D.s:** n/av
Graduate: 1896 men, 1973 women	**Student/Faculty:** 15 to 1
Year: 4-1-4, summer session	**Tuition:** $35,305
Application Deadline:	**Room & Board:** $8986
Freshman Class: 5540 applied, 4774 accepted, 1368 enrolled	
SAT CR/M: 580/590 **ACT:** 25	**VERY COMPETITIVE**

The University of Saint Thomas, founded in 1885, is a private liberal arts institution affiliated with the Roman Catholic Church. There are 4 undergraduate schools and 8 graduate schools. In addition to regional accreditation, Saint Thomas has baccalaureate program accreditation with AACSB, ABET, CSWE, NASM, and NCATE. The 5 libraries contain 695,137 volumes, 1.1 million microform items, 76,383 audio/video tapes/CDs/DVDs, and subscribe to 193,510 periodicals including electronic. Computerized library services include interlibrary loans, database searching, and Wi-Fi capability. Special learning facilities include an art gallery, radio station, and TV station. The 78-acre campus is in an urban area 5 miles west of St. Paul and 5 miles east of Minneapolis.

Student Life: 78% of undergraduates are from Minnesota. Others are from states, and Canada. The average age of freshmen is 18; all undergraduates, 21. 12% do not continue beyond their first year; 88% remain to graduate.

Housing: College-sponsored housing includes single-sex dorms, on-campus apartments, and off-campus apartments. In addition, there are special-interest houses, chemical-free lifestyle, first-year experience, women in science housing, special housing for disabled students, theme housing, wellness housing, and housing options for Catholic women and Catholic men. On-campus housing is available on a first-come, first-served basis, and is available on a lottery system for upperclassmen. 61% of students commute. All students may keep cars.

Activities: There are no fraternities or sororities. There are 140 groups on campus, including band, choir, chorus, computers, dance, drama, ethnic, gay, honors, international, jazz band, literary magazine, newspaper, pep band, political, professional, radio and TV, religious, social, social service, student government, and yearbook.

Sports: There are 10 intercollegiate sports for men and 10 for women. Facilities include 180,000 square feet 2,000-seat basketball and volleyball arena, aquatic center containing an eight-lane swimming pool, diving area, and spectator seating field house with 200-meter, six-lane track, beneath the field house are locker rooms, meeting rooms, training rooms and other support facilities. West wing contains a fitness center, weight room and aerobics rooms on the first floor, and offices, classrooms and labs on the second and third floors.

Campus Safety and Security: Measures include 24-hour foot and vehicle patrol, emergency notification system, and security escort services. There are shuttle buses, emergency telephones, lighted pathways/sidewalks, and controlled access to dorms/residences.

Programs of Study: Saint Thomas confers B.A., B.S., B.S.M.E., B.S.E.E. and B.M. degrees. Master's and doctoral degrees are also awarded. Bachelor's degrees are awarded in Business is the largest.

Special: There are a freshman honors program.

Faculty/Classroom: No introductory courses are taught by graduate students.

Admissions: 86% of the 2013-2014 applicants were accepted.

Requirements: The SAT is recommended. AP and CLEP credits are accepted.

Procedure: Freshmen are admitted fall and spring. Entrance exams should be taken by the fall of the senior year. There are deferred admissions and rolling admissions plans. Application deadlines are open. Applications are accepted online.

Transfer: 271 transfer students enrolled in 2012-2013. Transfer applicants must have a minimum GPA of 2.3 in transferable college credits. 32 of 132 credits required for the bachelor's degree must be completed at Saint Thomas.

Visiting: There are regularly scheduled orientations for prospective students. There are guides for informal visits, visitors may sit in on classes, and stay overnight. To schedule a visit, contact the Visit Coordinator.

Financial Aid: The FAFSA is required. Check with the school for current application deadlines.

International Students: They must take the TOEFL or MELAB. They must also take the SAT or ACT.

Computers: All students may access the system any time. There are no time limits and no fees.

Graduates: From July 1, 2012 to June 30, 2013, 1283 bachelor's degrees were awarded.

Admissions Contact: Marla Friederichs, Associate Vice President for Enrollment Management. E-Mail: *admissions@stthomas.edu* Web: *www.stthomas.edu*

WINONA STATE UNIVERSITY D-5

Winona, MN 55987 (507) 457-5100
(800) DIAL-WSU; (507) 457-5620

Full-time: 2899 men, 4452 women	**Faculty:** n/av; IIA, -$
Part-time: 304 men, 599 women	**Ph.D.s:** n/av
Graduate: 122 men, 379 women	**Student/Faculty:** 24 to 1
Year: semesters, summer session	**Tuition:** $8730 ($14,230)
Application Deadline: 07 12	**Room & Board:** $7800
Freshman Class: 7212 applied, 4381 accepted, 1650 enrolled	
ACT: 23	**COMPETITIVE**

Winona State University, founded in 1858, is a mid-sized comprehensive regional university that is part of the Minnesota State Colleges and Universities system. There are 5 undergraduate schools and one graduate school. In addition to regional accreditation, WSU has baccalaureate program accreditation with AACSB, ABET, CSWE, NASM, NCATE, and TEAC. The library contains 479,521 volumes, 27,501 microform items, 21,446 audio/video tapes/CDs/DVDs, and subscribes to 34,393 periodicals including electronic. Computerized library services include interlibrary loans, database searching, Internet access, and Wi-Fi capability. Special learning facilities include an art gallery and radio station. The 125-acre campus is in a small town 120 miles southeast of Minneapolis and St. Paul. Including any residence halls, there are 35 buildings.

Student Life: 69% of undergraduates are from Minnesota. Others are from 36 states, 42 foreign countries, and Canada. 87% are White. The average age of freshmen is 18; all undergraduates, 22. 22% do not continue beyond their first year; 56% remain to graduate.

Housing: 2722 students can be accommodated in college housing, which

includes single-sex and coed dorms and on-campus apartments. In addition, there are special-interest houses. On-campus housing is guaranteed for the freshman year only, is available on a first-come, and first-served basis. 71% of students commute. Alcohol is not permitted. All students may keep cars.

Activities: There are 155 groups on campus, including art, band, cheerleading, chess, choir, chorale, chorus, computers, dance, debate, drama, environmental, ethnic, film, forensics, gay, honors, international, jazz band, literary magazine, musical theater, newspaper, orchestra, pep band, photography, political, professional, radio and TV, religious, social, social service, student government, and symphony. Popular campus events include Homecoming.

Sports: There are 5 intercollegiate sports for men and 10 for women, and 16 intramural sports for men and 16 for women. Facilities include a 4000-seat stadium, a baseball field, a softball field, 8 gyms in multiples buildings, a weight room, a gymnastic practice area, a swimming pool, 5 handball/ racquetball courts, a cardio-fitness center with 60 machines, and a walking/jogging inside track.

Disabled Students: 4% of the campus is accessible. Facilities include wheelchair ramps, elevators, special parking, specially equipped restrooms, special class scheduling, lowered drinking fountains, lowered telephones, and special housing.

Services: Counseling and information services are available, as is tutoring in most subjects.

Campus Safety and Security: Measures include 24-hour foot and vehicle patrol, emergency notification system, self-defense education, and security escort services. There are shuttle buses, emergency telephones, lighted pathways/sidewalks, and controlled access to dorms/residences.

Programs of Study: WSU confers B.A., B.S., B.S.E., B.S.N., B.S.W., B.A.S. and B.M. degrees. Associate, master's, and doctoral degrees are also awarded. Bachelor's degrees are awarded in BIOLOGICAL SCIENCE (biology/biological science), BUSINESS (accounting, banking and finance, business administration and management, business economics, human resources/organizational mgmt, management information systems, marketing, and recreation and leisure services), COMMUNICATIONS AND THE ARTS (broadcasting, communication studies, dramatic arts, English, fine arts, graphic design, journalism, music, music performance, Spanish, and speech/debate/rhetoric), COMPUTER AND PHYSICAL SCIENCE (applied science, chemistry, computer science, earth science, earth science / adolescence education, geology, mathematics, physics, and statistics), EDUCATION (art education, athletic training, business education, early childhood education, elementary education, foreign languages education, health education, mathematics education, music education, physical education, science education, secondary education, social studies education, special education, specific learning disabilities, and teaching English as a second/foreign language (TESOL/TEFOL)), ENGINEERING AND ENVIRONMENTAL DESIGN (materials engineering and preengineering), HEALTH PROFESSIONS (community health work, cytotechnology, exercise science, health care administration, movement science, nursing, predentistry, premedicine, preoptometry, prepharmacy, prephysical therapy, prepodiatry, preveterinary science, and public health), SOCIAL SCIENCE (criminal justice, economics, (Social Science) Global Studies, history, paralegal studies, physical fitness/movement, political science/government, prelaw, psychology, public administration, social work, sociology, and women & gender studies). Nursing, education, and engineering are the strongest academically. Nursing, elementary education, and biology have the largest enrollments.

Required: To graduate, students must complete 120 credit hours with a minimum GPA of 2.0. General education requirements include 3 credits in public speaking, 3 credits in English, 7 credits in natural sciences, 3 in math and logical reasoning, 9 in history and social sciences, 9 in humanities and fine arts, and 2 in phys ed. Majors average 46 credits, and some require a capstone experience.

Special: WSU offers cross-registration with St. Mary's University, study abroad in 12 countries, internships, work-study programs, student-designed majors, dual majors, pass/fail options, and credit for life, military, and work experience. Students may earn accelerated degrees in all majors and a general studies degree. There are 9 national honor societies and 6 departmental honors programs.

Faculty/Classroom: 38% of faculty are male; 62% are female. No introductory courses are taught by graduate students. The average class size in a regular course is 31.

Admissions: 61% of the 2013-2014 applicants were accepted. The ACT scores were 28% below 21, 41% between 21 and 23, 22% between 24 and 26, 6% between 27 and 28, and 3% above 28. 15% of the current freshmen were in the top fifth of their class; 23% were in the top two fifths.

Requirements: The ACT is required. Candidates should have completed 4 units of English, 1 of which may be speech; 3 each of math and science; 2 each of a foreign language and social studies; 1 of history; and 1 elective, preferably in world culture, the arts, or computer science. AP and CLEP credits are accepted. Important factors in the admissions decision are recommendations by school officials.

Procedure: Freshmen are admitted fall, spring, and summer. Entrance exams should be taken in the junior year. There is a rolling admissions plan. Applications should be filed by July for fall entry; 11 22 for spring entry. The fall 2013 application fee was $20. Applications are accepted online.

Transfer: 633 transfer students enrolled in 2012-2013. Applicants must have completed 24 semester hours of credit with a minimum GPA of 2.4. 30 of 120 credits required for the bachelor's degree must be completed at WSU.

Visiting: There are regularly scheduled orientations for prospective students, including daily tours and admissions visits from October through January on select Saturday mornings. There are guides for informal visits and visitors may sit in on classes. To schedule a visit, contact the Office of Admissions.

Financial Aid: In 2013-2014, 88% of all full-time freshmen and 81% of continuing full-time students received some form of financial aid. 61% of all full-time freshmen and 61% of continuing full-time students received need-based aid. 27% of undergraduate students work part-time. Average annual earnings from campus work are $2200. The average financial indebtedness of the 2013 graduate was $33,610. The FAFSA is required. The priority date for freshman financial aid applications for fall entry is May 1.

International Students: There are 273 international students enrolled. The school actively recruits these students. They must take the TOEFL with a minimum score of 520 on the paper-based TOEFL (PBT) or 68 on the Internet-based version (iBT).

Computers: All students may access the system 24 hours a day. There are no time limits. The fee is $103.

Graduates: From July 1, 2012 to June 30, 2013, 1672 bachelor's degrees were awarded. The most popular majors were nursing (15%), business administration (8%), and biology (6%). In an average class, 31% graduate in 4 years or less, 48% graduate in 5 years or less, and 56% graduate in 6 years or less. Of the 2012 graduating class, 69% were employed within 6 months of graduation.

Admissions Contact: Carl Stange, Director of Admissions. E-Mail: *admissions@winona.edu* Web: *www.winona.edu*

MISSISSIPPI

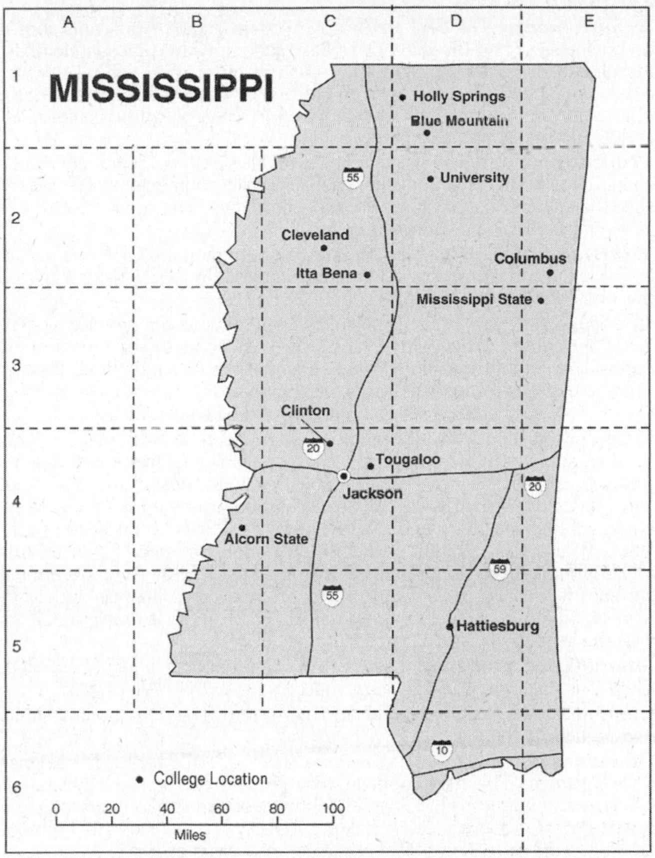

ALCORN STATE UNIVERSITY B-4

Alcorn State, MS 39096 **(601) 877-6147; (601) 877-6347**

Full-time: 980 men, 1725 women
Part-time: 60 men, 245 women
Graduate: 165 men, 505 women
Year: semesters, summer session
Application Deadline: open
Freshman Class: n/av
SAT: recommended

Faculty: n/av; IIB, --$
Ph.D.s: 64%
Student/Faculty: 17 to 1
Tuition: $4500 ($10,000)
Room & Board: $5000

ACT: required **COMPETITIVE**

Alcorn State University, founded in 1871, is a public institution offering programs in agriculture, the arts and sciences, business, engineering, and nursing. The figures in the above capsule and in this profile are approximate. There are 6 undergraduate schools and one graduate school. In addition to regional accreditation, has baccalaureate program accreditation with AACSB, ADA, AHEA, NASM, NCATE, and NLN. The library contains 225,423 volumes, 581,883 microform items, 17,200 audio/video tapes/CDs/DVDs, and subscribes to 40,741 periodicals including electronic. Computerized library services include interlibrary loans, database searching, Internet access, and Wi-Fi capability. Special learning facilities include a radio station. The 1756-acre campus is in a rural area 45 miles south of Vicksburg and 7 miles west of Lorman. Including any residence halls, there are 128 buildings.

Student Life: 81% of undergraduates are from Mississippi. Others are from 32 states, 13 foreign countries, and Canada. 95% are from public schools. 91% are African American. The average age of freshmen is 24; all undergraduates, 25. 28% do not continue beyond their first year; 45% remain to graduate.

Housing: 2495 students can be accommodated in college housing, which includes single-sex dorms. In addition, there are honors houses. On-campus housing is guaranteed for all 4 years. 56% of students commute. Alcohol is not permitted. All students may keep cars.

Activities: 7% of men belong to 4 local and 4 national fraternities; 10% of women belong to 4 local and 4 national sororities. There are 79 groups on campus, including band, cheerleading, choir, chorus, dance, drama, honors, jazz band, marching band, newspaper, photography, radio and TV, religious, student government, and yearbook. Popular campus events include High School Day and Career Development Day.

Sports: There are 8 intercollegiate sports for men and 10 for women, and 9 intramural sports for men and 9 for women. Facilities include a 10,000-seat stadium and a 5000-seat gym.

Disabled Students: 15% of the campus is accessible. Facilities include wheelchair ramps, elevators, special parking, specially equipped rest-rooms, and lowered drinking fountains.

Services: Counseling and information services are available, as is tutoring in most subjects. There is remedial math, reading, and writing.

Campus Safety and Security: Measures include 24-hour foot and vehicle patrol. There are lighted pathways/sidewalks.

Programs of Study: confers B.A., B.S., B.M., B.M.E. and B.S.N. degrees. Associate and master's degrees are also awarded. Bachelor's degrees are awarded in AGRICULTURE (agricultural business management and agricultural economics), BIOLOGICAL SCIENCE (biology/biological science and nutrition), BUSINESS (accounting, business administration and management, and recreation and leisure services), COMMUNICATIONS AND THE ARTS (communications, English, and music), COMPUTER AND PHYSICAL SCIENCE (applied science, chemistry, computer science, and mathematics), EDUCATION (elementary education and special education), ENGINEERING AND ENVIRONMENTAL DESIGN (computer technology), HEALTH PROFESSIONS (health science, nursing, and sports medicine), SOCIAL SCIENCE (child psychology/development, criminal justice, economics, history, political science/government, psychology, social work, and sociology). Business administration, biology, and elementary education have the largest enrollments.

Required: To graduate, students must complete at least 128 semester hours with a minimum GPA of 2.0. Core requirements include 12 hours of social science, 9 each of natural science and creative arts, 6 of English, 4 of phys ed or military science, and 3 each of math and oral communications, as well as 1 of student adjustment.

Special: The university offers, internships, and work-study programs. There are 1 national honor societies, including Phi Beta Kappa, a freshman honors program, and 5 departmental honors programs.

Faculty/Classroom: 55% of faculty are male; 45% are female. 92% teach undergraduates. No introductory courses are taught by graduate students.

Requirements: The ACT is required. The SAT is recommended. In addition, students must have graduated from an accredited high school with at least a C average and have completed 15 1/2 units of a college prep curriculum. A GPA of 2.0 is required. AP and CLEP credits are accepted.

Procedure: Freshmen are admitted to all sessions. Entrance exams should be taken so that scores may be submitted at the time application is made. There are early decision, deferred admissions, and rolling admissions plans. Application deadlines are open. Notification is sent on a rolling basis.

Transfer: 286 transfer students enrolled in 2012-2013. Applicants must have at least 6 hours each of composition and lab sciences, 3 hours of college algebra or above, and 9 other transferable elective hours and must have maintained an overall minimum GPA of 2.0. 104 of 128 credits required for the bachelor's degree must be completed at Alcorn.

Visiting: There are regularly scheduled orientations for prospective students. There are guides for informal visits, visitors may sit in on classes, and stay overnight.

Financial Aid: In 2013-2014, 42% of all full-time freshmen students received some form of financial aid. 31% of all full-time freshmen students received need-based aid. The average freshman award was $6,199. Need-based scholarships or need-based grants averaged $3,974 ($4,310 maximum); need-based self-help aid (loans and jobs) averaged $3,308 ($3,500 maximum); non-need-based athletic scholarships averaged $9,192 ($14,696 maximum); and other non-need-based awards and non-need-based scholarships averaged $5,162 ($9,550 maximum). 27% of undergraduate students work part-time. Average annual earnings from campus work are $1700. The average financial indebtedness of the 2013 graduate was $22,842. is a member of CSS. The FAFSA and the college's own financial statement are required. Check with the school for current application deadlines.

International Students: There are 30 international students enrolled. The school actively recruits these students. They must take the TOEFL with a minimum score of 525 on the paper-based TOEFL (PBT). They must also take the SAT or ACT, scoring 21.

Computers: All students may access the system. There are no time limits and no fees.

Graduates: From July 1, 2012 to June 30, 2013, 399 bachelor's degrees were awarded. The most popular majors were general studies (20%), biology (12%), and nursing (9%). 214 companies recruited on campus in 2012-2013. In an average class, 45% graduate in 6 years or less. Of the 2012 graduating class, 38% were enrolled in graduate school within 6 months of graduation, and 99% were employed.

Admissions Contact: Emanuel F. Barnes, Director of Admissions. E-Mail: *ebarnes@alcorn.edu* Web: *www.alcorn.edu*

BELHAVEN UNIVERSITY C-4

Jackson, MS 39202 (601) 968-5940
(800) 960-5940; (601) 968-8946

Full-time: 556 men, 685 women **Faculty:** n/av
Part-time: 425 men, 910 women **Ph.D.s:** 55%
Graduate: 376 men, 897 women **Student/Faculty:** 13 to 1
Year: semesters, summer session **Tuition:** $19,970
Application Deadline: **Room & Board:** $7200
Freshman Class: 2280 applied, 1074 accepted, 324 enrolled
SAT CR/M: 530/500 **ACT:** 22 **COMPETITIVE**

Belhaven University, formerly Belhaven College, was founded in 1883 and is a private liberal arts institution with a Presbyterian heritage. There is one graduate school. In addition to regional accreditation, Belhaven has baccalaureate program accreditation with NASAD and NASM. The library contains 118,374 volumes, 11,867 microform items, 3,815 audio/video tapes/CDs/DVDs, and subscribes to 15,117 periodicals including electronic. Computerized library services include interlibrary loans, database searching, Internet access, and Wi-Fi capability. Special learning facilities include an art gallery. The 42-acre campus is in an urban area in Jackson, MS. Including any residence halls, there are 17 buildings.

Student Life: 70% of undergraduates are from Mississippi. Others are from 29 states, and 28 foreign countries. 44% are African American; 38% White. 87% are Protestant. The average age of freshmen is 28; all undergraduates, 31. 28% do not continue beyond their first year; 57% remain to graduate.

Housing: 556 students can be accommodated in college housing, which includes single-sex dorms. On-campus housing is guaranteed for all 4 years, is available on a first-come, and first-served basis. 75% of students commute. Alcohol is not permitted. All students may keep cars.

Activities: There are no fraternities or sororities. There are 24 groups on campus, including art, band, cheerleading, choir, chorus, dance, drama, ethnic, honors, jazz band, literary magazine, marching band, musical theater, newspaper, orchestra, political, professional, religious, social service, student government, and yearbook. Popular campus events include Singing Christmas Tree, Concert and Lecture Series and Lake Day.

Sports: There are 8 intercollegiate sports for men and 7 for women, and 6 intramural sports for men and 6 for women. Facilities include a gym, 5 tennis courts, a lake, an intramural and soccer field, a baseball field, a football/soccer practice field, an athletic training facility, and an exercise, weight, and conditioning complex.

Disabled Students: 25% of the campus is accessible. Facilities include wheelchair ramps, elevators, special parking, specially equipped restrooms, special class scheduling, lowered drinking fountains, and special housing.

Services: There is remedial math, reading, and writing. Study halls for athletes.

Campus Safety and Security: Measures include 24-hour foot and vehicle patrol and security escort services. There are lighted pathways/sidewalks and controlled access to dorms/residences.

Programs of Study: Belhaven confers B.A., B.S., B.A.A., B.B.A., B.F.A., B.H.A. and B.S.M. degrees. Associate and master's degrees are also awarded. Bachelor's degrees are awarded in BIOLOGICAL SCIENCE (biology/biological science), BUSINESS (accounting and business administration and management), COMMUNICATIONS AND THE ARTS (art, arts administration/management, ballet, broadcasting, communications, creative writing, dance, dramatic arts, English, and music), COMPUTER AND PHYSICAL SCIENCE (chemistry, computer science, information sciences and systems, and mathematics), EDUCATION (athletic training and elementary education), HEALTH PROFESSIONS (exercise science and sports medicine), SOCIAL SCIENCE (biblical studies, history, humanities, interdisciplinary studies, international studies, philosophy, political science/government, psychology, religious music, and social work). Biology and chemistry is the strongest academically. Business administration and education have the largest enrollments.

Required: Requirements for graduation vary by degree, but students must complete at least 124 semester hours, including 25 hours of World View Curriculum courses, with a minimum 2.0 GPA.

Special: Students may participate in various internships, including one in Washington, D.C., or in 6 countries through the study-travel program. Belhaven also offers accelerated degree programs, dual majors, student-designed majors, nondegree study, pass/fail options, a 3-2 engineering degree with Mississippi State University, and work-study. 2 1-month summer sessions and 2 2-week minisessions offer additional opportunities for credit. There are 7 national honor societies, a freshman honors program, and 17 departmental honors programs.

Faculty/Classroom: 58% of faculty are male; 32% are female. All teach undergraduates. No introductory courses are taught by graduate students. The average class size in a regular course is 18.

Admissions: 47% of the 2013-2014 applicants were accepted. The SAT scores for the 2013-2014 freshman class were: Critical Reading--39% below 500, 31% between 500 and 599, 27% between 600 and 699, and 3% between 700 and 800; Math--45% below 500, 44% between 500 and 599, and 11% between 600 and 699. The ACT scores were 42% below 21, 28% between 21 and 23, 16% between 24 and 26, 7% between 27 and 28, and 7% above 28.

Requirements: The SAT or ACT is recommended. Applicants should be graduates of an accredited secondary school, with 16 academic units, including 4 of English, 2 of math, 1 each of history and natural science, a recommended 2 of a foreign language, and 6 of electives. A personal recommendation and essay are also required. A GPA of 2.0 is required. AP and CLEP credits are accepted.

Procedure: Freshmen are admitted to all sessions. Entrance exams should be taken in the junior year. There is a rolling admissions plan. Check with the school for current application deadlines. The application fee is $25. Applications are accepted online.

Transfer: Transfer applicants must have a minimum 2.0 GPA and submit all college transcripts. 31 of 124 credits required for the bachelor's degree must be completed at Belhaven.

Visiting: There are regularly scheduled orientations for prospective students, including Preview Days, which allow students to see the campus, meet students, interview with faculty and admissions, and attend classes. There are guides for informal visits, visitors may sit in on classes, and stay overnight. To schedule a visit, contact the Admissions Office.

Financial Aid: In 2013-2014, 57% of all full-time freshmen students received some form of financial aid. 56% of all full-time freshmen students received need-based aid. The average freshman award was $12,563. Need-based scholarships or need-based grants averaged $4,587; need-based self-help aid (loans and jobs) averaged $4,730; non-need-based athletic scholarships averaged $13,656; and other non-need-based awards and non-need-based scholarships averaged $11,436. Average annual earnings from campus work are $2031. The average financial indebtedness of the 2013 graduate was $31,000. The FAFSA is required. Check with the school for current application deadlines.

International Students: There are 82 international students enrolled. They must take the TOEFL. They must also take the SAT or ACT.

Computers: All students may access the system. There are no time limits and no fees.

Graduates: From July 1, 2012 to June 30, 2013, 475 bachelor's degrees were awarded. The most popular majors were business administration (37%), social sciences (11%), and healthcare administration and management (8%). In an average class, 32% graduate in 4 years or less, 47% graduate in 5 years or less, and 49% graduate in 6 years or less.

Admissions Contact: Suzanne Sullivan, Assistant VP for University Advancement. E-Mail: *admission@belhaven.edu* Web: *www.belhaven.edu*

BLUE MOUNTAIN COLLEGE D-1

Blue Mountain, MS 38610 (662) 685-4771
(800) 235-0136; (662) 685-4776

Full-time: 193 men, 260 women **Faculty:** 34
Part-time: 24 men, 43 women **Ph.D.s:** 76%
Graduate: 12 women **Student/Faculty:** 13 to 1
Year: semesters, summer session **Tuition:** $9470
Application Deadline: **Room & Board:** $4080
Freshman Class: 315 applied, 162 accepted, 85 enrolled
SAT CR/M/W: 540/470/450 **ACT:** 20 **LESS COMPETITIVE**

Blue Mountain College is a Christian liberal arts institution supported by the Mississippi Baptist Convention. Deeply committed to the education of it's students since it's founding in 1873, the College has continued to attract capable, confident students who desire to pursue knowledge through a Christian worldview in a caring, person-centered environment. There is one undergraduate school and one graduate school. The 2 libraries contain 80,566 volumes, 1 microform item, 1,444 audio/video tapes/CDs/DVDs, and subscribe to 95 periodicals including electronic. Computerized library services include interlibrary loans, database searching, Internet access, and Wi-Fi capability. The 44-acre campus is in a rural area 69 miles from Memphis, TN. Including any residence halls, there are 15 buildings.

Student Life: 81% of undergraduates are from Mississippi. Others are from 13 states, and 5 foreign countries. 85% are from public schools. 86% are White. 97% are Protestant. The average age of freshmen is 19; all undergraduates, 23. 30% do not continue beyond their first year; 51% remain to graduate.

Housing: 287 students can be accommodated in college housing, which includes single-sex dorms. On-campus housing is available on a first-come and first-served basis. 56% of students live on campus; of those, 25% remain on campus on weekends. Alcohol is not permitted. All students may keep cars.

Activities: There are no fraternities or sororities. There are 33 groups on campus, including art, choir, chorale, chorus, drama, honors, literary magazine, musical theater, professional, religious, social, student government, and yearbook. Popular campus events include Society Rush, Founder's Day, Homecoming on the Hill, Ministerial Alumni Day, Homecoming, and Topper Days.

Sports: There are 4 intercollegiate sports for men and 4 for women, and 7 intramural sports for men and 7 for women. Facilities include The athletic and recreation facilities are a gymnasium, a swimming pool, a sportsplex, and a fitness center.

Disabled Students: 95% of the campus is accessible. Facilities include wheelchair ramps, elevators, special parking, specially equipped restrooms, special class scheduling, lowered drinking fountains, and special housing.

Services: Counseling and information services are available, as is tutoring in most subjects. There is remedial math, reading, and writing.

Campus Safety and Security: Measures include 24-hour foot and vehicle patrol and emergency notification system. There are lighted pathways/sidewalks and controlled access to dorms/residences.

Programs of Study: BMC confers B.A., B.S., and B.S.Ed. degrees. Master's degrees are also awarded. Bachelor's degrees are awarded in BIOLOGICAL SCIENCE (biology/biological science), BUSINESS (business administration and management), COMMUNICATIONS AND THE ARTS (English, fine arts, music, Spanish, and speech/debate/rhetoric), COMPUTER AND PHYSICAL SCIENCE (mathematics), EDUCATION (elementary education, English education, foreign languages education, mathematics education, music education, physical education, science education, secondary education, and social science education), HEALTH PROFESSIONS (exercise science and medical technology), SOCIAL SCIENCE (biblical studies, history, and psychology). Elementary Education is the strongest academically. Elementary education, business administration, and biology have the largest enrollments.

Required: All students must take a minimum of 120 semester hours, with a minimum of 40 hours on the junior-senior level; 25% of total degree hours required must be earned at Blue Mountain. No more than 42 hours of course work carrying the same prefix may be credited toward the degree. Core curriculum requirements include 12 semester hours of English, 6 each of history and biblical studies, 4 of biological science, 3 each of psychology, fine arts, math, physical science, computer applications, and electives, and 2 of phys ed. A 2.0 GPA overall is required (2.5 for teacher education).

Special: The college offers dual majors and internships (maximum 6 credits); consortial relationship with Union University resulting in dual degrees in Biology/Nursing, Psychology/Nursing; a consortial relationship with Baptist Memorial College of Health Sciences resulting in dual degress in Biology/Nursing, Biology/Health Science and a joint program in Business Administration with concentration in Health Care Management; two online degree programs: Business Administration and Psychology. There are 5 national honor societies and 8 departmental honors programs.

Faculty/Classroom: 40% of faculty are male; 60% are female. All teach undergraduates. No introductory courses are taught by graduate students. The average class size in an introductory lecture is 16; in a laboratory is 16; and in a regular course is 13.

Admissions: 51% of the 2013-2014 applicants were accepted. The SAT scores for the 2013-2014 freshman class were: Critical Reading--33% below 500, 33% between 500 and 599, and 34% between 600 and 699; Math--100% below 500; Writing--66% below 500, and 34% between 500 and 599. The ACT scores were 53% below 21, 17% between 21 and 23, 17% between 24 and 26, 4% between 27 and 28, and 9% above 28. 25% of the current freshmen were in the top fifth of their class; 61% were in the top two fifths. 2 freshmen graduated first in their class.

Requirements: The SAT or ACT is required. BMC recommends that applicants for admission have completed 4 units of English, 3 each of math, science, and social studies, and 2 of a foreign language. BMC will accept either the ACT or the SAT; both are not required. A GPA of 2.0 is required. AP and CLEP credits are accepted. Important factors in the admissions decision are ability to finance college education, recommendations by alumni, and recommendations by school officials.

Procedure: Freshmen are admitted to all sessions. Entrance exams should be taken during junior or senior year. There are deferred admissions and rolling admissions plans. Application deadlines are open. Application fee is $10. Applications are accepted online. Application fees are waived if application is completed online.

Transfer: 73 transfer students enrolled in 2012-2013. Transfer students who have been enrolled in other colleges must submit official transcripts from each college attended and must be eligible to re-enter tha last college attended. A maximum of 64 semester hours of credit may be transferred from a community or junior college. 30 of 120 credits required for the bachelor's degree must be completed at BMC.

Visiting: There are regularly scheduled orientations for prospective students, consisting of days set aside prior to enrollment term/semester for transfers to meet with academic advisors and enroll in classes. Those who cannot come on designated days can make individual appointments through the Office of Admissions. There are guides for informal visits, visitors may sit in on classes, and stay overnight. To schedule a visit, contact Joan Herrington at (662) 685-4771 x.158.

Financial Aid: In 2013-2014, 97% of all full-time freshmen and 97% of continuing full-time students received some form of financial aid. 74% of all full-time freshmen and 89% of continuing full-time students received need-based aid. The average freshman award was $11,618. Need-based scholarships or need-based grants averaged $5,036 ($6,035 maximum); need-based self-help aid (loans and jobs) averaged $4,707 ($5,500 maximum); non-need-based athletic scholarships averaged $8,655 ($12,570 maximum); and other non-need-based awards and non-need-based scholarships averaged $2,516 ($5,500 maximum). 19% of undergraduate students work part-time. Average annual earnings from campus work are $1018. The average financial indebtedness of the 2013 graduate was $17,760. The FAFSA is required. The priority date for freshman financial aid applications for fall entry is April 1.

International Students: There are 8 international students enrolled. The school actively recruits these students. They must take the TOEFL with a minimum score of 500 on the paper-based TOEFL (PBT) or 61 on the Internet-based version (iBT). They must also take the SAT or ACT.

Computers: All students may access the system during regular school hours. There are no time limits and no fees.

Graduates: From July 1, 2012 to June 30, 2013, 128 bachelor's degrees were awarded. The most popular majors were Elementary Education (48%), Biblical Studies (17%), and Psychology (8%). 3 companies recruited on campus in 2012-2013. In an average class, 37% graduate in 4 years or less, 51% graduate in 5 years or less, and 51% graduate in 6 years or less. Of the 2012 graduating class, 27% were enrolled in graduate school within 6 months of graduation, and 59% were employed.

Admissions Contact: Austin Kimbrough, Interim Director of Admissions. E-Mail: *akimbrough@bmc.edu* Web: *www.bmc.edu*

DELTA STATE UNIVERSITY — C-2

Cleveland, MS 38733 — (662) 846-4020; (800) 468-6378; (662) 846-4683

Full-time: 921 men, 1332 women	**Faculty:** 165; IIA, --$
Part-time: 195 men, 308 women	**Ph.D.s:** 69%
Graduate: 558 men, 1449 women	**Student/Faculty:** 18 to 1
Year: semesters, summer session	**Tuition:** $5724 ($14,820)
Application Deadline: August 1	**Room & Board:** $6568
Freshman Class: 511 applied, 455 accepted, 332 enrolled	
SAT CR/M: 473/507 **ACT:** 20	**LESS COMPETITIVE**

Delta State University, founded in 1924, is a public liberal arts institution offering degrees in arts and sciences, business, education, and nursing. There are 4 undergraduate schools and one graduate school. In addition to regional accreditation, DSU has baccalaureate program accreditation with ACBSP, CSWE, NASAD, NASM, and NCATE. The library contains 374,284 volumes, 832,822 microform items, 20,028 audio/video tapes/CDs/DVDs, and subscribes to 24,018 periodicals including electronic. Computerized library services include interlibrary loans, database searching, and Internet access. Special learning facilities include an art gallery, natural history museum, planetarium, a performing arts center. The 274-acre campus is in a small town 110 miles south of Memphis, and 130 miles north of Jackson. Including any residence halls, there are 92 buildings.

Student Life: 89% of undergraduates are from Mississippi. Others are from 31 states, 20 foreign countries, and Canada. 60% are White; 33% African American. The average age of freshmen is 18; all undergraduates, 25. 38% do not continue beyond their first year; 45% remain to graduate.

Housing: 1094 students can be accommodated in college housing, which includes single-sex dorms, on-campus apartments, and married student housing. On-campus housing is guaranteed for all 4 years, is available on a first-come, and first-served basis. 71% of students commute. Alcohol is not permitted. All students may keep cars.

Activities: 16% of men belong to 8 national fraternities; 13% of women belong to 6 national sororities. There are 79 groups on campus, including art, band, cheerleading, choir, chorale, chorus, computers, dance, drama, ethnic, honors, international, jazz band, literary magazine, marching band, musical theater, newspaper, opera, orchestra, pep band, photography, political, professional, religious, social, social service, student government, and yearbook. Popular campus events include Springfest and Pig Pickin.

Sports: There are 7 intercollegiate sports for men and 6 for women, and 21 intramural sports for men and 21 for women. Facilities include a coliseum, indoor pool, gym, baseball field, softball field, football stadium, 9-hole golf course, outdoor tennis courts, 2 intramural fields, outdoor walking facility, and fitness center.

Disabled Students: 95% of the campus is accessible. Facilities include wheelchair ramps, elevators, special parking, specially equipped restrooms, special class scheduling, lowered drinking fountains, and lowered telephones.

Services: Counseling and information services are available, as is tutoring in every subject. There is remedial math, reading, and writing.

Campus Safety and Security: Measures include 24-hour foot and vehicle patrol, emergency notification system, self-defense education, and security escort services. There are emergency telephones and lighted pathways/sidewalks.

Programs of Study: DSU confers B.A., B.S., B.B.A., B.C.A., B.F.A., B.M., B.M.E., B.S.J.C., B.S.Ed., B.S.I.S., B.S.M.I.S., B.S.N. and B.S.W.

degrees. Master's and doctoral degrees are also awarded. Bachelor's degrees are awarded in BIOLOGICAL SCIENCE (biology/biological science), BUSINESS (accounting, business administration and management, hospitality management services, insurance, management science, and marketing/retailing/merchandising), COMMUNICATIONS AND THE ARTS (art, communications, English, journalism, music, and music business management), COMPUTER AND PHYSICAL SCIENCE (chemistry, information sciences and systems, and mathematics), EDUCATION (athletic training, elementary education, English education, foreign languages education, health education, mathematics education, music education, and social science education), ENGINEERING AND ENVIRONMENTAL DESIGN (aviation administration/management and environmental science), HEALTH PROFESSIONS (nursing and speech pathology/audiology), SOCIAL SCIENCE (criminal justice, family/consumer studies, history, interdisciplinary studies, political science/government, psychology, social science, and social work). Elementary education, biology, health, physical education and recreation have the largest enrollments.

Required: To graduate, students must complete 124 to 126 semester hours, including 30 to 54 in the major, depending on the program, with a minimum GPA of 2.0. General education requirements include 6 hours each of English composition, English literature, history, lab science, and social science, 3 hours each of fine arts, math, psychology, and speech, and 2 hours of personal development.

Special: DSU offers internships in several majors. An interdisciplinary studies degree and non-degree study are also available. There are 17 national honor societies, a freshman honors program, and 10 departmental honors programs.

Faculty/Classroom: 46% of faculty are male; 54% are female. 89% teach undergraduates. No introductory courses are taught by graduate students. The average class size in an introductory lecture is 21; in a laboratory is 17; and in a regular course is 17.

Admissions: 89% of the 2013-2014 applicants were accepted. The SAT scores for the 2013-2014 freshman class were: Critical Reading--59% below 500, 36% between 500 and 599, and 5% between 600 and 699; Math--32% below 500, 59% between 500 and 599, and 9% between 600 and 699. The ACT scores were 59% below 21, 21% between 21 and 23, 13% between 24 and 26, 3% between 27 and 28, and 4% above 28. 29% of the current freshmen were in the top fifth of their class; 65% were in the top two fifths.

Requirements: The ACT is required. In addition, Students may gain admission by completing the college prep curriculum with a minimum 3.2 GPA; by completing the college prep curriculum with a minimum of 2.5 GPA and scoring at least 16 on the ACT (650 on the SAT), by ranking in the upper 50% of the class and scoring at least 16 on the ACT (650 on the SAT); or by completing the college prep curriculum with a minimum 2.0 GPA and scoring 18 or higher on the ACT (740 on the SAT). The Nelson Denny Reading Test and Math Placement Test must also be taken. Applicants must be graduates of an accredited secondary school or have the GED. They should have completed 4 courses in English; 3 each in math, science, and social studies; 2 in a foreign language, world geography, or additional science/math; and .5 in computer applications. A GPA of 2.0 is required. AP and CLEP credits are accepted.

Procedure: Freshmen are admitted to all sessions. Entrance exams should be taken as early as possible. There is a rolling admissions plan. Applications should be filed by August 1 for fall entry; January 1 for spring entry. The fall 2013 application fee was $25. Applications are accepted online.

Transfer: 426 transfer students enrolled in 2012-2013. A minimum GPA of 2.0 is required, as is an associate degree and ACT or SAT scores; students must be in good standing with last college or university attended. 30 of 124 credits required for the bachelor's degree must be completed at DSU.

Visiting: There are regularly scheduled orientations for prospective students, including campus tours and introduction to faculty and staff. There are guides for informal visits, visitors may sit in on classes, and stay overnight. To schedule a visit, contact the Undergraduate Admissions Office.

Financial Aid: In 2013-2014, 89% of all full-time freshmen and 91% of continuing full-time students received some form of financial aid. 72% of all full-time freshmen and 75% of continuing full-time students received need-based aid. The average freshman award was $3,150. Need-based scholarships or need-based grants averaged $3,774 ($6,850 maximum); need-based self-help aid (loans and jobs) averaged $3,113 ($12,466 maximum); non-need-based athletic scholarships averaged $3,904 ($11,448 maximum); and other non-need-based awards and non-need-based scholarships averaged $1,052 ($7,448 maximum). 9% of undergraduate students work part-time. Average annual earnings from campus work are $1295. The FAFSA is required. The deadline for filing freshman financial aid applications for fall entry is March 1.

International Students: There are 52 international students enrolled. The school actively recruits these students. They must take the TOEFL with a minimum score of 525 on the paper-based TOEFL (PBT) or 71 on the Internet-based version (iBT). They must also take the SAT or ACT.

Computers: All students may access the system Monday to Thursday, 7:30 a.m. to 10 p.m.; Friday, 7:30 a.m. to 4 p.m.; Saturday, closed; Sunday 2 to 10 p.m. There are no time limits and no fees.

Graduates: From July 1, 2012 to June 30, 2013, 503 bachelor's degrees were awarded. The most popular majors were elementary education (11%), nursing (11%), and social work (8%). In an average class, 2% graduate in 3 years or less, 18% graduate in 4 years or less, 33% graduate in 5 years or less, and 37% graduate in 6 years or less.

Admissions Contact: Debbie Heslep, Dean of Enrollment Management. E-Mail: *admissions@deltastate.edu* Web: *www.deltastate.edu*

JACKSON STATE UNIVERSITY — C-4

Jackson, MS 39217 (601) 979-2100
(800) 848-6817; (601) 979-3445

Full-time: 2214 men, 3212 women	**Faculty:** n/av
Part-time: 351 men, 1125 women	**Ph.D.s:** 78%
Graduate: 639 men, 1593 women	**Student/Faculty:** 14 to 1
Year: semesters, summer session	**Tuition:** $6348 ($15,552)
Application Deadline: open	**Room & Board:** $7164
Freshman Class: 5325 applied, 3442 accepted, 1103 enrolled	
SAT: required **ACT:** 19	**LESS COMPETITIVE**

Jackson State University, founded in 1877, is a public institution with an emphasis on liberal arts, science, engineering, business, music, research and teacher preparation. There are 5 undergraduate schools and one graduate school. In addition to regional accreditation, JSU has baccalaureate program accreditation with AACSB, ABET, ACEJMC, CSWE, NASAD, NASM, and NCATE. The library contains 500,656 volumes, 654,601 microform items, 2,308 audio/video tapes/CDs/DVDs, and subscribes to 575,134 periodicals including electronic. Computerized library services include interlibrary loans, database searching, Internet access, and Wi-Fi capability. Special learning facilities include an art gallery, natural history museum, planetarium, radio station, and TV station. The 175-acre campus is in an urban area 190 miles north of New Orleans. Including any residence halls, there are 49 buildings.

Student Life: 82% of undergraduates are from Mississippi. Others are from 43 states, 55 foreign countries, and Canada. 90% are African American. The average age of freshmen is 22; all undergraduates, 25.

Housing: 2577 students can be accommodated in college housing, which includes single-sex dorms and on-campus apartments. On-campus housing is available on a first-come and first-served basis. 71% of students commute. Alcohol is not permitted. All students may keep cars.

Activities: 4% of men belong to 4 local and 5 national fraternities; 5% of women belong to 4 local and 4 national sororities. There are 71 groups on campus, including art, band, cheerleading, choir, computers, dance, drama, drill team, ethnic, honors, international, jazz band, marching band, musical theater, newspaper, opera, orchestra, pep band, political, radio and TV, religious, social service, student government, symphony, and yearbook.

Sports: There are 7 intercollegiate sports for men and 4 for women, and 2 intramural sports for men and 2 for women. Facilities include an Olympic-size swimming pool, a gym with 2 basketball courts, indoor and outdoor tennis courts, badminton and volleyball courts, a dance studio, a baseball diamond, soccer and athletic fields, a track, and a bowling alley.

Disabled Students: All of the campus is accessible. Facilities include wheelchair ramps, elevators, special parking, specially equipped restrooms, lowered drinking fountains, and lowered telephones.

Services: There is remedial math, reading, and writing.

Campus Safety and Security: Measures include 24-hour foot and vehicle patrol, emergency notification system, and self-defense education. There are shuttle buses, emergency telephones, lighted pathways/sidewalks, and controlled access to dorms/residences.

Programs of Study: JSU confers B.A., B.S., B.B.A, B.M., B.M.E., B.S.Ed. and B.S.W. degrees. Master's and doctoral degrees are also awarded. Bachelor's degrees are awarded in BIOLOGICAL SCIENCE (biology/biological science), BUSINESS (accounting, business administration and management, entrepreneurial studies, finance, and marketing/retailing/merchandising), COMMUNICATIONS AND THE ARTS (art, communications, English, languages, piano/organ, speech/debate/rhetoric, and Telecommunications Engineering Technology), COMPUTER AND PHYSICAL SCIENCE (atmospheric sciences and meteorology, chemistry, computer science, earth science, mathematics, and physics), EDUCATION (business education, elementary education, health education, mathematics education, music education, social science education, and special education), ENGINEERING AND ENVIRONMENTAL DESIGN (civil engineering, computer engineering, electrical/electronics engineering, and industrial engineering technology), HEALTH PROFESSIONS (health care administration and premedicine), SOCIAL SCIENCE (child care/child and family studies, communication sciences & disorders, corrections, criminal justice, economics, history, political science/government, psychology, social work, sociology, and urban studies). Biology, childcare and family education, elementary education, criminal justice, engineering, social work, professional interdisciplinary studies, computer science, and business administration are the strongest academically. Biology, childcare and family education, and criminal justice have the largest enrollments.

Required: To graduate, students must complete at least 128 semester hours with a minimum GPA of 2.0. At least 30 upper-division hours must be earned in the major. Distribution requirements include a total of 49 to 59 hours in communications, humanities and fine arts, social and behavioral sciences, natural sciences, health and phys ed, and concepts for success in college. Students must pass the Undergraduate English Proficiency Examination.

Special: Internships with various corporations, nondegree study, work-study programs, accelerated degrees, dual degree, B.A.-B.S. degrees, and a student-exchange program are available. There are 4 national honor societies, a freshman honors program, and 17 departmental honors programs.

Faculty/Classroom: 52% of faculty are male; 48% are female. No introductory courses are taught by graduate students.

Admissions: 65% of the 2013-2014 applicants were accepted. The ACT scores were 72% below 21, 19% between 21 and 23, 7% between 24 and 26, 2% between 27 and 28, and 1% above 28.

Requirements: The SAT or ACT is required. Applicants must be graduates of an accredited secondary school or have a GED certificate. They must have earned 15 Carnegie units, including 4 of English, 3 each of math, social studies, and sciences, 0.5 of computer applications, and 2 of advanced electives. A satisfactory ACT or SAT score exempts students from the specific high school unit requirements. An interview is recommended. A GPA of 2.0 is required. AP and CLEP credits are accepted. Important factors in the admissions decision are advanced placement or honors courses, ability to finance college education, and geographical diversity.

Procedure: Freshmen are admitted to all sessions. Entrance exams should be taken during the first semester of the senior year. There are early admissions, deferred admissions, and rolling admissions plans. Application deadlines are open. Notification is sent on a rolling basis. Applications are accepted online.

Transfer: 642 transfer students enrolled in 2012-2013. Applicants should submit an official transcript from each institution attended, be in good standing at the last college or university attended, and have a minimum cumulative GPA of 2.0. 30 of 128 credits required for the bachelor's degree must be completed at JSU.

Visiting: There are regularly scheduled orientations for prospective students. There are guides for informal visits, visitors may sit in on classes, and stay overnight. To schedule a visit, contact Andrea Jones at (601) 979-2913.

Financial Aid: JSU is a member of CSS. The FAFSA is required. Check with the school for current application deadlines.

International Students: There are 117 international students enrolled. The school actively recruits these students. They must take the TOEFL with a minimum score of 525 on the paper-based TOEFL (PBT) or 69 on the Internet-based version (iBT), and a placement test. They must also take the SAT or ACT, scoring 16.

Computers: All students may access the system 7 a.m. to 12 a.m., with access to PCs during business hours. There are no time limits and no fees.

Graduates: From July 1, 2012 to June 30, 2013, 1485 bachelor's degrees were awarded. The most popular majors were professional linguistics studies (13%), biology (8%), and criminal justice and correctional services (7%). In an average class, 45% graduate in 6 years or less. Of the 2012 graduating class, 51% were employed within 6 months of graduation.

Admissions Contact: Janieth Wilson-Adams, Interim Director of Admissions. E-Mail: *janieth.f.wilson_adams@jsums.edu* Web: *www.jsums.edu*

MILLSAPS COLLEGE — C-4

Jackson, MS 39210 — (601) 974-1050; (800) 352-1050; (601) 974-1059

Full-time: 384 men, 346 women	**Faculty:** 86; IIB, av$
Part-time: 5 men, 9 women	**Ph.D.s:** 95%
Graduate: 41 men, 19 women	**Student/Faculty:** 8 to 1
Year: semesters, summer session	**Tuition:** $32,520
Application Deadline: rolling	**Room & Board:** $11,368
Freshman Class: 1901 applied, 902 accepted, 171 enrolled	
SAT CR/M: 540/560	**ACT:** 26 **VERY COMPETITIVE+**

Millsaps College, founded in 1890, is an independent liberal arts institution affiliated with the United Methodist Church. Millsaps College is known for its academic strength, national-caliber faculty, small class size, and spirit of community service. There is one graduate school. In addition to regional accreditation, Millsaps has baccalaureate program accreditation with AACSB and NCATE. The library contains 200,396 volumes, 35,525 microform items, 8,984 audio/video tapes/CDs/DVDs, and subscribes to 38,588 periodicals including electronic. Computerized library services include interlibrary loans, database searching, Internet access, and Wi-Fi capability. Special learning facilities include an art gallery, an observatory, a multi-disciplinary laboratory, and a molecular biology/functional genomics research lab. The 100-acre campus is in an urban area in the capital city of Jackson. Including any residence halls, there are 33 buildings.

Student Life: 58% of undergraduates are from out of state, mostly the South. Students are from 25 states, 14 foreign countries, and Canada. 61% are from public schools. 76% are White. 51% claim no religious affiliation; 33% Protestant; 14% Catholic. The average age of freshmen is 18; all undergraduates, 20. 21% do not continue beyond their first year; 67% remain to graduate.

Housing: 950 students can be accommodated in college housing, which includes single-sex and coed dorms. In addition, there are special-interest houses, fraternity houses, designated housing for freshmen, special housing for diabled students, and a service learning residence hall dedicated to community service and leadership. On-campus housing is available on a first-come, first-served basis, and is available on a lottery system for upperclassmen. 88% of students live on campus; of those, 75% remain on campus on weekends. All students may keep cars.

Activities: 60% of men belong to 6 national fraternities; 64% of women belong to 4 national sororities. There are 80 groups on campus, including art, cheerleading, choir, chorale, chorus, computers, dance, debate, drama, environmental, ethnic, gay, honors, international, literary magazine, musical theater, newspaper, pep band, photography, political, professional, religious, social, social service, student government, and yearbook. Popular campus events include Major Madness, Project Midtown, and Homecoming.

Sports: There are 9 intercollegiate sports for men and 9 for women, and 9 intramural sports for men and 9 for women. Facilities include a 63,300-square-foot activities center containing a fitness center with basketball and volleyball courts, a cardio theater, an aerobics room, fitness and weight-training equipment, a free-weight room, an outdoor pool, racquetball and handball courts, and a squash court. Outdoor areas include 6 tennis courts, a sand volleyball court, and softball, baseball, football, soccer, and multipurpose fields.

Disabled Students: 90% of the campus is accessible. Facilities include wheelchair ramps, elevators, special parking, specially equipped restrooms, special class scheduling, lowered drinking fountains, lowered telephones, special housing. Other needs can be addressed through the ADA coordinator on an individual basis.

Services: Counseling and information services are available, as is tutoring in most subjects, by request, as needed. A writing center, a language lab, and a math lab are available.

Campus Safety and Security: Measures include 24-hour foot and vehicle patrol, emergency notification system, self-defense education, and security escort services. There are emergency telephones, lighted pathways/sidewalks, controlled access to dorms/residences, controlled access to all buildings during specified hours; entrances to campus are gated and staffed at night.

Programs of Study: Millsaps confers B.A., B.S. and B.B.A. degrees. Master's degrees are also awarded. Bachelor's degrees are awarded in BIOLOGICAL SCIENCE (biochemistry, biology/biological science, and neurosciences), BUSINESS (accounting and business administration and management), COMMUNICATIONS AND THE ARTS (art history and appreciation, classics, communications, creative writing, English, music, Spanish, and studio art), COMPUTER AND PHYSICAL SCIENCE (applied mathematics, chemistry, geology, mathematics, and physics), EDUCATION (education), SOCIAL SCIENCE (anthropology, economics, European studies, history, Latin American studies, philosophy, political science/government, psychology, public administration, religion, and sociology). Biology, chemistry and premed are the strongest academically. Business administration, biology and psychology have the largest enrollments.

Required: To graduate, students must complete 128 credit hours with 32 to 48 hours in the major and a minimum GPA of 2.0. The core curriculum includes 4 interdisciplinary courses in humanities and 4 in the sciences and math. Students must also take Introduction to Liberal Studies during the freshman year and reflections on Liberal Studies during the senior year. Other requirements include satisfactory completion of a 7-paper writing proficiency portfolio and a comprehensive exam in the specific field of study.

Special: Millsaps sponsors international studies programs in Africa, Asia, Europe, and Latin America. Direct exchange options are offered in Japan and Ireland. Students may also participate in a wide variety of field research, honors, internship, fellowships, and service learning programs. There are 28 national honor societies, including Phi Beta Kappa, and 19 departmental honors programs.

Faculty/Classroom: 50% of faculty are male; 50% are female. All teach undergraduates, and 90% do both. No introductory courses are taught by graduate students. The average class size in an introductory lecture is 20; in a laboratory is 20; and in a regular course is 13.

Admissions: 47% of the 2013-2014 applicants were accepted. The SAT scores for the 2013-2014 freshman class were: Critical Reading--25%

below 500, 39% between 500 and 599, 28% between 600 and 699, and 8% between 700 and 800; Math--17% below 500, 47% between 500 and 599, 33% between 600 and 699, and 3% between 700 and 800. The ACT scores were 9% below 21, 23% between 21 and 23, 27% between 24 and 26, 18% between 27 and 28, and 23% above 28. 48% of the current freshmen were in the top fifth of their class; 79% were in the top two fifths. 6 freshmen graduated first in their class.

Requirements: The SAT or ACT is required. Applicants should be graduates of an accredited secondary school or have a GED certificate, and have completed at least 14 academic units, including 4 in English, 3 in math, 2 in social studies, and 2 in histroy. An essay is required. A GPA of 2.5 is required. AP and CLEP credits are accepted. Important factors in the admissions decision are advanced placement or honors courses, extracurricular activities record, and recommendations by school officials.

Procedure: Freshmen are admitted fall and spring. Entrance exams should be taken in the spring of the junior year or fall of the senior year. There are early admissions, deferred admissions, and rolling admissions plans. Early decision applications should be filed by January 12. Notification is sent on a rolling basis. Applications are accepted online.

Transfer: 36 transfer students enrolled in 2012-2013. Applicants must have a minimum GPA of 2.75 and be in good standing at their previous school. Requirements include high school and college transcripts, an essay or personal statement, and ACT or SAT scores. 32 of 128 credits required for the bachelor's degree must be completed at Millsaps.

Visiting: There are regularly scheduled orientations for prospective students, including meetings with faculty and student services personneland tours of the campus. There are guides for informal visits, visitors may sit in on classes, and stay overnight. To schedule a visit, contact the Admissions Office.

Financial Aid: In 2013-2014, 99% of all full-time freshmen and 98% of continuing full-time students received some form of financial aid. 67% of all full-time freshmen and 57% of continuing full-time students received need-based aid. The average freshman award was $30,461. Need-based scholarships or need-based grants averaged $24,248 ($44,890 maximum); need-based self-help aid (loans and jobs) averaged $8,358 ($28,790 maximum); and other non-need-based awards and non-need-based scholarships averaged $20,865 ($44,890 maximum). 76% of undergraduate students work part-time. Average annual earnings from campus work are $175. The average financial indebtedness of the 2013 graduate was $27,926. The FAFSA, and FAFSA is required. The priority date for freshman financial aid applications for fall entry is March 1.

International Students: There are 23 international students enrolled. The school actively recruits these students. They must take the TOEFL with a minimum score of 550 on the paper-based TOEFL (PBT) or 80 on the Internet-based version (iBT), IELTS. They must also take the SAT or ACT, scoring 21. The SAT or ACT are accepted in lieu of the TOEFL.

Computers: All students may access the system at any time. There are no time limits and no fees.

Graduates: From July 1, 2012 to June 30, 2013, 202 bachelor's degrees were awarded. The most popular majors were biology (13%), accounting (13%), and business administration (12%). 276 companies recruited on campus in 2012-2013. In an average class, 1% graduate in 3 years or less, 62% graduate in 4 years or less, 66% graduate in 5 years or less, and 67% graduate in 6 years or less. Of the 2012 graduating class, 40% were enrolled in graduate school within 6 months of graduation, and 33% were employed.

Admissions Contact: Tammy Teixeira, Director of Admissions Operations. E-Mail: *admissions@millsaps.edu* Web: *www.millsaps.edu*

MISSISSIPPI COLLEGE — C-4

Clinton, MS 39058 — (601) 925-3800; (800) 738-1236; (601) 925-3950

Full-time: n/av	**Faculty:** n/av; IIA, -$
Part-time: n/av	**Ph.D.s:** n/av
Graduate: n/av	**Student/Faculty:** n/av
Year: semesters, summer session	**Tuition:** $14,848
Application Deadline: open	**Room & Board:** $7150
Freshman Class: 1763 applied, 1080 accepted, 466 enrolled	
SAT CR/M: 550/520 **ACT:** 23	**VERY COMPETITIVE**

Mississippi College, founded in 1826 and affiliated with the Southern Baptist Church, is a private institution offering degrees in liberal arts, business, education, and health sciences. There are 6 undergraduate schools and 2 graduate schools. In addition to regional accreditation, MC has baccalaureate program accreditation with ACBSP, CSWE, NASM, and NCATE. The 2 libraries contain 370,404 volumes, 540,471 microform items, 18,348 audio/video tapes/CDs/DVDs, and subscribe to 4,742 periodicals including electronic. Computerized library services include interlibrary loans, database searching, Internet access, and Wi-Fi capability. Special learning facilities include an art gallery, radio station, and TV station. The 320-acre campus is in a suburban area 5 miles west of Jackson. Including any residence halls, there are 30 buildings.

Student Life: 60% of undergraduates are from Mississippi. Others are from 39 states, and 29 foreign countries. 94% are Protestant. The average age of freshmen is 18; all undergraduates, 24.

Housing: 1800 students can be accommodated in college housing, which includes single-sex dorms, on-campus apartments, and off-campus apartments. On-campus housing is available on a first-come and first-served basis. 55% of students live on campus. Alcohol is not permitted. All students may keep cars.

Activities: There are 70 groups on campus, including art, band, cheerleading, chess, choir, chorale, chorus, computers, dance, debate, drama, environmental, ethnic, forensics, honors, international, jazz band, literary magazine, marching band, musical theater, newspaper, opera, pep band, political, professional, radio and TV, religious, social, social service, student government, symphony, and yearbook. Popular campus events include I Love America Day, Derby Day, and Spring Fever Week.

Sports: There are 9 intercollegiate sports for men and 8 for women, and 8 intramural sports for men and 8 for women. Facilities include a coliseum, an 8300-seat stadium, tennis courts, soccer and softball fields, a swimming pool, a 4000-seat gym, a fitness facility, and a campus weight-training facility.

Disabled Students: Facilities include wheelchair ramps, elevators, special parking, specially equipped restrooms, special class scheduling, lowered drinking fountains, lowered telephones, special housing. wide doors and special dorm rooms equipped for the physically disabled.

Services: Counseling and information services are available, as is tutoring in most subjects, and study skills classes There is remedial math, reading, and writing.

Campus Safety and Security: Measures include 24-hour foot and vehicle patrol, emergency notification system, self-defense education, and security escort services. There are shuttle buses, emergency telephones, lighted pathways/sidewalks, and controlled access to dorms/residences.

Programs of Study: MC confers B.A., B.S., B.M., B.M.Ed., B.S.B.A., B.S.Ed., B.S.N. and B.S.W. degrees. Master's and doctoral degrees are also awarded. Bachelor's degrees are awarded in BIOLOGICAL SCIENCE (biochemistry and biology/biological science), BUSINESS (accounting, business administration and management, and marketing/retailing/merchandising), COMMUNICATIONS AND THE ARTS (applied music, art, communications, English, French, graphic design, languages, modern language, music, music theory and composition, piano/organ, Spanish, voice, and winds), COMPUTER AND PHYSICAL SCIENCE (chemistry, computer science, mathematics, and physics), EDUCATION (art education, business education, elementary education, music education, and special education), ENGINEERING AND ENVIRONMENTAL DESIGN (engineering physics and interior design), HEALTH PROFESSIONS (nursing), SOCIAL SCIENCE (American studies, Christian studies, criminal justice, family/consumer studies, history, paralegal studies, political science/government, psychology, religious music, social studies, social work, and sociology). Biology and chemistry is the strongest academically. Business, nursing, and education have the largest enrollments.

Required: To graduate, students must complete 130 credit hours, with an average of C or better in the major. The core curriculum includes English, history, economics, computer science, religion, math, art, social science, phys ed, and chapel. 30 hours are usually required in the major; some majors require 36 to 45. Students must pass a writing proficiency exam. B.A. candidates and English majors must take 12 hours of a foreign language.

Special: Cooperative programs, including a 3-2 engineering degree and a program in agriculture, are offered with the University of Mississippi, Mississippi State University, and Auburn University. MC also offers study abroad in up to 10 countries, a 3-3 program with the School of Law, work-study programs, internships, B.A.-B.S. degrees, and credit for military experience and by exam. There are 25 national honor societies and a freshman honors program.

Faculty/Classroom: No introductory courses are taught by graduate students. The average class size in an introductory lecture is 30; in a laboratory is 25; and in a regular course is 25.

Admissions: 61% of the 2013-2014 applicants were accepted. The SAT scores for the 2013-2014 freshman class were: Critical Reading--43% below 500, 30% between 500 and 599, 24% between 600 and 699, and 4% between 700 and 800; Math--41% below 500, 33% between 500 and 599, 19% between 600 and 699, and 7% between 700 and 800. The ACT scores were 30% below 21, 23% between 21 and 23, 20% between 24 and 26, 12% between 27 and 28, and 16% above 28. 4 freshmen graduated first in their class.

Requirements: In addition to the application for admission, students must submit a 250-word essay, at least 1 letter of recommendation (3 are recommended for scholarship consideration), and a transcript from all schools previously attended. For freshmen, SAT or ACT scores must be submitted (ACT is preferred). A satisfactory ACT or SAT composite score is required for regular admission. Students scoring below these levels may be considered for acceptance into the developmental program. A well-rounded high school program is advisable. An interview is recommended, as is a portfolio or audition for some majors. A GPA of 2.0 is required. AP and CLEP credits are accepted. Important factors in the admissions decision are personality/intangible qualities, extracurricular activities record, and leadership record.

Procedure: Freshmen are admitted fall, spring, and summer. Entrance exams should be taken by December of the senior year. There are early decision, deferred admissions, and rolling admissions plans. Application deadlines are open. Notification is sent on a rolling basis. Applications are accepted online.

Transfer: 440 transfer students enrolled in 2012-2013. Applicants must be junior college graduates or students in good academic standing with the college they last attended. They must have a minimum GPA of 2.0. Transfer students will be considered as freshmen if fewer than 12 semester hours or 16 quarter hours have been completed. Applicants must submit transcripts from all schools previously attended. 33 of 130 credits required for the bachelor's degree must be completed at MC.

Visiting: There are regularly scheduled orientations for prospective students, Including attending classes, touring the campus, and meeting with administrators and departmental advisers. There are guides for informal visits, visitors may sit in on classes, and stay overnight. To schedule a visit, contact the Director of Admissions.

Financial Aid: In 2013-2014, 96% of all full-time freshmen and 95% of continuing full-time students received some form of financial aid. 56% of all full-time freshmen and 60% of continuing full-time students received need-based aid. The average freshman award was $12,363. Need-based scholarships or need-based grants averaged $4,118; need-based self-help aid (loans and jobs) averaged $1,774; and other non-need-based awards and non-need-based scholarships averaged $6,471. The average financial indebtedness of the 2013 graduate was $26,323. The FAFSA is required. The priority date for freshman financial aid applications for fall entry is March 1.

International Students: There are 76 international students enrolled. The school actively recruits these students. They must take the TOEFL and the college's own test.

Computers: Students who have been assigned an account may access the system. may access the system. There are no time limits and no fees.

Graduates: From July 1, 2012 to June 30, 2013, 522 bachelor's degrees were awarded. The most popular majors were business administration (15%), nursing (11%), and biology (10%). In an average class, 36% graduate in 4 years or less, 50% graduate in 5 years or less, and 52% graduate in 6 years or less.

Admissions Contact: Chad Phillips, Director of Admissions. E-Mail: *enrollment-services@mc.edu* Web: *www.mc.edu*

MISSISSIPPI STATE UNIVERSITY E-3

Mississippi State, MS 39762 **(662) 325-2224; (662) 325-7360**

Full-time: 7830 men, 7174 women	**Faculty:** 882; I, --$
Part-time: 696 men, 690 women	**Ph.D.s:** 76%
Graduate: 1966 men, 2009 women	**Student/Faculty:** 19 to 1
Year: semesters, summer session	**Tuition:** $6264 ($15,828)
Application Deadline: August 1	**Room & Board:** $8486
Freshman Class: 10449 applied, 7245 accepted, 2894 enrolled	
SAT: required	**ACT:** 23

Mississippi State University, founded in 1878 as a land-grant institution, offering degree programs in the arts and sciences, agriculture, business and industry, education, engineering, forest resources, architecture, accounting, and professional training in veterinary medicine. There are 9 undergraduate schools and one graduate school. In addition to regional accreditation, MSU has baccalaureate program accreditation with AACSB, ABET, ACCE, ADA, AHEA, ASLA, CSWE, FIDER, NAAB, NASAD, NASM, NCATE, and SAF. The 2 libraries contain 2.4 million volumes, 3.5 million microform items, 15,069 audio/video tapes/CDs/DVDs, and subscribe to 117,097 periodicals including electronic. Computerized library services include interlibrary loans, database searching, Internet access, and Wi-Fi capability. Special learning facilities include an art gallery, natural history museum, planetarium, radio station, TV station, Cullis & Gladys Wade Clock Museum, Dunn-Seiler Museum, Giles Hall Gallery, Lois Dowdle Cobb Museum, Mississippi Entomological Museum, and many others. The 4200-acre campus is in a small town 125 miles northeast of Jackson, MS. Including any residence halls, there are 192 buildings.

Student Life: 76% of undergraduates are from Mississippi. Others are from 50 states, 83 foreign countries, and Canada. 70% are White; 20% African American. The average age of freshmen is 18; all undergraduates, 21. 18% do not continue beyond their first year; 82% remain to graduate.

Housing: College-sponsored housing includes single-sex and coed dorms, on-campus apartments, and married student housing. In addition, there are honors houses, special-interest houses, fraternity houses, and sorority houses. On-campus housing is available on a first-come and first-served basis. 73% of students commute. Alcohol is not permitted. All students may keep cars.

Activities: 16% of men belong to 17 national fraternities; 21% of women belong to 1 local and 12 national sororities. There are 400 groups on campus, including art, band, cheerleading, chess, choir, chorale, chorus, communications, computers, dance, debate, drama, drill team, ethnic, film, gay, honors, international, jazz band, literary magazine, marching band, musical theater, newspaper, opera, orchestra, pep band, photography, political, professional, radio and TV, religious, social, social service, student government, symphony, and yearbook. Popular campus events include Pep Rallies, Concerts and Lyceum Series.

Sports: Facilities include a 52,000-seat football stadium, a 6,700-seat baseball park, a 9,200-seat multipurpose coliseum, a physical fitness complex, an all-weather track, 4 practice football fields, a 6-court tennis complex, an 18-hole golf course, 5 lighted tennis courts, the Sanderson Center, which consists of 7 basketball courts, 6 volleyball courts, 8 racquetball courts, 10000 square feet for strength and aerobic conditioning, 3 full size dance studios, an indoor rock climbing wall, a 1/8 mile walking track, and RecPlex, which is a multipurpose field complex with 4 softball, 2 soccer, and 6 flag football fields.

Disabled Students: 90% of the campus is accessible. Facilities include wheelchair ramps, elevators, special parking, specially equipped restrooms, special class scheduling, lowered drinking fountains, lowered telephones, special housing. phones equipped with TTY in the union and library.

Services: Counseling and information services are available, as is tutoring in every subject, math, English, chemistry, physics and study skills. There is a reader service for the blind, and remedial math, reading, and writing. writing effectiveness, study assistance, preparation for professional exams and credit courses in reading and study skills.

Campus Safety and Security: Measures include 24-hour foot and vehicle patrol, emergency notification system, self-defense education, and security escort services. There are shuttle buses, emergency telephones, and lighted pathways/sidewalks.

Programs of Study: MSU confers B.A., B.S., B.Accy., B.Arch., B.B.A., B.F.A., B.G.S., B.Land.Arch., B.Mus.Ed. and B.S.W. degrees. Master's and doctoral degrees are also awarded. Bachelor's degrees are awarded in AGRICULTURE (agricultural business management, agricultural economics, agriculture, agronomy, animal science, fishing and fisheries, forestry production and processing, horticulture, plant protection (pest management), poultry science, and wildlife management), BIOLOGICAL SCIENCE (biochemistry, biology/biological science, and microbiology), BUSINESS (accounting, banking and finance, business administration and management, insurance, marketing/retailing/merchandising, real estate, and trade and industrial supervision and management), COMMUNICATIONS AND THE ARTS (art, communications, English, and languages), COMPUTER AND PHYSICAL SCIENCE (chemistry, computer science, geoscience, information sciences and systems, mathematics, physics, and science), EDUCATION (agricultural education, business education, education, elementary education, music education, physical education, secondary education, special education, and technical education), ENGINEERING AND ENVIRONMENTAL DESIGN (aerospace studies, agricultural engineering technology, architecture, bioengineering, chemical engineering, civil engineering, computer engineering, electrical/electronics engineering, industrial engineering, industrial engineering technology, landscape architecture/design, and mechanical engineering), HEALTH PROFESSIONS (medical technology), SOCIAL SCIENCE (anthropology, economics, food science, history, interdisciplinary studies, liberal arts/general studies, philosophy, political science/government, psychology, social work, and sociology). Accounting, biochemistry, and physics are the strongest academically. General business administration, elementary education, and biology have the largest enrollments.

Required: The core curriculum includes 6 to 9 hours of math and natural science, 6 each of humanities, English composition, and social behavior, and 3 each of public speaking, computer literacy, and fine arts, and junior/senior-level writing. The total number of hours required for graduation and in the major varies. A minimum GPA of 2.0 must be maintained.

Special: Cooperative education, cross-registration with the Academic Common Market, internships, and study abroad in 15 countries are offered. Work-study programs, a Washington semester, accelerated degree programs, a general studies degree, nondegree study, student-designed majors, B.A.-B.S. degrees, and pass/fail options for some courses are available. There are 40 national honor societies, a freshman honors program, and 14 departmental honors programs.

Faculty/Classroom: 60% of faculty are male; 41% are female. 81% teach undergraduates, and 9% do research. No introductory courses are taught by graduate students.

Admissions: 69% of the 2013-2014 applicants were accepted. The SAT scores for the 2013-2014 freshman class were: Critical Reading--32% below 500, 38% between 500 and 599, 24% between 600 and 699, and 5% between 700 and 800; Math--27% below 500, 36% between 500 and 599, 30% between 600 and 699, and 7% between 700 and 800. The ACT scores were 31% below 21, 20% between 21 and 23, 21% between 24 and 26, 12% between 27 and 28, and 17% above 28. 27% of the current freshmen were in the top fifth of their class; 27% were in the top two fifths. There were 17 National Merit finalists.

Requirements: The SAT or ACT is required. Applicants should have completed 15 1/2 high school academic credits, including 4 in English, 3 each in math, science, and social science, 2 advanced electives (foreign language, world geography, 4th year lab-based science, or 4th year math), and 1/2 credit in the computer as a productivity tool (not keyboarding). Full admission is granted with all of the above and one of the following: minimum 3.2 GPA on required high school courses; 2.5 GPA on required high school classes or class standing in top 50% with ACT score of 16 or higher/SAT I combined score of 750 or higher; 2.0 GPA on required high school classes with ACT score of 18 or higher/SAT I combined 840 or higher; or satisfy National Collegiate Athletic Association standards for student-athletes who are full qualifiers under Division I guidelines. Students with a GED are accepted with the required ACT/SAT I score. A GPA of 2.0 is required. AP and CLEP credits are accepted.

Procedure: Freshmen are admitted fall, spring, and summer. Entrance exams should be taken in the spring of junior year or fall semester of senior year. There are deferred admissions and rolling admissions plans. Applications should be filed by August 1 for fall entry; November 15 for spring entry; and May 15 for summer entry. The fall 2013 application fee was $35. Notification is sent on a rolling basis. Applications are accepted online.

Transfer: 1754 transfer students enrolled in 2012-2013. Applicants must submit an official college transcript from each college attended, indicating a minimum GPA of 2.0 (some departents require 2.5), and must be in good standing at their previous school. 31 of 124 credits required for the bachelor's degree must be completed at MSU.

Visiting: There are regularly scheduled orientations for prospective students, including 2 day sessions for freshmen, and 1-day session for transfers. There are guides for informal visits, visitors may sit in on classes, and stay overnight. To schedule a visit, contact Recruitment and Campus Visit Program.

Financial Aid: 63% of all full-time freshmen and 62% of continuing full-time students received need-based aid. The average freshman award was $13,045. Need-based scholarships or need-based grants averaged $5,440 ; need-based self-help aid (loans and jobs) averaged $3,316; non-need-based athletic scholarships averaged $12,426; and other non-need-based awards and non-need-based scholarships averaged $3,161. The average financial indebtedness of the 2013 graduate was $24,535. The FAFSA, and State Grant/Scholarship Application is required. The deadline for filing freshman financial aid applications for fall entry is April 1.

International Students: There are 237 international students enrolled. The school actively recruits these students. They must take the TOEFL with a minimum score of 525 on the paper-based TOEFL (PBT) or 71 on the Internet-based version (iBT). They must also take the SAT.

Computers: All students may access the system 24 hours a day. There are no time limits and no fees.

Graduates: From July 1, 2012 to June 30, 2013, 2922 bachelor's degrees were awarded. The most popular majors were business/marketing (19%), education (18%), and engineering (13%). In an average class, 30% graduate in 4 years or less, 54% graduate in 5 years or less, and 60% graduate in 6 years or less.

Admissions Contact: Phil Bonfanti, Executive Director, Enrollment. E-Mail: *admit@msstate.edu* Web: *www.msstate.edu*

MISSISSIPPI UNIVERSITY FOR WOMEN — E-2

Columbus, MS 39701 — (662) 329-7106 (877) 462-8439; (662) 241-7481

Full-time: 300 men, 1600 women	**Faculty:** n/av; IIA, --$
Part-time: 300 men, 1000 women	**Ph.D.s:** 68%
Graduate: 20 men, 100 women	**Student/Faculty:** n/av
Year: semesters, summer session	**Tuition:** $5400 ($13,800)
Application Deadline: open	**Room & Board:** $6200
Freshman Class: n/av	
SAT or ACT: required	

LESS COMPETITIVE

Mississippi University for Women, founded in 1884, is a public institution offering degrees in liberal arts, education, business and communications, nursing, human sciences, science and math, health and kinesiology, and culinary arts. The figures given in the above capsule and in this profile are approximate. There are 8 undergraduate schools and 2 graduate schools. In addition to regional accreditation, MUW has baccalaureate program accreditation with AHEA, NASAD, NASM, NCATE, and NLN. The library contains 232,600 volumes, 569,400 microform items, 100 audio/video tapes/CDs/DVDs, and subscribes to 1600 periodicals including electronic. Computerized library services include interlibrary loans and database searching. Special learning facilities include a learning resource center, art gallery, radio station, TV station, and distance learning studio. The 110-acre campus is in a small town 120 miles west of Birmingham, Alabama. Including any residence halls, there are 53 buildings.

Student Life: 90% of undergraduates are from Mississippi. Others are from 20 states, 25 foreign countries, and Canada. 80% are from public schools. 70% are white; 25% African American. The average age of freshmen is 19; all undergraduates, 29. 30% do not continue beyond their first year; 40% remain to graduate.

Housing: 1100 students can be accommodated in college housing, which includes single-sex dorms, on-campus apartments, and married student housing. On-campus housing is available on a first-come, first-served basis. 77% of students commute. Alcohol is not permitted. All students may keep cars.

Activities: 10% of men belong to 2 local and 1 national fraternities; 20% of women belong to 12 local and 3 national sororities. There are 84 groups on campus, including art, band, choir, chorale, chorus, computers, dance, drama, ethnic, film, honors, international, jazz band, literary magazine, musical theater, newspaper, orchestra, photography, political, professional, radio and TV, religious, social, social service, student government, and yearbook. Popular campus events include Mardi Gras, Oktoberfest, and Nutcracker.

Sports: There are 4 intercollegiate sports for women, and 5 intramural sports for men and 5 for women. Facilities include 3 gyms, a softball field, tennis and racquetball courts, indoor and outdoor swimming pools, a gymnastics room, a weight room, a dance studio, a 3-hole pitch-and-putt golf course, a soccer and flag football field, and a Vita course.

Disabled Students: 95% of the campus is accessible. Facilities include wheelchair ramps, elevators, special parking, specially equipped restrooms, special class scheduling, lowered drinking fountains, and lowered telephones.

Services: Counseling and information services are available, as is tutoring in most subjects. There is remedial math, reading, and writing.

Campus Safety and Security: Measures include 24-hour foot and vehicle patrol and security escort services. There are lighted pathways/sidewalks, guard gates, and a freshman orientation class.

Programs of Study: MUW confers B.A., B.S., B.F.A., B.M., and B.S.N. degrees. Associate and master's degrees are also awarded. Bachelor's degrees are awarded in BIOLOGICAL SCIENCE (biology/biological science and microbiology), BUSINESS (accounting, business administration and management, fashion merchandising, and sports management), COMMUNICATIONS AND THE ARTS (communications, English, fine arts, music, and Spanish), COMPUTER AND PHYSICAL SCIENCE (chemistry, mathematics, and physical sciences), EDUCATION (art education, elementary education, and music education), HEALTH PROFESSIONS (nursing and speech pathology/audiology), SOCIAL SCIENCE (clothing and textiles management/production/services, food production/management/services, history, human development, paralegal studies, physical fitness/movement, political science/government, psychology, and social science). Biology, chemistry, and English are the strongest academically. Business, nursing, and elementary education have the largest enrollments.

Required: To graduate, students must complete 128 credit hours, including 30 to 39 in a major, with a minimum GPA of 2.0. The core curriculum requires 12 hours of English, 8 of lab-based science, 6 each of history and social sciences, 3 each of speech or philosophy, fine arts, and math, 2 of phys ed, and 1 of a freshman seminar. Students must also pass a comprehensive exam.

Special: Cross-registration and a 3-2 engineering degree are available with Mississippi State University. MUW also offers internships in all divisions, co-op and work-study programs, several combinations of dual majors, study abroad in 5 countries, credit for experience, nondegree study, and a pass/fail option. There are 15 national honor societies, a freshman honors program, and 3 departmental honors programs.

Faculty/Classroom: 40% of faculty are male; 60% are female. 90% teach undergraduates. No introductory courses are taught by graduate students.

Requirements: The SAT or ACT is required. In addition, prospective students should have completed 4 units of English; 3 each of math, science, and social studies courses in U.S. history, world history, government, and economics or geography; 2 of advanced electives, including foreign language or geography; and a course in computer applications. A GPA of 2.0 is required. AP and CLEP credits are accepted. Important factors in the admissions decision are recommendations by school officials, leadership record, and advanced placement or honors courses.

Procedure: Freshmen are admitted to all sessions. Entrance exams should be taken as early as possible. There are early decision, early admissions and rolling admissions plans. Application deadlines are open. Check with the school for the current fee.

Transfer: Applicants must have a GPA of 2.0 in 6 semester hours of both English composition and a lab science, 3 of college algebra or above, and 9 of transferable electives. High school and college transcripts are required. 32 of 128 credits required for the bachelor's degree must be completed at MUW.

Visiting: There are regularly scheduled orientations for prospective students, including talks with various student services officers and preregistration. There are guides for informal visits, and visitors may sit in on classes and stay overnight. To schedule a visit, contact Admissions.

Financial Aid: MUW is a member of CSS. The FAFSA is required. Check with the school for current application deadlines.

International Students: The school actively recruits these students.

They must take the TOEFL, IELTS, or PTE. They must also take the SAT or ACT, scoring 18 on the ACT.

Computers: All students may access the system 8 a.m. to 12 a.m. Monday through Friday. There are no time limits and no fees. It is strongly recommended that all students have a personal computer.

Admissions Contact: Admissions. E-Mail: *admissions@muw.edu* Web: *www.muw.edu*

MISSISSIPPI VALLEY STATE UNIVERSITY C-2

Itta Bena, MS 38941-1400 (662) 254-3347
(800) 844-6885; (662) 254-3759

Full-time: 800 men, 1600 women	**Faculty:** 116; IIB, --$
Part-time: 300 men and women	**Ph.D.s:** 61%
Graduate: 400 men and women	**Student/Faculty:** n/av
Year: semesters, summer session	**Tuition:** $10,500 (17,300)
Application Deadline: see profile	**Room & Board:** $6700
Freshman Class: n/av	
SAT or ACT: required	

LESS COMPETITIVE

Mississippi Valley State University, founded in 1946, is a public institution that offers programs in the arts and sciences, business, and education. The figures in the above capsule and in this profile are approximate. There are 5 undergraduate schools and 1 graduate school. In addition to regional accreditation, MVSU has baccalaureate program accreditation with AACSB, NASAD, NASM, and NCATE. The library contains 127,109 volumes, 295,500 microform items, 853 audio/video tapes/CDs/DVDs, and subscribes to 350 periodicals including electronic. Computerized library services include interlibrary loans, database searching, and Internet access. Special learning facilities include a learning resource center, art gallery, radio station, TV station, campus nursery/preschool, and writing lab. The 450-acre campus is in a small town 8 miles from Greenwood, MS. Including any residence halls, there are 37 buildings.

Student Life: 90% of undergraduates are from Mississippi. Students are from 26 states, 4 foreign countries, and Canada. 92% are from public schools. 94% are African American. The average age of freshmen is 18; all undergraduates, 20. 25% do not continue beyond their first year; 40% remain to graduate.

Housing: 1914 students can be accommodated in college housing, which includes single-sex dorms. In addition, there are honors houses. On-campus housing is available on a first-come and first-served basis. 72% of students commute. Alcohol is not permitted. All students may keep cars.

Activities: There are 44 groups on campus, including art, band, cheerleading, choir, chorus, computers, dance, debate, drama, drill team, environmental, forensics, honors, international, jazz band, literary magazine, marching band, newspaper, orchestra, pep band, performing, political, professional, radio and TV, religious, social, social service, student government, symphony, and yearbook. Popular campus events include Founders Day, Pride Day, and Black History Month.

Sports: There are 8 intercollegiate sports for men and 6 for women, and 10 intramural sports for men and 9 for women. Facilities include a stadium for football and track, a gymnastics room, a dance studio, an indoor pool, a 2200-seat gym, basketball arena, a weight-training room, and handball, squash, and paddleball courts.

Disabled Students: 99% of the campus is accessible. Facilities include wheelchair ramps, elevators, special parking, specially equipped restrooms, and lowered drinking fountains.

Services: Counseling and information services are available, as is tutoring in most subjects. There is a reader service for the blind, and remedial math, reading, and writing.

Campus Safety and Security: Measures include 24-hour foot and vehicle patrol. There are emergency telephones and lighted pathways/sidewalks.

Programs of Study: MVSU confers B.A., B.S., B.M.E., B.S.E, and B.S.W. degrees. Master's degrees are also awarded. Bachelor's degrees are awarded in BIOLOGICAL SCIENCE (biology/biological science), BUSINESS (accounting, business administration and management, and office supervision and management), COMMUNICATIONS AND THE ARTS (art, communications, English, fine arts, and speech/debate/rhetoric), COMPUTER AND PHYSICAL SCIENCE (chemistry, computer science, and mathematics), EDUCATION (early childhood education, elementary education, English education, mathematics education, music education, physical education, science education, and social science education), ENGINEERING AND ENVIRONMENTAL DESIGN (industrial engineering technology), HEALTH PROFESSIONS (environmental health science), SOCIAL SCIENCE (criminal justice, history, political science/government, public administration, social work, and sociology). Education, business, and early childhood education have the largest enrollments.

Required: General education requirements include 12 semester hours in English, 6 each in social studies and lab science, 3 each in college algebra, speech, fine arts, psychology, and health ed, and 2 in phys ed. To graduate, students must complete at least 124 credit hours with a minimum GPA of 2.0 overall and in the major.

Special: MVSU offers a special cooperative education program, B.A.-B.S. degree, internships in social work and environmental health, an accelerated degree program, work-study, and nondegree study. Credit may be granted for military experience. A pass/fail option is possible. There are 4 national honor societies and a freshman honors program.

Faculty/Classroom: 57% of faculty are male; 43% are female. All teach undergraduates. No introductory courses are taught by graduate students. The average class size in an introductory lecture is 30; in a laboratory is 25; and in a regular course is 30.

Admissions: 25% of a recent year's applicants were accepted. The ACT scores were 91% below 21, 6% between 21 and 23, and 3% between 24 and 26.

Requirements: The ACT is required for Mississippi residents. Out-of-state students may submit SAT scores. Applicants must be graduates of a secondary school or have a GED and have completed 4 credits in English, 3 each in math, natural sciences, and social sciences, and 2 in advanced electives, including foreign language. Recommendations are considered important. A GPA of 2.0 is required. AP and CLEP credits are accepted.

Procedure: Freshmen are admitted fall, spring, and summer. There are early admissions and rolling admissions plans. Check with the school for current application deadlines and fee. Applications are accepted online.

Transfer: 221 transfer students enrolled in a recent year. Transfers must have a minimum 2.0 GPA in at least 24 specified credit hours. 30 of 124 credits required for the bachelor's degree must be completed at MVSU.

Visiting: There are regularly scheduled orientations for prospective students. Student visits include campus tours with a student guide. There are guides for informal visits, visitors may sit in on classes, and stay overnight. To schedule a visit, contact Admissions.

Financial Aid: The CSS/Profile, FAFSA, and the college's own financial statement are required. Check with the school for current financial aid deadlines.

International Students: There were 23 international students enrolled in a recent year. The school actively recruits these students. They must take the TOEFL. They must also take the SAT or ACT.

Computers: Wireless access is available. All students may access the system at various times depending on location. There are no time limits and no fees. It is strongly recommended that all students have a personal computer.

Graduates: 346 bachelor's degrees were awarded in a recent year. The most popular majors were early childhood education (14%), social work (14%), and criminal justice (9%). In an average class, 19% graduate in 4 years or less, 15% graduate in 5 years or less, and 6% graduate in 6 years or less.

Admissions Contact: Admissions. E-Mail: *admsn@mvsu.edu* Web: *www.mvsu.edu*

RUST COLLEGE D-1

Holly Springs, MS 38635 (662) 252-8000, ext. 4059
(888) 886-8492, ext. 4059;
(662) 252-8895

Full-time: 300 men, 550 women	**Faculty:** n/av
Part-time: 60 men, 105 women	**Ph.D.s:** 47%
Graduate: n/av	**Student/Faculty:** n/av
Year: semesters, summer session	**Tuition:** $7400
Application Deadline:	**Room & Board:** $3200
Freshman Class: n/av	
SAT or ACT: required	

COMPETITIVE

Rust College, founded in 1866, is a private liberal arts college affiliated with the United Methodist Church. The academic year consists of semesters, each divided into two 8-week modules, plus a summer term. The library contains 123,055 volumes, and 106 audio/video tapes/CDs/DVDs, and subscribes to 340 periodicals including electronic. Computerized library services include interlibrary loans, database searching, and Internet access. Special learning facilities include a radio station, TV station, the Dr. Ron Trojak collection of African tribal art. The 126-acre campus is in a small town 35 miles southeast of Memphis, Tennessee. Including any residence halls, there are 23 buildings.

Student Life: 55% of undergraduates are from Mississippi. Others are from 24 states, and 6 foreign countries. 90% are from public schools. 93% are African American. 60% are Protestant; 29% claim no religious affiliation. The average age of freshmen is 19; all undergraduates, 22. 57% do not continue beyond their first year.

Housing: 856 students can be accommodated in college housing, which includes single-sex dorms. In addition, there are honors houses. On-campus housing is guaranteed for all 4 years. 65% of students live on campus; of those, 50% remain on campus on weekends. Alcohol is not permitted. All students may keep cars.

Activities: 2% of men belong to 3 local and 3 national fraternities; 6% of women belong to 4 local and 4 national sororities. There are 32 groups on campus, including band, cheerleading, choir, chorale, computers, drama, ethnic, honors, international, marching band, newspaper, political, radio and TV, religious, social, social service, and student government. Popular campus events include Career Day, Religious Emphasis Week, and African American Student Leadership Conference.

Sports: There are 7 intercollegiate sports for men and 7 for women. Facilities include a 2500-seat gym, a swimming pool, tennis courts, a track, a 2000-seat stadium, a bowling alley, pool tables, and the Magic Johnson Sports Arena.

Disabled Students: All of the campus is accessible. Facilities include wheelchair ramps, elevators, special parking, specially equipped restrooms, and lowered drinking fountains.

Services: Counseling and information services are available, as is tutoring in most subjects. There is remedial math, reading, and writing.

Campus Safety and Security: Measures include 24-hour foot and vehicle patrol and security escort services. There are lighted pathways/sidewalks.

Programs of Study: Rust confers B.A., B.S. and B.S.W. degrees. Associate degrees are also awarded. Bachelor's degrees are awarded in BIOLOGICAL SCIENCE (biology/biological science), BUSINESS (business administration and management), COMMUNICATIONS AND THE ARTS (communications, English, journalism, and music), COMPUTER AND PHYSICAL SCIENCE (chemistry, computer science, and mathematics), EDUCATION (business education, elementary education, English education, mathematics education, science education, secondary education, and social science education), HEALTH PROFESSIONS (health), SOCIAL SCIENCE (political science/government, social work, and sociology). Business administration and management is the strongest academically. Biology, computer science, and social work have the largest enrollments.

Required: All students must earn a minimum of 124 semester hours while maintaining a cumulative GPA of 2.0. Distribution requirements include 59 1/2 general education credits in the fields of education, humanities, science, and math and a required freshman program. A minimum of 50 credits constitutes a major, and comprehensive exams are given in all programs. Required courses in addition to the freshman program include math, biology, physical science, computer science, English, foreign language, literature, speech, social science, and history.

Special: Internships are available in all areas and may be required for some majors. On-campus work-study, study abroad, credit by examination, independent study, B.A.-B.S. degrees, and dual majors in a variety of programs are available. There are 3-2 degrees in preprofessional programs and medical technology and a 3-2 engineering degree with the student's school of choice. There are 3 national honor societies, a freshman honors program, and 5 departmental honors programs.

Faculty/Classroom: 67% of faculty are male; 33% are female. All teach undergraduates. No introductory courses are taught by graduate students. The average class size in an introductory lecture is 10; in a laboratory is 10; and in a regular course is 25.

Requirements: The SAT or ACT is required. Students must submit 19 academic credits, including 4 in English, 3 each in math, science, and social studies, and 6 electives. An audition, an interview, and 2 letters of recommendation are required. The GED is accepted. An essay and portfolio are recommended. A GPA of 2.0 is required. AP and CLEP credits are accepted. Important factors in the admissions decision are evidence of special talent, extracurricular activities record, and recommendations by school officials.

Procedure: Freshmen are admitted fall, spring, and summer. Entrance exams should be taken prior to the first semester of the freshman year. There is a rolling admissions plan. Check with the school for current application deadlines. The fall 2013 application fee was $10. Applications are accepted online.

Transfer: Transfer applicants with at least 15 semester hours of credit need not take the ACT or SAT. No credits for courses with a grade below C and no credits for any course that are not in keeping with the college's catalog will be accepted. 30 of 124 credits required for the bachelor's degree must be completed at Rust.

Visiting: There are regularly scheduled orientations for prospective students, including a campus tour, departmental visits, introduction to the application process, financial aid orientation, and question-and-answer session. There are guides for informal visits, visitors may sit in on classes, and stay overnight. To schedule a visit, contact Enrollment Services.

Financial Aid: The FFS and the college's own financial statement are required. Check with the school for current application deadlines.

International Students: They must take the TOEFL. They must also take the SAT or ACT.

Computers: All students may access the system. There are no time limits and no fees.

Admissions Contact: Johnny McDonald, Director Enrollment Services. E-Mail: *jbmcdonald@rustcollege.edu* Web: *www.rustcollege.edu*

TOUGALOO COLLEGE C-4

Tougaloo, MS 39174 **(601) 977-7768**
(888) 426-2500; (601) 977-6185

Full-time: 270 men, 600 women
Part-time: 20 men, 50 women
Graduate: n/av
Year: semesters, summer session
Application Deadline: open
Freshman Class: n/av
SAT or ACT: required
Faculty: n/av
Ph.D.s: 52%
Student/Faculty: n/av
Tuition: $10,275
Room & Board: $5000

NONCOMPETITIVE

Tougaloo College, founded in 1869, is a private arts and sciences institution affiliated with the United Church of Christ. The figures in the above capsule and in this profile are approximate. There are 5 undergraduate schools. In addition to regional accreditation, Tougaloo has baccalaureate program accreditation with NCATE. The library contains 117,000 volumes, 7,371 microform items, 3,600 audio/video tapes/CDs/DVDs, and subscribes to 126,934 periodicals including electronic. Computerized library services include interlibrary loans, database searching, Internet access, and Wi-Fi capability. Special learning facilities include an art gallery, manuscripts and archival materials, and the largest collection of civil rights archives in the South. The 500-acre campus is in a suburban area 1 mile north of Jackson. Including any residence halls, there are 35 buildings.

Student Life: 87% of undergraduates are from Mississippi. Others are from 23 states, and 2 foreign countries. 98% are from public schools. 97% are African American. 80% are Protestant; 20% Catholic. The average age of freshmen is 18; all undergraduates, 20. 18% do not continue beyond their first year; 68% remain to graduate.

Housing: 800 students can be accommodated in college housing, which includes single-sex dorms. On-campus housing is available on a first-come and first-served basis. 60% of students live on campus; of those, 80% remain on campus on weekends. Alcohol is not permitted. All students may keep cars.

Activities: 35% of men belong to 4 national fraternities; 40% of women belong to 4 national sororities. Groups on campus include art, cheerleading, choir, chorus, computers, dance, debate, drama, film, honors, international, jazz band, literary magazine, newspaper, photography, political, professional, radio and TV, religious, social, social service, student government, and yearbook. Popular campus events include Founders' Week, Humanities Festival, and Mr and Miss UNCF.

Sports: There are 5 intercollegiate sports for men and 5 for women, and 2 intramural sports for men and 2 for women. Facilities include a gym, tennis courts, baseball diamond, outdoor swimming pool, and access to a bowling alley and a golf course.

Disabled Students: 80% of the campus is accessible. Facilities include wheelchair ramps, elevators, special parking, specially equipped restrooms, and special housing.

Services: Counseling and information services are available, as is tutoring in every subject. There is remedial math, reading, and writing.

Campus Safety and Security: Measures include 24-hour foot and vehicle patrol, self-defense education, and security escort services. There are emergency telephones and lighted pathways/sidewalks.

Programs of Study: Tougaloo confers B.A., and B.S. degrees. Associate degrees are also awarded. Bachelor's degrees are awarded in BIOLOGICAL SCIENCE (biology/biological science), BUSINESS (hospitality management services and recreation and leisure services), COMMUNICATIONS AND THE ARTS (art, communications, English, journalism, and music performance), COMPUTER AND PHYSICAL SCIENCE (chemistry, computer science, mathematics, and physics), EDUCATION (elementary education, English education, mathematics education, music education, physical education, science education, and special education), SOCIAL SCIENCE (child psychology/development, economics, history, humanities, political science/government, psychology, religion, and sociology). Biology, chemistry, and economics are the strongest academically. Biology, economics, and psychology have the largest enrollments.

Required: To graduate, students must complete a minimum 124 credit hours, including 27 to 48 in the major, with a minimum GPA of 2.0 Students must fulfill about 56 hours of general education requirements, take computer science and phys ed courses, complete a senior paper, pass an English/writing proficiency exam, and complete 60 hours of community service.

Special: Tougaloo offers domestic exchange programs with Brown and Boston Universities, Smith College, Bowdoin College, and New York University as well as study abroad in African, European, South American, and Caribbean countries, a Washington semester in conjunction with American University and an internship in a congressman's office, other internships, work-study programs, credit for military service, and pass/fail options. There are 3 national honor societies, a freshman honors program, and 2 departmental honors programs.

Faculty/Classroom: 55% of faculty are male; 45% are female. All teach undergraduates, 20% do research, and 20% do both. No introductory

courses are taught by graduate students. The average class size in an introductory lecture is 30; in a laboratory is 15; and in a regular course is 15.
Requirements: The SAT or ACT is required. Candidates should be graduates of an accredited secondary school or have a GED certificate. They should have completed 3 credits of English, 2 each of math and science, and 1 each of history and social studies. An interview is recommended. A GPA of 2.0 is required. AP and CLEP credits are accepted. Important factors in the admissions decision are advanced placement or honors courses, evidence of special talent, and leadership record.
Procedure: Freshmen are admitted fall and spring. Entrance exams should be taken by March of the senior year. There is a rolling admissions plan. Application deadlines are open. The fall 2013 application fee was $25. Notification is sent on a rolling basis. Applications are accepted online.
Transfer: Applicants must submit transcripts of all college course work and have a minimum GPA of 2.0. 30 of 124 credits required for the bachelor's degree must be completed at Tougaloo.
Visiting: There are regularly scheduled orientations for prospective students, consisting of information on admission process, financial aid, campus tour, interview with departmental faculty if pre-scheduled; for music majors, auditions. There are guides for informal visits, visitors may sit in on classes, and stay overnight. To schedule a visit, contact the Office of Enrollment Management.
Financial Aid: Tougaloo is a member of CSS. The CCS/Profile, or FAFSA, or FFS, or SFS is required. Check with the school for current application deadlines.
International Students: They must take the TOEFL. They must also take the SAT or ACT.
Computers: All students may access the system. There are no time limits and no fees.
Admissions Contact: Director of Admissions. Web: *www.tougaloo.edu*

UNIVERSITY OF MISSISSIPPI D-2

University, MS 38677 (662) 915-7226
(800) OLE-MISS; (662) 915-1831

Full-time: 6680 men, 8253 women	**Faculty:** n/av; 1, --$
Part-time: 524 men, 603 women	**Ph.D.s:** 82%
Graduate: 1278 men, 1456 women	**Student/Faculty:** 19 to 1
Year: semesters, summer session	**Tuition:** $6282 ($16,266)
Application Deadline: July 1	**Room & Board:** $9200
Freshman Class: 13934 applied, 8507 accepted, 3373 enrolled	
SAT CR/M: 530/540	**ACT:** 24 **VERY COMPETITIVE**

The University of Mississippi, founded in 1844, is a public institution offering undergraduate and graduate programs in the liberal arts, business, pharmacy, engineering, accountancy, applied sciences, journalism, and education. There are 8 undergraduate schools and 3 graduate schools. In addition to regional accreditation, Ole Miss has baccalaureate program accreditation with AACSB, ABET, ACEJMC, CSWE, NASAD, NASM, NCATE, and NRPA. The 2 libraries contain 1.9 million volumes, 1.1 million microform items, 118,668 audio/video tapes/CDs/DVDs, and subscribe to 1,686,280 periodicals including electronic. Computerized library services include interlibrary loans, database searching, Internet access, and Wi-Fi capability. Special learning facilities include an art gallery, radio station, TV station, Mary Buie Museum; the Center for the Study of Southern Culture; the National Center for Physical Acoustics; Rowan Oak, the home of William Faulkner; the National Center for Development of Natural Products; the National Food Service Management Institute, and the Croft Institute for International Studies, Honors College. The 3350-acre campus is in a small town 70 miles southeast of Memphis, Tennessee.
Student Life: 63% of undergraduates are from Mississippi. Others are from 50 states, 70 foreign countries, and Canada. 75% are White; 17% African American. The average age of freshmen is 18; all undergraduates, 21. 19% do not continue beyond their first year; 54% remain to graduate.
Housing: 5268 students can be accommodated in college housing, which includes single-sex dorms, on-campus apartments, off-campus apartments, and married student housing. In addition, there are honors houses, special-interest houses, fraternity houses, sorority houses, living-learning communities and freshman interest groups. On-campus housing is guaranteed for the freshman year only, is available on a first-come, first-served basis, and is available on a lottery system for upperclassmen. Alcohol is not permitted. All students may keep cars.
Activities: 28% of men belong to 19 national fraternities; 34% of women belong to 13 national sororities. There are 216 groups on campus, including art, band, cheerleading, chess, choir, chorale, chorus, computers, dance, drama, drill team, ethnic, gay, honors, international, jazz band, literary magazine, marching band, musical theater, newspaper, orchestra, pep band, political, professional, radio and TV, religious, social, social service, student government, symphony, and yearbook. Popular campus events include Welcome Week, Red and Blue Week, The Big Event, Faulkner and Yoknapatawpha Conference and Oxford Conference for the Book.
Sports: There are 6 intercollegiate sports for men and 8 for women. Facilities include A 60,580-seat football stadium; a 8700-seat basketball coliseum; baseball stadium; intramural fields; women's soccer complex; softball complex; volleyball courts; an indoor tennis facility; golf course; track and field complex; athletic training center; and a fitness center with indoor pool, racquetball courts, and basketball courts.
Disabled Students: Facilities include wheelchair ramps, elevators, special parking, specially equipped restrooms, special class scheduling, lowered drinking fountains, lowered telephones.
Services: Counseling and information services are available, as is tutoring in every subject. There is a reader service for the blind, and remedial math and reading.
Campus Safety and Security: Measures include 24-hour foot and vehicle patrol, emergency notification system, self-defense education, and security escort services. There are shuttle buses, emergency telephones, lighted pathways/sidewalks, and controlled access to dorms/residences.
Programs of Study: Ole Miss confers B.A., B.A.Ed., B.A.J., B.A.P.R.M., B.Accy., B.B.A, B.F.A., B.G.S., B.M., B.P.S., B.S., B.S.C.E., B.S.C.J., B.S.Ch.E., B.S.C.S., B.S.E.E., B.S.E.S., B.S.F.C.S., B.S.G.E., B.S.J., B.S.M.E. and B.S.W. degrees. Master's and doctoral degrees are also awarded. Bachelor's degrees are awarded in BIOLOGICAL SCIENCE (biochemistry and biology/biological science), BUSINESS (accounting, banking and finance, business administration and management, business economics, finance, hospitality management services, insurance, management information systems, management science, marketing/retailing/merchandising, and real estate), COMMUNICATIONS AND THE ARTS (art, art history and appreciation, Chinese, communication science, English, French, German, journalism, linguistics, music, Spanish, and theatre arts), COMPUTER AND PHYSICAL SCIENCE (chemistry, computer science, geology, mathematics, and physics), EDUCATION (elementary education, English education, mathematics education, science education, social science education, and special education), ENGINEERING AND ENVIRONMENTAL DESIGN (chemical engineering, civil engineering, electrical/electronics engineering, geological engineering, and mechanical engineering), HEALTH PROFESSIONS (exercise science, medical technology, pharmaceutical science, speech pathology/audiology, and speech therapy), SOCIAL SCIENCE (African American studies, anthropology, area studies, classical/ancient civilization, dietetics, economics, family/consumer studies, forensic studies, history, international studies, liberal arts/general studies, paralegal studies, parks and recreation management, philosophy, political science/government, psychology, public administration, religion, social work, and sociology). Business and education have the largest enrollments.
Required: Students must maintain a minimum GPA of 2.0 (2.5 in teacher education) while taking 126 to 139 semester hours, including 24 to 42 in the major. Other requirements include 6 hours each of English composition and lab science and 3 each of college algebra and humanities and fine arts.
Special: Study abroad in numerous countries, internships and work-study programs within the college are offered. Online programs, dual majors, a general studies degree, credit by exam, special testing in music and languages, credit for military experience, and limited pass/fail options also are available. US internships in Washington, DC and New York, NY. International interships in Sydney, London, Dublin, Scottish Parliament, and South Africa. There are including Phi Beta Kappa and a freshman honors program.
Faculty/Classroom: 56% of faculty are male; 44% are female. No introductory courses are taught by graduate students. The average class size in an introductory lecture is 25 and in a laboratory is 25.
Admissions: 61% of the 2013-2014 applicants were accepted. The SAT scores for the 2013-2014 freshman class were: Critical Reading--31% below 500, 44% between 500 and 599, 20% between 600 and 699, and 5% between 700 and 800; Math--29% below 500, 43% between 500 and 599, 24% between 600 and 699, and 4% between 700 and 800. The ACT scores were 24% below 21, 25% between 21 and 23, 22% between 24 and 26, 12% between 27 and 28, and 17% above 28.
Requirements: Applicants need 15 academic credits, including 4 units in English, 3 each in math (4th recommended), 3 sciences with lab (4th recommended), and 3 social studies, 1 in foreign language, and 1/2 in computer applications. Electives should include 2nd year foreign language or world geography. A portfolio for art majors and an audition for theater and music majors are required. A GPA of 2.0 is required. AP and CLEP credits are accepted.
Procedure: Freshmen are admitted to all sessions. There are early admissions, deferred admissions, and rolling admissions plans. Applications should be filed by July 1 for fall entry, along with a $35 fee.
Transfer: 1490 transfer students enrolled in 2012-2013. Transfer students must have earned a minimum 2.0 GPA on previous college work. The SAT or ACT may be required depending on credits earned. 30 of 126 credits required for the bachelor's degree must be completed at Ole Miss.
Visiting: There are regularly scheduled orientations for prospective students, including academic information/student life discussions and tours. Class attendance and academic appointments can be arranged. There are guides for informal visits, visitors may sit in on classes, and stay overnight. To schedule a visit, contact the Office of Admissions.

Financial Aid: Ole Miss is a member of CSS. The FAFSA is required. Check with the school for current application deadlines.

International Students: The school actively recruits these students. They must take the TOEFL and the college's own test. They must also take the SAT or ACT.

Computers: All students may access the system 24 hours a day. There are no time limits and no fees.

Graduates: From July 1, 2012 to June 30, 2013, 2661 bachelor's degrees were awarded. The most popular majors were teacher education (13%), marketing (7%), and psychology (6%). In an average class, 37% graduate in 4 years or less, 55% graduate in 5 years or less, and 58% graduate in 6 years or less.

Admissions Contact: Whitman Smith, Director of Enrollment Services. E-Mail: *admissions@olemiss.edu* Web: *www.olemiss.edu*

UNIVERSITY OF SOUTHERN MISSISSIPPI D-5

Hattiesburg, MS 39406 **(601) 266-5000; (601) 266-5148**

Full-time: 4250 men, 7143 women **Faculty:** 687; I, --$
Part-time: 967 men, 1298 women **Ph.D.s:** 76%
Graduate: 1039 men, 1771 women **Student/Faculty:** 18 to 1
Year: semesters, summer session **Tuition:** $6336 ($14,440)
Application Deadline: June 30 **Room & Board:** $6834
Freshman Class: 4436 applied, 2473 accepted, 1787 enrolled
ACT: 22

COMPETITIVE

The University of Southern Mississippi, founded in 1910, is a public institution offering comprehensive undergraduate and graduate programs. There are 6 undergraduate schools and one graduate school. In addition to regional accreditation, Southern Miss has baccalaureate program accreditation with AACSB, ABET, ACEJMC, ADA, AHEA, ASLA, CAHEA, CSAB, CSWE, FIDER, NASAD, NASM, NCATE, NLN, and NRPA. The 2 libraries contain 122,428 volumes, 4.9 million microform items, 33,189 audio/video tapes/CDs/DVDs, and subscribe to 24,369 periodicals including electronic. Computerized library services include interlibrary loans, database searching, and Internet access. Special learning facilities include an art gallery, natural history museum, radio station, TV station, TV production studios, the Museum of Natural Science, and a music resource center. The 1090-acre campus is in a suburban area 90 miles southeast of Jackson, and 105 miles north of New Orleans. Including any residence halls, there are 176 buildings.

Student Life: 88% of undergraduates are from Mississippi. Others are from 50 states, 57 foreign countries, and Canada. 65% are White; 29% African American. The average age of freshmen is 18; all undergraduates, 23. 25% do not continue beyond their first year; 50% remain to graduate.

Housing: 3400 students can be accommodated in college housing, which includes single-sex dorms and married student housing. In addition, there are special-interest houses, fraternity houses, sorority houses, A section in 1 dorm is reserved for honor students. Freshmen are housed together. On-campus housing is available on a first-come and first-served basis. 72% of students commute. Alcohol is not permitted. All students may keep cars.

Activities: 15% of men belong to 14 national fraternities; 17% of women belong to 11 national sororities. There are 239 groups on campus, including art, band, cheerleading, choir, chorale, chorus, computers, dance, drama, drum and bugle corps, ethnic, film, gay, honors, international, jazz band, literary magazine, marching band, musical theater, newspaper, opera, orchestra, pep band, photography, political, professional, radio and TV, religious, social, social service, student government, and symphony.

Sports: There are 6 intercollegiate sports for men and 6 for women, and 36 intramural sports for men and 36 for women. Facilities include a recreational lake, a football stadium, a basketball coliseum, a baseball park, a softball stadium, a track and field stadium, a fitness institute, a natatorium, volleyball courts, and playing fields for softball, flag football, and soccer.

Disabled Students: 80% of the campus is accessible. Facilities include wheelchair ramps, elevators, special parking, specially equipped restrooms, special class scheduling, lowered drinking fountains, lowered telephones, special housing.

Services: Counseling and information services are available, as is tutoring in most subjects. There is a reader service for the blind, and remedial math, reading, and writing.

Campus Safety and Security: Measures include 24-hour foot and vehicle patrol, emergency notification system, self-defense education, and security escort services. There are shuttle buses, emergency telephones, lighted pathways/sidewalks, and controlled access to dorms/residences.

Programs of Study: Southern Miss confers B.A., B.S., B.F.A., B.M., B.M.E. and B.S.B.A degrees. Master's and doctoral degrees are also awarded. Bachelor's degrees are awarded in BIOLOGICAL SCIENCE (biology/biological science), BUSINESS (accounting, banking and finance, business administration and management, business economics, hotel/motel and restaurant management, international business management, marketing/retailing/merchandising, and personnel management), COMMUNICATIONS AND THE ARTS (advertising, communications, dance, design, dramatic arts, English, fine arts, journalism, languages, music, radio/television technology, and speech/debate/rhetoric), COMPUTER AND PHYSICAL SCIENCE (chemistry, computer science, geology, information sciences and systems, mathematics, physics, polymer science, and statistics), EDUCATION (art education, business education, early childhood education, elementary education, foreign languages education, guidance education, health education, home economics education, industrial arts education, middle school education, music education, science education, and secondary education), ENGINEERING AND ENVIRONMENTAL DESIGN (architectural technology, computer technology, construction technology, electrical/electronics engineering technology, engineering technology, and mechanical engineering technology), HEALTH PROFESSIONS (medical laboratory technology, nursing, predentistry, premedicine, and speech pathology/audiology), SOCIAL SCIENCE (anthropology, criminal justice, economics, geography, history, international studies, parks and recreation management, philosophy, political science/government, prelaw, psychology, social science, social work, and sociology). Curriculum instruction special education, human performance, and management international business have the largest enrollments.

Required: To graduate, students must complete at least 128 semester hours, including 64 at the senior college level, with a minimum GPA of 2.0. Core requirements include courses in reasoning and communication skills, English, including composition, history, humanities and fine arts, social and behavioral sciences, human wellness, and natural and applied sciences.

Special: USM offers many cooperative programs, internships, dual majors, nondegree study, limited pass/fail options, credit for life experience, and study abroad in 12 countries. The university also participates in the Title IV College Work-Study Program. Accelerated degrees, distance learning, ESL, independent study, and a teacher certification program are also available. There are 27 national honor societies and a freshman honors program.

Faculty/Classroom: 49% of faculty are male; 51% are female. 64% do both. No introductory courses are taught by graduate students.

Admissions: 56% of the 2013-2014 applicants were accepted. The SAT scores for the 2013-2014 freshman class were: Critical Reading--35% below 500, 43% between 500 and 599, 18% between 600 and 699, and 4% between 700 and 800; Math--42% below 500, 40% between 500 and 599, and 18% between 600 and 699. The ACT scores were 41% below 21, 24% between 21 and 23, 19% between 24 and 26, 7% between 27 and 28, and 9% above 28. There were 6 National Merit finalists.

Requirements: The ACT is required. In addition, Full admission will be granted to the following: 1. All students completing the College Preparatory Curriculum (CPC) with a minimum of a 3.2 high school GPA on the CPC and a submitted ACT (composite) or SAT score 2. All students completing the College Preparatory Curriculum (CPC) with a minimum of a 2.5 high school GPA on the CPC or a class rank in the top 50 percent, as well as a score of 16 or higher on the ACT (composite) or a combined SAT score of 760 3. All students completing the College Preparatory Curriculum (CPC) with a minimum of 2.0 high school GPA on the CPC and a score of 18 or higher on the ACT (composite) or a combined SAT score of 860 4. Students who satisfy the National Collegiate Athletic Association (NCAA) standards for student-athletes who are full qualifiers under Division I guidelines A GPA of 2.0 is required. AP and CLEP credits are accepted.

Procedure: Freshmen are admitted fall, spring, and summer. Entrance exams should be taken in the fall of the senior year. Applications should be filed by June 30 for fall entry; January 1 for spring entry; and May 1 for summer entry, along with a $35 fee. Notification is sent on a rolling basis. Applications are accepted online.

Transfer: 1787 transfer students enrolled in 2012-2013. Students must have either an associate degree intended for transfer from a regionally accredited institution or have completed the 30 semester hours of designated coursework outlined below with a minimum 2.0 cumulative grade point average for admission. • 6 semester hours of English Composition (English Composition I and II) • 3 semester hours of mathematics (college algebra, quantitative reasoning, or higher mathematics) • 6 semester hours of natural science (courses must be laboratory-based, with the lecture courses accompanied by the respective lab course) • 9 semester hours of humanities and fine arts (common examples of acceptable coursework are history, philosophy, religion, world literature, art, music) • 6 semester hours of social or behavioral sciences (common examples of acceptable coursework are anthropology, geography, sociology, psychology, and social work) 32 of 128 credits required for the bachelor's degree must be completed at Southern Miss.

Visiting: There are regularly scheduled orientations for prospective students, including campus tours and general session orientations. There are guides for informal visits and visitors may sit in on classes. To schedule a visit, contact Office of Admissions at (601) 266-5000.

Financial Aid: In 2013-2014, 66% of all full-time freshmen and 64% of continuing full-time students received some form of financial aid. 75% of all full-time freshmen and 70% of continuing full-time students received need-based aid. The average freshman award was $10,446. Need-based scholarships or need-based grants averaged $4,505 ; need-based self-help aid (loans and jobs) averaged $3,552; non-need-based athletic scholarships averaged $7,396; and other non-need-based awards and non-need-based scholarships averaged $5,568. The average financial indebtedness of the 2013 graduate was $29,502. The the college's own financial statement is required. Check with the school for current application deadlines.

International Students: The school actively recruits these students. They must take the TOEFL with a minimum score of 525 on the paper-based TOEFL (PBT). They must also take the SAT or ACT, scoring 18.

Computers: All students may access the system. at any time labs are open (departmental labs are for the department only). There are no time limits and no fees.

Graduates: From July 1, 2012 to June 30, 2013, 2520 bachelor's degrees were awarded. The most popular majors were nursing (9%), elementary education (6%), and psychology (6%). 918 companies recruited on campus in 2012-2013. In an average class, 8% graduate in 4 years or less, 43% graduate in 5 years or less, and 49% graduate in 6 years or less.

Admissions Contact: Amanda King, Admissions Office. E-Mail: *admissions@usm.edu* Web: *www.usm.edu*

WILLIAM CAREY UNIVERSITY D-5

Hattiesburg, MS 39401-5499 (601) 318-6103
(800) 962-5991; (601) 318-6454

Full-time: 500 men, 900 women	**Faculty:** 80
Part-time: 150 men, 300 women	**Ph.D.s:** 57%
Graduate: n/av	**Student/Faculty:** 17 to 1
Year: trimesters, summer session	**Tuition:** $9800
Application Deadline:	**Room & Board:** $4700
Freshman Class: n/av	
ACT: required	

LESS COMPETITIVE

William Carey University was founded in 1906 and is a private liberal arts college affiliated with the Mississippi Baptist Convention. The fgures in the above capsule and in this profile are approximate. There are 4 undergraduate schools and 2 graduate schools. In addition to regional accreditation, Carey has baccalaureate program accreditation with NASDTEC, NASM, and NLN. The 4 libraries contain 135,000 volumes, 30,000 microform items, 3000 audio/video tapes/CDs/DVDs, and subscribe to 600 periodicals including electronic. Computerized library services include interlibrary loans and database searching. Special learning facilities include a learning resource center and art gallery. The 120-acre campus is in a small town 100 miles from New Orleans, Louisiana. Including any residence halls, there are 15 buildings.

Student Life: The average age of freshmen is 18.

Housing: 400 students can be accommodated in college housing, which includes single-sex dorms and on-campus apartments. Alcohol is not permitted. All students may keep cars.

Activities: There is 1 national fraternity and 2 local and 1 national sororities. There are 20 groups on campus, including art, cheerleading, choir, chorale, drama, ethnic, honors, international, literary magazine, newspaper, pep band, professional, religious, social, social service, student government, and yearbook. Popular campus events include Hydromania and Mudbowl, Spring Fling Week, and Crawfish Boil.

Sports: There are 4 intercollegiate sports for men and 4 for women, and 3 intramural sports for men and 3 for women. Facilities include a gym, a baseball field, an intramural field, and tennis courts.

Disabled Students: 80% of the campus is accessible. Facilities include wheelchair ramps, special parking, specially equipped restrooms, and special class scheduling.

Services: Counseling and information services are available, as is tutoring in every subject. There is remedial math, reading, and writing.

Campus Safety and Security: Measures include 24-hour foot and vehicle patrol and security escort services. There are emergency telephonesand lighted pathways/sidewalks. Campus security personnel are on duty 24 hours a day.

Programs of Study: Carey confers B.A., B.S., B.F.A., B.G.S., B.L.S., B.M., B.S.B., and B.S.N. degrees. Master's degrees are also awarded. Bachelor's degrees are awarded in BIOLOGICAL SCIENCE (biology/biological science), BUSINESS (business administration and management), COMMUNICATIONS AND THE ARTS (art, communications, dramatic arts, English, music, music performance, and Spanish), COMPUTER AND PHYSICAL SCIENCE (chemistry, mathematics, and radiological technology), EDUCATION (elementary education, music education, and physical education), HEALTH PROFESSIONS (medical laboratory technology, music therapy, and nursing), SOCIAL SCIENCE (history, liberal arts/general studies, psychology, religion, religious music, and social science). Education, music, and nursing are the strongest academically. Education and nursing have the largest enrollments.

Required: Students must complete a core curriculum, including 6 credits each in religion, English, history, and social and behavioral science; 4 in lab science; 3 each in math, fine arts, communication, and literature; and 2 in phys ed. A total of 128 trimester hours, with a minimum 2.0 GPA overall and in the major, is needed to graduate.

Special: Internships are available in some disciplines, and nondegree study, a 3-2 program in forestry, and a 3-1 program in medical technology are also available. 2-year professional programs are possible in engineering, physical therapy, medical records administration, radiological technology, optometry, and pharmacy. Upperclassmen may choose 1 pass/fail option per trimester. There are 7 national honor societies and a freshman honors program.

Requirements: The ACT or SAT is required. Applicants must have earned 16 Carnegie units, including courses in English, foreign language, social studies, science, and math. The admissions committee also considers special skills or aptitudes and other evidence of academic potential. Recommendations from high school officials and college alumni, extracurricular activities, honors courses, leadership potential, and ability to pay also are considered. A GPA of 2.0 is required. AP and CLEP credits are accepted.

Procedure: Freshmen are admitted to all sessions. There are early admissions, deferred admissions, and rolling admissions plans. Check with the school for current application deadlines and fee. Notification is sent on a rolling basis.

Transfer: Transfer students must have a minimum GPA of 1.4 for freshmen, 1.7 for sophomores, and 2.0 for juniors. 30 of 128 credits required for the bachelor's degree must be completed at Carey.

Visiting: There are regularly scheduled orientations for prospective students, including panel discussions, campus tours, faculty advising, and financial aid seminars. There are guides for informal visits, and visitors may sit in on classes and stay overnight. To schedule a visit, contact the Admissions Office.

Financial Aid: The FAFSA is required. Check with the school for current application deadlines.

International Students: They must take the TOEFL or the MELAB and the college's own test. They must also take the SAT or ACT.

Computers: All students may access the system. There are no time limits and no fees.

Admissions Contact: the Admissions Office. Web: *www.wmcarey.edu*

MISSOURI

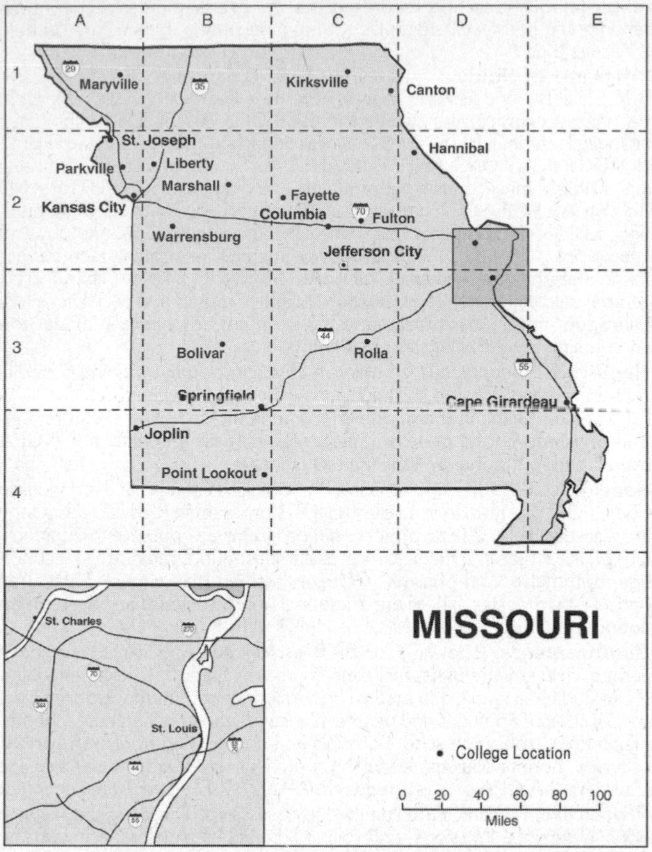

AVILA UNIVERSITY A-2

Kansas City, MO 64145

(816) 501-2400
(800) GO-AVILA; (816) 501-2453

Full-time: 320 men, 600 women	**Faculty:** n/av; IIB, --$
Part-time: 60 men, 150 women	**Ph.D.s:** 69%
Graduate: 230 men, 480 women	**Student/Faculty:** n/av
Year: semesters, summer session	**Tuition:** $24,050
Application Deadline: see profile	**Room & Board:** $6850
Freshman Class: n/av	
SAT or ACT: required	

COMPETITIVE

Avila University, founded in 1916, is a comprehensive liberal arts institution sponsored by the Sisters of St. Joseph of Carondelet. There are 7 undergraduate schools and 3 graduate schools. The figures in the above capsule and in this profile are approximate. In addition to regional accreditation, Avila has baccalaureate program accreditation with CAHEA and CSWE. The library contains 81,755 volumes, 493,760 microform items, and 2910 audio/video tapes/CDs/DVDs, and subscribes to 550 periodicals including electronic. Computerized library services include interlibrary loans, database searching, Internet access, and laptop Internet portals. Special learning facilities include a learning resource center, art gallery, TV station, 500-seat theater, interactive video library, video production facilities, Nursing Education and Resource Center, and dance studio. The 48-acre campus is in a suburban area in Kansas City. Including any residence halls, there are 11 buildings.

Student Life: 55% of undergraduates are from Missouri. Others are from 21 states, 34 foreign countries, and Canada. 87% are from public schools. 66% are white; 14% African American. 26% are Catholic. The average age of freshmen is 18; all undergraduates, 23. 33% do not continue beyond their first year; 51% remain to graduate.

Housing: 310 students can be accommodated in college housing, which includes single-sex and coed dorms and on-campus apartments. On-campus housing is guaranteed for the freshman year only, is available on a first-come, first-served basis, and is available on a lottery system for upperclassmen. Priority is given to out-of-town students. 71% of students commute. All students may keep cars.

Activities: There are no fraternities or sororities. There are 37 groups on campus, including art, cheerleading, choir, chorale, chorus, computers, dance, drama, ethnic, film, gay, honors, international, literary magazine, mock trial, musical theater, newspaper, photography, political, professional, radio and TV, religious, social, social service, and student government. Popular campus events include Student Appreciation Day, Organization Fair, and International Festival.

Sports: There are 4 intercollegiate sports for men and 7 for women. Facilities include a field house with basketball and volleyball courts, a training room, and weight and fitness equipment. There is also an athletic complex with baseball, softball, and soccer fields, tennis courts, and practice fields.

Disabled Students: 95% of the campus is accessible. Facilities include wheelchair ramps, elevators, special parking, specially equipped rest rooms, special class scheduling, lowered drinking fountains, and lowered telephones.

Services: Counseling and information services are available, as is tutoring in most subjects. There is a reader service for the blind and remedial math, reading, and writing.

Campus Safety and Security: Measures include 24-hour foot and vehicle patrol and security escort services. There are emergency telephones, lighted pathways/sidewalks, controlled access to dorms/residences, evening and night security patrols, and 24-hour closed-circuit television in residence hall entryways, computer labs, the student lounge, gym areas, and all university parking lot entrances.

Programs of Study: Avila confers B.A., B.S., B.F.A., B.S.B.A., B.S.N., and B.S.W. degrees. Master's degrees are also awarded. Bachelor's degrees are awarded in BIOLOGICAL SCIENCE (biology/biological science), BUSINESS (accounting, banking and finance, business administration and management, international business management, management science, and marketing/retailing/merchandising), COMMUNICATIONS AND THE ARTS (art, communications, dramatic arts, English, and music), COMPUTER AND PHYSICAL SCIENCE (chemistry, computer science, information sciences and systems, mathematics, and radiological technology), EDUCATION (business education, elementary education, middle school education, and special education), HEALTH PROFESSIONS (medical laboratory technology, nursing, premedicine, and sports medicine), SOCIAL SCIENCE (history, paralegal studies, political science/government, psychology, social work, sociology, and theological studies). Nursing, education, and communications are the strongest academically. Nursing, education, and radiologic technology have the largest enrollments.

Required: To graduate, students must complete at least 128 semester hours with a minimum 2.0 GPA. The 41- to 46-hour core curriculum consists of courses in composition, communication, math, history, literature, theology, philosophy, the arts, the sciences, and social institutions. The average hours in a major range from 36 to 60.

Special: Students may cross-register with the Kansas City Area Student Exchange, the Sisters of Saint Joseph College Consortium, and the Council of Independent Colleges Student Exchange. Avila also offers internships in business, communication, graphic design, paralegal, and other majors, work-study, a Washington center program, dual majors in science, math, and health professions, and accelerated degree programs in business administration and psychology. There are 6 national honor societies and 4 departmental honors programs.

Faculty/Classroom: 33% of faculty are male; 67% are female. All teach and do research. No introductory courses are taught by graduate students. The average class size in an introductory lecture is 22; in a laboratory, 25; and in a regular course, 14.

Requirements: The SAT or ACT is required. Applicants must be graduates of an accredited secondary school or have a GED certificate. They should have completed 16 academic units, including 4 in English, 3 in math, 2 to 4 in foreign language, 2 to 3 in natural and social sciences, and 1 to 2 in fine arts. A GPA of 2.5 is required. AP and CLEP credits are accepted. Important factors in the admissions decision are recommendations by school officials, extracurricular activities record, and leadership record.

Procedure: Freshmen are admitted to all sessions. Entrance exams should be taken in the spring or summer of the junior year. There is a rolling admissions plan. Application deadlines are open. Application fee is $25 (waived for online applications). Notification is sent on a rolling basis. Applications are accepted online.

Transfer: Applicants must have a minimum GPA of 2.0. 30 of 128 credits required for the bachelor's degree must be completed at Avila.

Visiting: There are regularly scheduled orientations for prospective students, including a visit with admissions and a faculty member, a campus tour, and an appointment with the athletics or performance grant manager. There are guides for informal visits, and visitors may sit in on classes and stay overnight. To schedule a visit, contact the Campus Visit Coordinator.

Financial Aid: The FAFSA is required. Check with the school for current application deadlines.

International Students: The school actively recruits these students. They must take the TOEFL with a minimum score of 500 on the paper-based TOEFL (PBT) or 61 on the Internet-based version (iBT).

Admissions Contact: Director of Admissions. E-mail *admission@avila.edu* Web: *www.avila.edu*

CENTRAL METHODIST UNIVERSITY C-2

Fayette, MO 65248 (660) 248-6251
(877) CMU-1854; (660) 248-1872

Full-time: 575 men, 583 women	**Faculty:** 63; IIB, --$
Part-time: 5 men, 10 women	**Ph.D.s:** 83%
Graduate: n/av	**Student/Faculty:** 16 to 1
Year: semesters, summer session	**Tuition:** $21,320
Application Deadline:	**Room & Board:** $6920
Freshman Class: n/av	
ACT: required	

VERY COMPETITIVE

Central Methodist University, founded in 1854, is a private liberal arts institution affiliated with the Methodist Church. In addition to regional accreditation, CMU has baccalaureate program accreditation with NASM. The library contains 102,695 volumes, 140,812 microform items, 3,736 audio/video tapes/CDs/DVDs, and subscribes to 447 periodicals including electronic. Computerized library services include interlibrary loans, database searching, Internet access, and Wi-Fi capability. Special learning facilities include an art gallery, natural history museum, radio station, TV station, an observatory. The 83-acre campus is in a small town 30 miles northwest of Columbia. Including any residence halls, there are 16 buildings.

Student Life: 90% of undergraduates are from Missouri. Others are from 23 states, 8 foreign countries, and Canada. 96% are from public schools. 85% are White. 86% are Protestant; 14% Catholic. The average age of freshmen is 18; all undergraduates, 21. 35% do not continue beyond their first year; 43% remain to graduate.

Housing: 700 students can be accommodated in college housing, which includes single-sex and coed dorms, off-campus apartments, and married student housing. On-campus housing is guaranteed for all 4 years. 59% of students live on campus. Alcohol is not permitted. All students may keep cars.

Activities: 21% of men belong to 3 local and 2 national fraternities; 24% of women belong to 4 local sororities. There are 37 groups on campus, including premed and criminal justice, band, cheerleading, choir, chorale, chorus, computers, dance, debate, drama, drill team, honors, jazz band, literary magazine, marching band, newspaper, opera, photography, political, prelaw, professional, radio and TV, religious, social, social service, and student government. Popular campus events include Music Festival.

Sports: There are 5 intercollegiate sports for men and 4 for women, and 10 intramural sports for men and 10 for women. Facilities include a field house with a 2000-seat gym, playing fields, and a recreation center.

Disabled Students: 65% of the campus is accessible. Facilities include wheelchair ramps, elevators, special parking, specially equipped restrooms, special class scheduling, and lowered drinking fountains.

Services: Counseling and information services are available, as is tutoring in some subjects. There is remedial reading.

Campus Safety and Security: Measures include 24-hour foot and vehicle patrol, emergency notification system, and security escort services. There are emergency telephones, lighted pathways/sidewalks, controlled access to dorms/residences, key-card access to student housing.

Programs of Study: CMU confers B.A., B.S., B.M., B.M.E., B.S.E. and B.S.N., B.G.S., B.A.S.M. and B.ACC. degrees. Associate and master's degrees are also awarded. Bachelor's degrees are awarded in BIOLOGICAL SCIENCE (biology/biological science and marine biology), BUSINESS (accounting, business administration and management, recreational facilities management, and sports management), COMMUNICATIONS AND THE ARTS (broadcasting, communications, dramatic arts, English, music, and Spanish), COMPUTER AND PHYSICAL SCIENCE (chemistry, computer science, mathematics, and physics), EDUCATION (athletic training, early childhood education, elementary education, middle school education, music education, physical education, social science education, and special education), ENGINEERING AND ENVIRONMENTAL DESIGN (environmental science), HEALTH PROFESSIONS (nursing), SOCIAL SCIENCE (criminal justice, history, interdisciplinary studies, philosophy, political science/government, psychology, religion, and sociology). Sciences, music, and preprofessional programs are the strongest academically. Business, education, and nursing have the largest enrollments.

Required: To graduate, students must complete 124 to 131 credit hours, including at least 24 in the major, depending on the degree. A minimum GPA of 2.0 is required for all but the athletic training and education programs, which require a 2.5. Students must complete 53 hours of a distribution curriculum, including computer literacy, computer science, phys ed, religion, philosophy, freshman orientation to college life, and a senior capstone.

Special: CMU offers cooperative programs in medical technology and physical therapy and 3-2 engineering degrees with the University of Missouri at Rolla, the University of Evansville, Stanford University, and Washington University in St. Louis. Work-study programs, internships, study abroad, dual majors, a general studies degree, and nondegree study are also available. There are 14 national honor societies and a freshman honors program.

Faculty/Classroom: 60% of faculty are male; 63% are female. All teach undergraduates. No introductory courses are taught by graduate students. The average class size in an introductory lecture is 30; in a laboratory is 24; and in a regular course is 12.

Admissions: 67% of the 2013-2014 applicants were accepted. 4 freshmen graduated first in their class.

Requirements: The ACT is required. A minimum score of 21 on the ACT is required. Those students with a GPA lower than 2.5 may request conditional admission. Applicants should be graduates of an accredited secondary school or have a GED certificate. Recommended preparatory courses include 4 units of English, 3 of math, and 2 each of science, social studies, and humanities. A GPA of 2.5 is required. AP and CLEP credits are accepted. Important factors in the admissions decision are advanced placement or honors courses, evidence of special talent, and extracurricular activities record.

Procedure: Freshmen are admitted to all sessions. There is a rolling admissions plan. Application deadlines are open. The fall 2013 application fee was $20. Applications are accepted online.

Transfer: 105 transfer students enrolled in 2012-2013. Transfer applicants must be in good academic standing at their previous college and have a 2.0 cumulative GPA. 30 of 124 credits required for the bachelor's degree must be completed at Central Methodist.

Visiting: There are regularly scheduled orientations for prospective students, including meeting with admissions and financial assistance staff, a campus tour, and visits with faculty members. There are guides for informal visits, visitors may sit in on classes, and stay overnight. To schedule a visit, contact the Admissions Office.

Financial Aid: In 2013-2014, 100% of all full-time freshmen and 96% of continuing full-time students received some form of financial aid. 89% of all full-time freshmen and 81% of continuing full-time students received need-based aid. The average freshman award was $17,813. Need-based scholarships or need-based grants averaged $5,030; need-based self-help aid (loans and jobs) averaged $3,187; non-need-based athletic scholarships averaged $4,725; other non-need-based awards and non-need-based scholarships averaged $8,871; and $3,467 from other forms of aid. 27% of undergraduate students work part-time. Average annual earnings from campus work are $1045. The average financial indebtedness of the 2013 graduate was $21,828. The FAFSA is required. Check with the school for current application deadlines.

International Students: There are 11 international students enrolled. They must take the TOEFL with a minimum score of 550 on the paper-based TOEFL (PBT).

Graduates: From July 1, 2012 to June 30, 2013, 149 bachelor's degrees were awarded. The most popular majors were health professions/related programs (19%), education (19%), and social sciences (15%). In an average class, 30% graduate in 4 years or less, 38% graduate in 5 years or less, and 42% graduate in 6 years or less.

Admissions Contact: Office of Admissions E-Mail: *admissions@centralmethodist.edu* Web: *www.centralmethodist.edu*

COLLEGE OF THE OZARKS B-4

Point Lookout, MO 65726 (417) 334-6411, ext. 4219
(800) 222-0525; (417) 335-2618

Full-time: 575 men, 740 women	**Faculty:** n/av; IIB, -$
Part-time: 20 men, 25 women	**Ph.D.s:** 58%
Graduate: n/av	**Student/Faculty:** n/av
Year: semesters	**Tuition:** see profile
Application Deadline: see profile	**Room & Board:** $6400
Freshman Class: n/av	
SAT or ACT: required	

VERY COMPETITIVE

College of the Ozarks, founded in 1906, is a private liberal arts college affiliated with the Presbyterian Church. Instead of paying tuition, students work a total of 560 hours in campus jobs and are responsible only for room and board, books, personal expenses, and a health/technology/services fee of $215 per semester. The figures in the above capsule and in this profile are approximate. In addition to regional accreditation, C of O has baccalaureate program accreditation with ADA. The library contains 117,125 volumes, 31,210 microform items, and 5764 audio/video tapes/CDs/DVDs. Computerized library services include interlibrary loans, database searching, and Internet access. Special learning facilities include a learning resource center, art gallery, radio station, museum, grist mill, weaving studio, firehouse, print shop, orchid greenhouses, fruitcake/jelly kitchens, day care center, and 3 farm operations. The 1000-acre campus is in a small town 40 miles south of Springfield, adjacent to the resort town of Branson. Including any residence halls, there are 82 buildings.

Student Life: 64% of undergraduates are from Missouri. Others are from 39 states and 13 foreign countries. 85% are from public schools. 94% are white. 74% are Protestant; 20% claim no religious affiliation. The average age of freshmen is 18; all undergraduates, 21. 22% do not continue beyond their first year; 78% remain to graduate.

Housing: 1031 students can be accommodated in college housing, which includes single-sex dorms. Student members of the volunteer fire department have living facilities in the campus fire station. On-campus housing is guaranteed for all 4 years. 68% of students live on campus; of those, 80% remain on campus on weekends. Alcohol is not permitted. All students may keep cars.

Activities: There are no fraternities or sororities. There are 49 groups on campus, including art, band, cheerleading, choir, chorale, computers, dance, departmental academic major clubs, drama, honors, international, jazz band, literary magazine, musical theater, orchestra, pep band, photography, political, professional, religious, social service, and student government. Popular campus events include Fourth of July, lectures, and concerts.

Sports: There are 2 intercollegiate sports for men and 2 for women, and 12 intramural sports for men and 12 for women. Facilities include an all-weather track, an indoor walking track, a horseshoe pit, softball and baseball fields, tennis courts, handball courts, volleyball and sand volleyball, badminton and table tennis facilities, an aerobics room, a rehabilitation training room, and a field house with a 4500-seat gym, 3 basketball courts, an Olympic-size pool, a weight-training room, racquetball courts, and a dance studio.

Disabled Students: 80% of the campus is accessible. Facilities include wheelchair ramps, elevators, special parking, specially equipped rest rooms, and special housing.

Services: Counseling and information services are available, as is tutoring in some subjects, including math and foreign language. There is also a center for writing and thinking. There is remedial math and writing.

Campus Safety and Security: Measures include 24-hour foot and vehicle patrol and emergency notification system. There are emergency telephones, lighted pathways/sidewalks, a parking lot security system, and a 24-hour paramedic service on campus. The front gate is locked at 1 a.m. daily, and women's dorms are locked at closing hours.

Programs of Study: C of O confers B.A. and B.S. degrees. Bachelor's degrees are awarded in AGRICULTURE (agricultural business management, agriculture, agronomy, animal science, conservation and regulation, and horticulture), BIOLOGICAL SCIENCE (biology/biological science), BUSINESS (accounting, business administration and management, business economics, hotel/motel and restaurant management, international business management, and marketing management), COMMUNICATIONS AND THE ARTS (art, broadcasting, communications, dramatic arts, English, journalism, media arts, music, music business management, musical theater, performing arts, public relations, Spanish, studio art, and theater design), COMPUTER AND PHYSICAL SCIENCE (chemistry, computer science, information sciences and systems, and mathematics), EDUCATION (agricultural education, art education, business education, early childhood education, elementary education, English education, foreign languages education, mathematics education, music education, physical education, recreation education, secondary education, social studies education, and vocational education), ENGINEERING AND ENVIRONMENTAL DESIGN (graphic arts technology and preengineering), HEALTH PROFESSIONS (health, medical technology, nursing, premedicine, prepharmacy, and preveterinary science), SOCIAL SCIENCE (child psychology/development, clothing and textiles management/production/services, corrections, criminal justice, criminology, dietetics, family/consumer studies, food science, gerontology, history, home economics, interdisciplinary studies, law enforcement and corrections, philosophy, prelaw, psychology, religion, religious music, social work, and sociology). Sciences, history, and education are the strongest academically. Business administration, education, and criminal justice have the largest enrollments.

Required: 42 to 48 hours of general education requirements include specific courses in English, speech, religion, history and political science, math, and phys ed. Students must also select courses from an arts and letters, social science, and physical science distribution. B.A. candidates must complete 8 credit hours of foreign language, and B.S. candidates must complete 6 to 8 credit hours of additional science, computer science, or math. To graduate, all students must complete at least 125 credit hours, including 36 upper-level and 30 in a major field, with a minimum GPA of 2.0 in the major as well as overall. A portfolio and comprehensive exam for psychology, education, and nursing are required.

Special: The college offers co-op programs, cross-registration with Focus on the Family Institute, internships, a 3-2 engineering degree program, and independent study/practicum courses. All students are required to work as part of the work education program. There are 6 national honor societies, a freshman honors program, and 7 departmental honors programs.

Faculty/Classroom: 71% of faculty are male; 29% are female. All teach undergraduates. The average class size in an introductory lecture is 35; in a laboratory, 20; and in a regular course, 21.

Requirements: The SAT or ACT is required. In addition, applicants must be graduates of accredited secondary schools, have a GED, or have an ACT score of 19 or better. A physical exam, financial aid application, 2 recommendations (preferably from school personnel), and an interview are required. C of O requires applicants to be in the upper 50% of their class. A GPA of 3.0 is required. AP and CLEP credits are accepted. Important factors in the admissions decision are ability to finance college education, leadership record, and advanced placement or honors courses.

Procedure: Freshmen are admitted fall and spring. Entrance exams should be taken in October or December of the senior year. There is a rolling admissions plan. Check with the school for current application deadlines. Applications are accepted online. A waiting list is maintained.

Transfer: Transfer applicants must present a minimum GPA of 2.0 and may not have a previous disciplinary or loan default record. The ACT or SAT is required if the applicant has completed fewer than 48 credit hours. An interview is required. The dean of students at the transfer college must complete a form attesting to the positive character of the applicant. All transfer students must submit a financial aid form. 45 of 125 credits required for the bachelor's degree must be completed at C of O.

Visiting: There are regularly scheduled orientations for prospective students Monday through Friday. There are guides for informal visits, and visitors may sit in on classes. To schedule a visit, contact the Admissions Office.

Financial Aid: The FAFSA is required. Check with the school for current application deadlines.

International Students: They must take the TOEFL with a minimum score of 556 on the paper-based TOEFL (PBT) or 79 on the Internet-based version (iBT); it is recommended that they also take the ACT or SAT.

Admissions Contact: Marci Linson, Dean of Admissions. E-Mail: *admiss4@cofo.edu* Web: *www.cofo.edu*

COLUMBIA COLLEGE C-2

Columbia, MO 65216 (573) 875-7352
(800) 231-7352; (573) 875-7506

Full-time: 329 men, 464 women	**Faculty:** 68; IIB, -$
Part-time: 71 men, 89 women	**Ph.D.s:** 72%
Graduate: 73 men, 167 women	**Student/Faculty:** 11 to 1
Year: semesters, summer session	**Tuition:** $17,950
Application Deadline: August 13	**Room & Board:** $6628
Freshman Class: 571 applied, 393 accepted, 148 enrolled	
SAT CR/M: 483/535 **ACT:** 23	**COMPETITIVE**

Columbia College, a private, coeducational institution, offers associate, baccalaureate and master's degrees that prepare students of differing backgrounds for entry level or advanced positions in various occupations and professions. Founded in 1851 by charter of the Missouri legislature and then named Christian Female College, Columbia College assumed its current name and became coeducational in 1970. Although it retains a covenant with the Christian Church (Disciples of Christ), Columbia College is a nonsectarian institution. The college is accredited by the Higher Learning Commission and is a member of the North Central Association of Colleges and Schools and holds specialized accreditation in its Education program. Students may enroll in day, evening or online education classes at the home campus in Columbia, Missouri, or in its Adult Higher Education Division at one of the many nationwide campuses. Columbia College educates 25,000 students each year and has more than 70,000 Columbia College alumni. There is one undergraduate school and one graduate school. In addition to regional accreditation, Columbia has baccalaureate program accreditation with CSWE. The library contains 63,273 volumes, 1,761 audio/video tapes/CDs/DVDs, and subscribes to 199 periodicals including electronic. Computerized library services include interlibrary loans, database searching, and Internet access. Special learning facilities include an art gallery. The 33-acre campus is in an urban area 120 miles east of Kansas City and 120 miles west of St. Louis. Including any residence halls, there are 27 buildings.

Student Life: 89% of undergraduates are from Missouri. Others are from 20 states, 30 foreign countries, and Canada. 73% are White. 65% claim no religious affiliation; 17% Baptist, Christian, Disciples of Christ, Lutheran and Methodist; 11% Catholic. The average age of freshmen is 18; all undergraduates, 22. 39% do not continue beyond their first year; 43% remain to graduate.

Housing: 395 students can be accommodated in college housing, which includes single-sex and coed dorms and on-campus apartments. Living Learning Communities. On-campus housing is guaranteed for all 4 years, is available on a first-come, and first-served basis. 66% of students commute. Alcohol is not permitted. All students may keep cars.

Activities: There are no fraternities or sororities. There are 35 groups on campus, including Model UN and student government, art, choir, chorale, dance, drama, drum and bugle corps, environmental, ethnic, forensics, gay, honors, international, international student, literary magazine, orchestra, photography, political, professional, religious, social, social service, and student government. Popular campus events include Ivy Chain, Holiday Lighting Ceremony and Schiffman Ethics.

Sports: There are 4 intercollegiate sports for men and 6 for women, and 16 intramural sports for men and 16 for women. Facilities include softball and soccer fields, a dance studio, indoor tennis courts, an exercise/weight room, and a gym and sports complex.

Disabled Students: 85% of the campus is accessible. Facilities include wheelchair ramps, elevators, special parking, specially equipped restrooms, special class scheduling, lowered drinking fountains, lowered telephones, and special housing.

Services: Counseling and information services are available, as is tutoring in some subjects, including American and world history, speech, introduction to computer information systems and ethics.

Campus Safety and Security: Measures include 24-hour foot and vehicle patrol, emergency notification system, and security escort services. There are emergency telephones, lighted pathways/sidewalks, and controlled access to dorms/residences.

Programs of Study: Columbia confers B.A., B.S., B.G.S. and B.F.A. degrees. Associate and master's degrees are also awarded. Bachelor's degrees are awarded in AGRICULTURE (environmental studies), BIOLOGICAL SCIENCE (biology/biological science), BUSINESS (accounting, banking and finance, business administration and management, finance, human resources, international business management, marketing/retailing/merchandising, and sports management), COMMUNICATIONS AND THE ARTS (art, ceramic art and design, communications, English, fine arts, graphic design, painting, photography, printmaking, and public relations), COMPUTER AND PHYSICAL SCIENCE (chemistry, computer science, information sciences and systems, and mathematics), EDUCATION (education, elementary education, middle school education, and secondary education), ENGINEERING AND ENVIRONMENTAL DESIGN (military science), HEALTH PROFESSIONS (health care administration and nursing), SOCIAL SCIENCE (American studies, criminal justice, fire services administration, forensic studies, history, human services, interdisciplinary studies, liberal arts/general studies, philosophy, political science/government, psychology, social work, and sociology). Psychology, chemisty, computer science, forensic science, mathmatics, and computer information systems are the strongest academically. Business administration has the largest enrollment.

Required: To graduate, students must complete 60 credit hours for an Associate's degree or 120 credit hours for a Bachelors degree with a minimum GPA of 2.0. Distribution requirements include 12 hours in basic skills (English Composition, Speech, Computer Information Systems and Math); six hours in humanities, history, social and behavioral science; 5-6 hours in math/science and three hours in ethics. Bachelor of Art degrees require six hours of a foreign language or culture and society courses, ethics course, and 39 hours of upper-level course work. Most majors require students to complete a capstone course with the exception of bachelor's in general studies and associates degrees.

Special: Columbia offers cross-registration with the University of Missouri/Columbia and Stephens College, internships, study abroad in more than 20 countries, B.A.-B.S. degrees in most disciplines, an interdisciplinary studies degree, student-designed and dual majors, nondegree study, and pass/fail options. Select students who complete a special 2-semester project earn a bachelor's degree with distinction (B.A.D.). There are 15 national honor societies, a freshman honors program, and 1 departmental honors program.

Faculty/Classroom: 54% of faculty are male; 46% are female. All teach undergraduates, and 50% do research. No introductory courses are taught by graduate students. The average class size in an introductory lecture is 15; in a laboratory is 14; and in a regular course is 16.

Admissions: 69% of the 2013-2014 applicants were accepted. The SAT scores for the 2013-2014 freshman class were: Critical Reading--58% below 500, 33% between 500 and 599, 8% between 600 and 699; Math--33% below 500, 42% between 500 and 599, 17% between 600 and 699, and 8% between 700 and 800. The ACT scores were 25% below 21, 28% between 21 and 23, 25% between 24 and 26, 11% between 27 and 28, and 10% above 28. 23% of the current freshmen were in the top fifth of their class; 46% were in the top two fifths. 4 freshmen graduated first in their class.

Requirements: The SAT or ACT and ACT Writing Test are recommended. Applicants must be graduates of an accredited secondary school or have a GED certificate. Students should have completed 4 units of English, 3 of math including 2 of algebra and 1 of geometry, and 3 each of natural science and social studies, and. 2 of foreign language A GPA of 2.5 is required. AP and CLEP credits are accepted.

Procedure: Freshmen are admitted to all sessions. Entrance exams should be taken In spring of the junior year or fall of the senior year. There are deferred admissions and rolling admissions plans. Applications should be filed by August 13 for fall entry; January 1 for spring entry, along with a $35 fee. Applications are accepted online.

Transfer: 182 transfer students enrolled in 2012-2013. Applicants must have a minimum GPA of 2.0 overall and in the last semester attended and must submit a high school transcript and SAT or ACT scores, and be in good standing from prior institution. 24 of 120 credits required for the bachelor's degree must be completed at Columbia.

Visiting: There are regularly scheduled orientations for prospective students, including a campus tour, a workshop in financial aid, an academic/organization fair, and a luncheon. There are guides for informal visits and visitors may sit in on classes. To schedule a visit, contact the Admissions Office at (800) 231-2391, ext. 7352.

Financial Aid: In 2013-2014, 62% of all full-time freshmen and 59% of continuing full-time students received some form of financial aid. 41% of all full-time freshmen and 43% of continuing full-time students received need-based aid. The average freshman award was $16,560. Need-based scholarships or need-based grants averaged $1,647 ($9,305 maximum); need-based self-help aid (loans and jobs) averaged $1,879 ($6,885 maximum); non-need-based athletic scholarships averaged $12,419 ($22,786 maximum); and other non-need-based awards and non-need-based scholarships averaged $6,740 ($23,536 maximum). 14% of undergraduate students work part-time. Average annual earnings from campus work are $2336. The average financial indebtedness of the 2013 graduate was $11,726. Columbia is a member of CSS. The FAFSA and the college's own financial statement are required. The priority date for freshman financial aid applications for fall entry is March 1. The deadline for filing freshman financial aid applications for fall entry is April 30.

International Students: There are 97 international students enrolled. The school actively recruits these students. They must take the TOEFL with a minimum score of 500 on the paper-based TOEFL (PBT) or 61 on the Internet-based version (iBT). They must also take the ACT.

Graduates: From July 1, 2012 to June 30, 2013, 177 bachelor's degrees were awarded. The most popular majors were business/marketing (42%), psychology (9%), and art (8%). 90 companies recruited on campus in 2012-2013. In an average class, 38% graduate in 5 years or less and 43% graduate in 6 years or less. Of the 2012 graduating class, 86% were enrolled in graduate school within 6 months of graduation.

Admissions Contact: Samantha White, Director of Admissions. E-Mail: *admissions@ccis.edu* Web: *www.ccis.edu*

COX COLLEGE B-3

Springfield, MO 65802 **(417) 269-3038**
(866) 898-5355; (417) 269-3586

Full-time: 20 men, 260 women	**Faculty:** n/av
Part-time: 30 men, 290 women	**Ph.D.s:** n/av
Graduate: n/av	**Student/Faculty:** 12 to 1
Year: semesters, summer session	**Tuition:** $11,500
Application Deadline:	**Room & Board:** $4500
Freshman Class: n/av	
ACT: recommended	

LESS COMPETITIVE

Cox College was founded in 1994, and is a private institution providing programs in nursing and health science. The figures in the above capsule and in this profile are approximate. In addition to regional accreditation, Cox College has baccalaureate program accreditation with NLN. The library contains 7000 volumes and subscribes to 440 periodicals including electronic. Computerized library services include interlibrary loans, database searching, and Internet access. Special learning facilities include a learning resource center, a nursing skills lab, and an audiovisual learning center. The campus is in an urban area in Springfield.

Student Life: 99% of undergraduates are from Missouri. 96% are white. The average age of all undergraduates is 27.

Housing: 60 students can be accommodated in college housing, which includes coed dorms. On-campus housing is available on a first-come, first-served basis. 90% of students commute. Alcohol is not permitted. All students may keep cars.

Activities: There are no fraternities or sororities. There are 3 groups on campus, including professional, religious, and student government. Popular campus events include Fall Fling, Wellness Days, and Diversity Day.

Sports: There is no sports program at Cox College.

Disabled Students: Facilities include wheelchair ramps, elevators, and special parking.

Services: Counseling and information services are available, as is tutoring in some subjects, including math and writing. There is remedial math, reading, and writing. Peer tutoring is available for most science courses.

Campus Safety and Security: Measures include 24-hour foot and vehicle patrol and security escort services. There are emergency telephones and lighted pathways/sidewalks.

Programs of Study: Cox College confers B.S.N. degrees. Associate and master's degrees are also awarded. Bachelor's degrees are awarded in HEALTH PROFESSIONS (nursing).

Required: A total of 122 credit hours and a minimum 2.5 GPA are required for the B.S.N.

Special: Cox College offers cross-registration with Evangel University, work-study programs, and an accelerated degree program in nursing.

Faculty/Classroom: All teach undergraduates. The average class size in an introductory lecture is 25; in a laboratory, 33; and in a regular course, 25.

Requirements: The ACT is recommended. A GPA of 2.5 is required. AP and CLEP credits are accepted.

Procedure: Freshmen are admitted fall, spring, and summer. There is an early decision admission plan. Entrance exams should be taken after admission, prior to registration. Check with the school for current application deadlines. Application fee is $45.

Transfer: A GPA of 2.5 or better is required, with 12 or more hours of credit. Only courses with a grade of C or better will be considered for transfer. Transfer applicants are not required to submit an ACT score. 30 of 122 credits required for the bachelor's degree must be completed at Cox College.

Visiting: There are guides for informal visits and visitors may sit in on classes.

Financial Aid: The FAFSA is required. Check with the school for current application deadlines.

International Students: They must take the TOEFL. They must also take the ACT, scoring 22.

Admissions Contact: Director of Admission. A campus DVD is available. E-Mail: *admissions@coxcollege.edu* Web: *www.coxcollege.edu*

CULVER-STOCKTON COLLEGE C-1

Canton, MO 63435 (573) 288-6331
(800) 537-1883; (573) 288-6618

Full-time: 401 men, 371 women	**Faculty:** 49
Part-time: 12 men, 46 women	**Ph.D.s:** 71%
Graduate: 7 men, 6 women	**Student/Faculty:** 13 to 1
Year: semesters, summer session	**Tuition:** $23,300
Application Deadline:	**Room & Board:** $7600
Freshman Class: 2040 applied, 1209 accepted, 220 enrolled	
SAT: recommended	**ACT:** 21 **COMPETITIVE**

Culver-Stockton College, established in 1853, is a private liberal arts institution affiliated with the Christian Church (Disciples of Christ). In addition to regional accreditation, C-SC has baccalaureate program accreditation with NASM and NLN. The library contains 211,393 volumes, 156 microform items, 6,000 audio/video tapes/CDs/DVDs, and subscribes to 25,561 periodicals including electronic. Computerized library services include interlibrary loans, database searching, Internet access, and Wi-Fi capability. Special learning facilities include an art gallery, planetarium, radio station, TV station, A phage genomics research facility with DNA sequencer, astronomy observation deck, biological research station, collegiate teaching greenhouse, rare books collection, a performing arts center with a multi-media editing suite and recording studio, a publications lab, a photography studio, a simulated classroom, mock trial courtroom with legal research library, 17 computer labs and a tutoring center. The 143-acre campus is in a small town 125 miles north of St. Louis. Including any residence halls, there are 21 buildings.

Student Life: 52% of undergraduates are from Missouri. Others are from 28 states, 13 foreign countries, and Canada. 95% are from public schools. 78% are White; 12% African American. 87% are Protestant; 45% Catholic; 27% claim no religious affiliation. The average age of freshmen is 18; all undergraduates, 20. 32% do not continue beyond their first year; 49% remain to graduate.

Housing: 719 students can be accommodated in college housing, which includes single-sex and coed dorms. In addition, there are fraternity houses and sorority houses. On-campus housing is guaranteed for all 4 years. 74% of students live on campus; of those, 50% remain on campus on weekends. All students may keep cars.

Activities: 36% of men belong to 5 national fraternities; 39% of women belong to 3 national sororities. There are 38 groups on campus, including art, band, cheerleading, choir, chorus, communications, dance, drama, environmental, ethnic, gay, honors, international, jazz band, literary magazine, musical theater, newspaper, orchestra, photography, political, professional, radio and TV, religious, social, social service, student government, and symphony. Popular campus events include National Collegiate Alcohol Awareness Week, Honors Day, Hillstock, Up 'til Dawn, Wildcat Welcome and Greek Week.

Sports: There are 8 intercollegiate sports for men and 8 for women, and 8 intramural sports for men and 8 for women. Facilities include a 2,000-seat football stadium, a soccer field, a baseball field, softball field,intramural fields, a dance studio, a weight room, exercise equipment, and a field house with basketball, volleyball, tennis, and racquetball courts. There is also a golf course, bowling alley, and swimming pool available off-campus for students.

Disabled Students: 40% of the campus is accessible. Facilities include wheelchair ramps, elevators, special parking, specially equipped restrooms, and lowered drinking fountains.

Services: Counseling and information services are available, as is tutoring in most subjects. There is remedial math and writing.

Campus Safety and Security: Measures include 24-hour foot and vehicle patrol, emergency notification system, self-defense education, and security escort services. There are emergency telephones, lighted pathways/sidewalks, and controlled access to dorms/residences.

Programs of Study: C-SC confers B.A., B.S., B.F.A., B.M.E. and B.S.N. degrees. Master's degrees are also awarded. Bachelor's degrees are awarded in BIOLOGICAL SCIENCE (biochemistry and biology/biological science), BUSINESS (accounting, business administration and management, finance, and sports management), COMMUNICATIONS AND THE ARTS (art, arts administration/management, communications, dramatic arts, English, fine arts, graphic design, music, and musical theater), COMPUTER AND PHYSICAL SCIENCE (mathematics), EDUCATION (art education, athletic training, drama education, education, elementary education, music education, and physical education), HEALTH PROFESSIONS (nursing), SOCIAL SCIENCE (criminal justice, history, legal studies, political science/government, psychology, and religion). Accounting, education and nursing are the strongest academically. Business, nursing and psychology have the largest enrollments.

Required: To graduate, students must complete 120 credit hours, including 30 to 72 in the major, with a minimum GPA of 2.0. Distribution requirements include 1 course each in western culture, creativity and arts, diverse populations, individual and society, natural science, and quantitative literacy. English composition, speech, religion, phys ed, and Academic and Cultural Events are also required.

Special: Culver-Stockton offers a joint-degree program in nursing in conjunction with Blessing-Rieman College of Nursing and a 3-2 occupational therapy degree with Washington University in St. Louis. Study abroad, internships, and individualized majors are also available. There are 11 national honor societies, a freshman honors program, and 9 departmental honors programs.

Faculty/Classroom: 52% of faculty are male; 48% are female. All teach undergraduates. No introductory courses are taught by graduate students. The average class size in an introductory lecture is 20; in a laboratory is 17; and in a regular course is 16.

Admissions: 59% of the 2013-2014 applicants were accepted. The SAT scores for the 2013-2014 freshman class were: Critical Reading--53% below 500, 40% between 500 and 599, and 7% between 600 and 699; Math--33% below 500, and 67% between 500 and 599. The ACT scores were 51% below 21, 26% between 21 and 23, 15% between 24 and 26, 5% between 27 and 28, and 3% above 28. 20% of the current freshmen were in the top fifth of their class; 50% were in the top two fifths. 4 freshmen graduated first in their class.

Requirements: The SAT or ACT is recommended. Requirements include secondary school records with GPA and SAT or ACT (preferred) scores. Recommended is a college preparatory program including 4 years of English, 2 to 4 of science, 3 years of social studies, and 2 of math. The GED is accepted. A GPA of 2.0 is required. AP and CLEP credits are accepted.

Procedure: Freshmen are admitted fall and spring. Entrance exams should be taken by April of the entering school year. There are deferred admissions and rolling admissions plans. Application deadlines are open. Applications are accepted online.

Transfer: 80 transfer students enrolled in 2012-2013. Transfer applicants must submit college transcripts and must have a minimum college GPA of 2.0. 30 of 120 credits required for the bachelor's degree must be completed at C-SC.

Visiting: There are regularly scheduled orientations for prospective students, includes meetings with professors, students, coaches,financial aid and extracurricular advisers, financial aid information, a student life panel, and campus tours. There are guides for informal visits, visitors may sit in on classes, and stay overnight. To schedule a visit, contact Gaye Redd at (800) 537-1883.

Financial Aid: In 2013-2014, 100% of all full-time freshmen and 100% of continuing full-time students received some form of financial aid. 95% of all full-time freshmen and 89% of continuing full-time students received need-based aid. The average freshman award was $20,644. Need-based scholarships or need-based grants averaged $17,372 ($30,900 maximum); need-based self-help aid (loans and jobs) averaged $3,678 ($34,952 maximum); non-need-based athletic scholarships averaged $5,239 ($9,000 maximum); and other non-need-based awards and non-need-based scholarships averaged $8,845 ($30,900 maximum). 45% of undergraduate students work part-time. Average annual earnings from campus work are $1295. The average financial indebtedness of the 2013 graduate was $22,975. C-SC is a member of CSS. The FAFSA is required. The priority date for freshman financial aid applications for fall entry is March 1. The deadline for filing freshman financial aid applications for fall entry is June 1.

International Students: There are 14 international students enrolled. The school actively recruits these students. They must take the TOEFL with a minimum score of 550 on the paper-based TOEFL (PBT) or 79 on the Internet-based version (iBT), International students are not required to take the TOEFL if they have resided in this country for 1 semester or submit SAT or ACT scores. They must also take the SAT or ACT.

Graduates: From July 1, 2012 to June 30, 2013, 124 bachelor's degrees were awarded. The most popular majors were business (12%), sport management (10%), and nursing (8%). 29 companies recruited on campus in 2012-2013. In an average class, 41% graduate in 4 years or less, 46%

graduate in 5 years or less, and 46% graduate in 6 years or less. Of the 2012 graduating class, 23% were enrolled in graduate school within 6 months of graduation, and 74% were employed.

Admissions Contact: Misty McBee, Director of Admission. E-Mail: *admissions@culver.edu* Web: *www.culver.edu*

DRURY UNIVERSITY B-3

Springfield, MO 65802 (417) 873-7205
(800) 922-2274; (417) 866-3873

Full-time: 725 men, 819 women
Part-time: 16 men, 10 women
Graduate: 117 men, 301 women
Year: semesters, summer session
Application Deadline: August 1
Freshman Class: 1244 applied, 909 accepted, 324 enrolled
ACT: 25
Faculty: 135; II B, -$
Ph.D.s: 94%
Student/Faculty: 11 to 1
Tuition: $22,295
Room & Board: $8024

VERY COMPETITIVE

Drury University is a private university for education and health sciences. There are 3 undergraduate schools and 7 graduate schools. In addition to regional accreditation, Drury has baccalaureate program accreditation with AACSB, ACBSP, NAAB, NASM, and NCATE. The library contains 194,988 volumes, 13,565 microform items, and 5,344 audio/video tapes/CDs/DVDs, and subscribes to 469 periodicals including electronic. Computerized library services include interlibrary loans, database searching, Internet access, and Wi-Fi capability. Special learning facilities include an art gallery, radio station, TV station, astronomical observatory, greenhouse, teleconference facility, art and architecture slide collection, speech communication center, and writing center. The 80-acre campus is in an urban area 200 miles southwest of St. Louis and 150 miles southeast of Kansas City. Including any residence halls, there are 44 buildings.

Student Life: 85% of undergraduates are from Missouri. Others are from 31 states, 38 foreign countries, and Canada. 85% are from public schools. 81% are White. 70% are Protestant; 16% Catholic. The average age of freshmen is 18; all undergraduates, 21. 16% do not continue beyond their first year; 64% remain to graduate.

Housing: 1022 students can be accommodated in college housing, which includes coed dorms, on-campus apartments, off-campus apartments, and married student housing. In addition, there are honors houses, fraternity houses, and leadership, and living-learning communities. On-campus housing is guaranteed for all 4 years. 52% of students live on campus; of those, 80% remain on campus on weekends. All students may keep cars.

Activities: 25% of men belong to 4 national fraternities; 26% of women belong to 4 national sororities. There are 100 groups on campus, including and academic interests., environment, leadership, student life, art, band, cheerleading, chess, choir, chorale, chorus, computers, dance, debate, drama, environmental, ethnic, film, forensics, gay, honors, international, jazz band, literary magazine, minority students, musical theater, newspaper, opera, orchestra, pep band, photography, political, professional, radio and TV, religious, social, social service, student government, and symphony. Popular campus events include Homecoming, Fireworks on Sunderland Field, Fall Festival, Earth Day and Christmas Vespers.

Sports: There are 9 intercollegiate sports for men and 10 for women, and 5 intramural sports for men and 5 for women. Facilities include An Gold LEED certified 3100-seat event center, a gym, lighted tennis court, racquetball courts, a soccer stadium also used for intramurals, a practice field for soccer, a baseball training center, baseball field (off-campus), a tennis stadium (off-campus), an Olympic-size pool, a fitness center, a running track, a Wellness Program with free massages and exercise classes.

Disabled Students: 95% of the campus is accessible. Facilities include wheelchair ramps, elevators, special parking, specially equipped restrooms, special class scheduling, lowered drinking fountains, and lowered telephones.

Services: Counseling and information services are available, as is tutoring in every subject. There is a reader service for the blind, and remedial writing. There is a math and reading learning center, a writing center, and a communications center.

Campus Safety and Security: Measures include 24-hour foot and vehicle patrol, emergency notification system, self-defense education, and security escort services. There are shuttle buses, emergency telephones, lighted pathways/sidewalks, controlled access to dorms/residences, lighted parking lots with security cameras.

Programs of Study: Drury confers B.A., B.Arch., B.M.E., B.M.T., B.B.A., M.E.D., A.S., B.M. and B.S.Ed. degrees. Master's degrees are also awarded. Bachelor's degrees are awarded in AGRICULTURE (environmental studies and natural resource management), BIOLOGICAL SCIENCE (biology/biological science), BUSINESS (accounting, banking and finance, business administration and management, management information systems, marketing management, organizational leadership and management, and sports management), COMMUNICATIONS AND THE ARTS (advertising, art history and appreciation, arts administration/management, communications, design, dramatic arts, English, fine arts, French, German, media arts, music, public relations, radio/television technology, Spanish, and visual design), COMPUTER AND PHYSICAL SCIENCE (chemistry, computer science, mathematics, and physics), EDUCATION (elementary education, music education, physical education, and secondary education), ENGINEERING AND ENVIRONMENTAL DESIGN (architecture and environmental science), HEALTH PROFESSIONS (environmental health science, exercise science, health science, music therapy, predentistry, premedicine, preoptometry, preosteopathy, prepharmacy, prephysical therapy, preveterinary science, and respiratory therapy), SOCIAL SCIENCE (American studies, criminal justice, criminology, economics, history, human services, international studies, philosophy, political science/government, prelaw, psychology, religion, sociology, and Spanish studies). Premedicine, business, and architecture are the strongest academically. Psychology, business/marketing, and biology have the largest enrollments.

Required: To graduate, students must complete 124 credit hours (150 for accounting and 170 for B.Arch.). They must also maintain a minimum GPA of 2.0 and complete 26 to 32 credit hours in the major (99 for architecture). Students pursue a broad curriculum called Global Perspectives that includes requirements in science, math, humanities, fine arts, fitness, foreign language, and social science, with specific classes in Alpha Seminar, Math and Science Inquiry, Global Awareness, Global Futures, and Values Analysis. All students who complete the curriculum are awarded a minor in global studies.

Special: Drury offers study abroad in Aigina, Greece and 19 other countries as well as cross-registration with colleges in 8 countries; 52% of students study abroad. Premedical early admission arrangements with St. Louis University, the University of Missouri, and Kirksville College of Osteopathic Medicine and a 3-2 engineering dual-degree program in conjunction with the University of Missouri and Washington University are available. Co-op programs include computer information systems and arts administration. 75% of students complete a professional internship; options include public and private sectors and a Washington semester. Work study, credit by exam, non-degree study, dual majors in most majors, and satisfactory/unsatisfactory options are also possible. There are 11 national honor societies, including Phi Beta Kappa, a freshman honors program, and 8 departmental honors programs.

Faculty/Classroom: 54% of faculty are male; 46% are female. All teach undergraduates, and 40% do both. No introductory courses are taught by graduate students. The average class size in an introductory lecture is 21; in a laboratory is 21; and in a regular course is 18.

Admissions: 73% of the 2013-2014 applicants were accepted. The SAT scores for the 2013-2014 freshman class were: Critical Reading--17% below 500, 39% between 500 and 599, 22% between 600 and 699, and 22% between 700 and 800; Math--13% below 500, 52% between 500 and 599, 30% between 600 and 699, and 5% between 700 and 800; Writing--43% below 500, 26% between 500 and 599, 22% between 600 and 699, and 9% between 700 and 800. The ACT scores were 10% below 21, 21% between 21 and 23, 35% between 24 and 26, 12% between 27 and 28, and 22% above 28. 61% of the current freshmen were in the top fifth of their class; 84% were in the top two fifths.

Requirements: The ACT is required. Applicants must be graduates of an accredited secondary school or have a GED certificate. Recommended high school credits include 4 units of English and at least 3 each of math through algebra II, natural science, and social studies. An essay and a reference from the high school counselor or principal are required. A GPA of 3.0 is required. AP and CLEP credits are accepted. Important factors in the admissions decision are ability to finance college education, recommendations by school officials, and personality/intangible qualities.

Procedure: Freshmen are admitted to all sessions. Entrance exams should be taken in the spring of the junior year or fall of the senior year. There are deferred admissions and rolling admissions plans. Applications should be filed by August 1 for fall entry; December 1 for spring entry, along with a $25 fee. Notifications are sent October 1. Applications are accepted online.

Transfer: 85 transfer students enrolled in 2012-2013. Applicants must have a minimum GPA of 2.0 in all college work completed and supply an essay or writing sample. 30 of 124 credits required for the bachelor's degree must be completed at Drury.

Visiting: There are regularly scheduled orientations for prospective students, including visit days for all students as well as visit days specialized for premed, architecture, preengineering, math, physics, computer sciences, arts and sciences, and social sciences students. There are guides for informal visits, visitors may sit in on classes, and stay overnight. To schedule a visit, contact Judy Stelzer at (417) 873-7205.

Financial Aid: In 2013-2014, 88% of all full-time freshmen and 98% of continuing full-time students received some form of financial aid. 83% of all full-time freshmen and 97% of continuing full-time students received need-based aid. The average freshman award was $12,303. Need-based scholarships or need-based grants averaged $9,893; need-based self-help aid (loans and jobs) averaged $4,000; non-need-based athletic scholarships averaged $20,656; and other non-need-based awards and non-need-based scholarships averaged $4,674. 74% of undergraduate students work part-time. Average annual earnings from campus work are $1500. The average financial indebtedness of the 2013 graduate was $24,950. Drury is a member of CSS. The FAFSA and the college's own financial statement are required. The priority date for freshman financial aid applications for fall entry is February 15. The deadline for filing freshman financial aid applications for fall entry is March 15.

International Students: There are 152 international students enrolled. The school actively recruits these students. They must take the TOEFL with a minimum score of 530 on the paper-based TOEFL (PBT) or 71 on the Internet-based version (iBT). They must also take the SAT or ACT. TOFEL or IELTS.

Graduates: From July 1, 2012 to June 30, 2013, 307 bachelor's degrees were awarded. The most popular majors were psychology (14%), business/marketing (12%), and biological/life sciences (10%). 50 companies recruited on campus in 2012-2013. In an average class, 1% graduate in 3 years or less, 47% graduate in 4 years or less, 63% graduate in 5 years or less, and 66% graduate in 6 years or less. Of the 2012 graduating class, 39% were enrolled in graduate school within 6 months of graduation.

Admissions Contact: Karen Chen, Dean of Admission. E-Mail: *druryad@drury.edu* Web: *www.drury.edu*

EVANGEL UNIVERSITY D-3

Springfield, MO 65802 (417) 865-2811
(800) EVANGEL; (417) 865-9599

Full-time: 710 men, 910 women
Part-time: 50 men, 50 women
Graduate: 60 men, 160 women
Year: semesters, summer session
Application Deadline: open
Freshman Class: n/av
SAT or ACT: recommended
Faculty: n/av
Ph.D.s: 74%
Student/Faculty: n/av
Tuition: $19,430
Room & Board: $7140

COMPETITIVE

Evangel University, established in 1955, is a private facility affiliated with the Assemblies of God. There is 1 graduate school. The figures in the above capsule and in this profile are approximate. In addition to regional accreditation, Evangel has baccalaureate program accreditation with CSWE, NASM, and NCATE. The library contains 96,487 volumes, 11,386 microform items, 6801 audio/video tapes/CDs/DVDs, and subscribes to 748 periodicals including electronic. Computerized library services include interlibrary loans, database searching, Internet access, and laptop Internet portals. Special learning facilities include a learning resource center, art gallery, radio station, and TV station. The 80-acre campus is in an urban area 225 miles west of St. Louis. Including any residence halls, there are 21 buildings.

Student Life: 55% of undergraduates are from Missouri. Others are from 49 states, 61 foreign countries, and Canada. 79% are from public schools. 74% claim no religious affiliation; 12% Protestant. The average age of freshmen is 18; all undergraduates, 21. 31% do not continue beyond their first year.

Housing: 1460 students can be accommodated in college housing, which includes single-sex and coed dorms and married student housing. In addition, there are honors communities. On-campus housing is guaranteed for all 4 years. 75% of students live on campus; of those, all remain on campus on weekends. Alcohol is not permitted. All students may keep cars.

Activities: There are no fraternities or sororities. There are 20 groups on campus, including band, cheerleading, choir, chorale, chorus, drama, forensics, honors, jazz band, musical theater, newspaper, orchestra, pep band, photography, political, professional, radio and TV, religious, student government, and yearbook. Popular campus events include College Weekend.

Sports: There are 5 intercollegiate sports for men and 6 for women, and 4 intramural sports for men and 4 for women. Facilities include a student activities center and a 2000-seat gym.

Disabled Students: All of the campus is accessible. Facilities include wheelchair ramps, elevators, special parking, specially equipped rest rooms, lowered drinking fountains, and lowered telephones.

Services: Counseling and information services are available, as is tutoring in every subject. There is a reader service for the blind, and remedial math, reading, and writing.

Campus Safety and Security: Measures include 24-hour foot and vehicle patrol, emergency notification system, and security escort services. There are emergency telephones, lighted pathways/sidewalks, and controlled access to dorms/residences.

Programs of Study: Evangel confers B.A., B.S., B.B.A., B.F.A., B.M., and B.S.W. degrees. Associate and master's degrees are also awarded. Bachelor's degrees are awarded in BIOLOGICAL SCIENCE (biology/biological science), BUSINESS (accounting, management science, and marketing/retailing/merchandising), COMMUNICATIONS AND THE ARTS (art, broadcasting, communications, design, dramatic arts, English, journalism, music, music performance, Spanish, and speech/debate/rhetoric), COMPUTER AND PHYSICAL SCIENCE (chemistry, computer science, and mathematics), EDUCATION (business education, early childhood education, elementary education, foreign languages education, music education, physical education, science education, secondary education, and special education), HEALTH PROFESSIONS (medical laboratory technology), SOCIAL SCIENCE (biblical studies, criminal justice, history, international studies, missions, parks and recreation management, political science/government, psychology, public administration, religion, religious music, social science, social work, and sociology). Science and technology and behavioral science are the strongest academically. Business has the largest enrollment.

Required: All students must complete 50 to 53 general education hours, including courses in phys ed, computer literacy, English composition, English literature, and Bible study. A minimum GPA of 2.0 is required for graduation. Students must complete 124 credit hours, 36 of which are upper division level, with approximately 30 credit hours in the major.

Special: There are 3-2 engineering degrees available in conjunction with the University of Missouri at Columbia. Other options include work-study, credit by exam, and a Washington semester. There are 9 national honor societies and 8 departmental honors programs.

Faculty/Classroom: 62% of faculty are male; 38% are female. All teach undergraduates. No introductory courses are taught by graduate students. The average class size in an introductory lecture, 40, and in a regular course, 20.

Requirements: The SAT or ACT is recommended. In addition, the recommended preparatory curriculum includes 3 credits in English, 2 each in math and social studies, and 1 in lab science. The GED is accepted. A GPA of 2.0 is required. AP and CLEP credits are accepted.

Procedure: Freshmen are admitted to all sessions. Entrance exams should be taken before high school graduation. There is a rolling admissions plan. Application deadlines are open. Application fee is $25. Applications are accepted online.

Transfer: 96 transfer students enrolled in a recent year. Transfer applicants must be in good standing with their previous institutions and have a cumulative GPA of 2.0. 30 of 124 credits required for the bachelor's degree must be completed at Evangel.

Visiting: There are regularly scheduled orientations for prospective students, consisting of scheduled visits every Friday and by appointment. There are guides for informal visits; visitors may sit in on classes and stay overnight. To schedule a visit, contact Office of Admissions.

Financial Aid: The FAFSA is required. Check with the school for current application deadlines.

International Students: There were 9 international students enrolled in a recent year. They must take the TOEFL. They must also take the SAT or ACT.

Graduates: In a recent year, 322 bachelor's degrees were awarded. The most popular majors were health professions and related sciences (22%), education (15%), and communications/journalism (12%). 88 companies recruited on campus in a recent year. In an average class, 25% graduate in 4 years or less, 36% graduate in 5 years or less, and 37% graduate in 6 years or less.

Admissions Contact: Director of Admissions. A campus DVD is available. E-Mail: *admissions@evangel.edu* Web: *www.evangel.edu*

FONTBONNE UNIVERSITY D-3

St. Louis, MO 63105 (314) 889-1413
(800) 205-5862; (314) 889-1451

Full-time: 460 men, 1075 women
Part-time: 160 men, 390 women
Graduate: 250 men, 645 women
Year: semesters, summer session
Application Deadline:
Freshman Class: n/av
SAT or ACT: required
Faculty: n/av
Ph.D.s: 69%
Student/Faculty: n/av
Tuition: $22,684
Room & Board: $8700

COMPETITIVE

Fontbonne University, a Catholic coeducational institution of higher learning sponsored by the Sisters of St. Joseph of Carondelet, is rooted in the Judeo-Christian tradition. The university is dedicated to the discovery, understanding, preservation and dissemination of truth. Undergraduate and graduate programs are offered in an atmosphere characterized by a commitment to open communication, personal concern and diversity. Fontbonne University seeks to educate students to think critically, to act ethically and to assume responsibility as citizens and leaders. There are 2 undergraduate schools and 19 graduate schools. In addition to regional accreditation, Fontbonne has baccalaureate program accreditation with ACBSP, ADA, CSWE, and NCATE. The library contains 91,172 volumes, 3,564 audio/video tapes/CDs/DVDs, and subscribes to 23,463 periodicals including electronic. Computerized library services include interlibrary loans, database searching, Internet access, and Wi-Fi capability. Special learning facilities include an art gallery, a biological green house, test and demo kitchens for dietetics, speech-language and audiology clinics. The 16-acre campus is in a suburban area in Clayton, Missouri, 1 mile west of St. Louis city limits. Including any residence halls, there are 10 buildings.

Student Life: 88% of undergraduates are from Missouri. Others are from

21 states, and 19 foreign countries. 55% are from public schools. 63% are White; 33% African American. 55% are Catholic; 23% Protestant. The average age of freshmen is 19; all undergraduates, 29. 42% do not continue beyond their first year; 51% remain to graduate.

Housing: 270 students can be accommodated in college housing, which includes coed dorms, on-campus apartments, and off-campus apartments. On-campus housing is available on a first-come and first-served basis. Priority is given to out-of-town students. 90% of students commute. All students may keep cars.

Activities: There are no fraternities or sororities. There are 32 groups on campus, including Griffn Gang (althletic support club), computers, dance, drama, environmental, ethnic, Fontbonne Activities Board (planning of on campus activites, gay, honors, international, literary magazine, musical theater, newspaper, photography, political, professional, religious, social, social service, and student government. Popular campus events include Spring Fest, Art Shows, International Bazaar, Lip Sync Contest, Comedy Nights and Musical Performances.

Sports: There are 9 intercollegiate sports for men and 9 for women. Facilities include a student activity center that houses a 1000-seat gym, weight room, track, aerobics room, and cafe.

Disabled Students: All of the campus is accessible. Facilities include wheelchair ramps, elevators, special parking, specially equipped restrooms, special class scheduling, lowered drinking fountains, and special housing.

Services: Counseling and information services are available, as is tutoring in every subject. There is remedial math, reading, and writing.

Campus Safety and Security: Measures include 24-hour foot and vehicle patrol, emergency notification system, and security escort services. There are shuttle buses and controlled access to dorms/residences.

Programs of Study: Fontbonne confers B.A., B.S., B.B.A. and B.F.A. degrees. Master's degrees are also awarded. Bachelor's degrees are awarded in BIOLOGICAL SCIENCE (biology/biological science and nutritional sciences), BUSINESS (accounting, apparel and accessories marketing, business administration and management, fashion merchandising, marketing management, marketing/retailing/merchandising, sports management, and supply chain management), COMMUNICATIONS AND THE ARTS (advertising, art, communications, dramatic arts, English, English literature, English Writing, fine arts, performing arts, theatre acting, theatre arts, theatre production, theater management, and writing), COMPUTER AND PHYSICAL SCIENCE (computer science, computer security and information assurance, information sciences and systems, and mathematics), EDUCATION (childhood education: 1-6, drama education, early childhood education, education, education of the deaf and hearing impaired, elementary education, English education, general studies, mathematics education, middle school education, secondary education, and special education), HEALTH PROFESSIONS (predentistry, premedicine, prephysical therapy, and speech pathology/audiology), SOCIAL SCIENCE (behavioral science, child care/child and family studies, communication sciences & disorders, dietetics, family/consumer studies, history, human services, liberal arts/general studies, prelaw, psychology, religion, religious studies, social work, and sociology). Education, computer science, and math are the strongest academically. Business administration, organizational studies, and education have the largest enrollments.

Required: To graduate, students must complete 128 credit hours, including 44 in general education requirements, with a minimum GPA of 2.0. The number of hours required for the major varies.

Special: Fontbonne offers cross-registration with several area colleges and a student exchange program with the Sisters of St. Joseph Consortium. There are also cooperative programs in all majors except education, internships with major companies, study abroad in 2 countries, work-study programs, student-designed and dual majors, credit by exam, nondegree study, pass/fail options, and B.A.-B.S. degrees. In addition, an accelerated degree program in business is available, as are 3-2 degrees in engineering and social work with Washington University. There is 1 national honor society and a freshman honors program.

Faculty/Classroom: No introductory courses are taught by graduate students. The average class size in an introductory lecture is 12; in a laboratory is 13; and in a regular course is 12.

Admissions: 1 freshman graduated first in the class.

Requirements: The SAT or ACT is required, with a satisfactory SAT or ACT score. Applicants must be graduates of an accredited secondary school or have a GED certificate. They must have completed 16 academic credits, including 4 in English, 3 in math, 2 each in science and social studies, and 1 in history. An audition or portfolio may be required. Fontbonne requires applicants to be in the upper 50% of their class. A GPA of 2.5 is required. AP and CLEP credits are accepted. Important factors in the admissions decision are advanced placement or honors courses, extracurricular activities record, and leadership record.

Procedure: Freshmen are admitted to all sessions. Entrance exams should be taken prior to registration. There are deferred admissions and rolling admissions plans. Check with the school for current application deadlines. The application fee is $25. Applications are accepted online.

Transfer: 233 transfer students enrolled in 2012-2013. Applicants must have a minimum GPA of 2.0 and either submit ACT or the SAT scores or take a placement test. Students with fewer than 30 credits must submit a high school transcript. An interview is recommended. 32 of 128 credits required for the bachelor's degree must be completed at Fontbonne.

Visiting: There are regularly scheduled orientations for prospective students, including a campus tour, a financial aid presentation, and visits with faculty and current students. There are guides for informal visits, visitors may sit in on classes, and stay overnight. To schedule a visit, contact the Admissions Office.

Financial Aid: The CSS/Profile, FAFSA, FFS, and the college's own financial statement are required. Check with the school for current application deadlines.

International Students: There are 26 international students enrolled. The school actively recruits these students. They must take the TOEFL.

Graduates: From July 1, 2012 to June 30, 2013, 466 bachelor's degrees were awarded. The most popular majors were business administration (37%), special education (10%), and organizational behavior studies (10%). 25 companies recruited on campus in 2012-2013. In an average class, 33% graduate in 4 years or less, 51% graduate in 5 years or less, and 54% graduate in 6 years or less.

Admissions Contact: Keith Quigley, Director of Freshman Recruitment. E-Mail: *kquigley@fontbonne.edu* Web: *www.fontbonne.edu*

HANNIBAL-LAGRANGE UNIVERSITY — D-2

Hannibal, MO 63401 — 573-629-4112
(800) HLG-1119; (573) 221-6594

Full-time: n/av	**Faculty:** 65
Part-time: n/av	**Ph.D.s:** n/av
Graduate: n/av	**Student/Faculty:** 12 to 1
Year: semesters, summer session	**Tuition:** $17,920
Application Deadline: August 29	**Room & Board:** $6570

Freshman Class: 696 applied, 448 accepted, 184 enrolled
ACT: required

COMPETITIVE

Hannibal-LaGrange University, founded in 1858, is a private facility affiliated with the Southern Baptist Church. There is one graduate school. In addition to regional accreditation, HLGU has baccalaureate program accreditation with NLN. The library contains 113,830 volumes, 21,944 microform items, and 6,226 audio/video tapes/CDs/DVDs, and subscribes to 12,443 periodicals including electronic. Computerized library services include interlibrary loans, database searching, and Internet access. Special learning facilities include an art gallery, theatre, mission center, sports complex, and nature trail. The 165-acre campus is in a small town 100 miles north of St. Louis. Including any residence halls, there are 22 buildings.

Student Life: 80% of undergraduates are from Missouri. Others are from 29 states, and 27 foreign countries. 83% are White. 80% are Protestant. 43% do not continue beyond their first year; 47% remain to graduate.

Housing: 550 students can be accommodated in college housing, which includes single-sex dorms and on-campus apartments. On-campus housing is available on a first-come and first-served basis. 53% of students commute. Alcohol is not permitted. All students may keep cars.

Activities: There are no fraternities or sororities. There are 24 groups on campus, including and women students, art, cheerleading, choir, chorus, drama, ethnic, honors, international, musical theater, newspaper, professional, radio and TV, religious, science, social, social service, student government, and yearbook. Popular campus events include Campus Visitation Days, Experience HLGU Day, Homecoming and Booster Banquet.

Sports: There are 8 intercollegiate sports for men and 8 for women, and 7 intramural sports for men and 7 for women. Facilities include baseball, softball, and soccer fields and a 41,000-square-foot sports complex that contains a gym, weight and aerobics rooms, and volleyball, tennis, and racquetball courts.

Disabled Students: 70% of the campus is accessible. Facilities include wheelchair ramps, elevators, special parking, specially equipped restrooms, special class scheduling, and special housing.

Services: Counseling and information services are available, as is tutoring in some subjects, based on available tutors There is remedial math and writing, and sign language for hearing-impaired students.

Campus Safety and Security: Measures include 24-hour foot and vehicle patrol, emergency notification system, self-defense education, and security escort services. There are emergency telephones, lighted pathways/sidewalks, and controlled access to dorms/residences.

Programs of Study: HLGU confers B.A., B.S., B.A.S., B.S.E. and B.S.N. degrees. Associate and master's degrees are also awarded. Bachelor's degrees are awarded in BIOLOGICAL SCIENCE (biology/biological science), BUSINESS (accounting, business administration and management, organizational behavior, and recreation and leisure services), COMMUNICATIONS AND THE ARTS (art, communications, dramatic arts, English, music, music performance, and speech/debate/rhetoric), COMPUTER AND PHYSICAL SCIENCE (computer programming, information sciences and systems, and mathematics), EDUCATION (Christian education, early childhood education, elementary education, and secondary education), HEALTH PROFESSIONS (nursing), SOCIAL SCIENCE (biblical studies, criminal justice, history, human services, liberal arts/general studies, missions, psychology, religious music, and sociology). Nursing, and education are the strongest academically. Education, criminal justice, nusing, business, and organizational management have the largest enrollments.

Required: All students must complete a minimum of 124 credit hours with a 2.0 GPA to graduate. The major usually requires 36 or more credit hours of study. General education requirements include 8 hours in natural science; 6 hours each in Bible, composition, literature, foreign language, history, fine arts, and social science; 3 hours each in speech and algebra; 2 hours in phys ed; and 1 hour in Success in Education. Different core requirements pertain to education and nursing students.

Special: Credit by examination, prior learning assessment, online courses, adult programs, and self-designed liberal arts degree There are 2 national honor societies, a freshman honors program, and 2 departmental honors programs.

Faculty/Classroom: All teach undergraduates. No introductory courses are taught by graduate students. The average class size in an introductory lecture is 25 and in a laboratory is 15.

Admissions: 64% of the 2013-2014 applicants were accepted. 21% of the current freshmen were in the top fifth of their class; 52% were in the top two fifths.

Requirements: The ACT is required. Applicants must be graduates of an accredited secondary school or have the GED. A GPA of 2.0 is required. AP and CLEP credits are accepted.

Procedure: Freshmen are admitted to all sessions. Entrance exams should be taken before registration. There is a rolling admissions plan. Applications should be filed by August 29 for fall entry; January 8 for spring entry. The fall 2013 application fee was $25. Applications are accepted online.

Transfer: 187 transfer students enrolled in 2012-2013. Applicants must submit transcripts from all colleges attended. Students applying with fewer than 30 credit hours must also submit a high school transcript along with ACT or SAT scores. 32 of 124 credits required for the bachelor's degree must be completed at HLGU.

Visiting: There are regularly scheduled orientations for prospective students, consisting of Encounter Days, which are organized tours of the campus covering financial aid, student affairs, and academic areas, and which include lunch in the cafeteria. There are guides for informal visits, visitors may sit in on classes, and stay overnight. To schedule a visit, contact the Admissions Office.

Financial Aid: 70% of undergraduate students work part-time. Average annual earnings from campus work are $1500. The FAFSA is required. Check with the school for current application deadlines.

International Students: There are 115 international students enrolled. The school actively recruits these students. They must take the TOEFL with a minimum score of 520 on the paper-based TOEFL (PBT) or 68 on the Internet-based version (iBT). They must also take the SAT or ACT, scoring 20.

Graduates: From July 1, 2012 to June 30, 2013, 257 bachelor's degrees were awarded. The most popular majors were education, nursing, and organizational management. In an average class, 39% graduate in 6 years or less. Of the 2012 graduating class, 33% were enrolled in graduate school within 6 months of graduation, and 55% were employed.

Admissions Contact: Ray Carty, Vice President of Enrollment Management. E-Mail: *rcarty@hlg.edu* Web: *www.hlg.edu*

HARRIS-STOWE STATE UNIVERSITY D-3

St. Louis, MO 63103 **(314) 340-3300; (314) 340-3555**

Full-time: 367 men, 617 women	**Faculty:** 45
Part-time: 91 men, 223 women	**Ph.D.s:** 66%
Graduate: n/av	**Student/Faculty:** 13 to 1
Year: semesters, summer session	**Tuition:** $5220 ($9853)
Application Deadline: July 31	**Room & Board:** $9140

Freshman Class: 541 applied, 541 accepted, 195 enrolled
SAT or ACT: required

NONCOMPETITIVE

Harris-Stowe State University, founded in 1857, is a state-supported institution offering undergraduate programs in areas such as business administration, teacher education, criminal justice, urban affairs, mathematics, and biology. There are 3 undergraduate schools. In addition to regional accreditation, Harris-Stowe has baccalaureate program accreditation with ACBSP and NCATE. The library contains 99,000 volumes, 32,124 microform items, and subscribes to 352 periodicals including electronic. Computerized library services include interlibrary loans, database searching, and Internet access. The 22-acre campus is in an urban area in metropolitan St. Louis. Including any residence halls, there are 8 buildings.

Student Life: 89% of undergraduates are from Missouri. Others are from 14 states, and 7 foreign countries. 83% are African American. The average age of freshmen is 19; all undergraduates, 26. 57% do not continue beyond their first year; 10% remain to graduate.

Housing: 428 students can be accommodated in college housing, which includes coed dorms. On-campus housing is available on a first-come and first-served basis. 115% of students live on campus. Alcohol is not permitted. All students may keep cars.

Activities: There are no fraternities or sororities. There are 43 groups on campus, including art, cheerleading, choir, chorale, dance, drama, ethnic, honors, international, literary magazine, newspaper, professional, religious, social, and student government. Popular campus events include President's Tailgate Party and Homecoming.

Sports: There are 3 intercollegiate sports for men and 4 for women.

Disabled Students: All of the campus is accessible. Facilities include wheelchair ramps, elevators, special parking, specially equipped restrooms, special class scheduling, lowered drinking fountains, and lowered telephones.

Services: Counseling and information services are available, as is tutoring in most subjects. There is remedial math, reading, and writing.

Campus Safety and Security: Measures include 24-hour foot and vehicle patrol and security escort services. There are shuttle buses, emergency telephones, lighted pathways/sidewalks, and controlled access to dorms/residences.

Programs of Study: Harris-Stowe confers B.S., B.S.B.A. and B.S.E.D. degrees. Bachelor's degrees are awarded in BIOLOGICAL SCIENCE (biology/biological science), BUSINESS (accounting, business administration and management, and hospitality management services), COMMUNICATIONS AND THE ARTS (information technology), COMPUTER AND PHYSICAL SCIENCE (mathematics), EDUCATION (early childhood education, education, elementary education, middle school education, and secondary education), HEALTH PROFESSIONS (health care administration), SOCIAL SCIENCE (criminal justice and liberal arts/general studies). Criminal justice, biology, and business administration are the strongest academically. Business administration, criminal justice, and elementary education have the largest enrollments.

Required: Students are required to complete a minimum 120 hours, including a 42-hour core curriculum of general education courses, and must maintain a minimum GPA of 2.5 (2.0 for non-teaching majors). Exit competency is dependent on the specific area of study.

Special: Opportunities are provided for internships as part of the degree in urban education, business administration, and criminal justice. Cross-registration with the University of Missouri-St. Louis and St. Louis University and student-designed majors are possible. There are 3 national honor societies.

Faculty/Classroom: 54% of faculty are male; 46% are female. All teach undergraduates. No introductory courses are taught by graduate students. The average class size in an introductory lecture is 14; in a laboratory is 12; and in a regular course is 14.

Admissions: 100% of the 2013-2014 applicants were accepted. The ACT scores were 88% below 21, 11% between 21 and 23, 2% between 24 and 26, 1% between 27 and 28, and % above 28.

Requirements: The SAT or ACT is required. Applicants should have graduated from high school or received a GED. Applicant that have not completed the ACT or that received a score of less than 18 in the subjects of English, reading, and math are required to take the Harris-Stowe State University Placement Test. AP and CLEP credits are accepted.

Procedure: Freshmen are admitted to all sessions. Entrance exams should be taken before the close of registration. There are deferred admissions and rolling admissions plans. Application deadlines are open. Application fee is $15. Notification is sent on a rolling basis.

Transfer: 173 transfer students enrolled in 2012-2013. Students must have completed 24 college-level credit hours. If they have fewer than 24 credit hours they may be required to take the Harris-Stowe State University Placement Test. 30 of 120 credits required for the bachelor's degree must be completed at Harris-Stowe.

Visiting: There are guides for informal visits and visitors may sit in on classes. To schedule a visit, contact the Admissions Office.

Financial Aid: In 2013-2014, 98% of all full-time freshmen and 93% of continuing full-time students received some form of financial aid. 88% of all full-time freshmen and 78% of continuing full-time students received need-based aid. The average freshman award was $10,674. Need-based scholarships or need-based grants averaged $4,846; need-based self-help aid (loans and jobs) averaged $5,370; and non-need-based athletic scholarships averaged $2,948. The average financial indebtedness of the 2013 graduate was $27,000. The FAFSA and the college's own financial statement are required. The deadline for filing freshman financial aid applications for fall entry is April 1.

International Students: There are 7 international students enrolled. They must take the TOEFL with a minimum score of 500 on the paper-based TOEFL (PBT). They must also take the SAT or ACT, and the college's own entrance exam.

Graduates: From July 1, 2012 to June 30, 2013, 132 bachelor's degrees

were awarded. The most popular majors were business administration (34%), criminal justice (17%), and educational studies (14%). In an average class, 2% graduate in 4 years or less, 7% graduate in 5 years or less, and 10% graduate in 6 years or less.

Admissions Contact: Meghan Sprung, Assistant Director of Admissions. E-Mail: *sprungm@hssc.edu* Web: *www.hssc.edu*

KANSAS CITY ART INSTITUTE — A-2

Kansas City, MO 64111 (816) 474-5224; (816) 802-3309

Full-time: 300 men, 400 women
Part-time: 10 men, 15 women
Graduate: n/av
Year: semesters, summer session
Application Deadline: February 1
Freshman Class: n/av
SAT or ACT: required
Faculty: n/av
Ph.D.s: n/av
Student/Faculty: n/av
Tuition: $29,000
Room & Board: $9000
SPECIAL

The Kansas City Art Institute, founded in 1885, is an independent college of art and design. In addition to regional accreditation, KCAI has baccalaureate program accreditation with NASAD. The library contains 32,000 volumes, and 38 audio/video tapes/CDs/DVDs, and subscribes to 96 periodicals including electronic. Computerized library services include interlibrary loans, database searching, Internet access, and Wi-Fi capability. Special learning facilities include an art gallery. The 15-acre campus is in an urban area in midtown Kansas City. Including any residence halls, there are 14 buildings.

Student Life: 57% of undergraduates are from out of state, mostly the Mid-West. Students are from 31 states, and 7 foreign countries. 90% are from public schools. 73% are White. The average age of freshmen is 18; all undergraduates, 21. 20% do not continue beyond their first year; 60% remain to graduate.

Housing: 180 students can be accommodated in college housing, which includes single-sex and coed dorms and off-campus apartments. The Student Affairs Office offers assistance finding off-campus housing. On-campus housing is guaranteed for the freshman year only, is available on a first-come, and first-served basis. 74% of students commute. Alcohol is not permitted. All students may keep cars.

Activities: There are no fraternities or sororities. There are 3 groups on campus, including ethnic, literary magazine, newspaper, and student government. Popular campus events include Dances, Film Series, and Poetry Readings.

Sports: There is no sports program at KCAI.

Disabled Students: 50% of the campus is accessible. Facilities include wheelchair ramps, elevators, special parking, specially equipped restrooms, and sign language interpreters.

Services: Counseling and information services are available, as is tutoring in every subject. There is remedial reading and writing.

Campus Safety and Security: Measures include 24-hour foot and vehicle patrol and security escort services. There are emergency telephones and lighted pathways/sidewalks.

Programs of Study: KCAI confers B.F.A. degrees. Bachelor's degrees are awarded in COMMUNICATIONS AND THE ARTS (animation, art history and appreciation, ceramic art and design, creative writing, design, digital communications, fiber/textiles/weaving, illustration, painting, photography, printmaking, and sculpture), COMPUTER AND PHYSICAL SCIENCE (digital arts/technology). Painting and graphic design has the largest enrollments.

Required: Students must maintain a minimum GPA of 2.0 overall and within their studio major. A total of 129 credit hours is needed, including 81 in studio classes; 45 distributed among courses in history of Western thought, art history, literature, humanities, and other liberal arts; and 3 in electives.

Special: KCAI offers internships with major corporations such as Hallmark and Disney, independent study, work-study programs, study abroad in 7 countries, cross-registration, an exchange program, and nondegree study. There is also a Community Arts and Service Learning (CASL) certificate program.

Faculty/Classroom: 57% of faculty are male; 43% are female. All teach undergraduates. No introductory courses are taught by graduate students. The average class size in an introductory lecture is 22; in a laboratory is 15; and in a regular course is 22.

Requirements: The SAT or ACT is required. Applicants must submit a portfolio consisting of 10 to 20 pieces of artwork, 2 letters of recommendation, and high school transcripts. The GED is accepted. A statement of purpose and an interview are required. A GPA of 2.5 is required. AP and CLEP credits are accepted. Important factors in the admissions decision are evidence of special talent, advanced placement or honors courses, and recommendations by school officials.

Procedure: Freshmen are admitted fall and spring. Entrance exams should be taken in spring of the junior year or fall of the senior year. There are deferred admissions and rolling admissions plans. Applications should be filed by February 1 for fall entry, along with a $35 fee. Notification is sent on a rolling basis. Applications are accepted online.

Transfer: 59 transfer students enrolled in 2012-2013. Transfer applicants must submit official transcripts and a portfolio. A minimum GPA of 2.0 is required. 66 of 129 credits required for the bachelor's degree must be completed at KCAI.

Visiting: There are regularly scheduled orientations for prospective students, consisting of information sessions offered every other Friday. There are guides for informal visits and visitors may sit in on classes. To schedule a visit, contact the Admissions Office.

Financial Aid: In 2013-2014, 100% of all full-time freshmen and 99% of continuing full-time students received some form of financial aid. 70% of all full-time freshmen and 69% of continuing full-time students received need-based aid. The average freshman award was $22,582. Need-based scholarships or need-based grants averaged $18,537 ($25,680 maximum); need-based self-help aid (loans and jobs) averaged $4,459 ($8,500 maximum); and other non-need-based awards and non-need-based scholarships averaged $4,588 ($25,680 maximum). 61% of undergraduate students work part-time. Average annual earnings from campus work are $1035. The average financial indebtedness of the 2013 graduate was $26,000. The FAFSA, and student and parent IRS tax forms, are required. Check with the school for current application deadlines.

International Students: There are 7 international students enrolled. They must take the TOEFL.

Graduates: From July 1, 2012 to June 30, 2013, 128 bachelor's degrees were awarded. The most popular majors were art history (23%), painting (17%), and fiber (14%). Of the 2012 graduating class, 11% were enrolled in graduate school within 6 months of graduation, and 50% were employed.

Admissions Contact: Bambi Burgard, Vice President for Enrollment Management. E-Mail: *admiss@kcai.edu* Web: *www.kcai.edu*

LINCOLN UNIVERSITY — C-2

Jefferson City, MO 65102 573-681-5599; 800-521-5052; 573-681-5889

Full-time: 893 men, 1034 women
Part-time: 370 men, 716 women
Graduate: 65 men, 127 women
Year: semesters, summer session
Application Deadline: July 15
Freshman Class: 2487 applied, 1059 accepted, 449 enrolled
SAT CR/M: 423/399
Faculty: n/av
Ph.D.s: n/av
Student/Faculty: 15 to 1
Tuition: $6725 ($12,725)
Room & Board: $5271
ACT: 18
NONCOMPETITIVE

Lincoln University is a historically black, 1890 land-grant, public comprehensive institution located in the capital city. There are 4 undergraduate schools and 1 graduate school. In addition to regional accreditation, LU has baccalaureate program accreditation with ACBSP, NASM, NCATE, and NLN. The library contains 151,643 volumes, 127,131 microform items, and 7,512 audio/video tapes/CDs/DVDs, and subscribes to 96 periodicals including electronic. Computerized library services include interlibrary loans, database searching, Internet access, and Wi-Fi capability. Special learning facilities include a radio station, TV station, ethnic studies center, 3 research farms, native plants outdoor laboratory. The 171-acre campus is in a small town 132 miles from St. Louis, 157 miles from Kansas City. Including any residence halls, there are 39 buildings.

Student Life: 84% of undergraduates are from Missouri. Others are from 36 states, 16 foreign countries, and Canada. 58% are White; 35% African American. The average age of freshmen is 19; all undergraduates, 22.

Housing: 923 students can be accommodated in college housing, which includes single-sex and coed dorms. In addition, there are honors houses, wellness housing. On-campus housing is available on a first-come and first-served basis. 78% of students commute. Alcohol is not permitted. All students may keep cars.

Activities: There are 17 groups on campus, including art, band, cheerleading, choir, chorale, dance, drama, honors, international, jazz band, literary magazine, marching band, newspaper, pep band, professional, radio and TV, religious, student government, and yearbook. Popular campus events include Black History Week, Homecoming and Spring Fest.

Sports: There are 5 intercollegiate sports for men and 6 for women. Facilities include a 5500-seat stadium and a 1500-seat gym; athletic weight room; baseball and softball fields; tennis courts.

Disabled Students: All of the campus is accessible. Facilities include wheelchair ramps, elevators, special parking, specially equipped restrooms, and lowered drinking fountains.

Services: Counseling and information services are available, as is tutoring in most subjects. There is a reader service for the blind, and remedial math, reading, and writing.

Campus Safety and Security: Measures include 24-hour foot and vehicle patrol and emergency notification system. There are emergency telephones, lighted pathways/sidewalks, and controlled access to dorms/residences.

Programs of Study: LU confers B.A., B.S., B.M.E. and B.S.Ed. degrees. Associate and master's degrees are also awarded. Bachelor's degrees are awarded in AGRICULTURE (agricultural business management and agriculture), BIOLOGICAL SCIENCE (biology/biological science), BUSINESS (accounting, business administration and management, and marketing/retailing/merchandising), COMMUNICATIONS AND THE ARTS (English, fine arts, journalism, and Spanish), COMPUTER AND PHYSICAL SCIENCE (chemistry, computer science, information sciences and systems, mathematics, and physics), EDUCATION (art education, business education, elementary education, English education, mathematics education, music education, physical education, social science education, and special education), ENGINEERING AND ENVIRONMENTAL DESIGN (civil engineering technology and environmental science), HEALTH PROFESSIONS (medical technology and nursing), SOCIAL SCIENCE (criminal justice, history, liberal arts/general studies, political science/government, psychology, public administration, social work, and sociology). Nursing, business administration and criminal justice have the largest enrollments.

Required: To graduate with a bachelor's degree, students must complete a minimum of 121 credit hours including at least 40 upper division credits of which 30 must be obtained in residence. Students must maintain a minimum GPA of 2.0. Course work is required in math, English, speech, humanities, history, social science, cultural diversity, life and physical science and physical education.

Special: LU offers cross registration with the University of Missouri-Columbia, William Woods University, and Westminster and Stephens Colleges. Credit by exam and a continuing education program are available. There are 5 national honor societies and a freshman honors program.

Faculty/Classroom: 49% of faculty are male; 51% are female. No introductory courses are taught by graduate students.

Admissions: 43% of the 2013-2014 applicants were accepted. The SAT scores for the 2013-2014 freshman class were: Critical Reading--70% below 500, 10% between 500 and 599, 20% between 600 and 699; Math--80% below 500, 20% between 500 and 599. The ACT scores were 79% below 21, 14% between 21 and 23, 5% between 24 and 26, and 2% between 27 and 28.

Requirements: The ACT is required. High school diploma is required and GED is accepted. A GPA of 2.0 is required. AP and CLEP credits are accepted.

Procedure: Freshmen are admitted fall, spring, and summer. Entrance exams should be taken prior to registration. There are deferred admissions and rolling admissions plans. Applications should be filed by July 15 for fall entry; December 1 for spring entry; and May 15 for summer entry. The fall 2013 application fee was $20. Notification is sent on a rolling basis.

Transfer: 208 transfer students enrolled in 2012-2013. Standardized test scores and high school transcripts required if applicant is transfering fewer thann 30 credit hours. Students with less than 2.0 GPA may be admitted on academic probation. 30 of 121 credits required for the bachelor's degree must be completed at LU.

Visiting: There are regularly scheduled orientations for prospective students, freshmen orientation sessions. There are guides for informal visits and visitors may sit in on classes. To schedule a visit, contact the Admissions Office.

Financial Aid: In 2013-2014, 90% of all full-time freshmen students received some form of financial aid. 88% of all full-time freshmen students received need-based aid. LU is a member of CSS. The FAFSA and the college's own financial statement are required. The priority date for freshman financial aid applications for fall entry is March 1.

International Students: There are 58 international students enrolled. They must take the TOEFL with a minimum score of 500 on the paper-based TOEFL (PBT) or 61 on the Internet-based version (iBT) or take the MELAB. They must also take the ACT.

Graduates: From July 1, 2012 to June 30, 2013, 302 bachelor's degrees were awarded. The most popular majors were business administration (12%), criminal justice (11%), and liberal studies (11%). In an average class, 9% graduate in 4 years or less, 20% graduate in 5 years or less, and 24% graduate in 6 years or less.

Admissions Contact: Annette Crowder, Director of Admissions. E-Mail: *enroll@lincolnu.edu* Web: *www.lincolnu.edu*

LINDENWOOD UNIVERSITY D-2

St. Charles, MO 63301-1695 **(636) 949-4949; (636) 949-4989**

Full-time: 2460 men, 3185 women	**Faculty:** n/av; IIA, --$
Part-time: 100 men, 160 women	**Ph.D.s:** n/av
Graduate: 1065 men, 2680 women	**Student/Faculty:** n/av
Year: semesters, summer session	**Tuition:** $14,380
Application Deadline: open	**Room & Board:** $7500
Freshman Class: n/av	
SAT or ACT: required	

COMPETITIVE

Lindenwood University, founded in 1827, is a private institution offering undergraduate and graduate degree programs in the arts and sciences, business, education, and preprofessional fields. There are 8 undergraduate schools and 5 graduate schools. Some figures in the above capsule and in this profile are approximate. In addition to regional accreditation, Lindenwood has baccalaureate program accreditation with TEAC. The library contains 171,562 volumes, 26,128 microform items, 1763 audio/video tapes/CDs/DVDs, and subscribes to 793 periodicals including electronic. Computerized library services include interlibrary loans, database searching, Internet access, and laptop Internet portals. Special learning facilities include a learning resource center, art gallery, radio station, TV station, greenhouse, wetlands program facility, success center, and the Boone Home historic site. The 500-acre campus is in a suburban area 25 miles west of St. Louis. Including any residence halls, there are 37 buildings.

Student Life: 73% of undergraduates are from Missouri. Others are from 43 states, 63 foreign countries, and Canada. 76% are white; 12% African American. The average age of freshmen is 19; all undergraduates, 25. 38% do not continue beyond their first year; 40% remain to graduate.

Housing: 3500 students can be accommodated in college housing, which includes single-sex dorms, on-campus apartments, and married student housing. In addition, there are sorority houses. On-campus housing is guaranteed for all 4 years. 68% of students live on campus; of those, 67% remain on campus on weekends. Alcohol is not permitted. All students may keep cars.

Activities: 1% of men belong to 1 local fraternity and 2 national fraternities; 1% of women belong to 1 national sorority. There are 71 groups on campus, including art, band, cheerleading, chess, choir, chorale, chorus, computers, dance, debate, drama, drill team, ethnic, film, forensics, honors, international, jazz band, literary magazine, marching band, musical theater, newspaper, pep band, photography, political, professional, radio and TV, religious, social, social service, and student government. Popular campus events include Spring Fling, Alumni Weekend, and Christmas Walk.

Sports: There are 20 intercollegiate sports for men and 19 for women, and 9 intramural sports for men and 9 for women. Facilities include an indoor pool, a gym, weight rooms, a 5000-seat stadium, a 3000-seat performance arena, a sand volleyball court, tennis courts, softball, baseball, and soccer fields, a state-of-the art all-weather track, and an 800-seat dual ice rink. Students may use the local golf course and bowling alley for a discounted fee.

Disabled Students: 50% of the campus is accessible. Facilities include wheelchair ramps, elevators, special parking, specially equipped rest rooms, special class scheduling, lowered drinking fountains, and lowered telephones.

Services: Counseling and information services are available, as is tutoring in every subject. There is a reader service for the blind and remedial math, reading, and writing.

Campus Safety and Security: Measures include 24-hour foot and vehicle patrol, emergency notification system, self-defense education, and security escort services. There are emergency telephones and lighted pathways/sidewalks.

Programs of Study: Lindenwood confers B.A., B.S., and B.F.A. degrees. Master's and doctoral degrees are also awarded. Bachelor's degrees are awarded in BIOLOGICAL SCIENCE (biology/biological science), BUSINESS (accounting, banking and finance, business administration and management, human resources, management information systems, marketing/retailing/merchandising, and sports management), COMMUNICATIONS AND THE ARTS (art history and appreciation, communications, creative writing, dance, dramatic arts, English, French, music, performing arts, Spanish, and studio art), COMPUTER AND PHYSICAL SCIENCE (chemistry, computer science, and mathematics), EDUCATION (athletic training, business education, early childhood education, elementary education, music education, physical education, science education, and secondary education), ENGINEERING AND ENVIRONMENTAL DESIGN (engineering), HEALTH PROFESSIONS (medical technology), SOCIAL SCIENCE (criminal justice, fashion design and technology, history, human services, international studies, liberal arts/general studies, ministries, political science/government, prelaw, psychology, public administration, religion, social work, and sociology). Biology, education, and mass communications are the strongest academically. Business, education, and mass communications have the largest enrollments.

Required: To graduate, students must complete a minimum of 128 credit hours, including at least 36 in the major and 42 in upper-division courses, with a minimum GPA of 2.0. Core curriculum courses include 10 hours of math and science, 9 each of social sciences, humanities, and civilization, 6 of English, and 3 each of fine arts and communications. Students must score at proficiency level on a writing assessment.

Special: The university offers internships in most majors, a co-op program in computer science, study abroad and a Washington semester for juniors, and cross-registration through a consortium of Greater St. Louis Colleges and Universities. Dual and student-designed majors, accelerated degree programs, 3-2 degrees in engineering with Washington University in St. Louis and the University of Missouri-Columbia, work-study programs, and nondegree study are also available. There are evening and weekend classes for working adults and 5-year bachelor's programs. There are 9 national honor societies, a freshman honors program, and 6 departmental honors programs.

Faculty/Classroom: 49% of faculty are male; 51% are female. 99%

teach undergraduates. No introductory courses are taught by graduate students. The average class size in an introductory lecture is 30; in a laboratory, 25; and in a regular course, 25.

Requirements: The SAT or ACT is required. Applicants must be graduates of an accredited secondary school or have a GED. High school preparation should include at least 16 academic units, including 4 years of English, 2 to 3 each of math, science, and social studies, 2 of a foreign language, and some study of fine or performing arts. An essay and an interview are recommended. Lindenwood requires applicants to be in the upper 50% of their class. A GPA of 2.5 is required. AP and CLEP credits are accepted. Important factors in the admissions decision are leadership record, evidence of special talent, and advanced placement or honors courses.

Procedure: Freshmen are admitted to all sessions. There are deferred admissions and rolling admissions plans. Application deadlines are open. Application fee is $30.

Transfer: Applicants must have a minimum GPA of 2.0 and should submit official college transcripts in order to transfer credits. 38 of 128 credits required for the bachelor's degree must be completed at Lindenwood.

Visiting: There are regularly scheduled orientations for prospective students, including an admissions interview, a campus tour, and advising. There are guides for informal visits; visitors may sit in on classes and stay overnight. To schedule a visit, contact the Office of Undergraduate Admissions.

Financial Aid: The FAFSA is required. Check with the school for current application deadlines.

International Students: The school actively recruits these students. They must take the TOEFL with a minimum score of 500 on the paper-based TOEFL (PBT) or 61 on the Internet-based version (iBT). They must also take the SAT or ACT.

Admissions Contact: Dean of Undergraduate Admissions. A campus DVD is available. E-Mail: *admissions@lindenwood.edu* Web: *www.lindenwood.edu*

MARYVILLE UNIVERSITY OF SAINT LOUIS D-3

St. Louis, MO 63141 (314) 529-9350
(800) 627-9855; (314) 529-9927

Full-time: 600 men, 1186 women	**Faculty:** 98; IIA, --$
Part-time: 225 men, 818 women	**Ph.D.s:** 86%
Graduate: 321 men, 1883 women	**Student/Faculty:** 18 to 1
Year: semesters, summer session	**Tuition:** $25,002
Application Deadline:	**Room & Board:** $9918

Freshman Class: 1595 applied, 1214 accepted, 409 enrolled
ACT: 25

VERY COMPETITIVE

Founded in 1872, Maryville University is a selective, comprehensive and nationally ranked private institution with over 5,000 students. Maryville offers more than 75 degrees at the undergraduate, masters and doctoral levels to students from 46 states and 30 countries. Maryville's athletics teams compete at the Division II level in the Great Lakes Valley Conference. There are 4 undergraduate schools and 5 graduate schools. In addition to regional accreditation, Maryville has baccalaureate program accreditation with ACBSP, FIDER, NASAD, NASM, and NCATE. The library contains 67,249 volumes, 443,597 microform items, 4,603 audio/video tapes/CDs/DVDs, and subscribes to 85,674 periodicals including electronic. Computerized library services include interlibrary loans, database searching, Internet access, and Wi-Fi capability. Special learning facilities include an art gallery, an observatory, a teaching lab, art and design labs, clinical labs for nursing, occupational therapy, and physical therapy, a communications lab, video conferencing facilities on all campuses, 50 multimedia-ready classrooms, and residence hall computer labs. The 130-acre campus is in a suburban area 20 miles west of downtown St. Louis. Including any residence halls, there are 30 buildings.

Student Life: 81% of undergraduates are from Missouri. Others are from 49 states, and 28 foreign countries. 91% are from public schools. 75% are White. 69% claim no religious affiliation; 13% Catholic. The average age of freshmen is 18; all undergraduates, 26. 13% do not continue beyond their first year; 70% remain to graduate.

Housing: 665 students can be accommodated in college housing, which includes single-sex and coed dorms and on-campus apartments. On-campus housing is available on a first-come, first-served basis, and is available on a lottery system for upperclassmen. 77% of students commute. All students may keep cars.

Activities: There are no fraternities or sororities. There are 70 groups on campus, including art, cheerleading, chorale, dance, environmental, ethnic, forensics, gay, honors, international, jazz band, literary magazine, newspaper, orchestra, pep band, political, professional, religious, social, social service, and student government. Popular campus events include Saturday Night Live Comedy Series, Fall Festival, and Bingo and Brew.

Sports: There are 7 intercollegiate sports for men and 9 for women, and 5 intramural sports for men and 5 for women. Facilities include soccer, softball, and baseball fields, wrestling facility, a gym, outdoor and indoor basketball hoops, an expanded fitness center, table tennis and billiards, and outdoor walking and hiking trails.

Disabled Students: All of the campus is accessible. Facilities include wheelchair ramps, elevators, special parking, specially equipped restrooms, special class scheduling, lowered drinking fountains, lowered telephones.

Services: Counseling and information services are available, as is tutoring in every subject. There is a reader service for the blind. There also is a writing center, learning styles inventory, and help with time management and test-taking skills, study skills materials, workshops, and individual consultations.

Campus Safety and Security: Measures include 24-hour foot and vehicle patrol, emergency notification system, self-defense education, and security escort services. There are emergency telephones, lighted pathways/sidewalks, video security systems in residence halls, and security key operated dorm entrances.

Programs of Study: Maryville confers B.A., B.S., B.F.A., B.S.C.L.S., B.S.M.T. and B.S.N. degrees. Master's and doctoral degrees are also awarded. Bachelor's degrees are awarded in AGRICULTURE (environmental studies), BIOLOGICAL SCIENCE (biochemistry and biology/biological science), BUSINESS (accounting, business administration and management, international business management, marketing management, organizational leadership and management, and sports management), COMMUNICATIONS AND THE ARTS (communications, English, graphic design, and studio art), COMPUTER AND PHYSICAL SCIENCE (actuarial science, chemistry, information sciences and systems, mathematics, and science), EDUCATION (art education, early childhood education, elementary education, middle school education, and secondary education), ENGINEERING AND ENVIRONMENTAL DESIGN (engineering, environmental science, and interior design), HEALTH PROFESSIONS (clinical science, health science, music therapy, nursing, occupational therapy, physical therapy, and rehabilitation therapy), SOCIAL SCIENCE (criminology, forensic studies, history, international studies, liberal arts/general studies, paralegal studies, psychology, and sociology). Actuarial science, education and physical therapy are the strongest academically. Nursing, business administration, and psychology have the largest enrollments.

Required: To graduate, all students must complete a minimum of 128 credit hours, with a minimum GPA of 2.0. The core curriculum consists of 12 credit hours each of humanities, math and science, and social and behavioral science, and 8 credit hours each of communication skills and fine arts. 48 upper-division credits must be completed.

Special: There is cross-registration with Missouri Baptist College and Fontbonne, Webster, and Lindenwood Universities. Students may choose internships in various fields, and cooperative programs are available with various employers Other options include dual and student-designed majors, study abroad in China, England, France, Italy, Japan, Spain, and other countries, a 3-2 engineering degree with Washington University, and a Washington semester. Accelerated degree programs are offered in actuarial science and nursing. A 3+4 B.S/O.D. optometry degree with the University of Missouri-St. Louis and a B.A. criminal justice/criminology degree in association with St. Louis County and Municipal Police Academy are possible. There are 6 national honor societies and a freshman honors program.

Faculty/Classroom: 32% of faculty are male; 68% are female. 75% teach undergraduates. No introductory courses are taught by graduate students. The average class size in an introductory lecture is 17 and in a laboratory is 13.

Admissions: 76% of the 2013-2014 applicants were accepted. The ACT scores were 7% below 21, 28% between 21 and 23, 31% between 24 and 26, 21% between 27 and 28, and 13% above 28. 51% of the current freshmen were in the top fifth of their class; 85% were in the top two fifths. 9 freshmen graduated first in their class.

Requirements: The ACT is required. Students must have graduated from an accredited secondary school with 22 academic credits or have the GED. Expected preparatory courses include 4 units of English, 3 of math, and 2 each of science and social studies, plus 3 additional units in any of the preceding areas or in a foreign language. Some majors have additional admission requirements. A GPA of 2.5 is required. AP and CLEP credits are accepted. Important factors in the admissions decision are recommendations by school officials, advanced placement or honors courses, and leadership record.

Procedure: Freshmen are admitted to all sessions. Entrance exams should be taken during the junior year. There is a rolling admissions plan. Check with the school for current application deadlines. The fall 2013 application fee was $30. Notification is sent on a rolling basis. Applications are accepted online.

Transfer: 319 transfer students enrolled in 2012-2013. A minimum GPA of 2.0, or higher for some majors, is required. Some majors may require ACT or SAT. 30 of 128 credits required for the bachelor's degree must be completed at Maryville.

Visiting: There are regularly scheduled orientations for prospective stu-

dents, including visiting the campus and arranging a personal interview with an admissions counselor. There are guides for informal visits, visitors may sit in on classes, and stay overnight. To schedule a visit, contact the Admissions Office.

Financial Aid: In 2013-2014, 81% of all full-time freshmen and 75% of continuing full-time students received some form of financial aid. 81% of all full-time freshmen and 74% of continuing full-time students received need-based aid. The average freshman award was $23,541. Need-based scholarships or need-based grants averaged $16,878; need-based self-help aid (loans and jobs) averaged $4,055; non-need-based athletic scholarships averaged $14,877; and other non-need-based awards and non-need-based scholarships averaged $14,933. 12% of undergraduate students work part-time. Average annual earnings from campus work are $2200. The average financial indebtedness of the 2013 graduate was $26,626. The FAFSA is required. The priority date for freshman financial aid applications for fall entry is March 1. The deadline for filing freshman financial aid applications for fall entry is April 1.

International Students: There are 71 international students enrolled. The school actively recruits these students. They must take the TOEFL with a minimum score of 500 on the paper-based TOEFL (PBT) or 61 on the Internet-based version (iBT).

Graduates: From July 1, 2012 to June 30, 2013, 662 bachelor's degrees were awarded. The most popular majors were nursing/health professions (41%), business administration (23%), and psychology (10%). 60 companies recruited on campus in 2012-2013. In an average class, 67% graduate in 6 years or less.

Admissions Contact: Shani Lenore-Jenkins, Associate Vice President of Enrollment. E-Mail: *admissions@maryville.edu* Web: *www.maryville.edu*

MISSOURI BAPTIST UNIVERSITY D-3

St. Louis, MO 63141 (314) 392-2296
(877) 434-1115; (314) 434-7596

Full-time: 669 men, 748 women	**Faculty:** n/av; IIB, --$
Part-time: 960 men, 1573 women	**Ph.D.s:** 52%
Graduate: 371 men, 1024 women	**Student/Faculty:** 12 to 1
Year: semesters, summer session	**Tuition:** $21,670
Application Deadline: open	**Room & Board:** $8640

Freshman Class: 840 applied, 512 accepted, 261 enrolled
ACT: 22

COMPETITIVE

Missouri Baptist University, established in 1964, is a private liberal arts institution. There is one undergraduate school and one graduate school. In addition to regional accreditation, MBU has baccalaureate program accreditation with NASM and NCATE. The library contains 71,704 volumes, 3,708 microform items, and 2,705 audio/video tapes/CDs/DVDs, and subscribes to 2,276 periodicals including electronic. Computerized library services include interlibrary loans, database searching, Internet access, and Wi-Fi capability. The 65-acre campus is in a suburban area 15 miles west of St. Louis. Including any residence halls, there are 15 buildings.

Student Life: 77% of undergraduates are from Missouri. Others are from 30 states, and Canada. 76% are White; 11% African American. 41% are Protestant; 39% claim no religious affiliation; 15% Catholic. The average age of freshmen is 19; all undergraduates, 21. 60% do not continue beyond their first year.

Housing: 346 students can be accommodated in college housing, which includes single-sex dorms, on-campus apartments, and off-campus apartments. On-campus housing is available on a first-come and first-served basis. 90% of students commute. Alcohol is not permitted. All students may keep cars.

Activities: There are no fraternities or sororities. There are 24 groups on campus, including band, business, cheerleading, choir, chorale, chorus, computers, dance, drama, film, international, jazz band, literary magazine, musical theater, opera, political, professional, radio and TV, religious, and student government. Popular campus events include Spring Musical, Christmas Concert, and Hanging of the Green.

Sports: There are 12 intercollegiate sports for men and 13 for women, and 6 intramural sports for men and 6 for women. Facilities include Our 47,000-square-foot Carl and Deloris Petty Sports and Recreation Complex includes a 1,000-seat gymnasium, a suspended indoor track, locker rooms, a concession area in Spartan Hall, state-of-the-art training and fitness centers. In addition the campus also has baseball, softball, and soccer fields.

Disabled Students: 80% of the campus is accessible. Facilities include wheelchair ramps, elevators, special parking, specially equipped restrooms, special class scheduling, lowered drinking fountains, and special housing.

Services: Counseling and information services are available, as is tutoring in some subjects. There is a reader service for the blind, and remedial math and writing. Walk-in tutoring in math, biology and chemistry

Campus Safety and Security: Measures include 24-hour foot and vehicle patrol, emergency notification system, self-defense education, and security escort services. There are shuttle buses, emergency telephones, lighted pathways/sidewalks, and controlled access to dorms/residences.

Programs of Study: MBU confers B.A., B.S., B.M., B.M.E., B.P.S. and B.S.E. degrees. Associate, master's, and doctoral degrees are also awarded. Bachelor's degrees are awarded in BIOLOGICAL SCIENCE (biochemistry, biology/biological science, and biotechnology), BUSINESS (accounting, business administration and management, management science, marketing management, and sports management), COMMUNICATIONS AND THE ARTS (communications, English, journalism, music, music performance, musical theater, public relations, and theatre arts), COMPUTER AND PHYSICAL SCIENCE (chemistry, information sciences and systems, and mathematics), EDUCATION (business education, early childhood education, elementary education, health education, middle school education, music education, physical education, and secondary education), HEALTH PROFESSIONS (exercise science, health care administration, and health science), SOCIAL SCIENCE (behavioral science, child psychology/development, Christian studies, criminal justice, history, human services, liberal arts/general studies, ministries, psychology, religion, religious music, and social science). Education, business and psychology have the largest enrollments.

Required: All students must take courses in the humanities/fine arts, social and behavioral sciences, natural sciences, phys ed, computer literacy, and Old and New Testament History. A minimum GPA of 2.0 is required (some majors require a GPA of 2.5 or better). To graduate, students must complete at least 128 credit hours, with a minimum of 30 hours in the major and 45 hours of upper-division courses; pass a general education exam and an exit exam or other assessment in the major; and complete a capstone project.

Special: There is cross-registration with Fontbonne, and Maryville, Lindenwood, and Webster Universities. Students may opt for credit by examination, non-degree study, and student-designed majors. A 3-2 engineering degree with the University of Missouri/Columbia or a 2-2 engineering degree with the University of Missouri/Rolla is available. Study abroad is possible at Harlaxton College in England and at Hong Kong Baptist University. MBU also offers internships in various disciplines and dual majors in some fields. There are 5 national honor societies and a freshman honors program.

Faculty/Classroom: 51% of faculty are male; 48% are female. No introductory courses are taught by graduate students. The average class size in an introductory lecture is 30; in a laboratory is 20; and in a regular course is 25.

Admissions: 61% of the 2013-2014 applicants were accepted.

Requirements: The ACT is required. Applicants must have a minimum score of 20 on the ACT or a satisfactory score on the SAT. Applicants must be graduates of an accredited secondary school. GED and home-schooled students are accepted. MBU requires applicants to be in the upper 50% of their class. A GPA of 2.0 is required. AP and CLEP credits are accepted. Important factors in the admissions decision are advanced placement or honors courses, leadership record, and evidence of special talent.

Procedure: Freshmen are admitted to all sessions. Entrance exams should be taken during the junior year. There is a rolling admissions plan. Application deadlines are open. Application fee is $35. Applications are accepted online.

Transfer: 445 transfer students enrolled in 2012-2013. Applicants must have a 2.0 GPA, with some programs requiring 2.5 or better. Students must submit official transcripts from all previous colleges attended, along with a character reference. 24 of 128 credits required for the bachelor's degree must be completed at MBU.

Visiting: There are regularly scheduled orientations for prospective students, Student visits include a Welcome Weekend, open houses, and campus tours. There are guides for informal visits, visitors may sit in on classes, and stay overnight. To schedule a visit, contact the Admissions Office at (314) 392-2290.

Financial Aid: In 2013-2014, 100% of all full-time freshmen and % of continuing full-time students received some form of financial aid. The FAFSA and the college's own financial statement are required. Check with the school for current application deadlines.

International Students: There are 48 international students enrolled. The school actively recruits these students. They must take the TOEFL with a minimum score of 550 on the paper-based TOEFL (PBT) or 80 on the Internet-based version (iBT). They must also take the ACT, scoring 20.

Computers: All students may access the system. There are no time limits and no fees.

Graduates: From July 1, 2012 to June 30, 2013, 393 bachelor's degrees were awarded.

Admissions Contact: Cynthia Sutton, Director of Admissions. E-Mail: *admissions@mobap.edu* Web: *www.mobap.edu*

MISSOURI SOUTHERN STATE UNIVERSITY A-4

Joplin, MO 64801 (417) 625-9379
(866) 818-6778; (417) 659-4429

Full-time: 1797 men, 2328 women **Faculty:** n/av; IIB, --$
Part-time: 557 men, 905 women **Ph.D.s:** 96%
Graduate: 9 men, 20 women **Student/Faculty:** 18 to 1
Year: semesters, summer session **Tuition:** $5797
Application Deadline: **Room & Board:** $6113
Freshman Class: 1726 applied, 1679 accepted, 808 enrolled
ACT: 21
COMPETITIVE

Missouri Southern State University, founded in 1937, is a public, primarily commuter institution offering undergraduate degree programs in the arts and sciences, business, education, psychology, and technology. There are 4 undergraduate schools. In addition to regional accreditation, Missouri Southern has baccalaureate program accreditation with ABET, ACBSP, ADA, NCATE, and NLN. The library contains 234,291 volumes, 754,023 microform items, 7,704 audio/video tapes/CDs/DVDs, and subscribes to 18,117 periodicals including electronic. Computerized library services include interlibrary loans, database searching, and Internet access. Special learning facilities include an art gallery, radio station, TV station, a biology pond, a child development center, a crime lab, a small business development center, a performing arts center, a greenhouse, and an international trade and quality center. The 365-acre campus is in a small town in the southwest corner of the state, 138 miles south of Kansas City. Including any residence halls, there are 41 buildings.

Student Life: 90% of undergraduates are from Missouri. Others are from 30 states, and 27 foreign countries. 90% are White. The average age of freshmen is 20; all undergraduates, 25. 36% do not continue beyond their first year; 29% remain to graduate.

Housing: 700 students can be accommodated in college housing, which includes single-sex dorms and on-campus apartments. On-campus housing is available on a first-come and first-served basis. 88% of students commute. Alcohol is not permitted. All students may keep cars.

Activities: 6% of men belong to 2 national fraternities. There are 95 groups on campus, including art, band, cheerleading, chess, choir, chorale, chorus, communications, computers, dance, debate, drama, ethnic, film, forensics, honors, international, jazz band, literary magazine, marching band, musical theater, newspaper, orchestra, pep band, photography, political, professional, radio and TV, religious, social, social service, student government, and symphony. Popular campus events include Spring Fling, Natural High, and International Semesters.

Sports: There are 7 intercollegiate sports for men and 7 for women, and 14 intramural sports for men and 14 for women. Facilities include a 10,000-seat Astroturf football stadium, a 4000-seat gym, a 4000-seat auditorium, a natatorium, a student life center, a black-box theater, a 3240-seat gym with basketball court, a 6-lane 200-meter indoor track, a training and weight room, a cross-country course, and soccer, softball, and baseball fields.

Disabled Students: 99% of the campus is accessible. Facilities include wheelchair ramps, elevators, special parking, specially equipped restrooms, special class scheduling, lowered drinking fountains, lowered telephones, and special housing.

Services: There is a reader service for the blind, and remedial math, reading, and writing. Assistance is also provided for improving time management and test-taking skills.

Campus Safety and Security: Measures include 24-hour foot and vehicle patrol and security escort services. There are lighted pathways/sidewalks, and courtesy services such as unlocking cars and providing jump starts.

Programs of Study: Missouri Southern confers B.A., B.S., B.G.S., B.S.B.A. and B.S.E. degrees. Associate and master's degrees are also awarded. Bachelor's degrees are awarded in BIOLOGICAL SCIENCE (biology/biological science, biotechnology, ecology, genetics, marine biology, and microbiology), BUSINESS (accounting, banking and finance, business administration and management, business economics, international business management, management information systems, management science, and marketing/retailing/merchandising), COMMUNICATIONS AND THE ARTS (art, communications, dramatic arts, English, fine arts, French, German, graphic design, music, Spanish, and speech/debate/rhetoric), COMPUTER AND PHYSICAL SCIENCE (chemistry, computer mathematics, computer science, information sciences and systems, mathematics, and physics), EDUCATION (art education, business education, drama education, early childhood education, elementary education, English education, foreign languages education, health education, mathematics education, middle school education, music education, physical education, reading education, science education, secondary education, social science education, social studies education, special education, teaching English as a second/foreign language (TESOL/TEFOL), and trade and industrial education), ENGINEERING AND ENVIRONMENTAL DESIGN (computer technology and manufacturing technology), HEALTH PROFESSIONS (environmental health science, medical laboratory technology, nursing, physical therapy, predentistry, premedicine, preoptometry, prepharmacy, and preveterinary science), SOCIAL SCIENCE (criminal justice, economics, history, international studies, liberal arts/general studies, political science/government, psychology, social science, social studies, and sociology). Biology, preengineering and economics and finance are the strongest academically. Business, education, and criminal justice have the largest enrollments.

Required: General education requirements include a total of 51 credit hours, with 15 in basic studies, 12 each in science and cultural studies, 9 in humanities, and 3 in international studies. Students must also demonstrate proficiency in computer skills and writing. To graduate, students must complete at least 124 credit hours, including a minimum of 40 in the major, and present a minimum GPA of 2.0 (2.75 for the B.S.E.).

Special: There are co-op programs in radiological and medical technology, respiratory therapy, paramedical studies, aviation, and engineering. Students may study abroad at Oxford or Cambridge and in 100 countries through ISEP. Missouri Southern also offers internships in many majors, accelerated degree programs in all majors, a 3-2 engineering degree with the University of Missouri-Rolla, a general studies degree, and credit for life experience. Nondegree study is possible. There are 14 national honor societies, a freshman honors program, and 1 departmental honors program.

Faculty/Classroom: 104% of faculty are male; 92% are female. All teach undergraduates. No introductory courses are taught by graduate students.

Admissions: 97% of the 2013-2014 applicants were accepted.

Requirements: The ACT is required. Applicants must be graduates of accredited secondary schools or have earned a GED. The college requires completion of 16 Carnegie units in core courses for high school graduates. Missouri Southern requires applicants to be in the upper 50% of their class. A GPA of 2.3 is required. AP and CLEP credits are accepted. Important factors in the admissions decision are advanced placement or honors courses.

Procedure: Freshmen are admitted to all sessions. Entrance exams should be taken during the junior or senior year of high school. There are deferred admissions and rolling admissions plans. Check with the school for current application deadlines. The application fee is $25. Notification is sent on a rolling basis. Applications are accepted online.

Transfer: 582 transfer students enrolled in 2012-2013. Applicants must have a GPA of 2.0 and must be able to return to their previous college. 30 of 124 credits required for the bachelor's degree must be completed at Missouri Southern.

Visiting: There are regularly scheduled orientations for prospective students, including a preenrollment tour during the summer. There are guides for informal visits, visitors may sit in on classes, and stay overnight. To schedule a visit, contact the Admissions Office.

Financial Aid: The average freshman award was $7,377. Need-based scholarships or need-based grants averaged $4,091; need-based self-help aid (loans and jobs) averaged $2,038; non-need-based athletic scholarships averaged $5,589; other non-need-based awards and non-need-based scholarships averaged $2,486; and $1,834 from other forms of aid. The average financial indebtedness of the 2013 graduate was $27,042. The FAFSA is required. Check with the school for current application deadlines.

International Students: The school actively recruits these students. They must take the TOEFL or MELAB. They must also take the ACT, scoring 18.

Computers: All students may access the system there are no time limits. The fee is $20.

Graduates: The most popular majors were business/marketing (20%), health professions and related programs (14%), and education (12%).

Admissions Contact: Derek S. Skaggs, Director of Admissions. E-Mail: *admissions@mssu.edu* Web: *www.mssu.edu*

MISSOURI STATE UNIVERSITY B-3

Springfield, MO 65897 (417) 836-5000
(800) 492-7900; (417) 836-6334

Full-time: 5834 men, 7631 women **Faculty:** n/av; IIA, --$
Part-time: 1790 men, 2179 women **Ph.D.s:** 71%
Graduate: 1251 men, 1944 women **Student/Faculty:** n/av
Year: semesters, summer session **Tuition:** $6792 ($13,138)
Application Deadline: July 20 **Room & Board:** $7204
Freshman Class: 7342 applied, 6113 accepted, 2566 enrolled
SAT: required **ACT:** 24 **VERY COMPETITIVE**

Missouri State University, founded in 1905, is a public institution offering undergraduate programs in arts and letters, business administration, humanities and social sciences, education and psychology, health and applied sciences, and science and math. There are 9 undergraduate schools and 1 graduate school. In addition to regional accreditation, MSU has baccalaureate program accreditation with AACSB, ABET, ACCE, APTA, CSAB, CSWE, NASM, NCATE, and NRPA. The library contains

701,592 volumes, 1.1 million microform items, 20,050 audio/video tapes/CDs/DVDs, and subscribes to 36,000 periodicals including electronic. Computerized library services include interlibrary loans, database searching, and Internet access. Special learning facilities include an art gallery, radio station, and TV station. The 225-acre campus is in a suburban area 220 miles southwest of St. Louis. Including any residence halls, there are 60 buildings.

Student Life: 89% of undergraduates are from Missouri. Others are from 50 states, 83 foreign countries, and Canada. 82% are White. The average age of freshmen is 18; all undergraduates, 21. 25% do not continue beyond their first year; 55% remain to graduate.

Housing: 4000 students can be accommodated in college housing, which includes coed dorms, on-campus apartments, and married student housing. In addition, there are honors houses, fraternity houses, sorority houses, wellness houses, and housing for international students, nontraditional students (age 23 and older), upperclassma and families. On-campus housing is guaranteed for all 4 years. 77% of students commute. Alcohol is not permitted. All students may keep cars.

Activities: There are 348 groups on campus, including art, band, cheerleading, chess, choir, chorale, chorus, communications, computers, dance, drama, drill team, environmental, ethnic, film, gay, honors, international, jazz band, literary magazine, marching band, musical theater, newspaper, opera, orchestra, pep band, political, professional, radio and TV, religious, social, social service, student government, and symphony. Popular campus events include Tent Theater, Spring Fling, Community Service Fair and Leadership Conference.

Sports: There are 6 intercollegiate sports for men and 10 for women, and 23 intramural sports for men and 22 for women. Facilities include A 16,600-seat stadium, an 11,000-seat arena, an 8,858 seat arena, a swimming pool, softball and practice fields, tennis courts, bowling lanes, and the newly constructed, and state-of-the-art Foster Recreation Center.

Disabled Students: All of the campus is accessible. Facilities include wheelchair ramps, elevators, special parking, specially equipped restrooms, special class scheduling, lowered drinking fountains, lowered telephones, and special housing.

Services: Counseling and information services are available, as is tutoring in some subjects. There is a reader service for the blind, and remedial math, reading, and writing. A math center and a writing center are available for student use. Proctors are available for tests given to those with disabilities.

Campus Safety and Security: Measures include 24-hour foot and vehicle patrol, emergency notification system, self-defense education, and security escort services. There are shuttle buses, emergency telephones, lighted pathways/sidewalks, and controlled access to dorms/residences.

Programs of Study: MSU confers B.S.A.T., B.A., B.A.S., B.F.A., B.M.U.S., B.M.E., B.S., B.S.Ed., B.S.N. and B.S.W. degrees. Master's and doctoral degrees are also awarded. Bachelor's degrees are awarded in AGRICULTURE (agriculture, animal science, environmental studies, plant science, and wildlife management), BIOLOGICAL SCIENCE (biology/biological science and cell biology), BUSINESS (accounting, apparel and textiles, business administration and management, entrepreneurial studies, fashion merchandising, finance, logistics, management science, marketing/retailing/merchandising, and recreation and leisure services), COMMUNICATIONS AND THE ARTS (art history, art, communications, communication science, design, English, French, German, information technology, journalism, Latin, music, musical theater, performing arts, Spanish, speech/debate/rhetoric, and theatre arts), COMPUTER AND PHYSICAL SCIENCE (chemistry, computer science, geology, mathematics, and natural sciences), EDUCATION (agricultural education, athletic training, business education, computer education, early childhood education, education administration, elementary education, middle school education, physical education, science education, and special education), ENGINEERING AND ENVIRONMENTAL DESIGN (construction management, interior design, and materials science), HEALTH PROFESSIONS (clinical science, exercise science, health care administration, health promotion, hospital administration, nursing, physical therapy, physician's assistant, radiological science, respiratory therapy, and speech pathology/audiology), SOCIAL SCIENCE (anthropology, child psychology/development, counseling/psychology, criminology, dietetics, economics, family/consumer studies, fashion design and technology, geography, gerontology, (Social Science) Global Studies, history, philosophy, political science/government, religion, social work, and sociology). Business and education have the largest enrollments.

Required: A total of 125 to 130 semester hours, including 30 to 60 in the major, and a minimum GPA of 2.0 are required. 45 general education semester hours are required, to include 8 in natural sciences, 6 to 9 each in social sciences and humanities, 6 in American studies, 4 in phys ed, 3 to 6 in English composition, 3 each in math and speech, and 1 in freshman orientation. Arts/fine arts and computer literacy classes are also required.

Special: MSU offers co-op programs, internships, study abroad in 40 countries, and work-study programs. Also available are B.A.-B.S. degrees in 12 majors, preprofessional programs in law and medicine, accelerated degree programs and student-designed and interdisciplinary majors, including antiquities, agriculture business and agriculture education, chemistry/biochemistry, communication management, and finance/real estate. A 3-2 engineering degree is available through the University of Missouri-Rolla. Credit for military experience and pass/not-pass options are offered. There are 27 national honor societies and a freshman honors program.

Faculty/Classroom: 52% of faculty are male; 48% are female. No introductory courses are taught by graduate students. The average class size in a regular course is 23.

Admissions: 83% of the 2013-2014 applicants were accepted. 37% of the current freshmen were in the top fifth of their class; 62% were in the top two fifths.

Requirements: Either SAT or ACT is required for admittance; the ACT is preferred. Admission is based on a sliding scale of rank or GPA and test score. Freshmen must also have a 17-unit high school core curriculum, including 4 in English, 3 each in math and social studies, 3 in science, 1 in visual and performing arts, and 3 electives. AP and CLEP credits are accepted. Important factors in the admissions decision are advanced placement or honors courses, extracurricular activities record, and personality/intangible qualities.

Procedure: Freshmen are admitted to all sessions. Entrance exams should be taken as early as possible. There is a rolling admissions plan. Applications should be filed by July 20 for fall entry, along with a $35 fee. Notification is sent on a rolling basis. Applications are accepted online.

Transfer: 1575 transfer students enrolled in 2012-2013. Applicants must present a minimum GPA of 2.0 on transferable courses. College transcripts are required. If they have completed less than 24 semester hours, they are also required to meet freshman admission requirements. 30 of 125 credits required for the bachelor's degree must be completed at MSU.

Visiting: There are regularly scheduled orientations for prospective students, Guests can request an appointment with an admissions advisor, an academic department, or other areas of interest.. There are guides for informal visits. To schedule a visit, contact the Admissions Office.

Financial Aid: In 2013-2014, 63% of all full-time freshmen and 58% of continuing full-time students received some form of financial aid. 56% of all full-time freshmen and 48% of continuing full-time students received need-based aid. The average freshman award was $6,093. Need-based scholarships or need-based grants averaged $8,164; need-based self-help aid (loans and jobs) averaged $5,897; non-need-based athletic scholarships averaged $11,563; and other non-need-based awards and non-need-based scholarships averaged $3,948. The average financial indebtedness of the 2013 graduate was $20,545. MSU is a member of CSS. The FAFSA is required. The priority date for freshman financial aid applications for fall entry is March 30. The deadline for filing freshman financial aid applications for fall entry is rolling.

International Students: The school actively recruits these students. They must take the TOEFL with a minimum score of 500 on the paper-based TOEFL (PBT) or 61 on the Internet-based version (iBT). They must also take the ACT.

Graduates: From July 1, 2012 to June 30, 2013, 3264 bachelor's degrees were awarded. The most popular majors were finance and general business (9%), childhood education and family studies (7%), and management (7%). 610 companies recruited on campus in 2012-2013. In an average class, 32% graduate in 4 years or less, 50% graduate in 5 years or less, and 55% graduate in 6 years or less. Of the 2012 graduating class, 70% were employed within 6 months of graduation.

Admissions Contact: Andrew Wright, Director of Admissions. E-Mail: *info@missouristate.edu* Web: *www.missouristate.edu*

MISSOURI UNIVERSITY OF SCIENCE AND TECHNOLOGY — C-3

Rolla, MO 65409 — (573) 341-4164; (800) 522-0938; (573) 341-4082

Full-time: 4227 men, 1245 women	**Faculty:** 361
Part-time: 487 men, 187 women	**Ph.D.s:** 89%
Graduate: 1577 men, 407 women	**Student/Faculty:** 15 to 1
Year: semesters, summer session	**Tuition:** $9510 ($24,675)
Application Deadline: July 1	**Room & Board:** $9145
Freshman Class: n/av	
SAT CR/M: 590/640	**ACT:** 28 — **VERY COMPETITIVE+**

Missouri University of Science and Technology, founded in 1870, is part of the University of Missouri system. A public research institution, it offers comprehensive undergraduate and graduate programs and confers degrees in arts and sciences, engineering, mines and metallurgy, and management and information systems. In addition to regional accreditation, Missouri S&T has baccalaureate program accreditation with AACSB, ABET, and CSAB. The library contains 479,874 volumes, 423,403 microform items, and 4,634 audio/video tapes/CDs/DVDs, and subscribes to 3,901 periodicals including electronic. Computerized library services include interlibrary loans, database searching, Internet access, and Wi-Fi capability. Special learning facilities include a radio station, a writing center, student design center, nuclear reactor, observatory, explosives testing labs, and underground mine, hot glass shop. The 284-acre campus is in a small town 100 miles southwest of St. Louis, MO and 100 miles northeast of Springfield, MO. Including any residence halls, there are 72 buildings.

Student Life: 77% of undergraduates are from Missouri. Others are from 49 states, 60 foreign countries, and Canada. 78% are White. The average age of freshmen is 18; all undergraduates, 21. 17% do not continue beyond their first year; 63% remain to graduate.

Housing: 2152 students can be accommodated in college housing, which includes coed dorms, on-campus apartments, and married student housing. In addition, there are honors houses, fraternity houses, sorority houses, residential college, learning community, and holistic community. On-campus housing is guaranteed for the freshman year only, is available on a first-come, and first-served basis. Alcohol is not permitted. All students may keep cars.

Activities: 21% of men belong to 23 national fraternities; 19% of women belong to 5 national sororities. There are 221 groups on campus, including art, band, cheerleading, chess, choir, chorale, chorus, computers, dance, drama, drill team, ethnic, gay, honors, international, jazz band, literary magazine, marching band, musical theater, newspaper, orchestra, pep band, political, professional, radio and TV, religious, social, social service, student government, symphony, and yearbook. Popular campus events include St. Patrick's Day, Homecoming, Campus Block Party and Celebration of Nations.

Sports: There are 8 intercollegiate sports for men and 7 for women, and 20 intramural sports for men and 19 for women. Facilities include a gym, weight room, pool, a nine hole golf course, track, racquetball and tennis courts, baseball and soccer fields, and a 5000-seat stadium.

Disabled Students: 95% of the campus is accessible. Facilities include wheelchair ramps, elevators, special parking, specially equipped restrooms, special class scheduling, lowered drinking fountains, lowered telephones, special housing.

Services: Counseling and information services are available, as is tutoring in most subjects. There is a reader service for the blind.

Campus Safety and Security: Measures include 24-hour foot and vehicle patrol, emergency notification system, self-defense education, and security escort services. There are shuttle buses, emergency telephones, lighted pathways/sidewalks, crime prevention and rape/sexual assault programs.

Programs of Study: Missouri S&T confers B.A., and B.S. degrees. Master's and doctoral degrees are also awarded. Bachelor's degrees are awarded in BIOLOGICAL SCIENCE (biology/biological science, environmental biology, and life science), BUSINESS (business administration and management and management information systems), COMMUNICATIONS AND THE ARTS (English and technical and business writing), COMPUTER AND PHYSICAL SCIENCE (applied mathematics, chemistry, computer science, geology, geophysics and seismology, information sciences and systems, mathematics, physics, and statistics), EDUCATION (secondary education), ENGINEERING AND ENVIRONMENTAL DESIGN (aeronautical engineering, architectural engineering, ceramic engineering, chemical engineering, civil engineering, computer engineering, electrical/electronics engineering, engineering management, engineering mechanics, environmental engineering, geological engineering, manufacturing engineering, materials engineering, mechanical engineering, metallurgical engineering, mining and mineral engineering, nuclear engineering, petroleum/natural gas engineering, and systems engineering), HEALTH PROFESSIONS (premedicine), SOCIAL SCIENCE (economics, history, philosophy, prelaw, and psychology). Engineering, science and technology are the strongest academically. Engineering, arts, sciences, mines and metallurgy have the largest enrollments.

Required: Candidates for graduation must maintain at least a 2.0 GPA. A total of 120 credits is required. A Senior assessment exam is required.

Special: MS&T offers internships in business and government, co-op programs in which students work and attend school on alternating schedules, and study abroad in more than 40 countries. Accelerated degrees in science and engineering, dual majors, B.A.-B.S. degrees, a 3-2 engineering degree, work-study programs, credit for life/military/work experience, and pass/fail options in certain courses are also available. There are 28 national honor societies, a freshman honors program, and 16 departmental honors programs.

Faculty/Classroom: 75% of faculty are male; 25% are female. No introductory courses are taught by graduate students.

Admissions: The SAT scores for the 2013-2014 freshman class were: Critical Reading--14% below 500, 35% between 500 and 599, 36% between 600 and 699, and 15% between 700 and 800; Math--5% below 500, 21% between 500 and 599, 54% between 600 and 699, and 21% between 700 and 800. The ACT scores were 1% below 21, 8% between 21 and 23, 26% between 24 and 26, 19% between 27 and 28, and 46% above 28. 60% of the current freshmen were in the top fifth of their class; 88% were in the top two fifths.

Requirements: The SAT or ACT is required. In addition, the sum of the high school student's class rank percentile and aptitude exam percentile must be 120 or higher. Candidates must be graduates of an accredited secondary school or have the GED. The applicant must have completed 16 academic credit units, including 4 each in English and math, 3 each in science and social studies, and 2 in a foreign language. Students may take the SAT or the ACT, however the ACT is recommended. A GPA of 2.0 is required. AP and CLEP credits are accepted. Important factors in the admissions decision are leadership record, extracurricular activities record, and advanced placement or honors courses.

Procedure: Freshmen are admitted fall, winter, and summer. Entrance exams should be taken late in the junior year or early in the senior year. There are deferred admissions and rolling admissions plans. Early decision applications should be filed by December 1; regular applications, by July 1 for fall entry; December 1 for spring entry; and May 1 for summer entry, along with a $50 fee. applicants were on the 2013 waiting list; were admitted. Applications are accepted online.

Transfer: 427 transfer students enrolled in 2012-2013. Applicants with fewer than 24 semester hours of college-level work must apply as freshmen; those with 24 or more must have attained at least a 2.0 GPA in all college-level courses. 60 of 120 credits required for the bachelor's degree must be completed at Missouri S&T.

Visiting: There are regularly scheduled orientations for prospective students, including a tour with a student, admissions and financial aid counseling, special interest contact, and a departmental visit with a faculty member. There are guides for informal visits, visitors may sit in on classes, and stay overnight. To schedule a visit, contact Admissions Office.

Financial Aid: In 2013-2014, 88% of all full-time freshmen and 90% of continuing full-time students received some form of financial aid. 43% of all full-time freshmen and 52% of continuing full-time students received need-based aid. The average freshman award was $11,773. Need-based scholarships or need-based grants averaged $9,131; need-based self-help aid (loans and jobs) averaged $3,755; non-need-based athletic scholarships averaged $5,569; and other non-need-based awards and non-need-based scholarships averaged $6,300. The average financial indebtedness of the 2013 graduate was $6,166. Missouri S&T is a member of CSS. The FAFSA is required. The priority date for freshman financial aid applications for fall entry is March 1.

International Students: There are 384 international students enrolled. The school actively recruits these students. They must take the TOEFL with a minimum score of 550 on the paper-based TOEFL (PBT) or 79 on the Internet-based version (iBT). They must also take the SAT or ACT.

Graduates: From July 1, 2012 to June 30, 2013, 1118 bachelor's degrees were awarded. The most popular majors were mechanical engineering (15%), civil engineering (12%), and electrical engineering (8%). 872 companies recruited on campus in 2012-2013. In an average class, 63% graduate in 6 years or less. Of the 2012 graduating class, 16% were enrolled in graduate school within 6 months of graduation, and 57% were employed.

Admissions Contact: Lynn Stichnote, Director. E-Mail: *admissions@mst.edu* Web: *www.futurestudents.mst.edu*

MISSOURI VALLEY COLLEGE B-2

Marshall, MO 65340 **(660) 831-4157; (660) 831-4233**

Full-time: 840 men, 550 women	**Faculty:** n/av
Part-time: 20 men, 20 women	**Ph.D.s:** n/av
Graduate: n/av	**Student/Faculty:** n/av
Year: semesters, summer session	**Tuition:** $18,280
Application Deadline: open	**Room & Board:** $7200
Freshman Class: n/av	
SAT or ACT: required	

COMPETITIVE

Missouri Valley College, founded in 1889, is a private liberal arts college affiliated with the Presbyterian Church, offering 27 majors. The figures in the above capsule and in this profile are approximate. In addition to regional accreditation, MVC has baccalaureate program accreditation with CAHEA. The 2 libraries contain 75,000 volumes, 27,000 microform items, 1600 audio/video tapes/CDs/DVDs, and subscribe to 250 periodicals including electronic. Computerized library services include interlibrary loans, database searching, Internet access, and laptop Internet portals. Special learning facilities include a learning resource center, radio station, and TV station. The 150-acre campus is in a small town 50 miles northwest of Columbia and 80 miles northeast of Kansas City. Including any residence halls, there are 17 buildings.

Student Life: 66% of undergraduates are from Missouri. Others are from 43 states, 26 foreign countries, and Canada. 75% are from public schools. 83% are white; 17% African American. 45% are Protestant; 14% Catholic. The average age of freshmen is 19; all undergraduates, 21. 48% do not continue beyond their first year; 20% remain to graduate.

Housing: 1100 students can be accommodated in college housing, which includes single-sex and coed dorms and on-campus apartments. In addition, there are honors houses, special-interest houses, fraternity houses, and sorority houses. On-campus housing is guaranteed for all 4 years. 72% of students live on campus; of those, 50% remain on campus on weekends. Alcohol is not permitted. All students may keep cars.

Activities: 15% of men belong to 4 national fraternities; 8% of women belong to 2 national sororities. There are 40 groups on campus, including art, cheerleading, choir, chorale, chorus, computers, dance, drama, ethnic, film, honors, international, jazz band, literary magazine, musical theater, newspaper, photography, radio and TV, religious, SADD, social, social service, student government, and yearbook. Popular campus events include Springfest, Maastricht Institute of Entrepreneurship, and Guerilla Film Festival.

Sports: There are 13 intercollegiate sports for men and 12 for women, and 7 intramural sports for men and 7 for women. Facilities include a 2000-seat gym, tennis and basketball courts, football and soccer fields, a 1000-seat stadium, and horse stables.

Disabled Students: 65% of the campus is accessible. Facilities include wheelchair ramps, elevators, special parking, specially equipped rest rooms, and special class scheduling.

Services: Counseling and information services are available, as is tutoring in most subjects. There is remedial math, reading, and writing.

Campus Safety and Security: Measures include emergency notification system and security escort services. There are shuttle buses, emergency telephones, and lighted pathways/sidewalks.

Programs of Study: MVC confers B.A., B.S., and B.F.A. degrees. Associate degrees are also awarded. Bachelor's degrees are awarded in BIOLOGICAL SCIENCE (biology/biological science), BUSINESS (accounting, business administration and management, and recreational facilities management), COMMUNICATIONS AND THE ARTS (art, communications, dramatic arts, English, and speech/debate/rhetoric), COMPUTER AND PHYSICAL SCIENCE (information sciences and systems and mathematics), EDUCATION (elementary education, physical education, and social studies education), HEALTH PROFESSIONS (exercise science), SOCIAL SCIENCE (addiction studies, anthropology, criminal justice, economics, history, human services, liberal arts/general studies, philosophy, political science/government, psychology, public administration, religion, and sociology). Education is the strongest academically. Business administration, phys ed, and psychology have the largest enrollments.

Required: Students must complete 128 hours, with 30 to 50 hours in the major and 40 hours in a core curriculum. A 2.0 GPA is also required.

Special: Accelerated degree programs, internships, study abroad, work-study, co-op programs, nondegree study, and pass/fail options are available. There are 3 national honor societies and 3 departmental honors programs.

Faculty/Classroom: 73% of faculty are male; 27% are female. All teach undergraduates. The average class size in an introductory lecture is 30; in a laboratory, 25; and in a regular course, 18.

Requirements: The SAT or ACT is required. Students must have graduated from an accredited secondary school or have the GED. Auditions are required for performance-based scholarships. MVC requires applicants to be in the upper 50% of their class. A GPA of 2.0 is required. AP and CLEP credits are accepted. Important factors in the admissions decision are advanced placement or honors courses, evidence of special talent, and extracurricular activities record.

Procedure: Freshmen are admitted to all sessions. Entrance exams should be taken as early as possible. There is a rolling admissions plan. Application deadlines are open. Application fee is $15. Notification is sent on a rolling basis. Applications are accepted online.

Transfer: A minimum GPA of 2.0 is recommended; D grades do not transfer. Official transcripts are required for all previous colleges attended. Students with fewer than 27 credits transferring must submit high school transcripts as well. 30 of 128 credits required for the bachelor's degree must be completed at MVC.

Visiting: There are regularly scheduled orientations for prospective students, including jump-start days in the summer and registration days during the school year. There are guides for informal visits, and visitors may sit in on classes and stay overnight. To schedule a visit, contact the Admission Coordinator.

Financial Aid: MVC is a member of CSS. The FAFSA is required. Check with the school for current application deadlines.

International Students: The school actively recruits these students. They must take the TOEFL. They must also take the SAT or ACT.

Computers: Wireless access is available. All students may access the system. There are no time limits and no fees. It is strongly recommended that all students have a personal computer. An IBM is recommended.

Admissions Contact: Director of Admissions. E-Mail: *admissions@moval.edu* Web: *www.moval.edu*

MISSOURI WESTERN STATE UNIVERSITY — A-2

St. Joseph, MO 64507 — (816) 271-4266; (800) 662-7041; (816) 271-5833

Full-time: 1550 men, 2260 women	**Faculty:** n/av; IIB, -$
Part-time: 550 men, 910 women	**Ph.D.s:** n/av
Graduate: n/av	**Student/Faculty:** n/av
Year: semesters, summer session	**Tuition:** $6174 ($10,935)
Application Deadline: see profile	**Room & Board:** $7296
Freshman Class: n/av	
SAT or ACT: required	

NONCOMPETITIVE

Missouri Western State University, founded in 1915, is a public institution offering undergraduate degrees in the arts and sciences, business administration, education, nursing, technology, and social work. There are 2 undergraduate schools. The figures in the above capsule and in this profile are approximate. In addition to regional accreditation, Western has baccalaureate program accreditation with ABET, CSWE, NASM, NCATE, and NLN. The library contains 210,000 volumes, 112,000 microform items, 16,000 audio/video tapes/CDs/DVDs, and subscribes to 1500 periodicals including electronic. Computerized library services include interlibrary loans and database searching. Special learning facilities include a learning resource center, planetarium, and biology nature study area. The 740-acre campus is in a suburban area 50 miles north of Kansas City. Including any residence halls, there are 15 buildings.

Student Life: 91% of undergraduates are from Missouri. Others are from 35 states, 10 foreign countries, and Canada. 86% are white; 11% African American. The average age of freshmen is 20; all undergraduates, 24. 44% do not continue beyond their first year; 29% remain to graduate.

Housing: 1050 students can be accommodated in college housing, which includes single-sex and coed dorms and on-campus apartments. On-campus housing is available on a first-come, first-served basis. 80% of students commute. Alcohol is not permitted. All students may keep cars.

Activities: 7% of men belong to 5 national fraternities; 3% of women belong to 7 national sororities. There are 51 groups on campus, including art, band, cheerleading, choir, dance, drama, drill team, ethnic, honors, international, jazz band, marching band, musical theater, newspaper, pep band, political, professional, religious, social, social service, student government, symphony, and yearbook. Popular campus events include Spring Fest, Fall Convocation, and Family Day.

Sports: There are 4 intercollegiate sports for men and 5 for women, and 20 intramural sports for men and 20 for women. Facilities include tennis and racquetball courts, a 6000-seat football stadium, a 468-seat auditorium, a swimming pool, a jogging/walking trail, a fitness center, baseball and softball fields, a trapshooting range, a volleyball area, a track, and 2 gyms, the larger seating 4000.

Disabled Students: 99% of the campus is accessible. Facilities include wheelchair ramps, elevators, special parking, specially equipped rest rooms, lowered drinking fountains, and lowered telephones.

Services: Counseling and information services are available, as is tutoring in some subjects. There is a reader service for the blind and remedial math, reading, and writing.

Campus Safety and Security: Measures include 24-hour foot and vehicle patrol, self-defense education, and security escort services. There are emergency telephones and lighted pathways/sidewalks.

Programs of Study: Western confers B.A., B.S., B.I.S., B.S.B.A., B.S.E., B.S.N., B.S.T., and B.S.W. degrees. Associate degrees are also awarded. Bachelor's degrees are awarded in BIOLOGICAL SCIENCE (biology/biological science), BUSINESS (accounting, business administration and management, and marketing/retailing/merchandising), COMMUNICATIONS AND THE ARTS (communications, English, fine arts, French, graphic design, music, Spanish, and speech/debate/rhetoric), COMPUTER AND PHYSICAL SCIENCE (chemistry, computer programming, computer science, information sciences and systems, mathematics, and natural sciences), EDUCATION (art education, early childhood education, elementary education, foreign languages education, music education, and secondary education), ENGINEERING AND ENVIRONMENTAL DESIGN (engineering technology), HEALTH PROFESSIONS (medical laboratory technology and nursing), SOCIAL SCIENCE (criminal justice, economics, history, parks and recreation management, political science/government, psychology, and social work). Physical sciences are the strongest academically. Education, nursing, and criminal justice have the largest enrollments.

Required: The core curriculum consists of 12 credit hours of basic skills (English composition, algebra, and speech), 9 to 10 of humanities, 9 of social sciences, 8 to 10 of natural sciences, and 4 of physical health. To graduate, students must complete at least 124 credit hours, including 45 to 71 in the major, with a minimum GPA of 2.0.

Special: MWSC offers internships, work-study programs with local employers, dual majors, a 3-2 engineering degree program with the University of Missouri-Rolla, credit for life experience, pass/fail options, and nondegree study. There are 6 national honor societies, a freshman honors program, and 12 departmental honors programs.

Faculty/Classroom: 60% of faculty are male; 40% are female. All teach undergraduates. The average class size in an introductory lecture is 35; in a laboratory, 25; and in a regular course, 25.

Requirements: The SAT or ACT is required. Applicants must be graduates of an accredited secondary school or have earned a GED. AP and CLEP credits are accepted.

Procedure: Freshmen are admitted to all sessions. Entrance exams should be taken at least 6 months prior to enrollment. Check with the school for current application deadlines. Application fee is $15. Applications are accepted online.

Transfer: The required GPA depends on the number of credit hours completed, but a minimum of 2.0 is standard. 30 of 124 credits required for the bachelor's degree must be completed at Western.

Visiting: There are regularly scheduled orientations for prospective students. There are guides for informal visits. To schedule a visit, contact the Admissions Office.

Financial Aid: The FAFSA is required. Check with the school for current application deadlines.

International Students: They must take the TOEFL. They must also take the ACT.

Computers: All students may access the system. There are no time limits.

Admissions Contact: Director of Admissions. A campus DVD is available. E-Mail: *admission@missouriwestern.edu* Web: *www.missouriwestern.edu*

NORTHWEST MISSOURI STATE UNIVERSITY — A-1

Maryville, MO 64468 — (660) 562-1146; (800) 633-1175; (660) 562-1121

Full-time: 2225 men, 2763 women	**Faculty:** 237
Part-time: 256 men, 298 women	**Ph.D.s:** 61%
Graduate: 441 men, 502 women	**Student/Faculty:** 22 to 1
Year: trimesters, summer session	**Tuition:** $5360 ($11,611)
Application Deadline: open	**Room & Board:** $8869
Freshman Class: 5619 applied, 4111 accepted, 1256 enrolled	
SAT CR/M: 420/460 **ACT:** 22	**COMPETITIVE**

Northwest Missouri State University, founded in 1905, is a public institution offering undergraduate courses in agriculture, science, arts and humanities, business, government, computer science, and education. There are 3 undergraduate schools and 1 graduate school. In addition to regional accreditation, Northwest has baccalaureate program accreditation with AACSB, ADA, AHEA, NASM, and NCATE. The library contains 359,371 volumes, 807,678 microform items, and 6,094 audio/video tapes/CDs/DVDs, and subscribes to 31,567 periodicals including electronic. Computerized library services include interlibrary loans, database searching, Internet access, and Wi-Fi capability. Special learning facilities include an art gallery, radio station, TV station, Missouri Arboretum, Mozingo Outdoor Education Recreation Area (observatory, ropes challenge course, trap and archery, canoes and kayaks), Horace Mann Laboratory School, R.T. Wright Farm (dairy operation, swine herd, horticulture complex, experimental farmland), Center for Innovation and Entrepreneurship (business incubator), Studio Theater and Black Box experimental theater, online Northwest History Museum, Science Museum, Agriculture Museum, Jean Jennings Bartik Computing Museum, Warren Stucki Museum of Broadcasting, Student Media Converged Newsroom, Joyce and Harvey White International Plaza. The 370-acre campus is in a small town 90 miles north of Kansas City. Including any residence halls, there are 34 buildings.

Student Life: 70% of undergraduates are from Missouri. Others are from 44 states, and 24 foreign countries. 97% are from public schools. 83% are White. The average age of freshmen is 18; all undergraduates, 20. 33% do not continue beyond their first year; 58% remain to graduate.

Housing: 2987 students can be accommodated in college housing, which includes single-sex and coed dorms, on-campus apartments, and married student housing. In addition, there are fraternity houses and sorority houses. On-campus housing is guaranteed for all 4 years and is guaranteed for the freshman year only. 61% of students commute. Alcohol is not permitted. All students may keep cars.

Activities: 21% of men belong to 9 national fraternities; 20% of women belong to 6 national sororities. There are 150 groups on campus, including band, cheerleading, choir, chorale, chorus, computers, dance, debate, drama, drill team, drum and bugle corps, ethnic, film, forensics, international, jazz band, literary magazine, marching band, newspaper, orchestra, pep band, photography, political, professional, radio and TV, religious, social, student government, symphony, and yearbook. Popular campus events include Pow-Wow, Mr. Northwest and MOSAIC.

Sports: There are 7 intercollegiate sports for men and 9 for women, and 12 intramural sports for men and 13 for women. Facilities include a 7000-seat stadium, a 3000-seat basketball arena, 3 gyms, 4 racquetball courts, a weight-lifting area, volleyball and tennis courts, dance areas.

Disabled Students: All of the campus is accessible. Facilities include wheelchair ramps, elevators, special parking, specially equipped restrooms, special class scheduling, lowered drinking fountains, and lowered telephones.

Services: Counseling and information services are available, as is tutoring in most subjects. There is a reader service for the blind, and remedial math, reading, and writing.

Campus Safety and Security: Measures include 24-hour foot and vehicle patrol, emergency notification system, self-defense education, and security escort services. There are lighted pathways/sidewalks and controlled access to dorms/residences.

Programs of Study: Northwest confers B.A., B.S., B.F.A., B.S.Ed., B.S.Med.Tech., B.S.N. and B.Tech. degrees. Master's degrees are also awarded. Bachelor's degrees are awarded in AGRICULTURE (agricultural business management, agricultural mechanics, agriculture, agronomy, animal science, conservation and regulation, forestry and related sciences, horticulture, and wildlife management), BIOLOGICAL SCIENCE (biology/biological science, botany, and zoology), BUSINESS (accounting, banking and finance, business administration and management, business economics, international business management, marketing/retailing/merchandising, and recreation and leisure services), COMMUNICATIONS AND THE ARTS (advertising, art, broadcasting, communications, dramatic arts, English, fine arts, journalism, music, public relations, Spanish, and speech/debate/rhetoric), COMPUTER AND PHYSICAL SCIENCE (chemistry, computer management, computer science, earth science, geology, information sciences and systems, mathematics, physics, science, and statistics), EDUCATION (agricultural education, art education, business education, early childhood education, education of the mentally handicapped, elementary education, mathematics education, middle school education, music education, physical education, recreation education, science education, secondary education, special education, and specific learning disabilities), ENGINEERING AND ENVIRONMENTAL DESIGN (preengineering), HEALTH PROFESSIONS (predentistry, premedicine, prepharmacy, and preveterinary science), SOCIAL SCIENCE (child care/child and family studies, economics, family/consumer resource management, food science, geography, history, humanities, industrial and organizational psychology, philosophy, political science/government, prelaw, psychology, public administration, social science, sociology, and textiles and clothing). Teacher education, business management and psychology are the strongest academically and have the largest enrollments.

Required: All students must maintain a minimum GPA of 2.0 while taking at least 124 credit hours. Distribution requirements include 9 hours each in social science and humanities, 8 in natural science, 6 in composition, 4 each in math and phys ed, 3 each in oral communications and behavioral sciences, and 1 in the freshman seminar.

Special: Campus-wide internships, study abroad in England and Mexico, and a Washington semester are available. Work-study programs, student designed majors, a 3-2 engineering degree with the Missouri University of Science and Technology, formerly the University of Missouri-Rolla, credit for military experience, service learning, nondegree study, and pass/fail options are possible. There are 3 national honor societies and a freshman honors program.

Faculty/Classroom: 53% of faculty are male; 47% are female. All teach undergraduates. No introductory courses are taught by graduate students. The average class size in an introductory lecture is 40; in a laboratory is 20; and in a regular course is 24.

Admissions: 73% of the 2013-2014 applicants were accepted. The ACT scores were 33% below 21, 30% between 21 and 23, 23% between 24 and 26, 9% between 27 and 28, and 5% above 28. 31% of the current freshmen were in the top fifth of their class; 61% were in the top two fifths. 43 freshmen graduated first in their class.

Requirements: The ACT is required, with a minimum composite score of 970 on the SAT or 21 on the ACT; if scores are below those levels, a combined percentile index obtained from the SAT or ACT score and high school rank will be used. A GPA of 2.0 is required. AP and CLEP credits are accepted. Important factors in the admissions decision are evidence of special talent and personality/intangible qualities.

Procedure: Freshmen are admitted fall, spring, and summer. Entrance exams should be taken in the fall of the senior year. There is a rolling admissions plan. Application deadlines are open. Application fee is $25. Notifications are sent September 1. Applications are accepted online.

Transfer: 236 transfer students enrolled in 2012-2013. Applicants must present a minimum GPA of 2.0. 30 of 124 credits required for the bachelor's degree must be completed at Northwest.

Visiting: There are regularly scheduled orientations for prospective students. There are guides for informal visits, visitors may sit in on classes, and stay overnight. To schedule a visit, contact the Admissions and Visitors Center.

Financial Aid: In 2013-2014, 70% of all full-time freshmen and 66% of continuing full-time students received some form of financial aid. 61% of all full-time freshmen and 52% of continuing full-time students received need-based aid. The average freshman award was $9,208. Need-based scholarships or need-based grants averaged $6,247; need-based self-help aid (loans and jobs) averaged $3,134; and non-need-based athletic scholarships averaged $5,363. 51% of undergraduate students work part-time. Average annual earnings from campus work are $2320. The FAFSA is required. The priority date for freshman financial aid applications for fall entry is April 1.

International Students: There are 126 international students enrolled. The school actively recruits these students. They must take the TOEFL with a minimum score of 500 on the paper-based TOEFL (PBT) or 61 on the Internet-based version (iBT).

Computers: All students may access the system 24 hours daily. There are no time limits and no fees.

Graduates: From July 1, 2012 to June 30, 2013, 1010 bachelor's degrees were awarded. The most popular majors were business (26%), education (21%), and psychology (9%). 180 companies recruited on campus in 2012-2013. In an average class, 28% graduate in 4 years or less, 46% graduate in 5 years or less, and 49% graduate in 6 years or less. Of the 2012 graduating class, 19% were enrolled in graduate school within 6 months of graduation, and 93% were employed.

Admissions Contact: Tamera Grow, Associate Director of Admissions. E-Mail: *tammi@nwmissouri.edu* Web: *www.nwmissouri.edu/admissions*

PARK UNIVERSITY — A-2

Parkville, MO 64152-9974 (816) 584-6215
(800) 745-7275, (816) 741-4462

Full-time: 490 men, 680 women	**Faculty:** n/av
Part-time: 5930 men, 5590 women	**Ph.D.s:** n/av
Graduate: 240 men, 350 women	**Student/Faculty:** n/av
Year: semesters, summer session	**Tuition:** $9950
Application Deadline: see profile	**Room & Board:** $7045
Freshman Class: n/av	
SAT or ACT: required	

COMPETITIVE

Park University, founded in 1875, is a private institution offering degree programs in the humanities, performing arts, natural and life sciences, and social and administrative sciences. There are 4 undergraduate schools and 1 graduate school. Some figures in the above capsule and in this profile are approximate. In addition to regional accreditation, Park has baccalaureate program accreditation with NLN. The library contains 141,870 volumes, 195,530 microform items, and 670 audio/video tapes/CDs/DVDs, and subscribes to 775 periodicals including electronic. Computerized library services include interlibrary loans and database searching. Special learning facilities include a learning resource center, art gallery, radio station, and TV station. The 700-acre campus is in a suburban area 12 miles north of Kansas City. Including any residence halls, there are 17 buildings.

Student Life: 82% of undergraduates are from Missouri. Others are from 49 states, 112 foreign countries, and Canada. 80% are from public schools. 58% are white; 21% African American; 15% Hispanic. 88% claim no religious affiliation. The average age of freshmen is 18; all undergraduates, 32. 36% do not continue beyond their first year; 38% remain to graduate.

Housing: 254 students can be accommodated in college housing, which includes coed dorms and on-campus apartments. In addition, there are honors houses. On-campus housing is guaranteed for all 4 years. 98% of students commute. Alcohol is not permitted. All students may keep cars.

Activities: There are no fraternities or sororities. There are 30 groups on campus, including cheerleading, computers, drama, ethnic, honors, international, literary magazine, newspaper, outdoor, photography, political, professional, radio and TV, religious, social, social service, and student government. Popular campus events include Fall Harvest Festival, Spring Fling, and International Week.

Sports: There are 6 intercollegiate sports for men and 7 for women, and 3 intramural sports for men and 3 for women. Facilities include 2 indoor gyms with basketball and volleyball courts, an all-weather outdoor track, soccer and softball fields, a sports medicine room, 4 tennis courts, and outdoor sand volleyball and basketball courts.

Disabled Students: 95% of the campus is accessible. Facilities include wheelchair ramps, elevators, special parking, specially equipped rest rooms, special class scheduling, and lowered drinking fountains.

Services: Counseling and information services are available, as is tutoring in most subjects. There is a reader service for the blind and remedial math, reading, and writing.

Campus Safety and Security: Measures include 24-hour foot and vehicle patrol and security escort services. There are lighted pathways/sidewalks.

Programs of Study: Park confers B.A., B.S., and B.P.A. degrees. Associate and master's degrees are also awarded. Bachelor's degrees are awarded in BIOLOGICAL SCIENCE (biology/biological science), BUSINESS (accounting, business administration and management, business economics, human resources, management information systems, and marketing management), COMMUNICATIONS AND THE ARTS (communications, dramatic arts, English, fine arts, graphic design, music, public relations, and Spanish), COMPUTER AND PHYSICAL SCIENCE (chemistry, computer science, information sciences and systems, mathematics, and natural sciences), EDUCATION (athletic training, early childhood education, and elementary education), ENGINEERING AND ENVIRONMENTAL DESIGN (aviation administration/management, computational sciences, engineering management, and interior design), HEALTH PROFESSIONS (health care administration), SOCIAL SCIENCE (child care/child and family studies, criminal justice, economics, fire protection, fire services administration, geography, history, human services, law, liberal arts/general studies, political science/government, psychology, public administration, social psychology, social work, and sociology). Management, management/computer information systems, and management/human resources are the largest.

Required: All students must complete core requirements, including 3 semesters of English composition and 1 of algebra, as well as 1 science course. They must also complete 24 to 27 hours of general education courses and 9 hours of liberal learning courses. Of the 120 credit hours needed for the bachelor's degree, 45 must be completed in upper-division work and 30 to 60 in the major, with a minimum GPA of 2.0.

Special: Cross-registration is available through a Kansas City consortium, and study abroad is possible through other schools. The university also offers internships in most majors, work-study programs with local companies, a Washington semester, credit for life and military experience, pass/fail options, and nondegree study. An accelerated degree program is offered in some majors. There are 2 national honor societies and a freshman honors program.

Faculty/Classroom: 52% of faculty are male; 48% are female. All teach undergraduates, and 80% do research. No introductory courses are taught by graduate students. The average class size in an introductory lecture is 20; in a laboratory, 10; and in a regular course, 15.

Requirements: The SAT or ACT is required. The GED is accepted with a minimum total score of 225 and no area less than 35. Park requires applicants to be in the upper 50% of their class. A GPA of 2.0 is required. AP and CLEP credits are accepted. Important factors in the admissions decision are advanced placement or honors courses, leadership record, and extracurricular activities record.

Procedure: Freshmen are admitted fall, spring, and summer. Entrance exams should be taken during the junior year or early in the senior year. There is a rolling admissions plan. Check with the school for current application deadlines. Application fee is $25. Notification is sent on a rolling basis. Applications are accepted online.

Transfer: The college requires a GPA of at least 2.0. A minimum ACT composite score of 20 is recommended but is waived for students age 25 or older. 24 of 120 credits required for the bachelor's degree must be completed at Park.

Visiting: There are regularly scheduled orientations for prospective students, including a campus tour, lunch, an information session with a student panel, sessions on admissions, scholarships, and financial aid, and a chance to attend a class and meet with a faculty member. There are guides for informal visits, and visitors may sit in on classes and stay overnight.

Financial Aid: The FAFSA and the college's own financial statement are required. Check with the school for current application deadlines.

International Students: The school actively recruits these students. They must take the TOEFL. They must also take the ACT.

Computers: Wireless access is available. All students may access the system Monday through Thursday, 8 a.m. to 11 p.m.; Friday, 8 a.m. to 5 p.m; Saturday, 10 a.m. to 5 p.m.; Sunday, noon to 5 p.m. There are no time limits and no fees.

Admissions Contact: Cathy Colapietro, Director of Admissions and Student Financial Services. E-Mail: *admissions@park.edu* Web: *www.park.edu*

RESEARCH COLLEGE OF NURSING — A-2

Kansas City, MO 64132 (816) 995-2812
(866) 855-0296; (816) 995-2813

Full-time: 20 men, 310 women	**Faculty:** 26
Part-time: 2 women	**Ph.D.s:** 23%
Graduate: 5 men, 100 women	**Student/Faculty:** n/av
Year: semesters, summer session	**Tuition:** $29,010
Application Deadline: see profile	**Room & Board:** $8379
Freshman Class: n/av	
ACT: required	

SPECIAL

Research College of Nursing, founded in 1980, is a private college of nursing affiliated with Rockhurst University of Kansas City, a Jesuit-run, 25-acre liberal arts college with an enrollment of about 1500 undergraduates. Located on the campus of the Research Medical Center, the Research College of Nursing offers classes on its home campus, on the Rockhurst campus, and in a variety of health-related settings in the Kansas City area. There is 1 graduate school. Some figures in the above capsule and in this profile are approximate. The library contains 109,000 volumes, 150,000 microform items, 1100 audio/video tapes/CDs/DVDs, and subscribes to 700 periodicals including electronic. Computerized library services include interlibrary loans, database searching, and Internet access. Special learning facilities include a learning resource center. The campus is in an urban area in Kansas City, Missouri. Including any residence halls, there are 2 buildings.

Student Life: 90% of undergraduates are from Missouri. Others are from 6 states and 1 foreign country. 55% are from public schools. 79% are white. 45% are Catholic; 17% Protestant. The average age of freshmen is 18; all undergraduates, 22. 30% do not continue beyond their first year; 63% remain to graduate.

Housing: 815 students can be accommodated in college housing, which includes single-sex and coed dorms, on-campus apartments, and married student housing. In addition, there are fraternity houses. On-campus housing is guaranteed for all 4 years. 65% of students live on campus; of those, 60% remain on campus on weekends. Alcohol is not permitted. All students may keep cars.

Activities: 27% of men belong to 3 national fraternities; 12% of women belong to 3 national sororities. There are 35 groups on campus, including art, cheerleading, chess, choir, chorus, computers, drama, drill team, ethnic, gay, honors, international, literary magazine, musical theater, newspaper, political, professional, radio and TV, religious, social, social service, student government, and yearbook. Popular campus events include the Mass of the Holy Spirit.

Sports: There are 6 intercollegiate sports for men and 5 for women, and 30 intramural sports for men and 30 for women. Facilities include tennis courts, a gym, an exercise facility, a fitness center, and racquetball courts.

Disabled Students: 80% of the campus is accessible. Facilities include wheelchair ramps, elevators, special parking, specially equipped rest rooms, lowered drinking fountains, and lowered telephones.

Services: Counseling and information services are available, as is tutoring in some subjects, primarily freshman- and sophomore-level courses. There is remedial writing. The learning center offers assistance with college writing tasks and study strategies.

Campus Safety and Security: Measures include 24-hour foot and vehicle patrol, self-defense education, and security escort services. There are emergency telephones, lighted pathways/sidewalks, and controlled access to dorms/residences.

Programs of Study: Research College confers B.S.N. degrees. Master's degrees are also awarded. Bachelor's degrees are awarded in HEALTH PROFESSIONS (nursing).

Required: To earn the B.S.N., students must complete a total of 128 semester hours, with 66 in liberal arts and sciences and 62 in the nursing major. A 2.0 GPA overall and in all nursing course work is required to graduate.

Special: Work-study, co-op, and accelerated degree programs, study abroad in 7 countries, and a Washington semester are available. There is a chapter of Phi Beta Kappa, a freshman honors program, and 1 departmental honors program.

Faculty/Classroom: 2% of faculty are male; 98% are female. 81% teach undergraduates. No introductory courses are taught by graduate students.

Admissions: 68% of a recent year's applicants were accepted. 33% of a recent year's freshmen were in the top fifth of their class; 67% were in the top two fifths.

Requirements: The ACT is required, with a minimum composite score of 20 on each area of the ACT. A satisfactory score on the SAT may be substituted. Applicants should graduate from an accredited secondary school or have the GED. An interview is recommended. Applicants should have completed 3 years of high school math, including algebra II, 3 years of English, and 2 years of science, including chemistry. Research College requires applicants to be in the upper 50% of their class. A GPA of 2.5 is required. AP and CLEP credits are accepted. Important factors in the admissions decision are advanced placement or honors courses, recommendations by school officials, and leadership record.

Procedure: Freshmen are admitted to all sessions. Entrance exams should be taken during the junior or senior year of high school. There are deferred admissions and rolling admissions plans. Check with the school for current application deadlines and fee. Notification is sent on a rolling basis.

Transfer: 25 transfer students enrolled in a recent year. A minimum GPA of 2.7 is required to interview for the Research/Rockhurst Joint B.S.N. Program. Students must complete the sophomore-level nursing course before entering the junior-level clinical; this course is offered only in the spring. Admission requires an interview along with all official transcripts. Admission for transfers is very limited. 30 of 128 credits required for the bachelor's degree must be completed at Research College.

Visiting: There are regularly scheduled orientations for prospective students, consisting of 5 weekend programs for students and their parents. There are guides for informal visits; visitors may sit in on classes and stay overnight. To schedule a visit, contact Rockhurst Admission and Financial Aid Office.

Financial Aid: Research College is a member of CSS. The FAFSA is required. Check with the school for current application deadlines.

International Students: There was 1 international student enrolled in a recent year. They must take the TOEFL with a minimum score of 550 on the paper-based TOEFL (PBT) or 79 on the Internet-based version (iBT). They must also take the ACT, scoring 20. The school will accept the SAT but prefers the ACT.

Computers: Wireless access is available to all students, faculty, and staff, and there is 24/7 access to 2 computers. All students may access the system. There are no time limits and no fees. It is strongly recommended that all students have a personal computer.

Admissions Contact: Director of Admissions. Web: *www.researchcollege.edu*

ROCKHURST UNIVERSITY — A-2

Kansas City, MO 64110-2561 — (816) 501-4100; (800) 842-6776; (816) 501-4241

Full-time: 620 men, 850 women	**Faculty:** n/av; IIA, --$
Part-time: 320 men, 540 women	**Ph.D.s:** n/av
Graduate: 340 men, 480 women	**Student/Faculty:** n/av
Year: semesters, summer session	**Tuition:** $29,010
Application Deadline: see profile	**Room & Board:** $8500
Freshman Class: n/av	
SAT or ACT: required	

COMPETITIVE

Rockhurst University, founded in 1910, is a private Catholic Jesuit institution that offers undergraduate programs in the arts and sciences, education, nursing, and business. There are 4 undergraduate schools and 2 graduate schools. The figures in the above capsule and in this profile are approximate. In addition to regional accreditation, Rockhurst has baccalaureate program accreditation with APTA, CAHEA, NLN, and TEAC. The library contains 314,890 volumes, 596,850 microform items, and 8078 audio/video tapes/CDs/DVDs, and subscribes to 38,934 periodicals including electronic. Computerized library services include interlibrary loans, database searching, Internet access, and laptop Internet portals. Special learning facilities include a learning resource center, art gallery, and multimedia classrooms. The 55-acre campus is in an urban area in Kansas City. Including any residence halls, there are 19 buildings.

Student Life: 58% of undergraduates are from Missouri. Others are from 17 states. 49% are from public schools. 82% are white. 46% are Catholic; 34% Buddhist, Hindu, Muslim/Islamic, and other; 20% Protestant. The average age of freshmen is 18; all undergraduates, 21. 11% do not continue beyond their first year; 66% remain to graduate.

Housing: 815 students can be accommodated in college housing, which includes single-sex and coed dorms and on-campus apartments. In addition, there are honors houses and special-interest houses. On-campus housing is available on a first-come, first-served basis. Priority is given to out-of-town students. 61% of students live on campus; of those, 45% remain on campus on weekends. All students may keep cars.

Activities: 7% of men belong to 4 national fraternities; 7% of women belong to 2 national sororities. There are 55 groups on campus, including art, cheerleading, choir, chorale, chorus, computers, drama, ethnic, honors, international, literary magazine, musical theater, newspaper, photography, political, professional, radio and TV, religious, social, social service, and student government. Popular campus events include fraternity socials, coffee house events, and Rockstock (live bands).

Sports: There are 5 intercollegiate sports for men and 5 for women, and 12 intramural sports for men and 12 for women. Facilities include athletic and soccer fields, tennis, handball, racquetball, badminton, basketball, and volleyball courts, a weight and exercise room, gymnastics facilities, and an NCAA baseball field.

Disabled Students: 90% of the campus is accessible. Facilities include wheelchair ramps, elevators, special parking, specially equipped rest rooms, lowered drinking fountains, and lowered telephones.

Services: Counseling and information services are available, as is tutoring in most subjects. The Learning Center offers tutoring in many subjects, assistance with writing and study strategies, SI courses, and support for various professional tests.

Campus Safety and Security: Measures include 24-hour foot and vehicle patrol, self-defense education, and security escort services. There are shuttle buses, emergency telephones, lighted pathways/sidewalks, formal presentations, and a full in-house security program geared toward integration of security into the overall campus operation.

Programs of Study: Rockhurst confers B.A., B.S., B.S.B.A., and B.S.N. degrees. Master's and doctoral degrees are also awarded. Bachelor's degrees are awarded in BIOLOGICAL SCIENCE (biochemistry, bioinformatics, and biology/biological science), BUSINESS (business administration and management, business communications, business economics, and nonprofit/public organization management), COMMUNICATIONS AND THE ARTS (communications, English, French, and Spanish), COMPUTER AND PHYSICAL SCIENCE (chemistry, computer science, mathematics, and physics), EDUCATION (elementary education, foreign languages education, and secondary education), ENGINEERING AND ENVIRONMENTAL DESIGN (computer technology), HEALTH PROFES-

SIONS (clinical science, nursing, and speech pathology/audiology), SOCIAL SCIENCE (economics, history, international relations, philosophy, political science/government, psychology, and theological studies). Nursing and business administration are the strongest academically.

Required: Students must complete 128 credit hours with a minimum of 18 in the major, with at least a 2.0 GPA. 52 prescribed semester hours in philosophy, theology, history, literature, science, social studies, and the arts are required. Students must also demonstrate proficiency in oral and written communication and math.

Special: Students may obtain career-related work experience through the Cooperative Education Program. Internships for credit and salary are available. Students are encouraged to study abroad in 1 of 5 countries for a semester, to take a semester in New York at Fordham University, or to participate in a congressional intern/study program in Washington, D.C., through Marquette University. B.A.-B.S. degrees are available in business administration. Work-study and an accelerated degree in nursing are also available. Students may pursue dual majors, a 3-2 engineering degree, and interdisciplinary majors. There are 7 national honor societies, including Phi Beta Kappa, a freshman honors program, and 12 departmental honors programs.

Faculty/Classroom: 52% of faculty are male; 48% are female. 87% teach undergraduates. No introductory courses are taught by graduate students. The average class size in an introductory lecture is 20; in a laboratory, 14; and in a regular course, 21.

Requirements: The SAT or ACT is required. An applicant must be a graduate of an accredited secondary school or have earned a GED. The university requires completion of 15 academic credits, including 4 years of English, 3 to 4 of history/social science, 3 of math, 2 to 4 of a foreign language, and 1 of visual or performing arts. An interview is recommended, and a recommendation is required. Rockhurst requires applicants to be in the upper 50% of their class. A GPA of 2.0 is required. AP and CLEP credits are accepted. Important factors in the admissions decision are advanced placement or honors courses, recommendations by school officials, and leadership record.

Procedure: Freshmen are admitted to all sessions. Entrance exams should be taken in April or June of the junior year or October, December, or February of the senior year. There are deferred admissions and rolling admissions plans. Check with the school for current application deadlines. Application fee is $25 (waived for online applications).

Transfer: Transfer applicants must have a GPA of at least 2.25. An interview is recommended. All college transcripts must be submitted; a high school transcript and test scores are required if the applicant has completed fewer than 24 college semester hours. 30 of 128 credits required for the bachelor's degree must be completed at Rockhurst.

Visiting: There are regularly scheduled orientations for prospective students, including a campus tour, an interview with an admissions counselor, and a classroom visit or meeting with a faculty member. There are guides for informal visits, and visitors may sit in on classes and stay overnight. To schedule a visit, contact Admissions.

Financial Aid: The FAFSA is required. Check with the school for current application deadlines.

International Students: The school actively recruits these students. They must take the TOEFL with a minimum score of 550 on the paper-based TOEFL (PBT) or 79 on the Internet-based version (iBT). They must also take the SAT or ACT, scoring 20 on the ACT.

Computers: All students may access the system 24 hours a day. There are no time limits.

Admissions Contact: Director of Admissions. E-Mail: *admission@rockhurst.edu* Web: *www.rockhurst.edu*

SAINT LOUIS UNIVERSITY — D-2

St. Louis, MO 63103 — **(314) 977-2500**
(800) SLUFORU; (314) 977-7136

Full-time: 3283 men, 4512 women	**Faculty:** 709; I, --$
Part-time: 269 men, 623 women	**Ph.D.s:** 98%
Graduate: 1993 men, 2825 women	**Student/Faculty:** 12 to 1
Year: semesters, summer session	**Tuition:** $36,726
Application Deadline: December 1	**Room & Board:** $9868
Freshman Class: 13091 applied, 8327 accepted, 1578 enrolled	
SAT: required	**ACT:** 28 **VERY COMPETITIVE+**

Saint Louis University, founded in 1818, is a private institution affiliated with the Jesuit Order of the Roman Catholic Church. There are 9 undergraduate schools and 6 graduate schools. In addition to regional accreditation, SLU has baccalaureate program accreditation with AACSB, ABET, ADA, CSWE, NASAD, and NCATE. The 3 libraries contain 1.9 million volumes, 2.7 million microform items, 75,424 audio/video tapes/CDs/DVDs, and subscribe to 7,735 periodicals including electronic. Computerized library services include interlibrary loans, database searching, Internet access, and Wi-Fi capability. Special learning facilities include an art gallery, radio station, TV station, the Vatican Manuscripts microfilm library, biological station, entrepreneurial studies center, earthquake research center, performing arts center, supersonic wind tunnel, airport, flight simulators, sculpture/ceramics studio, and physiology/gait research labs, Madrid Campus, demonstration clinics, 8 lane NCAA regulation track & field, 3 student unions, LEED Certified Research Facility, Doisy Research Center, Chaifetz Arena. The 271-acre campus is in an urban area midtown section of St. Louis, approximately 4 miles west of the Gateway Arch. Including any residence halls, there are 134 buildings.

Student Life: 61% of undergraduates are from out of state, mostly the Mid-West. Students are from 48 states, 75 foreign countries, and Canada. 64% are White. 40% claim no religious affiliation; 35% Catholic; 18% Protestant. The average age of freshmen is 18; all undergraduates, 20. 15% do not continue beyond their first year; 73% remain to graduate.

Housing: 3870 students can be accommodated in college housing, which includes single-sex and coed dorms and on-campus apartments. In addition, there are honors houses, language houses, special-interest houses, fraternity houses, sorority houses, women's dorms, men's dorms, special housing for disabled students, learning community houses. On-campus housing is guaranteed for the freshman year only, is available on a first-come, first-served basis, and is available on a lottery system for upperclassmen. 50% of students commute. All students may keep cars.

Activities: 12% of men belong to 8 national fraternities; 16% of women belong to 6 national sororities. There are 134 groups on campus, including improvisational comedy, minority student groups, model UN, singing groups, sports/fitness club, student union, wilderness outdoor program, art, band, cheerleading, chess, choir, chorale, chorus, computers, dance, debate, drama, drill team, environmental, ethnic, games/hobbies, gay, honors, international, jazz band, literary magazine, musical theater, newspaper, pep band, photography, political, professional, radio and TV, religious, social, social service, and student government. Popular campus events include Make a Difference Day, SLU Involvement Fair, and International Banquet, Homecoming/Welcome Week, Sunday Night Mass, midnight breakfast at finals, SLU basketball games, comedians, concerts, Billikens After Dark Events, Atlas Week, Relay for Life.

Sports: There are 8 intercollegiate sports for men and 10 for women, and 23 intramural sports for men and 23 for women. Facilities include Chaifetz Arena (men's/women's basketball home court) and Chaifetz Pavilion, a two-court practice facility (which accommodates volleyball home matches & volleyball/basketball practices); Robert R. Hermann Stadium (men's and women's soccer playing field) and an adjacent practice soccer field; Billiken Sports Center includes a baseball field and softball diamond; Simon Recreation Center includes various facilities for student use, but specifically includes a pool utilized by our swimming and diving teams; Dwight Davis Tennis Center/Sunset Hills Tennis Center is outdoor/indoor tennis courts utilized by our tennis teams; St. Louis Soccer Park includes an astroturf field utilized by our field hockey team.

Disabled Students: 95% of the campus is accessible. Facilities include wheelchair ramps, elevators, special parking, specially equipped restrooms, special class scheduling, lowered drinking fountains, lowered telephones, and special housing.

Services: Counseling and information services are available, as is tutoring in most subjects.

Campus Safety and Security: Measures include 24-hour foot and vehicle patrol, emergency notification system, self-defense education, and security escort services. There are shuttle buses, emergency telephones, lighted pathways/sidewalks, controlled access to dorms/residences, video cameras, identification of valuables, 24 hour campus security, foot and vehicle patrols, smoke detectors in halls, informal discussions, bike patrols, prevention/awareness programs, mobile security patrols, motorist assistance, security officers who have police powers on campus including power to arrest individuals.

Programs of Study: SLU confers B.A., and B.S. degrees. Master's and doctoral degrees are also awarded. Bachelor's degrees are awarded in BIOLOGICAL SCIENCE (biochemistry, biology/biological science, nutrition, and nutritional sciences), BUSINESS (accounting, business administration and management, business economics, finance, hospitality management services, international business, knowledge management, management information systems, marketing, and organizational behavior), COMMUNICATIONS AND THE ARTS (art history, classical languages, classics, dramatic arts, English, English literature, fine arts, french and francophone studies, Germanic languages and literature, Italian, music, Russian languages and literature, Spanish, and studio art), COMPUTER AND PHYSICAL SCIENCE (atmospheric sciences and meteorology, chemistry, clinical laboratory science, computer information systems, earth science, geology, geophysics and seismology, mathematics, and physics), EDUCATION (athletic training, education, elementary education, general studies, health information management, middle school education, special education, and sports and wellness studies), ENGINEERING AND ENVIRONMENTAL DESIGN (aeronautical engineering, aeronautical technology, aerospace studies, airline piloting and navigation, aviation administration/management, bioengineering, biomedical engineering, civil engineering, computer engineering, electrical/electronics engineering, emergency/disaster science, engineering, engineering physics, environmental science, food services technology, mechanical engineering, and nuclear medicine technology), HEALTH PROFESSIONS (biology, clinical science, cytotechnology, exercise science, health care administration, kinesiology, medical laboratory science, nursing, nutrition and dietetics, occupational therapy, preventive/wellness health care, public health, radiation therapy, radiologic imaging modalities, and speech pathology/audiology), SOCIAL SCIENCE (African American studies, American studies, anthropology, corrections, criminal justice, food production/management/services, food science, history, humanities, international relations, Latin American studies, legal studies, liberal arts/general studies, philosophy, political science/government, psychology, social work, sociology, theology, theological studies, urban studies, and women's studies). Psychology, physician's assistant, physical therapy, center for dental education are the strongest academically. Nursing, physical therapy, and biology have the largest enrollments.

Required: Students must maintain a 2.0 GPA while completing a minimum of 120 credit hours. The core curriculum includes courses in English, philosophy, theology, math, and cultural diversity.

Special: Students may study abroad in 24 countries. Cross-registration with Washington University and the University of Missouri at St. Louis, internships, work-study programs on campus, an accelerated degree program in nursing, a 3-2 engineering degree program with Washington University in St. Louis, dual majors, student-designed majors, a Washington semester, and pass/fail options are also possible. Students may also participate in university-sponsored mission trips. There are 3 national honor societies, including Phi Beta Kappa, a freshman honors program, and 1 departmental honors programs.

Faculty/Classroom: 61% of faculty are male; 39% are female. 40% teach undergraduates, 43% do research, and 24% do both. Graduate students teach 13% of introductory courses. The average class size in an introductory lecture is 23; in a laboratory is 19; and in a regular course is 22.

Admissions: 64% of the 2013-2014 applicants were accepted. The SAT scores for the 2013-2014 freshman class were: Critical Reading--13% below 500, 40% between 500 and 599, 36% between 600 and 699, and 11% between 700 and 800; Math--8% below 500, 4% between 500 and 599, 41% between 600 and 699, and 31% between 700 and 800. The ACT scores were 2% below 21, 10% between 21 and 23, 27% between 24 and 26, 20% between 27 and 28, and 41% above 28. 65% of the current freshmen were in the top fifth of their class; 87% were in the top two fifths. There were 6 National Merit finalists.

Requirements: The SAT or ACT is required. A complete application is required for admission consideration, which consists of an application, an essay, high school transcript, and test scores. Auditions and portfolios are required for the music and art programs. A GPA of 2.5 is required. AP and CLEP credits are accepted. Important factors in the admissions decision are advanced placement or honors courses, leadership record, and extracurricular activities record.

Procedure: Freshmen are admitted fall, spring, and summer. Entrance exams should be taken in the junior or senior year. Junior is recommended. There are deferred admissions and rolling admissions plans. Applications should be filed by December 1 for fall entry; January 1 for spring entry; and June 1 for summer entry. Notification is sent on a rolling basis. 131 applicants were on the 2013 waiting list. Applications are accepted online.

Transfer: 405 transfer students enrolled in 2012-2013. The university requires a minimum GPA of at least 2.5 (on a scale of 4.0). 30 of 120 credits required for the bachelor's degree must be completed at SLU.

Visiting: There are regularly scheduled orientations for prospective students, consisting of a campus tour, individual and group visits to a class or an academic department, and admissions and financial aid counseling. There are guides for informal visits, visitors may sit in on classes, and stay overnight. To schedule a visit, contact Andrea Hitsman at admission@slu.edu.

Financial Aid: In 2013-2014, 95% of all full-time freshmen and 93% of continuing full-time students received some form of financial aid. 56% of all full-time freshmen and 59% of continuing full-time students received need-based aid. 22% of undergraduate students work part-time. Average annual earnings from campus work are $5842. The average financial indebtedness of the 2013 graduate was $39,919. SLU is a member of CSS. The FAFSA is required. The priority date for freshman financial aid applications for fall entry is March 1. The deadline for filing freshman financial aid applications for fall entry is May 1.

International Students: There are 665 international students enrolled. The school actively recruits these students. They must take the TOEFL with a minimum score of 550 on the paper-based TOEFL (PBT) or 80 on the Internet-based version (iBT) and the college's own test, IELTS.

Computers: All students may access the system. There are no time limits and no fees.

Graduates: From July 1, 2012 to June 30, 2013, 1798 bachelor's degrees were awarded. The most popular majors were nursing (7%), psychology (6%), and accounting (5%). 266 companies recruited on campus in 2012-2013. In an average class, 60% graduate in 4 years or less, 72% graduate in 5 years or less, and 73% graduate in 6 years or less. Of the 2012 graduating class, 39% were enrolled in graduate school within 6 months of graduation, and 55% were employed.

Admissions Contact: Jean M. Gilman, Dean of Admissions. E-Mail: *admission@slu.edu* Web: *www.slu.edu*

SOUTHEAST MISSOURI STATE UNIVERSITY E-3

Cape Girardeau, MO 63701 **573-651-2539; 573-651-5936**

Full-time: 3566 men, 4528 women	**Faculty:** 383; IIA, --$
Part-time: 1096 men, 1565 women	**Ph.D.s:** 75%
Graduate: 391 men, 771 women	**Student/Faculty:** 21 to 1
Year: semesters, summer session	**Tuition:** $6863 ($12,195)
Application Deadline: July 1	**Room & Board:** $8120
Freshman Class: 4388 applied, 3750 accepted, 1729 enrolled	
SAT: required **ACT:** 23	**LESS COMPETITIVE**

Southeast Missouri State University, founded in 1873, is a public institution offering undergraduate and graduate programs in arts and sciences, agriculture, business, education, health and human services, and technology. It includes a school of visual and performing arts. There are 7 undergraduate schools and 1 graduate school. In addition to regional accreditation, Southeast has baccalaureate program accreditation with AACSB, ABET, ACEJMC, CSWE, NASM, NCATE, and NRPA. The library contains 439,445 volumes, 1.3 million microform items, and 16,933 audio/video tapes/CDs/DVDs, and subscribes to 71,045 periodicals including electronic. Computerized library services include interlibrary loans, database searching, Internet access, and Wi-Fi capability. Special learning facilities include an art gallery, radio station, museum of archaeological items and artworks, center for regional history, school of visual and performing arts, center for innovation and entrepreneurship, agriculture research center, horticulture greenhouse. The 400-acre campus is in a small town 120 miles south of St. Louis. Including any residence halls, there are 87 buildings.

Student Life: 80% of undergraduates are from Missouri. Others are from 31 states, 56 foreign countries, and Canada. 76% are White. The average age of freshmen is 19; all undergraduates, 22. 26% do not continue beyond their first year; 54% remain to graduate.

Housing: 3106 students can be accommodated in college housing, which includes single-sex and coed dorms. In addition, there are honors houses, special-interest houses, fraternity houses, sorority houses, Honors program students and transfer students may choose to live in honors or transfer housing. A variety of other learning and theme communities are available for students. Examples include education, science, business, and health care. On-campus housing is guaranteed for the freshman year only, and is available on a first-come, and first-served basis. 73% of students commute. Alcohol is not permitted. All students may keep cars.

Activities: 14% of men belong to 11 national fraternities; 11% of women belong to 7 national sororities. There are 150 groups on campus, including and residence hall association, student activities council, art, band, cheerleading, choir, chorus, dance, debate, drama, drill team, ethnic, Fraternities and sororities, gay, honors, international, jazz band, literary magazine, marching band, musical theater, newspaper, opera, orchestra, pep band, photography, political, professional, radio and TV, religious, social, social service, student government, and symphony. Popular campus events include Family Weekend, Homecoming, Late Night Breakfast, Spring Fling, Ice Cream PigOut and International Week.

Sports: There are 5 intercollegiate sports for men and 8 for women, and 30 intramural sports for men and 30 for women. Facilities include Two student recreation centers housing indoor tracks, a climbing wall, six racquetball courts, indoor basketball courts, a weight room, volleyball courts, bicycle and rowing machines, strength-training equipment, stair climbers, and elliptical machines. There is also a student aquatic center with 25-yd lap pool, hot tub, and a leisure pool with volleyball court, basketball hoop, climbing wall, zip line and rope swing.

Disabled Students: All of the campus is accessible. Facilities include wheelchair ramps, elevators, special parking, specially equipped restrooms, special class scheduling, lowered drinking fountains, lowered telephones, special housing.

Services: Counseling and information services are available, as is tutoring in most subjects. There is a reader service for the blind, and remedial math, reading, and writing.

Campus Safety and Security: Measures include 24-hour foot and vehicle patrol, emergency notification system, self-defense education, and security escort services. There are shuttle buses, emergency telephones, lighted pathways/sidewalks, and controlled access to dorms/residences.

Programs of Study: Southeast confers B.A., B.F.A., B.G.S., B.S., B.S.B.A., B.S.Ed., B.F.C.S.E., B.M.E., B.M. and B.S.N. degrees. Associate and master's degrees are also awarded. Bachelor's degrees are awarded in AGRICULTURE (agricultural business management, animal science, horticulture, and plant science), BIOLOGICAL SCIENCE (biology/biological science), BUSINESS (accounting, business administration and management, finance, hospitality management services, international business management, marketing management, recreation and leisure services, and sports management), COMMUNICATIONS AND THE ARTS (advertising, art, communication rhetoric/communication, English, historic preservation, journalism, English and Professional Communication, music, photography, public relations, radio/television technology, theatre arts, video, and visual and performing arts), COMPUTER AND PHYSICAL SCIENCE (chemistry, computer science, mathematics, and physics), EDUCATION (agricultural education, art education, athletic training, business education, early childhood education, education of the exceptional child, elementary education, English education, foreign languages education, health information management, industrial arts education, mathematics education, middle school education, music education, physical education, science education, secondary education, and social studies education), ENGINEERING AND ENVIRONMENTAL DESIGN (engineering physics, engineering technology, environmental science, and technological management), HEALTH PROFESSIONS (medical technology and nursing), SOCIAL SCIENCE (corrections, criminal justice, criminology, economics, family/consumer studies, French studies, German area studies, (Social Science) Global Studies, history, interdisciplinary studies, law enforcement and corrections, philosophy, political science/government, psychology, social work, and Spanish studies). Nursing, general studies, and psychology have the largest enrollments.

Required: Students must complete 120 credit hours (24 to 97 hours in the major). The core includes 51 credit hours in the University Studies program, as well as in interdisciplinary studies, English, and math. Minimum GPAs (at least 2.0) and other graduation requirements vary by program. Students must also pass a writing exam and complete 4 career proficiency checks and, at the freshman and senior level, Measure of Academic Proficiency and Progress (MAPP).

Special: Southeast offers a Cooperative Doctorate of Education in Educational Leadership with the University of Missouri/Columbia and Cooperative Master of Science in Criminal Justice with Missouri Southern State University. Opportunities are provided for individually arranged internships and work-study, study abroad in 40 countries, a general studies degree, dual and student-designed majors (interdisciplinary studies), credit by exam, nondegree study, and pass/fail options. A 3-2 engineering degree is possible in conjunction with the University of Missouri at Rolla or at Columbia. A 3-3 doctor of chiropractic degree is possible in conjunction with Logan College of Chiropractic in Chesterfield. There is cross registration with Three Rivers College to facilitate completion of an AA degree and transfer to a Southeast four-year degree program. There are preprofessional programs in architecture, chiropractic, dentistry, engineering, law, medicine, optometry, pharmacy, physical therapy, occupational therapy, and veterinary medicine. There are 28 national honor societies and a freshman honors program.

Faculty/Classroom: 47% of faculty are male; 53% are female. All teach and do research. Graduate students teach 5% of introductory courses. The average class size in an introductory lecture is 27; in a laboratory is 21; and in a regular course is 26.

Admissions: 85% of the 2013-2014 applicants were accepted. The ACT scores were 31% below 21, 30% between 21 and 23, 20% between 24 and 26, 9% between 27 and 28, and 9% above 28. 27% of the current freshmen were in the top fifth of their class; 48% were in the top two fifths. 39 freshmen graduated first in their class.

Requirements: The SAT or ACT is required. Graduation from an accredited secondary school is required; the GED is accepted. Applicants should submit an academic record with 4 units in English, 2 units in social studies, 1 unit in history, 3 units in mathematics, 3 units in science (1 unit must be lab course), 1 unit in visual and performing arts, and 3 units of academic electives. A GPA of 2.0 is required. AP and CLEP credits are accepted.

Procedure: Freshmen are admitted fall, spring, and summer. Entrance exams should be taken in the spring of the junior year or fall of the senior year. There is a rolling admissions plan. Applications should be filed by July 1 for fall entry; November 1 for spring entry; and May 1 for summer entry, along with a $30 fee. Applications are accepted online.

Transfer: 643 transfer students enrolled in 2012-2013. Transcripts from the student's previous college must be submitted, listing at least 24 credits earned and a minimum GPA of 2.0. The ACT is required for those students who have fewer than 24 credit hours. 30 of 120 credits required for the bachelor's degree must be completed at Southeast.

Visiting: There are regularly scheduled orientations for prospective students, Includes academic advising and other university information. There are guides for informal visits. To schedule a visit, contact the Office of Admissions.

Financial Aid: In 2013-2014, 92% of all full-time freshmen and 89% of continuing full-time students received some form of financial aid. 62% of all full-time freshmen and 58% of continuing full-time students received need-based aid. The average freshman award was $9,457. Need-based scholarships or need-based grants averaged $4,261 ($12,500 maximum); need-based self-help aid (loans and jobs) averaged $3,236 ($8,963 maximum); non-need-based athletic scholarships averaged $11,369 ($24,686 maximum); other non-need-based awards and non-need-based scholarships averaged $3,601 ($23,714 maximum); and $4,560 from other forms of aid. 18% of undergraduate students work part-time. Average annual earnings from campus work are $1810. The average financial indebtedness of the 2013 graduate was $24,204. The FAFSA is required. The priority date for freshman financial aid applications for fall entry is March 1.

International Students: There are 683 international students enrolled. The school actively recruits these students. They must take the TOEFL with a minimum score of 500 on the paper-based TOEFL (PBT) or 61 on the Internet-based version (iBT). They must also take the SAT or ACT, scoring 18.

Computers: All students may access the system. There are no time limits and no fees.

Graduates: From July 1, 2012 to June 30, 2013, 1634 bachelor's degrees were awarded. The most popular majors were general studies (8%), nursing (7%), and elementary education (3%). In an average class, 28% graduate in 4 years or less, 49% graduate in 5 years or less, and 49% graduate in 6 years or less.

Admissions Contact: Lenell Hahn, Director of Admissions. E-Mail: *admissions@semo.edu* Web: *www.semo.edu*

SOUTHWEST BAPTIST UNIVERSITY B-3

Bolivar, MO 65613 (417) 328-1817
(800) 526-5859; (417) 328-1514

Full-time: 833 men, 1232 women
Part-time: 244 men, 700 women
Graduate: 313 men, 542 women
Year: 4-1-4, summer session
Application Deadline:
Freshman Class: n/av
SAT or ACT: required
Faculty: n/av; IIA, --$
Ph.D.s: 71%
Student/Faculty: n/av
Tuition: $18,360
Room & Board: $6350

COMPETITIVE

Southwest Baptist University, founded in 1878, is a private liberal arts institution affiliated with the Southern Baptist Convention. There are 6 undergraduate schools and 3 graduate schools. In addition to regional accreditation, SBU has baccalaureate program accreditation with ACBSP, NASM, and NLN. The library contains 724,203 volumes, 482,190 microform items, and 11,451 audio/video tapes/CDs/DVDs, and subscribes to 22,679 periodicals including electronic. Computerized library services include interlibrary loans, database searching, Internet access, and Wi-Fi capability. Special learning facilities include an art gallery. The 180-acre campus is in a small town 28 miles north of Springfield Missouri. Including any residence halls, there are 26 buildings.

Student Life: 71% of undergraduates are from Missouri. Others are from 40 states, 19 foreign countries, and Canada. 73% are White. 87% are Protestant. The average age of freshmen is 18; all undergraduates, 21. 28% do not continue beyond their first year.

Housing: 1071 students can be accommodated in college housing, which includes single-sex dorms and on-campus apartments. On-campus housing is guaranteed for all 4 years. 62% of students live on campus; of those, 65% remain on campus on weekends. Alcohol is not permitted. All students may keep cars.

Activities: There are no fraternities or sororities. There are 36 groups on campus, including art, band, cheerleading, choir, chorale, chorus, computers, debate, drama, forensics, honors, international, jazz band, musical theater, newspaper, opera, orchestra, pep band, photography, political, professional, religious, social service, and student government. Popular campus events include Welcome Week, Concerts and Courtwarming.

Sports: Facilities include a Jane and Ken Meyer Wellness and Sports Center, which houses intramural basketball courts, racquetball courts, a rock-climbing wall, weight rooms, an aerobics room, an indoor walking/jogging track, health and phys ed classrooms, and an Olympic-size swimming pool. The sports arena has seating for 2800 people.

Disabled Students: 95% of the campus is accessible. Facilities include wheelchair ramps, elevators, special parking, specially equipped restrooms, special class scheduling, and lowered drinking fountains.

Services: Counseling and information services are available, as is tutoring in every subject. There is remedial math, reading, and writing.

Campus Safety and Security: Measures include 24-hour foot and vehicle patrol. There are emergency telephones and lighted pathways/sidewalks.

Programs of Study: SBU confers B.A., B.S., B.A.S., B.M. and B.S.N. degrees. Associate, master's, and doctoral degrees are also awarded. Bachelor's degrees are awarded in BIOLOGICAL SCIENCE (biology/biological science), BUSINESS (accounting, business administration and management, international business management, marketing and distribution, recreation and leisure services, and sports management), COMMUNICATIONS AND THE ARTS (art, communications, English, journalism, music, performing arts, and Spanish), COMPUTER AND PHYSICAL SCIENCE (chemistry, computer science, information sciences and systems, and mathematics), EDUCATION (art education, athletic training, early childhood education, elementary education, health education, mathematics education, middle school education, music education, physical education, secondary education, and social studies education), ENGINEERING AND ENVIRONMENTAL DESIGN (commercial art and occupational safety and health), HEALTH PROFESSIONS (medical technology and nursing), SOCIAL SCIENCE (biblical studies, criminal justice, economics, history, human services, interdisciplinary studies, ministries, missions, parks and recreation management, pastoral studies, political science/government, psychology, religious education, religious music, and sociology). Education, psychology, and business administration have the largest enrollments.

Required: To graduate, students must complete 128 credit hours, with 40 in upper-division courses and 52 in general education requirements, and maintain a 2.0 GPA. The number of hours in the major varies.

Special: SBU offers internships, study abroad in 80 countries, an Oxford honors program, a Washington semester, work-study programs. There are also American studies, contemporary music, family film, and journalism programs. There are a freshman honors program.

Faculty/Classroom: 80% teach undergraduates. No introductory courses are taught by graduate students. The average class size in an introductory lecture is 40; in a laboratory is 20; and in a regular course is 20.

Requirements: The SAT or ACT is required. An SBU applicant must present either proof of graduation from an accredited or approved high school or a homeschool transcript. Additionally, students must meet 2 of the following 3 qualifiers: 2.5 high school GPA on a 4.0 scale; 21 ACT or satisfactory SAT composite score; or top 50% of high school rank. Applicants are recommended to have 13 academic credits, including a recommended 4 credits in English, 3 in math, 2 each in natural science and history or social science, and 2 elective units. AP and CLEP credits are accepted.

Procedure: Freshmen are admitted to all sessions. Entrance exams should be taken at any time prior to admission. There are deferred admissions and rolling admissions plans. Application deadlines are open. Application fee is $30. Applications are accepted online.

Transfer: 114 transfer students enrolled in 2012-2013. Applicants must submit official college and high school transcripts and have a minimum GPA of 2.0. An interview is encouraged. Students who have not yet met SBU's English and math requirements must present scores from the ACT, SAT, or other approved placement test. Only 6 hours of D credit can be transferred. 30 of 128 credits required for the bachelor's degree must be completed at SBU.

Visiting: There are regularly scheduled orientations for prospective students, including fall and spring visitation days. There are guides for informal visits, visitors may sit in on classes, and stay overnight. To schedule a visit, contact the Director of Admissions at (800) 526-5859.

Financial Aid: The FAFSA and the college's own financial statement are required. Check with the school for current application deadlines.

International Students: There are 30 international students enrolled. They must take the TOEFL. They must also take the SAT or ACT.

Computers: All students may access the system. Computer labs are open from 8 a.m. to 1:30 a.m. daily. There are no time limits. There is a fee.

Graduates: From July 1, 2012 to June 30, 2013, 419 bachelor's degrees were awarded. In an average class, 41% graduate in 4 years or less, 50% graduate in 5 years or less, and 53% graduate in 6 years or less.

Admissions Contact: Darren Crowder, Director of Admissions. E-Mail: *dcrowder@sbuniv.edu* Web: *www.sbuniv.edu*

STEPHENS COLLEGE

C-2

Columbia, MO 65215

(573) 876-7207
(800) 876-7207; (573) 876-7237

Full-time: 15 men, 560 women	**Faculty:** n/av
Part-time: 15 men, 170 women	**Ph.D.s:** 83%
Graduate: 10 men, 60 women	**Student/Faculty:** n/av
Year: semesters, summer session	**Tuition:** $27,120
Application Deadline: open	**Room & Board:** $9500
Freshman Class: n/av	
SAT or ACT: required	

VERY COMPETITIVE

Stephens College, founded in 1833, is a private college primarily for women and offering undergraduate programs in the arts and sciences, business, education, and fine arts. There are 2 undergraduate schools and 2 graduate schools. The figures in the above capsule and in this profile are approximate. The library contains 129,915 volumes, 11,322 microform items, and 1254 audio/video tapes/CDs/DVDs, and subscribes to 9836 periodicals including electronic. Computerized library services include interlibrary loans, database searching, and Internet access. Special learning facilities include a learning resource center, art gallery, radio station, and TV station. The 86-acre campus is in an urban area 120 miles west of St. Louis. Including any residence halls, there are 35 buildings.

Student Life: 55% of undergraduates are from out of state, mostly the Midwest. Students are from 44 states and 3 foreign countries. 80% are from public schools. 87% are white. The average age of freshmen is 18; all undergraduates, 20. 27% do not continue beyond their first year; 58% remain to graduate.

Housing: 842 students can be accommodated in college housing, which includes single-sex dorms and on-campus apartments. In addition, there are honors houses, special-interest houses for intercultural scholars and fine arts majors, and houses with designated academic floors, nonsmoking floors, and pet floors. On-campus housing is guaranteed for all 4 years. 75% of students live on campus; of those, 90% remain on campus on weekends. All students may keep cars.

Activities: There are no fraternities; 8% of women belong to 2 national sororities. There are 45 groups on campus, including art, choir, chorale, chorus, dance, drama, ethnic, gay, honors, international, literary magazine, musical theater, newspaper, photography, political, professional, radio and TV, religious, social, social service, student government, and yearbook. Popular campus events include the opening convocation, Honors Convocation, and performing arts events.

Sports: There are 4 intercollegiate sports for women. Facilities include a 300-seat gym, an Olympic-size pool, and tennis courts.

Disabled Students: 80% of the campus is accessible. Facilities include wheelchair ramps, elevators, special parking, specially equipped rest rooms, special class scheduling, lowered drinking fountains, and special housing.

Services: Counseling and information services are available, as is tutoring in most subjects, including English and courses with written expectations. There is remedial writing.

Campus Safety and Security: Measures include 24-hour foot and vehicle patrol, self-defense education, and security escort services. There are emergency telephones and lighted pathways/sidewalks.

Programs of Study: Stephens confers B.A., B.S., and B.F.A. degrees. Associate and master's degrees are also awarded. Bachelor's degrees are awarded in AGRICULTURE (equine science), BIOLOGICAL SCIENCE (biology/biological science), BUSINESS (accounting, business administration and management, and fashion merchandising), COMMUNICATIONS AND THE ARTS (creative writing, dance, dramatic arts, English, film arts, graphic design, public relations, and theater design), EDUCATION (early childhood education and elementary education), ENGINEERING AND ENVIRONMENTAL DESIGN (interior design), SOCIAL SCIENCE (fashion design and technology, liberal arts/general studies, and prelaw). Education and biology are the strongest academically. Performing arts, fashion, and biology have the largest enrollments.

Required: All students must complete 6 hours of English and a distribution of 9 courses in lower-division work, including 6 hours of social sciences and 3 hours each of math, science, literary studies, history, cultural studies, and ethics. The bachelor's degree requires completion of at least 120 semester hours, including 30 to 72 in a major field, with a minimum GPA of 2.0.

Special: Students may study abroad in England, Italy, Mexico, France, Ecuador, South Korea, and Spain. Stephens also offers cross-registration with the Mid-Missouri Association of Colleges and Universities, many internships, a Washington semester, dual and student-designed majors, a 3-2 occupational therapy degree program with Washington University, accelerated degree programs in dance and theater arts, and pass/fail options for electives. There are 8 national honor societies and a freshman honors program.

Faculty/Classroom: 40% of faculty are male; 60% are female. 92% teach undergraduates, and all do research. No introductory courses are taught by graduate students. The average class size in an introductory lecture is 30; in a laboratory, 12; and in a regular course, 20.

Requirements: The SAT or ACT is required. In addition, applicants must be graduates of accredited secondary schools or have earned a GED. An essay is required, and an interview is recommended. A GPA of 2.5 is required. AP and CLEP credits are accepted. Important factors in the admissions decision are advanced placement or honors courses, leadership record, and recommendations by school officials.

Procedure: Freshmen are admitted fall and spring. There are deferred admissions and rolling admissions plans. Application deadlines are open. Application fee is $25. Applications are accepted online.

Transfer: Applicants must submit official transcripts from all college work attempted or completed as well as a recommendation from an academic college instructor. Transfers must submit an official high school transcript. 36 of 120 credits required for the bachelor's degree must be completed at Stephens.

Visiting: There are regularly scheduled orientations for prospective students, consisting of attendance at classes, a campus tour, an appointment with instructors, and an interview. There are guides for informal visits, and visitors may sit in on classes and stay overnight. To schedule a visit, contact the campus visit coordinator.

Financial Aid: The FAFSA is required. Check with the school for current application deadlines.

International Students: The school actively recruits these students. They must take the TOEFL.

Computers: Wireless access is available. There are wireless computer labs, and wireless access is available in residence halls and academic buildings. All students may access the system. There are no time limits and no fees.

Admissions Contact: Director of Admissions. E-Mail: *apply@stephens.edu* Web: *www.stephens.edu*

TRUMAN STATE UNIVERSITY C-1

Kirksville, MO 63501 **(660) 785-4114; (660) 785-7456**

Full-time: 2233 men, 3126 women	**Faculty:** 339; IIA, --$
Part-time: 53 men, 56 women	**Ph.D.s:** 82%
Graduate: 87 men, 192 women	**Student/Faculty:** 16 to 1
Year: semesters, summer session	**Tuition:** $6692 ($11,543)
Application Deadline: March 1	**Room & Board:** $6854

Freshman Class: 4608 applied, 3333 accepted, 1342 enrolled

SAT CR/M: 600/610 **ACT:** 27 **HIGHLY COMPETITIVE**

Truman State University, founded in 1867, is a public liberal arts institution offering undergraduate and graduate degree programs in business and accountaning, arts and sciences, and education. There are 5 undergraduate schools and 5 graduate schools. In addition to regional accreditation, Truman has baccalaureate program accreditation with AACSB, NASM, and NCATE. The library contains 483,708 volumes, 1.5 million microform items, and 37,797 audio/video tapes/CDs/DVDs, and subscribes to 3,942 periodicals including electronic. Computerized library services include interlibrary loans, database searching, Internet access, and Wi-Fi capability. Special learning facilities include an art gallery, radio station, an independent learning center for nursing students, an observatory, a greenhouse chamber, a speech and hearing clinic, a broadcasting studio, language learning center, student success center, and various labs for science programs. The 140-acre campus is in a small town 170 miles northeast of Kansas City, MO and 200 miles north of St. Louis, MO. Including any residence halls, there are 35 buildings.

Student Life: 77% of undergraduates are from Missouri. Others are from 36 states, and 43 foreign countries. 73% are from public schools. 75% are White. 37% are unknown affiliation; 36% Protestant; 26% Catholic. The average age of freshmen is 18; all undergraduates, 20. 16% do not continue beyond their first year; 71% remain to graduate.

Housing: 2853 students can be accommodated in college housing, which includes single-sex and coed dorms, on-campus apartments, and married student housing. All residence halls are designated residential colleges that provide professional advisers to all freshmen, classrooms, and academic centers within the colleges, a low student-to-adviser ratio, and an integrative living-learning environment. A Romance Languages House is available in MO Hall. On-campus housing is guaranteed for the freshman year only, is available on a first-come, first-served basis, and is available on a lottery system for upperclassmen. 52% of students commute. Alcohol is not permitted. All students may keep cars.

Activities: 25% of men belong to 14 national fraternities; 17% of women belong to 1 local and 5 national sororities. There are 272 groups on campus, including art, band, cheerleading, chess, choir, chorale, chorus, computers, dance, drama, drill team, environmental, ethnic, forensics, gay, honors, international, jazz band, literary magazine, marching band, musical theater, orchestra, pep band, political, professional, religious, social, social service, and student government. Popular campus events include Final Blowout, Kohlenberg Lyceum Series, and the Big Event.

Sports: There are 11 intercollegiate sports for men and 10 for women, and 31 intramural sports for men and 31 for women. Facilities include a 5,000-seat football stadium, a soccer field, tennis and racquetball courts, a softball diamond, a baseball diamond, a 3,000-seat arena with 3 basketball courts, an Olympic-size pool, weight training rooms, indoor and outdoor track facilities, and a 60,000-square-foot student recreation center.

Disabled Students: 98% of the campus is accessible. Facilities include wheelchair ramps, elevators, special parking, specially equipped restrooms, special class scheduling, lowered drinking fountains, lowered telephones, special housing. The swimming pool is equipped with a lift to assist physically disabled swimmers.

Services: Counseling and information services are available, as is tutoring in most subjects, services for the hearing impaired, and a braille scanner and printer. There is a reader service for the blind, and remedial math and writing. Disability Services provides note taking and test taking accomodations for students, as well as many other services for qualified individuals.

Campus Safety and Security: Measures include 24-hour foot and vehicle patrol, emergency notification system, self-defense education, and security escort services. There are emergency telephones, lighted pathways/sidewalks, and controlled access to dorms/residences.

Programs of Study: Truman confers B.A., B.S., B.F.A., B.M. and B.S.N. degrees. Master's degrees are also awarded. Bachelor's degrees are awarded in AGRICULTURE (agricultural business management, agriculture, agronomy, animal science, equine science, and horticulture), BIOLOGICAL SCIENCE (biology/biological science), BUSINESS (accounting, business administration and management, and international business management), COMMUNICATIONS AND THE ARTS (art, art history and appreciation, classics, communications, dramatic arts, English, fine arts, French, German, journalism, linguistics, music, music performance, romance languages and literature, Russian, Spanish, studio art, and visual design), COMPUTER AND PHYSICAL SCIENCE (chemistry, computer science, mathematics, and physics), EDUCATION (athletic training and physical education), ENGINEERING AND ENVIRONMENTAL DESIGN (preengineering), HEALTH PROFESSIONS (clinical science, exercise science, health science, nursing, physical therapy, predentistry, premedicine, prepharmacy, preveterinary science, public health, and speech pathology/audiology), SOCIAL SCIENCE (anthropology, criminal justice, economics, history, interdisciplinary studies, philosophy, physical fitness/movement, political science/government, prelaw, psychology, religion, and sociology). Chemistry, political science, and accounting are the strongest academically. Business administration, biology, and English have the largest enrollments.

Required: All students must complete 63 hours of course work in the liberal arts, 16 of which must be in written and oral communication, math and statistics, computer literacy, and personal well-being, and 23 of which must be in history, science, social science, philosophy/religion, math, and aesthetics. Elementary proficiency in a foreign language is required of all majors. The B.A., B.F.A., and B.M. degree require intermediate proficiency in one foreign language, and the B.S. and B.S.N. require additional course work in science, math, statistics, computer science, social sciences, or logic. Skills such as writing, quantitative analysis, problem solving, and critical thinking are reinforced throughout the curriculum, and all seniors end their studies with a capstone, or culminating experience, in their majors. Students must also complete a nationally normed exam in their subject areas as part of Truman's assessment program.

Special: Study abroad in 51 countries is offered through Truman's own programs and those of the College Consortium for International Studies, the Council on International Educational Exchange, and the International Student Exchange Program. The university requires internships in education and health and exercise science. Voluntary legislative internships are offered to all students at the state capitol, and internships through the Washington Center. There is a 3-2 engineering program with the University of Missouri-Rolla. Work-study programs, B.A.-B.S. degrees, dual majors, student-designed majors in health and exercise science, biology, history, and agricultural science, credit for military experience, pass/fail options for internships, and nondegree study are available. There are 18 national honor societies, including Phi Beta Kappa, a freshman honors program, and 19 departmental honors programs.

Faculty/Classroom: 60% of faculty are male; 40% are female. 98% teach undergraduates. Graduate students teach 3% of introductory courses. The average class size in an introductory lecture is 36; in a laboratory is 20; and in a regular course is 26.

Admissions: 72% of the 2013-2014 applicants were accepted. The SAT scores for the 2013-2014 freshman class were: Critical Reading--12% below 500, 40% between 500 and 599, 34% between 600 and 699, and 14% between 700 and 800; Math--12% below 500, 28% between 500 and 599, 49% between 600 and 699, and 11% between 700 and 800. The ACT scores were 3% below 21, 14% between 21 and 23, 29% between 24 and 26, 16% between 27 and 28, and 38% above 28. 71% of the current freshmen were in the top fifth of their class; 94% were in the top two fifths. There were 19 National Merit finalists. 156 freshmen graduated first in their class.

Requirements: Truman prefers the ACT, but accepts either the ACT or SAT. Applicants should have completed 4 units of English, 3 each of science and social studies, 2 of foreign language, and 1 of art or music. 4 units of math are strongly recommended. An essay is required and a visit is recommended. AP and CLEP credits are accepted. Important factors in the admissions decision are leadership record, advanced placement or honors courses, and extracurricular activities record.

Procedure: Freshmen are admitted to all sessions. Entrance exams should be taken during the spring or summer following the junior year. There are deferred admissions and rolling admissions plans. Applications should be filed by March 1 for fall entry; November 15 for spring entry; and March 1 for summer entry. Notification is sent on a rolling basis. Applications are accepted online.

Transfer: 176 transfer students enrolled in 2012-2013. Transfer applicants are considered for admission through a competitive individualized review process that emphasizes preparedness for study based upon a variety of criteria. Cumulative grade point average in transferable college credit, strength of college curriculum, the admission essay, and the graded college paper are considered for all transfer admission candidates. Cumulative high school record and ACT/SAT scores will also be reviewed for applicants who have completed fewer than 24 hours of transferable post high school college credit at the time of application. 45 of 124 credits required for the bachelor's degree must be completed at Truman.

Visiting: There are regularly scheduled orientations for prospective students, Campus visits include a personalized meeting with an admission counselor, a student-led campus tour, and appointments with a faculty member in the student's major or in any areas of special interest upon request. There are guides for informal visits, visitors may sit in on classes, and stay overnight. To schedule a visit, contact the Admissions Office.

Financial Aid: In 2013-2014, 94% of all full-time freshmen and 76% of continuing full-time students received some form of financial aid. 35% of all full-time freshmen and 30% of continuing full-time students received need-based aid. The average freshman award was $8,875. Need-based scholarships or need-based grants averaged $3,821 ($7,960 maximum);

need-based self-help aid (loans and jobs) averaged $3,391 ($11,000 maximum); non-need-based athletic scholarships averaged $2,585 ($17,772 maximum); and other non-need-based awards and non-need-based scholarships averaged $4,926 ($21,700 maximum). 18% of undergraduate students work part-time. Average annual earnings from campus work are $1677. The average financial indebtedness of the 2013 graduate was $21,858. The FAFSA and the college's own financial statement are required. The priority date for freshman financial aid applications for fall entry is February 15. The deadline for filing freshman financial aid applications for fall entry is April 1.

International Students: There are 279 international students enrolled. The school actively recruits these students. They must take the TOEFL with a minimum score of 550 on the paper-based TOEFL (PBT) or 79 on the Internet-based version (iBT) and the Comprehensive English Language Test. They must also take the SAT or ACT.

Computers: All students may access the system 24/7. There are no time limits and no fees.

Graduates: From July 1, 2012 to June 30, 2013, 1217 bachelor's degrees were awarded. The most popular majors were business administration (10%), English and linguistics (10%), and biology (9%). 170 companies recruited on campus in 2012-2013. In an average class, 1% graduate in 3 years or less, 47% graduate in 4 years or less, 66% graduate in 5 years or less, and 71% graduate in 6 years or less.

Admissions Contact: Melody Chambers, Director of Admissions. E-Mail: *admissions@truman.edu* Web: *www.truman.edu*

UNIVERSITY OF CENTRAL MISSOURI B-2

Warrensburg, MO 64093 (660) 543-4290; (660) 543-8517

Full-time: 3764 men, 4428 women	**Faculty:** 452; IIA, --$
Part-time: 680 men, 867 women	**Ph.D.s:** 67%
Graduate: 810 men, 1399 women	**Student/Faculty:** 17 to 1
Year: semesters, summer session	**Tuition:** $7647 ($13,935)
Application Deadline: open	**Room & Board:** $7958

Freshman Class: 4700 applied, 3800 accepted, 1787 enrolled

ACT: 22

COMPETITIVE

University of Central Missouri, founded in 1871, is a public liberal arts institution offering a comprehensive range of degree programs. There are 4 undergraduate schools and one graduate school. In addition to regional accreditation, Central has baccalaureate program accreditation with AACSB, ABET, ACCE, ADA, ASLA, CSWE, NASAD, NASM, NCATE, and NLN. The library contains 2.2 million volumes, 815,787 microform items, 20,544 audio/video tapes/CDs/DVDs, and subscribes to 783 periodicals including electronic. Computerized library services include interlibrary loans, database searching, Internet access, and Wi-Fi capability. Special learning facilities include an art gallery, natural history museum, planetarium, radio station, TV station, an instructional airport, a 200-acre farm, a driving/safety range, a speech and hearing clinic, a child development lab, and an English Language Center. The 1561-acre campus is in a small town 50 miles southeast of Kansas City. Including any residence halls, there are 107 buildings.

Student Life: 89% of undergraduates are from Missouri. Others are from 42 states, 59 foreign countries, and Canada. 92% are from public schools. 85% are White. 54% are Protestant; 20% Catholic; 12% claim no religious affiliation. The average age of freshmen is 19; all undergraduates, 22. 32% do not continue beyond their first year; 51% remain to graduate.

Housing: 3540 students can be accommodated in college housing, which includes single-sex and coed dorms, on-campus apartments, off-campus apartments, and married student housing. In addition, there are honors houses, special-interest houses, fraternity houses, sorority houses, and quiet dorms. On-campus housing is guaranteed for the freshman year only, is available on a first-come, and first-served basis. 72% of students commute. All students may keep cars.

Activities: 6% of men belong to 12 national fraternities; 6% of women belong to 11 national sororities. There are 250 groups on campus, including art, band, cheerleading, chess, choir, chorale, chorus, computers, dance, debate, drama, drill team, ethnic, film, forensics, gay, honors, international, jazz band, literary magazine, marching band, musical theater, newspaper, opera, orchestra, pep band, photography, political, professional, radio and TV, religious, social, social service, student government, and symphony. Popular campus events include Performing Arts Series, Technology Fair, and Repertory Theater.

Sports: There are 7 intercollegiate sports for men and 7 for women, and 32 intramural sports for men and 32 for women. Facilities include a stadium seating more than 12,000, 3 gyms, baseball, softball, women's soccer, and practice fields, a bowling alley, tennis courts, and a multipurpose building that contains a swimming pool, weight rooms, and courts for basketball, racquetball, and volleyball. A nearby outdoor recreation area has an 18-hole golf course and facilities for swimming and other activities. The Student Recreation and Wellness Center includes 3 fitness rooms for aerobics, spinning, kickboxing, 3 new sport courts, a free weight room, 4 additional fitness areas that houses nearly a half-million dollars of fitness equipment, a passive recreation room, inside walking track, outside patio area for lounging, climbing wall, and Einstein's bagels.

Disabled Students: 95% of the campus is accessible. Facilities include wheelchair ramps, elevators, special parking, specially equipped restrooms, special class scheduling, lowered drinking fountains, lowered telephones, and special housing.

Services: Counseling and information services are available, as is tutoring in some subjects, for a fee including math, chemistry, physics, biology, accounting, economics, and business. There is a reader service for the blind, and remedial math. Writing and learning labs are available for all students. Tutoring is available through TRIO Student Support Services.

Campus Safety and Security: Measures include 24-hour foot and vehicle patrol, emergency notification system, self-defense education, and security escort services. There are emergency telephones, lighted pathways/sidewalks, a bike patrol, and a canine patrol.

Programs of Study: Central confers B.A., B.S., B.F.A., B.M., B.M.E., B.S.B.A., B.S.Ed. and B.S.W. degrees. Associate and master's degrees are also awarded. Bachelor's degrees are awarded in AGRICULTURE (agricultural business management and conservation and regulation), BIOLOGICAL SCIENCE (biology/biological science), BUSINESS (accounting, business administration and management, hotel/motel and restaurant management, human resources, management science, marketing/retailing/merchandising, organizational behavior, recreation and leisure services, and tourism), COMMUNICATIONS AND THE ARTS (broadcasting, communications, English, French, German, journalism, music, photography, public relations, Spanish, speech/debate/rhetoric, studio art, and theater design), COMPUTER AND PHYSICAL SCIENCE (actuarial science, chemistry, computer science, earth science, geology, information sciences and systems, mathematics, and physics), EDUCATION (agricultural education, art education, business education, early childhood education, elementary education, English education, foreign languages education, industrial arts education, mathematics education, middle school education, music education, physical education, science education, secondary education, social studies education, and special education), ENGINEERING AND ENVIRONMENTAL DESIGN (agricultural engineering technology, automotive technology, aviation computer technology, commercial art, construction management, drafting and design technology, electrical/electronics engineering, electrical/electronics engineering technology, engineering, engineering technology, graphic arts technology, industrial engineering technology, interior design, manufacturing technology, and occupational safety and health), HEALTH PROFESSIONS (medical laboratory technology, nursing, predentistry, premedicine, preveterinary science, and speech pathology/audiology), SOCIAL SCIENCE (criminal justice, dietetics, economics, geography, history, political science/government, prelaw, psychology, safety management, social work, sociology, and textiles and clothing). School of technology, elementary education and early childhood. Criminal justice and nursing have the largest enrollments.

Required: To graduate, students must complete a minimum of 120 hours, including 35 to 64 in the major, and have a minimum GPA of 2.0; several majors require a higher cumulative GPA. General education requirements include a total of 39 to 45 hours in humanities, social sciences, multicultural studies, technology, English and oral communications, math, science, and individual development. A comprehensive exam may be part of the exit assessment in selected majors.

Special: Central offers cross-registration with the Midwest Student Exchange program, credit and non-credit internships, study abroad in more than 15 countries, a B.A. - B.S. degree, dual and student-designed majors, credit for military service, pass/fail options, nondegree study, and a 3-2 engineering degree with the University of Missouri at Columbia and at Rolla and with the University of Indiana. There are 25 national honor societies, a freshman honors program, and 7 departmental honors programs.

Faculty/Classroom: 54% of faculty are male; 46% are female. No introductory courses are taught by graduate students. The average class size in an introductory lecture is 30 and in a regular course is 23.

Admissions: 24% of the current freshmen were in the top fifth of their class; 55% were in the top two fifths. 20 freshmen graduated first in their class.

Requirements: The ACT is required. Applicants must have completed 16 academic credits, including 4 in English with a writing emphasis, 3 each in math (algebra and beyond) and social science, 2 in natural sciences, and 1 in fine or performing arts, as well as 3 in academic electives. A foreign language is recommended. The GED is accepted. A GPA of 2.0 is required. AP and CLEP credits are accepted.

Procedure: Freshmen are admitted to all sessions. Entrance exams should be taken in the junior year of high school. There is a rolling admissions plan. Application deadlines are open. Application fee is $30. Notification is sent on a rolling basis. Applications are accepted online.

Transfer: 1006 transfer students enrolled in 2012-2013. Applicants must have a minimum GPA of 2.0, as indicated by an official college transcript. 30 of 120 credits required for the bachelor's degree must be completed at Central.

Visiting: There are regularly scheduled orientations for prospective students, including orientation sessions on housing, general education requirements, and enrollment for fall classes. There are guides for informal visits, visitors may sit in on classes, and stay overnight. To schedule a visit, contact the Office of Admissions.

Financial Aid: In 2013-2014, 94% of all full-time freshmen and 71% of continuing full-time students received some form of financial aid. 66% of all full-time freshmen and 62% of continuing full-time students received need-based aid. The average freshman award was $9,825. 11% of undergraduate students work part-time. Average annual earnings from campus work are $3300. The average financial indebtedness of the 2013 graduate was $23,766. Central is a member of CSS. The FAFSA is required. The priority date for freshman financial aid applications for fall entry is April 1.

International Students: There are 540 international students enrolled. The school actively recruits these students. They must take the TOEFL with a minimum score of 500 on the paper-based TOEFL (PBT), participate in institutional assessment. They must also take the ACT.

Computers: All students may access the system 24 hours a day. There are no time limits and no fees.

Graduates: From July 1, 2012 to June 30, 2013, 1805 bachelor's degrees were awarded. The most popular majors were technology (8%), criminal justice (7%), and elementary and early childhood education (6%). 330 companies recruited on campus in 2012-2013. In an average class, 28% graduate in 4 years or less, 45% graduate in 5 years or less, and 49% graduate in 6 years or less. Of the 2012 graduating class, 18% were enrolled in graduate school within 6 months of graduation, and 91% were employed.

Admissions Contact: Dr. Richard Sluder, Assistant Provost of Enrollment Management. E-Mail: *admit@ucmo.edu* Web: *www.ucmo.edu*

UNIVERSITY OF MISSOURI SYSTEM

The University of Missouri System, established in 1963, is a public system in Missouri. It is governed by a board of curators, whose chief administrator is the president. The primary goal of the system is teaching, research, extension, and public service. The main priorities are access to quality learning, teaching, academic and research achievement, and quality community-university engagement. The total student enrollment of all 4 campuses is usually 72,000, with 8000 faculty members. Altogether there are 236 baccalaureate, 219 master's, and 135 doctoral programs offered in University of Missouri System. 4-year campuses are located in Columbia, Kansas City, Rolla, and St. Louis. Profiles of the 4-year campuses are included in this section.

UNIVERSITY OF MISSOURI/COLUMBIA C-2

Columbia, MO 65211 **(573) 882-7786; (573) 882-7887**

Full-time: 12097 men, 13081 women	**Faculty:** 1241; I, -$
Part-time: 924 men, 894 women	**Ph.D.s:** 93%
Graduate: 3290 men, 4462 women	**Student/Faculty:** 20 to 1
Year: semesters, summer session	**Tuition:** $9257 ($23,366)
Application Deadline: May 1	**Room & Board:** $8944
Freshman Class: n/av	
ACT: required	

MOST COMPETITIVE

The University of Missouri/Columbia, established in 1839, offers a comprehensive array of undergraduate and graduate programs as well as professional training in law, medicine, and veterinary medicine. There are 16 undergraduate schools and 19 graduate schools. In addition to regional accreditation, Mizzou has baccalaureate program accreditation with AACSB, ABET, ACEJMC, ADA, APTA, CAHEA, CSWE, FIDER, NASM, NCATE, NRPA, and SAF. The 11 libraries contain 2.7 million volumes, 8.1 million microform items, and 35,711 audio/video tapes/CDs/DVDs. Computerized library services include interlibrary loans, database searching, Internet access, and Wi-Fi capability. Special learning facilities include an art gallery, natural history museum, radio station, TV station, astronomy observatory, freedom of information center; herbarium, State Historical Society of Missouri, Western Historical Manuscripts, and anthropology, fishery, wildlife collections. The 1262-acre campus is in a suburban area 120 miles west of St. Louis and 120 miles east of Kansas City. Including any residence halls, there are 350 buildings.

Student Life: 71% of undergraduates are from Missouri. Others are from 50 states, 115 foreign countries, and Canada. 81% are White. The average age of freshmen is 18; all undergraduates, 20. 16% do not continue beyond their first year; 71% remain to graduate.

Housing: 7177 students can be accommodated in college housing, which includes single-sex and coed dorms, off-campus apartments, and married student housing. In addition, there are honors houses, language houses, special-interest houses, fraternity houses, sorority houses, international houses, quiet houses, graduate/professional houses, and learning/living communities by major. 74% of students commute. Alcohol is not permitted. All students may keep cars.

Activities: 22% of men belong to 32 national fraternities; 28% of women belong to 18 national sororities. There are 700 groups on campus, including art, band, cheerleading, chess, choir, chorale, chorus, computers, dance, debate, drama, drill team, drum and bugle corps, environmental, ethnic, film, gay, honors, international, jazz band, literary magazine, marching band, musical theater, newspaper, orchestra, pep band, photography, political, professional, radio and TV, religious, social, social service, student government, symphony, and yearbook. Popular campus events include Big Twelve athletics, academic weeks, and Meet Mizzou Day.

Sports: There are 8 intercollegiate sports for men and 10 for women, and 35 intramural sports for men and 37 for women. Facilities include recreation complex with a 50-meter competition pool and diving well, a club pool, a high-tech fitness club, a heavy-lifting gym, a climbing and bouldering wall, multicourts, racquetball courts, and an indoor track. There is a 62,000-seat stadium, a 1,300-seat indoor gym, and an 18,000-seat auditorium.

Disabled Students: All of the campus is accessible. Facilities include wheelchair ramps, elevators, special parking, specially equipped restrooms, special class scheduling, lowered drinking fountains, lowered telephones, and special housing.

Services: Counseling and information services are available, as is tutoring in some subjects. There is a reader service for the blind.

Campus Safety and Security: Measures include 24-hour foot and vehicle patrol, emergency notification system, self-defense education, and security escort services. There are shuttle buses, emergency telephones, lighted pathways/sidewalks, a 24-hour bicycle patrol.

Programs of Study: Mizzou confers B.A., B.S., B.E.S., B.F.A., B.G.S., B.H.S., B.J., B.M., B.S.Acc., B.S.B.A., B.S.B.E., B.S.ChE., B.S.CiE., B.O.S., B.S.E.E., B.S.Ed., B.S.F., B.S.F.W., B.S.H.E.S., B.S.I.E., B.S.M.E., B.S.N. and B.S.W. degrees. Master's and doctoral degrees are also awarded. Bachelor's degrees are awarded in AGRICULTURE (agricultural business management, agricultural economics, agriculture, animal science, fishing and fisheries, forestry and related sciences, plant science, and soil science), BIOLOGICAL SCIENCE (biochemistry, biology/biological science, microbiology, and nutrition), BUSINESS (accounting, banking and finance, business administration and management, business economics, hotel/motel and restaurant management, marketing/retailing/merchandising, real estate, and tourism), COMMUNICATIONS AND THE ARTS (advertising, art, art history and appreciation, broadcasting, classics, communications, creative writing, design, dramatic arts, English, English literature, French, German, journalism, linguistics, music, Russian, and Spanish), COMPUTER AND PHYSICAL SCIENCE (atmospheric sciences and meteorology, chemistry, computer science, geology, mathematics, physics, and statistics), EDUCATION (art education, early childhood education, education, education administration, elementary education, English education, mathematics education, middle school education, music education, science education, secondary education, and social studies education), ENGINEERING AND ENVIRONMENTAL DESIGN (biomedical engineering, chemical engineering, civil engineering, computer engineering, electrical/electronics engineering, engineering, industrial engineering, and mechanical engineering), HEALTH PROFESSIONS (nursing, occupational therapy, physical therapy, public health, radiological science, respiratory therapy, and veterinary science), SOCIAL SCIENCE (anthropology, archeology, child care/child and family studies, counseling/psychology, early childhood studies, economics, family/consumer resource management, food science, geography, history, human development, international studies, liberal arts/general studies, parks and recreation management, philosophy, political science/government, psychology, public administration, public affairs, religion, rural sociology, social science, social work, sociology, and textiles and clothing). Biological sciences, accounting, and journalism are the strongest academically. Business administration, journalism, and biological sciences have the largest enrollments.

Required: To graduate, students must maintain a minimum 2.0 GPA and complete at least 120 credits, of which at least 30 must be in their major, although credit requirements can vary by degree program. All students must take English, plus 2 additional writing-intensive courses, demonstrate competency in college algebra, take 1 additional course in development math and reasoning skills, and complete a course in American history or government. Students must complete 9 hours in social and behavioral sciences, 9 in physical and biological sciences (including 1 lab course), and 9 in humanities and fine arts. A capstone experience is also required.

Special: Available academic programs include co-op programs and cross-registration with other schools, internships, study abroad, a Washington semester, and work-study programs. Special degrees or studies include an accelerated degree, dual majors, a general studies degree, and student-designed majors. For highly motivated students, there is an honors college and the possibility of early admission to the schools of law and medicine. There are 25 national honor societies, including Phi Beta Kappa, a freshman honors program, and 34 departmental honors programs.

Faculty/Classroom: 63% of faculty are male; 37% are female. No introductory courses are taught by graduate students.

Admissions: The ACT scores were 6% below 21, 23% between 21 and 23, 31% between 24 and 26, 18% between 27 and 28, and 23% above

28. There were 29 National Merit finalists. 235 freshmen graduated first in their class.

Requirements: The ACT is required. Students may gain probationary admission with sufficient GED scores. The usual requirements are completion of 17 Carnegie units, including 4 each in English and math, 3 each in social studies and science, 2 in a foreign language, and 1 in fine arts. Admission is determined by these units and a combination of class rank and ACT score. AP and CLEP credits are accepted. Important factors in the admissions decision are advanced placement or honors courses and evidence of special talent.

Procedure: Freshmen are admitted to all sessions. Entrance exams should be taken late in the junior year or in the senior year. There are deferred admissions and rolling admissions plans. Applications should be filed by May 1 for fall entry, along with a $50 fee. Notification is sent on a rolling basis. Applications are accepted online.

Transfer: 1407 transfer students enrolled in 2012-2013. Transfer students must present 24 hours of completed college-level course work with a minimum 2.5 GPA. Students must also complete college algebra or equivalent as well as freshman English or equivalent with a C- or better. 30 of 120 credits required for the bachelor's degree must be completed at Mizzou.

Visiting: There are regularly scheduled orientations for prospective students, consisting of a campus tour, a visit with an admissions representative, and a visit with an academic representative on request. There are guides for informal visits and visitors may sit in on classes. To schedule a visit, contact the Admissions Office.

Financial Aid: In 2013-2014, 52% of all full-time freshmen and 48% of continuing full-time students received some form of financial aid. 46% of all full-time freshmen and 39% of continuing full-time students received need-based aid. The average financial indebtedness of the 2013 graduate was $23,588. The FAFSA is required. The priority date for freshman financial aid applications for fall entry is March 1.

International Students: There are 798 international students enrolled. The school actively recruits these students. They must take the TOEFL.

Computers: All students may access the system. 24 hours daily by modem; lab hours vary, but labs are open 7 days a week. There are no time limits and no fees.

Graduates: From July 1, 2012 to June 30, 2013, 5528 bachelor's degrees were awarded. The most popular majors were business (17%), journalism (12%), and health professions and related sciences (10%). 1786 companies recruited on campus in 2012-2013. In an average class, 46% graduate in 4 years or less, 67% graduate in 5 years or less, and 71% graduate in 6 years or less.

Admissions Contact: Barbara Rupp, Director of Undergraduate Admissions. E-Mail: *MU4U@missouri.edu* Web: *www.missouri.edu*

UNIVERSITY OF MISSOURI-KANSAS CITY — A-2

Kansas City, MO 64110 — **(816) 235-1111; 1-800-775-8652; (816) 235-5544**

Full-time: 2950 men, 3863 women	**Faculty:** n/av; 1, -$
Part-time: 1386 men, 2048 women	**Ph.D.s:** 85%
Graduate: 2519 men, 2980 women	**Student/Faculty:** 13 to 1
Year: semesters, summer session	**Tuition:** $8103 ($20,850)
Application Deadline: open	**Room & Board:** $11,500

Freshman Class: 4462 applied, 29193009 accepted, 1078 enrolled
SAT M/W: 570/540

COMPETITIVE

The University of Missouri/Kansas City, which opened in 1933, is a public institution offering undergraduate and graduate programs in the arts and sciences, engineering, business, education, health fields, preprofessional, and professional studies. There are 10 undergraduate schools and 12 graduate schools. In addition to regional accreditation, UMKC has baccalaureate program accreditation with AACSB, ABET, ACPE, ADA, NASM, NCATE, and NLN. The 4 libraries contain 1.1 million volumes, 1.2 million microform items, 353,243 audio/video tapes/CDs/DVDs, and subscribe to 7,222 periodicals including electronic. Computerized library services include interlibrary loans, database searching, and Internet access. Special learning facilities include a planetarium and radio station. The 149-acre campus is in an urban area in Kansas City. Including any residence halls, there are 68 buildings.

Student Life: 73% of undergraduates are from Missouri. Others are from 42 states, 42 foreign countries, and Canada. 60% are White; 14% African American. The average age of freshmen is 18; all undergraduates, 23. 27% do not continue beyond their first year; 73% remain to graduate.

Housing: 1399 students can be accommodated in college housing, which includes coed dorms, on-campus apartments, and married student housing. In addition, there are fraternity houses and sorority houses. On-campus housing is available on a first-come and first-served basis. 95% of students commute. Alcohol is not permitted. All students may keep cars.

Activities: 4% of men belong to 6 national fraternities; 6% of women belong to 2 local and 7 national sororities. There are 255 groups on campus, including art, band, cheerleading, chess, choir, chorale, chorus, computers, dance, debate, drama, ethnic, gay, honors, international, jazz band, literary magazine, newspaper, opera, orchestra, photography, political, professional, radio and TV, religious, social, social service, student government, and yearbook. Popular campus events include International Food and Culture Night, Welcome Back Week and Spring Fling, Homecoming and CourtWarming.

Sports: There are 6 intercollegiate sports for men and 8 for women, and 13 intramural sports for men and 13 for women. Facilities include a recreation center with 5 gyms, an indoor/outdoor pool, indoor and outdoor tracks, a fitness center, and handball, racquetball, and squash courts. There are also recreation facilities at the University Center.

Disabled Students: 95% of the campus is accessible. Facilities include wheelchair ramps, elevators, special parking, specially equipped restrooms, special class scheduling, lowered drinking fountains, lowered telephones, and special housing.

Services: Counseling and information services are available, as is tutoring in some subjects, accounting, biology, chemistry, foreign languages, writing, and math and statistics. There is a reader service for the blind.

Campus Safety and Security: Measures include 24-hour foot and vehicle patrol, emergency notification system, self-defense education, and security escort services. There are shuttle buses, emergency telephones, lighted pathways/sidewalks, and controlled access to dorms/residences.

Programs of Study: UMKC confers B.A., B.S., B.B.A., B.F.A., B.I.T., B.L.A., B.M., B.M.E., B.S.C.I.E., B.S.D.H., B.S.E.E., B.S.M.E., B.H.S. and B.S.N. degrees. Master's and doctoral degrees are also awarded. Bachelor's degrees are awarded in BIOLOGICAL SCIENCE (bioinformatics, biology/biological science, and biotechnology), BUSINESS (accounting and business administration and management), COMMUNICATIONS AND THE ARTS (art history and appreciation, communications, dance, dramatic arts, English, French, German, information technology, music, music performance, music theory and composition, performing arts, Spanish, and studio art), COMPUTER AND PHYSICAL SCIENCE (chemistry, computer science, geology, mathematics, and physics), EDUCATION (early childhood education, elementary education, middle school education, music education, and secondary education), ENGINEERING AND ENVIRONMENTAL DESIGN (civil engineering, electrical/electronics engineering, environmental science, and mechanical engineering), HEALTH PROFESSIONS (dental hygiene, health, health science, music therapy, and nursing), SOCIAL SCIENCE (criminal justice, economics, geography, history, Judaic studies, liberal arts/general studies, philosophy, political science/government, psychology, sociology, and urban studies). Health sciences and performing arts are the strongest academically. Liberal arts has the largest enrollment.

Required: Most candidates for the B.A. and B.S. degrees must complete a core curriculum that consists of courses in English, a foreign language, math, philosophy, fine arts, history, literature, natural sciences, and social sciences. They must complete 120 credit hours, including 30 in their major, with a 2.0 GPA.

Special: Special academic programs include co-op programs and internships in several majors, study abroad in 8 countries, an accelerated degree program, and dual majors. Special degrees include a B.A.-B.S. degree in the computer science program and a liberal arts degree offered by the adult program. The pass/fail option is available in some courses. Freshmen may enter 6-year medical and dental programs. There are 4 national honor societies, a freshman honors program, and 1 departmental honors program.

Faculty/Classroom: 54% of faculty are male; 46% are female. No introductory courses are taught by graduate students. The average class size in an introductory lecture is 30; in a laboratory is 16; and in a regular course is 24.

Admissions: The SAT scores for the 2013-2014 freshman class were: Math--24% below 500, 34% between 500 and 599, 25% between 600 and 699, and 17% between 700 and 800; Writing--19% below 500, 43% between 500 and 599, 19% between 600 and 699, and 17% between 700 and 800. The ACT scores were 22% below 21, 25% between 21 and 23, 24% between 24 and 26, 11% between 27 and 28, and 18% above 28. 44% of the current freshmen were in the top fifth of their class; 77% were in the top two fifths.

Requirements: The ACT is required. In addition, a combination of the student's test score and class rank determines admissibility; if the rank is 47 or below, the ACT score must be 23 or higher. Graduation from an accredited secondary school is a requirement for admission; the GED is also accepted. Required high school subjects include 4 units each of English and math, 3 each of social studies and science, 1 of arts, and 2 of a foreign language. A portfolio is required for art majors, an audition for music majors, and an interview for only those students applying for the pharmacy degree or the 6-year medical and dental programs. AP and CLEP credits are accepted.

Procedure: Freshmen are admitted to all sessions. Entrance exams should be taken by March of the senior year. There is a rolling admissions plan. Application deadlines are open. Application fee is $45. Applications are accepted online.

Transfer: 1371 transfer students enrolled in 2012-2013. Transfer Students need to have an overall 2.0 GPA on a 4.0 scale in all coursework, which includes repeated coursework, attempted at previous institutions. Transfer students must send in all official college transcripts from all colleges and universities where coursework was attempted. Transfer students with fewer than 24 hours of transferable college credit must also send in official high school transcripts. Some academic units and departments have specific admission requirements in addition to general university requirements. 30 of 120 credits required for the bachelor's degree must be completed at UMKC.

Visiting: There are regularly scheduled orientations for prospective students, consisting of a 1-day program for new freshmen or a half-day optional program for transfer students. There are guides for informal visits. To schedule a visit, contact the UMKC Welcome Center at (816) 235-8652.

Financial Aid: In 2013-2014, 69% of all full-time freshmen received some form of financial aid. 66% of all full-time freshmen received need-based aid. The average freshman award was $10,463. Need-based scholarships or need-based grants averaged $7,401; and need-based self-help aid (loans and jobs) averaged $6,935. The FAFSA is required. The priority date for freshman financial aid applications for fall entry is March 1.

International Students: There are 822 international students enrolled. The school actively recruits these students. They must take the TOEFL with a minimum score of 550 on the paper-based TOEFL (PBT) or 79 on the Internet-based version (iBT).

Computers: All students may access the system 24 hours, 7 days a week. There are no time limits and no fees.

Graduates: From July 1, 2012 to June 30, 2013, 1759 bachelor's degrees were awarded. The most popular majors were liberal arts (14%), business administration (11%), and nursing (10%). In an average class, 2% graduate in 3 years or less, 23% graduate in 4 years or less, 40% graduate in 5 years or less, and 47% graduate in 6 years or less.

Admissions Contact: Tamara Byland, Director of Admissions. E-Mail: *admit@umkc.edu* Web: *www.umkc.edu/admissions*

UNIVERSITY OF MISSOURI-ST. LOUIS D-2

St. Louis, MO 63121	(314) 516-UMSL; (314) 516-5310
Full-time: 2591 men, 3444 women	**Faculty:** 716; I, --$
Part-time: 3113 men, 4426 women	**Ph.D.s:** 75%
Graduate: 1104 men, 2136 women	**Student/Faculty:** 16 to 1
Year: semesters, summer session	**Tuition:** $9474 ($24,429)
Application Deadline: July 1	**Room & Board:** $8830
Freshman Class: 1753 applied, 1300 accepted, 482 enrolled	
SAT CR/M/W: 550/580/510 **ACT:** 24	**VERY COMPETITIVE**

The University of Missouri/St. Louis, founded in 1963, is a public institution offering undergraduate and graduate programs and conferring degrees in arts and sciences, business, nursing, education, engineering, and optometry. There are 7 undergraduate schools and 5 graduate schools. In addition to regional accreditation, UMSL has baccalaureate program accreditation with AACSB, ABET, CSWE, NASM, and NCATE. The 3 libraries contain 1.3 million volumes, 1.3 million microform items, and 4,030 audio/video tapes/CDs/DVDs, and subscribe to 2,606 periodicals including electronic. Computerized library services include interlibrary loans, database searching, Internet access, and Wi-Fi capability. Special learning facilities include an art gallery, planetarium, radio station, and TV station. The 350-acre campus is in an urban area 10 miles north of downtown St. Louis, Missouri. Including any residence halls, there are 44 buildings.

Student Life: 84% of undergraduates are from Missouri. Others are from 44 states, 68 foreign countries, and Canada. 80% are from public schools. 69% are White; 14% African American. The average age of freshmen is 18; all undergraduates, 26. 25% do not continue beyond their first year; 46% remain to graduate.

Housing: 1202 students can be accommodated in college housing, which includes coed dorms, on-campus apartments, off-campus apartments, and married student housing. In addition, there are honors houses, language houses, special-interest houses, fraternity houses, sorority houses, Theme, wellness, students over 21 apartments, and graduate/professional school housing. On-campus housing is available on a first-come and first-served basis. Priority is given to out-of-town students. 92% of students commute. All students may keep cars.

Activities: 3% of men belong to 3 national fraternities; 2% of women belong to 3 national sororities. There are 96 groups on campus, including art, band, cheerleading, choir, chorale, chorus, computers, dance, debate, drama, environmental, ethnic, forensics, gay, honors, international, jazz band, literary magazine, newspaper, opera, pep band, photography, political, professional, radio and TV, religious, social, social service, and student government. Popular campus events include Expo, Weeks of Welcome, Family Weekend, MLK Day of Service, and Mirthday.

Sports: There are 5 intercollegiate sports for men and 6 for women, and 12 intramural sports for men and 12 for women. Facilities include indoor jogging track, fitness center, handball/racquetball, basketball, volleyball, and badminton courts; wrestling, dance, and conditioning rooms, and a swimming pool; outdoors, there are intramural fields and facilities for baseball, soccer, handball, racquetball, and tennis.

Disabled Students: All of the campus is accessible. Facilities include wheelchair ramps, elevators, special parking, specially equipped restrooms, special class scheduling, lowered drinking fountains, lowered telephones, and special housing.

Services: Counseling and information services are available, as is tutoring in most subjects, math and writing labs. There is remedial math.

Campus Safety and Security: Measures include 24-hour foot and vehicle patrol, emergency notification system, self-defense education, and security escort services. There are shuttle buses, emergency telephones, lighted pathways/sidewalks, controlled access to dorms/residences, and criminal investigations.

Programs of Study: UMSL confers B.A., B.S., B.F.A., B.L.S., B.M., B.M.E., B.M, B.S.Acc., B.S.B.A., B.S.C.I.E., B.S.Ed., B.S.E.E., B.S.M.E., B.E.S., B.S.N., B.S.P.P.A., B.S.W., B.I.S. and B.S.I.S. degrees. Master's and doctoral degrees are also awarded. Bachelor's degrees are awarded in BIOLOGICAL SCIENCE (biochemistry, biology/biological science, and biotechnology), BUSINESS (accounting, business administration and management, finance, international business management, logistics, management information systems, marketing management, and operations management), COMMUNICATIONS AND THE ARTS (art history and appreciation, communications, dance, dramatic arts, English, French, German, Germanic languages and literature, Japanese, media arts, music, Spanish, and studio art), COMPUTER AND PHYSICAL SCIENCE (chemistry, computer science, information sciences and systems, mathematics, and physics), EDUCATION (early childhood education, education, elementary education, music education, physical education, secondary education, and special education), ENGINEERING AND ENVIRONMENTAL DESIGN (civil engineering, electrical/electronics engineering, and mechanical engineering), HEALTH PROFESSIONS (nursing), SOCIAL SCIENCE (anthropology, criminal justice, economics, history, interdisciplinary studies, liberal arts/general studies, philosophy, political science/government, psychology, public administration, social work, and sociology). CCJ, biology, chemistry, biochem/biotech, nursing, and international business are the strongest academically. Business, education, and nursing have the largest enrollments.

Required: To graduate, students must complete 120 credit hours, 42 of which must be in the area of general education. They must maintain a 2.0 GPA. The number of hours required for the major varies.

Special: Cross-registration with Washington University, St. Louis University, and St. Louis Community College and cooperative programs in all majors are offered. Study abroad in 32 countries, including England, France, and Germany is available. Most degree programs are available through the Evening Courses. Some work-study is available. There is an accelerated nursing degree program and student-designed majors for the B.L.S. There are 24 national honor societies and a freshman honors program.

Faculty/Classroom: 56% of faculty are male; 44% are female. 38% teach undergraduates, 13% do research, and 19% do both. Graduate students teach 23% of introductory courses. The average class size in an introductory lecture is 31; in a laboratory is 17; and in a regular course is 20.

Admissions: 74% of the 2013-2014 applicants were accepted. The SAT scores for the 2013-2014 freshman class were: Critical Reading--50% below 500, 28% between 500 and 599, 11% between 600 and 699, and 11% between 700 and 800; Math--22% below 500, 56% between 500 and 599, 22% between 600 and 699; Writing--44% below 500, 44% between 500 and 599, 6% between 600 and 699, and 6% between 700 and 800. The ACT scores were 15% below 21, 31% between 21 and 23, 25% between 24 and 26, 12% between 27 and 28, and 12% above 28. 54% of the current freshmen were in the top fifth of their class; 80% were in the top two fifths.

Requirements: The SAT or ACT is required. Applicants are required to have a total of 17 units, including 4 each in English and math, 3 each in social studies and science, 2 in the same foreign language, and 1 in fine arts. Class rank and test scores are used to determine eligibility for admission. A GPA of 2.0 is required. AP and CLEP credits are accepted.

Procedure: Freshmen are admitted fall, spring, and summer. Entrance exams should be taken in the junior year. There is a rolling admissions plan. Application deadlines are open. Application fee is $35. Notification is sent on a rolling basis. Applications are accepted online.

Transfer: 1626 transfer students enrolled in 2012-2013. Transfer students must have earned a minimum of 24 credit hours and maintained a minimum 2.0 GPA. 30 of 120 credits required for the bachelor's degree must be completed at UMSL.

Visiting: There are regularly scheduled orientations for prospective students, 20-minute info session, special appointments if needed and a campus walking tour. There are guides for informal visits, visitors may sit in on classes, and stay overnight. To schedule a visit, contact Yolanda Weathersby at (314) 516-6877.

Financial Aid: The average freshman award was $14,384. Need-based scholarships or need-based grants averaged $6,186 ($13,045 maximum); need-based self-help aid (loans and jobs) averaged $3,624 ($8,000 maximum); non-need-based athletic scholarships averaged $9,973 ($22,737 maximum); and other non-need-based awards and non-need-based scholarships averaged $9,644 ($33,444 maximum). Average annual earnings from campus work are $3727. The average financial indebtedness of the 2013 graduate was $23,617. The FAFSA is required. The priority date for freshman financial aid applications for fall entry is March 1.

International Students: There are 392 international students enrolled. The school actively recruits these students. They must take the TOEFL with a minimum score of 500 on the paper-based TOEFL (PBT) or 61 on the Internet-based version (iBT) and the college's own test.

Computers: All students may access the system. There are no time limits and no fees.

Graduates: From July 1, 2012 to June 30, 2013, 1974 bachelor's degrees were awarded. The most popular majors were business administration (22%), education (12%), and health professions (12%). 320 companies recruited on campus in 2012-2013. In an average class, 20% graduate in 3 years or less, 18% graduate in 4 years or less, 7% graduate in 5 years or less, and 46% graduate in 6 years or less. Of the 2012 graduating class, 14% were enrolled in graduate school within 6 months of graduation, and 74% were employed.

Admissions Contact: Jerry D. Hoffman, Associate Director of Admissions. E-Mail: *admissions@umsl.edu* Web: *www.umsl.edu*

WASHINGTON UNIVERSITY IN ST. LOUIS D-3

St. Louis, MO 63130 (314) 935-6000
(800) 638-0700; (314) 935-4290

Full-time: 3211 men, 3161 women	**Faculty:** 818; I, +$
Part-time: 296 men, 571 women	**Ph.D.s:** 98%
Graduate: 3275 men, 3394 women	**Student/Faculty:** 8 to 1
Year: semesters, summer session	**Tuition:** $41,992
Application Deadline: January 15	**Room & Board:** $13,119

Freshman Class: 28823 applied, 4763 accepted, 1488 enrolled
SAT or ACT: required

MOST COMPETITIVE

Washington University, founded in 1853, is a private institution offering undergraduate and graduate programs in arts and sciences, business, architecture, engineering, art, and professional programs in law, medicine (including physical therapy and occupational therapy), and social work. There are 5 undergraduate schools and 8 graduate schools. In addition to regional accreditation, Washington U. has baccalaureate program accreditation with AACSB, ABET, and NASAD. The 12 libraries contain 5.1 million volumes, 3.5 million microform items, and 72,256 audio/video tapes/CDs/DVDs, and subscribe to 94,826 periodicals including electronic. Computerized library services include interlibrary loans, database searching, Internet access, and Wi-Fi capability. Special learning facilities include an art gallery, planetarium, radio station, TV station, a dance studio, a professional theater, observatory, and studio theater. The 169-acre campus is in a suburban area 7 miles west of St. Louis, MO. Including any residence halls, there are 112 buildings.

Student Life: 93% of undergraduates are from out of state, mostly the Mid-West. Students are from 50 states, 47 foreign countries, and Canada. 57% are from public schools. 55% are White; 17% Asian American. The average age of freshmen is 18; all undergraduates, 21. 4% do not continue beyond their first year; 94% remain to graduate.

Housing: 5148 students can be accommodated in college housing, which includes single-sex and coed dorms, on-campus apartments, off-campus apartments, and married student housing. In addition, there are special-interest houses, fraternity houses, special-interest suites, upper-class housing, and small group housing for students who share common interests and goals. On-campus housing is guaranteed for the freshman year only and is available on a lottery system for upperclassmen. 67% of students live on campus; of those, 97% remain on campus on weekends. Upperclassmen may keep cars.

Activities: 25% of men belong to 11 national fraternities; 25% of women belong to 7 national sororities. There are 300 groups on campus, including art, band, cheerleading, chess, choir, chorale, chorus, computers, dance, debate, drama, environmental, ethnic, film, forensics, gay, honors, international, jazz band, literary magazine, musical theater, newspaper, opera, orchestra, pep band, photography, political, professional, radio and TV, religious, social, social service, student government, symphony, and yearbook. Popular campus events include Multicultural Celebrations, W.I.L.D. (concert festival), and student-run carnival.

Sports: There are 9 intercollegiate sports for men and 10 for women, and 33 intramural sports for men and 33 for women. Facilities include a swimming pool, tracks, a weight room, saunas, recreational playing fields, a football stadium, a fitness center, and racquetball, tennis, handball, wallyball, and squash courts.

Disabled Students: 95% of the campus is accessible. Facilities include wheelchair ramps, elevators, special parking, specially equipped restrooms, special class scheduling, lowered drinking fountains, lowered telephones.

Services: Counseling and information services are available, as is tutoring in every subject. There is a reader service for the blind.

Campus Safety and Security: Measures include 24-hour foot and vehicle patrol, emergency notification system, self-defense education, and security escort services. There are shuttle buses, emergency telephones, lighted pathways/sidewalks, and controlled access to dorms/residences.

Programs of Study: Washington U. confers B.A., B.S., B.F.A., B.M., B.S.B.A, B.S.B.M.E., B.S.C.E., B.S.Ch.E., B.S.C.S., B.S.Co.E., B.S.E.E., B.S.I.M., B.S.M.E., and B.S.S.S.E., degrees. Associate, master's, and doctoral degrees are also awarded. Bachelor's degrees are awarded in AGRICULTURE (environmental studies, natural resource management, and plant science), BIOLOGICAL SCIENCE (biochemistry, bioinformatics, biology/biological science, biomathematics, biophysics, ecology, and neurosciences), BUSINESS (accounting, banking and finance, business administration and management, business economics, entrepreneurial studies, human resources, international business management, international economics, marketing management, marketing/retailing/merchandising, and trade and industrial supervision and management), COMMUNICATIONS AND THE ARTS (advertising, American literature, Arabic, art history and appreciation, ceramic art and design, Chinese, classical languages, classics, communications, comparative literature, creative writing, dance, design, dramatic arts, drawing, East Asian languages and literature, English, English literature, film arts, fine arts, French, German, Germanic languages and literature, graphic design, Greek (classical), Hebrew, illustration, Italian, Japanese, journalism, languages, Latin, linguistics, literature, music, music theory and composition, painting, performing arts, photography, printmaking, romance languages and literature, sculpture, Spanish, studio art, and visual and performing arts), COMPUTER AND PHYSICAL SCIENCE (applied mathematics, chemistry, computer programming, computer science, earth science, geology, geophysics and seismology, information sciences and systems, mathematics, physical sciences, physics, and statistics), EDUCATION (art education, education, elementary education, foreign languages education, mathematics education, middle school education, science education, secondary education, social science education, and social studies education), ENGINEERING AND ENVIRONMENTAL DESIGN (architectural technology, architecture, bioengineering, biomedical engineering, chemical engineering, civil engineering, commercial art, computer engineering, electrical/electronics engineering, engineering, engineering mechanics, environmental science, mechanical engineering, systems engineering, and technology and public affairs), HEALTH PROFESSIONS (allied health, health care administration, health science, pharmacy, predentistry, premedicine, prepharmacy, and preveterinary science), SOCIAL SCIENCE (African studies, African American studies, American studies, anthropology, archeology, area studies, Asian/Oriental studies, biopsychology, East Asian studies, Eastern European studies, economics, ethnic studies, European studies, fashion design and technology, history, humanities, industrial and organizational psychology, interdisciplinary studies, international relations, international studies, Islamic studies, Judaic studies, Latin American studies, Middle Eastern studies, Near Eastern studies, philosophy, political science/government, psychology, religion, social science, South Asian studies, systems science, urban studies, Western European studies, and women's studies). Social sciences, engineering, business, biological/life sciences, and psychology are the strongest academically. Social sciences, engineering, and business are the largest.

Special: Opportunities are provided for cooperative programs with other schools, internships, work-study programs, study abroad, a Washington (D.C.) semester, accelerated degree programs, a B.A.-B.S. engineering degree, credit by examination, nondegree study, pass/fail options, and dual and student-designed majors. There are 18 national honor societies including Phi Beta Kappa.

Faculty/Classroom: 63% of faculty are male; 37% are female. No introductory courses are taught by graduate students. The average class size in an introductory lecture is 27; in a laboratory is 20; and in a regular course is 24.

Admissions: 16% of the 2013-2014 applicants were accepted. The SAT scores for the 2013-2014 freshman class were: Critical Reading--1% between 500 and 599, 24% between 600 and 699, and 75% between 700 and 800; Math--11% between 600 and 699, and 89% between 700 and 800; Writing--1% between 500 and 599, 24% between 600 and 699, and 75% between 700 and 800. The ACT scores were 1% between 27 and 28, and 99% above 28.

Requirements: The SAT or ACT is required. In addition, An essay is required from all applicants. Portfolios are required for students applying to the College of Art. Portfolios are encouraged for students applying to the College of Architecture. 4 years of english, math, science, and social studies are recommended. Up to 4 years of a foreign language and history are recommended. Also required are recommendations from a teacher and a counselor. SAT or ACT is required. AP credits are accepted.

Procedure: Freshmen are admitted fall. Entrance exams should be taken By December of the senior year. There are early decision and deferred admissions plans. Early decision applications should be filed by November 15; regular applications, by January 15 for fall entry, along with a $75 fee.

Notification of early decision is sent December 15; regular decision, April 1. 539 early decision candidates were accepted for the 2013-2014 class. Applications are accepted online.

Transfer: 38 transfer students enrolled in 2012-2013.

Visiting: There are regularly scheduled orientations for prospective students, student visits consist of group presentations followed by a campus tour, as well as class visits and meetings with current students and faculty. There are guides for informal visits, visitors may sit in on classes, and stay overnight. To schedule a visit, contact Office of Undergraduate Admissions at (800) 638-0700.

Financial Aid: In 2013-2014, 56% of all full-time freshmen and 53% of continuing full-time students received some form of financial aid. 41% of all full-time freshmen and 39% of continuing full-time students received need-based aid. Average annual earnings from campus work are $2139. Washington U. is a member of CSS. The CSS/Profile and FAFSA, and Finalized FAFSA using IRS Data Retrieval Tool are required. The deadline for filing freshman financial aid applications for fall entry is February 1.

International Students: There are 579 international students enrolled. The school actively recruits these students. They must take the TOEFL with a minimum score of 550 on the paper-based TOEFL (PBT) or 100 on the Internet-based version (iBT). They must also take the SAT or ACT.

Computers: All students may access the system. 24 hours per day, 7 days per week. There are no time limits and no fees.

Graduates: From July 1, 2012 to June 30, 2013, 1587 bachelor's degrees were awarded. The most popular majors were Biology and Psychology (18%), engineering (16%), and business (10%). 400 companies recruited on campus in 2012-2013. In an average class, 88% graduate in 4 years or less, 93% graduate in 5 years or less, and 94% graduate in 6 years or less. Of the 2012 graduating class, 33% were enrolled in graduate school within 6 months of graduation, and 62% were employed.

Admissions Contact: Office of Undergraduate Admissions E-Mail: *admissions@wustl.edu* Web: *www.wustl.edu*

WEBSTER UNIVERSITY D-2

St. Louis, MO 63119 **(314) 246-8793**

Full-time: 1136 men, 1322 women	**Faculty:** 200
Part-time: 215 men, 289 women	**Ph.D.s:** 82%
Graduate: 649 men, 1335 women	**Student/Faculty:** 12 to 1
Year: semesters, summer session	**Tuition:** $23,700
Application Deadline: August 1	**Room & Board:** $10,290

Freshman Class: 1769 applied, 1337 accepted, 496 enrolled
ACT: 24

COMPETITIVE+

Webster University is an independent institution with programs in fine and performing arts, liberal arts and sciences, media communications, education, nursing, and business. There are 5 undergraduate schools and 5 graduate schools. In addition to regional accreditation, Webster has baccalaureate program accreditation with ACBSP, NASM, NCATE, and NLN. The library contains 280,051 volumes, 137,600 microform items, and 27,007 audio/video tapes/CDs/DVDs, and subscribes to 1,622 periodicals including electronic. Computerized library services include interlibrary loans, database searching, Internet access, and Wi-Fi capability. Special learning facilities include an art gallery, radio station, TV station, a media center, a theater, and a community music school. The 47-acre campus is in a suburban area 6 miles southwest of St. Louis. Including any residence halls, there are 41 buildings.

Student Life: 77% of undergraduates are from Missouri. Others are from 41 states, 62 foreign countries, and Canada. 70% are White; 11% African American. The average age of freshmen is 19; all undergraduates, 23. 19% do not continue beyond their first year; 64% remain to graduate.

Housing: 730 students can be accommodated in college housing, which includes single-sex and coed dorms and on-campus apartments. In addition, there are special-interest houses. On-campus housing is available on a first-come, first-served basis, and is available on a lottery system for upperclassmen. Priority is given to out-of-town students. 75% of students commute. All students may keep cars.

Activities: There are no fraternities; 3% of women belong to 1 local sorority. There are 67 groups on campus, including and international, art, band, cheerleading, chess, choir, chorale, chorus, computers, dance, debate, departmental, drama, environmental, ethnic, film, forensics, gay, international, jazz band, literary magazine, musical theater, newspaper, opera, orchestra, photography, political, professional, radio and TV, religious, social, social service, student government, and symphony. Popular campus events include Homecoming, Webster Works Worldwide, and Spring Fest.

Sports: There are 7 intercollegiate sports for men and 7 for women, and 4 intramural sports for men and 4 for women. Facilities include a gym, an athletic training center, a sauna, a fitness center, a 25-yard 6-lane indoor swimming pool.

Disabled Students: 75% of the campus is accessible. Facilities include wheelchair ramps, elevators, special parking, specially equipped restrooms, special class scheduling, lowered drinking fountains, lowered telephones, special housing. telephones for the hearing impaired, automatic door openers, a reading machine, computer for paraplegic students, reading and writing software, deaf interpreters, note takers, and textbooks on tape. All TV monitors in classrooms have closed caption capabilities.

Services: Counseling and information services are available, as is tutoring in most subjects. There is a reader service for the blind. Peer tutoring and study skills training are available.

Campus Safety and Security: Measures include 24-hour foot and vehicle patrol, emergency notification system, self-defense education, and security escort services. There are emergency telephones, lighted pathways/sidewalks, and controlled access to dorms/residences.

Programs of Study: Webster confers B.A., B.S., B.F.A., B.M., B.M.Ed. and B.S.N. degrees. Master's and doctoral degrees are also awarded. Bachelor's degrees are awarded in AGRICULTURE (environmental studies), BIOLOGICAL SCIENCE (biology/biological science), BUSINESS (accounting, business administration and management, finance, management science, and marketing management), COMMUNICATIONS AND THE ARTS (acting, advertising, animation, art history, art, art history and appreciation, audio technology, ballet, ceramic art and design, choral music, communications, costume design, creative writing, dance, digital communications, dramatic arts, English, film arts, French, German, graphic design, information technology, instrumental performance, instrumental music education, jazz, journalism, media arts, music, music performance, music theory and composition, musical theater, painting, photography, piano performance, playwriting/screenwriting, printmaking, public relations, scenic and lighting design, sculpture, Spanish, studio art, theater design, video, vocal performance, voice, and vocal music education), COMPUTER AND PHYSICAL SCIENCE (computer management, computer science, information sciences and systems, and mathematics), EDUCATION (art education, early childhood education, education, elementary education, foreign languages education, journalism education, mathematics education, middle school education, music education, secondary education, social studies education, social studies secondary school education, and special education), HEALTH PROFESSIONS (nursing), SOCIAL SCIENCE (American studies, area studies, cultural anthropology, economics, European studies, history, interdisciplinary studies, international relations, legal studies, philosophy, political science/government, psychology, religion, religious studies, social science, sociology, and women's studies). Fine arts is the strongest academically. Business has the largest enrollment.

Required: To graduate, students must complete at least 128 semester hours, with a minimum GPA of 2.0. They must successfully complete an approved major, which may or may not require more than 128 credit hours, and successfully complete the global citizenship program or general education program requirements. All new degree-seeking freshmen with fewer than 16 college credit hours are required to take a freshman seminar. At least 30 semester credits of a student's final 36 credits must be earned at Webster.

Special: Webster University offers co-op programs, work-study programs, internships, dual majors, student-designed majors, and a 3-2 engineering degree with the University of Missouri/Columbia and Washington University. Study abroad in 7 countries is available.

Faculty/Classroom: 55% of faculty are male; 45% are female. All teach undergraduates. No introductory courses are taught by graduate students. The average class size in an introductory lecture is 12; in a laboratory is 9; and in a regular course is 10.

Admissions: 76% of the 2013-2014 applicants were accepted. The ACT scores were 25% below 21, 24% between 21 and 23, 24% between 24 and 26, 12% between 27 and 28, and 15% above 28. 33% of the current freshmen were in the top fifth of their class; 59% were in the top two fifths. 7 freshmen graduated first in their class.

Requirements: The ACT is required. Applicants must be graduates of an accredited secondary school. The GED is accepted. Webster recommends that students complete 16 high school academic units, including 4 units of English, 3 each of social studies/history and math, and 2 each of foreign language, science, and electives. An essay is required of all students, and a portfolio or audition is required for art, dance, music, musical theater, and film. Webster requires applicants to be in the upper 50% of their class. A GPA of 2.5 is required. AP and CLEP credits are accepted. Important factors in the admissions decision are advanced placement or honors courses, leadership record, and recommendations by school officials.

Procedure: Freshmen are admitted fall, spring, and summer. Entrance exams should be taken in the spring of the junior year. There are deferred admissions and rolling admissions plans. Applications should be filed by August 1 for fall entry; December 1 for spring entry, along with a $35 fee. Notification is sent on a rolling basis. Applications are accepted online.

Transfer: 547 transfer students enrolled in 2012-2013. Applicants for transfer must have a minimum GPA of 2.0 for college credit completed. If they have fewer than 30 transferable hours, they must submit high school transcripts. 30 of 128 credits required for the bachelor's degree must be completed at Webster.

Visiting: There are regularly scheduled orientations for prospective students, consisting of an open house, which includes classes, meetings with faculty, a financial aid workshop, a tour of the university, and a student activities overview. There are guides for informal visits, visitors may sit in on classes, and stay overnight. To schedule a visit, contact the Visit Coordinator at (800) 753-6765.

Financial Aid: In 2013-2014, 82% of all full-time freshmen and 74% of continuing full-time students received some form of financial aid. 82% of all full-time freshmen and 73% of continuing full-time students received need-based aid. The average freshman award was $22,183. Need-based scholarships or need-based grants averaged $17,501; need-based self-help aid (loans and jobs) averaged $8,178; other non-need-based awards and non-need-based scholarships averaged $11,429; and $3,297 from other forms of aid. 20% of undergraduate students work part-time. Average annual earnings from campus work are $3840. The average financial indebtedness of the 2013 graduate was $30,330. Webster is a member of CSS. The FAFSA and the college's own financial statement are required. The priority date for freshman financial aid applications for fall entry is March 1. The deadline for filing freshman financial aid applications for fall entry is August 1.

International Students: There are 100 international students enrolled. The school actively recruits these students. They must take the TOEFL with a minimum score of 550 on the paper-based TOEFL (PBT) or 80 on the Internet-based version (iBT) and the Comprehensive English Language Test, written and oral/listening tests, and IELTS, SAT or ACT if they are graduates of U.S. high schools or international secondary schools that use English as the language of instruction.

Computers: All students may access the system 24/7. There are no time limits and no fees.

Graduates: From July 1, 2012 to June 30, 2013, 832 bachelor's degrees were awarded. The most popular majors were management (13%), art (6%), and media communications (5%). 52 companies recruited on campus in 2012-2013. In an average class, 1% graduate in 3 years or less, 42% graduate in 4 years or less, 55% graduate in 5 years or less, and 59% graduate in 6 years or less.

Admissions Contact: Robert Pampel, Director Undergraduate Admissions. E-Mail: *robertpampel63@webster.edu* Web: *www.webster.edu/admissions*

WESTMINSTER COLLEGE C-2

Fulton, MO 65251 (573) 592-5251
(800) 475-3361; (573) 592-5255

Full-time: 576 men, 460 women	**Faculty:** 63; IIB, --$
Part-time: 4 men, 4 women	**Ph.D.s:** 87%
Graduate: n/av	**Student/Faculty:** 14 to 1
Year: semesters, summer session	**Tuition:** $21,680
Application Deadline: open	**Room & Board:** $8810
Freshman Class: 1308 applied, 902 accepted, 257 enrolled	
SAT: recommended **ACT:** 24	**VERY COMPETITIVE**

Westminster College, founded in 1851, is a private liberal arts and sciences college affiliated with the Presbyterian Church. Westminster College offers learning opportunities through Mesa, AZ and Fulton, MO campuses. There is one undergraduate school. The 2 libraries contain 100,265 volumes, 6,912 microform items, and 9,691 audio/video tapes/CDs/DVDs, and subscribe to 30,201 periodicals including electronic. Computerized library services include interlibrary loans, database searching, Internet access, and Wi-Fi capability. The 87-acre campus is in a small town 20 miles east of Columbia and 25 miles north of Jefferson City. Including any residence halls, there are 26 buildings.

Student Life: 62% of undergraduates are from Missouri. Others are from 28 states, and 74 foreign countries. 75% are from public schools. 67% are White; 17% Foreign. 56% are Protestant; 20% Catholic; 15% claim no religious affiliation. The average age of freshmen is 18; all undergraduates, 20. 22% do not continue beyond their first year; 68% remain to graduate.

Housing: 863 students can be accommodated in college housing, which includes single-sex and coed dorms and off-campus apartments. In addition, there are special-interest houses and fraternity houses. On-campus housing is guaranteed for all 4 years. 85% of students live on campus; of those, 95% remain on campus on weekends. All students may keep cars.

Activities: 45% of men belong to 6 national fraternities; 34% of women belong to 4 national sororities. There are 65 groups on campus, including and Multicultural Club, International Club, art, Blue Blazers investment club, cheerleading, choir, chorale, chorus, computers, dance, drama, environmental, ethnic, gay, honors, international, jazz band, literary magazine, musical theater, newspaper, pep band, photography, political, professional, religious, social, social service, student government, and yearbook. Popular campus events include Alumni Weekend, Westminster Symposium, Undergraduate Scholars Forum, What if...? Conference and International Week.

Sports: There are 8 intercollegiate sports for men and 8 for women, and 16 intramural sports for men and 10 for women. Facilities include an 800-seat gym, an aerobic training center, weight room, and training room, football, baseball, softball, and soccer fields, a field sports area, tennis, racquetball, and sand volleyball courts, a swimming pool, an indoor rifle range, and a 1500-seat auditorium/arena.

Disabled Students: 80% of the campus is accessible. Facilities include wheelchair ramps, elevators, special parking, specially equipped restrooms, special class scheduling, lowered drinking fountains, and lowered telephones.

Services: Counseling and information services are available, as is tutoring in most subjects. There is remedial math, reading, and writing.

Campus Safety and Security: Measures include 24-hour foot and vehicle patrol, emergency notification system, self-defense education, and security escort services. There are emergency telephones and lighted pathways/sidewalks.

Programs of Study: Westminster confers B.A. degrees. Bachelor's degrees are awarded in BIOLOGICAL SCIENCE (biochemistry and biology/biological science), BUSINESS (accounting, business administration and management, business communications, international business management, and management information systems), COMMUNICATIONS AND THE ARTS (English, French, and Spanish), COMPUTER AND PHYSICAL SCIENCE (chemistry, computer science, mathematics, and physics), EDUCATION (elementary education, middle school education, physical education, and secondary education), ENGINEERING AND ENVIRONMENTAL DESIGN (environmental science), HEALTH PROFESSIONS (nursing), SOCIAL SCIENCE (anthropology, economics, history, international studies, philosophy, political science/government, psychology, religion, and sociology). English, biology, psychology, leadership studies, transnational/international studies are the strongest academically. Business administration, biology, psychology and education have the largest enrollments.

Required: To graduate, students must complete 122 credit hours, including a maximum of 40 hours in their major, with a minimum GPA of 2.0. All students are required to take Westminster seminar, academic writing, statistics or calculus, 4 hours of foreign language, and 1 hour of phys ed. Students must also take 6 to 10 hours (37 to 42 total) in scientific inquiry, historical awareness, fundamental questions, artistic expression, human behaviors and institutions, cultural diversity, and global interdependence. In addition, an integrative upper-level course, 2 writing intensive courses, and an upper-level course from a non-major academic division are required.

Special: Westminster offers co-op programs with colleges of the Mid-Missouri Associated Colleges and Universities, cross-registration with William Woods University, internships in all areas, study abroad in 15 countries, a Washington semester, a United Nations semester, and an urban studies program in Chicago. Student-designed majors are available as well as a dual degree nursing program with Golfarb School of Nursing at Barnes-Jewish College and a 3-2 engineering degree with Washington University in St. Louis. The pass/fail option and dual majors are available. There are 15 national honor societies, a freshman honors program, and 8 departmental honors programs.

Faculty/Classroom: 52% of faculty are male; 48% are female. All teach undergraduates, 75% do research, and 75% do both. No introductory courses are taught by graduate students. The average class size in an introductory lecture is 19; in a laboratory is 20; and in a regular course is 15.

Admissions: 69% of the 2013-2014 applicants were accepted. The ACT scores were 17% below 21, 28% between 21 and 23, 27% between 24 and 26, 13% between 27 and 28, and 14% above 28. 44% of the current freshmen were in the top fifth of their class; 66% were in the top two fifths. 11 freshmen graduated first in their class.

Requirements: The ACT is required. The SAT is recommended. Applicants must be graduates of an accredited secondary school. The GED is also accepted. Students must have completed 4 years each of social studies and English, 3 years each of math and science, and 2 years each of a foreign language and history. An essay is required and an interview is recommended. Westminster requires applicants to be in the upper 50% of their class. A GPA of 2.5 is required. AP and CLEP credits are accepted. Important factors in the admissions decision are advanced placement or honors courses, leadership record, and extracurricular activities record.

Procedure: Freshmen are admitted to all sessions. Entrance exams should be taken in the junior year of high school. There are early decision, deferred admissions, and rolling admissions plans. Application deadlines are open. Applications are accepted online.

Transfer: 65 transfer students enrolled in 2012-2013. Applicants must have taken either the ACT or the SAT and must complete at least 4 semesters at Westminster as full-time students. 60 of 122 credits required for the bachelor's degree must be completed at Westminster.

Visiting: There are regularly scheduled orientations for prospective students, including 1-day summer programs with a general orientation and class registration. There are guides for informal visits, visitors may sit in on classes, and stay overnight. To schedule a visit, contact Kelle Silvey, Director of Admissions at (573) 592-5195.

Financial Aid: In 2013 2014, 99% of all full-time freshmen and 99% of continuing full-time students received some form of financial aid. 53% of all full-time freshmen and 57% of continuing full-time students received need-based aid. The average freshman award was $20,155. Need-based scholarships or need-based grants averaged $15,940; and need-based self-help aid (loans and jobs) averaged $4,660. 66% of undergraduate students work part-time. Average annual earnings from campus work are $2000. The average financial indebtedness of the 2013 graduate was $26,723. The FAFSA is required. The priority date for freshman financial aid applications for fall entry is February 15.

International Students: There are 176 international students enrolled. The school actively recruits these students. They must take the TOEFL.

Computers: All students may access the system. There are no time limits and no fees.

Graduates: From July 1, 2012 to June 30, 2013, 231 bachelor's degrees were awarded. The most popular majors were business administration/management (26%), biology and psychology (17%), and education (15%). 71 companies recruited on campus in 2012-2013. In an average class, 48% graduate in 4 years or less, 64% graduate in 5 years or less, and 68% graduate in 6 years or less. Of the 2012 graduating class, 24% were enrolled in graduate school within 6 months of graduation, and 90% were employed.

Admissions Contact: Kille Silvey, Director of Admissions. E-Mail: *kelle.silvey@westminster-mo.edu* Web: *www.westminster-mo.edu*

WILLIAM JEWELL COLLEGE B-2

Liberty, MO 64068 **(816) 781-7700, ext. 5137 (800) 753-7009; (816) 415-5027**

Full-time: 410 men, 620 women	**Faculty:** 70; IIB, -$
Part-time: n/av	**Ph.D.s:** 86%
Graduate: n/av	**Student/Faculty:** n/av
Year: semesters, summer session	**Tuition:** $30,100
Application Deadline: see profile	**Room & Board:** $8060
Freshman Class: n/av	
SAT or ACT: required	

VERY COMPETITIVE+

William Jewell College, founded in 1849, is an academically selective liberal arts college. It offers undergraduate programs in the arts and sciences, business, education, and nursing fields. The figures in the above capsule and in this profile are approximate. In addition to regional accreditation, Jewell has baccalaureate program accreditation with NASM. The library contains 231,031 volumes, 1050 microform items, and 11,232 audio/video tapes/CDs/DVDs, and subscribes to 500 periodicals including electronic. Computerized library services include interlibrary loans, database searching, and Internet access. Special learning facilities include a learning resource center, art gallery, planetarium, and radio station. The 200-acre campus is in a suburban area 15 miles northeast of Kansas City. Including any residence halls, there are 28 buildings.

Student Life: 69% of undergraduates are from Missouri. Others are from 30 states and 11 foreign countries. 91% are from public schools. 82% are white. 51% are Protestant; 35% claim no religious affiliation; 11% Catholic. The average age of freshmen is 19; all undergraduates, 20. 22% do not continue beyond their first year; 63% remain to graduate.

Housing: 1013 students can be accommodated in college housing, which includes single-sex and coed dorms. In addition, there are honors houses, language houses, fraternity houses, and sorority houses. On-campus housing is guaranteed for all 4 years. 75% of students live on campus; of those, 60% remain on campus on weekends. Alcohol is not permitted. All students may keep cars.

Activities: 31% of men belong to 3 national fraternities; 34% of women belong to 4 national sororities. There are 60 groups on campus, including cheerleading, choir, chorale, chorus, computers, dance, debate, drama, drill team, ethnic, gay, honors, international, jazz band, ministries, musical theater, newspaper, orchestra, pep band, photography, political, professional, radio and TV, religious, social, social service, student government, and symphony. Popular campus events include Hanging of the Green/Lighting of the Quad and Family Weekend.

Sports: There are 9 intercollegiate sports for men and 9 for women, and 12 intramural sports for men and 12 for women. Facilities include a football and soccer stadium, a complex for baseball and softball, and a phys ed center with an indoor track, a dance room, and facilities for basketball, racquetball, swimming, indoor tennis, volleyball, and weight lifting. The total seating capacity of the stadium is 3200 and that of the indoor gym is 1000.

Disabled Students: 85% of the campus is accessible. Facilities include wheelchair ramps, elevators, special parking, specially equipped rest rooms, special class scheduling, lowered drinking fountains, lowered telephones, and special housing.

Services: Counseling and information services are available, as is tutoring in most subjects.

Campus Safety and Security: Measures include 24-hour foot and vehicle patrol, emergency notification system, and self-defense education. There are emergency telephones, lighted pathways/sidewalks, and controlled access to dorms/residences.

Programs of Study: Jewell confers B.A. and B.S. degrees. Bachelor's degrees are awarded in BIOLOGICAL SCIENCE (biochemistry and biology/biological science), BUSINESS (accounting, business administration and management, business economics, and international business management), COMMUNICATIONS AND THE ARTS (art, communications, dramatic arts, English, French, music, and Spanish), COMPUTER AND PHYSICAL SCIENCE (chemistry, mathematics, and physics), EDUCATION (elementary education, music education, and secondary education), HEALTH PROFESSIONS (medical laboratory technology and nursing), SOCIAL SCIENCE (history, international relations, Japanese studies, philosophy, political science/government, psychology, and religion). Business has the largest enrollment.

Required: To graduate, students must complete a minimum of 124 credits with a minimum 2.0 GPA, fulfilling the proper core requirements for their major and degree. All students must take The Responsible Self in their first year and must also take courses in oral and written communication, phys ed, math, and foreign language, interdisciplinary courses in 4 categories, and a core curriculum capstone course. Comprehensive exams in most majors are required.

Special: Internships for juniors or seniors, study abroad in Europe, Japan, Mexico, Australia, and Hong Kong, and a Washington semester are offered. B.A.-B.S. degrees, dual majors of any combination, internships, an accelerated degree in nursing, student-designed majors, and 3-2 engineering degrees with Washington University and the Universities of Missouri and Kansas are available. The Oxbridge Honors Program for major study is patterned after the teaching methods of Oxford and Cambridge and includes a year at either Oxford or Cambridge. Leadership and service learning programs are offered. There are 13 national honor societies, a freshman honors program, and 13 departmental honors programs.

Faculty/Classroom: 51% of faculty are male; 49% are female. 80% teach undergraduates. The average class size in an introductory lecture is 20; in a laboratory, 18; and in a regular course, 15.

Admissions: 55% of a recent year's applicants were accepted. 68% of a recent year's freshmen were in the top fifth of their class; 92% were in the top two fifths. 28 freshmen graduated first in their class.

Requirements: The SAT or ACT is required. Students must be graduates of an accredited secondary school; the GED is accepted. The college requires that applicants have taken 4 English courses and 4 academic electives, 3 courses each in math, social studies, and science (of these, 1 must be a lab), and 2 in foreign language. An interview is recommended. An audition is advised for music applicants. AP and CLEP credits are accepted. Important factors in the admissions decision are advanced placement or honors courses, extracurricular activities record, and leadership record.

Procedure: Freshmen are admitted fall, spring, and summer. Entrance exams should be taken in the junior year. There are deferred admissions and rolling admissions plans. Check with the school for current application deadlines. Application fee is $25 (waived for online applications). Notification is sent on a rolling basis.

Transfer: 44 transfer students enrolled in a recent year. Transfer students must have maintained a 2.5 GPA and be in good academic standing with their former schools and submit all college transcripts. Education majors must take the ACT, achieving a minimum score of 20. An interview is recommended for all students. 30 of 124 credits required for the bachelor's degree must be completed at Jewell.

Visiting: There are regularly scheduled orientations for prospective students, and personalized visits can be arranged upon request. There are guides for informal visits, and visitors may sit in on classes. To schedule a visit, contact the Admission Office.

Financial Aid: In a recent year, 99% of all full-time freshmen and 96% of continuing full-time students received some form of financial aid. 72% of all full-time freshmen and 69% of continuing full-time students received need-based aid. The average freshman award was $25,316. Need-based self-help aid (loans and jobs) averaged $6783 ($16,500 maximum). The average financial indebtedness of a recent year's graduate was $24,102. Jewell is a member of CSS. The FAFSA is required. Check with the school for current application deadlines.

International Students: There were 22 international students enrolled in a recent year. The school actively recruits these students. They must take the TOEFL with a minimum score of 550 on the paper-based TOEFL (PBT) or 80 on the Internet-based version (iBT) or take the MELAB.

Computers: Wireless access is available. All students may access the system. There are no time limits and no fees. It is strongly recommended that all students have a personal computer.

Graduates: In a recent year, 267 bachelor's degrees were awarded. The most popular majors were business/marketing (22%), health professions and related sciences (17%), and psychology (11%). 36 companies recruited on campus in a recent year. In an average class, 54% graduate in 4 years or less, 62% graduate in 5 years or less, and 63% graduate in 6 years or less. Of a recent year's graduating class, 25% were enrolled in graduate school within 6 months of graduation, and 75% were employed.

Admissions Contact: Director of Admissions. E-Mail: *admission@william.jewell.edu* Web: *www.jewell.edu*

WILLIAM WOODS UNIVERSITY C-2

Fulton, MO 65251 (573) 592-4221
(800) 995-3159; (573) 592-1146

Full-time: 207 men, 657 women **Faculty:** 56
Part-time: 51 men, 154 women **Ph.D.s:** 60%
Graduate: 512 men, 802 women **Student/Faculty:** 14 to 1
Year: semesters, summer session **Tuition:** $17,310
Application Deadline: open **Room & Board:** $6950
Freshman Class: 877 applied, 672 accepted, 243 enrolled
SAT CR/M: 560/510 **ACT:** 23 **COMPETITIVE**

William Woods University, founded in 1870, is an independent professions-oriented, liberal arts institution affiliated with the Christian Church (Disciples of Christ). Unique programs of study include an equestrian studies program and a four-year American Sign Language Interpreting program. Figures in the above capsule and in this profile are approximate. There is one undergraduate school and one graduate school. In addition to regional accreditation, William Woods has baccalaureate program accreditation with CSWE. The library contains 134,338 volumes, 11,072 microform items, and 28,711 audio/video tapes/CDs/DVDs, and subscribes to 15,796 periodicals including electronic. Computerized library services include interlibrary loans, database searching, and Internet access. Special learning facilities include an art gallery, radio station, 12 "smart classrooms" equipped with Smartboards and networked computers, labs for photography, foreign languages, art, and American Sign Language interpreting, equestrian studies stables, a model courtroom, and an observatory. The 170-acre campus is in a small town 100 miles west of St. Louis. Including any residence halls, there are 35 buildings.

Student Life: 70% of undergraduates are from Missouri. Others are from 44 states, 5 foreign countries, and Canada. 83% are White. 42% are Baptist, Christian, Methodist, Lutheran, Presbyterian, Pentecost; 30% claim no religious affiliation; 21% Catholic. The average age of freshmen is 19; all undergraduates, 21. 22% do not continue beyond their first year; 55% remain to graduate.

Housing: 760 students can be accommodated in college housing, which includes single-sex and coed dorms and on-campus apartments. In addition, there are special-interest houses, fraternity houses, sorority houses, and nonsmoking and independent housing. On-campus housing is guaranteed for all 4 years. 80% of students live on campus; of those, 60% remain on campus on weekends. All students may keep cars.

Activities: 22% of men belong to 2 national fraternities; 30% of women belong to 4 national sororities. There are 40 groups on campus, including art, cheerleading, choir, drama, honors, international, musical theater, newspaper, professional, radio and TV, religious, social, social service, and student government. Popular campus events include Salute to the Arts, Campus Involvement and Activities Fair, and Autumn at the Woods.

Sports: There are 5 intercollegiate sports for men and 6 for women, and 7 intramural sports for men and 7 for women. Facilities include a gym, a fitness center, a sand volleyball court, tennis courts, soccer, baseball, and softball fields, a weight room, a lake with a sand beach, table tennis and pool tables, a cross-country trail equipped with FitTrail stations, and a sauna.

Disabled Students: 85% of the campus is accessible. Facilities include wheelchair ramps, elevators, special parking, specially equipped restrooms, special class scheduling, lowered telephones. campus access to TTY phones.

Services: Counseling and information services are available, as is tutoring in most subjects. There is a reader service for the blind, and remedial math and writing. Interpreting is provided for the deaf upon request and receipt of supporting documentation.

Campus Safety and Security: Measures include 24-hour foot and vehicle patrol, self-defense education, and security escort services. There are emergency telephones and lighted pathways/sidewalks.

Programs of Study: William Woods confers B.A., B.S., B.F.A. and B.S.W. degrees. Associate and master's degrees are also awarded. Bachelor's degrees are awarded in AGRICULTURE (equine science), BIOLOGICAL SCIENCE (biology/biological science), BUSINESS (accounting and business administration and management), COMMUNICATIONS AND THE ARTS (art, communications, dramatic arts, English, graphic design, journalism, and studio art), COMPUTER AND PHYSICAL SCIENCE (computer science, information sciences and systems, mathematics, and science), EDUCATION (athletic training, early childhood education, elementary education, middle school education, physical education, and special education), SOCIAL SCIENCE (family/juvenile justice, history, interdisciplinary studies, international studies, interpreter for the deaf, paralegal studies, political science/government, psychology, and social work). Business, equestrian studies, and education are the strongest academically and have the largest enrollments.

Required: Students must complete a minimum of 122 credits to graduate, including at least 30 in the major and 52 in Common Studies, with 7 in the natural sciences, 6 each in English, the humanities, and behavioral and social sciences, 3 each in oral communication, math, and fine or performing arts, and 2 in freshman seminar. They must have maintained a minimum GPA of 2.0. An internship or other culimating project is required for many majors.

Special: William Woods University offers cross-registration with schools in the Mid-Missouri Association of Colleges and Universities, internships in various fields, including equestrian studies and computer information systems, study abroad, a Washington semester, and work-study. An accelerated degree program in most majors, B.A.-B.S. degrees, and student-designed and dual majors are possible. Credit for life, military, and work experience and pass/fail are available. The LEAD (Leading, Educating, Achieving, and Developing) program provides awards ($5000 to residential students) to any incoming student who makes a commitment to attend a minimum number of campus activities and participate within the surrounding community. There are 12 national honor societies and a freshman honors program.

Faculty/Classroom: 46% of faculty are male; 54% are female. All teach undergraduates. No introductory courses are taught by graduate students. The average class size in an introductory lecture is 25; in a laboratory is 15; and in a regular course is 20.

Admissions: 77% of the 2013-2014 applicants were accepted. The SAT scores for the 2013-2014 freshman class were: Critical Reading--30% below 500, 39% between 500 and 599, 29% between 600 and 699, and 2% between 700 and 800; Math--44% below 500, 44% between 500 and 599, and 12% between 600 and 699. The ACT scores were 37% below 21, 22% between 21 and 23, 20% between 24 and 26, 9% between 27 and 28, and 12% above 28. 29% of the current freshmen were in the top fifth of their class; 58% were in the top two fifths. 5 freshmen graduated first in their class.

Requirements: The SAT or ACT is required. In addition, , with a score of 870 on the SAT or 18 on the ACT. Students must graduate within the top 50% of an accredited high school class to be admitted. The GED is also accepted. They must have completed 16 course units, 11 of which must be distributed among English, a foreign language, math, natural sciences, and social sciences. 2 references are required, and an interview is recommended. William Woods requires applicants to be in the upper 50% of their class. A GPA of 2.5 is required. AP and CLEP credits are accepted. Important factors in the admissions decision are personality/intangible qualities, leadership record, and recommendations by school officials.

Procedure: Freshmen are admitted to all sessions. Entrance exams should be taken in the spring of the junior year or the fall of the senior year. There are deferred admissions and rolling admissions plans. Application deadlines are open. Application fee is $25. Applications are accepted online.

Transfer: 114 transfer students enrolled in 2012-2013. Transfer students must submit high school transcripts or GED and all college transcripts. They must also provide 2 references and be in good standing with their previous institution. 30 of 122 credits required for the bachelor's degree must be completed at William Woods.

Visiting: There are regularly scheduled orientations for prospective students, including the opportunity to talk with an academic adviser and an extensive student development-directed orientation to campus life. There are guides for informal visits, visitors may sit in on classes, and stay overnight. To schedule a visit, contact the Office of Enrollment Services.

Financial Aid: In 2013-2014, 100% of all full-time freshmen and 95% of continuing full-time students received some form of financial aid. 70% of all full-time freshmen and 70% of continuing full-time students received need-based aid. The average freshman award was $16,124. Need-based scholarships or need-based grants averaged $12,823; need-based self-help aid (loans and jobs) averaged $4,324; and non-need-based athletic scholarships averaged $6,415. 41% of undergraduate students work part-time. Average annual earnings from campus work are $1000. The average financial indebtedness of the 2013 graduate was $18,969. The FAFSA and the college's own financial statement are required. The deadline for filing freshman financial aid applications for fall entry is March 1.

International Students: There are 8 international students enrolled. The school actively recruits these students. They must take the TOEFL with a minimum score of 500 on the paper-based TOEFL (PBT) or 61 on the Internet-based version (iBT), or pass the STEP-EIKEN Grade Pre-1 Test. They must also take the SAT or ACT, scoring 19.

Computers: All students may access the system 7 days a week. There are no time limits and no fees.

Graduates: From July 1, 2012 to June 30, 2013, 215 bachelor's degrees were awarded. The most popular majors were business (29%), education (16%), and equestrian studies/equestrian (16%). 50 companies recruited on campus in 2012-2013. In an average class, 44% graduate in 4 years or less and 48% graduate in 6 years or less.

Admissions Contact: Sarah Munns, Dean of Enrollment Services. E-Mail: *admissions@williamwoods.edu* Web: *www.williamwoods.edu*

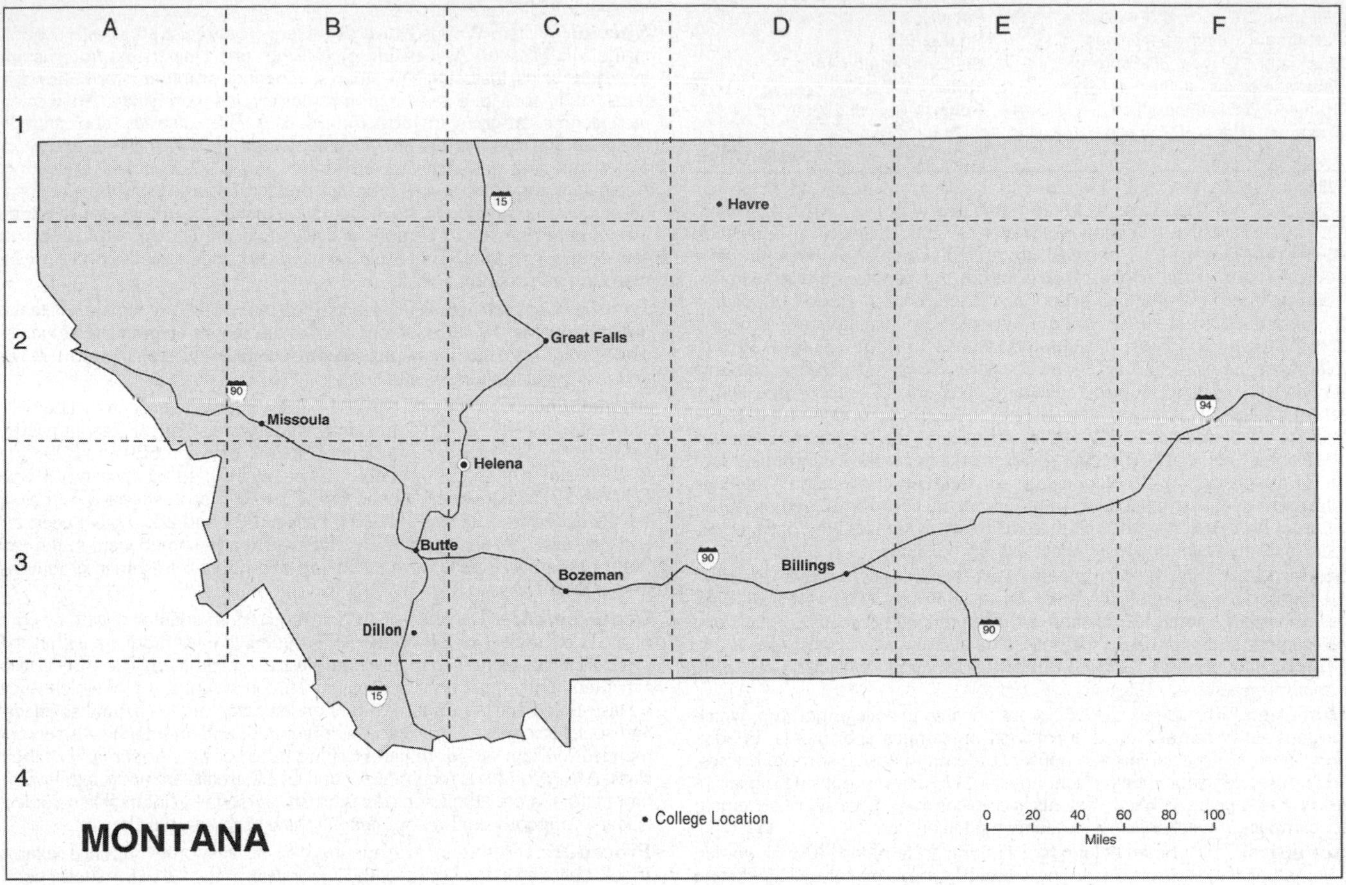

CARROLL COLLEGE C-3

Helena, MT 59625-0002 (406) 447-4384
(800) 992-3648; (406) 447-4533

Full-time: 575 men, 750 women
Part-time: 95 men, 130 women
Graduate: n/av
Year: semesters, summer session
Application Deadline: June 1
Freshman Class: n/av
SAT or ACT: required
Faculty: n/av
Ph.D.s: n/av
Student/Faculty: n/av
Tuition: $21,500
Room & Board: $7500

COMPETITIVE

Carroll College, founded in 1909, is a small liberal arts college affiliated with the Roman Catholic Church. It offers undergraduate programs in arts and sciences, business, engineering, nursing, education, religion, and selected preprofessional training. Some figures in the above capsule and in this profile are approximate. In addition to regional accreditation, Carroll has baccalaureate program accreditation with CAHEA, CSWE, NLN, and NRPA. The library contains 89,003 volumes, 64,500 microform items, 3890 audio/video tapes/CDs/DVDs, and subscribes to 504 periodicals including electronic. Computerized library services include interlibrary loans, database searching, and Internet access. Special learning facilities include a learning resource center, radio station, civil engineering lab, nursing lab (SimMan), performing arts theater, and astronomical observatory. The 64-acre campus is in a small town 110 miles east of Missoula and 100 miles west of Bozeman. Including any residence halls, there are 16 buildings.

Student Life: 64% of undergraduates are from Montana. Others are from 30 states, 11 foreign countries, and Canada. 81% are from public schools. 67% are white. 67% are Catholic; 31% Lutheran, Methodist, Baptist. The average age of freshmen is 18; all undergraduates, 21. 21% do not continue beyond their first year; 60% remain to graduate.

Housing: 830 students can be accommodated in college housing, which includes single-sex and coed dorms and on-campus apartments. In addition, there is a freshman dorm. On-campus housing is guaranteed for all 4 years. 54% of students live on campus; of those, 95% remain on campus on weekends. All students may keep cars.

Activities: There are no fraternities or sororities. There are 35 groups on campus, including art, cheerleading, choir, dance, drama, drill team, ethnic, film, forensics, honors, international, jazz band, literary magazine, musical theater, newspaper, pep band, political, professional, radio and TV, religious, social, social service, student government, and yearbook. Popular campus events include theme dances, casino night, and softball tournament.

Sports: There are 3 intercollegiate sports for men and 5 for women, and 10 intramural sports for men and 10 for women. Facilities include basketball, tennis, and racquetball courts, weight-lifting, aerobics, and dance rooms, a swimming pool, a football stadium, a soccer field, a fitness center, and a 4200-seat gym.

Disabled Students: 90% of the campus is accessible. Facilities include wheelchair ramps, elevators, special parking, specially equipped rest rooms, special class scheduling, and lowered drinking fountains.

Services: Counseling and information services are available, as is tutoring in most subjects, including writing, math, statistics, economics, chemistry, accounting, anatomy, and physiology. There is remedial math, reading, and writing.

Campus Safety and Security: Measures include security escort services. There are lighted pathways/sidewalks.

Programs of Study: Carroll confers B.A. degrees. Associate degrees are also awarded. Bachelor's degrees are awarded in BIOLOGICAL SCIENCE (biology/biological science), BUSINESS (accounting and business administration and management), COMMUNICATIONS AND THE ARTS (classical languages, communications, creative writing, dramatic arts, English, French, performing arts, public relations, and Spanish), COMPUTER AND PHYSICAL SCIENCE (chemistry, computer science, and mathematics), EDUCATION (elementary education, foreign languages education, physical education, secondary education, and teaching English as a second/foreign language (TESOL/TEFOL)), ENGINEERING AND ENVIRONMENTAL DESIGN (civil engineering and environmental science), HEALTH PROFESSIONS (clinical science, health care administration, nursing, predentistry, premedicine, preoptometry, prepharmacy, and preveterinary science), SOCIAL SCIENCE (history, international relations, philosophy, political science/government, prelaw, psychology, public administration, religion, social science, and sociology). Business, nursing, and biology have the largest enrollment.

Required: To graduate, students must complete 122 semester hours and maintain the specific GPA and credit concentration required by their major. The college's general liberal arts requirements include courses in writing, communications, history, math, natural and social sciences, philosophy, theology, and fine arts.

Special: Carroll College offers a 3-2 engineering program leading to acceptance to any of 6 cooperating universities. In addition, internships, study abroad in Paris, Japan, Spain, Germany, Korea, and many other countries through a consortium for international studies, and work-study programs in certain fields are available. Students may take a dual major in any two fields of study, select an interdisciplinary major such as health information management, earn credit for life, military, and work experience, or pursue nondegree study. The pass/fail option is available. There are 6 national honor societies, including Phi Beta Kappa, a freshman honors program, and 5 departmental honors programs.

Faculty/Classroom: 62% of faculty are male; 38% are female. All teach undergraduates. The average class size in an introductory lecture is 22; in a laboratory, 13; and in a regular course, 17.

Requirements: The SAT or ACT is required. Students must be graduates of an accredited secondary school or have a GED. An essay is required. A GPA of 2.5 is required. AP and CLEP credits are accepted. Important factors in the admissions decision are advanced placement or honors courses, recommendations by school officials, and leadership record.

Procedure: Freshmen are admitted fall and spring. Entrance exams should be taken in the fall of the senior year. There are deferred admissions and rolling admissions plans. Check with the school for current application deadlines. Application fee is $35. Notification is sent on a rolling basis. Applications are accepted online.

Transfer: Transfer students need a 2.5 GPA and must submit ACT or SAT scores if fewer than 30 college credits have been completed. Letters of recommendation are required. 30 of 122 credits required for the bachelor's degree must be completed at Carroll.

Visiting: There are regularly scheduled orientations for prospective students. There are guides for informal visits; visitors may sit in on classes and stay overnight. To schedule a visit, contact the Admissions Office.

Financial Aid: The FAFSA is required. Check with the school for current application deadlines.

International Students: The school actively recruits these students. They must take the TOEFL. English-speaking students must submit SAT or ACT scores.

Computers: Wireless access is available. All students may access the system. There are no time limits and no fees.

Admissions Contact: Director of Admissions. A campus DVD is available. E-Mail: *enroll@carroll.edu* Web: *www.carroll.edu*

MONTANA STATE UNIVERSITY C-3

Bozeman, MT 59717 (406) 994-2452
888-MSU-CATS; (406) 994-1923

Full-time: 5269 men, 4246 women	**Faculty:** 592
Part-time: 1049 men, 1015 women	**Ph.D.s:** 79%
Graduate: 911 men, 1069 women	**Student/Faculty:** 17 to 1
Year: semesters, summer session	**Tuition:** $6668 ($18,791)
Application Deadline: open	**Room & Board:** $8400
Freshman Class: 5786 accepted, 2623 enrolled	
SAT CR/M/W: 550/560/540 **ACT:** 24	**VERY COMPETITIVE**

Montana State University-Bozeman, founded in 1893, is a public, land-grant institution providing a challenging and richly diverse learning environment in which the entire university community is fully engaged in supporting student success. The school also provides an environment that promotes the exploration, discovery, and dissemination of new knowledge. In addition, Montana State University provide a collegial environment for faculty and students in which discovery and learning are closely integrated and highly valued. It serves the people and communities of Montana by sharing our expertise and collaborating with others to improve the lives and prosperity of Montanans. In accomplishing our mission, we remain committed to the wise stewardship of resources through meaningful assessment and public accountability. There are 9 undergraduate schools and 1 graduate school. In addition to regional accreditation, MSU has baccalaureate program accreditation with AACSB, ABET, ADA, CSAB, NAAB, NASAD, NASM, NCATE, and NLN. The 2 libraries contain 744,989 volumes, 2.2 million microform items, 13,446 audio/video tapes/CDs/DVDs, and subscribe to 10,131 periodicals including electronic. Computerized library services include interlibrary loans, database searching, and Internet access. Special learning facilities include a learning resource center, art gallery, natural history museum, planetarium, radio station, TV station, Center for Biofilm Engineering, Burns Telecommunication Center, and a geographic information and analysis center. The 1781-acre campus is in a small town 140 miles west of Billings and 90 miles north of Yellowstone National Park. Including any residence halls, there are 90 buildings.

Student Life: 69% of undergraduates are from Montana. Others are from 50 states, 65 foreign countries, and Canada. 84% are white. The average age of freshmen is 19; all undergraduates, 22. 29% do not continue beyond their first year; 47% remain to graduate.

Housing: 5400 students can be accommodated in college housing, which includes coed dorms and married student housing. In addition, there are honors houses, floors for older students, nonsmoking floors, and wellness floors. On-campus housing is guaranteed for the freshman year only, is available on a first-come, and first-served basis. 75% of students commute. All students may keep cars.

Activities: 3% of men belong to 7 national fraternities; 3% of women belong to 4 national sororities. There are 150 groups on campus, including art, band, cheerleading, chess, choir, chorale, chorus, computers, dance, drama, drill team, environmental, ethnic, film, gay, honors, international, jazz band, marching band, musical theater, newspaper, orchestra, pep band, photography, political, professional, radio and TV, religious, social, social service, student government, and symphony. Popular campus events include International Food Bazaar and Native American Pow-Wow.

Sports: There are 6 intercollegiate sports for men and 7 for women, and 38 intramural sports for men and 40 for women.

Disabled Students: 90% of the campus is accessible. Facilities include wheelchair ramps, elevators, special parking, specially equipped restrooms, special class scheduling, lowered drinking fountains, lowered telephones. Services through the resource center, and a taping service for the blind.

Services: Counseling and information services are available, as is tutoring in most subjects. There is a reader service for the blind, and remedial math, reading, and writing.

Campus Safety and Security: Measures include 24-hour foot and vehicle patrol, emergency notification system, self-defense education, and security escort services. There are emergency telephones, lighted pathways/sidewalks, and controlled access to dorms/residences.

Programs of Study: MSU confers B.A., B.S., B.F.A., and B.Mus.Ed. degrees. Master's and doctoral degrees are also awarded. Bachelor's degrees are awarded in AGRICULTURE (agricultural business management, animal science, horticulture, natural resource management, and plant science), BIOLOGICAL SCIENCE (biology/biological science, biotechnology, cell biology, microbiology, and neurosciences), BUSINESS (business administration and management), COMMUNICATIONS AND THE ARTS (art, English, fine arts, media arts, modern language, and music), COMPUTER AND PHYSICAL SCIENCE (chemistry, computer science, earth science, mathematics, and physics), EDUCATION (agricultural education, elementary education, music education, secondary education, and technical education), ENGINEERING AND ENVIRONMENTAL DESIGN (agricultural engineering technology, chemical engineering, civil engineering, computer engineering, construction engineering, electrical/electronics engineering, environmental design, environmental science, industrial engineering, land use management and reclamation, mechanical engineering, and mechanical engineering technology), HEALTH PROFESSIONS (health and nursing), SOCIAL SCIENCE (anthropology, economics, history, human development, liberal arts/general studies, philosophy, political science/government, psychology, and sociology). Engineering, physical science, and architecture are the strongest academically. Business, education, and nursing are the largest.

Required: To graduate, students must complete a core curriculum of 8 credits of natural sciences, 6 credits each of multicultural studies, humanities, social science, and communications, and 3 credits each of fine arts and math. The total number of credits required varies by program, with 120 being the minimum; at least one third must be in upper-division courses. A minimum 2.0 GPA is needed. Students must be officially registered in their chosen curriculum for at least 2 semesters before graduation.

Special: Montana State University offers internships in selected majors, study in 40 countries, cross-registration in selected programs, B.A.-B.S. degrees, dual and interdisciplinary majors, nondegree study, and pass/fail options. There are 23 national honor societies and a freshman honors program.

Faculty/Classroom: 62% of faculty are male; 38% are female. All teach and do research. Graduate students teach 21% of introductory courses. The average class size in an introductory lecture is 66; in a laboratory is 18; and in a regular course is 22.

Admissions: The SAT scores for a recent freshman class were: Critical Reading--27% below 500, 39% between 500 and 599, 27% between 600 and 700, and 6% above 700; Math--24% below 500, 39% between 500 and 599, 29% between 600 and 700, and 7% above 700; Writing--31% below 500, 43% between 500 and 599, 21% between 600 and 700, and 4% above 700. The ACT scores were 21% below 21, 24% between 21 and 23, 23% between 24 and 26, 13% between 27 and 28, and 19% above 28. There were 6 National Merit finalists. 114 freshmen graduated first in their class.

Requirements: The SAT or ACT is required. In addition, MSU requires applicants to have a minimum GPA of 2.5, rank in the upper 50% of their graduating class or have minimum composite scores of 24 on the ACT or a satisfactory score on the SAT. They must be graduates of an accredited secondary school. The GED is accepted. Students should have completed 4 years of English, 3 years each of social studies and math, 2 years of lab science, and 2 years of language, computer science, visual and performing arts, or vocational education. MSU requires applicants to be in the upper 50% of their class. A GPA of 2.5 is required. AP and CLEP credits are accepted.

Procedure: Freshmen are admitted fall, spring, and summer. Entrance exams should be taken in the fall of the senior year. There are deferred admissions and rolling admissions plans. Application deadlines are open. The fall application fee was $30. Notification is sent on a rolling basis. Applications are accepted online.

Transfer: 790 transfer students enrolled in a recent year. Applicants must have a minimum GPA of 2.0; grades of D or better transfer for credit. 30 of 120 credits required for the bachelor's degree must be completed at MSU.

Visiting: There are regularly scheduled orientations for prospective students. There are guides for informal visits, visitors may sit in on classes, and stay overnight. To schedule a visit, contact the Office of New Student Services.

Financial Aid: In a recent year, 54% of all full-time freshmen and 56% of continuing full-time students received some form of financial aid. 50% of undergraduate students work part-time. The average financial indebtedness of a recent graduate was $24,421. The FAFSA is required. Check with the school for current application deadlines.

International Students: The school actively recruits these students. They must take the TOEFL with a minimum score of 525 on the paper-based TOEFL (PBT), Students must also submit proof of American Cultural Exchange Language Institute Level 6 (available at MSU).

Computers: All students may access the system. There are no time limits. There is a fee. Students enrolled in environmental design must have a personal computer.

Graduates: The most popular majors were engineering (12%), business (12%), and health professions and related sciences (10%). 126 companies recruited on campus in a recent year. In an average class, 17% graduate in 4 years or less, 40% graduate in 5 years or less, and 47% graduate in 6 years or less. Of a recent graduating class, 15% were enrolled in graduate school within 6 months of graduation, and 95% were employed.

Admissions Contact: Ronda Russell, Director, Admissions. A campus DVD is available. E-Mail: *admissions@montana.edu* Web: *www.montana.edu*

MONTANA STATE UNIVERSITY-BILLINGS — D-3

Billings, MT 59101 — (406) 657-2158; (800) 565-MSUB; (406) 657-2302

Full-time: 1339 men, 1825 women	**Faculty:** 161; IIA, --$
Part-time: 416 men, 885 women	**Ph.D.s:** 86%
Graduate: 129 men, 375 women	**Student/Faculty:** 18 to 1
Year: semesters, summer session	**Tuition:** $5745 ($17,092)
Application Deadline: open	**Room & Board:** $6680
Freshman Class: n/av	

LESS COMPETITIVE

Montana State University-Billings, founded in 1927, is a comprehensive, regional, public university offering instructional and learning opportunities in the arts and sciences as well as professional programs in business, technology, human services, rehabilitation, health professions, and education. The figures in the above capsule and in this profile are approximate. There are 5 undergraduate schools and one graduate school. In addition to regional accreditation, MSU-Billings has baccalaureate program accreditation with AACSB, NASAD, NASM, and NCATE. The 2 libraries contain 228,225 volumes, 549,194 microform items, 2,275 audio/video tapes/CDs/DVDs, and subscribe to 790 periodicals including electronic. Computerized library services include interlibrary loans, database searching, Internet access, and Wi-Fi capability. Special learning facilities include an art gallery, radio station, a scientific field station, a small business institute, an urban institute, a special education learning center, a disabilities center, a center for business enterprise, and a center for applied economic research. The 92-acre campus is in an urban area in Billings. Including any residence halls, there are 22 buildings.

Student Life: 91% of undergraduates are from Montana. Others are from 39 states, 21 foreign countries, and Canada. 97% are from public schools. 83% are White. The average age of freshmen is 21; all undergraduates, 25. 42% do not continue beyond their first year; 33% remain to graduate.

Housing: 558 students can be accommodated in college housing, which includes single-sex and coed dorms and married student housing. On-campus housing is available on a first-come and first-served basis. 81% of students commute. All students may keep cars.

Activities: There are no fraternities or sororities. There are 53 groups on campus, including art, band, cheerleading, choir, chorale, chorus, computers, drama, ethnic, honors, international, jazz band, literary magazine, newspaper, orchestra, pep band, political, professional, radio and TV, religious, social, social service, and student government. Popular campus events include Powwow and Native American Day.

Sports: There are 6 intercollegiate sports for men and 7 for women, and 6 intramural sports for men and 5 for women. Facilities include a phys ed building with an Olympic-size pool, 2 gyms, a running track, weight-training equipment, 6 racquetball courts, and a soccer/softball field.

Disabled Students: All of the campus is accessible. Facilities include wheelchair ramps, elevators, special parking, specially equipped restrooms, special class scheduling, lowered drinking fountains, lowered telephones, a Disability Support Services Office.

Services: Counseling and information services are available, as is tutoring in most subjects. There is a reader service for the blind, and remedial math, reading, and writing. Academic support center.

Campus Safety and Security: Measures include 24-hour foot and vehicle patrol, emergency notification system, self-defense education, and security escort services. There are shuttle buses, emergency telephones, lighted pathways/sidewalks, and controlled access to dorms/residences.

Programs of Study: MSU-Billings confers B.A., B.S., B.A., B.A.S., B.S.Ed., B.S.H.S. and B.S.L.S. degrees. Associate and master's degrees are also awarded. Bachelor's degrees are awarded in BIOLOGICAL SCIENCE (biology/biological science), BUSINESS (business administration and management), COMMUNICATIONS AND THE ARTS (art, communications, dramatic arts, English, music, music performance, and public relations), COMPUTER AND PHYSICAL SCIENCE (chemistry, information sciences and systems, and mathematics), EDUCATION (art education, early childhood education, education, elementary education, health education, mathematics education, middle school education, music education, physical education, science education, secondary education, social science education, social studies education, and special education), ENGINEERING AND ENVIRONMENTAL DESIGN (environmental science), HEALTH PROFESSIONS (health care administration and rehabilitation therapy), SOCIAL SCIENCE (criminal justice, history, human services, liberal arts/general studies, political science/government, psychology, sociology, and Spanish studies). The sciences, business, and education are the strongest academically. Education and business have the largest enrollments.

Required: To graduate, students must have earned a minimum of 120 semester credits, including 30 in their major. They must maintain a minimum 2.0 GPA; education and human services majors must maintain a minimum 2.7 GPA. General education requirements must also be fulfilled.

Special: MSU-Billings offers co-op programs in business, human services, and liberal arts, internships, work-study programs, B.A.-B.S. degrees, dual majors, nondegree study, and pass/fail options. There are 10 national honor societies, a freshman honors program, and 1 departmental honors programs.

Faculty/Classroom: 58% of faculty are male; 42% are female. All teach undergraduates. No introductory courses are taught by graduate students. The average class size in an introductory lecture is 30 and in a laboratory is 19.

Admissions: 31% of the current freshmen were in the top fifth of their class; 62% were in the top two fifths.

Requirements: The SAT or ACT is required. Applicants must be graduates of an accredited secondary school; the GED is also accepted. The applicant must have taken 4 years of English, 3 each of social science and math, and 2 each of science, foreign languages, or humanities. Students need to meet 1 of 3 criteria: be in the upper 50% of their class; have a GPA of 2.0 or better; or have minimum composite scores of 22 on the ACT or satisfactory scores on the SAT. A GPA of 2.0 is required. AP and CLEP credits are accepted. Important factors in the admissions decision are advanced placement or honors courses, geographical diversity, and evidence of special talent.

Procedure: Freshmen are admitted to all sessions. Entrance exams should be taken in the senior year of high school. There are deferred admissions and rolling admissions plans. Application deadlines are open. The fall 2013 application fee was $30. Notification is sent on a rolling basis. Applications are accepted online.

Transfer: 426 transfer students enrolled in 2012-2013. Out-of-state transfer students must have earned a 2.0 GPA; in-state transfer students must be in good academic standing. 32 of 120 credits required for the bachelor's degree must be completed at MSU-Billings.

Visiting: There are regularly scheduled orientations for prospective students. There are guides for informal visits, visitors may sit in on classes, and stay overnight. To schedule a visit, contact Tammi Watson at (406) 657-2044.

Financial Aid: In 2013-2014, 80% of all full-time freshmen and 79% of continuing full-time students received some form of financial aid. 68% of all full-time freshmen and 67% of continuing full-time students received need-based aid. The average freshman award was $9,086. Need-based scholarships or need-based grants averaged $5,116; need-based self-help aid (loans and jobs) averaged $2,956; non-need-based athletic scholarships averaged $3,313; and other non-need-based awards and non-need-based scholarships averaged $2,878. 75% of undergraduate students work part-time. Average annual earnings from campus work are $1340. The average financial indebtedness of the 2013 graduate was $29,035. The FAFSA and the college's own financial statement are required. The priority date for freshman financial aid applications for fall entry is March 1. The deadline for filing freshman financial aid applications for fall entry is September 30.

International Students: There are 156 international students enrolled. The school actively recruits these students. They must take the TOEFL with a minimum score of 515 on the paper-based TOEFL (PBT) or 68 on the Internet-based version (iBT). They must also take the SAT or ACT.

Computers: All students may access the system 24 hours a day. There are no time limits. The fee is $2.65 per credit hour.

Graduates: From July 1, 2012 to June 30, 2013, 568 bachelor's degrees were awarded. The most popular majors were business (24%), education (23%), and liberal arts (11%). 100 companies recruited on campus in 2012-2013. In an average class, 14% graduate in 4 years or less, 12% graduate in 5 years or less, and 7% graduate in 6 years or less. Of the 2012 graduating class, 9% were enrolled in graduate school within 6 months of graduation, and 90% were employed.

Admissions Contact: Cheri Johanenes, Director of Admissions and Records and Registrar. E-Mail: *cjohannes@msubillings.edu* Web: *www.msubillings.edu*

MONTANA STATE UNIVERSITY-NORTHERN D-1

Havre, MT 59501 (406) 265-3704
(800) 662-6132; (406) 265-3792

Full-time: 610 men, 510 women	**Faculty:** n/av
Part-time: 110 men, 210 women	**Ph.D.s:** n/av
Graduate: 55 men, 110 women	**Student/Faculty:** n/av
Year: semesters, summer session	**Tuition:** $6000 ($15,000)
Application Deadline: open	**Room & Board:** $6500
Freshman Class: n/av	
SAT or ACT: required	**NONCOMPETITIVE**

Montana State University-Northern, founded in 1929, is part of the Montana University System and offers programs in the liberal arts, teacher education, business, and technology. There are 2 undergraduate schools and one graduate school. In addition to regional accreditation, MSU-Northern has baccalaureate program accreditation with ABET, NCATE, and NLN. The library contains 100,000 volumes, 600,000 microform items, and subscribes to 650 periodicals including electronic. Computerized library services include interlibrary loans, database searching, Internet access, and Wi-Fi capability. Special learning facilities include an art gallery and radio station. The 105-acre campus is in a small town 115 miles north of Great Falls. Including any residence halls, there are 21 buildings.

Student Life: The average age of freshmen is 21; all undergraduates, 28.

Housing: 450 students can be accommodated in college housing, which includes single-sex and coed dorms, on-campus apartments, and married student housing. On-campus housing is guaranteed for all 4 years. All students may keep cars.

Activities: There are no fraternities or sororities. There are 30 groups on campus, including dance, ethnic, musical theater, newspaper, pep band, religious, social service, student government, and yearbook. Popular campus events include Concerts, Dances, and Theatrical Productions.

Sports: There are 3 intercollegiate sports for men and 3 for women, and 11 intramural sports for men and 9 for women. Facilities include tennis courts, a swimming pool, weight and wrestling rooms, and 2 gyms, the larger seating 2500. Nearby Glacier National Park offers outdoor facilities.

Disabled Students: Facilities include wheelchair ramps, elevators, special parking, and specially equipped restrooms.

Services: Counseling and information services are available, as is tutoring in every subject. There is remedial math, reading, and writing.

Campus Safety and Security: There are lighted pathways/sidewalks.

Programs of Study: MSU-Northern confers B.A., B.S., B.S.Ed. and B.T. degrees. Associate and master's degrees are also awarded. Bachelor's degrees are awarded in AGRICULTURE (agricultural mechanics), BIOLOGICAL SCIENCE (biology/biological science and ecology), COMMUNICATIONS AND THE ARTS (communications, dramatic arts, English, fine arts, French, and music), COMPUTER AND PHYSICAL SCIENCE (chemistry), EDUCATION (business education, elementary education, industrial arts education, physical education, science education, secondary education, and social science education), ENGINEERING AND ENVIRONMENTAL DESIGN (automotive technology, civil engineering technology, construction technology, drafting and design technology, electrical/electronics engineering technology, engineering technology, environmental science, and manufacturing technology), HEALTH PROFESSIONS (nursing), SOCIAL SCIENCE (history, humanities, interdisciplinary studies, Native American studies, and social science). Business technology, nursing, and education have the largest enrollments.

Required: To graduate, students must complete at least 128 credits with a minimum GPA of 2.0 overall and 2.25 in their major and minor. Distribution requirements include 12 credits each of humanities, social science, math/science, and technology/applied arts. Students also must demonstrate proficiency in computing and in written and oral communication.

Special: B.A.-B.S. and other dual-degree programs, pass/fail options, cooperative programs in most disciplines, independent study, dual majors, and work-study programs are available.

Faculty/Classroom: All teach undergraduates. No introductory courses are taught by graduate students.

Requirements: The SAT or ACT is required, with a minimum composite scores of 20. Applicants must be graduates of an accredited high school or have a GED certificate. They should have completed 4 years of English, 3 each of math, social science, and history, including global studies and U.S. history, and 2 each of lab science and electives. A GPA of 2.5 is required. CLEP credits are accepted.

Procedure: Freshmen are admitted to all sessions. There are early admissions and rolling admissions plans. Application deadlines are open. Application fee is $30. Notification is sent on a rolling basis.

Transfer: Nonresidents must have a minimum GPA of 2.0. Any applicant with fewer than 12 transfer credits must submit a transcript of college work completed and meet standard freshman requirements. 36 of 128 credits required for the bachelor's degree must be completed at MSU-Northern.

Visiting: There are regularly scheduled orientations for prospective students. There are guides for informal visits, visitors may sit in on classes, and stay overnight. To schedule a visit, contact the Admissions Office.

Financial Aid: The the college's own financial statement is required. Check with the school for current application deadlines.

International Students: The school actively recruits these students. They must take the TOEFL.

Computers: All students may access the system, when the buildings are open. There are no time limits. There is a fee.

Admissions Contact: Stacey Gonsalez, Admissions Counselor. E-Mail: *msunadmit@msun.edu* Web: *www.msun.edu*

MONTANA TECH OF THE UNIVERSITY OF MONTANA B-3

Butte, MT 59701 (406) 496-4568
(800) 445-TECH; (406) 496-4710

Full-time: 1421 men, 769 women	**Faculty:** n/av; IIB, -$
Part-time: 243 men, 324 women	**Ph.D.s:** 60%
Graduate: 106 men, 60 women	**Student/Faculty:** n/av
Year: semesters, summer session	**Tuition:** $6722 ($19,500)
Application Deadline: open	**Room & Board:** $7928
Freshman Class: 877 applied, 773 accepted, 441 enrolled	
SAT CR/M/W: 545/610/530 **ACT:** 24	**VERY COMPETITIVE**

Montana Tech possesses an internationally esteemed, century-old tradition of excellence in higher education. The university offers degrees and certificates focused in areas such as nursing, health and safety, responsible development of natural resources, engineering, ecology and restoration, business, information technology, energy, and workforce development. Montana Tech has a long-standing reputation for producing outstanding graduates. There are 3 undergraduate schools and one graduate school. In addition to regional accreditation, Montana Tech has baccalaureate program accreditation with ABET and CSAB. The library contains 140,851 volumes, 60,390 microform items, 5,329 audio/video tapes/CDs/DVDs, and subscribes to 41,874 periodicals including electronic. Computerized library services include interlibrary loans, database searching, Internet access, and Wi-Fi capability. Special learning facilities include a radio station, a mineral museum, and METNET 2-way interactive communication studio. The 56-acre campus is in a small town in Butte, Montana. Including any residence halls, there are 19 buildings.

Student Life: 77% of undergraduates are from Montana. Others are from 42 states, 20 foreign countries, and Canada. 82% are White. 37% do not continue beyond their first year; 44% remain to graduate.

Housing: College-sponsored housing includes coed dorms, off-campus apartments, and married student housing. On-campus housing is guaranteed for the freshman year only, is available on a first-come, and first-served basis. Priority is given to out-of-town students. 89% of students commute. All students may keep cars.

Activities: There are no fraternities or sororities. There are 50 groups on campus, including band, cheerleading, chess, choir, chorale, computers, environmental, ethnic, gay, honors, international, newspaper, pep band, political, professional, radio and TV, religious, social, social service, and student government. Popular campus events include M-Day, and Homecoming.

Sports: There are 3 intercollegiate sports for men and 3 for women. Facilities include The HPER contains Kelvin Sampson Court, cardio room, weight room, racquetball courts, locker rooms, classrooms, and offices. The Alumni Coliseum provides an outstanding football experience for Digger home games.

Disabled Students: 75% of the campus is accessible. Facilities include wheelchair ramps, elevators, special parking, specially equipped restrooms, special class scheduling, lowered drinking fountains, lowered telephones, and special housing.

Services: Counseling and information services are available, as is tutoring in most subjects, accounting, algebra, basic math, biology, business, calculus, chemistry, differential equations, dynamics, E-circuits, engineering economics, fluids, nursing, physics, psychology, statics, strengths, survey of metallurgical & materials and engineering There is a reader service for the blind, and remedial math and writing. Career exploration, student/parent mentoring program, financial management workshops and study skills workshops

Campus Safety and Security: Measures include 24-hour foot and vehicle patrol, emergency notification system, self-defense education, and security escort services. There are emergency telephones and lighted pathways/sidewalks.

Programs of Study: Montana Tech confers B.S., and B.A.S degrees. Associate and master's degrees are also awarded. Bachelor's degrees are awarded in BIOLOGICAL SCIENCE (biology/biological science), BUSINESS (business systems analysis), COMMUNICATIONS AND THE ARTS (communications and communications technology), COMPUTER AND PHYSICAL SCIENCE (chemistry, computer programming, computer science, mathematics, science, and statistics), EDUCATION (health information management), ENGINEERING AND ENVIRONMENTAL DESIGN (computer engineering, engineering, environmental engineering, geological engineering, geophysical engineering, metallurgical engineering, mining and mineral engineering, occupational safety and health, and petroleum/natural gas engineering), HEALTH PROFESSIONS (nursing), SOCIAL SCIENCE (liberal arts/general studies).

Required: For graduation, students must complete at least 120 semester credits (more for engineering degrees) and maintain a minimum 2.0 GPA. Requirements include 6 hours each of communications, humanities/fine arts, mathematical sciences, and social sciences, and 6 to 7 hours of physical and life sciences with a lab required for 1 course. Engineering students must satisfy specific requirements within the individual curriculum.

Special: 3-2 liberal arts-engineering program with Carroll College, dual enrollment agreement with Flathead Valley Community College, collaborative programs with UM Helena (BAS Business, BS BIT, BAS General Studies), UM Western (Elementary Education Certification and Secondary Education Certification in Biological Sciences, General Sciences, and Mathematical Sciences), and UM-COT (AAS Surgical Technology)Additionally, Tech offers double majors, honors program, independent study, internships, and work study. There are 3 national honor societies, including Phi Beta Kappa, and a freshman honors program.

Faculty/Classroom: 61% of faculty are male; 39% are female. No introductory courses are taught by graduate students.

Admissions: 88% of the 2013-2014 applicants were accepted. The SAT scores for the 2013-2014 freshman class were: Critical Reading--25% below 500, 44% between 500 and 599, 26% between 600 and 699, and 4% between 700 and 800; Math--11% below 500, 31% between 500 and 599, 46% between 600 and 699, and 13% between 700 and 800; Writing--38% below 500, 36% between 500 and 599, 24% between 600 and 699, and 3% between 700 and 800. The ACT scores were 14% below 21, 31% between 21 and 23, 31% between 24 and 26, 12% between 27 and 28, and 12% above 28. 24 freshmen graduated first in their class.

Requirements: The SAT or ACT is required. The ACT Optional Writing test is also required. In addition, applicants must be graduates of an accredited secondary school. The GED is accepted. 14 academic credits are required, including English, 4 years; math and social studies, 3 years each; science, 2 years; plus 2 years chosen from foreign language, computer science, visual and performing arts, or vocational education. Applicants must have minimum composite scores of 22 on the ACT or satisfactory scores on the SAT or a 2.5 GPA, or be in the top half of their graduating class. Other factors regarding admissions are considered only if the preceding standards are not met. Montana Tech requires applicants to be in the upper 50% of their class. A GPA of 2.5 is required. AP and CLEP credits are accepted.

Procedure: Freshmen are admitted to all sessions. Entrance exams should be taken in the senior year. There are deferred admissions and rolling admissions plans. Application deadlines are open. Application fee is $30. Notification is sent on a rolling basis. Applications are accepted online.

Transfer: 226 transfer students enrolled in 2012-2013. Transfer applicants must have a minimum GPA of 2.0. Grades of C and above transfer for credit.

Visiting: There are regularly scheduled orientations for prospective students, There is an official fall orientation, though visits are welcome any time. There are guides for informal visits, visitors may sit in on classes, and stay overnight. To schedule a visit, contact the Enrollment Services at (406) 496-4256.

Financial Aid: In 2013-2014, 63% of all full-time freshmen and 61% of continuing full-time students received some form of financial aid. 60% of all full-time freshmen and 54% of continuing full-time students received need-based aid. The average freshman award was $9,725. Need-based scholarships or need-based grants averaged $5,496; need-based self-help aid (loans and jobs) averaged $3,239; non-need-based athletic scholarships averaged $7,534; and other non-need-based awards and non-need-based scholarships averaged $3,230. The FAFSA and the college's own financial statement are required. Check with the school for current application deadlines.

International Students: There are 183 international students enrolled. The school actively recruits these students. They must take the TOEFL with a minimum score of 525 on the paper-based TOEFL (PBT) or 71 on the Internet-based version (iBT). They must also take the SAT or ACT, scoring 22.

Computers: All students may access the system any time. There are no time limits. The fee is $12/credit.

Graduates: From July 1, 2012 to June 30, 2013, 278 bachelor's degrees were awarded. The most popular majors were petroleum engineering (21%), general engineering (17%), and businees (15%). 127 companies recruited on campus in 2012-2013. In an average class, 18% graduate in 4 years or less, 42% graduate in 5 years or less, and 48% graduate in 6 years or less.

Admissions Contact: Stephanie Crowe, Director of Recruiting. E-Mail: *enrollment@mtech.edu* Web: *www.mtech.edu*

MONTANA UNIVERSITY SYSTEM

The Montana University System, established in 1972, is a private system in Montana. It is governed by a Board of Regents, whose chief administrator is the commissioner of higher education. The goal of the system is teaching first, then research and public service. The main priorities are funding, system structure, and transfer articulation. The total student enrollment is usually about 28,000 with 1200 faculty members. Altogether there are 148 baccalaureate, 92 master's, and 26 doctoral programs offered in the Montana University System. Profiles of the 4-year campuses are included in this section.

ROCKY MOUNTAIN COLLEGE — D-3

Billings, MT 59102 — **(406) 657-1000 or 657-1026 (800) 877-6259; (406) 657-1189**

Full-time: 490 men, 457 women	**Faculty:** 65; IIB, --$
Part-time: 23 men, 18 women	**Ph.D.s:** 85%
Graduate: 37 men, 43 women	**Student/Faculty:** 12 to 1
Year: semesters, summer session	**Tuition:** $24,530
Application Deadline:	**Room & Board:** $7712
Freshman Class: 1396 applied, 933 accepted, 238 enrolled	
SAT CR/M/W: 510/500/480 **ACT:** 22	**COMPETITIVE**

Rocky Mountain College is a private college founded on the unique practice of joining the liberal arts tradition along with practical training for professional development. Established in 1878, RMC functions on a mission of educating students through liberal arts and professional programs that cultivate critical thinking, creative expression, ethical decision-making, informed citizenship, and professional excellence. The College supports its mission through core themes of academic excellence, transformational learning, and shared responsibility and stewardship. There is one undergraduate school and one graduate school. The library contains 107,128 volumes, 1,266 microform items, 1,627 audio/video tapes/CDs/DVDs, and subscribes to 30,609 periodicals including electronic. Computerized library services include interlibrary loans, database searching, Internet access, and Wi-Fi capability. Special learning facilities include an art gallery, a flight school, and equestrian facilities. The 60-acre campus is in a suburban area in a residential section of Billings, MT. Including any residence halls, there are 16 buildings.

Student Life: 52% of undergraduates are from Montana. Others are from 47 states, 19 foreign countries, and Canada. 80% are White. The average age of freshmen is 19; all undergraduates, 21. 31% do not continue beyond their first year; 69% remain to graduate.

Housing: 525 students can be accommodated in college housing, which includes coed dorms, on-campus apartments, and married student housing. On-campus housing is guaranteed for the freshman year only, is available on a first-come, and first-served basis. 52% of students commute. Alcohol is not permitted. All students may keep cars.

Activities: There are no fraternities or sororities. There are 13 groups on campus, including and equestrian., aviation, band, cheerleading, choir, chorale, chorus, computers, debate, drama, environmental, forensics, gay, honors, international, jazz band, literary magazine, marching band, musical theater, newspaper, pep band, photography, professional, religious, social, social service, student government, symphony, and yearbook. Popular campus events include Convocations, and Intercollegiate Athletics.

Sports: There are 7 intercollegiate sports for men and 7 for women, and 10 intramural sports for men and 10 for women. Facilities include The athletic and recreational facilities include a football stadium, a soccer field, a gymnasium, auxiliary exercise areas, a swimming pool, and a climbing wall.

Disabled Students: 75% of the campus is accessible. Facilities include wheelchair ramps, elevators, special parking, specially equipped restrooms, special class scheduling, lowered drinking fountains, and special housing.

Services: Counseling and information services are available, as is tutoring in most subjects. There is a reader service for the blind, and remedial math, reading, and writing. Note taking is available for qualified students.

Campus Safety and Security: Measures include emergency notification system, self-defense education, and security escort services. There are lighted pathways/sidewalks, controlled access to dorms/residences, security cameras, and eletronic access systems.

Programs of Study: Rocky confers B.A., and B.S. degrees. Associate and master's degrees are also awarded. Bachelor's degrees are awarded in AGRICULTURE (environmental studies and equine science), BIOLOGICAL SCIENCE (biochemistry and biology/biological science), BUSINESS (accounting, business administration and management, and business economics), COMMUNICATIONS AND THE ARTS (art, communications, dramatic arts, literature, and music performance), COMPUTER AND PHYSICAL SCIENCE (chemistry, computer science, geology, mathematics, and natural sciences), EDUCATION (art education, education, elementary education, English education, mathematics education, music education, physical education, psychology education, science education, social science education, and social studies education), ENGINEERING AND ENVIRONMENTAL DESIGN (aeronautical science, aviation administration/management, and environmental science), SOCIAL SCIENCE (anthropology, history, philosophy, political science/government, psychology, religion, and sociology). Business, biology, physical education and health, education and aviation have the largest enrollments.

Required: To graduate, students must complete a minimum of 124 credit hours, complete all major requirements with a minimum overall GPA of 2.0 and 2.25 in the major. If a minor area is chosen, a minimum of 18 hours is required. There are general education requirements in fine arts, humanities, communication, and the natural and social sciences, as well as writing, communication, and math.

Special: The college offers internships, study abroad in 49 countries, dual majors, individualized programs of study, and credit for life, military, and work experience. Juniors and seniors may elect to take 1 course on a pass/fail basis each semester. There are 1 national honor societies, a freshman honors program, and 1 departmental honors programs.

Faculty/Classroom: 54% of faculty are male; 46% are female. All teach undergraduates, and 5% do research. No introductory courses are taught by graduate students. The average class size in an introductory lecture is 14; in a laboratory is 12; and in a regular course is 14.

Admissions: 67% of the 2013-2014 applicants were accepted. The SAT scores for the 2013-2014 freshman class were: Critical Reading--43% below 500, 38% between 500 and 599, 17% between 600 and 699, and 2% between 700 and 800; Math--46% below 500, 36% between 500 and 599, 16% between 600 and 699, and 3% between 700 and 800; Writing--58% below 500, 34% between 500 and 599, and 8% between 600 and 699. The ACT scores were 32% below 21, 30% between 21 and 23, 24% between 24 and 26, 9% between 27 and 28, and 2% above 28. 25% of the current freshmen were in the top fifth of their class; 58% were in the top two fifths. 6 freshmen graduated first in their class.

Requirements: The SAT or ACT is required. Applicants must be graduates of an accredited secondary school. The GED is also accepted. Students must have completed 4 units of English, 4 units of Math, 3 units in the Natural Sciences, 3 units in the socal sciences, and 2 units of history. The school recommends a portfolio for admission to the art program, an audition for admission to the music or theater program, and an interview for academically challenged students. A GPA of 2.5 is required. AP and CLEP credits are accepted. Important factors in the admissions decision are extracurricular activities record, parents or siblings attended your school, and recommendations by school officials.

Procedure: Freshmen are admitted fall, spring, and summer. Entrance exams should be taken during the first half of the senior year. There are early admissions, deferred admissions, and rolling admissions plans. Application deadlines are open. Application fee is $35. Applications are accepted online.

Transfer: 69 transfer students enrolled in 2012-2013. Transfer students must have a minimum GPA of 2.0, and grades of 2.0 and higher transfer for credit. Transfers are admitted every term. 30 of 124 credits required for the bachelor's degree must be completed at Rocky.

Visiting: There are regularly scheduled orientations for prospective students, Students may visit in the fall, winter, and spring. There are guides for informal visits, visitors may sit in on classes, and stay overnight. To schedule a visit, contact Kristin Mullaney at (406) 657-1026.

Financial Aid: In 2013-2014, 99% of all full-time freshmen and 99% of continuing full-time students received some form of financial aid. 80% of all full-time freshmen and 76% of continuing full-time students received need-based aid. The average freshman award was $23,726. Need-based scholarships or need-based grants averaged $15,470; need-based self-help aid (loans and jobs) averaged $6,330; and non-need-based athletic scholarships averaged $8,308. 32% of undergraduate students work part-time. Average annual earnings from campus work are $871. The average financial indebtedness of the 2013 graduate was $30,948. The FAFSA and the college's own financial statement are required. The priority date for freshman financial aid applications for fall entry is March 1.

International Students: There are 46 international students enrolled. The school actively recruits these students. They must take the TOEFL with a minimum score of 525 on the paper-based TOEFL (PBT) or 72 on the Internet-based version (iBT) or take the MELAB, IELTS. They must also take the SAT or ACT.

Computers: All students may access the system. There are no time limits and no fees.

Graduates: From July 1, 2012 to June 30, 2013, 175 bachelor's degrees were awarded. The most popular majors were business (19%), physical education and health (14%), and education (10%). In an average class, 28% graduate in 4 years or less, 46% graduate in 5 years or less, and 50% graduate in 6 years or less. Of the 2012 graduating class, 16% were enrolled in graduate school within 6 months of graduation, and 80% were employed.

Admissions Contact: Kelly Edwards, Vice President for Enrollment Management. E-Mail: *admissions@rocky.edu* Web: *www.rocky.edu*

UNIVERSITY OF GREAT FALLS — C-2

Great Falls, MT 59405 (406) 791-5200
(800) 856-9544; (406) 791-5209

Full-time: 210 men, 310 women	**Faculty:** n/av
Part-time: 110 men, 210 women	**Ph.D.s:** n/av
Graduate: 40 men, 110 women	**Student/Faculty:** n/av
Year: semesters, summer session	**Tuition:** $17,970
Application Deadline:	**Room & Board:** $7000
Freshman Class: n/av	
SAT or ACT: recommended	

COMPETITIVE

The University of Great Falls, established in 1932, is a private, liberal arts institution affiliated with the Roman Catholic Church. The figures in the above capsule and in this profile are approximate. There are 2 undergraduate schools and 1 graduate school. The library contains 106,135 volumes, 124,608 microform items, and 3,894 audio/video tapes/CDs/DVDs, and subscribes to 587 periodicals including electronic. Computerized library services include interlibrary loans and database searching. Special learning facilities include an art gallery. The 40-acre campus is in an urban area. Including any residence halls, there are 13 buildings.

Student Life: 93% of undergraduates are from Montana. Others are from 20 states, and Canada. 99% are from public schools. 80% are White. 28% are Catholic; 22% claim no religious affiliation; 19% Protestant. The average age of freshmen is 26; all undergraduates, 33. 46% do not continue beyond their first year; 20% remain to graduate.

Housing: 189 students can be accommodated in college housing, which includes single-sex and coed dorms, off-campus apartments, and married student housing. On-campus housing is guaranteed for the freshman year only, is available on a first-come, and first-served basis. Priority is given to out-of-town students. 88% of students commute. Alcohol is not permitted. All students may keep cars.

Activities: There are no fraternities or sororities. There are 15 groups on campus, including art, cheerleading, chess, choir, chorus, computers, drama, ethnic, forensics, honors, literary magazine, musical theater, newspaper, orchestra, photography, professional, religious, social, social service, student government, Students in Free Enterprise (SIFE), and symphony. Popular campus events include Orientation Barbecue, Halloween Dance, and Intramural Festival.

Sports: There are 1 intercollegiate sports for men and 2 for women, and 7 intramural sports for men and 7 for women. Facilities include a gym, Olympic-size pool, a game room, and workout room.

Disabled Students: All of the campus is accessible. Facilities include wheelchair ramps, elevators, special parking, specially equipped restrooms, special class scheduling, and lowered drinking fountains.

Services: Counseling and information services are available, as is tutoring in some subjects, 100-level courses, 200-level courses, and selected 300-level courses. There is a reader service for the blind, and remedial math, reading, and writing. Tutoring in basic skills.

Campus Safety and Security: Measures include 24-hour foot and vehicle patrol, self-defense education, and security escort services. There are emergency telephones and lighted pathways/sidewalks.

Programs of Study: UGF confers B.A., and B.S. degrees. Associate and master's degrees are also awarded. Bachelor's degrees are awarded in BIOLOGICAL SCIENCE (biology/biological science, botany, microbiology, molecular biology, and physiology), BUSINESS (accounting, business administration and management, management science, and marketing/retailing/merchandising), COMMUNICATIONS AND THE ARTS (art, English, and fine arts), COMPUTER AND PHYSICAL SCIENCE (computer management, computer programming, computer science, mathematics, physical sciences, and science), EDUCATION (education of the exceptional child, elementary education, health education, mathematics education, middle school education, physical education, reading education, science education, secondary education, social studies education, and special education), ENGINEERING AND ENVIRONMENTAL DESIGN (computer graphics), HEALTH PROFESSIONS (health care administration, predentistry, and premedicine), SOCIAL SCIENCE (counseling/psychology, criminal justice, history, human services, law enforcement and corrections, paralegal studies, political science/government, prelaw, psychology, religion, social science, sociology, and theological studies). Biology, paralegal studies, and computer science are the strongest academically. Education, criminal justice, and business have the largest enrollments.

Required: Students must complete 128 credit hours, including 30 to 65 in the major, plus 15 to 21 minor credits, maintaining a minimum GPA of 2.0. The 52-credit-hour core curriculum includes math, computer science, art, behavioral science, history, literature, philosophy, science, writing, theology, and religion. Specific disciplines required include human nature, intellectual inquiry, and religious dimension.

Special: Internships are offered in sociology, criminal justice, paralegal studies, health care administration, and chemical-dependency counseling. Opportunities are provided for work-study programs, B.A.-B.S. degrees in most majors, dual majors, a general studies degree, credit by exam or for military service, and nondegree study. A 3-2 engineering degree for applied computer science and applied math majors is offered with Montana State University-Bozeman. Specialized instruction is available through the use of videotape and telephone discussions in 14 locations throughout Montana and Canada. There are 1 national honor societies.

Faculty/Classroom: 59% of faculty are male; 42% are female. All teach undergraduates. No introductory courses are taught by graduate students. The average class size in an introductory lecture is 15; in a laboratory is 10; and in a regular course is 14.

Requirements: The SAT or ACT is recommended. Graduation from an accredited secondary school is required; the GED is accepted. Applicants should have 4 years of English, 3 of math, and 2 each of social studies, science, and electives, including foreign language, art, music, and vocational education. An interview is recommended. A GPA of 2.0 is required. AP and CLEP credits are accepted.

Procedure: Freshmen are admitted fall, spring, and summer. Entrance exams should be taken prior to registration. There is a rolling admissions plan. Check with the school for current application deadlines. The fall 2013 application fee was $25.

Transfer: Transfer applicants must be in good academic standing from another accredited college or university, and must submit official transcripts from all colleges or universities attended. Those without a bachelor's degree must also submit an official high school transcript. 30 of 128 credits required for the bachelor's degree must be completed at UGF.

Visiting: There are regularly scheduled orientations for prospective students, including meeting with prospective advisers and staff, financial aid presentation, campus tour, and lunch. There are guides for informal visits, visitors may sit in on classes, and stay overnight. To schedule a visit, contact the Office of Admissions.

Financial Aid: UGF is a member of CSS. The FAFSA is required. Check with the school for current application deadlines.

International Students: The school actively recruits these students. They must take the TOEFL.

Computers: All students may access the system 7 days a week. There are no time limits and no fees.

Admissions Contact: Director of Admissions E-Mail: *enroll@ugf.edu* Web: *www.ugf.edu*

UNIVERSITY OF MONTANA — B-2

Missoula, MT 59812 — (406) 243-6266, (800) 462-8636; (406) 243-5711

Full-time: 4465 men, 4981 women	**Faculty:** n/av; I, --$
Part-time: 1211 men, 1597 women	**Ph.D.s:** 80%
Graduate: 947 men, 1324 women	**Student/Faculty:** 18 to 1
Year: semesters, summer session	**Tuition:** $6045 ($21,719)
Application Deadline: March 1	**Room & Board:** $7625
Freshman Class: n/av	
SAT or ACT: required	

COMPETITIVE

The University of Montana, founded in 1893, is a public institution with programs in arts and sciences, business administration, fine arts, education, forestry, journalism, and pharmacy and allied health sciences. It is part of the Montana University System. The figures in the above capsule and in this profile are approximate. There are 8 undergraduate schools and 2 graduate schools. In addition to regional accreditation, U of M has baccalaureate program accreditation with AACSB, ACCE, ACPE, APTA, CAHEA, CSAB, CSWE, NASAD, NASDTEC, NASM, NCATE, and SAF. The 4 libraries contain 1.4 million volumes, 343,000 microform items, 70,000 audio/video tapes/CDs/DVDs, and subscribe to 5,000 periodicals including electronic. Computerized library services include interlibrary loans, database searching, Internet access, and Wi-Fi capability. Special learning facilities include an art gallery, radio station, TV station, experimental forest, biological station, ranch, center for people and forests, geology field camp, international language lab, wilderness institute, observatory, and freshwater research center. The 220-acre campus is in an urban area 200 miles east of Spokane. Including any residence halls, there are 57 buildings.

Student Life: 74% of undergraduates are from Montana. Others are from 50 states, 58 foreign countries, and Canada. 80% are from public schools. 77% are White. The average age of freshmen is 19; all undergraduates, 25. 26% do not continue beyond their first year; 48% remain to graduate.

Housing: 3430 students can be accommodated in college housing, which includes single-sex and coed dorms, off-campus apartments, and married student housing. In addition, there are honors houses, special-interest houses, an international house, and nontraditional houses. On-campus housing is guaranteed for the freshman year only. 75% of students commute. All students may keep cars.

Activities: 10% of men belong to 9 national fraternities; 8% of women belong to 4 national sororities. There are 130 groups on campus, including academic, and forestry, art, band, cheerleading, chess, choir, chorale, chorus, computers, creative writing, dance, drill team, ethnic, gay, honors, international, jazz band, literary magazine, marching band, newspaper, opera, orchestra, pep band, political, professional, radio and TV, religious, social, social service, student government, and symphony. Popular campus events include Foresters Day, Founders Day, and International Week.

Sports: There are 6 intercollegiate sports for men and 9 for women, and 16 intramural sports for men and 12 for women. Facilities include a field house, a 10,000-seat arena, a 26,000-seat stadium, a fitness center, a golf course, soccer and rugby fields, an Olympic-size pool, a game room, a climbing wall, weight rooms, and mountain trails.

Disabled Students: 75% of the campus is accessible. Facilities include wheelchair ramps, elevators, special parking, specially equipped restrooms, special class scheduling, lowered drinking fountains, lowered telephones, special housing.

Services: Counseling and information services are available, as is tutoring in every subject. There is a reader service for the blind, and remedial math, reading, and writing. Mentors and note takers are available, as are books on tape for LD students.

Campus Safety and Security: Measures include 24-hour foot and vehicle patrol, self-defense education, and security escort services. There are emergency telephones and lighted pathways/sidewalks.

Programs of Study: U of M confers B.A., B.S., B.A.E., B.S.H.P.E. and B.S.M. degrees. Associate, master's, and doctoral degrees are also awarded. Bachelor's degrees are awarded in AGRICULTURE (environmental studies and forestry and related sciences), BIOLOGICAL SCIENCE (biology/biological science, botany, microbiology, wildlife biology, and zoology), BUSINESS (accounting, banking and finance, business administration and management, marketing/retailing/merchandising, personnel management, and small business management), COMMUNICATIONS AND THE ARTS (classics, communications, dramatic arts, English, fine arts, French, German, Japanese, journalism, music, music performance, radio/television technology, Russian, and Spanish), COMPUTER AND PHYSICAL SCIENCE (chemistry, computer science, geology, mathematics, and physics), EDUCATION (elementary education, music education, physical education, science education, and secondary education), HEALTH PROFESSIONS (medical technology and pharmacy), SOCIAL SCIENCE (anthropology, economics, geography, history, liberal arts/general studies, Native American studies, philosophy, political science/government, psychology, social work, sociology, and women's studies). Journalism, forestry, and liberal arts are the strongest academically. Business, forestry, and education have the largest enrollments.

Required: A total of 120 credits is required for graduation in most majors. The number of hours in the major varies; some majors require a thesis. There are competency requirements in writing, math, and foreign language or symbolic systems. Juniors must pass writing exams. Distribution requirements include courses in expressive arts, literary and artistic studies, historical and cultural studies, social sciences, ethical and human values, and natural sciences. A minimum GPA of 2.0 must be maintained.

Special: Students may cross-register with Montana Tech and Western Montana College. Co-op programs exist in business, communications, economics, management, and liberal studies; internships in most majors, work-study programs with nonprofit organizations, and study abroad in 12 countries are available. The school offers a B.A.-B.S. degree in chemistry, pass/fail options in classes other than major requirements, and dual majors in physics and computer science as well as history and political science. There are 7 national honor societies, including Phi Beta Kappa, a freshman honors program, and 5 departmental honors programs.

Faculty/Classroom: 57% of faculty are male; 43% are female. All teach and do research. Graduate students teach 2% of introductory courses. The average class size in an introductory lecture is 35; in a laboratory is 25; and in a regular course is 35.

Requirements: The SAT or ACT is required with a minimum composite ACT score of 22 or a satisfactory SAT verbal-math-writing composite score. Applicants must be graduates of an accredited secondary school. The GED is accepted. Students should have completed 4 years of English, 3 of math, 3 of social studies, 2 of lab science, and 2 from foreign language, computer science, visual arts, or vocational education. U of M requires applicants to be in the upper 50% of their class. A GPA of 2.5 is required. AP and CLEP credits are accepted. Important factors in the admissions decision are advanced placement or honors courses, evidence of special talent, and geographical diversity.

Procedure: Freshmen are admitted to all sessions. There are deferred admissions and rolling admissions plans. Applications should be filed by March 1 for fall entry; November 15 for spring entry, along with a $30 fee. Notification is sent on a rolling basis. Applications are accepted online.

Transfer: Applicants must have a minimum GPA of 2.0. Grades of 2.0 or better transfer for credit. 30 of 120 credits required for the bachelor's degree must be completed at U of M.
Visiting: There are regularly scheduled orientations for prospective students, including placement testing, advising, workshops, and social events. There are guides for informal visits and visitors may sit in on classes. To schedule a visit, contact the Office of Admissions.
Financial Aid: U of M is a member of CSS. The FAFSA is required. Check with the school for current application deadlines.
International Students: The school actively recruits these students. They must take the TOEFL.
Computers: All students may access the system any time. There are no time limits. The fee is $3 per credit.
Admissions Contact: Jed Liston, Assistant VP for Enrollment. E-Mail: *admiss@umontana.edu* Web: *www.umt.edu*

UNIVERSITY OF MONTANA-WESTERN B-3

Dillon, MT 59725 (406) 683-7331
877-683-7331; (406) 683-7493

Full-time: 514 men, 527 women	**Faculty:** 61; IIB, --$
Part-time: 45 men, 157 women	**Ph.D.s:** 75%
Year: semesters, summer session	**Student/Faculty:** 15 to 1
Application Deadline: July 1	**Tuition:** $4743 ($13,494)
	Room & Board: $6010

Freshman Class: 478 applied, 449 accepted, 237 enrolled
SAT CR/M: 460/470 **ACT:** 20 **LESS COMPETITIVE**

The University of Montana-Western, established in 1893, is a public institution, part of the University of Montana system. The college is learning in block scheduling/teaching/learning/approach called experience one. The figures in the above capsule and in this profile are approximate. There are 2 undergraduate schools. In addition to regional accreditation, Montana Western has baccalaureate program accreditation with NCATE. The library contains 60,416 volumes, 5,792 microform items, 6,920 audio/video tapes/CDs/DVDs, and subscribes to 22,427 periodicals including electronic. Computerized library services include interlibrary loans, database searching, Internet access, and Wi-Fi capability. Special learning facilities include an art gallery and radio station. The 34-acre campus is in a small town 60 miles south of Butte and 150 miles from Yellowstone National Park. Including any residence halls, there are 25 buildings.
Student Life: 79% of undergraduates are from Montana. Others are from 34 states, and 2 foreign countries. 87% are from public schools. 89% are White. The average age of freshmen is 19; all undergraduates, 24. 26% do not continue beyond their first year; 28% remain to graduate.
Housing: 424 students can be accommodated in college housing, which includes single-sex and coed dorms, on-campus apartments, and married student housing. On-campus housing is guaranteed for all 4 years. 78% of students commute. Alcohol is not permitted. All students may keep cars.
Activities: There are no fraternities or sororities. There are 24 groups on campus, including art, band, choir, chorale, dance, drama, environmental, ethnic, gay, honors, jazz band, musical theater, pep band, political, radio and TV, religious, social, social service, and student government. Popular campus events include Welcome Fair, Super Bowl Party, and Wellness Fair.
Sports: There are 4 intercollegiate sports for men and 4 for women, and 7 intramural sports for men and 7 for women. Facilities include a gym, 3 basketball and 4 racquetball courts, weight rooms, an aerobics room, circuit training, an indoor arena, and a 3000-seat stadium.
Disabled Students: 98% of the campus is accessible. Facilities include wheelchair ramps, elevators, special parking, specially equipped restrooms, special class scheduling, lowered drinking fountains, and lowered telephones.
Services: Counseling and information services are available, as is tutoring in most subjects. There is a reader service for the blind, and remedial math.
Campus Safety and Security: Measures include 24-hour foot and vehicle patrol, emergency notification system, and security escort services. There are emergency telephones and lighted pathways/sidewalks.
Programs of Study: Montana Western confers B.A., B.S.Business, B.Applied Sc., and B.S. Elementary and Secondary Education degrees. Associate degrees are also awarded. Bachelor's degrees are awarded in AGRICULTURE (animal science, environmental studies, equine science, fish and game management, and natural resource management), BIOLOGICAL SCIENCE (biomathematics, cell biology, physiology, and wildlife biology), BUSINESS (management information systems, small business management, sports management, and tourism), COMMUNICATIONS AND THE ARTS (art, arts administration/management, communications, creative writing, dramatic arts, English, English literature, illustration, music, technical and business writing, and visual and performing arts), COMPUTER AND PHYSICAL SCIENCE (applied mathematics, geology, geoscience, and mathematics), EDUCATION (art education, athletic training, business education, computer education, drama education, early childhood education, education, elementary education, English education, environmental education, health education, industrial arts education, mathematics education, middle school education, music education, physical education, science education, secondary education, social science education, social studies education, special education, sports and wellness studies, and sports studies), ENGINEERING AND ENVIRONMENTAL DESIGN (environmental science), HEALTH PROFESSIONS (art therapy, preveterinary science, and veterinary science), SOCIAL SCIENCE (anthropology, criminal justice, history, liberal arts/general studies, political science/government, prelaw, social science, sociology, Western civilization/culture, and women's studies). Elementary education, secondary education, business, biology have the largest enrollments.
Required: For graduation, students must complete 120 credit hours (128 for education) and maintain a minimum GPA of 2.0. Other requirements vary by major.
Special: Experience One prepares students to enter the work force or graduate studies with 4 years of hands on and interactive learning in majors.The college offers co-op programs, work-study programs, B.A.-B.S. degrees, dual majors, and pass/fail options. The Rural Education Program is designed to prepare students for teaching in smaller rural school settings. There are 2 national honor societies, including Phi Beta Kappa, and a freshman honors program.
Faculty/Classroom: 52% of faculty are male; 48% are female. All teach undergraduates. No introductory courses are taught by graduate students. The average class size in an introductory lecture is 18; in a laboratory is 18; and in a regular course is 18.
Admissions: 94% of the 2013-2014 applicants were accepted. The SAT scores for the 2013-2014 freshman class were: Critical Reading--68% below 500, 20% between 500 and 599, 10% between 600 and 699, and 2% between 700 and 800; Math--63% below 500, 29% between 500 and 599, and 8% between 600 and 699. The ACT scores were 62% below 21, 23% between 21 and 23, 13% between 24 and 26, and 3% between 27 and 28. 15% of the current freshmen were in the top fifth of their class; 37% were in the top two fifths. 6 freshmen graduated first in their class.
Requirements: The SAT or ACT is required. The ACT Optional Writing test is also required. Applicants must be graduates of an accredited secondary school. The GED is accepted. Students should have completed 4 years of English, 3 each of social studies and math, 2 years of lab science, and 2 years of science, and 2 years of electives. Montana Western requires applicants to be in the upper 50% of their class. A GPA of 2.5 is required. AP and CLEP credits are accepted.
Procedure: Freshmen are admitted to all sessions. There are deferred admissions and rolling admissions plans. Applications should be filed by July 1 for fall entry; December 1 for spring entry; and May 1 for summer entry, along with a $30 fee. Applications are accepted online.
Transfer: 196 transfer students enrolled in 2012-2013. Transfers must have attempted a minimum of 12 credit hours and have a cumulative GPA of 2.0. Credits earned at any accredited college can be used to satisfy curriculum or degree requirements only after evaluation. 30 of 120 credits required for the bachelor's degree must be completed at Montana Western.
Visiting: There are regularly scheduled orientations for prospective students, including pre-orientation days during summer months, two day orientation prior to the first day of school in the fall. the three days prior to the first day of school in the fall. Spring semester registration day and orientation are abbreviated. There are guides for informal visits and visitors may sit in on classes. To schedule a visit, contact the Admissions Office.
Financial Aid: In 2013-2014, 92% of all full-time freshmen and 84% of continuing full-time students received some form of financial aid. 74% of all full-time freshmen and 72% of continuing full-time students received need-based aid. The average freshman award was $5,713. Need-based scholarships or need-based grants averaged $2,987 ($5,950 maximum); need-based self-help aid (loans and jobs) averaged $2,725 ($7,500 maximum); and non-need-based athletic scholarships averaged $2,075 ($9,097 maximum). 45% of undergraduate students work part-time. Average annual earnings from campus work are $1943. The average financial indebtedness of the 2013 graduate was $24,410. The FAFSA is required. The priority date for freshman financial aid applications for fall entry is March 1.
International Students: There are 6 international students enrolled. They must take the TOEFL with a minimum score of 500 on the paper-based TOEFL (PBT) or 61 on the Internet-based version (iBT). The ACT or SAT is required for Canadian high school students.
Computers: All students may access the system from 8 a.m. to 10 p.m. There are no time limits. The fee is $85.
Graduates: From July 1, 2012 to June 30, 2013, 128 bachelor's degrees were awarded. The most popular majors were secondary education (30%), business (27%), and elementary education (27%). In an average class, 12% graduate in 4 years or less, 26% graduate in 5 years or less, and 28% graduate in 6 years or less.
Admissions Contact: Catherine Redhead, Director of Admissions. E-Mail: *admissions@umwestern.edu* Web: *www.umwestern.edu*

NEBRASKA

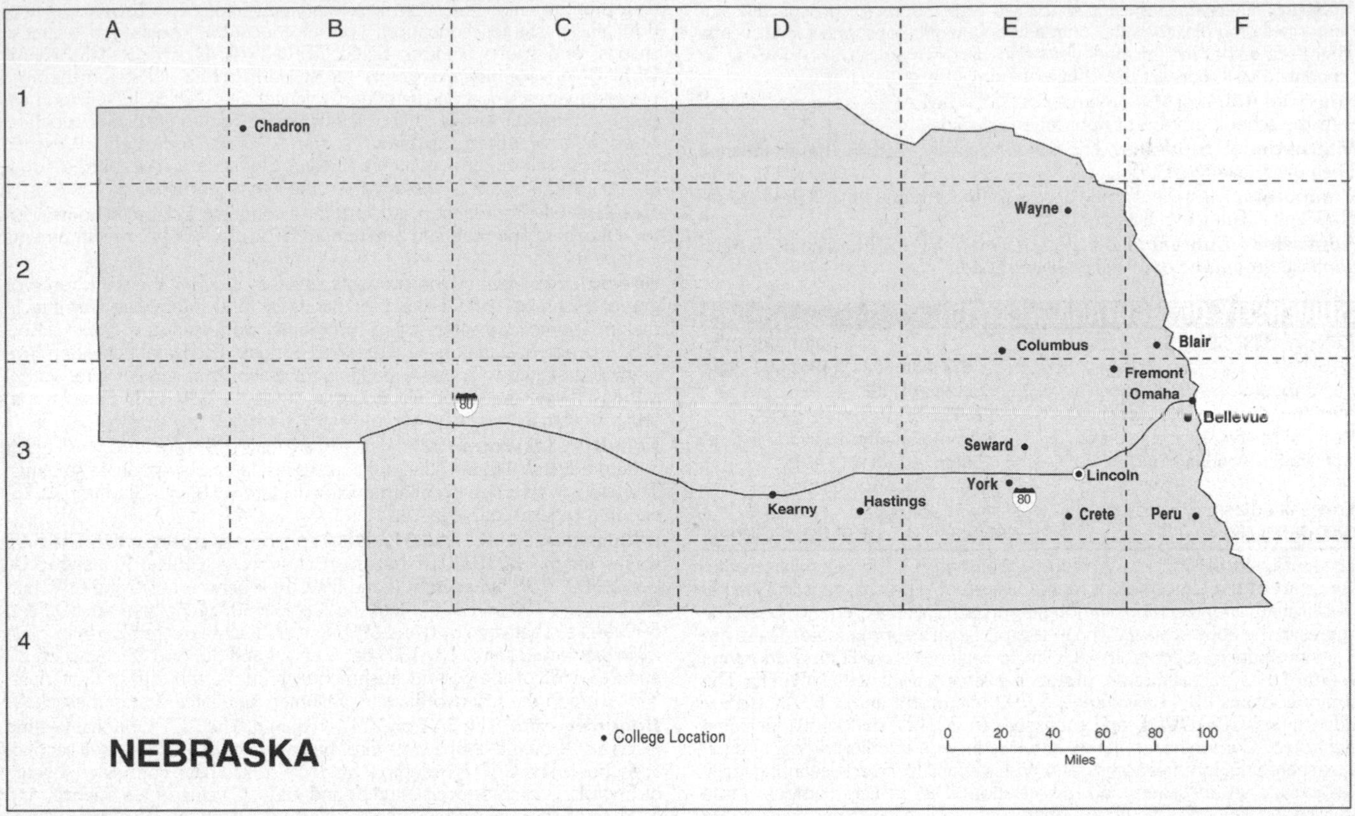

BELLEVUE UNIVERSITY F-3

Bellevue, NE 68005 (402) 293-2000
(800) 756-7920; (402) 557-7230

Full-time: 1300 men, 1200 women
Part-time: 600 men, 675 women
Graduate: 550 men, 655 women
Year: semesters, summer session
Application Deadline: open
Freshman Class: n/av
SAT or ACT: required
Faculty: n/av; IIA, --$
Ph.D.s: n/av
Student/Faculty: n/av
Tuition: $8450
Room & Board: n/app

NONCOMPETITIVE

Bellevue University, established in 1966, is a private commuter institution offering undergraduate degrees in arts and sciences, professional studies, and business. There are 3 undergraduate schools and 1 graduate school. Computerized library services include interlibrary loans and database searching. Special learning facilities include a learning resource center and art gallery. The 19-acre campus is in a suburban area 5 miles south of Omaha. There are 6 buildings.

Student Life: 95% of undergraduates are from Nebraska. 90% are from public schools. 86% are white. The average age of all undergraduates is 25. 12% do not continue beyond their first year; 40% remain to graduate.

Housing: There are no residence halls. All students commute.

Activities: There are no fraternities or sororities. There are 3 groups on campus, including cheerleading, newspaper, and professional. Popular campus events include Halloween and Christmas parties, Black History Month, and Spring Bash.

Sports: There are 2 intercollegiate sports for men and 1 for women. Facilities include racquetball, basketball, and volleyball courts, and weight-lifting equipment.

Disabled Students: All of the campus is accessible.

Services: Counseling and information services are available, as is tutoring in most subjects.

Campus Safety and Security: Measures include self-defense education. There are lighted pathways/sidewalks.

Programs of Study: Bellevue confers B.A., B.S., and B.F.A. degrees. Master's degrees are also awarded. Bachelor's degrees are awarded in BUSINESS (accounting, business administration and management, and personnel management), COMMUNICATIONS AND THE ARTS (communications, English, fine arts, and photography), COMPUTER AND PHYSICAL SCIENCE (information sciences and systems), EDUCATION (physical education), SOCIAL SCIENCE (criminal justice, geography, history, philosophy, political science/government, psychology, social science, sociology, and urban studies). Business administration is the strongest academically.

Required: To graduate, students must complete the core curriculum, with course work in communicative arts, a foreign language, art, English literature, foreign language literature, culture, civilization, music, philosophy, biology, chemistry, geology, math, geography, physics, psychology, sociology, economics, history, and political science. The required distribution of core credits varies by degree program from 63 to 66, and the total number of hours in the major varies by major. Students must earn 127 to 132 credits, depending on the degree. The minimum required GPA is 2.0 overall and 2.5 in the major.

Special: Bellevue University offers co-op programs with Buena Vista University and Grace College of the Bible, internships, and work-study. Students may earn B.A.-B.S. degrees, and an accelerated degree program is possible in professional studies. The college permits dual majors, and composite, interdisciplinary majors are available in the social sciences and urban studies. Credit may be conferred for military experience. Nondegree study is possible. The Lockstep Degree Competition Program offers an alternative to the traditional academic structure. The School of Arts and Sciences operates on a 4-day academic week to provide flexibility. There is 1 national honor society.

Faculty/Classroom: 91% teach undergraduates. No introductory courses are taught by graduate students. The average class size in an introductory lecture is 35; in a laboratory, 25; and in a regular course, 25.

Requirements: The ACT or SAT is required, with a recommended minimum score of 19 on the ACT, for those entering college within 2 years after high school graduation; submission of ACT/SAT scores is recommended for all others. Applicants must be graduates of an accredited secondary school or have a GED. Interviews are recommended. AP and CLEP credits are accepted.

Procedure: Freshmen are admitted to all sessions. Entrance exams should be taken in April. There are early decision, early admissions, and rolling admissions plans. Application deadlines are open. Application fee is $50.

Transfer: 30 of 127 to 132 credits required for the bachelor's degree must be completed at Bellevue.

Visiting: There are regularly scheduled orientations for prospective stu-

dents. There are guides for informal visits, and visitors may sit in on classes. To schedule a visit, contact the Admissions Office.

Financial Aid: The FAFSA is required. Check with the school for current application deadlines.

International Students: The school actively recruits these students. They must take the TOEFL or MELAB. They must also take the ACT.

Admissions Contact: Director of Admissions. E-Mail: *info@bellevue.edu* Web: *www.bellevue.edu*

CHADRON STATE COLLEGE B-1

Chadron, NE 69337 (308) 432-6263
(800) CHADRON; (308) 432-6229

Full-time: 770 men, 1020 women
Part-time: 200 men, 370 women
Graduate: 130 men, 310 women
Year: semesters, summer session
Application Deadline: open
Freshman Class: n/av
SAT or ACT: recommended
Faculty: n/av
Ph.D.s: n/av
Student/Faculty: n/av
Tuition: $5831 ($9888)
Room & Board: $5050

NONCOMPETITIVE

Chadron State College, founded in 1911, is a public college offering programs in liberal arts and professional training. There are 2 undergraduate schools and 1 graduate school. In addition to regional accreditation, CSC has baccalaureate program accreditation with CSWE and NCATE. Computerized library services include interlibrary loans and database searching. Special learning facilities include a learning resource center, natural history museum, planetarium, and radio station. The 281-acre campus is in a small town 100 miles south of Rapid City, South Dakota. Including any residence halls, there are 27 buildings.

Student Life: 72% of undergraduates are from Nebraska. 97% are from public schools. 90% are white. 45% are Protestant; 40% Catholic; 13% claim no religious affiliation. The average age of freshmen is 18; all undergraduates, 22. 35% do not continue beyond their first year; 33% remain to graduate.

Housing: 1200 students can be accommodated in college housing, which includes single-sex and coed dorms and married student housing. In addition, there are honors houses. On-campus housing is guaranteed for all 4 years. 65% of students commute. Alcohol is not permitted. All students may keep cars.

Activities: There are no fraternities or sororities. There are 71 groups on campus, including art, band, cheerleading, choir, dance, ethnic, gay, honors, international, jazz band, musical theater, newspaper, orchestra, pep band, photography, political, radio and TV, science fiction, student government, symphony, and video. Popular campus events include Spring Daze.

Sports: There are 5 intercollegiate sports for men and 5 for women, and 46 intramural sports for men and 46 for women. Facilities include a 3000-seat stadium, a gym, a swimming pool, and an activity center.

Disabled Students: All of the campus is accessible.

Services: Counseling and information services are available, as is tutoring in most subjects. There is a reader service for the blind, and remedial math, reading, and writing.

Campus Safety and Security: Measures include 24-hour foot and vehicle patrol and self-defense education. There are emergency telephones and lighted pathways/sidewalks.

Programs of Study: CSC confers B.A., B.S., and B.S.E. degrees. Master's degrees are also awarded. Bachelor's degrees are awarded in BIOLOGICAL SCIENCE (biology/biological science), BUSINESS (business administration and management), COMMUNICATIONS AND THE ARTS (art, dramatic arts, English, music, and speech/debate/rhetoric), COMPUTER AND PHYSICAL SCIENCE (chemistry, mathematics, and physics), EDUCATION (early childhood education, elementary education, health education, science education, and secondary education), ENGINEERING AND ENVIRONMENTAL DESIGN (industrial engineering technology), HEALTH PROFESSIONS (predentistry and premedicine), SOCIAL SCIENCE (criminal justice, history, political science/government, prelaw, psychology, social science, social work, and sociology). Education, business, and health professions are the strongest academically. Education, business, and justice studies have the largest enrollments.

Required: For graduation, students must complete 125 credit hours, including 47 hours of general education courses, and maintain a 2.0 GPA for the B.A. and a 2.5 GPA for the B.S.E. Other requirements vary by major.

Special: The college offers internships, a Washington semester, and work-study programs. Dual majors, co-op programs, and credit for life, military, and work experience are possible. There are 12 national honor societies and a freshman honors program.

Faculty/Classroom: 72% of faculty are male; 28% are female. All teach undergraduates. Graduate students teach 2% of introductory courses. The average class size in an introductory lecture is 36; in a laboratory, 19; and in a regular course, 25.

Requirements: The SAT or ACT is recommended unless the applicant has been out of high school for more than 5 years. Applicants need not be graduates of an accredited secondary school. The GED is accepted. High school work should include a minimum of 15 academic units, with at least 3 units in English and others in math, science, social studies, and foreign language. AP and CLEP credits are accepted. Important factors in the admissions decision are advanced placement or honors courses, evidence of special talent, and leadership record.

Procedure: Freshmen are admitted to all sessions. There is a rolling admissions plan. Application deadlines are open. Application fee is $15. Applications are accepted online.

Transfer: A maximum of 66 semester credits earned at an accredited 2-year college may be transferred. The registrar will evaluate credit earned at a 3- or 4-year college to determine the student's classification. All passing credit obtained from an institution is accepted in programs offered by Chadron State. Transfers are admitted every term. 30 of 125 credits required for the bachelor's degree must be completed at CSC.

Visiting: There are regularly scheduled orientations for prospective students, including visits with faculty, tours of the campus, meetings with financial aid and housing advisers, and complimentary meals. There are guides for informal visits; visitors may sit in on classes and stay overnight. To schedule a visit, contact the Admissions Office.

Financial Aid: The FAFSA is required. Check with the school for current application deadlines.

International Students: They must take the TOEFL. They must also take the SAT or ACT.

Admissions Contact: Director of Admissions. E-Mail: *inquire@csc.edu* Web: *www.csc.edu*

CLARKSON COLLEGE F-3

Omaha, NE 68131 (402) 552-3041
(800) 647-5500; (402) 552-6057

Full-time: 500 men and women
Part-time: 200 men and women
Graduate: 140 men and women
Year: semesters, summer session
Application Deadline: open
Freshman Class: n/av
SAT or ACT: required
Faculty: n/av
Ph.D.s: n/av
Student/Faculty: n/av
Tuition: $14,405
Room & Board: $7200

VERY COMPETITIVE

Clarkson College, established in 1888 and affiliated with the Episcopal Church, offers undergraduate and graduate degrees in the health care professions and business. There are 3 undergraduate schools and 2 graduate schools. The figures in the above capsule and in this profile are approximate. In addition to regional accreditation, Clarkson has baccalaureate program accreditation with NLN. Computerized library services include interlibrary loans, database searching, and Internet access. Special learning facilities include a learning resource center and a regional medical center. The 3-acre campus is in an urban area in Omaha. Including any residence halls, there are 4 buildings.

Student Life: 61% of undergraduates are from Nebraska. Others are from 13 states and 2 foreign countries. 90% are from public schools. 90% are white. 50% are Catholic; 45% Protestant. The average age of all undergraduates is 22.

Housing: 140 students can be accommodated in college housing, which includes coed on-campus apartments. On-campus housing is available on a first-come, first-served basis. Priority is given to out-of-town students. 90% of students commute. Alcohol is not permitted. All students may keep cars.

Activities: There are no fraternities or sororities. There are 12 groups on campus, including newspaper, professional, religious, social, social service, and student government. Popular campus events include talent show, game nights, and intramural volleyball.

Sports: There is no sports program at Clarkson. There is an exercise room available 24 hours, and a small gym area with basketball hoops and volleyball courts.

Disabled Students: 95% of the campus is accessible.

Services: Counseling and information services are available, as is tutoring in every subject.

Campus Safety and Security: Measures include 24-hour foot and vehicle patrol, emergency notification system, self-defense education, and security escort services. There are emergency telephones and lighted pathways/sidewalks.

Programs of Study: Clarkson confers B.S. and B.S.N. degrees. Associate and master's degrees are also awarded. Bachelor's degrees are awarded in BUSINESS (business administration and management), COMPUTER AND PHYSICAL SCIENCE (radiological technology), HEALTH PROFESSIONS (nursing and radiograph medical technology). Radiological technology and nursing are the strongest academically. Nursing has the largest enrollment.

Required: To graduate, students must complete 128 credit hours, including 68 in the major, and maintain a minimum GPA of 2.0. General education requirements include courses in the humanities, English, behavioral and social sciences, science and math, and phys ed. A 9-hour core curriculum is also required.

Special: A co-op program in nursing, work-study programs, and dual majors are available. Credit is given for military experience, and nondegree study is possible. The distance education option allows advanced placement students living a distance from the campus to complete their studies at home. There is 1 national honor society.

Faculty/Classroom: 16% of faculty are male; 84% are female. All teach undergraduates. No introductory courses are taught by graduate students. The average class size in an introductory lecture is 30; in a laboratory, 20; and in a regular course, 20.

Requirements: The SAT or ACT is required, with a minimum composite score of 20 on the ACT or a satisfactory score on the SAT. The ACT is preferred. Tests are not required for applicants more than 2 years out of high school. Applicants must be graduates of an accredited secondary school, with 3 years of English and 2 each of social science, algebra, and science (including lab science). The GED is accepted. Clarkson requires applicants to be in the upper 50% of their class. A GPA of 2.5 is required. AP and CLEP credits are accepted. Important factors in the admissions decision are advanced placement or honors courses, extracurricular activities record, and evidence of special talent.

Procedure: Freshmen are admitted to all sessions. Entrance exams should be taken during the junior year or first semester of the senior year. There is a deferred admissions plan. Application deadlines are open. Application fee is $35. A waiting list is maintained.

Transfer: Transfer students must have a minimum GPA of 2.5. Grades of C or better transfer for credit. Transfers are admitted for fall and spring. An interview is sometimes required. 64 of 128 credits required for the bachelor's degree must be completed at Clarkson.

Visiting: There are regularly scheduled orientations for prospective students. There are guides for informal visits, and visitors may sit in on classes. To schedule a visit, contact the Admissions Office.

Financial Aid: Clarkson is a member of CSS. The FAFSA and the college's own financial statement are required. Check with the school for current application deadlines.

International Students: They must take the TOEFL. They must also take the SAT or ACT.

Admissions Contact: Denise Work, Director of Admissions. E-Mail: *admiss@clarksoncollege.edu* Web: *www.clarksoncollege.edu*

COLLEGE OF SAINT MARY — F-3

Omaha, NE 68106 — **402-399-2407**
(800) 926-5534; (402) 399-2412

Full-time: no men, 639 women	**Faculty:** 53
Part-time: 10 men, 86 women	**Ph.D.s:** 62%
Graduate: 21 men, 214 women	**Student/Faculty:** 13 to 1
Year: semesters, summer session	**Tuition:** $27,434
Application Deadline: open	**Room & Board:** $7900

Freshman Class: 206 applied, 189 accepted, 89 enrolled
ACT: 22

COMPETITIVE

College of Saint Mary, founded in 1923, is a women's college committed to the works, values and aspirations of the Sisters of Mercy and dedicated to the education of women in an environment that calls forth potential and fosters leadership. There is one undergraduate school and one graduate school. In addition to regional accreditation, CSM has baccalaureate program accreditation with NLN. Computerized library services include interlibrary loans, database searching, Internet access, and Wi-Fi capability. Special learning facilities include an art gallery, cadaver lab; digital piano lab; native fish acquarium; nursing/occupational therapy/physician assistant laboratories;lecture capture system; online learning platform. The 40-acre campus is in an urban area within metro Omaha. Including any residence halls, there are 9 buildings.

Student Life: 92% of undergraduates are from Nebraska. Others are from 18 states, and 7 foreign countries. 82% are from public schools. 80% are White. 59% are unknown religion; 41% Catholic. The average age of freshmen is 20; all undergraduates, 24. 21% do not continue beyond their first year; 40% remain to graduate.

Housing: 289 students can be accommodated in college housing, which includes single-sex dorms. a residence hall for single student mothers with children. On-campus housing is guaranteed for all 4 years. 70% of students commute. All students may keep cars.

Activities: There are no fraternities or sororities. There are 20 groups on campus, including and campus activities board, business, green team, art, choir, chorus, dance, drama, environmental, ethnic, forensics, honors, international, multicultural, professional, religious, social, social service, and student government. Popular campus events include Heritage Week, Queen of Hearts Celebration, Casino and Comedian Night.

Sports: There are 8 intercollegiate sports for women, and 5 intramural sports for women. Facilities include a gym, a 6-lane swimming pool, weight room, an elevated running track, exercise room, a training room, 2 soccer fields, and 2 softball fields.

Disabled Students: All of the campus is accessible.

Services: Counseling and information services are available, as is tutoring in most subjects. There is a reader service for the blind, and remedial math, reading, and writing. There are also study groups and learning circles.

Campus Safety and Security: Measures include 24-hour foot and vehicle patrol, emergency notification system, self-defense education, and security escort services. There are lighted pathways/sidewalks, controlled access to dorms/residences, camera-monitored entrances to residence halls.

Programs of Study: CSM confers B.A., B.S., B.B.L.M, B.G.S. and B.R.S. degrees. Associate, master's, and doctoral degrees are also awarded. Bachelor's degrees are awarded in BIOLOGICAL SCIENCE (biology/biological science), BUSINESS (business administration and management and business intelligence and analytics), COMMUNICATIONS AND THE ARTS (art, English, language arts, and Spanish), COMPUTER AND PHYSICAL SCIENCE (chemistry, mathematics, and natural sciences), EDUCATION (early childhood education, education, and elementary education), HEALTH PROFESSIONS (medical laboratory technology, nursing, occupational therapy, and physician's assistant), SOCIAL SCIENCE (applied psychology, humanities, liberal arts/general studies, paralegal studies, psychology, social science, and theological studies). Biology, chemistry, occupational therapy and nursing are the strongest academically. Occupational therapy, nursing, education, business and biology have the largest enrollments.

Required: To graduate, students must complete 128 semester hours, with a minimum of 30 hours in the major and a 2.0 GPA in the major and overall. Required general education courses total 47 hours, with 10 in quantitative reasoning and science, 6 each in English and theology, 3 each in communications, moral reasoning, fine arts, global cultural diversity, history, philosophy, and social science, and 1 in a core seminar. Each student prior to graduation completes and presents a research project in her major either individually or with a team.

Special: Students may pursue internships in any major, including research courses in the sciences. CSM also offers dual majors, study abroad, nondegree study, pass/fail options, an accelerated degree program in business leadership, and credit for life, military, and work experience. There are 2 national honor societies, a freshman honors program, and 30 departmental honors programs.

Faculty/Classroom: 21% of faculty are male; 79% are female. 95% teach undergraduates, and 10% do research. No introductory courses are taught by graduate students. The average class size in an introductory lecture is 18; in a laboratory is 13; and in a regular course is 16.

Admissions: 92% of the 2013-2014 applicants were accepted. The ACT scores were 33% below 21, 30% between 21 and 23, 18% between 24 and 26, 13% between 27 and 28, and 6% above 28. 42% of the current freshmen were in the top fifth of their class; 74% were in the top two fifths. 2 freshmen graduated first in their class.

Requirements: The ACT is required. Students are accepted with a minimum composite score of 18 on the ACT or comparable SAT score. Students must also have a GPA of at least 2.0. Applicants must be graduates of an accredited secondary school. The GED is accepted. Students should have completed 16 academic units, including 4 years of English and 2 each of math, social studies, and science, with biology and chemistry required for the various health profession majors. An interview is recommended. A GPA of 2.0 is required. AP and CLEP credits are accepted.

Procedure: Freshmen are admitted to all sessions. Entrance exams should be taken in the junior or senior year. There are deferred admissions and rolling admissions plans. Application deadlines are open. Application fee is $30. Applications are accepted online.

Transfer: 119 transfer students enrolled in 2012-2013. Applicants should have a minimum GPA of 2.0 and submit official transcripts from previous colleges attended. Students with fewer than 12 credit hours must also submit ACT or SAT scores. Grades of C or better transfer for credit. Students are admitted every term. 30 of 128 credits required for the bachelor's degree must be completed at CSM.

Visiting: There are regularly scheduled orientations for prospective students, consisting of a tour of the campus, a meeting with a financial aid representative, student-life presentations, and lunch. There are guides for informal visits, visitors may sit in on classes, and stay overnight. To schedule a visit, contact Valyn Gipson at (402) 399-2355.

Financial Aid: In 2013-2014, 100% of all full-time freshmen and 99% of continuing full-time students received some form of financial aid. 76% of all full-time freshmen and 90% of continuing full-time students received need-based aid. The average freshman award was $27,324. Need-based scholarships or need-based grants averaged $8,160; need-based self-help aid (loans and jobs) averaged $5,575; non-need-based athletic scholarships averaged $5,979; and other non-need-based awards and non-need-based scholarships averaged $16,079. 75% of undergraduate students work part-time. Average annual earnings from campus work are $1162. The average financial indebtedness of the 2013 graduate was $40,026. The

FAFSA is required. The priority date for freshman financial aid applications for fall entry is March 15.

International Students: There are 4 international students enrolled. They must take the TOEFL with a minimum score of 550 on the paper-based TOEFL (PBT) or 79 on the Internet-based version (iBT), . They must also take the SAT or ACT, scoring 18.

Graduates: From July 1, 2012 to June 30, 2013, 148 bachelor's degrees were awarded. The most popular majors were rehabilitation studies/occupational therapy (36%), nursing (23%), and business (12%). 15 companies recruited on campus in 2012-2013. In an average class, 28% graduate in 4 years or less, 37% graduate in 5 years or less, and 40% graduate in 6 years or less. Of the 2012 graduating class, 3% were enrolled in graduate school within 6 months of graduation, and 92% were employed.

Admissions Contact: Greg Fritz, VP Enrollment Services. E-Mail: *enroll@csm.edu* Web: *www.csm.edu*

CONCORDIA UNIVERSITY NEBRASKA — E-3

Seward, NE 68434 — (402) 643-7233; (800) 535-5494; (402) 643-4073

Full-time: n/av
Part-time: n/av
Graduate: n/av
Year: semesters, summer session
Application Deadline:
Freshman Class: n/av
SAT or ACT: required
Faculty: n/av; IIB, --$
Ph.D.s: n/av
Student/Faculty: n/av
Tuition: $20,000
Room & Board: $6000

VERY COMPETITIVE

Concordia University Nebraska, founded in 1894, is a private university owned and operated by the Lutheran Church-Missouri Synod, with degree programs in professional education and liberal arts. Among Concordia's major programs are those for professional work in the Lutheran Church: teacher education, director of Christian education, preseminary pastoral training, and church music. There is one graduate school. In addition to regional accreditation, Concordia has baccalaureate program accreditation with NCATE. Computerized library services include database searching. Special learning facilities include an art gallery, natural history museum, an observatory. The 120-acre campus is in a small town 25 miles west of Lincoln. Including any residence halls, there are 26 buildings.

Student Life: 59% of undergraduates are from out of state, mostly the Mid-West. Students are from 37 states, and 9 foreign countries. 95% are White. 95% are Protestant. The average age of freshmen is 18; all undergraduates, 21. 22% do not continue beyond their first year; 48% remain to graduate.

Housing: 815 students can be accommodated in college housing, which includes single-sex dorms, off-campus apartments, and married student housing. On-campus housing is guaranteed for all 4 years. 85% of students live on campus; of those, 90% remain on campus on weekends. Alcohol is not permitted. All students may keep cars.

Activities: There are no fraternities or sororities. There are 35 groups on campus, including band, cheerleading, choir, chorale, chorus, computers, dance, debate, drama, drill team, ethnic, forensics, honors, international, jazz band, literary magazine, musical theater, newspaper, orchestra, pep band, photography, professional, religious, social, social service, student government, and yearbook. Popular campus events include Spring Weekend and Multicultural Awareness Week.

Sports: There are 8 intercollegiate sports for men and 8 for women, and 7 intramural sports for men and 7 for women. Facilities include a gym, a weight-training room, an indoor pool, football, baseball, and soccer fields, and a track and field stadium.

Disabled Students: 35% of the campus is accessible.

Services: Counseling and information services are available, as is tutoring in every subject. There is a reader service for the blind. talking books and tape recorders

Campus Safety and Security: Measures include 24-hour foot and vehicle patrol, self-defense education, and security escort services. There are emergency telephones, lighted pathways/sidewalks, vehicle and bicycle registration, and a possession ID engraving program.

Programs of Study: Concordia confers B.A., B.S., B.F.A., B.S.Med.Tech., B.Mus. and B.Sacred Music degrees. Master's degrees are also awarded. Bachelor's degrees are awarded in BIOLOGICAL SCIENCE (biology/biological science), BUSINESS (accounting, business administration and management, and sports management), COMMUNICATIONS AND THE ARTS (communications, dramatic arts, English, fine arts, music, speech/debate/rhetoric, and studio art), COMPUTER AND PHYSICAL SCIENCE (chemistry, computer science, mathematics, natural sciences, and physical sciences), EDUCATION (business education, Christian education, early childhood education, elementary education, home economics education, industrial arts education, middle school education, music education, physical education, science education, secondary education, and special education), HEALTH PROFESSIONS (exercise science, health, medical laboratory technology, predentistry, and premedicine), SOCIAL SCIENCE (behavioral science, geography, history, physical fitness/movement, prelaw, psychology, and theological studies). Education, business, and art are the strongest academically. Education has the largest enrollments.

Required: To graduate, students must complete a minimum of 128 credits with a GPA of at least 2.0. Required general education courses include 12 hours of theology, 9 hours each of English/speech, social science, and science, 6 of fine arts, 3 each of math and health and phys ed, 2 to 3 of electives, and 1 hour minimum of computer literacy.

Special: Concordia offers cross-registration with the University of Nebraska in Lincoln. Internships are available in education, business, and Christian education. B.A.-B.S. degrees, student-designed majors, dual majors, study abroad in England and China, nondegree studies, and pass/fail options are available. There is an accelerated degree program in organizational management. There are a freshman honors program.

Faculty/Classroom: 71% of faculty are male; 29% are female. All teach undergraduates. Graduate students teach 1% of introductory courses. The average class size in an introductory lecture is 20; in a laboratory is 15; and in a regular course is 15.

Requirements: The SAT or ACT is required. A minimum composite score of 18 is recommended for the ACT. Applicants need not be graduates of an accredited secondary school. The GED is accepted. The school strongly encourages high school courses in art, English, foreign language, history, math, music, phys ed, science, and social studies. An interview is recommended. A GPA of 2.8 is required. AP and CLEP credits are accepted. Important factors in the admissions decision are ability to finance college education, leadership record, and recommendations by alumni.

Procedure: Freshmen are admitted to all sessions. Entrance exams should be taken in the junior or senior year. There is a rolling admissions plan. Application deadlines are open. Applications are accepted online.

Transfer: 58 transfer students enrolled in 2012-2013. Applicants should have a minimum GPA of 2.5 and a minimum ACT score of 18. An interview is recommended. Passing grades transfer for credit. Transfers are admitted every term. 30 of 128 credits required for the bachelor's degree must be completed at Concordia.

Visiting: There are regularly scheduled orientations for prospective students, including a campus tour, visits with professors/coaches, and an admission interview. There are guides for informal visits, visitors may sit in on classes, and stay overnight. To schedule a visit, contact the Office of Admission.

Financial Aid: In 2013-2014, 98% of all full-time freshmen received some form of financial aid. The FAFSA and the college's own financial statement are required. Check with the school for current application deadlines.

International Students: There are 9 international students enrolled. They must take the TOEFL. They must also take the SAT or ACT.

Admissions Contact: Office of Admission E-Mail: *admiss@cune.edu* Web: *www.cune.edu*

CREIGHTON UNIVERSITY — F-3

Omaha, NE 68178 — (402) 280-2703; (800) 282-5835; (402) 280-2685

Full-time: 1545 men, 2270 women
Part-time: 119 men, 142 women
Graduate: 1801 men, 2142 women
Year: semesters, summer session
Application Deadline: February 15
Freshman Class: 5336 applied, 4090 accepted, 966 enrolled
SAT CR/M/W: 580/600/560
ACT: 27
Faculty: 290; IIA, +$
Ph.D.s: 89%
Student/Faculty: 13 to 1
Tuition: $34,330
Room & Board: $9728

VERY COMPETITIVE+

Creighton University, founded in 1878, is a private Jesuit Catholic institution offering undergraduate programs in arts and sciences, business administration, and nursing as well as graduate, dental, medical, law, pharmacy, physical therapy, and occupational therapy programs. There are 3 undergraduate schools and 1 graduate school. In addition to regional accreditation, Creighton has baccalaureate program accreditation with AACSB, ACPE, ADA, CSWE, and NCATE. Computerized library services include interlibrary loans, database searching, Internet access, and Wi-Fi capability. Special learning facilities include an art gallery, TV station, University archives; largest solar array in the state of Nebraska used for prototype testing of solar cells. The 139-acre campus is in an urban area near downtown Omaha Nebraska. It is near, yet set apart from, the city's urban center. Including any residence halls, there are 61 buildings.

Student Life: 70% of undergraduates are from out of state, mostly the Mid-West. Students are from 50 states, 45 foreign countries, and Canada. 50% are from public schools. 73% are White. 58% are Catholic; 21% Protestant; 18% Jewish (0.2%), Hinduism, Buddhism, Islam and Unknown. The average age of freshmen is 18; all undergraduates, 21. 9% do not continue beyond their first year; 75% remain to graduate.

Housing: 2444 students can be accommodated in college housing, which includes single-sex and coed dorms, on-campus apartments, and married student housing. In addition, there are honors houses, special-interest houses, the Cortina Community and Freshman Leadership Program housing. On-campus housing is available on a first-come, first-served basis, and is available on a lottery system for upperclassmen. 62% of students live on campus; of those, 90% remain on campus on weekends. All students may keep cars.

Activities: 30% of men belong to 5 national fraternities; 33% of women belong to 7 national sororities. There are 212 groups on campus, including art, band, cheerleading, chess, choir, chorale, chorus, computers, dance, debate, drama, drill team, environmental, ethnic, forensics, gay, honors, international, jazz band, literary magazine, musical theater, newspaper, orchestra, pep band, photography, political, professional, radio and TV, religious, social, social service, student government, and symphony. Popular campus events include Diversity Week, Fallapalooza Concert, CUNITY Week, Spring Fling Week, Luau, Pow Wow, Greek Week, FLP Thanksgiving Dinner, and Greek Philanthropies.

Sports: There are 6 intercollegiate sports for men and 8 for women, and 22 intramural sports for men and 22 for women. Facilities include Creighton has a sports complex (an outdoor artificial turf area) along with a baseball/softball facility, an intercollegiate soccer facility, and 2 physical fitness centers with space for basketball, volleyball, badminton, soccer and open recreational play, a weight room and a jogging track. Another facility houses an arena for women's basketball and volleyball as well as locker rooms, athletic training rooms and offices for the coaching staff. Creighton is in the process of building a new basketball practice facility to replace its existing practice arena.

Disabled Students: 85% of the campus is accessible.

Services: Counseling and information services are available, as is tutoring in most subjects.

Campus Safety and Security: Measures include 24-hour foot and vehicle patrol, emergency notification system, self-defense education, and security escort services. There are shuttle buses, emergency telephones, lighted pathways/sidewalks, controlled access to dorms/residences, an pedestrian escort service, full-time crime prevention officer, violence intervention and prevention center, electronic card access systems, and surveillance camera.

Programs of Study: Creighton confers B.A., B.F.A., B.S., B.S.Atmospheric Science, B.S.B.A., B.S.Chemistry, B.S.Dental Hygiene, B.S.Emergency Medical Services, B.S.Environmental Science, B.S.Health Sciences, B.S. Mathematics, B.S.N., B.S.Physics and B.S.W. degrees. Associate, master's, and doctoral degrees are also awarded. Bachelor's degrees are awarded in BIOLOGICAL SCIENCE (biochemistry and biology/biological science), BUSINESS (accounting, banking and finance, business administration and management, business intelligence and analytics, entrepreneurial studies, integrated leadership studies, international business management, management information systems, management science, and marketing/retailing/merchandising), COMMUNICATIONS AND THE ARTS (art history, art, classical languages, communication studies, dance, dramatic arts, English, fine arts, french and francophone studies, german studies, graphic design & media, Greek, journalism, Latin, music, musical theater, studio art, theatre arts, and visual and performing arts), COMPUTER AND PHYSICAL SCIENCE (applied physics, chemistry, computer science, energy science, informatics and computer science, mathematics, physical sciences, and physics), EDUCATION (elementary education and secondary education), ENGINEERING AND ENVIRONMENTAL DESIGN (computational sciences, energy management technology, and environmental science), HEALTH PROFESSIONS (dental hygiene, emergency medical services, exercise science, health administration and policy, health science, and nursing), SOCIAL SCIENCE (African studies, American studies, anthropology, classical and near eastern civilization, cultural anthropology, economics, history, international relations, justice and society, medical anthropology, Native American studies, Near Eastern studies, peace studies, philosophy, political science/government, psychology, social work, sociology, Spanish studies, spanish and hispanic studies, and theology). Business, science/health science, nursing, biological sciences and psychology are the strongest academically, and have the largest enrollments.

Required: For graduation, students must complete a minimum of 128 credit hours and maintain a GPA of 2.0. Each school has general education requirements. Total number of hours required in major and specific disciplines varies by college and major.

Special: The University offers study abroad in 56 countries, a Washington semester, and numerous internship opportunities. Students may take an accelerated degree program in organizational communication and creative writing. B.A.-B.S. degrees and dual majors are possible as well as a 3-2 engineering degree with the University of Detroit Mercy. Army ROTC is offered on campus; Air Force ROTC is available through an arrangement with University of Nebraska Omaha. There are 15 national honor societies, including Phi Beta Kappa, and a freshman honors program.

Faculty/Classroom: 54% of faculty are male; 46% are female. All teach and do research. No introductory courses are taught by graduate students. The average class size in an introductory lecture is 22; in a laboratory is 9; and in a regular course is 21.

Admissions: 77% of the 2013-2014 applicants were accepted. The SAT scores for the 2013-2014 freshman class were: Critical Reading--14% below 500, 45% between 500 and 599, 32% between 600 and 699, and 9% between 700 and 800; Math--8% below 500, 38% between 500 and 599, 40% between 600 and 699, and 14% between 700 and 800; Writing--21% below 500, 42% between 500 and 599, 31% between 600 and 699, and 6% between 700 and 800. The ACT scores were 4% below 21, 16% between 21 and 23, 29% between 24 and 26, 17% between 27 and 28, and 34% above 28. 64% of the current freshmen were in the top fifth of their class; 87% were in the top two fifths. There were 3 National Merit finalists. 55 freshmen graduated first in their class.

Requirements: The SAT or ACT is required. Applicants must be graduates of an accredited secondary school. The GED is accepted. Students should have completed 16 credits including 4 credits in English, 3 each in math and electives, and 2 each in foreign language, science, and social studies. Home-schooled students are welcome. Creighton requires applicants to be in the upper 50% of their class. A GPA of 2.5 is required. AP and CLEP credits are accepted. Important factors in the admissions decision are advanced placement or honors courses, extracurricular activities record, and recommendations by school officials.

Procedure: Freshmen are admitted fall, spring, and summer. Entrance exams should be taken Fall of the senior year. There are deferred admissions and rolling admissions plans. Applications should be filed by February 15 for fall entry; December 15 for spring entry, along with a $40 fee. Notification is sent on a rolling basis. Applications are accepted online. Application fees are waived if application is completed online.

Transfer: 46 transfer students enrolled in 2012-2013. Applicants must have a 2.0 minimum GPA in a regionally accredited school. A minimum score of 21 on the ACT or 990 on the SAT is recommended. Grades of C or better transfer for credit. Transfers are admitted every semester. 48 of 128 credits required for the bachelor's degree must be completed at Creighton.

Visiting: There are regularly scheduled orientations for prospective students, consisting of open house programs with various presentations and campus tours. A daily visit can be scheduled by either calling the Admissions office or completing online request at http:/admissions.creighton.edu/visit/schedule-visit. There are guides for informal visits, visitors may sit in on classes, and stay overnight. To schedule a visit, contact the Admissions Office.

Financial Aid: In 2013-2014, 99% of all full-time freshmen and 96% of continuing full-time students received some form of financial aid. 62% of all full-time freshmen and 57% of continuing full-time students received need-based aid. The average freshman award was $27,298. Need-based scholarships or need-based grants averaged $21,989; need-based self-help aid (loans and jobs) averaged $6,220; non-need-based athletic scholarships averaged $24,871; and $15,527 from other forms of aid. 19% of undergraduate students work part-time. Average annual earnings from campus work are $2372. The average financial indebtedness of the 2013 graduate was $35,510. The FAFSA is required. The priority date for freshman financial aid applications for fall entry is April 1.

International Students: There are 79 international students enrolled. The school actively recruits these students. They must take the TOEFL with a minimum score of 550 on the paper-based TOEFL (PBT) or 80 on the Internet-based version (iBT), TOEFL or IELTS.

Graduates: From July 1, 2012 to June 30, 2013, 1011 bachelor's degrees were awarded. The most popular majors were health professions and related programs (29%), business/marketing (15%), and biological/life sciences (9%). 250 companies recruited on campus in 2012-2013. In an average class, 1% graduate in 3 years or less, 67% graduate in 4 years or less, 75% graduate in 5 years or less, and 76% graduate in 6 years or less. Of the 2012 graduating class, 32% were enrolled in graduate school within 6 months of graduation, and 56% were employed.

Admissions Contact: Sarah Richardson, Director of Admissions and Scholarships. E-Mail: *SarahRichardson@creighton.edu* Web: *www.creighton.edu/admissions*

DOANE COLLEGE — E-3

Crete, NE 68333 — **(402) 826-8222**
(800) 333-6263; (402) 826-8600

Full-time: 553 men, 553 women	**Faculty:** 80; IIB, --$
Part-time: 3 men, 4 women	**Ph.D.s:** 81%
Graduate: n/av	**Student/Faculty:** 12 to 1
Year: 4-1-4	**Tuition:** $26,180
Application Deadline:	**Room & Board:** $7550
Freshman Class: 1822 applied, 1307 accepted, 289 enrolled	
SAT: recommended	**ACT:** 23 **VERY COMPETITIVE**

Doane College, founded in 1872, is a private liberal arts and science college. There are 3 undergraduate schools and 3 graduate schools. In addition to regional accreditation, Doane has baccalaureate program accreditation with NCATE. Computerized library services include interlibrary loans, database searching, Internet access, and Wi-Fi capability. Special learning facilities include an art gallery, radio station, TV station, an observatory. The 300-acre campus is in a small town 25 miles southwest of Lincoln. Including any residence halls, there are 28 buildings.

Student Life: 80% of undergraduates are from Nebraska. Others are from 22 states, 7 foreign countries, and Canada. 75% are from public schools. 86% are White. 22% are Catholic. The average age of freshmen is 18; all undergraduates, 20. 23% do not continue beyond their first year; 77% remain to graduate.

Housing: 832 students can be accommodated in college housing, which includes single-sex and coed dorms and on-campus apartments. In addition, there are honors houses and special-interest houses. On-campus housing is guaranteed for all 4 years. 75% of students live on campus; of those, 79% remain on campus on weekends. All students may keep cars.

Activities: 34% of men belong to 5 local fraternities; 25% of women belong to 4 local sororities. There are 50 groups on campus, including alternative spring break, and wildlife/conservation, Hanson Leadership Program, investment, art, band, cheerleading, choir, chorale, chorus, computers, dance, drama, ethnic, forensics, gay, honors, international, jazz band, literary magazine, marching band, musical theater, newspaper, pep band, photography, political, professional, radio and TV, religious, social, social service, speech team, and student government. Popular campus events include Parents Day, Stop Day, Christmas Festival and Concert.

Sports: There are 6 intercollegiate sports for men and 6 for women, and 4 intramural sports for men and 4 for women. Facilities include a phys ed building, a field house, a sports field, a fitness center, a gym, a pool, nature and cross-country trails, a challenge course, and indoor and outdoor tracks.

Disabled Students: 60% of the campus is accessible.

Services: Counseling and information services are available, as is tutoring in every subject. There is remedial math, reading, and writing.

Campus Safety and Security: Measures include security escort services. There are emergency telephones, lighted pathways/sidewalks, evening patrols by trained security personnel.

Programs of Study: Doane confers B.A., and B.S. degrees. Bachelor's degrees are awarded in BIOLOGICAL SCIENCE (biochemistry and biology/biological science), BUSINESS (accounting and business administration and management), COMMUNICATIONS AND THE ARTS (art, dramatic arts, English, English as a second/foreign language, French, German, journalism, music, and Spanish), COMPUTER AND PHYSICAL SCIENCE (chemistry, computer science, information sciences and systems, mathematics, natural sciences, physical sciences, and physics), EDUCATION (business education, elementary education, physical education, and special education), ENGINEERING AND ENVIRONMENTAL DESIGN (environmental science), SOCIAL SCIENCE (economics, history, international studies, philosophy, political science/government, psychology, public administration, religion, and sociology). Biology and economics (emphasis business, management) are the strongest academically. Education and business administration have the largest enrollments.

Required: The Doane Plan requires students to complete 60 to 70 credits in heritage studies, contemporary issues, international/multicultural perspective, natural science, quantitative reasoning, communication, aesthetic perspective, health and well-being, and community and leadership. Students are also required to complete 2 hours of phys ed, demonstrate computer skills in word processing, and in most disciplines, complete a senior seminar. Students must complete 132 credit hours and have a minimum GPA of 2.0 in the major to graduate.

Special: Internships for sophomores through seniors, a Washington semester, and study abroad in numerous countries are possible. A 3-2 engineering program in conjunction with Washington at St. Louis and Columbia Universities, work-study, student-designed and interdisciplinary majors, dual majors and accelerated degrees in all areas, credit by exam, nondegree study, and pass/fail options are available. Doane also offers the HELPS program, designed for Doane College graduates who wish to return as full-time students to seek further education in preparation for career advancement. Students may pursue a 3-2 environmental studies/forestry degree in conjunction with Duke University. Doane's Lincoln campus, designed for adults, offers intensive 8-week classes in the evening and on weekends in both undergraduate and graduate programs. Doane offers an honors program, leadership development program, and the opportunity to conduct summer research projects with faculty. There are 7 national honor societies, a freshman honors program, and 3 departmental honors programs.

Faculty/Classroom: 49% of faculty are male; 51% are female. All teach undergraduates. No introductory courses are taught by graduate students. The average class size in an introductory lecture is 24; in a laboratory is 16; and in a regular course is 18.

Admissions: 72% of the 2013-2014 applicants were accepted. The ACT scores were 23% below 21, 27% between 21 and 23, 27% between 24 and 26, 11% between 27 and 28, and 12% above 28. 38% of the current freshmen were in the top fifth of their class; 88% were in the top two fifths. There were 2 National Merit finalists. 9 freshmen graduated first in their class.

Requirements: The ACT is required. The SAT is recommended. Applicants must be graduates of an accredited secondary school. The GED is accepted. It is recommended that 4 units of English and 3 units each of math, science, and the social sciences be completed. An interview is recommended. Art students must submit a portfolio, and music and drama students must audition. A GPA of 2.0 is required. AP and CLEP credits are accepted. Important factors in the admissions decision are advanced placement or honors courses, leadership record, parents or siblings attended your school, evidence of special talent, personality/intangible qualities, extracurricular activities record, recommendations by alumni, geographical diversity, recommendations by school officials, and ability to finance college education.

Procedure: Freshmen are admitted fall, winter, and spring. Entrance exams should be taken by spring of the junior year or early senior year. There are deferred admissions and rolling admissions plans. Application deadlines are open. Notification is sent on a rolling basis. Applications are accepted online.

Transfer: 51 transfer students enrolled in 2012-2013. Transfer students must submit a transcript from previously attended colleges and have been in good standing. The SAT or ACT is usually required. Grades of 2.0 or higher generally transfer for credit. 30 of 132 credits required for the bachelor's degree must be completed at Doane.

Visiting: There are regularly scheduled orientations for prospective students, including 4 scheduled half-day visits that incorporate a parents program. There are guides for informal visits, visitors may sit in on classes, and stay overnight. To schedule a visit, contact the Admissions Office.

Financial Aid: In 2013-2014, 100% of all full-time freshmen and 98% of continuing full-time students received some form of financial aid. 90% of all full-time freshmen and 89% of continuing full-time students received need-based aid. The average freshman award was $21,353. Need-based scholarships or need-based grants averaged $17,884 ($25,560 maximum); need-based self-help aid (loans and jobs) averaged $4,641 ($9,150 maximum); non-need-based athletic scholarships averaged $10,509 ($23,000 maximum); and other non-need based awards and non-need-based scholarships averaged $8,638 ($25,560 maximum). 43% of undergraduate students work part-time. Average annual earnings from campus work are $920. The average financial indebtedness of the 2013 graduate was $24,578. The FAFSA is required. The deadline for filing freshman financial aid applications for fall entry is March 1.

International Students: There are 11 international students enrolled. The school actively recruits these students. They must take the TOEFL with a minimum score of 525 on the paper-based TOEFL (PBT) or 70 on the Internet-based version (iBT), IELTS with a minimum score of 5.5. They must also take the SAT or ACT, scoring 21. 21 on the ACT English subsection, or a satisfactory score on the SAT.

Graduates: From July 1, 2012 to June 30, 2013, 239 bachelor's degrees were awarded. The most popular majors were elementary education (24%), biology (16%), and business (13%). 45 companies recruited on campus in 2012-2013. In an average class, 1% graduate in 3 years or less, 60% graduate in 4 years or less, 63% graduate in 5 years or less, and 66% graduate in 6 years or less. Of the 2012 graduating class, 20% were enrolled in graduate school within 6 months of graduation, and 77% were employed.

Admissions Contact: Joel Weyand, Vice President for Enrollment . E-Mail: *admissions@doane.edu* Web: *www.doane.edu*

HASTINGS COLLEGE

D-3

Hastings, NE 68901 (402) 461-7403
(800) 532-7642; (402) 461-7490

Full-time: 564 men, 519 women	**Faculty:** 86; IIB, --$
Part-time: 10 men, 11 women	**Ph.D.s:** 72%
Graduate: 22 men, 28 women	**Student/Faculty:** 13 to 1
Year: semesters, summer session	**Tuition:** $23,325
Application Deadline: August 1	**Room & Board:** $8,228
Freshman Class: 11186 applied, 1126 accepted, 289 enrolled	
SAT: required	**ACT:** 24 COMPETITIVE+

Hastings College, founded in 1882 and affiliated with the Presbyterian Church, offers programs in the liberal arts and sciences, education, business, and pre-health professions. There is 1 graduate school. In addition to regional accreditation, Hastings College has baccalaureate program accreditation with NASM and NCATE. Computerized library services include interlibrary loans, database searching, Internet access, and laptop Internet portals. Special learning facilities include a learning resource center, art gallery, radio station, TV station, an observatory, and a glass blowing studio, greenhouse, and infant study lab. The 109-acre campus is in a rural area 150 miles west of Omaha. Including any residence halls, there are 42 buildings.

Student Life: 69% of undergraduates are from Nebraska. Others are from 31 states, 8 foreign countries, and Canada. 86% are from public schools. 89% are white. 38% are Protestant; 34% claim no religious affiliation; 21% Catholic. The average age of freshmen is 19; all undergraduates, 21. 27% do not continue beyond their first year; 63% remain to graduate.

Housing: 842 students can be accommodated in college housing, which includes single-sex and coed dorms and on-campus apartments. In addition, there are honors houses, non-honors houses. On-campus housing is guaranteed for the freshman year only, is available on a first-come, and first-served basis. Priority is given to out-of-town students. 73% of students live on campus; of those, 60% remain on campus on weekends. All students may keep cars.

Activities: 30% of men belong to 4 local fraternities; 30% of women belong to 4 local sororities. There are 80 groups on campus, including and public relations, health advisory council, nontraditional students, peer educators, art, band, cheerleading, choir, chorus, computers, dance, debate, drama, environmental, ethnic, flag team, forensics, gay, honors, international, jazz band, literary magazine, marching band, musical theater, newspaper, orchestra, pep band, photography, political, professional, radio and TV, religious, social, social service, student government, and symphony. Popular campus events include May Fete, Festival of Lessons and Carols, and Artist Lecture Series.

Sports: There are 9 intercollegiate sports for men and 10 for women, and 12 intramural sports for men and 12 for women. Facilities include a physical fitness center, a pool, a weight room, indoor and outdoor tennis courts, a 3000-seat stadium, a 2500-seat gym, a wellness center, and an all-weather track.

Disabled Students: 90% of the campus is accessible.

Services: Counseling and information services are available, as is tutoring in most subjects, all core subjects and most lower-division courses.

Campus Safety and Security: Measures include emergency notification system and security escort services. There are emergency telephones, lighted pathways/sidewalks, and a night security patrol.

Programs of Study: Hastings College confers B.A. and B.M. degrees. Master's degrees are also awarded. Bachelor's degrees are awarded in BIOLOGICAL SCIENCE (biology/biological science), BUSINESS (accounting and business administration and management), COMMUNICATIONS AND THE ARTS (broadcasting, communications, dramatic arts, English, fine arts, German, music, Spanish, and speech/debate/rhetoric), COMPUTER AND PHYSICAL SCIENCE (chemistry, computer science, mathematics, and physics), EDUCATION (art education, business education, elementary education, foreign languages education, music education, science education, secondary education, and special education), HEALTH PROFESSIONS (health care administration), SOCIAL SCIENCE (economics, history, human services, philosophy, political science/government, psychology, religion, social science, and sociology). Physics, mathematics, and religion are the strongest academically. Business administration, teacher education, and biology have the largest enrollments.

Required: Students are required to take courses in written and oral communication, physical and life science, foreign language, history, social and political science, literature, philosophy, religion, health/wellness, computer science, the fine arts, and phys ed. A minimum 2.0 GPA and 127 credit hours, with 30 to 36 in the major, are required to graduate.

Special: There is a co-op nursing program, a 3-2 engineering program with Columbia and Washington Universities and Georgia Institute of Technology, and a 3-2 degree in occupational therapy with Boston and Washington Universities. Internships, study abroad in England, Spain, Russia, Ireland, Holland, and Germany, dual majors in all areas, and student-designed majors are possible. There are 12 national honor societies.

Faculty/Classroom: 56% of faculty are male; 44% are female. All teach undergraduates, and 25% do both. No introductory courses are taught by graduate students. The average class size in an introductory lecture is 25; in a laboratory is 24; and in a regular course is 23.

Admissions: 10% of a recent year, applicants were accepted. The ACT scores were 37% below 21, 23% between 21 and 23, 20% between 24 and 26, 10% between 27 and 28, and 10% above 28. 36% of the current freshmen were in the top fifth of their class; 64% were in the top two fifths. 18 freshmen graduated first in their class.

Requirements: The SAT or ACT is required. Applicants should graduate from an accredited secondary school with a minimum of 4 academic credits in English and 2 each in math, science, social studies, and a foreign language. Generally, placement in the upper half of the graduating class, a minimum GPA of 2.0, or a composite score of 20 on the enhanced ACT, is a minimal requirement for consideration for admission. Hastings College requires applicants to be in the upper 50% of their class. A GPA of 2.0 is required. AP and CLEP credits are accepted. Important factors in the admissions decision are advanced placement or honors courses, leadership record, and personality/intangible qualities.

Procedure: Freshmen are admitted to all sessions. Entrance exams should be taken before November. There is a rolling admissions plan. Applications should be filed by August 1 for fall entry; December 1 for winter entry; January 1 for spring entry; and May 15 for summer entry. The fall application fee was $20. Applications are accepted online.

Transfer: 48 transfer students enrolled in a recent year. Transfer students must have completed course work equivalent by description to that of Hastings and have earned grades of C or better. 30 of 127 credits required for the bachelor's degree must be completed at Hastings College.

Visiting: There are regularly scheduled orientations for prospective students, including academic department presentations, a financial aid session, a student panel discussion, a student guided tour, and an activities fair. There are guides for informal visits, visitors may sit in on classes, and stay overnight. To schedule a visit, contact the Admissions Office.

Financial Aid: In a recent year, 99% of all full-time freshmen and 99% of continuing full-time students received some form of financial aid. 78% of all full-time freshmen and 73% of continuing full-time students received need-based aid. 40% of undergraduate students work part-time. Average annual earnings from campus work are $1200. The average financial indebtedness of a recent graduate was $22,882. Hastings College is a member of CSS. The FAFSA is required. The deadline for filing freshman financial aid applications for fall entry is May 1.

International Students: There are 16 international students enrolled. The school actively recruits these students. They must take the TOEFL. International athletes should take a standardized test for athletic eligibility.

Graduates: In a recent year, 238 bachelor's degrees were awarded. The most popular majors were business administration (9%), psychology (9%), and biology (8%). 80 companies recruited on campus in 2010-2011. In an average class, 52% graduate in 4 years or less, 62% graduate in 5 years or less, and 63% graduate in 6 years or less. Of a recent year graduating class, 27% were enrolled in graduate school within 6 months of graduation, and 71% were employed.

Admissions Contact: Director of Admissions. A campus DVD is available. *www.hastings.edu*

MIDLAND UNIVERSITY — E-3

Fremont, NE 68025 (402) 941-6501
(800) 642-8382; (402)-941-6513

Full-time: n/av	**Faculty:** n/av
Part-time: n/av	**Ph.D.s:** n/av
Graduate: n/av	**Student/Faculty:** n/av
Year: 4-1-4, summer session	**Tuition:** $27,000
Application Deadline:	**Room & Board:** $7000
Freshman Class: n/av	
SAT or ACT: required	

COMPETITIVE

Midland University is a private liberal arts institution located just 30 minutes from Omaha, NE. Affiliated with the ELCA, Midland offers more than 40 programs of study, 27 varsity sports, a plethora of ARTS opportunities, and several student organizations. There are 2 graduate schools. In addition to regional accreditation, Midland has baccalaureate program accreditation with NLN. Computerized library services include interlibrary loans, database searching, Internet access, and Wi-Fi capability. Special learning facilities include an art gallery and planetarium. The 27-acre campus is in an urban area 30 minutes northwest of Omaha. Including any residence halls, there are 18 buildings.

Student Life: 75% of undergraduates are from Nebraska. Others are from 23 states, 10 foreign countries, and Canada. 94% are from public schools. 91% are White. 57% are Protestant; 32% Catholic. The average age of freshmen is 18; all undergraduates, 20. 16% do not continue beyond their first year; 56% remain to graduate.

Housing: 600 students can be accommodated in college housing, which includes single-sex and coed dorms, on-campus apartments, and off-campus apartments. On-campus housing is available on a first-come, first-served basis, and is available on a lottery system for upperclassmen. 30% of students commute. Alcohol is not permitted. All students may keep cars.

Activities: 20% of men belong to 4 local fraternities; 20% of women belong to 4 local sororities. There are 36 groups on campus, including art, band, cheerleading, choir, chorale, chorus, computers, drama, drill team, drum and bugle corps, ethnic, film, forensics, gay, honors, jazz band, literary magazine, musical theater, newspaper, orchestra, pep band, photography, political, professional, radio and TV, religious, social, social service, student government, and yearbook. Popular campus events include Greek Games, Snow Week, and Martin Luther King Day, Midland U's Got Talent, and Festival of the ARTS,.

Sports: There are 12 intercollegiate sports for men and 15 for women. Facilities include a phys ed center, an athletic practice field, an indoor pool, an indoor track, and a weight room. Students also have access to the second largest YMCA in the world at no cost to them.

Disabled Students: 90% of the campus is accessible.

Services: Counseling and information services are available, as is tutoring in every subject. There is remedial reading and writing.

Campus Safety and Security: Measures include 24-hour foot and vehicle patrol, emergency notification system, and security escort services. There are lighted pathways/sidewalks and controlled access to dorms/residences.

Programs of Study: Midland confers B.A., B.S., B.S.B.A. and B.S.N. degrees. Master's degrees are also awarded. Bachelor's degrees are awarded in BIOLOGICAL SCIENCE (biology/biological science), BUSINESS (accounting, business administration and management, business economics, management information systems, and marketing/retailing/merchandising), COMMUNICATIONS AND THE ARTS (advertising, communications, English, fine arts, journalism, and music), COMPUTER

AND PHYSICAL SCIENCE (chemistry, computer programming, computer science, and mathematics), EDUCATION (art education, business education, early childhood education, elementary education, middle school education, music education, science education, and secondary education), HEALTH PROFESSIONS (nursing, predentistry, and premedicine), SOCIAL SCIENCE (community services, economics, history, parks and recreation management, prelaw, psychology, religion, social science, and sociology). Business, journalism, and education are the strongest academically. Business, education, and nursing have the largest enrollments.

Required: To graduate, students need a total of 120 credit hours, with 33 of these in distribution requirements of the student's selection. 1 English, speech, and math courses are required, as well as 1 year of foreign language on the high school or college level. The total number of hours in the major varies from 34 to 48, and students must maintain a GPA of at least 2.0 overall and 2.25 in the major, with some departments requiring a higher minimum GPA.

Special: There is cross-registration with Dana College in Blair, internships in business, public relations, journalism, and art, study abroad in 3 countries, student-designed majors, work-study programs, and a 3-2 engineering degree with Washington University. Other options include dual majors, independent study, directed study, and the pass/no credit grading system. There are 2 national honor societies.

Faculty/Classroom: 60% of faculty are male; 40% are female. All teach undergraduates. No introductory courses are taught by graduate students. The average class size in a laboratory is 20 and in a regular course is 20.

Requirements: The SAT or ACT is required. Applicants should be graduates of an accredited secondary school. The GED is accepted. Recommended preparation includes 3 units of English, 2 each of math, and foreign language, and 10 of electives. An interview is recommended. AP and CLEP credits are accepted. Important factors in the admissions decision are leadership record, extracurricular activities record, and evidence of special talent.

Procedure: Freshmen are admitted fall and winter. Entrance exams should be taken during the fall of the senior year. There are deferred admissions and rolling admissions plans. Application deadlines are open. Notification is sent on a rolling basis. Applications are accepted online.

Transfer: 125 transfer students enrolled in 2012-2013. Applicants must be in good standing at their previous college and generally have a 2.0 minimum GPA. Grades of C or higher transfer for credit. 30 of 120 credits required for the bachelor's degree must be completed at Midland.

Visiting: There are regularly scheduled orientations for prospective students, Campus visits are scheduled on an individual basis and as much as possible include visits with faculty, students, and financial aid counselors. There are guides for informal visits, visitors may sit in on classes, and stay overnight. To schedule a visit, contact the Admissions Office.

Financial Aid: In 2013-2014, 98% of all full-time freshmen and 97% of continuing full-time students received some form of financial aid. Midland is a member of CSS. The FAFSA and FFS are required. Check with the school for current application deadlines.

International Students: The school actively recruits these students. They must take the TOEFL.

Admissions Contact: Eliza Ferzely, VP for Admissions & Enrollment Mgmnt. E-Mail: *Ferzely@MidlandU.edu* Web: *www.MidlandU.edu*

NEBRASKA METHODIST COLLEGE OF NURSING AND ALLIED HEALTH F-3

Omaha, NE 68114 (402) 354-7200
(800) 335-5510; (402) 354-7020

Full-time: 41 men, 401 women	**Faculty:** 46
Part-time: 25 men, 255 women	**Ph.D.s:** 31%
Graduate: 25 men, 175 women	**Student/Faculty:** 10 to 1
Year: semesters, summer session	**Tuition:** $15,840
Application Deadline: March 1	**Room & Board:** $7032
Freshman Class: n/av	
ACT: required	**SPECIAL**

Nebraska Methodist College, founded in 1891, is a private non-profit institution offering education opportunities in healthcare careers. The College enrolls more than 900 students in short term certificate programs, AS and BS degrees, as well as online master's degree programs. The library contains 13,600 volumes, 1,722 microform items, 500 audio/video tapes/CDs/DVDs, and subscribes to 640 periodicals including electronic. Computerized library services include interlibrary loans, database searching, Internet access, and Wi-Fi capability. Special learning facilities include a The 7-acre campus is in a suburban area in the center of Omaha. Including any residence halls, there are 19 buildings.

Student Life: 95% of undergraduates are from Nebraska. Others are from 32 states, and 2 foreign countries. 95% are from public schools. 83% are White. The average age of freshmen is 25; all undergraduates, 26. 14% do not continue beyond their first year; 72% remain to graduate.

Housing: 101 students can be accommodated in college housing, which includes coed on-campus apartments. On-campus housing is available on a first-come and first-served basis. Priority is given to out-of-town students. 89% of students commute. Alcohol is not permitted. All students may keep cars.

Activities: There are no fraternities; 5% of women belong to 1 local sororities. There are 12 groups on campus, including ethnic, gay, professional, religious, social, social service, and student government. Popular campus events include Honors Convocation, Pledging Ceremonies, Fall Carnival and Veteran's Day Activities.

Sports: There is no sports program at Nebraska Methodist College. Facilities include NMC has an on-campus fitness center available to students, faculty and staff.

Disabled Students: 80% of the campus is accessible. Facilities include elevators, special parking, specially equipped restrooms, and lowered drinking fountains.

Services: Counseling and information services are available, as is tutoring in most subjects. There is remedial math, reading, and writing. A reader service for the blind is available in the metropolitan area.

Campus Safety and Security: Measures include 24-hour foot and vehicle patrol, emergency notification system, self-defense education, and security escort services. There are emergency telephones, lighted pathways/sidewalks, and controlled access to dorms/residences.

Programs of Study: Nebraska Methodist College confers B.S., and B.S.N. degrees. Associate and master's degrees are also awarded. Bachelor's degrees are awarded in COMPUTER AND PHYSICAL SCIENCE (radiological technology), HEALTH PROFESSIONS (allied health, health care administration, nursing, and respiratory therapy). Nursing has the largest enrollments.

Required: All NMC undergraduate students are required to complete Arts & Science courses in our Educated Citizen Core Curriculum (45 credits for BS degrees; 21 credits for AS degrees). These courses are divided into four categories: communications; humanities; social sciences; natural and applied sciences. An NMC graduate is an educated citizen who is a competent practitioner and engaged citizen who responds productively to the complex dynamics of the world and who utilizes a diversity of disciplines and perspectives. Our goal as an institution is that graduates of NMC will be able to articulate and demonstrate growth in the following areas: as reflective individuals; as effective communicators; as change agents in an increasingly educated citizenry.

Special: NMC has a 15-month Accelerated BS in Nursing degree. There are 1 national honor societies and 2 departmental honors programs.

Faculty/Classroom: 9% of faculty are male; 91% are female. 89% teach undergraduates. No introductory courses are taught by graduate students. The average class size in a regular course is 19.

Admissions: 22% of the current freshmen were in the top fifth of their class; 35% were in the top two fifths. 1 freshman graduated first in the class.

Requirements: The ACT is required. Students must be graduates of an accredited secondary school with the number of academic credits required under Nebraska state law. The GED is accepted. Students should have completed 4 years of English and 2 years each of math (including algebra) and science (including biology and chemistry) and social science. An essay and an interview are required for admissions consideration. A GPA of 2.5 is required. AP and CLEP credits are accepted. Important factors in the admissions decision are personality/intangible qualities, advanced placement or honors courses, and leadership record.

Procedure: Freshmen are admitted fall and spring. Entrance exams should be taken as early as possible. There is a rolling admissions plan. Applications should be filed by March 1 for fall entry; October 1 for spring entry, along with a $25 fee. Notifications are sent April 15. Applications are accepted online.

Transfer: 135 transfer students enrolled in 2012-2013. Applicants must have a GPA above 2.5. Grades of C and above can be transferred for credit. An interview is required. 30 of 127 credits required for the bachelor's degree must be completed at Nebraska Methodist College.

Visiting: There are regularly scheduled orientations for prospective students. There are guides for informal visits and visitors may sit in on classes. To schedule a visit, contact the Admissions Office.

Financial Aid: In 2013-2014, 84% of all full-time freshmen and 94% of continuing full-time students received some form of financial aid. 81% of all full-time freshmen and 67% of continuing full-time students received need-based aid. The average freshman award was $10,113. Need-based scholarships or need-based grants averaged $6,878; need-based self-help aid (loans and jobs) averaged $3,791; and other non-need-based awards and non-need-based scholarships averaged $4,584. 68% of undergraduate students work part-time. Average annual earnings from campus work are $1900. The average financial indebtedness of the 2013 graduate was $41,742. The FAFSA and the college's own financial statement are required. The priority date for freshman financial aid applications for fall entry is April 1.

International Students: There are 3 international students enrolled. They must take the TOEFL with a minimum score of 550 on the paper-based TOEFL (PBT) or 80 on the Internet-based version (iBT). They must also take the ACT, scoring 20.

Graduates: From July 1, 2012 to June 30, 2013, 164 bachelor's degrees were awarded. The most popular majors were nursing (96%), healthcare administration/applied clinical operations (2%), and respiratory care (2%). In an average class, 67% graduate in 4 years or less, 76% graduate in 5 years or less, and 79% graduate in 6 years or less. Of the 2012 graduating class, 98% were employed within 6 months of graduation.

Admissions Contact: Admissions Representative E-Mail: *admissions@methodistcollege.edu* Web: *www.methodistcollege.edu*

NEBRASKA WESLEYAN UNIVERSITY E-3

Lincoln, NE 68504 **(402) 465-2144; (402) 465-2179**

Full-time: 690 men, 980 women	**Faculty:** 105; IIB, --$
Part-time: 78 men, 155 women	**Ph.D.s:** 89%
Graduate: 66 men, 179 women	**Student/Faculty:** 12 to 1
Year: semesters, summer session	**Tuition:** $23,974
Application Deadline: May 1	**Room & Board:** $6800
Freshman Class: n/av	
SAT: required	**ACT:** 25 **COMPETITIVE+**

Nebraska Wesleyan University, founded in 1887, is a private liberal arts institution affiliated with the United Methodist Church. There are 18 undergraduate schools and 3 graduate schools. In addition to regional accreditation, NWU has baccalaureate program accreditation with ACBSP, CSWE, NASM, NCATE, and NLN. The library contains 221,084 volumes, 4,897 microform items, 8,826 audio/video tapes/CDs/DVDs, and subscribes to 832 periodicals including electronic. Computerized library services include interlibrary loans, database searching, Internet access, and laptop Internet portals. Special learning facilities include a learning resource center, art gallery, planetarium, radio station, laboratory theater, sleep lab, greenhouse, herbarium, and nuclear magnetic resonance lab. The 50-acre campus is in a suburban area 50 miles west of Omaha. Including any residence halls, there are 31 buildings. The figures in the above capsule and in this profile are approximate.

Student Life: 88% of undergraduates are from Nebraska. Others are from 25 states, 14 foreign countries, and Canada. 93% are white. 36% are Protestant; 24% Catholic; 14% claim no religious affiliation. The average age of freshmen is 18; all undergraduates, 20. 18% do not continue beyond their first year; 70% remain to graduate.

Housing: 1055 students can be accommodated in college housing, which includes single-sex and coed dorms, on-campus apartments, and off-campus apartments. In addition, there are fraternity houses and sorority houses. On-campus housing is guaranteed for all 4 years. 65% of students live on campus; of those, 70% remain on campus on weekends. All students may keep cars.

Activities: 12% of men belong to 1 local and 3 national fraternities; 19% of women belong to 2 local and 2 national sororities. There are 80 groups on campus, including art, band, cheerleading, choir, chorus, computers, debate, drama, drill team, ethnic, forensics, gay, honors, international, jazz band, literary magazine, musical theater, newspaper, opera, orchestra, pep band, political, professional, religious, social, social service, student government, and yearbook. Popular campus events include international dinners, Mosaic Week (week emphasizing multicultural activities), and Visions.

Sports: There are 8 intercollegiate sports for men and 8 for women, and 8 intramural sports for men and 8 for women. Facilities include a recreation and fitness center, a field house and gym, a football/soccer stadium, a swimming pool, an outdoor track, football and baseball fields, tennis courts, racquetball courts, and volleyball courts.

Disabled Students: 92% of the campus is accessible. Facilities include wheelchair ramps, elevators, special parking, specially equipped restrooms, special class scheduling, lowered drinking fountains, lowered telephones, special housing. All academic programs can be moved or adapted as needed to accommodate students.

Services: Counseling and information services are available, as is tutoring in some subjects, sciences, social sciences, humanities, and math.

Campus Safety and Security: Measures include emergency notification system and security escort services. There are emergency telephones, lighted pathways/sidewalks, controlled access to dorms/residences, security service, night time foot patrol, and a uniformed police officer during the day.

Programs of Study: NWU confers B.A., B.S., B.F.A., B.M., and B.S.N. degrees. Master's degrees are also awarded. Bachelor's degrees are awarded in BIOLOGICAL SCIENCE (biochemistry, biology/biological science, and molecular biology), BUSINESS (accounting, business administration and management, international business management, and sports management), COMMUNICATIONS AND THE ARTS (applied music, art, communications, dramatic arts, English, French, German, language arts, music, Spanish, and studio art), COMPUTER AND PHYSICAL SCIENCE (chemistry, computer science, information sciences and systems, mathematics, and physics), EDUCATION (athletic training, elementary education, English education, middle school education, music education, physical education, science education, social science education, and special education), HEALTH PROFESSIONS (exercise science, health, and nursing), SOCIAL SCIENCE (biopsychology, economics, history, international studies, paralegal studies, philosophy, political science/government, psychology, religion, social work, sociology, and women's studies). Business administration, biology, and psychology have the largest enrollments.

Required: To graduate, students must complete approximately 42 to 48 hours of general education requirements, including 9 hours in First-year Experience, 8 in Developing Foundations courses, 7 in Scientific Inquiry, 6 in U.S. Culture and Society, 3 to 11 in Global Perspectives, 3 in Western Intellectual and Religious Traditions, and 3 in Fine Arts. At least 126 credit hours, including 30 in the major, must be completed with a minimum GPA of 2.0. A senior comprehensive is also needed, consisting of a comprehensive exam in the major discipline, a thesis or independent study, or an internship, presentation, or performance.

Special: NWU offers the Capitol Hill Internship Program; study abroad in 38 countries through the International Student Exchange Program and sister schools in Mexico, Japan, and Estonia; a global studies major; and many other interdisciplinary studies majors and minors. Internships are available in most departments and required in many. Natural sciences majors can complete summer research fellowships at labs, universities, and agencies nationwide and internationally. Other options include pass/fail options, dual majors, credit by exam, and a 3-2 engineering degree in conjunction with Washington and Columbia Universities. There are 25 national honor societies.

Faculty/Classroom: 45% of faculty are male; 55% are female. All teach undergraduates. No introductory courses are taught by graduate students. The average class size in an introductory lecture is 22; in a laboratory is 17; and in a regular course is 19.

Admissions: The ACT scores were 10% below 21, 27% between 21 and 23, 28% between 24 and 26, 18% between 27 and 28, and 17% above 28. 48% of the current freshmen were in the top fifth of their class; 79% were in the top two fifths. 22 freshmen graduated first in their class.

Requirements: The SAT or ACT is required. Freshmen must be graduates of an accredited secondary school or submit the GED. A campus visit is recommended. NWU requires applicants to be in the upper 50% of their class. AP and CLEP credits are accepted.

Procedure: Freshmen are admitted fall and spring. Entrance exams should be taken no later than December of the senior year. There are early decision and deferred admissions plans. Early decision applications should be filed by November 15; regular applications, by May 1 for fall entry; December 15 for spring entry; and April 15 for summer entry, along with a $20 fee. Notification of early decision is sent December 15; regular decision, January 15. Applications are accepted online.

Transfer: Applicants must be in good standing at their previous school and have a 2.0 GPA or higher. Grades of C- or better transfer for credit. 30 of 126 credits required for the bachelor's degree must be completed at NWU.

Visiting: There are regularly scheduled orientations for prospective students, consisting of a tour, classroom visits, and meetings with faculty, financial aid and admissions personnel, and current students. There are guides for informal visits, visitors may sit in on classes, and stay overnight. To schedule a visit, contact the Admissions Office.

Financial Aid: In a recent year, 99% of all full-time freshmen and 96% of continuing full-time students received some form of financial aid. 77% of all full-time freshmen and 71% of continuing full-time students received need-based aid. The average freshman award was $16,769. Need-based scholarships or need-based grants averaged $10,040 ($28,500 maximum); need-based self-help aid (loans and jobs) averaged $3,648 ($16,541 maximum); and other non-need-based awards and non-need-based scholarships averaged $2,690 ($19,625 maximum). Average annual earnings from campus work are $1318. The average financial indebtedness of the 2011 graduate was $19,636. The FAFSA is required. The priority date for freshman financial aid applications for fall entry is rolling. The deadline for filing freshman financial aid applications for fall entry is rolling.

International Students: There are 33 international students enrolled. The school actively recruits these students. They must take the TOEFL with a minimum score of 525 on the paper-based TOEFL (PBT) or 71 on the Internet-based version (iBT). The SAT or ACT is recommended.

Graduates: In a recent year, 403 bachelor's degrees were awarded. The most popular majors were business administration (23%), nursing (13%), and education (9%). In an average class, 1% graduate in 3 years or less, 52% graduate in 4 years or less, 64% graduate in 5 years or less, and 70% graduate in 6 years or less.

Admissions Contact: Director of Admissions. A campus DVD is available. E-Mail: *admissions@nebrwesleyan.edu* Web: *www.nebrwesleyan.edu*

PERU STATE COLLEGE F-3

Peru, NE 68421-0010
(402) 872-2221
(800) 742-4412; (402) 872-2296

Full-time: 430 men, 470 women
Part-time: 250 men, 335 women
Graduate: 50 men, 140 women
Year: semesters, summer session
Application Deadline: open
Freshman Class: n/av
SAT or ACT: required
Faculty: n/av
Ph.D.s: n/av
Student/Faculty: n/av
Tuition: $5871
Room & Board: $6420

NONCOMPETITIVE

Peru State College, established in 1867 and a part of the Nebraska State College System, is a public institution offering curricula in the arts, business, military studies, teacher preparation, and technical studies. There is 1 graduate school. The figures in the above capsule and in this profile are approximate. In addition to regional accreditation, Peru State College has baccalaureate program accreditation with NCATE. The library contains 102,432 volumes, 494,101 microform items, and 10,403 audio/video tapes/CDs/DVDs, and subscribes to 313 periodicals including electronic. Computerized library services include interlibrary loans and database searching. Special learning facilities include a learning resource center and art gallery. The 103-acre campus is in a rural area 60 miles south of Omaha. Including any residence halls, there are 21 buildings.

Student Life: 85% of undergraduates are from Nebraska. Others are from 12 states, 8 foreign countries, and Canada. 98% are from public schools. 87% are white. The average age of freshmen is 18; all undergraduates, 22. 28% do not continue beyond their first year; 35% remain to graduate.

Housing: 590 students can be accommodated in college housing, which includes single-sex dorms, on-campus apartments, and married student housing. In addition, there are substance-free facilities. On-campus housing is guaranteed for all 4 years. 65% of students live on campus; of those, 27% remain on campus on weekends. Alcohol is not permitted. All students may keep cars.

Activities: There are no fraternities or sororities. There are 27 groups on campus, including art, band, cheerleading, choir, chorus, computers, drama, ethnic, gay, honors, jazz band, pep band, photography, professional, religious, social, social service, student government, and yearbook. Popular campus events include Spring Break Trip.

Sports: There are 3 intercollegiate sports for men and 3 for women, and 7 intramural sports for men and 7 for women. Facilities include a playing field, an activity trail, a 2500-seat stadium, and a health and recreation complex containing basketball and tennis courts, an indoor track, and an Olympic-size swimming pool.

Disabled Students: 80% of the campus is accessible. Facilities include wheelchair ramps, elevators, special parking, specially equipped rest rooms, special class scheduling, lowered drinking fountains, and lowered telephones.

Services: Counseling and information services are available, as is tutoring in most subjects. There is a reader service for the blind, and remedial math, reading, and writing.

Campus Safety and Security: Measures include 24-hour foot and vehicle patrol and security escort services. There are lighted pathways/sidewalks.

Programs of Study: Peru State College confers B.A., B.S., and B.T. degrees. Master's degrees are also awarded. Bachelor's degrees are awarded in AGRICULTURE (wildlife management), BIOLOGICAL SCIENCE (biology/biological science), BUSINESS (accounting, business administration and management, marketing/retailing/merchandising, and sports management), COMMUNICATIONS AND THE ARTS (English, music, and music business management), COMPUTER AND PHYSICAL SCIENCE (computer management, computer programming, computer science, mathematics, nuclear technology, and physical sciences), EDUCATION (art education, elementary education, music education, physical education, science education, secondary education, and special education), ENGINEERING AND ENVIRONMENTAL DESIGN (preengineering), HEALTH PROFESSIONS (premedicine, prepharmacy, and preveterinary science), SOCIAL SCIENCE (history, prelaw, psychology, social science, and sociology).

Required: To graduate, students must complete 45 to 53 hours of general education requirements in literature, communications, fine arts, social and behavioral sciences, health and hygiene, computer science, and natural sciences, as well as a phys ed requirement. Teacher education majors must have a GPA of 2.5; all others must have a GPA of 2.0. The college requires 125 credit hours for graduation.

Special: The college offers cooperative programs, internships, B.A.-B.S. degrees, dual majors, work-study programs, and nondegree study. Credit may be granted for military experience. There are 2 national honor societies and a freshman honors program.

Faculty/Classroom: 79% of faculty are male; 21% are female. All teach undergraduates. No introductory courses are taught by graduate students. The average class size in an introductory lecture is 40; in a laboratory, 25; and in a regular course, 25.

Requirements: The SAT or ACT is required. Applicants who have graduated from an accredited Nebraska secondary school will be admitted; holders of the GED will be considered. Out-of-state applicants should have earned 16 Carnegie units. A GPA of 2.0 is required. AP and CLEP credits are accepted.

Procedure: Freshmen are admitted to all sessions. There are deferred admissions and rolling admissions plans. Application deadlines are open. Notification is sent on a rolling basis. Applications are accepted online.

Transfer: Transfer students must be in good standing with the previously attended institution. 30 of 125 credits required for the bachelor's degree must be completed at Peru State College.

Visiting: There are regularly scheduled orientations for prospective students. There are guides for informal visits; visitors may sit in on classes and stay overnight. To schedule a visit, contact the Admissions Office.

Financial Aid: The FAFSA is required. Check with the school for current application deadlines.

International Students: They must take the TOEFL.

Admissions Contact: Director of Admissions. E-Mail: *admissions@oakmail.peru.edu* Web: *www.peru.edu*

UNION COLLEGE E-3

Lincoln, NE 68506
(402) 486-2504
(800) 228-4600; (402) 486-2895

Full-time: 280 men, 380 women
Part-time: 50 men, 70 women
Graduate: 20 men, 50 women
Year: semesters, summer session
Application Deadline: open
Freshman Class: n/av
SAT or ACT: required
Faculty: 53
Ph.D.s: 52%
Student/Faculty: n/av
Tuition: $19,280
Room & Board: $6520

VERY COMPETITIVE

Union College, established in 1891, is a private liberal arts institution affiliated with the Seventh-day Adventist Church. The figures in the above capsule and in this profile are approximate. In addition to regional accreditation, Union has baccalaureate program accreditation with CSWE and NCATE. The library contains 161,728 volumes, 1938 microform items, 2066 audio/video tapes/CDs/DVDs, and subscribes to 604 periodicals including electronic. Computerized library services include interlibrary loans, database searching, Internet access, and laptop Internet portals. Special learning facilities include a learning resource center, art gallery, and state-run natural arboretum. The 26-acre campus is in a suburban area in southeast Lincoln. Including any residence halls, there are 11 buildings.

Student Life: 86% of undergraduates are from out of state, mostly the Midwest. Students are from 45 states, 21 foreign countries, and Canada. 30% are from public schools. 72% are white. The average age of freshmen is 18; all undergraduates, 22. 35% do not continue beyond their first year; 54% remain to graduate.

Housing: 642 students can be accommodated in college housing, which includes single-sex dorms, on-campus apartments, and married student housing. On-campus housing is guaranteed for the freshman year only. 52% of students commute. Alcohol is not permitted. All students may keep cars.

Activities: There are no fraternities or sororities. There are 18 groups on campus, including art, band, choir, chorale, chorus, computers, drama, ethnic, honors, international, literary magazine, newspaper, orchestra, photography, religious, social, student government, and yearbook.

Sports: There are 2 intercollegiate sports for men and 3 for women, and 8 intramural sports for men and 8 for women. Facilities include an Olympic-size indoor swimming pool, a weight room, tennis courts, and a sandlot volleyball court.

Disabled Students: 75% of the campus is accessible. Facilities include wheelchair ramps, elevators, special parking, specially equipped rest rooms, and lowered telephones.

Services: Counseling and information services are available, as is tutoring in most subjects. There is a reader service for the blind and remedial math, reading, and writing. Tutoring is available upon request.

Campus Safety and Security: Measures include 24-hour foot and vehicle patrol and security escort services. There are emergency telephones and lighted pathways/sidewalks.

Programs of Study: Union confers B.A., B.S., B.A.T., B.Ed., B.M., B.S.W., and B.T. degrees. Associate and master's degrees are also awarded. Bachelor's degrees are awarded in BIOLOGICAL SCIENCE (biology/biological science), BUSINESS (accounting, banking and finance, business administration and management, management science, marketing and distribution, and small business management), COMMUNICATIONS AND THE ARTS (communications, English, French, German, graphic design, journalism, literature, music, music performance, public relations, Spanish, and studio art), COMPUTER AND PHYSICAL SCIENCE (chemistry, computer science, mathematics, physics, and science), EDUCATION (art education, business education, computer education, elementary education, English education, mathematics education, music education, physical education, secondary education, and social science education), HEALTH PROFESSIONS (medical laboratory technology, nursing, and physician's assistant), SOCIAL SCIENCE (history, international public service, international studies, pastoral studies, physical fitness/movement, psychology, religion, religious education, social science, social work, and theological studies). Physician's assistant and physical science are the strongest academically. Nursing and international rescue and relief have the largest enrollments.

Required: Students must complete 128 semester hours, with fulfillment of a major and maintain a minimum GPA of 2.0. There are 56 hours of core classes, including those in art/fine arts, computer science, English, history, math, science, and philosophy/religion. Courses in phys ed are also required.

Special: Special academic programs include study abroad in 7 countries, co-op programs with 9 Adventist institutions abroad, and cross-registration with the University of Nebraska, Nebraska Wesleyan University, and Southeast Community College. Student-designed majors are available through the Personalized Bachelor's Degree Program. There are pass/fail options in electives for upperclassmen with a minimum cumulative GPA of 2.0. Some internships are available. There is a freshman honors program.

Faculty/Classroom: 55% of faculty are male; 45% are female. No introductory courses are taught by graduate students. The average class size in an introductory lecture is 21; in a regular course, 16.

Admissions: 32% of a recent year's freshmen were in the top fifth of their class; 69% were in the top two-fifths.

Requirements: The SAT or ACT is required. Freshmen with a high school GPA below 2.5 and/or an ACT composite score below the 20th percentile will be enrolled in the freshman development program. Applicants must have graduated from an accredited secondary school with 18 academic credits, including 3 units of English and 1 unit each of math, science, and history. For math and science programs, 2 units of algebra and 1 unit each of geometry and trigonometry are recommended. For majors in nursing, biology, chemistry, physics, or engineering, applicants should complete physics and chemistry courses. The GED is also accepted. An essay and interview are advised, and music students should audition. A GPA of 2.5 is required. AP and CLEP credits are accepted.

Procedure: Freshmen are admitted fall and spring. Entrance exams should be taken by fall of the senior year. There is a rolling admissions plan. Application deadlines are open.

Transfer: Transfer students must have a minimum GPA of 2.0. The ACT is required, and high school and college transcripts must be submitted. 30 of 128 credits required for the bachelor's degree must be completed at Union.

Visiting: There are regularly scheduled orientations for prospective students. There are guides for informal visits; visitors may sit in on classes and stay overnight. To schedule a visit, contact the Admissions Office Campus Hostess.

Financial Aid: The FAFSA is required. Check with the school for current application deadlines.

International Students: The school actively recruits these students. They must take the TOEFL with a minimum score of 550 on the paper-based TOEFL (PBT) or 80 on the Internet-based version (iBT). They must also take the ACT, scoring 18.

Graduates: In a recent year, 170 bachelor's degrees were awarded. The most popular majors were nursing (16%), business administration (15%), and elementary education (8%). 32 companies recruited on campus in a recent year. In an average class, 29% graduate in 4 years or less and 57% graduate in 6 years or less. Of a recent year's graduating class, 15% were enrolled in graduate school within 6 months of graduation and 80% were employed.

Admissions Contact: Huda McClelland, Director of Admissions. E-Mail: *ucenroll@ucollege.edu* Web: *www.ucollege.edu*

UNIVERSITY OF NEBRASKA SYSTEM

The University of Nebraska System, established in 1869, is a public system in Nebraska. It is governed by a board of regents and a central administration, whose chief administrator is the president. The primary mission and priorities of the system are teaching, research, and service. The total student enrollment of all 5 campuses is usually 49,500, with 4230 faculty members. Altogether there are 449 baccalaureate, 169 master's, and 51 doctoral programs offered in the University of Nebraska System. 4-year campuses are located in Kearney, Lincoln, and Omaha. Profiles of the 4-year campuses are included in this section.

UNIVERSITY OF NEBRASKA - LINCOLN E-3

Lincoln, NE 68588 (402) 472-2023
(800) 742-8800; (402) 472-0670

Full-time: 9697 men, 8405 women	**Faculty:** 1043; I, -$
Part-time: 741 men, 533 women	**Ph.D.s:** 94%
Graduate: 2454 men, 2615 women	**Student/Faculty:** 17 to 1
Year: semesters, summer session	**Tuition:** $8475 ($26,302)
Application Deadline: May 1	**Room & Board:** $10,032
Freshman Class: 10929 applied, 6999 accepted, 4420 enrolled	
SAT CR/M: 580/600 **ACT:** 25	**VERY COMPETITIVE**

The University of Nebraska–Lincoln is a public institution, founded in 1869 as a land-grant facility. UNL is an educational institution of international stature, listed by the Carnegie Foundation within the "Research Universities (very high research activity)" category. UNL is a land-grant university and a member of the Association of Public and Land-grant Universities (APLU). The university is accredited by the Higher Learning Commission of the North Central Association of Colleges and Schools. Programs are offered through the Colleges of Agricultural Sciences and Natural Resources, Architecture, Arts and Sciences, Business Administration, Education and Human Sciences, Engineering, Fine and Performing Arts, Journalism and Mass Communications, and Law; and the Exploratory and Pre-Professional Advising Center. Its 624-acre campus is located in Lincoln, 55 miles southwest of Omaha. There are 8 undergraduate schools and 1 graduate school. In addition to regional accreditation, UNL has baccalaureate program accreditation with AACSB, ABET, ACCE, ACEJMC, ADA, ASLA, FIDER, NAAB, NASAD, NASM, and TEAC. The 8 libraries contain 2.6 million volumes, 0 microform items, and 454,000 audio/video tapes/CDs/DVDs, and subscribe to 62,500 periodicals including electronic. Computerized library services include interlibrary loans, database searching, Internet access, and Wi-Fi capability. Special learning facilities include an art gallery, natural history museum, planetarium, radio station, TV station, Nebraska State Museum, International Quilt Study Center and Museum, Sheldon Museum of Art, Diocles Laser/Extreme Light Lab, Krueger Collection of Miniatures, Jackie Gaughan Multicultural Center, Larsen Tractor Test and Power Museum, Great Plains Art Museum, Behlen Observatory, Midwest Roadside Safety Facility. The 622-acre campus is in an urban area 55 miles southwest of Omaha. Including any residence halls, there are 237 buildings.

Student Life: 81% of undergraduates are from Nebraska. Others are from 50 states, 101 foreign countries, and Canada. 80% are White. The average age of freshmen is 18; all undergraduates, 21. 16% do not continue beyond their first year; 67% remain to graduate.

Housing: 9200 students can be accommodated in college housing, which includes single-sex and coed dorms, on-campus apartments, off-campus apartments, and married student housing. In addition, there are honors houses, special-interest houses, fraternity houses, sorority houses, floors for scholars, engineering, science, music, writing, design, advertising, education, agribusiness, and journalism. On-campus housing is guaranteed for the freshman year only, is available on a first-come, and first-served basis. 61% of students commute. Alcohol is not permitted. All students may keep cars.

Activities: 18% of men belong to 30 national fraternities; 22% of women belong to 20 national sororities. There are 629 groups on campus, including art, band, cheerleading, chess, choir, chorale, chorus, communications, computers, dance, debate, drama, drill team, environmental, ethnic, film, forensics, gay, honors, international, jazz band, literary magazine, marching band, musical theater, newspaper, opera, orchestra, pep band, photography, political, professional, radio and TV, religious, social, social service, student government, and symphony. Popular campus events include Homecoming, Big Red Welcome, The Big Event, Dance Marathon and football games.

Sports: There are 9 intercollegiate sports for men and 13 for women, and 80 intramural sports for men and 78 for women. Facilities include campus recreation center, athlietic conditioning and training center, football stadium, indoor and outdoor practice facilities, soccer fields, track, tennis courts, swimming pools, also arena and baseball/softball stadiums shared with city of Lincoln.

Disabled Students: All of the campus is accessible. Facilities include wheelchair ramps, elevators, special parking, specially equipped restrooms, special class scheduling, lowered drinking fountains, lowered telephones, special housing. assistance from Services for Students with Disabilities.

Services: There is a reader service for the blind.

Campus Safety and Security: Measures include 24-hour foot and vehicle patrol, emergency notification system, self-defense education, and security escort services. There are shuttle buses, emergency telephones, lighted pathways/sidewalks, and controlled access to dorms/residences.

Programs of Study: UNL confers B.A., B.S., B.F.A., B.J., B.M., B.M.Ed. and B.L.A. degrees. Master's and doctoral degrees are also awarded. Bachelor's degrees are awarded in AGRICULTURE (agricultural business management, agricultural communications, agricultural economics, agricultural mechanics, agriculture, agronomy, animal science, environmental studies, fish and game management, food technology for companion animals, great plains studies, horticulture, natural resource/environmental economics, natural resource management, plant science, ranch management, range/farm management, turfgrass and landscape management, and wildlife management), BIOLOGICAL SCIENCE (biochemistry, biology/biological science, entomology, forensic science, life science secondary school education, microbiology, and nutrition), BUSINESS (accounting, apparel and accessories marketing, apparel and textiles, banking and finance, business administration and management, business economics, entrepreneurial studies, fashion merchandising, finance, hospitality management services, human resources, insurance and risk management, international business management, investments and securities, management science, marketing management, marketing/retailing/merchandising, organizational leadership and management, and supply chain management), COMMUNICATIONS AND THE ARTS (advertising, apparel design, art history, art, art history and appreciation, broadcasting, classical languages, classics, communications, communication rhetoric/communication, dance, dramatic arts, English, English as a second/foreign language, film arts, film, television and digital media, fine arts, French, German, information technology, journalism, language arts, Latin, music, public relations, Russian, Spanish, speech/debate/rhetoric, studio art, theatre arts, and theater design), COMPUTER AND PHYSICAL SCIENCE (actuarial science, applied science, astronomy, atmospheric sciences and meteorology, chemistry, chemistry/adolescence education, computer science, earth science / adolescence education, geology, mathematics, physics, and physics with astrophysics option), EDUCATION (agricultural education, athletic training, business education, (Education) Childhood Education, computer education, drama education, early childhood education, education, education of the deaf and hearing impaired, elementary education, English education, foreign languages education, golf enterprise management, home economics education, journalism education, marketing and distribution education, mathematics education, music education, physical science secondary school education, science education, secondary education, social science education, special education, and teaching English as a second/foreign language (TESOL/TEFOL)), ENGINEERING AND ENVIRONMENTAL DESIGN (agricultural engineering, architectural engineering, architecture, bioengineering, chemical engineering, civil engineering, computer engineering, construction engineering, construction management, electrical/electronics engineering, environmental science, interior design, landscape architecture, landscape architecture/design, and mechanical engineering), HEALTH PROFESSIONS (exercise science, health science, predentistry, premedicine, prepharmacy, speech pathology/audiology, and veterinary science), SOCIAL SCIENCE (anthropology, architectural studies, child care/child and family studies, classical/ancient civilization, culinary arts, dietetics, early childhood studies, economics, ethnic studies, European studies, family/consumer studies, food production/management/services, food science, geography, (Social Science) Global Studies, history, interdisciplinary studies, international studies, Latin American studies, liberal arts/general studies, medieval studies, parks and recreation management, philosophy, political science/government, prelaw, psychology, religious studies, sociology, textiles and clothing, water resources, and women and gender studies). Agriculture, biochemistry, biological sciences, business administration, early childhood development, economics, natural resource and environmental economics, engineering , psychology and water science are the strongest academically. Psychology, business administration, and finance have the largest enrollments.

Required: All students must complete the general education requirements for the Achievement-Centered Education (ACE) program. The program is based on a set of four institutional objectives and 10 student learning outcomes. Students complete the equivalent of 3 credit hours for each of the ten student learning outcomes. A minimum GPA of 2.0 is required. Each college and major has its own requirements; few graduation requirements apply to all students.

Special: There is cross-registration with many schools, and co-op programs are available in the Colleges of Engineering and Agriculture. Through membership in the International Student Exchange Program, the university can place students in more than 90 universities around the world. Internship opportunities abound, as do work-study programs and undergraduate research opportunities. Accelerated degree programs, a Washington semester, B.A.-B.S. degrees, dual majors, combined preprofessional programs, student-designed majors, credit by exam, nondegree study, and pass/fail options are also available. There are 37 national honor societies, including Phi Beta Kappa, a freshman honors program, and 42 departmental honors programs.

Faculty/Classroom: 70% of faculty are male; 30% are female. 95% teach undergraduates, 90% do research, and 86% do both. No introductory courses are taught by graduate students. The average class size in an introductory lecture is 38; in a laboratory is 21; and in a regular course is 27.

Admissions: 64% of the 2013-2014 applicants were accepted. The SAT scores for the 2013-2014 freshman class were: Critical Reading--26% below 500, 30% between 500 and 599, 28% between 600 and 699, and 17% between 700 and 800; Math--16% below 500, 33% between 500 and 599, 36% between 600 and 699, and 15% between 700 and 800. The ACT scores were 13% below 21, 23% between 21 and 23, 26% between 24 and 26, 13% between 27 and 28, and 25% above 28. 44% of the current freshmen were in the top fifth of their class; 73% were in the top two fifths. 300 freshmen graduated first in their class.

Requirements: The SAT or ACT is recommended. Applicants must be graduates of an accredited secondary school. The GED is accepted. Students must have completed 4 years each of English and math, 3 years of science and social studies, and 2 years of a foreign language. Applicants must have a minimum composite ACT score of 20, or a combined SAT score of 950, or rank in the top 50% of their high school class. UNL requires applicants to be in the upper 50% of their class. AP and CLEP credits are accepted. Important factors in the admissions decision are advanced placement or honors courses, recommendations by school officials, and evidence of special talent.

Procedure: Freshmen are admitted to all sessions. Entrance exams should be taken in April of the junior year. There is a rolling admissions plan. Applications should be filed by May 1 for fall entry; December 1 for spring entry; and May 1 for summer entry, along with a $45 fee. Applications are accepted online.

Transfer: 995 transfer students enrolled in 2012-2013. Transfer students must have a 2.0 GPA for both the cumulative average of all post-secondary facilities attended and for the most recent term of attendance. In certain majors, a higher GPA and/or extra course work may be required.

Visiting: There are regularly scheduled orientations for prospective students, a campus tour, an information session about academics, scholarships and financial aid, living and dining options, how to get involved, Greek Life and career connections for your future. There are guides for informal visits, visitors may sit in on classes, and stay overnight. To schedule a visit, contact the Admissions Office at (402) 472-2023.

Financial Aid: In 2013-2014, 87% of all full-time freshmen and 69% of continuing full-time students received some form of financial aid. 55% of all full-time freshmen and 43% of continuing full-time students received need-based aid. The average freshman award was $14,319. Need-based scholarships or need-based grants averaged $7,651; need-based self-help aid (loans and jobs) averaged $3,875; non-need-based athletic scholarships averaged $10,242; and other non-need-based awards and non-need-based scholarships averaged $5,589. 100% of undergraduate students work part-time. Average annual earnings from campus work are $4447. The average financial indebtedness of the 2013 graduate was $21,802. The FAFSA is required. The priority date for freshman financial aid applications for fall entry is April 1.

International Students: There are 1095 international students enrolled. The school actively recruits these students.

Graduates: From July 1, 2012 to June 30, 2013, 3716 bachelor's degrees were awarded. The most popular majors were business marketing (22%), engineering (10%), and education (9%). 153 companies recruited on campus in 2012-2013. In an average class, 32% graduate in 4 years or less, 61% graduate in 5 years or less, and 67% graduate in 6 years or less. Of the 2012 graduating class, 26% were enrolled in graduate school within 6 months of graduation, and 72% were employed.

Admissions Contact: Amber Williams, Associate Dean of Enrollment Management. E-Mail: *admissions@unl.edu* Web: *http:/admissions.unl.edu*

UNIVERSITY OF NEBRASKA AT KEARNEY D-3

Kearney, NE 68849 (308) 865-8526
(800) KEARNEY; (308) 865-8987

Full-time: 2339 men, 3163 women	**Faculty:** 305; IIA, --$
Part-time: n/av	**Ph.D.s:** 76%
Graduate: 499 men, 1051 women	**Student/Faculty:** 16 to 1
Year: semesters, summer session	**Tuition:** $6521 ($12,348)
Application Deadline: open	**Room & Board:** $8334
Freshman Class: 2815 applied, 2402 accepted, 1136 enrolled	
SAT: required **ACT:** 23	**LESS COMPETITIVE**

The University of Nebraska at Kearney, founded in 1905, is Nebraska's premier, undergraduate residential, medium sized, public university. There are 4 undergraduate schools and 1 graduate school. In addition to regional accreditation, UNK has baccalaureate program accreditation with AACSB, ADA, CSWE, NASM, NCATE, and NLN. The library contains 287,000 volumes, 985,000 microform items, 1,300 audio/video tapes/CDs/DVDs, and subscribes to 1,650 periodicals including electronic. Computerized library services include interlibrary loans, database searching, Internet access, and Wi-Fi capability. Special learning facilities include an art gallery, planetarium, radio station, Learning Commons (tutoring & writing center) and Museum of Nebraska Art. The 514-acre campus is in a rural area UNK is located in the center of Nebraska right along Interstate 80. Including any residence halls, there are 48 buildings.

Student Life: 83% of undergraduates are from Nebraska. Others are from

50 states, 56 foreign countries, and Canada. 79% are White. The average age of freshmen is 20; all undergraduates, 21. 20% do not continue beyond their first year; 56% remain to graduate.

Housing: 2000 students can be accommodated in college housing, which includes single-sex and coed dorms, off-campus apartments, and married student housing. In addition, there are honors houses, special-interest houses, fraternity houses, and sorority houses. On-campus housing is guaranteed for the freshman year only, is available on a first-come, and first-served basis. 60% of students commute. Alcohol is not permitted. All students may keep cars.

Activities: 10% of men belong to 4 national fraternities; 10% of women belong to 4 national sororities. There are 180 groups on campus, including art, band, cheerleading, choir, chorale, chorus, computers, dance, debate, drama, drill team, ethnic, forensics, gay, honors, international, jazz band, literary magazine, marching band, musical theater, newspaper, opera, orchestra, pep band, photography, political, professional, radio and TV, religious, social, social service, student government, and symphony. Popular campus events include Welcome Week, Bike Bowl, and the Midwest Conference on World Affairs.

Sports: There are 8 intercollegiate sports for men and 9 for women, and 14 intramural sports for men and 14 for women. Facilities include a field, tennis courts, and a health and sports facility.

Disabled Students: Facilities include wheelchair ramps, elevators, special parking, specially equipped restrooms, lowered drinking fountains, and special housing.

Services: Counseling and information services are available, as is tutoring in most subjects. There is a reader service for the blind, and remedial math and writing.

Campus Safety and Security: Measures include 24-hour foot and vehicle patrol, emergency notification system, self-defense education, and security escort services. There are emergency telephones, lighted pathways/sidewalks, and controlled access to dorms/residences.

Programs of Study: UNK confers B.A., B.S., B.A.Ed., B.F.A., B.G.S. and B.S.Ed. degrees. Master's degrees are also awarded. Bachelor's degrees are awarded in BIOLOGICAL SCIENCE (biology/biological science), BUSINESS (accounting, banking and finance, business administration and management, business economics, marketing/retailing/merchandising, and personnel management), COMMUNICATIONS AND THE ARTS (advertising, broadcasting, communications, dramatic arts, English, fine arts, French, German, journalism, music, Spanish, speech/debate/rhetoric, and telecommunications), COMPUTER AND PHYSICAL SCIENCE (chemistry, computer programming, computer science, information sciences and systems, mathematics, physics, and statistics), EDUCATION (art education, business education, early childhood education, elementary education, foreign languages education, health education, middle school education, music education, physical education, science education, secondary education, special education, and teaching English as a second/foreign language (TESOL/TEFOL)), ENGINEERING AND ENVIRONMENTAL DESIGN (aviation administration/management, construction management, industrial administration/management, and interior design), HEALTH PROFESSIONS (nursing, predentistry, and premedicine), SOCIAL SCIENCE (criminal justice, economics, family/consumer studies, geography, history, human development, international studies, political science/government, prelaw, psychology, social science, social work, and sociology). Education, business, communication, and psychology are the strongest academically. Industrial distribution, elementary education, and special education have the largest enrollments.

Required: To graduate, all students must complete courses in humanities, communications, civilization, math, natural sciences, and social and behavioral sciences. A minimum of 120 credit hours is required, with approximately 60 in the major. Students must maintain a GPA of 2.0 or higher.

Special: Special arrangements include internships, work-study programs, study at other U.S. colleges and universities under the auspices of the National Student Exchange Program, and study abroad in more than 40 countries through the International Student Exchange Program. Cooperative programs in some health science majors and a credit/no credit grading option are available. There are a freshman honors program.

Faculty/Classroom: 49% of faculty are male; 51% are female. 99% teach undergraduates. No introductory courses are taught by graduate students. The average class size in an introductory lecture is 32; in a laboratory is 25; and in a regular course is 20.

Admissions: 85% of the 2013-2014 applicants were accepted. The SAT scores for the 2013-2014 freshman class were: Critical Reading--37% below 500, 42% between 500 and 599, 16% between 600 and 699, and 5% between 700 and 800; Math--11% below 500, 42% between 500 and 599, 42% between 600 and 699, and 5% between 700 and 800. The ACT scores were 30% below 21, 29% between 21 and 23, 22% between 24 and 26, 9% between 27 and 28, and 10% above 28. 30% of the current freshmen were in the top fifth of their class; 47% were in the top two fifths.

Requirements: The SAT or ACT is required. Applicants must be graduates of an accredited secondary school. The GED is accepted. They should have completed 4 years of high school English, 3 years each of math, science, and social studies, 2 years of the same foreign language, and 1 year of an academic elective. They should score 20 or above on the ACT or 950 on the SAT (critical reading and math) or be in the top half of their graduating class. UNK requires applicants to be in the upper 50% of their class. AP and CLEP credits are accepted. Important factors in the admissions decision are recommendations by school officials, evidence of special talent, and advanced placement or honors courses.

Procedure: Freshmen are admitted fall, spring, and summer. Entrance exams should be taken at the end of the junior year or beginning of the senior year. There is a rolling admissions plan. Application deadlines are open. Application fee is $45. Notification is sent on a rolling basis. Applications are accepted online.

Transfer: 315 transfer students enrolled in 2012-2013. Transfer students must supply transcripts from previous institutions. If the GPA from the previous school is lower than 2.0, students will be evaluated by the Admissions Director. Transfers must show proof of honorable dismissal from the last institution attended. Grades of C and above transfer for credit. 32 of 120 credits required for the bachelor's degree must be completed at UNK.

Visiting: There are regularly scheduled orientations for prospective students, including registration for classes and campus orientation. There are guides for informal visits, visitors may sit in on classes, and stay overnight. To schedule a visit, contact the Admissions Office at BeALoper@unk.edu.

Financial Aid: In 2013-2014, 87% of all full-time freshmen and 90% of continuing full-time students received some form of financial aid. 60% of all full-time freshmen and 65% of continuing full-time students received need-based aid. 80% of undergraduate students work part-time. The FAFSA and the college's own financial statement are required. Check with the school for current application deadlines.

International Students: There are 401 international students enrolled. The school actively recruits these students. They must take the TOEFL with a minimum score of 500 on the paper-based TOEFL (PBT) or 61 on the Internet-based version (iBT).

Graduates: From July 1, 2012 to June 30, 2013, 881 bachelor's degrees were awarded. The most popular majors were business (23%), education (18%), and visual and performing arts (6%). In an average class, 1% graduate in 3 years or less, 22% graduate in 4 years or less, 48% graduate in 5 years or less, and 56% graduate in 6 years or less.

Admissions Contact: Dusty Newton, Director of Admissions. E-Mail: *BeALoper@unk.edu* Web: *www.unk.edu*

UNIVERSITY OF NEBRASKA AT OMAHA F-3

Omaha, NE 68182 **(402) 554-2393; (402) 554-3472**

Full-time: 4000 men, 4730 women	**Faculty:** n/av; IIA, av$
Part-time: 1300 men, 1500 women	**Ph.D.s:** n/av
Graduate: 1090 men, 1720 women	**Student/Faculty:** n/av
Year: semesters, summer session	**Tuition:** $6780 ($16,390)
Application Deadline: see profile	**Room & Board:** $8640
Freshman Class: n/av	
SAT or ACT: required	

COMPETITIVE

The University of Nebraska at Omaha, established in 1908, is a public institution and part of the University of Nebraska system. There are 9 undergraduate schools and 1 graduate school. The figures in the above capsule and in this profile are approximate. In addition to regional accreditation, UNO has baccalaureate program accreditation with AACSB, ABET, CSWE, NASAD, NASM, and NCATE. The library contains 700,000 volumes, 2 million microform items, 7000 audio/video tapes/CDs/DVDs, and subscribes to 3000 periodicals including electronic. Computerized library services include interlibrary loans, database searching, and Internet access. Special learning facilities include an art gallery, radio station, and TV station. The 158-acre campus is in a suburban area within the Omaha city limits. Including any residence halls, there are 46 buildings.

Student Life: 93% of undergraduates are from Nebraska. Others are from 34 states, 78 foreign countries, and Canada. 86% are from public schools. 82% are white. The average age of freshmen is 18; all undergraduates, 23. 29% do not continue beyond their first year; 39% remain to graduate.

Housing: 1212 students can be accommodated in college housing, which includes single-sex and coed dorms and on-campus apartments. In addition, there are honors houses. On-campus housing is available on a first-come, first-served basis. 91% of students commute. Alcohol is not permitted. All students may keep cars.

Activities: 2% of men belong to 7 national fraternities; 2% of women belong to 9 national sororities. There are 112 groups on campus, including band, cheerleading, chess, choir, chorale, chorus, dance, drama, drill team, ethnic, film, gay, honors, international, jazz band, literary magazine, marching band, musical theater, newspaper, opera, orchestra, pep band, political, professional, radio and TV, religious, social, social service, student government, and symphony. Popular campus events include Celebrate UNO, International Week, and Black History Month.

Sports: There are 5 intercollegiate sports for men and 8 for women, and

16 intramural sports for men and 16 for women. Facilities include a football field, a field house, and a recreation building housing basketball and volleyball courts, weight rooms, and a swimming pool.

Disabled Students: 99% of the campus is accessible. Facilities include wheelchair ramps, elevators, special parking, specially equipped rest rooms, special class scheduling, lowered drinking fountains, and lowered telephones.

Services: Counseling and information services are available, as is tutoring in some subjects, including math and psychology. There is a reader service for the blind.

Campus Safety and Security: Measures include 24-hour foot and vehicle patrol, self-defense education, and security escort services. There are shuttle buses, emergency telephones, and lighted pathways/sidewalks.

Programs of Study: UNO confers B.A., B.S., B.A.A.H., B.A.S.A., B.A.T.H., B.F.A., B.I.S., B.G.S., B.M., B.S.B.A., B.S.C.N., B.S.C.S., B.S.E.D., B.S.P.A., and B.S.S.W. degrees. Master's and doctoral degrees are also awarded. Bachelor's degrees are awarded in AGRICULTURE (environmental studies), BIOLOGICAL SCIENCE (bioinformatics, biology/biological science, and biotechnology), BUSINESS (accounting, banking and finance, business communications, management information systems, management science, marketing/retailing/merchandising, real estate, and recreation and leisure services), COMMUNICATIONS AND THE ARTS (art, art history and appreciation, broadcasting, communications, creative writing, dramatic arts, English, fine arts, French, German, journalism, music, Spanish, and speech/debate/rhetoric), COMPUTER AND PHYSICAL SCIENCE (chemistry, computer science, geology, information sciences and systems, mathematics, and physics), EDUCATION (elementary education, library science, physical education, and secondary education), ENGINEERING AND ENVIRONMENTAL DESIGN (aviation administration/management and engineering physics), HEALTH PROFESSIONS (community health work and health care administration), SOCIAL SCIENCE (African American studies, criminal justice, economics, geography, history, interdisciplinary studies, international studies, Latin American studies, liberal arts/general studies, philosophy, political science/government, psychology, public administration, social work, sociology, and women's studies). Elementary education, criminal justice, and marketing management have the largest enrollments.

Required: To graduate, students must complete 30 hours of distribution requirements in natural and physical sciences, humanities and fine arts, and social and behavioral sciences; 15 hours in fundamental academic skills in English writing, math, and public speaking; and 6 hours in cultural diversity.

Special: UNO offers internships for business students, cooperative programs, and credit by exam. Students may study abroad in various European countries. There are 15 national honor societies, a freshman honors program, and 10 departmental honors programs.

Faculty/Classroom: 59% of faculty are male; 41% are female. 97% teach undergraduates. Graduate students teach 4% of introductory courses. The average class size in an introductory lecture is 38; in a laboratory, 12; and in a regular course, 21.

Requirements: The SAT or ACT is required. Students must be graduates of an accredited secondary school. The GED is accepted. Students must have completed 4 units of English and 2 each of math, social sciences, and sciences. UNOmaha requires applicants to be in the upper 50% of their class. A GPA of 2.0 is required. AP and CLEP credits are accepted. Important factors in the admissions decision are recommendations by school officials, evidence of special talent, and personality/intangible qualities.

Procedure: Freshmen are admitted fall, spring, and summer. Entrance exams should be taken by the senior year. There is a rolling admissions plan. Check with the school for current application deadlines. Application fee is $45. Applications are accepted online.

Transfer: Applicants must present evidence of good standing at the last institution they attended. Grades of C or better transfer for credit. A minimum GPA of 2.0 is required. 30 of 125 credits required for the bachelor's degree must be completed at UNO.

Visiting: There are regularly scheduled orientations for prospective students. There are guides for informal visits, and visitors may sit in on classes. To schedule a visit, contact the Office of Orientation.

Financial Aid: The FAFSA is required. Check with the school for current application deadlines.

International Students: The school actively recruits these students. They must take the TOEFL.

Admissions Contact: Jolene Adams, Director of Admissions. E-Mail: *unoadm@unomaha.edu* Web: *www.unomaha.edu*

WAYNE STATE COLLEGE

E-2

Wayne, NE 68787

(402) 375-7000
(800) 228-9972; (402) 375-7204

Full-time: 1173 men, 1562 women	**Faculty:** n/av; IIA, --$
Part-time: 104 men, 152 women	**Ph.D.s:** 81%
Graduate: 231 men, 284 women	**Student/Faculty:** 20 to 1
Year: semesters, summer session	**Tuition:** $5574 ($9774)
Application Deadline: open	**Room & Board:** $6190

Freshman Class: 2070 applied, 2070 accepted, 691 enrolled
ACT: 21

NONCOMPETITIVE

Wayne State College, founded in 1910, is a public liberal arts institution. There are 4 undergraduate schools and 2 graduate schools. In addition to regional accreditation, Wayne State has baccalaureate program accreditation with NASAD, NASM, and NCATE. The library contains 348,951 volumes, 620,128 microform items, 19,820 audio/video tapes/CDs/DVDs, and subscribes to 45,026 periodicals including electronic. Computerized library services include interlibrary loans, database searching, Internet access, and Wi-Fi capability. Special learning facilities include an art gallery, natural history museum, planetarium, radio station, TV station, an arboretum. The 128-acre campus is in a rural area 45 miles southwest of Sioux City. Including any residence halls, there are 25 buildings.

Student Life: 87% of undergraduates are from Nebraska. Others are from 27 states, 18 foreign countries, and Canada. 79% are White. The average age of freshmen is 18; all undergraduates, 21. 38% do not continue beyond their first year; 53% remain to graduate.

Housing: 1571 students can be accommodated in college housing, which includes coed dorms. On-campus housing is guaranteed for the freshman year only, is available on a first-come, and first-served basis. 54% of students commute. Alcohol is not permitted. All students may keep cars.

Activities: There are 100 groups on campus, including art, band, cheerleading, chess, choir, chorale, chorus, computers, dance, drama, drill team, ethnic, forensics, gay, honors, international, jazz band, marching band, musical theater, newspaper, orchestra, pep band, political, professional, radio and TV, religious, social, student government, and symphony. Popular campus events include International Dinner, Elizabethan Dinners and Greek Olympics.

Sports: There are 6 intercollegiate sports for men and 7 for women, and 37 intramural sports for men and 37 for women. Facilities include tennis courts; softball, flag football, and soccer fields; a gym; a 33,000-square-foot recreation center, which has an indoor track, weight room, pool, and handball, volleyball, basketball, and tennis courts; a football stadium; an outdoor track; and a baseball/softball complex.

Disabled Students: Facilities include wheelchair ramps, elevators, special parking, specially equipped restrooms, special class scheduling, lowered drinking fountains, lowered telephones, special housing, and a pool equipped with special steps.

Services: Counseling and information services are available, as is tutoring in most subjects. There is a reader service for the blind.

Campus Safety and Security: Measures include 24-hour foot and vehicle patrol, emergency notification system, and security escort services. There are emergency telephones and lighted pathways/sidewalks.

Programs of Study: Wayne State confers B.A., and B.S. degrees. Master's degrees are also awarded. Bachelor's degrees are awarded in BIOLOGICAL SCIENCE (biology/biological science and life science), BUSINESS (business administration and management and sports management), COMMUNICATIONS AND THE ARTS (art, communications, dramatic arts, English, graphic design, modern language, music, Spanish, and speech/debate/rhetoric), COMPUTER AND PHYSICAL SCIENCE (chemistry, computer science, and mathematics), EDUCATION (elementary education, health education, home economics education, industrial arts education, middle school education, music education, science education, and special education), ENGINEERING AND ENVIRONMENTAL DESIGN (technological management), HEALTH PROFESSIONS (exercise science), SOCIAL SCIENCE (counseling/psychology, criminal justice, early childhood studies, family/consumer studies, geography, history, interdisciplinary studies, political science/government, psychology, social science, and sociology). Business, elementary education, and criminal justice have the largest enrollments.

Required: Students must complete a specified 44-credit general education curriculum. A minimum of 120 credit hours is required for graduation, of which at least 40 must be in upper-level courses. Students must maintain at least a 2.0 overall GPA for nonteaching majors and a 2.5 overall GPA for teaching majors.

Special: Pass/fail options, internships, study abroad, credit by exam, any combination of dual majors, a B.A.-B.S. degree in certain instances, and some student-designed majors. There is also a Regional Health Opportunities Program. There are a freshman honors program and 14 departmental honors programs.

Faculty/Classroom: 55% of faculty are male; 45% are female. No introductory courses are taught by graduate students.

Admissions: 100% of the 2013-2014 applicants were accepted. The

ACT scores were 45% below 21, 26% between 21 and 23, 15% between 24 and 26, 8% between 27 and 28, and 6% above 28.

Requirements: Applicants must be graduates of an accredited secondary school. The GED is accepted. Entering freshmen should have completed 18 credits, with a recommended 4 units of English, 3 each of math and social studies, and 2 each of science, foreign language, computer science, and visual/performing arts. AP and CLEP credits are accepted.

Procedure: Freshmen are admitted to all sessions. Entrance exams should be taken in the spring of the junior year or fall of the senior year. There are deferred admissions and rolling admissions plans. Application deadlines are open. Applications are accepted online.

Transfer: 184 transfer students enrolled in 2012-2013. Transfer students must have a minimum GPA of 2.0. Grades of C and above transfer for credit. 30 of 120 credits required for the bachelor's degree must be completed at Wayne State.

Visiting: There are regularly scheduled orientations for prospective students. There are guides for informal visits, visitors may sit in on classes, and stay overnight. To schedule a visit, contact the Admissions Office.

Financial Aid: The FAFSA is required. The priority date for freshman financial aid applications for fall entry is April 1.

International Students: They must take the TOEFL with a minimum score of 550 on the paper-based TOEFL (PBT).

Graduates: From July 1, 2012 to June 30, 2013, 522 bachelor's degrees were awarded. The most popular majors were education (28%), business (15%), and psychology (9%). In an average class, 27% graduate in 4 years or less, 48% graduate in 5 years or less, and 53% graduate in 6 years or less.

Admissions Contact: Director of Admissions. E-Mail: *admit1@wsc.edu* Web: *www.wsc.edu*

YORK COLLEGE — E-3

York, NE 68467-2699 — **(402) 363-5627; (800) 950-YORK; (402) 363-5623**

Full-time: 180 men, 190 women
Part-time: 25 men, 20 women
Graduate: n/av
Year: semesters, summer session
Application Deadline: see profile
Freshman Class: n/av
ACT: recommended
Faculty: n/av
Ph.D.s: n/av
Student/Faculty: n/av
Tuition: $15,300
Room & Board: $5850

COMPETITIVE

York College, founded in 1890, is an independent undergraduate college affiliated with the Churches of Christ. The figures in the above capsule and in this profile are approximate. In addition to regional accreditation, York has baccalaureate program accreditation with NCATE. The library contains 126,086 volumes, 21,578 microform items, 7017 audio/video tapes/CDs/DVDs, and subscribes to 301 periodicals including electronic. Computerized library services include interlibrary loans and database searching. The 40-acre campus is in a small town 45 miles west of Lincoln. Including any residence halls, there are 18 buildings.

Student Life: 67% of undergraduates are from out of state, mostly the Midwest. Students are from 30 states, 5 foreign countries, and Canada. 90% are from public schools. 87% are white. 22% are Protestant. The average age of freshmen is 18; all undergraduates, 21. 15% do not continue beyond their first year; 50% remain to graduate.

Housing: 472 students can be accommodated in college housing, which includes single-sex dorms and on-campus apartments. On-campus housing is guaranteed for all 4 years. 72% of students live on campus; of those, 85% remain on campus on weekends. Alcohol is not permitted. All students may keep cars.

Activities: 57% of men belong to 4 local fraternities; 62% of women belong to 4 local sororities. There are 25 groups on campus, including art, choir, chorus, computers, drama, honors, international, literary magazine, musical theater, newspaper, photography, political, professional, religious, social, social service, student government, and yearbook. Popular campus events include High School Days, Fall Musical, and All School Banquet.

Sports: There are 4 intercollegiate sports for men and 3 for women, and 6 intramural sports for men and 6 for women. Facilities include basketball and volleyball courts, a gym, soccer, baseball, and intramural fields, a weight room, and an indoor track.

Disabled Students: 50% of the campus is accessible. Facilities include wheelchair ramps, elevators, special parking, specially equipped rest rooms, lowered drinking fountains, lowered telephones, and special housing.

Services: Counseling and information services are available, as is tutoring in most subjects. There is remedial math, reading, and writing, and a peer tutoring program.

Campus Safety and Security: Measures include self-defense education. There are emergency telephones, lighted pathways/sidewalks, and an evening/night foot patrol.

Programs of Study: York confers B.A., B.S., B.B.A., and B.Mus. degrees. Associate degrees are also awarded. Bachelor's degrees are awarded in BIOLOGICAL SCIENCE (biology/biological science), BUSINESS (accounting, business administration and management, and human resources), COMMUNICATIONS AND THE ARTS (communications, English, music performance, and voice), COMPUTER AND PHYSICAL SCIENCE (natural sciences), EDUCATION (drama education, education, elementary education, English education, middle school education, music education, psychology education, science education, secondary education, social science education, and special education), SOCIAL SCIENCE (biblical studies, biopsychology, history, human services, liberal arts/general studies, psychology, and youth ministry). Education, natural science, and psychology are the strongest academically. Education and business have the largest enrollments.

Required: To graduate, students must complete a minimum of 128 credits with a 2.0 GPA. Course work includes a general education requirement of 18 hours of humanities, 16 of Bible, 12 of social science, 6 of science, and 3 of math or computer science. The major requirements vary according to concentration; typically, 40 hours or more are required. Some majors and minors require a 2.5 GPA.

Special: Summer internships are required in biblical studies and psychology, and work-study is available on campus. Honors and independent study are available as adjuncts to a normal course load. There are 2 national honor societies, a freshman honors program, and 2 departmental honors programs.

Faculty/Classroom: 67% of faculty are male; 33% are female. All teach undergraduates. The average class size in an introductory lecture is 30; in a laboratory, 20; and in a regular course, 25.

Requirements: The ACT is recommended. In addition, for regular acceptance, students must meet 2 of the following 3 requirements: a 2.0 cumulative GPA; graduate in the top half of their graduating class; satisfactory scores on the ACT or SAT. AP and CLEP credits are accepted. Important factors in the admissions decision are ability to finance college education, personality/intangible qualities, and evidence of special talent.

Procedure: Freshmen are admitted to all sessions. Entrance exams should be taken before April. There is a rolling admissions plan. Application deadlines are open. Application fee is $20 (waived for online applications).

Transfer: Transfer students with less than 24 semester hours must have a high school transcript, ACT scores, college transcripts, and 1 reference. Transfers with 24 to 60 hours must have proof of high school graduation (diploma or final), a college transcript, and 1 reference. Transfers with more than 60 hours must have a college transcript and 1 reference letter. 30 of 128 credits required for the bachelor's degree must be completed at York.

Visiting: There are regularly scheduled orientations for prospective students, including a campus tour, a visit with financial aid and admissions representatives, and a visit with the registrar and possibly with a faculty member within the student's major area of concentration. There are guides for informal visits; visitors may sit in on classes and stay overnight.

Financial Aid: The FAFSA is required. Check with the school for current application deadlines.

International Students: They must take the TOEFL. They must also take the SAT or ACT.

Admissions Contact: Director of Admissions. E-Mail: *enroll@york.edu* Web: *www.york.edu*

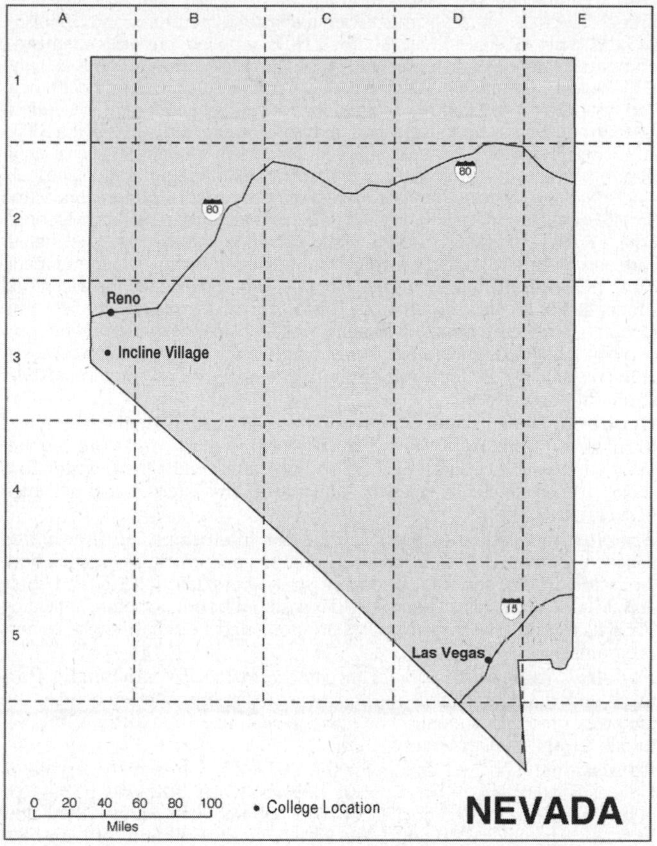

SIERRA NEVADA COLLEGE A-3

Incline Village, NV 89451 (775) 831-1314
(866) 412-4636; (775) 831-6223

Full-time: 70 men, 90 women
Part-time: 25 men, 10 women
Graduate: 95 men, 245 women
Year: semesters, summer session
Application Deadline: February 15
Freshman Class: n/av
ACT: required

Faculty: n/av
Ph.D.s: n/av
Student/Faculty: n/av
Tuition: $24,200
Room & Board: $9500

VERY COMPETITIVE

Sierra Nevada College, founded in 1969, is a private institution offering programs in liberal arts, fine arts, business, hotel resort management, ski business management, environmental science, and teacher education. The figures in the above capsule and in this profile are approximate. There are 7 undergraduate schools. The library contains 20,000 volumes, 10,000 microform items, and subscribes to 100 periodicals including electronic. Computerized library services include interlibrary loans, database searching, Internet access, and Wi-Fi capability. Special learning facilities include an art gallery, an observatory, and a recording studio. The 17-acre campus is in a rural area 25 miles west of Reno. Including any residence halls, there are 7 buildings.

Student Life: 70% of undergraduates are from out of state, mostly the West. Students are from 35 states, 8 foreign countries, and Canada. 60% are from public schools. 93% are White. The average age of freshmen is 19; all undergraduates, 22. 14% do not continue beyond their first year; 62% remain to graduate.

Housing: 120 students can be accommodated in college housing, which includes coed dorms and on-campus apartments. On-campus housing is guaranteed for all 4 years. 60% of students commute. Alcohol is not permitted. All students may keep cars.

Activities: There are no fraternities or sororities. Groups on campus include art, choir, chorale, chorus, computers, dance, environmental, ethnic, honors, international, musical theater, newspaper, political, professional, social, social service, student government, and yearbook. Popular campus events include Bohemia Night, Nevada Day, and Game Show Take-off.

Sports: There are 2 intercollegiate sports for men and 2 for women, and 2 intramural sports for men and 2 for women. Facilities include nearby ski areas, hiking and mountain biking trails, volleyball and softball areas, community tennis courts and golf courses, and sites for water sports and beach volleyball at Lake Tahoe.

Disabled Students: All of the campus is accessible. Facilities include wheelchair ramps, elevators, special parking, specially equipped restrooms, special class scheduling, and special housing.

Services: Counseling and information services are available, as is tutoring in every subject. There is remedial math, reading, and writing.

Campus Safety and Security: Measures include 24-hour foot and vehicle patrol, emergency notification system, and security escort services. There are lighted pathways/sidewalks and controlled access to dorms/residences.

Programs of Study: SNC confers B.A., B.S. and B.F.A. degrees. Bachelor's degrees are awarded in BUSINESS (business administration and management and recreational facilities management), COMMUNICATIONS AND THE ARTS (fine arts and music), COMPUTER AND PHYSICAL SCIENCE (science), ENGINEERING AND ENVIRONMENTAL DESIGN (environmental science), SOCIAL SCIENCE (humanities). Environmental science/ecology are the strongest academically. Business administration has the largest enrollment.

Required: All students must complete at least 120 semester hours, including 40 in upper-division courses with a minimum GPA of 2.0. Students also must pass the writing proficiency exam and meet distribution requirements in 4 interdisciplinary themes: symbols, relationships with nature and humans, memberships in groups and institutions, and ethics, values, and beliefs.

Special: Business administration concentrations are offered in ski business and resort management and in hotel, restaurant, and resort management. Student-designed majors, work-study programs, internships, credit for life experiences and volunteer community work, and nondegree study are available.

Faculty/Classroom: 60% of faculty are male; 40% are female. All teach undergraduates, 15% do research, and 25% do both. No introductory courses are taught by graduate students. The average class size in an introductory lecture is 12; in a laboratory is 8; and in a regular course is 12.

Requirements: The ACT is required. The ACT Optional Writing test is also required. All applicants are reviewed individually. Official transcripts, an essay, and 2 letters of recommendation are required, and an interview is recommended. AP and CLEP credits are accepted. Important factors in the admissions decision are advanced placement or honors courses, recommendations by school officials, and personality/intangible qualities.

Procedure: Freshmen are admitted to all sessions. Entrance exams should be taken in the spring of junior year or fall of senior year. There are early decision, early admissions, deferred admissions, and rolling admissions plans. Applications should be filed by February 15 for fall entry. Notification is sent on a rolling basis. Applications are accepted online.

Transfer: 46 transfer students enrolled in 2012-2013. The college accepts applications from students who have completed course work at an accredited post-secondary institution. If fewer than 15 credits have been earned, the high school transcript and standardized test scores are also required. Transfer applicants are expected to be in good academic standing at their college or university. 96 of 120 credits required for the bachelor's degree must be completed at Sierra.

Visiting: There are regularly scheduled orientations for prospective students, including a student-led campus tour that is available by appointment and 1-night overnight stays. There are guides for informal visits, visitors may sit in on classes, and stay overnight. To schedule a visit, contact the Office of Admissions.

Financial Aid: In 2013-2014, 80% of all full-time freshmen and 80% of continuing full-time students received some form of financial aid. 80% of all full-time freshmen and 80% of continuing full-time students received need-based aid. The average freshman award was $15,000. Need-based scholarships or need-based grants averaged $7,000 ($16,000 maximum); need-based self-help aid (loans and jobs) averaged $3,800 ($7,500 maximum); and other non-need-based awards and non-need-based scholarships averaged $3,000 ($10,000 maximum). 37% of undergraduate students work part-time. The FAFSA and the college's own financial statement are required. Check with the school for current application deadlines.

International Students: The school actively recruits these students. They must take the TOEFL, or take any other English proficiency test.

Computers: All students may access the system 8 a.m. to 9 p.m. daily. There are no time limits and no fees.

Admissions Contact: Admissions Department, Dean of Admission and Financial Aid. E-Mail: *admissions@sierranevada.edu* Web: *www.sierranevada.edu*

UNIVERSITY AND COMMUNITY COLLEGE SYSTEM OF NEVADA

The University and Community College System of Nevada, established in

1865, is a public system in Nevada. It is governed by a board of regents, whose chief administrator is the chancellor. The primary goal of the system is teaching, research, and public service. The main priorities are to provide all public programs of postsecondary instruction in Nevada, to sponsor programs of basic and applied research that contribute to the cultural, economic, and social development of Nevada, and to sponsor programs of public service for citizens of the state. The total student enrollment for all seven campuses is usually about 64,000 with 1750 faculty members. Altogether there are approximate 135 baccalaureate, 97 master's, 34 doctoral programs offered in the University and Community College System of Nevada. Profiles of the 4-year campuses are included in this section.

UNIVERSITY OF NEVADA, LAS VEGAS D-5

Las Vegas, NV 89154 **(702) 774-UNLV; (702) 774-8008**

Full-time: 7372 men, 9019 women
Part-time: 3451 men, 2866 women
Graduate: 2201 men, 3355 women
Year: semesters, summer session
Application Deadline: February 1
Freshman Class: n/av
Faculty: 676; I, -$
Ph.D.s: 95%
Student/Faculty: 24 to 1
Tuition: $4783 ($17,123)
Room & Board: $12,250

COMPETITIVE

University of Nevada, Las Vegas, established in 1957, is a state-supported institution offering undergraduate and graduate programs in business, education, health science, engineering, science and math, hotel administration, fine arts, liberal arts, urban affairs, and honors. There are 10 undergraduate schools and 1 graduate school. In addition to regional accreditation, UNLV has baccalaureate program accreditation with AACSB, ABET, ACCE, ADA, APTA, ASLA, CSAB, CSWE, FIDER, NAAB, NASAD, NASM, NCATE, and NLN. The 6 libraries contain 950,600 volumes, 1.8 million microform items, and 13,500 audio/video tapes/CDs/DVDs, and subscribe to 1,759 periodicals including electronic. Computerized library services include interlibrary loans, database searching, Internet access, and Wi-Fi capability. Special learning facilities include an art gallery, natural history museum, and radio station. The 353-acre campus is in an urban area on the southern tip of Nevada, just east of the Las Vegas strip. Including any residence halls, there are 90 buildings.

Student Life: 80% of undergraduates are from Nevada. Others are from 50 states, 57 foreign countries, and Canada. 46% are White; 18% Asian American; 14% Hispanic. The average age of freshmen is 18; all undergraduates, 25. 26% do not continue beyond their first year; 39% remain to graduate.

Housing: 2500 students can be accommodated in college housing, which includes single-sex and coed dorms. In addition, there are honors houses, special-interest houses, substance-free, study-intensive recess housing, major-specific houses, a global house, and a leadership focus house. On-campus housing is guaranteed for the freshman year only, is available on a first-come, and first-served basis. Priority is given to out-of-town students. 90% of students commute. All students may keep cars.

Activities: 5% of men belong to 18 national fraternities; 3% of women belong to 11 national sororities. There are 160 groups on campus, including art, band, cheerleading, chess, choir, chorus, computers, dance, debate, drama, drill team, ethnic, film, gay, honors, international, jazz band, literary magazine, marching band, musical theater, newspaper, orchestra, pep band, photography, political, professional, radio and TV, religious, social, social service, student government, and symphony. Popular campus events include Weeks of Welcome, Premier UNLV, and Unityfest.

Sports: There are 8 intercollegiate sports for men and 9 for women, and 47 intramural sports for men and 47 for women. Facilities include a recreation and wellness center that includes a lap pool, cardio machines, weight room, running track, racquetball courts, and 5 multiuse courts. There is a 19,000-seat indoor arena for basketball, a 3,000-seat arena for basketball and volleyball, a 40,000-seat football stadium, football practice fields, tennis courts, a softball stadium, a baseball stadium, soccer fields, track facilities, a boxing gym, and separate athletic/training facilities and weight room facilities for intercollegiate athletes.

Disabled Students: All of the campus is accessible. Facilities include wheelchair ramps, elevators, special parking, specially equipped restrooms, special class scheduling, lowered drinking fountains, lowered telephones, and special housing.

Services: Counseling and information services are available, as is tutoring in every subject. There is a reader service for the blind, and remedial math, reading, and writing.

Campus Safety and Security: Measures include 24-hour foot and vehicle patrol, emergency notification system, self-defense education, and security escort services. There are shuttle buses, emergency telephones, and lighted pathways/sidewalks.

Programs of Study: UNLV confers B.A., B.S. and B.F.A. degrees. Master's and doctoral degrees are also awarded. Bachelor's degrees are awarded in BIOLOGICAL SCIENCE (biology/biological science), BUSINESS (accounting, banking and finance, hotel/motel and restaurant management, human resources, international business management, management information systems, management science, marketing/retailing/merchandising, real estate, and recreational facilities management), COMMUNICATIONS AND THE ARTS (art history and appreciation, communications, dance, dramatic arts, English, film arts, fine arts, French, German, music, romance languages and literature, and Spanish), COMPUTER AND PHYSICAL SCIENCE (applied physics, chemistry, computer science, earth science, geology, mathematics, physics, and radiological technology), EDUCATION (elementary education, health education, physical education, recreation education, secondary education, special education, and trade and industrial education), ENGINEERING AND ENVIRONMENTAL DESIGN (architectural engineering, civil engineering, computer engineering, construction management, electrical/electronics engineering, environmental science, interior design, landscape architecture/design, mechanical engineering, and urban planning technology), HEALTH PROFESSIONS (clinical science, exercise science, health care administration, nuclear medical technology, nursing, and sports medicine), SOCIAL SCIENCE (anthropology, criminal justice, economics, food production/management/services, history, interdisciplinary studies, philosophy, physical fitness/movement, political science/government, psychology, public administration, social science, social work, sociology, and women's studies). Hotel administration, fine arts, and engineering are the strongest academically.

Required: Students must complete 124 credits, with 45 in the major, and maintain a minimum GPA of 2.0. All students must meet core requirements that include courses in English, logic and math, the Constitution, social science, fine arts, science, humanities, and international and multicultural diversity.

Special: Opportunities are provided for internships, an accelerated degree program, B.A.-B.S. degrees, dual majors, credit by examination, credit for military service, nondegree study, pass/fail options, and study abroad in 25 countries. There are 16 national honor societies, including Phi Beta Kappa, a freshman honors program, and 11 departmental honors programs.

Faculty/Classroom: 65% of faculty are male; 35% are female. 95% teach undergraduates, and 5% do research. No introductory courses are taught by graduate students. The average class size in an introductory lecture is 21 and in a laboratory is 20.

Admissions: The SAT scores for the 2013-2014 freshman class were: Critical Reading--50% below 500, 36% between 500 and 599, 13% between 600 and 699, and 1% between 700 and 800; Math--42% below 500, 38% between 500 and 599, 17% between 600 and 699, and 3% between 700 and 800. The ACT scores were 16% below 21, 52% between 21 and 23, 15% between 24 and 26, 14% between 27 and 28, and 3% above 28. 52% of the current freshmen were in the top fifth of their class; 85% were in the top two fifths. There were 3 National Merit finalists.

Requirements: Graduation from an accredited secondary school is required. Applicants must also meet the academic core requirements, which include 4 credits in English and 3 each in history, social studies, math, and science. A GPA of 3.0 is required. AP and CLEP credits are accepted. Important factors in the admissions decision are recommendations by school officials, advanced placement or honors courses, and geographical diversity.

Procedure: Freshmen are admitted to all sessions. Entrance exams should be taken by February 1. There is a rolling admissions plan. Applications should be filed by February 1 for fall entry; October 1 for spring entry; and February 1 for summer entry, along with a $60 fee. Applications are accepted online.

Transfer: 1934 transfer students enrolled in 2012-2013. Applicants should present a minimum GPA of 2.5 and a minimum of 24 credits for transfer. The SAT or the ACT is recommended. Applicants must be in good academic standing and eligible to return to the educational institution last attended. 30 of 124 credits required for the bachelor's degree must be completed at University of Nevada.

Visiting: There are regularly scheduled orientations for prospective students, consisting of a complete introduction to the campus, student services, and parent orientation. There are guides for informal visits and visitors may sit in on classes. To schedule a visit, contact the Office of Admissions.

Financial Aid: The average freshman award was $4,711. Need-based scholarships or need-based grants averaged $3,791; and need-based self-help aid (loans and jobs) averaged $3,336. 75% of undergraduate students work part-time. UNLV is a member of CSS. The CCS/Profile, or FAFSA, or FFS, or SFS and the college's own financial statement, and Singlefile Form are required. The priority date for freshman financial aid applications for fall entry is February 1.

International Students: They must take the TOEFL with a minimum score of 500 on the paper-based TOEFL (PBT) or 61 on the Internet-based version (iBT) or take the MELAB, IELTS, or prove English proficiency by other means.

Computers: All students may access the system 24 hours a day, 7 days a week. There are no time limits and no fees.

Graduates: The most popular majors were education (9%), psychology (7%), and communications/journalism (6%).

Admissions Contact: Wendell Staszkow, Assistant Director of Admissions. Web: *www.unlv.edu*

UNIVERSITY OF NEVADA/RENO A-3

Reno, NV 89557 **(775) 784-1110; (775) 784-4283**

Full-time: 4810 men, 5540 women
Part-time: 1380 men, 1390 women
Graduate: 1350 men, 1915 women
Year: semesters, summer session
Application Deadline: February 1
Freshman Class: n/av
SAT or ACT: required
Faculty: n/av; I, -$
Ph.D.s: 93%
Student/Faculty: n/av
Tuition: $4500 ($15,500)
Room & Board: $10,000

NONCOMPETITIVE

The University of Nevada/Reno, established in 1874, is a land-grant institution and part of the Nevada System of Higher Education. It offers programs in agriculture, arts and science, business administration, education, engineering, human and community sciences, journalism, medicine, and mining, as well as interdisciplinary studies. The figures in the above capsule and in this profile are approximate. There are 10 undergraduate schools and one graduate school. In addition to regional accreditation, Nevada has baccalaureate program accreditation with AACSB, ABET, ACEJMC, AHEA, CSWE, NASM, NCATE, and NLN. The 6 libraries contain 1.2 million volumes, 3.3 million microform items, and 49,433 audio/video tapes/CDs/DVDs, and subscribe to 19,058 periodicals including electronic. Computerized library services include interlibrary loans, database searching, and Internet access. Special learning facilities include an art gallery, planetarium, radio station, TV station, the Nevada Historical Society Museum. The 200-acre campus is in an urban area 200 miles east of San Francisco, 35 miles from Lake Tahoe. Including any residence halls, there are 105 buildings.

Student Life: 82% of undergraduates are from Nevada. Others are from 47 states, 77 foreign countries, and Canada. 69% are White. The average age of freshmen is 18; all undergraduates, 22. 22% do not continue beyond their first year.

Housing: 1835 students can be accommodated in college housing, which includes single-sex and coed dorms, on-campus apartments, off-campus apartments, and married student housing. In addition, there are honors houses. On-campus housing is available on a first-come and first-served basis. 89% of students commute. Alcohol is not permitted. All students may keep cars.

Activities: 7% of men belong to 2 local and 11 national fraternities; 7% of women belong to 4 national sororities. There are 100 groups on campus, including art, band, cheerleading, chess, choir, chorale, chorus, computers, dance, debate, drama, drill team, ethnic, film, forensics, gay, honors, international, jazz band, literary magazine, marching band, musical theater, newspaper, orchestra, pep band, photography, political, professional, radio and TV, religious, social, social service, student government, and symphony. Popular campus events include Mackay Week.

Sports: There are 7 intercollegiate sports for men and 8 for women, and 14 intramural sports for men and 11 for women. Facilities include a recreation center, a 30,000-seat stadium, a 2,200-seat gym, a 3,000-seat baseball field, a 200-seat movie theater, and an 11,600-seat indoor events center.

Disabled Students: 99% of the campus is accessible. Facilities include wheelchair ramps, elevators, special parking, specially equipped restrooms, special class scheduling, lowered drinking fountains, lowered telephones, special housing, and automatic door openers.

Services: Counseling and information services are available, as is tutoring in most subjects. There is a reader service for the blind, and remedial math, reading, and writing. Students are mainstreamed with special services for the disabled.

Campus Safety and Security: Measures include 24-hour foot and vehicle patrol, emergency notification system, self-defense education, and security escort services. There are shuttle buses, emergency telephones, lighted pathways/sidewalks, and controlled access to dorms/residences.

Programs of Study: Nevada confers B.A., B.S., B.A.C.J., B.A.Ed., B.F.A., B.G.S., B.M., B.S.Bus.Ad., B.S.C.E., B.S.Chem.E., B.S.Chem., B.S.C.S., B.S.Ed., B.S.E.E., B.S.E.P., B.S.Geog., B.S.Geol., B.S.Geol.E., B.S.Geophys., B.S.M.E., B.S.Met.E., B.S.Min.E., B.S.Nurs. and B.S.Vet.Sc. degrees. Master's and doctoral degrees are also awarded. Bachelor's degrees are awarded in AGRICULTURE (agricultural economics, animal science, and natural resource management), BIOLOGICAL SCIENCE (biochemistry, biology/biological science, and nutrition), BUSINESS (accounting, banking and finance, business economics, management science, and marketing/retailing/merchandising), COMMUNICATIONS AND THE ARTS (applied music, art, dramatic arts, English, French, German, journalism, music, Spanish, and speech/debate/rhetoric), COMPUTER AND PHYSICAL SCIENCE (chemistry, computer science, geology, geophysics and seismology, hydrology, information sciences and systems, mathematics, and physics), EDUCATION (elementary education, music education, secondary education, and special education), ENGINEERING AND ENVIRONMENTAL DESIGN (chemical engineering, civil engineering, electrical/electronics engineering, engineering physics, environmental science, geological engineering, interior design, mechanical engineering, metallurgical engineering, and mining and mineral engineering), HEALTH PROFESSIONS (nursing and speech pathology/audiology), SOCIAL SCIENCE (anthropology, child care/child and family studies, criminal justice, geography, history, human ecology, international relations, liberal arts/general studies, philosophy, political science/government, psychology, social work, and sociology). Biology, psychology, and English have the largest enrollments.

Required: To graduate, all students must complete 124 to 138 semester credits and earn a GPA of 2.0. The core curriculum includes 9 credits of Western Traditions, 6 each of capstone courses and natural science, 3 to 6 of writing, 3 each of math, social science, and fine arts, and fulfillment of the diversity requirement.

Special: Students may study abroad in 24 countries, pursue internships, and complete dual majors in many subject areas. There are 1 national honor societies and a freshman honors program.

Faculty/Classroom: 58% of faculty are male; 42% are female. All teach and do research. Graduate students teach 10% of introductory courses. The average class size in an introductory lecture is 43; in a laboratory is 19; and in a regular course is 31.

Requirements: The SAT or ACT is required. However, test scores are used for placement purposes only. Applicants should have completed 13 1/2 academic credits, including 4 in English, 3 each in math, science, and social studies/history, and a half credit in computer literacy. The GED is not accepted. A GPA of 3.0 is required. AP and CLEP credits are accepted. Important factors in the admissions decision are advanced placement or honors courses, recommendations by school officials, and leadership record.

Procedure: Freshmen are admitted fall and spring. Entrance exams should be taken in October of the senior year. There are deferred admissions and rolling admissions plans. Applications should be filed by February 1 for fall entry; November 1 for spring entry. The fall 2013 application fee was $60. Notification is sent on a rolling basis.

Transfer: 1279 transfer students enrolled in 2012-2013. Applicants should have a GPA of 2.5 and 24 transferable credits. College transcripts are required. 32 of 124 credits required for the bachelor's degree must be completed at Nevada.

Visiting: There are regularly scheduled orientations for prospective students, Meetings with academic representatives. Campus tours include visiting residence halls. There are guides for informal visits and visitors may sit in on classes. To schedule a visit, contact the Office for Prospective Students.

Financial Aid: In 2013-2014, 27% of all full-time freshmen and 32% of continuing full-time students received some form of financial aid. 25% of all full-time freshmen and 29% of continuing full-time students received need-based aid. The average financial indebtedness of the 2013 graduate was $12,285. The FAFSA is required. Check with the school for current application deadlines.

International Students: There are 260 international students enrolled. The school actively recruits these students. They must take the TOEFL. The SAT or ACT may also be submitted.

Computers: All students may access the system. There are no time limits. The fee varies per class laboratory session.

Graduates: From July 1, 2012 to June 30, 2013, 1962 bachelor's degrees were awarded. The most popular majors were social sciences (9%), biological/life sciences (9%), and education (9%). In an average class, 14% graduate in 4 years or less, 39% graduate in 5 years or less, and 46% graduate in 6 years or less.

Admissions Contact: Dr. Melisa N. Choroszy, Assistant Vice President, Records/Enrollment Services. E-Mail: *asknevada@unr.edu* Web: *www.unr.edu*

NEW HAMPSHIRE

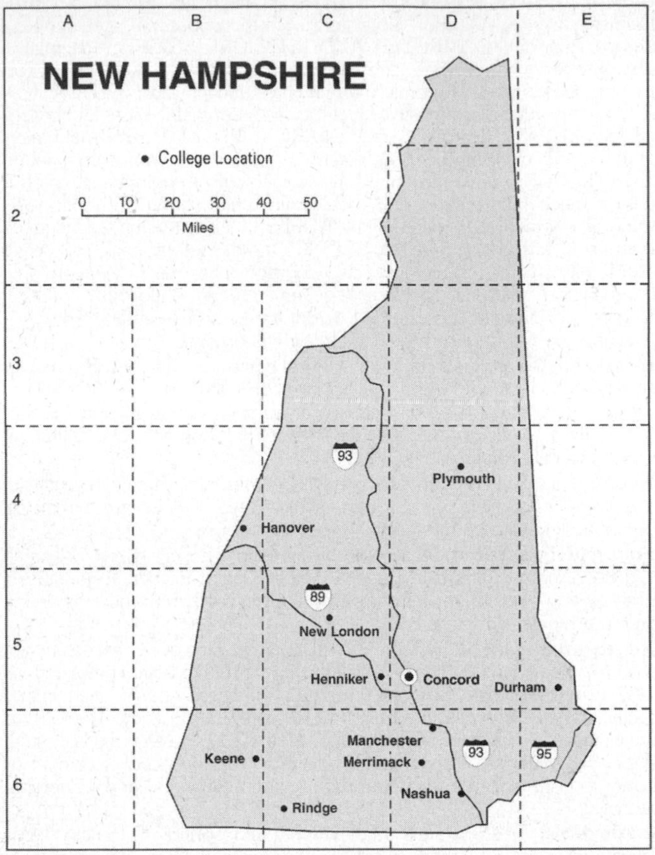

COLBY-SAWYER COLLEGE — C-5

New London, NH 03257

(603) 526-3700
(800) 272-1015; (603) 526-3452

Full-time: 1,415 men and women
Part-time: 15 men, 10 women
Graduate: n/av
Year: semesters
Application Deadline: open
Freshman Class: n/av
SAT or ACT: required

Faculty: n/av; IIB, --$
Ph.D.s: n/av
Student/Faculty: 14 to 1
Tuition: $35,810
Room & Board: $12,060

COMPETITIVE

Colby-Sawyer College, established in 1837, is a private, independent institution offering programs of study that innovatively integrate liberal arts and sciences with professional preparation. Undergraduate majors include environmental studies, graphic design, child development, education, exercise and sport sciences, studio arts, nursing, business, biology, English, psychology, communications, and history, society, and culture, as well as education certification. The library contains 93,861 volumes, 204,109 microform items, and 2,400 audio/video tapes/CDs/DVDs, and subscribes to 32,019 periodicals including electronic. Computerized library services include interlibrary loans, database searching, and Internet access. Special learning facilities include an art gallery, radio station, academic development center, laboratory school (K-3), weather station, and the Curtis L. Ivey Science Center. The 200-acre campus is in a small town 90 minutes north of Boston. Including any residence halls, there are 30 buildings.

Student Life: 68% of undergraduates are from out of state, mostly the Northeast. Students are from 22 states, 29 foreign countries, and Canada. 83% are from public schools. 89% are White. The average age of freshmen is 18; all undergraduates, 19. 19% do not continue beyond their first year; 64% remain to graduate.

Housing: 870 students can be accommodated in college housing, which includes single-sex and coed dorms. a substance-free residence hall. On-campus housing is guaranteed for all 4 years. 90% of students live on campus; of those, 70% remain on campus on weekends. All students may keep cars.

Activities: There are no fraternities or sororities. There are 40 groups on campus, including and student academic counselors, key association (campus tour guides), art, chorus, dance, drama, environmental, film, gay, honors, international, literary magazine, musical theater, newspaper, outing, photography, political, professional, radio and TV, religious, social, social service, and student government. Popular campus events include Fall and Spring Weekends and Mountain Day.

Sports: There are 8 intercollegiate sports for men and 9 for women, and 15 intramural sports for men and 15 for women. Facilities include 6 outdoor and 3 indoor tennis courts, a fitness center, an NCAA-approved swimming pool, a suspended indoor track, squash and racquetball courts, 4 outdoor competitive fields, and nearby golf courses, ski and biking trails, and an indoor riding arena.

Disabled Students: 50% of the campus is accessible. Facilities include wheelchair ramps, elevators, special parking, specially equipped restrooms, special class scheduling, and special housing.

Services: Counseling and information services are available, as is tutoring in every subject. There is a reader service for the blind, and remedial math, reading, and writing.

Campus Safety and Security: Measures include 24-hour foot and vehicle patrol, emergency notification system, self-defense education, and security escort services. There are shuttle buses, emergency telephones, lighted pathways/sidewalks, controlled access to dorms/residences, and monthly meetings between students and campus safety personnel.

Programs of Study: Colby-Sawyer confers B.A., B.S. and B.F.A. degrees. Associate degrees are also awarded. Bachelor's degrees are awarded in AGRICULTURE (environmental studies), BIOLOGICAL SCIENCE (biology/biological science), BUSINESS (business administration and management and sports management), COMMUNICATIONS AND THE ARTS (art, communications, creative writing, English, graphic design, performing arts, and studio art), COMPUTER AND PHYSICAL SCIENCE (natural sciences), EDUCATION (art education, athletic training, early childhood education, English education, social science education, and social studies education), ENGINEERING AND ENVIRONMENTAL DESIGN (environmental science), HEALTH PROFESSIONS (exercise science, nursing, and public health), SOCIAL SCIENCE (child psychology/development, history, humanities, philosophy, psychology, and sociology). Exercise and sport sciences, business administration and nursing have the largest enrollments.

Required: Required courses include writing, math, and computer literacy. Each pathway is a set of five courses that all relate to a theme. Each student is required to take a total of eight Exploration courses: 1 course each in fne and performing arts, history, humanities, literature, social sciences, and laboratory science course, and 1 course from 2 of the following areas: environmental literacy, media literacy, global perspectives, and wellness. Most majors must also complete an internship or a senior research project. A total of 120 credit hours, with a minimum GPA of 2.0, is required for graduation.

Special: There is cross-registration through the New Hampshire College and University Council. Students may choose internships (required in some majors) and may study abroad in Australia, Canada, and several European countries. A Washington semester with American University is available. Other options include education certification, credit by exam, and interdisciplinary majors such as history, society, and culture. There are 4 national honor societies and a freshman honors program.

Faculty/Classroom: 48% of faculty are male; 52% are female. All teach undergraduates. No introductory courses are taught by graduate students. The average class size in a regular course is 17.

Requirements: The SAT or ACT is required. The ACT Optional Writing test is also required. The GED is accepted. A minimum of 15 college preparatory credits is recommended for admission, including 4 years of English, 3 or more of social studies, 3 of math, 2 of the same foreign language, and 3 or more of lab science. An essay is required, as are 2 letters of recommendation. Interviews are strongly recommended. A GPA of 2.0 is required. AP and CLEP credits are accepted.

Procedure: Freshmen are admitted fall and spring. Entrance exams should be taken in the fall of the senior year. There are early decision, deferred admissions, and rolling admissions plans. Early decision applications should be filed by December 1, along with a $45 fee. Notification of early decision is sent December 15. Applications are accepted online.

Transfer: 17 transfer students enrolled in 2012-2013. College-level work will be emphasized. College transcripts, course descriptions, and a dean's form are required in addition to the standard requirements. 60 of 120 credits required for the bachelor's degree must be completed at Colby-Sawyer.

Visiting: There are regularly scheduled orientations for prospective students, including tours and interviews. Open house programs offer tours as well as academic, athletic, campus life, career development, and academic development presentations; several visiting-day programs offer tours, interviews, and class visits. There are guides for informal visits, visitors may sit in on classes, and stay overnight. To schedule a visit, contact the Admissions Office.

Financial Aid: In 2013-2014, 97% of all full-time freshmen and 78% of continuing full-time students received some form of financial aid. 81% of all full-time freshmen and 78% of continuing full-time students received need-based aid. The average freshman award was $24,043.. The average financial indebtedness of the 2013 graduate was $13,578. Colby-Sawyer is a member of CSS. The FAFSA is required. Check with the school for current application deadlines.

International Students: There are 13 international students enrolled. The school actively recruits these students. They must take the TOEFL.

Graduates: From July 1, 2012 to June 30, 2013, 216 bachelor's degrees were awarded. The most popular majors were business administration (22%), health and phusical education (13%), and teacher education (11%). In an average class, 51% graduate in 4 years or less, 59% graduate in 5 years or less, and 60% graduate in 6 years or less. Of the 2012 graduating class, 11% were enrolled in graduate school within 6 months of graduation, and 90% were employed.

Admissions Contact: Admissions Office E-Mail: *admissions@colby-sawyer.edu* Web: *www.colby-sawyer.edu*

DANIEL WEBSTER COLLEGE D-6

Nashua, NH 03063 (603) 577-6600; (800) 325-6876; (603) 577-6001

Full-time: 555 men, 135 women	**Faculty:** n/av
Part-time: 25 men, 10 women	**Ph.D.s:** n/av
Graduate: 75 men, 70 women	**Student/Faculty:** 16 to 1
Year: semesters, summer session	**Tuition:** $15,090
Application Deadline: open	**Room & Board:** $10,290
Freshman Class: n/av	
SAT: required	

COMPETITIVE

Daniel Webster College, founded in 1965, is a non-denominational private college offering study in the fields of aviation, business, computer sciences, engineering, sports management, and social sciences. The figures in the above capsule and in this profile are approximate. There are 4 undergraduate schools and 1 graduate school. The library contains 32,000 volumes, 55,294 microform items, 1,457 audio/video tapes/CDs/DVDs, and subscribes to 390 periodicals including electronic. Computerized library services include interlibrary loans, database searching, and Internet access. Special learning facilities include a The 54-acre campus is in a suburban area in Southern New Hampshire in Nashua, 36 miles to Boston and 20 miles to Manchester, NH. Including any residence halls, there are 14 buildings.

Student Life: 66% of undergraduates are from out of state, mostly the Northeast. Students are from 22 states, 15 foreign countries, and Canada. 91% are White. The average age of freshmen is 18; all undergraduates, 21. 24% do not continue beyond their first year.

Housing: 500 students can be accommodated in college housing, which includes single-sex and coed dorms and on-campus apartments. Suites, quiet floors in residence halls, smoke-free areas, and a substance-free, 10-month housing option. On-campus housing is guaranteed for all 4 years. 68% of students live on campus; of those, 80% remain on campus on weekends. All students may keep cars.

Activities: There are no fraternities or sororities. There are 26 groups on campus, including golf and culinary club., ski club, computers, drama, film, honors, jazz band, newspaper, off reading club, professional, religious, social, social service, student government, and yearbook. Popular campus events include Ski Day, Family Weekend, and Whitewater Rafting Trip.

Sports: There are 7 intercollegiate sports for men and 7 for women, and 6 intramural sports for men and 5 for women. Facilities include an indoor basketball/volleyball court, a weight room, soccer, lacrosse, and softball fields, and cross-country trails.

Disabled Students: 75% of the campus is accessible. Facilities include wheelchair ramps, elevators, special parking, specially equipped restrooms, special class scheduling, and lowered drinking fountains.

Services: Counseling and information services are available, as is tutoring in every subject. There is remedial math and writing. study skills and test skills workshops, study groups, a math/science center, a writing center, and accommodations for students with learning disabilities.

Campus Safety and Security: Measures include 24-hour foot and vehicle patrol, emergency notification system, self-defense education, and security escort services. There are emergency telephones, lighted pathways/sidewalks, and controlled access to dorms/residences.

Programs of Study: DWC confers B.S., and M.B.A. degrees. Associate and master's degrees are also awarded. Bachelor's degrees are awarded in BUSINESS (business administration and management, management information systems, marketing management, and sports management), COMPUTER AND PHYSICAL SCIENCE (computer science and information sciences and systems), ENGINEERING AND ENVIRONMENTAL DESIGN (aeronautical engineering, air traffic control, airline piloting and navigation, aviation administration/management, computer technology, and mechanical engineering), SOCIAL SCIENCE (psychology and social science). Aviation, computer science, and information systems are the strongest academically. Aviation has the largest enrollment.

Required: Students must complete general education courses in communication, computer literacy, math, natural science, the humanities, and the social sciences. At least 120 credits, with 45 to 58 in the major, are required for graduation. Students must maintain a minimum overall GPA of 2.0. and grades of C or better in their major.

Special: There is cross-registration with the New Hampshire College and University Council. All programs offer credit by exam. Interdisciplinary majors, including aviation flight operations and aviation management/air traffic management are available. Study abroad, internships in aviation, business management, computer sciences, and sport management, a general studies degree, and a 2-2 engineering program with the universities of New Hampshire and Massachusetts at Lowell, Kettering University, and Clarkson University are additional options. There is 1 national honor society and 1 departmental honors program.

Faculty/Classroom: 80% of faculty are male; 20% are female. All teach and do research. No introductory courses are taught by graduate students. The average class size in an introductory lecture is 17; in a laboratory is 12; and in a regular course is 20.

Requirements: The SAT is required. Applicants must be graduates of an accredited secondary school or submit the GED. Students should have taken 4 years of English, 3 of math, 2 each of social studies and science, and 1 of history. An essay and an interview are recommended. A GPA of 2.0 is required. AP and CLEP credits are accepted. Important factors in the admissions decision are advanced placement or honors courses, recommendations by school officials, and leadership record.

Procedure: Freshmen are admitted to all sessions. There are early decision, deferred admissions, and rolling admissions plans. Application deadlines are open. Application fee is $35. Applications are accepted online.

Transfer: Transfer students must have a minimum college GPA of 2.0. The SAT is required. Grades of C or better transfer for credit. 30 of 120 credits required for the bachelor's degree must be completed at Daniel Webster College.

Visiting: There are regularly scheduled orientations for prospective students, including a tour and an admissions interview; also available are meetings with faculty and coaches and an aerial tour of the campus as well as sitting in on class. There are guides for informal visits, visitors may sit in on classes, and stay overnight. To schedule a visit, contact the Office of Admissions.

Financial Aid: The FAFSA and the college's own financial statement are required. Check with the school for current application deadlines.

International Students: They must take the TOEFL. They must also take the SAT or ACT.

Admissions Contact: Daniel P. Monahan, Dean of Admissions. E-Mail: *admissions@dwc.edu* Web: *www.dwc.edu*

DARTMOUTH COLLEGE B-4

Hanover, NH 03755 (603) 646-2875; (603) 646-1216

Full-time: 2064 men, 2037 women	**Faculty:** 482; I, +$
Part-time: 25 men, 21 women	**Ph.D.s:** n/av
Graduate: 988 men, 713 women	**Student/Faculty:** 8 to 1
Year: quarters, summer session	**Tuition:** $45,042
Application Deadline: January 1	**Room & Board:** $12,954
Freshman Class: 18132 applied, 2279 accepted, 1094 enrolled	
SAT or ACT: required	

MOST COMPETITIVE

Dartmouth College, chartered in 1769, is a private liberal arts institution offering a wide range of graduate and undergraduate programs. There is a year-round academic calendar of 4 10-week terms. There are 4 graduate schools. The 10 libraries contain 2.5 million volumes, 2.6 million microform items, and 772,660 audio/video tapes/CDs/DVDs, and subscribe to 42,116 periodicals including electronic. Computerized library services include interlibrary loans, database searching, Internet access, and Wi-Fi capability. Special learning facilities include an art gallery, radio station, creative and performing arts center, life sciences lab, physical and social sciences centers, and observatory. The 269-acre campus is in a rural area 140 miles northwest of Boston. Including any residence halls, there are 160 buildings.

Student Life: 96% of undergraduates are from out of state, mostly the Middle Atlantic. Students are from 50 states, 80 foreign countries, and Canada. 62% are from public schools. 53% are White; 14% Asian American. 30% are Protestant; 28% claim no religious affiliation; 23% Catholic; 11% Jewish. The average age of freshmen is 18; all undergraduates, 20. 2% do not continue beyond their first year; 95% remain to graduate.

Housing: 3500 students can be accommodated in college housing, which includes coed dorms, on-campus apartments, off-campus apartments, and married student housing. In addition, there are language houses, special-interest houses, fraternity houses, sorority houses, substance- and smoke-free residence halls, and faculty-in-residence and academic affinity programs. On-campus housing is guaranteed for the freshman year only and is available on a lottery system for upperclassmen. 85% of students live on campus. Upperclassmen may keep cars.

Activities: 39% of men belong to 9 local and 5 national fraternities; 34% of women belong to 3 local and 6 national sororities. There are 300 groups on campus, including and outing., art, band, cheerleading, chess, choir, chorale, chorus, computers, dance, debate, drama, environmental, ethnic, film, forensics, gay, honors, international, jazz band, literary magazine, marching band, musical theater, newspaper, opera, orchestra, pep band, photography, political, professional, radio and TV, religious, social, social service, student government, symphony, and yearbook. Popular campus events include Dartmouth Night/Homecoming Weekend, Winter Carnival and Green Key Service Weekend.

Sports: There are 17 intercollegiate sports for men and 17 for women, and 25 intramural sports for men and 25 for women. Facilities include a 2100-seat arena, a 16,000-square-foot fitness center, squash and racquetball courts, a dance studio, a 5000-seat ice-hockey arena, a gym, a 20,000-seat football stadium, a boat house, a tennis center with indoor and outdoor courts, a golf course, a ski slope with 3 chairlifts, and a riding farm.

Disabled Students: All of the campus is accessible. Facilities include wheelchair ramps, elevators, special parking, specially equipped restrooms, special class scheduling, lowered drinking fountains, lowered telephones, and special housing.

Services: Counseling and information services are available, as is tutoring in every subject. There is a reader service for the blind. There is an academic skills center for all students. Readers, note takers, tape recorders and support for learning-disabled students are available.

Campus Safety and Security: Measures include 24-hour foot and vehicle patrol, emergency notification system, self-defense education, and security escort services. There are shuttle buses, emergency telephones, and lighted pathways/sidewalks.

Programs of Study: Dartmouth confers B.A., and B.Eng. degrees. Master's and doctoral degrees are also awarded. Bachelor's degrees are awarded in AGRICULTURE (environmental studies), BIOLOGICAL SCIENCE (biochemistry, biology/biological science, genetics, and neurosciences), COMMUNICATIONS AND THE ARTS (Arabic, art history and appreciation, Chinese, classical languages, classics, comparative literature, dramatic arts, English, film arts, French, German, Italian, linguistics, music, Portuguese, romance languages and literature, Russian, Spanish, and studio art), COMPUTER AND PHYSICAL SCIENCE (astrophysics, chemistry, computer science, earth science, mathematics, and physics), ENGINEERING AND ENVIRONMENTAL DESIGN (engineering and applied science, engineering physics, and environmental science), SOCIAL SCIENCE (African American studies, anthropology, Asian/Oriental studies, classical/ancient civilization, cognitive science, economics, French studies, geography, German area studies, history, Latin American studies, Middle Eastern studies, Native American studies, philosophy, psychology, religion, Russian and Slavic studies, sociology, Spanish studies, and women's studies). Economics, government, and psychological and brain sciences have the largest enrollments.

Required: All students must pass 35 courses, 10 of which must be distributed in the following fields: arts; social analysis; literature; quantitative or deductive science; philosophical, religious, or historical analysis; natural science; technology or applied science; and international or comparative study. 3 world culture courses are required from the U.S., Europe, and at least 1 non-Western society. A multidisciplinary or interdisciplinary course, a freshman seminar, a senior project, and foreign language proficiency are also required.

Special: Students may design programs using the college's unique Dartmouth Plan, which divides the academic calendar into 4 10-week terms, based on the seasons. The plan permits greater flexibility for vacations and for the 45 study-abroad programs in 23 countries in Latin America, Europe, Asia, and Africa. Cross-registration is offered through the Twelve College Exchange Network. Exchange programs also exist with the University of California at San Diego, Stanford, Oxford, and McGill Universities, selected German universities, Keio University in Tokyo, and Beijing Normal University in China. Students may design their own interdisciplinary majors involving multiple departments, take dual majors in all fields, or create a modified major involving 2 departments, with emphasis in 1. Hands-on computer science education, internships, and work-study programs also are available. A 3-2 engineering degree is offered with Dartmouth's Thayer School of Engineering. There are 3 national honor societies including Phi Beta Kappa.

Faculty/Classroom: 62% of faculty are male; 38% are female. All teach and do research. No introductory courses are taught by graduate students. The average class size in an introductory lecture is 34; in a laboratory is 16; and in a regular course is 23.

Admissions: 13% of the 2013-2014 applicants were accepted. 95% of the current freshmen were in the top fifth of their class; 100% were in the top two fifths. 323 freshmen graduated first in their class.

Requirements: The SAT or ACT is required. The ACT Optional Writing test is also required. Evidence of intellectual capacity, motivation, and personal integrity are important factors in the highly competitive admissions process, which also considers talent, accomplishment, and involvement in nonacademic areas. Course requirements are flexible, but students are urged to take English, foreign language, math, lab science, and history. The GED is accepted. AP credits are accepted.

Procedure: Freshmen are admitted fall. Entrance exams should be taken no later than November or January of the senior year. There are early decision and deferred admissions plans. Early decision applications should be filed by November 1; regular applications, by January 1 for fall entry. The fall 2013 application fee was $70. Notification of early decision is sent December 15; regular decision, April 1. 958 applicants were on the 2013 waiting list; 95 were admitted. Applications are accepted online.

Transfer: 23 transfer students enrolled in 2012-2013. Applicants must demonstrate high achievement and intellectual motivation through college transcripts as well as standardized test scores and high school transcripts. 18 of 35 credits required for the bachelor's degree must be completed at Dartmouth.

Visiting: There are regularly scheduled orientations for prospective students, including a campus tour, a group information session, and a student forum. There are guides for informal visits, visitors may sit in on classes, and stay overnight. To schedule a visit, contact the Office of Admissions.

Financial Aid: In 2013-2014, 49% of all full-time freshmen and 53% of continuing full-time students received some form of financial aid. 49% of all full-time freshmen and 53% of continuing full-time students received need-based aid. The average freshman award was $37,055. Need-based scholarships or need-based grants averaged $34,927; and need-based self-help aid (loans and jobs) averaged $2,870. The average financial indebtedness of the 2013 graduate was $18,095. Dartmouth is a member of CSS. The CSS/Profile and FAFSA, and parents' and student's federal income tax returns. are required. The deadline for filing freshman financial aid applications for fall entry is February 1.

International Students: There are 286 international students enrolled. The school actively recruits these students. They must take the TOEFL. They must also take the SAT or ACT.

Graduates: From July 1, 2012 to June 30, 2013, 1084 bachelor's degrees were awarded. The most popular majors were economics, government, and psychological and brain sciences. In an average class, 95% graduate in 6 years or less.

Admissions Contact: Maria Laskaris, Dean of Admissions. E-Mail: *admissions.office@dartmouth.edu* Web: *www.dartmouth.edu*

FRANKLIN PIERCE UNIVERSITY C-6

Rindge, NH 03461 **(603) 899-4050**
(800) 437-0048; (603) 899-4394

Full-time: 591 men, 716 women	**Faculty:** 71; IIB, -$
Part-time: 95 men, 285 women	**Ph.D.s:** 70%
Graduate: 205 men, 324 women	**Student/Faculty:** 14 to 1
Year: semesters, summer session	**Tuition:** $31,000
Application Deadline:	**Room & Board:** $11,598
Freshman Class: 4419 applied, 3681 accepted, 450 enrolled	

COMPETITIVE

Franklin Pierce University, founded in 1962, is a private liberal arts institution with an extensive continuing education program. The main campus in Rindge, New Hampshire is home to 1,400 undergraduate students. Adult undergraduate and graduate students take classes online and at locations in Concord, Lebanon, Manchester, and Portsmouth, New Hampshire, and in Goodyear, Arizona. Many degrees are offered with emphasis in health care, business, education, mass communications, psychology, humanities, visual and performing arts, and leadership studies. There are 2 undergraduate schools and 1 graduate school. The library contains 144,770 volumes, 26,182 microform items, and 10,312 audio/video tapes/CDs/DVDs, and subscribes to 10,275 periodicals including electronic. Computerized library services include interlibrary loans, database searching, Internet access, and Wi-Fi capability. Special learning facilities include an art gallery, radio station, TV station, computer labs, theaters, recording studios, athletic training facility, glassblowing hut. The 1200-acre campus is in a rural area 65 miles northwest of Boston. Including any residence halls, there are 30 buildings.

Student Life: 78% of undergraduates are from out of state, mostly the Northeast. Students are from 34 states, 29 foreign countries, and Canada. 83% are from public schools. 78% are White; 13% race unknown. The average age of freshmen is 18; all undergraduates, 20. 31% do not continue beyond their first year; 52% remain to graduate.

Housing: 1492 students can be accommodated in college housing, which includes coed dorms, on-campus apartments, and off-campus apartments. In addition, there are special-interest houses, Wellness living, and apartments for single student. On-campus housing is guaranteed for all 4 years. 94% of students live on campus; of those, 70% remain on campus on weekends. All students may keep cars.

Activities: There are no fraternities or sororities. There are 35 groups

on campus, including art, cheerleading, choir, chorale, chorus, computers, dance, drama, environmental, ethnic, film, forensics, gay, honors, international, jazz band, literary magazine, musical theater, newspaper, outing, photography, political, professional, radio and TV, religious, social, social service, student government, and yearbook. Popular campus events include Winter Carnival, Spring and Fall Weekend and Up All Night Mardi Gras.

Sports: There are 9 intercollegiate sports for men and 11 for women, and 32 intramural sports for men and 32 for women. Facilities include a 72,000-square-foot airframe activity center, (with tennis courts, indoor turf soccer field, basketball courts, track, fitness center, and volleyball courts) a field house, a fitness center, an 800-seat gym, an athletic training facility, playing fields including an artificial turf baseball field, and artificial turf soccer/lacrosse and field hockey field, a softball field, and another all-purpose field, a lake with a beach, a fleet of sailboats and kayaks, cross-country and hiking trails, and courts for tennis, basketball, and volleyball.

Disabled Students: 70% of the campus is accessible. Facilities include wheelchair ramps, elevators, special parking, specially equipped restrooms, special class scheduling, and special housing.

Services: Counseling and information services are available, as is tutoring in every subject. There is a reader service for the blind, and remedial math, reading, and writing, note takers, a professional reading specialist, alternative testing, reduced course loads, study skills workshops, and content-area study skills courses

Campus Safety and Security: Measures include 24-hour foot and vehicle patrol, emergency notification system, self-defense education, and security escort services. There are shuttle buses, emergency telephones, lighted pathways/sidewalks, On campus student-run Fire Department and EMS squad.

Programs of Study: FPU confers B.A., and B.S. degrees. Associate, master's, and doctoral degrees are also awarded. Bachelor's degrees are awarded in BIOLOGICAL SCIENCE (biology/biological science), BUSINESS (accounting, banking and finance, business administration and management, management science, marketing/retailing/merchandising, and sports management), COMMUNICATIONS AND THE ARTS (arts administration/management, communications, dance, dramatic arts, English, fine arts, graphic design, music, and theatre arts), COMPUTER AND PHYSICAL SCIENCE (mathematics), EDUCATION (education, elementary education, and secondary education), ENGINEERING AND ENVIRONMENTAL DESIGN (environmental science), HEALTH PROFESSIONS (health care administration, health science, and nursing), SOCIAL SCIENCE (American studies, anthropology, criminal justice, history, interdisciplinary studies, political science/government, psychology, and social work). Anthropology, health sciences, biology and history are the strongest academically. Biology, health sciences, criminal justice, psychology, education and management have the largest enrollments.

Required: Students must complete 120 semester hours with a cumulative GPA of at least 2.0 and pass exams for writing and math competency. General and liberal education core curricular requirements include mastery of an established set of learning outcomes in the following areas: Knowledge and Understanding, Intellectual and Practical Skills, Personal and Social Responsibility, Engaged Learning and Thinking. These learning outcomes focus on preparing our students for life and careers in an increasingly complex and challenging 21st-century world.

Special: Cross-registration is offered in nearly every subject through the New Hampshire College and University Council, a 13-member consortium of area institutions. Study abroad in 9 countries, Pierce on the Camino, internships in most majors on or off campus, a Washington semester, and work-study through the college are possible. In addition, accelerated degree programs in all majors, dual majors in most fields, student-designed majors, credit for life experience, and nondegree study are available. Pathway programs from undergraduate to M.D. and D.V.M. programs at St. George's University in Grenada afford students special graduate study opportunities, along with pathways and consideration to Franklin Pierce's Doctor of Physical Therapy and Master of Physician Assistant Studies programs. Pathway and accelerated Franklin Pierce M.B.A., M.Ed., and M.S. in Information Technology Management degree programs provide additional options. There are 7 national honor societies and a freshman honors program.

Faculty/Classroom: 48% of faculty are male; 52% are female. All teach undergraduates, and 50% do both. No introductory courses are taught by graduate students. The average class size in an introductory lecture is 60; in a laboratory is 16; and in a regular course is 16.

Admissions: 83% of the 2013-2014 applicants were accepted. The SAT scores for the 2013-2014 freshman class were: Critical Reading--58% below 500, 36% between 500 and 599, 6% between 600 and 699, Math--54% below 500, 37% between 500 and 599, 7% between 600 and 699, Writing--63% below 500, 32% between 500 and 599, 5% between 600 and 699. The ACT scores were 9% below 21, 72% between 21 and 23 and 19% above 28. 44% of the current freshmen were in the top fifth of their class; 56% were in the top two fifths.

Requirements: The SAT is required. The ACT and ACT Writing Test are recommended. Applicants must have earned 10 academic units or 16 Carnegie units in high school, including 4 years of English, 3 each in math and social studies, and 3 in science. An interview is recommended. The GED is accepted. FPU requires applicants to be in the upper 60% of their class. A GPA of 2.9 is required. AP and CLEP credits are accepted. Important factors in the admissions decision are recommendations by school officials, advanced placement or honors courses, and extracurricular activities record.

Procedure: Freshmen are admitted to all sessions. Entrance exams should be taken in the spring of junior year or the fall of the senior year. There are deferred admissions and rolling admissions plans. Application deadlines are open. Application fee is $40. Notification is sent on a rolling basis. Applications are accepted online.

Transfer: 21 transfer students enrolled in 2012-2013. A minimum 2.0 GPA in college work is required. Students with fewer than 30 credits must submit SAT results (no minimum score) and official high school transcripts. A personal recommendation is necessary, and an interview is recommended. 30 of 120 credits required for the bachelor's degree must be completed at Franklin Pierce.

Visiting: There are regularly scheduled orientations for prospective students, including open houses held each spring and fall and interviews and tours available weekdays and most Saturdays. There are guides for informal visits, visitors may sit in on classes, and stay overnight. To schedule a visit, contact the Admissions Office.

Financial Aid: In 2013-2014, 86% of all full-time freshmen and 85% of continuing full-time students received some form of financial aid. 86% of all full-time freshmen and 85% of continuing full-time students received need-based aid. The average freshman award was $23,887. Need-based scholarships or need-based grants averaged $19,445; need-based self-help aid (loans and jobs) averaged $5,484; non-need-based athletic scholarships averaged $12,919; and other non-need-based awards and non-need-based scholarships averaged $13,304. 50% of undergraduate students work part-time. Average annual earnings from campus work are $618. The average financial indebtedness of the 2013 graduate was $36,087. FPU is a member of CSS. The FAFSA is required. The priority date for freshman financial aid applications for fall entry is March 1.

International Students: There are 25 international students enrolled. The school actively recruits these students. They must take the TOEFL with a minimum score of 61 on the Internet-based version (iBT), and also take ELS Level 109. The SAT or ACT may be substituted for the TOEFL. either TOEFL, SAT, or ACT.

Graduates: From July 1, 2012 to June 30, 2013, 378 bachelor's degrees were awarded. The most popular majors were business/marketing (18%), health professions and related sciences (14%), and biological/life sciences (7%). In an average class, 2% graduate in 3 years or less, 37% graduate in 4 years or less, 48% graduate in 5 years or less, and 50% graduate in 6 years or less. Of the 2012 graduating class, 37% were enrolled in graduate school within 6 months of graduation, and 79% were employed.

Admissions Contact: Linda Quimby, Director. E-Mail: *admissions@franklinpierce.edu* Web: *www.franklinpierce.edu/admissions*

GRANITE STATE COLLEGE D-5

Concord, NH 03301-7317 **(603) 513-1320**
(888) 228-3000; (603) 513-1387

Full-time: 215 men, 472 women	**Faculty:** n/av
Part-time: 195 men, 636 women	**Ph.D.s:** 25%
Graduate: 35 men, 1652211 women	**Student/Faculty:** n/av
Year: trimesters, summer session	**Tuition:** $6695 ($7055)
Application Deadline: open	**Room & Board:** n/app
Freshman Class: 746 applied, 746 accepted, 492 enrolled	**SPECIAL**

Since 1972, Granite State College, has been the University System of New Hampshire's leader in providing access to public higher education for adults. The figures given in the above capsule and in this profile are approximate. The college features online degrees, community-based academic centers, and innovative programs such as self-designed bachelor degrees. Computerized library services include interlibrary loans, database searching, and Internet access. Special learning facilities include a learning resource center and a virtual library that serves all 9 Centers and online students. The campus is in a small town.

Student Life: 90% of undergraduates are from New Hampshire. Others are from 32 states. 90% are white. The average age of all undergraduates is 36.

Housing: There are no residence halls. All students commute.

Activities: There are no fraternities or sororities.

Sports: There is no sports program at GSC.

Disabled Students: All of the campus is accessible. Facilities include wheelchair ramps, special parking, and specially equipped restrooms.

Services: Counseling and information services are available, as is tutoring in every subject. There is remedial math, reading, and writing. Other accommodations may be requested.

Campus Safety and Security: Measures include an emergency notification system. There are lighted pathways/sidewalks and controlled access to dorms/residences.

Programs of Study: GSC confers B.A. and B.S. degrees. Associate degrees are also awarded. Bachelor's degrees are awarded in BUSINESS (management science), COMPUTER AND PHYSICAL SCIENCE (applied science), EDUCATION (early childhood education), SOCIAL SCIENCE (behavioral science, criminal justice, and liberal arts/general studies). Individualized studies majors and business management have the largest enrollments.

Required: Students must complete 124 credits, at least 32 to 39 in the major, and must maintain a minimum GPA of 2.0. All students are required to complete general education courses in critical thinking, written communication, quantitative reasoning, oral communication, information technology literacy, arts and culture, literature and ideas, history and politics, social science, science, and global perspectives.

Special: Opportunities are provided for internships, cross-registration with all USNH schools, student-designed majors, credit by exam, nondegree study, and pass/fail options (for degree students only). GSC offers programs throughout the state through a network of 9 local Academic Centers. There is 1 national honor society.

Faculty/Classroom: 42% of faculty are male; 58% are female. All teach undergraduates. No introductory courses are taught by graduate students. The average class size in a regular course is 10.

Admissions: All of a recent year's applicants were accepted.

Requirements: Applicants must self-certify that they have received a high school diploma or GED. An essay is required, and an advising interview is recommended. The college no longer requires the taking of the Accuplacer for admissions; instead, the tests are used for skills assessment and placement purposes. AP and CLEP credits are accepted.

Procedure: Freshmen are admitted to all sessions. There is a rolling admissions plan. Application deadlines are open. The fall 2011 application fee was $45. Notification is sent on a rolling basis. Applications are accepted online.

Transfer: 246 transfer students enrolled in a recent year. Transfer credits will be accepted via transcript if they are from a regionally accredited institution and will be evaluated to determine whether they contribute toward meeting GSC degree requirements. Minimum grade for transferred course credits is a C. There is no time limit on past college credits. 30 of 124 credits required for the bachelor's degree must be completed at GSC.

Visiting: There are regularly scheduled orientations for prospective students, consisting of an overview of college programs, financial aid, services, and transfer policies. Visitors may sit in on classes. To schedule a visit, contact the Academic Center.

Financial Aid: The average financial indebtedness of recent graduates was $21,500. The FAFSA is required. Check with the school for current application deadlines.

International Students: They must submit acceptable TOEFL, IELTS, or Accuplacer scores.

Graduates: 221 bachelor's degrees were awarded in a recent year. The most popular majors were individualized studies (31%), business management (27%), and behavioral science (18%). In an average class, 51% graduate in 6 years or less.

Admissions Contact: Ruth Nawn, Associate Director of Admissions. A campus DVD is available. E-Mail: *ruth.nawn@granite.edu* Web: *www.granite.edu*

KEENE STATE COLLEGE B-6

Keene, NH 03435 (603) 358-2276
(800) KSC-1909; (603) 358-2767

Full-time: 1916 men, 2608 women	**Faculty:** 199; IIA, av$
Part-time: 57 men, 67 women	**Ph.D.s:** 83%
Graduate: 20 men, 65 women	**Student/Faculty:** 17 to 1
Year: semesters, summer session	**Tuition:** $12,776 ($20,161)
Application Deadline: April 1	**Room & Board:** $9008

Freshman Class: 6144 applied, 5029 accepted, 1258 enrolled
SAT CR/M/W: 430/440/430

COMPETITIVE

Keene State College, founded in 1909, is part of the public University System of New Hampshire and offers a liberal arts program that includes teacher preparation, art, and business emphases. There are 3 undergraduate schools and 1 graduate school. In addition to regional accreditation, KSC has baccalaureate program accreditation with NASM and NCATE. The library contains 298,672 volumes, 231,025 microform items, and 16,739 audio/video tapes/CDs/DVDs, and subscribes to 50,242 periodicals including electronic. Computerized library services include interlibrary loans, database searching, Internet access, and Wi-Fi capability. Special learning facilities include an art gallery, radio station, TV station, the Cohen Center for Holocaust Studies/Holocaust Resource Center. The 150-acre campus is in a small town 90 miles northwest of Boston and 100 miles north of Hartford, CT. Including any residence halls, there are 70 buildings.

Student Life: 52% of undergraduates are from out of state, mostly the Northeast. Students are from 30 states, and 6 foreign countries. 82% are White; 12% race unknown. The average age of freshmen is 18; all undergraduates, 20. 24% do not continue beyond their first year; 63% remain to graduate.

Housing: 2664 students can be accommodated in college housing, which includes single-sex and coed dorms, on-campus apartments, and married student housing. In addition, there are honors houses, special-interest houses, fraternity houses, sorority houses, Learning Communities: Equity and Social Justice, Mind, Body, and Character, Citizens and Service, Excellence inTeaching, learning, and scholarship. On-campus housing is available on a lottery system for upperclassmen. 55% of students live on campus; of those, 65% remain on campus on weekends. Upperclassmen may keep cars.

Activities: 8% of men belong to 6 national fraternities; 5% of women belong to 4 national sororities. There are 127 groups on campus, including art, band, cheerleading, choir, chorale, chorus, computers, dance, debate, drama, environmental, ethnic, film, gay, honors, international, jazz band, literary magazine, musical theater, newspaper, orchestra, photography, political, professional, radio and TV, religious, social, social service, student government, and yearbook. Popular campus events include Spring Weekend, Pumpkin Festival and Alternative Spring Break.

Sports: There are 8 intercollegiate sports for men and 10 for women, and 13 intramural sports for men and 12 for women. Facilities include a 46,000-square foot recreational center, a 2100-seat gym, a 1300 seat stadium for soccer, field hockey, baseball and softball diamonds, and lacrosse, an indoor pool, a fitness center, racquetball, tennis, squash, basketball, volleyball, and indoor soccer courts, a jogging track, and a training room.

Disabled Students: 95% of the campus is accessible. Facilities include wheelchair ramps, elevators, special parking, specially equipped restrooms, lowered drinking fountains, and lowered telephones.

Services: Counseling and information services are available, as is tutoring in most subjects, There is a writing process center, a reading center, and a math center. There is a reader service for the blind, and remedial math, reading, and writing.

Campus Safety and Security: Measures include 24-hour foot and vehicle patrol, emergency notification system, self-defense education, and security escort services. There are shuttle buses, emergency telephones, lighted pathways/sidewalks, and controlled access to dorms/residences.

Programs of Study: KSC confers B.A., B.S., B.F.A. and B.M. degrees. Master's degrees are also awarded. Bachelor's degrees are awarded in AGRICULTURE (environmental studies), BIOLOGICAL SCIENCE (biology/biological science and nutrition), BUSINESS (business administration and management), COMMUNICATIONS AND THE ARTS (art history, art, communications, dance, English, English literature, English Writing, film arts, French, graphic design, journalism, music, music composition, music performance, music technology, Spanish, studio art, theatre arts, and theater design), COMPUTER AND PHYSICAL SCIENCE (chemistry, computer mathematics, computer science, earth science, geology, mathematics, physics, science, and software engineering), EDUCATION (athletic training, dance education, early childhood education, education, elementary education, mathematics education, music education, physical education, physical science secondary school education, science education, secondary education, and special education), ENGINEERING AND ENVIRONMENTAL DESIGN (architecture and occupational safety and health), HEALTH PROFESSIONS (exercise science, health promotion, and nursing), SOCIAL SCIENCE (addiction studies, American studies, anthropology, criminal justice, economics, geography, history, philosophy, political science/government, psychology, social science, and women and gender studies). Safety and occupational health applied sciences, chemistry and holocaust and genocide studies are the strongest academically. Education, safety and occupational health applied sciences and psychology have the largest enrollments.

Required: Education in the liberal arts and sciences and in several professional fields is provided through bachelor degree programs. These programs include three basic components:Integrative Studies – requirements, established by the College, purposefully and intentionally help students engage ethical issues, approach global issues from multiple perspectives, apply diverse perspectives to their thinking and their actions, and analyze key social and environmental issues confronting us all Major/Option/Specialization or Concentration Requirements, specified by discipline faculty, offer depth of scholarship through specialization in a field of interest. Electives, selected by the student, provide the opportunity to develop a minor, to fulfill teacher certification requirements, or to take courses in other areas for personal and professional growth.

Special: Internships and co-op programs in most areas of study, study abroad anywhere in the world, and work-study at the college are available. Student teaching is required for education majors. Students also may pursue dual majors, a general studies degree, individualized majors, accelerated degrees in the psychology honors program, and a 3-2 engineering degree with Clarkson University or the University of New Hampshire. In addition, there are pass/fail options and credit for life experience. There are 19 national honor societies and a freshman honors program.

Faculty/Classroom: 51% of faculty are male; 48% are female. 91% teach undergraduates. No introductory courses are taught by graduate stu-

dents. The average class size in an introductory lecture is 22; in a laboratory is 14; and in a regular course is 20.

Admissions: 82% of the 2013-2014 applicants were accepted. The SAT scores for the 2013-2014 freshman class were: Critical Reading--56% below 500, 35% between 500 and 599, 8% between 600 and 699, and 1% between 700 and 800; Math--55% below 500, 38% between 500 and 599, 7% between 600 and 699, and 1% between 700 and 800; Writing--56% below 500, 36% between 500 and 599, and 8% between 600 and 699. 13% of the current freshmen were in the top fifth of their class; 40% were in the top two fifths.

Requirements: The SAT is required. Applicants must submit completed application with fee, official high school transcript including first marking period grades for senior year, SAT test scores (or ACT test scores), essay, and a letter of recommendation. Applicants need at least 14 academic credits, including 4 years of English, and 3 years each of math and science, 2 years each of social studies, and academic electives or GED. A portfolio or an audition is required for certain programs. A GPA of 2.0 is required. AP and CLEP credits are accepted.

Procedure: Freshmen are admitted fall and spring. Entrance exams should be taken during the spring of the junior year or fall of the senior year. There are deferred admissions and rolling admissions plans. Applications should be filed by April 1 for fall entry; December 1 for spring entry, along with a $50 fee. Notifications are sent December 1. Applications are accepted online.

Transfer: 163 transfer students enrolled in 2012-2013. Applicants must submit completed application with fee, official school transcripts from all previous colleges, SAT test scores (or ACT test scores), essay, and a letter of reference from a college administrator. A portfolio or an audition is required for certain programs. 30 of 120 credits required for the bachelor's degree must be completed at KSC.

Visiting: There are regularly scheduled orientations for prospective students. The overview with Admissions counselor and tour of campus takes about 2 hrs. There are guides for informal visits and visitors may sit in on classes.

Financial Aid: In 2013-2014, 67% of all full-time freshmen received some form of financial aid. 49% of all full-time freshmen students received need-based aid. The average freshman award was $2,091. 23% of undergraduate students work part-time. Average annual earnings from campus work are $1689. The average financial indebtedness of the 2013 graduate was $23,205. The FAFSA, and IRS tax returns is required. The priority date for freshman financial aid applications for fall entry is March 1. The deadline for filing freshman financial aid applications for fall entry is March 1.

International Students: There are 12 international students enrolled. They must take the TOEFL with a minimum score of 550 on the paper-based TOEFL (PBT) or 213 on the Internet-based version (iBT). International students living in the US for 2 or more years attending High School must take SAT.

Graduates: From July 1, 2012 to June 30, 2013, 1200 bachelor's degrees were awarded. The most popular majors were education (18%), psychology (11%), and social sciences (10%). In an average class, 52% graduate in 4 years or less, 62% graduate in 5 years or less, and 62% graduate in 6 years or less.

Admissions Contact: Peggy Richmond, Director of Admissions. E-Mail: *admissions@keene.edu* Web: *www.keene.edu*

NEW ENGLAND COLLEGE C-5

Henniker, NH 03242 **(603) 428-2223**
(800) 521-7642; (608) 428-3155

Full-time: 690 men, 885 women	**Faculty:** 62
Part-time: 28 men, 30 women	**Ph.D.s:** 71%
Graduate: 262 men, 518 women	**Student/Faculty:** 24 to 1
Year: varies, summer session	**Tuition:** $33,500
Application Deadline: open	**Room & Board:** $13,430

Freshman Class: 5843 applied, 5251 accepted, 398 enrolled

LESS COMPETITIVE

New England College, founded in 1946, is an independent liberal arts institution emphasizing small classes and a cocurricular leadership program. There is one undergraduate school and one graduate school. The library contains 110,000 volumes, 36,000 microform items, and 2,000 audio/video tapes/CDs/DVDs, and subscribes to 700 periodicals including electronic. Computerized library services include interlibrary loans, database searching, Internet access, and Wi-Fi capability. Special learning facilities include an art gallery, radio station, the Center for Educational Innovation, and a high-tech classroom building. The 225-acre campus is in a small town 17 miles west of Concord and 80 miles north of Boston, Massachusetts. Including any residence halls, there are 31 buildings.

Student Life: 76% of undergraduates are from out of state, mostly the Northeast. Students are from 50 states, 19 foreign countries, and Canada. 83% are from public schools. 58% are White; 19% African American; 13% race unknown. 100% claim no religious affiliation The average age of freshmen is 20; all undergraduates, 27. 41% do not continue beyond their first year; 38% remain to graduate.

Housing: 685 students can be accommodated in college housing, which includes coed dorms and on-campus apartments. In addition, there are special-interest houses, cooperative substance-free housing. On-campus housing is guaranteed for all 4 years and is available on a lottery system for upperclassmen. 68% of students commute. All students may keep cars.

Activities: 5% of men belong to 2 local and 1 national fraternities; 10% of women belong to 3 local and 1 national sororities. There are 36 groups on campus, including cheerleading, chorus, dance, drama, environmental, ethnic, film, gay, honors, international, literary magazine, newspaper, photography, political, professional, radio and TV, religious, social, social service, sports, student government, and yearbook. Popular campus events include International Week, Snow Day, and Spring Weekend.

Sports: There are 6 intercollegiate sports for men and 7 for women, and 7 intramural sports for men and 7 for women. Facilities include a gym, a field house, 26 acres of playing fields, indoor and outdoor basketball and tennis courts, cross-country ski trails, Alpine skiing at a local ski area, turf field, and a fitness center.

Disabled Students: 80% of the campus is accessible. Facilities include wheelchair ramps, elevators, special parking, specially equipped restrooms, and special class scheduling.

Services: Counseling and information services are available, as is tutoring in most subjects. There is remedial math and writing. The mentor program provides both academic and life coaching.

Campus Safety and Security: Measures include 24-hour foot and vehicle patrol, emergency notification system, and security escort services. There are shuttle buses, emergency telephones, lighted pathways/sidewalks, and controlled access to dorms/residences.

Programs of Study: NEC confers B.A., and B.S. degrees. Associate, master's, and doctoral degrees are also awarded. Bachelor's degrees are awarded in BIOLOGICAL SCIENCE (biology/biological science), BUSINESS (business administration and management, recreation and leisure services, and sports management), COMMUNICATIONS AND THE ARTS (art history and appreciation, communications, comparative literature, creative writing, dramatic arts, English literature, and fine arts), COMPUTER AND PHYSICAL SCIENCE (computer science and mathematics), EDUCATION (education, elementary education, physical education, secondary education, and special education), ENGINEERING AND ENVIRONMENTAL DESIGN (environmental science), HEALTH PROFESSIONS (health science), SOCIAL SCIENCE (criminal justice, law, legal studies, philosophy, physical fitness/movement, political science/government, psychology, sociology, and women's studies). Business, education, biology/health science, and psychology are the strongest academically. Business, education, and biology/health science have the largest enrollments.

Required: All students must earn a minimum GPA of 2.0 and take 120 credit hours, including an average of 50 in their major. 8 credits of college writing; one Math course; LAS 1 On Being Human; LAS 2 Communities in America; LAS 3 The Creative Arts; LAS 4 The Scientific Process; LAS 5 Laboratory Science; LAS 6 Humanities; and LAS 7 Global Perspectives.

Special: Cross-registration is available with the New Hampshire College and University Council. Also available are internships for juniors and seniors with a GPA of 2.5, study abroad in most countries, work-study programs, dual majors, student-designed majors, interdisciplinary majors, nondegree study, pass/fail options, and a 3-2 engineering degree with Clarkson University. A 4+1 MBA at Union University; and 3+3 Law program at New York Law School are also offered. Washington semeste; Double majors; Individually designed majors; Work Study on and off campus; fully online programs both at undergraduate and graduate levels. There are 1 national honor societies, a freshman honors program, and 32 departmental honors programs.

Faculty/Classroom: 49% of faculty are male; 51% are female. 65% teach undergraduates, and 20% do both. No introductory courses are taught by graduate students. The average class size in an introductory lecture is 14; in a laboratory is 14; and in a regular course is 14.

Admissions: 90% of the 2013-2014 applicants were accepted. 12% of the current freshmen were in the top fifth of their class; 24% were in the top two fifths.

Requirements: 4 years of English, 3 years each of math and social studies, and 2 years each of science and electives are recommended. An essay is required and an interview is recommended. A GPA of 2.0 is required. AP and CLEP credits are accepted. Important factors in the admissions decision are personality/intangible qualities, extracurricular activities record, and leadership record.

Procedure: Freshmen are admitted to all sessions. There are deferred admissions and rolling admissions plans. Application deadlines are open. Application fee is $30. Notification is sent on a rolling basis. Applications are accepted online.

Transfer: 180 transfer students enrolled in 2012-2013. Transfer students should have a 2.0 minimum GPA from the previous college. A recommendation from the dean of students is required. An interview is recommended. 30 of 120 credits required for the bachelor's degree must be completed at NEC.

Visiting: There are regularly scheduled orientations for prospective students, including class registration and meeting faculty and other students. There are guides for informal visits, visitors may sit in on classes, and stay overnight. To schedule a visit, contact the Admissions Office.

Financial Aid: In 2013-2014, 99% of all full-time freshmen and 85% of continuing full-time students received some form of financial aid. 92% of all full-time freshmen and 78% of continuing full-time students received need-based aid. The average freshman award was $28,657. Need-based scholarships or need-based grants averaged $7,046 ($281,145 maximum); need-based self-help aid (loans and jobs) averaged $9,937 ($40,496 maximum); and other non-need-based awards and non-need-based scholarships averaged $18,545 ($38,295 maximum). 94% of undergraduate students work part-time. Average annual earnings from campus work are $1935. The average financial indebtedness of the 2013 graduate was $35,309. The FAFSA and the college's own financial statement are required. The priority date for freshman financial aid applications for fall entry is March 1. The deadline for filing freshman financial aid applications for fall entry is September 5.

International Students: There are 68 international students enrolled. The school actively recruits these students. They must take the TOEFL or MELAB, the Comprehensive English Language Test, and the college's own test.

Computers: All students may access the system 24 hours a day, 7 days a week. There are no time limits and no fees.

Graduates: From July 1, 2012 to June 30, 2013, 159 bachelor's degrees were awarded. The most popular majors were business (15%), education (14%), and health sciences (8%). 32 companies recruited on campus in 2012-2013. In an average class, 2% graduate in 3 years or less, 36% graduate in 4 years or less, 37% graduate in 5 years or less, and 37% graduate in 6 years or less. Of the 2012 graduating class, 19% were enrolled in graduate school within 6 months of graduation, and 84% were employed.

Admissions Contact: Office of Admission, Yasin Alsaidi. E-Mail: *admission@nec.nec.edu* Web: *www.nec.edu*

PLYMOUTH STATE UNIVERSITY D-4

Plymouth, NH 03264 (603) 535-2237
(800) 842-6900; (603) 535-2714

Full-time: 1974 men, 1820 women	**Faculty:** n/av; IIA
Part-time: 144 men, 126 women	**Ph.D.s:** n/av
Graduate: 380 men, 792 women	**Student/Faculty:** n/av
Year: semesters, summer session	**Tuition:** $12,610 ($20,030)
Application Deadline: April 1	**Room & Board:** $10,538
Freshman Class: 5120 applied, 3967 accepted, 930 enrolled	
SAT CR/M: 479/484	**ACT:** 20 **LESS COMPETITIVE**

Plymouth State University, founded in 1871, is a comprehensive regional university located in central New Hampshire at the gateway to the White Mountains and Lakes Region and offering programs in business, education, and liberal arts and sciences. There are 3 undergraduate schools and one graduate school. In addition to regional accreditation, PSU has baccalaureate program accreditation with ABET, ACBSP, CSWE, and NCATE. The library contains 346,207 volumes, 325,000 microform items, 7,043 audio/video tapes/CDs/DVDs, and subscribes to 54,212 periodicals including electronic. Computerized library services include interlibrary loans, database searching, Internet access, and Wi-Fi capability. Special learning facilities include an art gallery, planetarium, radio station, a major performing arts center, NAEYC-accredited lab school for children ages 2 to 6, Geographic information systems lab, Meteorology lab, Graphic design, Computer labs, MIDI lab, Weather technology evaluation center, Museum of The White Mountains, Welcome Center & Ice Arena. The 170-acre campus is in a small town 2 hours north of Boston. Including any residence halls, there are 47 buildings.

Student Life: 59% of undergraduates are from New Hampshire. Others are from 13 states, 26 foreign countries, and Canada. 78% are White; 13% race unknown. The average age of freshmen is 18; all undergraduates, 20. 38% do not continue beyond their first year; 55% remain to graduate.

Housing: 2475 students can be accommodated in college housing, which includes coed dorms, on-campus apartments, and married student housing. In addition, there are special-interest houses, The mission of the Plymouth State University EcoHouse is to demonstrate environmentally sustainable technology in a residential setting, to provide hands-on experiential learning opportunities to PSU students and the surrounding region, to collect and disseminate information about sustainability, and to help others live in more sustainable ways.There is a wellness residence hall and special interest areas in the residence halls for skiing, snowboarding, biking, hiking, music/theater, fine arts, community service, fitness, and quiet study/academic. On-campus housing is guaranteed for all 4 years and is available on a lottery system for upperclassmen. 52% of students live on campus; of those, 70% remain on campus on weekends. All students may keep cars.

Activities: There are no fraternities; 3% of women belong to 1 local and 2 national sororities. There are 100 groups on campus, including art, band, cheerleading, choir, chorale, chorus, communications, computers, dance, debate, drama, ethnic, film, gay, honors, international, jazz band, literary magazine, musical theater, newspaper, pep band, political, professional, radio and TV, religious, social, social service, student government, symphony, and yearbook. Popular campus events include Spring Fling, Homecoming, Earth Jam, Winter Carnival and PRIDE Drag show.

Sports: There are 9 intercollegiate sports for men and 11 for women, and 15 intramural sports for men and 15 for women. Facilities include Our atheletic facility has a 2500-seat stadium, a 2000-seat gym, playing fields, basketball, racquetball, indoor soccer, swimming, tennis, volleyball, softball, and lacrosse. In addition there is also a recreation student center separate from athletics. We also have a ropes course. Our ice arena is also home to our new welcome center.

Disabled Students: 75% of the campus is accessible. Facilities include wheelchair ramps, elevators, special parking, specially equipped restrooms, lowered drinking fountains, lowered telephones, special housing. The shuttle service is wheelchair-accessible, and there are handicap-accessible student apartment units, ADA compliant alarm systems, and TDD/TTY.

Services: Counseling and information services are available, as is tutoring in most subjects, 100 and 200-level courses and some upper-level courses There is remedial writing. Peer tutoring is available.

Campus Safety and Security: Measures include 24-hour foot and vehicle patrol, emergency notification system, self-defense education, and security escort services. There are shuttle buses, emergency telephones, lighted pathways/sidewalks, there are also programs in defensive driving, alcohol awareness, drug identification, and personal safety.

Programs of Study: PSU confers B.A., B.S. and B.F.A. degrees. Master's degrees are also awarded. Bachelor's degrees are awarded in AGRICULTURE (environmental studies), BIOLOGICAL SCIENCE (biology/biological science, biotechnology, and environmental biology), BUSINESS (accounting, business administration and management, marketing management, recreation and leisure services, and tourism), COMMUNICATIONS AND THE ARTS (art history, art, communications, English, French, graphic design, music, performing arts, Spanish, and theatre arts), COMPUTER AND PHYSICAL SCIENCE (atmospheric sciences and meteorology, chemistry, computer science, information sciences and systems, and mathematics), EDUCATION (art education, athletic training, health education, music education, physical education, recreation education, and science education), ENGINEERING AND ENVIRONMENTAL DESIGN (city/community/regional planning), HEALTH PROFESSIONS (nursing), SOCIAL SCIENCE (anthropology, child care/child and family studies, criminal justice, early childhood studies, economics, geography, history, humanities, interdisciplinary studies, philosophy, political science/government, psychology, public administration, social science, and social work). Business, education, health and human performance have the largest enrollments.

Required: All students must maintain a minimum GPA of 2.0 while enrolled in 120 semester hours, including 1 course each in composition and math foundations, a 3-credit first year seminar, and the general education program, which requires 6 credits each in creative thought, scientific inquiry, and self and society directions, and 3 credits each in diversity, global awareness, integration, and wellness connections. Also required are quantitative reasoning in the disciplines as well as technology and writing connections in the major.

Special: Cross-registration with the New Hampshire College and University Council is available. Internships, study abroad in 3 countries, and college work-study programs are available. Dual majors, an accelerated degree program, offering an undergraduate business and M.B.A. degree in 5 years, and student-designed majors are possible. There are 15 national honor societies, a freshman honors program, and 12 departmental honors programs.

Faculty/Classroom: No introductory courses are taught by graduate students.

Admissions: 77% of the 2013-2014 applicants were accepted. The SAT scores for the 2013-2014 freshman class were: Critical Reading--62% below 500, 31% between 500 and 599, 7% between 600 and 699; Math--57% below 500, 34% between 500 and 599, 8% between 600 and 699, and 1% between 700 and 800; Writing--65% below 500, 30% between 500 and 599, 5% between 600 and 699. The ACT scores were 59% below 21, 20% between 21 and 23, 14% between 24 and 26, 4% between 27 and 28, and 1% above 28.

Requirements: The SAT is required. The ACT is recommended. PSU requires that applicants have completed 4 units of English, 3 of math, 2 of social studies and science (1 lab) and 1 of history, and recommends 2 in foreign language. An audition or portfolio is required for certain programs, and an essay is required. The GED is accepted. AP and CLEP credits are accepted. Important factors in the admissions decision are advanced placement or honors courses, recommendations by school officials, and leadership record.

Procedure: Freshmen are admitted fall and spring. Entrance exams

should be taken in November of the senior year. There are deferred admissions and rolling admissions plans. Applications should be filed by April 1 for fall entry; December 1 for spring entry, along with a $50 fee. Notification is sent on a rolling basis. Applications are accepted online.

Transfer: 223 transfer students enrolled in 2012-2013. Transfer students must have a minimum GPA of 2.0 on prior work to be considered. 30 of 120 credits required for the bachelor's degree must be completed at PSU.

Visiting: There are regularly scheduled orientations for prospective students, Admission presentation, a tour of the campus, and a meal in the dining hall. There are guides for informal visits and visitors may sit in on classes. To schedule a visit, contact the Admission Office.

Financial Aid: The FAFSA is required. The priority date for freshman financial aid applications for fall entry is March 1.

International Students: There are 56 international students enrolled. The school actively recruits these students. They must take the TOEFL with a minimum score of 520 on the paper-based TOEFL (PBT) or 68 on the Internet-based version (iBT), Proof of English proficiency during secondary education.

Computers: All students may access the system. There are no time limits. There is a fee.

Graduates: From July 1, 2012 to June 30, 2013, 905 bachelor's degrees were awarded. The most popular majors were business (22%), education (14%), and parks and recreation (8%). 100 companies recruited on campus in 2012-2013. In an average class, 75% graduate in 3 years or less, 67% graduate in 4 years or less, 62% graduate in 5 years or less, and 16% graduate in 6 years or less.

Admissions Contact: Andrew Palumbo , Director or Admissions. E-Mail: *plymouthadmit@plymouth.edu* Web: *www.plymouth.edu*

RIVIER COLLEGE D-6

Nashua, NH 03060 (603) 897-8507
(800) 44-RIVIER; (603) 891-1799

Full-time: 310 men, 610 women	**Faculty:** n/av
Part-time: 205 men, 505 women	**Ph.D.s:** n/av
Graduate: 255 men, 625 women	**Student/Faculty:** n/av
Year: semesters, summer session	**Tuition:** $26,000
Application Deadline: open	**Room & Board:** $9000
Freshman Class: n/av	
SAT: required	**VERY COMPETITIVE**

Rivier College, founded in 1933 by the Sisters of the Presentation of Mary, is a private Roman Catholic college offering a liberal arts and professional curriculum. The figures in the above capsule and in this profile are approximate. There is one graduate school. In addition to regional accreditation, Rivier has baccalaureate program accreditation with NLN. The library contains 107,200 volumes, 89,572 microform items, 29,094 audio/video tapes/CDs/DVDs, and subscribes to 480 periodicals including electronic. Computerized library services include interlibrary loans and database searching. Special learning facilities include an art gallery, radio station, TV station, education curriculum resources center, legal reference center, early childhood center/laboratory school, and language lab. The 68-acre campus is in a suburban area 45 miles north of Boston. Including any residence halls, there are 44 buildings.

Student Life: 68% of undergraduates are from New Hampshire. Others are from 13 states, 13 foreign countries, and Canada. 80% are from public schools. 93% are White. 80% are Catholic. The average age of freshmen is 18; all undergraduates, 28. 29% do not continue beyond their first year.

Housing: 425 students can be accommodated in college housing, which includes coed dorms. a substance-free/wellness residence hall. On-campus housing is guaranteed for all 4 years, is available on a first-come, and first-served basis. 56% of students commute. All students may keep cars.

Activities: There are no fraternities or sororities. There are 32 groups on campus, including and nursing, behavioral sciences, history, paralegal, art, chorus, computers, debate, drama, ethnic, honors, international, literary magazine, newspaper, political, professional, religious, social, social sciences, social service, student government, and yearbook. Popular campus events include Spirit Week, Black History Month, and Women's History Month.

Sports: There are 5 intercollegiate sports for men and 5 for women, and 7 intramural sports for men and 7 for women. Facilities include a 300-seat gym, a weight room, and soccer and softball fields.

Disabled Students: 75% of the campus is accessible. Facilities include wheelchair ramps, elevators, special parking, specially equipped restrooms, and lowered drinking fountains.

Services: Counseling and information services are available, as is tutoring in some subjects, math, English, business, and languages. Tutoring is available in other subjects. There is remedial math and writing. There is a full-service writing center.

Campus Safety and Security: Measures include 24-hour foot and vehicle patrol and security escort services. There are emergency telephones, lighted pathways/sidewalks, 24-hour access by telephone or walkie-talkie, and electronically operated dorm entrances using security cards.

Programs of Study: Rivier confers B.A., B.S. and B.F.A. degrees. Associate and master's degrees are also awarded. Bachelor's degrees are awarded in BIOLOGICAL SCIENCE (biology/biological science), BUSINESS (business administration and management, management information systems, and management science), COMMUNICATIONS AND THE ARTS (communications, English, graphic design, illustration, and studio art), COMPUTER AND PHYSICAL SCIENCE (computer science and mathematics), EDUCATION (art education, early childhood education, elementary education, English education, mathematics education, secondary education, and social studies education), HEALTH PROFESSIONS (nursing, predentistry, premedicine, and preveterinary science), SOCIAL SCIENCE (history, human development, liberal arts/general studies, political science/government, prelaw, psychology, and sociology). Art, education, and nursing are the strongest academically. Education, psychology, and business have the largest enrollments.

Required: A writing sample is required at entry, and a demonstration of writing proficiency must be shown prior to graduation. Students must complete at least 120 credit hours, ordinarily consisting of 40 3-credit courses with 35 to 60 credits in the student's major, and they must maintain a minimum GPA of 2.0. Distribution requirements include 17 core courses in basic skills of writing and math, the humanities, and the sciences. These courses include religious studies, philosophy, physical and life sciences, fine arts, modern languages, literature, behavioral and social sciences, and Western civilization.

Special: Rivier offers cross-registration through the New Hampshire College and University Council, internships in most majors, an accelerated master's program in English, dual majors, a liberal studies degree, credit by challenge examination, nondegree study, and pass/fail options. There are 1 national honor societies and a freshman honors program.

Faculty/Classroom: 38% of faculty are male; 62% are female. 88% teach undergraduates. No introductory courses are taught by graduate students. The average class size in an introductory lecture is 25; in a laboratory is 20; and in a regular course is 17.

Requirements: The SAT is required. Applicants must be high school graduates or hold the GED. The recommended college preparatory curriculum includes 4 years of English, 3 of math, 2 or more each of foreign language and social studies, 1 of lab science, and 4 academic electives. An essay and 1 or 2 letters of recommendation are required, and an interview is highly recommended. Prospective art majors must submit a portfolio. A GPA of 2.5 is required. AP and CLEP credits are accepted. Important factors in the admissions decision are advanced placement or honors courses, recommendations by school officials, and extracurricular activities record.

Procedure: Freshmen are admitted fall and spring. Entrance exams should be taken in the junior or senior year. There are deferred admissions and rolling admissions plans. Application deadlines are open. The fall 2013 application fee was $25. Notification of early decision is sent December 1; regular decision, on a rolling basis. Applications are accepted online.

Transfer: Transfer applicants should have a minimum GPA of 2.5 and submit SAT I or ACT scores if they have earned fewer than 12 credits at the previous institution. Official college transcripts are required and an interview is recommended. 60 of 120 credits required for the bachelor's degree must be completed at Rivier.

Visiting: There are regularly scheduled orientations for prospective students, including an opportunity to interview, a tour, class visits, and opportunities to meet with faculty, coaches, and current students. There are guides for informal visits, visitors may sit in on classes, and stay overnight. To schedule a visit, contact the Office of Undergraduate Admissions.

Financial Aid: Rivier is a member of CSS. The FAFSA is required. Check with the school for current application deadlines.

International Students: The school actively recruits these students. They must take the TOEFL and the college's own test.

Computers: All students may access the system 24 hours a day. There are no time limits. The fee is $varies.

Admissions Contact: David A. Boisvert, Director of Undergraduate Admissions. E-Mail: *rivadmit@rivier.edu* Web: *www.rivier.edu*

SAINT ANSELM COLLEGE D-6

Manchester, NH 03102 (603) 641-7500
(888)-4-ANSELM; (603) 641-7550

Full-time: 762 men, 1116 women	**Faculty:** n/av; IIB, av$
Part-time: 17 men, 28 women	**Ph.D.s:** n/av
Graduate: n/av	**Student/Faculty:** n/av
Year: semesters, summer session	**Tuition:** $35,634
Application Deadline: February 1	**Room & Board:** $12,690
Freshman Class: 3829 applied, 2820 accepted, 508 enrolled	
SAT CR/M/W: 574/572/574 **ACT:** 25	**VERY COMPETITIVE**

Saint Anselm College, founded in 1889, is a private Roman Catholic institution offering a liberal arts education. In addition to regional accreditation,

Saint Anselm has baccalaureate program accreditation with NLN. The library contains 219,000 volumes, 65,000 microform items, 8,000 audio/video tapes/CDs/DVDs, and subscribes to 3,900 periodicals including electronic. Computerized library services include interlibrary loans, database searching, and Internet access. Special learning facilities include an art gallery, planetarium, radio station, and TV station. The 404-acre campus is in a suburban area 50 miles north of Boston. Including any residence halls, there are 63 buildings.

Student Life: 80% of undergraduates are from out of state, mostly the Northeast. Students are from 28 states, 21 foreign countries, and Canada. 67% are from public schools. 78% are White; 13% race unknown. 55% are Catholic. The average age of freshmen is 18; all undergraduates, 20. 12% do not continue beyond their first year; 75% remain to graduate.

Housing: 1644 students can be accommodated in college housing, which includes single-sex and coed dorms and on-campus apartments. In addition, there are special-interest houses, substance-free housing. On-campus housing is guaranteed for all 4 years. 92% of students live on campus; of those, 95% remain on campus on weekends. All students may keep cars.

Activities: There are no fraternities or sororities. There are 65 groups on campus, including art, band, cheerleading, chess, choir, chorale, chorus, computers, dance, debate, drama, environmental, ethnic, honors, international, jazz band, literary magazine, musical theater, newspaper, orchestra, pep band, photography, political, professional, radio and TV, religious, social, social service, student government, and yearbook. Popular campus events include Winter Weekend, Family Weekend, and Road for Hope.

Sports: There are 10 intercollegiate sports for men and 10 for women, and 13 intramural sports for men and 13 for women. Facilities include a 1500-seat gym, an ice hockey arena, an activity center that houses basketball, volleyball, tennis, and racquetball courts, and weight and training rooms; a 2500-seat football stadium; a 500-seat baseball stadium; and athletic fields.

Disabled Students: 60% of the campus is accessible. Facilities include wheelchair ramps, elevators, special parking, specially equipped restrooms, special class scheduling, and lowered drinking fountains.

Services: Counseling and information services are available, as is tutoring in most subjects. There is a reader service for the blind.

Campus Safety and Security: Measures include 24-hour foot and vehicle patrol. There are emergency telephones, lighted pathways/sidewalks, security escort upon request.

Programs of Study: Saint Anselm confers B.A., and B.S.N. degrees. Bachelor's degrees are awarded in BIOLOGICAL SCIENCE (biochemistry and biology/biological science), BUSINESS (accounting, banking and finance, and business administration and management), COMMUNICATIONS AND THE ARTS (classics, English, fine arts, French, and Spanish), COMPUTER AND PHYSICAL SCIENCE (chemistry, computer science, mathematics, and natural sciences), EDUCATION (secondary education), ENGINEERING AND ENVIRONMENTAL DESIGN (engineering and environmental science), HEALTH PROFESSIONS (nursing, predentistry, and premedicine), SOCIAL SCIENCE (criminal justice, economics, history, liberal arts/general studies, philosophy, political science/government, prelaw, psychology, sociology, and theological studies). Nursing, psychology, biology have the largest enrollments.

Required: All students must maintain a GPA of 2.0 in the major while completing at least 40 semester courses, including 4 semesters in the humanities, 3 each in philosophy and theology, 2 each in English and lab science, and 2 to 4 in foreign language; 10 to 13 courses are required in the major area of study.

Special: Saint Anselm offers a 5-year liberal arts and a 3-2 engineering program in cooperation with Manhattan College, University of Notre Dame, University of Massachusetts Lowell, and Catholic University of America. Cross-registration is possible. In addition, internships, work-study, a Washington semester, a New York City semester, study abroad, and nondegree study are available. There are 11 national honor societies, a freshman honors program, and 20 departmental honors programs.

Faculty/Classroom: 60% of faculty are male; 40% are female. All teach undergraduates. No introductory courses are taught by graduate students. The average class size in an introductory lecture is 20; in a laboratory is 14; and in a regular course is 24.

Admissions: 74% of the 2013-2014 applicants were accepted. The SAT scores for the 2013-2014 freshman class were: Critical Reading--10% below 500, 57% between 500 and 599, 29% between 600 and 699, and 4% between 700 and 800; Math--11% below 500, 51% between 500 and 599, 36% between 600 and 699, and 2% between 700 and 800; Writing--11% below 500, 51% between 500 and 599, 34% between 600 and 699, and 4% between 700 and 800. The ACT scores were 6% below 21, 23% between 21 and 23, 37% between 24 and 26, 22% between 27 and 28, and 12% above 28. 56% of the current freshmen were in the top fifth of their class; 87% were in the top two fifths. 2 freshmen graduated first in their class.

Requirements: Applicants must have 16 academic credits and 16 Carnegie units, including 4 years of English, 3 each of math and science, 2 of foreign language, and 1 each of history and social studies. An essay is required, and an interview is recommended. The GED is accepted. AP and CLEP credits are accepted. Important factors in the admissions decision are advanced placement or honors courses, leadership record, extracurricular activities record, recommendations by school officials, parents or siblings attended your school, evidence of special talent, personality/intangible qualities, recommendations by alumni, and geographical diversity.

Procedure: Freshmen are admitted fall and spring. Entrance exams should be taken during the spring of the junior year or fall of the senior year. There are early admissions and deferred admissions plans. Early decision applications should be filed by November 15; regular applications, by February 1 for fall entry; and November 15 for spring entry, along with a $50 fee. Notifications are sent March 10. 196 applicants were on the 2013 waiting list; 38 were admitted. Applications are accepted online.

Transfer: 21 transfer students enrolled in 2012-2013. 20 of 40 credits required for the bachelor's degree must be completed at Saint Anselm.

Visiting: There are regularly scheduled orientations for prospective students, consisting of daily individual interviews and/or group information sessions followed by a campus tour. There are guides for informal visits and visitors may sit in on classes. To schedule a visit, contact the Office of Admission.

Financial Aid: In 2013-2014, 97% of all full-time freshmen and 97% of continuing full-time students received some form of financial aid. The average freshman award was $22,490. Need-based scholarships or need-based grants averaged $17,940. Saint Anselm is a member of CSS. The CSS/Profile and FAFSA are required. The deadline for filing freshman financial aid applications for fall entry is March 15.

International Students: There are 12 international students enrolled. They must take the TOEFL with a minimum score of 80 on the Internet-based version (iBT), International students must submit either scores from the SAT or TOEFL if they have not taken the SAT. They must also take the SAT or ACT.

Computers: All students may access the system 8:30 a.m. to 12 a.m., Monday through Friday; 10 a.m. to 6 p.m. Saturday; 1 p.m. to 12 a.m. Sunday. There are no time limits and no fees.

Graduates: From July 1, 2012 to June 30, 2013, 438 bachelor's degrees were awarded. The most popular majors were social sciences (20%), business/marketing (19%), and health professions and related programs (19%). In an average class, 71% graduate in 4 years or less, 74% graduate in 5 years or less, and 75% graduate in 6 years or less.

Admissions Contact: Eric Nichols, Director of Admission. E-Mail: *admission@anselm.edu* Web: *www.anselm.edu*

SOUTHERN NEW HAMPSHIRE UNIVERSITY D-6

Manchester, NH 03106 (603) 645-9611
(800) 642-4968; (603) 645-9693

Full-time: 870 men, 1070 women	**Faculty:** n/av; IIA, av$
Part-time: 25 men, 30 women	**Ph.D.s:** n/av
Graduate: 965 men, 1415 women	**Student/Faculty:** n/av
Year: semesters, summer session	**Tuition:** $28,380
Application Deadline:	**Room & Board:** $9720
Freshman Class: n/av	
SAT or ACT: required	

COMPETITIVE

Southern New Hampshire University, founded in 1932, is a private university offering academic programs in business, education, liberal arts, culinary arts, and community economic development. SNHU also has continuing education and online education programs. There are 5 undergraduate schools and 4 graduate schools. In addition to regional accreditation, SNHU has baccalaureate program accreditation with ACBSP. The library contains 94,042 volumes, 378,319 microform items, and 3,170 audio/video tapes/CDs/DVDs, and subscribes to 755 periodicals including electronic. Computerized library services include interlibrary loans, database searching, Internet access, and Wi-Fi capability. Special learning facilities include an art gallery, radio station, a center for financial studies, an advertising agency (on campus), an audiovisual studio, a psychology observation lab, a career development center, and an iMAC graphics lab. The 280-acre campus is in a suburban area 55 miles north of Boston. Including any residence halls, there are 28 buildings.

Student Life: 54% of undergraduates are from out of state, mostly the Northeast. Students are from 28 states, 54 foreign countries, and Canada. 88% are from public schools. 77% are White. 36% are Catholic; 29% claim no religious affiliation; 20% Protestant. The average age of freshmen is 19; all undergraduates, 20. 25% do not continue beyond their first year; 50% remain to graduate.

Housing: 1668 students can be accommodated in college housing, which includes single-sex and coed dorms and on-campus apartments. In addition, there are special-interest houses, and a wellness housing area. On-campus housing is guaranteed for all 4 years. 76% of students live on campus; of those, 65% remain on campus on weekends. All students may keep cars.

Activities: 4% of men belong to 2 national fraternities; 5% of women belong to 3 local and 1 national sororities. There are 52 groups on campus, including and field hockey, crew club, cheerleading, chess, chorus, dance, debate, drama, ethnic, gay, honors, international, musical theater, newspaper, political, professional, radio and TV, religious, social, social service, sports club, student government, and yearbook. Popular campus events include Fall, Winter, and Spring Weekends, International Night, and Trips Abroad (Italy, Greece, and England).

Sports: There is no sports program at SNHU. Facilities include 2 gyms, an Olympic-sized swimming pool, 4 lighted tennis courts, a lighted artificial surface game field, a fitness room, natural grass baseball , softball, and practice fields, a racquetball court, and an aerobic/excercise room.

Disabled Students: 80% of the campus is accessible. Facilities include wheelchair ramps, elevators, special parking, specially equipped restrooms, special class scheduling, lowered drinking fountains, lowered telephones, special housing, and automatic door openers.

Services: Counseling and information services are available, as is tutoring in every subject. There is a reader service for the blind, and remedial math and writing. Peer mentoring and structured learning assistance services are also available. There is also a Jump Start program available for the summer of pre-college.

Campus Safety and Security: Measures include 24-hour foot and vehicle patrol, emergency notification system, and security escort services. There are emergency telephones, lighted pathways/sidewalks, controlled access to dorms/residences, winter driving seminars for international students, and public safety officers.

Programs of Study: SNHU confers B.A., B.S. and B.A.S.H.A. degrees. Associate, master's, and doctoral degrees are also awarded. Bachelor's degrees are awarded in AGRICULTURE (environmental studies), BUSINESS (accounting, business administration and management, fashion merchandising, hospitality management services, international business management, marketing management, marketing/retailing/merchandising, retailing, sports management, and tourism), COMMUNICATIONS AND THE ARTS (advertising, communications, creative writing, English, English as a second/foreign language, English literature, and graphic design), COMPUTER AND PHYSICAL SCIENCE (computer science, digital arts/technology, and information sciences and systems), EDUCATION (business education, early childhood education, education, elementary education, English education, secondary education, social studies education, and special education), ENGINEERING AND ENVIRONMENTAL DESIGN (technological management), SOCIAL SCIENCE (child psychology/development, culinary arts, history, liberal arts/general studies, political science/government, psychology, public affairs, and social science). Business administration is the strongest academically. Business administration, sports management, and psychology have the largest enrollments.

Required: To graduate, students must complete a minimum of 120 credit hours, including 39 in their majors, with a GPA of 2.0. Distribution requirements total 45 credits from the college core, including 2 to 3 courses in writing, and 2 math, information technology, public speaking, statistics, behavioral, social and natural sciences, courses and electives in fine arts and literature.

Special: There are co-ops available, a choice of over 35 study abroad opportunities through the University Studies Abroad Consortium, work-study positions throughout the campus, dual majors, and a 3-year bachelor's degree that is an accelerated degree program in business administration. There are 6 national honor societies, a freshman honors program, and 1 departmental honors programs.

Faculty/Classroom: 60% of faculty are male; 40% are female. 90% teach undergraduates, 78% do research, and 73% do both. No introductory courses are taught by graduate students. The average class size in an introductory lecture is 20; in a laboratory is 15; and in a regular course is 21.

Requirements: The SAT or ACT is required. The ACT Optional Writing test is also required. Students must have completed 4 years of English and 3 of math. An essay, high school transcript, SAT or ACT (with writing), and a letter of recommendation from a guidance counselor or 2 teachers are required. An interview is strongly recommended. The GED is accepted. A GPA of 2.0 is required. AP and CLEP credits are accepted.

Procedure: Freshmen are admitted fall and spring. There are deferred admissions and rolling admissions plans. Application deadlines are open. Application fee is $40. Notification is sent on a rolling basis. Applications are accepted online.

Transfer: 164 transfer students enrolled in 2012-2013. Transfer applicants must submit a completed application, essay, official high school transcript, official college transcripts, supplemental transfer form, and a letter of recommendation. An interview is also highly recommended. Most successful applicants for transfer admission have a cumulative GPA of 2.5 or higher 30 of 120 credits required for the bachelor's degree must be completed at SNHU.

Visiting: There are regularly scheduled orientations for prospective students, including a greeting from college administrators, campus tours with students, and informal presentation/discussions with faculty and staff. There are guides for informal visits and visitors may sit in on classes. To schedule a visit, contact the Admission Office.

Financial Aid: In 2013-2014, 95% of all full-time freshmen and 92% of continuing full-time students received some form of financial aid. 76% of all full-time freshmen and 68% of continuing full-time students received need-based aid. SNHU is a member of CSS. The FAFSA is required. Check with the school for current application deadlines.

International Students: There are 89 international students enrolled. The school actively recruits these students. They must take the TOEFL.

Computers: All students may access the system 8 a.m. to 12 p.m. daily; extended hours during final exams. There are no time limits and no fees.

Graduates: From July 1, 2012 to June 30, 2013, 1141 bachelor's degrees were awarded. The most popular majors were business administration (42%), psychology (6%), and accounting (6%). 75 companies recruited on campus in 2012-2013. In an average class, 40% graduate in 4 years or less, 48% graduate in 5 years or less, and 50% graduate in 6 years or less. Of the 2012 graduating class, 11% were enrolled in graduate school within 6 months of graduation, and 85% were employed.

Admissions Contact: Steven Soba, Director of Admission. E-Mail: *admission@snhu.edu* Web: *www.snhu.edu*

THOMAS MORE COLLEGE OF LIBERAL ARTS D-6

Merrimack, NH 03054 (603) 880-8308
(800) 880-8308; (603) 880-9280

Full-time: 52 men, 44 women	**Faculty:** 5
Part-time: n/av	**Ph.D.s:** 100%
Graduate: n/av	**Student/Faculty:** 14 to 1
Year: semesters	**Tuition:** $19,200
Application Deadline: open	**Room & Board:** $9400
Freshman Class: n/av	
SAT or ACT: required	

COMPETITIVE

Thomas More College of Liberal Arts, founded in 1978 by Roman Catholic educators, is an undergraduate institution that combines intensive reading of the Great Books with lectures and seminar discussions placing those works in their historical, cultural, and theological context. Thomas More welcomes students of all faiths. There is one undergraduate school. In addition to regional accreditation, Thomas More College has baccalaureate program accreditation with AALE. The library contains 50,000 and subscribes to 20 periodicals including electronic. Computerized library services include Internet access. The 17-acre campus is in a small town between Nashua and Manchester, 40 miles north of Boston. Including any residence halls, there are 5 buildings.

Student Life: 81% of undergraduates are from out of state, mostly the Northeast. Students are from 20 states, 2 foreign countries, and Canada. 84% are White. The average age of freshmen is 18; all undergraduates, 20. 9% do not continue beyond their first year.

Housing: College-sponsored housing includes single-sex dorms. On-campus housing is guaranteed for all 4 years. Alcohol is not permitted. All students commute. All students may keep cars.

Activities: There are no fraternities or sororities. Groups on campus include art, choir, chorale, chorus, dance, debate, drama, literary magazine, musical theater, newspaper, photography, radio and TV, and yearbook. Popular campus events include St. Patrick's Day.

Disabled Students: 70% of the campus is accessible. Facilities include wheelchair ramps, special parking, and specially equipped restrooms.

Services: Counseling and information services are available, as is tutoring in most subjects. Informal tutoring is available by request.

Campus Safety and Security: Measures include security escort services. There are lighted pathways/sidewalks.

Programs of Study: Thomas More College confers B.A. degrees. Bachelor's degrees are awarded in SOCIAL SCIENCE (liberal arts/general studies).

Required: To graduate, students in the classes of 2013 and beyond must complete 121 credit hours, including 32 in humanities, 12 each in classical languages, tutorials, philosophy, and Sacred Scripture, 9 in writing/rhetoric/poetics, 7 in fine arts, and 6 each in math, natural science, and theology. In addition, students must complete a junior project of independent study and a senior thesis and seminar.

Special: A semester in Rome for sophomores is required. Internships are available at Vatican Radio, Zenit News, and the United Nations.

Faculty/Classroom: 80% of faculty are male; 20% are female. All teach undergraduates, 80% do research, and 80% do both. No introductory courses are taught by graduate students.

Admissions: There were 2 National Merit finalists.

Requirements: The SAT or ACT is required. Applicants should be high school graduates with 4 college preparatory units of English, 3 of math, and 2 each of foreign language, social science, and lab science. The GED is accepted. An essay and 2 letters of recommendation are required. An interview is strongly recommended. Important factors in the admissions decision are personality/intangible qualities, evidence of special talent, and leadership record.

Procedure: Freshmen are admitted fall and spring. There is a rolling admissions plan. Application deadlines are open. Applications are accepted online.

Transfer: 4 transfer students enrolled in 2012-2013. Applicants must submit a transcript from all higher institutions attended.

Visiting: There are regularly scheduled orientations for prospective students. There are guides for informal visits, visitors may sit in on classes, and stay overnight. To schedule a visit, contact Director of Admissions.

Financial Aid: In 2013-2014, 80% of all full-time freshmen and 90% of continuing full-time students received some form of financial aid. 65% of all full-time freshmen and 77% of continuing full-time students received need-based aid. The average freshman award was $8,768. 59% of undergraduate students work part-time. Average annual earnings from campus work are $1960. The average financial indebtedness of the 2013 graduate was $13,056. Thomas More College is a member of CSS. The FAFSA is required. Check with the school for current application deadlines.

International Students: There are 2 international students enrolled. The school actively recruits these students.

Computers: All students may access the system during library hours. There are no time limits and no fees.

Graduates: From July 1, 2012 to June 30, 2013, 12 bachelor's degrees were awarded. The most popular majors were liberal arts (100%). In an average class, 100% graduate in 4 years or less. Of the 2012 graduating class, 27% were enrolled in graduate school within 6 months of graduation, and 73% were employed.

Admissions Contact: Mark Schwerdt, Director of Admissions. E-Mail: *admissions@thomasmorecollege.edu* Web: *www.thomasmorecollege.edu*

UNIVERSITY OF NEW HAMPSHIRE — E-5

Durham, NH 03824	**(603) 862-1360; (603) 862-0077**
Full-time: 5481 men, 6628 women	**Faculty:** 616; I, av$
Part-time: 268 men, 232 women	**Ph.D.s:** 93%
Graduate: 1094 men, 1469 women	**Student/Faculty:** 20 to 1
Year: semesters, summer session	**Tuition:** $15,250 ($28,570)
Application Deadline: February 1	**Room & Board:** $9452
Freshman Class: 17344 applied, 12863 accepted, 2949 enrolled	
SAT CR/M/W: 540/560/540 **ACT:** 24	**VERY COMPETITIVE**

The University of New Hampshire, founded in 1866, is part of the public university system of New Hampshire and offers degree programs in liberal arts, engineering, physical sciences, business, economics, life sciences, agriculture, and health and human services. There are 6 undergraduate schools and 1 graduate school. In addition to regional accreditation, UNH has baccalaureate program accreditation with AACSB, ABET, ADA, CSWE, NASM, NRPA, SAF, and TEAC. The 5 libraries contain 1.6 million volumes, 3.0 million microform items, and 27,375 audio/video tapes/CDs/DVDs, and subscribe to 64,222 periodicals including electronic. Computerized library services include interlibrary loans, database searching, Internet access, and laptop Internet portals. Special learning facilities include a learning resource center, art gallery, radio station, TV station, optical observatory, marine research labs, interoperability lab, flow physics facility, experiential learning center, electron microscope, child development center, journalism lab, various agricultural and equine facilities, sawmill, language labs, performing arts center, and survey center. The 2600-acre campus is in a small town 50 miles north of Boston. Including any residence halls, there are 183 buildings.

Student Life: 60% of undergraduates are from New Hampshire. Others are from 42 states, 29 foreign countries, and Canada. 80% are from public schools. 85% are white. The average age of freshmen is 18; all undergraduates, 20. 13% do not continue beyond their first year; 77% remain to graduate.

Housing: 7500 students can be accommodated in college housing, which includes coed dorms, on-campus apartments, and married student housing. In addition, there are honors houses, language houses, special-interest houses, international and substance-free residence halls. On-campus housing is guaranteed for the freshman year only, is available on a first-come, and first-served basis. 59% of students live on campus; of those, 65% remain on campus on weekends. Upperclassmen may keep cars.

Activities: 7% of men belong to 10 national fraternities; 10% of women belong to 7 national sororities. There are 249 groups on campus, including art, band, cheerleading, chess, choir, chorale, chorus, computers, dance, debate, drama, environmental, ethnic, film, gay, honors, international, jazz band, literary magazine, marching band, musical theater, newspaper, orchestra, pep band, political, professional, radio and TV, religious, social, social service, student government, symphony, and yearbook. Popular campus events include Jukebox, student activities fair, concerts and comedians, Winter carnival, athletic events, and MUB lecture series.

Sports: There are 33 intercollegiate sports for men and 34 for women, and 28 intramural sports for men and 29 for women. Facilities include indoor and outdoor swimming pools, tracks, tennis courts, gyms, wrestling and gymnastics rooms, a dance studio, playing fields, an indoor ice rink, and cross-country ski trails. A 3-story recreation and sports complex, which seats 6,500 for hockey and 7,500 for basketball games and special events, includes a fitness center, jogging track, weight room, racquetball courts, international squash court, aerobics and martial arts studios, multipurpose courts, and basketball courts.

Disabled Students: 88% of the campus is accessible. Facilities include wheelchair ramps, elevators, special parking, specially equipped restrooms, special class scheduling, lowered drinking fountains, lowered telephones, special housing. Accommodations made on a case-by-case basis include sign language interpreters, reduced course loads, extended exam time, accessible transportation, academic modifications, note takers, text on tape, and note takers.

Services: Counseling and information services are available, as is tutoring in most subjects. Instruction in learning strategies, study skills, time management, and organizational skills is available. The university writing center offers free assistance by trained consultants.

Campus Safety and Security: Measures include 24-hour foot and vehicle patrol, emergency notification system, self-defense education, and security escort services. There are shuttle buses, emergency telephones, lighted pathways/sidewalks, controlled access to dorms/residences, prevention awareness programs.

Programs of Study: UNH confers B.A., B.F.A., B.Mus., B.S., and B.S.Forestry degrees. Associate, master's, and doctoral degrees are also awarded. Bachelor's degrees are awarded in AGRICULTURE (animal science, dairy science, environmental studies, forestry and related sciences, horticulture, plant science, soil science, and wildlife management), BIOLOGICAL SCIENCE (biochemistry, biology/biological science, genetics, microbiology, molecular biology, neurosciences, nutrition, and zoology), BUSINESS (business administration and management, hospitality management services, hotel/motel and restaurant management, recreation and leisure services, and tourism), COMMUNICATIONS AND THE ARTS (classics, communications, English, English literature, fine arts, French, German, Greek, Latin, linguistics, music, music performance, music theory and composition, Russian, Spanish, studio art, and voice), COMPUTER AND PHYSICAL SCIENCE (chemistry, computer science, earth science, geology, information sciences and systems, mathematics, and physics), EDUCATION (athletic training, English education, environmental education, mathematics education, music education, physical education, recreation education, and science education), ENGINEERING AND ENVIRONMENTAL DESIGN (chemical engineering, city/community/regional planning, civil engineering, computer engineering, electrical/electronics engineering, environmental engineering, environmental science, and mechanical engineering), HEALTH PROFESSIONS (biomedical science, health care administration, health science, medical laboratory science, nursing, occupational therapy, preveterinary science, and speech pathology/audiology), SOCIAL SCIENCE (anthropology, economics, European studies, family/consumer studies, French studies, history, humanities, philosophy, physical fitness/movement, political science/government, psychology, social work, sociology, water resources, and women's studies). Business, engineering, and English are the strongest academically. Business, psychology, English, and communications have the largest enrollments.

Required: To graduate, all students must maintain a GPA of 2.0 and complete at least 128 credits, with a minimum of 36 credits and 10 classes in the major. General education requirements include 4 writing-intensive courses, including freshman composition; 3 courses in biological/physical science, 1 course each in quantitative reasoning, historical perspectives, social science, fine arts, foreign culture, and philosophy/literature. Honors students and most seniors write a thesis or complete a project.

Special: Joint programs with Cornell University in marine science are available. Extensive cross-registration is possible through the New Hampshire College and University Council Consortium. There also is nationwide study through the National Student Exchange and worldwide study through the Center for International Education. Internships, study abroad throughout the world, a Washington semester, work-study, and B.A.-B.S. degrees, dual majors, a general studies degree, student-designed majors, extensive 3-2 B.S./M.B.A. programs and other bachelor's/graduate degree plans, nondegree study, and pass/fail options are also available. A 3-2 engineering degree is offered with the New Hampshire Technical Institute, Vermont Technical College, Keene State College, and other institutions. There are 18 national honor societies, including Phi Beta Kappa, a freshman honors program, and 41 departmental honors programs.

Faculty/Classroom: 54% of faculty are male; 46% are female. 90% teach undergraduates, all do research. Graduate students teach 2% of introductory courses. The average class size in an introductory lecture is 54; in a laboratory is 22; and in a regular course is 25.

Admissions: 74% of a recent year applicants were accepted. The SAT scores for a recent freshman class were: Critical Reading--26% below 500, 50% between 500 and 599, 21% between 600 and 700, and 3% above 700; Math--20% below 500, 47% between 500 and 599, 30% between

600 and 700, and 3% above 700; Writing--24% below 500, 52% between 500 and 599, 22% between 600 and 700, and 2% above 700. The ACT scores were 13% below 21, 30% between 21 and 23, 30% between 24 and 26, 14% between 27 and 28, and 13% above 28. 43% of the current freshmen were in the top fifth of their class; 82% were in the top two fifths. 53 freshmen graduated first in their class.

Requirements: The SAT or ACT is required. The ACT Optional Writing test is also required. In addition, required: 15 academic units: 4 English, 3 Mathematics, 3 Science (at least 2 must include lab), 2 Foreign Language, 3 Social Studies. Recommended: 19 academic units: 4 English, 4 Mathematics, 4 Science (3 that include lab), 3 Foreign Language, 3 Social Studies, 1 Visual/Performing Arts. Essay required for all students. Audition is required for music students. AP credits are accepted. Important factors in the admissions decision are advanced placement or honors courses, recommendations by school officials, and evidence of special talent.

Procedure: Freshmen are admitted fall and spring. Entrance exams should be taken before February 1 of the senior year. There are early decision and deferred admissions plans. Early decision applications should be filed by November 15; regular applications, by February 1 for fall entry; and October 15 for spring entry. The fall application fee is $65. Notification of early decision is sent January 15; regular decision, April 15. Applications are accepted online.

Transfer: 529 transfer students enrolled in a recent year. Applicants must submit an overall minimum GPA of 2.8 in a general education curriculum. The SAT or the ACT is required unless waived. An essay is required. A letter of recommendation is optional. 32 of 128 credits required for the bachelor's degree must be completed at University of New Hampshire.

Visiting: There are regularly scheduled orientations for prospective students, including campus tours, group information session, and open house programs. There are guides for informal visits and visitors may sit in on classes. To schedule a visit, contact the Admissions Office.

Financial Aid: In a recent year, 86% of all full-time freshmen and 80% of continuing full-time students received some form of financial aid. 64% of all full-time freshmen and 60% of continuing full-time students received need-based aid. The average freshman award was $19,420. Need-based scholarships or need-based grants averaged $8,991 ($28,658 maximum); need-based self-help aid (loans and jobs) averaged $6,145 ($8,000 maximum); non-need-based athletic scholarships averaged $22,713 ($35,587 maximum); and other non-need-based awards and non-need-based scholarships averaged $9,590 ($36,000 maximum). 42% of undergraduate students work part-time. Average annual earnings from campus work are $2485. The average financial indebtedness of a recent graduate was $32,323. The FAFSA is required. The deadline for filing freshman financial aid applications for fall entry is March 1.

International Students: There are 79 international students enrolled. The school actively recruits these students. They must take the TOEFL with a minimum score of 550 on the paper-based TOEFL (PBT) or 80 on the Internet-based version (iBT). They must also take the SAT or ACT.

Graduates: In a recent year, 2671 bachelor's degrees were awarded. The most popular majors were business administration (12%), psychology (7%), and communication (5%). 200 companies recruited on campus in a recent year. In an average class, 64% graduate in 4 years or less, 76% graduate in 5 years or less, and 77% graduate in 6 years or less. Of the 2010 graduating class, 30% were enrolled in graduate school within 6 months of graduation, and 50% were employed.

Admissions Contact: Robert McGann, Director of Admissions. E-Mail: *admissions@unh.edu* Web: *www.unh.edu*

UNIVERSITY SYSTEM OF NEW HAMPSHIRE

The University System of New Hampshire, established in 1963, is a public system in New Hampshire. It is governed by a board of trustees, whose chief administrator is the chancellor. The primary goal of the system is to serve the higher educational needs of the people of New Hampshire. The main priorities are to provide a well-coordinated system of higher education, student access and diversity, and quality programs with a commitment to excellence. The total student enrollment of all four campuses is usually about 29,286 with 1080 faculty members. Altogether there are 131 baccalaureate, 68 master's, and 21 doctoral programs offered in the University System of New Hampshire. Profiles of the 4-year campuses are included in this section.

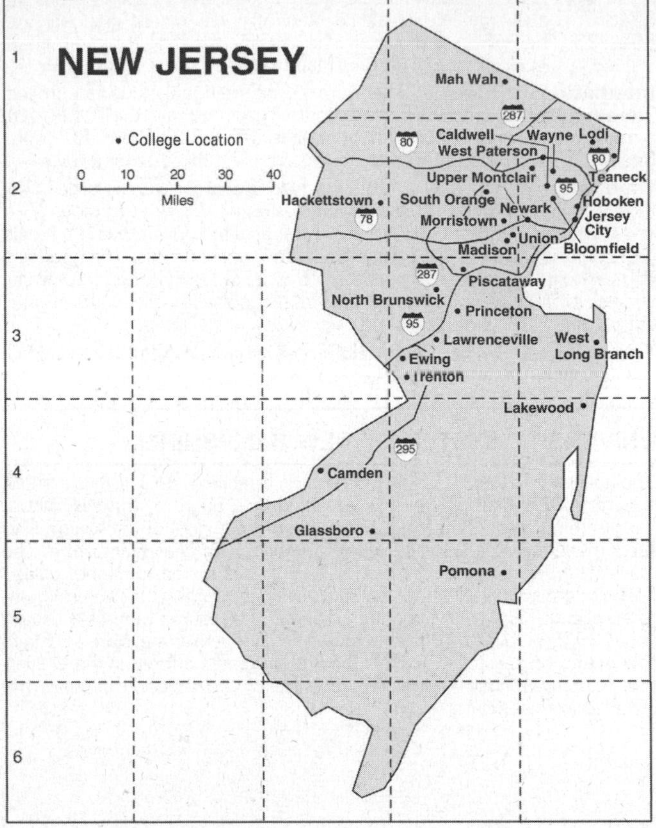

BERKELEY COLLEGE/NEW JERSEY E-2

West Paterson, NJ 07424 (973) 278-5400
(800) 446-5400; (273) 278-9141

Full-time: 788 men, 1841 women
Part-time: 68 men, 355 women
Graduate: n/av
Year: trimesters
Application Deadline: open
Freshman Class: n/av
SAT or ACT: required
Faculty: n/av
Ph.D.s: n/av
Student/Faculty: n/av
Tuition: $18,800
Room & Board: $9500

LESS COMPETITIVE

Berkeley College of New Jersey, founded in 1931, is a private institution offering undergraduate programs in business. Figures in the above capsule and this profile are approximate. The library contains 11,000 volumes and subscribes to 130 periodicals including electronic. Computerized library services include interlibrary loans and database searching. Special learning facilities include a learning resource center. The campus is in a suburban area in West Paterson, approximately 20 miles from New York City. Including any residence halls, there are 2 buildings.

Student Life: 93% of undergraduates are from New Jersey. Others are from 4 states and 4 foreign countries. 34% are African American; 23% white; 23% Hispanic.

Housing: College-sponsored housing includes dorms. 96% of students commute.

Activities: There are no fraternities or sororities.

Sports: There is no sports program at Berkeley.

Services: Counseling and information services are available, as is tutoring in most subjects. There is remedial math, reading, and writing.

Programs of Study: Berkeley confers B.B.A. degrees. Associate degrees are also awarded. Bachelor's degrees are awarded in BUSINESS (accounting, business administration and management, international business management, and marketing/retailing/merchandising), HEALTH PROFESSIONS (health care administration).

Requirements: The SAT or ACT is required. In addition, graduation from an accredited high school or the GED, and an entrance exam or SAT or ACT scores are basic requirements for admission. A personal interview is strongly recommended. AP and CLEP credits are accepted.

Procedure: Freshmen are admitted to all sessions. Entrance exams should be taken any time. There are deferred admissions and rolling admissions plans. Application deadlines are open. The application fee is $50. Notification is sent on a rolling basis. Applications are accepted online.

Transfer: A transcript from each college or university attended must be submitted to receive credit. 60 of 180 credits required for the bachelor's degree must be completed at Berkeley.

Visiting: There are guides for informal visits.

Financial Aid: The FAFSA, the college's own financial statement, and state income tax form are required. Check with the school for current application deadlines.

International Students: The school actively recruits these students. They must take the TOEFL.

Computers: All students may access the system. There are no time limits and no fees.

Graduates: In a recent year, 242 bachelor's degrees were awarded.

Admissions Contact: Admissions Officer E-mail: *info@berkeleycollege.edu* Web: *www.berkeleycollege.edu*

BLOOMFIELD COLLEGE E-2

Bloomfield, NJ 07003 (973) 748-9000, ext. 1390
(800) 848-4555; (973) 748-0916

Full-time: 630 men, 1135 women
Part-time: 55 men, 149 women
Graduate: 3 men, 5 women
Year: semesters, summer session
Application Deadline: August 1
Freshman Class: n/av
Faculty: 72; IIB, av$
Ph.D.s: 72%
Student/Faculty: 25 to 1
Tuition: $26,060
Room & Board: $10,900
ACT: required

COMPETITIVE

Bloomfield College, founded in 1868 and affiliated with the Presbyterian Church, is an independent institution offering programs in liberal arts and sciences, creative arts and technology, professional studies, and the clinical and health sciences. There is one undergraduate school and one graduate school. In addition to regional accreditation, Bloomfield has baccalaureate program accreditation with NLN. The library contains 56,416 volumes, and 2,966 audio/video tapes/CDs/DVDs, and subscribes to 460 periodicals including electronic. Computerized library services include interlibrary loans, database searching, Internet access, and Wi-Fi capability. Special learning facilities include an art gallery, radio station, electronic classrooms. The 12-acre campus is in a suburban area 15 miles from New York City. Including any residence halls, there are 38 buildings.

Student Life: 91% of undergraduates are from New Jersey. Others are from 19 states, and 6 foreign countries. 65% are from public schools. 50% are African American; 22% Hispanic; 13% White. The average age of freshmen is 19; all undergraduates, 23. 36% do not continue beyond their first year; 36% remain to graduate.

Housing: 505 students can be accommodated in college housing, which includes single-sex and coed dorms and on-campus apartments and off-campus hotel. On-campus housing is available on a first-come, first-served basis, and is available on a lottery system for upperclassmen. Priority is given to out-of-town students. 74% of students commute. Alcohol is not permitted. All students may keep cars.

Activities: 4% of men belong to 7 national fraternities; 2% of women belong to 9 national sororities. There are 42 groups on campus, including communications, dance, drama, environmental, ethnic, honors, international, literary magazine, professional, radio and TV, religious, social, social service, and student government. Popular campus events include Welcome Back BBQ, Spring Formal, Midnight Madness, and Quad Wars.

Sports: There are 5 intercollegiate sports for men and 5 for women, and 2 intramural sports for men and 2 for women. Facilities include a 500-seat gym, weight-lifting facilities, basketball and volleyball court.

Disabled Students: 55% of the campus is accessible. Facilities include wheelchair ramps, elevators, special parking, specially equipped restrooms, lowered drinking fountains, special housing.

Services: There is a reader service for the blind.

Campus Safety and Security: Measures include 24-hour foot and vehicle patrol, emergency notification system, and security escort services. There are lighted pathways/sidewalks, security cameras are installed in all high-traffic areas.

Programs of Study: Bloomfield confers B.A., and B.S. degrees. Bachelor's degrees are awarded in BIOLOGICAL SCIENCE (biology/biological science), BUSINESS (accounting and business administration and management), COMMUNICATIONS AND THE ARTS (English and fine arts), COMPUTER AND PHYSICAL SCIENCE (applied mathematics, chemistry, information sciences and systems, and mathematics), EDUCATION (education), ENGINEERING AND ENVIRONMENTAL DESIGN (graphic arts technology), HEALTH PROFESSIONS (allied health, clinical science, and nursing), SOCIAL SCIENCE (history, philosophy, political science/

government, psychology, religion, and sociology). Nursing and education is the strongest academically. Pre-nursing, nursing, sociology and criminal justice have the largest enrollments.

Required: All degree candidates must successfully complete at least 32 course units at the 100 level or above, and at least 16 course units at an advanced level (i.e., 200 or above). The course units include general education core courses, general education electives, required major and minor courses, and other electives.

Special: Internships, study abroad, and work-study programs are available. Double majors and contract majors are also possible. There are 4 national honor societies, a freshman honors program, and 21 departmental honors programs.

Faculty/Classroom: 52% of faculty are male; 48% are female. All teach undergraduates. No introductory courses are taught by graduate students. The average class size in an introductory lecture is 17; in a laboratory is 13; and in a regular course is 15.

Admissions: 15% of the current freshmen were in the top fifth of their class; 43% were in the top two fifths.

Requirements: The SAT or ACT is required. The college requires at least 14 academic units, which should include English, math, history, and lab science. An essay and 2 personal recommendations are required. A GPA of 2.5 is required. AP and CLEP credits are accepted. Important factors in the admissions decision are advanced placement or honors courses, recommendations by school officials, and extracurricular activities record.

Procedure: Freshmen are admitted fall, spring, and summer. Entrance exams should be taken during the senior year. There are early admissions, deferred admissions, and rolling admissions plans. Applications should be filed by August 1 for fall entry; January 10 for spring entry; and May 1 for summer entry, along with a $40 fee. Notification is sent on a rolling basis. 366 early decision candidates were accepted for the 2013-2014 class. 120 applicants were on the 2013 waiting list; 63 were admitted. Applications are accepted online.

Transfer: 195 transfer students enrolled in 2012-2013. Applicants must present a minimum GPA of 2.0 from an accredited institution and submit official transcripts from all previously attended colleges. 8 of 33 credits required for the bachelor's degree must be completed at Bloomfield.

Visiting: There are regularly scheduled orientations for prospective students, consisting of a campus tour, an admissions interview, and other activities by request. There are guides for informal visits, visitors may sit in on classes, and stay overnight. To schedule a visit, contact Nicole Cibelli at nicole_cibelli@bloomfield.edu.

Financial Aid: In 2013-2014, 98% of all full-time freshmen and 97% of continuing full-time students received some form of financial aid. 93% of all full-time freshmen and 92% of continuing full-time students received need-based aid. The average freshman award was $29,688. Need-based scholarships or need-based grants averaged $16,186 ($36,780 maximum); need-based self-help aid (loans and jobs) averaged $2,376 ($2,400 maximum); non need-based athletic scholarships averaged $12,588 ($30,000 maximum); and other non-need-based awards and non-need-based scholarships averaged $11,897 ($36,934 maximum). 13% of undergraduate students work part-time. Average annual earnings from campus work are $1273. The average financial indebtedness of the 2013 graduate was $10,543. The FAFSA is required. The priority date for freshman financial aid applications for fall entry is March 15. The deadline for filing freshman financial aid applications for fall entry is June 1.

International Students: There are 62 international students enrolled. The school actively recruits these students. They must take the TOEFL with a minimum score of 550 on the paper-based TOEFL (PBT) or 79 on the Internet-based version (iBT). SAT or TOEFL.

Computers: All students may access the system. There are no time limits and no fees.

Graduates: From July 1, 2012 to June 30, 2013, 293 bachelor's degrees were awarded. The most popular majors were visual and performing arts (20%), sociology (17%), and psychology (14%). 151 companies recruited on campus in 2012-2013. In an average class, 7% graduate in 4 years or less, 24% graduate in 5 years or less, and 36% graduate in 6 years or less. Of the 2012 graduating class, 14% were enrolled in graduate school within 6 months of graduation, and 60% were employed.

Admissions Contact: Nicole Cibelli, Director of Admissions. E-Mail: *admission@bloomfield.edu* Web: *www.bloomfield.edu*

CALDWELL COLLEGE — E-2

Caldwell, NJ 07006 — (973) 618-3000; (888) 864-9516; (973) 618-3600

Full-time: 380 men, 700 women	**Faculty:** n/av; IIB, av$
Part-time: 165 men, 460 women	**Ph.D.s:** n/av
Graduate: 120 men, 460 women	**Student/Faculty:** n/av
Year: semesters, summer session	**Tuition:** $26,102
Application Deadline: open	**Room & Board:** $10,500
Freshman Class: 120 applied, 990 accepted, 286 enrolled	
SAT CR/M/W: 490/480/490 **ACT:** 21	**LESS COMPETITIVE**

Caldwell College, founded in 1939, is a private school offering programs in liberal arts, science, business, fine arts, and education. It is affiliated with the Roman Catholic Church. The figures in the above capsule and in this profile are approximate. There is 1 graduate school. In addition to regional accreditation, Caldwell has baccalaureate program accreditation with ACBSP and TEAC. The library contains 144,909 volumes, 6,228 microform items, 2,112 audio/video tapes/CDs/DVDs, and subscribes to 370 periodicals including electronic. Computerized library services include interlibrary loans, database searching, and Internet access. Special learning facilities include a learning resource center and art gallery. The 80-acre campus is in a suburban area 20 miles west of New York City. Including any residence halls, there are 9 buildings.

Student Life: 87% of undergraduates are from New Jersey. Others are from 14 states, 31 foreign countries, and Canada. 75% are from public schools. 68% are white; 13% African American. The average age of freshmen is 18; all undergraduates, 34. 27% do not continue beyond their first year; 56% remain to graduate.

Housing: 380 students can be accommodated in college housing, which includes coed dorms. On-campus housing is guaranteed for all 4 years. 61% of students commute. All students may keep cars.

Activities: There are no fraternities or sororities. There are 21 groups on campus, including art, band, cheerleading, choir, ethnic, honors, international, literary magazine, newspaper, orchestra, professional, religious, social, social service, student government, and yearbook. Popular campus events include Founders Day, Freshman Investiture, and Fall Festival.

Sports: There are 5 intercollegiate sports for men and 5 for women, and 4 intramural sports for men and 4 for women. Facilities include a multipurpose gym, a training room, tennis courts, weight rooms, playing fields, and a pool.

Disabled Students: 85% of the campus is accessible. Facilities include wheelchair ramps, elevators, special parking, specially equipped restrooms, special class scheduling, lowered drinking fountains, and lowered telephones.

Services: Counseling and information services are available, as is tutoring in most subjects. There is a reader service for the blind, and remedial math, reading, and writing.

Campus Safety and Security: Measures include 24-hour foot and vehicle patrol, self-defense education, and security escort services. There are emergency telephones and lighted pathways/sidewalks.

Programs of Study: Caldwell confers B.A., B.S., and B.F.A. degrees. Master's and doctoral degrees are also awarded. Bachelor's degrees are awarded in BIOLOGICAL SCIENCE (biology/biological science), BUSINESS (accounting, business administration and management, international business management, management science, and marketing and distribution), COMMUNICATIONS AND THE ARTS (art, communications, English, fine arts, French, music, Spanish, and studio art), COMPUTER AND PHYSICAL SCIENCE (chemistry, computer management, computer science, information sciences and systems, and mathematics), EDUCATION (elementary education), HEALTH PROFESSIONS (medical laboratory technology and nursing), SOCIAL SCIENCE (criminal justice, history, political science/government, psychology, social studies, sociology, and theological studies). Liberal arts, education, and sciences are the strongest academically. Business, education, and psychology have the largest enrollments.

Required: Students must maintain a minimum GPA of 2.0 while taking 120 credit hours, including a minimum of 30 in the major. The 55-credit core includes 15 credits in religion/philosophy, 6 each in history, English, language, social science, math and computer science, and fine arts, and 2 in communication arts. Students must participate in an outcome assessment that is unique for each department. It is a comprehensive exam for some.

Special: Caldwell offers co-op and internship programs in all majors; study abroad in 6 countries; a Washington semester; 1-semester internships; and work-study with Dominican Adult Day Care, Hill Top Day Care, and Family and Child Services of North Essex. B.A.-B.S. degrees in 29 fields, dual majors in all majors, credit for life experience in adult education, nondegree study,student-designed majors, and pass/fail options are possible. The Continuing Education Program offers adults (23 years or older) a chance to complete degree requirements in the evening and Saturdays, and the External Degree Program gives adults an opportunity to earn a degree off without attending on-campus classes. There are 15 national honor societies and a freshman honors program.

Faculty/Classroom: 49% of faculty are male; 51% are female. 89% teach undergraduates. No introductory courses are taught by graduate students. The average class size in an introductory lecture is 15; in a laboratory is 13; and in a regular course is 12.

Admissions: In a recent year, 83% applicants were accepted. The SAT scores for a recent freshman class were: Critical Reading--60% below 500, 30% between 500 and 599, 9% between 600 and 700, and 1% above 700; Math--50% below 500, 37% between 500 and 599, 12% between 600 and 700, and 1% above 700; Writing--52% below 500, 39% between 500 and 599, 9% between 600 and 700, and 1% above 700. The ACT scores were 46% below 21, 31% between 21 and 23, 20% between 24 and 26, 3% between 27 and 28. 29% of the current freshmen were in the top fifth of their class; 59% were in the top two fifths.

Requirements: The SAT is required. Applicants need 16 academic credits or 16 Carnegie units, including 4 years in English, 2 each in foreign language, math, and science, and 1 in history. A written recommendation from a high school counselor is required. A portfolio, audition, and interview are recommended, depending on the field of study. The GED is accepted. A GPA of 2.0 is required. AP and CLEP credits are accepted. Important factors in the admissions decision are leadership record, recommendations by school officials, and advanced placement or honors courses.

Procedure: Freshmen are admitted to all sessions. Entrance exams should be taken in fall of the senior year. There are early admissions and rolling admissions plans. Application deadlines are open. Application fee is $40. Applications are accepted online.

Transfer: In a recent year, 91 transfer students enrolled. Transfer students must have a minimum GPA of 2.0 (2.5 in teacher education) and 12 transferable credits. 45 of 120 credits required for the bachelor's degree must be completed at Caldwell.

Visiting: There are regularly scheduled orientations for prospective students, including a brief presentation by faculty and students, followed by a tour. There are guides for informal visits, visitors may sit in on classes, and stay overnight. To schedule a visit, contact the Admissions Office.

Financial Aid: In a recent year, 91% of all full-time freshmen and 85% of continuing full-time students received some form of financial aid. 82% of all full-time freshmen and 78% of continuing full-time students received need-based aid. The average freshman award was $20,863. Need-based scholarships or need-based grants averaged $17,992 ($26,468 maximum); need-based self-help aid (loans and jobs) averaged $3,650 ($4,700 maximum); non-need-based athletic scholarships averaged $6,631 ($35,000 maximum); and other non-need-based awards and non-need-based scholarships averaged $7,720 ($24,752 maximum). 32% of undergraduate students work part-time. Average annual earnings from campus work are $1816. The average financial indebtedness of a recent year graduate was $18,369. Caldwell is a member of CSS. The FAFSA and the college's own financial statement are required. The priority date for freshman financial aid applications for fall entry is April 1.

International Students: The school actively recruits these students. They must take the TOEFL with a minimum score of 550 on the paper-based TOEFL (PBT) or 70 on the Internet-based version (iBT). They must also take the SAT or ACT.

Computers: All students may access the system Monday to Thursday 9 a.m. to 9:30 p.m., Friday 10:30 a.m. to 4 p.m., and weekends, 12 p.m. to 5 p.m. There are no time limits and no fees.

Admissions Contact: Stephen Quinn, Executive Director of Admissions. A campus DVD is available. E-Mail: *admissions@caldwell.edu* Web: *www.caldwell.edu*

CENTENARY COLLEGE C-2

Hackettstown, NJ 07840 (908) 852-1400
(800) 236-8679; (908) 852-3454

Full-time: 680 men, 1160 women	**Faculty:** 72; IIB, -$
Part-time: 58 men, 95 women	**Ph.D.s:** 54%
Graduate: 229 men, 472 women	**Student/Faculty:** 26 to 1
Year: semesters, summer session	**Tuition:** $29,390
Application Deadline: open	**Room & Board:** $10,220
Freshman Class: 753 applied, 672 accepted, 272 enrolled	
SAT CR/M: 465/463	**ACT:** 21 **LESS COMPETITIVE**

Centenary College, founded in 1867, is a private institution affiliated with the United Methodist Church. The college offers undergraduate and graduate programs in liberal arts, business, international studies, education, equine studies, fashion, and fine arts. There is 1 graduate school. In addition to regional accreditation, Centenary has baccalaureate program accreditation with CSWE, NASDTEC, and TEAC. The library contains 68,000 volumes, 20,000 microform items, 5,000 audio/video tapes/CDs/DVDs, and subscribes to 375 periodicals including electronic. Computerized library services include interlibrary loans, database searching, Internet access, and laptop Internet portals. Special learning facilities include a learning resource center, radio station, TV station, an equestrian center, CAD lab, wireless network. The 42-acre campus is in a suburban area 55 miles west of New York City. Including any residence halls, there are 22 buildings.

Student Life: 88% of undergraduates are from New Jersey. Others are from 21 states, 8 foreign countries, and Canada. 85% are from public schools. 66% are white. The average age of freshmen is 18; all undergraduates, 24. 24% do not continue beyond their first year; 51% remain to graduate.

Housing: 756 students can be accommodated in college housing, which includes single-sex and coed dorms and on-campus apartments. On-campus housing is available on a first-come, first-served basis, and is available on a lottery system for upperclassmen. 54% of students live on campus; of those, 70% remain on campus on weekends. All students may keep cars.

Activities: 3% of men belong to 1 local fraternity; 5% of women belong to 3 local sororities. There are 30 groups on campus, including art, chorus, dance, debate, drama, environmental, ethnic, gay, honors, international, literary magazine, newspaper, photography, political, professional, radio and TV, religious, social, social service, student government, and yearbook. Popular campus events include President's Ball, Community Plunge, and Tis the Season.

Sports: There are 7 intercollegiate sports for men and 7 for women. Facilities include a gym, a fitness center and indoor pool, tennis courts, playing fields, and an equine center and stables.

Disabled Students: 60% of the campus is accessible. Facilities include wheelchair ramps, special parking, specially equipped restrooms, special class scheduling, and lowered telephones.

Services: Counseling and information services are available, as is tutoring in every subject, as requested. There is remedial math, reading, and writing. Learning associates provide personalized subject matter support.

Campus Safety and Security: Measures include 24-hour foot and vehicle patrol, emergency notification system, and security escort services. There are emergency telephones, lighted pathways/sidewalks, and controlled access to dorms/residences.

Programs of Study: Centenary confers B.A., B.F.A., and B.S. degrees. Associate and master's degrees are also awarded. Bachelor's degrees are awarded in AGRICULTURE (equine science), BIOLOGICAL SCIENCE (biology/biological science), BUSINESS (accounting and business administration and management), COMMUNICATIONS AND THE ARTS (applied art, communications, dramatic arts, and English), COMPUTER AND PHYSICAL SCIENCE (mathematics), EDUCATION (elementary education and secondary education), SOCIAL SCIENCE (criminal justice, fashion design and technology, history, interdisciplinary studies, international studies, political science/government, psychology, and sociology). Equine studies, business, and education are the strongest academically.

Required: Students must complete a distribution of 40 to 46 semester hours in core courses, including college seminars, and 9 credits in liberal arts studies, as well as the required number of credits, usually 48, for their majors. At least 128 semester hours and a minimum GPA of 2.0 are needed to earn the bachelor's degree.

Special: Centenary offers internships in every major. The college offers study abroad in England and other countries, dual majors, as long as they are covered under the same degree, an accelerated degree program in liberal arts and business administration, student-designed majors, work-study on-campus, and a pass/fail option. Students ages 25 or older may earn life experience credits. There is 1 national honor society and a freshman honors program.

Faculty/Classroom: 44% of faculty are male; 56% are female. All teach and do research. No introductory courses are taught by graduate students. The average class size in an introductory lecture is 25; in a laboratory is 20; and in a regular course is 15.

Admissions: In a recent year, 89% of the applicants were accepted. The SAT scores for a recent freshman class were: Critical Reading--67% below 500, 25% between 500 and 599, 7% between 600 and 700, and 1% above 700; Math--65% below 500, 30% between 500 and 599, and 5% between 600 and 700. The ACT scores were 29% below 21, 43% between 21 and 23, 7% between 24 and 26, 7% between 27 and 28, and 14% above 28.

Requirements: The SAT or ACT is required. Minimum scores include a satisfactory SAT score or an ACT composite of 18. Applicants must be graduates of accredited secondary schools or have earned a GED. Centenary requires 16 academic credits or Carnegie units, based on 4 years of English, math, and science, and 2 years each of foreign language and history. An essay is required for freshmen, and an interview is recommended. Applicants to specific fine arts programs must also submit a portfolio. A GPA of 2.0 is required. AP and CLEP credits are accepted. Important factors in the admissions decision are advanced placement or honors courses, leadership record, and ability to finance college education.

Procedure: Freshmen are admitted fall and spring. Entrance exams should be taken as early as possible in the senior year. There are deferred admissions and rolling admissions plans. Application deadlines are open. Application fee is $30. Notification is sent on a rolling basis. Applications are accepted online.

Transfer: In a recent year, 178 transfer students enrolled. Applicants must have a minimum college GPA of 2.0 and submit proof of high school graduation or the equivalent. 32 of 128 credits required for the bachelor's degree must be completed at Centenary.

Visiting: There are regularly scheduled orientations for prospective students, including basic skills testing, advising, registration, and social events. Visitors may sit in on classes and stay overnight. To schedule a visit, contact the Admissions Office.

Financial Aid: In a recent year, 85% of all full-time freshmen and 88% of continuing full-time students received some form of financial aid. 84% of all full-time freshmen and 85% of continuing full-time students received need-based aid. The average freshman award was $19,100. Need-based scholarships or need-based grants averaged $14,806; and need-based self-help aid (loans and jobs) averaged $5,279. 75% of undergraduate students work part-time. The FAFSA and other forms as requested are required. Check with the school for recent application deadlines and fees.

International Students: There are 54 international students enrolled. The school actively recruits these students. They must take the TOEFL with a minimum score of 520 on the paper-based TOEFL (PBT) or 80 on the Internet-based version (iBT), or IELTS with a score of 5.0. They must also take the SAT or ACT.

Computers: Wireless access is available. All full-time undergraduates are provided with laptops. Computer facilities are also available throughout the campus. All students may access the system. Computer and CAD lab use depends on lab hours. The fee is $700. It is strongly recommended that all students have a personal computer.

Graduates: In a recent year, 524 bachelor's degrees were awarded. The most popular majors were business administration (51%), social sciences (9%), and psychology (8%). In an average class, 51% graduate in 4 years or less, 51% graduate in 5 years or less, and 52% graduate in 6 years or less. Of a recent graduating class, 10% were enrolled in graduate school within 6 months of graduation, and 75% were employed.

Admissions Contact: Glenna Warren, Dean of Admissions and Financial Aid. E-Mail: *admissions@centenarycollege.edu* Web: *www.centenarycollege.edu*

COLLEGE OF NEW JERSEY D-3

Ewing, NJ 08628 (609) 771-2131
(800) 624-0967; (609) 637-5174

Full-time: 2775 men, 3680 women
Part-time: 76 men, 122 women
Graduate: 107 men, 580 women
Year: semesters, summer session
Application Deadline: January 15
Freshman Class: 11145 applied, 4828 accepted, 1404 enrolled
SAT CR/M/W: 610/640/620
Faculty: 342; IIA, ++$
Ph.D.s: 88%
Student/Faculty: 13 to 1
Tuition: $14,730 ($25,135)
Room & Board: $11,343

HIGHLY COMPETITIVE

The College of New Jersey, founded in 1855, is a public institution offering programs in the liberal arts, sciences, business, engineering, nursing, and education. There are 7 undergraduate schools and one graduate school. In addition to regional accreditation, TCNJ has baccalaureate program accreditation with AACSB, ABET, NASM, NCATE, and NLN. The library contains 694,144 volumes, 426,253 microform items, and 40,127 audio/video tapes/CDs/DVDs, and subscribes to 73,733 periodicals including electronic. Computerized library services include interlibrary loans, database searching, Internet access, and Wi-Fi capability. Special learning facilities include an art gallery, planetarium, radio station, TV station, electron microscopy lab, nuclear magnetic resonance lab, optical spectroscopy lab, observatory, planetarium, and greenhouse. The 289-acre campus is in a suburban area between Princeton and Trenton, NJ. Including any residence halls, there are 61 buildings.

Student Life: 94% of undergraduates are from New Jersey. Others are from 23 states, 30 foreign countries, and Canada. 70% are from public schools. 66% are White; 11% Hispanic. 48% are Catholic; 17% Protestant; 15% claim no religious affiliation; 15% Eastern Orthodox, Buddhist, Muslim, Islamic and Quaker. The average age of freshmen is 18; all undergraduates, 20. 6% do not continue beyond their first year; 86% remain to graduate.

Housing: 4000 students can be accommodated in college housing, which includes single-sex and coed dorms, on-campus apartments, and off-campus apartments. On-campus housing is guaranteed for the freshman year only and is available on a lottery system for upperclassmen. 52% of students commute. Upperclassmen may keep cars.

Activities: 9% of men belong to 14 national fraternities; 11% of women belong to 13 national sororities. There are 226 groups on campus, including foreign language, art, band, cheerleading, chess, choir, chorale, chorus, computers, dance, drama, environmental, ethnic, film, forensics, gay, honors, international, jazz band, literary magazine, musical theater, newspaper, opera, orchestra, pep band, photography, political, professional, radio and TV, recreational, religious, social, social service, student government, symphony, and yearbook. Popular campus events include Lallanobozza, Mystique of the EAST, and TCNJ Later Nighter.

Sports: There are 9 intercollegiate sports for men and 9 for women, and 14 intramural sports for men and 14 for women. Facilities include a 5000-seat stadium with an Astroturf field, an aquatic center, baseball and softball diamonds, a Sportexe-surface soccer/multipurpose field, an all-weather track, a sand volleyball court, 5 grass playing fields, a 1200-seat gym, a physical enhancement center, a student recreation center, tennis, racquetball, and basketball/volleyball courts, and a free weight room.

Disabled Students: 90% of the campus is accessible. Facilities include wheelchair ramps, elevators, special parking, specially equipped restrooms, special class scheduling, lowered drinking fountains, lowered telephones, special housing.

Services: Counseling and information services are available, as is tutoring in most subjects. There is a reader service for the blind, and remedial math, reading, and writing.

Campus Safety and Security: Measures include 24-hour foot and vehicle patrol, emergency notification system, self-defense education, and security escort services. There are emergency telephones, lighted pathways/sidewalks, and controlled access to dorms/residences.

Programs of Study: TCNJ confers B.A., B.S., B.A.B.M.E., B.F.A., B.M., B.S.C.E., B.S.Co.E., B.S.E.E., B.S.M.E. and B.S.N. degrees. Master's degrees are also awarded. Bachelor's degrees are awarded in BIOLOGICAL SCIENCE (biology/biological science), BUSINESS (accounting and business administration and management), COMMUNICATIONS AND THE ARTS (art, art history and appreciation, communications, English, fine arts, graphic design, multimedia, music, and Spanish), COMPUTER AND PHYSICAL SCIENCE (chemistry, computer science, digital arts/technology, mathematics, and physics), EDUCATION (art education, early childhood education, education of the deaf and hearing impaired, elementary education, English education, health education, mathematics education, music education, physical education, science education, social science education, social studies education, special education, and technical education), ENGINEERING AND ENVIRONMENTAL DESIGN (biomedical engineering, civil engineering, computer engineering, electrical/electronics engineering, engineering and applied science, and mechanical engineering), HEALTH PROFESSIONS (exercise science and nursing), SOCIAL SCIENCE (criminal justice, economics, history, international studies, philosophy, political science/government, psychology, sociology, and women's studies). Biology, education, and engineering are the strongest academically. Psychology, biology, and elementary education have the largest enrollments.

Required: To graduate, students must complete a liberal learning curriculum of 128 to 136 credit hours that includes at least 1 major, as well as a suite of courses that address 3 interdependent structural elements: intellectual and scholarly growth; civic responsibilities; and the broad sectors of human inquiry within the arts and humanities, social sciences, natural sciences, and quantitative reasoning.

Special: TCNJ offers cross-registration with the New Jersey Marine Science Consortium, a limited number of overseas internship possibilities, numerous internships in the public and private sectors, a Washington semester, and study abroad in more than a dozen countries. Pass/fail options and some dual majors are possible. Specially designed research courses allow students to participate in collaborative scholarly projects with members of the faculty, and the Bonner Center offers opportunities for community-engaged initiatives. Combined advanced and accelerated degree programs are offered in education of the deaf and hard of hearing, special education, medicine, and optometry. There are 16 national honor societies, including Phi Beta Kappa, a freshman honors program, and 40 departmental honors programs.

Faculty/Classroom: 49% of faculty are male; 51% are female. All teach undergraduates, and 85% do both. No introductory courses are taught by graduate students. The average class size in an introductory lecture is 25; in a laboratory is 17; and in a regular course is 21.

Admissions: 43% of the 2013-2014 applicants were accepted. The SAT scores for the 2013-2014 freshman class were: Critical Reading--7% below 500, 38% between 500 and 599, 43% between 600 and 699, and 12% between 700 and 800; Math--4% below 500, 27% between 500 and 599, 51% between 600 and 699, and 18% between 700 and 800; Writing--8% below 500, 32% between 500 and 599, 44% between 600 and 699, and 16% between 700 and 800. 87% of the current freshmen were in the top fifth of their class; 98% were in the top two fifths. 13 freshmen graduated first in their class.

Requirements: The SAT is required. Applicants must have earned 16 academic credits in high school, consisting of 4 in English, 3 each in math and science, 2 each in foreign language and social studies, and 6 others distributed among math, science, social studies, and a foreign language. An essay is required. Art majors must submit a portfolio, and music majors must audition. The GED is accepted. A GPA of 2.0 is required. AP and CLEP credits are accepted. Important factors in the admissions decision are advanced placement or honors courses, leadership record, and evidence of special talent.

Procedure: Freshmen are admitted fall and spring. Entrance exams should be taken by the end of the junior year or early in the senior year. There are early decision and rolling admissions plans. Early decision applications should be filed by November 15; regular applications, by January 15 for fall entry; and November 15 for spring entry, along with a $75 fee. Notification of early decision is sent December 15; regular decision, January 15. 344 early decision candidates were accepted for the 2013-2014 class. 529 applicants were on the 2013 waiting list; 37 were admitted. Applications are accepted online.

Transfer: 258 transfer students enrolled in 2012-2013. Transfer students must have a minimum GPA of 2.5, and those with fewer than 33 credits must submit SAT scores. An associate degree is recommended. All transfer students must submit high school transcripts. 12 of 34 credits required for the bachelor's degree must be completed at TCNJ.

Visiting: There are regularly scheduled orientations for prospective stu-

dents, consisting of an admissions presentation and a tour of campus. Reservations are required. There are guides for informal visits, visitors may sit in on classes, and stay overnight. To schedule a visit, contact the Admissions Office.

Financial Aid: In 2013-2014, 70% of all full-time freshmen and 62% of continuing full-time students received some form of financial aid. 55% of all full-time freshmen and 52% of continuing full-time students received need-based aid. The average freshman award was $11,034. Need-based scholarships or need-based grants averaged $14,369; need-based self-help aid (loans and jobs) averaged $3,636; and other non-need-based awards and non-need-based scholarships averaged $5,798. 21% of undergraduate students work part-time. Average annual earnings from campus work are $2400. The average financial indebtedness of the 2013 graduate was $21,032. TCNJ is a member of CSS. The FAFSA, and copies of students' and parents' tax returns as applicable is required. The priority date for freshman financial aid applications for fall entry is March 1. The deadline for filing freshman financial aid applications for fall entry is October 1.

International Students: There are 23 international students enrolled. They must take the TOEFL with a minimum score of 550 on the paper-based TOEFL (PBT) or 90 on the Internet-based version (iBT). They must also take the SAT or ACT. The SAT is required for merit scholarship consideration.

Computers: All students may access the system. There are no time limits. The fee is $212.50.

Graduates: From July 1, 2012 to June 30, 2013, 1568 bachelor's degrees were awarded. The most popular majors were business/finance (18%), psychology (7%), and education (3%). 400 companies recruited on campus in 2012-2013. In an average class, 1% graduate in 3 years or less, 76% graduate in 4 years or less, 87% graduate in 5 years or less, and 87% graduate in 6 years or less. Of the 2012 graduating class, 33% were enrolled in graduate school within 6 months of graduation, and 95% were employed.

Admissions Contact: Grecia Montero, Director of Admissions. E-Mail: *tcnjinfo@tcnj.edu* Web: *www.tcnj.edu*

COLLEGE OF SAINT ELIZABETH — D-2

Morristown, NJ 07960 — (973) 290-4700
(800) 210-7900; (973) 290-4710

Full-time: 20 men, 534 women	**Faculty:** 49
Part-time: 55 men, 378 women	**Ph.D.s:** 87%
Graduate: 103 men, 462 women	**Student/Faculty:** 9 to 1
Year: semesters, summer session	**Tuition:** $31,095
Application Deadline: March 1	**Room & Board:** $12,744

Freshman Class: 1386 applied, 798 accepted, 146 enrolled
SAT CR/M/W: 431/437/440

LESS COMPETITIVE

The College of St. Elizabeth, founded in 1899, is a private Roman Catholic college primarily for women. Undergraduate programs are offered in the arts and sciences, business administration, education, and foods and nutrition, psychology and theology. There is also an upper-level nursing program where RNs with an associates degree can earn a BSN. There are masters programs in education, health care management, nutrition, psychology, and theology. Doctoral programs include an Ed.D. in School Leadership and a Psychology Doctorate PsyD. Adult undergraduate degree programs and graduate programs are coed. There is one graduate school. In addition to regional accreditation, CSE has baccalaureate program accreditation with ADA, NLN, and TEAC. The library contains 128,890 volumes, 142,451 microform items, and 2,599 audio/video tapes/CDs/DVDs, and subscribes to 1,048 periodicals including electronic. Computerized library services include interlibrary loans, database searching, Internet access, and Wi-Fi capability. Special learning facilities include an art gallery, a television studio. The 200-acre campus is in a suburban area one hour from New York City. Including any residence halls, there are 10 buildings.

Student Life: 96% of undergraduates are from New Jersey. Others are from 13 states, and 10 foreign countries. 34% are from public schools. 39% are White; 26% African American; 15% Hispanic; 11% race unknown. 51% are Hindu, Islamic, 35% Catholic; 13% Protestant and unknown religion. The average age of freshmen is 19; all undergraduates, 23. 28% do not continue beyond their first year; 62% remain to graduate.

Housing: 411 students can be accommodated in college housing, which includes single-sex dorms. On-campus housing is guaranteed for all 4 years. 67% of students commute. All students may keep cars.

Activities: There are no fraternities or sororities. There are 15 groups on campus, including chorale, dance, drama, ethnic, honors, international, literary magazine, newspaper, professional, religious, social, social service, and student government. Popular campus events include Rathskellers, Oktoberfest, and International Night.

Sports: There are 8 intercollegiate sports for women. Facilities include a student center that houses a swimming pool, a weight room, an archery range, and a gym. Tennis courts are also available, as is a bike and fitness trail.

Disabled Students: 75% of the campus is accessible. Facilities include wheelchair ramps, elevators, special parking, specially equipped restrooms, special class scheduling, and handrails.

Services: Counseling and information services are available, as is tutoring in most subjects. There is remedial math, reading, and writing. Other services include books on tape, large monitor computers, and note takers.

Campus Safety and Security: Measures include 24-hour foot and vehicle patrol, emergency notification system, and security escort services. There are emergency telephones and lighted pathways/sidewalks.

Programs of Study: CSE confers B.A., B.S. and B.S.N. degrees. Master's and doctoral degrees are also awarded. Bachelor's degrees are awarded in BIOLOGICAL SCIENCE (biochemistry, biology/biological science, and nutrition), BUSINESS (business administration and management), COMMUNICATIONS AND THE ARTS (art, communications, English, fine arts, music, and Spanish), COMPUTER AND PHYSICAL SCIENCE (chemistry, computer science, and mathematics), EDUCATION (education and elementary education), HEALTH PROFESSIONS (nursing), SOCIAL SCIENCE (American studies, economics, history, international studies, philosophy, psychology, sociology, and theological studies). Math, chemistry, and education are the strongest academically. Nursing, education, and business administration have the largest enrollments.

Required: To graduate, students must complete 120 semester hours, with a minimum of 32 in the major, while maintaining a GPA of 2.0, or 2.75 for education majors. Core requirements 32 credits with an additional six credits for writing that students may require.

Special: There is cross-registration with Drew and Fairleigh Dickinson Universities. CSE also offers internships in business, law, technology, health, government, sports, and television. On-campus work-study, accelerated degree programs, dual majors, student-designed majors, study abroad, credit for life experience, pass/fail options, and non-degree study are also available. Continuing studies programs are are offered in the evening and on weekends to accommodate the the adult working student. There are 10 national honor societies, a freshman honors program, and 1 departmental honors programs.

Faculty/Classroom: 34% of faculty are male; 66% are female. 71% teach undergraduates. No introductory courses are taught by graduate students. The average class size in an introductory lecture is 15; in a laboratory is 12; and in a regular course is 15.

Admissions: 58% of the 2013-2014 applicants were accepted. The SAT scores for the 2013-2014 freshman class were: Critical Reading--78% below 500, 17% between 500 and 599, 4% between 600 and 699, and 1% between 700 and 800; Math--77% below 500, 16% between 500 and 599, 6% between 600 and 699, and 1% between 700 and 800; Writing--74% below 500, 19% between 500 and 599, 5% between 600 and 699, and 2% between 700 and 800. 29% of the current freshmen were in the top fifth of their class; 57% were in the top two fifths.

Requirements: The SAT is required. Applicants must be graduates of an accredited secondary school or have earned a GED. The college requires 16 academic units, including 3 each in English and math/science, 2 in foreign language, and 1 in history. An essay and 2 letters of recommendation are required, and an interview is recommended. A GPA of 2.0 is required. AP and CLEP credits are accepted. Important factors in the admissions decision are advanced placement or honors courses, recommendations by school officials, and leadership record.

Procedure: Freshmen are admitted fall and spring. Entrance exams should be taken early in the senior year. There are deferred admissions and rolling admissions plans. Applications should be filed by March 1 for fall entry; November 1 for spring entry, along with a $35 fee. Notifications are sent November 15. Applications are accepted online.

Transfer: 56 transfer students enrolled in 2012-2013. Applicants must present a minimum GPA of 2.0 in course work from an accredited college. SAT and an interview are also recommended. 32 of 128 credits required for the bachelor's degree must be completed at CSE.

Visiting: There are regularly scheduled orientations for prospective students, including interviews, tours, and class visitation. There are guides for informal visits, visitors may sit in on classes, and stay overnight. To schedule a visit, contact Donna Tatarka at (973) 290-4705.

Financial Aid: In 2013-2014, 78% of all full-time freshmen and 66% of continuing full-time students received some form of financial aid. 31% of undergraduate students work part-time. Average annual earnings from campus work are $4350. CSE is a member of CSS. The FAFSA is required. The priority date for freshman financial aid applications for fall entry is March 1. The deadline for filing freshman financial aid applications for fall entry is September 1.

International Students: There are 41 international students enrolled. The school actively recruits these students. They must take the TOEFL, or other approved assessment tests. Applicants from English-speaking countries may submit scores from either the TOEFL or the SAT.

Computers: All students may access the system. There are no time limits and no fees.

Graduates: From July 1, 2012 to June 30, 2013, 257 bachelor's degrees were awarded. The most popular majors were nursing (34%), business (7%), and communication (4%). In an average class, 44% graduate in 4 years or less, 53% graduate in 5 years or less, and 54% graduate in 6 years or less.

Admissions Contact: Donna Tatarka, Dean of Admissions. E-Mail: *apply@www.cse.edu* Web: *www.cse.edu*

DREW UNIVERSITY/COLLEGE OF LIBERAL ARTS D-2

Madison, NJ 07940 **(973) 408-DREW; (973) 408-3068**

Full-time: 547 men, 887 women	**Faculty:** 128; IIA, +$
Part-time: 25 men, 34 women	**Ph.D.s:** 99%
Graduate: 365 men, 441 women	**Student/Faculty:** 9 to 1
Year: semesters, summer session	**Tuition:** $43,918
Application Deadline: February 15	**Room & Board:** $11,944
Freshman Class: n/av	
SAT or ACT: required	

VERY COMPETITIVE

The College of Liberal Arts was added to Drew University in 1928 and is part of an educational complex that includes a theological school and a graduate school. Drew is a private, independent institution. There is 1 undergraduate school and 2 graduate schools. The library contains 621,365 volumes, 507,462 microform items, and 2,832 audio/video tapes/CDs/DVDs, and subscribes to 47,034 periodicals including electronic. Computerized library services include interlibrary loans, database searching, Internet access, and Wi-Fi capability. Special learning facilities include an art gallery, radio station, TV station, observatory, photography gallery, and TV satellite dish. The 186-acre campus is in a suburban area 30 miles west of New York City. Including any residence halls, there are 57 buildings.

Student Life: 69% of undergraduates are from New Jersey. Others are from 38 states, and 20 foreign countries. 56% are White; 14% Hispanic; 11% African American. The average age of freshmen is 18; all undergraduates, 20. 83% remain to graduate.

Housing: 1457 students can be accommodated in college housing, which includes single-sex and coed dorms, on-campus apartments, and married student housing. In addition, there are language houses and special-interest houses. On-campus housing is guaranteed for all 4 years. 88% of students live on campus; of those, 70% remain on campus on weekends. Upperclassmen may keep cars.

Activities: There are no fraternities or sororities. There are 80 groups on campus, including an a cappella ensemble, 36 Madison Avenue, art, cheerleading, choir, chorale, chorus, computers, dance, drama, environmental, ethnic, film, gay, honors, international, jazz band, literary magazine, newspaper, orchestra, photography, political, professional, radio and TV, religious, social, social service, and student government. Popular campus events include Drew Forum Lecture Series, First Annual Picnic, Holiday Ball, JamFest a Capella Concert, Chamber Music Society of Lincoln Center Concert Series, Drew Theatre productions, MedFest - That Medieval Thing.

Sports: There are 11 intercollegiate sports for men and 12 for women, and 12 intramural sports for men and 12 for women. Facilities include an artificial turf athletic field with a 1000-seat gym, a 1000-seat auditorium, a swimming pool, a lighted tennis complex, a weight training room, a game room, an indoor track, a forest preserve, and an arboretum.

Disabled Students: Facilities include wheelchair ramps, elevators, special parking, specially equipped restrooms, special class scheduling, lowered drinking fountains, lowered telephones, special housing. The main dining facility, the student center and commons, and the ground floor of every dorm and classroom building are accessible to students with physical disabilities.

Services: Counseling and information services are available, as is tutoring in most subjects. There is a reader service for the blind.

Campus Safety and Security: Measures include 24-hour foot and vehicle patrol, emergency notification system, self-defense education, and security escort services. There are shuttle buses, emergency telephones, lighted pathways/sidewalks, and controlled access to dorms/residences.

Programs of Study: Drew confers B.A. degrees. Master's and doctoral degrees are also awarded. Bachelor's degrees are awarded in AGRICULTURE (environmental studies), BIOLOGICAL SCIENCE (biochemistry, biology/biological science, and neurosciences), COMMUNICATIONS AND THE ARTS (art, art history and appreciation, Chinese, classics, English, French, German, music, Spanish, and theatre arts), COMPUTER AND PHYSICAL SCIENCE (chemistry, computer science, mathematics, and physics), SOCIAL SCIENCE (African studies, anthropology, economics, history, philosophy, political science/government, psychology, religion, sociology, and women's studies). Theatre, and business studies are the strongest academically. Psychology, business/economics, political science, and English have the largest enrollments.

Required: To graduate, students must earn at least 128 credits, of which at least 64 must be beyond the lower level and at least 32 must be at the upper level. All students must fulfill the requirements of a major and those of the general education program. For graduation, the cumulative GPA, both overall and in the major, must be at least 2.0. General education requirements include a first-year seminar, demonstration of writing competency, at least 8 credits in foreign language and fulfillment of a language-in-context requirement, and completion of at least 4 credits in each of 2 different departments in the following 4 divisions: natural and mathematical sciences, social sciences, humanities, and arts and literature. Each student may also complete a minor.

Special: Drew offers co-op programs with Duke University, as well as cross registration with the College of Saint Elizabeth and Fairleigh Dickinson University. There are also dual majors, study abroad, a Wall Street semester, a Washington semester, student-designed majors, internships, 3-2 engineering programs with Washington University in St. Louis, the Stevens Institute of Technology, and Columbia University in New York City, and a 7-year B.A.-M.D. program in medicine with UMDNJ. There are 11 national honor societies, including Phi Beta Kappa, a freshman honors program, and 12 departmental honors programs.

Faculty/Classroom: 48% of faculty are male; 52% are female. All teach undergraduates, 5% do research, and 5% do both. No introductory courses are taught by graduate students. The average class size in an introductory lecture is 25; in a laboratory is 20; and in a regular course is 17.

Admissions: The SAT scores for the 2013-2014 freshman class were: Critical Reading--21% below 500, 41% between 500 and 599, 31% between 600 and 699, and 7% between 700 and 800; Math--26% below 500, 44% between 500 and 599, 26% between 600 and 699, and 4% between 700 and 800; Writing--21% below 500, 41% between 500 and 599, 31% between 600 and 699, and 7% between 700 and 800. The ACT scores were 9% below 21, 31% between 21 and 23, 34% between 24 and 26, 13% between 27 and 28, and 13% above 28.

Requirements: The SAT or ACT is required. In addition, The university strongly recommends 18 academic credits or Carnegie units, including 4 in English, 3 in math, 3 in the same foreign language, 3 in science including 2 lab courses, 3 in history, with the remaining 2 in other academic courses. An essay is also required, and an interview is recommended. AP and CLEP credits are accepted. Important factors in the admissions decision are extracurricular activities record, recommendations by school officials, and advanced placement or honors courses.

Procedure: Freshmen are admitted fall and spring. Entrance exams should be taken by January of the senior year. There are early decision, early admissions, and deferred admissions plans. Early decision applications should be filed by December 1; regular applications, by February 15 for fall entry; and January 1 for spring entry, along with a $60 fee. Notification of early decision is sent December 15; regular decision, March 30. Applications are accepted online.

Transfer: 40 transfer students enrolled in 2012-2013. Applicants must submit official high school and college transcripts, a personal essay, and a statement of good standing from previous schools attended. An interview also may be required. Students with fewer then 12 credits must apply as entering freshman. 48 of 128 credits required for the bachelor's degree must be completed at Drew.

Visiting: There are regularly scheduled orientations for prospective students, Traditionally, open houses begin early in the morning and run through early afternoon. The day includes campus tours, information sessions about admissions and financial assistance, and presentations about student life and academics. There are guides for informal visits and visitors may sit in on classes. To schedule a visit, contact the Office of College Admissions.

Financial Aid: Drew is a member of CSS. The FAFSA is required. The deadline for filing freshman financial aid applications for fall entry is February 15.

International Students: The school actively recruits these students. They must take the TOEFL with a minimum score of 550 on the paper-based TOEFL (PBT) or 80 on the Internet-based version (iBT).

Computers: All students may access the system. There are no time limits and no fees.

Graduates: 78 companies recruited on campus in 2012-2013.

Admissions Contact: Mark Kopenski, Vice President of Enrollment Management. E-Mail: *cadm@drew.edu* Web: *www.drew.edu*

FAIRLEIGH DICKINSON UNIVERSITY SYSTEM

The Fairleigh Dickinson University System, established in 1942, is a private system in New Jersey. It is governed by a board of trustees, whose chief administrator is the president. The primary goal of the system is teaching/research. The main priorities are to provide an academically challenging learning experience to prepare students for employment or enrollment in graduate and professional schools; to promote independent thinking and collaborative learning in students; to cultivate a holistic, integrated living-learning experience as part of the educational process; and to foster the ideals of good citizenship and community service. The total student enrollment is usually about 11,500 with 700 faculty members. Altogether there are 38 baccalaureate, 51 master's, and 1 doctoral program offered in the Fairleigh Dickinson University System. Profiles of the 4-year campuses are included in this section.

FAIRLEIGH DICKINSON UNIVERSITY/COLLEGE AT FLORHAM D-2

Madison, NJ 07940 (973) 443-8900
(800) 338-8803; (973) 443-8088

Full-time: 1076 men, 1205 women **Faculty:** n/av
Part-time: 98 men, 101 women **Ph.D.s:** n/av
Graduate: 512 men, 517 women **Student/Faculty:** n/av
Year: semesters, summer session **Tuition:** $31,584
Application Deadline: open **Room & Board:** $11,558
Freshman Class: 3907 applied, 2601 accepted, 646 enrolled
SAT CR/M/W: 520/530/520 **ACT:** required **COMPETITIVE**

Fairleigh Dickinson University/College at Florham, founded in 1942, is an independent university offering undergraduate, graduate, and professional level programs. Figures in the above capsule and in this profile are approximate. Studies are rooted in the liberal arts but also offer hands-on opportunities in business and professional internships, cooperative education, and global studies abroad. There are 3 undergraduate schools and 2 graduate schools. In addition to regional accreditation, College at Florham has baccalaureate program accreditation with AACSB and NASDTEC. The library contains 149,850 volumes, 19,236 microform items, 689 audio/video tapes/CDs/DVDs, and subscribes to 1182 periodicals including electronic. Computerized library services include interlibrary loans, database searching, Internet access, and laptop Internet portals. Special learning facilities include a learning resource center, art gallery, radio station, web-lab, ITV multimedia classrooms, and theaters. The 166-acre campus is in a suburban area 27 miles west of New York City. Including any residence halls, there are 36 buildings.

Student Life: 85% of undergraduates are from New Jersey. Others are from 27 states, 12 foreign countries, and Canada. 69% are white. The average age of freshmen is 18; all undergraduates, 20. 25% do not continue beyond their first year; 52% remain to graduate.

Housing: 1500 students can be accommodated in college housing, which includes coed dorms. In addition, there are honors houses and special-interest houses. On-campus housing is available on a first-come, first-served basis. Priority is given to out-of-town students. 60% of students live on campus; of those, 75% remain on campus on weekends. Upperclassmen may keep cars.

Activities: There are 6 national fraternities and 4 national sororities. There are 44 groups on campus, including cheerleading, chorale, computers, dance, environmental, ethnic, gay, honors, international, literary magazine, newspaper, political, professional, radio and TV, religious, social, social service, and student government. Popular campus events include Florham Fest and Haunted Mansion.

Sports: There are 9 intercollegiate sports for men and 9 for women, and 7 intramural sports for men and 5 for women. Facilities include a state-of-the-art synthetic turf field for football, field hockey, soccer, and lacrosse.

Disabled Students: 34% of the campus is accessible. Facilities include wheelchair ramps, elevators, special parking, specially equipped restrooms, special class scheduling, lowered drinking fountains, lowered telephones, and special housing.

Services: Counseling and information services are available, as is tutoring in most subjects. There is a reader service for the blind, remedial math, reading, and writing, and oral interpretation for the hearing impaired. Workshops also offer assistance with study skills and time management, and support services for basic skills students and freshmen are available. There is a Regional Center for College Students with Learning Disabilities that offers comprehensive support to students admitted to the program.

Campus Safety and Security: Measures include 24-hour foot and vehicle patrol, emergency notification system, self-defense education, and security escort services. There are shuttle buses, emergency telephones, and lighted pathways/sidewalks.

Programs of Study: College at Florham confers B.A., B.S., B.S.A.H.T, B.S.C.L.S., and B.S.N. degrees. Master's degrees are also awarded. Bachelor's degrees are awarded in BIOLOGICAL SCIENCE (biochemistry and biology/biological science), BUSINESS (accounting, banking and finance, business administration and management, entrepreneurial studies, hotel/motel and restaurant management, and marketing/retailing/merchandising), COMMUNICATIONS AND THE ARTS (animation, communications, creative writing, dramatic arts, film arts, fine arts, literature, and video), COMPUTER AND PHYSICAL SCIENCE (chemistry, computer science, mathematics, and radiological technology), HEALTH PROFESSIONS (allied health, clinical science, medical laboratory technology, and nursing), SOCIAL SCIENCE (economics, French studies, history, humanities, liberal arts/general studies, philosophy, political science/government, psychology, sociology, and Spanish studies). Psychology, business management, and communications have the largest enrollments.

Required: To graduate, students must complete a 120 to 128 credits, including 30 to 44 in the major, with an overall minimum 2.0 GPA (2.5 in the major). Distribution requirements include courses in English, communications, math, phys ed, foreign language, humanities, social and behavioral sciences, lab and computer science, an integrated, interdisciplinary university core sequence, and freshman seminar.

Special: The college offers co-op programs in most majors, internships, and study abroad. A Washington semester, work-study, accelerated degrees, and student-designed majors in the humanities and general studies are possible. Prepharmacy and joint baccalaureate dental programs are available. There are 10 national honor societies, a freshman honors program, and 11 departmental honors programs.

Faculty/Classroom: No introductory courses are taught by graduate students.

Admissions: 67% of a recent year's applicants were accepted. The SAT scores for a recent freshman class were: Critical Reading--36% below 500, 51% between 500 and 599, 13% between 600 and 700, and 1% above 700; Math--31% below 500, 49% between 500 and 599, 18% between 600 and 700, and 1% above 700; Writing--36% below 500, 50% between 500 and 599, 13% between 600 and 700, and 1% above 700. 32% of recent freshmen were in the top fifth of their class; 62% were in the top two fifths. 5 freshmen graduated first in their class.

Requirements: The SAT or ACT is required. Applicants should be graduates of an accredited high school or have a GED certificate. They should have completed a minimum of 16 academic units, including 4 in English, 3 each in math and science, 2 each in history and foreign language, and 4 units of electives. Those students applying to science and health sciences programs must meet additional requirements. An interview may be requested. AP and CLEP credits are accepted. Important factors in the admissions decision are leadership record, recommendations by school officials, and extracurricular activities record.

Procedure: Freshmen are admitted to all sessions. Entrance exams should be taken May of their junior year. There are early admissions, deferred admissions, and rolling admissions plans. Application deadlines are open; March 1 is recommended for fall entry. Check with the school for current application fee. Notification is sent on a rolling basis. Applications are accepted online.

Transfer: 131 transfer students enrolled in a recent year. All transfer applicants must submit official transcripts for all college work taken. Those students with fewer than 24 credits must also submit a high school transcript or a copy of their state department of education's equivalency score and SAT scores. 32 of 120 to 128 credits required for the bachelor's degree must be completed at College at Florham.

Visiting: There are regularly scheduled orientations for prospective students, including standardized placement testing, faculty advisement, class registration, and educational and social activities to prepare students for entrance. There are guides for informal visits; visitors may sit in on classes and stay overnight. To schedule a visit, contact the Admissions Office.

Financial Aid: The FAFSA is required. The priority date for freshman financial aid applications for fall entry is January 15.

International Students: There were 14 international students enrolled in a recent year. The school actively recruits these students. They must take the TOEFL, IELTS, or PTE-A, with a minimum score of 550 on the paper-based TOEFL (PBT) or 79 on the Internet-based version (iBT). The SAT or ACT is required for scholarship consideration.

Computers: Wireless access is available. All students may access the system. There are no time limits. The fee is $692. It is strongly recommended that all students have a personal computer. An IBM ThinkPad or NetVista is recommended.

Graduates: 522 bachelor's degrees were awarded in a recent year. The most popular majors were psychology (14%), business/marketing (12%), and communications (8%). 200 companies recruited on campus in a recent year. In an average class, 35% graduate in 4 years or less, 48% graduate in 5 years or less, and 52% graduate in 6 years or less.

Admissions Contact: Admissions, E-mail: *admissions@fdu.edu* Web: *www.fdu.edu*

FAIRLEIGH DICKINSON UNIVERSITY/METROPOLITAN CAMPUS E-2

Teaneck, NJ 07666 (201) 692-2553
(800) 338-8803; (201) 692-7319

Full-time: 983 men, 1488 women **Faculty:** n/av
Part-time: 1567 men, 2006 women **Ph.D.s:** n/av
Graduate: 1126 men, 1634 women **Student/Faculty:** n/av
Year: semesters, summer session **Tuition:** $30,500
Application Deadline: March 15 **Room & Board:** $12,200
Freshman Class: 5108 applied, 2916 accepted, 711 enrolled
SAT CR/M/W: 510/530/500 **ACT:** required **COMPETITIVE**

Fairleigh Dickinson University/Metropolitan Campus, founded in 1942, is an independent university offering undergraduate and graduate degrees in business, arts and sciences, professional studies, public administration, and hotel, restaurant, and tourism management. There are 3 undergraduate schools and 3 graduate schools. In addition to regional accreditation, FDU has baccalaureate program accreditation with AACSB, ABET, and TEAC. The 3 libraries contain 196,703 volumes, 103,808 microform items, 1,311 audio/video tapes/CDs/DVDs, and subscribe to 1,601 periodicals including electronic. Computerized library services include interlibrary loans, database searching, and Internet access. Special learning facilities include a learning resource center, art gallery, radio station, computer labs, ITV multimedia classrooms, photonics lab, theater, art galleries, web-lab, cyber crime lab, and the Regional Center for College Students with Learning Disabilities. The 92-acre campus is in a suburban area 13 miles from midtown Manhattan, New York City. Including any residence halls, there are 55 buildings. The figures in the above capsule and in this profile are approximate.

Student Life: 87% of undergraduates are from New Jersey. Others are from 25 states, 64 foreign countries, and Canada. 33% are white; 20% Hispanic; 18% African American. The average age of freshmen is 18; all undergraduates, 22. 27% do not continue beyond their first year; 40% remain to graduate.

Housing: 982 students can be accommodated in college housing, which includes single-sex and coed dorms. In addition, there are honors houses, special-interest houses, L.I.F.E. house and Global Scholar houses. On-campus housing is available on a first-come, first-served basis, and is available on a lottery system for upperclassmen. 79% of students commute. Alcohol is not permitted. All students may keep cars.

Activities: 1% of men belong to 5 national fraternities; 1% of women belong to 7 national sororities. There are 72 groups on campus, including cheerleading, chorus, computers, dance, drama, environmental, ethnic, film, gay, honors, international, literary magazine, newspaper, pep band, photography, political, professional, radio and TV, religious, social, social service, student government, and student programming board. Popular campus events include Welcome Back Week, Spring Fest, and dances.

Sports: There are 7 intercollegiate sports for men and 10 for women, and 7 intramural sports for men and 7 for women. Facilities include a 5,000-seat facility with a 6-lane, 200-meter track, 4 full basketball courts, 2 volleyball courts, 4 racquetball courts, and a fully equipped weight room; 6 outdoor tennis courts; a baseball field and soccer field with bleachers; 2 training room facilities; a softball field; and a state-of-the-art fitness center with aerobics room, selectorized weight room, and cardio room.

Disabled Students: 41% of the campus is accessible. Facilities include wheelchair ramps, elevators, special parking, specially equipped restrooms, special class scheduling, lowered drinking fountains, lowered telephones, special housing. oral interpretation for the hearing impaired.

Services: Counseling and information services are available, as is tutoring in every subject. There is a reader service for the blind, and remedial math, reading, and writing. Workshops offer assistance with academic study skills, time management, and advanced reading and writing. Support services for basic skills students and freshmen are available. There is also a Regional Center for College Students with Learning Disabilities that offers comprehensive support to students admitted to the program.

Campus Safety and Security: Measures include 24-hour foot and vehicle patrol, emergency notification system, self-defense education, and security escort services. There are emergency telephones and lighted pathways/sidewalks.

Programs of Study: FDU confers B.A., B.S., B.S.Civ.E.T., B.S.C.L.S., B.S.Con.E.T., B.S.E.E., B.S.E.E.T., B.S.M.E.T., and B.S.N. degrees. Associate, master's, and doctoral degrees are also awarded. Bachelor's degrees are awarded in BIOLOGICAL SCIENCE (biochemistry, biology/biological science, and marine biology), BUSINESS (accounting, business administration and management, business economics, entrepreneurial studies, hotel/motel and restaurant management, and marketing/retailing/merchandising), COMMUNICATIONS AND THE ARTS (communications, English literature, and fine arts), COMPUTER AND PHYSICAL SCIENCE (chemistry, computer science, information sciences and systems, mathematics, radiological technology, and science), ENGINEERING AND ENVIRONMENTAL DESIGN (civil engineering technology, construction engineering, electrical/electronics engineering, electrical/electronics engineering technology, and mechanical engineering technology), HEALTH PROFESSIONS (allied health, clinical science, medical laboratory technology, nursing, and physical therapy), SOCIAL SCIENCE (criminal justice, economics, history, humanities, interdisciplinary studies, international studies, liberal arts/general studies, philosophy, political science/government, psychology, and Spanish studies). Nursing, psychology, and business management have the largest enrollments.

Required: To graduate, students must complete 120 to 128 credits, including 30 to 44 in the major, with an overall minimum 2.0. GPA. Students must complete a 4-semester interdisciplinary sequence and 1 course in freshman seminar. The core curriculum includes 6 credits in English, 12 in university core, and 3 each in math and computer science.

Special: FDU offers co-op programs in most majors, cross-registration, internships, and study abroad in England and Vancouver. A Washington semester, work-study, accelerated degrees, and student-designed majors in the humanities and general studies are possible. A 7-year medical program is available with Karol Marcinkowski School of Medicine in Poland, as is an accelerated chiropractic program with New York Chiropractic College and Logan Chiropractic College (B.S.,B.A./M.A.T.). There are 12 national honor societies, a freshman honors program, and 16 departmental honors programs.

Faculty/Classroom: No introductory courses are taught by graduate students.

Admissions: In a recent year, 57% of the applicants were accepted. The SAT scores for a recent freshman class were: Critical Reading--42% below 500, 46% between 500 and 599, 11% between 600 and 700, and % above 700; Math--30% below 500, 52% between 500 and 599, 16% between 600 and 700, and 2% above 700; Writing--43% below 500, 49% between 500 and 599, 8% between 600 and 700, and % above 700. 30% of the current freshmen were in the top fifth of their class; 62% were in the top two fifths. 1 freshman graduated first in the class.

Requirements: The SAT or ACT is required. Applicants should be graduates of an accredited high school or have a GED certificate. They should have completed a minimum of 16 academic units, including 4 in English, 3 in math, 2 each in history, foreign language, and lab science (3 are recommended), and 3 in electives. Those students applying to science, engineering, and health sciences programs must meet additional requirements. An interview may be required. AP and CLEP credits are accepted. Important factors in the admissions decision are leadership record, recommendations by school officials, and extracurricular activities record.

Procedure: Freshmen are admitted to all sessions. Entrance exams should be taken by May of the junior year. There are deferred admissions and rolling admissions plans. Applications should be filed by March 15 for fall entry, along with a $40 fee. Notification is sent on a rolling basis. Applications are accepted online.

Transfer: In a recent year, 499 transfer students enrolled. All applicants must submit official transcripts for all college work taken. Those students with fewer than 24 credits must also submit a high school transcript or a copy of their state department of education's equivalency score and SAT scores. 32 of 128 credits required for the bachelor's degree must be completed at FDU.

Visiting: There are regularly scheduled orientations for prospective students, including standardized placement testing, faculty advisement, class registration, and educational and social activities to prepare students for entrance. There are guides for informal visits, visitors may sit in on classes, and stay overnight. To schedule a visit, contact the Admissions Office.

Financial Aid: Check with the school for current application deadlines.

International Students: There are 243 international students enrolled. The school actively recruits these students. They must take the TOEFL with a minimum score of 550 on the paper-based TOEFL (PBT) or 79 on the Internet-based version (iBT) or IELTS. The ACT or SAT is highly recommended.

Computers: Wireless access is available. All students may access the system. There are no time limits. The fee is $692. It is strongly recommended that all students have a personal computer. A IBM ThinkPad or NetVista is recommended.

Graduates: In a recent year, 784 bachelor's degrees were awarded. The most popular majors were psychology (7%), nursing (6%), and criminal justice (6%). 201 companies recruited on campus in a recent year. In an average class, 21% graduate in 4 years or less, 37% graduate in 5 years or less, and 40% graduate in 6 years or less.

Admissions Contact: Jonathan Wexler, Associate Vice President of Enrollment Management. E-Mail: *globaleducation@fdu.edu* Web: *www.fdu.edu*

FELICIAN COLLEGE E-2

Lodi, NJ 07644 **(201) 559-6131; (201) 559-6188**

Full-time: 390 men, 950 women	**Faculty:** 100
Part-time: 57 men, 224 women	**Ph.D.s:** n/av
Graduate: 54 men, 258 women	**Student/Faculty:** 15 to 1
Year: semesters, summer session	**Tuition:** $29,990
Application Deadline: open	**Room & Board:** $11,650

Freshman Class: 2207 applied, 1382 accepted, 153 enrolled

COMPETITIVE

Felician College, founded in 1942, is a private, Roman Catholic, liberal arts school with concentrations in health science, teacher education, and arts and sciences. There are 4 undergraduate schools and 4 graduate schools. In addition to regional accreditation, Felician has baccalaureate program accreditation with CAHEA and NLN. The 2 libraries contain 132,184 volumes, 89,191 microform items, and 1,624 audio/video tapes/CDs/DVDs, and subscribe to 22,721 periodicals including electronic. Computerized library services include interlibrary loans, database searching, Internet access, and Wi-Fi capability. Special learning facilities include a radio station, a nursing clinical lab; drama theater. The 37-acre campus is in a suburban area 12 miles west of New York City. Including any residence halls, there are 15 buildings.

Student Life: 92% of undergraduates are from New Jersey. Others are from 13 states, 25 foreign countries, and Canada. 65% are from public schools. 40% are White; 23% Hispanic; 20% African American. The average age of freshmen is 19; all undergraduates, 26. 27% do not continue beyond their first year; 42% remain to graduate.

Housing: 520 students can be accommodated in college housing, which includes single-sex and coed dorms. On-campus housing is guaranteed for all 4 years. 85% of students commute. Alcohol is not permitted. Upperclassmen may keep cars.

Activities: There are no fraternities or sororities. There are 17 groups on campus, including and karate, free enterprise, science, art, cheerleading, chess, choir, computers, drama, education, ethnic, honors, international, jazz band, literary magazine, professional, religious, social service, and student government. Popular campus events include College Festival, Springfest, and Sibling Weekend.

Sports: There are 5 intercollegiate sports for men and 5 for women. Facilities include 2 fitness centers and a gym.

Disabled Students: 90% of the campus is accessible. Facilities include wheelchair ramps, elevators, special parking, specially equipped restrooms, lowered drinking fountains, lowered telephones, special housing, and wheelchair lifts.

Services: Counseling and information services are available, as is tutoring in most subjects. There is remedial math, reading, and writing.

Campus Safety and Security: Measures include 24-hour foot and vehicle patrol, emergency notification system, and self-defense education. There are shuttle buses, emergency telephones, and lighted pathways/sidewalks.

Programs of Study: Felician confers B.A., B.S. and B.S.N. degrees. Associate, master's, and doctoral degrees are also awarded. Bachelor's degrees are awarded in BIOLOGICAL SCIENCE (biology/biological science), BUSINESS (accounting, business administration and management, international business management, and marketing management), COMMUNICATIONS AND THE ARTS (art, communications, English, fine arts, graphic design, journalism, and music), COMPUTER AND PHYSICAL SCIENCE (computer security and information assurance, information sciences and systems, mathematics, and natural sciences), EDUCATION (early childhood education, education, elementary education, secondary education, and special education), HEALTH PROFESSIONS (allied health and nursing), SOCIAL SCIENCE (criminal justice, history, humanities, liberal arts/general studies, philosophy, psychology, religion, and social science). Education and nursing is the strongest academically.

Required: All students must earn a minimum GPA of 2.0 (2.5 in medical lab technology, 2.75 in nursing, and 3.0 in education), while taking 120 credit hours (128 to 130 in education), with 39 to 57 hours in their majors. Distribution requirements include 45 to 47 hours from a core curriculum, including courses in English, philosophy, religious studies, humanities, historical tradition, science, and social-cultural studies.

Special: Co-op programs are available in clinical lab sciences with the University of Medicine and Dentistry of New Jersey and with SUNY College of Optometry, New York Chiropractic College, New York College of Podiatric Medicine, and Bloomsburg University of Pennsylvania (Audiology Program). In addition, internships for credit, work-study at the college, dual majors in education, an interdisciplinary studies degree, an accelerated degree in nursing, student-designed majors within humanities and social and behavioral sciences, and pass/fail options are possible. There is a freshman honors program.

Faculty/Classroom: 43% of faculty are male; 57% are female. No introductory courses are taught by graduate students. The average class size in an introductory lecture is 25; in a laboratory is 20; and in a regular course is 15.

Admissions: 63% of the 2013-2014 applicants were accepted. 17% of the current freshmen were in the top fifth of their class; 44% were in the top two fifths.

Requirements: The SAT is required, with a minimum composite score of 850 recommended (critical reading and math). The college also recommends that applicants have 16 academic credits, including 4 in English, 2 to 3 each in math, science, and social studies, and 3 to 6 in academic electives, including foreign language. An interview is recommended. The GED is accepted. A GPA of 2.0 is required. AP and CLEP credits are accepted. Important factors in the admissions decision are recommendations by school officials, advanced placement or honors courses, and extracurricular activities record.

Procedure: Freshmen are admitted fall and spring. There is a rolling admissions plan. Application deadlines are open. Application fee is $30. Notification is sent on a rolling basis. Applications are accepted online.

Transfer: 84 transfer students enrolled in 2012-2013. Applicants must have maintained a minimum GPA of 2.5 (2.75 in nursing and 3.0 in education). An interview is recommended. Nursing majors require previous college-level lab science. 30 of 120 credits required for the bachelor's degree must be completed at Felician.

Visiting: There are regularly scheduled orientations for prospective students. There are guides for informal visits and visitors may sit in on classes. To schedule a visit, contact the Office of Undergraduate Admission.

Financial Aid: In 2013-2014, 97% of all full-time freshmen and 85% of continuing full-time students received some form of financial aid. 80% of all full-time freshmen and 69% of continuing full-time students received need-based aid. 97% of undergraduate students work part-time. Average annual earnings from campus work are $3000. The average financial indebtedness of the 2013 graduate was $38,598. The FAFSA and the college's own financial statement are required. Check with the school for current application deadlines.

International Students: There are 42 international students enrolled. The school actively recruits these students. They must take the TOEFL with a minimum score of 500 on the paper-based TOEFL (PBT) or 61 on the Internet-based version (iBT), the IELTS.

Computers: All students may access the system. There are no time limits and no fees.

Graduates: From July 1, 2012 to June 30, 2013, 357 bachelor's degrees were awarded. The most popular majors were nursing (35%), arts and sciences (33%), and business (18%). 17 companies recruited on campus in 2012-2013. In an average class, 23% graduate in 4 years or less, 37% graduate in 5 years or less, and 42% graduate in 6 years or less.

Admissions Contact: Steve Goetsch, AVP Undergraduate Enrollment Services. E-Mail: *goetschs@felician.edu* Web: *www.felician.edu*

GEORGIAN COURT UNIVERSITY — E-4

Lakewood, NJ 08701 — **(800) 458-8422**

Full-time: 175 men, 1086 women	**Faculty:** 100; IIA, -$
Part-time: 126 men, 180 women	**Ph.D.s:** 88%
Graduate: 119 men, 571 women	**Student/Faculty:** 13 to 1
Year: semesters, summer session	**Tuition:** $29,606
Application Deadline: August 1	**Room & Board:** $10,120
Freshman Class: n/av	
SAT CR/M/W: 440/450/440	**ACT:** recommended

LESS COMPETITIVE

Georgian Court University, founded in 1908, is an independent Roman Catholic university. Undergraduate programs are offered in the arts and sciences, business, and education. There are 3 undergraduate schools and 3 graduate schools. In addition to regional accreditation, The Court has baccalaureate program accreditation with ACBSP, CSWE, and TEAC. Computerized library services include interlibrary loans, database searching, Internet access, and Wi-Fi capability. Special learning facilities include an art gallery, an arboretum. The 156-acre campus is in a suburban area 60 miles south of New York City and 60 miles east of Philadelphia. Including any residence halls, there are 27 buildings.

Student Life: 94% of undergraduates are from New Jersey. Others are from 19 states, 15 foreign countries, and Canada. 48% are White; 22% race unknown; 14% African American; 11% Hispanic. The average age of freshmen is 18; all undergraduates, 22. 29% do not continue beyond their first year; 51% remain to graduate.

Housing: 447 students can be accommodated in college housing, which includes coed dorms. On-campus housing is guaranteed for the freshman year only, is available on a first-come, first-served basis, and is available on a lottery system for upperclassmen. 72% of students commute. All students may keep cars.

Activities: There are no fraternities or sororities. There are 50 groups on campus, including art, band, choir, chorale, chorus, dance, ethnic, gay, honors, international, jazz band, literary magazine, newspaper, orchestra, professional, religious, social, social service, and student government. Popular campus events include Latin Night, Diversifest, and Comedy Night.

Sports: There are 4 intercollegiate sports for men and 8 for women. Facilities include a wellness center and athletic complex with fitness and aerobic facilities as well as a dance studio.

Disabled Students: 77% of the campus is accessible. Facilities include wheelchair ramps, elevators, special parking, specially equipped restrooms, special class scheduling, lowered drinking fountains, lowered telephones, and special equipment for the visually and hearing impaired.

Services: Counseling and information services are available, as is tutoring in most subjects. There is remedial math, reading, and writing.

Campus Safety and Security: Measures include 24-hour foot and vehicle patrol, emergency notification system, and security escort services. There are shuttle buses, emergency telephones, lighted pathways/sidewalks, and controlled access to dorms/residences.

Programs of Study: The Court confers B.A., B.S., B.S.N., B.F.A. and B.S.W. degrees. Master's degrees are also awarded. Bachelor's degrees are awarded in BIOLOGICAL SCIENCE (biochemistry and biology/biological science), BUSINESS (accounting and business administration and management), COMMUNICATIONS AND THE ARTS (applied art, art, communications, dance, English, and Spanish), COMPUTER AND PHYSICAL SCIENCE (chemistry, mathematics, and natural sciences), EDUCATION (education), HEALTH PROFESSIONS (allied health, clinical science, exercise science, health, medical records administration/services, and nursing), SOCIAL SCIENCE (criminal justice, history, humanities, psychology, religion, and social work). Psychology, nursing and education are the strongest academically. Psychology, nursing, and English have the largest enrollments.

Required: All students must complete 120 total credit hours.

Special: Georgian Court offers internships, study abroad, dual majors with education. There are 18 national honor societies and a freshman honors program.

Faculty/Classroom: 35% of faculty are male; 65% are female. All teach undergraduates. No introductory courses are taught by graduate students. The average class size in an introductory lecture is 18 and in a regular course is 14.

Admissions: The SAT scores for the 2013-2014 freshman class were: Critical Reading--73% below 500, 24% between 500 and 599, 3% between 600 and 699, Math--69% below 500, 26% between 500 and 599, 4% between 600 and 699, and 1% between 700 and 800; Writing--73% below 500, 24% between 500 and 599, 3% between 600 and 700, 22% of the current freshmen were in the top fifth of their class; 51% were in the top two fifths.
Requirements: The SAT is required. The ACT and ACT Writing Test are recommended. Applicants must be graduates of accredited secondary schools or have earned a GED. The university requires 16 academic credits or Carnegie units based on 6 years of academic electives, 4 of English, 2 each of foreign language and math, and 1 each of history and a lab science. An interview is recommended for all students, and an audition is required for applied music and dance majors. AP and CLEP credits are accepted.
Procedure: Freshmen are admitted fall and spring. Entrance exams should be taken by January of the senior year. There is a rolling admissions plan. Applications should be filed by August 1 for fall entry; January 1 for spring entry. The fall 2013 application fee was $40. Notification is sent on a rolling basis. Applications are accepted online.
Transfer: 213 transfer students enrolled in 2012-2013. Applicants with fewer than 24 credits must fulfill freshman requirements. 30 of 120 credits required for the bachelor's degree must be completed at The Court.
Visiting: There are regularly scheduled orientations for prospective students, including visits with faculty and students and a tour of facilities. There are guides for informal visits, visitors may sit in on classes, and stay overnight. To schedule a visit, contact Tracey Howard-Ubelhoer.
Financial Aid: In 2013-2014, 99% of all full-time freshmen and 95% of continuing full-time students received some form of financial aid. The average freshman award was $27,849. The Court is a member of CSS. The FAFSA and the college's own financial statement, and parent and student 1040 tax forms are required. Check with the school for current application deadlines.
International Students: There are 13 international students enrolled. The school actively recruits these students. They must take the TOEFL.
Computers: All students may access the system. There are no time limits and no fees.
Graduates: From July 1, 2012 to June 30, 2013, 391 bachelor's degrees were awarded. The most popular majors were psychology (34%), English (12%), and business (8%). In an average class, 25% graduate in 4 years or less, 49% graduate in 5 years or less, and 54% graduate in 6 years or less.
Admissions Contact: John Mc Auliffe, VP Enrollment Management. E-Mail: *admissions@georgian.edu* Web: *www.georgian.edu*

KEAN UNIVERSITY D-2

Union, NJ 07083 **(908) 737-7100; (908) 737-7105**

Full-time: 3801 men, 5450 women
Part-time: 990 men, 1837 women
Graduate: 558 men, 1768 women
Year: semesters, summer session
Application Deadline: May 31
Faculty: n/av; IIA, ++$
Ph.D.s: 87%
Student/Faculty: 17 to 1
Tuition: $10,918 ($17,141)
Room & Board: $11,142
Freshman Class: 4952 applied, 3980 accepted, 1525 enrolled
SAT: required

LESS COMPETITIVE

Kean University is a public university serving undergraduate and graduate students in the liberal arts, the sciences, and the professions. There are 6 undergraduate schools and one graduate school. In addition to regional accreditation, Kean has baccalaureate program accreditation with NASAD, NASM, NCATE, and NLN. The library contains 224,487 volumes, and subscribes to 47,721 periodicals including electronic. Computerized library services include interlibrary loans, database searching, Internet access, and Wi-Fi capability. Special learning facilities include an art gallery, planetarium, radio station, TV station, New Jersey Center for Science, Technology, and Mathematics; Holocaust Resource Center; Wynona Moore Lipman Ethnic Studies Center; Liberty Hall Museum; Human Rights Institute and New Jersey Highlands. The 185-acre campus is in a suburban area in Union, NJ additional locations in Toms River, NJ and Wenzhou, China. Including any residence halls, there are 44 buildings.
Student Life: 98% of undergraduates are from New Jersey. Others are from 25 states, 53 foreign countries, and Canada. 34% are White; 23% Hispanic; 18% African American; 17% race unknown. The average age of freshmen is 18; all undergraduates, 24. 26% do not continue beyond their first year; 46% remain to graduate.
Housing: 2036 students can be accommodated in college housing, which includes single-sex and coed dorms and on-campus apartments. In addition, there are special-interest houses, freshman housing, and women-only floor, living learning communities for SIMS (Success in Math and Science), GREEN (Gearing Residents toward Environment, Exercise and Nutrition) and WELL (Women Empowered toward Leadership and Learning). On-campus housing is available on a first-come and first-served basis. 86% of students commute. Alcohol is not permitted. Upperclassmen may keep cars.
Activities: Men belong to 5 local and 9 national fraternities; Women belong to 5 local and 10 national sororities. There are 127 groups on campus, including art, band, choir, chorale, chorus, communications, computers, dance, drama, environmental, ethnic, gay, honors, international, jazz band, literary magazine, musical theater, newspaper, opera, orchestra, pep band, photography, political, professional, radio and TV, religious, social, social service, student government, symphony, and yearbook. Popular campus events include Homecoming, Campus Awareness Festival, Comedy Show, Unity Week, Concerts, Class Events and Meet the Greeks, Food Bank Luncheon, Student Group Expo, and Martin Luther King Jr. Day of Service.
Sports: There are 6 intercollegiate sports for men and 7 for women, and 6 intramural sports for men and 6 for women. Facilities include 5300-seat stadium, an 8-lane track, 800-seat soccer stadium, 350-seat baseball stadium, 250-seat softball stadium, practice fields, 3000-seat arena, 5 indoor basketball courts, 2 outdoor basketball courts, 10 outdoor tennis courts, indoor swimming pool, 3 fitness rooms and pool tables.
Disabled Students: All of the campus is accessible. Facilities include wheelchair ramps, elevators, special parking, specially equipped restrooms, special class scheduling, lowered drinking fountains, lowered telephones, and special housing.
Services: Counseling and information services are available, as is tutoring in most subjects. There is a reader service for the blind, and remedial math, reading, and writing.
Campus Safety and Security: Measures include 24-hour foot and vehicle patrol, emergency notification system, self-defense education, and security escort services. There are shuttle buses, emergency telephones, lighted pathways/sidewalks, controlled access to dorms/residences, all residence halls have surveillance cameras in floors, lounges, elevators and exit doors; All residence halls have fire sprinkler systems.
Programs of Study: Kean confers B.A., B.S., B.F.A., B.I.D. and B.S.N. degrees. Master's and doctoral degrees are also awarded. Bachelor's degrees are awarded in BIOLOGICAL SCIENCE (biology/biological science), BUSINESS (accounting, finance, international business, management science, marketing management, recreational facilities management, and sustainable management), COMMUNICATIONS AND THE ARTS (art history and appreciation, broadcasting, communications, English, film arts, fine arts, industrial design, information technology, media arts, music, music performance, performing arts, Spanish, studio art, theatre arts, theater design, and visual and performing arts), COMPUTER AND PHYSICAL SCIENCE (chemistry, computer science, earth science, information sciences and systems, mathematics, and science and technology studies), EDUCATION (athletic training, early childhood education, elementary education, health information management, middle school education, music education, physical education, secondary education, and special education), ENGINEERING AND ENVIRONMENTAL DESIGN (interior design), HEALTH PROFESSIONS (medical technology, nursing, and speech pathology/audiology), SOCIAL SCIENCE (Asian/Oriental studies, criminal justice, economics, history, political science/government, psychology, public administration, and sociology). science/technology and education is the strongest academically. Business and education have the largest enrollments.
Special: There are 27 national honor societies, a freshman honors program, and 8 departmental honors programs.
Faculty/Classroom: 48% of faculty are male; 52% are female. No introductory courses are taught by graduate students. The average class size in a regular course is 22.
Admissions: 80% of the 2013-2014 applicants were accepted. 22% of the current freshmen were in the top fifth of their class; 52% were in the top two fifths.
Requirements: The SAT is required. Applicants must be graduates of accredited secondary schools or have earned a GED. College preparatory study includes 4 courses in English, 3 in math, 2 each in lab science and history, and 5 in academic electives. An essay and 2 letters of recommendation, official transcript and SAT/ACT are also required. AP and CLEP credits are accepted.
Procedure: Freshmen are admitted fall and spring. Entrance exams should be taken junior & senior year. There are deferred admissions and rolling admissions plans. Applications should be filed by May 31 for fall entry; December 1 for spring entry, along with a $75 fee. Notifications are sent November 1. Applications are accepted online.
Transfer: 1505 transfer students enrolled in 2012-2013. NACES evaluation of transcripts for any foreign institution attended. The minimum number of credits to transfer with a 2.0 is 30. Between 15-30 credit (semester) hours students must have a 3.0 GPA. 32 of 124 credits required for the bachelor's degree must be completed at Kean.
Visiting: There are regularly scheduled orientations for prospective students. There are guides for informal visits and visitors may sit in on classes. To schedule a visit, contact the Office of Undergraduate Admissions.
Financial Aid: In 2013-2014, 79% of all full-time freshmen received some form of financial aid. 73% of all full-time freshmen received need-based aid. The average freshman award was $9,968. Need-based scholarships or need-based grants averaged $8,125; need-based self-help aid

(loans and jobs) averaged $3,602; and other non-need-based awards and non-need-based scholarships averaged $3,379. 7% of undergraduate students work part-time. Average annual earnings from campus work are $4320. The average financial indebtedness of the 2013 graduate was $29,667. The FAFSA is required. The priority date for freshman financial aid applications for fall entry is April 17.

International Students: There are 126 international students enrolled. The school actively recruits these students. They must take the TOEFL with a minimum score of 550 on the paper-based TOEFL (PBT) or 75 on the Internet-based version (iBT). They must also take the SAT or ACT. SAT or ACT is required of some applicants.

Computers: All students may access the system. There are no time limits and no fees.

Graduates: From July 1, 2012 to June 30, 2013, 2705 bachelor's degrees were awarded. The most popular majors were psychology (14%), management science (8%), and criminal justice (6%). 186 companies recruited on campus in 2012-2013. In an average class, 19% graduate in 4 years or less, 39% graduate in 5 years or less, and 46% graduate in 6 years or less.

Admissions Contact: Valerie Winslow, Director of Admissions. E-Mail: *admitme@kean.edu* Web: *www.kean.edu*

MONMOUTH UNIVERSITY — E-3

West Long Branch, NJ 07764 (732) 571-3456
(800) 543-9671; (732) 263-5166

Full-time: 1761 men, 2543 women	**Faculty:** 249; IIA, +$
Part-time: 120 men, 183 women	**Ph.D.s:** 81%
Graduate: 404 men, 1305 women	**Student/Faculty:** 17 to 1
Year: semesters, summer session	**Tuition:** $31,018
Application Deadline: March 1	**Room & Board:** $11,234
Freshman Class: 5537 applied, 4314 accepted, 906 enrolled	
SAT CR/M/W: 520/540/520 **ACT:** 23	**COMPETITIVE**

Monmouth University, founded in 1933, is a private comprehensive institution offering both undergraduate and graduate programs in the arts and sciences, business, education, nursing, technology, and professional training. There are 7 undergraduate schools and one graduate school. In addition to regional accreditation, Monmouth has baccalaureate program accreditation with AACSB, ABET, CSWE, NCATE, and NLN. The library contains 343,000 volumes, 950 audio/video tapes/CDs/DVDs, and subscribes to 49,000 periodicals including electronic. Computerized library services include interlibrary loans, database searching, Internet access, and Wi-Fi capability. Special learning facilities include an art gallery, radio station, TV station, including a theater, greenhouse and a community garden. The 159-acre campus is in a suburban area 55 miles from New York City, and 75 miles from Philadelphia. Including any residence halls, there are 65 buildings.

Student Life: 87% of undergraduates are from New Jersey. Others are from 29 states, 28 foreign countries, and Canada. 85% are from public schools. 77% are White. The average age of freshmen is 18; all undergraduates, 21. 20% do not continue beyond their first year; 61% remain to graduate.

Housing: 1924 students can be accommodated in college housing, which includes coed dorms, on-campus apartments, and off-campus apartments. In addition, there are honors houses. On-campus housing is available on a first-come, first-served basis, and is available on a lottery system for upperclassmen. Priority is given to out-of-town students. 59% of students commute. All students may keep cars.

Activities: 5% of men belong to 6 national fraternities; 8% of women belong to 8 local and 7 national sororities. There are 80 groups on campus, including art, band, cheerleading, choir, chorus, computers, dance, debate, drama, environmental, ethnic, gay, honors, international, jazz band, literary magazine, musical theater, newspaper, pep band, photography, political, professional, radio and TV, religious, social, social service, student government, veterans, and yearbook. Popular campus events include Springfest, Ebony Night, and Winter Ball.

Sports: There are 10 intercollegiate sports for men and 11 for women, and 8 intramural sports for men and 9 for women. Facilities include a 4100 seat competition arena, 200 meter 6-lane indoor track, a 2500-seat gym, a 4600-seat football field, outdoor tennis courts, 3 basketball courts, an 8-lane all-weather track, an indoor Olympic-size pool, exercise, and weight rooms, and baseball, softball, soccer, and field hockey fields.

Disabled Students: 95% of the campus is accessible. Facilities include wheelchair ramps, elevators, special parking, specially equipped restrooms, special class scheduling, lowered drinking fountains, special housing. academic assistance provided within the classroom.

Services: Counseling and information services are available, as is tutoring in every subject. There is a reader service for the blind, and remedial math, reading, and writing.

Campus Safety and Security: Measures include 24-hour foot and vehicle patrol, emergency notification system, self-defense education, and security escort services. There are emergency telephones, lighted pathways/sidewalks, controlled access to dorms/residences.

Programs of Study: Monmouth confers B.A., B.S., B.F.A., B.S.N. and B.S.W. degrees. Associate, master's, and doctoral degrees are also awarded. Bachelor's degrees are awarded in BIOLOGICAL SCIENCE (biology/biological science and marine biology), BUSINESS (accounting, banking and finance, business administration and management, business economics, international business management, marketing management, and real estate), COMMUNICATIONS AND THE ARTS (art, art history and appreciation, communications, English, graphic design, modern language, music, music business management, Spanish, and theatre arts), COMPUTER AND PHYSICAL SCIENCE (chemistry, clinical laboratory science, computer science, mathematics, and software engineering), EDUCATION (art education, English education, foreign languages education, health education, mathematics education, music education, physical education, science education, secondary education, and special education), ENGINEERING AND ENVIRONMENTAL DESIGN (computer graphics), HEALTH PROFESSIONS (medical laboratory science, medical laboratory technology, nursing, and premedicine), SOCIAL SCIENCE (anthropology, criminal justice, history, homeland security, political science/government, prelaw, psychology, social work, and sociology). Business, education, and communication have the largest enrollments.

Required: To graduate, students must earn at least 128 credits, including 30 to 81 in a major, with a minimum GPA of 2.0 overall and 2.1 in the major. Education majors are required to have a cumulative GPA of 2.75.

Special: Students may study abroad in England, Australia, Italy, and Spain. There are cooperative and internship programs and a Washington semester. Five year Baccalaureate/Mater's programs in many academice areas. Monmouth also offers work-study programs, dual majors, flexible studies programs, and credit for life experience. Nondegree study is possible. There are 22 national honor societies and a freshman honors program.

Faculty/Classroom: 46% of faculty are male; 54% are female. 92% teach undergraduates, 92% do research, and 92% do both. No introductory courses are taught by graduate students. The average class size in an introductory lecture is 24; in a laboratory is 17; and in a regular course is 21.

Admissions: 78% of the 2013-2014 applicants were accepted. The SAT scores for the 2013-2014 freshman class were: Critical Reading--37% below 500, 49% between 500 and 599, 13% between 600 and 699, and 1% between 700 and 800; Math--28% below 500, 50% between 500 and 599, 21% between 600 and 699, and 1% between 700 and 800; Writing--35% below 500, 48% between 500 and 599, 16% between 600 and 699, and 1% between 700 and 800. The ACT scores were 11% below 21, 40% between 21 and 23, 34% between 24 and 26, 11% between 27 and 28, and 3% above 28. 38% of the current freshmen were in the top fifth of their class; 72% were in the top two fifths.

Requirements: The SAT or ACT is required. The ACT Optional Writing test is also required. In addition, applicants must be graduates of accredited secondary schools or have earned a GED. The college requires 16 Carnegie units, based on 4 years of English, 3 of math, and 2 each of history and science, with the remaining 5 units in academic electives. An essay and a letter of recommendation are required. AP and CLEP credits are accepted. Important factors in the admissions decision are advanced placement or honors courses, leadership record, and extracurricular activities record.

Procedure: Freshmen are admitted fall and spring. Entrance exams should be taken by December of the senior year. There is a deferred admissions plan. Applications should be filed by March 1 for fall entry; January 1 for spring entry, along with a $50 fee. Notifications are sent April 1. Applications are accepted online.

Transfer: 474 transfer students enrolled in 2012-2013. Transfer applicants with fewer than 24 transferable college credits must provide a high school transcript and SAT or ACT scores. All transfer applicants must submit college transcripts and a statement of good standing. A 2.25 minimum college GPA is required for general admission consideration,does not guarantee acceptance. For education majors, a minimum cumulative GPA of 2.75 is required. 32 of 128 credits required for the bachelor's degree must be completed at Monmouth.

Visiting: There are regularly scheduled orientations for prospective students, Students visits include campus tours. There are guides for informal visits and visitors may sit in on classes. To schedule a visit, contact the Admission Office.

Financial Aid: In 2013-2014, 100% of all full-time freshmen and 96% of continuing full-time students received some form of financial aid. 61% of all full-time freshmen and 57% of continuing full-time students received need-based aid. The average freshman award was $28,095. Need-based scholarships or need-based grants averaged $12,908 ($16,594 maximum); need-based self-help aid (loans and jobs) averaged $5,106 ($4,000 maximum); non-need-based athletic scholarships averaged $19,530 ($42,000 maximum); other non-need-based awards and non-need-based scholarships averaged $10,200 ($31,538 maximum); and $11,419 from other forms of aid. 29% of undergraduate students work part-time. Average annual earnings from campus work are $1234. The average financial indebtedness of the 2013 graduate was $22,999. The FAFSA and the state aid form are required. Check with the school for current application deadlines.

International Students: There are 38 international students enrolled. The school actively recruits these students. They must take the TOEFL with a minimum score of 550 on the paper-based TOEFL (PBT) or 79 on the Internet-based version (iBT) or take the MELAB, the IELTS, or the Cambridge ESOL (CAE). They must also take the SAT or ACT, scoring varies by student profile. Students from English speaking countries must take the SAT or ACT.

Computers: All students may access the system 24 hours a day, 7 days a week. There are no time limits and no fees.

Graduates: From July 1, 2012 to June 30, 2013, 1118 bachelor's degrees were awarded. The most popular majors were business (24%), education (12%), and communication (12%). 110 companies recruited on campus in 2012-2013. In an average class, 50% graduate in 4 years or less, 66% graduate in 5 years or less, and 61% graduate in 6 years or less. Of the 2012 graduating class, 47% were enrolled in graduate school within 6 months of graduation, and 44% were employed.

Admissions Contact: Victoria Bobik, Director of Undergraduate Admission. E-Mail: *admission@monmouth.edu* Web: *www.monmouth.edu*

MONTCLAIR STATE UNIVERSITY E-2

Montclair, NJ 07042 (973) 655-4444
(800) 331-9205; (973) 655-7700

Full-time: 4784 men, 7596 women	**Faculty:** n/av; IIA, ++$
Part-time: 829 men, 1223 women	**Ph.D.s:** 92%
Graduate: 1066 men, 2884 women	**Student/Faculty:** 17 to 1
Year: semesters, summer session	**Tuition:** $11,058 ($20,136)
Application Deadline: March 1	**Room & Board:** $11,556
Freshman Class: n/av	
SAT CR/M/W: 487/502/497	

COMPETITIVE

Montclair State University, established in 1908, is a public institution offering programs in liberal arts and sciences, business administration, fine and performing arts, and professional studies. There are 5 undergraduate schools and 1 graduate school. In addition to regional accreditation, Montclair has baccalaureate program accreditation with AACSB, ABET, ADA, CSAB, NASAD, NASDTEC, NASM, NCATE, and NRPA. The library contains 459,034 volumes, 1.2 million microform items, and 21,145 audio/video tapes/CDs/DVDs, and subscribes to 21,145 periodicals including electronic. Computerized library services include interlibrary loans, database searching, and Internet access. Special learning facilities include an art gallery, radio station, and TV station. The 275-acre campus is in a suburban area 14 miles west of New York City. Including any residence halls, there are 66 buildings.

Student Life: 97% of undergraduates are from New Jersey. Others are from 33 states, 110 foreign countries, and Canada. 53% are White; 21% Hispanic. The average age of freshmen is 19; all undergraduates, 22. 63% remain to graduate.

Housing: 5200 students can be accommodated in college housing, which includes single-sex and coed dorms and on-campus apartments. In addition, there are honors houses, special-interest houses, living learning communities. On-campus housing is available on a first-come and first-served basis. Priority is given to out-of-town students. 74% of students commute. Alcohol is not permitted. Upperclassmen may keep cars.

Activities: 5% of men belong to 2 local and 13 national fraternities; 4% of women belong to 4 local and 12 national sororities. There are 142 groups on campus, including band, cheerleading, choir, chorus, dance, drama, environmental, ethnic, film, gay, honors, international, jazz band, literary magazine, marching band, musical theater, newspaper, orchestra, pep band, political, professional, radio and TV, religious, social, social service, student government, and yearbook. Popular campus events include Fall Frenzy, Homecoming, Greek Week and World's Fair.

Sports: There are 8 intercollegiate sports for men and 9 for women, and 12 intramural sports for men and 12 for women. Facilities include Panzer Athletic Center is the home of intercollegiate athletics and physical education classes. The athletic center has a pool, competition gymnasium, auxiliary gymnasium, offices, athletic training facility and locker rooms. There is a turf multi-purpose stadium called Sprague Field, which is the home to field hockey, football, and men's and women's lacrosse. Pit taser Field is a turf soccer park, home to men's and women's soccer. Intramurals are also played on Sprague Field. There is a baseball stadium and a softball stadium and an 8 lane track.

Disabled Students: 90% of the campus is accessible. Facilities include wheelchair ramps, elevators, special parking, specially equipped restrooms, special class scheduling, lowered drinking fountains, lowered telephones, special housing. curb cuts, speaker phones, special building signs, TDDs, and priority registration. There is a disability resource center on campus.

Services: Counseling and information services are available, as is tutoring in most subjects. There is a reader service for the blind, and remedial math, reading, and writing. Audio textbooks are available.

Campus Safety and Security: Measures include 24-hour foot and vehicle patrol, emergency notification system, self-defense education, and security escort services. There are shuttle buses, emergency telephones, lighted pathways/sidewalks, controlled access to dorms/residences, and a crime prevention programs.

Programs of Study: Montclair confers B.A., B.S., B.F.A., B.S./M.S., B.S./M.A.T., and B.Mus. degrees. Master's and doctoral degrees are also awarded. Bachelor's degrees are awarded in BIOLOGICAL SCIENCE (biochemistry, biology/biological science, environmental biology, marine science, molecular biology, and nutrition), BUSINESS (accounting, banking and finance, business administration and management, business economics, hospitality management services, international business management, management information systems, marketing management, recreation and leisure services, retailing, and tourism), COMMUNICATIONS AND THE ARTS (art, art history and appreciation, broadcasting, classics, communications, communications technology, creative writing, dance, dramatic arts, English, film arts, fine arts, French, graphic design, Italian, Latin, linguistics, music, music performance, music theory and composition, musical theater, public relations, Spanish, speech/debate/rhetoric, studio art, and theater design), COMPUTER AND PHYSICAL SCIENCE (applied mathematics, astronomy, chemistry, computer science, geoscience, information sciences and systems, mathematics, and physics), EDUCATION (art education, athletic training, business education, early childhood education, health education, home economics education, middle school education, music education, and physical education), HEALTH PROFESSIONS (allied health, community health work, music therapy, predentistry, premedicine, prepharmacy, and public health), SOCIAL SCIENCE (anthropology, criminal justice, dietetics, economics, family and community services, food production/management/services, geography, gerontology, history, home economics, human ecology, humanities, law, paralegal studies, parks and recreation management, philosophy, political science/government, psychology, religion, sociology, and women's studies). Business administration, family and child studies, and psychology have the largest enrollments.

Required: Students must successfully complete a minimum of 120 semester hours, with 33 to 82 in the major, while maintaining a minimum GPA of 2.0. General education requirements include courses in communications, contemporary issues, art appreciation, a foreign language, humanities, math, natural/physical science, social sciences, and multicultural awareness, as well as 1 semester hour in phys ed and 3 semester hours in computer science.

Special: Internships, co-op programs in all majors, credit by exam, pass/fail options, work-study, credit for life experience, independent study, and study abroad in 51 countries are offered. Joint-degree programs are offered in practical anthropology and applied economics, and a 5-year B.A.-B.Mus. program in music is available, as is an articulated medical, dental, physical therapy, and physician assistant program with the University of Medicine and Dentistry of New Jersey and an articulated program leading to a Pharm.D. with Rutgers University. There are 28 national honor societies, a freshman honors program, and 3 departmental honors programs.

Faculty/Classroom: 47% of faculty are male; 53% are female. All teach undergraduates. No introductory courses are taught by graduate students. The average class size in an introductory lecture is 25; in a laboratory is 18; and in a regular course is 24.

Admissions: The SAT scores for the 2013-2014 freshman class were: Critical Reading--58% below 500, 34% between 500 and 599, 7% between 600 and 699, and 1% between 700 and 800; Math--48% below 500, 42% between 500 and 599, 9% between 600 and 699, and 1% between 700 and 800; Writing--52% below 500, 39% between 500 and 599, 8% between 600 and 699, and 1% between 700 and 800. 32% of the current freshmen were in the top fifth of their class; 70% were in the top two fifths.

Requirements: The SAT is required. Applicants must submit 16 Carnegie units, including 4 in English, 3 to 4 in math (including algebra I and II and geometry), 2 each in lab science, social studies, and a foreign language, and the remainder in additional courses in these fields. The GED is accepted. A portfolio, audition, or interview is required for students planning to major in fine arts, music, speech, or theater. Admission to computer science requires 4 years of math, including trigonometry. AP and CLEP credits are accepted. Important factors in the admissions decision are advanced placement or honors courses, recommendations by school officials, and leadership record.

Procedure: Freshmen are admitted fall and spring. Entrance exams should be taken October, November, or December of the senior year. There is a rolling admissions plan. Applications should be filed by March 1 for fall entry; November 1 for spring entry, along with a $65 fee. Notification is sent on a rolling basis. Applications are accepted online.

Transfer: 1379 transfer students enrolled in 2012-2013. Applicants must have completed a minimum of 15 credits from an accredited college. A cumulative GPA of 2.5 is required for most majors, with higher required in select programs. Applicants must have completed English composition. High school and college transcripts are required. 32 of 128 credits required for the bachelor's degree must be completed at Montclair.

Visiting: There are regularly scheduled orientations for prospective stu-

dents, Students engage in activities, registration, learn MSU policies and procedures, learn about connecting in and out of the classroom, and obtain an MSU ID. There are guides for informal visits. To schedule a visit, contact the Admissions Office.

Financial Aid: In 2013-2014, 83% of all full-time freshmen and 53% of continuing full-time students received some form of financial aid. 80% of all full-time freshmen and 67% of continuing full-time students received need-based aid. The average freshman award was $8,461. Need-based scholarships or need-based grants averaged $8,868 ($15,268 maximum); need-based self-help aid (loans and jobs) averaged $3,435 ($8,500 maximum); and other non-need-based awards and non-need-based scholarships averaged $10,454 ($12,000 maximum). 13% of undergraduate students work part-time. Average annual earnings from campus work are $1661. The average financial indebtedness of the 2013 graduate was $20,993. The FAFSA is required. The priority date for freshman financial aid applications for fall entry is March 1.

International Students: There are 282 international students enrolled. The school actively recruits these students. They must take the TOEFL with a minimum score of 80 on the Internet-based version (iBT). They must also take the SAT.

Computers: All students may access the system. There are no time limits and no fees.

Graduates: From July 1, 2012 to June 30, 2013, 314 bachelor's degrees were awarded. The most popular majors were business administration (14%), family and child studies (14%), and psychology (9%). In an average class, 1% graduate in 3 years or less, 35% graduate in 4 years or less, 58% graduate in 5 years or less, and 63% graduate in 6 years or less. Of the 2012 graduating class, 16% were enrolled in graduate school within 6 months of graduation.

Admissions Contact: Lisa Kasper, Director of Admissions. E-Mail: *msuadm@mail.montclair.edu* Web: *www.montclair.edu*

NEW JERSEY CITY UNIVERSITY E-2

Jersey City, NJ 07305 (201) 200-3234
(888) 441-NJCU; (201) 200-2044

Full-time: 1980 men, 2798 women
Part-time: 585 men, 1075 women
Graduate: 571 men, 1434 women
Year: semesters, summer session
Application Deadline: April 1
Faculty: 240; IIB, ++$
Ph.D.s: 91%
Student/Faculty: 15 to 1
Tuition: $10,653 ($19,065)
Room & Board: $10,407
Freshman Class: 4183 applied, 1727 accepted, 649 enrolled
SAT CR/M: 450/480

COMPETITIVE+

New Jersey City University, founded in 1927, is a public institution offering undergraduate and graduate programs in the arts and sciences, business administration, education, health science, upper-level nursing, and other professional fields. There are 3 undergraduate schools and 1 graduate school. In addition to regional accreditation, NJCU has baccalaureate program accreditation with ACBSP, NASAD, NASM, NCATE, NLN, and TEAC. The library contains 298,326 volumes, 1.8 million microform items, and 4,417 audio/video tapes/CDs/DVDs, and subscribes to 24,214 periodicals including electronic. Computerized library services include interlibrary loans, database searching, Internet access, and Wi-Fi capability. Special learning facilities include an art gallery, radio station, a media arts center, and a lab school for special education instruction. The 57-acre campus is in an urban area 5 miles west of New York City. Including any residence halls, there are 19 buildings.

Student Life: 99% of undergraduates are from New Jersey. Others are from 15 states. 32% are Hispanic; 29% White; 20% African American. The average age of freshmen is 18; all undergraduates, 26.

Housing: 265 students can be accommodated in college housing, which includes coed dorms. On-campus housing is guaranteed for all 4 years. 96% of students commute. Alcohol is not permitted. All students may keep cars.

Activities: 1% of men belong to 2 local and 7 national fraternities; 1% of women belong to 2 local and 5 national sororities. There are 24 groups on campus, including art, band, choir, chorale, chorus, computers, dance, drama, ethnic, film, gay, honors, international, jazz band, literary magazine, musical theater, newspaper, opera, orchestra, photography, political, professional, radio and TV, religious, social, social service, student government, and symphony.

Sports: There are 6 intercollegiate sports for men and 6 for women. Facilities include an athletic and fitness center with a 2000-seat arena, a jogging track, fitness facilities, a 6-lane pool, sauna, racquetball courts, a soccer, tennis, baseball, and softball facilities.

Disabled Students: All of the campus is accessible. Facilities include wheelchair ramps, elevators, special parking, specially equipped restrooms, special class scheduling, lowered drinking fountains, and lowered telephones.

Services: Counseling and information services are available, as is tutoring in most subjects. There is remedial math, reading, and writing.

Campus Safety and Security: Measures include 24-hour foot and vehicle patrol, emergency notification system, and security escort services. There are shuttle buses, emergency telephones, lighted pathways/sidewalks, and controlled access to dorms/residences.

Programs of Study: NJCU confers B.A., B.F.A., B.S., B.S.N. and accelerated B.S.N. degrees. Master's and doctoral degrees are also awarded. Bachelor's degrees are awarded in BIOLOGICAL SCIENCE (biology/biological science), BUSINESS (accounting and business administration and management), COMMUNICATIONS AND THE ARTS (English, fine arts, media arts, music, photography, and Spanish), COMPUTER AND PHYSICAL SCIENCE (chemistry, computer science, geology, mathematics, and physics), EDUCATION (art education, early childhood education, elementary education, health education, music education, secondary education, and special education), HEALTH PROFESSIONS (nursing and public health), SOCIAL SCIENCE (criminal justice, economics, geography, history, philosophy, political science/government, psychology, sociology, and women & gender studies). Nursing, accelerated nursing, early childhood education, national securty service, and fire science are the strongest academically. Business, criminal justice, psychology, and education have the largest enrollments.

Required: Students must complete 66 semester hours in general education courses, satisfy college requirements in English, communication, and math, and complete the introductory career exploration and computer usage courses. The bachelor's degree requires completion of at least 128 semester hours, including 36 to 54 in a major field, with a minimum GPA of 2.0. Distribution requirements include 9 credits each in natural science, social science, humanities, and fine and performing arts and 6 credits in communications and contemporary world.

Special: Co-op programs in all majors and internships in some are available. NJCU also offers study abroad, work-study programs, numerous health science programs, and some programs affiliated with New Jersey College of Medicine and Dentistry in Newark. Nondegree study and dual majors are possible. There is an accelerated degree program in nursing. There are 4 national honor societies, a freshman honors program, and 1 departmental honors program.

Faculty/Classroom: 54% of faculty are male; 46% are female. All teach undergraduates. No introductory courses are taught by graduate students. The average class size in a regular course is 19.

Admissions: 41% of the 2013-2014 applicants were accepted. The SAT scores for the 2013-2014 freshman class were: Critical Reading--72% below 500, 25% between 500 and 599, and 3% between 600 and 699; Math--60% below 500, 34% between 500 and 599, and 6% between 600 and 699. 13% of the current freshmen were in the top fifth of their class; and 29% were in the top two fifths.

Requirements: The SAT is required. In addition, Applicants must be graduates of accredited secondary schools or have earned a GED. The college requires 16 Carnegie units, including 4 in English, 3 in math, and 2 each in social studies and a lab science, with the remaining 5 units in a foreign language and additional academic courses. An essay is also required, and an interview is recommended. NJCU requires applicants to be in the upper 50% of their class. A GPA of 2.5 is required. AP and CLEP credits are accepted. Important factors in the admissions decision are advanced placement or honors courses, evidence of special talent, and recommendations by school officials.

Procedure: Freshmen are admitted fall and spring. Entrance exams should be taken in the spring of the junior year or fall of the senior year. There are deferred admissions and rolling admissions plans. Applications should be filed by April 1 for fall entry, along with a $50 fee. Notifications are sent January 1. Applications are accepted online.

Transfer: 973 transfer students enrolled in 2012-2013. Applicants must present a minimum GPA of 2.0 in at least 12 credit hours completed at the college level. Students transferring fewer than 12 credits must also submit SAT scores of at least 480 verbal and 440 math. An interview is recommended for all transfers. A basic skills test is required for transfers who have fewer than 30 credits or have not taken English or math at their previous school. College transcript is required. 36 of 128 credits required for the bachelor's degree must be completed at NJCU.

Visiting: There are regularly scheduled orientations for prospective students, including a financial aid workshop, guided tours, and open house. There is a summer orientation. There are guides for informal visits and visitors may sit in on classes. To schedule a visit, contact the Office of Admissions.

Financial Aid: In 2013-2014, 83% of all full-time freshmen and 78% of continuing full-time students received some form of financial aid. 76% of all full-time freshmen and 83% of continuing full-time students received need-based aid. The average freshman award was $11,446. Need-based scholarships or need-based grants averaged $8,819; need-based self-help aid (loans and jobs) averaged $3,039; and other non-need-based awards and non-need-based scholarships averaged $5,243. 4% of undergraduate students work part-time. Average annual earnings from campus work are $1600. The average financial indebtedness of the 2013 graduate was $18,865. The FAFSA is required. The priority date for freshman financial aid applications for fall entry is April 15.

International Students: There are 26 international students enrolled.

They must take the TOEFL with a minimum score of 173 on the paper-based TOEFL (PBT) or 61 on the Internet-based version (iBT). They must also take the SAT or ACT.

Computers: All students may access the system, 24 hours a day. There are no time limits and no fees.

Graduates: From July 1, 2012 to June 30, 2013, 1211 bachelor's degrees were awarded. The most popular majors were business administration (12%), psychology (10%), and criminal justice (8%). 350 companies recruited on campus in 2012-2013. In an average class, 6% graduate in 4 years or less, 22% graduate in 5 years or less, and 32% graduate in 6 years or less.

Admissions Contact: Jose Balda, Director of Admissions. E-Mail: *admissions@njcu.edu* Web: *www.njcu.edu*

NEW JERSEY INSTITUTE OF TECHNOLOGY E-2

Newark, NJ 07102 **(973) 596-3300; (973) 596-3461**

Full-time: 4352 men, 1177 women	**Faculty:** 418; I, +$
Part-time: 1072 men, 510 women	**Ph.D.s:** 100%
Graduate: 1948 men, 885 women	**Student/Faculty:** 13 to 1
Year: semesters, summer session	**Tuition:** $14,740 ($27,140)
Application Deadline: June 1	**Room & Board:** $11,750

Freshman Class: 4216 applied, 2684 accepted, 1626 enrolled

SAT CR/M/W: 549/614/540

VERY COMPETITIVE

New Jersey Institute of Technology is a public research university providing instruction, research, and public service in engineering, computer science, management, architecture, engineering technology, applied sciences, and related fields. There are 6 undergraduate schools and 1 graduate school. In addition to regional accreditation, NJIT has baccalaureate program accreditation with AACSB, ABET, and NAAB. The 2 libraries contain 171,180 volumes, 7,650 microform items, and 100,502 audio/video tapes/CDs/DVDs. Computerized library services include interlibrary loans and database searching. Special learning facilities include an art gallery, radio station, 3 TV studios. NJIT is home to many government- and industry-sponsored labs and research centers, including the EPA Northeast Hazardous Substance Research Center, the National Center for Transportation and Industrial Productivity, the Center for Manufacturing Systems, the Emission Reduction Research Center, the Microelectronics Research Center, the Center for Microwave and Lightwave Engineering, and the Multi-Lifecycle Engineering Center. The 45-acre campus is in an urban area 10 miles west of New York City. Including any residence halls, there are 27 buildings.

Student Life: 93% of undergraduates are from New Jersey. Others are from 24 states, 86 foreign countries, and Canada. 80% are from public schools. 35% are White; 21% Asian American; 14% Hispanic. The average age of freshmen is 18; all undergraduates, 22. 18% do not continue beyond their first year; 54% remain to graduate.

Housing: 1663 students can be accommodated in college housing, which includes coed dorms. On-campus housing is available on a first-come, first-served basis, and is available on a lottery system for upperclassmen. Priority is given to out-of-town students. 74% of students commute. All students may keep cars.

Activities: 8% of men belong to 19 local and 10 national fraternities; 5% of women belong to 4 local and 5 national sororities. There are 92 groups on campus, including art, chess, computers, drama, drum and bugle corps, ethnic, gay, honors, international, musical theater, newspaper, photography, professional, radio and TV, religious, social, social service, student government, and yearbook. Popular campus events include Miniversity, International Students Food Festival, and Leadership Training Weekend.

Sports: There are 9 intercollegiate sports for men and 6 for women, and 13 intramural sports for men and 7 for women. Facilities include a 1000-seat stadium, a fitness center with an indoor track, a 6-lane swimming pool, 4 tennis courts, 4 racquet sport courts, playing fields, bowling lanes, a table tennis and billiards area, and 3 gyms, the largest of which seats 1200.

Disabled Students: 95% of the campus is accessible. Facilities include wheelchair ramps, elevators, special parking, specially equipped restrooms, special class scheduling, lowered drinking fountains, and lowered telephones.

Services: Counseling and information services are available, as is tutoring in most subjects. There is a reader service for the blind, and remedial math, reading, and writing.

Campus Safety and Security: Measures include 24-hour foot and vehicle patrol, self-defense education, and security escort services. There are shuttle buses, emergency telephones, and lighted pathways/sidewalks.

Programs of Study: NJIT confers B.A., B.S. and B.Arch. degrees. Master's and doctoral degrees are also awarded. Bachelor's degrees are awarded in BIOLOGICAL SCIENCE (biology/biological science), BUSINESS (management science), COMMUNICATIONS AND THE ARTS (communications and technical and business writing), COMPUTER AND PHYSICAL SCIENCE (applied mathematics, applied physics, chemistry, computer management, computer science, information sciences and systems, and mathematics), ENGINEERING AND ENVIRONMENTAL DESIGN (architecture, biomedical engineering, chemical engineering, civil engineering, computer engineering, computer technology, electrical/electronics engineering, engineering and applied science, engineering technology, environmental engineering, environmental science, geophysical engineering, industrial engineering, manufacturing engineering, mechanical engineering, technological management, and technology and public affairs), SOCIAL SCIENCE (history). Engineering, computer science and architecture are the strongest academically.

Required: General university requirements include 9 credits of humanities and social science electives, 7 of natural sciences, 6 each of math, cultural history, basic social sciences, and engineering technology, 3 each of English and management, and 2 of computer science. Students must also complete 2 courses in phys ed. To graduate, students must earn between 124 and 164 credits, depending on the program, including 50 in the major, with a minimum GPA of 2.0 in upper-level major courses.

Special: Cross-registration is offered in conjunction with Essex County College, Rutgers University's Newark campus, and the University of Medicine and Dentistry of New Jersey. Cooperative programs, available in all majors, include two 6-month internships. There are 3-2 engineering degree programs with Stockton State College and Lincoln and Seton Hall Universities. NJIT also offers work-study programs, study abroad in 18 countries, dual and interdisciplinary majors, accelerated degree programs, distance learning, and nondegree study. There is 1 national honor society, a freshman honors program, and 17 departmental honor programs.

Faculty/Classroom: 82% of faculty are male; 18% are female. All teach undergraduates, all do research, and 74% do both. Graduate students teach 10% of introductory courses. The average class size in an introductory lecture is 30; in a laboratory is 27; and in a regular course is 25.

Admissions: 64% of the 2013-2014 applicants were accepted. The SAT scores for the 2013-2014 freshman class were: Critical Reading--34% below 500, 40% between 500 and 599, 21% between 600 and 699, and 5% between 700 and 800; Math--4% below 500, 43% between 500 and 599, 40% between 600 and 699, and 13% between 700 and 800; Writing--37% below 500, 41% between 500 and 599, 18% between 600 and 699, and 4% between 700 and 800. 40% of the current freshmen were in the top fifth of their class; 73% were in the top two fifths.

Requirements: The SAT is required. The SAT: Subject test in math I or II is also required. Applicants should have completed 16 secondary school units, including 4 each in English and math, 2 in a lab science, and 6 in a distribution of social studies, foreign language, math, and science courses. NJIT requires applicants to be in the upper 30% of their class. AP and CLEP credits are accepted. Important factors in the admissions decision are advanced placement or honors courses, recommendations by school officials, and geographical diversity.

Procedure: Freshmen are admitted fall and spring. Entrance exams should be taken in May of the junior year or November of the senior year. There is a rolling admissions plan. Applications should be filed by June 1 for fall entry; November 15 for spring entry, along with a $70 fee. Notifications are sent January 2. Applications are accepted online.

Transfer: 616 transfer students enrolled in 2012-2013. A minimum college GPA of 2.0 is required, but 2.5 or higher is recommended. Students must submit transcripts of all attempted postsecondary academic work. Applicants with fewer than 30 credits may be asked to provide scores on the SAT and the SAT: Subject test in math, as well as high school transcripts. Engineering technology students must present an associate degree. Admission to the School of Architecture is very competitive for transfer students. 33 of 124 credits required for the bachelor's degree must be completed at NJIT.

Visiting: There are regularly scheduled orientations for prospective students, including tours and meetings with admissions personnel, students, and faculty. There are guides for informal visits, visitors may sit in on classes, and stay overnight. To schedule a visit, contact the Director of Admissions.

Financial Aid: In 2013-2014, 94% of all full-time freshmen and 71% of continuing full-time students received some form of financial aid. 88% of all full-time freshmen and 66% of continuing full-time students received need-based aid. The average freshman award was $16,000. Need-based scholarships or need-based grants averaged $11,792 ($31,190 maximum); need-based self-help aid (loans and jobs) averaged $3,392 ($5,500 maximum); non-need-based athletic scholarships averaged $28,016 ($28,285 maximum); and other non-need-based awards and non-need-based scholarships averaged $7,579 ($38,120 maximum). 100% of undergraduate students work part-time. Average annual earnings from campus work are $2293. The average financial indebtedness of the 2013 graduate was $32,000. The priority date for freshman financial aid applications for fall entry is March 15.

International Students: There are 271 international students enrolled. The school actively recruits these students. They must take the TOEFL with a minimum score of 550 on the paper-based TOEFL (PBT) or 79 on the Internet-based version (iBT). They must also take the SAT, scoring 1100.

Computers: All students may access the system. There are no time limits and no fees.

Graduates: From July 1, 2012 to June 30, 2013, 1006 bachelor's degrees were awarded. The most popular majors were architecture (10%), mechanical engineering (9%), and civil engineering (7%). 170 companies recruited on campus in 2012-2013. In an average class, 1% graduate in 3 years or less, 23% graduate in 4 years or less, 46% graduate in 5 years or less, and 54% graduate in 6 years or less. Of the 2012 graduating class, 27% were enrolled in graduate school within 6 months of graduation, and 51% were employed.

Admissions Contact: Kathy Kelly, Director of Admissions. E-Mail: *admissions@njit.edu* Web: *www.njit.edu*

PRINCETON UNIVERSITY D-3

Princeton, NJ 08544 **609-258-3060; (609) 258-6743**

Full-time: 2673 men, 2571 women	**Faculty:** 904; I, ++$
Part-time: n/av	**Ph.D.s:** 94%
Graduate: 1675 men, 1016 women	**Student/Faculty:** 6 to 1
Year: semesters	**Tuition:** $40,715
Application Deadline: January 1	**Room & Board:** $13,080
Freshman Class: 26498 applied, 1963 accepted, 1285 enrolled	
SAT CR/M/W: 740/760/750	**ACT:** 33 **MOST COMPETITIVE**

Princeton University, established in 1746, is a private institution offering degrees in the liberal arts and sciences, engineering, applied science, architecture, public and international affairs, interdisciplinary and regional studies, and the creative arts. There are 4 graduate schools. In addition to regional accreditation, Princeton has baccalaureate program accreditation with ABET and NAAB. The 11 libraries contain 8.2 million volumes, 395,285 microform items, 120,600 audio/video tapes/CDs/DVDs, and subscribe to 84,283 periodicals including electronic. Computerized library services include interlibrary loans, database searching, Internet access, and Wi-Fi capability. Special learning facilities include an art gallery, natural history museum, radio station, a music center, a visual and performing arts center, several theaters, an observatory, a plasma physics lab, and a center for environmental and energy studies. The 500-acre campus is in a small town 50 miles south of New York City. Including any residence halls, there are 160 buildings.

Student Life: 84% of undergraduates are from out of state, mostly the Middle Atlantic. Students are from 50 states, 88 foreign countries, and Canada. 47% are White; 20% Asian American; 11% Foreign. The average age of freshmen is 18; all undergraduates, 20. 2% do not continue beyond their first year; 96% remain to graduate.

Housing: 6729 students can be accommodated in college housing, which includes single-sex and coed dorms, on-campus apartments, off-campus apartments, and married student housing. Freshmen and sophomores are assigned to 1 of 6 residential colleges; most juniors and seniors live in upper-class dorms and select from among such dining options as co-ops and private clubs. On-campus housing is guaranteed for all 4 years. 98% of students live on campus. Upperclassmen may keep cars.

Activities: There are no fraternities or sororities. There are 250 groups on campus, including art, band, cheerleading, chess, choir, chorale, chorus, communications, computers, dance, debate, drama, environmental, ethnic, forensics, gay, honors, international, jazz band, literary magazine, marching band, Model UN, musical theater, newspaper, opera, orchestra, pep band, photography, political, professional, religious, social, social service, student government, symphony, and yearbook. Popular campus events include Communiversity.

Sports: There are 20 intercollegiate sports for men and 18 for women, and 20 intramural sports for men and 20 for women. Facilities include a 250,000-square-foot gymnasium for intercollegiate sports; a gymnasium for recreational sports; a fitness center; an Olympic-size pool with complete diving facilities; separate stadiums for football (28,000 seats), track and field, and lacrosse and field hockey; a hockey rink; and outdoor facilities such as tennis courts, an 18-hole golf course, and more than 50 acres of fields for baseball, lacrosse, rugby, soccer, and softball.

Disabled Students: Facilities include wheelchair ramps, elevators, special parking, specially equipped restrooms, lowered drinking fountains, lowered telephones, special housing. Each student's needs are assessed individually. Accommodations may include additional testing time, sign language translators, and dietary accommodations for food allergies. Princeton has an Office of Disability Services.

Services: Counseling and information services are available, as is tutoring in every subject. There is a reader service for the blind. Princeton's McGraw Center for Teaching and Learning offers workshops and individual consultations in which students can learn to manage large reading loads, problem-solve, take effective notes and create study tools, prepare for long-term projects and oral presentations; prepare for exams, manage time, and overcome test anxiety. Princeton's Writing Program works to ensure freshmen and others can master college-level writing.

Campus Safety and Security: Measures include 24-hour foot and vehicle patrol, emergency notification system, self-defense education, and security escort services. There are shuttle buses, emergency telephones, lighted pathways/sidewalks, and controlled access to dorms/residences.

Programs of Study: Princeton confers A.B., and B.S.E. degrees. Master's and doctoral degrees are also awarded. Bachelor's degrees are awarded in BIOLOGICAL SCIENCE (ecology, evolutionary biology, and molecular biology), BUSINESS (operations research), COMMUNICATIONS AND THE ARTS (classics, comparative literature, English, French, German, Italian, music, Portuguese, Slavic languages, and Spanish), COMPUTER AND PHYSICAL SCIENCE (astrophysics, chemistry, computer science, geoscience, mathematics, and physics), ENGINEERING AND ENVIRONMENTAL DESIGN (aeronautical engineering, architectural engineering, architecture, chemical engineering, civil engineering, electrical/electronics engineering, and mechanical engineering), SOCIAL SCIENCE (anthropology, archeology, East Asian studies, economics, history, international relations, Near Eastern studies, philosophy, political science/government, psychology, religion, and sociology). Economics, politics, and public policy have the largest enrollments.

Required: To graduate, students must complete 8 semesters, or academic units. Candidates for the A.B. degree must demonstrate proficiency in English composition and a foreign language and they must complete distribution requirements in 7 academic areas. Candidates for the B.S.E. must satisfy the English composition requirement and complete a minimum of 7 courses in the humanities and social sciences spread over 4 distribution areas. A junior project and senior thesis are required of virtually all students.

Special: Princeton offers independent study, accelerated degree programs, student-proposed courses and majors, field study, community-based learning courses that enrich course work with related service projects, study abroad, freshman seminars, and independent work in the junior and senior year. They also offer a Program in Teacher Preparation. There are 2 national honor societies including Phi Beta Kappa.

Faculty/Classroom: 68% of faculty are male; 32% are female. All teach and do research. No introductory courses are taught by graduate students.

Admissions: 7% of the 2013-2014 applicants were accepted. The SAT scores for the 2013-2014 freshman class were: Critical Reading--3% between 500 and 599, 21% between 600 and 699, and 76% between 700 and 800; Math--1% between 500 and 599, 19% between 600 and 699, and 80% between 700 and 800; Writing--3% between 500 and 599, 18% between 600 and 699, and 79% between 700 and 800. The ACT scores were 1% between 24 and 26, 6% between 27 and 28, and 93% above 28. 98% of the current freshmen were in the top fifth of their class; 99% were in the top two fifths. 137 freshmen graduated first in their class.

Requirements: The SAT or ACT is required. The ACT is accepted in lieu of SAT Reasoning test when every other school to which the student applies requires only the ACT. Three SAT Subject tests are also required for all applicants. Recommended college preparatory courses include 4 years each of English, math, science, and a foreign language; 2 years each of lab science and history; and some study of art and music. Essays are required as part of the application and an interview is recommended. Students with special talent in visual or performing arts may supplement tapes, CDs or DVDs. AP credits are accepted. Important factors in the admissions decision are personality/intangible qualities, recommendations by school officials, and advanced placement or honors courses.

Procedure: Freshmen are admitted fall. Entrance exams should be taken by January of the senior year at the latest. There are early admissions and deferred admissions plans. Applications should be filed by January 1 for fall entry, along with a $65 fee. Notifications are sent April 1. 1395 applicants were on the 2013 waiting list; 33 were admitted. Applications are accepted online.

Transfer: Princeton does not have a transfer admissions option.

Visiting: There are regularly scheduled orientations for prospective students, Including information sessions on Monday to Friday within the Admission Office, and some Saturdays in the fall. Also, Princeton has an open campus, with many free and public events, and students are welcome to attend such events. Visitors may sit in on classes. To schedule a visit, contact the Undergraduate Admission Office.

Financial Aid: Princeton is a member of CSS. Check with the school for current application deadlines.

International Students: There are 569 international students enrolled. The school actively recruits these students. They must take the TOEFL, The SAT: Writing Test may be substituted for the TOEFL. They must also take the SAT or ACT. Students must take the SAT or ACT, plus three SAT Subject Tests.

Computers: All students may access the system. There are no time limits and no fees.

Graduates: From July 1, 2012 to June 30, 2013, 1271 bachelor's degrees were awarded. The most popular majors were social science (26%), engineering (20%), and life sciences (10%). In an average class, 88% graduate in 4 years or less, 95% graduate in 5 years or less, and 97% graduate in 6 years or less.

Admissions Contact: Janet Lavin Rapelye, Dean of Admissions. E-Mail: *uaoffice@princeton.edu* Web: *http:/www.princeton.edu/admission/*

RAMAPO COLLEGE OF NEW JERSEY D-1

Mahwah, NJ 07430 (201) 684-7300
(800) 9-RAMAPO; (201) 684-7964

Full-time: 2239 men, 2702 women	**Faculty:** 218
Part-time: 196 men, 273 women	**Ph.D.s:** 94%
Graduate: 82 men, 156 women	**Student/Faculty:** 18 to 1
Year: semesters, summer session	**Tuition:** $13,388 ($22,038)
Application Deadline: March 1	**Room & Board:** $11,550
Freshman Class: 6297 applied, 3480 accepted, 889 enrolled	
SAT CR/M/W: 540/555/530 **ACT:** 23	**COMPETITIVE+**

Ramapo College, founded in 1969, is a public institution offering undergraduate programs in the arts and sciences, American and international studies, business administration, and human services. Personal interaction is incorporated throughout the curriculum as is an international and multicultural component including telecommunications and computer technology. There are 5 undergraduate schools and 3 graduate schools. In addition to regional accreditation, Ramapo has baccalaureate program accreditation with AACSB, CSWE, and TEAC. The library contains 191,031 volumes, 2,500 microform items, 9,373 audio/video tapes/CDs/DVDs, and subscribes to 488 periodicals including electronic. Computerized library services include interlibrary loans, database searching, Internet access, and Wi-Fi capability. Special learning facilities include a radio station, TV station, astronomical observatory, international telecommunications satellite center, the Marge Roukema Center for International Education and Entrepreneurship, a solar greenhouse center, a spirituality center, and a sustainability education center. The 314-acre campus is in a suburban area 25 miles northwest of New York City. Including any residence halls, there are 62 buildings.

Student Life: 96% of undergraduates are from New Jersey. Others are from 19 states, and 77 foreign countries. 72% are White; 11% Hispanic. The average age of freshmen is 18; all undergraduates, 22. 12% do not continue beyond their first year; 72% remain to graduate.

Housing: 3062 students can be accommodated in college housing, which includes coed dorms and on-campus apartments. In addition, there are honors houses, special-interest houses, Blocks of rooms are reserved for scholars and honors students. On-campus housing is guaranteed for all 4 years, is available on a first-come, and first-served basis. 53% of students live on campus. All students may keep cars.

Activities: 17% of men belong to 15 national fraternities; 17% of women belong to 13 national sororities. There are 100 groups on campus, including theme housing, environmental clubs, cheerleading, choir, chorale, chorus, computers, dance, debate, drama, environmental, ethnic, film, gay, honors, international, jazz band, literary magazine, musical theater, newspaper, pep band, photography, political, professional, radio and TV, religious, social, social service, student government, volunteer/community service, and yearbook. Popular campus events include LollaNoBooza, Octoberfest, and Stress Busters.

Sports: There are 8 intercollegiate sports for men and 10 for women, and 16 intramural sports for men and 16 for women. Facilities include 10% Varsity and 80% Intramural participation. Facilities include a 1200-seat stadium that includes an 8-lane, 400-meter track and a FieldTurf field, 12 lighted tennis courts, and baseball, softball, field hockey, and soccer fields. A 1457-seat competition arena houses basketball and volleyball courts, and there is an auxiliary gym for intramurals and recreation. A 5000-square-foot fitness center includes cardio machines, machine weight stations, and free weights. Also available is a new athletic training room, a 6-lane swimming pool, and multiple locker rooms.

Disabled Students: All of the campus is accessible. Facilities include wheelchair ramps, elevators, special parking, specially equipped restrooms, special class scheduling, lowered drinking fountains, lowered telephones, and special housing.

Services: Counseling and information services are available, as is tutoring in every subject. There is a reader service for the blind, and remedial math, reading, and writing. Students have access to resources at the Center for Academic Success

Campus Safety and Security: Measures include 24-hour foot and vehicle patrol, emergency notification system, and security escort services. There are shuttle buses, emergency telephones, lighted pathways/sidewalks, surveillance cameras.

Programs of Study: Ramapo confers B.A., B.S., B.S.N. and B.S.W. degrees. Master's degrees are also awarded. Bachelor's degrees are awarded in AGRICULTURE (environmental studies), BIOLOGICAL SCIENCE (biochemistry, bioinformatics, and biology/biological science), BUSINESS (accounting, business administration and management, and international business management), COMMUNICATIONS AND THE ARTS (art, communications, dramatic arts, literature, music, and visual and performing arts), COMPUTER AND PHYSICAL SCIENCE (chemistry, computer science, information sciences and systems, and mathematics), ENGINEERING AND ENVIRONMENTAL DESIGN (engineering physics and environmental science), HEALTH PROFESSIONS (allied health, clinical science, and nursing), SOCIAL SCIENCE (African studies, American studies, economics, history, international studies, law, liberal arts/general studies, political science/government, psychology, science and society, social science, social work, sociology, and Spanish studies). Physics, bioinformatics, and biology. are the strongest academically. Business administration, psychology, and communication arts have the largest enrollments.

Required: Students must complete general education requirements of approximately 50 credits in science, social science, humanities, and English composition, as well as core requirements in their school of study and their particular major. A senior seminar is also required. To graduate, students must earn at least 128 credits with a minimum GPA of 2.0.

Special: Ramapo's curriculum emphasizes the interdependence of global society and includes an international dimension in all academic programs. Students may study abroad in many countries. Cooperative programs are available with various corporations and in foreign countries. Cross-registration is possible with local state colleges. Ramapo offers accelerated degree programs, dual and student-designed majors, credit for life experience, pass/fail options, internships, work-study programs, and certificate programs in gerontology and substance abuse. A teachers education program is offered. There are 23 national honor societies, a freshman honors program, and 5 departmental honors programs.

Faculty/Classroom: 51% of faculty are male; 49% are female. All teach undergraduates. No introductory courses are taught by graduate students. The average class size in an introductory lecture is 26; in a laboratory is 19; and in a regular course is 23.

Admissions: 55% of the 2013-2014 applicants were accepted. The SAT scores for the 2013-2014 freshman class were: Critical Reading--29% below 500, 51% between 500 and 599, 18% between 600 and 699, and 3% between 700 and 800; Math--21% below 500, 49% between 500 and 599, 25% between 600 and 699, and 5% between 700 and 800; Writing-32% below 500, 47% between 500 and 599, 18% between 600 and 699, and 3% between 700 and 800. The ACT scores were 12% below 21, 42% between 21 and 23, 40% between 24 and 26, and 6% above 28. 57% of the current freshmen were in the top fifth of their class; 89% were in the top two fifths. 2 freshmen graduated first in their class.

Requirements: The SAT is required. In addition, applicants must be graduates of an accredited secondary schools or have earned a GED. The college requires 18 academic credits, including 4 in English, 3 each in math, science, and social studies, 2 in foreign language, and the remaining 3 in academic electives. Students must also submit an essay. An interview is recommended. AP and CLEP credits are accepted. Important factors in the admissions decision are advanced placement or honors courses, recommendations by school officials, and evidence of special talent.

Procedure: Freshmen are admitted fall and spring. Entrance exams should be taken during the senior year. There are early admissions, deferred admissions, and rolling admissions plans. Applications should be filed by March 1 for fall entry; December 1 for spring entry. The fall 2013 application fee was $60. Notification is sent on a rolling basis. Applications are accepted online.

Transfer: 596 transfer students enrolled in 2012-2013. Applicants must supply a completed admission application, official transcripts from all previously attended colleges, and an official high school transcript (if fewer than 60 credits from another college attempted). 48 of 128 credits required for the bachelor's degree must be completed at Ramapo.

Visiting: There are regularly scheduled orientations for prospective students, Student visits include orientation, advisement, registration, and immediate decision days (that follow the early action plan). There are guides for informal visits and visitors may sit in on classes. To schedule a visit, contact the Admissions Office at admissions@ramapo.edu.

Financial Aid: In 2013-2014, 80% of all full-time freshmen and 82% of continuing full-time students received some form of financial aid. 60% of all full-time freshmen and 50% of continuing full-time students received need-based aid. The average freshman award was $11,368. Need-based scholarships or need-based grants averaged $10,305; need-based self-help aid (loans and jobs) averaged $4,525; other non-need-based awards and non-need-based scholarships averaged $4,437; and $10,254 from other forms of aid. 4% of undergraduate students work part-time. Average annual earnings from campus work are $2000. The average financial indebtedness of the 2013 graduate was $22,309. The FAFSA is required. The priority date for freshman financial aid applications for fall entry is March 1. The deadline for filing freshman financial aid applications for fall entry is March 15.

International Students: There are 77 international students enrolled. The school actively recruits these students. They must take the TOEFL with a minimum score of 550 on the paper-based TOEFL (PBT) or 90 on the Internet-based version (iBT) and the Comprehensive English Language Test. They must also take the SAT.

Computers: All students may access the system according to posted schedules for lab times. There are no time limits and no fees.

Graduates: From July 1, 2012 to June 30, 2013, 1325 bachelor's degrees were awarded. The most popular majors were business/marketing (21%), psychology (15%), and communication arts (11%). 130 companies recruited on campus in 2012-2013. In an average class, 2% graduate in

3 years or less, 60% graduate in 4 years or less, 70% graduate in 5 years or less, and 72% graduate in 6 years or less.

Admissions Contact: Peter Rice, Director of Admissions. E-Mail: *admissions@ramapo.edu* Web: *www.ramapo.edu*

RICHARD STOCKTON COLLEGE OF NEW JERSEY D-5

Pomona, NJ 08240-0195 (609) 652-4261
(866) RSC-2885; (609) 626-5541

Full-time: 2500 men, 3400 women	**Faculty:** n/av; IIA, +$
Part-time: 350 men, 600 women	**Ph.D.s:** n/av
Graduate: 200 men, 400 women	**Student/Faculty:** n/av
Year: semesters, summer session	**Tuition:** $12,500 ($18,700)
Application Deadline: see profile	**Room & Board:** $11,100
Freshman Class: n/av	
SAT or ACT: required	

VERY COMPETITIVE

Richard Stockton College of New Jersey, founded in 1969, is a public liberal arts college with 28 undergraduate programs and 6 graduate specialty areas. The figures in the above capsule and in this profile are approximate. There is 1 graduate school. In addition to regional accreditation, Stockton has baccalaureate program accreditation with APTA, CSWE, NASDTEC, and NLN. The library contains 627,300 volumes, 1.1 million microform items, and 15,300 audio/video tapes/CDs/DVDs, and subscribes to 26,400 periodicals including electronic. Computerized library services include interlibrary loans, database searching, and Internet access. Special learning facilities include a learning resource center, art gallery, radio station, TV station, astronomical observatory, marine science field lab, marina with a fleet of small boats, Holocaust resource center, educational technology, training center, and performing arts center. The 1600-acre campus is in a suburban area 12 miles northwest of Atlantic City. Including any residence halls, there are 55 buildings.

Student Life: 98% of undergraduates are from New Jersey. Others are from 21 states, 10 foreign countries, and Canada. 74% are from public schools. 78% are white. The average age of freshmen is 18; all undergraduates, 22. 17% do not continue beyond their first year; 67% remain to graduate.

Housing: 2081 students can be accommodated in college housing, which includes coed dorms and on-campus apartments. In addition, there are special-interest houses, and wellness, substance-free, academic, and smoke-free housing. On-campus housing is guaranteed for the freshman year only, is available on a first-come, first-served basis, and is available on a lottery system for upperclassmen. 68% of students commute. All students may keep cars.

Activities: 4% of men belong to 11 national fraternities; 5% of women belong to 10 national sororities. There are 94 groups on campus, including art, band, cheerleading, chess, choir, chorale, chorus, computers, dance, drama, ethnic, gay, honors, international, jazz band, literary magazine, newspaper, orchestra, pep band, photography, political, professional, radio and TV, religious, social, social service, and student government. Popular campus events include Spring Concert, Spring Fling, and Black History Month.

Sports: There are 7 intercollegiate sports for men and 10 for women, and 10 intramural sports for men and 10 for women. Facilities include an indoor 6-lane swimming pool, an outdoor track, a weight-lifting gym, 2 multipurpose gyms, a sauna, steam baths, and dance studios, as well as playing fields, a 60-acre lake for fishing and canoeing, cross-country courses, bike trails, an all-weather track, and tennis, racquetball, and basketball courts. There are 9 club sports in addition to intramurals.

Disabled Students: 99% of the campus is accessible. Facilities include wheelchair ramps, elevators, special parking, specially equipped restrooms, special class scheduling, lowered drinking fountains, and lowered telephones.

Services: Counseling and information services are available, as is tutoring in most subjects. There is a reader service for the blind, and remedial math, reading, and writing. In addition, there is a skills center and a learning access program for learning-disabled students.

Campus Safety and Security: Measures include 24-hour foot and vehicle patrol, emergency notification system, self-defense education, and security escort services. There are emergency telephones, lighted pathways/sidewalks, and a fully commissioned police department.

Programs of Study: Stockton confers B.A., B.S., and B.S.N. degrees. Master's and doctoral degrees are also awarded. Bachelor's degrees are awarded in BIOLOGICAL SCIENCE (biochemistry, biology/biological science, and marine science), BUSINESS (accounting, banking and finance, business administration and management, and management science), COMMUNICATIONS AND THE ARTS (communications, dance, dramatic arts, fine arts, languages, literature, and music), COMPUTER AND PHYSICAL SCIENCE (chemistry, computer science, geology, information sciences and systems, mathematics, and physics), EDUCATION (education), ENGINEERING AND ENVIRONMENTAL DESIGN (computational sciences, environmental science, and preengineering), HEALTH PROFESSIONS (nursing, physical therapy, public health, and speech pathology/audiology), SOCIAL SCIENCE (anthropology, criminal justice, economics, history, liberal arts/general studies, philosophy, political science/government, psychology, and social work). Sciences are the strongest academically. Business, psychology, and criminal justice have the largest enrollments.

Required: To graduate, students must earn 128 credit hours, with 32 in the general studies curriculum and maintain a minimum GPA of 2.0. 3 quantitative reasoning and 4 writing courses as well as freshman seminar are required.

Special: Stockton offers internships in all fields with a wide variety of companies, work-study with various government agencies and corporations, a Washington semester, independent study, and study abroad in 53 countries. Dual majors in all programs, student-designed majors, an accelerated degree in medicine and criminal justice, 3-2 engineering degrees with the New Jersey Institute of Technology and Rutgers University, and general studies degrees are also offered. Nondegree study, pass/fail options, and credit for life, military, and work experience are possible. There are 5 national honor societies and a freshman honors program.

Faculty/Classroom: 54% of faculty are male; 46% are female. No introductory courses are taught by graduate students.

Requirements: The SAT or ACT is required. Applicants must be high school graduates; the GED is accepted. 16 academic credits are required, including 4 years in English, 3 each in math and social studies, 2 in science, and 4 additional years of any of the above or a foreign language, or both. An essay and an interview are recommended, and a portfolio or audition is necessary where appropriate. AP and CLEP credits are accepted. Important factors in the admissions decision are advanced placement or honors courses, leadership record, and evidence of special talent.

Procedure: Freshmen are admitted fall and spring. Entrance exams should be taken once in the junior year and again before January in the senior year. There is a rolling admissions plan. Check with the school for current application deadlines and fee. Notification is sent on a rolling basis. Applications are accepted online. A waiting list is maintained.

Transfer: Transfer students must have earned at least 16 credits at other colleges and must submit college and high school transcripts as well as SAT scores. 32 of 128 credits required for the bachelor's degree must be completed at Stockton.

Visiting: There are regularly scheduled orientations for prospective students, including academic advising and orientation. There are guides for informal visits and visitors may sit in on classes. To schedule a visit, contact Admissions.

Financial Aid: The FAFSA is required. Check with the school for current application deadlines.

International Students: They must take the TOEFL, SAT, or ACT.

Computers: Wireless access is available. All students have access to the wireless network from their personally owned computers. All residential students have access to the campus network through a hard-wired Ethernet connection. All students have access to the network from 850 computers in 40 different computer labs. Three of these labs (64 computers) are open 24/7. The remaining labs are open 94 hours per week. All students may access the system 24 hours a day. There are no time limits and no fees.

Admissions Contact: Admissions. E-Mail: *admissions@stockton.edu* Web: *www.stockton.edu*

RIDER UNIVERSITY D-3

Lawrenceville, NJ 08648 (609) 896-5042
(800) 257-9026; (609) 895-6645

Full-time: 1648 men, 2280 women	**Faculty:** 237; IIA, ++$
Part-time: 246 men, 375 women	**Ph.D.s:** 98%
Graduate: 329 men, 607 women	**Student/Faculty:** 17 to 1
Year: semesters, summer session	**Tuition:** $33,420
Application Deadline:	**Room & Board:** $12,340
Freshman Class: 7903 applied, 5701 accepted, 919 enrolled	
SAT CR/M/W: 510/520/520	**ACT:** 22

COMPETITIVE

Rider University, founded in 1865, is a private institution offering undergraduate programs in the areas of business administration, liberal arts, education, sciences, and continuing studies. Westminster Choir College, located in nearby Princeton, is Rider's fourth college. There are 4 undergraduate schools and 2 graduate schools. In addition to regional accreditation, Rider has baccalaureate program accreditation with AACSB, NASM, and NCATE. The library contains 448,025 volumes, 657,600 microform items, 5,444 audio/video tapes/CDs/DVDs, and subscribes to 50,594 periodicals including electronic. Computerized library services include interlibrary loans, database searching, Internet access, and Wi-Fi capability. Special learning facilities include an art gallery, radio station, TV station, journalism and sociology labs, and a holocaust/genocide center. The 280-acre campus is in a suburban area 3 miles north of Trenton and 7 miles south of Princeton. Including any residence halls, there are 41 buildings.

Student Life: 78% of undergraduates are from New Jersey. Others are from 51 states, 64 foreign countries, and Canada. 66% are White. The average age of freshmen is 18; all undergraduates, 22. 23% do not continue beyond their first year; 66% remain to graduate.

Housing: 2515 students can be accommodated in college housing, which includes single-sex and coed dorms and on-campus apartments. In addition, there are honors houses, language houses, special-interest houses, fraternity houses, sorority houses, learning community, wellness, quiet, science area, and first-year experience housing. On-campus housing is available on a lottery system for upperclassmen. 57% of students live on campus; of those, 50% remain on campus on weekends. All students may keep cars.

Activities: 5% of men belong to 4 national fraternities; 9% of women belong to 8 national sororities. There are 130 groups on campus, including art, band, cheerleading, choir, chorale, chorus, computers, dance, drama, environmental, ethnic, film, gay, honors, international, jazz band, literary magazine, musical theater, newspaper, opera, orchestra, pep band, photography, political, professional, religious, social, social service, student government, symphony, and yearbook. Popular campus events include Cranberry Fest, Family Day and Unity Day.

Sports: There are 10 intercollegiate sports for men and 10 for women, and 10 intramural sports for men and 6 for women. Facilities include a recreation center with basketball, volleyball, and tennis courts, and an elevated jogging/walking track, and a fitness center with cardio equipment, weight room machines, and free weights.

Disabled Students: 75% of the campus is accessible. Facilities include wheelchair ramps, elevators, special parking, specially equipped restrooms, special class scheduling, lowered drinking fountains, and lowered telephones.

Services: Counseling and information services are available, as is tutoring in most subjects. There is remedial math, reading, and writing.

Campus Safety and Security: Measures include 24-hour foot and vehicle patrol, emergency notification system, self-defense education, and security escort services. There are shuttle buses, emergency telephones, lighted pathways/sidewalksa shuttle car, a staffed kiosk at the entrance, a security system in residence halls, video camera surveillance, bike patrol, and a property ID program.

Programs of Study: Rider confers B.A., B.M., B.S. and B.S.B.A. degrees. Associate and master's degrees are also awarded. Bachelor's degrees are awarded in BIOLOGICAL SCIENCE (biochemistry, biology/biological science, and marine science), BUSINESS (accounting, banking and finance, business administration and management, business economics, human resources, international business management, management science, marketing/retailing/merchandising, and office supervision and management), COMMUNICATIONS AND THE ARTS (advertising, communications, dance, dramatic arts, English, English literature, fine arts, French, German, journalism, multimedia, music, piano/organ, public relations, Russian, Spanish, and voice), COMPUTER AND PHYSICAL SCIENCE (actuarial science, chemistry, geoscience, information sciences and systems, mathematics, and physics), EDUCATION (business education, early childhood education, elementary education, English education, foreign languages education, marketing and distribution education, mathematics education, music education, science education, secondary education, and social studies education), ENGINEERING AND ENVIRONMENTAL DESIGN (environmental science), HEALTH PROFESSIONS (premedicine), SOCIAL SCIENCE (American studies, biopsychology, economics, history, liberal arts/general studies, philosophy, political science/government, prelaw, psychology, and sociology). Elementary education, accounting, and business administration have the largest enrollments.

Required: To graduate, all students must maintain a minimum GPA of 2.0 while taking 120 semester hours. Students also must fulfill core curriculum requirements, including 9 hours in humanities, 7 to 8 in science, 6 each in English writing and foreign language (may be waived if proficiency is demonstrated), social sciences/communications, and history, and 3 in math. 30 to 76 credits are required in the major. A thesis is required in the honors program and some science majors.

Special: Internships in many programs, a co-op program in retail marketing, work-study, study abroad in 14 countries, a B.A.-B.S. degree in all liberal arts and sciences, dual majors in education, a liberal studies degree, and nondegree study are possible. There are 24 national honor societies, a freshman honors program, and 17 departmental honors programs.

Faculty/Classroom: 56% of faculty are male; 44% are female. All teach and do research. No introductory courses are taught by graduate students. The average class size in an introductory lecture is 26; in a laboratory is 14; and in a regular course is 20.

Admissions: 72% of the 2013-2014 applicants were accepted. The SAT scores for the 2013-2014 freshman class were: Critical Reading--44% below 500, 42% between 500 and 599, 12% between 600 and 699, and 2% between 700 and 800; Math--35% below 500, 44% between 500 and 599, 18% between 600 and 699, and 2% between 700 and 800; Writing--43% below 500, 40% between 500 and 599, 14% between 600 and 699, and 2% between 700 and 800.

Requirements: The SAT or ACT is required. Applicants need 16 Carnegie units, including 4 years of English and 2 of math. 3 units of math are required for prospective math, science, and business majors. An essay is recommended. An audition is required for theater scholarships. The GED is accepted. AP and CLEP credits are accepted. Important factors in the admissions decision are advanced placement or honors courses, extracurricular activities record, and leadership record.

Procedure: Freshmen are admitted fall and spring. Entrance exams should be taken by January of the senior year. There are deferred admissions and rolling admissions plans. Application deadlines are open. Application fee is $50. Notification is sent on a rolling basis. 70 applicants were on the 2013 waiting list; 49 were admitted. Applications are accepted online.

Transfer: 262 transfer students enrolled in 2012-2013. A GPA of 2.5 or better is required for applicants. If students have fewer than 30 credits, they also must submit high school transcripts and SAT scores. An essay or personal statement is required, and an interview is recommended. 30 of 120 credits required for the bachelor's degree must be completed at Rider.

Visiting: There are regularly scheduled orientations for prospective students, including 3 open houses, Saturday information sessions and other programs that consist of a welcome, a campus tour, and a variety of formal and informal activities to meet faculty, staff, current students, and alumni. There are guides for informal visits and visitors may sit in on classes. To schedule a visit, contact the Office of Admissions.

Financial Aid: In 2013-2014, 78% of all full-time freshmen and 71% of continuing full-time students received some form of financial aid. 77% of all full-time freshmen and 69% of continuing full-time students received need-based aid. The average freshman award was $25,177. Need-based scholarships or need-based grants averaged $20,455; need-based self-help aid (loans and jobs) averaged $5,627; and $3,226 from other forms of aid. The average financial indebtedness of the 2013 graduate was $32,718. The FAFSA is required. The priority date for freshman financial aid applications for fall entry is March 1.

International Students: There are 74 international students enrolled. The school actively recruits these students. They must take the TOEFL with a minimum score of 550 on the paper-based TOEFL (PBT) or 80 on the Internet-based version (iBT). They must also take the SAT or ACT.

Computers: All students may access the system. during regular lab hours and at any time in residence halls. There are no time limits. The fee is $300/year.

Graduates: From July 1, 2012 to June 30, 2013, 865 bachelor's degrees were awarded. The most popular majors were business (35%), education (15%), and English (12%). 150 companies recruited on campus in 2012-2013. In an average class, 57% graduate in 4 years or less, 65% graduate in 5 years or less, and 67% graduate in 6 years or less.

Admissions Contact: Susan C. Christian, Director of Admissions. E-Mail: *admissions@rider.edu* Web: *www.rider.edu*

ROWAN UNIVERSITY C-4

Glassboro, NJ 08028 (855) 256-4200
1.877.RU.ROWAN; (856) 256-4430

Full-time: 4895 men, 4453 women	**Faculty:** 385
Part-time: 638 men, 965 women	**Ph.D.s:** 82%
Graduate: 950 men, 1448 women	**Student/Faculty:** 16 to 1
Year: semesters, summer session	**Tuition:** $12,380 ($20,186)
Application Deadline: March 1	**Room & Board:** $11,190

Freshman Class: 9142 applied, 5472 accepted, 1777 enrolled
SAT CR/M/W: 586/614/562

VERY COMPETITIVE

A leading state-designated comprehensive public research institution, Rowan University combines liberal education with professional preparation from the baccalaureate through the doctorate. Rowan provides a collaborative, learning-centered environment in which highly qualified and diverse faculty, staff, and students integrate teaching, research, scholarship, creative activity, and community service. Colleges include Business, Biomedical Sciences, Communication and Creative Arts, Education, Engineering, Graduate and Continuing Education, Humanities and Social Sciences, Performing Arts, Science & Mathematics, Camden Campus, Cooper Medical School of Rowan University (an MD-granting medical school), Rowan University School of Osteopathic Medicine (a DO-granting medical school), Graduate School of Biomedical Sciences. There are 9 undergraduate schools and one graduate school. In addition to regional accreditation, Rowan has baccalaureate program accreditation with AACSB, ABET, CSAB, NASAD, NASDTEC, NASM, and NCATE. The 4 libraries contain 541,767 volumes, 519,817 microform items, and 18,934 audio/video tapes/CDs/DVDs, and subscribe to 88,154 periodicals including electronic. Computerized library services include interlibrary loans, database searching, Internet access, and Wi-Fi capability. Special learning facilities include an art gallery, planetarium, radio station, TV station, virtual reality cave, exercise science research laboratory, Rowan university assessment and learning center, Whitney center apartments and Bantivoglio honors program. The 200-acre campus is in a suburban area 20 miles southeast of Philadelphia. Including any residence halls, there are 85 buildings.

Student Life: 96% of undergraduates are from New Jersey. Others are from 15 states, and 8 foreign countries. 90% are from public schools. 72%

are White. The average age of freshmen is 18; all undergraduates, 22. 17% do not continue beyond their first year; 67% remain to graduate.

Housing: 3932 students can be accommodated in college housing, which includes coed dorms and on-campus apartments. In addition, there are honors houses and special-interest houses. On-campus housing is guaranteed for the freshman year only and is available on a lottery system for upperclassmen. Priority is given to out-of-town students. 65% of students commute. Upperclassmen may keep cars.

Activities: 8% of men belong to 16 national fraternities; 7% of women belong to 10 national sororities. There are 150 groups on campus, including and concert band, art, band, cheerleading, chess, choir, chorale, chorus, communications, computers, dance, drama, environmental, ethnic, film, gay, honors, international, jazz band, literary magazine, music ensembles, musical theater, newspaper, opera, orchestra, pep band, photography, political, professional, radio and TV, religious, social, social service, student government, symphony, and yearbook. Popular campus events include Prof Stock, Back to the Boro, Senior Send Off, Home Coming, and Leadership Conference.

Sports: There are 8 intercollegiate sports for men and 10 for women, and 15 intramural sports for men and 15 for women. Facilities include an 5,500-seat stadium, a 1,800 seat gym, a 1,000 seat auditorium, 110 lockers for football and four locker rooms with 30 lockers for men's and women's soccer , field hockey and women's lacrosse. This also has a state of the art equipment room and athletic training room. The stadium has brand new turf in 2013. The NCAA sports are for men are football, soccer, cross country, basketball, swimming, indoor track, outdoor track and baseball. For women there are volleyball, cross country, field hockey, soccer, basketball, indoor track, swimming, lacrosse, outdoor track and softball. Regarding men's and women's intramural sports breakdown: Many of our sports are either open to either gender or we have co-rec or co-ed divisions available: The majority of open divisions are men's teams – such as Wiffleball, Bowling, Billiards, Racquetball, Ping pong, Tennis, Badminton, Dodgeball, Battleship, HORSE, Golf, Sand Volleyball, Punt, Pass & Kick, Free Throw & 3 Point Competition (15 offerings) *Men's specific – Basketball, Outdoor Soccer, Softball, Volleyball, Flag Football, Indoor Soccer, 1 on 1 Basketball, Kickball, Regional Dodgeball (9 offerings) *Women's specific – Basketball, Outdoor Soccer, Softball, Volleyball, Flag Football, Indoor Soccer, 1 on 1 Basketball, Regional Dodgeball (8 offerings) 76,000 square foot student recreation center including: Two 25 yard competition pools, 3 court recreational multi-purpose wood courts, indoor jogging track, group fitness studio, cycling studio, 4 racquetball courts, free weight room, cardiovascular and selectorized equipment areas, multi-purpose outdoor recreational field, and café area.

Disabled Students: 95% of the campus is accessible. Facilities include wheelchair ramps, elevators, special parking, specially equipped restrooms, special class scheduling, lowered drinking fountains, lowered telephones, and special housing.

Services: Counseling and information services are available, as is tutoring in every subject. There is a reader service for the blind, and remedial math, reading, and writing.

Campus Safety and Security: Measures include 24-hour foot and vehicle patrol, emergency notification system, self-defense education, and security escort services. There are shuttle buses, emergency telephones, lighted pathways/sidewalks, controlled access to dorms/residences, Rowan Dept. of Public Safety also has an EMS service which include 2 ambulances.

Programs of Study: Rowan confers B.A., B.S., B.S.N., B.F.A. and B.M. degrees. Master's and doctoral degrees are also awarded. Bachelor's degrees are awarded in AGRICULTURE (environmental studies), BIOLOGICAL SCIENCE (biochemistry, bioinformatics, and biology/biological science), BUSINESS (accounting, business administration and management, entrepreneurial studies, human resources, marketing/retailing/merchandising, personnel management, and small business management), COMMUNICATIONS AND THE ARTS (advertising, art, broadcasting, communications, dramatic arts, English, fine arts, jazz, journalism, music, public relations, radio/television technology, Spanish, speech/debate/rhetoric, and theatre arts), COMPUTER AND PHYSICAL SCIENCE (chemistry, computer science, mathematics, physical sciences, and physics), EDUCATION (art education, athletic training, collaborative education, early childhood education, education, elementary education, foreign languages education, music education, and science education), ENGINEERING AND ENVIRONMENTAL DESIGN (biomedical engineering, chemical engineering, civil engineering, engineering, and mechanical engineering), HEALTH PROFESSIONS (health and nursing), SOCIAL SCIENCE (African studies, American studies, criminal justice, economics, geography, history, liberal arts/general studies, philosophy and religion, political science/government, psychology, and sociology). Engineering, communications, and business administration are the strongest academically. Biological science, psychology, and law/justice have the largest enrollments.

Required: General education requirements include 6-12 credits of social and behavior sciences; 6-12 credits of history, humanities and language; 7-15 credits of math and science (one science course must be 4 credits with a lab component), 9 credits of communication, and 6 credits in non-program courses. Students also take requirements in the Rowan Experience, which includes the Rowan Seminar and courses with the following designations: Multicultural/Global, Artistic/Creative Experience, Literature, and Writing Intensive. The bachelor's degree requires 120-132 semester hours, including 30-42 in a major field, with a minimum GPA of 2.0.

Special: Honors program (please reference question number 80 below) is a special interdisciplinary program that is not housed in any department per se; rather departments provide courses to the stand alone honors program. Hence, the zero entered in question 80. Students may study abroad in 50 countries. Internships are available in all majors both with and without pay. Rowan also offers accelerated degree programs and 3-2 degrees in optometry, podiatry, and pharmacy as well as a 4-1 degree in business. There are dual majors, pass/fail options, and credit for military experience. There are 12 national honor societies and a freshman honors program.

Faculty/Classroom: 52% of faculty are male; 48% are female. All teach undergraduates. No introductory courses are taught by graduate students. The average class size in an introductory lecture is 22; in a laboratory is 16; and in a regular course is 22.

Admissions: 60% of the 2013-2014 applicants were accepted. The SAT scores for the 2013-2014 freshman class were: Critical Reading--5% below 500, 55% between 500 and 599, 33% between 600 and 699, and 7% between 700 and 800; Math--2% below 500, 39% between 500 and 599, 46% between 600 and 699, and 13% between 700 and 800; Writing--15% below 500, 56% between 500 and 599, 26% between 600 and 699, and 3% between 700 and 800. 56% of the current freshmen were in the top fifth of their class; 83% were in the top two fifths.

Requirements: Students are required to take the SAT and score an 1080, or no less than 500 on either part. Students submitting ACT scores should have a minimum composite score of 23. Applicants must be graduates of accredited secondary schools or have earned a GED. Rowan requires 16 academic credits or Carnegie units, including 4 in English, 3 each in math and college preparatory electives, and 2 each in foreign language, history, and lab science. A portfolio or audition is required for specific majors. A GPA of 3.0 is required. AP and CLEP credits are accepted. Important factors in the admissions decision are advanced placement or honors courses, evidence of special talent, and leadership record.

Procedure: Freshmen are admitted fall and spring. Entrance exams should be taken by May or June of the junior year, or by December of the sen. There is a deferred admissions plan. Applications should be filed by March 1 for fall entry; November 1 for spring entry, along with a $65 fee. Notifications are sent April 15. 150 applicants were on the 2013 waiting list; 56 were admitted. Applications are accepted online.

Transfer: 1296 transfer students enrolled in 2012-2013. Applicants must have a minimum GPA of 2.0, but should present a GPA of 2.5 to be competitive. An associate degree is recommended. Students who have earned fewer than 24 semester hours must also submit a high school transcript and SAT I results. 30 of 120 credits required for the bachelor's degree must be completed at Rowan.

Visiting: There are regularly scheduled orientations for prospective students, Visiting students may participate in a 2-day summer program providing schedule confirmation/adjustment, student activities updates, and workshops for students and parents. There are guides for informal visits and visitors may sit in on classes. To schedule a visit, contact the Admissions Office.

Financial Aid: In 2013-2014, 68% of all full-time freshmen and 66% of continuing full-time students received some form of financial aid. 64% of all full-time freshmen and 63% of continuing full-time students received need-based aid. The average freshman award was $9,868. Need-based scholarships or need-based grants averaged $9,868 ; need-based self-help aid (loans and jobs) averaged $3,405; and other non-need-based awards and non-need-based scholarships averaged $8,566. 10% of undergraduate students work part-time. Average annual earnings from campus work are $1200. The average financial indebtedness of the 2013 graduate was $31,515. The FAFSA is required. The priority date for freshman financial aid applications for fall entry is January 1. The deadline for filing freshman financial aid applications for fall entry is March 15.

International Students: There are 86 international students enrolled. The school actively recruits these students. They must take the TOEFL with a minimum score of 550 on the paper-based TOEFL (PBT) or 79 on the Internet-based version (iBT), IELTS. They must also take the SAT or ACT. SAT for Students whose first language is English and all engineering Majors.

Computers: All students may access the system 24 hours a day. There are no time limits and no fees.

Graduates: From July 1, 2012 to June 30, 2013, 2556 bachelor's degrees were awarded. The most popular majors were elementary education (7%), psychology (7%), and law/justice (5%). 106 companies recruited on campus in 2012-2013. In an average class, 43% graduate in 4 years or less, 63% graduate in 5 years or less, and 67% graduate in 6 years or less. Of the 2012 graduating class, 72% were enrolled in graduate school within 6 months of graduation.

Admissions Contact: Albert Betts, Director of Admissions. E-Mail: *admissions@rowan.edu* Web: *www.rowan.edu/sem/admissions/*

RUTGERS, THE STATE UNIVERSITY OF NEW JERSEY

Rutgers, the State University of New Jersey, established in 1766, is a public system in New Jersey. It is governed by a board of governors, whose chief administrator is the president. The primary goal of the system is instruction, research, and service. The main priorities are to continue development as a distinguished comprehensive public university, to enhance undergraduate education, to strengthen graduate education and research, and to develop and improve programs to serve society New Jersey's needs. The total student enrollment is usually about 49,000 with 1,900 faculty members. Altogether there are approximately 117 baccalaureate, 116 master's, and 83 doctoral programs offered by the school. Profiles of the 4-year campuses are included in this section.

RUTGERS, THE STATE UNIVERSITY OF NEW JERSEY/CAMDEN CAMPUS C-4

Camden, NJ 08102 (856) 225-6104

Full-time: 1824 men, 2115 women | **Faculty:** 299; IIA, ++$
Part-time: 359 men, 544 women | **Ph.D.s:** 99%
Graduate: 812 men, 610 women | **Student/Faculty:** 13 to 1
Year: semesters, summer session | **Tuition:** $13,348 ($26,908)
Application Deadline: open | **Room & Board:** $10,906
Freshman Class: 7437 applied, 4357 accepted, 497 enrolled
SAT CR/M/W: 520/540/510 | **ACT:** required | **COMPETITIVE**

Rutgers, The State University of New Jersey/Camden Campus was founded in 1926. On July 1, 2013, the New Jersey Medical and Health Sciences Education Restructuring Act went into effect, integrating Rutgers, The State University of New Jersey, with all units of the University of Medicine and Dentistry of New Jersey (UMDNJ), except University Hospital in Newark and the School of Osteopathic Medicine in Stratford. The integration of the legacy elements of UMDNJ into Rutgers has created a fourth unit, Rutgers Biomedical and Health Sciences (RBHS), which consists of a number of schools and units located on various sites but closely aligned with the campuses in Newark and New Brunswick. The campus is comprised of 4 undergraduate, degree-granting schools: College of the Arts and Sciences, University College--Camden, the School of Nursing-Camden and the School of Business--Camden. Each school has individual requirements, policies, and fees. There are 4 undergraduate schools and 4 graduate schools. In addition to regional accreditation, RU-Camden has baccalaureate program accreditation with AACSB, APTA, CSWE, and TEAC. The 2 libraries contain 729,987 volumes, 974,491 microform items, 591 audio/video tapes/CDs/DVDs, and subscribe to 15,013 periodicals including electronic. Computerized library services include interlibrary loans, database searching, and Internet access. Special learning facilities include an art gallery and radio station. The 32-acre campus is in an urban area 1 mile east of Philadelphia. Including any residence halls, there are 47 buildings.

Student Life: 98% of undergraduates are from New Jersey. Others are from 22 states, 18 foreign countries, and Canada. 56% are White; 17% African American; 11% Hispanic. The average age of freshmen is 18; all undergraduates, 22. 18% do not continue beyond their first year; 82% remain to graduate.

Housing: 566 students can be accommodated in college housing, which includes coed dorms and on-campus apartments. In addition, there are fraternity houses, sorority houses. 91% of students commute. Alcohol is not permitted.

Activities: There are no fraternities or sororities. There are 75 groups on campus, including computers, drama, ethnic, gay, honors, international, newspaper, political, professional, radio and TV, religious, social, social service, student government, and yearbook. Popular campus events include Raptor Day, Springfest and Basketball Team Sports.

Sports: There are 6 intercollegiate sports for men and 6 for women.

Disabled Students: 95% of the campus is accessible. Facilities include wheelchair ramps, elevators, special parking, specially equipped restrooms, special class scheduling, lowered drinking fountains, lowered telephones, special housing. Facilities vary from building to building. However, all classes are scheduled in accessible locations for disabled students.

Services: Counseling and information services are available, as is tutoring in some subjects, introductory classes There is a reader service for the blind, and remedial math, reading, and writing.

Campus Safety and Security: Measures include 24-hour foot and vehicle patrol, emergency notification system, self-defense education, and security escort services. There are shuttle buses, emergency telephones, lighted pathways/sidewalks, the police department is supplemented by security guards.

Programs of Study: RU-Camden confers B.A., B.S. and B.H.M. degrees. Master's and doctoral degrees are also awarded. Bachelor's degrees are awarded in BIOLOGICAL SCIENCE (biochemistry and biology/biological science), BUSINESS (accounting, banking and finance, hospitality management services, management science, and marketing/retailing/merchandising), COMMUNICATIONS AND THE ARTS (art, art history and appreciation, dramatic arts, English, French, German, music, and Spanish), COMPUTER AND PHYSICAL SCIENCE (chemistry, computer science, mathematics, physics, and science), HEALTH PROFESSIONS (medical laboratory technology and nursing), SOCIAL SCIENCE (African American studies, child care/child and family studies, criminal justice, economics, history, interdisciplinary studies, liberal arts/general studies, philosophy, political science/government, psychology, religion, social work, sociology, and urban studies). Management, psychology, and nursing have the largest enrollments.

Required: To graduate, students must complete 120 credits, with 30 to 48 in the major, and maintain a minimum GPA of 2.0. A core curriculum of 60 credits is required, including 3 credits each in literary masterpieces, art, music or theater arts, and a foreign language, with an additional 3 credits in English or a foreign language; and 3 credits in math, with an additional 3 credits in math, computer science, or statistics. 1 interdisciplinary course is required, as are 9 credits from social science disciplines, 6 credits in English composition, 6 credits in history, 6 credits in the natural science disciplines, and an additional 9 credits in courses offered outside the major department.

Special: The University offers a cooperative baccalaureate program in engineering with School of Engineering (New Brunswick Campus). Interdisciplinary programs in African-American studies, general science. Cooperative baccalaureate in medical technology with approved hospital. B.A./M.A. in Childhood Studies, English, history, liberal studies or psychology; B.A./M.S. in biology, chemistry or mathematics (with the Graduate School-Camden). B.A. in economics or political science/Master of Public Administration (with the Graduate School-Camden); BS/Master of Business and Science (MBS). In addition, there is an 8-year B.A./M.D. program and many combined bachelor's and master's programs. There are distance learning, English as a Second Language, honors and independent study programs. There is a freshman honors program.

Faculty/Classroom: 54% of faculty are male; 46% are female. No introductory courses are taught by graduate students. The average class size in an introductory lecture is 30; in a laboratory is 20; and in a regular course is 30.

Admissions: 59% of the 2013-2014 applicants were accepted. The SAT scores for the 2013-2014 freshman class were: Critical Reading--37% below 500, 47% between 500 and 599, 15% between 600 and 699, and 1% between 700 and 800; Math--28% below 500, 53% between 500 and 599, 16% between 600 and 699, and 3% between 700 and 800; Writing--39% below 500, 48% between 500 and 599, 12% between 600 and 699, and 1% between 700 and 800. 34% of the current freshmen were in the top fifth of their class; 70% were in the top two fifths.

Requirements: The SAT or ACT is required, except for students who have been out of high school for 2 years or more. SAT: Subject tests are required of students without a high school diploma from an accredited high school and from some GED holders. A high school diploma is required; the GED is accepted. Students must have completed a general college-preparatory program, including 16 academic credits or Carnegie units, with 4 years of English, 3 years of math (4 recommended), and 2 years each of a foreign language and science, plus 5 in electives. AP and CLEP credits are accepted. Important factors in the admissions decision are advanced placement or honors courses, evidence of special talent, and leadership record.

Procedure: Freshmen are admitted fall. Entrance exams should be taken by December of senior year is recommended, but not required. There are early admissions and rolling admissions plans. Application deadlines are open. Application fee is $65. Notifications are sent March 1. Applications are accepted online.

Transfer: 837 transfer students enrolled in 2012-2013. Applicants must have a minimum of 12 credit hours. Grades of C or better in courses that correspond in content and credit to those offered by the college transfer for credit. Transfer students are admitted in the fall and spring semesters. All high school and previous college transcripts are required. 30 of 120 credits required for the bachelor's degree must be completed at RU-Camden.

Visiting: There are regularly scheduled orientations for prospective students, including an information session with an admissions officer and a campus tour. Visitors may sit in on classes. To schedule a visit, contact the Admissions Office (Camden).

Financial Aid: In 2013-2014, 93% of all full-time freshmen and 93% of continuing full-time students received some form of financial aid. 69% of all full-time freshmen and 73% of continuing full-time students received need-based aid. The average freshman award was $7,998. Need-based scholarships or need-based grants averaged $9,146; need-based self-help aid (loans and jobs) averaged $4,676; and other non-need-based awards and non-need-based scholarships averaged $7,998. Average annual earnings from campus work are $1424. The average financial indebtedness of the 2013 graduate was $25,483. The FAFSA is required. The priority date for freshman financial aid applications for fall entry is March 15. The deadline for filing freshman financial aid applications for fall entry is open.

International Students: There are 60 international students enrolled.

They must take the TOEFL with a minimum score of 550 on the paper-based TOEFL (PBT) or 79 on the Internet-based version (iBT). They must also take the SAT or ACT, or the IELTS, scoring 7.

Computers: All students may access the system. Public labs are open whenever the building housing lab is open. There are no time limits. The fee is $307.

Graduates: From July 1, 2012 to June 30, 2013, 1071 bachelor's degrees were awarded. The most popular majors were business/marketing (27%), psychology (15%), and social sciences (9%). In an average class, 58% graduate in 5 years or less and 63% graduate in 6 years or less.

Admissions Contact: Rodney Morrison, Assoc Chancellor for Enroll Management. E-Mail: *admissions@ugadm.rutgers.edu* Web: *www.rutgers.edu*

RUTGERS, THE STATE UNIVERSITY OF NEW JERSEY/NEW BRUNSWICK D-3

Piscataway, NJ 08854 **(732) 932-4636; (732) 445-0237**

Full-time: 15975 men, 15784 women	**Faculty:** 2007; I, av$
Part-time: 881 men, 1260 women	**Ph.D.s:** 99%
Graduate: 5408 men, 8720 women	**Student/Faculty:** 16 to 1
Year: semesters, summer session	**Tuition:** $13,499 ($27,523)
Application Deadline:	**Room & Board:** $11,578
Freshman Class: 30631 applied, 18230 accepted, 6337 enrolled	
SAT CR/M/W: 590/640/610	**ACT:** required **VERY COMPETITIVE**

Rutgers, The State University of New Jersey, New Brunswick was founded in 1766. On July 1, 2013, the New Jersey Medical and Health Sciences Education Restructuring Act went into effect, integrating Rutgers, The State University of New Jersey, with all units of the University of Medicine and Dentistry of New Jersey (UMDNJ), except University Hospital in Newark and the School of Osteopathic Medicine in Stratford. The integration of the legacy elements of UMDNJ into Rutgers has created a fourth unit, Rutgers Biomedical and Health Sciences (RBHS), which consists of a number of schools and units located on various sites but closely aligned with the campus in New Brunswick. The campus is comprised of 12 undergraduate units. Undergraduate students in New Brunswick enroll in the School of Arts and Sciences, the liberal arts college, and/or in one of the professional schools: School of Environmental and Biological Sciences (formerly Cook College); Mason Gross School of the Arts; Rutgers Business School: Undergraduate-New Brunswick; School of Communication, and Information; School of Engineering; Edward J. Bloustein School of Planning and Public Policy; the School of Management and Labor Relations; Ernest Mario School of Pharmacy; College of Nursing; School of Nursing; School of Health Related Professions; or the School of Public Health. Some schools located in New Brunswick and/or Newark are also part of the Rutgers Biomedical and Health Sciences unit and are listed for each campus. Each school has individual requirements, policies, and fees. There are 12 undergraduate schools and 17 graduate schools. In addition to regional accreditation, RU-New Brunswick has baccalaureate program accreditation with AACSB, ABET, ACPE, ADA, APTA, ASLA, CSWE, NASM, and TEAC. The 15 libraries contain 5.5 million volumes, 3.6 million microform items, 57,166 audio/video tapes/CDs/DVDs, and subscribe to 195,296 periodicals including electronic. Computerized library services include interlibrary loans, database searching, Internet access, and Wi-Fi capability. Special learning facilities include an art gallery, radio station, TV station, a geology museum, and various research centers. The 2688-acre campus is in an urban area 33 miles south of New York City. Including any residence halls, there are 670 buildings.

Student Life: 90% of undergraduates are from New Jersey. Others are from 44 states, 54 foreign countries, and Canada. 45% are White; 25% Asian American; 12% Hispanic. The average age of freshmen is 18; all undergraduates, 21. 9% do not continue beyond their first year; 91% remain to graduate.

Housing: 15733 students can be accommodated in college housing, which includes single-sex and coed dorms and married student housing. In addition, there are language houses, special-interest houses, fraternity houses, sorority houses, substance-free house, Math/Science/Engineering House for women, first-year residence, transfer center, and residence for single mothers and children. 53% of students live on campus. Alcohol is not permitted. Upperclassmen may keep cars.

Activities: 9% of men belong to 27 national fraternities. There are 400 groups on campus, including art, band, cheerleading, chess, choir, chorale, chorus, computers, dance, drama, drill team, ethnic, film, gay, honors, international, jazz band, literary magazine, marching band, musical theater, newspaper, opera, orchestra, pep band, photography, political, professional, radio and TV, religious, social, social service, student government, symphony, and yearbook. Popular campus events include Theater Trips, Rutgers Day, Football and Basketball.

Sports: There are 9 intercollegiate sports for men and 13 for women, and 50 intramural sports for men and 50 for women.

Disabled Students: Facilities include wheelchair ramps, elevators, special parking, specially equipped restrooms, special class scheduling, lowered drinking fountains, lowered telephones, special housing. Facilities vary from building to building. However, all classes are scheduled in accessible locations for disabled students.

Services: Counseling and information services are available, as is tutoring in most subjects, with specific assistance in difficult first- and second-level courses, as well as reading assistance There is remedial math, reading, and writing. There is computer software with aids, library technology, and assistance.

Campus Safety and Security: Measures include 24-hour foot and vehicle patrol, self-defense education, and security escort services. There are shuttle buses, emergency telephones, lighted pathways/sidewalks, the police department is supplemented by security guards and student safety officers.

Programs of Study: RU-New Brunswick confers B.A., B.S., B.F.A. and B.Mus. and B.S.N. degrees. Associate, master's, and doctoral degrees are also awarded. Bachelor's degrees are awarded in AGRICULTURE (agriculture, animal science, natural resource/environmental economics, natural resource management, and plant science), BIOLOGICAL SCIENCE (biochemistry, biology/biological science, biomathematics, biotechnology, botany, cell biology, ecology, evolutionary biology, genetics, marine science, microbiology, molecular biology, nutrition, and physiology), BUSINESS (accounting, banking and finance, business administration and management, finance, human resources, labor studies, management information systems, management science, marketing, and marketing/retailing/merchandising), COMMUNICATIONS AND THE ARTS (art, art history and appreciation, Chinese, classics, communications, comparative literature, dance, dramatic arts, East Asian languages and literature, English, French, German, Italian, journalism, Latin, linguistics, music, Portuguese, Russian, Spanish, and visual and performing arts), COMPUTER AND PHYSICAL SCIENCE (astrophysics, atmospheric sciences and meteorology, chemistry, computer science, geology, information sciences and systems, mathematics, physics, and statistics), EDUCATION (health information management), ENGINEERING AND ENVIRONMENTAL DESIGN (biomedical engineering, bioresource engineering, ceramic engineering, chemical engineering, civil engineering, electrical/electronics engineering, engineering and applied science, environmental design, environmental science, industrial engineering, materials science and engineering, and mechanical engineering), HEALTH PROFESSIONS (allied health, biomedical science, exercise science, medical technology, nursing, pharmacy, and public health), SOCIAL SCIENCE (African American studies, American studies, anthropology, Asian/Oriental studies, criminal justice, economics, food science, geography, Hispanic American studies, history, humanities, Judaic studies, Latin American studies, medieval studies, Middle Eastern studies, philosophy, political science/government, psychology, religion, Russian and Slavic studies, social work, sociology, urban studies, and women's studies). Management, pharmacy, and nursing have the largest enrollments.

Required: To graduate, students must complete 120 credits, with a minimum GPA of 2.0. A liberal arts core requirement includes Writing (6 credits); Quantitative Reasoning (6 credits); Natural Sciences (6 credits); Social Sciences and Humanities (12 credits); Diversity (3 credits); and Global Awareness (3 credits). Check with the individual college for specific program requirements.

Special: 5-year B.A. or B.S./MBA program in Rutgers Business School; BS in Business Discipline/MBA; BA or BS in Science Discipline/MBA; 8-year Bachelor/Medical Dual Degree program with Robert Wood Johnson Medical School; 5-year BS/BS in Bioenvironmental engineering with the School of Engineering; 5-year accelerated baccalaureate-M.B.A with Rutgers Business School.; Bureau of Engineering Research, supported by the university, industry, state and federal government, provides research opportunities for students and faculty; Continuing professional education; Exchange program between School of Engineering and the City University of London for qualified students majoring in civil, electrical, or mechanical engineering; 5-year (BA/BS degree) program in liberal arts and engineering; 5-year BA or BS/M.Ed. with the Graduate School of Education; Interdepartmental programs and certificate programs are available; Study Abroad in England, France, Italy, Ireland, Germany, Greece, Mexico, Israel, Australia, India, Japan, Netherlands, Scotland, South Africa, South Korea, Spain and several others; Alumnae externship program; Language and Cultural House Program; B.A. in Religion/M.A. in Religious Studies; B.A./Master of Communication and Information Studies (with SC&I); B.A./MLER (with School of Management and Labor Relations); Baccalaureate/M.C.R.P., or M.P.P with EJB School of Planning and Public Policy;Baccalaureate in Business major/Master of Human Resource Management (with School of Management and Labor Relations-SMLR); BS/Master of Business and Science (MBS). Pharm.D./MBA program with Rutgers Business School; Pharm.D./M.P.H.;Pharm.D./Ph.D.in Pharmaceutical Science; Pharm.D./Ph.D. in Toxicology; Pharm.D./M.D. There are 2 national honor societies, including Phi Beta Kappa, and a freshman honors program.

Faculty/Classroom: 52% of faculty are male; 48% are female. No introductory courses are taught by graduate students. The average class size in an introductory lecture is 30; in a laboratory is 20; and in a regular course is 30.

Admissions: 60% of the 2013-2014 applicants were accepted. The SAT scores for the 2013-2014 freshman class were: Critical Reading--7% below 500, 44% between 500 and 599, 37% between 600 and 699, and 12% between 700 and 800; Math--2% below 500, 28% between 500 and 599, 45% between 600 and 699, and 25% between 700 and 800; Writing--5% below 500, 40% between 500 and 599, 40% between 600 and 699, and 15% between 700 and 800. 64% of the current freshmen were in the top fifth of their class; 92% were in the top two fifths.

Requirements: The SAT or ACT is required. A high school diploma is required. The GED is accepted. Students must have completed a general college-preparatory program, including 16 academic credits or Carnegie units, with 4 years of English, 3 years of math 4 recommended, including (algebra I and II, and geometry), 2 years each of a foreign language and science, and 5 in electives. Engineering students need 4 years of math and must take chemistry and physics for sciences; nursing and pharmacy students must take biology and chemistry. SAT: Subject tests are required for students without a high school diploma from an accredited high school and from some GED holders. AP and CLEP credits are accepted. Important factors in the admissions decision are evidence of special talent, extracurricular activities record, and ability to finance college education.

Procedure: Freshmen are admitted fall. Entrance exams should be taken December of senior year is recommended but not required. There are early admissions and rolling admissions plans. Application deadlines are open. Application fee is $65. Notifications are sent March 1. Applications are accepted online.

Transfer: 2581 transfer students enrolled in 2012-2013. Applicant must have a minimum of 12 credit hours earned. High school and college transcripts are required. Transfers are admitted in the fall or spring. 30 of 120 credits required for the bachelor's degree must be completed at RU-New Brunswick.

Visiting: There are regularly scheduled orientations for prospective students, including a preadmission orientation for prospective students. To schedule a visit, contact the University Undergraduate Admissions.

Financial Aid: In 2013-2014, 58% of all full-time freshmen students received some form of financial aid. 52% of all full-time freshmen and 60% of continuing full-time students received need-based aid. The average freshman award was $22,212. Need-based scholarships or need-based grants averaged $10,236; need-based self-help aid (loans and jobs) averaged $4,851; non-need-based athletic scholarships averaged $20,641; and other non-need-based awards and non-need-based scholarships averaged $8,664. The average financial indebtedness of the 2013 graduate was $26,656. The FAFSA is required. The priority date for freshman financial aid applications for fall entry is March 15.

International Students: There are 1330 international students enrolled. They must take the TOEFL with a minimum score of 550 on the paper-based TOEFL (PBT) or 79 on the Internet-based version (iBT). Student's are required to take the IELTS, scoring 7.

Computers: All students may access the system 24 hours per day. There are no time limits. The fee is $307.

Graduates: From July 1, 2012 to June 30, 2013, 6912 bachelor's degrees were awarded. The most popular majors were social sciences (13%), business, management, marketing (11%), biological/life sciences, communications, and engineering (10%). 1000 companies recruited on campus in 2012-2013. In an average class, 76% graduate in 5 years or less and 79% graduate in 6 years or less.

Admissions Contact: Office of University Undergraduate Admissions E-Mail: *admissions@ugadm.rutgers.edu* Web: *www.rutgers.edu*

RUTGERS, THE STATE UNIVERSITY OF NEW JERSEY/NEWARK CAMPUS — E-2

Newark, NJ 07102 — **(973) 353-5205; (973) 353-1440**

Full-time: 2929 men, 2898 women	**Faculty:** 449; I, +$
Part-time: 648 men, 742 women	**Ph.D.s:** 99%
Graduate: 2265 men, 1730 women	**Student/Faculty:** 12 to 1
Year: semesters, summer session	**Tuition:** $12,998 ($27,022)
Application Deadline: open	**Room & Board:** $12,379

Freshman Class: 13282 applied, 7173 accepted, 988 enrolled

SAT CR/M/W: 510/550/520 **ACT:** required **COMPETITIVE**

Rutgers, The State University of New Jersey/Newark Campus was founded in 1908. On July 1, 2013, the New Jersey Medical and Health Sciences Education Restructuring Act went into effect, integrating Rutgers, The State University of New Jersey, with all units of the University of Medicine and Dentistry of New Jersey (UMDNJ), except University Hospital in Newark and the School of Osteopathic Medicine in Stratford. The integration of the legacy elements of UMDNJ into Rutgers has created a fourth unit, Rutgers Biomedical and Health Sciences (RBHS), which consists of a number of schools and units located on various sites but closely aligned with the campus in New Brunswick. The campus is comprised of 5 undergraduate, degree-granting schools: Newark College of Arts and Sciences, University College-Newark, Rutgers Business School, Undergraduate-Newark, College of Nursing, School of Nursing, School of Criminal Justice and the School of Public Affairs and Administration. Some schools located in Newark and/or New Brunswick are also part of the Rutgers Biomedical and Health Sciences unit and are listed for each campus. Each school has individual requirements, policies, and fees. There are 5 undergraduate schools and 5 graduate schools. In addition to regional accreditation, RU-Newark has baccalaureate program accreditation with AACSB, CSWE, and TEAC. The 4 libraries contain 729,987 volumes, 974,491 microform items, 591 audio/video tapes/CDs/DVDs, and subscribe to 15,013 periodicals including electronic. Computerized library services include interlibrary loans, database searching, and Internet access. Special learning facilities include an art gallery, radio station, a molecular and behavioral neuroscience center, and institutes of jazz and animal behavior. The 106-acre campus is in an urban area 7 miles west of New York City. Including any residence halls, there are 51 buildings.

Student Life: 96% of undergraduates are from New Jersey. Others are from 25 states, 41 foreign countries, and Canada. 25% are White; 23% Hispanic; 22% Asian American; 18% African American. The average age of freshmen is 18; all undergraduates, 23. 11% do not continue beyond their first year; 89% remain to graduate.

Housing: 1720 students can be accommodated in college housing, which includes coed dorms and on-campus apartments. In addition, there are fraternity houses. 91% of students commute. Alcohol is not permitted.

Activities: There are no fraternities or sororities. There are 85 groups on campus, including chess, chorale, chorus, drama, newspaper, outreach, radio and TV, and student government. Popular campus events include Alpha Sigma Lambda, Black History Month and Honors Convocation.

Sports: There are 7 intercollegiate sports for men and 7 for women. Facilities include The mission of the Rutgers-Newark Department of Athletics and Recreation is to provide University constituencies, including students, faculty, staff, alumni, and the community at-large with a diverse range of programs and activities to enhance the overall quality of life and participation in the "Rutgers Experience." The department mission supports the Rutgers-Newark tradition of providing a "first-rate education to students of modest means, to first-generation college attendees, and to students of diverse racial, ethnic and religious backgrounds." The program addresses the varied interests of constituents participating in intercollegiate competition, practices, and instruction as well as social and tournament play. The Rutgers-Newark intercollegiate athletics program gives undergraduate students an opportunity to participate and represent their institution in competition while providing all constituencies the chance to witness and support on-campus events. The athletics program provides the campus community with a high degree of visibility, enhancing the stature of the institution and its programs while conducting affairs within the moral and ethical principles of the University and the spirit of fair play. Rutgers-Newark is committed to providing its student-athletes with qualified professionals and facilities to support their athletic endeavors, and experienced educational support to enhance their academic progress, regardless of sport or gender. The department places the welfare of the student above any consideration, with the primary concern being the overall development of the participant, leading to the completion of a degree. The Rutgers-Newark recreation program offers a multitude of programs designed to encourage participation and enhance individual health, wellness and overall quality of life. The programs and activities offered are designed to enhance institutional and community relationships, emphasizing the educational, health, social and recreational values of individual and competitive sports. Athletics facilities, utilized by varsity sports and recreation, are available to all members of the Rutgers community. The facilities complement the diversified program offerings. Rutgers-Newark pledges to provide its constituencies modern facilities and equipment in sufficient numbers that conform to optimum standards for health and safety.

Disabled Students: 80% of the campus is accessible. Facilities include wheelchair ramps, elevators, special parking, specially equipped restrooms, special class scheduling, lowered drinking fountains, lowered telephones, special housing. Facilities vary from building to building. However, all classes are scheduled in accessible locations for disabled students.

Services: Counseling and information services are available, as is tutoring in most subjects. There is a reader service for the blind, and remedial math, reading, and writing.

Campus Safety and Security: Measures include 24-hour foot and vehicle patrol, self-defense education, and security escort services. There are shuttle buses, emergency telephones, lighted pathways/sidewalks, Security guards assist Rutgers police in providing public safety services. There is also a student marshal program.

Programs of Study: RU-Newark confers B.A., B.S. and B.F.A. degrees. Master's and doctoral degrees are also awarded. Bachelor's degrees are awarded in BIOLOGICAL SCIENCE (biology/biological science, botany, and zoology), BUSINESS (accounting, banking and finance, business administration and management, finance, management science, marketing, marketing/retailing/merchandising, and supply chain management), COMMUNICATIONS AND THE ARTS (art, dramatic arts, English, French, German, Italian, journalism, music, Portuguese, Spanish, and visual and performing arts), COMPUTER AND PHYSICAL SCIENCE (applied mathematics, applied physics, chemistry, computer science, geology, geoscience, information sciences and systems, mathematics, and physics), ENGINEERING AND ENVIRONMENTAL DESIGN (environmental science and geological engineering), HEALTH PROFESSIONS (allied health, clinical science, medical laboratory technology, and nursing), SOCIAL SCIENCE (African American studies, American studies, anthropology, area studies, classical/ancient civilization, criminal justice, Eastern European studies, economics, history, interdisciplinary studies, medieval studies, philosophy, political science/government, psychology, public administration, Puerto Rican studies, science and society, social work, sociology, and women's studies). Accounting, criminal justice, and finance are the largest.

Required: To graduate, students must complete 124 credits with a minimum GPA of 2.0. Distribution requirements include 8 credits in natural science/math or 3 courses in nonlab science, math, or computer science; 6 credits each in history, literature, social sciences, humanities, and fine arts; 1 course in critical thinking; and 15 credits of electives. All students must take English composition and demonstrate math proficiency either by exam or by successfully completing a college algebra course or any other advanced course in math, a college calculus course, (with a grade of C or better) or a precalculus course (with a grade of B or better).

Special: Students may cross-register with the New Jersey Institute of Technology. Internships are available. The school offers study abroad in over 30 countries, accelerated degree programs in business administration and criminal justice, co-op programs, independent study, distance learning, English as a Second Language, dual majors, student-designed majors, nondegree study, and pass/fail options. Contact the school for information on the Honors College. 5-year baccalaureate-MBA with Rutgers Business School; BS in Business Discipline/MBA; BA or BS in Science Discipline/MBA; Baccalaureate/M.A. in Criminal Justice with the School of Criminal Justice; Baccalaureate/MPA with the School of Public Affairs and Administration; Cooperative baccalaureate program with School of Engineering (New Brunswick campus); Cooperative baccalaureate in medical technology with affiliated hospitals; Interdisciplinary programs in archaeology, international affairs, legal studies, women's studies; continuing professional education; Baccalaureate in Business Major/Master of Human Resource Management (with School of Management and Labor Relations in New Brunswick); Baccalaureate-master's dual degree programs with the School of Criminal Justice and Rutgers Business School; BA or BS in Biology/MS in Biology; BA in Chemistry/MS in Chemistry; BA in Economics/MA in Economics; BS in Environmental Sciences/MS In Environmental Geology; BS in Environmental Sciences/MS in Environmental Sciences; BA in Political Science, Sociology or Anthropology/MS in Global Affairs; BA in History/MA in History; BA in History, Sociology or Anthropology/MA in Jazz History and Research; BA in Political Science/MA in Political Science; BA/MA in Peace and Conflict Studies; BS in Computer Science or Information Science/Master of Information Technology; BS in Accounting/Master of Accountancy (Governmental Accounting or Financial Accounting); BS in Accounting/MBA in Professional Accounting; BS in Finance/Master of Quantitative Finance; BS/Master of Business and Science (MBS). The College of Nursing offers a program on the New Brunswick Campus. Students are admitted in the fall semester only; BS in Nursing/MS in Nursing. Pharm.D./M.B.A. program with Rutgers Business School. There are 12 national honor societies, including Phi Beta Kappa, and a freshman honors program.

Faculty/Classroom: 62% of faculty are male; 38% are female. All teach and do research. No introductory courses are taught by graduate students. The average class size in an introductory lecture is 30; in a laboratory is 20; and in a regular course is 30.

Admissions: 54% of the 2013-2014 applicants were accepted. The SAT scores for the 2013-2014 freshman class were: Critical Reading--37% below 500, 49% between 500 and 599, 12% between 600 and 699, and 2% between 700 and 800; Math--21% below 500, 48% between 500 and 599, 26% between 600 and 699, and 5% between 700 and 800; Writing--33% below 500, 50% between 500 and 599, 14% between 600 and 699, and 3% between 700 and 800. 44% of the current freshmen were in the top fifth of their class; 78% were in the top two fifths.

Requirements: The SAT or ACT is required. In addition, a high school diploma is required; the GED is accepted. SAT: Subject tests are required of students without a high school diploma from an accredited high school and from some GED holders. Students should have completed 16 high school academic credits or Carnegie units, with 4 years of English, 3 years of math, (4 recommended) 2 years each of science, a general college-preparatory program, including and a foreign language, and 5 electives. Biology and chemistry are required for nursing students. AP and CLEP credits are accepted. Important factors in the admissions decision are advanced placement or honors courses, evidence of special talent, and leadership record.

Procedure: Freshmen are admitted fall. Entrance exams should be taken by December of senior year is recommended, but not required. There are early admissions and rolling admissions plans. Application deadlines are open. Application fee is $65. Notifications are sent March 1. Applications are accepted online.

Transfer: 779 transfer students enrolled in 2012-2013. Students who have completed at least 12 credit hours at another college with a cumulative GPA of 2.0 are considered for admission as transfer students. Transfers are admitted in the fall and spring. High school and college transcripts are required. 30 of 124 credits required for the bachelor's degree must be completed at RU-Newark.

Visiting: There are regularly scheduled orientations for prospective students, including an information session with an admissions counselor and a tour of the campus. There are guides for informal visits and visitors may sit in on classes. To schedule a visit, contact the Admissions Office (Newark).

Financial Aid: In 2013-2014, 85% of all full-time freshmen and 89% of continuing full-time students received some form of financial aid. 71% of all full-time freshmen and 83% of continuing full-time students received need-based aid. Average annual earnings from campus work are $1272. The average financial indebtedness of the 2013 graduate was $24,837. The FAFSA is required. The priority date for freshman financial aid applications for fall entry is March 15. The deadline for filing freshman financial aid applications for fall entry is open.

International Students: There are 187 international students enrolled. They must take the TOEFL with a minimum score of 550 on the paper-based TOEFL (PBT) or 79 on the Internet-based version (iBT) and the college's own test.

Computers: All students may access the system. There are no time limits. The fee is $307.

Graduates: From July 1, 2012 to June 30, 2013, 1609 bachelor's degrees were awarded. The most popular majors were business/marketing (35%), criminal justice (13%), and health professions and related programs (10%). In an average class, 56% graduate in 5 years or less and 61% graduate in 6 years or less.

Admissions Contact: Director of Admissions-Newark E-Mail: *admissions@ugadm.rutgers.edu* Web: *www.rutgers.edu*

SAINT PETER'S COLLEGE — E-2

Jersey City, NJ 07306 — (201) 915-9213, (888) SPC-9933; (201) 432-5860

Full-time: 825 men, 1077 women	**Faculty:** n/av; IIA, -$
Part-time: 101 men, 314 women	**Ph.D.s:** n/av
Graduate: 282 men, 446 women	**Student/Faculty:** 12 to 1
Year: semesters, summer session	**Tuition:** $31,222
Application Deadline: open	**Room & Board:** $13,020
Freshman Class: 3256 applied, 1973 accepted, 393 enrolled	
SAT or ACT: required	**COMPETITIVE**

Saint Peter's College, founded in 1872, is a private liberal arts and business college affiliated with the Roman Catholic Church and known as New Jersey's Jesuit College. There are 2 undergraduate schools and 3 graduate schools. In addition to regional accreditation, SPC has baccalaureate program accreditation with NLN. The 2 libraries contain 285,000 volumes, 70,000 microform items, 3,800 audio/video tapes/CDs/DVDs, and subscribe to 1,800 periodicals including electronic. Computerized library services include interlibrary loans and database searching. Special learning facilities include an art gallery, radio station, and TV station. The 15-acre campus is in an urban area 2 miles west of New York City. Including any residence halls, there are 29 buildings.

Student Life: 87% of undergraduates are from New Jersey. Others are from 26 states, and 10 foreign countries. 56% are from public schools. 44% are White; 27% Hispanic; 21% African American. 68% are Catholic. The average age of freshmen is 18; all undergraduates, 24. 23% do not continue beyond their first year; 51% remain to graduate.

Housing: 863 students can be accommodated in college housing, which includes single-sex and coed dorms and on-campus apartments. In addition, there are special-interest houses, community service houses. On-campus housing is guaranteed for all 4 years. 50% of students commute. Upperclassmen may keep cars.

Activities: There are no fraternities or sororities. There are 50 groups on campus, including cheerleading, chess, chorus, computers, debate, drama, ethnic, forensics, honors, international, literary magazine, newspaper, pep band, political, professional, radio and TV, religious, social, social service, and student government. Popular campus events include International Day, Career Fairs and SpringFest.

Sports: There are 10 intercollegiate sports for men and 8 for women, and 20 intramural sports for men and 18 for women. Facilities include a recreational center, a 2000-seat gym, and an athletic field.

Disabled Students: 80% of the campus is accessible. Facilities include wheelchair ramps, elevators, special parking, specially equipped restrooms, special class scheduling, lowered drinking fountains, lowered telephones.

Services: Counseling and information services are available, as is tutoring in every subject. There is a reader service for the blind, and remedial math, reading, and writing.

Campus Safety and Security: Measures include 24-hour foot and

vehicle patrol, self-defense education, and security escort services. There are shuttle buses, emergency telephones, security desk monitoring of access to residence halls.

Programs of Study: SPC confers B.A., B.S. and B.S.N. degrees. Associate, master's, and doctoral degrees are also awarded. Bachelor's degrees are awarded in BIOLOGICAL SCIENCE (biochemistry and biology/biological science), BUSINESS (accounting, business administration and management, international business management, and marketing/retailing/merchandising), COMMUNICATIONS AND THE ARTS (art history and appreciation, classical languages, communications, English, fine arts, graphic design, modern language, Spanish, and visual and performing arts), COMPUTER AND PHYSICAL SCIENCE (chemistry, computer science, mathematics, natural sciences, and physics), EDUCATION (elementary education and secondary education), HEALTH PROFESSIONS (biomedical science, health care administration, medical laboratory technology, nursing, predentistry, and premedicine), SOCIAL SCIENCE (African American studies, American studies, classical/ancient civilization, criminal justice, economics, history, humanities, interdisciplinary studies, international studies, Latin American studies, philosophy, political science/government, prelaw, psychology, social science, sociology, theological studies, and urban studies). Natural sciences and accounting is the strongest academically. Business management, accounting, and computer sciences have the largest enrollments.

Required: To graduate, students must complete 129 credit hours, including 57 in the core curriculum, 12 in core electives, between 30 and 45 in the major, and the rest in subjects related to the major. The core curriculum requires 9 credits of natural sciences, 6 to 8 of math, and 3 each of social science, philosophy, history, literature, a modern language, fine arts, and composition. Students must earn a GPA of 2.0.

Special: There are co-op programs with local companies, as well as departmental programs, and many internships available in Jersey City and nearby New York City. A Washington semester and study abroad in any of 60 countries are offered. There are preprofessional programs in dentistry, pharmacy, physician assistant, and physical therapy. The college also offers dual majors and student-designed majors, credit for life, military, and work experience, nondegree study, and pass/fail options. There are 9 national honor societies, a freshman honors program, and 1 departmental honors programs.

Faculty/Classroom: 50% of faculty are male; 50% are female. All teach undergraduates. No introductory courses are taught by graduate students. The average class size in an introductory lecture is 23; in a laboratory is 14; and in a regular course is 16.

Admissions: 61% of the 2013-2014 applicants were accepted.

Requirements: The SAT or ACT is required. Applicants must be high school graduates or submit the GED certificate. Students should have completed 16 Carnegie units of high school study, including 4 years of English, 3 of math, 2 each of science, history, and a foreign language, and another 3 of additional work in any of these subjects. An essay and 2 letters of recommendation are required, and an interview is recommended. SPC requires applicants to be in the upper 97% of their class. A GPA of 3.1 is required. AP and CLEP credits are accepted. Important factors in the admissions decision are advanced placement or honors courses, extracurricular activities record, and recommendations by school officials.

Procedure: Freshmen are admitted fall and spring. Entrance exams should be taken by the fall of the senior year. There are early admissions, deferred admissions, and rolling admissions plans. Application deadlines are open. Notification is sent on a rolling basis. 299 applicants were on the 2013 waiting list; 290 were admitted. Applications are accepted online.

Transfer: 164 transfer students enrolled in 2012-2013. The school requires a 2.0 college GPA of transfer students, as well as a high school transcript and a satisfactory composite SAT score for students less than 2 years out of high school. An interview is recommended. 30 of 129 credits required for the bachelor's degree must be completed at SPC.

Visiting: There are regularly scheduled orientations for prospective students, including open houses, weekend and weekday visit days with a tour and class and information sessions, as well as tours and interviews by appointment. There are guides for informal visits, visitors may sit in on classes, and stay overnight. To schedule a visit, contact the Admissions Office.

Financial Aid: SPC is a member of CSS. The FAFSA is required. Check with the school for current application deadlines.

International Students: The school actively recruits these students. They must take the TOEFL.

Computers: All students may access the system. The system may be used for remote access 24 hours a day; for local access, about 94 hours a week.

Graduates: From July 1, 2012 to June 30, 2013, 489 bachelor's degrees were awarded. The most popular majors were business/marketing (29%), biological/life sciences (10%), and health professions and related programs (9%). In an average class, 53% graduate in 6 years or less.

Admissions Contact: Joseph Giglio, Director of Admissions. E-Mail: *admissions@spc.edu* Web: *www.spc.edu*

SETON HALL UNIVERSITY — D-2

South Orange, NJ 07079 — (973) 313-6146; (800) THE-HALL; (973) 275-2040

Full-time: 1939 men, 2698 women	**Faculty:** 339; I, -$
Part-time: 189 men, 322 women	**Ph.D.s:** 88%
Graduate: 1992 men, 2516 women	**Student/Faculty:** 14 to 1
Year: semesters, summer session	**Tuition:** $33,490
Application Deadline: March 1	**Room & Board:** $12,412

Freshman Class: 6436 applied, 5474 accepted, 993 enrolled

SAT CR/M/W: 530/540/550 **ACT:** 23 **COMPETITIVE**

Seton Hall University, founded in 1856, is a major Catholic University. Seton Hall's 58 acre campus is located in South Orange, New Jersey, only 14 miles from New York City. The University is home to 10,000 students and eight schools that offer degrees at the baccalaureate, master, and doctoral and professional levels. There are 6 undergraduate schools and 8 graduate schools. In addition to regional accreditation, Seton Hall has baccalaureate program accreditation with AACSB, CSWE, and NCATE. The 2 libraries contain 629,978 volumes, 500,000 microform items, and 5,340 audio/video tapes/CDs/DVDs, and subscribe to 29,000 periodicals including electronic. Computerized library services include interlibrary loans, database searching, Internet access, and Wi-Fi capability. Special learning facilities include an art gallery, radio station, TV station, various institutes, and centers for learning and research. Including any residence halls, there are 35 buildings.

Student Life: 76% of undergraduates are from New Jersey. Others are from 43 states, 46 foreign countries, and Canada. 69% are from public schools. 51% are White; 14% Hispanic; 13% African American. 69% are Catholic; 14% Protestant. The average age of freshmen is 18; all undergraduates, 21. 19% do not continue beyond their first year; 65% remain to graduate.

Housing: 2236 students can be accommodated in college housing, which includes coed dorms and off-campus apartments. In addition, there are honors houses and special-interest houses. On-campus housing is available on a lottery system for upperclassmen. Priority is given to out-of-town students. 58% of students commute. Upperclassmen may keep cars.

Activities: 7% of men belong to 11 national fraternities; 11% of women belong to 14 national sororities. There are 124 groups on campus, including recreation, student Ambassador Society, art, cheerleading, chess, choir, chorus, commuter council, computers, dance, drama, drill team, environmental, ethnic, film, forensics, honors, international, literary magazine, musical theater, newspaper, pep band, photography, political, professional, radio and TV, religious, social, social service, and student government. Popular campus events include University Day, Theatre-in-the-Round, and Career Day.

Sports: There are 6 intercollegiate sports for men and 8 for women, and 13 intramural sports for men and 13 for women. Facilities include A 2000-seat on-campus arena, recreational field house, indoor track, indoor pool, fitness and aerobics rooms, a soccer and baseball field, a softball field, and tennis and racquetball courts; men's basketball also uses the Prudential Center, which seats 10,000.

Disabled Students: 95% of the campus is accessible. Facilities include wheelchair ramps, elevators, special parking, specially equipped restrooms, special class scheduling, lowered drinking fountains, and special housing.

Services: Counseling and information services are available, as is tutoring in most subjects. There is a reader service for the blind, and remedial math, reading, and writing. The Academic Resource Center also offers support for students interested in national scholarship opportunities and aids students who are pursuing interdisciplinary and pre-professional majors.

Campus Safety and Security: Measures include 24-hour foot and vehicle patrol, emergency notification system, self-defense education, and security escort services. There are shuttle buses, emergency telephones, lighted pathways/sidewalks, controlled access to dorms/residences, security attendants are posted at residence hall entrances.

Programs of Study: Seton Hall confers B.A., B.S., B.A.B.A., B.S.B., B.S.E., B.S.I.R. and B.S.N. degrees. Master's and doctoral degrees are also awarded. Bachelor's degrees are awarded in AGRICULTURE (environmental studies), BIOLOGICAL SCIENCE (biochemistry and biology/biological science), BUSINESS (accounting, business administration and management, business economics, finance, management information systems, marketing management, and sports management), COMMUNICATIONS AND THE ARTS (applied music, art history, broadcasting, classics, communications, creative writing, English, fine arts, French, graphic design, Italian, journalism, modern language, music, Spanish, and theatre arts), COMPUTER AND PHYSICAL SCIENCE (chemistry, computer science, mathematics, and physics), EDUCATION (elementary education, secondary education, and special education), HEALTH PROFESSIONS (nursing), SOCIAL SCIENCE (African American studies, anthropology, Asian/Oriental studies, criminal justice, economics, history, international relations, Latin American studies, liberal arts/general studies, philosophy, political science/government, psychology, religion, social science, social work, sociology, and theological studies). Business, biology, and diplomacy are the strongest academically. Nursing has the largest enrollment.

Required: To graduate, students must complete the University Core Curriculum and complete at least 120 credit hours earning a minimum GPA of 2.0.

Special: Co-op and work-study are possible through the College of Arts & Sciences and the School of Business; internships are available through the College of Arts & Sciences and School of Diplomacy. Education majors go into the field during their sophomore year. Engineering 3+2 degrees are available with the New Jersey Institute of Technology. Study abroad is available in 15 countries. An accelerated B.S.N. degree is offered. There are a total of 17 bachelor/graduate dual degree programs. Non-degree study is permitted. There are 27 national honor societies, a freshman honors program, and 5 departmental honors programs.

Faculty/Classroom: 53% of faculty are male; 47% are female. No introductory courses are taught by graduate students. The average class size in an introductory lecture is 26; in a laboratory is 17; and in a regular course is 21.

Admissions: 85% of the 2013-2014 applicants were accepted. The SAT scores for the 2013-2014 freshman class were: Critical Reading--29% below 500, 49% between 500 and 599, 21% between 600 and 699, and 1% between 700 and 800; Math--26% below 500, 49% between 500 and 599, 24% between 600 and 699, and 2% between 700 and 800; Writing--24% below 500, 48% between 500 and 599, 26% between 600 and 699, and 2% between 700 and 800. The ACT scores were 20% below 21, 33% between 21 and 23, 27% between 24 and 26, 8% between 27 and 28, and 13% above 28. 48% of the current freshmen were in the top fifth of their class; 72% were in the top two fifths. 1 freshman graduated first in the class.

Requirements: The SAT or ACT is required. Seton Hall recommends a satisfactory score on the SAT or a minimum composite score on the ACT. Applicants must supply high school transcripts or a GED certificate. Students should have completed 16 Carnegie units of high school study, including 4 years of English, 3 of Math, 2 each of a foreign language and either History or Social Studies, 1 of Science, and 4 academic electives. An essay is required and an interview is recommended. AP and CLEP credits are accepted. Important factors in the admissions decision are advanced placement or honors courses, leadership record, and parents or siblings attended your school.

Procedure: Freshmen are admitted fall and spring. Entrance exams should be taken by January of the senior year. There are early admissions, deferred admissions, and rolling admissions plans. Application deadlines are open. Application fee is $55. Notification is sent on a rolling basis. Applications are accepted online.

Transfer: 315 transfer students enrolled in 2012-2013. Applicants should have earned 30 hours of college credit, with a minimum GPA of 2.5, or 2.8 for the business and science schools. The SAT is required for students with fewer than 30 credits of college-level work at the time of application, and an interview is recommended. 30 of 120 credits required for the bachelor's degree must be completed at Seton Hall.

Visiting: There are regularly scheduled orientations for prospective students, Including campus tours weekdays and Saturdays during the academic year and on weekdays during the summer. Open houses for prospective applicants are available each fall. Visitors may sit in on classes. To schedule a visit, contact the Enrollment Services Office at (973) 761-9332.

Financial Aid: The FAFSA is required. The priority date for freshman financial aid applications for fall entry is March 1. The deadline for filing freshman financial aid applications for fall entry is open.

International Students: There are 90 international students enrolled. The school actively recruits these students. They must take the TOEFL with a minimum score of 550 on the paper-based TOEFL (PBT) or 79 on the Internet-based version (iBT). They must also take the SAT.

Computers: All students may access the system. Public labs are available until 11 p.m.; there is 24-hour remote network access. There are no time limits and no fees.

Graduates: From July 1, 2012 to June 30, 2013, 993 bachelor's degrees were awarded. The most popular majors were nursing (10%), finance (7%), and biology (7%). 400 companies recruited on campus in 2012-2013. In an average class, 51% graduate in 4 years or less, 62% graduate in 5 years or less, and 65% graduate in 6 years or less. Of the 2012 graduating class, 29% were enrolled in graduate school within 6 months of graduation, and 77% were employed.

Admissions Contact: Wendy Lin-Cook, Assistant Vice President for Admissions. E-Mail: *thehall@shu.edu* Web: *www.shu.edu*

STEVENS INSTITUTE OF TECHNOLOGY E-2

Hoboken, NJ 07030 **(201) 216-5194**
(800) 458-5323; (201) 216-8348

Full-time: 1654 men, 579 women	**Faculty:** 226
Part-time: 1 men	**Ph.D.s:** 90%
Graduate: 2761 men, 867 women	**Student/Faculty:** 10 to 1
Year: semesters, summer session	**Tuition:** $37,980
Application Deadline: February 1	**Room & Board:** $12,150
Freshman Class: 3232 applied, 1609 accepted, 614 enrolled	
SAT CR/M/W: 600/670/600	**ACT:** 27 **HIGHLY COMPETITIVE**

Stevens Institute of Technology, founded in 1870, is a private institution offering programs of study in science, computer science, engineering, business, and humanities. There are 4 undergraduate schools and 3 graduate schools. In addition to regional accreditation, Stevens has baccalaureate program accreditation with ABET and CSAB. The library contains 123,063 volumes, and subscribes to 39,500 periodicals including electronic. Computerized library services include interlibrary loans, database searching, Internet access, and Wi-Fi capability. Special learning facilities include a radio station, TV station, a lab for ocean and coastal engineering, an environmental lab, a design and manufacturing institute, a technology center, a telecommunications institute, a computer vision lab, an ultrafast laser spectroscopy and high-speed communications lab, and a wireless network security center. The 55-acre campus is in an urban area on the banks of the Hudson River, overlooking the Manhattan skyline. Including any residence halls, there are 25 buildings.

Student Life: 60% of undergraduates are from New Jersey. Others are from 42 states, 30 foreign countries, and Canada. 80% are from public schools. 54% are White; 11% Asian American. The average age of freshmen is 18; all undergraduates, 20. 10% do not continue beyond their first year; 76% remain to graduate.

Housing: 1358 students can be accommodated in college housing, which includes coed dorms, on-campus apartments, off-campus apartments, and married student housing. In addition, there are special-interest houses, fraternity houses, and sorority houses. On-campus housing is guaranteed for all 4 years. 85% of students live on campus; of those, 70% remain on campus on weekends. Alcohol is not permitted. Upperclassmen may keep cars.

Activities: 19% of men belong to 11 national fraternities; 20% of women belong to 1 local and 3 national sororities. There are 105 groups on campus, including anime, gamers, paintball, SAE, art, band, chess, choir, chorus, computers, dance, debate, drama, Engineers without Borders, environmental, ethnic, film, honors, international, jazz band, literary magazine, musical theater, newspaper, pep band, photography, political, professional, radio and TV, religious, social, social service, and student government. Popular campus events include Fall Tech Fest, Spring Boken Festival and Midnight Breakfast.

Sports: There are 13 intercollegiate sports for men and 13 for women, and 12 intramural sports for men and 12 for women. Facilities include a 60,000-square-foot complex with an NCAA regulation swimming pool, a 1,400-seat basketball arena, fitness rooms, racquetball/squash courts, a playing field, a student union, and several outdoor courts.

Disabled Students: All of the campus is accessible. Facilities include wheelchair ramps, elevators, special parking, specially equipped restrooms, lowered drinking fountains, and special housing.

Services: Counseling and information services are available, as is tutoring in every subject.

Campus Safety and Security: Measures include 24-hour foot and vehicle patrol, emergency notification system, self-defense education, and security escort services. There are emergency telephones, lighted pathways/sidewalks, and controlled access to dorms/residences.

Programs of Study: Stevens confers B.A., B.S. and B.E. degrees. Master's and doctoral degrees are also awarded. Bachelor's degrees are awarded in BIOLOGICAL SCIENCE (biochemistry and bioinformatics), BUSINESS (business administration and management), COMMUNICATIONS AND THE ARTS (literature and music technology), COMPUTER AND PHYSICAL SCIENCE (chemistry, computer science, computer security and information assurance, digital arts/technology, information sciences and systems, mathematics, physics, and science technology), ENGINEERING AND ENVIRONMENTAL DESIGN (biomedical engineering, chemical engineering, civil engineering, computational sciences, computer engineering, electrical/electronics engineering, engineering management, engineering physics, environmental engineering, mechanical engineering, naval architecture and marine engineering, and systems engineering), SOCIAL SCIENCE (history and philosophy). Engineering is the strongest academically. Mechanical engineering, civil engineering, and business have the largest enrollments.

Required: To graduate, the student must have earned 122 to 150 credit hours (dependent on program) with a minimum 2.0 GPA; the total hours in the major vary by program. The core curriculum includes courses in engineering, science, computer science, math, liberal arts, and phys ed.

Special: Stevens offers cross-registration and a 3-2 engineering degree with New York University, a work-study program within the school, co-op programs, corporate and research internships through the Undergraduate Projects in Technology and Medicine, study abroad in 7 countries, and pass/fail options for extra courses. Students may undertake dual majors as well as accelerated degree programs in medicine, dentistry, and law and can receive a B.A.-B.E. degree or a B.A.-B.S. degree in all majors. Undergraduates may take graduate courses. There are 9 national honor societies and a freshman honors program.

Faculty/Classroom: 80% of faculty are male; 20% are female. 75% do both. No introductory courses are taught by graduate students. The average class size in an introductory lecture is 75; in a laboratory is 20; and in a regular course is 25.

Admissions: 50% of the 2013-2014 applicants were accepted. The SAT scores for the 2013-2014 freshman class were: Critical Reading--9% below 500, 41% between 500 and 599, 41% between 600 and 699, and 9% between 700 and 800; Math--14% between 500 and 599, 58% between 600 and 699, and 28% between 700 and 800; Writing--11% below 500, 39% between 500 and 599, 41% between 600 and 699, and 9% between 700 and 800. The ACT scores were 18% between 21 and 23, 58% between 27 and 28, and 24% above 28. 78% of the current freshmen were in the top fifth of their class; 95% were in the top two fifths. 9 freshmen graduated first in their class.

Requirements: The SAT or ACT is required. Applicants must provide official high school transcripts. Students should have taken 4 years of English, math, and science. An interview, essay, and 2 letters of recommendation are required. AP credits are accepted. Important factors in the admissions decision are advanced placement or honors courses, extracurricular activities record, and personality/intangible qualities.

Procedure: Freshmen are admitted fall. Entrance exams should be taken by February of the senior year. There are early decision and deferred admissions plans. Early decision applications should be filed by November 15; regular applications, by February 1 for fall entry; and December 1 for spring entry, along with a $55 fee. Notification of early decision is sent December 15; regular decision, March 21. 338 early decision candidates were accepted for the 2013-2014 class. 481 applicants were on the 2013 waiting list; 30 were admitted. Applications are accepted online.

Transfer: 45 transfer students enrolled in 2012-2013. Applicants should have a minimum GPA of 3.0. They must submit all college transcripts, including course descriptions; SAT or ACT scores are required of those students with fewer than 30 hours of college credit. 50 of 122 credits required for the bachelor's degree must be completed at Stevens.

Visiting: There are regularly scheduled orientations for prospective students, including interviews and campus tours. There are guides for informal visits, visitors may sit in on classes, and stay overnight. To schedule a visit, contact the Admissions Office.

Financial Aid: In 2013-2014, 93% of all full-time freshmen and 90% of continuing full-time students received some form of financial aid. 84% of all full-time freshmen and 80% of continuing full-time students received need-based aid. 24% of undergraduate students work part-time. Average annual earnings from campus work are $1202. The average financial indebtedness of the 2013 graduate was $1,587. Stevens is a member of CSS. The CSS/Profile and FAFSA are required. The priority date for freshman financial aid applications for fall entry is February 15.

International Students: There are 92 international students enrolled. The school actively recruits these students. They must take the TOEFL with a minimum score of 550 on the paper-based TOEFL (PBT) or 83 on the Internet-based version (iBT). They must also take the SAT or ACT.

Computers: All students may access the system at all times. There are no time limits and no fees.

Graduates: From July 1, 2012 to June 30, 2013, 419 bachelor's degrees were awarded. The most popular majors were mechanical engineering (18%), electrical engineering (12%), and business (11%). 380 companies recruited on campus in 2012-2013. In an average class, 25% graduate in 4 years or less, 72% graduate in 5 years or less, and 76% graduate in 6 years or less. Of the 2012 graduating class, 20% were enrolled in graduate school within 6 months of graduation, and 75% were employed.

Admissions Contact: Daniel Gallagher, Dean of University Admissions. E-Mail: *admissions@stevens.edu* Web: *www.stevens.edu*

THOMAS EDISON STATE COLLEGE — D-3

Trenton, NJ 08608 — **(888) 442-8372; (609) 984-8447**

Full-time: n/av	**Faculty:** n/av
Part-time: 10434 men, 9162 women	**Ph.D.s:** n/av
Graduate: 382 men, 899 women	**Student/Faculty:** n/av
Year: other	**Tuition:** n/av
Application Deadline: open	**Room & Board:** n/app
Freshman Class: n/av	**SPECIAL**

Thomas Edison State College, founded in 1972, is a public institution of higher education. The college provides many ways to complete a degree in more than 100 areas of study, including credit by examination, assessment of experiential learning, guided independent study, and credit for corporate and military training. The college offers multiple tuitions plans. There are 4 undergraduate schools. In addition to regional accreditation, Thomas Edison State College has baccalaureate program accreditation with ABET and NLN. Special learning facilities include a The 2-acre campus is in an urban area 40 miles north of Philadelphia. Including any residence halls, there are 4 buildings.

Student Life: 55% of undergraduates are from out of state, mostly the South. Students are from 50 states, 64 foreign countries, and Canada. 58% are White; 15% African American; 11% race unknown. The average age of all undergraduates is 35.

Housing: Alcohol is not permitted.

Activities: There are no fraternities or sororities.

Sports: There is no sports program at Thomas Edison State College.

Disabled Students: Facilities include wheelchair ramps, elevators, special parking, specially equipped restrooms, lowered drinking fountains. interpreter services for the hearing-impaired, and examinations formatted to accommodate the student's need.

Campus Safety and Security: Measures include emergency notification system and security escort services. There are lighted pathways/sidewalks, a guard on the premises 7 a.m. to 8 p.m., and the perimeter is patrolled by the New Jersey state police.

Programs of Study: Thomas Edison State College confers B.A., B.S., B.S.A.S.T., B.S.B.A., B.S.H.S., B.S.He.S., B.S.O.L., B.S.HiS, B.S.MiS and B.S.N. degrees. Associate and master's degrees are also awarded. Bachelor's degrees are awarded in AGRICULTURE (environmental studies), BUSINESS (accounting, accounting/CPA, entrepreneurial studies, finance, financial institutions management, global/general management, hospitality management services, human resources/organizational mgmt, international business, labor studies, military technology leadership, operations management, organizational leadership and management, and real estate), COMMUNICATIONS AND THE ARTS (Arabic, art, Chinese, communications, English, foreign language, French, German, Hebrew, information technology, Italian, Japanese, journalism, Korean, music, photography, Russian, Spanish, theatre arts, and yiddish), COMPUTER AND PHYSICAL SCIENCE (clinical laboratory science, computer information systems, mathematics, and natural sciences/mathematics), EDUCATION (health information management, learner designed area of study, and technical education), ENGINEERING AND ENVIRONMENTAL DESIGN (air traffic control, automotive technology, aviation flight technology, aviation maintenance technology, biomedical electronics, construction, electrical technology, electrical/electronics engineering technology, energy systems technology, energy utility technology, environmental science, fire protection science, kitchen and bath design, nuclear energy engineering technology, nuclear engineering technology, and nuclear medicine technology), HEALTH PROFESSIONS (biology, cardiac sonography, dental education, dental hygiene, diagnostic medical sonography, health services technology, hospital administration, imaging sciences, laboratory animal science, medical imaging, nuclear medicine, nursing, nutrition and dietetics, radiation therapy, radiologic imaging modalities, respiratory therapy, and vascular sonography), SOCIAL SCIENCE (anthropology, criminal justice, dietetics, economics, history, homeland security/emergency preparedness, human services, humanities, international studies, liberal arts/general studies, philosophy, political science/government, psychology, public administration, radiation protection, religion, social science, and sociology). Nursing, liberal studies, and general management have the largest enrollments.

Required: The baccalaureate student must complete a General Education requirement that includes courses in English composition, humanities, social sciences, natural sciences, and math for a total of approximately 60 general education credits. To graduate, 120 semester hours are required, with a minimum GPA of 2.0. Some degree programs require more than 120 semester hours of credit.

Special: Thomas Edison State College provides high-quality, collegiate learning opportunities for self-directed adults and offers flexible learning methods ranging from online courses and prior learning assessment to credit transfer and credit-bearing exams. New undergraduate terms begin every month, 12 months a year. The College offers courses in a variety of formats that are accessible to students at their convenience without requiring them to log on at set times. Most courses are structured on a 12-week schedule. The College offers several bachelor's to master's degree programs, enabling students to apply 9 credits they earn at the College to both their bachelor's and master's degrees at the College. The College partners with the School of Health Related Professions at Rutgers to offer Bachelor of Science programs in Health Information Management, Health Sciences, Medical Imaging Sciences and Nutrition and Dietetics. The College also has been selected to partner with the Medical Education and Training Campus (METC) at Fort Sam Houston in San Antonio, Texas, to provide a degree completion program for the Interservice Respiratory Therapy Program (IRTP). For experienced RNs, the College offers a Bachelor's in Nursing (BSN) degree or a BSN/MSN program in which students can earn both a Bachelor and Master of Science degree in Nursing with preparation as a nurse educator. The Accelerated 2nd Degree BSN Program at the College is a one-year BSN degree program for those who previously have earned

a bachelor's degree (non-nursing) and are interested in becoming RNs. The College also offers Learner Designed Areas of Study for students to customize studies within a discipline or blend of disciplines. There are 1 national honor societies.
Faculty/Classroom: No introductory courses are taught by graduate students.
Requirements: Applicants must have a high school diploma or the equivalent and be at least 21 years old. Applicants under the age of 21 may be accepted on a case-by-case basis, or if they are a member of a special population, such as a corporate partner or a member of the U.S. Military. Certain health-related and other areas of study are limited to persons holding appropriate certification. Admission to the bachelor's degree nursing program is limited to registered nurses (RNs) who are currently licensed in the United States. Admission to Master of Arts in Educational Leadership degree is limited to persons with valid Teacher's Certificate. AP and CLEP credits are accepted.
Procedure: Freshmen are admitted to all sessions. There is a rolling admissions plan. Application deadlines are open. Application fee is $75. Applications are accepted online.
Transfer: Students may transfer previously earned credits that have been awarded by regionally accredited colleges and universities. Students may transfer up to 80 credits from regionally-accredited community colleges and up to 120 credits from regionally-accredited four-year institutions.
Visiting: There are regularly scheduled orientations for prospective students, consisting of three on-campus information sessions are offered in addition to an online admissions Video Guide. To schedule a visit, contact the Office of Admissions.
Financial Aid: Thomas Edison State College is a member of CSS. The FAFSA and the college's own financial statement are required. Check with the school for current application deadlines.
International Students: They must take the TOEFL with a minimum score of 550 on the paper-based TOEFL (PBT) or 79 on the Internet-based version (iBT).
Computers: There are no time limits. The fee is $121.
Graduates: From July 1, 2012 to June 30, 2013, 2497 bachelor's degrees were awarded. The most popular majors were liberal studies (18%), nursing (10%), and general management (6%).
Admissions Contact: Mr. David Hoftiezer, Director of Admissions. E-Mail: *admissions@tesc.edu* Web: *www.tesc.edu*

WESTMINSTER CHOIR COLLEGE D-3

Princeton, NJ 08540 **(609) 921-7100; (800) 962-4647**

Full-time: 100 men, 200 women	**Faculty:** n/av
Part-time: 15 men and women	**Ph.D.s:** n/av
Graduate: 100 men and women	**Student/Faculty:** n/av
Year: semesters, summer session	**Tuition:** $31,400
Application Deadline: open	**Room & Board:** $11,800
Freshman Class: n/av	
SAT or ACT: required	**SPECIAL**

Westminster Choir College is a residential college of music located on a 23 acre campus in Princeton, N.J. offering a Bachelors in Music, a Bachelor of Arts in Music and a Master"s of Music. WCC also offers two summer study degree programs: Masters of Music Education and Voice Pedagogy. The figures in the above capsule and in this profile are approximate. There is 1 graduate school. In addition to regional accreditation, Westminster has baccalaureate program accreditation with NASDTEC, NASM, and NCATE. The library contains 455,809 volumes, 874,019 microform items, and 20,890 audio/video tapes/CDs/DVDs, and subscribes to 21,931 periodicals including electronic. Special learning facilities include a TV station. The campus is in a suburban area 50 miles south of New York City. Including any residence halls, there are 13 buildings.
Student Life: 56% of undergraduates are from out of state, mostly the Middle Atlantic. Students are from 26 states and 10 foreign countries. 80% are white. The average age of freshmen is 19. 21% do not continue beyond their first year.
Housing: College-sponsored housing includes single-sex and coed dorms. In addition, there are special-interest houses. On-campus housing is available on a first-come, first-served basis, and is available on a lottery system for upperclassmen. 57% of students live on campus. Upperclassmen may keep cars.
Activities: There are no fraternities or sororities. Groups on campus include choir, chorale, chorus, ethnic, gay, honors, international, musical theater, newspaper, opera, professional, religious, social, social service, and student government. Popular campus events include Family Day and Spring Fling.
Sports: There is no sports program at Westminster.
Disabled Students: 43% of the campus is accessible. Facilities include elevators, special parking, and specially equipped restrooms.
Services: Counseling and information services are available, as is tutoring in most subjects. There is remedial math, reading, writing, music theory, and music history.
Campus Safety and Security: Measures include 24-hour foot and vehicle patrol, self-defense education, and security escort services. There are emergency telephones and lighted pathways/sidewalks.
Programs of Study: confers B.A.M. and B.M. degrees. Master's degrees are also awarded. Bachelor's degrees are awarded in COMMUNICATIONS AND THE ARTS (music, music theory and composition, musical theater, piano/organ, and voice), EDUCATION (music education).
Required: To graduate, all students must maintain a minimum GPA of 2.0 while taking 120 semester hours.
Special: Internships in many programs, work study, summer study in Europe, and dual majors are available. There is a freshman honors program.
Faculty/Classroom: No introductory courses are taught by graduate students.
Requirements: The SAT or ACT is required. Undergraduate students must submit official high school transcripts. All undergraduate applicants must complete an academic course of study in high school. The GED is accepted. Two letters of recommendation, at least one of which must be from a music reference, are required, as is a personal essay. Graduate students must submit official college transcripts showing proof of graduation. All applicants must audition.
Procedure: Application deadlines are open. Check with the school for current fees.
Visiting: There are guides for informal visits. To schedule a visit, contact the Office of Admissions.
Financial Aid: Check with the school for current application deadlines.
International Students: They must take the TOEFL or IELTS.
Admissions Contact: Admissions. E-Mail: *wccadmission@wcc.edu* Web: *www.wcc.edu*

WILLIAM PATERSON UNIVERSITY OF NEW JERSEY E-2

Wayne, NJ 07470 **(973) 720-2125; (973) 720-2910**

Full-time: 3814 men, 4522 women	**Faculty:** 400; IIA, ++$	
Part-time: 755 men, 935 women	**Ph.D.s:** 92%	
Graduate: 322 men, 1004 women	**Student/Faculty:** 21 to 1	
Year: semesters, summer session	**Tuition:** $12,194 ($19,594)	
Application Deadline: June 1	**Room & Board:** $10,500	
Freshman Class: 6968 applied, 4234 accepted, 1240 enrolled		
SAT CR/M: 517/526	**ACT:** required	**COMPETITIVE**

William Paterson University of New Jersey, founded in 1855 as a college, is a public institution comprised of the colleges of Arts and Communication; Education; Humanities, and Social Sciences; Science and Health; and Business. There are 5 undergraduate schools and 5 graduate schools. In addition to regional accreditation, WPUNJ has baccalaureate program accreditation with ASLA, NASM, NCATE, and NLN. The library contains 300,000 volumes, 1,000,000 microform items, 20,000 audio/video tapes/CDs/DVDs, and subscribes to 5,000 periodicals including electronic. Computerized library services include interlibrary loans and database searching. Special learning facilities include an art gallery, radio station, TV station, a speech and hearing clinic, an academic support center, a computerized writing center, and a teleconference center. The 370-acre campus is in a suburban area 25 miles west of New York City. Including any residence halls, there are 35 buildings.
Student Life: 98% of undergraduates are from New Jersey. Others are from 22 states, 58 foreign countries, and Canada. 75% are from public schools. 63% are White; 15% Hispanic; 12% African American. The average age of freshmen is 18; all undergraduates, 24.
Housing: College-sponsored housing includes coed dorms and on-campus apartments. In addition, there are honors houses. On-campus housing is guaranteed for all 4 years. 77% of students commute. Upperclassmen may keep cars.
Activities: 2% of men belong to 13 national fraternities; 3% of women belong to 12 national sororities. There are 100 groups on campus, including art, cheerleading, chorus, computers, dance, drama, ethnic, film, gay, honors, international, jazz band, literary magazine, musical theater, newspaper, opera, orchestra, photography, political, professional, radio and TV, religious, social, social service, student government, and yearbook. Popular campus events include Pioneer Pride Week, Latin Heritage Celebration, Welcome Week, African Heritage Celebration, WinterFest, Springfest and Meet the Greeks.
Sports: There are 7 intercollegiate sports for men and 7 for women, and 24 intramural sports for men and 24 for women. Facilities include a recreation center with courts for basketball, tennis, racquetball, volleyball, and badminton, weight and exercise rooms, saunas and whirlpools, and a 4000-seat auditorium. The university also offers an Olympic-size pool, 8 additional tennis courts, and an athletic complex with fields for baseball, field hockey, football, soccer, softball, and track.
Disabled Students: Facilities include wheelchair ramps, elevators, special parking, specially equipped restrooms, special class scheduling, lowered drinking fountains, lowered telephones, and special housing.
Services: Counseling and information services are available, as is tutoring

in most subjects. There is remedial math, reading, and writing. There is a science enrichment center, a writing center, and a business tutorial lab.

Campus Safety and Security: Measures include emergency notification system, and security escort services. There are shuttle buses, emergency telephones, lighted pathways/sidewalks, and controlled access to dorms/residences.

Programs of Study: WPUNJ confers B.A., B.S., B.F.A. and B.M. degrees. Master's and doctoral degrees are also awarded. Bachelor's degrees are awarded in BIOLOGICAL SCIENCE (biology/biological science and biotechnology), BUSINESS (accounting, banking and finance, and business administration and management), COMMUNICATIONS AND THE ARTS (art history and appreciation, communications, dramatic arts, English, fine arts, music, Spanish, and studio art), COMPUTER AND PHYSICAL SCIENCE (chemistry, computer science, and mathematics), EDUCATION (health education, music education, physical education, and special education), ENGINEERING AND ENVIRONMENTAL DESIGN (environmental science), HEALTH PROFESSIONS (community health work, health science, and nursing), SOCIAL SCIENCE (African American studies, anthropology, economics, geography, history, philosophy, political science/government, psychology, and sociology). Biology/biotechnology, computer science, and English are the strongest academically. Management, communications, and education have the largest enrollment.

Required: All students must maintain a cumulative GPA of at least 2.0 and take 120 credit hours, typically including 30 to 40 in their major. The University Core Curriculum (the Core) will be the general education program of William Paterson University for students entering Fall 2011 or later. It is a 40 credit program, which constitutes a third of the entire undergraduate curriculum. Students create their Core experience by choosing a sequence of 13 (thirteen) courses from each of the following six areas of study. Each area and sub-area will have a variety of courses to choose from. Also required are 1 course in health or movement science, 1 course dealing with racism or sexism. Courses in Areas Four, Five and Six (Diversity and Justice, Community and Civic Engagement, and Global Awareness) may be within student majors. Such courses can thus be used to satisfy both, Core and major requirements. Students at WPU are required to complete four (4) Writing Intensive (WI) courses and two (2) Technology Intensive (TI) courses. These courses are not additional "stand-alone" courses but any course within the Core, or any major or any minor or any free elective that has been designated as a WI or TI course.

Special: Study abroad in 33 countries, cross-registration, internships, work-study programs on campus, accelerated degree programs, dual majors, individual curriculum design, and credit for military experience are available. Nondegree study and some pass/fail options are also possible. In the Learning Clusters Project, students experience how 3 general education courses, taken together, reinforce and better integrate each other. There is a professional program in teacher education leading to certification in early childhood, elementary, middle, and secondary education. There are 19 national honor societies, a freshman honors program, and 11 departmental honors programs.

Faculty/Classroom: 51% of faculty are male; 49% are female. All teach undergraduates, all do research, and all teach and do research. No introductory courses are taught by graduate students. The average class size in an introductory lecture is 32; in a laboratory is 24; and in a regular course is 19.

Admissions: 61% of the 2013-2014 applicants were accepted. The SAT scores for the 2013-2014 freshman class were: Critical Reading--49% below 500, 39% between 500 and 599, 9% between 600 and 699, and 2% between 700 and 800; Math--42% below 500, 46% between 500 and 599, and 12% between 600 and 699.

Requirements: The SAT or ACT is required. Applicants must have 16 academic credits or Carnegie units, including 4 in English, 3 in math, 2 each in science lab and social studies, and 5 electives such as foreign language and history. An essay and interview are recommended for some applicants, as are a portfolio and audition. The GED is accepted. AP and CLEP credits are accepted. Important factors in the admissions decision are advanced placement or honors courses, recommendations by school officials, and evidence of special talent.

Procedure: Freshmen are admitted fall and spring. Entrance exams should be taken by January 31. There are early admissions, deferred admissions, and rolling admissions plans. Applications should be filed by June 1 for fall entry; December 1 for spring entry, along with a $50 fee. Notification is sent on a rolling basis. Applications are accepted online.

Transfer: Transfer students must present at least 12 college level credits with a minimum 2.0 GPA. Nursing Majors are encouraged to have a minimum of a 3.0 GPA or higher. Communication Disorders must have a minimum GPA of 3.5. Allied Health, Public Health, and Business Majors have specific requirements for admission please check our website, www.wpunj.edu for those requirements. 30 of 120 credits required for the bachelor's degree must be completed at WPUNJ.

Visiting: There are regularly scheduled orientations for prospective students, including a campus tour, guest speakers, and dissemination of printed information. There are guides for informal visits and visitors may sit in on classes. To schedule a visit, contact the Admissions Office.

Financial Aid: In 2013-2014, 86% of all full-time freshmen and 84% of continuing full-time students received some form of financial aid. 64% of all full-time freshmen and 66% of continuing full-time students received need-based aid. The average freshman award was $13,247. Need-based scholarships or need-based grants averaged $8,359 ($13,800 maximum); need-based self-help aid (loans and jobs) averaged $3,285 ($5,000 maximum); and other non-need-based awards and non-need-based scholarships averaged $5,622 ($18,000 maximum). 72% of undergraduate students work part-time. Average annual earnings from campus work are $1500. The average financial indebtedness of the 2013 graduate was $29,906. WPUNJ is a member of CSS. The FAFSA is required. The priority date for freshman financial aid applications for fall entry is April 1.

International Students: There are 99 international students enrolled. They must take the TOEFL with a minimum score of 550 on the paper-based TOEFL (PBT) or 80 on the Internet-based version (iBT), IELTS - Overall band score of 6.0 or higher. TOEFL could be waived based on submission of sufficient SAT/ACT scores.

Computers: All students may access the system at all times. There are no time limits. The fee is $168.77.

Graduates: From July 1, 2012 to June 30, 2013, 1984 bachelor's degrees were awarded. The most popular majors were business/marketing (19%), education (13%), and psychology (11%). In an average class, 14% graduate in 4 years or less, 40% graduate in 5 years or less, and 47% graduate in 6 years or less.

Admissions Contact: Rohan Howell, Director of Undergraduate Admissions. E-Mail: *admissions@wpunj.edu* Web: *www.wpunj.edu*

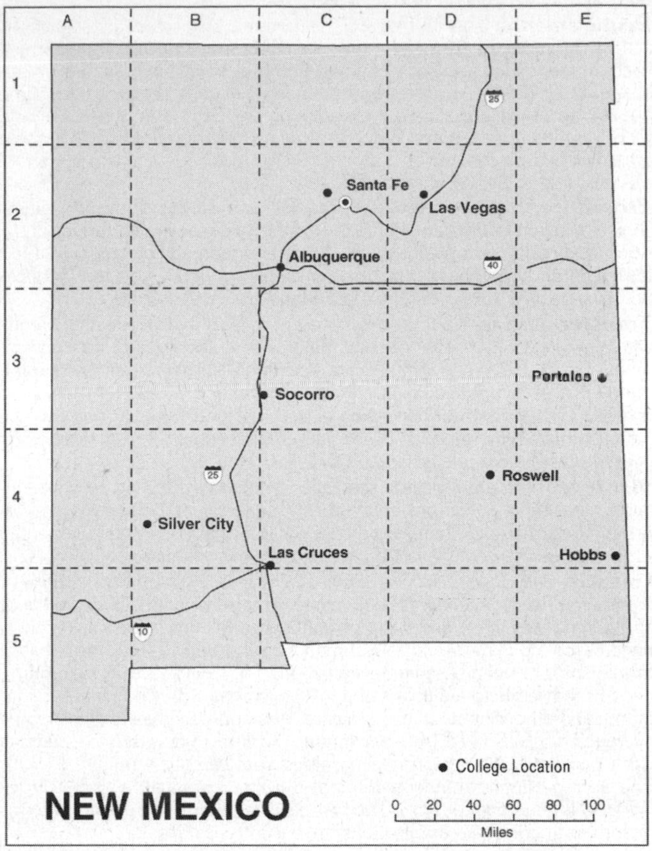

EASTERN NEW MEXICO UNIVERSITY E-3

Portales, NM 88130 (575) 562-2178
(800) 367-3668; (575) 562-2118

Full-time: 1204 men, 1555 women	**Faculty:** 151
Part-time: 796 men, 1017 women	**Ph.D.s:** 80%
Graduate: 324 men, 959 women	**Student/Faculty:** 17 to 1
Year: semesters, summer session	**Tuition:** $4592 ($9862)
Application Deadline: open	**Room & Board:** $6090
Freshman Class: 2291 applied, 1515 accepted, 709 enrolled	
SAT CR/M: 470/490 **ACT:** 21	**COMPETITIVE**

Eastern New Mexico University, founded in 1934, is a public institution offering programs in the liberal arts and sciences, as well as education, business, fine arts, and vocational and technical fields. There are 4 undergraduate schools and one graduate school. In addition to regional accreditation, Eastern has baccalaureate program accreditation with ACBSP, ASLA, CSWE, NASM, NCATE, NLN, and TEAC. The 3 libraries contain 329,003 volumes, 467,017 microform items, 28,321 audio/video tapes/CDs/DVDs, and subscribe to 62,670 periodicals including electronic. Computerized library services include interlibrary loans, database searching, and Internet access. Special learning facilities include an art gallery, natural history museum, radio station, TV station, Eastern New Mexico University is home to a broadcasting center, with one of the largest viewing areas in the nation, and serves as a PBS and NPR affiliate. ENMU also has a science fiction library, a teacher education library, a mineral museum, an anthropology museum, an archeological dig site, and a corresponding museum to the dig site at Blackwater Draw. The 400-acre campus is in a small town in Portales, NM. Including any residence halls, there are 40 buildings.

Student Life: 80% of undergraduates are from New Mexico. Others are from 47 states, 16 foreign countries, and Canada. 47% are White; 33% Hispanic. The average age of freshmen is 19; all undergraduates, 25. 39% do not continue beyond their first year.

Housing: 1098 students can be accommodated in college housing, which includes single-sex and coed dorms, on-campus apartments, and married student housing. In addition, there are sorority houses, female freshmen-only living areas. On-campus housing is guaranteed for all 4 years, is guaranteed for the freshman year only, is available on a first-come, and first-served basis. Priority is given to out-of-town students. 67% of students commute. Alcohol is not permitted. All students may keep cars.

Activities: There are 55 groups on campus, including art, band, cheerleading, choir, chorus, communications, computers, dance, debate, drama, drill team, environmental, ethnic, film, forensics, gay, honors, international, jazz band, marching band, musical theater, newspaper, pep band, photography, political, professional, radio and TV, religious, social, social service, student government, symphony, and yearbook. Popular campus events include Green and Silver Preview, and Dawg Days (freshman orientation).

Sports: There are 7 intercollegiate sports for men and 7 for women, and 15 intramural sports for men and 15 for women. Facilities include an indoor 4,800-seat arena, a 5,000-seat outdoor stadium, indoor/outdoor tennis courts, handball and racquetball courts, and an indoor pool.

Disabled Students: All of the campus is accessible. Facilities include wheelchair ramps, elevators, special parking, specially equipped restrooms, special class scheduling, lowered drinking fountains, special housing. ADA compliant campus, reserved parking, automatic doors, curb cuts, and elevators.

Services: Counseling and information services are available, as is tutoring in every subject, Limited upper division tutoring for selected majors. There is a reader service for the blind, and remedial math, reading, and writing.

Campus Safety and Security: Measures include 24-hour foot and vehicle patrol, emergency notification system, self-defense education, and security escort services. There are emergency telephones, lighted pathways/sidewalks, controlled access to dorms/residences, new security cameras to deter crime/theft.

Programs of Study: Eastern confers B.A., B.S., B.A.E., B.B.A., B.F.A., B.M., B.M.E., B.S.E., B.U.S., B.A.A.S., B.S.N., B.S.W. and B.O.E. degrees. Associate and master's degrees are also awarded. Bachelor's degrees are awarded in AGRICULTURE (agricultural business management, agriculture, animal science, and wildlife management), BIOLOGICAL SCIENCE (avian sciences, biochemistry, and biology/biological science), BUSINESS (accounting, business administration and management, and marketing/retailing/merchandising), COMMUNICATIONS AND THE ARTS (art, communications, dramatic arts, English, music, Spanish, and visual design), COMPUTER AND PHYSICAL SCIENCE (chemistry, computer science, geology, information sciences and systems, and mathematics), EDUCATION (agricultural education, business education, early childhood education, elementary education, home economics education, music education, physical education, special education, and technical education), ENGINEERING AND ENVIRONMENTAL DESIGN (electrical/electronics engineering technology and environmental science), HEALTH PROFESSIONS (medical laboratory technology, nursing, and speech pathology/audiology), SOCIAL SCIENCE (anthropology, counseling/psychology, criminal justice, forensic studies, history, human services, political science/government, psychology, religion, social studies, social work, and sociology). Elementary education, business administration, nursing (BSN only) and biology are the strongest academically. Business, education, criminal justice and biology have the largest enrollments.

Required: To graduate, students must earn 128 credit hours, 36 in the major, 40 total upper division, with a minimum GPA of 2.0. Minimum 32 hours must be from ENMU-Main campus; 15 of final 33 hours must be upper division.

Special: The school offers co-op programs in wildlife and fisheries and communication, internships, work-study programs, student-designed majors, a general studies degree, credit for military experience, and nondegree study. There are 2 national honor societies.

Faculty/Classroom: 49% of faculty are male; 51% are female. 93% teach undergraduates, all do research, and 93% do both. Graduate students teach 10% of introductory courses. The average class size in an introductory lecture is 30; in a laboratory is 15; and in a regular course is 19.

Admissions: 66% of the 2013-2014 applicants were accepted. The SAT scores for the 2013-2014 freshman class were: Critical Reading--60% below 500, 23% between 500 and 599, and 9% between 600 and 699; Math--54% below 500, 33% between 500 and 599, 9% between 600 and 699, and 1% between 700 and 800. The ACT scores were 56% below 21, 25% between 21 and 23, 15% between 24 and 26, 2% between 27 and 28, and 2% above 28. 36% of the current freshmen were in the top fifth of their class; 68% were in the top two fifths. 14 freshmen graduated first in their class.

Requirements: The SAT or ACT is required. A minimum composite score of 17 on the ACT or 810 on the SAT, or a GPA of 2.5, is required. Applicants must be high school graduate or possess a GED certificate and be in good standing with all previously attended institutions. A GPA of 2.5 is required. AP and CLEP credits are accepted.

Procedure: Freshmen are admitted fall, spring, and summer. Entrance exams should be taken in the junior or senior year of high school. There is a rolling admissions plan. Application deadlines are open. Applications are accepted online.

Transfer: 615 transfer students enrolled in 2012-2013. Transfer stu-

dents must have a minimum cumulative college GPA of 2.0 and be in good standing with all previously attended institutions. 32 of 128 credits required for the bachelor's degree must be completed at Eastern.

Visiting: There are regularly scheduled orientations for prospective students, including meetings with admissions, financial aid, meeting advisor/faculty in field of interest, a tour of campus, and a meal in the dining hall. There are guides for informal visits, visitors may sit in on classes, and stay overnight. To schedule a visit, contact the Admissions Office.

Financial Aid: In 2013-2014, 98% of all full-time freshmen and 89% of continuing full-time students received some form of financial aid. 42% of all full-time freshmen and 44% of continuing full-time students received need-based aid. The average freshman award was $10,356. Need-based scholarships or need-based grants averaged $4,736; need-based self-help aid (loans and jobs) averaged $3,892; non-need-based athletic scholarships averaged $3,382; other non-need-based awards and non-need-based scholarships averaged $4,213; and $2,905 from other forms of aid. The average financial indebtedness of the 2013 graduate was $14,821. The FAFSA and the college's own financial statement, and institutional scholarship application are required. The priority date for freshman financial aid applications for fall entry is March 1. The deadline for filing freshman financial aid applications for fall entry is August 15.

International Students: There are 151 international students enrolled. They must take the TOEFL with a minimum score of 550 on the paper-based TOEFL (PBT) or 61 on the Internet-based version (iBT).

Computers: All students may access the system. There are no time limits and no fees.

Graduates: From July 1, 2012 to June 30, 2013, 615 bachelor's degrees were awarded. The most popular majors were university studies (9%), elementary education (9%), and applied arts and science (9%). 91 companies recruited on campus in 2012-2013. In an average class, 11% graduate in 4 years or less, 24% graduate in 5 years or less, and 29% graduate in 6 years or less.

Admissions Contact: Cody Spitz, Director of Enrollment Services. E-Mail: *enrollment.services@enmu.edu* Web: *www.enmu.edu*

NEW MEXICO HIGHLANDS UNIVERSITY D-2

Las Vegas, NM 87701 (505) 454-3434
(800) 338-6648; (505) 454-3552

Full-time: 753 men, 893 women	**Faculty:** n/av
Part-time: 213 men, 537 women	**Ph.D.s:** n/av
Graduate: 408 men, 886 women	**Student/Faculty:** 15 to 1
Year: semesters, summer session	**Tuition:** $4000
Application Deadline: open	**Room & Board:** $5720
Freshman Class: 1575 applied, 1575 accepted, 348 enrolled	
SAT CR/M/W: 430/435/430 **ACT:** 18	**NONCOMPETITIVE**

New Mexico Highlands University, founded in 1893, is a state-supported institution offering undergraduate programs in liberal and fine arts, science and engineering, and professional studies. There are 4 undergraduate schools and 4 graduate schools. In addition to regional accreditation, Highlands University has baccalaureate program accreditation with ACBSP, CSWE, and NCATE. The library contains 616,364 volumes, 184,454 microform items, 139 audio/video tapes/CDs/DVDs, and subscribes to 747 periodicals including electronic. Computerized library services include interlibrary loans, database searching, and Internet access. Special learning facilities include an art gallery, radio station, TV station, a video production studio. The 248-acre campus is in a small town 65 miles northeast of Santa Fe. Including any residence halls, there are 45 buildings.

Student Life: 92% of undergraduates are from New Mexico. Others are from 31 states, 10 foreign countries, and Canada. 98% are from public schools. 55% are Hispanic; 27% White. The average age of freshmen is 18; all undergraduates, 26. 24% remain to graduate.

Housing: 480 students can be accommodated in college housing, which includes single-sex and coed dorms, on-campus apartments, and married student housing. In addition, there are special-interest houses, special housing for disabled students. On-campus housing is guaranteed for the freshman year only, is available on a first-come, and first-served basis. All students may keep cars.

Activities: There are no fraternities or sororities. There are 45 groups on campus, including art, band, cheerleading, choir, chorale, dance, drama, ethnic, film, gay, honors, international, literary magazine, musical theater, newspaper, pep band, photography, political, professional, radio and TV, religious, social, social service, student government, and yearbook. Popular campus events include Multicultural Week, Career Day, and Welcome Back Weeks.

Sports: There are 4 intercollegiate sports for men and 3 for women, and 8 intramural sports for men and 8 for women. Facilities include a 5000-seat football stadium, a 3600-seat arena, an indoor swimming pool, a weight room, athletic fields, a 9-hole golf course, and tennis, racquetball, and basketball courts. Hiking and skiing are nearby.

Disabled Students: All of the campus is accessible. Facilities include wheelchair ramps, elevators, special parking, specially equipped restrooms, special class scheduling, lowered drinking fountains, lowered telephones, special housing.

Services: Counseling and information services are available, as is tutoring in most subjects. There is remedial math, reading, and writing.

Campus Safety and Security: Measures include 24-hour foot and vehicle patrol, self-defense education, and security escort services.

Programs of Study: Highlands University confers B.A., B.S., B.B.A., B.F.A., B.S.E. and B.S.W. degrees. Associate and master's degrees are also awarded. Bachelor's degrees are awarded in AGRICULTURE (natural resource management), BIOLOGICAL SCIENCE (biology/biological science), BUSINESS (accounting, banking and finance, business administration and management, management information systems, marketing and distribution, and marketing/retailing/merchandising), COMMUNICATIONS AND THE ARTS (art, communications, English, graphic design, music, and Spanish), COMPUTER AND PHYSICAL SCIENCE (chemistry, computer science, mathematics, and physics), EDUCATION (early childhood education, elementary education, science education, and special education), ENGINEERING AND ENVIRONMENTAL DESIGN (engineering and environmental science), HEALTH PROFESSIONS (health), SOCIAL SCIENCE (anthropology, history, physical fitness/movement, political science/government, psychology, social work, and sociology). Physical sciences and psychology is the strongest academically. Education, business administration, and social work have the largest enrollments.

Required: Students must complete 40 to 51 credits of core curriculum requirements, including courses in English, history, science, social environment, thought and critical analysis, fine arts, literature, communicating skills, and phys ed. Proficiency in language and math must be demonstrated. A minimum of 128 credits, including at least 30 in the major, with a GPA of at least 2.0 is required to graduate.

Special: Highlands offers practicum, internship, study abroad in 2 countries, and field-study courses; cooperative programs in most majors; internships in education; minors in geology, physics, secondary education, philosophy, and theater; and credit for military training. There are 5 national honor societies, a freshman honors program, and 3 departmental honors programs.

Faculty/Classroom: 54% of faculty are male; 46% are female. All teach undergraduates, and 20% do both. No introductory courses are taught by graduate students. The average class size in an introductory lecture is 42; in a laboratory is 15; and in a regular course is 18.

Admissions: 100% of the 2013-2014 applicants were accepted. The SAT scores for the 2013-2014 freshman class were: Critical Reading--76% below 500, 23% between 500 and 599, 1% between 600 and 699, Math--76% below 500, 19% between 500 and 599, 6% between 600 and 699, Writing--81% below 500, 19% between 500 and 599.

Requirements: The ACT is required. SAT scores may be substituted. Scores are used for placement purposes. Applicants should be graduates of an accredited secondary school; the GED is accepted. A GPA of 2.0 is required. AP and CLEP credits are accepted. Important factors in the admissions decision are advanced placement or honors courses, evidence of special talent, and recommendations by school officials.

Procedure: Freshmen are admitted to all sessions. There are early decision, deferred admissions, and rolling admissions plans. Application deadlines are open. The fall 2013 application fee was $15. Notification is sent on a rolling basis. Applications are accepted online.

Transfer: 477 transfer students enrolled in 2012-2013. Transfer applicants with 16 or more semester credit hours must have at least a 2.0 GPA. 32 of 128 credits required for the bachelor's degree must be completed at Highlands University.

Visiting: There are regularly scheduled orientations for prospective students, available on a call-in basis. There are guides for informal visits, visitors may sit in on classes, and stay overnight. To schedule a visit, contact the Admissions Office.

Financial Aid: The average freshman award was $1,816. Need-based scholarships or need-based grants averaged $1,886 ; need-based self-help aid (loans and jobs) averaged $2,360; and non-need-based athletic scholarships averaged $2,436. The FAFSA is required. Check with the school for current application deadlines.

International Students: There are 9 international students enrolled. They must take the TOEFL, or IELTS.

Computers: All students may access the system 24 hours daily. There are no time limits and no fees.

Graduates: From July 1, 2012 to June 30, 2013, 432 bachelor's degrees were awarded. The most popular majors were health professions and related programs (29%), education (22%), and business/marketing (15%). In an average class, 18% graduate in 6 years or less.

Admissions Contact: John Coca, Director of Admissions. E-Mail: *admissions@nmhu.edu* Web: *www.nmhu.edu*

NEW MEXICO INSTITUTE OF MINING AND TECHNOLOGY C-3

Socorro, NM 87801 (575) 835-5424
(800) 428-TECH; (575) 835-5989

Full-time: 997 men, 362 women **Faculty:** n/av
Part-time: 52 men, 14 women **Ph.D.s:** 97%
Graduate: 252 men, 156 women **Student/Faculty:** 12 to 1
Year: semesters, summer session **Tuition:** $5714 ($17,073)
Application Deadline: August 1 **Room & Board:** $7178
Freshman Class: 1188 applied, 369 accepted, 348 enrolled
SAT CR/M: 600/630 **ACT:** 27 **HIGHLY COMPETITIVE**

New Mexico Institute of Mining and Technology, founded in 1889 as the New Mexico School of Mines, is a science and engineering university. It has 4 research-associated divisions: the New Mexico Bureau of Geology and Mineral Resources, the Energetic Materials Research and Testing Center, the Petroleum Recovery Research Center, and the Langmuir Laboratory for Atmospheric Research. There is one undergraduate school and one graduate school. In addition to regional accreditation, New Mexico Tech has baccalaureate program accreditation with ABET. The library contains 385,987 volumes, 79,926 microform items, and 2,899 audio/video tapes/CDs/DVDs, and subscribes to 50,000 periodicals including electronic. Computerized library services include interlibrary loans, database searching, Internet access, and Wi-Fi capability. Special learning facilities include a radio station, a mineral museum, a seismic research mine, and a campus astronomical observatory. The 320-acre campus is in a small town 75 miles south of Albuquerque. Including any residence halls, there are 28 buildings.

Student Life: 81% of undergraduates are from New Mexico. Others are from 50 states, 38 foreign countries, and Canada. 60% are White; 26% Hispanic. The average age of freshmen is 18; all undergraduates, 22. 26% do not continue beyond their first year; 49% remain to graduate.

Housing: 807 students can be accommodated in college housing, which includes single-sex and coed dorms, on-campus apartments, off-campus apartments, and married student housing. On-campus housing is available on a first-come and first-served basis. 50% of students commute. Alcohol is not permitted. All students may keep cars.

Activities: There are no fraternities or sororities. There are 55 groups on campus, including art, band, chess, chorus, computers, drama, ethnic, gay, honors, international, jazz band, musical theater, orchestra, political, professional, radio and TV, religious, social, social service, student government, and yearbook. Popular campus events include 49ers, Spring Fling, and International Student Exhibit.

Sports: There are 9 intramural sports for men and 9 for women. Facilities include a swimming pool, two gyms, an 18-hole golf course, an athletic field, a climbing wall, a weight/fitness room, racquetball/squash, tennis courts, sand volleyball court, a Ping-Pong area, and a martial arts/combative room.

Disabled Students: Facilities include wheelchair ramps, elevators, special parking, specially equipped restrooms, lowered drinking fountains, lowered telephones. The majority of the campus is wheelchair accessible.

Services: Counseling and information services are available, as is tutoring in most subjects. There is a reader service for the blind.

Campus Safety and Security: Measures include 24-hour foot and vehicle patrol, self-defense education, and security escort services. There are emergency telephones and lighted pathways/sidewalks.

Programs of Study: New Mexico Tech confers B.S., and B.G.S. degrees. Associate, master's, and doctoral degrees are also awarded. Bachelor's degrees are awarded in BIOLOGICAL SCIENCE (biology/biological science), BUSINESS (business administration and management), COMMUNICATIONS AND THE ARTS (technical and business writing), COMPUTER AND PHYSICAL SCIENCE (chemistry, computer science, earth science, information sciences and systems, mathematics, and physics), ENGINEERING AND ENVIRONMENTAL DESIGN (chemical engineering, civil engineering, electrical/electronics engineering, environmental engineering, environmental science, materials engineering, mechanical engineering, mining and mineral engineering, and petroleum/natural gas engineering), SOCIAL SCIENCE (liberal arts/general studies and psychology). Physics and electrical engineering is the strongest academically. Mechanical engineering, computer science, and electrical engineering have the largest enrollments.

Required: Students must earn at least 130 credit hours to graduate, including 42 hours of basic science, consisting in part of 10 hours of physics and 8 each of chemistry, calculus, and biology/geology/engineering. Further distribution requirements include 9 hours each of written and spoken English, 18 hours of literature, philosophy, the arts, and social science, and a senior seminar or senior design project. The credit hours required in the major vary by program. The student must also maintain a cumulative GPA of 2.0.

Special: New Mexico Tech offers co-op programs in computer science and all engineering majors, internships in technical communications, and cross-registration with New Mexico State, University of New Mexico, and Los Alamos National Laboratories in the WERC consortium. Dual majors are offered in engineering, computer science, physics, and math. Work-study, student-designed majors in environmental science, general studies, and basic science, nondegree study, and pass/fail options are also available. There are 4 national honor societies.

Faculty/Classroom: 80% of faculty are male; 20% are female. 95% do both. No introductory courses are taught by graduate students. The average class size in an introductory lecture is 18; in a laboratory is 12; and in a regular course is 18.

Admissions: 31% of the 2013-2014 applicants were accepted. The SAT scores for the 2013-2014 freshman class were: Critical Reading--13% below 500, 34% between 500 and 599, 36% between 600 and 699, and 17% between 700 and 800; Math--5% below 500, 32% between 500 and 599, 43% between 600 and 699, and 20% between 700 and 800. The ACT scores were 5% below 21, 21% between 21 and 23, 24% between 24 and 26, 20% between 27 and 28, and 30% above 28. 60% of the current freshmen were in the top fifth of their class; 81% were in the top two fifths. 6 freshmen graduated first in their class.

Requirements: The SAT or ACT is required. The ACT is recommended. In addition, students must have a minimum score of 21 on the ACT. Applicants must be high school graduates or present a GED certificate. Students should have earned 15 academic credits, consisting of 4 units of English, 3 each of social science and math (2 beyond general math), 2 of lab science, and electives. A GPA of 2.5 is required. AP credits are accepted. Important factors in the admissions decision are advanced placement or honors courses, evidence of special talent, and extracurricular activities record.

Procedure: Freshmen are admitted to all sessions. Entrance exams should be taken by December of the senior year. There are early decision, early admissions, deferred admissions, and rolling admissions plans. Applications should be filed by August 1 for fall entry; December 1 for spring entry, along with a $15 fee. Notifications are sent March 1.

Transfer: 104 transfer students enrolled in 2012-2013. Transfer students must have a GPA of 2.0 and have completed 30 semester hours of transferable credit. Those who have fewer than 30 credit hours, or who have not completed freshman English, must present a minimum ACT score of 21, as well as high school transcripts. 30 of 130 credits required for the bachelor's degree must be completed at New Mexico Tech.

Visiting: There are regularly scheduled orientations for prospective students, including 2 days of get-acquainted social activities, information sessions for parents and students, and transition sessions for parents. There are guides for informal visits, visitors may sit in on classes, and stay overnight. To schedule a visit, contact The Admission Office at admissions@admin.nmt.edu.

Financial Aid: The average financial indebtedness of the 2013 graduate was $18,834. The FAFSA is required. The priority date for freshman financial aid applications for fall entry is March 1. The deadline for filing freshman financial aid applications for fall entry is May 1.

International Students: There are 38 international students enrolled. They must take the TOEFL with a minimum score of 540 on the paper-based TOEFL (PBT) or 76 on the Internet-based version (iBT).

Computers: All students may access the system 16 1/2 hours a day on site; 24 hours a day via network. There are no time limits. The fee is $2 per semester.

Graduates: From July 1, 2012 to June 30, 2013, 194 bachelor's degrees were awarded. The most popular majors were mechanical engineering (26%), biology (10%), and chemical engineering (8%). In an average class, 17% graduate in 4 years or less, 42% graduate in 5 years or less, and 49% graduate in 6 years or less.

Admissions Contact: Tony Ortiz, Director of Admission. E-Mail: *tortiz@admin.nmt.edu* Web: *www.nmt.edu*

NEW MEXICO STATE UNIVERSITY C-4

Las Cruces, NM 88003 (505) 646-3121
(800) 662-6678; (505) 646-6330

Full-time: 5366 men, 5931 women **Faculty:** 567
Part-time: 999 men, 1286 women **Ph.D.s:** 79%
Graduate: 1325 men, 1858 women **Student/Faculty:** 20 to 1
Year: semesters, summer session **Tuition:** $6220 ($19,644)
Application Deadline: open **Room & Board:** $7735
Freshman Class: 5365 applied, 4571 accepted, 1918 enrolled
SAT CR/M/W: 470/480/460 **ACT:** 21 **LESS COMPETITIVE**

New Mexico State University, founded in 1888, is a public institution offering undergraduate and graduate programs that include study in liberal arts, agriculture, business, engineering, health science, education, and visual and performing arts. There are 6 undergraduate schools and 1 graduate school. In addition to regional accreditation, NMSU has baccalaureate program accreditation with AACSB, ABET, ADA, CSWE, NASM, and NCATE. The library contains 1.9 million volumes, 1.5 million microform items, and 17,048 audio/video tapes/CDs/DVDs, and subscribes to 70,796 periodicals including electronic. Computerized library services include interlibrary loans, database searching, Internet access, and Wi-Fi capability. Special learning facilities include an art gallery, natural history museum, radio station, TV station, a 289-acre experimental farm and orchard, a 61,760-acre cattle and experimental ranch, and a 2160-acre recreational area in the Organ Mountains. The 900-acre campus is in a small town 40 miles north of El Paso. Including any residence halls, there are 294 buildings.

Student Life: 72% of undergraduates are from New Mexico. Others are from 49 states, 53 foreign countries, and Canada. 49% are Hispanic; 33% White. The average age of freshmen is 19; all undergraduates, 24. 26% do not continue beyond their first year; 74% remain to graduate.

Housing: 3385 students can be accommodated in college housing, which includes single-sex and coed dorms, on-campus apartments, and married student housing. In addition, there are honors houses, fraternity houses, and sorority houses. On-campus housing is guaranteed for all 4 years, is available on a first-come, and first-served basis. 84% of students commute. All students may keep cars.

Activities: 2% of men belong to 10 national fraternities; 2% of women belong to 6 national sororities. There are 256 groups on campus, including art, band, cheerleading, choir, chorale, chorus, computers, dance, drama, drill team, drum and bugle corps, environmental, ethnic, gay, honors, international, jazz band, literary magazine, marching band, musical theater, newspaper, opera, orchestra, pep band, photography, political, professional, radio and TV, religious, social, social service, student government, and symphony. Popular campus events include Fiestas Latinas, American Indian Week, and Noche De Luminarias, Greek Week, Halloween Howl and NMSU Homecoming.

Sports: There are 6 intercollegiate sports for men and 10 for women, and 7 intramural sports for men and 7 for women. Facilities include a game room, a natatorium, tennis courts, playing fields, a gym, and rodeo grounds. One campus stadium seats 30,342 while the other seats more than 13,000.

Disabled Students: 95% of the campus is accessible. Facilities include wheelchair ramps, elevators, special parking, specially equipped restrooms, lowered drinking fountains, lowered telephones.

Services: Counseling and information services are available, as is tutoring in most subjects. There is a reader service for the blind. Remedial classes are offered at the Dona Ana Branch Community College. There is also an interpreter for the hearing impaired.

Campus Safety and Security: Measures include 24-hour foot and vehicle patrol, emergency notification system, self-defense education, and security escort services. There are shuttle buses, lighted pathways/sidewalks, recycled phones with 911 programmed in for emergencies.

Programs of Study: NMSU confers B.A., and B.S. degrees. Associate, master's, and doctoral degrees are also awarded. Bachelor's degrees are awarded in AGRICULTURE (agricultural business management, agricultural economics, agriculture, agronomy, animal science, horticulture, natural resource management, range/farm management, and soil science), BIOLOGICAL SCIENCE (biochemistry, biology/biological science, ecology, genetics, microbiology, nutrition, plant pathology, and wildlife biology), BUSINESS (accounting, business administration and management, business economics, fashion merchandising, hotel/motel and restaurant management, international business management, management information systems, marketing/retailing/merchandising, and tourism), COMMUNICATIONS AND THE ARTS (animation, art, communications, dance, dramatic arts, English, film arts, fine arts, journalism, languages, music, music performance, video, and visual and performing arts), COMPUTER AND PHYSICAL SCIENCE (chemistry, computer science, geology, information sciences and systems, mathematics, and physics), EDUCATION (agricultural education, athletic training, early childhood education, elementary education, home economics education, music education, physical education, secondary education, and special education), ENGINEERING AND ENVIRONMENTAL DESIGN (aerospace studies, agricultural engineering, chemical engineering, city/community/regional planning, civil engineering, computer technology, electrical/electronics engineering, engineering physics, engineering technology, environmental engineering, environmental science, industrial engineering, mechanical engineering, and surveying engineering), HEALTH PROFESSIONS (clinical science, community health work, environmental health science, nursing, and speech pathology/audiology), SOCIAL SCIENCE (anthropology, child psychology/development, community services, criminal justice, economics, family/consumer studies, geography, history, philosophy, physical fitness/movement, political science/government, psychology, social work, sociology, textiles and clothing, and women's studies). Criminal justice, nursing, and psychology have the largest enrollments.

Required: All students must complete a minimum of 128 credits, including at least 50 upper-division credits. A minimum GPA of 2.0 is needed. Distribution requirements include communications, humanities, math, natural sciences, and social sciences.

Special: Internships, cooperative programs in engineering, math, science, teacher education, business, agriculture, social services, health, government, and other majors, dual majors, study abroad in 56 countries, work-study, and B.A.-B.S. degrees are available. WICHE and National Student Exchange are also available. There are 25 national honor societies, a freshman honors program, and 18 departmental honors programs.

Faculty/Classroom: 50% of faculty are male; 50% are female. Graduate students teach 22% of introductory courses. The average class size in an introductory lecture is 39 and in a laboratory is 21.

Admissions: 85% of the 2013-2014 applicants were accepted. The SAT scores for the 2013-2014 freshman class were: Critical Reading--57% below 500, 33% between 500 and 599, 9% between 600 and 699, and 1% between 700 and 800; Math--56% below 500, 32% between 500 and 599, 11% between 600 and 699, and 1% between 700 and 800; Writing--66% below 500, 27% between 500 and 599, 6% between 600 and 699, and 1% between 700 and 800. The ACT scores were 47% below 21, 26% between 21 and 23, 16% between 24 and 26, 7% between 27 and 28, and 4% above 28. 38% of the current freshmen were in the top fifth of their class; 67% were in the top two fifths. 35 freshmen graduated first in their class.

Requirements: The ACT is required. Applicants must score 20 on the ACT or may take the SAT (accepted, but not recommended) and submit a composite score of 780. The GED is accepted. Minimum high school preparation includes 4 units of English, 3 of math, 2 beyond general science, and 1 foreign language/fine arts. A GPA of 2.0 is required. AP and CLEP credits are accepted.

Procedure: Freshmen are admitted to all sessions. Entrance exams should be taken during the high school junior or senior year. There is a rolling admissions plan. Application deadlines are open. Application fee is $20. Notification is sent on a rolling basis. Applications are accepted online.

Transfer: 1715 transfer students enrolled in 2012-2013. Applicants must have a minimum GPA of 2.0. 30 credits are required to avoid freshman admission requirements. If the applicant has earned 30 academic credit hours or more, the ACT score will be waived. If the applicant has earned 48 academic credit hours or more, the high school transcript will be waived. 30 of 128 credits required for the bachelor's degree must be completed at NMSU.

Visiting: There are regularly scheduled orientations for prospective students, including a tour of the campus and meetings with admissions counselors, faculty members, and financial aid advisers. There are guides for informal visits, visitors may sit in on classes, and stay overnight. To schedule a visit, contact the Office of Admissions.

Financial Aid: In 2013-2014, 96% of all full-time freshmen and 86% of continuing full-time students received some form of financial aid. 66% of all full-time freshmen and 61% of continuing full-time students received need-based aid. The average freshman award was $9,387. Need-based scholarships or need-based grants averaged $6,352 ($24,642 maximum); need-based self-help aid (loans and jobs) averaged $4,620 ($12,500 maximum); non-need-based athletic scholarships averaged $10,161 ($15,022 maximum); and other non-need-based awards and non-need-based scholarships averaged $4,048 ($15,326 maximum). 7% of undergraduate students work part-time. The average financial indebtedness of the 2013 graduate was $19,199. The FAFSA is required. The deadline for filing freshman financial aid applications for fall entry is March 1.

International Students: There are 565 international students enrolled. The school actively recruits these students. They must take the TOEFL with a minimum score of 550 on the paper-based TOEFL (PBT) or 79 on the Internet-based version (iBT) or take the MELAB.

Computers: All students may access the system at any time. There are no time limits and no fees.

Graduates: From July 1, 2012 to June 30, 2013, 2599 bachelor's degrees were awarded. The most popular majors were criminal justice (7%), individualized studies (5%), and psychology (5%). 318 companies recruited on campus in 2012-2013. In an average class, 15% graduate in 4 years or less, 37% graduate in 5 years or less, and 44% graduate in 6 years or less.

Admissions Contact: Valerie Pickett, Director of Admissions. E-Mail: *admissions@nmsu.edu* Web: *www.nmsu.edu*

SANTA FE UNIVERSITY OF ART AND DESIGN — C-2

Santa Fe, NM 87505 — **505-473-6652**

Full-time: 256 men, 285 women	**Faculty:** 27
Part-time: 2 men, 1 women	**Ph.D.s:** 24%
Graduate: n/av	**Student/Faculty:** 20 to 1
Year: semesters, summer session	**Tuition:** $30,682
Application Deadline:	**Room & Board:** $8984
Freshman Class: n/av	
SAT or ACT: required	**SPECIAL**

Santa Fe University of Art and Design is an accredited institution located in Santa Fe, New Mexico, one of the world's leading centers for art and design. The university offers degrees in arts management, contemporary music, creative writing, digital arts, graphic design, film, performing arts, photography and studio art. Faculty members are practicing artists who teach students in small groups, following a unique interdisciplinary curriculum that combines hands-on experience with core theory and prepares graduates to become well-rounded, creative, problem-solving professionals. As a Laureate International Universities Center of Excellence in Art, Architecture and Design, the university boasts an international student body and opportunities to study abroad, encouraging students to develop a global perspective on the arts. There are 8 undergraduate schools. The 3 libraries contain 170,000 volumes, 90,500 microform items, 19,517 audio/video tapes/CDs/DVDs, and subscribe to 25,706 periodicals including electronic. Computerized library services include interlibrary loans, database searching, Internet access, and Wi-Fi capability. Special learning facilities include an art gallery, Located on the campus of Santa Fe University of Art and Design, Garson Studios provides professional internship and learning opportunities to students in The Film School and other programs. Garson Studios are professional soundstages that have been hosting the production of independent and feature films, television series and commercials since 1989. That includes recent productions such as True Grit, Cowboys and Aliens and Longmire, and classics like City Slickers. Films made at Garson have won five Oscars including Best Picture No Country for Old Men and been nominated for 18 others. SFUAD also boasts a visual arts center, Greer Garson Theatre, digital arts laboratories, and recording studios. The 66-acre campus is in a suburban area 60 miles north of Albuquerque. Including any residence halls, there are 25 buildings.

Student Life: 70% of undergraduates are from out of state, mostly the Southwest. Students are from 40 states, 12 foreign countries, and Canada. 45% are White; 22% Hispanic; 12% Foreign. The average age of freshmen is 18; all undergraduates, 21. 40% do not continue beyond their first year; 48% remain to graduate.

Housing: 812 students can be accommodated in college housing, which includes single-sex and coed dorms and on-campus apartments. On-campus housing is available on a first-come and first-served basis. 70% of students live on campus; of those, 70% remain on campus on weekends. Alcohol is not permitted. All students may keep cars.

Activities: There are no fraternities or sororities. There are 20 groups on campus, including art, chorus, communications, drama, environmental, film, gay, international, jazz band, literary magazine, musical theater, photography, social, and student government. Popular campus events include commUNITY Focus Day, Fiesta, Vampire Ball, Pancake Flip, Date Auction, Casino Night, Quadstock and Cultural Fusion,.

Sports: There is no sports program at SFUAD. Facilities include Students have access to the Driscoll Fitness Center, with racquetball/squash courts, weight room, multipurpose exercise room, yoga and dance classes, gym and other amenities.

Disabled Students: 90% of the campus is accessible. Facilities include wheelchair ramps, elevators, special parking, specially equipped restrooms, lowered drinking fountains, special housing. Lowered light switches and controls in residence halls.

Services: Counseling and information services are available, as is tutoring in every subject. There is a reader service for the blind. For students with documentation of a disability, we provide: interpreters for people with hearing impairments, testing accommodations, printed materials in alternative formats, readers/scribes, note takers and other accommodations.

Campus Safety and Security: Measures include 24-hour foot and vehicle patrol, emergency notification system, and security escort services. There are emergency telephones, lighted pathways/sidewalks, and controlled access to dorms/residences.

Programs of Study: SFUAD confers B.A., B.B.A. and B.F.A. degrees. Bachelor's degrees are awarded in COMMUNICATIONS AND THE ARTS (animation, applied art, creative writing, dance, dramatic arts, English literature, film arts, fine arts, graphic design, music, music performance, music technology, music theory and composition, musical theater, painting, performing arts, photography, sculpture, studio art, theater design, and theater management), COMPUTER AND PHYSICAL SCIENCE (digital arts/technology). Film, performing arts, contemporary music and creative writing are the strongest academically. Performing arts, film and studio arts are the largest.

Special: SFUAD offers internships in all areas of study, in addition to extensive study abroad opportunities. SFUAD belongs to the Laureate International Universities network, which unites a global network of accredited online and campus-based institutions comprising more than 60 universities in 30 countries, including Milan, Italy, Turkey, and New Zealand. We offer work-study programs, dual majors, student-designed majors, a pass/fail option. There is 1 national honor society.

Faculty/Classroom: 64% of faculty are male; 36% are female. All teach undergraduates. No introductory courses are taught by graduate students. The average class size in an introductory lecture is 13; in a laboratory is 8; and in a regular course is 13.

Requirements: The SAT or ACT is required. Graduation from an accredited secondary school is required. The GED is accepted. Applicants must have 18 academic credits, including 4 years of English, 2 each of math, science, and social studies, and the remainder in college-prep courses. In addition to high school transcripts, students must submit a goal statement and SAT or ACT scores. A portfolio or audition is required for specific majors. AP and CLEP credits are accepted. Important factors in the admissions decision are evidence of special talent and advanced placement or honors courses.

Procedure: Freshmen are admitted to all sessions. Entrance exams should be taken In the junior year of high school. There are early admissions, deferred admissions, and rolling admissions plans. Application deadlines are open. Application fee is $50. Notification is sent on a rolling basis. Applications are accepted online.

Transfer: 67 transfer students enrolled in 2012-2013. Applicants must submit an official transcripts from all previous colleges and a goal statement. 32 of 120 credits required for the bachelor's degree must be completed at SFUAD.

Visiting: There are regularly scheduled orientations for prospective students, including campus tours, departmental receptions, a meeting with an admissions counselor, a theatrical performance or music event, panel discussions for students and parents, portfolio review and auditions. There are guides for informal visits, visitors may sit in on classes, and stay overnight. To schedule a visit, contact the Enrollment Office.

Financial Aid: In 2013-2014, 80% of all full-time freshmen and 95% of continuing full-time students received some form of financial aid. 63% of all full-time freshmen and 67% of continuing full-time students received need-based aid. The average freshman award was $23,713. Need-based scholarships or need-based grants averaged $4,554 ($7,750 maximum); need-based self-help aid (loans and jobs) averaged $6,443 ($15,500 maximum); and other non-need-based awards and non-need-based scholarships averaged $37,931 ($45,698 maximum). The FAFSA is required. Check with the school for current application deadlines.

International Students: There are 64 international students enrolled. The school actively recruits these students. They must take the TOEFL with a minimum score of 72 on the Internet-based version (iBT), IELTS. They must also take the SAT or ACT.

Computers: All students may access the system. There are no time limits and no fees.

Graduates: From July 1, 2012 to June 30, 2013, 68 bachelor's degrees were awarded. The most popular majors were moving image arts (25%), contemporary music (13%), and photography (13%). In an average class, 42% graduate in 4 years or less, 47% graduate in 5 years or less, and 48% graduate in 6 years or less.

Admissions Contact: Christine Guevara, Executive Director of Student Operations. E-Mail: *admissions@santafeuniversity.edu* Web: *www.santafeuniversity.edu*

ST. JOHN'S COLLEGE, SANTA FE C-2

Santa Fe, NM 87505 (505) 984-6060
(800) 331-5232; (505) 984-6162

Full-time: 198 men, 147 women	**Faculty:** 66
Part-time: 1 men, 3 women	**Ph.D.s:** 53%
Graduate: 56 men, 25 women	**Student/Faculty:** 8 to 1
Year: semesters, summer session	**Tuition:** $45,004
Application Deadline: March 1	**Room & Board:** $9994

Freshman Class: 251 applied, 211 accepted, 100 enrolled
SAT CR/M: 680/630 **ACT:** 28 **HIGHLY COMPETITIVE+**

St. John's College, founded in 1696, offers a curriculum based on the great books of western civilization in which students and faculty learn together in small discussion-based classes. The interdisciplinary curriculum features 4 years of seminar (the study of literature, Biblical literature,philosophy, history, political theory, economics, and psychology); 4 years of language (ancient Greek and French); 4 years of math; 3 years of lab science; and 1 year of music. There is one graduate school. The library contains 67,800 volumes, 4,192 audio/video tapes/CDs/DVDs, and subscribes to 95 periodicals including electronic. Computerized library services include interlibrary loans, database searching, and Internet access. Special learning facilities include an art gallery, music practice rooms, Ptolemy stone, and laboratories. The 250-acre campus is in a suburban area in Santa Fe, New Mexico. Including any residence halls, there are 31 buildings.

Student Life: 94% of undergraduates are from out of state, mostly the Southwest. Students are from 46 states, 17 foreign countries, and Canada. 68% are from public schools. 74% are White. The average age of freshmen is 20; all undergraduates, 21. 10% do not continue beyond their first year; 60% remain to graduate.

Housing: 327 students can be accommodated in college housing, which includes single-sex and coed dorms, on-campus apartments, and married student housing. In addition, there are special-interest houses, substance free residences, and green/sustainable housing. On-campus housing is guaranteed for the freshman year only and is available on a lottery system for upperclassmen. 75% of students live on campus; of those, 75% remain on campus on weekends. All students may keep cars.

Activities: There are no fraternities or sororities. There are 27 groups on campus, including fencing, art, chess, chorus, dance, drama, environmental, film, gay, international, literary magazine, musical theater, newspaper, orchestra, photography, religious, search and rescue, social service, and student government. Popular campus events include Oktoberfest, Halloween and Christmas parties.

Sports: 5 intramural sports for men and 5 for women. Facilities include soccer field, track, outdoor tennis courts, gym with weight room and cardio equipment, racquetball, squash, and basketball courts, nearby mountains, a ski mountain 30 minutes from campus, hiking trails which depart from campus.

Disabled Students: 75% of the campus is accessible. Facilities include wheelchair ramps, elevators, special parking, specially equipped restrooms, special class scheduling, and special housing.

Services: Counseling and information services are available, as is tutoring in every subject.

Campus Safety and Security: Measures include 24-hour foot and vehicle patrol, emergency notification system, self-defense education, and security escort services. There are shuttle buses, emergency telephones, lighted pathways/sidewalks, controlled access to dorms/residences, informal discussions and pamphlets/posters/films.

Programs of Study: St. John's confers B.A. degrees. Master's degrees are also awarded. Bachelor's degrees are awarded in COMPUTER AND PHYSICAL SCIENCE (mathematics and science), SOCIAL SCIENCE (liberal arts/general studies and philosophy).

Required: The college has 1 curriculum, based on the great books of western civilization for a total of 136 credits. Students attend seminars, preceptorials on specific works or topics, language, music, and math tutorials, and a 3-year science lab. Students take oral exams each semester and write annual essays. Sophomores take a math exam and seniors write a final essay and take an oral exam.

Special: Internships with alumni in a wide range of fields are available and students may transfer between the Santa Fe and Annapolis campuses. Ariel Internship Program provides stipends to undergraduates for a limited number of summer intership opportunities. Work study programs are available with the state government, museums, galleries, the Santa Fe Institute, businesses, and schools. Pre-medical studies at universities around the country.

Faculty/Classroom: 75% of faculty are male; 25% are female. All teach undergraduates. No introductory courses are taught by graduate students. The average class size in a laboratory is 15 and in a regular course is 15.

Admissions: 84% of the 2013-2014 applicants were accepted. The SAT scores for the 2013-2014 freshman class were: Critical Reading--4% below 500, 19% between 500 and 599, 29% between 600 and 699, and 48% between 700 and 800; Math--20% below 500, 21% between 500 and 599, 40% between 600 and 699, and 19% between 700 and 800. There were 2 National Merit finalists.

Requirements: Applicants must write 3 personal essays and submit 2 teacher references, a secondary school report including a reference from a school official, and transcripts of all academic work in high school and college. A campus visit and interview are recommended. Three years of math and 2 years of foreign language are required; 4 years each of math, foreign language, and English, and 3 years of science are recommended. The GED is accepted.

Procedure: Freshmen are admitted fall and spring. There are deferred admissions and rolling admissions plans. Application deadlines are open. Applications are accepted online.

Transfer: 21 transfer students enrolled in 2012-2013. St. John's accepts transfer students only for its freshman class; no previous college credit is recognized. Admission requirements are the same as for freshmen. 136 of 136 credits required for the bachelor's degree must be completed at St. John's.

Visiting: There are regularly scheduled orientations for prospective students, Student-led walking tour of the campus, audit a seminar and math and language tutorials, spend the night in student housing, interview with admission's counselor and faculty member. There are guides for informal visits, visitors may sit in on classes, and stay overnight. To schedule a visit, contact the Admissions Office.

Financial Aid: In 2013-2014, 81% of all full-time freshmen and 75% of continuing full-time students received some form of financial aid. 80% of all full-time freshmen and 70% of continuing full-time students received need-based aid. The average freshman award was $36,445. Need-based scholarships or need-based grants averaged $31,970; need-based self-help aid (loans and jobs) averaged $7,200; other non-need-based awards and non-need-based scholarships averaged $5,250; and $25,328 from other forms of aid. 115% of undergraduate students work part-time. Average annual earnings from campus work are $2880. The average financial indebtedness of the 2013 graduate was $26,750. The CSS/Profile and FAFSA, and Business/FARM Supplement, Non-custodial Parent Statement are required. The priority date for freshman financial aid applications for fall entry is February 15.

International Students: There are 36 international students enrolled. The school actively recruits these students. They must take the TOEFL with a minimum score of 550 on the paper-based TOEFL (PBT).

Computers: All students may access the system. There are no time limits and no fees.

Graduates: From July 1, 2012 to June 30, 2013, 104 bachelor's degrees were awarded. The most popular majors were liberal arts/general studies (100%). 29 companies recruited on campus in 2012-2013. In an average class, 65% graduate in 4 years or less and 15% graduate in 5 years or less. Of the 2012 graduating class, 13% were enrolled in graduate school within 6 months of graduation, and 62% were employed.

Admissions Contact: Larry Clendenin, Director of Admissions. E-Mail: *admissions@sjcsf.edu* Web: *www.sjcsf.edu*

UNIVERSITY OF NEW MEXICO C-2

Albuquerque, NM 87131 **(505) 277-8900**
1-800-CALL UNM ext. 1; (505) 277-6809

Full-time: 7401 men, 8939 women
Part-time: 1875 men, 2637 women
Graduate: 2744 men, 3425 women
Year: semesters, summer session
Application Deadline: June 15
Faculty: n/av; I, --$
Ph.D.s: 85%
Student/Faculty: 20 to 1
Tuition: $6846 ($20,688)
Room & Board: $8454
Freshman Class: 11652 applied, 7350 accepted, 3518 enrolled
SAT or ACT: required

COMPETITIVE

The University of New Mexico, founded in 1889, is a public university offering instruction in liberal and fine arts, business, engineering, health science, teacher preparation, law, and technology. In addition to the Main Campus located in Albuquerque, there are four branch campuses. There are 10 undergraduate schools and 5 graduate schools. In addition to regional accreditation, UNM has baccalaureate program accreditation with AACSB, ABET, ACCE, ACEJMC, ACPE, ADA, CAHEA, NAAB, NASM, and NCATE. The 8 libraries contain 3.6 million volumes, 713,958 microform items, 54,238 audio/video tapes/CDs/DVDs, and subscribe to 71,932 periodicals including electronic. Computerized library services include interlibrary loans, database searching, Internet access, and Wi-Fi capability. Special learning facilities include an art gallery, planetarium, radio station, TV station, a robotics lab, lithography and meteoritic institutes, observatory, arts lab, and museums of geology, anthropology, biology, and art. The 783-acre campus is in an urban area within the city of Albuquerque. Including any residence halls, there are 339 buildings.

Student Life: 90% of undergraduates are from New Mexico. Others are from 50 states, 56 foreign countries, and Canada. 45% are Hispanic; 37% White. The average age of freshmen is 19; all undergraduates, 23. 22% do not continue beyond their first year; 48% remain to graduate.

Housing: 3700 students can be accommodated in college housing, which includes single-sex and coed dorms, on-campus apartments, and married student housing. In addition, there are honors houses, special-interest houses, fraternity houses, sorority houses, freshman living learning communities, scholar's wing, graduates and senior undergraduate unit, global learning community, and combined BA/MD degree program quarters. 89% of students commute. Alcohol is not permitted. All students may keep cars.

Activities: 2% of men belong to 15 national fraternities; 3% of women belong to 10 national sororities. There are 400 groups on campus, including art, band, cheerleading, chess, choir, chorale, chorus, communications, dance, drama, drill team, environmental, ethnic, gay, honors, international, jazz band, literary magazine, marching band, musical theater, opera, orchestra, pep band, political, professional, religious, social, social service, student government, and symphony. Popular campus events include Spring Fiesta, Welcome Back Days, and Hanging of the Greens.

Sports: There are 8 intercollegiate sports for men and 11 for women, and 5 intramural sports for men and 5 for women. Facilities include a football field, 2 gyms, 2 pools, weights, racquetball, basketball, and tennis courts. The stadium seats 38,370, the gym 7,000, and the largest arena 18,018.

Disabled Students: All of the campus is accessible. Facilities include wheelchair ramps, elevators, special parking, specially equipped restrooms, lowered drinking fountains, and special housing.

Services: Counseling and information services are available, as is tutoring in most subjects. There is remedial math, reading, and writing.

Campus Safety and Security: Measures include 24-hour foot and vehicle patrol, emergency notification system, self-defense education, and security escort services. There are shuttle buses, emergency telephones, lighted pathways/sidewalks, crime stoppers, jump starts, operation ID, bicycle registration, and a 911 emergency system.

Programs of Study: UNM confers B.A., B.S., B.A.A., B.A.E.P.D., B.A.Ed., B.A.F.A., B.B.A., B.F.A., B.I.S., B.L.A., B.M., B.M.E., B.S.C.E., B.S.Ch.E., B.S.Cp.E., B.S.Cn.E., B.S.C.S., B.S.D.H., B.S.E.E., B.S.Ed., B.S.M.E., B.S.M.L., B.S.N., B.S.D.H. and B.S.N.E degrees. Associate, master's, and doctoral degrees are also awarded. Bachelor's degrees are awarded in BIOLOGICAL SCIENCE (biochemistry, biology/biological science, and nutrition), BUSINESS (business administration and management), COMMUNICATIONS AND THE ARTS (American Sign Language, art history, art, classics, communications, comparative literature, dance, English, film, television and digital media, French, German, journalism, languages, linguistics, media arts, music, Portuguese, Russian, Spanish, studio art, theater design, and theatre studies), COM-

PUTER AND PHYSICAL SCIENCE (astrophysics, chemistry, computer science, earth science, mathematics, physics, and statistics), EDUCATION (art education, athletic training, drama education, early childhood education, elementary education, health education, music education, physical education, secondary education, special education, and technical education), ENGINEERING AND ENVIRONMENTAL DESIGN (architecture, chemical engineering, civil engineering, computer engineering, construction engineering, construction management, electrical/electronics engineering, environmental design, environmental science, mechanical engineering, and nuclear engineering), HEALTH PROFESSIONS (dental hygiene, emergency medical technologies, exercise science, health, medical laboratory technology, nursing, radiological science, and speech pathology/audiology), SOCIAL SCIENCE (Africana studies, American studies, anthropology, Asian/Oriental studies, child care/child and family studies, criminology, economics, European studies, family/consumer studies, geography, history, human development, human services, interdisciplinary studies, international studies, Latin American studies, liberal arts/general studies, Mexican-American/Chicano studies, Native American studies, philosophy, political science/government, psychology, religion, sociology, and women's studies). Business administration, psychology, and biology have the largest enrollments.

Required: All students must take 2 English courses or pass an English composition competence examination and complete the University Core Curriculum. A minimum of 128 credit hours is required, along with a GPA of 2.0.

Special: There is a 3-2 engineering program with the Anderson School of Management. Study abroad is available in 28 countries. The university offers cooperative programs in arts and sciences management, engineering, and fine arts, a Washington semester, work-study, dual and student-designed majors, a general studies degree, credit for military experience, nondegree study, and pass/fail options. There are 20 national honor societies, including Phi Beta Kappa, a freshman honors program, and 46 departmental honors programs.

Faculty/Classroom: 52% of faculty are male; 48% are female. No introductory courses are taught by graduate students.

Admissions: 63% of the 2013-2014 applicants were accepted. The ACT scores were 7% above 28.

Requirements: The SAT or ACT is required. A total of 13 academic credits is required, including 4 years of English, 3 years of math, and 2 years each of foreign language, natural science (1 lab), and social science (1 U.S. history). A GED is accepted. Freshman applicants must be graduates of a high school accredited by a regional accrediting association or by the state department of education or state university of the state in which the high school is located. The minimum GPA requirement for admission to bachelor degree programs is 2.25 (on a 4.00 scale) in all previous academic work from an accredited high school. Grades in all courses allowed toward high school graduation are computed in the average. A GPA of 2.5 is required. AP and CLEP credits are accepted.

Procedure: Freshmen are admitted fall, spring, and summer. Entrance exams should be taken during the summer following the junior year. There are early admissions, deferred admissions, and rolling admissions plans. June 15 for fall entry; November 15 for spring entry; and May 1 for summer entry. The fall 2013 application fee was $20. Notification is sent on a rolling basis. Applications are accepted online.

Transfer: 927 transfer students enrolled in 2012-2013. Applicants must have at least a 2.0 GPA in all transferable courses. Please note that admission requirements are subject to change. 30 of 128 credits required for the bachelor's degree must be completed at UNM.

Visiting: There are regularly scheduled orientations for prospective students, includes academic advisement and registration. There are guides for informal visits, visitors may sit in on classes, and stay overnight. To schedule a visit, contact Admissions and Recrutiment Services at (505) 277-2260.

Financial Aid: In 2013-2014, 85% of continuing full-time students received some form of financial aid. The FAFSA is required. Check with the school for current application deadlines.

International Students: There are 208 international students enrolled. The school actively recruits these students. They must take the TOEFL, University of Cambridge English Examination (CPE or CAE) and IELTS. They must also take the SAT or ACT.

Computers: All students may access the system. There are no time limits and no fees.

Graduates: From July 1, 2012 to June 30, 2013, 3493 bachelor's degrees were awarded. The most popular majors were business administration (20%), psychology (8%), and elementary education (6%). 414 companies recruited on campus in 2012-2013. In an average class, 48% graduate in 6 years or less.

Admissions Contact: Matthew Hulett, Director of Admissions. E-Mail: *apply@unm.edu* Web: *http:/www.unm.edu*

UNIVERSITY OF THE SOUTHWEST — E-4

Hobbs, NM 88240 — (505) 392-6563; (800) 530-4400; (505) 392-6006

Full-time: 150 men, 200 women
Part-time: 20 men, 55 women
Graduate: 40 men, 125 women
Year: semesters, summer session
Application Deadline: open
Freshman Class: n/av
SAT or ACT: required

Faculty: n/av
Ph.D.s: n/av
Student/Faculty: n/av
Tuition: $11,000
Room & Board: $4000

COMPETITIVE

University of the Southwest, founded in 1962, is an independent college offering undergraduate programs in arts and sciences, business, education, psychology, and criminal justice. Graduate programs are offered in education. There is one graduate school. The figures in the above capsule and in this profile are approximate. The library contains 76,450 volumes, 25,750 microform items, and 1,553 audio/video tapes/CDs/DVDs, and subscribes to 333 periodicals including electronic. Computerized library services include interlibrary loans, database searching, and Internet access. Special learning facilities include a The 162-acre campus is in a small town 110 miles southwest of Lubbock, TX. Including any residence halls, there are 11 buildings.

Student Life: 70% of undergraduates are from New Mexico. Others are from 11 states, 5 foreign countries, and Canada. 43% are White; 38% Hispanic. The average age of freshmen is 20; all undergraduates, 26. 35% do not continue beyond their first year; 35% remain to graduate.

Housing: 172 students can be accommodated in college housing, which includes single-sex and coed dorms and on-campus apartments. On-campus housing is available on a first-come and first-served basis. Priority is given to out-of-town students. 77% of students commute. Alcohol is not permitted. All students may keep cars.

Activities: There are no fraternities or sororities. There are 7 groups on campus, including debate, drama, honors, international, newspaper, professional, religious, and student government. Popular campus events include Annual Students in Free Enterprise Dinner and Award Presentation, Family Week, and Speakers' Presentations.

Sports: There are 4 intercollegiate sports for men and 6 for women, and 5 intramural sports for men and 5 for women. Facilities include A soccer and baseball fields, a game room, and a physical fitness center with a multipurpose gym, racquetball courts, and physiology lab.

Disabled Students: All of the campus is accessible. Facilities include wheelchair ramps, special parking, and specially equipped restrooms.

Services: Counseling and information services are available, as is tutoring in most subjects. There is remedial math and writing.

Campus Safety and Security: Measures include 24-hour foot and vehicle patrol.

Programs of Study: confers B.S., B.A.S.and B.B.A. degrees. Master's degrees are also awarded. Bachelor's degrees are awarded in BIOLOGICAL SCIENCE (biology/biological science), BUSINESS (accounting and business administration and management), COMMUNICATIONS AND THE ARTS (English and fine arts), COMPUTER AND PHYSICAL SCIENCE (mathematics), EDUCATION (elementary education, secondary education, and special education), SOCIAL SCIENCE (criminal justice, history, humanities, psychology, and sociology). Education and business are the strongest academically. Education, business, and criminal justice have the largest enrollments.

Required: To graduate, students must complete 128 semester hours with a minimum GPA of 2.0 (2.5 for education majors). General education requirements include 12 semester hours each of social science and math/science, 9 each of humanities/fine arts and communications, 6 of religion, and 3 of economics, as well as a course in free enterprise and a senior seminar in leadership and ethics.

Special: The school offers co-op programs in early childhood education. Internships are available for students majoring in business, psychology, and education. CSW also offers nondegree study and credit for military experience. There are 2 national honor societies and 1 departmental honors programs.

Faculty/Classroom: 51% of faculty are male; 49% are female. 99% teach undergraduates. No introductory courses are taught by graduate students. The average class size in an introductory lecture is 11; in a laboratory is 7; and in a regular course is 12.

Requirements: The SAT or ACT is required. The ACT Optional Writing test is also required. In addition, Students must have a minimum composite score of 18 on the ACT or a satisfactory score on the SAT. Applicants must be graduates of an accredited secondary school or have a GED certificate. requires applicants to be in the upper 50% of their class. A GPA of 2.0 is required. AP and CLEP credits are accepted. Important factors in the admissions decision are advanced placement or honors courses, extracurricular activities record, and ability to finance college education.

Procedure: Freshmen are admitted to all sessions. There is a rolling admissions plan. Application deadlines are open. Application fee is $25. Notification is sent on a rolling basis. Applications are accepted online.

Transfer: 135 transfer students enrolled in 2012-2013. Applicants must present a minimum GPA of 2.0 and official transcripts from all colleges attended.

Visiting: There are guides for informal visits, visitors may sit in on classes, and stay overnight. To schedule a visit, contact Coordinator of Admissions.

Financial Aid: In 2013-2014, 97% of all full-time freshmen and 88% of continuing full-time students received some form of financial aid. 64% of all full-time freshmen and 70% of continuing full-time students received need-based aid. 17% of undergraduate students work part-time. Average annual earnings from campus work are $2000. The FAFSA and the college's own financial statement are required. Check with the school for current application deadlines.

International Students: There are 27 international students enrolled. They must take the TOEFL. They must also take the SAT or ACT.

Computers: There are no time limits and no fees.

Graduates: From July 1, 2012 to June 30, 2013, 98 bachelor's degrees were awarded. The most popular majors were education (29%), psychology (11%), and accounting (10%). 10 companies recruited on campus in 2012-2013. In an average class, 19% graduate in 5 years or less. Of the 2012 graduating class, 5% were enrolled in graduate school within 6 months of graduation.

Admissions Contact: Ashley Taylor, Coordinator of Admissions. E-Mail: *ataylor@csw.edu* Web: *www.csw.edu*

WESTERN NEW MEXICO UNIVERSITY B-4

Silver City, NM 88061 (505) 538-6106
(800) 222-9668; (505) 538-6127

Full-time: 210 men, 310 women	**Faculty:** n/av
Part-time: 50 men, 90 women	**Ph.D.s:** n/av
Graduate: 80 men, 140 women	**Student/Faculty:** n/av
Year: semesters, summer session	**Tuition:** $3500 ($9000)
Application Deadline: July 21	**Room & Board:** $5000
Freshman Class: n/av	
SAT or ACT: required	

LESS COMPETITIVE

Western New Mexico University, founded in 1893, is a public institution offering vocational, liberal arts, science, and professional programs. The figures in above capsule and in this profile are approximate. There are 2 undergraduate schools and 3 graduate schools. The library contains 120,000 volumes, 500,000 microform items, 500 audio/video tapes/CDs/DVDs, and subscribes to 950 periodicals including electronic. Computerized library services include interlibrary loans and database searching. Special learning facilities include an art gallery, natural history museum, a instrumental-vocal music center with individual practice rooms. The 80-acre campus is in a small town 113 miles northwest of Las Cruces, NM. Including any residence halls, there are 40 buildings.

Housing: 285 students can be accommodated in college housing, which includes single-sex and coed dorms, on-campus apartments, and married student housing. Alcohol is not permitted. All students may keep cars.

Activities: Groups on campus include academic, band, cheerleading, choir, chorus, dance, drama, ethnic, honors, international, jazz band, marching band, musical theater, newspaper, orchestra, pep band, political, professional, religious, social, social service, and student government.

Sports: There is no sports program at WNMU. Facilities include an indoor swimming pool, locker rooms for public use, intramural gym, two athletic gyms (1 specifically for spectator sports), athletics only locker rooms, football stadium with attached free-weight/cardio facility and locker rooms, circuit training room, and an athletic training facility for athletics use.

Disabled Students: Facilities include wheelchair ramps, elevators, special parking, specially equipped restrooms, lowered drinking fountains, and special housing.

Services: Counseling and information services are available, as is tutoring in most subjects. There is a reader service for the blind, and remedial math, reading, and writing. Two tutoring facilities exist on campus for free student use.

Campus Safety and Security: Measures include 24 hour foot and vehicle patrol.

Programs of Study: WNMU confers B.A., B.S., B.B.A., B.S.V.T. and B.S.W. degrees. Associate and master's degrees are also awarded. Bachelor's degrees are awarded in AGRICULTURE (forestry and related sciences), BIOLOGICAL SCIENCE (biology/biological science, botany, and zoology), BUSINESS (accounting, business administration and management, international business management, management information systems, and marketing/retailing/merchandising), COMMUNICATIONS AND THE ARTS (English, fine arts, music, and Spanish), COMPUTER AND PHYSICAL SCIENCE (chemistry, computer science, mathematics, and science), EDUCATION (art education, business education, elementary education, physical education, science education, secondary education, special education, and vocational education), HEALTH PROFESSIONS (medical laboratory technology, predentistry, premedicine, prepharmacy, and public health), SOCIAL SCIENCE (Hispanic American studies, history, human services, humanities, law enforcement and corrections, psychology, public administration, social science, social work, and sociology). The school of Education is the strongest academically and has the largest enrollment.

Required: To graduate, students must earn at least 128 credit hours, including 30 to 54 in the major, with a minimum GPA of 2.0, and complete 51 hours of general education requirements.

Special: WNMU offers internships, dual and student-designed majors, and work-study programs. There are a freshman honors program.

Faculty/Classroom: No introductory courses are taught by graduate students.

Requirements: The SAT or ACT is required. Applicants should be graduates of an accredited secondary school or present a GED. Students should have completed at least 3 units of English, and 2 of social studies, including U.S. history, as well as 2 each of science and math. Intermediate algebra and plane geometry are advised for students planning to enter certain fields. WNMU recommends a 2.0 GPA, but lower averages will be considered if applicants' test scores and personal recommendations are strong. CLEP credits are accepted.

Procedure: Freshmen are admitted to all sessions. Entrance exams should be taken by the senior year. There is a rolling admissions plan. Applications should be filed by July 21 for fall entry. Notification is sent on a rolling basis.

Transfer: Transfer students must have a GPA of 2.0. Those with fewer than 32 hours of college credit must supply ACT or SAT scores and a high school transcript. 30 of 128 credits required for the bachelor's degree must be completed at WNMU.

Visiting: There are regularly scheduled orientations for prospective students. There are guides for informal visits, visitors may sit in on classes, and stay overnight. To schedule a visit, contact The Admissions Office.

Financial Aid: The FAFSA is required. Check with the school for current application deadlines.

International Students: The school actively recruits these students. They must take the TOEFL. They must also take the SAT or ACT.

Computers: There are no time limits and no fees.

Admissions Contact: Dan Tressler, Director of Admissions. Web: *www.wnmu.edu*

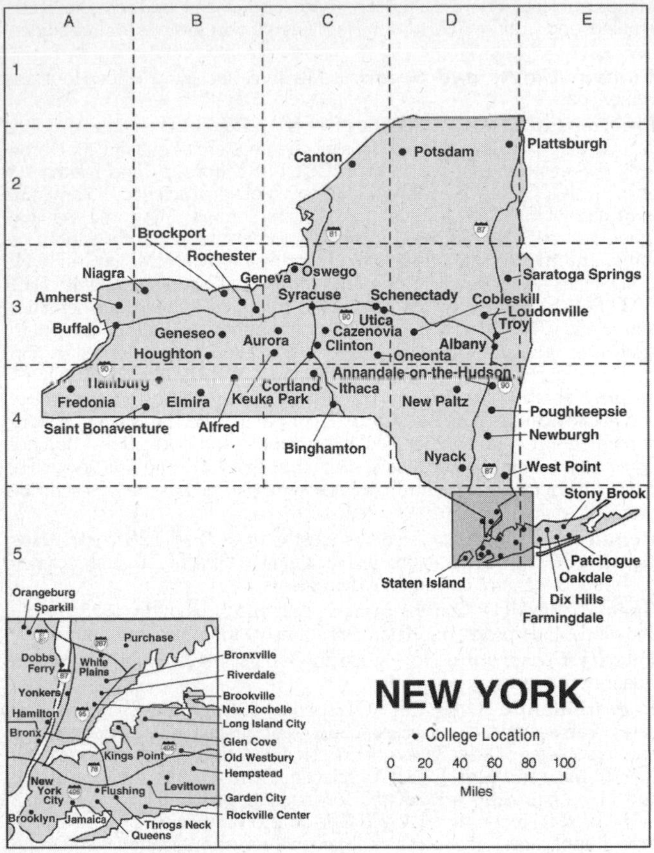

ADELPHI UNIVERSITY D-5

Garden City, NY 11530 (516) 877-3050
(800) ADELPHI; (516) 877-3039

Full-time: 1393 men, 3138 women	**Faculty:** 316; I, av$
Part-time: 145 men, 364 women	**Ph.D.s:** 87%
Graduate: 529 men, 2076 women	**Student/Faculty:** 12 to 1
Year: semesters, summer session	**Tuition:** $30,800
Application Deadline: open	**Room & Board:** $12,330

Freshman Class: 8654 applied, 5897 accepted, 918 enrolled

SAT CR/M/W: 553/564/575 **ACT:** 25 **VERY COMPETITIVE**

Adelphi University, founded in 1896, is a private institution. The figure for tuition and fees in the above capsule is for first-year students. There are 8 undergraduate schools and 7 graduate schools. In addition to regional accreditation, Adelphi has baccalaureate program accreditation with AACSB, CSWE, NCATE, and NLN. The library contains 605,791 volumes, 785,962 microform items, 26,472 audio/video tapes/CDs/DVDs, and subscribes to 1,068 periodicals including electronic. Computerized library services include interlibrary loans, database searching, Internet access, and Wi-Fi capability. Special learning facilities include an art gallery, radio station, an observatory, a theater, sculpture and ceramics studios, a bronze casting foundry, and language labs. The 75-acre campus is in a suburban area 20 miles east of New York City. Including any residence halls, there are 26 buildings.

Student Life: 92% of undergraduates are from New York. Others are from 38 states, 40 foreign countries, and Canada. 74% are from public schools. 61% are White; 15% Hispanic; 12% African American. 47% are Catholic; 17% Hindu, Buddhist, Muslim, Christian, and unknown; 16% claim no religious affiliation; 12% Jewish. The average age of freshmen is 18; all undergraduates, 23. 19% do not continue beyond their first year; 67% remain to graduate.

Housing: 1282 students can be accommodated in college housing, which includes coed dorms. In addition, there are special-interest houses, honors dorms. On-campus housing is available on a first-come, first-served basis, and is available on a lottery system for upperclassmen. Priority is given to out-of-town students. 77% of students commute. Alcohol is not permitted. All students may keep cars.

Activities: 11% of men belong to 7 national fraternities; 9% of women belong to 10 national sororities. There are 80 groups on campus, including art, band, cheerleading, chorale, chorus, computers, dance, debate, drama, environmental, ethnic, film, gay, honors, international, jazz band, literary magazine, musical theater, newspaper, opera, orchestra, political, professional, radio and TV, religious, social, social service, student government, and yearbook. Popular campus events include Family Week, Student Holiday Party, Spring-In Festival, Spring Concert and Commuter Appreciation Week.

Sports: There are 9 intercollegiate sports for men and 11 for women, and 14 intramural sports for men and 14 for women. Facilities include a 3000-seat stadium, a 600-seat gym, a 4-lane swimming pool, a finess center, racquetball, squash, and tennis courts, a dance studio, an indoor track, a baseball field, and a softball field.

Disabled Students: 95% of the campus is accessible. Facilities include wheelchair ramps, elevators, special parking, specially equipped restrooms, special class scheduling, lowered drinking fountains, lowered telephones, and special housing.

Services: Counseling and information services are available, as is tutoring in most subjects, a learning center offers tutoring in writing, quantitative skills and help with class assignments There is a reader service for the blind. A writing center is also available.

Campus Safety and Security: Measures include 24-hour foot and vehicle patrol, emergency notification system, self-defense education, and security escort services. There are shuttle buses, emergency telephones, lighted pathways/sidewalks, Dorm main entrances are videotaped and dorm doors are locked 24 hours a day.

Programs of Study: Adelphi confers B.A., B.S., B.B.A., B.F.A., B.S.Ed. and B.S.S.W. degrees. Associate, master's, and doctoral degrees are also awarded. Bachelor's degrees are awarded in AGRICULTURE (environmental studies), BIOLOGICAL SCIENCE (biochemistry and biology/ biological science), BUSINESS (accounting, banking and finance, business administration and management, human resources, and management information systems), COMMUNICATIONS AND THE ARTS (art history and appreciation, communications, dance, design, dramatic arts, English, fine arts, French, languages, music, performing arts, Spanish, and theater design), COMPUTER AND PHYSICAL SCIENCE (chemistry, computer science, mathematics, and physics), EDUCATION (art education and physical education), HEALTH PROFESSIONS (nursing and speech pathology/ audiology), SOCIAL SCIENCE (anthropology, criminal justice, economics, history, Latin American studies, philosophy, political science/government, psychology, social science, social work, and sociology). Nursing, business, and social work are the strongest academically. Nursing, biology, and psychology have the largest enrollments.

Required: To graduate, students need at least a 2.0 cumulative GPA (higher in some programs) and 120 credit hours with a minimum of 27 in the major. 6 credits each are required in the arts, humanities, and languages, natural sciences and math, and social sciences. Other course requirements include English composition, freshman seminar (3 credits each), and a 1-credit freshman orientation experience, and a capstone experience for seniors.

Special: Cross-registration is possible with New York University College of Dentistry, Tufts University School of Dental Medicine, Columbia University, New York Law School, SUNY State College of Optometry, and New York Medical College. Internships are available in accounting, banking and money management, and communications, among others. Study abroad is available in 65 countries, including Spain, France, Denmark, and England. A 5-year bachelor's/master's degree in a number of fields, including biology, social work, and education is offered. In addition, work-study programs, double majors, the B.A.-B.S. degree, an accelerated degree program, student-designed majors, and a Washington semester are available. A 3-2 engineering degree is offered with Rensselaer Polytechnic, Columbia, Polytechnic, and Stevens Institute of Technology, and joint degree programs are offered in computer science, dentistry, engineering, environmental studies, law, optometry, and physical therapy with other universities and technical institutions. Credit for life experience for adult students, nondegree study in special cases, and pass/fail options are possible. There are 27 national honor societies and a freshman honors program.

Faculty/Classroom: 46% of faculty are male; 54% are female. All teach undergraduates. No introductory courses are taught by graduate students. The average class size in a regular course is 20.

Admissions: 68% of the 2013-2014 applicants were accepted. The SAT scores for the 2013-2014 freshman class were: Critical Reading--25% below 500, 50% between 500 and 599, 20% between 600 and 699, and 5% between 700 and 800; Math--18% below 500, 48% between 500 and 599, 29% between 600 and 699, and 5% between 700 and 800; Writing--19% below 500, 47% between 500 and 599, 29% between 600 and 699, and 5% between 700 and 800. 46% of the current freshmen were in the top fifth of their class; 81% were in the top two fifths.

Requirements: Applicants should have 16 academic credits, including a recommended 4 units of English, history, and social studies, 3 each of math and science, and 2 or 3 of foreign language. An essay is required and an interview recommended for all applicants. A portfolio for art and technical theater candidates, an audition for music, dance, and theater candidates, and an interview for nursing, social work, and honors candidates are required. The SAT is recommended for the general studies and learning disabilities programs. A GPA of 2.5 is required. AP credits are accepted. Important factors in the admissions decision are advanced placement or honors courses, leadership record, and personality/intangible qualities.

Procedure: Freshmen are admitted fall and spring. Entrance exams should be taken in October of the senior year or May of the junior year. There are early admissions, deferred admissions, and rolling admissions plans. Application deadlines are open. The fall 2013 application fee was $40. Applications are accepted online.

Transfer: 541 transfer students enrolled in 2012-2013. A GPA of 2.5 is recommended in addition to an essay, an official high school transcript, and official records of all work completed or in progress from previous colleges and universities. An interview is required for students in social work and nursing, while an audition is needed for music, dance, and theater students and a portfolio for art and technical theater students. 30 of 120 credits required for the bachelor's degree must be completed at Adelphi.

Visiting: There are regularly scheduled orientations for prospective students, including a campus tour, an interview, and information sessions. There are guides for informal visits and visitors may sit in on classes. To schedule a visit, contact the Undergraduate Admissions at undergraduate@adelphi.edu.

Financial Aid: In 2013-2014, 99% of all full-time freshmen and 88% of continuing full-time students received some form of financial aid. 75% of all full-time freshmen and 72% of continuing full-time students received need-based aid. The average freshman award was $19,000. Need-based scholarships or need-based grants averaged $6,837; need-based self-help aid (loans and jobs) averaged $5,139; and non-need-based athletic scholarships averaged $13,490. 23% of undergraduate students work part-time. Average annual earnings from campus work are $2944. The average financial indebtedness of the 2013 graduate was $35,429. Adelphi is a member of CSS. The FAFSA and the state aid form are required. The priority date for freshman financial aid applications for fall entry is March 1. The deadline for filing freshman financial aid applications for fall entry is February 15.

International Students: There are 203 international students enrolled. The school actively recruits these students. They must take the TOEFL with a minimum score of 550 on the paper-based TOEFL (PBT) or 80 on the Internet-based version (iBT). They must also take the SAT or ACT.

Graduates: From July 1, 2012 to June 30, 2013, 1250 bachelor's degrees were awarded. The most popular majors were health professions (23%), business (13%), and social science (12%). 200 companies recruited on campus in 2012-2013. In an average class, 5% graduate in 3 years or less, 54% graduate in 4 years or less, 61% graduate in 5 years or less, and 66% graduate in 6 years or less. Of the 2012 graduating class, 41% were enrolled in graduate school within 6 months of graduation, and 88% were employed.

Admissions Contact: Christine Murphy, Director of Admissions. E-Mail: *admissions@adelphi.edu* Web: *www.adelphi.edu*

ALBANY COLLEGE OF PHARMACY AND HEALTH SCIENCES D-3

Albany, NY 12208	**(518) 694-7221; (518) 694-7322**
Full-time: 421 men, 636 women	**Faculty:** 95
Part-time: 6 men, 12 women	**Ph.D.s:** 84%
Graduate: 231 men, 331 women	**Student/Faculty:** n/av
Year: semesters, summer session	**Tuition:** $28,900
Application Deadline: February 1	**Room & Board:** $10,000
Freshman Class: 1556 applied, 1088 accepted, 281 enrolled	
SAT CR/M/W: 570/610/570 **ACT:** 26	**SPECIAL**

Established in 1881, Albany College of Pharmacy and Health Sciences is a private institution which offers a range of academic programs for students interested in careers in health care. There are 2 undergraduate schools. In addition to regional accreditation, ACPHS has baccalaureate program accreditation with ACPE. The 2 libraries contain 15,926 volumes, 28,388 microform items, 950 audio/video tapes/CDs/DVDs, and subscribe to 298 periodicals including electronic. Computerized library services include interlibrary loans, database searching, Internet access, and Wi-Fi capability. The 35-acre campus is in a small town in Albany, NY and a campus in Colchester, VT. Including any residence halls, there are 10 buildings.

Student Life: 73% of undergraduates are from New York. Others are from 23 states, 8 foreign countries, and Canada. The average age of freshmen is 18; all undergraduates, 21. 20% do not continue beyond their first year; 65% remain to graduate.

Housing: 750 students can be accommodated in college housing, which includes coed dorms and on-campus apartments. On-campus housing is guaranteed for the freshman year only and is available on a lottery system for upperclassmen. 55% of students commute. Alcohol is not permitted. All students may keep cars.

Activities: 3% of men belong to 2 national fraternities. There are 35 groups on campus, including and colleges against cancer, dance, multicultural, outdoors, ski, band, bowling, choir, chorus, dance, ethnic, honors, international, literary magazine, newspaper, photography, professional, religious, social service, student government, and yearbook. Popular campus events include Interview Day, White Coat Ceremony and Relay for Life.

Sports: There are 3 intercollegiate sports for men and 3 for women, and 4 intramural sports for men and 4 for women. Facilities include a gym, fitness center, an outdoor track, and a soccer field.

Disabled Students: 98% of the campus is accessible. Facilities include wheelchair ramps, elevators, special parking, specially equipped restrooms, lowered drinking fountains, and special housing.

Services: Counseling and information services are available, as is tutoring in most subjects, required math and science-based courses in all undergraduate and professional programs and writing assistance.

Campus Safety and Security: Measures include 24-hour foot and vehicle patrol and emergency notification system. There are emergency telephones, lighted pathways/sidewalks, and controlled access to dorms/residences.

Programs of Study: ACPHS confers B.S. degrees. Master's and doctoral degrees are also awarded. Bachelor's degrees are awarded in BIOLOGICAL SCIENCE (microbiology), COMPUTER AND PHYSICAL SCIENCE (chemistry), HEALTH PROFESSIONS (biomedical science, health science, medical laboratory science, and pharmaceutical science). Doctor of Pharmacy program is the strongest academically, and has the largest enrollment.

Required: To graduate, students must complete between 129 and 162 credits, depending on the degree program, including core curriculum courses, with a minimum GPA of 2.0. Doctor of Pharmacy program - a minimum GPA of 2.5 Masters - a minimum GPA of 3.0

Special: Students in the PharmD or BS programs may also enroll in a joint degree program with Union Graduate College for an MS in Clinical Leadership or an MBA in Health Systems Administration. There is 1 national honor society.

Faculty/Classroom: 53% of faculty are male; 47% are female. No introductory courses are taught by graduate students.

Admissions: 70% of the 2013-2014 applicants were accepted. The SAT scores for the 2013-2014 freshman class were: Critical Reading--11% below 500, 52% between 500 and 599, 36% between 600 and 699, and 2% between 700 and 800; Math--2% below 500, 35% between 500 and 599, 55% between 600 and 699, and 8% between 700 and 800; Writing--14% below 500, 50% between 500 and 599, 32% between 600 and 699, and 4% between 700 and 800. The ACT scores were 4% below 21, 18% between 21 and 23, 29% between 24 and 26, 21% between 27 and 28, and 28% above 28. 79% of the current freshmen were in the top fifth of their class; 98% were in the top two fifths. 9 freshmen graduated first in their class.

Requirements: The SAT or ACT is required. Applicants must be graduates of an accredited high school or have a GED. Applicants need to have completed at least 4 units in English, 4 units in Science, including Chemistry, and 3 units in Math. AP and CLEP credits are accepted. Important factors in the admissions decision are advanced placement or honors courses, extracurricular activities record, recommendations by school officials, personality/intangible qualities, and recommendations by alumni.

Procedure: Freshmen are admitted fall. Entrance exams should be taken by the junior year. There is a early decision plan. Early decision applications should be filed by November 1; regular applications, by February 1 for fall entry; and December 1 for spring entry, along with a $75 fee. Notification of early decision is sent December 15; regular decision, March 15. 95 early decision candidates were accepted for the 2013-2014 class. Applications are accepted online.

Transfer: 100 transfer students enrolled in 2012-2013. Applicants must have a GPA of 3.0.

Visiting: There are regularly scheduled orientations for prospective students, including a tour of the school and residence halls and a discussion of admissions requirements, financial aid, and student activities. There are guides for informal visits and visitors may sit in on classes. To schedule a visit, contact the Office of Admissions.

Financial Aid: In 2013-2014, 95% of all full-time freshmen and 85% of continuing full-time students received some form of financial aid. 86% of all full-time freshmen and 66% of continuing full-time students received need-based aid. The average freshman award was $14,937. Need-based scholarships or need-based grants averaged $4,339; need-based self-help aid (loans and jobs) averaged $3,222; and other non-need-based awards and non-need-based scholarships averaged $7,376. 24% of undergraduate students work part-time. ACPHS is a member of CSS. The CSS/Profile and FAFSA are required. The priority date for freshman financial aid applications for fall entry is February 1. The deadline for filing freshman financial aid applications for fall entry is May 1.

International Students: There are 63 international students enrolled.

They must take the TOEFL with a minimum score of 600 on the paper-based TOEFL (PBT) or 100 on the Internet-based version (iBT), or the TSE. They must also take the SAT or ACT.

Graduates: From July 1, 2012 to June 30, 2013, 27 bachelor's degrees were awarded. The most popular majors were pharmacy (84%), clinical laboratory sciences (8%), and pharmaceutical sciences (4%).

Admissions Contact: Matthew Stever, Director of Admissions. E-Mail: *matthew.stever@acphs.edu* Web: *www.acphs.edu*

ALBERT A. LIST COLLEGE OF JEWISH STUDIES D-5

New York, NY 10027 (212) 678-8832; (212) 678-8947

Full-time: 90 men, 90 women	**Faculty:** n/av
Part-time: 15 men, 15 women	**Ph.D.s:** n/av
Graduate: n/av	**Student/Faculty:** n/av
Year: semesters, summer session	**Tuition:** $12,100
Application Deadline:	**Room & Board:** $10,500
Freshman Class: n/av	
SAT or ACT: required	

Albert A. List College of Jewish Studies, the undergraduate division of the Jewish Theological Seminary, founded in 1886, is a private institution affiliated with the Conservative branch of the Jewish faith. List College offers programs in all aspects of Judaism, including Bible, Rabbinics, literature, history, philosophy, education, and communal service. There is also a combined liberal arts program with Columbia University and Barnard College. The figures in the above capsule and in this profile are approximate. The library contains 320,000 volumes, 3,500 microform items, and subscribes to 750 periodicals including electronic. Computerized library services include interlibrary loans and database searching. Special learning facilities include an art gallery, a music center, a Jewish education, research center, and the Jewish Museum Archives Center. The 1-acre campus is in an urban area in New York, NY. Including any residence halls, there are 6 buildings.

Student Life: 75% of undergraduates are from out of state, mostly the Middle Atlantic. Students are from 12 states, 3 foreign countries, and Canada. 70% are from public schools. 100% are White. 100% are Jewish. The average age of freshmen is 18; all undergraduates, 20. 96% remain to graduate.

Housing: 212 students can be accommodated in college housing, which includes coed dorms, on-campus apartments, off-campus apartments, and married student housing. kosher housing. On-campus housing is guaranteed for all 4 years. 93% of students live on campus; of those, 95% remain on campus on weekends. Alcohol is not permitted. All students may keep cars.

Activities: There are no fraternities or sororities. Groups on campus include art, band, choir, chorus, computers, dance, drama, ethnic, film, gay, honors, international, List College students have access to all clubs and organizations at Columbia and Barnard., literary magazine, musical theater, newspaper, orchestra, photography, political, professional, radio and TV, religious, social, social service, student government, and yearbook. Popular campus events include Purim, Simchat Torah and Orientation.

Sports: There are 3 intramural sports for men and 3 for women. Facilities include List College students may use the facilities at Columbia University.

Disabled Students: All of the campus is accessible. Facilities include wheelchair ramps, elevators, special parking, specially equipped restrooms, lowered drinking fountains, lowered telephones, and elevators with braille panels.

Services: Counseling and information services are available, as is tutoring in most subjects.

Campus Safety and Security: Measures include 24-hour foot and vehicle patrol and security escort services. There are emergency telephones and lighted pathways/sidewalks.

Programs of Study: List College confers B.A. degrees. Bachelor's degrees are awarded in Social Science (biblical studies and Judaic studies).

Required: Students must take a Hebrew language requirement, 24 credits in Jewish history, 9 in literature, and 6 each in Bible, Jewish philosophy, and Talmud. In addition, there are 60 required credits in liberal arts, including 6 credits each in English, history/philosophy/social science, and math or lab science to be completed at another college or university. A total of 156 credits (96 taken at List College) is required for graduation, with 21 in a major field.

Special: There is a joint program with Columbia University and a double-degree program with Barnard College, which enable students to earn 2 B.A. degrees in 4 to 4 1/2 years. Study abroad is available in Israel, England, France, and Spain. Student-designed majors, credit by exam, and nondegree study are also offered. There is a Phi Beta Kappa society, and a freshman honors program.

Faculty/Classroom: 68% of faculty are male; 32% are female. All teach and do research. No introductory courses are taught by graduate students. The average class size in an introductory lecture is 30 and in a regular course is 10.

Requirements: The SAT or ACT is required. Applicants must be graduates of an accredited secondary school or have the GED. An essay and 2 recommendations are required; an interview is strongly recommended. AP credits are accepted. Important factors in the admissions decision are advanced placement or honors courses, extracurricular activities record, and personality/intangible qualities.

Procedure: Freshmen are admitted fall and spring. Entrance exams should be taken in the spring of the junior year. There are early decision, early admissions, and deferred admissions plans. Early decision applications should be filed by November 15; regular applications, by November 1 for spring entry. The fall 2013 application fee was $60. Notification of early decision is sent December 15; regular decision, April 15.

Transfer: Applicants must submit SAT or ACT scores, an essay, high school and college transcripts, and 2 academic recommendations. A minimum college GPA of 2.5 is required. An interview is recommended. 48 of 156 credits required for the bachelor's degree must be completed at List College.

Visiting: There are regularly scheduled orientations for prospective students, including a tour of the campus and of Columbia University, an interview with the dean, and an overnight dormitory stay. There are guides for informal visits, visitors may sit in on classes, and stay overnight. To schedule a visit, contact the Admissions Office.

Financial Aid: List College is a member of CSS. The CSS/Profile and the college's own financial statement, and 1040 tax forms are required. Check with the school for current application deadlines.

International Students: They must take the TOEFL and the college's own test, the American Language English Placement Test. They must also take the SAT or ACT.

Admissions Contact: Reena Kamins, Director of Admissions. E-Mail: *lcadmissions@jtsa.edu* Web: *www.jtsa.edu*

ALFRED STATE / SUNY COLLEGE OF TECHNOLOGY B-4

Alfred, NY 14802 (607) 587-4215
(800) 4-ALFRED; (607) 587-4299

Full-time: n/av	**Faculty:** n/av	
Part-time: n/av	**Ph.D.s:** n/av	
Graduate: n/av	**Student/Faculty:** n/av	
Year: semesters, summer session	**Tuition:** $6874 ($16,124)	
Application Deadline:	**Room & Board:** $11,160	
Freshman Class: n/av		
SAT CR/M/W: 520/540/490	**ACT:** 23	**COMPETITIVE**

The State University of New York College of Technology at Alfred, founded in 1908, is a public institution conferring associate and bachelor's degrees. There are 3 undergraduate schools. In addition to regional accreditation, Alfred State College has baccalaureate program accreditation with ABET. The 2 libraries contain 61,500 volumes, and 8,148 audio/video tapes/CDs/DVDs, and subscribe to 5,500 periodicals including electronic. Computerized library services include interlibrary loans, database searching, Internet access, and Wi-Fi capability. Special learning facilities include an art gallery and radio station. The 150-acre campus is in a rural area 15 miles north of Pennsylvania, 75 miles south of Rochester, and 90 miles southeast of Buffalo. Including any residence halls, there are 50 buildings.

Student Life: 97% of undergraduates are from New York. Others are from 7 states, 12 foreign countries, and Canada. 73% are White; 11% African American. The average age of freshmen is 18; all undergraduates, 19. 67% remain to graduate.

Housing: College-sponsored housing includes coed dorms and on-campus apartments. In addition, there are honors houses, language houses, special-interest houses, wellness, computerized, and adult housing. On-campus housing is guaranteed for all 4 years. 70% of students live on campus; of those, 50% remain on campus on weekends. Alcohol is not permitted. All students may keep cars.

Activities: There are 90 groups on campus, including a rescue and response team, band, cheerleading, chess, choir, chorale, chorus, computers, dance, drama, environmental, ethnic, forensics, gay, honors, international, jazz band, literary magazine, musical theater, newspaper, orchestra, peer education network, pep band, professional, radio and TV, social, social service, student government, and yearbook. Popular campus events include Family Weekend and Hot Dog Day.

Sports: There are 9 intercollegiate sports for men and 7 for women, and 26 intramural sports for men and 23 for women. Facilities include a fitness center/weight room, an indoor swimming pool, a wrestling room, a full gym, tennis courts, an outdoor track, baseball and softball fields, and practice fields.

Disabled Students: All of the campus is accessible. Facilities include wheelchair ramps, elevators, special parking, specially equipped restrooms, special class scheduling, lowered drinking fountains, lowered telephones, and special housing.

Services: Counseling and information services are available, as is tutoring in most subjects. There is a reader service for the blind, and remedial math, reading, and writing.

Campus Safety and Security: Measures include 24-hour foot and vehicle patrol, emergency notification system, self-defense education, and

security escort services. There are shuttle buses, emergency telephones, lighted pathways/sidewalks, and controlled access to dorms/residences.

Programs of Study: Alfred State College confers B.S., B.B.A. and B.T. degrees. Associate degrees are also awarded. Bachelor's degrees are awarded in BUSINESS (banking and finance), COMPUTER AND PHYSICAL SCIENCE (information sciences and systems), ENGINEERING AND ENVIRONMENTAL DESIGN (architectural technology, computer technology, construction management, electrical/electronics engineering technology, manufacturing technology, mechanical engineering technology, survey and mapping technology, and technological management). Engineering technology program are the strongest academically and have the largest enrollment.

Required: To graduate, candidates for a bachelor's degree must complete a total of 120 credits. A core sequence, including courses in math, physical sciences, and liberal studies, and a year-long senior technical project, are required. A phys ed course is also required.

Special: Cross-registration is offered with Alfred University, Houghton College, Rochester area colleges, and the Western New York Consortium. On-campus work-study programs are available, as are summer internships. There are 2 national honor societies, a freshman honors program, and 52 departmental honors programs.

Faculty/Classroom: 66% of faculty are male; 34% are female. All teach undergraduates. No introductory courses are taught by graduate students. The average class size in an introductory lecture is 40; in a laboratory is 20; and in a regular course is 20.

Requirements: The SAT or ACT is required. Applicants must have graduated from an accredited secondary school or earned a GED. Specific course requirements vary by curriculum. A portfolio is required for applicants interested in computer art and design and Digital Media and Animation. AP and CLEP credits are accepted. Important factors in the admissions decision are advanced placement or honors courses, extracurricular activities record, and recommendations by school officials.

Procedure: Freshmen are admitted to all sessions. Entrance exams should be taken November 1 (rolling). There is a rolling admissions plan. Application deadlines are open. Application fee is $50. Notifications are sent November 1. Applications are accepted online.

Transfer: 263 transfer students enrolled in 2012-2013. Transfer applicants must have a minimum 2.4 GPA. 30 of 120 credits required for the bachelor's degree must be completed at Alfred State College.

Visiting: There are regularly scheduled orientations for prospective students, including open houses during the fall and spring semesters. All aspects of the campus are open for visitation, and accepted students are invited to participate in an overnight visit. There are guides for informal visits, visitors may sit in on classes, and stay overnight. To schedule a visit, contact the Admissions Office.

Financial Aid: In 2013-2014, 80% of all full-time freshmen received some form of financial aid. 80% of all full-time freshmen and 80% of continuing full-time students received need-based aid. Average annual earnings from campus work are $1000. The FAFSA is required. Check with the school for current application deadlines.

International Students: There are 50 international students enrolled. The school actively recruits these students. They must take the TOEFL.

Graduates: Of the 2012 graduating class, 99% were enrolled in graduate school within 6 months of graduation, and 99% were employed.

Admissions Contact: Deborah Goodrich, Associate Vice President for Enrollment Management. E-Mail: *admissions@alfredstate.edu* Web: *www.alfredstate.edu*

ALFRED UNIVERSITY B-4

Alfred, NY 14802 (607) 871-2115
(800) 541-9229; (607) 871-2198

Full-time: 939 men, 970 women	**Faculty:** 150; III, -$
Part-time: 24 men, 27 women	**Ph.D.s:** 93%
Graduate: 157 men, 314 women	**Student/Faculty:** 12 to 1
Year: semesters, summer session	**Tuition:** $28,774
Application Deadline: February 1	**Room & Board:** $11,618
Freshman Class: 3417 applied, 2385 accepted, 535 enrolled	
SAT CR/M/W: 530/550/510	**ACT:** 24 **VERY COMPETITIVE**

Alfred University, founded in 1836, is composed of the privately endowed College of Liberal Arts and Sciences, College of Professional Studies, School of Business and the New York State College of Ceramics (Inamori School of Engineering and School of Art and Design). Bachelors, masters, certificates of advanced study, and doctoral degrees are awarded as the culmination of Alfred University's academic and professional programs. There are 5 undergraduate schools and 1 graduate school. In addition to regional accreditation, AU has baccalaureate program accreditation with AACSB, ABET, NASAD, and TEAC. The 2 libraries contain 286,995 volumes, 79,704 microform items, and 179,255 audio/video tapes/CDs/DVDs, and subscribe to 93,502 periodicals including electronic. Computerized library services include interlibrary loans, database searching, Internet access, and Wi Fi capability. Special learning facilities include an art gallery, radio station, TV station, John L. Stull Observatory, and a Museum of Ceramic Art, Carillon. The 232-acre campus is in a rural area 70 miles south of Rochester, NY. Including any residence halls, there are 52 buildings.

Student Life: 76% of undergraduates are from New York. Others are from 42 states, 19 foreign countries, and Canada. 66% are White; 12% race unknown. The average age of freshmen is 18; all undergraduates, 20. 26% do not continue beyond their first year; 62% remain to graduate.

Housing: 1469 students can be accommodated in college housing, which includes single-sex and coed dorms and on-campus apartments. In addition, there are honors houses, language houses, special-interest houses, Theme housing. On-campus housing is guaranteed for the freshman year only, is available on a first-come, first-served basis, and is available on a lottery system for upperclassmen. 76% of students live on campus; of those, 90% remain on campus on weekends. All students may keep cars.

Activities: There are no fraternities or sororities. There are 90 groups on campus, including and honors, cultural, art, athletics, band, cheerleading, chorale, chorus, computers, dance, drama, environmental, ethnic, film, gay, honors, international, jazz band, literary magazine, musical theater, newspaper, orchestra, pep band, photography, political, professional, radio and TV, religious, social, social service, student government, and yearbook. Popular campus events include Homecoming Weekend, Family Weekend and Hot Dog Day.

Sports: There are 10 intercollegiate sports for men and 11 for women, and 14 intramural sports for men and 13 for women. Facilities include a multi-purpose field for football, soccer, and lacrosse; an Olympic-size pool; softball field; tennis courts; racquetball and squash courts; a weight room; and dance and exercise studios. Merrill Field seats approximately 5,000; the indoor gym seats approximately 3,500. There is also a fitness center, an equestrian center, many hiking trails, and easy access to cross-country skiing. We are currently building an addition to our gym that will house a four-lane indoor track, basketball courts, and storage and locker facilities.

Disabled Students: 45% of the campus is accessible. Facilities include wheelchair ramps, elevators, special parking, specially equipped restrooms, special class scheduling, lowered drinking fountains.

Services: Counseling and information services are available, as is tutoring in most subjects, depends on tutor availability. Time management, study skills workshops, and a writing center are available. There are also services for students with learning and physical disabilities.

Campus Safety and Security: Measures include emergency notification system and security escort services. There are emergency telephones, lighted pathways/sidewalks, controlled access to dorms/residences, vehicle and foot patrol.

Programs of Study: AU confers B.A., B.F.A. and B.S. degrees. Master's and doctoral degrees are also awarded. Bachelor's degrees are awarded in AGRICULTURE (environmental studies), BIOLOGICAL SCIENCE (biology/biological science), BUSINESS (accounting, business administration and management, and marketing/retailing/merchandising), COMMUNICATIONS AND THE ARTS (art history and appreciation, ceramic art and design, communications, dramatic arts, English, fine arts, glass, Spanish, and theatre arts), COMPUTER AND PHYSICAL SCIENCE (chemistry, geology, mathematics, physics, and science), EDUCATION (art education, athletic training, business education, early childhood education, mathematics education, science education, secondary education, and social studies education), ENGINEERING AND ENVIRONMENTAL DESIGN (ceramic engineering, materials engineering, and mechanical engineering), SOCIAL SCIENCE (criminal justice, crosscultural studies, gerontology, history, interdisciplinary studies, philosophy, political science/government, psychology, and sociology). Engineering is the strongest academically. Art and design, business administration, and mechanical engineering have the largest enrollments.

Required: To satisfy the requirements for a Bachelors Degree a student must: Complete all course requirements, including those required for the major, general education, and the minimum number of credits for the degree sought depending on the school or college of enrollment; Earn a cumulative GPA of at least 2.0; Satisfy the Global Perspective Requirement; Satisfy the Physical Education requirement; Request legal conferral of degree and satisfy financial obligations to the University; Earn at least 45 semester credit hours at AU; and be in residence at AU at least during the final 30 credit hours earned toward the degree.

Special: There are cooperative programs in engineering with Duke and Columbia Universities. AU participates in a cross-registration program with more than 15 area colleges and universities through the Rochester Area Colleges consortium. AU also offers study abroad, Washington and Albany semesters, student-designed majors, and a 4+1 MBA program for students majoring in Liberal Arts & Sciences or Engineering. There are 16 national honor societies, including Phi Beta Kappa.

Faculty/Classroom: 54% of faculty are male; 46% are female. 90% do both. No introductory courses are taught by graduate students. The average class size in an introductory lecture is 30; in a laboratory is 20; and in a regular course is 18.

Admissions: 70% of the 2013-2014 applicants were accepted. The SAT

scores for the 2013-2014 freshman class were: Critical Reading--27% below 500, 51% between 500 and 599, 19% between 600 and 699, and 3% between 700 and 800; Math--20% below 500, 49% between 500 and 599, 27% between 600 and 699, and 4% between 700 and 800; Writing--43% below 500, 40% between 500 and 599, 15% between 600 and 699, and 2% between 700 and 800. The ACT scores were 16% below 21, 28% between 21 and 23, 30% between 24 and 26, 15% between 27 and 28, and 11% above 28. 36% of the current freshmen were in the top fifth of their class; 70% were in the top two fifths. 3 freshmen graduated first in their class.

Requirements: The SAT or ACT is required. A GED is accepted. A minimum of 16 Carnegie units is required, including 4 years of English, 2 to 3 years each of math, history/social studies, and science. Depending on the school/college applied to, the remaining units may be either in a foreign language, the categories listed above, or business, art, or computer science. Official high school transcripts, one letter of recommendation, an essay, and a $50 fee (may be waived by visiting campus or with a NACAC or College Board waiver) is required of all applicants. Applicants to the School of Art & Design must submit a portfolio. Interviews are encouraged. AP credits are accepted. Important factors in the admissions decision are recommendations by school officials, extracurricular activities record, and leadership record.

Procedure: Freshmen are admitted fall and spring. Entrance exams should be taken spring of junior year. There are early decision, deferred admissions, and rolling admissions plans. Early decision applications should be filed by December 1; regular applications, by February 1 for fall entry; and December 1 for spring entry, along with a $50 fee. Notification of early decision is sent December 15; regular decision, on a rolling basis. 45 early decision candidates were accepted for the 2013-2014 class. 91 applicants were on the 2013 waiting list; 11 were admitted. Applications are accepted online.

Transfer: 80 transfer students enrolled in 2012-2013. Transfer applicants must have a GPA of at least 2.5 on a 4.0 scale. They must submit at least 1 letter of recommendation and official high school and college transcripts. Applicants to the School of Art and Design must also submit a portfolio. 45 of 120 credits required for the bachelor's degree must be completed at AU.

Visiting: There are regularly scheduled orientations for prospective students, Agenda is customized per student's needs. There are guides for informal visits, visitors may sit in on classes, and stay overnight. To schedule a visit, contact the Admissions Office.

Financial Aid: In 2013-2014, 88% of all full-time freshmen and 83% of continuing full-time students received some form of financial aid. 82% of all full-time freshmen and 88% of continuing full-time students received need-based aid. The average freshman award was $26,623. Need-based scholarships or need-based grants averaged $20,371; need-based self-help aid (loans and jobs) averaged $6,640; and $4,986 from other forms of aid. 40% of undergraduate students work part-time. Average annual earnings from campus work are $1800. The average financial indebtedness of the 2013 graduate was $33,467. AU is a member of CSS. The FAFSA, the state aid form, and the college's own financial statement, and the business/farm supplement, and the noncustodial parent statement are required. The priority date for freshman financial aid applications for fall entry is March 15. The deadline for filing freshman financial aid applications for fall entry is May 1.

International Students: There are 51 international students enrolled. The school actively recruits these students. They must take the TOEFL with a minimum score of 550 on the paper-based TOEFL (PBT) or 80 on the Internet-based version (iBT). They must also take the SAT or ACT.

Graduates: From July 1, 2012 to June 30, 2013, 356 bachelor's degrees were awarded. The most popular majors were fine arts (31%), engineering (17%), and biology (8%). 80 companies recruited on campus in 2012-2013. In an average class, 44% graduate in 4 years or less, 61% graduate in 5 years or less, and 62% graduate in 6 years or less.

Admissions Contact: Earl E. Pierce, VP for Enrollment Management.
E-Mail: *admissions@alfred.edu* Web: *www.alfred.edu*

BARD COLLEGE — D-4

Annandale-on-Hudson, NY 12504 — **(845) 758-7472; (845) 758-5208**

Full-time: 848 men, 1077 women	**Faculty:** 149; IIB, +$
Part-time: 47 men, 50 women	**Ph.D.s:** 96%
Graduate: 91 men, 165 women	**Student/Faculty:** 10 to 1
Year: 4-1-4	**Tuition:** $46,370
Application Deadline: January 1	**Room & Board:** $13,502

Freshman Class: 5466 applied, 2056 accepted, 489 enrolled
SAT CR/M: 650/620

HIGHLY COMPETITIVE

Bard College, founded in 1860, is an independent liberal arts and sciences institution affiliated historically with the Association of Episcopal Colleges. Discussion-oriented seminars and independent study are encouraged, tutorials are on a one-to-one basis, and most classes are kept small. There is 1 undergraduate school and 13 graduate schools. The library contains 372,669 volumes, 8,002 microform items, 5,337 audio/video tapes/CDs/DVDs, and subscribes to 37,293 periodicals including electronic. Computerized library services include interlibrary loans, database searching, Internet access, and Wi-Fi capability. Special learning facilities include an art gallery, radio station, an ecology field station, the Levy Economics Institute, the Institute for Writing and Thinking, the Institute for Advanced Theology, the Center for Curatorial Studies and Art in Contemporary Culture, and an archeological station. The 600-acre campus is in a rural area 100 miles north of New York City. Including any residence halls, there are 70 buildings.

Student Life: 65% of undergraduates are from out of state, mostly the Middle Atlantic. Students are from 47 states, 65 foreign countries, and Canada. 60% are from public schools. 60% are White; 15% race unknown; 12% Foreign. The average age of freshmen is 18; all undergraduates, 20. 13% do not continue beyond their first year; 74% remain to graduate.

Housing: 1450 students can be accommodated in college housing, which includes single-sex and coed dorms. In addition, there are special-interest houses, A single-sex dorm, suites, and quiet dorms. On-campus housing is guaranteed for the freshman year only and is available on a lottery system for upperclassmen. 73% of students live on campus; of those, 75% remain on campus on weekends. All students may keep cars.

Activities: There are no fraternities or sororities. There are 150 groups on campus, including and Model UN, art, band, Chamber groups, chess, choir, chorus, computers, dance, debate, drama, environmental, ethnic, film, forensics, gay, international, jazz band, literary magazine, musical theater, newspaper, opera, orchestra, photography, political, radio and TV, religious, social, social service, student government, and symphony. Popular campus events include Winter Carnival, Spring Festival and International Students Cultural Show.

Sports: There are 10 intercollegiate sports for men and 8 for women, and 9 intramural sports for men and 9 for women. Facilities include A gym and pool, baseball field, fitness and weight facilities, rugby, soccer and lacrosse fields, squash and tennis courts, cross-country trails, bike paths, and multi-purpose fields for activities such as ultimate frisbee and open recreation.

Disabled Students: 70% of the campus is accessible. Facilities include wheelchair ramps, elevators, special parking, specially equipped restrooms, lowered drinking fountains, and lowered telephones.

Services: Counseling and information services are available, as is tutoring in every subject. There is a reader service for the blind.

Campus Safety and Security: Measures include 24-hour foot and vehicle patrol, emergency notification system, self-defense education, and security escort services. There are shuttle buses, emergency telephones, lighted pathways/sidewalks, volunteer emergency medical technicians on call 24 hours a day, and Bard response to Rape and Associated Violence Education (BRAVE).

Programs of Study: Bard confers B.A., B.S., B.Music, and B.P.S. degrees. Associate, master's, and doctoral degrees are also awarded. Bachelor's degrees are awarded in AGRICULTURE (environmental studies), BIOLOGICAL SCIENCE (biology/biological science), COMMUNICATIONS AND THE ARTS (Arabic, art history and appreciation, Chinese, classical languages, creative writing, dance, dramatic arts, English literature, film arts, French, Germanic languages and literature, Hebrew, Italian, literature, music, photography, Russian, Spanish, studio art, and theatre arts), COMPUTER AND PHYSICAL SCIENCE (chemistry, computer science, mathematics, and physics), SOCIAL SCIENCE (African studies, American studies, anthropology, area studies, Asian/Oriental studies, Celtic studies, classical/ancient civilization, cognitive science, economics, French studies, gender studies, German area studies, history, interdisciplinary studies, international studies, Italian studies, Judaic studies, Latin American studies, medieval studies, Middle Eastern studies, philosophy, political science/government, psychology, religion, Russian and Slavic studies, Sanskrit and Indian studies, science and society, sociology, Spanish studies, theological studies, and Victorian studies). Social studies, visual and performing arts, languages and literatures have the largest enrollments.

Required: All students must complete a 3-week workshop in Language and Thinking (August of first year), a two and a half week Citizen Science program (January of first year); a first-year seminar; and a senior project. A conference in the junior year is required, and through a moderation process in the sophomore year, the student chooses a concentration in an academic department. A distribution of at least 1 course in each of the 9 academic areas is required, with 40 credits outside the division of the student's major and a total of 128 credit hours needed to graduate. "Rethinking Differences," a course fulfilling the diversity requirement, is also required.

Special: Bard offers opportunities for study abroad, internships, Washington and New York semesters, dual majors, student-designed majors, accelerated degree programs, and pass/fail options. A 3-2 engineering degree is available with the Columbia University, Washington University (St. Louis), and Dartmouth College Schools of Engineering. Other 3-2 degrees are available in forestry and environmental studies, social work, architecture, city and regional planning, public health, and business administration. There are also opportunities for independent study, multicultural and ethnic studies, area studies, human rights, and globalization and international affairs.

Faculty/Classroom: 58% of faculty are male; 42% are female. All teach and do research. No introductory courses are taught by graduate students. The average class size in a regular course is 17.

Admissions: 38% of the 2013 2014 applicants were accepted.

Requirements: Bard places strong emphasis on the academic background and intellectual curiosity of applicants, as well as indications of the student's commitment to social and environmental concerns, independent research, volunteer work, and other important extracurricular activities. Students applying for admission are expected to have graduated from an accredited secondary school (the GED is accepted) and must submit written essays with the application. The high school record should include a full complement of college-preparatory courses. Honors and advanced placement courses are also considered. A GPA of 3.0 is required. AP credits are accepted. Important factors in the admissions decision are advanced placement or honors courses, recommendations by school officials, and extracurricular activities record.

Procedure: Freshmen are admitted fall. There are early admissions and deferred admissions plans. Applications should be filed by January 1 for fall entry; November 1 for spring entry, along with a $50 fee. Notifications are sent April 1. 404 applicants were on the 2013 waiting list; 88 were admitted. Applications are accepted online.

Transfer: 61 transfer students enrolled in 2012-2013. Admission requirements are the same as for regular applicants. A minimum GPA of 3.0 and an interview are recommended. High School transcript (when less than 2 years of college-level study completed), transfer questionnaire, and dean's report are required. 64 of 128 credits required for the bachelor's degree must be completed at Bard.

Visiting: There are regularly scheduled orientations for prospective students, Consisting of regularly scheduled daily tours and information sessions. Visitors may sit in on classes. To schedule a visit, contact the Admissions Office.

Financial Aid: In 2013-2014, 70% of all full-time freshmen and 70% of continuing full-time students received some form of financial aid. 68% of all full-time freshmen and 68% of continuing full-time students received need-based aid. The average freshman award was $42,888. Need-based scholarships or need-based grants averaged $33,525; need-based self-help aid (loans and jobs) averaged $6,512; and other non-need-based awards and non-need-based scholarships averaged $21,973. 30% of undergraduate students work part-time. Average annual earnings from campus work are $2000. The average financial indebtedness of the 2013 graduate was $25,644. Bard is a member of CSS. The CSS/Profile, FAFSA, and the state aid form, and Non-custodial profile and/or Business/Farm supplement if applicable are required. The priority date for freshman financial aid applications for fall entry is February 1. The deadline for filing freshman financial aid applications for fall entry is February 15.

International Students: There are 237 international students enrolled. The school actively recruits these students. They must take the TOEFL with a minimum score of 600 on the paper-based TOEFL (PBT).

Graduates: From July 1, 2012 to June 30, 2013, 489 bachelor's degrees were awarded. The most popular majors were social studies (32%), visual and performing arts (31%), and language and literature (20%). In an average class, 60% graduate in 4 years or less, 72% graduate in 5 years or less, and 74% graduate in 6 years or less.

Admissions Contact: Mary Backlund, Director of Admissions. E-Mail: *admission@bard.edu* Web: *www.bard.edu*

BERKELEY COLLEGE OF NEW YORK CITY — D-5

New York, NY 10017 — (212) 986-4343; (800) 446-5400; (212) 697-3371

Full-time: 740 men, 1618 women	**Faculty:** n/av
Part-time: 70 men, 194 women	**Ph.D.s:** n/av
Graduate: n/av	**Student/Faculty:** n/av
Year: trimesters	**Tuition:** $18,300
Application Deadline: open	**Room & Board:** n/app
Freshman Class: n/av	
SAT or ACT: required	

LESS COMPETITIVE

Berkeley College of New York City, founded in 1931, is a private institution offering undergraduate programs in business. The figures in the above capsule and in this profile are approximate. The library contains 11,000 volumes, and subscribes to 130 periodicals including electronic. Computerized library services include interlibrary loans and database searching. The campus is in an urban area New York City, NY. Including any residence halls, there are 2 buildings.

Student Life: 76% of undergraduates are from New York. Others are from states. 24% are Hispanic; 23% African American; 18% Foreign; 15% White. The average age of freshmen is 20; all undergraduates, 24.

Housing: All students commute.

Activities: There are no fraternities or sororities.

Services: Counseling and information services are available, as is tutoring in most subjects. There is remedial math, reading, and writing.

Programs of Study: Associate degrees are also awarded. Bachelor's degrees are awarded in BUSINESS (accounting, business administration and management, international business management, and marketing/retailing/merchandising).

Faculty/Classroom: All teach undergraduates. No introductory courses are taught by graduate students.

Requirements: The SAT or ACT is required. Graduation from an accredited high school or the GED, and an entrance exam or SAT or ACT scores are basic requirements for admission. A personal interview is strongly recommended. AP and CLEP credits are accepted.

Procedure: Freshmen are admitted to all sessions. Entrance exams should be taken any time. There are deferred admissions and rolling admissions plans. Application deadlines are open. Application fee is $50. Notification is sent on a rolling basis. Applications are accepted online.

Transfer: A transcript from each college or university attended must be submitted to receive credit. 60 of 180 credits required for the bachelor's degree.

Visiting: There are guides for informal visits.

Financial Aid: In 2013-2014, 90% of all full-time, freshmen students received some form of financial aid. The FAFSA the college's own financial statement, and state income tax form are required. Check with the school for current application deadlines.

International Students: There are 130 international students enrolled. The school actively recruits these students. They must take the TOEFL.

Graduates: From July 1, 2012 to June 30, 2013, 311 bachelor's degrees were awarded. Of the 2012 graduating class, 94% were employed within 6 months of graduation.

Admissions Contact: Admissions Officer E-Mail: *info@berkeleycollege.edu* Web: *www.berkeleycollege.edu*

BERKELEY COLLEGE/WESTCHESTER CAMPUS — D-5

White Plains, NY 10601 — (914) 694-1122; (800) 446-5400; (914) 328-9469

Full-time: 170 men, 410 women	**Faculty:** n/av
Part-time: 15 men, 45 women	**Ph.D.s:** n/av
Graduate: n/av	**Student/Faculty:** n/av
Year: semesters	**Tuition:** $18,800
Application Deadline: open	**Room & Board:** $10,300
Freshman Class: n/av	

LESS COMPETITIVE

Berkeley College, established in 1945, is a private institution with 5 campuses in New York and New Jersey. Its programs are designed to prepare students for careers in business by providing an education that balances academic studies, professional training, and hands-on experience. The information in this profile refers to the Westchester campus. The figures in the above capsule and in this profile are approximate. The library contains 9,500 volumes and 800 audio/video tapes/CDs/DVDs, and subscribes to 80 periodicals including electronic. Computerized library services include interlibrary loans and database searching. Special learning facilities include a learning resource center. The 10-acre campus is in a suburban area. Including any residence halls, there are 3 buildings.

Student Life: 80% of undergraduates are from New York. Others are from 8 states, and 14 foreign countries. 66% are white; 16% African American; 11% Hispanic. The average age of freshmen is 19; all undergraduates, 20.

Housing: 96 students can be accommodated in college housing, which includes coed dorms. Priority is given to out-of-town students. 86% of students commute. Alcohol is not permitted. All students may keep cars.

Activities: There are no fraternities or sororities. There are 6 groups on campus, including international, newspaper, professional, social, social service, and student government. Popular campus events include Multicultural Month and Commuter Appreciation Day.

Sports: There is no sports program at Berkeley. Students have access to the sports and exercise facilities at nearby Manhattanville College.

Disabled Students: Facilities include wheelchair ramps, elevators, and special parking.

Services: Counseling and information services are available, as is tutoring in every subject. There is remedial math, reading, and writing.

Campus Safety and Security: There are lighted pathways/sidewalks and night patrols by trained security personnel.

Programs of Study: Berkeley confers B.B.A. degrees. Associates degrees are also awarded. Bachelor's degrees are awarded in BUSINESS (accounting, business administration and management, international business management, and marketing/retailing/merchandising).

Faculty/Classroom: No introductory courses are taught by graduate students.

Requirements: Graduation from an accredited high school or the equivalent (GED) and an entrance exam or the SAT or ACT scores are basic requirements for admission. A personal interview is strongly recommended. AP and CLEP credits are accepted.

Procedure: Freshmen are admitted to all sessions. Entrance exams

should be taken as soon as the application is submitted, if possible. There are deferred admissions and rolling admissions plans. Application deadlines are open. The fall 2011 application fee was $35. Notification is sent on a rolling basis. Applications are accepted online.

Transfer: Applicants must submit a transcript from each college attended and a high school transcript or equivalent (GED). 60 of 180 credits required for the bachelor's degree must be completed at Berkeley.

Visiting: There are guides for informal visits.

Financial Aid: The FAFSA, the college's own financial statement, and state income tax return are required. Check with the school for current application deadlines.

International Students: The school actively recruits these students. They must take the TOEFL.

Admissions Contact: Admissions Officer E-Mail: *info@berkeleycollege.edu* Web: *www.berkeleycollege.edu*

BINGHAMTON UNIVERSITY / THE STATE UNIVERSITY OF NEW YORK C-4

Binghamton, NY 13902 (607) 777-2171; (607) 777-4445

Full-time: 6687 men, 5872 women	**Faculty:** 641; I, -$
Part-time: 239 men, 199 women	**Ph.D.s:** 94%
Graduate: 1548 men, 1532 women	**Student/Faculty:** 20 to 1
Year: semesters, summer session	**Tuition:** $8144 ($18,464)
Application Deadline: January 15	**Room & Board:** $12,688
Freshman Class: 29067 applied, 12134 accepted, 2633 enrolled	
SAT CR/M/W: 630/670/620	**ACT:** 29 **HIGHLY COMPETITIVE+**

Part of the State University of New York (SUNY) system, Binghamton University was founded in 1946. The university offers programs in arts and sciences, education, nursing, business administration, engineering and applied science, and community and public affairs. There are 5 undergraduate schools and 2 graduate schools. In addition to regional accreditation, Binghamton University has baccalaureate program accreditation with AACSB, ABET, CSWE, NASM, and TEAC. The 3 libraries contain 2.5 million volumes, 1.9 million microform items, and 126,483 audio/video tapes/CDs/DVDs, and subscribe to 87,696 periodicals including electronic. Computerized library services include interlibrary loans, database searching, Internet access, and Wi-Fi capability. Special learning facilities include an art gallery, radio station, TV station, theaters, art/dance studios, sculpture foundry, art museum, nature preserve, teaching greenhouse, information commons/workstations, public archaeology facility, child development institute, GIS core facility, biotechnology start-up suites, innovative technologies complex, analytical diagnostics laboratory, electron microscopy laboratory, innovative practice center simulation lab, collaboratory, and centers for performing arts, learning and teaching, organized research, integrated electronics engineering, advanced microelectronics manufacturing and autonomous solar power. The 930-acre campus is in a suburban area 1 mile west of Binghamton. Including any residence halls, there are 102 buildings.

Student Life: 89% of undergraduates are from New York. Others are from 48 states, 117 foreign countries, and Canada. 88% are from public schools. 54% are White; 14% Asian American; 11% Foreign. The average age of freshmen is 18; all undergraduates, 20. 9% do not continue beyond their first year; 81% remain to graduate.

Housing: 7467 students can be accommodated in college housing, which includes coed dorms, on-campus apartments, and off-campus apartments. In addition, there are special-interest houses, chemical- and smoke-free housing, and living learning communities. On-campus housing is guaranteed for the freshman year only, is available on a first-come, first-served basis, and is available on a lottery system for upperclassmen. 59% of students live on campus; of those, 95% remain on campus on weekends. Upperclassmen may keep cars.

Activities: 10% of men belong to 34 national fraternities; 10% of women belong to 18 national sororities. There are 363 groups on campus, including club sports/intramurals, special interest groups, art, band, cheerleading, chess, choir, chorale, chorus, communications, computers, cultural, dance, debate, drama, environmental, ethnic, film, gay, honors, international, jazz band, literary magazine, musical theater, newspaper, opera, orchestra, pep band, photography, political, professional, radio and TV, religious, social, social service, student government, symphony, and yearbook. Popular campus events include Spring Fling, University Fest, China Night, Frost Fest, Welcome Weekend, Shabbat 1500 Dinner, Homecoming, Family Weekend, basketball/soccer/lacrosse games, concerts and stand-up comedian performances.

Sports: There are 11 intercollegiate sports for men and 10 for women, and 10 intramural sports for men and 10 for women. Facilities include a 5,000-seat events center with basketball and tennis courts and a 200-meter track. 2 additional gyms are equipped with swimming pools, fitness center, all-purpose courts for basketball, volleyball, and other activities, and racquetball and squash courts, dance and karate studios. The campus has a 2,500-seat soccer and lacrosse complex and separate facilities for baseball, softball, track and field, tennis, and cross-country. The campus also features a 190-acre nature preserve.

Disabled Students: 95% of the campus is accessible. Facilities include wheelchair ramps, elevators, special parking, specially equipped restrooms, lowered drinking fountains, lowered telephones, special housing, a comprehensive array of services for students with physical, learning, or other disabilities.

Services: Counseling and information services are available, as is tutoring in most subjects. There is a reader service for the blind. Walk-in and by appointment tutoring available 7 days per week

Campus Safety and Security: Measures include 24-hour foot and vehicle patrol, emergency notification system, self-defense education, and security escort services. There are shuttle buses, emergency telephones, lighted pathways/sidewalks, controlled access to dorms/residences, police officers, monitored entrance to campus with proper identification between midnight and 5 a.m., and formal personal safety programs.

Programs of Study: Binghamton University confers B.A., B.S. and Mus.B. degrees. Master's and doctoral degrees are also awarded. Bachelor's degrees are awarded in AGRICULTURE (environmental studies), BIOLOGICAL SCIENCE (biochemistry, biology/biological science, cell biology, environmental earth resources, evolutionary biology, molecular biology, and neurosciences), BUSINESS (accounting, business administration and management, entrepreneurial studies, finance, management information systems, management science, marketing management, and supply chain management), COMMUNICATIONS AND THE ARTS (Arabic, art history, art, classics, comparative literature, creative writing, dance, dramatic arts, English, English literature, film arts, French, German, Germanic languages and literature, Hebrew, Italian, Korean, Latin, linguistics, literature, music, music performance, Spanish, speech/debate/rhetoric, studio art, theatre arts, theater design, and visual and performing arts), COMPUTER AND PHYSICAL SCIENCE (actuarial mathematics, chemistry, computer science, environmental chemistry, environmental geology, geology, information sciences and systems, mathematics, and physics), ENGINEERING AND ENVIRONMENTAL DESIGN (bioengineering, computer engineering, electrical/electronics engineering, engineering, environmental design, environmental science, industrial engineering, mechanical engineering, and systems engineering), HEALTH PROFESSIONS (nursing and Pre-Health Studies), SOCIAL SCIENCE (africana studies, anthropology, Asian/American studies, Caribbean studies, Chinese Studies, classical/ancient civilization, East Asian studies, economics, geography, history, human development, interdisciplinary studies, international studies, Japanese studies, Judaic studies, Latin American studies, medieval studies, philosophy, political science/government, psychobiology, psychology, sociology, and South Asian studies). Business administration, political science, and biology are the strongest academically. Engineering, business administration, and psychology have the largest enrollments.

Required: To graduate, all students must complete 124 to 130 credit hours, with 36 to 72 in the major and a minimum GPA of 2.0. General education requirements include courses in language and communication, global vision, science, aesthetic perspective, foreign language, humanities, math, social science, physical activity/wellness, and pluralism. Other requirements vary by school.

Special: The university offers a number of accelerated programs (3-2 and 4-1) to earn bachelors and masters degrees; 600 study abroad opportunities in over 100 countries; internship opportunities in New York City and other major cities; dual and interdisciplinary majors such as philosophy, politics, and law; pre-health programs in medicine - dentistry, optometry, veterinary medicine, podiatry, nutrition, physical and occupational therapy, and chiropractic. Early assurance programs guarantee graduate admission at partner SUNY schools (Buffalo, Upstate Medical-Syracuse, and College of Optometry). There are 26 national honor societies, including Phi Beta Kappa, a freshman honors program, and 34 departmental honors programs.

Faculty/Classroom: 59% of faculty are male; 41% are female. All teach and do research. Graduate students teach 6% of introductory courses. The average class size in an introductory lecture is 58; in a laboratory is 20; and in a regular course is 35.

Admissions: 42% of the 2013-2014 applicants were accepted. The SAT scores for the 2013-2014 freshman class were: Critical Reading--5% below 500, 25% between 500 and 599, 55% between 600 and 699, and 15% between 700 and 800; Math--1% below 500, 13% between 500 and 599, 54% between 600 and 699, and 32% between 700 and 800; Writing--3% below 500, 21% between 500 and 599, 56% between 600 and 699, and 20% between 700 and 800. The ACT scores were 1% below 21, 5% between 21 and 23, 14% between 24 and 26, 25% between 27 and 28, and 55% above 28. 77% of the current freshmen were in the top fifth of their class; 93% were in the top two fifths.

Requirements: The SAT or ACT is required. The ACT Optional Writing test is also required. Applicants must be graduates of an accredited secondary school or have a GED certificate and complete 16 academic credits. These include 4 units of English, 3 units of 1 foreign language or 2 units each of 2 foreign languages, 3 of math, and 2 each of science and social studies. Students may submit slides of artwork, request an audition for music, prepare a videotape for dance or theater, or share athletic achievements. An essay is required. Binghamton University requires that each enrolling student fulfills the graduation requirements at their high school. AP and CLEP credits are accepted.

Procedure: Freshmen are admitted fall and spring. Entrance exams should be taken in the spring of the junior year or the fall of the senior year. There are early admissions, deferred admissions, and rolling admissions plans. Application deadlines are open. Application fee is $50. Notification is sent on a rolling basis. 2474 applicants were on the 2013 waiting list; 218 were admitted. Applications are accepted online.

Transfer: 1452 transfer students enrolled in 2012-2013. Applicants must submit college transcripts; students who wish to transfer after their first year of college must also submit their high school transcripts. 44 of 124 credits required for the bachelor's degree must be completed at Binghamton University.

Visiting: There are regularly scheduled orientations for prospective students, including an information session and a student-led tour of campus. To schedule a visit, contact the Office of Undergraduate Admissions.

Financial Aid: In 2013-2014, 82% of all full-time freshmen and 67% of continuing full-time students received some form of financial aid. 62% of all full-time freshmen and 56% of continuing full-time students received need-based aid. The average freshman award was $12,909. Need-based scholarships or need-based grants averaged $4,086; need-based self-help aid (loans and jobs) averaged $2,633; non-need-based athletic scholarships averaged $532; and other non-need-based awards and non-need-based scholarships averaged $7,221. 15% of undergraduate students work part-time. Average annual earnings from campus work are $1334. The average financial indebtedness of the 2013 graduate was $23,912. The FAFSA and the state aid form are required. The priority date for freshman financial aid applications for fall entry is February 1.

International Students: There are 1242 international students enrolled. The school actively recruits these students. They must take the TOEFL with a minimum score of 560 on the paper-based TOEFL (PBT) or 83 on the Internet-based version (iBT), If the student attends a high school where the primary language of instruction is English, SAT/ACT test required. The TOEFL replaces the SAT or ACT for nonnative speakers of English.

Graduates: From July 1, 2012 to June 30, 2013, 2915 bachelor's degrees were awarded. The most popular majors were management (12%), engineering (10%), and psychology (10%). 147 companies recruited on campus in 2012-2013. In an average class, 5% graduate in 3 years or less, 69% graduate in 4 years or less, 79% graduate in 5 years or less, and 81% graduate in 6 years or less. Of the 2012 graduating class, 35% were enrolled in graduate school within 6 months of graduation.

Admissions Contact: Randall Edouard, Asst Provost for Undergraduate Admission. E-Mail: *admit@binghamton.edu* Web: *www.binghamton.edu/admissions*

BORICUA COLLEGE D-5

New York, NY 10032 (212) 694-1000 or (718) 782-2200 (212) 694-1015 or (718) 782-2050

Full-time: 260 men, 910 women	**Faculty:** n/av
Part-time: n/av	**Ph.D.s:** n/av
Graduate: n/av	**Student/Faculty:** n/av
Year: 4-1-4, summer session	**Tuition:** $9100
Application Deadline:	**Room & Board:** n/app
Freshman Class: n/av	
	COMPETITIVE

Boricua College, founded in 1974, is a private college for bilingual students, designed to meet the needs of a Spanish-speaking population. There are 4 undergraduate schools and 2 graduate schools. The 4 libraries contain 128,727 volumes, and 3,000 audio/video tapes/CDs/DVDs, and subscribe to 227 periodicals including electronic. Computerized library services include database searching, Internet access, and Wi-Fi capability. Special learning facilities include an art gallery. The campus is in an urban area in the Bronx, Manhattan, and Brooklyn. Including any residence halls, there are 4 buildings.

Student Life: 100% of undergraduates are from New York. Others are from 1 states. 70% are from public schools. 85% are Hispanic. 85% are Catholic. The average age of freshmen is 29; all undergraduates, 32. 12% do not continue beyond their first year; 80% remain to graduate.

Housing: Alcohol is not permitted. No one may keep cars.

Activities: There are no fraternities or sororities. There are 5 groups on campus, including art, chorus, drama, newspaper, and student government. Popular campus events include Cultural Programs, Puerto Rican Discovery Day, Christmas and spring concerts with Chorus and Orchestra.

Sports: Facilities include a gym.

Disabled Students: Facilities include elevators and specially equipped restrooms.

Services: Counseling and information services are available, as is tutoring in most subjects.

Campus Safety and Security: There are shuttle buses, emergency telephones, and lighted pathways/sidewalks.

Programs of Study: Boricua confers B.A. degrees. Associate degrees are also awarded. Bachelor's degrees are awarded in BUSINESS (business administration and management), EDUCATION (elementary education), SOCIAL SCIENCE (human services and liberal arts/general studies). Applied science paralegal studies is the strongest academically. Human services has the largest enrollment.

Faculty/Classroom: No introductory courses are taught by graduate students.

Requirements: Boricua administers its own tests to prospective students, although either the SAT or ACT is accepted. Applicants must be graduates of an accredited secondary school or have a GED. 2 letters of recommendation and an admissions interview are required. Applicants must demonstrate a working knowledge of English and Spanish to a faculty panel. CLEP credits are accepted. Important factors in the admissions decision are leadership record, personality/intangible qualities, and recommendations by school officials.

Procedure: Freshmen are admitted fall, spring, and summer. Entrance exams should be taken when called by the admissions staff. There are early decision and rolling admissions plans. Application deadlines are open. Application fee is $30.

Transfer: Applicants with associate degrees may transfer up to 60 credits. All college credits passed with grade C and above are accepted. 80 of 124 credits required for the bachelor's degree must be completed at Boricua.

Visiting: There are regularly scheduled orientations for prospective students, Letters are sent to prospective students advising them of scheduled orientations. To schedule a visit, contact Abraham Cruzat or Miriam Preff-erat.

Financial Aid: In 2013-2014, 100% of all full-time freshmen and 100% of continuing full-time students received some form of financial aid. 100% of all full-time freshmen and 100% of continuing full-time students received need-based aid. The average freshman award was $100. Boricua is a member of CSS. The FAFSA and income tax forms are required. Check with the school for current application deadlines.

Graduates: From July 1, 2012 to June 30, 2013, 90 bachelor's degrees were awarded. The most popular majors were human services, early childhood education, and business administration. In an average class, 65% graduate in 4 years or less and 35% graduate in 5 years or less.

Admissions Contact: Abraham Cruz, Director of Student Services. E-Mail: *mpfeffer@boricuacolleg* Web: *www.boricuacollege.edu*

CANISIUS COLLEGE A-3

Buffalo, NY 14208 (716) 888-2200 (800) 843-1517; (716) 888-3230

Full-time: 1328 men, 1497 women	**Faculty:** 210; IIA, av$
Part-time: 205 men, 54 women	**Ph.D.s:** 97%
Graduate: 545 men, 908 women	**Student/Faculty:** 12 to 1
Year: semesters, summer session	**Tuition:** $33,332
Application Deadline: March 1	**Room & Board:** $12,270
Freshman Class: 4322 applied, 3134 accepted, 682 enrolled	
SAT CR/M: 520/500	**ACT:** 24 **VERY COMPETITIVE**

Canisius College, founded in 1870, is a private Roman Catholic college in the Jesuit tradition. It offers undergraduate programs in the liberal arts and sciences, business, education, and human services. There are 3 undergraduate schools and 3 graduate schools. In addition to regional accreditation, Canisius has baccalaureate program accreditation with AACSB, CAHEA, and NCATE. The library contains 464,755 volumes, 599,947 microform items, and 14,762 audio/video tapes/CDs/DVDs, and subscribes to 52,472 periodicals including electronic. Computerized library services include interlibrary loans, database searching, Internet access, and Wi-Fi capability. Special learning facilities include an art gallery, radio station, TV station, a television studio, foreign language lab, 85+ media-assisted classrooms, digital media lab, and musical instrument digital interface classroom. The 72-acre campus is in an urban area in Buffalo NY. Including any residence halls, there are 51 buildings.

Student Life: 92% of undergraduates are from New York. Others are from 29 states, 18 foreign countries, and Canada. 70% are from public schools. 73% are White. The average age of freshmen is 18; all undergraduates, 20. 20% do not continue beyond their first year; 68% remain to graduate.

Housing: 1422 students can be accommodated in college housing, which includes single-sex and coed dorms, on-campus apartments, and off-campus apartments. In addition, there are honors houses, special-interest houses, an intercultural hall, and townhouses plus an Honor's Dorm. On-campus housing is guaranteed for all 4 years, is available on a first-come, first-served basis, and is available on a lottery system for upperclassmen. 52% of students commute. All students may keep cars.

Activities: 1% of men belong to 1 national fraternity; 1% of women belong to 1 national sorority. There are 140 groups on campus, including art, band, cheerleading, chess, choir, chorale, computers, dance, drama, drill team, environmental, ethnic, gay, honors, international, jazz band, literary magazine, musical theater, newspaper, orchestra, pep band, political, professional, radio and TV, religious, social, social service, student government, and yearbook. Popular campus events include Fall Semiformal, International Fest, and Canisius Concert Series.

Sports: There are 8 intercollegiate sports for men and 9 for women, and 12 intramural sports for men and 12 for women. Facilities include an 1800-seat athletic center with a 25-yard pool, training rooms, a 1000-seat sports complex with Astroturf playing fields, a rifle range, and a mirrored dance studio.

Disabled Students: 90% of the campus is accessible. Facilities include wheelchair ramps, elevators, special parking, specially equipped restrooms, special class scheduling, lowered drinking fountains, lowered telephones. automatic doors, TDD, a shuttle service for students with disabilities, distraction-free testing spaces, and adjustable classroom desks.

Services: Counseling and information services are available, as is tutoring in every subject. There is a reader service for the blind, and remedial math, reading, and writing.

Campus Safety and Security: Measures include 24-hour foot and vehicle patrol, emergency notification system, self-defense education, and security escort services. There are shuttle buses, emergency telephones, lighted pathways/sidewalks, controlled access to dorms/residences, a crime prevention officer, bicycle patrols, and crime prevention programs. Also blue light emergency stations around campus.

Programs of Study: Canisius confers B.A., B.S., B.A.Ed. and B.S.Ed. degrees. Master's degrees are also awarded. Bachelor's degrees are awarded in AGRICULTURE (environmental studies), BIOLOGICAL SCIENCE (biochemistry, bioinformatics, biology/biological science, cell biology, neurosciences, and zoology), BUSINESS (accounting, banking and finance, business administration and management, business communications, business economics, entrepreneurial studies, fashion merchandising, finance, international business management, management information systems, management science, marketing management, marketing/retailing/merchandising, operations research, and sports management), COMMUNICATIONS AND THE ARTS (art history, classical languages, communications, creative writing, digital communications, English, fine arts, French, German, journalism, media arts, modern language, music, music performance, Spanish, speech/debate/rhetoric, and theatre arts), COMPUTER AND PHYSICAL SCIENCE (chemistry, computer science, information sciences and systems, mathematics, and physics), EDUCATION (athletic training, business education, (Education) Childhood Education, early childhood education, education, education administration, education of the deaf and hearing impaired, education of the exceptional child, elementary education, English education, foreign languages education, mathematics education, middle school education, physical education, science education, social studies education, special education, and teaching English as a second/foreign language (TESOL/TEFOL)), ENGINEERING AND ENVIRONMENTAL DESIGN (computational sciences, environmental science, and preengineering), HEALTH PROFESSIONS (clinical science, exercise science, medical laboratory technology, predentistry, premedicine, prepharmacy, preveterinary science, and sports medicine), SOCIAL SCIENCE (anthropology, biblical studies, cognitive science, criminal justice, European studies, gerontology, history, humanities and social science, international relations, Latin American studies, liberal arts/general studies, philosophy, prelaw, psychology, social science, sociology, urban studies, and women's studies). Accounting, biology, and finance are the strongest academically. Psychology, business administration/management, and communication studies have the largest enrollments.

Required: Students take 12 required courses and complete 6 knowledge and skills requirement areas to satisfy their requirements. In addition, students must take 10 3-credit courses in the major. A minimum of 120 credit hours and a GPA of 2.0 are required for graduation.

Special: Canisius offers internships, credit by exam, pass/fail options, dual majors, a Washington semester, work-study programs, and study abroad in over a dozen countries. Cooperative programs are available with the Fashion Institute of Technology in New York City. Cross-registration is permitted with the schools in the Western New York Consortium of Higher Education. Canisius also offers early assurance and joint degree programs, with SUNY health professions schools in Buffalo and Syracuse, and a 3-2 MBA. There are 16 national honor societies, a freshman honors program, and 5 departmental honors programs.

Faculty/Classroom: 55% of faculty are male; 45% are female. All teach and do research. No introductory courses are taught by graduate students. The average class size in an introductory lecture is 23; in a laboratory is 18; and in a regular course is 20.

Admissions: 73% of the 2013-2014 applicants were accepted. The SAT scores for the 2013-2014 freshman class were: Critical Reading--40% below 500, 40% between 500 and 599, 17% between 600 and 699, and 3% between 700 and 800; Math--35% below 500, 38% between 500 and 599, 23% between 600 and 699, and 4% between 700 and 800. The ACT scores were 21% below 21, 28% between 21 and 23, 23% between 24 and 26, 14% between 27 and 28, and 14% above 28. 39% of the current freshmen were in the top fifth of their class; 68% were in the top two fifths. 7 freshmen graduated first in their class.

Requirements: The SAT or ACT is required. All students must submit official high school transcript (or GED) and SAT or ACT results. College preparatory course work should include 4 units each of English and social science, 3 units each of math, science, and foreign language. Students with a B+ average and a satisfactory SAT score are most competitive. An essay and an interview are recommended. A GPA of 2.0 is required. AP and CLEP credits are accepted. Important factors in the admissions decision are leadership record, recommendations by school officials, and advanced placement or honors courses.

Procedure: Freshmen are admitted fall, spring, and summer. Entrance exams should be taken during the junior or senior year. There are deferred admissions and rolling admissions plans. Applications should be filed by March 1 for fall entry, along with a $40 fee. Notification is sent on a rolling basis. Applications are accepted online.

Transfer: 119 transfer students enrolled in 2012-2013. Applicants must present a minimum GPA of 2.0 and a Transfer Recommendation Form. 30 of 120 credits required for the bachelor's degree must be completed at Canisius.

Visiting: There are regularly scheduled orientations for prospective students, including an admissions interview or group session, campus tour, and financial aid appointment by request. Also available are summer visitations for families, selected Saturday visits, multiple Fall Open Houses and an Open House in the Spring, a Financial Aid Workshop Workshop in January, and overnights for admitted students. There are guides for informal visits and visitors may sit in on classes. To schedule a visit, contact the Admissions Office.

Financial Aid: In 2013-2014, 98% of all full-time freshmen and 97% of continuing full-time students received some form of financial aid. 86% of all full-time freshmen and 79% of continuing full-time students received need-based aid. The average freshman award was $31,604. Need-based scholarships or need-based grants averaged $10,219 ($42,332 maximum); need-based self-help aid (loans and jobs) averaged $4,888 ($7,800 maximum); non-need-based athletic scholarships averaged $17,946 ($47,900 maximum); and other non-need-based awards and non-need-based scholarships averaged $15,391 ($45,907 maximum). 19% of undergraduate students work part-time. Average annual earnings from campus work are $1662. The average financial indebtedness of the 2013 graduate was $37,903. Canisius is a member of CSS. The FAFSA is required. The priority date for freshman financial aid applications for fall entry is February 15.

International Students: There are 131 international students enrolled. The school actively recruits these students. They must take the TOEFL with a minimum score of 500 on the paper-based TOEFL (PBT) or 61 on the Internet-based version (iBT). IELTS or STEPs are also acceptable. They must also take the SAT or ACT.

Graduates: From July 1, 2012 to June 30, 2013, 682 bachelor's degrees were awarded. The most popular majors were business/marketing (27%), education (14%), and biological/life sciences (12%). 30 companies recruited on campus in 2012-2013. In an average class, 58% graduate in 4 years or less, 67% graduate in 5 years or less, and 68% graduate in 6 years or less.

Admissions Contact: Mollie Ballaro, Dean of Admissions. E-Mail: *admissions@canisius.edu* Web: *www.canisius.edu*

CAZENOVIA COLLEGE — C-3

Cazenovia, NY 13035 — (315) 655-7208; (800) 654-3210; (315) 655-2190

Full-time: 250 men, 700 women	**Faculty:** n/av; IIB,--$
Part-time: 35 men, 120 women	**Ph.D.s:** n/av
Graduate: n/av	**Student/Faculty:** n/av
Year: semesters, summer session	**Tuition:** $22,500
Application Deadline: open	**Room & Board:** $9800
Freshman Class: n/av	
SAT or ACT: recommended	

COMPETITIVE

Cazenovia College, founded in 1824, is a private institution offering degree programs in liberal arts and preprofessional studies. The figures in the above capsule and in this profile are approximate. The library contains 83,340 volumes, 14,727 microform items, and 4,160 audio/video tapes/CDs/DVDs, and subscribes to 61,000 periodicals including electronic. Computerized library services include interlibrary loans, database searching, Internet access, and laptop Internet portals. Special learning facilities include a learning resource center, art gallery, radio station, and a nearby campus farm with equine center. The 40-acre campus is in a small town 18 miles southeast of Syracuse. Including any residence halls, there are 26 buildings.

Student Life: 80% of undergraduates are from New York. Others are from 24 states, 4 foreign countries, and Canada. 90% are from public schools. 86% are white; 54% African American. The average age of freshmen is 18.

Housing: 817 students can be accommodated in college housing, which includes single-sex and coed dorms, on-campus apartments, and off-campus apartments. In addition, there are all-female residence hall, and

upperclass-only housing. 90% of students live on campus. Upperclassmen may keep cars.
Activities: There are no fraternities or sororities. There are 52 groups on campus, including art, band, cheerleading, choir, chorale, computers, debate, drama, environmental, ethnic, gay, honors, literary magazine, musical theater, newspaper, political, professional, religious, social, social service, student government, and yearbook.
Sports: There are 10 intercollegiate sports for men and 10 for women, and 9 intramural sports for men and 9 for women. Facilities include an athletic center with a pool, 2 gyms, a fitness center, outdoor tennis courts, and athletic fields.
Disabled Students: 86% of the campus is accessible. Facilities include wheelchair ramps, elevators, special parking, specially equipped restrooms, special class scheduling, lowered telephones, and special housing.
Services: Counseling and information services are available, as is tutoring in most subjects. There is a reader service for the blind, and remedial math, reading, and writing.
Campus Safety and Security: Measures include 24-hour foot and vehicle patrol, emergency notification system, and security escort services. There are emergency telephones, lighted pathways/sidewalks, and controlled access to dorms/residences.
Programs of Study: Cazenovia confers B.A., B.S., B.F.A., and B.P.S. degrees. Associates degrees are also awarded. Bachelor's degrees are awarded in AGRICULTURE (environmental studies), BUSINESS (business administration and management and management science), COMMUNICATIONS AND THE ARTS (communications, English, studio art, and visual design), EDUCATION (early childhood education and elementary education), ENGINEERING AND ENVIRONMENTAL DESIGN (commercial art and interior design), SOCIAL SCIENCE (criminology, fashion design and technology, human services, liberal arts/general studies, psychology, and social science). Interior design and equine management are the strongest academically. Management has the largest enrollment.
Required: A total of 120 semester credits and a GPA of 2.0 are required for the bachelor's degree. Students must take courses in speech, academic writing, diversity and social consciousness, science or math, visual literacy, communications, ethics, cultural literacy, and research methods. They must also demonstrate math proficiency and complete a senior capstone course.
Special: Cazenovia offers internships, a Washington semester, work-study, B.A.-B.S. degrees in liberal studies and liberal and professional studies. There is a study-abroad program at Canterbury Christ Church University in the United Kingdom. There are 3 national honor societies, a freshman honors program, and 2 departmental honors programs.
Faculty/Classroom: 40% of faculty are male; 60% are female. All teach undergraduates, and 1% do research. No introductory courses are taught by graduate students. The average class size in an introductory lecture is 20; in a laboratory is 15; and in a regular course is 16.
Requirements: The SAT or ACT is recommended. Applicants should be graduates of an accredited secondary school or the equivalent. A recommendation from a guidance counselor or teacher is required. AP and CLEP credits are accepted. Important factors in the admissions decision are advanced placement or honors courses and leadership record.
Procedure: Freshmen are admitted fall and spring. Entrance exams should be taken by the fall of the senior year. There are deferred admissions and rolling admissions plans. Application deadlines are open. Application fee is $30. Applications are accepted online. A waiting list is maintained.
Transfer: 66 transfer students enrolled in a recent year. Applicants must present at least 12 college credits, with a minimum GPA of 2.0, and official transcripts from previous colleges attended. Students with fewer than 24 credits must also submit a high school transcript. 30 of 120 credits required for the bachelor's degree must be completed at Cazenovia.
Visiting: There are regularly scheduled orientations for prospective students, consisting of a welcome by the president and deans, financial aid sessions, placement testing, academic advising, and registration. There are guides for informal visits; visitors may sit in on classes and stay overnight. To schedule a visit, contact the Admissions and Financial Aid Office.
Financial Aid: Cazenovia is a member of CSS. The FAFSA and Express TAP are required. Check with the school for current application deadlines.
International Students: There were 4 international students enrolled in a recent year. The school actively recruits these students. They must take the TOEFL.
Graduates: In a recent year, 163 bachelor's degrees were awarded. The most popular majors were management (39%), human services (25%), and visual communications (19%).
Admissions Contact: Robert A. Croot, Dean for Admissions and Financial Aid. E-Mail: *admission@cazcollege.edu* Web: *www.cazenovia.edu*

CITY UNIVERSITY OF NEW YORK

The City University of New York, established in 1847, is a public system in New York. It is governed by a board of trustees, whose chief administrator is the chancellor. The primary goal of the system is to maintain and expand its commitment to academic excellence and to provide equal access and opportunity. The main priorities are providing access for all students who seek to enroll, insuring student success, and enhancing instructional and research excellence. The total student enrollment for all 4 campuses is usually 269,144 with 7313 faculty members. Altogether there are 573 baccalaureate, 451 master's and 65 doctoral programs offered in the City University of New York System. Profiles of the 4-year campuses are included in this section.

CITY UNIVERSITY OF NEW YORK/BARUCH COLLEGE D-5

New York, NY 10010 **(646) 312-1400; (646) 312-1361**

Full-time: 5530 men, 4866 women	**Faculty:** n/av
Part-time: 1752 men, 1934 women	**Ph.D.s:** 59%
Graduate: 1632 men, 1791 women	**Student/Faculty:** 20 to 1
Year: semesters, summer session	**Tuition:** $6561 ($16,581)
Application Deadline: February 1	**Room & Board:** n/av

Freshman Class: 19423 applied, 5153 accepted, 1254 enrolled
SAT or ACT: required

VERY COMPETITIVE

Baruch College was founded in 1919 and became a separate unit of the City University of New York in 1968. It offers undergraduate programs in business and public administration and liberal arts and sciences. There are 3 undergraduate schools and 3 graduate schools. In addition to regional accreditation, Baruch has baccalaureate program accreditation with AACSB. The library contains 626,753 volumes, 2.1 million microform items, 52,020 audio/video tapes/CDs/DVDs, and subscribes to 89,951 periodicals including electronic. Computerized library services include interlibrary loans, database searching, Internet access, and Wi-Fi capability. Special learning facilities include an art gallery, radio station, journalism lab, newspaper lab. The 4-acre campus is in an urban area New York City. Including any residence halls, there are 6 buildings.
Student Life: 85% of undergraduates are from New York. Others are from 2 states, and 164 foreign countries. 62% are from public schools. 34% are Asian American; 30% White; 13% Hispanic; 12% Foreign. The average age of freshmen is 18; all undergraduates, 24. 12% do not continue beyond their first year; 66% remain to graduate.
Housing: 160 students can be accommodated in college housing, which includes dorms. On-campus housing is available on a lottery system for upperclassmen. Alcohol is not permitted. All students commute. No one may keep cars.
Activities: 1% of men belong to 2 national fraternities; 1% of women belong to 2 national sororities. There are 172 groups on campus, including cheerleading, chess, chorus, computers, dance, debate, drama, ethnic, gay, honors, international, literary magazine, newspaper, photography, political, professional, radio and TV, religious, social, social service, student government, and yearbook. Popular campus events include Club fairs, Relay for Life and Caribbean Week.
Sports: There are 7 intercollegiate sports for men and 7 for women, and 5 intramural sports for men and 5 for women. Facilities include a swimming pool, two gyms, a weight room, an exercise room, and racquetball courts.
Disabled Students: All of the campus is accessible. Facilities include wheelchair ramps, elevators, specially equipped restrooms, special class scheduling, lowered drinking fountains, and lowered telephones.
Services: Counseling and information services are available, as is tutoring in most subjects. There is a reader service for the blind, and remedial math and writing. Note takers and large-print computer screens are available. There are also interpreters for the deaf.
Campus Safety and Security: Measures include 24-hour foot and vehicle patrol, self-defense education, and security escort services. There are lighted pathways/sidewalks, controlled access to dorms/residences, There are fire safety directors and an ID system that uses card swipe in turnstiles for entry.
Programs of Study: Baruch confers B.A., B.S. and B.B.A. degrees. Master's degrees are also awarded. Bachelor's degrees are awarded in BUSINESS (accounting, investments and securities, management science, marketing management, marketing/retailing/merchandising, operations research, personnel management, and real estate), COMMUNICATIONS AND THE ARTS (advertising, communications, English, journalism, music, and Spanish), COMPUTER AND PHYSICAL SCIENCE (actuarial science, information sciences and systems, mathematics, and statistics), SOCIAL SCIENCE (economics, history, industrial and organizational psychology, philosophy, political science/government, psychology, public affairs, and sociology). Economics, English, and math are the strongest academically. Accounting, finance, and marketing have the largest enrollments.
Required: Students must complete a minimum of 120 credits for the B.A. or B.S. and 124 for the B.B.A., with at least 24 hours in the major, and maintain a GPA of 2.0 overall in the major. Students' core curriculum should include courses in English, literature, communications, history, philosophy, psychology, microeconomics, and fine and performing arts.
Special: Students may take courses at all CUNY schools. The college

offers internships and study abroad in Great Britain, France, Germany, Mexico, and Israel. Students may design their own liberal arts major. A federal work-study program is available, and pass/fail options are permitted for liberal arts majors. Students may combine any undergraduate major with a master's in accountancy. There are 4 national honor societies, a freshman honors program, and 17 departmental honors programs.

Faculty/Classroom: 60% of faculty are male; 40% are female. 93% teach undergraduates, and 89% do research. Graduate students teach 8% of introductory courses. The average class size in an introductory lecture is 275; in a laboratory is 20; and in a regular course is 35.

Admissions: 27% of the 2013-2014 applicants were accepted. The SAT scores for the 2013-2014 freshman class were: Critical Reading--12% below 500, 48% between 500 and 599, 31% between 600 and 699, and 8% between 700 and 800; Math--1% below 500, 21% between 500 and 599, 50% between 600 and 699, and 27% between 700 and 800.

Requirements: The SAT or ACT is required. Applicants must present an official high school transcript (a GED will be accepted) indicating a minimum average grade of 81% in academic subjects (minimum of 14 credits). A GPA of 81.0 is required. AP and CLEP credits are accepted. Important factors in the admissions decision are personality/intangible qualities, advanced placement or honors courses, and leadership record.

Procedure: Freshmen are admitted fall and spring. Entrance exams should be taken March 1. There are early decision and rolling admissions plans. Early decision applications should be filed by December 1; regular applications, by February 1 for fall entry; and October 1 for spring entry, along with a $65 fee. Notifications are sent February 1. Applications are accepted online.

Transfer: 1571 transfer students enrolled in 2012-2013. Applicants must have a minimum GPA of 2.5 for 12 to 34.9 credits submitted, a minimum GPA of 2.25 for 35 to 59.9 credits, and a minimum GPA of 2.0 for 60 or more credits. Business applicants must have a 2.75 GPA. Students applying for transfer with fewer than 12 credits earned must have a minimum GPA of 2.5 and a minimum high school average of 80%. 32 of 128 credits required for the bachelor's degree must be completed at Baruch.

Visiting: There are regularly scheduled orientations for prospective students, including a meeting with an admissions counselor. There are guides for informal visits. To schedule a visit, contact the Admissions Office.

Financial Aid: The FAFSA is required. Check with the school for current application deadlines.

International Students: There are 1669 international students enrolled. They must take the TOEFL. They must also take the SAT or ACT.

Graduates: From July 1, 2012 to June 30, 2013, 3042 bachelor's degrees were awarded. The most popular majors were finance and investment (23%), accounting (20%), and marketing (10%). 200 companies recruited on campus in 2012-2013. In an average class, 5% graduate in 4 years or less, 63% graduate in 5 years or less, and 67% graduate in 6 years or less.

Admissions Contact: Marybeth Murphy, Director of Undergraduate Admissions. E-Mail: *marybeth_murphy@baruch.cuny.edu* Web: *www.cuny.edu*

CITY UNIVERSITY OF NEW YORK/BROOKLYN COLLEGE D-5

Brooklyn, NY 11210 **(718) 951-5001; (718) 951-4506**

Full-time: 3852 men, 5386 women	**Faculty:** 543
Part-time: 1472 men, 2389 women	**Ph.D.s:** 96%
Graduate: 1169 men, 2256 women	**Student/Faculty:** 15 to 1
Year: semesters, summer session	**Tuition:** $5884 ($15,004)
Application Deadline: October 1	**Room & Board:** n/av
Freshman Class: n/av	
SAT or ACT: required	

COMPETITIVE+

Brooklyn College, established in 1930, is a publicly supported college of liberal arts, sciences, pre-professional, and professional studies. It is part of the City University of New York and serves the commuter student. There are 5 undergraduate schools and 5 graduate schools. In addition to regional accreditation, Brooklyn College has baccalaureate program accreditation with ADA and NCATE. The library contains 1.7 million volumes, 1.3 million microform items, and 130,093 audio/video tapes/CDs/DVDs, and subscribes to 185,516 periodicals including electronic. Computerized library services include interlibrary loans, database searching, and Internet access. Special learning facilities include an art gallery, radio station, TV station, three color studios, and a speech and hearing clinic. The 36-acre campus is in an urban area in Brooklyn, NY. Including any residence halls, there are 15 buildings.

Student Life: 99% of undergraduates are from New York. Others are from 10 states, 140 foreign countries, and Canada. 78% are from public schools. 40% are White; 25% African American; 16% Asian American; 14% Hispanic. The average age of freshmen is 18; all undergraduates, 23. 16% do not continue beyond their first year; 84% remain to graduate.

Housing: Alcohol is not permitted. All students commute. No one may keep cars.

Activities: 3% of men belong to 2 local and 6 national fraternities; 3% of women belong to 4 local and 4 national sororities. There are 161 groups on campus, including academic, art, chess, computers, dance, drama, ethnic, film, forensics, gay, honors, international, literary magazine, musical theater, newspaper, political, professional, radio and TV, religious, social, social service, student government, symphony, and yearbook. Popular campus events include Welcome Back Bash, Fall Festival and Make a Difference Day.

Sports: There are 6 intercollegiate sports for men and 7 for women, and 3 intramural sports for men and 3 for women. Facilities include a swimming pool, soccer field, softball field, volleyball, tennis, and basketball courts, a fitness center, and a jogging track.

Disabled Students: All of the campus is accessible. Facilities include wheelchair ramps, elevators, special parking, specially equipped restrooms, special class scheduling, and lowered drinking fountains.

Services: Counseling and information services are available, as is tutoring in every subject. There is a reader service for the blind.

Campus Safety and Security: Measures include 24-hour foot and vehicle patrol, emergency notification system, and security escort services. There are shuttle buses, emergency telephones, lighted pathways/sidewalks, CCTV cameras, and informational assistants.

Programs of Study: Brooklyn College confers B.A., B.S., B.F.A., B.B.A., and B.Mus. degrees. Master's degrees are also awarded. Bachelor's degrees are awarded in AGRICULTURE (environmental studies), BIOLOGICAL SCIENCE (biology/biological science), BUSINESS (accounting, banking and finance, business administration and management, business (dual major program), business information systems, and business systems analysis), COMMUNICATIONS AND THE ARTS (art, art history and appreciation, broadcasting, classics, communications, comparative literature, creative writing, English, film arts, French, Italian, journalism, linguistics, multimedia, music, music performance, music theory and composition, radio/television technology, Russian, Spanish, speech/debate/rhetoric, theater management, and visual and performing arts), COMPUTER AND PHYSICAL SCIENCE (chemistry, computer science, earth science, geology, information sciences and systems, mathematics, and physics), EDUCATION (art education, bilingual/bicultural education, (Education) Childhood Education, childhood education: 1-6, early childhood education, elementary education, English education, foreign languages education, mathematics education, music education, physical education, science education, secondary education, and social studies education), HEALTH PROFESSIONS (health science and speech pathology/audiology), SOCIAL SCIENCE (African studies, American studies, anthropology, Caribbean studies, child care/child and family studies, economics, Hispanic American studies, history, interdisciplinary studies, Judaic studies, Latin American studies, philosophy, political science/government, psychology, Puerto Rican studies, religion, sociology, and women's studies). Business, accounting, and education have the largest enrollments.

Required: There are 11 required, interrelated courses that cover the following core curriculum areas: classics, art, music, political science, sociology, history, literature, math, computer science, chemistry, physics, biology, geology, philosophy, and comparative cultures. There are basic skills requirements in reading, composition, speech, and math, as well as a foreign language requirement. A 2.0 GPA and a minimum of 120 credit hours, with 31 to 36 in the major (67 to 70 for chemistry), are required to graduate.

Special: There are numerous cross-registration programs with colleges and universities in the area. Many internships and work-study programs are available. Study abroad is possible in more than 29 countries. A B.A.-M.D., B.S.-M.P.S., and accelerated B.A.-M.A. programs are available. A number of B.A.-B.S. degrees, dual majors, a 3-2 engineering degree, and student-designed majors are possible. Credit by exam, credit for life experience, non-degree study, and pass/fail options are offered. There is a Latin and Greek Institute offered during the summer through the Graduate Center. There are 9 national honor societies, including Phi Beta Kappa, a freshman honors program, and 6 departmental honors programs.

Faculty/Classroom: 51% of faculty are male; 49% are female. No introductory courses are taught by graduate students. The average class size in a laboratory is 16 and in a regular course is 32.

Requirements: The SAT or ACT is required. Applicants applying directly from high school must have completed 81% GPA with 5 units of math and English with no less than 2 years of either combined (critical reading and math) SAT score or ACT equivalent of 1000 for regular freshmen admissions. Students will be admitted with GED score of 3000 and have the equivalent of 2 years of high school math. A GPA of 3.0 is required. AP and CLEP credits are accepted.

Procedure: Freshmen are admitted fall and spring. There are early admissions and rolling admissions plans. Applications should be filed by October 1 for fall entry; February 1 for spring entry, along with a $65 fee. Notification of early decision is sent December 15; regular decision, on a rolling basis. Applications are accepted online.

Transfer: 2879 transfer students enrolled in 2012-2013. Transfer students must have up to 24 credits and 2.5 GPA and freshman requirements are 25 and over credits and a 2.3 GPA. 30 of 120 credits required for the bachelor's degree must be completed at Brooklyn College.

Visiting: There are regularly scheduled orientations for prospective students, including campus tours, presentations, and meetings with faculty. There are guides for informal visits. To schedule a visit, contact Christopher Milton, Assistant Director for Recruitment at (718) 951-5001.

Financial Aid: In 2013-2014, 69% of all full-time freshmen and 76% of continuing full-time students received some form of financial aid. 61% of all full-time freshmen and 74% of continuing full-time students received need-based aid. The average freshman award was $7,500. Need-based scholarships or need-based grants averaged $3,300 ($10,500 maximum); need-based self-help aid (loans and jobs) averaged $3,200 ($3,500 maximum); and other non-need-based awards and non-need-based scholarships averaged $1,500 ($10,500 maximum). 71% of undergraduate students work part-time. Average annual earnings from campus work are $1200. The average financial indebtedness of the 2013 graduate was $12,300. The FAFSA is required. The priority date for freshman financial aid applications for fall entry is April 1.

International Students: There are 352 international students enrolled. The school actively recruits these students. They must take the TOEFL with a minimum score of 500 on the paper-based TOEFL (PBT) or 61 on the Internet-based version (iBT) and the college's own test.

Graduates: From July 1, 2012 to June 30, 2013, 2474 bachelor's degrees were awarded. The most popular majors were business (21%), psychology (13%), and accounting (11%). 330 companies recruited on campus in 2012-2013. In an average class, 46% graduate in 5 years or less and 54% graduate in 6 years or less.

Admissions Contact: Admissions Office E-Mail: *adminqry@brooklyn.cuny.edu* Web: *www.brooklyn.cuny.edu*

CLARKSON UNIVERSITY D-2

Potsdam, NY 13699	**(315) 268-6480; (315) 268-7647**
Full-time: 2214 men, 870 women	**Faculty:** 178; I, -$
Part-time: 15 men, 11 women	**Ph.D.s:** 89%
Graduate: 387 men, 229 women	**Student/Faculty:** 14 to 1
Year: semesters, summer session	**Tuition:** $40,540
Application Deadline: January 15	**Room & Board:** $12,998
Freshman Class: 6747 applied, 4320 accepted, 757 enrolled	
SAT CR/M/W: 560/620/550 **ACT:** 26	**HIGHLY COMPETITIVE**

Clarkson University, located just outside the Adirondack Park in Potsdam, NY, is a private, nationally ranked research university with 3,500 students pursuing 50+ academic programs in engineering, business, arts, sciences and health professions. There are 4 undergraduate schools and 4 graduate schools. In addition to regional accreditation, Clarkson has baccalaureate program accreditation with AACSB, ABET, and APTA. The 2 libraries contain 371,937 volumes, 256,398 microform items, and 458 audio/video tapes/CDs/DVDs, and subscribe to 23,962 periodicals including electronic. Computerized library services include interlibrary loans, database searching, Internet access, and Wi-Fi capability. Special learning facilities include a radio station. The 640-acre campus is in a rural area Clarkson is located in Potsdam, 135 miles northeast of Syracuse, 85 miles south of Ottawa, Canada and 69 miles northwest of the Olympic Village in Lake Placid. Including any residence halls, there are 71 buildings.

Student Life: 74% of undergraduates are from New York. Others are from 42 states, 29 foreign countries, and Canada. 85% are from public schools. 83% are White. The average age of freshmen is 18; all undergraduates, 20. 12% do not continue beyond their first year; 75% remain to graduate.

Housing: 2510 students can be accommodated in college housing, which includes single-sex and coed dorms, on-campus apartments, and off-campus apartments. In addition, there are honors houses, special-interest houses, fraternity houses, and sorority houses. On-campus housing is guaranteed for all 4 years and is available on a lottery system for upperclassmen. 84% of students live on campus; of those, 90% remain on campus on weekends. All students may keep cars.

Activities: 12% of men belong to 3 local and 8 national fraternities; 15% of women belong to 4 national sororities. There are 147 groups on campus, including cheerleading, chorus, computers, drama, drill team, environmental, ethnic, gay, honors, international, jazz band, musical theater, newspaper, orchestra, pep band, photography, political, professional, radio and TV, religious, social, social service, SPEED Teams (Student Projects for Engineering Experience & Design), student government, and yearbook. Popular campus events include Spring and WinterFest, World in Potsdam Diversity Festival, and NCAA Division I Championship hockey games.

Sports: There are 10 intercollegiate sports for men and 10 for women, and 6 intramural sports for men and 6 for women. Facilities include 3000-seat multipurpose ice arena, fitness center, gym, swimming pool, weight room, field house, tennis courts, and all-purpose indoor and outdoor turf fields.

Disabled Students: 85% of the campus is accessible. Facilities include wheelchair ramps, elevators, special parking, specially equipped restrooms, special class scheduling, lowered drinking fountains, lowered telephones, and special housing.

Services: Counseling and information services are available, as is tutoring in most subjects. There is a reader service for the blind, and remedial math and writing.

Campus Safety and Security: Measures include 24-hour foot and vehicle patrol, emergency notification system, and security escort services. There are emergency telephones, lighted pathways/sidewalks, and controlled access to dorms/residences.

Programs of Study: Clarkson confers B.S., and B.P.S. degrees. Master's and doctoral degrees are also awarded. Bachelor's degrees are awarded in BIOLOGICAL SCIENCE (biology/biological science and molecular biology), BUSINESS (accounting, business administration and management, business systems analysis, entrepreneurial studies, finance, management information systems, and supply chain management), COMMUNICATIONS AND THE ARTS (communications and technical and business writing), COMPUTER AND PHYSICAL SCIENCE (applied mathematics, chemistry, computer science, digital arts/technology, information sciences and systems, mathematics, physics, science, and software engineering), ENGINEERING AND ENVIRONMENTAL DESIGN (aeronautical engineering, chemical engineering, civil engineering, computer engineering, electrical/electronics engineering, engineering management, environmental engineering, environmental science, and mechanical engineering), HEALTH PROFESSIONS (environmental health science), SOCIAL SCIENCE (American studies, history, humanities, interdisciplinary studies, political science/government, psychology, and social science). Engineering, business, and physical/life sciences are the strongest academically. Engineering, and physical/life sciences have the largest enrollments.

Required: Students must complete a least 120 credit hours, 30 in a major field of study, with a minimum 2.0 cumulative GPA. Students must meet the requirements of the Clarkson Common Experience, which includes a professional experience such as a co op or internship, and any additional requirements determined by their major department. A student entering as a first-year freshman must have been in residence for at least four semesters including the final undergraduate semester or, if entering with advanced standing, have completed at least half the remaining upper-level undergraduate work in residence at Clarkson.

Special: Students can take advantage of many unique educational experiences at Clarkson. Students can sign up for the Washington Semester, Adirondack Semester or Semester at Sea. Students can cross-register at St. Lawrence University, SUNY Potsdam or SUNY Canton, or transfer to Clarkson through one of our many 3-2 engineering degree agreements. Our 3-2 agreements allow students to take their first 3 years of college at a 4-year liberal arts institution and then transfer with junior standing into one of Clarkson's 4-year engineering programs. Students can choose one of Clarkson's may pre-designed interdisciplinary majors, or design their own with a dual major or BPS degree. All Clarkson students are required to complete a professional experience, which usually takes place through a co-op or internship, with one of Clarkson's many industry partners including General Dynamics, General Electric, IBM, Lockheed Martin, and Proctor & Gamble. Many programs of study also require a study abroad experience, which can take place through instructor-led summer trips or a semester/year abroad in Australia, Austria, China, Denmark, France, Germany, Hong Kong, Hungary, India, Ireland, Japan, South Korea, Mexico, New Zealand, Singapore, Spain, Sweden, or the United Kingdom. Work-study programs are also available. There are 15 national honor societies, a freshman honors program, and 9 departmental honors programs.

Faculty/Classroom: 71% of faculty are male; 29% are female. 80% teach undergraduates, all do research, and 80% do both. No introductory courses are taught by graduate students. The average class size in an introductory lecture is 35; in a laboratory is 21; and in a regular course is 29.

Admissions: 64% of the 2013-2014 applicants were accepted. The SAT scores for the 2013-2014 freshman class were: Critical Reading--15% below 500, 50% between 500 and 599, 28% between 600 and 699, and 7% between 700 and 800; Math--5% below 500, 31% between 500 and 599, 51% between 600 and 699, and 13% between 700 and 800; Writing--23% below 500, 50% between 500 and 599, 22% between 600 and 699, and 4% between 700 and 800. The ACT scores were 4% below 21, 20% between 21 and 23, 32% between 24 and 26, 20% between 27 and 28, and 24% above 28. 67% of the current freshmen were in the top fifth of their class; 92% were in the top two fifths. 24 freshmen graduated first in their class.

Requirements: The SAT or ACT is required. SAT subject tests are recommended. Applicants must have graduated from an accredited secondary school or have a GED. A campus visit and interview are also recommended. AP and CLEP credits are accepted. Important factors in the admissions decision are advanced placement or honors courses, recommendations by school officials, and extracurricular activities record.

Procedure: Freshmen are admitted fall and spring. Entrance exams should be taken by November. There are early decision, early admissions, and deferred admissions plans. Early decision applications should be filed by December 1; regular applications, by January 15 for fall entry; and October 15 for spring entry, along with a $50 fee. Notification of early decision is sent January 1; regular decision, February 1. 120 early decision candidates were accepted for the 2013-2014 class. 159 applicants were on the 2013 waiting list; 17 were admitted. Applications are accepted online. Application fees are waived if application is completed online.

Transfer: 121 transfer students enrolled in 2012-2013. Transfer applicants must submit two letters of recommendation, including one from an academic professor or instructor. Applicants must also submit official secondary school transcripts if not earning an Associate's Degree, and SAT or ACT scores if less than 24 credits at time of application. Transfer applicants into engineering or other majors requiring calculus should have completed at least one college-level calculus course. International students whose first language is not English must submit TOEFL or IELTS scores. 30 of 120 credits required for the bachelor's degree must be completed at Clarkson.

Visiting: There are regularly scheduled orientations for prospective students, Visits are individually customized to your interests, and include a personalized tour with a Clarkson student and one-on-one meetings with admissions officers, faculty members, and coaches. There are guides for informal visits, visitors may sit in on classes, and stay overnight. To schedule a visit, contact the Undergraduate Admissions.

Financial Aid: In 2013-2014, 98% of all full-time freshmen and 99% of continuing full-time students received some form of financial aid. 81% of all full-time freshmen and 84% of continuing full-time students received need-based aid. The average freshman award was $37,165. Need-based scholarships or need-based grants averaged $30,384 ($57,848 maximum); need-based self-help aid (loans and jobs) averaged $5,015 ($10,700 maximum); non-need-based athletic scholarships averaged $40,705 ($53,728 maximum); and other non-need-based awards and non-need-based scholarships averaged $24,683 ($45,997 maximum). 38% of undergraduate students work part-time. Average annual earnings from campus work are $1476. The average financial indebtedness of the 2013 graduate was $26,832. The FAFSA is required. The priority date for freshman financial aid applications for fall entry is February 15. The deadline for filing freshman financial aid applications for fall entry is March 1.

International Students: There are 110 international students enrolled. The school actively recruits these students. They must take the TOEFL with a minimum score of 550 on the paper-based TOEFL (PBT) or 80 on the Internet-based version (iBT). They must also take the SAT or ACT.

Graduates: From July 1, 2012 to June 30, 2013, 639 bachelor's degrees were awarded. The most popular majors were mechanical engineering (16%), civil engineering (11%), and engineering management (9%). 251 companies recruited on campus in 2012-2013. In an average class, 1% graduate in 3 years or less, 63% graduate in 4 years or less, 75% graduate in 5 years or less, and 75% graduate in 6 years or less. Of the 2012 graduating class, 15% were enrolled in graduate school within 6 months of graduation, and 70% were employed.

Admissions Contact: Brian T. Grant, Dean of Admissions. E-Mail: *bgrant@clarkson.edu* Web: *www.clarkson.edu*

COLGATE UNIVERSITY — D-5

Hamilton, NY 13346 — **(315) 228-7401; (315) 228-7544**

Full-time: 1313 men, 1487 women	**Faculty:** 266; IIB, ++$
Part-time: 10 men, 15 women	**Ph.D.s:** 96%
Graduate: 4 men, 8 women	**Student/Faculty:** 11 to 1
Year: semesters	**Tuition:** $41,520
Application Deadline: January 15	**Room & Board:** $10,410
Freshman Class: 7816 applied, 2464 accepted, 750 enrolled	
SAT CR/M: 661/680	**ACT:** 30 **MOST COMPETITIVE**

Colgate University, founded in 1819, is a private liberal arts institution. There is 1 graduate school. The 2 libraries contain 734,812 volumes, 593,646 microform items, and subscribe to 36,752 periodicals including electronic. Computerized library services include interlibrary loans, database searching, Internet access, and laptop Internet portals. Special learning facilities include a learning resource center, art gallery, radio station, TV station, anthropology museum, and observatory. The 515-acre campus is in a rural area 45 miles southeast of Syracuse and 35 miles southwest of Utica. Including any residence halls, there are 87 buildings.

Student Life: 72% of undergraduates are from out of state, mostly the Northeast. Students are from 49 states, 35 foreign countries, and Canada. 62% are from public schools. 74% are white. The average age of freshmen is 18; all undergraduates, 20. 5% do not continue beyond their first year; 91% remain to graduate.

Housing: 2400 students can be accommodated in college housing, which includes coed dorms and on-campus apartments. In addition, there are language houses, special-interest houses, and fraternity houses. On-campus housing is guaranteed for all 4 years. 93% of students live on campus; of those, 96% remain on campus on weekends. All students may keep cars.

Activities: 40% of men belong to 6 national fraternities; 38% of women belong to 3 national sororities. Only sophomores, juniors, and seniors can join fraternties and sororities. There are 180 groups on campus, including art, band, cheerleading, chess, choir, chorale, chorus, computers, dance, debate, drama, environmental, ethnic, film, forensics, gay, honors, international, jazz band, literary magazine, musical threater, newspaper, orchestra, pep band, photography, political, professional, radio and TV, religious, social, social service, student government, symphony, and yearbook. Popular campus events include Winter Olympics, DanceFest, and Spring Party Weekend.

Sports: There are 11 intercollegiate sports for men and 12 for women, and 19 intramural sports for men and 19 for women. Facilities include numerous athletic fields, a softball diamond, an outdoor artificial surface field, a football stadium, an athletic center, a 3000-seat gym, a golf course, a field house, a 50-meter pool, a bowling center, a hockey rink, a 9000-square-foot fitness center, running trails, a trap range, and courts for basketball, tennis, squash, handball, and racquetball.

Disabled Students: 20% of the campus is accessible. Facilities include wheelchair ramps, elevators, special parking, specially equipped rest rooms, special class scheduling, and lowered drinking fountains.

Services: Counseling and information services are available, as is tutoring in every subject. There is a reader service for the blind and remedial writing. There is a note-taking service for students with learning and sensory disabilities and a writing center.

Campus Safety and Security: Measures include 24-hour foot and vehicle patrol, emergency notification system, self-defense education, and security escort services. There are shuttle buses, emergency telephones, and lighted pathways/sidewalks.

Programs of Study: Colgate confers B.A. degrees. Master's degrees are also awarded. Bachelor's degrees are awarded in BIOLOGICAL SCIENCE (biochemistry, biology/biological science, molecular biology, and neurosciences), COMMUNICATIONS AND THE ARTS (art history and appreciation, Chinese, classics, dramatic arts, English, French, German, Greek, Japanese, Latin, music, Russian, Spanish, and studio art), COMPUTER AND PHYSICAL SCIENCE (astronomy, astrophysics, chemistry, computer science, geology, geophysics and seismology, mathematics, natural sciences, physical sciences, and physics), EDUCATION (education), ENGINEERING AND ENVIRONMENTAL DESIGN (environmental science), SOCIAL SCIENCE (African studies, Asian/Oriental studies, economics, geography, history, humanities, international relations, Latin American studies, Native American studies, peace studies, philosophy, political science/government, psychology, religion, Russian and Slavic studies, social science, sociology, and women's studies). English, economics, and history have the largest enrollments.

Required: To graduate, students must complete a first-year seminar course and the core curriculum, including 4 general education courses and 2 courses each in the natural sciences, social sciences, and humanities. A total of 32 courses is required, with 8 to 12 courses in the major. Study in a foreign language, phys ed, and a swimming test are also required. Students need a minimum 2.0 GPA.

Special: Colgate offers various internships, semester and summer research opportunities with faculty, work-study, study abroad in 22 countries, accelerated degree programs, dual majors, and student-designed majors. A 3-2 engineering degree with Columbia and Washington Universities and Rensselaer Polytechnic Institute, an early assurance medical program with George Washington University, credit by exam, and pass/fail options are available. There are 12 national honor societies, including Phi Beta Kappa, and 10 departmental honors programs.

Faculty/Classroom: 57% of faculty are male; 43% are female. All teach and do research. No introductory courses are taught by graduate students. The average class size in an introductory lecture is 21; in a laboratory is 17; and in a regular course is 19.

Admissions: The SAT scores for a recent freshman class were: Critical Reading--4% below 500, 12% between 500 and 599, 47% between 600 and 700, and 37 above 700; Math--2% below 500, 11% between 500 and 599, 45% between 600 and 700, and 42% above 700. The ACT scores were 1% below 21, 3% between 21 and 23, 9% between 24 and 26, 13% between 27 and 28, and 76% above 28. 86% of the current freshmen were in the top fifth of their class; 98% were in the top two-fifths. 23 freshmen graduated first in their class.

Requirements: The SAT or ACT is required. 2 teacher recommendations and a counselor's report are required. An interview, though not evaluated, is recommended. Students should present 16 or more Carnegie credits, based on 4 years each of English and math and at least 3 of lab science, social science, and a foreign language, with electives in the arts. AP credits are accepted. Important factors in the admissions decision are advanced placement or honors courses, recommendations by school officials, and leadership record.

Procedure: Freshmen are admitted in the fall. Entrance exams should be taken in time for score reports to reach the university by January 15. There are early decision and deferred admissions plans. Early decision applications should be filed by November 15; regular applications, by January 15 for fall entry, along with a $55 fee. Notification of early decision is sent December 15; regular decision, April 1. Applications are accepted online. 709 applicants were on a recent waiting list, 22 were accepted.

Transfer: 22 transfer students enrolled in a recent year. Either the SAT or the ACT is required, as well as college and high school transcripts, a dean's report, and faculty recommendations. 16 of 32 credits required for the bachelor's degree must be completed at Colgate.

Visiting: There are regularly scheduled orientations for prospective students, including nonevaluative interviews, group information sessions, and student-led tours. There are guides for informal visits, visitors may sit in on classes and stay overnight. To schedule a visit, contact the Office of Admissions.

Financial Aid: In a recent year, 34% of all full-time freshmen and 35% of continuing full-time students received some form of financial aid, including need-based aid. The average freshmen award was $39,758. The average financial indebtedness of recent graduates was $14,170. Colgate is a member of CSS. The CSS/Profile and FAFSA are required. International students need the International Student's Financial Aid Application. The deadline for filing freshman financial aid applications for fall entry is January 15.

International Students: There were 133 international students enrolled in a recent year. The school actively recruits these students. They must take the TOEFL and the SAT or ACT.

Graduates: In a recent year, 704 bachelor's degrees were awarded. 200 companies recruited on campus in a recent year. In an average class, 1% graduate in 3 years or less, 88% graduate in 4 years or less, 90% graduate in 5 years or less, and 91% graduate in 6 years or less. Of a recent graduating class, 20% were enrolled in graduate school within 6 months of graduation, and 80% were employed.

Admissions Contact: Gary L. Ross, Dean of Admission. E-Mail: *admission@mail.colgate.edu* Web: *www.colgate.edu*

COLLEGE OF MOUNT SAINT VINCENT D-5

Riverdale, NY 10471 (718) 405-3304
(800) 665-CMSV; (718) 549-7945

Full-time: 305 men, 1105 women	**Faculty:** n/av; IIB, av$
Part-time: 30 men, 155 women	**Ph.D.s:** n/av
Graduate: 105 men, 310 women	**Student/Faculty:** n/av
Year: semesters, summer session	**Tuition:** $24,120
Application Deadline: April 2	**Room & Board:** $12,060
Freshman Class: n/av	
SAT or ACT: required	

MOST COMPETITIVE

The College of Mount Saint Vincent, founded as an academy in 1847 and chartered as a college in 1911, is a private liberal arts institution in the Catholic tradition. There is one undergraduate school and one graduate school. In addition to regional accreditation, The Mount has baccalaureate program accreditation with ACBSP and NLN. The library contains 129,000 volumes, 7,000 microform items, and 6,500 audio/video tapes/CDs/DVDs, and subscribes to 234 periodicals including electronic. Computerized library services include interlibrary loans, database searching, and Internet access. Special learning facilities include a radio station and TV station. The 70-acre campus is in an urban area 11 miles north of New York City. Including any residence halls, there are 11 buildings.

Student Life: 89% of undergraduates are from New York. Others are from 19 states, and 4 foreign countries. 46% are from public schools. 38% are White; 32% Hispanic; 14% African American. 81% are Catholic. The average age of freshmen is 18; all undergraduates, 22. 25% do not continue beyond their first year; 62% remain to graduate.

Housing: 778 students can be accommodated in college housing, which includes coed dorms. On-campus housing is guaranteed for all 4 years, is available on a first-come, first-served basis, and is available on a lottery system for upperclassmen. 54% of students live on campus; of those, 65% remain on campus on weekends. All students may keep cars.

Activities: There are no fraternities or sororities. There are 30 groups on campus, including art, cheerleading, chess, choir, chorus, computers, dance, debate, drama, ethnic, film, gay, honors, international, literary magazine, musical theater, newspaper, photography, professional, radio and TV, religious, social, social service, student government, and yearbook. Popular campus events include Phin Fest, Mount Madness, Brown Bag Bingo, Spring Concert and Theater Thursdays.

Sports: There are 8 intercollegiate sports for men and 7 for women, and 5 intramural sports for men and 5 for women. Facilities include two gyms (main Peter Jay Sharp Athletic and Recreation Center and a smaller upstairs gym in the same building), a weight room, a dance studio, a recreation room, a fitness center with aerobic and Nautilus facilities, basketball court, squash.

Disabled Students: 90% of the campus is accessible. Facilities include wheelchair ramps, elevators, special parking, specially equipped restrooms, lowered drinking fountains, and lowered telephones.

Services: Counseling and information services are available, as is tutoring in most subjects, computer science, math, chemistry, biology, languages, psychology, sociology, writing, and economics. There is a reader service for the blind, and remedial math, reading, and writing.

Campus Safety and Security: Measures include 24 hour foot and vehicle patrol and security escort services. There are shuttle buses, emergency telephones, lighted pathways/sidewalks, a college committee on safety and security on campus.

Programs of Study: The Mount confers B.A. and B.S. degrees. Associate and master's degrees are also awarded. Bachelor's degrees are awarded in BIOLOGICAL SCIENCE (biochemistry and biology/biological science), BUSINESS (business administration and management), COMMUNICATIONS AND THE ARTS (communications, English, French, modern language, and Spanish), COMPUTER AND PHYSICAL SCIENCE (chemistry, computer science, mathematics, and physics), EDUCATION (health education, physical education, and special education), HEALTH PROFESSIONS (allied health and nursing), SOCIAL SCIENCE (economics, history, liberal arts/general studies, philosophy, psychology, religion, sociology, and urban studies). Nursing and biology are the strongest academically. Nursing, psychology, and business have the largest enrollments.

Required: All students must complete a 49-credit core curriculum with courses in humanities, social sciences, math and computers, and natural sciences. A total of 120 credits for a B.A. or 126 credits for a B.S., with a minimum of 30 credits in the major, and a minimum GPA of 2.0 are required.

Special: Cross-registration with Manhattan College offers cooperative B.A. programs in international studies, philosophy, phys ed, physics, religious studies, and urban affairs. Internships, work-study, study abroad in 6 countries, a 3-2 engineering degree with Manhattan College, dual majors, and student-designed majors in liberal arts are available. B.A.-B.S. degrees in computer science, health education, math, and psychology, and teacher dual certification programs with special education and elementary, middle school, and secondary education are possible. There are 15 national honor societies, a freshman honors program, and 5 departmental honors programs.

Faculty/Classroom: 39% of faculty are male; 61% are female. All teach undergraduates, and 80% do both. No introductory courses are taught by graduate students. The average class size in an introductory lecture is 25; in a laboratory is 15; and in a regular course is 15.

Requirements: The SAT or ACT is required. Applicants should have completed 4 high school academic units of English, 3 of science, and 2 each of math, foreign language, and social sciences, as well as electives. An essay is required, and an interview is recommended. One letter of recommendation is required, and additional letters are encouraged. A GPA of 80.0 is required. AP and CLEP credits are accepted. Important factors in the admissions decision are advanced placement or honors courses, recommendations by school officials, and extracurricular activities record.

Procedure: Freshmen are admitted fall and spring. Entrance exams should be taken during the junior year and/or fall of the senior year. There are early admissions and rolling admissions plans. Early decision applications should be filed by November 15; regular applications, by April 2 for fall entry. The fall 2013 application fee was $35. Notification is sent on a rolling basis. Applications are accepted online.

Transfer: Transfer applicants should have a minimum GPA of 2.0. Those majoring in nursing, the sciences, math, or computer science need at least a 2.5 GPA. An interview is recommended. 45 of 120 credits required for the bachelor's degree must be completed at The Mount.

Visiting: There are regularly scheduled orientations for prospective students, Upon request, students may have an interview with an admissions counselor, sit in on classes, and tour the campus. All students are invited to an open house. Accepted students may have a one-on-one meeting with a student on campus. There are guides for informal visits, visitors may sit in on classes, and stay overnight. To schedule a visit, contact the Admissions Office.

Financial Aid: The Mount is a member of CSS. The FAFSA, and the TAP application for New York state residents is required. Check with the school for current application deadlines.

International Students: The school actively recruits these students. They must take the TOEFL, or complete ELS Level 109, available on campus. They must also take the SAT or ACT, scoring 900.

Admissions Contact: Timothy P. Nash, Dean of Admission and Financial Aid. E-Mail: *admissns@mountsaintvincent.edu* Web: *www.cmsv.edu*

THE COLLEGE OF NEW ROCHELLE D-5

New Rochelle, NY 10805 (914) 654-5452
(800) 933-5923; (914) 654-5464

Full-time: 25 men, 605 women	**Faculty:** n/av; IIA, +$
Part-time: 60 men, 335 women	**Ph.D.s:** n/av
Graduate: 105 men, 930 women	**Student/Faculty:** n/av
Year: semesters, summer session	**Tuition:** $25,500
Application Deadline: August 15	**Room & Board:** $9800
Freshman Class: n/av	
SAT: required	

VERY COMPETITIVE

The College of New Rochelle was founded in 1904 by the Ursuline order as the first Catholic college for women in New York State. Now independent, there are 3 undergraduate schools. The School of Arts and Sciences offers liberal arts baccalaureate education for women only and the School of Nursing is coeducational. The School of New Resources is described in a separate profile. The figures in the above profile and in this capsule are approximate. There are 3 undergraduate schools and one graduate school. In addition to regional accreditation, CNR has baccalaureate program accreditation with CSWE and NLN. The library contains 224,000 volumes, 277 microform items, and 5,700 audio/video tapes/CDs/DVDs, and subscribes to 1,432 periodicals including electronic. Computerized library services include interlibrary loans, database searching, and Internet access. Special learning facilities include an art gallery, a Learning Center for Nursing. The 20-acre campus is in a suburban area 12 miles north of New York City. Including any residence halls, there are 20 buildings.

Student Life: 87% of undergraduates are from New York. Others are from 17 states, and 10 foreign countries. 73% are from public schools. 52% are African American; 22% Hispanic; 18% White. 77% are Catholic; 18% Protestant. The average age of freshmen is 20; all undergraduates, 27. 29% do not continue beyond their first year; 71% remain to graduate.

Housing: 410 students can be accommodated in college housing, which includes single-sex dorms. On-campus housing is guaranteed for all 4 years. 56% of students live on campus; of those, 50% remain on campus on weekends. All students may keep cars.

Activities: There are no fraternities or sororities. There are 18 groups on campus, including art, cheerleading, choir, chorus, drama, environmental, ethnic, film, honors, international, literary magazine, musical theater, newspaper, photography, political, professional, religious, social, social service, and student government. Popular campus events include Junior Celebration, Family Weekend, and Strawberry Festival.

Sports: There are 6 intercollegiate sports for women. Facilities include a fitness center and tennis courts.

Disabled Students: 50% of the campus is accessible. Facilities include wheelchair ramps, elevators, special parking, specially equipped restrooms, and special class scheduling.

Services: Counseling and information services are available, as is tutoring in some subjects, science, languages There is remedial math, reading, and writing. Individual counseling and educational workshops about self-development and personal concerns are available, as are self-help materials.

Campus Safety and Security: Measures include 24-hour foot and vehicle patrol, self-defense education, and security escort services. There are shuttle buses, emergency telephones, lighted pathways/sidewalks, card access to dorms, and surveillance cameras.

Programs of Study: CNR confers B.A., B.S., B.F.A. and B.S.N. degrees. Master's degrees are also awarded. Bachelor's degrees are awarded in AGRICULTURE (environmental studies), BIOLOGICAL SCIENCE (biology/biological science), BUSINESS (business administration and management), COMMUNICATIONS AND THE ARTS (art history and appreciation, classics, communications, English, French, and Spanish), COMPUTER AND PHYSICAL SCIENCE (chemistry and mathematics), EDUCATION (art education), HEALTH PROFESSIONS (art therapy and nursing), SOCIAL SCIENCE (economics, history, international studies, philosophy, political science/government, psychology, religion, social work, sociology, and women's studies). Nursing, art, and psychology are the largest.

Required: Students must complete 120 credit hours, 60 to 90 in liberal arts courses, depending on the major, meet specific course distribution requirements, and maintain a minimum GPA of 2.0 to graduate. 4 phys ed courses are also required.

Special: CNR provides cooperative programs in all disciplines, work-study programs, dual majors in all majors, interdisciplinary studies, an accelerated degree program in nursing, a Washington semester, internships, study abroad in 9 countries, non-degree study, pass/fail options, student-designed majors, and a general studies degree. There is 1 national honor society and a freshman honors program.

Faculty/Classroom: 25% of faculty are male; 75% are female. All teach and do research. No introductory courses are taught by graduate students. The average class size in an introductory lecture is 25; in a laboratory is 10; and in a regular course is 15.

Requirements: The SAT is required. Graduation from an accredited secondary school is required. The GED is accepted. Applicants must have completed 15 academic credits, with 4 in English, 3 each in math, science, and social studies, and 2 in a foreign language. A portfolio is required for art majors. An essay and interview are recommended. AP and CLEP credits are accepted. Important factors in the admissions decision are advanced placement or honors courses, recommendations by school officials, and leadership record.

Procedure: Freshmen are admitted to all sessions. Entrance exams should be taken in the junior year or fall of the senior year. There are early decision, early admissions, deferred admissions, and rolling admissions plans. Early decision applications should be filed by November 1; regular applications, by August 15 for fall entry; and January 10 for spring entry. The fall 2013 application fee was $20. Notification of early decision is sent December 15; regular decision, on a rolling basis.

Transfer: 68 transfer students enrolled in 2012-2013. Transfer students must submit a transcript from their previous college showing courses completed and a minimum GPA of 2.0. High school records and SAT scores are required. An interview is recommended. 30 of 120 credits required for the bachelor's degree must be completed at CNR.

Visiting: There are regularly scheduled orientations for prospective students, including several open houses providing information on admission. There are guides for informal visits, visitors may sit in on classes, and stay overnight. To schedule a visit, contact the Office of Admissions.

Financial Aid: The FAFSA, CCS/Profile, the college's own financial statement, and income documentation are required. Check with the school for current application deadlines.

International Students: They must take the TOEFL, or the ESL Language Test. They must also take the SAT or ACT.

Graduates: From July 1, 2012 to June 30, 2013, 241 bachelor's degrees were awarded. The most popular majors were nursing (67%), psychology (9%), and commercial arts (4%). 27 companies recruited on campus in 2012-2013. In an average class, 50% graduate in 4 years or less, 51% graduate in 5 years or less, and 52% graduate in 6 years or less. Of the 2012 graduating class, 20% were enrolled in graduate school within 6 months of graduation, and 60% were employed.

Admissions Contact: Stephanie Decker, Director of Admission. E-Mail: *sdecker@cnr.edu* Web: *www.cnr.edu*

COLLEGE OF NEW ROCHELLE - SCHOOL OF NEW RESOURCES D-5

New Rochelle, NY 10805 (914) 654-5526
(800) 288-4767; (914) 654-5664

Full-time: 405 men, 3505 women	**Faculty:** n/av
Part-time: 50 men, 400 women	**Ph.D.s:** n/av
Graduate: n/av	**Student/Faculty:** n/av
Year: semesters, summer session	**Tuition:** n/av
Application Deadline: August 15	**Room & Board:** n/av
Freshman Class: n/av	

VERY COMPETITIVE

The College of New Rochelle's school of new resources is a liberal arts institution serving adult baccalaureate students. The figures in the above capsule and in this profile are approximate. The library contains 224,000 volumes, 277 microform items, and 5,700 audio/video tapes/CDs/DVDs, and subscribes to 1,432 periodicals including electronic. Computerized library services include interlibrary loans, database searching, and Internet access. Special learning facilities include an art gallery, and TV station. The campus is in an urban area 12 miles north of New York City. Including any residence halls, there are 20 buildings.

Student Life: 98% of undergraduates are from New York. Others are from 3 states, and 3 foreign countries. 82% are African American; 14% Hispanic. The average age of freshmen is 33; all undergraduates, 36. 35% do not continue beyond their first year; 65% remain to graduate.

Housing: Alcohol is not permitted. All students commute. All students may keep cars.

Activities: There are no fraternities or sororities. Groups on campus include drama, musical theater, religious, and student government. Popular campus events include Founders Day, College Bowl, and Women's and Ethnic Activities.

Sports: There is no sports program at SNR.

Services: Counseling and information services are available, as is tutoring in some subjects, including communication skills, problem solving, and math skills. There is remedial math, reading, and writing.

Campus Safety and Security: Measures include 24-hour foot and vehicle patrol, self-defense education, and security escort services. There are shuttle buses, emergency telephones, lighted pathways/sidewalks, surveillance cameras.

Programs of Study: SNR confers B.A. degrees. Bachelor's degrees are awarded in SOCIAL SCIENCE (liberal arts/general studies).

Required: Students must complete 120 credit hours, meet specific course distribution requirements, and maintain a minimum GPA of 2.0 to graduate. Entrance, core, and exit seminars are required, as are degree-planning courses.

Special: SNR provides a voluntary work-study program. Student-designed internships, courses, and degree plans are available. Credit for prior learning may be obtained.

Faculty/Classroom: 54% of faculty are male; 46% are female. All teach undergraduates. No introductory courses are taught by graduate students. The average class size in an introductory lecture is 15; in a laboratory is 10; and in a regular course is 15.

Requirements: Enrolling students must be age 21 or older, have a high school diploma or its equivalent, and have successfully completed an English assessment. Test scores are not required. New students are expected to attend an orientation workshop. AP and CLEP credits are accepted.

Procedure: Freshmen are admitted to all sessions. Entrance exams should be taken in the junior year or fall of the senior year. There is a rolling admissions plan. Early decision applications should be filed by November 1; regular applications, by August 15 for fall entry; and January 10 for spring entry. Notification of early decision is sent December 15; regular decision, on a rolling basis.

Transfer: Transfer students must obtain a transcript from their previous college. With some restrictions, course grades of C- or better will be accepted. 30 of 120 credits required for the bachelor's degree must be completed at SNR.

Financial Aid: The FAFSA, the college's own financial statement, and income documentation are required. The deadline for filing freshman financial aid applications for fall entry is open.

Admissions Contact: Director of Admissions E-Mail: *admission@cnr.edu* Web: *nyts.edu/college-of-new-rochelle*

THE COLLEGE OF SAINT ROSE D-3

Albany, NY 12203 (518) 454-5150
(800) 637-8556; (518) 454-2013

Full-time: 887 men, 1777 women	**Faculty:** 209; IIA, --$
Part-time: 82 men, 145 women	**Ph.D.s:** 96%
Graduate: 377 men, 1036 women	**Student/Faculty:** 13 to 1
Year: semesters, summer session	**Tuition:** $27,684
Application Deadline: February 1	**Room & Board:** $11,250
Freshman Class: 4651 applied, 3605 accepted, 621 enrolled	
SAT CR/M: 520/520 **ACT:** 23	**COMPETITIVE**

The College of Saint Rose offers students the benefits of an urban environment as well as a close-knit campus community. The College offers 70 undergraduate majors and 52 graduate programs through its four schools: School of Arts & Humanities, School of Business, School of Education, and School of Mathematics and Sciences. Saint Rose is distinguished by its rigorous academics taught in a highly personal learning environment in state-of-the-art facilities. There are 4 undergraduate schools and 4 graduate schools. In addition to regional accreditation, College of Saint Rose has baccalaureate program accreditation with ACBSP, ASLA, CSWE, NASAD, NASM, and NCATE. The 3 libraries contain 223,844 volumes, 313,339 microform items, and 5,010 audio/video tapes/CDs/DVDs, and subscribe to 562 periodicals including electronic. Computerized library services include interlibrary loans, database searching, Internet access, and Wi-Fi capability. Special learning facilities include an art gallery, radio station, TV station, internship office, entrepreneurship center, TV and radio studios, music recording studio, performance venue, music/video editing computer labs, recital hall, rehearsal rooms, and labs for geology, biology, chemistry, computer science and neuro-psychology. The 46-acre campus is in an urban area in the Capital Region of New York state. Including any residence halls, there are 88 buildings.

Student Life: 88% of undergraduates are from New York. Others are from 29 states, 22 foreign countries, and Canada. 72% are White. The average age of freshmen is 18; all undergraduates, 21. 25% do not continue beyond their first year; 66% remain to graduate.

Housing: 1408 students can be accommodated in college housing, which includes single-sex and coed dorms and on-campus apartments. Apartments for single students and special housing for disabled students are also available. On-campus housing is guaranteed for all 4 years, is available on a first-come, first-served basis, and is available on a lottery system for upperclassmen. 56% of students commute. Upperclassmen may keep cars.

Activities: There are no fraternities or sororities. There are 33 groups on campus, including and habitat for humanity, geology club, girls for God (G4G), student events board, adventure club, band, cheerleading, chorale, dance, drama, environmental, ethnic, international, jazz band, literary magazine, musical theater, newspaper, pep band, political, professional, radio and TV, religious, social, social service, student government, symphony, and yearbook. Popular campus events include Harvest Fest, Rose Rock Music Festival, Midnight Madnes and Dodgeball Madness.

Sports: There are 9 intercollegiate sports for men and 9 for women, and 9 intramural sports for men and 9 for women. Facilities include Nolan Gym has 1 full sized basketball court, 2 smaller basketball courts, 1 full sized volleyball court, 2 smaller sized volleyball courts, 4 lane indoor pool, and fitness center. Plumeri Sports Complex has 1 synthetic turf field lined for men's lacrosse and soccer, 1 grass NCAA baseball field, 1 grass NCAA softball field, and 1 grass practice field.

Disabled Students: 71% of the campus is accessible. Facilities include wheelchair ramps, elevators, special parking, specially equipped restrooms, lowered drinking fountains, lowered telephones, special housing.

Services: Counseling and information services are available, as is tutoring in every subject. There is a reader service for the blind, and remedial math, reading, and writing. There is also a full-time director of disabled student services.

Campus Safety and Security: Measures include 24-hour foot and vehicle patrol, emergency notification system, and security escort services. There are shuttle buses, emergency telephones, lighted pathways/sidewalks, and controlled access to dorms/residences.

Programs of Study: College of Saint Rose confers B.A., B.S. and B.F.A. degrees. Master's degrees are also awarded. Bachelor's degrees are awarded in BIOLOGICAL SCIENCE (biochemistry, bioinformatics, biology/adolescence education, biology/biological science, forensic psychology, and forensic science), BUSINESS (accounting and business administration and management), COMMUNICATIONS AND THE ARTS (communications, English, graphic design, information technology, music, music industry, Spanish, spanish/adolescence education, and studio art), COMPUTER AND PHYSICAL SCIENCE (chemistry, chemistry/adolescence education, computer science, earth science/adolescence education, geology, and mathematics), EDUCATION (art education, childhood education: 1-6, early childhood education, English education, mathematics education, music education, science education, social studies secondary school education, and special education), HEALTH PROFESSIONS (cytotechnology and medical technology), SOCIAL SCIENCE (American studies, communication sciences and disorders, criminal justice, economics, history, interdisciplinary studies, law, philosophy, political science/government, psychology, religion, social work, sociology, and women and gender studies). Communication sciences and disorders, art, music, education, and business administration are the strongest academically. Business administration, communications, special education/childhood education, communication sciences and disorders have the largest enrollments.

Required: To graduate, students must complete 122 credits with a minimum GPA of 2.0 overall and in the major; these requirements are higher for certain majors. Liberal education requirements consist of 4 credits in college writing and speech and 30 credits in the humanities, science and math, social science and business, English, computer literacy, foreign languages, history, philosophy, and the arts. Students must also complete 2 credits in physical education.

Special: CSR offers cross-registration with several local colleges, internships, work-study programs, study abroad in several countries, dual and student-designed majors, non-degree study, and pass/fail options. There are 3-2 engineering degree programs with Alfred and Clarkson Universities, Union College, and Rensselaer Polytechnic University, as well as a 6-year law program with Albany Law School. There are 14 national honor societies and 11 departmental honors programs.

Faculty/Classroom: 44% of faculty are male; 56% are female. All teach and do research. No introductory courses are taught by graduate students. The average class size in an introductory lecture is 19; in a laboratory is 18; and in a regular course is 13.

Admissions: 78% of the 2013-2014 applicants were accepted. The SAT scores for the 2013-2014 freshman class were: Critical Reading--37% below 500, 44% between 500 and 599, 17% between 600 and 699, and 2% between 700 and 800; Math--35% below 500, 47% between 500 and 599, 16% between 600 and 699, and 3% between 700 and 800. The ACT scores were 28% below 21, 23% between 21 and 23, 28% between 24 and 26, 11% between 27 and 28, and 11% above 28. 36% of the current freshmen were in the top fifth of their class; 68% were in the top two fifths. 1 freshman graduated first in the class.

Requirements: The SAT or ACT is recommended. Applicants must be graduates of an accredited secondary school or have a GED certificate. They should have completed college preparatory programs including 4 years of English and history, and 3 years of math, science, and foreign language. All students must submit a letter of recommendation and an essay. Art students must submit portfolios, and music students must audition. A GPA of 83.0 is required. AP and CLEP credits are accepted. Important factors in the admissions decision are advanced placement or honors courses, extracurricular activities record, and leadership record.

Procedure: Freshmen are admitted fall and spring. Entrance exams should be taken During the spring of junior year or the fall of senior year. There are early admissions, deferred admissions, and rolling admissions plans. Early decision applications should be filed by December 1; regular applications, by February 1 for fall entry; and December 1 for spring entry, along with a $40 fee. Notification is sent on a Rolling basis. Applications are accepted online.

Transfer: 248 transfer students enrolled in 2012-2013. Applicants must submit official transcripts from all colleges attended, a letter of recommendation, and an essay of the reasons for seeking transfer. An interview is recommended. Art majors must submit a portfolio, and music majors must audition. The minimum overall college GPA is a 2.5. 60 of 122 credits required for the bachelor's degree must be completed at College of Saint Rose.

Visiting: There are regularly scheduled orientations for prospective students, Tours begin at 8:30 a.m. followed by a formal presentation at 10:00 a.m. Tours of specific facilities and faculty presentations follow morning events. There are guides for informal visits, visitors may sit in on classes, and stay overnight. To schedule a visit, contact the Undergraduate Admissions.

Financial Aid: In 2013-2014, 98% of all full-time freshmen and 98% of

continuing full-time students received some form of financial aid. 95% of all full-time freshmen and 91% of continuing full-time students received need-based aid. The average freshman award was $23,415. Need-based scholarships or need-based grants averaged $11,730; need-based self-help aid (loans and jobs) averaged $3,963; non-need-based athletic scholarships averaged $15,545; and other non-need-based awards and non-need-based scholarships averaged $10,584. 70% of undergraduate students work part-time. Average annual earnings from campus work are $1700. The average financial indebtedness of the 2013 graduate was $25,780. College of Saint Rose is a member of CSS. The FAFSA is required. The priority date for freshman financial aid applications for fall entry is February 1. The deadline for filing freshman financial aid applications for fall entry is April 1.

International Students: There are 35 international students enrolled. The school actively recruits these students. Students must take the TOEFL with a minimum score of 80 on the paper-based TOEFL (PBT) or 82 on the Internet-based version (iBT), IELTS. Students must also take the SAT or ACT.

Graduates: From July 1, 2012 to June 30, 2013, 613 bachelor's degrees were awarded. The most popular majors were childhood education (10%), business administration (10%), and special education (9%). 59 companies recruited on campus in 2012-2013. In an average class, 47% graduate in 4 years or less, 64% graduate in 5 years or less, and 66% graduate in 6 years or less. Of the 2012 graduating class, 50% were enrolled in graduate school within 6 months of graduation, and 70% were employed.

Admissions Contact: Jeremy Bogan, Assistant VP of Undergraduate Admissions. E-Mail: *admit@strose.edu* Web: *www.strose.edu*

COLLEGE OF STATEN ISLAND / THE CITY UNIVERSITY OF NEW YORK — D-5

Staten Island, NY 10314 — **(718) 982-2190; (718) 982-2500**

Full-time: 4475 men, 5389 women — **Faculty:** 287
Part-time: 1508 men, 2026 women — **Ph.D.s:** 78%
Graduate: 228 men, 734 women — **Student/Faculty:** 34 to 1
Year: semesters, summer session — **Tuition:** $6158 ($14,978)
Application Deadline: — **Room & Board:** $10,620
Freshman Class: 12123 applied, 12123 accepted, 2751 enrolled
SAT CR/M/W: 490/525/479

NONCOMPETITIVE

The College of Staten Island (CSI) is a senior college of The City University of New York (CUNY) and boasts a modern, 204-acre campus that offers the serene and beautiful surroundings traditionally associated with academic life, and facilities that are among the most advanced of any college.

Student Life: 99% of undergraduates are from New York. Others are from 13 states, 70 foreign countries, and Canada. 77% are from public schools. 36% are White; 19% African American; 14% Hispanic; 11% Asian American. The average age of freshmen is 18.2; all undergraduates, 23. 18% do not continue beyond their first year; 82% remain to graduate.

Housing: 454 students can be accommodated in college housing, which includes coed on-campus apartments. On-campus housing is available on a first-come and first-served basis. Priority is given to out-of-town students. Alcohol is not permitted. All students may keep cars.

Activities: There are no fraternities or sororities. There are 45 groups on campus, including art, cheerleading, chorale, computers, dance, drama, environmental, ethnic, film, gay, honors, international, literary magazine, newspaper, photography, political, professional, radio and TV, religious, social, social service, and student government. Popular campus events include Spring Carnival and Club Festival, CSI's Got Talent, Relay for Life, Involvement Fair and Welcome Back Carnival.

Sports: There are 6 intercollegiate sports for men and 7 for women, and 16 intramural sports for men and 16 for women. The Sports and Recreation Center houses a full range of facilities and equipment for individual and team sports and games: a gymnasium with seating capacity for 1,200 spectators, an auxiliary gymnasium, two fitness rooms, volleyball courts, racquetball courts, and a 25-meter pool. Outdoor facilities include a track, tennis courts, baseball, softball and soccer fields.

Disabled Students: All of the campus is accessible. Facilities include wheelchair ramps, elevators, special parking, specially equipped restrooms, special class scheduling, lowered drinking fountains, lowered telephones, special housing.

Services: Counseling and information services are available, as is tutoring in most subjects. There is remedial math, reading, and writing.

Campus Safety and Security: Measures include 24-hour foot and vehicle patrol, emergency notification system, and security escort services. There are shuttle buses, emergency telephones, lighted pathways/sidewalks, controlled access to dorms/residences, radar-controlled traffic monitoring, and bicycle patrol.

Programs of Study: CSI confers B.A., and B.S. degrees. Associate, master's, and doctoral degrees are also awarded. Bachelor's degrees are awarded in BIOLOGICAL SCIENCE (biochemistry and biology/biological science), BUSINESS (accounting and business administration and management), COMMUNICATIONS AND THE ARTS (art, communications, dramatic arts, English, film arts, music, and Spanish), COMPUTER AND PHYSICAL SCIENCE (chemistry, computer science, mathematics, and physics), EDUCATION (secondary education), ENGINEERING AND ENVIRONMENTAL DESIGN (engineering and applied science), HEALTH PROFESSIONS (medical technology and nursing), SOCIAL SCIENCE (African American studies, American studies, economics, history, international studies, Italian studies, philosophy, political science/government, psychology, science and society, social work, sociology, and women and gender studies). Psychology, business, biology, science letters and society, and accounting have the largest enrollments.

Required: Skill proficiency, General Education Requirements, GPA of at least 2.0 though some programs require a higher GPA.

Special: Cross-registration is available with any other CUNY college. Internships are available in most fields. The College of Staten Island offers a wide range of study abroad and exchange programs for its students. Washington semester is available. There are interdisciplinary majors, including computer science-math, sociology-anthropology, political science-philosophy, and science, letters, and society. The Verrazano School program provides motivated and talented students with an exceptional baccalaureate experience. Macaulay Honors College at CSI: The Macaulay Honors College at CSI offers an outstanding education to academically gifted students. There are 11 national honor societies, a freshman honors program, and 17 departmental honors programs.

Faculty/Classroom: 50% of faculty are male; 50% are female. 88% teach undergraduates. No introductory courses are taught by graduate students.

Admissions: 100% of the 2013-2014 applicants were accepted. The SAT scores for the 2013-2014 freshman class were: Critical Reading--54% below 500, 38% between 500 and 599, 7% between 600 and 699, and 1% between 700 and 800; Math--84% below 500, 14% between 500 and 599, and 2% between 600 and 699; Writing--61% below 500, 31% between 500 and 599, 7% between 600 and 699, and 1% between 700 and 800.

Requirements: Admission into a baccalaureate program is based on an examination of an applicant's entire high school/secondary school academic record, which includes: academic units, grades/grade trends, and standardized test scores (SAT, ACT and NY State Regents). To be admitted into a four-year program, you must demonstrate college-level readiness in reading, writing and mathematics. Applicants who are not admitted to a bachelor's degree program may be eligible for admission to an associate degree program at the College. AP and CLEP credits are accepted.

Procedure: Freshmen are admitted fall, spring, and summer. Entrance exams should be taken as soon as possible after admission. There are deferred admissions and rolling admissions plans. Application deadlines are open. The fall 2013 application fee was $65. Applications are accepted online.

Transfer: 1066 transfer students enrolled in 2012-2013. Transfer students with less than 30 credits completed at the time of application must also fulfill our freshmen requirements and submit their high school documentation as part of the application process. In addition, the student's completed college work must have an overall GPA of 2.0. Transfer students with 30 or more credits completed at the time of application must have a minimum cumulative GPA of 2.0. 30 of 120 credits required for the bachelor's degree must be completed at CSI.

Visiting: There are regularly scheduled orientations for prospective students, includes pre-admission advisement, campus tours and presentations. There are guides for informal visits and visitors may sit in on classes. To schedule a visit, contact Holly Block at (718) 982-2259.

Financial Aid: The FAFSA and the state aid form are required. The priority date for freshman financial aid applications for fall entry is March 30.

International Students: The school actively recruits these students. They must take the TOEFL with a minimum score of 450 on the paper-based TOEFL (PBT) or 45 on the Internet-based version (iBT).

Graduates: From July 1, 2012 to June 30, 2013, 2298 bachelor's degrees were awarded. The most popular majors were liberal arts (14%), business (13%), and nursing (7%). 150 companies recruited on campus in 2012-2013. In an average class, 24% graduate in 4 years or less, 42% graduate in 5 years or less, and 47% graduate in 6 years or less. Of the 2012 graduating class, 5% were enrolled in graduate school within 6 months of graduation, and 41% were employed.

Admissions Contact: Emmanuel Esperance, Director of Recruitment and Admissions. E-Mail: *Emmanuel.Esperance@csi.cuny.edu* Web: *http:/www.csi.cuny.edu/admissions/*

COLUMBIA UNIVERSITY SYSTEM

The Columbia University System, established in 1754, is a public system in New York. It is governed by a board of trustees, whose chief administrator is the president. The primary goal of the system is teaching and research. The main priorities are providing outstanding undergraduate instruction; conducting research to develop new knowledge and methods;

and training of professionals in law, business, social work, and medicine. The total student enrollment is usually about 20,000 with 2500 faculty members. Altogether there are 110 baccalaureate, 159 master's, and 79 doctoral programs offered in the Columbia University System. Profiles of the 4-year campuses are included in this section.

COLUMBIA UNIVERSITY IN THE CITY OF NEW YORK D-5

New York, NY 10027 **(212) 854-2522; (212) 854 1209**

Full-time: 3174 men, 2910 women	**Faculty:** n/av; I, ++$
Part-time: n/av	**Ph.D.s:** n/av
Graduate: n/av	**Student/Faculty:** 6 to 1
Year: semesters, summer session	**Tuition:** $49,138
Application Deadline: January 1	**Room & Board:** $11,978
Freshman Class: 33531 applied, 2311 accepted, 1416 enrolled	
SAT CR/M/W: 740/750/750	**ACT:** 33 **MOST COMPETITIVE**

Columbia University in the City of New York was founded in 1754. 4,500 undergraduates study liberal arts and science programs in Columbia College and 1,500 major in The Fu Foundation School of Engineering and Applied Science. Students also have access to our more than a dozen graduate and professional schools, a traditional college campus in the neighborhood of Morningside Heights, and all that New York City has to offer professionally, socially, and culturally. The 25 libraries contain 9.5 million volumes. Computerized library services include interlibrary loans, database searching, Internet access, and Wi-Fi capability. Special learning facilities include an art gallery, planetarium, radio station, TV station, an observatory. The 36-acre campus is in an urban area in New York City. Including any residence halls, there are 50 buildings.

Student Life: 77% of undergraduates are from out of state, mostly the Middle Atlantic. Students are from 50 states, 90 foreign countries, and Canada. 36% are White; 22% Asian American; 13% Hispanic; 13% Foreign; 11% African American; and 3% Race Unknown. The average age of freshmen is 18; all undergraduates, 20. 1% do not continue beyond their first year; 99% remain to graduate.

Housing: 5606 students can be accommodated in college housing, which includes single-sex and coed dorms and on-campus apartments. In addition, there are language houses, special-interest houses, and fraternity houses. On-campus housing is guaranteed for all 4 years and is available on a lottery system for upperclassmen. 94% of students live on campus. All students may keep cars.

Activities: 19% of men belong to 22 national fraternities; 9% of women belong to 11 national sororities. There are 500 groups on campus, including and outdoor, art, band, cheerleading, chess, choir, chorale, chorus, communications, computers, dance, debate, drama, environmental, ethnic, film, forensics, gay, honors, international, jazz band, literary magazine, marching band, musical theater, newspaper, opera, orchestra, pep band, photography, political, professional, radio and TV, religious, social, social service, student government, symphony, and yearbook. Popular campus events include New Student Orientation Program, Orgo Night, Bacchanal Spring Concert and Tree Lighting Ceremony/Yule Log.

Sports: There are 14 intercollegiate sports for men and 15 for women, and 20 intramural sports for men and 20 for women. Facilities include a football stadium, indoor and outdoor track and field facilities, a baseball field, a soccer stadium, a recreational gym with a swimming pool, basketball/volleyball courts, aerobic, fencing, wrestling, martial arts, and weight rooms, a boat house, and tennis, squash, handball, and racquetball courts.

Disabled Students: All of the campus is accessible. Facilities include wheelchair ramps, elevators, special parking, specially equipped restrooms, special class scheduling, lowered drinking fountains, lowered telephones, special housing.

Services: Counseling and information services are available, as is tutoring in every subject. There is a reader service for the blind.

Campus Safety and Security: Measures include 24-hour foot and vehicle patrol, emergency notification system, self-defense education, and security escort services. There are shuttle buses, emergency telephones, lighted pathways/sidewalks, and controlled access to dorms/residences.

Programs of Study: Columbia confers B.A., and B.S. degrees. Master's and doctoral degrees are also awarded. Bachelor's degrees are awarded in BIOLOGICAL SCIENCE (biochemistry, biology/biological science, biophysics, environmental biology, and neurosciences), BUSINESS (operations research), COMMUNICATIONS AND THE ARTS (art history and appreciation, classics, comparative literature, dance, dramatic arts, English, film arts, French, German, Germanic languages and literature, Greek, Latin, linguistics, music, Russian, Spanish, and visual and performing arts), COMPUTER AND PHYSICAL SCIENCE (applied mathematics, applied physics, astronomy, astrophysics, chemistry, computer science, earth science, geochemistry, geology, geophysics and seismology, mathematics, physics, and statistics), EDUCATION (education), ENGINEERING AND ENVIRONMENTAL DESIGN (architecture, biomedical engineering, chemical engineering, civil engineering, computer engineering, electrical/electronics engineering, engineering management, engineering mechanics, environmental science, industrial engineering technology, materials science, mechanical engineering, metallurgical engineering, and mining and mineral engineering), SOCIAL SCIENCE (African American studies, American studies, anthropology, archeology, area studies, Asian/American studies, classical/ancient civilization, East Asian studies, economics, Hispanic American studies, history, Italian studies, Latin American studies, medieval studies, Middle Eastern studies, philosophy, political science/government, psychology, religion, Russian and Slavic studies, sociology, urban studies, and women's studies). Political science, economics, engineering, history, English, psychology have the largest enrollments.

Required: All students complete a core curriculum consisting of classes in Western and non-Western cultures, literature and philosophy, history, social science, art, sculpture and architecture, and music of the Western tradition and science; 2 courses in non-Western areas are also required. Distribution requirements include 2 years of foreign language (unless competency can be demonstrated), 2 semesters of science, 1 year of phys ed, and 1 semester of writing. A thesis may be required for departmental honors in certain departments. A total of 124 credit hours is required; usually 30 to 40 of these are in the major. The engineering students are required to take calculus, physics, chemistry, economics and specific introductory engineering design courses in addition to half of the Columbia College core. The minimum required GPA is 2.0.

Special: There is a study abroad program at more than 200 locations, including France, Oxford, Cambridge,Universities in England, and the Kyoto Center for Japanese Studies in Japan, and Biosphere 2 (Arizona). Cross-registration is possible with the Juilliard School and Barnard College. Combined B.A.-B.S. degrees are offered via 3-2 or 4-1 engineering programs. A 3-2 engineering degree is offered with Columbia's Fu Foundation School of Engineering and Applied Science. There is also a 5-year B.A./M.I.A. with Columbia's School of International and Public Affairs. The college offers work-study, internships, credit by exam, pass/fail options, and dual, student-designed, and interdisciplinary majors, including regional studies and ancient studies.

Faculty/Classroom: All teach and do research. No introductory courses are taught by graduate students.

Admissions: 7% of the 2013-2014 applicants were accepted. The SAT scores for the 2013-2014 freshman class were: Critical Reading--3% between 500 and 599, 21% between 600 and 699, and 76% between 700 and 800; Math--2% between 500 and 599, 20% between 600 and 699, and 78% between 700 and 800; Writing--2% between 500 and 599, 24% between 600 and 699, and 74% between 700 and 800. The ACT scores were 10% between 27 and 28, and 90% above 28.

Requirements: The SAT or ACT is required. The ACT Optional Writing test is also required. The admissions application consists of the Common Application and Columbia Supplement; HS transcript; SAT and 2 SAT Subject Tests or ACT with Writing; 3 letters of reference; and an essay. AP credits are accepted.

Procedure: Freshmen are admitted fall. Entrance exams should be taken by Jan. of the senior year (RD) or Nov. There are early decision and deferred admissions plans. Early decision applications should be filed by November 1; regular applications, by January 1 for fall entry, along with a $85 fee. Notification of early decision is sent December 15; regular decision, April 1. Applications are accepted online.

Transfer: 123 transfer students enrolled in 2012-2013. Applicants must have completed 1 full year of college (24 credits). They must submit high school and college transcripts. 60 of 128 credits required for the bachelor's degree must be completed at Columbia.

Visiting: There are regularly scheduled orientations for prospective students, consisting of group information sessions and student-led tours as well as special science tours and engineering tours. There are guides for informal visits, visitors may sit in on classes, and stay overnight. To schedule a visit, contact the Visitors Center at (212) 854-4900.

Financial Aid: 51% of all full-time freshmen and 52% of continuing full-time students received need-based aid. The average freshman award was $43,087. Need-based scholarships or need-based grants averaged $42,785; and need-based self-help aid (loans and jobs) averaged $2,263. Columbia is a member of CSS. The CSS/Profile, FAFSA, and the college's own financial statement, and federal tax returns, the business/farm supplement, and/or the divorced/separated parents statement, if applicable, are required. The deadline for filing freshman financial aid applications for fall entry is March 1.

International Students: The school actively recruits these students. They must take the TOEFL with a minimum score of 100 on the Internet-based version (iBT). They must also take the SAT or ACT.

Graduates: From July 1, 2012 to June 30, 2013, 1580 bachelor's degrees were awarded. The most popular majors were social sciences (22%), engineering (21%), and biological/life sciences (10%). 370 companies recruited on campus in 2012-2013. In an average class, 89% graduate in 4 years or less, 94% graduate in 5 years or less, and 96% graduate in 6 years or less.

Admissions Contact: Admissions Officer, Office of Undergraduate Admissions. E-Mail: *ugrad ask@columbia.edu* Web: *undergrad.admissions.columbia.edu*

COLUMBIA UNIVERSITY/BARNARD COLLEGE D-5

New York, NY 10027-6598 (212) 854-5262; (212) 854-6220

Full-time: 2300 women
Part-time: 55 women
Graduate: n/av
Year: semesters
Application Deadline: January 1
Freshman Class: n/av
SAT or ACT: required
Faculty: n/av
Ph.D.s: n/av
Student/Faculty: n/av
Tuition: $30,000
Room & Board: $13,000

MOST COMPETITIVE

Barnard College, founded in 1889, is an independent affiliate of Columbia University. It is an undergraduate womens' liberal arts college. Figures in the above capsule and in this profile are approximate. The library contains 204,906 volumes, 17,705 microform items, and 17,448 audio/video tapes/CDs/DVDs, and subscribes to 543 periodicals including electronic. Computerized library services include interlibrary loans, database searching, and Internet access. Special learning facilities include a learning resource center, art gallery, radio station, TV station, a greenhouse, history of physics lab, child development research and study center, dance studio, modern theater, womens' research archives within a womens' center, and multimedia labs and classrooms. The 4-acre campus is in an urban area occupying 4 city blocks of Manhattan's Upper West Side. Including any residence halls, there are 15 buildings.

Student Life: 68% of undergraduates are from out of state, mostly the Middle Atlantic. Students are from 48 states, 35 foreign countries, and Canada. 53% are from public schools. 66% are white; 16% Asian American. The average age of freshmen is 18; all undergraduates, 20. 5% do not continue beyond their first year; 84% remain to graduate.

Housing: 2057 students can be accommodated in college housing, which includes single-sex and coed dorms, on-campus apartments, and off-campus apartments. In addition, there are special-interest houses. On-campus housing is guaranteed for all 4 years. 90% of students live on campus; of those, 75% remain on campus on weekends. Alcohol is not permitted. All students may keep cars.

Activities: There are no fraternities or sororities. There are 100 groups on campus, including art, band, cheerleading, choir, chorale, chorus, dance, debate, drama, ethnic, film, gay, international, jazz band, literary magazine, marching band, Model UN, musical theater, newspaper, opera, orchestra, pep band, photography, political, professional, radio and TV, religious, social, social service, student government, symphony, and yearbook. Popular campus events include Spring and Winter Festivals, Founders Day, and Take Back the Night.

Sports: There are 15 intercollegiate sports for women, and 16 intramural sports for women. Facilities include pools, weight rooms, gyms, tennis courts, an indoor track, and a boat slip.

Disabled Students: 90% of the campus is accessible. Facilities include wheelchair ramps, elevators, special parking, specially equipped restrooms, special class scheduling, lowered drinking fountains, lowered telephones, and special housing. The Office of Disability Services provides a variety of support services to students with permanent and temporary disabilities.

Services: Counseling and information services are available, as is tutoring in every subject. There is a reader service for the blind. A student-staffed writing room is available for students of all levels of writing ability, and a math help room is also available to students in all math courses.

Campus Safety and Security: Measures include 24-hour foot and vehicle patrol and security escort services. There are shuttle buses, emergency telephones, lighted pathways/sidewalks, and safety and security education programs.

Programs of Study: Barnard College confers B.A. degrees. Bachelor's degrees are awarded in BIOLOGICAL SCIENCE (biochemistry and biology/biological science), COMMUNICATIONS AND THE ARTS (art history and appreciation, classics, comparative literature, dance, dramatic arts, English, film arts, French, German, Greek, Italian, Latin, linguistics, music, Russian, and Spanish), COMPUTER AND PHYSICAL SCIENCE (astronomy, chemistry, computer science, mathematics, physics, and statistics), ENGINEERING AND ENVIRONMENTAL DESIGN (architecture and environmental science), SOCIAL SCIENCE (American studies, anthropology, biopsychology, classical/ancient civilization, East Asian studies, economics, European studies, history, international studies, medieval studies, Middle Eastern studies, philosophy, political science/government, psychology, religion, sociology, urban studies, and women's studies). English, psychology, and economics have the largest enrollments.

Required: A total of 120 credits is required, with a minimum GPA of 2.0. All students must take 4 semesters each of a foreign language, humanities, or social sciences outside the major, and geographic and cultural diversity courses that may satisfy the major or other requirements, 2 semesters each of lab science and phys ed, and 1 semester each in first-year seminar, first-year English, and quantitative reasoning.

Special: Barnard offers cross-registration with Columbia University, more than 2500 internships with New York City firms and institutions, and study abroad worldwide. A 3-2 engineering program with the Columbia School of Engineering and double-degree programs with the Columbia University Schools of International and Public Affairs, Law, and Dentistry, the Juilliard School, and the Jewish Theological Seminary are possible. The college offers dual and student-designed majors and multidisciplinary majors, including economic history. There is 1 national honor society and Phi Beta Kappa.

Faculty/Classroom: 35% of faculty are male; 65% are female. All teach and do research. No introductory courses are taught by graduate students. The average class size in an introductory lecture is 30; in a laboratory is 11; and in a regular course is 13.

Requirements: The SAT or ACT is required. If taking the SAT, an applicant must also take 3 SAT subject tests, one of which must be in writing or literature. A GED is accepted. Applicants should prepare with 4 years of English, 3 of math and science, 3 or 4 of a foreign language, 2 of a lab science, and 1 of history. An interview is recommended. AP credits are accepted. Important factors in the admissions decision are advanced placement or honors courses, evidence of special talent, and extracurricular activities record.

Procedure: Freshmen are admitted fall. Entrance exams should be taken by January of the senior year. There are early decision, early admissions and deferred admissions plans. Early decision applications should be filed by November 15; regular applications, by January 1 for fall entry, along with a $55 fee. Notification of early decision is sent December 15; regular decision, April 1. Applications are accepted online. A waiting list is maintained.

Transfer: In a recent year, 80 transfer students enrolled. Applicants must complete at least 1 college course. The SAT or ACT is required. Deadline for transfer applicants is April 1 (fall term) and November 1 (spring term). They must submit high school and college transcripts. They must be in good standing from prior institutions attended and submit an essay or personal statement. 60 of 120 credits required for the bachelor's degree must be completed at Barnard College.

Visiting: There are regularly scheduled orientations for prospective students, consisting of open house programs for prospective students regularly scheduled throughout the fall. There are guides for informal visits; visitors may sit in on classes and stay overnight. To schedule a visit, contact the Office of Admissions.

Financial Aid: In a recent year, 44% of all full-time freshmen and 44% of continuing full-time students received some form of financial aid. 41% of all full-time freshmen and 42% of continuing full-time students received need-based aid. The average freshmen award was $30,644. 46% of undergraduate students worked part-time. Barnard College is a member of CSS. The CSS/Profile, FAFSA, the state aid form, the college's own financial statement, the parents' and student's federal tax returns, and the business and/or farm supplement are required. Check with the school for current application deadlines.

International Students: The school actively recruits these students. They must take the TOEFL. They must also take the SAT or ACT. Applicants who take the SAT must also take SAT subject tests in writing or literature and 2 others.

Graduates: In a recent year, 597 bachelor's degrees were awarded. The most popular majors were social sciences (25%), psychology (14%), and English (11%). In an average class, 2% graduate in 3 years or less, 82% graduate in 4 years or less, 88% graduate in 5 years or less, and 89% graduate in 6 years or less.

Admissions Contact: Jennifer Fondiller, Dean of Admissions. E-Mail: *admissions@barnard.edu* Web: *www.barnard.edu*

COLUMBIA UNIVERSITY/SCHOOL OF GENERAL STUDIES D-5

New York, NY 10027 (212) 854-2772
(800) 895-1169; (212) 854-6316

Full-time: 569 men, 360 women
Part-time: 254 men, 316 women
Graduate: n/av
Year: semesters, summer session
Application Deadline: June 1
Freshman Class: n/av
SAT or ACT: recommended
Faculty: 1823
Ph.D.s: 100%
Student/Faculty: 6 to 1
Tuition: $43,958
Room & Board: $10,125

MOST COMPETITIVE

The School of General Studies of Columbia University is a liberal arts college created specifically for returning and nontraditional students seeking a rigorous, traditional, Ivy League undergraduate degree full- or part-time. GS is also home to the oldest and largest Postbaccalaureate Premedical Program in the United States, the Joint Program with Jewish Theological Seminary, and the Dual BA Program Between Columbia University and Sciences Po. There are 3 undergraduate schools and 14 graduate schools. The 22 libraries contain 1.0 million volumes, 6.4 million microform items, and 156,717 audio/video tapes/CDs/DVDs, and subscribe to 144,787 periodicals including electronic. Computerized library services include interlibrary loans, database searching, Internet access, and Wi-Fi capability. Special learning facilities include an art gallery, planetarium, radio station, and TV station. The 36-acre campus is in an urban area on the upper west side of Manhattan in New York City.

Student Life: 57% of undergraduates are from New York. Others are from states, 82 foreign countries, and Canada. 37% are White; 15% Foreign. The average age of freshmen is 22; all undergraduates, 29.

Housing: 645 students can be accommodated in college housing, which includes single-sex and coed off-campus apartments and married student housing. In addition, there are special-interest houses, fraternity houses, an international house. On-campus housing is available on a first-come and first-served basis. Priority is given to out-of-town students. 57% of students commute. Alcohol is not permitted. No one may keep cars.

Activities: 1% of men belong to 17 national fraternities; 1% of women belong to 11 national sororities. There are 541 groups on campus, including and womens, art, band, cheerleading, chess, choir, chorale, chorus, computers, dance, debate, drama, environmental, ethnic, film, gay, honors, international, jazz band, literary magazine, marching band, musical theater, newspaper, opera, orchestra, photography, political, professional, radio and TV, religious, social, social service, student government, symphony, writers, and yearbook.

Sports: There are 14 intercollegiate sports for men and 15 for women, and 11 intramural sports for men and 11 for women. Facilities include 2 gyms, a swimming pool, tennis, squash, and racquetball courts, a training center, 2 dance/martial arts studios, a fencing room, a wrestling room, and an indoor track.

Disabled Students: All of the campus is accessible. Facilities include wheelchair ramps, elevators, specially equipped restrooms, lowered drinking fountains, and lowered telephones.

Services: Counseling and information services are available, as is tutoring in some subjects, English composition, math, languages, and sciences.

Campus Safety and Security: Measures include 24-hour foot and vehicle patrol, emergency notification system, self-defense education, and security escort services. There are shuttle buses, emergency telephones, and lighted pathways/sidewalks.

Programs of Study: GS confers B.A., and B.S. degrees. Bachelor's degrees are awarded in BIOLOGICAL SCIENCE (biology/biological science), COMMUNICATIONS AND THE ARTS (art history and appreciation, classics, comparative literature, dance, dramatic arts, English literature, film arts, French, German, Italian, literature, music, Slavic languages, Spanish, and visual and performing arts), COMPUTER AND PHYSICAL SCIENCE (applied mathematics, astronomy, chemistry, computer science, geoscience, mathematics, physics, and statistics), ENGINEERING AND ENVIRONMENTAL DESIGN (architecture and environmental science), SOCIAL SCIENCE (African American studies, anthropology, archeology, classical/ancient civilization, East Asian studies, economics, French studies, German area studies, Hispanic American studies, history, Italian studies, Latin American studies, Middle Eastern studies, philosophy, political science/government, psychology, religion, sociology, urban studies, and women's studies). Political science, economics, and English have the largest enrollments.

Required: All students must complete 124 credit hours, including 56 distribution requirement credits in literature, humanities, foreign language or literature, social science, science, and cultural diversity. Proficiency in English composition and math is required. A GPA of 2.0 is necessary to graduate.

Special: Pre-professional studies in allied health and medical fields and interdisciplinary majors, minors, and concentrations are offered. Internships in New York City, work-study programs on campus, study abroad, a 3-2 engineering degree at Columbia University School of Engineering and Applied Science, B.A.-B.S. degrees, and dual majors are available.

Faculty/Classroom: 66% of faculty are male; 34% are female. No introductory courses are taught by graduate students.

Requirements: The SAT or ACT is recommended. SAT, ACT, or Columbia's General Studies Admissions Exam scores should be submitted along with high school and all college transcripts. An autobiographical statement is required. An interview is encouraged. AP credits are accepted. Important factors in the admissions decision are personality/intangible qualities, extracurricular activities record, and evidence of special talent.

Procedure: Freshmen are admitted fall, spring, and summer. Entrance exams should be taken as early as possible. There are deferred admissions and rolling admissions plans. Early decision applications should be filed by March 1; regular applications, by June 1 for fall entry; November 1 for spring entry; and April 1 for summer entry, along with a $75 fee. Notification of early decision is sent May 1; regular decision, July 30. 20 applicants were on the 2013 waiting list; 7 were admitted. Applications are accepted online.

Transfer: 395 transfer students enrolled in 2012-2013. Most students come to GS with some college credit. 64 of 124 credits required for the bachelor's degree must be completed at GS.

Visiting: There are regularly scheduled orientations for prospective students, consisting of an admissions information session every other Wednesday, preceded by a campus tour. There are guides for informal visits and visitors may sit in on classes. To schedule a visit, contact the Office of Admissions and Financial Aid.

Financial Aid: The average freshman award was $8,000. 75% of undergraduate students work part-time. Average annual earnings from campus work are $2500. GS is a member of CSS. The FAFSA and the college's own financial statement are required. The priority date for freshman financial aid applications for fall entry is March 1. The deadline for filing freshman financial aid applications for fall entry is June 1.

International Students: There are 225 international students enrolled. The school actively recruits these students. They must take the TOEFL with a minimum score of 600 on the paper-based TOEFL (PBT) or 100 on the Internet-based version (iBT) and the college's own test, International students must take either the TOEFL or an English placement test administered by Columbia's American Language Program. Submission of recent SAT scores is encouraged. Students who have not taken the SAT must take the Columbia's General Studies Admissions Exam.

Graduates: From July 1, 2012 to June 30, 2013, 308 bachelor's degrees were awarded. The most popular majors were economics (14%), political science (8%), and history (8%). 300 companies recruited on campus in 2012-2013.

Admissions Contact: Curtis Rodgers, Dean of Admissions. E-Mail: *gsdegree@columbia.edu* Web: *www.gs.columbia.edu*

CONCORDIA COLLEGE NEW YORK D-5

Bronxville, NY 10708 (914) 337-9300

(800) 937-2655; (914) 395-4636

Full-time: 275 men, 355 women	**Faculty:** n/av
Part-time: 35 men, 70 women	**Ph.D.s:** n/av
Graduate: n/av	**Student/Faculty:** n/av
Year: semesters	**Tuition:** $23,000
Application Deadline: March 15	**Room & Board:** $9500
Freshman Class: n/av	
SAT or ACT: required	

VERY COMPETITIVE

Concordia College, founded in 1881, is a Christian liberal arts college offering undergraduate majors, including business, education, music, social work, and professional training in ministry. The figures in the above capsule and in this profile are approximate. In addition to regional accreditation, Concordia has baccalaureate program accreditation with CSWE and NCATE. The library contains 85,000 volumes, 25,000 microform items, and 8,750 audio/video tapes/CDs/DVDs, and subscribes to 350 periodicals including electronic. Computerized library services include interlibrary loans, database searching, Internet access, and Wi-Fi capability. Special learning facilities include an art gallery, education center, family center, and Lutheran education service. The 33-acre campus is in a suburban area 15 miles north of New York City. Including any residence halls, there are 21 buildings.

Student Life: 66% of undergraduates are from New York. Others are from 27 states, and 34 foreign countries. 54% are White; 11% African American. 40% are Protestant; 32% Catholic; 19% unknown denominations. The average age of freshmen is 18; all undergraduates, 24. 24% do not continue beyond their first year; 45% remain to graduate.

Housing: 424 students can be accommodated in college housing, which includes single-sex dorms. In addition, there are special-interest houses. On-campus housing is guaranteed for all 4 years. 66% of students live on campus; of those, 75% remain on campus on weekends. All students may keep cars.

Activities: 10% of men belong to 2 national fraternities; 10% of women belong to 2 national sororities. There are 25 groups on campus, including and organists guild, art, chamber and jazz ensembles, cheerleading, choir, chorus, drama, ethnic, honors, international, jazz band, literary magazine, musical theater, newspaper, orchestra, photography, professional, religious, social, social service, student government, symphony, and yearbook. Popular campus events include Guest Lectures, Dramatic Presentations, and Spring and Fall Festivals.

Sports: There are 5 intercollegiate sports for men and 6 for women, and 10 intramural sports for men and 10 for women. Facilities include an athletic center, a field house, indoor and outdoor tennis courts, squash and racquetball courts, a weight room, a fitness center, and 3 athletic fields.

Disabled Students: 50% of the campus is accessible. Facilities include wheelchair ramps, elevators, special parking, specially equipped restrooms, lowered drinking fountains, and lowered telephones.

Services: Counseling and information services are available, as is tutoring in most subjects. There is remedial math, reading, and writing.

Campus Safety and Security: Measures include 24-hour foot and vehicle patrol and security escort services. There are emergency telephones and lighted pathways/sidewalks.

Programs of Study: Concordia confers B.A., and B.S. degrees. Associate degrees are also awarded. Bachelor's degrees are awarded in BIOLOGICAL SCIENCE (biology/biological science), BUSINESS (business administration and management), COMMUNICATIONS AND THE ARTS (applied music, arts administration/management, English, and music), COMPUTER AND PHYSICAL SCIENCE (mathematics), EDUCATION (early childhood education, education, elementary education, mathematics education, music education, and social studies education), ENGINEERING AND ENVIRONMENTAL DESIGN (environmental science), SOCIAL SCIENCE (behavioral science, history, interdisciplinary studies, international studies, religion, religious music, and social work). Education, behavioral sciences, and social work are the strongest academically. Education, business administration, and behavioral sciences have the largest enrollments.

Required: To graduate, students must complete 122 semester hours with a minimum GPA of 2.0. General education requirements include 21 hours of integrated learning courses and 18 credits of discipline support courses. Students are required to take 3 credits each of phys ed. A thesis is required in some majors.

Special: A registered professional nurse program is offered in cooperation with Mount Vernon Hospital School of Nursing. Concordia also offers co-op programs in social work and education, cross-registration with a consortium of nearby colleges, internships, study abroad in England, B.A.-B.S. degrees, an interdisciplinary studies degree and credit for life experience. Accelerated degree programs are available in business administration and behavioral sciences. There is 1 national honor society, a freshman honors program, and 10 departmental honors programs.

Faculty/Classroom: 55% of faculty are male; 45% are female. All teach undergraduates. No introductory courses are taught by graduate students. The average class size in an introductory lecture is 19; in a laboratory is 12; and in a regular course is 12.

Requirements: The SAT or ACT is required. Applicants should be graduates of an accredited secondary school or have a GED certificate. Concordia prefers completion of 4 years of English, 3 of math,and 2 each of laboratory social studies, science and a foreign language. An interview is recommended, and those students applying to the music program must audition. A GPA of 2.5 is required. AP and CLEP credits are accepted. Important factors in the admissions decision are advanced placement or honors courses, evidence of special talent, and extracurricular activities record.

Procedure: Freshmen are admitted fall and spring. Entrance exams should be taken in the fall of the senior year. There are early decision, early admissions, and rolling admissions plans. Early decision applications should be filed by November 15; regular applications, by March 15 for fall entry; and December 30 for spring entry, along with a $40 fee. Notification of early decision is sent December 1; regular decision, January 15. Applications are accepted online.

Transfer: A 2.0 GPA is recommended. Applicants must submit official transcripts from previous colleges attended. Students must complete the last 30 credits at Concordia College. 30 of 122 credits required for the bachelor's degree must be completed at Concordia.

Visiting: There are regularly scheduled orientations for prospective students, Which include opportunities to interact with faculty, tour campus, learn about admission and financial aid, and discover academic and student life opportunities. There are guides for informal visits, visitors may sit in on classes, and stay overnight. To schedule a visit, contact the Admissions Office.

Financial Aid: The FAFSA is required. Check with the school for current application deadlines.

International Students: The school actively recruits these students. They must take the TOEFL, or take the SAT.

Admissions Contact: Donna Hoyt E-Mail: *admissions@concordia-ny.edu* Web: *www.concordia-ny.edu*

COOPER UNION FOR THE ADVANCEMENT OF SCIENCE AND ART D-5

New York, NY 10003	**(212) 353-4120; (212) 353-4342**
Full-time: 556 men, 307 women	**Faculty:** 50; IIB, av$
Part-time: 1 men, 4 women	**Ph.D.s:** 90%
Graduate: 36 men, 16 women	**Student/Faculty:** 17 to 1
Year: semesters, summer session	**Tuition:** $39,600
Application Deadline: January 1	**Room & Board:** $15,000
Freshman Class: 3193 applied, 247 accepted, 186 enrolled	
SAT CR/M: 650/730	**ACT:** 31 **MOST COMPETITIVE**

The Cooper Union for the Advancement of Science and Art is an all honors college that offers degrees in architecture, art, and engineering. There are 3 undergraduate schools and one graduate school. In addition to regional accreditation, Cooper Union has baccalaureate program accreditation with ABET, NAAB, and NASAD. The library contains 147,552 volumes, 24,217 microform items, and 2,228 audio/video tapes/CDs/DVDs, and subscribes to 9,730 periodicals including electronic. Computerized library services include interlibrary loans, database searching, and Internet access. Special learning facilities include an art gallery, a center for speaking and writing, an electronic resources center, and a visual resources center. The campus is in an urban area of New York City. Including any residence halls, there are 4 buildings.

Student Life: 55% of undergraduates are from New York. Others are from 39 states, 14 foreign countries, and Canada. 70% are from public schools. 37% are White; 19% Asian American; 14% race unknown. The average age of freshmen is 18; all undergraduates, 20. 5% do not continue beyond their first year; 81% remain to graduate.

Housing: 178 students can be accommodated in college housing, which includes coed dorms. On-campus housing is available on a first-come, first-served basis, and is available on a lottery system for upperclassmen. 80% of students commute. Some may keep cars.

Activities: 10% of men belong to 2 national fraternities. There are no sororities. There are 90 groups on campus, including art, band, chess, chorale, computers, dance, drama, environmental, ethnic, ethnic and musical, film, gay, honors, international, jazz band, literary magazine, musical theater, newspaper, orchestra, photography, political, professional, religious, social, social service, student government, and yearbook. Popular campus events include Annual Culture Show, Annual Talent Show, End-of-the-Year Student Art, Architecture and Engineering Exhibit and ongoing events in the Great Hall.

Sports: There are 5 intercollegiate sports for men and 3 for women, and 12 intramural sports for men and 12 for women. Facilities include access to local gyms on weekends, a nearby swimming pool, and basketball courts.

Disabled Students: 80% of the campus is accessible. Facilities include wheelchair ramps, elevators, specially equipped restrooms, special class scheduling, and special housing.

Services: Counseling and information services are available, as is tutoring in some subjects including, math, physics, speech, writing, and other forms of communication.

Campus Safety and Security: Measures include emergency notification system. There are emergency telephones, lighted pathways/sidewalks, controlled access to dorms/residences, There are security guards in all building lobbies and hand-scan technology in the residence hall.

Programs of Study: Cooper Union confers B.S., B.Arch., B.E. and B.F.A. degrees. Master's degrees are also awarded. Bachelor's degrees are awarded in COMMUNICATIONS AND THE ARTS (fine arts and graphic design), ENGINEERING AND ENVIRONMENTAL DESIGN (architecture, chemical engineering, civil engineering, electrical/electronics engineering, engineering, and mechanical engineering). Architecture, fine art and engineering are the strongest academically. Engineering has the largest enrollment.

Required: The 5-year architecture program requires 160 credits, including 30 in liberal arts and electives, for graduation. Art students must complete 128 credits, including 38 in liberal arts and electives. Engineering students are required to complete a minimum of 135 credits, including a computer programming course and approximately 12-28 credits in humanities and social sciences, with a minimum GPA of 2.0. All students must complete a four semester sequence of humanities and social science courses.

Special: Cross-registration with New School University, internships, formal study abroad for art and engineering students. Non-degree study is possible. An accelerated degree in engineering is also available (combined bachelors and masters degree program). Cooper Union also participates in a joint MEng/MD degree program with SUNY Downstate Medical Center. Students are permitted with approval, to take an elective leave to further pursue their interests and long term goals. There are 4 national honor societies and 1 departmental honors programs.

Faculty/Classroom: 73% of faculty are male; 27% are female. All teach and do research. No introductory courses are taught by graduate students. The average class size in an introductory lecture is 25; in a laboratory is 16; and in a regular course is 20.

Admissions: 8% of the 2013-2014 applicants were accepted. The SAT scores for the 2013-2014 freshman class were: Critical Reading--3% below 500, 19% between 500 and 599, 47% between 600 and 699, and 31% between 700 and 800; Math--9% below 500, 17% between 500 and 599, 18% between 600 and 699, and 57% between 700 and 800. The ACT scores were 25% between 27 and 28, and 75% above 28. 90% of the current freshmen were in the top fifth of their class; 95% were in the top two fifths. 10 freshmen graduated first in their class.

Requirements: The SAT or ACT is required. Engineering applicants must take SAT Subject Tests in mathematics I or II and physics or chemistry. Graduation from an approved secondary school is required. Applicants should have completed 16 to 18 high school academic credits, depending on their major. An essay is part of the application process. Art students must submit a portfolio. Art and architecture applicants must complete a project called the home test. AP credits are accepted. Important factors in the admissions decision are personality/intangible qualities, evidence of special talent, and advanced placement or honors courses.

Procedure: Freshmen are admitted fall. Entrance exams should be taken before February 1. There are early decision, early admissions, and deferred admissions plans. Early decision applications should be filed by December 1; regular applications, by January 1 for fall entry, along with a $70 fee. Notification of early decision is sent February 1; regular decision, April 1.

75 early decision candidates were accepted for the 2013-2014 class. 75 applicants were on the 2013 waiting list; 15 were admitted. Applications are accepted online.

Transfer: 20 transfer students enrolled in 2012-2013. Art and architecture transfer applicants must present a portfolio and a minimum of 24 credits in studio classes. Engineering transfer applicants must submit a transcript with grades of B or better in at least 24 credits of appropriate courses. 68 of 128 credits required for the bachelor's degree must be completed at Cooper Union.

Visiting: There are regularly scheduled orientations for prospective students, consisting of open house and portfolio review days for art and open house for engineering; architecture tours are by appointment. There are guides for informal visits and visitors may sit in on classes. To schedule a visit, contact the Office of Admissions and Records.

Financial Aid: In 2013-2014, 100% of all full-time freshmen and 100% of continuing full-time students received some form of financial aid. 36% of all full-time freshmen and 35% of continuing full-time students received need-based aid. The average freshman award was $37,500. Need-based scholarships or need-based grants averaged $5,254 ($5,500 maximum); need-based self-help aid (loans and jobs) averaged $3,217 ($3,768 maximum); and other non-need-based awards and non-need-based scholarships averaged $37,500 ($37,500 maximum). 47% of undergraduate students work part time. Average annual earnings from campus work are $1001. The average financial indebtedness of the 2013 graduate was $14,902. Cooper Union is a member of CSS. The CSS/Profile and FAFSA are required. The priority date for freshman financial aid applications for fall entry is April 15. The deadline for filing freshman financial aid applications for fall entry is May 1.

International Students: There are 86 international students enrolled. They must take the TOEFL with a minimum score of 600 on the paper-based TOEFL (PBT) or 100 on the Internet-based version (iBT). They must also take the SAT or ACT, and the college's own entrance exam. All freshman applicants must take the SAT; art and architecture students must also take the home test.

Graduates: From July 1, 2012 to June 30, 2013, 184 bachelor's degrees were awarded. The most popular majors were fine arts (30%), electrical engineering (16%), and mechanical engineering (15%). 110 companies recruited on campus in 2012-2013. In an average class, 1% graduate in 3 years or less, 70% graduate in 4 years or less, 81% graduate in 5 years or less, and 82% graduate in 6 years or less. Of the 2012 graduating class, 42% were enrolled in graduate school within 6 months of graduation, and 42% were employed.

Admissions Contact: Mitchell Lipton, Dean of Admissions and Records. E-Mail: *admissions@cooper.edu* Web: *http:/cooper.edu*

CORNELL UNIVERSITY — C-4

Ithaca, NY 14850 — **(607) 255-5241**

Full-time: 7050 men, 7343 women	**Faculty:** n/av
Part-time: n/av	**Ph.D.s:** n/av
Graduate: 4024 men, 3176 women	**Student/Faculty:** n/av
Year: semesters, summer session	**Tuition:** $45,359
Application Deadline: January 2	**Room & Board:** $13,678

Freshman Class: 39999 applied, 6222 accepted, 3223 enrolled
SAT or ACT: required

MOST COMPETITIVE

Cornell University was founded in 1865 as the federal land-grant institution of New York State. It a private endowed university, a member of the Ivy League/Ancient Eight, and a partner of the State University of New York. It has 7 undergraduate units and 4 graduate and professional units in Ithaca, 2 medical graduate and professional units in New York City, and 1 in Doha, Qatar. The Cornell NYC Tech Campus in New York City is the latest addition. There are 7 undergraduate schools and 4 graduate schools. In addition to regional accreditation, Cornell has baccalaureate program accreditation with AACSB, ABET, ASLA, and NAAB. The library contains 8.6 million volumes, 0 microform items, and 154,231 audio/video tapes/CDs/DVDs, and subscribes to 102,683 periodicals including electronic. Computerized library services include interlibrary loans, database searching, Internet access, and Wi-Fi capability. Special learning facilities include an art gallery, radio station, TV station, biotechnology institute, woods sanctuary, 4 designated national resource centers, 2 local optical observatories, Africana Studies and research center, arboretum, particle accelerator, supercomputers, national research centers, performing arts center, lab of ornithology, vertebrates museum, living and learning communities, campus orchard, dairy pilot plant, mineralogical museum, animal teaching hospital, 2 agricultural experiment stations, and a marine laboratory. The 745-acre campus is in a rural area 60 miles south of Syracuse, NY. Including any residence halls, there are 770 buildings.

Student Life: 64% of undergraduates are from out of state, mostly the Middle Atlantic. Students are from 49 states, 77 foreign countries, and Canada. 42% are White; 16% Asian American; 11% Hispanic. The average age of freshmen is 19; all undergraduates, 20. 3% do not continue beyond their first year; 93% remain to graduate.

Housing: 9203 students can be accommodated in college housing, which includes single-sex and coed dorms, on-campus apartments, and married student housing. In addition, there are language houses, special-interest houses, fraternity houses, and sorority houses. On-campus housing is available on a lottery system for upperclassmen. 55% of students live on campus; of those, 90% remain on campus on weekends. All students may keep cars.

Activities: 27% of men belong to 2 local and 48 national fraternities; 25% of women belong to 19 national sororities. There are 1017 groups on campus, including art, band, cheerleading, chess, choir, chorale, chorus, communications, computers, dance, debate, drama, drill team, environmental, ethnic, film, forensics, gay, honors, international, jazz band, literary magazine, marching band, musical theater, newspaper, orchestra, pep band, photography, political, professional, radio and TV, religious, social, social service, student government, symphony, and yearbook. Popular campus events include Dragon Day, New Student Reading Project, and Third World Festival of the Arts.

Sports: Facilities include indoor and outdoor tracks, a 5000-seat indoor gym, 3 swimming pools, a 25000-seat stadium, 16 intercollegiate fields, a bowling alley, intramural fields, a boat house, indoor and outdoor tennis courts, and the Lindseth climbing wall.

Disabled Students: Facilities include wheelchair ramps, elevators, special parking, specially equipped restrooms, special class scheduling, lowered drinking fountains, lowered telephones, special housing, alternative test arrangements, and bus passes or van transportation.

Services: Counseling and information services are available, as is tutoring in some subjects, Many introductory courses in math, the sciences, and economics. There is a reader service for the blind. Biology and math student support centers, and writing workshops are also available. In addition, supplemental instruction in introductory math, chemistry, biology, economics, and physics courses are provided.

Campus Safety and Security: Measures include 24-hour foot and vehicle patrol, emergency notification system, self-defense education, and security escort services. There are shuttle buses, emergency telephones, and lighted pathways/sidewalks.

Programs of Study: Cornell confers B.A., B.S., B.Arch. and B.F.A. degrees. Master's and doctoral degrees are also awarded. Bachelor's degrees are awarded in AGRICULTURE (agricultural sciences, animal science, international agriculture / rural development, natural resources, plant science, and viticulture and enology), BIOLOGICAL SCIENCE (biology/biological science, biology and society, biometrics and biostatistics, entomology, human biology, health, and society, and nutritional sciences), BUSINESS (applied economics / management, hotel and restaurant administration, industrial and labor relations, and policy analysis and management), COMMUNICATIONS AND THE ARTS (art history, classics, communication, comparative literature, dance, design and environmental analysis, English, fiber science and apparel design, film arts, fine arts, French, German, Italian, linguistics, music, Spanish, and theatre arts), COMPUTER AND PHYSICAL SCIENCE (astronomy, atmospheric sciences and meteorology, chemistry / chemical biology, computer science, information sciences and systems, information science, mathematics, physics, science of earth systems, science of natural and environmental systems, science and technology studies, and statistics), ENGINEERING AND ENVIRONMENTAL DESIGN (architecture, bioengineering, chemical engineering, civil engineering, electrical and computer engineering, engineering physics, environmental engineering, history of architecture / urban development, landscape architecture, materials science and engineering, mechanical engineering, and operations research and engineering), SOCIAL SCIENCE (africana studies, American studies, anthropology, archeology, asian studies, china asia-pacific studies, developmental sociology, economics, government, feminist, gender, sexuality studies, food science, German area studies, history, human development, Near Eastern studies, philosophy, psychology, religious studies, sociology, and urban studies). Engineering, business, agriculture, and life sciences have the largest enrollments.

Required: A student's college determines degree requirements such as residency, number of credits, distribution of credits, and grade averages. See the individual requirements listed by each college or school or contact the college registrar's office.

Special: Cornell's colleges and schools offer nearly unlimited opportunities for international study internships and exchanges. There are opportunities for dual-majors and minors throughout the university. Refer to information provided by the individual schools, colleges, and programs for details. There are 7 national honor societies, including Phi Beta Kappa.

Faculty/Classroom: No introductory courses are taught by graduate students.

Admissions: 16% of the 2013-2014 applicants were accepted. The SAT scores for the 2013-2014 freshman class were: Critical Reading--10% between 500 and 599, 40% between 600 and 699, and 50% between 700 and 800; Math--5% between 500 and 599, 29% between 600 and 699, and 66% between 700 and 800.

Requirements: The SAT or ACT is required. The ACT Optional Writing test is also required. In addition, An essay is required as part of the application process. Other requirements vary by division or program, including specific SAT Subject tests and selection of courses within the minimum 16 secondary-school academic units needed. An interview and/or portfolio is required for specific majors. AP credits are accepted.

Procedure: Freshmen are admitted fall. There are early decision and deferred admissions plans. Early decision applications should be filed by November 1; regular applications, by January 2 for fall entry, along with a $75 fee. Notifications are sent in April. 1247 early decision candidates were accepted for the 2013-2014 class. 1966 applicants were on the 2013 waiting list; 168 were admitted. Applications are accepted online.

Transfer: 542 transfer students enrolled in 2012-2013. All applicants must submit high school and college transcripts, as well as scores from the SAT or ACT if taken previously. Other admission requirements vary by program, including the number of credits that must be completed at Cornell. 60 of 120 credits required for the bachelor's degree must be completed at Cornell.

Visiting: There are regularly scheduled orientations for prospective students, Student visits consist of campus tours and information sessions. There are guides for informal visits, visitors may sit in on classes, and stay overnight. To schedule a visit, contact the Red Carpet Society at (607) 255-3447.

Financial Aid: The average freshman award was $42,439. Need-based scholarships or need-based grants averaged $36,604; and need-based self-help aid (loans and jobs) averaged $5,835. The average financial indebtedness of the 2013 graduate was $20,577. The CSS/Profile, FAFSA, and the college's own financial statement, are required. The deadline for filing freshman financial aid applications for fall entry is February 15.

International Students: There are 1418 international students enrolled. The school actively recruits these students. They must take the TOEFL with a minimum score of 600 on the paper-based TOEFL (PBT) or 100 on the Internet-based version (iBT). They must also take the SAT or ACT.

Graduates: From July 1, 2012 to June 30, 2013, 3577 bachelor's degrees were awarded. The most popular majors were engineering (18%), business (14%), and biological/life sciences (13%). In an average class, 9% graduate in 3 years or less, 87% graduate in 4 years or less, 92% graduate in 5 years or less, and 93% graduate in 6 years or less.

Admissions Contact: Jason Locke, Director of Undergraduate Admissions. E-Mail: *admissions@cornell.edu* Web: *admissions.cornell.edu*

CUNY-CITY COLLEGE D-5

New York, NY 10031 **(212) 650-6977; (212) 650-6417**

Full-time: 4398 men, 4876 women	**Faculty:** 510
Part-time: 1695 men, 1660 women	**Ph.D.s:** 87%
Graduate: 1201 men, 1634 women	**Student/Faculty:** 13 to 1
Year: semesters, summer session	**Tuition:** $5788 ($11,998)
Application Deadline: December 1	**Room & Board:** $13,788

Freshman Class: 26628 applied, 2648 accepted, 1444 enrolled
SAT CR/M: 510/550

HIGHLY COMPETITIVE+

City College, founded in 1847, is a public liberal arts college that is part of the City University of New York. The college offers programs through 4 undergraduate and 4 graduate schools and 2 professional centers. There are 6 undergraduate schools and 6 graduate schools. In addition to regional accreditation, CCNY has baccalaureate program accreditation with ABET, ABFSE, NAAB, and NCATE. The 47 libraries contain 1.8 million volumes, 901,300 microform items, and 225,480 audio/video tapes/CDs/DVDs, and subscribe to 56,476 periodicals including electronic. Computerized library services include interlibrary loans, database searching, Internet access, and Wi-Fi capability. Special learning facilities include an art gallery, planetarium, radio station, TV station, weather station, laser labs, microwave labs, and structural biology lab. The 35-acre campus is in an urban area in New York City. Including any residence halls, there are 14 buildings.

Student Life: 96% of undergraduates are from New York. Others are from 40 states, 158 foreign countries, and Canada. 84% are from public schools. 25% are Hispanic; 23% African American; 21% Asian American. The average age of freshmen is 19; all undergraduates, 24. 22% do not continue beyond their first year; 42% remain to graduate.

Housing: 580 students can be accommodated in college housing, which includes single-sex and coed on-campus apartments and married student housing. On-campus housing is available on a first-come and first-served basis. Priority is given to out-of-town students. 97% of students commute. Alcohol is not permitted. All students may keep cars.

Activities: There are 170 groups on campus, including art, band, cheerleading, chess, chorus, computers, debate, drama, ethnic, film, gay, honors, international, jazz band, literary magazine, newspaper, orchestra, photography, political, professional, radio and TV, religious, social, social service, student government, and yearbook. Popular campus events include Langston Hughes Poetry Contest, Dance Theater of Harlem Performances at Davis Center and Architecture Lecture Series.

Sports: There are 9 intercollegiate sports for men and 9 for women, and 9 intramural sports for men and 9 for women. Facilities include a weight room, swimming pools, and two gyms.

Disabled Students: 94% of the campus is accessible. Facilities include wheelchair ramps, elevators, special parking, specially equipped restrooms, special class scheduling, lowered drinking fountains, and lowered telephones.

Services: Counseling and information services are available, as is tutoring in most subjects. There is a reader service for the blind.

Campus Safety and Security: Measures include 24-hour foot and vehicle patrol, emergency notification system, and security escort services. There are shuttle buses, emergency telephones, lighted pathways/sidewalks, controlled access to dorms/residences, bicycle patrols, IDs, criminal investigations, and security systems.

Programs of Study: CCNY confers B.A., B.S., B.Arch., B.E., B.F.A., B.M.E. and B.S.Ed. degrees. Master's and doctoral degrees are also awarded. Bachelor's degrees are awarded in BIOLOGICAL SCIENCE (biology/biological science), BUSINESS (business administration and management), COMMUNICATIONS AND THE ARTS (art, communications, comparative literature, dramatic arts, English, film arts, fine arts, French, multimedia, music, performing arts, romance languages and literature, Spanish, and video), COMPUTER AND PHYSICAL SCIENCE (atmospheric sciences and meteorology, chemistry, computer science, earth science, geology, mathematics, physics, and quantitative methods), EDUCATION (art education, bilingual/bicultural education, early childhood education, education of the emotionally handicapped, education of the mentally handicapped, elementary education, English education, foreign languages education, mathematics education, secondary education, social studies education, and special education), ENGINEERING AND ENVIRONMENTAL DESIGN (architecture, biomedical engineering, chemical engineering, civil engineering, computer engineering, electrical/electronics engineering, environmental engineering, environmental science, landscape architecture/design, and mechanical engineering), HEALTH PROFESSIONS (biomedical science, physician's assistant, predentistry, and premedicine), SOCIAL SCIENCE (American studies, anthropology, area studies, Asian/Oriental studies, economics, ethnic studies, history, international studies, Latin American studies, philosophy, political science/government, prelaw, psychology, sociology, and urban studies). Engineering, architecture, and sciences are the strongest academically. Engineering, architecture, and psychology have the largest enrollments.

Required: Students must successfully complete 120 credits, with 32 to 48 in the major, and maintain a minimum GPA of 2.0. A core curriculum must be met,including courses in anthropology, art, English, psychology, and sociology. Students must complete a college proficiency exam.

Special: Cross-registration is permitted with other City University colleges. A 7-year biomedical education degree is available. Opportunities are provided for a co-op program in engineering, internships, a Washington semester, work-study programs, a wide variety of accelerated degree programs, dual majors, credit by exam, credit for life experience, study abroad in 12 countries, and a B.A.-B.S. degree in biomedical engineering, math, physics, and psychology. There are 2 national honor societies, including Phi Beta Kappa, a freshman honors program, and 100 departmental honors programs.

Faculty/Classroom: 56% of faculty are male; 44% are female. 77% teach undergraduates, 65% do research, and 53% do both. No introductory courses are taught by graduate students. The average class size in an introductory lecture is 29; in a laboratory is 15; and in a regular course is 19.

Admissions: 10% of the 2013-2014 applicants were accepted. The SAT scores for the 2013-2014 freshman class were: Critical Reading--9% below 500, 67% between 500 and 599, 17% between 600 and 699, and 7% between 700 and 800; Math--14% below 500, 43% between 500 and 599, 31% between 600 and 699, and 12% between 700 and 800. 60% of the current freshmen were in the top fifth of their class; 87% were in the top two fifths.

Requirements: The SAT is required. Students who apply should have a recommended satisfactory minimum SAT score or an ACT score of 22. Graduation from an accredited secondary school is generally required, but a GED will be accepted. 14 academic credits should be presented with a minimum grade average of 80%. AP credits are accepted.

Procedure: Freshmen are admitted to all sessions. Entrance exams should be taken prior to registration. There is a rolling admissions plan. Applications should be filed by December 1 for fall entry; October 15 for spring entry, along with a $65 fee. Notifications are sent January 15. Applications are accepted online.

Transfer: 1427 transfer students enrolled in 2012-2013. Transfer applicants must have earned a minimum of 24 credit hours and maintained a GPA of 2.0. Selected programs have more competitive requirements. 32 of 120 credits required for the bachelor's degree must be completed at CCNY.

Visiting: There are regularly scheduled orientations for prospective students. There are guides for informal visits and visitors may sit in on classes. To schedule a visit, contact the Admissions Office.

Financial Aid: In 2013-2014, 71% of all full-time freshmen and 75% of

continuing full-time students received some form of financial aid. 70% of all full-time freshmen and 73% of continuing full-time students received need-based aid. The average freshman award was $8,646. Need-based scholarships or need-based grants averaged $7,942; need-based self-help aid (loans and jobs) averaged $3,202; other non-need-based awards and non-need-based scholarships averaged $2,002; and $2,900 from other forms of aid. The average financial indebtedness of the 2013 graduate was $16,944. The FAFSA and the state aid form are required. The priority date for freshman financial aid applications for fall entry is April 1. The deadline for filing freshman financial aid applications for fall entry is rolling.

International Students: There are 1758 international students enrolled. They must take the TOEFL with a minimum score of 500 on the paper-based TOEFL (PBT) or 61 on the Internet-based version (iBT). They must also take the ACT and the CUNY Placement Exam.

Graduates: From July 1, 2012 to June 30, 2013, 1975 bachelor's degrees were awarded. The most popular majors were psychology (14%), engineering (13%), and social sciences (11%). 850 companies recruited on campus in 2012-2013. In an average class, 8% graduate in 4 years or less, 30% graduate in 5 years or less, and 42% graduate in 6 years or less. Of the 2012 graduating class, 18% were enrolled in graduate school within 6 months of graduation.

Admissions Contact: Joe Fantozzi, Director of Admissions. E-Mail: *admissions@admin.ccny.cuny.edu* Web: *www.ccny.cuny.edu*

DAEMEN COLLEGE A-3

Amherst, NY 14226 (716) 839-8225
(800) 462-7652; (716) 839-8370

Full-time: 390 men, 975 women	**Faculty:** n/av; IIB, --$
Part-time: 60 men, 260 women	**Ph.D.s:** n/av
Graduate: 125 men, 725 women	**Student/Faculty:** n/av
Year: semesters, summer session	**Tuition:** $22,00
Application Deadline: open	**Room & Board:** $11,000
Freshman Class: n/av	
SAT or ACT: required	

COMPETITIVE

Daemen College, founded in 1947, is a private institution offering undergraduate and graduate programs in the liberal and fine arts, business, education, allied health professions, and natural sciences. The figures in the above capsule and in this profile are approximate. There is 1 undergraduate school and 1 graduate school. In addition to regional accreditation, Daemen has baccalaureate program accreditation with APTA, CSWE, and NLN. The library contains 140,576 volumes, 28,055 microform items, and 2,354 audio/video tapes/CDs/DVDs, and subscribes to 31,925 periodicals including electronic. Computerized library services include interlibrary loans, database searching, Internet access, and laptop Internet portals. Special learning facilities include a learning resource center, art gallery, video conference center. The 35-acre campus is in a suburban area 9 miles northeast of downtown Buffalo. Including any residence halls, there are 18 buildings.

Student Life: 96% of undergraduates are from New York. Others are from 16 states, 4 foreign countries, and Canada. 85% are white. 42% are Catholic; 15% Protestant; 12% Student designated. The average age of freshmen is 18; all undergraduates, 23. 26% do not continue beyond their first year; 54% remain to graduate.

Housing: 524 students can be accommodated in college housing, which includes coed dorms and on-campus apartments. a quiet dorm. On-campus housing is guaranteed for all 4 years. 65% of students commute. All students may keep cars.

Activities: 6% of men belong to 1 local fraternity; 4% of women belong to 4 local sororities. There are 47 groups on campus, including Amnesty International, academic clubs, Pre-law association, student without borders, art, cheerleading, choir, dance, drama, environmental, ethnic, gay, honors, literary magazine, newspaper, professional, social, social service, student government, wellness club, and yearbook. Popular campus events include Homecoming, Battle of the Bands, and Spring Fest.

Sports: There are 4 intercollegiate sports for men and 4 for women, and 4 intramural sports for men and 2 for women. Facilities include a gym, weight and exercise rooms, saunas, and a volleyball sand court.

Disabled Students: 83% of the campus is accessible. Facilities include wheelchair ramps, elevators, special parking, specially equipped restrooms, lowered drinking fountains, and lowered telephones.

Services: Counseling and information services are available, as is tutoring in every subject. There is remedial math, reading, and writing.

Campus Safety and Security: Measures include 24-hour foot and vehicle patrol and security escort services. There are emergency telephones, lighted pathways/sidewalks, and video monitors.

Programs of Study: Daemen confers B.A., B.S., B.S./M.S., and B.F.A. degrees. Master's and doctoral degrees are also awarded. Bachelor's degrees are awarded in AGRICULTURE (environmental studies), BIOLOGICAL SCIENCE (biochemistry and biology/biological science), BUSINESS (accounting and business administration and management), COMMUNICATIONS AND THE ARTS (animation, applied art, art, arts administration/management, English, fine arts, French, graphic design, and Spanish), COMPUTER AND PHYSICAL SCIENCE (mathematics and natural sciences), EDUCATION (art education, early childhood education, elementary education, English education, foreign languages education, mathematics education, science education, and social studies education), HEALTH PROFESSIONS (health science, nursing, physician's assistant, and preventive/wellness health care), SOCIAL SCIENCE (history, paralegal studies, political science/government, psychology, religion, and social work). Physical therapy, physician assistant, and natural science are the strongest academically. Nursing, childhood education, physical therapy, and natural science have the largest enrollments.

Required: To graduate, students must complete 120 to 199 hours (depending on the degree program) with a minimum GPA of 2.0. Students are required to complete a minimum of 30 credit hours of course work in residence. The final semester's course work must be taken in residence.

Special: Daemen offers cooperative programs in all majors, internships, cross-registration within the Western New York Consortium of Colleges and Universities, student-designed majors, work-study programs, an accelerated degree program in nursing, dual majors, a Washington semester, and study abroad in 6 countries. There is an International Studies Program that leads to a minor in international studies. There are 8 national honor societies, a freshman honors program, and 20 departmental honors programs.

Faculty/Classroom: 40% of faculty are male; 60% are female. 64% teach undergraduates. No introductory courses are taught by graduate students. The average class size in an introductory lecture is 17; in a laboratory is 10; and in a regular course is 14.

Requirements: The SAT or ACT is required. Applicants must be graduates of an accredited secondary school or have the GED equivalent. Some departments have further admissions requirements, including a portfolio review for art majors, 3-year sequences of math and science for all natural science programs, and 2 essays, 3 letters of recommendation, and a supplemental application for the physician assistant program. A GPA of 2.0 is required. AP and CLEP credits are accepted. Important factors in the admissions decision are advanced placement or honors courses, leadership record, and evidence of special talent.

Procedure: Freshmen are admitted fall, spring, and summer. Entrance exams should be taken by the summer following the senior year. There are early admissions, deferred admissions, and rolling admissions plans. Application deadlines are open. Notification is sent on a rolling basis. Applications are accepted online.

Transfer: In a recent year, 243 transfer students enrolled. Applicants must present college transcripts and an indication of good standing from the last institution attended and a minimum GPA of 2.0. to 2.8. Physician assistant applicants should submit essays, 3 letters of recommendation, and supplemental applications. 30 of 120 credits required for the bachelor's degree must be completed at Daemen.

Visiting: There are regularly scheduled orientations for prospective students. Two 5-day orientations include a campus tour, an interview, and placement testing in math and English during July and August. Fall Open House in October, College Night in September, and Day at Daemen in September and November are other regularly scheduled admissions events. There are guides for informal visits, visitors may sit in on classes, and stay overnight. To schedule a visit, contact the Admissions Office.

Financial Aid: In a recent year, 88% of all full-time freshmen and 90% of continuing full-time students received some form of financial aid. 83% of all full-time freshmen and 82% of continuing full-time students received need-based aid. The average freshman award was $12,769. Need-based scholarships or need-based grants averaged $8,931; need-based self-help aid (loans and jobs) averaged $4,356; non-need-based athletic scholarships averaged $6,833; and other non-need-based awards and non-need-based scholarships averaged $3,149. 20% of undergraduate students work part-time. The FAFSA, the state aid form, and foreign student certification of finances are required. Check with the school for current application deadlines.

International Students: There are 10 international students enrolled. They must take the TOEFL.

Graduates: In a recent year, 279 bachelor's degrees were awarded. The most popular majors were nursing (18%), natural science (16%), and early childhood/childhood education (15%). In an average class, 35% graduate in 4 years or less, 50% graduate in 5 years or less, and 54% graduate in 6 years or less. Of a recent graduating class, 25% were enrolled in graduate school within 6 months of graduation, and 90% were employed.

Admissions Contact: Dean of Admissions. A campus DVD is available. E-Mail: *admissions@daemen.edu* Web: *www.daemen.edu*

DOMINICAN COLLEGE D-5

Orangeburg, NY 10962 (845) 848-7900
(866) 432-4636; (845) 365-3150

Full-time: 466 men, 897 women	**Faculty:** 64; IIA, --$
Part-time: 66 men, 248 women	**Ph.D.s:** 56%
Graduate: 64 men, 242 women	**Student/Faculty:** 21 to 1
Year: semesters, summer session	**Tuition:** $21,500
Application Deadline: open	**Room & Board:** $10,500
Freshman Class: 1474 applied, 1072 accepted, 375 enrolled	
SAT CR/M/W: 451/451/448 **ACT:** 18	**COMPETITIVE**

Dominican College, founded in 1952, is a private Catholic institution offering undergraduate and graduate programs in business, biology, education, liberal arts, nursing, premedicine, occupational therapy, and social sciences. There are 6 undergraduate schools and 5 graduate schools. In addition to regional accreditation, Dominican has baccalaureate program accreditation with CSWE and TEAC. The library contains 95,021 volumes, 17,000 microform items, and 1000 audio/video tapes/CDs/DVDs, and subscribes to 10,500 periodicals including electronic. Computerized library services include interlibrary loans, database searching, Internet access, and laptop Internet portals. Special learning facilities include a learning resource center. The 70-acre campus is in a suburban area 17 miles north of New York City. Including any residence halls, there are 16 buildings.

Student Life: 74% of undergraduates are from New York. Others are from 25 states, 18 foreign countries, and Canada. 70% are from public schools. 53% are white; 24% Hispanic; 20% African American; 12% Asian American. The average age of freshmen is 18; all undergraduates, 24. 34% do not continue beyond their first year; 47% remain to graduate.

Housing: 750 students can be accommodated in college housing, which includes coed dorms. On-campus housing is guaranteed for all 4 years. 52% of students live on campus; of those, 40% remain on campus on weekends. Alcohol is not permitted. All students may keep cars.

Activities: There are no fraternities or sororities. There are 27 groups on campus, including cheerleading, chorus, computers, debate, drama, ethnic, honors, literary magazine, musical theater, newspaper, professional, religious, social, social service, and student government. Popular campus events include Fire in the Sky, Family Day, and Fall Festival.

Sports: There are 5 intercollegiate sports for men and 7 for women, and 4 intramural sports for men and 4 for women. Facilities include a soccer and lacrosse field, a softball field, a practice field, a gym, an indoor track, a weight room, and a fitness center.

Disabled Students: All of the campus is accessible. Facilities include wheelchair ramps, special parking, specially equipped restrooms, lowered drinking fountains, and lowered telephones.

Services: Counseling and information services are available, as is tutoring in some subjects, including English and math. There is remedial math, reading, and writing. Content-based tutoring is also available.

Campus Safety and Security: Measures include 24-hour foot and vehicle patrol, emergency notification system, and security escort services. There are shuttle buses and lighted pathways/sidewalks.

Programs of Study: Dominican confers B.A., B.S., B.S.Ed., B.S.N., and B.S.W. degrees. Associates, master's, and doctoral degrees are also awarded. Bachelor's degrees are awarded in BIOLOGICAL SCIENCE (biology/biological science), BUSINESS (accounting, banking and finance, business administration and management, business economics, human resources, international business management, and marketing/retailing/merchandising), COMMUNICATIONS AND THE ARTS (English and Spanish), COMPUTER AND PHYSICAL SCIENCE (computer science, information sciences and systems, and mathematics), EDUCATION (athletic training, elementary education, mathematics education, science education, secondary education, and special education), HEALTH PROFESSIONS (health care administration, nursing, and occupational therapy), SOCIAL SCIENCE (criminal justice, history, humanities, psychology, social science, and social work). Occupational therapy, nursing, and physical therapy are the strongest academically. Nursing, occupational therapy, and biology have the largest enrollments.

Required: All students must complete courses in English and communications. Computer courses are required for business majors. To graduate, all students must complete 120 semester hours, including a general education curriculum of 36 to 39 credits. Distribution requirements include 12 to 15 credits in Communications and Analysis; 12 credits in Roots of Contemporary Life and Culture; and 12 credits in Issues in Contemporary Life and Culture. A minimum GPA of 2.7 must be maintained by nursing majors; 3.0 for occupational therapy majors. All other majors require a minimum of 2.0.

Special: There are internship opportunities available in various fields. A 3-2 engineering degree with Manhattan College is also offered. Dual teacher certification in elementary or secondary education and special education is available. Credit for life experience is granted through submission of a portfolio. An accelerated B.S.N. and B.S. degree are available as well as a combined B.S./M.S. in occupational therapy. Weekend College, offered on a trimester basis, is designed to meet the needs of working adults. There are 7 national honor societies and a freshman honors program.

Faculty/Classroom: 28% of faculty are male; 72% are female. 88% teach undergraduates. No introductory courses are taught by graduate students. The average class size in an introductory lecture is 24; in a laboratory, 16; and in a regular course, 18.

Admissions: The SAT scores for a recent freshman class were: Critical Reading--77% below 500, 20% between 500 and 599, 2% between 600 and 700, and 1% above 700; Math--75% below 500, 21% between 500 and 599, and 4% between 600 and 700; Writing--75% below 500, 21% between 500 and 599, 3% between 600 and 700, and 1% above 700. The ACT scores were 32% below 21, 58% between 21 and 23, 5% between 24 and 26, and 5% between 27 and 28.

Requirements: The SAT is required. The ACT Optional Writing test is also required. In addition, applicants should be graduates of an accredited secondary school or possess a GED equivalent. An interview and an essay are required for some professional programs. Recommended preparation includes 16 academic units of study distributed among English, math, natural sciences, and foreign language. AP and CLEP credits are accepted. Important factors in the admissions decision are advanced placement or honors courses, leadership record, and extracurricular activities record.

Procedure: Freshmen are admitted to all sessions. Entrance exams should be taken by November of the senior year. There are deferred admissions and rolling admissions plans. Application deadlines are open. The application fee is $35. Notification is sent on a rolling basis. Applications are accepted online.

Transfer: Applicants must submit a transcript from their previous school. A minimum GPA of 2.0 is required. An interview may be required. 30 of 120 credits required for the bachelor's degree must be completed at Dominican.

Visiting: There are regularly scheduled orientations for prospective students. There are guides for informal visits and visitors may sit in on classes. To schedule a visit, contact Admissions.

Financial Aid: In a recent year, 97% of all full-time freshmen and 84% of continuing full-time students received some form of financial aid. 91% of all full-time freshmen and 84% of continuing full-time students received need-based aid. The average freshmen award was $14,526, with $11,745 ($15,000 maximum) from need-based scholarships or need-based grants; $3834 ($4625 maximum) from need-based self-help aid (loans and jobs); and $9101 ($10,000 maximum) from non-need-based athletic scholarships. 85% of undergraduate students work part-time. Average annual earnings from campus work are $1500. The average financial indebtedness of recent graduates was $26,515. Dominican is a member of CSS. The FAFSA and the state aid form are required. The priority date for freshman financial aid applications for fall entry is February 15. Check with the school for the current deadline for filing freshman financial aid applications.

International Students: They must take the TOEFL. They must also take the SAT or ACT.

Graduates: In a recent year, 298 bachelor's degrees were awarded. The most popular majors were health (33%), business (24%), and social sciences (15%). 25 companies recruited on campus in a recent year. In an average class, 27% graduate in 4 years or less, 42% graduate in 5 years or less, and 48% graduate in 6 years or less.

Admissions Contact: Director of Admissions. E-Mail: *admissions@dc.edu* Web: *www.dc.edu*

DOWLING COLLEGE E-5

Oakdale, NY 11769-1999 (631) 244-3436
(800) DOWLING; (631) 563-3271

Full-time: 980 men, 1210 women	**Faculty:** n/av; IIB, -$
Part-time: 480 men, 765 women	**Ph.D.s:** n/av
Graduate: 850 men, 1550 women	**Student/Faculty:** n/av
Year: semesters, summer session	**Tuition:** $16,800
Application Deadline: see profile	**Room & Board:** $9800
Freshman Class: n/av	
	LESS COMPETITIVE

Dowling College, founded in 1955, is an independent comprehensive institution offering programs in the arts and sciences, aviation and transportation, business, and education. The figures in the above capsule and in this profile are approximate. There are 4 undergraduate schools and 3 graduate schools. In addition to regional accreditation, Dowling has baccalaureate program accreditation with NCATE. The 2 libraries contain 222,920 volumes, 394,000 microform items, and 2,843 audio/video tapes/CDs/DVDs, and subscribe to 961 periodicals including electronic. Computerized library services include interlibrary loans, database searching, Internet access, and laptop Internet portals. Special learning facilities include a learning resource center, art gallery, radio station, government documents, and the Federal Aviation Administration (FAA) Aviation Education Resource Center. The 156-acre campus is in a suburban area 50 miles east of New York City. Including any residence halls, there are 10 buildings.

Student Life: 88% of undergraduates are from New York. Others are from 31 states, 61 foreign countries, and Canada. 89% are from public schools. 61% are white. The average age of freshmen is 19; all undergraduates, 22. 33% do not continue beyond their first year; 48% remain to graduate.

Housing: 496 students can be accommodated in college housing, which includes coed on-campus apartments. On-campus housing is available on a first-come and first-served basis. Priority is given to out-of-town students. 82% of students commute. Alcohol is not permitted. All students may keep cars.

Activities: There are no fraternities or sororities. There are 39 groups on campus, including aeronautics, arts, cheerleading, choir, chorus, computers, drama, ethnic, gay, gospel choir, honors, international, literary magazine, martial arts, newspaper, orchestra, photography, professional, psychology, radio and TV, religious, social, and student government. Popular campus events include Freshman Mixer, Holiday Party, and Spring Cotillion.

Sports: There are 8 intercollegiate sports for men and 9 for women, and 1 intramural sports for men and 1 for women. Facilities include a basketball court, a weight room, tennis courts, and a fitness center.

Disabled Students: All of the campus is accessible. Facilities include wheelchair ramps, elevators, special parking, specially equipped restrooms, special class scheduling, lowered drinking fountains, and lowered telephones.

Services: Counseling and information services are available, as is tutoring in most subjects. There is remedial math, reading, and writing.

Campus Safety and Security: Measures include 24-hour foot and vehicle patrol and security escort services. There are shuttle buses, emergency telephones, and lighted pathways/sidewalks.

Programs of Study: Dowling confers B.A., B.S., and B.B.A. degrees. Master's and doctoral degrees are also awarded. Bachelor's degrees are awarded in BIOLOGICAL SCIENCE (biology/biological science and marine biology), BUSINESS (accounting, banking and finance, business administration and management, international business management, marketing/retailing/merchandising, sports management, tourism, and transportation management), COMMUNICATIONS AND THE ARTS (communications, English, fine arts, languages, music, romance languages and literature, speech/debate/rhetoric, and visual and performing arts), COMPUTER AND PHYSICAL SCIENCE (applied mathematics, computer science, information sciences and systems, mathematics, and natural sciences), EDUCATION (art education, elementary education, music education, secondary education, and special education), ENGINEERING AND ENVIRONMENTAL DESIGN (aeronautical science, aeronautical technology, and aviation administration/management), SOCIAL SCIENCE (economics, history, humanities, liberal arts/general studies, philosophy, political science/government, psychology, social science, and sociology). Business, education, and computer sciences have the largest enrollments.

Required: To graduate, students must complete 122 credits with a minimum GPA of 2.0. The required 36-credit general education core includes a senior seminar.

Special: Dowling offers a B.S. in professional and liberal studies, internships, independent study, work-study, and nondegree study. There are cooperative programs in several majors, including aeronautics and airway science majors, with the FAA. There are 10 national honor societies, a freshman honors program, and 3 departmental honors programs.

Faculty/Classroom: 58% of faculty are male; 42% are female. 63% teach undergraduates. No introductory courses are taught by graduate students. The average class size in an introductory lecture is 20; in a laboratory is 15; and in a regular course is 17.

Requirements: Applicants should be graduates of an accredited secondary school and have completed at least 16 Carnegie units, including 4 in English. An interview is strongly recommended. AP and CLEP credits are accepted. Important factors in the admissions decision are advanced placement or honors courses, evidence of special talent, and recommendations by school officials.

Procedure: Freshmen are admitted to all sessions. Entrance exams should be taken by January of the senior year. There are deferred admissions and rolling admissions plans. Application deadlines are open. Application fee is $25. Applications are accepted online.

Transfer: 617 transfer students enrolled in a recent year. Applicants must submit official transcripts from all colleges attended. Courses completed with a grade of C or better may transfer. 30 of 122 credits required for the bachelor's degree must be completed at Dowling.

Visiting: There are regularly scheduled orientations for prospective students, including a campus tour and meetings with enrollment services members, staff, and faculty. There are guides for informal visits; visitors may sit in on classes and stay overnight. To schedule a visit, contact the Enrollment Services Office.

Financial Aid: In a recent year, 89% of all full-time freshmen and 73% of continuing full-time students received some form of financial aid. 79% of all full-time freshmen and 70% of continuing full-time students received need-based aid. All of undergraduate students worked part-time. Average annual earnings from campus work were $2,874. Dowling is a member of CSS. The FAFSA and the college's own financial statement are required. Check with the school for current application deadlines.

International Students: There were 158 international students enrolled in a recent year. The school actively recruits these students. They must take the TOEFL.

Graduates: In a recent year, 505 bachelor's degrees were awarded. The most popular majors were education (18%), liberal arts/general studies (10%), and social science (8%). 100 companies recruited on campus in a recent year. In an average class, 3% graduate in 3 years or less, 20% graduate in 4 years or less, 31% graduate in 5 years or less, and 34% graduate in 6 years or less.

Admissions Contact: Associate VP for of Enrollment and Systems Management. Web: *www.dowling.edu*

D'YOUVILLE COLLEGE — A-3

Buffalo, NY 14201 — (716) 829-7600; (800) 777-3921; (716) 829-7900

Full-time: 404 men, 1063 women	**Faculty:** 146
Part-time: 77 men, 322 women	**Ph.D.s:** n/av
Graduate: 329 men, 776 women	**Student/Faculty:** 12 to 1
Year: semesters, summer session	**Tuition:** $20,050
Application Deadline:	**Room & Board:** $9800
Freshman Class: 822 applied, 791 accepted, 155 enrolled	
SAT CR/M/W: 520/530/510 **ACT:** 23	**COMPETITIVE**

D'Youville College, founded in 1908, is a private, nonsectarian liberal arts institution granting degrees at the Bachelors, Masters, First Professional and Doctoral levels. There is one graduate school. In addition to regional accreditation, D'Youville has baccalaureate program accreditation with ADA and APTA. The library contains 96,876 volumes, 205,411 micro form items, and 4,246 audio/video tapes/CDs/DVDs, and subscribes to 683 periodicals including electronic. Computerized library services include interlibrary loans, database searching, Internet access, and Wi-Fi capability. The 10-acre campus is in an urban area 1 mile north of Downtown Buffalo, and 1 mile from the Peace Bridge border crossing to Canada. Including any residence halls, there are 12 buildings.

Student Life: 95% of undergraduates are from New York. Others are from 20 states, 48 foreign countries, and Canada. 80% are from public schools. 65% are White; 12% African American. 46% are Anglican, Buddhist, Christian, and Hindu,; 25% Catholic. The average age of freshmen is 18; all undergraduates, 24. 27% do not continue beyond their first year; 63% remain to graduate.

Housing: 478 students can be accommodated in college housing, which includes single-sex and coed dorms and on-campus apartments. quiet floors, and 21 and older floors. On-campus housing is guaranteed for all 4 years. 87% of students commute. All students may keep cars.

Activities: There are no fraternities or sororities. There are 35 groups on campus, including cheerleading, chorus, computers, dance, drama, drill team, ethnic, gay, honors, international, literary magazine, newspaper, professional, religious, social, social service, and student government. Popular campus events include Moving Up Days, International Fiesta and Honors Convocation.

Sports: There are 7 intercollegiate sports for men and 7 for women. Facilities include a 500-seat gym that houses basketball and volleyball courts and an indoor batting cage, and a fitness facility with aerobic and free weights, swimming pool, and dance studio.

Disabled Students: 95% of the campus is accessible. Facilities include wheelchair ramps, elevators, special parking, specially equipped restrooms, lowered drinking fountains, and special housing.

Services: Counseling and information services are available, as is tutoring in some subjects based on tutor accessibility. There is a reader service for the blind, as well as remedial math, reading, and writing.

Campus Safety and Security: Measures include 24-hour foot and vehicle patrol, emergency notification system, self-defense education, and security escort services. There are emergency telephones, lighted pathways/sidewalks, a special focus program, and a security committee.

Programs of Study: D'Youville confers B.A., B.S., B.S./M.S. and B.S.N. degrees. Master's and doctoral degrees are also awarded. Bachelor's degrees are awarded in BIOLOGICAL SCIENCE (biology/biological science), BUSINESS (accounting and business administration and management), COMMUNICATIONS AND THE ARTS (English), COMPUTER AND PHYSICAL SCIENCE (information sciences and systems and mathematics), HEALTH PROFESSIONS (exercise science, health care administration, nursing, and physician's assistant), SOCIAL SCIENCE (dietetics, history, interdisciplinary studies, international studies, philosophy, psychology, and sociology). Education and health professions are the strongest academically. Health professions, business, and nursing have the largest enrollments.

Required: All students must complete general program and core curriculum requirements, including 5 courses in humanities, 2 each in English and natural sciences, and 1 each in ethics, philosophy or religion, history, sociology, psychology, economics or political science, math, and computer science. A minimum of 120 to 144 credit hours, varying by major, with a minimum GPA of 2.0, (higher for some programs), is required to graduate.

Special: D'Youville has cross-registration with member colleges of the Western New York Consortium. Internships, work-study programs, dual majors, study abroad in 5 countries, and pass/fail options are available. Accelerated 5-year B.S.-M.S. programs in occupational therapy, international business, elementary education, Physician's Assistant and nursing, and dietetics are offered. For freshmen with undecided majors, the Career Discovery Program offers special courses, internships, and faculty advisers. There are 3 national honor societies and 2 departmental honors programs.

Faculty/Classroom: 43% of faculty are male; 57% are female. All teach and do research. No introductory courses are taught by graduate students.

Admissions: 96% of the 2013-2014 applicants were accepted. The SAT scores for the 2013-2014 freshman class were: Critical Reading--44% below 500, 48% between 500 and 599, 8% between 600 and 699, Math--33% below 500, 53% between 500 and 599, 14% between 600 and 699, and 1% between 700 and 800; Writing--49% below 500, 46% between 500 and 599, 6% between 600 and 699. The ACT scores were 20% below 21, 37% between 21 and 23, 27% between 24 and 26, 10% between 27 and 28, and 7% above 28. 40% of the current freshmen were in the top fifth of their class; 80% were in the top two fifths.

Requirements: The SAT or ACT is required. Applicants should have completed 16 Carnegie units, including 4 years of high school English, 3 of social studies, and 1 each of math and science; some majors require additional years of math and science. The GED is accepted. A GPA of 2.0 is required. AP and CLEP credits are accepted.

Procedure: Freshmen are admitted fall and spring. Entrance exams should be taken by the end of the junior year. There are deferred admissions and rolling admissions plans. Application deadlines are open. Application fee is $25. Applications are accepted online.

Transfer: 235 transfer students enrolled in 2012-2013. Applicants need a minimum GPA of 2.0, or 2.5 for some programs. 30 of 120 credits required for the bachelor's degree must be completed at D'Youville.

Visiting: There are regularly scheduled orientations for prospective students. There are guides for informal visits, visitors may sit in on classes, and stay overnight. To schedule a visit, contact the Admissions Office.

Financial Aid: In 2013-2014, 86% of all full-time freshmen and 87% of continuing full-time students received some form of financial aid. 84% of all full-time freshmen and 84% of continuing full-time students received need-based aid. The average freshman award was $20,127. Need-based scholarships or need-based grants averaged $14,155 ($20,127 maximum); need-based self-help aid (loans and jobs) averaged $8,108 ($9,900 maximum); and other non-need-based awards and non-need-based scholarships averaged $11,709 ($9,900 maximum). The average financial indebtedness of the 2013 graduate was $31,401. The FAFSA and the state aid form are required. The priority date for freshman financial aid applications for fall entry is March 1. The deadline for filing freshman financial aid applications for fall entry is April 15.

International Students: There are 156 international students enrolled. The school actively recruits these students. They must take the TOEFL with a minimum score of 500 on the paper-based TOEFL (PBT) or 61 on the Internet-based version (iBT). They must also take the SAT or ACT, scoring 900.

Graduates: From July 1, 2012 to June 30, 2013, 318 bachelor's degrees were awarded. The most popular majors were health professions and related sciences (49%), business/marketing (20%), and interdisciplinary studies (10%). 92 companies recruited on campus in 2012-2013. In an average class, 40% graduate in 4 years or less, 63% graduate in 5 years or less, and 63% graduate in 6 years or less.

Admissions Contact: Steven Smith, Director of Undergraduate Admissions. E-Mail: *admiss@dyc.edu* Web: *www.dyc.edu*

EASTMAN SCHOOL OF MUSIC — B-3

Rochester, NY 14604 (585) 274-1060
(800) 388-9695; (585) 232-8601

Full-time: 265 men, 240 women	**Faculty:** n/av
Part-time: n/av	**Ph.D.s:** n/av
Graduate: 201 men, 188 women	**Student/Faculty:** n/av
Year: semesters	**Tuition:** $46,216
Application Deadline: December 1	**Room & Board:** $12,586

Freshman Class: 1100 applied, 362 accepted, 167 enrolled
SAT or ACT: recommended

SPECIAL

Eastman School of Music, founded in 1921, is a private professional school of music within the University of Rochester. In addition to regional accreditation, Eastman has baccalaureate program accreditation with NASM. The library contains 333,014 volumes, 14,116 microform items, and 78,154 audio/video tapes/CDs/DVDs, and subscribes to 620 periodicals including electronic. Computerized library services include interlibrary loans, database searching, Internet access, and Wi-Fi capability. The 3-acre campus is in an urban area in downtown Rochester, New York. Including any residence halls, there are 5 buildings.

Student Life: 80% of undergraduates are from out of state, mostly the Northeast. Students are from 40 states, 28 foreign countries, and Canada. 90% are from public schools. The average age of freshmen is 18; all undergraduates, 20.

Housing: 360 students can be accommodated in college housing, which includes single-sex and coed dorms. In addition, there are special-interest houses. On-campus housing is guaranteed for all 4 years. 72% of students live on campus; of those, 100% remain on campus on weekends. All students may keep cars.

Activities: 4% of women belong to 1 national sorority. There are 20 groups on campus, including art, band, choir, chorale, chorus, computers, dance, debate, drama, gay, international, jazz band, literary magazine, musical theater, newspaper, opera, orchestra, pep band, photography, professional, radio and TV, religious, social, social service, student government, symphony, and yearbook. There are over 900 performances on our campus annually.

Sports: There is no sports program at Eastman. Students at Eastman are welcome to utilize any of the facilities that are available on the River Campus at the University of Rochester.

Disabled Students: 95% of the campus is accessible. Facilities include wheelchair ramps, elevators, special parking, specially equipped restrooms, lowered drinking fountains, and lowered telephones.

Services: Counseling and information services are available, as is tutoring in every subject. There is a reader service for the blind, and remedial writing. English tutoring for nonnative English speakers is available.

Campus Safety and Security: Measures include 24-hour foot and vehicle patrol, emergency notification system, self-defense education, and security escort services. There are shuttle buses, emergency telephones, lighted pathways/sidewalks, controlled access to dorms/residences, and security cameras.

Programs of Study: Eastman confers B.M. degrees. Master's and doctoral degrees are also awarded. Bachelor's degrees are awarded in COMMUNICATIONS AND THE ARTS (jazz, music, music performance, and music theory and composition), EDUCATION (music education). Performance has the largest enrollment.

Required: All students must complete core requirements in a major instrument or voice, music theory, music history, and Western cultural tradition, as well as English and humanities electives. A total of 120 to 148 credit hours, varying by program, with a minimum GPA of 2.0, is required to graduate.

Special: The Eastman School of Music and the University of Rochester cooperatively offer the B.A. degree with a music concentration. All the facilities of the university are open to Eastman students. Cross-registration is also available with colleges in the Rochester Consortium. Dual majors are available in all areas of study. Internships, work-study, and study abroad (in 7 countries) are also possible. There is 1 national honor society.

Faculty/Classroom: All teach and do research. Graduate students teach 10% of introductory courses. The average class size in an introductory lecture is 30 and in a regular course is 15.

Admissions: 33% of the 2013-2014 applicants were accepted.

Requirements: The SAT or ACT is recommended. The SAT or ACT is required only of home-schooled applicants. Applicants should be graduates of an accredited secondary school with 16 academic credits, including 4 years of English. The GED is accepted. An audition and an interview are required, as are 3 letters of recommendation. Some majors have other specific requirements. Important factors in the admissions decision are evidence of special talent, personality/intangible qualities, and advanced placement or honors courses.

Procedure: Freshmen are admitted fall. Applications should be filed by December 1 for fall entry, along with a $125 fee. Notifications are sent April 15. Applications are accepted online.

Transfer: 12 transfer students enrolled in 2012-2013. Requirements include satisfactory academic standing at the previous institution, a successful audition, and an interview.

Visiting: There are regularly scheduled orientations for prospective students, includes a group information session and a tour of the facilities. To schedule a visit, contact the Admissions Office.

Financial Aid: In 2013-2014, 100% of all full-time freshmen received some form of financial aid. Eastman is a member of CSS. The CSS/Profile, FAFSA, the state aid form, and the college's own financial statement are required. Check with the school for current application deadlines.

International Students: The school actively recruits these students. They must take the TOEFL with a minimum score of 83 on the Internet-based version (iBT).

Computers: All students may access the system. There are no time limits and no fees.

Admissions Contact: Danielle Arnold, Senior Admissions Counselor. E-Mail: *admissions.esm.rochester.edu* Web: *www.esm.rochester.edu/admissions/*

ELMIRA COLLEGE B-4

Elmira, NY 14901 (607) 735-1724
(800) 935-6472; (607) 735-1718

Full-time: 347 men, 841 women	**Faculty:** 82
Part-time: 52 men, 168 women	**Ph.D.s:** 100%
Graduate: 12 men, 122 women	**Student/Faculty:** 14 to 1
Year: other, summer session	**Tuition:** $38,150
Application Deadline: rolling	**Room & Board:** $11,800
Freshman Class: 2083 applied, 1648 accepted, 396 enrolled	
SAT CR/M: 540/530 **ACT:** 24	**COMPETITIVE+**

Elmira College, founded in 1855, is a private liberal arts institution offering general and preprofessional programs. In addition to regional accreditation, Elmira has baccalaureate program accreditation with NLN. The library contains 203,343 volumes, 591,429 microform items, and 5,897 audio/video tapes/CDs/DVDs, and subscribes to 337 periodicals including electronic. Computerized library services include interlibrary loans, database searching, Internet access, and Wi-Fi capability. Special learning facilities include an art gallery, radio station, speech/hearing clinic and Mark Twain's study and exhibit. The 42-acre campus is in a suburban area 90 miles southwest of Syracuse and 50 miles west of Binghamton. Including any residence halls, there are 26 buildings.

Student Life: 52% of undergraduates are from out of state, mostly the Northeast. Students are from 35 states, 21 foreign countries, and Canada. 59% are from public schools. 71% are White. The average age of freshmen is 18; all undergraduates, 20. 25% do not continue beyond their first year; 66% remain to graduate.

Housing: 1097 students can be accommodated in college housing, which includes single-sex and coed dorms and on-campus apartments. quiet floors and alcohol- and tobacco-free floors. On-campus housing is guaranteed for all 4 years. 93% of students live on campus; of those, 90% remain on campus on weekends. All students may keep cars.

Activities: There are no fraternities or sororities. There are 119 groups on campus, including and hall council, model UN, orientation leaders, student alumni council, art, chorale, chorus, dance, drama, environmental, ethnic, gay, honors, international, literary magazine, musical theater, newspaper, photography, political, professional, religious, social, social service, Student activities board, student government, and yearbook. Popular campus events include Mountain Day, Finals breakfast, and May Days.

Sports: There are 8 intercollegiate sports for men and 11 for women, and 17 intramural sports for men and 17 for women. Facilities include 2500-seat and 950-seat gyms, indoor tennis facilities, a 3500-seat hockey arena, racquetball courts, a fitness center, a dance studio, and a swimming pool.

Disabled Students: 25% of the campus is accessible. Facilities include wheelchair ramps, elevators, special parking, specially equipped restrooms, special class scheduling, lowered drinking fountains, and special housing.

Services: Counseling and information services are available, as is tutoring in most subjects. There is a reader service for the blind. Tutoring in math and freshman English is available in each freshman dorm.

Campus Safety and Security: Measures include 24-hour foot and vehicle patrol, emergency notification system, and security escort services. There are emergency telephones, lighted pathways/sidewalks, and controlled access to dorms/residences.

Programs of Study: Elmira confers B.A., and B.S. degrees. Associate and master's degrees are also awarded. Bachelor's degrees are awarded in BIOLOGICAL SCIENCE (biochemistry and biology/biological science), BUSINESS (accounting, business administration and management, business economics, international business management, and marketing/retailing/merchandising), COMMUNICATIONS AND THE ARTS (art, classics, dramatic arts, English literature, fine arts, French, languages, music, and Spanish), COMPUTER AND PHYSICAL SCIENCE (chemistry and mathematics), EDUCATION (art education, elementary education, foreign languages education, science education, and secondary education), ENGINEERING AND ENVIRONMENTAL DESIGN (environmental science), HEALTH PROFESSIONS (medical laboratory technology, nursing, predentistry, premedicine, and speech pathology/audiology), SOCIAL SCIENCE (American studies, anthropology, criminal justice, history, human services, international studies, philosophy, political science/government, prelaw, psychology, and sociology). History, theater, and premedicine are the strongest academically. Psychology, business administration, and education have the largest enrollments.

Required: All students must complete general degree requirements, including communication skills, writing courses, math competency, and a core curriculum; distribution requirements in culture and civilization, contemporary social institutions, the scientific method, the creative process, and phys ed; and a field experience program. A total of 120 credit hours with a minimum GPA of 2.0 overall and in the major is required to graduate.

Special: The required field experience program provides a career-related internship as well as community service. A junior year abroad program, an accelerated degree program, a general studies degree, student-designed majors, and pass/fail options are available. A 3-2 chemical engineering degree is offered with Clarkson University. B.A.-B.S. degrees are offered in biochemistry, biology, chemistry, economics, education, environmental studies, history, math, political science, and psychology. There are 20 national honor societies, including Phi Beta Kappa.

Faculty/Classroom: 63% of faculty are male; 37% are female. All teach and do research. No introductory courses are taught by graduate students. The average class size in an introductory lecture is 24; in a laboratory is 10; and in a regular course is 16.

Admissions: 79% of the 2013-2014 applicants were accepted. The SAT scores for the 2013-2014 freshman class were: Critical Reading--37% below 500, 42% between 500 and 599, 16% between 600 and 699, and 5% between 700 and 800; Math--35% below 500, 46% between 500 and 599, 16% between 600 and 699, and 3% between 700 and 800. The ACT scores were 2% below 21, 5% between 21 and 23, 16% between 24 and 26, 20% between 27 and 28, and 7% above 28. 56% of the current freshmen were in the top fifth of their class; 91% were in the top two fifths. There were 2 National Merit finalists. 24 freshmen graduated first in their class.

Requirements: The SAT or ACT is required. Applicants should have completed 4 years of high school English, 3 of math, and 2 of science. An essay is part of the application process. An interview is strongly recommended. A GPA of 2.0 is required. AP and CLEP credits are accepted. Important factors in the admissions decision are advanced placement or honors courses, extracurricular activities record, and recommendations by school officials.

Procedure: Freshmen are admitted fall and winter. Entrance exams should be taken by January of the entry year. There are early decision, deferred admissions, and rolling admissions plans. Early decision applications should be filed by November 15, along with a $50 fee. Notification of early decision is sent December 15; regular decision, on a rolling basis. 71 early decision candidates were accepted for the 2013-2014 class. 26 applicants were on the 2013 waiting list; 2 were admitted. Applications are accepted online.

Transfer: 49 transfer students enrolled in 2012-2013. Applicants should have a minimum GPA of 2.0. An interview is strongly recommended. 30 of 120 credits required for the bachelor's degree must be completed at Elmira.

Visiting: There are regularly scheduled orientations for prospective students, consisting of an open house format and overview, a tour, lunch, a student panel, a faculty panel, general admissions and scholarship information, and an optional interview. Individual visits for interviews and tours are available year-round, including Saturday mornings. There are guides for informal visits, visitors may sit in on classes, and stay overnight. To schedule a visit, contact the Office of Admissions.

Financial Aid: In 2013-2014, 98% of all full-time freshmen and 98% of continuing full-time students received some form of financial aid. 87% of all full-time freshmen and 84% of continuing full-time students received need-based aid. The average freshman award was $30,064. Need-based scholarships or need-based grants averaged $26,776; and need-based self-help aid (loans and jobs) averaged $4,151. 50% of undergraduate students work part-time. Average annual earnings from campus work are $1500. The average financial indebtedness of the 2013 graduate was $27,426. The FAFSA and the state aid form are required. The priority date for freshman financial aid applications for fall entry is February 1. The deadline for filing freshman financial aid applications for fall entry is March 15.

International Students: There are 74 international students enrolled. The school actively recruits these students. They must take the TOEFL with a minimum score of 500 on the paper-based TOEFL (PBT) or 61 on the Internet-based version (iBT) and the Comprehensive English Language Test.

Computers: All students may access the system. There are no time limits and no fees.

Graduates: From July 1, 2012 to June 30, 2013, 274 bachelor's degrees were awarded. The most popular majors were education (19%), business administration (17%), and nursing (13%). 60 companies recruited on campus in 2012-2013. In an average class, 60% graduate in 4 years or less, 2% graduate in 5 years or less, and 1% graduate in 6 years or less.

Admissions Contact: Brett Moore, Director of Admissions. E-Mail: *admissions@elmira.edu* Web: *www.elmira.edu*

EUGENE LANG COLLEGE - THE NEW SCHOOL FOR LIBERAL ARTS D-5

New York, NY 10011 212.229.5150
800.292.3040; 212.229.5355

Full-time: 425 men, 930 women	**Faculty:** 65
Part-time: 42 men, 60 women	**Ph.D.s:** 80%
Graduate: n/av	**Student/Faculty:** 22 to 1
Year: semesters	**Tuition:** $39,976
Application Deadline: January 6	**Room & Board:** $15,674
Freshman Class: 1558 applied, 1193 accepted, 455 enrolled	
SAT CR/M/W: 560/555/570 **ACT:** 24	**VERY COMPETITIVE**

Eugene Lang College, established in 1978, is the liberal arts undergraduate division of the New School. There is one undergraduate school. The 3 libraries contain 15.7 million volumes, 1,184 microform items, and 17,426 audio/video tapes/CDs/DVDs, and subscribe to 76,012 periodicals including electronic. Computerized library services include interlibrary loans, database searching, Internet access, and Wi-Fi capability. Special learning facilities include an art gallery, a writing center. The 37-acre campus is in an urban area in Greenwich Village, Manhattan, New York City. Including any residence halls, there are 23 buildings.

Student Life: 72% of undergraduates are from out of state, mostly the Middle Atlantic. Students are from 43 states, 46 foreign countries, and Canada. 61% are from public schools. 57% are White; 13% Hispanic. The average age of freshmen is 19; all undergraduates, 20. 20% do not continue beyond their first year; 52% remain to graduate.

Housing: 1945 students can be accommodated in college housing, which includes coed dorms. In addition, there are special-interest houses, Honors community housing is focused more on Academics than an actual GPA. On-campus housing is available on a first-come, first-served basis, and is available on a lottery system for upperclassmen. 70% of students commute. Alcohol is not permitted. All students may keep cars.

Activities: There are no fraternities or sororities. There are 46 groups on campus, including dress practice collective, game clubs, international interest clubs (10), textile association, art, band, choir, chorus, communications, computers, dance, debate, drama, environmental, ethnic, film, gay, honors, international, jazz band, literary magazine, Museum Club, musical theater, newspaper, opera, orchestra, photography, political, professional, radio and TV, religious, social, social service, student government, and symphony. Popular campus events include; Welcome Back Block party, Seek Relief Week, Midnight Breakfast, 100 Nights Dinner, Leadership Retreat, Service Trips, Leadership Awards Banquet.

Sports: There are 4 intramural sports for men and 4 for women. Facilities include we do not have a fitness facility, but we do have a fitness room where we host group fitness classes and personal training.

Disabled Students: 95% of the campus is accessible. Facilities include wheelchair ramps, elevators, specially equipped restrooms, special class scheduling, lowered drinking fountains, and special housing.

Campus Safety and Security: Measures include self-defense education.

Programs of Study: Eugene Lang College confers B.A. degrees. Bachelor's degrees are awarded in AGRICULTURE (environmental studies), COMMUNICATIONS AND THE ARTS (dance, dramatic arts, literature, music, theatre acting, theater design, and theatre studies), EDUCATION (education and foreign languages education), SOCIAL SCIENCE (anthropology, Chinese Studies, economics, gender studies, history, interdisciplinary studies, philosophy, political science/government, psychology, religion, sociology, and urban studies). Creative writing, history, urban studies, and education are the strongest academically. Writing and cultural studies have the largest enrollments.

Required: To graduate, students must complete 120 credit hours, with a GPA of 2.0 and a minimum of 36 hours in 1 of 11 paths of study: writing, literature, the arts (includes dance and theater, urban studies, social and historical inquiry, cultural studies, media, philosophy, religious studies, psychology, education studies, and science, technology, and society. Also required are 88 credit hours in Lang College courses and 4 credits of senior work. Required courses include a first-year writing seminar and a freshman workshop program.

Special: Lang College offers a concentration rather than a traditional major; there is no core curriculum and students are instructed in small seminars. Students may cross-register with other New School divisions. A large variety of internships for credit, study abroad, B.A./M.A. and B.A./M.S.T. options, a B.A./B.F.A. degree with Parsons The New School for Design and The New School for Jazz and Contemporary Music Program, student-designed majors, and nondegree study are available.

Faculty/Classroom: 43% of faculty are male; 57% are female. All teach undergraduates. No introductory courses are taught by graduate students.

Requirements: Freshmen: Common App (online); 2 essays; secondary school transcript; counselor recommendation; teacher evaluation; SAT or ACT scores (or a graded academic paper); TOEFL score (for ESL students). Transfers: college transcripts. AP and CLEP credits are accepted. Important factors in the admissions decision are recommendations by school officials, advanced placement or honors courses, and extracurricular activities record.

Procedure: Freshmen are admitted fall and spring. Entrance exams should be taken in May of the junior year or October of the senior year. There are early decision and deferred admissions plans. Early decision applications should be filed by November 1; regular applications, by January 6 for fall entry; and November 1 for spring entry, along with a $50 fee. Notification of early decision is sent December 15; regular decision, April 1. Applications are accepted online. Application fees are waived if application is completed online.

Transfer: Applicants must have a minimum college GPA of 2.5 and must submit high school transcripts, ACT or SAT scores (if taken in the last 5 years), and 2 recommendations. An interview is recommended. Grades of C or better transfer for credit. 60 of 120 credits required for the bachelor's degree must be completed at Eugene Lang College.

Visiting: There are regularly scheduled orientations for prospective students, consisting of information sessions every weekday at 2 o'clock; tours every weekday at 3 o'clock. Walk in meetings with counselors available every weekday between 9 AM and 5 PM. There are guides for informal visits and visitors may sit in on classes. To schedule a visit, contact Denise Rodriguez at rodrigud@newschool.edu.

Financial Aid: In 2013-2014, 41% of all full-time freshmen students received need-based aid. The average financial indebtedness of the 2013 graduate was $23,170. Eugene Lang College is a member of CSS. The FAFSA and the state aid form are required. The priority date for freshman financial aid applications for fall entry is March 1. The deadline for filing freshman financial aid applications for fall entry is June 30.

International Students: There are 96 international students enrolled. The school actively recruits these students. They must take the TOEFL with a minimum score of 100 on the paper-based TOEFL (PBT) or 100 on the Internet-based version (iBT).

Computers: All students may access the system. There are no time limits and no fees.

Graduates: From July 1, 2012 to June 30, 2013, 420 bachelor's degrees were awarded. The most popular majors were liberal arts (32%), literary studies (16%), and arts (15%). In an average class, 39% graduate in 4 years or less, 48% graduate in 5 years or less, and 52% graduate in 6 years or less. Of the 2012 graduating class, 10% were enrolled in graduate school within 6 months of graduation, and 6% were employed.

Admissions Contact: Karen Williams, Director of Admissions. E-Mail: *lang@newschool.edu* Web: *www.newschool.edu/lang*

EXCELSIOR COLLEGE D-3

Albany, NY 12203-5159 (518) 464-8500
(888) 674-2388; (518) 464-8777

Full-time: n/av	**Faculty:** n/av
Part-time: n/av	**Ph.D.s:** n/av
Graduate: 325 men, 580 women	**Student/Faculty:** n/av
Year: summer session	**Tuition:** $1000
Application Deadline: see profile	**Room & Board:** n/av
Freshman Class: n/av	**SPECIAL**

Excelsior College, founded in 1971, offers 34 degree programs designed to meet the needs of working adults, among whom are approximately 6,200 members of the U.S. armed forces. The college is home to a competency-based nursing program and the largest school of nursing in the United States. The college offers nondegree certificate programs as well as a series of ACE evaluated college-level proficiency exams that students can use to earn credit toward a degree at hundreds of colleges around the country. Figures in the above capsule and in this profile are approximate. There are 5 undergraduate schools and 3 graduate schools. In addition to regional accreditation, Excelsior has baccalaureate program accreditation with ABET and NLN. Computerized library services include interlibrary loans, database searching, and Internet access. The campus is in a suburban area in Albany. Including any residence halls, there are 3 buildings.

Student Life: 91% of undergraduates are from out of state. Students are from 50 states, 52 foreign countries, and Canada. 67% are white; 19% African American. The average age of all undergraduates is 40.

Housing: There are no residence halls. All students commute.

Activities: There are no fraternities or sororities. Popular campus events include commencement.

Sports: There is no sports program at Excelsior.

Disabled Students: All of the campus is accessible. Facilities include wheelchair ramps, elevators, special parking, specially equipped restrooms, and lowered drinking fountains.

Services: Counseling and information services are available, as is tutoring in some subjects, including statistics and writing.

Programs of Study: Excelsior confers B.A., B.S., B.S.Comp.Tech, B.S.Elect.Tech, B.S.N., B.S.Nuc.T, and B.S.T. degrees. Associate and master's degrees are also awarded. Bachelor's degrees are awarded in BIOLOGICAL SCIENCE (biology/biological science), BUSINESS (accounting, banking and finance, business administration and management, human resources, insurance and risk management, international business management, management information systems, and marketing/retailing/merchandising), COMMUNICATIONS AND THE ARTS (communications, English literature, languages, and music), COMPUTER AND PHYSICAL SCIENCE (chemistry, geology, information sciences and systems, mathematics, nuclear technology, and physics), ENGINEERING AND ENVIRONMENTAL DESIGN (computer technology, electrical/electronics engineering technology, and technological management), HEALTH PROFESSIONS (health science and nursing), SOCIAL SCIENCE (criminal justice, economics, geography, history, liberal arts/general studies, philosophy, political science/government, psychology, and sociology). Nursing and liberal studies have the largest enrollments.

Required: To graduate, students must complete 120 credits with 30 in the major and a minimum 2.0 GPA. At least 50% of course work must be in the arts and sciences. The required core courses include 6 to 12 credits each in humanities, math/science, and social science/history and 1 credit in information literacy. The nursing program requires a different set of core courses as well as the nursing performance exams. All students must fulfill a written English requirement.

Special: B.A. or B.S. candidates may major in liberal studies or in most traditional academic disciplines. Faculty consultants design curricula, approve sources of credit, create exams, and assess student learning. Students receive academic advising by telephone, letter, computer, or in person. The flexibility of this alternate program enables adults to pursue an undergraduate degree independently. Exams are available. Pass/fail options are possible. There is 1 national honor society.

Faculty/Classroom: 40% of faculty are male; 60% are female. No introductory courses are taught by graduate students.

Requirements: There are no admissions requirements except for nursing students. Applicants need not be residents of New York State. Students without a high school diploma or equivalent are admitted as special students. Nursing enrollment is available only to students with certain health care backgrounds. AP and CLEP credits are accepted.

Procedure: Freshmen are admitted to all sessions. There is a rolling admissions plan. Check with school for current application deadlines and fees. Applications are accepted online.

Financial Aid: The FAFSA and the college's own financial statement are required. Check with the school for current application deadlines.

International Students: The school actively recruits these students.

Computers: All students may access the system 24 hours a day, 7 days a week, via the Internet. There are no time limits and no fees.

Admissions Contact: Prospective Student Adviser E-Mail: *info@excelsior.edu* Web: *www.excelsior.edu*

FARMINGDALE STATE COLLEGE — E-5

Farmingdale, NY 11735 — **(631) 420-2200; (631) 420-2633**

Full-time: 3651 men, 2423 women	**Faculty:** 203; IIB, +$
Part-time: 1045 men, 1044 women	**Ph.D.s:** 66%
Graduate: n/av	**Student/Faculty:** 29 to 1
Year: semesters, summer session	**Tuition:** $7125 ($16,575)
Application Deadline: January 1	**Room & Board:** $11,860
Freshman Class: 5214 applied, 2672 accepted, 1146 enrolled	
SAT CR/M/W: 497/534/485 — **ACT:** 22	**COMPETITIVE**

Farmingdale State College, is a public institution offering associate and bachelor's degrees in the applied sciences and technology. There are 4 undergraduate schools. In addition to regional accreditation, SUNY Farmingdale has baccalaureate program accreditation with ABET and NLN. The library contains 180,000 volumes, 27,000 microform items, and 1,446 audio/video tapes/CDs/DVDs, and subscribes to 706 periodicals including electronic. Computerized library services include interlibrary loans, database searching, Internet access, and Wi-Fi capability. Special learning facilities include an art gallery, radio station, dental hygiene clinic, CAD/CAM and CIM labs, fleet of multi- and single-engine airplanes, and a greenhouse complex. The 380-acre campus is in a suburban area on Long Island, about 35 miles east of New York City. Including any residence halls, there are 40 buildings.

Student Life: 98% of undergraduates are from New York. Others are from 12 states, 28 foreign countries, and Canada. 92% are from public schools. 63% are White; 14% Hispanic; 11% African American. The average age of freshmen is 18; all undergraduates, 24. 18% do not continue beyond their first year; 45% remain to graduate.

Housing: 600 students can be accommodated in college housing, which includes coed dorms. On-campus housing is available on a first-come and first-served basis. 92% of students commute. Alcohol is not permitted. All students may keep cars.

Activities: There are 57 groups on campus, including art, computers, ethnic, honors, musical theater, newspaper, professional, religious, social, social service, student government, and yearbook. Popular campus events include Homecoming Week, Bingo for Books, Casino Night, and Farewell to Farmingdale.

Sports: There are 9 intercollegiate sports for men and 9 for women, and 11 intramural sports for men and 11 for women. Facilities include basketball, badminton, volleyball, racquetball, handball, squash, and tennis courts, a wrestling room, bowling alleys, weight training rooms, an indoor and outdoor tracks, a golf driving range and 3-hole golf layout, a baseball, softball, soccer/lacrosse, and multipurpose fields.

Disabled Students: 90% of the campus is accessible. Facilities include wheelchair ramps, elevators, special parking, specially equipped restrooms, special class scheduling, lowered drinking fountains, and lowered telephones.

Services: Counseling and information services are available, as is tutoring in most subjects. There is a reader service for the blind, and remedial math, reading, and writing. There is a learning disabilities specialist counselor available.

Campus Safety and Security: Measures include 24-hour foot and vehicle patrol, emergency notification system, and security escort services. There are emergency telephones, lighted pathways/sidewalks, and controlled access to dorms/residences.

Programs of Study: SUNY Farmingdale confers B.S., and B.Tech. degrees. Associate degrees are also awarded. Bachelor's degrees are awarded in AGRICULTURE (horticulture), BIOLOGICAL SCIENCE (biology/biological science), BUSINESS (applied economics / management, business administration and management, and sports management), COMMUNICATIONS AND THE ARTS (English and Professional Communication, Telecommunications Engineering Technology, and visual design), COMPUTER AND PHYSICAL SCIENCE (applied mathematics, Computer Engineering Technology, computer programming, and information sciences and systems), ENGINEERING AND ENVIRONMENTAL DESIGN (aeronautical science, architectural technology, aviation administration/management, electrical/electronics engineering technology, engineering technology, industrial engineering technology, manufacturing technology, and mechanical engineering technology), HEALTH PROFESSIONS (dental hygiene, medical technology, and nursing), SOCIAL SCIENCE (applied psychology, criminal justice, and safety and security technology). Nursing, dental hygiene, and bioscience are the strongest academically. Business management, computer programming and information systems, and bioscience have the largest enrollments.

Required: To graduate, students must complete 120 to 130 credits with a minimum GPA of 2.0. The core curriculum includes at least 60 credits of liberal arts and sciences courses in the Bachelor of Science programs and 45 credits in the Bachelor of Technology programs, as well as credits in major coursework. One writing-intensive course and all general education requirements must be satisfactorily completed.

Special: Internships are available, as well as study abroad in Italy. There are 5 national honor societies.

Faculty/Classroom: 56% of faculty are male; 44% are female. No introductory courses are taught by graduate students. The average class size in an introductory lecture is 28; in a laboratory is 22; and in a regular course is 28.

Admissions: 51% of the 2013-2014 applicants were accepted. The SAT scores for the 2013-2014 freshman class were: Critical Reading--54% below 500, 40% between 500 and 599, 5% between 600 and 699, and 1% between 700 and 800; Math--28% below 500, 54% between 500 and 599, 17% between 600 and 699, and 1% between 700 and 800. The ACT scores were 27% below 21, 45% between 21 and 23, 21% between 24 and 26, 7% between 27 and 28, and 1% above 28.

Requirements: Applicants must be graduates of an accredited secondary school or have earned a GED. Specific entrance requirements vary by program, but recommended preparation includes 4 units of English and 3 each of math, science, and social science. A GPA of 3.0 is required. AP and CLEP credits are accepted. Important factors in the admissions decision are advanced placement or honors courses, recommendations by school officials, and extracurricular activities record.

Procedure: Freshmen are admitted fall and spring. There are deferred admissions and rolling admissions plans. Application deadlines are open. Application fee is $50. Notification is sent on a rolling basis. Applications are accepted online.

Transfer: 1391 transfer students enrolled in 2012-2013. Applicants must have a minimum GPA of 2.5. 30 of 120 credits required for the bachelor's degree must be completed at SUNY Farmingdale.

Visiting: There are regularly scheduled orientations for prospective students, including a tour of the campus and general information about the college, admissions, financial aid, and residence life. There are guides for informal visits. To schedule a visit, contact the Admissions Office.

Financial Aid: In 2013-2014, 79% of all full-time freshmen and 66% of continuing full-time students received some form of financial aid. 54% of all full-time freshmen and 48% of continuing full-time students received need-based aid. The average freshman award was $7,939. Need-based scholarships or need-based grants averaged $5,770 ($16,857 maximum); need-based self-help aid (loans and jobs) averaged $3,332 ($6,500 maximum); and other non-need-based awards and non-need-based scholarships averaged $1,825 ($12,627 maximum). The FAFSA, the state aid form, and the college's own financial statement are required. Check with the school for current application deadlines.

International Students: There are 208 international students enrolled. They must take the TOEFL with a minimum score of 520 on the paper-based TOEFL (PBT) or 68 on the Internet-based version (iBT). They must also take the SAT or ACT, scoring 1000.

Computers: All students may access the system during lab hours or 24 hours a day wireless. There are no time limits and no fees.

Graduates: From July 1, 2012 to June 30, 2013, 1088 bachelor's degrees were awarded. The most popular majors were business management (23%), liberal arts and sciences (14%), and computer programming and information systems (5%). 50 companies recruited on campus in 2012-2013. In an average class, 45% graduate in 6 years or less. Of the 2012 graduating class, 30% were employed within 6 months of graduation.

Admissions Contact: Jim Hall, Director of Admissions. E-Mail: *admissions@farmingdale.edu* Web: *www.farmingdale.edu*

FASHION INSTITUTE OF TECHNOLOGY/STATE UNIVERSITY OF NEW YORK — D-5

New York, NY 10001-5992 — (212) 217-7675; (800) Go To FIT; (212) 217-7401

Full-time: 1010 men, 5610 women	**Faculty:** n/av
Part-time: 810 men, 3310 women	**Ph.D.s:** n/av
Graduate: 20 men, 110 women	**Student/Faculty:** n/av
Year: semesters, summer session	**Tuition:** $7000 ($13,500)
Application Deadline: see profile	**Room & Board:** $12,590
Freshman Class: n/av	
	SPECIAL

The Fashion Institute of Technology, founded in 1944 as part of the State University of New York, is an art and design, business, and technology college that prepares students for careers in fashion and related design. The figures in the above capsule and in this profile are approximate. There is 1 graduate school. In addition to regional accreditation, FIT has baccalaureate program accreditation with FIDER and NASAD. The library contains 168,879 volumes, 4,712 microform items, and 244,335 audio/video tapes/CDs/DVDs, and subscribes to 502 periodicals including electronic. Computerized library services include interlibrary loans and database searching. Special learning facilities include an art gallery, radio station, design lab, lighting lab, quick response center, computer-aided design and communications facility, and the Annette Green Fragrance Foundation Studio Collections of the Museum at FIT. The 5-acre campus is in an urban area in Manhattan. Including any residence halls, there are 8 buildings.

Student Life: 63% of undergraduates are from New York. Others are from 49 states, 80 foreign countries, and Canada. 43% are white; 12% foreign nationals. The average age of freshmen is 22; all undergraduates, 29. 81% do not continue beyond their first year; 51% remain to graduate.

Housing: 1250 students can be accommodated in college housing, which includes single-sex and coed dorms and on-campus apartments. On-campus housing is available on a lottery system for upperclassmen. Priority is given to out-of-town students. 83% of students commute. Alcohol is not permitted. No one may keep cars.

Activities: There are no fraternities or sororities. There are 70 groups on campus, including art, cheerleading, choir, dance, drama, ethnic, gay, honors, literary magazine, musical theater, newspaper, photography, political, professional, radio and TV, religious, social, social service, student government, and yearbook. Popular campus events include fashion shows, a lecture series, and craft center events.

Sports: There are 4 intercollegiate sports for men and 4 for women, and 4 intramural sports for men and 4 for women. Facilities include 2 gyms, a dance studio, and a weight room.

Disabled Students: 95% of the campus is accessible. Facilities include wheelchair ramps, elevators, special parking, specially equipped restrooms, lowered drinking fountains, lowered telephones, services/facilities for the hearing impaired, and library tapes.

Services: Counseling and information services are available, as is tutoring in every subject. There is remedial math, reading, and writing. The school has a special program for the learning disabled.

Campus Safety and Security: Measures include 24-hour foot and vehicle patrol and self-defense education. There are emergency telephones, lighted pathways/sidewalks, and lectures by the New York City police department.

Programs of Study: FIT confers B.S. and B.F.A. degrees. Associates and master's degrees are also awarded. Bachelor's degrees are awarded in BUSINESS (apparel and accessories marketing, fashion merchandising, and marketing/retailing/merchandising), COMMUNICATIONS AND THE ARTS (advertising, design, fiber/textiles/weaving, graphic design, illustration, and toy design), ENGINEERING AND ENVIRONMENTAL DESIGN (computer graphics, interior design, and textile technology), SOCIAL SCIENCE (fashion design and technology, home furnishings and equipment management/production/services, and textiles and clothing). Fashion merchandising management, fashion design, and communication design have the largest enrollments.

Required: To graduate, students must complete the credit and course requirements for their majors with a 2.0 GPA. Students may qualify for a degree in two ways: by earning 60 credits, with half in the major while in residence at the upper-division level, or by earning 30 credits at the upper-division level in addition to an FIT associate degree. There is a 2-credit phys ed requirement.

Special: Internships are offered, and students may study abroad in 8 countries. Nondegree study is available. There is 1 departmental honors program.

Faculty/Classroom: 48% of faculty are male; 52% are female. All teach undergraduates. No introductory courses are taught by graduate students. The average class size in an introductory lecture is 25; in a laboratory is 18; and in a regular course is 25.

Requirements: Applicants must be high school graduates or have a GED certificate. An essay and, when appropriate, a portfolio are required. A GPA of 2.0 is required. AP and CLEP credits are accepted. Important factors in the admissions decision are personality/intangible qualities, leadership record, and evidence of special talent.

Procedure: Freshmen are admitted fall and spring. There are early decision and rolling admissions plans. Applications are accepted online. A waiting list is maintained. Check with the school for current application deadlines.

Transfer: Applicants must have a GPA of 2.0 and at least 30 college credits. An interview is required for art and design applicants, as well as a portfolio when appropriate. 30 of 60 credits required for the bachelor's degree must be completed at FIT.

Visiting: There are regularly scheduled orientations for prospective students, including a presentation and group information session with a counselor. To schedule a visit, contact the Admissions Office.

Financial Aid: FIT is a member of CSS. The FAFSA and the state aid form are required. Check with the school for current application deadlines.

International Students: They must take the TOEFL.

Computers: All students may access the system. There are no time limits and no fees.

Admissions Contact: Director of Admissions. E-Mail: *fitinfo@fitnyc.edu* Web: *www.fitnyc.edu*

FIVE TOWNS COLLEGE — E-5

Dix Hills, NY 11746 — (631) 656-2110; (631) 656-2172

Full-time: 479 men, 213 women	**Faculty:** 24
Part-time: 41 men, 16 women	**Ph.D.s:** 33%
Graduate: 29 men, 10 women	**Student/Faculty:** 14 to 1
Year: semesters, summer session	**Tuition:** $20,880
Application Deadline: rolling	**Room & Board:** $13,610
Freshman Class: 598 applied, 331 accepted, 239 enrolled	
SAT CR/M/W: 450/430/430 **ACT:** 21	**SPECIAL**

Five Towns College, founded in 1972, is a private institution offering undergraduate programs in music, music business, business, liberal arts, theater, elementary education, mass communication (broadcasting, journalism), audio recording technology, and film/video. Graduate programs in music, music education, and childhood education are also offered. There is one undergraduate school and one graduate school. In addition to regional accreditation, FTC has baccalaureate program accreditation with NCATE. The 2 libraries contain 44,771 volumes, 50 microform items, and 16,416 audio/video tapes/CDs/DVDs, and subscribe to 500 periodicals including electronic. Computerized library services include interlibrary loans, database searching, Internet access, and Wi-Fi capability. Special learning facilities include a radio station, 72-, 48-, and 24-track recording studios, a MIDI studio, and a film video/TV studio. The 40-acre campus is in a suburban area 48 miles east of New York City. Including any residence halls, there are 5 buildings.

Student Life: 94% of undergraduates are from New York. Others are from 9 states, and 1 foreign countries. 91% are from public schools. 51% are White; 20% African American; 13% Hispanic. The average age of freshmen is 19; all undergraduates, 21. 23% do not continue beyond their first year; 55% remain to graduate.

Housing: 200 students can be accommodated in college housing, which includes coed dorms. Priority is given to out-of-town students. 80% of students commute. Alcohol is not permitted. Upperclassmen may keep cars.

Activities: There are no fraternities or sororities. There are 16 groups on campus, including and broadcasting, barbershop quartets, hip-hop, music business, readers theater, theatrical concert, art, band, choir, chorale, chorus, dance, drama, film, international, jazz band, live audio, musical theater, newspaper, orchestra, professional, radio and TV, social, student government, symphony, and yearbook. Popular campus events include Lunch & Lecture Series, Annual Picnic and Spring and Fall Festivals.

Sports: There is no sports program at FTC. Facilities include a gym with basketball and volleyball courts, an outdoor baseball/soccer field, and a fitness center.

Disabled Students: All of the campus is accessible. Facilities include wheelchair ramps, special parking, specially equipped restrooms, and special housing.

Services: Counseling and information services are available, as is tutoring in most subjects. There is a reader service for the blind.

Campus Safety and Security: Measures include 24-hour foot and vehicle patrol, emergency notification system, and security escort services. There are shuttle buses, lighted pathways/sidewalks, and controlled access to dorms/residences.

Programs of Study: FTC confers B.S., B.F.A., B.P.S. and Mus.B. degrees. Associate, master's, and doctoral degrees are also awarded. Bachelor's degrees are awarded in COMMUNICATIONS AND THE ARTS (audio technology, communications, dramatic arts, jazz, music business management, music performance, music theory and composition, and video), EDUCATION (elementary education and music education). Music, business, and childhood education are the strongest academically. Business management with a concentration in audio recording technology, film, and video have the largest enrollments.

Required: To graduate, all students must complete a total of 134 credits for a Mus.B. or B.F.A. degree, 127 for a B.S. degree, or 121 for a B.P.S. degree. Students must maintain at least a C average in their major concentration and have a minimum GPA of 2.0 to graduate. Distribution requirements include 45 credits in core courses in liberal arts. The core curriculum consists of English Composition 101 and 102, Speech 101, 3 credits each of either psychology or sociology, and various upper-division liberal arts and social science courses. All music students must pass a jury exam. Music majors and elementary education majors must take a comprehensive exam.

Special: Internships are required in business management (concentrations in audio recording technology and music business), mass communication (concentrations in broadcasting and journalism), and are available for all other degree programs. There is 1 national honor society.

Faculty/Classroom: 56% of faculty are male; 42% are female. 98% teach undergraduates, 20% do research, and 20% do both. No introductory courses are taught by graduate students. The average class size in an introductory lecture is 30 and in a regular course is 15.

Admissions: 55% of the 2013-2014 applicants were accepted. The SAT scores for the 2013-2014 freshman class were: Critical Reading--67% below 500, 26% between 500 and 599, 5% between 600 and 699, and 2% between 700 and 800; Math--68% below 500, 24% between 500 and 599, 7% between 600 and 699, and 1% between 700 and 800; Writing--75% below 500, 21% between 500 and 599, 3% between 600 and 699, and 1% between 700 and 800. The ACT scores were 40% below 21, 45% between 21 and 23, 15% between 24 and 26. 15% of the current freshmen were in the top fifth of their class; 40% were in the top two fifths.

Requirements: The SAT or ACT is required. A minimum high school average of 80 is required. A GED with a minimum score of 2500 is accepted. An audition is required for students in music and theater. We recommend a 1350 on all three parts of the SAT and a 19 on the ACT. We offer an entrance exam for students that do not meet our academic standards. A GPA of 80.0 is required. AP and CLEP credits are accepted. Important factors in the admissions decision are evidence of special talent, recommendations by school officials, and extracurricular activities record.

Procedure: Freshmen are admitted fall, spring, and summer. Entrance exams should be taken prior to admission. There are early decision, deferred admissions, and rolling admissions plans. Early decision applications should be filed by December 1, along with a $35 fee. Notification is sent on a rolling basis. 5 early decision candidates were accepted for the 2013-2014 class. Applications are accepted online.

Transfer: 70 transfer students enrolled in 2012-2013. Students must be in good academic standing at their former school and have a minimum GPA of 2.5. 60 of 121 credits required for the bachelor's degree must be completed at FTC.

Visiting: There are regularly scheduled orientations for prospective students, including a campus tour, academic counseling, financial aid counseling, and educational workshops. Students also learn about student support services and how to become involved in student activities. There are guides for informal visits and visitors may sit in on classes. To schedule a visit, contact the Admissions Office at (631) 656-2110.

Financial Aid: In 2013-2014, 92% of all full-time freshmen and 90% of continuing full-time students received some form of financial aid. 73% of all full-time freshmen and 75% of continuing full-time students received need-based aid. The average freshman award was $14,000. Need-based scholarships or need-based grants averaged $3,900; need-based self-help aid (loans and jobs) averaged $4,000; and other non-need-based awards and non-need-based scholarships averaged $7,000. 90% of undergraduate students work part-time. Average annual earnings from campus work are $3000. The average financial indebtedness of the 2013 graduate was $22,000. The FAFSA and the college's own financial statement are required. The priority date for freshman financial aid applications for fall entry is March 31. The deadline for filing freshman financial aid applications for fall entry is August 25.

International Students: There are 7 international students enrolled. The school actively recruits these students. They must take the TOEFL with a minimum score of 520 on the paper-based TOEFL (PBT) or 79 on the Internet-based version (iBT).

Computers: All students may access the system 24 hours a day, 7 days a week. There are no time limits and no fees.

Graduates: From July 1, 2012 to June 30, 2013, 178 bachelor's degrees were awarded. The most popular majors were business management (48%), film and video (16%), and music (11%). 64 companies recruited on campus in 2012-2013. In an average class, 54% graduate in 4 years or less, 61% graduate in 5 years or less, and 75% graduate in 6 years or less. Of the 2012 graduating class, 15% were enrolled in graduate school within 6 months of graduation, and 81% were employed.

Admissions Contact: Jerry Cohen, Dean of Enrollment Services. E-Mail: *admissions@ftc.edu* Web: *www.ftc.edu*

FORDHAM UNIVERSITY SYSTEM

The Fordham University System, established in 1841, is a private system in New York affiliated with the Catholic Church in the Jesuit tradition. It is governed by a board of trustees, whose chief administrator is the president. The primary goal of the system is to foster the intellectual, moral, and religious development of its students and prepare them for leadership in a global society. The main priorities are excellence in undergraduate and graduate/professional programs, and commitment to teaching, research, and service. The total student enrollment in a recent year was 14,448 with 1403 faculty members. Altogether there are approximately 69 baccalaureate, 71 master's, and 25 doctoral programs offered in the Fordham University System. Profiles of the 4-year campuses are included in this section.

FORDHAM UNIVERSITY — D-5

Bronx, NY 10458 (718) 817-4000
(800) FORDHAM; (718) 367-9404

Full-time: 3654 men, 4056 women — **Faculty:** n/av; I, av$
Part-time: 255 men, 360 women — **Ph.D.s:** 94%
Graduate: 2664 men, 4181 women — **Student/Faculty:** 14 to 1
Year: semesters, summer session — **Tuition:** $43,092
Application Deadline: January 1 — **Room & Board:** $15,835
Freshman Class: 36111 applied, 17005 accepted, 1920 enrolled
SAT CR/M/W: 620/640/630 — **ACT:** required
HIGHLY COMPETITIVE

Fordham University, founded in 1841, is a private institution offering an education based on the Jesuit tradition, with 2 traditional campuses in New York: 1 in the Bronx and 1 in Manhattan near Lincoln Center. Fordham University also has a campus in Westchester which serves graduate and adult students. There are 3 undergraduate schools and 6 graduate schools. In addition to regional accreditation, has baccalaureate program accreditation with AACSB and NCATE. The 4 libraries contain 2.0 million volumes, 3.2 million microform items, and 64,833 audio/video tapes/CDs/DVDs, and subscribe to 68,957 periodicals including electronic. Computerized library services include interlibrary loans, database searching, and Internet access. Special learning facilities include an art gallery, radio station, a seismic station, an archeological site, and a biological field station. The 93-acre campus is in an urban area adjacent to the Bronx Zoo; The Lincoln Center campus is located at 60th Street and Columbus Avenue. Including any residence halls, there are 37 buildings.

Student Life: 52% of undergraduates are from New York. Others are from 46 states, 69 foreign countries, and Canada. 62% are White; 14% Hispanic. 55% are Catholic; 15% Buddhist, Greek Orthodox, Hindu, and Muslim. The average age of freshmen is 18.4; all undergraduates, 21. 12% do not continue beyond their first year; 88% remain to graduate.

Housing: 4307 students can be accommodated in college housing, which includes coed dorms, on-campus apartments, and off-campus apartments. integrated learning communities. On-campus housing is guaranteed for all 4 years, is available on a first-come, first-served basis, and is available on a lottery system for upperclassmen. 56% of students live on campus. All students may keep cars.

Activities: There are no fraternities or sororities. There are 165 groups on campus, including campus activities board, art, band, cheerleading, choir, chorale, chorus, computers, dance, debate, drama, environmental, ethnic, film, gay, honors, international, jazz band, literary magazine, marching band, musical theater, newspaper, orchestra, pep band, photography, political, professional, radio and TV, religious, social, social service, student admission ambassadors, student government, symphony, and yearbook. Popular campus events include Fall in Love with Fordham Festival, Spring Weekend, Spring Semiformal and Senior Week.

Sports: There are 12 intercollegiate sports for men and 10 for women, and 5 intramural sports for men and 5 for women. Facilities include a 6000-seat football stadium, an Olympic-size pool with a separate diving area, an indoor track, a 3200-seat gym, and tennis, squash, and racquetball courts, a newly renovated student workout room.

Disabled Students: 80% of the campus is accessible. Facilities include wheelchair ramps, elevators, special parking, specially equipped restrooms, special class scheduling, and lowered drinking fountains.

Services: Counseling and information services are available, as is tutoring in most subjects.

Campus Safety and Security: Measures include 24-hour foot and vehicle patrol, emergency notification system, and security escort services. There are shuttle buses, emergency telephones, and lighted pathways/sidewalks.

Programs of Study: confers B.A., B.S. and B.F.A. degrees. Master's and doctoral degrees are also awarded. Bachelor's degrees are awarded in BIOLOGICAL SCIENCE (biology/biological science and neurosciences), BUSINESS (accounting, business administration and management, business economics, finance, international business management, and marketing management), COMMUNICATIONS AND THE ARTS (art history, classical languages, classics, communication, communications, comparative literature, dance, dramatic arts, English, English literature, English Writing, fine arts, French, German, graphic design, Italian, journalism, Latin, music, music theory and composition, performing arts, Spanish, studio art, theatre acting, theater design, theatre production, and visual and performing arts), COMPUTER AND PHYSICAL SCIENCE (chemistry, computer science, information sciences and systems, mathematics, mathematics – economics, natural sciences, physics, science, and statistics), ENGINEERING AND ENVIRONMENTAL DESIGN (engineering physics and environmental science), SOCIAL SCIENCE (African studies, African American studies, American studies, anthropology, classical/ancient civilization, economics, French studies, German area studies, history, international studies, Italian studies, Latin American studies, medieval studies, Middle Eastern studies, philosophy, political science/government, psychology, religion, social science, social work, sociology, Spanish studies, theological studies, urban studies, and women's studies). Biology, political science, English, business administration, communication and media Studies are the strongest academically. Business, communication and media studies, and psychology have the largest enrollments.

Required: All students must complete a core curriculum, including 2 courses each in literature, history, philosophy, theology, natural sciences, social sciences, and foreign language competency and 1 each in math, English composition, and fine arts. A total of 124 credits with 30 in the major and a 2.0 minimum GPA are required for graduation. A thesis is required for the honors program.

Special: Fordham University offers career-oriented internships during the junior or senior year with New York City companies and institutions. A combined 3-2 engineering program is available with Columbia and Case Western Reserve Universities. Study abroad, accelerated degrees, dual and student-designed majors, and pass/fail options are available. Fordham additionally offers a B.F.A program in conjunction with the Alvin Ailey School of Dance and a B.A. program in theatre. There are 6 national honor societies, including Phi Beta Kappa, and a freshman honors program.

Faculty/Classroom: 55% of faculty are male; 45% are female. No introductory courses are taught by graduate students. The average class size in an introductory lecture is 23.

Admissions: 47% of the 2013-2014 applicants were accepted. The SAT scores for the 2013-2014 freshman class were: Critical Reading--5% below 500, 31% between 500 and 599, 48% between 600 and 699, and 16% between 700 and 800; Math--3% below 500, 26% between 500 and 599, 51% between 600 and 699, and 20% between 700 and 800; Writing--4% below 500, 27% between 500 and 599, 50% between 600 and 699, and 19% between 700 and 800.

Requirements: The SAT or ACT is required. Applicants should have completed 4 years of high school English and 3 each of math, science, social studies, history, and foreign language. Applicants should submit the Common Application which includes an essay and questions on the Fordham member screen. A guidance counselor recommendation is also required. Auditions are required for theatre and dance majors. AP credits are accepted. Important factors in the admissions decision are advanced placement or honors courses, leadership record, extracurricular activities record, parents or siblings attended your school, evidence of special talent, personality/intangible qualities, geographical diversity, and recommendations by school officials.

Procedure: Freshmen are admitted fall and spring. Entrance exams should be taken by January of the senior year. There are early admissions and deferred admissions plans. Early decision applications should be filed by November 1; regular applications, by January 1 for fall entry; and December 1 for spring entry, along with a $70 fee. Notification of early decision is sent December 15; regular decision, April 1. 1503 applicants were on the 2013 waiting list; 748 were admitted. Applications are accepted online.

Transfer: A 3.0 minimum GPA is recommended. Applicants with less than 1 full year of full-time course work at a post-secondary institution should submit SAT or ACT scores. 64 of 124 credits required for the bachelor's degree must be completed at Fordham.

Visiting: There are regularly scheduled orientations for prospective students. There are guides for informal visits and visitors may sit in on classes. To schedule a visit, contact the Office of Undergraduate Admission.

Financial Aid: The CSS/Profile and FAFSA, noncustodial profile, and business and farm supplement are required. The deadline for filing freshman financial aid applications for fall entry is February 10.

International Students: There are 459 international students enrolled. The school actively recruits these students. They must take the TOEFL with a minimum score of 90 on the Internet-based version (iBT) and the college's own test. They must also take the SAT or ACT.

Computers: All students may access the system. There are no time limits and no fees.

Graduates: The most popular majors were business administration (30%), social sciences (17%), and communication and media studies (11%). 500 companies recruited on campus in 2012-2013. In an average class, 1% graduate in 3 years or less, 77% graduate in 4 years or less, 80% graduate in 5 years or less, and 81% graduate in 6 years or less.

Admissions Contact: Patricia Peek, Ph.D., Director of Admissions. E-Mail: *enroll@fordham.edu* Web: *www.fordham.edu*

HAMILTON COLLEGE C-3

Clinton, NY 13323 (315) 859-4421
(800) 843-2655; (315) 859-4457

Full-time: 910 men, 958 women	**Faculty:** 188; IIB, ++$
Part-time: 7 men, 9 women	**Ph.D.s:** 94%
Graduate: n/av	**Student/Faculty:** 10 to 1
Year: semesters	**Tuition:** $44,350
Application Deadline: January 1	**Room & Board:** $11,270
Freshman Class: 5107 applied, 1389 accepted, 469 enrolled	
SAT CR/M/W: 700/700/700 **ACT:** 31	**MOST COMPETITIVE**

Hamilton College, chartered in 1812, is a private, nonsectarian, liberal arts school offering undergraduate programs in the arts and sciences. The 2 libraries contain 625,376 volumes, 293,834 microform items, and 35,217 audio/video tapes/CDs/DVDs, and subscribe to 4,546 periodicals including electronic. Computerized library services include interlibrary loans, database searching, Internet access, and laptop Internet portals. Special learning facilities include an art gallery, radio station, TV station, an observatory, electron microscope, Wellin Museum of Art. The 1300-acre campus is in a rural area 9 miles southwest of Utica. Including any residence halls, there are 106 buildings.

Student Life: 67% of undergraduates are from out of state, mostly the Middle Atlantic. Students are from 46 states, 39 foreign countries, and Canada. 61% are from public schools. 63% are white; 11% race unknown. 40% claim no religious affiliation; 24% Protestant; 21% Catholic. The average age of freshmen is 18; all undergraduates, 20. 4% do not continue beyond their first year; 91% remain to graduate.

Housing: 1835 students can be accommodated in college housing, which includes coed dorms, on-campus apartments, and married student housing. In addition, there are special-interest houses, quiet floors, and substance-free areas. On-campus housing is guaranteed for all 4 years. 98% of students live on campus; of those, 90% remain on campus on weekends. Upperclassmen may keep cars.

Activities: 26% of men belong to 11 national fraternities; 17% of women belong to 6 local and 1 national sororities. There are 189 groups on campus, including art, band, chess, choir, chorale, chorus, communications, computers, dance, debate, drama, environmental, ethnic, film, gay, honors, international, jazz band, literary magazine, musical theater, newspaper, orchestra, photography, political, professional, radio and TV, religious, social, social service, student government, and yearbook. Popular campus events include Class and Charter Day, and February Fest (Winter Carnival).

Sports: There are 14 intercollegiate sports for men and 15 for women, and 16 intramural sports for men and 16 for women. Facilities include a gym, a field house, a fitness and dance center, squash and racquetball courts, indoor and outdoor tennis courts, an artificial grass football stadium, a 9-hole golf course, a swimming pool, indoor and outdoor tracks, baseball and softball fields, numerous grass fields, an artificial turf field, paddle tennis courts, and an ice rink.

Disabled Students: Facilities include wheelchair ramps, elevators, special parking, specially equipped restrooms, special class scheduling, and special housing.

Services: Counseling and information services are available, as is tutoring in some subjects through the New York State Higher Education Opportunity Program (HEOP).

Campus Safety and Security: Measures include 24-hour foot and vehicle patrol, emergency notification system, self-defense education, and security escort services. There are shuttle buses, emergency telephones, lighted pathways/sidewalks, and controlled access to dorms/residences.

Programs of Study: Hamilton confers A.B. degrees. Bachelor's degrees are awarded in AGRICULTURE (environmental studies), BIOLOGICAL SCIENCE (biochemistry, biology/biological science, and neurosciences), COMMUNICATIONS AND THE ARTS (art, art history and appreciation, Chinese, classics, communications, comparative literature, creative writing, dance, dramatic arts, English, English literature, French, languages, music, and studio art), COMPUTER AND PHYSICAL SCIENCE (chemical physics, chemistry, computer science, geoscience, mathematics, and physics), SOCIAL SCIENCE (African studies, American studies, anthropology, archeology, Asian/Oriental studies, economics, German area studies, Hispanic American studies, history, interdisciplinary studies, international relations, philosophy, political science/government, psychobiology, psychology, public affairs, religion, Russian and Slavic studies, sociology, and women's studies). Economics, mathematics, and psychology have the largest enrollments.

Required: Students must successfully complete 128 credits, with 32 to 40 of these in the student's major, and must maintain at least a 72 average in half the courses taken.

Special: Cross-registration is permitted with Colgate University and Utica College. Opportunities are provided for a Washington semester and a New York City semester. Student-designed majors and study abroad in many countries are available, and 3-2 engineering degrees are offered with Washington University in St. Louis, Rensselaer Polytechnic Institute, and Columbia University. There are 8 national honor societies, including Phi Beta Kappa.

Faculty/Classroom: 57% of faculty are male; 43% are female. All teach undergraduates. No introductory courses are taught by graduate students. The average class size in a regular course is 16.

Admissions: 27% of the 2012-2013 applicants were accepted. The SAT scores for the 2012-2013 freshman class were: Critical Reading--1% below 500, 10% between 500 and 599, 38% between 600 and 699, and 51% between 700 and 800; Math--1% below 500, 7% between 500 and 599, 42% between 600 and 699, and 51% between 700 and 800; Writing--1% below 500, 11% between 500 and 599, 36% between 600 and 699, and 52% between 700 and 800. The ACT scores were 1% below 21, 1% between 21 and 23, 9% between 24 and 26, 8% between 27 and 28, and 82% above 28. 95% of the current freshmen were in the top fifth of their class; 100% were in the top two fifths. 20 freshmen graduated first in their class.

Requirements: The SAT or ACT is required. Although graduation from an accredited secondary school or a GED is desirable, and a full complement of college-preparatory courses is recommended, Hamilton will consider all highly recommended candidates who demonstrate an ability and desire to perform at intellectually demanding levels. Students can fulfill test requirements with the SAT, ACT, 3 SAT Subject tests, 3 AP exams, or any combination of these. An essay is required, and an interview is recommended. AP credits are accepted. Important factors in the admissions decision are advanced placement or honors courses, recommendations by school officials, and parents or siblings attended the school.

Procedure: Freshmen are admitted fall. Entrance exams should be taken prior to February of the senior year. There are early decision and deferred admissions plans. Early decision applications should be filed by November 15; regular applications, by January 1 for fall entry. The fall 2012 application fee was $60. Notification of early decision is sent December 15; regular decision, April 1. 251 early decision candidates were accepted for the 2012-2013 class. 1016 applicants were on the 2012 waiting list; 3 were admitted. Applications are accepted online.

Transfer: 14 transfer students enrolled in 2011-2012. Transfer applicants must submit high school and college transcripts, an essay or personal statement, and standardized test scores and must present a minimum GPA of 3.0 in all college-level work. 64 of 128 credits required for the bachelor's degree must be completed at Hamilton.

Visiting: There are regularly scheduled orientations for prospective students, consisting of an interview, tour, class visit, and open house program. There are guides for informal visits, visitors may sit in on classes, and stay overnight. To schedule a visit, contact the Office of Admission.

Financial Aid: 56% of undergraduate students work part-time. Average annual earnings from campus work are $1300. The CSS/Profile, FAFSA, the state aid form, and the college's own financial statement are required. The deadline for filing freshman financial aid applications for fall entry is February 8.

International Students: There are 90 international students enrolled. The school actively recruits these students. They must take the TOEFL. They must also take the SAT or ACT.

Computers: Over 1,700 College-owned computers available for use. Wireless access throughout campus. All students may access the system. There are no time limits and no fees.

Graduates: From July 1, 2011 to June 30, 2012, 462 bachelor's degrees were awarded. The most popular majors were economics (16%), mathematics (10%), and government (8%). In an average class, 85% graduate in 4 years or less, 90% graduate in 5 years or less, and 91% graduate in 6 years or less.

Admissions Contact: Monica Inzer, Vice President and Dean of Admission and Financial Aid. E-Mail: *admission@hamilton.edu* Web: *www.hamilton.edu*

HARTWICK COLLEGE D-3

Oneonta, NY 13820 (607) 431-4150
(888) HARTWICK; (607) 431-4102

Full-time: 645 men, 931 women
Part-time: 13 men, 26 women
Graduate: n/av
Year: 4-1-4
Application Deadline: rolling
Freshman Class: n/av
Faculty: 112; IIB, av$
Ph.D.s: 88%
Student/Faculty: 11 to 1
Tuition: $39,330
Room & Board: $10,485

COMPETITIVE+

Hartwick College, founded in 1797, is a private undergraduate liberal arts and sciences college. In addition to regional accreditation, Hartwick has baccalaureate program accreditation with NASAD, NASM, and TEAC. The library contains 300,832 volumes, 29,700 microform items, and 8,944 audio/video tapes/CDs/DVDs, and subscribes to 13,112 periodicals including electronic. Computerized library services include interlibrary loans, database searching, Internet access, and Wi-Fi capability. Special learning facilities include an art gallery, radio station, an art and culture museum, a 100-acre environmental campus, and an observatory. The 425-acre campus is in a small town 75 miles southwest of Albany, NY. Including any residence halls, there are 28 buildings.

Student Life: 70% of undergraduates are from New York. Others are from 29 states, 25 foreign countries, and Canada. 88% are from public schools. 69% are White; 14% race unknown. 33% claim no religious affiliation; 30% Protestant; 26% Catholic. The average age of freshmen is 18; all undergraduates, 20. 27% do not continue beyond their first year; 58% remain to graduate.

Housing: 1221 students can be accommodated in college housing, which includes single-sex and coed dorms and on-campus apartments. In addition, there are honors houses, fraternity houses, sorority houses, substance-free housing, and an environmental campus. On-campus housing is guaranteed for all 4 years and is available on a lottery system for upperclassmen. 78% of students live on campus; of those, 90% remain on campus on weekends. All students may keep cars.

Activities: 3% of men belong to 2 national fraternities; 5% of women belong to 2 local and 1 national sororities. There are 70 groups on campus, including art, band, cheerleading, choir, chorale, chorus, dance, drama, environmental, ethnic, gay, honors, international, jazz band, literary magazine, musical theater, newspaper, pep band, political, professional, radio and TV, religious, social, social service, student government, and yearbook. Popular campus events include Wick Wars, Oneonta State and Hartwick Fest (street fair and concert), and Scholar Showcase.

Sports: There are 7 intercollegiate sports for men and 10 for women, and 5 intramural sports for men and 5 for women. Facilities include 2 gyms, an indoor pool, a dance room, athletic and training facilities, a track, a fitness center, a lighted all-weather playing field, a lighted soccer field, an equestrian complex (off-campus), and courts for handball, racquetball, squash, and tennis.

Disabled Students: 50% of the campus is accessible. Facilities include wheelchair ramps, elevators, special parking, and specially equipped restrooms.

Services: Counseling and information services are available, as is tutoring in most subjects. There is a reader service for the blind, writing center, and an academic support center.

Campus Safety and Security: Measures include 24-hour foot and vehicle patrol, emergency notification system, self-defense education, and security escort services. There are emergency telephones, lighted pathways/sidewalks, and controlled access to dorms/residences.

Programs of Study: Hartwick confers B.A., and B.S. degrees. Bachelor's degrees are awarded in BIOLOGICAL SCIENCE (biochemistry and biology/biological science), BUSINESS (accounting and business administration and management), COMMUNICATIONS AND THE ARTS (art, art history and appreciation, dramatic arts, English, French, German, languages, music, and Spanish), COMPUTER AND PHYSICAL SCIENCE (chemistry, computer science, geology, information sciences and systems, mathematics, and physics), EDUCATION (music education), ENGINEERING AND ENVIRONMENTAL DESIGN (environmental science), HEALTH PROFESSIONS (medical technology and nursing), SOCIAL SCIENCE (anthropology, economics, history, philosophy, political science/government, psychology, religion, and sociology). Psychology, business administration/accounting, and nursing have the largest enrollments.

Required: Students must complete 120 credit hours with at least a 2.0 GPA. The core curriculum consists of Hartwick's Liberal Arts in Practice. Distribution requirements include a first-year seminar; 9 credits spread through humanities, physical and life sciences, and social and behavioral sciences; 3 credits in quantitative and formal reasoning; foreign language (intermediate-level proficiency); attainment of writing level 4; and a senior capstone.

Special: Hartwick's innovative approach emphasizes personalized instruction and practical experiences both inside and outside the classroom: study abroad, internships, collaborative research, and more. Hartwick offers more thane than 30 courses of study leading to a bachelor of arts (B.A.) or bachelor of science (B.S.) degree, four pre-professional programs, five cooperative programs, and a series of interesting minors and other options, including certification in education. Plus, you can design you own major. Within Hartwick's Three-Year Bachelor's Degree Program, there are 24 major areas of study leading to a bachelor of arts (B.A.) or bachelor of science (B.S.) degree. There is a 3-2 engineering program with Clarkson University or Columbia University, and a 3-3 program with Albany Law School. There are 10 national honor societies and a freshman honors program.

Faculty/Classroom: 55% of faculty are male; 45% are female. All teach undergraduates. No introductory courses are taught by graduate students. The average class size in an introductory lecture is 20; in a laboratory is 20; and in a regular course is 30.

Admissions: 47% of the current freshmen were in the top fifth of their class.

Requirements: Reporting of SAT and ACT scores is optional. The recommended secondary course of study includes 4 years of English and 3 years each of math, a foreign language, history, and lab science. Hartwick strongly recommends that applicants plan a campus visit and interview. Prospective art majors should submit a portfolio, and music majors must audition. A GPA of 2.5 is required. AP and CLEP credits are accepted. Important factors in the admissions decision are advanced placement or honors courses, recommendations by school officials, and ability to finance college education.

Procedure: Freshmen are admitted fall and spring. Entrance exams should be taken in the spring of the junior year and/or the fall of the senior year. There are early decision, deferred admissions, and rolling admissions plans. Application deadlines are open. Notification is sent on a rolling basis. 35 early decision candidates were accepted for the 2013-2014 class. 71 applicants were on the 2013 waiting list. Applications are accepted online.

Transfer: 36 transfer students enrolled in 2012-2013. Applicants should present a minimum GPA of 2.0. 60 of 120 credits required for the bachelor's degree must be completed at Hartwick.

Visiting: There are regularly scheduled orientations for prospective students, consisting of an interview and tour, lunch, departmental open houses, presentations on student life, off-campus programs, and a career planning process. There are guides for informal visits, visitors may sit in on classes, and stay overnight. To schedule a visit, contact the Admissions Office at admissions@hartwick.edu.

Financial Aid: In 2013-2014, 99% of all full-time freshmen and 99% of continuing full-time students received some form of financial aid. 66% of undergraduate students work part-time. Average annual earnings from campus work are $1640. The average financial indebtedness of the 2013 graduate was $30,751. Hartwick is a member of CSS. The FAFSA and the college's own financial statement are required. The deadline for filing freshman financial aid applications for fall entry is February 15.

International Students: There are 51 international students enrolled. The school actively recruits these students. They must take the TOEFL with a minimum score of 550 on the paper-based TOEFL (PBT) or 79 on the Internet-based version (iBT). They must also take the SAT.

Computers: All students may access the system 24 hours per day, 7 days per week. There are no time limits and no fees.

Graduates: From July 1, 2012 to June 30, 2013, 314 bachelor's degrees were awarded. The most popular majors were business administration (15%), nursilng (11%), and sociology (11%). In an average class, 54% graduate in 4 years or less, 60% graduate in 5 years or less, and 62% graduate in 6 years or less. Of the 2012 graduating class, 22% were enrolled in graduate school within 6 months of graduation, and 25% were employed.

Admissions Contact: David Conway, Vice President for Enrollment Management. E-Mail: *admissions@hartwick.edu* Web: *www.hartwick .edu*

HILBERT COLLEGE A-4

Hamburg, NY 14075 (716) 649-7900
(800) 649-8003; (716) 649-0702

Full-time: 404 men, 480 women	**Faculty:** 47; IIB, --$
Part-time: 52 men, 83 women	**Ph.D.s:** 53%
Graduate: 21 men, 29 women	**Student/Faculty:** 18 to 1
Year: semesters, summer session	**Tuition:** $19,900
Application Deadline:	**Room & Board:** $8650
Freshman Class: n/av	

COMPETITIVE

Hilbert College, located in suburban Hamburg, N.Y., south of Buffalo, is a private four-year college founded in 1957 in the Catholic Franciscan tradition. There is one undergraduate school and one graduate school. The library contains 36,076 volumes, 3,616 microform items, and 1,165 audio/video tapes/CDs/DVDs, and subscribes to 23,190 periodicals including electronic. Computerized library services include interlibrary loans, database searching, Internet access, and Wi-Fi capability. The 44-acre campus is in a suburban area about 10 miles south of Buffalo. Including any residence halls, there are 11 buildings.

Student Life: 95% of undergraduates are from New York. Others are from 12 states, 2 foreign countries, and Canada. 80% are from public schools. 73% are White. The average age of freshmen is 18; all undergraduates, 22. 25% do not continue beyond their first year; 39% remain to graduate.

Housing: 304 students can be accommodated in college housing, which includes coed dorms and on-campus apartments. On-campus housing is guaranteed for the freshman year only, is available on a first-come, first-served basis, and is available on a lottery system for upperclassmen. 71% of students commute. All students may keep cars.

Activities: There are no fraternities or sororities. There are 20 groups on campus, including and human services, criminal justice, psychology, and academic (e.g., cheerleading, ethnic, film, honors, literary magazine, newspaper, professional, religious, social, social service, and student government. Popular campus events include Quad Party, Fall Fest, and Fall Family Weekend.

Sports: There are 5 intercollegiate sports for men and 6 for women, and 4 intramural sports for men and 4 for women. Facilities include a soccer/lacrosse field, baseball and softball diamonds, a practice field, a fitness center, and a 900-seat NCAA regulation indoor athletic facility.

Disabled Students: 95% of the campus is accessible. Facilities include wheelchair ramps, elevators, special parking, specially equipped restrooms, special class scheduling, lowered drinking fountains, and lowered telephones.

Services: Counseling and information services are available, as is tutoring in some subjects. There is remedial math and writing.

Campus Safety and Security: Measures include 24-hour foot and vehicle patrol, emergency notification system, self-defense education, and security escort services. There are emergency telephones, lighted pathways/sidewalks, and controlled access to dorms/residences.

Programs of Study: Hilbert confers B.A., and B.S. degrees. Associate and master's degrees are also awarded. Bachelor's degrees are awarded in BIOLOGICAL SCIENCE (forensic science), BUSINESS (accounting, business administration and management, international business management, organizational leadership and management, and sports management), COMMUNICATIONS AND THE ARTS (digital communications and English), COMPUTER AND PHYSICAL SCIENCE (computer security and information assurance), HEALTH PROFESSIONS (rehabilitation therapy), SOCIAL SCIENCE (criminal justice, criminology, forensic studies, human services, liberal arts/general studies, paralegal studies, political science/government, and psychology). Paralegal studies, psychology, and accounting are the strongest academically. Criminal justice, forensic science, and business administration have the largest enrollments.

Required: To graduate, students must complete 120 credit hours, including at least 36 in the major and 60 in liberal arts, with a minimum 2.0 GPA. Students must fulfill General Education requirements in interdisciplinary studies,intercultural awareness, arts & literature, math, religious studies, moral reasoning, political science/geography/history, sociology/psychology/economics, and physical sciences.

Special: Hilbert offers study abroad, cross-registration with the 17-member Western New York College Consortium, internships in most majors, and work-study programs. The college maintains articulation agreements with 22 New York State community colleges. There are 4 national honor societies, a freshman honors program, and 3 departmental honors programs.

Faculty/Classroom: 51% of faculty are male; 49% are female. All teach undergraduates, and 10% do both. No introductory courses are taught by graduate students. The average class size in an introductory lecture is 20 and in a regular course is 15.

Requirements: The SAT or ACT is recommended. Admission is based upon past academic performance, demonstrated ability, and personal characteristics. Applicants must submit an official high school transcript or GED certificate. A GPA of 75.0 is required. AP and CLEP credits are accepted. Important factors in the admissions decision are leadership record, advanced placement or honors courses, and recommendations by school officials.

Procedure: Freshmen are admitted to all sessions. There are deferred admissions and rolling admissions plans. Application deadlines are open. Application fee is $25. Applications are accepted online. Application fees are waived if application is completed online.

Transfer: 301 transfer students enrolled in 2012-2013. Applicants must submit official transcripts from all colleges attended and, in somes cases, the high school transcript. 30 of 120 credits required for the bachelor's degree must be completed at Hilbert.

Visiting: There are regularly scheduled orientations for prospective students. There are guides for informal visits and visitors may sit in on classes. To schedule a visit, contact Office of Admissions.

Financial Aid: In 2013-2014, 88% of all full-time freshmen and 83% of continuing full-time students received some form of financial aid. 100% of all full-time freshmen and 98% of continuing full-time students received

need-based aid. The average freshman award was $15,206. Need-based scholarships or need-based grants averaged $11,620; need-based self-help aid (loans and jobs) averaged $3,971; and other non-need-based awards and non-need-based scholarships averaged $5,087. 7% of undergraduate students work part-time. Average annual earnings from campus work are $1735. Hilbert is a member of CSS. The FAFSA is required. The priority date for freshman financial aid applications for fall entry is March 1. The deadline for filing freshman financial aid applications for fall entry is December 1.

International Students: There are 6 international students enrolled. They must take the TOEFL.

Computers: All students may access the system. There are no time limits and no fees.

Graduates: From July 1, 2012 to June 30, 2013, 227 bachelor's degrees were awarded. The most popular majors were criminal justice (37%), forensic science/crime scene invetigation (22%), and business administration (8%). 50 companies recruited on campus in 2012-2013. In an average class, 36% graduate in 4 years or less, 38% graduate in 5 years or less, and 39% graduate in 6 years or less. Of the 2012 graduating class, 15% were enrolled in graduate school within 6 months of graduation, and 75% were employed.

Admissions Contact: Justin Rogers, Director of Admissions. E-Mail: *admissions@hilbert.edu* Web: *www.hilbert.edu*

HOBART AND WILLIAM SMITH COLLEGES B-3

Geneva, NY 14456-3397 **H: (315) 781-3622; (315) 781-3471**

Full-time: 880 men, 1015 women
Part-time: 5 men and women
Graduate: n/av
Year: semesters
Application Deadline: see profile
Freshman Class: n/av
SAT or ACT: required
Faculty: n/av; IIB, +$
Ph.D.s: n/av
Student/Faculty: n/av
Tuition: $42,915
Room & Board: $10000

VERY COMPETITIVE

Hobart College, a men's college founded in 1822, shares campus, classes, and faculty with William Smith College, a women's college founded in 1908. Together, these coordinate colleges offer degree programs in the liberal arts. Figures in the above capsule and in this profile are approximate. The library contains 375,762 volumes, 77,396 microform items, and 9,600 audio/video tapes/CDs/DVDs, and subscribes to 1,926 periodicals including electronic. Computerized library services include interlibrary loans, database searching, and Internet access. Special learning facilities include a learning resource center, art gallery, radio station, a 100-acre natural preserve, and a 70-foot research vessel. The 170-acre campus is in a small town 50 miles west of Syracuse and 50 miles east of Rochester, on the north shore of Seneca Lake. Including any residence halls, there are 95 buildings.

Student Life: 51% of undergraduates are from out of state, mostly the Northeast. Students are from 40 states, 19 foreign countries, and Canada. 65% are from public schools. 86% are white. 30% are Catholic; 30% Protestant; 20% claim no religious affiliation; 15% Jewish. The average age of freshmen is 18; all undergraduates, 20. 15% do not continue beyond their first year; 75% remain to graduate.

Housing: 1500 students can be accommodated in college housing, which includes single-sex and coed dorms and on-campus apartments. In addition, there are honors houses, language houses, special-interest houses, fraternity houses, cooperative houses in which students plan and prepare their own meals, and townhouses for upperclassmen. On-campus housing is guaranteed for all 4 years. 90% of students live on campus; of those, 93% remain on campus on weekends. All students may keep cars.

Activities: 15% of men belong to 5 national fraternities. There are no sororities. There are 70 groups on campus, including art, chess, choir, chorale, chorus, computers, dance, debate, drama, ethnic, film, forensics, gay, honors, international, jazz band, literary magazine, musical theater, newspaper, orchestra, photography, political, professional, radio and TV, religious, social, social service, student government, symphony, and yearbook. Popular campus events include Folk Festival, Charter Day, and Moving Up Day.

Sports: There are 11 intercollegiate sports for men and 11 for women, and 23 intramural sports for men and 23 for women. Facilities include a sport and recreation center, 2 gyms, numerous athletic fields, a swimming pool, 5 indoor tennis courts, 3 weight rooms, basketball and racquetball courts, an indoor track, international squash courts, a boathouse, and a crew facility.

Disabled Students: Facilities include wheelchair ramps, elevators, special parking, specially equipped restrooms, special class scheduling, and lowered drinking fountains.

Services: Counseling and information services are available, as is tutoring in every subject. There is a reader service for the blind, and remedial math, reading, and writing. There is a counseling center staffed by 5 therapists/counselors as well as various support groups and educational workshops.

Campus Safety and Security: Measures include 24-hour foot and vehicle patrol, self-defense education, and security escort services. There are shuttle buses, emergency telephones, and lighted pathways/sidewalks.

Programs of Study: HWS confers B.A. and B.S. degrees. Master's degrees are also awarded. Bachelor's degrees are awarded in BIOLOGICAL SCIENCE (biology/biological science), COMMUNICATIONS AND THE ARTS (art history and appreciation, classics, comparative literature, dance, English, fine arts, French, modern language, music, and studio art), COMPUTER AND PHYSICAL SCIENCE (chemistry, computer science, geoscience, mathematics, and physics), ENGINEERING AND ENVIRONMENTAL DESIGN (architecture and environmental science), SOCIAL SCIENCE (African studies, American studies, anthropology, Asian/Oriental studies, economics, European studies, history, international relations, Latin American studies, philosophy, political science/government, psychology, religion, Russian and Slavic studies, sociology, Spanish studies, urban studies, and women's studies). Natural sciences, environmental studies, and creative writing are the strongest academically. English, economics, and political science have the largest enrollments.

Required: All first-year students must take a seminar. Students should complete a major of 14 to 18 courses and a minor of 6 to 8 courses, or a second major. Of the major or the minor (or second major), one must be disciplinary and the other interdisciplinary. Minimum grade and GPA standards apply. In addition, all students must meet the 8 goals established by the faculty to ensure breadth across the disciplines as well as depth in the major.

Special: Students are encouraged to spend at least 1 term in a study-abroad program, offered in more than 29 countries and locales within the United States. Options include a United Nations term, a Washington semester, an urban semester, and prearchitecture semesters in New York, Paris, Florence, or Copenhagen. HWS offers dual and student-designed majors, internships, credit for life/military/work experience, nondegree study, and pass/fail options. There are also advanced business degree programs with Clarkson University and Rochester Institute of Technology and 3-2 engineering degrees with Columbia University, Rensselaer Polytechnic Institute, and Dartmouth College. There are 9 national honor societies, including Phi Beta Kappa, and all departments have honors programs.

Faculty/Classroom: 60% of faculty are male; 40% are female. All teach and do research. No introductory courses are taught by graduate students. The average class size in an introductory lecture 40; in a laboratory 18; and in a regular course 18.

Requirements: The SAT or ACT is required. SAT: subject tests are not required but will be considered if taken. A GED may be accepted. A total of 19 academic credits is required, including 4 years of English, 3 of math, and at least 3 each of lab science, foreign language, and history. An essay is required; an interview is recommended. AP credits are accepted. Important factors in the admissions decision are advanced placement or honors courses, evidence of special talent, and leadership record.

Procedure: Freshmen are admitted fall. Entrance exams should be taken no later than December of the senior year. There are early decision, early admissions and deferred admissions plans. Applications are accepted online. A waiting list is maintained. Check with the school for current application deadlines and fee.

Transfer: Applicants must have a 2.5 GPA and have completed 1 year of college study. They are required to take the SAT or ACT. An interview is recommended. 16 of 32 credits required for the bachelor's degree must be completed at HWS.

Visiting: There are regularly scheduled orientations for prospective students, including 7 open houses in the spring, summer, and fall and daily tours and personal interviews year round. Information sessions are offered February through April and on Saturdays in the summer. There are guides for informal visits; visitors may sit in on classes and stay overnight. To schedule a visit, contact the Office of Admissions.

Financial Aid: HWS is a member of CSS. The CSS/Profile and FAFSA are required. Check with the school for current application deadlines.

International Students: The school actively recruits these students. They must take the TOEFL. They must also take the SAT or ACT.

Computers: All students may access the system from 8 a.m. to 1 a.m., 7 days a week. There are no time limits and no fees. It is strongly recommended that all students have a personal computer. A Gateway Solo Laptop is recommended.

Admissions Contact: Director of Admissions. Web: *www.hws.edu*

HOFSTRA UNIVERSITY D-5

Hempstead, NY 11549 **(516) 463-6700**
(800) HOFSTRA; (516) 463-7660

Full-time: 2936 men, 3438 women
Part-time: 291 men, 228 women
Graduate: 1684 men, 2446 women
Year: semesters, summer session
Application Deadline: open
Faculty: 385; I, av$
Ph.D.s: 93%
Student/Faculty: 18 to 1
Tuition: $35,950
Room & Board: $12,070
Freshman Class: 22733 applied, 13346 accepted, 1488 enrolled
SAT CR/M: 580/590 **ACT:** 25 **VERY COMPETITIVE+**

Hofstra University, founded in 1935, is an independent institution offering programs in liberal arts and sciences, business, communications, education, engineering and applied sciences, health and human services, honors studies, law, and medicine. There are 7 undergraduate schools and 8 graduate schools. In addition to regional accreditation, Hofstra has baccalaureate program accreditation with AACSB, ABET, ACEJMC, and TEAC. The 3 libraries contain 1.1 million volumes, 3.5 million microform items, and 16,396 audio/video tapes/CDs/DVDs, and subscribe to 11,322 periodicals including electronic. Computerized library services include interlibrary loans, database searching, Internet access, and Wi-Fi capability. Special learning facilities include an art gallery, radio station, TV station, 100% wireless campus; State-of-the-art medical school; financial trading room; multi-media converged news room; comprehensive media production facility including a 24-hr radio station; multiple 3-D printers; digital language lab; science labs and new state-of-the-art bio-engineering labs; rooftop observatory; 6 theaters including a black box teaching theater; assessment centers for client observation and counseling; child care institute; cultural center; museum, arboretum, and bird sanctuary. The 240-acre campus is in a suburban area 25 miles east of New York City. Including any residence halls, there are 115 buildings.

Student Life: 62% of undergraduates are from New York. Others are from 46 states, 50 foreign countries, and Canada. 61% are White; 11% Hispanic. The average age of freshmen is 18; all undergraduates, 20. 22% do not continue beyond their first year; 61% remain to graduate.

Housing: 3800 students can be accommodated in college housing, which includes single-sex and coed dorms and on-campus apartments. In addition, there are honors houses, special-interest houses, There also is a living-learning center, quiet floors, women's floors, and freshman housing. On-campus housing is guaranteed for all 4 years, is available on a first-come, first-served basis, and is available on a lottery system for upperclassmen. Priority is given to out-of-town students. 51% of students commute. All students may keep cars.

Activities: 11% of men belong to 14 national fraternities; 9% of women belong to 2 local and 8 national sororities. There are 222 groups on campus, including Resident Student Association, art, band, cheerleading, chess, choir, chorale, chorus, Commuting Student Organization, computers, dance, debate, drama, drum and bugle corps, environmental, ethnic, film, forensics, gay, honors, international, jazz band, literary magazine, musical theater, newspaper, opera, orchestra, pep band, photography, political, professional, radio and TV, religious, social, social service, student government, symphony, and yearbook. Popular campus events include New Student Convocation, Welcome Week, Spring Week, Hofstra Celebrates the Holidays, Student Leadership Awards and Hofstra Music Festival.

Sports: There are 8 intercollegiate sports for men and 9 for women, and 5 intramural sports for men and 5 for women. Facilities include a 15,000-seat stadium, a 5,000-seat arena, a 1,600-seat soccer stadium, a physical education building, a swim center with an Olympic-size swimming pool and high-dive area, a softball stadium, intramural fields, and a fitness center with a multipurpose gym, an indoor track, cardio area, weight room, cycle studio, yoga studio, and aerobics studio.

Disabled Students: All of the campus is accessible. Facilities include wheelchair ramps, elevators, special parking, specially equipped restrooms, special class scheduling, lowered drinking fountains, lowered telephones, special housing.

Services: Counseling and information services are available, as is tutoring in most subjects. There is a reader service for the blind. Tutoring is offered in subjects such as English, math, reading, and writing

Campus Safety and Security: Measures include 24-hour foot and vehicle patrol, emergency notification system, self-defense education, and security escort services. There are shuttle buses, emergency telephones, lighted pathways/sidewalks, controlled access to dorms/residences, residence halls have security cameras, require card access to enter, and entrance is monitored by resident student safety representative 24/7 and CCTV; bike patrol; and a motorist assistance program.

Programs of Study: Hofstra confers B.A., B.S., B.B.A., B.E., B.F.A. and B.S.Ed. degrees. Master's and doctoral degrees are also awarded. Bachelor's degrees are awarded in AGRICULTURE (environmental studies), BIOLOGICAL SCIENCE (biochemistry and biology/biological science), BUSINESS (accounting, banking and finance, business administration and management, business economics, business law, entrepreneurial studies, international business management, labor studies, management information systems, marketing management, and supply chain management), COMMUNICATIONS AND THE ARTS (American literature, art history and appreciation, audio technology, ceramic art and design, Chinese, classics, comparative literature, creative writing, dance, design, dramatic arts, film arts, fine arts, French, German, Hebrew, Italian, jazz, journalism, Latin, linguistics, media arts, metal/jewelry, music, music business management, music history and appreciation, music performance, music theory and composition, painting, photography, public relations, publishing, radio/television technology, Russian, Spanish, speech/debate/rhetoric, theater design, theater management, video, and visual and performing arts), COMPUTER AND PHYSICAL SCIENCE (applied mathematics, applied physics, chemistry, computer science, geology, information sciences and systems, mathematics, physics, and Urban Ecology), EDUCATION (art education, athletic training, business education, (Education) Childhood Education, dance education, elementary education, English education, foreign languages education, health education, mathematics education, music education, physical education, science education, secondary education, and social studies education), ENGINEERING AND ENVIRONMENTAL DESIGN (biomedical engineering, civil engineering, computer engineering, electrical/electronics engineering, engineering and applied science, industrial engineering, manufacturing engineering, and mechanical engineering), HEALTH PROFESSIONS (allied health, community health work, exercise science, health science, Pre-Health Studies, predentistry, premedicine, preoptometry, preosteopathy, prepodiatry, preveterinary science, and speech pathology/audiology), SOCIAL SCIENCE (African studies, American studies, anthropology, Caribbean studies, Chinese Studies, china asia-pacific studies, criminology, economics, forensic studies, geography, (Social Science) Global Studies, Hispanic American studies, history, Judaic studies, Latin American studies, liberal arts/general studies, philosophy, political science/government, psychology, religion, sociology, and women's studies). Accounting, biology, and communication are the strongest academically. Biology, psychology, and education have the largest enrollments.

Required: A total of 124 to 152 credit hours is required for graduation, with approximately 30 to 60 in the major depending on degree program and a minimum GPA of 2.0. Students must pass Writing Studies and Composition (WSC) 1 and 2 and pass a writing proficiency exam. A minimum of 9 semester hours each is required in humanities, natural sciences/math/computer science, and in social science. Foreign language study is required for the B.A. the B.B.A. in International Business, and some B.S. programs.

Special: Internships in numerous career fields, SUNY Brockport/Washington Semester, utilization of the Washington Center for internship conferences and programming, an Albany Internship with the NY State Assembly, NY State Senate Internship, study abroad, and dual and student-designed majors are offered. Credit for prior learning and credit by exam are given with proper credentials. Hofstra offers non-degree study and pass/fail options. There are 33 national honor societies, including Phi Beta Kappa, a freshman honors program, and 35 departmental honors programs.

Faculty/Classroom: 56% of faculty are male; 44% are female. 81% teach undergraduates, all do research, and 81% do both. No introductory courses are taught by graduate students. The average class size in an introductory lecture is 27; in a laboratory is 15; and in a regular course is 21.

Admissions: 59% of the 2013-2014 applicants were accepted. The SAT scores for the 2013-2014 freshman class were: Critical Reading--9% below 500, 51% between 500 and 599, 36% between 600 and 699, and 4% between 700 and 800; Math--7% below 500, 48% between 500 and 599, 40% between 600 and 699, and 5% between 700 and 800. The ACT scores were 2% below 21, 24% between 21 and 23, 35% between 24 and 26, 20% between 27 and 28, and 19% above 28. 52% of the current freshmen were in the top fifth of their class; 78% were in the top two fifths. 5 freshmen graduated first in their class.

Requirements: Applicants should graduate from an accredited secondary school or have a GED. Preparatory work should include 4 years of English, 3 each of history and social studies, math, and science, and 2 of foreign language. Engineering students are required to have 4 years of math and 1 each of chemistry and physics. An essay is required. Interviews are recommended. One counselor or teacher recommendation is recommended. Standardized tests are not used or required for admission to New Opportunities at Hofstra (NOAH) or the School of University Studies, and not required for Program for Academic Learning Skills (PALS) or international applicants (TOEFL is required). AP and CLEP credits are accepted. Important factors in the admissions decision are advanced placement or honors courses, recommendations by school officials, and leadership record.

Procedure: Freshmen are admitted fall and spring. Entrance exams should be taken in the junior or senior year. There are early admissions, deferred admissions, and rolling admissions plans. Early decision applications should be filed by December 15, along with a $70 fee. Notification of early decision is sent January 15; regular decision, February 1. 56 applicants were on the 2013 waiting list; 31 were admitted. Applications are accepted online.

Transfer: 450 transfer students enrolled in 2012-2013. Admission is based primarily on prior college work. A maximum of 64 credits from a 2-year school or 94 credits from a 4-year school is accepted. There is a 30-credit maximum on AP/CLEP credits. 30 of 124 credits required for the bachelor's degree must be completed at Hofstra.

Visiting: There are regularly scheduled orientations for prospective students, A group information session, a campus tour and an optional interview with a admission counselor. There are guides for informal visits, visitors may sit in on classes, and stay overnight. To schedule a visit, contact Jessica Linck at (516) 463-6798.

Financial Aid: In 2013-2014, 94% of all full-time freshmen and 84% of continuing full-time students received some form of financial aid. 72% of all full-time freshmen and 62% of continuing full-time students received

need-based aid. The average freshman award was $20,000. Need-based scholarships or need-based grants averaged $17,000 ($63,000 maximum); need-based self-help aid (loans and jobs) averaged $4,000 ($13,000 maximum); non-need-based athletic scholarships averaged $21,000 ($41,000 maximum); and other non-need-based awards and non-need-based scholarships averaged $13,000 ($36,000 maximum). 28% of undergraduate students work part-time. Average annual earnings from campus work are $3129. The FAFSA and the state aid form are required. The priority date for freshman financial aid applications for fall entry is February 15.

International Students: There are 162 international students enrolled. The school actively recruits these students. They must take the TOEFL with a minimum score of 550 on the paper-based TOEFL (PBT) or 80 on the Internet-based version (iBT).

Computers: All students may access the system. There are no time limits. The fee is $105.

Graduates: From July 1, 2012 to June 30, 2013, 1701 bachelor's degrees were awarded. The most popular majors were marketing (8%), psychology (8%), and public relations (6%). 320 companies recruited on campus in 2012-2013. In an average class, 45% graduate in 4 years or less, 59% graduate in 5 years or less, and 61% graduate in 6 years or less. Of the 2012 graduating class, 27% were enrolled in graduate school within 6 months of graduation, and 79% were employed.

Admissions Contact: Jessica Eads, Vice President of Enrollment Management . E-Mail: *admission@hofstra.edu* Web: *www.hofstra.edu*

HOUGHTON COLLEGE B-3

Houghton, NY 14744 (585) 567-9353
(800) 777-2556; (585) 567-9522

Full-time: 363 men, 660 women	**Faculty:** 73
Part-time: 22 men, 36 women	**Ph.D.s:** 88%
Graduate: 12 men, 7 women	**Student/Faculty:** 14 to 1
Year: semesters, summer session	**Tuition:** $27,428
Application Deadline:	**Room & Board:** $8012
Freshman Class: 807 applied, 735 accepted, 223 enrolled	
SAT CR/M/W: 569/548/547	**ACT:** 25 **VERY COMPETITIVE**

Houghton College, founded in 1883, provides a residential educational experience integrating academic instruction with Christian faith. In addition to regional accreditation, Houghton has baccalaureate program accreditation with NASM and TEAC. The 2 libraries contain 314,183 volumes, 47,163 microform items, and 21,092 audio/video tapes/CDs/DVDs, and subscribe to 57,591 periodicals including electronic. Computerized library services include interlibrary loans, database searching, Internet access, and Wi-Fi capability. Special learning facilities include an art gallery, radio station, an equestrian center, a ropes course, digital media lab, greenhouse, outdoor classroom. The 1300-acre campus is in a rural area 65 miles southeast of Buffalo and 70 miles southwest of Rochester. Including any residence halls, there are 20 buildings.

Student Life: 58% of undergraduates are from New York. Others are from 36 states, 31 foreign countries, and Canada. 66% are from public schools. 84% are White. 95% are Protestant. The average age of freshmen is 18; all undergraduates, 22. 12% do not continue beyond their first year; 74% remain to graduate.

Housing: 1066 students can be accommodated in college housing, which includes single-sex dorms, on-campus apartments, and married student housing. In addition, there are special-interest houses, Equestrian students have the opportunity to live in housing on site. On-campus housing is guaranteed for all 4 years. Priority is given to out-of-town students. 87% of students live on campus; of those, 67% remain on campus on weekends. Alcohol is not permitted. All students may keep cars.

Activities: There are no fraternities or sororities. There are 50 groups on campus, including mission organizations, ministry, art, bagpipe, band, choir, chorale, chorus, communications, drama, environmental, ethnic, film, honors, international, jazz band, literary magazine, musical theater, newspaper, opera, orchestra, pep band, photography, political, professional, religious, social, social service, student government, symphony, volunteer service, and yearbook. Popular campus events include Christian Life Emphasis Week, Film Festival, SPOT Variety Show, Purple and Gold Week, Faith and Justice Symposium and Martin Luther King Jr. Service Day.

Sports: There are 7 intercollegiate sports for men and 9 for women, and 7 intramural sports for men and 7 for women. Facilities include 3 basketball and 4 racquetball courts, a swimming pool, an indoor track, a downhill ski slope, cross-country ski trails, 6 tennis courts, a climbing wall, an 8-lane all-weather track, a ropes course, and a 386-acre equestrian center with an indoor riding ring. The gym seats 1800; the auditorium, 1300, baseball and softball fields under construction along with new athletic complex/field house.

Disabled Students: 85% of the campus is accessible. Facilities include wheelchair ramps, elevators, special parking, specially equipped restrooms, special class scheduling, lowered drinking fountains, lowered telephones, and special housing.

Services: Counseling and information services are available, as is tutoring in some subjects, general education courses. There is a reader service for the blind. There is support for students with learning-related disabilities.

Campus Safety and Security: Measures include 24-hour foot and vehicle patrol, emergency notification system, and security escort services. There are emergency telephones, lighted pathways/sidewalks, controlled access to dorms/residences, Campus emergency preparedness plan includes agreements with local police departments, American Red Cross, and local schools/businesses for cooperative assistance as needed.

Programs of Study: Houghton confers B.A., B.S., B.F.A. and B.Mus. degrees. Associate and master's degrees are also awarded. Bachelor's degrees are awarded in AGRICULTURE (equine science), BIOLOGICAL SCIENCE (biochemistry, biology/adolescence education, biology/biological science, and environmental biology), BUSINESS (accounting, business administration and management, recreation and leisure services, and recreational facilities management), COMMUNICATIONS AND THE ARTS (art, communication, English, English as a second/foreign language, English literature, English Writing, instrumental performance, media arts, music, music performance, music theory and composition, organ performance, printmaking, Spanish, studio art, vocal performance, voice, vocal music education, and writing), COMPUTER AND PHYSICAL SCIENCE (applied physics, chemistry, chemistry/adolescence education, computer science, mathematics, physics, and science), EDUCATION (art education, (Education) Childhood Education, childhood education: 1-6, Christian education, education of the exceptional child, elementary education, English education, foreign languages education, general studies, health education, mathematics education, music education, physical education, science education, secondary education, special education, and teaching English as a second/foreign language (TESOL/TEFOL)), ENGINEERING AND ENVIRONMENTAL DESIGN (environmental science and preengineering), HEALTH PROFESSIONS (medical technology, predentistry, premedicine, preoptometry, prepharmacy, prephysical therapy, preveterinary science, and recreation therapy), SOCIAL SCIENCE (biblical studies, Christian studies, counseling/psychology, crosscultural studies, history, humanities, interdisciplinary studies, international studies, liberal arts/general studies, ministries, parks and recreation management, pastoral studies, philosophy, political science/government, prelaw, psychobiology, psychology, religion, religious education, religious studies, religious music, and sociology). Biology, religion, art, music, psychology, communications, and business administration are the strongest academically. Management/business administration, biology, and inclusive childhood education have the largest enrollments.

Required: Integrative studies courses are required in the following disciplines: writing, literature, Bible, foreign language, history, math, science, physical education, theology, philosophy, fine arts, social science, and humanities. A minimum GPA of 2.0 is required to graduate.

Special: Students may cross-register with members of the Western New York Consortium, the Christian College Consortium, and the Five College Committee. Internships are available in psychology, social work, business, educational ministries, physical fitness, political science, graphic design, communication, athletic training, recreation, English, and Christian education. Study abroad in 25 countries, a Washington semester, and dual majors. A 3-2 engineering degree with Clarkson and Washington Universities are available as well as a 4-1 BS/MBA degree with Alfred U, Clarkson U, Niagara U and Rochester Institute of Technology. A PharmD 3-4 degree program with University of Buffalo is also available. Students may design their own major as an Interdisciplinary Studies major. Credit for military experience and nondegree study are possible. There are 3 national honor societies, including Phi Beta Kappa, a freshman honors program, and 3 departmental honors programs.

Faculty/Classroom: 64% of faculty are male; 36% are female. All teach undergraduates, 20% do research, and 20% do both. No introductory courses are taught by graduate students. The average class size in an introductory lecture is 26; in a laboratory is 13; and in a regular course is 17.

Admissions: 91% of the 2013-2014 applicants were accepted. The SAT scores for the 2013-2014 freshman class were: Critical Reading--22% below 500, 41% between 500 and 599, 29% between 600 and 699, and 8% between 700 and 800; Math--27% below 500, 44% between 500 and 599, 25% between 600 and 699, and 4% between 700 and 800; Writing--32% below 500, 36% between 500 and 599, 28% between 600 and 699, and 4% between 700 and 800. The ACT scores were 17% below 21, 20% between 21 and 23, 26% between 24 and 26, 19% between 27 and 28, and 19% above 28. 51% of the current freshmen were in the top fifth of their class; 80% were in the top two fifths. There was 1 National Merit finalist. 8 freshmen graduated first in their class.

Requirements: The SAT or ACT is required. Applicants must graduate from an accredited secondary school, be home-schooled, or have a GED. A total of 16 academic credits is recommended, including 4 of English, 3 of social studies, and 2 each of foreign language, math, and science. An essay is required. Music students must audition. An interview is recommended. AP and CLEP credits are accepted. Important factors in the admissions decision are personality/intangible qualities, advanced placement or honors courses, and recommendations by school officials.

Procedure: Freshmen are admitted fall and spring. Entrance exams

should be taken in the spring of the junior year or fall of the senior year. There are deferred admissions and rolling admissions plans. Application deadlines are open. Application fee is $40. Notifications are sent January 1. Applications are accepted online.

Transfer: 60 transfer students enrolled in 2012-2013. Applicants should have a 2.75 or better GPA. A character recommendation and high school transcripts must be submitted. The essay, an SAT or ACT and an interview are optional but encouraged. 30 of 125 credits required for the bachelor's degree must be completed at Houghton.

Visiting: There are regularly scheduled orientations for prospective students, including a campus tour, an admissions interview, a financial aid session, a class visit, and an academic information session. There are guides for informal visits, visitors may sit in on classes, and stay overnight. To schedule a visit, contact the Visit Office at (800) 777-2556.

Financial Aid: In 2013-2014, 100% of all full-time freshmen and 97% of continuing full-time students received some form of financial aid. 85% of all full-time freshmen and 86% of continuing full-time students received need-based aid. The average freshman award was $22,221. Need-based scholarships or need-based grants averaged $7,116 ($14,000 maximum); need-based self-help aid (loans and jobs) averaged $4,232 ($5,500 maximum); other non-need-based awards and non-need-based scholarships averaged $8,468 ($26,924 maximum); and $2,405 from other forms of aid. 43% of undergraduate students work part-time. Average annual earnings from campus work are $1561. The average financial indebtedness of the 2013 graduate was $22,197. Houghton is a member of CSS. The FAFSA is required. The priority date for freshman financial aid applications for fall entry is March 1.

International Students: There are 64 international students enrolled. The school actively recruits these students. They must take the TOEFL with a minimum score of 550 on the paper-based TOEFL (PBT) or 80 on the Internet-based version (iBT).

Computers: All students may access the system. There are no time limits and no fees.

Graduates: From July 1, 2012 to June 30, 2013, 348 bachelor's degrees were awarded. The most popular majors were business administration (21%), education (13%), and biology (11%). 54 companies recruited on campus in 2012-2013. In an average class, 2% graduate in 3 years or less, 64% graduate in 4 years or less, 72% graduate in 5 years or less, and 74% graduate in 6 years or less. Of the 2012 graduating class, 18% were enrolled in graduate school within 6 months of graduation, and 86% were employed.

Admissions Contact: Eric Currie, Vice President for Enrollment Management. E-Mail: *admission@houghton.edu* Web: *www.houghton.edu*

HUNTER COLLEGE / THE CITY UNIVERSITY OF NEW YORK D-5

New York, NY 10065 **(212) 772-4490; (800) 772-4000**

Full-time: 4185 men, 7611 women	**Faculty:** 750
Part-time: 1664 men, 3178 women	**Ph.D.s:** 86%
Graduate: 1434 men, 4752 women	**Student/Faculty:** 15 to 1
Year: semesters, summer session	**Tuition:** $6129 ($15,699)
Application Deadline: open	**Room & Board:** $5300
Freshman Class: n/av	
SAT CR/M: 574/598	

VERY COMPETITIVE

Hunter College, a comprehensive, institution established in 1870, is part of the City University of New York and is both city and state-supported. Primarily a commuter college, it emphasizes liberal arts in its undergraduate and graduate programs. There are 3 undergraduate schools and 4 graduate schools. In addition to regional accreditation, Hunter has baccalaureate program accreditation with ADA, APTA, ASLA, CSWE, NCATE, and NLN. The library contains 865,240 volumes, 651,000 microform items, and 75,000 audio/video tapes/CDs/DVDs, and subscribes to 36,000 periodicals including electronic. Computerized library services include database searching. Special learning facilities include an art gallery, radio station, a geography/geology lab, on-campus elementary and secondary schools, and a theater. The 3-acre campus is in an urban area New York City. Including any residence halls, there are 6 buildings.

Student Life: 98% of undergraduates are from New York. Others are from 42 states, 151 foreign countries, and Canada. 71% are from public schools. 44% are White; 21% Asian American; 17% Hispanic; 12% African American. The average age of freshmen is 18; all undergraduates, 24. 17% do not continue beyond their first year.

Housing: 662 students can be accommodated in college housing, which includes coed dorms. On-campus housing is available on a first-come, first-served basis, and is available on a lottery system for upperclassmen. 99% of students commute. No one may keep cars.

Activities: 2% of men belong to 1 local and 1 national fraternities. There are 150 groups on campus, including art, band, cheerleading, choir, chorale, chorus, drama, ethnic, film, gay, honors, international, jazz band, literary magazine, musical theater, newspaper, orchestra, political, professional, radio and TV, religious, social, social service, student government, and symphony. Popular campus events include Major Day Fair.

Sports: There are 9 intercollegiate sports for men and 11 for women. Facilities include fencing, dance, and weight rooms, racquetball courts, a pool, outdoor tennis courts, and a gym.

Disabled Students: All of the campus is accessible. Facilities include wheelchair ramps, elevators, special parking, specially equipped restrooms, special class scheduling, lowered drinking fountains, lowered telephones.

Services: Counseling and information services are available, as is tutoring in every subject. There is a reader service for the blind, and remedial math, reading, and writing. Review of graduate-level papers through the writing center and a math tutoring center are available.

Campus Safety and Security: Measures include self-defense education. There are shuttle buses, emergency telephones, 24-hour foot patrol.

Programs of Study: Hunter confers B.A., B.S., B.F.A., B.Mus. and B.S.Ed degrees. Master's degrees are also awarded. Bachelor's degrees are awarded in BIOLOGICAL SCIENCE (biology/biological science and nutrition), BUSINESS (accounting), COMMUNICATIONS AND THE ARTS (Chinese, classics, comparative literature, creative writing, dance, dramatic arts, English, English literature, film arts, fine arts, French, German, Greek, Hebrew, Italian, languages, Latin, media arts, music, Russian, and Spanish), COMPUTER AND PHYSICAL SCIENCE (chemistry, computer science, mathematics, physics, and statistics), EDUCATION (art education, early childhood education, elementary education, foreign languages education, health education, middle school education, music education, science education, and secondary education), ENGINEERING AND ENVIRONMENTAL DESIGN (energy management technology, environmental science, and preengineering), HEALTH PROFESSIONS (medical laboratory technology, nursing, physical therapy, predentistry, premedicine, and public health), SOCIAL SCIENCE (African American studies, anthropology, archeology, economics, geography, Hispanic American studies, history, international relations, Judaic studies, Latin American studies, philosophy, political science/government, prelaw, psychology, religion, social science, sociology, urban studies, and women's studies). Nursing is the strongest academically. Psychology has the largest enrollment.

Required: To graduate, students must complete 120 credits. The total number of hours in a major varies from 24 credits for a liberal arts major to 63 credits for a professional concentration; a minimum GPA of 2.0 is needed overall and in the major. Distribution requirements include 12 credits of social sciences, up to 12 credits of a foreign language, 10 or more of math and science, 9 of humanities and the arts, 6 of literature, and 3 of English composition.

Special: Special academic programs include internships, student-designed majors, work-study, study abroad in 24 countries, and dual majors. There is cross-registration with the Brooklyn School of Law, Marymount Manhattan College, and the YIVO Institute. Through the National Student Exchange Program, Hunter students can study for 1 or 2 semesters at any of 150 U.S. campuses. Accelerated degree programs are offered in anthropology, biopharmacology, economics, English, history, math, physics, sociology, and social research. Exchange programs in Paris or Puerto Rico are possible. There are 2 national honor societies, including Phi Beta Kappa, a freshman honors program, and 19 departmental honors programs.

Faculty/Classroom: No introductory courses are taught by graduate students. The average class size in a laboratory is 20 and in a regular course is 30.

Admissions: The SAT scores for the 2013-2014 freshman class were: Critical Reading--12% below 500, 54% between 500 and 599, 26% between 600 and 699, and 8% between 700 and 800; Math--3% below 500, 50% between 500 and 599, 37% between 600 and 699, and 10% between 700 and 800.

Requirements: The SAT is required. Student admission is based on a combination of high school grade average, high school academic credits, including English and math, and SAT scores. AP and CLEP credits are accepted.

Procedure: Freshmen are admitted fall and spring. Entrance exams should be taken by October of the junior year. There are early admissions, deferred admissions, and rolling admissions plans. Application deadlines are open. Application fee is $65. Notification of early decision is sent December 15; regular decision, January 1. 4 early decision candidates were accepted for the 2013-2014 class. Applications are accepted online.

Transfer: 1877 transfer students enrolled in 2012-2013. Applicants must have at least a 2.0 GPA. All students must complete 30 of the 120 to 131 credits required for a bachelor's degree at the college, including half of those needed for both the major and the minor.

Visiting: There are regularly scheduled orientations for prospective students, presentations and tours every Friday. There are guides for informal visits and visitors may sit in on classes. To schedule a visit, contact the Admissions Office.

Financial Aid: The FAFSA and the college's own financial statement are required. The deadline for filing freshman financial aid applications for fall entry is May 1.

International Students: There are 1352 international students enrolled. They must take the TOEFL with a minimum score of 500 on the paper-based TOEFL (PBT) and the college's own test.

Computers: All students may access the system 24 hours a day. There are no time limits and no fees.

Graduates: From July 1, 2012 to June 30, 2013, 2707 bachelor's degrees were awarded. The most popular majors were psychology (21%), social sciences (18%), and English (14%). In an average class, 46% graduate in 6 years or less.

Admissions Contact: Bill Zlata, Director of Admissions. E-Mail: *admissions@hunter.cuny.edu* Web: *www.hunter.cuny.edu*

IONA COLLEGE D-5

New Rochelle, NY 10801 (914) 633-2502
(800) 231-IONA; (914) 633-2182

Full-time: 1267 men, 1660 women	**Faculty:** 169; IIA, +$
Part-time: 248 men, 287 women	**Ph.D.s:** 90%
Graduate: 320 men, 459 women	**Student/Faculty:** 17 to 1
Year: semesters, summer session	**Tuition:** $31,540
Application Deadline: February 15	**Room & Board:** $12,488

Freshman Class: 8741 applied, 7556 accepted, 722 enrolled
SAT CR/M: 500/500 **ACT:** 22 **COMPETITIVE**

Iona College, founded in 1940, is a private college offering programs through schools of general studies, arts and science, and business. It has a graduate campus in Rockland County in addition to the main campus in New Rochelle. There are 2 undergraduate schools and 2 graduate schools. In addition to regional accreditation, Iona has baccalaureate program accreditation with AACSB, ABET, ACEJMC, CSWE, and NCATE. The 3 libraries contain 268,476 volumes, 510,213 microform items, and 4,176 audio/video tapes/CDs/DVDs, and subscribe to 742 periodicals including electronic. Computerized library services include interlibrary loans, database searching, Internet access, and Wi-Fi capability. Special learning facilities include an art gallery, radio station, TV station, an electron microscope, and a speech and hearing clinic. The 43-acre campus is in a suburban area 17 miles northeast of New York City. Including any residence halls, there are 49 buildings.

Student Life: 76% of undergraduates are from New York. Others are from 34 states, 32 foreign countries, and Canada. 57% are White; 17% race unknown; 16% Hispanic. The average age of freshmen is 18; all undergraduates, 19. 19% do not continue beyond their first year; 65% remain to graduate.

Housing: 1358 students can be accommodated in college housing, which includes single-sex dorms, on-campus apartments, and off-campus apartments. Honors floor, in suite style residence hall; science floor, in suite style residence hall; an Education floor, in suite style residence hall. On-campus housing is available on a first-come, first-served basis, and is available on a lottery system for upperclassmen. 57% of students commute. Upperclassmen may keep cars.

Activities: 6% of men belong to 1 local and 2 national fraternities; 9% of women belong to 4 local and 1 national sororities. There are 70 groups on campus, including black student union, democracy matters, Gaelic society) club sports- (Rugby, Hispanic organization of Latin awareness, Italian society, karate club, national student speech and hearing/language association) general interest - (inter-residence hall council, students against destructive, students association) community sevice and Religious groups, students for veterans students for peace, bagpipe, cheerleading, cheerleading and dance) academic professional groups, public relations student society of America, chorale, computers, dance, debate, drama, environmental, film, gay, honors, literary magazine, multi cultural groups(students Caribbean ancestry, musical theater, newspaper, political, professional, radio and TV, religious, social, social service, student government, and yearbook. Popular campus events include Spring Weekend/Concert Event, Travel Series, Heritage Week, Fashion Show, Campus Coffee House, Homecoming Carnivel, Week of the Peacemaker and Make a Difference Week, Black History Month, Hispanic Heritage Month and Alcohol Awareness Week.

Sports: There are 10 intercollegiate sports for men and 11 for women, and 10 intramural sports for men and 10 for women. Facilities include Indoor facilities: 2 gymnasiums, 2 weight rooms, cardio room, core studio, aerobics studio, rowing tank and a swimming pool. Outdoor facilities: soccer/lacrosse field and softball field.

Disabled Students: 70% of the campus is accessible. Facilities include wheelchair ramps, elevators, special parking, specially equipped restrooms, special class scheduling, lowered drinking fountains, special housing. All classes are on the first floor.

Services: Counseling and information services are available, as is tutoring in most subjects. There is a reader service for the blind.

Campus Safety and Security: Measures include 24-hour foot and vehicle patrol, emergency notification system, and security escort services. There are shuttle buses, emergency telephones, lighted pathways/sidewalks, and controlled access to dorms/residences.

Programs of Study: Iona confers B.A., B.S., B.B.A. and B.P.S. degrees. Master's degrees are also awarded. Bachelor's degrees are awarded in BIOLOGICAL SCIENCE (biochemistry and biology/biological science), BUSINESS (accounting, business administration and management, finance, international business management, management science, and marketing management), COMMUNICATIONS AND THE ARTS (communications, English, French, Italian, Spanish, and speech/debate/rhetoric), COMPUTER AND PHYSICAL SCIENCE (applied mathematics, chemistry, computer science, information sciences and systems, mathematics, and physics), EDUCATION ((Education) Childhood Education and early childhood education), ENGINEERING AND ENVIRONMENTAL DESIGN (environmental science), HEALTH PROFESSIONS (speech pathology/audiology), SOCIAL SCIENCE (criminal justice, economics, history, international studies, liberal arts/general studies, philosophy, political science/government, psychology, religion, social work, and sociology). Psychology, marketing, and mass communication are the strongest academically. Mass communication, psychology, and criminal justice have the largest enrollments.

Required: All students are required to take courses in the humanities courses, social sciences, science and technology, natural and/or symbolic languages, and communication skills as a part of the College Core. Students enrolled in BBA programs, BS programs, and the Honors Program take specific core courses that are unique to each program. Students who earn BA degrees must take a total of 90 liberal arts credits; students who earn BS degrees must take a total of 60 liberal arts credits; and students who earn BBA degrees must take a total of 63 liberal arts credits in order to complete the bachelor's degree. Computer literacy is required. The total number of credits required to graduate is at least 120, depending on the major, with at least 30 in the major. The minimum GPA requirement is 2.0.

Special: There are internships available for students. Study abroad is available in 9 countries. Work-study positions are available in several locations throughout the College. Students may earn either a BA or BS degree in Adolescent Education, Computer Science, Economics, or Mathematics. There is an articulation agreement with New York Medical College for Physical Therapy. Five-year programs are offered in the following areas: Chemistry and Adolescent Education; Chemistry and Computer Science; Computer Science; Criminal Justice; English; History, Mathematics and Computer Science; and Psychology. There are 2 national honor societies, a freshman honors program, and 24 departmental honors programs.

Faculty/Classroom: 58% of faculty are male; 42% are female. 88% teach undergraduates. No introductory courses are taught by graduate students. The average class size in an introductory lecture is 25; in a laboratory is 17; and in a regular course is 14.

Admissions: 86% of the 2013-2014 applicants were accepted. The SAT scores for the 2013-2014 freshman class were: Critical Reading--49% below 500, 41% between 500 and 599, 9% between 600 and 699, and 1% between 700 and 800; Math--44% below 500, 42% between 500 and 599, 13% between 600 and 699, and 2% between 700 and 800. The ACT scores were 28% below 21, 37% between 21 and 23, 20% between 24 and 26, 6% between 27 and 28, and 10% above 28. 34% of the current freshmen were in the top fifth of their class; 66% were in the top two fifths.

Requirements: The SAT or ACT is required. Applicants must complete 16 academic credits, including 4 units of English, 3 of math,3 science, 2 each of foreign language and social studies, and 1 each of history, and academic electives. A GED is accepted. An essay is required, and an interview is recommended. AP and CLEP credits are accepted. Important factors in the admissions decision are recommendations by school officials, extracurricular activities record, and leadership record.

Procedure: Freshmen are admitted fall and spring. Entrance exams should be taken in the spring of the junior year. There are early admissions and deferred admissions plans. Applications should be filed by February 15 for fall entry; January 1 for spring entry, along with a $50 fee. 1184 applicants were on the 2013 waiting list; 1120 were admitted. Applications are accepted online.

Transfer: 161 transfer students enrolled in 2012-2013. Transfer applicants must have a GPA of at least 2.0 and must submit high school transcripts if they have earned fewer than 30 college credits. An interview is recommended. 30 of 120 credits required for the bachelor's degree must be completed at Iona.

Visiting: There are regularly scheduled orientations for prospective students, including a meeting with an admissions counselor, a campus tour, and a variety of on-campus programs during the summer and fall. There are guides for informal visits and visitors may sit in on classes. To schedule a visit, contact Elizabeth English at (914) 633-2622.

Financial Aid: In 2013-2014, 98% of all full-time freshmen and 96% of continuing full-time students received some form of financial aid. 72% of all full-time freshmen and 65% of continuing full-time students received need-based aid. The average freshman award was $27,908. Need-based scholarships or need-based grants averaged $6,704 ($20,400 maximum); need-based self-help aid (loans and jobs) averaged $3,871 ($9,800 maximum); non-need-based athletic scholarships averaged $17,643 ($49,102 maximum); and other non-need-based awards and non-need-based scholarships averaged $20,153 ($48,611 maximum). 15% of undergraduate students work part-time. Average annual earnings from campus work are $1261. The average financial indebtedness of the 2013 graduate was $31,960. Iona is a member of CSS. The FAFSA and the state aid form are required. The priority date for freshman financial aid applications for fall entry is April 15. The deadline for filing freshman financial aid applications for fall entry is April 15.

International Students: There are 48 international students enrolled. The school actively recruits these students. They must take the TOEFL with a minimum score of 550 on the paper-based TOEFL (PBT). They must also take the SAT or ACT.

Computers: All students may access the system. There is unlimited access. There are no fees.

Graduates: From July 1, 2012 to June 30, 2013, 727 bachelor's degrees were awarded. The most popular majors were business (38%), mass communication (17%), and education (10%). 65 companies recruited on campus in 2012-2013. In an average class, 1% graduate in 3 years or less, 56% graduate in 4 years or less, 63% graduate in 5 years or less, and 65% graduate in 6 years or less. Of the 2012 graduating class, 40% were enrolled in graduate school within 6 months of graduation, and 68% were employed.

Admissions Contact: Katherine Reilly, Director for Undergraduate Admissions. E-Mail: *admissions@iona.edu* Web: *www.iona.edu*

ITHACA COLLEGE C-4

Ithaca, NY 14850 (607) 274-3124
(800) 429-4274; (607) 274-1900

Full-time: 2670 men, 3461 women
Part-time: 55 men, 48 women
Graduate: 140 men, 349 women
Year: semesters, summer session
Application Deadline: February 1
Faculty: 489; IIA, av$
Ph.D.s: 94%
Student/Faculty: 11 to 1
Tuition: $38,400
Room & Board: $13,900
Freshman Class: 15658 applied, 10429 accepted, 1789 enrolled
SAT CR/M/W: 590/590/590

HIGHLY COMPETITIVE

Located in New York's Finger Lakes region, Ithaca College (IC) is home to 6,100 undergraduates and 400 graduate students and offers more than 100 degree programs in its schools. There are 5 undergraduate schools and one graduate school. In addition to regional accreditation, Ithaca has baccalaureate program accreditation with AACSB, APTA, NASM, and NRPA. The library contains 318,480 volumes, 21,143 microform items, and 34,988 audio/video tapes/CDs/DVDs, and subscribes to 60,197 periodicals including electronic. Computerized library services include interlibrary loans, database searching, Internet access, and Wi-Fi capability. Special learning facilities include an art gallery, radio station, and a TV station. The 669-acre campus is in a small town 250 miles northwest of New York City. Including any residence halls, there are 86 buildings.

Student Life: 56% of undergraduates are from out of state, mostly the Middle Atlantic. Students are from 47 states, 68 foreign countries, and Canada. 84% are from public schools. 69% are White; 11% race unknown. The average age of freshmen is 18; all undergraduates, 20. 13% do not continue beyond their first year; 76% remain to graduate.

Housing: 4694 students can be accommodated in college housing, which includes single-sex and coed dorms and on-campus apartments. In addition, there are honors houses, language houses, special-interest houses, first-year students only housing, quiet study residence hall, service and music honor fraternities, smoke-free buildings and floors, coed by buildings, honors floors, substance-free building, multicultural housing, and several freshman seminar groups housed together. On-campus housing is guaranteed for all 4 years. 70% of students live on campus; of those, 95% remain on campus on weekends. All students may keep cars.

Activities: 1% of men belong to 4 national fraternities; 1% of women belong to 1 local sorority. There are 200 groups on campus, including cultural and academic clubs, art, band, cheerleading, chess, choir, chorale, chorus, computers, dance, drama, drum and bugle corps, environmental, ethnic, film, forensics, gay, honors, international, jazz band, literary magazine, musical theater, newspaper, opera, orchestra, pep band, photography, political, professional, radio and TV, religious, social, social service, sports clubs, student government, and symphony. Popular campus events include Pep Rallies, Student Involvement Fair, and Various Multicultural Awareness Events.

Sports: There are 11 intercollegiate sports for men and 14 for women, and 24 intramural sports for men and 24 for women. Facilities include 5 gyms, 2 dance studios, a student union, indoor and outdoor pools, a fitness center and wellness clinic, tennis courts, and baseball, football, an athletics and events center has an indoor track, an aquatics pavilion and stadium seating for 6,700.

Disabled Students: Facilities include wheelchair ramps, elevators, special parking, specially equipped restrooms, special class scheduling, lowered drinking fountains, and lowered telephones.

Services: Nonremedial tutoring is available.

Campus Safety and Security: Measures include 24-hour foot and vehicle patrol, emergency notification system, and security escort services. There are emergency telephones, lighted pathways/sidewalks, crime prevention programs.

Programs of Study: Ithaca confers B.A., B.S., B.F.A. and Mus.B. degrees. Master's and doctoral degrees are also awarded. Bachelor's degrees are awarded in AGRICULTURE (environmental studies), BIOLOGICAL SCIENCE (biochemistry and biology/biological science), BUSINESS (accounting, applied economics / management, business administration and management, business communications, organizational behavior, recreation and leisure services, and sports management), COMMUNICATIONS AND THE ARTS (art history, art, art history and appreciation, audio technology, broadcasting, communication, communications, creative writing, dramatic arts, English, English literature, English Writing, film arts, fine arts, French, German, jazz, journalism, languages, media arts, modern language, music, music performance, music theory and composition, musical theater, performing arts, photography, piano pedagogy, public relations, Spanish, sports media, studio art, telecommunications, theater design, theater management, video, and visual and performing arts), COMPUTER AND PHYSICAL SCIENCE (chemistry, computer mathematics, computer science, information sciences and systems, mathematics, mathematics – economics, and physics), EDUCATION (art education, athletic training, education, education of the deaf and hearing impaired, English education, foreign languages education, health education, mathematics education, middle school education, music education, physical education, secondary education, social studies education, speech correction, sports and wellness studies, and sports studies), ENGINEERING AND ENVIRONMENTAL DESIGN (engineering chemistry, engineering physics, and environmental science), HEALTH PROFESSIONS (allied health, clinical science, community health work, exercise science, health, health science, occupational therapy, physical therapy, preallied health, Pre-Health Studies, predentistry, premedicine, preoptometry, public health, recreation therapy, rehabilitation therapy, speech pathology/audiology, speech therapy, and sports medicine), SOCIAL SCIENCE (anthropology, applied psychology, architectural studies, area studies, economics, German area studies, gerontology, history, industrial and organizational psychology, interdisciplinary studies, Italian studies, legal studies, liberal arts/general studies, philosophy, philosophy and religion, physical fitness/movement, political science/government, prelaw, psychology, social studies, and sociology). Physical therapy, theater, and music are the strongest academically. Music, business administration, and television/radio have the largest enrollments.

Required: Students must successfully complete a minimum of 120 credits including the course requirements of their specific major. Starting in Fall 2013, all entering students will participate in the Ithaca College's Integrative Core Curriculum (ICC). The centerpiece of the ICC is a "Themes and Perspectives" sequence where students take courses from natural science, creative arts, humanities, and social sciences, all focusing on a general theme such as "Inquiry, Imagination, and Innovation" or "Quest for a Sustainable Future". The Themes and Perspectives sequence kicks off with a first semester Ithaca Seminar, introducing students to the theme and helping them transition to college life and learning. Additional elements of the ICC include coursework in writing, diversity, and quantitative literacy, as well as a capstone experience and learning portfolio.

Special: Cross-registration is available with Cornell University and Wells College. Opportunities are also provided for internships, study abroad, a semester of study/internship in NYC, work-study programs, accelerated degree programs, dual majors, non-degree study, pass/fail options, and student-designed majors. A 3-2 engineering degree with Cornell University, Clarkson University, Rensselaer Polytechnic Institute, and Binghamton University is available. There is also a 4-1 B.S./M.B.A. program, a 3-1 optometry program, a pre-med and pre-law advisory program, and a one-semester program in marine biology with Duke University and the Sea Education Association. There are 32 national honor societies, a freshman honors program, and 33 departmental honors programs.

Faculty/Classroom: 51% of faculty are male; 49% are female. All teach undergraduates. Graduate students teach 6% of introductory courses. The average class size in an introductory lecture is 24.

Admissions: 67% of the 2013-2014 applicants were accepted. The SAT scores for the 2013-2014 freshman class were: Critical Reading--9% below 500, 46% between 500 and 599, 38% between 600 and 699, and 7% between 700 and 800; Math--9% below 500, 44% between 500 and 599, 41% between 600 and 699, and 6% between 700 and 800; Writing--11% below 500, 41% between 500 and 599, 41% between 600 and 699, and 7% between 700 and 800. 53% of the current freshmen were in the top fifth of their class; 82% were in the top two fifths. There were 6 National Merit finalists. 12 freshmen graduated first in their class.

Requirements: Applicants should be graduates of an accredited secondary school with a minimum of 16 Carnegie units, including 4 years of English, 3 each of math, science, and social studies, 2 of foreign language, and other college-preparatory electives. The GED is accepted. An essay is required, as is an audition for music and theater students. In some majors, a portfolio and an interview are recommended. AP and CLEP credits are accepted.

Procedure: Freshmen are admitted fall and spring. Entrance exams

should be taken in spring of the junior year or fall of the senior year. There are early decision, early admissions, deferred admissions, and rolling admissions plans. Early decision applications should be filed by November 1; regular applications, by February 1 for fall entry; and December 1 for spring entry, along with a $60 fee. Notification of early decision is sent December 15; regular decision, April 15. 160 early decision candidates were accepted for the 2013-2014 class. Applications are accepted online.

Transfer: 140 transfer students enrolled in 2012-2013. Transfer applicants must submit a high school transcript, transcripts from previously attended colleges, and a personal recommendation from their adviser or Dean of Students. A minimum college GPA of 2.75 is recommended. 30 of 120 credits required for the bachelor's degree must be completed at Ithaca.

Visiting: There are regularly scheduled orientations for prospective students, including a campus tour and an interview with an admissions counselor. Fall open house programs offering personal meetings with faculty are available by appointment. There are guides for informal visits and visitors may sit in on classes.

Financial Aid: In 2013-2014, 95% of all full-time freshmen and 90% of continuing full-time students received some form of financial aid. 71% of all full-time freshmen and 67% of continuing full-time students received need-based aid. The average freshman award was $34,366. Need-based scholarships or need-based grants averaged $23,407 ($53,695 maximum); need-based self-help aid (loans and jobs) averaged $7,371 ($14,100 maximum); and other non-need-based awards and non-need-based scholarships averaged $9,617 ($55,587 maximum). 39% of undergraduate students work part-time. Average annual earnings from campus work are $2361. Ithaca is a member of CSS. The CSS/Profile and FAFSA are required. The deadline for filing freshman financial aid applications for fall entry is February 1.

International Students: There are 124 international students enrolled. The school actively recruits these students. They must take the TOEFL with a minimum score of 550 on the paper-based TOEFL (PBT) or 80 on the Internet-based version (iBT).

Computers: All students may access the system 24 hours a day. There are no time limits and no fees.

Graduates: From July 1, 2012 to June 30, 2013, 1671 bachelor's degrees were awarded. The most popular majors were business administration (9%), television/radio (9%), and music (8%). 197 companies recruited on campus in 2012-2013. In an average class, 2% graduate in 3 years or less, 69% graduate in 4 years or less, 75% graduate in 5 years or less, and 76% graduate in 6 years or less. Of the 2012 graduating class, 35% were enrolled in graduate school within 6 months of graduation, and 44% were employed.

Admissions Contact: Gerard Turbide, Director of Admission. E-Mail: *admission@ithaca.edu* Web: *www.ithaca.edu*

JOHN JAY COLLEGE OF CRIMINAL JUSTICE / THE CITY UNIVERSITY OF NEW YORK D-5

New York, NY 10019 **(212) 237-8873**

Full-time: n/av
Part-time: n/av
Graduate: n/av
Year: semesters, summer session
Application Deadline: open
Freshman Class: n/av
SAT or ACT: required
Faculty: n/av
Ph.D.s: n/av
Student/Faculty: n/av
Tuition: $6059 ($15,629)
Room & Board: n/av

COMPETITIVE

John Jay College of Criminal Justice, established in 1964, is a liberal arts college and part of the City University of New York, with special emphasis in the fields of criminology, forensic science, correction administration, and other areas of the criminal justice system. Figures in the above capsule and in the this profile are approximate. The library contains 318,204 volumes, 220,385 microform items, and 4,500 audio/video tapes/CDs/DVDs, and subscribes to 14,284 periodicals including electronic. Computerized library services include interlibrary loans, database searching, Internet access, and Wi-Fi capability. Special learning facilities include an art gallery, radio station, TV station, a fire science lab, a security technology lab, and an explosion-proof forensic science/toxicology lab. The campus is in an urban area of New York City. Including any residence halls, there are 3 buildings.

Student Life: 95% of undergraduates are from New York. Others are from states. 80% are from public schools.. The average age of freshmen is 19; all undergraduates, 23. 26% do not continue beyond their first year; 40% remain to graduate.

Housing: College-sponsored housing includes off-campus apartments. All students commute. All students may keep cars.

Activities: There are no fraternities or sororities. There are 26 groups on campus, including art, cheerleading, chess, choir, chorale, chorus, computers, dance, drama, ethnic, film, gay, honors, international, literary magazine, musical theater, newspaper, photography, political, professional, radio and TV, religious, social, social service, student government, and yearbook.

Sports: There are 5 intercollegiate sports for men and 5 for women, and 15 intramural sports for men and 15 for women. Facilities include A fitness center, 2 gyms 2 racquetball courts, a swimming pool, a strength training center, and a rooftop outdoor tennis court and jogging track.

Disabled Students: 99% of the campus is accessible. Facilities include wheelchair ramps, elevators, special parking, specially equipped restrooms, special class scheduling, lowered drinking fountains, and lowered telephones.

Services: Counseling and information services are available, as is tutoring in most subjects, English, math and reading. There is a reader service for the blind, and remedial math, reading, and writing.

Campus Safety and Security: Measures include 24-hour foot and vehicle patrol and self-defense education. There are emergency telephones and lighted pathways/sidewalks.

Programs of Study: John Jay confers B.A. and B.S. degrees. Master's degrees are also awarded. Bachelor's degrees are awarded in COMMUNICATIONS AND THE ARTS (English), COMPUTER AND PHYSICAL SCIENCE (computer information technology), SOCIAL SCIENCE (criminal justice, criminology, economics, fire science, fire services administration, forensic studies, gender studies, humanities and social science, law, philosophy, political science/government, psychology, public administration, and safety management). Forensic psychology is the strongest academically. Criminal justice, forensic psychology, and public administration have the largest enrollments.

Required: Students are required to complete 128 credit hours, with 36 to 42 of these hours in the student's major, and must maintain a minimum GPA of 2.0. 1 credit in phys ed is required of all students.

Special: The school offers co-op programs, and cross-registration with other schools in the City University of New York. Internships are available with the Manhattan District Attorney, the Queens Supreme Court, the New York City Police Department, the United States Marshal's Service, and the New York City Corrections Department. Opportunities are provided for work-study programs, a Washington semester in public administration, interdisciplinary and student-designed majors, including forensic psychology, pass/fail options, non-degree study, credit for life experience, B.A.-M.A. programs in forensic psychology, criminal justice, and public administration, and study abroad in 5 countries, including England, Barbados, and Isreal. There is 1 national honor society and a freshman honors program.

Faculty/Classroom: 54% of faculty are male; 46% are female. 94% teach undergraduates, and 80% do both. Graduate students teach 5% of introductory courses. The average class size in an introductory lecture is 25; in a laboratory is 15; and in a regular course is 20.

Requirements: The SAT or ACT is required. The ACT Optional Writing test is also required. The SAT is recommended. In addition, applicants must have graduated from an accredited secondary school or a GED certificate will be accepted. Admission to baccalaureate degree program requires a minimum SAT I score of 1100 or a high school average of 80, and 14 academic units, with 4 units in English, 3 units in math, 2 units in each discipline, and 1 unit in visual arts. A GPA of 80.0 is required. AP and CLEP credits are accepted.

Procedure: Freshmen are admitted fall and spring. There are early admissions and rolling admissions plans. Application deadlines are open. Application fee is $65. Notification is sent on a rolling basis.

Transfer: Applicants must have completed 24 credits with a cumulative GPA of 2.0. If fewer than 24 credits are presented, a high school transcript should be presented. Half of the credits required for the major must be completed at John Jay.

Visiting: There are regularly scheduled orientations for prospective students, Consisting of a freshman/transfer workshop. There are guides for informal visits and visitors may sit in on classes.

Financial Aid: 85% of all full-time freshmen and 85% of continuing full-time students received need-based aid. The average freshman award was $9,445. Need-based scholarships or need-based grants averaged $2,954; and need-based self-help aid (loans and jobs) averaged $1,962. The FAFSA is required. The deadline for filing freshman financial aid applications for fall entry is open.

International Students: They must take the TOEFL.

Computers: All students may access the system. There are no time limits and no fees.

Admissions Contact: Stephanie Autenrieth, Director of Admissions. E-Mail: *sautenrieth@jjay.cuny.edu* Web: *www.jjay.cuny.edu*

JUILLIARD SCHOOL D-5

New York, NY 10023-6588 (212) 799-5000, ext. 223; (212) 724-6420

Full-time: 275 men, 230 women	**Faculty:** n/av
Part-time: n/av	**Ph.D.s:** n/av
Graduate: 190 men, 170 women	**Student/Faculty:** n/av
Year: semesters	**Tuition:** $34,130
Application Deadline: see profile	**Room & Board:** $13,270
Freshman Class: n/av	

SPECIAL

The Juilliard School, founded in 1905, is a private conservatory for dance, drama, and music. Figures in the above capsule and in this profile are approximate. The library contains 96,013 volumes, 1,399 microform items, and 25,960 audio/video tapes/CDs/DVDs, and subscribes to 230 periodicals including electronic. Computerized library services include interlibrary loans, database searching, Internet access, and laptop Internet portals. The campus is in an urban area at Lincoln Center in New York City. Including any residence halls, there are 2 buildings.

Student Life: 87% of undergraduates are from out of state, mostly the Northeast. Students are from 47 states, 47 foreign countries, and Canada. 50% are white; 25% foreign nationals; 15% Asian American. The average age of freshmen is 18; all undergraduates, 20. 3% do not continue beyond their first year; 80% remain to graduate.

Housing: 350 students can be accommodated in college housing, which includes single-sex dorms. In addition, there are special-interest houses, all floors are smoke-free. There are quiet, alcohol-free, and single sex (all female) floors. On-campus housing is guaranteed for the freshman year only, is available on a first-come, first-served basis, and is available on a lottery system for upperclassmen. 60% of students live on campus; of those, 95% remain on campus on weekends. No one may keep cars.

Activities: There are no fraternities or sororities. There are 15 groups on campus, including band, book discussion, choir, chorale, chorus, community service, dance, drama, environmental, ethnic, gay, international, jazz band, marching band, opera, orchestra, professional, recreation, religious, social, social service, student government, and symphony. Popular campus events include performances by the Juilliard orchestras at Lincoln Center, dance concerts, and drama and opera.

Sports: There is no sports program at Juilliard. Facilities include a fitness center in the residence hall.

Disabled Students: All of the campus is accessible. Facilities include wheelchair ramps, elevators, specially equipped restrooms, lowered drinking fountains, and lowered telephones.

Services: Counseling and information services are available, as is tutoring in some subjects, including ear training, literature and materials of music, and English.

Campus Safety and Security: Measures include 24-hour foot and vehicle patrol and self-defense education. There are emergency telephones, lighted pathways/sidewalks, and video cameras, and turnstiles with ID card access.

Programs of Study: Juilliard confers B.Mus. and B.F.A. degrees. Master's and doctoral degrees are also awarded. Bachelor's degrees are awarded in COMMUNICATIONS AND THE ARTS (dance, dramatic arts, and music). Piano, voice, and violin are the largest.

Required: Each division has its own requirements for graduation.

Special: A joint program with Columbia College and Barnard College (at Columbia University) allows students to obtain a 5-year B.A.-B.-MM. degree. Internships are available with cultural organizations in New York City. There is study abroad in music academy in England. There are work-study programs, accelerated degrees and dual majors in music.

Faculty/Classroom: 67% of faculty are male; 33% are female. No introductory courses are taught by graduate students.

Requirements: A high school diploma or GED is required. Students are accepted primarily on the basis of personal auditions rather than tests. Important factors in the admissions decision are evidence of special talent.

Procedure: Freshmen are admitted in the fall. Personal auditions should be completed in December for opera, January and February for drama; February and March for dance; March for music; February and March for jazz. Applications are accepted online. A waiting list is maintained. Check with the school for current application deadlines and fee.

Transfer: Transfer applicants must audition in person.

Visiting: There are regularly scheduled orientations for prospective students, including guided tours and question-and-answer sessions, Monday to Friday at noon. Visitors may sit in on classes. To schedule a visit, contact the Admissions Office.

Financial Aid: The FAFSA and the college's own financial statement are required. Check with the school for current application deadlines.

International Students: They must take the TOEFL and the college's own test, TWE. All students must audition in person.

Computers: Wireless access is available. All students may access the system. Students are limited to during lab hours. There are no fees.

Admissions Contact: Office of Admissions E-Mail: *admissions@juilliard.edu* Web: *www.juilliard.edu*

KEUKA COLLEGE B-3

Keuka Park, NY 14478 (315) 536-5254, ext. 254; (800) 33-KEUKA; (315) 536-5386

Full-time: 383 men, 1131 women	**Faculty:** 80; IIA, -$
Part-time: 34 men, 281 women	**Ph.D.s:** 75%
Graduate: 48 men, 156 women	**Student/Faculty:** 15 to 1
Year: 4-1-4, summer session	**Tuition:** $27,240
Application Deadline: open	**Room & Board:** $10,590

Freshman Class: 1375 applied, 1207 accepted, 224 enrolled
SAT or ACT: required

COMPETITIVE

Keuka College, founded in 1890, is an independent college affiliated with American Baptist Churches and offers instruction in the liberal arts. In addition to regional accreditation, Keuka has baccalaureate program accreditation with AHEA, CSWE, and NLN. The library contains 112,297 volumes, 4,190 microform items, and 4,190 audio/video tapes/CDs/DVDs, and subscribes to 18,151 periodicals including electronic. Computerized library services include interlibrary loans and database searching. Special learning facilities include an art gallery and radio station. The 203-acre campus is in a rural area 60 miles south of Rochester. Including any residence halls, there are 19 buildings.

Student Life: 94% of undergraduates are from New York. Others are from 26 states, 9 foreign countries, and Canada. 80% are from public schools. 90% are White. The average age of freshmen is 18; all undergraduates, 23. 27% do not continue beyond their first year; 52% remain to graduate.

Housing: 719 students can be accommodated in college housing, which includes single-sex and coed dorms. In addition, there are honors houses, special-interest houses, cooperative living, and leadership and wellness housing. On-campus housing is guaranteed for all 4 years. 55% of students live on campus; of those, 60% remain on campus on weekends. Alcohol is not permitted. Upperclassmen may keep cars.

Activities: There are no fraternities or sororities. There are 45 groups on campus, including and leadership, art, cheerleading, choir, chorale, community service, dance, drama, ethnic, gay, honors, international, literary magazine, newspaper, political, professional, religious, social, social service, student government, and yearbook. Popular campus events include Spring Weekend, May Day and Family Weekend.

Sports: There are 7 intercollegiate sports for men and 8 for women, and 8 intramural sports for men and 8 for women. Facilities include a gym, a fitness center, a weight room, and an outdoor athletic facility.

Disabled Students: 60% of the campus is accessible. Facilities include wheelchair ramps, elevators, special parking, specially equipped restrooms, special class scheduling, lowered drinking fountains, and special housing.

Services: Counseling and information services are available, as is tutoring in every subject. There is a reader service for the blind, and remedial math, reading, and writing. Individual and group tutoring is available free through the college's academic support services.

Campus Safety and Security: Measures include 24-hour foot and vehicle patrol and self-defense education. There are shuttle buses, emergency telephones, and lighted pathways/sidewalks.

Programs of Study: Keuka confers B.A., and B.S. degrees. Master's degrees are also awarded. Bachelor's degrees are awarded in BIOLOGICAL SCIENCE (biochemistry and biology/biological science), BUSINESS (accounting, business administration and management, hotel/motel and restaurant management, and marketing/retailing/merchandising), COMMUNICATIONS AND THE ARTS (American Sign Language, communications, and English), EDUCATION (elementary education and secondary education), ENGINEERING AND ENVIRONMENTAL DESIGN (environmental science), HEALTH PROFESSIONS (medical laboratory technology, nursing, occupational therapy, predentistry, premedicine, and preveterinary science), SOCIAL SCIENCE (criminal justice, political science/government, prelaw, psychology, social work, and sociology). Occupational therapy, biology, and education are the strongest academically. Occupational therapy, education, and management have the largest enrollments.

Required: Students must complete 1 field period combining academic study and professional experience for each year of enrollment. The core curriculum consists of 43 to 46 credits, including but not limited to required courses in phys ed, computer science, and integrative studies. A total of 120 credit hours is required for graduation with a minimum of 30 credits in the major and a major and cumulative GPA of 2.0.

Special: There are co-op programs with other members of the Rochester Area Colleges Consortium. The college offers internships, study abroad, a Washington semester, dual majors, and student-designed majors. Credit is also given by exam and for work experience. There are 16 national honor societies.

Faculty/Classroom: 32% of faculty are male; 68% are female. All teach undergraduates. No introductory courses are taught by graduate students. The average class size in an introductory lecture is 20; in a laboratory is 15; and in a regular course is 20.

Admissions: 88% of the 2013-2014 applicants were accepted. The SAT scores for the 2013-2014 freshman class were: Critical Reading--59% below 500, 36% between 500 and 599, and 5% between 600 and 699; Math--61% below 500, 31% between 500 and 599, and 8% between 600 and 699; Writing--73% below 500, 26% between 500 and 599, 1% between 600 and 699. The ACT scores were 79% below 21, 2% above 28. 26% of the current freshmen were in the top fifth of their class; 63% were in the top two fifths.

Requirements: The SAT or ACT is required. Students should graduate from an accredited secondary school with a minimum GPA of 2.8. The GED is accepted. A minimum of 15 Carnegie units is required, including 4 years of English, 3 of history, 2 to 3 of math and science, 2 of foreign language, and 1 of social studies. An essay is required, and an interview is recommended. AP and CLEP credits are accepted. Important factors in the admissions decision are recommendations by school officials, extracurricular activities record, and leadership record.

Procedure: Freshmen are admitted fall and spring. Entrance exams should be taken in the spring of the junior year or the fall of the senior year. There are early decision, deferred admissions, and rolling admissions plans. Check with the school for current application deadlines. The application fee is $50. Notification is sent on a rolling basis. Applications are accepted online.

Transfer: Applicants must take the SAT or ACT and submit transcripts. An interview is recommended. A minimum GPA of 2.5 is required in college work. 30 of 120 credits required for the bachelor's degree must be completed at Keuka.

Visiting: There are regularly scheduled orientations for prospective students, including open houses held in October and April, when students can speak with faculty, student affairs and financial aid representatives, and current students. There are guides for informal visits, visitors may sit in on classes, and stay overnight. To schedule a visit, contact the Admissions Office.

Financial Aid: In 2013-2014, 95% of all full-time freshmen and 93% of continuing full-time students received some form of financial aid. 93% of all full-time freshmen and 90% of continuing full-time students received need-based aid. The average freshman award was $22,711. Need-based scholarships or need-based grants averaged $14,206 ($7,852 maximum). 65% of undergraduate students work part-time. Average annual earnings from campus work are $1250. The average financial indebtedness of the 2013 graduate was $19,507. The FAFSA and the college's own financial statement are required. Check with the school for current application deadlines.

International Students: There are 76 international students enrolled. The school actively recruits these students. They must take the TOEFL.

Computers: All students may access the system. There are no time limits and no fees.

Graduates: From July 1, 2012 to June 30, 2013, 462 bachelor's degrees were awarded. The most popular majors were business (29%), nursing (16%), and criminal justice (14%). In an average class, 45% graduate in 4 years or less, 5% graduate in 5 years or less, and 1% graduate in 6 years or less. Of the 2012 graduating class, 39% were enrolled in graduate school within 6 months of graduation, and 90% were employed.

Admissions Contact: Gary Boyer, Director of Admissions. E-Mail: *admissions@mail.keuka.edu* Web: *www.keuka.edu*

LE MOYNE COLLEGE C-3

Syracuse, NY 13214 **(315) 445-4300**
(800) 333-4733; (315) 445-4711

Full-time: 1050 men, 1351 women **Faculty:** 143; IIA, av$
Part-time: 103 men, 281 women **Ph.D.s:** 94%
Graduate: 174 men, 360 women **Student/Faculty:** 15 to 1
Year: semesters, summer session **Tuition:** $30,460
Application Deadline: March 1 **Room & Board:** $11,740
Freshman Class: 5924 applied, 3667 accepted, 622 enrolled
SAT CR/M: 540/550 **ACT:** 24 **VERY COMPETITIVE**

Le Moyne College, founded in 1946, is a private liberal arts and sciences institution affiliated with the Roman Catholic Society of Jesus (Jesuit) and offers undergraduate and graduate degrees in a variety of disciplines. In addition to regional accreditation, Le Moyne has baccalaureate program accreditation with AACSB and TEAC. The library contains 223,345 volumes, 277,313 microform items, and 9,224 audio/video tapes/CDs/DVDs, and subscribes to 141,773 periodicals including electronic. Computerized library services include interlibrary loans, database searching, Internet access, and Wi-Fi capability. Special learning facilities include an art gallery, radio station, TV station, W. Carroll Coyne Performing Arts Center, and media center. The 161-acre campus is in a suburban area on the eastern edge of Syracuse. Including any residence halls, there are 42 buildings.

Student Life: 94% of undergraduates are from New York. Others are from 26 states, 34 foreign countries, and Canada. 81% are from public schools. 77% are White. 57% claim no religious affiliation; 31% Catholic. The average age of freshmen is 18; all undergraduates, 21. 12% do not continue beyond their first year; 74% remain to graduate.

Housing: 1581 students can be accommodated in college housing, which includes coed dorms, on-campus apartments, and off-campus apartments. In addition, there are special-interest houses, living learning communities. On-campus housing is guaranteed for all 4 years, is available on a first-come, first-served basis, and is available on a lottery system for upperclassmen. Priority is given to out-of-town students. 60% of students live on campus; of those, 85% remain on campus on weekends. All students may keep cars.

Activities: There are no fraternities or sororities. There are 90 groups on campus, including art, band, cheerleading, chess, choir, chorale, chorus, communications, computers, dance, drama, environmental, ethnic, film, gay, honors, international, jazz band, literary magazine, musical theater, newspaper, orchestra, pep band, photography, political, professional, radio and TV, religious, social, social service, student government, and yearbook. Popular campus events include Spring Olympics, Halloween Dance, Snow Ball Holiday Party and Senior Week Activities.

Sports: There are 8 intercollegiate sports for men and 9 for women, and 12 intramural sports for men and 12 for women. Facilities include a 2500-seat gym, an athletic weightroom, team rooms, a 25-yard lap pool with diving board, a fitness center, an athletic training room, a jogging track, racquetball courts, a recreational gym, and locker rooms. Outdoor facilities include fields for intercollegiate baseball, softball, soccer, and lacrosse, a cross-country trail, and several intramural and club sports fields.

Disabled Students: 98% of the campus is accessible. Facilities include wheelchair ramps, elevators, special parking, specially equipped restrooms, lowered drinking fountains, lowered telephones, special housing, automatic door openers, strobe fire alarm system, wheelchair tables in classrooms and braille signage.

Services: Counseling and information services are available, as is tutoring in some subjects, including math, biology, chemistry, physics, economics, philosophy, Spanish, French, German, Latin, Arabic and history. There is a reader service for the blind, and remedial math and writing. Study groups are available for selected courses. Writing tutor support for all subjects.

Campus Safety and Security: Measures include 24-hour foot and vehicle patrol, emergency notification system, self-defense education, and security escort services. There are shuttle buses, emergency telephones, lighted pathways/sidewalks, controlled access to dorms/residences, 8 blue light security phones, 170 stationary closed-circuit security cameras, AT&T campuswide card access, and 8 pan tilt zoom closed-circuit security cameras.

Programs of Study: Le Moyne confers B.A., and B.S. degrees. Master's degrees are also awarded. Bachelor's degrees are awarded in BIOLOGICAL SCIENCE (biochemistry, biology/biological science, and ecology), BUSINESS (accounting, banking and finance, business administration and management, human resources, management information systems, marketing management, operations management, and organizational leadership and management), COMMUNICATIONS AND THE ARTS (advertising, communications, creative writing, dramatic arts, English, film arts, French, journalism, literature, media arts, music, public relations, radio/television technology, and Spanish), COMPUTER AND PHYSICAL SCIENCE (actuarial science, applied mathematics, chemistry, computer programming, computer science, information sciences and systems, mathematics, physical sciences, physics, science, and statistics), EDUCATION (elementary education, English education, foreign languages education, mathematics education, science education, secondary education, social studies education, special education, and teaching English as a second/foreign language (TESOL/TEFOL)), ENGINEERING AND ENVIRONMENTAL DESIGN (environmental science and preengineering), HEALTH PROFESSIONS (nursing, predentistry, premedicine, preoptometry, prepharmacy, prepodiatry, and preveterinary science), SOCIAL SCIENCE (anthropology, criminal justice, criminology, economics, history, human services, international relations, international studies, law enforcement and corrections, peace studies, philosophy, political science/government, prelaw, psychology, religion, and sociology). Biology, psychology, and accounting are the strongest academically and have the largest enrollments.

Required: A core curriculum of courses in the humanities, natural sciences, and social sciences is required. Students must earn a GPA of 2.0. 30 hours in the major and 120 total credit hours to graduate.

Special: Internships are available to students in all majors. A campus work-study program, study abroad in 16 countries, dual majors, and a Washington semester are offered. A bachelor plus Master's partnership with L.C. Smith School of Engineering at Syracuse University. 3+3 partnership with Syracuse University College of Law. There are early assurance medical and dental programs; Direct entry Physician Assistant Studies program; 3-3 DPT with Upstate Medical University and 3-4 dental with University of Buffalo, podiatry and optometry programs are offered. Some pass/fail options are offered. There are 15 national honor societies, a freshman honors program, and 11 departmental honors programs.

Faculty/Classroom: 58% of faculty are male; 42% are female. All teach

and do research. No introductory courses are taught by graduate students. The average class size in an introductory lecture is 21; in a laboratory is 16; and in a regular course is 20.

Admissions: 62% of the 2013-2014 applicants were accepted. The SAT scores for the 2013-2014 freshman class were: Critical Reading--34% below 500, 46% between 500 and 599, 17% between 600 and 699, and 3% between 700 and 800; Math--22% below 500, 47% between 500 and 599, 24% between 600 and 699, and 7% between 700 and 800. The ACT scores were 18% below 21, 29% between 21 and 23, 24% between 24 and 26, 11% between 27 and 28, and 18% above 28. 41% of the current freshmen were in the top fifth of their class; 78% were in the top two fifths. 8 freshmen graduated first in their class.

Requirements: The SAT or ACT is required. Students should graduate from an accredited high school having completed 17 academic units that include 4 in English and social studies, 3 to 4 each in math and science, and 3 in foreign language. A personal statement and letters of recommendation from a teacher and a counselor are required. AP and CLEP credits are accepted. Important factors in the admissions decision are recommendations by school officials, advanced placement or honors courses, and extracurricular activities record.

Procedure: Freshmen are admitted fall and spring. Entrance exams should be taken in the spring of the junior year or fall of the senior year. There are early admissions, deferred admissions, and rolling admissions plans. Applications should be filed by March 1 for fall entry; December 1 for spring entry, along with a $35 fee. Notification is sent on a rolling basis. 93 applicants were on the 2013 waiting list; 19 were admitted. Applications are accepted online. Application fees are waived if application is completed online.

Transfer: 272 transfer students enrolled in 2012-2013. A 2.6 GPA is required for admission to most programs. A completed application for transfer admission, official college transcripts, and a personal statement must be submitted. Official high school transcripts and SAT or ACT scores are needed for students with fewer than 24 completed college credits at the time of application. 30 of 120 credits required for the bachelor's degree must be completed at Le Moyne.

Visiting: There are regularly scheduled orientations for prospective students, including a campus tour and an interview with admissions counselors. Accepted students are invited to attend class, meet with faculty and stay overnight in a residence hall. There are guides for informal visits, visitors may sit in on classes, and stay overnight. To schedule a visit, contact the Admission Office at (315) 445-4300.

Financial Aid: In 2013-2014, 93% of all full-time freshmen and 90% of continuing full-time students received some form of financial aid. 84% of all full-time freshmen and 84% of continuing full-time students received need-based aid. The average freshman award was $22,655. Need-based scholarships or need-based grants averaged $18,607 ($40,000 maximum); need-based self-help aid (loans and jobs) averaged $4,615 ($7,500 maximum); non-need-based athletic scholarships averaged $7,216 ($40,780 maximum); and other non-need-based awards and non-need-based scholarships averaged $7,004 ($22,500 maximum). 33% of undergraduate students work part-time. Average annual earnings from campus work are $975. The average financial indebtedness of the 2013 graduate was $27,126. Le Moyne is a member of CSS. The FAFSA and the state aid form are required. The deadline for filing freshman financial aid applications for fall entry is February 15.

International Students: There are 24 international students enrolled. The school actively recruits these students. They must take the TOEFL with a minimum score of 550 on the paper-based TOEFL (PBT) or 79 on the Internet-based version (iBT). They must also take the SAT or ACT.

Computers: All students may access the system. 24 hours a day. There are no time limits. The fee is $150.

Graduates: From July 1, 2012 to June 30, 2013, 590 bachelor's degrees were awarded. The most popular majors were psychology (21%), biology (12%), and management (7%). 210 companies recruited on campus in 2012-2013. In an average class, 59% graduate in 4 years or less, 72% graduate in 5 years or less, and 74% graduate in 6 years or less. Of the 2012 graduating class, 16% were enrolled in graduate school within 6 months of graduation, and 20% were employed.

Admissions Contact: Erin B. Craig, Director of Admission. E-Mail: *admission@lemoyne.edu* Web: *www.lemoyne.edu/admissions*

LEHMAN COLLEGE / THE CITY UNIVERSITY OF NEW YORK D-5

Bronx, NY 10468 (718) 960-8706
(877) LEHMAN-1; (718) 960-8712

Full-time: 1788 men, 3556 women — **Faculty:** n/av
Part-time: 1300 men, 2933 women — **Ph.D.s:** 76%
Graduate: 650 men, 1734 women — **Student/Faculty:** 14 to 1
Year: semesters, summer session — **Tuition:** $5430 ($11,640)
Application Deadline: — **Room & Board:** n/a
Freshman Class: 15518 applied, 3612 accepted, 551 enrolled
SAT CR/M/W: 470/490/460 — **ACT:** recommended
LESS COMPETITIVE

Lehman College, established in 1968 as an independent unit of the City University of New York, is a commuter institution offering programs in the arts and humanities, natural and social sciences, nursing, and professional studies. There are 5 undergraduate schools and 4 graduate schools. In addition to regional accreditation, Lehman has baccalaureate program accreditation with ADA, CSWE, NCATE, and NLN. The library contains 666,065 volumes, 713,912 microform items, and 6,735 audio/video tapes/CDs/DVDs, and subscribes to 9,665 periodicals including electronic. Computerized library services include database searching. Special learning facilities include an art gallery, radio station, TV station, a center for performing arts. The 37-acre campus is in an urban area pf the Bronx, New York. Including any residence halls, there are 15 buildings.

Student Life: 99% of undergraduates are from New York. Others are from 15 states, 138 foreign countries, and Canada. 74% are from public schools. 49% are Hispanic; 30% African American. 54% are Catholic; 14% claim no religious affiliation. The average age of freshmen is 21; all undergraduates, 34. 18% do not continue beyond their first year; 40% remain to graduate.

Housing: College-sponsored housing includes Alcohol is not permitted. All students commute. All students may keep cars.

Activities: There are no fraternities or sororities. There are 54 groups on campus, including art, band, chess, choir, chorus, computers, dance, drama, ethnic, film, honors, international, literary magazine, musical theater, newspaper, professional, radio and TV, religious, social, social service, student government, and yearbook.

Sports: There are 9 intercollegiate sports for men and 7 for women, and 9 intramural sports for men and 9 for women. Facilities include an exercise room, three gyms, a swimming pool, outdoor tennis courts, soccer and baseball fields, and a dance studio.

Disabled Students: 90% of the campus is accessible. Facilities include wheelchair ramps, elevators, special parking, specially equipped restrooms, and special class scheduling.

Services: Counseling and information services are available, as is tutoring in every subject. There is a reader service for the blind, and remedial math, reading, and writing. A writing center offers individual and small group tutorials and workshops.

Campus Safety and Security: Measures include 24-hour foot and vehicle patrol. There are emergency telephones and lighted pathways/sidewalks.

Programs of Study: Lehman confers B.A., B.S. and B.F.A. degrees. Master's degrees are also awarded. Bachelor's degrees are awarded in BIOLOGICAL SCIENCE (biology/biological science), BUSINESS (accounting, business administration and management, and management science), COMMUNICATIONS AND THE ARTS (communications, comparative literature, dance, English, fine arts, French, German, Greek, Hebrew, Italian, languages, Latin, linguistics, music, Russian, Spanish, and speech/debate/rhetoric), COMPUTER AND PHYSICAL SCIENCE (chemistry, computer science, geology, mathematics, and physics), EDUCATION (art education, business education, early childhood education, elementary education, foreign languages education, health education, science education, and secondary education), HEALTH PROFESSIONS (health care administration, nursing, predentistry, premedicine, and speech pathology/audiology), SOCIAL SCIENCE (African American studies, American studies, anthropology, dietetics, economics, geography, history, international relations, philosophy, political science/government, prelaw, psychology, social work, and sociology). Economics and accounting, education, nursing have the largest enrollments.

Required: To graduate, students must successfully complete 120 credits, including 64 in the major, with a minimum GPA of 2.0. Requirements include 17 credits of core courses, 8 of English composition, 3 to 10 of a foreign language, and 3 of oral communication, as well as 22 credits distributed among courses in comparative culture, historical studies, social science, natural science, literature, art, and knowledge, self, and values. Students must demonstrate proficiency in basic reading, writing, and math skills before entering the upper division.

Special: Lehman offers internships, study abroad, work-study programs, dual and student-designed majors, non-degree study, pass/fail options, and credit for life experience. A 3-2 social work degree is offered in conjunction with the senior college of CUNY, Bard, and Sarah Lawrence. Transfer programs in pre-engineering, pre-pharmacy, and pre-environmental science and forestry allow students to complete their degrees at specialized colleges of other New York universities. There are 21 national honor societies, including Phi Beta Kappa, a freshman honors program, and 60 departmental honors programs.

Faculty/Classroom: 51% of faculty are male; 49% are female. No introductory courses are taught by graduate students. The average class size in an introductory lecture is 25 and in a laboratory is 12.

Admissions: 23% of the 2013-2014 applicants were accepted. The SAT scores for the 2013-2014 freshman class were: Critical Reading--67% below 500, 26% between 500 and 599, 5% between 600 and 699, and 2% between 700 and 800; Math--51% below 500, 38% between 500 and 599, 9% between 600 and 699, and 2% between 700 and 800; Writing--69% below 500, 24% between 500 and 599, 5% between 600 and 699, and 2% between 700 and 800.

Requirements: The SAT or ACT is recommended. This requirement may also be satisfied by a satisfactory SAT score. Graduation from an accredited secondary school is required. A GED will be accepted as well. A GPA of 80.0 is required. AP and CLEP credits are accepted.

Procedure: Freshmen are admitted fall and spring. Entrance exams should be taken before registration. There are early decision, early admissions, deferred admissions, and rolling admissions plans. Check with the school for current application deadlines. The application fee is $40.

Transfer: 1259 transfer students enrolled in 2012-2013. Applicants must submit all educational records and show a minimum GPA of 2.0 in previous college work. Applicants with fewer than 13 college credits must also have a high school average of 80 in academic subjects. 38 of 120 credits required for the bachelor's degree must be completed at Lehman.

Visiting: There are regularly scheduled orientations for prospective students. There are guides for informal visits and visitors may sit in on classes. To schedule a visit, contact the Office of Student Recruitment.

Financial Aid: Average annual earnings from campus work are $7500. The average financial indebtedness of the 2013 graduate was $15,500. The the college's own financial statement is required. Check with the school for current application deadlines.

International Students: There are 2055 international students enrolled. They must take the TOEFL and the college's own test.

Computers: All students may access the system. There are no time limits and no fees.

Graduates: From July 1, 2012 to June 30, 2013, 1975 bachelor's degrees were awarded. The most popular majors were social work (5%), business administration (5%), and sociology (4%). In an average class, 12% graduate in 4 years or less, 28% graduate in 5 years or less, and 34% graduate in 6 years or less.

Admissions Contact: Laurie Austin, Director of Admissions. E-Mail: *Laurie.Austin@lehman.cuny.edu* Web: *www.lehman.cuny.edu*

LIM COLLEGE D-5

New York, NY 10022-5268 (212) 752-1530
(800) 677-1323; (212) 750-3432

Full-time: 76 men, 1226 women	**Faculty:** 26
Part-time: 6 men, 49 women	**Ph.D.s:** n/av
Graduate: n/av	**Student/Faculty:** 56 to 1
Year: semesters, summer session	**Tuition:** $22,725
Application Deadline: open	**Room & Board:** $19,850
Freshman Class: 1147 applied, 933 accepted, 331 enrolled	
SAT CR/M: 483/474	**ACT:** 20 **LESS COMPETITIVE**

LIM College, founded in 1939, is a private college offering programs in fashion merchandising, marketing, management, and visual merchandising. There is 1 graduate school. The library contains 83,000 volumes, and 1,200 audio/video tapes/CDs/DVDs, and subscribes to 10,000 periodicals including electronic. Computerized library services include database searching, Internet access, and laptop Internet portals. Special learning facilities include a learning resource center, color and materials lab, and CAD lab. The campus is in mid-town Manhattan. Including any residence halls, there are 5 buildings.

Student Life: 57% of undergraduates are from out of state, mostly the Middle Atlantic. Students are from 40 states, 8 foreign countries, and Canada. 80% are from public schools. 70% are white; 15% Hispanic. The average age of freshmen is 18; all undergraduates, 20. 31% do not continue beyond their first year; 54% remain to graduate.

Housing: 355 students can be accommodated in college housing, which includes coed dorms. On-campus housing is available on a first-come and first-served basis. 77% of students commute. Alcohol is not permitted. No one may keep cars.

Activities: There are no fraternities or sororities. Groups on campus include visual merchandising, activities board, BRAG, art, dance, ethnic, Fashion, newspaper, professional, social service, student government, and yearbook. Popular campus events include annual Fashion show, a Ski Trip, and various industry events.

Sports: There is no sports program at LIM College.

Disabled Students: All of the campus is accessible. Facilities include elevators and specially equipped restrooms.

Services: Counseling and information services are available, as is tutoring in most subjects. There is remedial math, reading, and writing.

Campus Safety and Security: Measures include emergency notification system. There is controlled access to dorms/residences.

Programs of Study: LIM College confers B.B.A. and B.P.S. degrees. Associate and master's degrees are also awarded. Bachelor's degrees are awarded in BUSINESS (business administration and management, fashion merchandising, and marketing management). Fashion merchandising has the largest enrollment.

Special: Internships are required in the first, second, and fourth years. Study abroad is available in China, Italy, Spain, France, and England. There are co-op programs as well as work-study programs with major department stores and specialty shops, manufacturers, showrooms, magazine publishers, and cosmetics companies.

Faculty/Classroom: 54% of faculty are male; 46% are female. All teach undergraduates. No introductory courses are taught by graduate students. The average class size in a regular course is 17.

Admissions: 81% of a recent year applicants were accepted. The SAT scores for a recent freshman class were: Critical Reading--61% below 500, 34% between 500 and 599, 5% between 600 and 700; Math--67% below 500, 28% between 500 and 599, 5% between 600 and 700. The ACT scores were 58% below 21, 29% between 21 and 23, 13% between 24 and 26.

Requirements: The SAT or ACT is required. The ACT Optional Writing test is also required. In addition, applicants should be high school graduates or hold the GED. An essay and letters of recommendation are required. AP and CLEP credits are accepted.

Procedure: Freshmen are admitted fall and spring. There are early admissions, deferred admissions, and rolling admissions plans. Application deadlines are open. Application fee is $40. Notification of early decision is sent December 15; regular decision, on a rolling basis. Applications are accepted online.

Transfer: 175 transfer students enrolled in a recent year. Applicants must also submit their official high school and all college transcripts. Students with fewer than 30 college credits must submit SAT or ACT scores. Essay and letters of recommendation are required of all applicants. 61 of 127 credits required for the bachelor's degree must be completed at LIM College.

Visiting: There are regularly scheduled orientations for prospective students, including tours and presentations on admissions, curriculum, career opportunities, and financial aid. There are guides for informal visits and visitors may sit in on classes. To schedule a visit, contact the Admissions Office.

Financial Aid: In a recent year, 79% of all full-time freshmen and 70% of continuing full-time students received some form of financial aid. 64% of all full-time freshmen and 53% of continuing full-time students received need-based aid. The FAFSA and the college's own financial statement are required. The priority date for freshman financial aid applications for fall entry is March 1.

International Students: There are 13 international students enrolled. They must take the TOEFL with a minimum score of 550 on the paper-based TOEFL (PBT) or 80 on the Internet-based version (iBT). They must also take the SAT or ACT.

Computers: There are 335 computers connected to the college network throughout campus, all with Internet access. All campus locations have wireless access. Housing facilities all have high-speed Internet access. All students may access the system. There are no time limits and no fees.

Graduates: In a recent year, 332 bachelor's degrees were awarded. The most popular majors were fashion merchandising (58%), marketing (27%), and visual merchandising (9%). 70 companies recruited on campus in 2010-2011. In an average class, 1% graduate in 3 years or less, 54% graduate in 4 years or less, 57% graduate in 5 years or less, and 64% graduate in 6 years or less. Of a recent graduating class, 94% were employed within 6 months of graduation.

Admissions Contact: Assistant Dean of Admissions. E-Mail: *admissions@limcollege.edu* Web: *www.limcollege.edu*

LONG ISLAND UNIVERSITY SYSTEM

The Long Island University System, established in 1886, is a private system in New York. It is governed by a board of trustees, whose chief administrator is the president. The primary goal of the system is to provide Long Island's communities with high-quality, humane, higher education. The main priorities are teaching in the liberal arts and professions, extending higher education to underrepresented populations, and providing every student with opportunities for cooperative education placements in a field related to his or her major. The total student enrollment is usually about 171,800 with 1500 faculty members. Altogether there are 179 baccalaureate, 148 master's, and 2 doctoral programs offered in the Long Island University System. Profiles of the 4-year campuses are included in this section.

LONG ISLAND UNIVERSITY/BROOKLYN CAMPUS D-5

Brooklyn, NY 11201 (718) 488-1292
(800) LIU-PLAN; (718) 797-2399

Full-time: 1310 men, 3010 women
Part-time: 260 men, 810 women
Graduate: 915 men, 1215 women
Year: semesters, summer session
Application Deadline: open
Freshman Class: n/av
SAT or ACT: recommended
Faculty: n/av; IIA, +$
Ph.D.s: n/av
Student/Faculty: n/av
Tuition: $20,500
Room & Board: $9000

COMPETITIVE

Long Island University/Brooklyn Campus, founded in 1926, is part of the Long Island University system. LIU is a private institution offering programs in liberal arts and sciences, pharmacy, health professions, education, business, nursing, and special programs. It is largely a commuter school. The figures in the above capsule and in this profile are approximate. There are 6 undergraduate schools and 5 graduate schools. In addition to regional accreditation, LIU has baccalaureate program accreditation with ACPE and NLN. The library contains 2.1 million volumes, 813,544 microform items, and 7,902 audio/video tapes/CDs/DVDs, and subscribes to 8,042 periodicals including electronic. Computerized library services include interlibrary loans. Special learning facilities include a learning resource center, art gallery, radio station, and TV station. The 10-acre campus is in an urban area. Including any residence halls, there are 11 buildings.

Student Life: 86% of undergraduates are from New York. Others are from 35 states, 21 foreign countries, and Canada. 75% are from public schools. 43% are African American; 27% white; 19% Hispanic; 11% Asian American. The average age of freshmen is 21; all undergraduates, 25. 36% do not continue beyond their first year; 61% remain to graduate.

Housing: 525 students can be accommodated in college housing, which includes single-sex and coed dorms and married student housing. On-campus housing is available on a first-come and first-served basis. 89% of students commute. Alcohol is not permitted. No one may keep cars.

Activities: There are 75 groups on campus, including band, cheerleading, chess, chorale, computers, dance, ethnic, honors, international, jazz band, literary magazine, newspaper, pep band, photography, political, radio and TV, religious, student government, and yearbook.

Sports: There are 7 intercollegiate sports for men and 6 for women, and 6 intramural sports for men and 6 for women. Facilities include a baseball/soccer field and a basketball gym.

Disabled Students: All of the campus is accessible. Facilities include wheelchair ramps, elevators, specially equipped restrooms, special class scheduling, lowered drinking fountains, and lowered telephones.

Services: Counseling and information services are available, as is tutoring in most subjects. There is remedial math, reading, and writing.

Campus Safety and Security: Measures include 24-hour foot and vehicle patrol. There are emergency telephones and lighted pathways/sidewalks.

Programs of Study: LIU confers B.A., B.S., and B.F.A. degrees. Associates, master's, and doctoral degrees are also awarded. Bachelor's degrees are awarded in BIOLOGICAL SCIENCE (biology/biological science), BUSINESS (accounting, banking and finance, business administration and management, and marketing/retailing/merchandising), COMMUNICATIONS AND THE ARTS (broadcasting, communications, English, fine arts, journalism, languages, music, and speech/debate/rhetoric), COMPUTER AND PHYSICAL SCIENCE (chemistry, computer science, information sciences and systems, and mathematics), EDUCATION (art education, business education, early childhood education, elementary education, music education, science education, secondary education, special education, and teaching English as a second/foreign language (TESOL/TEFOL)), HEALTH PROFESSIONS (nursing, occupational therapy, pharmacy, physical therapy, physician's assistant, predentistry, and premedicine), SOCIAL SCIENCE (anthropology, economics, history, philosophy, political science/government, prelaw, psychology, social science, social work, and sociology). Health professions, pharmacy, and liberal arts are the strongest academically. Health professions, liberal arts, and business have the largest enrollments.

Required: Proficiency courses include basic English and math, English composition, and speech. Distribution requirements are 6 credits each in foreign language, math, and science. Students must complete a core curriculum of 18 credits in the humanities, 12 in social sciences, 8 in natural sciences, and 6 in math. A total of 128 credits (197 for pharmacy) is required for graduation, with 36 credits in the major, and a GPA of 2.0.

Special: Accelerated degree programs are available in all majors. Students may cross-register with other LIU campuses. Internships in career-related jobs provide cooperative education credits. Study abroad, dual-majors, credit for life, military, and work experience, and pass/fail options are also offered. There is a freshman honors program.

Faculty/Classroom: All teach undergraduates. No introductory courses are taught by graduate students. The average class size in a regular course is 22.

Requirements: The SAT or ACT is recommended. LIU requires applicants to be in the upper 75% of their class. A GPA of 2.0 is required. AP and CLEP credits are accepted. Important factors in the admissions decision are recommendations by school officials, advanced placement or honors courses, and evidence of special talent.

Procedure: Freshmen are admitted to all sessions. Entrance exams should be taken by January of the senior year. There are deferred admissions and rolling admissions plans. Application deadlines are open. Application fee is $30. Notification is sent on a rolling basis. Applications are accepted online.

Transfer: A GPA of 2.5 is required. 32 of 128 credits required for the bachelor's degree must be completed at LIU.

Visiting: There are regularly scheduled orientations for prospective students. Visitors may sit in on classes. To schedule a visit, contact the Admissions Office.

Financial Aid: The CSS/Profile and the college's own financial statement are required. Check with the school for current application deadlines.

International Students: The school actively recruits these students. They must take the TOEFL. They must also take the SAT or ACT.

Computers: All students may access the system during library hours. There are no time limits and no fees.

Admissions Contact: Dean of Admissions. E-Mail: *attend@liu.edu*
Web: *www.liu.edu/campus/brooklyn*

LONG ISLAND UNIVERSITY/C.W. POST CAMPUS D-5

Brookville, NY 11548-1300 (516) 299-2900
(800) LIU-PLAN; (516) 299-2137

Full-time: 1610 men, 2410 women
Part-time: 1100 men, 1510 women
Graduate: 1010 men, 2610 women
Year: semesters, summer session
Application Deadline: open
Freshman Class: n/av
SAT or ACT: required
Faculty: n/av; IIA, +$
Ph.D.s: n/av
Student/Faculty: n/av
Tuition: $30,546
Room & Board: $12,340

COMPETITIVE

Long Island University/C.W. Post Campus, founded in 1954 as part of the private Long Island University system, offers 100 undergraduate and 63 graduate majors in education, liberal arts and sciences, accountancy, business, public service, health professions and nursing, and information and computer science. Figures in the above capsule and in this profile are approximate. There are 6 undergraduate schools and 6 graduate schools. In addition to regional accreditation, C.W. Post has baccalaureate program accreditation with AACSB, ADA, ASLA, CAHEA, CSWE, and NLN. The library contains 1.1 million volumes, 834,413 microform items, and 9606 audio/video tapes/CDs/DVDs, and subscribes to 10,999 periodicals including electronic. Computerized library services include interlibrary loans and database searching. Special learning facilities include a learning resource center, art gallery, radio station, TV station, art museum, tax institute, speech and hearing center, center for business research, federal depository, and multimedia computer center. The 307-acre campus is in a suburban area 25 miles east of New York City, on the former estate of Marjorie Merriweather Post. Including any residence halls, there are 53 buildings.

Student Life: 91% of undergraduates are from New York. Others are from 32 states, 46 foreign countries, and Canada. 71% are from public schools. 13% are white. The average age of freshmen is 18; all undergraduates, 21. 31% do not continue beyond their first year; 37% remain to graduate.

Housing: 1710 students can be accommodated in college housing, which includes single-sex and coed dorms. In addition, there is a quiet hall. On-campus housing is guaranteed for all 4 years. 60% of students commute. All students may keep cars.

Activities: 1% of men belong to 4 national fraternities; 3% of women belong to 9 national sororities. There are 80 groups on campus, including art, band, chamber singing, cheerleading, choir, chorale, chorus, dance, drama, equestrian, ethnic, film, gay, honors, international, jazz band, literary magazine, Madrigal, musical theater, newspaper, orchestra, pep band, photography, political, professional, radio and TV, religious, Renaissance music, social, social service, student government, and vocal jazz. Popular campus events include Theater Festival, Spring Fling, and Cereal Bowl: The Inter-Residential Hall Competition.

Sports: There are 7 intercollegiate sports for men and 10 for women, and 5 intramural sports for men and 5 for women. Facilities include a 5000-seat football stadium, an equestrian center, tennis courts, 70 acres of baseball, soccer, lacrosse, softball, and practice fields, a recreational center with an 8-lane swimming pool, 3 basketball courts with spectator seating for 3000, racquetball courts, an indoor track, and weight and aerobic rooms.

Disabled Students: 75% of the campus is accessible. Facilities include wheelchair ramps, elevators, special parking, specially equipped rest rooms, special class scheduling, lowered drinking fountains, lowered telephones, special housing, and electric doors.

Services: Counseling and information services are available, as is tutoring

in most subjects. There is a reader service for the blind, remedial math, reading, and writing, and an academic resource center for learning-disabled students.

Campus Safety and Security: Measures include 24-hour foot and vehicle patrol, self-defense education, and security escort services. There are shuttle buses, emergency telephones, lighted pathways/sidewalks, restricted night access to campus, card-access residence entrances, and an electronic keyless locking system for dorm rooms.

Programs of Study: C.W. Post confers B.A., B.F.A., B.S., and B.S.Ed. degrees. Associates, master's, and doctoral degrees are also awarded. Bachelor's degrees are awarded in AGRICULTURE (conservation and regulation), BIOLOGICAL SCIENCE (biology/biological science, molecular biology, and nutrition), BUSINESS (accounting, banking and finance, business administration and management, and marketing/retailing/merchandising), COMMUNICATIONS AND THE ARTS (arts administration/management, broadcasting, communications, dance, dramatic arts, English, film arts, fine arts, French, German, Italian, journalism, music, photography, public relations, and Spanish), COMPUTER AND PHYSICAL SCIENCE (chemistry, computer science, geology, information sciences and systems, mathematics, physics, and radiological technology), EDUCATION (art education, early childhood education, elementary education, English education, foreign languages education, health education, music education, science education, and secondary education), ENGINEERING AND ENVIRONMENTAL DESIGN (preengineering), HEALTH PROFESSIONS (art therapy, biomedical science, health care administration, medical laboratory technology, medical records administration/services, nursing, predentistry, premedicine, prepharmacy, and speech pathology/audiology), SOCIAL SCIENCE (criminal justice, economics, forensic studies, geography, history, international studies, philosophy, political science/government, prelaw, psychology, public administration, and social work). Accounting, radiologic technology, and biology are the strongest academically. Business, education, and media arts have the largest enrollments.

Required: Core requirements include 9 credits each of history and philosophy, 8 of lab science, 6 each of language and literature, arts, political science and economics, sociology, psychology, and geography or anthropology, and 3 of math. A minimum of 128 credits is required to graduate. GPA requirements range from 2.0 to 2.5 in most departments, 3.0 in interdisciplinary studies. Students must demonstrate competency in writing, quantitative skills, computer skills, oral communications, and library use.

Special: There is cross-registration with several other Long Island colleges. C.W. Post offers co-op programs in all majors, internships, study abroad in 11 countries, work-study in most departments, accelerated degree programs, and a Washington semester for outstanding criminal justice students. Dual and student-designed majors are available. There is a 3-2 engineering degree with Polytechnic University, Pratt Institute, and Arizona State University, and credit is available for life, military, and work experience. Nondegree study is available, as are pass/fail options. There are 14 national honor societies, a freshman honors program, and 16 departmental honors programs.

Faculty/Classroom: No introductory courses are taught by graduate students. The average class size in an introductory lecture is 26, in a laboratory, 20, and in a regular course, 19.

Requirements: The SAT or ACT is required, with a minimum composite SAT score of 900 or a minimum ACT score of 20. Applicants should be graduates of an accredited secondary school with a B average or have a GED. Preparatory work should include 4 years each of English and social science and 2 each of foreign language, college preparatory math, and lab science. A GPA of 75.0 is required. AP and CLEP credits are accepted. Important factors in the admissions decision are advanced placement or honors courses, recommendations by school officials, and evidence of special talent.

Procedure: Freshmen are admitted to all sessions. Entrance exams should be taken from May of the junior year through December of the senior year. There are early admissions, deferred admissions, and rolling admissions plans. Application deadlines are open. The application fee is $30. Applications are accepted online.

Transfer: Applicants should have appropriate high school credentials and a minimum college GPA of 2.25. 32 of 128 credits required for the bachelor's degree must be completed at C.W. Post.

Visiting: There are regularly scheduled orientations for prospective students, consisting of Post Preview Days, which include meeting the faculty, an admissions and financial aid overview, and a campus tour. There are guides for informal visits and visitors may sit in on classes. To schedule a visit, contact the Office of Admissions.

Financial Aid: C.W. Post is a member of CSS. The CSS/Profile and FAFSA are required. Check with the school for current application deadlines.

International Students: The school actively recruits these students. They must take the TOEFL. SAT or ACT scores are recommended to help evaluate students' admissions eligibility and enable students to be considered for scholarships.

Computers: All students may access the system Monday to Thursday 8 a.m. to 11 p.m. and Friday to Sunday 9 a.m. to 10 p.m. Dial-up capacity is available 24 hours a day There are no time limits and no fees.

Admissions Contact: Director of Admissions. E-Mail: *enroll@cwpost.liu.edu* Web: *www.liu.edu*

MANHATTAN COLLEGE D-5

Riverdale, NY 10471 **(718) 862-7200**
(800) 622-9235; (718) 862-8019

Full-time: 1713 men, 1428 women — **Faculty:** n/av
Part-time: 151 men, 59 women — **Ph.D.s:** 95%
Graduate: 196 men, 253 women — **Student/Faculty:** 12 to 1
Year: semesters, summer session — **Tuition:** $32,735
Application Deadline: March 1 — **Room & Board:** $12,220
Freshman Class: 6546 applied, 4555 accepted, 842 enrolled
SAT CR/M/W: 526/535/528 — **ACT:** 24 — **VERY COMPETITIVE**

Founded in 1853, Manhattan College offers an exceptional college education enriched by Lasallian Catholic values and access to New York City. There are 5 undergraduate schools and 3 graduate schools. In addition to regional accreditation, Manhattan has baccalaureate program accreditation with AACSB, ABET, AHEA, CAHEA, and TEAC. The library contains 292,438 volumes, 675,489 microform items, and 2,676 audio/video tapes/CDs/DVDs, and subscribes to 343 periodicals including electronic. Computerized library services include interlibrary loans, database searching, Internet access, and Wi-Fi capability. Special learning facilities include a radio station, TV station, research and learning center, 24-hour Internet cafe, Holocaust, Genocide and Interfaith Education Center, and Center for Academic Success. The 22-acre campus is in an urban area 10 miles north of midtown Manhattan. Including any residence halls, there are 21 buildings.

Student Life: 75% of undergraduates are from New York. Others are from 36 states, 46 foreign countries, and Canada. 60% are from public schools. 60% are White; 17% Hispanic. 55% are Catholic. The average age of freshmen is 18; all undergraduates, 21. 12% do not continue beyond their first year; 75% remain to graduate.

Housing: 2095 students can be accommodated in college housing, which includes coed dorms, on-campus apartments, off-campus apartments, and married student housing. Arches - a living/learning environment. On-campus housing is guaranteed for all 4 years. 65% of students live on campus; of those, 80% remain on campus on weekends. All students may keep cars.

Activities: 3% of men belong to 2 local and 1 national fraternities; 1% of women belong to 2 local sororities. There are 70 groups on campus, including bagpipe, cheerleading, choir, chorus, computers, dance, debate, drama, ethnic, honors, international, jazz band, literary magazine, musical theater, newspaper, orchestra, pep band, political, professional, radio and TV, religious, social, social service, student government, and yearbook. Popular campus events include Annual Springfest, Special Olympics and Jasper Jingle.

Sports: There are 8 intercollegiate sports for men and 8 for women, and 7 intramural sports for men and 7 for women. Facilities include Draddy Gym, which has 3 hardwood basketball courts an indoor track and weight room with free weights and weightlifting machines. Alumni Hall - has a fitness center with many different cardio machines and a dance studio use for dancing and fitness classes. Gaelic Park has a large turf field used for football, soccer, lacrosse, softball, and ultimate frisbee.

Disabled Students: All of the campus is accessible. Facilities include wheelchair ramps, elevators, special parking, specially equipped restrooms, and special housing.

Services: Counseling and information services are available, as is tutoring in every subject. The Center for Academic Success is comprised of 3 offices with open door policy and extended hours.

Campus Safety and Security: Measures include 24-hour foot and vehicle patrol and emergency notification system. There are emergency telephones, lighted pathways/sidewalks, and controlled access to dorms/residences.

Programs of Study: Manhattan confers B.A., B.S. and B.S.E. degrees. Master's degrees are also awarded. Bachelor's degrees are awarded in BIOLOGICAL SCIENCE (biochemistry and biology/biological science), BUSINESS (accounting, banking and finance, business economics, international business management, labor studies, and marketing/retailing/merchandising), COMMUNICATIONS AND THE ARTS (broadcasting, communications, English, French, journalism, and Spanish), COMPUTER AND PHYSICAL SCIENCE (chemistry, computer science, information sciences and systems, mathematics, and physics), EDUCATION (early childhood education, education, education of the emotionally handicapped, elementary education, foreign languages education, health education, middle school education, physical education, science education, secondary education, and special education), ENGINEERING AND ENVIRONMENTAL DESIGN (chemical engineering, civil engineering, electrical/electronics engineering, environmental engineering, and mechanical engineering), HEALTH PROFESSIONS (predentistry, premedicine, and radiological science), SOCIAL SCIENCE (economics, history, peace studies, philosophy, political science/government, prelaw, psychology, religion, sociology, and urban studies). Engineering and business are the strongest academically. Engineering, business, and arts have the largest enrollments.

Required: All students must take courses in English composition and literature, religious studies, philosophy, humanities, social science, science, math, and a modern foreign language. About 130 credit hours are required for graduation, with about 36 in the major. The minimum GPA is 2.0.

Special: Manhattan offers credit and non-credit based internships and experiential learning opportunities in for-profit, not-for-profit, social, cultural, educational, religious, government and non-government organizations. Students may enroll in numerous study abroad programs that are offered throughout the world. Five year Bachelors/Masters degrees in Business, Education and Engineering are offered and a dual major in international business, credit by exam, and non-degree study are also available. There are 22 national honor societies, including Phi Beta Kappa, a freshman honors program, and 28 departmental honors programs.

Faculty/Classroom: 60% of faculty are male; 40% are female. All teach undergraduates, and 80% do both. No introductory courses are taught by graduate students. The average class size in an introductory lecture is 15 and in a regular course is 22.

Admissions: 70% of the 2013-2014 applicants were accepted. The SAT scores for the 2013-2014 freshman class were: Critical Reading--38% below 500, 44% between 500 and 599, 16% between 600 and 699, and 2% between 700 and 800; Math--29% below 500, 40% between 500 and 599, 27% between 600 and 699, and 4% between 700 and 800; Writing--35% below 500, 45% between 500 and 599, 19% between 600 and 699, and 2% between 700 and 800. The ACT scores were 16% below 21, 27% between 21 and 23, 30% between 24 and 26, 12% between 27 and 28, and 15% above 28.

Requirements: The SAT or ACT is required. Applicants must graduate from an accredited secondary school or have earned a GED. 16 academic units are required, including 4 of English, 3 each of math and social studies, and 2 of foreign language, lab sciences, and electives. An essay is required and an interview is recommended. AP and CLEP credits are accepted. Important factors in the admissions decision are advanced placement or honors courses, leadership record, and recommendations by school officials.

Procedure: Freshmen are admitted fall and spring. Entrance exams should be taken in the spring of the junior year or the fall of the senior year. There are early decision, deferred admissions, and rolling admissions plans. Early decision applications should be filed by November 15; regular applications, by March 1 for fall entry; and December 1 for spring entry, along with a $60 fee. Notification of early decision is sent December 15; regular decision, December 15. 38 early decision candidates were accepted for the 2013-2014 class. 272 applicants were on the 2013 waiting list; 52 were admitted. Applications are accepted online.

Transfer: 143 transfer students enrolled in 2012-2013. Applicants must have a GPA of 2.5 and meet subject course requirements according to their course of study. They must submit transcripts from colleges and high schools attended. An interview is recommended. 66 of 130 credits required for the bachelor's degree must be completed at Manhattan.

Visiting: There are regularly scheduled orientations for prospective students, during 2 days in the summer, which include scheduling, parent workshops, loan seminars, and English and math testing. There are guides for informal visits, visitors may sit in on classes, and stay overnight. To schedule a visit, contact the Admission Center.

Financial Aid: In 2013-2014, 75% of all full-time freshmen and 72% of continuing full-time students received some form of financial aid. 74% of all full-time freshmen and 72% of continuing full-time students received need-based aid. The average freshman award was $22,566. Need-based scholarships or need-based grants averaged $14,551; need-based self-help aid (loans and jobs) averaged $4,900; and non-need-based athletic scholarships averaged $31,336. 26% of undergraduate students work part-time. Average annual earnings from campus work are $1500. The average financial indebtedness of the 2013 graduate was $34,375. The FAFSA and the college's own financial statement are required. The priority date for freshman financial aid applications for fall entry is February 15.

International Students: There are 85 international students enrolled. The school actively recruits these students. They must take the TOEFL with a minimum score of 550 on the paper-based TOEFL (PBT) or 80 on the Internet-based version (iBT). They must also take the SAT or ACT.

Computers: All students may access the system. 13 hours a day in the labs and 24 hours a day in residence halls or by modem. There are no time limits and no fees.

Graduates: From July 1, 2012 to June 30, 2013, 784 bachelor's degrees were awarded. The most popular majors were engineering (25%), business (22%), and education (13%). In an average class, 63% graduate in 4 years or less and 70% graduate in 6 years or less. Of the 2012 graduating class, 18% were enrolled in graduate school within 6 months of graduation, and 65% were employed.

Admissions Contact: William J. Bisset, Jr., Vice President for Enrollment Management. E-Mail: *admit@manhattan.edu* Web: *www.manhattan.edu*

MANHATTAN SCHOOL OF MUSIC D-5

New York, NY 10027 **(212) 749-2802, ext. 4501; (212) 749-3025**

Full-time: 210 men, 210 women	**Faculty:** n/av
Part-time: 5 men, 5 women	**Ph.D.s:** n/av
Graduate: 200 men, 245 women	**Student/Faculty:** n/av
Year: semesters	**Tuition:** $36,500
Application Deadline:	**Room & Board:** $9350
Freshman Class: n/av	
SAT or ACT: recommended	**SPECIAL**

The Manhattan School of Music, founded in 1917, is a private college offering undergraduate and graduate degrees in music performance and composition. There is one graduate school. The library contains 73,405 and 31,500 audio/video tapes/CDs/DVDs, and subscribes to 128 periodicals including electronic. Computerized library services include interlibrary loans, database searching, and Internet access. The 1-acre campus is in an urban area in New York City. Including any residence halls, there are 2 buildings.

Student Life: 83% of undergraduates are from out of state, mostly the Northeast. Students are from 31 states, 48 foreign countries, and Canada. 81% are from public schools. 36% are White; 36% Foreign. The average age of freshmen is 18; all undergraduates, 21. 9% do not continue beyond their first year; 54% remain to graduate.

Housing: 380 students can be accommodated in college housing, which includes single-sex and coed dorms. On-campus housing is guaranteed for the freshman year only and is available on a lottery system for upperclassmen. Priority is given to out-of-town students. 50% of students commute. All students may keep cars.

Activities: 10% of men belong to 2 local fraternities; 20% of women belong to 2 local sororities. There are 13 groups on campus, including choir, chorale, chorus, ethnic, gay, international, jazz band, musical theater, opera, orchestra, student government, and symphony. Popular campus events include Halloween Party, Christmas and Chanukah Party, and a Post-Opera Party.

Sports: There is no sports program at MSM.

Disabled Students: 70% of the campus is accessible. Facilities include wheelchair ramps, elevators, specially equipped restrooms, special class scheduling, and lowered telephones.

Services: Counseling and information services are available, as is tutoring in most subjects. There is a reader service for the blind.

Campus Safety and Security: Measures include 24-hour foot and vehicle patrol. There are lighted pathways/sidewalks.

Programs of Study: MSM confers B.Mus. degrees. Master's and doctoral degrees are also awarded. Bachelor's degrees are awarded in COMMUNICATIONS AND THE ARTS (jazz, music, music performance, music theory and composition, piano/organ, strings, and voice). Classical piano, classical voice, and jazz are the largest.

Required: All students must take 4 music theory courses, a 4-course core curriculum in the humanities, and 4 elective humanities courses and perform a final, senior-year recital. Composition majors must complete an original symphonic work. To graduate, students must earn 120 to 130 credit hours, including 90 to 100 in the major, with a minimum GPA of 2.0.

Special: There is cross-registration with Barnard College. Credit by exam in theory and music history is available.

Faculty/Classroom: 69% of faculty are male; 31% are female. All teach undergraduates. Graduate students teach 1% of introductory courses. The average class size in an introductory lecture is 20 and in a regular course is 15.

Requirements: The SAT or ACT is recommended. Applicants should graduate from an accredited high school. The GED is accepted. Admission is based on a performance audition, evaluation of scholastic achievements, and available openings in the major field. AP and CLEP credits are accepted. Important factors in the admissions decision are evidence of special talent, personality/intangible qualities, and extracurricular activities record.

Procedure: Freshmen are admitted fall. Check with the school for current application deadlines. The application fee is $100. Notifications are sent April 1.

Transfer: Applicants must audition and submit college transcripts. 60 of 120 credits required for the bachelor's degree must be completed at MSM.

Visiting: There are regularly scheduled orientations for prospective students, consisting of a tour of the facility and a discussion with a counselor. There are guides for informal visits and visitors may sit in on classes. To schedule a visit, contact the Office of Admission and Financial Aid.

Financial Aid: In 2013-2014, 52% of all full-time freshmen and 51% of continuing full-time students received some form of financial aid. 57% of all full-time freshmen and 44% of continuing full-time students received

need-based aid. The average freshman award was $18,263. Need-based scholarships or need-based grants averaged $14,494 ($36,000 maximum); and other non-need-based awards and non-need-based scholarships averaged $14,083 ($28,750 maximum). 19% of undergraduate students work part-time. Average annual earnings from campus work are $1443. The average financial indebtedness of the 2013 graduate was $17,658. The CSS/Profile, FAFSA, and the college's own financial statement are required. Check with the school for current application deadlines.

International Students: The school actively recruits these students. They must take the TOEFL. Applicants auditioning live whose first language is not English are required to take the English Placement Test (EPT). Applicants taking the EPT do not need to submit a TOEFL score. Applicants eligible for a recorded audition must submit a TOEFL score.

Computers: All students may access the system. There are no time limits and no fees.

Graduates: From July 1, 2012 to June 30, 2013, 85 bachelor's degrees were awarded. The most popular majors were voice (22%), piano (21%), and strings (16%). In an average class, 4% graduate in 3 years or less, 47% graduate in 4 years or less, 52% graduate in 5 years or less, and 54% graduate in 6 years or less.

Admissions Contact: Amy A. Anderson, Dean for Enrollment Management. E-Mail: *admission@msmnyc.edu* Web: *www.msmnyc.edu*

MANHATTANVILLE COLLEGE D-5

Purchase, NY 10577 (914) 323-5464
(800) 32 VILLE; (914) 694-1732

Full-time: 588 men, 1129 women	**Faculty:** 102; IIA, av$
Part-time: 48 men, 77 women	**Ph.D.s:** 99%
Graduate: 394 men, 745 women	**Student/Faculty:** 17 to 1
Year: semesters, summer session	**Tuition:** $32,760
Application Deadline: open	**Room & Board:** $13,500
Freshman Class: 4242 applied, 2240 accepted, 507 enrolled	
SAT CR/M: 530/540	**ACT:** 24 **VERY COMPETITIVE**

Manhattanville College, founded in 1841, is an independent liberal arts institution offering more than 45 undergraduate areas of study. The figures in the above capsule and in this profile are approximate. There is 1 undergraduate school and 2 graduate schools. In addition to regional accreditation, M'ville has baccalaureate program accreditation with NCATE. The library contains 250,209 volumes, 259,230 microform items, and 5,312 audio/video tapes/CDs/DVDs, and subscribes to 36,923 periodicals including electronic. Computerized library services include interlibrary loans, database searching, Internet access, and Wi-Fi capability. Special learning facilities include an art gallery, radio station, TV station, Environmental Sciences Building, and Heritage Halle. The 100-acre campus is in a suburban area 25 miles north of New York City. Including any residence halls, there are 18 buildings.

Student Life: 53% of undergraduates are from New York. Others are from 39 states, 56 foreign countries, and Canada. 51% are White; 15% Hispanic; 11% Foreign. The average age of freshmen is 18; all undergraduates, 20. 19% do not continue beyond their first year; 60% remain to graduate.

Housing: 1330 students can be accommodated in college housing, which includes single-sex and coed dorms. On-campus housing is guaranteed for all 4 years. 77% of students live on campus; of those, 75% remain on campus on weekends. All students may keep cars.

Activities: There are no fraternities or sororities. There are 60 groups on campus, including art, band, cheerleading, chess, choir, chorale, chorus, computers, dance, debate, drama, environmental, ethnic, film, gay, honors, international, jazz band, literary magazine, musical theater, newspaper, orchestra, pep band, photography, political, professional, radio and TV, religious, social, social service, student government, and yearbook. Popular campus events include Quad Jam, Fall Jam and The Global Pot.

Sports: There are 11 intercollegiate sports for men and 10 for women, and 5 intramural sports for men and 5 for women. Facilities include a 1000-seat gym, a 25-yard indoor pool, 6 deco-turf tennis courts, a health-works-wellness center, baseball, turf lacrosse, field hockey, softball fields, and batting cages.

Disabled Students: All of the campus is accessible. Facilities include wheelchair ramps, elevators, special parking, specially equipped restrooms, special class scheduling, lowered drinking fountains, lowered telephones, and special housing.

Services: Counseling and information services are available, as is tutoring in every subject. There is a program for students with documented learning disabilities.

Campus Safety and Security: Measures include 24-hour foot and vehicle patrol, emergency notification system, and security escort services. There are shuttle buses, emergency telephones, lighted pathways/sidewalks, and controlled access to dorms/residences.

Programs of Study: M'ville confers B.A., B.S., B.F.A. and B.Mus. degrees. Master's degrees are also awarded. Bachelor's degrees are awarded in BIOLOGICAL SCIENCE (biochemistry and biology/biological science), BUSINESS (banking and finance and management science), COMMUNICATIONS AND THE ARTS (art, art history and appreciation, communications, dance, dramatic arts, English, French, music, and Spanish), COMPUTER AND PHYSICAL SCIENCE (chemistry, computer science, mathematics, and physics), EDUCATION (education), SOCIAL SCIENCE (American studies, Asian/Oriental studies, economics, history, international studies, philosophy, political science/government, psychology, religion, and sociology). English, art, and psychology are the strongest academically. Psychology, management, and history have the largest enrollments.

Required: All Manhattanville undergraduates must complete the indicated credit requirement in all 4 of the following curricular distribution areas: Humanities (6 credits), Social Science (6 credits), Mathematical (3 credits) and Scientific (3 credits), and Fine Arts (6 credits). A total of 120 credit hours and a minimum GPA of 2.0 are needed to graduate.

Special: Manhattanville offers cross-registration with SUNY Purchase, internships in all majors for credit, a Washington semester, and study abroad in 15 countries. Accelerated degree programs in behavioral studies, organizational management, and communications management are offered. Dual, student-designed, and interdisciplinary majors and pass/fail options are also available. Under the portfolio degree plan, students develop an individualized program combining both academic and nonacademic training. There are a freshman honors program and 16 departmental honors programs.

Faculty/Classroom: 50% of faculty are male; 50% are female. All teach undergraduates. No introductory courses are taught by graduate students. The average class size in an introductory lecture is 15; in a laboratory is 12; and in a regular course is 10.

Admissions: 53% of the 2013-2014 applicants were accepted. The SAT scores for the 2013-2014 freshman class were: Critical Reading--5% below 500, 74% between 500 and 599, 20% between 600 and 699, and 1% between 700 and 800; Math--5% below 500, 67% between 500 and 599, 26% between 600 and 699, and 2% between 700 and 800. The ACT scores were 25% below 21, 33% between 21 and 23, 26% between 24 and 26, 8% between 27 and 28, and 8% above 28. 100 freshmen graduated first in their class.

Requirements: The SAT or ACT is required. Applicants should graduate in the upper 50% of their class with 4 years of English, 3 each of history, math, and science, including 2 of lab science, and 1 half-year each of art and music. The GED is accepted. Interviews are strongly encouraged. Art applicants must submit a portfolio; music applicants must audition. A GPA of 2.0 is required. AP and CLEP credits are accepted. Important factors in the admissions decision are leadership record, recommendations by alumni, and recommendations by school officials.

Procedure: Freshmen are admitted fall and spring. Entrance exams should be taken in the spring of the junior or fall of the senior year. There are early decision, early admissions, deferred admissions, and rolling admissions plans. Application deadlines are open. Application fee is $70. Notification of early decision is sent December 31; regular decision, 146 early decision candidates were accepted for the 2013-2014 class. 100 applicants were on the 2013 waiting list; 20 were admitted. Applications are accepted online.

Transfer: 104 transfer students enrolled in 2012-2013. Applicants must submit college transcripts. A minimum GPA of 2.5 and a statement of good standing are required. Applicants with fewer than 40 credits must submit all high school records and SAT scores. 60 of 120 credits required for the bachelor's degree must be completed at M'ville.

Visiting: There are regularly scheduled orientations for prospective students, including a campus tour and a meeting in Admissions. There are guides for informal visits, visitors may sit in on classes, and stay overnight. To schedule a visit, contact the Office of Admissions.

Financial Aid: In 2013-2014, 78% of all full-time freshmen and 76% of continuing full-time students received some form of financial aid. 63% of all full-time freshmen and 58% of continuing full-time students received need-based aid. The average freshman award was $24,828. 33% of undergraduate students work part-time. Average annual earnings from campus work are $1750. The average financial indebtedness of the 2013 graduate was $23,294. The FAFSA, the state aid form, and the college's own financial statement are required. The deadline for filing freshman financial aid applications for fall entry is March 1.

International Students: There are 222 international students enrolled. The school actively recruits these students. They must also take the SAT or ACT.

Computers: All students may access the system. Internet and intranet are usable 24 hours per day, 7 days a week. Computer labs are open about 64 to 70 hours throughout the week. There are no time limits and no fees.

Graduates: From July 1, 2012 to June 30, 2013, 345 bachelor's degrees were awarded. The most popular majors were management (17%), psychology (11%), and communications (11%). 102 companies recruited on campus in 2012-2013. In an average class, 56% graduate in 4 years or less, 60% graduate in 5 years or less, and 60% graduate in 6 years or less.

Of the 2012 graduating class, 32% were enrolled in graduate school within 6 months of graduation, and 28% were employed.

Admissions Contact: Jose Flores, Vice President, Enrollment Management. E-Mail: *admissions@mville.edu* Web: *www.manhattanville.edu*

MANNES COLLEGE NEW SCHOOL FOR MUSIC D-5

New York, NY 10024 (212) 580-0210, ext. 4805 (800) 292-3040; (212) 580-1738

Full-time: 70 men, 100 women
Part-time: 20 men, 20 women
Graduate: 75 men, 115 women
Year: semesters
Application Deadline: December 1
Freshman Class: n/av
Faculty: n/av
Ph.D.s: n/av
Student/Faculty: n/av
Tuition: $32,500
Room & Board: $12,000

COMPETITIVE

Mannes College New School for music formerly Mannes College of Music, was founded in 1916 and is a private Classical music conservatory. There is one graduate school. The 3 libraries contain 2.4 million volumes, 13,000 microform items, and 14,275 audio/video tapes/CDs/DVDs, and subscribe to 33,320 periodicals including electronic. Computerized library services include interlibrary loans, database searching, Internet access, and Wi-Fi capability. The campus is in an urban area in Manhattan.

Student Life: 78% of undergraduates are from out of state, mostly the Middle Atlantic. Students are from 25 states, 13 foreign countries, and Canada. 59% are from public schools. 46% are White; 28% Foreign; 11% Asian American. The average age of freshmen is 19; all undergraduates, 21. 9% do not continue beyond their first year.

Housing: College-sponsored housing includes coed dorms, on-campus apartments, and off-campus apartments. On-campus housing is guaranteed for all 4 years, is available on a first-come, first-served basis, and is available on a lottery system for upperclassmen. 86% of students commute. Alcohol is not permitted.

Activities: There are no fraternities or sororities. There are 30 groups on campus, including art, choir, chorus, dance, debate, environmental, ethnic, film, gay, honors, international, jazz band, literary magazine, newspaper, opera, orchestra, photography, political, professional, religious, social, social service, student government, and symphony. Popular campus events include Orchestra/Chorus Concerts, Christmas Parties, and Recitals.

Sports: There is no sports program at Mannes. Facilities include a recreation room. YMCA is also available for student use.

Disabled Students: 90% of the campus is accessible. Facilities include wheelchair ramps, elevators, specially equipped restrooms, lowered drinking fountains, and lowered telephones.

Services: Counseling and information services are available, as is tutoring in some subjects.

Programs of Study: Mannes confers B.S., and B.Mus. degrees. Master's degrees are also awarded. Bachelor's degrees are awarded in COMMUNICATIONS AND THE ARTS (applied music, choral music, guitar, music, music performance, music theory and composition, piano/organ, strings, voice, and winds). Piano, voice, and violin have the largest enrollments.

Required: Students majoring in instruments and voice must participate in various ensemble classes. Courses are also required in English, western civilization, art history, literature, and history of music. To graduate, performance majors must perform before a faculty jury, and composition majors must submit 5 original pieces for juried consideration.

Special: Mannes offers cross-registration with New School. Internships and work-study are available.

Faculty/Classroom: 60% of faculty are male; 40% are female. All teach undergraduates, 3% do research, and 3% do both. No introductory courses are taught by graduate students. The average class size in an introductory lecture is 11 and in a regular course is 8.

Requirements: Applicants must be graduates of an accredited secondary school or have a GED certificate. An audition, an interview, a letter of recommendation, and a written test in music theory and musicianship are required. A GPA of 2.0 is required. AP credits are accepted. Important factors in the admissions decision are evidence of special talent, personality/intangible qualities, and recommendations by school officials.

Procedure: Freshmen are admitted fall. Entrance exams should be taken at the time of the audition. There is a deferred admissions plan. Applications should be filed by December 1 for fall entry; November 1 for spring entry, along with a $100 fee. Notifications are sent April 15. 17 applicants were on the 2013 waiting list; 9 were admitted. Applications are accepted online.

Transfer: 11 transfer students enrolled in 2012-2013. Transfer applicants must complete the same procedures as entering freshmen and submit transcripts from all secondary schools and colleges attended. 67 credits required for the bachelor's degree must be completed at Mannes.

Visiting: There are regularly scheduled orientations for prospective students. There are guides for informal visits and visitors may sit in on classes. To schedule a visit, contact the Admissions Office.

Financial Aid: In 2013-2014, 61% of all full-time freshmen and 63% of continuing full-time students received some form of financial aid. 61% of all full-time freshmen and 63% of continuing full-time students received need-based aid. The average freshman award was $15,508. Other non-need-based awards and non-need-based scholarships averaged $14,502 ($29,800 maximum). Average annual earnings from campus work are $2000. The average financial indebtedness of the 2013 graduate was $17,938. Mannes is a member of CSS. The FAFSA, the state aid form, and the college's own financial statement are required. Check with the school for current application deadlines.

International Students: There are 64 international students enrolled. They must take the TOEFL and the college's own test.

Computers: All students may access the system. There are no time limits and no fees.

Graduates: From July 1, 2012 to June 30, 2013, 25 bachelor's degrees were awarded. The most popular majors were visual and performing (100%). In an average class, 47% graduate in 4 years or less, 66% graduate in 5 years or less, and 66% graduate in 6 years or less.

Admissions Contact: Georgia Schmitt, Director of Admissions. E-Mail: *mannesadmissions@mannes.edu* Web: *www.mannes.newschool.edu*

MARIST COLLEGE D-4

Poughkeepsie, NY 12601 (845) 575-3226 (800) 436-5483; (845) 575-3215

Full-time: 1910 men, 2610 women
Part-time: 200 men, 200 women
Graduate: 410 men, 500 women
Year: semesters, summer session
Application Deadline: see profile
Freshman Class: n/av
SAT or ACT: required
Faculty: n/av; IIA, -$
Ph.D.s: n/av
Student/Faculty: n/av
Tuition: $28,800
Room & Board: $12,600

COMPETITIVE

Marist College, founded in 1929, is private liberal arts college with a Catholic tradition. The figures in the above capsule and in this profile are approximate. There are 7 undergraduate schools and 4 graduate schools. In addition to regional accreditation, Marist has baccalaureate program accreditation with AACSB and CSWE. The library contains 207,750 volumes, 12,206 microform items, and 5,657 audio/video tapes/CDs/DVDs, and subscribes to 30,127 periodicals including electronic. Computerized library services include interlibrary loans, database searching, Internet access, and laptop Internet portals. Special learning facilities include a learning resource center, art gallery, radio station, TV station, a gallery of Lowell Thomas memorabilia, estuarine and environmental studies lab, public opinion institute, and economic research center. The 180-acre campus is in a suburban area 75 miles north of New York City on the Hudson River. Including any residence halls, there are 49 buildings.

Student Life: 59% of undergraduates are from New York. Others are from 39 states, 9 foreign countries, and Canada. 70% are from public schools. 77% are white. The average age of freshmen is 18; all undergraduates, 22. 9% do not continue beyond their first year; 78% remain to graduate.

Housing: 2858 students can be accommodated in college housing, which includes coed dorms, on-campus apartments, and off-campus apartments. In addition, there are special-interest houses, freshman dorms with mentors, and housing for upperclassmen. 72% of students live on campus; of those, 90% remain on campus on weekends. Alcohol is not permitted. Upperclassmen may keep cars.

Activities: 1% of men belong to 3 national fraternities; 3% of women belong to 1 local and 3 national sororities. There are 81 groups on campus, including art, band, cheerleading, chess, choir, chorale, chorus, computers, dance, debate, drama, ethnic, film, gay, honors, international, jazz band, literary magazine, marching band, musical theater, newspaper, orchestra, pep band, photography, political, professional, radio and TV, religious, social, social service, student government, and symphony. Popular campus events include Activities Fair, Foxfest, and Giving Tree Program.

Sports: There are 11 intercollegiate sports for men and 12 for women, and 4 intramural sports for men and 4 for women. Facilities include a boathouse, a 3600-seat basketball arena, a 5000-seat stadium, 30 acres of playing fields, a field house, a swimming pool, a diving well, racquetball courts, a tennis pavilion, a dance and aerobics studio, a weight room, intramural basketball courts, an all-purpose playing space, and a fitness center.

Disabled Students: All of the campus is accessible. Facilities include wheelchair ramps, elevators, special parking, specially equipped restrooms, special class scheduling, lowered drinking fountains, and lowered telephones.

Services: Counseling and information services are available, as is tutoring in every subject. There is a reader service for the blind, and remedial math, reading, and writing.

Campus Safety and Security: Measures include 24-hour foot and vehicle patrol and security escort services. There are emergency telephones and lighted pathways/sidewalks.

Programs of Study: Marist confers B.A., B.S., and B.P.S. degrees.

Master's degrees are also awarded. Bachelor's degrees are awarded in BIOLOGICAL SCIENCE (biology/biological science), BUSINESS (accounting, business administration and management, and fashion merchandising), COMMUNICATIONS AND THE ARTS (communications, English, fine arts, French, and Spanish), COMPUTER AND PHYSICAL SCIENCE (chemistry, computer mathematics, computer science, digital arts/technology, information sciences and systems, and mathematics), EDUCATION (athletic training and special education), ENGINEERING AND ENVIRONMENTAL DESIGN (environmental science), HEALTH PROFESSIONS (medical technology), SOCIAL SCIENCE (American studies, criminal justice, economics, fashion design and technology, history, interdisciplinary studies, philosophy, political science/government, psychology, and social work). Business administration, communications, and childhood/special education have the largest enrollments.

Required: To graduate, students must maintain a GPA of 2.0 in the major while taking 120 credits. A 30-credit core curriculum and 30 to 36 credits in a major are required. Distribution requirements include 6 credits each in natural sciences, social sciences, history, literature, and math and 3 credits each in fine arts and philosophy/religious studies. Specific course requirements include English writing skills and foundation courses in those areas defined by major programs.

Special: Marist offers cross-registration with schools in the Mid-Hudson Career Consortium and study abroad in 38 countries. The school also offers a 3 year degree in social work, co-op programs in computer science and computer information systems, information technology, accounting, and business, work-study programs, and dual and student-designed majors. There are internships available with more than 1100 organizations in the United States and abroad, including New York State Legislature and White House programs. There are 14 national honor societies and a freshman honors program.

Faculty/Classroom: 56% of faculty are male; 44% are female. 95% teach undergraduates, 68% do research, and 66% do both. No introductory courses are taught by graduate students. The average class size in an introductory lecture is 20; in a laboratory is 20; and in a regular course is 18.

Requirements: The SAT or ACT is required. The ACT Optional Writing test is also required. In addition, applicants should have 17 high school units, including at least 4 years in English, 3 each in math and science, 2 each in social studies, foreign language, and an elective, and 1 in American history. An essay and 2 letters of recommendation are also required. Marist requires applicants to be in the upper 50% of their class. AP and CLEP credits are accepted. Important factors in the admissions decision are advanced placement or honors courses, leadership record, and recommendations by school officials.

Procedure: Freshmen are admitted fall and spring. Entrance exams should be taken during the fall of the senior year. There are early decision and deferred admissions plans. Applications are accepted online. Check with the school for current application deadlines and fee.

Transfer: Applicants must have at least a 2.8 GPA (depending on the college and major program) in at least 30 college credits. Students with fewer than 25 credits will be treated as freshmen. Grades of C or better transfer. 30 of 120 credits required for the bachelor's degree must be completed at Marist.

Visiting: There are regularly scheduled orientations for prospective students, including 1-day June visits for freshmen and a 1-week welcome program. There are guides for informal visits; visitors may sit in on classes and stay overnight. To schedule a visit, contact the Admissions Office.

Financial Aid: The FAFSA is required. Check with the school for current application deadlines.

International Students: The school actively recruits these students. They must take the TOEFL and the college's own test. The IELTS is accepted.

Computers: Wireless access is available. All residence halls and classrooms are connected to the campus network and the Internet. Students can also access Marist's wireless network from their residence halls and classrooms, as well as the library, dining room, lounges, athletic center, stadium, and laundry rooms. There are 36 computer labs and clusters with a total of 646 for student access. Internet 2 is available to all students to share resources with other Internet 2 institutions. All students may access the system. There are no time limits and no fees. It is strongly recommended that all students have a personal computer.

Admissions Contact: Dean of Admission. E-Mail: *admissions@marist.edu* Web: *www.marist.edu*

MARITIME COLLEGE / STATE UNIVERSITY OF NEW YORK D-5

Throgs Neck, NY 10465 (718) 409-7221
(800) 642-1874; (718) 409-7465

Full-time: 1330 men, 140 women
Part-time: 100 men, 20 women
Graduate: 155 men, 35 women
Year: semesters, summer session
Application Deadline: open
Freshman Class: n/av
SAT or ACT: required

Faculty: n/av; IIA, -$
Ph.D.s: 49%
Student/Faculty: 21 to 1
Tuition: $6956 ($15,996)
Room & Board: $10,990

COMPETITIVE

The Maritime College of the State University of New York, founded in 1874, is a public institution that prepares students for the U.S. Merchant Marine officers' license and for bachelor's degrees in engineering, naval architecture, marine environmental science, and marine transportation/business administration The figures in the above capsule and in this profile are approximate. In addition to regional accreditation, New York Maritime has baccalaureate program accreditation with ABET. The library contains 85,984 volumes, 28,400 microform items, and 774 audio/video tapes/CDs/DVDs, and subscribes to 38,735 periodicals including electronic. Computerized library services include interlibrary loans, database searching, and Internet access. Special learning facilities include a learning resource center, a 17,000-ton training ship, a tug, a barge, and a center for simulated marine operations, which contains bridge, radar, tanker, and oil spill response simulators. The 52-acre campus is in a suburban area on the Throgs Neck peninsula where Long Island Sound meets the East River. Including any residence halls, there are 31 buildings.

Student Life: 65% of undergraduates are from New York. Others are from 28 states, and 20 foreign countries. 70% are from public schools. 71% are white. The average age of freshmen is 19; all undergraduates, 21. 23% do not continue beyond their first year; 77% remain to graduate.

Housing: 1281 students can be accommodated in college housing, which includes single-sex and coed dorms. On-campus housing is guaranteed for all 4 years, is available on a first-come, first-served basis. 82% of students live on campus; of those, 25% remain on campus on weekends. Alcohol is not permitted. Upperclassmen may keep cars.

Activities: There are no fraternities or sororities. There are 30 groups on campus, including art, bagpipe, band, chorus, computers, drill team, ethnic, honors, international, jazz band, marching band, newspaper, pep band, photography, political, professional, religious, social, social service, and student government. Popular campus events include Thursdays in the TIV, Ring Dance, and Super Bowl Party.

Sports: There are 9 intercollegiate sports for men and 9 for women, and 6 intramural sports for men and 6 for women. Facilities include an athletic center containing a 2000-seat gym, a swimming pool, exercise and weight rooms, a rifle and pistol range, and 3 handball/racquetball and squash courts; a sailing center; and football, baseball, lacrosse, and soccer fields.

Disabled Students: 81% of the campus is accessible. Facilities include wheelchair ramps, elevators, special parking, and specially equipped rest rooms.

Services: Counseling and information services are available, as is tutoring in every subject.

Campus Safety and Security: Measures include 24-hour foot and vehicle patrol, emergency notification system, self-defense education, and security escort services. There are emergency telephones, lighted pathways/sidewalks, and controlled access to dorms/residences.

Programs of Study: New York Maritime confers B.S. and B.E. degrees. Associates and master's degrees are also awarded. Bachelor's degrees are awarded in BIOLOGICAL SCIENCE (marine science), BUSINESS (business administration and management and transportation management), COMPUTER AND PHYSICAL SCIENCE (atmospheric sciences and meteorology), ENGINEERING AND ENVIRONMENTAL DESIGN (electrical/electronics engineering, engineering, environmental science, marine engineering, maritime science, and naval architecture and marine engineering), SOCIAL SCIENCE (humanities). Marine operations, marine environmental science, and electrical engineering are the strongest academically. Marine transportation, marine engineering, and international transportation and trade have the largest enrollments.

Required: Bachelor's degree candidates must earn 126 to 181 credit hours, with a GPA of 2.0 and distribution requirements vary by the major. If pursuing the U.S. Merchant Marine officers' license, all students must spend 3 summer semesters at sea acquiring hands-on experience aboard the college's training vessel.

Special: The college offers co-op programs in engineering, an accelerated degree program in marine transportation/transportation management, and internships as cadet observers aboard commercial ships. There are 2 national honor societies, a freshman honors program, and 2 departmental honors programs.

Faculty/Classroom: 89% of faculty are male; 11% are female. 96% teach undergraduates. No introductory courses are taught by graduate stu-

dents. The average class size in an introductory lecture is 28; in a laboratory is 16; and in a regular course is 30.

Requirements: The SAT is required. Applicants must be high school graduates or hold a GED. 16 Carnegie units are required, including 4 years of English, 3 of math (4 are preferred), and 1 of physics or chemistry. An essay is required and an interview is recommended. A GPA of 80.0 is required. AP and CLEP credits are accepted. Important factors in the admissions decision are advanced placement or honors courses, extracurricular activities record, and leadership record.

Procedure: Freshmen are admitted fall and spring. Entrance exams should be taken during the junior or senior year. There are early decision, early admissions, deferred admissions, and rolling admissions plans. Check with the school for current application deadlines. The application fee is $40. Notification of early decision is sent December 15. Applications are accepted online.

Transfer: 77 transfer students enrolled in a recent year. Transfer students must have a 2.5 GPA.

Visiting: There are regularly scheduled orientations for prospective students, including a tour of the campus and facilities and meetings with faculty and students. There are guides for informal visits, visitors may sit in on classes, and stay overnight. To schedule a visit, contact the Admissions Office.

Financial Aid: In a recent year, 77% of all full-time freshmen and 80% of continuing full-time students received some form of financial aid. 44% of all full-time freshmen and 47% of continuing full-time students received need-based aid. The FAFSA the college's own financial statement, and student and parent federal income tax returns are required. Check with the school for current application deadlines.

International Students: There were 94 international students enrolled in a recent year. The school actively recruits these students. They must take the TOEFL and the SAT or ACT.

Computers: Each student has access to 5 public computer labs within the science and engineering building, which is wireless. The library and fort classrooms are also wireless. All students may access the system from 8:30 a.m. to 11 p.m. The computer center stays open after 11 p.m. when there is sufficient demand. There are no time limits. The fee is $267 per year.

Graduates: In a recent year, 306 bachelor's degrees were awarded. The most popular majors were marine transportation (30%), international transportation and trade (18%), and naval architecture (9%). 22 companies recruited on campus in a recent year. In an average class, 31% graduate in 4 years or less, 47% graduate in 5 years or less, and 49% graduate in 6 years or less. Of a recent graduating class, 4% were enrolled in graduate school within 6 months of graduation, and 100% were employed.

Admissions Contact: Dean of Admissions. A campus DVD is available.
E-Mail: *sunymaritime.edu* Web: *www.sunymaritime.edu*

MARYMOUNT MANHATTAN COLLEGE D-5

New York, NY 10021 (212) 517-0555
(800) 627-9668; (212) 517-0448

Full-time: 450 men, 1300 women	**Faculty:** n/av; IIB, av$
Part-time: 25 men, 30 women	**Ph.D.s:** 91%
Graduate: n/av	**Student/Faculty:** n/av
Year: semesters, summer session	**Tuition:** $25,280
Application Deadline: open	**Room & Board:** $14,530
Freshman Class: n/av	
SAT or ACT: required	

VERY COMPETITIVE

Marymount Manhattan College is an urban, independent liberal arts college, offering programs in the arts and sciences for all ages, as well as substantial preprofessional preparation. The figures in the above capsule and in this profile are approximate. The library contains 75,000 volumes, 70 microform items, and 4,000 audio/video tapes/CDs/DVDs, and subscribes to 2,740 periodicals including electronic. Computerized library services include interlibrary loans, database searching, Internet access, and laptop Internet portals. Special learning facilities include a learning resource center, art gallery, radio station, TV station, and a communications arts multimedia suite featuring digital editing technology. The 1-acre campus is in an urban area in Manhattan. Including any residence halls, there are 3 buildings.

Student Life: 55% of undergraduates are from out of state, mostly the Middle Atlantic. Students are from 44 states, 26 foreign countries, and Canada. 57% are from public schools. 68% are white; 14% Hispanic; 12% African American. The average age of freshmen is 18; all undergraduates, 20. 38% do not continue beyond their first year; 49% remain to graduate.

Housing: 780 students can be accommodated in college housing, which includes single-sex and coed dorms and off-campus apartments. On-campus housing is available on a first-come, first-served basis, and is available on a lottery system for upperclassmen. Priority is given to out-of-town students. 64% of students commute. Alcohol is not permitted. All students may keep cars.

Activities: There are no fraternities; 1% of women belong to 2 national sororities. There are 29 groups on campus, including art, choir, computers, dance, drama, ethnic, film, gay, honors, international, literary magazine, musical theater, newspaper, photography, political, professional, radio and TV, religious, social, social service, and student government. Popular campus events include Strawberry Festival, Honors Day, and Holiday Soiree.

Sports: There are 3 intramural sports for men and 3 for women. Facilities include a 300-seat auditorium.

Disabled Students: All of the campus is accessible. Facilities include wheelchair ramps, elevators, specially equipped restrooms, special class scheduling, and lowered drinking fountains.

Services: Counseling and information services are available, as is tutoring in every subject. There is remedial math, reading, and writing.

Campus Safety and Security: Measures include 24-hour foot and vehicle patrol and self-defense education. There are shuttle buses, lighted pathways/sidewalks, security cameras, and photo ID check-in.

Programs of Study: MMC confers B.A., B.S., and B.F.A. degrees. Associate degrees are also awarded. Bachelor's degrees are awarded in BIOLOGICAL SCIENCE (biology/biological science), BUSINESS (accounting and business administration and management), COMMUNICATIONS AND THE ARTS (communications, dance, dramatic arts, English, and fine arts), COMPUTER AND PHYSICAL SCIENCE (information sciences and systems), EDUCATION (elementary education), HEALTH PROFESSIONS (premedicine and speech pathology/audiology), SOCIAL SCIENCE (history, international studies, liberal arts/general studies, philosophy and religion, political science/government, psychology, and sociology). Theater, communications, and business are the strongest academically.

Required: To graduate, students must complete 120 credit hours, including 31 to 71 in the major, with a minimum GPA of 2.0. The core plus shared curriculum totals 48 credits in the areas of critical thinking, psychology and philosophy, quantitative reasoning and science, the modern world, communications/language, and the arts.

Special: MMC offers study abroad, interdisciplinary courses, pass/fail options, nondegree study, credit for life experience, and some 250 internships in all majors. Cooperative programs in business and finance, dance, music, languages, nursing, and urban education are offered in conjunction with local colleges and institutes. There is a January mini-session, cross-registration with Hunter College, and the China Institute, and a 5-year masters in publishing with Pace University. There are 7 national honor societies and 5 departmental honors programs.

Faculty/Classroom: 51% of faculty are male; 49% are female. 65% teach undergraduates. No introductory courses are taught by graduate students. The average class size in an introductory lecture, 25, in a laboratory, 15, and in a regular course, 20.

Requirements: The SAT or ACT is required. Applicants should be graduates of an accredited secondary school or have a GED certificate. MMC recommends completion of 16 academic units, including 4 each in English and electives, and 3 each in language, math, social science, and science. Recommendations are required, and an interview is strongly advised. Applicants to the dance and acting programs must audition. A GPA of 2.5 is required. AP and CLEP credits are accepted. Important factors in the admissions decision are personality/intangible qualities, evidence of special talent, and leadership record.

Procedure: Freshmen are admitted to all sessions. Entrance exams should be taken as early as possible. There are deferred admissions and rolling admissions plans. Application deadlines are open. Notification is sent on a rolling basis. Applications are accepted online. A waiting list is maintained.

Transfer: 151 transfer students enrolled in a recent year. Applicants who have graduated from high school less then 5 years ago must meet standard freshman requirements and must submit official transcripts from all colleges attended. 30 of 120 credits required for the bachelor's degree must be completed at MMC.

Visiting: There are regularly scheduled orientations for prospective students, including an interview with an admissions counselor, a tour of the school and dorms, and a meeting with a financial aid adviser. There are guides for informal visits and visitors may sit in on classes. To schedule a visit, contact the Admissions Office.

Financial Aid: In a recent year, at least 72% of all full-time freshmen and 75% of continuing full-time students received some form of financial aid. At least 70% of all full-time freshmen and 59% of continuing full-time students received need-based aid. The average freshman award was $14,025. Need-based scholarships or need-based grants averaged $11,158; need-based self-help aid (loans and jobs) averaged $3,686. Institutional awards averaged $5,263. 75% of undergraduate students worked part-time. Average annual earnings from campus work were $2500. The FAFSA and TAP for (New York state residents) are required. Check with the school for current application deadlines.

International Students: In a recent year, there were 58 international students enrolled. The school actively recruits these students. They must take the TOEFL. They must also take the SAT or ACT.

Computers: Wireless access is available. There are 2 PC labs with 22 stations each in the main building, and 1 PC lab for general use in the library. These are specialized computer labs for communications students and arts students. Wireless access is available in the library and in the Nugent building. There are 100 laptops in the library that can be used to access the Internet. All students may access the system. There are no time limits and no fees.

Graduates: In a recent year, 338 bachelor's degrees were awarded. The most popular majors were visual/performing arts (37%), journalism (27%), and social sciences (12%). 37 companies recruited on campus in a recent year. In an average class, 39% graduate in 4 years or less, 48% graduate in 5 years or less, and 49% graduate in 6 years or less. Of a recent graduating class, 23% were enrolled in graduate school within 6 months of graduation, and 63% were employed.

Admissions Contact: Dean of Admissions. E-Mail: *admissions@mmm.edu* Web: *www.mmm.edu*

MEDAILLE COLLEGE A-1

Buffalo, NY 14214 **(716) 880-2200; (716) 880-2007**

Full-time: 580 men, 1069 women
Part-time: 42 men, 152 women
Graduate: 179 men, 611 women
Year: semesters, summer session
Application Deadline:
Freshman Class: 1497 applied, 895 accepted, 400 enrolled
SAT CR/M: 460/460

Faculty: n/av; IIB, --$
Ph.D.s: 62%
Student/Faculty: 16 to 1
Tuition: $23,812
Room & Board: $11,300
ACT: 21 **VERY COMPETITIVE**

Medaille College, founded in 1875, is a private, nonsectarian institution offering undergraduate programs in liberal arts, education, business, and sciences, and graduate programs in business and education, to a primarily commuter student body. There is one graduate school. The library contains 55,690 volumes, and 1,411 audio/video tapes/CDs/DVDs, and subscribes to 236 periodicals including electronic. Computerized library services include interlibrary loans, database searching, Internet access, and Wi-Fi capability. Special learning facilities include a radio station, TV station, new media institute. The 13-acre campus is in an urban area 3 miles from downtown Buffalo. Including any residence halls, there are 17 buildings.

Student Life: 92% of undergraduates are from New York. Others are from 17 states, 4 foreign countries, and Canada. 61% are White; 16% African American. The average age of freshmen is 18; all undergraduates, 24. 32% do not continue beyond their first year; 68% remain to graduate.

Housing: 420 students can be accommodated in college housing, which includes single-sex and coed dorms and on-campus apartments. On-campus housing is available on a first-come and first-served basis. 80% of students commute. All students may keep cars.

Activities: There are no fraternities or sororities. There are 26 groups on campus, including academic clubs, art, cheerleading, dance, drama, environmental, ethnic, gay, honors, literary magazine, musical theater, newspaper, photography, professional, radio and TV, social, and student government. Popular campus events include Founders Day, Silent Auction, Campus Carnival and Honors Convocation.

Sports: There are 7 intercollegiate sports for men and 8 for women, and 3 intramural sports for men and 3 for women. Facilities include an NCAA regulation gym located in the student center, and a softball and soccer field.

Disabled Students: All of the campus is accessible. Facilities include wheelchair ramps, elevators, special parking, specially equipped restrooms, lowered drinking fountains, and lowered telephones.

Services: Counseling and information services are available, as is tutoring in most subjects. There is a reader service for the blind, and remedial math, reading, and writing.

Campus Safety and Security: Measures include 24-hour foot and vehicle patrol, emergency notification system, self-defense education, and security escort services. There are shuttle buses, emergency telephones, lighted pathways/sidewalks, and controlled access to dorms/residences.

Programs of Study: Medaille confers B.A., B.S., B.B.A. and B.S.Ed. degrees. Associate and master's degrees are also awarded. Bachelor's degrees are awarded in BIOLOGICAL SCIENCE (biology/biological science), BUSINESS (business administration and management and sports management), COMMUNICATIONS AND THE ARTS (communications and English), EDUCATION (early childhood education, elementary education, and middle school education), HEALTH PROFESSIONS (veterinary science), SOCIAL SCIENCE (criminal justice, liberal arts/general studies, psychology, and social science). Education, business, communication, and veterinary technology are the strongest academically. Education, business administration, and veterinary technology have the largest enrollments.

Required: The bachelor's degree requires successful completion of 120 credit hours or 128 for elementary education and biology majors. In addition to specific course requirements for each major, students must maintain a minimum GPA of 2.0. Students must also complete a general education core curriculum of 30 required credits in Self and Others (3 credits); U.S. Colonial History (3 credits); Creative Expression (3 credits); Scientific Discovery, (3 credits); Mathematics (3 credits); Communication (9 credits) and 6 credits in baccalaureate capstone courses.

Special: Cross-registration is available with colleges in the Western New York Consortium. Most degree programs require internships. Opportunities are provided for student-designed majors, credit by examination, pass/fail options, accelerated degrees, dual majors, and credit for work experience. There are 2 national honor societies and a freshman honors program.

Faculty/Classroom: 50% of faculty are male; 50% are female. No introductory courses are taught by graduate students. The average class size in an introductory lecture is 20; in a laboratory is 10; and in a regular course is 14.

Admissions: 60% of the 2013-2014 applicants were accepted. The SAT scores for the 2013-2014 freshman class were: Critical Reading--80% below 500, 17% between 500 and 599, 2% between 600 and 699, and 1% between 700 and 800; Math--72% below 500, 22% between 500 and 599, and 6% between 600 and 699.

Requirements: The SAT is required. Applicants must be graduates of an accredited secondary school or hold the GED. An essay and an interview are required. A GPA of 70.0 is required. AP and CLEP credits are accepted. Important factors in the admissions decision are advanced placement or honors courses, personality/intangible qualities, and leadership record.

Procedure: Freshmen are admitted to all sessions. Entrance exams should be taken in May. There are deferred admissions and rolling admissions plans. Applications should be filed by January 15 for spring entry; May 15 for summer entry, along with a $25 fee. Notification is sent on a rolling basis. Applications are accepted online.

Transfer: 205 transfer students enrolled in 2012-2013. Transfer applicants must have a minimum GPA of 2.0 in their previous college work. An interview and recommendations are required. 30 of 120 credits required for the bachelor's degree must be completed at Medaille.

Visiting: There are regularly scheduled orientations for prospective students, including campus tours, academic program meetings, ice-breakers, and a review of policies and procedures. There are guides for informal visits, visitors may sit in on classes, and stay overnight. To schedule a visit, contact Karen McGrath at (716) 880-2200.

Financial Aid: In 2013-2014, 100% of all full-time freshmen and 98% of continuing full-time students received some form of financial aid. 100% of all full-time freshmen and 97% of continuing full-time students received need-based aid. The average freshman award was $13,473. 15% of undergraduate students work part-time. Average annual earnings from campus work are $1500. Medaille is a member of CSS. The FAFSA, the state aid form, and the college's own financial statement are required. The deadline for filing freshman financial aid applications for fall entry is March 1.

International Students: There are 4 international students enrolled. The school actively recruits these students. They must take the TOEFL with a minimum score of 550 on the paper-based TOEFL (PBT) or 61 on the Internet-based version (iBT). They must also take the SAT.

Computers: All students may access the system. There are no time limits and no fees.

Graduates: From July 1, 2012 to June 30, 2013, 316 bachelor's degrees were awarded. The most popular majors were business administration (34%), veterinary technology (18%), and education (9%). 75 companies recruited on campus in 2012-2013. In an average class, 35% graduate in 4 years or less, 41% graduate in 5 years or less, and 45% graduate in 6 years or less. Of the 2012 graduating class, 28% were enrolled in graduate school within 6 months of graduation, and 95% were employed.

Admissions Contact: Karen McGrath, Vice President for Enrollment Management. E-Mail: *admissionsug@medaille.edu* Web: *www.medaille.edu*

MEDGAR EVERS COLLEGE / THE CITY UNIVERSITY OF NEW YORK D-5

Brooklyn, NY 11225-2201 **(718) 270-6024; (718) 270-6198**

Full-time: 1250 men, 3400 women
Part-time: 510 men, 1920 women
Graduate: n/av
Year: semesters, summer session
Application Deadline: open
Freshman Class: n/av
SAT or ACT: required

Faculty: 179; IIB, +$
Ph.D.s: 55%
Student/Faculty: n/av
Tuition: $5432 ($14,102)
Room & Board: n/av
NONCOMPETITIVE

Medgar Evers College, established in 1969 as part of the City University of New York, is an undergraduate commuter institution offering programs in business, education, natural sciences and math, nursing, and social sciences. Some figures in the above capsule and in this profile are approximate. In addition to regional accreditation, MEC has baccalaureate program accreditation with NCATE and NLN. The library contains 120,000 volumes, 42,225 microform items, and 6000 audio/video tapes/CDs/DVDs, and subscribes to 36,282 periodicals including electronic. Computerized library services include interlibrary loans, database searching, and Internet access. Special learning facilities include a learning resource center, radio station, TV station, and a TV lab. The 8-acre campus is in an urban area located in Central Brooklyn of New York City. There are 3 buildings.

Student Life: 97% of undergraduates are from New York. Others are from 4 states, 75 foreign countries, and Canada. 99% are from public schools. 90% are African American. The average age of freshmen is 21; all undergraduates, 27.7. 58% do not continue beyond their first year; 10% remain to graduate.

Housing: There are no residence halls. All students commute.

Activities: There are no fraternities or sororities. There are 25 groups on campus, including cheerleading, choir, dance, drama, ethnic, gay, jazz band, newspaper, political, professional, radio and TV, religious, social, social service, and student government. Popular campus events include Kwanzaa and Black Solidarity Day.

Sports: There are 4 intercollegiate sports for men and 3 for women, and 5 intramural sports for men and 3 for women. Facilities include a swimming pool, a gym, and an exercise room.

Disabled Students: All of the campus is accessible. Facilities include wheelchair ramps, elevators, special parking, specially equipped rest rooms, lowered drinking fountains, and lowered telephones.

Services: Counseling and information services are available, as is tutoring in every subject. There is a reader service for the blind, and remedial math, reading, and writing.

Campus Safety and Security: Measures include 24-hour foot and vehicle patrol.

Programs of Study: MEC confers B.A. and B.S. degrees. Associate degrees are also awarded. Bachelor's degrees are awarded in BIOLOGICAL SCIENCE (biology/biological science), BUSINESS (accounting, business administration and management, and management information systems), COMMUNICATIONS AND THE ARTS (English), COMPUTER AND PHYSICAL SCIENCE (computer science and mathematics), EDUCATION (elementary education and special education), ENGINEERING AND ENVIRONMENTAL DESIGN (environmental science), HEALTH PROFESSIONS (nursing), SOCIAL SCIENCE (liberal arts/general studies, psychology, and public administration). Nursing is the strongest academically. Education has the largest enrollment.

Required: To graduate, students must complete 120 credits (depending on the program) with a minimum GPA of 2.0. The core curriculum requires a total of 42 credits in English, philosophy, speech, math, liberal arts, career planning, and phys ed. Students must demonstrate proficiency in basic reading, writing, and math skills prior to entering their junior year.

Special: MEC offers exchange programs with other CUNY institutions, evening and weekend classes, credit for military and prior learning experience, pass/fail options, and nondegree study. Study abroad in 3 countries is also possible. There is 1 national honor society, a freshman honors program, and 11 departmental honors programs.

Faculty/Classroom: 54% of faculty are male; 46% are female. All teach undergraduates, and 8% do research. The average class size in an introductory lecture is 26; in a laboratory, 20; and in a regular course, 25.

Admissions: 20% of a recent year's applicants were accepted.

Requirements: The SAT or ACT is required. MEC accepts all applicants who either are graduates of an accredited secondary school or have earned a GED with a score of 225 or higher. Students must meet the university's health standards. CLEP credits are accepted.

Procedure: Freshmen are admitted fall and spring. Entrance exams should be taken during the last year of high school. There is a rolling admissions plan. Application deadlines are open. Application fee is $65.

Transfer: 779 transfer students enrolled in a recent year. Applicants must have a minimum GPA of 2.0. Those students with fewer than 24 college credits must also submit a high school transcript. 32 of 120 credits required for the bachelor's degree must be completed at MEC.

Financial Aid: In a recent year, 85% of all full-time freshmen and 81% of continuing full-time students received some form of financial aid, including need-based aid. The average freshman award was $3406, with $3707 ($5225 maximum) from need-based scholarships or need-based grants and $710 ($1742 maximum) from need-based self-help aid (loans and jobs). 40% of undergraduate students work part-time. The FAFSA and CUNY Student Aid Form (CSAF) are required. Check with the school for current application deadlines.

International Students: There were 112 international students enrolled in a recent year. The school actively recruits these students. They must take the TOEFL with a minimum score of 475 on the paper-based TOEFL (PBT). They must also take the ACT and the college's own entrance exam.

Computers: Wireless access is available. Students can access PCs in any of the college's 3 computer labs and in the library. All students may access the system. There are no time limits. There is a fee.

Graduates: In a recent year, 329 bachelor's degrees were awarded. The most popular majors were public administration (17%), psychology (15%), and business (15%). 15 companies recruited on campus in a recent year. In an average class, 5% graduate in 4 years or less, 11% graduate in 5 years or less, and 19% graduate in 6 years or less.

Admissions Contact: Director of Admissions. E-Mail: *enroll@mec.cuny.edu* Web: *www.mec.cuny.edu*

MERCY COLLEGE — D-5

Dobbs Ferry, NY 10522 — (877) 637-2946
(877) MERCY-GO; 914-674-7382

Full-time: 1729 men, 3818 women
Part-time: 768 men, 1839 women
Graduate: 685 men, 2809 women
Year: semesters, summer session
Application Deadline: open
Freshman Class: 6394 applied, 4013 accepted, 837 enrolled
Faculty: 198; IIA, av$
Ph.D.s: 83%
Student/Faculty: 18 to 1
Tuition: $17,576
Room & Board: $12,390

COMPETITIVE

Mercy College, founded in 1950, is a private institution dedicated to offering a curriculum of liberal arts and sciences as well as preprofessional and professional programs. Graduate programs provide advanced preparation in selected disciplines. There are 5 undergraduate schools and 5 graduate schools. In addition to regional accreditation, Mercy has baccalaureate program accreditation with CSWE and NASAD. The 4 libraries contain 150,000 volumes, and 3,000 audio/video tapes/CDs/DVDs, and subscribe to 20,040 periodicals including electronic. Computerized library services include interlibrary loans, database searching, Internet access, and Wi-Fi capability. Special learning facilities include a TV station, a computer lab, reference library, and a digital arts center. The 64-acre campus is in a suburban area 12 miles north of New York City. Including any residence halls, there are 10 buildings.

Student Life: 93% of undergraduates are from New York. Others are from 42 states, 45 foreign countries, and Canada. 35% are White; 29% Hispanic; 24% African American. The average age of freshmen is 19; all undergraduates, 24. 30% do not continue beyond their first year; 35% remain to graduate.

Housing: 400 students can be accommodated in college housing, which includes coed dorms. On-campus housing is available on a first-come and first-served basis. Priority is given to out-of-town students. 93% of students commute. Alcohol is not permitted. All students may keep cars.

Activities: There are no fraternities or sororities. There are 18 groups on campus, including and PACT mentoring program, veterinary club, cheerleading, chess, communications, computers, dance, drama, environmental, ethnic, film, gay, honors, international, literary magazine, newspaper, political, professional, religious, social, social service, student government, and student military veteran club. Popular campus events include Veterans Day Activities, Founders Day, Open Houses, Major League Baseball Events, Broadway Shows, Spring Fling Festival, Poetry Readings and Club Fairs.

Sports: There are 4 intercollegiate sports for men and 6 for women, and 1 intramural sports for men and 2 for women. Facilities include a gym, a soccer/baseball/softball field, 3 swimming pools, 2 tennis courts, a track, a basketball/volleyball court and a fitness center.

Disabled Students: 75% of the campus is accessible. Facilities include wheelchair ramps, elevators, special parking, specially equipped restrooms, special class scheduling, and lowered drinking fountains.

Services: Counseling and information services are available, as is tutoring in every subject. There is a reader service for the blind.

Campus Safety and Security: Measures include 24-hour foot and vehicle patrol, emergency notification system, self-defense education, and security escort services. There are emergency telephones, lighted pathways/sidewalks, and controlled access to dorms/residences.

Programs of Study: Mercy confers B.A., B.F.A and B.S. degrees. Associate, master's, and doctoral degrees are also awarded. Bachelor's degrees are awarded in BIOLOGICAL SCIENCE (biology/biological science), BUSINESS (accounting, banking and finance, business administration and management, business (dual major program), and entrepreneurial studies), COMMUNICATIONS AND THE ARTS (broadcasting, communications, English, film, television and digital media, fine arts, journalism, media arts, music, music industry, music technology, and Spanish), COMPUTER AND PHYSICAL SCIENCE (computer science, digital arts/technology, information sciences and systems, and mathematics), EDUCATION (elementary education, special education, and teaching English as a second/foreign language (TESOL/TEFOL)), HEALTH PROFESSIONS (exercise science, health science, medical laboratory technology, nursing, speech pathology/audiology, and veterinary science), SOCIAL SCIENCE (behavioral science, communication sciences & disorders, criminal justice, history, interdisciplinary studies, legal studies, liberal arts/general studies, paralegal studies, political science/government, psychology, social work, and sociology). Health professions programs are the strongest academically. Business and education have the largest enrollments.

Required: To graduate, students must complete 120 semester hours with a minimum GPA of 2.0 overall. In total 30 semester hours must be completed at Mercy. The Mercy College General Education Curriculum includes: 6 English credits, 3 speech credits, 6 history credits, 9 social science credits, 3 philosophy/religion credits, 3 art/music credits, 3 foreign language credits, 3 math credits, 3 computer science credits, and 3 natural science credits.

Special: Mercy offers internships and cooperative education in each major, an on-campus employment program with a community service component, study abroad, dual majors and degrees, credit for life experience, non-degree study, and pass/fail options. There are 7 national honor societies, including Phi Beta Kappa, a freshman honors program, and 14 departmental honors programs.

Faculty/Classroom: 33% of faculty are male; 67% are female. All teach undergraduates. No introductory courses are taught by graduate students. The average class size in an introductory lecture is 18 and in a regular course is 18.

Admissions: 63% of the 2013-2014 applicants were accepted.

Requirements: Applicants must be graduates of an accredited secondary school or have a GED certificate. They should have completed at least 16 academic units. An essay and an interview is required and a letter of recommendation from the high school counselor or principal is required. A GPA of 2.5 is required. AP and CLEP credits are accepted. Important factors in the admissions decision are recommendations by school officials, personality/intangible qualities, and leadership record.

Procedure: Freshmen are admitted fall, spring, and summer. Entrance exams should be taken between January and August of their senior year. There are early decision, deferred admissions, and rolling admissions plans. Application deadlines are open. Application fee is $40. Notification is sent on a rolling basis. Applications are accepted online.

Transfer: 1011 transfer students enrolled in 2012-2013. Applicants must submit official transcripts from all colleges attended and must also submit their high school transcript. An interview is required. An essay is also required. 30 of 120 credits required for the bachelor's degree must be completed at Mercy.

Visiting: There are regularly scheduled orientations for prospective students, including spring and fall open houses and information sessions. There are guides for informal visits and visitors may sit in on classes. To schedule a visit, contact the Admissions Office.

Financial Aid: The average freshman award was $14,078. Need-based scholarships or need-based grants averaged $10,525; need based self-help aid (loans and jobs) averaged $3,430; non-need-based athletic scholarships averaged $4,694; and other non-need-based awards and non-need-based scholarships averaged $3,357. 1% of undergraduate students work part-time. The average financial indebtedness of the 2013 graduate was $19,745. The FAFSA is required. The priority date for freshman financial aid applications for fall entry is February 15.

International Students: There are 33 international students enrolled. The school actively recruits these students. They must take the TOEFL with a minimum score of 550 on the paper-based TOEFL (PBT) or 79 on the Internet-based version (iBT) and the college's own test.

Computers: All students may access the system. There are no time limits and no fees.

Graduates: From July 1, 2012 to June 30, 2013, 1183 bachelor's degrees were awarded. The most popular majors were behavioral science (31%), health science (22%), and business (14%). 212 companies recruited on campus in 2012-2013. In an average class, 23% graduate in 4 years or less, 32% graduate in 5 years or less, and 35% graduate in 6 years or less.

Admissions Contact: Dierdre Whitman, Vice President for Enrollment Management. E-Mail: *admissions@mercy.edu* Web: *www.mercy.edu*

METROPOLITAN COLLEGE OF NEW YORK D-5

New York, NY 10013 (212) 343-1234, ext. 5001; (212) 343-8470

Full-time: 631 men and women	**Faculty:** n/av
Part-time: 45 men and women	**Ph.D.s:** 84%
Graduate: 409 men and women	**Student/Faculty:** n/av
Year: semesters, summer session	**Tuition:** $17,000
Application Deadline: open	**Room & Board:** n/av

Freshman Class: 650 applied, 330 accepted, 126 enrolled

VERY COMPETITIVE

Metropolitan College of New York, founded in 1964, is a private commuter institution offering programs in human services and business management. All bachelor degree programs involve a combination of class work and field work and may be completed in 2 years and 8 months. Most master's degree programs can be completed in 1 year. There are 2 undergraduate schools and 2 graduate schools. The library contains 32,000 volumes and 1800 microform items, and subscribes to 3300 periodicals including electronic. Computerized library services include interlibrary loans, database searching, and Internet access. Special learning facilities include a learning resource center. The campus is in an urban area in New York City. There is 1 building.

Student Life: 99% of undergraduates are from New York. Others are from 4 states, 9 foreign countries, and Canada. 68% are from public schools. 63% are African American; 19% Hispanic. The average age of freshmen is 32; all undergraduates, 32. 40% do not continue beyond their first year; 43% remain to graduate.

Housing: There are no residence halls. All students commute.

Activities: There are no fraternities or sororities. There are 10 groups on campus, including computers, ethnic, gay, honors, newspaper, professional, social, social service, and student government. Popular campus events include career fairs, admissions open house, and dean's list ceremonies.

Sports: There is no sports program at the college.

Disabled Students: All of the campus is accessible. Facilities include wheelchair ramps, elevators, specially equipped restrooms, special class scheduling, lowered drinking fountains, and lowered telephones.

Services: Counseling and information services are available, as is tutoring in every subject. There is remedial math, reading, and writing.

Campus Safety and Security: Measures include 24-hour foot and vehicle patrol emergency notification system, lighted pathways/sidewalks, fire drills, and a fire escape stairwell.

Programs of Study: The college confers B.B.A. and B.P.S. degrees. Associate and master's degrees are also awarded. Bachelor's degrees are awarded in BUSINESS (business administration and management), EDUCATION (early childhood education), HEALTH PROFESSIONS (mental health/human services), SOCIAL SCIENCE (child care/child and family studies, community services, gerontology, human services, prelaw, psychology, and social work). Business management is the strongest academically. Human services has the largest enrollment.

Required: To graduate, students must complete 128 credit hours with a minimum GPA of 2.0. The curriculum is prescribed; no electives are featured. A constructive action document based on performance in the field and mastery of course work is required each semester.

Special: Internships include required weekly 14-hour field sites. Study abroad in 3 countries, work-study programs, B.A.-B.S. degrees, and accelerated degree programs in human services, business management, and American urban studies are offered, as well as credit by exam and credit for life experience.

Faculty/Classroom: 51% of faculty are male; 49% are female. 95% teach undergraduates, 10% do research, and 99% do both. No introductory courses are taught by graduate students. The average class size in a laboratory is 15 and in a regular course, 15.

Admissions: 51% of the 2011-2012 applicants were accepted.

Requirements: Students must take the ETS's Accuplacer Test in reading and math; recent high school graduates who have a satisfactory SAT score may present the SAT instead. Applicants must have graduated from an accredited secondary school. The GED is accepted. An essay and an interview are required. CLEP credits are accepted. Important factors in the admissions decision are evidence of special talent, leadership record, and personality/intangible qualities.

Procedure: Freshmen are admitted to all sessions. Entrance exams should be taken in the senior year. There are deferred admissions and rolling admissions plans. Applications should be filed by December 1 for spring entry and April 1 for summer entry, along with a $30 fee. Applications are accepted online.

Transfer: 45 transfer students enrolled in a recent year. Admission is based on current skills and abilities as measured on the entrance exam and essay. 64 of 128 credits required for the bachelor's degree must be completed at the college.

Visiting: There are regularly scheduled orientations for prospective students. There are guides for informal visits and visitors may sit in on classes. To schedule a visit, contact the Admissions Office.

Financial Aid: In a recent year, 96% of all full-time freshmen and 90% of continuing full-time students received some form of financial aid. The average freshman award was $13,611. Need-based scholarships or need-based grants averaged $10,154; need-based self-help aid (loans and jobs) averaged $3517. The CSS/Profile, FAFSA, and the New York State Higher Education Financial Statement are required. The priority date for freshman financial aid applications for fall entry is March. The deadline for filing freshman financial aid applications for fall entry is August 15.

International Students: The school actively recruits international students. They must take the TOEFL and the Accuplacer test.

Computers: All students may access the system whenever the college is open. There are no time limits. The fee is $100. It is strongly recommended that all students have a personal computer.

Graduates: In a recent year, 166 bachelor's degrees were awarded. 70 companies recruited on campus in a recent year. In an average class, 42% graduate in 4 years or less. Of a recent graduating class, 50% were enrolled in graduate school within 6 months of graduation, and 80% were employed.

Admissions Contact: Dean of Admissions. Web: *www.metropolitan.edu*

MOLLOY COLLEGE D-5

Rockville Centre, NY 11570 **(516) 323-4000; (516) 256-2247**

Full-time: 754 men, 1939 women
Part-time: 126 men, 556 women
Graduate: 228 men, 852 women
Year: 4-1-4, summer session
Application Deadline: open
Faculty: n/av; IIB, +$
Ph.D.s: 76%
Student/Faculty: 10 to 1
Tuition: $25,710
Room & Board: $13,240
Freshman Class: 3242 applied, 2356 accepted, 501 enrolled
SAT CR/M/W: 520/540/520 **ACT:** 23 **COMPETITIVE**

There are 6 graduate schools. In addition to regional accreditation, Molloy has baccalaureate program accreditation with CSWE, NCATE, and NLN. The library contains 143,300 volumes, and 4,600 audio/video tapes/CDs/DVDs, and subscribes to 36,000 periodicals including electronic. Computerized library services include interlibrary loans, database searching, and Internet access. Special learning facilities include an art gallery. The 30-acre campus is in a suburban area 20 miles east of New York City. Including any residence halls, there are 5 buildings.

Student Life: 99% of undergraduates are from New York. Others are from 14 states, and 7 foreign countries. 63% are White; 14% Hispanic; 13% African American. 64% are Catholic; 12% claim no religious affiliation. The average age of freshmen is 19; all undergraduates, 24. 11% do not continue beyond their first year; 66% remain to graduate.

Housing: 174 students can be accommodated in college housing, which includes coed dorms. Priority is given to out-of-town students. 95% of students commute. Alcohol is not permitted. All students may keep cars.

Activities: There are no fraternities or sororities. There are 48 groups on campus, including art, band, cheerleading, chess, chorus, dance, drama, ethnic, honors, international, jazz band, literary magazine, newspaper, professional, religious, social, social service, student government, and yearbook. Popular campus events include Scavenger Hunt, Halloween Party, Relay for Life, Safe Halloween, Hats and Stockings and Stuff a Bear.

Sports: There are 7 intercollegiate sports for men and 9 for women, and 3 intramural sports for men and 3 for women. Facilities include a gym, a dance studio, a weight room, sports fields, and basketball and tennis courts.

Disabled Students: All of the campus is accessible. Facilities include wheelchair ramps, elevators, special parking, specially equipped restrooms, special class scheduling, lowered drinking fountains, and lowered telephones.

Services: Counseling and information services are available, as is tutoring in every subject. There is a reader service for the blind, and remedial math, reading, and writing.

Campus Safety and Security: Measures include 24-hour foot and vehicle patrol, emergency notification system, and security escort services. There are shuttle buses, emergency telephones, lighted pathways/sidewalks, campus concerns committee.

Programs of Study: Molloy confers B.A., B.S., B.F.A. and B.S.W degrees. Associate, master's, and doctoral degrees are also awarded. Bachelor's degrees are awarded in BIOLOGICAL SCIENCE (biology/biological science), BUSINESS (accounting, business administration and management, and finance), COMMUNICATIONS AND THE ARTS (art, communications, English, music, and Spanish), COMPUTER AND PHYSICAL SCIENCE (computer science, information sciences and systems, and mathematics), EDUCATION (elementary education, secondary education, and special education), ENGINEERING AND ENVIRONMENTAL DESIGN (environmental science), HEALTH PROFESSIONS (health, music therapy, nursing, and speech pathology/audiology), SOCIAL SCIENCE (criminal justice, history, interdisciplinary studies, philosophy, political science/government, psychology, social work, sociology, and theological studies). Nursing, education, and business are the strongest academically.

Required: General Education requirements consist of 45 to 54 credits. A total of 128 to 137 credit hours is required for graduation.

Special: The college offers study abroad programs, dual degree programs, and other unique internship opportunities. There are 18 national honor societies and a freshman honors program.

Faculty/Classroom: 31% of faculty are male; 69% are female. No introductory courses are taught by graduate students. The average class size in an introductory lecture is 15; in a laboratory is 12; and in a regular course is 15.

Admissions: 73% of the 2013-2014 applicants were accepted. The SAT scores for the 2013-2014 freshman class were: Critical Reading--34% below 500, 53% between 500 and 599, 13% between 600 and 699, and 1% between 700 and 800; Math--25% below 500, 55% between 500 and 599, 20% between 600 and 699, and 1% between 700 and 800; Writing--39% below 500, 45% between 500 and 599, 15% between 600 and 699, and 1% between 700 and 800. The ACT scores were 27% below 21, 33% between 21 and 23, 27% between 24 and 26, 8% between 27 and 28, and 5% above 28.

Requirements: The SAT or ACT is required. The ACT Optional Writing test is also required. In addition, applicants should be graduates of a secondary school or have a GED. Preparation should include 4 units of English and social studies, 3 units of math, science, foreign language and history. An essay is required and an interview is recommended. Music students must audition and take a theory exam. AP and CLEP credits are accepted. Important factors in the admissions decision are advanced placement or honors courses, recommendations by school officials, and extracurricular activities record.

Procedure: Freshmen are admitted fall and spring. Entrance exams should be taken in the fall of the senior year. There are early admissions, deferred admissions, and rolling admissions plans. Application deadlines are open. Application fee is $30. Notifications are sent by October 15. Applications are accepted online.

Transfer: 384 transfer students enrolled in 2012-2013. A minimum college GPA of 2.0 is required, with some majors requiring a higher GPA. An interview is recommended. 30 of 128 credits required for the bachelor's degree must be completed at Molloy.

Visiting: There are regularly scheduled orientations for prospective students, including an address by the president of the college, department presentations, campus tours, and admissions, financial aid, and scholarship information. There are guides for informal visits and visitors may sit in on classes. To schedule a visit, contact the Admissions Office.

Financial Aid: Molloy is a member of CSS. The FAFSA is required. The priority date for freshman financial aid applications for fall entry is April 15. The deadline for filing freshman financial aid applications for fall entry is May 1.

International Students: There are 6 international students enrolled. They must take the TOEFL with a minimum score of 500 on the paper-based TOEFL (PBT).

Computers: All students may access the system. There are no time limits and no fees.

Graduates: From July 1, 2012 to June 30, 2013, 742 bachelor's degrees were awarded. The most popular majors were nursing (42%), education (13%), and business (8%). In an average class, 38% graduate in 4 years or less, 62% graduate in 5 years or less, and 66% graduate in 6 years or less.

Admissions Contact: Marguerite Lane, Dean of Admissions. E-Mail: *mlane@molloy.edu* Web: *www.molloy.edu*

MONROE COLLEGE D-5

Bronx, NY 10468 **(718) 933-6700**
(800) 55 MONROE; (718) 364-3552

Full-time: 1415 men, 3515 women
Part-time: 160 men, 410 women
Graduate: n/av
Year: varies, summer session
Application Deadline: see profile
Freshman Class: n/av
SAT: recommended
Faculty: n/av
Ph.D.s: n/av
Student/Faculty: n/av
Tuition: $11,640
Room & Board: $6500
COMPETITIVE

Monroe College, founded in 1933, offers bachelor's degrees in accounting, business management, computer information systems, criminal justice, hospitality management, and health services administration. The figures in the above capsule and in this profile are approximate. Computerized library services include interlibrary loans, database searching, Internet access, and laptop Internet portals. Special learning facilities include a learning resource center. The campus is located in the Fordham Road section of the Bronx. Including any residence halls, there are 5 buildings.

Student Life: 96% of undergraduates are from New York. 46% are African American; 42% Hispanic. The average age of freshmen is 23; all undergraduates, 26.

Housing: 620 students can be accommodated in college housing, which includes single-sex and coed dorms and off-campus apartments. In addition, there are honors houses. On-campus housing is guaranteed for all 4 years. 90% of students commute. All students may keep cars.

Activities: There are no fraternities or sororities. Groups on campus include cheerleading, computers, dance, drama, honors, literary magazine, newspaper, professional, and social service. Popular campus events include talent shows, President's and Deans' List Galas and cultural trips to New York City.

Sports: There is no sports program at Monroe.

Disabled Students: All of the campus is accessible. Facilities include wheelchair ramps, elevators, special parking, specially equipped restrooms, special class scheduling, lowered drinking fountains, lowered telephones, and special housing.

Services: Counseling and information services are available, as is tutoring in every subject. There is a reader service for the blind, and remedial math, reading, and writing.

Campus Safety and Security: Measures include 24-hour foot and vehicle patrol, self-defense education, and security escort services. There are shuttle buses, emergency telephones, and lighted pathways/sidewalks.

Programs of Study: confers B.S. and B.B.A. degrees. Associates and master's degrees are also awarded. Bachelor's degrees are awarded in BUSINESS (accounting, business administration and management, and hospitality management services), COMPUTER AND PHYSICAL SCI-

ENCE (information sciences and systems), HEALTH PROFESSIONS (health care administration), SOCIAL SCIENCE (criminal justice). Business management, criminal justice, and health services administration have the largest enrollments.

Required: To graduate, students must have 120 credit hours and at least a 2.0 GPA. The core curriculum includes courses in writing/literature, math, liberal arts, and business or technology.

Special: Co-op programs are available in all degree programs. Study abroad is available for culinary students interested in studying in Italy. There is 1 national honor society, a freshman honors program, and 1 departmental honors program.

Faculty/Classroom: All teach undergraduates. No introductory courses are taught by graduate students. The average class size in an introductory lecture is 30.

Requirements: The SAT is recommended, an application, an essay, and an interview are required. Monroe requires applicants to be in the upper 50% of their class. A GPA of 70.0 is required. AP and CLEP credits are accepted.

Procedure: Freshmen are admitted fall, winter, and spring. There are early decision and rolling admissions plans. Check with the school for current application deadlines.

Transfer: Transfer students must provide an official transcript from any prior institution they have attended in addition to the application and an essay. 30 of 120 credits required for the bachelor's degree must be completed at Monroe.

Visiting: There are regularly scheduled orientations for prospective students, including a variety of open houses during the semester in which applicants can tour the campus and talk with faculty and/pr chairs of individual departments. There are guides for informal visits; visitors may sit in on classes and stay overnight.

Financial Aid: The FAFSA, the state aid form, and the college's own financial statement are required. Check with the school for current application deadlines.

International Students: The school actively recruits these students.

Computers: Wireless access is available. There are a number of learning centers, libraries, and classrooms at both the Bronx and New Rochelle campuses where students have free use of more than 300 computers. Most of these computers have Internet access as well as access to the college's network. All students may access the system. There are no time limits and no fees.

Admissions Contact: Director of Admissions. A campus DVD is available. E-Mail: *admissions@monroecollege.edu* Web: *www.monroecollege.edu*

MOUNT SAINT MARY COLLEGE D-4

Newburgh, NY 12550 **(845) 569-3255**
(888) YES-MSMC; (845) 562-6762

Full-time: 538 men, 1024 women	**Faculty:** 92; IIB, av$
Part-time: 121 men, 340 women	**Ph.D.s:** 91%
Graduate: 95 men, 258 women	**Student/Faculty:** 20 to 1
Year: semesters, summer session	**Tuition:** $26,250
Application Deadline: open	**Room & Board:** $13,290
Freshman Class: 3551 applied, 3054 accepted, 449 enrolled	

COMPETITIVE

MSMC founded in 1959, is a private liberal arts college offering undergraduate programs leading to Bachelor of Arts and Bachelor of Science degrees, and graduate programs leading to the masters in education, nursing, and business administration. An accelerated evening program is offered for nontraditional and adult students. There are 3 graduate schools. In addition to regional accreditation, the Mount has baccalaureate program accreditation with NCATE. The 2 libraries contain 76,888 volumes, and 8,231 audio/video tapes/CDs/DVDs, and subscribe to 51,095 periodicals including electronic. Computerized library services include interlibrary loans, database searching, Internet access, and Wi-Fi capability. Special learning facilities include a radio station, elementary school, herbarium field station, and an arboretum. The 86-acre campus is in a suburban area 58 miles north of New York City. Including any residence halls, there are 41 buildings.

Student Life: 89% of undergraduates are from New York. Others are from 13 states. 76% are from public schools. 64% are White; 13% race unknown; 12% Hispanic. 49% are Baptist, Episcopalian, Lutheran or Methodist; 45% Catholic. The average age of freshmen is 18; all undergraduates, 23. 31% do not continue beyond their first year; 52% remain to graduate.

Housing: 1064 students can be accommodated in college housing, which includes single-sex and coed dorms. on-campus townhouses. On-campus housing is guaranteed for all 4 years. 54% of students commute. Upperclassmen may keep cars.

Activities: There are no fraternities or sororities. There are 37 groups on campus, including art, cheerleading, choir, computers, dance, drama, environmental, ethnic, gay, honors, literary magazine, musical theater, newspaper, photography, political, professional, radio and TV, religious, social, student government, and yearbook. Popular campus events include Spring Weekend, Siblings Weekend and Holiday Formal.

Sports: There are 9 intercollegiate sports for men and 9 for women, and 10 intramural sports for men and 10 for women. Facilities include The Elaine and William Kaplan Physical Recreation Center houses 3 regulation basketball courts, an elevated running track, a cardiovascular room, a fully equipped weight room, an aerobics studio, an indoor full-length swimming pool and a multipurpose room. The recently completed outdoor athletic complex features an all-weather, synthetic turf field, a natural grass field, and six hard court tennis courts.

Disabled Students: 95% of the campus is accessible. Facilities include wheelchair ramps, elevators, special parking, specially equipped restrooms, lowered telephones. Special equipment in the library and computer centers to accommodate students with poor vision.

Services: Counseling and information services are available, as is tutoring in every subject. There is remedial math, reading, and writing.

Campus Safety and Security: Measures include 24-hour foot and vehicle patrol, emergency notification system, self-defense education, and security escort services. There are shuttle buses, emergency telephones, lighted pathways/sidewalks, and controlled access to dorms/residences.

Programs of Study: the Mount confers B.A., B.S. and B.S.Ed. degrees. Master's degrees are also awarded. Bachelor's degrees are awarded in BIOLOGICAL SCIENCE (biology/biological science), BUSINESS (accounting and business administration and management), COMMUNICATIONS AND THE ARTS (English, information technology, media arts, and public relations), COMPUTER AND PHYSICAL SCIENCE (chemistry, mathematics, and science), EDUCATION (education), HEALTH PROFESSIONS (nursing), SOCIAL SCIENCE (Hispanic American studies, history, human services, interdisciplinary studies, political science/government, psychology, social science, social work, and sociology). Education, nursing, and business are the strongest academically and have the largest enrollments.

Required: A total of 120 credit hours is required for the B.A. or B.S., with 24 to 40 in the major and a minimum GPA of 2.0. Overall requirements are higher for nursing, medical technology, and education students. All students must achieve computer literacy before graduation.

Special: Co-op programs and internships are available in all majors. There is cross-registration with other mid-Hudson area colleges, as well as accelerated degree programs in business, accounting, and nursing, among others. There are several collaborative programs. The college also offers study abroad in more than 22 countries, a Washington semester, work-study, and dual and student-designed majors. Credit by exam and for life, military, and work experience is available for a maximum of 30 credits. There are 12 national honor societies and a freshman honors program.

Faculty/Classroom: 42% of faculty are male; 58% are female. 94% teach undergraduates. No introductory courses are taught by graduate students. The average class size in an introductory lecture is 20; in a laboratory is 11; and in a regular course is 19.

Admissions: 86% of the 2013-2014 applicants were accepted. 27% of the current freshmen were in the top fifth of their class; 61% were in the top two fifths.

Requirements: The SAT or ACT is required. Students should be graduates of an accredited secondary school. The GED is accepted. Applicants should prepare with 4 years each of English and history, and at least 3 each of math and science and 2 of foreign language. An essay and an interview are recommended. AP and CLEP credits are accepted. Important factors in the admissions decision are advanced placement or honors courses, evidence of special talent, and personality/intangible qualities.

Procedure: Freshmen are admitted to all sessions. Entrance exams should be taken by the junior year. There are deferred admissions and rolling admissions plans. Application deadlines are open. Application fee is $45. Notification is sent on a rolling basis. Applications are accepted online. Application fees are waived if application is completed online.

Transfer: 199 transfer students enrolled in 2012-2013. Applicants must have a GPA of at least 2.5 in all college work. The SAT or ACT, and an interview are recommended. 30 of 120 credits required for the bachelor's degree must be completed at the Mount.

Visiting: There are regularly scheduled orientations for prospective students, Student visits include 4 open houses per year, a summer orientation program, and Spend a Day with a Current Student program in the spring. There are guides for informal visits, visitors may sit in on classes, and stay overnight. To schedule a visit, contact the Admissions Office at admissions@msmc.edu.

Financial Aid: In 2013-2014, 97% of all full-time freshmen and 95% of continuing full-time students received some form of financial aid. 91% of all full-time freshmen and 87% of continuing full-time students received need-based aid. The average freshman award was $23,266. Need-based scholarships or need-based grants averaged $8,096 ($46,186 maximum); need-based self-help aid (loans and jobs) averaged $7,375 ($36,665 maximum); and other non-need-based awards and non-need-based scholarships averaged $10,897 ($38,110 maximum). 11% of undergraduate students work part-time. Average annual earnings from campus work are $1200.

The average financial indebtedness of the 2013 graduate was $28,645. The FAFSA is required. The priority date for freshman financial aid applications for fall entry is February 15. The deadline for filing freshman financial aid applications for fall entry is March 15.

International Students: They must take the TOEFL with a minimum score of 550 on the paper-based TOEFL (PBT) or 80 on the Internet-based version (iBT). They must also take the SAT or ACT, and the college's own entrance exam. Freshman students are required to take a standard placement test.

Computers: All students may access the system. Networks are available 24/7. There are no time limits and no fees.

Graduates: From July 1, 2012 to June 30, 2013, 554 bachelor's degrees were awarded. The most popular majors were nursing (19%), business (18%), and psychology (11%). 91 companies recruited on campus in 2012-2013. In an average class, 1% graduate in 3 years or less, 41% graduate in 4 years or less, 50% graduate in 5 years or less, and 52% graduate in 6 years or less. Of the 2012 graduating class, 26% were enrolled in graduate school within 6 months of graduation, and 84% were employed.

Admissions Contact: Nancy Scaffidi, Director of Admissions. E-Mail: *nancy.scaffidi@msmc.edu* Web: *www.msmc.edu*

NAZARETH COLLEGE OF ROCHESTER B-3

Rochester, NY 14618 **(585) 389-2860**
(800) 462-3944; (585) 389-2826

Full-time: 511 men, 1390 women **Faculty:** 163
Part-time: 37 men, 96 women **Ph.D.s:** 73%
Graduate: 168 men, 621 women **Student/Faculty:** 12 to 1
Year: semesters, summer session **Tuition:** $29,424
Application Deadline: February 1 **Room & Board:** $12,166
Freshman Class: 3838 applied, 2625 accepted, 423 enrolled
SAT CR/M/W: 540/540/520 **ACT:** 25 **VERY COMPETITIVE**

Nazareth College of Rochester, founded in 1924, is an independent institution offering programs in the liberal arts and sciences and preprofessional areas. There are 4 undergraduate schools and 4 graduate schools. In addition to regional accreditation, Nazareth has baccalaureate program accreditation with CSWE, NASM, and TEAC. The library contains 237,203 volumes, 470,000 microform items, and 181,114 audio/video tapes/CDs/DVDs, and subscribes to 86,321 periodicals including electronic. Computerized library services include interlibrary loans, database searching, Internet access, and Wi-Fi capability. Special learning facilities include an art gallery and radio station. The 150-acre campus is in a suburban area 7 miles east of Rochester. Including any residence halls, there are 29 buildings.

Student Life: 93% of undergraduates are from New York. Others are from 27 states, 22 foreign countries, and Canada. 88% are from public schools. 72% are White; 13% race unknown. The average age of freshmen is 18; all undergraduates, 21. 21% do not continue beyond their first year; 68% remain to graduate.

Housing: 1232 students can be accommodated in college housing, which includes single-sex and coed dorms and on-campus apartments. In addition, there are language houses, special-interest houses, substance-free floors, freshman experience floors, and honors floors. On-campus housing is guaranteed for all 4 years. 53% of students live on campus; of those, 88% remain on campus on weekends. All students may keep cars.

Activities: There are no fraternities or sororities. There are 48 groups on campus, including art, band, choir, chorale, chorus, communications, computers, dance, drama, ethnic, gay, honors, international, jazz band, literary magazine, musical theater, newspaper, opera, orchestra, political, professional, radio, religious, social, student government, and yearbook. Popular campus events include Springfest and Siblings Weekend, Welcome Week, Battle of the Beaks and Family Weekend Formal.

Sports: There are 11 intercollegiate sports for men and 13 for women, and 20 intramural sports for men and 20 for women. Facilities include a gym, a 25-meter swimming pool, soccer and lacrosse fields, including an outdoor turf field, tennis and racquetball courts, a fitness center, a sauna, a 2,200-seat stadium, and a 400-meter all-weather track.

Disabled Students: 80% of the campus is accessible. Facilities include wheelchair ramps, elevators, special parking, specially equipped restrooms, special class scheduling, lowered drinking fountains, and special housing.

Services: Counseling and information services are available, as is tutoring in every subject.

Campus Safety and Security: Measures include 24-hour foot and vehicle patrol, emergency notification system, and security escort services. There are shuttle buses, emergency telephones, lighted pathways/sidewalks, controlled access to dorms/residences, an alarm system, and security beepers free to all students.

Programs of Study: Nazareth confers B.A., B.S., B.F.A., and B.Mus. degrees. Master's and doctoral degrees are also awarded. Bachelor's degrees are awarded in BIOLOGICAL SCIENCE (biochemistry, biology/adolescence education, biology/biological science, and toxicology), BUSINESS (accounting, business administration and management, finance, international business management, and marketing and distribution), COMMUNICATIONS AND THE ARTS (art history, art, Chinese, communication rhetoric/communication, English, fine arts, French, German, information technology, Italian, literature, music, music business management, music history and appreciation, music performance, music theory and composition, musical theater, Spanish, spanish / adolescence education, studio art, theatre arts, and visual design), COMPUTER AND PHYSICAL SCIENCE (chemistry, chemistry/adolescence education, and mathematics), EDUCATION (art education, business education, elementary education, English education, foreign languages education, mathematics education, middle school education, music education, psychology education, and social science education), ENGINEERING AND ENVIRONMENTAL DESIGN (environmental science), HEALTH PROFESSIONS (health science, music therapy, nursing, and speech pathology/audiology), SOCIAL SCIENCE (American studies, anthropology, asian studies, communication sciences & disorders, economics, history, international studies, legal studies, peace studies, philosophy, political science/government, psychology, religion, social science, social work, sociology, and women's studies). Physical therapy and history are the strongest academically. Physical therapy, nursing, and business have the largest enrollments.

Required: Nazareth's new Core Curriculum is all about integration integrating the various ways that different disciplines explore Enduring Questions, engaging in three Integrative Studies courses that help you explore a question of your own, and participating in an Experiential Learning Pathway that helps you integrate what you have learned in the classroom with what is happening in the world. Additional requirements vary by major program. A total of 120 credit hours are required to graduate, with a minimum GPA of 2.0.

Special: Nazareth offers cross-registration with members of the Rochester Area College Consortium (about 15 colleges participate in this program). Full-time students can register for courses at any of these institutions. Internships are available in any of our academic programs and are arranged through the student's academic adviser and Director of Internships. Nazareth participates in the Washington and Albany internship programs. There is study abroad in France, Spain, Italy, and Germany, and there are exchange programs in Australia, Japan, Italy, France, Peru, United Kingdom, Hungary, Wales. There are 25 national honor societies, a freshman honors program, and 13 departmental honors programs.

Faculty/Classroom: 37% of faculty are male; 63% are female. 93% teach undergraduates. No introductory courses are taught by graduate students. The average class size in an introductory lecture is 21; in a laboratory is 11; and in a regular course is 19.

Admissions: 68% of the 2013-2014 applicants were accepted. The SAT scores for the 2013-2014 freshman class were: Critical Reading--29% below 500, 49% between 500 and 599, 20% between 600 and 699, and 2% between 700 and 800; Math--24% below 500, 49% between 500 and 599, 23% between 600 and 699, and 4% between 700 and 800; Writing--33% below 500, 45% between 500 and 599, 19% between 600 and 699, and 3% between 700 and 800. The ACT scores were 15% below 21, 26% between 21 and 23, 31% between 24 and 26, 14% between 27 and 28, and 14% above 28. 55% of the current freshmen were in the top fifth of their class; 81% were in the top two fifths. 6 freshmen graduated first in their class.

Requirements: Applicants should graduate from an accredited secondary school or have a GED. A minimum of 16 academic credits is required, including 4 years of English and 3 each of social studies, foreign language, math, and science. An essay is required, as is an audition for music and theater students and a portfolio for art students. An interview is recommended. Nazareth requires applicants to be in the upper 50% of their class. A GPA of 2.8 is required. AP and CLEP credits are accepted. Important factors in the admissions decision are geographical diversity, advanced placement or honors courses, and evidence of special talent.

Procedure: Freshmen are admitted fall and spring. Entrance exams should be taken by December of the senior year. There are early decision, early admissions, and deferred admissions plans. Early decision applications should be filed by November 1; regular applications, by February 1 for fall entry; and November 1 for spring entry, along with a $45 fee. Notification of early decision is sent December 1; regular decision, March 1. 59 early decision candidates were accepted for the 2013-2014 class. 58 applicants were on the 2013 waiting list; 6 were admitted. Applications are accepted online.

Transfer: 168 transfer students enrolled in 2012-2013. Applicants must have a college GPA of 2.5 (2.75 for education and physical therapy students). Those with fewer than 30 credits must submit high school transcripts. 30 of 120 credits required for the bachelor's degree must be completed at Nazareth.

Visiting: There are regularly scheduled orientations for prospective students, including individual appointments, group sessions, campus tours, open houses, and summer academic orientation. There are guides for informal visits, visitors may sit in on classes, and stay overnight. To schedule a visit, contact the Admissions Office.

Financial Aid: In 2013-2014, 100% of all full-time freshmen and 99%

of continuing full-time students received some form of financial aid. 81% of all full-time freshmen and 81% of continuing full-time students received need-based aid. The average freshman award was $25,702. Need-based scholarships or need-based grants averaged $17,253; need-based self-help aid (loans and jobs) averaged $4,991; and other non-need-based awards and non-need-based scholarships averaged $18,469. 25% of undergraduate students work part-time. Average annual earnings from campus work are $1009. The average financial indebtedness of the 2013 graduate was $28,938. Nazareth is a member of CSS. The FAFSA and the CSS Profile are required for early decision applicants only. The priority date for freshman financial aid applications for fall entry is February 1.

International Students: There are 62 international students enrolled. The school actively recruits these students. They must take the TOEFL with a minimum score of 550 on the paper-based TOEFL (PBT) or 79 on the Internet-based version (iBT).

Computers: All students may access the system. There are no time limits and no fees.

Graduates: From July 1, 2012 to June 30, 2013, 520 bachelor's degrees were awarded. The most popular majors were education (17%), health (17%), and business (10%). 36 companies recruited on campus in 2012-2013. In an average class, 59% graduate in 4 years or less, 67% graduate in 5 years or less, and 68% graduate in 6 years or less. Of the 2012 graduating class, 49% were enrolled in graduate school within 6 months of graduation, and 72% were employed.

Admissions Contact: Ian Mortimer, Vice President of Enrollment Management. E-Mail: *admissions@naz.edu* Web: *ww.naz.edu*

NEW YORK CITY COLLEGE OF TECHNOLOGY / THE CITY UNIVERSITY OF NEW YORK D-5

Brooklyn, NY 11201 **(718) 260-5500; (718) 260-5504**

Full-time: 5952 men, 4066 women
Part-time: 2992 men, 3197 women
Graduate: n/av
Year: semesters, summer session
Application Deadline: February 1
Freshman Class: n/av
Faculty: 417
Ph.D.s: n/av
Student/Faculty: 24 to 1
Tuition: $5769 ($14,899)
Room & Board: n/av

NONCOMPETITIVE

New York City College of Technology, founded in 1946 and made part of the City University of New York system in 1964, is an undergraduate commuter college offering day and evening programs in technology. The College's offerings encompass the preprofessional, professional and technical programs that respond to regional economic needs and provide access to higher education for all who seek fulfillment of career and economic goals through education. The 63 registered programs offered allow graduates to pursue careers in the architectural and engineering technologies, the computer, entertainment, and health professions, human services, advertising and publishing, hospitality, business, and law-related professions, as well as programs in career and technical teacher education. There are 3 undergraduate schools. In addition to regional accreditation, City Tech has baccalaureate program accreditation with ABET, ADA, NCATE, and NLN. The library contains 185,699 volumes, 14,007 microform items, and 88,527 audio/video tapes/CDs/DVDs, and subscribes to 170,071 periodicals including electronic. Computerized library services include interlibrary loans, database searching, Internet access, and Wi-Fi capability. Special learning facilities include an art gallery. The campus is in an urban area in downtown Brooklyn, NY. Including any residence halls, there are 9 buildings.

Student Life: 99% of undergraduates are from New York. Others are from 13 states. 35% are African American; 29% Hispanic; 17% Asian American; 14% White. The average age of freshmen is 19; all undergraduates, 24. 23% do not continue beyond their first year; 77% remain to graduate.

Housing: Alcohol is not permitted. All students commute. Some may keep cars.

Activities: There are no fraternities or sororities. There are 60 groups on campus, including computers, dance, drama, ethnic, gay, honors, international, literary magazine, musical theater, newspaper, professional, religious, social, social service, and student government. Popular campus events include Club Fair, Welcome Back Bash, Applefest and Straberryfest.

Sports: There are 10 intramural sports for men and 10 for women.

Disabled Students: All of the campus is accessible. Facilities include wheelchair ramps, elevators, specially equipped restrooms, lowered drinking fountains, and lowered telephones.

Services: Counseling and information services are available, as is tutoring in most subjects. There is a reader service for the blind, and remedial math, reading, and writing. Tutoring Services are available at the College Learning Center.

Campus Safety and Security: Measures include 24-hour foot and vehicle patrol and security escort services. There are emergency telephones and lighted pathways/sidewalks.

Programs of Study: City Tech confers B.S., B.S.Ed. and B.T. degrees. Associate degrees are also awarded. Bachelor's degrees are awarded in BIOLOGICAL SCIENCE (bioinformatics), BUSINESS (hospitality management services and institutional management), COMMUNICATIONS AND THE ARTS (communications and telecommunications), COMPUTER AND PHYSICAL SCIENCE (applied mathematics and information sciences and systems), EDUCATION (mathematics education, technical education, and vocational education), ENGINEERING AND ENVIRONMENTAL DESIGN (architectural technology, computer engineering, graphic and printing production, and mechanical engineering technology), HEALTH PROFESSIONS (health care administration, nursing, and radiological science), SOCIAL SCIENCE (human services and paralegal studies). Computer information systems, communication design, hospitality management have the largest enrollments.

Required: Students must receive CUNY certification in reading, writing, and math and complete associate degree requirements. General education requirements include selections from African-American, Puerto Rican, and Latin American studies, sciences, humanities,and social sciences. A total of 120 credits is required for the B.S., B.S.Ed or B.T. degree.

Special: B.A. and B.S. degrees are offered through CUNY's university wide bachelor's exchange credits program. An alternative format program for adults offers credit for life/work experience. Non-degree study is possible. Internships are required in most majors.

Faculty/Classroom: 57% of faculty are male; 43% are female. All teach undergraduates. No introductory courses are taught by graduate students. The average class size in a laboratory is 18 and in a regular course is 25.

Requirements: Applicants should be graduates of an accredited secondary school or have the GED equivalent and meet the university's immunization requirements. A GPA of 2.0 is required. AP and CLEP credits are accepted.

Procedure: Freshmen are admitted fall, spring, and summer. Entrance exams should be taken during the spring or summer prior to fall entrance. There are deferred admissions and rolling admissions plans. Applications should be filed by February 1 for fall entry; September 15 for spring entry, along with a $65 fee. Notification is sent on a rolling basis. Applications are accepted online.

Transfer: 1245 transfer students enrolled in 2012-2013. Candidates must have a 2.0 GPA. They must meet CUNY requirements in reading, writing, and math. 34 of 120 credits required for the bachelor's degree must be completed at City Tech.

Financial Aid: In 2013-2014, 81% of all full-time freshmen and 81% of continuing full-time students received some form of financial aid. The average freshman award was $8,985. Need-based scholarships or need-based grants averaged $8,730 ($13,619 maximum); need-based self-help aid (loans and jobs) averaged $1,534 ($10,935 maximum); and other non-need-based awards and non-need-based scholarships averaged $271 ($430 maximum). The FAFSA, and CUNY Student Aid Form (CSAF) is required. Check with the school for current application deadlines.

International Students: There are 402 international students enrolled. The school actively recruits these students. They must take the TOEFL with a minimum score of 500 on the paper-based TOEFL (PBT) or 61 on the Internet-based version (iBT).

Computers: All students may access the system. There are no time limits and no fees.

Graduates: From July 1, 2012 to June 30, 2013, 847 bachelor's degrees were awarded. The most popular majors were hospitality management (15%), information system (13%), and architectural technology (13%). In an average class, 23% graduate in 6 years or less.

Admissions Contact: Alexis Chaconis, Director of Admissions. E-Mail: *Achaconis@citytech.cuny.edu* Web: *www.citytech.cuny.edu*

NEW YORK INSTITUTE OF TECHNOLOGY D-5

Old Westbury, NY 11568 **(800) 345-NYIT (800) 345-NYIT; (516) 686-7613**

Full-time: 2501 men, 1516 women
Part-time: 442 men, 337 women
Graduate: 1416 men, 1671 women
Year: semesters, summer session
Application Deadline:
Freshman Class: 4314 accepted, 898 enrolled
SAT CR/M: 533/593
Faculty: n/av; IIA, ++$
Ph.D.s: n/av
Student/Faculty: n/av
Tuition: $28,940
Room & Board: $11,650
ACT: 25

VERY COMPETITIVE

NYIT offers more than 100 programs of study through seven schools and colleges: School of Architecture and Design, Education, Engineering and Computing Sciences, Health Professions, Management, Arts and Sciences, and the College of Osteopathic Medicine. There are 7 undergraduate schools and 7 graduate schools. In addition to regional accreditation, NYIT has baccalaureate program accreditation with ABET, ADA, FIDER, NAAB, and NCATE. The 4 libraries contain 135,630 volumes, 699,846 microform items, and 242 audio/video tapes/CDs/DVDs, and subscribe to 2,308 periodicals including electronic. Computerized library services include interlibrary loans, database searching, Internet access, and Wi-Fi capability. Special learning facilities include an art gallery, radio station, and

TV station. The 215-acre campus is in a suburban area is 25 miles east of New York City, 10 miles from Queens. Including any residence halls, there are 57 buildings.

Student Life: 85% of undergraduates are from New York. Others are from 48 states, 109 foreign countries, and Canada. 33% are White; 23% Foreign; 16% Asian American; 15% Hispanic; 12% African American. The average age of freshmen is 19; all undergraduates, 23. 30% do not continue beyond their first year; 46% remain to graduate.

Housing: 712 students can be accommodated in college housing, which includes coed dorms, on-campus apartments, and off-campus apartments. On-campus housing is guaranteed for all 4 years and is available on a lottery system for upperclassmen. Priority is given to out-of-town students. 85% of students commute. Alcohol is not permitted. All students may keep cars.

Activities: 3% of men belong to 1 local and 7 national fraternities; 2% of women belong to 1 local and 5 national sororities. There are 70 groups on campus, including special interest, student media, academic, art, cheerleading, chorale, computers, dance, drama, environmental, ethnic, film, honors, international, literary magazine, musical theater, newspaper, political, professional, radio and TV, religious, social, social service, student government, and yearbook. Popular campus events include May Fest, Club Fair Day, Earth Day, Relay for Life and Festival of Lights.

Sports: There are 12 intercollegiate sports for men and 12 for women, and 7 intramural sports for men and 7 for women. Facilities include The indoor gym is used for intercollegiate Athletics and recreation, seating 300. The field turf lacrosse/soccer field seating 1500. Field turf baseball field seating 500 Grass softball field, seating 100. Weight room & recreation room (pool tables and ping pong).

Disabled Students: All of the campus is accessible. Facilities include wheelchair ramps, elevators, special parking, specially equipped restrooms, lowered drinking fountains, and special housing.

Services: Counseling and information services are available, as is tutoring in every subject. There is remedial math, reading, and writing.

Campus Safety and Security: Measures include 24-hour foot and vehicle patrol, emergency notification system, and security escort services. There are shuttle buses, emergency telephones, lighted pathways/sidewalks, controlled access to dorms/residences, Automatic text system for emergency weather conditions.

Programs of Study: NYIT confers B.A., B.S., B.Arch., B.F.A., B.P.S. and B.Tech. degrees. Associate, master's, and doctoral degrees are also awarded. Bachelor's degrees are awarded in BIOLOGICAL SCIENCE (biology/biological science, life science, and nutrition), BUSINESS (accounting, banking and finance, business administration and management, hospitality management services, marketing and distribution, and marketing/retailing/merchandising), COMMUNICATIONS AND THE ARTS (advertising, communications, English, fine arts, graphic design, technical and business writing, and telecommunications), COMPUTER AND PHYSICAL SCIENCE (chemistry, computer science, mathematics, and physics), EDUCATION (art education, business education, education, elementary education, health education, middle school education, science education, secondary education, technical education, and trade and industrial education), ENGINEERING AND ENVIRONMENTAL DESIGN (aeronautical engineering, architecture, biomedical engineering, computer engineering, computer graphics, electrical/electronics engineering, electrical/electronics engineering technology, engineering technology, environmental design, environmental engineering technology, industrial engineering, interior design, manufacturing engineering, mechanical engineering, and technological management), HEALTH PROFESSIONS (clinical science, nursing, occupational therapy, physical therapy, physician's assistant, and preosteopathy), SOCIAL SCIENCE (behavioral science, interdisciplinary studies, political science/government, prelaw, social studies, and sociology). Life sciences, and architectural technology have the largest enrollmets.

Required: All students take a new core curriculum –NYIT Discovery Core, implemented in fall of 2010. This new core curriculum is outcome rather than subject based, and it is sequenced to build core competences that today's employers demand: Literacy, Critical thinking, Global Awareness, Interdisciplinary Mindset, Ethical and Moral Citizenship and understanding of Nature and Process of Sciences.

Special: Combined, accelerated bachelor's/master's programs in Accounting, Architecture, Energy Management, Communication arts as well as combined bachelor's/Doctor of Osteopathy and bachelor's/Doctor of Physical Therapy programs. Interdisciplinary study between programs in the School of Health Professions the NYIT College of Osteopathic Medicine, as well the Center for Gerontology and Geriatrics and the Center for Global Health. Experiential learning opportunities include: Semester- or year-long study abroad in China, Canada, United Arab Emirates; summers abroad (France, Italy, Germany, Spain, Greece, Egypt, Turkey, Israel, Turkey, China); short-term faculty-led trips; service learning (New York City); alternative spring break (Peru); corporate challenge; student advisory boards; student/faculty research projects. Student-managed Community Service Centers (CSC) that promote participation and organization of community service and volunteering opportunities. Internship Certificate Programs provided by the Career Services Office offer credit-bearing internship courses for qualified students, leading to the creation of a professional portfolio and one-on-one guidance in job seeking. The Institute for Clinical Competence provides state-of-the-art clinical learning and skills assessment of health professions students using simulations that include Standardized Patients (simulated medical conditions), mannequin-based simulators and a staff trained in simulation and medical education and test development. There is a freshman honors program.

Faculty/Classroom: 63% of faculty are male; 37% are female. No introductory courses are taught by graduate students.

Admissions: The SAT scores for the 2013-2014 freshman class were: Critical Reading--29% below 500, 48% between 500 and 599, 17% between 600 and 699, and 4% between 700 and 800; Math--8% below 500, 45% between 500 and 599, 36% between 600 and 699, and 11% between 700 and 800.

Requirements: The SAT is required. AP and CLEP credits are accepted.

Procedure: Freshmen are admitted fall, spring, and summer. Entrance exams should be taken in spring for fall enrollment. There are early decision, early admissions, deferred admissions, and rolling admissions plans. Early decision applications should be filed by December 17. The fall 2013 application fee was $50. Notification is sent on a rolling basis. Applications are accepted online.

Transfer: 471 transfer students enrolled in 2012-2013. 30 of 120 credits required for the bachelor's degree must be completed at NYIT.

Visiting: There are regularly scheduled orientations for prospective students, They include the following: open houses in fall and spring, with campus tours, a president's address, financial aid seminars, honors receptions, sessions with faculty advisers, and major-specific receptions. There are guides for informal visits and visitors may sit in on classes. To schedule a visit, contact the Admissions Office.

Financial Aid: In 2013-2014, 78% of all full-time freshmen and 77% of continuing full-time students received some form of financial aid. 56% of all full-time freshmen and 60% of continuing full-time students received need-based aid. The average freshman award was $18,712. Need-based scholarships or need-based grants averaged $5,326; and need-based self-help aid (loans and jobs) averaged $3,635. The FAFSA and NYS TAP form are required. Check with the school for current application deadlines.

International Students: There are 579 international students enrolled. The school actively recruits these students. They must take the TOEFL with a minimum score of 550 on the paper-based TOEFL (PBT) or 79 on the Internet-based version (iBT) and the college's own test. They must also take the SAT or ACT.

Computers: All students may access the system. There are no time limits and no fees.

Graduates: From July 1, 2012 to June 30, 2013, 1626 bachelor's degrees were awarded. The most popular majors were business administration (28%), osteopathic medicine (10%), and electrical engineering (8%). 118 companies recruited on campus in 2012-2013. In an average class, 1% graduate in 3 years or less, 24% graduate in 4 years or less, 41% graduate in 5 years or less, and 46% graduate in 6 years or less. Of the 2012 graduating class, 42% were enrolled in graduate school within 6 months of graduation, and 94% were employed.

Admissions Contact: Jacquelyn Nealon, Dean of Admissions and Financial Aid. E-Mail: *admissions@nyit.edu* Web: *www.nyit.edu*

NEW YORK UNIVERSITY D-5

New York, NY 10011 **(212) 998-4500; (212) 995-4902**

Full-time: 8567 men, 12798 women	**Faculty:** n/av
Part-time: 499 men, 751 women	**Ph.D.s:** n/av
Graduate: 9553 men, 12431 women	**Student/Faculty:** n/av
Year: semesters, summer session	**Tuition:** $44,848
Application Deadline: January 1	**Room & Board:** $16,622

Freshman Class: 45329 applied, 14423 accepted, 4984 enrolled

SAT CR/M/W: 670/680/680 **ACT:** 30 **MOST COMPETITIVE**

New York University, founded in 1831, is the largest private university in the United States. NYU, which is composed of 18 schools, colleges, and divisions, occupies 5 major centers in Manhattan and operates branch campus and research programs in other parts of the United States and abroad. There are 9 undergraduate schools and 11 graduate schools. In addition to regional accreditation, NYU has baccalaureate program accreditation with AACSB, ACEJMC, ADA, CSWE, and NLN. Computerized library services include interlibrary loans, database searching, Internet access, and Wi-Fi capability. Special learning facilities include an art gallery, radio station, TV station, a speech-language-hearing clinic, and a center for students with disabilities. The campus is in an urban area in New York City's Greenwich Village. Including any residence halls, there are 82 buildings.

Student Life: 70% of undergraduates are from out of state, mostly the Northeast. Students are from 50 states, 144 foreign countries, and Canada. 39% are White; 18% Asian American; 14% Foreign; 11% race unknown. The average age of freshmen is 18; all undergraduates, 21. 8% do not continue beyond their first year; 84% remain to graduate.

Housing: 10774 students can be accommodated in college housing, which includes coed dorms and on-campus apartments. In addition, there are special-interest houses, fraternity houses, SAFE (Substance and Alcohol-Free Environment), First Year Residential Experience, Sophomore Residential Experience, and Explorations Learning Communities. On-campus housing is guaranteed for all 4 years. 52% of students commute. All students may keep cars.

Activities: 7% of men belong to 19 national fraternities; 5% of women belong to 12 national sororities. Groups on campus include art, bagpipe, band, cheerleading, chess, choir, chorale, chorus, computers, dance, debate, drama, environmental, ethnic, film, forensics, gay, honors, international, jazz band, literary magazine, marching band, musical theater, newspaper, opera, orchestra, pep band, photography, political, professional, radio and TV, religious, social, social service, student government, and symphony. Popular campus events include Spring Strawberry Festival, Grad Alley and Career Services Fair.

Sports: There are 10 intercollegiate sports for men and 9 for women, and 9 intramural sports for men and 9 for women. Facilities include 2 state-of-the-art sports and recreation facilities. The sports center houses multipurpose courts for basketball, volleyball, tennis, and badminton, squash courts, handball and racquetball courts, rooftop tennis courts and running track, a 25-meter swimming pool, a diving tank, saunas, weight-training facilities, an aerobic fitness room, rooms for wrestling, judo, fencing, physical fitness, exercise prescription, and dance, and a rock-climbing wall. The athletic center is equipped with a 25-yard swimming pool, basketball/activities courts, a foot aerobic fitness room with cardio equipment, and a 30-foot indoor climbing center.

Disabled Students: 95% of the campus is accessible. Facilities include wheelchair ramps, elevators, specially equipped restrooms, special class scheduling, lowered drinking fountains, lowered telephones, special housing, buses with hydraulic lifts, adaptive computer equipment, CART or C-print services, a CTV enlargement system, a JAWS speech synthesizer, Dragon Dictate Voice Recognition, and Kurzweil Personal Readers.

Services: Counseling and information services are available, as is tutoring in every subject. There is a reader service for the blind. Services include sign language interpreters, scribes, research aides, and note takers for special needs.

Campus Safety and Security: Measures include 24-hour foot and vehicle patrol, emergency notification system, self-defense education, and security escort services. There are shuttle buses, emergency telephones, lighted pathways/sidewalks, 24-hour security in residence halls, and a neighborhood-merchant emergency help service.

Programs of Study: NYU confers B.A., B.S., B.F.A., B.S./B.E. and Mus.B. degrees. Associate, master's, and doctoral degrees are also awarded. Bachelor's degrees are awarded in AGRICULTURE (environmental studies), BIOLOGICAL SCIENCE (biochemistry, biology/biological science, cell biology, microbiology, neurosciences, and nutrition), BUSINESS (accounting, banking and finance, business administration and management, business economics, business law, finance, hotel/motel and restaurant management, human resources, industrial and labor relations, international business management, management information systems, management science, marketing management, marketing/retailing/merchandising, operations management, operations research, organizational behavior, property management, real estate, recreation and leisure services, and sports management), COMMUNICATIONS AND THE ARTS (American literature, animation, Arabic, art history, art history and appreciation, arts administration/management, classical languages, classics, communications, communications technology, comparative literature, creative writing, dance, design, digital communications, dramatic arts, English, English literature, film arts, fine arts, French, German, Germanic languages and literature, graphic design, Greek, Greek (classical), Greek (modern), Hebrew, information technology, instrumental performance, Italian, journalism, languages, Latin, linguistics, literature, media arts, music, music business management, music composition, music performance, music technology, music theory and composition, performing arts, photography, piano performance, Portuguese, public relations, publishing, radio/television technology, romance languages and literature, Russian, Slavic languages, Spanish, speech/debate/rhetoric, studio art, technical and business writing, theater management, vocal performance, voice, and writing), COMPUTER AND PHYSICAL SCIENCE (actuarial science, chemistry, Computer Engineering Technology, computer mathematics, computer science, digital arts/technology, earth science, information sciences and systems, mathematics, mathematics – economics, physics, and statistics), EDUCATION (art education, bilingual/bicultural education, (Education) Childhood Education, childhood education: 1-6, dance education, early childhood education, education, elementary education, English education, foreign languages education, general studies, mathematics education, music education, nursing education, school psychology, science education, secondary education, social science education, social studies education, social studies secondary school education, special education, and speech correction), ENGINEERING AND ENVIRONMENTAL DESIGN (biomedical engineering, chemical engineering, civil engineering, computational sciences, computer engineering, construction management, electrical and computer engineering, electrical/electronics engineering, engineering, engineering chemistry, engineering mechanics, engineering physics, graphic arts technology, mechanical engineering, and urban design), HEALTH PROFESSIONS (art therapy, dental hygiene, environmental health science, health care administration, music therapy, nursing, nursing home administration, occupational therapy, pharmacology, physical therapy, Pre-Health Studies, predentistry, premedicine, public health, and speech pathology/audiology), SOCIAL SCIENCE (African studies, africana studies, African American studies, American studies, anthropology, applied psychology, architectural studies, area studies, Asian/American studies, Asian/Oriental studies, asian studies, child care/child and family studies, classical/ancient civilization, counseling/psychology, developmental psychology, early childhood studies, East Asian studies, economics, ethnic studies, European studies, French studies, gender studies, (Social Science) Global Studies, history, humanities, humanities and social science, Iberian studies, international relations, Islamic studies, Italian studies, Japanese studies, Judaic studies, Latin American studies, law, Luso-Brazilian studies, medieval studies, Middle Eastern studies, Pacific area studies, philosophy, philosophy and religion, political science/government, psychology, public administration, religion, religious studies, Russian and Slavic studies, social science, social studies, social work, sociology, and urban studies). Business, individualized major, and theatre have the largest enrollments.

Required: All students must complete a minimum of 128 credit hours and maintain a minimum GPA of 2.0. A course in expository writing is required. Students must complete a core liberal arts curriculum in addition to major and elective credit.

Special: A vast array of internships is available, as well as study worldwide at NYU's 10 sites: Berlin, Buenos Aires, Florence, Ghana, London, Madrid, Paris, Prague, Shanghai, and Tel Aviv. B.A.-B.S. degree options, accelerated degrees in more than 230 majors, dual and student designed majors, credit by exam, and pass/fail options are also available. A Washington semester is available to political science majors. There are exchange programs with several historically black colleges. There is a Phi Beta Kappa chapter and a freshman honors program.

Faculty/Classroom: No introductory courses are taught by graduate students.

Admissions: 32% of the 2013-2014 applicants were accepted. The SAT scores for the 2013-2014 freshman class were: Critical Reading--1% below 500, 14% between 500 and 599, 50% between 600 and 699, and 35% between 700 and 800; Math--1% below 500, 13% between 500 and 599, 43% between 600 and 699, and 43% between 700 and 800; Writing--1% below 500, 10% between 500 and 599, 47% between 600 and 699, and 42% between 700 and 800. The ACT scores were 1% between 21 and 23, 10% between 24 and 26, 18% between 27 and 28, and 71% above 28.

Requirements: The SAT or ACT is required. The ACT Optional Writing test is also required. Applicants must graduate from an accredited secondary school. The GED is accepted. Students must present at least 16 Carnegie units, including 4 in English. Some majors require an audition or submission of a creative portfolio. All applicants must submit an essay and 2 letters of recommendation. Applicants can submit the SAT and 2 SAT: Subject tests; the ACT with Writing; the SAT and 2 Advanced Placement (AP) exam scores; 3 SAT: Subject tests (1 in literature or the humanities, 1 in math/science, and 1 in any non-language area); or 3 AP exam scores (1 in literature/humanities, 1 in math/science, and 1 in any non-language area). AP credits are accepted.

Procedure: Freshmen are admitted fall and spring. Entrance exams should be taken by November of the senior year. There is a early decision plan. Early decision applications should be filed by November 1; regular applications, by January 1 for fall entry, along with a $70 fee. Notification of early decision is sent December 15; regular decision, April 1. 1967 early decision candidates were accepted for the 2013-2014 class. Applications are accepted online.

Transfer: 607 transfer students enrolled in 2012-2013. Students must submit official college transcripts from all postsecondary institutions attended, a final high school transcript, and SAT scores. 64 of 128 credits required for the bachelor's degree must be completed at NYU.

Visiting: There are regularly scheduled orientations for prospective students, including campus tours and weekday information sessions by appointment. There are also 2 fall open house visits. Contact Office of Admissions.

Financial Aid: The CSS/Profile, FAFSA, and the state aid form are required. The deadline for filing freshman financial aid applications for fall entry is February 15.

International Students: There are 3024 international students enrolled. The school actively recruits these students. They must take the TOEFL and the college's own test, or take the IELTS or have ESL testing. They must also take the SAT or ACT.

Computers: All students may access the system 24 hours a day, 7 days a week. There are no time limits and no fees.

Graduates: From July 1, 2012 to June 30, 2013, 6310 bachelor's

degrees were awarded. The most popular majors were social science (38%), visual and performing arts (16%), culture, education, and human development (12%). 800 companies recruited on campus in 2012-2013. In an average class, 77% graduate in 4 years or less, 82% graduate in 5 years or less, and 84% graduate in 6 years or less.

Admissions Contact: Office of Undergraduate Admissions Web: *http:/ www.nyu.edu/admissions/undergraduate-admissions.html*

NIAGARA UNIVERSITY A-3

Niagara University, NY 14109 (716) 286-8700
(800) 462-2111; (716) 286-8710

Full-time: 1183 men, 1682 women
Part-time: 110 men, 252 women
Graduate: 304 men, 590 women
Year: semesters, summer session
Application Deadline:
Freshman Class: n/av
Faculty: n/av; IIA, -$
Ph.D.s: n/av
Student/Faculty: 12 to 1
Tuition: $28,200
Room & Board: $11,600

COMPETITIVE

Niagara University, founded in 1856 by the Vincentian fathers and brothers, is a private institution rooted in a Roman Catholic tradition. Programs offered include those in liberal arts, business, education, nursing, and travel, hotel, and restaurant administration. The figures in the above capsule and in this profile are approximate. There are 4 undergraduate schools and 3 graduate schools. In addition to regional accreditation, Niagara has baccalaureate program accreditation with AACSB, ACCE, CSWE, NCATE, and NLN. The library contains 185,706 volumes, 6,438 microform items, and 5,979 audio/video tapes/CDs/DVDs, and subscribes to 23,500 periodicals including electronic. Computerized library services include interlibrary loans, database searching, Internet access, and Wi-Fi capability. Special learning facilities include an art gallery, radio station, TV station, 2 theaters, and a greenhouse. The 160-acre campus is in a suburban area 4 miles north of Niagara Falls, 20 miles north of Buffalo, 90 miles from Toronto, Canada. Including any residence halls, there are 32 buildings.

Student Life: 78% of undergraduates are from New York. Others are from 35 states, 28 foreign countries, and Canada. 64% are White; 17% Foreign. 61% are Catholic; 15% Protestant; 12% claim no religious affiliation. The average age of freshmen is 19; all undergraduates, 22. 19% do not continue beyond their first year; 66% remain to graduate.

Housing: 1442 students can be accommodated in college housing, which includes single-sex and coed dorms and on-campus apartments. In addition, there are honors houses, special-interest houses, International housing. On-campus housing is guaranteed for all 4 years and is available on a lottery system for upperclassmen. 56% of students commute. All students may keep cars.

Activities: There are 81 groups on campus, including art, cheerleading, choir, chorale, computers, dance, drama, drill team, environmental, ethnic, film, honors, international, musical theater, newspaper, pep band, political, professional, radio and TV, religious, social, social service, student government, and yearbook. Popular campus events include Orientation, CARE, and Family Weekend.

Sports: There are 8 intercollegiate sports for men and 10 for women, and 25 intramural sports for men and 25 for women. Facilities include a 3400-seat gym, a 6-lane swimming and diving pool, exercise and weight rooms, saunas and dance areas, outdoor tennis courts, baseball and soccer fields, rugby pitch, basketball and racquetball courts, a hockey arena, and multipurpose courts with an indoor track. Hiking and biking trails are nearby.

Disabled Students: 75% of the campus is accessible. Facilities include wheelchair ramps, elevators, special parking, specially equipped restrooms, special class scheduling, lowered drinking fountains.

Services: Counseling and information services are available, as is tutoring in most subjects. There is a reader service for the blind, and remedial math, reading, and writing. Study skills development, note taking, and escort-assistance services are available, as are educational assistant services for the vision-impaired, educational/classroom assistance and machines for the hearing-impaired, and services for the learning disabled

Campus Safety and Security: Measures include 24-hour foot and vehicle patrol, emergency notification system, self-defense education, and security escort services. There are emergency telephones, lighted pathways/sidewalks, controlled access to dorms/residences, A campus security advisory board.

Programs of Study: Niagara confers B.A., B.S., B.B.A. and B.F.A. degrees. Associate, master's, and doctoral degrees are also awarded. Bachelor's degrees are awarded in BIOLOGICAL SCIENCE (biochemistry, biology/biological science, and life science), BUSINESS (accounting, business administration and management, business economics, hotel/motel and restaurant management, human resources, marketing/retailing/ merchandising, tourism, and transportation management), COMMUNICATIONS AND THE ARTS (communications, dramatic arts, English, French, and Spanish), COMPUTER AND PHYSICAL SCIENCE (chemistry, computer science, information sciences and systems, and mathematics), EDUCATION (business education, early childhood education, elementary education, English education, foreign languages education, mathematics education, middle school education, science education, secondary education, social studies education, and special education), ENGINEERING AND ENVIRONMENTAL DESIGN (preengineering), HEALTH PROFESSIONS (nursing, predentistry, and premedicine), SOCIAL SCIENCE (criminal justice, history, international studies, liberal arts/general studies, philosophy, political science/government, prelaw, psychology, religion, social science, social work, and sociology). Business, Social sciences, and biology are the strongest academically. Business administration, hospitality, tourism, and education have the largest enrollments.

Required: To graduate, students must earn 120 to 126 credit hours and a GPA of at least 2.0; 60 to 66 such hours are required in the major, 20 in specific disciplines, and 20 in liberal arts classes. A comprehensive exam is required in some majors; a thesis is required of honor students and some majors.

Special: Niagara offers a Washington semester, a semester at the state capitol in Albany, on-campus work-study, internships in most majors with such companies as the Big 6 accounting firms and Walt Disney World, and co-op programs in all areas except nursing, education, and social work. Students may study abroad in 8 countries and cross-register through the Western New York Consortium. An accelerated degree program in business, B.A.-B.S. degrees, dual majors, non-degree study, credit for life, military, and work experience, pass/fail options, and research are also available. There is also an academic exploration program for undeclared majors. There are 18 national honor societies and a freshman honors program.

Faculty/Classroom: 59% of faculty are male; 41% are female. No introductory courses are taught by graduate students. The average class size in a regular course is 21.

Requirements: The SAT or ACT is required. Applicants should be graduates of an accredited high school. The GED is accepted. The high school program should include 16 academic credits, with 4 in English and 2 each in foreign language, history, math, science, and social studies, as well as academic electives. Science, math, and computer majors should have 3 credits each in math and science. A GPA of 80.0 is required. AP and CLEP credits are accepted. Important factors in the admissions decision are advanced placement or honors courses, parents or siblings attended your school, and recommendations by school officials.

Procedure: Freshmen are admitted to all sessions. Entrance exams should be taken In the junior year or fall of the senior year. There are early decision, early admissions, deferred admissions, and rolling admissions plans. Check with the school for current application deadlines. The fall 2013 application fee was $30. Notification is sent on a rolling basis. Applications are accepted online.

Transfer: 200 transfer students enrolled in 2012-2013. Applicants must have a minimum GPA of 2.0 in travel, hotel, and restaurant administration, arts and sciences, and academic exploration (except for 2.25 in business and 2.5 for nursing and education majors) and submit all high school and college transcripts. The SAT or ACT is recommended. 30 of 120 credits required for the bachelor's degree must be completed at Niagara.

Visiting: There are regularly scheduled orientations for prospective students, Includes individual interviews and campus tours. Other arrangements can be made individually, such as to attend a class, eat in the student cafeteria, and/or speak with a faculty member. There are guides for informal visits, visitors may sit in on classes, and stay overnight. To schedule a visit, contact the Admissions Office.

Financial Aid: Niagara is a member of CSS. The FAFSA is required. Check with the school for current application deadlines.

International Students: There are 460 international students enrolled. The school actively recruits these students. They must take the TOEFL with a minimum score of 550 on the paper-based TOEFL (PBT) or 79 on the Internet-based version (iBT).

Computers: All students may access the system. There are no time limits and no fees.

Graduates: From July 1, 2012 to June 30, 2013, 657 bachelor's degrees were awarded. The most popular majors were business (23%), hospitality and tourism (16%), and education (15%). 139 companies recruited on campus in 2012-2013. In an average class, 2% graduate in 3 years or less, 56% graduate in 4 years or less, 62% graduate in 5 years or less, and 63% graduate in 6 years or less. Of the 2012 graduating class, 32% were enrolled in graduate school within 6 months of graduation, and 96% were employed.

Admissions Contact: Harry Gong, Director of Admissions. E-Mail: *admissions@niagara.edu* Web: *www.niagara.edu*

NYACK COLLEGE D-4

Nyack, NY 10960 (845) 675-4401
(800) 336-9225; (845) 358-3047

Full-time: 600 men, 915 women
Part-time: 121 men, 195 women
Graduate: 551 men, 700 women
Year: semesters, summer session
Application Deadline:
Freshman Class: n/av
SAT or ACT: required

Faculty: 87
Ph.D.s: 75%
Student/Faculty: n/av
Tuition: $23,350
Room & Board: $8650

COMPETITIVE

Nyack College, founded in 1882, is a private, Christian, liberal arts institution affiliated with the Christian and Missionary Alliance. There are 6 undergraduate schools and 4 graduate schools. In addition to regional accreditation, Nyack has baccalaureate program accreditation with CSWE, NASM, and NCATE. The 3 libraries contain 169,062 volumes, 34,744 microform items, and 7,876 audio/video tapes/CDs/DVDs, and subscribe to 428 periodicals including electronic. Computerized library services include interlibrary loans, database searching, Internet access, and Wi-Fi capability. Special learning facilities include a radio station. The 125-acre campus is in a suburban area in Nyack, NY (20 miles north of New York City) and lower Manhattan. Including any residence halls, there are 40 buildings.

Student Life: 64% of undergraduates are from New York. Others are from 39 states, 57 foreign countries, and Canada. 32% are African American; 26% Hispanic; 20% White; 12% Asian American. 95% are Protestant. The average age of freshmen is 24; all undergraduates, 27. 33% do not continue beyond their first year.

Housing: College-sponsored housing includes single-sex dorms, on-campus apartments, and married student housing. On-campus housing is guaranteed for all 4 years. Priority is given to out-of-town students. Alcohol is not permitted. Upperclassmen may keep cars.

Activities: There are no fraternities or sororities. There are 40 groups on campus, including band, cheerleading, chorale, dance, drama, ethnic, honors, international, jazz band, literary magazine, Ministry teams, musical theater, newspaper, opera, orchestra, professional, radio and TV, religious, social, social service, and student government. Popular campus events include Homecoming, Spiritual Emphasis Week, Christmas Concert, and Midnight Breakfast.

Sports: There are 5 intercollegiate sports for men and 6 for women, and 7 intramural sports for men and 7 for women. Facilities include a gym, soccer field, a fitness center, field house, baseball and softball fields, and tennis courts.

Campus Safety and Security: Measures include 24-hour foot and vehicle patrol. There are emergency telephones and lighted pathways/sidewalks.

Programs of Study: Nyack confers B.A., B.S., B.Mus., S.M.B. and B.P.S degrees. Associate, master's, and doctoral degrees are also awarded. Bachelor's degrees are awarded in BIOLOGICAL SCIENCE (biology/biological science), BUSINESS (accounting, business administration and management, and organizational leadership and management), COMMUNICATIONS AND THE ARTS (communications, communication rhetoric/communication, English, music, music performance, music theory and composition, piano/organ, and voice), COMPUTER AND PHYSICAL SCIENCE (computer science and mathematics), EDUCATION ((Education) Childhood Education, early childhood education, elementary education, music education, secondary education, and teaching English as a second/foreign language (TESOL/TEFOL)), HEALTH PROFESSIONS (nursing), SOCIAL SCIENCE (biblical studies, criminal justice, crosscultural studies, history, interdisciplinary studies, pastoral studies, philosophy, philosophy and religion, psychology, religion, religious music, social work, sociology, theological studies, and youth ministry). Psychology, education, ministry-related programs, nursing, and business have the largest enrollments.

Special: There is a freshman honors program.

Faculty/Classroom: 54% of faculty are male; 46% are female. No introductory courses are taught by graduate students.

Requirements: The SAT or ACT is required. High School graduation or its equivalent is essential. Completion of 16 academic credits is highly recommended: 4 units of English, 3 of mathematics, 3 of science, 3 of social science, and 2 of a foreign language. Students must demonstrate sound Christian character through personal testimony and recommendations. An interview may be required. A GPA of 2.0 is required. AP and CLEP credits are accepted.

Procedure: Freshmen are admitted fall, spring, and summer. There are deferred admissions and rolling admissions plans. Application deadlines are open. Application fee is $25. Notification is sent on a rolling basis. Applications are accepted online.

Transfer: Applicants must provide all transcripts from previous schools attended. 30 of 120 credits required for the bachelor's degree must be completed at Nyack.

Visiting: There are regularly scheduled orientations for prospective students. There are guides for informal visits, visitors may sit in on classes, and stay overnight. To schedule a visit, contact the Office of Admissions at admissions@nyack.edu.

Financial Aid: The FAFSA and the college's own financial statement are required. Check with the school for current application deadlines.

International Students: The school actively recruits these students. They must take the TOEFL with a minimum score of 550 on the paper-based TOEFL (PBT) or 83 on the Internet-based version (iBT). They must also take the SAT or ACT.

Computers: All students may access the system. There are no time limits and no fees.

Graduates: From July 1, 2012 to June 30, 2013, 429 bachelor's degrees were awarded. The most popular majors were organizational management, interdisciplinary studies, and psychology.

Admissions Contact: Dinesh Mahtani, Director of Admissions. E-Mail: *admissions@nyack.edu* Web: *www.nyack.edu*

OSWEGO / STATE UNIVERSITY OF NEW YORK C-3

Oswego, NY 13126 (315) 312-2250; (315) 312-3260

Full-time: 3361 men, 3593 women
Part-time: 192 men, 182 women
Graduate: 320 men, 469 women
Year: semesters, summer session
Application Deadline: January 15
Freshman Class: 9746 applied, 4719 accepted, 1270 enrolled
SAT CR/M: 540/560

Faculty: n/av; IIA, -$
Ph.D.s: 88%
Student/Faculty: 18 to 1
Tuition: $6510 ($15,560)
Room & Board: $12,610
ACT: 24

VERY COMPETITIVE

State University of New York at Oswego, founded in 1861, is a comprehensive institution offering more than 110 cooperative, preprofessional, and graduate programs through the College of Liberal Arts and Sciences, School of Business, School of Communication, Media and the Arts and School of Education. There are 4 undergraduate schools and one graduate school. In addition to regional accreditation, Oswego has baccalaureate program accreditation with AACSB, NASAD, NASM, and NCATE. The library contains 554,986 volumes, 1.6 million microform items, and 31,384 audio/video tapes/CDs/DVDs, and subscribes to 52,600 periodicals including electronic. Computerized library services include interlibrary loans, database searching, Internet access, and Wi-Fi capability. Special learning facilities include an art gallery, planetarium, radio station, TV station, 330-acre biological Rice Creek Field Station. The 696-acre campus is in a small town on the southeast shore of Lake Ontario, 35 miles northwest of Syracuse. Including any residence halls, there are 40 buildings.

Student Life: 96% of undergraduates are from New York. Others are from 26 states, 15 foreign countries, and Canada. 90% are from public schools. 79% are White. The average age of freshmen is 18; all undergraduates, 21. 18% do not continue beyond their first year; 62% remain to graduate.

Housing: 4600 students can be accommodated in college housing, which includes coed dorms and on-campus apartments. In addition, there are special-interest houses, resident hall living and learning communities, a freshmen-only building, upperclassmen suites and upperclassmen townhouses. On-campus housing is guaranteed for all 4 years. 65% of students live on campus; of those, 90% remain on campus on weekends. All students may keep cars.

Activities: 7% of men belong to 7 local and 10 national fraternities; 6% of women belong to 5 local and 7 national sororities. There are 186 groups on campus, including cheerleading and Equestrian Teams, ice hockey, rugby, art, athletics: crew, band, cheerleading, choir, chorale, chorus, communications, computers, dance, drama, environmental, ethnic, film, gay, honors, international, jazz band, literary magazine, musical theater, newspaper, opera, orchestra, pep band, photography, political, professional, radio and TV, religious, social, social service, student government, symphony, and yearbook. Popular campus events include Honors Convocations, Quest, May Day, Fall and Spring Concerts, Family and Friends Weekend and Hockey Nights in Oswego.

Sports: There are 12 intercollegiate sports for men and 12 for women, and 21 intramural sports for men and 21 for women. Facilities include an ice hockey rink, a field house with an artificial-grass practice area, 18 tennis courts, an outdoor track, 3 soccer and 3 lacrosse fields, baseball and softball fields, numerous basketball courts, racquetball and squash courts, 2 indoor pools, and a diving well. The gym seats 3500. There are also 2 membership fitness centers and weight rooms, a cross-country ski lodge, and a martial arts/dance studio.

Disabled Students: 85% of the campus is accessible. Facilities include wheelchair ramps, elevators, special parking, specially equipped restrooms, special class scheduling, lowered drinking fountains, lowered telephones, special housing, and a student support group.

Services: Counseling and information services are available, as is tutoring in every subject. There is a reader service for the blind, and remedial math, reading, and writing. In addition, the Office of Disablility Services provides general foundation support.

Campus Safety and Security: Measures include 24-hour foot and

vehicle patrol, emergency notification system, self-defense education, and security escort services. There are shuttle buses, emergency telephones, lighted pathways/sidewalks, controlled access to dorms/residences, and an electronic device that locates students and alerts the police when pressed.

Programs of Study: Oswego confers B.A., B.S. and B.F.A. degrees. Master's degrees are also awarded. Bachelor's degrees are awarded in BIOLOGICAL SCIENCE (biochemistry, biology/adolescence education, biology/biological science, (Biological) Pre-Health Studies, and zoology), BUSINESS (accounting, business administration and management, finance, human resources, insurance and risk management, management science, marketing/retailing/merchandising, operations management, and recreational facilities management), COMMUNICATIONS AND THE ARTS (art, broadcasting, communications, creative writing, dramatic arts, English, English as a second/foreign language, English Writing, film arts, French, German, graphic design, journalism, linguistics, music, musical theater, public relations, Spanish, spanish / adolescence education, theatre acting, theatre arts, and theatre production), COMPUTER AND PHYSICAL SCIENCE (applied mathematics, atmospheric sciences and meteorology, chemistry, computer science, earth science, earth science / adolescence education, environmental geology, geochemistry, geology, information sciences and systems, mathematics, physics, and software engineering), EDUCATION (agricultural education, business education, (Education) Childhood Education, elementary education, English education, foreign languages education, mathematics education, secondary education, social studies education, teaching English as a second/foreign language (TESOL/TEFOL), technical education, trade and industrial education, and vocational education), ENGINEERING AND ENVIRONMENTAL DESIGN (electrical and computer engineering, preengineering, and technological management), HEALTH PROFESSIONS (Pre-Health Studies, predentistry, premedicine, preoptometry, prephysical therapy, and preveterinary science), SOCIAL SCIENCE (American studies, anthropology, cognitive science, criminal justice, economics, family/consumer studies, French studies, history, human development, international studies, philosophy, political science/government, prelaw, psychology, sociology, women and gender studies, and women's studies). Biological sciences, chemistry, computer science, meteorology, education, and accounting are the strongest academically. Childhood/adolescence education, business administration, and biological sciences have the largest enrollments.

Required: To graduate, all students must complete 30 to 33 general education credits, including 9-12 in writing, mathematics, foreign language, natural science and 15 credits from areas of natural sciences, social & behavior sciences, american history, western civilization, humanities, fine & performing arts and world awareness. Students must have a minimum 2.0 GPA and complete 122 total credit hours (127 hours for technology and vocational education students). The total number of hours in the major varies from 33 to 95.

Special: Oswego offers cross-registration with ACUSNY-Visiting Student Program. More than 1000 internships are available with business, social, cultural, and government agencies. In addition 12 departments offer co-op opportunities as well. The university also offers a Washington semester, study abroad in more than 80 programs, a 5-year accounting B.S./M.B.A. program, dual majors, B.A.-B.S. degrees in several sciences and a B.A.-B.F.A. in art, credit for military experience, nondegree study, and pass/fail options. A pre-engineering option is available. A 3-4 degree in optometry with SUNY College of Optometry, and 2+2 medical imaging/ 3+3 physical therapy with SUNY Upstate Medical Center are also possible. There are 21 national honor societies, a freshman honors program, and 9 departmental honors programs.

Faculty/Classroom: 53% of faculty are male; 47% are female. 96% teach undergraduates. No introductory courses are taught by graduate students. The average class size in an introductory lecture is 40; in a laboratory is 15; and in a regular course is 24.

Admissions: 48% of the 2013-2014 applicants were accepted. The SAT scores for the 2013-2014 freshman class were: Critical Reading--22% below 500, 58% between 500 and 599, 18% between 600 and 699, and 2% between 700 and 800; Math--16% below 500, 59% between 500 and 599, 23% between 600 and 699, and 2% between 700 and 800. The ACT scores were 11% below 21, 40% between 21 and 23, 29% between 24 and 26, 15% between 27 and 28, and 5% above 28. 51% of the current freshmen were in the top fifth of their class; 80% were in the top two fifths.

Requirements: The SAT or ACT is required. Applicants must be graduates of an accredited secondary school or have a GED certificate. 18 academic units are required, preferring 4 years each of English and social studies, 7 years combined of math and science, and 2 of a foreign language. An essay and interview are strongly recommended. A GPA of 82.0 is required. AP and CLEP credits are accepted. Important factors in the admissions decision are advanced placement or honors courses, extracurricular activities record, and personality/intangible qualities.

Procedure: Freshmen are admitted fall and spring. Entrance exams should be taken during the spring of the junior year and fall of the senior year. There are early decision, early admissions, deferred admissions, and rolling admissions plans. Early decision applications should be filed by November 29; regular applications, by January 15 for fall entry, along with a $50 fee. Notification of early decision is sent December 15; regular decision, in January. 140 early decision candidates were accepted for the 2013-2014 class. Applications are accepted online.

Transfer: 762 transfer students enrolled in 2012-2013. Applicants must submit official transcripts from previously attended colleges. Students with a minimum GPA of 2.3 are encouraged to apply. SUNY associate degree holders are given preference. Secondary school records may be required for 1-year transfers. 30 of 122 credits required for the bachelor's degree must be completed at Oswego.

Visiting: There are regularly scheduled orientations for prospective students, usually including a campus tour and a meeting/presentation with a counselor. There are guides for informal visits, visitors may sit in on classes, and stay overnight. To schedule a visit, contact the Office of Admissions at admiss@oswego.edu.

Financial Aid: In 2013-2014, 70% of all full-time freshmen and 70% of continuing full-time students received some form of financial aid. 65% of all full-time freshmen and 66% of continuing full-time students received need-based aid. The average freshman award was $7,044. Need-based scholarships or need-based grants averaged $6,391; need-based self-help aid (loans and jobs) averaged $3,843; other non-need-based awards and non-need-based scholarships averaged $3,728; and $3,204 from other forms of aid. 65% of undergraduate students work part time. Average annual earnings from campus work are $1500. The average financial indebtedness of the 2013 graduate was $26,611. Oswego is a member of CSS. The FAFSA and the state aid form are required. The priority date for freshman financial aid applications for fall entry is March 1.

International Students: There are 147 international students enrolled. The school actively recruits these students. They must take the TOEFL with a minimum score of 550 on the paper-based TOEFL (PBT) or 80 on the Internet-based version (iBT).

Computers: All students may access the system anytime once the user becomes a student. There are no time limits. The fee is $98.

Graduates: From July 1, 2012 to June 30, 2013, 1668 bachelor's degrees were awarded. The most popular majors were education (23%), business (23%), and communications (11%). 150 companies recruited on campus in 2012-2013. In an average class, 38% graduate in 4 years or less, 54% graduate in 5 years or less, and 58% graduate in 6 years or less. Of the 2012 graduating class, 26% were enrolled in graduate school within 6 months of graduation, and 95% were employed.

Admissions Contact: Daniel Griffin, Interim Director of Admissions. E-Mail: *admiss@oswego.edu* Web: *www.oswego.edu*

PACE UNIVERSITY D-5

New York, NY 10038 (212) 346-1323 or (914) 773-3746 (800) 874-PACE; (212) 346-1040 or (914) 773-3851

Full-time: 2825 men, 4291 women	**Faculty:** 419; I, av$
Part-time: 573 men, 600 women	**Ph.D.s:** 88%
Graduate: 1588 men, 2747 women	**Student/Faculty:** 16 to 1
Year: semesters, summer session	**Tuition:** $38,069
Application Deadline: February 15	**Room & Board:** $13,130
Freshman Class: 14550 applied, 11838 accepted, 1758 enrolled	
SAT CR/M: 547/548	**ACT:** required **VERY COMPETITIVE**

Pace University, founded in 1906, is a private institution offering programs in arts and sciences, business, nursing, education, and computer and information science on 3 campuses, with undergraduate studies in New York City and Pleasantville and graduate studies and the Law School in White Plains. There are 5 undergraduate schools and 6 graduate schools. In addition to regional accreditation, Pace has baccalaureate program accreditation with AACSB, ABET, and NCATE. The 3 libraries contain 811,488 volumes, 53,441 microform items, and 5,552 audio/video tapes/CDs/DVDs, and subscribe to 182,533 periodicals including electronic. Computerized library services include interlibrary loans, database searching, Internet access, and Wi-Fi capability. Special learning facilities include an art gallery, radio station, TV station, 2 art galleries, a performing arts center, biological research labs, an environmental center, a language lab, and computer labs. The 265-acre campus is in an urban area of New York. Including any residence halls, there are 65 buildings.

Student Life: 57% of undergraduates are from New York. Others are from 46 states, 97 foreign countries, and Canada. 75% are from public schools. 47% are White; 16% Hispanic; 11% African American. The average age of freshmen is 18; all undergraduates, 22. 24% do not continue beyond their first year; 54% remain to graduate.

Housing: 3291 students can be accommodated in college housing, which includes coed dorms and on-campus apartments. In addition, there are honors houses, special-interest houses, and a wellness floor. 56% of students commute. Some may keep cars.

Activities: 4% of men belong to 1 local and 11 national fraternities; 5% of women belong to 3 local and 11 national sororities. There are 92 groups on campus, including art, cheerleading, chorus, computers, dance, debate, drama, environmental, ethnic, film, gay, honors, international, literary magazine, musical theater, newspaper, photography, political, professional, radio and TV, religious, social, social service, student government, and yearbook. Popular campus events include Homecoming, CariCulture and Live Love Laugh.

Sports: There are 6 intercollegiate sports for men and 6 for women, and 8 intramural sports for men and 8 for women. Facilities include the civic center gym in New York City, tennis courts, playing fields, and a health, fitness, and recreation center at the Pleasantville/Briarcliff Manor campus.

Disabled Students: 70% of the campus is accessible. Facilities include wheelchair ramps, elevators, special parking, special class scheduling, lowered drinking fountains, lowered telephones, and other facilities that vary by campus; there is no student parking.

Services: Counseling and information services are available, as is tutoring in every subject. There is remedial math, reading, and writing. All services are provided in the University's Center for Academic Excellence.

Campus Safety and Security: Measures include 24-hour foot and vehicle patrol, emergency notification system, and security escort services. There are shuttle buses, emergency telephones, lighted pathways/sidewalks, controlled access to dorms/residences, closed circuit TV.

Programs of Study: Pace confers B.A., B.S., B.B.A., B.F.A. and B.S.N. degrees. Associate, master's, and doctoral degrees are also awarded. Bachelor's degrees are awarded in AGRICULTURE (environmental studies), BIOLOGICAL SCIENCE (biology/adolescence education, biology/biological science, and forensic science), BUSINESS (accounting, banking and finance, business administration and management, business economics, entrepreneurial studies, finance, hospitality management services, international business management, and marketing/retailing/merchandising), COMMUNICATIONS AND THE ARTS (advertising, art history, art, art history and appreciation, communications, dance, English, film arts, fine arts, modern language, musical theater, Spanish, theatre acting, theatre arts, theater design, and theater management), COMPUTER AND PHYSICAL SCIENCE (chemistry, computer science, computer security and information assurance, information sciences and systems, and mathematics), EDUCATION (elementary education), ENGINEERING AND ENVIRONMENTAL DESIGN (environmental science), HEALTH PROFESSIONS (nursing and speech pathology/audiology), SOCIAL SCIENCE (American studies, applied psychology, biopsychology, criminal justice, economics, forensic studies, history, Latin American studies, philosophy, philosophy and religion, political science/government, psychology, social science, sociology, women and gender studies, and women's studies). Accounting is the strongest academically. Business and finance have the largest enrollments.

Required: To graduate students must complete 128 to 133 credit hours, including 32 to 50 in the major, with a minimum GPA of 2.0. A core curriculum of 60 credits and an introductory computer science course are required as well as a community-based learning experience and 2 enhanced writing courses.

Special: Internships, study abroad, and a cooperative education program in all majors are available. Pace also offers accelerated degree programs, B.A.-B.S. degrees, dual majors, general studies degrees, and 3-2 engineering degrees with Manhattan College and Rensselaer Polytechnic Institute. Credit for life, military, and work experience, nondegree study, and pass/fail options are available. There are 25 national honor societies, a freshman honors program, and 19 departmental honors programs.

Faculty/Classroom: 54% of faculty are male; 46% are female. 84% teach undergraduates, and 24% do research. No introductory courses are taught by graduate students. The average class size in an introductory lecture is 35; in a laboratory is 11; and in a regular course is 23.

Admissions: 81% of the 2013-2014 applicants were accepted. The SAT scores for the 2013-2014 freshman class were: Critical Reading--20% below 500, 58% between 500 and 599, 20% between 600 and 699, and 2% between 700 and 800; Math--22% below 500, 54% between 500 and 599, 22% between 600 and 699, and 2% between 700 and 800. The ACT scores were 6% below 21, 33% between 21 and 23, 33% between 24 and 26, 15% between 27 and 28, and 13% above 28. 39% of the current freshmen were in the top fifth of their class; 76% were in the top two fifths.

Requirements: The SAT or ACT is required. Applicants should be graduates of an accredited secondary school with at least 16 academic credits, including 4 in English, 3 to 4 each in math, science, and history, and 2 to 3 in foreign language. The GED is accepted. An essay is required. A GPA of 3.0 is required. AP and CLEP credits are accepted. Important factors in the admissions decision are advanced placement or honors courses, recommendations by school officials, and leadership record.

Procedure: Freshmen are admitted fall and spring. Entrance exams should be taken by December of the senior year. There are early admissions, deferred admissions, and rolling admissions plans. Early decision applications should be filed by December 1; regular applications, by February 15 for fall entry, along with a $50 fee. Notifications are sent December 15. Applications are accepted online.

Transfer: 589 transfer students enrolled in 2012-2013. Applicants are admitted in the fall or spring. A college GPA of 2.5 is required. Grades of C or better transfer for credit. A maximum of 68 credits will be accepted from a 2-year school. Students who transfer with less than 32 credits also need to submit SAT or ACT scores 32 of 128 credits required for the bachelor's degree must be completed at Pace.

Visiting: There are regularly scheduled orientations for prospective students, including student-for-a-day programs and overnight visits by appointment. There are guides for informal visits, visitors may sit in on classes, and stay overnight. To schedule a visit, contact the Office of Undergraduate Admission.

Financial Aid: In 2013-2014, 82% of all full-time freshmen and 76% of continuing full-time students received some form of financial aid. 82% of all full-time freshmen and 75% of continuing full-time students received need-based aid. The average freshman award was $30,563. Need-based scholarships or need-based grants averaged $25,057; need-based self-help aid (loans and jobs) averaged $5,971; non-need-based athletic scholarships averaged $29,084; and other non-need-based awards and non-need-based scholarships averaged $13,059. Average annual earnings from campus work are $2156. The average financial indebtedness of the 2013 graduate was $35,095. The FAFSA is required. The deadline for filing freshman financial aid applications for fall entry is February 15.

International Students: There are 477 international students enrolled. The school actively recruits these students. They must take the TOEFL with a minimum score of 570 on the paper-based TOEFL (PBT) or 89 on the Internet-based version (iBT) and the college's own test.

Computers: All students may access the system 24 hours a day. There are no time limits and no fees.

Graduates: From July 1, 2012 to June 30, 2013, 1577 bachelor's degrees were awarded. The most popular majors were finance (11%), accounting (9%), and communication studies (8%). 321 companies recruited on campus in 2012-2013. In an average class, 2% graduate in 3 years or less, 38% graduate in 4 years or less, 52% graduate in 5 years or less, and 54% graduate in 6 years or less. Of the 2012 graduating class, 20% were enrolled in graduate school within 6 months of graduation, and 77% were employed.

Admissions Contact: Donna J. Grand Pre, Dean of Admissions. E-Mail: *infoctr@pace.edu* Web: *www.pace.edu*

PARSONS THE NEW SCHOOL FOR DESIGN D-5

New York, NY 10011 **(212) 229-5150**

Full-time: n/av	**Faculty:** n/av
Part-time: n/av	**Ph.D.s:** n/av
Graduate: n/av	**Student/Faculty:** 9 to 1
Year: semesters, summer session	**Tuition:** $41,520
Application Deadline: open	**Room & Board:** $15,090
Freshman Class: n/av	
SAT or ACT: required	
	SPECIAL

Parsons The New School for Design, founded in 1896, is a private professional art school and is part of The New School, a leading university in New York City. Parsons offers degrees in creative commercial fields in NYC and Paris campuses. There are 5 undergraduate schools and 5 graduate schools. In addition to regional accreditation, Parsons has baccalaureate program accreditation with NAAB and NASAD. The 4 libraries contain 2.4 million volumes, 13,000 microform items, and 14,275 audio/video tapes/CDs/DVDs, and subscribe to 2,085,673 periodicals including electronic. Computerized library services include interlibrary loans, database searching, Internet access, and Wi-Fi capability. Special learning facilities include an art gallery. The campus is in an urban area in New York City and Paris. Including any residence halls, there are 9 buildings.

Student Life: 44% of undergraduates are from out of state, mostly the Middle Atlantic. Students are from 51 states, 108 foreign countries, and Canada. 39% are Foreign; 28% White; 15% Asian American. The average age of freshmen is 19; all undergraduates, 21. 17% do not continue beyond their first year; 65% remain to graduate.

Housing: 1460 students can be accommodated in college housing, which includes coed dorms, on-campus apartments, and off-campus apartments. On-campus housing is guaranteed for all 4 years. Alcohol is not permitted. All students may keep cars.

Activities: There are no fraternities or sororities. There are 30 groups on campus, including art, choir, chorus, communications, dance, debate, environmental, ethnic, gay, honors, international, jazz band, literary magazine, newspaper, opera, orchestra, photography, political, professional, religious, social, social service, student government, and symphony.

Sports: There are 3 intramural sports for men and 3 for women. Facilities include The New School does not have an athletic facility but does have a Recreation Department. Intramural sports take place at offsite locations, including the YMCA which has a regulation size basketball court, locker room/changing area, weight room and a 25 meter swimming pool. Recreation classes take place on and off campus in multipurpose rooms that can accommodate 20 to 35 participants and sites throughout the city.

Disabled Students: 90% of the campus is accessible. Facilities include

wheelchair ramps, elevators, specially equipped restrooms, lowered drinking fountains, and lowered telephones.

Services: Counseling and information services are available, as is tutoring in some subjects including, English and art history. There is remedial reading and writing.

Programs of Study: Parsons confers A.A.S., B.A/B.F.A, B.A., B.S., B.F.A. and B.B.A. degrees. Associate and master's degrees are also awarded. Bachelor's degrees are awarded in BUSINESS (marketing/retailing/merchandising), COMMUNICATIONS AND THE ARTS (advertising, design, fine arts, graphic design, illustration, industrial design, photography, and studio art), COMPUTER AND PHYSICAL SCIENCE (digital arts/technology), ENGINEERING AND ENVIRONMENTAL DESIGN (architectural engineering, interior design, and urban design), SOCIAL SCIENCE (fashion design and technology). Fashion design, communication design, and design management have the largest enrollments.

Required: To graduate, students must complete 120 credit hours, with a minimum GPA of 2.0. Parsons requires a minimum of 30 credits in liberal arts and 12 in art history.

Special: Students have increasing opportunities to enroll in courses offered by other divisions of The New School. Students may study abroad at the Parsons campus in Paris as well as several other programs. The 5-year combined B.A.-B.F.A. degree requires 180 credits for graduation.

Faculty/Classroom: 54% of faculty are male; 46% are female. All teach undergraduates, 13% do research, and 13% do both. No introductory courses are taught by graduate students. The average class size in an introductory lecture is 16 and in a regular course is 15.

Requirements: The SAT or ACT is required. Applicants must be graduates of an accredited secondary school. The GED is accepted. Applicants should have completed 4 years each of art, English, history, and social studies. A portfolio and home exam are required, and an interview is recommended. A GPA of 3.0 is required. AP credits are accepted. Important factors in the admissions decision are personality/intangible qualities, leadership record, advanced placement or honors courses, evidence of special talent, and extracurricular activities record.

Procedure: Freshmen are admitted fall and spring. Entrance exams should be taken by spring of the junior year. There are deferred admissions and rolling admissions plans. Application deadlines are open. Application fee is $50. Notification is sent on a rolling basis. Applications are accepted online.

Transfer: 655 transfer students enrolled in 2012-2013. Applicants will receive credit for grade C work or better in college courses that are similar in content, purpose, and standards to the courses offered at Parsons. A high school transcript is required for undergraduates, and the SAT or ACT is recommended. All students must present a portfolio and Parsons Challenge. Transfers are admitted in the fall, and to selected programs in the spring. Any student attending an international college must get a W.E.S. credit summary and submit it to the admission office if they would like to receive credit. 60 of 120 credits required for the bachelor's degree must be completed at Parsons.

Visiting: There are regularly scheduled orientations for prospective students. There are guides for informal visits. To schedule a visit, contact the Office of Admissions at thinkparsons@newschool.edu.

Financial Aid: In 2013-2014, 76% of all full-time freshmen students received some form of financial aid. 76% of all full-time freshmen students received need-based aid. The average freshman award was $22,815. Need-based scholarships or need-based grants averaged $8,548 ($30,270 maximum); and need-based self-help aid (loans and jobs) averaged $3,358 ($5,500 maximum). Average annual earnings from campus work are $2000. The average financial indebtedness of the 2013 graduate was $17,339. Parsons is a member of CSS. The FAFSA, the state aid form, and the college's own financial statement are required. The priority date for freshman financial aid applications for fall entry is January 1. The deadline for filing freshman financial aid applications for fall entry is March 1.

International Students: There are 1664 international students enrolled. The school actively recruits these students. They must take the TOEFL with a minimum score of 580 on the paper-based TOEFL (PBT) or 92 on the Internet-based version (iBT), IELTS. They must also take the SAT or ACT.

Computers: All students may access the system. There are no time limits and no fees.

Graduates: 212 companies recruited on campus in 2012-2013. In an average class, 53% graduate in 4 years or less, 66% graduate in 5 years or less, and 69% graduate in 6 years or less. Of the 2012 graduating class, 92% were employed within 6 months of graduation.

Admissions Contact: Carolina Wheat, Director of Undergraduate Admissions. E-Mail: *thinkparsons@newschool.edu* Web: *www.parsons.newschool..edu*

POLYTECHNIC INSTITUTE OF NEW YORK UNIVERSITY D-5

Brooklyn, NY 11201 (718) 260-3100
(800) 765-8324; (718) 260-3446

Full-time: 1517 men, 435 women	**Faculty:** 157; I, av$
Part-time: 88 men, 31 women	**Ph.D.s:** n/av
Graduate: 1946 men, 635 women	**Student/Faculty:** 14 to 1
Year: semesters, summer session	**Tuition:** $39,564
Application Deadline:	**Room & Board:** $13,500

Freshman Class: 3284 applied, 2453 accepted, 495 enrolled
SAT CR/M/W: 600/680/600 **ACT:** 28 **HIGHLY COMPETITIVE+**

Polytechnic Institute of New York University is the nation's second oldest private engineering institution. There is one undergraduate school and one graduate school. In addition to regional accreditation, NYU-Poly has baccalaureate program accreditation with ABET and CSAB. The library contains 120,863 volumes, 20,000 microform items, and 460 audio/video tapes/CDs/DVDs, and subscribes to 43,500 periodicals including electronic. Computerized library services include interlibrary loans, database searching, Internet access, and Wi-Fi capability. Special learning facilities include a radio station. The 3-acre campus is in an urban area 2 miles from New York City. Including any residence halls, there are 6 buildings.

Student Life: 68% of undergraduates are from New York. Others are from 26 states, 31 foreign countries, and Canada. 88% are from public schools. 38% are Foreign; 21% White; 20% Asian American. The average age of freshmen is 18; all undergraduates, 20. 14% do not continue beyond their first year; 55% remain to graduate.

Housing: 400 students can be accommodated in college housing, which includes coed dorms. On-campus housing is available on a first-come and first-served basis. Priority is given to out-of-town students. 75% of students commute. Alcohol is not permitted. No one may keep cars.

Activities: 2% of men belong to 2 local and 3 national fraternities; 1% of women belong to 1 national sorority. There are 46 groups on campus, including chess, computers, dance, ethnic, film, honors, international, literary magazine, newspaper, photography, professional, radio and TV, religious, social, social service, student government, and yearbook. Popular campus events include Chinese New Year, Film Festivals and International Food Fair.

Sports: There are 7 intercollegiate sports for men and 7 for women, and 13 intramural sports for men and 12 for women. Facilities include soccer, lacrosse, and baseball fields, basketball courts, Ping-Pong tables, and 2 student centers.

Disabled Students: All of the campus is accessible. Facilities include wheelchair ramps, elevators, special parking, specially equipped restrooms, lowered drinking fountains, and lowered telephones.

Services: Counseling and information services are available, as is tutoring in every subject. There is remedial math and writing.

Campus Safety and Security: Measures include 24-hour foot and vehicle patrol. There are emergency telephones and lighted pathways/sidewalks.

Programs of Study: NYU-Poly confers B.S. degrees. Master's and doctoral degrees are also awarded. Bachelor's degrees are awarded in BIOLOGICAL SCIENCE (molecular biology), BUSINESS (business administration and management), COMPUTER AND PHYSICAL SCIENCE (chemistry, computer science, information sciences and systems, mathematics, and physics), ENGINEERING AND ENVIRONMENTAL DESIGN (chemical engineering, civil engineering, computer engineering, construction management, electrical/electronics engineering, and mechanical engineering), SOCIAL SCIENCE (humanities, liberal arts/general studies, and social science). Electrilcal engineering, mechanical engineering, and civil engineering have the largest enrollments.

Required: Students must complete all university and departmental course requirements, including 24 credits in Humanities/Social Science, 16 in Math, 12 in Chemistry/Physics, 4 in Engineering Design, and 3 in Programming Methodology. A total of 120 to 128 credits must be earned, with 32 in the major, and a minimum GPA of 2.0 is required to graduate. A senior design project is also required of engineering students.

Special: Cooperative programs are available in all majors. Opportunities are provided for internships, work-study programs, study abroad, accelerated degree programs in engineering and computer science, dual majors, student-designed majors, and nondegree study. There are 9 national honor societies, a freshman honors program, and 3 departmental honors programs.

Faculty/Classroom: 80% of faculty are male; 20% are female. 68% teach undergraduates. No introductory courses are taught by graduate students. The average class size in an introductory lecture is 29; in a laboratory is 16; and in a regular course is 22.

Admissions: 75% of the 2013-2014 applicants were accepted. The SAT scores for the 2013-2014 freshman class were: Critical Reading--11% below 500, 38% between 500 and 599, 40% between 600 and 699, and 11% between 700 and 800; Math--1% below 500, 10% between 500 and

599, 45% between 600 and 699, and 44% between 700 and 800; Writing--9% below 500, 40% between 500 and 599, 41% between 600 and 699, and 10% between 700 and 800. The ACT scores were 25% between 24 and 26, 26% between 27 and 28, and 48% above 28.

Requirements: The SAT is required. Graduation from an accredited secondary school is required; a GED will be accepted. The preferred secondary school course of study is: Four Course Years of English, four of Science (Chemistry is required and physics is strongly recommended), and four of Mathematics (Sequential I, II, III, precalculus, calculus). An essay and an interview are recommended. AP credits are accepted. Important factors in the admissions decision are advanced placement or honors courses, leadership record, and evidence of special talent.

Procedure: Freshmen are admitted fall, spring, and summer. Entrance exams should be taken by November of the senior year. There are early admissions, deferred admissions, and rolling admissions plans. Application deadlines are open. Application fee is $65. Notification is sent on a rolling basis. Applications are accepted online.

Transfer: 81 transfer students enrolled in 2012-2013. Transfer applicants must have a 2.5 cumulative GPA. Students with fewer than 30 credits must submit SAT scores and secondary school transcripts in addition to official college-level transcripts. 64 of 124 credits required for the bachelor's degree must be completed at NYU-Poly.

Visiting: There are regularly scheduled orientations for prospective students, Including a keynote speaker, major presentations, financial aid and scholarship sessions, and student life and career services sessions. There are guides for informal visits and visitors may stay overnight. To schedule a visit, contact the Dean of Admissions.

Financial Aid: In 2013-2014, 73% of all full-time freshmen and 75% of continuing full-time students received some form of financial aid. 67% of all full-time freshmen and 71% of continuing full-time students received need-based aid. The average freshman award was $28,428. Need-based scholarships or need-based grants averaged $14,348; need-based self-help aid (loans and jobs) averaged $3,817; and other non-need-based awards and non-need-based scholarships averaged $13,261. 30% of undergraduate students work part-time. Average annual earnings from campus work are $6360. The average financial indebtedness of the 2013 graduate was $36,574. NYU-Poly is a member of CSS. The FAFSA and the college's own financial statement are required. The priority date for freshman financial aid applications for fall entry is March 1.

International Students: There are 207 international students enrolled. The school actively recruits these students. They must take the TOEFL with a minimum score of 550 on the paper-based TOEFL (PBT) or 80 on the Internet-based version (iBT). They must also take the SAT or ACT.

Computers: All students may access the system 24-hour dial-up service is available. There are no time limits and no fees.

Graduates: From July 1, 2012 to June 30, 2013, 276 bachelor's degrees were awarded. The most popular majors were electrical engineering (17%), civil engineering (15%), and mechanical engineering (12%). 285 companies recruited on campus in 2012-2013. In an average class, 41% graduate in 4 years or less, 58% graduate in 5 years or less, and 62% graduate in 6 years or less. Of the 2012 graduating class, 20% were enrolled in graduate school within 6 months of graduation, and 64% were employed.

Admissions Contact: Joy Colelli, Dean of Undergraduate Admissions. E-Mail: *uadmit@poly.edu* Web: *www.poly.edu*

PRATT INSTITUTE — D-5

Brooklyn, NY 11205 — (718) 636-3514
(800) 331-0834; (718) 636-3670

Full-time: 1035 men, 1838 women	**Faculty:** n/av
Part-time: 68 men, 80 women	**Ph.D.s:** n/av
Graduate: 468 men, 1233 women	**Student/Faculty:** n/av
Year: semesters, summer session	**Tuition:** $39,310
Application Deadline: January 5	**Room & Board:** $10,210
Freshman Class: 4247 applied, 2541 accepted, 608 enrolled	
SAT CR/M/W: 585/605/595	**ACT:** 26 — **SPECIAL**

Pratt Institute, founded in 1887, is a private institution offering undergraduate and graduate programs in architecture, art and design education, art history, art therapy, critical and visual studies, industrial, interior, and communication design, fine arts, design management, arts and cultural management, writing and library science. There are 3 undergraduate schools and 3 graduate schools. In addition to regional accreditation, Pratt has baccalaureate program accreditation with FIDER, NAAB, NASAD, and TEAC. The library contains 176,674 volumes, 50,000 microform items, and 3,500 audio/video tapes/CDs/DVDs, and subscribes to 700 periodicals including electronic. Computerized library services include database searching, Internet access, and Wi-Fi capability. Special learning facilities include an art gallery, radio station, foundry and woodshop. The 25-acre campus is in an urban area 3 miles east of downtown Manhattan. Including any residence halls, there are 28 buildings.

Student Life: 69% of undergraduates are from out of state, mostly the Middle Atlantic. Students are from 48 states, 77 foreign countries, and Canada. 48% are White; 18% Asian American; 17% Foreign. The average age of freshmen is 18; all undergraduates, 21. 17% do not continue beyond their first year; 62% remain to graduate.

Housing: 1612 students can be accommodated in college housing, which includes single-sex and coed dorms and on-campus apartments. In addition, there are special-interest houses, special interest communities include: healthy choices, global learning, community service, quiet floor and gender blind. On-campus housing is guaranteed for the freshman year only, is available on a first-come, first-served basis, and is available on a lottery system for upperclassmen. Priority is given to out-of-town students. 53% of students live on campus. All students may keep cars.

Activities: There are 50 groups on campus, including art, environmental, ethnic, film, gay, honors, international, literary magazine, martial arts, newspaper, photography, professional, radio and TV, religious, social, social service, student government, and yearbook. Popular campus events include Springfest, International Food Fair, and Holiday Ball.

Sports: There are 6 intercollegiate sports for men and 4 for women, and 3 intramural sports for men and 1 for women. Facilities include an activities resource center containing 5 indoor tennis courts, a 200-meter indoor track, volleyball and basketball courts, a weight room, and 2 dance studios.

Disabled Students: 75% of the campus is accessible. Facilities include wheelchair ramps, elevators, special parking, specially equipped restrooms, lowered drinking fountains, and special housing.

Services: Counseling and information services are available, as is tutoring in some subjects including, math, English, science, social science, and art history. There is a reader service for the blind. Individual tutoring and testing services are also available.

Campus Safety and Security: Measures include 24-hour foot and vehicle patrol, emergency notification system, and security escort services. There are emergency telephones, lighted pathways/sidewalks, controlled access to dorms/residences, orientation safety workshops.

Programs of Study: Pratt confers B.Arch., B.F.A., B.I.D. and B.P.S. degrees. Associate and master's degrees are also awarded. Bachelor's degrees are awarded in COMMUNICATIONS AND THE ARTS (art history and appreciation, communications, creative writing, film arts, fine arts, industrial design, and photography), EDUCATION (art education), ENGINEERING AND ENVIRONMENTAL DESIGN (architecture, computer graphics, construction management, and interior design), SOCIAL SCIENCE (fashion design and technology). Architecture, interior design, fine arts, industrial design, and communications design are the strongest academically. Architecture and communications design have the largest enrollments.

Required: The number of credits needed for graduation varies with the major, but a minimum of 132 is required, one quarter of which must be in liberal arts. Undergraduates must maintain a GPA of 2.0. All students must take 13 credits (15 for architecture majors) of liberal arts electives, 6 credits each of social sciences or philosophy, English, and cultural history, and 3 credits of science.

Special: Internships, study abroad in 4 countries Denmark, Italy, Japan, and Greece, dual degree programs, work-study programs on capmus, credit for work experience, non-degree study, and pass/fail options are available. There are 4 national honor societies.

Faculty/Classroom: 58% of faculty are male; 42% are female. 92% teach undergraduates. No introductory courses are taught by graduate students. The average class size in an introductory lecture is 22; in a laboratory is 20; and in a regular course is 15.

Admissions: 60% of the 2013-2014 applicants were accepted. The SAT scores for the 2013-2014 freshman class were: Critical Reading--14% below 500, 38% between 500 and 599, 39% between 600 and 699, and 9% between 700 and 800; Math--10% below 500, 31% between 500 and 599, 47% between 600 and 699, and 12% between 700 and 800; Writing--7% below 500, 41% between 500 and 599, 44% between 600 and 699, and 8% between 700 and 800. The ACT scores were 3% below 21, 16% between 21 and 23, 37% between 24 and 26, 23% between 27 and 28, and 21% above 28.

Requirements: The SAT or ACT is required. The ACT Optional Writing test is also required. SAT: subject tests in writing and mathematics level I or II are recommended for architecture applicants. Applicants must be graduates of an accredited secondary school. The GED is accepted. Students should have completed 4 years of English, 4 of math, and 2 each of science and history, and 1 of social studies. A portfolio is required. An interview is recommended but not required. A GPA of 2.8 is required. AP and CLEP credits are accepted. Important factors in the admissions decision are evidence of special talent, advanced placement or honors courses, and recommendations by school officials.

Procedure: Freshmen are admitted fall and spring. Entrance exams should be taken by November of the senior year. There is a deferred admissions plan. Early decision applications should be filed by November 1; regular applications, by January 5 for fall entry; and October 1 for spring entry, along with a $50 fee. Notifications are sent April 1. 150 applicants were on the 2013 waiting list; 30 were admitted. Applications are accepted online.

Transfer: 147 transfer students enrolled in 2012-2013. Applicants

should present college transcripts and recommendations. All transfer applicants without an associate degree must submit high school transcripts as well. A portfolio is required for architecture, writing, and art and design students. Applicants must have a statement of good standing from prior institution(s). 48 of 132 credits required for the bachelor's degree must be completed at Pratt.

Visiting: There are regularly scheduled orientations for prospective students, campus tour, schoolwide presentations, departmental presentations, and financial aid workshops. There are guides for informal visits and visitors may sit in on classes. To schedule a visit, contact the Office of Admissions.

Financial Aid: Pratt is a member of CSS. The CSS/Profile, FAFSA, and the college's own financial statement, and the parents' and students' tax returns are required. The deadline for filing freshman financial aid applications for fall entry is February 1.

International Students: There are 516 international students enrolled. The school actively recruits these students. They must take the TOEFL and the college's own test.

Computers: All students may access the system 24 hours a day, 7 days a week. There are no time limits and no fees.

Graduates: From July 1, 2012 to June 30, 2013, 527 bachelor's degrees were awarded. The most popular majors were visual and performing arts (78%), architecture (15%), and liberal arts (3%).

Admissions Contact: Judith Aaron, Vice President for Enrollment. E-Mail: *jaaron@pratt.edu* Web: *www.pratt.edu*

PURCHASE COLLEGE / STATE UNIVERSITY OF NEW YORK — D-5

Purchase, NY 10577-1400 — **(914) 251-6306; (914) 251-6314**

Full-time: 1605 men, 2010 women	**Faculty:** n/av; IIB, av$
Part-time: 100 men, 125 women	**Ph.D.s:** 100%
Graduate: 55 men, 75 women	**Student/Faculty:** n/av
Year: semesters, summer session	**Tuition:** $7500 ($15,431)
Application Deadline: see profile	**Room & Board:** $11,196
Freshman Class: n/av	
SAT or ACT: required	

COMPETITIVE

State University of New York/College at Purchase (also known as Purchase College SUNY), founded in 1967, is a public institution that offers programs in visual arts, music, acting, dance, film, theater/stage design technology, natural science, social science, and humanities. The figures in the above capsule and in this profile are approximate. There is 1 graduate school. In addition to regional accreditation, Purchase College SUNY has baccalaureate program accreditation with NASAD and NASM. The library contains 241,984 volumes, 257,609 microform items, and 18,273 audio/video tapes/CDs/DVDs, and subscribes to 37,153 periodicals including electronic. Computerized library services include interlibrary loans, database searching, Internet access, and laptop Internet portals. Special learning facilities include a learning resource center, radio station, TV station, listening and viewing center, science and photography labs, music practice rooms and instruments, multitrack synthesizers, music composition labs, digital video editing labs, typesetting and computer graphics labs, experimental stage, a performing arts complex, an electron microscope, and the Children's Center. The 500-acre campus is in a suburban area 35 miles north of midtown Manhattan. Including any residence halls, there are 40 buildings.

Student Life: 80% of undergraduates are from New York. Others are from 43 states, 27 foreign countries, and Canada. 55% are white. The average age of freshmen is 18; all undergraduates, 22. 18% do not continue beyond their first year; 51% remain to graduate.

Housing: 2600 students can be accommodated in college housing, which includes single-sex and coed dorms and on-campus apartments. In addition, there are special-interest houses, transfer student units, nontraditional-aged student units, wellness halls, presidential scholars halls, sophomore communities, conservatory halls, and learning community halls. On-campus housing is guaranteed for the freshman year only and is available on a first-come, first-served basis. 67% of students live on campus; of those, 75% remain on campus on weekends. All students may keep cars.

Activities: There are no fraternities or sororities. There are more than 40 groups on campus, including art, band, cheerleading, choir, chorale, computers, dance, drama, environmental, ethnic, jazz band, literary magazine, opera, orchestra, photography, political, professional, religious, social, social service, student government, symphony, and visual arts. Popular campus events include Spring Concert, Alcohol Awareness Week, and film programs.

Sports: There are 7 intercollegiate sports for men and 6 for women, and 20 intramural sports for men and 20 for women. Facilities include a fitness center, 6-lane pool, aerobics studio, 3 basketball courts, 4 racquetball courts, 2 squash courts, 10 tennis courts, outdoor climbing wall, 5 soccer fields, baseball field, softball field, and 4-lane bowling alley.

Disabled Students: All of the campus is accessible. Facilities include wheelchair ramps, elevators, special parking, and specially equipped restrooms. There are note takers, extended test times, quiet rooms for tests, interpreters for the hearing impaired, readers for the visually impaired, a reading machine in the library, and special note-taking paper.

Services: Counseling and information services are available, as is tutoring in every subject. There is a reader service for the blind, and remedial math, reading, and writing. There are drop-in sessions for math and writing.

Campus Safety and Security: Measures include 24-hour foot and vehicle patrol and security escort services. There are emergency telephones and lighted pathways/sidewalks.

Programs of Study: Purchase College SUNY confers B.A., B.S., B.A.L.A., B.F.A., and Mus. B. degrees. Master's degrees are also awarded. Bachelor's degrees are awarded in BIOLOGICAL SCIENCE (biology/biological science), COMMUNICATIONS AND THE ARTS (art history and appreciation, creative writing, dance, dramatic arts, film arts, journalism, literature, music, theater design, and visual and performing arts), COMPUTER AND PHYSICAL SCIENCE (chemistry and mathematics), ENGINEERING AND ENVIRONMENTAL DESIGN (environmental science), SOCIAL SCIENCE (anthropology, economics, ethnic studies, history, liberal arts/general studies, philosophy, political science/government, psychology, sociology, and women's studies). Biology and journalism are the strongest academically. Visual arts, music, and liberal studies have the largest enrollments.

Required: A minimum 2.0 GPA is required with a minimum of 120 credits. Students majoring in the arts complete a minimum of 90 professional credits and the SUNY general education curriculum. Students majoring in the liberal arts and sciences complete the general education curriculum and major requirements and must complete a senior thesis.

Special: Purchase College offers cross-registration with Empire State colleges, internships with corporations, newspapers, and local agencies, and student-designed majors, dual majors, study abroad, work-study, nondegree study, and pass/fail options. There is also an arts conservatory program.

Faculty/Classroom: 54% of faculty are male; 46% are female. All teach undergraduates. No introductory courses are taught by graduate students. The average class size in an introductory lecture is 27; in a laboratory, 12; and in a regular course, 14.

Requirements: The SAT or ACT is required, with minimum required composite scores of 1100 on the SAT or 23 on the ACT. Applicants must be graduates of an accredited secondary school and have completed 16 academic credits and 16 Carnegie units. The GED is accepted. Visual arts students must submit an essay and portfolio and have an interview. Film students need an essay and an interview. Design technology students need a portfolio and an interview. Performing arts students must audition. A GPA of 2.0 is required. AP and CLEP credits are accepted. Important factors in the admissions decision are evidence of special talent, recommendations by school officials, and personality/intangible qualities.

Procedure: Freshmen are admitted fall and spring. Entrance exams should be taken by the fall of the senior year. There are early decision, early admissions, deferred admissions, and rolling admissions plans. Notification of early decision is sent December 15; regular decision, sent on a rolling basis. Applications are accepted online. A waiting list is maintained. Check with the school for current application deadlines and fee.

Transfer: Students transferring to the School of Arts (visual or performing arts) must pass an audition or portfolio review. Transfer credit is limited; students can contact the Office of Admission to get a preliminary credit evaluation. Students transferring to programs in liberal arts and sciences must have a minimum 2.0 G.P.A. if they have completed 30 or more semester hours; if they have fewer than 30 semester hours, the high school transcript is also reviewed. Liberal arts and science transfers can transfer a maximum of 90 semester hours from 4-year colleges and 75 semester hours from 2-year colleges. 30 of 120 credits required for the bachelor's degree must be completed at Purchase College SUNY.

Visiting: There are regularly scheduled orientations for prospective students, including group question-and-answer sessions followed by a tour of the campus. To schedule a visit, contact the Admissions Office.

Financial Aid: Purchase College SUNY is a member of CSS. The FAFSA is required. Check with the school for current deadlines.

International Students: The school actively recruits international students. They must take the TOEFL with a minimum score of 550 on the paper-based TOEFL (PBT) or 80 on the Internet-based version (iBT), or score 430 on the SAT: verbal test, or take the IELTS.

Computers: There are no time limits. The fee is $150 per semester. It is strongly recommended that all students have a personal computer.

Admissions Contact: Dennis Craig, Vice President of Admissions. E-mail: *dennis.craig@purchase.edu* Web: *www.purchase.edu*

QUEENS COLLEGE / THE CITY UNIVERSITY OF NEW YORK D-5

Flushing, NY 11367 **(718) 997-5608; (718) 997-5617**

Full-time: 4631 men, 6138 women **Faculty:** n/av
Part-time: 1832 men, 2750 women **Ph.D.s:** 85%
Graduate: 1003 men, 2620 women **Student/Faculty:** 16 to 1
Year: semesters, summer session **Tuition:** $6207 ($15,027)
Application Deadline: February 1 **Room & Board:** $10,900
Freshman Class: 19032 applied, 7045 accepted, 890 enrolled
SAT CR/M: 540/574

VERY COMPETITIVE

At its founding in 1937, Queens College was hailed by the people of the borough as "the college of the future." Now part of the City University of New York (CUNY), Queens College offers a rigorous education in the liberal arts and sciences under the guidance of a faculty dedicated to both teaching and research. There is one undergraduate school and one graduate school. In addition to regional accreditation, Queens has baccalaureate program accreditation with ADA, NASM, NCATE, and TEAC. The library contains 1.1 million volumes, 978,608 microform items, 41,563 audio/video tapes/CDs/DVDs, and subscribes to 42,000 periodicals including electronic. Computerized library services include interlibrary loans, database searching, Internet access, and Wi-Fi capability. Special learning facilities include an art gallery, radio station, TV station, a small museums, and a theater. The 92-acre campus is in an urban area 12 miles from Manhattan. Including any residence halls, there are 17 buildings.

Student Life: 99% of undergraduates are from New York. Others are from 15 states, 90 foreign countries, and Canada. 70% are from public schools. 45% are White; 26% Asian American; 16% Hispanic. The average age of freshmen is 19; all undergraduates, 24. 13% do not continue beyond their first year; 55% remain to graduate.

Housing: 494 students can be accommodated in college housing, which includes coed dorms. On-campus housing is available on a first-come and first-served basis. 97% of students commute. Alcohol is not permitted. All students may keep cars.

Activities: 1% of men belong to 3 national fraternities. There are 81 groups on campus, including art, band, choir, chorus, communications, computers, dance, debate, drama, environmental, ethnic, film, gay, honors, international, jazz band, literary magazine, musical theater, newspaper, orchestra, political, professional, radio and TV, religious, social, social service, student government, symphony, and yearbook. Popular campus events include Fall and Spring Campus Fests, Spring Job Fair and Transfer Student Day.

Sports: There are 9 intercollegiate sports for men and 12 for women, and 9 intramural sports for men and 9 for women. Facilities include a gym complex, swimming pool, dance studios, weight rooms, outdoor quarter-mile track, soccer, lacrosse, and baseball fields, and 18 tennis courts.

Disabled Students: All of the campus is accessible. Facilities include wheelchair ramps, elevators, special parking, specially equipped restrooms, special class scheduling, lowered drinking fountains, lowered telephones, and special housing.

Services: Counseling and information services are available, as is tutoring in most subjects. There is a reader service for the blind.

Campus Safety and Security: Measures include 24-hour foot and vehicle patrol and emergency notification system. There are emergency telephones, lighted pathways/sidewalks, and controlled access to dorms/residences.

Programs of Study: Queens confers B.A.,B.S., B.B.A., B.F.A. and B.Mus. degrees. Master's degrees are also awarded. Bachelor's degrees are awarded in AGRICULTURE (environmental studies), BIOLOGICAL SCIENCE (biology/biological science, environmental biology, neurosciences, and nutrition), BUSINESS (accounting, banking and finance, business administration and management, international business management, and labor studies), COMMUNICATIONS AND THE ARTS (art, art history and appreciation, Chinese, comparative literature, dance, dramatic arts, English, film arts, French, German, graphic design, Greek (modern), Hebrew, Italian, linguistics, media arts, music, music performance, Russian, Spanish, and studio art), COMPUTER AND PHYSICAL SCIENCE (actuarial science, chemistry, computer science, environmental geology, geology, mathematics, and physics), EDUCATION (art education, early childhood education, home economics education, music education, physical education, and science education), ENGINEERING AND ENVIRONMENTAL DESIGN (environmental science), HEALTH PROFESSIONS (exercise science and speech pathology/audiology), SOCIAL SCIENCE (African studies, American studies, anthropology, classical/ancient civilization, East Asian studies, economics, family/consumer studies, history, home economics, interdisciplinary studies, Judaic studies, Latin American studies, philosophy, political science/government, psychology, religion, sociology, urban studies, and women's studies). Accounting, psychology, and economics have the largest enrollments.

Required: To graduate, students must complete 120 credits with a minimum GPA of 2.0. They must fulfill requirements in the major and liberal arts core curriculum. Effective Fall 2013, entering freshmen and transfer students will follow a revised liberal arts curriculum to meet the requirements of the CUNY Pathways Initiative. The Pathways General Education framework is common to all CUNY colleges. This guarantees that the core curriculum requirements fulfilled at one CUNY college will carry over seamesly if a student transfers to another CUNY college.

Special: Queens offers co-op programs, cross-registration with other CUNY campuses, internships in business, liberal arts, journalism, and social sciences, study abroad, work-study, accelerated degrees, dual majors, pass/fail options, and nondegree study. There are preprofessional programs in engineering, law, and prehealth. The SEEK program provides financial and educational resources for underprepared freshmen. There are 15 national honor societies, including Phi Beta Kappa, and a freshman honors program.

Faculty/Classroom: 52% of faculty are male; 48% are female. Graduate students teach 1% of introductory courses.

Admissions: 37% of the 2013-2014 applicants were accepted. The SAT scores for the 2013-2014 freshman class were: Critical Reading--35% below 500, 47% between 500 and 599, 13% between 600 and 699, and 5% between 700 and 800; Math--6% below 500, 60% between 500 and 599, 28% between 600 and 699, and 6% between 700 and 800; Writing--39% below 500, 45% between 500 and 599, 13% between 600 and 699, and 4% between 700 and 800.

Requirements: The SAT is required. High school preparation should include 4 years each of English and social studies, 3 each of math and foreign language, and 2 of lab science. A GPA of 3.0 is required. AP and CLEP credits are accepted.

Procedure: Freshmen are admitted fall and spring. Entrance exams should be taken in the spring of the junior year or the fall of the senior year. There are early admissions and rolling admissions plans. Application deadlines are open. Application fee is $65. Notifications are sent February 1.

Transfer: 3431 transfer students enrolled in 2012-2013. Admissions requirements vary depending on the number of credits to be transferred; students should consult with the Admissions Office. 45 of 120 credits required for the bachelor's degree must be completed at Queens.

Visiting: There are regularly scheduled orientations for prospective students, including information sessions and a campus tour. Visitors may sit in on classes. To schedule a visit, contact the Admissions Office.

Financial Aid: In 2013-2014, 65% of all full-time freshmen and 46% of continuing full-time students received some form of financial aid. 68% of all full-time freshmen and 46% of continuing full-time students received need-based aid. The average freshman award was $4,500. Need-based scholarships or need-based grants averaged $6,000; need-based self-help aid (loans and jobs) averaged $4,857; and non-need-based athletic scholarships averaged $5,000. 2% of undergraduate students work part-time. Average annual earnings from campus work are $3474. The average financial indebtedness of the 2013 graduate was $20,000. The FAFSA and the state aid form are required. The priority date for freshman financial aid applications for fall entry is February 15.

International Students: There are 736 international students enrolled. They must take the TOEFL with a minimum score of 600 on the paper-based TOEFL (PBT) or 62 on the Internet-based version (iBT). They must also take the SAT or the CUNY Skills Assessment Test.

Computers: All students may access the system during day and evening hours, 7 days a week. There are no time limits. The fee is $100 per semester.

Graduates: From July 1, 2012 to June 30, 2013, 3207 bachelor's degrees were awarded. The most popular majors were psychology (18%), accounting (14%), and economics/ sociology (10%). 55 companies recruited on campus in 2012-2013. In an average class, 4% graduate in 3 years or less, 25% graduate in 4 years or less, 45% graduate in 5 years or less, and 55% graduate in 6 years or less. Of the 2012 graduating class, 25% were enrolled in graduate school within 6 months of graduation, and 67% were employed.

Admissions Contact: Dr. Vincent J. Angrisani, Executive Director of Admissions, Marketing, and Sholarship. E-Mail: *vincent.angrisani@qc.cuny.edu* Web: *http://www.qc.cuny.edu/admissions*

RENSSELAER POLYTECHNIC INSTITUTE D-3

Troy, NY 12180 **(518) 276-6216**
(800) 448-6562; (518) 276-4072

Full-time: 3819 men, 1604 women **Faculty:** 404; I, av$
Part-time: 21 men, 8 women **Ph.D.s:** 99%
Graduate: 1112 men, 431 women **Student/Faculty:** 15 to 1
Year: semesters, summer session **Tuition:** $46,269
Application Deadline: January 15 **Room & Board:** $12,960
Freshman Class: 16150 applied, 6654 accepted, 1411 enrolled
SAT CR/M: 660/720 **ACT:** 29 **MOST COMPETITIVE**

Rensselaer Polytechnic Institute, founded in 1824, is a private institution that offers bachelor's, master's and doctoral degrees in engineering, the sciences, information technology, architecture, management, and the humanities and social sciences. Institute programs serve undergraduates, graduate students, and working professionals around the world. There are 5 undergraduate schools and 5 graduate schools. In addition to regional accreditation, Rensselaer has baccalaureate program accreditation with AACSB, ABET, and NAAB. The 2 libraries contain 476,510 volumes, 125,616 microform items, and 137,094 audio/video tapes/CDs/DVDs, and subscribe to 21,036 periodicals including electronic. Computerized library services include interlibrary loans, database searching, Internet access, and Wi-Fi capability. Special learning facilities include an art gallery, radio station, TV station, an observatory. The 295-acre campus is in a suburban area 10 miles north of Albany. Including any residence halls, there are 200 buildings.

Student Life: 66% of undergraduates are from out of state, mostly the Northeast. Students are from 49 states, 63 foreign countries, and Canada. 71% are from public schools. 65% are White. The average age of freshmen is 18; all undergraduates, 20. 7% do not continue beyond their first year; 85% remain to graduate.

Housing: 3400 students can be accommodated in college housing, which includes single-sex and coed dorms, on-campus apartments, and married student housing. In addition, there are fraternity houses. On-campus housing is available on a first-come, first-served basis, and is available on a lottery system for upperclassmen. 57% of students live on campus. Upperclassmen may keep cars.

Activities: 30% of men belong to 1 local and 31 national fraternities; 16% of women belong to 1 local and 4 national sororities. There are 161 groups on campus, including Biomedical Engineering Society, Entrepreneurship, Finance, Rensselaer Biotechnology Students Association, art, Astrophysical Society, band, cheerleading, chess, choir, chorale, chorus, computers, dance, drama, drill team, environmental, ethnic, film, gay, honors, international, jazz band, literary magazine, musical theater, orchestra, pep band, photography, political, professional, radio and TV, religious, social, social service, student government, and symphony. Popular campus events include Winter Carnival and Big Red Freak-out.

Sports: There are 12 intercollegiate sports for men and 11 for women, and 22 intramural sports for men and 21 for women. Facilities include a field house, pool, stadium, 5 gyms, a sports and recreation center, several playing fields, 2 weight rooms, a fitness center, 6 tennis courts, 7 handball/squash courts, 3 artificial turf fields, an indoor track, an ice hockey rink, a stadium and a arena.

Disabled Students: Facilities include wheelchair ramps, elevators, special parking, specially equipped restrooms, special class scheduling, lowered drinking fountains, and lowered telephones.

Services: Counseling and information services are available, as is tutoring in every subject. There is a reader service for the blind, and remedial math, reading, and writing. There is a writing center and an advising and learning assistance center.

Campus Safety and Security: Measures include 24-hour foot and vehicle patrol, self-defense education, and security escort services. There are shuttle buses, emergency telephones, lighted pathways/sidewalks, card-access residence halls, on-campus bicycle patrol, and a student volunteer program.

Programs of Study: Rensselaer confers B.S., and B.Arch. degrees. Master's and doctoral degrees are also awarded. Bachelor's degrees are awarded in BIOLOGICAL SCIENCE (biochemistry, biology/biological science, and biophysics), BUSINESS (management information systems, management science, and recreation and leisure services), COMMUNICATIONS AND THE ARTS (communications and media arts), COMPUTER AND PHYSICAL SCIENCE (applied physics, chemistry, computer science, geology, hydrogeology, mathematics, physics, and science technology), ENGINEERING AND ENVIRONMENTAL DESIGN (aeronautical engineering, architecture, biomedical engineering, chemical engineering, civil engineering, computer engineering, construction engineering, electrical/electronics engineering, engineering, engineering physics, environmental engineering, industrial engineering, materials engineering, mechanical engineering, and nuclear engineering), HEALTH PROFESSIONS (premedicine), SOCIAL SCIENCE (economics, interdisciplinary studies, philosophy, prelaw, and psychology). Engineering, sciences, and architecture are the strongest academically. General engineering, computer science, and management have the largest enrollments.

Required: For graduation, students must earn at least 124 credits in all majors except engineering (128 needed) and the B.Arch. Program (168 needed). The core curriculum includes 48 credits in math, science, humanities, and social sciences. Students must maintain a minimum GPA of 1.8 and must fulfill a writing requirement.

Special: Rensselaer offers co-op programs, internships, study abroad/exchange program, and pass/fail options are available. Students may pursue dual and student-designed majors, a 3-2 engineering degree with more than 40 universities, 2-2 agreements, an accelerated degree program in physician-scientist, law and MBA. There are 14 national honor societies and 8 departmental honors programs.

Faculty/Classroom: 77% of faculty are male; 23% are female. No introductory courses are taught by graduate students. The average class size in an introductory lecture is 35; in a laboratory is 18; and in a regular course is 28.

Admissions: 41% of the 2013-2014 applicants were accepted. The SAT scores for the 2013-2014 freshman class were: Critical Reading--1% below 500, 17% between 500 and 599, 48% between 600 and 699, and 34% between 700 and 800; Math--3% between 500 and 599, 33% between 600 and 699, and 64% between 700 and 800. The ACT scores were 5% between 21 and 23, 18% between 24 and 26, 21% between 27 and 28, and 56% above 28. 88% of the current freshmen were in the top fifth of their class; 98% were in the top two fifths. 43 freshmen graduated first in their class.

Requirements: The SAT or ACT is required. SAT subject tests in critical reading, math and science are required for accelerated-program applicants or ACT, which must include the optional writing component in lieu of SAT and SAT. AP credits are accepted. Important factors in the admissions decision are advanced placement or honors courses, recommendations by school officials, and leadership record.

Procedure: Freshmen are admitted fall, spring, and summer. Entrance exams should be taken in the junior or senior year. There are early decision and deferred admissions plans. Early decision applications should be filed by November 1; regular applications, by January 15 for fall entry; and November 1 for spring entry, along with a $70 fee. Notification of early decision is sent December 14; regular decision, March 8. 340 early decision candidates were accepted for the 2013-2014 class. 3787 applicants were on the 2013 waiting list; 2475 were admitted. Applications are accepted online.

Transfer: 126 transfer students enrolled in 2012-2013. Applicants should have completed 12 or more transferable college credits, and must be in good academic standing at the institutions they are attending or attended. 60 of 120 credits required for the bachelor's degree must be completed at Rensselaer.

Visiting: There are regularly scheduled orientations for prospective students, Mon-Friday Info session at 9am, tour 10 am M-F 8:30-5:00 pm, and Saturday 10 am March-Nov only. There are guides for informal visits and visitors may sit in on classes. To schedule a visit, contact the Admissions Office at (518) 276-6216.

Financial Aid: In 2013-2014, 93% of all full-time freshmen and 95% of continuing full-time students received some form of financial aid. 70% of all full-time freshmen and 65% of continuing full-time students received need-based aid. The average freshman award was $35,747. Need-based scholarships or need-based grants averaged $30,108; need-based self-help aid (loans and jobs) averaged $5,656; non-need-based athletic scholarships averaged $50,841; and other non-need-based awards and non-need-based scholarships averaged $14,902. Average annual earnings from campus work are $2500. The average financial indebtedness of the 2013 graduate was $32,000. Rensselaer is a member of CSS. The CSS/Profile and FAFSA are required. The priority date for freshman financial aid applications for fall entry is February 1.

International Students: There are 396 international students enrolled. The school actively recruits these students. They must take the TOEFL with a minimum score of 570 on the paper-based TOEFL (PBT) or 88 on the Internet-based version (iBT). They must also take the SAT or ACT.

Computers: All students may access the system. There are no time limits and no fees.

Graduates: From July 1, 2012 to June 30, 2013, 1244 bachelor's degrees were awarded. The most popular majors were engineering (53%), computer science (9%), and management (7%). 370 companies recruited on campus in 2012-2013. In an average class, 60% graduate in 4 years or less, 83% graduate in 5 years or less, and 84% graduate in 6 years or less. Of the 2012 graduating class, 22% were enrolled in graduate school within 6 months of graduation, and 49% were employed.

Admissions Contact: Paul P Marthers, VP Enrollment. E-Mail: *admissions@rpi.edu* Web: *www.rpi.edu*

ROBERTS WESLEYAN COLLEGE — B-3

Rochester, NY 14624 — **(585) 594-6400**
(800) 777-4792; (585) 594-6371

Full-time: 358 men, 819 women	**Faculty:** 87
Part-time: 50 men, 96 women	**Ph.D.s:** 71%
Graduate: 91 men, 338 women	**Student/Faculty:** 14 to 1
Year: semesters, summer session	**Tuition:** $27,754
Application Deadline: February 1	**Room & Board:** $9630
Freshman Class: 1928 applied, 897 accepted, 210 enrolled	
SAT CR/M: 542/533 **ACT:** 24	**COMPETITIVE+**

Roberts Wesleyan College, founded in 1866, is a private institution affiliated with the Free Methodist Church. The curriculum offers a Christian liberal arts education. In addition to regional accreditation, Roberts has baccalaureate program accreditation with ACBSP, CSWE, NASAD, NASM, and NLN. The library contains 142,268 volumes, 117,854 microform items, and 2,373 audio/video tapes/CDs/DVDs, and subscribes to 33,000 periodicals including electronic. Computerized library services include interlibrary loans, database searching, Internet access, and Wi-Fi capability. Special learning facilities include an art gallery. The 188-acre campus is in a suburban area 8 miles southwest of Rochester. Including any residence halls, there are 32 buildings.

Student Life: 91% of undergraduates are from New York. Others are from 27 states, 33 foreign countries, and Canada. 75% are White; 12% African American. 86% are Protestant; 14% Catholic. The average age of freshmen is 18; all undergraduates, 25. 20% do not continue beyond their first year; 59% remain to graduate.

Housing: 792 students can be accommodated in college housing, which includes single-sex dorms, on-campus apartments, and off-campus apartments. On-campus housing is guaranteed for all 4 years. 65% of students live on campus; of those, 60% remain on campus on weekends. Alcohol is not permitted. All students may keep cars.

Activities: There are no fraternities or sororities. Groups on campus include band, choir, chorale, chorus, dance, drama, ethnic, honors, international, jazz band, musical theater, newspaper, opera, orchestra, pep band, religious, social, social service, student government, symphony, and yearbook. Popular campus events include Winter Weekend, Spring Formal, Talent and Variety Shows.

Sports: There are 7 intercollegiate sports for men and 7 for women, and 6 intramural sports for men and 6 for women. Facilities include an athletic center with facilities for basketball, volleyball, tennis, badminton, track, soccer, weight lifting, walleyball, racquetball, flag football, ultimate frisbee, and swimming.

Disabled Students: 71% of the campus is accessible. Facilities include wheelchair ramps, elevators, special parking, specially equipped restrooms, special class scheduling, lowered drinking fountains, and lowered telephones.

Services: Counseling and information services are available, as is tutoring in every subject. Note takers for the hearing impaired are available. There is a reader service for the blind, and remedial math, reading, and writing.

Campus Safety and Security: Measures include 24-hour foot and vehicle patrol, emergency notification system, self-defense education, and security escort services. There are emergency telephones, lighted pathways/sidewalks, controlled access to dorms/residences, personal-safety education programs.

Programs of Study: Roberts confers B.A., and B.S. degrees. Associate and master's degrees are also awarded. Bachelor's degrees are awarded in BIOLOGICAL SCIENCE (biochemistry and biology/biological science), BUSINESS (accounting, business administration and management, international business management, and marketing/retailing/merchandising), COMMUNICATIONS AND THE ARTS (applied art, applied music, art, communications, English, fine arts, graphic design, music, music performance, Spanish, and studio art), COMPUTER AND PHYSICAL SCIENCE (chemistry, computer science, mathematics, and physics), EDUCATION (art education, early childhood education, elementary education, English education, mathematics education, music education, physical education, secondary education, and special education), ENGINEERING AND ENVIRONMENTAL DESIGN (preengineering), HEALTH PROFESSIONS (nursing, pharmacy, premedicine, prepharmacy, and preveterinary science), SOCIAL SCIENCE (biblical studies, Christian studies, criminal justice, history, humanities, interdisciplinary studies, liberal arts/general studies, philosophy, prelaw, psychology, religion, and social work). Music, education, and social work are the strongest academically. Elementary education and nursing have the largest enrollments.

Required: To graduate, students must complete a minimum of 124 credit hours, with a minimum of 30 hours in the major. Required courses include first-year experience, phys ed, modern technology, world issues, speech, writing, history, Bible, and philosophy.

Special: Students may cross-register with members of the Rochester Area Colleges consortium. Internships, study abroad in 8 countries, a Washington semester, co-op programs, B.A.-B.S. degrees, dual majors, and 3-2 engineering degrees with Clarkson University, Rensselaer Polytechnic Institute, and Rochester Institute of Technology are available. Nondegree study and credit for life, military, and work experience are also offered. The organizational management program, geared to adults, consists of 4-hour weekly sessions, with reliance on out-of-class work. There is a freshman honors program and 100 departmental honors programs.

Faculty/Classroom: 44% of faculty are male; 56% are female. 85% teach undergraduates. No introductory courses are taught by graduate students. The average class size in an introductory lecture is 38; in a laboratory is 15; and in a regular course is 23.

Admissions: 47% of the 2013-2014 applicants were accepted. The SAT scores for the 2013-2014 freshman class were: Critical Reading--35% below 500, 39% between 500 and 599, 21% between 600 and 699, and 5% between 700 and 800; Math--40% below 500, 39% between 500 and 599, 17% between 600 and 699, and 4% between 700 and 800; Writing--51% below 500, 31% between 500 and 599, 14% between 600 and 699, and 4% between 700 and 800. The ACT scores were 23% below 21, 18% between 21 and 23, 18% between 24 and 26, 23% between 27 and 28, and 18% above 28. 49% of the current freshmen were in the top fifth of their class; 85% were in the top two fifths. 8 freshmen graduated first in their class.

Requirements: The SAT or ACT is required. Applicants must be graduates of an accredited secondary school. The GED is accepted. At least 12 academic credits are required, including 4 years of English and 2 years each of math and science. A foreign language and 3 years of social studies are recommended. The chosen major may modify requirements. An essay is required, and an interview is recommended. Roberts requires applicants to be in the upper 50% of their class. A GPA of 2.5 is required. AP and CLEP credits are accepted. Important factors in the admissions decision are advanced placement or honors courses, personality/intangible qualities, and extracurricular activities record.

Procedure: Freshmen are admitted fall, spring, and summer. There are deferred admissions and rolling admissions plans. Applications should be filed by February 1 for fall entry; December 1 for spring entry, along with a $35 fee. Notification is sent on a rolling basis. Applications are accepted online.

Transfer: 93 transfer students enrolled in 2012-2013. Applicants must submit transcripts from all previous institutions attended. Credit is usually accepted for courses with grade C or better. 30 of 124 credits required for the bachelor's degree must be completed at Roberts.

Visiting: There are regularly scheduled orientations for prospective students, including a campus tour, class visits, admissions overview, meetings with faculty, and a financial aid presentation. There are guides for informal visits, visitors may sit in on classes, and stay overnight. To schedule a visit, contact the Admissions Office.

Financial Aid: In 2013-2014, 98% of all full-time freshmen and 98% of continuing full-time students received some form of financial aid. 90% of all full-time freshmen and 90% of continuing full-time students received need-based aid. The average freshman award was $23,673. Need-based scholarships or need-based grants averaged $18,934; need-based self-help aid (loans and jobs) averaged $5,513; and other non-need-based awards and non-need-based scholarships averaged $4,319. 35% of undergraduate students work part-time. Average annual earnings from campus work are $1020. Roberts is a member of CSS. The FAFSA and TAP (New York residents only) are required. The priority date for freshman financial aid applications for fall entry is March 15. The deadline for filing freshman financial aid applications for fall entry is rolling.

International Students: There are 66 international students enrolled. They must take the TOEFL with a minimum score of 540 on the paper-based TOEFL (PBT) or 75 on the Internet-based version (iBT). International students who take the SAT or ACT and score high enough do not need to take the TOEFL or IELTS.

Computers: All students may access the system 24 hours a day, 7 days a week. There are no time limits and no fees.

Graduates: From July 1, 2012 to June 30, 2013, 361 bachelor's degrees were awarded. The most popular majors were nursing (18%), education (14%), and psychology (9%). In an average class, 48% graduate in 4 years or less, 57% graduate in 5 years or less, and 67% graduate in 6 years or less. Of the 2012 graduating class, 24% were enrolled in graduate school within 6 months of graduation, and 93% were employed.

Admissions Contact: JP Anderson, Associate Vice President for UG Admiss.. E-Mail: *anderson_JP@roberts.edu* Web: *www.roberts.edu*

ROCHESTER INSTITUTE OF TECHNOLOGY B-3

Rochester, NY 14623 **(585) 475-6631; (585) 475-7424**

Full-time: 8531 men, 4212 women **Faculty:** n/av; IIA, +$
Part-time: 950 men, 531 women **Ph.D.s:** 70%
Graduate: 1959 men, 1023 women **Student/Faculty:** 13 to 1
Year: quarters, summer session **Tuition:** $32,037
Application Deadline: March 1 **Room & Board:** $10,413
Freshman Class: 14097 applied, 8465 accepted, 2612 enrolled
SAT or ACT: required

VERY COMPETITIVE+

Rochester Institute of Technology (RIT) is one of the world's leading career-oriented, technological universities. RIT offers more than ninety undergraduate programs in areas such as engineering, computing, information technology, engineering technology, business, hospitality, science, art, design, photography, biomedical sciences, game design and development, and the liberal arts including psychology, advertising and public relations, and public policy. Students may choose from more than ninety different minors to develop personal and professional interests that complement their academic program. Experiential education is integrated into many programs through cooperative education, internships, study abroad, and undergraduate research. As home to the National Technical Institute for the Deaf (NTID), RIT is a leader in providing access services for deaf and hard-of-hearing students. RIT enrolls students from every state and more than one-hundred countries. There are 9 undergraduate schools and 9 graduate schools. In addition to regional accreditation, RIT has baccalaureate program accreditation with AACSB, ABET, ADA, CAHEA, CSAB, CSWE, FIDER, and NASAD. The library contains 422,281 volumes,

498,703 microform items, and 54,935 audio/video tapes/CDs/DVDs, and subscribes to 21,208 periodicals including electronic. Computerized library services include interlibrary loans, database searching, Internet access, and Wi-Fi capability. Special learning facilities include an art gallery, radio station, TV station, a computer chip manufacturing facility, a student-operated restaurant, an electronic prepress lab, an imaging science facility, and an observatory. The 1300-acre campus is in a suburban area 5 miles south of Rochester. Including any residence halls, there are 195 buildings.

Student Life: 51% of undergraduates are from New York. Others are from 50 states, 107 foreign countries, and Canada. 85% are from public schools. 70% are White. The average age of freshmen is 18; all undergraduates, 21. 8% do not continue beyond their first year; 69% remain to graduate.

Housing: 7144 students can be accommodated in college housing, which includes single-sex and coed dorms, on-campus apartments, and married student housing. In addition, there are honors houses, special-interest houses, fraternity houses, and sorority houses. On-campus housing is guaranteed for the freshman year only, is available on a first-come, and first-served basis. 68% of students live on campus; of those, 90% remain on campus on weekends. All students may keep cars.

Activities: 5% of men belong to 17 national fraternities; 5% of women belong to 12 national sororities. There are 207 groups on campus, including art, band, cheerleading, chess, choir, chorale, chorus, computers, dance, drama, environmental, ethnic, film, gay, gospel choir, honors, international, jazz band, literary magazine, newspaper, orchestra, pep band, photography, political, professional, radio and TV, religious, social, social service, and student government. Popular campus events include Fall, Spring, and Winter Weekends and Martin Luther King Celebration.

Sports: There are 11 intercollegiate sports for men and 12 for women, and 13 intramural sports for men and 13 for women. Facilities include 3 gyms, an ice rink, 2 swimming pools, 9 tennis courts, a field house, athletic fields, and a student life center with 8 racquetball courts, dance facilities, weight training facilities, and an indoor track.

Disabled Students: 95% of the campus is accessible. Facilities include wheelchair ramps, elevators, special parking, specially equipped restrooms, special class scheduling, lowered drinking fountains, lowered telephones, special housing.

Services: Counseling and information services are available, as is tutoring in most subjects. There is a reader service for the blind. There are comprehensive support services for students with physical or learning disabilities and for first-generation college students.

Campus Safety and Security: Measures include 24-hour foot and vehicle patrol, emergency notification system, self-defense education, and security escort services. There are shuttle buses, emergency telephones, lighted pathways/sidewalks, and controlled access to dorms/residences.

Programs of Study: RIT confers B.S. and B.F.A. degrees. Associate, master's, and doctoral degrees are also awarded. Bachelor's degrees are awarded in BIOLOGICAL SCIENCE (biochemistry, bioinformatics, biology/biological science, biotechnology, and nutrition), BUSINESS (accounting, banking and finance, business administration and management, business systems analysis, hotel/motel and restaurant management, international business management, management information systems, management science, marketing management, and tourism), COMMUNICATIONS AND THE ARTS (animation, applied art, ceramic art and design, communications, communications technology, crafts, design, film arts, fine arts, glass, graphic design, illustration, industrial design, metal/jewelry, photography, publishing, sculpture, studio art, telecommunications, and video), COMPUTER AND PHYSICAL SCIENCE (applied mathematics, chemistry, computer mathematics, computer science, information sciences and systems, mathematics, physics, polymer science, software engineering, statistics, and systems analysis), EDUCATION (education of the deaf and hearing impaired), ENGINEERING AND ENVIRONMENTAL DESIGN (aerospace studies, biomedical engineering, chemical engineering, civil engineering technology, computer engineering, computer graphics, computer technology, electrical/electronics engineering, electrical/electronics engineering technology, engineering, engineering technology, environmental engineering technology, environmental science, furniture design, graphic arts technology, graphic and printing production, industrial engineering, interior design, manufacturing engineering, manufacturing technology, materials science, mechanical engineering, mechanical engineering technology, military science, printing technology, and woodworking), HEALTH PROFESSIONS (allied health, physician's assistant, predentistry, premedicine, preveterinary science, and ultrasound technology), SOCIAL SCIENCE (criminal justice, dietetics, economics, food production/management/services, interpreter for the deaf, philosophy, prelaw, psychology, and public affairs). Mechanical engineering, computer science, and film and animation are the strongest academically. Engineering, information technology, and photography have the largest enrollments.

Required: Students must have a GPA of 2.0 and have completed 180 quarter credit hours to graduate. Distribution requirements include 36 credits in the liberal arts (writing, humanities, and social sciences). B.S. programs also require a minimum of 20 quarter credit hours in science and math. There are no general science or math requirements for the B.F.A. programs in art, design, photography, or film/video.

Special: RIT offers internships in social science and allied health majors, and cooperative education programs with 1900 co-op employers. Cooperative education is required or recommended in most programs and provides full-time paid work experience. Cross-registration with Rochester-area colleges is available. There are accelerated dual degree (BS/MS, BS/ME, BS/MBA) programs in science, engineering, public policy, math, computer science, materials science, imaging science, and business. Students may study abroad in 15 countries, and student-designed majors are permitted in applied arts and sciences. There is an Honors Program in general education and home colleges. There are 6 national honor societies, a freshman honors program, and 7 departmental honors programs.

Faculty/Classroom: 65% of faculty are male; 35% are female. 97% teach undergraduates, 3% do research, and 90% do both. No introductory courses are taught by graduate students. The average class size in an introductory lecture is 30; in a laboratory is 16; and in a regular course is 20.

Admissions: 60% of the 2013-2014 applicants were accepted. 60% of the current freshmen were in the top fifth of their class; 85% were in the top two fifths.

Requirements: The SAT or ACT is required. Applicants must be high school graduates or have a GED certificate. Applicants are required to submit an essay, and an interview is recommended. The School of Art, the School of Design, and the School for American Crafts emphasize a required portfolio of artwork. Required high school math and science credits vary by program, with 3 years in each area generally acceptable. RIT requires applicants to be in the upper 50% of their class. AP and CLEP credits are accepted. Important factors in the admissions decision are advanced placement or honors courses, recommendations by school officials, and extracurricular activities record.

Procedure: Freshmen are admitted to all sessions. Entrance exams should be taken during the junior or senior year. There are early decision and deferred admissions plans. Early decision applications should be filed by December 1; regular applications, by March 1 for fall entry, along with a $50 fee. Notification of early decision is sent January 15; regular decision, March 15. Applications are accepted online.

Transfer: 1079 transfer students enrolled in 2012-2013. Transfer students must have a GPA of 2.5 for admission to most programs; those with fewer than 30 college credits must supply a high school transcript. Other requirements vary by program. 45 of 180 credits required for the bachelor's degree must be completed at RIT.

Visiting: There are regularly scheduled orientations for prospective students, including academic advising and information on housing and student services. There are guides for informal visits, visitors may sit in on classes, and stay overnight. To schedule a visit, contact the Admissions Receptionist at (585) 475-6736.

Financial Aid: In 2013-2014, 85% of all full-time freshmen and 89% of continuing full-time students received some form of financial aid. 81% of all full-time freshmen and 83% of continuing full-time students received need-based aid. The average freshman award was $18,900. Need-based scholarships or need-based grants averaged $16,500; and need-based self-help aid (loans and jobs) averaged $5,000. 70% of undergraduate students work part-time. Average annual earnings from campus work are $2500. The average financial indebtedness of the 2013 graduate was $23,800. The FAFSA is required. The priority date for freshman financial aid applications for fall entry is March 1.

International Students: There are 545 international students enrolled. The school actively recruits these students. They must take the TOEFL with a minimum score of 550 on the paper-based TOEFL (PBT) or 79 on the Internet-based version (iBT). They must also take the SAT or ACT.

Computers: All students may access the system 7 days per week, 24-hour access. There are no time limits and no fees.

Graduates: From July 1, 2012 to June 30, 2013, 2432 bachelor's degrees were awarded. The most popular majors were business administration (7%), mechanical engineering (5%), and information technology (5%). 900 companies recruited on campus in 2012-2013. In an average class, 69% graduate in 6 years or less. Of the 2012 graduating class, 15% were enrolled in graduate school within 6 months of graduation, and 80% were employed.

Admissions Contact: Daniel Shelley, Director of Admissions. E-Mail: *admissions@rit.edu* Web: *www.rit.edu*

RUSSELL SAGE COLLEGE D-3

Troy, NY 12180 (518) 244-2217
(888) Very-Sage; (518) 244-6880

Full-time: 10 men, 772 women
Part-time: 9 men, 32 women
Graduate: n/av
Year: semesters, summer session
Application Deadline:
Freshman Class: n/av
Faculty: 61; IIA, --$
Ph.D.s: 90%
Student/Faculty: 10 to 1
Tuition: $28,000
Room & Board: $11,370

COMPETITIVE

Russell Sage College is a comprehensive college for women nestled within the historic district of Troy, NY. RSC offers liberal arts and professional degree programs in an environment aimed at empowering students to become women of influence in their careers and their communities. There are 2 undergraduate schools and 1 graduate school. In addition to regional accreditation, Russell Sage has baccalaureate program accreditation with ADA, APTA, NASAD, NCATE, and NLN. The library contains 164,946 volumes, 18,514 microform items, and 6,419 audio/video tapes/CDs/DVDs, and subscribes to 65,391 periodicals including electronic. Computerized library services include interlibrary loans and database searching. Special learning facilities include a The 14-acre campus is in an urban area 10 miles from Albany and Schenectady. Including any residence halls, there are 38 buildings.

Student Life: 93% of undergraduates are from New York. Others are from 16 states, and 1 foreign countries. 67% are White; 12% race unknown. The average age of freshmen is 18; all undergraduates, 21. 10% do not continue beyond their first year; 73% remain to graduate.

Housing: 738 students can be accommodated in college housing, which includes single-sex dorms and on-campus apartments. In addition, there are language houses and special-interest houses. On-campus housing is guaranteed for all 4 years and is available on a lottery system for upperclassmen. 52% of students commute. Alcohol is not permitted. All students may keep cars.

Activities: There are no fraternities or sororities. There are 26 groups on campus, including choir, chorus, dance, drama, ethnic, gay, honors, literary magazine, musical theater, newspaper, political, religious, social, student government, and yearbook. Popular campus events include Spirit of Sage River Cruise, Rally Day, Sage Fest, and Family Weekend.

Sports: There are 7 intercollegiate sports for men and 8 for women, and 7 intramural sports for men and 8 for women. Facilities include Neff Athletic Center, Robison Athletic Center, a weight and fitness center, swimming pool, tennis courts, a practice field, 2 gyms, and a large multipurpose room for indoor recreation.

Disabled Students: 75% of the campus is accessible. Facilities include wheelchair ramps, elevators, and special parking.

Services: Counseling and information services are available, as is tutoring in most subjects. There is remedial math, reading, and writing.

Campus Safety and Security: Measures include 24-hour foot and vehicle patrol, self-defense education, and security escort services. There are emergency telephones, lighted pathways/sidewalks, an evening escort service, and monitored video cameras.

Programs of Study: Russell Sage confers B.A., and B.S. degrees. Master's degrees are also awarded. Bachelor's degrees are awarded in BIOLOGICAL SCIENCE (biochemistry, biology/biological science, and nutrition), COMMUNICATIONS AND THE ARTS (English, musical theater, and Spanish), COMPUTER AND PHYSICAL SCIENCE (chemistry and mathematics), EDUCATION (elementary education), ENGINEERING AND ENVIRONMENTAL DESIGN (environmental science), HEALTH PROFESSIONS (art therapy, nursing, occupational therapy, and physical therapy), SOCIAL SCIENCE (applied psychology, criminal justice, forensic studies, history, interdisciplinary studies, international studies, political science/government, psychology, and sociology). Nursing, nutrition, health sciences, education, and psychology are the strongest academically. Health and rehabilitative sciences, education and psychology have the largest enrollments.

Required: A minimum of 120 credit hours is required for the baccalaureate degree. Students must complete at least half the major at Sage. Furthermore, 30 of the last 45 credits must be completed in residence (i.e. at Sage or through the Hudson Mohawk Association). Students must satisfy general education as well as major requirements and must maintain satisfactory standards of scholarship to be eligible for graduation. A Bachelor of Arts degree must include a minimum of 90 credit hours in the liberal arts. A Bachelor of Science degree must include a minimum of 60 credit hours in the liberal arts. Students must achieve a 2.2 grade point average in the major and a 2.0 overall cumulative grade point average. Some majors require a higher grade point average for graduation. The ultimate responsibility for fulfilling graduation requirements rests with the individual student.

Special: Students may cross-register with the 14 area schools of the Hudson-Mohawk Association of Colleges. A theater major is offered in conjunction with Sage Theater Institute. Study abroad, internships, and work-study programs are available. RSC has several accelerated 5-year programs; 3 + 2 M.S., in Occupational Therapy, a 3-2 engineering degree with nearby Rensselaer Polytechnic Institute and our accelerated 4+3 D.P.T. program. The college confers credit for life, military, or work experience. Non-degree study, student-designed majors, dual majors, and pass/fail options are also available. There are 14 national honor societies and a freshman honors program.

Faculty/Classroom: 28% of faculty are male; 72% are female. All teach and do research. No introductory courses are taught by graduate students. The average class size in an introductory lecture is 19; in a laboratory is 9; and in a regular course is 16.

Requirements: Applicants must be graduates of an accredited secondary school or have a GED. A minimum of 16 academic units are required. An essay, for applicants still in high school, is required, and an interview is recommended. A GPA of 2.0 is required. AP and CLEP credits are accepted. Important factors in the admissions decision are advanced placement or honors courses, recommendations by school officials, leadership record, recommendations by alumni, parents or siblings attended your school, evidence of special talent, extracurricular activities record, and geographical diversity.

Procedure: Freshmen are admitted fall and spring. Entrance exams should be taken during spring of the junior year or fall of the senior year. There are early admissions, deferred admissions, and rolling admissions plans. Early decision applications should be filed by December 1, along with a $30 fee. Notification of early decision is sent December 15; regular decision, on a rolling basis. Applications are accepted online.

Transfer: 84 transfer students enrolled in 2012-2013. Applicants must have a minimum GPA of 2.5. Interviews are strongly encouraged and may be required in some instances. 45 of 120 credits required for the bachelor's degree must be completed at Russell Sage.

Visiting: There are regularly scheduled orientations for prospective students, including meetings with faculty, a campus tour, a financial aid session, and an admissions interview. There are guides for informal visits, visitors may sit in on classes, and stay overnight. To schedule a visit, contact Thomas Barresi at rscadm@sage.edu.

Financial Aid: In 2013-2014, 94% of all full-time freshmen and 91% of continuing full-time students received some form of financial aid. 79% of all full-time freshmen and 74% of continuing full-time students received need-based aid. The FAFSA is required. Check with the school for current application deadlines.

International Students: There are 4 international students enrolled. The school actively recruits these students. They must take the TOEFL. They must also take the SAT or ACT.

Computers: All students may access the system. The public computer labs are open 14 hours per day, 7 days a week; dial-in access is available 24 hours a day. There are no time limits and no fees.

Graduates: From July 1, 2012 to June 30, 2013, 212 bachelor's degrees were awarded. The most popular majors were nursing (23%), health sciences (9%), and education (9%). 20 companies recruited on campus in 2012-2013. In an average class, 65% graduate in 4 years or less, 71% graduate in 5 years or less, and 73% graduate in 6 years or less. Of the 2012 graduating class, 32% were enrolled in graduate school within 6 months of graduation, and 65% were employed.

Admissions Contact: Elizabeth Robertson, Associate Vice President for Admissions. E-Mail: *rscadm@sage.edu* Web: *www.sage.edu*

SARAH LAWRENCE COLLEGE D-5

Bronxville, NY 10708 (914) 395-2510
(800) 888-2858; (914) 395-2515

Full-time: 330 men, 930 women
Part-time: 20 men, 70 women
Graduate: 60 men, 315 women
Year: semesters
Application Deadline: see profile
Freshman Class: n/av
Faculty: n/av; IIB, ++$
Ph.D.s: n/av
Student/Faculty: n/av
Tuition: $37,000
Room & Board: $13,000

HIGHLY COMPETITIVE

Sarah Lawrence College, established in 1926, is an independent institution conferring liberal arts degrees. The academic structure is based on the British don system. Students meet biweekly with professors in tutorials and are enrolled in small seminars. While there are no formal majors, students develop individual concentrations that are usually interdisciplinary. Figures in the above capsule and in this profile are approximate. There is 1 graduate school. The 3 libraries contain 282,676 volumes, 24,218 microform items, and 9,319 audio/video tapes/CDs/DVDs, and subscribe to 916 periodicals including electronic. Computerized library services include interlibrary loans, database searching, and Internet access. Special learning facilities include an art gallery, radio station, a slide library with 75,000 slides of art and architecture, early childhood center, electronic music studio; music library, student-run theater and student-run art gallery. The 41-acre campus is in a suburban area 15 miles north of midtown Manhattan. Including any residence halls, there are 50 buildings.

Student Life: 81% of undergraduates are from out of state, mostly the

Middle Atlantic. Students are from 46 states, 25 foreign countries, and Canada. 65% are from public schools. 70% are white. The average age of freshmen is 18; all undergraduates, 20. 7% do not continue beyond their first year; 72% remain to graduate.

Housing: 965 students can be accommodated in college housing, which includes single-sex and coed dorms and on-campus apartments. In addition there is a French Interest House, the Perkins Art Co-op, and the Good Life House. On-campus housing is guaranteed for all 4 years. 87% of students live on campus; of those, 90% remain on campus on weekends. Upperclassmen may keep cars.

Activities: There are no fraternities or sororities. There are 30 groups on campus, including art, choir, chorale, chorus, computers, dance, drama, ethnic, film, gay, human rights, international, jazz band, literary magazine, musical theater, newspaper, orchestra, philosophy, photography, poetry, political, radio and TV, religious, social, social service, student government, and yearbook. Popular campus events include Mayfair.

Sports: There are 5 intercollegiate sports for men and 6 for women, and 9 intramural sports for men and 9 for women. Facilities include a sports center with a gym, a jogging track, a 6-lane swimming pool, a rowing tank, a multipurpose studio, and 3 squash courts; a fitness center and weight room; tennis courts; and a number of open fields and lawns. Off-campus, the college has the use of a boat house and stables.

Disabled Students: 50% of the campus is accessible. Facilities include wheelchair ramps, elevators, special parking, specially equipped restrooms, special class scheduling, lowered drinking fountains, and lowered telephones.

Services: Counseling and information services are available, as is tutoring in writing. There is a reader service for the blind.

Campus Safety and Security: Measures include 24-hour foot and vehicle patrol, self-defense education, and security escort services. There are shuttle buses, emergency telephones, and lighted pathways/sidewalks.

Programs of Study: Sarah Lawrence confers B.A. degrees. Master's degrees are also awarded. Bachelor's degrees are awarded in BIOLOGICAL SCIENCE (biology/biological science), COMMUNICATIONS AND THE ARTS (art history and appreciation, classics, creative writing, dance, dramatic arts, English, film arts, fine arts, French, German, Greek, Italian, Latin, literature, music, Russian, Spanish, and visual and performing arts), COMPUTER AND PHYSICAL SCIENCE (chemistry and mathematics), HEALTH PROFESSIONS (premedicine), SOCIAL SCIENCE (anthropology, Asian/Oriental studies, economics, history, liberal arts/general studies, philosophy, political science/government, psychology, religion, Russian and Slavic studies, sociology, and women's studies).

Required: To graduate, students must complete 120 credit hours and meet distribution requirements in 3 of 4 academic areas, including history and social sciences, creative and performing arts, natural science and math, and humanities. Students must fulfill a first-year studies requirement in one of 18 areas and meet a phys ed requirement. Students must also take 2 lecture courses, where the average class size is 40.

Special: Internships are available in a variety of fields, with the school offering proximity to New York City art galleries and agencies. Study abroad in many countries, work-study programs, dual concentrations, a 3-2 engineering degree with Columbia, and a general degree may be pursued. All concentrations are self-designed and can be combined.

Faculty/Classroom: 49% of faculty are male; 51% are female. All teach and do research. No introductory courses are taught by graduate students. The average class size in a regular course is 11.

Requirements: Important academic requirements are: secondary school record, teacher recommendation(s), and essay; class rank is considered. Nonacademic requirements include character and personality qualities; extracurricular activities, talent/ability, volunteer work, and work experience. Campus interview, alumnae relations, geographical residence, and minority status are considered. AP credits are accepted.

Procedure: Freshmen are admitted in the fall. There are early decision, early admissions, and deferred admissions plans. Check with the school for current application deadlines. Notification of early decision is sent December 15; regular decision, April 1. Applications are accepted online. A waiting list is maintained.

Transfer: Applicants must submit high school and college transcripts, and a statement of good standing from prior institution(s). A GPA of 3.0 is required and transfer applicants must have a minimum of 30 credits completed, or the equivalent of 2 semesters of full-time college work. An interview is recommended, but not required. November 15 is the application deadline for spring entry. 60 of 120 credits required for the bachelor's degree must be completed at Sarah Lawrence.

Visiting: There are regularly scheduled orientations for prospective students, consisting of a full day of faculty and student panels, lectures, tours, and discussion with admissions officers, offered twice per year during the fall. There are guides for informal visits; visitors may sit in on classes and stay overnight. To schedule a visit, contact the Admissions Office.

Financial Aid: Sarah Lawrence is a member of CSS. The CSS/Profile, FAFSA, and non-custodial parent statement are required. Check with the school for current application deadlines.

International Students: The school actively recruits these students. They must take the TOEFL or SAT II: English as a second language test.

Computers: All students may access the system 24 hours a day. There are no time limits and no fees.

Admissions Contact: Dean of Admission E-Mail: *slcadmit@alc.edu* Web: *www.sarahlawrence.edu*

SCHOOL OF VISUAL ARTS — D-5

New York, NY 10010-3994 — (212) 592-2100; (800) 436-4204; (212) 592-2116

Full-time: 1485 men, 1740 women	**Faculty:** n/av
Part-time: 60 men, 80 women	**Ph.D.s:** n/av
Graduate: 180 men, 170 women	**Student/Faculty:** n/av
Year: semesters, summer session	**Tuition:** $24,608
Application Deadline: see profile	**Room & Board:** $11,000
Freshman Class: n/av	
SAT or ACT: required	**SPECIAL**

The School of Visual Arts, established in 1947, is a private college of art and design conferring undergraduate and graduate degrees in fine and commercial arts. The figures in the above capsule and in this profile are approximate. There is 1 graduate school. In addition to regional accreditation, SVA has baccalaureate program accreditation with FIDER and NASAD. The library contains 70,000 volumes, 1,070 microform items, and 3,168 audio/video tapes/CDs/DVDs, and subscribes to 307 periodicals including electronic. Computerized library services include database searching, Internet access, and laptop Internet portals. Special learning facilities include a learning resource center, art gallery, radio station, a design study center and archive, 5 student galleries, 3 media arts workshops, 3 film and 2 video studios, numerous editing facilities, animation studio with 3 pencil test facilities, digital audio room, tape transfer room, and multimedia facility with digital printing and editing systems. The campus is in an urban area in mid-Manhattan. Including any residence halls, there are 14 buildings.

Student Life: 55% of undergraduates are from out of state, mostly the Middle Atlantic. Students are from 47 states, 45 foreign countries, and Canada. 53% are white; 13% Asian American; 13% foreign nationals. The average age of freshmen is 18; all undergraduates, 21. 16% do not continue beyond their first year; 66% remain to graduate.

Housing: 1150 students can be accommodated in college housing, which includes single-sex and coed dorms. On-campus housing is available on a first-come and first-served basis. 70% of students commute. Alcohol is not permitted. All students may keep cars.

Activities: There are no fraternities or sororities. There are 20 groups on campus, including art, drama, ethnic, film, gay, honors, international, literary magazine, photography, political, professional, radio and TV, religious, social, social service, student government, and yearbook. Popular campus events include an annual ski trip and a Halloween party.

Sports: There is no sports program at SVA.

Disabled Students: All of the campus is accessible. Facilities include wheelchair ramps, elevators, specially equipped restrooms, special class scheduling, and lowered telephones.

Services: There is remedial reading and writing.

Campus Safety and Security: Measures include 24-hour foot and vehicle patrol. There are shuttle buses, emergency telephones, lighted pathways/sidewalks, and controlled access to dorms/residences.

Programs of Study: SVA confers B.F.A. degrees. Master's degrees are also awarded. Bachelor's degrees are awarded in COMMUNICATIONS AND THE ARTS (advertising, animation, film arts, fine arts, graphic design, illustration, photography, video, and visual effects), ENGINEERING AND ENVIRONMENTAL DESIGN (computer graphics and interior design). Visual and critical studies, computer art, computer animation and special effects are the strongest academically. Graphic design, film/video and photography are the largest.

Required: To graduate, students must complete 120 credits, including at least 72 in the major, with a minimum GPA of 2.0. These credits must include 30 in humanities and sciences, 12 in art history, and 6 in electives. Students must complete 2 introductory courses in literature and writing and must pass a proficiency exam in the first semester. A thesis is required in most programs.

Special: SVA offers for-credit internships with more than 200 media-related, design, and advertising firms, including DC Comics, MTV, and Pentagram Design. A summer internship with Walt Disney Studios is possible for illustration/cartooning majors. There is a freshman honors program.

Faculty/Classroom: 64% of faculty are male; 36% are female. 86% teach undergraduates. No introductory courses are taught by graduate students. The average class size in a regular course is 20.

Requirements: The SAT or ACT is required. In addition, applicants must graduate from an accredited secondary school or have a GED. A statement of intent is required of all students. A portfolio is also required. A personal interview and letters of recommendation are considered helpful. A GPA of 2.7 is required. AP and CLEP credits are accepted. Important factors in the admissions decision are personality/intangible qualities, extracurricular activities record, and evidence of special talent.

Procedure: Freshmen are admitted in the fall. There are early decision, deferred admissions and rolling admissions plans. Notification of early decision is sent January 15. Applications are accepted online. Check with the school for current application deadlines.

Transfer: College transcripts from all previously attended accredited colleges or universities, portfolio, admissions essay, and high school transcripts are required, letters of recommendation are encouraged. 60 of 120 credits required for the bachelor's degree must be completed at SVA.

Visiting: There are regularly scheduled orientations for prospective students, including Saturday open house receptions and weekly tours. There are guides for informal visits. To schedule a visit, contact the Office of Admissions.

Financial Aid: The FAFSA is required. Check with the school for current application deadlines.

International Students: The school actively recruits these students. They must take the TOEFL and the college's own test, or earn a minimum score of 6 in all categories of the NYU English proficiency exam.

Computers: Wireless access is available. Every student is given a log-in ID to the college's internal network, including web-based e-mail account SVA has over 700 PCs and Macs available for student use, including in the library, public areas on campus, and the writing resource center. All students may access the system during normal operating hours of the library and the writing resource center. There are no time limits and no fees. It is strongly recommended that all students have a personal computer. An Intel- based Mac is recommended.

Admissions Contact: Adam Rogers, Director of Admissions. E-Mail: *admissions@sva.edu* Web: *www.schoolofvisualarts.edu*

SIENA COLLEGE — D-3

Loudonville, NY 12211 (518) 783-2423 (888) AT SIENA; (518) 783-2436

Full-time: 1400 men, 1608 women	**Faculty:** 210; IIB, +$
Part-time: 86 men, 67 women	**Ph.D.s:** 89%
Graduate: 35 men, 20 women	**Student/Faculty:** 12 to 1
Year: semesters, summer session	**Tuition:** $31,368
Application Deadline: February 15	**Room & Board:** $12,495
Freshman Class: 9438 applied, 5428 accepted, 765 enrolled	
SAT CR/M/W: 540/550/530 **ACT:** 25	**VERY COMPETITIVE**

Siena College, founded in 1937, is a learning community advancing the ideals of a liberal arts education, rooted in its identity as a Franciscan and Catholic Institution. There are 3 undergraduate schools and 1 graduate school. In addition to regional accreditation, Siena has baccalaureate program accreditation with AACSB, CSWE, and NCATE. The library contains 369,191 volumes, 27,739 microform items, and 5,922 audio/video tapes/CDs/DVDs, and subscribes to 280 periodicals including electronic. Computerized library services include interlibrary loans, database searching, Internet access, and Wi-Fi capability. Special learning facilities include an art gallery, radio station, TV station, and the Hickey Financial Technology Center, which features real-time capital market trading room with stock ticker, data screens, workstations, and access to financial information sources and accounting labs. The 175-acre campus is in a suburban area 2 miles north of Albany. Including any residence halls, there are 33 buildings.

Student Life: 78% of undergraduates are from New York. Others are from 33 states, 14 foreign countries, and Canada. 78% are White. The average age of freshmen is 18; all undergraduates, 20. 14% do not continue beyond their first year; 77% remain to graduate.

Housing: 2502 students can be accommodated in college housing, which includes coed dorms and on-campus apartments. In addition, there are special-interest houses. On-campus housing is available on a lottery system for upperclassmen. 81% of students live on campus. Upperclassmen may keep cars.

Activities: There are no fraternities or sororities. There are 70 groups on campus, including and community service, cheerleading, chorus, computers, dance, debate, drama, ethnic, film, gay, honors, international, literary magazine, musical theater, newspaper, opera, orchestra, pep band, political, professional, radio and TV, religious, social, social service, student government, and yearbook. Popular campus events include Charity Week, Sienafest and Family Weekend.

Sports: There are 7 intercollegiate sports for men and 11 for women, and 7 intramural sports for men and 7 for women. Facilities include an athletic complex with free weights, a training facility, an indoor track, an 8-lane, 25-meter pool, fitness equipment, life cycles, 4 multipurpose courts, 6 outdoor tennis courts, 5 outdoor fields, 2 squash courts, and racquetball courts.

Disabled Students: 90% of the campus is accessible. Facilities include wheelchair ramps, elevators, special parking, specially equipped restrooms, special class scheduling, special housing, and an office for students with disabilities that provides various resources.

Services: Counseling and information services are available, as is tutoring in most subjects. There is a reader service for the blind, and remedial math and writing. and a writing center that offers free one-to-one assistance.

Campus Safety and Security: Measures include 24-hour foot and vehicle patrol, emergency notification system, and security escort services. There are emergency telephones, lighted pathways/sidewalks, a card access system for residence halls, radio dispatch, and a 911 on-campus telephone system.

Programs of Study: Siena confers B.A., and B.S degrees. Master's degrees are also awarded. Bachelor's degrees are awarded in BIOLOGICAL SCIENCE (biochemistry and biology/biological science), BUSINESS (accounting, banking and finance, business administration and management, and marketing management), COMMUNICATIONS AND THE ARTS (classics, English, French, Spanish, and visual and performing arts), COMPUTER AND PHYSICAL SCIENCE (actuarial science, chemistry, computer science, mathematics, and physics), ENGINEERING AND ENVIRONMENTAL DESIGN (environmental science), SOCIAL SCIENCE (American studies, economics, history, philosophy, political science/government, psychology, religion, social work, and sociology). accounting, pyschology, and biology are the largest.

Required: To graduate, students must earn 120 credits, including 30 to 39 depending on major, with at least a 2.0 GPA. At least a C-grade in every major field course used to satisfy the credit hour requirement of the major. The required core curriculum is 42 credits.

Special: The College has opportunities for cross-registration through the Hudson-Mohawk Association. Domestic and international internships, study abroad in 23 countries, a Washington semester, and work-study programs are available. The College offers dual majors in different divisions and a B.A.-B.S. degree in math, economics, and biology as well as a 3-2 engineering degree with Rensselaer Polytechnic Institute, Catholic University, Clarkson University, Manhattan College, SUNY Binghamton, and Western New England College. A 4-4 medical program with Albany Medical College is also offered. There are 15 national honor societies, a freshman honors program, and 4 departmental honors programs.

Faculty/Classroom: 58% of faculty are male; 42% are female. All teach undergraduates. No introductory courses are taught by graduate students.

Admissions: 58% of the 2013-2014 applicants were accepted. The SAT scores for the 2013-2014 freshman class were: Critical Reading--31% below 500, 44% between 500 and 599, 20% between 600 and 699, and 5% between 700 and 800; Math--29% below 500, 38% between 500 and 599, 27% between 600 and 699, and 6% between 700 and 800; Writing--30% below 500, 45% between 500 and 599, 22% between 600 and 699, and 3% between 700 and 800. The ACT scores were 16% below 21, 24% between 21 and 23, 27% between 24 and 26, 13% between 27 and 28, and 20% above 28. 48% of the current freshmen were in the top fifth of their class; 81% were in the top two fifths.

Requirements: The SAT or ACT is required. The ACT Optional Writing test is also required. AP and CLEP credits are accepted. Important factors in the admissions decision are advanced placement or honors courses, personality/intangible qualities, and extracurricular activities record.

Procedure: Freshmen are admitted fall and spring. Entrance exams should be taken during spring of the junior year or fall of the senior year. There are early decision, early admissions, and deferred admissions plans. Early decision applications should be filed by December 1; regular applications, by February 15 for fall entry; January 15 for spring entry; and May 1 for summer entry. The fall 2013 application fee was $50. 76 early decision candidates were accepted for the 2013-2014 class. 835 applicants were on the 2013 waiting list; 29 were admitted. Applications are accepted online.

Transfer: 132 transfer students enrolled in 2012-2013. Applicants must have a minimum 2.5 GPA. An interview is recommended. At least half of the major field requirements must be completed at Siena. 30 of 120 credits required for the bachelor's degree must be completed at Siena.

Visiting: There are regularly scheduled orientations for prospective students, students may interview with an admissions counselor, tour campus, or attend a group information session. There are guides for informal visits and visitors may sit in on classes. To schedule a visit, contact Admissions Office at admissions@siena.edu.

Financial Aid: In 2013-2014, 97% of all full-time freshmen and 96% of continuing full-time students received some form of financial aid. 72% of all full-time freshmen and 64% of continuing full-time students received need-based aid. The average freshman award was $18,731. Need-based scholarships or need-based grants averaged $9,995 ($33,356 maximum); need-based self-help aid (loans and jobs) averaged $6,000 ($11,500 maximum); non-need-based athletic scholarships averaged $19,522 ($47,121 maximum); and other non-need-based awards and non-need-based scholarships averaged $10,723 ($28,000 maximum). The FAFSA and the state aid form are required. The priority date for freshman financial aid applications for fall entry is February 15. The deadline for filing freshman financial aid applications for fall entry is May 1.

International Students: There are 37 international students enrolled. The school actively recruits these students. They must take the TOEFL with a minimum score of 550 on the paper-based TOEFL (PBT) or 79 on the Internet-based version (iBT). They must also take the SAT or ACT.

Computers: All students may access the system. 24 hours per day. There are no time limits and no fees.

Graduates: From July 1, 2012 to June 30, 2013, 769 bachelor's degrees were awarded. The most popular majors were accounting (14%), psychology (10%), and marketing (9%). 678 companies recruited on campus in 2012-2013. In an average class, 1% graduate in 3 years or less, 72% graduate in 4 years or less, 79% graduate in 5 years or less, and 80% graduate in 6 years or less.

Admissions Contact: Heather Renault, Associate Vice President for Admissions. E-Mail: *admissions@siena.edu* Web: *www.siena.edu*

SKIDMORE COLLEGE — D-3

Saratoga Springs, NY 12866 — (518) 580-5570; (800) 867-6007; (518) 580-5584

Full-time: 1035 men, 1661 women	**Faculty:** 260
Part-time: 17 men, 21 women	**Ph.D.s:** 88%
Graduate: 5 men, 13 women	**Student/Faculty:** 9 to 1
Year: semesters, summer session	**Tuition:** $42,380
Application Deadline: January 15	**Room & Board:** $12,202
Freshman Class: 8285 applied, 2904 accepted, 660 enrolled	
SAT CR/M/W: 020/020/000	**ACT:** 28 **HIGHLY COMPETITIVE**

Skidmore College, established in 1903, is an independent institution offering undergraduate programs in liberal arts and sciences, as well as preprofessional programs (business, social work, education, studio art, dance, and theater). There is one undergraduate school and one graduate school. In addition to regional accreditation, Skidmore has baccalaureate program accreditation with CSWE and NASAD. Computerized library services include interlibrary loans, database searching, and Internet access. Special learning facilities include an art gallery, radio station, TV station, an electronic music studio, music and art studios, theater teaching facility, anthropology lab, and special biological habitats on campus. The 890-acre campus is in a small town 30 miles north of Albany. Including any residence halls, there are 50 buildings.

Student Life: 69% of undergraduates are from out of state, mostly the Northeast. Students are from 44 states, 63 foreign countries, and Canada. 58% are from public schools. 63% are White; 54% two or more races. The average age of freshmen is 18; all undergraduates, 21. 7% do not continue beyond their first year; 86% remain to graduate.

Housing: College-sponsored housing includes single-sex and coed dorms and on-campus apartments. theme housing; wellness housing; housing for disabled students. On-campus housing is guaranteed for all 4 years and is available on a lottery system for upperclassmen. 87% of students live on campus. All students may keep cars.

Activities: There are no fraternities or sororities. There are 86 groups on campus, including art, band, chorale, chorus, computers, dance, debate, drama, environmental, ethnic, film, gay, honors, international, jazz band, literary magazine, musical theater, newspaper, opera, orchestra, photography, political, professional, radio and TV, religious, social, social service, student government, symphony, and yearbook. Popular campus events include Martin Luther King Week, Oktoberfest, and Spring Fling.

Sports: There are 9 intercollegiate sports for men and 10 for women. Facilities include Facilities include sports and recreation center (main gymnasium with three basketball/volleyball courts, intramural and recreation gyms, swimming pool and diving well,racquetball courts, athletic training room, human-performance laboratory, aerobics and fitness area, and weight room); nine tennis courts (four lighted); new artificial-surface field for field hockey; new softball diamond with Field Turf outfield; lighted stadium with 1,400 seats, all-weather track, and Field Turf playing field for soccer, lacrosse, and intramurals; baseball diamond; golf driving range; heated barn, indoor and outdoor riding rings, hunter course, and riding trails; rowing boathouse; and ice hockey rink (owned by City of Saratoga Springs).

Disabled Students: 98% of the campus is accessible. Facilities include wheelchair ramps, elevators, special parking, specially equipped restrooms, lowered drinking fountains, and special housing.

Services: Counseling and information services are available, as is tutoring in most subjects. There is a reader service for the blind. Diagnostic services, note takers, and books on tape are also offered.

Campus Safety and Security: Measures include 24-hour foot and vehicle patrol, emergency notification system, and security escort services. There are shuttle buses, emergency telephones, lighted pathways/sidewalks, controlled access to dorms/residences, a special security alert system, rigorous fire response procedures, and a lock system on dorm entrances.

Programs of Study: Skidmore confers B.A., and B.S. degrees. Master's degrees are also awarded. Bachelor's degrees are awarded in AGRICULTURE (environmental studies), BIOLOGICAL SCIENCE (biochemistry, biology/biological science, and neurosciences), BUSINESS (business administration and management and business economics), COMMUNICATIONS AND THE ARTS (art, art history and appreciation, classics, dance, dramatic arts, English, French, German, music, and Spanish), COMPUTER AND PHYSICAL SCIENCE (chemistry, computer science, geology, mathematics, and physics), EDUCATION (elementary education), HEALTH PROFESSIONS (exercise science), SOCIAL SCIENCE (American studies, anthropology, Asian/Oriental studies, economics, French studies, gender studies, history, international relations, liberal arts/general studies, philosophy, political science/government, psychology, religion, social science, social work, and sociology). Social sciences, visual and performing arts, business/marketing, English, and psychology have the largest enrollments.

Required: To graduate, students must complete 120 credits, including at least 24 at the 300 level, with a minimum GPA of 2.0 overall and in the major. B.A. candidates require 90 credits in the liberal arts to graduate; B.S. candidates require 60 credits. Students must fulfill all core curriculum, distribution, and major requirements.

Special: Skidmore offers cross-registration with the Hudson-Mohawk Consortium, individually designed internships, various study-abroad programs, a Washington semester in conjunction with American University, dual and student-designed majors, credit for life and experience, and pass/fail options, as well as a nondegree study program for senior citizens. There are cooperative programs with other schools in engineering, business administration, and health. There are 9 national honor societies, including Phi Beta Kappa, and a freshman honors program.

Faculty/Classroom: 44% of faculty are male; 56% are female. All teach undergraduates, all do research, and all teach and do research. No introductory courses are taught by graduate students. The average class size in a regular course is 16.

Admissions: 35% of the 2013-2014 applicants were accepted. The SAT scores for the 2013-2014 freshman class were: Critical Reading--7% below 500, 31% between 500 and 599, 43% between 600 and 699, and 19% between 700 and 800; Math--4% below 500, 34% between 500 and 599, 45% between 600 and 699, and 17% between 700 and 800; Writing--5% below 500, 29% between 500 and 599, 46% between 600 and 699, and 20% between 700 and 800. The ACT scores were 2% below 21, 8% between 21 and 23, 19% between 24 and 26, 28% between 27 and 28, and 43% above 28. 69% of the current freshmen were in the top fifth of their class; 92% were in the top two fifths.

Requirements: The SAT or ACT is required. SAT subject tests are recommended. AP and CLEP credits are accepted. Important factors in the admissions decision are advanced placement or honors courses, recommendations by school officials, and evidence of special talent.

Procedure: Freshmen are admitted fall. Entrance exams should be taken by December of the senior year. There are early decision, early admissions, and deferred admissions plans. Early decision applications should be filed by November 15; regular applications, by January 15 for fall entry, along with a $65 fee. Notification of early decision is sent December 15; regular decision, April 1. 283 early decision candidates were accepted for the 2013-2014 class. 430 applicants were on the 2013 waiting list; 21 were admitted. Applications are accepted online.

Transfer: 33 transfer students enrolled in 2012-2013. Transfer students must have a GPA of 2.7 and must submit a high school transcript, all college transcripts, an essay or personal statement, test scores, and a statement of good standing from prior institutions. At least one professor recommendation from the current institution and a mid-term report are also required. 60 of 120 credits required for the bachelor's degree must be completed at Skidmore.

Visiting: There are regularly scheduled orientations for prospective students, including full-day open-house programs. There are guides for informal visits, visitors may sit in on classes, and stay overnight. To schedule a visit, contact the Admissions Office at (800) 867-6007.

Financial Aid: In 2013-2014, 51% of all full-time freshmen and 51% of continuing full-time students received some form of financial aid. 46% of all full-time freshmen and 48% of continuing full-time students received need-based aid. The average freshman award was $38,700. Need-based scholarships or need-based grants averaged $35,600 ($58,750 maximum); need-based self-help aid (loans and jobs) averaged $3,900 ($5,500 maximum); and other non-need-based awards and non-need-based scholarships averaged $12,500 ($15,000 maximum). 48% of undergraduate students work part-time. Average annual earnings from campus work are $2220. The average financial indebtedness of the 2013 graduate was $24,371. Skidmore is a member of CSS. The CSS/Profile and FAFSA are required. The deadline for filing freshman financial aid applications for fall entry is February 1.

International Students: There are 182 international students enrolled. The school actively recruits these students. They must take the TOEFL with a minimum score of 590 on the paper-based TOEFL (PBT) or 96 on the Internet-based version (iBT). They must also take the SAT or ACT.

Computers: All students may access the system 24 hours per day. There are no time limits and no fees.

Graduates: From July 1, 2012 to June 30, 2013, 616 bachelor's degrees were awarded. The most popular majors were social sciences (17%), visual and performing arts (15%), and business/marketing (12%). 51 companies recruited on campus in 2012-2013. In an average class, 83% graduate in

4 years or less, 85% graduate in 5 years or less, and 86% graduate in 6 years or less. Of the 2012 graduating class, 16% were enrolled in graduate school within 6 months of graduation, and 80% were employed.

Admissions Contact: Mary Lou Bates, Director of Admissions. E-Mail: *admissions@skidmore.edu* Web: *www.skidmore.edu*

ST. BONAVENTURE UNIVERSITY B-4

St. Bonaventure, NY 14778 (716) 375-2400
(800) 462-5050; (716) 375-4005

Full-time: 890 men, 992 women	**Faculty:** 141
Part-time: 35 men, 34 women	**Ph.D.s:** 79%
Graduate: 185 men, 316 women	**Student/Faculty:** 13 to 1
Year: semesters, summer session	**Tuition:** $28,727
Application Deadline: July 1	**Room & Board:** $10,104
Freshman Class: 2545 applied, 2045 accepted, 489 enrolled	
SAT CR/M/W: 520/530/510 **ACT:** 23	**COMPETITIVE**

Saint Bonaventure University, founded in 1858, is a private Roman Catholic institution in the Franciscan tradition, offering programs in the arts and sciences, education, business, and journalism and mass communication. There are 4 undergraduate schools and 1 graduate school. In addition to regional accreditation, SBU has baccalaureate program accreditation with AACSB and NCATE. The library contains 349,443 volumes, 16,950 microform items, and 14,808 audio/video tapes/CDs/DVDs, and subscribes to 56,082 periodicals including electronic. Computerized library services include interlibrary loans, database searching, Internet access, and Wi-Fi capability. Special learning facilities include an art gallery, radio station, TV station, observatory. The 500-acre campus is in a small town 75 miles southeast of Buffalo. Including any residence halls, there are 30 buildings.

Student Life: 75% of undergraduates are from out of state, mostly the Northeast. Students are from 33 states, 34 foreign countries, and Canada. 82% are from public schools. 68% are White. The average age of freshmen is 18; all undergraduates, 20. 20% do not continue beyond their first year; 63% remain to graduate.

Housing: 1644 students can be accommodated in college housing, which includes single-sex and coed dorms and on-campus apartments. In addition, there are special-interest houses, Living/learning communities. On-campus housing is guaranteed for all 4 years. 76% of students live on campus; of those, 100% remain on campus on weekends. All students may keep cars.

Activities: There are no fraternities or sororities. There are 65 groups on campus, including academic, art, band, cheerleading, choir, chorale, chorus, computers, dance, drama, environmental, ethnic, gay, honors, international, jazz band, literary magazine, newspaper, pep band, photography, political, professional, radio and TV, religious, social, social service, student government, and yearbook. Popular campus events include Family Weekend, and Spring and Winter Weekends.

Sports: There are 7 intercollegiate sports for men and 7 for women, and 10 intramural sports for men and 9 for women. Facilities include a 5500-seat basketball arena, an indoor swimming pool, a 9-hole golf course, weight facilities and free weights, and a fitness center with state-of-the-art strength, aerobics and conditioning areas, an indoor track, 3 multi-use courts, and a rock climbing wall. There is also a 77-acre area on campus with soccer, baseball, softball, rugby, and intramural fields, and a recreation trail that winds through campus.

Disabled Students: 90% of the campus is accessible. Facilities include wheelchair ramps, elevators, special parking, and specially equipped restrooms.

Services: Counseling and information services are available, as is tutoring in most subjects.

Campus Safety and Security: Measures include 24-hour foot and vehicle patrol, emergency notification system, and security escort services. There are shuttle buses, emergency telephones, and lighted pathways/sidewalks.

Programs of Study: SBU confers B.A., B.S., B.B.A. and B.S.Ed. degrees. Master's degrees are also awarded. Bachelor's degrees are awarded in BIOLOGICAL SCIENCE (biochemistry, bioinformatics, biology/biological science, and biophysics), BUSINESS (accounting, banking and finance, management information systems, management science, and marketing/retailing/merchandising), COMMUNICATIONS AND THE ARTS (art history, classical languages, communications, dramatic arts, English, French, journalism, music, Spanish, and visual and performing arts), COMPUTER AND PHYSICAL SCIENCE (chemistry, computer science, mathematics, and physics), EDUCATION (education, elementary education, physical education, special education, and sports studies), ENGINEERING AND ENVIRONMENTAL DESIGN (engineering physics and environmental science), SOCIAL SCIENCE (child care/child and family studies, gerontology, history, international studies, philosophy, political science/government, psychology, sociology, theological studies, and women's studies). Journalism/mass communication, biology, accounting, and elementary/special education have the largest enrollments.

Required: To graduate, students must complete 120 credit hours, 30 of them in the major, with a minimum GPA of 2.0. Students must also demonstrate writing competency through testing or course work.

Special: Internships are available in business, mass communication, political science, psychology, sociology. Study abroad in 18 countries, B.A.-B.S. degrees, accelerated degree programs, dual and student-designed majors, a Washington semester with American University, and pass/fail options are offered. Dual admissions with George Washington University School of Medicine, Lake Erie College of Osteopathic Medicine, University at Buffalo School of Dental Medicine, Lake Erie College of Osteopathic Medicine School of Pharmacy, and SUNY-Upstate Medical are also possible. There are 10 national honor societies and a freshman honors program.

Faculty/Classroom: 64% of faculty are male; 36% are female. 92% teach undergraduates. No introductory courses are taught by graduate students. The average class size in an introductory lecture is 21; in a laboratory is 14; and in a regular course is 18.

Admissions: 80% of the 2013-2014 applicants were accepted. The SAT scores for the 2013-2014 freshman class were: Critical Reading--38% below 500, 42% between 500 and 599, 18% between 600 and 699, and 2% between 700 and 800; Math--32% below 500, 45% between 500 and 599, 20% between 600 and 699, and 3% between 700 and 800; Writing--41% below 500, 41% between 500 and 599, 14% between 600 and 699, and 4% between 700 and 800. The ACT scores were 27% below 21, 25% between 21 and 23, 26% between 24 and 26, 9% between 27 and 28, and 13% above 28. 37% of the current freshmen were in the top fifth of their class; 64% were in the top two fifths. 6 freshmen graduated first in their class.

Requirements: The SAT is required. The ACT is recommended. A satisfactory score on the SAT or 24 on the ACT is required. Applicants must be graduates of an accredited secondary school or have a GED. 16 academic credits are required, including 4 years each of English and social studies, 3 each of math and science, and 2 of a foreign language. An essay and an interview are recommended. AP and CLEP credits are accepted.

Procedure: Freshmen are admitted to all sessions. Entrance exams should be taken during the spring of the junior year or the fall of the senior year. There are early admissions, deferred admissions, and rolling admissions plans. Applications should be filed by July 1 for fall entry; October 15 for spring entry, along with a $30 fee. Notification is sent on a rolling basis. Applications are accepted online.

Transfer: 117 transfer students enrolled in 2012-2013. Applicants must have a minimum 2.0 GPA. High school and college transcripts, essay, and a letter of recommendation are required. 60 of 120 credits required for the bachelor's degree must be completed at SBU.

Visiting: There are regularly scheduled orientations for prospective students, including interviews, tours, class visits, and meetings with professors. There are guides for informal visits, visitors may sit in on classes, and stay overnight. To schedule a visit, contact the Admissions Office.

Financial Aid: In 2013-2014, 98% of all full-time freshmen and 95% of continuing full-time students received some form of financial aid. 80% of all full-time freshmen and 76% of continuing full-time students received need-based aid. The average freshman award was $21,777. Need-based scholarships or need-based grants averaged $7,463; need-based self-help aid (loans and jobs) averaged $6,886; non-need-based athletic scholarships averaged $9,752; and other non-need-based awards and non-need-based scholarships averaged $12,923. The average financial indebtedness of the 2013 graduate was $28,282. The FAFSA is required. The priority date for freshman financial aid applications for fall entry is February 15.

International Students: There are 43 international students enrolled. The school actively recruits these students. They must take the TOEFL with a minimum score of 550 on the paper-based TOEFL (PBT) or 79 on the Internet-based version (iBT).

Computers: All students may access the system 24 hours per day via residence hall rooms or at designated lab hours. There are no time limits and no fees.

Graduates: From July 1, 2012 to June 30, 2013, 436 bachelor's degrees were awarded. The most popular majors were business (29%), communications/journalism (15%), and education (13%). In an average class, 1% graduate in 3 years or less, 48% graduate in 4 years or less, 62% graduate in 5 years or less, and 63% graduate in 6 years or less.

Admissions Contact: Monica Emery, Director of Recruitment. E-Mail: *admissions@sbu.edu* Web: *www.sbu.edu*

ST. FRANCIS COLLEGE D-5

Brooklyn, NY 11201 **(718) 489-5200; (718) 802-0453**

Full-time: 1088 men, 1368 women
Part-time: 129 men, 179 women
Graduate: 31 men, 24 women
Year: semesters, summer session
Application Deadline: April 1
Freshman Class: n/av
SAT CR/M: 474/472
Faculty: 80; IIB, +$
Ph.D.s: 86%
Student/Faculty: 18 to 1
Tuition: $20,700
Room & Board: $13,500

LESS COMPETITIVE

St. Francis College, founded in 1859 by the Franciscan Brothers of Brooklyn, is located in Brooklyn Heights, NY. Since its founding, the College has pursued its Franciscan mission to provide an affordable, high-quality education to students from New York City's five boroughs and beyond. In addition to regional accreditation, St. Francis has baccalaureate program accreditation with TEAC. The library contains 140,000 volumes, 10,440 microform items, and 2,050 audio/video tapes/CDs/DVDs, and subscribes to 14,300 periodicals including electronic. Computerized library services include interlibrary loans, database searching, Internet access, and Wi-Fi capability. Special learning facilities include an art gallery, HDTV television studio, nursing lab with multiple simulators (SYMBaby, SYM Man), greenhouse. The 1-acre campus is in an urban area Brooklyn Heights, NY. Including any residence halls, there are 6 buildings.

Student Life: 98% of undergraduates are from New York. Others are from 8 states, 50 foreign countries, and Canada. 49% are from public schools. 37% are White; 22% Hispanic; 19% African American. 51% are Catholic; 29% Protestant; 14% claim no religious affiliation. The average age of freshmen is 19; all undergraduates, 21. 22% do not continue beyond their first year; 52% remain to graduate.

Housing: 173 students can be accommodated in college housing, which includes coed dorms. Students may apply for housing with EHS. On-campus housing is available on a first-come and first-served basis. 100% of students commute. Alcohol is not permitted. All students commute. Some may keep cars.

Activities: 10% of men belong to 3 national fraternities; 6% of women belong to 3 local and 1 national sororities. There are 40 groups on campus, including art, cheerleading, choir, chorus, communications, computers, dance, debate, drama, ethnic, honors, international, literary magazine, musical theater, newspaper, photography, political, professional, radio and TV, religious, social, social service, student government, and yearbook. Popular campus events include Terrier Tuesday, Sports Events, Community Day, Valentines Day Auction, Family Day, Battle of Brooklyn, Welcome Back BBQ.

Sports: There are 9 intercollegiate sports for men and 10 for women, and 5 intramural sports for men and 5 for women. Facilities include a full sized basketball court, a competition-size swimming pool, a weight-training room, and the Genovesi Center, which is a multipurpose facility used for athletic, college, and community events. Home soccer games are played on a brand new field on a pier at Brooklyn Bridge Park.

Disabled Students: All of the campus is accessible. Facilities include wheelchair ramps, elevators, specially equipped restrooms, lowered drinking fountains, and lowered telephones.

Services: Counseling and information services are available, as is tutoring in most subjects. There is a reader service for the blind, and remedial math, reading, and writing. there are workshops in academic skills such as note taking, test taking, and study skills.

Campus Safety and Security: Measures include 24-hour foot and vehicle patrol and emergency notification system.

Programs of Study: St. Francis confers B.A., and B.S. degrees. Associate and master's degrees are also awarded. Bachelor's degrees are awarded in BIOLOGICAL SCIENCE (biology/biological science), BUSINESS (accounting, business administration and management, and management science), COMMUNICATIONS AND THE ARTS (communications, English, and Spanish), COMPUTER AND PHYSICAL SCIENCE (chemistry, information sciences and systems, and mathematics), EDUCATION (education, elementary education, middle school education, physical education, and secondary education), HEALTH PROFESSIONS (health care administration, health science, medical laboratory technology, nursing, physician's assistant, and radiological science), SOCIAL SCIENCE (criminal justice, economics, history, international studies, liberal arts/general studies, philosophy, political science/government, psychology, religion, social studies, and sociology). Accounting, management, psychology, and teacher education are the strongest academically. Management, psychology and communications have the largest enrollments.

Required: The core curriculum varies according to the major, but all baccalaureate degree programs require courses in communications, english, fine arts, phys ed, history, philosophy, sociology, and science or math. A minimum 2.0 GPA and 128 credit hours are required to graduate.

Special: There are co-op programs in physical therapy, nursing, and computer science. Work-study with Methodist Hospital or the borough president's office, and there are preprofessional health programs with the State University of New York Health Science Center, Methodist Hospital, and St. Vincent's Catholic Medical Center. Study abroad in several countries, dual majors, pass/fail options, and credit for life experience are possible. There are 16 national honor societies, a freshman honors program, and 21 departmental honors programs.

Faculty/Classroom: 59% of faculty are male; 41% are female. All teach and do research. No introductory courses are taught by graduate students. The average class size in an introductory lecture is 22; in a laboratory is 22; and in a regular course is 22.

Requirements: The SAT is required. Applicants should graduate from an accredited secondary school or have a GED. An entrance essay is required, as well as the submission of SAT scores and recommendation letters, official high transcript or GED. AP and CLEP credits are accepted. Important factors in the admissions decision are advanced placement or honors courses, extracurricular activities record, and recommendations by school officials.

Procedure: Freshmen are admitted to all sessions. Entrance exams should be taken In spring of the junior year and fall of the senior year. There are deferred admissions and rolling admissions plans. Applications should be filed by April 1 for fall entry; November 1 for winter entry, along with a $35 fee. Notification is sent on a rolling basis. Applications are accepted online. Application fees are waived if application is completed online.

Transfer: 183 transfer students enrolled in 2012-2013. A minimum 2.0 GPA is required for transfer students. Official transcripts from previous colleges and high school transcripts, or a graduation certificate, is also required. 30 of 128 credits required for the bachelor's degree must be completed at St. Francis.

Visiting: There are regularly scheduled orientations for prospective students, Visiting students can participate in a student guided tour of the college, and meetings with faculty if desired. There are guides for informal visits and visitors may sit in on classes. To schedule a visit, contact The Office of Admissions at admissions@sfc.edu.

Financial Aid: In 2013-2014, 98% of all full-time freshmen and 83% of continuing full-time students received some form of financial aid. 66% of all full-time freshmen and 58% of continuing full-time students received need-based aid. The average freshman award was $14,300. Need-based scholarships or need-based grants averaged $6,000 ($12,100 maximum); need-based self-help aid (loans and jobs) averaged $7,800 ($29,400 maximum); non-need-based athletic scholarships averaged $9,800 ($32,600 maximum); and other non-need-based awards and non-need-based scholarships averaged $8,300 ($20,700 maximum). 10% of undergraduate students work part-time. Average annual earnings from campus work are $2600. The FAFSA, the state aid form, and the college's own financial statement are required. The priority date for freshman financial aid applications for fall entry is February 15.

International Students: There are 154 international students enrolled. The school actively recruits these students. They must take the TOEFL with a minimum score of 500 on the paper-based TOEFL (PBT) or 61 on the Internet-based version (iBT). They must also take the SAT or ACT.

Computers: All students may access the system. The college's portal is available 24/7 as is the wireless network. There are no time limits. The fee is $150.

Graduates: From July 1, 2012 to June 30, 2013, 578 bachelor's degrees were awarded. The most popular majors were communications (18%), management (13%), and nursing (12%). 20 companies recruited on campus in 2012-2013. In an average class, 1% graduate in 3 years or less, 31% graduate in 4 years or less, 51% graduate in 5 years or less, and 52% graduate in 6 years or less. Of the 2012 graduating class, 37% were enrolled in graduate school within 6 months of graduation, and 51% were employed.

Admissions Contact: Joseph Cummings, AVP Enrollment Services. E-Mail: *admissions@sfc.edu* Web: *www.sfc.edu*

ST. JOHN FISHER COLLEGE B-3

Rochester, NY 14618 **(585) 385-8064**
(800) 444-4640; (585) 385-8386

Full-time: 1101 men, 1637 women
Part-time: 85 men, 136 women
Graduate: 355 men, 673 women
Year: semesters, summer session
Application Deadline: Rolling
Faculty: 161; IIB, av$
Ph.D.s: 91%
Student/Faculty: 13 to 1
Tuition: $28,430
Room & Board: $10,940
Freshman Class: 4016 applied, 2521 accepted, 521 enrolled
SAT CR/M/W: 520/550/510 **ACT:** 24 **COMPETITIVE+**

St. John Fisher College is an independent, liberal arts institution in the Catholic tradition of American higher education. Guided since its inception in 1948 by the educational philosophy of the Congregation of St. Basil, the college emphasizes liberal learning for students in traditional academic disciplines, as well as for those in more directly career-oriented fields. There are 4 undergraduate schools and 5 graduate schools. In addition to regional accreditation, Fisher has baccalaureate program accreditation with

AACSB, ACPE, and NCATE. The library contains 171,467 volumes, 52,323 microform items, and 7,968 audio/video tapes/CDs/DVDs, and subscribes to 75,357 periodicals including electronic. Computerized library services include interlibrary loans, database searching, and Internet access. Special learning facilities include an art gallery, radio station, TV station, a multimedia center, "wet" and "dry" multidisciplinary science labs, animal labs, growth chambers, campus center, and athletics fitness facility. The 154-acre campus is in a suburban area 6 miles southeast of Rochester. Including any residence halls, there are 25 buildings.

Student Life: 97% of undergraduates are from New York. Others are from 25 states, 10 foreign countries, and Canada. 84% are from public schools. 83% are White. The average age of freshmen is 18; all undergraduates, 21. 17% do not continue beyond their first year; 72% remain to graduate.

Housing: 1400 students can be accommodated in college housing, which includes single-sex and coed dorms. On-campus housing is guaranteed for the freshman year only and is available on a lottery system for upperclassmen. Priority is given to out-of-town students. 54% of students commute. Upperclassmen may keep cars.

Activities: There are no fraternities or sororities. There are 70 groups on campus, including commuter council, resident student association, student senate SGA, art, cheerleading, choir, chorus, computers, dance, drama, environmental, ethnic, gay, honors, international, literary magazine, musical theater, newspaper, photography, political, professional, radio and TV, religious, social, social service, Student Activities Board, student government, and yearbook. Popular campus events include Spring Event, Senior Week, and TEDDI 24-hour Dance Marathon for Charity.

Sports: There are 11 intercollegiate sports for men and 12 for women, and 4 intramural sports for men and 4 for women. Facilities include Fisher's Student Life Center includes a field house, the Manning & Napier Varsity Gymnasium for men's and women's basketball teams, a fitness center/weight room, training facilities, and team locker rooms. Growney Stadium, a 2100-seat stadium is home to the football, soccer, and lacrosse teams and is used by many of the college's intramural teams. The Polisseni Track & Field complex features an eight-lane, 400-meter competition track with a grass infield; Dugan Yard baseball complex is home to the men's baseball team. Additional athletic facilitites include a softball complex, outdoor tennis courts, regulation-size grass practice fields, and a 9-hole golf course.

Disabled Students: All of the campus is accessible. Facilities include wheelchair ramps, elevators, special parking, specially equipped restrooms, special class scheduling, lowered drinking fountains, lowered telephones. Accessible dorm rooms are available.

Services: Counseling and information services are available, as is tutoring in most subjects. There is a reader service for the blind. Math and writing centers provide help to students at all levels. Peer tutoring is available to all students in most undergraduate subject areas.

Campus Safety and Security: Measures include 24-hour foot and vehicle patrol, emergency notification system, self-defense education, and security escort services. There are shuttle buses, emergency telephones, lighted pathways/sidewalks, controlled access to dorms/residences. Access to the residence halls is controlled by the ID card access system. Residence halls are patrolled and monitored 24 hours a day by security officers or resident advisers. All other campus facilities are locked and unlocked according to established schedules.

Programs of Study: Fisher confers B.A., and B.S. degrees. Master's and doctoral degrees are also awarded. Bachelor's degrees are awarded in BIOLOGICAL SCIENCE (biology/biological science), BUSINESS (accounting, business administration and management, marketing management, and sports management), COMMUNICATIONS AND THE ARTS (communications, digital communications, English, French, and Spanish), COMPUTER AND PHYSICAL SCIENCE (chemistry, computer science, mathematics, physics, and statistics), EDUCATION (elementary education, English education, foreign languages education, mathematics education, middle school education, science education, secondary education, social studies education, and special education), HEALTH PROFESSIONS (nursing), SOCIAL SCIENCE (American studies, anthropology, criminology, economics, history, interdisciplinary studies, international studies, legal studies, philosophy, political science/government, psychology, religion, and sociology). Sciences is the strongest academically. Management, nursing, and biological sciences have the largest enrollments.

Required: To graduate, students must complete at least 120 credit hours, including at least 30 in the major, and maintain a 2.0 minimum GPA. The core curriculum consists of 15 courses that students must successfully complete to graduate; the core is composed of 2 tiers of study: Foundations courses and Perspectives courses. Freshmen must participate in one of the integrative learning communities.

Special: The college has cooperative programs and cross-registration with Rochester area colleges. The college offers internships in most majors, independent research in various majors, study abroad, accelerated degree programs in specific majors, Washington semesters, dual and student-designed majors, and degrees in interdisciplinary studies. A 3-2 engineering degree is offered. Navy and Marine ROTC are available at the University of Rochester and Air Force and Army ROTC is available at Rochester Institute of Technology. There are 10 national honor societies, a freshman honors program, and 8 departmental honors programs.

Faculty/Classroom: 43% of faculty are male; 57% are female. 88% teach undergraduates. No introductory courses are taught by graduate students. The average class size in an introductory lecture is 22 and in a laboratory is 13.

Admissions: 63% of the 2013-2014 applicants were accepted. The SAT scores for the 2013-2014 freshman class were: Critical Reading--34% below 500, 52% between 500 and 599, 14% between 600 and 699, and 1% between 700 and 800; Math--45% below 500, 42% between 500 and 599, 12% between 600 and 699, and 1% between 700 and 800; Writing--45% below 500, 42% between 500 and 599, 12% between 600 and 699, and 1% between 700 and 800. The ACT scores were 7% below 21, 33% between 21 and 23, 34% between 24 and 26, 21% between 27 and 28, and 6% above 28. 51% of the current freshmen were in the top fifth of their class; 83% were in the top two fifths. 2 freshmen graduated first in their class.

Requirements: The SAT or ACT is required. Applicants are required to submit either SAT or ACT standardized test scores for admission to the College. Applicants must be graduates of an accredited secondary school and have completed 16 academic credits including 4 years each in English and history/social studies, 3 years each in math and science, and 2 years in a foreign language. Interviews are recommended. A GPA of 85.0 is required. AP and CLEP credits are accepted. Important factors in the admissions decision are advanced placement or honors courses, extracurricular activities record, and leadership record.

Procedure: Freshmen are admitted fall. There are early decision, deferred admissions, and rolling admissions plans. Application deadlines are open. Application fee is $30. Notification of early decision is sent January 15; regular decision, on a Rolling basis. 111 early decision candidates were accepted for the 2013-2014 class. Applications are accepted online.

Transfer: 258 transfer students enrolled in 2012-2013. Applicants must have a minimum GPA of 2.0 to be considered (mean GPA is 2.8). A high school transcript is required for students with fewer than 24 college credits. Interviews are recommended. 30 of 120 credits required for the bachelor's degree must be completed at Fisher.

Visiting: There are regularly scheduled orientations for prospective students, Prospective students can schedule a campus tour; an interview with a member of the admissions staff; a meeting with faculty and coaches; and lunch on campus. There are guides for informal visits, visitors may sit in on classes, and stay overnight. To schedule a visit, contact the Office of Freshman Admissions at (585) 385-8064.

Financial Aid: In 2013-2014, 100% of all full-time freshmen and 99% of continuing full-time students received some form of financial aid. 85% of all full-time freshmen and 83% of continuing full-time students received need-based aid. The average freshman award was $20,384. Need-based scholarships or need-based grants averaged $16,531 ($34,000 maximum); and need-based self-help aid (loans and jobs) averaged $4,671 ($8,000 maximum). 22% of undergraduate students work part-time. Average annual earnings from campus work are $510. The average financial indebtedness of the 2013 graduate was $32,157. The FAFSA and the state aid form are required. The priority date for freshman financial aid applications for fall entry is February 15.

International Students: There are 5 international students enrolled. They must take the TOEFL with a minimum score of 550 on the paper-based TOEFL (PBT) or 80 on the Internet-based version (iBT). They must also take the SAT or ACT.

Computers: All students may access the system 24 hours per day. There are no time limits. The fee is $50/year.

Graduates: From July 1, 2012 to June 30, 2013, 685 bachelor's degrees were awarded. The most popular majors were business (27%), nursing (21%), and education (13%). In an average class, 1% graduate in 3 years or less, 65% graduate in 4 years or less, 72% graduate in 5 years or less, and 72% graduate in 6 years or less.

Admissions Contact: Stacy Ledermann, Director of Freshman Admissions. E-Mail: *admissions@sjfc.edu* Web: *www.sjfc.edu*

ST. JOHN'S UNIVERSITY D-5

Queens, NY 11439 (718) 990-2000
(888) 9ST-JOHNS; (718) 990-2096

Full-time: 5164 men, 5744 women	**Faculty:** 598
Part-time: 2006 men, 2859 women	**Ph.D.s:** 93%
Graduate: 1885 men, 3071 women	**Student/Faculty:** 19 to 1
Year: semesters, summer session	**Tuition:** $37,260
Application Deadline: open	**Room & Board:** $15,580
Freshman Class: 51207 applied, 26932 accepted, 2794 enrolled	
SAT CR/M: 540/550	**ACT:** 24 **COMPETITIVE+**

St. John's University, founded in 1870 by the Vincentian Fathers, is a private Roman Catholic institution offering programs in the arts and sciences, education, business, pharmacy and health sciences, theology, and professional studies. There are 5 undergraduate schools and 7 graduate schools. In addition to regional accreditation, St. John's has baccalaureate program accreditation with AACSB, ACPE, NASAD, and TEAC. The 4 libraries contain 1.0 million volumes, 376,579 microform items, and 9,354 audio/video tapes/CDs/DVDs, and subscribe to 72,204 periodicals including electronic. Computerized library services include interlibrary loans, database searching, Internet access, and Wi-Fi capability. Special learning facilities include an art gallery, radio station, TV station, health education resource center, model pharmacy, speech and hearing clinic, instructional materials center, instructional media center, institute of Asian studies, global language and culture center, financial information lab, Chappell Players Little Theatre, a math learning center and a writing center. The 97-acre campus is in a suburban area in a residential section of Queens. There is also a 16-acre branch campus in Staten Island, a campus in downtown Manhattan, a campus in Rome, Italy, and a 175-acre location in Oakdale, Long Island. Including any residence halls, there are 52 buildings.

Student Life: 76% of undergraduates are from New York. Others are from 47 states, 98 foreign countries, and Canada. 62% are from public schools. 41% are White; 16% Asian American; 16% Hispanic; 15% African American. 48% are Catholic; 18% claim no religious affiliation; 18% Muslim, Hindu, Buddhist, Mormon, Greek and Russian Orthodox; 13% Protestant. The average age of freshmen is 18; all undergraduates, 20. 20% do not continue beyond their first year; 55% remain to graduate.

Housing: 3947 students can be accommodated in college housing, which includes coed dorms, on-campus apartments, and off-campus apartments. In addition, there are honors houses, special-interest houses, Honors housing (certain beds allocated), and special interest housing (learning communities). On-campus housing is available on a first-come, first-served basis, and is available on a lottery system for upperclassmen. Priority is given to out-of-town students. 78% of students commute. Alcohol is not permitted. Upperclassmen may keep cars.

Activities: 9% of men belong to 1 local and 16 national fraternities; 8% of women belong to 2 local and 16 national sororities. There are 180 groups on campus, including cheerleading, choir, chorus, computers, dance, debate, drama, environmental, ethnic, film, honors, international, jazz band, literary magazine, musical theater, newspaper, pep band, photography, political, professional, radio and TV, religious, social, social service, student government, and yearbook. Popular campus events include Fall Activities Fair, Spring Fling, Winter Carnival, Pep Rallys and Tailgates and DAC after Dark.

Sports: There are 7 intercollegiate sports for men and 9 for women, and 14 intramural sports for men and 12 for women. Facilities include gyms; tennis courts; weight and exercise rooms; baseball and softball diamonds; fields for football/lacrosse and soccer; basketball courts; outdoor track.

Disabled Students: 95% of the campus is accessible. Facilities include wheelchair ramps, elevators, special parking, specially equipped restrooms, special class scheduling, lowered drinking fountains, and lowered telephones.

Services: Counseling and information services are available, as is tutoring in most subjects. There is a reader service for the blind. Note-taking services, tape recorders, assistance in study skills, and a program for at-risk freshmen are available.

Campus Safety and Security: Measures include 24-hour foot and vehicle patrol, emergency notification system, self-defense education, and security escort services. There are shuttle buses, emergency telephones, lighted pathways/sidewalks, controlled access to dorms/residences, and a crime prevention awareness program.

Programs of Study: St. John's confers B.A., B.S., B.F.A. and B.S.Ed. degrees. Associate, master's, and doctoral degrees are also awarded. Bachelor's degrees are awarded in AGRICULTURE (environmental studies), BIOLOGICAL SCIENCE (biology/adolescence education, biology/biological science, and toxicology), BUSINESS (accounting, business administration and management, business economics, finance, funeral home services, hospitality management services, information & communication technology, insurance and risk management, management information systems, management science, marketing management, and sports management), COMMUNICATIONS AND THE ARTS (advertising, communications, dramatic arts, English, film, television and digital media, fine arts, French, graphic design, illustration, Italian, journalism, languages, photography, public relations, radio/television technology, Spanish, speech/debate/rhetoric, and telecommunications), COMPUTER AND PHYSICAL SCIENCE (actuarial science, chemistry, computer science, computer security and information assurance, mathematics, physical sciences, and physics), EDUCATION (childhood education: 1-6, early childhood education, education, elementary education, English education, foreign languages education, mathematics education, middle school education, science education, secondary education, social studies education, and special education), HEALTH PROFESSIONS (clinical science, health care administration, pharmacy, physician's assistant, premedicine, radiological science, and speech pathology/audiology), SOCIAL SCIENCE (anthropology, Asian/Oriental studies, criminal justice, economics, history, homeland security, human services, legal studies, liberal arts/general studies, philosophy, political science/government, prelaw, psychology, public administration, social studies, sociology, and theological studies). Pharmacy, biology, and psychology are the strongest academically. Pharmacy has the largest enrollment.

Required: To graduate, students must complete at least 126 credit hours, including core courses and distribution requirements, with a minimum GPA of 2.0 overall and in the major. Other requirements vary by program. Core courses include English, theology, philosophy, Discover NY, history, scientific inquiry, and speech. Distribution requirements include a second language, fine arts, language and culture, math, philosophy, theology, and social sciences.

Special: St. John's offers internships, cross-registration, study abroad in Europe, Central and South America, Australia, the Caribbean, Africa, and Asia, accelerated degree programs in many majors, B.A.-B.S. degrees, dual majors and combined degree programs, pass/fail options, and some credit for life, military, and work experience. There are cooperative programs in engineering with Manhattan College, funeral service administration with the McAllister Institute, Dramatic Arts, Film and Television with the American Academy of Dramatic Arts, Biomedical Engineering with Polytechnic University, and Optometry with SUNY College of Optometry. St. John's Staten Island campus offers 14 different 3-year bachelor degree program opportunities. There is a 6-year doctor of pharmacy program for incoming freshmen. Many combined degree programs are available. Eligible students may participate in the University Honors Program. There are 15 national honor societies and a freshman honors program.

Faculty/Classroom: 58% of faculty are male; 42% are female. 91% teach undergraduates. No introductory courses are taught by graduate students.

Admissions: 53% of the 2013-2014 applicants were accepted. The SAT scores for the 2013-2014 freshman class were: Critical Reading--29% below 500, 48% between 500 and 599, 20% between 600 and 699, and 3% between 700 and 800; Math--24% below 500, 43% between 500 and 599, 24% between 600 and 699, and 9% between 700 and 800. The ACT scores were 20% below 21, 30% between 21 and 23, 25% between 24 and 26, 10% between 27 and 28, and 15% above 28. 34% of the current freshmen were in the top fifth of their class; 61% were in the top two fifths.

Requirements: The SAT or ACT is required. Admissions decisions are made by committee and are based on several criteria, including standardized test scores, academic curriculum, and high school average. AP and CLEP credits are accepted. Important factors in the admissions decision are advanced placement or honors courses, recommendations by school officials, and extracurricular activities record.

Procedure: Freshmen are admitted fall, spring, and summer. Entrance exams should be taken late in the junior year or early in the senior year. There are early admissions, deferred admissions, and rolling admissions plans. Application deadlines are open. Application fee is $50. Notification is sent on a rolling basis. Applications are accepted online. Application fees are waived if application is completed online.

Transfer: 715 transfer students enrolled in 2012-2013. Applicants must present official transcripts of high school and college work, as well as a list of courses in progress. If the student has been out of school a semester or more, a letter of explanation is also required. Admissions requirements for transfer students to the 6-year pharmacy program are stricter, and placement is limited. 30 of 126 credits required for the bachelor's degree must be completed at St. John's.

Visiting: There are regularly scheduled orientations for prospective students, including small group presentations and a tour of the campus. Accepted students may also participate in overnight visits scheduled during the Spring semester. There are guides for informal visits and visitors may sit in on classes. To schedule a visit, contact the Office of Admissions.

Financial Aid: In 2013-2014, 98% of all full-time freshmen and 95% of continuing full-time students received some form of financial aid. 90% of all full-time freshmen and 84% of continuing full-time students received need-based aid. The average freshman award was $45,957. Need-based scholarships or need-based grants averaged $11,236 ($26,645 maximum); need-based self-help aid (loans and jobs) averaged $8,074 ($9,500 maximum); non-need-based athletic scholarships averaged $33,336 ($52,030 maximum); other non-need-based awards and non-need-based scholarships averaged $15,552 ($36,450 maximum); and $21,169 from other forms of aid. 9% of undergraduate students work part-time. Average annual earnings from campus work are $4000. The average financial indebtedness of the 2013 graduate was $32,477. The FAFSA is required. The priority date for freshman financial aid applications for fall entry is February 1. The deadline for filing freshman financial aid applications for fall entry is March 1.

International Students: There are 621 international students enrolled. The school actively recruits these students. They must take the TOEFL with a minimum score of 600 on the paper-based TOEFL (PBT) or 100 on the Internet-based version (iBT). They must also take the SAT or ACT, scoring 1000. This requirement may be waived for international students educated outside of the United States.

Computers: All students may access the system. There are no time limits and no fees.

Graduates: From July 1, 2012 to June 30, 2013, 2252 bachelor's degrees were awarded. The most popular majors were business/marketing (22%), communications/journalism (11%), and health professions (9%). 250 companies recruited on campus in 2012-2013. In an average class, 1% graduate in 3 years or less, 36% graduate in 4 years or less, 47% graduate in 5 years or less, and 55% graduate in 6 years or less. Of the 2012 graduating class, 46% were enrolled in graduate school within 6 months of graduation, and 55% were employed.

Admissions Contact: David S. Follick, Director, Admissions - Queens. E-Mail: *admhelp@stjohns.edu* Web: *www.stjohns.edu/admission*

ST. JOSEPH'S COLLEGE, NEW YORK / BROOKLYN CAMPUS D-5

Brooklyn, NY 11205 (718) 940-5820

Full-time: 305 men, 615 women
Faculty: 60
Part-time: 83 men, 228 women
Ph.D.s: 87%
Graduate: 41 men, 189 women
Student/Faculty: 15 to 1
Year: semesters, summer session
Tuition: $21,878
Application Deadline: August 15
Room & Board: n/app
Freshman Class: 1572 applied, 1140 accepted, 162 enrolled
SAT CR/M/W: 490/480/470 **ACT:** 23 **COMPETITIVE**

St. Joseph's, Brooklyn, is a private, liberal arts college. Founded as a women's college in 1916, it adopted coeducation in 1969. There are 2 undergraduate schools and 2 graduate schools. The library contains 143,419 volumes, 367 microform items, and 3,024 audio/video tapes/CDs/DVDs, and subscribes to 46,112 periodicals including electronic. Computerized library services include interlibrary loans, database searching, Internet access, and Wi-Fi capability. Special learning facilities include an art gallery, and a Dillon Child Study Center. The 5-acre campus is in an urban area 5 miles from midtown Manhattan. Including any residence halls, there are 8 buildings.

Student Life: 96% of undergraduates are from New York. Others are from 16 states, and 35 foreign countries. 40% are from public schools. 39% are White; 27% African American; 15% Hispanic. The average age of freshmen is 18; all undergraduates, 26. 13% do not continue beyond their first year; 87% remain to graduate.

Housing: College-sponsored housing includes coed On-campus housing is available on a first-come and first-served basis. 99% of students commute. Alcohol is not permitted. All students may keep cars.

Activities: 1% of men belong to 1 local fraternity; 5% of women belong to 2 local sororities. There are 42 groups on campus, including art, cheerleading, chess, chorus, computers, dance, drama, environmental, ethnic, film, gay, honors, international, jazz band, literary magazine, musical theater, newspaper, orchestra, political, professional, religious, social, social service, student government, symphony, and yearbook. Popular campus events include Student Leadership Experience, Fashion Show and Multicultural Fair.

Sports: There are 6 intercollegiate sports for men and 7 for women, and 7 intramural sports for men and 6 for women. Facilities include off campus availability are baseball, softball, tennis, soccer and swimming venues. On campus is a fitness center-cardio and strength features.

Disabled Students: Facilities include wheelchair ramps, elevators, special parking, specially equipped restrooms, and lowered drinking fountains.

Services: Counseling and information services are available, as is tutoring in most subjects including math, chemistry, biology, speech, psychology, French, Italian, Spanish, computers, economics, business, and philosophy. There is remedial math, reading, and writing.

Campus Safety and Security: Measures include 24-hour foot and vehicle patrol, emergency notification system, and security escort services.

Programs of Study: St. Joseph's College confers B.A., B.S., B.S./M.S., B.S./M.B.A. degrees. Master's degrees are also awarded. Bachelor's degrees are awarded in BIOLOGICAL SCIENCE (biology/biological science), BUSINESS (accounting, business administration and management, hotel/motel and restaurant management, human resources, marketing management, organizational leadership and management, and recreation and leisure services), COMMUNICATIONS AND THE ARTS (English, journalism, Spanish, and speech/debate/rhetoric), COMPUTER AND PHYSICAL SCIENCE (chemistry, computer information technology, computer science, and mathematics), EDUCATION (education, elementary education, secondary education, and special education), HEALTH PROFESSIONS (health care administration, medical technology, and nursing), SOCIAL SCIENCE (child psychology/development, community services, criminal justice, history, human services, liberal arts/general studies, parks and recreation management, philosophy and religion, political science/government, psychology, social science, and sociology). Child study and secondary education is the strongest academically. Child study, business administration and psychology have the largest enrollments.

Required: To graduate, students must complete 8 courses in humanities. Students with a B.A. Degree need 90 credits of core curriculum and 60 credits for those with a B.S. Degree. The minimum GPA is 2.0. Students must earn 128 credits, with 30 credits in the major.

Special: We have an interdisciplinary major in human relations. We offer B.A. and B.S. degrees, and a dual major program in Child Study, elementary and special education. The college offers internship programs in English, history, political science, psychology, sociology, speech, and business/accounting. Adult students may pursue a general studies degree in which the college allows credit for life, military, and work experience. Study abroad in Nicaragua, Paris, Greece, Rome and Argentina. There are 5 national honor societies, a freshman honors program, and 1 departmental honors program.

Faculty/Classroom: 47% of faculty are male; 53% are female. All teach undergraduates. No introductory courses are taught by graduate students. The average class size in an introductory lecture is 14; in a laboratory is 12; and in a regular course is 13.

Admissions: 73% of the 2013-2014 applicants were accepted. The SAT scores for the 2013-2014 freshman class were:. Critical Reading--53% below 500, 40% between 500 and 599, and 8% between 600 and 699; Math--53% below 500, 38% between 500 and 599, 8% between 600 and 699, and 1% between 700 and 800; Writing--59% below 500, 30% between 500 and 599, 10% between 600 and 699, and 1% between 700 and 800. The ACT scores were 29% below 21, 21% between 21 and 23, 43% between 24 and 26, 4% between 27 and 28, and 4% above 28.

Requirements: The SAT or ACT is required. On the SAT a minimum composite score of 900. Applicants must graduate from an accredited secondary school or earn a GED. 16 Carnegie units are required, including 4 units of English and Social Studies, 3 of math, 2 of languages and science, and 3 elective units. Interviews are recommended. A GPA of 2.5 is required. AP and CLEP credits are accepted. Important factors in the admissions decision are advanced placement or honors courses, recommendations by school officials, and leadership record.

Procedure: Freshmen are admitted fall and spring. There are early admissions and deferred admissions plans. Applications should be filed by August 15 for fall entry, along with a $25 fee. Notification of early decision is sent November 1; regular decision. Applications are accepted online.

Transfer: 103 transfer students enrolled in 2012-2013. 24 of 128 credits required for the bachelor's degree must be completed at St. Joseph's College.

Visiting: There are regularly scheduled orientations for prospective students. There are guides for informal visits and visitors may sit in on classes. To schedule a visit, contact the Admissions Office.

Financial Aid: In 2013-2014, 98% of all full-time freshmen and 92% of continuing full-time students received some form of financial aid. 72% of all full-time freshmen and 67% of continuing full-time students received need-based aid. The average freshman award was $17,064. Need-based scholarships or need-based grants averaged $6,276 ($16,624 maximum); need-based self-help aid (loans and jobs) averaged $3,538 ($5,500 maximum); and other non-need-based awards and non-need-based scholarships averaged $12,442 ($35,600 maximum). 9% of undergraduate students work part-time. Average annual earnings from campus work are $1902. The average financial indebtedness of the 2013 graduate was $22,047. The FAFSA and the state aid form are required. The priority date for freshman financial aid applications for fall entry is February 25.

International Students: There are 29 international students enrolled. They must take the TOEFL with a minimum score of 550 on the paper-based TOEFL (PBT) or 79 on the Internet-based version (iBT). They must also take the SAT or ACT.

Computers: All students may access the system. There are no time limits and no fees.

Graduates: From July 1, 2012 to June 30, 2013, 267 bachelor's degrees were awarded. The most popular majors were child study (24%), business administration and accounting (13%), and nursing (9%). 80 companies recruited on campus in 2012-2013. In an average class, 63% graduate in 4 years or less, 71% graduate in 5 years or less, and 72% graduate in 6 years or less. Of the 2012 graduating class, 24% were enrolled in graduate school within 6 months of graduation, and 13% were employed.

Admissions Contact: Theresa LaRocca Meyer, Vice President for Enrollment Management. E-Mail: *tlaroccameyer@sjcny.edu* Web: *www.sjcny.edu*

ST. JOSEPH'S COLLEGE, NEW YORK / SUFFOLK CAMPUS E-5

Patchogue, NY 11772 (631) 687-4500

Full-time: 854 men, 1817 women
Faculty: 120
Part-time: 183 men, 444 women
Ph.D.s: 76%
Graduate: 155 men, 440 women
Student/Faculty: 22 to 1
Year: semesters, summer session
Tuition: $21,878
Application Deadline: August 15
Room & Board: n/app
Freshman Class: 1576 applied, 1233 accepted, 385 enrolled
SAT CR/M/W: 520/540/510 **ACT:** 23 **VERY COMPETITIVE**

St. Joseph's, Patchogue, founded in 1916, is a private, liberal arts college. It's campus, established in 1976, was redesignated as Suffolk Campus in 1979. There are 2 undergraduate schools and 2 graduate schools. The library contains 190,016 volumes, 1,375 microform items, and 2,527 audio/video tapes/CDs/DVDs, and subscribes to 37,525 periodicals including electronic. Computerized library services include interlibrary loans, database searching, Internet access, and Wi-Fi capability. Special learning facilities include an art gallery and radio station. The 51-acre campus is in a suburban area 55 miles from midtown Manhattan. Including any residence halls, there are 10 buildings.

Student Life: 100% of undergraduates are from New York. Others are from 8 states, and 35 foreign countries. 85% are from public schools. 70% are White; 13% race unknown. The average age of freshmen is 18; all undergraduates, 24. 18% do not continue beyond their first year; 82% remain to graduate.

Housing: Alcohol is not permitted. All students commute. All students may keep cars.

Activities: 1% of men belong to 2 local fraternities; 4% of women belong to 3 local sororities. There are 52 groups on campus, including art, cheerleading, chess, chorus, computers, dance, drama, environmental, ethnic, film, gay, honors, international, jazz band, literary magazine, musical theater, newspaper, orchestra, political, professional, radio and TV, religious, social, social service, student government, symphony, and yearbook. Popular campus events include Annual Concert, Student Leadership Experience and Club Fair.

Sports: There are 8 intercollegiate sports for men and 11 for women, and 13 intramural sports for men and 13 for women. Facilities include Baseball, sofball fields and artificial turf soccer/lacrosse fields; indoor and outdoor tracks, tennis courts, basketball arena, weight and aerobics rooms, swimming pool.

Disabled Students: Facilities include wheelchair ramps, elevators, special parking, specially equipped restrooms, and lowered drinking fountains.

Services: Counseling and information services are available, as is tutoring in most subjects. There is a reader service for the blind, and remedial math, reading, and writing.

Campus Safety and Security: Measures include 24-hour foot and vehicle patrol, emergency notification system, and security escort services. There are lighted pathways/sidewalks.

Programs of Study: St. Joseph's College confers B.A., B.S., B.A./M.A., B.S./M.A., B.S./M.S., B.S./M.B.A. degrees. Master's degrees are also awarded. Bachelor's degrees are awarded in BIOLOGICAL SCIENCE (biology/biological science), BUSINESS (accounting, business administration and management, hospitality management services, human resources, marketing management, organizational leadership and management, recreation and leisure services, and tourism), COMMUNICATIONS AND THE ARTS (English, journalism, Spanish, and speech/debate/rhetoric), COMPUTER AND PHYSICAL SCIENCE (chemistry, computer information technology, computer science, information sciences and systems, and mathematics), EDUCATION (education, secondary education, and special education), HEALTH PROFESSIONS (health care administration, medical technology, and public health), SOCIAL SCIENCE (child psychology/development, community services, criminal justice, history, human development, human services, liberal arts/general studies, philosophy and religion, political science/government, psychology, social science, and sociology). Child study and secondary education are the strongest academically. Child Study, business administration and psychology have the largest enrollments.

Required: To graduate, students must complete 8 courses in humanities. Students with a B.A. Degree need 90 credits of core curriculum and 60 credits for those with a B.S. Degree. The minimum GPA is 2.0. Students must earn 128 credits, with 30 credits in the major.

Special: We have an interdisciplinary major in human relations. We offer B.A. and B.S. degrees, and a dual major in Child Study, elementary and special education. The college offers internship programs in English, history, political science, psychology, sociology, speech, and business/accounting. Adult students may pursue a general studies degree in which the college allows credit for life, military, and work experience. Study abroad in Ireland, Nicaragua, Greece, Rome, Costa Rica, Argentina, Romania, Germany and Poland. There are 7 national honor societies, a freshman honors program, and 6 departmental honors programs.

Faculty/Classroom: 40% of faculty are male; 60% are female. All teach undergraduates. No introductory courses are taught by graduate students. The average class size in an introductory lecture is 16; in a laboratory is 14; and in a regular course is 16.

Admissions: 78% of the 2013-2014 applicants were accepted. The SAT scores for the 2013-2014 freshman class were: Critical Reading--34% below 500, 50% between 500 and 599, 15% between 600 and 699, and 1% between 700 and 800; Math--23% below 500, 52% between 500 and 599, 21% between 600 and 699, and 3% between 700 and 800; Writing--40% below 500, 46% between 500 and 599, 14% between 600 and 699, and 1% between 700 and 800. The ACT scores were 20% below 21, 34% between 21 and 23, 29% between 24 and 26, 13% between 27 and 28, and 4% above 28.

Requirements: The SAT or ACT is required. The ACT Optional Writing test is also required. For acceptance, students typically have a GPA of at least 80 and a combined CR+M SAT of 1050/ACT 22. Course work should include four years of English and Social Studies, three years of Math and lab Science (four years required for Math and Science majors) and at least one year of foreign language. Letters of recommendation and admissions essay are requested. An interview is strongly recommended. Also considered are rank in class (if provided), trends in grades, competitiveness of curriculum, and contributions to school and community through activities, leadership experiences and community service. A GPA of 2.8 is required. AP and CLEP credits are accepted. Important factors in the admissions decision are advanced placement or honors courses, extracurricular activities record, and leadership record.

Procedure: Freshmen are admitted fall and spring. Entrance exams should be taken spring of junior year and fall of senior year. There are early admissions, deferred admissions, and rolling admissions plans. Application deadlines are open. Application fee is $25. Notification of early decision is sent November 1. Applications are accepted online.

Transfer: 396 transfer students enrolled in 2012-2013. 2.8 GPA required for child study and secondary education majors. 24 of 128 credits required for the bachelor's degree must be completed at St. Joseph's College.

Visiting: There are regularly scheduled orientations for prospective students, 1-day orientation in August just prior to start of classes. There are guides for informal visits and visitors may sit in on classes. To schedule a visit, contact the Admissions Office.

Financial Aid: In 2013-2014, 96% of all full-time freshmen and 92% of continuing full-time students received some form of financial aid. 70% of all full-time freshmen and 66% of continuing full-time students received need-based aid. The average freshman award was $16,347. Need-based scholarships or need-based grants averaged $5,379 ($21,850 maximum); need-based self-help aid (loans and jobs) averaged $3,386 ($5,500 maximum); and other non-need-based awards and non-need-based scholarships averaged $12,185 ($29,950 maximum). 5% of undergraduate students work part-time. Average annual earnings from campus work are $2217. The average financial indebtedness of the 2013 graduate was $23,801. The FAFSA and the state aid form are required. The priority date for freshman financial aid applications for fall entry is February 25.

International Students: There are 10 international students enrolled. They must take the TOEFL with a minimum score of 550 on the paper-based TOEFL (PBT) or 79 on the Internet-based version (iBT). They must also take the SAT or ACT.

Computers: All students may access the system. There are no time limits and no fees.

Graduates: From July 1, 2012 to June 30, 2013, 873 bachelor's degrees were awarded. The most popular majors were child study (27%), business administration and accounting (12%), and psychology (8%). 107 companies recruited on campus in 2012-2013. In an average class, 1% graduate in 3 years or less, 52% graduate in 4 years or less, 69% graduate in 5 years or less, and 71% graduate in 6 years or less. Of the 2012 graduating class, 21% were enrolled in graduate school within 6 months of graduation, and 17% were employed.

Admissions Contact: Gigi Lamens, Assoc Vice President for Enrollment Mgmt. E-Mail: *glamens@sjcny.edu* Web: *www.sjcny.edu*

ST. LAWRENCE UNIVERSITY C-2

Canton, NY 13617 (315) 229-5261
(800) 285-1856; (315) 229-5818

Full-time: 1978 men, 1257 women	**Faculty:** 166; IIB, +$
Part-time: 12 men, 14 women	**Ph.D.s:** 98%
Graduate: 38 men, 58 women	**Student/Faculty:** 14 to 1
Year: semesters, summer session	**Tuition:** $43,235
Application Deadline: February 1	**Room & Board:** $11,505
Freshman Class: 4273 applied, 1855 accepted, 647 enrolled	
SAT CR/M/W: 618/602/620	

HIGHLY COMPETITIVE

St. Lawrence University, established in 1856, is a private liberal arts institution. There is one graduate school. The 2 libraries contain 612,057 volumes, 599,822 microform items, and 7,513 audio/video tapes/CDs/DVDs, and subscribe to 41,900 periodicals including electronic. Computerized library services include interlibrary loans, database searching, and Internet access. Special learning facilities include a learning resource center, art gallery, radio station, a science field station. The 1000-acre campus is in a small town 80 miles south of Ottawa, Canada. Including any residence halls, there are 30 buildings.

Student Life: 52% of undergraduates are from out of state, mostly the Northeast. Students are from 40 states, 45 foreign countries, and Canada. 69% are from public schools. 83% are white. The average age of freshmen is 18; all undergraduates, 20. 10% do not continue beyond their first year; 79% remain to graduate.

Housing: 2162 students can be accommodated in college housing, which includes coed dorms and on-campus apartments. In addition, there are special-interest houses, fraternity houses, sorority houses, and theme cottages, such as Habitat for Humanity. On-campus housing is guaranteed for all 4 years. 98% of students live on campus; of those, 90% remain on campus on weekends. All students may keep cars.

Activities: 4% of men belong to 2 national fraternities; 19% of women belong to 1 local and 3 national sororities. There are 100 groups on campus, including art, choir, chorus, computers, dance, drama, environmental, ethnic, forensics, gay, honors, international, jazz band, literary magazine, newspaper, orchestra, photography, political, professional, radio and TV, religious, social, social service, student government, and yearbook. Popular campus events include Moving Up Day, 100th Night, and Candlelight Service.

Sports: There are 16 intercollegiate sports for men and 16 for women, and 11 intramural sports for men and 11 for women. Facilities include basketball, squash, and tennis courts, a swimming pool, and a 133-station fitness center. There are also 2 field houses, an arena, an artificial ice rink,an 18-hole golf course, riding stables, jogging and cross-country ski trails, indoor and outdoor competition tracks, and soccer, baseball, and softball fields.

Disabled Students: 75% of the campus is accessible. Facilities include wheelchair ramps, elevators, special parking, specially equipped restrooms, special class scheduling, lowered drinking fountains, and visual fire alarms.

Services: Counseling and information services are available, as is tutoring in every subject. There is a reader service for the blind. a writing center, and science and technology counseling.

Campus Safety and Security: Measures include 24-hour foot and vehicle patrol, emergency notification system, self-defense education, and security escort services. There are emergency telephones, lighted pathways/sidewalks, student patrols.

Programs of Study: St. Lawrence confers B.A. and B.S. degrees. Master's degrees are also awarded. Bachelor's degrees are awarded in AGRICULTURE (conservation and regulation and environmental studies), BIOLOGICAL SCIENCE (biochemistry, biology/biological science, biophysics, and neurosciences), BUSINESS (international economics), COMMUNICATIONS AND THE ARTS (art, art history and appreciation, communications, creative writing, dramatic arts, English, fine arts, French, German, languages, modern language, music, Spanish, studio art, and visual and performing arts), COMPUTER AND PHYSICAL SCIENCE (chemistry, computer science, geology, mathematics, and physics), ENGINEERING AND ENVIRONMENTAL DESIGN (environmental science), SOCIAL SCIENCE (African studies, anthropology, Asian/Oriental studies, Canadian studies, economics, history, interdisciplinary studies, international studies, philosophy, political science/government, psychology, religion, and sociology). Psychology, economics, and government have the largest enrollments.

Required: To graduate, students must maintain a minimum GPA of 2.0 and complete 120 course hours, with 29 to 43 in the major. Freshmen must take a first-year program, a 2-semester team-taught course. Requirements also include 1 course in arts/expression, 1 in humanities, 1 in social science, 1 in math or foreign language, 2 in natural science/science studies, and 2 in diversity.

Special: Students may cross-register with the Associated Colleges of the St. Lawrence Valley. Internships are available through the sociology, psychology, and English departments and through a service learning program. Study-abroad in 15 countries and a Washington semester are offered. Dual majors and student-designed majors can be arranged. Students may earn 3-2 engineering degrees in conjunction with 7 engineering schools. Nondegree study and pass/fail options are available. An Adirondack semester is also offered. There are 20 national honor societies, including Phi Beta Kappa, and 17 departmental honors programs.

Faculty/Classroom: 55% of faculty are male; 45% are female. 99% teach undergraduates, and all do research. No introductory courses are taught by graduate students. The average class size in a regular course is 16.

Admissions: 43% of a recent year applicants were accepted. The SAT scores for a recent year freshman class were: Critical Reading--3% below 500, 35% between 500 and 599, 50% between 600 and 700, and 12% above 700; Math--3% between 500 and 599, 60% between 600 and 700, and 9% above 700; Writing--6% below 500, 32% between 500 and 599, 49% between 600 and 700, and 12% above 700. 71% of the current freshmen were in the top fifth of their class; 91% were in the top two fifths. 14 freshmen graduated first in their class.

Requirements: Applicants must be graduates of an accredited high school. 16 or more academic credits are required, including 4 years of English and 3 years each of foreign languages, math, science, and social studies. Essays are required and interviews are recommended for all applicants. Submissions of standardized test scores is optional. AP credits are accepted. Important factors in the admissions decision are advanced placement or honors courses, extracurricular activities record, and recommendations by school officials.

Procedure: Freshmen are admitted fall and spring. Entrance exams should be taken during the spring of the junior year or the fall of the senior year. There are early decision and deferred admissions plans. Early decision applications should be filed by November 1; regular applications, by February 1 for fall entry; and December 1 for spring entry, along with a $60 fee. Notification of early decision is sent December 15; regular decision, March 30. In a recent year, 351 applicants were on the waiting list; 18 were admitted. Applications are accepted online.

Transfer: 24 transfer students enrolled in in a recent year. The high school transcript and SAT scores will be evaluated, but college work is more important. High school and college recommendations are required.

Visiting: There are regularly scheduled orientations for prospective students, including interviews and tours. There are guides for informal visits, visitors may sit in on classes, and stay overnight. To schedule a visit, contact the Admissions Office.

Financial Aid: In a recent year, 92% of all full-time freshmen and 88% of continuing full-time students received some form of financial aid. 63% of all full-time freshmen and 66% of continuing full-time students received need-based aid. The average freshman award was $32,003. Need-based scholarships or need-based grants averaged $37,659; need-based self-help aid (loans and jobs) averaged $6,654; non-need-based athletic scholarships averaged $49,898; and other non-need-based awards and non-need-based scholarships averaged $17,838. 33% of undergraduate students work part-time. St. Lawrence is a member of CSS. The CSS/Profile, FAFSA, and nocustodial profile are required. Check with the school for current deadlines for filing freshman financial aid applications.

International Students: There are 126 international students enrolled. The school actively recruits these students.

Computers: Wireless access is available. There are 660 public access computers. Wireless access is available throughout the campus. All students may access the system 24 hours per day. There are no time limits and no fees.

Graduates: In a recent year, 444 bachelor's degrees were awarded. The most popular majors were psychology (17%), economics (14%), and environmental studies (10%). In an average class, 1% graduate in 3 years or less, 78% graduate in 4 years or less, 80% graduate in 5 years or less, and 81% graduate in 6 years or less. Of the 2010 graduating class, 24% were enrolled in graduate school within 6 months of graduation, and 72% were employed.

Admissions Contact: Dean of Admissions and Financial Aid. E-Mail: *admissions@stlawu.edu* Web: *www.stlwu.edu*

ST. THOMAS AQUINAS COLLEGE — D-5

Sparkill, NY 10976 — (914) 398-4100; (800) 999-STAC; (914) 398-4224

Full-time: 1410 men and women	**Faculty:** n/av; IIB, +$
Part-time: 810 men and women	**Ph.D.s:** n/av
Graduate: 80 men, 130 women	**Student/Faculty:** n/av
Year: semesters, summer session	**Tuition:** $24,606
Application Deadline: see profife	**Room & Board:** $10,500
Freshman Class: n/av	
SAT or ACT: required	

COMPETITIVE

Saint Thomas Aquinas College, founded in 1952, is an independent liberal arts institution. Figures in above capsule and in this profile are approximate. There are 2 graduate schools. The library contains 102,943 volumes, and 45,900 microform items, and subscribes to 108 periodicals including electronic. Computerized library services include interlibrary loans and database searching. Special learning facilities include a learning resource center, radio station, and TV station. The 43-acre campus is in a suburban area 15 miles north of New York City. Including any residence halls, there are 12 buildings.

Student Life: 75% of undergraduates are from New York. Others are from 6 states, 8 foreign countries, and Canada. 80% are from public schools. 84% are white. 62% are Catholic; 23% Protestant. The average age of freshmen is 18; all undergraduates, 23. 16% do not continue beyond their first year; 62% remain to graduate.

Housing: 450 students can be accommodated in college housing, which includes single-sex dorms and on-campus apartments. On-campus housing is guaranteed for all 4 years. 65% of students commute. Alcohol is not permitted. All students may keep cars.

Activities: There are no fraternities or sororities. There are 15 groups on campus, including cheerleading, chorus, computers, drama, honors, international, literary magazine, musical theater, newspaper, professional, radio and TV, religious, social service, student government, and yearbook. Popular campus events include trips to Broadway shows and Halloween and Christmas mixers.

Sports: There are 5 intercollegiate sports for men and 4 for women, and 6 intramural sports for men and 5 for women. Facilities include an auditorium, a 750-seat gym, a weight room, and basketball and tennis courts.

Disabled Students: 90% of the campus is accessible. Facilities include wheelchair ramps, elevators, special parking, specially equipped restrooms, special class scheduling, and lowered telephones.

Services: Counseling and information services are available, as is tutoring in most subjects. There is remedial math and writing.

Campus Safety and Security: Measures include 24-hour foot and vehicle patrol and security escort services. There are emergency telephones and lighted pathways/sidewalks.

Programs of Study: STAC confers B.A., B.S., and B.S.E. degrees. Associates and master's degrees are also awarded. Bachelor's degrees are awarded in BUSINESS (accounting, banking and finance, business administration and management, marketing/retailing/merchandising, and recreation and leisure services), COMMUNICATIONS AND THE ARTS (communications, English, fine arts, romance languages and literature, and Spanish), EDUCATION (art education, bilingual/bicultural education, elementary education, foreign languages education, science education, secondary education, and special education), ENGINEERING AND ENVIRONMENTAL DESIGN (commercial art), HEALTH PROFESSIONS (medical laboratory technology and premedicine), SOCIAL SCIENCE (criminal justice, history, philosophy, prelaw, psychology, religion, and social science). Education, business administration, and natural sciences are the strongest academically. Business administration has the largest enrollment.

Required: To graduate, all students must complete a total of 120 credit hours, with 36 to 54 in the major and a minimum GPA of 2.0. A core curriculum of 51 credits in liberal arts courses is required.

Special: The college offers cross-registration with Barry University and Aquinas College and internships in business, criminal justice, commercial design, recreation and leisure, and communications. Study abroad in Europe and Asia, a 3-2 engineering degree with George Washington University and Manhattan College, and in physical therapy with New York Medical College, and work-study programs are available. Nondegree study and pass/fail options are possible. There are 7 national honor societies, including Phi Beta Kappa, and a freshman honors program.

Faculty/Classroom: 55% of faculty are male; 45% are female. 99% teach undergraduates, 50% do research, and 50% do both. No introductory courses are taught by graduate students. The average class size in an introductory lecture is 35; in a laboratory is 15; and in a regular course is 20.

Requirements: The SAT or ACT is required. Applicants must be graduates of an accredited secondary school or have a GED certificate. 16 Carnegie units are recommended, including 4 years of English, and social science, 2 years of math, foreign language, and science, including 2 years of lab science. A GPA of 2.2 is required. AP and CLEP credits are accepted. Important factors in the admissions decision are leadership record, extracurricular activities record, and advanced placement or honors courses.

Procedure: Freshmen are admitted fall and spring. Entrance exams should be taken by the spring of the junior year. There are early decision, early admissions, deferred admissions, and rolling admissions plans. Check with the school for current application deadlines and fee. Notification is sent on a rolling basis. Applications are accepted online.

Transfer: Applicants must have a 2.0 GPA from the previous school. 30 of 120 credits required for the bachelor's degree must be completed at STAC.

Visiting: There are guides for informal visits; visitors may sit in on classes and stay overnight. To schedule a visit, contact the Admissions Office.

Financial Aid: STAC is a member of CSS. The FAFSA is required. Check with the school for current application deadlines.

International Students: The school actively recruits these students. They must take the TOEFL.

Computers: All students may access the system. There are no time limits. The fee is $100.

Admissions Contact: Tracey A. Howard-Ubelhoer, Director of Admissions. A campus DVD is available. E-Mail: *thoward@stac.edu* Web: *www.stac.edu*

STATE UNIVERSITY OF NEW YORK

The State University of New York, established in 1948, is a public system in New York. It is governed by a board of trustees, whose chief administrator is the chancellor. The primary goal of the system is teaching, research, and public service. The main priorities are to educate the largest number of people possible at the highest level, including educationally disadvantaged groups; to provide students with enhanced educational skills and techniques; and to enhance the quality of life for all New Yorkers. The total student enrollment is usually about 412,355 with 27000 faculty members. Altogether there are 1423 baccalaureate, 860 master's, and 278 doctoral programs offered in the State University of New York System. Profiles of the 4-year campuses are included in this section.

STATE UNIVERSITY OF NEW YORK / COLLEGE OF ENVIRONMENTAL SCIENCE AND FORESTRY C-3

Syracuse, NY 13210-2779 **(315) 470-6600; (315) 470-6933**

Full-time: 910 men, 620 women	**Faculty:** n/av; I, --$
Part-time: 305 men, 350 women	**Ph.D.s:** 96%
Graduate: 320 men, 315 women	**Student/Faculty:** n/av
Year: semesters	**Tuition:** $5941 ($15,569)
Application Deadline: see profile	**Room & Board:** $14,078
Freshman Class: n/av	
SAT or ACT: required	

HIGHLY COMPETITIVE

The SUNY College of Environmental Science and Forestry, founded in 1911, is the nation's oldest and largest college focused exclusively on the science, design, engineering, and management of our environment and natural resources. The figures in the above capsule and in this profile are approximate. The college offers 21 undergraduate and 28 graduate degree programs, including 8 Ph.D. programs. Students also benefit from a special partnership with Syracuse University (SU) that provides access to courses, housing, and student organizations. There is 1 undergraduate school and 1 graduate school. In addition to regional accreditation, ESF has baccalaureate program accreditation with ABET, ASLA, and SAF. The library contains 135,305 volumes, 200,090 microform items, and 1,118 audio/video tapes/CDs/DVDs, and subscribes to 2,001 periodicals including electronic. Computerized library services include interlibrary loans, database searching, Internet access, and laptop Internet portals. Special learning facilities include a learning resource center, art gallery, natural history museum, radio station, and TV station. The 12-acre campus is in an urban area in Syracuse with 25,000 additional acres in New York State used for teaching and research. Including any residence halls, there are 7 buildings.

Student Life: 86% of undergraduates are from New York. Others are from 28 states and 6 foreign countries. 85% are from public schools. 85% are white. The average age of freshmen is 18; all undergraduates, 21. 22% do not continue beyond their first year; 65% remain to graduate.

Housing: 475 students can be accommodated in college housing, which includes single-sex and coed dorms, on-campus apartments, and off-campus apartments. In addition, there are special-interest houses, fraternity houses, sorority houses, and substance-free floors, quiet floors, and learning communities. On-campus housing is guaranteed for all 4 years and is available on a lottery system for upperclassmen. 3% of students commute. Alcohol is not permitted. Upperclassmen may keep cars.

Activities: 3% of men belong to 20 national fraternities; 3% of women belong to 20 national sororities. There are 300 groups on campus, including art, bagpipe, band, cheerleading, choir, chorale, chorus, computers, dance, debate, drama, environmental, ethnic, film, gay, honors, international, jazz band, literary magazine, marching band, musical theater, newspaper, orchestra, pep band, photography, political, professional, radio and TV, religious, social, social service, student government, symphony, and yearbook. Popular campus events include Earth Week, Awards Banquet, and December Soiree.

Sports: There are 4 intercollegiate sports for men and 3 for women, and 15 intramural sports for men and 15 for women. ESF has soccer, golf, cross-country, and woodsman's teams. Students can participate in all Syracuse University club teams, intramural sports, and recreational activities.

Disabled Students: 95% of the campus is accessible. Facilities include wheelchair ramps, elevators, special parking, specially equipped restrooms, lowered drinking fountains, lowered telephones, and special housing.

Services: Counseling and information services are available, as is tutoring in most subjects. There is a reader service for the blind.

Campus Safety and Security: Measures include 24-hour foot and vehicle patrol, emergency notification system, self-defense education, and security escort services. There are shuttle buses, emergency telephones, lighted pathways/sidewalks, and controlled access to dorms/residences.

Programs of Study: ESF confers B.S. and B.L.A. degrees. Associates, master's, and doctoral degrees are also awarded. Bachelor's degrees are awarded in AGRICULTURE (animal science, environmental studies, fishing and fisheries, forest engineering, forestry and related sciences, natural resource management, plant science, soil science, and wood science), BIOLOGICAL SCIENCE (biology/biological science, biotechnology, botany, ecology, entomology, environmental biology, microbiology, molecular biology, plant genetics, plant pathology, plant physiology, and wildlife biology), COMPUTER AND PHYSICAL SCIENCE (chemistry and polymer science), EDUCATION (environmental education and science education), ENGINEERING AND ENVIRONMENTAL DESIGN (chemical engineering, construction management, environmental design, environmental engineering, environmental science, landscape architecture/design, paper and pulp science, paper engineering, and survey and mapping technology), HEALTH PROFESSIONS (predentistry, premedicine, and prepharmacy), SOCIAL SCIENCE (prelaw). Engineering, chemistry, and biology are the strongest academically. Environmental and forest biology, landscape architecture, and environmental science have the largest enrollments.

Required: Students must complete 125 to 130 credit hours for the B.S.

(160 for the B.L.A.), including 60 in the major, with a minimum 2.0 GPA. Courses in chemistry, English, math, and biology or physics are required.

Special: Cross-registration is offered with Syracuse University. Co-op programs, internships, and dual options in forest ecosystem science are available. Study abroad is available in landscape architecture and through Syracuse University. There is an honors program for outstanding students. There is 1 national honor society, a freshman honors program, and 8 departmental honors programs.

Faculty/Classroom: 72% of faculty are male; 28% are female. All teach and do research. No introductory courses are taught by graduate students. The average class size in a regular course is 25.

Requirements: The SAT or ACT is required. Applicants are required to have a minimum of 3 years of math and science, including chemistry, in a college preparatory curriculum. A supplemental application form, essay and results of SAT or ACT exams are required. A campus visit, letters of recommendation, and a personal portfolio or resume are recommended. ESF requires applicants to be in the upper 50% of their class. A GPA of 85.0 is required. AP and CLEP credits are accepted. Important factors in the admissions decision are advanced placement or honors courses, leadership record, and extracurricular activities record.

Procedure: Freshmen are admitted fall and spring. Entrance exams should be taken by October of the senior year. There are early admissions, deferred admissions, and rolling admissions plans. Check with the school for current application deadlines and fee. Notifications are sent March 1. Applications are accepted online.

Transfer: 226 transfer students enrolled in a recent year. Transfer requirements vary by major. Students must successfully complete prerequisite course work and must have a 2.5 or higher GPA to be considered. 24 of 125 credits required for the bachelor's degree must be completed at ESF.

Visiting: There are regularly scheduled orientations for prospective students, including a fall open house, which provides campus tours, faculty sessions, an activities fair, and student affairs presentations. There are guides for informal visits and visitors may sit in on classes. To schedule a visit, contact the Admissions Office.

Financial Aid: In a recent year, 85% of all full-time freshmen and 85% of continuing full-time students received some form of financial aid. 80% of all full-time freshmen and 80% of continuing full-time students received need-based aid. The average freshmen award was $7,200, with $1,500 ($3,000 maximum) from need-based scholarships or need-based grants; $4,250 ($5,500 maximum) from need-based self-help aid (loans and jobs); and $4,500 ($6,000 maximum) from other non-need-based awards and non-need-based scholarships. 75% of undergraduate students worked part-time. ESF is a member of CSS. The FAFSA is required. Check with the school for current application deadlines.

International Students: There were 11 international students enrolled in a recent year. They must take the TOEFL with a minimum score of 550 on the paper-based TOEFL (PBT) or 79 on the Internet-based version (iBT). They must also take the SAT or ACT.

Computers: All ESF students are provided e-mail addresses. All student housing has wireless and Internet access. Wireless is accessible at several locations on campus. The college has over 120 computers available in 4 computing labs for student use. All students may access the system any time. There are no time limits and no fees. Students enrolled in landscape architecture must have a personal computer.

Graduates: In a recent year, 286 bachelor's degrees were awarded. The most popular majors were environmental and forest biology (47%), environmental studies (20%), and landscape architecture (9%). 40 companies recruited on campus in a recent year. In an average class, 3% graduate in 3 years or less, 60% graduate in 4 years or less, 71% graduate in 5 years or less, and 72% graduate in 6 years or less. Of a recent graduating class, 16% were enrolled in graduate school within 6 months of graduation, and 61% were employed.

Admissions Contact: Director of Admissions and Inter-Institutional Relations. A campus DVD is available. E-Mail: *esfinfo@esf.edu* Web: *www.esf.edu*

STATE UNIVERSITY OF NEW YORK INSTITUTE OF TECHNOLOGY AT UTICA / ROME C-3

Utica, NY 13502 (315) 792-7500
1-866-2SUNYIT; (315) 792-7837

Full-time: 802 men, 471 women	**Faculty:** 78
Part-time: 114 men, 301 women	**Ph.D.s:** 76%
Graduate: 296 men, 387 women	**Student/Faculty:** 18 to 1
Year: semesters, summer session	**Tuition:** $6764 ($16,014)
Application Deadline: August 1	**Room & Board:** $10,290

Freshman Class: 1884 applied, 732 accepted, 198 enrolled
SAT CR/M: 510/550 **ACT:** 22 **COMPETITIVE**

The State University of New York/Institute of Technology, founded in 1966, is a public institution offering programs in technology and professional studies. There are 7 undergraduate schools and 6 graduate schools. In addition to regional accreditation, SUNYIT has baccalaureate program accreditation with AACSB and ABET. The library contains 148,670 volumes, and 1,502 audio/video tapes/CDs/DVDs, and subscribes to 1,401 periodicals including electronic. Computerized library services include interlibrary loans, database searching, Internet access, and Wi-Fi capability. Special learning facilities include an art gallery, radio station, and TV station. The 800-acre campus is in a suburban area at the western end of Mohawk Valley. Including any residence halls, there are 10 buildings.

Student Life: 98% of undergraduates are from New York. Others are from 11 states, and 12 foreign countries. 73% are White. The average age of freshmen is 19; all undergraduates, 27. 30% do not continue beyond their first year; 50% remain to graduate.

Housing: 584 students can be accommodated in college housing, which includes coed dorms. In addition, there are special-interest houses. On-campus housing is available on a first-come, first-served basis, and is available on a lottery system for upperclassmen. Priority is given to out-of-town students. 80% of students commute. All students may keep cars.

Activities: There are no fraternities or sororities. There are 38 groups on campus, including computers, environmental, ethnic, international, jazz band, newspaper, professional, radio and TV, social, and student government. Popular campus events include Fall Fest Weekend, Diwali and Holi Festivals, and Apocalypse Week.

Sports: There are 6 intercollegiate sports for men and 6 for women, and 10 intramural sports for men and 10 for women. Facilities include an indoor and outdoor facilities, a fitness center, fitness trail, and a gym with indoor track, field house, lighted turf field, grass baseball, softball and soccer fields.

Disabled Students: 99% of the campus is accessible. Facilities include wheelchair ramps, elevators, special parking, specially equipped restrooms, lowered drinking fountains, lowered telephones, and special housing.

Services: Counseling and information services are available, as is tutoring in most subjects. There is a reader service for the blind, and remedial math, reading, and writing.

Campus Safety and Security: Measures include 24-hour foot and vehicle patrol, emergency notification system, self-defense education, and security escort services. There are emergency telephones, lighted pathways/sidewalks, and emergency call boxes.

Programs of Study: SUNYIT confers B.A., B.S., B.B.A. and B.P.S. degrees. Master's degrees are also awarded. Bachelor's degrees are awarded in BUSINESS (accounting, banking and finance, and business administration and management), COMMUNICATIONS AND THE ARTS (communications technology and telecommunications), COMPUTER AND PHYSICAL SCIENCE (applied mathematics and computer science), ENGINEERING AND ENVIRONMENTAL DESIGN (civil engineering technology, computer technology, electrical/electronics engineering, electrical/electronics engineering technology, industrial engineering, and mechanical engineering technology), HEALTH PROFESSIONS (health, health care administration, and nursing), SOCIAL SCIENCE (criminal justice, liberal arts/general studies, psychology, and sociology). Engineering, technology, computer science, business, and nursing have the largest enrollments.

Required: Students must meet general education requirements and complete 124 to 128 credit hours to graduate.

Special: SUNYIT offers cross-registration with the Mohawk Valley Consortium, internships, and work study. An accelerated degree program in nursing, communications and information design and computer information science is possible, and there is a joint partnership (1+2+1) with St. Elizabeth College of Nursing. There are 2 national honor societies.

Faculty/Classroom: 66% of faculty are male; 34% are female. No introductory courses are taught by graduate students. The average class size in an introductory lecture is 24 and in a regular course is 18.

Admissions: 39% of the 2013-2014 applicants were accepted. The SAT scores for the 2013-2014 freshman class were: Critical Reading--42% below 500, 40% between 500 and 599, 14% between 600 and 699, and 1% between 700 and 800; Math--19% below 500, 50% between 500 and 599, 25% between 600 and 699, and 3% between 700 and 800. The ACT scores were 2% below 21, 29% between 21 and 23, 29% between 24 and 26, and 3% above 28. 34% of the current freshmen were in the top fifth of their class; 80% were in the top two fifths. 2 freshmen graduated first in their class.

Requirements: The SAT or ACT is required. Official transcripts, test scores, essay, and supplemental application are required. A GPA of 3.0 is required. AP and CLEP credits are accepted. Important factors in the admissions decision are advanced placement or honors courses, evidence of special talent, and recommendations by school officials.

Procedure: Freshmen are admitted fall and spring. Entrance exams should be taken by April of year applicant intends to enroll. There are early admissions, deferred admissions, and rolling admissions plans. Applications should be filed by August 1 for fall entry; December 1 for spring entry, along with a $50 fee. Notifications are sent December 15. Applications are accepted online.

Transfer: 301 transfer students enrolled in 2012-2013. Transfer stu-

dents generally must present a minimum cumulative GPA of 2.7 or better. Applicants presenting a GPA below 2.5 will be considered on an individual basis. 30 of 124 credits required for the bachelor's degree must be completed at SUNYIT.

Visiting: There are regularly scheduled orientations for prospective students, registration and orientation to campus. There are guides for informal visits, visitors may sit in on classes, and stay overnight. To schedule a visit, contact the Admissions Office at (315) 792-7500.

Financial Aid: In 2013-2014, 81% of all full-time freshmen and 78% of continuing full-time students received some form of financial aid. 71% of all full-time freshmen and 74% of continuing full-time students received need-based aid. 9% of undergraduate students work part-time. Average annual earnings from campus work are $1470. The FAFSA and the state aid form are required. The priority date for freshman financial aid applications for fall entry is March 1.

International Students: There are 10 international students enrolled. The school actively recruits these students. They must take the TOEFL with a minimum score of 550 on the paper-based TOEFL (PBT) or 79 on the Internet-based version (iBT), Can also take IELTS (International English Language Testing Service). They must also take the SAT or ACT, scoring 900. for first-time, full-time students only.

Computers: All students may access the system anytime. There are no time limits and no fees.

Graduates: From July 1, 2012 to June 30, 2013, 433 bachelor's degrees were awarded. The most popular majors were business administration (17%), nursing (17%), and computer science (9%). 68 companies recruited on campus in 2012-2013.

Admissions Contact: Jennifer Phelan-Ninh, Director of Admissions. E-Mail: *admissions@sunyit.edu* Web: *www.sunyit.edu*

STATE UNIVERSITY OF NEW YORK/EMPIRE STATE COLLEGE D-3

Saratoga Springs, NY 12866 **(518) 587-2100, ext. 2214 (800) 847-3000; (518) 580-9759**

Full-time: 1290 men, 2941 women	**Faculty:** 164
Part-time: 2825 men, 3795 women	**Ph.D.s:** 96%
Graduate: 348 men, 650 women	**Student/Faculty:** 26 to 1
Year: other, summer session	**Tuition:** $6315 ($15,765)
Application Deadline: June 1	**Room & Board:** n/app
Freshman Class: n/av	**SPECIAL**

Empire State College, founded in 1971, part of the State University of New York, offers degree programs in the arts and sciences through its statewide network of regional centers and units. It operates on a five-term calendar, with September, November, January, March, and May terms. The needs of adult learners are met through guided independent study, distance learning, study groups, cross-registration, and credit for lifelong learning. There is one graduate school. In addition to regional accreditation, Empire State College has baccalaureate program accreditation with TEAC. The library contains 1,000,000 audio/video tapes/CDs/DVDs. Computerized library services include interlibrary loans and database searching.

Student Life: 93% of undergraduates are from New York. Others are from 49 states, 28 foreign countries, and Canada. 68% are White; 16% African American. The average age of freshmen is 35; all undergraduates, 36.

Housing: Alcohol is not permitted. All students commute. All students may keep cars.

Activities: There are no fraternities or sororities. There are 2 groups on campus, including literary magazine and student government. Popular campus events include outside speakers throughout the year.

Sports: There is no sports program at Empire State College.

Disabled Students: All of the campus is accessible. Facilities include wheelchair ramps, elevators, and special parking.

Services: Counseling and information services are available, as is tutoring in every subject.

Campus Safety and Security: Measures include emergency notification system.

Programs of Study: Empire State College confers B.A., B.S. and B.P.S. degrees. Associate and master's degrees are also awarded. Bachelor's degrees are awarded in BUSINESS (accounting, business administration and management, human resources, labor studies, management information systems, management science, and marketing and distribution), COMPUTER AND PHYSICAL SCIENCE (computer science, information sciences and systems, mathematics, and science), EDUCATION (education), HEALTH PROFESSIONS (health care administration and nursing), SOCIAL SCIENCE (child care/child and family studies, community services, counseling/psychology, criminal justice, early childhood studies, economics, fire services administration, history, human development, humanities and social science, interdisciplinary studies, liberal arts/general studies, psychology, public affairs, and sociology). Business, management, and economics have the largest enrollments.

Required: Students must earn 128 credits, including 24 in their major and 30 credits that meet SUNY general education requirements, to graduate. Degree programs are customized and will vary in content.

Special: Empire State College offers cross-registration with numerous consortiums and institutions in New York State, internships in government, business, nonprofits, and academia, and study abroad in Greece, Lebanon, Czech Republic, Albania, and Dominican Republic. Accelerated degrees and dual and student-designed majors are possible in all programs. Nondegree study, credit for life, military, and work experience is possible.

Faculty/Classroom: 36% of faculty are male; 64% are female. No introductory courses are taught by graduate students.

Requirements: Applicants must be high school graduates, have a GED, or show ability to succeed at the college level. Empire State College also considers the ability of a learning location to meet individual needs. AP and CLEP credits are accepted. Important factors in the admissions decision are recommendations by school officials and personality/intangible qualities.

Procedure: Freshmen are admitted to all sessions. There is a rolling admissions plan. Applications should be filed by June 1 for fall entry; November 1 for winter entry; January 1 for spring entry; and March 1 for summer entry. Applications are accepted online.

Transfer: Empire State College offers maximum flexibility to transfer applicants, who must provide official transcripts from previous colleges attended. 32 of 128 credits required for the bachelor's degree must be completed at Empire State College.

Visiting: There are regularly scheduled orientations for prospective students, by invitation, after students attend an information session. There are guides for informal visits. To schedule a visit, contact Melanie Kaiser at (518) 587-2100.

Financial Aid: The FAFSA is required. Check with the school for current application deadlines.

International Students: They must take the TOEFL.

Computers: All students may access the system 24 hours a day. There are no time limits and no fees.

Graduates: From July 1, 2012 to June 30, 2013, 2437 bachelor's degrees were awarded. The most popular majors were business, management, and economics (37%), community and human services (24%), and human development (8%).

Admissions Contact: Jennifer D'Agostino, Director of Admissions. E-Mail: *admissions@esc.edu* Web: *www.esc.edu*

STONY BROOK UNIVERSITY / STATE UNIVERSITY OF NEW YORK E-5

Stony Brook, NY 11794 **(631) 632-6868; 631) 632-9898**

Full-time: 8126 men, 6879 women		**Faculty:** 939; I, av$
Part-time: 549 men, 605 women		**Ph.D.s:** 97%
Graduate: 3649 men, 4553 women		**Student/Faculty:** 18 to 1
Year: semesters, summer session		**Tuition:** $7995 ($19,935)
Application Deadline: January 15		**Room & Board:** $11,364
Freshman Class: 30300 applied, 11963 accepted, 2709 enrolled		
SAT CR/M/W: 600/660/610	**ACT:** 28	**HIGHLY COMPETITIVE**

Stony Brook University, founded in 1957, and part of the State University of New York, is a public institution offering degree programs in arts and sciences, engineering and applied sciences, business, journalism, atmospheric and marine sciences, sustainability studies, public health, nursing, health technology and management, and social work. Professional programs in medicine and dental medicine are offered at the graduate level. There are 9 undergraduate schools and 12 graduate schools. In addition to regional accreditation, Stony Brook University has baccalaureate program accreditation with ABET, ADA, APTA, CAHEA, CSWE, NCATE, and NLN. The 7 libraries contain 2.1 million volumes, 3.8 million microform items, and 44,986 audio/video tapes/CDs/DVDs, and subscribe to 89,222 periodicals including electronic. Computerized library services include interlibrary loans, database searching, and Internet access. Special learning facilities include an art gallery, radio station, TV station, the Museum of Long Island Natural Sciences, and the Fine Arts Center, which has an 1100-seat main theater, a 400-seat recital hall, and 3 experimental theaters. The 1450-acre campus is in a suburban area on Long Island, 55 miles from New York City. Including any residence halls, there are 200 buildings.

Student Life: 82% of undergraduates are from New York. Others are from 52 states, 110 foreign countries, and Canada. 89% are from public schools. 37% are White; 24% Asian American; 11% Foreign. The average age of freshmen is 18; all undergraduates, 21. 8% do not continue beyond their first year; 70% remain to graduate.

Housing: 9554 students can be accommodated in college housing, which includes coed dorms, on-campus apartments, and married student housing. In addition, there are honors houses, special-interest houses, A choice of undergraduate colleges that integrate academic experience with living environments. On-campus housing is guaranteed for all 4 years. 60% of students live on campus; of those, 65% remain on campus on weekends. Alcohol is not permitted. Upperclassmen may keep cars.

Activities: 2% of men belong to 1 local and 18 national fraternities; 2% of women belong to 2 local and 18 national sororities. There are 341 groups on campus, including band, cheerleading, choir, chorale, dance, drama, ethnic, film, gay, honors, international, jazz band, literary magazine, marching band, musical theater, newspaper, opera, orchestra, pep band, photography, political, professional, radio and TV, religious, social, and student government. Popular campus events include Fall Fest, Opening Week Activities, and Caribbean Weekend.

Sports: There are 10 intercollegiate sports for men and 10 for women, and 10 intramural sports for men and 10 for women. Facilities include an indoor sports complex housing a 4000-seat arena, a 1800-seat gym, swimming pool, 2 squash and 5 racquetball courts, a dance studio, and exercise and universal gym rooms. Outdoor facilities include an 8100-seat stadium, a 500-seat softball facility, a 1000-seat baseball facility, 12 tennis courts, 2 multi-sport practice facilities, 2 recreational basketball and 4 handball courts, 2 recreational softball fields, and a multi-sport recreational area.

Disabled Students: 85% of the campus is accessible. Facilities include wheelchair ramps, elevators, special parking, specially equipped restrooms, special class scheduling, lowered drinking fountains, lowered telephones, special housing, and automatic door openers.

Services: There is a reader service for the blind, and remedial math and writing.

Campus Safety and Security: Measures include 24-hour foot and vehicle patrol, emergency notification system, self-defense education, and security escort services. There are shuttle buses, emergency telephones, lighted pathways/sidewalks, controlled access to dorms/residences, a campus crime stoppers program, building access through use of cards, and controlled campus access after midnight.

Programs of Study: Stony Brook University confers B.A., B.S. and B.E. degrees. Master's and doctoral degrees are also awarded. Bachelor's degrees are awarded in AGRICULTURE (environmental studies), BIOLOGICAL SCIENCE (biochemistry, biology/biological science, ecology, and marine biology), BUSINESS (business administration and management), COMMUNICATIONS AND THE ARTS (art history and appreciation, comparative literature, dramatic arts, English, film arts, Germanic languages and literature, linguistics, music, Russian languages and literature, and studio art), COMPUTER AND PHYSICAL SCIENCE (applied mathematics, astronomy, atmospheric sciences and meteorology, chemistry, computer science, earth science, geology, information sciences and systems, mathematics, and physics), EDUCATION (athletic training), ENGINEERING AND ENVIRONMENTAL DESIGN (biomedical engineering, chemical engineering, computer engineering, electrical/electronics engineering, engineering and applied science, engineering chemistry, environmental design, environmental science, mechanical engineering, and technological management), HEALTH PROFESSIONS (clinical science, cytotechnology, health science, nursing, occupational therapy, pharmacology, physical therapy, and respiratory therapy), SOCIAL SCIENCE (African studies, American studies, anthropology, Asian/American studies, economics, ethnic studies, European studies, French studies, history, humanities, interdisciplinary studies, Italian studies, liberal arts/general studies, philosophy, political science/government, psychology, religion, social science, social work, sociology, Spanish studies, and women's studies). Biology, business management, and economics are the strongest academically. Biology, psychology, and health science have the largest enrollments.

Required: To graduate, students must have a minimum 2.0 GPA in 120 credit hours (B.A. and B.S.) or 128 (B.E.). The required number of hours in the major varies. At least 39 credits must be earned in upper-division courses. Students must complete at least 30 credits of general education, through which they are expected to demonstrate versatility, explore interconnectedness, pursue deeper understanding, and prepare for life-long learning. Arts and sciences majors must fulfill a foreign language requirement, unless completed through advanced high-school study. Other requirements vary by school.

Special: The university offers a variety of internships in government, including a Washington semester, as well as internships in business and industry, with hospitals and clinics, and in legal and social agencies. The URECA Program promotes undergraduate research and creative projects, both on and off campus -- including nearby Brookhaven National Laborary, which is co-managed by Stony Brook University. A fast-track MBA program and more than thirty additional combined degree programs are available to undergraduates. Scholars for Medicine, Engineering Scholars for Medicine, and Scholars for Dental Medicine are highly selective programs in which a small number of freshmen are admitted to eight-year combined degree programs in medicine and dental medicine. Women in Science and Engineering, the Honors College, and University Scholars programs provide additional experiences to challenge, inspire, and sustain our most academically talent students.Students may declare double majors or pursue dual degrees. The multidisciplinary studies major is student-designed. Students have the opportunity to study at another college or university through the national student exchange program or our study abroad programs in more than 20 countries, including China, New Zealand, France, Sweden, Taiwan, Denmark, England, Korea, Madagascar, Australia, Costa Rica, Jamaica, Tanzania, Kenya, Spain, Norway, Russia, Japan, Italy, Greece, and Germany. Cross-registration may be arranged through the Long Island Regional Advisory Council for Higher Education. There are 6 national honor societies, including Phi Beta Kappa, a freshman honors program, and 30 departmental honors programs.

Faculty/Classroom: 60% of faculty are male; 40% are female. No introductory courses are taught by graduate students. The average class size in an introductory lecture is 42; in a laboratory is 24; and in a regular course is 36.

Admissions: 39% of the 2013-2014 applicants were accepted. The SAT scores for the 2013-2014 freshman class were: Critical Reading--7% below 500, 37% between 500 and 599, 45% between 600 and 699, and 11% between 700 and 800; Math--1% below 500, 16% between 500 and 599, 57% between 600 and 699, and 26% between 700 and 800; Writing--7% below 500, 37% between 500 and 599, 46% between 600 and 699, and 10% between 700 and 800. The ACT scores were 1% below 21, 5% between 21 and 23, 28% between 24 and 26, 24% between 27 and 28, and 42% above 28. 66% of the current freshmen were in the top fifth of their class; 88% were in the top two fifths. There were 2 National Merit finalists. 23 freshmen graduated first in their class.

Requirements: The SAT is required. Applicants must be graduates of an accredited secondary school or have a GED certificate. 16 or 17 academic credits are required, including 4 years each of English and social studies, 3 or 4 of math, 3 of science (4 for engineering majors), and 2 or 3 of a foreign language. One letter of recommendation and supplemental application, including and essay are required. 3 SAT Subject tests, an essay, and an interview are recommended. AP and CLEP credits are accepted. Important factors in the admissions decision are advanced placement or honors courses, extracurricular activities record, and evidence of special talent.

Procedure: Freshmen are admitted fall and spring. Entrance exams should be taken during the junior year or in the fall of the senior year. There is a deferred admissions plan. Applications should be filed by January 15 for fall entry; November 1 for spring entry. The fall 2013 application fee was $50. Notifications are sent April 1. 2176 applicants were on the 2013 waiting list; 187 were admitted. Applications are accepted online.

Transfer: 2235 transfer students enrolled in 2012-2013. Applicants must have a minimum 2.5 GPA. An associate degree and an interview are recommended. Other requirements vary by program. Applicants who have earned fewer than 24 college credits must submit a high school transcript. 36 of 120 credits required for the bachelor's degree must be completed at Stony Brook University.

Visiting: There are regularly scheduled orientations for prospective students, Informative sessions about campus life. There are guides for informal visits and visitors may sit in on classes. To schedule a visit, contact the Admissions Office.

Financial Aid: In 2013-2014, 76% of all full-time freshmen and 68% of continuing full-time students received some form of financial aid. 56% of all full-time freshmen and 57% of continuing full-time students received need-based aid. The average freshman award was $9,790. Need-based scholarships or need-based grants averaged $7,125 ($13,245 maximum); need-based self-help aid (loans and jobs) averaged $3,774 ($10,500 maximum); non-need-based athletic scholarships averaged $15,300 ($268,575 maximum); and other non-need-based awards and non-need-based scholarships averaged $3,290 ($22,230 maximum). 13% of undergraduate students work part-time. Average annual earnings from campus work are $2330. The average financial indebtedness of the 2013 graduate was $20,385. Stony Brook University is a member of CSS. The FAFSA and the state aid form are required. The priority date for freshman financial aid applications for fall entry is March 1.

International Students: There are 1729 international students enrolled. They must take the TOEFL with a minimum score of 550 on the paper-based TOEFL (PBT) or 80 on the Internet-based version (iBT).

Computers: All students may access the system 24 hours a day. There are no time limits and no fees.

Graduates: From July 1, 2012 to June 30, 2013, 3643 bachelor's degrees were awarded. The most popular majors were health sciences (18%), biology (13%), and psychology (12%). 404 companies recruited on campus in 2012-2013. In an average class, 2% graduate in 3 years or less, 47% graduate in 4 years or less, 65% graduate in 5 years or less, and 70% graduate in 6 years or less. Of the 2012 graduating class, 34% were enrolled in graduate school within 6 months of graduation, and 76% were employed.

Admissions Contact: Judith Burke-Berhanan, Dean of Admissions . E-Mail: *enroll@stonybrook.edu* Web: *www.stonybrook.edu*

SUNY COLLEGE AT GENESEO B-3

Geneseo, NY 14454 **(585) 245-5571; (585) 245-5550**

Full-time: 2225 men, 3052 women **Faculty:** 255; IIA, av$
Part-time: 51 men, 60 women **Ph.D.s:** 83%
Graduate: 39 men, 130 women **Student/Faculty:** 19 to 1
Year: semesters, summer session **Tuition:** $7095 ($16,345)
Application Deadline: January 1 **Room & Board:** $10,960
Freshman Class: 9069 applied, 4786 accepted, 1132 enrolled
SAT CR/M: 630/639 **ACT:** 28 **HIGHLY COMPETITIVE+**

The State University of New York/at Geneseo, founded in 1871, is a public institution offering liberal arts, business, and accounting programs, and teaching certification. There are 2 undergraduate schools and 1 graduate school. In addition to regional accreditation, Geneseo has baccalaureate program accreditation with AACSB and NCATE. The library contains 484,071 volumes, 206,937 microform items, 22,356 audio/video tapes/CDs/DVDs, and subscribes to 4,126 periodicals including electronic. Computerized library services include interlibrary loans, database searching, Internet access, and Wi-Fi capability. Special learning facilities include an art gallery, planetarium, radio station, TV station, 4 theaters, electron microscopes, integrated science center, particle accelerator, and a wave tank. The 220-acre campus is in a small town 30 miles south of Rochester. Including any residence halls, there are 46 buildings.

Student Life: 98% of undergraduates are from New York. Others are from 34 states, 42 foreign countries, and Canada. 82% are from public schools. 75% are White. 18% are Catholic. The average age of freshmen is 18; all undergraduates, 20. 10% do not continue beyond their first year; 79% remain to graduate.

Housing: 3293 students can be accommodated in college housing, which includes coed dorms and on-campus apartments. In addition, there are honors houses, special-interest houses, and town houses. On-campus housing is guaranteed for all 4 years, is guaranteed for the freshman year only, is available on a first-come, and first-served basis. 54% of students live on campus; of those, 98% remain on campus on weekends. All students may keep cars.

Activities: 15% of men belong to 8 local and 3 national fraternities; 23% of women belong to 8 local and 7 national sororities. There are 191 groups on campus, including art, band, cheerleading, chess, choir, chorale, chorus, computers, dance, debate, drama, environmental, ethnic, gay, honors, international, jazz band, literary magazine, musical theater, newspaper, orchestra, pep band, political, professional, radio and TV, religious, social, social service, student government, and symphony. Popular campus events include Siblings Weekend, Blue and White Day, Student Organization Expo, Geneseo Recognizing Excellence, Achievement and Talent Day, Great Day, Relay for Life and Weeks of Welcome.

Sports: There are 8 intercollegiate sports for men and 11 for women, and 16 intramural sports for men and 16 for women. Facilities include an ice arena, a swimming pool, 2 gyms, 3 squash and 8 tennis courts,4 racquetball courts, an indoor jogging area, nautilus and weight rooms, an outdoor track, and several playing fields.

Disabled Students: 95% of the campus is accessible. Facilities include wheelchair ramps, elevators, special parking, specially equipped restrooms, special class scheduling, lowered drinking fountains, lowered telephones, special housing, and fire alarms for hearing-impaired students.

Services: Counseling and information services are available, as is tutoring in some subjects, Foreign languages There is a reader service for the blind. Tutoring offered through some departments. Also a Writing Center and a Math Center for all students.

Campus Safety and Security: Measures include 24-hour foot and vehicle patrol, emergency notification system, self-defense education, and security escort services. There are shuttle buses, emergency telephones, lighted pathways/sidewalks, and controlled access to dorms/residences.

Programs of Study: Geneseo confers B.A., B.S. and B.S.Ed. degrees. Master's degrees are also awarded. Bachelor's degrees are awarded in BIOLOGICAL SCIENCE (biochemistry, biology/biological science, and biophysics), BUSINESS (accounting and business administration and management), COMMUNICATIONS AND THE ARTS (art history and appreciation, communications, comparative literature, English, French, music, musical theater, performing arts, Spanish, and theater design), COMPUTER AND PHYSICAL SCIENCE (applied physics, chemistry, geochemistry, geology, geophysics and seismology, mathematics, natural sciences, and physics), EDUCATION (early childhood education, elementary education, and special education), SOCIAL SCIENCE (African American studies, American studies, anthropology, economics, geography, history, international relations, philosophy, political science/government, psychology, and sociology). Education, biology, business administration, psychology, and English have the largest enrollments.

Required: To graduate, students must complete 120 credit hours with a minimum 2.0 GPA. The required core curriculum includes 2 courses each in humanities, fine arts, social sciences, and natural sciences and 1 course each in non-Western tradition, critical writing/reading, numeric and symbolic reasoning, U.S. history, and foreign language proficiency.

Special: The college offers a cooperative 3-2 engineering degree with Alfred, Case Western Reserve, Clarkson, Columbia, Penn State, and Syracuse Universities, SUNY at Binghamton and Buffalo, and the University of Rochester, as well as a 3-3 degree with Rochester Institute of Technology and Upstate Medical University. Cross-registration is available with the Rochester Area Colleges Consortium. Geneseo offers internships, study abroad, a Washington semester, dual majors, and work-study programs. There is a Phi Beta Kappa chapter and a freshman honors program.

Faculty/Classroom: 56% of faculty are male; 44% are female. All teach undergraduates. No introductory courses are taught by graduate students. The average class size in an introductory lecture is 30; in a laboratory is 17; and in a regular course is 27.

Admissions: 53% of the 2013-2014 applicants were accepted. The SAT scores for the 2013-2014 freshman class were: Critical Reading--6% below 500, 24% between 500 and 599, 49% between 600 and 699, and 21% between 700 and 800; Math--6% below 500, 19% between 500 and 599, 57% between 600 and 699, and 18% between 700 and 800. The ACT scores were 4% below 21, 81% between 27 and 28, and 15% above 28. 19 freshmen graduated first in their class.

Requirements: The SAT or ACT is required. Applicants must be graduates of an accredited secondary school or have a GED certificate. The academic program must have included 4 years each of English, math, science, and social studies and 4 years of a foreign language. An essay is required. A portfolio or audition for certain programs and an interview are recommended. SAT or ACT standardized test score required. Rigor of secondary school reviewed. AP and CLEP credits are accepted. Important factors in the admissions decision are advanced placement or honors courses, leadership record, and ability to finance college education.

Procedure: Freshmen are admitted fall and spring. Entrance exams should be taken during the spring of the junior year. There are early decision and deferred admissions plans. Early decision applications should be filed by November 15; regular applications, by January 1 for fall entry; and December 15 for spring entry, along with a $50 fee. Notification of early decision is sent December 15; regular decision, March 1. 133 early decision candidates were accepted for the 2013-2014 class. 1350 applicants were on the 2013 waiting list; 47 were admitted. Applications are accepted online.

Transfer: 325 transfer students enrolled in 2012-2013. Applicants must provide transcripts from all previously attended colleges. A minimum 3.0 GPA is required. Students with fewer than 24 credit hours must submit SAT or ACT scores. 30 of 120 credits required for the bachelor's degree must be completed at Geneseo.

Visiting: There are regularly scheduled orientations for prospective students, generally including a 90-minute campus tour and a 45-minute information session. Students may also elect to sit in on classes, visit faculty and coaches, or stay overnight. There are guides for informal visits, visitors may sit in on classes, and stay overnight. To schedule a visit, contact the Office of Admissions at admissions@geneseo.edu.

Financial Aid: In 2013-2014, 65% of all full-time freshmen students received some form of financial aid. 60% of all full-time freshmen students received need-based aid. The average freshman award was $10,658. Need-based scholarships or need-based grants averaged $5,593; need-based self-help aid (loans and jobs) averaged $5,082; other non-need-based awards and non-need-based scholarships averaged $2,465; and $4,746 from other forms of aid. 17% of undergraduate students work part-time. Average annual earnings from campus work are $4950. The average financial indebtedness of the 2013 graduate was $20,790. Geneseo is a member of CSS. The FAFSA is required. The priority date for freshman financial aid applications for fall entry is February 15.

International Students: There are 188 international students enrolled. The school actively recruits these students. They must take the TOEFL with a minimum score of 525 on the paper-based TOEFL (PBT) or 71 on the Internet-based version (iBT). They must also take the SAT or ACT.

Computers: All students may access the system 24 hours a day. There are no time limits. The fee is $216.

Graduates: From July 1, 2012 to June 30, 2013, 1304 bachelor's degrees were awarded. The most popular majors were education (20%), social science (15%), and biological/life sciences (12%). 38 companies recruited on campus in 2012-2013. In an average class, 67% graduate in 4 years or less, 78% graduate in 5 years or less, and 79% graduate in 6 years or less. Of the 2012 graduating class, 42% were enrolled in graduate school within 6 months of graduation, and 58% were employed.

Admissions Contact: Kristine Shay, Director of Admissions. E-Mail: *admissions@geneseo.edu* Web: *www.geneseo.edu/admissions*

SUNY COLLEGE AT OLD WESTBURY D-5

Old Westbury, NY 11568-0210 (516) 876-3073; (516) 876-3307

Full-time: 1467 men, 2094 women
Part-time: 289 men, 380 women
Graduate: 125 men, 104 women
Year: semesters, summer session
Application Deadline: open
Freshman Class: n/av
SAT: required
Faculty: 138; IIB, +$
Ph.D.s: 83%
Student/Faculty: 24 to 1
Tuition: $6324 ($15,374)
Room & Board: $9700

COMPETITIVE

The State University of New York/College at Old Westbury, founded in 1965, is a public institution offering degree programs in the arts and sciences, business, education, fine arts, and health science. There are 3 undergraduate schools and 3 graduate schools. In addition to regional accreditation, SUNY Old Westbury has baccalaureate program accreditation with NCATE. The library contains 240,986 volumes, 19,421 microform items, and 2,466 audio/video tapes/CDs/DVDs, and subscribes to 1,345 periodicals including electronic. Computerized library services include interlibrary loans, database searching, Internet access, and laptop Internet portals. Special learning facilities include a learning resource center, art gallery, radio station, TV studio. The 604-acre campus is in a suburban area 20 miles east of New York City. Including any residence halls, there are 22 buildings.

Student Life: 97% of undergraduates are from New York. Others are from 17 states, and 32 foreign countries. 35% are white; 33% African American; 20% Hispanic. The average age of freshmen is 18; all undergraduates, 23. 24% do not continue beyond their first year; 39% remain to graduate.

Housing: 1500 students can be accommodated in college housing, which includes coed dorms. In addition, there are honors houses. On-campus housing is available on a first come and first-served basis. Priority is given to out-of-town students. 77% of students commute. Alcohol is not permitted. All students may keep cars.

Activities: 1% of men belong to 6 national fraternities; 1% of women belong to 4 national sororities. There are 60 groups on campus, including art, cheerleading, choir, chorale, computers, dance, drama, ethnic, film, gay, honors, international, newspaper, photography, political, professional, radio and TV, religious, social, social service, and student government. Popular campus events include Welcome Back Festival, Wellness at Old Westbury, and Panther Pride Week.

Sports: There are 5 intercollegiate sports for men and 5 for women, and 7 intramural sports for men and 7 for women. Facilities include a 3000-seat gym, an auxiliary gym, a cross-country course, playing fields, a swimming pool, a fitness center, a weight room, jogging trails, a student union building, and courts for tennis, paddleball, handball, racquetball, and squash.

Disabled Students: 90% of the campus is accessible. Facilities include wheelchair ramps, elevators, special parking, specially equipped restrooms, special class scheduling, lowered drinking fountains, lowered telephones, limited volunteer transportation.

Services: Counseling and information services are available, as is tutoring in most subjects. There is a reader service for the blind, and remedial math, reading, and writing.

Campus Safety and Security: Measures include 24-hour foot and vehicle patrol, emergency notification system, and security escort services. There are shuttle buses, emergency telephones, lighted pathways/sidewalks. An officer patrols dormitories from 6 p.m. to 2 a.m.

Programs of Study: SUNY Old Westbury confers B.A., B.S., and B.P.S. degrees. Master's degrees are also awarded. Bachelor's degrees are awarded in BIOLOGICAL SCIENCE (biochemistry and biology/biological science), BUSINESS (accounting, banking and finance, business administration and management, labor studies, management information systems, and marketing/retailing/merchandising), COMMUNICATIONS AND THE ARTS (communications, media arts, Spanish, and visual and performing arts), COMPUTER AND PHYSICAL SCIENCE (chemistry, computer science, information sciences and systems, and mathematics), EDUCATION (bilingual/bicultural education, early childhood education, elementary education, foreign languages education, mathematics education, middle school education, science education, secondary education, social studies education, and special education), HEALTH PROFESSIONS (community health work and health), SOCIAL SCIENCE (American studies, criminology, economics, history, humanities, international studies, philosophy, political science/government, psychology, religion, and sociology). Teacher education, business, and psychology are the strongest academically. Education, business and psychology are the largest.

Required: To graduate, students must maintain a GPA of 2.0 to 3.0, depending on the major, in 120 or 128 semester credits (accounting and special education majors require 128 credits). General education requirements include courses in writing and reasoning skills, creative arts, ideas and ideology, cross-cultural perspectives, U.S. society and history, physical or life science, and foreign language. A senior project or capstone course is required, based on major.

Special: SUNY Old Westbury offers cross-registration with SUNY Empire State, Lirache, and colleges in Nassau and Suffolk counties, internships in teacher education, extensive study-abroad programs, a B.A.-B.S. in psychology, chemistry, industrial labor and relations, and sociology, dual majors, and a 3-2 engineering degree with SUNY at Stony Brook and SUNY Maritime College. Credit for military and life experience, nondegree study, and pass/fail options are available. There are 5 national honor societies, a freshman honors program, and 6 departmental honors programs.

Faculty/Classroom: 47% of faculty are male; 53% are female. All teach undergraduates, 12% do research, and 11% do both. No introductory courses are taught by graduate students. The average class size in an introductory lecture is 25; in a laboratory is 20; and in a regular course is 25.

Admissions: 45% of the current freshmen were in the top fifth of their class; 80% were in the top two fifths.

Requirements: The SAT is required. In addition, applicants must be graduates of an accredited secondary school or have a GED. An essay, portfolio, and interview are also recommended. Students are evaluated according to qualifying categories of academic achievement, special knowledge and creative ability, paid work experience, and social or personal experience. AP and CLEP credits are accepted. Important factors in the admissions decision are leadership record, recommendations by school officials, and evidence of special talent.

Procedure: Freshmen are admitted fall and spring. There are early decision, deferred admissions, and rolling admissions plans. Application deadlines are open. Application fee is $50. Notification is sent on a rolling basis. Applications are accepted online.

Transfer: 1395 transfer students enrolled in 2010-2011. Applicants must submit official transcripts from all colleges attended. Those students with fewer than 24 college credits must also submit a high school transcript. The college requires a minimum overall GPA of 2.0. Specific academic majors may require a higher GPA. 48 of 120 credits required for the bachelor's degree must be completed at SUNY Old Westbury.

Visiting: There are regularly scheduled orientations for prospective students. There are guides for informal visits. To schedule a visit, contact Enrollment Services.

Financial Aid: In 2011-2012, 69% of all full-time freshmen and 62% of continuing full-time students received some form of financial aid. 65% of all full-time freshmen and 57% of continuing full-time students received need-based aid. The average freshman award was $7,207. Need-based scholarships or need-based grants averaged $7,016; need-based self-help aid (loans and jobs) averaged $7,351; and other non-need-based awards and non-need-based scholarships averaged $1,971. Average annual earnings from campus work are $902. The average financial indebtedness of the 2011 graduate was $17,340. The FAFSA, the college's own financial statement, the IFAA (institutional application), and previous year's household income are required. The deadline for filing freshman financial aid applications for fall entry is April 19.

International Students: There are 72 international students enrolled. The school actively recruits these students. They must take the TOEFL with a minimum score of 513 on the paper-based TOEFL (PBT) or 80 on the Internet-based version (iBT) and the college's own test.

Computers: Wireless access is available. The college supports a network spanning the entire campus including high speed Internet access in dorm rooms. The wireless network is fully accessible in all academic buildings including the library, student union, and administrative building. There are 450+ public computers spread among 8 locations split between public access and departmental labs dedicated to specific disciplines. All students receive e-mail and computer accounts and have access to printers. All students may access the system daily. There are no time limits and no fees. It is strongly recommended that all students have a personal computer.

Graduates: From July 1, 2010 to June 30, 2011, 739 bachelor's degrees were awarded. The most popular majors were accounting (16%), psychology (13%), and childhood education (8%). 50 companies recruited on campus in 2010-2011. In an average class, 2% graduate in 3 years or less, 23% graduate in 4 years or less, 36% graduate in 5 years or less, and 39% graduate in 6 years or less.

Admissions Contact: Mary Marquez Bell, Vice President for Enrollment Services. A campus DVD is available. E-Mail: *enroll@oldwestbury.edu* Web: *www.oldwestbury.edu*

SUNY CORTLAND / THE STATE UNIVERSITY OF NEW YORK C-4

Cortland, NY 13045 (607) 753-4711; (607) 753-5998

Full-time: n/av
Part-time: n/av
Graduate: n/av
Year: semesters, summer session
Application Deadline:
Freshman Class: 11518 applied, 5394 accepted, 1211 enrolled
SAT or ACT: required
Faculty: n/av; IIA, -$
Ph.D.s: n/av
Student/Faculty: n/av
Tuition: $7327 ($16,777)
Room & Board: $11,790

COMPETITIVE

The State University of New York College at Cortland, founded in 1868, is a public institution offering academic programs leading to baccalaureate and master's degrees in liberal arts and professional studies. There are 3 undergraduate schools and 3 graduate schools. In addition to regional accreditation, SUNY Cortland has baccalaureate program accreditation with CAHEA, NCATE, and NRPA. The library contains 423,158 volumes, 844,222 microform items, and 2,947 audio/video tapes/CDs/DVDs, and subscribes to 428 periodicals including electronic. Computerized library services include interlibrary loans, database searching, Internet access, and Wi-Fi capability. Special learning facilities include an art gallery, planetarium, radio station, TV station, a greenhouse, a center for speech and hearing disorders, classrooms equipped with integrated technologies (multimedia enhanced instruction), and many specialized labs to support various program offerings. The 191-acre campus is in a small town 18 miles north of Ithaca and 29 miles south of Syracuse.

Housing: 3223 students can be accommodated in college housing, which includes coed dorms and off-campus apartments. In addition, there are special-interest houses, fraternity houses, sorority houses, wellness floor in a residence hall, 24-hour quiet floor in a residence hall, green building, leadership house, winter athlete housing, and buildings for students age 21+. All students may keep cars.

Activities: There are 100 groups on campus, including art, band, cheerleading, chess, choir, chorale, chorus, computers, dance, drama, ethnic, film, gay, honors, international, jazz band, literary magazine, musical theater, newspaper, orchestra, political, professional, radio and TV, religious, social, social service, student government, symphony, and yearbook. Popular campus events include Cortland-Ithaca College Football Game, Winterfest, and Multicultural Festival.

Sports: There are 10 intercollegiate sports for men and 13 for women, and 55 intramural sports for men and 55 for women. Facilities include an outdoor multupurpose stadium complex, an Olympic-size pool, gym, ice arena, gymnastics arena, wrestling and weight romms, dance studio, handball/racquetball courts, squash courts, athletic training facility, fitness centers, free-swimming pool, track, baseball field, football/lacrosse/track field, lighted soccer field, field house and 50 acres of athletic fields.

Disabled Students: 75% of the campus is accessible. Facilities include wheelchair ramps, elevators, special parking, specially equipped restrooms, special class scheduling, lowered drinking fountains, and lowered telephones.

Services: Counseling and information services are available, as is tutoring in some subjects. There is a reader service for the blind. There is a fully staffed Academic Support and Achievement Program for writing, math, study skills, and learning strategies. Specific course tutoring is available with peer tutors.

Campus Safety and Security: Measures include self-defense education, and security escort services. There are shuttle buses, emergency telephones, lighted pathways/sidewalks, State University police maintain a web site with safety information and inks. University police also have a Silent Witness program for reporting crimes anonymously.

Programs of Study: SUNY Cortland confers B.A., B.S., B.S.Ed. and B.F.A. degrees. Master's degrees are also awarded. Bachelor's degrees are awarded in BIOLOGICAL SCIENCE (biology/biological science), BUSINESS (management science and sports management), COMMUNICATIONS AND THE ARTS (art, communications, English, film arts, and musical theater), COMPUTER AND PHYSICAL SCIENCE (chemistry, geochemistry, geology, geophysics and seismology, mathematics, and physics), EDUCATION (athletic training, education services, foreign languages education, health education, middle school education, physical education, recreation education, and secondary education), ENGINEERING AND ENVIRONMENTAL DESIGN (environmental science), HEALTH PROFESSIONS (health science and speech pathology/audiology), SOCIAL SCIENCE (African American studies, anthropology, economics, geography, history, human services, international studies, philosophy, political science/government, psychology, and sociology). Biology, political science, and speech pathology/audiology are the strongest academically. Elementary education, phys ed, and communication studies have the largest enrollments.

Required: To graduate, undergraduates must complete 6 hours in English Composition, and at least 6 hours of writing-intensive courses, with 3 of those in the major. One course meeting the Quantitative Skills criteria must also be passed; 28 to 29 hours of courses in the General Education program must also be completed, with no more than 2 courses taken in any one of the 8 disciplines in the program. A major of 30 to 36 hours, with no more than 45 credits in discipline-specific courses must be completed. Completion of 90 credits of Liberal Arts and Science courses toward a B.A., 60 credits toward a B.S.E., or 75 credits toward a B.S. is required. A 2.0 GPA, both overall and in all minors and concentrations, must be maintained. Special requirements may be designated by each school of the college.

Special: Cortland offers cross-registration with Tompkins Cortland Comumuninty College and has cooperative programs with the State University of New York College of Environmental Science and Forestry, and Centers at Binghamton and Buffalo, and Cornell and Case Western Reserve Universities. Students may study abroad in 11 countries, and they may enroll in a Washington semester. Work-study programs are available. The college confers an individualized studies degree and allows dual majors. Students may pursue a 3-2 engineering degree in conjunction with Alfred, Case Western Reserve, and Clarkson Universities, and the State University of New York Centers at Binghamton, Buffalo, and Stony Brook. Cortland offers nondegree study opportunities. There are 19 national honor societies, including Phi Beta Kappa, a freshman honors program, and 5 departmental honors programs.

Faculty/Classroom: All teach undergraduates, 15% do research, and 15% do both. No introductory courses are taught by graduate students.

Admissions: 47% of the 2013-2014 applicants were accepted.

Requirements: The SAT or ACT is required. Applicants must graduate from an accredited secondary school or have a GED. They must have earned 16 Carnegie units and 16 to 20 academic credits, including 4 units each in English and history or social studies and 2 (3 units preferred) each in math and science; the other 4 units must be taken in areas listed above or in a foreign language. Essays and recommendations are required, and in some cases auditions as well. Interviews are strongly recommended. AP and CLEP credits are accepted. Important factors in the admissions decision are advanced placement or honors courses, extracurricular activities record, and recommendations by school officials.

Procedure: Freshmen are admitted fall and spring. Entrance exams should be taken during the spring of the junior year or fall of the senior year. There are early decision, early admissions, deferred admissions, and rolling admissions plans. Early decision applications should be filed by November 15, along with a $40 fee. Notification of early decision is sent December 15; regular decision, on a rolling basis. Applications are accepted online.

Transfer: 606 transfer students enrolled in 2012-2013. Applicants must have a minimum GPA of 2.5. Some programs are more competitive. Interviews are encouraged. 45 of 124 credits required for the bachelor's degree must be completed at SUNY Cortland.

Visiting: There are regularly scheduled orientations for prospective students, consisting of Autumn Preview Days for prospective students as well as Spring Open House for accepted students. There are guides for informal visits and visitors may sit in on classes. To schedule a visit, contact the Admissions Office.

Financial Aid: The FAFSA and NYS TAP application are required. The deadline for filing freshman financial aid applications for fall entry is April 1.

International Students: The school actively recruits these students. They must take the TOEFL, the SAT I or a General Certificate of Education is acceptable in lieu of the TOEFL. They must also take the SAT or ACT.

Computers: All students may access the system 24 hours per day in some labs connected to the campus network. There are no time limits and no fees.

Admissions Contact: Mark Yacavone, Assistant VP, Enrollment Management. E-Mail: *admissions@cortland.edu* Web: *http:/www2.cortland.edu/admissions/*

SUNY FREDONIA / THE STATE UNIVERSITY OF NEW YORK AT FREDONIA — A-4

Fredonia, NY 14063 — **(716) 673-3251**
(800) 252-1212; (716) 673-3249

Full-time: 2215 men, 2743 women	**Faculty:** 251; IIA, -$
Part-time: 72 men, 72 women	**Ph.D.s:** 88%
Graduate: 68 men, 234 women	**Student/Faculty:** 16 to 1
Year: semesters, summer session	**Tuition:** $7358 ($16,808)
Application Deadline: open	**Room & Board:** $11,344
Freshman Class: 6146 applied, 3261 accepted, 1106 enrolled	
SAT CR/M: 540/545	**ACT:** 24 **VERY COMPETITIVE**

The State University of New York at Fredonia, established in 1826, is a public institution offering undergraduate programs in the arts and sciences, business and professional curricula, teacher preparation, and the fine and performing arts. There are 5 undergraduate schools and 1 graduate school. In addition to regional accreditation, Fredonia has baccalaureate program accreditation with CSWE, NASAD, NASM, and NCATE. The library contains 391,121 volumes, 1.1 million microform items, and 26,574 audio/video tapes/CDs/DVDs, and subscribes to 1,983 periodicals including electronic. Computerized library services include interlibrary loans, database searching, Internet access, and Wi-Fi capability. Special learning facilities include an art gallery, natural history museum, radio station, TV station, a greenhouse, a day-care center, a speech clinic, and the Rockefeller arts center. The 266-acre campus is in a small town 50 miles south of Buffalo and 45 miles north of Erie, Pennsylvania. Including any residence halls, there are 50 buildings.

Student Life: 95% of undergraduates are from New York. Others are from 25 states, 11 foreign countries, and Canada. 92% are from public schools. 80% are White. The average age of freshmen is 17.9; all undergraduates, 20.3. 14% do not continue beyond their first year; 64% remain to graduate.

Housing: 2733 students can be accommodated in college housing, which

includes single-sex and coed dorms and on-campus apartments. In addition, there are honors houses, special-interest houses, Living space for fraternities and sororities is available in residence halls. In addition, there are special interest houses for computer and athletics students and quiet-hour centers. On-campus housing is guaranteed for the freshman year only, is available on a first-come, first-served basis, and is available on a lottery system for upperclassmen. Priority is given to out-of-town students. 56% of students live on campus; of those, 96% remain on campus on weekends. All students may keep cars.

Activities: 2% of men belong to 2 national fraternities; 4% of women belong to 3 national sororities. There are 150 groups on campus, including and Spectrum Entertainment Board, art, band, cheerleading, choir, chorale, chorus, communications, computers, dance, debate, drama, drill team, environmental, ethnic, film, gay, honors, international, jazz band, literary magazine, musical theater, newspaper, opera, orchestra, pep band, photography, political, professional, radio and TV, religious, Ski Club, social, social service, student government, and symphony. Popular campus events include various art center presentations, Fred-Fest, and Little Siblings Weekend.

Sports: There are 8 intercollegiate sports for men and 9 for women, and 15 intramural sports for men and 15 for women. Facilities include A basketball arena, an ice rink, a swimming pool, two gyms and weight rooms, dance studios, soccer fields, indoor and outdoor tracks, racquetball, tennis, and volleyball courts, and a soccer/lacrosse stadium.

Disabled Students: 85% of the campus is accessible. Facilities include wheelchair ramps, elevators, special parking, specially equipped restrooms, special class scheduling, lowered drinking fountains, lowered telephones, and special housing.

Services: Counseling and information services are available, as is tutoring in most subjects. There is a reader service for the blind.

Campus Safety and Security: Measures include 24-hour foot and vehicle patrol, emergency notification system, self-defense education, and security escort services. There are shuttle buses, emergency telephones, lighted pathways/sidewalks, controlled access to dorms/residences, and card swipe access to residence halls.

Programs of Study: Fredonia confers B.A., B.F.A., B.S., B.S.Ed. and Mus.B. degrees. Master's degrees are also awarded. Bachelor's degrees are awarded in BIOLOGICAL SCIENCE (biochemistry, biology/biological science, and genetics), BUSINESS (accounting, business administration and management, business economics, finance, institutional management, and sports management), COMMUNICATIONS AND THE ARTS (animation, arts administration/management, audio technology, communications, dance, dramatic arts, English, fine arts, French, graphic design, journalism, media arts, music, music performance, music theory and composition, musical theater, painting, photography, Spanish, theatre arts, theater design, and video), COMPUTER AND PHYSICAL SCIENCE (chemistry, computer science, earth science, geology, mathematics, and physics), EDUCATION (early childhood education, education, elementary education, English education, foreign languages education, middle school education, music education, science education, and secondary education), ENGINEERING AND ENVIRONMENTAL DESIGN (environmental science), HEALTH PROFESSIONS (health care administration, medical laboratory technology, music therapy, predentistry, premedicine, preoptometry, and speech pathology/audiology), SOCIAL SCIENCE (early childhood studies, economics, history, interdisciplinary studies, philosophy, political science/government, prelaw, psychology, social work, sociology, and women's studies). Music, theatre, visual arts, and natural sciences (bio, chem, physics, geo) are the strongest academically. Education, business, and psycholgy have the largest enrollments.

Required: To graduate, students must complete 120 hours, including 36 to 90 or more in the major, with a 2.0 GPA. Students must take specific courses in English and math and complete 50 hours of general education courses, including writing, statistical/quantitative abilities, oral communication, natural and social sciences, humanities, and arts.

Special: Cooperative programs are available with many other institutions. Students may cross-register with colleges in the Western New York Consortium. Fredonia offers a variety of internships, study-abroad programs in more than 60 countries, and a Washington semester. Accelerated degrees, a general studies degree, dual and student-designed majors, a 3-2 engineering degree program with 14 universities, nondegree study, and pass/fail grading options are available. There are 19 national honor societies, a freshman honors program, and 19 departmental honors programs.

Faculty/Classroom: 53% of faculty are male; 47% are female. All teach and do research. No introductory courses are taught by graduate students. The average class size in an introductory lecture is 35; in a laboratory is 16; and in a regular course is 23.

Admissions: 53% of the 2013-2014 applicants were accepted. The SAT scores for the 2013-2014 freshman class were: Critical Reading--28% below 500, 54% between 500 and 599, 16% between 600 and 699, and 2% between 700 and 800; Math--23% below 500, 58% between 500 and 599, 17% between 600 and 699, and 3% between 700 and 800. The ACT scores were 8% below 21, 39% between 21 and 23, 31% between 24 and 26, 12% between 27 and 28, and 10% above 28. 34% of the current freshmen were in the top fifth of their class; 71% were in the top two fifths. 5 freshmen graduated first in their class.

Requirements: The SAT or ACT is required. Applicants must possess a high school diploma or have a GED. 16 academic credits are recommended, including 4 credits each in English and social studies and 3 each in math, science, and a foreign language. 4 years of math and science are encouraged. Essays are required. Where applicable, an audition or portfolio is required. AP and CLEP credits are accepted. Important factors in the admissions decision are advanced placement or honors courses, leadership record, parents or siblings attended your school, evidence of special talent, personality/intangible qualities, extracurricular activities record, recommendations by alumni, geographical diversity, recommendations by school officials, and ability to finance college education.

Procedure: Freshmen are admitted fall and spring. Entrance exams should be taken Spring of the junior year or fall of the senior year. There are early decision, early admissions, deferred admissions, and rolling admissions plans. Early decision applications should be filed by November 1, along with a $50 fee. Notification of early decision is sent December 1; regular decision, December 5. 60 early decision candidates were accepted for the 2013-2014 class. Applications are accepted online.

Transfer: 442 transfer students enrolled in 2012-2013. Applicants should have a minimum GPA of 2.0. and appropriate academic course work to be considered. An interview is recommended. 45 of 120 credits required for the bachelor's degree must be completed at Fredonia.

Visiting: There are regularly scheduled orientations for prospective students, including various open house programs and information sessions and tours Monday through Friday, morning and afternoon, and varied Saturday tours. Visitors may sit in on classes and stay overnight. To schedule a visit, contact The Office of Admissions.

Financial Aid: In 2013-2014, 83% of all full-time freshmen and 77% of continuing full-time students received some form of financial aid. 68% of all full-time freshmen and 68% of continuing full-time students received need-based aid. The average freshman award was $9,280. Need-based scholarships or need-based grants averaged $4,534; need-based self-help aid (loans and jobs) averaged $5,090; and other non-need-based awards and non-need-based scholarships averaged $527. Average annual earnings from campus work are $1287. The average financial indebtedness of the 2013 graduate was $20,574. The FAFSA and the state aid form, and Express TAP Application (ETA) are required. The priority date for freshman financial aid applications for fall entry is February 1.

International Students: There are 134 international students enrolled. The school actively recruits these students. They must take the TOEFL with a minimum score of 500 on the paper-based TOEFL (PBT) or 62 on the Internet-based version (iBT).

Computers: All students may access the system. There are no time limits and no fees.

Graduates: From July 1, 2012 to June 30, 2013, 1523 bachelor's degrees were awarded. The most popular majors were education (25%), business administration (13%), and music (10%). 69 companies recruited on campus in 2012-2013. In an average class, 47% graduate in 4 years or less, 62% graduate in 5 years or less, and 64% graduate in 6 years or less.

Admissions Contact: Chris Dearth, Director of Admissions. E-Mail: *admissions@fredonia.edu* Web: *www.fredonia.edu*

SUNY NEW PALTZ — D-4

New Paltz, NY 12561-2443 — **(845) 257-3200; (845) 257-3209**

Full-time: 1690 men, 3585 women
Part-time: 295 men, 560 women
Graduate: 490 men, 940 women
Year: semesters, summer session
Application Deadline: April 1
Freshman Class: n/av
SAT or ACT: required

Faculty: n/av; IIA, -$
Ph.D.s: n/av
Student/Faculty: n/av
Tuition: $6510 ($13,910)
Room & Board: $9500

COMPETITIVE

State University of New York/University at New Paltz, founded in 1828, is a public institution offering undergraduate and graduate programs in the liberal arts and sciences, business, education, engineering, fine and performing arts, and the health professions. The figures in the above capsule and in this profile are approximate. There are 5 undergraduate schools and 1 graduate school. In addition to regional accreditation, SUNY New Paltz has baccalaureate program accreditation with ABET, CSAB, NASAD, NASM, and NCATE. The library contains 499,048 volumes, 1.2 million microform items, and 4,030 audio/video tapes/CDs/DVDs, and subscribes to 32,361 periodicals including electronic. Computerized library services include interlibrary loans, database searching, Internet access, and laptop Internet portals. Special learning facilities include a learning resource center, planetarium, radio station, TV station, greenhouse, robotics lab, electron microscope facility, speech and hearing clinic, art museum, music therapy training facility, observatory, Fournier transform mass spectrometer, honors center, electronic media center, electronic classroom, and an IBM e-business virtual lab. The 216-acre campus is in a small town 100 miles north of New York City and 65 miles south of Albany. Including any residence halls, there are 53 buildings.

Student Life: 92% of undergraduates are from New York. Others are from 28 states, 48 foreign countries, and Canada. 90% are from public schools. 58% are white. The average age of freshmen is 18; all undergraduates, 20. 16% do not continue beyond their first year; 59% remain to graduate.

Housing: 2800 students can be accommodated in college housing, which includes coed dorms. In addition, there are special-interest houses. On-campus housing is guaranteed for the freshman year only, is available on a first-come, and first-served basis. Priority is given to out-of-town students. 51% of students live on campus; of those, 90% remain on campus on weekends. Upperclassmen may keep cars.

Activities: 3% of men belong to 5 local and 5 national fraternities; 2% of women belong to 5 local and 8 national sororities. There are 136 groups on campus, including art, band, cheerleading, chess, choir, chorale, chorus, computers, dance, drama, ethnic, gay, honors, international, jazz band, literary magazine, musical theater, newspaper, orchestra, photography, political, professional, radio and TV, religious, social, social service, student government, and yearbook. Popular campus events include Spirit Weekend, New Paltz Summer Repertory Theater, and Rainbow Month.

Sports: There are 9 intercollegiate sports for men and 11 for women, and 12 intramural sports for men and 9 for women. Facilities include a gym with a swimming pool, numerous playing fields, a 35,000-square-foot air-supported structure for tennis, jogging, volleyball, and basketball, and 24 outdoor tennis courts.

Disabled Students: 90% of the campus is accessible. Facilities include wheelchair ramps, elevators, special parking, specially equipped restrooms, special class scheduling, lowered drinking fountains, lowered telephones, and special housing.

Services: Counseling and information services are available, as is tutoring in most subjects. There is a reader service for the blind, and remedial math, reading, and writing.

Campus Safety and Security: Measures include 24-hour foot and vehicle patrol, self-defense education, and security escort services. There are emergency telephones, lighted pathways/sidewalks, a bicycle patrol, locked residence halls, and a campus 911 system.

Programs of Study: SUNY New Paltz confers B.A., B.S., and B.F.A. degrees. Master's degrees are also awarded. Bachelor's degrees are awarded in BIOLOGICAL SCIENCE (biology/biological science), BUSINESS (accounting, banking and finance, business administration and management, international business management, and marketing/retailing/merchandising), COMMUNICATIONS AND THE ARTS (art history and appreciation, communications, dramatic arts, English, French, German, graphic design, journalism, metal/jewelry, music, painting, photography, sculpture, Spanish, speech/debate/rhetoric, studio art, theater design, and visual and performing arts), COMPUTER AND PHYSICAL SCIENCE (chemistry, computer science, environmental geology, geology, mathematics, and physics), EDUCATION (art education, early childhood education, elementary education, English education, foreign languages education, mathematics education, middle school education, science education, secondary education, and social studies education), ENGINEERING AND ENVIRONMENTAL DESIGN (computer engineering, electrical/electronics engineering, and woodworking), HEALTH PROFESSIONS (music therapy, nursing, and speech pathology/audiology), SOCIAL SCIENCE (African American studies, anthropology, Asian/Oriental studies, economics, geography, history, international relations, Latin American studies, liberal arts/general studies, philosophy, political science/government, psychology, social science, sociology, and women's studies). Business, computer science, and math are the strongest academically. Business, visual arts, and elementary education have the largest enrollments.

Required: To graduate, students must complete a minimum of 120 credits with a 2.0 GPA. The core curriculum of 16 to 17 credits includes courses in English composition, math and analytical skills, and modern world studies. The number of credits required in the major varies. Distribution requirements include courses in cultures and civilizations, American experience, social sciences, physical and biological sciences, foreign languages, and aesthetic expression, 1 writing-intensive course in the major, and 60 credits in upper-division courses. New York State Teacher Competency Exams are required of education majors. Engineering students must complete a senior project, and art majors must show their work in a senior exhibition.

Special: There is cross-registration with the Mid-Hudson Consortium of Colleges. The university offers co-op programs and internships in most majors, work-study programs on campus and at the Children's Center of New Paltz, and opportunities for student-designed or dual majors. Students may study abroad in 18 countries. A 3-2 advanced degree in environmental biology is offered with SUNY Environmental Science and Forestry. There are 7-year medical and optometry accelerated degree programs. B.A.-B.S. degrees are offered in liberal arts and science, education, business, science and, engineering, and fine and performing arts. There are 4 national honor societies, a freshman honors program, and 6 departmental honors programs.

Faculty/Classroom: 45% of faculty are male; 55% are female. Graduate students teach 1% of introductory courses. The average class size in an introductory lecture is 19; in a laboratory is 10; and in a regular course is 19.

Requirements: The SAT or ACT is required. In addition, 4 units each of English, and social studies, 3 to 4 units each of mathematics and science, including 2 units of lab science, and 2 to 4 units of foreign language are required. The GED is accepted but must be accompanied by a high school transcript and SAT or ACT scores. SUNY New Paltz requires applicants to be in the upper 50% of their class. A GPA of 3.0 is required. AP and CLEP credits are accepted. Important factors in the admissions decision are advanced placement or honors courses, recommendations by school officials, and evidence of special talent.

Procedure: Freshmen are admitted in the fall. Entrance exams should be taken before December 31. There are early admissions, deferred admissions, and rolling admissions plans. Applications should be filed by April 1 for fall entry. Notification is sent on a rolling basis. Applications are accepted online. A waiting list is maintained.

Transfer: 1011 transfer students enrolled in a recent year. To be considered, applicants must have maintained a minimum GPA of 2.75 in all previous college work at accredited institutions. Some programs require a higher GPA for consideration. 30 of 120 credits required for the bachelor's degree must be completed at SUNY New Paltz.

Visiting: There are regularly scheduled orientations for prospective students, including daily information sessions and campus tours. Visitors may sit in on classes. To schedule a visit, contact the Admissions Office.

Financial Aid: In a recent year, 70% of all full-time freshmen and 75% of continuing full-time students received some form of financial aid. 55% of all full-time freshmen and 75% of continuing full-time students received need-based aid. The FAFSA is required. Check with the school for current application deadlines.

International Students: There were 219 international students enrolled in a recent year. The school actively recruits these students. They must take the TOEFL with a minimum score of 550 on the paper-based TOEFL (PBT) or 80 on the Internet-based version (iBT), or take the SAT, or demonstrate English Proficiency. Conditional acceptance is available to both graduate and undergraduate programs. Accepted students must take a placement test upon arrival at SUNY New Paltz. If the student is not yet proficient, he or she must take ESL courses until required proficiency is achieved.

Computers: Wireless access is available. All students may access the system 24 hours a day. There are no time limits and no fees. It is strongly recommended that all students have a personal computer.

Graduates: In recent year, 1592 bachelor's degrees were awarded. The most popular majors were education (21%), business and marketing (14%), and social science (11%). 135 companies recruited on campus in a recent year. In an average class, 36% graduate in 4 years or less, 59% graduate in 5 years or less, and 61% graduate in 6 years or less.

Admissions Contact: Kimberly Lavoie, Director of Freshman/International Admissions. E-Mail: *admissions@newpaltz.edu* Web: *www.newpaltz.edu*

SUNY ONEONTA / STATE UNIVERSITY OF NEW YORK D-3

Oneonta, NY 13820 (607) 436-2524
(800) 786-9123; (607) 436-3074

Full-time: 2294 men, 3430 women	**Faculty:** 251; IIA, --$
Part-time: 65 men, 74 women	**Ph.D.s:** 86%
Graduate: 43 men, 163 women	**Student/Faculty:** 18 to 1
Year: semesters, summer session	**Tuition:** $6887 ($13,137)
Application Deadline: open	**Room & Board:** $10,032

Freshman Class: 12031 applied, 5190 accepted, 1146 enrolled
SAT CR/M: 538/563 **ACT:** 24 **VERY COMPETITIVE**

The State University of New York/College at Oneonta, founded in 1889, offers undergraduate and graduate programs in the arts and sciences with a campus-wide emphasis on student engagement, diversity and community service. There is one undergraduate school and one graduate school. In addition to regional accreditation, SUNY Oneonta has baccalaureate program accreditation with AACSB, ADA, NASM, and NCATE. The library contains 482,408 volumes, 1.2 million microform items, and 19,174 audio/video tapes/CDs/DVDs, and subscribes to 50,000 periodicals including electronic. Computerized library services include interlibrary loans, database searching, Internet access, and Wi-Fi capability. Special learning facilities include an art gallery, planetarium, radio station, TV station, digital planetarium, science discovery center, community service center, college camp, children's center, and off-campus biological field station. The 250-acre campus is in a rural area 75 miles southwest of Albany and 55 miles northeast of Binghamton. Including any residence halls, there are 36 buildings.

Student Life: 98% of undergraduates are from New York. Others are from 25 states, and 18 foreign countries. 81% are White. The average age of freshmen is 18; all undergraduates, 20. 16% do not continue beyond their first year; 67% remain to graduate.

Housing: 3557 students can be accommodated in college housing, which includes coed dorms and on-campus apartments. freshman housing and special-interest groupings within residence halls. On-campus housing is guaranteed for the freshman year only, is available on a first-come, first-served basis, and is available on a lottery system for upperclassmen. 59% of students live on campus; of those, 60% remain on campus on weekends. Alcohol is not permitted. Upperclassmen may keep cars.

Activities: 1% of men belong to 5 national fraternities; 1% of women belong to 8 national sororities. There are 112 groups on campus, including academic, cultural and special-interest organizations, and a variety of volunteer, art, band, cheerleading, choir, chorale, chorus, computers, dance, debate, drama, environmental, ethnic, film, gay, honors, international, jazz band, literary magazine, musical theater, newspaper, opera, orchestra, photography, political, professional, radio and TV, religious, social, social service, student government, and yearbook. Popular campus events include Into the Streets Day of Service, OH-Fest, Battle of the Red Dragons, Red Day and Passing through the Pillars.

Sports: There are 10 intercollegiate sports for men and 11 for women, and 13 intramural sports for men and 13 for women. Facilities include a gym, field house, dance studios, weight rooms, pool, indoor racquetball courts, tennis courts, indoor and outdoor tracks, athletic fields, and a lighted all-weather field.

Disabled Students: 90% of the campus is accessible. Facilities include wheelchair ramps, elevators, special parking, specially equipped restrooms, special class scheduling, lowered drinking fountains. All academic buildings and most residence halls are accessible.

Services: Counseling and information services are available, as is tutoring in most subjects. There is a reader service for the blind, and remedial math, reading, and writing. Tutoring is also available in all introductory-level courses and most upper-level courses.

Campus Safety and Security: Measures include 24-hour foot and vehicle patrol, emergency notification system, self-defense education, and security escort services. There are shuttle buses, emergency telephones, lighted pathways/sidewalks, and controlled access to dorms/residences.

Programs of Study: SUNY Oneonta confers B.A., and B.S. degrees. Master's degrees are also awarded. Bachelor's degrees are awarded in BIOLOGICAL SCIENCE (biology/biological science), BUSINESS (accounting, business economics, and fashion merchandising), COMMUNICATIONS AND THE ARTS (art, communications, dramatic arts, English, fine arts, French, music, music business management, and Spanish), COMPUTER AND PHYSICAL SCIENCE (atmospheric sciences and meteorology, chemistry, computer science, earth science, geology, mathematics, physics, and statistics), EDUCATION (business education, elementary education, English education, foreign languages education, home economics education, mathematics education, science education, secondary education, and social science education), ENGINEERING AND ENVIRONMENTAL DESIGN (environmental science), HEALTH PROFESSIONS (predentistry and premedicine), SOCIAL SCIENCE (African studies, anthropology, child care/child and family studies, criminal justice, dietetics, economics, geography, gerontology, Hispanic American studies, history, home economics, international studies, philosophy, political science/government, prelaw, psychology, sociology, and water resources). Physical and natural sciences, business economics, and education are the strongest academically. Elementary education, adolescent education, business, music industry, and fashion have the largest enrollments.

Required: Students must complete 122 semester hours, with 30 to 36 hours in the major. A minimum GPA of 2.0 (2.5 for education majors) must be maintained. In addition, students must complete a 36-hour general education requirement including courses in math, natural sciences, social sciences, American history, Western civilization, humanities, the arts, foreign language and basic communications. Students must also pass a writing exam.

Special: Oneonta offers limited cross-registration with Hartwick College, internships in most fields, and dual majors. Students can study abroad through eight exchange programs in Ghana, Finland, Germany, Sweden, Japan and South Korea, as well as more than 500 study abroad programs around the world through the SUNY network. A 3-1 fashion program with the Fashion Institute of Technology, 3-2 engineering degree,and other cooperative programs are offered. There are 20 national honor societies.

Faculty/Classroom: 50% of faculty are male; 50% are female. 96% teach undergraduates. No introductory courses are taught by graduate students. The average class size in an introductory lecture is 28; in a laboratory is 18; and in a regular course is 23.

Admissions: 43% of the 2013-2014 applicants were accepted. The SAT scores for the 2013-2014 freshman class were: Critical Reading--23% below 500, 62% between 500 and 599, 14% between 600 and 699, and 1% between 700 and 800; Math--14% below 500, 59% between 500 and 599, 25% between 600 and 699, and 2% between 700 and 800.

Requirements: The SAT or ACT is required. Applicants should be graduates of an accredited secondary school and have 19 academic credits, including 4 years each of English, social studies, mathematics and science, including lab. Three units of foreign language is required, and four units is recommended. The GED is accepted. AP and CLEP credits are accepted. Important factors in the admissions decision are advanced placement or honors courses, evidence of special talent, and leadership record.

Procedure: Freshmen are admitted fall and spring. Entrance exams should be taken in the spring of the junior year or the fall of the senior year. There are deferred admissions and rolling admissions plans. Application deadlines are open. Application fee is $50. Notifications are sent December 1. Applications are accepted online.

Transfer: 465 transfer students enrolled in 2012-2013. Official transcripts of all previous college work must be submitted. A minimum of 15 semester hours of transferable credit and a GPA of 2.0 (2.5 for education majors) are required. 45 of 122 credits required for the bachelor's degree must be completed at SUNY Oneonta.

Visiting: There are regularly scheduled orientations for prospective students, open houses, Friday and Saturday information sessions and individual appointments for prospective students; Academic Exploration Day and summer orientation sessions for admitted students. There are guides for informal visits and visitors may sit in on classes. To schedule a visit, contact the Admissions Office at (800) SUNY-123.

Financial Aid: In 2013-2014, 83% of all full-time freshmen and 66% of continuing full-time students received some form of financial aid. 42% of all full-time freshmen and 59% of continuing full-time students received need-based aid. The average freshman award was $8,818. Need-based scholarships or need-based grants averaged $6,510; need-based self-help aid (loans and jobs) averaged $3,999; and other non-need-based awards and non-need-based scholarships averaged $2,841. The average financial indebtedness of the 2013 graduate was $15,373. The FAFSA and the state aid form are required. Check with the school for current application deadlines.

International Students: There are 111 international students enrolled. The school actively recruits these students. They must take the TOEFL with a minimum score of 500 on the paper-based TOEFL (PBT) or 61 on the Internet-based version (iBT).

Computers: All students may access the system anytime. There are no time limits and no fees.

Graduates: From July 1, 2012 to June 30, 2013, 1206 bachelor's degrees were awarded. The most popular majors were education (18%), human ecology (10%), and English (9%). In an average class, 50% graduate in 4 years or less, 63% graduate in 5 years or less, and 64% graduate in 6 years or less.

Admissions Contact: Karen Brown, Director of Admissions. E-Mail: *admissions@oneonta.edu* Web: *www.oneonta.edu*

SUNY PLATTSBURGH / STATE UNIVERSITY OF NEW YORK D-2

Plattsburgh, NY 12901 (518) 564-2040
(888) 673-0012; (518) 564-2045

Full-time: 2311 men, 2875 women	**Faculty:** n/av; IIA, -$
Part-time: 159 men, 294 women	**Ph.D.s:** 81%
Graduate: 107 men, 305 women	**Student/Faculty:** 16 to 1
Year: semesters, summer session	**Tuition:** $7159 ($16,609)
Application Deadline: August 1	**Room & Board:** $10,924
Freshman Class: n/av	

VERY COMPETITIVE

The State University of New York/College at Plattsburgh, founded in 1889, is a public institution offering degree programs in the liberal arts and professional programs. There are 3 undergraduate schools and 2 graduate schools. In addition to regional accreditation, SUNY Plattsburgh has baccalaureate program accreditation with AACSB, ADA, CSWE, NLN, and TEAC. The library contains 541,609 volumes, 723,474 microform items, and 25,698 audio/video tapes/CDs/DVDs, and subscribes to 114,144 periodicals including electronic. Computerized library services include interlibrary loans, database searching, Internet access, and Wi-Fi capability. Special learning facilities include an art gallery, planetarium, radio station, TV station, an environmental science institute, a child care center, a research institute, a teacher resource center, a speech and hearing clinic, the Alzheimer's Disease Assistance Center, auditory research labs, a virtual reality simulator, and distance learning facilities. The 300-acre campus is in a suburban area 150 miles north of Albany, 25 miles west of Burlington, Vermont, and 65 miles south of Montreal, Canada. Including any residence halls, there are 36 buildings.

Student Life: 90% of undergraduates are from New York. Others are from 27 states, 67 foreign countries, and Canada. 95% are from public schools. 71% are White. The average age of freshmen is 18; all undergraduates, 21. 22% do not continue beyond their first year; 61% remain to graduate.

Housing: 2682 students can be accommodated in college housing, which includes single-sex and coed dorms and on-campus apartments. In addi-

tion, there are special-interest houses, adult student halls/floors, wellness floors, a substance-free building, and vacation housing. On-campus housing is available on a first-come, first-served basis, and is available on a lottery system for upperclassmen. 56% of students commute. All students may keep cars.

Activities: 6% of men belong to 1 local and 11 national fraternities; 5% of women belong to 1 local and 8 national sororities. There are 120 groups on campus, including art, band, cheerleading, choir, chorale, chorus, computers, dance, debate, drama, ethnic, film, gay, honors, international, jazz band, literary magazine, musical theater, newspaper, orchestra, pep band, photography, political, professional, radio and TV, religious, social, social service, student government, and yearbook. Popular campus events include Volunteer Opportunities (Relay for Life, Up 'til Dawn), Family Weekend, Night of Nations, President's Gala, Plattsburgh's Best Dance Crew and Plattsburgh's Got Talent Competitions.

Sports: There are 7 intercollegiate sports for men and 8 for women, and 9 intramural sports for men and 9 for women. Facilities include a 3500-seat ice arena, a 1500-seat gym, an indoor track, soccer and volleyball areas, an indoor swimming pool, exercise and weight rooms, an aerobics studio, racquetball courts, lighted tennis courts, softball, lacrosse, and rugby fields, and a fitness center.

Disabled Students: 95% of the campus is accessible. Facilities include wheelchair ramps, elevators, special parking, specially equipped restrooms, special class scheduling, lowered drinking fountains, lowered telephones, special housing.

Services: Counseling and information services are available, as is tutoring in every subject. There is a reader service for the blind, and remedial math, reading, and writing.

Campus Safety and Security: Measures include 24-hour foot and vehicle patrol, emergency notification system, self-defense education, and security escort services. There are shuttle buses, emergency telephones, lighted pathways/sidewalks, controlled access to dorms/residences, bicycle patrols, combination locks on student rooms, a computerized keyless entry system for residence hall access, door viewers, and basement and ground-level security windows in residence halls.

Programs of Study: SUNY Plattsburgh confers B.A., B.S., B.F.A. and B.S.Ed. degrees. Master's degrees are also awarded. Bachelor's degrees are awarded in BIOLOGICAL SCIENCE (biochemistry, biology/adolescence education, biology/biological science, ecology, and nutrition), BUSINESS (accounting, business administration and management, entrepreneurial studies, finance, hotel/motel and restaurant management, international business management, management information systems, marketing/retailing/merchandising, and supply chain management), COMMUNICATIONS AND THE ARTS (art, communications, English, English literature, English Writing, French, journalism, music, public relations, Spanish, and spanish / adolescence education), COMPUTER AND PHYSICAL SCIENCE (chemistry, chemistry/adolescence education, computer science, geology, mathematics, and physics), EDUCATION (childhood education: 1-6, English education, mathematics education, special education, and sports and wellness studies), ENGINEERING AND ENVIRONMENTAL DESIGN (environmental science), HEALTH PROFESSIONS (cytotechnology, medical laboratory technology, medical technology, and nursing), SOCIAL SCIENCE (anthropology, Canadian studies, child care/child and family studies, communication sciences & disorders, criminal justice, economics, French studies, gender studies, geography, history, home economics, human development, interdisciplinary studies, Latin American studies, philosophy, political science/government, psychology, social work, sociology, and women's studies). Adolescence education, multimedia journalism, global supply, and chain management are the strongest academically. Psychology, education, business, criminal justice, and nursing have the largest enrollments.

Required: To graduate students must have a 2.0 GPA and complete at least 120 semester hours. Core curriculum courses total 41 to 46 credits. In addition, all students must demonstrate proficiency in writing by completion of English composition and an advanced writing requirement. Specific courses such as library research skills and computer science are offered. A comprehensive exam in some majors and a thesis in the upper-division honors program. Many majors require practicum and/or internship experience to complete a degree.

Special: The college offers cross-registration with Clinton Community College and Empire State College, internships, study abroad in 10 countries, cooperative programs in all majors, B.A.-B.S. degrees, dual and student-designed majors, an accelerated degree program in any major except nursing, and B.A./M.S.T. and B.S./MSED combined undergraduate and graduate programs. A 3-2 engineering degree is offered with SUNY Stony Brook and Binghamton, Clarkson, Syracuse, and McGill Universities, and the University of Vermont. There are 31 national honor societies and a freshman honors program.

Faculty/Classroom: 48% of faculty are male; 52% are female. All teach and do research. No introductory courses are taught by graduate students. The average class size in an introductory lecture is 27; in a laboratory is 17; and in a regular course is 24.

Admissions: 34% of the current freshmen were in the top fifth of their class; 75% were in the top two fifths.

Requirements: The SAT or ACT is required. Applicants must have at least 12 academic credits, including 4 years of English, 5 combined years of math and science, and 3 years of social studies. An essay, portfolio, audition, and interview may be recommended in some programs. The GED is accepted. SUNY Plattsburgh requires applicants to be in the upper 50% of their class. A GPA of 78.0 is required. AP and CLEP credits are accepted. Important factors in the admissions decision are advanced placement or honors courses, recommendations by school officials, and leadership record.

Procedure: Freshmen are admitted fall and spring. Entrance exams should be taken during the second half of the junior year or the beginning of the senior year. There is a rolling admissions plan. Early decision applications should be filed by November 15; regular applications, by August 1 for fall entry; and November 1 for spring entry, along with a $50 fee. Notification of early decision is sent December 15; regular decision, January 15. 310 applicants were on the 2013 waiting list; 26 were admitted. Applications are accepted online.

Transfer: 612 transfer students enrolled in 2012-2013. Applicants must have a minimum 2.0 GPA. Most academic programs require a 2.5 GPA or better. 36 of 120 credits required for the bachelor's degree must be completed at SUNY Plattsburgh.

Visiting: There are regularly scheduled orientations for prospective students, including a group, student-led tour, and either a group or individual interview. Special overnight events for accepted freshmen include meals with students and faculty, classroom visits, discussions with faculty, and special workshops. There are guides for informal visits, visitors may sit in on classes, and stay overnight. To schedule a visit, contact the Admissions Office.

Financial Aid: In 2013-2014, 65% of all full-time freshmen students received some form of financial aid. 58% of all full-time freshmen and 59% of continuing full-time students received need-based aid. The average freshman award was $11,845. Need-based scholarships or need-based grants averaged $7,093; need-based self-help aid (loans and jobs) averaged $6,510; and other non-need-based awards and non-need-based scholarships averaged $6,227. 34% of undergraduate students work part-time. Average annual earnings from campus work are $1520. The average financial indebtedness of the 2013 graduate was $26,894. The FAFSA is required. The priority date for freshman financial aid applications for fall entry is February 15.

International Students: There are 308 international students enrolled. The school actively recruits these students. They must take the TOEFL with a minimum score of 450 on the paper-based TOEFL (PBT) or 45 on the Internet-based version (iBT).

Computers: All students may access the system. There are no time limits. The fee is $50 per semester.

Graduates: From July 1, 2012 to June 30, 2013, 1417 bachelor's degrees were awarded. The most popular majors were business/marketing (22%), communication/journalism (10%), and education (10%). 120 companies recruited on campus in 2012-2013. In an average class, 1% graduate in 3 years or less, 40% graduate in 4 years or less, 17% graduate in 5 years or less, and 1% graduate in 6 years or less. Of the 2012 graduating class, 12% were enrolled in graduate school within 6 months of graduation, and 79% were employed.

Admissions Contact: Richard Higgins, Director of Admissions. E-Mail: *higginrj@.plattsburgh.edu* Web: *www.plattsburgh.edu*

SYRACUSE UNIVERSITY — C-3

Syracuse, NY 13244 — **(315) 443-3611**

Full-time: 6448 men, 7974 women	**Faculty:** n/av; I, -$
Part-time: 307 men, 368 women	**Ph.D.s:** 86%
Graduate: 3034 men, 3136 women	**Student/Faculty:** n/av
Year: semesters, summer session	**Tuition:** $40,458
Application Deadline: January 1	**Room & Board:** $14,054

Freshman Class: 28269 applied, 13990 accepted, 3487 enrolled

SAT or ACT: required

HIGHLY COMPETITIVE

Founded in 1870, Syracuse University is a private institution offering undergraduate degree programs in liberal arts (social sciences, physical sciences, humanities); architecture; education; engineering and computer science; human ecology (including child and family studies, health and wellness, hospitality management, marriage and family therapy, nutrition sciences and dietetics, sport management, and social work); information management and technology; management; public communications; and visual and performing arts, (including art, design, music, drama, and communication and rhetorical studies). There are 9 undergraduate schools and 11 graduate schools. In addition to regional accreditation, Syracuse has baccalaureate program accreditation with ABET, ACEJMC, CSWE, FIDER, NAAB, NASAD, NASM, and NCATE. The 4 libraries contain 4.5 million volumes, 105,291 microform items, and 228,454 audio/video tapes/CDs/DVDs, and subscribe to 33,187 periodicals including electronic. Computerized library services include interlibrary loans, database searching, Internet access, and Wi-Fi capability. Special learning facilities include an art gallery, radio station, and TV station. The 708-acre campus is in an urban area Syracuse University is situated in the city of Syracuse, the heart of Central New York. Including any residence halls, there are 272 buildings.

Student Life: 56% of undergraduates are from out of state, mostly the Northeast. Students are from 49 states, 86 foreign countries, and Canada. 68% are from public schools. 55% are White; 11% Hispanic. 47% claim no religious affiliation; 22% Catholic; 13% Protestant; 11% Jewish. The average age of freshmen is 18; all undergraduates, 20. 8% do not continue beyond their first year; 82% remain to graduate.

Housing: 8270 students can be accommodated in college housing, which includes coed dorms and on-campus apartments. In addition, there are special-interest houses, fraternity houses, sorority houses, Theme/wellness housing; special housing for students with disabilities. On-campus housing is available on a lottery system for upperclassmen. 75% of students live on campus; of those, 85% remain on campus on weekends. Upperclassmen may keep cars.

Activities: 22% of men belong to 33 national fraternities; 27% of women belong to 24 national sororities. There are 300 groups on campus, including art, band, cheerleading, chess, choir, chorale, chorus, computers, dance, debate, drama, environmental, ethnic, film, forensics, gay, honors, international, jazz band, literary magazine, marching band, musical theater, newspaper, opera, orchestra, pep band, photography, political, professional, radio and TV, religious, social, social service, special interest, student government, and yearbook. Popular campus events include Syracuse Welcome, Winter Welcome, Winter Carnival, Senior Celebration, Dance Works Annual Production, 1st Year Players Annual Production, Block Party, Juice Jam, Homecoming, Univ. Lectures, PULSE Performing Arts, Mayfest, Syracuse Showcase.

Sports: There are 8 intercollegiate sports for men and 12 for women, and 15 intramural sports for men and 15 for women. Facilities include 5 fitness centers, 2 swimming pools, ice skating pavilion, fencing room, racquetball and squash courts, basketball courts, dance studios, volleyball facilities, table-tennis,weight rooms, tennis courts, exercise rooms, indoor track, grass playing fields, multiple outdoor artificial turf fields, an outdoor track, ropes challenge course and zip line, indoor challenge course, soccer stadium, softball stadium, football complex, athlete weight room, fitness classes, country club, golf course, boathouse/rowing facilities, multipurpose domed stadium seats 50,000 for football and 30,000 for basketball.

Disabled Students: 76% of the campus is accessible. Facilities include wheelchair ramps, elevators, special parking, specially equipped restrooms, lowered drinking fountains, lowered telephones.

Services: Counseling and information services are available, as is tutoring in most subjects. There is a reader service for the blind. A variety of services are offered by Syracuse University Tutoring Services including subject specific help, tutoring by academic program, study resources, and the tutoring and study center.

Campus Safety and Security: Measures include 24-hour foot and vehicle patrol, emergency notification system, self-defense education, and security escort services. There are shuttle buses, emergency telephones, lighted pathways/sidewalks, controlled access to dorms/residences.

Programs of Study: Syracuse confers B.A., B.S., B.Arch., B.F.A, B.I.D. and B. Mus. degrees. Associate, master's, and doctoral degrees are also awarded. Bachelor's degrees are awarded in BIOLOGICAL SCIENCE (biochemistry, biology/biological science, biophysics, biotechnology, neurosciences, and nutrition), BUSINESS (accounting, entrepreneurial studies, finance, management science, marketing management, real estate, retailing, sports management, and supply chain management), COMMUNICATIONS AND THE ARTS (advertising, art history, art, broadcasting, ceramic art and design, classics, communications, comparative literature, digital communications, dramatic arts, English, English literature, film arts, fine arts, French, Germanic languages and literature, graphic design, Greek, illustration, industrial design, journalism, linguistics, media arts, metal/jewelry, modern language, music, music business management, music history and appreciation, music performance, music theory and composition, musical theater, painting, percussion, photography, piano/organ, printmaking, public relations, Russian languages and literature, sculpture, speech/debate/rhetoric, strings, telecommunications, theater design, theater management, video, voice, winds, and writing), COMPUTER AND PHYSICAL SCIENCE (chemistry, Computer Engineering Technology, computer science, earth science, energy science, geology, information sciences and systems, mathematics, and physics), EDUCATION (art education, early childhood education, education, elementary education, English education, health education, mathematics education, middle school education, music education, physical education, science education, social studies education, and special education), ENGINEERING AND ENVIRONMENTAL DESIGN (aeronautical engineering, architectural history, architecture, bioengineering, chemical engineering, civil engineering, computer engineering, computer graphics, electrical/electronics engineering, environmental design, environmental engineering, and mechanical engineering), HEALTH PROFESSIONS (health science, predentistry, premedicine, preveterinary science, public health, and speech pathology/audiology), SOCIAL SCIENCE (African American studies, anthropology, child care/child and family studies, classical/ancient civilization, economics, ethics, politics, and social policy, European studies, fashion design and technology, forensic studies, geography, history, international relations, Italian studies, Judaic studies, Latin American studies, liberal arts/general studies, Middle Eastern studies, philosophy, political science/government, prelaw, psychology, religion, Russian and Slavic studies, social work, sociology, Spanish studies, and women & gender studies). Architecture, public communications, management, life sciences, sport management, drama, and recording and allied entertainment industries are the strongest academically. Psychology, information management and technology, and architecture have the largest enrollments.

Required: Portions of the liberal arts core are required by all colleges. New students are required to take a writing course. Liberal arts core is required in most majors: writing skills; foreign language or quantitative skills; humanities, natural sciences and mathematics, social sciences; and critical reflections on ethical and social issues. A minimum of 120 credit hours to graduate, but it varies by college or major(s).

Special: Co-op programs exist for aerospace engineering, bioengineering, chemical engineering, civil engineering, computer engineering, computer science, electric engineering, environmental engineering, mechanical engineering, and systems and information science. SU students are encouraged to undertake internships during both the academic year and summers in the Syracuse community, across the nation and at times internationally. There are 14 national honor societies, including Phi Beta Kappa, and a freshman honors program.

Faculty/Classroom: 59% of faculty are male; 41% are female. No introductory courses are taught by graduate students. The average class size in an introductory lecture is 207; in a laboratory is 19; and in a regular course is 24.

Admissions: 49% of the 2013-2014 applicants were accepted. The SAT scores for the 2013-2014 freshman class were: Critical Reading--21% below 500, 45% between 500 and 599, 29% between 600 and 699, and 5% between 700 and 800; Math--12% below 500, 37% between 500 and 599, 40% between 600 and 699, and 11% between 700 and 800; Writing--18% below 500, 43% between 500 and 599, 33% between 600 and 699, and 6% between 700 and 800. 62% of the current freshmen were in the top fifth of their class; 88% were in the top two fifths.

Requirements: The SAT or ACT is required. The ACT Optional Writing test is also required. Applicants to Syracuse University must submit the Common Application and Syracuse University Supplement; scores for either the SAT or ACT (for those applicants only taking the ACT, the optional writing test is required); secondary school transcript; counselor evaluation; two academic recommendations; an essay and short written answers to questions. Applicants should have a strong college preparatory record from an accredited secondary school or have a GED equivalent. A portfolio is required for art and architecture majors, and an audition is required for music and drama majors. The SAT and ACT are optional for international applicants studying outside the U.S. who are not prospective student-athletes and not attending an American-system school. AP and CLEP credits are accepted.

Procedure: Freshmen are admitted fall and spring. Entrance exams should be taken Prior to Jan. of the senior year for regular decision. There are early decision and deferred admissions plans. Early decision applications should be filed by November 15; regular applications, by January 1 for fall entry; and November 15 for spring entry. The fall 2013 application fee was $75. Notification of early decision is sent January 1; regular decision, March 15. 961 early decision candidates were accepted for the 2013-2014 class. 1732 applicants were on the 2013 waiting list; 681 were admitted. Applications are accepted online.

Transfer: 422 transfer students enrolled in 2012-2013. Online common application form; $75 application fee; official academic transcript; two academic recommendations; and common application supplement. For applicants with fewer than 30 college credit hours completed, submit SAT or ACT scores and secondary school transcript. A portfolio is required for art and architecture applicants, and an audition for music and drama applicants. TOEFL scores are required for students whose native language is not English. Additional requirements may apply to international students.

Visiting: There are regularly scheduled orientations for prospective students. There are guides for informal visits, visitors may sit in on classes, and stay overnight. To schedule a visit, contact Office of Admissions.

Financial Aid: In 2013-2014, 73% of all full-time freshmen and 74% of continuing full-time students received some form of financial aid. 57% of all full-time freshmen and 58% of continuing full-time students received need-based aid. The average freshman award was $34,700. Need-based scholarships or need-based grants averaged $27,370; and need-based self-help aid (loans and jobs) averaged $7,330. 70% of undergraduate students work part-time. Average annual earnings from campus work are $2700. The average financial indebtedness of the 2013 graduate was $33,455. Syracuse is a member of CSS. The CSS/Profile, FAFSA, and noncustodial profile are required. The deadline for filing freshman financial aid applications for fall entry is February 1.

International Students: There are 1397 international students enrolled.

The school actively recruits these students. They must take the TOEFL with a minimum score of 550 on the paper-based TOEFL (PBT) or 85 on the Internet-based version (iBT). The SAT and ACT are optional for international students who have not studied in an American-based system.

Computers: All students may access the system 24 hours per day. There are no time limits and no fees.

Graduates: From July 1, 2012 to June 30, 2013, 3146 bachelor's degrees were awarded. The most popular majors were business and marketing (16%), communications/journalism (13%), and social sciences (12%). 154 companies recruited on campus in 2012-2013. In an average class, 68% graduate in 4 years or less, 79% graduate in 5 years or less, and 81% graduate in 6 years or less. Of the 2012 graduating class, 21% were enrolled in graduate school within 6 months of graduation, and 91% were employed.

Admissions Contact: Office of Admissions E-Mail: *orange@syr.edu* Web: *http:/admissions.syr.edu*

STATE UNIVERSITY OF NEW YORK / THE COLLEGE AT BROCKPORT B-3

Brockport, NY 14420 **(585) 395-2751; (585) 395-5452**

Full-time: 2928 men, 3483 women	**Faculty:** 313; IIA, av$
Part-time: 273 men, 406 women	**Ph.D.s:** 90%
Graduate: 341 men, 697 women	**Student/Faculty:** 21 to 1
Year: semesters, summer session	**Tuition:** $7222 ($16,672)
Application Deadline: open	**Room & Board:** $11,140
Freshman Class: n/av	

VERY COMPETITIVE

The State University of New York/College at Brockport, established in 1835, is a comprehensive public liberal arts college with offerings including 47 undergraduate majors and more than 50 graduate programs, post-master's and advanced certificate programs, teacher certification in 23 areas and combined bachelor's/master's programs. There are 5 undergraduate schools and 1 graduate school. In addition to regional accreditation, SUNY Brockport has baccalaureate program accreditation with AACSB, ABET, CSAB, CSWE, NCATE, and NRPA. The library contains 525,631 volumes, 18,892 microform items, and 15,525 audio/video tapes/CDs/DVDs, and subscribes to 31,163 periodicals including electronic. Computerized library services include interlibrary loans, database searching, Internet access, and Wi-Fi capability. Special learning facilities include an art gallery, planetarium, radio station, and TV station. The 454-acre campus is in a small town 16 miles west of Rochester. Including any residence halls, there are 68 buildings.

Student Life: 98% of undergraduates are from New York. Others are from 29 states, 11 foreign countries, and Canada. 74% are White. The average age of freshmen is 18; all undergraduates, 23. 19% do not continue beyond their first year; 50% remain to graduate.

Housing: 2705 students can be accommodated in college housing, which includes coed dorms and on-campus apartments. In addition, there are special-interest houses, special residence hall communities for first-year students, and academic excellence floors. On-campus housing is guaranteed for the freshman year only. 63% of students commute. All students may keep cars.

Activities: 2% of men belong to 2 national fraternities; 2% of women belong to 3 national sororities. There are 119 groups on campus, including outdoors, criminal justice, art, Business, cheerleading, chess, choir, chorus, computers, dance, drama, ethnic, film, gay, honors, international, jazz band, literary magazine, musical theater, newspaper, photography, political, professional, radio and TV, religious, social, social service, and student government. Popular campus events include Scholar's Day, Honors Convocation and Health Week.

Sports: There are 12 intercollegiate sports for men and 13 for women, and 28 intramural sports for men and 25 for women. Facilities include field hockey, baseball, and softball fields; a soccer pitch; a swimming pool; 6 gyms; a gymnastics area; wrestling and weight rooms; handball, squash, tennis, and racquetball courts; an ice arena; and a Special Olympics stadium with a football field and track.

Disabled Students: 95% of the campus is accessible. Facilities include wheelchair ramps, elevators, special parking, specially equipped restrooms, special class scheduling, lowered drinking fountains, lowered telephones, special housing.

Services: Counseling and information services are available, as is tutoring in some subjects, which vary from semester to semester. Study skills support is available to all students.

Campus Safety and Security: Measures include 24-hour foot and vehicle patrol, emergency notification system, and security escort services. There are shuttle buses, emergency telephones, lighted pathways/sidewalks, controlled access to dorms/residences, a community policing program, bicycle patrols, and 24-hour locked residence halls.

Programs of Study: SUNY Brockport confers B.A., B.S., B.F.A. and B.S.N. degrees. Master's degrees are also awarded. Bachelor's degrees are awarded in BIOLOGICAL SCIENCE (biology/biological science), BUSINESS (accounting, business administration and management, finance, international business management, marketing management, recreation and leisure services, and sports management), COMMUNICATIONS AND THE ARTS (communications, dance, English, French, journalism, Spanish, studio art, and theatre acting), COMPUTER AND PHYSICAL SCIENCE (atmospheric sciences and meteorology, chemistry, computer science, earth science, geology, mathematics, and physics), EDUCATION (physical education), ENGINEERING AND ENVIRONMENTAL DESIGN (computational sciences and environmental science), HEALTH PROFESSIONS (exercise science, health science, medical technology, and nursing), SOCIAL SCIENCE (African studies, African American studies, anthropology, criminal justice, history, interdisciplinary studies, international studies, philosophy, political science/government, psychology, social work, sociology, water resources, and women's studies). Business administration, nursing, and education have the largest enrollments.

Required: To graduate, students must complete a minimum of 120 credits, including 30 or more credits in the major, with a 2.0 GPA. The core curriculum includes the SUNY-wide general education requirements (1 course each in math, natural sciences, social sciences, American history, Western civilization, world (non-Western) civilization, humanities, the arts, foreign language, and basic communication). All students must take courses in contemporary issues, diversity, and perspectives on women and pass the appropriate competency exams. An academic planning seminar is required of entering freshmen.

Special: Co-op programs, internships in most majors, and work-study programs in education are available. Brockport offers cross-registration with Rochester area colleges, a Washington semester, study abroad in 16 countries, accelerated degree programs, and an interdisciplinary major in arts for children, emphasizing art, dance, music, and theater. Credit for military and work experience, nondegree study, and pass/fail grading options are available. An alternative general education program, Delta College, is an interdisciplinary program that emphasizes global issues and provides opportunities for work or study in other countries, as well as locally, regionally, and nationally. There are 32 national honor societies, a freshman honors program, and 1 departmental honors program.

Faculty/Classroom: 46% of faculty are male; 54% are female. 93% teach undergraduates. No introductory courses are taught by graduate students.

Admissions: The SAT scores for the 2013-2014 freshman class were: Critical Reading--6% below 500, 57% between 500 and 599, 15% between 600 and 699, and 2% between 700 and 800; Math--17% below 500, 57% between 500 and 599, 24% between 600 and 699, and 2% between 700 and 800; Writing--40% below 500, 48% between 500 and 599, and 12% between 600 and 699. The ACT scores were 12% below 21, 36% between 21 and 23, 32% between 24 and 26, 13% between 27 and 28, and 6% above 28. 49% of the current freshmen were in the top fifth of their class; 80% were in the top two fifths. 3 freshmen graduated first in their class.

Requirements: The SAT or ACT is required. SUNY Brockport seeks students who have demonstrated academic success and who show persistence. Applicants must have a high school diploma (preferably from the New York State Regents Program) or have completed a minimum of 18 academic units: 4 each in English and social studies, 4 in academic electives, 3 each in math and science (1 with lab). An essay and letters of recommendation are encouraged. An audition is required for dance and theater applicants. A GPA of 85.0 is required. AP and CLEP credits are accepted. Important factors in the admissions decision are advanced placement or honors courses, leadership record, and extracurricular activities record.

Procedure: Freshmen are admitted fall and spring. Entrance exams should be taken during the spring of the junior year and fall of the senior year. There are deferred admissions and rolling admissions plans. Application deadlines are open. Application fee is $50. Notification is sent on a rolling basis. 93 applicants were on the 2013 waiting list; 93 were admitted. Applications are accepted online.

Transfer: 1338 transfer students enrolled in 2012-2013. Applicants must have a minimum GPA of 2.25. Many departments specify prerequisite courses and a higher GPA. SUNY Brockport recommends that transfer applicants have an associate degree or 54 credit hours, with preference given to degree holders. 30 of 120 credits required for the bachelor's degree must be completed at SUNY Brockport.

Visiting: There are regularly scheduled orientations for prospective students, including daily admissions information presentations and campus tours. Visits may be arranged on selected Saturdays and holidays. There are guides for informal visits, visitors may sit in on classes, and stay overnight. To schedule a visit, contact the Office of Undergraduate Admissions.

Financial Aid: In 2013-2014, 90% of all full-time freshmen and 84% of continuing full-time students received some form of financial aid. 68% of all full-time freshmen and 71% of continuing full-time students received need-based aid. The average freshman award was $13,417. Need-based scholarships or need-based grants averaged $5,945 ($14,945 maximum); need-based self-help aid (loans and jobs) averaged $4,979 ($9,395 maximum); and other non-need-based awards and non-need-based scholarships averaged $6,869 ($28,766 maximum). 34% of undergraduate students work part-time. Average annual earnings from campus work are $1428. The average financial indebtedness of the 2013 graduate was $27,844. SUNY Brockport is a member of CSS. The FAFSA is required. The deadline for filing freshman financial aid applications for fall entry is February 15.

International Students: There are 53 international students enrolled. The school actively recruits these students. They must take the TOEFL with a minimum score of 530 on the paper-based TOEFL (PBT) or 71 on the Internet-based version (iBT) or take the MELAB. They must also take the SAT or ACT.

Computers: All students may access the system 24 hours per day. There are no time limits. The fee is $167.50.

Graduates: From July 1, 2012 to June 30, 2013, 1771 bachelor's degrees were awarded. The most popular majors were health professions and related sciences (16%), business administration (16%), and psychology (8%). 140 companies recruited on campus in 2012-2013. In an average class, 3% graduate in 3 years or less, 48% graduate in 4 years or less, 64% graduate in 5 years or less, and 66% graduate in 6 years or less.

Admissions Contact: Megan Ryan, Associate Director of Admissions. E-Mail: *admit@brockport.edu* Web: *www.brockport.edu*

THE STATE UNIVERSITY OF NEW YORK AT POTSDAM — D-2

Potsdam, NY 13676	**(315) 267-2180; (315) 267-2163**
Full-time: 1534 men, 2062 women	**Faculty:** 274; IIA, --$
Part-time: 45 men, 66 women	**Ph.D.s:** 67%
Graduate: 82 men, 253 women	**Student/Faculty:** 13 to 1
Year: semesters, summer session	**Tuition:** $7174 ($16,624)
Application Deadline: rolling	**Room & Board:** $10,580
Freshman Class: 4764 applied, 3257 accepted, 821 enrolled	
SAT CR/M: 520/520	**ACT:** 23 **COMPETITIVE**

The State University of New York at Potsdam, founded in 1816, joined the state university system in 1948. SUNY Potsdam offers over 50 programs in Arts and Sciences, 6 in The Crane School of Music and over 20 in The School of Education and Professional Studies as well as programs in Interdisciplinary Studies. Bachelor Degrees are offered in Arts, Science, Fine Arts and Music and Master's degrees in Arts, Education, Science and Music. SUNY Potsdam offers dual degrees with a number of other Universities. There are 3 undergraduate schools and 1 graduate school. In addition to regional accreditation, SUNY Potsdam has baccalaureate program accreditation with NASM and NCATE. The 2 libraries contain 437,228 volumes, 772,929 microform items, and 13,901 audio/video tapes/CDs/DVDs, and subscribe to 59,000 periodicals including electronic. Computerized library services include interlibrary loans, database searching, Internet access, and Wi-Fi capability. Special learning facilities include an art gallery, natural history museum, planetarium and radio station. The 240-acre campus is in a rural area 30 miles from Massena and Ogdensburg, and 140 miles northeast of Syracuse and 80 miles from Montreal, Canada. Including any residence halls, there are 56 buildings.

Student Life: 96% of undergraduates are from New York. Others are from 28 states, 16 foreign countries, and Canada. 88% are from public schools. 72% are White. The average age of freshmen is 18; all undergraduates, 21. 26% do not continue beyond their first year; 51% remain to graduate.

Housing: 2715 students can be accommodated in college housing, which includes single-sex and coed dorms, on-campus apartments, and off-campus apartments. In addition, there are honors houses, special-interest houses, First year experience, quiet study, international house, transfer student housing, sustainability housing,gender neutral,. On-campus housing is guaranteed for all 4 years. 61% of students live on campus; of those, 70% remain on campus on weekends. All students may keep cars.

Activities: 1% of men belong to 3 local and 2 national fraternities; 2% of women belong to 7 local and 3 national sororities. There are 81 groups on campus, including art, band, cheerleading, choir, chorale, chorus, computers, dance, drama, environmental, environmental awareness, ethnic, gay, honors, international, jazz band, literary magazine, musical theater, newspaper, opera, orchestra, photography, political, professional, radio and TV, religious, social, social service, student government, and symphony. Popular campus events include Welcome Weekend Carnival, Spring Fest and Crane Candlelight Concert.

Sports: There are 7 intercollegiate sports for men and 9 for women, and 10 intramural sports for men and 2 for women. Maxcy Hall is the center of the sports world on campus. Maxcy is surrounded by 50 acres of athletic fields and courts for tennis and basketball and a quarter-mile track. There is a new field for softball and a modern turf field for soccer, lacrosse, and intramural competition.

Disabled Students: 95% of the campus is accessible. Facilities include wheelchair ramps, elevators, special parking, specially equipped restrooms, special class scheduling, lowered drinking fountains, lowered telephones, special housing, and electric doors.

Services: Counseling and information services are available, as is tutoring in every subject. There is a reader service for the blind.

Campus Safety and Security: Measures include 24-hour foot and vehicle patrol, emergency notification system, self-defense education, and security escort services. There are emergency telephones, lighted pathways/sidewalks, controlled access to dorms/residences, educational programs, campus rescue squad, portable jump-start packs, vehicle lockouts, and parking management.

Programs of Study: SUNY Potsdam confers B.A., B.F.A., B.M. and B.S. degrees. Master's degrees are also awarded. Bachelor's degrees are awarded in AGRICULTURE (environmental studies), BIOLOGICAL SCIENCE (biochemistry and biology/biological science), BUSINESS (business administration and management and business economics), COMMUNICATIONS AND THE ARTS (art history, art, creative writing, dance, English, English literature, English Writing, fine arts, French, literature, music, music business management, music performance, music theory and composition, Spanish, studio art, theatre arts, and visual and performing arts), COMPUTER AND PHYSICAL SCIENCE (chemistry, computer science, geology, mathematics, and physics), EDUCATION (early childhood education, elementary education, English education, mathematics education, music education, and social studies education), HEALTH PROFESSIONS (community health work), SOCIAL SCIENCE (anthropology, archeology, criminal justice, economics, French studies, history, philosophy, political science/government, psychology, sociology, Spanish studies, and women's studies). Music, anthropology and geology are the strongest academically. Music education, childhood education and psychology have the largest enrollments.

Required: To graduate, Student must complete a major and earn at least a 2.0 in 30 hours of major coursework (some majors have higher standards). A student must complete the general education requirements and must graduate with an overall G.P.A. of 2.0. Out of a total 120 credits, 45 of those must be designated as upper division courses (level 300 or higher).

Special: Cross-registration is offered with Clarkson University, St. Lawrence University, and SUNY Canton. Over 530 internships available. SUNY Postdam also offers work-study opportunities, a 3-2 engineering degree with Clarkson University, study abroad, 3-2 management and accounting degrees, student-designed majors, dual majors in interdisciplinary natural science, non-degree study, and pass/fail options.Handcrafted education for students who enroll in the Honors Program or engage in Research through the UG Research and Presidential Scholars programs. There are 22 national honor societies, a freshman honors program, and 19 departmental honors programs.

Faculty/Classroom: 19% of faculty are male; 51% are female. All teach undergraduates. No introductory courses are taught by graduate students.

Admissions: 68% of the 2013-2014 applicants were accepted. The SAT scores for the 2013-2014 freshman class were: Critical Reading--38% below 500, 41% between 500 and 599, 16% between 600 and 699, and 5% between 700 and 800; Math--37% below 500, 44% between 500 and 599, 18% between 600 and 699, and 1% between 700 and 800. The ACT scores were 34% below 21, 19% between 21 and 23, 27% between 24 and 26, 7% between 27 and 28, and 13% above 28.

Requirements: Applicants must be high school graduates in a college preparatory program or hold a GED. 4 years each of English and social studies, 3 years each of math, foreign language, and science, and 1 year of art or music recommended. An interview is important; an audition when appropriate is required. The majority of our applicants will NOT have to submit an SAT or ACT score. If you would like to have your scores submitted as part of your application, you must request your scores be sent directly from the testing agency. Also, you must submit an SAT or ACT score to be considered for our Mount Emmons Scholarship. Minimum scores for scholarship consideration are a 1300 on the SAT or a 29 on the ACT. AP and CLEP credits are accepted. Important factors in the admissions decision are advanced placement or honors courses, recommendations by school officials, and extracurricular activities record.

Procedure: Freshmen are admitted fall and spring. Entrance exams should be taken in the junior year or early senior year. There are early admissions, deferred admissions, and rolling admissions plans. Application deadlines are open. Application fee is $50. Notifications are sent October 1. Applications are accepted online.

Transfer: 257 transfer students enrolled in 2012-2013. Applicants must have earned 12 hours of college credit. Transfers with fewer than 24 credit hours must submit a high school transcript. College transcript required and essay or personal statement required. 30 of 124 credits required for the bachelor's degree must be completed at SUNY Potsdam.

Visiting: There are regularly scheduled orientations for prospective students, Individual Campus Visit available Monday through Friday, and Spring Open House March 19 and April 16. There are guides for informal visits and visitors may sit in on classes. To schedule a visit, contact the Admissions Office - Lisa Martin at visit@potsdam.edu.

Financial Aid: In 2013-2014, 92% of all full-time freshmen and 86% of continuing full-time students received some form of financial aid. 74% of all full-time freshmen and 70% of continuing full-time students received need-based aid. The average freshman award was $15,182. Need-based scholarships or need-based grants averaged $6,660 ($18,590 maximum);

need-based self-help aid (loans and jobs) averaged $4,066 ($10,200 maximum); and other non-need-based awards and non-need-based scholarships averaged $2,788 ($21,455 maximum). The average financial indebtedness of the 2013 graduate was $20,910. The FAFSA and the state aid form are required. The priority date for freshman financial aid applications for fall entry is March 1. The deadline for filing freshman financial aid applications for fall entry is May 1.

International Students: There are 39 international students enrolled. They must take the TOEFL with a minimum score of 550 on the paper-based TOEFL (PBT) or 79 on the Internet-based version (iBT), IELTS.

Computers: All students may access the system 7 days a week. There are no time limits. The fee is $192.50.

Graduates: From July 1, 2012 to June 30, 2013, 748 bachelor's degrees were awarded. The most popular majors were childhood education (12%), music education (8%), and business administration (8%). 39 companies recruited on campus in 2012-2013. In an average class, 30% graduate in 4 years or less, 49% graduate in 5 years or less, and 51% graduate in 6 years or less. Of the 2012 graduating class, 38% were enrolled in graduate school within 6 months of graduation, and 58% were employed.

Admissions Contact: Thomas Nesbitt, Director of Admissions. E-Mail: *admissions@potsdam.edu* Web: *www.potsdam.edu*

THE STATE UNIVERSITY OF NEW YORK COLLEGE OF AGRICULTURE AND TECH AT COBLESKILL D-3

Cobleskill, NY 12043 (518) 255-5525 (800) 295-8988; (518) 255-6769

Full-time: 1119 men, 1202 women
Part-time: 62 men, 87 women
Graduate: n/av
Year: semesters, summer session
Application Deadline: August
Freshman Class: n/av
Faculty: 97
Ph.D.s: n/av
Student/Faculty: 24 to 1
Tuition: $7149 ($16,559)
Room & Board: $11,720

VERY COMPETITIVE

The State University of New York/College of Agriculture and Technology at Cobleskill, established in 1916, is a comprehensive public institution offering bachelors and associate degrees and a certificate program. There are 2 undergraduate schools. The library contains 68,000 volumes, 32,165 microform items, and 4,462 audio/video tapes/CDs/DVDs, and subscribes to 22,228 periodicals including electronic. Computerized library services include interlibrary loans, database searching, Internet access, and Wi-Fi capability. Special learning facilities include an art gallery, an arboretum, greenhouses, an equestrian center, dairy barns, fish hatchery, and a plant nursery. The 750-acre campus is in a rural area 35 miles south of Albany. Including any residence halls, there are 53 buildings.

Student Life: 90% of undergraduates are from New York. Others are from 16 states, and 11 foreign countries. 98% are from public schools. 74% are White; 11% African American. The average age of freshmen is 18; all undergraduates, 20. 26% do not continue beyond their first year; 52% remain to graduate.

Housing: 1771 students can be accommodated in college housing, which includes single-sex and coed dorms. special interest floors in residence halls. On-campus housing is guaranteed for the freshman year only, is available on a first-come, first-served basis, and is available on a lottery system for upperclassmen. 60% of students live on campus. Alcohol is not permitted. All students may keep cars.

Activities: There are no fraternities or sororities. There are 45 groups on campus, including cheerleading, choir, chorus, drama, environmental, ethnic, gay, honors, international, jazz band, musical theater, newspaper, one departmental, photography, professional, radio and TV, religious, social, social service, and student government. Popular campus events include Alumni Weekend.

Sports: There are 10 intercollegiate sports for men and 10 for women, and 4 intramural sports for men and 4 for women. Facilities include indoor and outdoor basketball and tennis courts, playing fields, a gym, a fitness center, a swimming pool, bowling lanes, a field house, badminton, volleyball, and handball courts, archery and golf driving areas, a quarter-mile track, a ski center, and a fitness trail.

Disabled Students: 25% of the campus is accessible. Facilities include wheelchair ramps, elevators, special parking, specially equipped restrooms, special class scheduling, and special housing.

Services: Counseling and information services are available, as is tutoring in most subjects. There is a reader service for the blind, and remedial math, reading, and writing. There is also an academic support center.

Campus Safety and Security: Measures include 24-hour foot and vehicle patrol, self-defense education, and security escort services. There are emergency telephones, lighted pathways/sidewalks, and controlled access to dorms/residences.

Programs of Study: SUNY Cobleskill confers B.S., B.B.A. and B.T. degrees. Associate degrees are also awarded. Bachelor's degrees are awarded in AGRICULTURE (agricultural business management, agricultural mechanics, animal science, fishing and fisheries, plant science, and wildlife management), BIOLOGICAL SCIENCE (biotechnology), BUSINESS (business administration and management), COMMUNICATIONS AND THE ARTS (communications and graphic design), COMPUTER AND PHYSICAL SCIENCE (information sciences and systems), ENGINEERING AND ENVIRONMENTAL DESIGN (landscape architecture/design and technological management), SOCIAL SCIENCE (applied psychology, child care/child and family studies, and culinary arts). Health science studies, fisheries and wildlife, and agricultural biotechnology are the strongest academically. Social science, animal science, and business administration have the largest enrollments.

Required: Degree requirements include completion of 126 credit hours. Students must maintain a minimum 2.0 GPA.

Special: The college sponsors internship programs and cross-registration is possible with the Hudson-Mohawk Area Consortium. Study abroad options are also available. There is 1 national honor society, a freshman honors program, and 1 departmental honors program.

Faculty/Classroom: 52% of faculty are male; 48% are female. All teach undergraduates, 10% do research, and 10% do both. No introductory courses are taught by graduate students. The average class size in an introductory lecture is 19; in a laboratory is 15; and in a regular course is 19.

Requirements: The SAT or ACT is recommended. Applicants must have graduated from an accredited secondary school or earned a GED, and are encouraged to have completed college-preparatory courses. A GPA of 75.0 is required. AP and CLEP credits are accepted. Important factors in the admissions decision are advanced placement or honors courses, evidence of special talent, and leadership record.

Procedure: Freshmen are admitted fall and spring. There are early admissions, deferred admissions, and rolling admissions plans. Application deadlines are open. Application fee is $50. Notification of early decision is sent November 1; regular decision, Applications are accepted online.

Transfer: 295 transfer students enrolled in 2012-2013. Applicants must have a minimum GPA of 2.0. 45 of 126 credits required for the bachelor's degree must be completed at SUNY Cobleskill.

Visiting: There are regularly scheduled orientations for prospective students. There are guides for informal visits, visitors may sit in on classes, and stay overnight. To schedule a visit, contact the Office of Admissions.

Financial Aid: In 2013-2014, 89% of all full-time freshmen and 83% of continuing full-time students received some form of financial aid. 60% of all full-time freshmen and 57% of continuing full-time students received need-based aid. The average freshman award was $19,095. 12% of undergraduate students work part-time. Average annual earnings from campus work are $735. The average financial indebtedness of the 2013 graduate was $8,025. SUNY Cobleskill is a member of CSS. The FAFSA and the college's own financial statement, are required. Check with the school for current application deadlines.

International Students: There are 37 international students enrolled. The school actively recruits these students. They must take the TOEFL with a minimum score of 500 on the paper-based TOEFL (PBT).

Computers: All students may access the system 24 hours a day/7 days a week (where wireless and in residence halls). There are no time limits. The fee is $295.

Graduates: From July 1, 2012 to June 30, 2013, 343 bachelor's degrees were awarded. The most popular majors were animal sciences (20%), business administration (13%), and early childhood education (10%). In an average class, 39% graduate in 4 years or less, 48% graduate in 5 years or less, and 48% graduate in 6 years or less.

Admissions Contact: Robert Blanchet, Director of Admissions. E-Mail: *admissions@cobleskill.edu* Web: *http:/www.cobleskill.edu/admissions/*

TOURO COLLEGE D-5

New York, NY 10010 (718) 252-7800, ext. 299 or 320 (718) 253-9455

Full-time: 2810 men, 5110 women
Part-time: 910 men, 910 women
Graduate: 2285 men, 4580 women
Year: semesters, summer session
Application Deadline: open
Faculty: n/av
Ph.D.s: n/av
Student/Faculty: n/av
Tuition: $13,550
Room & Board: $9600
Freshman Class: 1076 applied, 875 accepted, 389 enrolled
SAT CR/M/W: 580/550/560 **ACT:** 24 **VERY COMPETITIVE**

Touro College, founded in 1971, is a private institution offering undergraduate programs primarily through the Lander College of Liberal Arts and Sciences, the School of General Studies, and the School of Health Sciences. Campuses are in midtown Manhattan, Brooklyn, and Queens. The figures in the above capsule and in this profile are approximate. There are 6 undergraduate schools and 8 graduate schools. In addition to regional accreditation, Touro College and University System has baccalaureate program accreditation with APTA and CAHEA. The 11 libraries contain 271,509 volumes, 14,100 microform items, and 4,054 audio/video tapes/CDs/DVDs, and subscribe to 3,163 periodicals including electronic. Computerized library services include interlibrary loans, database searching, Internet access, and Wi-Fi capability. The campus is in an urban area. Including any residence halls, there are 12 buildings.

Student Life: 95% of undergraduates are from New York. Others are from 25 states, 30 foreign countries, and Canada. 27% do not continue beyond their first year; 47% remain to graduate.

Housing: 200 students can be accommodated in college housing, which includes single-sex dorms, on-campus apartments, and off-campus apartments. On-campus housing is available on a first-come and first-served basis. Priority is given to out-of-town students. Alcohol is not permitted. All students may keep cars.

Activities: There are no fraternities or sororities. There are 8 groups on campus, including computers, debate, literary magazine, newspaper, political, professional, religious, social, student government, and yearbook. Popular campus events include student-sponsored lecture series and student-faculty social events.

Sports: There is no sports program at Touro College and University System. Facilities include 1 baseball field, 2 tennis courts, and 2 basketball courts.

Disabled Students: All of the campus is accessible. Facilities include wheelchair ramps, elevators, specially equipped restrooms, lowered drinking fountains, and lowered telephones.

Services: Counseling and information services are available, as is tutoring in some subjects, accounting, math, English, and natural sciences. There is remedial math, reading, and writing.

Campus Safety and Security: Measures include 24-hour foot and vehicle patrol and emergency notification system. There are shuttle buses, lighted pathways/sidewalks, and controlled access to dorms/residences.

Programs of Study: Touro College and University System confers B.A., B.S., B.S.N., and B.P.S. degrees. Associate, master's, and doctoral degrees are also awarded. Bachelor's degrees are awarded in BIOLOGICAL SCIENCE (biology/biological science), BUSINESS (accounting, banking and finance, business administration and management, management science, and marketing/retailing/merchandising), COMMUNICATIONS AND THE ARTS (English, Hebrew, literature, and speech/debate/rhetoric), COMPUTER AND PHYSICAL SCIENCE (chemistry, computer science, mathematics, and physics), EDUCATION (elementary education and special education), HEALTH PROFESSIONS (nursing, occupational therapy, physical therapy, predentistry, and premedicine), SOCIAL SCIENCE (economics, history, human services, interdisciplinary studies, Judaic studies, liberal arts/general studies, philosophy, political science/government, prelaw, psychology, social science, and sociology). Business/accounting, education, and health sciences are the strongest academically. Psychology, education, and business have the largest enrollments.

Required: To graduate, all students must complete at least 120 credit hours (varies by major), with 30 to 70 in the major; 45 of the 120 credits must be from Touro and 1/2 of the student's major has to be completed with Touro. A minimum 2.0 GPA is required, with 2.3 in the major. Specific disciplines include Judaic studies or ethnic studies. Required courses include English composition, history, literature, math, and social and natural sciences.

Special: The college offers cross-registration with the Fashion Institute of Technology, internships for juniors and seniors, study abroad in Israel, work-study programs, interdisciplinary majors, an accelerated degree program, credit for life, military, and work experience, pass/fail options, and dual majors. Early and/or preferential admission to professional programs is also possible. There are 2 national honor societies, a freshman honors program, and 5 departmental honors programs.

Faculty/Classroom: 49% of faculty are male; 51% are female. No introductory courses are taught by graduate students. The average class size in an introductory lecture is 16; in a laboratory is 12; and in a regular course is 15.

Admissions: 81% of the 2013-2014 applicants were accepted. The SAT scores for the 2013-2014 freshman class were: Critical Reading--8% below 500, 46% between 500 and 599, 34% between 600 and 699, and 12% between 700 and 800; Math--17% below 500, 48% between 500 and 599, 27% between 600 and 699, and 8% between 700 and 800; Writing--15% below 500, 44% between 500 and 599, 32% between 600 and 699, and 9% between 700 and 800. The ACT scores were 3% below 21, 45% between 21 and 23, 31% between 24 and 26, 13% between 27 and 28, and 8% above 28.

Requirements: The SAT or ACT is recommended. Applicants must be graduates of an accredited secondary school with a satisfactory high school average. A satisfactory SAT score is recommended. A GPA of 3.0 is required. AP and CLEP credits are accepted. Important factors in the admissions decision are advanced placement or honors courses, recommendations by school officials, and extracurricular activities record.

Procedure: Freshmen are admitted fall, spring, and summer. Entrance exams should be taken in May of the junior year or fall of the senior year. There are early admissions, deferred admissions, and rolling admissions plans. Early decision applications should be filed by 11 19, along with a $50 fee. Notification of early decision is sent December 1.

Transfer: 299 transfer students enrolled in 2012-2013. A 2.5 GPA is required. If the student has less than 60 credits, high school documentation is also required. 45 of 120 credits required for the bachelor's degree must be completed at Touro College and University System.

Visiting: There are regularly scheduled orientations for prospective students. There are guides for informal visits, visitors may sit in on classes, and stay overnight. To schedule a visit, contact Steven Toplan at steven.toplan@touro.edu.

Financial Aid: The CSS/Profile is required. Check with the school for current application deadlines.

International Students: There are 159 international students enrolled. They must take the TOEFL with a minimum score of 550 on the paper-based TOEFL (PBT) or 80 on the Internet-based version (iBT) and the college's own test.

Computers: All students may access the system. There are no time limits and no fees.

Graduates: From July 1, 2012 to June 30, 2013, 1584 bachelor's degrees were awarded. 32 companies recruited on campus in 2012-2013.

Admissions Contact: Steven Toplan, Director of Admissions. E-Mail: *admissions.lander@touro.edu* Web: *www.touro.edu*

UNION COLLEGE C-3

Schenectady, NY 12308 (518) 388-6112
(888) 843-6688; (518) 388-6986

Full-time: 1199 men, 1026 women
Part-time: 11 men, 10 women
Graduate: n/av
Year: trimesters
Application Deadline: January 15
Freshman Class: 1134 accepted, 559 enrolled
Faculty: n/av
Ph.D.s: n/av
Student/Faculty: n/av
Tuition: n/av
Room & Board: n/av

MOST COMPETITIVE

Union College, founded in 1795, is an independent liberal arts and engineering college. In addition to regional accreditation, Union has baccalaureate program accreditation with ABET. The library contains 617,945 volumes, 803,952 microform items, and 14,366 audio/video tapes/CDs/DVDs, and subscribes to 10,053 periodicals including electronic. Computerized library services include interlibrary loans, database searching, Internet access, and Wi-Fi capability. Special learning facilities include a radio station, a theater, high-tech classroom, lab center, multimedia auditorium, music center, and an art, science, history gallery. The 100-acre campus is in a small town 15 miles west of Albany. Including any residence halls, there are 100 buildings.

Student Life: 60% of undergraduates are from out of state, mostly the Northeast. Students are from states, and Canada. The average age of freshmen is 19; all undergraduates, 20.

Housing: 1975 students can be accommodated in college housing, which includes single-sex and coed dorms and on-campus apartments. In addition, there are language houses, special-interest houses, fraternity houses, sorority houses, Minerva Houses: Up to 45 students live in each of seven distinct houses. All students and faculty members have house affiliations. Each house contributes intellectual, cultural, and social events to the campus. On-campus housing is available on a lottery system for upperclassmen. Upperclassmen may keep cars.

Activities: Groups on campus include art, band, cheerleading, chess, choir, computers, dance, debate, drama, environmental, ethnic, gay, honors, international, jazz band, literary magazine, newspaper, orchestra, pep band, photography, political, professional, radio and TV, religious, social, social service, and student government. Popular campus events include Spring Fest, lectures and concerts.

Sports: Facilities include a field house for volleyball, recreational basketball, indoor track, and intramural activities, 2 synthetic grass fields for soccer, football, field hockey, lacrosse, intramurals, and recreation, basketball/volleyball facility, an ice rink, a gym, that includes a weight room, a fitness center, racquetball/squash courts, aerobics room, and swimming pool, 8 outdoor tennis courts, an outdoor basketball/street hockey court, and boathouse and docks.

Disabled Students: 80% of the campus is accessible. Facilities include wheelchair ramps, elevators, special parking, specially equipped restrooms, special class scheduling, lowered drinking fountains, lowered telephones, and special housing.

Services: Counseling and information services are available, as is tutoring in most subjects, science and math. A writing center and a language center are available.

Campus Safety and Security: Measures include 24-hour foot and vehicle patrol, emergency notification system, self-defense education, and security escort services. There are shuttle buses, emergency telephones, lighted pathways/sidewalks, controlled access to dorms/residences, 24-hour locked residence halls, emergency medical assistance, awareness programs, a bicycle patrol, a trolley escort service, a shuttle van, and a security measures sheet.

Programs of Study: Union confers B.A., and B.S degrees. Bachelor's degrees are awarded in AGRICULTURE (environmental studies), BIOLOGICAL SCIENCE (biochemistry, biology/biological science, and neurosciences), COMMUNICATIONS AND THE ARTS (classics, English, fine arts, modern language, and studio art), COMPUTER AND PHYSICAL

SCIENCE (astronomy, chemistry, computer science, geology, mathematics, physics, and science), ENGINEERING AND ENVIRONMENTAL DESIGN (bioengineering, computer engineering, electrical/electronics engineering, environmental science, and mechanical engineering), SOCIAL SCIENCE (American studies, anthropology, Asian/Oriental studies, Caribbean studies, economics, French studies, German area studies, history, humanities, interdisciplinary studies, liberal arts/general studies, philosophy, political science/government, psychology, religion, social science, sociology, Spanish studies, and women's studies). Chemistry, geology, classics, and philosophy are the strongest academically.

Required: Students must complete a minimum of 36 term courses (engineering may require up to 40), requirements in the major field, degree program, or interdepartmental major, including the major field examination and/or thesis, as applicable, and attain a minimum GPA of 1.8 and 2.0 in the major (2.0 in the minor if a minor has been declared).

Special: Cross-registration is permitted with the Hudson Mohawk Consortium. Opportunities are provided for legislative internships in Albany and Washington, D.C., pass/fail options, B.A.-B.S. degrees, dual and student-designed majors, accelerated degree programs in law and medicine, and study abroad in 38 countries. There are 15 national honor societies, including Phi Beta Kappa, a freshman honors program, and 19 departmental honors programs.

Faculty/Classroom: No introductory courses are taught by graduate students.

Admissions: The SAT scores for the 2013-2014 freshman class were: Critical Reading--3% below 500, 25% between 500 and 599, 54% between 600 and 699, and 18% between 700 and 800; Math--12% between 500 and 599, 49% between 600 and 699, and 38% between 700 and 800; Writing--25% between 500 and 599, 54% between 600 and 699, and 21% between 700 and 800.

Requirements: Testing is optional except for combined programs. Leadership in Medicine program applicants must submit the SAT I and SAT II or the ACT; Law and Public Policy program applicants must submit the SAT I or the ACT. Applicants to these programs must complete the necessary tests no later than December of the senior year. International students are required to submit the SAT or the ACT, and the TOEFL or IELTS if English is not the first language. Applicants must submit a minimum of 16 full-year credits, distributed as follows: 4 years of English, 2 of a foreign language, 2 1/2 to 3 1/2 years of math, 2 years each of science and social studies, and the remainder in college-preparatory courses. Engineering and math majors are expected to have completed additional math and science courses beyond the minimum requirements. An essay is also required and an interview is recommended. AP credits are accepted. Important factors in the admissions decision are advanced placement or honors courses, extracurricular activities record, and recommendations by school officials.

Procedure: Freshmen are admitted fall, winter, and spring. Entrance exams should be taken by January of the senior year. There are early decision, early admissions, and deferred admissions plans. Early decision applications should be filed by November 15; regular applications, by January 15 for fall entry. Notification of early decision is sent December 15; regular decision, April 1. 259 early decision candidates were accepted for the 2013-2014 class. 851 applicants were on the 2013 waiting list; 18 were admitted. Applications are accepted online.

Transfer: 22 transfer students enrolled in 2012-2013. A 3.0 GPA and 1 full year of college academic work are required. Transfer students must study at Union for at least 2 years. 18 of 36 credits required for the bachelor's degree must be completed at Union.

Visiting: There are regularly scheduled orientations for prospective students, including interviews and a tour of the campus. There are guides for informal visits and visitors may sit in on classes. To schedule a visit, contact the Admissions Office, Grant Hall at (518) 388-6112.

Financial Aid: The average freshman award was $39,353. Need-based scholarships or need-based grants averaged $34,489; need-based self-help aid (loans and jobs) averaged $48,097; and other non-need-based awards and non-need-based scholarships averaged $3,694. Union is a member of CSS. The CSS/Profile, FAFSA, the state aid form, and noncustodial profile are required. The deadline for filing freshman financial aid applications for fall entry is February 1.

International Students: The school actively recruits these students. They must take the TOEFL. International students are required to submit the SAT or ACT.

Computers: All students may access the system at any time. There are no time limits and no fees.

Graduates: From July 1, 2012 to June 30, 2013, 539 bachelor's degrees were awarded. The most popular majors were biology (10%), psychology (10%), and political science (8%). 82 companies recruited on campus in 2012-2013. In an average class, 76% graduate in 4 years or less, 82% graduate in 5 years or less, and 83% graduate in 6 years or less. Of the 2012 graduating class, 30% were enrolled in graduate school within 6 months of graduation, and 60% were employed.

Admissions Contact: Ann Fleming Brown, Director of Admission. E-Mail: *admissions@union.edu* Web: *www.union.edu*

UNITED STATES MERCHANT MARINE ACADEMY — D-5

Kings Point, NY 11024 (516) 726-5641
(866) 546-4778; (516) 773-5390

Full-time: 851 men, 136 women — **Faculty:** 120
Part-time: n/av — **Ph.D.s:** 34%
Graduate: 23 men, 2 women — **Student/Faculty:** 11 to 1
Year: trimesters — **Tuition:** see profile
Application Deadline: March 1 — **Room & Board:** n/app
Freshman Class: 2252 applied, 354 accepted, 237 enrolled
SAT CR/M: 614/643 — **ACT:** required
HIGHLY COMPETITIVE+

The United States Merchant Marine Academy, founded in 1943, is a publicly supported institution offering maritime, military, and engineering programs for the purpose of training officers for the U.S. merchant marine, the maritime industry, and the armed forces. Students make no conventional tuition and room/board payments. Required fees for freshmen are approximately $7,020; costs in subsequent years are less. In addition to regional accreditation, Kings Point has baccalaureate program accreditation with ABET. The library contains 209,217 volumes, 21,306 microform items, and 4,750 audio/video tapes/CDs/DVDs, and subscribes to 573 periodicals including electronic. Computerized library services include interlibrary loans, database searching, Internet access, and Wi-Fi capability. Special learning facilities include a planetarium, a maritime museum. The 82-acre campus is in a suburban area 19 miles east of midtown New York City. Including any residence halls, there are 28 buildings.

Student Life: 88% of undergraduates are from out of state, mostly the Middle Atlantic. Students are from 50 states, and 2 foreign countries. 77% are from public schools. 84% are White. 48% are Catholic; 42% Protestant. The average age of freshmen is 19; all undergraduates, 21. 8% do not continue beyond their first year; 92% remain to graduate.

Housing: 930 students can be accommodated in college housing, which includes coed dorms. On-campus housing is guaranteed for all 4 years. Alcohol is not permitted. Upperclassmen may keep cars.

Activities: There are no fraternities or sororities. There are 51 groups on campus, including band, choir, chorus, computers, dance, debate, drill team, drum and bugle corps, ethnic, marching band, newspaper, pep band, photography, professional, religious, and student government. Popular campus events include Regimental Thanksgiving and Holiday Dinners, Battle Standard Dinner, Lanier Lecture Dinners, Ring Dance, Festival of Lights, Holiday Dance, Valentines Dance and Midshipman Appreciation Day.

Sports: There are 14 intercollegiate sports for men and 9 for women, and 10 intramural sports for men and 10 for women. Facilities include a gymnasium with a swimming pool, basketball and racquetball courts and outdoor track and football field.

Disabled Students: 5% of the campus is accessible. Facilities include wheelchair ramps, elevators, special parking, and specially equipped restrooms.

Services: Counseling and information services are available, as is tutoring in most subjects.

Campus Safety and Security: Measures include 24-hour foot and vehicle patrol. There are lighted pathways/sidewalks.

Programs of Study: Kings Point confers B.S. degrees. Master's degrees are also awarded. Bachelor's degrees are awarded in ENGINEERING AND ENVIRONMENTAL DESIGN (marine engineering, marine engineering/shipyard management, marine engineering systems, marine transportation, and maritime logistics & security). Marine engineering systems is the strongest academically and have the largest enrollments.

Required: To graduate, students must complete a minimum of 163 credit hours according to the new curriculum with a minimum cumulative and major GPA of 2.0. The required curriculum includes courses in math, science, computer science, English, humanities, history, naval science, phys ed, and ship's medicine. Students must complete one year of sea service on U.S flag merchant ships. All students must pass resident and sea project courses, U.S. Coast Guard licensing exam and all required certificates, and the academy physical fitness test. Students must apply for and accept, if offered, a commission in the U.S. uniformed services.

Special: The college offers internships in the maritime industry and work-study programs with U.S. shipping companies.

Faculty/Classroom: 87% of faculty are male; 13% are female. All teach undergraduates, and 25% do both. No introductory courses are taught by graduate students. The average class size in an introductory lecture is 28; in a laboratory is 16; and in a regular course is 28.

Admissions: 16% of the 2013-2014 applicants were accepted. The SAT scores for the 2013-2014 freshman class were: Critical Reading--4% below 500, 40% between 500 and 599, 45% between 600 and 699, and 11% between 700 and 800; Math--15% between 500 and 599, 66% between 600 and 699, and 19% between 700 and 800. The ACT scores were 2% between 21 and 23, 35% between 24 and 26, 35% between 27 and 28, and 28% above 28. 57% of the current freshmen were in the top fifth of their class; 38% were in the top two fifths. There were 13 National Merit finalists. 4 freshmen graduated first in their class.

Requirements: The SAT or ACT is required. Candidates for admission to the academy must be nominated by a member of the U.S. Congress. They must be between the ages of 17 and 25, U.S. citizens (except by special arrangement), and in excellent physical condition. Applicants should be graduates of an accredited secondary school or have a GED equivalent. 18 academic credits are required, including 4 in English, 3 in math, 1 credit in physics or chemistry with a lab, and 10 in electives. An essay is required. AP credits are accepted. Important factors in the admissions decision are advanced placement or honors courses, leadership record, and extracurricular activities record.

Procedure: Freshmen are admitted fall. Entrance exams should be taken SATs must be taken through January. ACTs through February. There is a rolling admissions plan. Applications should be filed by March 1 for fall entry. Notifications are sent April 1. 263 applicants were on the 2013 waiting list. Applications are accepted online.

Transfer: College-level applicants must submit college transcipts (and must have at least a 2.5 cumulative GPA in college level work), and must submit two (2) letters of recommendation from college instructors/ professors. 172 of 172 credits required for the bachelor's degree must be completed at Kings Point.

Visiting: There are guides for informal visits, visitors may sit in on classes, and stay overnight. To schedule a visit, contact the Admissions Office.

Financial Aid: In 2013-2014, 14% of all full-time freshmen and 11% of continuing full-time students received some form of financial aid. 9% of all full-time freshmen and 7% of continuing full-time students received need-based aid. The average freshman award was $4,187. Need-based scholarships or need-based grants averaged $4,071 ($5,550 maximum); need-based self-help aid (loans and jobs) averaged $1,916 ($2,673 maximum); and other non-need-based awards and non-need-based scholarships averaged $3,420 ($5,446 maximum). The FAFSA is required. The deadline for filing freshman financial aid applications for fall entry is May 1.

International Students: There are 15 international students enrolled. They must take the TOEFL with a minimum score of 540 on the paper-based TOEFL (PBT) or 76 on the Internet-based version (iBT). They must also take the SAT or ACT.

Computers: All students may access the system 24 hours per day. There are no time limits and no fees.

Graduates: From July 1, 2012 to June 30, 2013, 201 bachelor's degrees were awarded. The most popular majors were marine engineering (23%), marine transportation (22%), and logistics and intermodal transportation (21%). 78 companies recruited on campus in 2012-2013. In an average class, 77% graduate in 4 years or less and 83% graduate in 5 years or less. Of the 2012 graduating class, 100% were employed within 6 months of graduation.

Admissions Contact: CPT. Robert E. Johnson, Director of Admissions and Financial Aid. E-Mail: *admissions@usmma.edu* Web: *www.usmma.edu*

UNITED STATES MILITARY ACADEMY — D-4

West Point, NY 10996 (845) 938-4041; (845) 938-8121

Full-time: 3540 men, 645 women	**Faculty:** n/av
Part-time: n/av	**Ph.D.s:** 39%
Graduate: n/av	**Student/Faculty:** n/av
Year: semesters, summer session	**Tuition:** see profile
Application Deadline: see profile	**Room & Board:** see profile
Freshman Class: n/av	
SAT or ACT: required	

MOST COMPETITIVE

The United States Military Academy, founded in 1802, offers military, engineering, and comprehensive arts and sciences programs leading to a bachelor's degree and a commission as a second lieutenant in the U.S. Army, with a 5-year active duty service obligation. All students receive free tuition and room and board as well as an annual salary of $10,148. An initial deposit of $2900 is required. Figures in this profile are approximate. In addition to regional accreditation, West Point has baccalaureate program accreditation with ABET. The library contains 442,169 volumes, 748,443 microform items, and 12,378 audio/video tapes/CDs/DVDs, and subscribes to 1,963 periodicals including electronic. Computerized library services include interlibrary loans and database searching. Special learning facilities include a learning resource center, art gallery, radio station, TV station, and military museum. Cadets may conduct research in conjunction with the academic departments through the Operations Research Center, the Photonics Research Center, the Mechanical Engineering Research Center, and the Office of Artificial Intelligence, Analysis, and Evaluation. There is also a visiting artist program featuring painting, sculpture, and photography. The 16,080-acre campus is in a small town 56 miles north of New York City. Including any residence halls, there are 902 buildings.

Student Life: 92% of undergraduates are from out of state, mostly the Northeast. Students are from 50 states and 19 foreign countries. 81% are from public schools. 81% are white. 49% are Protestant; 33% Catholic; 15% claim no religious affiliation. The average age of freshmen is 18; all undergraduates, 20. 8% do not continue beyond their first year; 82% remain to graduate.

Housing: 4500 students can be accommodated in college housing. All cadets live in cadet barracks. On-campus housing is guaranteed for all 4 years. Upperclassmen may keep cars.

Activities: There are no fraternities or sororities. There are 105 groups on campus, including art, astronomy, bagpipe, band, cheerleading, chess, choir, chorale, chorus, computers, dance, debate, debate, drama, drill team, drum and bugle corps, ethnic, film, flying, forensics, honors, international, language, literary magazine, marching band, musical theater, newspaper, pep band, photography, professional, radio and TV, religious, social, social service, student government, and yearbook. Popular campus events include Ring Weekend, 100th Night for Seniors, 500th Night for Juniors, and Plebe-Parent Weekend for Freshmen.

Sports: There are 15 intercollegiate sports for men and 9 for women, and 18 intramural sports for men and 14 for women. Facilities include a 40,000-seat football stadium, baseball fields, a 2500-seat hockey rink, a 5000-seat basketball arena, a gymnasium with 5 gyms for squash, handball, tennis, and racquetball, 3 swimming pools, and workout areas, a field house, indoor/outdoor tracks, a golf course, a ski slope, and hunting, fishing, and boating facilities.

Disabled Students: Facilities include wheelchair ramps, elevators, special parking, specially equipped restrooms, lowered drinking fountains, and lowered telephones.

Services: Counseling and information services are available, as is tutoring in every subject. The Center for Enhanced Performance offers 2 courses that provide cadets an opportunity to learn and enhance reading, study, and mental skills.

Campus Safety and Security: Measures include 24-hour foot and vehicle patrol and self-defense education. There are shuttle buses and lighted pathways/sidewalks.

Programs of Study: West Point confers B.S. degrees. Bachelor's degrees are awarded in BIOLOGICAL SCIENCE (life science), BUSINESS (management science and operations research), COMMUNICATIONS AND THE ARTS (languages and literature), COMPUTER AND PHYSICAL SCIENCE (chemistry, computer science, mathematics, and physics), ENGINEERING AND ENVIRONMENTAL DESIGN (civil engineering, electrical/electronics engineering, engineering management, engineering physics, environmental engineering, mechanical engineering, military science, nuclear engineering, and systems engineering), SOCIAL SCIENCE (behavioral science, economics, geography, history, international studies, law, philosophy, and political science/government). Engineering, behavioral sciences, and history have the largest enrollments.

Required: All cadets must complete a core of 31 courses and 9 academic electives pertinent to their field of study. The major requires an additional 1 to 3 electives to the field. In addition, all cadets must complete 4 courses each in phys ed and military science and a senior thesis or design project in the major. A total of 140 credits, including 127 academic, 6 military, and 7 physical, with at least a C average, are required to graduate.

Special: Junior and senior cadets may participate in 3-week summer educational experiences, including Operations Crossroads Africa, research work in technical areas throughout the country, medical internships at Walter Reed Medical Center, workfellow positions with federal and Department of Defense agencies, language training in foreign countries, and study at other military and civilian institutions. There are 7 national honor societies, including Phi Beta Kappa, a freshman honors program, and 5 departmental honors programs.

Faculty/Classroom: 88% of faculty are male; 12% are female. 40% do research, and 40% do both. No introductory courses are taught by graduate students. The average class size in an introductory lecture is 15, in a laboratory, 15, and in a regular course, 15.

Requirements: The SAT or ACT is required. Applicants must be qualified academically, physically, and medically. Candidates must be nominated for admission by members of the U.S. Congress or executive sources. West Point recommends that applicants have 4 years each of English and math, 2 years each of foreign language and lab science, such as chemistry and physics, and 1 year of U.S. history. Courses in geography, government, and economics are also suggested. An essay is required, and an interview is recommended. The GED is accepted. Applicants must be 17 to 22 years old, a U.S. citizen at the time of enrollment (except by agreement with another country), unmarried, and not pregnant or legally obligated to support children. AP credits are accepted. Important factors in the admissions decision are leadership record, extracurricular activities record, and recommendations by school officials.

Procedure: Freshmen are admitted summer. Entrance exams should be taken in the spring of the junior year and not later than the fall of the senior year. There are early decision, early admissions and rolling admissions plans. Check with the school for current application deadlines. A waiting list is maintained.

Transfer: All applicants must enter as freshmen. 140 of 140 credits required for the bachelor's degree must be completed at West Point.

Visiting: There are regularly scheduled orientations for prospective stu-

dents. Candidates will be escorted by a cadet, attend class, have lunch with the Corps of Cadets, and talk with cadets about all phases of West Point life. There are guides for informal visits; visitors may sit in on classes and stay overnight. To schedule a visit, contact the Admissions Office.

Financial Aid: Check with the school for current application deadlines.

International Students: They must take the TOEFL. They must also take the SAT or ACT.

Computers: All students may access the system 24 hours daily. There are no time limits and no fees. All students are required to have a personal computer.

Admissions Contact: Colonel Michael L. Jones, Director of Admissions. A campus DVD is available. E-Mail: *admissions@usma.edu* Web: *www.usma.edu*

UNIVERSITY AT ALBANY / SUNY — D-3

Albany, NY 12222 — **(518) 956-8220; (518) 442-5383**

Full-time: 6177 men, 5791 women	**Faculty:** 701; I, av$
Part-time: 322 men, 252 women	**Ph.D.s:** 95%
Graduate: 1755 men, 2761 women	**Student/Faculty:** 17 to 1
Year: semesters, summer session	**Tuition:** $8040 ($18,360)
Application Deadline: August 1	**Room & Board:** $10,634
Freshman Class: 21591 applied, 12028 accepted, 2560 enrolled	
SAT CR/M: 540/560	**ACT:** 24 **VERY COMPETITIVE**

The State University of New York/University at Albany, established in 1844, is a public institution conferring undergraduate and graduate degrees in humanities and fine arts, science and math, social and behavioral sciences, business, public policy, education, and social welfare. There are 8 undergraduate schools and 9 graduate schools. In addition to regional accreditation, University at Albany has baccalaureate program accreditation with AACSB, CSWE, and TEAC. The 3 libraries contain 2.2 million volumes, 2.9 million microform items, and 13,718 audio/video tapes/CDs/DVDs, and subscribe to 75,570 periodicals including electronic. Computerized library services include interlibrary loans, database searching, Internet access, and Wi-Fi capability. Special learning facilities include an art gallery, radio station, linear accelerator, sophisticated weather data system, national lightning detection system, interactive media center, extensive art studios, state-of-the-art electronic library, and the Northeast Regional Forensic Institute (NERFI). The 560-acre campus is in a suburban area about 5 miles west of downtown Albany. Including any residence halls, there are 185 buildings.

Student Life: 95% of undergraduates are from New York. Others are from 37 states, 54 foreign countries, and Canada. 58% are White; 11% African American; 11% Hispanic. The average age of freshmen is 18; all undergraduates, 21. 16% do not continue beyond their first year; 65% remain to graduate.

Housing: 7900 students can be accommodated in college housing, which includes coed dorms, on-campus apartments, and married student housing. In addition, there are honors houses, language houses, and special-interest houses. On-campus housing is available on a first-come, first-served basis, and is available on a lottery system for upperclassmen. Priority is given to out-of-town students. 61% of students live on campus. Alcohol is not permitted. Upperclassmen may keep cars.

Activities: 4% of men belong to 18 national fraternities; 4% of women belong to 1 local and 18 national sororities. There are 209 groups on campus, including chamber singers, percussion ensemble, art, band, cheerleading, chess, chorale, chorus, computers, dance, debate, drama, electronic music ensemble, environmental, ethnic, film, gay, honors, international, jazz band, literary magazine, marching band, musical theater, newspaper, orchestra, pep band, photography, political, professional, radio and TV, religious, social, social service, student government, symphony, and yearbook. Popular campus events include Relay for Life and New York State Writer's Series.

Sports: There are 8 intercollegiate sports for men and 11 for women, and 8 intramural sports for men and 8 for women. Facilities include a gym with an olympic-size pool, an ancillary gym with a quarter-mile track, football stadium, softball, soccer, and practice fields, an all-weather lacrosse field, and a 5000-seat recreation and convocation center.

Disabled Students: 99% of the campus is accessible. Facilities include wheelchair ramps, elevators, special parking, specially equipped restrooms, lowered drinking fountains, lowered telephones. disabled student services provides a broad range of personalized services to people with disabilities, including preadmission information and accessible housing information.

Services: Counseling and information services are available, as is tutoring in most subjects. There is a reader service for the blind. The Excel program provides low-income and first-generation college students with a variety of mentoring, tutorial, and counseling services.

Campus Safety and Security: Measures include 24-hour foot and vehicle patrol, emergency notification system, self-defense education, and security escort services. There are shuttle buses, emergency telephones, lighted pathways/sidewalks, controlled access to dorms/residences, 5-Quad ambulance service.

Programs of Study: University at Albany confers B.A., and B.S. degrees. Master's and doctoral degrees are also awarded. Bachelor's degrees are awarded in AGRICULTURE (environmental studies), BIOLOGICAL SCIENCE (biochemistry, biology/biological science, and molecular biology), BUSINESS (accounting and business administration and management), COMMUNICATIONS AND THE ARTS (art history and appreciation, Chinese, communications, English, fine arts, linguistics, music, Spanish, and studio art), COMPUTER AND PHYSICAL SCIENCE (actuarial science, applied mathematics, atmospheric sciences and meteorology, chemistry, computer science, earth science, information sciences and systems, mathematics, and physics), ENGINEERING AND ENVIRONMENTAL DESIGN (materials engineering, materials science, and urban design), HEALTH PROFESSIONS (predentistry and premedicine), SOCIAL SCIENCE (African American studies, anthropology, Asian/Oriental studies, Caribbean studies, criminal justice, East Asian studies, economics, geography, Hispanic American studies, history, interdisciplinary studies, Latin American studies, medieval studies, philosophy, political science/government, prelaw, psychology, religion, social work, sociology, and women's studies). Criminal justice, accounting, public administration and policy are the strongest academically. Business, psychology, communication and rhetoric have the largest enrollments.

Required: To graduate, students must complete a total of 120 credits with a 2.0 GPA in their major and minor, including 30 to 36 credits required in the major for a B.A. degree and 30 to 42 credits for a B.S. degree. B.A. degree candidates must complete 90 credits in liberal arts courses and B.S. candidates must complete 60. The general education program at the University at Albany consists of a minimum of 30 credits of course work in the following areas: disciplinary perspectives, cultural and historical perspectives, and communication and reasoning competencies.

Special: Cross-registration is available with Rensselaer Polytechnic Institute, Albany Law School, and Union, Siena, and Russell Sage Colleges. Internships may be arranged with state government agencies and private organizations. Study abroad in many countries, a Washington semester, B.A.-B.S. degrees, and work-study programs are offered. Dual and student-designed majors, nondegree study, and pass/fail grading options are available. There are accelerated 5-year bachelor's/master's programs in 40 fields; most arts and sciences fields may be combined with an accelerated M.B.A. A 3-2 engineering degree with 1 of 4 institutions is also possible. There are 15 national honor societies, including Phi Beta Kappa, a freshman honors program, and 30 departmental honors programs.

Faculty/Classroom: 59% of faculty are male; 41% are female. 96% teach undergraduates, and 76% do research. Graduate students teach 13% of introductory courses. The average class size in an introductory lecture is 31; in a laboratory is 15; and in a regular course is 22.

Admissions: 56% of the 2013-2014 applicants were accepted. The SAT scores for the 2013-2014 freshman class were: Critical Reading--25% below 500, 59% between 500 and 599, 15% between 600 and 699, and 2% between 700 and 800; Math--16% below 500, 54% between 500 and 599, 26% between 600 and 699, and 4% between 700 and 800. The ACT scores were 8% below 21, 33% between 21 and 23, 35% between 24 and 26, 14% between 27 and 28, and 10% above 28.

Requirements: The SAT or ACT is required. Applicants must be graduates of an accredited secondary school or have a GED. 18 academic credits are required, including 2 to 3 units of math, 2 units of lab sciences, and 1 unit of foreign language study. Either SAT or ACT required. AP and CLEP credits are accepted. Important factors in the admissions decision are advanced placement or honors courses, personality/intangible qualities, and leadership record.

Procedure: Freshmen are admitted fall, spring, and summer. Entrance exams should be taken by November of the senior year. There are early decision, deferred admissions, and rolling admissions plans. Early decision applications should be filed by November 15; regular applications, by August 1 for fall entry; December 1 for spring entry; and April 1 for summer entry, along with a $50 fee. Notification of early decision is sent January 1; regular decision. Applications are accepted online.

Transfer: 1387 transfer students enrolled in 2012-2013. Admission to certain programs is competitive and based not only on a required GPA but also on completion of a certain set of prerequisite core courses. A grade average of B or better is required for applicants to the accounting, business administration, criminal justice, and social welfare programs. 30 of 120 credits required for the bachelor's degree must be completed at University at Albany.

Visiting: There are regularly scheduled orientations for prospective students, including a 2-day summer orientation session. There are guides for informal visits and visitors may sit in on classes. To schedule a visit, contact the Undergraduate Admissions Office.

Financial Aid: In 2013-2014, 62% of all full-time freshmen and 63% of continuing full-time students received some form of financial aid. 62% of all full-time freshmen and 63% of continuing full-time students received need-based aid. The average freshman award was $9,925. Need-based scholarships or need-based grants averaged $6,988; need-based self-help aid (loans and jobs) averaged $4,069; non-need-based athletic scholarships averaged $11,201; and other non-need-based awards and non-need-based scholarships averaged $3,097. 9% of undergraduate students work part-time. The FAFSA is required. The priority date for freshman financial aid applications for fall entry is March 15.

International Students: There are 615 international students enrolled. The school actively recruits these students. They must take the TOEFL with a minimum score of 550 on the paper-based TOEFL (PBT) or 79 on the Internet-based version (iBT). They must also take the SAT or ACT.

Computers: All students may access the system. There are no time limits and no fees.

Graduates: From July 1, 2012 to June 30, 2013, 2944 bachelor's degrees were awarded. The most popular majors were English (13%), business (11%), and psychology (11%). 140 companies recruited on campus in 2012-2013. In an average class, 53% graduate in 4 years or less, 64% graduate in 5 years or less, and 65% graduate in 6 years or less.

Admissions Contact: Timothy Lee, Director of Undergraduate Admissions. E-Mail: *ugadmissions@albany.edu* Web: *www.albany.edu*

UNIVERSITY AT BUFFALO / THE STATE UNIVERSITY OF NEW YORK A-3

Buffalo, NY 14214 **(716) 645-6900**
(888) UB-ADMIT; (716) 645-6411

Full-time: 9785 men, 8118 women	**Faculty:** n/av; I, av$
Part-time: 780 men, 822 women	**Ph.D.s:** 96%
Graduate: 4622 men, 4825 women	**Student/Faculty:** n/av
Year: semesters, summer session	**Tuition:** $8426 ($20,366)
Application Deadline:	**Room & Board:** $11,857
Freshman Class: 23207 applied, 13134 accepted	
SAT CR/M: 550/601	**ACT:** 26 **VERY COMPETITIVE**

The University at Buffalo, State University of New York, established in 1846, is a public institution offering more than 300 bachelor's, master's, and doctoral degree programs. UB is a comprehensive research-extensive university and the largest in the 64-campus State University of New York system. There are 8 undergraduate schools and 12 graduate schools. In addition to regional accreditation, UB has baccalaureate program accreditation with AACSB, ABET, ACPE, ADA, APTA, CSWE, NAAB, and NASAD. The 11 libraries contain 4.2 million volumes, 6.2 million microform items, and 283,577 audio/video tapes/CDs/DVDs. Computerized library services include interlibrary loans, database searching, Internet access, and Wi-Fi capability. Special learning facilities include an art gallery, radio station, TV station, an earthquake engineering research center, an arts center, a bio-informatics and life sciences center, a document analysis and recognition center, a concert hall, an anthropology research center, a computational research center, a poetry and rare books collection, a virtual site museum, center for engineering design and industrial innovation, an electronic poetry center, an archeological center, a pharmacy museum, and a clinical and translational research center. The 1350-acre campus is in a suburban area 3 miles north of Buffalo. Including any residence halls, there are 181 buildings.

Student Life: 86% of undergraduates are from New York. Others are from 46 states, 80 foreign countries, and Canada. 52% are White; 16% Foreign; 12% Asian American. The average age of freshmen is 18; all undergraduates, 21. 13% do not continue beyond their first year; 70% remain to graduate.

Housing: 7019 students can be accommodated in college housing, which includes coed dorms, on-campus apartments, and married student housing. In addition, there are honors houses, special-interest houses, freshmen-only housing and cultural interest housing. On-campus housing is guaranteed for all 4 years, is guaranteed for the freshman year only, is available on a first-come, first-served basis, and is available on a lottery system for upperclassmen. 65% of students commute. All students may keep cars.

Activities: 2% of men belong to 2 local and 22 national fraternities; 2% of women belong to 16 national sororities. There are 250 groups on campus, including art, band, cheerleading, chess, choir, chorale, chorus, computers, dance, debate, drama, drill team, environmental, ethnic, film, gay, honors, international, jazz band, literary magazine, marching band, musical theater, newspaper, orchestra, pep band, photography, political, professional, radio and TV, religious, social, social service, student government, and symphony. Popular campus events include Homecoming, Family Weekend and Fallfest.

Sports: There are 9 intercollegiate sports for men and 9 for women, and 8 intramural sports for men and 8 for women. Facilities include racquetball, squash, tennis, basketball, volleyball, badminton, and handball courts, baseball, soccer, hockey, and multipurpose fields, a football and track and field stadium, an indoor jogging track; an Olympic-size pool and diving well; a triple gym; weight training and wrestling rooms; dance studios; and a spinning room.

Disabled Students: 90% of the campus is accessible. Facilities include wheelchair ramps, elevators, special parking, specially equipped restrooms, special class scheduling, lowered drinking fountains, lowered telephones, special housing.

Services: Counseling and information services are available, as is tutoring in most subjects. There is a reader service for the blind, and remedial math, reading, and writing. Peer tutoring and some computer-assisted instruction are also available.

Campus Safety and Security: Measures include 24-hour foot and vehicle patrol, emergency notification system, self-defense education, and security escort services. There are shuttle buses, emergency telephones, lighted pathways/sidewalks, controlled access to dorms/residences, an alarm system, routine patrols, student aides in residence halls, some security cameras, blue-light phones, and a university-wide safety committee.

Programs of Study: UB confers B.A., B.S., B.F.A. and Mus.B. degrees. Master's and doctoral degrees are also awarded. Bachelor's degrees are awarded in AGRICULTURE (environmental studies), BIOLOGICAL SCIENCE (biochemistry, bioinformatics, biology/biological science, and biotechnology), BUSINESS (business administration and management), COMMUNICATIONS AND THE ARTS (art, art history and appreciation, classics, communications, dance, English, film arts, French, German, Italian, linguistics, media arts, music, musical theater, Spanish, studio art, and theatre arts), COMPUTER AND PHYSICAL SCIENCE (chemistry, computer science, geology, mathematics, and physics), ENGINEERING AND ENVIRONMENTAL DESIGN (aerospace studies, architecture, biomedical engineering, chemical engineering, civil engineering, computational sciences, computer engineering, electrical/electronics engineering, engineering physics, environmental design, environmental engineering, industrial engineering, and mechanical engineering), HEALTH PROFESSIONS (biomedical science, exercise science, medical technology, nuclear medical technology, nursing, occupational therapy, pharmaceutical science, pharmacology, pharmacy, physical therapy, and speech pathology/audiology), SOCIAL SCIENCE (African American studies, American studies, anthropology, Asian/Oriental studies, cognitive science, economics, geography, history, legal studies, philosophy, political science/government, psychology, social science, sociology, and women's studies). Engineering, business administration, and psychology have the largest enrollments.

Required: To graduate, students must complete 120 semester hours with a minimum GPA of 2.0. General education requirements include writing skills, mathematical sciences, library skills, world civilizations, American pluralism, natural sciences, language, humanities, arts, social and behavioral sciences, and depth requirement. The total number of hours in the major varies.

Special: Students may cross-register with the Western New York Consortium. Internships are available, and students may study abroad in 29 countries. UB offers a Washington semester, work-study programs, accelerated degree programs, B.A.-B.S. degrees, dual, student-designed, and interdisciplinary majors, and credit for military experience. A 3-2 engineering degree can be pursued. Students may choose a successful/unsuccessful (S/U) grading option for selected courses. There is an early assurance of admission program to medical school for undergraduate sophomore students who possess a minimum approximate overall and science GPA of 3.75 and complete particular science courses. There are 34 national honor societies, including Phi Beta Kappa, and a freshman honors program.

Faculty/Classroom: 61% of faculty are male; 39% are female. No introductory courses are taught by graduate students.

Admissions: 57% of the 2013-2014 applicants were accepted. The SAT scores for the 2013-2014 freshman class were: Critical Reading--23% below 500, 50% between 500 and 599, 23% between 600 and 699, and 4% between 700 and 800; Math--8% below 500, 40% between 500 and 599, 40% between 600 and 699, and 12% between 700 and 800.

Requirements: The SAT is required. Freshmen are evaluated based on secondary school performance, strength of curriculum, standardized test scores, and, in some cases, a supplemental application. A high school diploma is required and the GED is accepted. Dance, music theatre, theatre & music applicants must audition. Architecture requires a portfolio. AP and CLEP credits are accepted. Important factors in the admissions decision are advanced placement or honors courses, recommendations by school officials, and evidence of special talent.

Procedure: Freshmen are admitted fall and spring. Entrance exams should be taken during the spring of the junior year or the fall of the senior year. There are early decision and rolling admissions plans. Early decision applications should be filed by November 1. The fall 2013 application fee was $50. Notification of early decision is sent December 15; regular decision, in February. 319 early decision candidates were accepted for the 2013-2014 class. 55 applicants were on the 2013 waiting list; 25 were admitted. Applications are accepted online.

Transfer: 1897 transfer students enrolled in 2012-2013. Transfer applicants with fewer than 24 credit hours must supply high school transcripts, SAT and/or ACT test scores, and the previous college academic record. It is recommended that students present a strong record of college study, with a 2.5 GPA. Entry at junior level requires a higher GPA for some programs. Credit may be awarded for military experience and other nontraditional sources. 30 of 120 credits required for the bachelor's degree must be completed at UB.

Visiting: There are regularly scheduled orientations for prospective students, including the Visit UB program, in which visitors tour the campus and attend an information session to learn about application procedures, admissions criteria, housing, financial aid, and scholarship programs. The program is offered, with some exceptions, Monday through Friday year-round and on selected Saturdays during the academic year. Reservations are required. Visitors may sit in on classes. To schedule a visit, contact the Office of Admissions at ub-admissions@buffalo.edu.

Financial Aid: The average freshman award was $9,505. Need-based scholarships or need-based grants averaged $5,770; need-based self-help aid (loans and jobs) averaged $3,675; non-need-based athletic scholarships averaged $17,420; and other non-need-based awards and non-need-based scholarships averaged $6,025. The FAFSA is required. The priority date for freshman financial aid applications for fall entry is March 1.

International Students: There are 2574 international students enrolled. The school actively recruits these students. They must take the TOEFL with a minimum score of 550 on the paper-based TOEFL (PBT) or 79 on the Internet-based version (iBT). The SAT or ACT is strongly recommended.

Computers: All students may access the system. any time. There are no time limits and no fees.

Graduates: From July 1, 2012 to June 30, 2013, 4496 bachelor's degrees were awarded. The most popular majors were business administration (22%), social sciences (14%), and psychology (12%). 274 companies recruited on campus in 2012-2013. In an average class, 3% graduate in 3 years or less, 44% graduate in 4 years or less, 65% graduate in 5 years or less, and 70% graduate in 6 years or less.

Admissions Contact: Barry Taylor, Director of Admissions. E-Mail: *ubadmissions@buffalo.edu* Web: *www.buffalo.edu*

UNIVERSITY OF ROCHESTER B-3

Rochester, NY 14627 (585) 275-3221
(888) 822-2256; (585) 461-4595

Full-time: 2732 men, 2780 women	**Faculty:** n/av; I, av$
Part-time: 66 men, 207 women	**Ph.D.s:** 88%
Graduate: 2357 men, 2368 women	**Student/Faculty:** 10 to 1
Year: semesters, summer session	**Tuition:** $45,372
Application Deadline: January 1	**Room & Board:** $13,128

Freshman Class: 14987 applied, 5370 accepted, 1228 enrolled

MOST COMPETITIVE

The University of Rochester, founded in 1850, is a private institution offering programs in the arts and sciences, engineering and applied science, nursing, medicine and dentistry, business administration, music, and education. There are 4 undergraduate schools and 7 graduate schools. In addition to regional accreditation, UR has baccalaureate program accreditation with AACSB, ABET, ACPE, ADA, NASM, and NCATE. The 7 libraries contain 4.1 million volumes, 4.7 million microform items, and 137,751 audio/video tapes/CDs/DVDs, and subscribe to 40,879 periodicals including electronic. Computerized library services include interlibrary loans, database searching, and Internet access. Special learning facilities include a learning resource center, art gallery, radio station, Labs for nuclear structure research and laser energetics; a center for visual science; the Strong Memorial Hospital, an art center, an observatory, an institute of optics, a center for electronic imaging systems, and the National Science Foundation Center for Photoinduced Charge Transfer. The 655-acre campus is in a suburban area 2 miles south of downtown Rochester, NY. Including any residence halls, there are 159 buildings.

Student Life: 64% of undergraduates are from out of state, mostly the Middle Atlantic. Students are from 50 states, 73 foreign countries, and Canada. 75% are from public schools. 56% are White; 13% Foreign; 11% Asian American. 37% claim no religious affiliation; 19% Catholic; 13% Jewish. The average age of freshmen is 18; all undergraduates, 20. 4% do not continue beyond their first year; 85% remain to graduate.

Housing: 3709 students can be accommodated in college housing, which includes coed dorms, on-campus apartments, and married student housing. In addition, there are language houses, special-interest houses, and fraternity houses. On-campus housing is guaranteed for the freshman year only and is available on a lottery system for upperclassmen. 83% of students live on campus; of those, 90% remain on campus on weekends. Upperclassmen may keep cars.

Activities: 19% of men belong to 16 national fraternities; 20% of women belong to 15 national sororities. There are 250 groups on campus, including art, band, campus activities board, cheerleading, chess, choir, chorale, chorus, computers, dance, debate, drama, drill team, environmental, ethnic, film, gay, honors, international, jazz band, literary magazine, marching band, musical theater, newspaper, opera, orchestra, pep band, photography, political, professional, radio and TV, religious, social, social service, student government, symphony, and yearbook. Popular campus events include Meliora Weekend, Yellowjacket Day and Boar's Head Dinner.

Sports: There are 11 intercollegiate sports for men and 12 for women, and 7 intramural sports for men and 7 for women. Facilities include an 11,000-square-foot athletic center, a 5,000-seat stadium, a field house, an ice rink, courts for handball, racquetball, squash, and tennis, an indoor track, a fitness center and weight room, a jogging path, and an aquatic center.

Disabled Students: 90% of the campus is accessible. Facilities include wheelchair ramps, elevators, special parking, specially equipped restrooms, special class scheduling, lowered drinking fountains, lowered telephones, and special housing.

Services: Counseling and information services are available, as is tutoring in most subjects. There is access to screen reading and adaptive software.

Campus Safety and Security: Measures include 24-hour foot and vehicle patrol, emergency notification system, self-defense education, and security escort services. There are shuttle buses, emergency telephones, lighted pathways/sidewalks, and controlled access to dorms/residences.

Programs of Study: UR confers B.A., B.S. and B.M. degrees. Master's and doctoral degrees are also awarded. Bachelor's degrees are awarded in AGRICULTURE (environmental studies), BIOLOGICAL SCIENCE (biochemistry, biology/biological science, cell biology, ecology, microbiology, molecular biology, and neurosciences), BUSINESS (business administration and management), COMMUNICATIONS AND THE ARTS (American Sign Language, art history and appreciation, audio technology, classics, comparative literature, English, English literature, film arts, French, German, Japanese, jazz, linguistics, media arts, music, music performance, music theory and composition, Russian, Spanish, studio art, and theatre arts), COMPUTER AND PHYSICAL SCIENCE (applied mathematics, astronomy, chemistry, computer science, geology, mathematics, optics, physics, and statistics), EDUCATION (music education), ENGINEERING AND ENVIRONMENTAL DESIGN (biomedical engineering, chemical engineering, electrical/electronics engineering, engineering and applied science, environmental science, geological engineering, mechanical engineering, and optical engineering), HEALTH PROFESSIONS (health, nursing, and public health), SOCIAL SCIENCE (African American studies, American studies, anthropology, archeology, cognitive science, economics, history, interdisciplinary studies, international relations, philosophy, political science/government, psychology, religion, Russian and Slavic studies, and women's studies). Biomedical engineering, optics, and political science are the strongest academically. Biology, economics, and engineering have the largest enrollments.

Required: Students focus on the humanities, social sciences, and natural sciences; one of the three areas will be their major, and they select a 3-course cluster in each of the other two. A total of 128 credit hours with a minimum GPA of 2.0 is required to graduate. Additionally, all students satisfy a freshman writing requirement and take two upper-level courses in their major that are writing intensive.

Special: Cross-registration is offered with Rochester Area Colleges. Selective programs for exceptional undergraduates in medicine (REMS), engineering (GEAR), and education (GRADE) guarantee admission to professional or graduate school upon completion of the bachelor's degree. The Take Five Scholars Program allows students to stay tuition-free for a fifth year of study. Rochester offers 3-2 programs in business, human development, neuroscience, physics and astronomy, and public health. Study abroad is possible in more than 40 countries. Internships, a Washington semester, B.A.-B.S. degrees, accelerated degree programs, dual and student-designed majors, nondegree study, and pass/fail options are available. There are 8 national honor societies, including Phi Beta Kappa, a freshman honors program, and 13 departmental honors programs.

Faculty/Classroom: 64% of faculty are male; 36% are female. No introductory courses are taught by graduate students. The average class size in an introductory lecture is 75; in a laboratory is 20; and in a regular course is 20.

Admissions: 36% of the 2012-2013 applicants were accepted. The SAT scores for the 2012-2013 freshman class were: Critical Reading--1% below 500, 23% between 500 and 599, 48% between 600 and 699, and 28% between 700 and 800; Math--1% below 500, 11% between 500 and 599, 43% between 600 and 699, and 46% between 700 and 800; Writing--2% below 500, 21% between 500 and 599, 51% between 600 and 699, and 27% between 700 and 800. The ACT scores were 1% between 21 and 23, 9% between 24 and 26, 14% between 27 and 28, and 75% above 28. 86% of the current freshmen were in the top fifth of their class; 97% were in the top two fifths. There were 25 National Merit finalists. 8 freshmen graduated first in their class.

Requirements: The SAT or ACT is recommended. In addition, applicants should be graduates of an accredited secondary school or have a GED equivalent. An essay or personal statement and recommendations are required. An interview is recommended. An audition is required for music majors. Applicants should complete the Common Application. Admission to the College of Arts, Sciences, and Engineering is based on a holistic review process that includes a "test-flexible" philosophy. As we seek to enroll a diverse and talented class each year, our review procedures incorporate a variety of factors, including many kinds of academic records. In addition to submitting a record of courses and grades during secondary school, applicants must show evidence of preparation through examination results. A wide variety of test results can fulfill this countries), Gao Kao (China), and results from many other national secondary exams. AP credits are accepted. Important factors in the admissions decision are advanced placement or honors courses, personality/intangible qualities, and recommendations by school officials.

Procedure: Freshmen are admitted fall and spring. Entrance exams

should be taken by December of the senior year. There are early decision and deferred admissions plans. Early decision applications should be filed by November 1; regular applications, by January 1 for fall entry; and October 1 for spring entry, along with a $70 fee. Notification of early decision is sent December 15; regular decision, April 1. 272 early decision candidates were accepted for the 2012-2013 class. 1630 applicants were on the 2012 waiting list; 56 were admitted. Applications are accepted online.

Transfer: 127 transfer students enrolled in 2011-2012. The most important criterion is an applicant's college record. 64 of 128 credits required for the bachelor's degree must be completed at UR.

Visiting: There are regularly scheduled orientations for prospective students, group information session, campus tour, and interview (optional for seniors). There are guides for informal visits, visitors may sit in on classes, and stay overnight. To schedule a visit, contact the Office of Admissions at (888) 822-2256.

Financial Aid: In 2012-2013, 84% of all full-time freshmen and 83% of continuing full-time students received some form of financial aid. 56% of all full-time freshmen and 55% of continuing full-time students received need-based aid. The average freshman award was $37,988. 60% of undergraduate students work part-time. Average annual earnings from campus work are $2500. The average financial indebtedness of the 2012 graduate was $27,601. UR is a member of CSS. The CSS/Profile, FAFSA, and the state aid form are required. The deadline for filing freshman financial aid applications for fall entry is February 1.

International Students: There are 740 international students enrolled. The school actively recruits these students. They must take the TOEFL with a minimum score of 600 on the paper-based TOEFL (PBT) or 100 on the Internet-based version (iBT). They must also take the SAT or ACT.

Computers: Wireless access is available. There are 572 computers/terminals and 4,000 ports available on campus for general student use. High-speed Internet access is available in the residence halls. Wireless access is available in all academic areas. All students may access the system 24 hours daily. There are no time limits and no fees.

Graduates: From July 1, 2011 to June 30, 2012, 1463 bachelor's degrees were awarded. The most popular majors were psychology (13%), biology/biological sciences (12%), and engineering (10%). 1000 companies recruited on campus in 2011-2012. In an average class, 74% graduate in 4 years or less, 83% graduate in 5 years or less, and 85% graduate in 6 years or less. Of the 2011 graduating class, 31% were enrolled in graduate school within 6 months of graduation, and 56% were employed.

Admissions Contact: Jonathan Burdick, Dean of Admissions and Financial Aid. A campus DVD is available. E-Mail: *admit@admissions.rochester.edu* Web: *www.rochester.edu*

UTICA COLLEGE C-3

Utica, NY 13502 (315) 792-3006
(800) 782-8884; (315) 792-3003

Full-time: 982 men, 1248 women	**Faculty:** 143; IIB, -$
Part-time: 147 men, 504 women	**Ph.D.s:** 85%
Graduate: 466 men, 681 women	**Student/Faculty:** 11 to 1
Year: semesters, summer session	**Tuition:** $32,800
Application Deadline: open	**Room & Board:** $11,934
Freshman Class: n/av	
SAT or ACT: recommended	

COMPETITIVE

Utica College is a private, comprehensive institution founded by Syracuse University in 1946. There are 4 undergraduate schools and one graduate school. In addition to regional accreditation, UC has baccalaureate program accreditation with APTA and NLN. The library contains 145,412 volumes, 34,282 microform items, and 10,260 audio/video tapes/CDs/DVDs, and subscribes to 657 periodicals including electronic. Computerized library services include interlibrary loans, database searching, Internet access, and Wi-Fi capability. Special learning facilities include an art gallery, radio station, TV station, an early childhood education lab, and a math and writing center. The 128-acre campus is in a suburban area 50 miles east of Syracuse. Including any residence halls, there are 18 buildings.

Student Life: 85% of undergraduates are from New York. Others are from 43 states, 19 foreign countries, and Canada. 80% are from public schools. 69% are White. The average age of freshmen is 18; all undergraduates, 21. 29% do not continue beyond their first year; 47% remain to graduate.

Housing: 1046 students can be accommodated in college housing, which includes single-sex and coed dorms. In addition, there are special-interest houses. On-campus housing is guaranteed for all 4 years and is available on a lottery system for upperclassmen. 56% of students commute. All students may keep cars.

Activities: 2% of men belong to 2 local and 3 national fraternities; 2% of women belong to 2 local and 3 national sororities. There are 86 groups on campus, including art, band, cheerleading, chess, choir, chorus, communications, computers, dance, drama, environmental, ethnic, film, gay, honors, international, jazz band, literary magazine, musical theater, newspaper, orchestra, pep band, photography, political, professional, radio and TV, religious, social, social service, student government, and yearbook. Popular campus events include outdoor concerts, mock elections, and winter weekend.

Sports: There are 10 intercollegiate sports for men and 11 for women, and 28 intramural sports for men and 28 for women. Facilities include a 2200-seat gym, a competition-size swimming pool, tennis, racquetball, handball, and squash courts, a sauna, Nautilus and weight rooms, dance and aerobic rooms, playing fields, a stadium, and hockey facilities.

Disabled Students: 85% of the campus is accessible. Facilities include wheelchair ramps, elevators, special parking, specially equipped restrooms, lowered drinking fountains.

Services: Counseling and information services are available, as is tutoring in most subjects. There is a reader service for the blind, and remedial math, reading, and writing.

Campus Safety and Security: Measures include 24-hour foot and vehicle patrol, emergency notification system, and security escort services. There are shuttle buses, emergency telephones, lighted pathways/sidewalks, and controlled access to dorms/residences.

Programs of Study: UC confers B.A., and B.S. degrees. Master's and doctoral degrees are also awarded. Bachelor's degrees are awarded in BIOLOGICAL SCIENCE (biochemistry and biology/biological science), BUSINESS (accounting, business administration and management, business economics, and insurance and risk management), COMMUNICATIONS AND THE ARTS (communications, English, journalism, and public relations), COMPUTER AND PHYSICAL SCIENCE (chemistry, computer science, computer security and information assurance, geoscience, mathematics, and physics), EDUCATION (education and foreign languages education), ENGINEERING AND ENVIRONMENTAL DESIGN (construction management), HEALTH PROFESSIONS (nursing, occupational therapy, physical therapy, and recreation therapy), SOCIAL SCIENCE (child psychology/development, criminal justice, economics, gerontology, history, liberal arts/general studies, philosophy, political science/government, psychology, social studies, and sociology). Occupational therapy, psychology, and biology are the strongest academically. Health studies and criminal justice have the largest enrollments.

Required: To graduate, students must complete a total of 120 to 128 hours with a minimum 2.0 GPA. They must complete a general education requirement including basic skills and distribution requirements.

Special: UC offers co-op programs, internships, work-study programs in all majors, accelerated degrees, dual majors, and cross-registration with Hamilton College and the Mohawk Valley Consortium. Study abroad may be arranged in 9 countries. There is a 3-2 engineering degree with Syracuse University. There are 5 national honor societies and a freshman honors program.

Faculty/Classroom: 49% of faculty are male; 51% are female. All teach and do research. No introductory courses are taught by graduate students. The average class size in an introductory lecture is 23; in a laboratory is 11; and in a regular course is 17.

Requirements: The SAT or ACT and ACT Writing Test are recommended. Graduation from an accredited secondary school or satisfactory scores on the GED are required. Recommended high school courses include 4 years of English, 3 years each of math and social studies, and 2 years each of foreign language and science. An essay and an interview are also recommended. AP and CLEP credits are accepted. Important factors in the admissions decision are advanced placement or honors courses, extracurricular activities record, and leadership record.

Procedure: Freshmen are admitted fall and spring. Entrance exams should be taken during the junior year. There are deferred admissions and rolling admissions plans. Application deadlines are open. Application fee is $40. Notification of early decision is sent December 15; regular decision, on a rolling basis. Applications are accepted online.

Transfer: 174 transfer students enrolled in 2012-2013. Applicants must have a minimum GPA of 2.0. 30 of 128 credits required for the bachelor's degree must be completed at UC.

Visiting: There are regularly scheduled orientations for prospective students, including an interview, financial aid information, and a tour of the campus. There are guides for informal visits, visitors may sit in on classes, and stay overnight. To schedule a visit, contact the Admissions Office at admiss@utica.edu.

Financial Aid: In 2013-2014, 90% of all full-time freshmen and 91% of continuing full-time students received some form of financial aid. 90% of all full-time freshmen and 90% of continuing full-time students received need-based aid. The average freshman award was $29,665. Need-based scholarships or need-based grants averaged $9,740; and need-based self-help aid (loans and jobs) averaged $3,985. Average annual earnings from campus work are $1500. UC is a member of CSS. The FAFSA is required. The priority date for freshman financial aid applications for fall entry is February 15. The deadline for filing freshman financial aid applications for fall entry is April 1.

International Students: There are 88 international students enrolled. The school actively recruits these students. They must take the TOEFL with

a minimum score of 525 on the paper-based TOEFL (PBT) or 69 on the Internet-based version (iBT) and the Comprehensive English Language Test, or take the IELTS, APIEL, or MELAB. The SAT is recommended if the student's primary language is English.

Computers: All students may access the system during posted hours. Time limits are imposed only during peak hours. The fee is $200.

Graduates: From July 1, 2012 to June 30, 2013, 558 bachelor's degrees were awarded. The most popular majors were health studies (36%), criminal justice (21%), and business and marketing (9%). In an average class, 33% graduate in 4 years or less, 45% graduate in 5 years or less, and 47% graduate in 6 years or less.

Admissions Contact: Jeffery Gates, Vice President for Enrollment Management. E-Mail: *admiss@utica.edu* Web: *www.utica.edu*

VASSAR COLLEGE D-4

Poughkeepsie, NY 12604 **(845) 437-7300**
(800) 827-7270; (845) 437-7063

Full-time: 1034 men, 1336 women **Faculty:** 279; IIB, +$
Part-time: 17 men, 19 women **Ph.D.s:** 96%
Graduate: n/av **Student/Faculty:** 9 to 1
Year: semesters **Tuition:** $47,500
Application Deadline: January 1 **Room & Board:** $11,180
Freshman Class: 7908 applied, 1806 accepted, 659 enrolled
SAT CR/M/W: 704/690/700 **ACT:** 31 **MOST COMPETITIVE**

Vassar College, founded in 1861, is a private, independent college of liberal arts and sciences. There is one undergraduate school and one graduate school. The 3 libraries contain 995,578 volumes, 611,076 microform items, and 23,590 audio/video tapes/CDs/DVDs, and subscribe to 4,001 periodicals including electronic. Computerized library services include interlibrary loans, database searching, Internet access, and Wi-Fi capability. Special learning facilities include an art gallery, radio station, studio art building with studios, geological museum, large astronomical observatory, 3 theaters, concert hall, environmental field station, intercultural center, and many teaching and research-oriented lab facilities for natural sciences. The 1000-acre campus is in a suburban area 75 miles north of New York City. Including any residence halls, there are 100 buildings.

Student Life: 73% of undergraduates are from out of state, mostly the Middle Atlantic. Students are from 50 states, 60 foreign countries, and Canada. 60% are from public schools. 62% are White; 11% Hispanic. The average age of freshmen is 18; all undergraduates, 20. 4% do not continue beyond their first year; 92% remain to graduate.

Housing: 2305 students can be accommodated in college housing, which includes single-sex and coed dorms, on-campus apartments, off-campus apartments, and married student housing. There is 1 all-women residence hall and 1 cooperative living unit. On-campus housing is guaranteed for all 4 years. 100% of students live on campus; of those, 90% remain on campus on weekends. All students may keep cars.

Activities: There are no fraternities or sororities. There are 125 groups on campus, including art, band, chess, choir, chorale, chorus, computers, dance, debate, drama, environmental, ethnic, film, gay, honors, international, jazz band, literary magazine, musical theater, newspaper, opera, orchestra, photography, political, radio and TV, religious, social, social service, student government, symphony, and yearbook. Popular campus events include Founders Day, Spring and Fall Formals and All Parents Weekend.

Sports: There are 12 intercollegiate sports for men and 13 for women, and 18 intramural sports for men and 18 for women. Facilities include a field house with a swimming pool, 5 indoor tennis courts, a weight and conditioning room, a gym with squash and racquetball courts and basketball facilities, a 9-hole golf course, 13 outdoor tennis courts, an all-weather track, 2 soccer fields, a baseball diamond, a rugby field, club and intramural fields, a competition basketball gym, a banked running track, and a 5000-square-foot exercise and fitness center.

Disabled Students: 70% of the campus is accessible. Facilities include wheelchair ramps, elevators, special parking, specially equipped restrooms, special class scheduling, lowered drinking fountains. There is an Office of Disability and Support Services, signage in braille, and assisted listening devices.

Services: Counseling and information services are available, as is tutoring in most subjects. There is a reader service for the blind, and remedial math and writing.

Campus Safety and Security: Measures include 24-hour foot and vehicle patrol, emergency notification system, self-defense education, and security escort services. There are shuttle buses, emergency telephones, lighted pathways/sidewalks, and controlled access to dorms/residences.

Programs of Study: Vassar confers B.A. degrees. Master's degrees are also awarded. Bachelor's degrees are awarded in AGRICULTURE (environmental studies), BIOLOGICAL SCIENCE (biochemistry, biology/biological science, and neurosciences), COMMUNICATIONS AND THE ARTS (art, Chinese, dramatic arts, English, film arts, French, German, Germanic languages and literature, Japanese, languages, media arts, music, and Russian languages and literature), COMPUTER AND PHYSICAL SCIENCE (astronomy, chemistry, computer science, earth science, geology, mathematics, and physics), EDUCATION (foreign languages education), ENGINEERING AND ENVIRONMENTAL DESIGN (technology and public affairs), HEALTH PROFESSIONS (premedicine), SOCIAL SCIENCE (African studies, American studies, anthropology, Asian/Oriental studies, biopsychology, classical/ancient civilization, cognitive science, economics, geography, Hispanic American studies, history, international studies, Judaic studies, Latin American studies, medieval studies, philosophy, political science/government, prelaw, psychology, religion, social studies, sociology, Spanish studies, urban studies, Victorian studies, and women's studies). Art, mathematics, English, psychology, biology, economics, and political science have the largest enrollments.

Required: To graduate, students must have a total of 34 units equivalent to 120 credit hours, with a minimum GPA of 2.0. Of this total, no more than 17 units may be in a single field of concentration and 8 1/2 units must be outside the major field. Entering freshmen must take the freshman course. All students must meet the foreign language proficiency requirement and must take a quantitative skills course before their third year. A thesis is required in most departments.

Special: The school offers fieldwork in social agencies and schools, dual majors, independent majors, student-designed majors, cross-registration within the College Consortium, and non-recorded grade options. Vassar runs study-abroad programs in 7 countries and students also study in other approved programs around the world. A 3-2 engineering degree with Dartmouth College is offered.

Faculty/Classroom: 54% of faculty are male; 46% are female. All teach undergraduates, all do research, and all teach and do research. No introductory courses are taught by graduate students. The average class size in an introductory lecture is 21; in a laboratory is 7; and in a regular course is 17.

Admissions: 23% of the 2013-2014 applicants were accepted. The SAT scores for the 2013-2014 freshman class were: Critical Reading--7% between 500 and 599, 35% between 600 and 699, and 58% between 700 and 800; Math--5% between 500 and 599, 48% between 600 and 699, and 47% between 700 and 800; Writing--7% between 500 and 599, 38% between 600 and 699, and 54% between 700 and 800. The ACT scores were 2% between 24 and 26, 11% between 27 and 28, and 87% above 28. 90% of the current freshmen were in the top fifth of their class; 99% were in the top two fifths.

Requirements: The SAT or ACT is required. The ACT Optional Writing test is also required. In addition, 2 SAT Subject tests, or the ACT, are required. Graduation from an accredited secondary school or satisfactory scores on the GED are required for admission. The high school program should typically include 4 years each of English, social studies, math, foreign language, and science. An essay and a writing sample are required. AP credits are accepted. Important factors in the admissions decision are advanced placement or honors courses, recommendations by school officials, and extracurricular activities record.

Procedure: Freshmen are admitted fall. Entrance exams should be taken as early as possible but no later than December of the senior year. There are early decision and deferred admissions plans. Early decision applications should be filed by November 15; regular applications, by January 1 for fall entry, along with a $70 fee. Notification of early decision is sent December 15; regular decision, February 1. 260 early decision candidates were accepted for the 2013-2014 class. 1340 applicants were on the 2013 waiting list; 29 were admitted. Applications are accepted online.

Transfer: 9 transfer students enrolled in 2012-2013. Applicants must have a high level of achievement in both high school and college work. 17 of 34 credits required for the bachelor's degree must be completed at Vassar.

Visiting: There are regularly scheduled orientations for prospective students, including a campus tour, an information session, and a class visit when possible. There are guides for informal visits, visitors may sit in on classes, and stay overnight. To schedule a visit, contact the Admissions Office at (845)437-7300.

Financial Aid: In 2013-2014, 67% of all full-time freshmen and 67% of continuing full-time students received some form of financial aid. 58% of all full-time freshmen and 59% of continuing full-time students received need-based aid. The average freshman award was $45,236. Need-based scholarships or need-based grants averaged $42,101; need-based self-help aid (loans and jobs) averaged $3,135; and other non-need-based awards and non-need-based scholarships averaged $1,630. The average financial indebtedness of the 2013 graduate was $19,000. Vassar is a member of CSS. The CSS/Profile, FAFSA, FFS, and the college's own financial statement are required. Check with the school for current application deadlines.

International Students: There are 168 international students enrolled. The school actively recruits these students. They must take the TOEFL with a minimum score of 100 on the Internet-based version (iBT). They must also take the SAT or ACT.

Computers: All students may access the system 24 hours per day. There are no time limits and no fees.

Graduates: From July 1, 2012 to June 30, 2013, 597 bachelor's degrees

were awarded. The most popular majors were sciences and mathematics (33%), social sciences (16%), and visual and performing arts (16%). In an average class, 90% graduate in 4 years or less, 3% graduate in 5 years or less, and 1% graduate in 6 years or less. Of the 2012 graduating class, 54% were enrolled in graduate school within 6 months of graduation, and 28% were employed.

Admissions Contact: David Borus, Dean of Admission and Financial Aid. E-Mail: *admissions@vassar.edu* Web: *www.vassar.edu*

VAUGHN COLLEGE OF AERONAUTICS AND TECHNOLOGY — D-5

Flushing, NY 11369 — (718) 429-6600 ext 117; (718) 779-2231

Full-time: 1190 men, 172 women — **Faculty:** 41
Part-time: 376 men, 61 women — **Ph.D.s:** 54%
Graduate: 9 men, 4 women — **Student/Faculty:** 33 to 1
Year: semesters, summer session — **Tuition:** $19,460
Application Deadline: open — **Room & Board:** $11,900
Freshman Class: 723 applied, 618 accepted, 321 enrolled
SAT CR/M: 498/547 — **ACT:** 22 — **SPECIAL**

Vaughn College of Aeronautics and Technology, founded in 1932, is a private non-profit institution located in New York City, offering undergraduate and masters degrees in Engineering, Engineering Technology, Management, and Aviation. In addition to regional accreditation, Vaughn has baccalaureate program accreditation with ABET. The library contains 37,455 volumes, and 4,252 audio/video tapes/CDs/DVDs, and subscribes to 80,000 periodicals including electronic. Computerized library services include inter-library loans, database searching, and Internet access. The 6-acre campus is in an urban area Queens, New York. Including any residence halls, there are 2 buildings.

Student Life: 89% of undergraduates are from New York. Others are from 27 states, and 20 foreign countries. 96% are from public schools. 38% are Hispanic; 19% African American; 17% White. The average age of freshmen is 19; all undergraduates, 23. 20% do not continue beyond their first year; 57% remain to graduate.

Housing: 200 students can be accommodated in college housing, which includes coed dorms. In addition, there are special-interest houses. On-campus housing is available on a first-come and first-served basis. Priority is given to out-of-town students. 90% of students commute. Alcohol is not permitted. All students may keep cars.

Activities: There are no fraternities or sororities. There are 16 groups on campus, including computers, dance, ethnic, gay, honors, international, professional, religious, social, social service, and student government. Popular campus events include career and internship fairs, and Springfest.

Sports: There are 4 intercollegiate sports for men and 3 for women. Facilities include state-of-the-art fitness center.

Disabled Students: All of the campus is accessible. Facilities include wheelchair ramps, elevators, special parking, specially equipped restrooms, special class scheduling, lowered drinking fountains, and lowered telephones.

Services: Counseling and information services are available, as is tutoring in most subjects. There is remedial math, reading, and writing.

Campus Safety and Security: Measures include 24-hour foot and vehicle patrol, emergency notification system, and security escort services. There are shuttle buses, lighted pathways/sidewalks, and controlled access to dorms/residences.

Programs of Study: Vaughn confers B.S. degrees. Associate and master's degrees are also awarded. Bachelor's degrees are awarded in BUSINESS (business administration and management), ENGINEERING AND ENVIRONMENTAL DESIGN (air traffic control, aircraft mechanics, airline piloting and navigation, aviation administration/management, electrical/electronics engineering technology, mechanical engineering technology, and Mechatronics Engineering). Mechatronic engineering, mechanical engineering technology, and electronic engineering technology are the strongest academically. Aircraft operation (flight), airport management, and mechanical engineering technology have the largest enrollments.

Required: All students must satisfy English, math, and science requirements and fulfill appropriate licensing requirements while maintaining a GPA of at least 2.0. Students with advanced credit must complete 30 credits in residency.

Special: Work-study programs are available with Vaughn College, and internships may be arranged through the career development office. B.S. degrees are offered.

Faculty/Classroom: 88% of faculty are male; 12% are female. All teach undergraduates. No introductory courses are taught by graduate students. The average class size in an introductory lecture is 25; in a laboratory is 20; and in a regular course is 20.

Admissions: 85% of the 2013-2014 applicants were accepted. The SAT scores for the 2013-2014 freshman class were: Critical Reading--54% below 500, 37% between 500 and 599, 8% between 600 and 699, and 1% between 700 and 800; Math--25% below 500, 48% between 500 and 599, 24% between 600 and 699, and 3% between 700 and 800. The ACT scores were 16% below 21, 67% between 21 and 23, % between 24 and 26, and 17% above 28.

Requirements: The SAT is recommended. SAT or ACT scores are required for all applicants to bachelor of science degree programs. The average SAT score for the engineering program is 1160. The average SAT score for Engineering Technology, Management, and Aircraft Operations programs is 1040. A GPA of 2.0 is required. AP credits are accepted. Important factors in the admissions decision are evidence of special talent, advanced placement or honors courses, and personality/intangible qualities.

Procedure: Freshmen are admitted fall and spring. Entrance exams should be taken March 1. There is a rolling admissions plan. Application deadlines are open. The fall 2013 application fee was $40. Notification is sent on a rolling basis.

Transfer: 245 transfer students enrolled in 2012-2013. A minimum 2.0 GPA is required. 30 of 134 credits required for the bachelor's degree must be completed at Vaughn.

Visiting: There are regularly scheduled orientations for prospective students, scheduled prior to registration, which include a tour and academic advisement. There are guides for informal visits and visitors may sit in on classes. To schedule a visit, contact the Admissions Office at admitme@vaughn.edu.

Financial Aid: In 2013-2014, 95% of all full-time freshmen and 95% of continuing full-time students received some form of financial aid. 80% of all full-time freshmen and 80% of continuing full-time students received need-based aid. 60% of undergraduate students work part-time. The average financial indebtedness of the 2013 graduate was $32,500. The CSS/Profile, FAFSA, and the college's own financial statement are required. Check with the school for current application deadlines.

International Students: There are 40 international students enrolled. The school actively recruits these students. They must take the TOEFL with a minimum score of 80 on the paper-based TOEFL (PBT) or 112 on the Internet-based version (iBT). They must also take the SAT. TOEFL accepted in place of SAT for applicants from non-English speaking countries.

Computers: All students may access the system. There are no time limits and no fees.

Graduates: From July 1, 2012 to June 30, 2013, 138 bachelor's degrees were awarded. The most popular majors were airport management (65%), electronic engineering technology (14%), and mechanical engineering technology (11%). 45 companies recruited on campus in 2012-2013. In an average class, 35% graduate in 4 years or less, 52% graduate in 5 years or less, and 57% graduate in 6 years or less.

Admissions Contact: David Griffey, Director of Admissions. E-Mail: *admitme@vaughn.edu* Web: *www.vaughn.edu*

WAGNER COLLEGE — D-5

Staten Island, NY 10301 — (718) 390-3411; (800) 221-1010; (718) 390-3105

Full-time: 610 men, 1131 women — **Faculty:** 102; IIA, -$
Part-time: 23 men, 54 women — **Ph.D.s:** 85%
Graduate: 128 men, 259 women — **Student/Faculty:** 13 to 1
Year: semesters, summer session — **Tuition:** $37,440
Application Deadline: February 15 — **Room & Board:** $11,160
Freshman Class: 2652 applied, 1907 accepted, 426 enrolled
SAT CR/M/W: 560/540/530 — **ACT:** 25 — **VERY COMPETITIVE**

Wagner College, founded in 1883, is a private liberal arts institution. There is one undergraduate school and one graduate school. In addition to regional accreditation, Wagner has baccalaureate program accreditation with AACSB, ACBSP, NCATE, and NLN. The library contains 158,160 volumes, 218 microform items, and 2,453 audio/video tapes/CDs/DVDs, and subscribes to 56,399 periodicals including electronic. Computerized library services include interlibrary loans, database searching, Internet access, and Wi-Fi capability. Special learning facilities include an art gallery, planetarium, radio station, Nursing Resource Center. The 105-acre campus is in a suburban area 10 miles from Manhattan. Including any residence halls, there are 19 buildings.

Student Life: 52% of undergraduates are from New York. Others are from 40 states, 20 foreign countries, and Canada. 62% are from public schools. 77% are White; 11% race unknown. The average age of freshmen is 18; all undergraduates, 20. 17% do not continue beyond their first year; 70% remain to graduate.

Housing: 1600 students can be accommodated in college housing, which includes coed dorms and off-campus apartments. In addition, there are honors houses, special-interest houses, Greek floors, Honors building and floor, quiet floors, medical floors, and themed communities in dorms, senior year housing. On-campus housing is guaranteed for all 4 years and is available on a lottery system for upperclassmen. 67% of students live on campus; of those, 70% remain on campus on weekends. All students may keep cars.

Activities: 15% of menand 13 of women belong to 2 local and 2 national fraternities; 13% of women belong to 1 local and 3 national sororities. There are 65 groups on campus, including women's, academic, art, band, cheerleading, chess, choir, chorale, chorus, communications, computers, dance, debate, drama, environmental, ethnic, gay, honors, international, jazz band, literary magazine, marching band, musical theater, newspaper, opera, pep band, political, professional, religious, social, social service, student government, symphony, and yearbook. Popular campus events include Songfest, WagnerStock, Homecoming, Spring Fling Week, Fall Fest and Family Weekend.

Sports: There are 8 intercollegiate sports for men and 10 for women, and 5 intramural sports for men and 4 for women. Facilities include a football stadium, a gym, a regulation-sized pool, a fitness center, a track, and a basketball arena, soccer/softball/baseball field.

Disabled Students: 25% of the campus is accessible. Facilities include wheelchair ramps, elevators, special parking, specially equipped restrooms, special class scheduling, and lowered drinking fountains.

Services: Counseling and information services are available, as is tutoring in every subject. There is a reader service for the blind, and remedial math, reading, and writing.

Campus Safety and Security: Measures include 24-hour foot and vehicle patrol, emergency notification system, and security escort services. There are shuttle buses, emergency telephones, lighted pathways/sidewalks, controlled access to dorms/residences, and ID card access into residence halls.

Programs of Study: Wagner confers B.A., and B.S. degrees. Master's degrees are also awarded. Bachelor's degrees are awarded in BIOLOGICAL SCIENCE (biology/biological science and microbiology), BUSINESS (accounting and business administration and management), COMMUNICATIONS AND THE ARTS (arts administration/management, dramatic arts, English, fine arts, music, theater design, and visual and performing arts), COMPUTER AND PHYSICAL SCIENCE (chemistry, computer science, mathematics, and physics), EDUCATION (elementary education, middle school education, and secondary education), HEALTH PROFESSIONS (nursing and physician's assistant), SOCIAL SCIENCE (anthropology, history, philosophy, political science/government, psychology, public administration, and sociology). Natural sciences and health professions are the strongest academically. Business, nursing, psychology, visual and performing arts have the largest enrollments.

Required: To graduate, students must complete 36 units with 12 to 18 in the major and a minimum GPA of 2.0. All students must take courses in English, math, and multidisciplinary studies. In addition, students must fulfill distribution requirements in physical science, life science, math and computers, history, literature, philosophy and religion, foreign culture, aesthetics, and human behavior. All students are required to enroll in Learning Communities.

Special: Internships or field-based research is required of all majors. Students may earn B.A.-B.S. degrees in psychology. Student-designed and dual majors, credit for life experience, a Washington semester, nondegree study, and pass/fail options are available. Study abroad in most countries is possible. Learning Communities for freshmen, sophomores/juniors, and seniors. There are 11 national honor societies and a freshman honors program.

Faculty/Classroom: 45% of faculty are male; 55% are female. All teach undergraduates. No introductory courses are taught by graduate students. The average class size in an introductory lecture is 21; in a laboratory is 13; and in a regular course is 19.

Admissions: 72% of the 2013-2014 applicants were accepted. The SAT scores for the 2013-2014 freshman class were: Critical Reading--9% below 500, 42% between 500 and 599, 42% between 600 and 699, and 7% between 700 and 800; Math--10% below 500, 40% between 500 and 599, 42% between 600 and 699, and 7% between 700 and 800; Writing--11% below 500, 39% between 500 and 599, 42% between 600 and 699, and 7% between 700 and 800. The ACT scores were 5% below 21, 28% between 21 and 23, 42% between 24 and 26, 17% between 27 and 28, and 8% above 28. 38% of the current freshmen were in the top fifth of their class; 86% were in the top two fifths.

Requirements: Graduation from an accredited secondary school is required, with 18 academic credits or Carnegie units, including 4 years of English, 3 years each of history and math, 2 years each of foreign language, science, and social studies, and 1 year each of art and music. An essay is required, and an interview is strongly recommended. Auditions are required for music and theater applicants. An interview is required for the Physician Assistant Program. A GPA of 3.0 is required. AP and CLEP credits are accepted. Important factors in the admissions decision are advanced placement or honors courses, recommendations by school officials, and extracurricular activities record.

Procedure: Freshmen are admitted fall and spring. Entrance exams should be taken by December of the senior year. There are early decision and deferred admissions plans. Early decision applications should be filed by December 1; regular applications, by February 15 for fall entry; and November 1 for spring entry, along with a $50 fee. Notification of early decision is sent December 15; regular decision, March 1. 76 early decision candidates were accepted for the 2013-2014 class. 48 applicants were on the 2013 waiting list; 10 were admitted. Applications are accepted online.

Transfer: 96 transfer students enrolled in 2012-2013. Transfer students should have a minimum of 30 credit hours earned with a GPA of 2.5. Applicants must submit all college and high school transcripts, a letter of recommendation, and a personal statement. An interview is recommended. SAT or ACT scores taken within the past 5 years may be submitted. 9 of 36 credits required for the bachelor's degree must be completed at Wagner.

Visiting: There are regularly scheduled orientations for prospective students, including a presentation by the Admissions Office, a tour of the campus, and meetings with faculty and staff. There are guides for informal visits, visitors may sit in on classes, and stay overnight. To schedule a visit, contact the Admissions Office.

Financial Aid: In 2013-2014, 91% of all full-time freshmen and 90% of continuing full-time students received some form of financial aid. 72% of all full-time freshmen and 66% of continuing full-time students received need-based aid. The average freshman award was $26,233. Need-based scholarships or need-based grants averaged $16,613 ($48,600 maximum); need-based self-help aid (loans and jobs) averaged $4,468 ($10,000 maximum); non-need-based athletic scholarships averaged $33,317 ($52,076 maximum); and other non-need-based awards and non-need-based scholarships averaged $15,507 ($48,600 maximum). 19% of undergraduate students work part-time. Average annual earnings from campus work are $1004. Wagner is a member of CSS. The FAFSA and the state aid form are required. The priority date for freshman financial aid applications for fall entry is February 15.

International Students: There are 36 international students enrolled. The school actively recruits these students. They must take the TOEFL with a minimum score of 550 on the paper-based TOEFL (PBT) or 79 on the Internet-based version (iBT).

Computers: All students may access the system. There are no time limits and no fees.

Graduates: From July 1, 2012 to June 30, 2013, 417 bachelor's degrees were awarded. The most popular majors were nursing and physician assistants (18%), visual/performing arts (18%), and business administration (17%). 60 companies recruited on campus in 2012-2013. In an average class, 60% graduate in 4 years or less, 64% graduate in 5 years or less, and 66% graduate in 6 years or less. Of the 2012 graduating class, 20% were enrolled in graduate school within 6 months of graduation, and 79% were employed.

Admissions Contact: Robert Herr, Dean of Admissions. E-Mail: *admissions@wagner.edu* Web: *www.wagner.edu*

WEBB INSTITUTE D-5

Glen Cove, NY 11542 **(516) 671-2213; (516) 674-9838**

Full-time: 70 men, 25 women	**Faculty:** n/av
Part-time: n/av	**Ph.D.s:** 50%
Graduate: n/av	**Student/Faculty:** n/av
Year: semesters	**Tuition:** $9500
Application Deadline: see profile	**Room & Board:** n/av
Freshman Class: n/av	
SAT: required	

MOST COMPETITIVE

Webb Institute, founded in 1889, is a private engineering school devoted to professional knowledge of ship construction, design, and motive power. All students receive 4-year, full-tuition scholarships. Figures in the above capsule and in this profile are approximate. In addition to regional accreditation, Webb has baccalaureate program accreditation with ABET. The library contains 50,598 volumes, 1,633 microform items, and 1,851 audio/video tapes/CDs/DVDs, and subscribes to 267 periodicals including electronic. Computerized library services include interlibrary loans, database searching, and Internet access. The 26-acre campus is in a suburban area 24 miles east of New York City. Including any residence halls, there are 11 buildings.

Student Life: 76% of undergraduates are from out of state, mostly the Northeast. Students are from 22 states and 1 foreign country. 70% are from public schools. 96% are white. The average age of freshmen is 18; all undergraduates, 20. 4% do not continue beyond their first year; 73% remain to graduate.

Housing: 110 students can be accommodated in college housing, which includes single-sex dorms. On-campus housing is guaranteed for all 4 years. All students may keep cars.

Activities: There are no fraternities or sororities. Groups on campus include chorale, drama, orchestra, professional, social, student government, yachting, and yearbook. Popular campus events include Parents Day and Webbstock.

Sports: There are 6 intercollegiate sports for men and 6 for women, and 2 intramural sports for men and 2 for women. Facilities include a 60-seat gym, tennis courts, an athletic field, a boat house, and a beach-front dock.

Disabled Students: 90% of the campus is accessible. Facilities include elevators and special parking.

Services: Counseling and information services are available, as is tutoring in most subjects.
Campus Safety and Security: Measures include emergency telephones, lighted pathways/sidewalks, and student and professional security services.
Programs of Study: Webb confers B.S. degrees. Bachelor's degrees are awarded in ENGINEERING AND ENVIRONMENTAL DESIGN (naval architecture and marine engineering).
Required: The curriculum is prescribed, with all students taking the same courses in each of the 4 years. The Webb program has 4 practical 8-week paid work periods: freshman year, a helper mechanic in a shipyard; sophomore year, a cadet in the engine room of a ship; and junior and senior years, a draftsman or junior engineer in a design office. All students must complete a senior seminar, thesis, and technical reports, as well as make engineering inspection visits. A total of 146 credits with a minimum passing grade of 70% is required to graduate.
Special: All students are employed 2 months each year through co-op programs.
Faculty/Classroom: All of faculty are male. All teach undergraduates, and 40% do both. The average class size in an introductory lecture is 25, in a laboratory, 9, and in a regular course, 25.
Requirements: The SAT is required, with a minimum satisfactory score. Applicants should be graduates of an accredited secondary school with 16 academic credits completed, including 4 each in English and math, 2 each in history and science, 1 in foreign language, and 3 in electives. 3 SAT Subject tests in writing, math level I or II, and physics or chemistry are required, as is an interview. Candidates must be U.S. citizens. Webb requires applicants to be in the upper 20% of their class. A GPA of 3.2 is required. Important factors in the admissions decision are advanced placement or honors courses, evidence of special talent, and personality/intangible qualities.
Procedure: Freshmen are admitted fall. Entrance exams should be taken by January of the senior year. There is an early decision admissions plan. Check with the school for current application deadlines and fee.
Transfer: Transfers must enter as freshmen. A 3.2 GPA is required. SAT scores and an interview are required. 146 of 146 credits required for the bachelor's degree must be completed at Webb.
Visiting: There are regularly scheduled orientations for prospective students, including a weekend open house in October. There are guides for informal visits; visitors may sit in on classes and stay overnight. To schedule a visit, contact the Admissions Office.
Financial Aid: The CSS/Profile and the college's own financial statement are required. Check with the school for current application deadlines.
Computers: Wireless access is available. The school provides laptops for all students. All students may access the system 24 hours per day.
Admissions Contact: Director of Admissions. E-Mail: *admissions@webb-institute.edu* Web: *www.webb-institute.edu*

WELLS COLLEGE C-3

Aurora, NY 13026 (315) 364-3264
(800) 952-9355; (315) 364-3227

Full-time: 130 men, 415 women	**Faculty:** n/av; IIB, av$
Part-time: 10 men, 20 women	**Ph.D.s:** 100%
Graduate: n/av	**Student/Faculty:** n/av
Year: semesters	**Tuition:** $32,410
Application Deadline: see profile	**Room & Board:** $11,940
Freshman Class: n/av	
SAT or ACT: required	

VERY COMPETITIVE

Wells College is a private liberal arts institution, founded in 1868. Historically a women's college, it became coeducational in 2005. Figures in the above capsule and in this profile are approximate. The library contains 218,002 volumes, 14,882 microform items, and 1,154 audio/video tapes/CDs/DVDs, and subscribes to 371 periodicals including electronic. Computerized library services include interlibrary loans, database searching, Internet access, and laptop Internet portals. Special learning facilities include a learning resource center, art gallery, radio station, and the Book Arts Center. The 365-acre campus is in a small town on Cayuga Lake, 30 miles north of Ithaca. Including any residence halls, there are 22 buildings.
Student Life: 67% of undergraduates are from New York. Others are from 32 states and 14 foreign countries. 93% are from public schools. 68% are white. The average age of freshmen is 18; all undergraduates, 20. 20% do not continue beyond their first year; 60% remain to graduate.
Housing: 450 students can be accommodated in college housing, which includes single-sex and coed dorms and off-campus apartments. In addition, there are special-interest houses and housing for nontraditional-age students. On-campus housing is guaranteed for all 4 years. 85% of students live on campus. All students may keep cars.
Activities: There are no fraternities or sororities. There are 42 groups on campus, including bell ringers, choir, chorale, communications, dance, drama, environmental, ethnic, forensics, gay, international, jazz band, literary magazine, newspaper, photography, political, professional, religious, social, social service, student government, WILL (Women In Lifelong Learning), and women's resource center. Popular campus events include the Odd-Even Basketball Game, Spring Weekend, and 100 Days for Seniors.
Sports: There are 5 intercollegiate sports for men and 7 for women, and 10 intramural sports for men and 10 for women. Facilities include a competition-size swimming pool, a gym, a fitness center with weight and cardio equipment, an athletic training room, 2 indoor tennis courts/practice space, a dance studio, a 9-hole golf course, 4 all-weather tennis courts, a skinned infield softball field, 2 game fields for soccer and lacrosse, a field hockey field, and a boat house and dock with canoes, kayaks, and sailboats.
Disabled Students: 51% of the campus is accessible. Facilities include wheelchair ramps, elevators, special parking, specially equipped restrooms, special class scheduling, lowered telephones, and special housing.
Services: Counseling and information services are available, as is tutoring in every subject. Assistance is provided on an individual, as-needed basis. Untimed and extended-time testing options are available.
Campus Safety and Security: Measures include 24-hour foot and vehicle patrol, self-defense education, and security escort services. There are shuttle buses, emergency telephones, and lighted pathways/sidewalks. All students must escort their guests on campus at all times; blue light phones are provided.
Programs of Study: Wells confers B.A. degrees. Bachelor's degrees are awarded in AGRICULTURE (environmental studies), BIOLOGICAL SCIENCE (biochemistry, biology/biological science, and molecular biology), BUSINESS (business administration and management), COMMUNICATIONS AND THE ARTS (dance, dramatic arts, English, fine arts, French, German, language arts, music, Spanish, and visual and performing arts), COMPUTER AND PHYSICAL SCIENCE (chemistry, computer science, mathematics, and physics), EDUCATION (elementary education), SOCIAL SCIENCE (American studies, anthropology, economics, ethics, politics, and social policy, history, international studies, philosophy, political science/government, psychology, public affairs, religion, sociology, and women's studies). Psychology, English, and biological and chemical sciences have the largest enrollments.
Required: To graduate, students must complete a total of 120 credit hours, including 33 to 63 in the major, with a minimum GPA of 2.0 overall and in the major. All students must complete 2 first-year experience courses, a comprehensive exam, 3 January intersession internships/courses, and a senior project/thesis. Distribution requirements include 4 courses in phys ed and wellness, 3 each in natural and social sciences and in arts and humanities, 2 in a foreign language, and 1 in formal reasoning.
Special: Wells offers cross-registration with Cornell University, Cayuga Community College, and Ithaca College, a Washington semester with American University, internships, and accelerated degree programs in all majors. Study abroad in 13 countries is permitted. A 3-2 engineering degree is available with Columbia, Clarkson, and Cornell Universities. Students may also earn 3-2 degrees in business and community health with the University of Rochester and a 3-4 degree in veterinary medicine with Cornell University. Student-designed majors and pass-fail options are available. Work-study, B.A.-B.S. degrees, and dual majors are also available. There are 2 national honor societies, including Phi Beta Kappa.
Faculty/Classroom: 44% of faculty are male; 56% are female. All teach undergraduates. No introductory courses are taught by graduate students. The average class size in an introductory lecture is 25, in a laboratory, 16, and in a regular course, 13.
Requirements: The SAT or ACT is required. In addition, graduation from an accredited secondary school should include 20 academic credits or Carnegie units. High school courses must include 4 years of English, 3 each of a foreign language and math, and 2 each of history and lab science. 2 teacher recommendations and an essay/personal statement are required, and an interview is strongly recommended. AP and CLEP credits are accepted. Important factors in the admissions decision are recommendations by school officials, extracurricular activities record, and advanced placement or honors courses.
Procedure: Freshmen are admitted fall. Entrance exams should be taken prior to application. There are early decision and deferred admissions plans. Check with the school for current application deadlines. The application fee is $40. Applications are accepted online.
Transfer: Applicants must be in good standing at the institution last attended. A minimum GPA of 2.0 is required. Wells requires official college and high school transcripts, a personal statement, standardized test scores, and a recommendation from a professor. An interview is strongly recommended. 60 of 120 credits required for the bachelor's degree must be completed at Wells.
Visiting: There are regularly scheduled orientations for prospective students, including tours, interviews, class attendance, presentations, open houses, an overnight host program, and meetings with faculty and coaches. There are guides for informal visits; visitors may sit in on classes and stay overnight. To schedule a visit, contact the Admissions Office.
Financial Aid: Wells is a member of CSS. The FAFSA is required. Early

decision applicants must also submit the CSS Profile. Check with the school for current deadlines.

International Students: The school actively recruits these students. They must take the TOEFL with a minimum score of 550 on the paper-based TOEFL (PBT) or 80 on the Internet-based version (iBT). They must also take the SAT or ACT.

Computers: All residence hall rooms have Internet connectivity. All students may access the system. It is strongly recommended that all students have a personal computer.

Admissions Contact: Susan Sloan, Director of Admissions. A campus DVD is available. E-Mail: *admissions@wells.edu* Web: *www.wells.edu*

YESHIVA UNIVERSITY D-5

New York, NY 10033 (212) 960-5277; (212) 960-0086

Full-time: 1438 men, 1379 women
Part-time: 36 men, 16 women
Graduate: 1701 men, 2183 women
Year: semesters, summer session
Application Deadline:
Freshman Class: n/av
SAT CR/M/W: 619/622/610 **ACT.** 20

Faculty: n/av; I, +$
Ph.D.s: 79%
Student/Faculty: n/av
Tuition: $36,500
Room & Board: $10,750

VERY COMPETITIVE+

Yeshiva University, founded in 1886, is an independent liberal arts institution offering undergraduate programs through Yeshiva College, its undergraduate college for men, Stern College for Women, and Sy Syms School of Business. There are 7 graduate schools. In addition to regional accreditation, YU has baccalaureate program accreditation with CSWE. The 7 libraries contain 900,000 volumes, 759,000 microform items, and 980 audio/video tapes/CDs/DVDs, and subscribe to 7,790 periodicals including electronic. Computerized library services include interlibrary loans and database searching. Special learning facilities include an art gallery, radio station, museum. The 26-acre campus is in an urban area.

Student Life: 44% of undergraduates are from out of state. Students are from 31 states, 16 foreign countries, and Canada. 14% are from public schools. The average age of freshmen is 17; all undergraduates, 19. 8% do not continue beyond their first year; 92% remain to graduate.

Housing: 1600 students can be accommodated in college housing, which includes single-sex dorms and off-campus apartments. On-campus housing is guaranteed for all 4 years. 85% of students live on campus. Alcohol is not permitted. All students may keep cars.

Activities: There are no fraternities or sororities. There are 70 groups on campus, including radio, art, choir, computers, drama, honors, international, jazz band, literary magazine, musical theater, newspaper, political, professional, religious, social service, special interest, student government, and yearbook. Popular campus events include holiday and dramatic presentations and parents day.

Sports: There are 8 intercollegiate sports for men and 2 for women, and 5 intramural sports for men and 4 for women. Facilities include The athletic center at Yeshiva College houses a variety of facilities, including a 1000-seat gym.

Disabled Students: 95% of the campus is accessible. Facilities include wheelchair ramps and elevators.

Services: There is remedial reading and writing. There is also a writing center, which helps students with composition and verbal skills.

Campus Safety and Security: Measures include 24-hour foot and vehicle patrol and security escort services. There are shuttle buses, lighted pathways/sidewalks, ID cards, vulnerability surveys, fire drills, alarm systems, emergency telephone numbers, and transportation for routine and special events.

Programs of Study: YU confers B.A., and B.S. degrees. Associate degrees are also awarded. Bachelor's degrees are awarded in BIOLOGICAL SCIENCE (biology/biological science), BUSINESS (accounting, business administration and management, and marketing/retailing/merchandising), COMMUNICATIONS AND THE ARTS (classical languages, communications, English, French, Hebrew, music, and speech/debate/rhetoric), COMPUTER AND PHYSICAL SCIENCE (chemistry, computer science, and mathematics), ENGINEERING AND ENVIRONMENTAL DESIGN (preengineering), HEALTH PROFESSIONS (health science), SOCIAL SCIENCE (economics, history, philosophy, political science/government, psychology, religion, and sociology). The dual program of liberal arts and Jewish studies is the strongest academically. Accounting, psychology, and economics have the largest enrollments.

Required: To graduate, students must complete a total of 128 credit hours. Under the dual program, students pursue a liberal arts or business curriculum together with courses in Hebrew language, literature, and culture. Courses in Jewish learning are geared to the student's level of preparation.

Special: YU offers a 3-2 degree in occupational therapy with Columbia and New York Universities; a 3-4 degree in podiatry with the New York College of Podiatric Medicine; and a 3-2 or 4-2 degree in engineering with Columbia University. Stern College students may take courses in advertising, photography, and design at the Fashion Institute of Technology. Study-abroad programs may be arranged in Israel. The school offers independent study options and an optional pass/no credit system. There are 9 national honor societies and 20 departmental honors programs.

Faculty/Classroom: 73% of faculty are male; 27% are female. 58% teach undergraduates, 60% do research, and 28% do both. No introductory courses are taught by graduate students. The average class size in an introductory lecture is 38; in a laboratory is 15; and in a regular course is 18.

Admissions: 69% of the 2013-2014 applicants were accepted.

Requirements: The SAT or ACT is required. Graduation from an accredited secondary school with 16 academic credits is required for admission. The GED is accepted under limited and specific circumstances. The SAT Subject test in Hebrew is recommended for placement purposes. An interview and an essay are required. A GPA of 3.3 is required. AP and CLEP credits are accepted. Important factors in the admissions decision are extracurricular activities record, personality/intangible qualities, and evidence of special talent.

Procedure: Freshmen are admitted to all sessions. There are early admissions, deferred admissions, and rolling admissions plans. Check with the school for current application deadlines. The application fee is $70.

Transfer: 95 of 128 credits required for the bachelor's degree must be completed at YU.

Visiting: There are regularly scheduled orientations for prospective students, YU holds open houses for high school students. There are guides for informal visits, visitors may sit in on classes, and stay overnight. To schedule a visit, contact the Office of Admissions.

Financial Aid: YU is a member of CSS. The CSS/Profile and the college's own financial statement are required. Check with the school for current application deadlines.

International Students: The school actively recruits these students. They must take the TOEFL. They must also take the SAT or ACT.

Computers: All students may access the system 24 hours per day via modem or when buildings are open. There are no time limits and no fees.

Graduates: From July 1, 2012 to June 30, 2013, 631 bachelor's degrees were awarded. The most popular majors were business(27%), psychology (17%), and biology (14%).

Admissions Contact: Michael Kranzler, Director of Undergraduate Admissions. E-Mail: *yuadmit@ymail.yu.edu* Web: *www.yu.edu*

YORK COLLEGE / CITY UNIVERSITY OF NEW YORK D-5

Jamaica, NY 11451 (718) 262-2165; (718) 262-2601

Full-time: 1817 men, 3510 women
Part-time: 990 men, 2033 women
Graduate: 4 men, 35 women
Year: semesters, summer session
Application Deadline: open
Freshman Class: 13319 applied, 8038 accepted, 1111 enrolled

Faculty: 201
Ph.D.s: n/av
Student/Faculty: 19 to 1
Tuition: $5496 ($11,406)
Room & Board: n/app

NON COMPETITIVE

York College, established in 1966, is a public liberal arts commuter college and part of the City University of New York. There are 3 undergraduate schools. In addition to regional accreditation, York has baccalaureate program accreditation with CAHEA, CSWE, NCATE, and NLN. The library contains 184,799 volumes, 140,461 microform items, and 4,613 audio/video tapes/CDs/DVDs, and subscribes to 7,613 periodicals including electronic. Computerized library services include interlibrary loans and database searching. Special learning facilities include an art gallery, TV station, a cardio-pneumo simulator, flight simulator, and a theater. The 50-acre campus is in an urban area in New York City. Including any residence halls, there are 5 buildings.

Student Life: 90% of undergraduates are from New York. Others are from 6 states, 77 foreign countries, and Canada. 34% are African American; 27% race unknown; 18% Hispanic; 16% Asian American. The average age of freshmen is 19; all undergraduates, 24. 23% do not continue beyond their first year; 77% remain to graduate.

Housing: Alcohol is not permitted. All students commute. All students may keep cars.

Activities: There are no fraternities or sororities. There are 50 groups on campus, including art, cheerleading, choir, chorus, computers, drama, ethnic, honors, international, jazz band, literary magazine, musical theater, newspaper, political, professional, radio and TV, religious, social, social service, and student government. Popular campus events include club fairs, talent shows, and ethnic fairs.

Sports: There are 9 intercollegiate sports for men and 8 for women, and 9 intramural sports for men and 8 for women. Facilities include a 1200-seat gym, a 25-meter, 6-lane swimming pool with diving boards, a health risk appraisal center, an exercise therapy room, outdoor track; tennis courts; soccer field; indoor walking/jogging track; weight room; aerobics room; handball courts; and multipurpose room.

Disabled Students: All of the campus is accessible. Facilities include wheelchair ramps, elevators, special parking, specially equipped restrooms, special class scheduling, lowered drinking fountains, and lowered telephones.

Services: Counseling and information services are available, as is tutoring in every subject. There is a reader service for the blind, and remedial math, reading, and writing.

Campus Safety and Security: Measures include 24-hour foot and vehicle patrol and security escort services. There are emergency telephones and lighted pathways/sidewalks.

Programs of Study: York confers B.A., and B.S. degrees. Master's degrees are also awarded. Bachelor's degrees are awarded in BIOLOGICAL SCIENCE (biology/biological science and biotechnology), BUSINESS (accounting, business administration and management, and marketing/retailing/merchandising), COMMUNICATIONS AND THE ARTS (art history and appreciation, dramatic arts, English, French, music, Spanish, speech/debate/rhetoric, and studio art), COMPUTER AND PHYSICAL SCIENCE (chemistry, geology, information sciences and systems, mathematics, and physics), EDUCATION (physical education), HEALTH PROFESSIONS (community health work, environmental health science, exercise science, medical laboratory technology, nursing, occupational therapy, and pharmaceutical science), SOCIAL SCIENCE (African American studies, anthropology, economics, gerontology, history, liberal arts/general studies, philosophy, political science/government, psychology, social work, and sociology). Liberal studies, business administration, and accounting have largest enrollments.

Required: All students are required to complete 120 credits and maintain a minimum GPA of 2.0. The core curriculum of 36-42 credits includes courses in humanities, behavioral science, cultural diversity, math, natural science. Students must also take a 2-credit physical education course, complete 2 semesters of English, 2 writing intensive courses in the lower division of the curriculum (at the 100 or 200 level), and one writing intensive course in the upper division of the curriculum (at the 300 level or above) within the major discipline.

Special: Cross-registration with all schools in the City University of New York is permitted. Also provided are work-study programs, credit by exam, dual majors in physics and math, nondegree study, pass/fail options, credit for life experience, internships, cooperative programs with other schools, and student-designed majors. There are 6 national honor societies and 4 departmental honors programs.

Faculty/Classroom: 51% of faculty are male; 49% are female. All teach undergraduates, and 7% do both. No introductory courses are taught by graduate students.

Admissions: 60% of the 2013-2014 applicants were accepted.

Requirements: Students should achieve a satisfactory score on the SAT. Applicants must have graduated from an accredited secondary school or present a GED certificate. An audition is recommended for music majors. A GPA of 80.0 is required. AP and CLEP credits are accepted.

Procedure: Freshmen are admitted fall and spring. There are early admissions, deferred admissions, and rolling admissions plans. Application deadlines are open. The fall 2013 application fee was $65. Applications are accepted online.

Transfer: 894 transfer students enrolled in 2012-2013. Students must present a minimum GPA of 2.0. 40 of 120 credits required for the bachelor's degree must be completed at York.

Visiting: There are regularly scheduled orientations for prospective students, including workshops and group meetings with faculty and staff on matriculation; registration; financial aid, degree requirements; and advisement for classes. Visitors may sit in on classes. To schedule a visit, contact Michel Hodge at mhodge@york.cuny.edu.

Financial Aid: In 2013-2014, 69% of all full-time freshmen and 53% of continuing full-time students received some form of financial aid. 24% of all full-time freshmen and 14% of continuing full-time students received need-based aid. The average freshman award was $6,275.. The FAFSA and the college's own financial statement are required. The priority date for freshman financial aid applications for fall entry is April 1. The deadline for filing freshman financial aid applications for fall entry is June 1.

International Students: There are 120 international students enrolled. They must take the TOEFL. They must also take the SAT or ACT, scoring 1100.

Computers: All students may access the system during hours of operation of college facilities. There are no time limits and no fees.

Graduates: From July 1, 2012 to June 30, 2013, 1000 bachelor's degrees were awarded. The most popular majors were business administration (20%), psychology (18%), and health professions (18%). 100 companies recruited on campus in 2012-2013. In an average class, 24% graduate in 4 years or less, 84% graduate in 5 years or less, and 56% graduate in 6 years or less.

Admissions Contact: Michel Hodge, Director of Admissions and Enrollment. E-Mail: *admissions@york.cuny.edu* Web: *www.york.cuny.edu*

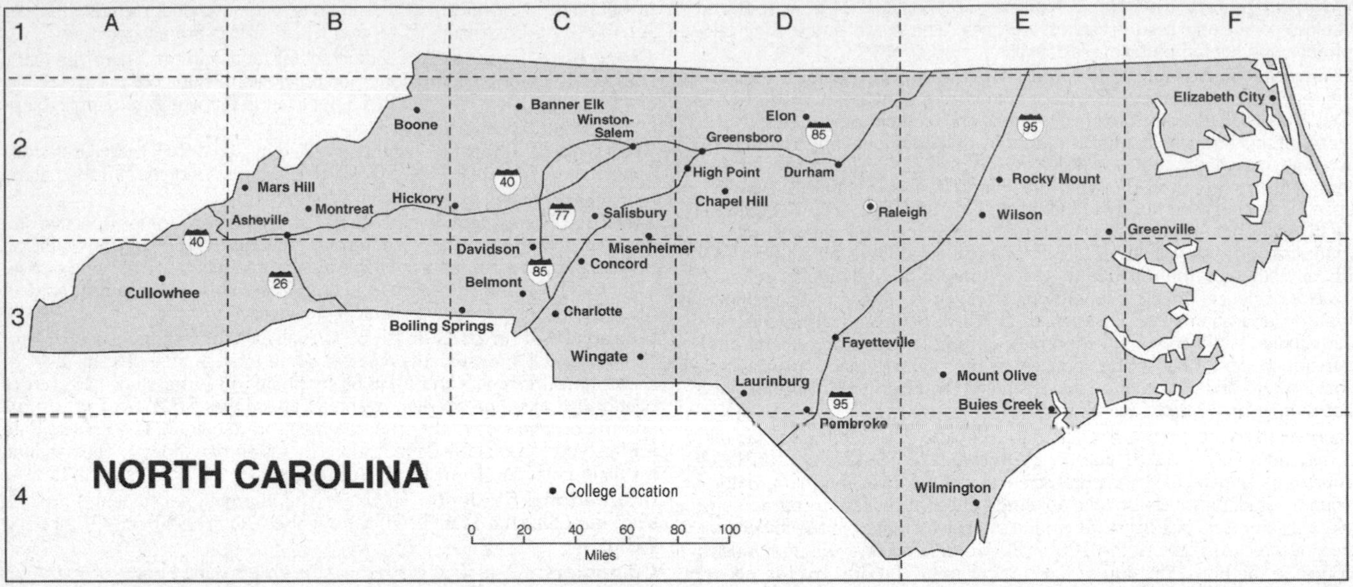

APPALACHIAN STATE UNIVERSITY B-2

Boone, NC 28608 **(828) 262-2120; (828) 262-3296**

Full-time: 7097 men, 7740 women **Faculty:** 814; IIA, -$
Part-time: 354 men, 521 women **Ph.D.s:** 99%
Graduate: 554 men, 1323 women **Student/Faculty:** 16 to 1
Year: semesters, summer session **Tuition:** $5859 ($17,907)
Application Deadline: March 15 **Room & Board:** $7060
Freshman Class: 12248 applied, 7744 accepted, 3028 enrolled
SAT CR/M/W: 572/581/548 **ACT:** 26 **VERY COMPETITIVE**

Appalachian State University, founded in 1899 and a member of the University of North Carolina system, is a comprehensive university offering undergraduate and graduate programs in the arts and sciences, business, teacher education, fine and applied arts, music, and health sciences. There are 8 undergraduate schools and 1 graduate school. In addition to regional accreditation, App State has baccalaureate program accreditation with AACSB, CSAB, CSWE, NASAD, NASM, NCATE, and NRPA. The 2 libraries contain 937,956 volumes, 1.5 million microform items, 72,813 audio/video tapes/CDs/DVDs, and subscribe to 23,861 periodicals including electronic. Computerized library services include interlibrary loans, database searching, and Internet access. Special learning facilities include an art gallery, radio station, dark sky observatory. The 1300-acre campus is in a small town in northwestern North Carolina. Including any residence halls, there are 90 buildings.

Student Life: 92% of undergraduates are from North Carolina. Others are from 46 states, 61 foreign countries, and Canada. 88% are from public schools. 87% are White; 12% race unknown. The average age of freshmen is 18; all undergraduates, 21. 12% do not continue beyond their first year; 66% remain to graduate.

Housing: 5775 students can be accommodated in college housing, which includes single-sex and coed dorms. In addition, there are sorority houses, learning communities. On-campus housing is guaranteed for the freshman year only and is available on a lottery system for upperclassmen. 67% of students commute. All students may keep cars.

Activities: 7% of men belong to 13 national fraternities; 11% of women belong to 9 national sororities. There are 289 groups on campus, including art, band, cheerleading, chess, choir, chorale, chorus, communications, computers, dance, debate, drama, drill team, environmental, ethnic, film, forensics, gay, honors, international, jazz band, literary magazine, marching band, musical theater, newspaper, opera, orchestra, pep band, photography, political, professional, radio and TV, religious, social, social service, student government, and symphony. Popular campus events include Football and Basketball Games, Annual Diversity Celebration, Legends Concerts, and Greek Week.

Sports: There are 10 intercollegiate sports for men and 10 for women, and 20 intramural sports for men and 20 for women. Facilities include a 9,000-seat convocation center, a 7,000-seat varsity gym, an 18,000-seat stadium, 3 fitness and recreation centers, facilities for football, soccer, field hockey, basketball, volleyball, wrestling, indoor and outdoor track, golf course, baseball field, tennis courts, 50-meter pool, 50-ft climbing wall, racquetball courts, aerobics studio, weight room, and cardio equipment.

Disabled Students: All of the campus is accessible. Facilities include wheelchair ramps, elevators, special parking, specially equipped restrooms, special class scheduling, lowered drinking fountains, lowered telephones, and special housing.

Services: Counseling and information services are available, as is tutoring in most subjects. There is a reader service for the blind, and remedial math, reading, and writing.

Campus Safety and Security: Measures include 24-hour foot and vehicle patrol, emergency notification system, self-defense education, and security escort services. There are shuttle buses, emergency telephones, lighted pathways/sidewalks, and controlled access to dorms/residences.

Programs of Study: App State confers B.A., B.S., B.F.A., B.M., B.S.B.A., B.S.C.J., B.S.N. and B.S.W. degrees. Master's and doctoral degrees are also awarded. Bachelor's degrees are awarded in AGRICULTURE (agricultural business management and environmental studies), BIOLOGICAL SCIENCE (biology/biological science, ecology, molecular biology, and nutrition), BUSINESS (accounting, banking and finance, hospitality management services, insurance and risk management, international business management, management engineering, marketing/retailing/merchandising, and recreational facilities management), COMMUNICATIONS AND THE ARTS (advertising, apparel design, art, arts administration/management, communications, dance, dramatic arts, English, French, graphic design, industrial design, journalism, music business management, music performance, performing arts, photography, public relations, Spanish, and studio art), COMPUTER AND PHYSICAL SCIENCE (actuarial science, chemistry, computer science, geology, mathematics, physics, and statistics), EDUCATION (art education, athletic training, business education, computer education, drama education, education, elementary education, English education, foreign languages education, health education, mathematics education, middle school education, music education, physical education, science education, secondary education, social science education, social studies education, and special education), ENGINEERING AND ENVIRONMENTAL DESIGN (architecture, computer technology, construction management, construction technology, electrical/electronics engineering technology, engineering technology, environmental science, graphic arts technology, industrial engineering technology, and interior design), HEALTH PROFESSIONS (exercise science, health care administration, health science, music therapy, nursing, preventive/wellness health care, and speech pathology/audiology), SOCIAL SCIENCE (anthropology, area studies, child psychology/development, criminal justice, East Asian studies, economics, family/consumer studies, French studies, geography, German area studies, history, interdisciplinary studies, Latin American studies, Middle Eastern studies, philosophy, political science/government, psychology, religion, social work, sociology, South Asian studies, Third World studies, and women's studies). Business/marketing, elementary education, and social sciences have the largest enrollments.

Required: To graduate, students must complete 122 credit hours for most programs, including 60 in the major, with a minimum 2.0 GPA. General education requirements include courses in math, science, history, phys ed, English, social sciences, and humanities.

Special: App State offers dual degree in Communications with Universidad de las Americas Puebla, a private university in Mexico, a 3-2 engineering degree with Clemson and Auburn Universities, internships, work-study programs, B.A.-B.S. degrees, dual majors, and study abroad. There are 16 national honor societies, a freshman honors program, and 25 departmental honors programs.

Faculty/Classroom: 53% of faculty are male; 47% are female. 88% teach undergraduates. Graduate students teach 6% of introductory courses. The average class size in a laboratory is 22 and in a regular course is 33.

Admissions: 63% of the 2013-2014 applicants were accepted. The SAT scores for the 2013-2014 freshman class were: Critical Reading--11% below 500, 55% between 500 and 599, 30% between 600 and 699, and 4% between 700 and 800; Math--6% below 500, 52% between 500 and 599, 38% between 600 and 699, and 4% between 700 and 800; Writing--22% below 500, 55% between 500 and 599, 21% between 600 and 699, and 2% between 700 and 800. The ACT scores were 3% below 21, 14% between 21 and 23, 47% between 24 and 26, 19% between 27 and 28, and 17% above 28. 45% of the current freshmen were in the top fifth of their class; 80% were in the top two fifths.

Requirements: The SAT or ACT is required. The ACT Optional Writing test is also required. Applicants must be graduates of an accredited secondary school; Applicants must have completed 4 course units in high school English and math, 3 in science, and 2 in foreign languages and social studies. AP and CLEP credits are accepted. Important factors in the admissions decision are advanced placement or honors courses, extracurricular activities record, and evidence of special talent.

Procedure: Freshmen are admitted fall, spring, and summer. Entrance exams should be taken by November 15, if possible. There are deferred admissions and rolling admissions plans. Applications should be filed by March 15 for fall entry, along with a $55 fee. 630 applicants were on the 2013 waiting list; 200 were admitted. Applications are accepted online.

Transfer: 1153 transfer students enrolled in 2012-2013. Transfer students must have earned a minimum 2.0 GPA on collegiate work. They must have a minimum of 30 semester credits or else apply as a freshman. 30 of 128 credits required for the bachelor's degree must be completed at App State.

Visiting: There are regularly scheduled orientations for prospective students, starting at the end of May for all new students. There are guides for informal visits and visitors may sit in on classes.

Financial Aid: In 2013-2014, 67% of all full-time freshmen and 64% of continuing full-time students received some form of financial aid. 47% of all full-time freshmen and 46% of continuing full-time students received need-based aid. The average freshman award was $10,345. Need-based scholarships or need-based grants averaged $7,710 ($30,679 maximum); need-based self-help aid (loans and jobs) averaged $3,292 ($6,577 maximum); non-need-based athletic scholarships averaged $10,948 ($25,727 maximum); and other non-need-based awards and non need based scholarships averaged $2,235 ($12,929 maximum). The average financial indebtedness of the 2013 graduate was $20,016. The FAFSA is required. Check with the school for current application deadlines.

International Students: There are 145 international students enrolled. The school actively recruits these students. They must take the TOEFL with a minimum score of 525 on the paper-based TOEFL (PBT) or 75 on the Internet-based version (iBT), IELTS or TOEFL required if SAT or ACT not taken. The SAT or ACT may be accepted in lieu of the TOEFL.

Computers: All students may access the system anytime. There are no time limits and no fees.

Graduates: From July 1, 2012 to June 30, 2013, 3435 bachelor's degrees were awarded. The most popular majors were business/ marketing (20%), education (17%), and social sciences (8%). 499 companies recruited on campus in 2012-2013. In an average class, 2% graduate in 3 years or less, 44% graduate in 4 years or less, 65% graduate in 5 years or less, and 66% graduate in 6 years or less.

Admissions Contact: Lloyd Scott, Director of Admissions. E-Mail: *admissions@appstate.edu* Web: *www.appstate.edu*

BARTON COLLEGE E-2

Wilson, NC 27893 (252) 399-6315
(800) 345-4973; (252) 399-6572

Full-time: 300 men, 580 women
Part-time: 35 men, 250 women
Graduate: n/app
Year: semesters, summer session
Application Deadline: open
Freshman Class: n/av
SAT or ACT: required
Faculty: n/av; IIB, --$
Ph.D.s: 69%
Student/Faculty: n/av
Tuition: $21,756
Room & Board: $8132

COMPETITIVE

Barton College, founded in 1902, is a private baccalaureate college affiliated with the Christian Church (Disciples of Christ) offering professional and liberal arts degrees. The figures in the above capsule and in this profile are approximate. There are 5 undergraduate schools. In addition to regional accreditation, Barton has baccalaureate program accreditation with CSWE, NCATE, and NLN. The library contains 135,994 volumes, 333,118 microform items, 4798 audio/video tapes/CDs/DVDs, and subscribes to 19,096 periodicals including electronic. Computerized library services include interlibrary loans, database searching, and Internet access. Special learning facilities include a learning resource center, art gallery, TV station, writing center, and theater. The 65-acre campus is in a suburban area 45 miles east of Raleigh. Including any residence halls, there are 28 buildings.

Student Life: 86% of undergraduates are from North Carolina. Others are from 24 states, 10 foreign countries, and Canada. 64% are white; 28% African American. 62% are Protestant; 32% claim no religious affiliation. The average age of freshmen is 19; all undergraduates, 26. 33% do not continue beyond their first year; 40% remain to graduate.

Housing: 638 students can be accommodated in college housing, which includes single-sex and coed dorms and sorority floors. On-campus housing is guaranteed for the freshman year only and is available on a first-come, first-served basis. 52% of students live on campus; of those, 65% remain on campus on weekends. All students may keep cars.

Activities: 16% of men belong to 3 national fraternities; 11% of women belong to 3 national sororities. There are 52 groups on campus, including academic, art, band, cheerleading, choir, chorus, dance, drama, environmental, ethnic, film, honors, international, literary magazine, musical theater, newspaper, orchestra, photography, political, professional, radio and TV, religious, social, social service, student government, and symphony. Popular campus events include Pre-exam Jam, Lighting of the Luminaries Christmas Celebration, and Welcome Back Barton Day.

Sports: There are 6 intercollegiate sports for men and 6 for women, and 10 intramural sports for men and 10 for women. Facilities include a recreation gym for activities, a workout room, an indoor pool and track, and a basketball gym as well as a tennis complex and baseball, softball, and soccer fields.

Disabled Students: 95% of the campus is accessible. Facilities include wheelchair ramps, elevators, special parking, specially equipped restrooms, special class scheduling, lowered drinking fountains, and special housing.

Services: Counseling and information services are available, as is tutoring in core courses for freshman and sophomores. Tutoring for all subjects is available upon request and dependent on the availability of tutors. There is remedial math, reading, and writing. In-class interpreting for hearing-impaired students is available upon request, as are in-class note takers for certain circumstances.

Campus Safety and Security: Measures include 24-hour foot and vehicle patrol, emergency notification system, self-defense education, and security escort services. There are emergency telephones, lighted pathways/sidewalks, controlled access to dorms/residences, campus-wide surveillance cameras, peephole doors to residence rooms, and a city police substation on campus.

Programs of Study: Barton confers B.A., B.S., B.F.A., B.L.S., B.S.N., and B.S.W. degrees. Bachelor's degrees are awarded in BIOLOGICAL SCIENCE (biology/biological science), BUSINESS (accounting, business administration and management, human resources, and sports management), COMMUNICATIONS AND THE ARTS (communications, dramatic arts, English, graphic design, painting, and studio art), COMPUTER AND PHYSICAL SCIENCE (chemistry, information sciences and systems, and mathematics), EDUCATION (art education, athletic training, education of the deaf and hearing impaired, elementary education, middle school education, physical education, and specific learning disabilities), ENGINEERING AND ENVIRONMENTAL DESIGN (environmental science), HEALTH PROFESSIONS (exercise science and nursing), SOCIAL SCIENCE (criminal justice, economics, gerontology, history, political science/ government, psychology, religion, social studies, social work, and Spanish studies). Nursing and education are the strongest academically. Business, nursing, and education have the largest enrollments.

Required: All students must complete a minimum of 126 credit hours, including 36 in the major and 45 to 48 in the core curriculum, with a minimum GPA of 2.0. Core requirements include 12 semester hours in humanities and fine arts, 6 to 9 in global and cross-cultural perspective, 7 in natural sciences, 6 in social sciences, 6 in writing proficiency, 3 each in math, computer proficiency, and first-year seminar (for freshmen), and 2 in sports science.

Special: Barton offers internships, a Washington semester, a general studies degree, dual majors, work study, and credit by exam in entry-level courses. Preprofessional programs are offered in law, engineering, and a variety of health-related fields, as are 3-2 engineering degrees with North Carolina State and North Carolina Agricultural and Technical State Universities and the University of North Carolina at Charlotte. There are 4 national honor societies, a freshman honors program, and 1 departmental honors program.

Faculty/Classroom: 42% of faculty are male; 58% are female. All teach undergraduates. No introductory courses are taught by graduate students.

The average class size in an introductory lecture is 22; in a laboratory, 12; and in a regular course, 16.

Requirements: The SAT or ACT is required. Applicants must be high school graduates with at least 13 college preparatory credits. Barton recommends 4 units of English, 3 of social science, 3 of math (including algebra), and 2 of natural science (including lab science). A foreign language is encouraged. Admission criteria vary for Weekend College. A GPA of 2.0 is required. AP and CLEP credits are accepted.

Procedure: Freshmen are admitted to all sessions. There is a rolling admissions plan. Application deadlines are open. Application fee is $25. Notification is sent on a rolling basis. Applications are accepted online.

Transfer: 136 transfer students enrolled in a recent year. Applicants must have a college GPA of 2.0 and be eligible to return to the school they last attended. 45 of 126 credits required for the bachelor's degree must be completed at Barton.

Visiting: There are regularly scheduled orientations for prospective students, including visiting classes, financial aid and freshman advising workshops, tours of the campus, and meeting with administrators, faculty, and students. There are guides for informal visits, and visitors may stay overnight. To schedule a visit, contact the Admissions Office.

International Students: There are 16 international students enrolled. The school actively recruits these students. They must take the TOEFL with a minimum score of 525 on the paper-based TOEFL (PBT) or 71 on the Internet-based version (iBT).

Computers: Wireless access is available. All students may access the system 24 hours a day, 7 days a week. There are no time limits and no fees.

Graduates: In a recent year, 230 bachelor's degrees were awarded. The most popular majors were business administration (20%), nursing (16%), and elementary education (10%). In an average class, 2% graduate in 3 years or less, 31% graduate in 4 years or less, 41% graduate in 5 years or less, and 44% graduate in 6 years or less.

Admissions Contact: Director of Admissions. E-mail: *enroll@barton.edu* Web: *www.barton.edu*

BELMONT ABBEY COLLEGE C-3

Belmont, NC 28012 (704) 461-6665
(888) BAC-0110; (704) 461-6220

Full-time: 663 men, 927 women	**Faculty:** 76; IIB, --$
Part-time: 33 men, 83 women	**Ph.D.s:** 70%
Graduate: n/av	**Student/Faculty:** 16 to 1
Year: semesters, summer session	**Tuition:** $27,622
Application Deadline:	**Room & Board:** $10,094
Freshman Class: 1843 applied, 1185 accepted, 303 enrolled	
SAT CR/M: 510/510 **ACT:** 23	**COMPETITIVE**

Belmont Abbey College, founded in 1876, is a private, liberal arts college affiliated with the Roman Catholic Church. In addition to regional accreditation, Belmont Abbey has baccalaureate program accreditation with NCATE. The library contains 118,827 volumes, 116,173 microform items, 7,418 audio/video tapes/CDs/DVDs, and subscribes to 275 periodicals including electronic. Computerized library services include interlibrary loans, database searching, Internet access, and Wi-Fi capability. Special learning facilities include a The 650-acre campus is in a suburban area 12 miles southwest of Charlotte. Including any residence halls, there are 20 buildings.

Student Life: 70% of undergraduates are from North Carolina. Others are from 43 states, 24 foreign countries, and Canada. 35% are White; 31% race unknown; 27% African American. 57% are Catholic; 47% claim no religious affiliation. The average age of freshmen is 20; all undergraduates, 28. 37% do not continue beyond their first year; 63% remain to graduate.

Housing: 747 students can be accommodated in college housing, which includes single-sex and coed dorms, on-campus apartments, and off-campus apartments. In addition, there are special-interest houses, and a quiet residence hall. Single-occupancy housing is available for all students. On-campus housing is guaranteed for all 4 years. 57% of students commute. All students may keep cars.

Activities: 6% of men belong to 1 local and 2 national fraternities; 5% of women belong to 4 local sororities. There are 21 groups on campus, including cheerleading, chess, choir, chorus, computers, drama, honors, international, literary magazine, newspaper, political, professional, religious, social, social service, and student government. Popular campus events include Spring Weekend, Special Olympics and Greek Week.

Sports: There are 8 intercollegiate sports for men and 8 for women. Facilities include a phys ed center with a 1200-seat gym and a college union with a 225-seat auditorium.

Disabled Students: 60% of the campus is accessible. Facilities include wheelchair ramps, elevators, special parking, specially equipped restrooms, special class scheduling, and lowered drinking fountains.

Services: Counseling and information services are available, as is tutoring in some subjects, including math, English, and accounting. There is a reader service for the blind.

Campus Safety and Security: Measures include 24-hour foot and vehicle patrol, self-defense education, and security escort services. There are emergency telephones and lighted pathways/sidewalks.

Programs of Study: Belmont Abbey confers B.A., and B.S. degrees. Bachelor's degrees are awarded in BIOLOGICAL SCIENCE (biology/biological science), BUSINESS (accounting, business administration and management, and sports management), COMMUNICATIONS AND THE ARTS (English), COMPUTER AND PHYSICAL SCIENCE (mathematics), EDUCATION (education and elementary education), SOCIAL SCIENCE (applied psychology, criminal justice, history, liberal arts/general studies, parks and recreation management, philosophy, political science/government, psychology, and theological studies). Psychology, elementary education, and English are the strongest academically. Business administration, education, and elementary education have the largest enrollments.

Required: To graduate, all students must complete a minimum of 120 credits, including 60 credits of core curriculum and 30 upper-level credits in the major. Among the core requirements are history, math, natural sciences, theology, philosophy, English, fine arts, and rhetoric. A minimum 2.0 GPA must be maintained. Honors students must submit a thesis.

Special: Cross-registration is offered through the Charlotte Area Educational Consortium. There are internships in many majors, including required internships in educational studies, as well as on-campus work-study, accelerated degree programs, nondegree study, dual majors, and study abroad in Guatemala, Germany, and France. There are 5 national honor societies and a freshman honors program.

Faculty/Classroom: 55% of faculty are male; 45% are female. All teach undergraduates, and 60% do both. No introductory courses are taught by graduate students. The average class size in an introductory lecture is 16; in a laboratory is 15; and in a regular course is 4.

Admissions: 64% of the 2013-2014 applicants were accepted. The SAT scores for the 2013-2014 freshman class were: Critical Reading--54% below 500, 29% between 500 and 599, 13% between 600 and 699, and 3% between 700 and 800; Math--42% below 500, 39% between 500 and 599, 17% between 600 and 699, and 2% between 700 and 800. The ACT scores were 27% below 21, 33% between 21 and 23, 28% between 24 and 26, 4% between 27 and 28, and 7% above 28. 20% of the current freshmen were in the top fifth of their class; 46% were in the top two fifths. 3 freshmen graduated first in their class.

Requirements: The SAT is required. Candidates must be graduates of an accredited secondary school and a 2.0 high school GPA. A minimum of 16 academic credits must be completed, including 4 in English, 3 each in math and electives, and 2 each in foreign language, history, and science. A GPA of 2.0 is required. AP and CLEP credits are accepted. Important factors in the admissions decision are advanced placement or honors courses, extracurricular activities record, and leadership record.

Procedure: Freshmen are admitted fall and spring. Entrance exams should be taken by October of the senior year. There are deferred admissions and rolling admissions plans. Check with the school for current application deadlines. The application fee is $35. Applications are accepted online.

Transfer: 185 transfer students enrolled in 2012-2013. Students with 24 or more credit hours must submit all college transcripts, and those with fewer than 24 credit hours must also submit a high school transcript and SAT scores. All candidates must have a minimum 2.0 GPA and be eligible to return to the last college attended. An interview is recommended. 30 of 120 credits required for the bachelor's degree must be completed at Belmont Abbey.

Visiting: There are regularly scheduled orientations for prospective students, consisting of a campus tour and meetings with a financial aid adviser, faculty, and students. There are guides for informal visits, visitors may sit in on classes, and stay overnight. To schedule a visit, contact the Admissions Office.

Financial Aid: In 2013-2014, 98% of all full-time freshmen and 94% of continuing full-time students received some form of financial aid. 72% of all full-time freshmen and 79% of continuing full-time students received need-based aid. The average freshman award was $20,296. Need-based scholarships or need-based grants averaged $17,293 ($20,000 maximum); need-based self-help aid (loans and jobs) averaged $4,023 ($125,800 maximum); non-need-based athletic scholarships averaged $5,053 ($21,000 maximum); and other non-need-based awards and non-need-based scholarships averaged $2,156 ($10,500 maximum). 12% of undergraduate students work part-time. Average annual earnings from campus work are $1800. The average financial indebtedness of the 2013 graduate was $19,516. Belmont Abbey is a member of CSS. The FAFSA and the state aid form are required. The priority date for freshman financial aid applications for fall entry is April 1. The deadline for filing freshman financial aid applications for fall entry is July 1.

International Students: There are 46 international students enrolled. The school actively recruits these students. They must take the TOEFL with a minimum score of 550 on the paper-based TOEFL (PBT) or 79 on the Internet-based version (iBT). They must also take the SAT or ACT, scoring 900.

Computers: All students may access the system at any time. There are no time limits and no fees.

Graduates: From July 1, 2012 to June 30, 2013, 379 bachelor's degrees were awarded. The most popular majors were business management (39%), education (15%), and elementary education (13%). 90 companies recruited on campus in 2012-2013. In an average class, 40% graduate in 4 years or less, 45% graduate in 5 years or less, and 46% graduate in 6 years or less. Of the 2012 graduating class, 16% were enrolled in graduate school within 6 months of graduation, and 88% were employed.

Admissions Contact: Roger Jones, Director of Admissions. E-Mail: *RogerJones@BAC.edu* Web: *www.belmontabbeycollege.edu*

BENNETT COLLEGE D-2

Greensboro, NC 27401 **(336) 517-2167; (800) 413-5323**

Full-time: 709 women	**Faculty:** 55; IIB, --$
Part-time: 57 women	**Ph.D.s:** 55%
Graduate: n/av	**Student/Faculty:** 13 to 1
Year: semesters	**Tuition:** $15,234
Application Deadline: open	**Room & Board:** $6736
Freshman Class: n/av	

LESS COMPETITIVE

Bennett College, founded in 1873, is a private, historically African American women's liberal arts institution affiliated with the United Methodist Church. In addition to regional accreditation, Bennett has baccalaureate program accreditation with ADA, CSWE, and NCATE. The library contains 121,390 volumes, 300 microform items, and 2,436 audio/video tapes/CDs/DVDs, and subscribes to 259 periodicals including electronic. Computerized library services include interlibrary loans, database searching, and Internet access. Special learning facilities include an art gallery, and the Women's Leadership Institute. The 55-acre campus is in an urban area approximately 1 mile from downtown Greensboro. Including any residence halls, there are 38 buildings.

Student Life: 65% of undergraduates are from out of state, mostly the Middle Atlantic. Students are from 31 states, and 5 foreign countries. 97% are African American. 13% claim no religious affiliation. The average age of freshmen is 19; all undergraduates, 20.

Housing: 536 students can be accommodated in college housing, which includes dorms. On-campus housing is guaranteed for all 4 years. 89% of students live on campus; of those, 50% remain on campus on weekends. Alcohol is not permitted. Upperclassmen may keep cars.

Activities: There are no fraternities; 10% of women belong to 4 national sororities. There are 84 groups on campus, including cheerleading, choir, computers, dance, drama, ethnic, film, honors, international, literary magazine, newspaper, orchestra, political, professional, religious, social service, and student government. Popular campus events include Convocatum Est and Spring Festival.

Sports: There are 1 intercollegiate sports for women, and 5 intramural sports for women. Facilities include a gym, a pool, exercise facilities, an athletic field, and basketball courts.

Disabled Students: 25% of the campus is accessible. Facilities include wheelchair ramps, special parking, specially equipped restrooms, and special class scheduling.

Services: Counseling and information services are available, as is tutoring in every subject. There is remedial math, reading, and writing.

Campus Safety and Security: Measures include 24-hour foot and vehicle patrol, emergency notification system, self-defense education, and security escort services. There are shuttle buses, lighted pathways/sidewalks, and controlled access to dorms/residences.

Programs of Study: Bennett confers B.A., B.S., B.A.S.I.S., B.F.A. and B.S.W. degrees. Bachelor's degrees are awarded in BIOLOGICAL SCIENCE (biology/biological science), BUSINESS (accounting and business administration and management), COMMUNICATIONS AND THE ARTS (arts administration/management, communications, English, music, and visual and performing arts), COMPUTER AND PHYSICAL SCIENCE (chemistry, computer science, and mathematics), EDUCATION (elementary education, English education, mathematics education, middle school education, music education, science education, and special education), SOCIAL SCIENCE (interdisciplinary studies, political science/government, psychology, and social work). Biology, business administration, and psychology are the strongest academically.

Required: All students must take 54 to 64 semester hours of general education courses in communication, humanities, math, natural science, reading, history, foreign language, philosophy, phys ed, religion, and women's studies. A total of 124 semester hours, with 60 to 64 in the major, and at least a 2.0 GPA are required for graduation. Comprehensive exams in math and English are required.

Special: Students may cross-register at member colleges of the Greensboro Regional Consortium, study off campus through exchange programs, take a Washington semester, and study abroad. Bennett offers student-designed majors, nondegree study, a 3-1 nursing program, a B.A.-B.S. degree in interdisciplinary studies, and a 3-2 engineering degree with North Carolina Agricultural and Technical State University. There are 7 national honor societies and 7 departmental honors programs.

Faculty/Classroom: 71% of faculty are male; 29% are female. All teach undergraduates. No introductory courses are taught by graduate students. The average class size in an introductory lecture is 15; in a laboratory is 15; and in a regular course is 20.

Admissions: 5% of the current freshmen were in the top fifth of their class; 13% were in the top two fifths.

Requirements: In addition, applicants must be graduates of accredited high schools or have earned the GED. Secondary preparation should include 4 years of English, 3 each of math and natural science, 2 each and social science and foreign language, and 5 electives. A personal essay is required, and an interview is recommended. A GPA of 2.0 is required. AP and CLEP credits are accepted. Important factors in the admissions decision are recommendations by school officials, parents or siblings attended your school, and evidence of special talent.

Procedure: Freshmen are admitted fall and spring. Entrance exams should be taken preferably during the senior year. There are deferred admissions and rolling admissions plans. Application deadlines are open. Application fee is $30. Applications are accepted online.

Transfer: 13 transfer students enrolled in 2012-2013. An official transcript and a catalog from each college previously attended, 2 letters of recommendation, a statement of honorable dismissal from previous colleges, and a personal essay are required. 64 of 124 credits required for the bachelor's degree must be completed at Bennett.

Visiting: There are regularly scheduled orientations for prospective students, including a campus tour and meetings with a financial aid officer and an academic program director. There are guides for informal visits, visitors may sit in on classes, and stay overnight. To schedule a visit, contact Director of Admissions.

Financial Aid: 4% of undergraduate students work part-time. Average annual earnings from campus work are $2000. Bennett is a member of CSS. The FAFSA and FFS are required. The priority date for freshman financial aid applications for fall entry is March 1.

International Students: There are 5 international students enrolled. The school actively recruits these students. They must take the TOEFL. They must also take the SAT or ACT.

Computers: All students may access the system at any time. There are no time limits and no fees.

Graduates: From July 1, 2012 to June 30, 2013, 99 bachelor's degrees were awarded. The most popular majors were psychology (15%), social work (15%), and mass communications (13%).

Admissions Contact: Jocelyn Bigg, Director of Admissions. E-Mail: *jbiggs@bennett.edu* Web: *www.bennett.edu*

CABARRUS COLLEGE OF HEALTH SCIENCES C-3

Concord, NC 28025-2405 **(704) 783-1555; (704) 783-2077**

Full-time: 30 men, 210 women	**Faculty:** n/av
Part-time: 20 men, 120 women	**Ph.D.s:** n/av
Graduate: n/app	**Student/Faculty:** n/av
Year: semesters	**Tuition:** $10,450
Application Deadline: see profile	**Room & Board:** n/av
Freshman Class: n/av	
SAT or ACT: required	**SPECIAL**

Cabarrus College of Health Sciences, founded in 1942, is a private institution specializing in health science. The figures in the above capsule and in this profile are approximate. The library contains 6370 volumes and 776 audio/video tapes/CDs/DVDs, and subscribes to 263 periodicals including electronic. Computerized library services include database searching and Internet access. Special learning facilities include a learning resource center. The campus is in a suburban area.

Student Life: All undergraduates are from North Carolina. 90% are white. The average age of freshmen is 25; all undergraduates, 26.

Housing: There are no residence halls. All students commute.

Activities: There are no fraternities or sororities. Groups on campus include honors, professional, and student government.

Sports: There is no sports program at Cabarrus.

Disabled Students: All of the campus is accessible. Facilities include wheelchair ramps, elevators, special parking, specially equipped restrooms, lowered drinking fountains, and lowered telephones.

Campus Safety and Security: Measures include 24-hour foot and vehicle patrol. There are emergency telephones and lighted pathways/sidewalks.

Programs of Study: Cabarrus confers B.S. degrees. Associates degrees are also awarded. Bachelor's degrees are awarded in HEALTH PROFESSIONS (health care administration and nursing).

Special: There is 1 national honor society.

Faculty/Classroom: All teach undergraduates. No introductory courses are taught by graduate students. The average class size in an introductory lecture is 20, in a laboratory, 15, and in a regular course, 20.

Requirements: The SAT or ACT is required. AP and CLEP credits are accepted.

Procedure: Freshmen are admitted fall and spring. Check with the school for current application deadlines. The application fee is $50. Applications are accepted online. A waiting list is maintained.

Visiting: There are regularly scheduled orientations for prospective students.

Financial Aid: Check with the school for current application deadlines.

International Students: They must take the SAT or ACT.

Computers: Wireless access is available.

Admissions Contact: Mark Ellison, Director of Admissions. E-Mail: *mellison@cabarruscollege.edu* Web: *www.cabarruscollege.edu*

CAMPBELL UNIVERSITY E-3

Buies Creek, NC 27506 (800) 334-4111, ext. 1320; (910) 893-1288

Full-time: 1310 men, 1450 women	**Faculty:** n/av
Part-time: 115 men, 70 women	**Ph.D.s:** 92%
Graduate: 680 men, 945 women	**Student/Faculty:** 30 to 1
Year: semesters, summer session	**Tuition:** $20,000
Application Deadline: n/av	**Room & Board:** $6500
Freshman Class: n/av	
SAT or ACT: required	**COMPETITIVE**

Campbell University, founded in 1887, is a private nonsectarian institution affiliated with the North Carolina Baptist Convention and offering degree programs in liberal arts and sciences, business, and education. Figures in the above capsule and in this profile are approximate. There are 6 undergraduate schools and 5 graduate schools. In addition to regional accreditation, Campbell has baccalaureate program accreditation with ACPE, CSWE, and NCATE. The 4 libraries contain 332,000 volumes, 1253 microform items, and 5033 audio/video tapes/CDs/DVDs, and subscribe to 15,665 periodicals including electronic. Computerized library services include interlibrary loans, database searching, Internet access, and laptop Internet portals. Special learning facilities include a learning resource center, art gallery, radio station, computer labs, computerized music lab, family and consumer sciences lab, athletic learning resources center, drug information center for the School of Pharmacy, pharmacy research facility, and the Lundy-Fetterman Museum. The 850-acre campus is in a rural area 28 miles south of Raleigh and 30 miles north of Fayetteville. Including any residence halls, there are 84 buildings.

Student Life: 77% of undergraduates are from North Carolina. Others are from 50 states, 42 foreign countries, and Canada. 90% are from public schools. 75% are white; 12% African American. 76% are Protestant. The average age of freshmen is 18; all undergraduates, 20. 13% do not continue beyond their first year; 45% remain to graduate.

Housing: 1500 students can be accommodated in college housing, which includes single-sex dorms, on-campus apartments, off-campus apartments, and married student housing. In addition, there are honors houses. On-campus housing is guaranteed for the freshman year only. 65% of students live on campus; of those, 85% remain on campus on weekends. Alcohol is not permitted. All students may keep cars.

Activities: There are no fraternities or sororities. There are 49 groups on campus, including art, band, cheerleading, choir, chorale, chorus, computers, debate, drama, ethnic, honors, international, jazz band, literary magazine, musical theater, newspaper, orchestra, pep band, photography, political, professional, religious, social, social service, and student government. Popular campus events include the Staley Lecture Series, Spring Fling, and spring and Christmas formals.

Sports: There are 8 intercollegiate sports for men and 9 for women, and 23 intramural sports for men and 23 for women. Facilities include a 1000-seat gym for intramural sports, an athletic complex, 2 golf courses, a nature trail, 2 running tracks, 3 workout facilities, tennis courts, baseball, softball, and soccer fields, and an indoor pool.

Disabled Students: 95% of the campus is accessible. Facilities include wheelchair ramps, elevators, special parking, specially equipped restrooms, special class scheduling, lowered drinking fountains, lowered telephones, and special housing.

Services: Counseling and information services are available, as is tutoring in most subjects. There is remedial math and writing.

Campus Safety and Security: Measures include 24-hour foot and vehicle patrol, emergency notification system, self-defense education, and security escort services. There are emergency telephones and lighted pathways/sidewalks.

Programs of Study: Campbell confers B.A., B.S., B.Applied Sci., B.B.A., B.H.S., and B.S.W. degrees. Associates, master's, and doctoral degrees are also awarded. Bachelor's degrees are awarded in BIOLOGICAL SCIENCE (biochemistry and biology/biological science), BUSINESS (accounting, business administration and management, international business management, investments and securities, and sports management), COMMUNICATIONS AND THE ARTS (advertising, art, communications, dramatic arts, English, French, journalism, music, and Spanish), COMPUTER AND PHYSICAL SCIENCE (chemistry, computer science, information sciences and systems, and mathematics), EDUCATION (athletic training, elementary education, and middle school education), ENGINEERING AND ENVIRONMENTAL DESIGN (military science and preengineering), HEALTH PROFESSIONS (clinical science and prepharmacy), SOCIAL SCIENCE (criminal justice, economics, family/consumer studies, history, physical fitness/movement, political science/government, prelaw, psychology, religion, and social work). Life and health science, trust management, and teacher education are the strongest academically. Education, pharmacy, and biology are the largest.

Required: To graduate, students must complete 128 credit hours with a minimum GPA of 2.0 overall and in the major. All students must take a core curriculum of 45 to 65 hours including English, math, science, social science, religion, fine arts, phys ed, and the Cultural Enrichment Program.

Special: Campbell offers co-op programs, internships, study abroad in 7 countries, a Washington semester, numerous apprenticeships, accelerated degrees, dual majors, and a general studies degree. There is credit for military and work experience. Cross-registration with the North Carolina Model Teacher Education Consortium is possible. There are 14 national honor societies, a freshman honors program, and all departments have honors programs.

Faculty/Classroom: 67% of faculty are male; 33% are female. 62% teach undergraduates, and 40% do research. No introductory courses are taught by graduate students. The average class size in an introductory lecture is 30; in a laboratory, 25, and in a regular course, 25.

Requirements: The SAT or ACT is required. Students with less than satisfactory test scores on the math and verbal sections will be eligible for full admission if they have a respectable high school GPA but will be monitored. Applicants should have completed 12 high school academic credits, including 4 credits of English, 3 of math, and 2 each of history or social studies, science, and foreign language. An essay, an interview, and a portfolio are recommended. An audition is required for some majors. Campbell requires applicants to be in the upper 50% of their class. A GPA of 2.7 is required. AP and CLEP credits are accepted. Important factors in the admissions decision are advanced placement or honors courses, leadership record, and personality/intangible qualities.

Procedure: Freshmen are admitted to all sessions. Entrance exams should be taken during the junior year or the fall of the senior year. There are deferred admissions and rolling admissions plans. Application deadlines are open. The application fee is $50. Applications are accepted online.

Transfer: Applicants should have a minimum GPA of 2.0 and supply transcripts from previously attended colleges. 36 of 128 credits required for the bachelor's degree must be completed at Campbell.

Visiting: There are regularly scheduled orientations for prospective students, including a campus tour, student panel, and department visits. There are guides for informal visits; visitors may sit in on classes and stay overnight. To schedule a visit, contact the Admissions Office.

Financial Aid: The FAFSA is required. Check with the school for current deadlines.

International Students: The school actively recruits these students. They must take the TOEFL, with a minimum score of 500 on the paper-based TOEFL (PBT) or 63 on the Internet-based version (iBT), or take the IELTS. They must also take the SAT or ACT.

Computers: Wireless access is available. All students may access the system during posted student hours, generally Monday through Thursday, 8 a.m. to 11 p.m, with extended hours Friday through Sunday. There are no time limits and no fees. It is strongly recommended that all students have a personal computer.

Admissions Contact: Herbert V. Kerner, Jr., Dean of Admissions. A campus DVD is available. E-Mail: *adm@campbell.edu* Web: *www.campbell.edu*

CATAWBA COLLEGE C-2

Salisbury, NC 28144 (704) 637-4402; (800) 228-2922; (704) 637-4444

Full-time: 595 men, 615 women	**Faculty:** 68; IIB, --$
Part-time: 23 men, 65 women	**Ph.D.s:** 84%
Graduate: 12 women	**Student/Faculty:** 17 to 1
Year: semesters, summer session	**Tuition:** $27,360
Application Deadline:	**Room & Board:** $9745
Freshman Class: 3226 applied, 1309 accepted, 342 enrolled	
SAT CR/M: 490/500 **ACT:** 21	**COMPETITIVE**

Catawba College, founded in 1851, is an independent institution affiliated with the United Church of Christ that offers undergraduate programs in the arts and sciences, business, education, performing arts, environmental science, social and behavioral sciences, and physical education. There are 5 undergraduate schools and 1 graduate school. In addition to regional accreditation, Catawba has baccalaureate program accreditation with NCATE. The 2 libraries contain 187,236 volumes, 647,109 microform items, and 8,823 audio/video tapes/CDs/DVDs, and subscribe to 1,307 periodicals including electronic. Computerized library services include interlibrary loans, database searching, Internet access, and Wi-Fi capability.

The 276-acre campus is in a small town 40 miles northeast of Charlotte. Including any residence halls, there are 35 buildings.

Student Life: 82% of undergraduates are from North Carolina. Others are from 33 states, 18 foreign countries, and Canada. 88% are from public schools. 70% are White; 21% African American. 56% are Protestant; 36% claim no religious affiliation. The average age of freshmen is 18; all undergraduates, 23. 30% do not continue beyond their first year; 52% remain to graduate.

Housing: 762 students can be accommodated in college housing, which includes single-sex and coed dorms. nonsmoking and alcohol-free dorms. On-campus housing is guaranteed for all 4 years. 65% of students live on campus; of those, 75% remain on campus on weekends. All students may keep cars.

Activities: There are no fraternities or sororities. There are 26 groups on campus, including art, band, cheerleading, chess, choir, chorale, chorus, computers, dance, drama, drill team, drum and bugle corps, ethnic, honors, literary magazine, musical theater, newspaper, orchestra, pep band, political, professional, religious, social, social service, student government, and yearbook. Popular campus events include Winterfest, Inaugural Ball and Parents Weekend.

Sports: There are 8 intercollegiate sports for men and 8 for women, and 4 intramural sports for men and 4 for women. Facilities include a 5000-seat stadium and a 3500-seat gym, football, baseball, softball, soccer, and field hockey fields, tennis, volleyball, and racquetball courts, a weight lifting room, a swimming pool, a challenge course, and table tennis and billiards.

Disabled Students: 95% of the campus is accessible. Facilities include wheelchair ramps, elevators, special parking, specially equipped restrooms, lowered drinking fountains, and lowered telephones.

Services: Counseling and information services are available, as is tutoring in most subjects.

Campus Safety and Security: Measures include 24-hour foot and vehicle patrol, emergency notification system, self-defense education, and security escort services. There are emergency telephones, lighted pathways/sidewalks, and controlled access to dorms/residences.

Programs of Study: Catawba confers B.A., B.A.E., B.S., B.B.A. and B.F.A. degrees. Master's degrees are also awarded. Bachelor's degrees are awarded in AGRICULTURE (environmental studies), BIOLOGICAL SCIENCE (biology/biological science), BUSINESS (accounting, business administration and management, international business management, marketing management, recreation and leisure services, sports management, and sustainable management), COMMUNICATIONS AND THE ARTS (communications, English, language arts, music, musical theater, Spanish, theatre arts, theater management, and writing), COMPUTER AND PHYSICAL SCIENCE (chemistry, computer science, information sciences and systems, and mathematics), EDUCATION (athletic training, education, elementary education, environmental education, mathematics education, middle school education, music education, physical education, science education, and social studies education), ENGINEERING AND ENVIRONMENTAL DESIGN (environmental science), HEALTH PROFESSIONS (medical technology and recreation therapy), SOCIAL SCIENCE (administration of justice , economics, history, philosophy, political science/government, prelaw, psychology, public administration, religion, and sociology). Business, education, and theater arts have the largest enrollments.

Required: To graduate, students must complete at least 120 credit hours, including up to 54 in their major, with a minimum GPA of 2.0. General education requirements include 9 semester hours in humanities, 7 in natural sciences, 6 each in social sciences, English composition, and fine arts, 4 to 6 in math, and 1 in physical fitness and foreign language through the intermediate level. Students must demonstrate proficiency in writing.

Special: There are cooperative programs in forestry and environmental science with Duke University, and physician assistant and medical technician training with Wake Forest University. Cross-registration is possible through the Charlotte Area Educational Consortium. Catawba also offers internships, study abroad in Costa Rica, work-study programs, accelerated degree programs, dual majors, pass/fail options, and student-designed majors. There are 13 national honor societies, a freshman honors program, and 8 departmental honors programs.

Faculty/Classroom: 54% of faculty are male; 46% are female. All teach undergraduates, 40% do research, and 40% do both. No introductory courses are taught by graduate students. The average class size in an introductory lecture is 18; in a laboratory is 16; and in a regular course is 16.

Admissions: 41% of the 2013-2014 applicants were accepted. The SAT scores for the 2013-2014 freshman class were: Critical Reading--60% below 500, 31% between 500 and 599, 6% between 600 and 699, and 3% between 700 and 800; Math--55% below 500, 32% between 500 and 599, 12% between 600 and 699, and 1% between 700 and 800. The ACT scores were 45% below 21, 28% between 21 and 23, 16% between 24 and 26, 6% between 27 and 28, and 4% above 28. 19% of the current freshmen were in the top fifth of their class; 34% were in the top two fifths. 5 freshmen graduated first in their class.

Requirements: The SAT or ACT and ACT Writing Test are recommended. SAT and ACT scores are optional. Applicants must be graduates of an accredited secondary school or have a GED. They must have completed 16 academic credits, of which 12 must be Carnegie units. An essay is required, and an interview is encouraged for all students. An audition is required for music and drama scholarships. A GPA of 2.5 is required. AP and CLEP credits are accepted. Important factors in the admissions decision are evidence of special talent, recommendations by school officials, and extracurricular activities record.

Procedure: Freshmen are admitted to all sessions. Entrance exams should be taken by December of the senior year. There are deferred admissions and rolling admissions plans. Application deadlines are open. Notification is sent on a rolling basis. Applications are accepted online. Application fees are waived if application is completed online.

Transfer: 117 transfer students enrolled in 2012-2013. Applicants must present a GPA of 2.0 or better. 30 of 120 credits required for the bachelor's degree must be completed at Catawba.

Visiting: There are regularly scheduled orientations for prospective students, including campus tours, lunches, meetings with faculty, and financial aid and athletic workshops. There are guides for informal visits and visitors may sit in on classes. To schedule a visit, contact the Office of Admissions at (704) 637-4442.

Financial Aid: In 2013-2014, 100% of all full-time freshmen and 97% of continuing full-time students received some form of financial aid. 78% of all full-time freshmen and 75% of continuing full-time students received need-based aid. The average freshman award was $27,836. Need-based scholarships or need-based grants averaged $7,900 ($15,145 maximum); need-based self-help aid (loans and jobs) averaged $5,159 ($11,500 maximum); non-need-based athletic scholarships averaged $8,673 ($23,730 maximum); and other non-need-based awards and non-need-based scholarships averaged $16,550 ($40,743 maximum). 27% of undergraduate students work part-time. Average annual earnings from campus work are $700. The average financial indebtedness of the 2013 graduate was $26,445. The FAFSA and the college's own financial statement are required. The deadline for filing freshman financial aid applications for fall entry is March 15.

International Students: There are 35 international students enrolled. They must take the TOEFL with a minimum score of 525 on the paper-based TOEFL (PBT) or 69 on the Internet-based version (iBT).

Computers: All students may access the system. There are no time limits and no fees.

Graduates: From July 1, 2012 to June 30, 2013, 157 bachelor's degrees were awarded. The most popular majors were business administration (37%), education (20%), and performing arts (10%). 15 companies recruited on campus in 2012-2013. In an average class, 46% graduate in 4 years or less, 48% graduate in 5 years or less, and 54% graduate in 6 years or less.

Admissions Contact: Lois Williams, Vice President for Enrollment. E-Mail: *lhwillia@catawba.edu* Web: *www.catawba.edu*

DAVIDSON COLLEGE — C-3

Davidson, NC 28035 — **(704) 894-2230** — **(800) 768-0380; (704) 894-2016**

Full-time: 889 men, 899 women	**Faculty:** 174; IIB, +$
Part-time: n/av	**Ph.D.s:** 97%
Graduate: n/av	**Student/Faculty:** 10 to 1
Year: semesters	**Tuition:** $42,849
Application Deadline: January 2	**Room & Board:** $11,834
Freshman Class: 4745 applied, 1215 accepted, 483 enrolled	
SAT CR/M/W: 675/660/660 **ACT:** 31	**MOST COMPETITIVE**

Davidson College, founded in 1837, is a private liberal arts institution affiliated with the Presbyterian Church. There is one undergraduate school. In addition to regional accreditation, Davidson has baccalaureate program accreditation with NCATE. The 3 libraries contain 561,427 volumes, 601,821 microform items, and 17,878 audio/video tapes/CDs/DVDs, and subscribe to 108,090 periodicals including electronic. Computerized library services include interlibrary loans, database searching, Internet access, and Wi-Fi capability. Special learning facilities include an art gallery, radio station, arboretum. The 665-acre campus is in a small town 19 miles north of Charlotte. Including any residence halls, there are 124 buildings.

Student Life: 78% of undergraduates are from out of state, mostly the South. Students are from 47 states, 42 foreign countries, and Canada. 44% are from public schools. 69% are White. The average age of freshmen is 18; all undergraduates, 20. 4% do not continue beyond their first year; 95% remain to graduate.

Housing: 1749 students can be accommodated in college housing, which includes single-sex and coed dorms, on-campus apartments, and off-campus apartments. In addition, there are special-interest houses, substance-free housing. On-campus housing is guaranteed for the freshman year only and is available on a lottery system for upperclassmen. 92% of students live on campus. All students may keep cars.

Activities: 34% of men belong to 6 national fraternities; 1% of women

belong to 4 local and 2 national sororities. There are 200 groups on campus, including art, cheerleading, choir, chorale, chorus, computers, dance, drama, ethnic, gay, honors, international, jazz band, literary magazine, musical theater, newspaper, opera, orchestra, outing, pep band, political, professional, radio and TV, religious, social, social service, student government, symphony, and yearbook. Popular campus events include Fall Concert, Spring Concert, and Convocations.

Sports: There are 11 intercollegiate sports for men and 10 for women. Facilities include John M. Belk basketball arena, Wilson baseball field, indoor and outdoor tennis courts, 3 racquetball courts, a squash court, a natatorium with a diving well, 2 Nautilus rooms, a gym, a wrestling room, a dance studio, a golf course, a cross-country course and trail, a football and soccer stadium, various other playing fields, and facilities for sailing, swimming, water skiing, and canoeing at the Lake campus.

Disabled Students: 90% of the campus is accessible. Facilities include wheelchair ramps, elevators, special parking, specially equipped restrooms, special class scheduling, lowered drinking fountains, and lowered telephones.

Services: Counseling and information services are available, as is tutoring in some subjects, Tutoring is available as needed through the Student Affairs Office. There is a reader service for the blind. Center for Teaching and Learning also provides student support

Campus Safety and Security: Measures include 24-hour foot and vehicle patrol, emergency notification system, self-defense education, and security escort services. There are shuttle buses, emergency telephones, lighted pathways/sidewalks, and controlled access to dorms/residences.

Programs of Study: Davidson confers A.B., and B.S. degrees. Bachelor's degrees are awarded in AGRICULTURE (environmental studies), BIOLOGICAL SCIENCE (biology/biological science), COMMUNICATIONS AND THE ARTS (art, classics, dramatic arts, English, French, German, music, and Spanish), COMPUTER AND PHYSICAL SCIENCE (chemistry, mathematics, and physics), SOCIAL SCIENCE (africana studies, anthropology, economics, gender studies, history, interdisciplinary studies, Latin American studies, philosophy, political science/government, psychology, religion, and sociology). Political science, biology, and psychology have the largest enrollments.

Required: Students must complete 32 courses, including 10 to 12 in the major, with a 2.0 GPA in order to graduate. Core curriculum requirements include courses in literature, fine arts, history, religion and philosophy, natural science, math, and social sciences. In addition, students must meet foreign language, composition, cultural diversity, and phys ed requirements. Comprehensive exams and a thesis are required in some majors.

Special: Davidson offers interdisciplinary international and South Asian studies programs and study abroad in 12 countries as well as through other schools' study-abroad programs. A 3-2 engineering program may be arranged with Georgia Institute of Technology and Columbia, Duke, North Carolina State, and Washington (St. Louis) Universities. Students may design their own majors and cross-register with any college in the Charlotte Area Educational Consortium. There are 15 national honor societies, including Phi Beta Kappa, and 20 departmental honors programs.

Faculty/Classroom: 59% of faculty are male; 41% are female. All teach and do research. No introductory courses are taught by graduate students. The average class size in an introductory lecture is 15; in a laboratory is 12; and in a regular course is 15.

Admissions: 26% of the 2013-2014 applicants were accepted. The SAT scores for the 2013-2014 freshman class were: Critical Reading--1% below 500, 13% between 500 and 599, 47% between 600 and 699, and 39% between 700 and 800; Math--3% below 500, 20% between 500 and 599, 46% between 600 and 699, and 31% between 700 and 800; Writing--2% below 500, 18% between 500 and 599, 47% between 600 and 699, and 33% between 700 and 800. The ACT scores were 1% between 21 and 23, 6% between 24 and 26, 10% between 27 and 28, and 83% above 28. 73% of the current freshmen were in the top fifth of their class; 100% were in the top two fifths.

Requirements: The SAT or ACT is required. SAT Subject Tests are strongly recommended. At least 16 high school units are required, although 20 units are recommended. These should include 4 units of English, 3 units of math, 2 units of the same foreign language, 2 units of science, and 2 units of history/social studies. It is strongly recommended that high school students continue for the third and fourth years in science and in the same foreign language, continue math through calculus, and take additional courses in history. AP credits are accepted. Important factors in the admissions decision are advanced placement or honors courses, recommendations by school officials, and leadership record.

Procedure: Freshmen are admitted fall. Entrance exams should be taken by the end of the junior year. There are early decision and deferred admissions plans. Early decision applications should be filed by November 15; regular applications, by January 2 for fall entry. The fall 2013 application fee was $50. Notification of early decision is sent December 15; regular decision, April 1. 256 early decision candidates were accepted for the 2013-2014 class. Applications are accepted online.

Transfer: 20 transfer students enrolled in 2012-2013. Applicants must have at least 1 full year of college work, generally with a 3.0 GPA. They must submit official college and high school transcripts, as well as required letters of recommendation, and be in good standing at their previous college. 16 of 32 credits required for the bachelor's degree must be completed at Davidson.

Visiting: There are guides for informal visits, visitors may sit in on classes, and stay overnight. To schedule a visit, contact the Office of Admission.

Financial Aid: In 2013-2014, 45% of all full-time freshmen students received some form of financial aid. 44% of all full-time freshmen students received need-based aid. The average freshman award was $36,168. Need-based scholarships or need-based grants averaged $33,367; need-based self-help aid (loans and jobs) averaged $2,801; non-need-based athletic scholarships averaged $17,219; and other non-need-based awards and non-need-based scholarships averaged $18,347. 45% of undergraduate students work part-time. The CSS/Profile, FAFSA, the college's own financial statement, and noncustodial (divorced/separated) parent's statement; corporate tax return and/or noncustodial parent tax return (if app are required. The deadline for filing freshman financial aid applications for fall entry is February 15.

International Students: There are 99 international students enrolled. The school actively recruits these students. They must take the TOEFL with a minimum score of 600 on the paper-based TOEFL (PBT) or 100 on the Internet-based version (iBT). They must also take the SAT or ACT.

Computers: All students may access the system 24 hours per day. There are no time limits and no fees.

Graduates: From July 1, 2012 to June 30, 2013, 461 bachelor's degrees were awarded. The most popular majors were political science (13%), economics (11%), and English (10%). 688 companies recruited on campus in 2012-2013. In an average class, 92% graduate in 4 years or less, 95% graduate in 5 years or less, and 95% graduate in 6 years or less. Of the 2012 graduating class, 21% were enrolled in graduate school within 6 months of graduation, and 69% were employed.

Admissions Contact: Christopher J. Gruber, Dean of Admission and Financial Aid. E-Mail: *admission@davidson.edu* Web: *www.davidson.edu*

DUKE UNIVERSITY — D-2

Durham, NC 27706 — **(919) 684-3214; (919) 681-8941**

Full-time: 3275 men, 2990 women	**Faculty:** n/av; I, ++$
Part-time: 915 men, 920 women	**Ph.D.s:** 97%
Graduate: 3850 men, 3380 women	**Student/Faculty:** n/av
Year: semesters, summer session	**Tuition:** $41,075
Application Deadline: see profile	**Room & Board:** $13,330
Freshman Class: n/av	
SAT or ACT: required	

MOST COMPETITIVE

Duke University, founded in 1838, is a private institution affiliated with the United Methodist Church and offering undergraduate programs in arts and sciences and engineering. The figures in the above capsule and in this profile are approximate. There are 2 undergraduate schools and 8 graduate schools. In addition to regional accreditation, Duke has baccalaureate program accreditation with AACSB, ABET, ACPE, AHEA, APTA, NCATE, NLN, and SAF. The 9 libraries contain 5.5 million volumes, 4.2 million microform items, and 61,281 audio/video tapes/CDs/DVDs, and subscribe to 33,934 periodicals including electronic. Computerized library services include interlibrary loans, database searching, and Internet access. Special learning facilities include a learning resource center, art gallery, radio station, TV station, marine lab at Beaufort, primate center, center for international studies, nuclear lab, free electron laser, science research center, institutes of the arts, statistics and decision sciences, policy sciences and public affairs, and centers for teaching and learning, community service, geometric computing, culture, and women. The 9727-acre campus is in a suburban area 285 miles southwest of Washington, D.C. Including any residence halls, there are 208 buildings.

Student Life: 86% of undergraduates are from out of state, mostly the South. Students are from 50 states, 55 foreign countries, and Canada. 60% are from public schools. 56% are white; 14% Asian American. 37% are Protestant; 23% Catholic; 16% claim no religious affiliation. The average age of freshmen is 18; all undergraduates, 20. 4% do not continue beyond their first year; 94% remain to graduate.

Housing: 5481 students can be accommodated in college housing, which includes single-sex and coed dorms, on-campus apartments, and married student housing. In addition, there are language houses, special-interest houses, and theme houses in women's studies, the arts, and community service (APO). On-campus housing is guaranteed for all 4 years. 82% of students live on campus. All students may keep cars.

Activities: 29% of men belong to 17 national fraternities; 42% of women belong to 10 national sororities. There are 400 groups on campus, including art, band, cheerleading, chess, choir, chorale, chorus, communications, computers, dance, debate, drama, drill team, ethnic, film, gay, honors, international, jazz band, literary magazine, marching band, musical theater, newspaper, opera, orchestra, pep band, photography, political, professional, radio and TV, religious, social, social service, student government, and symphony. Popular campus events include College Bowl, Oktoberfest, and Springfest.

Sports: There are 12 intercollegiate sports for men and 11 for women, and 21 intramural sports for men and 19 for women. Facilities include stadiums for baseball, basketball/volleyball, football, and soccer/lacrosse; squash, racquetball, and tennis courts; an aquatic center; training and weight rooms; a golf course; cross-country and jogging trails; and practice and intramural sport club fields.

Disabled Students: The campus is accessible. Facilities include wheelchair ramps, elevators, special parking, specially equipped restrooms, special class scheduling, lowered drinking fountains, lowered telephones, and special housing. In addition, activities such as concerts can be moved to accessible facilities upon request.

Services: Counseling and information services are available, as is tutoring in every subject. There is a reader service for the blind.

Campus Safety and Security: Measures include 24-hour foot and vehicle patrol, self-defense education, and security escort services. There are shuttle buses, emergency telephones, lighted pathways/sidewalks, and a crime prevention program.

Programs of Study: Duke confers B.S., A.B., and B.S.E. degrees. Master's and doctoral degrees are also awarded. Bachelor's degrees are awarded in BIOLOGICAL SCIENCE (anatomy and biology/biological science), COMMUNICATIONS AND THE ARTS (African languages, art history and appreciation, classical languages, dramatic arts, English, Germanic languages and literature, linguistics, literature, music, Slavic languages, Spanish, and visual and performing arts), COMPUTER AND PHYSICAL SCIENCE (chemistry, computer science, geology, mathematics, and physics), ENGINEERING AND ENVIRONMENTAL DESIGN (biomedical engineering, civil engineering, electrical/electronics engineering, environmental science, materials science, and mechanical engineering), SOCIAL SCIENCE (African studies, African American studies, anthropology, area studies, Asian/Oriental studies, Canadian studies, classical/ancient civilization, economics, French studies, history, Italian studies, medieval studies, philosophy, political science/government, psychology, public affairs, religion, sociology, and women's studies). Public policy studies, political science, and economics are the strongest academically. Biology, psychology, and history have the largest enrollments.

Required: A minimum of 34 course credits is required for graduation, including courses in natural sciences, quantitative reasoning, and social sciences. No more than 17 course credits are allowed in a major for the B.A. and no more than 19 for the B.S. At least 12 courses must be at or above the 100 level. At least 3 courses designated as seminars, tutorials, independent study, or thesis completion are required. Computer proficiency must be demonstrated by engineering students.

Special: Duke offers cross-registration with the University of North Carolina/Chapel Hill and North Carolina State and North Carolina Central Universities. Also available are internships through the Career Development Center, study abroad in 36 countries, and a Washington semester. An accelerated degree program is possible, achieving graduation in 3 years or combining the senior year with the first graduate year of the law, business, or environment schools. Several 3-2 and 4-1 medical technology programs (degree completed at Duke) are available. Project Calc, an innovative program in calculus, is also offered. Dual majors of any combination, student-designed majors, nondegree study, and pass/fail options are possible. There are 4 national honor societies, including Phi Beta Kappa, and 38 departmental honors programs.

Faculty/Classroom: 76% of faculty are male; 24% are female. All teach and do research. Graduate students teach 2% of introductory courses. The average class size in an introductory lecture is 39 and in a regular course, 21.

Requirements: The SAT or ACT is required. The ACT Optional Writing test is also required. In addition, 3 SAT subject tests, including writing, are required. Applicants must be graduates of an accredited secondary school and have completed 15 academic credits, with 4 in English and 3 each in math, science, and foreign language; an additional 2 in social studies or history are recommended. Engineering students must have 4 credit units in math and 1 in physics or chemistry. An essay is required and an interview is recommended. A portfolio or audition is advised in appropriate instances. AP credits are accepted. Important factors in the admissions decision are advanced placement or honors courses, recommendations by school officials, and extracurricular activities record.

Procedure: Freshmen are admitted fall and spring. Entrance exams should be taken in October of the junior year for early decision applicants and by January of the senior year for regular decision. There are early decision, early admissions and deferred admissions plans. Check with the school for current application deadlines. The application fee is $75. A waiting list is maintained.

Transfer: A minimum 3.6 GPA is recommended. The SAT, plus 3 SAT subject tests, or the ACT is required. 17 of 34 credits required for the bachelor's degree must be completed at Duke.

Visiting: There are regularly scheduled orientations for prospective students, including student-led tours, counselor-led group information sessions, class visits, and lunch with students. There are guides for informal visits, visitors may sit in on classes, and stay overnight. To schedule a visit, contact Undergraduate Admissions.

Financial Aid: The CSS/Profile and FAFSA are required. Check with the school for current deadlines.

International Students: The school actively recruits these students. They must also take the SAT or ACT.

Computers: All students may access the system 24 hours a day. There are no time limits and no fees. It is strongly recommended that all students have a personal computer.

Admissions Contact: Christoph Guttentag, Director, Undergraduate Admissions. A campus DVD is available. E-Mail: *askduke@admiss.duke.edu* Web: *www.duke.edu*

EAST CAROLINA UNIVERSITY — E-2

Greenville, NC 27858 — (252) 328-6640; (252) 328-6945

Full-time: 7637 men, 10680 women	**Faculty:** n/av; IIA, -$
Part-time: 1114 men, 1867 women	**Ph.D.s:** 81%
Graduate: 1981 men, 3668 women	**Student/Faculty:** 18 to 1
Year: semesters, summer session	**Tuition:** $5869 ($19,683)
Application Deadline: March 15	**Room & Board:** $8300
Freshman Class: 15535 applied, 9658 accepted, 4015 enrolled	
SAT CR/M/W: 510/540/490 **ACT:** 22	**COMPETITIVE**

East Carolina University, founded in 1907, is a state-supported institution offering degree programs in the arts and sciences, business, education, fine arts and communication, health and human performance, human ecology, technology and computer science, medicine, allied health sciences, and nursing. There are 11 undergraduate schools and 1 graduate school. In addition to regional accreditation, ECU has baccalaureate program accreditation with AACSB, ACCE, ADA, APTA, CSWE, FIDER, NASAD, NASM, NCATE, NLN, and NRPA. The 2 libraries contain 2.4 million volumes, 1.2 million microform items, and 69,251 audio/video tapes/CDs/DVDs, and subscribe to 73,498 periodicals including electronic. Computerized library services include interlibrary loans, database searching, and Wi-Fi capability. Special learning facilities include an art gallery and radio station. The 1401-acre campus is in an urban area 90 miles east of Raleigh. Including any residence halls, there are 239 buildings.

Student Life: 88% of undergraduates are from North Carolina. Others are from 42 states, 54 foreign countries, and Canada. 80% are White; 16% African American. The average age of freshmen is 18; all undergraduates, 23. 22% do not continue beyond their first year; 58% remain to graduate.

Housing: 5497 students can be accommodated in college housing, which includes single-sex and coed dorms. In addition, there are honors houses, fraternity houses, sorority houses, a first-year students' floor, a leadership hall, an extended-quiet-hours floor, a substance-free hall, a nonsmoking floor, and an academic-year hall. On-campus housing is guaranteed for the freshman year only, is available on a first-come, and first-served basis. 76% of students commute. Alcohol is not permitted. All students may keep cars.

Activities: 9% of men belong to 24 national fraternities; 8% of women belong to 14 national sororities. There are 399 groups on campus, including and recreation., military, academic, art, band, cheerleading, choir, chorale, chorus, communications, computers, dance, drama, drill team, environmental, ethnic, gay, honors, international, jazz band, literary magazine, marching band, musical theater, newspaper, opera, orchestra, pep band, photography, political, professional, radio and TV, religious, social, social service, student government, symphony, and yearbook. Popular campus events include Barefoot on the Mall, Midnight Madness and Pirate Palooza.

Sports: There are 9 intercollegiate sports for men and 9 for women, and 14 intramural sports for men and 14 for women. Facilities include a 43,000-seat stadium, an 8,000-seat basketball coliseum, a baseball and softball field, a track, and a natatorium. The Student Recreation Center is 150,000 square feet, and includes a 6-court multipurpose sports area(basketball courts), a 2 cardiovascular rooms and a weight lifting/training area, 3 exercise studios, indoor and outdoor pools, an indoor track, a 30-ft. climbing wall, 7 racquetball courts, a wellness center, and a fitness assessment center. The Blount Recreational Sports Complex includes 10 football/soccer fields, 5 softball fields, a ropes challenge course, and a 50-foot Alpine climbing tower.

Disabled Students: 95% of the campus is accessible. Facilities include wheelchair ramps, elevators, special parking, specially equipped restrooms, special class scheduling, lowered drinking fountains, lowered telephones, automatic doors, and state-of-the art adaptive equipment.

Services: Counseling and information services are available, as is tutoring in most subjects. There is a reader service for the blind, and remedial math and reading. Tutoring is established on a department-by- department basis. Several learning centers and labs have established hours of operation, or arrangements can be made by appointment.

Campus Safety and Security: Measures include 24-hour foot and

vehicle patrol, emergency notification system, self-defense education, and security escort services. There are shuttle buses, emergency telephones, lighted pathways/sidewalks, controlled access to dorms/residences, residence hall doors locked , biccle patrols, bicycle registration, motorist assistance lost and found, operation ID, the Residence Hall Liason Officer Program, on-and off campus crime prevention safety tips, staff and faculty eyes (SAFE) campus community watch program, and alcohol awareness.

Programs of Study: ECU confers B.A., B.S., B.F.A., B.M., B.S.A., B.S.A.P., B.S.B.A., B.S.B.E., B.S.N. and B.S.W. degrees. Master's and doctoral degrees are also awarded. Bachelor's degrees are awarded in BIOLOGICAL SCIENCE (biochemistry, biology/biological science, and nutrition), BUSINESS (accounting, banking and finance, business administration and management, hospitality management services, management information systems, marketing management, marketing/retailing/merchandising, and recreational facilities management), COMMUNICATIONS AND THE ARTS (art, art history and appreciation, communications, dance, design, dramatic arts, English, French, German, music performance, music theory and composition, speech/debate/rhetoric, and studio art), COMPUTER AND PHYSICAL SCIENCE (applied physics, atmospheric sciences and meteorology, chemistry, computer science, geology, information sciences and systems, mathematics, and physics), EDUCATION (art education, athletic training, business education, dance education, drama education, early childhood education, education of the emotionally handicapped, education of the mentally handicapped, elementary education, English education, foreign languages education, health education, home economics education, marketing and distribution education, mathematics education, middle school education, music education, physical education, science education, social studies education, and special education), ENGINEERING AND ENVIRONMENTAL DESIGN (city/community/regional planning, construction management, electrical/electronics engineering technology, engineering, environmental engineering technology, industrial engineering technology, and interior design), HEALTH PROFESSIONS (environmental health science, exercise science, health care administration, medical records administration/services, medical technology, music therapy, nursing, occupational therapy, public health, recreation therapy, rehabilitation therapy, and speech pathology/audiology), SOCIAL SCIENCE (African American studies, anthropology, applied social science, child care/child and family studies, clothing and textiles management/production/services, criminal justice, dietetics, economics, family and community services, geography, Hispanic American studies, history, liberal arts/general studies, parks and recreation management, philosophy, physical fitness/movement, political science/government, psychology, public history/archives, social work, sociology, and women's studies). Allied health, art, and music are the strongest academically. Elementary education, management, and communication have the largest enrollments.

Required: To graduate, students must complete 120 to 128 semester hours with a minimum GPA of 2.0 overall and in the major. General education requirements include 12 hours of social science, 10 of humanities and fine arts, 8 of science, 6 of English, 3 of math, and 3 of health and exercise and sport science. The total must include 12 hours of writing-intensive courses and a course in cultural diversity.

Special: ECU offers cooperative programs in most majors, internships, study abroad in 42 countries, a Washington semester, accelerated degrees, a B.A.-B.S. in accounting, dual majors, work-study, and a student-designed major in multidisciplinary studies. There are 18 national honor societies, including Phi Beta Kappa, a freshman honors program, and 39 departmental honors programs.

Faculty/Classroom: 48% of faculty are male; 52% are female. No introductory courses are taught by graduate students. The average class size in an introductory lecture is 42; in a laboratory is 26; and in a regular course is 35.

Admissions: 62% of the 2013-2014 applicants were accepted. The SAT scores for the 2013-2014 freshman class were: Critical Reading--49% below 500, 43% between 500 and 599, 7% between 600 and 699, and 1% between 700 and 800; Math--32% below 500, 55% between 500 and 599, 12% between 600 and 699, and 1% between 700 and 800; Writing--57% below 500, 37% between 500 and 599, and 6% between 600 and 699. The ACT scores were 18% below 21, 55% between 21 and 23, 19% between 24 and 26, 6% between 27 and 28, and 3% above 28. 35% of the current freshmen were in the top fifth of their class; 68% were in the top two fifths.

Requirements: The SAT or ACT is required. The ACT Optional Writing test is also required. Applicants must be graduates of an accredited secondary school. All degree-seeking students are required to complete 20 academic units, including 4 in English, 4 in math, 3 in science with 1 lab course, 2 in social studies with 1 in U.S. history, and 2 units in a foreign language. 1 unit in fine arts is recommended. 1 unit each in foreign language, natural science, and math should be taken in the senior year. Special circumstances exist for applicants with a GED. A GPA of 2.3 is required. AP and CLEP credits are accepted.

Procedure: Freshmen are admitted to all sessions. Entrance exams should be taken in the spring of the junior year or the fall of the senior year. There are deferred admissions and rolling admissions plans. Applications should be filed by March 15 for fall entry; November 1 for spring entry; and March 15 for summer entry, along with a $70 fee. Notifications are sent April 15. Applications are accepted online.

Transfer: 1427 transfer students enrolled in 2012-2013. Applicants must submit official transcripts from high school and all colleges attended and have a satisfactory GPA in courses attempted. Applicants who will have completed less than 30 semester hours will also be required to meet the freshmen requirements.

Visiting: There are regularly scheduled orientations for prospective students, including information sessions and campus tours. There are guides for informal visits. To schedule a visit, contact the Admissions Office.

Financial Aid: In 2013-2014, 60% of all full-time freshmen and 58% of continuing full-time students received some form of financial aid. 55% of all full-time freshmen and 31% of continuing full-time students received need-based aid. The average freshman award was $9,614. Need-based scholarships or need-based grants averaged $8,031; need-based self-help aid (loans and jobs) averaged $3,834; non-need-based athletic scholarships averaged $11,120; and other non-need-based awards and non-need-based scholarships averaged $4,532. The average financial indebtedness of the 2013 graduate was $25,983. ECU is a member of CSS. The FAFSA is required. The priority date for freshman financial aid applications for fall entry is March 1.

International Students: There are 200 international students enrolled. The school actively recruits these students. They must take the TOEFL with a minimum score of 80 on the Internet-based version (iBT), or IELTS. SAT or ACT scores are required if the student will receive an athletic scholarship or if the student will graduate from a U.S. high school.

Computers: All students may access the system at all times. There are no time limits and no fees.

Graduates: From July 1, 2012 to June 30, 2013, 4315 bachelor's degrees were awarded. The most popular majors were nursing (7%), communication (7%), and elementary education (6%). In an average class, 33% graduate in 4 years or less, 53% graduate in 5 years or less, and 58% graduate in 6 years or less.

Admissions Contact: James Coker, AssociateDirector of Undergraduate Admissions. E-Mail: *admis@ecu.edu* Web: *www.ecu.edu/admissions*

ELIZABETH CITY STATE UNIVERSITY F-2

Elizabeth City, NC 27909 (252) 335-3400
(800) 347-ECSU; (252) 335-3537

Full-time: 1035 men, 1474 women	**Faculty:** 113; IIB, -$
Part-time: 68 men, 183 women	**Ph.D.s:** 68%
Graduate: 29 men, 89 women	**Student/Faculty:** 16 to 1
Year: semesters, summer session	**Tuition:** $4426 ($15,283)
Application Deadline:	**Room & Board:** $7212
Freshman Class: 3925 applied, 2243 accepted, 527 enrolled	
SAT or ACT: required	

COMPETITIVE

Elizabeth City State University, founded in 1891 as part of the University of North Carolina System, is a public institution offering undergraduate programs in liberal arts and sciences, education, and business. The library contains 174,566 volumes, 486,884 microform items, and 1,220 audio/video tapes/CDs/DVDs, and subscribes to 1,698 periodicals including electronic. Computerized library services include interlibrary loans. Special learning facilities include an art gallery, planetarium, radio station, TV station, farm, and 639-acre educational research tract. The 829-acre campus is in a small town 55 miles from Norfolk, Virginia.

Student Life: 90% of undergraduates are from North Carolina. Others are from 25 states. 73% are African American; 12% White. 12% are race and ethnicity unknown. 25% do not continue beyond their first year; 50% remain to graduate.

Housing: 1019 students can be accommodated in college housing, which includes single-sex dorms and on-campus apartments. In addition, there are honors houses, Wellness housing. On-campus housing is guaranteed for all 4 years. 52% of students commute. Alcohol is not permitted. All students may keep cars.

Activities: Groups on campus include band, cheerleading, choir, chorus, dance, drama, honors, international, jazz band, literary magazine, marching band, musical theater, newspaper, pep band, radio and TV, religious, social, student government, symphony, and yearbook.

Sports: Facilities include a 4500-seat gym, a 3500-seat stadium, an all-weather track, a golf range, an Olympic pool, a weight room, 8 tennis courts, dance and exercise studios, handball and racquetball courts, and playing fields.

Disabled Students: Facilities include wheelchair ramps, elevators, special parking, specially equipped restrooms, and lowered drinking fountains.

Services: In addition to vocational counseling services, tutoring is available.

Campus Safety and Security: There are emergency telephones. ECSU has its own police department on campus.

Programs of Study: ECSU confers B.A., B.S. and B.S.Ed. degrees.

Master's degrees are also awarded. Bachelor's degrees are awarded in BIOLOGICAL SCIENCE (biology/biological science), BUSINESS (accounting and business administration and management), COMMUNICATIONS AND THE ARTS (art, English, and music), COMPUTER AND PHYSICAL SCIENCE (chemistry, computer science, geology, mathematics, and physics), EDUCATION (business education, elementary education, industrial arts education, middle school education, physical education, special education, and technical education), ENGINEERING AND ENVIRONMENTAL DESIGN (industrial engineering technology), SOCIAL SCIENCE (criminal justice, history, political science/government, psychology, social science, social work, and sociology).

Required: Students must have maintained a minimum GPA of 2.0, fulfilled a major, and completed the requirements of general education courses in the fields of grammar, composition, and literature.

Special: Opportunities are provided for internships, dual majors, weekend/evening degree completion programs, work-study, and credit by exam and for military service. There are 5 national honor societies and a freshman honors program.

Faculty/Classroom: 50% of faculty are male; 50% are female. All teach undergraduates. No introductory courses are taught by graduate students.

Admissions: 57% of the 2013-2014 applicants were accepted. The SAT scores for the 2013-2014 freshman class were: Critical Reading--89% below 500, 10% between 500 and 599, 1% between 600 and 699; Math--83% below 500, 16% between 500 and 599, 1% between 600 and 699; Writing--92% below 500, 8% between 500 and 599.

Requirements: The SAT or ACT is required. Graduation from an accredited secondary school is required; the GED is accepted. Applicants should submit an academic record with 4 courses in English, 3 each in math and 2 in science, and 2 in social studies; it is recommended that applicants have at least 2 course units in foreign languages. Students must also pass the NC Competency Examination or its equivalent. A GPA of 2.0 is required. AP and CLEP credits are accepted.

Procedure: Freshmen are admitted fall, spring, and summer. Entrance exams should be taken as early as possible. There are early admissions and deferred admissions plans. Application deadlines are open. Application fee is $30.

Transfer: 201 transfer students enrolled in 2012-2013. Applicants must have a minimum college GPA of 2.0 and submit high school and college transcripts. Those with fewer than 30 credit hours must meet both freshman and transfer admission requirements. 30 credits required for the bachelor's degree must be completed at ECSU.

Visiting: There are regularly scheduled orientations for prospective students. There are guides for informal visits. To schedule a visit, contact the Admissions Office.

Financial Aid: The FAFSA the college's own financial statement, and income tax forms are required. Check with the school for current application deadlines.

International Students: There are 6 international students enrolled. They must take the TOEFL or MELB. They must also take the SAT or ACT.

Computers: Students in computer-related courses may access the system. There are no time limits and no fees.

Graduates: From July 1, 2012 to June 30, 2013, 379 bachelor's degrees were awarded. The most popular majors were business/marketing (21%), education (15%), and homeland security (13%). In an average class, 33% graduate in 4 years or less, 46% graduate in 5 years or less, and 49% graduate in 6 years or less. Of the 2012 graduating class, 79% were enrolled in graduate school within 6 months of graduation.

Admissions Contact: Bridgett Golham, Director of Admissions and Recruitment. E-Mail: *admissions@alpha.ecsu.edu* Web: *www.ecsu.edu*

ELON UNIVERSITY D-2

Elon, NC 27244 (336) 278-3566
(800) 334-8448; (336) 278-7699

Full-time: 2224 men, 3240 women	**Faculty:** 347; II A, av$
Part-time: 61 men, 74 women	**Ph.D.s:** 86%
Graduate: 303 men, 403 women	**Student/Faculty:** 15 to 1
Year: 4-1-4, summer session	**Tuition:** $28,980
Application Deadline: January 10	**Room & Board:** $9480

Freshman Class: 10241 applied, 5293 accepted, 1425 enrolled
SAT CR/M/W: 615/614/616 **ACT:** 27 **HIGHLY COMPETITIVE**

Elon University is a selective, private university renowned as a national model for engaged learning, along with excellence in the liberal arts and sciences and professional programs. There are 4 undergraduate schools and 5 graduate schools. In addition to regional accreditation, Elon has baccalaureate program accreditation with AACSB, ACEJMC, and NCATE. The library contains 478,302 volumes, 461,323 microform items, and 24,171 audio/video tapes/CDs/DVDs, and subscribes to 51,886 periodicals including electronic. Computerized library services include interlibrary loans, database searching, Internet access, and Wi-Fi capability. Special learning facilities include a radio station, TV station, a writing center, botanical preserve, a protected Elon Forest, art collection walk, and observatory. The 620-acre campus is in a suburban area adjacent to Burlington and 17 miles east of Greensboro. Including any residence halls, there are 160 buildings.

Student Life: 78% of undergraduates are from out of state, mostly the Middle Atlantic. Students are from 47 states, 49 foreign countries, and Canada. 60% are from public schools. 82% are White. 38% are Protestant; 26% Catholic. The average age of freshmen is 18; all undergraduates, 20. 10% do not continue beyond their first year; 82% remain to graduate.

Housing: 3460 students can be accommodated in college housing, which includes single-sex and coed dorms, on-campus apartments, and off-campus apartments. In addition, there are honors houses, language houses, special-interest houses, fraternity houses, sorority houses, theme suites, and academic living-learning communities. On-campus housing is guaranteed for the freshman year only and is available on a lottery system for upperclassmen. 62% of students live on campus; of those, 75% remain on campus on weekends. All students may keep cars.

Activities: 23% of men belong to 12 national fraternities; 38% of women belong to 12 national sororities. There are 220 groups on campus, including art, band, cheerleading, chess, choir, chorale, chorus, communications, computers, dance, debate, drama, drill team, environmental, ethnic, film, gay, honors, international, jazz band, literary magazine, marching band, musical theater, newspaper, orchestra, pep band, photography, political, professional, radio and TV, religious, social, social service, student government, symphony, and yearbook. Popular campus events include Family Weekend, Homecoming, Greek Week, Spring Undergraduate Research Forum (SURF Day), College Coffee and CELEBRATE!, a week-long celebration of student achievements in academics and the arts.

Sports: There are 7 intercollegiate sports for men and 11 for women, and 21 intramural sports for men and 21 for women. Facilities include an 8250-seat stadium, lighted tennis courts, a softball field, a baseball stadium, a field house, and 15 athletic fields. The athletic center has racquetball courts, aerobic rooms, a human performance lab, a weight room, a two-story fitness center, 2 gyms, a driving range, and an indoor swimming pool.

Disabled Students: 85% of the campus is accessible. Facilities include wheelchair ramps, elevators, special parking, specially equipped restrooms, special class scheduling, lowered drinking fountains, lowered telephones, special housing.

Services: Counseling and information services are available, as is tutoring in most subjects, lower-level courses. Preparatory courses are offered, which count as elective credit toward graduation. We offer texts in alternative formats for students with print disabilities (both learning and visual disabilities).

Campus Safety and Security: Measures include 24-hour foot and vehicle patrol, emergency notification system, and security escort services. There are shuttle buses, emergency telephones, lighted pathways/sidewalks, controlled access to dorms/residences, over 200 cameras on campus, annual fire inspections through the county fire marshall's office. Campus safety & police operates 24 hours/day 7 days/week.

Programs of Study: Elon confers B.A., B.S., B.F.A. and B.S.B.A degrees. Master's and doctoral degrees are also awarded. Bachelor's degrees are awarded in AGRICULTURE (environmental studies), BIOLOGICAL SCIENCE (biochemistry and biophysics), BUSINESS (accounting, business administration and management, entrepreneurial studies, finance, international business management, international economics, management information systems, marketing, marketing management, and sports management), COMMUNICATIONS AND THE ARTS (acting, art history, art, arts administration/management, broadcasting, communications, creative writing, dance, dramatic arts, English, film arts, French, journalism, literature, media arts, music, music performance, music technology, musical theater, Spanish, strategic communication, theatre acting, theatre arts, theater design, theatre production, and theatre studies), COMPUTER AND PHYSICAL SCIENCE (applied mathematics, chemistry, computer science, digital arts/technology, information sciences and systems, mathematics, physics, and statistics), EDUCATION (early childhood education, education, elementary education, foreign languages education, health education, mathematics education, middle school education, music education, physical education, science education, secondary education, and special education), ENGINEERING AND ENVIRONMENTAL DESIGN (biomedical engineering, chemical engineering, computer engineering, engineering, engineering physics, environmental engineering, and environmental science), HEALTH PROFESSIONS (biology, exercise science, public health, and sports medicine), SOCIAL SCIENCE (anthropology, economics, history, human services, international studies, philosophy, political science/government, psychology, public administration, religious studies, and sociology). Business, music theater, education, biology, psychology, international studies, and communications are the strongest academically. Business, strategic communications, and psychology are the largest.

Required: To graduate, students must complete 132 semester hours, including 32 to 68 in the major, with a minimum GPA of 2.0. All students must fulfill the requirements of the General Studies program, which includes a first-year core, experiential learning, liberal studies, and advanced studies, for a total of 59 semester hours, and must satisfactorily complete a comprehensive exam in the major.

Special: Elon offers co-op programs in most majors, dual majors, student-designed majors, cross-registration with 6 other colleges and universities in North Carolina, paid and unpaid internships, more than 100 study abroad programs, Study USA programs, a Washington semester, a Los Angeles semester, work-study programs, pass/fail options, and 3-2 dual engineering degree programs. The month-long January term includes extensive international study opportunities as well as courses focused on domestic travel. There are 31 national honor societies, including Phi Beta Kappa, a freshman honors program, and 25 departmental honors programs.

Faculty/Classroom: 53% of faculty are male; 47% are female. 90% teach undergraduates, 65% do research, and 65% do both. No introductory courses are taught by graduate students. The average class size in an introductory lecture is 23; in a laboratory is 19; and in a regular course is 21.

Admissions: 54% of the 2013-2014 applicants were accepted. The SAT scores for the 2013-2014 freshman class were: Critical Reading--8% below 500, 43% between 500 and 599, 40% between 600 and 699, and 9% between 700 and 800; Math--8% below 500, 36% between 500 and 599, 48% between 600 and 699, and 8% between 700 and 800; Writing--8% below 500, 38% between 500 and 599, 43% between 600 and 699, and 11% between 700 and 800. The ACT scores were 4% below 21, 11% between 21 and 23, 29% between 24 and 26, 24% between 27 and 28, and 32% above 28. 51% of the current freshmen were in the top fifth of their class; 80% were in the top two fifths. There were 11 National Merit finalists. 11 freshmen graduated first in their class.

Requirements: The SAT or ACT is required. The ACT Optional Writing test is also required. In addition, Students must be graduates of an accredited secondary school or have a GED certificate. They should have completed 4 credits of english, 3 or more in math (must include algebra 1 and 2, and geometry), 2 or more in a foreign language, 2 or more in science, including at least 1 lab science, and 2 or more in social studies, including U.S. history. AP and CLEP credits are accepted.

Procedure: Freshmen are admitted fall and spring. Entrance exams should be taken in the spring of the junior year and the fall of the senior year. There are early decision, early admissions, and deferred admissions plans. Early decision applications should be filed by November 1; regular applications, by January 10 for fall entry; and December 1 for spring entry, along with a $50 fee. Notification of early decision is sent December 1; regular decision, March 15. 484 early decision candidates were accepted for the 2013-2014 class. 3072 applicants were on the 2013 waiting list; 27 were admitted. Applications are accepted online.

Transfer: 102 transfer students enrolled in 2012-2013. Applicants must present a high school transcript, 12 credit hours of college transferable classes in the liberal arts and sciences, and a minimum GPA of 2.7 from a two-year or four-year accredited institution. An interview is recommended. A dean's evaluation form is required from all colleges or universities attended, and the applicant must be eligible to return to that institution. 60 of 132 credits required for the bachelor's degree must be completed at Elon.

Visiting: There are regularly scheduled orientations for prospective students, consisting of 2 weekends in spring for deposited freshmen or a spring open house for nondeposited students. There are guides for informal visits and visitors may sit in on classes. To schedule a visit, contact the Admissions Office at (336) 278-3566.

Financial Aid: In 2013-2014, 73% of all full-time freshmen and 63% of continuing full-time students received some form of financial aid. 32% of all full-time freshmen and 38% of continuing full-time students received need-based aid. The average freshman award was $16,608. Need-based scholarships or need-based grants averaged $10,387 ($40,046 maximum); need-based self-help aid (loans and jobs) averaged $4,641 ($9,500 maximum); non-need-based athletic scholarships averaged $24,821 ($41,981 maximum); and other non-need-based awards and non-need-based scholarships averaged $6,144 ($34,250 maximum). 33% of undergraduate students work part-time. Average annual earnings from campus work are $4500. The average financial indebtedness of the 2013 graduate was $28,237. Elon is a member of CSS. The CSS/Profile, FAFSA, and the college's own financial statement are required. The priority date for freshman financial aid applications for fall entry is February 15.

International Students: There are 99 international students enrolled. The school actively recruits these students. They must take the TOEFL with a minimum score of 550 on the paper-based TOEFL (PBT) or 79 on the Internet-based version (iBT). They must also take the SAT or ACT, scoring 1330.

Computers: All students may access the system 24 hours a day.

Graduates: From July 1, 2012 to June 30, 2013, 1332 bachelor's degrees were awarded. The most popular majors were communications (10%), psychology (7%), and marketing (6%). 210 companies recruited on campus in 2012-2013. In an average class, 77% graduate in 4 years or less, 81% graduate in 5 years or less, and 82% graduate in 6 years or less. Of the 2012 graduating class, 24% were enrolled in graduate school within 6 months of graduation, and 66% were employed.

Admissions Contact: Lisa Keegan, Dean of Admissions. E-Mail: *admissions@elon.edu* Web: *www.elon.edu*

FAYETTEVILLE STATE UNIVERSITY — D-3

Fayetteville, NC 28301 — **(910) 672-1371**; **(800) 222-2594; (910) 672-1414**

Full-time: 1297 men, 2619 women	**Faculty:** 276; IIA, -$
Part-time: 323 men, 1048 women	**Ph.D.s:** n/av
Graduate: 186 men, 587 women	**Student/Faculty:** 16 to 1
Year: semesters, summer session	**Tuition:** $4674 ($15,378)
Application Deadline:	**Room & Board:** $6142
Freshman Class: n/av	
SAT or ACT: required	

COMPETITIVE

Fayetteville State University, founded in 1867 and today part of the University of North Carolina system, is a public institution offering degree programs in the arts and sciences, business, and teacher preparation. There are 3 undergraduate schools and 1 graduate school. In addition to regional accreditation, FSU has baccalaureate program accreditation with NCATE. The library contains 335,922 volumes, 1.0 million microform items, and 20,676 audio/video tapes/CDs/DVDs. Computerized library services include interlibrary loans and database searching. Special learning facilities include a planetarium and radio station. The 156-acre campus is in an urban area 60 miles south of Raleigh. Including any residence halls, there are 43 buildings.

Student Life: 95% of undergraduates are from North Carolina. Others are from states. 76% are African American; 20% White. The average age of freshmen is 19; all undergraduates, 27. 24% do not continue beyond their first year; 31% remain to graduate.

Housing: 1298 students can be accommodated in college housing, which includes single-sex and coed dorms and on-campus apartments. honors dorm. On-campus housing is available on a first-come and first-served basis. 71% of students commute. Alcohol is not permitted. All students may keep cars.

Activities: 1% of men belong to 4 local and 4 national fraternities; 1% of women belong to 3 national sororities. There are 30 groups on campus, including band, cheerleading, choir, chorus, dance, drama, film, honors, international, jazz band, literary magazine, marching band, newspaper, pep band, political, radio and TV, religious, social service, student government, and yearbook. Popular campus events include The Lyceum, Martin Luther King Day and Black History Month.

Sports: There are 8 intercollegiate sports for men and 8 for women, and 7 intramural sports for men and 5 for women. Facilities include 2 gyms, a stadium, tennis courts, a bowling alley, a dance studio, a swimming pool, and playing fields.

Disabled Students: 75% of the campus is accessible. Facilities include wheelchair ramps, elevators, special parking, specially equipped restrooms, and lowered drinking fountains.

Services: Counseling and information services are available, as is tutoring in some subjects. There is remedial math, reading, and writing.

Campus Safety and Security: Measures include 24-hour foot and vehicle patrol and security escort services. There are lighted pathways/sidewalks.

Programs of Study: FSU confers B.A., and B.S. degrees. Master's and doctoral degrees are also awarded. Bachelor's degrees are awarded in BIOLOGICAL SCIENCE (biology/biological science), BUSINESS (accounting, banking and finance, business administration and management, business economics, management information systems, and office supervision and management), COMMUNICATIONS AND THE ARTS (dramatic arts, English, Spanish, speech/debate/rhetoric, and visual and performing arts), COMPUTER AND PHYSICAL SCIENCE (chemistry, computer science, and mathematics), EDUCATION (business education, early childhood education, elementary education, health education, marketing and distribution education, middle school education, music education, secondary education, and social science education), HEALTH PROFESSIONS (medical laboratory technology and nursing), SOCIAL SCIENCE (criminal justice, economics, geography, history, political science/government, psychology, public administration, social science, social work, and sociology).

Required: To graduate, students must complete 120 credit hours with a minimum GPA of 2.0 overall and in the major. The core curriculum includes 8 to 11 credits in natural science, 6 to 15 in humanities, 6 to 7 in math, 3 to 9 in social science, 3 each in critical thinking and speech, and 2 each in phys ed/health and university seminar.

Special: FSU offers cooperative programs in business, math, and biological and physical sciences with North Carolina State University, internships, B.A.-B.S. degrees, dual majors, 3-2 engineering degree programs, credit for military experience, and nondegree study. There are 17 national honor societies, a freshman honors program, and 7 departmental honors programs.

Faculty/Classroom: 54% of faculty are male; 46% are female. All teach

and do research. No introductory courses are taught by graduate students. The average class size in an introductory lecture is 30; in a laboratory is 20; and in a regular course is 30.

Requirements: The SAT or ACT is required. Successful scores are also required on the North Carolina Competency Exam. Applicants must be graduates of an accredited secondary school or have the GED. They should have completed 4 academic units of English, 3 each of math and science with 1 lab course, and 2 of social studies; also recommended are 2 units of a foreign language and completion of 1 unit each of foreign language and math in the senior year. A GPA of 2.0 is required. AP and CLEP credits are accepted. Important factors in the admissions decision are advanced placement or honors courses, recommendations by school officials, and leadership record.

Procedure: Freshmen are admitted to all sessions. Entrance exams should be taken in November. There are early decision, early admissions, deferred admissions, and rolling admissions plans. Check with the school for current application deadlines. The application fee is $35. Notification is sent on a rolling basis.

Transfer: 670 transfer students enrolled in 2012-2013. Applicants must submit official transcripts from all colleges attended, have a minimum GPA of 2.0, and be eligible to return to their previous institution. 33 of 120 credits required for the bachelor's degree must be completed at FSU.

Visiting: There are regularly scheduled orientations for prospective students, including a campus tour, recreational activity, placement tests, preregistration, and orientation to FSU services. There are guides for informal visits, visitors may sit in on classes, and stay overnight. To schedule a visit, contact the Director of Enrollment Management at (910) 672-1784.

Financial Aid: FSU is a member of CSS. The FAFSA is required. Check with the school for current application deadlines.

International Students: They must take the TOEFL, or other English proficiency exam administered in their country. They must also take the SAT or ACT, scoring 800.

Computers: All students may access the system 24 hours a day. There are no time limits and no fees.

Graduates: From July 1, 2012 to June 30, 2013, 991 bachelor's degrees were awarded. The most popular majors were criminal justice (16%), psychology (16%), and business administration (14%).

Admissions Contact: Ulisa E. Bowles, Director of Admissions. E-Mail: *admissions@uncfsu.edu* Web: *www.uncfsu.edu*

GARDNER-WEBB UNIVERSITY C-3

Boiling Springs, NC 28017 **(704) 406-4495**
(800) 253-6472; (704) 406-4488

Full-time: 779 men, 1309 women	**Faculty:** 122; IIA, --$
Part-time: 118 men, 366 women	**Ph.D.s:** 79%
Graduate: 594 men, 1470 women	**Student/Faculty:** 17 to 1
Year: semesters, summer session	**Tuition:** $25,930
Application Deadline: open	**Room & Board:** $8445

Freshman Class: 5456 applied, 2640 accepted, 434 enrolled
SAT or ACT: required

COMPETITIVE+

Gardner-Webb University, founded in 1905, is an independent institution affiliated with the Baptist Convention of North Carolina and offering undergraduate programs in the arts and sciences, business, education, nursing, and professional studies. There are 4 undergraduate schools and 3 graduate schools. In addition to regional accreditation, Webb has baccalaureate program accreditation with ACBSP, NASM, NCATE, and NLN. The library contains 244,133 volumes, 653,778 microform items, and 12,494 audio/video tapes/CDs/DVDs, and subscribes to 108,251 periodicals including electronic. Computerized library services include interlibrary loans, database searching, Internet access, and Wi-Fi capability. Special learning facilities include an art gallery, radio station, observatory. The 250-acre campus is in a small town 50 miles west of Charlotte, NC. Including any residence halls, there are 46 buildings.

Student Life: 78% of undergraduates are from North Carolina. Others are from 35 states, 21 foreign countries, and Canada. 70% are from public schools. 69% are White; 20% African American. 64% are Protestant. The average age of freshmen is 18; all undergraduates, 21. 26% do not continue beyond their first year; 48% remain to graduate.

Housing: 1368 students can be accommodated in college housing, which includes single-sex dorms and on-campus apartments. In addition, there are honors houses. On-campus housing is guaranteed for all 4 years. 77% of students live on campus; of those, 50% remain on campus on weekends. Alcohol is not permitted. All students may keep cars.

Activities: There are no fraternities or sororities. There are 65 groups on campus, including art, band, cheerleading, choir, chorale, chorus, debate, drama, drill team, film, honors, international, jazz band, literary magazine, marching band, musical theater, newspaper, opera, orchestra, pep band, photography, political, professional, radio and TV, religious, social, social service, student government, symphony, and yearbook. Popular campus events include Festival of Lights, Bulldog Madness and Spring's Alive.

Sports: There are 11 intercollegiate sports for men and 10 for women, and 28 intramural sports for men and 28 for women. Facilities include Athletic and recreation facilities include an 8,500-seat stadium, 2 gyms, tennis and racquetball courts, a weight room, a swimming pool, playing fields for softball, soccer, football, and baseball, a 5500-seat arena, an aerobics room, and a ropes course.

Disabled Students: All of the campus is accessible. Facilities include wheelchair ramps, elevators, special parking, specially equipped restrooms, special class scheduling, lowered drinking fountains, and special housing.

Services: Counseling and information services are available, as is tutoring in every subject. There is a reader service for the blind, and remedial math, reading, and writing.

Campus Safety and Security: Measures include 24-hour foot and vehicle patrol, emergency notification system, self-defense education, and security escort services. There are emergency telephones, lighted pathways/sidewalks, controlled access to dorms/residences, police foot patrol inside of dorms is also provided.

Programs of Study: Webb confers B.A., B.S., B.F.A., B.M. and B.S.N. degrees. Associate, master's, and doctoral degrees are also awarded. Bachelor's degrees are awarded in BIOLOGICAL SCIENCE (biology/biological science), BUSINESS (accounting, business administration and management, international business management, and sports management), COMMUNICATIONS AND THE ARTS (American Sign Language, art, communications, English, French, music, and Spanish), COMPUTER AND PHYSICAL SCIENCE (chemistry, computer science, information sciences and systems, and mathematics), EDUCATION (athletic training, elementary education, foreign languages education, health education, middle school education, music education, physical education, and secondary education), ENGINEERING AND ENVIRONMENTAL DESIGN (industrial administration/management), HEALTH PROFESSIONS (health care administration, medical technology, nursing, and physician's assistant), SOCIAL SCIENCE (history, interpreter for the deaf, psychology, religion, religious music, social science, and sociology). Nursing, music, biology, and education are the strongest academically. Business, social science, education, and nursing have the largest enrollments.

Required: To graduate, students must complete 128 credit hours, including 24 to 36 in the major, with a minimum GPA of 2.0. The required core curriculum consists of 44 hours of general education, and liberal arts courses.

Special: The university offers work-study programs, internships, and study abroad in 11 countries. There are 11 national honor societies, a freshman honors program, and 3 departmental honors programs.

Faculty/Classroom: 51% of faculty are male; 49% are female. All teach undergraduates. No introductory courses are taught by graduate students. The average class size in an introductory lecture is 25; in a laboratory is 9; and in a regular course is 18.

Admissions: 48% of the 2013-2014 applicants were accepted. 42% of the current freshmen were in the top fifth of their class; 66% were in the top two fifths. 3 freshmen graduated first in their class.

Requirements: The SAT or ACT is required. In addition, candidates should be graduates of an accredited secondary school or have a GED certificate. The recommended preparatory curriculum includes 4 units of English, 3 of math, and 2 each of social science, natural science, a foreign language, and electives. One standardized test, either the SAT or the ACT, is required. Webb requires applicants to be in the upper 50% of their class. A GPA of 2.5 is required. AP and CLEP credits are accepted. Important factors in the admissions decision are leadership record, extracurricular activities record, and recommendations by school officials.

Procedure: Freshmen are admitted to all sessions. Entrance exams should be taken During the junior or senior year of high school. There are deferred admissions and rolling admissions plans. Application deadlines are open. Application fee is $40. Applications are accepted online.

Transfer: 114 transfer students enrolled in 2012-2013. Applicants must submit the standard application and fee, official high school and college transcripts, and SAT or ACT scores. High school transcripts and test scores are waived for applicants with 15 or more semester credits and a GPA of 2.25 and submission of a college tanscript. 32 of 128 credits required for the bachelor's degree must be completed at Webb.

Visiting: There are regularly scheduled orientations for prospective students, including a campus tour, and meet with an admissions counselor. There are guides for informal visits, visitors may sit in on classes, and stay overnight. To schedule a visit, contact the Visit Coordinator.

Financial Aid: In 2013-2014, 100% of all full-time freshmen and 98% of continuing full-time students received some form of financial aid. The average freshman award was $18,540. Need-based scholarships or need-based grants averaged $7,336; need-based self-help aid (loans and jobs) averaged $4,283; non-need-based athletic scholarships averaged $15,287; and other non-need-based awards and non-need-based scholarships averaged $11,745. Average annual earnings from campus work are $1303. The average financial indebtedness of the 2013 graduate was $19,725. Webb is a member of CSS. The FAFSA the state aid form, and federal tax returns are required. The priority date for freshman financial aid applications for fall entry is March 1.

International Students: There are 67 international students enrolled. The school actively recruits these students. They must take the TOEFL with a minimum score of 500 on the paper-based TOEFL (PBT) or 61 on the Internet-based version (iBT). They must also take the SAT or ACT, scoring 870.

Computers: All students may access the system. Wireless and network Internet access is always available, but the computer labs may be accessed from 7a.m. to 11p.m. except when a class is in progress. There are no time limits and no fees.

Graduates: From July 1, 2012 to June 30, 2013, 645 bachelor's degrees were awarded. The most popular majors were business administration (27%), social sciences (21%), and nursing and other health related majors (12%). In an average class, 9% graduate in 3 years or less, 37% graduate in 4 years or less, 47% graduate in 5 years or less, and 48% graduate in 6 years or less.

Admissions Contact: Angela Sundell, Assistant Vice President of Admissions. E-Mail: *admissions@gardner-webb.edu* Web: *www.gardner-webb.edu*

GREENSBORO COLLEGE D-2

Greensboro, NC 27401-1875 (336) 272-7102, ext. 211
(800) 346-8226; (336) 378-0154

Full-time: 500 men, 450 women
Part-time: 40 men, 110 women
Graduate: 15 men, 50 women
Year: semesters, summer session
Application Deadline: open
Freshman Class: n/av
SAT or ACT: recommended
Faculty: n/av; IIB, --$
Ph.D.s: 81%
Student/Faculty: n/av
Tuition: $25,200
Room & Board: $8830

LESS COMPETITIVE

Greensboro College, founded in 1838, is a private institution affiliated with the United Methodist Church and offering undergraduate programs in the arts and sciences, business, education, health sciences, and preprofessional studies and graduate programs in education and teaching English to speakers of other languages. The figures in the above capsule and in this profile are approximate. In addition to regional accreditation, Greensboro has baccalaureate program accreditation with NCATE. The library contains 109,896 volumes, 2981 microform items, and 2737 audio/video tapes/CDs/DVDs, and subscribes to 491 periodicals including electronic. Computerized library services include interlibrary loans, database searching, and Internet access. Special learning facilities include a learning resource center, an art gallery, and the Brock Museum of Greensboro College History. The 46-acre campus is in an urban area bordering downtown Greensboro. Including any residence halls, there are 23 buildings.

Student Life: 71% of undergraduates are from North Carolina. Others are from 30 states, 14 foreign countries, and Canada. 79% are white; 17% African American. 47% are Protestant; 33% claim no religious affiliation; 11% Catholic. The average age of freshmen is 18; all undergraduates, 23. 31% do not continue beyond their first year; 46% remain to graduate.

Housing: 620 students can be accommodated in college housing, which includes single-sex and coed dorms and on-campus apartments. On-campus housing is guaranteed for all 4 years. 52% of students commute. All students may keep cars.

Activities: 3% of men belong to 2 local and 1 national fraternity; 4% of women belong to 2 local sororities. There are 40 groups on campus, including art, band, cheerleading, choir, chorale, community service, computers, dance, drama, ethnic, honors, international, jazz band, literary magazine, marching band, musical theater, newspaper, opera, pep band, photography, political, professional, programming, religious, social, social service, and student government. Popular campus events include Winter Rose Formal, Festival of Lessons and Carols, and Spring Fling.

Sports: There are 8 intercollegiate sports for men and 8 for women, and 5 intramural sports for men and 5 for women. Facilities include an athletic field for soccer and lacrosse and tennis and basketball courts.

Disabled Students: 80% of the campus is accessible. Facilities include wheelchair ramps, elevators, special parking, specially equipped restrooms, special class scheduling, and lowered drinking fountains.

Services: Counseling and information services are available, as is tutoring in most subjects. There is remedial math and writing, a computerized writing center, and a Writing Across the Curriculum program to strengthen communication skills. Professional math and writing tutors are available to all students.

Campus Safety and Security: Measures include 24-hour foot and vehicle patrol, self-defense education, and security escort services. There are emergency telephones, lighted pathways/sidewalks, security entrances to residence halls, and controlled access to computer labs.

Programs of Study: confers B.A. B.S., B.B.A., and B.M.E. degrees. Master's degrees are also awarded. Bachelor's degrees are awarded in BIOLOGICAL SCIENCE (biology/biological science), BUSINESS (accounting and business administration and management), COMMUNICATIONS AND THE ARTS (art, dramatic arts, English, French, music, and Spanish), COMPUTER AND PHYSICAL SCIENCE (chemistry and mathematics), EDUCATION (art education, athletic training, drama education, early childhood education, elementary education, English education, foreign languages education, mathematics education, middle school education, music education, physical education, science education, secondary education, social studies education, and special education), HEALTH PROFESSIONS (exercise science), SOCIAL SCIENCE (history, political science/government, psychology, religion, and sociology). Business, education, and sociology are the strongest academically.

Required: To graduate, students must complete 124 credit hours, including 32 to 48 in the major. They must take courses in social science, fine arts, lab science, English and literature, religion, history, phys ed, math, and foreign language. They must also take at least 1 course designated as global awareness and demonstrate competency in writing, oral communication, and computing.

Special: The college offers cross-registration with members of the Greater Greensboro Consortium, Writing Across the Curriculum, and Allied Health programs in medical and radiologic technology, an accelerated degree program in business administration, and internships in all majors, B.A., B.S., B.M.E., and B.B.A degrees, work-study programs, study abroad, dual majors, pass/fail options, and credit for life, military, and work experience. Greensboro's Ethics Across the Curriculum program exposes students to ethical issues in a range of disciplines to promote the study and living of ethical principles at the college. Other special programs include the George Center for Honors Studies, First Year Seminar, International Studies, and Women's and Gender Studies. There are 12 national honor societies and a freshman honors program.

Faculty/Classroom: 50% of faculty are male; 50% are female. All teach undergraduates, 50% do research, and 50% do both. No introductory courses are taught by graduate students. The average class size in an introductory lecture is 21; in a laboratory is 16; and in a regular course is 11.

Requirements: The SAT or ACT is recommended. In addition, applicants must be graduates of an accredited secondary school or have a GED certificate. An essay is required and an interview is recommended. Selected majors must audition or present a portfolio. AP and CLEP credits are accepted. Important factors in the admissions decision are advanced placement or honors courses, leadership record, and evidence of special talent.

Procedure: Freshmen are admitted to all sessions. Entrance exams should be taken in the spring of the junior year. There are early admissions, deferred admissions, and rolling admissions plans. Check with the school for current application deadlines. The application fee is $35. Notification is sent on a rolling basis. Applications are accepted online.

Transfer: Official transcripts from any college attended are required. Standardized test scores and high school records are required of applicants with fewer than 30 semester hours. An essay is required, and an interview is recommended. 31 of 124 credits required for the bachelor's degree must be completed at Greensboro.

Visiting: There are regularly scheduled orientations for prospective students, including an interview, a campus tour, and meetings with faculty and students. There are guides for informal visits; visitors may sit in on classes and stay overnight. To schedule a visit, contact the Admissions Office.

Financial Aid: Greensboro is a member of CSS. The FAFSA, the state aid form, and the college's own financial statement are required. Check with the school for current application deadlines.

International Students: They must take the TOEFL with a minimum score of 550 on the paper-based TOEFL (PBT). They must also take the SAT or ACT.

Computers: Wireless access is available. Computer labs can be found in all classroom buildings, the Reynolds Family Student Center, the library, and the main building. Students may use the college network from their residence halls as well as from off-campus locations. Wireless access is available from most places on campus. All students may access the system 24 hours a day. There are no time limits and no fees. It is strongly recommended that all students have a personal computer.

Admissions Contact: Director of Admissions. A campus DVD is available. E-Mail: *admissions@greensborocollege.edu* Web: *www.greensborocollege.edu*

GUILFORD COLLEGE D-2

Greensboro, NC 27410 (336) 316-2220
(800) 992-7759; (336) 316-2954

Full-time: 897 men, 1159 women
Part-time: 143 men, 263 women
Graduate: n/av
Year: 4-1-4, summer session
Application Deadline: February 15
Freshman Class: 2549 applied, 2040 accepted, 322 enrolled
SAT CR/M/W: 550/540/520
Faculty: 124; IIB, --$
Ph.D.s: 91%
Student/Faculty: 17 to 1
Tuition: $30,430
Room & Board: $8270
ACT: 23

COMPETITIVE

Guilford's purpose is to provide a transformative, practical, and excellent liberal arts education that produces critical thinkers in an inclusive, diverse environment, guided by Quaker testimonies of community, equality, integrity, peace, and simplicity and emphasizing the creative problem-solving skills, experiences, enthusiasm, and international perspectives necessary to promote positive change in the world, In addition to regional accreditation, has baccalaureate program accreditation with NCATE. The library contains 256,465 volumes, 21,543 microform items, 5,119 audio/video tapes/CDs/DVDs, and subscribes to 30,561 periodicals including electronic. Computerized library services include interlibrary loans, database searching, Internet access, and Wi-Fi capability. Special learning facilities include an art gallery, planetarium, radio station, Cline Observatory (physics & astronomy); photography studio, outdoor sculpture studio, Guilford College Farm, community garden, and Friends Historical Collection. The 340-acre campus is in a suburban area in the western residential area of Greensboro, NC. Including any residence halls, there are 31 buildings.

Student Life: 72% of undergraduates are from North Carolina. Others are from 40 states, 15 foreign countries, and Canada. 72% are from public schools. 62% are White; 25% African American. 50% claim no religious affiliation. The average age of freshmen is 18; all undergraduates, 22. 29% do not continue beyond their first year; 59% remain to graduate.

Housing: 1043 students can be accommodated in college housing, which includes single-sex and coed dorms and on-campus apartments. In addition, there are special-interest houses, In addition to dormitory and on-campus apartment housing, Guilford offers the opportunity for groups of students to live together in special interest housing or theme houses. These are four houses that accommodate six to ten students and are organized around common social or academic interests, such as the study of languages, science, environmental sustainability, cultural themes, or a community service focus. Students may apply as a group each spring for special interest housing for the following academic year. The houses are not available for first–year students. 81% of students live on campus; of those, 80% remain on campus on weekends. All students may keep cars.

Activities: There are no fraternities or sororities. There are 43 groups on campus, including and Yachting, Bayard Rustin Center for LGBTQA Activism, Community Aids Awareness Project, Fencing Club, Guilford Peace Society, Inter–Club Council, Men and Women Rugby, Poetry Club, Archery Club, art, cheerleading, chess, choir, chorale, chorus, computers, dance, debate, drama, environmental, ethnic, film, gay, honors, international, jazz band, literary magazine, musical theater, newspaper, pep band, photography, political, professional, radio and TV, religious, social, social service, and student government. Popular campus events include Serendipity Spring Festival, Bryan Lecture Series in the Arts, Hip Hop Conference, Eastern Music Festival, International Dinner & Dance Holiday Choir Concerts.

Sports: There are 8 intercollegiate sports for men and 8 for women, and 3 intramural sports for men and 3 for women. Facilities include Athletic facilities include: 3500-seat football/track stadium with lights (also lacrosse, soccer); 1560-seat field house gymnasium with multiple courts for basketball and volleyball; baseball field; cross–country courses; swimming pool; lighted intramural field; additional playing fields for varsity and club sports; tennis courts; weight room; cardio room.

Disabled Students: 95% of the campus is accessible. Facilities include wheelchair ramps, elevators, special parking, specially equipped restrooms, special class scheduling, lowered drinking fountains, lowered telephones. an ATM machine.

Services: Counseling and information services are available, as is tutoring in every subject. There is a reader service for the blind, and remedial math, reading, and writing. Faculty tutoring for skills development; student tutoring for course-specific help; non–remedial writing.

Campus Safety and Security: Measures include 24-hour foot and vehicle patrol, emergency notification system, self-defense education, and security escort services. There are emergency telephones, lighted pathways/sidewalks, controlled access to dorms/residences, and a whistle program.

Programs of Study: confers A.B., B.S., and B.F.A. degrees. Bachelor's degrees are awarded in AGRICULTURE (environmental studies), BIOLOGICAL SCIENCE (biology/biological science), BUSINESS (accounting, business administration and management, information & communication technology, international business management, and sports management), COMMUNICATIONS AND THE ARTS (art, dramatic arts, English, French, German, music, Spanish, theatre arts, and visual and performing arts), COMPUTER AND PHYSICAL SCIENCE (chemistry, geology, information sciences and systems, mathematics, and physics), EDUCATION (education and sports studies), ENGINEERING AND ENVIRONMENTAL DESIGN (computer technology), HEALTH PROFESSIONS (exercise science and health science), SOCIAL SCIENCE (African American studies, anthropology, community services, criminal justice, economics, forensic studies, gender studies, history, interdisciplinary studies, international studies, peace studies, philosophy, political science/government, psychology, religion, sociology, and women's studies). Natural sciences, accounting, psychology, English, art, theater, forensic biology, and community justice are the strongest academically. Business management, psychology, and criminal justice have the largest enrollments.

Required: Students must fulfill requirements in Fine Arts, English, Humanities, Sciences, Social Sciences, and Foreign Language. They must take a first-year experience and an interdisciplinary capstone course, and courses in historical perspectives, intercultural studies, social justice and environmental responsibility, diversity, business and policy studies, and quantitative literacy. A minimum GPA of 2.0 is required. 128 credit hours must be completed with at least 32 in the major.

Special: Guilford offers 3-2 degree programs in forestry and environmental studies with Duke University, and in physician assistant training with Bowman Gray School of Medicine at Wake Forest University. Guilford also offers many internships, a Washington semester, work-study programs, accelerated degree programs, dual majors, student-designed majors, study abroad in 13 countries, B.A.-B.S. degrees, and cross-registration with members of the Greater Greensboro Consortium. There are 2 national honor societies and a freshman honors program.

Faculty/Classroom: 50% of faculty are male; 50% are female. All teach undergraduates. No introductory courses are taught by graduate students. The average class size in an introductory lecture is 19; in a laboratory is 17; and in a regular course is 19.

Admissions: 80% of the 2013-2014 applicants were accepted. The SAT scores for the 2013-2014 freshman class were: Critical Reading--29% below 500, 41% between 500 and 599, 25% between 600 and 699, and 5% between 700 and 800; Math--29% below 500, 47% between 500 and 599, 21% between 600 and 699, and 3% between 700 and 800; Writing--36% below 500, 37% between 500 and 599, 23% between 600 and 699, and 4% between 700 and 800. The ACT scores were 24% below 21, 28% between 21 and 23, 24% between 24 and 26, 10% between 27 and 28, and 14% above 28. 38% of the current freshmen were in the top fifth of their class; 70% were in the top two fifths. 1 freshman graduated first in the class.

Requirements: The SAT is recommended. A minimum SAT composite score of 1000 or ACT score of 22 is recommended. Applicants should have completed 20 Carnegie Units, including 4 in English, 2 each in foreign language and science, and 1 each in history and social studies. The GED is accepted. An essay is required and an interview is recommended. A GPA of 2.0 is required. AP and CLEP credits are accepted. Important factors in the admissions decision are advanced placement or honors courses, leadership record, and evidence of special talent.

Procedure: Freshmen are admitted fall and spring. Entrance exams should be taken in spring of the junior year or fall of the senior year. There are early decision, early admissions, and deferred admissions plans. Early decision applications should be filed by November 15; regular applications, by February 15 for fall entry; and February 15 for spring entry, along with a $25 fee. Notification of early decision is sent February 15; regular decision, April 1. Applications are accepted online.

Transfer: 459 transfer students enrolled in 2012-2013. Applicants for transfer must have a minimum GPA of 2.5 in at least 12 credit hours, submit either SAT or ACT scores, and provide a letter from the academic adviser or dean of the previous school. An interview is recommended. Transfer applicants are evaluated according to the same criteria used for freshman applicants. Consideration is given to the academic reputation of the former college. 32 of 128 credits required for the bachelor's degree must be completed at Guilford.

Visiting: There are regularly scheduled orientations for prospective students, Visits can be scheduled throughout the year. A typical visit includes an information session led by an Admission Counselor followed by a student–led tour. Class visits, professor meetings, and lunch buddies are available when classes are in session. There are guides for informal visits and visitors may sit in on classes. To schedule a visit, contact the Admission Office.

Financial Aid: In 2013-2014, 99% of all full-time freshmen and 87% of continuing full-time students received some form of financial aid. 82% of all full-time freshmen students received need-based aid. The average freshman award was $22,998. Need-based scholarships or need-based grants averaged $20,643 ($30,000 maximum); need-based self-help aid (loans and jobs) averaged $14,646; and other non-need-based awards and non-need-based scholarships averaged $9,351. 18% of undergraduate students work part-time. Average annual earnings from campus work are $1500. The average financial indebtedness of the 2013 graduate was $25,025. The FAFSA is required. The deadline for filing freshman financial aid applications for fall entry is March 1.

International Students: There are 23 international students enrolled. The school actively recruits these students. They must take the TOEFL with a minimum score of 550 on the paper-based TOEFL (PBT) or 80 on the Internet-based version (iBT).

Computers: All students may access the system 24 hours a day. There are no time limits and no fees.

Graduates: From July 1, 2012 to June 30, 2013, 539 bachelor's degrees were awarded. The most popular majors were business management (18%), psychology (11%), and criminal justice (10%). 183 companies recruited on campus in 2012-2013. In an average class, 50% graduate in 4 years or less, 56% graduate in 5 years or less, and 57% graduate in 6 years or less. Of the 2012 graduating class, 36% were enrolled in graduate school within 6 months of graduation, and 65% were employed.

Admissions Contact: Andy Strickler, Director of Admissions . E-Mail: *admission@guilford.edu* Web: *www.guilford.edu*

HIGH POINT UNIVERSITY D-2

High Point, NC 27262 (336) 841-9216
(800) 345-6993; (336) 888-6382

Full-time: 1506 men, 2308 women **Faculty:** 212; IIB, --$
Part-time: 60 men, 90 women **Ph.D.s:** 77%
Graduate: 64 men, 177 women **Student/Faculty:** 15 to 1
Year: semesters, summer session **Tuition:** $39,800
Application Deadline: March 15 **Room & Board:** n/app
Freshman Class: 4529 applied, 3228 accepted, 1030 enrolled
SAT CR/M/W: 530/545/530 **ACT:** 22 **COMPETITIVE**

Situated on 300 beautifully landscaped acres in the heart of North Carolina's Piedmont Triad, High Point University combines the warmth and intimacy of a small liberal arts college with the academic offerings and amenities of a large state university. There are 6 undergraduate schools and 1 graduate school. In addition to regional accreditation, High Point has baccalaureate program accreditation with NCATE. The library contains 288,473 volumes, 84,000 microform items, 12,500 audio/video tapes/CDs/DVDs, and subscribes to 34,000 periodicals including electronic. Computerized library services include interlibrary loans, database searching, and Internet access. Special learning facilities include an art gallery, radio station, and TV station. The 300-acre campus is in a suburban area 15 miles southeast of Winston-Salem and 12 miles southwest of Greensboro. Including any residence halls, there are 59 buildings.

Student Life: 69% of undergraduates are from out of state, mostly the Middle Atlantic. Students are from 46 states, 29 foreign countries, and Canada. 63% are from public schools. 81% are White. 59% are Protestant; 26% Catholic; 11% claim no religious affiliation. The average age of freshmen is 18; all undergraduates, 20. 20% do not continue beyond their first year; 60% remain to graduate.

Housing: 3004 students can be accommodated in college housing, which includes single-sex and coed dorms, on-campus apartments, and off-campus apartments. In addition, there are honors houses, special-interest houses, fraternity houses, sorority houses, wellness halls, honors housing, discipline-specific housing. On-campus housing is guaranteed for all 4 years. 93% of students live on campus; of those, 90% remain on campus on weekends. All students may keep cars.

Activities: 15% of men belong to 4 national fraternities; 25% of women belong to 1 local and 4 national sororities. There are 109 groups on campus, including art, band, cheerleading, choir, chorale, chorus, computers, dance, debate, drama, environmental, ethnic, film, honors, international, literary magazine, musical theater, newspaper, orchestra, pep band, political, professional, radio and TV, religious, social, social service, and student government.

Sports: There are 7 intercollegiate sports for men and 7 for women, and 6 intramural sports for men and 6 for women. Facilities include intramural fields, tennis courts, an intramural gym, a recreation center featuring a swimming pool, racquetball courts, an aerobics center, a weight room, and a 2500-seat arena. Newly constructed are a 45,000-square-foot student activities center, a soccer stadium and track, a sports center, and a new university park with amphitheater.

Disabled Students: 98% of the campus is accessible. Facilities include wheelchair ramps, elevators, special parking, specially equipped restrooms, special class scheduling, and lowered drinking fountains.

Services: Counseling and information services are available, as is tutoring in every subject. There is remedial math, reading, and writing.

Campus Safety and Security: Measures include 24-hour foot and vehicle patrol, emergency notification system, self-defense education, and security escort services. There are shuttle buses, emergency telephones, lighted pathways/sidewalks, controlled access to dorms/residences, 24-hour secured residence halls and student bike patrols. Valet parking service.

Programs of Study: High Point confers B.A., B.S. and B.S.B.A. degrees. Master's and doctoral degrees are also awarded. Bachelor's degrees are awarded in BIOLOGICAL SCIENCE (biochemistry and biology/biological science), BUSINESS (accounting, business administration and management, international business management, and nonprofit/public organization management), COMMUNICATIONS AND THE ARTS (art, communications, English literature, English Writing, fine arts, French, graphic design, music, Spanish, and theatre arts), COMPUTER AND PHYSICAL SCIENCE (actuarial science, chemistry, computer science, mathematics, and mathematics – economics), EDUCATION (athletic training, elementary education, middle school education, physical education, and special education), ENGINEERING AND ENVIRONMENTAL DESIGN (interior design), HEALTH PROFESSIONS (exercise science), SOCIAL SCIENCE (criminal justice, history, home furnishings and equipment management/production/services, human services, industrial and organizational psychology, international relations, philosophy, political science/government, psychology, religion, and sociology). Business administration, exercise and sport science, education, psychology, biology, interior design, communications have the largest enrollments.

Required: To graduate, students must complete a minimum of 128 credit hours with a minimum GPA of 2.0. The core curriculum consists of 1 course in each of the following subject areas: English, foreign language, mathematics, and ethical reasoning, as well as a First Year Seminar course, President's Seminar, and a PE activity course. Distribution requirements include 2 courses in the social sciences and 1 course in each of the following areas: performing or visual arts, literature, history, religion, and natural science with laboratory.

Special: There is cross-registration with the University of North Carolina at Greensboro, North Carolina Agricultural and Technical State University, and Greensboro, Elon, Guilford, and Bennett Colleges. High Point also offers study abroad in many countries, the Student Career Internship Program, accelerated degree programs, unique programs in home furnishings marketing/management studies, work-study programs, student-designed majors, and a 3-2 engineering program with Vanderbilt and Virginia Tech. There are 5 national honor societies, a freshman honors program, and 5 departmental honors programs.

Faculty/Classroom: 52% of faculty are male; 48% are female. All teach undergraduates. No introductory courses are taught by graduate students. The average class size in an introductory lecture is 20; in a laboratory is 18; and in a regular course is 18.

Admissions: 71% of the 2013-2014 applicants were accepted. The SAT scores for the 2013-2014 freshman class were: Critical Reading--30% below 500, 52% between 500 and 599, 16% between 600 and 699, and 2% between 700 and 800; Math--32% below 500, 49% between 500 and 599, 18% between 600 and 699, and 1% between 700 and 800; Writing--31% below 500, 52% between 500 and 599, 16% between 600 and 699, and 1% between 700 and 800. The ACT scores were 28% below 21, 37% between 21 and 23, 24% between 24 and 26, 7% between 27 and 28, and 5% above 28. 32% of the current freshmen were in the top fifth of their class; 62% were in the top two fifths. 7 freshmen graduated first in their class.

Requirements: The SAT or ACT is required. The SAT is preferred. Applicants should be graduates of an accredited secondary school or have a GED certificate. They should have completed 14 academic units, including 4 in English, 3 in math, 2 each in science, social studies, and history, and 1 elective. A GPA of 2.0 is required. AP and CLEP credits are accepted.

Procedure: Freshmen are admitted fall, spring, and summer. Entrance exams should be taken prior to high school graduation. There are early decision, early admissions, deferred admissions, and rolling admissions plans. Early decision applications should be filed by November 6; regular applications, by March 15 for fall entry, along with a $40 fee. Notification of early decision is sent November 27; regular decision, on a rolling basis. 283 early decision candidates were accepted for the 2013-2014 class. Applications are accepted online.

Transfer: 50 transfer students enrolled in 2012-2013. Applicants must submit official transcripts from colleges and high schools previously attended, as well as SAT or ACT scores, if available. Generally, a minimum GPA of 2.0 is required. 31 of 124 credits required for the bachelor's degree must be completed at High Point.

Visiting: There are regularly scheduled orientations for prospective students, students may visit during approved hours during the weekend and weekday. There are guides for informal visits and visitors may sit in on classes. To schedule a visit, contact the Admissions Office.

Financial Aid: In 2013-2014, 91% of all full-time freshmen and 78% of continuing full-time students received some form of financial aid. 56% of all full-time freshmen and 56% of continuing full-time students received need-based aid. The average freshman award was $10,875. Need-based scholarships or need-based grants averaged $2,555 ($6,000 maximum); need-based self-help aid (loans and jobs) averaged $4,000 ($4,125 maximum); non-need-based athletic scholarships averaged $17,160 ($19,026 maximum); and other non-need-based awards and non-need-based scholarships averaged $8,576 ($12,000 maximum). 67% of undergraduate students work part-time. Average annual earnings from campus work are $1500. The average financial indebtedness of the 2013 graduate was $11,280. High Point is a member of CSS. The FAFSA and the state aid form are required. The priority date for freshman financial aid applications for fall entry is March 1.

International Students: There are 65 international students enrolled. The school actively recruits these students. The SAT or ACT is required of students who wish to play on varsity athletic teams.

Computers: All students may access the system. There are no time limits.

Graduates: From July 1, 2012 to June 30, 2013, 513 bachelor's degrees were awarded. The most popular majors were business (42%), education (9%), and human relations (8%). 15 companies recruited on campus in 2012-2013. In an average class, 50% graduate in 4 years or less, 55% graduate in 5 years or less, and 56% graduate in 6 years or less. Of the 2012 graduating class, 22% were enrolled in graduate school within 6 months of graduation, and 95% were employed.

Admissions Contact: Beth McCarthy, Director of Admissions. E-Mail: *admiss@highpoint.edu* Web: *www.highpoint.edu*

JOHNSON AND WALES UNIVERSITY/CHARLOTTE CAMPUS C-3

Charlotte, NC 28202 (866) 598-2427; (950) 598-1111

Full-time: 968 men, 1524 women	**Faculty:** 88
Part-time: 23 men, 22 women	**Ph.D.s:** n/av
Graduate: n/av	**Student/Faculty:** 27 to 1
Year: quarters, summer session	**Tuition:** $25,107
Application Deadline: open	**Room & Board:** $10,314
Freshman Class: 5662 applied, 4331 accepted, 733 enrolled	
	COMPETITIVE

Johnson & Wales University/Charlotte Campus, founded in 2004, offers degree programs in its College of Business, College of Culinary Arts, and Hospitality College. The figures in the above capsule and in this profile are approximate. There are 3 undergraduate schools. The library contains 28,690 volumes, and 8,474 audio/video tapes/CDs/DVDs, and subscribes to 196 periodicals including electronic. Computerized library services include interlibrary loans, database searching, Internet access, and laptop Internet portals. Including any residence halls, there are 6 buildings.

Student Life: 61% of undergraduates are from out of state, mostly the South. Students are from 47 states, 22 foreign countries, and Canada. 39% are white; 28% African American. The average age of freshmen is 18; all undergraduates, 19. 75% remain to graduate.

Housing: College-sponsored housing includes coed dorms and on-campus apartments. On-campus housing is available on a lottery system for upperclassmen. 51% of students live on campus. Alcohol is not permitted. All students may keep cars.

Activities: There are no fraternities or sororities. There are 36 groups on campus, including cheerleading, gay, honors, international, newspaper, photography, religious, social, student government, and yearbook. Popular campus events include Welcome Week, Western Day, and Spring Week.

Disabled Students: All of the campus is accessible. Facilities include wheelchair ramps, elevators, special parking, specially equipped restrooms, special class scheduling, lowered drinking fountains, lowered telephones, and special housing.

Services: Counseling and information services are available, as is tutoring in every subject.

Campus Safety and Security: Measures include 24-hour foot and vehicle patrol, self-defense education, and security escort services. There are shuttle buses, emergency telephones, and lighted pathways/sidewalks.

Programs of Study: JWU confers B.S. degrees. Associate degrees are also awarded. Bachelor's degrees are awarded in BUSINESS (accounting, business administration and management, entrepreneurial studies, hospitality management services, hotel/motel and restaurant management, marketing and distribution, marketing management, marketing/retailing/merchandising, sports management, and tourism), ENGINEERING AND ENVIRONMENTAL DESIGN (food services technology), SOCIAL SCIENCE (clothing and textiles management/production/services, food production/management/services, and parks and recreation management).

Required: To graduate, students must complete 180 quarter credit hours, including at least 36 in the major, with a minimum GPA of 2.0. Required classes include English, math, history, economics, science, psychology, sociology, and professional development.

Special: The university offers co-op programs, accelerated degree programs, dual majors, study abroad, and worldwide work-study opportunities in business, hospitality, technology, and culinary arts. Most majors require 11-week internships. There is a freshman honors program.

Faculty/Classroom: All teach undergraduates. No introductory courses are taught by graduate students.

Admissions: 76% of the 2011-2012 applicants were accepted.

Requirements: Although SAT and ACT scores are required only for students applying for honors admissions, students who have taken these tests are encouraged to submit their scores. AP and CLEP credits are accepted. Important factors in the admissions decision are advanced placement or honors courses, extracurricular activities record, parents or siblings attended your school, and recommendations by school officials.

Procedure: Freshmen are admitted to all sessions. There are deferred admissions and rolling admissions plans. Application deadlines are open. Applications are accepted online.

Transfer: 223 transfer students enrolled in a recent year. Applicants are required to submit official high school and college transcripts and must have earned a minimum college GPA of 2.0. 45 of 180 credits required for the bachelor's degree must be completed at JWU.

Visiting: There are regularly scheduled orientations for prospective students, including an introduction to the academic and social aspects of the campus experience through interactive sessions. There are guides for informal visits, visitors may sit in on classes, and stay overnight. To schedule a visit, contact Admissions.

Financial Aid: JWU is a member of CSS. The FAFSA is required. The priority date for freshman financial aid applications for fall entry is March 1.

International Students: There are 46 international students enrolled. The school actively recruits these students. They must take the TOEFL with a minimum score of 550 on the paper-based TOEFL (PBT) or 80 on the Internet-based version (iBT).

Computers: There are 5 computer labs. 4 are located in the Academic Center, with more than 160 workstations; 1 is located in the library, with 30 workstations. All students may access the system. There are no time limits and no fees.

Admissions Contact: Joseph Campos, Director of Admissions. A campus DVD is available. E-Mail: *admissions.clt@jwu.edu* Web: *www.jwu.edu*

JOHNSON C. SMITH UNIVERSITY C-3

Charlotte, NC 28216 (704) 378-1010; (800) 782-7303; (704) 378-1242

Full-time: 544 men, 780 women	**Faculty:** 101
Part-time: 23 men, 40 women	**Ph.D.s:** 83%
Graduate: n/av	**Student/Faculty:** 11 to 1
Year: semesters, summer session	**Tuition:** $18,236
Application Deadline:	**Room & Board:** $7100
Freshman Class: 4777 applied, 1752 accepted, 232 enrolled	
SAT CR/M: 420/420 **ACT:** 17	**LESS COMPETITIVE**

Johnson C. Smith University continues to be a leader among private liberal arts colleges in the nation and serves as Charlotte's premier independent urban university. Founded in 1867 as Biddle Memorial Institute, the university enrolls approximately 1,500 students and confers bachelor's degrees to hundreds of students each year in 27 different majors. The university's service learning component, which combines academics and community service, has become a national model to other higher education institutions. Extensive career development opportunities abound through co-op programs and internships with more than 90 companies. There are 4 undergraduate schools. In addition to regional accreditation, JCSU has baccalaureate program accreditation with CSWE. The library contains 114,796 volumes, 4,068 microform items, and 1,635 audio/video tapes/CDs/DVDs, and subscribes to 11,295 periodicals including electronic. Computerized library services include interlibrary loans, database searching, Internet access, and Wi-Fi capability. Special learning facilities include a radio station. The 100-acre campus is in an urban area in Charlotte, NC. Including any residence halls, there are 26 buildings.

Student Life: 54% of undergraduates are from North Carolina. Others are from 31 states, 5 foreign countries, and Canada. 75% are African American; 14% race unknown. The average age of freshmen is 18; all undergraduates, 23. 56% do not continue beyond their first year; 44% remain to graduate.

Housing: 1316 students can be accommodated in college housing, which includes single-sex and coed dorms and on-campus apartments. In addition, there are honors houses. On-campus housing is available on a first-come and first-served basis. 53% of students commute. Alcohol is not permitted. Upperclassmen may keep cars.

Activities: 1% of men belong to 5 national fraternities; 2% of women belong to 4 national sororities. There are 60 groups on campus, including art, band, cheerleading, chess, choir, chorale, chorus, communications, computers, dance, debate, drama, ethnic, film, gay, honors, international, jazz band, literary magazine, marching band, newspaper, orchestra, pep band, photography, political, professional, radio and TV, religious, social, social service, student government, and yearbook. Popular campus events include Homecoming, Bullfest Spring Festival and CIAA.

Sports: There are 6 intercollegiate sports for men and 7 for women. Facilities include a 3200-seat gym, a pool, tennis and basketball courts, baseball field, a weight room, a training room, an Olympic-size track, a football field, and an on-campus stadium seating 4500.

Disabled Students: Facilities include wheelchair ramps, elevators, special parking, specially equipped restrooms, special class scheduling, and lowered drinking fountains.

Services: Counseling and information services are available, as is tutoring in every subject.

Campus Safety and Security: Measures include 24-hour foot and vehicle patrol, self-defense education, and security escort services. There are emergency telephones, lighted pathways/sidewalks, controlled access to dorms/residences, emergency alert stations.

Programs of Study: JCSU confers B.A., B.S. and B.S.W degrees. Bachelor's degrees are awarded in BIOLOGICAL SCIENCE (biology/biological science), BUSINESS (business administration and management and business economics), COMMUNICATIONS AND THE ARTS (communications, English, music business management, and Spanish), COMPUTER AND PHYSICAL SCIENCE (applied mathematics, chemistry, computer science, mathematics, physics, and science), EDUCATION (health education and physical education), ENGINEERING AND ENVIRONMENTAL DESIGN (computer engineering, engineering, and preengineering),

HEALTH PROFESSIONS (community health work, nursing, pharmacy, predentistry, and premedicine), SOCIAL SCIENCE (criminal justice, economics, history, liberal arts/general studies, political science/government, prelaw, psychology, religious music, social science, social work, and sociology). Business administration has the largest enrollment.

Required: Candidates for the bachelor's degree must complete at least on hundred-twenty-two credit hours; earn a minimum overall Grade Point Average of 2.00; earn a minimum grade of C in any course that counts toward the major; satisfy all requirements of the curriculum in the Liberal Studies; complete all requirements for Community Service and the Senior Investigative Paper.

Special: JCSU offers cooperative programs in all majors, student-designed majors, 3+3 dual degree program with Charlotte Law School, cross-registration with the Charlotte Area Educational Consortium, and internships with local businesses, work-study programs, study abroad, and a B.A.-B.S. degree in all majors except Social Work, who receive a B.S.W. JCSU also offers non-degree study in continuing education. There are 12 national honor societies, a freshman honors program, and 9 departmental honors programs.

Faculty/Classroom: 46% of faculty are male; 54% are female. All teach undergraduates. No introductory courses are taught by graduate students.

Admissions: 37% of the 2013-2014 applicants were accepted. The SAT scores for the 2013-2014 freshman class were: Critical Reading--83% below 500, 14% between 500 and 599, and 2% between 600 and 699; Math--90% below 500, 9% between 500 and 599, and 1% between 600 and 699. The ACT scores were 87% below 21, 9% between 21 and 23, 4% between 24 and 15% of the current freshmen were in the top fifth of their class; 33% were in the top two fifths. 1 freshman graduated first in the class.

Requirements: The SAT or ACT is required. Applicants should have completed 18 Carnegie units, including 4 in English, 3 each in math, 3 in social science, 3 in science, and 3 in electives. The GED is accepted. An essay and recommendation letters are suggested. AP credits are accepted.

Procedure: Freshmen are admitted fall and spring. Entrance exams should be taken prior to application. There are deferred admissions and rolling admissions plans. Application deadlines are open. Application fee is $25. Notification is sent on a Rolling basis. Applications are accepted online.

Transfer: 84 transfer students enrolled in 2012-2013. Applicants need a minimum GPA of 2.0 in 12 semester hours of transferable course work. 32 of 122 credits required for the bachelor's degree must be completed at JCSU.

Visiting: There are regularly scheduled orientations for prospective students, a campus tour, a classroom visit, and a financial aid meeting. There are guides for informal visits, visitors may sit in on classes, and stay overnight. To schedule a visit, contact the Office of Admissions at (704) 378-1010.

Financial Aid: In 2013-2014, 95% of all full-time freshmen and 84% of continuing full-time students received some form of financial aid. 92% of all full-time freshmen and 79% of continuing full-time students received need-based aid. The average freshman award was $15,717. Need-based scholarships or need-based grants averaged $12,039; need-based self-help aid (loans and jobs) averaged $4,600; non-need-based athletic scholarships averaged $16,366; and other non-need-based awards and non-need-based scholarships averaged $20,349. JCSU is a member of CSS. The FAFSA and the state aid form are required. The priority date for freshman financial aid applications for fall entry is March 1.

International Students: There are 35 international students enrolled. The school actively recruits these students. They must take the TOEFL. They must also take the SAT or ACT.

Computers: All students may access the system any time. There are no time limits and no fees.

Graduates: From July 1, 2012 to June 30, 2013, 252 bachelor's degrees were awarded. The most popular majors were business administration (22%), mass communication/media studies (12%), and criminology (9%). In an average class, 30% graduate in 4 years or less, 39% graduate in 5 years or less, and 44% graduate in 6 years or less.

Admissions Contact: Mr. James Burrell, Director of Admissions. E-Mail: *admissions@jcsu.edu* Web: *http:/www.jcsu.edu/admissions*

LEES-MCRAE COLLEGE C-2

Banner Elk, NC 28604

828-898-2417
800-280-4562; 828-898-8707

Full-time: 347 men, 536 women	**Faculty:** 45
Part-time: 6 men, 1 women	**Ph.D.s:** 64%
Graduate: n/av	**Student/Faculty:** 15 to 1
Year: semesters, summer session	**Tuition:** $24,150
Application Deadline:	**Room & Board:** $9474
Freshman Class: n/av	

COMPETITIVE

Lees-McRae is a four-year, coeducational residential college offering diverse baccalaureate degrees, strong athletic programs and outstanding faculty. The College offers online programs and degree-completion opportunities in surrounding communities to nontraditional learners. All academic programs incorporate a broad core curriculum and field-specific career preparation and experiential learning with an emphasis in leadership and service. In addition to regional accreditation, Lees-McRae has baccalaureate program accreditation with TEAC. The library contains 216,747 volumes, 7,194 microform items, and 1,488 audio/video tapes/CDs/DVDs. Computerized library services include interlibrary loans, database searching, Internet access, and Wi-Fi capability. Special learning facilities include an art gallery, wildlife rehabilitation center, academic success center. Including any residence halls, there are 43 buildings.

Student Life: 70% of undergraduates are from North Carolina. Others are from 34 states, 9 foreign countries, and Canada. The average age of freshmen is 19; all undergraduates, 24.

Housing: 705 students can be accommodated in college housing, which includes single-sex and coed dorms and on-campus apartments. In addition, there are honors houses, special-interest houses, substance-free, pet-friendly. On-campus housing is guaranteed for all 4 years and is available on a lottery system for upperclassmen. 64% of students live on campus. All students may keep cars.

Activities: There are no fraternities or sororities. Groups on campus include art, cheerleading, chorus, communications, dance, drama, environmental, honors, international, musical theater, photography, professional, religious, social, social service, and student government. Popular campus events include Mountain Day and Stephenson Lecture Series.

Sports: There are 7 intercollegiate sports for men and 8 for women. Facilities include a main gym that seats 2,000 with basketball/volleyball courts, a match field for soccer/lacrosse, 4 practice fields, a softball field with batting cages, 2 indoor tennis courts, 6 outdoor tennis courts, a secondary gym for intramurals, an indoor Olympic-size pool, a fitness center, a weight room facility, an outdoor basketball court.

Disabled Students: Facilities include wheelchair ramps, special parking, specially equipped restrooms, special class scheduling, and special housing.

Services: Counseling and information services are available, as is tutoring in most subjects. There is remedial math, reading, and writing.

Campus Safety and Security: Measures include 24-hour foot and vehicle patrol, emergency notification system, and security escort services. There are emergency telephones, lighted pathways/sidewalks, and controlled access to dorms/residences.

Programs of Study: Lees-McRae confers B.A., B.S., B.A.A.S and B.F.A. degrees. Bachelor's degrees are awarded in BIOLOGICAL SCIENCE (biology/biological science and wildlife biology), BUSINESS (business administration and management and sports management), COMMUNICATIONS AND THE ARTS (art, communications, design, dramatic arts, English, musical theater, performing arts, and visual and performing arts), COMPUTER AND PHYSICAL SCIENCE (mathematics), EDUCATION (athletic training, drama education, education, and elementary education), HEALTH PROFESSIONS (premedicine and preveterinary science), SOCIAL SCIENCE (criminal justice, humanities, interdisciplinary studies, psychology, and religion). Wildlife biology, nursing, and education have the largest enrollments.

Special: There is a freshman honors program.

Faculty/Classroom: 45% of faculty are male; 55% are female. All teach undergraduates. No introductory courses are taught by graduate students.

Admissions: The SAT scores for the 2013-2014 freshman class were: Critical Reading--59% below 500, 34% between 500 and 599, 6% between 600 and 699, and 1% between 700 and 800; Math--53% below 500, 35% between 500 and 599, 12% between 600 and 699.

Requirements: Applicants must have completed 18 units of secondary school academic courses, including 6 of academic electives, 4 of English, 3 of math, 2 of science (1 with lab work), and 1 each of social studies and history. AP and CLEP credits are accepted.

Procedure: Freshmen are admitted to all sessions. There is a rolling admissions plan. Application deadlines are open. Applications are accepted online.

Transfer: 167 transfer students enrolled in 2012-2013. Applicants must submit a college GPA of 2.0 and be in good standing at the previous or current institution. Students who have completed 24 semester hours or more must submit a dean's evaluation form; those with fewer than 24 must also submit high school transcripts. 32 of 124 credits required for the bachelor's degree must be completed at Lees-McRae.

Visiting: There are regularly scheduled orientations for prospective students. There are guides for informal visits, visitors may sit in on classes, and stay overnight. To schedule a visit, contact Candace Silver at (828) 898-8723.

Financial Aid: In 2013-2014, 88% of all full-time freshmen and 80% of continuing full-time students received some form of financial aid. Lees-McRae is a member of CSS. The FAFSA is required. The priority date for freshman financial aid applications for fall entry is April 15.

International Students: There are 19 international students enrolled. The school actively recruits these students. They must take the TOEFL.

Computers: All students may access the system 24 hours a day. There are no time limits and no fees.

Graduates: From July 1, 2012 to June 30, 2013, 185 bachelor's degrees were awarded. The most popular majors were health professions (25%), education (19%), and social sciences (19%). In an average class, 30% graduate in 4 years or less, 38% graduate in 5 years or less, and 38% graduate in 6 years or less.

Admissions Contact: Ginger Hansen, Vice President of Enrollment Management. E-Mail: *admissions@lmc.edu* Web: *www.lmc.edu*

LENOIR-RHYNE COLLEGE C-2

Hickory, NC 28603 (828) 328-7300
(800) 277-5721; (828) 328-7378

Full-time: 569 men, 891 women	**Faculty:** 107; IIA, --$
Part-time: 31 men, 73 women	**Ph.D.s:** 73%
Graduate: 72 men, 201 women	**Student/Faculty:** 13 to 1
Year: semesters, summer session	**Tuition:** $26,524
Application Deadline: open	**Room & Board:** $9370
Freshman Class: 3316 applied, 2882 accepted, 406 enrolled	
SAT CR/M: 480/500 **ACT:** 21	**COMPETITIVE**

Lenoir-Rhyne College, founded in 1891, is a private institution affiliated with the Lutheran Church, offering liberal arts programs that focus on business, education, and allied health sciences. The figures in the above capsule and in this profile are approximate. There is 1 graduate school. In addition to regional accreditation, Lenoir-Rhyne has baccalaureate program accreditation with NCATE and NLN. The library contains 145,960 volumes, 462,878 microform items, and 40,379 audio/video tapes/CDs/DVDs, and subscribes to 5,376 periodicals including electronic. Computerized library services include interlibrary loans and database searching. Special learning facilities include a learning resource center, radio station, TV station, and observatory. The 100-acre campus is in a suburban area 45 miles northwest of Charlotte. Including any residence halls, there are 30 buildings.

Student Life: 70% of undergraduates are from North Carolina. Others are from 30 states, 9 foreign countries, and Canada. 89% are from public schools. 87% are white. 68% are Protestant; 23% claim no religious affiliation. The average age of freshmen is 18; all undergraduates, 22. 20% do not continue beyond their first year; 63% remain to graduate.

Housing: 900 students can be accommodated in college housing, which includes single-sex and coed dorms and on-campus apartments. In addition, there are special-interest houses, fraternity houses, sorority houses, honors housing, hearing-impaired housing, special interest that varies by year. On-campus housing is guaranteed for all 4 years and is available on a lottery system for upperclassmen. 65% of students live on campus; of those, 70% remain on campus on weekends. All students may keep cars.

Activities: 23% of men belong to 3 national fraternities; 27% of women belong to 4 national sororities. There are 50 groups on campus, including art, band, cheerleading, choir, chorus, computers, dance, debate, drama, environmental, ethnic, gay, honors, international, jazz band, literary magazine, musical theater, newspaper, Outdoor adventure club, pep band, photography, political, professional, radio and TV, religious, social, social service, student government, symphony, and yearbook. Popular campus events include Spring Fling, Advent Candlelight Service, and Opening of School.

Sports: There are 10 intercollegiate sports for men and 10 for women, and 14 intramural sports for men and 14 for women. Facilities include an 8500-seat football stadium, a 3600-seat gym, practice fields, racquetball courts, weight rooms, a sauna, a 25-meter swimming pool, 2 intramural fields, and baseball, softball, and soccer fields, world class mondotrack track.

Disabled Students: All of the campus is accessible. Facilities include wheelchair ramps, elevators, special parking, specially equipped restrooms, lowered drinking fountains.

Services: Counseling and information services are available, as is tutoring in every subject. There is remedial math and writing. and interpreters and note takers for hearing-impaired students

Campus Safety and Security: Measures include 24-hour foot and vehicle patrol, emergency notification system, self-defense education, and security escort services. There are emergency telephones, lighted pathways/sidewalks, and controlled access to dorms/residences.

Programs of Study: Lenoir-Rhyne confers B.A., B.S., and B.Mus.Ed. degrees. Master's degrees are also awarded. Bachelor's degrees are awarded in AGRICULTURE (environmental studies), BIOLOGICAL SCIENCE (biology/biological science), BUSINESS (accounting, business administration and management, international business management, management information systems, and sports management), COMMUNICATIONS AND THE ARTS (applied music, communications, dramatic arts, English, English as a second/foreign language, French, German, graphic design, journalism, music, music performance, piano/organ, and Spanish), COMPUTER AND PHYSICAL SCIENCE (chemistry, computer science, mathematics, and physics), EDUCATION (athletic training, Christian education, early childhood education, elementary education, English education, foreign languages education, health education, middle school education, music education, science education, and secondary education), ENGINEERING AND ENVIRONMENTAL DESIGN (preengineering), HEALTH PROFESSIONS (exercise science, medical laboratory technology, nursing, occupational therapy, predentistry, premedicine, preoptometry, and preveterinary science), SOCIAL SCIENCE (American studies, economics, history, human services, philosophy, political science/government, prelaw, psychology, religion, religious education, religious music, sociology, theological studies, and youth ministry). Business and nursing have the largest enrollments.

Required: To graduate, students must complete 128 credit hours, including 56 to 57 in liberal arts courses, with a minimum GPA of 2.0. The total number of hours in a major varies by program.

Special: Lenoir-Rhyne offers study abroad in more than 25 countries and with the nationally known ISEP program, a Washington semester at American University and through the Lutheran College Washington Consortium, internships in most majors, a general studies degree, work-study programs, 3-2 enginering degrees with North Carolina State, North Carolina Agricultural and Technical, and Clemson Universities and the University of North Carolina at Charlotte, pass/fail options, and auditing for most courses. In addition, the Broyhill institute for Business Leadership offers programs to promote understanding of the business community. The university offers an honors program for outstanding students. There are 12 national honor societies, a freshman honors program, and 18 departmental honors programs.

Faculty/Classroom: 55% of faculty are male; 45% are female. All teach undergraduates. No introductory courses are taught by graduate students. The average class size in an introductory lecture is 26; in a laboratory is 20; and in a regular course is 20.

Admissions: 87% of the 2011-2012 applicants were accepted. The SAT scores for the 2011-2012 freshman class were: Critical Reading--57% below 500, 33% between 500 and 599, and 10% between 600 and 700; Math--46% below 500, 39% between 500 and 599, 14% between 600 and 700, and 1% above 700. The ACT scores were 74% below 21, 6% between 21 and 23, 17% between 24 and 26, 2% between 27 and 28, and 1% above 28. 42% of the current freshmen were in the top fifth of their class; 75% were in the top two fifths.

Requirements: The SAT or ACT is required. Applicants need 16 academic credits and should have 4 units in English, 3 in math (algebra 1, geometry, and algebra 2), 2 in the same foreign language, and 1 each in American history and a lab science. An interview is recommended for all students. Music majors must also audition. A GPA of 2.5 is required. AP and CLEP credits are accepted. Important factors in the admissions decision are advanced placement or honors courses, personality/intangible qualities, and leadership record.

Procedure: Freshmen are admitted to all sessions. Entrance exams should be taken in the spring of the junior year and thereafter. There are early admissions, deferred admissions, and rolling admissions plans. Application deadlines are open. Application fee is $35. Notification is sent on a Rolling basis. 30 applicants were on the 2011 waiting list; 5 were admitted. Applications are accepted online.

Transfer: 143 transfer students enrolled in 2010-2011. Applicants with more than 30 semester hours need a 2.0 minimum GPA in general studies programs or a 2.5 minimum GPA in nursing or education programs. Those with fewer than 30 semester hours must meet freshman entrance criteria. 32 of 128 credits required for the bachelor's degree must be completed at Lenoir-Rhyne.

Visiting: There are regularly scheduled orientations for prospective students, including a meeting with an admissions counselor and a student-guided tour of the campus. There are guides for informal visits, visitors may sit in on classes, and stay overnight. To schedule a visit, contact the Enrollment Management Office.

Financial Aid: In 2011-2012, 99% of all full-time freshmen and 92% of continuing full-time students received some form of financial aid. 40% of all full-time freshmen and 55% of continuing full-time students received need-based aid. 35% of undergraduate students work part-time. Average annual earnings from campus work are $1000. The average financial indebtedness of the 2011 graduate was $30,000. The FAFSA is required. The deadline for filing freshman financial aid applications for fall entry is March 15.

International Students: There are 19 international students enrolled. The school actively recruits these students. They must take the TOEFL with a minimum score of 550 on the paper-based TOEFL (PBT) or 79 on the Internet-based version (iBT).

Computers: Internet access and an email address is provided for all students. The entire campus has wireless access. There are 116 computers in labs throughout the campus. All students may access the system 24 hours per day via modem; computer lab hours are 8 a.m. to 11:30 p.m. There are no time limits and no fees.

Admissions Contact: Karen Feezor, Director of Admissions. E-Mail: *admission@lr.edu* Web: *www.lr.edu*

LIVINGSTONE COLLEGE C-2

Salisbury, NC 28144 (704) 216-6005
(800) 835-3435; (704) 216-6215

Full-time: 470 men, 410 women
Part-time: 30 men, 15 women
Graduate: n/av
Year: semesters
Application Deadline: see profile
Freshman Class: n/av
SAT or ACT: required
Faculty: n/av
Ph.D.s: n/av
Student/Faculty: n/av
Tuition: $15,908
Room & Board: $7262

LESS COMPETITIVE

Livingstone College, founded in 1879 and affiliated with the African Methodist Episcopal Zion Church, is a private institution offering programs in business, engineering, liberal arts, music, and professional and religious training. The figures in the above capsule and in this profile are approximate. There are 4 undergraduate schools. In addition to regional accreditation, LC has baccalaureate program accreditation with CSWE. The library contains 80,457 volumes, 1000 microform items, and 1451 audio/video tapes/CDs/DVDs, and subscribes to 423 periodicals including electronic. Computerized library services include interlibrary loans, database searching, Internet access, and laptop Internet portals. Special learning facilities include a learning resource center and natural history museum. The 272-acre campus is in a small town between Greensboro and Charlotte. Including any residence halls, there are 22 buildings.

Student Life: 55% of undergraduates are from North Carolina. Others are from 22 states and 7 foreign countries. 92% are from public schools. 93% are African American. 59% are Protestant. The average age of freshmen is 18; all undergraduates, 19. 39% do not continue beyond their first year; 49% remain to graduate.

Housing: 631 students can be accommodated in college housing, which includes single-sex dorms and off-campus apartments. In addition, there are honors houses. On-campus housing is guaranteed for all 4 years. 59% of students live on campus; of those, 50% remain on campus on weekends. Alcohol is not permitted. All students may keep cars.

Activities: 40% of men belong to 4 national fraternities; 45% of women belong to 4 national sororities. There are 14 groups on campus, including band, cheerleading, choir, chorus, communications, computers, drama, honors, jazz band, marching band, newspaper, pep band, religious, student government, and yearbook. Popular campus events include Open House, Career Day, and Book Fair.

Sports: There are 4 intercollegiate sports for men and 4 for women, and 5 intramural sports for men and 4 for women. Facilities include a gym and a 4000-seat stadium.

Disabled Students: 90% of the campus is accessible. Facilities include wheelchair ramps, special parking, specially equipped rest rooms, special class scheduling, and lowered drinking fountains.

Services: Counseling and information services are available, as is tutoring in every subject. There is remedial math, reading, and writing.

Campus Safety and Security: Measures include 24-hour foot and vehicle patrol and security escort services. There are lighted pathways/sidewalks.

Programs of Study: LC confers B.A., B.S., and B.S.W. degrees. Bachelor's degrees are awarded in BIOLOGICAL SCIENCE (biology/biological science), BUSINESS (accounting, business administration and management, and sports management), COMMUNICATIONS AND THE ARTS (dramatic arts, English, and music), COMPUTER AND PHYSICAL SCIENCE (chemistry, computer science, and mathematics), EDUCATION (early childhood education, elementary education, music education, science education, and secondary education), HEALTH PROFESSIONS (predentistry and premedicine), SOCIAL SCIENCE (criminal justice, history, political science/government, prelaw, psychology, social work, sociology, and theological studies). Business administration, criminal justice, and education have the largest enrollments.

Required: At least 125 semester hours with a minimum GPA of 2.0 are required for graduation. Required courses include freshman English and religion, 2 semesters each of foreign language and phys ed, 8 hours each of natural science, math, and social science, and 9 hours chosen from offerings in art, literature, music, and philosophy. 80 hours of community service are also required.

Special: Upperclassmen are eligible for a cooperative education program. Cross-registration for a dual engineering degree is available with North Carolina Agricultural and Technical State University. There are 6 national honor societies and a freshman honors program.

Faculty/Classroom: 56% of faculty are male; 44% are female. All teach undergraduates. No introductory courses are taught by graduate students. The average class size in an introductory lecture is 28 and in a regular course is 20.

Requirements: The SAT or ACT is required. The ACT optional writing test is also required. Applicants should be high school graduates or have earned the GED. Secondary preparation should include 4 academic credits in English, 2 each in history, math, and music, and 1 each in social studies, science, and art. A GPA of 2.0 is required. AP and CLEP credits are accepted. Important factors in the admissions decision are evidence of special talent, leadership record, and extracurricular activities record.

Procedure: Freshmen are admitted fall and spring. Entrance exams should be taken by summer orientation. There are early decision and rolling admissions plans. Check with the school for current application deadlines. The application fee is $25. A waiting list is maintained.

Transfer: Transfers should have at least a 2.0 GPA in 30 hours of previous college work. Those with fewer hours must meet freshman requirements. 45 of 125 credits required for the bachelor's degree must be completed at LC.

Visiting: There are regularly scheduled orientations for prospective students. There are guides for informal visits; visitors may sit in on classes and stay overnight. To schedule a visit, contact the Office of Enrollment Management and Admissions.

Financial Aid: LC is a member of CSS. The FAFSA and FFS are required. Check with the school for current application deadlines.

International Students: The school actively recruits these students. They must take the TOEFL. They must also take the SAT or ACT.

Computers: Wireless access is available. All students may access the system. There are no time limits and no fees.

Admissions Contact: Nicole Daniels, Director of Admissions. A campus DVD is available. E-Mail: *ndandiels@livingstone.edu* Web: *www.livingstone.edu*

MARS HILL COLLEGE B-2

Mars Hill, NC 28754 (828) 689-1201
(800) 543-1514; (828) 689-1473

Full-time: 510 men, 610 women
Part-time: 45 men, 110 women
Graduate: n/av
Year: semesters, summer session
Application Deadline: open
Freshman Class: n/av
SAT or ACT: required
Faculty: n/av; IIB, --$
Ph.D.s: n/av
Student/Faculty: n/av
Tuition: $23,818
Room & Board: $8582

LESS COMPETITIVE

Mars Hill College, founded in 1856, is a private institution affiliated with the Baptist Church and offers undergraduate programs in the arts and sciences, business, education, and preprofessional studies. The figures in the above capsule and in this profile are approximate. In addition to regional accreditation, Mars Hill has baccalaureate program accreditation with CSWE, NASM, and NCATE. The library contains 98,150 volumes, 1050 microform items, 6180 audio/video tapes/CDs/DVDs, and subscribes to 650 periodicals including electronic. Computerized library services include interlibrary loans and database searching. Special learning facilities include an art gallery, radio station, the Southern Appalachian Center of Regional History and Culture, and the Rural Life Museum. The 180-acre campus is in a rural area 18 miles north of Asheville. Including any residence halls, there are 47 buildings.

Student Life: 60% of undergraduates are from North Carolina. Others are from 19 states, 20 foreign countries, and Canada. 14% are African American. 81% are Protestant; 13% claim no religious affiliation. The average age of freshmen is 18; all undergraduates, 21. 20% do not continue beyond their first year; 49% remain to graduate.

Housing: College-sponsored housing includes single-sex dorms, on-campus apartments, and married student housing. In addition, there are honors houses. On-campus housing is guaranteed for all 4 years. 80% of students live on campus; of those, 33% remain on campus on weekends. Alcohol is not permitted. All students may keep cars.

Activities: 30% of men belong to 4 local and 2 national fraternities; 12% of women belong to 4 local and 1 national sorority. There are 80 groups on campus, including art, band, cheerleading, choir, chorale, chorus, dance, drama, ethnic, honors, international, jazz band, literary magazine, marching band, musical theater, newspaper, orchestra, photography, political, professional, radio and TV, religious, social, social service, student government, and yearbook. Popular campus events include Culturefest, Spring Fling, and the Bascom Lamar Lunsford Festival.

Sports: There are 7 intercollegiate sports for men and 6 for women, and 5 intramural sports for men and 5 for women. Facilities include a 5000-seat stadium, a 3500-seat gym, an indoor Olympic-size swimming pool, and a 10-acre complex that has a track, baseball diamond, soccer field, all-purpose playing field, and 6 tennis courts.

Disabled Students: 41% of the campus is accessible. Facilities include wheelchair ramps, elevators, special parking, and specially equipped rest rooms.

Services: Counseling and information services are available, as is tutoring in every subject. There is remedial math, reading, and writing.

Campus Safety and Security: Measures include 24-hour foot and vehicle patrol, self-defense education, and security escort services. There are emergency telephones and lighted pathways/sidewalks.

Programs of Study: Mars Hill confers B.A., B.S., B.F.A., B.M., and

B.S.W. degrees. Bachelor's degrees are awarded in BIOLOGICAL SCIENCE (biology/biological science, botany, and zoology), BUSINESS (accounting, business administration and management, fashion merchandising, and recreation and leisure services), COMMUNICATIONS AND THE ARTS (art history and appreciation, communications, dramatic arts, English, music, music performance, musical theater, performing arts, and Spanish), COMPUTER AND PHYSICAL SCIENCE (chemistry, computer science, and mathematics), EDUCATION (art education, athletic training, drama education, elementary education, mathematics education, middle school education, music education, physical education, science education, and social studies education), HEALTH PROFESSIONS (allied health, physician's assistant, predentistry, premedicine, prepharmacy, and preveterinary science), SOCIAL SCIENCE (history, international studies, political science/government, prelaw, psychology, religion, social work, and sociology). Music, education, and science are the strongest academically. Education has the largest enrollment.

Required: To graduate, students must complete at least 128 semester hours with a minimum GPA of 2.0. Distribution requirements include courses in fine arts, literature, American culture, foreign culture, math, natural science, social/behavioral science, ethics, and phys ed.

Special: Mars Hill offers cooperative programs with the Bowman Gray School of Medicine at Wake Forest, internships, study abroad, B.A.-B.S. degrees, dual majors, student-designed majors, and credit for life experience. The Community Life program promotes student involvement in culture and community activities. There are 4 national honor societies and a freshman honors program.

Faculty/Classroom: 58% of faculty are male; 42% are female. All teach undergraduates. No introductory courses are taught by graduate students. The average class size in an introductory lecture is 20, in a laboratory, 15, and in a regular course, 15.

Requirements: The SAT or ACT is required. Applicants need at least 18 academic credits, including 4 in English, 3 in math, and 2 each in history, science, and foreign language. The GED is accepted. A GPA of 2.0 is required. AP and CLEP credits are accepted. Important factors in the admissions decision are advanced placement or honors courses, leadership record, and extracurricular activities record.

Procedure: Freshmen are admitted to all sessions. There are early decision, early admissions and rolling admissions plans. Application deadlines are open. The application fee is $25.

Transfer: Transfer applicants must be eligible to return to their previous college or have been out of school for at least 1 semester. They must have a minimum GPA of 2.0 for at least 30 semester credit hours. Remedial and developmental hours do not apply. 32 of 128 credits required for the bachelor's degree must be completed at Mars Hill.

Visiting: There are regularly scheduled orientations for prospective students, consisting of a 2-day program during which a variety of special programs are offered. Individual students and their families may visit anytime throughout the year. There are guides for informal visits, visitors may sit in on classes and stay overnight. To schedule a visit, contact the Admissions Office.

Financial Aid: Mars Hill is a member of CSS. The FAFSA is required. Check with the school for current application deadlines.

International Students: The school actively recruits these students. They must take the TOEFL.

Computers: All students may access the system during library hours. Students are limited to up to 2 hours at a time. There are no fees.

Admissions Contact: Office of Admissions E-Mail: *admissions@mhc.edu* Web: *www.mhc.edu*

MEREDITH COLLEGE D-2

Raleigh, NC 27607 (919) 760-8581
(800) MEREDITH; (919) 760-2348

Full-time: 1766 women	**Faculty:** 138; IIA, --$
Part-time: 9 men, 192 women	**Ph.D.s:** 91%
Graduate: 32 men, 263 women	**Student/Faculty:** 13 to 1
Year: semesters, summer session	**Tuition:** $24,400
Application Deadline: February 15	**Room & Board:** $7020

Freshman Class: 1614 applied, 1047 accepted, 1481 enrolled

SAT CR/M: 519/520 **ACT:** 21 **COMPETITIVE**

Meredith College, founded in 1891, is a private college for women offering a comprehensive undergraduate program with a strong emphasis on the liberal arts. Graduate programs in business, music, education, and nutrition are offered to both women and men. The figures in the above capsule and in this profile are approximate. There are 6 undergraduate schools and one graduate school. In addition to regional accreditation, Meredith has baccalaureate program accreditation with ADA, CSWE, FIDER, NASM, and NCATE. The 2 libraries contain 155,165 volumes, 16,116 microform items, and 14,671 audio/video tapes/CDs/DVDs, and subscribe to 2,867 periodicals including electronic. Computerized library services include interlibrary loans, database searching, and Internet access. Special learning facilities include an art gallery, child-care lab, greenhouse, experimental and clinical psychology labs including one on autism, an electron microscope suite, astronomy observation deck, student/faculty research labs, and language lab. The 225-acre campus is in an urban area Raleigh, NC. Including any residence halls, there are 30 buildings.

Student Life: 90% of undergraduates are from North Carolina. Others are from 36 states, and 17 foreign countries. 77% are White; 11% African American. The average age of freshmen is 18; all undergraduates, 22. 24% do not continue beyond their first year; 76% remain to graduate.

Housing: 1150 students can be accommodated in college housing, which includes single-sex dorms and on-campus apartments, with all nonsmoking halls. On-campus housing is guaranteed for all 4 years. 56% of students commute. Alcohol is not permitted. All students may keep cars.

Activities: There are no fraternities or sororities. There are 91 groups on campus, including and nutrition and wellness, environmental, foreign language, art, chorale, chorus, commuter, computers, dance, drama, ethnic, gay, honors, international, literary magazine, musical theater, newspaper, orchestra, photography, political, professional, religious, social, social service, student government, and symphony. Popular campus events include Academics and Leadership Awards Day, White Iris Ball, and Undergraduate Research Conference.

Sports: There are 6 intercollegiate sports for women. Facilities include an indoor swimming pool, a dance studio, a fitness center, a horseshoe pit, a putting green and driving range, a softball diamond, tennis courts, a soccer field, and a gym with basketball, volleyball, and badminton courts.

Disabled Students: 81% of the campus is accessible. Facilities include wheelchair ramps, elevators, special parking, specially equipped restrooms, special class scheduling, lowered drinking fountains, special housing, a handicap lift in the swimming pool, and lowered fire alarms.

Services: Counseling and information services are available, as is tutoring in some subjects including math, writing, computer lab, French, Spanish, biology, chemistry, study skills, German, GRE prep, Praxis prep, and grammar There is a reader service for the blind.

Campus Safety and Security: Measures include 24-hour foot and vehicle patrol, self-defense education, and security escort services. There are emergency telephones, lighted pathways/sidewalks, controlled campus access at night, and 24-hour locked residence halls.

Programs of Study: Meredith confers B.A., B.S., B.M. and B.S.W. degrees. Master's degrees are also awarded. Bachelor's degrees are awarded in AGRICULTURE (environmental studies), BIOLOGICAL SCIENCE (biology/biological science and nutrition), BUSINESS (accounting, business administration and management, fashion merchandising, and international business management), COMMUNICATIONS AND THE ARTS (applied music, art, communications, dance, dramatic arts, English, fine arts, French, music, music performance, musical theater, and Spanish), COMPUTER AND PHYSICAL SCIENCE (chemistry, computer science, information sciences and systems, and mathematics), EDUCATION (music education), ENGINEERING AND ENVIRONMENTAL DESIGN (interior design), HEALTH PROFESSIONS (exercise science), SOCIAL SCIENCE (American studies, child psychology/development, economics, family/consumer studies, history, international studies, political science/government, psychology, public affairs, religion, social work, and sociology). Interior design, psychology, and biology have the largest enrollments.

Required: To graduate, students must complete a total of 124 credit hours, including general education requirements, a major field, and electives, with a minimum GPA of 2.0. General Education is comprised of a core curriculum focusing on understanding diverse cultures, fields of knowledge that ensure breadth in the liberal arts, and across-the-curriculum threads and independent learning experiences that build competencies. Some major fields offer or require a concentration, and contract majors are possible. Electives may be used to complete a second major, a minor, teacher licensure, or to explore areas of personal, career or pre-professional interest.

Special: Meredith offers cooperative programs, cross-registration with Cooperating Raleigh Colleges, internships, study abroad in Europe and Asia, a Washington semester at American University, a U.N. semester at Drew University, and work-study programs on campus. Dual majors, interdisciplinary and student-designed majors, preprofessional programs, and pass/fail options are available. Certification in social work and licensure for teaching are possible. Business administration, management, and social work majors can be completed through evening classes. There are 19 national honor societies and a freshman honors program.

Faculty/Classroom: 31% of faculty are male; 69% are female. All teach undergraduates. No introductory courses are taught by graduate students. The average class size in an introductory lecture is 20; in a laboratory is 11; and in a regular course is 17.

Admissions: 65% of the 2013-2014 applicants were accepted. The SAT scores for the 2013-2014 freshman class were: Critical Reading--41% below 500, 42% between 500 and 599, 16% between 600 and 699, and 1% between 700 and 800; Math--39% below 500, 43% between 500 and 599, 17% between 600 and 699, and 1% between 700 and 800. The ACT scores were 47% below 21, 24% between 21 and 23, 21% between 24 and 26, 5% between 27 and 28, and 6% above 28. 43% of the current freshmen were in the top fifth of their class; 72% were in the top two fifths. 5 freshmen graduated first in their class.

Requirements: The SAT or ACT is required. The ACT Optional Writing test is also required. Applicants who submit SAT scores are preferred. Applicants must also have a minimum of 16 units of credit, including 4 in English, 3 each in math, history/social studies, and science, 2 in foreign language, and 1 elective. The student is expected to rank in the top half of her class, and grades in academic subjects are very important. An interview may be requested as part of the evaluation process. Meredith requires applicants to be in the upper 50% of their class. A GPA of 2.0 is required. AP and CLEP credits are accepted. Important factors in the admissions decision are recommendations by school officials, advanced placement or honors courses, and evidence of special talent.

Procedure: Freshmen are admitted fall and spring. Entrance exams should be taken by January of the senior year. There are early decision, deferred admissions, and rolling admissions plans. Early decision applications should be filed by October 15; regular applications, by February 15 for fall entry, along with a $40 fee. Notification of early decision is sent November 1; regular decision, on a rolling basis. 121 early decision candidates were accepted for the 2013-2014 class. Applications are accepted online.

Transfer: 74 transfer students enrolled in 2012-2013. Applicants must have a minimum GPA of 2.0, be eligible to return to the last college attended, and be recommended by college officials. Those students with fewer than 30 hours of credit must also meet freshman admission requirements. 31 of 124 credits required for the bachelor's degree must be completed at Meredith.

Visiting: There are regularly scheduled orientations for prospective students students. There are guides for informal visits, visitors may sit in on classes, and stay overnight. To schedule a visit, contact the Admissions Office.

Financial Aid: Meredith is a member of CSS. The FAFSA is required. The priority date for freshman financial aid applications for fall entry is February 15.

International Students: There are 26 international students enrolled. The school actively recruits these students. They must take the TOEFL. If English is the student's native language or primary language of instruction, the SAT should be taken instead.

Computers: All students may access the system 24 hours per day in residence halls and one lab; 7 a.m. to midnight in other labs.

Graduates: From July 1, 2012 to June 30, 2013, 430 bachelor's degrees were awarded. The most popular majors were psychology (10%), interior design (9%), and child development (7%). In an average class, 14% graduate in 3 years or less, 44% graduate in 4 years or less, 55% graduate in 5 years or less, and 57% graduate in 6 years or less.

Admissions Contact: Cristan Trahey Harris, Director of Admissions. E-Mail: *admissions@meredith.edu* Web: *www.meredith.edu*

METHODIST UNIVERSITY D-3

Fayetteville, NC 28311 (910) 630-7027
(800) 488-7110; (910) 630-7285

Full-time: 1059 men, 960 women	**Faculty:** 142
Part-time: 109 men, 152 women	**Ph.D.s:** 79%
Graduate: 83 men, 113 women	**Student/Faculty:** 13 to 1
Year: semesters, summer session	**Tuition:** $27,082
Application Deadline:	**Room & Board:** $10,063
Freshman Class: 3823 applied, 2315 accepted, 488 enrolled	
SAT CR/M/W: 484/510/466 **ACT:** 21	**COMPETITIVE**

Methodist University, formerly Methodist College, founded in 1956, is a private institution affiliated with the United Methodist Church. The University offers programs in the arts and sciences, education, business, and professional training. There are 4 undergraduate schools and 3 graduate schools. In addition to regional accreditation, Methodist has baccalaureate program accreditation with ACBSP, CSWE, and NCATE. The library contains 181,833 volumes, 57,759 microform items, and 13,412 audio/video tapes/CDs/DVDs, and subscribes to 587 periodicals including electronic. Computerized library services include interlibrary loans, database searching, Internet access, and Wi-Fi capability. Special learning facilities include an art gallery, radio station, 18 hole golf course and pro shop for professional golf and tennis management programs. The 620-acre campus is in a suburban area 5 miles north of Fayetteville. Including any residence halls, there are 38 buildings.

Student Life: 56% of undergraduates are from North Carolina. Others are from 44 states, 31 foreign countries, and Canada. 86% are from public schools. 65% are White; 20% African American. 41% are Protestant; 16% Catholic. The average age of freshmen is 19; all undergraduates, 24. 33% do not continue beyond their first year; 44% remain to graduate.

Housing: 1095 students can be accommodated in college housing, which includes single-sex dorms and on-campus apartments. In addition, there are honors houses, fraternity houses, sorority houses, first year experience, and a health and wellness hall. On-campus housing is guaranteed for all 4 years. 57% of students live on campus; of those, 70% remain on campus on weekends. Alcohol is not permitted. All students may keep cars.

Activities: 6% of men belong to 1 local and 1 national fraternities; 6% of women belong to 2 local and 1 national sororities. There are 104 groups on campus, including art, band, cheerleading, choir, chorale, chorus, computers, dance, debate, drama, environmental, ethnic, forensics, honors, international, jazz band, literary magazine, marching band, musical theater, newspaper, orchestra, pep band, photography, political, professional, radio and TV, religious, social, social service, student government, and symphony. Popular campus events include Show You Care Day, Annual Woodcutting, and Spring Fest.

Sports: There are 9 intercollegiate sports for men and 10 for women, and 7 intramural sports for men and 4 for women. Facilities include the Nimocks Fitness center, a 1200-seat stadium, a 1500-seat gym, a golf course, a track and field area, tennis courts, and fields for baseball, softball, and soccer.

Disabled Students: 90% of the campus is accessible. Facilities include wheelchair ramps, elevators, special parking, specially equipped restrooms, and lowered drinking fountains.

Services: Counseling and information services are available, as is tutoring in most subjects. There is a reader service for the blind, and remedial math and writing.

Campus Safety and Security: Measures include 24-hour foot and vehicle patrol, emergency notification system, self-defense education, and security escort services. There are shuttle buses, emergency telephones, lighted pathways/sidewalks, and controlled access to dorms/residences.

Programs of Study: Methodist confers B.A., B.S., B.F.A, B.M. and B.S.W. degrees. Associate and master's degrees are also awarded. Bachelor's degrees are awarded in BIOLOGICAL SCIENCE (biology/biological science), BUSINESS (accounting, business administration and management, marketing/retailing/merchandising, organizational behavior, and sports management), COMMUNICATIONS AND THE ARTS (art, communications, creative writing, dramatic arts, English, French, music, music performance, and Spanish), COMPUTER AND PHYSICAL SCIENCE (chemistry, computer science, and mathematics), EDUCATION (art education, athletic training, elementary education, middle school education, music education, physical education, secondary education, and special education), ENGINEERING AND ENVIRONMENTAL DESIGN (computer technology), HEALTH PROFESSIONS (nursing, physician's assistant, and predentistry), SOCIAL SCIENCE (criminal justice, economics, history, international studies, political science/government, prelaw, psychology, religion, social studies, social work, and sociology). Business administration, biology, and education are the strongest academically, and have the largest enrollments.

Required: To graduate, students must complete at least 124 semester hours, including core requirements, with a minimum GPA of 2.0. A liberal arts core, ranging from 36 to 62 hours, is required in all majors.

Special: Methodist offers internships in political science and social work, study abroad in 4 countries, a Washington semester, a general studies degree, a 3-2 engineering degree with North Carolina State University, pass/fail options, dual majors, and nondegree study. The business administration major offers concentrations in professional golf, tennis, and resort management with specialized facilities and co-op programs. There are 7 national honor societies, a freshman honors program, and 5 departmental honors programs.

Faculty/Classroom: 52% of faculty are male; 48% are female. All teach undergraduates. No introductory courses are taught by graduate students. The average class size in an introductory lecture is 23; in a laboratory is 20; and in a regular course is 20.

Admissions: 61% of the 2013-2014 applicants were accepted. The SAT scores for the 2013-2014 freshman class were: Critical Reading--59% below 500, 34% between 500 and 599, 6% between 600 and 699, and 1% between 700 and 800; Math--45% below 500, 40% between 500 and 599, 14% between 600 and 699, and 1% between 700 and 800; Writing--60% below 500, 33% between 500 and 599, 6% between 600 and 699, and 1% between 700 and 800. The ACT scores were 50% below 21, 30% between 21 and 23, 10% between 24 and 26, 6% between 27 and 28, and 4% above 28. 27% of the current freshmen were in the top fifth of their class; 54% were in the top two fifths. 4 freshmen graduated first in their class.

Requirements: The SAT or ACT is required. Applicants should be graduates of an accredited secondary school or have a GED certificate. They must have 16 academic credits, including 4 in English and 3 each in history, math, and science. 2 years of foreign language are recommended. An essay and interview are also recommended. AP and CLEP credits are accepted. Important factors in the admissions decision are recommendations by school officials, evidence of special talent, and advanced placement or honors courses.

Procedure: Freshmen are admitted fall, spring, and summer. There are deferred admissions and rolling admissions plans. Application deadlines are open. Application fee is $25. Applications are accepted online.

Transfer: 292 transfer students enrolled in 2012-2013. Applicants must

have a minimum GPA of 2.0. They must also submit a high school transcript, college transcripts, and the SAT or ACT scores. 30 of 124 credits required for the bachelor's degree must be completed at Methodist.

Visiting: There are regularly scheduled orientations for prospective students, 3 days prior to the first day of fall semester. There are guides for informal visits, visitors may sit in on classes, and stay overnight. To schedule a visit, contact the Admissions Office.

Financial Aid: In 2013-2014, 92% of all full-time freshmen and 92% of continuing full-time students received some form of financial aid. 92% of all full-time freshmen and 85% of continuing full-time students received need-based aid. The average freshman award was $9,780. 60% of undergraduate students work part-time. Average annual earnings from campus work are $1000. The average financial indebtedness of the 2013 graduate was $20,026. The FAFSA is required. The priority date for freshman financial aid applications for fall entry is March 15.

International Students: There are 70 international students enrolled. The school actively recruits these students. They must take the TOEFL with a minimum score of 500 on the paper-based TOEFL (PBT) or 60 on the Internet-based version (iBT). They must also take the SAT or ACT. The student may take the SAT or ACT in place of the TOEFL if English proficiency is demonstrated.

Computers: All students may access the system during specified hours.

Graduates: From July 1, 2012 to June 30, 2013, 290 bachelor's degrees were awarded. The most popular majors were business (46%), social sciences (11%), and education (7%). 180 companies recruited on campus in 2012-2013. In an average class, 1% graduate in 3 years or less, 33% graduate in 4 years or less, 38% graduate in 5 years or less, and 40% graduate in 6 years or less. Of the 2012 graduating class, 24% were enrolled in graduate school within 6 months of graduation, and 70% were employed.

Admissions Contact: Jamie Legg, Director of Admissions. E-Mail: *jlegg@methodist.edu* Web: *www.methodist.edu*

MONTREAT COLLEGE B-2

Montreat, NC 28757 **(828) 669-8012, ext. 3717**
(800) 622-6968; (828) 669-0120

Full-time: 227 men, 235 women	**Faculty:** 31
Part-time: 93 men, 188 women	**Ph.D.s:** 48%
Graduate: 55 men, 128 women	**Student/Faculty:** 30 to 1
Year: semesters, summer session	**Tuition:** $23,520
Application Deadline: open	**Room & Board:** $7778
Freshman Class: 718 applied, 388 accepted, 112 enrolled	
SAT CR/M/W: 475/466/445	**ACT:** required **VERY COMPETITIVE**

Montreat College, founded in 1916, is a private liberal arts institution affiliated with the Association of Presbyterian Colleges & Universities, and committed to the integration of faith and learning. In addition to regional accreditation, Montreat has baccalaureate program accreditation with NCATE. The library contains 79,165 volumes, 117,155 microform items, and 3,119 audio/video tapes/CDs/DVDs, and subscribes to 485 periodicals including electronic. Computerized library services include interlibrary loans, database searching, and Internet access. Special learning facilities include an art gallery. The 100-acre campus is in a rural area 15 miles east of Asheville. Including any residence halls, there are 18 buildings.

Student Life: 79% of undergraduates are from North Carolina. Others are from 21 states, and 12 foreign countries. 55% are from public schools. 70% are White; 18% African American. The average age of freshmen is 18. 28% do not continue beyond their first year.

Housing: 392 students can be accommodated in college housing, which includes single-sex dorms and on-campus apartments. On-campus housing is guaranteed for all 4 years. 91% of students live on campus; of those, 50% remain on campus on weekends. Alcohol is not permitted. All students may keep cars.

Activities: There are no fraternities or sororities. There are 25 groups on campus, including art, band, choir, chorus, drama, honors, literary magazine, musical theater, newspaper, photography, political, professional, religious, social, social service, and student government.

Sports: There are 6 intercollegiate sports for men and 6 for women, and 4 intramural sports for men and 4 for women. Facilities include standard athletic facilities complemented by opportunities for outdoor recreation activities such as hiking, skiing, whitewater sports, mountain climbing, and camping.

Disabled Students: 75% of the campus is accessible. Facilities include wheelchair ramps, elevators, special parking, specially equipped restrooms, special class scheduling, and lowered telephones.

Services: Counseling and information services are available, as is tutoring in most subjects.

Campus Safety and Security: Measures include 24-hour foot and vehicle patrol and emergency notification system. There are lighted pathways/sidewalks and controlled access to dorms/residences.

Programs of Study: Montreat confers B.A., B.S., B.B.A. and B.M. degrees. Associate and master's degrees are also awarded. Bachelor's degrees are awarded in BUSINESS (business administration and management), COMMUNICATIONS AND THE ARTS (English, music business management, and music performance), COMPUTER AND PHYSICAL SCIENCE (mathematics), EDUCATION (elementary education), ENGINEERING AND ENVIRONMENTAL DESIGN (environmental science), SOCIAL SCIENCE (American studies, biblical studies, history, human services, liberal arts/general studies, and religion). English, and biology are the strongest academically. Business, outdoor education, and psychology/human services have the largest enrollments.

Required: VETo graduate, students must complete 126 credit hours with a minimum GPA of 2.0. 50-53 credits in general education courses are required, including competencies in reading, writing, math, computer skills, and oral communication skills. A thesis is required for some majors.

Special: Montreat offers internships in all majors, study abroad,a work-study program, individualized majors, and dual majors. There are 2 national honor societies, a freshman honors program, and 3 departmental honors programs.

Faculty/Classroom: 58% of faculty are male; 42% are female. All teach undergraduates. No introductory courses are taught by graduate students. The average class size in an introductory lecture is 30; in a laboratory is 15; and in a regular course is 10.

Admissions: 54% of the 2013-2014 applicants were accepted. The SAT scores for the 2013-2014 freshman class were: Critical Reading--20% below 500, 73% between 500 and 599, 7% between 600 and 699, and 1% between 700 and 800; Math--16% below 500, 76% between 500 and 599, 7% between 600 and 699, and 1% between 700 and 800.

Requirements: The SAT or ACT is required, and is rated on a sliding scale with the GPA, with a minimum 860 SAT I score or 18 ACT score needed. Applicants must be graduates of an accredited secondary school and have completed 4 years of English, 3 each of math, science, and social studies, and 1 of foreign language. The GED is accepted. A counselor or teacher recommendation is required, and short autobiographical essay is required unless the student has been interviewed. A GPA of 2.3 is required. CLEP credits are accepted. Important factors in the admissions decision are advanced placement or honors courses, extracurricular activities record, and evidence of special talent.

Procedure: Freshmen are admitted to all sessions. There is a rolling admissions plan. Application deadlines are open. Application fee is $30. Notification is sent on a rolling basis.

Transfer: 155 transfer students enrolled in 2012-2013. Applicants must submit official college transcripts, be in good standing at their previous institution, and have completed at least 24 semester hours of college credit with a minimum GPA of 2.0. Students with fewer credits must also submit high school transcripts and SAT I or ACT scores. 18 of 126 credits required for the bachelor's degree must be completed at Montreat.

Visiting: There are regularly scheduled orientations for prospective students, including a campus tour, faculty introduction, and student program. There are guides for informal visits, visitors may sit in on classes, and stay overnight. To schedule a visit, contact the Admissions Office.

Financial Aid: In 2013-2014, 98% of all full-time freshmen and 98% of continuing full-time students received some form of financial aid. 71% of all full-time freshmen and 75% of continuing full-time students received need-based aid. The average freshman award was $21,854. Need-based scholarships or need-based grants averaged $21,414; need-based self-help aid (loans and jobs) averaged $5,345; non-need-based athletic scholarships averaged $8,508; other non-need-based awards and non-need-based scholarships averaged $10,261; and $4,643 from other forms of aid. 30% of undergraduate students work part-time. Average annual earnings from campus work are $1700. The average financial indebtedness of the 2013 graduate was $27,843. Montreat is a member of CSS. The FAFSA and the college's own financial statement are required. The priority date for freshman financial aid applications for fall entry is April 15.

International Students: There are 12 international students enrolled. The school actively recruits these students. They must take the TOEFL.

Computers: All students may access the system during computer lab hours or all times via personal devices. There are no time limits and no fees.

Graduates: From July 1, 2012 to June 30, 2013, 145 bachelor's degrees were awarded. The most popular majors were business/marketing (55%), public administration and social services (7%), and natural resources and conservation/philosophy and religious studies/psychology (6%). In an average class, 26% graduate in 4 years or less, 38% graduate in 5 years or less, and 42% graduate in 6 years or less.

Admissions Contact: Jeff Holliday, Director of Enrollment Management. E-Mail: *admissions@montreat.edu* Web: *www.montreat.edu*

MOUNT OLIVE COLLEGE E-3

Mount Olive, NC 28365 (919) 658-2502
(800) 653-0854; (919) 658-7180

Full-time: 815 men, 1660 women
Part-time: 230 men, 415 women
Graduate: n/av
Year: semesters, summer session
Application Deadline: see profile
Freshman Class: n/av
SAT or ACT: required
Faculty: n/av
Ph.D.s: n/av
Student/Faculty: n/av
Tuition: $15,000
Room & Board: $6100

COMPETITIVE

Mount Olive College, founded in 1951, is a private liberal arts institution affiliated with the Original Free Will Baptist Church. The figures in the above capsule and in this profile are approximate. The 2 libraries contain 77,545 volumes, 48,735 microform items, and 2005 audio/video tapes/CDs/DVDs, and subscribe to 5979 periodicals including electronic. Computerized library services include interlibrary loans and database searching. Special learning facilities include a learning resource center, art gallery, and church archives collection. The 123-acre campus is in a small town 65 miles southeast of Raleigh. Including any residence halls, there are 16 buildings.

Student Life: 92% of undergraduates are from North Carolina. Others are from 21 states, 7 foreign countries, and Canada. 93% are from public schools. 55% are white; 32% African American. The average age of freshmen is 22; all undergraduates, 33. 36% do not continue beyond their first year.

Housing: 306 students can be accommodated in college housing, which includes single-sex dorms and on-campus apartments. On-campus housing is guaranteed for the freshman year only. 90% of students commute. Alcohol is not permitted. All students may keep cars.

Activities: There are no fraternities or sororities. There are 20 groups on campus, including art, cheerleading, choir, chorale, chorus, drama, honors, international, literary magazine, newspaper, orchestra, pep band, photography, political, professional, religious, and student government. Popular campus events include Founders Day, Pickle Classic Weekend, and the North Carolina Pickle Festival.

Sports: There are 6 intercollegiate sports for men and 6 for women, and 10 intramural sports for men and 8 for women. Facilities include a gym, racquetball and tennis courts, a track, wrestling/gymnastics and weight rooms, an athletic field, outdoor basketball areas, a student center, and baseball, softball, and soccer fields.

Disabled Students: 90% of the campus is accessible. Facilities include wheelchair ramps, elevators, special parking, specially equipped rest rooms, and special class scheduling.

Services: Counseling and information services are available, as is tutoring in most subjects, including math, English, and science. There is remedial math and reading.

Campus Safety and Security: There are lighted pathways/sidewalks and evening and weekend patrols.

Programs of Study: Mount Olive confers B.A., B.S., and B.AppliedSc. degrees. Associates degrees are also awarded. Bachelor's degrees are awarded in BIOLOGICAL SCIENCE (biology/biological science), BUSINESS (accounting, business administration and management, human resources, and recreation and leisure services), COMMUNICATIONS AND THE ARTS (art, communications, English, fine arts, and music), COMPUTER AND PHYSICAL SCIENCE (computer management, information sciences and systems, and mathematics), EDUCATION (middle school education and secondary education), ENGINEERING AND ENVIRONMENTAL DESIGN (environmental science), SOCIAL SCIENCE (criminal justice, history, human services, liberal arts/general studies, ministries, psychology, and religion). Business, accounting, and psychology are the strongest academically. Business, psychology, and recreation have the largest enrollments.

Required: To graduate, students must have completed a total of 126 credit hours, with a minimum 2.0 overall GPA in 63 credit hours for the B.A. or B.S. or in 53 hours for the B.AppliedSc. Distribution requirements include 30 to 36 hours in humanities, 18 in science/math, and 12 in social science. Specific course work includes 6 hours of religion, 4 of phys ed, and 3 hours of computer competency.

Special: Mount Olive offers co-op programs and internships in all majors, work-study, B.A.-B.S. degrees, dual majors, and accelerated degree programs in business, accounting, and criminal justice administration. Cross-registration with James Sprunt Community College and Wayne Community College, study abroad, and credit for life, military, and work experience are also possible. Professional degree completion programs run continuously for 55 to 57 weeks. There is 1 national honor society and a freshman honors program.

Faculty/Classroom: 58% of faculty are male; 42% are female. All teach undergraduates, 14% do research, and 14% do both. No introductory courses are taught by graduate students.

Requirements: The SAT or ACT is required. Applicants must be graduates of an accredited secondary school or have a GED certificate. They must have completed 4 units of English, 3 each of math and science, and 2 of history. An essay and interview are suggested. A GPA of 2.0 is required. AP and CLEP credits are accepted.

Procedure: Freshmen are admitted to all sessions. Entrance exams should be taken in the junior or senior year. There are deferred admissions and rolling admissions plans. Application deadlines are open. Notification is sent on a rolling basis. Applications are accepted online.

Transfer: 548 transfer students enrolled in a recent year. Applicants must have a minimum GPA of 2.0 and submit an official transcript from the previous institution. An interview may be required. 32 of 126 credits required for the bachelor's degree must be completed at Mount Olive.

Visiting: There are regularly scheduled orientations for prospective students, consisting of 2 days of advising, sports, and entertainment. There are guides for informal visits and visitors may sit in on classes. To schedule a visit, contact the Admissions Office.

Financial Aid: In a recent year, 83% of all full-time freshmen and 79% of continuing full-time students received some form of financial aid. 89% of all full-time freshmen and 77% of continuing full-time students received need-based aid. The average freshmen award was $8679. The average financial indebtedness of a recent graduate was $12,450. The FAFSA and the college's own financial statement are required. Check with the school for current application deadlines.

International Students: The school actively recruits these students. They must take the TOEFL with a minimum score of 513 on the paper-based TOEFL (PBT) or 65 on the Internet-based version (iBT). They must also take the SAT or ACT.

Computers: All students may access the system 8 a.m. to 10 p.m. Monday through Friday and during scheduled hours on weekends. There are no fees. It is strongly recommended that all students have a personal computer.

Graduates: In a recent year, 629 bachelor's degrees were awarded. The most popular majors were business (52%), criminal justice administration (15%), and education (12%).

Admissions Contact: Tim Woodard, Director of Admissions. A campus DVD is available. E-Mail: *admissions@moc.edu* Web: *www.moc.edu*

NORTH CAROLINA AGRICULTURAL AND TECHNICAL STATE UNIVERSITY D-2

Greensboro, NC 27411 (336) 334-7946
(800) 443-8964; (336) 334-7136

Full-time: 3655 men, 4447 women
Part-time: 407 men, 363 women
Graduate: 733 men, 956 women
Year: semesters, summer session
Application Deadline:
Freshman Class: 7368 applied, 4049 accepted, 1827 enrolled
SAT CR/M/W: 450/460/16
Faculty: 493; IIA, -$
Ph.D.s: 96%
Student/Faculty: 13 to 1
Tuition: $6795 ($17,875)
Room & Board: $6379
ACT: 18

LESS COMPETITIVE

North Carolina Agricultural and Technical State University, founded in 1891, is a public institution within the University of North Carolina System. A & T offers programs in arts and sciences, education, business and economics, agriculture, nursing, engineering, and technology. There are 7 undergraduate schools and 1 graduate school. In addition to regional accreditation, A & T has baccalaureate program accreditation with AACSB, ABET, ACCE, CSWE, NCATE, and NLN. The library contains 507,036 volumes, 1.0 million microform items, and 34,025 audio/video tapes/CDs/DVDs, and subscribes to 5,446 periodicals including electronic. Computerized library services include interlibrary loans and database searching. Special learning facilities include an art gallery, planetarium, radio station, TV station, and an African Heritage Center. The 191-acre campus is in an urban area 90 miles northeast of Charlotte. Including any residence halls, there are 107 buildings.

Student Life: 82% of undergraduates are from North Carolina. Others are from 39 states, and 25 foreign countries. 89% are African American. The average age of freshmen is 18; all undergraduates, 22. 20% do not continue beyond their first year; 49% remain to graduate.

Housing: 2959 students can be accommodated in college housing, which includes single-sex and coed dorms. In addition, there are honors houses. On-campus housing is available on a first-come, first-served basis, and is available on a lottery system for upperclassmen. 53% of students commute. Alcohol is not permitted. All students may keep cars.

Activities: 1% of men belong to 5 national fraternities; 1% of women belong to 4 national sororities. There are 150 groups on campus, including art, band, cheerleading, choir, chorus, computers, dance, drama, drill team, ethnic, film, honors, international, jazz band, marching band, newspaper, orchestra, pep band, photography, political, professional, radio and TV, religious, social, social service, student government, symphony, and yearbook. Popular campus events include Graduation, Martin Luther King's Birthday, and Ron McNair Commemoration.

Sports: There are 7 intercollegiate sports for men and 9 for women, and 12 intramural sports for men and 12 for women. Facilities include a gym, a sports center, a stadium, tennis courts, a student union, a field house, and softball/baseball facilities.

Disabled Students: 85% of the campus is accessible. Facilities include wheelchair ramps, elevators, special parking, specially equipped restrooms, special class scheduling, lowered drinking fountains, and lowered telephones.

Services: Counseling and information services are available, as is tutoring in every subject. There is a reader service for the blind, and remedial math, reading, and writing.

Campus Safety and Security: Measures include 24-hour foot and vehicle patrol, self-defense education, and security escort services. There are shuttle buses, emergency telephones, and lighted pathways/sidewalks.

Programs of Study: A & T confers B.A., B.S., B.F.A., B.S.I.E., B.S.M.E., B.S.N. and B.S.W. degrees. Master's and doctoral degrees are also awarded. Bachelor's degrees are awarded in AGRICULTURE (agricultural business management, agricultural economics, and animal science), BIOLOGICAL SCIENCE (biology/biological science), BUSINESS (accounting and business administration and management), COMMUNICATIONS AND THE ARTS (communications, dramatic arts, English, French, music, and speech/debate/rhetoric), COMPUTER AND PHYSICAL SCIENCE (chemistry, computer science, mathematics, and physics), EDUCATION (agricultural education, art education, business education, early childhood education, English education, home economics education, industrial arts education, mathematics education, music education, physical education, social science education, and special education), ENGINEERING AND ENVIRONMENTAL DESIGN (architectural engineering, chemical engineering, civil engineering, electrical/electronics engineering, engineering physics, industrial engineering, landscape architecture/design, mechanical engineering, and occupational safety and health), HEALTH PROFESSIONS (nursing), SOCIAL SCIENCE (child psychology/development, clothing and textiles management/production/services, economics, history, political science/government, psychology, social work, and sociology). Business, accounting, and electronics and computer technology are the strongest academically. Psychology, sports recreation, and biology have the largest enrollments.

Required: To graduate, students must complete a minimum of 124 credit hours, including at least 80 in the major, with an overall GPA of 2.0 or better. Specific course work is required in English, math, natural science, social science, humanities, and health or phys ed.

Special: A & T offers cross-registration with the Greensboro Regional Consortium, internships, B.A.-B.S. degrees, cooperative programs in most majors, study abroad in 5 countries, work-study programs, and dual majors. There are 3 national honor societies, a freshman honors program, and 13 departmental honors programs.

Faculty/Classroom: 65% of faculty are male; 35% are female. All teach undergraduates. No introductory courses are taught by graduate students. The average class size in an introductory lecture is 26; in a laboratory is 17; and in a regular course is 24.

Admissions: 55% of the 2013-2014 applicants were accepted. The SAT scores for the 2013-2014 freshman class were: Critical Reading--78% below 500, 20% between 500 and 599, and 2% between 600 and 699; Math--72% below 500, 24% between 500 and 599, and 4% between 600 and 699; Writing--88% below 500, and 11% between 500 and 599, and 1% between 700 and 800. The ACT scores were 44% below 21, 49% between 21 and 23, and 6% between 24 and 26.

Requirements: The SAT or ACT is required, with a minimum composite score of 750 on the SAT I or 17 on the ACT. Applicants must be graduates of an accredited secondary school or have a GED certificate. They must have completed at least 16 academic credits, including 4 in English, 3 each in math and science, 2 each in music and social sciences, and a foreign language. An audition is required of fine arts majors, and a portfolio is recommended. An interview is suggested for all applicants. A GPA of 2.0 is required. AP and CLEP credits are accepted. Important factors in the admissions decision are geographical diversity, advanced placement or honors courses, and personality/intangible qualities.

Procedure: Freshmen are admitted to all sessions. Entrance exams should be taken before April 1. There are deferred admissions and rolling admissions plans. Applications should be filed by December 1 for spring entry. The fall 2013 application fee was $35.

Transfer: 430 transfer students enrolled in 2012-2013. Applicants must have a minimum GPA of 2.0 in at least 24 semester hours and must be in good standing at their previous school. Specifically, 6 hours of English, history, college algebra, and science are required. 62 of 124 credits required for the bachelor's degree must be completed at A & T.

Visiting: There are regularly scheduled orientations for prospective students. There are guides for informal visits and visitors may sit in on classes. To schedule a visit, contact the Admissions Office.

Financial Aid: In 2013-2014, 56% of all full-time freshmen students received some form of financial aid. 80% of all full-time freshmen and 80% of continuing full-time students received need-based aid. The average freshman award was $13,873. Need-based scholarships or need-based grants averaged $5,109; need-based self-help aid (loans and jobs) averaged $4,131; other non-need-based awards and non-need-based scholarships averaged $7,333; and $4,062 from other forms of aid. The average financial indebtedness of the 2013 graduate was $15,008. A & T is a member of CSS. The FAFSA is required. The deadline for filing freshman financial aid applications for fall entry is March 15.

International Students: There are 71 international students enrolled. They must take the TOEFL. They must also take the SAT or ACT.

Computers: All students may access the system. There are no time limits and no fees.

Graduates: From July 1, 2012 to June 30, 2013, 127 bachelor's degrees were awarded. The most popular majors were enginering (14%), business/marketing (10%), and psychology (9%). In an average class, 19% graduate in 4 years or less, 34% graduate in 5 years or less, and 42% graduate in 6 years or less.

Admissions Contact: John Smith, Admissions Director. E-Mail: *uadmit@ncat.edu* Web: *www.ncat.edu*

NORTH CAROLINA CENTRAL UNIVERSITY D-2

Durham, NC 27707 (919) 560-6298
(919) 530-7625 or (919) 560-5462

Full-time: 1505 men, 2705 women
Part-time: 305 men, 805 women
Graduate: 505 men, 1305 women
Year: semesters, summer session
Application Deadline: see profile
Freshman Class: n/av
SAT or ACT: required
Faculty: n/av; IIA, +$
Ph.D.s: n/av
Student/Faculty: n/av
Tuition: $5568 ($15,203)
Room & Board: $7146

LESS COMPETITIVE

North Carolina Central University, founded in 1909, is a publicly funded liberal arts institution in the University of North Carolina system. The figures in the above capsule and in this profile are approximate. There are 3 undergraduate schools and 2 graduate schools. In addition to regional accreditation, NCCU has baccalaureate program accreditation with NCATE and NLN. The 6 libraries contain 663,913 volumes, 1.2 million microform items, and 10,991 audio/video tapes/CDs/DVDs, and subscribe to 6688 periodicals including electronic. Computerized library services include database searching. Special learning facilities include a learning resource center and art gallery. The 103-acre campus is in an urban area 2 miles from the center of Durham. Including any residence halls, there are 57 buildings.

Student Life: 89% of undergraduates are from North Carolina. Others are from 39 states, and 17 foreign countries. 80% are African American; 14% white. The average age of freshmen is 19; all undergraduates, 24.

Housing: 2377 students can be accommodated in college housing, which includes single-sex and coed dorms and on-campus apartments. In addition, there are honors houses. On-campus housing is available on a first-come, first-served basis and is available on a lottery system for upperclassmen. 63% of students commute. Alcohol is not permitted. All students may keep cars.

Activities: There are 4 national fraternities and 4 national sororities. There are 45 groups on campus, including art, band, cheerleading, chess, choir, computers, dance, drama, drill team, ethnic, honors, international, jazz band, literary magazine, marching band, newspaper, political, professional, radio and TV, religious, social, social service, student government, symphony, and yearbook.

Sports: There are 6 intercollegiate sports for men and 5 for women. Facilities include a 12,000-seat stadium, a 4500-seat gym, a swimming pool, handball and tennis courts, a track, a bowling alley, dance studios, and a weight room.

Disabled Students: 90% of the campus is accessible. Facilities include wheelchair ramps, elevators, special parking, specially equipped rest rooms, special class scheduling, lowered drinking fountains, and lowered telephones.

Services: There is a reader service for the blind, remedial math, reading, and writing, and assistance for students in obtaining needed documentations, registering, and other appropriate individual accommodations and assistance as needed.

Campus Safety and Security: Measures include 24-hour foot and vehicle patrol and security escort services. There are emergency telephones and lighted pathways/sidewalks.

Programs of Study: NCCU confers B.A., B.S., B.B.A., B.M., B.S.N., and B.S.W. degrees. Master's degrees are also awarded. Bachelor's degrees are awarded in BIOLOGICAL SCIENCE (biology/biological science and nutrition), BUSINESS (accounting and business administration and management), COMMUNICATIONS AND THE ARTS (art, dramatic arts, English, French, jazz, music, and Spanish), COMPUTER AND PHYSICAL SCIENCE (chemistry, computer science, mathematics, and physics), EDUCATION (elementary education, health education, middle school education, and physical education), ENGINEERING AND ENVIRONMENTAL DESIGN (environmental science), HEALTH PROFESSIONS (nursing), SOCIAL SCIENCE (child care/child and family studies, child psychology/

development, criminal justice, geography, history, human services, political science/government, psychology, social work, and sociology). Criminal justice and business are the strongest academically. Business, biology, and political science have the largest enrollments.

Required: To graduate, students must complete 124 semester hours, including 30 in the major, with a minimum GPA of 2.0. Core requirements include courses in communications, math and natural science, social science, humanities, and health and phys ed.

Special: NCCU offers internships, study abroad, a Washington semester, work-study programs, dual majors, and nondegree study. There are 10 national honor societies, a freshman honors program, and 10 departmental honors programs.

Faculty/Classroom: 53% of faculty are male; 47% are female. All teach undergraduates. No introductory courses are taught by graduate students.

Requirements: The SAT or ACT is required. Applicants must be graduates of an accredited secondary school or have a GED certificate. They must have completed 11 academic credits based on 4 years of English, 3 each of math and science, and 2 each of a foreign language and social studies. Music applicants must audition. A GPA of 2.0 is required. AP and CLEP credits are accepted. Important factors in the admissions decision are advanced placement or honors courses, leadership record, and evidence of special talent.

Procedure: Entrance exams should be taken in the spring of the junior year. There is a rolling admissions plan. Check with the school for current application deadlines. The application fee is $40. Applications are accepted online.

Transfer: Applicants must have a minimum GPA of 2.0 in all college-level courses. 30 of 124 credits required for the bachelor's degree must be completed at NCCU.

Visiting: There are regularly scheduled orientations for prospective students. There are guides for informal visits; visitors may sit in on classes and stay overnight.

Financial Aid: The FAFSA is required. Check with the school for current application deadlines.

International Students: They must take the TOEFL. They must also take the SAT or ACT, unless these tests are not administered in their country.

Computers: All students may access the system 9 a.m. to 5 p.m. Monday through Friday. The computing center also has dial-in service. There are no time limits and no fees. It is strongly recommended that all students have a personal computer.

Admissions Contact: Director of Admissions. A campus DVD is available. Web: *www.nccu.edu*

NORTH CAROLINA STATE UNIVERSITY D-2

Raleigh, NC 27695 **(919) 515-2434; (919) 515-5039**

Full-time: 12264 men, 9557 women	**Faculty:** 1723; I, -$
Part-time: 1744 men, 1268 women	**Ph.D.s:** 91%
Graduate: 5168 men, 4339 women	**Student/Faculty:** 12 to 1
Year: semesters, summer session	**Tuition:** $7788 ($20,953)
Application Deadline: November 1	**Room & Board:** $8414
Freshman Class: 20298 applied, 10124 accepted, 4225 enrolled	
SAT CR/M/W: 590/630/570	**ACT:** 26 **HIGHLY COMPETITIVE**

North Carolina State University, founded in 1887, is a member of the University of North Carolina System. Its degree programs emphasize the arts and sciences, agriculture, business, education, engineering, and preprofessional training. There are 10 undergraduate schools and 9 graduate schools. In addition to regional accreditation, NC State has baccalaureate program accreditation with ABET, CSAB, CSWE, NAAB, NCATE, NRPA, and SAF. The 5 libraries contain 4.6 million volumes, 66,571 microform items, and 177,538 audio/video tapes/CDs/DVDs, and subscribe to 66,000 periodicals including electronic. Computerized library services include interlibrary loans, database searching, Internet access, and Wi-Fi capability. Special learning facilities include an art gallery, radio station, TV station, nuclear reactor, phytotron, electron microscope facilities, Materials Research Center, Integrated Manufacturing Systems Engineering Institute, Japan Center, and Precision Engineering Center. The 2110-acre campus is in an urban area Raleigh, NC. Including any residence halls, there are 218 buildings.

Student Life: 88% of undergraduates are from North Carolina. Others are from 50 states, 119 foreign countries, and Canada. 91% are from public schools. 70% are White. The average age of freshmen is 18; all undergraduates, 21. 8% do not continue beyond their first year; 72% remain to graduate.

Housing: 7300 students can be accommodated in college housing, which includes single-sex and coed dorms, on-campus apartments, off-campus apartments, and married student housing. In addition, there are honors houses, special-interest houses, fraternity houses, sorority houses, international, arts and creative living, computer theme, and first-year-experience halls. On-campus housing is guaranteed for all 4 years. 66% of students commute. Alcohol is not permitted. Upperclassmen may keep cars.

Activities: 8% of men belong to 32 national fraternities; 14% of women belong to 19 national sororities. There are 560 groups on campus, including art, bagpipe, band, cheerleading, chess, choir, chorale, chorus, computers, dance, drama, drill team, drum and bugle corps, environmental, ethnic, gay, honors, international, jazz band, literary magazine, marching band, musical theater, orchestra, pep band, photography, political, professional, religious, social, social service, student government, symphony, and yearbook. Popular campus events include Pan African Festival, Wolfstock, and Greek Week.

Sports: There are 20 intercollegiate sports for men and 16 for women, and 28 intramural sports for men and 26 for women. Facilities include a 55,000-seat football stadium, a 20,000-seat sports arena, a 5000-seat soccer stadium, a baseball stadium, a 12,500-seat gym, a tennis complex, areas for track, 2 indoor pools, and an indoor rock-climbing wall.

Disabled Students: 78% of the campus is accessible. Facilities include wheelchair ramps, elevators, special parking, specially equipped restrooms, special class scheduling, lowered drinking fountains, lowered telephones, and van transportation.

Services: Counseling and information services are available, as is tutoring in most subjects. There is a reader service for the blind, and remedial math and writing.

Campus Safety and Security: Measures include 24-hour foot and vehicle patrol, emergency notification system, self-defense education, and security escort services. There are shuttle buses, emergency telephones, lighted pathways/sidewalks, and bicycle patrol.

Programs of Study: NC State confers B.A., B.S., B.Arch., B.E.D.A., B.L.A. and B.S.W. degrees. Associate, master's, and doctoral degrees are also awarded. Bachelor's degrees are awarded in AGRICULTURE (agricultural business management, agricultural economics, agriculture, agronomy, animal science, conservation and regulation, fishing and fisheries, forestry and related sciences, horticulture, natural resource management, poultry science, soil science, and wood science), BIOLOGICAL SCIENCE (biochemistry, biology/biological science, botany, microbiology, and zoology), BUSINESS (accounting, business administration and management, business economics, and recreation and leisure services), COMMUNICATIONS AND THE ARTS (communications, design, English, French, graphic design, industrial design, and Spanish), COMPUTER AND PHYSICAL SCIENCE (atmospheric sciences and meteorology, chemistry, computer science, earth science, geology, mathematics, physics, and statistics), EDUCATION (agricultural education, education, foreign languages education, industrial arts education, marketing and distribution education, mathematics education, middle school education, science education, secondary education, social studies education, technical education, and vocational education), ENGINEERING AND ENVIRONMENTAL DESIGN (aeronautical engineering, agricultural engineering, architecture, chemical engineering, civil engineering, computer engineering, construction management, electrical/electronics engineering, engineering, environmental design, environmental engineering, environmental science, furniture design, industrial engineering, landscape architecture/design, materials science, mechanical engineering, nuclear engineering, paper and pulp science, and textile engineering), HEALTH PROFESSIONS (medical laboratory technology, predentistry, premedicine, preveterinary science, and speech pathology/audiology), SOCIAL SCIENCE (clothing and textiles management/production/services, criminal justice, economics, food science, history, interdisciplinary studies, parks and recreation management, philosophy, political science/government, prelaw, psychology, religion, social science, social work, sociology, and textiles and clothing). Electrical engineering, chemical engineering, and architecture are the strongest academically. Business management, mechanical engineering, and electrical engineering have the largest enrollments.

Required: To graduate, students must complete 120 to 142 semester hours, including 60 to 70 in the major, with a minimum GPA of 2.0. Distribution requirements include 12 to 18 hours in humanities and social sciences, 6 to 8 each in math and science, 6 in English composition, and 4 in phys ed.

Special: NC State offers cross-registration within the Cooperating Raleigh Colleges network, study abroad in more than 90 countries, internships, work-study programs, an accelerated degree plan, dual majors within any program, a general studies degree in education, a 3-2 engineering degree with the University of North Carolina at Asheville, student-designed multidisciplinary studies majors, credit by examination, nondegree study, and pass/fail options. There are 15 national honor societies, including Phi Beta Kappa, a freshman honors program, and 44 departmental honors programs.

Faculty/Classroom: 71% of faculty are male; 29% are female. All teach and do research. Graduate students teach 8% of introductory courses. The average class size in an introductory lecture is 35; in a laboratory is 20; and in a regular course is 30.

Admissions: 50% of the 2013-2014 applicants were accepted. The SAT scores for the 2013-2014 freshman class were: Critical Reading--7% below 500, 47% between 500 and 599, 28% between 600 and 699, and 8% between 700 and 800; Math--3% below 500, 27% between 500 and 599, 54% between 600 and 699, and 16% between 700 and 800; Writing--13% below 500, 52% between 500 and 599, 30% between 600 and

699, and 5% between 700 and 800. 78% of the current freshmen were in the top fifth of their class; 98% were in the top two fifths. 110 freshmen graduated first in their class.

Requirements: The SAT or ACT is required. The ACT Optional Writing test is also required. In addition, the SAT: Math test is recommended. Applicants must be graduates of an accredited secondary school or have a GED certificate. They must have completed 20 academic credits, including 4 units of English, 3 each of science and math (4 of math is advised), 2 each of social studies and foreign language, and 1 of history. An essay is recommended for all applicants. A portfolio and interview are required for the School of Design. AP and CLEP credits are accepted. Important factors in the admissions decision are advanced placement or honors courses, leadership record, and evidence of special talent.

Procedure: Freshmen are admitted to all sessions. Entrance exams should be taken in the spring of the junior year and the fall of the senior year. There is a deferred admissions plan. Early decision applications should be filed by October 15; regular applications, by November 1 for fall entry; November 1 for spring entry; and February 1 for summer entry, along with a $70 fee. Notification of early decision is sent January 30; regular decision, March 15. Applications are accepted online.

Transfer: 1027 transfer students enrolled in 2012-2013. Applicants must have completed 30 semester hours of college-level work with a minimum GPA of 2.0. Priority is given to students who have completed 60 hours of relevant course work. An associate degree and an interview are recommended. Applicants must have math, English, and foreign language proficiency. 30 of 120 credits required for the bachelor's degree must be completed at NC State.

Visiting: There are regularly scheduled orientations for prospective students, consisting of admissions information sessions. There are guides for informal visits and visitors may sit in on classes. To schedule a visit, contact the Admissions Office.

Financial Aid: In 2013-2014, 98% of all full-time freshmen and 97% of continuing full-time students received some form of financial aid. 96% of all full-time freshmen and 94% of continuing full-time students received need-based aid. The average financial indebtedness of the 2013 graduate was $15,823. The FAFSA and the college's own financial statement are required. The deadline for filing freshman financial aid applications for fall entry is March 1.

International Students: There are 313 international students enrolled. The school actively recruits these students. They must take the TOEFL. They must also take the SAT or ACT if it is available to students in their country.

Computers: All students may access the system. Time limits vary by class. The fee is $100.

Graduates: The most popular majors were engineering (24%), business/marketing (15%), and biological/life sciences (10%). In an average class, 37% graduate in 4 years or less, 67% graduate in 5 years or less, and 72% graduate in 6 years or less. Of the 2012 graduating class, 20% were enrolled in graduate school within 6 months of graduation, and 59% were employed.

Admissions Contact: Thomas Griffin, Director of Admissions. E-Mail: *undergrad_admissions@ncsu.edu* Web: *www.ncsu.edu*

NORTH CAROLINA WESLEYAN COLLEGE E-2

Rocky Mount, NC 27804 **(252) 985-5200**
(800) 488-NCWC; (252) 985-5295

Full-time: 620 men, 520 women	**Faculty:** n/av; IIB, --$
Part-time: 290 men, 340 women	**Ph.D.s:** 45%
Graduate: n/av	**Student/Faculty:** n/av
Year: semesters, summer session	**Tuition:** $23,050
Application Deadline: open	**Room & Board:** $7890
Freshman Class: n/av	
SAT or ACT: required	

COMPETITIVE

North Carolina Wesleyan College, founded in 1956, is a private liberal arts institution affiliated with the United Methodist Church. The figures in the above capsule and in this profile are approximate. In addition to regional accreditation, NCWC has baccalaureate program accreditation with NCATE. The library contains 65,721 volumes, 2,830 microform items, and 4,200 audio/video tapes/CDs/DVDs, and subscribes to 4,645 periodicals including electronic. Computerized library services include interlibrary loans and database searching. Special learning facilities include a learning resource center, art gallery, and a performing arts center. The 200-acre campus is in a suburban area 57 miles east of Raleigh. Including any residence halls, there are 18 buildings.

Student Life: 85% of undergraduates are from North Carolina. Others are from 24 states, and 9 foreign countries. 70% are from public schools. 45% are African American; 43% white. 70% are Protestant; 16% Catholic; 14% claim no religious affiliation. The average age of freshmen is 19; all undergraduates, 26. 36% do not continue beyond their first year; 26% remain to graduate.

Housing: 504 students can be accommodated in college housing, which includes single-sex and coed dorms and off-campus apartments. In addition, there are single-occupancy residence halls with kitchens on each floor and smoke/substance free housing. On-campus housing is guaranteed for all 4 years. 68% of students commute. All students may keep cars.

Activities: 1% of men belong to 3 national fraternities; 1% of women belong to 3 national sororities. There are 23 groups on campus, including cheerleading, chess, choir, chorus, computers, drama, ethnic, gay, honors, international, literary magazine, musical theater, newspaper, political, professional, religious, social, social service, and student government. Popular campus events include Spring Fling, Parents Weekend, and Alumni Homecoming.

Sports: There are 5 intercollegiate sports for men and 5 for women, and 13 intramural sports for men and 13 for women. Facilities include a 1200-seat gym with areas for basketball, volleyball, and indoor soccer matches; tennis courts; a skeet range; and fields for intramural and for varsity baseball, softball, and soccer.

Disabled Students: 90% of the campus is accessible. Facilities include wheelchair ramps, elevators, special parking, specially equipped restrooms, special class scheduling, lowered drinking fountains, lowered telephones, and special housing.

Services: Counseling and information services are available, as is tutoring in most subjects. There is remedial math, reading, and writing.

Campus Safety and Security: Measures include 24-hour foot and vehicle patrol and security escort services. There are emergency telephones and lighted pathways/sidewalks.

Programs of Study: NCWC confers B.A. and B.S. degrees. Bachelor's degrees are awarded in BIOLOGICAL SCIENCE (biology/biological science), BUSINESS (accounting, business administration and management, and hotel/motel and restaurant management), COMMUNICATIONS AND THE ARTS (dramatic arts and English), COMPUTER AND PHYSICAL SCIENCE (chemistry, information sciences and systems, and mathematics), EDUCATION (elementary education and middle school education), ENGINEERING AND ENVIRONMENTAL DESIGN (environmental science), HEALTH PROFESSIONS (exercise science and premedicine), SOCIAL SCIENCE (criminal justice, history, political science/government, psychology, religion, and sociology). Business administration, justice studies, and computer information systems have the largest enrollments.

Required: To graduate, students must complete 124 semester hours, including 30 to 54 in the major, with a minimum GPA of 2.0. Distribution requirements consist of 6 semester hours of English composition or demonstrated proficiency; 4 each of biological and physical science; 3 each of ethics, non-Western culture, math, history, social science, psychology or sociology, religion, literature, and fine arts; 2 of phys ed; and 2 of introduction to college life. Some majors require a thesis.

Special: NCWC offers cooperative programs in all majors, internships, work-study programs through the college offices, credit for military experience, nondegree study, and pass/fail options. The B.A.-B.S. degree may be earned in all majors. There are 2 national honor societies and a freshman honors program.

Faculty/Classroom: 62% of faculty are male; 38% are female. All teach undergraduates. No introductory courses are taught by graduate students. The average class size in an introductory lecture, 23, in a laboratory, 15, and in a regular course, 18.

Requirements: The SAT or ACT is required, with a satisfactory SAT composite score or ACT score of 19 recommended. Applicants should be graduates of an accredited secondary school or have a GED. They should have completed at least 13 academic courses, including 4 in English, 3 in math, and 2 each in foreign language, social studies, and lab sciences. An essay and an interview are advised. AP and CLEP credits are accepted. Important factors in the admissions decision are advanced placement or honors courses, extracurricular activities record, and leadership record.

Procedure: Freshmen are admitted fall and spring. Entrance exams should be taken in spring of the junior year or fall or winter of the senior year. There are deferred admissions and rolling admissions plans. Application deadlines are open. Application fee is $25. Applications are accepted online.

Transfer: Applicants must have a minimum GPA of 2.0 in their college courses. They must submit transcripts of all high school and college work, along with proof of high school graduation. 31 of 124 credits required for the bachelor's degree must be completed at NCWC.

Visiting: There are regularly scheduled orientations for prospective students, including an individual campus tour, an interview, a financial aid session, and meetings with faculty and coaches. There are guides for informal visits; visitors may sit in on classes and stay overnight. To schedule a visit, contact the Admissions Office.

Financial Aid: NCWC is a member of CSS. The FAFSA is required. Check with the school for application deadlines.

International Students: They must take the TOEFL. They must also take the SAT.

Computers: There are no time limits and no fees.

Admissions Contact: Cecelia Summers, Director of Admissions. E-Mail: *adm@ncwc.edu* Web: *www.ncwc.edu*

PFEIFFER UNIVERSITY C-2

Misenheimer, NC 28109 (704) 463-3057
(800) 338-2060; (704) 463-1363

Full-time: 350 men, 505 women	**Faculty:** 81
Part-time: 27 men, 66 women	**Ph.D.s:** 78%
Graduate: 240 men, 665 women	**Student/Faculty:** 14 to 1
Year: semesters, summer session	**Tuition:** $24,210
Application Deadline: August 25	**Room & Board:** $9490

Freshman Class: 1684 applied, 774 accepted, 213 enrolled

SAT CR/M/W: 460/500/450 **ACT:** 20 **COMPETITIVE**

Pfeiffer University, founded in 1885, is a private institution of liberal arts and sciences affiliated with the United Methodist Church. There are 2 undergraduate schools and 1 graduate school. In addition to regional accreditation, Pfeiffer has baccalaureate program accreditation with NASM and NCATE. The library contains 135,235 volumes, 30,980 microform items, 2,656 audio/video tapes/CDs/DVDs, and subscribes to 29,662 periodicals including electronic. Computerized library services include interlibrary loans, database searching, Internet access, and Wi-Fi capability. The 321-acre campus is in a rural area 44 miles east of Charlotte. Including any residence halls, there are 47 buildings.

Student Life: 75% of undergraduates are from North Carolina. Others are from 34 states, 18 foreign countries, and Canada. 57% are White; 18% African American; 15% race unknown. 45% are Protestant; 44% claim no religious affiliation. The average age of freshmen is 18; all undergraduates, 21. 71% do not continue beyond their first year; 45% remain to graduate.

Housing: 533 students can be accommodated in college housing, which includes single-sex and coed dorms and on-campus apartments. In addition, there are special-interest houses, gender-specific. On-campus housing is available on a first-come, first-served basis, and is available on a lottery system for upperclassmen. 63% of students live on campus; of those, 60% remain on campus on weekends. All students may keep cars.

Activities: There are no fraternities or sororities. There are 39 groups on campus, including band, cheerleading, chess, choir, chorale, chorus, communications, computers, drama, environmental, ethnic, honors, international, jazz band, literary magazine, newspaper, pep band, photography, political, professional, religious, social, social service, and student government. Popular campus events include AprilFest, Homecoming Week, Campus Week of Dialogue, Servant Leadership Week, Dry Night and Cultural Hour (weekly).

Sports: There are 9 intercollegiate sports for men and 9 for women, and 6 intramural sports for men and 3 for women. Facilities include Athletic Complex. The athletics complex includes a 2200-seat gymnasium with 25-yard, six-lane AAU pool, weight, exercise and training rooms, classrooms, a sports medicine laboratory, an auxiliary gymnasium, baseball, softball, lacrosse, and soccer fields, along with 6 tennis courts. These facilities are available, not only for intercollegiate sports, but for intramural play as well. In addition, the nationally-recognized Old North State Club at Uwharrie Point is the Pfeiffer golf team's home course. Joseph S. Ferebee Field The Pfeiffer baseball program is proud to call Joseph S. Ferebee Field its home field. Named in honor of legendary Pfeiffer coach Joe Ferebee, this spacious park, located on the east end of campus, has been the home of the Falcons since 1974. Over the last two decades Ferebee Field has seen its share of conference championships and college All-Americans. Set in the shadow of scenic Gibson Lake, with a bermuda grass playing surface, this park is quickly being established as one of the finest small college fields in the Carolinas. A brand new press box and seating capacity for over 500 fans combine to make Ferebee Field a great place to see exciting college baseball. Knapp Tennis Center The Knapp Tennis center serves as the home of the Varsity Men's and Women's Tennis teams at Pfeiffer University. The center was completed in 1997 as a result of a gift from the Knapp family. It includes a player lounge and spectator seating on the veranda.

Disabled Students: 90% of the campus is accessible. Facilities include wheelchair ramps, elevators, special parking, specially equipped restrooms, special class scheduling, lowered drinking fountains, and special housing.

Services: Counseling and information services are available, as is tutoring in most subjects. There is a reader service for the blind, and remedial math and reading.

Campus Safety and Security: Measures include 24-hour foot and vehicle patrol, emergency notification system, self-defense education, and security escort services. There are lighted pathways/sidewalks and controlled access to dorms/residences.

Programs of Study: Pfeiffer confers B.A., and B.S. degrees. Master's degrees are also awarded. Bachelor's degrees are awarded in BIOLOGICAL SCIENCE (biology/biological science), BUSINESS (accounting, business administration and management, international business management, and sports management), COMMUNICATIONS AND THE ARTS (art, communications, creative writing, and English literature), COMPUTER AND PHYSICAL SCIENCE (chemistry, information sciences and systems, and mathematics), EDUCATION (Christian education, elementary education, English education, health education, physical education, science education, secondary education, social studies education, and special education), ENGINEERING AND ENVIRONMENTAL DESIGN (environmental science and preengineering), HEALTH PROFESSIONS (exercise science, nursing, and premedicine), SOCIAL SCIENCE (criminal justice, history, human services, political science/government, psychology, religion, religious education, religious music, and social studies). Nursing, pre-med, and biology are the strongest academically. Business administration, criminal justice, and elementary education have the largest enrollments.

Required: All students must complete 120 to 124 semester hours, including 37 credits in literary studies, historical perspective, writing, religion, visual and performing arts, social and behavioral arts, natural science, mathematics, and global awareness. Students must maintain an overall minimum GPA of 2.0 and complete 42 to 72 hours in the major. A freshman seminar and senior capstone course in the major are required, as well as participation in the cultural program and basic competency in computer technology.

Special: Cross registration with the Charlotte Area Education Consortium. 3-2 Program in Business Management and Leadership. Internships are available in all majors. There are 5 national honor societies, a freshman honors program, and 10 departmental honors programs.

Faculty/Classroom: 51% of faculty are male; 49% are female. 85% teach undergraduates, 25% do research, and 25% do both. No introductory courses are taught by graduate students. The average class size in an introductory lecture is 24; in a laboratory is 18; and in a regular course is 12.

Admissions: 46% of the 2013-2014 applicants were accepted. The SAT scores for the 2013-2014 freshman class were: Critical Reading--63% below 500, 31% between 500 and 599, 6% between 600 and 699; Math--49% below 500, 40% between 500 and 599, 11% between 600 and 699; Writing--71% below 500, 26% between 500 and 599, 2% between 600 and 699, and 1% between 700 and 800. The ACT scores were 55% below 21, 32% between 21 and 23, 7% between 24 and 26, and 5% between 27 and 28. 45% of the current freshmen were in the top fifth of their class; 66% were in the top two fifths.

Requirements: The SAT is required. The ACT is recommended. All applicants are required to have completed 4 years of English and 3 years of math, including algebra I. The GED is accepted. Pfeiffer requires applicants to be in the upper 50% of their class. A GPA of 2.0 is required. AP and CLEP credits are accepted. Important factors in the admissions decision are advanced placement or honors courses, leadership record, and extracurricular activities record.

Procedure: Freshmen are admitted to all sessions. Entrance exams should be taken by January of the senior year. There are early admissions, deferred admissions, and rolling admissions plans. Applications should be filed by August 25 for fall entry; January 20 for spring entry, along with a $35 fee. Notification is sent on a rolling basis. Applications are accepted online.

Transfer: 37 transfer students enrolled in 2012-2013. Applicants should be eligible for readmission to the last college attended and have a minimum GPA of 2.0 45 of 120 credits required for the bachelor's degree must be completed at Pfeiffer.

Visiting: There are regularly scheduled orientations for prospective students, including meetings with faculty/staff, a question-and-answer session, a tour, and a lunch. There are guides for informal visits, visitors may sit in on classes, and stay overnight. To schedule a visit, contact Michelle Inman, Campus Guest Coordinator at (704) 463-3055.

Financial Aid: In 2013-2014, 96% of all full-time freshmen and 97% of continuing full-time students received some form of financial aid. 79% of all full-time freshmen and 81% of continuing full-time students received need-based aid. The average freshman award was $24,650. Need-based scholarships or need-based grants averaged $2,771 ($5,234 maximum); need-based self-help aid (loans and jobs) averaged $3,820 ($7,561 maximum); non-need-based athletic scholarships averaged $6,790 ($12,237 maximum); and other non-need-based awards and non-need-based scholarships averaged $7,536 ($8,039 maximum). 29% of undergraduate students work part-time. Average annual earnings from campus work are $1037. The average financial indebtedness of the 2013 graduate was $24,687. The FAFSA is required. The priority date for freshman financial aid applications for fall entry is March 15. The deadline for filing freshman financial aid applications for fall entry is open.

International Students: There are 30 international students enrolled. They must also take the SAT and ACT, scoring 900. TOEFL or IELTS.

Computers: All students may access the system. There are no time limits and no fees.

Graduates: From July 1, 2012 to June 30, 2013, 192 bachelor's degrees were awarded. The most popular majors were business administration (24%), criminal justice (15%), and psychology (8%). In an average class, 4% graduate in 3 years or less, 30% graduate in 4 years or less, 38% graduate in 5 years or less, and 40% graduate in 6 years or less.

Admissions Contact: Terry Parker-Jeffries, Director of Admissions. E-Mail: *admissions@pfeiffer.edu* Web: *www.pfeiffer.edu*

QUEENS UNIVERSITY OF CHARLOTTE C-3

Charlotte, NC 28274 (704) 337-2212
(800) 849-0202; (704) 337-2403

Full-time: 408 men, 997 women
Part-time: 66 men, 232 women
Graduate: 183 men, 368 women
Year: semesters, summer session
Application Deadline: rolling
Faculty: n/av
Ph.D.s: 79%
Student/Faculty: 12 to 1
Tuition: $29,045
Room & Board: $10,498
Freshman Class: 1949 applied, 1498 accepted, 316 enrolled
SAT CR/M/W: 520/520/510 **ACT:** 24 **VERY COMPETITIVE**

Queens University of Charlotte is a private, co-ed, comprehensive university with a commitment to both liberal arts and professional studies. There are 5 undergraduate schools and 1 graduate school. In addition to regional accreditation, Queens has baccalaureate program accreditation with AACSB, ACBSP, NASM, NCATE, and NLN. The library contains 42,081 volumes, 97,670 audio/video tapes/CDs/DVDs, and subscribes to 74 periodicals including electronic. Computerized library services include interlibrary loans, database searching, Internet access, and Wi-Fi capability. Special learning facilities include an art gallery, Platiumn LEED Science Building, photographic lab, ceramics studio, and recital hall. The 30-acre campus is in a suburban area 2 miles south of uptown Charlotte. Including any residence halls, there are 38 buildings.

Student Life: 59% of undergraduates are from North Carolina. Others are from 36 states, 21 foreign countries, and Canada. 80% are from public schools. 59% are White; 13% African American; 12% race unknown. 17% are Protestant; 13% Catholic. The average age of freshmen is 18; all undergraduates, 20. 30% do not continue beyond their first year; 52% remain to graduate.

Housing: 916 students can be accommodated in college housing, which includes coed dorms and off-campus apartments. On-campus housing is guaranteed for all 4 years, is available on a first-come, first-served basis, and is available on a lottery system for upperclassmen. 83% of students live on campus. All students may keep cars.

Activities: 13% of men belong to 2 national fraternities; 21% of women belong to 5 national sororities. There are 72 groups on campus, including art, cheerleading, choir, chorale, chorus, dance, drama, environmental, ethnic, gay, honors, international, jazz band, literary magazine, musical theater, newspaper, pep band, political, professional, religious, social, social service, and student government. Popular campus events include Casino Night, Midnight on Ice, Spring Carnival, Exam Break Breakfast, Homecoming Week, Welcome Back Week, Moravian Love Feast, Boar's Head, International Week, and Queens After Dark.

Sports: There are 9 intercollegiate sports for men and 11 for women, and 6 intramural sports for men and 6 for women. Facilities include The Sports Complex is home to the Men's and Women's Lacrosse teams as well as the Men's and Women's Soccer teams. The Queens Sports Complex at Mario Diehl Park is one of the largest athletic venues in the region. It offers world class multi-sport champion field, cross country, a grass practice field, and a 14,000 square foot conference center.

Disabled Students: 70% of the campus is accessible. Facilities include wheelchair ramps, special parking, specially equipped restrooms, special class scheduling, lowered drinking fountains.

Services: Counseling and information services are available, as is tutoring in most subjects, math, science, social sciences, foreign languages, nursing, and core classes. The center for student success offers free individual peer tutoring, review sessions, knowledge workshops, academic success strategies, individual academic assistance and guidance, access to the writing center, and referrals to the Office of Disability Services.

Campus Safety and Security: Measures include 24-hour foot and vehicle patrol, emergency notification system, self-defense education, and security escort services. There are shuttle buses, emergency telephones, lighted pathways/sidewalks, and controlled access to dorms/residences.

Programs of Study: Queens confers B.A., B.B.A., B.S., B.Mus and B.S.N. degrees. Master's degrees are also awarded. Bachelor's degrees are awarded in AGRICULTURE (environmental studies), BIOLOGICAL SCIENCE (biochemistry and biology/biological science), BUSINESS (accounting, business administration and management, finance, and sports management), COMMUNICATIONS AND THE ARTS (art, communications, creative writing, digital communications, dramatic arts, English literature, French, graphic design, music, romance languages and literature, and Spanish), COMPUTER AND PHYSICAL SCIENCE (chemistry and mathematics), EDUCATION (elementary education), ENGINEERING AND ENVIRONMENTAL DESIGN (environmental science and interior design), HEALTH PROFESSIONS (exercise science, music therapy, and nursing), SOCIAL SCIENCE (community services, history, human services, philosophy, political science/government, psychology, religion, and sociology). Liberal arts and sciences, business and nursing are the strongest academically. Business, nursing, and communications have the largest enrollments.

Required: To graduate, students must complete a total of 122 credit hours with a minimum GPA of 2.0. For the B.A., between 30 and 40 hours are required in the student's major; for the B.S., 32 are required. 2 courses in English composition, 2 in phys ed, and 1 in lab science are required. If entering freshmen do not pass the placement exams given in math and a foreign language, additional courses will be required. Some majors require a thesis or research project.

Special: Required Internships in all majors, cross-registration with colleges of the Charlotte Area Educational Consortium, dual majors, nondegree study, and pass/fail options are available. The school offers a Washington semester. Study tours in over 14 countries(included in the cost of tuition) may be arranged through the school's John Belk International Program. There are 5 national honor societies and a freshman honors program.

Faculty/Classroom: 33% of faculty are male; 67% are female. All teach undergraduates. No introductory courses are taught by graduate students. The average class size in an introductory lecture is 15; in a laboratory is 10; and in a regular course is 15.

Admissions: 77% of the 2013-2014 applicants were accepted. The SAT scores for the 2013-2014 freshman class were: Critical Reading--41% below 500, 44% between 500 and 599, 11% between 600 and 699, and 3% between 700 and 800; Math--39% below 500, 43% between 500 and 599, 17% between 600 and 699, and 1% between 700 and 800; Writing--45% below 500, 37% between 500 and 599, 15% between 600 and 699, and 3% between 700 and 800. The ACT scores were 22% below 21, 26% between 21 and 23, 29% between 24 and 26, 13% between 27 and 28, and 10% above 28. 32% of the current freshmen were in the top fifth of their class; 64% were in the top two fifths.

Requirements: The SAT or ACT is required. The ACT Optional Writing test is also required. Applicants should have a college preparatory background in an accredited secondary school. The GED is accepted. High school courses should include 4 years of English, 3 of math, 2 each of history or social studies and a foreign language, and 2 years of science, including 1 of lab science. An interview is recommended. An audition or portfolio is recommended for art and music students. A GPA of 2.5 is required. AP and CLEP credits are accepted. Important factors in the admissions decision are recommendations by school officials, advanced placement or honors courses, and leadership record.

Procedure: Freshmen are admitted fall, spring, and summer. Entrance exams should be taken in the junior year or as early as possible in the senior year. There are early admissions, deferred admissions, and rolling admissions plans. Application deadlines are open. Application fee is $40. Notifications are sent September 15. Applications are accepted online. Application fees are waived if application is completed online.

Transfer: 163 transfer students enrolled in 2012-2013. Transfer students are accepted in all but the senior class. A college GPA of 2.0 is required for all previous college-level work. 45 of 122 credits required for the bachelor's degree must be completed at Queens.

Visiting: There are regularly scheduled orientations for prospective students, including a sampling of classes, campus tours, a college overview, a question/answer segment, a meet-the-faculty session, and a scholarship/financial aid session. There are guides for informal visits and visitors may sit in on classes. To schedule a visit, contact TUG Admissions.

Financial Aid: In 2013-2014, 97% of all full-time freshmen and 97% of continuing full-time students received some form of financial aid. 58% of all full-time freshmen and 58% of continuing full-time students received need-based aid. The average freshman award was $26,550. Need-based scholarships or need-based grants averaged $9,074 ($24,446 maximum); need-based self-help aid (loans and jobs) averaged $4,763 ($8,732 maximum); non-need-based athletic scholarships averaged $9,839 ($33,800 maximum); and other non need-based awards and non-need-based scholarships averaged $12,377 ($28,800 maximum). 15% of undergraduate students work part-time. Average annual earnings from campus work are $1700. The average financial indebtedness of the 2013 graduate was $28,507. Queens is a member of CSS. The FAFSA is required. The priority date for freshman financial aid applications for fall entry is March 1.

International Students: They must take the TOEFL with a minimum score of 550 on the paper-based TOEFL (PBT). They must also take the SAT or ACT.

Computers: All students may access the system 24/7. There are no time limits and no fees.

Graduates: From July 1, 2012 to June 30, 2013, 414 bachelor's degrees were awarded. The most popular majors were health professions and related programs (30%), business (12%), and communications (11%). 325 companies recruited on campus in 2012-2013. In an average class, 44% graduate in 4 years or less, 51% graduate in 5 years or less, and 52% graduate in 6 years or less.

Admissions Contact: Woody O'Cain, Assoc. Vice President, Dean of Admission. E-Mail: *admissions@queens.edu* Web: *www.queens.edu*

SAINT AUGUSTINE'S UNIVERSITY D-2

Raleigh, NC 27610 (919) 516-4000
(800) 948-1126; (919) 516-5805

Full-time: 505 men, 705 women
Part-time: 50 men, 100 women
Graduate: n/av
Year: semesters, summer session
Application Deadline:
Freshman Class: n/av
SAT or ACT: required
Faculty: 87
Ph.D.s: 59%
Student/Faculty: 16 to 1
Tuition: $10,000
Room & Board: $5000

COMPETITIVE

Saint Augustine's College, founded in 1867, is a historically black liberal arts institution affiliated with the Episcopal Church. Computerized library services include database searching. Special learning facilities include a The 110-acre campus is in an urban area 1 mile northeast of downtown Raleigh. Including any residence halls, there are 37 buildings.

Student Life: 51% of undergraduates are from North Carolina. Others are from 34 states, 16 foreign countries, and Canada. 99% are from public schools. 90% are African American. 58% are Protestant; 39% claim no religious affiliation. The average age of freshmen is 18; all undergraduates, 22. 38% do not continue beyond their first year; 27% remain to graduate.

Housing: 1143 students can be accommodated in college housing, which includes single-sex dorms. In addition, there are honors houses. On-campus housing is guaranteed for all 4 years. 62% of students live on campus; of those, 75% remain on campus on weekends. Alcohol is not permitted. All students may keep cars.

Activities: 6% of men belong to 5 national fraternities; 12% of women belong to 4 national sororities. There are 20 groups on campus, including band, cheerleading, chorale, dance, drama, ethnic, honors, international, newspaper, photography, professional, radio and TV, religious, social service, student government, and yearbook. Popular campus events include Opening Convocation each Semester, CIAA Tournament, and Career/Job Fairs.

Sports: There are 5 intercollegiate sports for men and 4 for women, and 4 intramural sports for men and 3 for women. Facilities include a 1700-seat gym, a track, baseball fields, and tennis and basketball courts.

Disabled Students: 64% of the campus is accessible. Facilities include wheelchair ramps, elevators, special parking, and specially equipped restrooms.

Services: There is remedial math, reading, and writing. Help with writing and test-taking skills is available.

Campus Safety and Security: Measures include 24-hour foot and vehicle patrol. There are emergency telephones and lighted pathways/sidewalks.

Programs of Study: confers B.A., and B.S. degrees. Bachelor's degrees are awarded in BIOLOGICAL SCIENCE (biology/biological science), BUSINESS (accounting, business administration and management, and international business management), COMMUNICATIONS AND THE ARTS (communications, English, fine arts, French, music, music business management, Spanish, and visual and performing arts), COMPUTER AND PHYSICAL SCIENCE (applied mathematics, chemistry, computer science, information sciences and systems, and mathematics), EDUCATION (business education, education of the exceptional child, elementary education, English education, mathematics education, music education, physical education, science education, and social studies education), ENGINEERING AND ENVIRONMENTAL DESIGN (industrial administration/management and industrial engineering), HEALTH PROFESSIONS (industrial hygiene, medical laboratory technology, and premedicine), SOCIAL SCIENCE (African American studies, criminal justice, history, physical fitness/movement, political science/government, prelaw, psychology, sociology, and urban studies). Engineering, math, premedicine, and chemistry are the strongest academically. Computer science, business administration, and communications have the largest enrollments.

Required: Students must complete at least 120 hours with a minimum 2.0 GPA for graduation. All students must complete a 50 to 55 credit core curriculum that includes courses in reading and communication, foreign language, science, math, philosophy, ethics, humanities, world civilization, psychology, and phys ed. Seniors must pass written and oral examinations in their major fields. Total credit hours required for a degree in offered majors range from 124 to 154.

Special: Students may cross-register at any of 5 area colleges, study abroad, or pursue a 3-2 engineering program with North Carolina State University. There is an accelerated degree program in organizational management for adult learners. Field experience programs, nondegree study, internships, work-study, cooperative programs, and credit for military service are offered. There are 1 national honor societies and a freshman honors program.

Faculty/Classroom: 60% of faculty are male; 40% are female. All teach undergraduates. No introductory courses are taught by graduate students. The average class size in an introductory lecture is 22; in a laboratory is 13; and in a regular course is 14.

Requirements: The SAT or ACT is required. Applicants must be graduates of an accredited secondary school with a C+ average in at least 18 academic units, including 4 in English, 3 in math, and 2 each in social studies and science. A GPA of 2.0 is required. AP credits are accepted. Important factors in the admissions decision are geographical diversity, evidence of special talent, and leadership record.

Procedure: Freshmen are admitted to all sessions. There are deferred admissions and rolling admissions plans. Check with the school for current application deadlines. The fall 2013 application fee was $25.

Transfer: 43 transfer students enrolled in 2012-2013. Transfers must submit high school and college transcripts and must be eligible to reenter the last institution attended. 30 of 124 credits required for the bachelor's degree must be completed at SAU.

Visiting: There are guides for informal visits and visitors may sit in on classes. To schedule a visit, contact the Admissions Office.

Financial Aid: In 2013-2014, 95% of all full-time freshmen and 90% of continuing full-time students received some form of financial aid. 87% of all full-time freshmen and 80% of continuing full-time students received need-based aid. The average freshman award was $10,474.. 69% of undergraduate students work part-time. Average annual earnings from campus work are $1572. The average financial indebtedness of the 2013 graduate was $12,850. is a member of CSS. The FAFSA is required. The deadline for filing freshman financial aid applications for fall entry is April 15.

International Students: There are 133 international students enrolled. The school actively recruits these students. They must take the TOEFL. They must also take the SAT or ACT.

Computers: All students may access the system. The system may be used during the operating hours of the library, the science building, and the business building. There are no time limits and no fees.

Graduates: From July 1, 2012 to June 30, 2013, 242 bachelor's degrees were awarded. The most popular majors were business (28%), psychology (12%), and criminal justice (8%). 25 companies recruited on campus in 2012-2013. In an average class, 1% graduate in 3 years or less, 12% graduate in 4 years or less, 25% graduate in 5 years or less, and 27% graduate in 6 years or less. Of the 2012 graduating class, 23% were enrolled in graduate school within 6 months of graduation, and 60% were employed.

Admissions Contact: Tim Chapman, Interim Director of Admissions. E-Mail: *admissions@es.st.aug.edu* Web: *www.st-aug.edu*

SALEM COLLEGE C-2

Winston-Salem, NC 27101 (336) 721-2621
(800) 327-2536; (336) 917-5572

Full-time: 15 men, 700 women
Part-time: 125 men, 160 women
Graduate: 20 men, 230 women
Year: semesters, summer session
Application Deadline: open
Freshman Class: n/av
SAT or ACT: required
Faculty: n/av; IIB, --$
Ph.D.s: n/av
Student/Faculty: n/av
Tuition: $22,860
Room & Board: $12,264

VERY COMPETITIVE

Salem College was begun as a school for girls in 1772 by the Moravians, an early Protestant denomination. Today the private college, which retains a historical relationship with the church, offers a liberal arts education primarily for women. The figures in the above capsule and in this profile are approximate. There is 1 graduate school. In addition to regional accreditation, Salem has baccalaureate program accreditation with NASM and NCATE. The 2 libraries contain 135,000 volumes, 302,534 microform items, and 13,553 audio/video tapes/CDs/DVDs, and subscribe to 15,000 periodicals including electronic. Computerized library services include interlibrary loans and database searching. Special learning facilities include a learning resource center, art gallery, radio station, and learning lab (computer lab with multimedia capability). The 64-acre campus is in an urban area in the center of Old Salem, a restored 18th-century village. Including any residence halls, there are 17 buildings.

Student Life: 51% of undergraduates are from North Carolina. Others are from 23 states and 17 foreign countries. 80% are from public schools. 65% are white; 18% African American. The average age of freshmen is 18; all undergraduates, 27. 25% do not continue beyond their first year; 55% remain to graduate.

Housing: 488 students can be accommodated in college housing, which includes single-sex dorms, on-campus apartments, and off-campus apartments. On-campus housing is guaranteed for all 4 years. 86% of students live on campus; of those, 55% remain on campus on weekends. All students may keep cars.

Activities: There are no fraternities or sororities. There are 41 groups on campus, including band, chorale, chorus, dance, drama, ethnic, gay, honors, international, literary magazine, marching band, musical theater, newspaper, orchestra, political, professional, radio and TV, religious, social, social service, student government, and yearbook. Popular campus events include Fall Fest, April Arts, and dance weekends.

Sports: There are 7 intercollegiate sports for women, and 7 intramural sports for women. Facilities include multiple athletic fields, a swimming pool, 2 gyms (1 practice, 1 regular), tennis courts, a dance studio,a softball field, and a universal weight room.

Disabled Students: 75% of the campus is accessible. Facilities include special parking, specially equipped rest rooms, special class scheduling, and lowered drinking fountains. Many buildings are historic, so disability access is limited to individual areas that have had recent renovations or were already accessible.

Services: Counseling and information services are available, as is tutoring in every subject. There is a writing center.

Campus Safety and Security: Measures include 24-hour foot and vehicle patrol and security escort services. There are emergency telephones and lighted pathways/sidewalks.

Programs of Study: Salem confers B.A., B.S., B.M., and B.S.B.A. degrees. Master's degrees are also awarded. Bachelor's degrees are awarded in BIOLOGICAL SCIENCE (biology/biological science), BUSINESS (accounting, business administration and management, and international business management), COMMUNICATIONS AND THE ARTS (art history and appreciation, arts administration/management, communications, English, French, German, music, Spanish, and studio art), COMPUTER AND PHYSICAL SCIENCE (chemistry and mathematics), ENGINEERING AND ENVIRONMENTAL DESIGN (interior design), HEALTH PROFESSIONS (medical laboratory technology), SOCIAL SCIENCE (American studies, economics, history, international relations, philosophy, psychology, religion, and sociology). Sociology, business, and communication have the largest enrollments.

Required: To graduate, students must complete a total of 36 courses, or 144 semester hours, with a minimum GPA of 2.0 both cumulative and in the major. All traditional students must complete 4 January-term courses and 2 terms of phys ed. Bachelor of arts degree students must complete the following general ed courses: 3 in a modern foreign language, 3 in math/science (including at least 1 math and at least 1 lab science), 2 each in English, social science, and history, and 1 each in fine arts and philosophy/religion.

Special: Salem offers an extensive internship program in all majors, cross-registration with Wake Forest University, and study abroad at various locations, including a summer program in Oxford, England. A Washington semester, student-designed and interdisciplinary majors, B.A.-B.S. degrees, nondegree study, and pass/fail options during the January term are available. A 3-2 engineering degree is available with Duke and Vanderbilt Universities. Students may participate in a model U.N. program directed by Drew University in Madison, New Jersey. Interdisciplinary majors are offered in American studies, arts management, and international relations. There are 9 national honor societies and a freshman honors program.

Faculty/Classroom: 47% of faculty are male; 53% are female. All teach and do research. No introductory courses are taught by graduate students. The average class size in an introductory lecture is 18, in a laboratory, 15, and in a regular course, 15.

Requirements: The SAT or ACT is required. Graduation from an accredited secondary school or the GED is required. Students must have 12 academic credits plus electives, including 4 years of high school English, 3 each of math and science, and 2 each of a foreign language and history. An essay is required for all students. Music students must audition. A GPA of 2.0 is also required. AP and CLEP credits are accepted. Important factors in the admissions decision are advanced placement or honors courses, leadership record, and evidence of special talent.

Procedure: Freshmen are admitted fall and spring. Entrance exams should be taken by January of the senior year. There are early admissions, deferred admissions, and rolling admissions plans. Application deadlines are open. Applications are accepted online.

Transfer: Applicants must have a minimum GPA of 2.0 in all previous college work and must submit a statement of good standing from the Dean of Students of the college previously attended, 2 letters of recommendation from teachers, a high school transcript, and a transcript and catalog from each college attended. SAT or ACT scores may be required on an individual basis. An interview is recommended. 36 of 144 credits required for the bachelor's degree must be completed at Salem.

Visiting: There are regularly scheduled orientations for prospective students. There are guides for informal visits; visitors may sit in on classes and stay overnight. To schedule a visit, contact the Admissions Office.

Financial Aid: The FAFSA and the college's own financial statement are required. Check with the school for current application deadlines.

International Students: The school actively recruits these students. They must take the TOEFL. They must also take the SAT or ACT.

Computers: Wireless access is available in various locations on campus; computers are available in 2 labs and in the library. All residence hall rooms and classrooms have Internet access ports. All students may access the system 24 hours a day. There are no time limits and no fees.

Admissions Contact: Dean of Admissions and Financial Aid. E-Mail: *admissions@salem.edu* Web: *www.salem.edu*

SHAW UNIVERSITY

D-2

Raleigh, NC 27601

(919) 546-8275
(800) 214-6683; (919) 546-8271

Full-time: 875 men, 1425 women	**Faculty:** n/av; IIB, --$
Part-time: 100 men, 195 women	**Ph.D.s:** n/av
Graduate: 100 men, 110 women	**Student/Faculty:** n/av
Year: semesters, summer session	**Tuition:** $12,676
Application Deadline: see profile	**Room & Board:** $8000
Freshman Class: n/av	
SAT or ACT: required	

LESS COMPETITIVE

Shaw University, founded in 1865, is a private liberal arts university affiliated with the Baptist Church. The figures in the above capsule and in this profile are approximate. There is 1 graduate school. In addition to regional accreditation, Shaw has baccalaureate program accreditation with NCATE. The library contains 153,304 volumes, 138,950 microform items, and 1306 audio/video tapes/CDs/DVDs, and subscribes to 15,357 periodicals including electronic. Computerized library services include interlibrary loans, database searching, and Internet access. Special learning facilities include a learning resource center, radio station, praxis lab, Academic Assessment and Achievement Center (AAA), and kinesiotherapy clinic. The 30-acre campus is in an urban area in downtown Raleigh. Including any residence halls, there are 23 buildings.

Student Life: 73% of undergraduates are from North Carolina. Others are from 32 states and 10 foreign countries. 94% are African American. The average age of freshmen is 24; all undergraduates, 28.

Housing: 1293 students can be accommodated in college housing, which includes single-sex dorms. On-campus housing is available on a first-come, first-served basis. 62% of students commute. Alcohol is not permitted. Upperclassmen may keep cars.

Activities: 4% of men belong to 4 national fraternities; 5% of women belong to 4 national sororities. There are 30 groups on campus, including band, cheerleading, choir, chorus, criminal justice and business, dance, drama, ethnic, honors, international, jazz band, marching band, musical theater, newspaper, pep band, professional, radio and TV, religious, social, social service, student government, and yearbook. Popular campus events include Career Day, Awards Day, and Religious Emphasis Week.

Sports: There are 7 intercollegiate sports for men and 7 for women, and 5 intramural sports for men and 4 for women.

Disabled Students: Facilities include wheelchair ramps, elevators, special parking, specially equipped rest rooms, lowered drinking fountains, and labels in braille.

Services: Counseling and information services are available, as is tutoring in some subjects, including English, math, biology, chemistry, physical science, statistics, and social science. There is remedial math, reading, and writing. There is peer tutoring in accounting.

Campus Safety and Security: Measures include 24-hour foot and vehicle patrol, self-defense education, and security escort services. There are lighted pathways/sidewalks and 24-hour electronic surveillance.

Programs of Study: Shaw confers B.A. and B.S. degrees. Associates and master's degrees are also awarded. Bachelor's degrees are awarded in BIOLOGICAL SCIENCE (biology/biological science), BUSINESS (accounting, business administration and management, and recreation and leisure services), COMMUNICATIONS AND THE ARTS (broadcasting, English, and visual and performing arts), COMPUTER AND PHYSICAL SCIENCE (chemistry, computer science, mathematics, and physics), EDUCATION (athletic training, elementary education, English education, mathematics education, physical education, science education, secondary education, social studies education, and special education), ENGINEERING AND ENVIRONMENTAL DESIGN (environmental science and preengineering), HEALTH PROFESSIONS (recreation therapy, rehabilitation therapy, and speech pathology/audiology), SOCIAL SCIENCE (African studies, criminal justice, gerontology, international relations, international studies, liberal arts/general studies, political science/government, psychology, public administration, religion, social work, and sociology). Business administration/management, criminal justice, and sociology have the largest enrollments.

Required: To graduate (in most majors), students must earn 120 credits, maintain a minimum GPA of 2.0, and successfully complete competency exams in math and English. The general core curriculum includes a total of 54 credits in college orientation, English, math, ethics, humanities, natural sciences, and social sciences.

Special: Shaw offers cross-registration with 4 other North Carolina colleges, internships, a work-study program, a 3-2 engineering degree with North Carolina State University and North Carolina Agricultural and Technical State University, dual and student-designed majors, independent study, and an external degree program for working adults. There are 4 national honor societies and a freshman honors program.

Faculty/Classroom: 94% teach undergraduates. No introductory courses are taught by graduate students. The average class size in a laboratory is 8 and in a regular course is 13.

Requirements: The SAT or ACT is required. In addition, applicants must be graduates of an accredited secondary school or have a GED certificate. They should have completed 3 units of English, 2 each of math, natural science (with 1 in a lab course), and social science, and 4 of academic electives. Admission to the Teacher Education Program follows separate guidelines. A GPA of 2.0 is required. AP and CLEP credits are accepted. Important factors in the admissions decision are advanced placement or honors courses, personality/intangible qualities, and recommendations by school officials.

Procedure: Freshmen are admitted to all sessions. Entrance exams should be taken prior to enrollment. There are deferred admissions and rolling admissions plans. Check with the school for current application deadlines. Applications are accepted online.

Transfer: Applicants must submit official transcripts from all colleges attended. Transfer credit is given only for course work of grade C or better completed at an accredited degree-granting institution. 30 of 120 credits required for the bachelor's degree must be completed at Shaw.

Visiting: There are regularly scheduled orientations for prospective students, consisting of parent visitation, tours, general administration, and registration. There are guides for informal visits and visitors may sit in on classes. To schedule a visit, contact the Admissions Office.

Financial Aid: The FAFSA is required. Check with the school for current application deadlines.

International Students: The school actively recruits these students. They must take the SAT or ACT.

Computers: All students may access the system. There are no time limits. It is strongly recommended that all students have a personal computer.

Admissions Contact: Alfonzo Carter, Interim Dean of Enrollment. E-Mail: *alcarter@shaw.edu* Web: *www.shawuniversity.edu*

ST. ANDREWS UNIVERSITY — D-3
Saint Andrews Presbyterian College

Laurinburg, NC 28352 (910) 277-5555; (800) 763-0198; (910) 277-5087

Full-time: 201 men, 237 women	**Faculty:** 27
Part-time: 6 men, 16 women	**Ph.D.s:** 60%
Graduate: 3 men, 11 women	**Student/Faculty:** 13 to 1
Year: semesters, summer session	**Tuition:** $22,674
Application Deadline: open	**Room & Board:** $9376
Freshman Class: 599 applied, 442 accepted, 142 enrolled	
SAT CR/M: 460/480	**ACT:** 19 **LESS COMPETITIVE**

St. Andrews University, formerly St. Andrews Presbyterian College, founded in 1896, is a private liberal arts institution affiliated with the Presbyterian Church. Recently merged with Webber International University. The library contains 110,105 volumes, 14,204 microform items, and 1,676 audio/video tapes/CDs/DVDs, and subscribes to 416 periodicals including electronic. Computerized library services include interlibrary loans and database searching. Special learning facilities include an art gallery, a 20,000-square-foot science lab, an artronics lab, and a writing lab. The 600-acre campus is in a small town about 100 miles from Charlotte. Including any residence halls, there are 17 buildings.

Student Life: 57% of undergraduates are from out of state, mostly the South. Students are from 35 states, 9 foreign countries, and Canada. 92% are from public schools. 69% are White; 19% African American. 40% are Protestant. The average age of freshmen is 18; all undergraduates, 20. 38% do not continue beyond their first year; 62% remain to graduate.

Housing: 766 students can be accommodated in college housing, which includes single-sex and coed dorms. On-campus housing is guaranteed for all 4 years. 75% of students live on campus; of those, 90% remain on campus on weekends. All students may keep cars.

Activities: There are no fraternities or sororities. There are 27 groups on campus, including art, bagpipe, choir, chorale, chorus, computers, debate, drama, environmental, ethnic, film, forensics, gay, honors, international, literary magazine, musical theater, newspaper, political, professional, radio and TV, religious, social, social service, student government, and yearbook. Popular campus events include Writers' Forum, Extravaganza Weekend and Springfest.

Sports: There are 8 intercollegiate sports for men and 8 for women, and 9 intramural sports for men and 9 for women. Facilities include a basketball and volleyball arena, equestrian facilities, a pool, soccer, baseball, and softball fields.

Disabled Students: 90% of the campus is accessible. Facilities include wheelchair ramps, elevators, special parking, specially equipped restrooms, lowered drinking fountains, lowered telephones, and personal aides.

Services: Counseling and information services are available, as is tutoring in most subjects.

Campus Safety and Security: Measures include 24-hour foot and vehicle patrol, emergency notification system, and security escort services. There are lighted pathways/sidewalks.

Programs of Study: St. Andrews confers B.A, B.S. and B.F.A. degrees. Master's degrees are also awarded. Bachelor's degrees are awarded in BIOLOGICAL SCIENCE (biology/biological science), BUSINESS (business administration and management), COMMUNICATIONS AND THE ARTS (creative writing and visual and performing arts), EDUCATION (elementary education, physical education, and sports studies), SOCIAL SCIENCE (forensic studies, humanities, interdisciplinary studies, psychology, social science, and therapeutic riding). Business and economics, equine studies, and biology are the strongest academically. Elementary education and physical education have the largest enrollments.

Required: To graduate, students must complete a total of 120 hours with a minimum GPA of 2.0. Between 10 and 15 courses are required in the student's major. All students must complete 16 hours in the interdisciplinary St. Andrews general education core program. In addition, students must satisfy breadth requirements in the creative arts, lab sciences, American Foundations, Literature Classics, and foreign language

Special: St. Andrew's offers disciplinary and student-designed majors for contract, nondegree study, on-campus work-study, and pass/fail options. Students may study abroad in 11 countries. There is a 3-2 engineering program with North Carolina State University and there are year-long, semester-long, and summer-term internships in all majors. There are 4 national honor societies, a freshman honors program, and 8 departmental honors programs.

Faculty/Classroom: 40% of faculty are male, 60% are female. All teach undergraduates. No introductory courses are taught by graduate students. The average class size in an introductory lecture is 15; in a laboratory is 15; and in a regular course is 15.

Admissions: 74% of the 2013-2014 applicants were accepted. The SAT scores for the 2013-2014 freshman class were: Critical Reading--67% below 500, 27% between 500 and 599, 4% between 600 and 699; Math--66% below 500, 29% between 500 and 599, 5% between 600 and 699.

Requirements: The SAT or ACT is required, with a satisfactory score on the SAT. Graduation from an accredited secondary school or the GED is required for admission. High school courses should include 3 units of English, 3 each of science and math, and 1 of a foreign language, 3 units of social studies and electives. A GPA of 2.5 is required. AP and CLEP credits are accepted. Important factors in the admissions decision are personality/intangible qualities, recommendations by school officials, and evidence of special talent.

Procedure: Freshmen are admitted to all sessions. Entrance exams should be taken as early as possible. There are deferred admissions and rolling admissions plans. Application deadlines are open. Application fee is $30. Applications are accepted online.

Transfer: 47 transfer students enrolled in 2012-2013. Transfer students must have a minimum GPA of 2.0. Up to 65 semester or 97 quarter hours may be transferred from a 2-year college and 90 semester or 135 quarter hours from a 4-year college. 30 of 120 credits required for the bachelor's degree must be completed at St. Andrews.

Visiting: There are regularly scheduled orientations for prospective students, including activities, fairs, information sessions, summer orientation sessions with activities, and preregistration. There are guides for informal visits and visitors may sit in on classes. To schedule a visit, contact the Admissions Office.

Financial Aid: In 2013-2014, 99% of all full-time freshmen and 99% of continuing full-time students received some form of financial aid. 80% of all full-time freshmen and 60% of continuing full-time students received need-based aid. The average freshman award was $14,920. Need-based scholarships or need-based grants averaged $4,458 ($7,554 maximum); need-based self-help aid (loans and jobs) averaged $2,884 ($11,300 maximum); non-need-based athletic scholarships averaged $5,000 ($21,000 maximum); and other non-need-based awards and non-need-based scholarships averaged $10,284 ($14,500 maximum). 42% of undergraduate students work part-time. Average annual earnings from campus work are $1800. The average financial indebtedness of the 2013 graduate was $31,648. The FAFSA is required. The priority date for freshman financial aid applications for fall entry is May 1. The deadline for filing freshman financial aid applications for fall entry is August 15.

International Students: There are 31 international students enrolled. The school actively recruits these students. They must take the TOEFL.

Computers: All students may access the system every day, 24 hours a day. There are no time limits and no fees.

Graduates: From July 1, 2012 to June 30, 2013, 135 bachelor's degrees were awarded. The most popular majors were education (14%), business administration (13%), and biology (12%). In an average class, 1% graduate in 3 years or less, 33% graduate in 4 years or less, 36% graduate in 5 years or less, and 38% graduate in 6 years or less. Of the 2012 graduating class, 25% were enrolled in graduate school within 6 months of graduation, and 50% were employed.

Admissions Contact: Jeff Bennett, Vice President for Enrollment and Student Services. E-Mail: *admissions@sapc.edu* Web: *www.sapc.edu*

UNIVERSITY OF NORTH CAROLINA SYSTEM

The University of North Carolina System, established in 1931, is a public system in North Carolina. It is governed by the University of North Carolina board of governors, whose chief administrator is the president. The primary goal of the system is to discover, create, transmit, and apply knowledge to address the needs of North Carolina and its people. The main priorities are teaching/instruction, research/scholarship/creative activities, public service (solving societal problems and enriching quality of life). The student enrollment for all 16 campuses is usually 155,800, with 9000 faculty members. Altogether there are 647 baccalaureate, 451 master's, and 138 doctoral programs offered in the University of North Carolina System. Profiles of the 4-year campuses are included in this section.

UNIVERSITY OF NORTH CAROLINA AT ASHEVILLE B-2

Asheville, NC 28804 **(828) 251-6481**
(800) 531-9842; (828) 251-6482

Full-time: 1316 men, 1738 women | **Faculty:** 213; IIB, av$
Part-time: 234 men, 405 women | **Ph.D.s:** 84%
Graduate: 20 men, 38 women | **Student/Faculty:** 14 to 1
Year: semesters, summer session | **Tuition:** $5916 ($19,732)
Application Deadline: February 15 | **Room & Board:** $7584
Freshman Class: 3018 applied, 1926 accepted, 553 enrolled
SAT CR/M/W: 600/590/570 **ACT:** 25 **VERY COMPETITIVE+**

The University of North Carolina at Asheville is the designated public liberal arts university in the 16-campus UNC system. There is one graduate school. In addition to regional accreditation, UNC Asheville has baccalaureate program accreditation with AACSB and NCATE. The library contains 280,449 volumes, 182,062 microform items, and 8,494 audio/video tapes/CDs/DVDs, and subscribes to 78,979 periodicals including electronic. Computerized library services include interlibrary loans, database searching, Internet access, and Wi-Fi capability. Special learning facilities include an art gallery, and radio station, The 365-acre campus is in an urban area approximately one mile north of downtown Asheville. Including any residence halls, there are 34 buildings.

Student Life: 88% of undergraduates are from North Carolina. Others are from 40 states, 23 foreign countries, and Canada. 85% are White. The average age of freshmen is 18; all undergraduates, 23. 22% do not continue beyond their first year; 55% remain to graduate.

Housing: 1266 students can be accommodated in college housing, which includes single-sex and coed dorms. In addition, there are honors houses, quiet dorms, and substance-free housing. On-campus housing is guaranteed for the freshman year only. 62% of students commute. Upperclassmen may keep cars.

Activities: 3% of men belong to 2 national fraternities; 3% of women belong to 2 national sororities. There are 66 groups on campus, including art, band, cheerleading, choir, chorus, computers, dance, departmental, drama, environmental, ethnic, gay, honors, international, jazz band, literary magazine, newspaper, pep band, political, professional, religious, social, social service, and student government. Popular campus events include Homecoming, Lawn Party, Family Weekend and Rockypalooza.

Sports: There are 8 intercollegiate sports for men and 8 for women, and 17 intramural sports for men and 18 for women. Facilities include a sports and health complex with a state-of-the-art weight/cardio room, educational kitchen, Wellness Café, 4 basketball courts, volleyball and racquetball courts, multiple dance and group exercise studios, an indoor swimming pool, basketball arena, indoor and outdoor tracks, soccer and baseball fields, and disc golf course. Campus Recreation Department also hosts outings for mountain biking, paddling, hiking and other outdoor activities. The campus features more than 5 miles of wooded hiking/walking trails.

Disabled Students: 97% of the campus is accessible. Facilities include wheelchair ramps, elevators, special parking, specially equipped restrooms, special class scheduling, lowered drinking fountains, lowered telephones, special housing.

Services: Counseling and information services are available, as is tutoring in most subjects. There is a reader service for the blind.

Campus Safety and Security: Measures include 24-hour foot and vehicle patrol, emergency notification system, self-defense education, and security escort services. There are shuttle buses, emergency telephones, lighted pathways/sidewalks, and controlled access to dorms/residences.

Programs of Study: UNC Asheville confers B.A., B.S. and B.F.A. degrees. Master's degrees are also awarded. Bachelor's degrees are awarded in BIOLOGICAL SCIENCE (biology/biological science), BUSINESS (accounting and business administration and management), COMMUNICATIONS AND THE ARTS (art, classics, communications, dramatic arts, fine arts, French, German, literature, multimedia, music, music technology, and Spanish), COMPUTER AND PHYSICAL SCIENCE (atmospheric sciences and meteorology, chemistry, computer science, mathematics, and physics), ENGINEERING AND ENVIRONMENTAL DESIGN (engineering, engineering management, environmental science, and industrial administration/management), HEALTH PROFESSIONS (health and health promotion), SOCIAL SCIENCE (anthropology, economics, history, liberal arts/general studies, philosophy, political science/government, psychology, religion, sociology, and women's studies). Psychology, environmental studies, and literature have the largest enrollments.

Required: To graduate, students must complete a minimum of 120 credit hours, including at least 27 hours in the major, to include a senior capstone experience. The core curriculum requires a 3 hour Liberal Studies Introductory Colloquium; 12 hours of humanities; 3 hours of interdisciplinary arts; a minimum of 7 hours of natural science including lab; 3 hours of social science; up to 6 hours of foreign language; 4 hours of math; 4 hours of academic writing; 2 hours of health and wellness; and a 4 hour Liberal Studies Senior Colloquium. Students take their non-lab natural science and social science courses with an additional liberal arts elective, within an integrative topical cluster. In addition, students are required to do intensive course work in writing, information literacy quantitative reasoning, and diversity. these courses can be taken in the major, in general education, or in electives, and need not add credit hours to the students program.

Special: UNC Asheville participates in a consortium with Warren Wilson and Mars Hill Colleges, and there is cross-registration with a number of North Carolina universities and colleges. Study-abroad programs are available in 46 countries. The school offers internships, dual majors, student-designed interdisciplinary majors, and a 2-2 engineering degree and joint engineering degree with North Carolina State University. Nondegree study is available. There are 16 national honor societies, a freshman honors program, and 13 departmental honors programs.

Faculty/Classroom: 55% of faculty are male; 45% are female. All teach undergraduates. No introductory courses are taught by graduate students. The average class size in an introductory lecture is 22; in a laboratory is 18; and in a regular course is 17.

Admissions: 64% of the 2013-2014 applicants were accepted. The SAT scores for the 2013-2014 freshman class were: Critical Reading--7% below 500, 41% between 500 and 599, 42% between 600 and 699, and 11% between 700 and 800; Math--5% below 500, 46% between 500 and 599, 42% between 600 and 699, and 7% between 700 and 800; Writing--15% below 500, 47% between 500 and 599, 31% between 600 and 699, and 6% between 700 and 800. The ACT scores were 5% below 21, 22% between 21 and 23, 39% between 24 and 26, 17% between 27 and 28, and 18% above 28. 46% of the current freshmen were in the top fifth of their class; 82% were in the top two fifths. 4 freshmen graduated first in their class.

Requirements: The SAT or ACT is required. The ACT Optional Writing test is also required. Graduation from an accredited secondary school is required. UNC Asheville requires a minimum of 16 high school academic units, including 4 of English, 4 of math (algebra I, geometry, algebra II, and a class beyond algebra II), 3 science (biology, physical science, and a lab course), 2 of social studies/history, and 2 of a foreign language which needs to be a sequence (Spanish I & II, French I & II, etc). Applicants are evaluated primarily on their academic achievement record, extracurricular activities that support academic achievement, and SAT or ACT scores. AP and CLEP credits are accepted. Important factors in the admissions decision are advanced placement or honors courses, leadership record, and evidence of special talent.

Procedure: Freshmen are admitted fall and spring. Entrance exams should be taken at the end of the junior year or the beginning of the senior year. There are early decision, early admissions, deferred admissions, and rolling admissions plans. Early decision applications should be filed by November 15; regular applications, by February 15 for fall entry; and October 15 for spring entry, along with a $50 fee. Notification of early decision is sent December 15; regular decision, on a rolling basis. Applications are accepted online.

Transfer: 325 transfer students enrolled in 2012-2013. Applicants under 24 years of age or with fewer than 24 semester or 36 quarter credit hours must submit high school transcripts and SAT or ACT scores. 30 of 120 credits required for the bachelor's degree must be completed at UNC Asheville.

Visiting: There are regularly scheduled orientations for prospective students, including meetings with admissions counselors, faculty, or other departments, information session for students and families, and a campus tour. Preregistration is prior to fall enrollment during the summer months. There are guides for informal visits, visitors may sit in on classes, and stay overnight. To schedule a visit, contact the Office of Admissions, Visit Coordinator at (828) 350-4553.

Financial Aid: In 2013-2014, 74% of all full-time freshmen and 71% of continuing full-time students received some form of financial aid. 62% of all full-time freshmen and 62% of continuing full-time students received need-based aid. The average freshman award was $9,522. Need-based scholarships or need-based grants averaged $5,687 ($17,227 maximum); need-based self-help aid (loans and jobs) averaged $4,032 ($21,100 maximum); non-need-based athletic scholarships averaged $9,007 ($28,509 maximum); and other non-need-based awards and non-need-based scholarships averaged $3,153 ($9,500 maximum). 17% of undergraduate students work part-time. Average annual earnings from campus work are $2600. The average financial indebtedness of the 2013 graduate was $17,600. The FAFSA is required. The priority date for freshman financial aid applications for fall entry is March 1.

International Students: There are 41 international students enrolled. The school actively recruits these students. They must take the TOEFL with a minimum score of 550 on the paper-based TOEFL (PBT) or 79 on the Internet-based version (iBT). They must also take the SAT or ACT.

Computers: All students may access the system 24 hours a day. There are no time limits and no fees.

Graduates: From July 1, 2012 to June 30, 2013, 713 bachelor's degrees were awarded. The most popular majors were psychology (15%), health and wellness promotion (7%), and literature (7%). 130 companies recruited on campus in 2012-2013. In an average class, 38% graduate in 4 years or less, 53% graduate in 5 years or less, and 58% graduate in 6 years or less. Of the 2012 graduating class, 19% were enrolled in graduate school within 6 months of graduation.

Admissions Contact: Shannon Earle, Director of Admissions. E-Mail: *admissions@unca.edu* Web: *www.unca.edu/admissions*

UNIVERSITY OF NORTH CAROLINA AT CHAPEL HILL D-2

Chapel Hill, NC 27599 (919) 962-3621; (919) 962-3045

Full-time: 7296 men, 10274 women	**Faculty:** 1044; I, av$
Part-time: 400 men, 400 women	**Ph.D.s:** 90%
Graduate: 4746 men, 6011 women	**Student/Faculty:** 14 to 1
Year: semesters, summer session	**Tuition:** $8340 ($30,122)
Application Deadline: January 7	**Room & Board:** $10,008

Freshman Class: 28437 applied, 7847 accepted, 3915 enrolled

SAT CR/M/W: 640/660/640 **ACT:** 29 **MOST COMPETITIVE**

Carolina's vibrant people and programs attest to the University's long-standing place among leaders in higher education since it was chartered in 1789 and opened its doors for students in 1795 as the nation's first public university. There are 9 undergraduate schools and 13 graduate schools. In addition to regional accreditation, UNC-Chapel Hill has baccalaureate program accreditation with AACSB, ACEJMC, ACPE, ADA, APTA, CSWE, NCATE, and NLN. The 15 libraries contain 7.6 million volumes, 5.3 million microform items, and 476,644 audio/video tapes/CDs/DVDs, and subscribe to 113,065 periodicals including electronic. Computerized library services include interlibrary loans, database searching, Internet access, and Wi-Fi capability. Special learning facilities include an art gallery, planetarium, radio station, TV station, botanical garden and theater. The 729-acre campus is in a suburban area 25 miles west of Raleigh. Including any residence halls, there are 683 buildings.

Student Life: 82% of undergraduates are from North Carolina. Others are from 50 states, 106 foreign countries, and Canada. 82% are from public schools. 66% are White. The average age of freshmen is 17; all undergraduates, 19. 4% do not continue beyond their first year; 90% remain to graduate.

Housing: 10223 students can be accommodated in college housing, which includes single-sex and coed dorms, on-campus apartments, off-campus apartments, and married student housing. In addition, there are honors houses, language houses, special-interest houses, fraternity houses, sorority houses, and substance-free housing. On-campus housing is guaranteed for the freshman year only and is available on a lottery system for upperclassmen. 53% of students live on campus; of those, 80% remain on campus on weekends. Upperclassmen may keep cars.

Activities: 17% of men belong to 32 national fraternities; 17% of women belong to 23 national sororities. There are 671 groups on campus, including and public/community service, games/e-sports, Greek alliance council, panhellenic council, academic, art, band, cheerleading, chess, choir, chorale, chorus, computers, dance, debate, drama, drill team, environmental, ethnic, film, forensics, gay, honors, international, jazz band, literary magazine, marching band, musical theater, newspaper, opera, orchestra, pep band, photography, political, professional, radio and TV, religious, social, social service, student government, symphony, and yearbook. Popular campus events include FallFest, SpringFest, Derby Days, Homecoming, Unity Conference and Midnight Madness Basketball.

Sports: There are 13 intercollegiate sports for men and 15 for women, and 38 intramural sports for men and 34 for women. Facilities include a 60,000-seat football stadium, 3 swimming pools, a 21,000-seat sports and student activities center, tennis courts, lacrosse and soccer fields, golf course, boathouse, gym facilities, softball fields, and a student recreation center with aerobics, weights, and wellness programs.

Disabled Students: 97% of the campus is accessible. Facilities include wheelchair ramps, elevators, special parking, lowered drinking fountains, and special housing.

Services: Counseling and information services are available, as is tutoring in most subjects. There is a reader service for the blind.

Campus Safety and Security: Measures include 24-hour foot and vehicle patrol, emergency notification system, self-defense education, and security escort services. There are shuttle buses, emergency telephones, lighted pathways/sidewalks, controlled access to dorms/residences, building security surveys.

Programs of Study: UNC-Chapel Hill confers B.A., B.S., B.A.E.D., B.A.J.M.C., B.F.A., B.M.U.S., B.S.B.A., B.S.N., B.S.P.H., B.S.Ph.S. and B.S.I.S. degrees. Master's and doctoral degrees are also awarded. Bachelor's degrees are awarded in AGRICULTURE (environmental studies), BIOLOGICAL SCIENCE (biology/biological science, biometrics and biostatistics, and nutrition), BUSINESS (business administration and management, management science, and recreational facilities management), COMMUNICATIONS AND THE ARTS (art history and appreciation, classics, communications, comparative literature, dramatic arts, English, German, journalism, linguistics, music, music performance, romance languages and literature, Russian, and studio art), COMPUTER AND PHYSICAL SCIENCE (applied mathematics, applied science, chemistry, computer science, geology, information sciences and systems, mathematics, and physics), EDUCATION (elementary education and middle school education), ENGINEERING AND ENVIRONMENTAL DESIGN (environmental science), HEALTH PROFESSIONS (clinical science, dental hygiene, environmental health science, exercise science, health care administration, nursing, pharmaceutical science, and radiological science), SOCIAL SCIENCE (African American studies, American studies, anthropology, archeology, Asian/Oriental studies, child care/child and family studies, economics, European studies, geography, history, interdisciplinary studies, international studies, Latin American studies, peace studies, philosophy, political science/government, psychology, public affairs, religion, Russian and Slavic studies, sociology, and women's studies). Psychology, biology, journalism/mass communication and business administration have the largest enrollments.

Required: To graduate, students must complete 120 credits (more for some B.S. degrees) with a 2.0 GPA. The general education requirements fall under 3 categories: Foundations, Approaches, and Connections. B.A. degree candidates must satisfy a supplemental education requirement by completing a second major or a minor, by completing - in addition to a student's major requirements - 9 credit hours outside the home department of the major, or by completing a concentration outside a professional school as part of the degree requirements for graduating from that school.

Special: Students may participate in joint programs with Duke University, North Carolina State University, and the National University of Singapore (NUS). Internships at home and abroad, a Washington semester focusing on international affairs, study abroad in 70 countries, B.A.-B.S. degrees, a Sea Semester, and student-designed majors are available. There are pass/fail options and non-degree study. There are 28 national honor societies, including Phi Beta Kappa, a freshman honors program, and 53 departmental honors programs.

Faculty/Classroom: 57% of faculty are male; 43% are female. 58% teach undergraduates. Graduate students teach 42% of introductory courses. The average class size in an introductory lecture is 43; in a laboratory is 20; and in a regular course is 36.

Admissions: 28% of the 2013-2014 applicants were accepted. The SAT scores for the 2013-2014 freshman class were: Critical Reading--3% below 500, 24% between 500 and 599, 47% between 600 and 699, and 27% between 700 and 800; Math--2% below 500, 19% between 500 and 599, 49% between 600 and 699, and 30% between 700 and 800; Writing--4% below 500, 24% between 500 and 599, 47% between 600 and 699, and 24% between 700 and 800. The ACT scores were 1% below 21, 7% between 21 and 23, 19% between 24 and 26, 19% between 27 and 28, and 53% above 28. 94% of the current freshmen were in the top fifth of their class; 99% were in the top two fifths. There were 99 National Merit finalists. 204 freshmen graduated first in their class.

Requirements: The SAT or ACT is required. The ACT Optional Writing test is also required. Applicants should present a minimum of 16 units of high school coursework within the 5 traditional academic areas (literature, math, physical and biological sciences, social sciences, and foreign languages), including 4 units of English; at least 4 units of college preparatory mathematics (2 algebra, 1 geometry, and a higher level math course for which algebra II is a prerequisite); at least 2 units of a single foreign language; 3 units in science, including at least 1 unit in a life or biological science and at least 1 in a physical science, and including at least 1 lab course; and 2 units of social science, including United States history. AP credits are accepted.

Procedure: Freshmen are admitted fall. Entrance exams should be taken in the junior or senior year. There are early admissions and deferred admissions plans. Early decision applications should be filed by October 15; regular applications, by January 7 for fall entry, along with a $80 fee. Notification of early decision is sent January 30; regular decision, March 20. 2445 applicants were on the 2013 waiting list; 384 were admitted. Applications are accepted online.

Transfer: 845 transfer students enrolled in 2012-2013. Sophomore transfers need at least 30 credit hours and a minimum GPA of 2.0; junior transfers need at least 60 credit hours and a minimum GPA of 2.0. High school diploma or equivalent, meeting minimum course requirements, also required. 45 of 120 credits required for the bachelor's degree must be completed at UNC-Chapel Hill.

Visiting: There are regularly scheduled orientations for prospective students, including campus tours and information sessions, offered twice each weekday. Visitors may sit in on classes. To schedule a visit, contact the Office of Undergraduate Admissions.

Financial Aid: In 2013-2014, 69% of all full-time freshmen and 63% of continuing full-time students received some form of financial aid. 41% of all full-time freshmen and 42% of continuing full-time students received need-based aid. The average freshman award was $13,995. Need-based scholarships or need-based grants averaged $12,428 ($51,640 maximum); need-based self-help aid (loans and jobs) averaged $3,459 ($9,271 maximum); non-need-based athletic scholarships averaged $21,365 ($48,628 maximum); other non-need-based awards and non-need-based scholarships averaged $4,672 ($44,726 maximum); and $5,742 from other forms of aid. Average annual earnings from campus work are $1839. The average financial indebtedness of the 2013 graduate was $16,983. UNC-Chapel Hill is a member of CSS. The CSS/Profile and FAFSA are required. The priority date for freshman financial aid applications for fall entry is March 1.

International Students: There are 476 international students enrolled. The school actively recruits these students. They must take the TOEFL with a minimum score of 600 on the paper-based TOEFL (PBT) or 100 on the Internet-based version (iBT). They must also take the SAT or ACT.

Computers: All students may access the system 24 hours a day. There are no time limits. The fee is $435.

Graduates: From July 1, 2012 to June 30, 2013, 4627 bachelor's degrees were awarded. The most popular majors were psychology (10%), biology (9%), and journalism and mass communication (8%). 216 companies recruited on campus in 2012-2013. In an average class, 2% graduate in 3 years or less, 81% graduate in 4 years or less, 89% graduate in 5 years or less, and 90% graduate in 6 years or less. Of the 2012 graduating class, 26% were enrolled in graduate school within 6 months of graduation, and 60% were employed.

Admissions Contact: Office of Undergraduate Admisstions E-Mail: *unchelp@admissions.unc.edu* Web: *www.admissions.unc.edu*

UNIVERSITY OF NORTH CAROLINA AT CHARLOTTE C-3

Charlotte, NC 28223 **(704) 687-5507; (704) 687-6483**

Full-time: 9549 men, 8760 women
Part-time: 1535 men, 1659 women
Graduate: 2069 men, 2999 women
Year: semesters, summer session
Application Deadline: July 1
Faculty: n/av; I, --$
Ph.D.s: 69%
Student/Faculty: n/av
Tuition: $6107 ($18,636)
Room & Board: $9740
Freshman Class: 13742 applied, 9416 accepted, 3541 enrolled
SAT CR/M/W: 520/540/500 **ACT:** 22 **COMPETITIVE**

UNC Charlotte is a vibrant urban research university committed to high quality undergraduate and graduate education. There are 8 undergraduate schools and 1 graduate school. In addition to regional accreditation, UNC-Charlotte has baccalaureate program accreditation with AACSB, ABET, CSWE, NAAB, and NCATE. The library contains 1.1 million volumes, 2.2 million microfilm items, 32,948 audio/video tapes/CDs/DVDs, and subscribes to 57,471 periodicals including electronic. Computerized library services include interlibrary loans, database searching, Internet access, and Wi-Fi capability. Special learning facilities include an art gallery, radio station, and TV station. The 1000-acre campus is in a suburban area 8 miles north of uptown Charlotte, North Carolina. Including any residence halls, there are 109 buildings. There are 8 undergraduate schools and one graduate school. Including any residence halls, there are 32 buildings.

Student Life: 94% of undergraduates are from North Carolina. Others are from 47 states, 88 foreign countries, and Canada. 61% are White; 17% African American. The average age of freshmen is 18; all undergraduates, 22. 20% do not continue beyond their first year; 80% remain to graduate.

Housing: 5643 students can be accommodated in college housing, which includes single-sex and coed dorms and on-campus apartments. In addition, there are honors houses, special-interest houses, fraternity houses, and sorority houses. On-campus housing is available on a first-come, first-served basis, and is available on a lottery system for upperclassmen. 76% of students commute. All students may keep cars.

Activities: 3% of men belong to 21 national fraternities; 4% of women belong to 15 national sororities. There are 375 groups on campus, including art, cheerleading, chess, choir, chorale, chorus, communications, computers, dance, debate, drama, environmental, ethnic, film, forensics, gay, honors, international, jazz band, literary magazine, musical theater, newspaper, opera, pep band, photography, political, professional, radio and TV, religious, social, social service, and student government. Popular campus events include Week of Welcome, Greek Week, International Festival and Homecoming.

Sports: There are 9 intercollegiate sports for men and 8 for women, and 24 intramural sports for men and 24 for women. Facilities include The Belk Gymnasium has multiple basketball courts, two racquetball and three squash courts, and a Olympic-size swimming pool. The James H. Barnhardt Student Activity Center contains a jogging track, recreational courts, climbing wall, weight room, group fitness room, training center and a 10,000 seat event arena. There are also 8 outdoor recreational fields along with tennis, sand volleyball, and basketball courts.

Disabled Students: 90% of the campus is accessible. Facilities include wheelchair ramps, elevators, special parking, specially equipped restrooms, special class scheduling, lowered drinking fountains, lowered telephones, special housing. The Disability Services Office assists students with all academic and physical accommodations.

Services: Counseling and information services are available, as is tutoring in some subjects. There is a reader service for the blind.

Campus Safety and Security: Measures include 24-hour foot and vehicle patrol, emergency notification system, self-defense education, and security escort services. There are shuttle buses, emergency telephones, and lighted pathways/sidewalks.

Programs of Study: UNC-Charlotte confers B.A., B.S., B.Arch., B.F.A., B.M., B.S.B.A, B.S.C.E., B.S.Cp.E, B.S.C.M., B.S.E.E., B.S.E.T., B.S.P.H. B.S.R.T., B.S.M.E., B.S.N. and B.S.W. degrees. Master's and doctoral degrees are also awarded. Bachelor's degrees are awarded in BIOLOGICAL SCIENCE (biology/biological science), BUSINESS (accounting, banking and finance, business administration and management, business economics, finance, international business management, management information systems, marketing, marketing/retailing/merchandising, real estate, and supply chain management), COMMUNICATIONS AND THE ARTS (art, art history and appreciation, communications, dance, dramatic arts, English, fine arts, French, German, music, music performance, Spanish, and theatre arts), COMPUTER AND PHYSICAL SCIENCE (atmospheric sciences and meteorology, chemistry, computer science, earth science, geology, mathematics, physics, and software engineering), EDUCATION (art education, athletic training, dance education, drama education, education of the mentally handicapped, elementary education, English education, foreign languages education, mathematics education, middle school education, music education, science education, social studies education, and special education), ENGINEERING AND ENVIRONMENTAL DESIGN (architecture, civil engineering, civil engineering technology, computer engineering, construction management, electrical/electronics engineering, electrical/electronics engineering technology, engineering technology, industrial administration/management, mechanical engineering, mechanical engineering technology, and systems engineering), HEALTH PROFESSIONS (exercise science, medical technology, nursing, public health, and respiratory therapy), SOCIAL SCIENCE (African American studies, anthropology, child care/child and family studies, child psychology/development, criminal justice, economics, fire control and safety technology, geography, history, international studies, Japanese studies, Latin American studies, liberal arts/general studies, philosophy, physical fitness/movement, political science/government, psychology, religion, religious studies, social work, and sociology). Engineering, business, and education are the strongest academically. Business, psychology, and biology have the largest enrollments.

Required: Students must complete a minimum of 120 credit hours with an overall minimum GPA of 2.0. Between 30 and 42 hours are required in the major with a minimum GPA of 2.0 in major and minor courses. All students must complete core requirements in the 6 interrelated areas of communication, problem solving, values, science and technology, arts, literature and ideas, and the individual, society, and culture.

Special: Cross-registration is available through the Charlotte Area Educational Consortium. Also available are cooperative programs in numerous majors and internships of 1 semester arranged with public and private community organizations. There are 23 national honor societies, a freshman honors program, and 21 departmental honors programs.

Faculty/Classroom: 51% of faculty are male; 49% are female. No introductory courses are taught by graduate students.

Admissions: 69% of the 2013-2014 applicants were accepted. The SAT scores for the 2013-2014 freshman class were: Critical Reading--36% below 500, 50% between 500 and 599, 13% between 600 and 699, and 1% between 700 and 800; Math--21% below 500, 53% between 500 and 599, 23% between 600 and 699, and 3% between 700 and 800; Writing--44% below 500, 46% between 500 and 599, 9% between 600 and 699, and 1% between 700 and 800. The ACT scores were 28% below 21, 35% between 21 and 23, 24% between 24 and 26, 7% between 27 and 28, and 6% above 28. 23% of the current freshmen were in the top fifth of their class; 43% were in the top two fifths. There were 257 National Merit finalists.

Requirements: The SAT or ACT is required. In addition, graduation from an accredited secondary school or the GED is required. The school requires 14 academic credits, including 4 years each of English, and math, 3 of science (including 1 of physical science), 2 of a foreign language, and 2 of social studies, including 1 of U.S. history. Seniors should select a challenging academic schedule that includes English, math, science, social studies or history and foreign language. A portfolio and interview are required for art and architecture students only. A GPA of 2.0 is required. AP and CLEP credits are accepted. Important factors in the admissions decision are advanced placement or honors courses, leadership record, and recommendations by school officials.

Procedure: Freshmen are admitted fall, spring, and summer. Entrance exams should be taken the end of the junior year or by December of the senior year. There are early admissions and rolling admissions plans. Applications should be filed by July 1 for fall entry; November 15 for spring entry; and May 1 for summer entry, along with a $60 fee. Notifications are sent December 15. Applications are accepted online.

Transfer: 2407 transfer students enrolled in 2012-2013. Transfer students must have a minimum GPA of 2.0 on all college courses attempted.

Certain majors have limited space and require a higher GPA and/or prerequisites. Applicants with fewer than 24 hours of transferable credit must meet both transfer and freshman admissions requirements. An interview is required only for architecture students. 30 of 120 credits required for the bachelor's degree must be completed at UNC-Charlotte.

Visiting: There are regularly scheduled orientations for prospective students, including tours. There are guides for informal visits, visitors may sit in on classes, and stay overnight. To schedule a visit, contact the Undergraduate Admissions Office.

Financial Aid: In 2013-2014, 63% of all full-time freshmen and 65% of continuing full-time students received some form of financial aid. 58% of all full-time freshmen and 57% of continuing full-time students received need-based aid. The average freshman award was $8,679. Need-based scholarships or need-based grants averaged $5,840; need-based self-help aid (loans and jobs) averaged $3,348; non-need-based athletic scholarships averaged $14,221; and other non-need-based awards and non-need-based scholarships averaged $7,434. 18% of undergraduate students work part-time. Average annual earnings from campus work are $2235. The average financial indebtedness of the 2013 graduate was $23,720. UNC-Charlotte is a member of CSS. The FAFSA is required. The priority date for freshman financial aid applications for fall entry is March 1.

International Students: There are 466 international students enrolled. They must take the TOEFL with a minimum score of 507 on the paper-based TOEFL (PBT) or 64 on the Internet-based version (iBT) or take the MELAB. They must also take the SAT or ACT. Students with a score of 450 or higher on the verbal part of the SAT are not required to take the TOEFL or other English Proficiency exam.

Computers: All students may access the system 24 hours per day. There are no time limits and no fees.

Graduates: From July 1, 2012 to June 30, 2013, 3964 bachelor's degrees were awarded. The most popular majors were business (20%), social sciences/psychology (8%), and health professions (8%). 290 companies recruited on campus in 2012-2013. In an average class, 1% graduate in 3 years or less, 26% graduate in 4 years or less, 47% graduate in 5 years or less, and 53% graduate in 6 years or less. Of the 2012 graduating class, 10% were enrolled in graduate school within 6 months of graduation, and 80% were employed.

Admissions Contact: Claire Kirby, Director of Admissions. E-Mail: *admissions@uncc.edu* Web: *www.uncc.edu*

UNIVERSITY OF NORTH CAROLINA AT GREENSBORO D-2

Greensboro, NC 27412 **(336) 334-5243; (336) 334-4180**

Full-time: 4481 men, 8429 women	**Faculty:** n/av; I, --$
Part-time: 581 men, 1183 women	**Ph.D.s:** 73%
Graduate: 1154 men, 2344 women	**Student/Faculty:** n/av
Year: semesters, summer session	**Tuition:** $6148 ($19,946)
Application Deadline: March 1	**Room & Board:** $6700
Freshman Class: n/av	

COMPETITIVE

The University of North Carolina at Greensboro, founded in 1891, is a publicly funded liberal arts institution in the University of North Carolina system. There are 7 undergraduate schools and 7 graduate schools. In addition to regional accreditation, UNCG has baccalaureate program accreditation with AACSB, ABET, ADA, NASAD, NASM, and NCATE. The 2 libraries contain 1.1 million volumes, 327,316 microform items, 53,052 audio/video tapes/CDs/DVDs, and subscribe to 52,691 periodicals including electronic. Computerized library services include interlibrary loans, database searching, Internet access, and Wi-Fi capability. Special learning facilities include an art gallery and radio station. The 210-acre campus is in an urban area in central Greensboro. Including any residence halls, there are 111 buildings.

Student Life: 94% of undergraduates are from North Carolina. Others are from 40 states, 27 foreign countries, and Canada. 59% are White; 25% African American. The average age of freshmen is 18; all undergraduates, 22. 24% do not continue beyond their first year; 54% remain to graduate.

Housing: 5014 students can be accommodated in college housing, which includes coed dorms, on-campus apartments, and off-campus apartments. In addition, there are special-interest houses, an international house, and a residential college program. On-campus housing is guaranteed for all 4 years, is available on a first-come, and first-served basis. 70% of students commute. All students may keep cars.

Activities: 4% of men belong to 10 national fraternities; 4% of women belong to 9 national sororities. There are 192 groups on campus, including art, band, chess, choir, chorale, chorus, communications, dance, drama, ethnic, film, gay, honors, international, jazz band, literary magazine, musical theater, newspaper, opera, orchestra, pep band, photography, political, professional, radio and TV, religious, social, social service, student government, and symphony. Popular campus events include Spring Fling, Fall Kickoff, and a International Festival.

Sports: There are 8 intercollegiate sports for men and 9 for women, and 12 intramural sports for men and 10 for women. Facilities include Baseball Stadium, softball stadium, soccer stadium, gymnasium, tennis courts, campus recreation center, and the 44-acre Piney Lake Field Campus, which includes 2 lakes for swimming, boating, and fishing.

Disabled Students: 80% of the campus is accessible. Facilities include wheelchair ramps, elevators, special parking, specially equipped restrooms, special class scheduling, special housing.

Services: Counseling and information services are available, as is tutoring in most subjects. There is a reader service for the blind.

Campus Safety and Security: Measures include 24-hour foot and vehicle patrol, emergency notification system, self-defense education, and security escort services. There are shuttle buses, emergency telephones, lighted pathways/sidewalks, and controlled access to dorms/residences.

Programs of Study: UNCG confers B.A., B.S., B.F.A., B.M., B.S.N. and B.S.W. degrees. Master's and doctoral degrees are also awarded. Bachelor's degrees are awarded in BIOLOGICAL SCIENCE (biochemistry, biology/biological science, and nutrition), BUSINESS (accounting, apparel and accessories marketing, banking and finance, business administration and management, business economics, entrepreneurial studies, finance, hospitality management services, international business management, and marketing/retailing/merchandising), COMMUNICATIONS AND THE ARTS (art, classical languages, communications, dance, dramatic arts, English, fine arts, French, German, information technology, jazz, media arts, music, music performance, music theory and composition, and Spanish), COMPUTER AND PHYSICAL SCIENCE (chemistry, computer science, mathematics, and physics), EDUCATION (art education, dance education, drama education, early childhood education, education of the deaf and hearing impaired, elementary education, English education, foreign languages education, mathematics education, middle school education, music education, physical education, science education, social science education, social studies education, and special education), ENGINEERING AND ENVIRONMENTAL DESIGN (interior design), HEALTH PROFESSIONS (exercise science, nursing, public health, and speech pathology/audiology), SOCIAL SCIENCE (African American studies, anthropology, child care/child and family studies, economics, geography, history, human development, liberal arts/general studies, parks and recreation management, philosophy, political science/government, psychology, religion, social work, sociology, and women's studies). Business administration, elementary education (K-6), and psychology have the largest enrollments.

Required: In order to graduate, students must complete a minimum of 122 credit hours with a GPA of at least 2.0. Major requirements vary from a minimum of 12 credit hours. The general education curriculum for all students requires at least 36 to 37 credit hours chosen from specified courses in the humanities, math and physical sciences, social and behavioral sciences, and a foreign language. Students must take 36 hours at the upper-division level and earn 31 hours of resident credit.

Special: Internships, and accelerated degree programs can be arranged in all majors. Cross-registration is offered with the Greater Greensboro Consortium. Students may study abroad in more than 40 countries. Dual and student-designed majors are also available. The Residential College, a 2-year program for freshmen and sophomores, offers an interdisciplinary curriculum, with faculty and students living in the same residence. Students in this program participate in independent study, community work, and workshops. There is a Phi Beta Kappa chapter and a freshman honors program.

Faculty/Classroom: 44% of faculty are male; 56% are female. No introductory courses are taught by graduate students. The average class size in an introductory lecture is 30; in a laboratory is 19; and in a regular course is 21.

Admissions: 40% of the current freshmen were in the top fifth of their class; 70% were in the top two fifths.

Requirements: The SAT is required. The ACT Optional Writing test is also required. Graduation from an accredited secondary school or the GED is required. High school courses must include 4 credits each of English, and math, 3 credits of science, 2 of a foreign language, 1 each of U.S. history and social studies, and an elective. A portfolio or audition is required of art and music students. A GPA of 2.0 is required. AP and CLEP credits are accepted. Important factors in the admissions decision are advanced placement or honors courses, leadership record, and evidence of special talent.

Procedure: Freshmen are admitted to all sessions. Entrance exams should be taken in June of the junior year or in the fall of the senior year. There is a rolling admissions plan. Applications should be filed by March 1 for fall entry; December 1 for spring entry, along with a $55 fee. Notification is sent on a rolling basis. Applications are accepted online.

Transfer: 1687 transfer students enrolled in 2012-2013. Transfer students must have a minimum GPA of 2.0. Students having fewer than 30 semester hours from a regionally accredited institution must meet requirements under both transfer and freshman admissions programs. 31 of 122 credits required for the bachelor's degree must be completed at UNCG.

Visiting: There are regularly scheduled orientations for prospective students. There are guides for informal visits. To schedule a visit, contact the Office of Undergraduate Admissions.

Financial Aid: In 2013-2014, 72% of all full-time freshmen and 70% of

continuing full-time students received some form of financial aid. 77% of all full-time freshmen and 73% of continuing full-time students received need-based aid. The average freshman award was $9,665. Need-based scholarships or need-based grants averaged $5,850 ($16,650 maximum); need-based self-help aid (loans and jobs) averaged $3,229 ($9,500 maximum); non-need-based athletic scholarships averaged $16,225 ($29,675 maximum); and other non-need-based awards and non-need-based scholarships averaged $4,600 ($15,000 maximum). The average financial indebtedness of the 2013 graduate was $24,199. The FAFSA is required. The priority date for freshman financial aid applications for fall entry is March 1.

International Students: There are 218 international students enrolled. They must take the TOEFL with a minimum score of 550 on the paper-based TOEFL (PBT) or 79 on the Internet-based version (iBT) or take the MELAB. They must also take the SAT or ACT.

Computers: All students may access the system, until late-night hours in labs and 24 hours a day via personal computer. There are no time limits and no fees.

Graduates: From July 1, 2012 to June 30, 2013, 2958 bachelor's degrees were awarded. The most popular majors were business/marketing (17%), education (13%), and health professions and related programs (11%). In an average class, 1% graduate in 3 years or less, 28% graduate in 4 years or less, 49% graduate in 5 years or less, and 54% graduate in 6 years or less.

Admissions Contact: Lise Keller, Director, Undergraduate Admissions. E-Mail: *admissions@uncg.edu* Web: *www.uncg.edu*

UNIVERSITY OF NORTH CAROLINA AT PEMBROKE D-3

Pembroke, NC 28372 910 521-6262
800 949-UNCP 8627; 910 521-6497

Full-time: 1874 men, 2558 women	**Faculty:** 303; IIA, --$
Part-time: 257 men, 815 women	**Ph.D.s:** 74%
Graduate: 209 men, 556 women	**Student/Faculty:** 15 to 1
Year: semesters, summer session	**Tuition:** $4857 ($14,064)
Application Deadline: July 15	**Room & Board:** $7010
Freshman Class: 3087 applied, 2224 accepted, 1020 enrolled	
SAT CR/M/W: 455/470/435	**ACT:** 19

UNC Pembroke, founded in 1887, is part of the University of North Carolina state-supported system. It provides a liberal arts education that includes art, business, health sciences, music, teacher preparation, and preprofessional studies. There are 4 undergraduate schools and one graduate school. In addition to regional accreditation, UNCP has baccalaureate program accreditation with AACSB, CSWE, NASM, and NCATE. The library contains 399,465 volumes, 709,797 microform items, and 16,029 audio/video tapes/CDs/DVDs, and subscribes to 65,210 periodicals including electronic. Computerized library services include interlibrary loans, database searching, Internet access, and Wi-Fi capability. Special learning facilities include an art gallery, radio station, TV station, a Native American resource center. The 200-acre campus is in a small town 31 miles south of Fayetteville, and 83 miles south of Raleigh. Including any residence halls, there are 75 buildings.

Student Life: 96% of undergraduates are from North Carolina. Others are from 26 states, 19 foreign countries, and Canada. 94% are from public schools. 38% are White; 35% African American; 14% American Indian/Alaska Native. The average age of freshmen is 18; all undergraduates, 25. 69% do not continue beyond their first year; 38% remain to graduate.

Housing: 1705 students can be accommodated in college housing, which includes single-sex and coed dorms and on-campus apartments. On-campus housing is guaranteed for the freshman year only, is available on a first-come, first-served basis, and is available on a lottery system for upperclassmen. 73% of students commute. All students may keep cars.

Activities: 7% of men belong to 10 national fraternities; 4% of women belong to 1 local and 10 national sororities. There are 97 groups on campus, including art, band, cheerleading, choir, chorale, chorus, computers, dance, debate, drama, ethnic, gay, honors, international, jazz band, literary magazine, marching band, musical theater, newspaper, orchestra, pep band, political, professional, radio and TV, religious, social, social service, student government, and yearbook. Popular campus events include Performing Arts Cultural Series, Miss UNCP Scholarship Pageant and Pembroke Day.

Sports: There are 8 intercollegiate sports for men and 8 for women, and 13 intramural sports for men and 13 for women. Facilities include a 3,200-seat gym, an auxiliary gym, a track, tennis courts, a natatorium with 1 swimming pool, and a diving tank, weight rooms, a bowling alley, a 1,600-seat auditorium, fields for soccer, baseball, and softball, a 2,500-seat football stadium, and a wellness center.

Disabled Students: 98% of the campus is accessible. Facilities include wheelchair ramps, elevators, special parking, specially equipped restrooms, special class scheduling, lowered drinking fountains, and lowered telephones.

Services: Counseling and information services are available, as is tutoring in most subjects. There is a reader service for the blind, and remedial math, reading, and writing. as well as Americans with Disabilities services.

Campus Safety and Security: Measures include 24-hour foot and vehicle patrol, emergency notification system, self-defense education, and security escort services. There are shuttle buses, emergency telephones, lighted pathways/sidewalks, and controlled access to dorms/residences.

Programs of Study: UNCP confers B.A., B.M., B.S., B.I.S., B.S.N. and B.S.W. degrees. Master's degrees are also awarded. Bachelor's degrees are awarded in AGRICULTURE (environmental studies), BIOLOGICAL SCIENCE (biology/biological science and biotechnology), BUSINESS (accounting and business administration and management), COMMUNICATIONS AND THE ARTS (communications, dramatic arts, English, fine arts, music, music performance, and Spanish), COMPUTER AND PHYSICAL SCIENCE (chemistry, computer science, information sciences and systems, mathematics, and physics), EDUCATION (athletic training, early childhood education, education, education administration, elementary education, English education, health education, mathematics education, middle school education, music education, physical education, reading education, science education, secondary education, social studies education, and special education), ENGINEERING AND ENVIRONMENTAL DESIGN (environmental science), HEALTH PROFESSIONS (nursing), SOCIAL SCIENCE (American Indian studies, American studies, counseling/psychology, criminal justice, history, interdisciplinary studies, philosophy and religion, political science/government, psychology, public administration, social work, and sociology). Education, business administration, and physical sciences are the strongest academically. Education, business, and social science have the largest enrollments.

Required: All students are required to complete 120 to 128 total credits, which include 44 semester hours of general education courses, 39 to 69 hours in a major, and a university orientation class before entrance. A minimum GPA of 2.0 must be maintained.

Special: Co-op programs, cross-registration, internships, study abroad in 40 countries, a Washington semester, and work-study programs are available.The B.A.-B.S. degree is available in American Indian studies or with the B.S.A.S. degree. In addition, dual majors, credit for military experience, and nondegree study are offered. There are 14 national honor societies, a freshman honors program, and 9 departmental honors programs.

Faculty/Classroom: 50% of faculty are male; 50% are female. 93% teach undergraduates. No introductory courses are taught by graduate students. The average class size in an introductory lecture is 24; in a laboratory is 13; and in a regular course is 23.

Admissions: 72% of the 2013-2014 applicants were accepted. The SAT scores for the 2013-2014 freshman class were: Critical Reading--80% below 500, 17% between 500 and 599, and 3% between 600 and 699; Math--73% below 500, 22% between 500 and 599, 4% between 600 and 699; Writing--87% below 500, 11% between 500 and 599, 1% between 600 and 699, and 1% between 700 and 800. The ACT scores were 78% below 21, 12% between 21 and 23, 5% between 24 and 26, 3% between 27 and 28, and 2% above 28. 3% of the current freshmen were in the top fifth of their class; 16% were in the top two fifths.

Requirements: The SAT or ACT is required. Applicants must be graduates of an accredited secondary school with 20 academic credits, including 4 courses in English, 4 in math, 3 in science, 2 in the same foreign language, and 2 in history. An essay and an interview are recommended. Students also must submit an official high school transcript that shows their class rank and GPA. The College Opportunity Program is designed to admit a limited number of students who meet most, but not all, of the regular admissions standards. Students who receive the GED should consult an admissions counselor. A GPA of 2.5 is required. AP and CLEP credits are accepted. Important factors in the admissions decision are advanced placement or honors courses, recommendations by school officials, parents or siblings attended your school, evidence of special talent, personality/intangible qualities, extracurricular activities record, recommendations by alumni, and geographical diversity.

Procedure: Freshmen are admitted fall, spring, and summer. Entrance exams should be taken During the high school junior and senior years. There are deferred admissions and rolling admissions plans. Application deadlines are open. Application fee is $45. Notification is sent on a rolling basis. Applications are accepted online.

Transfer: 499 transfer students enrolled in 2012-2013. Applicants must have a minimum GPA of 2.0, submit transcripts from high school and from all previous colleges, and be eligible to return to the last institution attended. The SAT and an interview are recommended. 30 of 128 credits required for the bachelor's degree must be completed at UNCP.

Visiting: There are regularly scheduled orientations for prospective students, Includes open houses in the fall, spring, and summer. There are guides for informal visits and visitors may sit in on classes. To schedule a visit, contact the Office of Undergraduate Admissions at admissions@uncp.edu.

Financial Aid: In 2013-2014, 68% of all full-time freshmen and 77% of continuing full-time students received some form of financial aid. 65% of all full-time freshmen and 70% of continuing full-time students received

need-based aid. The average freshman award was $6,656. Need-based scholarships or need-based grants averaged $6,656 ; and need-based self-help aid (loans and jobs) averaged $3,397. 2% of undergraduate students work part-time. Average annual earnings from campus work are $1854. The FAFSA is required. The deadline for filing freshman financial aid applications for fall entry is March 15.

International Students: There are 39 international students enrolled. The school actively recruits these students. They must take the TOEFL with a minimum score of 550 on the paper-based TOEFL (PBT) or 80 on the Internet-based version (iBT) and the Comprehensive English Language Test. They must also take the SAT or ACT.

Computers: All students may access the system at any time. There are no time limits and no fees.

Graduates: From July 1, 2012 to June 30, 2013, 905 bachelor's degrees were awarded. The most popular majors were education (14%), business/marketing (12%), and social sciences (11%). 50 companies recruited on campus in 2012-2013. In an average class, 1% graduate in 3 years or less, 16% graduate in 4 years or less, 29% graduate in 5 years or less, and 34% graduate in 6 years or less. Of the 2012 graduating class, 7% were enrolled in graduate school within 6 months of graduation.

Admissions Contact: Natalya Freeman Locklear, Interim Director of U.G. Admissions. E-Mail: *admissions@uncp.edu* Web: *www.uncp.edu*

UNIVERSITY OF NORTH CAROLINA AT WILMINGTON E-4

Wilmington, NC 28403-5904 **(910) 962-3243; (910) 962-3038**

Full-time: 4346 men, 6314 women	**Faculty:** 588; IIA, av$
Part-time: 388 men, 722 women	**Ph.D.s:** 86%
Graduate: 488 men, 813 women	**Student/Faculty:** 16 to 1
Year: semesters, summer session	**Tuition:** $5672 ($17,492)
Application Deadline: February 1	**Room & Board:** $7900

Freshman Class: 11397 applied, 5457 accepted, 1981 enrolled
SAT CR/M/W: 592/605/561 **ACT:** 26 **VERY COMPETITIVE+**

The University of North Carolina Wilmington, founded in 1947, is a publicly funded institution offering programs in the liberal arts and sciences, education, and business. It is a part of the University of North Carolina System. There are 4 undergraduate schools and 1 graduate school. In addition to regional accreditation, UNCW has baccalaureate program accreditation with NCATE and NLN. The library contains 1.0 million volumes, 1.0 million microform items, and 82,023 audio/video tapes/CDs/DVDs, and subscribes to 24,081 periodicals including electronic. Computerized library services include interlibrary loans, database searching, Internet access, and laptop Internet portals. Special learning facilities include a learning resource center, art gallery, radio station, TV station, wildflower preserve, nature preserve, museum of world cultures, and the research vessel Cape Fear, used for a marine biology labs and for research out of the Center for Marine Science, the university's privately owned and operated research center. The 660-acre campus is in a suburban area 125 miles southeast of Raleigh. Including any residence halls, there are 127 buildings.

Student Life: 82% of undergraduates are from North Carolina. Others are from 42 states, 53 foreign countries, and Canada. 86% are white. The average age of freshmen is 18; all undergraduates, 22. 13% do not continue beyond their first year; 67% remain to graduate.

Housing: 4143 students can be accommodated in college housing, which includes single-sex and coed dorms and on-campus apartments. In addition, there are honors houses, special-interest houses, fraternity houses, sorority houses, and an international student dorm. On-campus housing is guaranteed for all 4 years, is available on a first-come, and first-served basis. 61% of students commute. All students may keep cars.

Activities: 6% of men belong to 14 national fraternities; 4% of women belong to 13 national sororities. There are 200 groups on campus, including art, band, cheerleading, choir, chorale, chorus, computers, dance, debate, drama, environmental, ethnic, film, forensics, gay, honors, international, jazz band, literary magazine, musical theater, newspaper, orchestra, pep band, photography, political, professional, radio and TV, religious, social, social service, student government, and symphony. Popular campus events include Business Week, Greek Week, and Spring Week.

Sports: There are 10 intercollegiate sports for men and 11 for women, and 47 intramural sports for men and 47 for women. Facilities include a 6000-seat coliseum, an collegiate-size swimming pool and separate diving tank, a track and field complex, and basketball, tennis, and volleyball courts. A Student Recreation Center with basketball courts, exercise equipment and exercise classes, indoor track, and a rock climbing wall. As well, each of our upperclassmen apartment complexes have a recreational outdoor pool and clubhouse.

Disabled Students: 98% of the campus is accessible. Facilities include wheelchair ramps, elevators, special parking, specially equipped restrooms, special class scheduling, lowered drinking fountains, lowered telephones, special housing.

Services: Counseling and information services are available, as is tutoring in most subjects. There is a reader service for the blind, and remedial math, reading, and writing.

Campus Safety and Security: Measures include 24-hour foot and vehicle patrol, emergency notification system, self-defense education, and security escort services. There are shuttle buses, emergency telephones, lighted pathways/sidewalks, controlled access to dorms/residences, rape awareness defense (RAD) training, counseling services and the university police.

Programs of Study: UNCW confers B.A., B.S., B.F.A., B.S.W., and B.A. in Music. degrees. Master's and doctoral degrees are also awarded. Bachelor's degrees are awarded in BIOLOGICAL SCIENCE (biochemistry, biology/biological science, marine biology, and marine science), BUSINESS (accounting, banking and finance, business administration and management, business economics, business systems analysis, and marketing/retailing/merchandising), COMMUNICATIONS AND THE ARTS (art, art history and appreciation, communications, creative writing, dramatic arts, English, film arts, French, German, music, music performance, Spanish, speech/debate/rhetoric, studio art, and theater design), COMPUTER AND PHYSICAL SCIENCE (chemistry, computer science, geology, mathematics, physics, and statistics), EDUCATION (athletic training, early childhood education, elementary education, middle school education, music education, physical education, secondary education, and special education), ENGINEERING AND ENVIRONMENTAL DESIGN (environmental science and preengineering), HEALTH PROFESSIONS (clinical science, nursing, physical therapy, predentistry, premedicine, preoptometry, prepharmacy, prephysical therapy, prepodiatry, preveterinary science, and recreation therapy), SOCIAL SCIENCE (anthropology, criminal justice, economics, geography, German area studies, history, parks and recreation management, philosophy and religion, political science/government, prelaw, psychology, religion, social work, and sociology).

Required: Students may qualify for the bachelor's degree by successfully completing the university studies requirements, an approved course of study in an academic major, a minimum of 124 semester hours of credit, and a minimum quality point average of 2.0. The final 31 semester hours of course credit, including the final 15 semester hours in the major, must be completed at the University of North Carolina at Wilmington.

Special: UNC Wilmington offer internships, over 500 study abroad programs in 50 different countries, mentored research, and work-study programs. Dual majors may be pursued if requirements are met, and credit is given for military experience. There is a Phi Beta Kappa chapter and a freshman honors program.

Faculty/Classroom: 53% of faculty are male; 47% are female. 96% teach undergraduates, 62% do research, and 60% do both. No introductory courses are taught by graduate students. The average class size in a regular course is 21.

Admissions: 48% of the 2011-2012 applicants were accepted. The SAT scores for the 2011-2012 freshman class were: Critical Reading--6% below 500, 56% between 500 and 599, 35% between 600 and 700, and 3% above 700; Math--4% below 500, 50% between 500 and 599, 42% between 600 and 700, and 4% above 700; Writing--16% below 500, 56% between 500 and 599, 26% between 600 and 700, and 2% above 700. The ACT scores were 10% below 21, 30% between 21 and 23, 39% between 24 and 26, 14% between 27 and 28, and 8% above 28. 44% of the current freshmen were in the top fifth of their class; 70% were in the top two fifths.

Requirements: The SAT or ACT is required. The ACT Optional Writing test is also required. Graduation from an accredited secondary school or the GED is required for admission. High school courses must include 4 years of English, 4 years of math (algebra I, II, and geometry),and a math beyond Algebra II, 3 units of science (1 year each of biology, physical science, and a lab course), 2 years of social studies, including 1 year of U.S. history and 2 years of a foreign language. AP and CLEP credits are accepted.

Procedure: Freshmen are admitted fall and summer. Entrance exams should be taken during the junior or senior year. There are early admissions and deferred admissions plans. Early decision applications should be filed by November 1; regular applications, by February 1 for fall entry. The fall 2011 application fee was $60. Notification of early decision is sent January 20; regular decision, April 1. Applications are accepted online.

Transfer: 1280 transfer students enrolled in a recent year. Transfer students must have a minimum GPA of 2.5 and be eligible to return to the institution last attended. Prior to admission, transfer applicants must have successfully completed 1 year of freshman-level English, 1 unit of college-level math and have completed at least 24 semesters or 36 quarter hours of credit. 31 of 124 credits required for the bachelor's degree must be completed at UNCW.

Visiting: There are regularly scheduled orientations for prospective students. There are guides for informal visits. To schedule a visit, contact the Admissions Office.

Financial Aid: In a recent year, 60% of all full-time freshmen and 67% of continuing full-time students received some form of financial aid. 53% of all full-time freshmen and 58% of continuing full-time students received need-based aid. The average freshman award was $8,896. Need-based scholarships or need-based grants averaged $6,692; need-based self-help aid (loans and jobs) averaged $3,121; non-need-based athletic scholarships averaged $7,219; and other non-need-based awards and non-need-based scholarships averaged $2,211. 9% of undergraduate students work part-time. Average annual earnings from campus work are $1017. The average financial indebtedness of a recent graduate is $16,980. The FAFSA is required. The priority date for freshman financial aid applications for fall entry is March 1. The deadline for filing freshman financial aid applications for fall entry is December 31.

International Students: There are 211 international students enrolled. The school actively recruits these students. They must take the TOEFL with a minimum score of 525 on the paper-based TOEFL (PBT) or 71 on the Internet-based version (iBT). They must also take the SAT or ACT.

Computers: Wireless access is available. UNCW has is a laptop program that provides students with access to laptops equipped with wireless cards. Though provided by the centralized Information Technology Systems Division, these are available in distributed locations such as the library, the Union, and the Technology Support Center. Students personal computers are signed onto the network when they arrive on campus their Freshman year. Students who live off of campus also have access to wireless and network services. Students can also purchase laptops through the Student Laptop Initiative, which provides laptops to incoming students. The program is through ITSD, and students have access to free computer repair services through ITSD with this program. All students may access the system. from 8 a.m. to 11 p.m. at on-campus clusters and 24-hours daily via the Internet. There are no time limits and no fees. It is strongly recommended that all students have a personal computer. A Dell laptop is recommended.

Graduates: In a recent year, 2628 bachelor's degrees were awarded. 153 companies recruited on campus in a recent year. In an average class, 45% graduate in 4 years or less and 67% graduate in 6 years or less.

Admissions Contact: Director of Admissions. A campus DVD is available. E-Mail: *admissions@uncw.edu* Web: *www.uncw.edu*

UNIVERSITY OF NORTH CAROLINA SCHOOL OF THE ARTS C-2
North Carolina School of the Arts
Winston-Salem, NC 27127-2188 **(336) 770-3290; (336) 770-3370**

Full-time: 775 men and women	**Faculty:** n/av
Part-time: 20 men and women	**Ph.D.s:** n/av
Graduate: 110 men and women	**Student/Faculty:** n/av
Year: trimesters	**Tuition:** $5500 ($17,665)
Application Deadline: see profile	**Room & Board:** $7922
Freshman Class: n/av	
SAT or ACT: required	**SPECIAL**

University of North Carolina School of the Arts, formerly North Carolina School of the Arts, was founded in 1963 and is part of the University of North Carolina system. It is a public conservatory offering professional training in the performing arts. Figures in the above capsule and in this profile are approximate. There are 5 undergraduate schools and 2 graduate schools. The library contains 114,050 volumes, 25,053 microform items, and 73,025 audio/video tapes/CDs/DVDs, and subscribes to 490 periodicals including electronic. Computerized library services include interlibrary loans and database searching. Special learning facilities include a learning resource center, art gallery, numerous performance theaters, screening rooms, and CAD studios. The 67-acre campus is in an urban area in Winston-Salem. Including any residence halls, there are 65 buildings.

Student Life: 50% of undergraduates are from out of state, mostly the Middle Atlantic. Students are from 44 states, 28 foreign countries, and Canada. 80% are from public schools. 88% are white. The average age of freshmen is 19; all undergraduates, 25. 25% do not continue beyond their first year.

Housing: 300 students can be accommodated in college housing, which includes coed dorms and on-campus apartments. On-campus housing is available on a first-come, first-served basis. Priority is given to out-of-town students. 58% of students live on campus; of those, 90% remain on campus on weekends. Alcohol is not permitted. All students may keep cars.

Activities: There are no fraternities or sororities. Groups on campus include art, band, choir, chorale, chorus, dance, drama, ethnic, film, gay, international, jazz band, musical theater, newspaper, opera, orchestra, radio and TV, student government, and symphony.

Sports: There is no sports program at UNCSA. Facilities include a gym, fitness and weight rooms, a swimming pool, a soccer and touch football field, a golf course, and courts for tennis, basketball, and volleyball.

Disabled Students: 85% of the campus is accessible. Facilities include wheelchair ramps, elevators, special parking, specially equipped restrooms, and lowered drinking fountains.

Services: Counseling and information services are available, as is tutoring in every subject. There is remedial math, reading, and writing. Private tutoring is also offered on a fee basis.

Campus Safety and Security: Measures include 24-hour foot and vehicle patrol. There are emergency telephones and lighted pathways/sidewalks.

Programs of Study: NCSA confers B.F.A. and B.M. degrees. Master's degrees are also awarded. Bachelor's degrees are awarded in COMMUNICATIONS AND THE ARTS (ballet, dance, dramatic arts, film arts, music, performing arts, and theater design).

Required: To earn a bachelor's degree, students must demonstrate satisfactory skills in reading, writing, oral communication, and math; take courses in foundations of Western thought; complete studies in fine arts and humanities, social and behavioral sciences, and math and natural science; and meet all requirements in their arts major.

Special: UNCSA offers work-study programs, a general studies major, independent study, and design and production apprenticeships. An accelerated degree program is available to high school students in dance, drama, music, and visual arts.

Faculty/Classroom: 70% of faculty are male; 30% are female. All teach undergraduates. No introductory courses are taught by graduate students. The average class size in a regular course is 10.

Requirements: The SAT or ACT is required. The ACT Optional Writing test is also required. Applicants must be graduates of an accredited secondary school or have a GED certificate. They should have completed 4 units in English, 3 in math, 3 in science with 1 in a lab course, and 2 in social studies with 1 in U.S. history. Also recommended are 2 units in a foreign language and 1 unit each in foreign language and math in the senior year. An audition or interview demonstrating evidence of special talent is the primary admissions criterion. Applicants to the School of Design and Production must submit a portfolio. Film making applicants must submit a creative writing sample. AP and CLEP credits are accepted. Important factors in the admissions decision are recommendations by school officials, evidence of special talent, and recommendations by alumni.

Procedure: Freshmen are admitted fall and winter. There is a rolling admissions plan. Check with the school for current application deadlines. The application fee is $60. Applications are accepted online.

Transfer: Evidence of special talent and good academic standing are required. Placement is based on ability and experience, prior courses, and interviews and auditions.

Visiting: There are regularly scheduled orientations for prospective students, including tours on audition days and question-and-answer sessions with administration and faculty. Visitors may sit in on classes. To schedule a visit, contact the Admissions Office.

Financial Aid: Check with the school for current application deadlines.

International Students: The school actively recruits these students. They must take the Comprehensive English Language Test.

Computers: All students may access the system. There are no time limits and no fees. Students enrolled in film must have a personal computer; an Apple is recommended.

Admissions Contact: Director of Admissions. E-Mail: *admissions@uncsa.edu* Web: *www.uncsa.edu*

WAKE FOREST UNIVERSITY C-2
Winston-Salem, NC 27109 **(336) 758-5201**

Full-time: 2255 men, 2491 women	**Faculty:** 461; IIA, ++$
Part-time: 40 men, 29 women	**Ph.D.s:** 87%
Graduate: 1380 men, 1237 women	**Student/Faculty:** 11 to 1
Year: semesters, summer session	**Tuition:** $43,200
Application Deadline: January 15	**Room & Board:** $7800
Freshman Class: 11407 applied, 3875 accepted, 1234 enrolled	
	MOST COMPETITIVE

Wake Forest University, established in 1834, is a private institution offering undergraduate programs in the liberal arts and sciences, education, and preprofessional fields. There are 2 undergraduate schools and 6 graduate schools. In addition to regional accreditation, Wake Forest has baccalaureate program accreditation with AACSB and NCATE. The 3 libraries contain 2.1 million volumes, 2.2 million microform items, and 38,265 audio/video tapes/CDs/DVDs, and subscribe to 51,262 periodicals including electronic. Computerized library services include interlibrary loans, data base searching, Internet access, and Wi-Fi capability. Special learning facilities include an art gallery, radio station, TV station, fine arts center, anthropology museum, and laser research facility. The 340-acre campus is in a suburban area 4 miles northwest of Winston-Salem. Including any residence halls, there are 47 buildings.

Student Life: 77% of undergraduates are from out of state, mostly the South. Students are from 48 states, 28 foreign countries, and Canada. 60% are from public schools. 76% are White. 40% are Protestant; 28% Muslim, Hindu, Buddhist, Mormon and Greek Orthodox.; 25% Catholic. The average age of freshmen is 19; all undergraduates, 20. 6% do not continue beyond their first year; 86% remain to graduate.

Housing: 3380 students can be accommodated in college housing, which includes coed dorms and on-campus apartments. In addition, there are special-interest houses, fraternity houses, sorority houses, Theme and Wellness housing. On-campus housing is guaranteed for all 4 years. 68% of students live on campus; of those, 70% remain on campus on weekends. Upperclassmen may keep cars.

Activities: 38% of men belong to 16 national fraternities; 52% of women belong to 11 national sororities. There are 160 groups on campus, including art, band, cheerleading, choir, chorale, chorus, computers, dance, debate, drama, drill team, environmental, ethnic, film, gay, honors, international, jazz band, literary magazine, marching band, musical theater, newspaper, orchestra, pep band, photography, political, professional, radio and TV, religious, social, social service, student government, symphony, women's and environmental, and yearbook. Popular campus events include Project Pumpkin, Springfest and President's Ball.

Sports: There are 8 intercollegiate sports for men and 8 for women, and 18 intramural sports for men and 15 for women. Facilities include Indoor sports are played at Reynolds Gym and outdoor sports are played on Water Tower Field, Water Tower Courts, and Leighton Tennis Courts.

Disabled Students: 85% of the campus is accessible. Facilities include wheelchair ramps, elevators, special parking, specially equipped restrooms, special class scheduling, lowered drinking fountains, lowered telephones, and special housing.

Services: Counseling and information services are available, as is tutoring in some subjects, primarily in the sciences, math, and foreign languages There is a reader service for the blind. The Learning Assistance Center offers instructional support and skill development in writing, reading, and study strategies.

Campus Safety and Security: Measures include 24-hour foot and vehicle patrol, emergency notification system, self-defense education, and security escort services. There are shuttle buses, emergency telephones, lighted pathways/sidewalks, There are gatehouses at 2 of the university's 3 entrances that operate from 6 p.m. to 6 a.m. During those hours, the third entrance is closed.

Programs of Study: Wake Forest confers B.A., and B.S. degrees. Master's and doctoral degrees are also awarded. Bachelor's degrees are awarded in BIOLOGICAL SCIENCE (biology/biological science), BUSINESS (accounting, banking and finance, and business administration and management), COMMUNICATIONS AND THE ARTS (art history, art, Chinese, classics, communications, English, French, German, Greek, Japanese, Latin, music, Russian, Spanish, studio art, and theatre studies), COMPUTER AND PHYSICAL SCIENCE (chemistry, computer science, mathematics, mathematics – economics, and physics), EDUCATION (education), HEALTH PROFESSIONS (exercise science), SOCIAL SCIENCE (anthropology, economics, history, philosophy, political science/ government, psychology, religion, and sociology). Business and enterprise management, psychology, political science, communication, and finance have the largest enrollments.

Required: To graduate, students must complete a total of 120 credits with a minimum GPA of 2.0. The number of hours required in the major varies. All students must take 1 semester of a writing seminar, a first-year seminar, and 1 course in foreign language literature. In addition, students must complete 2 courses each in natural sciences and math, social and behavioral sciences, and history, religion, and philosophy; 1 course in literature; and 1 course in fine arts.

Special: Wake Forest offers cooperative programs in engineering with any other schools of engineering accredited by ABET; political science majors who minor in Latin American studies have the opportunity to pursue a 5-year cooperative B.A./M.A. program with Georgetown University. Cross-registration with Salem College is available for full-time students. Wake Forest sponsors study-abroad semester programs in 13 countries. Other special opportunities include internships, work-study programs, dual majors, and a minor in entrepreneurship and social enterprise. Students can also be certified in Spanish language translation and interpreting. An accelerated degree program may be arranged in medical technology. Interdisciplinary honors courses and the Open Curriculum program are available for selected students. Wake Forest owns residences in London, Venice, and Vienna where students and professors attend semester-long courses in a variety of disciplines. A semester-long program in Washington, D.C., is also offered. There are 11 national honor societies, including Phi Beta Kappa, a freshman honors program, and 23 departmental honors programs.

Faculty/Classroom: 57% of faculty are male; 43% are female. 86% teach undergraduates, and 73% do research. No introductory courses are taught by graduate students. The average class size in a regular course is 21.

Admissions: 34% of the 2013-2014 applicants were accepted. 94% of the current freshmen were in the top fifth of their class; 98% were in the top two fifths. 35 freshmen graduated first in their class.

Requirements: In addition, SAT Subject Tests, are considered if submitted. Graduation from an accredited secondary school or the GED is required. The school requires 16 academic credits, including 4 credits of English, 3 of math, 2 each of a foreign language, history, and social studies, and 1 of science. 1 credit each of art and music is recommended. All students must submit an essay. AP and CLEP credits are accepted. Important factors in the admissions decision are recommendations by school officials, leadership record, and advanced placement or honors courses.

Procedure: Freshmen are admitted fall and spring. There are early decision and deferred admissions plans. Early decision applications should be filed by November 15; regular applications, by January 15 for fall entry; and November 15 for spring entry, along with a $50 fee. Notification of early decision is sent December 15; regular decision, April 1. 337 early decision candidates were accepted for the 2013-2014 class. applicants were on the 2013 waiting list; were admitted. Applications are accepted online.

Transfer: 51 transfer students enrolled in 2012-2013. Transfer students must have a minimum GPA of 2.0 on all college work attempted. 60 of 120 credits required for the bachelor's degree must be completed at Wake Forest.

Visiting: There are regularly scheduled orientations for prospective students, including group information sessions and tours by appointment. There are guides for informal visits, visitors may sit in on classes, and stay overnight. To schedule a visit, contact the Admissions Office at (336) 758-5201.

Financial Aid: In 2013-2014, 39% of all full-time freshmen and 41% of continuing full-time students received some form of financial aid. 33% of all full-time freshmen and 38% of continuing full-time students received need-based aid. The average freshman award was $34,647. Need-based scholarships or need-based grants averaged $32,846; need-based self-help aid (loans and jobs) averaged $6,060, non-need based athletic scholarships averaged $42,041; other non-need-based awards and non-need-based scholarships averaged $17,809; and $17,809 from other forms of aid. 44% of undergraduate students work part-time. Average annual earnings from campus work are $1267. The average financial indebtedness of the 2013 graduate was $33,262. Wake Forest is a member of CSS. The CSS/ Profile, FAFSA, the state aid form, and noncustodial profile are required. The priority date for freshman financial aid applications for fall entry is February 15. The deadline for filing freshman financial aid applications for fall entry is March 1.

International Students: There are 143 international students enrolled. The school actively recruits these students. They must take the TOEFL. They must also take the SAT or ACT.

Computers: All students may access the system 24 hours per day. There are no time limits and no fees.

Graduates: From July 1, 2012 to June 30, 2013, 1112 bachelor's degrees were awarded. The most popular majors were social science (21%), business/marketing (20%), and psychology (9%). In an average class, 85% graduate in 4 years or less, 90% graduate in 5 years or less, and 88% graduate in 6 years or less. Of the 2012 graduating class, 26% were enrolled in graduate school within 6 months of graduation, and 68% were employed.

Admissions Contact: Martha B. Allman, Director of Admissions. E-Mail: *admissions@wfu.edu* Web: *www.wfu.edu*

WARREN WILSON COLLEGE — B-2

Asheville, NC 28815-9000 — **(828) 771-2073** **(800) 934-3536; (828) 298-1440**

Full-time: 345 men, 530 women	**Faculty:** n/av; IIB, -_$
Part-time: 10 men, 10 women	**Ph.D.s:** n/av
Graduate: 30 men, 55 women	**Student/Faculty:** n/av
Year: semesters	**Tuition:** $28,240
Application Deadline: see profile	**Room & Board:** $9056
Freshman Class: n/av	
SAT or ACT: required	

VERY COMPETITIVE

Warren Wilson College, founded in 1894, is a liberal arts institution affiliated with the Presbyterian Church and known for its triad of academics, work, and service. All students work 15 hours per week in jobs related to the operation and maintenance of the college. In exchange, room and board is provided at a low rate. The figures in the above capsule and in this profile are approximate. There is 1 graduate school. In addition to regional accreditation, Warren Wilson College has baccalaureate program accreditation with CSWE and NCATE. The library contains 110,702 volumes, 34,046 microform items, and 3,338 audio/video tapes/CDs/DVDs, and subscribes to 11,076 periodicals including electronic. Computerized library services include interlibrary loans, database searching, and Internet access. Special learning facilities include a learning resource center, art gallery, radio station, and outdoor adventure learning lab. The 1135-acre campus is in a small town 5 miles east of Asheville. Including any residence halls, there are 62 buildings.

Student Life: 83% of undergraduates are from out of state, mostly the Northeast. Students are from 46 states, 14 foreign countries, and Canada. 74% are from public schools. 91% are white. 50% claim no religious affiliation The average age of freshmen is 18; all undergraduates, 20. 34% do not continue beyond their first year; 45% remain to graduate.

Housing: 750 students can be accommodated in college housing, which includes single-sex and coed dorms. In addition, there is a wellness house, and an eco-dorm. On-campus housing is guaranteed for all 4 years. 85% of students live on campus; of those, 95% remain on campus on weekends. Upperclassmen may keep cars.

Activities: There are no fraternities or sororities. Groups on campus include art, chess, choir, chorus, computers, dance, drama, environmental, ethnic, film, gay, honors, international, jazz band, literary magazine, musical theater, newspaper, orchestra, outdoor activities, photography, political, professional, radio and TV, religious, social, social justice, social service, and student government. Popular campus events include International Fair, Work Day, and Service Day.

Sports: There are 6 intercollegiate sports for men and 6 for women, and 5 intramural sports for men and 5 for women. Facilities include 2 gyms, an aquatic center, weight and fitness rooms, tennis courts, playing fields, 25 miles of hiking/biking trails, kayak slalom gates, an indoor climbing wall, an alpine tower, a mountain bike skills area, and an outdoor basketball court.

Disabled Students: 90% of the campus is accessible. Facilities include wheelchair ramps, elevators, special parking, specially equipped rest rooms, special class scheduling, lowered drinking fountains, lowered telephones, and special housing.

Services: Counseling and information services are available, as is tutoring in most subjects. Tutoring is available through the Peer Assistance Center and the Writing Center. ESL tutoring is also available.

Campus Safety and Security: Measures include 24-hour foot and vehicle patrol and security escort services. There are emergency telephones and lighted pathways/sidewalks.

Programs of Study: confers B.A. and B.S. degrees. Master's degrees are also awarded. Bachelor's degrees are awarded in AGRICULTURE (environmental studies), BIOLOGICAL SCIENCE (biology/biological science), BUSINESS (business economics), COMMUNICATIONS AND THE ARTS (art, creative writing, English, and Spanish), COMPUTER AND PHYSICAL SCIENCE (chemistry and mathematics), EDUCATION (elementary education, English education, middle school education, and recreation education), SOCIAL SCIENCE (anthropology, behavioral science, history, humanities, international studies, philosophy, psychology, social work, sociology, and women's studies). Biology is the strongest academically. Environmental studies, biology, and English have the largest enrollments.

Required: To graduate, students must complete a total of 128 semester hours with a minimum GPA of 2.0. Between 32 and 40 hours are required in the student's major. All students must complete 36 hours in the core curriculum. All students must also complete 100 hours of community service over 4 years. A first-year seminar and college composition are required.

Special: Cross-registration is offered with Mars Hill College and the University of North Carolina at Asheville. Internships related to the major may be arranged. Study-abroad programs in South America, Europe, Japan, and India are available. The college offers an accelerated degree program in education, student-designed majors, nondegree study, and pass/fail options. There are dual majors in history/political science and English/theater arts. Cooperative programs are available in engineering with Washington University in St. Louis and with Duke University. There are 3 departmental honors programs.

Faculty/Classroom: 54% of faculty are male; 46% are female. All teach and do research. No introductory courses are taught by graduate students. The average class size in an introductory lecture is 16, in a laboratory, 15, and in a regular course, 11.

Requirements: The SAT or ACT is required, with a score of 500 on each section of the SAT or a composite score of 21 on the ACT. Graduation from an accredited secondary school or the GED is required. Applicants should have a total of 12 academic credits. An essay and an interview are recommended. A GPA of 2.8 is required. AP credits are accepted. Important factors in the admissions decision are advanced placement or honors courses, evidence of special talent, and recommendations by school officials.

Procedure: Freshmen are admitted fall and winter. Entrance exams should be taken by January 20 of the senior year. There are early decision and deferred admissions plans. Notification of early decision is sent December 1. Check with the school for current application deadlines and fee.

Transfer: Applicants must have a minimum GPA of 2.75. A year of residence at Warren Wilson is required for graduation. Applicants must be eligible to return to their previous institutions. 32 of 128 credits required for the bachelor's degree must be completed at Warren Wilson.

Visiting: There are guides for informal visits; visitors may sit in on classes, and stay overnight. To schedule a visit, contact the campus visit coordinator.

Financial Aid: The FAFSA and the college's own financial statement are required. Check with the school for current application deadlines.

International Students: The school actively recruits these students. They must take the TOEFL.

Computers: Wireless access is available. PCs are located in 1 30-seat lab and 4 smaller teaching labs. There is wireless access in 3 dorms, the library, and a computer lab. All students may access the system. There are no time limits and no fees. It is strongly recommended that all students have a personal computer.

Admissions Contact: Richard Blomgren, Dean of Admission. A campus DVD is available. E-Mail: *rickb@warren-wilson.edu* Web: *www.warren-wilson.edu*

WESTERN CAROLINA UNIVERSITY — A-3

Cullowhee, NC 28723 — (828) 227-7317; (877) WCU4YOU; (828) 227-7319

Full-time: 3216 men, 3579 women	**Faculty:** 420; IIA, -$
Part-time: 504 men, 680 women	**Ph.D.s:** 70%
Graduate: 543 men, 1086 women	**Student/Faculty:** 16 to 1
Year: semesters, summer session	**Tuition:** \$6479 (\$16,076)
Application Deadline: March 1	**Room & Board:** \$7477

Freshman Class: 15234 applied, 5739 accepted, 1560 enrolled

SAT CR/M/W: 515/526/486 **ACT:** 22 **COMPETITIVE+**

Western Carolina University, founded in 1889 and part of the University of North Carolina system, is a public-funded institution offering undergraduate programs in the arts, sciences, technology, business, and humanities. There are 7 undergraduate schools and one graduate school. In addition to regional accreditation, WCU has baccalaureate program accreditation with AACSB, ABET, ACCE, ADA, APTA, CSWE, FIDER, NASM, NCATE, and NLN. The library contains 626,918 volumes, 1.6 million microform items, and 17,043 audio/video tapes/CDs/DVDs, and subscribes to 12,465 periodicals including electronic. Computerized library services include interlibrary loans, database searching, Internet access, and Wi-Fi capability. Special learning facilities include an art gallery, natural history museum, radio station, TV station, the Mountain Heritage Center, the Fine and Performing Arts Center, and the Center for Applied Technology. The 682-acre campus is in a rural area 150 miles northeast of Atlanta, Georgia, and 50 miles west of Asheville. Including any residence halls, there are 91 buildings.

Student Life: 93% of undergraduates are from North Carolina. Others are from 40 states, 13 foreign countries, and Canada. 95% are from public schools. 83% are White. The average age of freshmen is 18; all undergraduates, 23. 16% do not continue beyond their first year; 48% remain to graduate.

Housing: 4023 students can be accommodated in college housing, which includes single-sex and coed dorms, on-campus apartments, and married student housing. In addition, there are honors houses, language houses, fraternity houses, and sorority houses. On-campus housing is guaranteed for all 4 years. 51% of students commute. All students may keep cars.

Activities: 9% of men belong to 13 national fraternities; 7% of women belong to 9 national sororities. There are 150 groups on campus, including art, band, cheerleading, choir, chorale, chorus, computers, dance, debate, drama, drill team, environmental, ethnic, film, gay, honors, international, jazz band, literary magazine, marching band, musical theater, newspaper, pep band, photography, political, professional, radio and TV, religious, social, social service, and student government. Popular campus events include Mountain Heritage Day, Greek Week, and Fine and Performing Arts Season.

Sports: There are 6 intercollegiate sports for men and 8 for women, and 33 intramural sports for men and 34 for women. Facilities include a football stadium, baseball diamond, track/tennis complex, 2 intramural softball fields, 2 intramural flag football fields, disc golf course, soccer field, 5 gyms, field house, jogging trails, picnic areas, game rooms, weight training room, swimming pool, golf driving range, golf putting green, and a 73,000-sq-ft student recreation center with 2 multipurpose courts, climbing wall, 9800-sq-ft area for strength training, cardiovascular equipment, 3-lane indoor track, 2500-sq-ft group exercise studio, fitness assessment rooms, locker rooms, and administrative offices.

Disabled Students: 90% of the campus is accessible. Facilities include wheelchair ramps, elevators, special parking, specially equipped restrooms, special class scheduling, lowered drinking fountains, lowered telephones, and special housing.

Services: Counseling and information services are available, as is tutoring in most subjects. There is a reader service for the blind, and remedial math, reading, and writing.

Campus Safety and Security: Measures include 24-hour foot and vehicle patrol and emergency notification system. There are shuttle buses, emergency telephones, lighted pathways/sidewalks, controlled access to dorms/residences, and crime-prevention education programs.

Programs of Study: WCU confers B.A., B.S., B.F.A., B.M., B.S.B.A., B.S.Ed., B.S.E.E., B.S.N. and B.S.W. degrees. Master's and doctoral degrees are also awarded. Bachelor's degrees are awarded in AGRICULTURE (natural resource management), BIOLOGICAL SCIENCE (biology/biological science), BUSINESS (accounting, banking and finance, business law, entrepreneurial studies, hospitality management services, international business management, management science, marketing and distribution, and sports management), COMMUNICATIONS AND THE ARTS (art, communications, dramatic arts, English, French, German, music, Spanish, and speech/debate/rhetoric), COMPUTER AND PHYSICAL SCIENCE (chemistry, computer science, geology, and mathematics), EDUCATION (art education, early childhood education, elementary education, English education, foreign languages education, mathematics education, middle school education, music education, physical education, science education, secondary education, social science education, special education, speech correction, and teaching English as a second/foreign language (TESOL/TEFOL)), ENGINEERING AND ENVIRONMENTAL DESIGN (construction management, electrical/electronics engineering, electrical/ electronics engineering technology, emergency/disaster science, engineering technology, interior design, manufacturing technology, and preengineering), HEALTH PROFESSIONS (emergency medical technologies, environmental health science, health care administration, medical laboratory science, medical records administration/services, nursing, predentistry, premedicine, preoptometry, prepharmacy, prephysical therapy, preveterinary science, recreation therapy, and sports medicine), SOCIAL SCIENCE (anthropology, criminal justice, dietetics, forensic studies, geography, history, liberal arts/general studies, parks and recreation management, philosophy, political science/government, prelaw, psychology, social science, social work, and sociology). Elementary and middle school education, criminal justice, and nursing have the largest enrollments.

Required: In order to graduate, students must complete a total of 120 to 128 credit hours with a minimum GPA of 2.0. Between 27 and 64 hours are required in the major. All students must fulfill liberal studies requirements in writing, oral communication, wellness, social sciences, physical and biological sciences, math, humanities, history, fine and performing arts, world cultures, the freshman seminar, and 1 course in upper-level perspectives outside the major. Most degree plans include a minimum of 12 hours of free electives.

Special: WCU offers cooperative education programs in most majors, extensive internship opportunities, an accelerated degree in nursing, B.A.-B.S. degrees, dual and student designed majors, nondegree study, pass/fail options in designated courses, and credit for life experience. Study-abroad programs may be arranged in 14 countries and a Washington internship is available to a select few junior- or senior-level students each semester. A joint degree program in electrical engineering with the University of North Carolina-Charlotte is offered. There are 12 national honor societies and a freshman honors program.

Faculty/Classroom: 51% of faculty are male; 49% are female. 81% teach undergraduates. Graduate students teach 5% of introductory courses.

Admissions: 38% of the 2013-2014 applicants were accepted. The SAT scores for the 2013-2014 freshman class were: Critical Reading--43% below 500, 43% between 500 and 599, 13% between 600 and 699, and 1% between 700 and 800; Math--36% below 500, 47% between 500 and 599, 16% between 600 and 699, and 1% between 700 and 800; Writing--60% below 500, 32% between 500 and 599, 7% between 600 and 699, and 1% between 700 and 800. The ACT scores were 34% below 21, 38% between 21 and 23, 16% between 24 and 26, 6% between 27 and 28, and 6% above 28. 28% of the current freshmen were in the top fifth of their class; 62% were in the top two fifths.

Requirements: The SAT is required. Graduation from an accredited secondary school or the GED is required. High school courses must include 4 units of English, 4 units of math, 3 units of lab science, 2 of social studies, including 1 of U.S. history, and 2 units of a foreign language. 5 units of academic electives are also required. A GPA of 2.5 is required. AP and CLEP credits are accepted. Important factors in the admissions decision are advanced placement or honors courses, recommendations by school officials, and evidence of special talent.

Procedure: Freshmen are admitted fall, spring, and summer. Entrance exams should be taken during the spring of the junior year or the fall of the senior year. There are early decision, early admissions, and rolling admissions plans. Early decision applications should be filed by November 15; regular applications, by March 1 for fall entry; November 15 for spring entry; and April 15 for summer entry, along with a $55 fee. Notification of early decision is sent December 15; regular decision, on a rolling basis. Applications are accepted online.

Transfer: 784 transfer students enrolled in 2012-2013. Transfer students must have a minimum GPA of 2.0 and meet freshman admissions requirements 32 of 128 credits required for the bachelor's degree must be completed at WCU.

Visiting: There are regularly scheduled orientations for prospective students, consisting of 6 open houses and 8 regional tour events annually and twice-daily campus tours every Monday, Tuesday, Thursday, and Friday. There are guides for informal visits, visitors may sit in on classes, and stay overnight. To schedule a visit, contact the Admissions Office.

Financial Aid: In 2013-2014, 66% of all full-time freshmen and 66% of continuing full-time students received some form of financial aid. 65% of all full-time freshmen and 64% of continuing full-time students received need-based aid. The average freshman award was $8,551. Need-based scholarships or need-based grants averaged $6,214; need-based self-help aid (loans and jobs) averaged $3,386; non-need-based athletic scholarships averaged $9,802; and other non-need-based awards and non-need-based scholarships averaged $3,071. 15% of undergraduate students work part-time. Average annual earnings from campus work are $4350. The average financial indebtedness of the 2013 graduate was $22,608. The FAFSA and the college's own financial statement are required. The priority date for freshman financial aid applications for fall entry is March 15.

International Students: There are 81 international students enrolled. The school actively recruits these students. They must take the TOEFL with a minimum score of 550 on the paper-based TOEFL (PBT) or 79 on the Internet-based version (iBT). They must also take the SAT.

Computers: All students may access the system 24 hours a day. There are no time limits and no fees.

Graduates: From July 1, 2012 to June 30, 2013, 1783 bachelor's degrees were awarded. The most popular majors were criminal justice (10%), nursing (7%), and elementary and middle grades education (7%). 300 companies recruited on campus in 2012-2013. In an average class, 1% graduate in 3 years or less, 28% graduate in 4 years or less, 44% graduate in 5 years or less, and 48% graduate in 6 years or less.

Admissions Contact: Undergraduate Admissions E-Mail: *admiss@wcu.edu* Web: *www.wcu.edu/admissions/*

WILLIAM PEACE UNIVERSITY — D-2

Raleigh, NC 27604 — **(919) 508-2000; (919) 508-2306**

Full-time: 118 men, 582 women	**Faculty:** 25
Part-time: 18 men, 73 women	**Ph.D.s:** 84%
Graduate: n/av	**Student/Faculty:** 28 to 1
Year: semesters, summer session	**Tuition:** $23,900
Application Deadline:	**Room & Board:** $9000
Freshman Class: 814 applied, 755 accepted, 232 enrolled	
SAT CR/M: 440/440	**ACT:** 18 — **LESS COMPETITIVE**

William Peace University, founded in 1857 and affiliated with the Presbyterian Church, is a women's undergraduate college of arts and sciences. There are 2 undergraduate schools. The library contains 49,950 volumes, 2,000 microform items, and 1,749 audio/video tapes/CDs/DVDs, and subscribes to 30,600 periodicals including electronic. Computerized library services include interlibrary loans, database searching, Internet access, and Wi-Fi capability. The 21-acre campus is in an urban area in Raleigh. Including any residence halls, there are 15 buildings.

Student Life: 94% of undergraduates are from North Carolina. Others are from 17 states, and 2 foreign countries. 42% are White; 36% African American; 13% race unknown. The average age of freshmen is 19; all undergraduates, 23. 65% do not continue beyond their first year; 45% remain to graduate.

Housing: 530 students can be accommodated in college housing, which includes single-sex and coed dorms, on-campus apartments, and off-campus apartments. On-campus housing is guaranteed for the freshman year only. 51% of students live on campus. All students may keep cars.

Activities: There are no fraternities; 4% of women belong to 1 national sorority. There are 36 groups on campus, including art, cheerleading, choir, chorus, dance, drama, environmental, ethnic, gay, honors, international, literary magazine, musical theater, newspaper, photography, political, professional, religious, social, social service, student government, and yearbook. Popular campus events include Late Night Breakfast, Red Rose Ball, Student Showcase, Family Weekend and Homecoming.

Sports: There are 5 intercollegiate sports for men and 6 for women, and 4 intramural sports for men and 4 for women. Facilities include A 500-seat gym for basketball and volleyball, an indoor pool, 3 lighted and 3 unlighted tennis courts, and a fitness room with weight-lifting and cardio equipment.

Disabled Students: 75% of the campus is accessible. Facilities include wheelchair ramps, elevators, special parking, specially equipped restrooms, lowered drinking fountains, and special housing.

Services: Counseling and information services are available, as is tutoring in some subjects.

Campus Safety and Security: Measures include 24-hour foot and vehicle patrol, emergency notification system, and self-defense education. There are shuttle buses, emergency telephones, lighted pathways/ sidewalks, controlled access to dorms/residences, security cameras.

Programs of Study: confers B.A., B.F.A. and B.S. degrees. Bachelor's degrees are awarded in BIOLOGICAL SCIENCE (biology/biological science), BUSINESS (business administration and management), COMMUNICATIONS AND THE ARTS (communications, English, game design and development, musical theater, and theatre arts), EDUCATION (education), SOCIAL SCIENCE (liberal arts/general studies, political science/ government, prelaw, and psychology).

Required: To graduate, all students must complete a minimum of 120 credit hours, with 30 or more in the major, and must maintain a minimum GPA of 2.0 in all academic courses. The liberal education requirements (49 credit hours) include courses in writing, empirical reasoning, ethical reasoning, critical thinking about culture and society, and professional readiness. A senior internship or research is required for most majors.

Special: Students may cross-register with North Carolina and Shaw Universities, and with Meredith and St. Augustine Colleges. Study abroad is offered as part of the cross-cultural requirement. On-campus work-study is available, and dual majors are possible, as is international baccalaureate credit. There are 7 national honor societies and a freshman honors program.

Faculty/Classroom: 48% of faculty are male; 52% are female. All teach undergraduates. No introductory courses are taught by graduate students.

Admissions: 93% of the 2013-2014 applicants were accepted. The SAT

scores for the 2013-2014 freshman class were: Critical Reading--72% below 500, 23% between 500 and 599, 5% between 600 and 699; Math--73% below 500, 24% between 500 and 599, 3% between 600 and 699. The ACT scores were 64% below 21, 10% between 21 and 23, 15% between 24 and 26, 3% between 27 and 28, and 8% above 28.

Requirements: The SAT or ACT is required. Recommended academic preparation includes 4 units of English, 3-4 of math (algebra I and II and geometry), 3 of science, 2 of social studies and 2 of a foreign language. AP and CLEP credits are accepted.

Procedure: Freshmen are admitted fall and spring. Entrance exams should be taken by or during orientation in July. There are early admissions, deferred admissions, and rolling admissions plans. Application deadlines are open. Application fee is $25. Applications are accepted online.

Transfer: 51 transfer students enrolled in 2012-2013. Transfer applicants must submit transcripts from all previously attended colleges or universities, as well as a dean's evaluation from the last attended. 30 of 120 credits required for the bachelor's degree must be completed at.

Visiting: There are regularly scheduled orientations for prospective students, including open house tours, meetings with faculty, and student lunch-socials. There are guides for informal visits and visitors may sit in on classes. To schedule a visit, contact the Admissions Office.

Financial Aid: In 2013-2014, 91% of all full-time freshmen and 89% of continuing full-time students received some form of financial aid. 91% of all full-time freshmen and 85% of continuing full-time students received need-based aid. The average freshman award was $23,939. Need-based scholarships or need-based grants averaged $20,850; and other non-need-based awards and non-need-based scholarships averaged $6,666. 6% of undergraduate students work part-time. Average annual earnings from campus work are $1319. The FAFSA is required. The deadline for filing freshman financial aid applications for fall entry is March 15.

International Students: There are 2 international students enrolled. The school actively recruits these students. They must take the TOEFL with a minimum score of 550 on the paper-based TOEFL (PBT) or 80 on the Internet-based version (iBT). They must also take the SAT or ACT, scoring 800.

Computers: All students may access the system 24 hours a day, 7 days a week. There are no time limits and no fees.

Graduates: From July 1, 2012 to June 30, 2013, 159 bachelor's degrees were awarded. The most popular majors were business administration (31%), psychology (15%), and communication (8%). 40 companies recruited on campus in 2012-2013. In an average class, 32% graduate in 4 years or less, 45% graduate in 5 years or less, and 45% graduate in 6 years or less.

Admissions Contact: Jenny Peacock, Director of Admissions. E-Mail: *admissions@peace.edu* Web: *www.peace.edu*

WINGATE UNIVERSITY C-3

Wingate, NC 28174 (704) 233-8200
(800) 755-5550; (704) 233-8110

Full-time: 713 men, 1001 women	**Faculty:** 87; IIB, -$
Part-time: 23 men, 36 women	**Ph.D.s:** 94%
Graduate: 395 men, 480 women	**Student/Faculty:** 14 to 1
Year: semesters, summer session	**Tuition:** $25,040
Application Deadline:	**Room & Board:** $9950

Freshman Class: 4862 applied, 3933 accepted, 548 enrolled
SAT CR/M/W: 500/520/490 **ACT:** 22 **COMPETITIVE**

Wingate University, founded in 1896, is a private liberal arts institution. There are 4 undergraduate schools and 4 graduate schools. In addition to regional accreditation, Wingate has baccalaureate program accreditation with ACBSP, ACPE, NASM, and NCATE. The library contains 103,397 volumes, 7,024 microform items, and 9,317 audio/video tapes/CDs/DVDs, and subscribes to 28,532 periodicals including electronic. Computerized library services include interlibrary loans, database searching, Internet access, and Wi-Fi capability. Special learning facilities include an art gallery, TV station, student newspaper and a fine arts center. The 330-acre campus is in a small town 25 miles east of Charlotte. Including any residence halls, there are 35 buildings.

Student Life: 80% of undergraduates are from North Carolina. Others are from 33 states, 17 foreign countries, and Canada. 90% are from public schools. 61% are White; 15% African American; 11% race unknown. 75% are Protestant; 15% Catholic. The average age of freshmen is 18; all undergraduates, 20. 25% do not continue beyond their first year; 52% remain to graduate.

Housing: 1560 students can be accommodated in college housing, which includes single-sex dorms, on-campus apartments, and married student housing. In addition, there are fraternity houses and sorority houses. On-campus housing is guaranteed for all 4 years. 80% of students live on campus; of those, 60% remain on campus on weekends. All students may keep cars.

Activities: 4% of men belong to 4 national fraternities; 10% of women belong to 4 national sororities. There are 53 groups on campus, including art, band, cheerleading, choir, chorale, chorus, computers, ethnic, honors, international, jazz band, literary magazine, musical theater, newspaper, opera, pep band, photography, political, professional, radio and TV, religious, social, social service, and student government. Popular campus events include Spring Fling and Fall Festival at Campus Lake and Name-band Concerts.

Sports: There are 10 intercollegiate sports for men and 10 for women, and 13 intramural sports for men and 13 for women. Facilities include Wingate has an athletic complex with a gym, swimming pool, racquetball courts, weight room, and tennis courts. The student center has an exercise room, table tennis, pool, and a game room. The university also has a football stadium, and baseball, soccer, and softball fields.

Disabled Students: 95% of the campus is accessible. Facilities include wheelchair ramps, elevators, special parking, specially equipped restrooms, special class scheduling, and lowered drinking fountains.

Services: Counseling and information services are available, as is tutoring in every subject. Additional academic support is available for students with learning disabilities.

Campus Safety and Security: Measures include 24-hour foot and vehicle patrol, emergency notification system, self-defense education, and security escort services. There are emergency telephones, lighted pathways/sidewalks, and controlled access to dorms/residences.

Programs of Study: Wingate confers B.A., B.S., B.F.A., B.S.N., B.L.S. and B.M.E. degrees. Master's and doctoral degrees are also awarded. Bachelor's degrees are awarded in BIOLOGICAL SCIENCE (biology/biological science and environmental biology), BUSINESS (accounting, business administration and management, finance, marketing management, and sports management), COMMUNICATIONS AND THE ARTS (communications, English, fine arts, journalism, music, and public relations), COMPUTER AND PHYSICAL SCIENCE (chemistry and mathematics), EDUCATION (athletic training, elementary education, English education, mathematics education, middle school education, music education, physical education, reading education, science education, and social science education), ENGINEERING AND ENVIRONMENTAL DESIGN (preengineering), HEALTH PROFESSIONS (nursing, predentistry, premedicine, prepharmacy, and preveterinary science), SOCIAL SCIENCE (criminal justice, history, human services, liberal arts/general studies, parks and recreation management, philosophy, political science/government, prelaw, psychology, religion, and sociology). Communications, management, education, biology, psychology, marketing, sport management have the largest enrollments.

Required: To graduate, students must complete a minimum of 125 credit hours with a GPA of 2.0. At least 30 hours must be completed in the student's major. All students must complete the Core Curriculum, which includes 24 hours of Global Perspectives.

Special: Cross-registration through the Charlotte Area Education Consortium, in Army and Air Force ROTC programs, internships, a liberal studies degree, B.A. B.S. degrees, and nondegree study are available. Wingate conducts foreign study semesters in London, Denmark, and China. The school also sponsors Winternational, a semester seminar with a 10-day trip to a foreign country for which students earn academic credit at little personal cost. Dual majors are offered in biology and education, history and education, art and education, English and education, math and education, and chemistry and business.Students can earn a B.S. in biology ans pharm.D. through a 3 + 1 program. There are 11 national honor societies and a freshman honors program.

Faculty/Classroom: 48% of faculty are male; 52% are female. 70% teach undergraduates. No introductory courses are taught by graduate students. The average class size in an introductory lecture is 26; in a laboratory is 15; and in a regular course is 16.

Admissions: 81% of the 2013-2014 applicants were accepted. The SAT scores for the 2013-2014 freshman class were: Critical Reading--49% below 500, 39% between 500 and 599, 11% between 600 and 699, and 1% between 700 and 800; Math--37% below 500, 42% between 500 and 599, 21% between 600 and 699, and 1% between 700 and 800; Writing--53% below 500, 37% between 500 and 599, 9% between 600 and 699, and 1% between 700 and 800. The ACT scores were 34% below 21, 35% between 21 and 23, 19% between 24 and 26, 6% between 27 and 28, and 6% above 28. 40% of the current freshmen were in the top fifth of their class; 73% were in the top two fifths. 6 freshmen graduated first in their class.

Requirements: Graduation from an accredited secondary school or the GED is required. High school curriculum must include 4 courses in English, 3 in math, 2 each in history and science, and 1 in social studies. 2 courses in a foreign language are recommended. An essay is required of all applicants, and an interview is recommended in some cases. The SAT or ACT is also required. A GPA of 2.7 is required. AP and CLEP credits are accepted. Important factors in the admissions decision are advanced placement or honors courses, leadership record, and recommendations by school officials.

Procedure: Freshmen are admitted fall, spring, and summer. Entrance exams should be taken In spring of the junior year or fall of the senior year.

There is a rolling admissions plan. Application deadlines are open. The fall 2013 application fee was $30. Applications are accepted online.

Transfer: 90 transfer students enrolled in 2012-2013. Applicants must have a minimum GPA of 2.0 and must be eligible to return to the institution last attended. The SAT or ACT is required if a student has been out of high school for less than 5 years or has fewer than 24 transferable hours. An interview may be recommended in some cases. 30 of 125 credits required for the bachelor's degree must be completed at Wingate.

Visiting: There are regularly scheduled orientations for prospective students, Saturday preview day 4 times a year, campus tours and presentations of travel programs, academic life, athletics, and student life. New student orientation takes place during one of several summer sessions according to student's declared major. There are guides for informal visits, visitors may sit in on classes, and stay overnight. To schedule a visit, contact the Admissions Office.

Financial Aid: In 2013-2014, 79% of all full-time freshmen and 83% of continuing full-time students received some form of financial aid. 79% of all full-time freshmen and 82% of continuing full-time students received need-based aid. The average freshman award was $22,406. Need-based scholarships or need-based grants averaged $19,076; need-based self-help aid (loans and jobs) averaged $4,233; non-need-based athletic scholarships averaged $8,128; and other non-need-based awards and non-need-based scholarships averaged $3,822. 20% of undergraduate students work part-time. Average annual earnings from campus work are $1200. The average financial indebtedness of the 2013 graduate was $24,785. The FAFSA is required. The deadline for filing freshman financial aid applications for fall entry is May 1.

International Students: There are 65 international students enrolled. They must take the TOEFL with a minimum score of 550 on the paper-based TOEFL (PBT). They must also take the SAT and ACT.

Computers: All students may access the system. Internet access is available 24/7. There are no time limits. The fee is $295.

Graduates: From July 1, 2012 to June 30, 2013, 276 bachelor's degrees were awarded. The most popular majors were business/marketing (22%), sport management (14%), and biology (12%). 50 companies recruited on campus in 2012-2013. In an average class, 38% graduate in 4 years or less, 43% graduate in 5 years or less, and 45% graduate in 6 years or less. Of the 2012 graduating class, 20% were enrolled in graduate school within 6 months of graduation, and 80% were employed.

Admissions Contact: Gabe Hollingsworth, Director of Admissions. E-Mail: *admit@wingate.edu* Web: *www.wingate.edu*

WINSTON-SALEM STATE UNIVERSITY C-2

Winston-Salem, NC 27110 (336) 750-2070
(800) 257-4052; (336) 750-2079

Full-time: 1428 men, 3404 women
Part-time: 148 men, 478 women
Graduate: 94 men, 318 women
Year: semesters, summer session
Application Deadline: open
Freshman Class: 2270 accepted, 969 enrolled
SAT M/W: 440/420
Faculty: 269; IIA, --$
Ph.D.s: 67%
Student/Faculty: 18 to 1
Tuition: $3748 ($12,388)
Room & Board: $5670

LESS COMPETITIVE

Winston-Salem State University, founded in 1892, is a state-supported liberal arts institution offering undergraduate programs through divisions of arts and sciences, business and economics, education, and nursing and allied health. The figures in the above capsule and this profile are approximate. There is one graduate school. In addition to regional accreditation, WSSU has baccalaureate program accreditation with NASM, NCATE, and NLN. The library contains 223,496 volumes, 348,178 microform items, and 5,275 audio/video tapes/CDs/DVDs, and subscribes to 28,240 periodicals including electronic. Computerized library services include interlibrary loans and database searching. Special learning facilities include an art gallery, radio station, TV station, a PLATO lab, and an enrichment center. The 117-acre campus is in a suburban area in Winston-Salem. Including any residence halls, there are 36 buildings.

Student Life: 92% of undergraduates are from North Carolina. Others are from 26 states, and 8 foreign countries. 79% are African American; 15% White. The average age of freshmen is 19; all undergraduates, 22. 23% do not continue beyond their first year; 10% remain to graduate.

Housing: 2133 students can be accommodated in college housing, which includes single-sex and coed dorms. On-campus housing is guaranteed for the freshman year only, is available on a first-come, and first-served basis. 64% of students commute. Alcohol is not permitted. All students may keep cars.

Activities: There are 70 groups on campus, including art, band, cheerleading, choir, computers, dance, drama, drill team, ethnic, honors, international, jazz band, marching band, newspaper, photography, political, radio and TV, social, and student government.

Sports: There are 4 intercollegiate sports for men and 5 for women. Facilities include 2 gyms, tennis courts, an indoor swimming pool, a track, and a weight training room.

Disabled Students: 90% of the campus is accessible. Facilities include wheelchair ramps, elevators, special parking, specially equipped restrooms, lowered drinking fountains, and lowered telephones.

Services: Counseling and information services are available, as is tutoring in most subjects. There is remedial math, reading, and writing.

Campus Safety and Security: Measures include 24-hour foot and vehicle patrol and security escort services. There are shuttle buses, emergency telephones, and lighted pathways/sidewalks.

Programs of Study: WSSU confers B.A., B.S., B.S.App.Sci., B.S.Med.Tech., B.S.N. and B.S.P.T. degrees. Master's degrees are also awarded. Bachelor's degrees are awarded in BIOLOGICAL SCIENCE (biology/biological science), BUSINESS (accounting, business administration and management, management information systems, and sports management), COMMUNICATIONS AND THE ARTS (art, communications, English, music business management, and Spanish), COMPUTER AND PHYSICAL SCIENCE (chemistry, computer science, and mathematics), EDUCATION (elementary education, music education, physical education, and special education), HEALTH PROFESSIONS (medical technology, nursing, physical therapy, and recreation therapy), SOCIAL SCIENCE (economics, history, political science/government, psychology, public administration, and sociology). Phys ed, computer science, and math are the strongest academically. Nursing, business administration, and education have the largest enrollments.

Required: Students must complete a minimum of 121 semester hours, with 40 of these hours in upper-level courses, and must maintain an overall minimum GPA of 2.0. All students must also complete the general education core requirement, which includes courses in English composition, social sciences, math and natural sciences, humanities, and phys ed or military science.

Special: Opportunities are provided for cooperative programs, internships, work-study programs, a B.A.-B.S. degree, a general studies degree, and credit for military experience. The nursing division offers flexible scheduling for employed RNs. There are a freshman honors program.

Faculty/Classroom: 46% of faculty are male; 54% are female. All teach undergraduates. No introductory courses are taught by graduate students. The average class size in an introductory lecture is 60; in a laboratory is 25; and in a regular course is 43.

Admissions: The SAT scores for the 2013-2014 freshman class were: Math--78% below 500, 12% between 500 and 599, and 1% between 600 and 699; Writing--79% below 500, 7% between 500 and 599, and 1% between 600 and 699. 4% of the current freshmen were in the top fifth of their class; 18% were in the top two fifths.

Requirements: The SAT or ACT is required with a minimum composite score of 700 on the SAT recommended. Graduation from an accredited secondary school is required; a GED will be accepted. Applicants should submit an academic record including 4 credits in English, 3 each in math and science, 2 in a foreign language, and 1 each in U.S. history, social studies, and phys ed and health. A GPA of 2.0 is required. AP and CLEP credits are accepted. Important factors in the admissions decision are advanced placement or honors courses, leadership record, and recommendations by school officials.

Procedure: Freshmen are admitted to all sessions. Entrance exams should be taken in the summer or early fall of the senior year in high school. There are deferred admissions and rolling admissions plans. Application deadlines are open. The fall 2013 application fee was $40. Notification is sent on a rolling basis. Applications are accepted online.

Transfer: 376 transfer students enrolled in 2012-2013. Transfer applicants must submit official transcripts from all colleges previously attended, showing no grade lower than C. No more than 64 semester hours (96 quarter hours) will be accepted for transfer. Those applicants transferring fewer than 29 credits will be admitted as freshmen and must meet all freshman admission requirements. 30 of 121 credits required for the bachelor's degree must be completed at WSSU.

Visiting: There are regularly scheduled orientations for prospective students, including summer and fall orientation. There are guides for informal visits and visitors may sit in on classes. To schedule a visit, contact the Admissions Office.

Financial Aid: In 2013-2014, 79% of all full-time freshmen and 75% of continuing full-time students received some form of financial aid. 79% of all full-time freshmen and 73% of continuing full-time students received need-based aid. The average financial indebtedness of the 2013 graduate was $10,300. WSSU is a member of CSS. The CSS/Profile, FFS, and the college's own financial statement are required. The deadline for filing freshman financial aid applications for fall entry is March 15.

International Students: They must take the TOEFL.

Computers: All students may access the system.

Graduates: From July 1, 2012 to June 30, 2013, 740 bachelor's degrees were awarded. The most popular majors were nursing (36%), business administration (10%), and interdisciplinary studies (7%). In an average class, 22% graduate in 4 years or less and 40% graduate in 5 years or less.

Admissions Contact: Tomikia LeGrande, Director of Undergraduate Admissions. E-Mail: *LeGrande@wssu.edu* Web: *www.wssu.edu*

NORTH DAKOTA

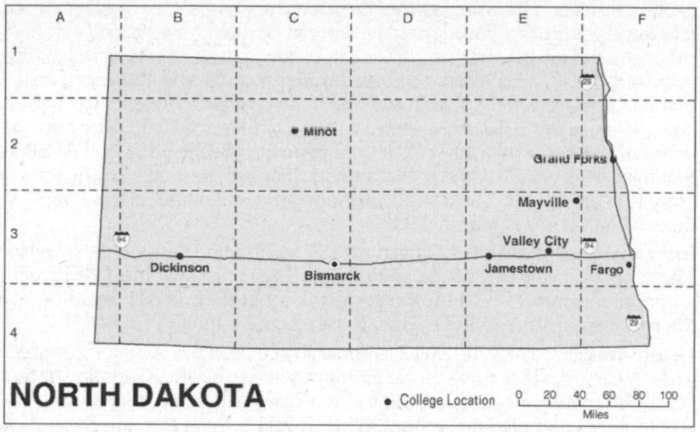

DICKINSON STATE UNIVERSITY — B-3

Dickinson, ND 58601-4896 — (701) 483-2175
(800) 279-4295; (701) 483-2409

Full-time: 765 men, 1025 women
Part-time: 345 men, 555 women
Graduate: n/av
Year: semesters, summer session
Application Deadline: see profile
Freshman Class: n/av
SAT or ACT: required
Faculty: n/av; IIB, --$
Ph.D.s: n/av
Student/Faculty: n/av
Tuition: $5800 ($12,695)
Room & Board: $4994

NONCOMPETITIVE

Dickinson State University is a public, regional institution offering undergraduate programs in teacher education, the liberal arts, business, health sciences, agriculture, and computer science. There are 2 undergraduate schools. In addition to regional accreditation, DSU has baccalaureate program accreditation with NCATE and NLN. The library contains 91,870 volumes, 8941 microform items, 5493 audio/video tapes/CDs/DVDs, and subscribes to 1748 periodicals including electronic. Computerized library services include interlibrary loans and database searching. Special learning facilities include a learning resource center and art gallery. The 100-acre campus is in a rural area 100 miles west of Bismarck. Including any residence halls, there are 15 buildings.

Student Life: 66% of undergraduates are from North Dakota. Others are from 37 states, 30 foreign countries, and Canada. 95% are from public schools. 71% are white. 50% are Catholic; 50% Protestant. The average age of freshmen is 19; all undergraduates, 22. 2% do not continue beyond their first year; 28% remain to graduate.

Housing: 655 students can be accommodated in college housing, which includes single-sex and coed dorms and married student housing. In addition, there are honors houses. On-campus housing is guaranteed for the freshman year only. 70% of students commute. Alcohol is not permitted. All students may keep cars.

Activities: There are no fraternities or sororities. There are 49 groups on campus, including art, band, cheerleading, choir, chorale, chorus, computers, dance, drama, drill team, ethnic, film, forensics, honors, international, jazz band, literary magazine, marching band, musical theater, newspaper, pep band, political, professional, religious, social, and student government. Popular campus events include Winter, Spring, and Back to School Weeks, and Family Weekend.

Sports: There are 9 intercollegiate sports for men and 8 for women, and 5 intramural sports for men and 3 for women. Facilities include a gym, an outdoor stadium, an indoor/outdoor rodeo arena, and an indoor track.

Disabled Students: 90% of the campus is accessible. Facilities include wheelchair ramps, elevators, special parking, specially equipped rest rooms, special class scheduling, lowered drinking fountains, and lowered telephones.

Services: Counseling and information services are available, as is tutoring in every subject. There is a reader service for the blind and remedial math, reading, and writing.

Campus Safety and Security: There are lighted pathways/sidewalks and 10-hour-a-day security.

Programs of Study: DSU confers B.A., B.S., B.A.S.T., B.S.E., B.S.N., and B.U.S. degrees. Associates degrees are also awarded. Bachelor's degrees are awarded in AGRICULTURE (agricultural business management), BIOLOGICAL SCIENCE (biology/biological science), BUSINESS (accounting, business administration and management, and personnel management), COMMUNICATIONS AND THE ARTS (communications, English, fine arts, journalism, music, Spanish, and speech/debate/rhetoric), COMPUTER AND PHYSICAL SCIENCE (chemistry, computer programming, computer science, earth science, and mathematics), EDUCATION (art education, business education, early childhood education, elementary education, middle school education, music education, science education, and secondary education), HEALTH PROFESSIONS (nursing), SOCIAL SCIENCE (geography, history, political science/government, social work, and sociology). Elementary education, math, and business are the strongest academically. Education, business, and nursing have the largest enrollments.

Required: To graduate, students must complete 128 semester hours, with 36 in the major and maintain a minimum GPA of 2.0. General education requirements: 10 hours in scientific inquiry, 9 hours each in expressions of human civilizations, understanding human civilization, and communication, 2 hours in phys ed, and 1 computer science course.

Special: DSU offers a co-op program in social work with the University of North Dakota and in agriculture with North Dakota State University. An additional co-op program exists with Bismarck State College and Williston State College. Cross-registration is available within the North Dakota University System. Internships in business and social work, study abroad in 3 countries, credit for life experience, and pass/fail options are available. Student-designed majors are possible through the Bachelor of University Studies program. There are 5 national honor societies, including Phi Beta Kappa, and a freshman honors program.

Faculty/Classroom: 47% of faculty are male; 53% are female. All teach undergraduates, and 5% do research. No introductory courses are taught by graduate students. The average class size in an introductory lecture is 40, in a laboratory, 25, and in a regular course, 20.

Requirements: The SAT or ACT is required; the ACT is preferred. Graduation from an accredited secondary school is recommended. The GED is accepted. Students must have 20 academic credits. An essay is not required. AP and CLEP credits are accepted.

Procedure: Freshmen are admitted to all sessions. Entrance exams should be taken in the spring before fall entrance. There is a rolling admissions plan. Application deadlines are open. The application fee is $35. Applications are accepted online.

Transfer: Transfer students must have a minimum GPA of 2.0. The ACT is preferred, but applicants may submit SAT scores. 32 of 128 credits required for the bachelor's degree must be completed at DSU.

Visiting: There are regularly scheduled orientations for prospective students, consisting of two 2-day orientations and two 1-day sessions in July and August. There are guides for informal visits; visitors may sit in on classes and stay overnight. To schedule a visit, contact the Office of Enrollment Services.

Financial Aid: The FAFSA is required. Check with the school for current application deadlines.

International Students: The school actively recruits these students. They must take the TOEFL with a minimum score of 525 on the paper-based TOEFL (PBT) or 71 on the Internet-based version (iBT).

Admissions Contact: Director of Enrollment Services. E-Mail: *dsu.hawk@dsu.nodak.edu* Web: *www.dickinsonstate.com*

MAYVILLE STATE UNIVERSITY — E-3

Mayville, ND 58257 — 701-788-4667
(800) 437-4104; (701) 788-4656

Full-time: 301 men, 286 women
Part-time: 151 men, 298 women
Graduate: 6 men, 23 women
Year: semesters, summer session
Application Deadline: open
Freshman Class: 317 applied, 163 accepted, 134 enrolled
ACT: 19
Faculty: 40; IIB, --$
Ph.D.s: 38%
Student/Faculty: 15 to 1
Tuition: $6353 ($8675)
Room & Board: $5048

NONCOMPETITIVE

Mayville State University, founded in 1889, is a public institution that emphasizes teacher education, business, and information technology. The figures in the above capsule and in this profile are approximate. There are 5 undergraduate schools. In addition to regional accreditation, Mayville State has baccalaureate program accreditation with NCATE. The library contains 93,685 volumes, 15,224 microform items, and 9,057 audio/video tapes/CDs/DVDs, and subscribes to 505 periodicals including electronic. Computerized library services include interlibrary loans, database searching, Internet access, and Wi-Fi capability. Special learning facilities include an art gallery, radio station, a learning services center. The 55-acre campus is in a rural area 58 miles north of Fargo and 42 miles south of Grand Forks. Including any residence halls, there are 19 buildings.

Student Life: 60% of undergraduates are from North Dakota. Others are from 37 states, 7 foreign countries, and Canada. 88% are from public schools. 79% are White. 36% are Protestant; 21% Catholic. The average age of freshmen is 18. 46% do not continue beyond their first year; 36% remain to graduate.

Housing: 294 students can be accommodated in college housing, which includes single-sex and coed dorms, on-campus apartments, and married student housing. On-campus housing is guaranteed for the freshman year only, is available on a first-come, and first-served basis. 59% of students commute. Alcohol is not permitted. All students may keep cars.

Activities: There are 24 groups on campus, including band, cheerleading, choir, chorus, debate, drama, ethnic, forensics, international, jazz band, musical theater, newspaper, pep band, political, professional, radio and TV, religious, social service, and student government. Popular campus events include Spring Fling, and Homecoming.

Sports: There are 3 intercollegiate sports for men and 3 for women, and 10 intramural sports for men and 9 for women. Facilities include a 4500-seat football stadium, a track and practice field, a baseball diamond, tennis courts, a swimming pool, a soccer field, a fitness center, and handball and racquetball courts.

Disabled Students: 75% of the campus is accessible. Facilities include elevators, special parking, special class scheduling, lowered drinking fountains, and lowered telephones.

Services: Counseling and information services are available, as is tutoring in some subjects. There is remedial math and writing.

Campus Safety and Security: There are lighted pathways/sidewalks, controlled access to dorms/residences, a nighttime foot patrol.

Programs of Study: Mayville State confers B.A., B.S., B.A.S., B.U.S. and B.S.Ed. degrees. Associate degrees are also awarded. Bachelor's degrees are awarded in BIOLOGICAL SCIENCE (biology/biological science), BUSINESS (business administration and management and sports management), COMMUNICATIONS AND THE ARTS (communications and English), COMPUTER AND PHYSICAL SCIENCE (chemistry, computer management, computer programming, mathematics, physical sciences, and science), EDUCATION (early childhood education, education, education of the exceptional child, elementary education, English education, health education, mathematics education, physical education, science education, secondary education, and social science education), HEALTH PROFESSIONS (medical laboratory technology and premedicine), SOCIAL SCIENCE (applied psychology, child care/child and family studies, early childhood studies, liberal arts/general studies, prelaw, social science, and social studies). Business administration, computer information science, and elementary education are the strongest academically. Business and elementary education have the largest enrollments.

Required: To graduate, students must complete 120 semester hours with a minimum overall GPA of 2.0 in most programs and 2.75 in education. General requirements include 8 semester hours of science, 6 each of humanities and social science, 6 of English, up to 3 of math, 3 each of speech and phys ed.; plus 1 credit in Computer Information Systems.

Special: Residents of all contiguous states, and Canadian provinces, and selected states in the MHEC and WUE consortiums pay a reduced out-of-state tuition. Mayville State also offers preprofessional programs, internships, work-study programs, B.A.-B.S. degrees, dual majors, a general studies degree, credit for life experience, nondegree study, and pass/fail options. Co-op programs are available, including a certified education program for all subject areas. There is also a 4-year major in early childhood education and applied psychology. There is 1 national honor society and a freshman honors program.

Faculty/Classroom: 52% of faculty are male; 48% are female. All teach undergraduates. No introductory courses are taught by graduate students. The average class size in an introductory lecture is 25; in a laboratory is 15; and in a regular course is 20.

Admissions: 51% of the 2013-2014 applicants were accepted. The ACT scores were 68% below 21, 20% between 21 and 23, 7% between 24 and 26, 3% between 27 and 28, and 2% above 28.

Requirements: The ACT is required. Applicants must be graduates of an accredited secondary school or have a GED certificate. Required core courses include 4 in English, and 3 each in math (algebra I or higher), sciences, and social sciences. A GPA of 2.0 is required. AP and CLEP credits are accepted.

Procedure: Freshmen are admitted fall, spring, and summer. Entrance exams should be taken during the senior year. There are early admissions and rolling admissions plans. Application deadlines are open. Application fee is $35. Applications are accepted online.

Transfer: 98 transfer students enrolled in 2012-2013. Applicants must submit official transcripts from all colleges attended and should have a minimum GPA of 2.0, with scores on the SAT or ACT also recommended. 30 of 120 credits required for the bachelor's degree must be completed at Mayville State.

Visiting: There are regularly scheduled orientations for prospective students, including a campus tour, meetings with faculty in fields of interest, and meetings with the financial aid director if needed. There are guides for informal visits, visitors may sit in on classes, and stay overnight. To schedule a visit, contact the Office of Enrollment Services at charlotte.anderson@mayvillestate.edu.

Financial Aid: In 2013-2014, 64% of all full-time freshmen and 62% of continuing full-time students received some form of financial aid. 55% of all full-time freshmen and 50% of continuing full-time students received need-based aid. The average freshman award was $13,275. Need-based scholarships or need-based grants averaged $5,223; need-based self-help aid (loans and jobs) averaged $5,550; non-need-based athletic scholarships averaged $656; and other non-need-based awards and non-need-based scholarships averaged $1,307. 20% of undergraduate students work part-time. Average annual earnings from campus work are $1200. The average financial indebtedness of the 2013 graduate was $22,558. The FAFSA is required. The priority date for freshman financial aid applications for fall entry is February 15. The deadline for filing freshman financial aid applications for fall entry is March 15.

International Students: There are 34 international students enrolled. The school actively recruits these students. They must take the TOEFL with a minimum score of 520 on the paper-based TOEFL (PBT) or 68 on the Internet-based version (iBT). They must also take the SAT or ACT.

Graduates: From July 1, 2012 to June 30, 2013, 137 bachelor's degrees were awarded. The most popular majors were business administration (22%), elementary education (20%), and early childhood education (9%). 3 companies recruited on campus in 2012-2013. In an average class, 21% graduate in 4 years or less, 31% graduate in 5 years or less, and 36% graduate in 6 years or less. Of the 2012 graduating class, 6% were enrolled in graduate school within 6 months of graduation, and 98% were employed.

Admissions Contact: Misti Wuori, Director of Admissions . E-Mail: *MaSU.admissions@mayvillestate.edu* Web: *www.mayvillestate.edu*

MINOT STATE UNIVERSITY — C-2

Minot, ND 58707 (701) 858-4347
(800) 777-0750; (701) 839-6933

Full-time: 840 men, 1338 women | **Faculty:** 159; IIA, --$
Part-time: 438 men, 682 women | **Ph.D.s:** 60%
Graduate: 77 men, 185 women | **Student/Faculty:** 16 to 1
Year: semesters, summer session | **Tuition:** $5921
Application Deadline: | **Room & Board:** $4994
Freshman Class: 1003 applied, 538 accepted, 399 enrolled
SAT or ACT: required

COMPETITIVE

Minot State University, founded in 1913, is a public institution offering undergraduate and graduate programs in arts and sciences, education, business, nursing, and human services. The figures in the above capsule and in this profile are approximate. There are 3 undergraduate schools and 1 graduate school. In addition to regional accreditation, MSU has baccalaureate program accreditation with CSWE, NASM, NCATE, and NLN. The library contains 411,678 volumes, 687,708 microform items, and 12,722 audio/video tapes/CDs/DVDs, and subscribes to 802 periodicals including electronic. Computerized library services include interlibrary loans and database searching. Special learning facilities include an art gallery, natural history museum, radio station, and TV station. The 103-acre campus is in a small town. Including any residence halls, there are 21 buildings.

Student Life: 83% of undergraduates are from North Dakota. Others are from 44 states, 18 foreign countries, and Canada. 95% are from public schools. 84% are White. The average age of freshmen is 19; all undergraduates, 21. 36% do not continue beyond their first year; 32% remain to graduate.

Housing: 643 students can be accommodated in college housing, which includes single-sex and coed dorms, on-campus apartments, and married student housing. In addition, there are language houses and special-interest houses. On-campus housing is guaranteed for the freshman year only, is available on a first-come, first-served basis, and is available on a lottery system for upperclassmen. 88% of students commute. Alcohol is not permitted. All students may keep cars.

Activities: There are no fraternities or sororities. There are 60 groups on campus, including art, band, Campus Ministries, choir, chorale, chorus, drama, ethnic, honors, international, marching band, musical theater, newspaper, orchestra, pep band, political, professional, radio and TV, religious, social service, student government, and symphony. Popular campus events include Welcome Week, Final Frenzy and Native American Awareness Week.

Sports: There are 6 intercollegiate sports for men and 6 for women, and 4 intramural sports for men and 4 for women. Facilities include a 10,000-seat field house, a 2800-seat football stadium, and a 3000-seat gym.

Disabled Students: 99% of the campus is accessible. Facilities include wheelchair ramps, elevators, special parking, specially equipped restrooms, special class scheduling, lowered drinking fountains, lowered telephones, and special housing.

Services: Counseling and information services are available, as is tutoring in most subjects. Special services are offered for disabled students.

Campus Safety and Security: Measures include self-defense education. There are emergency telephones and lighted pathways/sidewalks.

Programs of Study: MSU confers B.A., B.S., B.A.S., B.G.S., B.S. Ed.,

B.S.N. and B.S.W. degrees. Associate and master's degrees are also awarded. Bachelor's degrees are awarded in BIOLOGICAL SCIENCE (biology/biological science), BUSINESS (accounting, banking and finance, international business management, management information systems, management science, and marketing/retailing/merchandising), COMMUNICATIONS AND THE ARTS (art, broadcasting, communications, English, French, German, multimedia, music, and Spanish), COMPUTER AND PHYSICAL SCIENCE (chemistry, computer science, earth science, geology, mathematics, physical sciences, physics, and radiological technology), EDUCATION (business education, drama education, education of the deaf and hearing impaired, education of the exceptional child, education of the mentally handicapped, elementary education, English education, foreign languages education, mathematics education, music education, physical education, and science education), HEALTH PROFESSIONS (dental laboratory technology, nursing, and speech pathology/audiology), SOCIAL SCIENCE (addiction studies, criminal justice, economics, history, liberal arts/general studies, physical fitness/movement, psychology, social science, social work, and sociology). Communication disorders, special education, and elementary education are the strongest academically. Business, criminal justice, and education have the largest enrollments.

Required: Students must take a number of courses in humanities, history, communication, math, natural sciences, social and behavioral sciences, and leisure-time education. They must complete at least 128 semester hours, with 30 to 37 in the major and a minimum GPA of 2.0.

Special: A general studies degree, independent research, internships, work-study, and unique programs of study, including student-designed majors, are available. Cross-registration through the North Dakota University System, co-op programs in all majors, and study including student-designed majors, abroad in 3 countries also are offered. Preliminary programs are available in dental hygiene, dentistry, engineering, law, medicine, and many other areas. There is a freshman honors program.

Faculty/Classroom: 49% of faculty are male; 51% are female. All teach undergraduates, and 20% do research. No introductory courses are taught by graduate students. The average class size in an introductory lecture is 60; in a laboratory is 20; and in a regular course is 16.

Admissions: 54% of the 2013-2014 applicants were accepted.

Requirements: The SAT or ACT is required. Applicants must submit a high school diploma or GED certificate. Core course requirements include 4 years of English and 3 each of math, social studies, and science. AP and CLEP credits are accepted.

Procedure: Freshmen are admitted to all sessions. Entrance exams should be taken any time. There are deferred admissions and rolling admissions plans. Application deadlines are open. Application fee is $35. Applications are accepted online.

Transfer: 291 transfer students enrolled in 2012-2013. Transfers must submit transcripts from each college attended. 30 of 128 credits required for the bachelor's degree must be completed at MSU.

Visiting: There are regularly scheduled orientations for prospective students, prior to the beginning of the fall term. There are guides for informal visits and visitors may sit in on classes. To schedule a visit, contact the Enrollment Services.

Financial Aid: In 2013-2014, 67% of all full-time freshmen and 66% of continuing full-time students received some form of financial aid. 64% of all full-time freshmen and 66% of continuing full-time students received need-based aid. 1% of undergraduate students work part-time. Average annual earnings from campus work are $1260. The average financial indebtedness of the 2013 graduate was $25,117. The FAFSA is required. The priority date for freshman financial aid applications for fall entry is March 15. The deadline for filing freshman financial aid applications for fall entry is October 15.

International Students: There are 41 international students enrolled. The school actively recruits these students. They must take the TOEFL.

Graduates: From July 1, 2012 to June 30, 2013, 740 bachelor's degrees were awarded. The most popular majors were business/marketing (31%), health professions and related sciences (19%), and education (15%). 105 companies recruited on campus in 2012-2013. In an average class, 37% graduate in 6 years or less. Of the 2012 graduating class, 11% were enrolled in graduate school within 6 months of graduation, and 89% were employed.

Admissions Contact: Alexis Hendricks, Enrollment Services Representative. E-Mail: *alexis@minotstateu.edu* Web: *www.minotstateu.edu*

NORTH DAKOTA STATE UNIVERSITY F-3

Fargo, ND 58102 (701) 231-8643
(800) 488-NDSU; (701) 231-8802

Full-time: 6076 men, 4631 women	**Faculty:** n/av; I, --$
Part-time: 600 men, 641 women	**Ph.D.s:** 72%
Graduate: 1280 men, 1401 women	**Student/Faculty:** 18 to 1
Year: semesters, summer session	**Tuition:** $7540 ($18,122)
Application Deadline: August 1	**Room & Board:** $7102
Freshman Class: 5142 applied, 4888 accepted, 2553 enrolled	
SAT CR/M/W: 557/569/523 **ACT:** 23	**COMPETITIVE**

North Dakota is a student-focused, land grant, research university an economic engine that educates students, conducts primary research, creates new knowledge, and advances technology. We provide affordable access to an excellent education at a top-ranked research institution that combines teaching and research in a rich learning environment, educating future leaders who will create solutions to national and global challenges that will shape a better world. There are 8 undergraduate schools and 1 graduate school. In addition to regional accreditation, NDSU has baccalaureate program accreditation with AACSB, ABET, ACCE, ACPE, ADA, AHEA, CAHEA, CSAB, FIDER, NAAB, NASAD, NASM, and NCATE. The 5 libraries contain 784,978 volumes, 444,951 microform items, and 2,873 audio/video tapes/CDs/DVDs, and subscribe to 5,090 periodicals including electronic. Computerized library services include interlibrary loans, database searching, Internet access, and Wi-Fi capability. Special learning facilities include an art gallery, radio station, and TV station. The 258-acre campus is in an urban area 229 miles northwest of Minneapolis-St. Paul. Including any residence halls, there are 97 buildings.

Student Life: 56% of undergraduates are from North Dakota. Others are from 47 states, 78 foreign countries, and Canada. 87% are White. The average age of freshmen is 18; all undergraduates, 21. 20% do not continue beyond their first year; 50% remain to graduate.

Housing: 4996 students can be accommodated in college housing, which includes single-sex and coed dorms, on-campus apartments, and married student housing, learning communities and first-year student halls. On-campus housing is guaranteed for the freshman year only. 66% of students commute. Alcohol is not permitted. All students may keep cars.

Activities: 4% of men belong to 11 national fraternities; 2% of women belong to 3 national sororities. There are 280 groups on campus, including academic, and leisure learning , art, band, cheerleading, choir, chorus, computers, dance, debate, drama, drill team, ethnic, forensics, gay, honors, international, jazz band, marching band, musical theater, newspaper, pep band, political, professional, radio and TV, recreational, religious, social, social service, and student government. Popular campus events include International Students' Week, Spring Blast and Multicultural Activities.

Sports: There are 8 intercollegiate sports for men and 8 for women, and 5 intramural sports for men and 6 for women. Facilities include a sports arena, indoor and outdoor tracks, baseball and softball fields, wrestling and weight rooms, a multipurpose fitness room, volleyball, tennis, basketball, and racquetball courts, and a wellness center.

Disabled Students: All of the campus is accessible. Facilities include wheelchair ramps, elevators, special parking, specially equipped restrooms, special class scheduling, lowered drinking fountains, and lowered telephones.

Services: Counseling and information services are available, as is tutoring in most subjects. There is a reader service for the blind, and remedial math, reading, and writing.

Campus Safety and Security: Measures include 24-hour foot and vehicle patrol, emergency notification system, self-defense education, and security escort services. There are shuttle buses, emergency telephones, lighted pathways/sidewalks, and controlled access to dorms/residences.

Programs of Study: NDSU confers B.A., B.F.A., B.L.A., B.Mus., B.S., B.S.A.B.En., B.S.Arch., B.S.C.E., B.S.Cpr.E., B.S.Con.E., B.S.Cons.M., B.S.E.E., B.S.I.E.Mgt., B.S.Mfg.E., B.S.M.E., B.S.N. and B.U.S. degrees. Master's and doctoral degrees are also awarded. Bachelor's degrees are awarded in AGRICULTURE (agricultural business management, agricultural communications, agricultural economics, agricultural mechanics, agriculture, animal science, equine science, horticulture, natural resource management, plant protection (pest management), plant science, range/farm management, and soil science), BIOLOGICAL SCIENCE (biology/biological science, biotechnology, botany, microbiology, nutrition, and zoology), BUSINESS (accounting, business administration and management, finance, hospitality management services, hotel and restaurant administration, hotel/motel and restaurant management, institutional management, management information systems, recreation and leisure services, and sports management), COMMUNICATIONS AND THE ARTS (apparel design, art, communications, dramatic arts, English, French, instrumental music education, music, performing arts, Spanish, and theatre arts), COMPUTER AND PHYSICAL SCIENCE (actuarial science, chemistry, computer science, earth science, geology, mathematics, physics, radiological technology, and statistics), EDUCATION (agricultural education, athletic training, elementary education, health education, home economics education, music education, physical education, secondary education, and social science education), ENGINEERING AND ENVIRONMENTAL DESIGN (agricultural engineering, agricultural engineering technology, architecture, biomedical engineering, civil engineering, computer engineering, construction engineering, construction management, electrical/electronics engineering, emergency/disaster science, engineering management, environmental design, industrial engineering, interior design, landscape architecture/design, manufacturing engineering, and mechanical engineering), HEALTH PROFESSIONS (clinical science, nursing, pharmacy, preveterinary science, respiratory therapy, and veterinary science), SOCIAL SCIENCE (anthropology, child care/child and family studies, criminal justice, dietetics, economics, food science, history, human development, humanities, international studies, philosophy and religion, physical fitness/movement, political science/government, psychology, social science, sociology, textiles and clothing, water resources, and women and gender studies). Sciences are the strongest academically. Sciences, engineering, and human development have the largest enrollments.

Required: Students must complete at least 122 semester credits, with at least 24 in the major, and maintain at least a 2.0 GPA. General education requirements include 10 credits in science and technology, including a 1-credit lab course, 12 credits in communication, which includes freshman English and public speaking, 6 credits each in humanities and fine arts and in social and behavioral science, 3 credits in quantitative reasoning, at least 2 credits in a wellness course, and a first-year experience course. Included in these courses must be 1 course designated as a cultural diversity course and 1 designated as a global perspectives course.

Special: Special academic programs include cooperative work programs and internships. There is cross-registration with the Tri-college Consortium and all North Dakota State institutions. Student-designed and dual majors, study abroad, a B.A.-B.S. degree, nondegree study, and pass/fail options are possible. There are 22 national honor societies and a freshman honors program.

Faculty/Classroom: 62% of faculty are male; 38% are female. No introductory courses are taught by graduate students. The average class size in a laboratory is 26 and in a regular course is 42.

Admissions: 95% of the 2013-2014 applicants were accepted. The SAT scores for the 2013-2014 freshman class were: Critical Reading--26% below 500, 39% between 500 and 599, 27% between 600 and 699, and 8% between 700 and 800; Math--25% below 500, 37% between 500 and 599, 29% between 600 and 699, and 9% between 700 and 800; Writing--42% below 500, 36% between 500 and 599, 17% between 600 and 699, and 5% between 700 and 800. There were 6 National Merit finalists.

Requirements: The SAT or ACT is required. Applicants must have completed 4 units of English, and 3 each of math (algebra I or above), lab science, and social science. The GED is accepted, with a minimum score of 45 and no subject score lower than 40. A GPA of 2.5 is required. AP and CLEP credits are accepted.

Procedure: Freshmen are admitted to all sessions. Entrance exams should be taken in the spring of the junior year or in the fall of the senior year. There are deferred admissions and rolling admissions plans. Applications should be filed by August 1 for fall entry; December 11 for spring entry; and May 20 for summer entry, along with a $35 fee.

Transfer: Transfer students must have a minimum GPA of 2.0; ACT or SAT scores are required if the applicant has fewer than 24 semester credits. 36 of 122 credits required for the bachelor's degree must be completed at NDSU.

Visiting: There are regularly scheduled orientations for prospective students, including tours of the campus, academic appointments, and meetings with admissions counselors and financial aid counselors. There are guides for informal visits and visitors may sit in on classes. To schedule a visit, contact the Office of Admission at ndsu.admission@ndsu.edu.

Financial Aid: The average financial indebtedness of the 2013 graduate was $30,274. The FAFSA is required. The priority date for freshman financial aid applications for fall entry is March 15.

International Students: There are 1101 international students enrolled. The school actively recruits these students. They must take the TOEFL with a minimum score of 525 on the paper-based TOEFL (PBT) or 70 on the Internet-based version (iBT).

Graduates: From July 1, 2012 to June 30, 2013, 2136 bachelor's degrees were awarded. The most popular majors were business (17%), engineering (14%), health professions and related sciences (11%). In an average class, 25% graduate in 4 years or less, 46% graduate in 5 years or less, and 53% graduate in 6 years or less.

Admissions Contact: Jobey Lichtblau, Director of Admission. E-Mail: *ndsu.admission@ndsu.edu* Web: *www.ndsu.edu*

UNIVERSITY OF JAMESTOWN — E-3

Jamestown, ND 58405 — **(701) 252-3467, ext. 5415; (800) 336-2554; (701) 253-4318**

Full-time: 416 men, 466 women
Part-time: 25 men, 31 women
Graduate: 17 men, 25 women
Year: semesters, summer session
Application Deadline: open
Freshman Class: 898 applied, 602 accepted, 233 enrolled
SAT CR/M: 498/495
Faculty: 57; IIB, --$
Ph.D.s: 54%
Student/Faculty: 13 to 1
Tuition: $18,494
Room & Board: $6244
ACT: 22
COMPETITIVE

University of Jamestown, founded in 1883, is a private, institution founded by the Presbyterian Church. There is 1 undergraduate school and 2 graduate schools. In addition to regional accreditation, has baccalaureate program accreditation with NLN. The library contains 112,169 volumes, 9,000 microform items, and 5,518 audio/video tapes/CDs/DVDs, and subscribes to 18,610 periodicals including electronic. Computerized library services include interlibrary loans, database searching, and Internet access. Special learning facilities include an art gallery and TV station. The 110-acre campus is in a small town The campus is located, 100 miles west of Fargo, 350 miles west of Minneapolis. Including any residence halls, there are 25 buildings.

Student Life: 55% of undergraduates are from out of state, mostly the Mid-West. Students are from 37 states, 15 foreign countries, and Canada. 83% are White. 50% are Protestant; 27% claim no religious affiliation; 19% Catholic. The average age of freshmen is 18; all undergraduates, 21. 39% do not continue beyond their first year; 52% remain to graduate.

Housing: 744 students can be accommodated in college housing, which includes coed dorms, on-campus apartments, off-campus apartments, and married student housing. On-campus housing is guaranteed for the freshman year only, is available on a first-come, first-served basis, and is available on a lottery system for upperclassmen. 65% of students live on campus; of those, 65% remain on campus on weekends. Alcohol is not permitted. All students may keep cars.

Activities: There are no fraternities or sororities. There are 35 groups on campus, including art, band, choir, chorale, chorus, computers, drama, environmental, film, honors, international, jazz band, literary magazine, musical theater, newspaper, orchestra, pep band, political, professional, radio and TV, religious, social, social service, and student government. Popular campus events include Jimmie Jive Week, Homecoming, and Character in Leadership Fall Conference.

Sports: There are 8 intercollegiate sports for men and 8 for women, and 6 intramural sports for men and 6 for women. Facilities include an athletics center with a basketball court and wrestling and volleyball practice and composition area; a football stadium with an all-weather track; a soccer field; and a sports center with a swimming pool, weight room, running track, YMCA, and basketball, handball, and racquetball courts. Nearby facilities include a civic arena, softball field, baseball stadium, swimming pool, tennis courts, municipal golf course, and winter sports complex.

Disabled Students: 51% of the campus is accessible. Facilities include wheelchair ramps, elevators, special parking, specially equipped restrooms, special class scheduling, lowered drinking fountains, lowered telephones, and special housing.

Services: Counseling and information services are available, as is tutoring in most subjects. There is remedial math, reading, and writing.

Campus Safety and Security: Measures include emergency notification system, self-defense education, and security escort services. There are lighted pathways/sidewalks and controlled access to dorms/residences.

Programs of Study: confers B.A., B.S. and B.S.N. degrees. Master's and doctoral degrees are also awarded. Bachelor's degrees are awarded in BIOLOGICAL SCIENCE (biochemistry and biology/biological science), BUSINESS (accounting, business administration and management, and management information systems), COMMUNICATIONS AND THE ARTS (communications, English, fine arts, French, German, music, and Spanish), COMPUTER AND PHYSICAL SCIENCE (chemistry, computer science, information sciences and systems, mathematics, and radiological technology), EDUCATION (elementary education and physical education), HEALTH PROFESSIONS (clinical science, exercise science, and nursing), SOCIAL SCIENCE (criminal justice, history, history of science, psychology, religion, and religious education). Business, nursing, and physical sciences are the strongest academically. Business, nursing, and education have the largest enrollments.

Required: To graduate, students must have a minimum of 128 semester credits, at least 48 of which must be at the upper-division level, with an average of 48 semester credits in the major, and maintain at least a 2.0 GPA.

Special: Special academic options include co-op programs in business, nursing, computer science, and criminal justice, on-campus work-study, internships, study abroad, dual majors within any of the concentrations, and student-designed majors. There is a 3-2 engineering program with North Dakota State University. There are 5 national honor societies and 10 departmental honors programs.

Faculty/Classroom: 54% of faculty are male; 46% are female. All teach

undergraduates. No introductory courses are taught by graduate students. The average class size in an introductory lecture is 26; in a laboratory is 15; and in a regular course is 20.

Admissions: 67% of the 2013-2014 applicants were accepted. The SAT scores for the 2013-2014 freshman class were: Critical Reading--55% below 500, 28% between 500 and 599, 13% between 600 and 699, and 2% between 700 and 800; Math--57% below 500, 28% between 500 and 599, 11% between 600 and 699, and 2% between 700 and 800. The ACT scores were 32% below 21, 32% between 21 and 23, 24% between 24 and 26, 8% between 27 and 28, and 4% above 28. 42% of the current freshmen were in the top fifth of their class; 67% were in the top two fifths. 17 freshmen graduated first in their class.

Requirements: The ACT is recommended. Other admissions requirements include graduation from an accredited secondary school; the GED is also accepted. An interview is highly recommended. requires applicants to be in the upper 50% of their class. A GPA of 2.5 is required. AP and CLEP credits are accepted. Important factors in the admissions decision are evidence of special talent, extracurricular activities record, and leadership record.

Procedure: Freshmen are admitted to all sessions. Entrance exams should be taken before or during the fall of the senior year. There is a rolling admissions plan. Application deadlines are open. Applications are accepted online.

Transfer: 50 transfer students enrolled in 2012-2013. Applicants must have at least a 2.0 GPA and be in good standing with their previous college; Applicants are required to submit official high school and college transcripts. 35 of 128 credits required for the bachelor's degree must be completed at Jamestown.

Visiting: There are regularly scheduled orientations for prospective students, including a campus tour and faculty visits. There are guides for informal visits, visitors may sit in on classes, and stay overnight. To schedule a visit, contact the Admissions Office.

Financial Aid: In 2013-2014, 100% of all full-time freshmen and 100% of continuing full-time students received some form of financial aid. 57% of all full-time freshmen and 52% of continuing full-time students received need-based aid. The average freshman award was $18,372. Need-based scholarships or need-based grants averaged $4,040 ($7,993 maximum); need-based self-help aid (loans and jobs) averaged $3,700 ($11,000 maximum); non-need-based athletic scholarships averaged $4,136 ($14,974 maximum); and other non-need-based awards and non-need-based scholarships averaged $7,940 ($17,974 maximum). 24% of undergraduate students work part-time. Average annual earnings from campus work are $550. The average financial indebtedness of the 2013 graduate was $25,785. The FAFSA is required. The priority date for freshman financial aid applications for fall entry is March 15.

International Students: There are 43 international students enrolled. The school actively recruits these students. They must take the TOEFL with a minimum score of 525 on the paper-based TOEFL (PBT) or 70 on the Internet-based version (iBT) or take the MELAB.

Graduates: From July 1, 2012 to June 30, 2013, 154 bachelor's degrees were awarded. The most popular majors were nursing (19%), business (12%), and elementry education (9%). 25 companies recruited on campus in 2012-2013. In an average class, 34% graduate in 4 years or less, 50% graduate in 5 years or less, and 52% graduate in 6 years or less. Of the 2012 graduating class, 13% were enrolled in graduate school within 6 months of graduation, and 80% were employed.

Admissions Contact: Tena Lawrence, Dean of Enrollment Management. E-Mail: *admissions@jc.edu* Web: *www.jc.edu*

UNIVERSITY OF MARY C-3

Bismarck, ND 58504-9652 **(701) 355-8190**
(800) 288-6279; (701) 255-7687

Full-time: 655 men, 1010 women
Part-time: 195 men, 235 women
Graduate: 280 men, 455 women
Year: semesters, summer session
Application Deadline: see profile
Freshman Class: n/av
SAT or ACT: recommended

Faculty: n/av
Ph.D.s: n/av
Student/Faculty: n/av
Tuition: $13,700
Room & Board: $7500

COMPETITIVE

The University of Mary, founded in 1959, is a private institution affiliated with the Roman Catholic Church. Undergraduate and graduate programs emphasize liberal arts, humanities, social sciences, business, health science, music, professional training, philosophy and religious studies, and teacher preparation. The figures in the above capsule and in this profile are approximate. There are 8 undergraduate schools and 4 graduate schools. In addition to regional accreditation, Mary has baccalaureate program accreditation with CAHEA and CSWE. The library contains 78,137 volumes, 2 microform items, and 7,866 audio/video tapes/CDs/DVDs, and subscribes to 6997 periodicals including electronic. Computerized library services include interlibrary loans, database searching, Internet access, and laptop Internet portals. Special learning facilities include a learning resource center, art gallery, and radio station. The 107-acre campus is in a suburban area 7 miles south of Bismarck. Including any residence halls, there are 13 buildings.

Student Life: 70% of undergraduates are from North Dakota. Others are from 33 states, 23 foreign countries, and Canada. 95% are from public schools. 87% are white. 60% are Catholic; 30% Protestant. The average age of freshmen is 18; all undergraduates, 25. 26% do not continue beyond their first year; 51% remain to graduate.

Housing: 791 students can be accommodated in college housing, which includes single-sex dorms and on campus apartments. On-campus housing is guaranteed for all 4 years. 61% of students commute. Alcohol is not permitted. All students may keep cars.

Activities: There are no fraternities or sororities. There are 22 groups on campus, including band, cheerleading, choir, chorale, chorus, computers, drama, drill team, environmental, ethnic, forensics, jazz band, musical theater, newspaper, orchestra, pep band, photography, political, professional, radio and TV, religious, social, social service, student government, and symphony. Popular campus events include intramural sports and the Convocation Series.

Sports: There are 8 intercollegiate sports for men and 7 for women, and 10 intramural sports for men and 10 for women. Facilities include an activity center housing a 1200-seat gym, basketball and racquetball courts, wrestling and weight rooms, and a swimming pool. The field house includes an indoor track, 3 basketball/volleyball/tennis courts, and a climbing wall. There are also track/football, intramural, and softball fields, tennis courts, a fitness center, and a 1200-seat stadium.

Disabled Students: All of the campus is accessible. Facilities include wheelchair ramps, elevators, special parking, specially equipped rest rooms, special class scheduling, lowered drinking fountains, lowered telephones, and special housing.

Services: Counseling and information services are available, as is tutoring in every subject. There is a reader service for the blind and remedial math, reading, and writing.

Campus Safety and Security: Measures include emergency notification system and security escort services. There are emergency telephones, lighted pathways/sidewalks, and controlled access to dorms/residences.

Programs of Study: Mary confers B.A., B.S., and B.Univ.Studies degrees. Master's degrees are also awarded. Bachelor's degrees are awarded in BIOLOGICAL SCIENCE (biology/biological science), BUSINESS (accounting, business administration and management, business communications, and management information systems), COMMUNICATIONS AND THE ARTS (communications, English, and music), COMPUTER AND PHYSICAL SCIENCE (information sciences and systems, mathematics, and radiological technology), EDUCATION (athletic training, early childhood education, elementary education, English education, mathematics education, music education, physical education, social science education, and special education), ENGINEERING AND ENVIRONMENTAL DESIGN (engineering and applied science), HEALTH PROFESSIONS (exercise science, nursing, occupational therapy, physical therapy, premedicine, and respiratory therapy), SOCIAL SCIENCE (addiction studies, behavioral science, criminal justice, liberal arts/general studies, ministries, pastoral studies, prelaw, psychology, social science, social work, and theological studies). Business administration, education, and nursing are the strongest academically. Business, nursing, and elementary education have the largest enrollments.

Required: To graduate, students must complete 128 semester hours, with 32 to 56 in the major and 44 at the 300 to 400 level, and have a minimum GPA of 2.0. At least 56 semester hours must be in liberal arts courses. In addition, a B.A. degree requires 16 semester hours of a foreign language or 20 semester hours of philosophy/theology, with 12 such hours at the 300 to 400 level. All students must take 3 courses each in humanities, math/science, philosophy/theology, and social sciences.

Special: A co-op program in engineering is available as is cross-registration with the University of Minnesota. Special academic programs include internships in all fields and all programs, study abroad in France, Germany, and Spain, on-campus work-study, and a general studies degree. Dual majors include elementary education/early childhood, elementary education/special education, athletic training/biology, athletic training/phys ed, business/accounting, and business/computer information systems. There are accelerated degree programs in several majors and a 3-2 engineering program with the University of Minnesota. There are 3 national honor societies, a freshman honors program, and 2 departmental honors programs.

Faculty/Classroom: 48% of faculty are male; 52% are female. 95% teach undergraduates. No introductory courses are taught by graduate students. The average class size in an introductory lecture is 15, in a laboratory, 20, and in a regular course, 20.

Requirements: The SAT or ACT and ACT Writing Test are recommended. Applicants should be graduates of an accredited secondary school; the GED is accepted. For automatic acceptance, 3 requirements must be met: a minimum 2.5 GPA, an 18 or higher score on the ACT, and a rank in the upper half of the graduating class. The school's own testing can also be used to determine acceptance. A recommendation from a school counselor, teacher, or employer is requested. A GPA of 2.5 is required. AP and CLEP credits are accepted. Important factors in the admissions decision are evidence of special talent, leadership record, and advanced placement or honors courses.

Procedure: Freshmen are admitted fall and spring. Entrance exams should be taken in the fall of the senior year. There are early admissions, deferred admissions, and rolling admissions plans. Check with the school for current application deadlines. The application fee is $25. Applications are accepted online.

Transfer: Transfer students should have a 2.0 minimum GPA and should present a recommendation from a school counselor, instructor, or employer. 32 of 128 credits required for the bachelor's degree must be completed at Mary.

Visiting: There are regularly scheduled orientations for prospective students, including a campus tour and meetings with individual professors, coaches, students, and music instructors. There are guides for informal visits; visitors may sit in on classes and stay overnight. To schedule a visit, contact the Admissions Office.

Financial Aid: The FAFSA is required. Check with the school for current application deadlines.

International Students: The school actively recruits these students.

Graduates: In a recent year, 502 bachelor's degrees were awarded. The most popular majors were business (40%), nursing (19%), and education (10%). In an average class, 5% graduate in 3 years or less, 39% graduate in 4 years or less, 50% graduate in 5 years or less, and 1% graduate in 6 years or less. Of a recent graduating class, 17% were enrolled in graduate school within 6 months of graduation, and 80% were employed.

Admissions Contact: Dave Heringer, Vice President for Enrollment. A campus DVD is available. E-Mail: *heringer@umary.edu* Web: *www.umary.edu*

UNIVERSITY OF NORTH DAKOTA — E-2

Grand Forks, ND 58202 — **701-777 3000**
1-800-CALL-UND; (701) 777-2721

Full-time: 5126 men, 4259 women	**Faculty:** 662; I, --$
Part-time: 1514 men, 825 women	**Ph.D.s:** 94%
Graduate: 1378 men, 2041 women	**Student/Faculty:** 20 to 1
Year: semesters, summer session	**Tuition:** $7508 ($17,793)
Application Deadline: July 1	**Room & Board:** $6586
Freshman Class: 5408 applied, 3984 accepted, 2360 enrolled	
SAT: required **ACT:** 23	**COMPETITIVE**

UND enrolls 15,143 students from every state and more than 80 countries in more than 240 fields of study, from baccalaureate through doctoral and professional degrees, including law and medicine. There are 8 undergraduate schools and 3 graduate schools. In addition to regional accreditation, UND has baccalaureate program accreditation with ABET, ADA, CSWE, NASAD, NASM, and NCATE. The 2 libraries contain 1.4 million volumes, 1.1 million microform items, and 20,118 audio/video tapes/CDs/DVDs, and subscribe to 48,508 periodicals including electronic. Computerized library services include interlibrary loans, database searching, Internet access, and Wi-Fi capability. Special learning facilities include an art gallery, natural history museum, planetarium, radio station, TV station, an entrepreneur center, an atmospherium, and an art museum and gallery. The 548-acre campus is in an urban area 4 hours from Minneapolis/St. Paul, and 2 hours from Winnipeg, Manitoba. Including any residence halls, there are 240 buildings.

Student Life: 58% of undergraduates are from out of state, mostly the Mid-West. Students are from 50 states, 65 foreign countries, and Canada. 95% are from public schools. 81% are White. The average age of freshmen is 18; all undergraduates, 22. 26% do not continue beyond their first year; 74% remain to graduate.

Housing: 4267 students can be accommodated in college housing, which includes single-sex and coed dorms, on-campus apartments, and married student housing. In addition, there are special-interest houses. On-campus housing is guaranteed for all 4 years. 69% of students commute. Alcohol is not permitted. All students may keep cars.

Activities: 9% of men belong to 13 national fraternities; 11% of women belong to 6 national sororities. There are 275 groups on campus, including and special interest, art, band, cheerleading, chess, choir, chorale, chorus, computers, dance, debate, departmental, drama, drill team, ethnic, film, gay, honors, international, jazz band, literary magazine, marching band, musical theater, newspaper, opera, orchestra, pep band, photography, political, professional, radio and TV, religious, social, social service, student government, and symphony. Popular campus events include The Big Event, and athletic events, and Potato Bowl.

Sports: There are 9 intercollegiate sports for men and 10 for women, and 8 intramural sports for men and 4 for women. Facilities include a golf course, a 15,000-seat stadium, a 11,700-seat hockey arena, a 6,100-seat basketball center, a sports/field house with racquetball and basketball courts, weight rooms and a dance studio. The wellness center houses a three-court gymnasium, multi-activity court, cardiovascular and weight rooms, a 200-meter running track, and a 28-foot-high rock-climbing wall.

Disabled Students: 99% of the campus is accessible. Facilities include wheelchair ramps, elevators, special parking, specially equipped restrooms, special class scheduling, lowered drinking fountains, lowered telephones, special housing. accessible transportation, and academic and personal support services.

Services: Counseling and information services are available, as is tutoring in every subject. There is a reader service for the blind.

Campus Safety and Security: Measures include 24-hour foot and vehicle patrol, emergency notification system, self-defense education, and security escort services. There are shuttle buses, emergency telephones, lighted pathways/sidewalks, and emergency phones throughout the campus.

Programs of Study: UND confers B.A., B.Acc., B.B.A., B.F.A., B.G.S., B.M., B.S., B.S.A., B.S.A.T., B.S.AtSc, B.S.C.E., B.S.C.H.E., B.S.Chem., B.S.C.J.S., B.S.C.L.S., B.S.C.N., B.S.C.S.C.I., B.S.Cyto., B.S.D., B.S.E.E., B.S.E.D., B.S.E.G., B.S.F.W.B., B.S.G.D.T., B.S.G.E., B.S.Geol., B.S.I.T., B.S.M.E., B.S.N., B.S.O.S.E.H., B.S.P.A., B.S.P.X.W., B.S.R.T.S., B.S.R.H.S., B.S.S.W. and B.S.PTE degrees. Master's and doctoral degrees are also awarded. Bachelor's degrees are awarded in AGRICULTURE (environmental studies and fishing and fisheries), BIOLOGICAL SCIENCE (biology/biological science), BUSINESS (accounting, banking and finance, business economics, entrepreneurial studies, human resources, investments and securities, marketing management, and operations management), COMMUNICATIONS AND THE ARTS (Chinese, classical languages, communications, English, French, German, graphic design, music, music performance, musical theater, Norwegian, Spanish, and visual and performing arts), COMPUTER AND PHYSICAL SCIENCE (atmospheric sciences and meteorology, chemistry, computer science, geology, information sciences and systems, mathematics, natural sciences, physics, and science), EDUCATION (athletic training, business education, early childhood education, elementary education, middle school education, music education, and physical education), ENGINEERING AND ENVIRONMENTAL DESIGN (air traffic control, aviation maintenance management, chemical engineering, civil engineering, electrical/electronics engineering, geological engineering, industrial engineering technology, mechanical engineering, occupational safety and health, and petroleum/natural gas engineering), HEALTH PROFESSIONS (clinical science, cytotechnology, music therapy, nursing, and physical therapy), SOCIAL SCIENCE (anthropology, criminal justice, dietetics, early childhood studies, economics, forensic studies, geography, history, interdisciplinary studies, international studies, philosophy, political science/government, psychology, public administration, religion, social science, social work, sociology, and textiles and clothing). Science technologies, philosophy/religion, mathematics and stats are the strongest academically. Health professions, engineering, business have the largest enrollments.

Required: To graduate, students must complete at least 125 credit hours, 30 in the major, with a minimum GPA of 2.0. At least 36 credits must be numbered 300 or above, and at least 60 credits must be from a 4-year institution. Distribution requirements include 12 credits of math, science, and technology, 9 each of social sciences and arts, and humanities, and 6 of English composition. One course in social science or arts and humanities must meet the world cultures designation.

Special: Special academic programs include cooperative programs, accelerated degree programs in most majors, internships in many majors, study abroad in at least 20 countries, work-study, and dual majors in all areas. Also offered are a general studies degree, honors programs, student-designed majors, B.A.-B.S. degrees, nondegree study, and pass/fail options. Alternative academic programs include the Division of Continuing Education's correspondence study, the Integrated Studies Program, which offers a means of fulfilling general education requirements by a semester of related course work, and study via telecommunications. Cross-registration with all North Dakota 2- and 4-year public institutions is possible. There are 28 national honor societies, including Phi Beta Kappa, and a freshman honors program.

Faculty/Classroom: 56% of faculty are male; 44% are female. 90% teach undergraduates. No introductory courses are taught by graduate students. The average class size in an introductory lecture is 27; in a laboratory is 16; and in a regular course is 25.

Admissions: 74% of the 2013-2014 applicants were accepted. The ACT scores were 18% below 21, 31% between 21 and 23, 26% between 24 and 26, 8% between 27 and 28, and 11% above 28. 32% of the current freshmen were in the top fifth of their class; 61% were in the top two fifths. There were 7 National Merit finalists. 55 freshmen graduated first in their class.

Requirements: The SAT or ACT is required.The ACT is preferred, but the SAT will be accepted. Applicants must be graduates of an accredited secondary school or have passed the GED with an average of 50. A GPA of 2.5 is required. AP and CLEP credits are accepted.

Procedure: Freshmen are admitted to all sessions. Entrance exams

should be taken in spring of the junior year or fall of the senior year. There are early decision and rolling admissions plans. Applications should be filed by July 1 for fall entry. The fall 2013 application fee was $35. Notification is sent on a rolling basis.

Transfer: 825 transfer students enrolled in 2012-2013. Transfer students must have a minimum GPA of 2.0 and be in good academic standing. A higher GPA may be required in specific programs. 30 of 125 credits required for the bachelor's degree must be completed at UND.

Visiting: There are regularly scheduled orientations for prospective students, including a visit with an admissions counselor, a campus tour, an academic appointment, and an athletic appointment (if applicable). There are guides for informal visits, visitors may sit in on classes, and stay overnight. To schedule a visit, contact the Office of Admissions at (707) 777-3000.

Financial Aid: UND is a member of CSS. The FAFSA is required. Check with the school for current application deadlines.

International Students: There are 354 international students enrolled. They must take the TOEFL. They must also take the SAT or ACT.

Graduates: From July 1, 2012 to June 30, 2013, 1736 bachelor's degrees were awarded. The most popular majors were nursing (8%), psychology (6%), and commercial aviation (5%). 254 companies recruited on campus in 2012-2013. In an average class, 23% graduate in 4 years or less, 48% graduate in 5 years or less, and 54% graduate in 6 years or less. Of the 2012 graduating class, 16% were enrolled in graduate school within 6 months of graduation, and 81% were employed.

Admissions Contact: Sue Sholes, Asst Director Admissions. E-Mail: *und.admissions@und.edu* Web: *www.go.und.edu*

VALLEY CITY STATE UNIVERSITY — E-3

Valley City, ND 58072 — (701) 845-7101; (800) 532-8641; (701) 845-7299

Full-time: 378 men, 381 women	**Faculty:** 66; IIB, --$
Part-time: 156 men, 296 women	**Ph.D.s:** 38%
Graduate: 49 men, 106 women	**Student/Faculty:** 12 to 1
Year: semesters, summer session	**Tuition:** $6516 ($14,596)
Application Deadline: open	**Room & Board:** $5770
Freshman Class: 345 applied, 286 accepted, 186 enrolled	
SAT CR/M: 444/460	**ACT:** 20 — **LESS COMPETITIVE**

Valley City State University, founded in 1890, is a state-supported institution offering degree programs in the arts and sciences, business, and teacher education. In addition to regional accreditation, VCSU has baccalaureate program accreditation with NASM and NCATE. The library contains 150,000 volumes, 250 microform items, and 6,300 audio/video tapes/CDs/DVDs, and subscribes to 27,700 periodicals including electronic. Computerized library services include interlibrary loans, database searching, Internet access, and Wi-Fi capability. Special learning facilities include an art gallery and planetarium. The 64-acre campus is in a small town 58 miles west of Fargo, ND. Including any residence halls, there are 29 buildings.

Student Life: 62% of undergraduates are from North Dakota. Others are from 38 states, 9 foreign countries, and Canada. 83% are White. The average age of freshmen is 18; all undergraduates, 22. 35% do not continue beyond their first year.

Housing: 465 students can be accommodated in college housing, which includes single-sex and coed dorms and married student housing. On-campus housing is guaranteed for all 4 years. 76% of students commute. Alcohol is not permitted. All students may keep cars.

Activities: 1% of men belong to 1 local fraternity; 1% of women belong to 1 local sorority. There are 30 groups on campus, including art, band, cheerleading, choir, chorale, chorus, computers, drama, honors, international, jazz band, musical theater, newspaper, pep band, photography, political, professional, religious, social, student government, and yearbook. Popular campus events include Sno Daze, and Medicine Wheel Seasonal Celebrations.

Sports: There are 6 intercollegiate sports for men and 6 for women. Facilities include a 2500-seat football stadium with an all-weather track, a 2500-seat arena, an indoor pool, a field house, tennis and racquetball courts, a cross-country course, softball and baseball fields, a golf course, weight rooms, and a fitness room.

Disabled Students: 97% of the campus is accessible. Facilities include wheelchair ramps, elevators, special parking, specially equipped restrooms, special class scheduling, lowered drinking fountains, lowered telephones, and special housing.

Services: Counseling and information services are available, as is tutoring in most subjects. There is remedial writing.

Campus Safety and Security: Measures include 24-hour foot and vehicle patrol and self-defense education. There are lighted pathways/sidewalks, a night patrol, and surveillance cameras.

Programs of Study: VCSU confers B.A., B.S., B.S.Ed., and B.University Studies. degrees. Master's degrees are also awarded. Bachelor's degrees are awarded in BIOLOGICAL SCIENCE (biology/biological science), BUSINESS (business administration and management, human resources, and office supervision and management), COMMUNICATIONS AND THE ARTS (art, English, music, and Spanish), COMPUTER AND PHYSICAL SCIENCE (chemistry, information sciences and systems, mathematics, and science), EDUCATION (business education, elementary education, health education, physical education, technical education, and vocational education), SOCIAL SCIENCE (history and social science). Education, business, fisheries and wildlife science are the strongest academically. Elementary education, business, fisheries and wildlife science have the largest enrollments.

Required: To graduate, students must complete at least 120 semester hours with a minimum GPA of 2.0, or 2.5 for a B.S.Ed. degree. Except for those pursuing the Bachelor of University Studies degree, all students must complete the foundation studies curriculum, which includes 9 hours in communication, 6 in aesthetic engagement, 5 in global perspective, 12 in problem solving, 6 in wellness, 3 in technology, and 15 to 16 in foreign language. Students must complete 48 hours in their major if they do not have a minor, or 36 hours in their major if they have a minor. All students must complete a digital portfolio specific to their major.

Special: VCSU offers internships, dual majors, on-campus work-study, study abroad in 2 countries, pass/fail options for some courses, and credit for life, military, and work experience. There are 6 national honor societies and 4 departmental honors programs.

Faculty/Classroom: 43% of faculty are male; 57% are female. All teach undergraduates, 25% do research, and 25% do both. No introductory courses are taught by graduate students. The average class size in an introductory lecture is 40; in a laboratory is 20; and in a regular course is 25.

Admissions: 83% of the 2013-2014 applicants were accepted. The SAT scores for the 2013-2014 freshman class were: Critical Reading--90% below 500, and 10% between 600 and 699; Math--56% below 500, 27% between 500 and 599, and 17% between 600 and 699. The ACT scores were 58% below 21, 24% between 21 and 23, 12% between 24 and 26, 4% between 27 and 28, and 2% above 28. 19% of the current freshmen were in the top fifth of their class; 45% were in the top two fifths.

Requirements: The ACT is required. Applicants must be graduates of an accredited secondary school or have a GED certificate. Core curriculum requirements include 4 units of English and 3 units each of math, lab science, and social science. AP and CLEP credits are accepted.

Procedure: Freshmen are admitted to all sessions. There are deferred admissions and rolling admissions plans. Application deadlines are open. Application fee is $35. Notification is sent on a rolling basis. Applications are accepted online.

Transfer: Applicants must be in good academic standing, have a minimum GPA of 2.0, and be eligible to return to their previous institution. Official transcripts from all colleges attended are required. Some students may be required to submit high school transcripts and standardized test scores. 30 of 120 credits required for the bachelor's degree must be completed at VCSU.

Visiting: There are regularly scheduled orientations for prospective students. There are guides for informal visits, visitors may sit in on classes, and stay overnight.

Financial Aid: In 2013-2014, 89% of all full-time freshmen and 95% of continuing full-time students received some form of financial aid. 64% of all full-time freshmen and 64% of continuing full-time students received need-based aid. The average freshman award was $8,553. Need-based scholarships or need-based grants averaged $4,631; need-based self-help aid (loans and jobs) averaged $5,372; non-need-based athletic scholarships averaged $1,119; and other non-need-based awards and non-need-based scholarships averaged $2,239. The average financial indebtedness of the 2013 graduate was $30,484. VCSU is a member of CSS. The FAFSA is required. The priority date for freshman financial aid applications for fall entry is March 15. The deadline for filing freshman financial aid applications for fall entry is April 15.

International Students: There are 46 international students enrolled.

Graduates: From July 1, 2012 to June 30, 2013, 241 bachelor's degrees were awarded. The most popular majors were elementary edudcation (61%), business administration (14%), and fisheries and wildlife science (5%).

Admissions Contact: Charlene Stenson, Director of Enrollment Services. E-Mail: *enrollment.services@vcsu.edu* Web: *www.vcsu.edu*

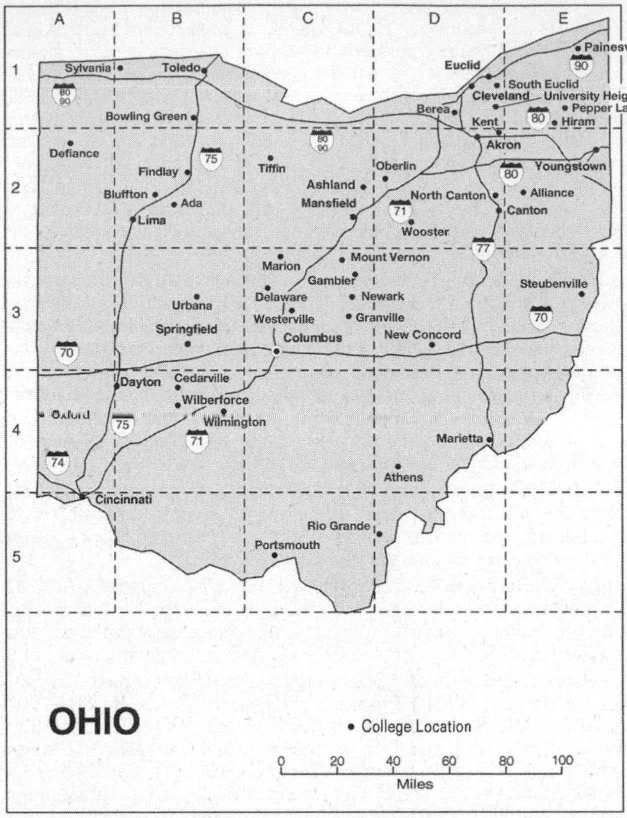

ART ACADEMY OF CINCINNATI — A-5

Cincinnati, OH 45202-7106
(513) 562-8744
(800) 323-5692; (513) 562-8778

Full-time: 55 men, 85 women
Part-time: 10 men, 15 women
Graduate: 5 men, 5 women
Year: semesters, summer session
Application Deadline: see profile
Freshman Class: n/av
SAT or ACT: required
Faculty: n/av
Ph.D.s: n/av
Student/Faculty: n/av
Tuition: $23,650
Room & Board: $7100

SPECIAL

The Art Academy of Cincinnati, founded in 1887, is a private professional college offering B.F.A. degrees in fine art, communication arts, and art history, an associate degree in graphic design, and a master's degree in art education. The figures in the above capsule and in this profile are approximate. There is 1 graduate school. In addition to regional accreditation, the Art Academy has baccalaureate program accreditation with NASAD. Special learning facilities include a learning resource center and art gallery. The 184-acre campus is in an urban area 1 mile north of downtown Cincinnati. Including any residence halls, there are 3 buildings.

Student Life: 70% of undergraduates are from Ohio. Others are from 6 states and 5 foreign countries. 86% are white. The average age of freshmen is 20; all undergraduates, 21. 20% do not continue beyond their first year; 53% remain to graduate.

Housing: College housing includes a coed dorm.

Activities: There are no fraternities or sororities. Groups on campus include art, literary magazine, student government, and yearbook. Popular campus events include field trips, career week, and performance day.

Sports: There is 1 coed intramural sport (soccer).

Disabled Students: All of the campus is accessible. Facilities include wheelchair ramps, elevators, special parking, specially equipped rest rooms, and lowered drinking fountains.

Services: Counseling and information services are available, as is tutoring in some subjects, including drawing and most academics. There is remedial writing.

Campus Safety and Security: Measures include 24-hour foot and vehicle patrol, self-defense education, and security escort services. There are lighted pathways/sidewalks and controlled access to dorms/residences.

Programs of Study: The Art Academy confers B.F.A. degrees. Associates and master's degrees are also awarded. Bachelor's degrees are awarded in COMMUNICATIONS AND THE ARTS (art history and appreciation, drawing, fine arts, graphic design, illustration, painting, photography, printmaking, sculpture, and visual design), COMPUTER AND PHYSICAL SCIENCE (digital arts/technology). Art history is the strongest academically. Visual communication and illustration have the largest enrollments.

Required: To graduate, students must complete 123 semester hours, including 30 to 45 in the major, with a GPA of 2.0. The foundation curriculum is required of all students, as are a senior thesis and a senior exhibition.

Special: Students may cross-register with member institutions of the Greater Cincinnati Consortium. Internships are available in communication arts, illustration, and art history. Work-study programs are available with various local graphic design firms.

Faculty/Classroom: 40% of faculty are male; 60% are female. All teach undergraduates. No introductory courses are taught by graduate students. The average class size in a regular course is 12.

Requirements: The SAT or ACT is required. Applicants should be graduates of an accredited secondary school. The GED is accepted. A portfolio review, interview, artist statement, ACT or SAT score, and 1 letter of recommendation are necessary. A GPA of 2.0 is required. AP and CLEP credits are accepted. Important factors in the admissions decision are evidence of special talent, personality/intangible qualities, and recommendations by school officials.

Procedure: Freshmen are admitted fall. There are deferred admissions and rolling admissions plans. Check with the school for current application deadlines. Applications are accepted online.

Transfer: Applicants must present college academic transcripts, an artist statement, and 1 letter or recommendation and undergo a portfolio review and an interview. 63 of 123 credits required for the bachelor's degree must be completed at the Art Academy.

Visiting: There are guides for informal visits and visitors may sit in on classes. To schedule a visit, contact Admissions.

Financial Aid: The FAFSA is required. Check with the school for current application deadlines.

International Students: They must take the TOEFL with a minimum score of 550 on the paper-based TOEFL (PBT) or 80 on the Internet-based version (iBT). They must also take the SAT or ACT.

Computers: There are 80 PCs available in 4 different labs, open 24 hours a day, all with Internet access. All students may access the system. There are no time limits and no fees.

Admissions Contact: Director of Admissions. E-Mail: *admissions@artacademy.edu* Web: *artacademy.edu*

ASHLAND UNIVERSITY — C-2

Ashland, OH 44805
(419) 289-5052
(800) 882-1548; (419) 289-5333

Full-time: 1000 men, 1450 women
Part-time: 100 men, 275 women
Graduate: 1475 men, 2480 women
Year: semesters, summer session
Application Deadline: open
Freshman Class: n/av
SAT or ACT: required
Faculty: n/av; IIA, --$
Ph.D.s: n/av
Student/Faculty: n/av
Tuition: $28,154
Room & Board: $9852

COMPETITIVE

Ashland University, founded in 1878, is a private liberal arts institution affiliated with the Brethren Church and offering undergraduate and graduate programs in the arts and sciences, business, education, and health services. The figures in the above capsule and in this profile are approximate. There are 3 undergraduate schools and 3 graduate schools. In addition to regional accreditation, AU has baccalaureate program accreditation with AACSB, AHEA, CSWE, NASM, NCATE, and NLN. The 2 libraries contain 270,000 volumes, 250,000 microform items, 8800 audio/video tapes/CDs/DVDs, and subscribe to 700 periodicals including electronic. Computerized library services include interlibrary loans and database searching. Special learning facilities include a learning resource center, art gallery, radio station, TV station, writing center, media center, and theater. The 150-acre campus is in a small town midway between Cleveland and Columbus. Including any residence halls, there are 38 buildings.

Student Life: 94% of undergraduates are from Ohio. Others are from 29 states, 13 foreign countries, and Canada. 86% are white. 46% claim no religious affiliation; 34% Protestant; 14% Catholic. The average age of freshmen is 18; all undergraduates, 23. 42% do not continue beyond their first year; 58% remain to graduate.

Housing: 1620 students can be accommodated in college housing, which includes single-sex and coed dorms and on-campus apartments. In addition, there are honors houses, fraternity houses, honors floors, sorority suites, and a resource management residence. On-campus housing is guaranteed for all 4 years. 72% of students live on campus. Alcohol is not permitted. All students may keep cars.

Activities: 14% of men belong to 4 national fraternities; 22% of women belong to 5 national sororities. There are 100 groups on campus, including art, band, cheerleading, choir, chorus, dance, drama, drill team, ethnic, health and environmental, honors, international, jazz band, literary magazine, marching band, musical theater, newspaper, orchestra, pep band, photography, political, professional, radio and TV, religious, social, social service, student government, symphony, and yearbook. Popular campus events include Spectrum Series, plays, and Little Sibs Weekend.

Sports: There are 10 intercollegiate sports for men and 9 for women, and 20 intramural sports for men and 20 for women. Facilities include a 5800-seat stadium, a 3000-seat gym, an all-weather track, a field house, a weight-training center, an 8-lane swimming pool with diving board, saunas, exercise rooms, 3 basketball courts, 2 handball/racquetball courts, playing fields, a fitness center, and a soccer complex with 2 full-size fields.

Disabled Students: 5% of the campus is accessible. Facilities include wheelchair ramps, elevators, special parking, specially equipped rest rooms, special class scheduling, lowered drinking fountains, lowered telephones, and special housing.

Services: Counseling and information services are available, as is tutoring in every subject. There is a reader service for the blind.

Campus Safety and Security: Measures include 24-hour foot and vehicle patrol, self-defense education, and security escort services. There are emergency telephones, lighted pathways/sidewalks, encoded student identification cards, and an electronic-access system in residence halls.

Programs of Study: AU confers B.A., B.S., B.M., B.S.B.A., B.S.Ed., B.S.N., and B.S.W. degrees. Associates, master's, and doctoral degrees are also awarded. Bachelor's degrees are awarded in BIOLOGICAL SCIENCE (biology/biological science and toxicology), BUSINESS (accounting, banking and finance, business administration and management, business economics, fashion merchandising, hotel/motel and restaurant management, management information systems, marketing/retailing/merchandising, and recreational facilities management), COMMUNICATIONS AND THE ARTS (art, broadcasting, communications, creative writing, dramatic arts, English, fine arts, French, journalism, media arts, music, musical theater, Spanish, and speech/debate/rhetoric), COMPUTER AND PHYSICAL SCIENCE (chemistry, computer science, geology, mathematics, and physics), EDUCATION (art education, athletic training, early childhood education, education administration, education of the exceptional child, elementary education, English education, foreign languages education, health education, home economics education, music education, physical education, science education, and secondary education), ENGINEERING AND ENVIRONMENTAL DESIGN (commercial art and environmental science), HEALTH PROFESSIONS (predentistry, premedicine, preoptometry, preveterinary science, and recreation therapy), SOCIAL SCIENCE (American studies, child care/child and family studies, criminal justice, economics, food science, history, international studies, philosophy, physical fitness/movement, political science/government, prelaw, psychology, religion, social science, social work, and sociology). Preprofessional science is the strongest academically. Business and teacher education have the largest enrollments.

Required: To graduate, students must complete at least 128 semester hours with a minimum GPA of 2.0 overall and 2.25 in the major. All students must complete 3 semester hours of freshman studies and 44 semester hours of interdisciplinary studies, including courses in English, phys ed, religion, speech, business or economics, fine arts, humanities, science, and social science.

Special: Opportunities are provided for internships, co-op programs in all business majors, work-study programs, dual majors, credit by exam, study abroad in 27 countries, a Washington semester, and pass/fail options. There are 17 national honor societies, a freshman honors program, and 10 departmental honors programs.

Faculty/Classroom: 61% of faculty are male; 39% are female. 81% teach undergraduates. No introductory courses are taught by graduate students. The average class size in an introductory lecture is 20, in a laboratory, 11, and in a regular course, 18.

Requirements: The SAT or ACT is required. Applicants must be graduates of an accredited secondary school. The GED is accepted. The recommended preparatory program includes 4 units of English, 3 each of science, social studies, and math, and 2 of foreign language. An interview is recommended. A GPA of 2.5 is required. AP and CLEP credits are accepted. Important factors in the admissions decision are advanced placement or honors courses, evidence of special talent, and leadership record.

Procedure: Freshmen are admitted to all sessions. Entrance exams should be taken in the spring of the junior year. There are deferred admissions and rolling admissions plans. Application deadlines are open. The application fee is $50. Applications are accepted online.

Transfer: Official transcripts from all previous colleges, showing course credits and a minimum GPA of 2.25, must be submitted when applying for transfer. Generally, if the student has successfully completed a minimum of 1 year of college, the SAT or ACT will not be required. 32 of 128 credits required for the bachelor's degree must be completed at AU.

Visiting: There are regularly scheduled orientations for prospective students. There are guides for informal visits; visitors may sit in on classes and stay overnight. To schedule a visit, contact the Office of Admissions.

Financial Aid: The FAFSA, the college's own financial statement, and federal tax returns are required. Check with the school for current application deadlines.

International Students: The school actively recruits these students. They must take the TOEFL.

Computers: All students may access the system. There are no time limits. The fee is $1.50 per credit hour.

Admissions Contact: Office of Admissions E-Mail: *enrollme@ashland.edu* Web: *www.ashland.edu*

BALDWIN WALLACE UNIVERSITY — D-1

Berea, OH 44017 — (440) 826-2222; 1-877-292-7759; (440) 826-3830

Full-time: 1395 men, 1608 women	**Faculty:** 172; IIB, av$
Part-time: 141 men, 281 women	**Ph.D.s:** 77%
Graduate: 259 men, 370 women	**Student/Faculty:** 20 to 1
Year: semesters, summer session	**Tuition:** $27,840
Application Deadline:	**Room & Board:** $9140
Freshman Class: 4220 applied, 2699 accepted, 762 enrolled	
SAT CR/M: 540/540	**ACT:** 24 — **VERY COMPETITIVE**

Baldwin Wallace University, established in 1845, is an independent liberal arts institution that blends the hallmarks of the liberal arts with an emphasis on professional and career preparation through undergraduate and graduate degree programs. There is 1 undergraduate school and 2 graduate schools. In addition to regional accreditation, BW has baccalaureate program accreditation with NASM and NCATE. The 3 libraries contain 302,751 volumes, 11,000 microform items, 20,781 audio/video tapes/CDs/DVDs, and subscribe to 44,000 periodicals including electronic. Computerized library services include interlibrary loans, database searching, and Internet access. Special learning facilities include an art gallery, radio station, a neuroscience lab, and an observatory. The 120-acre campus is in a suburban area 14 miles southwest of Cleveland, OH. Including any residence halls, there are 78 buildings.

Student Life: 84% of undergraduates are from Ohio. Others are from 41 states, 23 foreign countries, and Canada. 78% are from public schools. 80% are White. 46% are Protestant; 33% Catholic; 14% Baha'i, Buddhist, Hindu, Mormon, Muslim, Orthodox, Unitarian. The average age of freshmen is 18; all undergraduates, 20. 21% do not continue beyond their first year; 92% remain to graduate.

Housing: 1817 students can be accommodated in college housing, which includes coed dorms and on-campus apartments. In addition, there are honors houses, special-interest houses, inclding student-directed learning comm, themed housing, special housing disabled and international students, fraternities/sororities. On-campus housing is available on a first-come, first-served basis, and is available on a lottery system for upperclassmen. 61% of students live on campus; of those, 50% remain on campus on weekends. All students may keep cars.

Activities: 12% of men belong to 7 national fraternities; 19% of women belong to 7 national sororities. There are 117 groups on campus, including art, band, cheerleading, choir, chorale, chorus, computers, dance, drama, drill team, environmental, ethnic, film, forensics, gay, honors, international, jazz band, literary magazine, marching band, musical theater, newspaper, opera, orchestra, pep band, political, professional, radio and TV, religious, social, social service, student government, symphony, and yearbook. Popular campus events include Culture Night, Dance Marathon and April Reign.

Sports: There are 12 intercollegiate sports for men and 11 for women, and 28 intramural sports for men and 28 for women. Facilities include an 8,000-seat stadium with polyturf & all-weather track, a 3,000-seat gym, new athletic field (Tressel Field), baseball fields, and a 6-court tennis complex. The recreation center houses a 200-meter track, swimming pool, dance studio, athletic training/rehab facility, wrestling/gymnastics/weight rooms, fitness complex, and facilities for basketball, racquetball, tennis,volleyball, and a fitness and wellness programs/activities.

Disabled Students: 80% of the campus is accessible. Facilities include wheelchair ramps, elevators, special parking, specially equipped restrooms, special class scheduling, lowered telephones, special housing.

Services: Counseling and information services are available, as is tutoring in most subjects. There is remedial math, reading, and writing. Software for students who have difficulty reading or with visual impairments; access to Learning Ally and Bookshare which both come with a downloadable reader.

Campus Safety and Security: Measures include 24-hour foot and vehicle patrol, emergency notification system, self-defense education, and security escort services. There are emergency telephones, lighted pathways/sidewalks, controlled access to dorms/residences, more than 100 exterior/interior security cameras.

Programs of Study: BW confers B.A., B.S., B.M., B.M.E, B.S.Ed. and B.S.N degrees. Master's degrees are also awarded. Bachelor's degrees are awarded in BIOLOGICAL SCIENCE (biology/biological science and neurosciences), BUSINESS (accounting, business administration and management, entrepreneurial studies, finance, human resources, international business, marketing, organizational leadership and management, sports management, and sustainable management), COMMUNICATIONS AND THE ARTS (applied music, art history, broadcasting, communication studies, creative writing, English, film, television and digital media, French, German, instrumental performance, keyboard - piano concentration, music, music composition, music history and appreciation, music performance, music theory and composition, musical theater, public relations, Spanish, studio art, theatre acting, theater design, theater management, and voice), COMPUTER AND PHYSICAL SCIENCE (chemistry, computer science, computer security and information assurance, digital arts/technology, mathematics, mathematics - economics, physics, software engineering, and systems analysis), EDUCATION (art education, athletic training, early childhood education, middle school education, music education, physical education, science education, and specific learning disabilities), ENGINEERING AND ENVIRONMENTAL DESIGN (preengineering), HEALTH PROFESSIONS (exercise science, health care administration, health promotion, music therapy, nursing, predentistry, premedicine, prepharmacy, prephysical therapy, preveterinary science, and public health), SOCIAL SCIENCE (communication sciences & disorders, criminal justice, economics, history, industrial and organizational psychology, international studies, philosophy, political science/government, psychology, religion, and sociology). Biology, accounting, and business administration have the largest enrollments.

Required: All students must complete 124 semester hours and have at least a 2.0 GPA. A total of 43 semester hours must be taken in the liberal arts core, including 14 in humanities, 8 in social science, 7 in natural science, 6 in liberal arts and sciences, 3 each in math and English, and 2 in health and phys ed. All students must complete a minor and coursework in International Studies, Diversity Studies and Experiential Learning. Common courses all students must take include: Liberal Arts and Sciences (LAS 200), English 111, 131 (Composition), a math requirement and HPE-110W (Wellness). Comprehensive exams are required in some majors.

Special: Special academic programs include internships that can qualify for credit, work-study programs and study abroad. There is cross-registration with 7 participating institutions within the Greater Cleveland area, as well as a 3-2 program in social work with Case Western Reserve University, 3-2 master's program in accounting, human resources, & computer science/information systems, & a 3-2 program in engineering with Case Western Reserve and Columbia University. BW also offers the Consortium for Music Therapy, accelerated degree programs, a B.A.-B.S. degree, dual and student-designed majors, credit for life, military, and work experience, and pass/fail options. The Adult and Continuing Education Program offers degrees through evening and weekend colleges. 3+1 or 4+1 medical technology-based affiliation with Southwest General Health Center. Pre-professional programs are available in dentistry, law, medicine, pharmacy, and veterinary. Study abroad in Argentina, Australia, Austria, Ecuador, England, France, Germany, Ghana, India, Ireland, Italy, Japan, Mexico, Morocco, Scotland, South Korea, Spain, Sweden & Switzerland. There are 23 national honor societies and a freshman honors program.

Faculty/Classroom: 56% of faculty are male; 44% are female. 91% teach undergraduates. No introductory courses are taught by graduate students. The average class size in an introductory lecture is 20; in a laboratory is 16; and in a regular course is 17.

Admissions: 64% of the 2013-2014 applicants were accepted. The SAT scores for the 2013-2014 freshman class were: Critical Reading--33% below 500, 39% between 500 and 599, 20% between 600 and 699, and 8% between 700 and 800; Math--31% below 500, 46% between 500 and 599, 20% between 600 and 699, and 3% between 700 and 800. The ACT scores were 20% below 21, 24% between 21 and 23, 28% between 24 and 26, 15% between 27 and 28, and 13% above 28. 42% of the current freshmen were in the top fifth of their class; 71% were in the top two fifths. 19 freshmen graduated first in their class.

Requirements: The SAT or ACT is recommended. Applicants must be graduates of an accredited secondary school or have earned a GED. Applicants must have completed 16 academic credits, including 4 in English, 3 each in math, natural science, and social science, and 2 in a foreign language; however, alternative distributions are considered. A teacher's recommendation is required. BW does not require students to submit test scores for admission consideration. BW requires applicants to be in the upper 50% of their class. A GPA of 2.8 is required. AP and CLEP credits are accepted. Important factors in the admissions decision are advanced placement or honors courses, extracurricular activities record, and recommendations by school officials.

Procedure: Freshmen are admitted fall and spring. Entrance exams should be taken during junior year or early in senior year. There are deferred admissions and rolling admissions plans. Application deadlines are open. Applications are accepted online.

Transfer: 294 transfer students enrolled in 2012-2013. Students must be in good academic and social standing at prior institution(s). 32 of 124 credits required for the bachelor's degree must be completed at BW.

Visiting: There are regularly scheduled orientations for prospective students, Student visits include an interview, a tour, and classroom visits. There are guides for informal visits, visitors may sit in on classes, and stay overnight. To schedule a visit, contact the Admission Office.

Financial Aid: In 2013-2014, 100% of all full-time freshmen and 98% of continuing full-time students received some form of financial aid. 99% of all full-time freshmen and 100% of continuing full-time students received need-based aid. The average freshman award was $25,639. Need-based scholarships or need-based grants averaged $17,594 ($27,840 maximum); need-based self-help aid (loans and jobs) averaged $8,056 ($12,900 maximum); and other non-need-based awards and non-need-based scholarships averaged $11,840 ($27,840 maximum). 44% of undergraduate students work part-time. Average annual earnings from campus work are $972. The average financial indebtedness of the 2013 graduate was $27,204. The FAFSA is required. The priority date for freshman financial aid applications for fall entry is May 1. The deadline for filing freshman financial aid applications for fall entry is September 1.

International Students: There are 48 international students enrolled. The school actively recruits these students. They must take the TOEFL with a minimum score of 550 on the paper-based TOEFL (PBT) or 79 on the Internet-based version (iBT) and the college's own test, IELTS, and ELS Language Centers Level 12. They must also take the SAT or ACT.

Computers: All students may access the system 24 hours a day. There are no time limits and no fees.

Graduates: From July 1, 2012 to June 30, 2013, 734 bachelor's degrees were awarded. The most popular majors were accounting (6%), biology (6%), and business administration (5%). 95 companies recruited on campus in 2012-2013. In an average class, 2% graduate in 3 years or less, 55% graduate in 4 years or less, 69% graduate in 5 years or less, and 71% graduate in 6 years or less.

Admissions Contact: Susan Dileno, Vice President of Enrollment Management. E-Mail: *sdileno@bw.edu* Web: *www.bw.edu*

BLUFFTON UNIVERSITY B-2

Bluffton, OH 45817 (419) 358-3257
(800) 488-3257; (419) 358-3232

Full-time: 426 men, 407 women	**Faculty:** 56; IIB, --$
Part-time: 91 men, 153 women	**Ph.D.s:** 82%
Graduate: 51 men, 70 women	**Student/Faculty:** 14 to 1
Year: semesters, summer session	**Tuition:** $28,504
Application Deadline: May 31	**Room & Board:** $9360

Freshman Class: 1784 applied, 947 accepted, 250 enrolled

SAT CR/M: 495/510 **ACT:** 22 **COMPETITIVE**

Bluffton University, founded in 1899, is a private, Christian, liberal arts institution affiliated with the Mennonite Church. There is one graduate school. In addition to regional accreditation, Bluffton has baccalaureate program accreditation with ADA, CSWE, NASM, and NCATE. The library contains 263,537 volumes, 83,831 microform items, and 5,677 audio/video tapes/CDs/DVDs, and subscribes to 21,870 periodicals including electronic. Computerized library services include interlibrary loans, database searching, Internet access, and Wi-Fi capability. Special learning facilities include an art gallery, radio station, the Lion and Lamb Peace Arts center, and a nature preserve. The 65-acre campus is in a small town 60 miles south of Toledo and 75 miles north of Dayton. Including any residence halls, there are 26 buildings.

Student Life: 83% of undergraduates are from Ohio. Others are from 23 states, 7 foreign countries, and Canada. 91% are from public schools. 85% are White. 34% are Protestant; 23% unknown religion. The average age of freshmen is 18; all undergraduates, 22. 31% do not continue beyond their first year; 61% remain to graduate.

Housing: 732 students can be accommodated in college housing, which includes single-sex and coed dorms. In addition, there are special-interest houses, All full-time students must live in residence halls unless commuting from the home of their parents. On-campus housing is guaranteed for all 4 years. 81% of students live on campus; of those, 60% remain on campus on weekends. Alcohol is not permitted. All students may keep cars.

Activities: There are no fraternities or sororities. There are 40 groups on campus, including and Youth Ministries, Student Senate, art, band, cheerleading, choir, chorale, chorus, dance, drama, ethnic, gay, honors, international, International Connection, jazz band, literary magazine, musical theater, newspaper, pep band, political, professional, radio and TV, religious, social, social service, student government, and yearbook. Popular campus events include International Week, Spiritual Emphasis Weeks, and Artist Series.

Sports: There are 7 intercollegiate sports for men and 7 for women, and 8 intramural sports for men and 8 for women. Facilities include A new recreation and fitness center that includes a basketball/volleyball court, well-equipped fitness center, an athletic complex with baseball, softball, soccer and 2600 seat football stadium. Another building for indoor sports and intramurals.

Disabled Students: 75% of the campus is accessible. Facilities include wheelchair ramps, elevators, special parking, specially equipped restrooms, special class scheduling, lowered drinking fountains, lowered telephones. special computers for visually impaired students.

Services: Counseling and information services are available, as is tutoring in every subject. There is a reader service for the blind, and remedial math, reading, and writing. Tutoring is available for most students, as are classes at the student's request and/or faculty designation.

Campus Safety and Security: Measures include emergency notification system and self-defense education. There are emergency telephones, lighted pathways/sidewalks, controlled access to dorms/residences, In a town of only 4000, village police cruisers regularly patrol the campus during night hours. There are also 2 night security officers who communicate directly with village police and routinely patrol campus at night.

Programs of Study: Bluffton confers B.A. degrees. Master's degrees are also awarded. Bachelor's degrees are awarded in BIOLOGICAL SCIENCE (biology/biological science), BUSINESS (accounting, business administration and management, fashion merchandising, human resources, marketing/retailing/merchandising, organizational leadership and management, recreational facilities management, and sports management), COMMUNICATIONS AND THE ARTS (art, broadcasting, communications, creative writing, English, music, public relations, and Spanish), COMPUTER AND PHYSICAL SCIENCE (chemistry, computer science, information sciences and systems, mathematics, physical sciences, and physics), EDUCATION (early childhood education, home economics education, middle school education, music education, physical education, and special education), HEALTH PROFESSIONS (premedicine), SOCIAL SCIENCE (biblical studies, child psychology/development, criminal justice, early childhood studies, economics, family/consumer studies, fashion design and technology, food science, history, ministries, psychology, social science, social studies, social work, sociology, and youth ministry). Social work, education, and business have the largest enrollments.

Required: To graduate, students must complete 124 semester hours with 40 to 60 in the major and have a minimum GPA of 2.0. The general education requirements must be met, and satisfactory achievement in departmental senior comprehensives demonstrated. Distribution requirements are approximately one third for general education requirements, including 6 hours of religion, and one third to one half for the major.

Special: Special arrangements include internships in business, recreation, social work, and education, a Washington semester through the Council for Christian Colleges and Universities, and study abroad. Student-designed majors and independent study are possible, as is credit for prior learning and for learning in voluntary service. There is an accelerated degree program in organizational management and human resource management. Nondegree study and pass/fail options are offered. There are 2 national honor societies, a freshman honors program, and 14 departmental honors programs.

Faculty/Classroom: 64% of faculty are male; 36% are female. 99% teach undergraduates. No introductory courses are taught by graduate students. The average class size in an introductory lecture is 23; in a laboratory is 8; and in a regular course is 20.

Admissions: 53% of the 2013-2014 applicants were accepted. The SAT scores for the 2013-2014 freshman class were: Critical Reading--48% below 500, 33% between 500 and 599, 11% between 600 and 699, and 8% between 700 and 800; Math--51% below 500, 23% between 500 and 599, 20% between 600 and 699, and 3% between 700 and 800. The ACT scores were 45% below 21, 26% between 21 and 23, 19% between 24 and 26, 5% between 27 and 28, and 6% above 28. 25% of the current freshmen were in the top fifth of their class; 58% were in the top two fifths. 9 freshmen graduated first in their class.

Requirements: The SAT or ACT is required. To be considered for regular admission to Bluffton University as an undergraduate student, you need to have earned a score of 920 on the SAT (critical reading plus math) or 19 on the ACT. Other admissions requirements include graduation from an accredited secondary school with a 2.3 GPA or class rank above 50%. Recommended courses include 4 units of English and 3 units each of math, science, social studies, and a foreign language. The GED is accepted. A personal campus visit and an interview are strongly recommended. Music students must audition and art students submit a portfolio. Bluffton requires applicants to be in the upper 50% of their class. A GPA of 2.3 is required. AP and CLEP credits are accepted. Important factors in the admissions decision are leadership record, recommendations by school officials, and extracurricular activities record.

Procedure: Freshmen are admitted to all sessions. Entrance exams should be taken in the spring of the junior year or fall of the senior year. There are deferred admissions and rolling admissions plans. Applications should be filed by May 31 for fall entry, along with a $20 fee. Applications are accepted online.

Transfer: 129 transfer students enrolled in 2012-2013. Transfer students must have a minimum college GPA of 2.0, meet eligibility criteria from previous institutions, and have met their financial obligations at the former institution. A signed transfer recommendation must be submitted from each college attended. 30 of 124 credits required for the bachelor's degree must be completed at Bluffton.

Visiting: There are regularly scheduled orientations for prospective students, Personal visits are scheduled according to students' specific interests and may include obsesrving a class, visit with faculty and a tour of campus. Group visits are scheduled regularly throughout the year. Listed on website with online registration. There are guides for informal visits, visitors may sit in on classes, and stay overnight. To schedule a visit, contact Amy Tabler at (800) 488-3257.

Financial Aid: In 2013-2014, 100% of all full-time freshmen and 100% of continuing full-time students received some form of financial aid. 94% of all full-time freshmen and 82% of continuing full-time students received need-based aid. The average freshman award was $26,384. Need-based scholarships or need-based grants averaged $20,914 ($28,054 maximum); need-based self-help aid (loans and jobs) averaged $6,136 ($11,540 maximum); and other non-need-based awards and non-need-based scholarships averaged $14,603 ($23,709 maximum). 65% of undergraduate students work part-time. Average annual earnings from campus work are $2400. The average financial indebtedness of the 2013 graduate was $35,682. The FAFSA is required. The priority date for freshman financial aid applications for fall entry is May 1. The deadline for filing freshman financial aid applications for fall entry is October 1.

International Students: There are 11 international students enrolled. The school actively recruits these students. They must take the TOEFL with a minimum score of 500 on the paper-based TOEFL (PBT) or 64 on the Internet-based version (iBT). They must also take the SAT, scoring 920, and the college's own entrance exam. The SAT can substitute for the TOEFL.

Computers: All students may access the system any time. There are no time limits and no fees.

Graduates: From July 1, 2012 to June 30, 2013, 307 bachelor's degrees were awarded. The most popular majors were business/marketing (44%), education (15%), and social work (9%). 56 companies recruited on campus in 2012-2013. In an average class, 1% graduate in 3 years or less, 52% graduate in 4 years or less, 58% graduate in 5 years or less, and 60% graduate in 6 years or less. Of the 2012 graduating class, 20% were enrolled in graduate school within 6 months of graduation, and 80% were employed.

Admissions Contact: Derek Stemen, Director of Admissions. E-Mail: *admissions@bluffton.edu* Web: *www.bluffton.edu/admissions*

BOWLING GREEN STATE UNIVERSITY B-1

Bowling Green, OH 43403 **(419) 372-BGSU**
1-866-CHOOSE BGSU; (419) 372-6955

Full-time: 5788 men, 7599 women	**Faculty:** 747; I, --$
Part-time: 545 men, 545 women	**Ph.D.s:** 78%
Graduate: 965 men, 1516 women	**Student/Faculty:** 18 to 1
Year: semesters, summer session	**Tuition:** $10,726 ($24,438)
Application Deadline: July 15	**Room & Board:** $8244
Freshman Class: 15689 applied, 11370 accepted, 3348 enrolled	
SAT CR/M/W: 510/510/490	**ACT:** 23 **COMPETITIVE**

Bowling Green State University, founded in 1910, is a public institution. There are 7 undergraduate schools and one graduate school. In addition to regional accreditation, BGSU has baccalaureate program accreditation with AACSB, ACCE, ACEJMC, ADA, CSWE, NASAD, NASM, NCATE, and NRPA. The library contains 1.8 million volumes, 2.7 million microform items, 236,129 audio/video tapes/CDs/DVDs, and subscribes to 1,580 periodicals including electronic. Computerized library services include interlibrary loans, database searching, Internet access, and Wi-Fi capability. Special learning facilities include an art gallery, planetarium, radio station, and TV station. The 1338-acre campus is in a small town 23 miles south of Toledo, adjacent to Interstate 75. Including any residence halls, there are 119 buildings.

Student Life: 86% of undergraduates are from Ohio. Others are from 54 states, 44 foreign countries, and Canada. 78% are White. The average age of freshmen is 19; all undergraduates, 21. 30% do not continue beyond their first year; 58% remain to graduate.

Housing: 7017 students can be accommodated in college housing, which includes single-sex and coed dorms and on-campus apartments. In addition, there are honors houses, language houses, special-interest houses, fraternity houses, sorority houses, no-alcohol wings, residential/theme communities, and gender-neutral housing. 56% of students commute. All students may keep cars.

Activities: 11% of men belong to 20 national fraternities; 15% of women belong to 19 national sororities. There are 314 groups on campus, including art, band, cheerleading, chess, choir, chorale, chorus, communications, computers, dance, debate, drama, drill team, environmental, ethnic, film, gay, honors, international, jazz band, literary magazine, marching band, musical theater, newspaper, opera, pep band, photography, political, professional, radio and TV, religious, social, social service, student government, symphony, and yearbook. Popular campus events include Homecoming, Campus Fest, Move-in Weekend and Week of Welcome.

Sports: There are 7 intercollegiate sports for men and 10 for women, and 13 intramural sports for men and 15 for women.

Disabled Students: 92% of the campus is accessible. Facilities include wheelchair ramps, elevators, special parking, specially equipped restrooms, special class scheduling, lowered drinking fountains, lowered telephones, special housing, a shuttle van with lift capabilities.

Services: Counseling and information services are available, as is tutoring in some subjects, writing, math & stats, and any subject that has been requested by students for help. There is a reader service for the blind, and remedial math, reading, and writing.

Campus Safety and Security: Measures include 24-hour foot and vehicle patrol, emergency notification system, self-defense education, and security escort services. There are shuttle buses, emergency telephones, lighted pathways/sidewalks, controlled access to dorms/residences, in-room safes, and a campus 911.

Programs of Study: BGSU confers B.A., B.F.A., B.A.H.S., B.L.S., B.Mus., B.M.A. and B.S. degrees. Master's and doctoral degrees are also awarded. Bachelor's degrees are awarded in AGRICULTURE (environmental studies), BIOLOGICAL SCIENCE (avian sciences, biology/biological science, life science, and nutrition), BUSINESS (accounting, business administration and management, business statistics, management information systems, supply chain management, and tourism), COMMUNICATIONS AND THE ARTS (apparel design, art history, art, classics, communications, communications technology, crafts, creative writing, design, drawing, East Asian languages and literature, English, English literature, English Writing, film arts, fine arts, French, German, graphic design, jazz, journalism, languages, Latin, linguistics, literature, music, music history and appreciation, Technical Communication, music performance, music theory and composition, painting, performing arts, piano/organ, radio/television technology, romance languages and literature, Russian, sculpture, Spanish, strings, studio art, technical and business writing, telecommunications, theatre arts, visual and performing arts, visual design, and voice), COMPUTER AND PHYSICAL SCIENCE (chemistry, computer science, digital arts/technology, earth science, geology, mathematics, natural sciences, physical sciences, physics, science, and statistics), EDUCATION (art education, athletic training, business education, (Education) Childhood Education, drama education, early childhood education, education, education of the deaf and hearing impaired, education of the multiply handicapped, elementary education, English education, foreign languages education, mathematics education, middle school education, music education, physical education, reading education, science education, secondary education, social science education, social studies education, special education, sports studies, and technical education), ENGINEERING AND ENVIRONMENTAL DESIGN (construction technology, electrical/electronics engineering technology, engineering technology, interior design, and printing technology), HEALTH PROFESSIONS (exercise science, health science, medical laboratory science, nursing, premedicine, and public health), SOCIAL SCIENCE (African studies, American studies, architectural studies, area studies, Asian/Oriental studies, behavioral science, clothing and textiles management/production/services, criminal justice, crosscultural studies, dietetics, economics, ethnic studies, family and community services, fashion design and technology, fire services administration, food science, geography, gerontology, (Social Science) Global Studies, history, human development, human services, humanities, interdisciplinary studies, international studies, law enforcement and corrections, legal studies, liberal arts/general studies, philosophy, physical fitness/movement, political science/government, prelaw, psychology, social science, social studies, social work, sociology, textiles and clothing, Western civilization/culture, and women's studies). Education, has the largest enrollment.

Required: Earn a minimum of 122 semester hours of credit and at least 30 credit hours must be BGSU courses; earn an accumulative grade point average of at least 2.0 ("C" average) for all coursework attempted; complete the BG perspective requirements; complete at least 40 hours of credit in courses numbered 3000 and above; satisfy all college requirements for a degree; file an application for graduation.

Special: Special academic programs include co-op programs in all majors with the National Student Exchange, internships, a Washington semester, work-study, and study abroad. Dual majors are available in all programs, and a B.A.-B.S. degree is offered in computer science, geology, math, psychology, statistics, scientific and technical communication, and individualized planned program. Student-designed majors, independent study, credit for experience, nondegree study, and pass/fail options are possible. There are 23 national honor societies, including Phi Beta Kappa, and a freshman honors program.

Faculty/Classroom: 50% of faculty are male; 50% are female. 92% teach undergraduates. No introductory courses are taught by graduate students. The average class size in an introductory lecture is 34; in a laboratory is 21; and in a regular course is 33.

Admissions: 72% of the 2013-2014 applicants were accepted. The SAT scores for the 2013-2014 freshman class were: Critical Reading--42% below 500, 42% between 500 and 599, 14% between 600 and 699, and 1% between 700 and 800; Math--40% below 500, 46% between 500 and 599, 13% between 600 and 699, and 1% between 700 and 800; Writing--52% below 500, 40% between 500 and 599, 8% between 600 and 699, and 1% between 700 and 800. The ACT scores were 28% below 21, 32% between 21 and 23, 25% between 24 and 26, 9% between 27 and 28, and 7% above 28. 28% of the current freshmen were in the top fifth of their class; 60% were in the top two fifths. 36 freshmen graduated first in their class.

Requirements: The ACT is required. The SAT is recommended. Freshman AP and CLEP credits are accepted.

Procedure: Freshmen are admitted fall, spring, and summer. Entrance exams should be taken in the junior year. There are deferred admissions and rolling admissions plans. Applications should be filed by July 15 for fall entry; December 15 for spring entry; and May 15 for summer entry, along with a $45 fee. Notifications are sent 10 1. Applications are accepted online.

Transfer: 885 transfer students enrolled in 2012-2013. 30 of 122 credits required for the bachelor's degree must be completed at Bowling Green.

Visiting: There are regularly scheduled orientations for prospective students. There are guides for informal visits and visitors may sit in on classes. To schedule a visit, contact the Office of Admissions.

Financial Aid: 12% of undergraduate students work part-time. Average annual earnings from campus work are $1957. BGSU is a member of CSS. The FAFSA is required. Check with the school for current application deadlines.

International Students: There are 241 international students enrolled. The school actively recruits these students. They must take the TOEFL with a minimum score of 500 on the paper-based TOEFL (PBT) or 61 on the Internet-based version (iBT) or take the MELAB. SAT and ACT scores are considered if submitted.

Computers: All students may access the system. There are no time limits and no fees.

Graduates: From July 1, 2012 to June 30, 2013, 2801 bachelor's degrees were awarded. The most popular majors were Early Childhood Education (5%), Liberal Studies (5%), Education, and other (4%). In an average class, 1% graduate in 3 years or less, 31% graduate in 4 years or less, 51% graduate in 5 years or less, and 54% graduate in 6 years or less.

Admissions Contact: Castellano,Cecilia Ann, Interim Director, Admissions. E-Mail: *choosebgsu@bgsu.edu* Web: *http:/choose.bgsu.edu/admissions/apply*

CAPITAL UNIVERSITY — C-3

Columbus, OH 43209 — (614) 236-6101; 866-544-6175; (614) 236-6926

Full-time: 1075 men, 1373 women	**Faculty:** 145; IIA, av$
Part-time: 87 men, 185 women	**Ph.D.s:** 77%
Graduate: 426 men, 438 women	**Student/Faculty:** 13 to 1
Year: semesters, summer session	**Tuition:** $31,364
Application Deadline: May 1	**Room & Board:** $8460
Freshman Class: 3844 applied, 2880 accepted, 670 enrolled	
SAT CR/M/W: 545/542/545 — **ACT:** 24	**VERY COMPETITIVE**

Capital University, established in 1830, is a private institution affiliated with the Evangelical Lutheran Church in America. Its undergraduate and graduate programs emphasize the liberal arts and sciences, music, and nursing along with professional studies such as business. There are 5 undergraduate schools and 3 graduate schools. In addition to regional accreditation, Capital has baccalaureate program accreditation with ACBSP, CSWE, NASM, and NCATE. The library contains 220,594 volumes, 148,096 microform items, 103,078 audio/video tapes/CDs/DVDs, and subscribes to 162,236 periodicals including electronic. Computerized library services include interlibrary loans, database searching, Internet access, and Wi-Fi capability. Special learning facilities include an art gallery, radio station, and TV station. The 48-acre campus is in a suburban area 5 miles east of downtown Columbus. Including any residence halls, there are 24 buildings.

Student Life: 90% of undergraduates are from Ohio. Others are from 33 states, 12 foreign countries, and Canada. 82% are White. 30% are Protestant; 20% Catholic; 13% claim no religious affiliation. The average age of freshmen is 18; all undergraduates, 22. 25% do not continue beyond their first year; 59% remain to graduate.

Housing: 1546 students can be accommodated in college housing, which includes coed dorms, on-campus apartments, and off-campus apartments. In addition, there are honors houses, special-interest floors, substance-free floors, Greek organization floors, and a self-governing unit. On-campus housing is guaranteed for all 4 years and is available on a lottery system for upperclassmen. 57% of students live on campus; of those, 50% remain on campus on weekends. All students may keep cars.

Activities: 17% of men belong to 5 local and 5 national fraternities; 19% of women belong to 6 local and 6 national sororities. There are 63 groups on campus, including art, band, cheerleading, choir, chorale, chorus, communications, dance, debate, drama, environmental, ethnic, gay, honors, international, jazz band, literary magazine, musical theater, newspaper, opera, orchestra, political, professional, radio and TV, religious, social, social service, student government, and symphony. Popular campus events include Symposium on Undergraduate Scholarship, Honors Convocation, Greek Week, Martin Luther King Jr. Day of Learning, and Kids and Sibs Weekend.

Sports: There are 9 intercollegiate sports for men and 9 for women, and 9 intramural sports for men and 9 for women. Facilities include a 2500-seat football stadium, a 2400-seat gym, tennis courts, and weight and game rooms. The recreation center offers bowling, billiards, and other game facilities.

Disabled Students: All of the campus is accessible. Facilities include wheelchair ramps, elevators, special parking, and specially equipped restrooms.

Services: Counseling and information services are available, as is tutoring in most subjects. There is remedial math and writing.

Campus Safety and Security: Measures include 24-hour foot and vehicle patrol, emergency notification system, self-defense education, and security escort services. There are shuttle buses, lighted pathways/sidewalks, and controlled access to dorms/residences.

Programs of Study: Capital confers B.A., B.M., B.S.N. and B.S.W. degrees. Master's and doctoral degrees are also awarded. Bachelor's degrees are awarded in BIOLOGICAL SCIENCE (biochemistry and biology/biological science), BUSINESS (accounting and business administration and management), COMMUNICATIONS AND THE ARTS (art, communications, creative writing, dramatic arts, English, French, music, public relations, Spanish, speech/debate/rhetoric, and theatre studies), COMPUTER AND PHYSICAL SCIENCE (chemistry, computer science, and mathematics), EDUCATION (art education, athletic training, elementary education, middle school education, physical education, and secondary education), ENGINEERING AND ENVIRONMENTAL DESIGN (environmental science), HEALTH PROFESSIONS (art therapy, exercise science, nursing, predentistry, premedicine, and sports medicine), SOCIAL SCIENCE (behavioral science, criminal justice, economics, history, international relations, philosophy, physical fitness/movement, political science/government, prelaw, psychology, religion, social work, and sociology). Nursing, business, education have the largest enrollments.

Required: To graduate, all students must complete at least 124 semester hours, with a varying number of hours in the major, and maintain a minimum 2.0 GPA. The university core, 36 semester hours, must be followed in an ordered sequence throughout the 4 years; considered an assessment program, it includes specific courses in reading and writing, communication, health, art, science, social science, the humanities, ethics, and religion.

Special: Special academic programs include cross-registration with the Higher Education Council of Columbus, semester internships in most majors, and a Washington semester. Study abroad in 21 countries on 5 continents includes opportunities in Jamaica and at the Kodaly Institute of Music in Hungary. Also possible are a general studies degree and student-designed majors. A dual degree in engineering is offered with Case Western Reserve University and Washington University in St. Louis. Credit for life, military, and work experience may be granted, and nondegree study and pass/fail options are offered. There are 17 national honor societies and a freshman honors program.

Faculty/Classroom: 49% of faculty are male; 51% are female. 86% teach undergraduates. No introductory courses are taught by graduate students. The average class size in an introductory lecture is 30; in a laboratory is 12; and in a regular course is 17.

Admissions: 75% of the 2013-2014 applicants were accepted. The SAT scores for the 2013-2014 freshman class were: Critical Reading--33% below 500, 39% between 500 and 599, 21% between 600 and 699, and 7% between 700 and 800; Math--30% below 500, 40% between 500 and 599, 24% between 600 and 699, and 6% between 700 and 800; Writing--44% below 500, 36% between 500 and 599, 16% between 600 and 699, and 4% between 700 and 800. The ACT scores were 17% below 21, 29% between 21 and 23, 25% between 24 and 26, 15% between 27 and 28, and 14% above 28. 39% of the current freshmen were in the top fifth of their class; 70% were in the top two fifths. 14 freshmen graduated first in their class.

Requirements: The SAT or ACT is required. In addition, other admissions requirements include graduation from an accredited secondary school with 16 academic credits, including 4 units of English, 3 each of math, science, and social science, 2 units of a foreign language, and 1 of electives; nursing applicants need chemistry. The GED is accepted. High school students must submit recommendations from their guidance counselor. An interview is recommended. Students must audition for entry to the Conservatory of Music. A GPA of 2.6 is required. AP and CLEP credits are accepted. Important factors in the admissions decision are advanced placement or honors courses, recommendations by school officials, and evidence of special talent.

Procedure: Freshmen are admitted fall, spring, and summer. Entrance exams should be taken by December of the senior year. There are deferred admissions and rolling admissions plans. Applications should be filed by May 1 for fall entry, along with a $25 fee. Notifications are sent September 30. Applications are accepted online.

Transfer: 85 transfer students enrolled in 2012-2013. Transfer students must have a minimum college GPA of 2.25. The SAT or ACT is recommended, as is an interview. 30 of 124 credits required for the bachelor's degree must be completed at Capital.

Visiting: There are regularly scheduled orientations for prospective students, including an interview with a counselor and a campus tour. There are guides for informal visits, visitors may sit in on classes, and stay overnight. To schedule a visit, contact the Admissions Office.

Financial Aid: In 2013-2014, 91% of all full-time freshmen and 93% of continuing full-time students received some form of financial aid. 76% of all full-time freshmen and 75% of continuing full-time students received need-based aid. The average freshman award was $25,942. 33% of undergraduate students work part-time. Average annual earnings from campus work are $3400. The average financial indebtedness of the 2013 graduate was $45,814. The FAFSA is required. The priority date for freshman financial aid applications for fall entry is February 28.

International Students: There are 20 international students enrolled. The school actively recruits these students. They must take the TOEFL with a minimum score of 500 on the paper-based TOEFL (PBT) or 61 on the Internet-based version (iBT).

Computers: All students may access the system 24 hours per day. There are no time limits and no fees.

Graduates: From July 1, 2012 to June 30, 2013, 560 bachelor's degrees were awarded. The most popular majors were nursing (18%), education (15%), and business (13%). 27 companies recruited on campus in 2012-2013. In an average class, 50% graduate in 4 years or less, 58% graduate in 5 years or less, and 59% graduate in 6 years or less. Of the 2012 graduating class, 20% were enrolled in graduate school within 6 months of graduation, and 69% were employed.

Admissions Contact: Amanda Sohl, Director of Admission. E-Mail: *admission@capital.edu* Web: *www.capital.edu*

CASE WESTERN RESERVE UNIVERSITY D-1

Cleveland, OH 44106	**(216) 368-4450; (216) 368-5111**
Full-time: 2500 men, 2028 women	**Faculty:** 650; I, av$
Part-time: 55 men, 78 women	**Ph.D.s:** 91%
Graduate: 2676 men, 2988 women	**Student/Faculty:** 10 to 1
Year: semesters, summer session	**Tuition:** $42,280
Application Deadline: January 15	**Room & Board:** $12,898
Freshman Class: 18418 applied, 7713 accepted, 1252 enrolled	
SAT CR/M/W: 660/720/670	**ACT:** 31 **MOST COMPETITIVE**

Case Western Reserve University, founded in 1826, is a private institution offering undergraduate, graduate, and professional programs in arts and sciences, dentistry, engineering, law, management, medicine, nursing, and social work. There are 4 undergraduate schools and 8 graduate schools. In addition to regional accreditation, Case has baccalaureate program accreditation with AACSB, ABET, CSAB, NASM, NLN, and TEAC. The 7 libraries contain 2.9 million volumes, 2.2 million microform items, 28,771 audio/video tapes/CDs/DVDs, and subscribe to 111,270 periodicals including electronic. Computerized library services include interlibrary loans, database searching, Internet access, and Wi-Fi capability. Special learning facilities include an art gallery, natural history museum, planetarium, radio station, a biology field station. The 178-acre campus is in an urban area 4 miles east of downtown Cleveland, OH. Including any residence halls, there are 182 buildings.

Student Life: 62% of undergraduates are from out of state, mostly the Middle Atlantic. Students are from 49 states, 36 foreign countries, and Canada. 70% are from public schools. 53% are White; 18% Asian American. The average age of freshmen is 18; all undergraduates, 20. 6% do not continue beyond their first year; 80% remain to graduate.

Housing: 3874 students can be accommodated in college housing, which includes coed dorms and on-campus apartments. In addition, there are special-interest houses, fraternity houses, sorority houses, Recovery house, and residential colleges for first year students. On-campus housing is guaranteed for the freshman year only, is available on a first-come, first-served basis, and is available on a lottery system for upperclassmen. 89% of students live on campus; of those, 89% remain on campus on weekends. All students may keep cars.

Activities: 40% of men belong to 16 national fraternities; 37% of women belong to 8 national sororities. There are 176 groups on campus, including symphonic winds ensemble and percussion ensemble, art, band, cheerleading, chess, choir, chorale, chorus, communications, computers, dance, debate, drama, environmental, ethnic, film, gay, honors, international, jazz band, literary magazine, marching band, musical theater, newspaper, orchestra, pep band, photography, political, professional, radio, religious, social, social service, student government, and symphony. Popular campus events include Hudson Relays, Relay-for-Life, Thwing Study Over and Springfest.

Sports: There are 12 intercollegiate sports for men and 8 for women, and

30 intramural sports for men and 12 for women. Facilities include a gym with multipurpose courts and rock climbing wall, football and soccer fields, baseball/softball ballpark, indoor and all-weather tracks, softball diamonds, 2 swimming pools, weight, and wrestling rooms, basketball, badminton, volleyball, squash, tennis, and racquetball courts, a multipurpose aerobics room, cardio exercise room, rock climbing wall, and an archery range.

Disabled Students: 90% of the campus is accessible. Facilities include wheelchair ramps, elevators, special parking, specially equipped restrooms, special class scheduling, lowered drinking fountains, lowered telephones. TDD, special testing arrangements, note-taking assistance, individualized academic counseling and planning, adaptive equipment, interpreters, and access to audiotaped text materials.

Services: Counseling and information services are available, as is tutoring in every subject. There is a reader service for the blind. In addition, supplemental instruction is available in designated courses in biology, chemistry, math, and physics, and the writing resource center.

Campus Safety and Security: Measures include 24-hour foot and vehicle patrol, emergency notification system, self-defense education, and security escort services. There are shuttle buses, emergency telephones, lighted pathways/sidewalks, controlled access to dorms/residences, property crime prevention programs, bicycle lock rental, vehicle ID etching, and equipment bolting.

Programs of Study: Case confers B.A., B.S., B.S.E. and B.S.N. degrees. Master's and doctoral degrees are also awarded. Bachelor's degrees are awarded in BIOLOGICAL SCIENCE (biochemistry, biology/biological science, evolutionary biology, and nutrition), BUSINESS (accounting, business administration and management, finance, and marketing management), COMMUNICATIONS AND THE ARTS (art history and appreciation, classics, comparative literature, dance, dramatic arts, English, French, German, music, and Spanish), COMPUTER AND PHYSICAL SCIENCE (applied mathematics, astronomy, chemistry, chemistry / chemical biology, computer science, fluid and thermal science, geology, mathematics, natural sciences, physics, polymer science, and statistics), EDUCATION (art education, education, and music education), ENGINEERING AND ENVIRONMENTAL DESIGN (aeronautical engineering, architecture, biomedical engineering, chemical engineering, civil engineering, computer engineering, electrical/electronics engineering, engineering, engineering physics, environmental science, materials science, mechanical engineering, and systems engineering), HEALTH PROFESSIONS (nursing and speech pathology/audiology), SOCIAL SCIENCE (American studies, anthropology, Asian/Oriental studies, cognitive science, economics, French studies, German area studies, gerontology, history, history of science, international studies, Japanese studies, philosophy, political science/government, psychology, religion, sociology, systems science, and women's studies). Engineering, biology, management, and music are the strongest academically. Engineering, psychology, and biology have the largest enrollments.

Required: To graduate, students must complete a minimum of 120 semester hours, with at least 30 hours in the major, and maintain a minimum GPA of 2.0. Students must complete the SAGES (Seminar Approach to General Education and Scholarship) core curriculum and two semesters of physical education.

Special: Case offers co-op programs with nearly 200 employers, and students may alternate classroom study with full-time employment. Cross-registration with 13 institutions in the Cleveland area is available, as well as internships in government, corporations, and nonprofit agencies. Students may participate in study abroad, a Washington semester, work-study programs, and accelerated-degree programs. B.A.-B.S. degrees, dual and student-designed majors, 3-2 engineering degrees, non-degree study, independent study, and pass/fail options are possible. There are extensive opportunities for undergraduates to work with faculty on research projects. Pre-professional Scholars Programs in medicine, dental medicine, social work, and law are available. Interdisciplinary majors, such as environmental geology, and intradisciplinary majors, such as nutritional biochemistry and metabolism, are available. There are 8 national honor societies, including Phi Beta Kappa, and 16 departmental honors programs.

Faculty/Classroom: 57% of faculty are male; 43% are female. 75% teach undergraduates, 95% do research, and 77% do both. Graduate students teach 6% of introductory courses. The average class size in an introductory lecture is 35; in a laboratory is 23; and in a regular course is 28.

Admissions: 42% of the 2013-2014 applicants were accepted. The SAT scores for the 2013-2014 freshman class were: Critical Reading--1% below 500, 22% between 500 and 599, 44% between 600 and 699, and 33% between 700 and 800; Math--5% between 500 and 599, 32% between 600 and 699, and 63% between 700 and 800; Writing--16% between 500 and 599, 50% between 600 and 699, and 34% between 700 and 800. The ACT scores were 9% between 24 and 26, 12% between 27 and 28, and 79% above 28. 87% of the current freshmen were in the top fifth of their class; 99% were in the top two fifths. There were 71 National Merit finalists. 116 freshmen graduated first in their class.

Requirements: The SAT or ACT is required. The ACT Optional Writing test is also required. In addition, SAT Subject tests in writing plus 2 others of the student's choice are strongly recommended for students who take the SAT. Applicants must be graduates of an accredited secondary school. However, the GED is accepted. 16 high school academic credits are required, including 4 years of English, 3 of math, (4 for science, math, and engineering majors), and 2 of lab science (3 for science and math majors and premedical students). 2 to 4 years of foreign language are strongly recommended. Engineering, math, and science students should take the SAT: Subject tests in math I/IC of IIC and physics and/or chemistry. A writing sample of the student's choice is required, and an interview is recommended. AP credits are accepted. Important factors in the admissions decision are advanced placement or honors courses, leadership record, and recommendations by school officials.

Procedure: Freshmen are admitted fall, spring, and summer. Entrance exams should be taken by the fall of the senior year. There is a deferred admissions plan. Applications should be filed by January 15 for fall entry. Notifications are sent March 20. 3004 applicants were on the 2013 waiting list; 480 were admitted. Applications are accepted online.

Transfer: 60 transfer students enrolled in 2012-2013. Transfer students should have a minimum GPA of 3.2 and meet all high school requirements. Grades of C or better transfer for credit. 60 of 120 credits required for the bachelor's degree must be completed at Case.

Visiting: There are regularly scheduled orientations for prospective students. There are guides for informal visits, visitors may sit in on classes, and stay overnight. To schedule a visit, contact the Office of Undergraduate Admission.

Financial Aid: In 2013-2014, 87% of all full-time freshmen and 88% of continuing full-time students received some form of financial aid. 59% of all full-time freshmen and 62% of continuing full-time students received need-based aid. The average freshman award was $34,434. Need-based scholarships or need-based grants averaged $30,008 ($60,305 maximum); and need-based self-help aid (loans and jobs) averaged $7,663 ($35,278 maximum). 37% of undergraduate students work part-time. Average annual earnings from campus work are $3000. The average financial indebtedness of the 2013 graduate was $34,988. Case is a member of CSS. The CSS/Profile, FAFSA, and the college's own financial statement are required. The priority date for freshman financial aid applications for fall entry is February 15.

International Students: There are 395 international students enrolled. The school actively recruits these students. They must take the TOEFL with a minimum score of 577 on the paper-based TOEFL (PBT) or 90 on the Internet-based version (iBT). They must also take the SAT or ACT.

Computers: All students may access the system 24 hours a day. There are no time limits and no fees.

Graduates: From July 1, 2012 to June 30, 2013, 898 bachelor's degrees were awarded. The most popular majors were biomedical engineering (10%), biology (8%), and psychology (8%). 205 companies recruited on campus in 2012-2013. In an average class, 2% graduate in 3 years or less, 63% graduate in 4 years or less, 77% graduate in 5 years or less, and 80% graduate in 6 years or less. Of the 2012 graduating class, 38% were enrolled in graduate school within 6 months of graduation, and 48% were employed.

Admissions Contact: Robert McCullough, Director of Undergraduate Admissions. E-Mail: *admission@case.edu* Web: *www.case.edu*

CEDARVILLE UNIVERSITY B-4

Cedarville, OH 45314 **(937) 766-7700**
(800) CEDARVILLE; (937) 766-2760

Full-time: 1435 men, 1612 women	**Faculty:** 228; IIB, --$
Part-time: 77 men, 96 women	**Ph.D.s:** 68%
Graduate: 42 men, 118 women	**Student/Faculty:** 14 to 1
Year: semesters, summer session	**Tuition:** n/av
Application Deadline: open	**Room & Board:** $5540
Freshman Class: 3347 applied, 2523 accepted, 832 enrolled	
SAT CR/M/W: 590/600/580 **ACT:** 26	**VERY COMPETITIVE+**

Cedarville University, founded in 1887, is a private Baptist college of arts and sciences offering programs in engineering, nursing, accounting, computer information systems, and education. The school is known for its religious commitment, conservative values, and community outreach programs. There are 4 undergraduate schools and 3 graduate schools. In addition to regional accreditation, Cedarville has baccalaureate program accreditation with ABET, ACBSP, ACPE, CSWE, NCATE, and NLN. The library contains 239,169 volumes, 16,862 microform items, 9,254 audio/video tapes/CDs/DVDs, and subscribes to 9,094 periodicals including electronic. Computerized library services include interlibrary loans, database searching, Internet access, and Wi-Fi capability. Special learning facilities include a radio station, media resource center, observatory, state-of-the-art simulation labs for nursing and pharmacy students. The 400-acre campus is in a small town 12 miles south of Springfield. Including any residence halls, there are 45 buildings.

Student Life: 61% of undergraduates are from out of state, mostly the Mid-West. Students are from 48 states, 16 foreign countries, and Canada. 53% are from public schools. 92% are White. 81% are Protestant. The average age of freshmen is 18; all undergraduates, 20. 15% do not continue beyond their first year; 61% remain to graduate.

Housing: 2517 students can be accommodated in college housing, which includes single-sex dorms and married student housing. On-campus housing is guaranteed for all 4 years. 76% of students live on campus; of those, 83% remain on campus on weekends. Alcohol is not permitted. All students may keep cars.

Activities: There are no fraternities or sororities. There are 77 groups on campus, including band, cheerleading, chess, choir, chorale, chorus, dance, debate, drama, environmental, ethnic, forensics, honors, international, jazz band, musical theater, newspaper, orchestra, pep band, photography, political, professional, radio and TV, religious, social, social service, student government, and yearbook. Popular campus events include Junior and Senior Banquet, and Lil' Sibs Weekend.

Sports: There are 8 intercollegiate sports for men and 8 for women, and 12 intramural sports for men and 12 for women. Facilities include a 3500-seat gym, 5 volleyball and badminton courts, a fitness center with 3 racquetball courts, a climbing wall, an exercise studio, a free weight room, Nautilus strength training areas and cardiovascular areas, a field house with a 200-meter track, basketball, volleyball, tennis, and indoor soccer courts, indoor batting cages, and a training room, and outdoor facilities including tennis and sand volleyball courts, a track, soccer, baseball, and softball fields, a golf driving range, and intramural sports playing fields.

Disabled Students: 90% of the campus is accessible. Facilities include wheelchair ramps, elevators, special parking, specially equipped restrooms, special class scheduling, lowered drinking fountains, lowered telephones, and special housing.

Services: Counseling and information services are available, as is tutoring in some subjects, specific social science, calculus, and science courses. There is a reader service for the blind, and remedial math, reading, and writing.

Campus Safety and Security: Measures include 24-hour foot and vehicle patrol, emergency notification system, self-defense education, and security escort services. There are emergency telephones, lighted pathways/sidewalks, and controlled access to dorms/residences.

Programs of Study: Cedarville confers B.A., B.S., B.M., B.M.E., B.S.E.E., B.S.M.E., B.S.N. and Cp.E. degrees. Master's and doctoral degrees are also awarded. Bachelor's degrees are awarded in BIOLOGICAL SCIENCE (biology/biological science and molecular biology), BUSINESS (accounting, business administration and management, finance, management information systems, marketing/retailing/merchandising, and sports management), COMMUNICATIONS AND THE ARTS (broadcasting, church music, communications, English, graphic design, industrial design, information technology, journalism, keyboard - piano concentration, multimedia, music, music composition, Technical Communication, Spanish, technical and business writing, and theatre arts), COMPUTER AND PHYSICAL SCIENCE (chemistry, computer science, geology, geoscience, information sciences and systems, mathematics, and physics), EDUCATION (athletic training, Christian education, early childhood education, elementary education, English education, foreign languages education, mathematics education, middle school education, music education, physical education, science education, social studies education, and special education), ENGINEERING AND ENVIRONMENTAL DESIGN (computer engineering, electrical/electronics engineering, engineering, environmental science, and mechanical engineering), HEALTH PROFESSIONS (allied health, exercise science, nursing, and pharmacy), SOCIAL SCIENCE (American studies, applied psychology, biblical studies, criminal justice, forensic studies, history, international studies, liberal arts/general studies, missions, pastoral studies, philosophy, political science/government, prelaw, psychology, public administration, social work, sociology, and youth ministry). Nursing, mechanical engineering, pre-pharmacy, psychology, and early childhood education have the largest enrollments.

Required: To graduate, all students must maintain a minimum GPA of 2.0 while taking 128 semester hours, with a minimum of 32 in specific disciplines, 52 in core curriculum, and 36 in major. Specific courses required include English composition, fundamentals of speech, politics and American culture, and physical activity and the Christian life.

Special: Internships, study abroad in 97 countries, a Washington semester, dual majors, student-designed majors, B.A.-B.S. degrees in biology, physics, chemistry, and math, and work-study programs with the college are available. Cross-registration with the Southwest Ohio Consortium for Higher Education and the Ohio Learning Network is possible. Cooperative Learning Agreement with the International Center for Creativity for the Industrial and Innovative Design major. There are 5 national honor societies, a freshman honors program, and 10 departmental honors programs.

Faculty/Classroom: 63% of faculty are male; 37% are female. All teach undergraduates. No introductory courses are taught by graduate students. The average class size in an introductory lecture is 20; in a laboratory is 20; and in a regular course is 20.

Admissions: 75% of the 2013-2014 applicants were accepted. The SAT scores for the 2013-2014 freshman class were: Critical Reading--10% below 500, 41% between 500 and 599, 35% between 600 and 699, and 14% between 700 and 800; Math--13% below 500, 37% between 500 and 599, 40% between 600 and 699, and 10% between 700 and 800; Writing--16% below 500, 42% between 500 and 599, 32% between 600 and 699, and 11% between 700 and 800. The ACT scores were 7% below 21, 19% between 21 and 23, 29% between 24 and 26, 19% between 27 and 28, and 26% above 28. 54% of the current freshmen were in the top fifth of their class; 81% were in the top two fifths. There were 16 National Merit finalists. 55 freshmen graduated first in their class.

Requirements: The SAT or ACT (preferred) is required, with scores above the national average preferred. The college recommends that applicants have 4 years of English, 3 to 4 of math, and 3 each of social studies, math, science, and a foreign language. The GED is accepted. Recommendations from a local pastor and a high school counselor are required. An interview is recommended. Cedarville requires applicants to be in the upper 50% of their class. A GPA of 3.0 is required. AP and CLEP credits are accepted. Important factors in the admissions decision are personality/intangible qualities, recommendations by school officials, and advanced placement or honors courses.

Procedure: Freshmen are admitted to all sessions. Entrance exams should be taken by late junior year or early senior year. There are early admissions, deferred admissions, and rolling admissions plans. Application deadlines are open. Application fee is $30. Applications are accepted online.

Transfer: 90 transfer students enrolled in 2012-2013. Applicants must have a minimum college GPA of 3.0. The SAT or ACT (preferred) is strongly recommended. 32 of 128 credits required for the bachelor's degree must be completed at Cedarville.

Visiting: There are regularly scheduled orientations for prospective students, including campus tours, chapel services, class visits, and meetings with faculty, coaches, and admissions counselors. There are guides for informal visits, visitors may sit in on classes, and stay overnight. To schedule a visit, contact the Admissions Office.

Financial Aid: In 2013-2014, 97% of all full-time freshmen and 95% of continuing full-time students received some form of financial aid. 67% of all full-time freshmen and 67% of continuing full-time students received need-based aid. The average freshman award was $23,073. Need-based scholarships or need-based grants averaged $7,522 ($32,708 maximum); need-based self-help aid (loans and jobs) averaged $5,584 ($14,000 maximum); non-need-based athletic scholarships averaged $5,763 ($31,000 maximum); and other non-need-based awards and non-need-based scholarships averaged $18,066 ($45,033 maximum). 58% of undergraduate students work part-time. Average annual earnings from campus work are $840. The average financial indebtedness of the 2013 graduate was $41,468. The FAFSA and the college's own financial statement are required. The deadline for filing freshman financial aid applications for fall entry is March 1.

International Students: There are 27 international students enrolled. The school actively recruits these students. They must take the TOEFL with a minimum score of 80 on the Internet-based version (iBT). They must also take the SAT or ACT, scoring 22.

Computers: All students may access the system. 24 hours a day for dorm rooms or up to 93 hours a week in the labs. There are no time limits and no fees.

Graduates: From July 1, 2012 to June 30, 2013, 622 bachelor's degrees were awarded. The most popular majors were nursing (12%), mechanical engineering (6%), and early childhood education (5%). 214 companies recruited on campus in 2012-2013. In an average class, 2% graduate in 3 years or less, 57% graduate in 4 years or less, 71% graduate in 5 years or less, and 72% graduate in 6 years or less. Of the 2012 graduating class, 11% were enrolled in graduate school within 6 months of graduation, and 84% were employed.

Admissions Contact: Amy Holderby, Director of Admissions. E-Mail: *admissions@cedarville.edu* Web: *www.cedarville.edu*

CENTRAL STATE UNIVERSITY — B-4

Wilberforce, OH 45384 — (937) 376-6348
(800) 388-CSU1; (937) 376-6648

Full-time: 565 men, 655 women	**Faculty:** n/av
Part-time: 60 men, 75 women	**Ph.D.s:** n/av
Graduate: 35 men, 60 women	**Student/Faculty:** n/av
Year: trimesters, summer session	**Tuition:** $6172 ($13,148)
Application Deadline: see profile	**Room & Board:** $8984
Freshman Class: n/av	
ACT: required	

COMPETITIVE

Central State University, founded in 1887, is a public institution offering programs in liberal arts, business, engineering, teacher preparation, and professional training. The figures in the above capsule and in this profile are approximate. There are 3 undergraduate schools and 1 graduate school. In addition to regional accreditation, Central State has baccalaureate program accreditation with ABET and NASM. The library contains 179,241 volumes, 622,727 microform items, 500 audio/video tapes/

CDs/DVDs, and subscribes to 26,316 periodicals including electronic. Computerized library services include interlibrary loans and database searching. Special learning facilities include a learning resource center, art gallery, radio station, and the National Afro-American Museum and Cultural Center. The 60-acre campus is in a rural area 18 miles east of Dayton. Including any residence halls, there are 34 buildings.

Student Life: 77% of undergraduates are from Ohio. Others are from 24 states and 2 foreign countries. 96% are African American. The average age of freshmen is 18; all undergraduates, 22. 42% do not continue beyond their first year; 23% remain to graduate.

Housing: 745 students can be accommodated in college housing, which includes single-sex dorms. On-campus housing is guaranteed for the freshman year only and is available on a first-come, first-served basis. 57% of students live on campus. Alcohol is not permitted. All students may keep cars.

Activities: 1% of men belong to 2 national fraternities; 1% of women belong to 2 national sororities. There are 30 groups on campus, including art, band, cheerleading, choir, chorale, chorus, communications, drama, drill team, ethnic, honors, jazz band, marching band, pep band, political, professional, radio and TV, religious, social, and student government. Popular campus events include Career Day and May Week.

Sports: There are 3 intercollegiate sports for men and 4 for women, and 8 intramural sports for men and 7 for women. Facilities include 2 gyms, a stadium, a swimming pool, a pool room, a baseball diamond, tennis courts, and a weight room.

Disabled Students: All of the campus is accessible. Facilities include wheelchair ramps, elevators, special parking, specially equipped rest rooms, lowered drinking fountains, and lowered telephones.

Services: Counseling and information services are available, as is tutoring in most subjects.

Campus Safety and Security: Measures include 24-hour foot and vehicle patrol. There are lighted pathways/sidewalks.

Programs of Study: Central State confers B.A., B.S., B.M., B.S.Ed., and B.S.M.E. degrees. Master's degrees are also awarded. Bachelor's degrees are awarded in BIOLOGICAL SCIENCE (biology/biological science), BUSINESS (accounting, banking and finance, business administration and management, and marketing/retailing/merchandising), COMMUNICATIONS AND THE ARTS (advertising, broadcasting, English, journalism, and music), COMPUTER AND PHYSICAL SCIENCE (chemistry, computer science, and mathematics), EDUCATION (art education, elementary education, health education, music education, physical education, secondary education, and special education), ENGINEERING AND ENVIRONMENTAL DESIGN (graphic arts technology and manufacturing engineering), SOCIAL SCIENCE (economics, history, political science/government, psychology, public administration, social work, sociology, and water resources). Communication, music, and education are the strongest academically. Business administration has the largest enrollment.

Required: To graduate, students must complete 186 quarter credits, with a minimum GPA of 2.0 (2.5 in education). Required university core courses include 64 credits in English composition, math, computer skills, humanities, natural sciences, social sciences, health and phys ed, and African American history.

Special: Central State offers co-op programs in all majors, cross-registration with 15 area colleges, study abroad in 3 countries, internships, on-campus work-study programs, and B.A.-B.S. degrees. There is a freshman honors program.

Faculty/Classroom: 77% of faculty are male; 23% are female. All teach undergraduates, and 75% teach and do research. No introductory courses are taught by graduate students. The average class size in an introductory lecture is 25, in a laboratory, 20, and in a regular course, 15.

Requirements: The ACT is required; the SAT is accepted. Applicants must be graduates of an accredited secondary school. The GED is accepted. Students should have completed 4 years of high school English, 3 years each of math, science, and social studies, and 2 years of the same foreign language. Ohio applicants should have a GPA of 2.0 and a minimum ACT composite score of 15 or SAT score of 720. Criteria are higher for out-of-state applicants. A GPA of 2.0 is required. AP and CLEP credits are accepted.

Procedure: Freshmen are admitted to all sessions. There are early admissions, deferred admissions, and rolling admissions plans. Check with the school for current application deadlines. The application fee is $20. Applications are accepted online.

Transfer: Applicants should have a minimum college GPA of 2.0. Grades of C or better transfer for credit. Transfer students with fewer than 47 quarter hours must submit high school transcripts and test scores. Transfers are admitted every term. 45 of 186 credits required for the bachelor's degree must be completed at Central State.

Visiting: There are regularly scheduled orientations for prospective students. There are guides for informal visits and visitors may sit in on classes. To schedule a visit, contact the Admissions Office.

Financial Aid: The FAFSA and the college's own financial statement are required. Check with the school for current application deadlines.

International Students: They must take the TOEFL. They must also take the SAT or ACT, scoring 19 on the ACT.

Computers: All students may access the system.

Admissions Contact: Thandabantu Maceo, Director of Admissions. A campus DVD is available. E-Mail: *admissions@csu.ces.edu* Web: *www.centralstate.edu*

CHANCELLOR UNIVERSITY — D-1

Cleveland, OH 44114 — (216) 432-8992; (888) 316-9377; (216) 696-6430

Full-time: 135 men, 450 women	**Faculty:** n/av
Part-time: 200 men, 340 women	**Ph.D.s:** 23%
Graduate: 55 men, 40 women	**Student/Faculty:** n/av
Year: semesters, summer session	**Tuition:** $12,500
Application Deadline: open	**Room & Board:** n/app
Freshman Class: n/av	
SAT or ACT: required	

COMPETITIVE

Chancellor University, founded in 1848, is a private institution offering undergraduate programs in business to commuting students. The figures in the above capsule and in this profile are approximate. The library contains 13,250 volumes, 616 microform items, 471 audio/video tapes/CDs/DVDs, and subscribes to 140 periodicals including electronic. Computerized library services include interlibrary loans and database searching. Special learning facilities include a learning resource center. The 2-acre campus is in an urban area in Cleveland. There is 1 building.

Student Life: 45% of students are African American; 42% white. The average age of all undergraduates is 26.

Housing: There are no residence halls. All students commute.

Activities: There are no fraternities or sororities. Groups on campus include chorale, student government, and yearbook.

Sports: There is no sports program at Chancellor.

Disabled Students: All of the campus is accessible. Facilities include wheelchair ramps, elevators, specially equipped restrooms, special class scheduling, lowered drinking fountains, and lowered telephones.

Services: Counseling and information services are available, as is tutoring in most subjects. There is a reader service for the blind and remedial math, reading, and writing.

Programs of Study: Chancellor confers B.S. degrees. Associates and master's degrees are also awarded. Bachelor's degrees are awarded in BUSINESS (accounting, business administration and management, marketing/retailing/merchandising, office supervision and management, real estate, retailing, and secretarial studies/office management), COMPUTER AND PHYSICAL SCIENCE (information sciences and systems), ENGINEERING AND ENVIRONMENTAL DESIGN (industrial administration/management), HEALTH PROFESSIONS (health care administration), SOCIAL SCIENCE (economics, paralegal studies, public administration, and social science).

Required: All students must complete 51 hours of general education requirements and 27 hours in the business core, plus major requirements and electives. A minimum of 120 semester hours with a minimum GPA of 2.0 is required to graduate.

Special: The external degree program enables working adults to earn a bachelor's degree in a nontraditional manner, including credit by exam and credit for life/work experience. Work-study programs, co-op programs in 7 majors, internships, dual majors, pass/fail options, and cross-registration with other area colleges are offered. Evening and Saturday classes are also available.

Faculty/Classroom: 72% of faculty are male; 28% are female. All teach undergraduates. No introductory courses are taught by graduate students. The average class size in an introductory lecture is 11; in a laboratory, 16; and in a regular course, 11.

Requirements: The SAT or ACT is required for recent high school graduates. Applicants should have completed 19 Carnegie units, including 4 years of high school English, 3 each of math and science, and 2 each of social studies and history. The GED is accepted. An interview is recommended. AP and CLEP credits are accepted. Important factors in the admissions decision are ability to finance college education, advanced placement or honors courses, and recommendations by school officials.

Procedure: Freshmen are admitted to all sessions. Entrance exams should be taken by March of the senior year. There are deferred admissions and rolling admissions plans. Application deadlines are open. The application fee is $25. Notification is sent on a rolling basis.

Transfer: Applicants should have a minimum GPA of 2.0 in at least 24 semester hours. An associate's degree and an interview are recommended. 30 of 126 credits required for the bachelor's degree must be completed at Chancellor.

Visiting: There are guides for informal visits and visitors may sit in on classes. To schedule a visit, contact Admissions Services.

Financial Aid: Chancellor is a member of CSS. The FAFSA is required. Check with the school for current application deadlines.

International Students: They must take the TOEFL.

Computers: All students may access the system on or off campus. There are no time limits and no fees.

Admissions Contact: Admission Services. E-Mail: *cuadmissions@chancellor.edu* Web: *www.chancellor.edu*

CINCINNATI COLLEGE OF MORTUARY SCIENCE A-5

Cincinnati, OH 45224-1462 (513) 761-2020
(888) 377-8433; (513) 761-3333

Full-time: 85 men, 60 women	**Faculty:** n/av
Part-time: 2 men, 2 women	**Ph.D.s:** 33%
Graduate: n/av	**Student/Faculty:** n/av
Year: trimesters, summer session	**Tuition:** $12,500
Application Deadline: see profile	**Room & Board:** n/app
Freshman Class: n/av	
SAT or ACT: required	**SPECIAL**

The Cincinnati College of Mortuary Science, founded in 1882, is the oldest private mortuary college in the country. The curriculum encompasses the embalming sciences, funeral directing, and the liberal arts. The figures in the above capsule and in this profile are approximate. In addition to regional accreditation, CCMS has baccalaureate program accreditation with ABFSE. The 2 libraries contain 6,000 volumes. The 16-acre campus is in an urban area 8 miles from downtown Cincinnati. There is 1 building.

Student Life: 50% of undergraduates are from out of state, mostly the Midwest. Students are from 15 states. 93% are white. The average age of all undergraduates is 24. 15% do not continue beyond their first year; 85% remain to graduate.

Housing: There are no residence halls. All students commute.

Activities: There are no fraternities or sororities. Groups on campus include student government and yearbook. Popular campus events include field trips, guest lectures, and welcoming and farewell parties.

Sports: There is no sports program at CCMS.

Disabled Students: All of the campus is accessible. Facilities include wheelchair ramps, elevators, special parking, and specially equipped restrooms.

Campus Safety and Security: There are emergency telephones and lighted pathways/sidewalks.

Programs of Study: CCMS confers B.M.S. degrees. Associates degrees are also awarded. Bachelor's degrees are awarded in BUSINESS (funeral home services).

Required: To graduate, students must complete 180 quarter credit hours, including 90 in the major, with a minimum GPA of 2.0. General education requirements consist of 18 quarter hours each in natural science/math, social science, and humanities/arts and 12 each in English composition and literature, business management, and free electives.

Special: Limited credit may be given for life, military, and work experience.

Faculty/Classroom: 87% of faculty are male; 13% are female. All teach undergraduates. The average class size in an introductory lecture is 50 and in a laboratory is 20.

Requirements: The SAT or ACT is required. Applicants must be graduates of an accredited secondary school. The GED is accepted. Students must complete 16 high school units, including 8 of electives, 3 of English, 2 each of science and history, and 1 of math. An interview is recommended. A GPA of 2.0 is required. AP and CLEP credits are accepted. Important factors in the admissions decision are leadership record, recommendations by alumni, and parents or siblings who attended the school.

Procedure: Freshmen are admitted fall and spring. There is a rolling admissions plan. Check with the school for current application deadlines. The application fee is $40. Applications are accepted online.

Transfer: Applicants must submit transcripts from all colleges attended. Grades of D+ or better transfer for credit if students have a GPA of 2.0. Transfers are admitted for the fall and spring terms. 90 of 180 credits required for the bachelor's degree must be completed at CCMS.

Visiting: There are regularly scheduled orientations for prospective students, including open house programs in August and February. There are guides for informal visits. To schedule a visit, contact the Enrollment Management Coordinator.

Financial Aid: CCMS is a member of CSS. The CSS/Profile is required. Check with the school for current application deadlines.

Computers: All students may access the system during supervised lab hours. There are no fees.

Admissions Contact: Enrollment Management. E-Mail: *dburke@ccms.edu* Web: *www.ccms.edu*

CLEVELAND INSTITUTE OF ART D-1

Cleveland, OH 44106 (216) 421-7418
(800) 223-4700; (216) 754-3634

Full-time: 238 men, 320 women	**Faculty:** 43
Part-time: 3 men, 7 women	**Ph.D.s:** 70%
Graduate: n/av	**Student/Faculty:** 13 to 1
Year: semesters	**Tuition:** $37,009
Application Deadline: March 1	**Room & Board:** $12,632
Freshman Class: n/av	
SAT CR/M/W: 550/520/500 **ACT:** 22	**SPECIAL**

Cleveland Institute of Art, founded in 1882, is an independent professional school of art and design offering a 4-year B.F.A. degree. In addition to regional accreditation, CIA has baccalaureate program accreditation with NASAD. The library contains 51,000 volumes, 3,305 microform items, 1,577 audio/video tapes/CDs/DVDs, and subscribes to 139 periodicals including electronic. Computerized library services include interlibrary loans, database searching, Internet access, and Wi-Fi capability. Special learning facilities include an art gallery, radio station, CIA has a movie cinema on campus. The 5-acre campus is in an urban area 4 miles east of downtown Cleveland, adjacent to the Case Western Reserve University campus. Including any residence halls, there are 3 buildings.

Student Life: 68% of undergraduates are from Ohio. Others are from 28 states, 11 foreign countries, and Canada. 83% are from public schools. 75% are White. The average age of freshmen is 18; all undergraduates, 21. 20% do not continue beyond their first year; 65% remain to graduate.

Housing: 132 students can be accommodated in college housing, which includes single-sex and coed dorms and on-campus apartments. On-campus housing is guaranteed for the freshman year only, is available on a first-come, first-served basis, and is available on a lottery system for upperclassmen. Priority is given to out-of-town students. 74% of students commute. Alcohol is not permitted. Upperclassmen may keep cars.

Activities: There are 15 groups on campus, including and survey student gallery. Some of the Institute's social and educational student organizations also collaborate with similar student organizations at Case Western Reserve University and the Cleveland Institute of Music, student activities program board, student artist association, student leadership council, art, artists for Christ, band, ethnic, gay, international, musical theater, photography, professional, religious, social, social service, and student government. Popular campus events include Museum Trips, Annual Cookout, Spring Break, Halloween Party, Holiday Art Sale and Student Art Exhibits.

Sports: There are 9 intramural sports for men and 8 for women. Facilities include For a fee, students may use the recreation facilities of Case Western Reserve University.

Disabled Students: 90% of the campus is accessible. Facilities include wheelchair ramps, elevators, special parking, specially equipped restrooms, and lowered drinking fountains.

Services: Counseling and information services are available, as is tutoring in some subjects, English, Art History, and Academic Electives.

Campus Safety and Security: Measures include security escort services. There are shuttle buses, emergency telephones, lighted pathways/sidewalks, controlled access to dorms/residences, security officers present during building-occupied hours.

Programs of Study: CIA confers B.F.A. degrees. Bachelor's degrees are awarded in COMMUNICATIONS AND THE ARTS (animation, ceramic art and design, drawing, game design and development, glass, graphic design, illustration, industrial design, metal/jewelry, painting, photography, printmaking, and sculpture), COMPUTER AND PHYSICAL SCIENCE (biomedical art), ENGINEERING AND ENVIRONMENTAL DESIGN (architecture and interior architecture). Industrial Design, Painting, and Biomedical Art are the strongest academically. Industrial design, illustration, biomedical art, and painting have the largest enrollments.

Required: To graduate, students must complete 126 to 129 credit hours, with 42 to 51 in the major, and must maintain a minimum GPA of 2.0. Distribution requirements call for 87 studio credits and 42 liberal arts credits. A thesis is required, which is encompassed in the B.F.A. show that each student mounts in the spring of the final year.

Special: Cross-registration with selected colleges in Northeast Ohio, internships for upperclassmen with business and industry, and study abroad in 5 countries are available. There are joint programs with Case Western Reserve University in Art Education and Biomedical Art.

Faculty/Classroom: 60% of faculty are male; 40% are female. All teach undergraduates. No introductory courses are taught by graduate students. The average class size in an introductory lecture is 16 and in a regular course is 13.

Admissions: The SAT scores for the 2013-2014 freshman class were: Critical Reading--27% below 500, 40% between 500 and 599, 28% between 600 and 699, and 5% between 700 and 800; Math--41% below 500, 32% between 500 and 599, 22% between 600 and 699, and 5% between 700 and 800; Writing--44% below 500, 32% between 500 and 599, 22% between 600 and 699, and 2% between 700 and 800. The ACT scores were 33% below 21, 28% between 21 and 23, 17% between

24 and 26, 10% between 27 and 28, and 12% above 28. 30% of the current freshmen were in the top fifth of their class; 60% were in the top two fifths.

Requirements: The SAT or ACT is required. Applicants must be graduates of an accredited secondary school. The GED is accepted. An essay and a portfolio are required. An interview is strongly recommended. A GPA of 2.0 is required. AP and CLEP credits are accepted. Important factors in the admissions decision are evidence of special talent, personality/intangible qualities, and leadership record.

Procedure: Freshmen are admitted fall. Entrance exams should be taken during the junior year. There are early admissions and rolling admissions plans. Applications should be filed by March 1 for fall entry; November 15 for spring entry, along with a $30 fee. Notifications are sent March 15. Applications are accepted online.

Transfer: 29 transfer students enrolled in 2012-2013. Applicants must have a 2.0 GPA and must submit a portfolio. Those who have 30 to 36 credits in comparable studio courses or a strong portfolio will be reviewed by department faculty. Grades of C or better transfer for credit. 30 of 126 credits required for the bachelor's degree must be completed at CIA.

Visiting: There are regularly scheduled orientations for prospective students, consists of a tour, interview, and classrooms visits. There are guides for informal visits and visitors may sit in on classes. To schedule a visit, contact Arlene Thomas at (216) 421-7418.

Financial Aid: In 2013-2014, 99% of all full-time freshmen and 96% of continuing full-time students received some form of financial aid. 71% of all full-time freshmen and 75% of continuing full-time students received need-based aid. The average freshman award was $34,199. Need-based scholarships or need-based grants averaged $3,101 ($14,500 maximum); need-based self-help aid (loans and jobs) averaged $4,168 ($7,513 maximum); and other non-need-based awards and non-need-based scholarships averaged $11,211 ($31,500 maximum). 40% of undergraduate students work part-time. Average annual earnings from campus work are $1158. The average financial indebtedness of the 2013 graduate was $30,703. The FAFSA is required. The priority date for freshman financial aid applications for fall entry is March 15. The deadline for filing freshman financial aid applications for fall entry is March 15.

International Students: There are 29 international students enrolled. The school actively recruits these students. They must take the TOEFL with a minimum score of 525 on the paper-based TOEFL (PBT) or 71 on the Internet-based version (iBT), or complete Level 112 at an ELS center. They must also take the SAT or ACT.

Computers: All students may access the system. There are no time limits and no fees.

Graduates: From July 1, 2012 to June 30, 2013, 106 bachelor's degrees were awarded. The most popular majors were industrial design (21%), illustration (18%), and painting (8%). 400 companies recruited on campus in 2012-2013. In an average class, 60% graduate in 4 years or less, 64% graduate in 5 years or less, and 65% graduate in 6 years or less. Of the 2012 graduating class, 4% were enrolled in graduate school within 6 months of graduation, and 90% were employed.

Admissions Contact: Joanne Landers, Director of Admissions. E-Mail: *admissions@.cia.edu* Web: *www.cia.edu*

CLEVELAND INSTITUTE OF MUSIC D-1

Cleveland, OH 44106 **(216) 795-3107; (216) 795-3161**

Full-time: 105 men, 135 women	**Faculty:** n/av
Part-time: n/av	**Ph.D.s:** 9%
Graduate: 80 men, 110 women	**Student/Faculty:** n/av
Year: semesters, summer session	**Tuition:** $44,039
Application Deadline:	**Room & Board:** $12,843
Freshman Class: n/av	
SAT or ACT: required	

SPECIAL

The Cleveland Institute of Music, founded in 1920, is a private music conservatory offering education and training in performance, composition, and related musical disciplines. In addition to regional accreditation, CIM has baccalaureate program accreditation with NASM. The library contains 82,263 volumes, 28,600 audio/video tapes/CDs/DVDs. Computerized library services include interlibrary loans, database searching, Internet access, and Wi-Fi capability. The -acre campus is in an urban area 4 miles east of downtown Cleveland. Including any residence halls, there are 3 buildings.

Student Life: 68% of undergraduates are from out of state, mostly the Mid-West. Students are from 40 states, 21 foreign countries, and Canada. 95% are from public schools. 71% are White; 20% Foreign. The average age of freshmen is 18; all undergraduates, 21. 2% do not continue beyond their first year; 85% remain to graduate.

Housing: College-sponsored housing includes coed dorms. Alcohol is not permitted. All students may keep cars.

Activities: There are no fraternities or sororities. There are 8 groups on campus, including chorale, chorus, jazz band, opera, orchestra, religious, student government, and symphony. Popular campus events include Concerts by the Cleveland Orchestra.

Sports: There is no sports program at CIM. Facilities include Athletic facilities and a fitness center are available.

Disabled Students: Facilities include wheelchair ramps, elevators, special parking, specially equipped restrooms, and lowered drinking fountains.

Services: Counseling and information services are available, as is tutoring in some subjects.

Campus Safety and Security: Measures include 24-hour foot and vehicle patrol and security escort services. There are shuttle buses, emergency telephones, and lighted pathways/sidewalks.

Programs of Study: CIM confers B.M., and B.A.Mus.Ed. degrees. Master's and doctoral degrees are also awarded. Bachelor's degrees are awarded in COMMUNICATIONS AND THE ARTS (music), EDUCATION (music education).

Required: The Bachelor of Music program offers an intensive and comprehensive preparation for a professional career in music. All courses revolve around a core of studies in music theory, music history, and literature, with the additional educational breadth afforded by selected general education subjects.

Special: Students majoring in performance, composition, or eurhythmics may add a second major in audio recording technology. In addition, a wide variety of double-degree opportunities exist through a cooperative program with adjacent Case Western Reserve University. CIM also provides cross-registration possibilities with member schools in the Northeast Ohio Council on Higher Education. There are 2 national honor societies.

Faculty/Classroom: 68% of faculty are male; 32% are female. All teach undergraduates. No introductory courses are taught by graduate students.

Requirements: The SAT or ACT is required. An audition is required, at which time applicants must complete admission testing in music theory and ear training. The examinations determine each applicant's knowledge of key signatures and scale patterns, part-writing skills, and the ability to hear and identify intervals and triads. Applicants in composition must submit for prescreening copies of original scores (also recordings, if available). Other factors that weigh in making admissions decision include GPA, class rank, standardized test scores, and letters of recommendation. The GED is accepted in lieu of a diploma for applicants who are homeschooled. AP credits are accepted.

Procedure: Freshmen are admitted fall and spring. Entrance exams should be taken at the time of the entrance audition. Check with the school for current application deadlines. The fall 2013 application fee was $100. Applications are accepted online.

Transfer: 14 transfer students enrolled in 2012-2013. Applicants must meet the same criteria as entering freshmen and submit transcripts and letters of recommendation. 48 of 120 credits required for the bachelor's degree must be completed at CIM.

Visiting: Visitors may sit in on classes. To schedule a visit, contact the Admission Office.

Financial Aid: In 2013-2014, 96% of all full-time freshmen and 96% of continuing full-time students received some form of financial aid. 79% of all full-time freshmen and 83% of continuing full-time students received need-based aid. The average freshman award was $24,325. Need-based scholarships or need-based grants averaged $15,026 ($30,190 maximum); need-based self-help aid (loans and jobs) averaged $3,225 ($10,500 maximum); and other non-need-based awards and non-need-based scholarships averaged $6,075 ($22,170 maximum). 51% of undergraduate students work part-time. Average annual earnings from campus work are $948. The average financial indebtedness of the 2013 graduate was $20,000. CIM is a member of CSS. The FAFSA is required. Check with the school for current application deadlines.

International Students: There are 31 international students enrolled. They must take the TOEFL with a minimum score of 550 on the paper-based TOEFL (PBT) or 80 on the Internet-based version (iBT) or take the MELAB. They must also take the SAT or ACT, and the college's own entrance exam, and the student must also audition.

Computers: All students may access the system. There are no time limits and no fees.

Graduates: From July 1, 2012 to June 30, 2013, 59 bachelor's degrees were awarded. In an average class, 2% graduate in 3 years or less, 80% graduate in 4 years or less, and 81% graduate in 5 years or less.

Admissions Contact: Admission Office E-Mail: *admission@cim,edu* Web: *www.cim.edu*

CLEVELAND STATE UNIVERSITY D-1

Cleveland, OH 44115 (216) 523-7284
1 (800) CSU-OHIO; (216) 687-9210

Full-time: 4187 men, 4840 women	**Faculty:** 511
Part-time: 1469 men, 1880 women	**Ph.D.s:** 84%
Graduate: 2261 men, 3104 women	**Student/Faculty:** 20 to 1
Year: semesters, summer session	**Tuition:** $9499 ($12,678)
Application Deadline:	**Room & Board:** $11,858

Freshman Class: 6768 applied, 4255 accepted, 1727 enrolled
SAT CR/M: 510/520 **ACT:** 22 **COMPETITIVE**

Cleveland State University, founded in 1964, is a primarily commuter public institution offering undergraduate and graduate programs through the colleges of arts and sciences, business administration, education, engineering, law, and urban affairs. There are 8 undergraduate schools and 8 graduate schools. In addition to regional accreditation, CSU has baccalaureate program accreditation with AACSB, ABET, CSWE, NCATE, and NLN. The 2 libraries contain 1.9 million volumes, 725,281 microform items, 38,822 audio/video tapes/CDs/DVDs, and subscribe to 11,148 periodicals including electronic. Computerized library services include interlibrary loans, database searching, Internet access, and Wi-Fi capability. Special learning facilities include an art gallery and radio station. The 85-acre campus is in an urban area in downtown Cleveland, Ohio. Including any residence halls, there are 48 buildings.

Student Life: 92% of undergraduates are from Ohio. Others are from 40 states, 79 foreign countries, and Canada. 62% are White; 19% African American. The average age of freshmen is 22; all undergraduates, 25. 33% do not continue beyond their first year; 34% remain to graduate.

Housing: 1186 students can be accommodated in college housing, which includes coed dorms, on-campus apartments, and off-campus apartments. law, quiet study, and first-year experience floors. On-campus housing is available on a first come and first-served basis. 92% of students commute. All students may keep cars.

Activities: 1% of men belong to 6 local and 4 national fraternities; 1% of women belong to 3 local and 7 national sororities. There are 254 groups on campus, including art, cheerleading, chess, choir, chorale, chorus, computers, dance, drama, environmental, ethnic, film, gay, honors, international, jazz band, literary magazine, musical theater, newspaper, opera, orchestra, pep band, photography, political, professional, radio and TV, religious, social, social service, student government, and symphony. Popular campus events include Weeks of Welcome and Springfest.

Sports: There are 7 intercollegiate sports for men and 9 for women, and 5 intramural sports for men and 5 for women. Facilities include a gym, gymnastics and weight rooms, a dance studio, a swimming pool, a fitness trail, an indoor track, handball and squash courts, a 2500-seat soccer stadium, and a convocation center.

Disabled Students: All of the campus is accessible. Facilities include wheelchair ramps, elevators, special parking, specially equipped restrooms, lowered drinking fountains, and special housing.

Services: Counseling and information services are available, as is tutoring in most subjects. There is a reader service for the blind, and remedial math, reading, and writing.

Campus Safety and Security: Measures include 24-hour foot and vehicle patrol, emergency notification system, and security escort services. There are emergency telephones, lighted pathways/sidewalks, a campus watch organization for faculty and staff.

Programs of Study: CSU confers B.A., B.S., B.B.A., B.C.E., B.Ch.E., B.E.E., B.M., B.M.E., B.S.C.I.S., B.S.Ed., B.S.I.E., B.S.N. and B.S.T. degrees. Master's and doctoral degrees are also awarded. Bachelor's degrees are awarded in BIOLOGICAL SCIENCE (biology/biological science), BUSINESS (accounting, business economics, finance, labor studies, management information systems, management science, and marketing/retailing/merchandising), COMMUNICATIONS AND THE ARTS (art, communications, dramatic arts, English, film, television and digital media, French, linguistics, music, and Spanish), COMPUTER AND PHYSICAL SCIENCE (chemistry, computer science, geology, information sciences and systems, mathematics, and physics), EDUCATION (early childhood education, elementary education, health education, physical education, secondary education, and special education), ENGINEERING AND ENVIRONMENTAL DESIGN (chemical engineering, civil engineering, electrical/electronics engineering, electrical/electronics engineering technology, environmental science, mechanical engineering, and mechanical engineering technology), HEALTH PROFESSIONS (exercise science, health science, medical technology, nursing, occupational therapy, pharmaceutical science, physical therapy, premedicine, speech pathology/audiology, and speech therapy), SOCIAL SCIENCE (anthropology, classical/ancient civilization, criminology, economics, history, international relations, liberal arts/general studies, philosophy, political science/government, psychology, religion, social science, social studies, social work, sociology, urban studies, and women's studies). Business, communications, and psychology have the largest enrollments.

Required: Students must complete at least 120 semester hours with a minimum 2.0 GPA for graduation. Requirements include a core curriculum containing courses in English composition, arts and humanities, social science, natural sciences, math and logic, non-Western culture and civilization, Western culture and civilization, and human diversity and the African American experience.

Special: CSU offers a developmental program for Ohio students not qualified for regular freshman admission. There are also cooperative education programs, nondegree study, work-study programs, accelerated degree programs, internships, pass/fail options, and cross-registration at other Cleveland area colleges. Student designed and dual majors, study abroad in 10 countries, and volunteer opportunities are available, as well as a combined liberal arts and engineering degree and a 3-2 engineering degree. There are 6 national honor societies, a freshman honors program, and 38 departmental honors programs.

Faculty/Classroom: 53% of faculty are male; 47% are female. No introductory courses are taught by graduate students.

Admissions: 63% of the 2013-2014 applicants were accepted. The SAT scores for the 2013-2014 freshman class were: Critical Reading--43% below 500, 40% between 500 and 599, 16% between 600 and 699, and 2% between 700 and 800; Math--39% below 500, 39% between 500 and 599, 20% between 600 and 699, and 2% between 700 and 800.

Requirements: The SAT or ACT is required. A high school diploma is required or the GED is accepted. Students should have completed the following academic credits: 4 years of English, 3 of math, social studies, and science (1 must be a lab), and 2 of a foreign language. A general college-preparatory program is recommended. A GPA of 2.3 is required. AP and CLEP credits are accepted.

Procedure: Freshmen are admitted to all sessions. Entrance exams should be taken prior to application. There are deferred admissions and rolling admissions plans. Check with the school for current application deadlines. The application fee is $30. Notification is sent on a rolling basis. Applications are accepted online.

Transfer: 2313 transfer students enrolled in 2012-2013. Applicants must have a minimum GPA of 2.0 and submit previous college transcripts. Transfer students entering with fewer than 24 semester hours must submit official high school transcripts and test scores if they have been out of high school less than 5 years. 30 of 120 credits required for the bachelor's degree must be completed at CSU.

Visiting: There are regularly scheduled orientations for prospective students, including general visitation days for the university (in the fall) and each of the colleges (in the spring). There are guides for informal visits, visitors may sit in on classes, and stay overnight. To schedule a visit, contact the Office of Undergraduate Admissions.

Financial Aid: In 2013-2014, 74% of all full-time freshmen and 77% of continuing full-time students received some form of financial aid. 62% of all full-time freshmen and 60% of continuing full-time students received need-based aid. The average freshman award was $9,460. Need-based scholarships or need-based grants averaged $6,974; need-based self-help aid (loans and jobs) averaged $4,293; non-need-based athletic scholarships averaged $11,588; and other non-need-based awards and non-need-based scholarships averaged $5,561. The FAFSA is required. The priority date for freshman financial aid applications for fall entry is February 15.

International Students: There are 450 international students enrolled. They must take the TOEFL with a minimum score of 525 on the paper-based TOEFL (PBT) or 65 on the Internet-based version (iBT).

Computers: All students may access the system. Hours vary by input center. Modem access is available 24 hours per day. There are no time limits and no fees.

Graduates: From July 1, 2012 to June 30, 2013, 2117 bachelor's degrees were awarded. The most popular majors were business (19%), health professions/related (15%), and social sciences (11%). 50 companies recruited on campus in 2012-2013. In an average class, 10% graduate in 4 years or less, 26% graduate in 5 years or less, and 34% graduate in 6 years or less.

Admissions Contact: Rob Spademan, Interim Director, Undergrad. Admissions. E-Mail: *admissions@csuohio.edu* Web: *http:/www.engagecsu.com/*

COLLEGE OF MOUNT SAINT JOSEPH A-5

Cincinnati, OH 45233 (513) 244-4531
(800) 654-9314; (513) 244-4851

Full-time: 548 men, 675 women	**Faculty:** n/av
Part-time: 114 men, 458 women	**Ph.D.s:** 71%
Graduate: 136 men, 395 women	**Student/Faculty:** 11 to 1
Year: semesters, summer session	**Tuition:** $25,800
Application Deadline:	**Room & Board:** $8080

Freshman Class: 1180 applied, 1036 accepted, 321 enrolled
SAT CR/M: 475/468 **ACT:** 22 **COMPETITIVE**

The College of Mount St. Joseph, founded in 1920, is a private Catholic college offering 34 undergraduate and 5 graduate degree programs. There is one graduate school. In addition to regional accreditation, the Mount has baccalaureate program accreditation with CSWE, NASM, NLN, and TEAC. The library contains 95,428 volumes, 340,000 microform items, 4,149 audio/video tapes/CDs/DVDs, and subscribes to 3,906 periodicals including electronic. Computerized library services include interlibrary loans, database searching, Internet access, and Wi-Fi capability. Special learning facilities include an art gallery. The 92-acre campus is in a suburban area 7 miles west of downtown Cincinnati. Including any residence halls, there are 9 buildings.

Student Life: 85% of undergraduates are from Ohio. Others are from 25 states, and 4 foreign countries. 68% are from public schools. 76% are White. The average age of freshmen is 19; all undergraduates, 26. 31% do not continue beyond their first year; 69% remain to graduate.

Housing: 537 students can be accommodated in college housing, which includes coed dorms. On-campus housing is guaranteed for all 4 years. 79% of students commute. All students may keep cars.

Activities: There are no fraternities or sororities. There are 46 groups on campus, including and departmental clubs, art, band, cheerleading, choir, chorale, chorus, computers, dance, drama, ethnic, gay, honors, international, jazz band, literary magazine, marching band, musical theater, newspaper, orchestra, pep band, photography, professional, religious, social, social service, and student government. Popular campus events include MLK Luncheon, Spring Formal, Homecoming Pep Rally, and Little Sibs Weekend.

Sports: There are 10 intercollegiate sports for men and 9 for women, and 7 intramural sports for men and 7 for women. Facilities include a sports complex and field for football, soccer, lacrosse, and track and field with an 8-lane track and athletic training facilities. The student center houses 2 gyms used for basketball, volleyball, and wrestling and includes a running track, handball/racquetball courts, a fitness center, an athletic training center, and a wellness center. Facilities also include tennis courts, a softball field, and practice fields for soccer, lacrosse, and baseball.

Disabled Students: 95% of the campus is accessible. Facilities include wheelchair ramps, elevators, special parking, specially equipped restrooms, special class scheduling, lowered drinking fountains, lowered telephones, special housing. special door openings for wheelchair access, and a chairlift between levels where the science building and classroom building meet.

Services: Counseling and information services are available, as is tutoring in every subject. There is remedial math and writing, peer tutoring, and services to students with learning disabilities, math and writing centers are also available.

Campus Safety and Security: Measures include 24-hour foot and vehicle patrol, emergency notification system, and security escort services. There are emergency telephones, lighted pathways/sidewalks, crime prevention programs, assistance with vehicle trouble and first aid.

Programs of Study: Mount confers B.A., B.S., B.F.A. and B.S.N. degrees. Associate, master's, and doctoral degrees are also awarded. Bachelor's degrees are awarded in BIOLOGICAL SCIENCE (biochemistry, biology/biological science, and neurosciences), BUSINESS (accounting, business administration and management, organizational leadership and management, and sports management), COMMUNICATIONS AND THE ARTS (art history, art, communications, English, fine arts, graphic design, and music), COMPUTER AND PHYSICAL SCIENCE (chemistry and mathematics), EDUCATION (art education, athletic training, early childhood education, elementary education, general studies, health information management, middle school education, and special education), HEALTH PROFESSIONS (nursing), SOCIAL SCIENCE (criminology, history, liberal arts/general studies, paralegal studies, psychology, religion, religious education, social work, and sociology). Nursing, business administration, and sport management are the strongest academically. Business administration, nursing, and graphic design have the largest enrollments.

Required: To graduate, students must complete a minimum of 120 credits with a minimum GPA of 2.0 overall and in the major. 46-49 core curriculum total hours are required. All students must take 12-15 credit hours on the common good, and 34 credit hours of a discipline-specific core, and a capstone synthesis reflection.

Special: The college offers co-op programs in all majors, cross-registration with the Greater Cincinnati Consortium of Colleges and Universities, internships, credit for experiential learning, and study abroad in 3 countries. Also available are work-study programs, accelerated degree programs in 11 majors, dual majors, cultural immersion courses in the United States and abroad, a dual enrollment program (for transfer students), service learning, and off-campus study for RNs in area hospitals. The Mount also has a program for students with learning disabilities (Project EXCEL). There are 14 national honor societies, a freshman honors program, and 13 departmental honors programs.

Faculty/Classroom: 36% of faculty are male; 65% are female. No introductory courses are taught by graduate students. The average class size in an introductory lecture is 23; in a laboratory is 19; and in a regular course is 19.

Admissions: 88% of the 2013-2014 applicants were accepted. The SAT scores for the 2013-2014 freshman class were: Critical Reading--62% below 500, 30% between 500 and 599, 7% between 600 and 699, and 1% between 700 and 800; Math--61% below 500, 30% between 500 and 599, and 9% between 600 and 699. The ACT scores were 40% below 21, 29% between 21 and 23, 22% between 24 and 26, 6% between 27 and 28, and 3% above 28. 23% of the current freshmen were in the top fifth of their class; 51% were in the top two fifths. 3 freshmen graduated first in their class.

Requirements: The SAT or ACT is required. The College of Mount St. Joseph conducts a comprehensive and individualized review of every candidate's credentials for admission including but not limited to the following: a college prep high school curriculum, strong GPA, standardized test scores, evidence of leadership, and extracurricular involvement. An ACT score at or above the national average is recommended. In addition, students' personal background, attributes, and individual life circumstances are taken into consideration. A GPA of 2.5 is required. AP and CLEP credits are accepted.

Procedure: Freshmen are admitted to all sessions. There is a rolling admissions plan. Check with the school for current application deadlines. The application fee is $25. Notification is sent on a rolling basis. Applications are accepted online.

Transfer: 97 transfer students enrolled in 2012-2013. Transfer students must have a college GPA of 2.0 or better in a minimum of 12 semester or 18 quarter hours. All college hours must be presented. 30 of 120 credits required for the bachelor's degree must be completed at the Mount.

Visiting: There are regularly scheduled orientations for prospective students, including a meeting with an admissions counselor, a student-guided tour, a visit to financial aid, and a meeting with a faculty member and/or athletic coach, if requested. There are guides for informal visits, visitors may sit in on classes, and stay overnight. To schedule a visit, contact the Office of Admission.

Financial Aid: In 2013-2014, 100% of all full-time freshmen and 98% of continuing full-time students received some form of financial aid. 84% of all full-time freshmen and 81% of continuing full-time students received need-based aid. The average freshman award was $20,218. Need-based scholarships or need-based grants averaged $16,336 ($32,485 maximum); need-based self-help aid (loans and jobs) averaged $4,969 ($7,000 maximum); and other non-need-based awards and non-need-based scholarships averaged $12,022 ($27,400 maximum). 16% of undergraduate students work part-time. The FAFSA is required. The priority date for freshman financial aid applications for fall entry is March 1.

International Students: There are 4 international students enrolled. They must also take the SAT or ACT.

Computers: All students may access the system 24 hours a day. There are no time limits and no fees.

Graduates: From July 1, 2012 to June 30, 2013, 380 bachelor's degrees were awarded. The most popular majors were nursing (23%), general studies (9%), and business administration (8%). 75 companies recruited on campus in 2012-2013. In an average class, 57% graduate in 6 years or less. Of the 2012 graduating class, 17% were enrolled in graduate school within 6 months of graduation, and 82% were employed.

Admissions Contact: Peggy Minnich, Director of Admission. E-Mail: *admission@mail.msj.edu* Web: *www.msj.edu*

COLLEGE OF WOOSTER — D-2

Wooster, OH 44691 (330) 263-2322
(800) 877-9905; (330) 263-2621

Full-time: 865 men, 955 women	**Faculty:** n/av; IIB, -$
Part-time: 10 men, 10 women	**Ph.D.s:** 91%
Graduate: n/av	**Student/Faculty:** n/av
Year: semesters, summer session	**Tuition:** $38,790
Application Deadline: see profile	**Room & Board:** $9810
Freshman Class: n/av	
SAT or ACT: required	

VERY COMPETITIVE

The College of Wooster, founded in 1866, is a private liberal arts college. The figures in the above capsule and in this profile are approximate. In addition to regional accreditation, Wooster has baccalaureate program accreditation with NASM. The 3 libraries contain 622,672 volumes, 210,094 microform items, and 24,149 audio/video tapes/CDs/DVDs, and subscribe to 6696 periodicals including electronic. Computerized library services include interlibrary loans and database searching. Special learning facilities include a learning resource center, art gallery, and radio station. The 240-acre campus is in a suburban area 55 miles southwest of Cleveland. Including any residence halls, there are 37 buildings.

Student Life: 52% of undergraduates are from Ohio. Others are from 44 states, 35 foreign countries, and Canada. 74% are from public schools. 76% are white. The average age of freshmen is 19; all undergraduates, 20. 12% do not continue beyond their first year; 68% remain to graduate.

Housing: 1859 students can be accommodated in college housing, which includes single-sex and coed dorms. In addition, there are language houses, special-interest houses, fraternity houses, sorority houses, and almost 3 dozen small house residential options, most of which are associated with community service/volunteer programs. On-campus housing is guaranteed for all 4 years. 99% of students live on campus; of those, 80% remain on campus on weekends. All students may keep cars.

Activities: 10% of men belong to 3 local fraternities; 17% of women belong to 6 local sororities. There are 11 groups on campus, including art, bagpipe, band, cheerleading, chess, choir, chorale, chorus, dance, debate, drama, ethnic, film, forensics, gay, honors, international, jazz band, literary magazine, marching band, musical theater, newspaper, orchestra, pep band, photography, political, religious, social service, student government, symphony, and yearbook. Popular campus events include Party on the Green, Winter Gala, and Scot Spirit Day.

Sports: There are 11 intercollegiate sports for men and 11 for women, and 11 intramural sports for men and 11 for women. Facilities include a phys ed center, a stadium, a golf course, tennis courts, a track, baseball and softball fields, a soccer field, a hockey and lacrosse field, a natatorium, and a fitness center.

Disabled Students: 95% of the campus is accessible. Facilities include wheelchair ramps, elevators, special parking, specially equipped restrooms, special class scheduling, and lowered drinking fountains.

Services: Counseling and information services are available, as is tutoring in every subject. There is a reader service for the blind and remedial math, reading, and writing.

Campus Safety and Security: Measures include 24-hour foot and vehicle patrol and security escort services. There are emergency telephones and lighted pathways/sidewalks.

Programs of Study: Wooster confers B.A., B.Mus., and B.Mus.Ed. degrees. Bachelor's degrees are awarded in BIOLOGICAL SCIENCE (biochemistry and biology/biological science), BUSINESS (business economics), COMMUNICATIONS AND THE ARTS (communications, comparative literature, dramatic arts, English, fine arts, French, German, Greek (classical), Latin, music, and Spanish), COMPUTER AND PHYSICAL SCIENCE (chemistry, computer science, geology, mathematics, and physics), SOCIAL SCIENCE (African American studies, anthropology, archeology, area studies, economics, history, interdisciplinary studies, international relations, philosophy, political science/government, psychology, religion, Russian and Slavic studies, sociology, urban studies, and women's studies). Chemistry, history, and English are the strongest academically. History, English, and sociology have the largest enrollments.

Required: To graduate students must complete 32 course credits, with 9 to 13 in the major and a minimum GPA of 2.0. All students must take 1 course each in critical inquiry, studies in cultural differences, religious perspectives, and quantitative reasoning and demonstrate basic writing and foreign language proficiency. 2 courses each in English, foreign languages, social science/history, natural science/math, and arts/humanities are required.

Special: A 3-2 engineering degree is offered in conjunction with Case Western Reserve and Washington Universities. A B.A.-B.S. degree is offered in music/music education. Cross-registration is possible with off-campus programs of the Great Lakes Colleges Association. Internships are available in American politics in Washington, D.C., the Ohio State Legislature, and the U.S. State Department, as well as in professional theater and economics. Student-designed majors, dual majors, study abroad in 50 countries, a Washington semester, accelerated degree programs, nondegree study, and pass/fail options for a limited number of courses are available. All seniors participate in a 2-term independent-study project in the major. The student chooses the topic and works on a one-to-one basis with a faculty mentor. A sophomore research program is available by application. There are 12 national honor societies, including Phi Beta Kappa.

Faculty/Classroom: 55% of faculty are male; 45% are female. All teach and do research. The average class size in an introductory lecture is 15 and in a regular course is 20.

Requirements: The SAT or ACT is required. In addition, applicants should be graduates of an accredited secondary school. The GED is accepted. Students should have completed a minimum of 17 high school academic credits. The school also requires an essay and recommends an interview. AP credits are accepted. Important factors in the admissions decision are advanced placement or honors courses, recommendations by school officials, and leadership record.

Procedure: Freshmen are admitted fall and winter. Entrance exams should be taken in the fall of the senior year. There are early decision, early admissions and deferred admissions plans. Check with the school for current application deadlines. The application fee is $40. Applications are accepted online. A waiting list is maintained.

Transfer: Applicants for transfer must have a minimum GPA of 2.5 and must submit either the SAT or ACT scores as well as a dean's reference, a high school transcript, and an essay or personal statement. An interview is recommended. Grades of C or better transfer for credit. Transfers are admitted every semester. 17 of 32 credits required for the bachelor's degree must be completed at Wooster.

Visiting: There are regularly scheduled orientations for prospective students, including an interview, tour, class visits, and meetings with faculty and coaches. There are guides for informal visits, and visitors may sit in on classes and stay overnight. To schedule a visit, contact the Admissions Office.

Financial Aid: Wooster is a member of CSS. The CSS/Profile, FAFSA, and the college's own financial statement are required. Check with the school for current application deadlines.

International Students: The school actively recruits these students. They must take the TOEFL, MELAB, or American Language Institute test. They must also take the SAT or ACT, scoring 900 on the SAT.

Computers: All students may access the system any time.

Admissions Contact: Admissions Office. A campus DVD is available.
E-Mail: *admissions@wooster.edu* Web: *www.wooster.edu*

COLUMBUS COLLEGE OF ART AND DESIGN C-3

Columbus, OH 43215 **(614) 222-3261**
(877) 997-CCAD (2223); (614) 232-8344

Full-time: 454 men, 758 women	**Faculty:** 72
Part-time: 49 men, 72 women	**Ph.D.s:** 69%
Graduate: 15 men, 16 women	**Student/Faculty:** 11 to 1
Year: semesters, summer session	**Tuition:** $29,992
Application Deadline: August 15	**Room & Board:** $7740
Freshman Class: n/av	**SPECIAL**

Columbus College of Art and Design, founded in 1879, is a private institution offering undergraduate and graduate programs in art and design. There are 2 undergraduate schools and 1 graduate school. In addition to regional accreditation, CCAD has baccalaureate program accreditation with NASAD. The library contains 41,396 volumes, 13,475 microform items, and subscribes to 254 periodicals including electronic. Computerized library services include interlibrary loans, database searching, Internet access, and Wi-Fi capability. Special learning facilities include an art gallery. The 9-acre campus is in an urban area in Columbus, Ohio. Including any residence halls, there are 14 buildings.

Student Life: 73% of undergraduates are from Ohio. Others are from states, and Canada. 69% are White. The average age of freshmen is 19; all undergraduates, 21. 19% do not continue beyond their first year; 55% remain to graduate.

Housing: 435 students can be accommodated in college housing, which includes coed dorms and on-campus apartments. On-campus housing is guaranteed for the freshman year only, is available on a first-come, first-served basis, and is available on a lottery system for upperclassmen. 69% of students commute. Alcohol is not permitted. All students may keep cars.

Activities: There are no fraternities or sororities. There are 27 groups on campus, including art, environmental, ethnic, film, gay, honors, international, literary magazine, newspaper, photography, professional, religious, social, social service, and student government. Popular campus events include Local and National International Art Exhibitions, Art Fairs, Big Boo! Halloween Party, Alumni/Family Weekend, and Welcome Fest.

Sports: There are 4 intramural sports for men and 4 for women. Facilities include Soccer, basketball, dodgeball, yoga, and zumba; game room in student center, fitness/workout facility in Schottenstein Hall.

Disabled Students: 50% of the campus is accessible. Facilities include wheelchair ramps, elevators, special parking, specially equipped restrooms, special class scheduling, lowered drinking fountains, and lowered telephones.

Services: Counseling and information services are available, as is tutoring in most subjects. There is a reader service for the blind, and remedial math, reading, and writing.

Campus Safety and Security: Measures include 24-hour foot and vehicle patrol, emergency notification system, and security escort services. There are emergency telephones, lighted pathways/sidewalks, and controlled access to dorms/residences.

Programs of Study: CCAD confers B.F.A. degrees. Master's degrees are also awarded. Bachelor's degrees are awarded in COMMUNICATIONS AND THE ARTS (advertising, animation, film arts, fine arts, graphic design, illustration, industrial design, and photography), ENGINEERING AND ENVIRONMENTAL DESIGN (interior design), SOCIAL SCIENCE (fashion design and technology).

Required: Students must complete a minimum of 120 credit hours in required courses, have a cumulative GPA of 2.0 or better, present an approved portfolio, and complete a minimum of 60 credit hours at CCAD in order to graduate from CCAD. Of the total credit hours, about 60 percent is studio coursework and 40 percent is liberal arts.

Special: CCAD offers cross-registration, distance learning, double majors, ESL, domestic student exchange, internships, and study abroad. There are 9 departmental honors programs.

Faculty/Classroom: 53% of faculty are male; 47% are female. All teach undergraduates. No introductory courses are taught by graduate students. The average class size in a regular course is 19.

Admissions: 10% of the current freshmen were in the top fifth of their class; 44% were in the top two fifths.

Requirements: The SAT or ACT is required. Applicants should be graduates of an accredited secondary school or have the GED. A portfolio of artwork indicative of abilities must be submitted. An interview is advised. A GPA of 2.0 is required. AP credits are accepted. Important factors in the admissions decision are recommendations by alumni, recommendations by school officials, and evidence of special talent.

Procedure: Freshmen are admitted fall and spring. There are early decision, early admissions, deferred admissions, and rolling admissions plans. Early decision applications should be filed by December 1; regular applications, by August 15 for fall entry, along with a $40 fee. Notification of early decision is sent December 20; regular decision, April 1. 197 early decision candidates were accepted for the 2013-2014 class. 25 applicants were on the 2013 waiting list; 4 were admitted. Applications are accepted online.

Transfer: 76 transfer students enrolled in 2012-2013. Applicants must submit an acceptable portfolio of artwork as well as all high school and college transcripts. A minimum GPA of 2.0 is required. An interview is recommended. 60 of 120 credits required for the bachelor's degree must be completed at CCAD.

Visiting: There are regularly scheduled orientations for prospective students, Visits include a personal interview, a portfolio review, and a tour. There are guides for informal visits. To schedule a visit, contact the Admissions Office.

Financial Aid: In 2013-2014, 92% of all full time freshmen and 85% of continuing full-time students received some form of financial aid. 92% of all full-time freshmen and 90% of continuing full-time students received need-based aid. The average freshman award was $19,100. Need-based scholarships or need-based grants averaged $13,200; need-based self-help aid (loans and jobs) averaged $5,400; and $500 from other forms of aid. The average financial indebtedness of the 2013 graduate was $27,000. CCAD is a member of CSS. The FAFSA is required. The priority date for freshman financial aid applications for fall entry is February 28. The deadline for filing freshman financial aid applications for fall entry is March 1.

International Students: There are 101 international students enrolled. The school actively recruits these students. They must take the TOEFL with a minimum score of 500 on the paper-based TOEFL (PBT) or 61 on the Internet-based version (iBT). They must also take the SAT or ACT.

Computers: All students may access the system. There are no time limits and no fees.

Graduates: From July 1, 2012 to June 30, 2013, 262 bachelor's degrees were awarded. The most popular majors were advertising and graphic design (19%), media arts (16%), and fine arts (16%). In an average class, 44% graduate in 4 years or less, 54% graduate in 5 years or less, and 55% graduate in 6 years or less.

Admissions Contact: Densil R.R. Porteous II, Director of Admissions. E-Mail: *admissions@ccad.edu* Web: *www.ccad.edu/admissions*

DEFIANCE COLLEGE — A-2

Defiance, OH 43512 — **(419) 783-2365**
(800) 520-GODC; (419) 783-2468

Full-time: 410 men, 355 women	**Faculty:** n/av; IIB, --$
Part-time: 60 men, 150 women	**Ph.D.s:** 60%
Graduate: 40 men, 80 women	**Student/Faculty:** n/av
Year: semesters, summer session	**Tuition:** $25,800
Application Deadline: open	**Room & Board:** $8950
Freshman Class: n/av	
SAT or ACT: required	

COMPETITIVE

Defiance College is an independent, coeducational institution affiliated with the United Church of Christ and home to the McMaster School for Advancing Humanity. The figures in the above capsule and in this profile are approximate. There is 1 graduate school. In addition to regional accreditation, Defiance has baccalaureate program accreditation with CSWE and NCATE. The library contains 182,812 volumes, 7387 microform items, 3336 audio/video tapes/CDs/DVDs, and subscribes to 7673 periodicals including electronic. Computerized library services include interlibrary loans, database searching, Internet access, and laptop Internet portals. Special learning facilities include a learning resource center, an art gallery, the Thoreau Wildlife Sanctuary, a greenhouse, and a learning commons. The 150-acre campus is in a small town 55 miles southwest of Toledo and 50 miles east of Fort Wayne. Including any residence halls, there are 24 buildings.

Student Life: 85% of undergraduates are from Ohio. Others are from 15 states and 3 foreign countries. 97% are from public schools. 86% are white. 23% are Protestant; 23% claim no religious affiliation; 15% Catholic. The average age of freshmen is 18. 32% do not continue beyond their first year; 50% remain to graduate.

Housing: 505 students can be accommodated in college housing, which includes single-sex and coed dorms and on-campus apartments. In addition, there are academic floors in the residence halls with additional academic programming and resources. On-campus housing is guaranteed for all 4 years. 66% of students live on campus; of those, 50% remain on campus on weekends. All students may keep cars.

Activities: 6% of men belong to 1 national fraternity; 6% of women belong to 2 national sororities. There are 33 groups on campus, including academic, art, band, choir, chorale, chorus, dance, drama, ethnic, gay, honors, international, literary magazine, musical theater, newspaper, pep band, political, professional, religious, social, social service, student government, and yearbook. Popular campus events include Freshman Service Day, Arts on the Quad, and Thanksgiving Dinner.

Sports: There are 9 intercollegiate sports for men and 9 for women, and 10 intramural sports for men and 10 for women. Facilities include a 4000-seat stadium, baseball, softball, and soccer fields, a cross-country course, a gym, racquetball courts, an indoor track, a weight-lifting room, basketball courts, tennis courts, an 8-lane all-weather outdoor track, and a fitness center.

Disabled Students: 80% of the campus is accessible. Facilities include wheelchair ramps, elevators, special parking, specially equipped restrooms, special class scheduling, lowered drinking fountains, and lowered telephones.

Services: Counseling and information services are available, as is tutoring in every subject. There is a reader service for the blind.

Campus Safety and Security: Measures include emergency notification system and security escort services. There are lighted pathways/sidewalks, nighttime security guards in residence halls, security cameras in residence hall entrances, and a security guard on the grounds from dusk to dawn.

Programs of Study: Defiance confers B.A. and B.S. degrees. Associate and master's degrees are also awarded. Bachelor's degrees are awarded in BIOLOGICAL SCIENCE (biology/biological science and ecology), BUSINESS (accounting, banking and finance, business administration and management, human resources, management science, marketing/retailing/merchandising, organizational leadership and management, and sports management), COMMUNICATIONS AND THE ARTS (art, communications, and graphic design), COMPUTER AND PHYSICAL SCIENCE (information sciences and systems and mathematics), EDUCATION (art education, athletic training, Christian education, early childhood education, elementary education, health education, mathematics education, physical education, reading education, science education, secondary education, and social studies education), ENGINEERING AND ENVIRONMENTAL DESIGN (environmental science), HEALTH PROFESSIONS (medical laboratory technology and nursing), SOCIAL SCIENCE (criminal justice, forensic studies, history, humanities, international studies, physical fitness/movement, psychology, religion, and social work). Education and sciences are the strongest academically. Business, forensic sciences, and education have the largest enrollments.

Required: All students must fulfill general education requirements, including communication skills, arts and humanities, natural science, and social science. Freshman Seminar, Fitness for Life, as well as senior assessment in the major are also required. A total of 120 semester credits, with at least 30 in the major, and a minimum GPA of 2.0 are required to graduate. Service is required in all majors; computer proficiency must be demonstrated.

Special: Co-op programs and internships are available in all majors, as are B.A.-B.S. degrees and dual majors. Work study and student-designed majors are also available. The McMaster School for Advancing Humanity allows students and faculty to more closely examine global issues and how they affect the human condition. There is 1 national honor society, a freshman honors program, and 4 departmental honors programs.

Faculty/Classroom: 61% of faculty are male; 39% are female. All teach undergraduates, and 30% both teach and do research. No introductory courses are taught by graduate students. The average class size in an introductory lecture is 22; in a laboratory, 18; and in a regular course, 16.

Requirements: The ACT is required. The SAT is recommended. Applicants should be graduates of an accredited secondary school or have a GED, with 15 Carnegie units completed, including 4 in English, 3 each in math, science, and social studies, and 2 in foreign language. An essay and an interview are recommended. A GPA of 2.3 is required. AP and CLEP credits are accepted. Important factors in the admissions decision are personality/intangible qualities, advanced placement or honors courses, and leadership record.

Procedure: Freshmen are admitted to all sessions. Entrance exams should be taken in the spring of the junior year or the fall of the senior year. There are early admissions, deferred admissions, and rolling admissions plans. Application deadlines are open. The application fee is $25. Applications are accepted online.

Transfer: 61 transfer students enrolled in a recent year. A high school diploma, GED certificate, or equivalent; official transcript from each college or university attended; minimum college GPA of 2.0 from the last college attended; and a record indicating good standing socially from each college or university attended are required. An interview is recommended. 30 of 120 credits required for the bachelor's degree must be completed at Defiance.

Visiting: There are regularly scheduled orientations for prospective students, including admissions, financial aid, and special interest sessions, a campus tour, complimentary lunch, meetings with faculty, and observing a class in session. Interested applicants can meet with a coach. There are guides for informal visits, and visitors may sit in on classes and stay overnight. To schedule a visit, contact the Office of Admission.

Financial Aid: The FAFSA and the college's own financial statement are required. Check with the school for current application deadlines.

International Students: There were 3 international students enrolled in a recent year. The school actively recruits these students. They must take the TOEFL, with a minimum score of 550 on the paper-based TOEFL (PBT) or 79 on the Internet-based version (iBT), or take the MELAB. They must also take the SAT or ACT, scoring 18 on the ACT.

Computers: Wireless access is available. All students may access the system 24 hours a day, every day. There are no time limits. The fee is $280 per semester.

Graduates: In a recent year, 148 bachelor's degrees were awarded. The most popular majors were business adminstration (13%), criminal justice (11%), and social work (11%). In an average class, 42% graduate in 4 years or less, 48% graduate in 5 years or less, and 50% graduate in 6 years or less. Of a recent graduating class, 10% were enrolled in graduate school within 6 months of graduation and 92% were employed.

Admissions Contact: Brad Harsha, Director of Admissions. E-Mail: *admissions@defiance.edu* Web: *www.defiance.edu*

DENISON UNIVERSITY C-3

Granville, OH 43023 (740) 587-6276
(800) DENISON; (740) 587-6306

Full-time: 971 men, 1334 women
Part-time: 11 men, 20 women
Graduate: n/av
Year: semesters
Application Deadline: January 15
Freshman Class: 4757 applied, 2355 accepted, 629 enrolled
SAT CR/M: 647/639
Faculty: 230; IIB, av$
Ph.D.s: 99%
Student/Faculty: 10 to 1
Tuition: $43,910
Room & Board: $10,760
ACT: 29 **HIGHLY COMPETITIVE+**

Denison University, founded in 1831, is a private independent institution of liberal arts and sciences. The library contains 1.3 million volumes, 128,175 microform items, 37,365 audio/video tapes/CDs/DVDs, and subscribes to 21,805 periodicals including electronic. Computerized library services include interlibrary loans, database searching, Internet access, and Wi-Fi capability. Special learning facilities include an art gallery, planetarium, radio station, TV station, an observatory, a multimedia MIX lab, a field research station in a 350-acre biological reserve, a high-resolution spectrometer, economics computer labs, and a modern languages lab. The 900-acre campus is in a small town 25 miles east of Columbus. Including any residence halls, there are 62 buildings.

Student Life: 70% of undergraduates are from out of state, mostly the Mid-West. Students are from 48 states, 29 foreign countries, and Canada. 70% are from public schools. 71% are White. 36% are Protestant; 30% Catholic; 28% Muslim, Hindu, Buddhist, and Nondenominational. The average age of freshmen is 19; all undergraduates, 21. 8% do not continue beyond their first year; 80% remain to graduate.

Housing: 2188 students can be accommodated in college housing, which includes single-sex and coed dorms and on-campus apartments. In addition, there are honors houses, special-interest houses, a first-year center, substance-free dorms, quiet dorms, all-women dorms, suite-style dorms, and apartments for juniors and seniors with high GPAs. On-campus housing is guaranteed for all 4 years and is available on a lottery system for upperclassmen. 98% of students live on campus; of those, 92% remain on campus on weekends. All students may keep cars.

Activities: 35% of men belong to 10 national fraternities; 41% of women belong to 8 national sororities. There are 180 groups on campus, including art, cheerleading, choir, chorale, chorus, communications, computers, dance, drama, ethnic, film, gay, honors, international, jazz band, literary magazine, musical theater, newspaper, orchestra, pep band, photography, political, professional, religious, social, social service, student government, and symphony. Popular campus events include Community Picnic and Fair, Gala, Academic Awards Convocation and Vail Series.

Sports: There are 10 intercollegiate sports for men and 11 for women, and 15 intramural sports for men and 13 for women. Facilities include 6000-seat stadium, 1000 seat aquatic center, 1500-seat gym, 12 outdoor tennis courts, squash courts, 8-lane quarter-mile track, field house with a 200-meter track and 4 tennis courts, baseball/softball fields, recreation gym with 3 volleyball/basketball courts, weight, aerobic, fitness rooms, soccer and men's lacrosse stadium, women's field hockey and lacrosse field, and multiple practice fields.

Disabled Students: 70% of the campus is accessible. Facilities include wheelchair ramps, elevators, special parking, specially equipped restrooms, special class scheduling, lowered drinking fountains, and lowered telephones.

Services: Counseling and information services are available, as is tutoring in most subjects. There is a reader service for the blind. A reading and writing center is available, as are study sessions for math, chemistry, and some languages, reduced course loads, special counselor services, note-taking services, oral tests, extended time for tests, untimed tests, talking books, tape recorders, and readers.

Campus Safety and Security: Measures include 24-hour foot and vehicle patrol, emergency notification system, self-defense education, and security escort services. There are emergency telephones, lighted pathways/sidewalks, Residence halls are locked 24 hours a day with entry through a card access system.

Programs of Study: Denison confers B.A., B.F.A. and B.S. degrees. Bachelor's degrees are awarded in AGRICULTURE (environmental studies), BIOLOGICAL SCIENCE (biochemistry and biology/biological science), COMMUNICATIONS AND THE ARTS (art history and appreciation, communications, dance, dramatic arts, English, film arts, fine arts, French, German, languages, Latin, media arts, music, Spanish, speech/debate/rhetoric, and studio art), COMPUTER AND PHYSICAL SCIENCE (chemistry, computer science, geology, mathematics, and physics), EDUCATION (education and physical education), SOCIAL SCIENCE (African American studies, anthropology, classical/ancient civilization, East Asian studies, economics, history, international studies, Latin American studies, philosophy, political science/government, psychology, religion, sociology, Western European studies, and women's studies). Psychology, biology, and sociology/anthropology are the strongest academically. Communication, biology, psychology and economics have the largest enrollments.

Required: General education requirements include 2 first-year seminars, 2 courses each from fine arts, sciences, social sciences, and humanities, an interdisciplinary and world issues requirement, and foreign language. A total of 127 semester hours, with 36 in the major and a minimum GPA of 2.0, is required to graduate.

Special: Work-study programs, a Washington semester, study-abroad programs in more than 35 countries, student-designed majors, a dual major in education and various other majors, a philosophy, political science, and economics interdisciplinary major, and pass/fail options are available. A 3-2 engineering program is offered with Rensselaer Polytechnic Institute and Case Western Reserve, Columbia, and Washington Universities. A May-term internship is available at more than 200 U.S. locations. A B.A.-B.S. degree, accelerated degree programs, a media technology and arts interdisciplinary major, and nondegree study are possible. There are 15 national honor societies including Phi Beta Kappa.

Faculty/Classroom: 55% of faculty are male; 45% are female. All teach and do research. No introductory courses are taught by graduate students. The average class size in an introductory lecture is 18; in a laboratory is 21; and in a regular course is 20.

Admissions: 50% of the 2013-2014 applicants were accepted. The SAT scores for the 2013-2014 freshman class were: Critical Reading--3% below 500, 22% between 500 and 599, 44% between 600 and 699, and 31% between 700 and 800; Math--37% between 500 and 599, 42% between 600 and 699, and 21% between 700 and 800. The ACT scores were 1% below 21, 1% between 21 and 23, 13% between 24 and 26, 36% between 27 and 28, and 49% above 28. 83% of the current freshmen were in the top fifth of their class; 100% were in the top two fifths. There were 25 National Merit finalists. 15 freshmen graduated first in their class.

Requirements: The SAT or ACT is recommended. Denison operates under a test optional admissions policy. Applicants should have completed 19 Carnegie units, including 4 each in English, math, and science, 3 in foreign language, 2 in social studies, and 1 each in history and academic electives. An essay is part of the application process. An interview is advised, and a portfolio or an audition is recommended for art and music majors, respectively. AP and CLEP credits are accepted. Important factors in the admissions decision are personality/intangible qualities, evidence of special talent, and advanced placement or honors courses.

Procedure: Freshmen are admitted fall. Entrance exams should be taken by December of the senior year. There are early decision, early admissions, and deferred admissions plans. Early decision applications should be filed by December 1; regular applications, by January 15 for fall entry, along with a $40 fee. Notification of early decision is sent January 1; regular decision, April 1. 84 early decision candidates were accepted for the 2013-2014 class. 207 applicants were on the 2013 waiting list; 2 were admitted. Applications are accepted online.

Transfer: 10 transfer students enrolled in 2012-2013. A minimum GPA of 2.75 is required. SAT or ACT scores should be submitted, as well as high school and college transcripts, an essay, and a statement of good standing from previous institutions. An interview is recommended. 64 of 127 credits required for the bachelor's degree must be completed at Denison.

Visiting: There are regularly scheduled orientations for prospective students, including orientation programs, class visits, tours, and interviews. There are guides for informal visits, visitors may sit in on classes, and stay overnight. To schedule a visit, contact the Admissions Office.

Financial Aid: In 2013-2014, 97% of all full-time freshmen and 96% of continuing full-time students received some form of financial aid. 56% of all full-time freshmen and 52% of continuing full-time students received need-based aid. The average freshman award was $37,445. Need-based scholarships or need-based grants averaged $32,388; need-based self-help aid (loans and jobs) averaged $5,154; and other non-need-based awards and non-need-based scholarships averaged $23,165. 45% of undergraduate students work part-time. Average annual earnings from campus work are $2430. The average financial indebtedness of the 2013 graduate was $20,162. Denison is a member of CSS. The FAFSA is required. The deadline for filing freshman financial aid applications for fall entry is February 15.

International Students: There are 153 international students enrolled. The school actively recruits these students. They must take the TOEFL with a minimum score of 550 on the paper-based TOEFL (PBT) or 80 on the Internet-based version (iBT).

Computers: All students may access the system 24 hours a day. There are no time limits and no fees.

Graduates: From July 1, 2012 to June 30, 2013, 513 bachelor's degrees were awarded. The most popular majors were economics (13%), communications (11%), and biology (10%). 138 companies recruited on campus in 2012-2013. In an average class, 81% graduate in 4 years or less, 83% graduate in 5 years or less, and 85% graduate in 6 years or less. Of the 2012 graduating class, 26% were enrolled in graduate school within 6 months of graduation, and 64% were employed.

Admissions Contact: Perry Robinson, Vice President and Director of Admissions. E-Mail: *admissions@denison.edu* Web: *www.denison.edu*

FRANCISCAN UNIVERSITY OF STEUBENVILLE E-3

Steubenville, OH 43952-1763 (740) 283-6226
(800) 783-6220; (740) 284-5456

Full-time: 765 men, 1140 women
Part-time: 65 men, 90 women
Graduate: 170 men, 245 women
Year: semesters, summer session
Application Deadline: open
Freshman Class: n/av
SAT or ACT: required
Faculty: n/av; IIA, --$
Ph.D.s: 71%
Student/Faculty: n/av
Tuition: $21,720
Room & Board: $7600

VERY COMPETITIVE

Franciscan University of Steubenville, founded in 1946 by the Franciscan Friars, is a private liberal arts institution committed to the Catholic Church and its renewal. The figures in the above capsule and in this profile are approximate. There are 7 graduate schools. In addition to regional accreditation, Franciscan University has baccalaureate program accreditation with CSWE and NLN. The library contains 235,387 volumes, 250,968 microform items, 892 audio/video tapes/CDs/DVDs, and subscribes to 5874 periodicals including electronic. Computerized library services include interlibrary loans, database searching, and Internet access. Special learning facilities include an art gallery and radio station. The 220-acre campus is in a small town 40 miles west of Pittsburgh. Including any residence halls, there are 25 buildings.

Student Life: 78% of undergraduates are from out of state, mostly the Midwest. Others are from 50 states, 18 foreign countries, and Canada. 59% are from public schools. 86% are white. 97% are Catholic. The average age of freshmen is 19; all undergraduates, 21. 13% do not continue beyond their first year; 70% remain to graduate.

Housing: 1157 students can be accommodated in college housing, which includes single-sex dorms. In addition, there rae Christian faith houses in residence halls. On-campus housing is available on a first-come, first-served basis. 56% of students live on campus; of those, 70% remain on campus on weekends. Upperclassmen may keep cars.

Activities: There are no fraternities; there is 1 national sorority. There are 35 groups on campus, including choir, chorale, chorus, computers, drama, ethnic, honors, international, literary magazine, newspaper, orchestra, political, pro-life, professional, radio and TV, religious, social, social service, student government, and yearbook. Popular campus events include the Feast of St. Francis, Pro-Life Rally, and all-school Evangelism events.

Sports: There are 6 intercollegiate sports for men and 6 for women, and 9 intramural sports for men and 8 for women. Facilities include a campus athletic center, which houses 2 full-size basketball courts, racquetball courts, saunas, whirlpools, and locker rooms and provides indoor seating for 2000. Outdoor athletic facilities include a sand volleyball court and baseball, softball, flag football, and soccer fields.

Disabled Students: 80% of the campus is accessible. Facilities include wheelchair ramps, elevators, special parking, specially equipped restrooms, special class scheduling, lowered drinking fountains, and lowered telephones.

Services: Counseling and information services are available, as is tutoring in most subjects. There is a reader service for the blind and remedial reading and writing. Tutoring and counseling are available for learning-disabled students. Tutoring is also available for students on academic probation.

Campus Safety and Security: Measures include 24-hour foot and vehicle patrol, emergency notification system, self-defense education, and security escort services. There are shuttle buses, emergency telephones, lighted pathways/sidewalks, and controlled access to dorms/residences.

Programs of Study: Franciscan University confers B.A., B.S., and B.S.N. degrees. Associates and master's degrees are also awarded. Bachelor's degrees are awarded in BIOLOGICAL SCIENCE (biology/biological science), BUSINESS (accounting and business administration and management), COMMUNICATIONS AND THE ARTS (classics, communications, dramatic arts, English, French, German, and Spanish), COMPUTER AND PHYSICAL SCIENCE (chemistry, computer science, information sciences and systems, and mathematics), EDUCATION (elementary education), HEALTH PROFESSIONS (mental health/human services and nursing), SOCIAL SCIENCE (anthropology, economics, history, humanities and social science, law, philosophy, political science/government, psychology, religious music, social work, sociology, and theological studies). Theology, catechesis, and nursing are the strongest academically and have the largest enrollments.

Required: All students must complete core liberal arts courses, including 15 credits each in humanities and communications and 6 credits each in theology, social science, and natural science. A 1-credit thesis or seminar is required in all majors. A total of 124 credit hours, with at least 31 in the major, and a minimum GPA of 2.0 are required to graduate.

Special: Dual majors and internships for up to 6 credit hours are available in most majors. A humanities and Catholic culture major in Western tradition and minors in human life studies, film studies, Franciscan studies, and music are offered. Study abroad is offered through the university's course location in Gaming, Austria, where students spend a semester studying humanities as well as traveling through Europe. There are 5 national honor societies, a freshman honors program, and 25 departmental honors programs.

Faculty/Classroom: 65% of faculty are male; 35% are female. 94% teach undergraduates. No introductory courses are taught by graduate students. The average class size in an introductory lecture is 28; in a laboratory, 15; and in a regular course, 21.

Requirements: The SAT or ACT is required. Applicants should have completed 15 academic high school units, including 10 in 4 of the 5 following areas: English, foreign language, social science, math, and natural sciences. The GED is accepted. An essay is required and an interview is recommended. A GPA of 2.4 is required. AP and CLEP credits are accepted. Important factors in the admissions decision are advanced placement or honors courses, evidence of special talent, and leadership record.

Procedure: Freshmen are admitted fall, spring, and summer. Entrance exams should be taken in the spring of the junior year or the fall of the senior year. There is a rolling admissions plan. Application deadlines are open. Notification is sent on a rolling basis. Applications are accepted online. A waiting list is maintained.

Transfer: A minimum 2.0 college GPA is required. High school and college transcripts must be submitted. An interview is recommended. 30 of 124 credits required for the bachelor's degree must be completed at Franciscan University.

Visiting: There are regularly scheduled orientations for prospective students, including tours, interviews with professors, admissions, and financial aid officers, and class scheduling. There are guides for informal visits; visitors may sit in on classes and stay overnight. To schedule a visit, contact the Admissions Office.

Financial Aid: The FAFSA is required. Check with the school for current application deadlines.

International Students: They must take the TOEFL.

Computers: All students may access the system. There are no time limits and no fees.

Admissions Contact: Admissions Office. A campus DVD is available. E-Mail: *admissions@franciscan.edu* Web: *www.franciscan.edu*

FRANKLIN UNIVERSITY C-3

Columbus, OH 43215-5399 (614) 797-4700
(877) 341-6300; (614) 224-8027

Full-time: 995 men, 1640 women
Part-time: 1910 men, 2525 women
Graduate: 400 men, 515 women
Year: trimesters, summer session
Application Deadline: open
Freshman Class: n/av
Faculty: n/av
Ph.D.s: 57%
Student/Faculty: n/av
Tuition: $8500
Room & Board: n/app

SPECIAL

Franklin University is a student-centered, independent, regional institution of lifelong higher education (undergraduate and graduate) working in partnership with Central Ohio's business and professional community in a global context. The figures in the above capsule and in this profile are approximate. The library contains 15,000 volumes, 7,920 microform items, 132 audio/video tapes/CDs/DVDs, and subscribes to 200 periodicals including electronic. Computerized library services include interlibrary loans and database searching. Special learning facilities include a learning resource center and art gallery. The 14-acre campus is in an urban area located in downtown Columbus. There are 7 buildings.

Student Life: 75% of undergraduates are from Ohio. Others are from 48 states, 106 foreign countries, and Canada. 67% are white; 22% African American. The average age of freshmen is 28; all undergraduates, 32.

Housing: There are no residence halls. All students commute.

Activities: There are no fraternities or sororities. There are 6 groups on campus, including computers, international, and professional. Popular campus events include New student orientation, awards/scholarship reception, and opening week activities.

Sports: There is no sports program at Franklin.

Disabled Students: All of the campus is accessible. Facilities include wheelchair ramps, elevators, special parking, specially equipped rest rooms, special class scheduling, lowered drinking fountains, and lowered telephones.

Services: Counseling and information services are available, as is tutoring in most subjects. There is a reader service for the blind, and remedial math, reading, and writing.

Campus Safety and Security: Measures include security escort services.

Programs of Study: Franklin confers B.S. degrees. Associates and master's degrees are also awarded. Bachelor's degrees are awarded in BUSINESS (accounting, banking and finance, business administration and management, human resources, management science, marketing and distribution, and organizational behavior), COMPUTER AND PHYSICAL SCIENCE (computer science), ENGINEERING AND ENVIRONMENTAL DESIGN (technological management), HEALTH PROFESSIONS (health care administration), SOCIAL SCIENCE (applied psychology and safety management). Business administration and computer science have the largest enrollments.

Required: Students must complete general education core requirements in communication, math, humanities, social and behavioral sciences, and science. A total of 122 to 132 semester hours with a minimum GPA of 2.0 (2.25 for some majors) is required to graduate.

Special: Cross-registration is possible with other area colleges and universities through the Higher Education Council of Columbus. Internships are available for accounting, finance, marketing, business administration, computer science, human resources management, and management information sciences. Student-designed majors, ESL, and some pass/fail courses are offered. Bachelor of Science degree completion programs are available through alliances with community colleges in the United States and Canada. Accelerated delivery of specific courses is possible, as are integrated B.S./B.A. degrees in accounting, organizational leadership, financial management, and business administration.

Faculty/Classroom: 60% of faculty are male; 40% are female. 84% teach undergraduates. No introductory courses are taught by graduate students. The average class size in a regular course is 18.

Requirements: Applicants should be graduates of an accredited secondary school or have a GED. AP and CLEP credits are accepted.

Procedure: Freshmen are admitted fall, winter, and summer. There are early admissions, deferred admissions, and rolling admissions plans. Application deadlines are open. Notification is sent on a rolling basis.

Transfer: The open admission policy applies to transfer students as well as freshmen. 40 of 122 credits required for the bachelor's degree must be completed at Franklin.

Visiting: There are guides for informal visits and visitors may sit in on classes. To schedule a visit, contact the Admission Office.

Financial Aid: In a recent year, 3% of all full-time freshmen and 2% of continuing full-time students received some form of financial aid. The FAFSA and the college's own financial statement are required. Check with the school for current application deadlines.

International Students: There were 172 international students enrolled in a recent year. The school actively recruits these students. They must take the TOEFL or MELAB.

Computers: All students may access the system. There are no time limits and no fees.

Graduates: In a recent year, 1477 bachelor's degrees were awarded. The most popular majors were business administration (39%), accounting (11%), and computer science (9%).

Admissions Contact: Student Services Office E-Mail: *register@franklin.edu* Web: *www.franklin.edu*

HEIDELBERG UNIVERSITY C-2

Tiffin, OH 44883-2434 **(419) 448-2330; (419) 448-2334**

Full-time: 630 men, 555 women	**Faculty:** n/av; IIB, --$
Part-time: 10 men, 25 women	**Ph.D.s:** 82%
Graduate: 65 men, 150 women	**Student/Faculty:** n/av
Year: semesters, summer session	**Tuition:** $28,500
Application Deadline: see profile	**Room & Board:** $9208
Freshman Class: n/av	
SAT or ACT: required	

COMPETITIVE

Heidelberg University was founded in 1850 by the German Reformed Church (now United Church of Christ) and is a private liberal arts institution offering undergraduate and graduate degrees. The figures in the above capsule and in this profile are approximate. There is 1 graduate school. In addition to regional accreditation, Heidelberg has baccalaureate program accreditation with NASM. The library contains 260,055 volumes, 108,640 microform items, and 8300 audio/video tapes/CDs/DVDs, and subscribes to 829 periodicals including electronic. Computerized library services include interlibrary loans, database searching, Internet access, and laptop Internet portals. Special learning facilities include a learning resource center, radio station, TV station, media center, anthropology museum, human cadaver lab, water quality lab, archeology lab, physiology lab, and computer-assisted writing classroom. The 120-acre campus is in a small town 50 miles south of Toledo. Including any residence halls, there are 27 buildings.

Student Life: 90% of undergraduates are from Ohio. Others are from 27 states, 6 foreign countries, and Canada. 61% are from public schools. 84% are white. 61% are Protestant; 33% Catholic. The average age of freshmen is 18; all undergraduates, 23. 20% do not continue beyond their first year; 56% remain to graduate.

Housing: 900 students can be accommodated in college housing, which includes single-sex and coed dorms and on-campus apartments. In addition, there are special-interest houses. On-campus housing is guaranteed for all 4 years. 85% of students live on campus; of those, 80% remain on campus on weekends. All students may keep cars.

Activities: 30% of men belong to 5 local fraternities; 36% of women belong to 4 local sororities. There are 73 groups on campus, including art, band, cheerleading, chess, choir, chorale, chorus, computers, dance, drama, drill team, environmental, ethnic, film, forensics, gay, honors, international, jazz band, literary magazine, musical theater, newspaper, opera, orchestra, pep band, political, professional, radio and TV, religious, social, social service, student government, symphony, and yearbook. Popular campus events include Greek Sing, Battle of the Bands, and T-Bridge.

Sports: There are 9 intercollegiate sports for men and 9 for women, and 9 intramural sports for men and 8 for women. Facilities include a wrestling arena, an all-weather track, indoor courts for volleyball, basketball, racquetball, and tennis, a weight room and fitness area, a sports medicine clinic, and outdoor tennis, soccer, and football facilities. A YMCA adjacent to the college provides additional recreation options.

Disabled Students: 20% of the campus is accessible. Facilities include wheelchair ramps, elevators, special parking, specially equipped restrooms, special class scheduling, and lowered drinking fountains.

Services: Counseling and information services are available, as is tutoring in most subjects. There is remedial math and reading.

Campus Safety and Security: Measures include 24-hour foot and vehicle patrol, emergency notification system, self-defense education, and security escort services. There are emergency telephones and lighted pathways/sidewalks.

Programs of Study: Heidelberg confers B.A., B.S., and B.Mus. degrees. Master's degrees are also awarded. Bachelor's degrees are awarded in BIOLOGICAL SCIENCE (biochemistry, biology/biological science, and environmental biology), BUSINESS (accounting, business administration and management, business economics, management science, and sports management), COMMUNICATIONS AND THE ARTS (communications, dramatic arts, English, German, music, public relations, and Spanish), COMPUTER AND PHYSICAL SCIENCE (chemistry, computer science, information sciences and systems, mathematics, and physics), EDUCATION (athletic training, elementary education, foreign languages education, middle school education, music education, physical education, science education, and secondary education), ENGINEERING AND ENVIRONMENTAL DESIGN (preengineering), HEALTH PROFESSIONS (predentistry and premedicine), SOCIAL SCIENCE (anthropology, criminal justice, economics, forensic studies, history, international studies, philosophy, political science/government, prelaw, psychology, public administration, religion, social science, and water resources). Business administration, education, and sciences are the strongest academically. Business administration, physical sciences, and education have the largest enrollments.

Required: Students must fulfill 40 semester hours of general education requirements, including English composition and public speaking, arts, languages and literature, civilization, religion and philosophy, social sciences, natural sciences, and math, and 40 semester hours each in the major and electives. 4 units of health and phys ed are needed. A total of 120 semester hours with a minimum GPA of 2.0 overall and 2.5 in the major is required to graduate.

Special: Cross-registration with Terra Community College and North Central Community College and a 3-4 degree in osteropathic medicine with Lake Erie College of Osteopathic Medicine are offered. Study abroad is possible in Heidelberg, Germany, Seville, Spain, Mexico, the United Kingdom, and other countries. A Washington semester is available at American University. Dual majors in any combination, an honors program, credit for life experience, internships, and pass/fail options are possible. There are 10 national honor societies, a freshman honors program, and 15 departmental honors programs.

Faculty/Classroom: 57% of faculty are male; 43% are female. 97% teach undergraduates. No introductory courses are taught by graduate students. The average class size in an introductory lecture is 20; in a laboratory, 15; and in a regular course, 15.

Requirements: The SAT or ACT is required. Applicants should have completed 22 high school academic credits, including 4 years each of English and social studies, 3 each of math and science, and 2 of a foreign language. An audition is required for music majors. Recommendations and an interview are recommended. A GPA of 2.5 is required. AP and CLEP credits are accepted. Important factors in the admissions decision are recommendations by school officials, extracurricular activities record, and advanced placement or honors courses.

Procedure: Freshmen are admitted to all sessions. Entrance exams should be taken by the end of the junior year or the beginning of the senior year. There are deferred admissions and rolling admissions plans. Applications are accepted online. Check with the school for current application deadlines and fee.

Transfer: 41 transfer students enrolled in a recent year. A minimum GPA of 2.0 and a character reference from the institution most recently attended are required. 30 of 120 credits required for the bachelor's degree must be completed at Heidelberg.

Visiting: There are regularly scheduled orientations for prospective students, including coach and faculty sessions, academic overview, student panel, admissions, and financial aid presentations, a tour of the college, and lunch. There are guides for informal visits, and visitors may sit in on classes and stay overnight. To schedule a visit, contact the Office of Admission.

Financial Aid: In a recent year, 98% of all full-time freshmen and 99% of continuing full-time students received some form of financial aid. 90% of all full-time freshmen and 61% of continuing full-time students received need-based aid. 65% of undergraduate students worked part-time. Average annual earnings from campus work were $850. The FAFSA is required. Check with the school for current application deadlines.

International Students: There were 25 international students enrolled in a recent year. The school actively recruits these students. They must take the TOEFL with a minimum score of 550 on the paper-based TOEFL (PBT) or 80 on the Internet-based version (iBT) and the college's own test.

Computers: Wireless access is available. The main buildings are wireless, as are some housing facilities. Many PCs are available. Students may check out laptops in the library, and server space is given to all students. All students may access the system. There are no time limits and no fees.

Graduates: In a recent year, 262 bachelor's degrees were awarded. The most popular majors were business (22%), education (19%), and sport management (13%).

Admissions Contact: Lindsay Sooy, Director of Admission. E-mail: *adminfo@l.heidelberg.edu* Web: *www.heidelberg.edu*

HIRAM COLLEGE — E-1

Hiram, OH 44234 — (330) 569-5169; (800) 362-5280; (330) 569-5944

Full-time: 560 men, 635 women	**Faculty:** n/av; IIB, --$
Part-time: 55 men, 125 women	**Ph.D.s:** 92%
Graduate: 10 men, 25 women	**Student/Faculty:** n/av
Year: see profile, summer session	**Tuition:** $28,500
Application Deadline: open	**Room & Board:** $9960
Freshman Class: n/av	
SAT or ACT: required	

VERY COMPETITIVE

Hiram College, founded in 1850, is a private, residential liberal arts and sciences institution. The figures in the above capsule and in this profile are approximate. In addition to regional accreditation, Hiram has baccalaureate program accreditation with NASM. The library contains 506,792 volumes, 131 microform items, 22,786 audio/video tapes/CDs/DVDs, and subscribes to 8890 periodicals including electronic. Computerized library services include interlibrary loans, database searching, and Internet access. Special learning facilities include a learning resource center, art gallery, planetarium, radio station, a 260-acre biological field station, and a field station in the Upper Peninsula of Michigan. The 110-acre campus is in a rural area 35 miles southeast of Cleveland. Including any residence halls, there are 39 buildings.

Student Life: 75% of undergraduates are from Ohio. Others are from 33 states, 19 foreign countries, and Canada. 62% are white. The average age of freshmen is 18; all undergraduates, 20. 22% do not continue beyond their first year.

Housing: 1040 students can be accommodated in college housing, which includes single-sex and coed dorms and on-campus apartments. In addition, there is an international theme house. On-campus housing is guaranteed for all 4 years. 82% of students live on campus; of those, 60% remain on campus on weekends. All students may keep cars.

Activities: There are no fraternities or sororities. There are 90 groups on campus, including art, band, cheerleading, choir, chorale, chorus, computers, dance, drama, ethnic, gay, honors, international, jazz band, literary magazine, marching band, musical theater, newspaper, opera, orchestra, photography, political, professional, radio and TV, religious, social, social service, student government, and yearbook. Popular campus events include Campus Days, Springfest, and Madrigal Revels.

Sports: There are 7 intercollegiate sports for men and 7 for women, and 10 intramural sports for men and 10 for women. Facilities include a sports center with a 2000-seat gym, courts for tennis, volleyball, basketball, and baseball, an elevated 3-lane track, a multipurpose activity court, a 25-meter, 6-lane pool, a fitness center, a weight room, an aerobics studio, 2 racquetball courts, and a training room. Outdoor facilities include football, baseball, soccer, and softball fields, practice fields, and 3 tennis courts.

Disabled Students: 55% of the campus is accessible. Facilities include wheelchair ramps, elevators, special parking, and specially equipped restrooms.

Services: Counseling and information services are available, as is tutoring in every subject. There is a reader service for the blind. Note takers are available for most classes.

Campus Safety and Security: Measures include 24-hour foot and vehicle patrol, emergency notification system, self-defense education, and security escort services. There are emergency telephones and lighted pathways/sidewalks.

Programs of Study: Hiram confers B.A., and B.S.N. degrees. Master's degrees are also awarded. Bachelor's degrees are awarded in BIOLOGICAL SCIENCE (biochemistry, biology/biological science, and neurosciences), BUSINESS (accounting and management science), COMMUNICATIONS AND THE ARTS (art, communications, creative writing, dramatic arts, English, French, music, Spanish, and studio art), COMPUTER AND PHYSICAL SCIENCE (chemistry, computer science, mathematics, and physics), EDUCATION (education), ENGINEERING AND ENVIRONMENTAL DESIGN (environmental science), HEALTH PROFESSIONS (biomedical science and nursing), SOCIAL SCIENCE (economics, history, philosophy, political science/government, psychology, religion, social studies, and sociology). Management, accounting, and biology have the largest enrollments.

Required: All students must complete courses in a core curriculum and at least 120 semester hours (135 for B.S. in nursing) with a GPA of 2.0 overall and in the major. A capstone project is required in all undergraduate majors.

Special: There is cross-registration through the Cleveland Commission on Higher Education and a 3-2 engineering program with Case Western Reserve and Washington Universities. There is a Washington semester and study abroad in many countries with courses taught by Hiram faculty. Double majors and individually arranged internships in all fields, student-designed majors, and pass/no credit options are possible. An accelerated degree program in biomedical humanities is possible. There are 6 national honor societies, including Phi Beta Kappa. In addition, all departments have honors programs.

Faculty/Classroom: 54% of faculty are male; 46% are female. All teach undergraduates. No introductory courses are taught by graduate students. The average class size in an introductory lecture is 19; in a laboratory, 11; and in a regular course, 13.

Requirements: The SAT or ACT is required. In addition, applicants should have completed 16 academic units or the GED equivalent. An essay is required. A portfolio, audition, and interview are recommended. A GPA of 2.6 is required. AP and CLEP credits are accepted.

Procedure: Freshmen are admitted fall and spring. Entrance exams should be taken no later than the fall of the senior year. There are deferred admissions and rolling admissions plans. Application deadlines are open. Notification is sent on a rolling basis. Applications are accepted online.

Transfer: 27 transfer students enrolled in a recent year. Applicants should have at least a 2.75 GPA and be in good academic and social standing with the previous institution. An interview is recommended. 60 of 120 credits required for the bachelor's degree must be completed at Hiram.

Visiting: There are regularly scheduled orientations for prospective students, consisting of campus day visits and prospective student overnights while school is still in session. There are guides for informal visits; visitors may sit in on classes and stay overnight. To schedule a visit, contact the Admissions Office.

Financial Aid: In a recent year, 94% of all full-time freshmen and 93% of continuing full-time students received some form of financial aid. 82% of all full-time students received need-based aid. Hiram is a member of CSS. The FAFSA is required. Check with the school for current application deadlines.

International Students: There were 83 international students enrolled in a recent year. The school actively recruits these students. They must take the TOEFL, scoring 500 (550 for direct entry without language support classes) on the paper-based version or 61 (80 for direct entry without language support classes) on the Internet-based version. They must also take the SAT or ACT, scoring 17 on the ACT.

Computers: Wireless access is available. Students can use wireless networking in the classrooms, academic buildings, and residence halls. Hiram has 120 wireless access points. All students may access the system 24 hours a day, 7 days per week. There are no time limits and no fees. All students are required to have a personal computer. Dell laptops are recommended.

Graduates: In a recent year, 260 bachelor degrees were awarded. The most popular majors were management (8%), accounting/financial management (8%), and biology (7%). 30 companies recruited on campus in a recent year. In an average class, 64% graduate in 4 years or less, 67% graduate in 5 years or less, and 69% graduate in 6 years or less. Of a recent graduating class, 25% to 30% were enrolled in graduate school within 6 months of graduation and 60% were employed.

Admissions Contact: Sherman C. Dean II, Director of Admission. A campus DVD is available. E-mail: *admission@hiram.edu* Web: *www.hiram.edu*

JOHN CARROLL UNIVERSITY D-1

University Heights, OH 44118 **(216) 397-4294**
(888) 335-6800; (216) 397-4981

Full-time: 1531 men, 1431 women — **Faculty:** 193
Part-time: 59 men, 31 women — **Ph.D.s:** 96%
Graduate: 201 men, 470 women — **Student/Faculty:** 13 to 1
Year: semesters, summer session — **Tuition:** $34,480
Application Deadline: February 1 — **Room & Board:** $10,040
Freshman Class: 3721 applied, 3101 accepted, 792 enrolled
SAT CR/M/W: 540/550/540 — **ACT:** 24 — **COMPETITIVE+**

John Carroll is a private, coeducational, Jesuit Catholic university providing programs in the liberal arts, sciences, and business at the undergraduate and master's levels. As a Jesuit Catholic university, John Carroll inspires its students to excel in learning, leadership, and service in the region and in the world. Our unique size, structure, culture, and environment make us very successful at providing an outstanding education for our students and helping them become John Carroll graduates in four years. As evidence of that commitment John Carroll students who do not graduate after four years are eligible for full tuition scholarship consideration for their fifth year (view details on the website under Admission). There are 2 undergraduate schools and 2 graduate schools. In addition to regional accreditation, John Carroll has baccalaureate program accreditation with AACSB and NCATE. The library contains 465,699 volumes, 701,525 microform items, 12,770 audio/video tapes/CDs/DVDs, and subscribes to 9,894 periodicals including electronic. Computerized library services include interlibrary loans, database searching, Internet access, and Wi-Fi capability. Special learning facilities include a radio station, TV station, a learning commons/academic resource center, computer commons, a digital media center, and group study rooms. The 62-acre campus is in a suburban area in University Heights, Ohio, 10 miles east of Cleveland. Including any residence halls, there are 21 buildings.

Student Life: 69% of undergraduates are from Ohio. Others are from 34 states, 16 foreign countries, and Canada. 63% are from public schools. 83% are White. 64% are Catholic; 17% claim no religious affiliation. The average age of freshmen is 18; all undergraduates, 20. 12% do not continue beyond their first year; 75% remain to graduate.

Housing: 1600 students can be accommodated in college housing, which includes coed dorms. In addition, there are honors houses, fraternity/sorority, ROTC, wellness, special housing for disabled students. On-campus housing is guaranteed for the freshman year only and is available on a lottery system for upperclassmen. 54% of students live on campus; of those, 60% remain on campus on weekends. Some may keep cars.

Activities: 6% of men belong to 4 national fraternities; 11% of women belong to 5 national sororities. There are 110 groups on campus, including band, cheerleading, chess, choir, chorale, chorus, communications, computers, dance, debate, drama, drill team, environmental, ethnic, film, forensics, gay, honors, international, jazz band, literary magazine, musical theater, newspaper, pep band, photography, political, professional, radio and TV, religious, social, social service, student government, symphony, and yearbook. Popular campus events include Celebration of Scholarship, Winter Formal, Christmas Carroll Eve, Relay for Life, Carroll Fest (concert), Homecoming, Senior Week, Greek Week, Grad Fair and Spring Concert.

Sports: There are 11 intercollegiate sports for men and 11 for women, and 7 intramural sports for men and 6 for women. Facilities include A swimming pool and diving well, a 3,800-seat football stadium and track, a baseball stadium, soccer and softball fields, an indoor track, tennis, volleyball, racquetball, and basketball courts, a wrestling room, a weight room, and a fitness center. Club sports include hockey, rugby, lacrosse, field hockey, crew, women's basketball, ultimate frisbee, volleyball and sailing.

Disabled Students: 96% of the campus is accessible. Facilities include wheelchair ramps, elevators, special parking, specially equipped restrooms, special class scheduling, lowered drinking fountains, lowered telephones, and special housing.

Services: Counseling and information services are available, as is tutoring in some subjects, accounting, biology, chemistry, Chinese, economics, finance, French, German, Spanish, physics, psychology, and Theology/Religion. There is a reader service for the blind, and remedial writing.

Campus Safety and Security: Measures include 24-hour foot and vehicle patrol, emergency notification system, self-defense education, and security escort services. There are shuttle buses, emergency telephones, lighted pathways/sidewalks, and controlled access to dorms/residences.

Programs of Study: John Carroll confers B.A., B.S., B.A.Classics, B.S.B.A. and B.S.Econ. degrees. Master's degrees are also awarded. Bachelor's degrees are awarded in BIOLOGICAL SCIENCE (biochemistry, biology/biological science, cell biology, molecular biology, and (Biological) Pre-Health Studies), BUSINESS (accounting, banking and finance, business administration and management, business (dual major program), business data processing, entrepreneurial studies, finance, human resources, international business management, logistics, management information systems, and marketing/retailing/merchandising), COMMUNICATIONS AND THE ARTS (art history, art history and appreciation, classical languages, classics, communications, English, French, German, Greek, Latin, literature, modern language, Spanish, theatre arts, and theatre studies), COMPUTER AND PHYSICAL SCIENCE (chemistry, computer science, mathematics, natural sciences, and physics), EDUCATION (early childhood education, education, health information management, mathematics education, middle school education, physical education, and secondary education), ENGINEERING AND ENVIRONMENTAL DESIGN (engineering physics and environmental science), HEALTH PROFESSIONS (exercise science), SOCIAL SCIENCE (Asian/Oriental studies, criminal justice, criminology, East Asian studies, economics, European studies, gender studies, history, humanities, liberal arts/general studies, peace studies, philosophy, political science/government, psychology, religion, sociology, theological studies, and women's studies). communication and theatre arts, biology, accountancy, sociology and criminology are the strongest academically. Communication, theatre arts, biology, psychology, marketing, accountancy, education, finance, English, management, chemistry, political science, sociology and criminology have the largest enrollments.

Required: All students must take a first-year seminar and writing and speech courses. They may choose from nearly 500 courses across five divisions to meet the remaining liberal arts core curriculum requirements. A total of 128 credit hours with a minimum GPA of 2.0 is required for graduation.

Special: Cross-registration is offered with 9 area colleges, universities, and institutes. Study abroad is possible in 16 countries. Joint engineering degrees are offered with Case Western Reserve University or the University of Detroit Mercy. Other dual-degree options: after two years of study at JCU students can enter the University of Toledo College of Medicine MED-Start program; Biology majors can spend 3 years at JCU and then enroll in the Bolton School of Nursing at Case Western Reserve University towards a Doctor of Nursing Practice. Work-study programs with local corporations, internships, a Washington semester, student-designed majors, dual majors, and some pass/fail options are available. We offer 24 Study Abroad programs in the following countries: Australia, China, Costa Rica, England, France, Germany, Greece, Ireland, Italy, Japan, South Africa, Turkey. There are 15 national honor societies and a freshman honors program.

Faculty/Classroom: 53% of faculty are male; 47% are female. 97% teach undergraduates, 95% do research, and 95% do both. Graduate students teach 1% of introductory courses. The average class size in an introductory lecture is 19; in a laboratory is 15; and in a regular course is 19.

Admissions: 83% of the 2013-2014 applicants were accepted. The SAT scores for the 2013-2014 freshman class were: Critical Reading--28% below 500, 48% between 500 and 599, 21% between 600 and 699, and 3% between 700 and 800; Math--21% below 500, 51% between 500 and 599, 26% between 600 and 699, and 2% between 700 and 800; Writing--29% below 500, 45% between 500 and 599, 24% between 600 and 699, and 2% between 700 and 800. The ACT scores were 14% below 21, 25% between 21 and 23, 32% between 24 and 26, 14% between 27 and 28, and 15% above 28. 16% of the current freshmen were in the top fifth of their class; 39% were in the top two fifths. 11 freshmen graduated first in their class.

Requirements: The SAT or ACT is required. Applicants should be graduates of an accredited secondary school with a minimum of 16 academic credits, including 4 in English, 3 in math, 2 each in foreign language, lab science, and social studies, and 3 in electives. An essay is part of the application process, and an interview is highly encouraged for students concerned about admissions standards. We accept either the ACT or SAT. A GPA of 2.0 is required. AP and CLEP credits are accepted. Important factors in the admissions decision are advanced placement or honors courses, extracurricular activities record, and recommendations by school officials.

Procedure: Freshmen are admitted fall, spring, and summer. Entrance exams should be taken in the spring of the junior year or the fall of the senior year. There are deferred admissions and rolling admissions plans. Applications should be filed by February 1 for fall entry. Notification is sent on a rolling basis. Applications are accepted online.

Transfer: 97 transfer students enrolled in 2012-2013. Students must be in good standing at the time of application. The most recent term average and the cumulative average at the home school must be 2.0 or better to be considered for admission, and the cumulative average for all schools attended must be 2.0 or better. A GPA of at least 2.5 is preferred. 33 of 128 credits required for the bachelor's degree must be completed at John Carroll.

Visiting: There are regularly scheduled orientations for prospective students, consisting of open houses, admission and financial aid presentations, campus and Cleveland tours, and opportunities to meet faculty, coaches, and other campus officials. There are guides for informal visits and visitors may sit in on classes. To schedule a visit, contact the Office of Admission.

Financial Aid: In 2013-2014, 97% of all full-time freshmen and 92% of continuing full-time students received some form of financial aid. 78% of all full-time freshmen and 73% of continuing full-time students received need-based aid. The average freshman award was $28,910. Need-based scholarships or need-based grants averaged $10,057 ($25,675 maximum); need-based self-help aid (loans and jobs) averaged $15,186 ($13,300 maximum); other non-need-based awards and non-need-based scholarships averaged $5,000 ($33,500 maximum); and $1,808 from other forms of aid. 33% of undergraduate students work part-time. Average annual earnings from campus work are $1722. The average financial indebtedness of the 2013 graduate was $31,802. The FAFSA is required. The priority date for freshman financial aid applications for fall entry is March 15. The deadline for filing freshman financial aid applications for fall entry is August 1.

International Students: There are 32 international students enrolled. The school actively recruits these students. They must take the TOEFL with a minimum score of 550 on the paper-based TOEFL (PBT) or 79 on the Internet-based version (iBT). They must also take the SAT or ACT.

Computers: All students may access the system 24 hours a day. There are no time limits. The fee is $$450.

Graduates: From July 1, 2012 to June 30, 2013, 661 bachelor's degrees were awarded. The most popular majors were psychology (11%), communications (10%), and marketing (9%). 795 companies recruited on campus in 2012-2013. In an average class, 1% graduate in 3 years or less, 66% graduate in 4 years or less, 74% graduate in 5 years or less, and 75% graduate in 6 years or less. Of the 2012 graduating class, 30% were enrolled in graduate school within 6 months of graduation, and 78% were employed.

Admissions Contact: Steven P. Vitatoe, Executive Director of Enrollment. E-Mail: *http:/sites.jcu.edu/admission/* Web: *www.jcu.edu*

KENT STATE UNIVERSITY D-2

Kent, OH 44242 (330) 672-2444
(800) 988-KENT; (330) 672-2499

Full-time: 8255 men, 11610 women	**Faculty:** n/av; I, --$
Part-time: 1253 men, 1850 women	**Ph.D.s:** 71%
Graduate: 2174 men, 3856 women	**Student/Faculty:** 21 to 1
Year: semesters, summer session	**Tuition:** $9816 ($17,776)
Application Deadline:	**Room & Board:** $9536
Freshman Class: 16083 applied, 13368 accepted, 4355 enrolled	
SAT CR/M/W: 520/520/500 **ACT:** 22	**COMPETITIVE**

Kent State University, founded in 1910, is a public university offering degree programs in liberal and fine arts, business, health science, public health, teacher and professional training, and aviation. There are 11 undergraduate schools and 11 graduate schools. In addition to regional accreditation, KSU has baccalaureate program accreditation with AACSB, ABET, ACBSP, ACEJMC, ADA, FIDER, NAAB, NASAD, NASM, NCATE, NLN, and NRPA. The 6 libraries contain 2.6 million volumes, 1.3 million microform items, 10,400 audio/video tapes/CDs/DVDs, and subscribe to 12,000 periodicals including electronic. Computerized library services include interlibrary loans, database searching, Internet access, and Wi-Fi capability. Special learning facilities include an art gallery, planetarium, radio station, TV station, Fashion Museum, Liquid Crystal Institute. The 866-acre campus is in a suburban area 45 miles southeast of Cleveland. Including any residence halls, there are 138 buildings.

Student Life: 83% of undergraduates are from Ohio. Others are from 49 states, 69 foreign countries, and Canada. 75% are White. The average age of freshmen is 19; all undergraduates, 24. 22% do not continue beyond their first year; 51% remain to graduate.

Housing: 6200 students can be accommodated in college housing, which includes single-sex and coed dorms, on-campus apartments, and married student housing. In addition, there are honors houses and special-interest houses. On-campus housing is available on a first-come and first-served basis. 72% of students commute. Alcohol is not permitted. All students may keep cars.

Activities: 7% of men belong to 23 national fraternities; 6% of women belong to 9 national sororities. There are 200 groups on campus, including academic, art, band, cheerleading, chess, choir, chorale, chorus, communications, computers, dance, drama, environmental, ethnic, film, gay, honors, international, jazz band, literary magazine, marching band, musical theater, newspaper, opera, orchestra, pep band, photography, political, professional, radio and TV, religious, social, social service, and student government. Popular campus events include Black Squirrel Festival, Folk Festival, FlashFest and Back to School Blastoff.

Sports: There are 8 intercollegiate sports for men and 10 for women, and 18 intramural sports for men and 16 for women. Facilities include a gym, a recreation and wellness center, a football stadium, a field house, 2 fitness circuits, a golf course, a bowling alley, tennis courts, lighted basketball courts, an ice arena, a pool, a weight room, soccer, lacrosse, rugby, baseball, softball, and field hockey fields, an indoor track, an outdoor track, and a wrestling room.

Disabled Students: 95% of the campus is accessible. Facilities include wheelchair ramps, elevators, special parking, specially equipped restrooms, special class scheduling, lowered drinking fountains, lowered telephones, special housing.

Services: Counseling and information services are available, as is tutoring in some subjects. There is a reader service for the blind, and remedial math, reading, and writing. math, writing, foreign languages, and computer instruction.

Campus Safety and Security: Measures include 24-hour foot and vehicle patrol, emergency notification system, and security escort services. There are shuttle buses, emergency telephones, lighted pathways/sidewalks, controlled access to dorms/residences, a 24-hour campus police department, overnight security guards, and a 2-key system for residence halls.

Programs of Study: KSU confers B.A., B.S., B.A.R.C., B.B.A., B.F.A., B.G.S., B.M., B.R.I.T., B.S.E. and B.S.N. degrees. Associate, master's, and doctoral degrees are also awarded. Bachelor's degrees are awarded in AGRICULTURE (conservation and regulation), BIOLOGICAL SCIENCE (biology/biological science, biotechnology, botany, life science, nutrition, and zoology), BUSINESS (accounting, banking and finance, business administration and management, electronic business, fashion merchandising, hospitality management services, marketing and distribution, marketing management, operations management, recreation and leisure services, recreational facilities management, and sports management), COMMUNICATIONS AND THE ARTS (advertising, American Sign Language, apparel design, art history and appreciation, ceramic art and design, classics, communications, crafts, dance, dramatic arts, English, French, German, Latin, music, photography, public relations, Spanish, visual and performing arts, and visual design), COMPUTER AND PHYSICAL SCIENCE (applied mathematics, chemistry, computer science, earth science, geology, mathematics, physical sciences, physics, and radiological technology), EDUCATION (art education, athletic training, early childhood education, general studies, middle school education, music education, physical education, social studies education, teaching English as a second/foreign language (TESOL/TEFOL), and trade and industrial education), ENGINEERING AND ENVIRONMENTAL DESIGN (aeronautical science, aeronautical technology, air traffic control, architecture, computer technology, industrial engineering technology, and interior design), HEALTH PROFESSIONS (community health work, medical laboratory technology, nursing, predentistry, premedicine, preosteopathy, preveterinary science, public health, and speech pathology/audiology), SOCIAL SCIENCE (African studies, American studies, anthropology, Eastern European studies, economics, ethnic studies, fashion design and technology, geography, history, human development, international relations, Latin American studies, paralegal studies, philosophy, political science/government, psychology, Russian and Slavic studies, and sociology). Architecture, education, and fashion design and merchandising are the strongest academically. Business, psychology, and fashion merchandising have the largest enrollments.

Required: Students are required to complete 121 credit hours, of which 39 must be upper division. Distribution requirements include 9 hours each in humanities/fine arts and social sciences and 6 hours each in basic sciences, composition, math, logic, and foreign languages. Students must maintain an overall GPA of 2.0.

Special: A co-op program is available with the School of Technology, and cross-registration is available with the University of Akron, Cleveland State University, and Northeastern Ohio University's College of Medicine (NEOUCOM). Work-study programs and internships are offered. Study abroad in 22 countries, a Washington semester, an accelerated medical degree program, B.A.-B.S. degrees, dual majors, a general studies degree, student-designed majors, credit for military education, nondegree study, and pass/fail options are also possible. The Honors College provides honors course work in all majors. Dual admission with Cuyahoga Community, Lakeland Community, NEOUCOM, and Lorain County Community Colleges is available. Kent is a member of the national student exchange program. There are 15 national honor societies, including Phi Beta Kappa, and a freshman honors program.

Faculty/Classroom: 45% of faculty are male; 55% are female. Graduate students teach 5% of introductory courses. The average class size in an introductory lecture is 35 and in a laboratory is 20.

Admissions: 83% of the 2013-2014 applicants were accepted. The SAT scores for the 2013-2014 freshman class were: Critical Reading--35% below 500, 44% between 500 and 599, 18% between 600 and 699, and 3% between 700 and 800; Math--35% below 500, 45% between 500 and 599, 18% between 600 and 699, and 2% between 700 and 800; Writing--44% below 500, 41% between 500 and 599, 14% between 600 and 699, and 2% between 700 and 800. The ACT scores were 26% below 21, 35% between 21 and 23, 23% between 24 and 26, 9% between 27 and 28, and 7% above 28. 30% of the current freshmen were in the top fifth of their class; 61% were in the top two fifths. 52 freshmen graduated first in their class.

Requirements: The ACT is required. Applicants most likely to be admitted will have at least a 2.5 cumulative GPA (on a 4.0 scale) in a solid college-preparatory program and an ACT composite score of at least 21. A GPA of 2.5 is required. AP and CLEP credits are accepted.

Procedure: Freshmen are admitted fall, spring, and summer. Entrance exams should be taken in the spring of the junior year or the fall of the senior year. There is a rolling admissions plan. Application deadlines are open. Application fee is $40. Notification is sent on a rolling basis. Applications are accepted online.

Transfer: 1234 transfer students enrolled in 2012-2013. Applicants must present a minimum GPA of 2.0 on completed college course work. For students with fewer than 24 semester hours or 36 quarter hours, a high school transcript and ACT or SAT scores are also required. 30 of 121 credits required for the bachelor's degree must be completed at KSU.

Visiting: There are regularly scheduled orientations for prospective students, including information sessions (financial aid, residence halls, student panel), a campus tour, and meetings with academic representatives. There are guides for informal visits. To schedule a visit, contact the Admissions Office.

Financial Aid: In 2013-2014, 71% of all full-time freshmen students received some form of financial aid. 64% of all full-time freshmen students received need-based aid. The average freshman award was $10,340. Need-based scholarships or need-based grants averaged $6,569; need-based self-help aid (loans and jobs) averaged $3,986; non-need-based athletic scholarships averaged $17,294; and other non-need-based awards and non-need-based scholarships averaged $4,737. The average financial indebtedness of the 2013 graduate was $31,543. The FAFSA is required. The priority date for freshman financial aid applications for fall entry is March 3.

International Students: There are 1580 international students enrolled. The school actively recruits these students. They must take the TOEFL with a minimum score of 525 on the paper-based TOEFL (PBT) or 71 on the Internet-based version (iBT) or take the MELAB, IELTS.

Computers: All students may access the system 24 hours a day, 7 days a week. There are no time limits and no fees.

Graduates: From July 1, 2012 to June 30, 2013, 4739 bachelor's degrees were awarded. The most popular majors were nursing (13%), business management (6%), and psychology (5%). In an average class, 32% graduate in 4 years or less, 50% graduate in 5 years or less, and 51% graduate in 6 years or less.

Admissions Contact: Nancy Dellavecchia, Director of Admissions. E-Mail: *kentadm@kent.edu* Web: *www.kent.edu/admissions*

KENYON COLLEGE C-3

Gambier, OH 43022 **(740) 427-5776**
(800) 848-2468; (740) 427-5770

Full-time: 786 men, 909 women	**Faculty:** 166; IIB, +$
Part-time: 3 men, 7 women	**Ph.D.s:** 100%
Graduate: n/av	**Student/Faculty:** 10 to 1
Year: semesters	**Tuition:** $45,640
Application Deadline: January 15	**Room & Board:** $11,170

Freshman Class: 3473 applied, 1555 accepted, 480 enrolled
SAT CR/M/W: 680/650/670 **ACT:** 30 **MOST COMPETITIVE**

Kenyon College, among the nation's finest liberal arts institutions, takes pride in its exceptionally strong academic programs, especially in English (Kenyon is the home of the internationally known Kenyon Review), the sciences, and fine arts. Student-faculty interaction, both in and out of the classroom, and a strong sense of community are hallmarks of the Kenyon experience. Kenyon students, who come from all 50 states and 40 countries, enjoy an active extracurricular life, with more than 150 student organizations. The Kenyon campus is known for its beauty and the quality of its facilities, including a new science center, studio art center, art gallery, and top-rated recreation/athletic center. There is one undergraduate school. The library contains 550,832 volumes, 147,806 microform items, and 30,317 audio/video tapes/CDs/DVDs, and subscribes to 11,660 periodicals including electronic. Computerized library services include interlibrary loans, database searching, Internet access, and Wi-Fi capability. Special learning facilities include an art gallery, radio station, an observatory and an environmental center. The 1000-acre campus is in a rural area 50 miles northeast of Columbus, OH. Including any residence halls, there are 142 buildings.

Student Life: 86% of undergraduates are from out of state, mostly the Middle Atlantic. Students are from 50 states, 41 foreign countries, and Canada. 50% are from public schools. 75% are White. The average age of freshmen is 18; all undergraduates, 20. 5% do not continue beyond their first year; 89% remain to graduate.

Housing: 1696 students can be accommodated in college housing, which includes single-sex and coed dorms and on-campus apartments. In addition, there are special-interest houses, and special interest floors, including community service or social group halls, a substance-free hall, a wellness hall, an international wing, Kosher living, and Township Fire Department. On-campus housing is guaranteed for all 4 years. 99% of students live on campus; of those, 99% remain on campus on weekends. All students may keep cars.

Activities: 10% of men belong to 2 local and 7 national fraternities; 10% of women belong to 4 local sororities. There are 128 groups on campus; student lectureships, art, band, chess, choir, chorale, chorus, dance, debate, drama, environmental, environmental/conservation, ethnic, film, gay, honors, international, jazz band, literary magazine, musical theater, newspaper, opera, orchestra, pep band, photography, political, professional, radio and TV, religious, social, social service, student government, and symphony. Popular campus events include Founder's Day/ Matriculation, Convocation, Summer Send-Off, Fandango, Honors Day, Family Weekend, and Martin Luther King, Jr. Day.

Sports: There are 12 intercollegiate sports for men and 12 for women, and 12 intramural sports for men and 12 for women. Facilities include a athletic/recreation/fitness center, and 70 acres of playing, football, softball, and soccer fields, a 50-yard pool, a field house, a nautilus center and weight rooms, and basketball, tennis, squash, and racquetball courts.

Disabled Students: 70% of the campus is accessible. Facilities include wheelchair ramps, elevators, special parking, specially equipped restrooms, special class scheduling, lowered drinking fountains, lowered telephones, special housing.

Services: Counseling and information services are available, as is tutoring in some subjects, upon request There is a reader service for the blind, and remedial writing. peer note-taking services, oral test option, extended time on tests, use of computer for essay based tests or notes, advance syllabus access, priority registration, priority seating, permission to use digital audio recordings, digital text format and content specific tutors are provided.

Campus Safety and Security: Measures include 24-hour foot and vehicle patrol, emergency notification system, self-defense education, and security escort services. There are emergency telephones, lighted pathways/sidewalks, controlled access to dorms/residences, formal safety awareness events, and student patrols.

Programs of Study: Kenyon confers A.B. degrees. Bachelor's degrees are awarded in BIOLOGICAL SCIENCE (biochemistry, biology/biological science, molecular biology, and neurosciences), COMMUNICATIONS AND THE ARTS (art history, art, classics, dance, dramatic arts, English, film arts, French, German, Greek (classical), Latin, modern language, music, and Spanish), COMPUTER AND PHYSICAL SCIENCE (chemistry, mathematics, and physics), SOCIAL SCIENCE (American studies, anthropology, Asian studies, economics, history, international studies, philosophy, political science/government, psychology, religious studies, sociology, and women & gender studies). English, economics, and psychology have the largest enrollments.

Required: Students are required to complete a total of 16 units, including 4 to 7 units in the major, 1 unit in each of 4 divisions representing the arts, humanities, natural sciences, and social sciences, 1 unit of foreign language, and 1/2 unit of quantitative reasoning. Students must maintain a minimum GPA of 2.0 and complete the senior exercise in their major. A thesis is required for honor students.

Special: Kenyon offers more than 200 off-campus study programs. The college also offers dual and student-designed majors, pass/fail options, internships, winter and/or spring break externship programs, a Washington semester consisting of apprenticeships in any of several U.S. programs, and a 3-2 engineering degree with Case Western Reserve, Washington University in St. Louis, and Rensselaer Polytechnic Institute, as well as a 3-2 environmental studies program with Duke University. 3-2 or 4-1 master's (certification) programs with The Bank Street College of Education are also possible. There is Phi Beta Kappa and 25 departmental honors programs.

Faculty/Classroom: 55% of faculty are male; 45% are female. All teach undergraduates, all do research. No introductory courses are taught by graduate students. The average class size in an introductory lecture is 17 and in a regular course is 17.

Admissions: 45% of the 2013-2014 applicants were accepted. The SAT scores for the 2013-2014 freshman class were: Critical Reading--1% below 500, 15% between 500 and 599, 43% between 600 and 699, and 42% between 700 and 800; Math--1% below 500, 22% between 500 and 599, 56% between 600 and 699, and 22% between 700 and 800; Writing--1% below 500, 13% between 500 and 599, 49% between 600 and 699, and 37% between 700 and 800. The ACT scores were 61% above 28. 85% of the current freshmen were in the top fifth of their class; 95% were in the top two fifths. There were 13 National Merit finalists. 17 freshmen graduated first in their class.

Requirements: The SAT or ACT is required. Applicants should be graduates of an accredited secondary school. Candidates are encouraged to exceed the minimum requirements (4 units of English and math, 3 units of science, foreign language and social studies), especially in math and science, and to take advance placement or honors work in at least 2 subjects. Kenyon recommends 4 units each of English, math, foreign language, science, and 3 units of social studies. An interview is important criteria in the admissions decision. Talent in music, theater, art, writing, and athletics is given extra consideration. AP credits are accepted. Important factors in the admissions decision are advanced placement or honors courses, evidence of special talent, and leadership record.

Procedure: Freshmen are admitted fall. Entrance exams should be taken in the fall of the senior year. There are early decision, early admissions, and deferred admissions plans. Early decision applications should be filed by November 15; regular applications, by January 15 for fall entry, along with a $50 fee. Notification of early decision is sent February 1; regular decision, April 1. 210 early decision candidates were accepted for the 2013-2014 class. 366 applicants were on the 2013 waiting list; 6 were admitted. Applications are accepted online.

Transfer: 13 transfer students enrolled in 2012-2013. Transfer applicants must have a minimum college GPA of 3.0 and a high school record suggesting ability and potential. In addition, Kenyon requires a letter of recommendation from a professor, the Transfer Common Application, and the Transfer Supplement. 8 of 16 credits required for the bachelor's degree must be completed at Kenyon.

Visiting: There are regularly scheduled orientations for prospective students, It includes interviews with staff, a campus tour, and a class visit. Students may also request to meet with faculty and coaches. Kenyon students are also available to host a prospective student overnight in the dorm. There are guides for informal visits, visitors may sit in on classes, and stay overnight. To schedule a visit, contact the Admissions Office.

Financial Aid: In 2013-2014, 40% of all full-time freshmen and 53% of continuing full-time students received some form of financial aid. 39% of all full-time freshmen and 51% of continuing full-time students received need-based aid. The average freshman award was $37,979. Need-based scholarships or need-based grants averaged $36,344; need-based self-help aid (loans and jobs) averaged $4,211; other non-need-based awards and non-need-based scholarships averaged $14,336; and $2,982 from other forms of aid. The average financial indebtedness of the 2013 graduate was $18,902. Kenyon is a member of CSS. The CSS/Profile and FAFSA, and tax returns and non-custodial parent income are required. The priority date for freshman financial aid applications for fall entry is February 15. The deadline for filing freshman financial aid applications for fall entry is February 15.

International Students: There are 74 international students enrolled. The school actively recruits these students. They must take the TOEFL with a minimum score of 600 on the paper-based TOEFL (PBT) or 100 on the Internet-based version (iBT). They must also take the SAT or ACT.

Computers: All students may access the system 24 hours a day. There are no time limits and no fees.

Graduates: From July 1, 2012 to June 30, 2013, 410 bachelor's degrees were awarded. The most popular majors were English (18%), economics (10%), and political science (10%). In an average class, 1% graduate in 3 years or less, 87% graduate in 4 years or less, 89% graduate in 5 years or less, and 90% graduate in 6 years or less.

Admissions Contact: Jennifer Delahunty, Dean of Admissions and Financial Aid. E-Mail: *admissions@kenyon.edu* Web: *www.kenyon.edu*

LAKE ERIE COLLEGE — E-1

Painesville, OH 44077	**(855) GOSTORM; (440) 375-7005**
Full-time: 483 men, 462 women	**Faculty:** 41
Part-time: 29 men, 60 women	**Ph.D.s:** 71%
Graduate: 95 men, 72 women	**Student/Faculty:** 23 to 1
Year: semesters, summer session	**Tuition:** $27,368
Application Deadline: August 1	**Room & Board:** $8336
Freshman Class: 1509 applied, 953 accepted, 276 enrolled	
SAT CR/M/W: 485/510/460 **ACT:** 21	**COMPETITIVE**

Lake Erie College, founded in 1856, is a private liberal arts institution offering 37 undergraduate majors and master's degrees in business administration and education. The college is nationally recognized for its equine studies programs. There are 5 undergraduate schools and 2 graduate schools. The library contains 65,120 volumes, 7,360 microform items, 1,277 audio/video tapes/CDs/DVDs. Computerized library services include interlibrary loans, database searching, Internet access, and Wi-Fi capability. Special learning facilities include an art gallery, a fine arts theater, equestrian center, music hall, athletic trainng facilities. The 270-acre campus is in a small town 30 miles east of Cleveland. Including any residence halls, there are 21 buildings.

Student Life: 74% of undergraduates are from Ohio. Others are from 30 states, 14 foreign countries, and Canada. 81% are White. 100% are Unknown. The average age of freshmen is 19; all undergraduates, 21. 36% do not continue beyond their first year; 48% remain to graduate.

Housing: 530 students can be accommodated in college housing, which includes single-sex and coed dorms and off-campus apartments. On-campus housing is guaranteed for the freshman year only, is available on a first-come, first-served basis, and is available on a lottery system for upperclassmen. Priority is given to out-of-town students. 56% of students live on campus; of those, 45% remain on campus on weekends. All students may keep cars.

Activities: 2% of men belong to 1 national fraternity; 7% of women belong to 1 national sorority. There are 31 groups on campus, including art, cheerleading, chorus, dance, drama, environmental, equestrian, ethnic, gay, honors, international, marching band, musical theater, political, professional, religious, social, social service, and student government. Popular campus events include Prix de Ville of North America, Class Receptions, and Mountain Day.

Sports: There are 12 intercollegiate sports for men and 11 for women, and 6 intramural sports for men and 6 for women. Facilities include on campus soccer and softball fields, a nearby off-campus baseball field and an 85-acre equestrian center, including a competition arena. The college also has an athletic and wellness center with an indoor basketball/volleyball arena, a multi-purpose practice/intramural and recreational gym with a suspended indoor jogging track, and a 4000-square foot fitness center and weight room. Football, tennis, and baseball may be played at nearby Paineville Park.

Disabled Students: 45% of the campus is accessible. Facilities include wheelchair ramps, elevators, special parking, specially equipped restrooms, special class scheduling, lowered drinking fountains, and lowered telephones.

Services: Counseling and information services are available, as is tutoring in most subjects. There is a reader service for the blind, and remedial math, reading, and writing.

Campus Safety and Security: Measures include 24-hour foot and vehicle patrol, emergency notification system, and security escort services. There are emergency telephones, lighted pathways/sidewalks, and controlled access to dorms/residences.

Programs of Study: LEC confers B.A., B.S. and B.F.A. degrees. Master's degrees are also awarded. Bachelor's degrees are awarded in AGRICULTURE (equine science and range/farm management), BIOLOGICAL SCIENCE (biology/biological science), BUSINESS (accounting, business administration and management, entrepreneurial studies, finance, human resources, international business management, marketing and distribution, and sports management), COMMUNICATIONS AND THE ARTS (arts administration/management, communications, English, fine arts, language arts, and media arts), COMPUTER AND PHYSICAL SCIENCE (chemistry, digital arts/technology, and mathematics), EDUCATION (early childhood education, middle school education, and special education), SOCIAL SCIENCE (criminal justice, French studies, German area studies, history, interdisciplinary studies, Italian studies, paralegal studies, political science/government, psychology, social science, and Spanish studies). Biology, equine science, and business are the strongest academically. Biology, business administration, sports management, criminal justice, and psychology have the largest enrollments.

Required: General education requirements include 4 hours each of math, English, 8 hours of a foreign language, and 2 hours of public speaking. A computer literacy course is required. There are specific core requirements for 25 additional semester hours. Students must complete 128 credits, including an average of 64 in the major, with a minimum GPA of 2.0.

Special: Students may choose either national or international internships or study abroad in the Netherlands, France, Germany, Spain, England, Italy, or another country, as arranged by the student, B.A.-B.S. degrees, including a B.F.A. in fine arts, music, dance, or an individual major, student-designed majors, and potential credit for life, military, or work experience are offered. Cross-registration is available with the Northeast Ohio Commission on Higher Education. 128 credits are required. There are 3 national honor societies, a freshman honors program, and 4 departmental honors programs.

Faculty/Classroom: 50% of faculty are male; 50% are female. All teach undergraduates. No introductory courses are taught by graduate students. The average class size in an introductory lecture is 20; in a laboratory is 20; and in a regular course is 13.

Admissions: 63% of the 2013-2014 applicants were accepted. The SAT scores for the 2013-2014 freshman class were: Critical Reading--52% below 500, 33% between 500 and 599, 9% between 600 and 699, and 5% between 700 and 800; Math--41% below 500, 50% between 500 and 599, 6% between 600 and 699, and 2% between 700 and 800; Writing--62% below 500, 26% between 500 and 599, 9% between 600 and 699, and 1% between 700 and 800. The ACT scores were 49% below 21, 13% between 21 and 23, 10% between 24 and 26, 5% between 27 and 28, and 7% above 28. 38% of the current freshmen were in the top fifth of their class; 70% were in the top two fifths.

Requirements: The SAT or ACT is required. The ACT Optional Writing test is also required. Applicants should be graduates of an accredited secondary school with a minimum GPA of 2.5. The high school program should include 4 years each of English, 3 years each of math and science (including 2 years of lab science), and 3 years each of history and social studies, with 2 years of a foreign language. Two letters of recommendation are required, with at least one being from a guidance counselor or teacher. A 500-word essay is required. A GED is required for home-schooled students. A campus visit is strongly encouraged. A GPA of 2.5 is required. AP and CLEP credits are accepted.

Procedure: Freshmen are admitted fall, spring, and summer. Entrance

exams should be taken by November of the senior year. There are deferred admissions and rolling admissions plans. Early decision applications should be filed by May 1; regular applications, by August 1 for fall entry; and January 1 for spring entry, along with a $30 fee. Notification is sent on a rolling basis. Applications are accepted online.

Transfer: 54 transfer students enrolled in 2012-2013. Applicants should submit transcripts from all schools attended and show a GPA of 2.5 in all college work, plus 2 letters of recommendation and proof of high school graduation (copy of diploma or transcripts). 32 of 128 credits required for the bachelor's degree must be completed at LEC.

Visiting: There are regularly scheduled orientations for prospective students, including a campus tour, a financial aid information session, classroom observation, and faculty or department head interviews. There are guides for informal visits, visitors may sit in on classes, and stay overnight. To schedule a visit, contact the Admissions Office.

Financial Aid: In 2013-2014, 83% of all full-time freshmen and 82% of continuing full-time students received some form of financial aid. 83% of all full-time freshmen and 81% of continuing full-time students received need-based aid. The average freshman award was $22,233. Need-based scholarships or need-based grants averaged $19,076; and need-based self-help aid (loans and jobs) averaged $3,615. 19% of undergraduate students work part-time. Average annual earnings from campus work are $2000. The FAFSA is required. The priority date for freshman financial aid applications for fall entry is March 1. The deadline for filing freshman financial aid applications for fall entry is August 1.

International Students: There are 40 international students enrolled. The school actively recruits these students. They must take the TOEFL with a minimum score of 550 on the paper-based TOEFL (PBT). They must also take the SAT or ACT.

Computers: All students may access the system. There are no time limits and no fees.

Graduates: From July 1, 2012 to June 30, 2013, 226 bachelor's degrees were awarded. The most popular majors were business administration (12%), biology (8%), and criminal justice (6%). In an average class, 36% graduate in 4 years or less, 46% graduate in 5 years or less, and 48% graduate in 6 years or less. Of the 2012 graduating class, 23% were enrolled in graduate school within 6 months of graduation, and 43% were employed.

Admissions Contact: Christopher Harris, Dean of Admissions and Financial Aid. E-Mail: *admissions@lec.edu* Web: *http:/www.lec.edu/admissions*

LOURDES UNIVERSITY B-1

Sylvania, OH 43560 — **419-885-5291**; **800-878-3210; 419-824-3916**

Full-time: 386 men, 909 women	**Faculty:** 79
Part-time: 162 men, 661 women	**Ph.D.s:** 55%
Graduate: 59 men, 283 women	**Student/Faculty:** 16 to 1
Year: semesters, summer session	**Tuition:** $17,655
Application Deadline: open	**Room & Board:** $8400
Freshman Class: 1231 applied, 879 accepted, 266 enrolled	
SAT CR/M: 422/438	**ACT:** 20 **LESS COMPETITIVE**

Located in Sylvania, OH, Lourdes University provides a values-centered education with a diverse campus life. Rooted in the Catholic Franciscan tradition, Lourdes offers baccalaureate degrees in more than 30 academic fields and graduate degrees in business, education, liberal arts, nursing, organizational leadership and theology. At Lourdes, students will find dynamic social, recreational and educational activities for every interest. A member of the NAIA, Lourdes students can also compete in a variety of men's and women's sports. Named "Best Midwestern College," Lourdes is a nationally accredited, veteran and transfer-friendly institution. There are 5 undergraduate schools and one graduate school. In addition to regional accreditation, Lourdes has baccalaureate program accreditation with CSWE and TEAC. The library contains 187,314 volumes, 1,747 audio/video tapes/CDs/DVDs, and subscribes to 68,916 periodicals including electronic. Computerized library services include interlibrary loans, database searching, Internet access, and Wi-Fi capability. Special learning facilities include an art gallery and planetarium. The 113-acre campus is in a suburban area 10 miles west of Toledo. Including any residence halls, there are 21 buildings.

Student Life: 87% of undergraduates are from Ohio. Others are from 16 states, and Canada. 71% are White; 17% African American. 37% are Catholic; 12% claim no religious affiliation. The average age of freshmen is 19; all undergraduates, 28. 38% do not continue beyond their first year; 20% remain to graduate.

Housing: 432 students can be accommodated in college housing, which includes coed on-campus apartments. On-campus housing is guaranteed for all 4 years. 84% of students commute. All students may keep cars.

Activities: There are no fraternities or sororities. There are 24 groups on campus, including art, cheerleading, choir, chorus, dance, drama, environmental, ethnic, gay, honors, literary magazine, pep band, political, professional, religious, social service, and student government. Popular campus events include Spike the Spirit, Fall Fest and Spring Fling.

Sports: There are 6 intercollegiate sports for men and 6 for women, and 7 intramural sports for men and 7 for women. Facilities include a gym, fitness center, and baseball/softball fields.

Disabled Students: 95% of the campus is accessible. Facilities include wheelchair ramps, elevators, special parking, specially equipped restrooms, special class scheduling, lowered drinking fountains.

Services: Counseling and information services are available, as is tutoring in most subjects. There is remedial math, reading, and writing.

Campus Safety and Security: Measures include 24-hour foot and vehicle patrol, emergency notification system, self-defense education, and security escort services. There are shuttle buses, lighted pathways/sidewalks, and controlled access to dorms/residences.

Programs of Study: Lourdes confers B.A., B.S., B.I.S. and B.S.N. degrees. Associate and master's degrees are also awarded. Bachelor's degrees are awarded in BIOLOGICAL SCIENCE (biology/biological science), BUSINESS (accounting, business administration and management, finance, human resources, and marketing management), COMMUNICATIONS AND THE ARTS (art, art history and appreciation, and English), EDUCATION (education), ENGINEERING AND ENVIRONMENTAL DESIGN (environmental science), HEALTH PROFESSIONS (health care administration and nursing), SOCIAL SCIENCE (criminal justice, history, interdisciplinary studies, psychology, social work, sociology, and theological studies). Nursing, business, and education have the largest enrollments.

Required: Students are required to maintain a minimum 2.0 GPA for all college level courses. Some departments have further minimum GPA requirements for courses in the major. The number of credit hours required vary according to degree sought.

Special: Lourdes University offers baccalaureate degrees in more than 30 academic fields and graduate degrees in business, education, liberal arts, nursing, organizational leadership, and theology. There are 9 national honor societies and 8 departmental honors programs.

Faculty/Classroom: 33% of faculty are male; 67% are female. 91% teach undergraduates. No introductory courses are taught by graduate students. The average class size in an introductory lecture is 19; in a laboratory is 8; and in a regular course is 15.

Admissions: 71% of the 2013-2014 applicants were accepted. The SAT scores for the 2013-2014 freshman class were: Critical Reading--79% below 500, and 21% between 500 and 599; Math--80% below 500, 13% between 500 and 599, and 7% between 600 and 699. The ACT scores were 63% below 21, 25% between 21 and 23, 10% between 24 and 26, and 3% between 27 and 28. 19% of the current freshmen were in the top fifth of their class; 41% were in the top two fifths.

Requirements: The SAT or ACT is required. Entrance into Lourdes University requires either an earned diploma from an accredited high school, a home school program in a college preparatory course of study, or a GED certificate. Faculty recommend four units of English, three units of mathematics, three units of social studies, three units in science, and two units of foreign language. AP and CLEP credits are accepted.

Procedure: Freshmen are admitted to all sessions. There are early admissions, deferred admissions, and rolling admissions plans. Application deadlines are open. Application fee is $25. Notification is sent on a rolling basis. Applications are accepted online.

Transfer: 328 transfer students enrolled in 2012-2013. Transfer students need to submit official transcripts from all previously attended colleges, regardless of hours completed, earned, or attempted, and regardless of cumulative GPA. Students with less than 12 college semester hours (18 quarter hours) are required to submit official high school transcripts or GED along with transcripts from all previously attended colleges. 30 of 120 credits required for the bachelor's degree must be completed at Lourdes.

Visiting: There are guides for informal visits and visitors may sit in on classes. To schedule a visit, contact the Office of Admissions.

Financial Aid: In 2013-2014, 85% of all full-time freshmen and 84% of continuing full-time students received some form of financial aid. 70% of all full-time freshmen and 65% of continuing full-time students received need-based aid. The average freshman award was $14,715. Need-based scholarships or need-based grants averaged $6,048 ($14,106 maximum); need-based self-help aid (loans and jobs) averaged $3,529 ($7,466 maximum); non-need-based athletic scholarships averaged $3,761 ($8,500 maximum); and other non-need-based awards and non-need-based scholarships averaged $9,915 ($22,272 maximum). 4% of undergraduate students work part-time. Average annual earnings from campus work are $2016. The FAFSA is required. The priority date for freshman financial aid applications for fall entry is March 1.

International Students: They must take the TOEFL with a minimum score of 500 on the paper-based TOEFL (PBT).

Computers: All students may access the system. There are no time limits and no fees.

Graduates: From July 1, 2012 to June 30, 2013, 258 bachelor's degrees were awarded. The most popular majors were nursing (42%), business (21%), and education (11%). In an average class, 11% graduate in 4 years or less, 15% graduate in 5 years or less, and 20% graduate in 6 years or less.

Admissions Contact: Amy Houston, Associate Director of Admissions. E-Mail: *AdmissionLCAdmits@lourdes.edu* Web: *www.lourdes.edu*

MALONE UNIVERSITY D-2

Canton, OH 44709 (330) 471-8145
(800) 521-1146; (330) 471-8149

Full-time: 654 men, 799 women	**Faculty:** 96; IIA, --$
Part-time: 51 men, 152 women	**Ph.D.s:** 78%
Graduate: 139 men, 301 women	**Student/Faculty:** 16 to 1
Year: semesters, summer session	**Tuition:** $25,678
Application Deadline:	**Room & Board:** $8656
Freshman Class: 1333 applied, 957 accepted, 316 enrolled	
SAT CR/M: 520/510	**ACT:** 22 COMPETITIVE

Malone University, founded in 1892, is a private Christian university for the arts, sciences, and professions in the liberal arts tradition. The mission of Malone University is to provide students with an education based on biblical faith in order to develop men and women in intellectual maturity, wisdom, and Christian faith who are committed to serving the church, community, and world. There are 4 undergraduate schools and 4 graduate schools. In addition to regional accreditation, Malone has baccalaureate program accreditation with ACBSP, CSWE, and NCATE. The library contains 171,402 volumes, 654,486 microform items, 13,258 audio/video tapes/CDs/DVDs, and subscribes to 45,907 periodicals including electronic. Computerized library services include interlibrary loans, database searching, and Internet access. Special learning facilities include an art gallery, a writing lab; subject area tutoring; a TV production studio, a radio producing studio and a number of other production spaces in the Student Media Center. The 96-acre campus is in a suburban area 56 miles southeast of Cleveland. Including any residence halls, there are 23 buildings.

Student Life: 86% of undergraduates are from Ohio. Others are from 30 states, 16 foreign countries, and Canada. 81% are from public schools. 85% are White. 77% are Protestant; 15% claim no religious affiliation. The average age of freshmen is 18; all undergraduates, 23. 27% do not continue beyond their first year; 58% remain to graduate.

Housing: 1197 students can be accommodated in college housing, which includes single-sex dorms. special topic/discipleship floors for upperclassmen. On-campus housing is guaranteed for the freshman year only, is available on a first-come, first-served basis, and is available on a lottery system for upperclassmen. 55% of students live on campus; of those, 40% remain on campus on weekends. Alcohol is not permitted. All students may keep cars.

Activities: There are no fraternities or sororities. There are 50 groups on campus, including 12 of the approximately 50 organizations are honor societies, art, band, cheerleading, choir, chorale, communications, computers, dance, drama, drill team, environmental, ethnic, film, forensics, honors, international, jazz band, literary magazine, marching band, musical theater, newspaper, opera, photography, political, professional, radio and TV, religious, social, social service, student government, and yearbook. Popular campus events include Little Sibs Weekend, Christmas Celebration and Worldview Forums.

Sports: There are 10 intercollegiate sports for men and 10 for women, and 5 intramural sports for men and 5 for women. Facilities include a gym, a wellness center with a strength room and a cardio room, an outdoor track, baseball, softball, and soccer fields, practice soccer and football fields, intramural fields, a cross-country course, and outdoor volleyball and basketball courts.

Disabled Students: Facilities include wheelchair ramps, elevators, special parking, specially equipped restrooms, special class scheduling, lowered drinking fountains, lowered telephones, and special housing.

Services: Counseling and information services are available, as is tutoring in most subjects. There is a reader service for the blind, and remedial math, reading, and writing. There are also disability support services such as a distraction-reduced testing room.

Campus Safety and Security: Measures include 24-hour foot and vehicle patrol, emergency notification system, and security escort services. There are emergency telephones, lighted pathways/sidewalks, and controlled access to dorms/residences.

Programs of Study: Malone confers B.A., B.S.Ed. and B.S.N. degrees. Master's degrees are also awarded. Bachelor's degrees are awarded in BIOLOGICAL SCIENCE (biology/biological science, life science, and zoology), BUSINESS (accounting, business administration and management, and sports management), COMMUNICATIONS AND THE ARTS (art, broadcasting, communications, creative writing, English, journalism, language arts, music, music technology, public relations, Spanish, and theatre studies), COMPUTER AND PHYSICAL SCIENCE (chemistry, computer science, mathematics, and physical sciences), EDUCATION (art education, Christian education, early childhood education, foreign languages education, health education, middle school education, music education, physical education, science education, secondary education, social studies education, and special education), HEALTH PROFESSIONS (community health work, exercise science, medical laboratory technology, nursing, and public health), SOCIAL SCIENCE (biblical studies, history, international studies, liberal arts/general studies, ministries, philosophy, political science/government, psychology, religious music, social work, theological studies, and youth ministry). Nursing, business administration, and communications have the largest enrollments.

Required: Students must maintain a GPA of 2.0 overall and 2.25 to 2.75 in the major, depending upon the major. At least 30 hours in the major and 39 hours at the 300 or 400 level are required. To graduate, all students must complete at least 124 credit hours. The 50- to 54-hour general education curriculum includes 13 hours of Faith Learning courses, 9 to 10 hours of Foundational Skills courses, and 28 to 31 hours of Engaging God's World courses. Courses in English composition and literature, communication skills, world history, and lab science are also required.

Special: Students may participate in co-op programs and internships in many majors and may cross-register within the Christian College Consortium. Malone offers study abroad in England, China, Costa Rica, Israel, India, Australia, Uganda, and Kenya as well as Hollywood (Film Studies), Nashville (Contemporary Music), or Washington semesters through the Council for Christian Colleges and Universities. Approximately 20 other study abroad opportunities are available through Brethren Colleges Abroad (BCA). A liberal arts degree, dual and student-designed majors, and credit for life, military, or work experience are also available. The Malone Management Program(MMP)offers accelerated degree completion for students with 5 years of work experience and 40 to 88 transfer hours. MMP offers 5 majors: Organizational Management, Project Management, Marketing Management, Health Services Management, and Environmental Management. There are 12 national honor societies and a freshman honors program.

Faculty/Classroom: 49% of faculty are male; 51% are female. 87% teach undergraduates. No introductory courses are taught by graduate students. The average class size in an introductory lecture is 28; in a laboratory is 14; and in a regular course is 19.

Admissions: 72% of the 2013-2014 applicants were accepted. The SAT scores for the 2013-2014 freshman class were: Critical Reading--36% below 500, 44% between 500 and 599, 16% between 600 and 699, and 5% between 700 and 800; Math--38% below 500, 47% between 500 and 599, 16% between 600 and 699. The ACT scores were 36% below 21, 26% between 21 and 23, 19% between 24 and 26, 7% between 27 and 28, and 13% above 28. 34% of the current freshmen were in the top fifth of their class; 60% were in the top two fifths. 10 freshmen graduated first in their class.

Requirements: The ACT is preferred; the SAT is accepted. Applicants should be graduates of an accredited secondary school with a minimum GPA of 2.5. The GED is accepted. A GPA of 2.5 is required. AP and CLEP credits are accepted. Important factors in the admissions decision are advanced placement or honors courses, leadership record, and extracurricular activities record.

Procedure: Freshmen are admitted fall, spring, and summer. Entrance exams should be taken in the junior year. There are early admissions, deferred admissions, and rolling admissions plans. Application deadlines are open. Application fee is $20. Notifications are sent September 1. Applications are accepted online.

Transfer: 108 transfer students enrolled in 2012-2013. Applicants must submit a transfer reference form from the last institution attended. 30 of 124 credits required for the bachelor's degree must be completed at Malone.

Visiting: There are regularly scheduled orientations for prospective students, Discover Days are large group visit days that include two information sessions, devotional with the campus Ministries staff, a student panel, group tours, and a group lunch with a faculty member from your desired major. There are guides for informal visits, visitors may sit in on classes, and stay overnight. To schedule a visit, contact Jody Dimit at (330) 471-8147.

Financial Aid: In 2013-2014, 100% of all full-time freshmen and 94% of continuing full-time students received some form of financial aid. 81% of all full-time freshmen and 73% of continuing full-time students received need-based aid. The average freshman award was $28,296. Need-based scholarships or need-based grants averaged $9,322 ($22,594 maximum); need-based self-help aid (loans and jobs) averaged $4,925 ($9,000 maximum); non-need-based athletic scholarships averaged $10,334 ($26,334 maximum); other non-need-based awards and non-need-based scholarships averaged $13,004 ($31,625 maximum); and $12,820 from other forms of aid. 22% of undergraduate students work part-time. Average annual earnings from campus work are $1975. The average financial indebtedness of the 2013 graduate was $30,124. The FAFSA, and verification docs if chosen is required. The priority date for freshman financial aid applications for fall entry is March 1. The deadline for filing freshman financial aid applications for fall entry is July 31.

International Students: There are 24 international students enrolled. They must take the TOEFL with a minimum score of 550 on the paper-based TOEFL (PBT) or 79 on the Internet-based version (iBT). They must also take the ACT, scoring 18. not required of all international students; but definitely athletes due to NCAA requirements.

Computers: All students may access the system 24/7. There are no time limits and no fees.

Graduates: From July 1, 2012 to June 30, 2013, 519 bachelor's degrees

were awarded. The most popular majors were business administration/management (28%), nursing and other health professions and related programs (20%), and education (16%). In an average class, 2% graduate in 3 years or less, 44% graduate in 4 years or less, 56% graduate in 5 years or less, and 58% graduate in 6 years or less.

Admissions Contact: Linda K. Hoffman, Director of Admissions. E-Mail: *admissions@malone.edu* Web: *www.malone.edu*

MARIETTA COLLEGE D-5

Marietta, OH 45750 (740) 376-4600
(800) 331-7896; (740) 376-8888

Full-time: 816 men, 602 women	**Faculty:** 110; IIB, --$
Part-time: 27 men, 42 women	**Ph.D.s:** 92%
Graduate: 26 men, 109 women	**Student/Faculty:** 12 to 1
Year: semesters, summer session	**Tuition:** $32,265
Application Deadline: April 15	**Room & Board:** $9870

Freshman Class: 4157 applied, 2811 accepted, 395 enrolled
SAT CR/M/W: 539/555/517 **ACT:** 24 **VERY COMPETITIVE**

Marietta College, founded in 1835, is a private liberal arts college. There is 1 undergraduate school and 4 graduate schools. In addition to regional accreditation, Marietta has baccalaureate program accreditation with ABET, NASM, and NCATE. The library contains 449,123 volumes, 146,583 microform items, 5,031 audio/video tapes/CDs/DVDs, and subscribes to 13,557 periodicals including electronic. Computerized library services include interlibrary loans, database searching, and Internet access. Special learning facilities include an art gallery, planetarium, radio station, TV station, an observatory, a greenhouse, and a geology annex. The 90-acre campus is in a small town 115 miles southeast of Columbus. Including any residence halls, there are 40 buildings.

Student Life: 64% of undergraduates are from Ohio. Others are from 40 states, 15 foreign countries, and Canada. 89% are from public schools. 71% are White. The average age of freshmen is 18; all undergraduates, 20. 22% do not continue beyond their first year; 56% remain to graduate.

Housing: 1276 students can be accommodated in college housing, which includes single-sex and coed dorms and on-campus apartments. In addition, there are honors houses, special-interest houses, fraternity houses, and sorority houses. On-campus housing is guaranteed for all 4 years. 76% of students live on campus; of those, 80% remain on campus on weekends. All students may keep cars.

Activities: 23% of men belong to 3 national fraternities; 41% of women belong to 3 national sororities. There are 80 groups on campus, including and arts and humanities, Circle K, art, athletic training, band, cheerleading, choir, chorale, chorus, computers, dance, debate, drama, drill team, environmental, ethnic, film, forensics, gay, honors, international, jazz band, literary magazine, musical theater, newspaper, orchestra, pep band, photography, political, professional, radio and TV, religious, social, social service, student government, and yearbook. Popular campus events include DooDah Day, Little Sibs Weekend and Welcome Back Bash.

Sports: There are 9 intercollegiate sports for men and 9 for women, and 12 intramural sports for men and 12 for women. Facilities include a 7000-seat stadium, a 1500-seat performance gym, a 3500-seat field house, baseball, softball, and soccer fields, a boat house, a cross-country course, tennis courts, and a recreational center housing a 200-meter track, multipurpose and racquetball courts, an ergometer training room, cardio equipment, and a climbing wall.

Disabled Students: 90% of the campus is accessible. Facilities include wheelchair ramps, elevators, special parking, specially equipped restrooms, special class scheduling, lowered drinking fountains, lowered telephones, and special housing.

Services: Counseling and information services are available, as is tutoring in most subjects. There is a reader service for the blind, remedial math and writing, and a peer tutoring program.

Campus Safety and Security: Measures include 24-hour foot and vehicle patrol, emergency notification system, self-defense education, and security escort services. There are shuttle buses, emergency telephones, lighted pathways/sidewalks, controlled access to dorms/residences, and airport shuttles available upon request.

Programs of Study: Marietta confers B.A., B.S. and B.F.A. degrees. Associate and master's degrees are also awarded. Bachelor's degrees are awarded in AGRICULTURE (environmental studies), BIOLOGICAL SCIENCE (biochemistry and biology/biological science), BUSINESS (accounting, banking and finance, business administration and management, human resources, international business management, management information systems, marketing/retailing/merchandising, and sports management), COMMUNICATIONS AND THE ARTS (advertising, broadcasting, communications, dramatic arts, English, graphic design, journalism, music, public relations, Spanish, speech/debate/rhetoric, and studio art), COMPUTER AND PHYSICAL SCIENCE (applied physics, chemistry, computer science, geology, information sciences and systems, mathematics, and physics), EDUCATION (athletic training, early childhood education, and music education), ENGINEERING AND ENVIRONMENTAL DESIGN (environmental science and petroleum/natural gas engineering), HEALTH PROFESSIONS (health science and physician's assistant), SOCIAL SCIENCE (Asian/Oriental studies, economics, history, interdisciplinary studies, political science/government, and psychology). Petroleum engineering is the strongest academically. Petroleum engineering, advertising public relations, and psychology have the largest enrollments

Required: To graduate, students must complete at least 120 total credit hours, with general education requirements. The minimum number of hours required for a major is 36. A minimum GPA of 2.0 must be maintained. Seniors must complete a capstone project in their major.

Special: There are 3-2 binary engineering programs with Case Western Reserve, Columbia, and Ohio Universities. Internships are available in many majors, and students may study abroad in numerous countries and participate in a Washington semester through American University. Work-study programs, B.A.-B.S. degrees in all majors, and student-designed majors are also available. There are 23 national honor societies, including Phi Beta Kappa, a freshman honors program, and 17 departmental honors programs.

Faculty/Classroom: 51% of faculty are male; 49% are female. All teach undergraduates, and 30% do both. No introductory courses are taught by graduate students. The average class size in an introductory lecture is 19; in a laboratory is 13; and in a regular course is 16.

Admissions: 68% of the 2013-2014 applicants were accepted. The SAT scores for the 2013-2014 freshman class were: Critical Reading 33% below 500, 40% between 500 and 599, 25% between 600 and 699, and 2% between 700 and 800; Math--27% below 500, 36% between 500 and 599, 34% between 600 and 699, and 3% between 700 and 800; Writing--40% below 500, 42% between 500 and 599, 17% between 600 and 699, and 1% between 700 and 800. The ACT scores were 23% below 21, 27% between 21 and 23, 23% between 24 and 26, 13% between 27 and 28, and 15% above 28. 49% of the current freshmen were in the top fifth of their class; 79% were in the top two fifths. 9 freshmen graduated first in their class.

Requirements: The SAT or ACT is required. Students seeking admission should have completed 4 years of English and 3 of history, math, and science; 2 years of a foreign language is also recommended. An interview is strongly recommended. A GPA of 2.0 is required. AP and CLEP credits are accepted. Important factors in the admissions decision are advanced placement or honors courses, evidence of special talent, and leadership record.

Procedure: Freshmen are admitted fall and spring. Entrance exams should be taken no later than February of the senior year. There is a rolling admissions plan. Applications should be filed by April 15 for fall entry, along with a $25 fee. Notification is sent on a rolling basis. Applications are accepted online.

Transfer: 46 transfer students enrolled in 2012-2013. A minimum GPA of 2.5, a recommendation, and an essay are required. 36 of 120 credits required for the bachelor's degree must be completed at Marietta.

Visiting: There are regularly scheduled orientations for prospective students, including fall and spring open houses, tours, and meetings with faculty, coaches, and financial aid representatives. There are guides for informal visits, visitors may sit in on classes, and stay overnight. To schedule a visit, contact the Office of Admissions.

Financial Aid: In 2013-2014, 96% of all full-time freshmen and 93% of continuing full-time students received some form of financial aid. 84% of all full-time freshmen and 79% of continuing full-time students received need-based aid. The average freshman award was $27,091. Need-based scholarships or need-based grants averaged $9,561 ($19,220 maximum); need-based self-help aid (loans and jobs) averaged $3,602 ($7,500 maximum); and other non-need-based awards and non-need-based scholarships averaged $8,650 ($35,112 maximum). 30% of undergraduate students work part-time. Average annual earnings from campus work are $2000. The average financial indebtedness of the 2013 graduate was $20,911. The FAFSA is required. The deadline for filing freshman financial aid applications for fall entry is March 1.

International Students: There are 155 international students enrolled. The school actively recruits these students. They must take the TOEFL with a minimum score of 550 on the paper-based TOEFL (PBT) or 79 on the Internet-based version (iBT) and the college's own test, IELTS. They must also take the SAT or ACT.

Computers: All students may access the system. There are no time limits and no fees.

Graduates: From July 1, 2012 to June 30, 2013, 222 bachelor's degrees were awarded. The most popular majors were petroleum engineering (7%), advertising/public relations (7%), and psychology (6%). 60 companies recruited on campus in 2012-2013. In an average class, 3% graduate in 3 years or less, 46% graduate in 4 years or less, 55% graduate in 5 years or less, and 56% graduate in 6 years or less. Of the 2012 graduating class, 24% were enrolled in graduate school within 6 months of graduation, and 95% were employed.

Admissions Contact: Jason Turley, Dean of Admission. E-Mail: *admit@mcnet.marietta.edu* Web: *www.marietta.edu*

MIAMI UNIVERSITY A-4

Oxford, OH 45056 **(513) 529-2531; (513) 529-1550**

Full-time: 7017 men, 7640 women
Faculty: 841; I, av$
Part-time: 215 men, 209 women
Ph.D.s: 89%
Graduate: 783 men, 1819 women
Student/Faculty: 17 to 1
Year: semesters, summer session
Tuition: $13,595 ($29,159)
Application Deadline: February 1
Room & Board: $10,596
Freshman Class: 20314 applied, 14788 accepted, 3734 enrolled
SAT CR/M: 580/610 **ACT:** 27 **HIGHLY COMPETITIVE**

Miami University provides a rigorous academic experience in the quintessential collegiate setting of Oxford, Ohio. Here, the best and brightest students prepare for success as they are given the opportunities of a large university while experiencing the personalized teaching, attention, and sense of community found in the best small colleges. A public university, Miami offers a wide range of academic programs. The bachelor's degree is offered in more than 100 areas of study, the master's degree in more than 50 and doctoral programs in 10 disciplines. Dedicated to fostering an environment of teaching for more than 200 years, Miami faculty guide both undergraduates and graduate students in conducting significant research, completing projects with real-world clients, and fostering leadership skills. With a long-standing dedication to global learning, complete with a European center in Luxembourg, Miami ranks first among public colleges nationwide for the rate of undergraduate students who study abroad. Miami students and faculty have an intense appreciation for a global view and multicultural approaches to learning. Retention and graduation rates are some of the highest in NCAA Division I schools, as is our students' successful entry into top graduate programs and professional schools. Additionally, nearly twice as many employers recruit at Miami as at comparable universities and conduct four times as many on-campus interviews. As a result, Miami is regularly cited by national publications as a best value in higher education. The Oxford campus encompasses more than 2,000 acres and, with its distinctive modified Georgian architecture, is widely regarded as one of the most beautiful campuses in America. Enrollment is approximately 15,000 undergraduates and 2,500 graduate students; an additional 6,000 students are enrolled at Miami's regional facilities in Hamilton, Middletown, and West Chester, Ohio. Founded in 1809, the university is located in the Miami Valley region of Ohio and is proud of the ties maintained with the Miami Tribe, now located in Oklahoma. There are 5 undergraduate schools and 1 graduate school. In addition to regional accreditation, has baccalaureate program accreditation with AACSB, ABET, CSAB, CSWE, FIDER, NAAB, NASAD, NCATE, and NLN. The 4 libraries contain 4.2 million volumes, 276,385 microform items, 2.2 million audio/video tapes/CDs/DVDs, and subscribe to 109,477 periodicals including electronic. Computerized library services include interlibrary loans, database searching, Internet access, and Wi-Fi capability. Special learning facilities include an art gallery, natural history museum, radio station, and TV station. The 2138-acre campus is in a small town 35 miles north of Cincinnati, OH. Including any residence halls, there are 119 buildings.

Student Life: 70% of undergraduates are from Ohio. Others are from 50 states, 73 foreign countries, and Canada. 74% are from public schools. 82% are White. 38% are Protestant; 36% Catholic; 19% claim no religious affiliation. The average age of freshmen is 18; all undergraduates, 20. 11% do not continue beyond their first year; 80% remain to graduate.

Housing: 7138 students can be accommodated in college housing, which includes single-sex and coed dorms, on-campus apartments, and married student housing. In addition, there are honors houses, language houses, special-interest houses, sorority houses, international housing and first-year only housing. On-campus housing is guaranteed for the freshman year only and is available on a lottery system for upperclassmen. 52% of students commute. All students may keep cars.

Activities: 24% of men belong to 29 national fraternities; 25% of women belong to 21 national sororities. There are 344 groups on campus, including art, bagpipe, band, cheerleading, chess, choir, chorale, chorus, communications, computers, dance, debate, drama, drill team, environmental, ethnic, film, forensics, gay, honors, international, jazz band, literary magazine, marching band, musical theater, newspaper, opera, orchestra, pep band, photography, political, professional, radio and TV, religious, social, social service, student government, symphony, and yearbook. Popular campus events include Parents Weekend, Kidsfest Weekend, and Unity Fest.

Sports: There are 8 intercollegiate sports for men and 10 for women, and 17 intramural sports for men and 16 for women. Facilities include A 25,000-seat football stadium, a 170,000 sf ice arena, 70 acres of playing fields, 30 outdoor tennis courts, a recreational sports center, 10 indoor basketball/volleyball courts, racquetball, handball, and squash courts, a floor hockey/indoor soccer court, a climbing wall, equestrian stables and dressage course, a world-class aquatic center containing 3 indoor swimming pools, jogging paths, a par course, sand volleyball courts, aerobics and weight rooms, and a Frisbee golf course.

Disabled Students: All of the campus is accessible. Facilities include wheelchair ramps, elevators, special parking, specially equipped restrooms, special class scheduling, lowered drinking fountains, lowered telephones, and special housing.

Services: Counseling and information services are available, as is tutoring in most subjects. Assistance in study skills is available.

Campus Safety and Security: Measures include 24-hour foot and vehicle patrol, emergency notification system, self-defense education, and security escort services. There are shuttle buses, emergency telephones, lighted pathways/sidewalks, and controlled access to dorms/residences.

Programs of Study: confers A.B., B.S., B.F.A., B.Mus., A.B.Arc., A.B.Art., A.B.The., B.I.S., B.S.Aps., B.S.Art., B.S.AT., B.S.Bus., B.S.Cj., B.S.Cs., B.S.Ed., B.S.Egr., B.S.Ff., B.S.IT., B.S.Knh., B.W.Se., B.S.Swk. degrees. Associate, master's, and doctoral degrees are also awarded. Bachelor's degrees are awarded in BIOLOGICAL SCIENCE (biochemistry, botany, microbiology, nutrition, and zoology), BUSINESS (accounting, banking and finance, business economics, management information systems, management science, marketing/retailing/merchandising, sports management, sports marketing, and supply chain management), COMMUNICATIONS AND THE ARTS (art, art history and appreciation, classical languages, classics, communications, dramatic arts, East Asian languages and literature, English, French, German, graphic design, journalism, linguistics, media arts, music, music performance, Russian, Spanish, and speech/debate/rhetoric), COMPUTER AND PHYSICAL SCIENCE (chemistry, computer science, earth science, geology, mathematics, physics, software engineering, and statistics), EDUCATION (art education, athletic training, early childhood education, elementary education, foreign languages education, health information management, middle school education, music education, science education, secondary education, special education, and sports studies), ENGINEERING AND ENVIRONMENTAL DESIGN (architectural history, architecture, bioengineering, chemical engineering, computer engineering, electrical/electronics engineering, engineering, engineering management, engineering physics, engineering technology, environmental science, interior design, manufacturing engineering, mechanical engineering, and paper and pulp science), HEALTH PROFESSIONS (clinical science, health promotion, nursing, and speech pathology/audiology), SOCIAL SCIENCE (African American studies, American studies, anthropology, criminal justice, economics, family/consumer studies, geography, gerontology, history, interdisciplinary studies, international relations, international studies, Italian studies, Latin American studies, philosophy, physical fitness/movement, political science/government, psychology, public administration, religion, social work, sociology, urban studies, and women's studies). Marketing, finance, accountancy, zoology and psychology have the largest enrollments.

Required: To graduate students must complete 128 semester hours, with a minimum 2.0 GPA. At least 32 semester hours must be from Miami University. Students must fulfill all requirements for either the Miami Plan (i.e., liberal education requirements) or the Honors Plan. The Miami plan includes 36 semester hours of foundation courses, 9 semester hours in a thematic sequence, and a 3 hour capstone experience.

Special: The university offers cross-registration with Cincinnati area colleges, study abroad in multiple countries, co-op programs in the School of Applied Science, internships in health and sport studies and applied science, a 3-2 engineering degree with Case Western Reserve and Columbia Universities, and a 3-2 forestry degree with Duke University. Students may pursue student-designed majors through the Western Program or interdisciplinary majors. There are 21 national honor societies, including Phi Beta Kappa, and a freshman honors program.

Faculty/Classroom: 56% of faculty are male; 44% are female. All teach undergraduates. No introductory courses are taught by graduate students. The average class size in a regular course is 32.

Admissions: 73% of the 2013-2014 applicants were accepted. The SAT scores for the 2013-2014 freshman class were: Critical Reading--11% below 500, 46% between 500 and 599, 34% between 600 and 699, and 9% between 700 and 800; Math--7% below 500, 35% between 500 and 599, 45% between 600 and 699, and 13% between 700 and 800. The ACT scores were 3% below 21, 13% between 21 and 23, 33% between 24 and 26, 21% between 27 and 28, and 29% above 28. 59% of the current freshmen were in the top fifth of their class; 89% were in the top two fifths. 69 freshmen graduated first in their class.

Requirements: Applicants must complete either the ACT or the SAT. Candidates for admission must ordinarily be graduates of accredited secondary schools or hold the GED. Students should have completed 4 units of English, 3 each of math, science, and social studies/history, 2 of a foreign language, and 1 of fine arts. An audition, a portfolio, or an interview are required for direct admission to majors in the School of Fine Arts. AP and CLEP credits are accepted.

Procedure: Freshmen are admitted to all sessions. Entrance exams should be taken by December of the senior year. There are early decision and deferred admissions plans. Early decision applications should be filed by November 15; regular applications, by February 1 for fall entry; and November 1 for spring entry. The fall 2013 application fee was $50. Notification of early decision is sent December 15; regular decision, March 15. 692 early decision candidates were accepted for the 2013-2014 class. 629

applicants were on the 2013 waiting list; 6 were admitted. Applications are accepted online.

Transfer: 224 transfer students enrolled in 2012-2013. A limited number of transfer students will be accepted. A GPA of 2.00 or higher is necessary. 32 of 128 credits required for the bachelor's degree must be completed at Miami.

Visiting: There are regularly scheduled orientations for prospective students, Information sessions and guided tours are available throughout the year. There are guides for informal visits and visitors may sit in on classes. To schedule a visit, contact the Office of Admissions.

Financial Aid: In 2013-2014, 71% of all full-time freshmen and 66% of continuing full-time students received some form of financial aid. 42% of all full-time freshmen and 41% of continuing full-time students received need-based aid. The average freshman award was $10,647. Need-based scholarships or need-based grants averaged $7,326; need-based self-help aid (loans and jobs) averaged $3,741; non-need-based athletic scholarships averaged $19,975; and other non-need-based awards and non-need-based scholarships averaged $6,673. 38% of undergraduate students work part-time. Average annual earnings from campus work are $4320. The average financial indebtedness of the 2013 graduate was $22,579. The FAFSA is required. The priority date for freshman financial aid applications for fall entry is February 15.

International Students: There are 827 international students enrolled. The school actively recruits these students. They must take the TOEFL with a minimum score of 550 on the paper-based TOEFL (PBT) or 80 on the Internet-based version (iBT) or take the MELAB, IELTS or alternative proof of English language proficiency. They must also take the SAT or ACT. The SAT or ACT is required only for Canadian applicants, athletes, and those students who have followed a U.S. high school curriculum.

Computers: All students may access the system. There are no time limits. The fee is $276.

Graduates: From July 1, 2012 to June 30, 2013, 4121 bachelor's degrees were awarded. The most popular majors were finance (7%), accountancy (6%), and marketing (6%). 336 companies recruited on campus in 2012-2013. In an average class, 68% graduate in 4 years or less, 79% graduate in 5 years or less, and 80% graduate in 6 years or less.

Admissions Contact: Ann Larson, Director of Admissions. E-Mail: *admission@MiamiOH.edu* Web: *www.MiamiOH.edu/apply*

MOUNT VERNON NAZARENE UNIVERSITY C-3

Mount Vernon, OH 43050 **(740) 392-6868 ext. 4511 (866) 462-MVNU; (740) 393-0511**

Full-time: 522 men, 926 women	**Faculty:** 82; IIA, --$
Part-time: 96 men, 212 women	**Ph.D.s:** 62%
Graduate: 172 men, 339 women	**Student/Faculty:** 18 to 1
Year: 4-1-4, summer session	**Tuition:** $22,890
Application Deadline: May 1	**Room & Board:** $6700
Freshman Class: 1000 applied, 733 accepted, 290 enrolled	
SAT CR/M: 493/524	**ACT:** 23 **COMPETITIVE**

Mount Vernon Nazarene University, founded in 1968, is a private liberal arts college affiliated with the Church of the Nazarene. There are 6 undergraduate schools and 3 graduate schools. In addition to regional accreditation, MVNU has baccalaureate program accreditation with ACBSP, CSWE, NASM, and NCATE. The library contains 107,246 volumes, 11,439 microform items, 6,212 audio/video tapes/CDs/DVDs, and subscribes to 17,411 periodicals including electronic. Computerized library services include interlibrary loans, database searching, Internet access, and Wi-Fi capability. Special learning facilities include an art gallery, radio station, An academic support center and a nature center. The 406-acre campus is in a small town 45 miles northeast of Columbus. Including any residence halls, there are 51 buildings.

Student Life: 92% of undergraduates are from Ohio. Others are from 33 states, 5 foreign countries, and Canada. 74% are from public schools. 85% are White. 50% are Unknown Religious Affiliation. The average age of freshmen is 18; all undergraduates, 25. 24% do not continue beyond their first year; 76% remain to graduate.

Housing: 1146 students can be accommodated in college housing, which includes single-sex dorms and on-campus apartments. On-campus housing is guaranteed for all 4 years, is guaranteed for the freshman year only, is available on a first-come, and first-served basis. 80% of students live on campus; of those, 50% remain on campus on weekends. Alcohol is not permitted. All students may keep cars.

Activities: There are no fraternities or sororities. There are 55 groups on campus, including art, band, cheerleading, choir, chorale, chorus, communications, computers, drama, environmental, ethnic, honors, international, jazz band, literary magazine, musical theater, newspaper, orchestra, pep band, photography, political, professional, radio and TV, religious, social, social service, student government, symphony, and yearbook. Popular campus events include Friday Night Live, Battle of the Bands, Sonfest, Annual Luau and all Cougars Sporting Events.

Sports: There are 5 intercollegiate sports for men and 6 for women, and 11 intramural sports for men and 11 for women. Facilities include a main gym, an intramural/practice gym, a weight room, game room, a fitness/exercise facility, tennis courts, intramural, baseball, softball, soccer fields, and a baseball/softball batting facility.

Disabled Students: 95% of the campus is accessible. Facilities include wheelchair ramps, elevators, special parking, specially equipped restrooms, special class scheduling, lowered drinking fountains, lowered telephones, and special housing.

Services: Counseling and information services are available, as is tutoring in most subjects. There is a reader service for the blind, and remedial math, reading, and writing. Students in the at-risk program are required to take University Success Strategies.

Campus Safety and Security: Measures include 24-hour foot and vehicle patrol, emergency notification system, self-defense education, and security escort services. There are shuttle buses, emergency telephones, lighted pathways/sidewalks, controlled access to dorms/residences, Fire safety training with Student Leadership, and blood-borne pathogen seminars. Campus-wide sexual harassment training is required of all faculty, staff, and students, and there is a Campus Safety and Security Review Committee.

Programs of Study: MVNU confers B.A., B.S., B.S.W. and B.B.A. degrees. Associate and master's degrees are also awarded. Bachelor's degrees are awarded in BIOLOGICAL SCIENCE (biology/biological science and life science), BUSINESS (accounting, business administration and management, business data processing, finance, international business management, management information systems, management science, marketing/retailing/merchandising, and sports management), COMMUNICATIONS AND THE ARTS (art, broadcasting, communications, dramatic arts, English, graphic design, journalism, music, public relations, and Spanish), COMPUTER AND PHYSICAL SCIENCE (chemistry, Computer Engineering Technology, computer science, and mathematics), EDUCATION (art education, business education, early childhood education, English education, mathematics education, middle school education, music education, physical education, science education, social studies education, and special education), ENGINEERING AND ENVIRONMENTAL DESIGN (preengineering), HEALTH PROFESSIONS (exercise science, medical technology, nursing, premedicine, prepharmacy, and prephysical therapy), SOCIAL SCIENCE (biblical studies, criminal justice, family/consumer studies, history, ministries, missions, pastoral studies, philosophy, political science/government, prelaw, psychology, religion, religious education, religious music, social work, sociology, theological studies, and youth ministry). Biology, nursing, and education are the strongest academically. Nursing, business, and education have the largest enrollments.

Required: Students must complete 124 semester hours, at least 40 in upper-division courses, and maintain a minimum GPA of 2.0. Students must also complete the 43- to 46-hour B.A. general education core requirements and the general education and major assessment programs. Additional preparatory courses may be required (0-12 hours). Students who desire two or more majors are required to complete the assessment in each major.

Special: MVNU offers internships with local businesses and organizations, on-campus work-study programs, study abroad in 20 countries, dual majors, a general studies degree, and nondegree study. Cross-registration is available with Nazarene Universities, and the Council for Christian College and Universities program. There are 5 national honor societies, a freshman honors program, and 21 departmental honors programs.

Faculty/Classroom: 58% of faculty are male; 42% are female. 85% teach undergraduates. No introductory courses are taught by graduate students. The average class size in an introductory lecture is 20; in a laboratory is 16; and in a regular course is 16.

Admissions: 73% of the 2013-2014 applicants were accepted. The SAT scores for the 2013-2014 freshman class were: Critical Reading--34% below 500, 39% between 500 and 599, 20% between 600 and 699, and 6% between 700 and 800; Math--39% below 500, 37% between 500 and 599, and 24% between 600 and 699. The ACT scores were 26% below 21, 28% between 21 and 23, 20% between 24 and 26, 15% between 27 and 28, and 12% above 28. 32% of the current freshmen were in the top fifth of their class; 53% were in the top two fifths. 10 freshmen graduated first in their class.

Requirements: The ACT is required. Applicants should be graduates of an accredited high school or home-school program and have ACT composite and subscores of 19 or above, or comparable SAT scores. Recommended preparatory courses include 4 units in English and 4 units each in math (algebra I and II,geometry, other), social studies, science, lab science, and 3 foreign language. An essay is required. Applicants not meeting minimum academic standards may be granted conditional admission with additional course requirements. A GPA of 2.5 is required. AP and CLEP credits are accepted. Important factors in the admissions decision are recommendations by school officials, personality/intangible qualities, and leadership record.

Procedure: Freshmen are admitted fall, winter, and spring. Entrance exams should be taken in early fall. There are deferred admissions and rolling admissions plans. Applications should be filed by May 1 for fall entry; December 1 for winter entry; December 1 for spring entry; and May 15 for summer entry, along with a $25 fee. Applications are accepted online.

Transfer: 42 transfer students enrolled in 2012-2013. Transfer students must be in good standing academically and financially. Official transcripts from all colleges attended must be submitted. 30 of 124 credits required for the bachelor's degree must be completed at MVNU.

Visiting: There are regularly scheduled orientations for prospective students, MVNYou Visit Days - held throughout the year. There are guides for informal visits, visitors may sit in on classes, and stay overnight. To schedule a visit, contact the Admissions Office.

Financial Aid: In 2013-2014, 100% of all full-time freshmen and 99% of continuing full-time students received some form of financial aid. 96% of all full-time freshmen and 96% of continuing full-time students received need-based aid. The average freshman award was $19,942. Need-based scholarships or need-based grants averaged $12,919 ($29,590 maximum); need-based self-help aid (loans and jobs) averaged $7,107 ($18,054 maximum); non-need-based athletic scholarships averaged $6,701 ($14,950 maximum); and other non-need-based awards and non-need-based scholarships averaged $5,753 ($15,250 maximum). 46% of undergraduate students work part-time. Average annual earnings from campus work are $1800. The average financial indebtedness of the 2013 graduate was $25,313. The FAFSA and the college's own financial statement are required. The priority date for freshman financial aid applications for fall entry is March 15. The deadline for filing freshman financial aid applications for fall entry is August 8.

International Students: There are 7 international students enrolled. They must take the TOEFL with a minimum score of 550 on the paper-based TOEFL (PBT) or 80 on the Internet-based version (iBT) and the Comprehensive English Language Test. They must also take the SAT or ACT.

Computers: All students may access the system 24 hours, 7 days a week. There are no time limits and no fees.

Graduates: From July 1, 2012 to June 30, 2013, 673 bachelor's degrees were awarded. The most popular majors were business (59%), public administration and social services (8%), and education (7%). 18 companies recruited on campus in 2012-2013. In an average class, 46% graduate in 4 years or less, 54% graduate in 5 years or less, and 54% graduate in 6 years or less. Of the 2012 graduating class, 16% were enrolled in graduate school within 6 months of graduation, and 88% were employed.

Admissions Contact: James Smith, Director of Admissions. E-Mail: *admissions@mvnu.edu* Web: *www.mvnu.edu*

MUSKINGUM UNIVERSITY D-3

New Concord, OH 43762 **(740) 826-8137**
(800) 752-6082; (740) 826-8100

Full-time: 802 men, 771 women	**Faculty:** 99; IIB, -$
Part-time: 44 men, 132 women	**Ph.D.s:** 87%
Graduate: 146 men, 395 women	**Student/Faculty:** 14 to 1
Year: semesters, summer session	**Tuition:** $22,462
Application Deadline:	**Room & Board:** $8940

Freshman Class: 2134 applied, 1656 accepted, 438 enrolled
SAT CR/M: 491/513 **ACT:** 22 **COMPETITIVE**

Muskingum University, formerly Muskingum College, was founded in 1837 and is a private liberal arts and sciences institution affiliated with the Presbyterian Church. There is one graduate school. In addition to regional accreditation, Muskingum has baccalaureate program accreditation with NASM and NCATE. The library contains 209,220 volumes, 171,964 microform items, 3,471 audio/video tapes/CDs/DVDs, and subscribes to 14,127 periodicals including electronic. Computerized library services include interlibrary loans, database searching, and Internet access. Special learning facilities include an art gallery, radio station, TV station, greenhouse. The 245-acre campus is in a small town 9 miles west of Cambridge and 50 miles east of Columbus. Including any residence halls, there are 35 buildings.

Student Life: 86% of undergraduates are from Ohio. Others are from 28 states, and 10 foreign countries. 85% are from public schools. 87% are White. 42% are Protestant; 30% claim no religious affiliation; 16% Catholic. The average age of freshmen is 18; all undergraduates, 20. 33% do not continue beyond their first year; 55% remain to graduate.

Housing: 1200 students can be accommodated in college housing, which includes single-sex and coed dorms and on-campus apartments. In addition, there are language houses, special-interest houses, fraternity houses, and upperclassmen apartments and townhouses. On-campus housing is guaranteed for all 4 years. 87% of students live on campus; of those, 60% remain on campus on weekends. All students may keep cars.

Activities: 24% of men belong to 3 local and 2 national fraternities; 37% of women belong to 4 local and 2 national sororities. There are 90 groups on campus, including and dance team, art, band, cheerleading, choir, chorus, computers, dance, debate, drama, environmental, ethnic, forensics, gay, honors, international, jazz band, literary magazine, marching band, musical theater, newspaper, orchestra, pep band, political, professional, radio and TV, religious, social, social service, student government, symphony, and yearbook. Popular campus events include Li'l Sibs Weekend and Muskiepalooza.

Sports: There are 9 intercollegiate sports for men and 8 for women, and 8 intramural sports for men and 8 for women. Facilities include gyms, weight lifting/training rooms, an aerobics room, a baseball batting cage, a swimming pool, a walking/jogging trail, an all-weather track, football, baseball, and soccer fields, and tennis, basketball, and racquetball courts.

Disabled Students: 40% of the campus is accessible. Facilities include wheelchair ramps, elevators, special parking, specially equipped restrooms, and lowered drinking fountains.

Services: Counseling and information services are available, as is tutoring in every subject. There is a reader service for the blind. The PLUS program is available for learning-disabled and disabled students.

Campus Safety and Security: Measures include 24-hour foot and vehicle patrol, emergency notification system, and security escort services. There are emergency telephones, lighted pathways/sidewalks, and controlled access to dorms/residences.

Programs of Study: Muskingum confers B.A., and B.S. degrees. Master's degrees are also awarded. Bachelor's degrees are awarded in AGRICULTURE (conservation and regulation), BIOLOGICAL SCIENCE (biology/biological science, molecular biology, and neurosciences), BUSINESS (accounting, business administration and management, and international business management), COMMUNICATIONS AND THE ARTS (art, communications, digital communications, dramatic arts, English, French, German, journalism, music, Spanish, and speech/debate/rhetoric), COMPUTER AND PHYSICAL SCIENCE (chemistry, computer science, earth science, geology, mathematics, and physics), EDUCATION (Christian education, early childhood education, elementary education, foreign languages education, music education, physical education, reading education, science education, secondary education, and special education), ENGINEERING AND ENVIRONMENTAL DESIGN (engineering and environmental science), HEALTH PROFESSIONS (nursing), SOCIAL SCIENCE (American studies, criminal justice, economics, history, international relations, philosophy, political science/government, psychology, public affairs, religion, religious education, social science, and sociology). Sciences and education is the strongest academically. Education, business, psychology, and nursing have the largest enrollments.

Required: To graduate, students must complete a minimum of 124 credit hours, including at least 30 in a major and 40 in upper-level courses. Students must maintain a GPA of at least 2.0 and must also complete the 50 to 55 credit hours of Liberal Arts Essentials, with courses in writing, speech, math, arts and humanities, religion and ethics, science, social science, American studies, and phys ed. A senior capstone experience is required in all areas.

Special: Internships, both national and regional, work-study programs, study abroad in 13 countries, and a Washington semester are possible. Dual and student-designed majors, nondegree study, pass/fail options, and credit for life, military, or work experience are also available. There are 18 national honor societies.

Faculty/Classroom: 56% of faculty are male; 44% are female. 98% teach undergraduates, and 85% do both. No introductory courses are taught by graduate students. The average class size in an introductory lecture is 25; in a laboratory is 16; and in a regular course is 22.

Admissions: 78% of the 2013-2014 applicants were accepted. The SAT scores for the 2013-2014 freshman class were: Critical Reading--50% below 500, 43% between 500 and 599, 5% between 600 and 699, and 2% between 700 and 800; Math--45% below 500, 36% between 500 and 599, 14% between 600 and 699, and 5% between 700 and 800. The ACT scores were 40% below 21, 28% between 21 and 23, 19% between 24 and 26, 6% between 27 and 28, and 6% above 28. 39% of the current freshmen were in the top fifth of their class; 59% were in the top two fifths. 11 freshmen graduated first in their class.

Requirements: The SAT or ACT is required. Candidates for admission must have a high school diploma or its equivalent and should have 4 years of English, 3 years of college preparatory math, and 2 years each of science, social science, and foreign language. A GPA of 2.0 is required. AP and CLEP credits are accepted. Important factors in the admissions decision are advanced placement or honors courses, extracurricular activities record, and leadership record.

Procedure: Freshmen are admitted fall and spring. Entrance exams should be taken in the junior year or the fall of the senior year. There are deferred admissions and rolling admissions plans. Check with the school for current application deadlines. Applications are accepted online.

Transfer: 61 transfer students enrolled in 2012-2013. Applicants must submit an official college transcript and be in good academic standing at their previous institution. 32 of 124 credits required for the bachelor's degree must be completed at Muskingum.

Visiting: There are regularly scheduled orientations for prospective students, consisting of an admission presentation, faculty panel, student panel, and class attendance. There are guides for informal visits, visitors may sit in on classes, and stay overnight. To schedule a visit, contact the Admission Office.

Financial Aid: In 2013-2014, 99% of all full-time freshmen and 98% of continuing full-time students received some form of financial aid. 84% of all full-time freshmen and 82% of continuing full-time students received need-based aid. The average freshman award was $19,518. Need-based scholarships or need-based grants averaged $15,314 ($30,500 maximum); and need-based self-help aid (loans and jobs) averaged $4,204 ($8,500 maximum). 45% of undergraduate students work part-time. Average annual earnings from campus work are $1000. The average financial indebtedness of the 2013 graduate was $34,207. Muskingum is a member of CSS. The FAFSA is required. The priority date for freshman financial aid applications for fall entry is March 1.

International Students: There are 41 international students enrolled. The school actively recruits these students. They must take the TOEFL with a minimum score of 550 on the paper-based TOEFL (PBT) or 79 on the Internet-based version (iBT). Either the SAT or the ACT is recommended.

Computers: All students may access the system 24 hours a day. There are no time limits and no fees.

Graduates: From July 1, 2012 to June 30, 2013, 268 bachelor's degrees were awarded. The most popular majors were business (23%), education (21%), and biology (8%). 25 companies recruited on campus in 2012-2013. In an average class, 1% graduate in 3 years or less, 38% graduate in 4 years or less, 54% graduate in 5 years or less, and 55% graduate in 6 years or less. Of the 2012 graduating class, 15% were enrolled in graduate school within 6 months of graduation, and 93% were employed.

Admissions Contact: Beth DaLonzo, Senior Director of Admission and Student Financial Services. E-Mail: *adminfo@muskingum.edu* Web: *www.muskingum.edu*

NOTRE DAME COLLEGE D-1

South Euclid, OH 44121 (216) 373-5351
(800) NDC-OHIO; (216) 937-0357

Full-time: n/av	**Faculty:** n/av
Part-time: n/av	**Ph.D.s:** n/av
Graduate: n/av	**Student/Faculty:** n/av
Year: semesters, summer session	**Tuition:** $26,344
Application Deadline: August	**Room & Board:** $8598
Freshman Class: n/av	
SAT or ACT: required	**VERY COMPETITIVE**

Notre Dame College, founded in 1922, is a private liberal arts and sciences college affiliated with the Roman Catholic Church. There is one undergraduate school and one graduate school. In addition to regional accreditation, NDC has baccalaureate program accreditation with ADA and NCATE. The library contains 89,292 volumes, 14,200 microform items, 1,768 audio/video tapes/CDs/DVDs, and subscribes to 300 periodicals including electronic. Computerized library services include interlibrary loans and database searching. Special learning facilities include an art gallery, Tolerance Resource Center, Academic Support Center for Students with Learning Disabilities. The 53-acre campus is in a suburban area Off of the 271 Cedar/Brainard Exit just past Beachwood Mall and Legacy Village. It is located 13 miles east of Cleveland. Including any residence halls, there are 10 buildings.

Student Life: Students are from 20 states, 12 foreign countries, and Canada. 65% are from public schools. 65% are White; 23% African American. 55% are Catholic; 20% Baptist, and Muslim; 15% Protestant. The average age of freshmen is 18; all undergraduates, 26. 34% do not continue beyond their first year; 52% remain to graduate.

Housing: 650 students can be accommodated in college housing, which includes single-sex and coed dorms and on-campus apartments. Nonsmoking floors, quiet floors, gender specific for underclassman dorms. On-campus housing is guaranteed for all 4 years, is guaranteed for the freshman year only, and is available on a lottery system for upperclassmen. 60% of students live on campus. Alcohol is not permitted. All students may keep cars.

Activities: There are no fraternities or sororities. There are 32 groups on campus, including indoor colorguard, indoor percussions ensemble, art, band, cheerleading, choir, chorus, computers, dance, drama, ethnic, gay, honors, international, jazz band, literary magazine, marching band, marching band, newspaper, pep band, political, professional, religious, social, social service, and student government. Popular campus events include Founders Weekend, Welcome Weekend and Spring Fest Week.

Sports: There are 11 intercollegiate sports for men and 11 for women. Facilities include A 500-seat gym, a pool, and a fitness center.

Disabled Students: 75% of the campus is accessible. Facilities include wheelchair ramps, elevators, special parking, specially equipped restrooms, lowered drinking fountains, and lowered telephones.

Services: Counseling and information services are available, as is tutoring in every subject, Notre Dame offers free peer tutoring within our Dwyer Learning Center. We also have an Academic Support Center for Students with Learning Differences. There is remedial math, reading, and writing.

Campus Safety and Security: Measures include 24-hour foot and vehicle patrol, emergency notification system, self-defense education, and security escort services. There are emergency telephones, lighted pathways/sidewalks, controlled access to dorms/residences, Notre Dame offers 24/7 campus security that work hand in had with the South Euclid Police Department.

Programs of Study: NDC confers B.A., and B.S. degrees. Associate and master's degrees are also awarded. Bachelor's degrees are awarded in BIOLOGICAL SCIENCE (biology/biological science), BUSINESS (accounting, business economics, human resources, management science, and marketing/retailing/merchandising), COMMUNICATIONS AND THE ARTS (art, communications, English, graphic design, public relations, studio art, and visual and performing arts), COMPUTER AND PHYSICAL SCIENCE (chemistry, information sciences and systems, and mathematics), EDUCATION (early childhood education, elementary education, middle school education, secondary education, and special education), ENGINEERING AND ENVIRONMENTAL DESIGN (environmental science), HEALTH PROFESSIONS (nursing and physical therapy), SOCIAL SCIENCE (economics, history, ministries, political science/government, psychology, and theological studies). Business, education, and science are the strongest academically. Business administration, education, and sciences have the largest enrollments.

Required: To graduate, students must complete 128 semester hours with a minimum GPA of 2.0. Students must have successfully completed courses fulfilling in the General Education Requirements and those pertaining to their field of study. The following must be completed at NDC: 50% of major coursework, 50% of the last 32 credits at NDC. Have at least 45 upper-biennium courses. Have attended NDC for at least 1 semster and have completed a minimum of 32 semester credits at NDC.

Special: There is a freshman honors program.

Faculty/Classroom: All teach undergraduates. No introductory courses are taught by graduate students. The average class size in an introductory lecture is 16.

Requirements: The SAT or ACT is required. Applicants should be graduates of an accredited secondary school with 15 academic credits, including 4 of English, 2 of foreign language, 1 each of math, social studies, and science, plus 5 electives. The GED is accepted. An interview is recommended. A GPA of 2.5 is required. AP and CLEP credits are accepted.

Procedure: Freshmen are admitted fall and spring. There are deferred admissions and rolling admissions plans. Application deadlines are open. Notification is sent on a rolling basis. Applications are accepted online.

Transfer: Applicants must have a college GPA of at least 2.5. Perspective students must submit all college transcripts as well as high school. 32 of 128 credits required for the bachelor's degree must be completed at NDC.

Visiting: There are regularly scheduled orientations for prospective students, Students and their families will meet with an admissions counselor individually to discuss admissions, financial aid, and any other questions they may have. They also have the options of taking a tour of campus or meeting with a professor. There are guides for informal visits, visitors may sit in on classes, and stay overnight. To schedule a visit, contact The Admissions Office.

Financial Aid: In 2013-2014, 99% of all full-time freshmen received some form of financial aid. The FAFSA is required. Check with the school for current application deadlines.

International Students: The school actively recruits these students. They must take the TOEFL, or take the ELS Proficiency Test 109.

Computers: All students may access the system. There are no time limits. There is a fee.

Admissions Contact: Beth Ford, Director of Admissions/Financial Aid. E-Mail: *admissions@ndc.edu* Web: *www.notredamecollege.com*

OBERLIN COLLEGE D-2

Oberlin, OH 44074 (440) 775-8411
(800) 622-6243; (440) 775-6905

Full-time: 1310 men, 1579 women	**Faculty:** 290; IIB, +$
Part-time: 19 men, 22 women	**Ph.D.s:** 96%
Graduate: 8 men, 6 women	**Student/Faculty:** 10 to 1
Year: 4-1-4	**Tuition:** $44,905
Application Deadline: January 15	**Room & Board:** $12,120
Freshman Class: 7172 applied, 2248 accepted, 764 enrolled	
SAT CR/M/W: 700/670/700 **ACT:** 30	**MOST COMPETITIVE**

Oberlin College, founded in 1833, is a private institution offering degree programs in the liberal arts and sciences, and music. There are 2 undergraduate schools. In addition to regional accreditation, Oberlin has baccalaureate program accreditation with NASM. The 4 libraries contain 2.3 million volumes, 356,864 microform items, 104,227 audio/video tapes/CDs/DVDs, and subscribe to 30,750 periodicals including electronic. Computerized library services include interlibrary loans, database searching, and Internet access. Special learning facilities include an art gallery, radio station, an observatory, art museum, art library, arboretum, a conservatory of music, a music library, a science library, learning center specializing in foreign language education. The 440-acre campus is in a small town 35 miles southwest of Cleveland, OH. Including any residence halls, there are 68 buildings.

Student Life: 91% of undergraduates are from out of state, mostly the Middle Atlantic. Students are from 48 states, 49 foreign countries, and Canada. 65% are from public schools. 71% are White. The average age of freshmen is 18; all undergraduates, 20. 6% do not continue beyond their first year; 87% remain to graduate.

Housing: 2700 students can be accommodated in college housing, which includes single-sex and coed dorms and on-campus apartments. In addition, there are language houses, special-interest houses, co-ops. On-campus housing is guaranteed for all 4 years. All students may keep cars.

Activities: There are no fraternities or sororities. There are 200 groups on campus, including art, band, chess, choir, chorale, chorus, communications, computers, dance, debate, drama, environmental, ethnic, film, forensics, gay, honors, international, jazz band, literary magazine, marching band, musical theater, newspaper, opera, orchestra, photography, political, professional, radio and TV, religious, social, social service, student government, and symphony. Popular campus events include the Big Parade, Earth Day and Drag Ball.

Sports: There are 11 intercollegiate sports for men and 11 for women, and 10 intramural sports for men and 10 for women. Facilities include new field house; stadium; indoor 6-lane, 200-meter track; 8-lane outdoor track; 12 outdoor and 4 indoor tennis courts; cross-country course; fitness trail; swimming pool; Nautilus center; free-weight room; 22 practice/play fields; indoor space for football, soccer, and lacrosse practice.

Disabled Students: 90% of the campus is accessible. Facilities include wheelchair ramps, elevators, special parking, specially equipped restrooms, special class scheduling, lowered drinking fountains, lowered telephones, special housing. an indoor/outdoor lift.

Services: Counseling and information services are available, as is tutoring in every subject. There is a reader service for the blind, and remedial math, reading, and writing. computer-assisted services for hearing and visually impaired students.

Campus Safety and Security: Measures include 24-hour foot and vehicle patrol, emergency notification system, self-defense education, and security escort services. There are emergency telephones, lighted pathways/sidewalks, controlled access to dorms/residences, a full-time crime prevention officer, a 24-hour headquarters facility staffed by professional dispatchers, and an electronic card-access system in all dorms.

Programs of Study: Oberlin confers B.A., and B.Mus. degrees. Master's degrees are also awarded. Bachelor's degrees are awarded in AGRICULTURE (environmental studies), BIOLOGICAL SCIENCE (biochemistry, biology/biological science, and neurosciences), COMMUNICATIONS AND THE ARTS (art history, art, classics, comparative literature, creative writing, dance, dramatic arts, English, film arts, fine arts, French, German, Germanic languages and literature, music, music history and appreciation, music performance, music theory and composition, romance languages and literature, Russian, Russian languages and literature, and Spanish), COMPUTER AND PHYSICAL SCIENCE (applied mathematics, astronomy, chemistry, computer science, geology, mathematics, and physics), EDUCATION (music education), SOCIAL SCIENCE (African American studies, American studies, anthropology, archeology, East Asian studies, Eastern European studies, economics, gender studies, history, humanities, Judaic studies, Latin American studies, law, Near Eastern studies, philosophy, political science/government, psychology, religion, sociology, and women's studies). Sciences, art, and humanities are the strongest academically. English, biology, and history, politics have the largest enrollments.

Required: Students are required to complete 32 full courses, including 2 in each of the 3 academic divisions (arts/humanities, social/behavioral sciences, natural science/math), 3 courses dealing with cultural diversity, plus 3 winter term projects. In addition, they must earn a writing and quantitative proficiency certification.

Special: Internships are available through the Business Initiatives Program. Students may study abroad in 38 countries. Three-quarters of Oberlin students spend time abroad for study or service. The college offers independent and dual majors, 3-2 engineering programs with other institutions, non-degree study for special and visiting students, and a 5-year B.A.-B.Mus. double degree. Pass/no credit options are available to all students. There are 4 national honor societies, including Phi Beta Kappa, and 25 departmental honors programs.

Faculty/Classroom: 62% of faculty are male; 38% are female. All teach and do research. No introductory courses are taught by graduate students. The average class size in a laboratory is 14 and in a regular course is 20.

Admissions: 31% of the 2013-2014 applicants were accepted. The SAT scores for the 2013-2014 freshman class were: Critical Reading--1% below 500, 9% between 500 and 599, 41% between 600 and 699, and 49% between 700 and 800; Math--1% below 500, 13% between 500 and 599, 48% between 600 and 699, and 38% between 700 and 800; Writing--1% below 500, 11% between 500 and 599, 47% between 600 and 699, and 41% between 700 and 800. The ACT scores were 4% between 21 and 23, 38% between 27 and 28, and 58% above 28. 86% of the current freshmen were in the top fifth of their class; 100% were in the top two fifths.

Requirements: The SAT or ACT is required. The ACT Optional Writing test is also required. Candidates for admission should have completed 4 years each of English and math, and 3 each of science, social studies, and a foreign language. Either the SAT or ACT Plus Writing is required. International students must also submit TOEFL or IELTS exam scores. AP credits are accepted. Important factors in the admissions decision are leadership record, personality/intangible qualities, and advanced placement or honors courses.

Procedure: Freshmen are admitted fall. Entrance exams should be taken in the junior year or early in the senior year. There are early decision, early admissions, and deferred admissions plans. Early decision applications should be filed by November 15; regular applications, by January 15 for fall entry; and November 15 for spring entry, along with a $35 fee. Notification of early decision is sent December 15; regular decision, April 1. 250 early decision candidates were accepted for the 2013-2014 class. 1106 applicants were on the 2013 waiting list; 50 were admitted. Applications are accepted online.

Transfer: 34 transfer students enrolled in 2012-2013. Applicants should submit official transcripts of all college work completed, plus a list of current courses and midterm grades. An average of B or better should be presented. A high school transcript, recommendations, and standardized test scores are also required. 16 of 32 credits required for the bachelor's degree must be completed at Oberlin.

Visiting: There are regularly scheduled orientations for prospective students, campus tour, information session, class visits, interview, and an overnight stay in the dorm. There are guides for informal visits, visitors may sit in on classes, and stay overnight. To schedule a visit, contact the Campus Visit Office at (800) 622-6243.

Financial Aid: In 2013-2014, 87% of all full-time freshmen and 64% of continuing full-time students received some form of financial aid. 56% of all full-time freshmen and 78% of continuing full-time students received need-based aid. The average freshman award was $31,983. Need-based scholarships or need-based grants averaged $27,516; need-based self-help aid (loans and jobs) averaged $4,934; and other non-need-based awards and non-need-based scholarships averaged $13,169. 59% of undergraduate students work part-time. Average annual earnings from campus work are $2100. The average financial indebtedness of the 2013 graduate was $17,085. Oberlin is a member of CSS. The CSS/Profile, FAFSA, and the college's own financial statement are required. The deadline for filing freshman financial aid applications for fall entry is February 15.

International Students: There are 181 international students enrolled. The school actively recruits these students. They must take the TOEFL with a minimum score of 600 on the paper-based TOEFL (PBT) or 100 on the Internet-based version (iBT), IELTS. They must also take the SAT or ACT. International students whose native language is English must take the SAT or ACT Plus Writing.

Computers: All students may access the system. There are no time limits and no fees.

Graduates: From July 1, 2012 to June 30, 2013, 719 bachelor's degrees were awarded. The most popular majors were english (11%), politics (9%), and biology (8%). 45 companies recruited on campus in 2012-2013. In an average class, 1% graduate in 3 years or less, 70% graduate in 4 years or less, 83% graduate in 5 years or less, and 85% graduate in 6 years or less. Of the 2012 graduating class, 16% were enrolled in graduate school within 6 months of graduation, and 80% were employed.

Admissions Contact: Debra Chermonte, Vice President and Dean of Admissions and Financial Aid. E-Mail: *college.admissions@oberlin.edu* Web: *www.oberlin.edu*

OHIO DOMINICAN UNIVERSITY C-3

Columbus, OH 43219 **(614) 251-4500**
(800) 955-OHIO; (614) 252-0776

Full-time: 611 men, 780 women	**Faculty:** n/av
Part-time: 239 men, 375 women	**Ph.D.s:** 91%
Graduate: 178 men, 390 women	**Student/Faculty:** 12 to 1
Year: semesters, summer session	**Tuition:** $28,402
Application Deadline: open	**Room & Board:** $9978

Freshman Class: 2652 applied, 1310 accepted
ACT: required

COMPETITIVE+

Ohio Dominican University, founded in 1911 by the Dominican Sisters of St. Mary of the Springs, is a private liberal arts university affiliated with the Roman Catholic Church. There are 2 undergraduate schools and 1 graduate school. In addition to regional accreditation, ODU has baccalaureate program accreditation with ACBSP, CSWE, and NCATE. The library contains 161,704 volumes, 10,878 microform items, 4,422 audio/video tapes/CDs/DVDs, and subscribes to 13,282 periodicals including electronic. Computerized library services include interlibrary loans, database searching, Internet access, and Wi-Fi capability. Special learning facilities include an art gallery and radio station. The 98-acre campus is in an urban area 5 miles from downtown Columbus. Including any residence halls, there are 16 buildings.

Student Life: 96% of undergraduates are from Ohio. Others are from 16 states, 12 foreign countries, and Canada. 82% are from public schools. 67% are White; 23% African American. 37% are Catholic; 34% Protestant. The average age of freshmen is 18; all undergraduates, 24. 34% do not continue beyond their first year; 66% remain to graduate.

Housing: 620 students can be accommodated in college housing, which includes single-sex and coed dorms. In addition, there are honors houses. On-campus housing is available on a first-come and first-served basis. 73% of students commute. Alcohol is not permitted. All students may keep cars.

Activities: There are no fraternities or sororities. There are 40 groups on campus; academic, black student union, commuter, religious clubs, student government PhiAlpha club, art, association of resident students, band, cheerleading, choir, dance, drama, drill team, environmental, ethnic, honors, international, literary magazine, newspaper, panther players, pep band, political, professional, radio and TV, religious, social, social service, social woork, St. Alberts club, and student government. Popular campus events include Black History Week, International Student Week, and ODU Day in the Spring.

Sports: There are 8 intercollegiate sports for men and 8 for women, and 5 intramural sports for men and 5 for women. Facilities include an athletic center, a gym, a footlball stadium, baseball and softball field, a soccer field, outdoor basketball courts, and outdoor tennis courts.

Disabled Students: 90% of the campus is accessible. Facilities include wheelchair ramps, elevators, special parking, specially equipped restrooms, special class scheduling, and lowered drinking fountains.

Services: Counseling and information services are available, as is tutoring in most subjects. There is remedial math, reading, and writing. The Academic Center is a support unit designed to help all students meet their academic commitment and improve their learning skills. The staff offers workshops in study-related topics, and provides professional and peer tutoring.

Campus Safety and Security: Measures include 24-hour foot and vehicle patrol, emergency notification system, and security escort services. There are shuttle buses, emergency telephones, and lighted pathways/sidewalks.

Programs of Study: ODU confers B.A., B.S. and B.S.Ed. degrees. Associate and master's degrees are also awarded. Bachelor's degrees are awarded in AGRICULTURE (environmental studies), BIOLOGICAL SCIENCE (biology/biological science), BUSINESS (accounting, banking and finance, business administration and management, international business management, management information systems, and sports management), COMMUNICATIONS AND THE ARTS (art, communications, English, graphic design, and public relations), COMPUTER AND PHYSICAL SCIENCE (chemistry, computer science, and mathematics), EDUCATION (early childhood education, middle school education, and special education), HEALTH PROFESSIONS (exercise science), SOCIAL SCIENCE (criminal justice, economics, history, interdisciplinary studies, liberal arts/general studies, peace studies, philosophy, political science/government, psychology, social work, sociology, and theological studies). Business, education, and psychology have the largest enrollments.

Required: Core curriculum requirements include 9 semester hours in arts and ideas, 6 each in English and behavioral science, 6 each in philosophy and theology, 3 each in literature, math, and science, 3 or 6 in language, 3 addressing diversity, and 4 core curriculum seminars. All students beyond the freshman year must maintain a GPA of 2.0. Students must complete 120 semester credits. Individual departments set the total hours in the major.

Special: Students may cross-register with members of the Higher Education Council of Columbus Consortium, study abroad in various countries, and participate in a Washington semester. Internships are required in some majors. ODU offers dual majors and pass/fail options in some courses. Nondegree study and credit for life, military, and work experience are available. There is an accelerated degree program in business administration. There are 2 national honor societies and a freshman honors program.

Faculty/Classroom: 54% of faculty are male; 46% are female. All teach undergraduates. No introductory courses are taught by graduate students. The average class size in an introductory lecture is 20 and in a regular course is 20.

Admissions: 49% of the 2013-2014 applicants were accepted. The SAT scores for the 2013-2014 freshman class were: Critical Reading--53% below 500, 28% between 500 and 599, 14% between 600 and 699, and 5% between 700 and 800; Math--35% below 500, 42% between 500 and 599, and 23% between 600 and 699. The ACT scores were 33% below 21, 33% between 21 and 23, 22% between 24 and 26, 7% between 27 and 28, and 4% above 28. 36% of the current freshmen were in the top fifth of their class; 68% were in the top two fifths. 7 freshmen graduated first in their class.

Requirements: The ACT is required. Candidates for admission should have completed 4 units of English and 3 units each of a foreign language, math, science, and social studies. The freshman applicant is required to submit a completed application and transcripts of secondary courses and grades. An essay and an interview (in-state applicants) are required. A GPA of 2.0 is required. AP and CLEP credits are accepted.

Procedure: Freshmen are admitted to all sessions. There are deferred admissions and rolling admissions plans. Application deadlines are open. Application fee is $25. Applications are accepted online.

Transfer: 114 transfer students enrolled in 2012-2013. A completed application, an interview, and transcripts of all college work are required of transfer applicants. 32 of 124 credits required for the bachelor's degree must be completed at ODU.

Visiting: There are regularly scheduled orientations for prospective students, including an August orientation for fall entry and a January orientation for the second semester. Individual appointments can be arranged. There are guides for informal visits, visitors may sit in on classes, and stay overnight. To schedule a visit, contact the Director of Admissions.

Financial Aid: In 2013-2014, 100% of all full-time freshmen and 98% of continuing full-time students received some form of financial aid. 88% of all full-time freshmen and 87% of continuing full-time students received need-based aid. The average freshman award was $23,000. Need-based scholarships or need-based grants averaged $4,200 ($6,000 maximum); need-based self-help aid (loans and jobs) averaged $5,200 ($8,000 maximum); and other non-need-based awards and non-need-based scholarships averaged $7,000 ($13,000 maximum). 35% of undergraduate students work part-time. Average annual earnings from campus work are $1500. The FAFSA is required. Check with the school for current application deadlines.

International Students: There are 17 international students enrolled. The school actively recruits these students. They must take the TOEFL with a minimum score of 550 on the paper-based TOEFL (PBT) or 79 on the Internet-based version (iBT). They must also take the ACT.

Computers: All students may access the system. There are no time limits and no fees.

Graduates: From July 1, 2012 to June 30, 2013, 338 bachelor's degrees were awarded. The most popular majors were business (41%), early childhood education (14%), and criminal justice (5%). 15 companies recruited on campus in 2012-2013. In an average class, 1% graduate in 3 years or less, 29% graduate in 4 years or less, 40% graduate in 5 years or less, and 42% graduate in 6 years or less.

Admissions Contact: Nicole Evans, Director of Admissions. E-Mail: *admissions@ohiodominican.edu* Web: *www.ohiodominican.edu*

OHIO NORTHERN UNIVERSITY — B-2

Ada, OH 45810 (419) 772-2260
(800) 408-4668; (419) 772-2313

Full-time: 1190 men, 1055 women	**Faculty:** n/av; IIB, av$
Part-time: 40 men, 35 women	**Ph.D.s:** 82%
Graduate: 425 men, 580 women	**Student/Faculty:** n/av
Year: trimesters, summer session	**Tuition:** $34,640
Application Deadline: see profile	**Room & Board:** $10,344
Freshman Class: n/av	
SAT or ACT: required	

VERY COMPETITIVE

Ohio Northern University, founded in 1871, is a private institution affiliated with the United Methodist Church. Undergraduate programs are offered in arts and sciences, business administration, engineering, and pharmacy. The figures in the above capsule and in this profile are approximate. There are 4 undergraduate schools and 1 graduate school. In addition to regional accreditation, ONU has baccalaureate program accreditation with ABET, ACPE, NASM, and NCATE. The 2 libraries contain 250,518 volumes, 72,067 microform items, 10,815 audio/video tapes/CDs/DVDs, and subscribe to 1038 periodicals including electronic. Computerized library services include interlibrary loans and database searching. Special learning facilities include a learning resource center, art gallery, radio station, TV station, and pharmacy museum. The 285-acre campus is in a small town about 75 miles south of Toledo. Including any residence halls, there are 39 buildings.

Student Life: 86% of undergraduates are from Ohio. Others are from 42 states, 17 foreign countries, and Canada. 82% are from public schools. 95% are white. 43% are Baptist, Muslim, Lutheran, Presbyterian, United Church of Christ; 26% Catholic; 12% claim no religious affiliation. The average age of freshmen is 18; all undergraduates, 20. 18% do not continue beyond their first year; 66% remain to graduate.

Housing: 1915 students can be accommodated in college housing, which includes single-sex and coed dorms, on-campus apartments, and off-campus apartments. In addition, there are honors houses, special-interest houses, fraternity houses, and sorority houses. On-campus housing is guaranteed for all 4 years. 64% of students live on campus; of those, 70% remain on campus on weekends. All students may keep cars.

Activities: 25% of men belong to 8 national fraternities; 22% of women belong to 4 national sororities. There are 170 groups on campus, including art, band, cheerleading, chess, choir, chorale, chorus, computers, dance, debate, drama, drill team, ethnic, honors, international, jazz band, literary magazine, marching band, musical theater, newspaper, orchestra, pep band, political, professional, radio and TV, religious, social, social service, student government, symphony, and yearbook. Popular campus events include Tunes on the Tundra, International Week, and Little Sibs Weekend.

Sports: There are 11 intercollegiate sports for men and 10 for women, and 12 intramural sports for men and 11 for women. Facilities include a 6-lane pool, a wrestling room, weight rooms, indoor/outdoor tennis courts, 3 basketball courts, a football stadium, a training room, bowling lanes, a billiards room, a dance room, a fitness lab, a 200-meter indoor track, an 8-lane, 400-meter outdoor track, 3 racquetball courts, a nautilus room, and a 2 1/2-mile jogging/walking path.

Disabled Students: 95% of the campus is accessible. Facilities include wheelchair ramps, elevators, special parking, specially equipped restrooms, special class scheduling, lowered drinking fountains, and lowered telephones.

Services: Counseling and information services are available, as is tutoring in most subjects. There is a reader service for the blind and remedial math and writing.

Campus Safety and Security: Measures include 24-hour foot and vehicle patrol, self-defense education, and security escort services. There are emergency telephones and lighted pathways/sidewalks.

Programs of Study: ONU confers B.A., B.S., B.F.A., B.M., B.S.B.A., B.S.C.E., B.S.C.P.E., B.S.E.E., B.S.M.E., B.S.M.T., and B.S.Ph. degrees. Doctoral degrees are also awarded. Bachelor's degrees are awarded in AGRICULTURE (environmental studies), BIOLOGICAL SCIENCE (biochemistry, biology/biological science, and molecular biology), BUSINESS (accounting, business administration and management, business economics, international business management, management science, and sports management), COMMUNICATIONS AND THE ARTS (broadcasting, ceramic art and design, communications, creative writing, dramatic arts, English, fine arts, French, graphic design, journalism, language arts, literature, music, music business management, music performance, music theory and composition, public relations, and Spanish), COMPUTER AND PHYSICAL SCIENCE (chemistry, computer science, mathematics, physics, and statistics), EDUCATION (athletic training, early childhood education, health education, middle school education, music education, and physical education), ENGINEERING AND ENVIRONMENTAL DESIGN (civil engineering, computer engineering, electrical/electronics engineering, mechanical engineering, and technological management), HEALTH PROFESSIONS (health, medical technology, and pharmacy), SOCIAL SCIENCE (criminal justice, history, international studies, philosophy, political science/government, psychology, religion, social studies, sociology, and youth ministry). Chemistry, engineering, and pharmacy are the strongest academically. Pharmacy, engineering, and biology have the largest enrollments.

Required: To graduate, students must complete a minimum of 182 quarter hours, maintain a cumulative GPA of 2.0, and fulfill all departmental/college core requirements. Also, students must submit a formal application for graduation.

Special: Co-op programs are available in civil, electrical, computer, and mechanical engineering and technology, computer science, and math. Students may take internships in pharmacy, engineering, and business and may study abroad in 15 countries. B.A.-B.S. degrees and dual majors are available in arts/engineering, arts/pharmacy, and arts/business. The university also offers pass/fail options and work-study programs. There are 38 national honor societies, a freshman honors program, and 21 departmental honors programs.

Faculty/Classroom: 67% of faculty are male; 33% are female. 90% teach undergraduates. No introductory courses are taught by graduate students. The average class size in an introductory lecture is 29; in a laboratory, 14; and in a regular course, 25.

Requirements: The SAT or ACT is required. In addition, the preparatory program should include 4 years of English, 3 of math, and 2 each of science, social studies, art, history, and music; 2 years of foreign language are recommended. ONU requires applicants to be in the upper 50% of their class. A GPA of 2.5 is required. AP and CLEP credits are accepted. Important factors in the admissions decision are advanced placement or honors courses, leadership record, and extracurricular activities record.

Procedure: Freshmen are admitted to all sessions. Entrance exams should be taken in the spring of the junior year or the fall of the senior year. There are deferred admissions and rolling admissions plans. Check with the school for current application deadlines. Notification is sent on a rolling basis. Applications are accepted online.

Transfer: Applicants should have a minimum college GPA of 2.0 and submit official transcripts from all the schools they have attended. 45 of 182 credits required for the bachelor's degree must be completed at ONU.

Visiting: There are regularly scheduled orientations for prospective students, including a tour, lunch, and appointments in academics, admissions, and financial aid. A meeting with a coach can also be arranged. There are guides for informal visits, and visitors may sit in on classes and stay overnight. To schedule a visit, contact the Admissions Office.

Financial Aid: ONU is a member of CSS. The FAFSA and the college's own financial statement are required. Check with the school for current application deadlines.

International Students: The school actively recruits these students. They must take the TOEFL or the MELAB.

Computers: All students may access the system during building hours and 24 hours a day via modem. There are no time limits and no fees.

Admissions Contact: Deborah Miller, Director of Admissions. A campus DVD is available. E-Mail: *d-miller@onu.edu* Web: *www.onu.edu*

OHIO STATE UNIVERSITY SYSTEM

The Ohio State University System, established in 1870, is a land-grant system in Ohio. It is governed by the Ohio Board of Regents, whose chief administrator is the president. The primary goal of the system is teaching, research, and public service. The main priorities are to enhance the quality of human life by developing individual capacity for understanding, thinking, and acting; to serve as a natural resource; and to shape society for the common good. The total student enrollment is usually about 70,000 with 4558 faculty members. Altogether there are 220 baccalaureate, 132 master's, and 100 doctoral programs offered in the Ohio State University System. Profiles of the 4-year campuses are included in this section.

OHIO STATE UNIVERSITY AT LIMA — B-2

Lima, OH 45804 — **(419) 995-8396**

Full-time: 403 men, 469 women	**Faculty:** n/av; IIB, av$
Part-time: 75 men, 112 women	**Ph.D.s:** 97%
Graduate: 3 men, 15 women	**Student/Faculty:** n/av
Year: quarters, summer session	**Tuition:** $7140 ($22,860)
Application Deadline:	**Room & Board:** n/av
Freshman Class: 994 applied, 978 accepted, 394 enrolled	
SAT CR/M/W: 480/520/450 **ACT:** 22	**COMPETITIVE**

Ohio State University at Lima, founded in 1960, is a regional commuter campus in the Ohio State University system. At Lima, students may earn a bachelor's degree in education, English, and psychology as well as 1 to 3 years of credit toward any degree conferred by OSU. The student may finish the degree at the Columbus campus or transfer to another institution. In addition to regional accreditation, Ohio State Lima has baccalaureate program accreditation with AACSB, ABET, ACPE, ADA, AHEA, APTA, ASLA, CSAB, CSWE, FIDER, NAAB, NASAD, NASM, and NCATE. The library contains 81,572 volumes, 3,218 microform items, 1,111 audio/video tapes/CDs/DVDs, and subscribes to 276 periodicals including electronic. Computerized library services include interlibrary loans, database searching, Internet access, and Wi-Fi capability. Special learning facilities include a The 565-acre campus is in a suburban area 3 miles east of Lima, OH. Including any residence halls, there are 8 buildings.

Student Life: 100% of undergraduates are from Ohio. Others are from 3 states, and 1 foreign countries. 94% are from public schools. 87% are White. The average age of freshmen is 18; all undergraduates, 21. 62% remain to graduate.

Housing: All students commute. All students may keep cars.

Activities: There are no fraternities or sororities. There are 30 groups on campus, including art, band, choir, chorale, chorus, dance, drama, drill team, film, forensics, honors, international, literary magazine, musical theater, newspaper, pep band, political, professional, radio and TV, social, social service, student government, and yearbook. Popular campus events include May Week, Involvement Fair, Walking Taco Day, Blood Drives and Comic Book Day.

Sports: There are 3 intercollegiate sports for men and 3 for women, and 5 intramural sports for men and 5 for women. Facilities include Cook Hall gymnasium (The Hanger) 634 seating; Baron's baseball field, five indoor facilities and over 70 acres of outdoor parks.

Disabled Students: All of the campus is accessible. Facilities include wheelchair ramps, elevators, special parking, specially equipped restrooms, special class scheduling, lowered drinking fountains, lowered telephones, and special housing.

Services: Counseling and information services are available, as is tutoring in most subjects. There is a reader service for the blind, and remedial math, reading, and writing.

Campus Safety and Security: Measures include 24-hour foot and vehicle patrol, emergency notification system, self-defense education, and security escort services. There are emergency telephones and lighted pathways/sidewalks.

Programs of Study: Ohio State Lima confers B.A., B.S. and B.S.Ed. degrees. Associate and master's degrees are also awarded. Bachelor's degrees are awarded in BIOLOGICAL SCIENCE (biology/biological science), BUSINESS (business administration and management), COMMUNICATIONS AND THE ARTS (English), EDUCATION (education and health information management), HEALTH PROFESSIONS (dental hygiene and nursing), SOCIAL SCIENCE (family/consumer resource management, history, and psychology). Early and middle childhood education, psychology, and history have the largest enrollments.

Required: To graduate, all students must complete an average of 120 semester hours, with a minimum GPA of 2.0, and fulfill the general education curriculum requirements.

Special: Co-op programs and internships are available in some majors, and study abroad is available in some departments. Cross-registration is possible with Ohio State Main Campus and there is work-study with Ohio State. Dual and student-designed majors and nondegree study are possible, and pass/fail options are available. co-op programs, extensive study abroad in about 40 countries, work-study programs, dual and student-designed majors, a general degree, an accelerated degree, credit by exam, nondegree study, and pass/fail options. Co-Op programs, extensive study abroad in about 40 countries, work-study programs, dual and student-designed majors, a general degree, an accelerated degree, credit by exam, nondegree study, and pass/fail options. There are a freshman honors program and 4 departmental honors programs.

Faculty/Classroom: 55% of faculty are male; 45% are female. No introductory courses are taught by graduate students.

Admissions: 98% of the 2013-2014 applicants were accepted. The SAT scores for the 2013-2014 freshman class were: Critical Reading--39% below 500, 39% between 500 and 599, 18% between 600 and 699, and 4% between 700 and 800; Math--48% below 500, 26% between 500 and 599, and 26% between 600 and 699; Writing--48% below 500, 39% between 500 and 599, and 13% between 600 and 699. 8% of the current freshmen were in the top fifth of their class; 30% were in the top two fifths.

Requirements: The SAT or ACT is required. Candidates should be high school graduates with 4 years of English, 3 of math, 2 each of foreign language, science, and social studies, 1 of visual or performing arts, and 2 additional years of any of the above subjects. AP and CLEP credits are accepted.

Procedure: Freshmen are admitted fall and spring. Entrance exams should be taken in the spring of the junior year or early fall of the senior year. There is a rolling admissions plan. Application deadlines are open. Application fee is $60. Notifications are sent November 15. Applications are accepted online.

Transfer: 65 transfer students enrolled in 2012-2013. 2.0 or 45+ quarter hours; applicants with less than 45 qtr hrs considered for admission based on college and/or high school performance where the criteria vary by hours earned 30 of 120 credits required for the bachelor's degree must be completed at Ohio State Lima.

Visiting: There are regularly scheduled orientations for prospective students. There are guides for informal visits and visitors may sit in on classes. To schedule a visit, contact The Office of Admissions.

Financial Aid: In 2013-2014, 79% of all full-time freshmen and 79% of continuing full-time students received some form of financial aid. 71% of all full-time freshmen and 65% of continuing full-time students received need-based aid. The average freshman award was $7,389. Need-based scholarships or need-based grants averaged $3,757; need-based self-help aid (loans and jobs) averaged $4,396; and other non-need-based awards and non-need-based scholarships averaged $3,678. Average annual earnings from campus work are $1187. The FAFSA is required. The priority date for freshman financial aid applications for fall entry is February 15.

International Students: There are 2 international students enrolled. They must take the TOEFL with a minimum score of 527 on the paper-based TOEFL (PBT) or 71 on the Internet-based version (iBT). They must also take the SAT or ACT.

Computers: All students may access the system 24 hours, 7 days a week. There are no time limits and no fees.

Graduates: 45 companies recruited on campus in 2012-2013. In an average class, 2% graduate in 3 years or less, 19% graduate in 4 years or less, and 39% graduate in 5 years or less.

Admissions Contact: Beth Keehn, MBA, Associate Director of Enrollment Service. Web: *www.lima.osu.edu*

OHIO STATE UNIVERSITY AT MANSFIELD C-2

Mansfield, OH 44906 **419-755-4317**

Full-time: 440 men, 527 women	**Faculty:** n/av; IIB, av$
Part-time: 79 men, 109 women	**Ph.D.s:** 99%
Graduate: 2 men, 47 women	**Student/Faculty:** 19 to 1
Year: quarters, summer session	**Tuition:** $7140 ($22,860)
Application Deadline:	**Room & Board:** $6020
Freshman Class: 1309 applied, 1300 accepted, 503 enrolled	
SAT CR/M/W: 530/520/490 **ACT:** 22	**COMPETITIVE**

Ohio State University at Mansfield, founded in 1958, is a regional commuter campus of the Ohio State University system. At Mansfield, students may earn an undergraduate degree in elementary education. In addition to regional accreditation, OSU Mansfield has baccalaureate program accreditation with AACSB, ABET, ACPE, ADA, AHEA, APTA, CSAB, CSWE, FIDER, NAAB, NASM, and NCATE. The library contains 51,680 volumes, 1,674 audio/video tapes/CDs/DVDs. Computerized library services include interlibrary loans, database searching, Internet access, and Wi-Fi capability. Special learning facilities include a radio station and TV station. The 640-acre campus is in an urban area 2 miles from Mansfield, OH. Including any residence halls, there are 20 buildings.

Student Life: 100% of undergraduates are from Ohio. Others are from 4 states, and 2 foreign countries. 90% are from public schools. 85% are White. The average age of freshmen is 18; all undergraduates, 22. 70% remain to graduate.

Housing: 191 students can be accommodated in college housing, which includes coed on-campus apartments. apartments for single students. On-campus housing is guaranteed for the freshman year only, is available on a first-come, first-served basis, and is available on a lottery system for upperclassmen. 83% of students commute. All students may keep cars.

Activities: There are no fraternities or sororities. There are 50 groups on campus, including art, cheerleading, chorus, computers, dance, drama, environmental, ethnic, film, gay, international, music ensembles, musical theater, political, professional, religious, social, and student government. Popular campus events include Tuesday Afternoon Get Together, Black History Month, Indian Awarenss Weeek, Halloween Trick or Treating, May Day and Buckeye Week.

Sports: There are 12 intramural sports for men and 12 for women. Facilities include a gym and a weight room.

Disabled Students: All of the campus is accessible. Facilities include wheelchair ramps, elevators, special parking, specially equipped restrooms, special class scheduling, lowered drinking fountains, lowered telephones, special housing. Lift equipped buses in addition to partransit; adaptive recreation equipment.

Services: Counseling and information services are available, as is tutoring in most subjects. There is a reader service for the blind, and remedial math, reading, and writing.

Campus Safety and Security: Measures include 24-hour foot and vehicle patrol, emergency notification system, and security escort services. There are emergency telephones and lighted pathways/sidewalks.

Programs of Study: OSU Mansfield confers B.A., and B.S.Ed degrees. Associate and master's degrees are also awarded. Bachelor's degrees are awarded in BUSINESS (business administration and management), COMMUNICATIONS AND THE ARTS (English), EDUCATION (elementary education), HEALTH PROFESSIONS (nursing), SOCIAL SCIENCE (history and psychology). Early and middle childhood education, psychology, and English have the largest enrollments.

Required: To graduate, all students must complete 181 to 220 quarter hours, with a minimum GPA of 2.0. General education curriculum requirements must be met.

Special: OSU Mansfield offers co-op programs, study abroad, internships, a general studies degree (no major), nondegree study, pass/fail options, and work-study programs. There are 3 national honor societies, a freshman honors program, and 2 departmental honors programs.

Faculty/Classroom: 40% of faculty are male; 60% are female. No introductory courses are taught by graduate students.

Admissions: 99% of the 2013-2014 applicants were accepted. The SAT scores for the 2013-2014 freshman class were: Critical Reading--41% below 500, 49% between 500 and 599, and 10% between 600 and 699; Math--34% below 500, 38% between 500 and 599, 23% between 600 and 699, and 5% between 700 and 800; Writing--62% below 500, 28% between 500 and 599, and 10% between 600 and 699. The ACT scores were 38% below 21, 28% between 21 and 23, 16% between 24 and 26, 16% between 27 and 28, and 2% above 28. 26% of the current freshmen were in the top fifth of their class; 62% were in the top two fifths.

Requirements: The SAT or ACT is required. Candidates should be high school graduates with 4 years of English, 3 of math, 2 each of foreign language, science, and social studies, 1 of visual or performing arts, and 2 additional years of any of the above subjects. AP and CLEP credits are accepted.

Procedure: Freshmen are admitted fall and spring. Entrance exams should be taken spring of the junoir year or early fall ofthe senior year. There is a rolling admissions plan. Application deadlines are open. Application fee is $60. Notifications are sent November 15. Applications are accepted online.

Transfer: 51 transfer students enrolled in 2012-2013. 30 of 120 credits required for the bachelor's degree must be completed at OSU Mansfield.

Visiting: There are regularly scheduled orientations for prospective students. There are guides for informal visits, visitors may sit in on classes, and stay overnight. To schedule a visit, contact Pamela Leonard, Coordinator at (419) 755-4317.

Financial Aid: In 2013-2014, 76% of all full-time freshmen and 78% of continuing full-time students received some form of financial aid. 60% of all full-time freshmen and 60% of continuing full-time students received need-based aid. The average freshman award was $7,338. Need-based scholarships or need-based grants averaged $4,664; need-based self-help aid (loans and jobs) averaged $4,207; other non-need-based awards and non-need-based scholarships averaged $3,577; and $1,858 from other forms of aid. OSU Mansfield is a member of CSS. The FAFSA is required. The priority date for freshman financial aid applications for fall entry is February 15.

International Students: There are 1 international students enrolled. They must take the TOEFL with a minimum score of 527 on the paper-based TOEFL (PBT) or 71 on the Internet-based version (iBT). They must also take the SAT or ACT.

Computers: All students may access the system 24 hours, 7 days a week. There are no time limits and no fees.

Graduates: The most popular majors were early and middle childhood studies, psychology and religious studies, and English. 2 companies recruited on campus in 2012-2013. In an average class, 1% graduate in 3 years or less, 21% graduate in 4 years or less, 34% graduate in 5 years or less, and 39% graduate in 6 years or less.

Admissions Contact: Office of Admission E-Mail: *galat.12@osu.edu* Web: *http:/mansfield.osu.edu/HTML/admissions/admissions.html*

OHIO STATE UNIVERSITY AT MARION — C-3

Marion, OH 43302 (740) 725-6242; (740) 725-6258

Full-time: 20,989 men, 19,031 women | **Faculty:** n/av; IIB, av$
Part-time: 2293 men, 1888 women | **Ph.D.s:** 99%
Graduate: 6139 men, 7126 women | **Student/Faculty:** 19 to 1
Year: quarters, summer session | **Tuition:** $9850 ($22,860)
Application Deadline: | **Room & Board:** n/av
Freshman Class: 31359 applied, 48772 accepted, 7130 enrolled
SAT CR/M/W: 600/665/605 | **ACT:** 29 | **MOST COMPETITIVE**

Ohio State University at Marion, founded in 1957, is a commuter campus of the Ohio State University system. At Marion, students may earn a bachelor's degree in elementary education, English, history, business management, and psychology as well as 1 to 3 years of credit applicable to any other degree, including more than 170 academic programs, conferred by OSU, provided the program is completed at the main campus in Columbus. In addition to regional accreditation, OSU Marion has baccalaureate program accreditation with AACSB, ABET, ACPE, ADA, AHEA, APTA, CSAB, CSWE, FIDER, NAAB, NASM, and NCATE. The library contains 6.3 million volumes, 3,611 microform items, 90,951 audio/video tapes/CDs/DVDs, and subscribes to 79,751 periodicals including electronic. Computerized library services include interlibrary loans, database searching, Internet access, and Wi-Fi capability. Special learning facilities include an art gallery, planetarium, radio station, TV station, natural reconstructed prairie site, greenhouse, psychology lab, and early childhood education center. The 188-acre campus is in a rural area 45 miles north of Columbus, OH. Including any residence halls, there are 9 buildings.

Student Life: 100% of undergraduates are from Ohio. Others are from 5 states, and 1 foreign countries. 93% are from public schools. 82% are White. The average age of freshmen is 18; all undergraduates, 21. 33% do not continue beyond their first year; 67% remain to graduate.

Housing: Alcohol is not permitted. All students commute. All students may keep cars.

Activities: There are no fraternities or sororities. There are 25 groups on campus, including art, choir, chorus, dance, drama, ethnic, honors, international, jazz band, literary magazine, musical theater, newspaper, political, professional, religious, social, social service, and student government. Popular campus events include Buckeye Week, May Day and Cultural Events.

Sports: There are 2 intercollegiate sports for men, and 5 intramural sports for men. Facilities include General student center which includes gym, weightroom, aerobic room, game room and lounge.

Disabled Students: All of the campus is accessible. Facilities include wheelchair ramps, elevators, special parking, specially equipped restrooms, special class scheduling, lowered drinking fountains, and lowered telephones.

Services: Counseling and information services are available, as is tutoring in most subjects. There is a reader service for the blind, and remedial math, reading, and writing.

Campus Safety and Security: Measures include emergency notification system and security escort services. There are shuttle buses, emergency telephones, and lighted pathways/sidewalks.

Programs of Study: OSU Marion confers B.A., B.S. and B.S.Ed. degrees. Associate and master's degrees are also awarded. Bachelor's degrees are awarded in BUSINESS (business administration and management), COMMUNICATIONS AND THE ARTS (English), EDUCATION (education and elementary education), HEALTH PROFESSIONS (nursing), SOCIAL SCIENCE (history and psychology). Psychology, English, and history have the largest enrollments.

Required: To graduate, students must complete an average of 120 semester hours,with a minimum GPA of 2.0. The core curriculum consists of courses in writing skills, quantitative and logical skills, foreign language, the sciences, math, and the arts. Distribution requirements include 5 courses in arts and humanities, 4 to 5 courses in natural science, and 3 in social science.

Special: OSU Marion offers cross-registration with Ohio State University Columbus, various co-op and work-study programs, nondegree study in continuing education, and pass/fail options. There are a freshman honors program and 3 departmental honors programs.

Faculty/Classroom: 52% of faculty are male; 48% are female. No introductory courses are taught by graduate students.

Admissions: The SAT scores for the 2013-2014 freshman class were: Critical Reading--13% below 500, 32% between 500 and 599, 41% between 600 and 699, and 14% between 700 and 800; Math--2% below 500, 18% between 500 and 599, 46% between 600 and 699, and 34% between 700 and 800; Writing--9% below 500, 35% between 500 and 599, 44% between 600 and 699, and 12% between 700 and 800. The ACT scores were 6% between 21 and 23, and 94% above 28. 28% of the current freshmen were in the top fifth of their class; 70% were in the top two fifths.

Requirements: The SAT or ACT is required. In addition, OSU Marion follows an open admissions policy for in-state students. Applicants should be high school graduates with 4 units of English, 3 of math, 2 each of foreign language, history or social studies, and science, and 1 of art or music. AP and CLEP credits are accepted. Important factors in the admissions decision are advanced placement or honors courses, evidence of special talent, and extracurricular activities record.

Procedure: Freshmen are admitted fall and summer. Entrance exams should be taken by fall of the senior year in high school. There is a rolling admissions plan. Application deadlines are open. Application fee is $60. Notifications are sent November 15. Applications are accepted online.

Transfer: 2513 transfer students enrolled in 2012-2013. 30 of 120 credits required for the bachelor's degree must be completed at OSU Marion.

Visiting: There are regularly scheduled orientations for prospective students. There are guides for informal visits and visitors may sit in on classes. To schedule a visit, contact the Office of Admissions.

Financial Aid: In 2013-2014, 67% of all full-time freshmen and 70% of continuing full-time students received some form of financial aid. 70% of all full-time freshmen and 68% of continuing full-time students received need-based aid. The average freshman award was $12,183. Need-based scholarships or need-based grants averaged $9,032; need-based self-help aid (loans and jobs) averaged $5,107; non-need-based athletic scholarships averaged $22,992; other non-need-based awards and non-need-based scholarships averaged $6,027; and $5,443 from other forms of aid. The average financial indebtedness of the 2013 graduate was $22,472. The FAFSA is required. The priority date for freshman financial aid applications for fall entry is February 15.

International Students: They must take the TOEFL with a minimum score of 527 on the paper-based TOEFL (PBT) or 71 on the Internet-based version (iBT). They must also take the SAT or ACT.

Computers: All students may access the system 24/7. There are no time limits and no fees.

Graduates: From July 1, 2012 to June 30, 2013, 9548 bachelor's degrees were awarded. The most popular majors were business/marketing (17%), engineering (12%), and social sciences (11%). 61 companies recruited on campus in 2012-2013. In an average class, 2% graduate in 3 years or less, 13% graduate in 4 years or less, 29% graduate in 5 years or less, and 37% graduate in 6 years or less.

Admissions Contact: Mathieu Moreau, Director of Admissions and Financial Aid. E-Mail: *moreau.1@osu.edu* Web: *www.marion.osu.edu*

OHIO STATE UNIVERSITY AT NEWARK — C-3

Newark, OH 43055 (740) 366-9333; (740) 366-9460

Full-time: 910 men, 973 women | **Faculty:** n/av; IIB, av$
Part-time: 183 men, 197 women | **Ph.D.s:** 99%
Graduate: 4 men, 48 women | **Student/Faculty:** 24 to 1
Year: quarters, summer session | **Tuition:** $7140 ($22,860)
Application Deadline: | **Room & Board:** $10,373
Freshman Class: 2772 applied, 2733 accepted, 1092 enrolled
SAT CR/M/W: 500/510/480 | **ACT:** 22 | **COMPETITIVE**

The Ohio State University at Newark, founded in 1957, is a regional public commuter campus of the Ohio State University system. At Newark, students may earn a bachelor's degree in elementary education, psychology, history, or English as well as 1 to 3 years of credit applicable to any other degree, including 219 academic programs, conferred by OSU, provided the program is completed at the main campus in Columbus. In addition to regional accreditation, OSU Newark has baccalaureate program accreditation with AACSB, ABET, ACPE, ADA, AHEA, APTA, CSAB, CSWE, FIDER, NAAB, NASM, and NCATE. The library contains 47,000 volumes, 2,000 audio/video tapes/CDs/DVDs. Computerized library services include interlibrary loans, database searching, Internet access, and Wi-Fi capability. Special learning facilities include an art gallery. The 106-acre campus is in a suburban area 40 miles east of Columbus, OH. Including any residence halls, there are 7 buildings.

Student Life: 100% of undergraduates are from Ohio. Others are from 9 states. 92% are from public schools. 74% are White; 13% African American. The average age of freshmen is 18; all undergraduates, 21. 61% remain to graduate.

Housing: College-sponsored housing includes coed dorms and on-campus apartments. On-campus housing is available on a first-come and first-served basis. 92% of students commute. All students may keep cars.

Activities: There are no fraternities or sororities. There are 25 groups

on campus, including cheerleading, choir, chorale, chorus, drama, ethnic, gay, honors, professional, religious, social, social service, and student government. Popular campus events include Welcome Week, Spring Fling, and Community Service Programs.

Sports: There are 4 intercollegiate sports for men and 5 for women, and 8 intramural sports for men and 8 for women. Facilities include Small cardio room; small weight room; 2 full size gym floors with basketball courts; 2 grass flag football fields, 1 grass soccer field, 1 outdoor basketball court, 1 baseball field; paved biking/walking path arena, an archery range, a running track, sand volleyball courts, a cricket field, an in-line hockey rink, weight rooms, swimming pools, basketball, volleyball, and racquetball courts, field houses for tennis, volleyball, basketball, and soccer, and baseball and softball fields, five indoor facilities and over 70 acres of outdoor parks.

Disabled Students: All of the campus is accessible. Facilities include wheelchair ramps, elevators, special parking, specially equipped restrooms, special class scheduling, and lowered drinking fountains.

Services: Counseling and information services are available, as is tutoring in most subjects. There is a reader service for the blind, and remedial math and writing.

Campus Safety and Security: Measures include 24-hour foot and vehicle patrol, emergency notification system, self-defense education, and security escort services. There are emergency telephones.

Programs of Study: OSU Newark confers B.A., and B.S.Ed. degrees. Associate and master's degrees are also awarded. Bachelor's degrees are awarded in BUSINESS (business administration and management), COMMUNICATIONS AND THE ARTS (English), EDUCATION (elementary education), HEALTH PROFESSIONS (nursing), SOCIAL SCIENCE (history and psychology). Psychology, English and history have the largest enrollments.

Required: To graduate, students must complete on avereage 120 semester hours, with a minimum GPA of 2.0. The core curriculum consists of courses in writing skills, quantitative and logical skills, foreign language, the sciences, math, and the arts. Distribution requirements include 5 courses in arts and humanities, 4 to 5 courses in natural science, and 3 in social science.

Special: Co-op programs and internships are available in some majors, and study abroad is available in some departments. Cross-registration is possible with Central Ohio Technical College and HECC member schools, and there is work-study with Ohio State. B.A.-B.S. degrees are offered in elementary education, general business, English, history, and psychology. Dual and student-designed majors and nondegree study are possible, and pass/fail options are available. There are 4 national honor societies, a freshman honors program, and 4 departmental honors programs.

Faculty/Classroom: 51% of faculty are male; 49% are female. No introductory courses are taught by graduate students.

Admissions: 99% of the 2013-2014 applicants were accepted. The SAT scores for the 2013-2014 freshman class were: Critical Reading--45% below 500, 42% between 500 and 599, 10% between 600 and 699, and 3% between 700 and 800; Math--46% below 500, 35% between 500 and 599, 17% between 600 and 699, and 2% between 700 and 800; Writing--59% below 500, 30% between 500 and 599, 10% between 600 and 699, and 1% between 700 and 800. 22% of the current freshmen were in the top fifth of their class; 59% were in the top two fifths. 43 freshmen graduated first in their class.

Requirements: OSU Newark follows an open admissions policy for in-state students. Applicants should be high school graduates with 4 units of English, 3 of math, 2 each of science, foreign language, and history or social studies, and 1 of visual or performing arts. OSU Newark follows an open admissions policy for Ohio resident applicants. AP and CLEP credits are accepted.

Procedure: Freshmen are admitted fall and spring. Entrance exams should be taken before Autumn of senior year. There is a rolling admissions plan. Check with the school for current application deadlines. The application fee is $60. Notifications are sent November 15. Applications are accepted online.

Transfer: 131 transfer students enrolled in 2012-2013. A GPA of 2.0 is required. 30 of 120 credits required for the bachelor's degree must be completed at OSU Newark.

Visiting: There are regularly scheduled orientations for prospective students, Visits include a campus tour, meeting with faculty, financial aid, and student services, a placement test, and class scheduling. There are guides for informal visits, visitors may sit in on classes, and stay overnight. To schedule a visit, contact the Office of Admissions - Newark.

Financial Aid: In 2013-2014, 70% of all full-time freshmen and 71% of continuing full-time students received some form of financial aid. 70% of all full-time freshmen and 67% of continuing full-time students received need-based aid. The average freshman award was $7,777. Need-based scholarships or need-based grants averaged $3,962; need-based self-help aid (loans and jobs) averaged $4,167; and other non-need-based awards and non-need-based scholarships averaged $3,484. The FAFSA is required. The priority date for freshman financial aid applications for fall entry is February 15.

International Students: They must take the TOEFL with a minimum score of 527 on the paper-based TOEFL (PBT) or 71 on the Internet-based version (iBT) or take the MELAB.

Computers: All students may access the system 24/7. There are no time limits and no fees.

Graduates: 47 companies recruited on campus in 2012-2013. In an average class, 1% graduate in 3 years or less, 14% graduate in 4 years or less, 31% graduate in 5 years or less, and 38% graduate in 6 years or less.

Admissions Contact: Ann Donahue, Director of Enrollment. E-Mail: *donahue.5@osu.edu* Web: *www.newark.osu.edu*

OHIO UNIVERSITY D-4

Athens, OH 45701 **(740) 593-4100; (740) 593-0560**

Full-time: 8131 men, 8666 women	**Faculty:** 852
Part-time: 1297 men, 5425 women	**Ph.D.s:** 81%
Graduate: 2407 men, 2796 women	**Student/Faculty:** 18 to 1
Year: semesters, summer session	**Tuition:** $10,446 ($19,410)
Application Deadline: February 1	**Room & Board:** $10,230

Freshman Class: 20765 applied, 15149 accepted, 4244 enrolled

SAT CR/M/W: 540/540/520 **ACT:** 24 **VERY COMPETITIVE**

Ohio University, founded in 1804, is a public university offering programs in liberal and fine arts, aviation, business, communication, engineering, health science, osteopathic medicine, professional training, sciences, and teacher preparation. There are 9 undergraduate schools and 11 graduate schools. In addition to regional accreditation, Ohio has baccalaureate program accreditation with AACSB, ABET, ACEJMC, ADA, CSWE, NASAD, NASM, NCATE, and NRPA. The 3 libraries contain 3.3 million volumes. Computerized library services include interlibrary loans, database searching, Internet access, and Wi-Fi capability. Special learning facilities include an art gallery, radio station, TV station, a quarterly magazine, an accelerator lab, a hearing and speech and other wellness (physical and mental) clinics, integrated technology labs, specialized academic labs within buildings, land labs, and recreational facilities and fields. The 1774-acre campus is in a small town 75 miles southeast of Columbus. Including any residence halls, there are 214 buildings.

Student Life: 86% of undergraduates are from Ohio. Others are from 48 states, 62 foreign countries, and Canada. 82% are from public schools. 83% are White. 47% are Protestant; 34% Catholic; 14% claim no religious affiliation. The average age of freshmen is 18; all undergraduates, 20. 21% do not continue beyond their first year; 64% remain to graduate.

Housing: 8065 students can be accommodated in college housing, which includes single-sex and coed dorms. In addition, there are honors houses, special-interest houses, fraternity houses, and sorority houses. On-campus housing is guaranteed for the freshman year only and is available on a lottery system for upperclassmen. 60% of students commute. Upperclassmen may keep cars.

Activities: 8% of men belong to 19 national fraternities; 8% of women belong to 12 national sororities. There are 480 groups on campus, including art, band, cheerleading, chess, choir, chorale, chorus, computers, dance, drama, ethnic, film, forensics, gay, honors, international, jazz band, literary magazine, marching band, musical theater, newspaper, opera, orchestra, pep band, photography, political, professional, radio and TV, religious, social, social service, student government, symphony, and yearbook. Popular campus events include Performing Arts Series, Kennedy Lecture Series, and University Program Council.

Sports: There are 6 intercollegiate sports for men and 10 for women, and 28 intramural sports for men and 28 for women. Facilities include a recreation center, a football stadium with artificial turf, a convocation center (accommodating basketball, volleyball, and wrestling), an aquatic center, an ice rink, tennis courts, a golf course, an intramural gym, a running track, a fitness and aerobic center, baseball, softball, and soccer fields, a hockey field with a track, and 2 large outdoor recreation facilities (one can accommodate 4 flag football fields or 3 slow-pitch softball fields and the other can accommodate 2 full-size soccer or rugby fields).

Disabled Students: 89% of the campus is accessible. Facilities include wheelchair ramps, elevators, special parking, specially equipped restrooms, special class scheduling, lowered drinking fountains, lowered telephones, and special housing.

Services: Counseling and information services are available, as is tutoring in most subjects. There is a reader service for the blind, and remedial math, reading, and writing.

Campus Safety and Security: Measures include 24-hour foot and vehicle patrol, emergency notification system, self-defense education, and security escort services. There are shuttle buses, emergency telephones, lighted pathways/sidewalks, and controlled access to dorms/residences.

Programs of Study: Ohio confers A.B., B.A., B.B.A., B.C.J., B.F.A., B.Mus., B.S., B.S.A., B.A.H.C.S., B.S.A.M., B.S.A.T., B.S.C., B.S.C.E., B.S.C.S.,B.S.C.F.S., B.S.Ch.E., B.S.C.S.D., B.S.Ed., B.S.E.E., B.S.E.H., B.S.E.T.M, B.S.F.N.S., B.S.H., B.S.H.C.S., B.S.H.S.L.S., B.S.I.H., B.S.I.S.E., B.S.J., B.S.M.E., B.S.N., B.S.O.H.S., B.S.P.E., B.S.P.E.X., B.S.R.S., B.S.S., B.S.S.P.S., B.S.V.C., B.S.W., B.T.A.S. and

B.F.A.-DA. degrees. Associate, master's, and doctoral degrees are also awarded. Bachelor's degrees are awarded in BIOLOGICAL SCIENCE (biochemistry, biology/biological science, biotechnology, botany, cell biology, ecology, environmental biology, life science, marine biology, microbiology, molecular biology, neurosciences, nutrition, wildlife biology, and zoology), BUSINESS (accounting, banking and finance, business administration and management, business economics, business law, fashion merchandising, finance, hotel/motel and restaurant management, international business management, management information systems, management science, marketing management, recreation and leisure services, recreational facilities management, retailing, sports management, and tourism), COMMUNICATIONS AND THE ARTS (advertising, art history, art, art history and appreciation, audio technology, broadcasting, ceramic art and design, choral music, classics, communications, communications technology, creative writing, dance, design, digital communications, dramatic arts, English, film arts, French, German, graphic design, Greek, Greek (classical), illustration, journalism, language arts, Latin, linguistics, literature, media arts, modern language, multimedia, music, music history and appreciation, music performance, music theory and composition, painting, performing arts, photography, piano/organ, playwriting/screenwriting, printmaking, public relations, radio/television technology, Russian, sculpture, Spanish, speech/debate/rhetoric, studio art, telecommunications, theater design, theater management, video, visual and performing arts, and voice), COMPUTER AND PHYSICAL SCIENCE (actuarial science, applied mathematics, applied physics, astrophysics, atmospheric sciences and meteorology, chemistry, computer science, digital arts/technology, earth science, environmental geology, geology, geoscience, mathematics, physics, and statistics), EDUCATION (athletic training, business education, early childhood education, mathematics education, music education, nutrition education, physical education, science education, social studies education, and special education), ENGINEERING AND ENVIRONMENTAL DESIGN (aeronautical technology, airline piloting and navigation, aviation administration/management, bioengineering, chemical engineering, civil engineering, computer engineering, electrical/electronics engineering, energy management technology, engineering physics, engineering technology, environmental engineering, industrial engineering technology, interior design, materials engineering, and mechanical engineering), HEALTH PROFESSIONS (community health work, environmental health science, exercise science, health care administration, industrial hygiene, nursing, nursing home administration, physical therapy, predentistry, premedicine, prepharmacy, public health, speech pathology/audiology, and sports medicine), SOCIAL SCIENCE (African studies, African American studies, anthropology, Asian/American studies, Asian/Oriental studies, child care/child and family studies, classical/ancient civilization, community services, criminal justice, criminology, dietetics, Eastern European studies, economics, European studies, family and community services, family/consumer resource management, family/consumer studies, forensic studies, gender studies, geography, history, human development, international studies, Latin American studies, parks and recreation management, philosophy, political science/government, prelaw, psychology, public administration, religion, social work, sociology, and women's studies). Biological sciences, journalism, and psychology have the largest enrollments.

Required: Ohio University has two sets of graduation requirements: University-wide requirements, which all students must complete, and college-level requirements, which include the requirements for completing a major or minor. In general, you must have a minimum of 120 semester hours of credit for a bachelor's degree, with all other requirements met. All baccalaureate students (except Honors Tutorial College students) also must complete Ohio University's General Education requirements. Ohio University believes that, as an educated person, you need certain intellectual skills in order to participate effectively in society. These include the following: the ability to communicate effectively through the written word and the ability to use quantitative or symbolic reasoning, broad knowledge of the major fields of learning and a capacity for evaluation and synthesis.

Special: The university offers co-op programs in engineering and computer science, internships, study abroad, work-study programs, and an accelerated degree program for students in the Honors Tutorial College. Students may earn a B.A.- B.S. degree in most arts and sciences majors, or a general studies degree. Dual and student-designed majors, nondegree study, limited pass/fail options, and credit for life, military, or work experience are also available. There are 23 national honor societies and a freshman honors program.

Faculty/Classroom: 56% of faculty are male; 44% are female. All teach and do research. Graduate students teach 14% of introductory courses. The average class size in an introductory lecture is 46; in a laboratory is 21; and in a regular course is 31.

Admissions: 73% of the 2013-2014 applicants were accepted. The SAT scores for the 2013-2014 freshman class were: Critical Reading--30% below 500, 44% between 500 and 599, 20% between 600 and 699, and 6% between 700 and 800; Math--28% below 500, 46% between 500 and 599, 22% between 600 and 699, and 4% between 700 and 800; Writing--35% below 500, 44% between 500 and 599, 19% between 600 and 699, and 2% between 700 and 800. The ACT scores were 14% below 21, 34% between 21 and 23, 30% between 24 and 26, 11% between 27 and 28, and 11% above 28. 33% of the current freshmen were in the top fifth of their class; 68% were in the top two fifths. There were 6 National Merit finalists. 54 freshmen graduated first in their class.

Requirements: The SAT or ACT is required. Applicants should graduate with 4 units each of English and math, 3 each of science and social studies, 2 of foreign language, and 5 academic electives (which includes 1 unit of visual/performing arts). AP and CLEP credits are accepted. Important factors in the admissions decision are advanced placement or honors courses, recommendations by school officials, and extracurricular activities record.

Procedure: Freshmen are admitted fall, spring, and summer. Entrance exams should be taken in spring of the junior year or fall of the senior year. There are deferred admissions and rolling admissions plans. Applications should be filed by February 1 for fall entry; December 1 for spring entry; and February 1 for summer entry, along with a $45 fee. Notifications are sent September 15. Applications are accepted online.

Transfer: 518 transfer students enrolled in 2012-2013. Transfer students are evaluated individually, but must have a GPA of at least 2.0 and 20 semester hours of transferable college credit. Business and journalism majors usually require a GPA of 3.0 or higher. 30 of 120 credits required for the bachelor's degree must be completed at Ohio.

Visiting: There are regularly scheduled orientations for prospective students, including information sessions and campus tours conducted daily Monday through Friday and Saturday by appointment. Visitors may sit in on classes. To schedule a visit, contact the Undergraduate Admissions.

Financial Aid: In 2013-2014, 84% of all full-time freshmen and 86% of continuing full-time students received some form of financial aid. 51% of all full-time freshmen and 46% of continuing full-time students received need-based aid. The average freshman award was $13,577. Need-based scholarships or need-based grants averaged $6,380 ($13,715 maximum); need-based self-help aid (loans and jobs) averaged $3,304 ($7,285 maximum); non-need-based athletic scholarships averaged $19,607 ($38,204 maximum); and other non-need-based awards and non-need-based scholarships averaged $9,228 ($34,880 maximum). 37% of undergraduate students work part-time. Average annual earnings from campus work are $1883. The average financial indebtedness of the 2013 graduate was $26,928. The FAFSA is required. The priority date for freshman financial aid applications for fall entry is March 15.

International Students: There are 1047 international students enrolled. The school actively recruits these students. They must take the TOEFL, or IELTS.

Computers: All students may access the system. There are no time limits and no fees.

Graduates: From July 1, 2012 to June 30, 2013, 6070 bachelor's degrees were awarded. The most popular majors were nursing (30%), health administration (6%), and communication studies (5%). 376 companies recruited on campus in 2012-2013. In an average class, 44% graduate in 4 years or less, 60% graduate in 5 years or less, and 64% graduate in 6 years or less. Of the 2012 graduating class, 27% were enrolled in graduate school within 6 months of graduation, and 78% were employed.

Admissions Contact: Candace Boeninger, A.V. Provost for Enroll Mgmt & Dir of Ad. E-Mail: *admissions@ohio.edu* Web: *www.ohio.edu*

OHIO WESLEYAN UNIVERSITY C-3

Delaware, OH 43015 **(740) 368-3020**
(800) 922-8953; (740) 368-3314

Full-time: 816 men, 990 women	**Faculty:** 142; IIB, av$
Part-time: 8 men, 7 women	**Ph.D.s:** 100%
Graduate: n/av	**Student/Faculty:** 12 to 1
Year: semesters, summer session	**Tuition:** $39,150
Application Deadline: March 1	**Room & Board:** $10,310

Freshman Class: 3030 applied, 2823 accepted, 541 enrolled
SAT CR/M: 569/581 **ACT:** 26 **COMPETITIVE+**

Ohio Wesleyan University, founded in 1842, is an independent liberal arts institution affiliated with the United Methodist Church. There is one undergraduate school. In addition to regional accreditation, OWU has baccalaureate program accreditation with NASM and NCATE. The 3 libraries contain 540,937 volumes, 85,447 microform items, 9,174 audio/video tapes/CDs/DVDs, and subscribe to 66,994 periodicals including electronic. Computerized library services include interlibrary loans, database searching, Internet access, and Wi-Fi capability. Special learning facilities include an art gallery, radio station, an astronomical observatory. The 200-acre campus is in a small town 20 miles north of Columbus. Including any residence halls, there are 55 buildings.

Student Life: 53% of undergraduates are from Ohio. Others are from 41 states, 45 foreign countries, and Canada. 76% are White. The average age of freshmen is 18; all undergraduates, 20. 16% do not continue beyond their first year; 68% remain to graduate.

Housing: 1720 students can be accommodated in college housing, which includes single-sex and coed dorms and on-campus apartments. In addi-

tion, there are honors houses, language houses, special-interest houses, fraternity houses, Students are invited to submit theme proposals to run a residential house for 10 to 15 students. On-campus housing is guaranteed for all 4 years. 90% of students live on campus. All students may keep cars.

Activities: 40% of men belong to 8 national fraternities; 32% of women belong to 5 national sororities. There are 100 groups on campus, including art, cheerleading, chess, choir, chorale, chorus, communications, computers, dance, drama, ethnic, gay, honors, international, jazz band, literary magazine, musical theater, newspaper, opera, orchestra, pep band, political, professional, radio and TV, religious, social, social service, student government, symphony, and yearbook. Popular campus events include Sagan National Colloquium, Fallfest, Black Family, and Alumni Weekend Celebration.

Sports: There are 11 intercollegiate sports for men and 11 for women, and 17 intramural sports for men and 17 for women. Facilities include a gym, a football and lacrosse stadium, field hockey and soccer fields, practice fields, a weight room, indoor and outdoor tracks, handball and squash courts, an indoor pool, an exercise facility, and weight resistance equipment.

Disabled Students: 60% of the campus is accessible. Facilities include wheelchair ramps, elevators, special parking, specially equipped restrooms, special class scheduling, lowered drinking fountains, lowered telephones, and special housing.

Services: Counseling and information services are available, as is tutoring in most subjects. Students with learning disabilities may receive special help in writing and organization and in quantitive areas.

Campus Safety and Security: Measures include 24-hour foot and vehicle patrol, emergency notification system, self-defense education, and security escort services. There are emergency telephones and lighted pathways/sidewalks.

Programs of Study: OWU confers B.A., B.F.A. and B.M. degrees. Bachelor's degrees are awarded in BIOLOGICAL SCIENCE (biochemistry, biology/biological science, botany, genetics, microbiology, and zoology), BUSINESS (accounting, business economics, and international business management), COMMUNICATIONS AND THE ARTS (dramatic arts, English, fine arts, French, German, journalism, music, and Spanish), COMPUTER AND PHYSICAL SCIENCE (chemistry, computer science, earth science, geology, mathematics, and physics), EDUCATION (art education, early childhood education, elementary education, foreign languages education, middle school education, music education, physical education, and science education), ENGINEERING AND ENVIRONMENTAL DESIGN (environmental science), HEALTH PROFESSIONS (predentistry, premedicine, and preveterinary science), SOCIAL SCIENCE (African American studies, anthropology, economics, geography, history, international relations, philosophy, political science/government, prelaw, psychology, religion, social science, sociology, and women's studies). Economics and business, biological sciences, and psychology have the largest enrollments.

Required: Students are required to complete at least 34 units, including 3 units each of humanities/English, social sciences, and science, 2 units of foreign languages, and 1 unit of fine or performing arts. Each unit equals a full course and 3.75 semester hours. All students must also take 8 to 12 units in the major, maintain a minimum GPA of 2.0, and satisfy the university writing skills requirements.

Special: Cross-registration is available with members of the Great Lakes Colleges Association. Students may study abroad in 20 countries or participate in a Washington semester or a departmental internship. Students may also take dual majors in any combination, design their own majors, or pursue a 3-2 engineering degree in conjunction with 4 major universities. Nondegree study and pass/fail options are available. There are 27 national honor societies, including Phi Beta Kappa, a freshman honors program, and 22 departmental honors programs.

Faculty/Classroom: 60% of faculty are male; 40% are female. All teach undergraduates, all do research, and all teach and do research. No introductory courses are taught by graduate students. The average class size in an introductory lecture is 30; in a laboratory is 19; and in a regular course is 16.

Admissions: 93% of the 2013-2014 applicants were accepted. The SAT scores for the 2013-2014 freshman class were: Critical Reading--20% below 500, 44% between 500 and 599, 26% between 600 and 699, and 10% between 700 and 800; Math--13% below 500, 41% between 500 and 599, 36% between 600 and 699, and 10% between 700 and 800. The ACT scores were 11% below 21, 23% between 21 and 23, 26% between 24 and 26, 19% between 27 and 28, and 25% above 28. 29% of the current freshmen were in the top fifth of their class; 42% were in the top two fifths. 20 freshmen graduated first in their class.

Requirements: The SAT or ACT is required. Candidates for admission should complete a recommended 4 units of English and 3 each of math, foreign language, social studies, and science. AP credits are accepted. Important factors in the admissions decision are advanced placement or honors courses, extracurricular activities record, and recommendations by school officials.

Procedure: Freshmen are admitted fall and spring. Entrance exams should be taken in the spring of the junior year or fall of the senior year. There are early decision, early admissions, deferred admissions, and rolling admissions plans. Early decision applications should be filed by November 15; regular applications, by March 1 for fall entry. Notification of early decision is sent November 30; regular decision, on a rolling basis. 182 applicants were on the 2013 waiting list; 77 were admitted. Applications are accepted online.

Transfer: 29 transfer students enrolled in 2012-2013. Applicants should have better than a 2.5 college GPA. High school and college transcripts and an essay are required, along with a statement of good standing from the previous institution. An interview is recommended. 16 of 34 credits required for the bachelor's degree must be completed at OWU.

Visiting: There are regularly scheduled orientations for prospective students, The visit is approximately two hours and 15 minutes and includes a short presentation, a walking/riding tour of campus, and a conversation with an admission counselor. Optional class visit, meet professor or coach, and/or lunch on campus available. There are guides for informal visits, visitors may sit in on classes, and stay overnight. To schedule a visit, contact the Office of Admission.

Financial Aid: In 2013-2014, 99% of all full-time freshmen and 98% of continuing full-time students received some form of financial aid. 59% of all full-time freshmen and 63% of continuing full-time students received need-based aid. The average freshman award was $32,580. Need-based scholarships or need-based grants averaged $28,175; and need-based self-help aid (loans and jobs) averaged $5,065. 45% of undergraduate students work part-time. Average annual earnings from campus work are $2366. The average financial indebtedness of the 2013 graduate was $31,489. OWU is a member of CSS. The FAFSA is required. The priority date for freshman financial aid applications for fall entry is February 15. The deadline for filing freshman financial aid applications for fall entry is May 1.

International Students: There are 142 international students enrolled. The school actively recruits these students. They must take the TOEFL with a minimum score of 550 on the paper-based TOEFL (PBT) or 80 on the Internet-based version (iBT), IELTS. They must also take the SAT or ACT.

Computers: All students may access the system 24 hours a day. There are no time limits and no fees.

Graduates: From July 1, 2012 to June 30, 2013, 471 bachelor's degrees were awarded. The most popular majors were biological science (12%), psychology (10%), and economics management (9%). In an average class, 1% graduate in 3 years or less, 61% graduate in 4 years or less, 67% graduate in 5 years or less, and 68% graduate in 6 years or less.

Admissions Contact: Alisha Couch, Director of Admission. E-Mail: *owuadmit@owu.edu* Web: *choose.owu.edu*

OTTERBEIN COLLEGE — C-3

Westerville, OH 43081 — (614) 823-1500; (800) 488-8144; (614) 823-1200

Full-time: 830 men, 1470 women	**Faculty:** n/av; IIB, -$
Part-time: 135 men, 310 women	**Ph.D.s:** n/av
Graduate: 80 men, 325 women	**Student/Faculty:** n/av
Year: trimesters, summer session	**Tuition:** $30,050
Application Deadline: see profile	**Room & Board:** $8752
Freshman Class: n/av	
SAT or ACT: required	

COMPETITIVE

Otterbein College, founded in 1847, is an independent institution affiliated with the United Methodist Church. The college provides a solid liberal arts education combined with professional/career preparation. There are 4 graduate schools. The figures in the above capsule and in this profile are approximate. In addition to regional accreditation, Otterbein has baccalaureate program accreditation with NASM, NCATE, and NLN. The library contains 300,000 volumes. Computerized library services include interlibrary loans and database searching. Special learning facilities include a learning resource center, art gallery, planetarium, radio station, TV station, equine facility, 2 theaters, and recital hall. The 142-acre campus is in a suburban area 12 miles northeast of Columbus. Including any residence halls, there are 28 buildings.

Student Life: 91% of undergraduates are from Ohio. Others are from 29 states, 28 foreign countries, and Canada. 87% are white. 26% claim no religious affiliation; 22% Catholic. The average age of freshmen is 18; all undergraduates, 22. 27% do not continue beyond their first year; 73% remain to graduate.

Housing: 1183 students can be accommodated in college housing, which includes single-sex and coed dorms and on-campus apartments. In addition, there are honors houses, special-interest houses, fraternity houses, and sorority houses. On-campus housing is guaranteed for the freshman year only, is available on a first-come, first-served basis, and is available on a lottery system for upperclassmen. Priority is given to out-of-town students. 53% of students live on campus; of those, 55% remain on campus on weekends. Alcohol is not permitted. All students may keep cars.

Activities: 28% of men belong to 7 local and 1 national fraternity; 28%

of women belong to 6 local sororities. There are 90 groups on campus, including art, band, cheerleading, choir, chorale, chorus, communications, dance, debate, drama, drill team, equestrian, ethnic, forensics, gay, honors, international, jazz band, literary magazine, marching band, musical theater, newspaper, opera, orchestra, pep band, photography, political, professional, radio and TV, religious, social, social service, student government, symphony, and yearbook.

Sports: There are 8 intercollegiate sports for men and 8 for women, and 11 intramural sports for men and 11 for women. Facilities include a basketball and volleyball center, a football stadium, a soccer field, a weight room, tennis courts, a cross-country course, and a student recreation center.

Disabled Students: 81% of the campus is accessible. Facilities include wheelchair ramps, elevators, special parking, specially equipped restrooms, special class scheduling, lowered drinking fountains, and lowered telephones.

Services: Counseling and information services are available, as is tutoring in every subject. There is a reader service for the blind, and remedial math, reading, and writing.

Campus Safety and Security: Measures include 24-hour foot and vehicle patrol, self-defense education, and security escort services. There are emergency telephones, lighted pathways/sidewalks, controlled access to dorms/residences, and 24-hour locked dorm facilities.

Programs of Study: Otterbein confers B.A., B.S., B.F.A., B.M., B.Mus.Ed., B.S.E., and B.S.N. degrees. Master's degrees are also awarded. Bachelor's degrees are awarded in AGRICULTURE (equine science), BIOLOGICAL SCIENCE (biochemistry, life science, and molecular biology), BUSINESS (accounting and business administration and management), COMMUNICATIONS AND THE ARTS (art, broadcasting, communications, dramatic arts, English, French, journalism, music, music performance, musical theater, public relations, Spanish, speech/debate/rhetoric, and visual and performing arts), COMPUTER AND PHYSICAL SCIENCE (chemistry, computer science, mathematics, and physics), EDUCATION (athletic training, elementary education, health education, music education, and physical education), HEALTH PROFESSIONS (nursing), SOCIAL SCIENCE (economics, history, international studies, liberal arts/general studies, philosophy, political science/government, psychology, religion, and sociology). Life science, chemistry, and athletic training are the strongest academically. Business, education, and communications have the largest enrollments.

Required: All students must complete 180 quarter hours, including 50 to 100 in the major, with a minimum GPA of 2.0. The liberal arts core includes 15 hours in English composition and literature, 10 hours each in natural and social sciences, 5 hours each in religion/philosophy, fine arts, and non-Western cultures, and 3 in phys ed.

Special: Students may cross-register with members of the Higher Education Council of Columbus, study abroad in 9 countries, have an internship in most majors, or participate in a Washington semester. B.A.-B.S. degrees, 3-2 engineering degrees with Case Western Reserve and Washington Universities, credit for military experience, student-designed majors, nondegree study, and limited pass/fail options are also available. There are 9 national honor societies and a freshman honors program.

Faculty/Classroom: 52% of faculty are male; 48% are female. All teach undergraduates. No introductory courses are taught by graduate students. The average class size in an introductory lecture is 20; in a laboratory, 10; and in a regular course, 20.

Requirements: The SAT or ACT is required. Applicants should be graduates of an accredited secondary school. The recommended preparatory program includes 4 units of English, 3 to 4 units each of math, science, and social studies, 2 to 3 units of foreign language, and 1 to 2 units of performing arts. A high school GPA of 2.5 or better is recommended. Otterbein requires applicants to be in the upper 50% of their class. AP and CLEP credits are accepted. Important factors in the admissions decision are advanced placement or honors courses, evidence of special talent, and recommendations by school officials.

Procedure: Freshmen are admitted to all sessions. Entrance exams should be taken in the spring of the junior year. There are deferred admissions and rolling admissions plans. Notification is sent on a rolling basis. Applications are accepted online (no fee). Check with the school for current application deadlines and fee.

Transfer: Applicants should present a college GPA of 2.5. 60 of 180 credits required for the bachelor's degree must be completed at Otterbein.

Visiting: There are regularly scheduled orientations for prospective students, including a conference with an admissions counselor and a campus tour. There are guides for informal visits; visitors may sit in on classes and stay overnight. To schedule a visit, contact the Admissions Office.

Financial Aid: The FAFSA is required. Check with the school for current application deadlines.

International Students: The school actively recruits these students. They must take the TOEFL with a minimum score of 523 on the paper-based TOEFL (PBT) or 69 on the Internet-based version (iBT). They must also take the SAT or ACT.

Computers: All students may access the system. There are no time limits and no fees.

Admissions Contact: Dr. Cass Johnson, Director of Admissions. E-Mail: *uotterb@otterbein.edu* Web: *www.otterbein.edu*

SHAWNEE STATE UNIVERSITY C-5

Portsmouth, OH 45662 **(740) 351-2778**
(800) 959-2778; (740) 351-3111

Full-time: 1589 men, 2046 women	**Faculty:** 146; IIB, --$
Part-time: 190 men, 430 women	**Ph.D.s:** 58%
Graduate: 18 men, 68 women	**Student/Faculty:** 19 to 1
Year: semesters, summer session	**Tuition:** $7177 ($12,291)
Application Deadline:	**Room & Board:** $9368
Freshman Class: 4426 applied, 3688 accepted, 1104 enrolled	
SAT CR/M/W: 510/515/460 **ACT:** 20	**NONCOMPETITIVE**

Shawnee State University, founded in 1975, is a public institution offering programs in arts and sciences, business, engineering, health sciences, and education. There are 2 undergraduate schools and one graduate school. In addition to regional accreditation, Shawnee State has baccalaureate program accreditation with ADA, NCATE, and NLN. The library contains 160,254 volumes, 265,965 microform items, 19,825 audio/video tapes/CDs/DVDs, and subscribes to 79,003 periodicals including electronic. Computerized library services include interlibrary loans, database searching, Internet access, and Wi-Fi capability. Special learning facilities include an art gallery and planetarium. The 50-acre campus is in a small town 90 miles south of Columbus. Including any residence halls, there are 30 buildings.

Student Life: 89% of undergraduates are from Ohio. Others are from 25 states, and 17 foreign countries. 86% are White. The average age of freshmen is 19; all undergraduates, 23. 48% do not continue beyond their first year; 24% remain to graduate.

Housing: 970 students can be accommodated in college housing, which includes coed on-campus apartments. In addition, there are special-interest houses, gaming. On-campus housing is available on a first-come and first-served basis. 78% of students commute. Alcohol is not permitted. All students may keep cars.

Activities: 1% of men belong to 2 national fraternities; 1% of women belong to 1 local and 1 national sororities. There are 31 groups on campus, including academic, art, cheerleading, choir, chorus, computers, drama, ethnic, gay, honors, international, literary magazine, musical theater, newspaper, pep band, photography, political, professional, religious, social, social service, and student government. Popular campus events include Fall Fest, Spring Fest and Scare Week.

Sports: There are 5 intercollegiate sports for men and 6 for women, and 9 intramural sports for men and 9 for women. Facilities include a soccer field, an activities center with basketball and volleyball courts, and a sports center with racquetball courts, Nautilus and weight rooms, a pool, a sauna, and a whirlpool.

Disabled Students: All of the campus is accessible. Facilities include wheelchair ramps, elevators, special parking, specially equipped restrooms, lowered drinking fountains, and lowered telephones.

Services: Counseling and information services are available, as is tutoring in most subjects. There is a reader service for the blind, and remedial math, reading, and writing.

Campus Safety and Security: Measures include 24-hour foot and vehicle patrol and emergency notification system. There are emergency telephones and lighted pathways/sidewalks.

Programs of Study: Shawnee State confers B.A., B.S., B.F.A., B.I.S., B.S.E., B.S.S.S. and B.S.N. degrees. Associate and master's degrees are also awarded. Bachelor's degrees are awarded in BIOLOGICAL SCIENCE (biology/biological science), BUSINESS (business administration and management and sports management), COMMUNICATIONS AND THE ARTS (English and fine arts), COMPUTER AND PHYSICAL SCIENCE (chemistry, Computer Engineering Technology, computer game design/development, mathematics, and natural sciences), EDUCATION (athletic training, early childhood education, education, elementary education, and special education), ENGINEERING AND ENVIRONMENTAL DESIGN (engineering technology, environmental engineering technology, and plastics technology), HEALTH PROFESSIONS (nursing and premedicine), SOCIAL SCIENCE (history, humanities, interdisciplinary studies, international relations, philosophy and religion, prelaw, psychology, social science, and sociology). Nursing is the strongest academically. Psychology and business administration has the largest enrollments.

Required: To graduate, students must complete a general education program of at least 34 semester hours and a senior seminar. A total of 120 to 135 semester hours including 40 hours in the major is required along with a 2.0 GPA in all course work and in the major.

Special: Study abroad available in several countries, internships in sports studies, business, psychology, and health management, and student-designed programs are available. Cross-registration with Miami University, a Washington semester, and 2+2 programs are also possible as well as a 3+2 program in psychology and occupational therapy. There are 1 national honor societies and a freshman honors program.

Faculty/Classroom: 55% of faculty are male; 45% are female. All teach undergraduates. No introductory courses are taught by graduate students.

Admissions: 83% of the 2013-2014 applicants were accepted. The SAT scores for the 2013-2014 freshman class were: Critical Reading--44% below 500, 33% between 500 and 599, 21% between 600 and 699, and 2% between 700 and 800; Math--44% below 500, 31% between 500 and 599, 25% between 600 and 699; Writing--65% below 500, 33% between 500 and 599, 2% between 600 and 699. The ACT scores were 54% below 21, 23% between 21 and 23, 15% between 24 and 26, 5% between 27 and 28, and 3% above 28. 24% of the current freshmen were in the top fifth of their class; 52% were in the top two fifths. 12 freshmen graduated first in their class.

Requirements: Applicants must graduate from an accredited high school or have a GED. AP and CLEP credits are accepted.

Procedure: Freshmen are admitted to all sessions. Entrance exams should be taken in late spring or early summer. There is a rolling admissions plan. Application deadlines are open. Applications are accepted online.

Transfer: 230 transfer students enrolled in 2012-2013. A completed application and college and high school transcripts sent directly to SSU from previous institutions are required. 45 of 120 credits required for the bachelor's degree must be completed at Shawnee State.

Visiting: There are regularly scheduled orientations for prospective students, including fall and spring visitation days, which consist of small sessions with deans and faculty, orientation by student affairs offices, and tours with current college students. There are guides for informal visits and visitors may sit in on classes. To schedule a visit, contact the Office of Admissions.

Financial Aid: The average financial indebtedness of the 2013 graduate was $25,563. Shawnee State is a member of CSS. The FAFSA is required. Check with the school for current application deadlines.

International Students: There are 38 international students enrolled. The school actively recruits these students. They must take the TOEFL with a minimum score of 500 on the paper-based TOEFL (PBT) or 60 on the Internet-based version (iBT) or take the MELAB.

Computers: All students may access the system. There are no time limits and no fees.

Graduates: From July 1, 2012 to June 30, 2013, 419 bachelor's degrees were awarded. The most popular majors were business administration (13%), fine art (9%), and psychology (8%). In an average class, 13% graduate in 4 years or less, 22% graduate in 5 years or less, and 24% graduate in 6 years or less.

Admissions Contact: Rick Merb, Interim Director of Admissions . E-Mail: *To_SSU@shawnee.edu* Web: *www.shawnee.edu*

THE OHIO STATE UNIVERSITY C-3

Columbus, OH 43210 **(614) 292-3980; (614) 292-4818**

Full-time: 20989 men, 19031 women	**Faculty:** n/av; I, av$
Part-time: 2293 men, 1888 women	**Ph.D.s:** 99%
Graduate: 6139 men, 7126 women	**Student/Faculty:** n/av
Year: semesters, summer session	**Tuition:** $10,037 ($25,757)
Application Deadline: May 1	**Room & Board:** $9850
Freshman Class: 31359 applied, 17413 accepted, 7130 enrolled	
SAT CR/M/W: 600/660/600	**ACT:** 29 **MOST COMPETITIVE**

The Ohio State University is one of America's largest and most comprehensive academic institutions. More than 56,000 students on the Columbus campus select from 14 colleges, 175 undergraduate majors and 240 master's, doctoral and professional degree programs. More than 6,500 additional students attend Ohio State's regional campuses in Lima, Mansfield, Marion and Newark, and the Agricultural Technical Institute in Wooster. As Ohio's best and one of the nation's top-20 public universities, Ohio State is further recognized by a top-rated academic medical center and a premier cancer hospital and research center. Founded as a federal land-grant institution in 1870, the university has awarded 681,223 degrees since 1878. Its legacy extends to more than half a million living alumni. There are 16 undergraduate schools and one graduate school. In addition to regional accreditation, Ohio State, OSU has baccalaureate program accreditation with AACSB, ABET, ACPE, ADA, ASLA, CSWE, FIDER, NAAB, NASAD, and NCATE. The 21 libraries contain 7.1 million volumes, 6.2 million microform items, 526,075 audio/video tapes/CDs/DVDs, and subscribe to 26,297 periodicals including electronic. Computerized library services include interlibrary loans, database searching, Internet access, and Wi-Fi capability. Special learning facilities include an art gallery, planetarium, radio station, TV station, the Museum of Biological Diversity, the John Glenn Institute for Public Service and Public Policy, and the Cartoon Research Library. The 1777-acre campus is in an urban area 2 miles north of downtown Columbus, OH. Including any residence halls, there are 594 buildings.

Student Life: 81% of undergraduates are from Ohio. Others are from 50 states, 81 foreign countries, and Canada. 85% are from public schools. 72% are White. The average age of freshmen is 18; all undergraduates, 20. 8% do not continue beyond their first year; 92% remain to graduate.

Housing: 11149 students can be accommodated in college housing, which includes single-sex and coed dorms, on-campus apartments, off-campus apartments, and married student housing. In addition, there are honors houses, language houses, special-interest houses, Veterans house, international houses, language floors, and an alumnae scholarship house. On-campus housing is guaranteed for the freshman year only, is available on a first-come, and first-served basis. 74% of students commute. All students may keep cars.

Activities: 6% of men belong to 39 national fraternities; 6% of women belong to 26 national sororities. There are 916 groups on campus, including art, band, cheerleading, chess, choir, chorale, chorus, communications, computers, dance, debate, drama, environmental, ethnic, film, forensics, gay, honors, international, jazz band, literary magazine, marching band, musical theater, newspaper, opera, orchestra, pep band, photography, political, professional, radio and TV, religious, social, social service, student government, symphony, and yearbook. Popular campus events include OSU, African American Heritage Festival, Greek Week and May Week.

Sports: There are 17 intercollegiate sports for men and 18 for women, and 16 intramural sports for men and 16 for women. Facilities include a 100,000-seat football stadium, a 17,500-to-21,000-seat multipurpose event center, a 13,000-seat arena, an archery range, a running track, sand volleyball courts, a cricket field, an in-line hockey rink, weight rooms, swimming pools, basketball, volleyball, and racquetball courts, field houses for tennis, volleyball, basketball, and soccer, and baseball and softball fields.

Disabled Students: 96% of the campus is accessible. Facilities include wheelchair ramps, elevators, special parking, specially equipped restrooms, special class scheduling, lowered drinking fountains, lowered telephones, special housing. Campus bus system is fully lift equiped and suplimented by paratransit. Adaptive recreation faciliites are available.

Services: Counseling and information services are available, as is tutoring in most subjects. There is a reader service for the blind, and remedial math, reading, and writing.

Campus Safety and Security: Measures include 24-hour foot and vehicle patrol, emergency notification system, self-defense education, and security escort services. There are shuttle buses, emergency telephones, lighted pathways/sidewalks, , including crisis action teams, and off-campus patrols in cooperation with the city police.

Programs of Study: Ohio State, OSU confers B.A., B.S., B.A.E., B.F.A., B.Mus. and B.Mus.Ed. degrees. Associate, master's, and doctoral degrees are also awarded. Bachelor's degrees are awarded in AGRICULTURE (agricultural business management, agricultural economics, animal science, fishing and fisheries, forestry and related sciences, natural resource management, and plant science), BIOLOGICAL SCIENCE (avian sciences, biochemistry, biology/biological science, ecology, entomology, evolutionary biology, microbiology, molecular biology, neurosciences, nutrition, plant physiology, and zoology), BUSINESS (accounting, banking and finance, business administration and management, fashion merchandising, hospitality management services, human resources, insurance and risk management, international business management, logistics, management information systems, marketing and distribution, operations management, real estate, and transportation management), COMMUNICATIONS AND THE ARTS (Arabic, art, Chinese, classics, communications, dance, English, fine arts, French, German, Germanic languages and literature, Greek, Hebrew, industrial design, Italian, Japanese, jazz, journalism, Korean, linguistics, music, music history and appreciation, music performance, music theory and composition, piano/organ, Portuguese, Russian, Spanish, theatre arts, theater design, and visual design), COMPUTER AND PHYSICAL SCIENCE (actuarial science, astronomy, astrophysics, atmospheric sciences and meteorology, chemistry, computer science, earth science, geology, information sciences and systems, mathematics, and physics), EDUCATION (agricultural education, art education, athletic training, dance education, education, environmental education, health information management, middle school education, music education, physical education, and technical education), ENGINEERING AND ENVIRONMENTAL DESIGN (aeronautical engineering, architecture, biomedical engineering, chemical engineering, city/community/regional planning, civil engineering, computer engineering, construction management, electrical/electronics engineering, engineering physics, environmental engineering, environmental science, industrial engineering, interior design, landscape architecture/design, materials engineering, materials science, mechanical engineering, and welding engineering), HEALTH PROFESSIONS (biomedical science, dental hygiene, exercise science, health science, medical laboratory science, medical technology, nursing, occupational therapy, pharmaceutical science, physical therapy, radiograph medical technology, respiratory therapy, speech pathology/audiology, and speech therapy), SOCIAL SCIENCE (African American studies, anthropology, community services, criminal justice, criminology, economics, family/consumer resource management, family/consumer studies, French studies, geography, history, human development, human ecology, industrial and organizational psychology, international studies, Islamic studies, Judaic studies, medieval studies, philosophy, physical fitness/movement, political science/government, psychology, public affairs, social work, sociology, and women's studies). Biology, psychology and finance have the largest enrollments.

Required: To graduate, students must complete 120 or more semester hours, depending on major, including 30 to 40 in the major, with a minimum GPA of 2.0. The core curriculum consists of courses in writing skills, quantitative and logical skills, foreign language, the sciences, math, and the arts. Distribution requirements include 5 courses in arts and humanities, 4 to 5 courses in natural science, and 3 in social science.

Special: Students may cross-register with all central Ohio colleges. OSU offers internships, co-op programs, extensive study abroad in about 40 countries, work-study programs, dual and student-designed majors, a general degree, an accelerated degree, credit by exam, nondegree study, and pass/fail options. There are 39 national honor societies, including Phi Beta Kappa, a freshman honors program, and 15 departmental honors programs.

Faculty/Classroom: 59% of faculty are male; 41% are female. No introductory courses are taught by graduate students.

Admissions: 56% of the 2013-2014 applicants were accepted. The SAT scores for the 2013-2014 freshman class were: Critical Reading--13% below 500, 32% between 500 and 599, 41% between 600 and 699, and 14% between 700 and 800; Math--2% below 500, 18% between 500 and 599, 46% between 600 and 699, and 34% between 700 and 800; Writing--9% below 500, 35% between 500 and 599, 44% between 600 and 699, and 12% between 700 and 800. The ACT scores were 38% above 28. 90% of the current freshmen were in the top fifth of their class; 98% were in the top two fifths. There were 86 National Merit finalists. 349 freshmen graduated first in their class.

Requirements: The SAT or ACT is required. Applicants must complete high school with at least 19 academic credits, including 4 in English, 3 in math, 2 each in foreign language, science, and history or social studies, and 1 in art or music. The GED is accepted. AP and CLEP credits are accepted. Important factors in the admissions decision are advanced placement or honors courses, evidence of special talent, and extracurricular activities record.

Procedure: Freshmen are admitted fall, spring, and summer. Entrance exams should be taken by October of the senior year. There is a rolling admissions plan. Early decision applications should be filed by November 1; regular applications, by May 1 for fall entry; October 1 for spring entry; and March 1 for summer entry, along with a $60 fee. 1010 applicants were on the 2013 waiting list. Applications are accepted online.

Transfer: 2513 transfer students enrolled in 2012-2013. High school graduates with 30 hours of college credit and a minimum GPA of 2.0 are admitted for transfer. Students with fewer than 30 hours apply on a competitive basis. 30 of 120 credits required for the bachelor's degree must be completed at OSU.

Visiting: There are regularly scheduled orientations for prospective students, including campus tours, placement tests, course scheduling, and special sessions designed for parents. There are guides for informal visits, visitors may sit in on classes, and stay overnight. To schedule a visit, contact The Student Visitor Center at campusvisit@osu.edu.

Financial Aid: In 2013-2014, 81% of all full-time freshmen and 84% of continuing full-time students received some form of financial aid. 67% of all full-time freshmen and 70% of continuing full-time students received need-based aid. The average freshman award was $13,115. Need-based scholarships or need-based grants averaged $10,072; need-based self-help aid (loans and jobs) averaged $3,929; and other non-need-based awards and non-need-based scholarships averaged $3,633. The average financial indebtedness of the 2013 graduate was $26,472. Ohio State, OSU is a member of CSS. The FAFSA is required. The priority date for freshman financial aid applications for fall entry is February 15.

International Students: There are 3343 international students enrolled. The school actively recruits these students. They must take the TOEFL with a minimum score of 527 on the paper-based TOEFL (PBT) or 79 on the Internet-based version (iBT). They must also take the SAT or ACT.

Computers: All students may access the system 24/7. There are no time limits and no fees.

Graduates: From July 1, 2012 to June 30, 2013, 9548 bachelor's degrees were awarded. The most popular majors were business/marketing (18%), social sciences (12%), and engineering (10%). 1000 companies recruited on campus in 2012-2013. In an average class, 2% graduate in 3 years or less, 51% graduate in 4 years or less, 75% graduate in 5 years or less, and 80% graduate in 6 years or less.

Admissions Contact: Undergraduate Admissions and First Year Experience E-Mail: *askabuckeye@osu.edu* Web: *http:/undergrad.osu.edu/contact-us/index.html*

TIFFIN UNIVERSITY C-2

Tiffin, OH 44883 (800) 968-6446
(800) 968-6446; (419) 443-5006

Full-time: 1012 men, 1133 women	**Faculty:** 86
Part-time: 532 men, 1087 women	**Ph.D.s:** 60%
Graduate: 463 men, 727 women	**Student/Faculty:** 20 to 1
Year: semesters, summer session	**Tuition:** $20,700
Application Deadline: open	**Room & Board:** $9573
Freshman Class: n/av	

LESS COMPETITIVE

Tiffin University, established in 1888, is a private institution emphasizing degree programs in business, arts and science, and criminal justice. There are 3 undergraduate schools and 1 graduate school. In addition to regional accreditation, TU has baccalaureate program accreditation with ACBSP. The library contains 42,102 volumes, 36,239 microform items, 486 audio/video tapes/CDs/DVDs, and subscribes to 21,648 periodicals including electronic. Computerized library services include interlibrary loans, database searching, Internet access, and Wi-Fi capability. Special learning facilities include an art gallery. The 110-acre campus is in a small town 90 miles north of Columbus and 60 miles southeast of Toledo. Including any residence halls, there are 75 buildings.

Student Life: 66% of undergraduates are from Ohio. Others are from 50 states, 40 foreign countries, and Canada. 40% are race unknown; 33% White; 17% African American. The average age of freshmen is 19; all undergraduates, 27. 35% do not continue beyond their first year; 43% remain to graduate.

Housing: 1040 students can be accommodated in college housing, which includes single-sex and coed dorms, on-campus apartments, and off-campus apartments. In addition, there are honors houses, fraternity houses, sorority houses, student development housing for students who are involved in a number of activities and maintain a 3.2 GPA. On-campus housing is guaranteed for all 4 years. 75% of students commute. All students may keep cars.

Activities: 1% of men belong to 3 local and 1 national fraternities; 1% of women belong to 4 local and 2 national sororities. There are 40 groups on campus, including art, band, cheerleading, choir, chorale, chorus, communications, computers, dance, drama, drill team, ethnic, gay, honors, international, jazz band, marching band, musical theater, newspaper, pep band, political, professional, religious, social, social service, student government, and symphony. Popular campus events include Late Night Breakfast, International Dinner, and Faculty vs. Student Basketball Game.

Sports: There are 10 intercollegiate sports for men and 10 for women, and 10 intramural sports for men and 10 for women. Facilities include a recreation center for volleyball and basketball, a center for weight training and conditioning, and an athletic complex for softball, baseball, soccer, track, and cross country.

Disabled Students: 90% of the campus is accessible. Facilities include wheelchair ramps, elevators, special parking, specially equipped restrooms, special class scheduling, lowered drinking fountains, and lowered telephones.

Services: Counseling and information services are available, as is tutoring in most subjects. There is a reader service for the blind, and remedial math, reading, and writing.

Campus Safety and Security: Measures include self-defense education and security escort services. There are lighted pathways/sidewalks, controlled access to dorms/residences, and in-room safes.

Programs of Study: TU confers B.A., B.B.A., B.S. and B.C.J. degrees. Associate and master's degrees are also awarded. Bachelor's degrees are awarded in BUSINESS (accounting, banking and finance, business administration and management, marketing, and marketing/retailing/merchandising), COMMUNICATIONS AND THE ARTS (arts administration/management, communication studies, communications, English, and music business management), COMPUTER AND PHYSICAL SCIENCE (information sciences and systems and science), EDUCATION (English education and social studies education), SOCIAL SCIENCE (corrections, criminal justice, forensic studies, history, law enforcement and corrections, paralegal studies, and psychobiology). Management, criminal justice, and accounting are the strongest academically.

Required: To graduate, all students must complete 121 semester hours, including at least 48 in the major, with a GPA of 2.0 cumulatively and 2.5 in the major. The 49-semester-hour integrated core curriculum includes courses in computer systems, speech and writing, math and statistics, economics, psychology, and sociology, history, literature, philosophy, and cultural heritage. Open electives are required to complete the degree with a minimum of 15 hours at the 200-400 level.

Special: Internships are required for most majors and recommended for all students. Work-study programs, study abroad in 10 countries, and accelerated degree completion in professional studies, organizational management, and justice administration are available. There are 2 national honor societies and a freshman honors program.

Faculty/Classroom: 55% of faculty are male; 45% are female. All teach

undergraduates. No introductory courses are taught by graduate students. The average class size in an introductory lecture is 20; in a laboratory is 12; and in a regular course is 20.

Requirements: The SAT or ACT is required. Candidates should be graduates of an accredited secondary school, with 4 units of English, 3 of math, 2 each of science and social studies, and 5 of electives. The GED is accepted. An interview is recommended. AP and CLEP credits are accepted. Important factors in the admissions decision are leadership record, recommendations by school officials, and extracurricular activities record.

Procedure: Freshmen are admitted to all sessions. Entrance exams should be taken as early as possible. There is a rolling admissions plan. Application deadlines are open. The fall 2013 application fee was $20. Notification is sent on a rolling basis. Applications are accepted online.

Transfer: 340 transfer students enrolled in 2012-2013. Applicants with 12 or more hours of credit must have a minimum college GPA of 2.0. The SAT or ACT and an interview are recommended. Official transcripts from other institutions will be reviewed to determine the number of credit hours that can be transferred. 30 of 121 credits required for the bachelor's degree must be completed at Tiffin.

Visiting: There are regularly scheduled orientations for prospective students, consisting of placement testing, tours of the campus, lunch with advisers, and an appointment with an individual adviser to schedule fall classes. There are guides for informal visits, visitors may sit in on classes, and stay overnight. To schedule a visit, contact the Admissions Office.

Financial Aid: In 2013-2014, 90% of all full-time freshmen and 87% of continuing full-time students received some form of financial aid. 88% of all full-time freshmen and 86% of continuing full-time students received need-based aid. The average freshman award was $18,112. Need-based scholarships or need-based grants averaged $13,857; need-based self-help aid (loans and jobs) averaged $4,879; and non-need-based athletic scholarships averaged $12,981. 12% of undergraduate students work part-time. Average annual earnings from campus work are $800. The FAFSA is required. Check with the school for current application deadlines.

International Students: There are 94 international students enrolled. The school actively recruits these students. They must take the TOEFL with a minimum score of 500 on the paper-based TOEFL (PBT) or 61 on the Internet-based version (iBT).

Computers: All students may access the system. There are no time limits. The fee is $45.

Graduates: From July 1, 2012 to June 30, 2013, 406 bachelor's degrees were awarded. The most popular majors were business/management/accounting (42%), criminal justice/security services (34%), and psychology (10%).

Admissions Contact: Michael Herdlick, Dean of Students/Director of IR. E-Mail: *herdlickm@tiffin.edu* Web: *www.tiffin.edu*

UNION INSTITUTE & UNIVERSITY — A-5

Cincinnati, OH 45206-1925 — (513) 861-6400, (800) 486-3116; (513) 861-0779

Full-time: 185 men, 510 women	**Faculty:** n/av
Part-time: 190 men, 270 women	**Ph.D.s:** n/av
Graduate: 380 men, 885 women	**Student/Faculty:** n/av
Year: semesters, summer session	**Tuition:** $14,690
Application Deadline: see profile	**Room & Board:** n/app
Freshman Class: n/av	**SPECIAL**

The Union Institute and University, established in 1964, serves the academic needs of mature working adults seeking to earn the B.A. or B.S. degree. The figures in the above capsule and in this profile are approximate. In addition to the main Cincinnati campus, there are learning centers in Miami, Los Angeles, San Diego, and Sacramento. The Institute's Center for Distance Learning enables individuals to earn their degrees through a computer-based educational delivery system. There are 2 undergraduate schools and 2 graduate schools. The library contains 45,000 volumes 450 audio/video tapes/CDs/DVDs, and subscribes to 150 periodicals including electronic. Computerized library services include database searching. Special learning facilities include a learning resource center and art gallery. The campus is in an urban area 2 miles from downtown Cincinnati. Including any residence halls, there are 3 buildings.

Student Life: 77% of undergraduates are from Ohio. Others are from 45 states, 6 foreign countries, and Canada. 52% are white; 26% African American. The average age of freshmen is 38; all undergraduates, 38.

Housing: There are no residence halls. All students commute.

Activities: There are no fraternities or sororities.

Sports: There is no sports program at Union.

Disabled Students: All of the campus is accessible. Facilities include wheelchair ramps, elevators, special parking, specially equipped restrooms, lowered drinking fountains, lowered telephones.

Services: Scholar skills development is available.

Campus Safety and Security: There are lighted pathways/sidewalks and a security guard during operating hours.

Programs of Study: Union confers B.A. and B.S. degrees. Master's and doctoral degrees are also awarded. Bachelor's degrees are awarded in BUSINESS (business administration and management), COMMUNICATIONS AND THE ARTS (communications), COMPUTER AND PHYSICAL SCIENCE (computer science), EDUCATION (education), HEALTH PROFESSIONS (health), SOCIAL SCIENCE (criminal justice, liberal arts/general studies, psychology, public administration, social science, and social work).

Required: To graduate, students must complete a total of 128 semester credit hours. Distribution requirements include a minimum of 16 semester credits each in humanities and arts, social sciences, language and communications, and natural sciences and math, plus 64 credits in electives and the area of concentration. A senior project, including an oral presentation and thesis, is required.

Special: Programs are designed to meet individual learning needs, with tutorial-based courses, often one-on-one. Scheduling is flexible, and there are part-time enrollment options. Dual majors and student-designed majors are offered.

Faculty/Classroom: No introductory courses are taught by graduate students.

Requirements: Applicants must show evidence of ability to do college-level work, to be highly motivated, and to have the capacity for self-directed learning. All applicants should present 2 letters of recommendation, a structured personal essay, and transcripts of any previous college work. An interview is required. AP and CLEP credits are accepted. Important factors in the admissions decision are evidence of special talent, personality/intangible qualities, and leadership record.

Procedure: Freshmen are admitted to all sessions. There are deferred admissions and rolling admissions plans. Check with the school for current application deadlines and fee. Applications are accepted online.

Transfer: Grades of C or better from a regionally accredited institution may be transferable. 30 of 120 credits required for the bachelor's degree must be completed at Union.

Visiting: There are guides for informal visits and visitors may sit in on classes. To schedule a visit, contact the Admissions Office.

Financial Aid: The FAFSA and the college's own financial statement are required. Check with the school for current application deadlines.

Computers: All students may access the system. There are no time limits and no fees. It is strongly recommended that all students have a personal computer.

Admissions Contact: Admissions Office. E-Mail: *cinti.admissions@myunion.edu* Web: *www.myunion.edu*

UNIVERSITY OF AKRON — D-2

Akron, OH 44325 — (330) 972-7100, (800) 655-4884; (330) 972-7022

Full-time: 8413 men, 7456 women	**Faculty:** 718; I, --$
Part-time: 2334 men, 2378 women	**Ph.D.s:** 81%
Graduate: 1948 men, 2512 women	**Student/Faculty:** 21 to 1
Year: semesters, summer session	**Tuition:** $10,054 ($18,418)
Application Deadline: August 11	**Room & Board:** $10,382
Freshman Class: 10575 applied, 10204 accepted, 3812 enrolled	
SAT CR/M: 520/540 **ACT:** 21	**COMPETITIVE**

The University of Akron is the public research university for northern Ohio. Home to the nation's largest academic program for polymer science and polymer engineering, The University of Akron also earned national recognition in several other undergraduate and graduate degree programs. Serving 26,000 students, the university offers approximately 300 associate, bachelor's, master's, doctoral, and law degree programs and 100 certificate programs at sites in Summit, Wayne, Holmes, Medina and Cuyahoga counties. There are 7 undergraduate schools and 8 graduate schools. In addition to regional accreditation, UA has baccalaureate program accreditation with AACSB, ABET, ADA, CSWE, NASAD, NASM, and NCATE. The 3 libraries contain 2.3 million volumes, 1.7 million microform items, and 45,516 audio/video tapes/CDs/DVDs, and subscribe to 560,388 periodicals including electronic. Computerized library services include interlibrary loans, database searching, Internet access, and Wi-Fi capability. Special learning facilities include an art gallery, radio station, TV station, a nursing center, speech and hearing center, dance institute, educational media lab, and synchro hours learning classrooms. The 223-acre campus is in an urban area in downtown Akron, 40 miles south of Cleveland. Including any residence halls, there are 89 buildings.

Student Life: 95% of undergraduates are from Ohio. Others are from 50 states, 78 foreign countries, and Canada. 72% are White; 12% African American. The average age of freshmen is 19; all undergraduates, 23. 34% do not continue beyond their first year; 41% remain to graduate.

Housing: 3345 students can be accommodated in college housing, which includes single-sex and coed dorms and on-campus apartments. In addition, there are honors houses, special-interest houses, fraternity houses, sorority houses, private apartment-type halls and private residence halls. On-campus housing is available on a first-come and first-served basis. Priority is given to out-of-town students. 86% of students commute. Alcohol is not permitted. All students may keep cars.

Activities: 4% of men belong to 1 local and 14 national fraternities; 4% of women belong to 9 national sororities. There are 250 groups on campus, including art, band, cheerleading, chess, choir, chorale, chorus, computers, dance, drama, ethnic, gay, honors, international, jazz band, marching band, musical theater, newspaper, opera, orchestra, pep band, photography, political, professional, radio and TV, religious, social, social service, student government, and symphony. Popular campus events include Celebrating Akron Traditions and Zips Fest.

Sports: There are 8 intercollegiate sports for men and 10 for women, and 12 intramural sports for men and 12 for women. Facilities include a recreation and wellness center with features that include a 56-foot rock climbing wall and aerobics/dance studio, a natatorium with an Olympic-sized pool, and the athletic fieldhouse and indoor varsity golf practice facility, which includes a 120-yard football field and a 6-lane, 300 meter track. Facilities include a 5500-seat basketball/volleyball arena, a 30,000-seat on-campus weight room and athletic training room, an outdoor 100-yard astro play practice field, an 8-lane outdoor track, an outdoor soccer field, and a baseball field.

Disabled Students: 90% of the campus is accessible. Facilities include wheelchair ramps, elevators, special parking, specially equipped restrooms, special class scheduling, lowered drinking fountains, lowered telephones, special housing. city/campus bus service, residence hall accommodations, and priority registration for disabled students.

Services: Counseling and information services are available, as is tutoring in most subjects. There is a reader service for the blind, and remedial math, reading, and writing. TDDs are available.

Campus Safety and Security: Measures include 24-hour foot and vehicle patrol, emergency notification system, self-defense education, and security escort services. There are shuttle buses, emergency telephones, lighted pathways/sidewalks, controlled access to dorms/residences, in-room safes, security cameras.

Programs of Study: UA confers B.A., B.S., B.F.A., B.E., B.A.S.W., B.B.A., B.M., B.S.A., B.S.A.T., B.S.C.S., B.S.E., B.S.N. and B.S.T. degrees. Associate, master's, and doctoral degrees are also awarded. Bachelor's degrees are awarded in BIOLOGICAL SCIENCE (biology/biological science), BUSINESS (accounting, banking and finance, business administration and management, business communications, fashion merchandising, international business management, labor studies, management science, and marketing/retailing/merchandising), COMMUNICATIONS AND THE ARTS (art, classics, dance, English, French, media arts, music, music history and appreciation, music performance, music theory and composition, musical theater, public relations, Spanish, studio art, and theater management), COMPUTER AND PHYSICAL SCIENCE (applied mathematics, chemistry, computer science, computer security and information assurance, environmental geology, geology, geophysics and seismology, mathematics, natural sciences, physics, and statistics), EDUCATION (art education, athletic training, early childhood education, education, home economics education, middle school education, music education, physical education, special education, and technical education), ENGINEERING AND ENVIRONMENTAL DESIGN (automotive technology, biomedical engineering, chemical engineering, civil engineering, computer engineering, construction technology, electrical/electronics engineering, electrical/electronics engineering technology, emergency/disaster science, engineering, geological engineering, interior design, mechanical engineering, mechanical engineering technology, and survey and mapping technology), HEALTH PROFESSIONS (exercise science, nursing, physical therapy, respiratory therapy, and speech pathology/audiology), SOCIAL SCIENCE (anthropology, criminal justice, criminology, dietetics, economics, family/consumer studies, family/juvenile justice, geography, history, interdisciplinary studies, philosophy, political science/government, psychology, social science, social work, and sociology). Engineering, nursing, and business are the strongest academically. Business, education, and engineering have the largest enrollments.

Required: To graduate, all students must complete at least 128 credits, with a varying number of hours in the major, and maintain a GPA of 2.0. Specific course requirements include English composition, oral communications, Western cultural traditions, math, natural science, social science, humanities, speech, cultural diversity, and phys ed.

Special: UA offers co-op programs with local and out-of-state employers, study abroad in 22 countries, internships and work-study opportunities with community employers, a 6-year accelerated B.S.-M.D. program, B.A.-B.S. degrees in 10 majors, credit for military experience, nondegree study, and pass/fail options. There are 26 national honor societies, a freshman honors program, and 46 departmental honors programs.

Faculty/Classroom: 51% of faculty are male; 49% are female. 95% teach undergraduates. Graduate students teach 8% of introductory courses. The average class size in an introductory lecture is 26; in a laboratory is 24; and in a regular course is 26.

Admissions: 96% of the 2013-2014 applicants were accepted. The SAT scores for the 2013-2014 freshman class were: Critical Reading--38% below 500, 39% between 500 and 599, 20% between 600 and 699, and 3% between 700 and 800; Math--34% below 500, 36% between 500 and 599, 25% between 600 and 699, and 5% between 700 and 800. The ACT scores were 41% below 21, 24% between 21 and 23, 17% between 24 and 26, 8% between 27 and 28, and 10% above 28. 28% of the current freshmen were in the top fifth of their class; 51% were in the top two fifths. There were 2 National Merit finalists. 35 freshmen graduated first in their class.

Requirements: The SAT or ACT is required. Admission to the University of Akron is competitive. Students who demonstrate outstanding college preparation through completion of a college prep curriculum may be admitted directly to a specific academic program. Criteria considered include high school GPA, test scores, class rank, and some majors/programs additional information is reviewed, such as activities, leadership, recommendations, essays, portfolios, and auditions. AP and CLEP credits are accepted. Important factors in the admissions decision are advanced placement or honors courses, leadership record, and evidence of special talent.

Procedure: Freshmen are admitted to all sessions. Entrance exams should be taken received by November 1 for scholarship consideration. There are deferred admissions and rolling admissions plans. Applications should be filed by August 11 for fall entry, along with a $45 fee. Notification is sent on a rolling basis. Applications are accepted online.

Transfer: 1699 transfer students enrolled in 2012-2013. Applicants should present a minimum college GPA of 2.0. There are other requirements for direct admission to specific academic programs. 32 of 128 credits required for the bachelor's degree must be completed at Akron.

Visiting: There are regularly scheduled orientations for prospective students, including small groups for information on financial aid, student organizations, campus tours, and meetings with college faculty. There are guides for informal visits, visitors may sit in on classes, and stay overnight. To schedule a visit, contact the Office of Undergraduate Admissions.

Financial Aid: In 2013-2014, 76% of all full-time freshmen and 72% of continuing full-time students received some form of financial aid. 63% of all full-time freshmen and 61% of continuing full-time students received need-based aid. The average freshman award was $7,429. Need-based scholarships or need-based grants averaged $4,557; need-based self-help aid (loans and jobs) averaged $3,124; non-need-based athletic scholarships averaged $10,585; and other non-need-based awards and non-need-based scholarships averaged $4,521. 11% of undergraduate students work part-time. Average annual earnings from campus work are $4800. The average financial indebtedness of the 2013 graduate was $18,515. The FAFSA is required. The priority date for freshman financial aid applications for fall entry is February 1. The deadline for filing freshman financial aid applications for fall entry is June 30.

International Students: There are 386 international students enrolled. The school actively recruits these students. They must take the TOEFL with a minimum score of 550 on the paper-based TOEFL (PBT) or 71 on the Internet-based version (iBT) or take the MELAB, the International English Language Testing System (IELTS). They must also take the SAT or ACT. The English proficiency tests are in lieu of the SAT or ACT unless they are interested in scholarships and the scholarships requires it.

Computers: All students may access the system from 7 a.m. to 1 a.m. There are no time limits and no fees.

Graduates: From July 1, 2012 to June 30, 2013, 2967 bachelor's degrees were awarded. The most popular majors were nursing (8%), accounting (5%), and psychology (4%). 300 companies recruited on campus in 2012-2013. In an average class, 15% graduate in 4 years or less, 34% graduate in 5 years or less, and 41% graduate in 6 years or less. Of the 2012 graduating class, 20% were enrolled in graduate school within 6 months of graduation, and 81% were employed.

Admissions Contact: Diane Raybuck, Director of Admissions. E-Mail: *admissions@uakron.edu* Web: *www.uakron.edu*

UNIVERSITY OF CINCINNATI — A-5

Cincinnati, OH 45221-0127 — **(513) 556-1100; (513) 556-1105**

Full-time: 10160 men, 9211 women	**Faculty:** 1201; I, -$
Part-time: 1134 men, 2388 women	**Ph.D.s:** 80%
Graduate: 6041 men, 4395 women	**Student/Faculty:** 17 to 1
Year: quarters, summer session	**Tuition:** $10,919 ($25,442)
Application Deadline: July 31	**Room & Board:** $10,280

Freshman Class: 17020 applied, 11020 accepted, 4268 enrolled

SAT CR/M/W: 560/580/535 **ACT:** 24 **VERY COMPETITIVE**

The University of Cincinnati, founded in 1819, is a state-supported institution offering undergraduate programs in art and architecture, business, engineering, health science, liberal arts and sciences, music, and technical training. There are 8 undergraduate schools and 12 graduate schools. In addition to regional accreditation, UC has baccalaureate program accreditation with AACSB and NCATE. Computerized library services include interlibrary loans, database searching, and Internet access. Special learning facilities include a learning resource center, art gallery, and radio station. The 270-acre campus is in an urban area downtown Cincinnati. Including any residence halls, there are 90 buildings.

Student Life: 86% of undergraduates are from Ohio. Others are from 50

states, 125 foreign countries, and Canada. 73% are white. The average age of freshmen is 18; all undergraduates, 24. 15% do not continue beyond their first year.

Housing: 3970 students can be accommodated in college housing, which includes coed dorms and on-campus apartments. In addition, there are honors houses. On-campus housing is guaranteed for the freshman year only. Priority is given to out-of-town students. 80% of students commute. Alcohol is not permitted. All students may keep cars.

Activities: 11% of men belong to 24 local fraternities; 10% of women belong to 11 local sororities. There are 31 groups on campus, including art, band, cheerleading, chess, choir, chorale, chorus, computers, dance, drama, ethnic, gay, honors, international, jazz band, literary magazine, marching band, musical theater, newspaper, opera, orchestra, pep band, photography, political, professional, radio and TV, religious, social, social service, student government, and symphony. Popular campus events include College Conservatory of Music productions.

Sports: There are 8 intercollegiate sports for men and 10 for women, and 32 intramural sports for men and 32 for women. Facilities include a 30,000-seat stadium, a field house, a 13,000-seat gym, indoor and outdoor tracks, a swimming pool, tennis courts, and athletic fields.

Disabled Students: 95% of the campus is accessible. Facilities include wheelchair ramps, elevators, special parking, specially equipped restrooms, special class scheduling, lowered drinking fountains, and lowered telephones.

Services: Counseling and information services are available, as is tutoring in most subjects. There is remedial math, reading, and writing. Other services offered include interpreting services for the hearing impaired and note taking and reading services for the blind.

Campus Safety and Security: Measures include security escort services. There are shuttle buses, emergency telephones, and lighted pathways/sidewalks.

Programs of Study: UC confers B.A., B.S., B.Arch., B.B.A., B.F.A., B.G.S., B.M., B.S.Des., B.S.E., B.S.I.M., B.S.N., B.S.Pharm., B.S.W, and B.U.P. degrees. Associate, master's, and doctoral degrees are also awarded. Bachelor's degrees are awarded in BIOLOGICAL SCIENCE (biochemistry and biology/biological science), BUSINESS (accounting, banking and finance, business administration and management, management science, marketing/retailing/merchandising, and real estate), COMMUNICATIONS AND THE ARTS (broadcasting, communications, comparative literature, dance, design, digital communications, dramatic arts, English, fine arts, French, German, jazz, linguistics, music, music history and appreciation, music theory and composition, piano/organ, Spanish, theater design, and voice), COMPUTER AND PHYSICAL SCIENCE (chemical technology, chemistry, computer science, geology, information sciences and systems, mathematics, physics, and quantitative methods), EDUCATION (art education, business education, early childhood education, elementary education, foreign languages education, guidance education, health education, industrial arts education, middle school education, music education, nutrition education, science education, secondary education, and special education), ENGINEERING AND ENVIRONMENTAL DESIGN (aeronautical engineering, architectural engineering, architectural technology, chemical engineering, city/community/regional planning, civil engineering, computer engineering, construction management, electrical/electronics engineering, electrical/electronics engineering technology, engineering, engineering mechanics, engineering technology, industrial administration/management, industrial engineering technology, materials engineering, mechanical engineering, mechanical engineering technology, metallurgical engineering, and nuclear engineering), HEALTH PROFESSIONS (medical laboratory technology, nuclear medical technology, nursing, pharmacy, predentistry, premedicine, and speech pathology/audiology), SOCIAL SCIENCE (African American studies, anthropology, Asian/Oriental studies, classical/ancient civilization, criminal justice, economics, geography, history, international studies, Judaic studies, Latin American studies, liberal arts/general studies, philosophy, political science/government, prelaw, psychology, social science, social work, sociology, and urban studies). Architecture, music, and engineering are the strongest academically. Marketing, communications, and psychology have the largest enrollments.

Required: All students must complete English and humanities requirements. A minimum of 185 quarter credits is required for the baccalaureate degree.

Special: The Professional Practice Program, a 5-year cooperative plan offering alternate work in academic subjects and industry, is available for students in engineering, business, arts and sciences, design, architecture, and art. Study abroad is available in 29 countries. Nondegree study is possible.

Faculty/Classroom: 58% of faculty are male; 42% are female. No introductory courses are taught by graduate students.

Admissions: 65% of a recent year applicants were accepted. The SAT scores for the 2011-2012 freshman class were: Critical Reading--24% below 500, 44% between 500 and 599, 25% between 600 and 700, and 7% above 700; Math--18% below 500, 40% between 500 and 599, 34% between 600 and 700, and 9% above 700; Writing--32% below 500, 44% between 500 and 599, 19% between 600 and 700, and 5% above 700. The ACT scores were 8% below 21, 29% between 21 and 23, 32% between 24 and 26, 15% between 27 and 28, and 16% above 28. 50% of the current freshmen were in the top fifth of their class; 83% were in the top two fifths. There were 45 National Merit finalists. 70 freshmen graduated first in their class.

Requirements: The SAT or ACT is required. Applicants should be graduates of an accredited secondary school with 4 units of high school English, 3 of math, 2 each of science, social science, foreign language, and electives, and 1 of fine arts. A GPA of 2.0 is required. AP and CLEP credits are accepted.

Procedure: Freshmen are admitted to all sessions. Entrance exams should be taken in May of the junior year or January or March of the senior year. There is a rolling admissions plan. Applications should be filed by July 31 for fall entry, along with a $50 fee.

Transfer: 1550 transfer students enrolled in a recent year. A GPA of 2.0 is required to apply from a 4-year college, a GPA of 2.5 or an associate degree if applying from a 2-year college.

Visiting: There are regularly scheduled orientations for prospective students. There are guides for informal visits, visitors may sit in on classes, and stay overnight. To schedule a visit, contact the Admissions Office.

Financial Aid: In a recent year, 80% of all full-time freshmen and 75% of continuing full-time students received some form of financial aid. 40% of all full-time freshmen and 38% of continuing full-time students received need-based aid. The average freshman award was $8,358. Need-based scholarships or need-based grants averaged $5,889; need-based self-help aid (loans and jobs) averaged $2,974; and non-need-based athletic scholarships averaged $22,029. The CSS/Profile and FAFSA are required. Check with the school for current application deadlines.

International Students: There are 350 international students enrolled. The school actively recruits these students. They must take the TOEFL, with a minimum score of 550 on the paper-based TOEFL (PBT) or 79 on the Internet-based version (iBT), IELTS, or SAT.

Computers: Wireless access is available. All students may access the system. There are no time limits and no fees.

Graduates: In a recent year, 4277 bachelor's degrees were awarded. The most popular majors were health professions and related programs (17%), business/marketing (16%), and engineering (10%). In an average class, 1% graduate in 3 years or less, 22% graduate in 4 years or less, 49% graduate in 5 years or less, and 59% graduate in 6 years or less.

Admissions Contact: Admissions Office. E-Mail: *admissions@uc.edu* Web: *www.uc.edu*

UNIVERSITY OF DAYTON — B-4

Dayton, OH 45469 — (937) 229-4411; (800) 837-7433; (937) 229-4729

Full-time: 3843 men, 3636 women	**Faculty:** 440; IIA, +$
Part-time: 319 men, 271 women	**Ph.D.s:** 89%
Graduate: 1483 men, 1634 women	**Student/Faculty:** 16 to 1
Year: semesters, summer session	**Tuition:** $33,400
Application Deadline: March 1	**Room & Board:** $10,350
Freshman Class: 15101 applied, 8336 accepted, 2043 enrolled	
SAT CR/M/W: 560/590/580 **ACT:** 26	**VERY COMPETITIVE**

The University of Dayton, founded in 1850, is a private comprehensive institution affiliated with the Roman Catholic Church. Part of the Southwestern Ohio Council for Higher Education, it has undergraduate and graduate programs emphasizing the arts and sciences, business administration, engineering, education, allied professions, and law. There are 4 undergraduate schools and 5 graduate schools. In addition to regional accreditation, UD has baccalaureate program accreditation with AACSB, ABET, NASAD, NASM, and NCATE. The 3 libraries contain 1.1 million volumes, 1.5 million microform items, 159,227 audio/video tapes/CDs/DVDs, and subscribe to 73,332 periodicals including electronic. Computerized library services include interlibrary loans, database searching, and Internet access. Special learning facilities include an art gallery, radio station, TV station, UD Research Institute, Bombeck Family Learning Center, a learning teaching center, and Davis Center for Portfolio Management. The 388-acre campus is in a suburban area 2 miles south of downtown Dayton. Including any residence halls, there are 58 buildings.

Student Life: 53% of undergraduates are from Ohio. Others are from 46 states, 37 foreign countries, and Canada. 46% are from public schools. 82% are White. 33% are Catholic; 12% Protestant. The average age of freshmen is 18; all undergraduates, 20. 12% do not continue beyond their first year; 78% remain to graduate.

Housing: 6100 students can be accommodated in college housing, which includes coed dorms and on-campus apartments. In addition, there are honors houses, special-interest houses, fraternity houses, and sorority houses. On-campus housing is available on a first-come, first-served basis, and is available on a lottery system for upperclassmen. 79% of students live on campus; of those, 100% remain on campus on weekends. Upperclassmen may keep cars.

Activities: 17% of men belong to 1 local and 10 national fraternities; 17% of women belong to 9 national sororities. There are 186 groups on campus, including art, band, cheerleading, chess, choir, chorale, chorus, computers, dance, debate, drama, drill team, environmental, ethnic, film, gay, honors, international, jazz band, literary magazine, marching band, musical theater, newspaper, orchestra, pep band, photography, political, professional, radio and TV, religious, social, social service, student government, symphony, and yearbook. Popular campus events include Christmas on Campus, Green Sweep and Weekend Scene.

Sports: There are 7 intercollegiate sports for men and 9 for women, and 17 intramural sports for men and 17 for women. Facilities include a 13,455-seat arena, an 11,000-seat football stadium with a track, a 2000-seat soccer field, a 5000-seat volleyball facility, a baseball stadium, a softball stadium, and a state-of-the-art recreational sports facility containing a 4-court main gym, an aquatic center, a climbing wall, a 2-court MAC gym, a juice bar, 3 racquetball courts, classrooms, fitness studios, a fitness center, and an indoor track.

Disabled Students: Facilities include wheelchair ramps, elevators, special parking, specially equipped restrooms, special class scheduling, lowered drinking fountains, special housing. The university provides access to programs and services through the Office of Learning Resources.

Services: Counseling and information services are available, as is tutoring in some subjects, walk-in tutoring and/or supplemental instruction (SI) are available for many entry-level courses and some high-attrition upper level courses. A list for the current semester can be found under Schedules at <go.udayton.edu/learning>. Curricular and tutoria. Support is available for writing at all levels.

Campus Safety and Security: Measures include 24-hour foot and vehicle patrol, emergency notification system, and security escort services. There are emergency telephones, lighted pathways/sidewalks, controlled access to dorms/residences, a bike patrol, electronic access control for residence hall access, about 1000 video cameras, an on-campus ambulance service, automated external debrillators in residence halls and key facilities, centrally monitored fire alarm systems in all residential facilities, and fire suppression in high-density residential facilities.

Programs of Study: UD confers B.A., B.S., B.C.E., B.Ch.E., B.E.E., B.F.A., B.G.S., B.M.E. and B.Mus. degrees. Master's and doctoral degrees are also awarded. Bachelor's degrees are awarded in BIOLOGICAL SCIENCE (biochemistry, biology/biological science, environmental biology, and nutrition), BUSINESS (accounting, banking and finance, business administration and management, business economics, entrepreneurial studies, international business management, management information systems, marketing/retailing/merchandising, operations research, and sports management), COMMUNICATIONS AND THE ARTS (art, art history and appreciation, communications, dramatic arts, English, fine arts, French, German, music, music performance, music theory and composition, photography, Spanish, and visual design), COMPUTER AND PHYSICAL SCIENCE (chemistry, computer science, environmental geology, geology, information sciences and systems, mathematics, mathematics – economics, physical sciences, and physics), EDUCATION (art education, early childhood education, elementary education, music education, secondary education, and special education), ENGINEERING AND ENVIRONMENTAL DESIGN (chemical engineering, civil engineering, computer engineering, computer technology, electrical/electronics engineering, electrical/electronics engineering technology, engineering technology, industrial engineering technology, manufacturing technology, mechanical engineering, and mechanical engineering technology), HEALTH PROFESSIONS (exercise science, music therapy, pharmaceutical chemistry, predentistry, premedicine, and prephysical therapy), SOCIAL SCIENCE (American studies, criminal justice, dietetics, early childhood studies, economics, ethics, politics, and social policy, history, international studies, liberal arts/general studies, philosophy, political science/government, psychology, religion, religious education, sociology, and women's studies). Engineering, business, and education are the strongest academically. Business, marketing, engineering and engineering technologies have the largest enrollments.

Required: To graduate, all students must complete a minimum of 120 semester hours with at least 30 hours of residence, and maintain a minimum GPA of 2.0. The curricula must include general education requirements, including 4 classes in religious studies and philosophy as well as basic skills requirements. Departmental requirements vary.

Special: Traditional co-op programs are available in the School of Engineering; however, any student in any discipline may co-op, and qualification is determined on a case-by-case basis. Internships are available in all majors. Cross-registration is available with the Southwestern Ohio Council for Higher Education. Study abroad, work-study programs, a Washington semester, accelerated degree programs, and B.A.-B.S. degrees in chemistry, math, economics, and psychology are available. For students who wish to have a dual major, almost all programs may be combined. Student-designed majors include general studies and interdisciplinary studies. An engineering curriculum agreement exists with Sinclair Community College. There are a freshman honors program.

Faculty/Classroom: 63% of faculty are male; 67% are female. 82% teach undergraduates, 43% do research, and 41% do both. Graduate students teach 11% of introductory courses. The average class size in an introductory lecture is 29; in a laboratory is 18; and in a regular course is 22.

Admissions: 55% of the 2013-2014 applicants were accepted. The SAT scores for the 2013-2014 freshman class were: Critical Reading--20% below 500, 48% between 500 and 599, 26% between 600 and 699, and 6% between 700 and 800; Math--15% below 500, 39% between 500 and 599, 38% between 600 and 699, and 8% between 700 and 800; Writing--19% below 500, 40% between 500 and 599, 31% between 600 and 699, and 10% between 700 and 800. The ACT scores were 4% below 21, 18% between 21 and 23, 30% between 24 and 26, 20% between 27 and 28, and 28% above 28. 48% of the current freshmen were in the top fifth of their class; 77% were in the top two fifths.

Requirements: The SAT or ACT is required. Applicants should be graduates of an accredited secondary school with 16 units in English, math, science, social studies, and academic electives. In addition, 2 units of foreign language are required for admission to the College of Arts and Sciences. The GED is accepted. High school transcripts must be submitted. An essay or personal statement, a recommendation from the high school guidance counselor, and an interview are recommended. Music students must audition. AP and CLEP credits are accepted. Important factors in the admissions decision are personality/intangible qualities, recommendations by school officials, and leadership record.

Procedure: Freshmen are admitted fall, winter, and summer. Entrance exams should be taken by December of the senior year. There are deferred admissions and rolling admissions plans. Applications should be filed by March 1 for fall entry. Notification is sent on a rolling basis. Applications are accepted online.

Transfer: 158 transfer students enrolled in 2012-2013. Attention is directed to college and high school GPA and course selection. The minimum grade point average is 2.0. The School of Education and Allied Professions requires a minimum 2.5 GPA in previous college work. Achievement of the minimum GPA does not guarantee admission. For students under 21 years of age, results of the SAT or ACT are required. All students applying to the School of Education and Allied Professions must submit SAT or ACT and Praxis I scores. 30 of 120 credits required for the bachelor's degree must be completed at Dayton.

Visiting: There are regularly scheduled orientations for prospective students, including an admission interview, financial aid consultation, campus tour, residence hall tour, and faculty or class visit. High school seniors who have been accepted to the university may participate in an overnight visit during the winter semester. There are guides for informal visits, visitors may sit in on classes, and stay overnight. To schedule a visit, contact the Office of Admission.

Financial Aid: In 2013-2014, 89% of all full-time freshmen and 99% of continuing full-time students received some form of financial aid. 64% of all full-time freshmen and 60% of continuing full-time students received need-based aid. The average freshman award was $23,496. Need-based scholarships or need-based grants averaged $10,682 ($20,670 maximum); need-based self-help aid (loans and jobs) averaged $4,288 ($9,300 maximum); non-need-based athletic scholarships averaged $18,239 ($40,190 maximum); and other non-need-based awards and non-need-based scholarships averaged $11,626 ($40,190 maximum). The average financial indebtedness of the 2013 graduate was $32,862. UD is a member of CSS. The FAFSA is required. The priority date for freshman financial aid applications for fall entry is March 31.

International Students: There are 524 international students enrolled. The school actively recruits these students. They must take the TOEFL, or English Language Proficiency Test, or Advanced Placement International English Language Examination.

Computers: All students may access the system 24 hours a day, 7 day a week. There are no time limits and no fees.

Graduates: From July 1, 2012 to June 30, 2013, 1917 bachelor's degrees were awarded. The most popular majors were marketing (7%), communication (7%), and finance (6%). 403 companies recruited on campus in 2012-2013. In an average class, 59% graduate in 4 years or less, 76% graduate in 5 years or less, and 78% graduate in 6 years or less. Of the 2012 graduating class, 22% were enrolled in graduate school within 6 months of graduation, and 68% were employed.

Admissions Contact: Robert F. Durkle, Director of Admission. E-Mail: *admission@udayton.edu* Web: *www.udayton.edu*

UNIVERSITY OF FINDLAY B-2

Findlay, OH 45840 (419) 424-4732
(800) 548-0932; (419) 424-4822

Full-time: 1055 men, 1810 women
Part-time: 480 men, 660 women
Graduate: 610 men, 710 women
Year: semesters, summer session
Application Deadline: see profile
Freshman Class: n/av
SAT or ACT: required
Faculty: n/av; IIA, --$
Ph.D.s: n/av
Student/Faculty: n/av
Tuition: $27,590
Room & Board: $9570

COMPETITIVE

The University of Findlay, founded in 1882, is a private, independent institution affiliated with the Churches of God, General Conference, offering liberal arts and sciences and career preparation programs. The figures in the above capsule and in this profile are approximate. There are 4 undergraduate schools and 1 graduate school. In addition to regional accreditation, Findlay has baccalaureate program accreditation with NCATE. The library contains 135,000 volumes, 90,000 microform items, 1200 audio/video tapes/CDs/DVDs, and subscribes to 2500 periodicals including electronic. Computerized library services include interlibrary loans, database searching, Internet access, and laptop Internet portals. Special learning facilities include a learning resource center, art gallery, planetarium, radio station, TV station, university-owned farm, equine facility, and emergency response training center. The 250-acre campus is in a small town 45 miles south of Toledo and 100 miles northwest of Columbus. Including any residence halls, there are 55 buildings.

Student Life: 80% of undergraduates are from Ohio. Others are from 45 states, 30 foreign countries, and Canada. 80% are from public schools. 85% are white. 60% are Protestant; 35% Catholic. The average age of freshmen is 18; all undergraduates, 22. 25% do not continue beyond their first year; 55% remain to graduate.

Housing: 1350 students can be accommodated in college housing, which includes single-sex dorms and on-campus apartments. In addition, there are honors houses, language houses, special-interest houses, fraternity houses, and sorority houses. On-campus housing is guaranteed for all 4 years. 65% of students commute. Alcohol is not permitted. All students may keep cars.

Activities: 4% of men belong to 3 national fraternities; 1% of women belong to 2 national sororities. There are 40 groups on campus, including art, band, cheerleading, choir, chorale, chorus, computers, drama, drum and bugle corps, equestrian, ethnic, honors, international, jazz band, literary magazine, marching band, musical theater, newspaper, pep band, political, preveterinary, professional, radio and TV, religious, social, social service, and student government. Popular campus events include International Night and Spring Bash.

Sports: There are 12 intercollegiate sports for men and 11 for women, and 15 intramural sports for men and 15 for women. Facilities include a fitness center, a 7200-seat stadium, a 25-meter pool, racquetball courts, a phys ed center with a 3200-seat gym, an ice arena, an indoor track, and a 4-court athletic building.

Disabled Students: 90% of the campus is accessible. Facilities include wheelchair ramps, elevators, special parking, specially equipped restrooms, special class scheduling, and lowered drinking fountains.

Services: Counseling and information services are available, as is tutoring in most subjects. There is a reader service for the blind, and remedial math, reading, and writing. Other services include assistance with note taking, test taking, and study skills, and assistive technology per student need.

Campus Safety and Security: Measures include 24-hour foot and vehicle patrol, emergency notification system, self-defense education, and security escort services. There are emergency telephones and lighted pathways/sidewalks.

Programs of Study: Findlay confers B.A., B.S., B.S.B.M., B.S.C.J., and B.S.E.M. degrees. Associate, master's, and doctoral degrees are also awarded. Bachelor's degrees are awarded in AGRICULTURE (equine science), BIOLOGICAL SCIENCE (biology/biological science), BUSINESS (accounting, banking and finance, business administration and management, business economics, business systems analysis, hospitality management services, human resources, international business management, and marketing/retailing/merchandising), COMMUNICATIONS AND THE ARTS (arts administration/management, broadcasting, communications, dramatic arts, English, English as a second/foreign language, illustration, Japanese, Spanish, studio art, and technical and business writing), COMPUTER AND PHYSICAL SCIENCE (chemistry, computer science, mathematics, and science), EDUCATION (art education, bilingual/bicultural education, elementary education, foreign languages education, middle school education, physical education, and secondary education), ENGINEERING AND ENVIRONMENTAL DESIGN (environmental science, occupational safety and health, and technological management), HEALTH PROFESSIONS (health science, nuclear medical technology, nursing, occupational therapy, physician's assistant, premedicine, and preveterinary science), SOCIAL SCIENCE (criminal justice, economics, forensic studies, history, international studies, philosophy, political science/government, prelaw, psychology, religion, social work, and sociology). Business administration, preveterinary medicine, and education are the strongest academically. Business administration, equestrian studies, and education have the largest enrollments.

Required: All students must complete 36 semester hours of general education requirements, including fine arts, humanities, natural science, math, social science, and religion or philosophy, and must take courses in wellness, computer science, and statistics. There are competency requirements in English composition and reading and a wellness course. A total of 124 semester hours with a minimum GPA of 2.0 is required to graduate.

Special: Co-op programs are available in accounting and occupational health and safety. There is cross-registration with Mount Carmel College of Nursing and Lourdes College. The field experience program provides up to 20 semester hours in field placement. Internships are available for many majors, including business, business education, communication, hazardous materials management, and theater majors. Through the College Consortium for International Studies, study abroad is possible in 16 countries. Work-study, a Washington semester, dual and student-designed majors, a general studies degree, pass/fail options, and credit for life experience are offered. Nondegree study is possible. There is a freshman honors program.

Faculty/Classroom: 53% of faculty are male; 47% are female. All teach undergraduates. No introductory courses are taught by graduate students. The average class size in an introductory lecture is 23; in a laboratory, 15; and in a regular course, 22.

Requirements: The SAT or ACT is required. The ACT Optional Writing test is also required. Applicants should have completed 16 high school credits or GED equivalents, including 4 years of English, 2 years of social studies/history, 3 to 4 math courses, and 2 to 3 science courses. A letter of recommendation and an essay are required for all applicants. A GPA of 2.3 is required. AP and CLEP credits are accepted. Important factors in the admissions decision are advanced placement or honors courses, evidence of special talent, and extracurricular activities record.

Procedure: Freshmen are admitted to all sessions. Entrance exams should be taken during fall of the senior year or the spring of the junior year. There are deferred admissions and rolling admissions plans. Notification is sent on a rolling basis. Applications are accepted online. Check with the school for current application deadlines.

Transfer: A minimum 2.25 GPA and eligibility to return to the current institution are required. An interview is recommended. 30 of 124 credits required for the bachelor's degree must be completed at Findlay.

Visiting: There are regularly scheduled orientations for prospective students, including a tour, interview, and coach/faculty visits. There are guides for informal visits; visitors may sit in on classes and stay overnight. To schedule a visit, contact the Admissions Office.

Financial Aid: Findlay is a member of CSS. The FAFSA is required. Check with the school for current deadlines.

International Students: The school actively recruits these students. They must take the TOEFL.

Computers: Wireless access is available. All students may access the system. There are no time limits and no fees.

Admissions Contact: Donna Gruber, Director of Undergraduate Admissions. A campus DVD is available. E-Mail: *admissions@findlay.edu* Web: *www.findlay.edu*

UNIVERSITY OF MOUNT UNION E-2
Mount Union College

Alliance, OH 44601 (330) 821-5320
(800) 992-6682; (330) 823-3457

Full-time: 1095 men, 1053 women
Part-time: 14 men, 13 women
Graduate: 18 men, 60 women
Year: semesters, summer session
Application Deadline: open
Freshman Class: 2333 applied, 2071 accepted, 705 enrolled
ACT: 22
Faculty: 124
Ph.D.s: 87%
Student/Faculty: 17 to 1
Tuition: $26,650
Room & Board: $8480

COMPETITIVE

University of Mount Union, formerly Mount Union College, founded in 1846, is a private, liberal arts college affiliated with the United Methodist Church. In addition to regional accreditation, Mount Union has baccalaureate program accreditation with NASM and NCATE. The 2 libraries contain 230,000 volumes, 43,000 microform items, 35,700 audio/video tapes/CDs/DVDs, and subscribe to 950 periodicals including electronic. Computerized library services include interlibrary loans, database searching, Internet access, and Wi-Fi capability. Special learning facilities include an art gallery, radio station, An astronomical observatory, a university theater, a playhouse, and a nature center. The 115-acre campus is in a suburban area 20 miles east of Canton. Including any residence halls, there are 37 buildings.

Student Life: 84% of undergraduates are from Ohio. Others are from 27 states, 17 foreign countries, and Canada. 89% are from public schools.

85% are White. 42% are Protestant; 29% claim no religious affiliation; 28% Catholic. The average age of freshmen is 18; all undergraduates, 20. 22% do not continue beyond their first year; 65% remain to graduate.

Housing: 1544 students can be accommodated in college housing, which includes single-sex and coed dorms and on-campus apartments. In addition, there are honors houses, special-interest houses, fraternity houses, and substance-free (tobacco/alcohol) houses. On-campus housing is guaranteed for the freshman year only, is available on a first-come, first-served basis, and is available on a lottery system for upperclassmen. 78% of students live on campus; of those, 60% remain on campus on weekends. All students may keep cars.

Activities: 21% of men belong to 4 national fraternities; 43% of women belong to 1 local and 3 national sororities. There are 80 groups on campus, including art, band, cheerleading, chess, choir, chorale, chorus, computers, dance, debate, drama, drill team, environmental, ethnic, forensics, gay, honors, international, jazz band, literary magazine, marching band, musical theater, newspaper, orchestra, pep band, political, professional, radio and TV, religious, social, social service, student government, and symphony. Popular campus events include Spring Fest, Greek Week and Schooler Lecture series.

Sports: There are 11 intercollegiate sports for men and 10 for women, and 8 intramural sports for men and 8 for women. Facilities include A gym, field house, stadium, tennis courts, wellness center, exercise and aerobics rooms, and the campus center.

Disabled Students: 98% of the campus is accessible. Facilities include wheelchair ramps, elevators, special parking, specially equipped restrooms, special class scheduling, lowered drinking fountains, and special housing.

Services: Counseling and information services are available, as is tutoring in most subjects, General education courses and most introductory courses There is a reader service for the blind, and remedial writing. and facilitated study groups for most general education courses that meet once a week.

Campus Safety and Security: Measures include 24-hour foot and vehicle patrol, emergency notification system, self-defense education, and security escort services. There are emergency telephones and lighted pathways/sidewalks.

Programs of Study: Mount Union confers B.A., B.S., B.Mus. and B.Mus.Ed. degrees. Master's degrees are also awarded. Bachelor's degrees are awarded in BIOLOGICAL SCIENCE (biochemistry, biology/biological science, and environmental biology), BUSINESS (accounting, business administration and management, human resources, international business management, and sports management), COMMUNICATIONS AND THE ARTS (art, communications, creative writing, dramatic arts, English, French, German, Japanese, media arts, music, music performance, and Spanish), COMPUTER AND PHYSICAL SCIENCE (astronomy, chemistry, computer science, geology, information sciences and systems, mathematics, and physics), EDUCATION (athletic training, early childhood education, elementary education, middle school education, music education, and physical education), ENGINEERING AND ENVIRONMENTAL DESIGN (civil engineering, environmental science, and mechanical engineering), HEALTH PROFESSIONS (exercise science, health, and medical technology), SOCIAL SCIENCE (American studies, cognitive science, criminal justice, economics, history, international studies, Near Eastern studies, philosophy, political science/government, psychology, religion, social science, and sociology). Business, early childhood education, and sports management have the largest enrollments.

Required: To graduate, students must complete a minimum of 120 semester hours, including 30 in upper division courses and up to 48 in the major, with a minimum GPA of 2.0. General requirements include 49 hours in a core curriculum encompassing communication skills, analytical skills, religion/philosophy, international studies, Western history, literature, fine arts, wellness, and the freshman liberal arts experience. Students must also complete a minor requirement and the senior year culminating experience.

Special: Mount Union offers internships for credit in many majors, study abroad in 26 countries, co-op programs in business, work-study programs with various employers, student-designed majors, and pass/fail options. Adults in the nontraditional study program may receive credit for life, military, or work experience. There are 18 national honor societies, a freshman honors program, and 19 departmental honors programs.

Faculty/Classroom: 59% of faculty are male; 41% are female. All teach undergraduates. No introductory courses are taught by graduate students. The average class size in an introductory lecture is 19; in a laboratory is 15; and in a regular course is 18.

Admissions: 89% of the 2013-2014 applicants were accepted. The ACT scores were 30% below 21, 34% between 21 and 23, 18% between 24 and 26, 11% between 27 and 28, and 7% above 28. 31% of the current freshmen were in the top fifth of their class; 59% were in the top two fifths. 8 freshmen graduated first in their class.

Requirements: The ACT is required. Preference is given to high school graduates who have completed a minimum of 15 academic units, including 4 in English, 3 each in math, social science, and lab science, and 2 in foreign language. A GPA of 2.0 is required. AP and CLEP credits are accepted. Important factors in the admissions decision are advanced placement or honors courses, recommendations by school officials, and personality/intangible qualities.

Procedure: Freshmen are admitted fall and spring. There are deferred admissions and rolling admissions plans. Application deadlines are open. Notification is sent on a rolling basis. Applications are accepted online.

Transfer: 36 transfer students enrolled in 2012-2013. Applicants must have a college GPA of 2.0 for consideration and must submit a statement of honorable dismissal and an official transcript from the last college attended. A personal statement must accompany the transfer application. 45 of 120 credits required for the bachelor's degree must be completed at Mount Union.

Visiting: There are regularly scheduled orientations for prospective students, including interviews, a campus tour, meetings with faculty, and classroom visits. There are guides for informal visits, visitors may sit in on classes, and stay overnight. To schedule a visit, contact The Office of Admissions.

Financial Aid: In 2013-2014, 94% of all full-time freshmen and 96% of continuing full-time students received some form of financial aid. 80% of all full-time freshmen and 82% of continuing full-time students received need-based aid. The average freshman award was $20,644. Need-based scholarships or need-based grants averaged $14,651 ($26,350 maximum); need-based self-help aid (loans and jobs) averaged $5,734 ($6,900 maximum); and other non-need-based awards and non-need-based scholarships averaged $9,883 ($26,350 maximum). 39% of undergraduate students work part-time. Average annual earnings from campus work are $1350. The average financial indebtedness of the 2013 graduate was $27,862. Mount Union is a member of CSS. The FAFSA is required. The priority date for freshman financial aid applications for fall entry is March 1. The deadline for filing freshman financial aid applications for fall entry is September 1.

International Students: There are 75 international students enrolled. The school actively recruits these students. They must take the TOEFL with a minimum score of 450 on the paper-based TOEFL (PBT) or 79 on the Internet-based version (iBT), (IELTS) or certification of completion of ELS. They must also take the SAT or ACT.

Computers: All students may access the system. There are no time limits. The fee is $300.

Graduates: From July 1, 2012 to June 30, 2013, 451 bachelor's degrees were awarded. The most popular majors were education (15%), business (15%), and sports management (8%). 50 companies recruited on campus in 2012-2013. In an average class, 1% graduate in 3 years or less, 52% graduate in 4 years or less, 63% graduate in 5 years or less, and 64% graduate in 6 years or less. Of the 2012 graduating class, 29% were enrolled in graduate school within 6 months of graduation, and 87% were employed.

Admissions Contact: Amy Tomko, Vice President, Enrollment Services.
E-Mail: *admission@mountunion.edu* Web: *www.mountunion.edu*

UNIVERSITY OF RIO GRANDE D-5

Rio Grande, OH 45674 (740) 245-5353
(800) 282-7201; (740) 245-7260

Full-time: 625 men, 910 women	**Faculty:** n/av
Part-time: 120 men, 225 women	**Ph.D.s:** n/av
Graduate: 30 men, 80 women	**Student/Faculty:** n/av
Year: trimesters, summer session	**Tuition:** $4500 ($20,020)
Application Deadline: see profile	**Room & Board:** $8720
Freshman Class: n/av	
ACT: required	

NONCOMPETITIVE

The University of Rio Grande, founded in 1876, is a private institution offering degree programs in the liberal arts and sciences, business, and education. The figures in above capsule and in this profile are approximate. There are 9 undergraduate schools and 1 graduate school. In addition to regional accreditation, Rio has baccalaureate program accreditation with CSWE, NASDTEC, and NLN. The library contains 96,731 volumes, 274,400 microform items, 1835 audio/video tapes/CDs/DVDs, and subscribes to 850 periodicals including electronic. Computerized library services include interlibrary loans and database searching. Special learning facilities include a learning resource center, art gallery, radio station, and TV station. The 194-acre campus is in a rural area 100 miles southeast of Columbus. Including any residence halls, there are 27 buildings.

Student Life: 94% of undergraduates are from Ohio. Others are from 12 states, 15 foreign countries, and Canada. 98% are from public schools. 97% are white. The average age of freshmen is 23; all undergraduates, 24.

Housing: 640 students can be accommodated in college housing, which includes single-sex and coed dorms. In addition, there are special-interest houses. On-campus housing is guaranteed for all 4 years. 76% of students commute. All students may keep cars.

Activities: 6% of men belong to 2 local and 2 national fraternities; 4% of women belong to 5 local sororities. There are 39 groups on campus, including band, cheerleading, choir, chorale, chorus, drama, ecology, ethnic, gay, honors, international, jazz band, musical theater, newspaper, orchestra, pep band, photography, political, professional, radio and TV, religious, social, social service, and student government. Popular campus events include Ethnofest, Bob Evans Farm Festival, and Community Service Day.

Sports: There are 5 intercollegiate sports for men and 5 for women, and 10 intramural sports for men and 10 for women. Facilities include 2 gyms, tennis courts, an indoor Olympic-size pool, an outdoor track, handball, racquetball, and sand volleyball courts, a fitness center, a cross-country track, and soccer, baseball, and softball fields.

Disabled Students: 70% of the campus is accessible. Facilities include wheelchair ramps, elevators, special parking, specially equipped restrooms, special class scheduling, lowered drinking fountains, lowered telephones, note takers, tape recorders, and closed-caption TV.

Services: Counseling and information services are available, as is tutoring in every subject. There is a reader service for the blind, and remedial math, reading, and writing. There is also an Accessibility Office.

Campus Safety and Security: Measures include 24-hour foot and vehicle patrol, security escort services, emergency telephones, and lighted pathways/sidewalks.

Programs of Study: Rio confers B.A., B.S., B.S.I.T., B.S.N., and B.S.W. degrees. Associates and master's degrees are also awarded. Bachelor's degrees are awarded in BIOLOGICAL SCIENCE (biology/biological science), BUSINESS (accounting, business administration and management, business economics, international business management, and marketing management), COMMUNICATIONS AND THE ARTS (art, communications, English, fine arts, music, and public relations), COMPUTER AND PHYSICAL SCIENCE (chemistry, computer science, mathematics, and physical sciences), EDUCATION (art education, business education, early childhood education, education of the mentally handicapped, elementary education, English education, health education, mathematics education, music education, physical education, psychology education, reading education, science education, secondary education, social science education, and social studies education), ENGINEERING AND ENVIRONMENTAL DESIGN (computer technology, drafting and design technology, electrical/electronics engineering technology, environmental science, industrial engineering technology, manufacturing technology, preengineering, and woodworking), HEALTH PROFESSIONS (medical technology, nursing, predentistry, premedicine, and preveterinary science), SOCIAL SCIENCE (American studies, behavioral science, economics, history, humanities, physical fitness/movement, political science/government, prelaw, psychology, social work, and sociology).

Required: Students must complete 190 to 198 quarter hours, including 47 to 53 in the major, with a minimum GPA of 2.0. The required general studies program, for all but teacher certification and industrial technology majors, includes 13 credit hours in communication skills, 12 hours each in the humanities, math, natural sciences, and social sciences, 3 hours in health and phys ed, and 1 hour in liberal arts.

Special: Rio offers internships in social work, communications, and business, a Washington semester, student-designed majors, limited pass/fail options, and credit for life, military, or work experience. Nondegree study for 1-year certificates in secretarial science and personal computer applications is also available. A community college on the same campus offers technical degree programs that are built into 4-year degrees. There are 3 national honor societies, a freshman honors program, and 1 departmental honors program.

Faculty/Classroom: No introductory courses are taught by graduate students. The average class size in an introductory lecture is 30; in a laboratory, 20; and in a regular course, 20.

Requirements: The ACT is required for applicants who are less than 5 years out of high school. Rio follows an open admissions policy for all applicants. A high school diploma or GED is required. A GPA of 2.0 is required. AP and CLEP credits are accepted.

Procedure: Freshmen are admitted to all sessions. Entrance exams should be taken no later than December of the senior year for those entering college the following fall. There are early admissions and rolling admissions plans. Check with the school for current application deadlines. Applications are accepted online.

Transfer: Candidates must submit a final transcript and a dean's evaluation form from the last school attended. 45 of 190 credits required for the bachelor's degree must be completed at Rio.

Visiting: There are regularly scheduled orientations for prospective students, with parents and students participating in 1- or 2-day sessions. The program includes half-day placement testing and presentations from various offices, campus e-mail, advising, and registration. Residential students stay in the dorms and have dinner with the president. There are guides for informal visits, and visitors may sit in on classes. To schedule a visit, contact the Admissions Office.

Financial Aid: Rio is a member of CSS. The FAFSA and the college's own financial statement are required. Check with the school for current application deadlines.

International Students: The school actively recruits these students. They must take the TOEFL.

Computers: All students may access the system. It is strongly recommended that all students have a personal computer.

Admissions Contact: Mark F. Abell, Executive Director, Admissions. E-Mail: *mabell@rio.edu* Web: *www.rio.edu*

UNIVERSITY OF TOLEDO — B-1

Toledo, OH 43606-3398 (419) 530-5704
(800) 5TOLEDO; (419) 530-1202

Full-time: 7355 men, 7162 women	**Faculty:** n/av; I, --$
Part-time: 1611 men, 1716 women	**Ph.D.s:** n/av
Graduate: 2132 men, 2634 women	**Student/Faculty:** n/av
Year: semesters, summer session	**Tuition:** $9288 ($18,408)
Application Deadline: open	**Room & Board:** $10,176

Freshman Class: 11633 applied, 11131 accepted, 3837 enrolled
SAT: recommended **ACT:** 22 **COMPETITIVE**

The University of Toledo, founded in 1872, is a public comprehensive institution emphasizing undergraduate degree programs in the liberal arts and sciences, business, engineering, teacher preparation, and health professions. Many graduate and professional degree programs, including medicine, are also offered. There are 12 undergraduate schools and 10 graduate schools. In addition to regional accreditation, UT has baccalaureate program accreditation with AACSB, ABET, ACPE, APTA, NASM, and NCATE. The 3 libraries contain 2.1 million volumes, 1.8 million microform items, and 42,941 audio/video tapes/CDs/DVDs. Computerized library services include interlibrary loans, database searching, Internet access, and laptop Internet portals. Special learning facilities include a learning resource center, art gallery, planetarium, and radio station. The 813-acre campus is in a suburban area 6 miles northwest of downtown Toledo. Including any residence halls, there are 107 buildings.

Student Life: 84% of undergraduates are from Ohio. Others are from 47 states, 92 foreign countries, and Canada. 67% are white; 21% African American. The average age of freshmen is 19; all undergraduates, 22. 32% do not continue beyond their first year; 45% remain to graduate.

Housing: 4001 students can be accommodated in college housing, which includes single-sex and coed dorms. In addition, there are honors houses, special-interest houses, fraternity houses, sorority houses, and an international house. On-campus housing is available on a first-come and first-served basis. 69% of students commute. All students may keep cars.

Activities: 5% of men belong to 17 local and 7 national fraternities; 4% of women belong to 13 local and 7 national sororities. There are 200 groups on campus, including art, band, cheerleading, chess, choir, chorale, chorus, computers, dance, drama, drill team, ethnic, film, gay, honors, international, jazz band, literary magazine, marching band, musical theater, newspaper, orchestra, pep band, photography, political, professional, radio and TV, religious, social, social service, student government, and symphony. Popular campus events include Songfest and Greek Week.

Sports: There are 6 intercollegiate sports for men and 9 for women, and 48 intramural sports for men and 48 for women. Facilities include a recreation center, a 27000-seat stadium, a 9000-seat arena, a field house, 3 pools, 12 tennis courts, an indoor/outdoor track, a 4-field recreational softball complex, and recreational/sport club fields.

Disabled Students: 96% of the campus is accessible. Facilities include wheelchair ramps, elevators, special parking, specially equipped restrooms, special class scheduling, lowered drinking fountains, and lowered telephones.

Services: Counseling and information services are available, as is tutoring in every subject. There is a reader service for the blind, and remedial math, reading, and writing.

Campus Safety and Security: Measures include 24-hour foot and vehicle patrol, self-defense education, and security escort services. There are shuttle buses, emergency telephones, and lighted pathways/sidewalks.

Programs of Study: UT confers B.A., B.A.Env.Studies, B.A. in Africana Studies, B.B.A., B.Ed., B.E.T., B.F.A., B.M., B.S.Admin.Svcs., B.S.C.E., B.S.Chem.Eng., B.S.Comp.Sci. and Eng., B.S.Const.Eng., B.S.Crim.Just., B.S.C.S.E., B.S.E., B.S.E.E., B.S.El.Eng.Tech., B.S.Eng.Phys., B.S.Env.Sci., B.S.Exer.Sci., B.S.Health Care Spvsn., B.S.I.E., B.S. in Bioeng., B.S. in Comp.Sci. and Eng.Tech., B.S.M.E., B.S.Med.Tech., B.S.N., B.S.Pharm., B.S.P.T., B.S.Rad.Sci., B.S.Resp.Care, B.S.W., and B.Voc.Ed. degrees. Associate, master's, and doctoral degrees are also awarded. Bachelor's degrees are awarded in BIOLOGICAL SCIENCE (biology/biological science), BUSINESS (accounting, banking and finance, business administration and management, marketing/retailing/merchandising, and recreation and leisure services), COMMUNICATIONS AND THE ARTS (art history and appreciation, communications, dramatic arts, English, film arts, fine arts, French, German, linguistics, music, and Spanish), COMPUTER AND PHYSICAL SCIENCE (chemistry, computer science, geology, information sciences and systems, mathematics, and physics), EDUCATION (art education, business education, early childhood education, elementary education, foreign languages education, health education, music education, physical education, science education, secondary education, special education, and vocational education), ENGINEERING AND ENVIRONMENTAL DESIGN (bioengineering, chemical engineering, civil engineering, computer engineering, electrical/electronics engineering, electromechanical technology, engineering, engineering technology, environmental science, industrial engineering, and mechanical engineering), HEALTH PROFESSIONS (nursing, pharmacy, physical therapy, and speech pathology/audiology), SOCIAL SCIENCE (anthropology, community services, criminal justice, economics, geography, history, humanities, international relations, philosophy, physical fitness/movement, political science/government, psychology, social work, sociology, and women's studies). Engineering, pharmacy, and business are the strongest academically. Pharmacy, nursing, and business have the largest enrollments.

Required: To graduate, all students must complete 124 to 169 hours of credit, with a minimum of 60 in the major, and maintain a minimum GPA of 2.0. A core curriculum is required of all students. A thesis is required in the honors program. The number of hours required in the major varies.

Special: Special academic programs include internships in most majors, study abroad in 25 countries, and on-campus employment through the Financial Aid Office. There is a co-op program with the College of Engineering and cross-registration with Bowling Green State University. The B.A.-B.S. degree and dual majors are available in many areas of study. A general studies degree, student-designed majors, an accelerated degree, credit for life, military, and work experience, nondegree study, and pass/fail options are also offered. There are 56 national honor societies, a freshman honors program, and 21 departmental honors programs.

Faculty/Classroom: 57% of faculty are male; 43% are female. No introductory courses are taught by graduate students. The average class size in an introductory lecture is 38; in a laboratory is 18; and in a regular course is 31.

Admissions: 96% of a recent year applicants were accepted. The ACT scores were 47% below 21, 25% between 21 and 23, 17% between 24 and 26, 6% between 27 and 28, and 5% above 28. 30% of the current freshmen were in the top fifth of their class; 56% were in the top two fifths.

Requirements: The SAT or ACT and ACT Writing Test are recommended. In addition, the university follows an open admissions policy for Ohio applicants. Students should be graduates of an accredited secondary school or hold the GED. The preparatory program should include 4 years of English, 3 each of math, natural science, and social studies, and 2 of a foreign language. A GPA of 2.0 is required. AP and CLEP credits are accepted.

Procedure: Freshmen are admitted to all sessions. Entrance exams should be taken by the junior year or early in the senior year. There are deferred admissions and rolling admissions plans. Application deadlines are open. Application fee is $40. Applications are accepted online.

Transfer: 1086 transfer students enrolled in a recent year. Applicants must have earned college credit at another regionally accredited college or university and a GPA of 2.0. An interview is recommended.

Visiting: There are regularly scheduled orientations for prospective students, including an interview with an admissions representative and a student-guided campus tour. Academic appointments are available by request. There are guides for informal visits, visitors may sit in on classes, and stay overnight. To schedule a visit, contact the Office of Undergraduate Admissions.

Financial Aid: In a recent year, 81% of all full-time freshmen and 71% of continuing full-time students received some form of financial aid. 65% of all full-time freshmen and 64% of continuing full-time students received need-based aid. The average freshman award was $11,006. Need-based scholarships or need-based grants averaged $8,377; need-based self-help aid (loans and jobs) averaged $3,661; non-need-based athletic scholarships averaged $15,697; and other non-need-based awards and non-need-based scholarships averaged $4,781. The average financial indebtedness of a recent year graduate was $27,378. UT is a member of CSS. The FAFSA is required. The priority date for freshman financial aid applications for fall entry is April 1.

International Students: There are 602 international students enrolled. The school actively recruits these students. They must take the TOEFL with a minimum score of 61 on the Internet-based version (iBT).

Computers: Wireless access is available. There are approximately 5000 computers/terminals available on campus for students' use with Internet availability. All students may access the system 24 hours per day, except from Saturday at 5 p.m. to Sunday at noon. There are no time limits and no fees.

Graduates: In a recent year, 2354 bachelor's degrees were awarded. The most popular majors were marketing (7%), multi- and interdisciplinary studies (7%), and pharmacy (5%). In an average class, 23% graduate in 4 years or less, 41% graduate in 5 years or less, and 45% graduate in 6 years or less.

Admissions Contact: Director of Undergraduate Admissions. A campus DVD is available. E-Mail: *enroll@utoledo.edu* Web: *www.utoledo.edu*

URBANA UNIVERSITY B-3

Urbana, OH 43078-2091 **(937) 484-1356; (937) 484-1322**

Full-time: 510 men, 410 women	**Faculty:** n/av
Part-time: 200 men, 355 women	**Ph.D.s:** n/av
Graduate: 35 men, 65 women	**Student/Faculty:** n/av
Year: semesters, summer session	**Tuition:** $21,396
Application Deadline: open	**Room & Board:** $9000
Freshman Class: n/av	
SAT or ACT: required	

COMPETITIVE

Urbana University, founded in 1850 and affiliated with the Swedenborgian Church, is a independent institution emphasizing programs in liberal arts, business, professional training, and teacher preparation. There are 2 undergraduate schools and 2 graduate schools. The figures in the above capsule and in this profile are approximate. The library contains 70,000 volumes, 8176 microform items, 2099 audio/video tapes/CDs/DVDs, and subscribes to 328 periodicals including electronic. Computerized library services include interlibrary loans, database searching, and Internet access. Special learning facilities include a learning resource center, TV station, rare book room, and history museum. The 128-acre campus is in a small town 40 miles west of Columbus and 50 miles north of Dayton. Including any residence halls, there are 30 buildings.

Student Life: 90% of undergraduates are from Ohio. Others are from 5 states and 5 foreign countries. 95% are from public schools. 79% are white; 17% African American. The average age of freshmen is 20; all undergraduates, 24. 23% do not continue beyond their first year; 35% remain to graduate.

Housing: 450 students can be accommodated in college housing, which includes single-sex and coed dorms. In addition, there are honors houses. On-campus housing is available on a lottery system for upperclassmen. 58% of students commute. All students may keep cars.

Activities: There are no fraternities or sororities. There are 20 groups on campus, including art, band, cheerleading, choir, chorus, drama, ethnic, honors, international, literary magazine, marching band, musical theater, newspaper, pep band, political, professional, religious, social service, and student government. Popular campus events include Spring Week, Founders Day, and Activities Fair.

Sports: There are 5 intercollegiate sports for men and 4 for women, and 6 intramural sports for men and 6 for women. Facilities include a community center with a 3500-seat gym, a pool, handball and racquetball courts, a weight room, and outdoor tennis courts.

Disabled Students: 30% of the campus is accessible. Facilities include wheelchair ramps, elevators, special parking, and special class scheduling.

Services: Counseling and information services are available, as is tutoring in most subjects. There is remedial math, reading, and writing. Taped textbooks, reading and writing labs, and study skills seminars are also available.

Campus Safety and Security: Measures include 24-hour foot and vehicle patrol, self-defense education, and security escort services. There are emergency telephones and lighted pathways/sidewalks.

Programs of Study: Urbana confers B.A., B.S. and B.S.Ed. degrees. Associates and master's degrees are also awarded. Bachelor's degrees are awarded in BUSINESS (business administration and management and sports management), COMMUNICATIONS AND THE ARTS (communications and English), COMPUTER AND PHYSICAL SCIENCE (science), EDUCATION (elementary education, middle school education, and secondary education), HEALTH PROFESSIONS (premedicine and sports medicine), SOCIAL SCIENCE (criminal justice, liberal arts/general studies, philosophy, physical fitness/movement, prelaw, psychology, and sociology).

Required: To graduate, all students must complete 126 semester hours, with a minimum overall GPA of 2.0 and 2.5 in the major. Distribution requirements in a 47- to 49-hour core curriculum include 12 to 13 credit hours in math and science, 12 each in humanities and social sciences, 9 in communications, and 2 to 3 in health, phys ed, and recreation. The number of hours in the major varies. The business program requires business seminars; education graduates must take the NTE.

Special: Special academic programs include internships, cross-registration with the Southwestern Ohio Council for Higher Education, study abroad, and accelerated degree programs in teacher certification. B.A.-B.S. degrees, dual and student-designed majors, credit for life, military, and work experience, and nondegree study are also available. There is 1 national honor society, a freshman honors program, and 4 departmental honors programs.

Faculty/Classroom: 60% of faculty are male; 40% are female. All teach undergraduates. No introductory courses are taught by graduate students. The average class size in an introductory lecture is 18; in a laboratory, 7; and in a regular course, 19.

Requirements: The SAT or ACT is required for applicants under 23 years of age, with the ACT preferred (minimum score 18). SAT score's must be satisfactory. Applicants must be graduates of an accredited secodary school with a GPA of 2.0. The GED is accepted. An essay is required of all applicants, and an interview is recommended. CLEP credits are accepted. Important factors in the admissions decision are advanced placement or honors courses, evidence of special talent, and extracurricular activities record.

Procedure: Freshmen are admitted to all sessions. Entrance exams should be taken during the junior or senior year. There are deferred admissions and rolling admissions plans. Application deadlines are open. The application fee is $25. Applications are accepted online.

Transfer: Applicants must have at least 30 college credits with a GPA of 2.25 and must be in good standing at their previous institution. 30 of 126 credits required for the bachelor's degree must be completed at Urbana.

Visiting: There are regularly scheduled orientations for prospective students, consisting of a campus tour and sessions on academics, athletics, performing arts, financial aid, and student life. There are guides for informal visits; visitors may sit in on classes and stay overnight. To schedule a visit, contact the Admissions Office.

Financial Aid: The FAFSA, the college's own financial statement, and the state aid form for residents are required. Check with the school for current application deadlines.

International Students: The school actively recruits these students. They must take the TOEFL.

Computers: All students may access the system. There are no time limits and no fees.

Admissions Contact: Brian Keese, Director of Admissions. E-Mail: *bkeese@urbana.edu* Web: *www.urbana.edu*

URSULINE COLLEGE — E-1

Pepper Pike, OH 44124 — (440) 442-4203; (888) URSULINE; (440) 684-6138

Full-time: 46 men, 539 women	**Faculty:** 60; IIB, --$
Part-time: 43 men, 325 women	**Ph.D.s:** 64%
Graduate: 69 men, 466 women	**Student/Faculty:** 8 to 1
Year: semesters, summer session	**Tuition:** $25,410
Application Deadline: open	**Room & Board:** $8788
Freshman Class: 172 applied, 154 accepted, 83 enrolled	
SAT CR/M/W: 456/459/441 **ACT:** 20	**LESS COMPETITIVE**

Ursuline College, established in 1871, is a private, liberal arts, primarily women's college affiliated with the Roman Catholic Church. There are 3 undergraduate schools and 2 graduate schools. In addition to regional accreditation, Ursuline has baccalaureate program accreditation with CSWE and NCATE. The library contains 186,555 volumes, 4,675 microform items, 8,929 audio/video tapes/CDs/DVDs, and subscribes to 42,513 periodicals including electronic. Computerized library services include interlibrary loans, database searching, and Internet access. Special learning facilities include a learning resource center, art gallery, a media center, and curriculum library. The 114-acre campus is in a suburban area 13 miles east of Cleveland. Including any residence halls, there are 16 buildings.

Student Life: 97% of undergraduates are from Ohio. Others are from 18 states, 9 foreign countries, and Canada. 87% are from public schools. 65% are white; 28% African American. 29% are Catholic; 25% Baptist, Budhist, and Muslim; 11% claim no religious affiliation. The average age of freshmen is 18; all undergraduates, 29. 30% do not continue beyond their first year; 48% remain to graduate.

Housing: 242 students can be accommodated in college housing, which includes single-sex and coed dorms. On-campus housing is guaranteed for all 4 years, is available on a first-come, first-served basis, and is available on a lottery system for upperclassmen. Priority is given to out-of-town students. 84% of students commute. Alcohol is not permitted. All students may keep cars.

Activities: There are no fraternities or sororities. There are 19 groups on campus, including choir, drama, ethnic, gay, international, literary magazine, professional, religious, social, social service, and student government. Popular campus events include All College Day, a Formal Dance, and Charity Benefits.

Sports: There are 10 intercollegiate sports for women. Facilities include a fitness center, a swimming pool, a gym, and a campus center.

Disabled Students: 90% of the campus is accessible. Facilities include wheelchair ramps, elevators, special parking, and specially equipped restrooms.

Services: Counseling and information services are available, as is tutoring in most subjects. There is a reader service for the blind, and remedial math, reading, and writing.

Campus Safety and Security: Measures include 24-hour foot and vehicle patrol and security escort services. There are emergency telephones and lighted pathways/sidewalks.

Programs of Study: Ursuline confers B.A., B.F.A., and B.S.N. degrees. Master's and doctoral degrees are also awarded. Bachelor's degrees are awarded in BIOLOGICAL SCIENCE (biology/biological science and biotechnology), BUSINESS (accounting, business administration and management, fashion merchandising, human resources, management information systems, and marketing management), COMMUNICATIONS AND THE ARTS (art, English, graphic design, historic preservation, and public relations), COMPUTER AND PHYSICAL SCIENCE (mathematics), EDUCATION (early childhood education, elementary education, middle school education, secondary education, and special education), HEALTH PROFESSIONS (health care administration, nursing, and premedicine), SOCIAL SCIENCE (fashion design and technology, history, humanities, law, philosophy, prelaw, psychology, religion, social work, and sociology). Nursing is the strongest academically. Nursing and business have the largest enrollments.

Required: To graduate, students must complete 128 semester hours for the B.A. and 129 for the B.S.N., with a minimum GPA of 2.0 (2.5 in education courses). All students must take 49 credits of general education courses, structured to develop progressive stages of learning.

Special: Ursuline offers co-op programs in business, public relations, and fashion merchandising and cross-registration with colleges in the NE Ohio Commission of Higher Education. Internships, a general studies degree, dual and student-designed majors, nondegree study, and accelerated degree programs in business management, health care administration, legal studies, and management information systems are available. Students may receive credit for life, military, or work experience. There are pass/fail options and a continuing studies program for nontraditional students. There are 2 national honor societies and 3 departmental honors programs.

Faculty/Classroom: 22% of faculty are male; 78% are female. 84% teach undergraduates. No introductory courses are taught by graduate students. The average class size in an introductory lecture is 18; in a laboratory is 10; and in a regular course is 11.

Admissions: 90% of the recent year applicants were accepted. The SAT scores for a recent year freshman class were: Critical Reading--68% below 500, 21% between 500 and 599, 11% between 600 and 700; Math--74% below 500, 21% between 500 and 599, 5% between 600 and 700; Writing--74% below 500, 21% between 500 and 599, 5% between 600 and 700. The ACT scores were 56% below 21, 26% between 21 and 23, 15% between 24 and 26, 2% between 27 and 28, and 2% above 28. 27% of the current freshmen were in the top fifth of their class; 49% were in the top two fifths. 1 freshman graduated first in the class.

Requirements: The SAT or ACT is required. In addition, students should be graduates of an accredited secondary school and have a GPA of 2.5. Recommended college preparatory courses include 4 units of English, 3 each of social studies, math, and science, 2 of a foreign language, and 1 each of fine/performing arts and phys ed/health. A recommendation from a teacher or counselor is required and an interview is encouraged. A GPA of 2.5 is required. AP and CLEP credits are accepted. Important factors in the admissions decision are advanced placement or honors courses, recommendations by school officials, and leadership record.

Procedure: Freshmen are admitted fall, spring, and summer. Entrance exams should be taken in the junior year. There are deferred admissions and rolling admissions plans. Application deadlines are open. Application fee is $25. Notification is sent on a rolling basis. Applications are accepted online.

Transfer: 144 transfer students enrolled in a recent year. Offical copies of all transcripts and a 2.5 GPA are required. Students with less than 24 semester hours must provide high school transcripts. 43 of 128 credits required for the bachelor's degree must be completed at Ursuline.

Visiting: There are regularly scheduled orientations for prospective students, including an open house and overnight visit. There are guides for informal visits, visitors may sit in on classes, and stay overnight. To schedule a visit, contact the Admissions Office.

Financial Aid: In a recent year, 93% of all full-time freshmen and 90% of continuing full-time students received some form of financial aid. 93% of all full-time freshmen and 79% of continuing full-time students received need-based aid. The average freshman award was $21,668. Need-based scholarships or need-based grants averaged $17,890 ($33,750 maximum); need-based self-help aid (loans and jobs) averaged $4,160 ($7,500 maximum); non-need-based athletic scholarships averaged $9,134 ($25,000 maximum); and other non-need-based awards and non-need-based scholarships averaged $4,872 ($11,000 maximum). 3% of undergraduate students work part-time. Average annual earnings from campus work are $2800. The average financial indebtedness of the 2011 graduate was $20,718. The FAFSA and the college's own financial statement are required. The deadline for filing freshman financial aid applications for fall entry is March 1.

International Students: There are 6 international students enrolled. They must take the TOEFL with a minimum score of 500 on the paper-based TOEFL (PBT) or 60 on the Internet-based version (iBT). They must also take the SAT or ACT.

Computers: Wireless access is available. Access to the college's network is available on 72 PCs in labs in 3 buildings and the library. Wired drops are available in the Pilla Center and library, and wireless aps are available in the Pilla Center, Science Building, and library. All students may access the system daily at designated hours. There are no time limits. The fee is $250.

Admissions Contact: Matthew McCaffrey, Director of Admissions. E-Mail: *admission@ursuline.edu* Web: *www.ursuline.edu*

WALSH UNIVERSITY D-2

North Canton, OH 44720 (330) 490-7172
(800) 362-9846; (330) 490-7165

Full-time: 781 men, 1135 women
Part-time: 143 men, 326 women
Graduate: 166 men, 412 women
Year: semesters, summer session
Application Deadline: August 25
Faculty: 118; IIB, --$
Ph.D.s: 65%
Student/Faculty: 13 to 1
Tuition: $25,840
Room & Board: $9260
Freshman Class: 1640 applied, 1265 accepted, 492 enrolled
SAT CR/M: 500/530 **ACT:** 22 **COMPETITIVE**

Walsh University was established in 1958 by the Brothers of Christian Instruction, a religious order of the Roman Catholic Church. The private institution offers undergraduate programs in liberal arts, business, communication, education, professional training, and nursing. There are 9 undergraduate schools and 6 graduate schools. In addition to regional accreditation, Walsh has baccalaureate program accreditation with NCATE and NLN. The library contains 299,111 volumes, 16,133 audio/video tapes/CDs/DVDs, and subscribes to 87,434 periodicals including electronic. Computerized library services include interlibrary loans, database searching, Internet access, and Wi-Fi capability. Special learning facilities include an art gallery, radio station, a child development center, a corporate museum, Hoover Park, which includes trails and recreation facilities, bioinformatics lab, and a community clinic with counseling and wellness programs for the underserved. The 143-acre campus is in a small town 20 miles south of Akron. Including any residence halls, there are 24 buildings.

Student Life: 94% of undergraduates are from Ohio. Others are from 18 states, 20 foreign countries, and Canada. 76% are from public schools. 78% are White. 40% are Catholic; 33% claim no religious affiliation; 24% Protestant. The average age of freshmen is 18; all undergraduates, 24. 25% do not continue beyond their first year; 65% remain to graduate.

Housing: 1050 students can be accommodated in college housing, which includes single-sex and coed dorms and on-campus apartments. In addition, there are honors houses, special-interest houses, study floors, and substance-free floors. On-campus housing is guaranteed for all 4 years. 56% of students commute. All students may keep cars.

Activities: There are no fraternities or sororities. There are 40 groups on campus, including special interest, art, band, cheerleading, choir, chorale, chorus, dance, drama, environmental, ethnic, honors, international, leadership honor societies, literary magazine, marching band, newspaper, pep band, political, professional, radio and TV, religious, social, social service, student government, and yearbook. Popular campus events include Walshfest, Spring Formal, and Improv.

Sports: There are 9 intercollegiate sports for men and 9 for women, and 10 intramural sports for men and 9 for women. Facilities include 2 gymnasiums, 1200-seat and 2,000 seat, outdoor basketball and tennis courts, a track, softball and baseball fields, practice and intramural fields, a lighted soccer field, a game room, student exercise and weight rooms, located around campus, including in the residence halls, and an all-purpose artifical practice field. Intercollegiate football games are played at Fawcett Stadium, next door to the National Pro Football Hall of Fame and site of the Annual Hall of Fame Game.

Disabled Students: All of the campus is accessible. Facilities include wheelchair ramps, elevators, special parking, specially equipped restrooms, special class scheduling, lowered drinking fountains, lowered telephones, and special housing.

Services: Counseling and information services are available, as is tutoring in every subject. There is remedial math, reading, and writing. One-on-one and group tutoring and a study skills course are available.

Campus Safety and Security: Measures include 24-hour foot and vehicle patrol, emergency notification system, self-defense education, and security escort services. There are emergency telephones, lighted pathways/sidewalks, and controlled access to dorms/residences.

Programs of Study: Walsh confers B.A., B.S., B.S.Ed. and B.S.N. degrees. Associate, master's, and doctoral degrees are also awarded. Bachelor's degrees are awarded in BIOLOGICAL SCIENCE (biochemistry, bioinformatics, and biology/biological science), BUSINESS (accounting, business administration and management, business communications, international business management, and marketing management), COMMUNICATIONS AND THE ARTS (communications, English, French, graphic design, and Spanish), COMPUTER AND PHYSICAL SCIENCE (chemistry, computer science, mathematics, and science), EDUCATION (early childhood education, education of the emotionally handicapped, education of the exceptional child, education of the mentally handicapped, education of the physically handicapped, elementary education, middle school education, museum studies, physical education, secondary education, and special education), ENGINEERING AND ENVIRONMENTAL DESIGN (environmental science), HEALTH PROFESSIONS (clinical science, exercise science, nursing, physical therapy, predentistry, premedicine, preoptometry, prepharmacy, prephysical therapy, and preveterinary science), SOCIAL SCIENCE (criminal justice, family/consumer studies, history, international relations, international studies, liberal arts/general studies, philosophy, political science/government, prelaw, psychology, science and society, sociology, and theological studies). Biology, nursing, and business are the strongest academically. Biology, nursing, and management have the largest enrollments.

Required: To graduate, students must complete 125 semester hours with a minimum 2.0 GPA. The number of hours required in the major varies. A core curriculum of 37 hours is required, including courses in English, art or music, science, social science, math, humanities, theology, philosophy, service learning, diversity, and a foreign language.

Special: Work-study programs are available to students having financial need. Walsh offers internships for most majors; study abroad in 14 countries, with a campus outside Rome, Italy and a partner school in Kisubi, Uganda; accelerated degree programs in nursing, business and management; pre-medical, pre-dental, pre-pharmacy, pre-veterinary, pre-physical therapy, graduate programs in business, physial therapy, education, counseling, theology, and nursing; evening and continuing education programs; and credit for life experience. Reduced core for transfer students. There are 11 national honor societies, a freshman honors program, and 11 departmental honors programs.

Faculty/Classroom: 45% of faculty are male; 55% are female. 90% teach undergraduates, 37% do research, and 20% do both. No introductory courses are taught by graduate students. The average class size in an introductory lecture is 15; in a laboratory is 14; and in a regular course is 16.

Admissions: 77% of the 2013-2014 applicants were accepted. The SAT scores for the 2013-2014 freshman class were: Critical Reading--50% below 500, 36% between 500 and 599, 13% between 600 and 699, and 1% between 700 and 800; Math--34% below 500, 47% between 500 and 599, and 19% between 600 and 699. The ACT scores were 30% below 21, 31% between 21 and 23, 23% between 24 and 26, 10% between 27 and 28, and 6% above 28. 37% of the current freshmen were in the top fifth of their class; 67% were in the top two fifths. 13 freshmen graduated first in their class.

Requirements: The ACT is required. The SAT is recommended. In addition, the applicant must be a graduate of an accredited secondary school; the GED is accepted. Walsh recommends completion of 4 units of English, 3 each of math, science, and social studies, 2 of foreign language, and 1 of fine or performing arts. An essay and an interview are recommended. A GPA of 2.4 is required. AP and CLEP credits are accepted. Important factors in the admissions decision are recommendations by school officials, leadership record, and extracurricular activities record.

Procedure: Freshmen are admitted to all sessions. Entrance exams should be taken during the junior year. There are deferred admissions and rolling admissions plans. Applications should be filed by August 25 for fall entry; January 1 for spring entry; and April 29 for summer entry, along with a $25 fee. Notification is sent on a rolling basis. Applications are accepted online.

Transfer: 213 transfer students enrolled in 2012-2013. Applicants must have a minimum GPA of 2.0 from previous colleges attended. 32 of 125 credits required for the bachelor's degree must be completed at Walsh.

Visiting: There are regularly scheduled orientations for prospective students, consisting of a campus tour, a session with financial aid and admissions staff, and an opportunity to meet with faculty, coaches, and other personnel. There are guides for informal visits, visitors may sit in on classes, and stay overnight. To schedule a visit, contact the Admissions Office.

Financial Aid: In 2013-2014, 99% of all full-time freshmen and 96% of continuing full-time students received some form of financial aid. 81% of all full-time freshmen and 75% of continuing full-time students received need-based aid. The average freshman award was $20,140. Need-based scholarships or need-based grants averaged $7,067 ($12,725 maximum); need-based self-help aid (loans and jobs) averaged $4,340 ($7,500 maximum); non-need-based athletic scholarships averaged $7,946 ($31,356 maximum); and other non-need-based awards and non-need-based scholarships averaged $9,086 ($24,569 maximum). 83% of undergraduate students work part-time. Average annual earnings from campus work are $849. The average financial indebtedness of the 2013 graduate was $24,851. Walsh is a member of CSS. The FAFSA and the college's own financial statement are required. The priority date for freshman financial aid applications for fall entry is February 14. The deadline for filing freshman financial aid applications for fall entry is rolling.

International Students: There are 80 international students enrolled. The school actively recruits these students. They must take the TOEFL with a minimum score of 500 on the paper-based TOEFL (PBT) or 61 on the Internet-based version (iBT), STEP.

Computers: All students may access the system. There are no time limits and no fees.

Graduates: From July 1, 2012 to June 30, 2013, 451 bachelor's degrees were awarded. The most popular majors were nursing (24%), management (19%), and biology (12%). 108 companies recruited on campus in 2012-2013. In an average class, 52% graduate in 4 years or less, 62% graduate in 5 years or less, and 64% graduate in 6 years or less. Of the 2012 graduating class, 24% were enrolled in graduate school within 6 months of graduation, and 63% were employed.

Admissions Contact: Brett Freshhour, Vice President for Enrollment Management. E-Mail: *admissions@walsh.edu* Web: *www.walsh.edu*

WILBERFORCE UNIVERSITY B-4

Wilberforce, OH 45384-1091 (937) 376-2911, ext. 721
(800) 367-8568; (937) 376-4751

Full-time: 310 men, 490 women	**Faculty:** n/av
Part-time: 15 men, 15 women	**Ph.D.s:** n/av
Graduate: n/av	**Student/Faculty:** n/av
Year: semesters	**Tuition:** $14,000
Application Deadline: open	**Room & Board:** $6200
Freshman Class: n/av	
SAT or ACT: recommended	

LESS COMPETITIVE

Wilberforce University, founded in 1856, is a private institution operated under the auspices of the African Methodist Episcopal Church; it was the first black college in America. Its programs emphasize the liberal arts, business, art and fine arts, engineering, and music. The library contains 60,000 volumes, 12,000 microform items, 200 audio/video tapes/CDs/DVDs, and subscribes to 350 periodicals including electronic. Special learning facilities include a learning resource center, radio station, and the nearby National Afro-American Museum. The 125-acre campus is in a rural area 20 miles east of Dayton. Including any residence halls, there are 21 buildings.

Student Life: 64% of undergraduates are from out of state, mostly the Mid-West. Students are from 32 states and 2 foreign countries. All are African American. The average age of freshmen is 18; all undergraduates, 20.

Housing: 775 students can be accommodated in college housing, which includes dorms and married student housing. In addition, there are honors houses. On-campus housing is guaranteed for all 4 years. Alcohol is not permitted. All students may keep cars.

Activities: 10% of men belong to 3 national fraternities; 10% of women belong to 3 national sororities. There are 30 groups on campus, including choir, computers, dance, ethnic, honors, international, literary magazine, newspaper, political, religious, social, student government, and yearbook. Popular campus events include Fall Festival and Dawn Dance.

Sports: There are 5 intercollegiate sports for men and 4 for women, and 4 intramural sports for men and 4 for women. Facilities include a 1500-seat gym, outdoor and cross-country track, a softball field, and basketball, volleyball, and tennis courts.

Disabled Students: 50% of the campus is accessible. Facilities include wheelchair ramps, special parking, specially equipped restrooms, and limited elevator service in classroom buildings only.

Services: Counseling and information services are available, as is tutoring in most subjects. There is a reader service for the blind, and remedial math, reading, and writing.

Programs of Study: Wilberforce confers B.A. and B.S. degrees. Bachelor's degrees are awarded in BIOLOGICAL SCIENCE (biology/biological science), BUSINESS (accounting, banking and finance, business administration and management, business economics, management science, and marketing/retailing/merchandising), COMMUNICATIONS AND THE ARTS (communications, fine arts, literature, and music), COMPUTER AND PHYSICAL SCIENCE (chemistry, computer science, information sciences and systems, mathematics, and science), ENGINEERING AND ENVIRONMENTAL DESIGN (preengineering), HEALTH PROFESSIONS (health care administration and rehabilitation therapy), SOCIAL SCIENCE (economics, liberal arts/general studies, political science/government, prelaw, psychology, social science, social work, and sociology).

Required: To graduate, students must complete 126 credit hours with a minimum GPA of 2.0 and no grade in the major below a C. To fulfill the general studies requirements, all students must complete a first-year program, which includes composition and computer literacy courses, and they must also take at least 1 course from each of the following areas: humanistic traditions, music, art, religion, communication arts, literature and language, non-Western studies, behavioral sciences, economics and political science, physical sciences, and life science. 2 credits in health and phys ed and completion of 2 cooperative education experiences are also required.

Special: Wilberforce offers a co-op arrangement with St. John's University School of Law and cross-registration through the Southwestern Ohio Council for Higher Education. B.A.-B.S. degrees are available in all majors, and there are dual majors in engineering along with a 3-2 engineering degree with the University of Dayton. Credit is given for the mandatory co-op education program, in which students participate in paid work experience in their chosen field. Nondegree study is possible in military science. There is 1 national honor society, a freshman honors program, and 4 departmental honors programs.

Faculty/Classroom: 50% of faculty are male; 50% are female. No introductory courses are taught by graduate students. The average class size in an introductory lecture is 12 and in a regular course, 18.

Requirements: The SAT or ACT is recommended. SAT subject tests are recommended. In addition, students should be graduates of an accredited secondary school and have 15 Carnegie units, including 4 units of English, 2 to 3 of math, including algebra, 2 to 3 of science, including a lab course, and 2 of social studies, including U.S. history. The GED is accepted with a score of 45 or better. A GPA of 2.0 is required. AP and CLEP credits are accepted. Important factors in the admissions decision are recommendations by school officials, advanced placement or honors courses, and evidence of special talent.

Procedure: Freshmen are admitted fall and spring. Entrance exams should be taken by the fall of the senior year. There are early decision, early admissions, and rolling admissions plans. Application deadlines are open. A waiting list is maintained.

Transfer: A minimum college GPA of 2.0 is required. 30 of 126 credits required for the bachelor's degree must be completed at Wilberforce.

Visiting: There are regularly scheduled orientations for prospective students. There are guides for informal visits. To schedule a visit, contact the Office of Admissions.

Financial Aid: Wilberforce is a member of CSS. The FAFSA, the college's own financial statement, and parent and student federal income tax returns are required. Check with the school for current application deadlines.

International Students: International students must take the TOEFL and also take the SAT or ACT.

Computers: Students enrolled in computer and engineering programs may access the system. There are no time limits and no fees.

Admissions Contact: Kenneth C. Christmon, Director of Admissions. E-Mail: *admissions@wilberforce.edu* Web: *www.wilberforce.edu*

WILMINGTON COLLEGE B-4

Wilmington, OH 45177 (937) 382-6661, ext. 260
(800) 341-9318; (937) 382-7077

Full-time: 530 men, 635 women	**Faculty:** n/av; IIB, --$
Part-time: 90 men, 150 women	**Ph.D.s:** 69%
Graduate: n/av	**Student/Faculty:** n/av
Year: semesters, summer session	**Tuition:** $26,840
Application Deadline: open	**Room & Board:** $9370
Freshman Class: n/av	
SAT or ACT: required	

COMPETITIVE

Wilmington College, established in 1870, is a private institution sponsored by the Society of Friends. The college offers programs in the liberal arts, business, health science, teacher preparation, agricultural studies, religious studies, and athletic training. There is 1 graduate school. In addition to regional accreditation, Wilmington has baccalaureate program accreditation with NCATE. The library contains 110,000 volumes, 42,000 microform items, 1400 audio/video tapes/CDs/DVDs, and subscribes to 400 periodicals including electronic. Computerized library services include interlibrary loans and database searching. Special learning facilities include a learning resource center, art gallery, Peace Resource Center, Quaker museum, observatory, greenhouse, and academic farm. The 65-acre campus is in a small town 50 miles from Cincinnati. Including any residence halls, there are 21 buildings.

Student Life: 98% of undergraduates are from Ohio. Others are from 13 states and 4 foreign countries. 67% are white; 11% African American. 40% claim no religious affiliation; 17% Catholic. The average age of freshmen is 18; all undergraduates, 21. 31% do not continue beyond their first year.

Housing: 842 students can be accommodated in college housing, which includes single-sex and coed dorms and on-campus apartments. In addition, there are fraternity houses. On-campus housing is guaranteed for all 4 years. 65% of students live on campus. All students may keep cars.

Activities: 8% of men belong to 4 local and 1 national fraternities; 8% of women belong to 4 local sororities. There are 63 groups on campus, including band, cheerleading, choir, chorale, drama, ethnic, gay, honors, international, literary magazine, musical theater, newspaper, orchestra, photography, political, professional, religious, social, social service, student government, and yearbook. Popular campus events include Community Day, Westheimer Peace Symposium, and Fall Fest.

Sports: There are 11 intercollegiate sports for men and 10 for women, and 8 intramural sports for men and 8 for women. Facilities include an Olympic-size pool, a Nautilus weight-training room, an exercise room, racquetball courts, a 4500-seat gym, and a 3000-seat stadium.

Disabled Students: 20% of the campus is accessible. Facilities include wheelchair ramps, elevators, special parking, specially equipped restrooms, and special class scheduling.

Services: Counseling and information services are available, as is tutoring in every subject. There is remedial math, reading, and writing.

Campus Safety and Security: Measures include 24-hour foot and vehicle patrol and security escort services. There are emergency telephones and lighted pathways/sidewalks.

Programs of Study: Wilmington confers B.A. and B.S. degrees. Master's degrees are also awarded. Bachelor's degrees are awarded in AGRICUL-

TURE (agricultural business management, agronomy, animal science, equine science, and range/farm management), BIOLOGICAL SCIENCE (bacteriology, biochemistry, biology/biological science, and environmental biology), BUSINESS (accounting, business administration and management, management science, marketing and distribution, marketing management, and sports management), COMMUNICATIONS AND THE ARTS (advertising, art, communications, dramatic arts, English, journalism, music, public relations, Spanish, and speech/debate/rhetoric), COMPUTER AND PHYSICAL SCIENCE (astronomy, chemistry, computer science, geology, information sciences and systems, mathematics, and planetary and space science), EDUCATION (agricultural education, athletic training, early childhood education, education, elementary education, English education, health education, mathematics education, middle school education, physical education, science education, secondary education, social science education, and social studies education), HEALTH PROFESSIONS (premedicine and preveterinary science), SOCIAL SCIENCE (criminal justice, economics, history, liberal arts/general studies, philosophy, political science/government, prelaw, psychology, religion, social science, social work, and sociology). Chemistry, biology, and athletic training are the strongest academically. Business, agriculture, and athletic training have the largest enrollments.

Required: To graduate, students must complete 124 semester hours, with no more than 60 hours in the major, with a minimum GPA of 2.0. At least 40 hours must be in upper-division work. General education requirements include courses in English and math competence, international knowledge, basic areas of thought and expression, and personal fitness.

Special: Special academic programs include work-study, internships, a Washington semester, and cross-registration with the Southwest Ohio Consortium. Study abroad may be arranged in Mexico, Austria, France, and other countries. Dual majors in any subject and student-designed majors are offered. Credit for experience, nondegree study, and pass/fail options are possible. There are 5 national honor societies, a freshman honors program, and 3 departmental honors programs.

Faculty/Classroom: 65% of faculty are male; 57% are female. All teach undergraduates. The average class size in an introductory lecture is 25 and in a regular course is 19.

Requirements: The SAT or ACT is required. In addition, applicants must be graduates of an accredited secondary school, with 4 units of English, 2 units each of math, science, and social studies, and a recommended 2 units of a foreign language. An additional 6 units is required in other areas. The GED is accepted. An interview is recommended. An essay may be required. A GPA of 3.0 is required. AP and CLEP credits are accepted. Important factors in the admissions decision are recommendations by school officials, parents or siblings who attended the school, and recommendations by alumni.

Procedure: Freshmen are admitted fall and spring. Entrance exams should be taken as early as possible. There are deferred admissions and rolling admissions plans. Application deadlines are open. The application fee is $25. Notification is sent on a rolling basis.

Transfer: 63 transfer students enrolled in a recent year. Applicants' college and high school transcripts are evaluated on an individual basis. They must have a 2.0 GPA and a completed transfer recommendation form. 30 of 124 credits required for the bachelor's degree must be completed at Wilmington.

Visiting: There are regularly scheduled orientations for prospective students, including meetings with faculty and a tour of the campus. There are guides for informal visits, and visitors may sit in on classes and stay overnight. To schedule a visit, contact the Admissions Office.

Financial Aid: The FAFSA is required. Check with the school for current application deadlines.

International Students: The school actively recruits these students. They must take the TOEFL with a minimum score of 500 on the paper-based TOEFL (PBT). The TOEFL is not required if the SAT is taken. Students who have been previously enrolled in a U.S. high school must take the SAT or ACT.

Computers: 156 workstations are available for student use in libraries and computer centers. All students may access the system at any time. There are no time limits and no fees.

Graduates: In a recent year, 340 bachelor's degrees were awarded. The most popular majors were education (25%), business/marketing (24%), and psychology (10%).

Admissions Contact: Tina Garland, Director of Admissions. E-mail: *admissions@wilmington.edu* Web: *www.wilmington.edu*

WITTENBERG UNIVERSITY — B-3

Springfield, OH 45501 — (937) 327-6377; (877) 206-0332; (937) 327-6379

Full-time: 819 men, 1034 women	**Faculty:** 131; IIB, -$
Part-time: 32 men, 74 women	**Ph.D.s:** 92%
Graduate: 20 women	**Student/Faculty:** 12 to 1
Year: semesters, summer session	**Tuition:** $38,530
Application Deadline: March 15	**Room & Board:** $10,236
Freshman Class: 5160 applied, 4612 accepted, 549 enrolled	
SAT CR/M: 560/580	**ACT:** 26 **VERY COMPETITIVE**

Wittenberg University, founded in 1845, is a private liberal arts and sciences institution affiliated with the Evangelical Lutheran Church in America. In addition to regional accreditation, Wittenberg has baccalaureate program accreditation with NASM and NCATE. The library contains 503,058 volumes, 82,850 microform items, 21,328 audio/video tapes/CDs/DVDs, and subscribes to 9,986 periodicals including electronic. Computerized library services include interlibrary loans, database searching, Internet access, and Wi-Fi capability. Special learning facilities include an art gallery, radio station, a geology museum, an observatory, a GIS lab with supercomputer, and a parallel processing lab. The 114-acre campus is in a suburban area 25 miles east of Dayton, 40 miles west of Columbus, and 75 miles from Cincinnati. Including any residence halls, there are 26 buildings.

Student Life: 71% of undergraduates are from Ohio. Others are from 40 states, 26 foreign countries, and Canada. 80% are from public schools. 81% are White. 36% claim no religious affiliation; 30% Protestant; 16% Catholic. The average age of freshmen is 18; all undergraduates, 21. 26% do not continue beyond their first year; 63% remain to graduate.

Housing: 1806 students can be accommodated in college housing, which includes single-sex and coed dorms, on-campus apartments, off-campus apartments, and married student housing. In addition, there are honors houses, language houses, special-interest houses, fraternity houses, sorority houses, a substance-free residence hall, and an international awareness house. On-campus housing is guaranteed for the freshman year only and is available on a lottery system for upperclassmen. 84% of students live on campus; of those, 84% remain on campus on weekends. All students may keep cars.

Activities: 25% of men belong to 6 national fraternities; 35% of women belong to 5 national sororities. There are 125 groups on campus, including and mock trail association, caving club, fishing club, outdoor club, anime club, art, band, cheerleading, choir, chorale, computers, dance, drama, ethnic, gay, honors, international, jazz band, literary magazine, musical theater, newspaper, opera, orchestra, pep band, photography, political, professional, radio and TV, religious, social, social service, and student government. Popular campus events include Wittenberg Series, International Festival and Wittfest.

Sports: There are 11 intercollegiate sports for men and 12 for women, and 12 intramural sports for men and 12 for women. Facilities include a multipurpose field house, a swimming pool, 6 racquetball/handball courts, a cardio fitness center, a strength center, and sports medicine rooms. There is also a 3,200-seat gym, a 3,200-seat stadium, 12 acres of playing fields, a 1,000-seat baseball stadium, a 120-seat softball field and rugby playing field, a 400-meter track, and 12 tennis courts.

Disabled Students: 81% of the campus is accessible. Facilities include wheelchair ramps, elevators, special parking, specially equipped restrooms, special class scheduling, lowered drinking fountains, and lowered telephones.

Services: Counseling and information services are available, as is tutoring in most subjects. There is also a math workshop and writing and oral communication centers.

Campus Safety and Security: Measures include 24-hour foot and vehicle patrol, emergency notification system, self-defense education, and security escort services. There are emergency telephones, lighted pathways/sidewalks, a bicycle patrol, and various prevention programs. City police support campus police during the evening. There is also a student Eyes and Ears Program and a campus security committee made up of students and faculty.

Programs of Study: Wittenberg confers B.A., B.F.A., B.M.E. and B.S. degrees. Master's degrees are also awarded. Bachelor's degrees are awarded in BIOLOGICAL SCIENCE (biology/biological science), BUSINESS (business administration and management), COMMUNICATIONS AND THE ARTS (communications, dramatic arts, English, fine arts, French, German, music, Russian, and Spanish), COMPUTER AND PHYSICAL SCIENCE (chemistry, computer science, geology, mathematics, and physics), EDUCATION (elementary education, foreign languages education, middle school education, music education, science education, secondary education, and special education), ENGINEERING AND ENVIRONMENTAL DESIGN (environmental science), SOCIAL SCIENCE (American studies, East Asian studies, economics, geography, history, international relations, philosophy, political science/government, psychology, religion, and sociology). Biology, communication, and psychology are the strongest academically. Business, psychology, and biology have the largest enrollments.

Required: To graduate, students must complete at least 130 credits and have a minimum GPA of 2.0. The required minimum GPA and number of hours in the major vary by department. All Wittenberg students complete a program of general education built on 16 learning goals. These include acquisition of foundations skills in writing, math, foreign language, speaking, research, and computing, the understanding of the different arts and sciences disciplines and their distinct methodological approaches to knowledge, and an introduction to non-Western culture, the diversity of human experience, and inter- and transdisciplinary knowledge. Students achieve each general education learning goal by completing 1 to 2 courses. As part of general education, students also complete 2 physical activity classes and perform 30 hours of community service.

Special: Special academic programs include internships, cross-registration through the Southwest Ohio Consortium, a Washington semester, work-study programs, study-abroad opportunities in many countries, accelerated degree programs, dual and student-designed majors, non-degree study, and pass/fail options. A 3-2 engineering degree is offered through Washington, Columbia, and Case Western Reserve Universities and Georgia Institute of Technology. There is also a 3-2 nursing program with Johns Hopkins University and an occupational therapy program with Washington University. There are 11 national honor societies, including Phi Beta Kappa, a freshman honors program, and 19 departmental honors programs.

Faculty/Classroom: 57% of faculty are male; 43% are female. All teach undergraduates. No introductory courses are taught by graduate students. The average class size in an introductory lecture is 25; in a laboratory is 20; and in a regular course is 18.

Admissions: 89% of the 2013-2014 applicants were accepted. The SAT scores for the 2013-2014 freshman class were: Critical Reading--15% below 500, 51% between 500 and 599, 24% between 600 and 699, and 10% between 700 and 800; Math--16% below 500, 41% between 500 and 599, 39% between 600 and 699, and 4% between 700 and 800. The ACT scores were 6% below 21, 21% between 21 and 23, 34% between 24 and 26, 19% between 27 and 28, and 20% above 28. 40% of the current freshmen were in the top fifth of their class; 72% were in the top two fifths.

Requirements: Students should have graduated from an accredited secondary school with 16 academic credits, including 4 units of English and 3 each of a foreign language, math, science, and social studies, which includes history. An essay is required and an interview advised. Art students must present a portfolio, and music students must audition. Wittenberg is test score optional. AP credits are accepted. Important factors in the admissions decision are advanced placement or honors courses, evidence of special talent, and extracurricular activities record.

Procedure: Freshmen are admitted to all sessions. Entrance exams should be taken by the fall of the senior year, but as early as possible. There are early decision, early admissions, deferred admissions, and rolling admissions plans. Early decision applications should be filed by November 15; regular applications, by March 15 for fall entry; and December 1 for spring entry, along with a $40 fee. Notification of early decision is sent January 1; regular decision, on a rolling basis. 152 early decision candidates were accepted for the 2013-2014 class. Applications are accepted online.

Transfer: 30 transfer students enrolled in 2012-2013. Applicants should have a minimum GPA of 2.0 at an accredited college and be in good academic and social standing. High school transcripts are required in some cases. An interview is recommended. 50 of 130 credits required for the bachelor's degree must be completed at Wittenberg.

Visiting: There are regularly scheduled orientations for prospective students, including a tour and interview. There are guides for informal visits, visitors may sit in on classes, and stay overnight. To schedule a visit, contact the Admissions Office.

Financial Aid: In 2013-2014, 83% of all full-time freshmen and 83% of continuing full-time students received some form of financial aid. The average freshman award was $31,935. Need-based scholarships or need-based grants averaged $26,638; need-based self-help aid (loans and jobs) averaged $5,810; and other non-need-based awards and non-need-based scholarships averaged $18,110. 46% of undergraduate students work part-time. Average annual earnings from campus work are $2400. The average financial indebtedness of the 2013 graduate was $30,748. The FAFSA is required. The deadline for filing freshman financial aid applications for fall entry is March 15.

International Students: There are 41 international students enrolled. The school actively recruits these students. They must take the TOEFL with a minimum score of 550 on the paper-based TOEFL (PBT) or 79 on the Internet-based version (iBT), or the SAT or ACT. Institutions math and language placement tests.

Computers: All students may access the system 24 hours a day. There are no time limits and no fees.

Graduates: From July 1, 2012 to June 30, 2013, 362 bachelor's degrees were awarded. The most popular majors were social sciences (16%), biology (16%), and communication (8%). 136 companies recruited on campus in 2012-2013. In an average class, 59% graduate in 4 years or less, 62% graduate in 5 years or less, and 63% graduate in 6 years or less.

Admissions Contact: Karen Hunt, Director of Admissions. E-Mail: *admission@wittenberg.edu* Web: *www.wittenberg.edu*

WRIGHT STATE UNIVERSITY — B-4

Dayton, OH 45435 — (937) 775-5700; (937) 775-4410

Full-time: 4900 men, 5424 women — **Faculty:** n/av; I, --$
Part-time: 1371 men, 1448 women — **Ph.D.s:** n/av
Graduate: 1602 men, 2035 women — **Student/Faculty:** 22 to 1
Year: semesters, summer session — **Tuition:** $8354 ($16,182)
Application Deadline: open — **Room & Board:** $8629
Freshman Class: 8112 applied, 5569 accepted, 2311 enrolled
SAT CR/M/W: 499/503/481 — **ACT:** 21 — **COMPETITIVE**

Wright State University, founded in 1964, is a state-supported institution offering undergraduate programs in business and administration, education and human services, engineering and computer science, liberal arts, math and science, and nursing and health. There are 6 undergraduate schools and 8 graduate schools. In addition to regional accreditation, Wright State has baccalaureate program accreditation with AACSB, ABET, CAHEA, CSWE, NASM, NCATE, and NLN. The library contains 842,026 volumes, 1.4 million microform items, 20,738 audio/video tapes/CDs/DVDs, and subscribes to 5,700 periodicals including electronic. Computerized library services include interlibrary loans, database searching, and Internet access. Special learning facilities include an art gallery, radio station, TV station, and a TV production studio. The Department of Archives and Special Collections houses one of the most complete depositories of information on the Wright Brothers in the world. The 557-acre campus is in a suburban area 10 miles northeast of Dayton. Including any residence halls, there are 60 buildings.

Student Life: 97% of undergraduates are from Ohio. Others are from 50 states, 66 foreign countries, and Canada. 85% are from public schools. 73% are White; 12% African American. The average age of freshmen is 18; all undergraduates, 23. 44% do not continue beyond their first year; 40% remain to graduate.

Housing: 3000 students can be accommodated in college housing, which includes coed dorms, on-campus apartments, and married student housing. In addition, there are honors houses and special-interest houses. On-campus housing is available on a first-come, first-served basis, and is available on a lottery system for upperclassmen. 81% of students commute. Alcohol is not permitted. All students may keep cars.

Activities: 3% of men belong to 11 local fraternities; 4% of women belong to 10 local sororities. There are 200 groups on campus, including band, cheerleading, chess, choir, chorale, chorus, computers, dance, drill team, ethnic, film, gay, honors, international, jazz band, literary magazine, newspaper, orchestra, pep band, political, professional, radio and TV, religious, social, social service, and student government. Popular campus events include Fall Fest, April Craze, Lunar New Year Celebration and Madrigal Dinner.

Sports: There are 7 intercollegiate sports for men and 8 for women, and 26 intramural sports for men and 23 for women. Facilities include an athletic and entertainment center with an arena seating 13,000 spectators, break-off rooms, an auxiliary gym, and baseball and practice fields. The student union houses a natatorium, climbing wall, weight rooms, workout center, game rooms, and playing courts.

Disabled Students: All of the campus is accessible. Facilities include wheelchair ramps, elevators, special parking, specially equipped restrooms, lowered drinking fountains, lowered telephones, special housing. An underground tunnel system connects all academic buildings. Adaptive technology is available.

Services: Counseling and information services are available, as is tutoring in most subjects. There is a reader service for the blind, and remedial math, reading, and writing.

Campus Safety and Security: Measures include 24-hour foot and vehicle patrol, emergency notification system, self-defense education, and security escort services. There are shuttle buses, emergency telephones, and lighted pathways/sidewalks.

Programs of Study: Wright State confers B.A., B.A.C.S., B.A.Mus., B.F.A., B.S., B.S.B., B.S.B.E., B.S.C.E., B.S.C.L.S., B.S.C.S., B.S.Ed., B.S.E.E., B.S.E.P., B.S.I.S.E., B.S.M.E., B.S.M.S.E., B.S.N., and B.T.A.S. degrees. Associate, master's, and doctoral degrees are also awarded. Bachelor's degrees are awarded in BIOLOGICAL SCIENCE (biology/biological science and life science), BUSINESS (accounting, banking and finance, business economics, management information systems, management science, marketing/retailing/merchandising, nonprofit/public organization management, organizational leadership and management, real estate finance, and supply chain management), COMMUNICATIONS AND THE ARTS (American Sign Language, art history, art, art history and appreciation, arts administration/management, classical languages, communications, creative writing, dance, dramatic arts, English, film arts, fine arts, French, German, Greek, guitar, instrumental performance, language arts, Latin, literature, modern language, music, music history and appreciation, music theory and composition, musical theater, organ performance, percussion, Spanish, strings, studio art, theatre acting, theater design, theatre studies, theater management, vocal performance, and winds), COMPUTER AND PHYSICAL SCIENCE (applied mathematics, chemistry, computer science, geology, geophysics and seismology, mathematics, physics, and statistics), EDUCATION (art education, athletic training, business education, (Education) Childhood Education, career, technical education & training, early childhood education, education, elementary education, foreign languages education, mathematics education, middle school education, music education, physical education, science education, secondary education, social science education, and special education), ENGINEERING AND ENVIRONMENTAL DESIGN (biomedical engineering, computer engineering, electrical/electronics engineering, engineering physics, environmental science, industrial engineering, materials engineering, mechanical engineering, systems engineering, and water and wastewater technology), HEALTH PROFESSIONS (clinical science, community health work, environmental health science, exercise science, medical laboratory technology, nursing, predentistry, premedicine, and rehabilitation therapy), SOCIAL SCIENCE (African American studies, anthropology, applied psychology, cognitive science, criminal justice, economics, geography, history, humanities, international relations, liberal arts/general studies, philosophy, political science/government, prelaw, psychology, religion, social work, sociology, and urban studies). Business education, theater arts, and engineering are the strongest academically. Elementary education, accounting, and nursing have the largest enrollments.

Required: To graduate, students must complete 183 quarter hours, with a minimum GPA of 2.0. All students are required to take 56 credit hours of general education courses in 4 areas: communication and math skills, the Western experience, the non-Western world, and understanding the contemporary world.

Special: B.A.-B.S. degrees are offered in computer science, geography, urban affairs, biological sciences, chemistry, geological sciences, math, and psychology. Cross-registration with other area colleges is available through the Southwestern Ohio Council for Higher Education. Dual majors, co-op programs, internships, study abroad, work-study programs, student-designed majors, nondegree study, and credit for military experience are available. There are 3 national honor societies, a freshman honors program, and 32 departmental honors programs.

Faculty/Classroom: 55% of faculty are male; 45% are female. No introductory courses are taught by graduate students. The average class size in an introductory lecture is 41; in a laboratory is 27; and in a regular course is 32.

Admissions: 69% of the 2013-2014 applicants were accepted. The SAT scores for the 2013-2014 freshman class were: Critical Reading--49% below 500, 35% between 500 and 599, 12% between 600 and 699, and 4% between 700 and 800; Math--47% below 500, 32% between 500 and 599, 18% between 600 and 699, and 3% between 700 and 800; Writing--56% below 500, 34% between 500 and 599, 9% between 600 and 699, and 1% between 700 and 800. The ACT scores were 46% below 21, 25% between 21 and 23, 17% between 24 and 26, 7% between 27 and 28, and 5% above 28. 27% of the current freshmen were in the top fifth of their class; 52% were in the top two fifths.

Requirements: The SAT or ACT is required. Applicants should be graduates of an accredited secondary school and have 4 units in English, 3 units each in math, science, and social studies, 2 units in a foreign language, and 1 unit in the arts. A portfolio is required for art majors, an audition for theater and music majors. The GED is accepted. A GPA of 2.0 is required. AP and CLEP credits are accepted.

Procedure: Freshmen are admitted to all sessions. Entrance exams should be taken in the spring of the junior year. There are deferred admissions and rolling admissions plans. Application deadlines are open. Application fee is $30. Applications are accepted online.

Transfer: 2371 transfer students enrolled in 2012-2013. Applicants must have a 2.0 GPA. 45 of 183 credits required for the bachelor's degree must be completed at Wright State.

Visiting: There are regularly scheduled orientations for prospective students, including a campus tour and information on academic and student services. There are guides for informal visits and visitors may sit in on classes. To schedule a visit, contact the Office of Undergraduate Admissions at (937) 775-5700.

Financial Aid: In 2013-2014, 83% of all full-time freshmen and 78% of continuing full-time students received some form of financial aid. 71% of all full-time freshmen and 69% of continuing full-time students received need-based aid. The average freshman award was $8,912. Need-based scholarships or need-based grants averaged $5,937; need-based self-help aid (loans and jobs) averaged $4,370; non-need-based athletic scholarships averaged $10,010; and other non-need-based awards and non-need-based scholarships averaged $3,132. 14% of undergraduate students work part-time. The average financial indebtedness of the 2013 graduate was $28,349. Wright State is a member of CSS. The FAFSA is required. The priority date for freshman financial aid applications for fall entry is March 1.

International Students: There are 479 international students enrolled. They must take the TOEFL with a minimum score of 500 on the paper-based TOEFL (PBT) or 61 on the Internet-based version (iBT).

Computers: All students may access the system. There are no time limits and no fees.

Graduates: From July 1, 2012 to June 30, 2013, 2589 bachelor's degrees were awarded. The most popular majors were organizational leadership (10%), nursing (9%), and accountancy (5%). In an average class, 2% graduate in 3 years or less, 21% graduate in 4 years or less, 35% graduate in 5 years or less, and 40% graduate in 6 years or less.

Admissions Contact: Undergraduate Admission. E-Mail: *admissions@wright.edu* Web: *www.wright.edu*

XAVIER UNIVERSITY — A-5

Cincinnati, OH 45207 — (513) 745-3301; (877) 982-3648; (513) 745-4319

Full-time: 1912 men, 2238 women	**Faculty:** 311
Part-time: 233 men, 269 women	**Ph.D.s:** 76%
Graduate: 786 men, 1233 women	**Student/Faculty:** 13 to 1
Year: semesters, summer session	**Tuition:** $33,000
Application Deadline: February 1	**Room & Board:** $10,740
Freshman Class: 10907 applied, 7631 accepted, 1289 enrolled	
SAT CR/M: 550/560	**ACT:** 25 **VERY COMPETITIVE**

Xavier University, founded in 1831, is a comprehensive Jesuit institution affiliated with the Roman Catholic Church. There are 3 undergraduate schools and 9 graduate schools. In addition to regional accreditation, XU has baccalaureate program accreditation with AACSB, CSWE, NASM, NCATE, and TEAC. The library contains 479,256 volumes, 752,229 microform items, 13,936 audio/video tapes/CDs/DVDs, and subscribes to 58,509 periodicals including electronic. Computerized library services include interlibrary loans, database searching, Internet access, and Wi-Fi capability. Special learning facilities include an art gallery, TV station, an observatory and a financial trading room. The 189-acre campus is in a small town 5 miles northeast of the center of Cincinnati in a residential area. Including any residence halls, there are 52 buildings.

Student Life: 51% of undergraduates are from Ohio. Others are from 46 states, 44 foreign countries, and Canada. 53% are from public schools. 71% are White. 63% are Catholic; 29% Protestant. The average age of freshmen is 18; all undergraduates, 21. 17% do not continue beyond their first year; 78% remain to graduate.

Housing: 2390 students can be accommodated in college housing, which includes coed dorms, on-campus apartments, and off-campus apartments. In addition, there are honors houses, Living-learning communities. On-campus housing is guaranteed for the freshman year only, is available on a first-come, first-served basis, and is available on a lottery system for upperclassmen. 51% of students live on campus; of those, 75% remain on campus on weekends. All students may keep cars.

Activities: There are no fraternities or sororities. There are 170 groups on campus, including art, cheerleading, chess, choir, chorale, chorus, communications, computers, dance, drama, environmental, ethnic, film, gay, honors, international, jazz band, literary magazine, musical theater, newspaper, opera, orchestra, pep band, photography, political, professional, radio and TV, religious, social, social service, student government, and symphony. Popular campus events include Family Weekend, Academic Day and Spirit Celebration.

Sports: There are 8 intercollegiate sports for men and 8 for women, and 13 intramural sports for men and 13 for women. Facilities include a field house, a sports center, basketball and volleyball courts, baseball, soccer, and softball fields, a rifle range, and tennis courts.

Disabled Students: 99% of the campus is accessible. Facilities include wheelchair ramps, elevators, special parking, specially equipped restrooms, special class scheduling, lowered drinking fountains, lowered telephones, and special housing.

Services: Counseling and information services are available, as is tutoring in every subject, Xavier has a Learning Assistance Center which provides individual and small group tutoring in almost all subjects and study skills assistance, a Math Lab, and a Writing Center. There is also an Efficient Reading and Study Skills course. There is a reader service for the blind, and remedial math, reading, and writing.

Campus Safety and Security: Measures include 24-hour foot and vehicle patrol, emergency notification system, self-defense education, and security escort services. There are shuttle buses, emergency telephones, lighted pathways/sidewalks, controlled access to dorms/residences, alcohol awareness, drug awareness, sexual assault programs, and presence of a Title IX Coordinator.

Programs of Study: XU confers B.A., B.S., Honors A.B., B.F.A., B.L.A., B.S.B.A., B.S.N. and B.S.W. degrees. Associate, master's, and doctoral degrees are also awarded. Bachelor's degrees are awarded in AGRICULTURE (agriculture), BIOLOGICAL SCIENCE (biology/

biological science, biophysics, and life science), BUSINESS (accounting, banking and finance, business administration and management, business economics, entrepreneurial studies, human resources, international business management, management science, marketing/retailing/merchandising, sports management, sports marketing, and sustainable management), COMMUNICATIONS AND THE ARTS (advertising, art, classics, communication rhetoric/communication, design, English, fine arts, French, German, media arts, modern language, music, public relations, Spanish, and theatre arts), COMPUTER AND PHYSICAL SCIENCE (actuarial science, applied physics, chemistry, computer science, information sciences and systems, mathematics, natural sciences, physics, and radiological technology), EDUCATION (athletic training, early childhood education, education, middle school education, music education, science education, and special education), ENGINEERING AND ENVIRONMENTAL DESIGN (environmental science), HEALTH PROFESSIONS (medical laboratory science, nursing, preallied health, and prepharmacy), SOCIAL SCIENCE (criminal justice, economics, gender studies, history, humanities, international studies, liberal arts/general studies, philosophy, political science/government, psychology, social work, sociology, and theological studies). Natural sciences; and the philosophy, politics, and the public honors program are the strongest academically. Business, liberal arts, and nursing have the largest enrollments.

Required: To graduate, students must complete a minimum of 120 credit hours with a minimum GPA of 2.0. The total number of hours required in the major varies. All students must take core curriculum courses in English composition, cultural diversity, math, science, social science, history, theology, philosophy, a foreign language, literature, fine arts, and an ethics/religion and society focus.

Special: Xavier offers internships related to some majors, cross-registration through the Greater Cincinnati Consortium, and co-op programs in business and computer science. Students may study abroad in over 100 countries through Xavier's network of program providers. A Washington semester and nondegree study are available. A 3-2 engineering degree is offered with the University of Cincinnati, and a 3-2 applied biology degree is offered with Duke University. A professional accountancy B.S.B.A and M.B.A program is also offered. There are 13 national honor societies, including Phi Beta Kappa, a freshman honors program, and 2 departmental honors programs.

Faculty/Classroom: 47% of faculty are male; 53% are female. 80% teach undergraduates. No introductory courses are taught by graduate students. The average class size in an introductory lecture is 21; in a laboratory is 17; and in a regular course is 21.

Admissions: 70% of the 2013-2014 applicants were accepted. The SAT scores for the 2013-2014 freshman class were: Critical Reading--23% below 500, 50% between 500 and 599, 21% between 600 and 699, and 6% between 700 and 800; Math--19% below 500, 47% between 500 and 599, 29% between 600 and 699, and 5% between 700 and 800; Writing--29% below 500, 47% between 500 and 599, 21% between 600 and 699, and 3% between 700 and 800. The ACT scores were 13% below 21, 29% between 21 and 23, 30% between 24 and 26, 14% between 27 and 28, and 14% above 28. 41% of the current freshmen were in the top fifth of their class; 70% were in the top two fifths. 2 freshmen graduated first in their class.

Requirements: The SAT or ACT is required. Graduation from an accredited secondary school or satisfactory scores on the GED are required for admission. The school requires 21 academic credits, including 4 years of English, 3 each of math, social studies, and science, 2 of foreign language, and 1 of health/phys ed, plus 5 electives, one essay no fewer than 250 words, at least one recommendation from a high school counselor (preferred) or teacher, satisfactory results on the ACT or the SAT, and a resume or list of activities. AP and CLEP credits are accepted. Important factors in the admissions decision are advanced placement or honors courses, leadership record, and extracurricular activities record.

Procedure: Freshmen are admitted fall and spring. Entrance exams should be taken by fall of the senior year. There is a deferred admissions plan. Applications should be filed by February 1 for fall entry, along with a $35 fee. Notifications are sent March 15. 118 applicants were on the 2013 waiting list; 22 were admitted. Applications are accepted online. Application fees are waived if application is completed online.

Transfer: 121 transfer students enrolled in 2012-2013. Transfer students must have a minimum GPA of 2.0 in all college-level work. An interview is also recommended. Students who transfer to Xavier with 30 or more semester hours are not required to submit results of the ACT or SAT tests, an essay, or a counselor recommendation. 30 of 120 credits required for the bachelor's degree must be completed at XU.

Visiting: There are regularly scheduled orientations for prospective students, including an interview and a tour of the campus. There are guides for informal visits, visitors may sit in on classes, and stay overnight. To schedule a visit, contact Diane Burton at (513) 745-2940.

Financial Aid: In 2013-2014, 99% of all full-time freshmen and 95% of continuing full-time students received some form of financial aid. 67% of all full-time freshmen and 58% of continuing full-time students received need-based aid. The average freshman award was $19,800. Need-based scholarships or need-based grants averaged $15,100 ($3,400 maximum); need-based self-help aid (loans and jobs) averaged $5,000 ($4,500 maximum); non-need-based athletic scholarships averaged $15,600 ($45,000 maximum); and other non-need-based awards and non-need-based scholarships averaged $14,200 ($34,000 maximum). 35% of undergraduate students work part-time. Average annual earnings from campus work are $2000. The average financial indebtedness of the 2013 graduate was $23,000. XU is a member of CSS. The FAFSA is required. The priority date for freshman financial aid applications for fall entry is February 15. The deadline for filing freshman financial aid applications for fall entry is February 15.

International Students: There are 80 international students enrolled. The school actively recruits these students. They must take the TOEFL with a minimum score of 530 on the paper-based TOEFL (PBT) or 71 on the Internet-based version (iBT). They must also take the SAT or ACT. or TOEFL.

Computers: All students may access the system 24 hours a day, 7 days a week. There are no time limits and no fees.

Graduates: From July 1, 2012 to June 30, 2013, 804 bachelor's degrees were awarded. The most popular majors were nursing (10%), marketing (7%), and psychology (6%). 278 companies recruited on campus in 2012-2013. In an average class, 1% graduate in 3 years or less, 67% graduate in 4 years or less, 75% graduate in 5 years or less, and 76% graduate in 6 years or less. Of the 2012 graduating class, 20% were enrolled in graduate school within 6 months of graduation, and 63% were employed.

Admissions Contact: Aaron Meis, Dean of Undergraduate Admissions.
E-Mail: *xuadmit@xavier.edu* Web: *www.xavier.edu*

YOUNGSTOWN STATE UNIVERSITY E-2

Youngstown, OH 44555 **(330) 941-2000**
(877) 468-6978; (330) 941-3674

Full-time: 4593 men, 4880 women	**Faculty:** 421; IIA, av$
Part-time: 1142 men, 1557 women	**Ph.D.s:** 89%
Graduate: 459 men, 743 women	**Student/Faculty:** 22 to 1
Year: semesters, summer session	**Tuition:** $7899 ($13,899)
Application Deadline: August 1	**Room & Board:** $8475
Freshman Class: 4343 applied, 3756 accepted, 2104 enrolled	
SAT CR/M/W: 460/470/440 **ACT:** 20	**LESS COMPETITIVE**

Youngstown State University, founded in 1908, is a publicly funded, primarily commuter institution offering undergraduate and graduate programs in education, business, creative arts and communication, health and human services, liberal arts and social sciences, science, technology, engineering, and mathematics. There are 6 undergraduate schools and one graduate school. In addition to regional accreditation, YSU has baccalaureate program accreditation with AACSB, ABET, ADA, CAHEA, CSWE, NASAD, NASM, NCATE, and NLN. The library contains 759,234 volumes, 1.0 million microform items, 19,322 audio/video tapes/CDs/DVDs, and subscribes to 40,135 periodicals including electronic. Computerized library services include interlibrary loans, database searching, Internet access, and Wi-Fi capability. Special learning facilities include an art gallery, natural history museum, planetarium, radio station, a center for historic preservation, University Archives and Special Collections, the Rose Melnick Medical Museum. The 278-acre campus is in a small town 65 miles southeast of Cleveland. Including any residence halls, there are 52 buildings.

Student Life: 89% of undergraduates are from Ohio. Others are from 35 states, 70 foreign countries, and Canada. 74% are White; 14% African American. The average age of freshmen is 19.28; all undergraduates, 23.99. 31% do not continue beyond their first year; 35% remain to graduate.

Housing: 1381 students can be accommodated in college housing, which includes single-sex and coed dorms, on-campus apartments, and off-campus apartments. In addition, there are honors houses, fraternity houses, and sorority houses. On-campus housing is guaranteed for all 4 years. 90% of students commute. All students may keep cars.

Activities: 2% of men belong to 6 national fraternities; 2% of women belong to 5 national sororities. There are 170 groups on campus, including and education, art, band, cheerleading, choir, chorale, chorus, computers, dance, drama, engineering, environmental, ethnic, film, forensics, gay, honors, international, jazz band, literary magazine, marching band, musical theater, newspaper, opera, orchestra, pep band, photography, political, professional, radio and TV, religious, social, social service, student government, and symphony. Popular campus events include Organizational Fair, Greek Sing, Homecoming and Welcome Week, Martin Luther King Jr. Breakfast and Cinco de Mayo.

Sports: There are 8 intercollegiate sports for men and 10 for women, and 8 intramural sports for men and 7 for women. Facilities include The Department of Campus Recreation is located in the Andrews Student Recreation and Wellness Center. This state-of-the art facility contains more than 140 pieces of strength and conditioning equipment. Located near the free-weight and cardio area is the Center's impressive rock wall, at 53 feet Ohio's tallest. Volleyball, basketball, and other activities are situated within the multi-purpose sports forum, which contains four courts. The spacious aerobic studios are home to many group exercise classes and are adjacent to the 1/8-mile indoor track, both on the top floor of the facility. The Andrews Center also includes a tranquil meditation studio, full-functioning locker rooms, and the Wellness Resource Center. In addition to the Andrews Student Recreation and Wellness Center, the Department supervises programs in Beeghly Physical Education Center, Stambaugh Stadium, and the outdoor complex. Located on an 18-acre site adjacent to Beeghly Physical Education Center, the All-Sports Complex includes Arnold D. Stambaugh Stadium and Beede Field, an artificial-turf sports field for football and soccer, with seating for more than 20,630 spectators; officials' dressing rooms; varsity athletic offices; classrooms, racquetball courts, gymnasiums, weight rooms and facilities for various other health and physical education activities. The Watson And Tressel Training Site (WATTS) is an indoor athletic facility containing a 300-meter competition track, a full-size football field, batting cages, a putting green, and locker rooms. This facility allows for year-round training for all athletic programs, as well as a competition site for the track and field teams.

Disabled Students: 98% of the campus is accessible. Facilities include wheelchair ramps, elevators, special parking, specially equipped restrooms, special class scheduling, lowered drinking fountains.

Services: Counseling and information services are available, as is tutoring in most subjects. There is a reader service for the blind, and remedial math, reading, and writing. A foreign language lab is also available.

Campus Safety and Security: Measures include 24-hour foot and vehicle patrol, emergency notification system, self-defense education, and security escort services. There are shuttle buses, emergency telephones, lighted pathways/sidewalks, controlled access to dorms/residences, night security posts in dorms, and concentrated security in parking and other critical areas.

Programs of Study: YSU confers B.A., B.S., B.E., B.F.A., B.G.S., B.M., B.S., B.S.A.S., B.S.B.A., B.S.Ed., B.S.N., B.S.R.C. and B.S.W degrees. Associate, master's, and doctoral degrees are also awarded. Bachelor's degrees are awarded in AGRICULTURE (environmental studies), BIOLOGICAL SCIENCE (biology/biological science and nutrition), BUSINESS (accounting, apparel and accessories marketing, banking and finance, business administration and management, business economics, fashion merchandising, hospitality management services, hotel/motel and restaurant management, human resources, management information systems, marketing management, marketing/retailing/merchandising, and retailing), COMMUNICATIONS AND THE ARTS (advertising, applied music, art history, art, art history and appreciation, broadcasting, communications, dance, design, dramatic arts, English, English literature, French, graphic design, information technology, Italian, jazz, journalism, keyboard - piano concentration, literature, music, music composition, music history and appreciation, music performance, music theory and composition, musical theater, painting, percussion, performing arts, photography, piano/organ, piano performance, printmaking, public relations, Spanish, strings, studio art, technical and business writing, telecommunications, theatre acting, theatre arts, theatre production, theatre studies, vocal performance, voice, vocal music education, and winds), COMPUTER AND PHYSICAL SCIENCE (actuarial mathematics, applied mathematics, astronomy and physics, chemistry, computer programming, computer science, computer security and information assurance, digital arts/ technology, geology, information sciences and systems, mathematics, physical sciences, physics, and statistics), EDUCATION (art education, (Education) Childhood Education, computer education, early childhood education, education, general studies, health education, mathematics education, middle school education, music education, physical education, physical science secondary school education, secondary education, social science education, social studies education, special education, and vocational education), ENGINEERING AND ENVIRONMENTAL DESIGN (chemical engineering, civil engineering, civil engineering technology, computer technology, electrical/electronics engineering, electrical/ electronics engineering technology, engineering, graphic and printing production, industrial engineering, mechanical engineering, and mechanical engineering technology), HEALTH PROFESSIONS (allied health, clinical science, dental hygiene, exercise science, nursing, nursing home administration, predentistry, premedicine, preoptometry, preosteopathy, preveterinary science, public health, and respiratory therapy), SOCIAL SCIENCE (African studies, American studies, anthropology, child care/ child and family studies, criminal justice, dietetics, early childhood studies, economics, family/consumer studies, food science, forensic studies, French studies, geography, gerontology, history, Italian studies, law enforcement and corrections, philosophy, philosophy and religion, political science/government, prelaw, psychology, religion, social studies, social work, sociology, and Spanish studies). Criminal justice, nursing, and early childhood education have the largest enrollments.

Required: A minimum of 124 semester hours must be successfully completed to earn a bachelor's degree, with a minimum GPA of 2.0. At least 60 semester hours must be completed in courses numbered 2600 or higher; at least 48 of these 60 hours must be in courses numbered 3700 or higher. All students must fulfill core requirements including requirements in English, speech, and math.

Special: YSU offers co-op programs in a variety of majors, as well as internships, work study, dual majors, credit for military experience, nondegree study, honors degree programs, distance learning, joint engineering program, accelerated degrees, and pass/fail options. Student-designed majors are available through the Individualized Curriculum Program, Washington Semester, study abroad in a variety of countries and cross registration opportunities and accelerated degree program. There are 16 national honor societies and a freshman honors program.

Faculty/Classroom: 57% of faculty are male; 43% are female. All teach undergraduates. No introductory courses are taught by graduate students.

Admissions: 86% of the 2013-2014 applicants were accepted. The SAT scores for the 2013-2014 freshman class were: Critical Reading--64% below 500, 28% between 500 and 599, 6% between 600 and 699, and 2% between 700 and 800; Math--61% below 500, 26% between 500 and 599, 12% between 600 and 699, and 1% between 700 and 800; Writing--72% below 500, 21% between 500 and 599, 6% between 600 and 699, and 1% between 700 and 800. The ACT scores were 52% below 21, 24% between 21 and 23, 13% between 24 and 26, 5% between 27 and 28, and 6% above 28. 24% of the current freshmen were in the top fifth of their class; 22% were in the top two fifths. 65 freshmen graduated first in their class.

Requirements: The SAT or ACT is required. In-state students may be admitted conditionally who do not meet minimum standards. Students who have been out of school for 2 or more years and who are not pursuing a restricted program of study are exempt from test requirements. Out-of-state applicants must rank in the upper two-thirds of their class or have a combined SAT score of 820 or higher or 17 or higher composite on the ACT. Graduation from an accredited secondary school or satisfactory scores on the GED are required for all applicants. High school courses recommended are 4 units of English, 3 each of math, science, and social studies, 2 of foreign language, and 1 of fine or performing arts. A GPA of 2.0 is required. AP and CLEP credits are accepted.

Procedure: Freshmen are admitted fall, spring, and summer. Entrance exams should be taken in spring of the junior year or fall of the senior year. There are deferred admissions and rolling admissions plans. Early decision applications should be filed by February 15; regular applications, by August 1 for fall entry; December 1 for spring entry; and April 15 for summer entry, along with a $40 fee. Notification is sent on a rolling basis. Applications are accepted online.

Transfer: 1056 transfer students enrolled in 2012-2013. Transfer applicants in good standing at the last institution attended with an aggregate cumulative point average of 2.0 or higher for all courses taken at other colleges or universities are admitted in good standing. Those with an aggregate cumulative point average of less than 2.0 or on probation may be considered for probationary transfer if their overall academic record, including high school grades and test scores, indicate potential success. Applicants suspended or dismissed from other institutions are not eligible for consideration (without appeal to the Office of Undergraduate Admission) until at least 1 semester has passed following the term in which the suspension occurred. 30 of 124 credits required for the bachelor's degree must be completed at YSU.

Visiting: There are regularly scheduled orientations for prospective students, including an official academic advising session, registration for classes, and complete overview of the university resources and services. There are guides for informal visits and visitors may sit in on classes. To schedule a visit, contact the Office of Admissions.

Financial Aid: In 2013-2014, 93% of all full-time freshmen and 91% of continuing full-time students received some form of financial aid. 79% of all full-time freshmen and 75% of continuing full-time students received need-based aid. The average freshman award was $9,579. 12% of undergraduate students work part-time. Average annual earnings from campus work are $8000. The average financial indebtedness of the 2013 graduate was $22,937. YSU is a member of CSS. The FAFSA and the college's own financial statement are required. The deadline for filing freshman financial aid applications for fall entry is February 15.

International Students: There are 111 international students enrolled. They must take the TOEFL with a minimum score of 500 on the paper-based TOEFL (PBT) or 61 on the Internet-based version (iBT) or take the MELAB, Minimum score of 80 is required on the MELAB.

Computers: All students may access the system. There are no time limits and no fees.

Graduates: From July 1, 2012 to June 30, 2013, 1503 bachelor's degrees were awarded. The most popular majors were criminal justice (7%), general studies (5%), and accounting (5%). 215 companies recruited on campus in 2012-2013. In an average class, 2% graduate in 3 years or less, 10% graduate in 4 years or less, 25% graduate in 5 years or less, and 35% graduate in 6 years or less. Of the 2012 graduating class, 54% were employed within 6 months of graduation.

Admissions Contact: Sue Davis, Director, Admissions. E-Mail: *enroll@ysu.edu* Web: *www.ysu.edu*

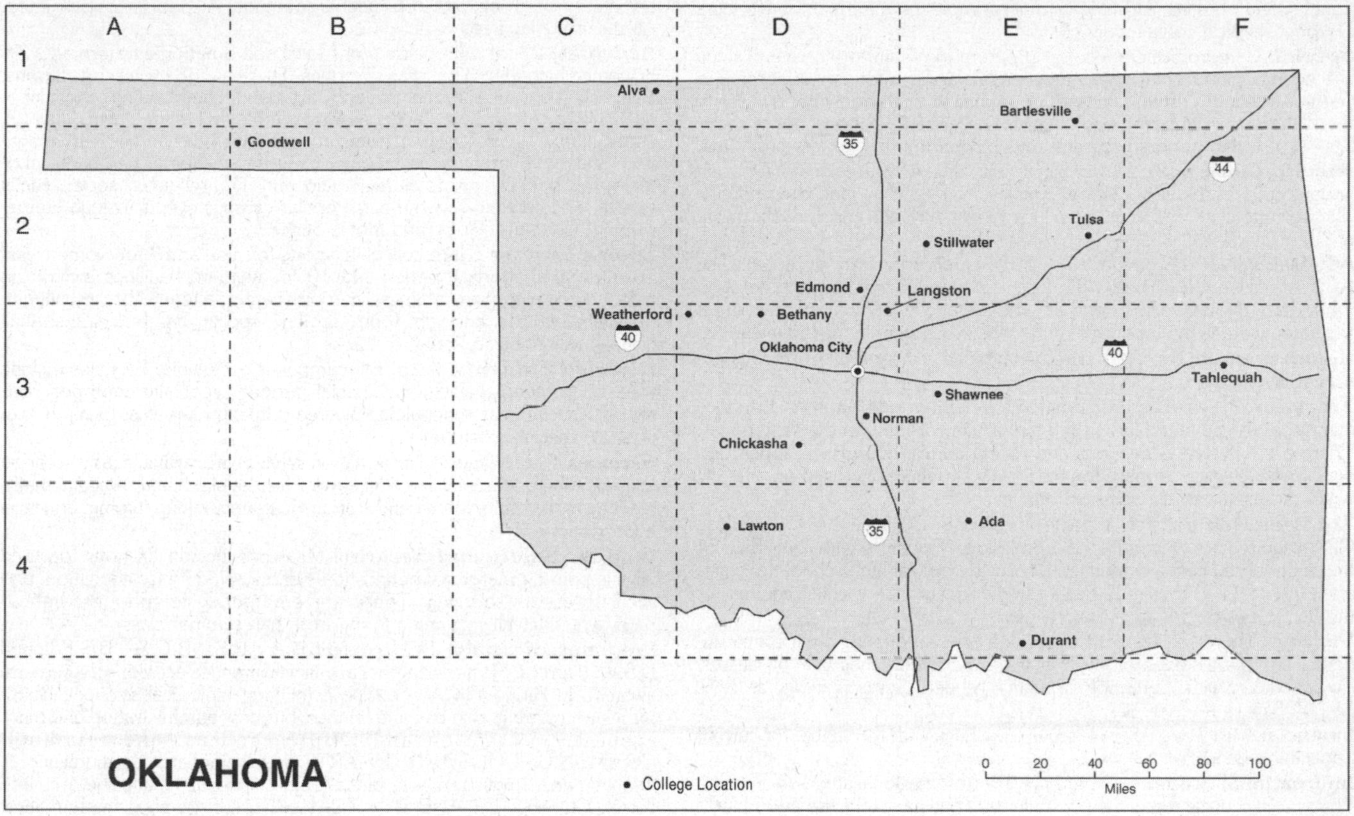

CAMERON UNIVERSITY D-4

Lawton, OK 73505 (580) 581-2289
(888) 454-7600; (580) 581-5514

Full-time: 1491 men, 2110 women
Part-time: 604 men, 1157 women
Graduate: 176 men, 363 women
Year: semesters, summer session
Application Deadline:
Freshman Class: 1346 applied, 1343 accepted, 946 enrolled
ACT: 19
Faculty: 189
Ph.D.s: 70%
Student/Faculty: 20 to 1
Tuition: $5055 ($12,495)
Room & Board: $4212

LESS COMPETITIVE

Founded in 1908, Cameron University is known for its student-centered approach to education and is committed to providing students the highest quality academic programs and a complete collegiate experience. Cameron understands that students want an education that prepares them to achieve career and life goals. Cameron's campus has been recently transformed with the completion of more than $60 million in capital improvements. There are 4 undergraduate schools. In addition to regional accreditation, Cameron has baccalaureate program accreditation with ACBSP, NASM, and NCATE. The library contains 253,453 volumes, 540,008 microform items, 21,638 audio/video tapes/CDs/DVDs, and subscribes to 30,794 periodicals including electronic. Computerized library services include interlibrary loans, database searching, Internet access, and Wi-Fi capability. Special learning facilities include an art gallery, radio station, and TV station. The 160-acre campus is in a suburban area 90 miles southwest of Oklahoma City. Including any residence halls, there are 35 buildings.

Student Life: 86% of undergraduates are from Oklahoma. Others are from 47 states, 51 foreign countries, and Canada. 44% are White; 16% African American. The average age of freshmen is 21; all undergraduates, 26. 39% do not continue beyond their first year; 20% remain to graduate.

Housing: 668 students can be accommodated in college housing, which includes single-sex and coed dorms and on-campus apartments. On-campus housing is available on a first-come and first-served basis. 90% of students commute. Alcohol is not permitted. All students may keep cars.

Activities: 2% of men belong to 4 national fraternities; 1% of women belong to 4 national sororities. There are 85 groups on campus, including art, band, cheerleading, choir, chorale, computers, dance, debate, drama, ethnic, film, forensics, gay, honors, international, jazz band, musical theater, newspaper, opera, orchestra, pep band, political, professional, radio and TV, religious, social, social service, student government, and symphony. Popular campus events include Homecoming, Welcome Week and Foam Dance.

Sports: There are 5 intercollegiate sports for men and 5 for women, and 9 intramural sports for men and 9 for women. Facilities include The Aggie Rec Center offers facilities and resources to fit into any type of fitness program, including a weight training area featuring free weights and weight-resistance machines; a cardio area with treadmills, ellipticals, ascent trainers, stationary bikes and a rower; a group fitness studio; a spin room; an indoor pool; basketball and racquetball courts; a stretch/personal DVD area; and an indoor track. The facility is also the start location of the Aggie Mile, a one-mile outdoor course contained within the Cameron campus.

Disabled Students: 99% of the campus is accessible. Facilities include wheelchair ramps, elevators, special parking, specially equipped restrooms, and lowered drinking fountains.

Services: Counseling and information services are available, as is tutoring in some subjects, writing, reading, accounting, math, communication, and physical sciences There is remedial math, reading, and writing.

Campus Safety and Security: Measures include 24-hour foot and vehicle patrol, emergency notification system, and security escort services. There are emergency telephones, lighted pathways/sidewalks, and controlled access to dorms/residences.

Programs of Study: Cameron confers B.A., B.S., B.Acct., B.B.A., B.F.A., B.M.E. and B.M. degrees. Associate and master's degrees are also awarded. Bachelor's degrees are awarded in AGRICULTURE (agriculture), BIOLOGICAL SCIENCE (biology/biological science), BUSINESS (accounting, business administration and management, organizational leadership and management, and sports management), COMMUNICATIONS AND THE ARTS (art, communications, English, information technology, languages, multimedia, music, and theatre arts), COMPUTER AND PHYSICAL SCIENCE (chemistry, computer science, mathematics, and physics), EDUCATION (early childhood education, elementary education, English education, foreign languages education, mathematics education, music education, physical education, science education, and social studies education), ENGINEERING AND ENVIRONMENTAL DESIGN (electrical/electronics engineering technology), HEALTH PROFESSIONS (medical technology), SOCIAL SCIENCE (child care/child and family studies, criminal justice, history, interdisciplinary studies, political science/government, psychology, and sociology). Business administration, psychology, and criminal justice have the largest enrollments.

Required: To graduate, students must complete all credit hours with a minimum GPA of 2.0. All students must take courses in English, math, science, U.S. history and government, humanities, behavioral science, economics, and phys ed. All students must complete a minimum of 40 hours of upper-division course work.

Special: Cameron offers a co-op program in respiratory care and study abroad in England. Dual majors in several fields, an interdisciplinary studies degree, nondegree study, degrees in organizational leadership, and credit for military experience are also offered. There are 23 national honor societies, a freshman honors program, and 1 departmental honors programs.

Faculty/Classroom: 53% of faculty are male; 47% are female. All teach undergraduates. No introductory courses are taught by graduate students. The average class size in an introductory lecture is 24 and in a laboratory is 23.

Admissions: 100% of the 2013-2014 applicants were accepted. The ACT scores were 59% below 21, 22% between 21 and 23, 13% between 24 and 26, 3% between 27 and 28, and 3% above 28. 22% of the current freshmen were in the top fifth of their class; 46% were in the top two fifths.

Requirements: The ACT is recommended. AP and CLEP credits are accepted.

Procedure: Freshmen are admitted fall, spring, and summer. Entrance exams should be taken late in the junior year or early in the senior year. There are deferred admissions and rolling admissions plans. Application deadlines are open. Application fee is $15. Notification is sent on a rolling basis. Applications are accepted online.

Transfer: 485 transfer students enrolled in 2012-2013. 2.0 College GPA required for unconditional admission. Transfers with less than 24 hours of earned college credits must provide official high school transcript and ACT/SAT (if under 21 years of age). 30 of 124 credits required for the bachelor's degree must be completed at Cameron.

Visiting: There are regularly scheduled orientations for prospective students. There are guides for informal visits and visitors may sit in on classes. To schedule a visit, contact Prospective Student Services Office at (580) 581-2987.

Financial Aid: The FAFSA is required. Check with the school for current application deadlines.

International Students: There are 199 international students enrolled. The school actively recruits these students. They must take the TOEFL with a minimum score of 500 on the paper-based TOEFL (PBT) or 61 on the Internet-based version (iBT). They must also take the SAT or ACT.

Computers: All students may access the system at any time. There are no time limits and no fees.

Graduates: From July 1, 2012 to June 30, 2013, 873 bachelor's degrees were awarded. The most popular majors were criminal justice (13%), business (13%), and interdisciplinary studies (12%). 110 companies recruited on campus in 2012-2013. In an average class, 1% graduate in 3 years or less, 8% graduate in 4 years or less, 17% graduate in 5 years or less, and 20% graduate in 6 years or less.

Admissions Contact: Zoe Du Rant, Director of Admissions. E-Mail: *admissions@cameron.edu* Web: *www.cameron.edu*

EAST CENTRAL UNIVERSITY — E-4

Ada, OK 74820 — **(580) 332-8000; (580) 559-5432**

Full-time: 1272 men, 1789 women	**Faculty:** n/av
Part-time: 216 men, 480 women	**Ph.D.s:** 65%
Graduate: 241 men, 589 women	**Student/Faculty:** 19 to 1
Year: semesters, summer session	**Tuition:** $5241 ($12,643)
Application Deadline: open	**Room & Board:** $4982

Freshman Class: 968 applied, 950 accepted, 612 enrolled

ACT: 20

LESS COMPETITIVE

East Central University, founded in 1909, is a publicly funded institution offering undergraduate programs in liberal arts and sciences, education, business, and health-related fields, and graduate programs in education, human resources, psychology. There are 4 undergraduate schools and 1 graduate school. In addition to regional accreditation, ECU has baccalaureate program accreditation with ACBSP, CSWE, NASM, NCATE, and NLN. The library contains 264,524 volumes, 355,809 microform items, and 11,302 audio/video tapes/CDs/DVDs, and subscribes to 40,969 periodicals including electronic. Computerized library services include interlibrary loans, database searching, Internet access, and Wi-Fi capability. Special learning facilities include an art gallery, radio station, an observatory. The 140-acre campus is in a small town 90 miles south of Oklahoma City.

Student Life: 93% of undergraduates are from Oklahoma. Others are from 28 states, 32 foreign countries, and Canada. 98% are from public schools. 58% are White; 16% American Indian/Alaska Native. The average age of freshmen is 19; all undergraduates, 24. 33% remain to graduate.

Housing: 1204 students can be accommodated in college housing, which includes single-sex and coed dorms, on-campus apartments, and married student housing. In addition, there are honors houses, special-interest houses, fraternity houses, living and learning communities: honors, athletic, music and general. On-campus housing is available on a first-come and first-served basis. 70% of students commute. Alcohol is not permitted. All students may keep cars.

Activities: 2% of men belong to 1 local and 3 national fraternities; 2% of women belong to 3 national sororities. There are 88 groups on campus, including and nontraditional students, art, band, cheerleading, choir, chorale, chorus, computers, dance, debate, drama, drill team, environmental, ethnic, film, forensics, gay, honors, international, jazz band, literary magazine, marching band, musical theater, newspaper, opera, pep band, photography, political, professional, radio and TV, religious, social, social service, and student government. Popular campus events include Homecoming, Concerts, Plays, and Movie Series.

Sports: There are 6 intercollegiate sports for men and 7 for women, and 10 intramural sports for men and 10 for women. Facilities include an indoor swimming pool, a fitness/aerobics center, a tennis, basketball, and racquetball courts, a weight room, football, soccer, baseball, and softball fields, and indoor and outdoor tracks.

Disabled Students: All of the campus is accessible. Facilities include wheelchair ramps, elevators, special parking, specially equipped restrooms, special class scheduling, lowered drinking fountains, lowered telephones, special housing.

Services: Counseling and information services are available, as is tutoring in every subject. There is a reader service for the blind, and remedial math, reading, and writing. Interpreters for the deaf, note taking/typing, and tape transcription.

Campus Safety and Security: Measures include 24-hour foot and vehicle patrol, emergency notification system, self-defense education, and security escort services. There are emergency telephones, lighted pathways/sidewalks, training in the freshman seminar class.

Programs of Study: ECU confers B.A., B.S., B.G.S., B.S.Ed. and B.S.W. degrees. Master's degrees are also awarded. Bachelor's degrees are awarded in BIOLOGICAL SCIENCE (biology/biological science), BUSINESS (accounting, banking and finance, business administration and management, recreation and leisure services, and retailing), COMMUNICATIONS AND THE ARTS (advertising, art, communications, dramatic arts, English, music, piano/organ, speech/debate/rhetoric, and voice), COMPUTER AND PHYSICAL SCIENCE (applied mathematics, chemistry, computer science, mathematics, and physics), EDUCATION (art education, athletic training, business education, early childhood education, elementary education, English education, mathematics education, music education, physical education, and special education), ENGINEERING AND ENVIRONMENTAL DESIGN (cartography), HEALTH PROFESSIONS (environmental health science, exercise science, medical technology, and nursing), SOCIAL SCIENCE (counseling/psychology, criminal justice, family/consumer resource management, family/consumer studies, history, human services, liberal arts/general studies, Native American studies, political science/government, prelaw, psychology, social work, and sociology). Nursing, accounting, and biology have the largest enrollments.

Required: To graduate, students must complete a minimum of 124 credit hours with a minimum GPA of 2.0. 60 hours must be from a 4-year college/university. At least 15 of his/her last semester before graduation or at least 50 percent of the hours required by the major must be earned from East Central University. All students must take 40 hours of upper-level courses, as well as 45 hours in general studies, and must meet computer proficiency requirements.

Special: The school offers co-op programs with the Ardmore Higher Education Center and is a member of the National Student Exchange Program. Internships are available in human resources, environmental health, political science, office technology, mass communications, and cartography. Students may participate in a work-study program with the Veterans Administration. Nondegree study, student designed majors, credit for military experience, and study abroad are available. The school offers special rates for nonresidents from approved states who wish to major in specialized fields. There are 9 national honor societies and a freshman honors program.

Faculty/Classroom: 51% of faculty are male; 49% are female. 97% teach undergraduates, 50% do research, and 50% do both. Graduate students teach 3% of introductory courses.

Admissions: 98% of the 2013-2014 applicants were accepted. The ACT scores were 52% below 21, 23% between 21 and 23, 16% between 24 and 26, 5% between 27 and 28, and 3% above 28.

Requirements: The ACT is required, with a minimum composite score of 20, the SAT will be accepted in place of the ACT. Applicants must be graduates of an accredited secondary school or have the GED. High school courses must include 4 years of English, 3 years of math, and 3 years of science (1 year must be a lab), 3 years of history and citizenship skills, and 2 years of subjects previously listed or selected from computer science, foreign language, or any Advanced Placement course except courses in the fine arts. ECU requires applicants to be in the upper 50% of their class. A GPA of 2.7 is required. AP and CLEP credits are accepted.

Procedure: Freshmen are admitted to all sessions. Entrance exams should be taken during the junior or senior year of high school. Application deadlines are open. Application fee is $20. Applications are accepted online.

Transfer: 392 transfer students enrolled in 2012-2013. Applicants having fewer than 24 credit hours must meet the criteria for entering freshmen. The required minimum GPA for transfer students is 2.0. 30 of 124 credits required for the bachelor's degree must be completed at ECU.

Visiting: There are regularly scheduled orientations for prospective students. There are guides for informal visits. To schedule a visit, contact the Student Development Office.

Financial Aid: The FAFSA and the college's own financial statement, and and federal tax returns are required. The priority date for freshman financial aid applications for fall entry is July 1.

International Students: There are 218 international students enrolled. The school actively recruits these students. They must take the TOEFL with a minimum score of 500 on the paper-based TOEFL (PBT) or 61 on the Internet-based version (iBT). They must also take the SAT or ACT. Students may be required to take the ACT upon arrival.

Computers: All students may access the system during hours of operation. There are no time limits and no fees.

Graduates: From July 1, 2012 to June 30, 2013, 711 bachelor's degrees were awarded. The most popular majors were registered nursing (13%), human services, general (11%), business administration and management, and general (9%). 88 companies recruited on campus in 2012-2013.

Admissions Contact: Pamla Armstrong, Registrar and Director of Admissions. E-Mail: *parmstro@ecok.edu* Web: *www.ecok.edu*

LANGSTON UNIVERSITY D-3

Langston, OK 73050 (405) 466-3224
(877) 466-2231; (405) 466-3381

Full-time: 1290 men, 1920 women	**Faculty:** n/av
Part-time: 290 men, 520 women	**Ph.D.s:** n/av
Graduate: 20 men, 40 women	**Student/Faculty:** n/av
Year: semesters, summer session	**Tuition:** $4618 ($10,808)
Application Deadline: see profile	**Room & Board:** $8002
Freshman Class: n/av	
SAT or ACT: required	

LESS COMPETITIVE

Langston University, founded in 1897, is a multiracial, public institution offering programs in liberal arts, business, allied health, and teacher preparation. The figures in the above capsule and in this profile are approximate. In addition to regional accreditation, Langston has baccalaureate program accreditation with ADA, APTA, NCATE, and NLN. The 6 libraries contain 110,248 volumes, 465,319 microform items, and subscribe to 80 periodicals including electronic. Computerized library services include interlibrary loans. Special learning facilities include a learning resource center, satellite teaching, a black heritage center, an institute for goat research, and a state research group in catfish production. The 40-acre campus is in a rural area 45 miles from Oklahoma City. Including any residence halls, there are 20 buildings.

Student Life: 66% of undergraduates are from Oklahoma. 98% are from public schools. 50% are white; 50% African American.

Housing: 676 students can be accommodated in college housing, which includes dorms and married student housing. Alcohol is not permitted. All students may keep cars.

Activities: 25% of men belong to 4 national fraternities; 30% of women belong to 4 national sororities. There are 30 groups on campus, including band, cheerleading, choir, drama, ethnic, international, jazz band, marching band, newspaper, professional, religious, social service, student government, and yearbook. Popular campus events include student theater productions and a performing arts series.

Sports: There are 4 intercollegiate sports for men and 2 for women, and 6 intramural sports for men and 5 for women. Facilities include a gym, tennis courts, a baseball field, and a track.

Disabled Students: 70% of the campus is accessible. Facilities include wheelchair ramps, elevators, special parking, specially equipped rest rooms, and special class scheduling.

Services: Counseling and information services are available, as is tutoring in some subjects. There is remedial math, reading, and writing.

Programs of Study: Langston confers B.A., B.S., B.B.A., B.S.Ed., and B.S.N. degrees. Associate and master's degrees are also awarded. Bachelor's degrees are awarded in AGRICULTURE (agricultural economics and animal science), BIOLOGICAL SCIENCE (biology/biological science and nutrition), BUSINESS (accounting, business administration and management, and management science), COMMUNICATIONS AND THE ARTS (dramatic arts, English, music, and speech/debate/rhetoric), COMPUTER AND PHYSICAL SCIENCE (chemistry, computer science, and mathematics), EDUCATION (business education, elementary education, home economics education, industrial arts education, mathematics education, physical education, and science education), ENGINEERING AND ENVIRONMENTAL DESIGN (industrial engineering technology), HEALTH PROFESSIONS (health care administration, medical laboratory technology, nursing, and physical therapy), SOCIAL SCIENCE (criminal justice, early childhood studies, economics, gerontology, history, home economics, psychology, social science, sociology, and urban studies).

Required: To graduate, students must complete a total of 124 semester hours, with a GPA of 2.0. The required general education core consists of 50 credits in English, math, computer science, biological and physical sciences, social science, and health and phys ed. 6 credits are required in American history and government, and all students must complete an internship or field experience.

Special: Work-study programs, internships, and nondegree and noncredit study are available. There are 6 national honor societies and a freshman honors program.

Faculty/Classroom: All teach undergraduates. No introductory courses are taught by graduate students.

Requirements: The SAT or ACT is required. Applicants should be graduates of accredited high schools with at least a C average (2.7 on a 4.0 scale) and rank in the upper 60% of their graduating classes. Required secondary preparation includes 4 years of English, 3 of math, and 2 each of lab science and history, including 1 of American history. 4 additional academic units, including a foreign language, are strongly recommended. There are alternative admission programs for students with varying backgrounds. AP and CLEP credits are accepted.

Procedure: Freshmen are admitted to all sessions. There is a rolling admissions plan. Application deadlines are open. Check with the school for the current application fee.

Transfer: Applicants should be in good standing and have earned at least a C average in previous college work. 30 of 124 credits required for the bachelor's degree must be completed at Langston.

Visiting: There are regularly scheduled orientations for prospective students. There are guides for informal visits; visitors may sit in on classes and stay overnight. To schedule a visit, contact the High School/College Relations Office.

Financial Aid: The FAFSA is required.

Computers: There are no time limits and no fees.

Admissions Contact: Director of Admissions and Enrollment Management. Web: *www.langston.edu*

NORTHEASTERN STATE UNIVERSITY F-3

Tahlequah, OK 74464 (918) 456-5511, ext. 2200
(800) 722-9614; (918) 458-2342

Full-time: 6130 men and women	**Faculty:** n/av; II A, --$
Part-time: 2060 men and women	**Ph.D.s:** 74%
Graduate: 1070 men and women	**Student/Faculty:** n/av
Year: semesters, summer session	**Tuition:** $5500 ($11,500)
Application Deadline: see profile	**Room & Board:** $5800
Freshman Class: n/av	
ACT: required	

VERY COMPETITIVE

Northeastern State University, founded in 1846, is a public institution offering programs in arts and sciences, professional training, teacher preparation, and business. There are 4 undergraduate schools and 5 graduate schools. The figures in the above capsule and in this profile are approximate. In addition to regional accreditation, NSU has baccalaureate program accreditation with ACBSP, ADA, ASLA, CSWE, NASM, NCATE, and NLN. The library contains 400,000 volumes, 766,300 microform items, and 8659 audio/video tapes/CDs/DVDs, and subscribes to 15,000 periodicals including electronic. Computerized library services include interlibrary loans, database searching, Internet access, and laptop Internet portals. Special learning facilities include a learning resource center. The 200-acre campus is in a small town 70 miles from Tulsa. Including any residence halls, there are 51 buildings.

Student Life: 93% of undergraduates are from Oklahoma. Others are from 34 states, 47 foreign countries, and Canada. 59% are white; 30% Native American/Eskimo. The average age of freshmen is 19; all undergraduates, 26. 30% do not continue beyond their first year.

Housing: 1653 students can be accommodated in college housing, which includes single-sex and coed dorms, on-campus apartments, married student housing, and rooming arrangements for special interest groups. On-campus housing is available on a first-come, first-served basis. 80% of students commute. Alcohol is not permitted. All students may keep cars.

Activities: 5% of men belong to 7 national fraternities; 2% of women belong to 5 national sororities. There are 80 groups on campus, including art, band, cheerleading, choir, chorus, dance, drama, drill team, ethnic, film, gay, honors, international, jazz band, literary magazine, marching band, musical theater, newspaper, orchestra, pep band, photography, political, professional, radio and TV, religious, social service, student government, and symphony. Popular campus events include Cherokee Seminaries, Symposium on the American Indian, and Sequoyah Institute shows.

Sports: There are 5 intercollegiate sports for men and 5 for women, and

16 intramural sports for men and 16 for women. Facilities include a 12,500-seat football stadium, an indoor practice facility, an exercise/ fitness track, baseball, softball, and soccer fields, tennis courts, a baseball field house, a soccer/softball field house, and a 1200-seat basketball gym and basketball court.

Disabled Students: 70% of the campus is accessible. Facilities include wheelchair ramps, elevators, special parking, specially equipped restrooms, special class scheduling, lowered drinking fountains, lowered telephones, and special housing.

Services: Counseling and information services are available, as is tutoring in most subjects. There is remedial math, reading, and writing.

Campus Safety and Security: Measures include 24-hour foot and vehicle patrol, self-defense education, and security escort services. There are shuttle buses, emergency telephones, lighted pathways/sidewalks, and a campus security police department.

Programs of Study: NSU confers B.A., B.S., B.A.Ed., B.B.A., B.S.Ed., B.S.Sci.Ed., B.S.N., and B.S.W. degrees. Master's and doctoral degrees are also awarded. Bachelor's degrees are awarded in BIOLOGICAL SCIENCE (biology/biological science), BUSINESS (accounting, banking and finance, business administration and management, and marketing/ retailing/merchandising), COMMUNICATIONS AND THE ARTS (advertising, communications, English, fine arts, journalism, music, Spanish, and speech/debate/rhetoric), COMPUTER AND PHYSICAL SCIENCE (chemistry, computer science, information sciences and systems, and mathematics), EDUCATION (art education, early childhood education, elementary education, health education, industrial arts education, music education, science education, secondary education, and special education), HEALTH PROFESSIONS (medical laboratory technology and nursing), SOCIAL SCIENCE (criminal justice, geography, history, political science/ government, social science, social work, and sociology).

Required: To graduate, students must complete at least 124 credit hours, with 24 to 50 in the major. General education requirements include 40 hours in language arts, social science, natural science, humanities, and phys ed. Freshman orientation and English proficiency are required.

Special: Internships are offered in business, mass communications, and education. There are 10 national honor societies, a freshman honors program, and 5 departmental honors programs.

Faculty/Classroom: 56% of faculty are male; 44% are female. 90% teach undergraduates. Graduate students teach 5% of introductory courses. The average class size in an introductory lecture is 60; in a laboratory, 24; and in a regular course, 20.

Requirements: The ACT is required, with a minimum composite score of 20. Applicants should be high school graduates or have a GED. Students should have completed 4 years of English, 3 of math, and 2 each of history and science. NSU requires applicants to be in the upper 50% of their class. A GPA of 2.7 is required. AP and CLEP credits are accepted.

Procedure: Freshmen are admitted to all sessions. There is a rolling admissions plan. Check with the school for current application deadlines. Application fee is $25. Notification is sent on a rolling basis.

Transfer: Transfer applicants must have a minimum GPA of 2.0, with 24 transfer hours completed, and be in good standing at the last institution attended. 30 of 124 credits required for the bachelor's degree must be completed at NSU.

Visiting: There are regularly scheduled orientations for prospective students, including a general campus visit with highlights presented by trained tour guides. Visitors may sit in on classes and stay overnight. To schedule a visit, contact High School and College Relations.

Financial Aid: The FAFSA and the college's own financial statement are required. Check with the school for current deadlines.

International Students: International students must take the TOEFL.

Computers: Wireless access is available. All students may access the system.

Admissions Contact: Admissions Office. E-Mail: *nsuinfo@nsuok.edu* Web: *www.nsuok.edu*

NORTHWESTERN OKLAHOMA STATE UNIVERSITY C-1

Alva, OK 73717 **(580) 327-8545; (580) 327-8413**

Full-time: 600 men, 775 women	**Faculty:** n/av
Part-time: 160 men, 290 women	**Ph.D.s:** n/av
Graduate: 50 men, 175 women	**Student/Faculty:** n/av
Year: semesters, summer session	**Tuition:** $5090 ($10,640)
Application Deadline: open	**Room & Board:** $4200
Freshman Class: n/av	
SAT or ACT: required	

NONCOMPETITIVE

Northwestern Oklahoma State University, founded in 1897, is a public institution offering programs in liberal and fine arts, agriculture, business, professional training, and teacher preparation. There are 2 undergraduate schools and 1 graduate school. The figures in the above capsule and in this profile are approximate. In addition to regional accreditation, Northwestern has baccalaureate program accreditation with NCATE and NLN. The 2 libraries contain 127,450 volumes, 1 million microform items, 4002 audio/video tapes/CDs/DVDs, and subscribe to 5782 periodicals including electronic. Computerized library services include interlibrary loans, database searching, and Internet access. Special learning facilities include a learning resource center, natural history museum, radio station, TV station, and cable channel. The 70-acre campus is in a small town 150 miles northwest of Oklahoma City. Including any residence halls, there are 36 buildings.

Student Life: 80% of undergraduates are from Oklahoma. Others are from 31 states, 20 foreign countries, and Canada. 86% are white. The average age of freshmen is 20; all undergraduates, 22. 35% do not continue beyond their first year; 35% remain to graduate.

Housing: 852 students can be accommodated in college housing, which includes single-sex dorms. On-campus housing is guaranteed for all 4 years. 75% of students commute. Alcohol is not permitted. All students may keep cars.

Activities: 1% of men belong to 1 national fraternity; 2% of women belong to 1 local sorority and 2 national sororities. There are 39 groups on campus, including art, band, cheerleading, choir, chorale, communications, computers, dance, drama, ethnic, forensics, honors, international, jazz band, marching band, musical theater, newspaper, pep band, photography, political, professional, radio and TV, religious, social, and student government. Popular campus events include Red Riot Week, Spirit Week, and Howdy Week.

Sports: There are 5 intercollegiate sports for men and 5 for women, and 8 intramural sports for men and 8 for women. Facilities include a field house, a wellness center, playing fields, a basketball court, a pool, and racquetball and tennis courts.

Disabled Students: Facilities include wheelchair ramps, elevators, special parking, specially equipped restrooms, special class scheduling, lowered drinking fountains, and special housing. Northwestern works with disabled students to accommodate their special academic needs.

Services: Counseling and information services are available, as is tutoring in most subjects. There is a reader service for the blind, and remedial math, reading, and writing.

Campus Safety and Security: Measures include 24-hour foot and vehicle patrol, emergency notification system, security escort services, and lighted pathways/sidewalks.

Programs of Study: Northwestern confers B.A., B.S., B.A.Ed., B.S.Ed., and B.S.N. degrees. Master's degrees are also awarded. Bachelor's degrees are awarded in AGRICULTURE (agricultural business management, agriculture, and conservation and regulation), BIOLOGICAL SCIENCE (biology/biological science), BUSINESS (accounting, business administration and management, and office supervision and management), COMMUNICATIONS AND THE ARTS (broadcasting, communications, dramatic arts, English, music, public relations, and speech/debate/ rhetoric), COMPUTER AND PHYSICAL SCIENCE (chemistry, computer science, mathematics, and physics), EDUCATION (business education, early childhood education, elementary education, English education, library science, mathematics education, music education, physical education, science education, secondary education, and special education), HEALTH PROFESSIONS (medical laboratory technology and nursing), SOCIAL SCIENCE (criminal justice, economics, history, political science/ government, psychology, social science, social work, and sociology). Education and business are the strongest academically.

Required: A total of 124 credit hours is required, including at least 40 in the major, with a minimum GPA of 2.0. General education courses total 54 hours, including 12 hours in communication and symbols, 12 in social, political, and economic systems, 10 to 12 hours in natural science, 7 hours in human heritage and culture, and 3 hours in values and beliefs. This general sequence totals 50 hours for education majors.

Special: Northwestern offers internships, study abroad, and credit by exam and for military experience. There are 4 national honor societies, a freshman honors program, and 7 departmental honors programs.

Faculty/Classroom: 46% of faculty are male; 54% are female. All teach undergraduates. No introductory courses are taught by graduate students. The average class size in an introductory lecture is 38; in a laboratory, 24; and in a regular course, 19.

Requirements: The SAT or ACT is required. Applicants must be graduates of an accredited secondary school or have earned a GED. Northwestern requires 20 academic credits, including 4 in English, 3 in math, and 2 each in history and lab science. Northwestern requires applicants to be in the upper 50% of their class. A GPA of 2.7 is required. CLEP credits are accepted.

Procedure: Freshmen are admitted to all sessions. Entrance exams should be taken in the junior or senior year. There is a rolling admissions plan. Application deadlines are open. Application fee is $15. Notification is sent on a rolling basis. Applications are accepted online.

Transfer: Applicants must have a GPA of at least 2.0. 40 of 124 credits required for the bachelor's degree must be completed at Northwestern.

Visiting: There are regularly scheduled orientations for prospective students, including Ranger Preview in the fall for all prospective students and their families. Students in attendance will receive a $400 scholarship. Freshman Connection in spring offers an early enrollment session for the incoming fall class. Freshman Orientation is held prior to the beginning of the fall semester. There are guides for informal visits; visitors may sit in on classes and stay overnight. To schedule a visit, contact the Recruitment Office.

Financial Aid: The FAFSA is required. Check with the school for current deadlines.

International Students: The school actively recruits these students. They must take the TOEFL with a minimum score of 500 on the paper-based TOEFL (PBT) or 61 on the Internet-based version (iBT).

Computers: Wireless access is available. There are numerous computer labs on all 3 campuses. Alva has 9 labs with 151 computers, Enid has 4 labs with 66 computers, and Woodward has 1 lab with 18 computers. All students may access the system 7:30 a.m. to midnight. There are no time limits and no fees.

Admissions Contact: Director of Recruitment. A campus DVD is available. E-Mail: *wmadair@nwosu.edu* Web: *www.nwosu.edu*

OKLAHOMA BAPTIST UNIVERSITY E-3

Shawnee, OK 74804 (405) 585-5120
(800) 654-3285; (405) 585-5105

Full-time: 731 men, 1137 women	**Faculty:** n/av
Part-time: 88 men, 63 women	**Ph.D.s:** n/av
Graduate: 34 men, 44 women	**Student/Faculty:** 15 to 1
Year: 4-1-4, summer session	**Tuition:** $21,842
Application Deadline: August 1	**Room & Board:** $6360

Freshman Class: 6560 applied, 3704 accepted, 580 enrolled
SAT CR/M: 536/536 **ACT:** 24 **VERY COMPETITIVE**

Oklahoma Baptist University, founded in 1910, is a liberal arts institution affiliated with the Southern Baptist Convention. OBU offers degrees in Christian service, business, nursing, fine arts, telecommunications, teacher education, and the traditional liberal arts areas. There are 6 undergraduate schools and one graduate school. In addition to regional accreditation, OBU has baccalaureate program accreditation with ACBSP, NASM, NCATE, and NLN. The library contains 290,000 volumes, 230,000 microform items, 1,500 audio/video tapes/CDs/DVDs, and subscribes to 600 periodicals including electronic. Computerized library services include interlibrary loans, database searching, Internet access, and Wi-Fi capability. Special learning facilities include an art gallery, planetarium, TV station, a language lab, and a Biblical research library. The 189-acre campus is in a small town 30 miles east of Oklahoma City and 90 miles southwest of Tulsa. Including any residence halls, there are 54 buildings.

Student Life: 70% of undergraduates are from Oklahoma. Others are from 34 states, 31 foreign countries, and Canada. 84% are from public schools. 70% are White. 93% are Protestant; 15% claim no religious affiliation. The average age of freshmen is 18; all undergraduates, 20. 26% do not continue beyond their first year; 56% remain to graduate.

Housing: 1391 students can be accommodated in college housing, which includes single-sex dorms, on-campus apartments, and married student housing. On-campus housing is guaranteed for all 4 years. 63% of students live on campus; 75% remain on campus on weekends. Alcohol is not permitted. All students may keep cars.

Activities: 1% of men belong to 1 local fraternity; 10% of women belong to 4 local sororities. There are 85 groups on campus, including art, band, cheerleading, choir, chorale, chorus, computers, drama, environmental, ethnic, film, honors, international, jazz band, literary magazine, marching band, musical theater, newspaper, opera, orchestra, pep band, photography, political, professional, radio and TV, religious, social, social service, student government, and yearbook. Popular campus events include Stampede of Stars, International Awareness Day and Hanging of the Green.

Sports: There are 10 intercollegiate sports for men and 12 for women, and 14 intramural sports for men and 14 for women. Facilities include a sports complex, which houses a 2500-seat arena; a 60,000-sqare-foot recreation and wellness center, which includes 3 basketball/volleyball courts, a 2 story rock climbing wall, state-of-the-art exercise and fitness equipment, weight rooms, a swimming pool, and a walking track on the top floor; an all-weather track; and baseball, softball, soccer, and sand volleyball facilities.

Disabled Students: 95% of the campus is accessible. Facilities include wheelchair ramps, elevators, special parking, specially equipped restrooms, lowered drinking fountains, lowered telephones, and special housing.

Services: Counseling and information services are available, as is tutoring in most subjects. There is a reader service for the blind, and remedial math, reading, and writing.

Campus Safety and Security: Measures include 24-hour foot and vehicle patrol, emergency notification system, self-defense education, and security escort services. There are emergency telephones, lighted pathways/sidewalks, and controlled access to dorms/residences.

Programs of Study: OBU confers B.A., B.S., B.B.A., B.F.A., B.Hum., B.M., B.M.A., B.Mus.Ed. and B.S.E. degrees. Associate and master's degrees are also awarded. Bachelor's degrees are awarded in BIOLOGICAL SCIENCE (biology/biological science), BUSINESS (accounting, banking and finance, business administration and management, and marketing/retailing/merchandising), COMMUNICATIONS AND THE ARTS (broadcasting, communications, dramatic arts, English, fine arts, French, German, journalism, music, Spanish, speech/debate/rhetoric, and telecommunications), COMPUTER AND PHYSICAL SCIENCE (chemistry, computer science, information sciences and systems, mathematics, and physics), EDUCATION (art education, early childhood education, elementary education, foreign languages education, music education, physical education, science education, and secondary education), HEALTH PROFESSIONS (nursing, physical therapy, predentistry, and premedicine), SOCIAL SCIENCE (history, political science/government, prelaw, psychology, religion, social science, social work, and sociology). Teacher education, biology, and religion are the strongest academically. Elementary education, and nursing have the largest enrollments.

Required: To graduate, students must complete a total of 128 credit hours, including 30 to 48 hours in the major, with a 2.0 GPA. Students are also required to complete 6 credits each of English, literature, history, science, Bible, social sciences, and language; 3 each in math, fine arts, and comparative civilization; 2 each in speech, philosophy, and phys ed; and 1 in computer literacy.

Special: OBU offers co-op programs in business, and a 3-2 engineering degree with Oklahoma State University. Students may study abroad in 15 countries in Europe, Central and South America, Asia, and Africa. Internships in several fields, student-designed majors, including an interdisciplinary program in humanities, and pass/fail options are available. There are 4 national honor societies and a freshman honors program.

Faculty/Classroom: 55% of faculty are male; 45% are female. All teach undergraduates. No introductory courses are taught by graduate students. The average class size in an introductory lecture is 25; in a laboratory is 19; and in a regular course is 15.

Admissions: 56% of the 2013-2014 applicants were accepted. The SAT scores for the 2013-2014 freshman class were: Critical Reading--32% below 500, 40% between 500 and 599, 23% between 600 and 699, and 5% between 700 and 800; Math--25% below 500, 47% between 500 and 599, 25% between 600 and 699, and 3% between 700 and 800. The ACT scores were 21% below 21, 27% between 21 and 23, 25% between 24 and 26, 12% between 27 and 28, and 15% above 28. 51% of the current freshmen were in the top fifth of their class; 78% were in the top two fifths. 28 freshmen graduated first in their class.

Requirements: The SAT or ACT is required. Admission is granted to students with composite scores of 950 on the SAT or 20 on the ACT, with a 3.0 GPA. Graduation from an accredited secondary school or satisfactory scores on the GED are required for admission. The recommended high school courses should include 4 units of English, 3 units of math, and 2 units each of social studies, lab science, and a foreign language. OBU requires applicants to be in the upper 50% of their class. A GPA of 3.0 is required. AP and CLEP credits are accepted. Important factors in the admissions decision are advanced placement or honors courses, recommendations by school officials, and leadership record.

Procedure: Freshmen are admitted to all sessions. Entrance exams should be taken during the spring of the junior year. There are deferred admissions and rolling admissions plans. Applications should be filed by August 1 for fall entry; December 15 for winter entry; January 15 for spring entry; and May 15 for summer entry. Applications are accepted online.

Transfer: 98 transfer students enrolled in 2012-2013. Transfer students must have a GPA of 2.5 for all college work attempted. 32 of 128 credits required for the bachelor's degree must be completed at OBU.

Visiting: There are regularly scheduled orientations for prospective students, including tours, faculty visits, and general information sessions. There are guides for informal visits, visitors may sit in on classes, and stay overnight. To schedule a visit, contact the OBU Admissions Office.

Financial Aid: In 2013-2014, 99% of all full-time freshmen and % of continuing full-time students received some form of financial aid. 75% of all full-time freshmen and 60% of continuing full-time students received need-based aid. The average freshman award was $19,681. Need-based scholarships or need-based grants averaged $5,846; need-based self-help aid (loans and jobs) averaged $3,223; non-need-based athletic scholarships averaged $5,551; and other non-need-based awards and non-need-based scholarships averaged $10,419. 95% of undergraduate students work part-time. Average annual earnings from campus work are $2000. The average financial indebtedness of the 2013 graduate was $26,557. The FAFSA is required. The priority date for freshman financial aid applications for fall entry is April 1.

International Students: There are 90 international students enrolled. The school actively recruits these students. They must take the TOEFL with a minimum score of 550 on the paper-based TOEFL (PBT) or 61 on the Internet-based version (iBT) or take the MELAB. They must also take the SAT or ACT.

Computers: All students may access the system 75 hours per week. There are no time limits and no fees.

Graduates: From July 1, 2012 to June 30, 2013, 302 bachelor's degrees were awarded. The most popular majors were health profession & related programs (19%), education (18%), and business/marketing (8%). In an average class, 41% graduate in 4 years or less and 56% graduate in 6 years or less.

Admissions Contact: Bruce Perkins, Dean of Enrollment Management. E-Mail: *admissions@okbu.edu* Web: *www.okbu.edu*

OKLAHOMA CHRISTIAN UNIVERSITY D-3

Oklahoma City, OK 73136 (405) 425-5050
(800) 877-5010; (405) 425-5069

Full-time: 979 men, 928 women	**Faculty:** 107
Part-time: 32 men, 27 women	**Ph.D.s:** 69%
Graduate: 267 men, 183 women	**Student/Faculty:** 18 to 1
Year: semesters, summer session	**Tuition:** $18,800
Application Deadline: open	**Room & Board:** $6175
Freshman Class: 1984 applied, 1254 accepted, 533 enrolled	
SAT CR/M/W: 520/535/510	**ACT:** 25 VERY COMPETITIVE

Oklahoma Christian University, founded in 1950, is a private liberal arts institution affiliated with the Church of Christ. There are 3 undergraduate schools and 3 graduate schools. In addition to regional accreditation, OC has baccalaureate program accreditation with ABET, ACBSP, NASM, and NCATE. The library contains 160,011 volumes, 686,736 microform items, 6,854 audio/video tapes/CDs/DVDs, and subscribes to 7,255 periodicals including electronic. Computerized library services include interlibrary loans, database searching, Internet access, and Wi-Fi capability. Special learning facilities include an art gallery, radio station, a journalism lab. The 200-acre campus is in a suburban area on the north side of Oklahoma City. Including any residence halls, there are 33 buildings.

Student Life: 45% of undergraduates are from out of state, mostly the Mid-West. Students are from 49 states, 55 foreign countries, and Canada. 66% are White; 15% Foreign; 14% African American. 22% are Protestant. The average age of freshmen is 18; all undergraduates, 22. 24% do not continue beyond their first year; 50% remain to graduate.

Housing: 2050 students can be accommodated in college housing, which includes single-sex dorms, on-campus apartments, and married student housing. In addition, there are honors houses. On-campus housing is guaranteed for all 4 years. 80% of students live on campus. Alcohol is not permitted. All students may keep cars.

Activities: There are no fraternities or sororities. There are 19 groups on campus, including band, cheerleading, choir, chorale, communications, computers, drama, ethnic, honors, international, jazz band, literary magazine, musical theater, newspaper, opera, orchestra, pep band, photography, political, professional, radio and TV, religious, social service, student government, symphony, and yearbook. Popular campus events include High School Day, Spring Sing, and Homecoming.

Sports: There are 7 intercollegiate sports for men and 7 for women, and 9 intramural sports for men and 8 for women. Facilities include basketball courts, a 25-meter six-lane swimming pool for recreational swimming, on campus baseball, softball, football, and soccer fields, a track and field facility, tennis courts, a 4,000-square-foot fitness center, and an auxiliary gym.

Disabled Students: 98% of the campus is accessible. Facilities include wheelchair ramps, elevators, special parking, specially equipped restrooms, special class scheduling, lowered drinking fountains, lowered telephones, and special housing.

Services: Counseling and information services are available, as is tutoring in some subjects, English, math, speech, chemistry, physics, business, education, and computer science. There is remedial math, reading, and writing.

Campus Safety and Security: Measures include 24-hour foot and vehicle patrol, emergency notification system, and security escort services. There are emergency telephones, lighted pathways/sidewalks, campus police.

Programs of Study: OC confers B.A., B.S., B.B.A., B.F.A., B.M.E., B.Mus.Ed., B.S.C.E., B.S.Ed., B.S.E., B.S.E.E. and B.S.M.E. degrees. Master's degrees are also awarded. Bachelor's degrees are awarded in BIOLOGICAL SCIENCE (biochemistry and biology/biological science), BUSINESS (accounting, business administration and management, and marketing/retailing/merchandising), COMMUNICATIONS AND THE ARTS (advertising, art, broadcasting, communications, creative writing, design, English, journalism, music, and Spanish), COMPUTER AND PHYSICAL SCIENCE (chemistry, computer science, information sciences and systems, and mathematics), EDUCATION (early childhood education, elementary education, English education, mathematics education, middle school education, music education, physical education, science education, social studies education, special education, and teaching English as a second/foreign language (TESOL/TEFOL)), ENGINEERING AND ENVIRONMENTAL DESIGN (computer engineering, electrical/electronics engineering, engineering physics, interior design, and mechanical engineering), HEALTH PROFESSIONS (medical laboratory technology and premedicine), SOCIAL SCIENCE (biblical studies, child care/child and family studies, history, liberal arts/general studies, ministries, missions, prelaw, psychology, religious education, and youth ministry). Health sciences, and nursing are the strongest academically. Business, education, and engineering have the largest enrollments.

Required: To graduate, students must have a minimum of 126 credit hours, including 30 to 104 in the major, with a GPA of 2.0. All students must complete 60 to 61 hours in the general education program, which includes courses in Bible, English, speech, American studies, math, literature, fine arts, economics, biology, physical science, philosophy, Western civilization, phys ed, personal development, and social science.

Special: OC offers a wide range of undergraduate degrees and many graduate programs in Accounting, Business, Theology, Ministry, and Engineering. Our ABET accredited engineering complements a full spectrum of majors across the arts, sciences, and humanities. Internships and practice are commonly required or offered in the nearby city. Students may study abroad in Austria, Japan, and China. Major-minor combinations and interdisciplinary studies options help students combine fields such as business, mass communications, family life, prelaw, advertising design, speech communication, education, English, music, math and others. An interdisciplinary Honors program serves students with high ACT/SAT scores. Many chapters of disciplinary societies, such as Sigma Tau Delta or Phil Alpha Theta achieve national awards for excellence. Cross-registration can be offered with the University of Central Oklahoma. There are 8 national honor societies, a freshman honors program, and 18 departmental honors programs.

Faculty/Classroom: 67% of faculty are male; 33% are female. All teach undergraduates, and 10% do both. No introductory courses are taught by graduate students. The average class size in an introductory lecture is 19; in a laboratory is 15; and in a regular course is 21.

Admissions: 63% of the 2013-2014 applicants were accepted. The SAT scores for the 2013-2014 freshman class were: Critical Reading--37% below 500, 32% between 500 and 599, 24% between 600 and 699, and 7% between 700 and 800; Math--36% below 500, 35% between 500 and 599, 20% between 600 and 699, and 9% between 700 and 800. The ACT scores were 17% below 21, 26% between 21 and 23, 22% between 24 and 26, 20% between 27 and 28, and 15% above 28. There were 10 National Merit finalists.

Requirements: The SAT or ACT is required. In addition, graduation from an accredited secondary school or satisfactory scores on the GED are required for admission. AP and CLEP credits are accepted.

Procedure: Freshmen are admitted to all sessions. There are deferred admissions and rolling admissions plans. Application deadlines are open. Application fee is $25. Notification is sent on a rolling basis.

Transfer: 115 transfer students enrolled in 2012-2013. Applicants must be eligible to return to the school from which they are transferring. 30 of 126 credits required for the bachelor's degree must be completed at OC.

Visiting: There are regularly scheduled orientations for prospective students, Comprehensive campus overview including academic conversations. There are guides for informal visits, visitors may sit in on classes, and stay overnight. To schedule a visit, contact the Admissions Office.

Financial Aid: In 2013-2014, 98% of all full-time freshmen and 90% of continuing full-time students received some form of financial aid. 32% of all full-time freshmen and 31% of continuing full-time students received need-based aid. The average freshman award was $21,425. Need-based scholarships or need-based grants averaged $3,105; need-based self-help aid (loans and jobs) averaged $3,224; and non-need-based athletic scholarships averaged $8,354. 18% of undergraduate students work part-time. Average annual earnings from campus work are $1872. The average financial indebtedness of the 2013 graduate was $21,298. The FAFSA is required. The priority date for freshman financial aid applications for fall entry is March 15. The deadline for filing freshman financial aid applications for fall entry is April 15.

International Students: There are 208 international students enrolled. The school actively recruits these students. They must take the TOEFL with a minimum score of 500 on the paper-based TOEFL (PBT) or 61 on the Internet-based version (iBT). They must also take the SAT or ACT.

Computers: All students may access the system 24 hours, 7 days a week. There are no time limits and no fees.

Graduates: From July 1, 2012 to June 30, 2013, 346 bachelor's degrees were awarded. The most popular majors were business (16%), engineering (11%), and education (7%). 50 companies recruited on campus in 2012-2013. In an average class, 31% graduate in 4 years or less, 44% graduate in 5 years or less, and 46% graduate in 6 years or less. Of the 2012 graduating class, 13% were enrolled in graduate school within 6 months of graduation, and 94% were employed.

Admissions Contact: Michael Mitchell, Director of Admissions & Recruiting. E-Mail: *info@oc.edu* Web: *www.oc.edu*

OKLAHOMA CITY UNIVERSITY D-3

Oklahoma City, OK 73106 (405) 208-5055
(800) 633-7242; (405) 208-5916

Full-time: 637 men, 1009 women	**Faculty:** 205; IIA, --$
Part-time: 42 men, 80 women	**Ph.D.s:** 76%
Graduate: 571 men, 641 women	**Student/Faculty:** 11 to 1
Year: semesters, summer session	**Tuition:** $29,426
Application Deadline: rolling	**Room & Board:** $4120

Freshman Class: 1432 applied, 1008 accepted, 354 enrolled
SAT: required **ACT:** 25 **VERY COMPETITIVE**

Oklahoma City University, founded in 1904, is a private, comprehensive university affiliated with the United Methodist Church, offering undergraduate and graduate programs in arts and sciences, business, music and performing arts, religion and church vocations, nursing, and law. There are 7 undergraduate schools and 6 graduate schools. In addition to regional accreditation, OCU has baccalaureate program accreditation with ACBSP, NASM, NCATE, and NLN. The 2 libraries contain 327,986 volumes, 1.0 million microform items, and 16,599 audio/video tapes/CDs/DVDs, and subscribe to 22,901 periodicals including electronic. Computerized library services include interlibrary loans, database searching, Internet access, and Wi-Fi capability. Special learning facilities include an art gallery and TV station. The 104-acre campus is in an urban area Within Oklahoma City. Including any residence halls, there are 36 buildings.

Student Life: 53% of undergraduates are from Oklahoma. Others are from 44 states, 58 foreign countries, and Canada. 89% are from public schools. 60% are White; 16% Foreign. 47% are Protestant; 27% claim no religious affiliation; 15% Hindu, Islamic, and Buddhist. The average age of freshmen is 19; all undergraduates, 22. 19% do not continue beyond their first year; 60% remain to graduate.

Housing: 1309 students can be accommodated in college housing, which includes single-sex and coed dorms, on-campus apartments, and married student housing. In addition, there are special-interest houses, fraternity houses, learning communities. On-campus housing is guaranteed for all 4 years. 53% of students live on campus. Alcohol is not permitted. All students may keep cars.

Activities: 27% of men belong to 3 national fraternities; 17% of women belong to 3 national sororities. There are 65 groups on campus, including art, band, cheerleading, choir, chorus, computers, dance, debate, drama, environmental, ethnic, film, gay, honors, international, jazz band, literary magazine, musical theater, newspaper, opera, orchestra, pep band, photography, political, professional, radio and TV, religious, social, social service, student government, symphony, and yearbook. Popular campus events include Midnight Breakfast, Movie Night, Oozeball, Homecoming, and Relay for Life.

Sports: There are 9 intercollegiate sports for men and 11 for women, and 9 intramural sports for men and 9 for women. Facilities include a baseball, softball, and soccer fields, and a wellness and activity center which houses basketball, volleyball, and wrestling.

Disabled Students: 98% of the campus is accessible. Facilities include wheelchair ramps, elevators, special parking, specially equipped restrooms, lowered drinking fountains, and lowered telephones.

Services: Counseling and information services are available, as is tutoring in most subjects. There is a reader service for the blind, and remedial math, reading, and writing. There are writing and learning enhancement centers and a math lab.

Campus Safety and Security: Measures include 24-hour foot and vehicle patrol, emergency notification system, and security escort services. There are emergency telephones, lighted pathways/sidewalks, controlled access to dorms/residences, an inner-campus bicycle patrol.

Programs of Study: OCU confers B.A., B.S., B.F.A., B.M., B.Perf.Arts, B.S.B., B.B.A., B.M., B.M.E. and B.S.N. degrees. Master's and doctoral degrees are also awarded. Bachelor's degrees are awarded in AGRICULTURE (environmental studies), BIOLOGICAL SCIENCE (biochemistry and cell biology), BUSINESS (accounting, banking and finance, business administration and management, management science, and marketing), COMMUNICATIONS AND THE ARTS (advertising, art, broadcasting, church music, communications, dance, English, film arts, French, guitar, instrumental performance, instrumental music education, instrumental music education, music, music composition, photography, piano/organ, public relations, Spanish, studio art, theatre acting, theatre arts, theater design, theatre production, and vocal performance), COMPUTER AND PHYSICAL SCIENCE (chemistry, mathematics, physics, science, and software engineering), EDUCATION (early childhood education, education, elementary education, music education, and secondary education), HEALTH PROFESSIONS (biology, biomedical science, exercise science, health care administration, nursing, and premedicine), SOCIAL SCIENCE (addiction studies, behavioral science, economics, history, humanities, liberal arts/general studies, philosophy, philosophy and religion, political science/government, prelaw, psychology, religion, religious education, and sociology). Nursing, sciences, and performing arts are the strongest academically. Sciences, performing arts, and liberal arts have the largest enrollments.

Required: To graduate, students must complete a total of 124 credit hours, including 30 to 80 in the major, with a minimum GPA of 2.0. Students must complete their last 15 hours, including the last 6 in the major, at OCU with a minimum GPA of 2.0. All students must take 43 hours in the core curriculum as specified by their college or department.

Special: OCU offers internships, a Washington semester, work-study programs, a general studies degree, dual and student-designed majors, credit for life experience, and study abroad programs in many countries. B.A.-B.S. degrees and an accelerated degree program in nursing and law are also available. There are 10 national honor societies, a freshman honors program, and 10 departmental honors programs.

Faculty/Classroom: 50% of faculty are male; 50% are female. 85% teach undergraduates. No introductory courses are taught by graduate students. The average class size in an introductory lecture is 18; in a laboratory is 12; and in a regular course is 13.

Admissions: 70% of the 2013-2014 applicants were accepted. The ACT scores were 11% below 21, 20% between 21 and 23, 31% between 24 and 26, 12% between 27 and 28, and 26% above 28. 37% of the current freshmen were in the top fifth of their class; 57% were in the top two fifths. There were 5 National Merit finalists. 16 freshmen graduated first in their class.

Requirements: The SAT or ACT is required. Graduation from an accredited secondary school or satisfactory scores on the GED is required for admission. High school courses must include 4 units of English, 2-3 units each of science (at least one should be lab), one unit of world history, one unit of state history and civics, one unit of US History, 2 units math, and 2 units of a foreign language. We look for a 3.0 unweighted GPA and 22 on the ACT or 1020 on the SAT. Additionally, we review the essay, letter of recommendation, and application materials. Dance and arts management, music, and theatre all require an audition. Studio art and photography require portfolio review. A GPA of 3.0 is required. AP and CLEP credits are accepted. Important factors in the admissions decision are evidence of special talent, advanced placement or honors courses, and leadership record.

Procedure: Freshmen are admitted to all sessions. Entrance exams should be taken by February of the senior year. There are deferred admissions and rolling admissions plans. Application deadlines are open. The fall 2013 application fee was $55. Notification is sent on a rolling basis. Applications are accepted online.

Transfer: 165 transfer students enrolled in 2012-2013. Applicants must submit a transcript from each college attended and must have a minimum cumulative GPA of 2.0 from an accredited institution. Applicants having fewer than 29 credit hours must submit a high school transcript and ACT or SAT scores. The application also requires an essay and recommendation from their Dean of Students. 30 of 124 credits required for the bachelor's degree must be completed at Oklahoma City.

Visiting: There are regularly scheduled orientations for prospective students, 9 am and 1 pm informational presentation and campus tour. There are guides for informal visits and visitors may sit in on classes. To schedule a visit, contact Tasha Casey-Loveless at tasha.loveless@okcu.edu.

Financial Aid: In 2013-2014, 95% of all full-time freshmen and 82% of continuing full-time students received some form of financial aid. 71% of all full-time freshmen and 56% of continuing full-time students received need-based aid. The average freshman award was $26,273. Need-based scholarships or need-based grants averaged $17,087 ($43,162 maximum); need-based self-help aid (loans and jobs) averaged $3,516 ($8,500 maximum); non-need-based athletic scholarships averaged $7,448 ($19,853 maximum); and other non-need-based awards and non-need-based scholarships averaged $15,598 ($33,558 maximum). 14% of undergraduate students work part-time. Average annual earnings from campus work are $2276. The average financial indebtedness of the 2013 graduate was $21,635. OCU is a member of CSS. The FAFSA, and and tax returns, if selected for verification is required. The priority date for freshman financial aid applications for fall entry is March 1. The deadline for filing freshman financial aid applications for fall entry is June 30.

International Students: There are 332 international students enrolled. The school actively recruits these students. They must take the TOEFL with a minimum score of 550 on the paper-based TOEFL (PBT) or 80 on the Internet-based version (iBT).

Computers: All students may access the system 24 hours a day. There are no time limits and no fees.

Graduates: From July 1, 2012 to June 30, 2013, 668 bachelor's degrees were awarded. The most popular majors were liberal arts and sciences (19%), business, marketing (16%), and nursing (13%). 96 companies recruited on campus in 2012-2013. In an average class, 47% graduate in 4 years or less, 58% graduate in 5 years or less, and 60% graduate in 6 years or less.

Admissions Contact: Michelle Cook, Director of Admissions Operations
E-Mail: *uadmissions@okcu.edu* Web: *www.okcu.edu*

OKLAHOMA PANHANDLE STATE UNIVERSITY B-2

Goodwell, OK 73939 (580) 349-1376
(800) 664-6778; (580) 349-1371

Full-time: 615 men, 501 women
Part-time: 82 men, 189 women
Graduate: n/av
Year: semesters, summer session
Application Deadline: open
Freshman Class: 316 applied, 316 accepted, 286 enrolled
SAT CR/M: 525/520
Faculty: 65; IIB, --$
Ph.D.s: 32%
Student/Faculty: 15 to 1
Tuition: $5844 ($11,403)
Room & Board: $4152
ACT: 22 **NONCOMPETITIVE**

Oklahoma Panhandle State University, founded in 1909, is a publicly funded institution offering undergraduate programs in the liberal arts, business and technology, education, agriculture, mathematics, sciences, and nursing. There are 5 undergraduate schools. In addition to regional accreditation, OPSU has baccalaureate program accreditation with NCATE and NLN. The library contains 123,026 volumes, 12,764 microform items, 7,159 audio/video tapes/CDs/DVDs, and subscribes to 275 periodicals including electronic. Computerized library services include interlibrary loans, database searching, and Internet access. Special learning facilities include a learning resource center, radio station, a writing lab, academic support lab, farm lab, children's collection library, and 2 instructional ITV facilities. The figures in the above capsule and in this profile are approximate. The 120-acre campus is in a rural area 100 miles north of Amarillo, Texas. Including any residence halls, there are 29 buildings.

Student Life: 50% of undergraduates are from out of state, mostly the Mid-West. Students are from 35 states, 15 foreign countries, and Canada. 98% are from public schools. 65% are white; 18% Hispanic. The average age of freshmen is 20; all undergraduates, 24. 42% do not continue beyond their first year; 38% remain to graduate.

Housing: 613 students can be accommodated in college housing, which includes single-sex and coed dorms, on-campus apartments, and married student housing. On-campus housing is guaranteed for the freshman year only, is available on a first-come, and first-served basis. 60% of students commute. Alcohol is not permitted. All students may keep cars.

Activities: 5% of men belong to 1 local fraternity. There are 40 groups on campus, including Ambassadors, block and bridle, FFA, soccer club, art, band, cheerleading, choir, chorale, computers, dance, drama, drill team, ethnic, honors, international, jazz band, marching band, musical theater, newspaper, pep band, photography, professional, radio and TV, religious, Rodeo Club, student government, and yearbook. Popular campus events include Mardi Gras, Talent Show, and Holiday Dinner.

Sports: There are 10 intercollegiate sports for men and 8 for women, and Facilities include a field house, an athletic field, a golf course, tennis courts, a gym, and an activity center. Water skiing and fishing spots are nearby.

Disabled Students: 97% of the campus is accessible. Facilities include wheelchair ramps, elevators, special parking, specially equipped restrooms, and special class scheduling.

Services: There is remedial math, reading, and writing. Free tutoring is provided through the peer counseling center.

Campus Safety and Security: Measures include emergency notification system. There are lighted pathways/sidewalks.

Programs of Study: OPSU confers B.A., B.S., B.B.A., B.F.A., B.I.T., B.M., B.S.N., and B.T. degrees. Associate degrees are also awarded. Bachelor's degrees are awarded in AGRICULTURE (agricultural business management, agronomy, animal science, and equine science), BIOLOGICAL SCIENCE (biology/biological science), BUSINESS (accounting and business administration and management), COMMUNICATIONS AND THE ARTS (English, fine arts, and music), COMPUTER AND PHYSICAL SCIENCE (chemistry, information sciences and systems, mathematics, and physical sciences), EDUCATION (agricultural education, business education, and physical education), ENGINEERING AND ENVIRONMENTAL DESIGN (industrial engineering technology and technological management), HEALTH PROFESSIONS (nursing), SOCIAL SCIENCE (history, psychology, and social studies). Biology, business administration, and nursing have the largest enrollments.

Required: To graduate, students must complete a total of 124 semester hours with a minimum GPA of 2.0. The number of hours required in the major varies. All students must complete 45 hours of general education courses, with at least 1 course at the upper-division level. Students must complete 40 upper-level hours and must have completed 60 hours at a 4-year institution.

Special: The university offers dual majors and B.A.-B.S. degrees in several majors. There is 1 national honor society and 1 departmental honors program.

Faculty/Classroom: 58% of faculty are male; 42% are female. All teach undergraduates. No introductory courses are taught by graduate students. The average class size in an introductory lecture is 30; in a laboratory is 20; and in a regular course is 20.

Admissions: 100% of a recent year applicants were accepted. The SAT scores for the recent freshman class were: Critical Reading--16% below 500, 67% between 500 and 599, and 17% between 600 and 700; Math--33% below 500, 50% between 500 and 599, and 17% between 600 and 700. The ACT scores were 25% below 21, 35% between 21 and 23, 28% between 24 and 26, 11% between 27 and 28, and 1% above 28.

Requirements: The SAT or ACT is recommended, with a minimum composite score on the ACT. Graduation from an accredited secondary school or satisfactory scores on the GED are required. High school courses must include 4 units of English, 3 units of math (beginning with Algebra I), 3 units of other courses such as foreign language or computer application courses, 2 units each of history (including 1 unit of American history) and lab science, and 1 unit of citizenship (for example, government, civics). AP and CLEP credits are accepted.

Procedure: Freshmen are admitted to all sessions. There is a rolling admissions plan. Application deadlines are open.

Transfer: An application for admission, a medical history form, college transcripts, high school transcripts, and ACT scores are required. If students are transferring in with a GPA below 2.0, they come in on academic probation. 30 of 124 credits required for the bachelor's degree must be completed at OPSU.

Visiting: There are regularly scheduled orientations for prospective students. There are guides for informal visits, visitors may sit in on classes, and stay overnight. To schedule a visit, contact High School and Community Relations.

Financial Aid: The FAFSA and the college's own financial statement are required. Check with the school for current application deadlines.

International Students: There are 42 international students enrolled. The school actively recruits these students. They must take the TOEFL with a minimum score of 500 on the paper-based TOEFL (PBT). They must also take the SAT or ACT.

Computers: Wireless access is available. All students may access the system. There are no time limits and no fees.

Graduates: In a recent year, 198 bachelor's degrees were awarded. The most popular majors were business administration (16%), registered nursing (12%), and biology (12%). In an average class, 38% graduate in 6 years or less.

Admissions Contact: Registrar and Director of Admissions. Web: *www.opsu.edu*

OKLAHOMA STATE SYSTEM OF HIGHER EDUCATION

The Oklahoma State System of Higher Education, established in 1941, is a public system in Oklahoma. It is governed by the Oklahoma State Regents for Higher Education, whose chief administrator is the chancellor. The primary mission of the system is to set academic standards, approve courses of study and grant degrees for all public colleges and universities, as well as recommend budget allocations and approve tuition and fees. The main priorities are to increase the number of college graduates, assure access to higher education, and achieve increasingly higher-quality education for students. The total student enrollment is usually about 207,905 with 5000 faculty members. Altogether there are 659 baccalaureate, 319 master's, and 110 doctoral programs offered in the Oklahoma State System of Higher Education. Profiles of the 4-year campuses are included in this section.

OKLAHOMA STATE UNIVERSITY E-2

Stillwater, OK 74078 (405) 744-5358
(800) 223-5019, ext.1; (405) 744-7092

Full-time: 9057 men, 8492 women
Part-time: 1381 men, 1124 women
Graduate: 2981 men, 2433 women
Year: semesters, summer session
Application Deadline:
Freshman Class: 12056 applied, 9351 accepted, 4289 enrolled
SAT CR/M: 540/560
Faculty: 808; I, --$
Ph.D.s: 91%
Student/Faculty: 20 to 1
Tuition: $7942 ($19,957)
Room & Board: $7368
ACT: 25 **VERY COMPETITIVE**

Oklahoma State University, founded in 1890, is a publicly funded land-grant institution, offering undergraduate programs in agricultural sciences and natural resources, arts and sciences, business, education, engineering, architecture, technology, and human environmental resources. There are 6 undergraduate schools and one graduate school. In addition to regional accreditation, OSU has baccalaureate program accreditation with AACSB, ABET, ACEJMC, ADA, AHEA, ASLA, FIDER, NAAB, NASM, NCATE, NRPA, and SAF. The 5 libraries contain 3.5 million volumes, 4.6 million microform items, 445,551 audio/video tapes/CDs/DVDs. Computerized library services include interlibrary loans, database searching, Internet access, and Wi-Fi capability. Special learning facilities include an art gallery and radio station. The 840-acre campus is in a small town 65 miles north of Oklahoma City.

Student Life: 74% of undergraduates are from Oklahoma. Others are from 48 states, 128 foreign countries, and Canada. 70% are White. The average age of freshmen is 19; all undergraduates, 22. 21% do not continue beyond their first year; 79% remain to graduate.

Housing: College-sponsored housing includes single-sex and coed dorms, on-campus apartments, off-campus apartments, and married student housing. In addition, there are honors houses, language houses, special-interest houses, fraternity houses, and sorority houses. On-campus housing is guaranteed for the freshman year only, is available on a first-come, and first-served basis. 55% of students commute. Alcohol is not permitted. All students may keep cars.

Activities: There are 400 groups on campus, including art, band, cheerleading, choir, chorale, chorus, computers, dance, drama, environmental, ethnic, gay, honors, international, jazz band, literary magazine, marching band, musical theater, newspaper, opera, orchestra, pep band, political, professional, radio and TV, religious, social, social service, student government, and symphony. Popular campus events include Freshmen Follies, Salsa Ball, and African Night.

Sports: There are 8 intercollegiate sports for men and 8 for women. Facilities include the recreation center, with more than 240,00 square feet of activity space, includes: 10 basketball-volleyball courts, a large multipurpose court, 30,000 square feet of weight and fitness equipment, cardiotheater, indoor climbing wall, golf practice area including 2 golf simulators, a 3-lane jogging track, indoor and outdoor swimming pools, and 12 racquetball-handball courts.

Disabled Students: 99% of the campus is accessible. Facilities include wheelchair ramps, elevators, special parking, specially equipped restrooms, special class scheduling, lowered drinking fountains, lowered telephones, special housing, and adaptive technology.

Services: Counseling and information services are available, as is tutoring in most subjects, math. Tutoring is not disability-specific There is a reader service for the blind, and remedial math, reading, and writing. Academic assessment and minority programs are also available.

Campus Safety and Security: Measures include 24-hour foot and vehicle patrol, emergency notification system, self-defense education, and security escort services. There are shuttle buses, emergency telephones, lighted pathways/sidewalks, and controlled access to dorms/residences.

Programs of Study: OSU confers B.A., B.S., B.Arch.,B.E.N., B.F.A., B.Land.Arch., B.M., B.S.A.E, B.S.A.G., B.S.B.A., B.S.B.E., B.S.C.H., B.S.C.P., B.S.C.V., B.S.E.E., B.S.E.T., B.S.I.E., B.S.M.E. and B.U.S. degrees. Master's and doctoral degrees are also awarded. Bachelor's degrees are awarded in AGRICULTURE (agricultural business management, agricultural communications, agricultural economics, animal science, horticulture, natural resource management, plant science, and soil science), BIOLOGICAL SCIENCE (biochemistry, biology/biological science, botany, cell biology, entomology, microbiology, molecular biology, nutrition, physiology, and zoology), BUSINESS (accounting, banking and finance, business administration and management, entrepreneurial studies, hotel/motel and restaurant management, international business management, management information systems, marketing/retailing/merchandising, and recreation and leisure services), COMMUNICATIONS AND THE ARTS (art, broadcasting, design, dramatic arts, English, French, German, journalism, music, Russian languages and literature, and Spanish), COMPUTER AND PHYSICAL SCIENCE (chemistry, computer science, geology, mathematics, physics, and statistics), EDUCATION (agricultural education, athletic training, education, elementary education, health education, music education, physical education, secondary education, and vocational education), ENGINEERING AND ENVIRONMENTAL DESIGN (aerospace studies, architectural engineering, architecture, bioengineering, chemical engineering, civil engineering, computer engineering, construction management, construction technology, electrical/electronics engineering, electrical/electronics engineering technology, environmental science, industrial administration/management, industrial engineering, landscape architecture/design, mechanical engineering, and mechanical engineering technology), HEALTH PROFESSIONS (speech pathology/audiology), SOCIAL SCIENCE (American studies, child care/child and family studies, economics, fire control and safety technology, food science, geography, history, human development, liberal arts/general studies, philosophy, political science/government, psychology, and sociology).

Required: To graduate, students must have a minimum GPA of 2.0 and at least 120 hours, including a minimum of 30 hours in the major for most programs. A higher GPA may be required in some majors. All students must take a minimum of 40 credit hours of core courses, including 6 each of English, humanities, analytical and quantitative thought, natural sciences, and social and behavioral sciences, 3 each of American history and government, and 1 each of scientific investigation and international studies.

Special: OSU offers cross-registration with Northern Oklahoma College and Tulsa Community College, a Washington semester, and an internship program. A B.A.-B.S. degree, dual majors, an individualized university studies degree, multidisciplinary majors in biosystems engineering and in cell and molecular biology, nondegree study, and pass/fail options are available. Students may study abroad in several countries. The school also sponsors Semester at Sea, a 1-semester program of study on a ship traveling to ports throughout the world. There is a freshman honors program.

Faculty/Classroom: 63% of faculty are male; 37% are female. Graduate students teach 19% of introductory courses. The average class size in an introductory lecture is 30 and in a laboratory is 21.

Admissions: 78% of the 2013-2014 applicants were accepted. The SAT scores for the 2013-2014 freshman class were: Critical Reading--27% below 500, 48% between 500 and 599, 21% between 600 and 699, and 4% between 700 and 800; Math--19% below 500, 42% between 500 and 599, 33% between 600 and 699, and 6% between 700 and 800. The ACT scores were 13% below 21, 23% between 21 and 23, 31% between 24 and 26, 14% between 27 and 28, and 19% above 28. 48% of the current freshmen were in the top fifth of their class; 78% were in the top two fifths. There were 16 National Merit finalists.

Requirements: The SAT or ACT is required. Freshman applicants must have a cumulative high school GPA of 3.0 and rank in the upper third of their graduating class; or achieve at least a 24 composite score on the ACT or 1090 on the SAT; or have a 3.0 GPA in the required 15 curricular units, which include 4 years of English, 3 of math (algebra I and above), 2 each of history and lab science, 1 of citizenship skills, and 3 more from any of the above or computer science or foreign language, along with an ACT score of 21 or SAT 980. OSU requires applicants to be in the upper 33% of their class. A GPA of 3.0 is required. AP and CLEP credits are accepted. Important factors in the admissions decision are advanced placement or honors courses, evidence of special talent, and recommendations by school officials.

Procedure: Freshmen are admitted fall, spring, and summer. Entrance exams should be taken during the junior or senior year. There is a rolling admissions plan. Application deadlines are open. Application fee is $40. Applications are accepted online.

Transfer: 1779 transfer students enrolled in 2012-2013. Applicants must submit official transcripts from all colleges attended. Students having fewer than 24 credit hours must also meet the requirements for entering freshmen and have a 2.25 GPA. Students that have earned 24-59 hours of college credit must achieve a minimum transfer GPA of 2.25 or higher in all college-level course work attempted. Students that have earned 60 or more hours of college credit must achieve a minimum transfer GPA of 2.0 or higher in all college-level course work attempted. 30 of 120 credits required for the bachelor's degree must be completed at OSU.

Visiting: There are regularly scheduled orientations for prospective students, including personal meetings and tours. Appointments are scheduled with other campus departments, as needed, to assist prospective students. There are guides for informal visits, visitors may sit in on classes, and stay overnight. To schedule a visit, contact the Undergraduate Admissions Office.

Financial Aid: The FAFSA and the college's own financial statement are required. The priority date for freshman financial aid applications for fall entry is February 1. The deadline for filing freshman financial aid applications for fall entry is rolling.

International Students: There are 757 international students enrolled. The school actively recruits these students. They must take the TOEFL with a minimum score of 500 on the paper-based TOEFL (PBT) or 61 on the Internet-based version (iBT). They must also take the SAT or ACT, scoring 24.

Computers: All students may access the system. There are no time limits. The fee is $9.40.

Graduates: From July 1, 2012 to June 30, 2013, 3775 bachelor's degrees were awarded. In an average class, 2% graduate in 3 years or less, 32% graduate in 4 years or less, 55% graduate in 5 years or less, and 61% graduate in 6 years or less.

Admissions Contact: Christine Crenshaw, Director Undergraduate Admissions. E-Mail: *admission@okstate.edu* Web: *www.okstate.edu*

OKLAHOMA WESLEYAN UNIVERSITY — E-1

Bartlesville, OK 74006 (918) 335-6219
(866) 222-8226; (918) 335-6229

Full-time: 280 men, 290 women	**Faculty:** n/av
Part-time: 160 men, 3290 women	**Ph.D.s:** n/av
Graduate: n/av	**Student/Faculty:** n/av
Year: semesters, summer session	**Tuition:** $20,160
Application Deadline: open	**Room & Board:** $6874
Freshman Class: n/av	
SAT or ACT: required	

COMPETITIVE

Oklahoma Wesleyan University, founded in 1909, is a private liberal arts institution affiliated with the Wesleyan Church. There are 5 undergraduate schools and 1 graduate school. The figures in the above capsule and in this profile are approximate. In addition to regional accreditation, OKWU has baccalaureate program accreditation with NCATE. The library contains 120,000 volumes, 20,000 microform items, 500 audio/video tapes/CDs/DVDs, and subscribes to 18,000 periodicals including electronic. Computerized library services include interlibrary loans and database searching. Special learning facilities include a learning resource center. The 101-acre campus is in a suburban area 40 miles north of Tulsa. Including any residence halls, there are 15 buildings.

Student Life: 73% of undergraduates are from Oklahoma. Others are from 33 states and 9 foreign countries. 80% are from public schools. 83%

are white. 74% are Protestant; 23% claim no religious affiliation. The average age of freshmen is 18; all undergraduates, 26. 20% do not continue beyond their first year; 60% remain to graduate.

Housing: 315 students can be accommodated in college housing, which includes single-sex dorms and honors houses. On-campus housing is guaranteed for all 4 years. 69% of students commute. Alcohol is not permitted. All students may keep cars.

Activities: There are no fraternities or sororities. There are more than 15 groups on campus, including band, cheerleading, choir, chorale, chorus, computers, drama, ethnic, honors, international, musical theater, photography, political, professional, religious, social service, and student government. Popular campus events include Spiritual Emphasis Week and Youth Conference.

Sports: There are 7 intercollegiate sports for men and 7 for women, and 10 intramural sports for men and 10 for women. Facilities include a 2000-seat indoor gym and an 8-acre athletic field.

Disabled Students: 73% of the campus is accessible. Facilities include wheelchair ramps, elevators, special parking, and specially equipped rest rooms.

Services: Counseling and information services are available, as is tutoring in most subjects. There is remedial math, reading, and writing.

Campus Safety and Security: There are lighted pathways/sidewalks and an evening patrol by a security guard.

Programs of Study: OKWU confers B.A. and B.S. degrees. Associate and master's degrees are also awarded. Bachelor's degrees are awarded in BIOLOGICAL SCIENCE (biology/biological science), BUSINESS (accounting, business administration and management, and human resources), COMMUNICATIONS AND THE ARTS (communications, English, and music), COMPUTER AND PHYSICAL SCIENCE (chemistry, mathematics, and science), EDUCATION (business education, elementary education, English education, mathematics education, middle school education, music education, physical education, science education, secondary education, and social studies education), HEALTH PROFESSIONS (predentistry and premedicine), SOCIAL SCIENCE (behavioral science, history, liberal arts/general studies, pastoral studies, political science/government, prelaw, religion, religious music, social studies, sociology, and youth ministry).

Required: To graduate, students must complete a total of 126 credit hours with a minimum GPA of 2.0. About 40 hours are required in the major. All students must take 9 hours of religion and a writing proficiency exam.

Special: OKWU offers cross-registration with Tri-County Tech, a Washington semester, a co-op program, internships, a general studies degree, credit for life experience, and an accelerated degree program in business and the B.S.N.

Faculty/Classroom: 65% of faculty are male; 35% are female. All teach undergraduates. The average class size in an introductory lecture is 20; in a laboratory, 20; and in a regular course, 20.

Requirements: The SAT or ACT is required. In addition, graduation from an accredited secondary school or satisfactory scores on the GED are required for admission. 18 academic credits must be completed, including 4 credits of English and 2 credits each of history, math, science, and social studies. A GPA of 2.0 is required. AP and CLEP credits are accepted.

Procedure: Freshmen are admitted to all sessions. Entrance exams should be taken during the senior year. There is a rolling admissions plan. Application deadlines are open. Check with the school for the current application fee. Applications are accepted online.

Transfer: Applicants must have a minimum GPA of 2.0. 24 of 126 credits required for the bachelor's degree must be completed at Oklahoma Wesleyan.

Visiting: There are regularly scheduled orientations for prospective students. There are guides for informal visits; visitors may sit in on classes and stay overnight. To schedule a visit, contact the Enrollment Services Office.

Financial Aid: The FAFSA and the college's own financial statement are required. Check with the school for current application deadlines.

International Students: They must take the TOEFL or MELAB.

Computers: Wireless access is available. All students may access the system. There are no time limits and no fees.

Admissions Contact: Director of Admissions. A campus DVD is available. E-Mail: *admissions@okwu.edu* Web: *www.okwu.edu*

ORAL ROBERTS UNIVERSITY — E-2

Tulsa, OK 74171 — (918) 495-6529
(800) 678-8876; (918) 495-6222

Full-time: 1102 men, 1443 women	**Faculty:** 135; IIA, --$
Part-time: 86 men, 151 women	**Ph.D.s:** 3%
Graduate: 249 men, 304 women	**Student/Faculty:** 15 to 1
Year: semesters, summer session	**Tuition:** $22,438
Application Deadline: open	**Room & Board:** $9296
Freshman Class: 1557 applied, 811 accepted, 480 enrolled	
SAT CR/M: 530/510 **ACT:** 22	**COMPETITIVE**

Oral Roberts University, founded in 1963, is a private (non-profit), Christian University located in Tulsa, Oklahoma. We offer more than 60 undergraduate degree programs, 13 master's degree programs and 2 doctoral degree programs. There are 6 undergraduate schools and 3 graduate schools. In addition to regional accreditation, ORU has baccalaureate program accreditation with ABET, ACBSP, CSWE, NASM, and NCATE. The library contains 487,000 volumes, 50,000 microform items, 18,000 audio/video tapes/CDs/DVDs, and subscribes to 65 periodicals including electronic. Computerized library services include interlibrary loans, database searching, Internet access, and Wi-Fi capability. Special learning facilities include a natural history museum, radio station, TV station, and a TV production studio. The 400-acre campus is in an urban area in Tulsa, Oklahoma. Including any residence halls, there are 29 buildings.

Student Life: 62% of undergraduates are from out of state, mostly the Mid-West. Students are from 48 states, 62 foreign countries, and Canada. 75% are from public schools. 42% are White; 11% African American. 98% are Protestant. The average age of freshmen is 19; all undergraduates, 22. 8% do not continue beyond their first year; 54% remain to graduate.

Housing: 2218 students can be accommodated in college housing, which includes single-sex dorms. honors wings of several dorms. On-campus housing is available on a first-come and first-served basis. 75% of students live on campus; of those, 99% remain on campus on weekends. Alcohol is not permitted. All students may keep cars.

Activities: There are no fraternities or sororities. There are 40 groups on campus, including and Leadership, art, band, cheerleading, choir, chorale, chorus, Community Outreach and Summer Mission, computers, dance, debate, drama, environmental, ethnic, film, honors, international, jazz band, musical theater, newspaper, opera, pep band, photography, political, professional, radio and TV, religious, social, social service, student government, symphony, and yearbook.

Sports: There are 8 intercollegiate sports for men and 8 for women, and 20 intramural sports for men and 20 for women. Facilities include Physical fitness center, track, tennis, racquetball, squash, volleyball, and basketball courts, and baseball and soccer fields.

Disabled Students: 90% of the campus is accessible. Facilities include wheelchair ramps, elevators, special parking, specially equipped restrooms, special class scheduling, lowered drinking fountains, and lowered telephones.

Services: Counseling and information services are available, as is tutoring in most subjects. There is a reader service for the blind, and remedial math, reading, and writing.

Campus Safety and Security: Measures include 24-hour foot and vehicle patrol, emergency notification system, self-defense education, and security escort services. There are shuttle buses, lighted pathways/sidewalks, and controlled access to dorms/residences.

Programs of Study: ORU confers B.A., B.S., B.M., B.Mus.Ed., B.S.E., B.S.N. and B.S.W. degrees. Master's and doctoral degrees are also awarded. Bachelor's degrees are awarded in BIOLOGICAL SCIENCE (biology/biological science), BUSINESS (accounting, banking and finance, business administration and management, international business management, management information systems, management science, marketing/retailing/merchandising, organizational behavior, and recreation and leisure services), COMMUNICATIONS AND THE ARTS (applied art, broadcasting, communications, dance, dramatic arts, English, English literature, film arts, French, German, literature, music, music performance, music theory and composition, Spanish, speech/debate/rhetoric, and studio art), COMPUTER AND PHYSICAL SCIENCE (chemistry, computer science, mathematics, and physics), EDUCATION (art education, business education, drama education, early childhood education, elementary education, English education, foreign languages education, health education, mathematics education, music education, physical education, recreation education, science education, social studies education, and special education), ENGINEERING AND ENVIRONMENTAL DESIGN (bioengineering, commercial art, computer engineering, electrical/electronics engineering, engineering, engineering management, mechanical engineering, and preengineering), HEALTH PROFESSIONS (biomedical science, health science, medical laboratory technology, nursing, optometry, predentistry, and premedicine), SOCIAL SCIENCE (biblical studies, history, international relations, international studies, liberal arts/general studies, ministries, philosophy, political science/government, prelaw, psychology, religion, religious education, religious music, and social work). All science programs, music and theology are the strongest academically. Nursing, media, business, psychology, Ministry and leadership have the largest enrollments.

Required: A minimum of 128 credit hours, with a minimum of 30 hours in the major, and a 2.0 GPA are required to graduate. All students must complete specific courses in the Bible, theology, and English, plus 12 hours in social sciences, 11 in biological, physical, and mathematical sciences, 6 to 7 in a modern foreign language, 3 in communication arts, and 2 in fine arts. 1 physical activity course is required per semester, along with regular, semiweekly chapel attendance. A senior paper must be completed in most majors.

Special: ORU offers combined B.A.-B.S. degrees, internships, 3-2 programs, a Washington semester, work-study programs, dual and student-designed majors, study abroad in 5 countries, independent study, nondegree study, an accelerated degree in business and education, and a liberal arts degree. An honors program/leadership academy is also offered. There are 4 national honor societies, a freshman honors program, and 12 departmental honors programs.

Faculty/Classroom: 56% of faculty are male; 44% are female. 84% do research. No introductory courses are taught by graduate students. The average class size in an introductory lecture is 30; in a laboratory is 20; and in a regular course is 20.

Admissions: 52% of the 2013-2014 applicants were accepted. The SAT scores for the 2013-2014 freshman class were: Critical Reading--32% below 500, 43% between 500 and 599, 19% between 600 and 699, and 7% between 700 and 800; Math--44% below 500, 33% between 500 and 599, 18% between 600 and 699, and 5% between 700 and 800. The ACT scores were 35% below 21, 28% between 21 and 23, 21% between 24 and 26, 9% between 27 and 28, and 8% above 28. 36% of the current freshmen were in the top fifth of their class; 64% were in the top two fifths. There were 7 National Merit finalists. 21 freshmen graduated first in their class.

Requirements: The SAT or ACT is required. In addition, students should be graduates of an accredited secondary school or hold a GED. High school preparation should include 4 years of English, 2 of math, including algebra and geometry or 2 years of algebra, and 2 each of foreign language, social studies, and science, including lab science. A recommendation from the student's minister is required. An academic recommendation and an interview are recommended. ORU requires applicants to be in the upper 40% of their class. A GPA of 2.6 is required. AP and CLEP credits are accepted. Important factors in the admissions decision are advanced placement or honors courses, evidence of special talent, and leadership record.

Procedure: Freshmen are admitted to all sessions. Entrance exams should be taken The last semester of the junior year or during senior year. There are deferred admissions and rolling admissions plans. Application deadlines are open. Application fee is $35. Applications are accepted online.

Transfer: 238 transfer students enrolled in 2012-2013. An official transcript showing honorable dismissal from each previous institution is required. 30 of 128 credits required for the bachelor's degree must be completed at ORU.

Visiting: There are regularly scheduled orientations for prospective students, College Weekend, which consists of visiting classes, meeting with faculty and staff, attending chapel services, and attending student life events. Visitors may sit in on classes and stay overnight. To schedule a visit, contact the Admissions Office at campusvisits@oru.edu.

Financial Aid: In 2013-2014, 75% of all full-time freshmen and 69% of continuing full-time students received some form of financial aid. 74% of all full-time freshmen and 66% of continuing full-time students received need-based aid. The average freshman award was $15,320. Need-based scholarships or need-based grants averaged $9,759; need-based self-help aid (loans and jobs) averaged $6,443; non-need-based athletic scholarships averaged $19,354; other non-need-based awards and non-need-based scholarships averaged $6,871; and $6,534 from other forms of aid. 100% of undergraduate students work part-time. Average annual earnings from campus work are $840. The average financial indebtedness of the 2013 graduate was $34,555. The FAFSA, and and the federal income tax return is required. The priority date for freshman financial aid applications for fall entry is March 15. The deadline for filing freshman financial aid applications for fall entry is July 30.

International Students: There are 167 international students enrolled. They must take the TOEFL with a minimum score of 500 on the paper-based TOEFL (PBT) or 61 on the Internet-based version (iBT). They must also take the SAT or ACT. either the TOEFL or the ACT/SAT.

Computers: All students may access the system at all times. There are no time limits. The fee is $10 per semester.

Graduates: From July 1, 2012 to June 30, 2013, 470 bachelor's degrees were awarded. The most popular majors were business marketing, theology and religious vocations, and communication/journalism.

Admissions Contact: Chris Belcher, Admissions. E-Mail: *admission@oru.edu* Web: *www.oru.edu*

SOUTHEASTERN OKLAHOMA STATE UNIVERSITY E-4

Durant, OK 74701 **(580) 745-2060**
(800) 435-1327; (580) 745-7502

Full-time: 1300 men, 1500 women
Part-time: 300 men, 500 women
Graduate: 175 men, 200 women
Year: semesters, summer session
Application Deadline: open
Freshman Class: n/av
SAT or ACT: required
Faculty: n/av; IIA, --$
Ph.D.s: 67%
Student/Faculty: n/av
Tuition: $5500 ($10,500)
Room & Board: $5600

COMPETITIVE

Southeastern Oklahoma State University, founded in 1909, is a public institution offering programs in the arts and sciences, business, education, music, and technology to a primarily commuter student body. There are 3 undergraduate schools and 1 graduate school. The figures in the above capsule and in this profile are approximate. In addition to regional accreditation, Southeastern has baccalaureate program accreditation with AACSB, ACBSP, NASM, and NCATE. The library contains 306,071 volumes, 591,277 microform items, 9254 audio/video tapes/CDs/DVDs, and subscribes to 841 periodicals including electronic. Computerized library services include interlibrary loans, database searching, and Internet access. Special learning facilities include a learning resource center, radio station, and herbarium. The 268-acre campus is in a rural area 90 miles north of Dallas. Including any residence halls, there are 46 buildings.

Student Life: 77% of undergraduates are from Oklahoma. Others are from 39 states, 25 foreign countries, and Canada. 99% are from public schools. The average age of freshmen is 21; all undergraduates, 25. 42% do not continue beyond their first year; 40% remain to graduate.

Housing: 648 students can be accommodated in college housing, which includes single-sex and coed dorms, on-campus apartments, and married student housing. In addition, there are special-interest houses. On-campus housing is guaranteed for all 4 years. 80% of students commute. Alcohol is not permitted. All students may keep cars.

Activities: 1% of men belong to 2 national fraternities; 5% of women belong to 2 national sororities. There are 70 groups on campus, including art, band, cheerleading, chess, choir, chorale, chorus, communications, computers, dance, debate, drama, drill team, environmental, ethnic, forensics, honors, international, jazz band, literary magazine, marching band, musical theater, newspaper, opera, pep band, photography, political, professional, radio and TV, religious, social, social service, student government, and yearbook. Popular campus events include Candlelighting and Springfest.

Sports: There are 6 intercollegiate sports for men and 6 for women, and 2 intramural sports for men and 1 for women. Facilities include a 4000-seat football stadium, a 2000-seat gym, baseball and softball fields, a track, tennis courts, playing fields, and a swimming pool.

Disabled Students: 90% of the campus is accessible. Facilities include wheelchair ramps, elevators, special parking, specially equipped rest rooms, special class scheduling, lowered drinking fountains, lowered telephones, and special housing.

Services: Counseling and information services are available, as is tutoring in every subject. There is a reader service for the blind, remedial math, reading, and writing, and tutoring in study skills.

Campus Safety and Security: Measures include 24-hour foot and vehicle patrol, emergency notification system, self-defense education, and security escort services. There are lighted pathways/sidewalks, in-room safes, and safety training.

Programs of Study: Southeastern confers B.A., B.S., B.A.A.S., B.B.A., B.G.S., B.M., and B.M.Ed. degrees. Master's degrees are also awarded. Bachelor's degrees are awarded in AGRICULTURE (conservation and regulation and environmental studies), BIOLOGICAL SCIENCE (biology/biological science and biotechnology), BUSINESS (accounting, business administration and management, recreation and leisure services, and secretarial studies/office management), COMMUNICATIONS AND THE ARTS (art, communications, dramatic arts, English, fine arts, music, and speech/debate/rhetoric), COMPUTER AND PHYSICAL SCIENCE (chemistry, computer science, information sciences and systems, mathematics, and physics), EDUCATION (art education, business education, early childhood education, education of the mentally handicapped, elementary education, mathematics education, music education, physical education, science education, secondary education, and social studies education), ENGINEERING AND ENVIRONMENTAL DESIGN (aviation administration/management and occupational safety and health), HEALTH PROFESSIONS (medical laboratory technology), SOCIAL SCIENCE (criminal justice, economics, gerontology, history, political science/government, psychology, social science, and sociology). Chemistry, history, and music are the strongest academically. Occupational safety and health, elementary education, and criminal justice have the largest enrollments.

Required: A total of 124 credit hours with a minimum GPA of 2.0 (2.5 for teacher education majors) is required for graduation. All students must complete 41 semester hours of general education requirements, including English, American history, government, humanities, arts, social and lab sciences, math, communications, and health education, and 3 hours of computer science.

Special: Internships, study abroad, credit for military experience, pass/fail options in some courses, and nondegree study are available. There are 15 national honor societies and 9 departmental honors programs.

Faculty/Classroom: No introductory courses are taught by graduate students. The average class size in an introductory lecture is 28; in a laboratory, 18; and in a regular course, 23.

Requirements: The SAT or ACT is required. Applicants should be graduates of an accredited secondary school or have earned a GED. High school courses must include 4 years of English, 3 of math, 2 each of lab science and history, 1 of citizenship skills (from the subjects of economics, geography, government, or non-Western culture), and 3 additional units of subjects previously listed or of computer science or foreign language. Southeastern requires applicants to be in the upper 50% of their class. A GPA of 2.7 is required. AP and CLEP credits are accepted.

Procedure: Freshmen are admitted to all sessions. Entrance exams should be taken by the fall of the senior year. There is a rolling admissions plan. Application deadlines are open. Application fee is $20. Notification is sent on a rolling basis. Applications are accepted online.

Transfer: Out-of-state applicants must have a 2.0 GPA. In-state applicants must have a 1.7 GPA with 24 to 36 credit hours earned, 1.8 with 37 to 72 hours, and 2.0 with 73 or more hours. 30 of 124 credits required for the bachelor's degree must be completed at Southeastern.

Visiting: There are guides for informal visits, and visitors may sit in on classes. To schedule a visit, contact Admissions and Recruitment Services.

Financial Aid: Southeastern is a member of CSS. The FAFSA and the college's own financial statement are required. Check with the school for current deadlines.

International Students: They must take the TOEFL with a minimum score of 500 on the paper-based TOEFL (PBT) or 61 on the Internet-based version (iBT). They must also take the SAT or ACT.

Computers: All students may access the system. There are no time limits.

Admissions Contact: Admissions and Records/Registrar. E-Mail: *admissions@se.edu* Web: *www.se.edu*

SOUTHERN NAZARENE UNIVERSITY — D-3

Bethany, OK 73008 — (405) 491-6324; (800) 648-9899; (405) 491-6320

Full-time: 760 men, 840 women	**Faculty:** 74
Part-time: 20 men, 30 women	**Ph.D.s:** 74%
Graduate: 180 men, 280 women	**Student/Faculty:** n/av
Year: semesters, summer session	**Tuition:** $20,294
Application Deadline: see profile	**Room & Board:** $8400
Freshman Class: n/av	
SAT or ACT: required	

NONCOMPETITIVE

Southern Nazarene University, founded in 1899, is a private institution affiliated with the Church of the Nazarene. It offers programs in liberal arts and sciences, health fields, business, and education. There are 3 undergraduate schools and 1 graduate school. The figures in the above capsule and in this profile are approximate. In addition to regional accreditation, SNU has baccalaureate program accreditation with NASM, NCATE, and NLN. The library contains 101,901 volumes, 332,461 microform items, 4360 audio/video tapes/CDs/DVDs. Computerized library services include interlibrary loans, database searching, Internet access, and laptop Internet portals. Special learning facilities include a learning resource center. The 40-acre campus is in a suburban area 10 miles northwest of Oklahoma City. Including any residence halls, there are 20 buildings.

Student Life: 70% of undergraduates are from Oklahoma. Others are from 36 states, 34 foreign countries, and Canada. 73% are white; 11% African American. 45% are Protestant; 32% are members of the school's denomination; 19% claim no religious affiliation. The average age of freshmen is 18; all undergraduates, 22. 12% do not continue beyond their first year; 49% remain to graduate.

Housing: 800 students can be accommodated in college housing, which includes single-sex dorms and on-campus apartments. On-campus housing is guaranteed for all 4 years. 68% of students live on campus; of those, 80% remain on campus on weekends. Alcohol is not permitted. All students may keep cars.

Activities: There are no fraternities or sororities. There are 40 groups on campus, including band, cheerleading, choir, chorale, chorus, computers, drama, drum and bugle corps, honors, international, jazz band, literary magazine, musical theater, newspaper, opera, orchestra, pep band, photography, political, professional, religious, social, social service, student government, symphony, and yearbook. Popular campus events include Valentine Banquet, Fall Fest, and Yule Feast.

Sports: There are 7 intercollegiate sports for men and 7 for women, and 3 intramural sports for men and 3 for women. Facilities include an 1824-seat phys ed center, gyms, a soccer complex, tennis courts, and a new athletic convocation center that seats 4000.

Disabled Students: All of the campus is accessible. Facilities include wheelchair ramps, elevators, special parking, specially equipped rest rooms, special class scheduling, lowered drinking fountains, and lowered telephones. Dorm rooms may be adapted for disabled students.

Services: Counseling and information services are available, as is tutoring in most subjects. There is remedial math, reading, and writing. Services may be arranged for deaf or learning-disabled students.

Campus Safety and Security: Measures include 24-hour foot and vehicle patrol, emergency notification system, self-defense education, and security escort services. There are lighted pathways/sidewalks and 24-hour controlled access into dorms.

Programs of Study: SNU confers B.S., A.B., and B.Mus.Ed. degrees. Associate and master's degrees are also awarded. Bachelor's degrees are awarded in AGRICULTURE (environmental studies), BIOLOGICAL SCIENCE (biochemistry, biology/biological science, and biophysics), BUSINESS (accounting, banking and finance, business administration and management, management information systems, management science, marketing/retailing/merchandising, sports management, and sports marketing), COMMUNICATIONS AND THE ARTS (communications, English, graphic design, journalism, music, music business management, music performance, Spanish, speech/debate/rhetoric, and sports media), COMPUTER AND PHYSICAL SCIENCE (chemistry, computer science, mathematics, physics, and science), EDUCATION (athletic training, Christian education, early childhood education, education, elementary education, English education, mathematics education, music education, physical education, science education, social studies education, and sports studies), ENGINEERING AND ENVIRONMENTAL DESIGN (aviation administration/management and systems engineering), HEALTH PROFESSIONS (exercise science and nursing), SOCIAL SCIENCE (American studies, history, human development, international studies, Latin American studies, missions, philosophy, physical fitness/movement, political science/government, psychology, religious music, sociology, Spanish studies, theological studies, urban studies, and youth ministry). Premedicine, physics, and theology are the strongest academically. Business and education have the largest enrollments.

Required: A total of 124 semester hours, including at least 32 hours in the major, with a minimum GPA of 2.0, is required to graduate. All students must complete 53 hours of general education requirements covering core areas of self and identity, faith and tradition, and service and society. Skills courses must be taken in computer science, composition, speech communication, math, natural science, citizenship, foreign language, and phys ed.

Special: Cross-registration and co-op programs are available through the Southwestern Colleges of Christian Ministry. Internships may be arranged in the major. A Washington semester, accelerated degree programs, study abroad in England, Russia, Costa Rica, Australia, China, and Egypt through the Council of Christian Colleges and Universities, work-study programs in sociology, and dual and student-designed majors are available. SNU offers nondegree study for life/military/work experience. There are 6 national honor societies, including Phi Beta Kappa, and a freshman honors program.

Faculty/Classroom: 50% of faculty are male; 50% are female. All teach undergraduates. No introductory courses are taught by graduate students. The average class size in an introductory lecture is 20; in a laboratory, 15.

Admissions: All of a recent year's applicants were accepted. 32% of a recent year's freshmen were in the top fifth of their class; 53% were in the top two fifths. There were 3 National Merit finalists.

Requirements: The SAT or ACT is required. Applicants must be graduates of an accredited secondary school or have a GED. AP and CLEP credits are accepted. Important factors in the admissions decision are advanced placement or honors courses, extracurricular activities record, and leadership record.

Procedure: Freshmen are admitted fall and spring. Entrance exams should be taken by April of the senior year or at orientation prior to the beginning of classes. There are early admissions, deferred admissions, and rolling admissions plans. Check with the school for current application deadlines. Application fee of $35 is waived for students who apply online before October 15.

Transfer: 92 transfer students enrolled in a recent year. Transfer applicants must have a 2.0 GPA and be in good standing at their previous college. 30 of 124 credits required for the bachelor's degree must be completed at SNU.

Visiting: There are regularly scheduled orientations for prospective students, including visits with faculty and students and seminars on financial aid and admissions. There are campus tours, group social activities, and small group mentoring throughout the fall semester. There are guides for informal visits, and visitors may sit in on classes and stay overnight. To schedule a visit, contact the Office of Admissions.

Financial Aid: In a recent year, 90% of all full-time students received some form of financial aid. The FAFSA is required. Check with the school for current application deadlines.

International Students: There were 52 international students enrolled in a recent year. They must take the TOEFL with a minimum score of 500 on the paper-based TOEFL (PBT) or 61 on the Internet-based version (iBT).

Computers: Wireless access is available. All students may access the system. There are no time limits and no fees. All students are required to have a personal computer.

Graduates: In a recent year, 540 bachelor's degrees were awarded. The most popular majors were organizational leadership (36%), business administration (11%), and nursing (10%). In an average class, 2% graduate in 3 years or less, 31% graduate in 4 years or less, 42% graduate in 5 years or less, and 49% graduate in 6 years or less.

Admissions Contact: Director of Admissions. A campus DVD is available. E-mail: *admissions@snu.edu* Web: *www.snu.edu*

SOUTHWESTERN OKLAHOMA STATE UNIVERSITY D-3

Weatherford, OK 73096 (580) 774-3009; (580) 774-3795

Full-time: 1655 men, 2044 women
Part-time: 256 men, 562 women
Graduate: 362 men, 461 women
Year: semesters, summer session
Application Deadline: open
Freshman Class: 1717 applied, 1585 accepted, 986 enrolled
ACT: 21
Faculty: 184; IIA, --$
Ph.D.s: 62%
Student/Faculty: 20 to 1
Tuition: $5300 ($11,360)
Room & Board: $4860

COMPETITIVE

Southwestern Oklahoma State University, founded in 1901, is a public institution offering programs in education, arts and sciences, business, health sciences, and pharmacy. There are 4 undergraduate schools and 3 graduate schools. In addition to regional accreditation, SWOSU has baccalaureate program accreditation with ABET, ABHES, ACBSP, ACPE, APTA, CAHEA, CSWE, NASM, NCATE, and NLN. The library contains 287,572 volumes, 1.2 million microform items, and 872 audio/video tapes/CDs/DVDs, and subscribes to 1,551 periodicals including electronic. Computerized library services include interlibrary loans and database searching. The figures in the above capsule and in this profile are approximate. The 73-acre campus is in a small town 70 miles west of Oklahoma City. Including any residence halls, there are 30 buildings.

Student Life: 11% of undergraduates are from out of state, mostly the Southwest. Students are from 37 states, 36 foreign countries, and Canada. 98% are from public schools. 79% are white. The average age of freshmen is 19; all undergraduates, 23. 36% do not continue beyond their first year; 32% remain to graduate.

Housing: 1255 students can be accommodated in college housing, which includes single-sex dorms and married student housing. On-campus housing is guaranteed for all 4 years. 75% of students commute. Alcohol is not permitted. All students may keep cars.

Activities: 7% of men belong to 2 local and 1 national fraternities; 5% of women belong to 3 local sororities. There are 66 groups on campus, including art, band, cheerleading, choir, chorale, chorus, computers, debate, drama, drill team, ethnic, forensics, honors, international, jazz band, marching band, musical theater, newspaper, opera, orchestra, pep band, political, professional, religious, social, social service, student government, and symphony. Popular campus events include Howdy Week, Miss Southwestern Pageant, and Panorama Series.

Sports: There are 6 intercollegiate sports for men and 6 for women, and 8 intramural sports for men and 8 for women. Facilities include a weight room, an indoor pool, an outdoor track, tennis courts, an outdoor football field and baseball diamond, 2 football practice fields, a rodeo arena, an exercise equipment room, a ropes course, and a lake. A soccer practice field, sand volleyball courts, and outdoor basketball courts are also available.

Disabled Students: 98% of the campus is accessible. Facilities include wheelchair ramps, elevators, special parking, specially equipped restrooms, special class scheduling, lowered drinking fountains, and lowered telephones.

Services: Counseling and information services are available, as is tutoring in some subjects, math, science, business, English, and social sciences There is remedial math, reading, and writing. A student development center offers counseling and tutoring on an individual basis.

Campus Safety and Security: Measures include 24-hour foot and vehicle patrol and self-defense education. There are emergency telephones and lighted pathways/sidewalks.

Programs of Study: SWOSU confers B.A., B.S., B.A.Ed., B.Art, B.B.A., B.Comm.Art, B.Gen.Tech., B.M., B.M.Ed., B.Rec., B.S.Ed., B.S.Eng.Tech., B.S.H.I.M., B.S.M.T., B.S.N., and B.S.P. degrees. Associate, master's, and doctoral degrees are also awarded. Bachelor's degrees are awarded in BIOLOGICAL SCIENCE (biology/biological science and biophysics), BUSINESS (accounting, banking and finance, business administration and management, management information systems, management science, marketing/retailing/merchandising, and recreational facilities management), COMMUNICATIONS AND THE ARTS (communications, English, and graphic design), COMPUTER AND PHYSICAL SCIENCE (chemistry, computer programming, computer science, information sciences and systems, mathematics, natural sciences, and physics), EDUCATION (art education, athletic training, education administration, elementary education, English education, health education, industrial arts education, mathematics education, music education, physical education, school psychology, science education, secondary education, social science education, special education, and technical education), ENGINEERING AND ENVIRONMENTAL DESIGN (computer engineering, electrical/electronics engineering technology, engineering physics, engineering technology, environmental engineering technology, industrial administration/management, industrial engineering technology, manufacturing engineering, and manufacturing technology), HEALTH PROFESSIONS (health care administration, health science, medical records administration/services, medical technology, music therapy, and nursing), SOCIAL SCIENCE (community psychology, criminal justice, history, political science/government, psychology, and social work). Chemistry is the strongest academically. Business and education have the largest enrollments.

Required: To graduate, students must complete 124 semester hours with a minimum GPA of 2.0. Distribution requirements include 8 hours in communication and natural sciences, 6 each in history and government, fine arts and humanities, and international and cultural studies, 3 each in economics, health and phys ed, behavioral/social science, and math, and 2 in computer applications.

Special: SWOSU offers work-study programs and a program allowing high school seniors to earn college credits. Preprofessional curricula are offered in numerous areas including medicine, law, engineering, and allied health professions. There are 4 national honor societies.

Faculty/Classroom: 58% of faculty are male; 42% are female. All teach undergraduates, 10% do research, and 10% do both. Graduate students teach 1% of introductory courses. The average class size in a laboratory is 15 and in a regular course is 27.

Admissions: 92% of a recent year applicants were accepted.

Requirements: The ACT is required. Applicants must have a minimum composite score of 19. Applicants should be graduates of an accredited secondary school. The GED is accepted. Students should present at least 15 academic credits, including 4 in English, 3 in math, 2 each in history and lab science, 1 in citizenship, and 3 additional units in computer science or foreign language. A GPA of 2.7 is required. AP and CLEP credits are accepted.

Procedure: Freshmen are admitted to all sessions. Entrance exams should be taken during the senior year. There is a rolling admissions plan. Check with the school for current application deadlines. The fall application fee was $15. Notification is sent on a rolling basis.

Transfer: Applicants must have a minimum college GPA of 2.0 and submit official transcripts from all institutions attended. 30 of 124 credits required for the bachelor's degree must be completed at SWOSU.

Visiting: There are regularly scheduled orientations for prospective students, including counseling sessions on careers, financial aid, social activities, and enrollment procedures. There are guides for informal visits, visitors may sit in on classes, and stay overnight. To schedule a visit, contact the Director.

Financial Aid: The FAFSA and the college's own financial statement are required. Check with the school for current application deadlines.

International Students: They must take the TOEFL. They must also take the SAT or ACT, scoring 19.

Computers: All students may access the system from 8 a.m. to midnight Monday through Thursday, 8 a.m. to 5 p.m. There are no time limits and no fees.

Graduates: In a recent year, 629 bachelor's degrees were awarded. The most popular majors were business/marketing (22%), health professions and related sciences (20%), and education (17%).

Admissions Contact: Admissions Coordinator. A campus DVD is available. Web: *www.swosu.edu*

ST. GREGORY'S UNIVERSITY E-3

Shawnee, OK 74804 (405) 878-5444
(888) 784-7347; (405) 878-5198

Full-time: 280 men, 335 women
Part-time: 65 men, 90 women
Graduate: n/av
Year: semesters, summer session
Application Deadline: open
Freshman Class: n/av
ACT: required
Faculty: 30
Ph.D.s: 57%
Student/Faculty: 20 to 1
Tuition: $12,923
Room & Board: $5320

NONCOMPETITIVE

Founded in 1875, St. Gregory's is a Roman Catholic University, offering through the master's degree level a liberal arts education that has been cherished and handed down in the educational institutions of the Benedictine Order. We promote the education of the whole person in the context of a Christian community in which students are encouraged to develop a love of learning and to live lives of balance, generosity and integrity. As Oklahoma's only Catholic university, St. Gregory's reaches out to members of other faiths who value the distinctive benefits which it offers. There are 5 undergraduate schools and 1 graduate school. The library contains 80,000 volumes, 3,526 microform items, and 450 audio/video tapes/CDs/DVDs, and subscribes to 150 periodicals including electronic. Computerized library services include interlibrary loans, database searching, Internet access, and Wi-Fi capability. Special learning facilities include an art gallery. The 300-acre campus is in a suburban area about 30 miles east of Oklahoma City. Including any residence halls, there are 12 buildings.

Student Life: 70% of undergraduates are from Oklahoma. Others are from 13 states, 15 foreign countries, and Canada. 80% are from public schools. 65% are White; 15% Foreign. 40% are Catholic; 24% claim no religious affiliation. The average age of freshmen is 18. 35% do not continue beyond their first year.

Housing: 415 students can be accommodated in college housing, which includes single-sex and coed dorms. In addition, there are honors houses and language houses. On-campus housing is guaranteed for the freshman year only, is available on a first-come, and first-served basis. Priority is given to out-of-town students. 70% of students live on campus; of those, 60% remain on campus on weekends. Alcohol is not permitted. All students may keep cars.

Activities: 10% of men belong to 3 local fraternities; 10% of women belong to 3 local sororities. There are 24 groups on campus, including art, cheerleading, choir, chorale, communications, computers, dance, drama, environmental, ethnic, history, honors, international, musical theater, newspaper, photography, professional, radio and TV, religious, social, social service, student government, and yearbook. Popular campus events include Sporting Events, Movie Nights and Dances.

Sports: There are 5 intercollegiate sports for men and 7 for women, and 4 intramural sports for men and 4 for women. Facilities include soccer, baseball, and softball facilities, a wellness center with 2 gyms, Cybex equipment, and a free-weight facility.

Disabled Students: 90% of the campus is accessible. Facilities include wheelchair ramps, elevators, special parking, specially equipped restrooms, special class scheduling, and lowered drinking fountains.

Services: Counseling and information services are available, as is tutoring in every subject, Partners in Learning is a program designed to aid those students with learning disabilities. There is a reader service for the blind, and remedial math, reading, and writing.

Campus Safety and Security: Measures include 24-hour foot and vehicle patrol, self-defense education, and security escort services. There are lighted pathways/sidewalks and controlled access to dorms/residences.

Programs of Study: St. Gregory's confers B.A.(Humanities), B.A.(Theology), B.S.(Business), B.S.(Natural Science), and B.S.(Social Science). Associate and master's degrees are also awarded. Bachelor's degrees are awarded in Life sciences, premedicine, and conservation biology are the strongest academically. Natural sciences, business, and social sciences are the largest.

Required: To graduate, students must complete 128 credits, including approximately 40 in the major, with a minimum 2.0 GPA. The core curriculum focuses on professional communication, creative thinking, self leadership, and informational technology, including specific courses in English, speech, math, life science, physical science, philosophy, and theology. Students must pass a comprehensive exam at the end of sophomore year and complete a senior research project.

Special: There are 4 national honor societies, a freshman honors program, and 100 departmental honors programs.

Faculty/Classroom: 45% of faculty are male; 55% are female. All teach undergraduates. No introductory courses are taught by graduate students. The average class size in an introductory lecture is 16; in a laboratory is 14; and in a regular course is 9.

Requirements: The ACT is required, with a minumum score requires applicants to be in the upper 50% of their class. A GPA of 2.8 is required. AP and CLEP credits are accepted. Important factors in the admissions decision are leadership record, parents or siblings attended your school, and recommendations by alumni.

Procedure: Freshmen are admitted to all sessions. Entrance exams should be taken in October. There are deferred admissions and rolling admissions plans. Application deadlines are open. Application fee is $25. Applications are accepted online.

Transfer: Applicants must have either an associate degree or a cumulative 2.0 GPA in all completed college courses. 30 of 128 credits required for the bachelor's degree must be completed at St. Gregory's.

Visiting: There are regularly scheduled orientations for prospective students, consisting of a private tour by an admissions counselor. There are guides for informal visits, visitors may sit in on classes, and stay overnight. To schedule a visit, contact the Office of Admissions.

Financial Aid: In 2013-2014, 62% of all full-time freshmen and 57% of continuing full-time students received some form of financial aid. 60% of all full-time freshmen and 56% of continuing full-time students received need-based aid. The average freshman award was $7,438. 38% of undergraduate students work part-time. Average annual earnings from campus work are $1000. The average financial indebtedness of the 2013 graduate was $17,959. The FAFSA is required. The deadline for filing freshman financial aid applications for fall entry is July 15.

International Students: The school actively recruits these students.

Computers: All students may access the system. There are no time limits and no fees.

Admissions Contact: Judy Chance, Office Manager. E-Mail: *jmchance@stgregorys.edu* Web: *www.stgregorys.edu*

UNIVERSITY OF CENTRAL OKLAHOMA D-2

Edmond, OK 73034 **(405) 974-2335**
(800) 254-4215; 405-974-3930

Full-time: 4782 men, 6199 women	**Faculty:** 466; IIA, --$
Part-time: 1862 men, 2524 women	**Ph.D.s:** 75%
Graduate: 526 men, 1324 women	**Student/Faculty:** 21 to 1
Year: semesters, summer session	**Tuition:** $5437 ($13,552)
Application Deadline:	**Room & Board:** $6856

Freshman Class: 4939 applied, 3945 accepted, 2223 enrolled
ACT: 21

COMPETITIVE

The University of Central Oklahoma, founded in 1890, is a state-supported institution offering undergraduate and graduate programs in the liberal arts and sciences, education, business, and music. There are 5 undergraduate schools and one graduate school. In addition to regional accreditation, UCO has baccalaureate program accreditation with ABET, ABFSE, ACBSP, ADA, NASM, NCATE, and NLN. The library contains 526,153 volumes, 578,619 microform items, 39,845 audio/video tapes/CDs/DVDs, and subscribes to 29,549 periodicals including electronic. Computerized library services include interlibrary loans, database searching, Internet access, and Wi-Fi capability. Special learning facilities include an art gallery, radio station, and TV station. The 200-acre campus is in a suburban area North of Oklahoma City. Including any residence halls, there are 51 buildings.

Student Life: 88% of undergraduates are from Oklahoma. Others are from 46 states, 86 foreign countries, and Canada. 83% are from public schools. 59% are White. The average age of freshmen is 20; all undergraduates, 24. 35% do not continue beyond their first year; 36% remain to graduate.

Housing: 1698 students can be accommodated in college housing, which includes single-sex and coed dorms, on-campus apartments, and married student housing. In addition, there are fraternity houses and sorority houses. On-campus housing is available on a first-come, first-served basis, and is available on a lottery system for upperclassmen. 91% of students commute. Alcohol is not permitted. All students may keep cars.

Activities: 6% of men belong to 11 national fraternities; 6% of women belong to 8 national sororities. There are 200 groups on campus, including art, band, cheerleading, choir, chorus, communications, computers, dance, debate, drama, drum and bugle corps, ethnic, film, gay, honors, international, jazz band, literary magazine, marching band, musical theater, newspaper, opera, orchestra, pep band, photography, political, professional, radio and TV, religious, social, student government, and yearbook. Popular campus events include Homecoming, Earth Day, May Day, The Big Event, Winterglow, International Festival, Big Pink Volleyball, and Miss UCO.

Sports: There are 5 intercollegiate sports for men and 9 for women, and 22 intramural sports for men and 22 for women. Facilities include a field house with a gym, a swimming pool, a track, a weight room, a stadium with a track and a softball field, and a wellness center with basketball courts, aerobic classes, cardiovascular equipment, weights, and various classes.

Disabled Students: Facilities include wheelchair ramps, elevators, special parking, specially equipped restrooms, special class scheduling, and lowered drinking fountains.

Services: Counseling and information services are available, as is tutoring in some subjects, English, math, reading, and writing There is a reader service for the blind, and remedial math.

Campus Safety and Security: Measures include 24-hour foot and vehicle patrol, emergency notification system, and security escort services. There are emergency telephones, lighted pathways/sidewalks, and a crime and terrorism tip line.

Programs of Study: UCO confers B.A., B.S., B.A.Ed., B.B.A., B.F.A., B.F.A.Ed., B.M.Ed., B.Mus., B.A.T., and B.S.Ed. degrees. Master's degrees are also awarded. Bachelor's degrees are awarded in BIOLOGICAL SCIENCE (biology/biological science, forensic psychology, forensic science, and nutrition), BUSINESS (accounting, banking and finance, business administration and management, fashion merchandising, finance, funeral home services, human resources, insurance, management information systems, and marketing/retailing/merchandising), COMMUNICATIONS AND THE ARTS (advertising, art history, art, broadcasting, communications, creative writing, dance, English, English as a second/foreign language, French, German, graphic design, journalism, music, photography, piano performance, public relations, Spanish, theatre acting, theatre arts, theater design, and theatre studies), COMPUTER AND PHYSICAL SCIENCE (actuarial science, applied mathematics, chemistry, computer science, and mathematics), EDUCATION (art education, athletic training, bilingual/bicultural education, dance education, early childhood education, elementary education, English education, foreign languages education, general studies, mathematics education, museum studies, music education, physical education, science education, secondary education, social studies education, and special education), ENGINEERING AND ENVIRONMENTAL DESIGN (biomedical engineering, electrical/electronics engineering, engineering, engineering physics, and interior design), HEALTH PROFESSIONS (allied health, art therapy, community health work, exercise science, industrial hygiene, nursing, predentistry, premedicine, preoptometry, and speech pathology/audiology), SOCIAL SCIENCE (addiction studies, child psychology/development, criminal justice, economics, family/consumer studies, forensic studies, geography, gerontology, history, humanities, legal studies, liberal arts/general studies, philosophy, physical fitness/movement, political science/government, psychology, public administration, and sociology). Nursing, speech/language pathology, educational leadership, and forensic science are the strongest academically. Nursing, accounting, and psychology have the largest enrollments.

Required: Students must complete 124 semester hours with a 2.00 GPA. Students must take 40 hours of upper division courses with at least 15 hours from the major. 10 hours of major course work must be earned from UCO. Students must also complete a maximum of 12 semester hours in general education requirements, including physical education. 60 hours must be earned from a bachelor's granting university.

Special: There is cross-registration with the Downtown Consortium. Opportunities are provided for internships, B.A.-B.S. degrees, dual majors, a general studies degree, credit by exam, nondegree study, and credit for military experience. Work-study programs may be arranged through the Federal College Work Study Program. There are 6 national honor societies.

Faculty/Classroom: 46% of faculty are male; 54% are female. Graduate students teach 2% of introductory courses. The average class size in an introductory lecture is 31 and in a laboratory is 26.

Admissions: 80% of the 2013-2014 applicants were accepted. The ACT scores were 35% below 21, 33% between 21 and 23, 19% between 24 and 26, 7% between 27 and 28, and 6% above 28. 29% of the current freshmen were in the top fifth of their class; 59% were in the top two fifths.

Requirements: The ACT is required. Minimum composite ACT of 20 or a 2.7 non-weighted, cumulative GPA and class ranking in the upper 50% of graduating class. Graduation from an accredited secondary school is required and a GED is accepted. The applicant's academic record should include 4 units of English; 3 units of math (first-year algebra and beyond); 3 units of lab science; and 3 units of history, of which 1 year must be in American history. Applicants must have a 2.7 GPA in the core curriculum courses. UCO requires applicants to be in the upper 50% of their class. A GPA of 2.7 is required. AP and CLEP credits are accepted. Important factors in the admissions decision are evidence of special talent, extracurricular activities record, and leadership record.

Procedure: Freshmen are admitted to all sessions. Entrance exams should be taken within 30 days of submitting the application. There are deferred admissions and rolling admissions plans. Application deadlines are open. Application fee is $40. Applications are accepted online.

Transfer: 1790 transfer students enrolled in 2012-2013. Applicants must submit official transcripts from all previously attended colleges and have a minimum GPA of 1.7 if the student has 30 or less credit hours or a 2.0 GPA for students with 31 or more credit hours. Students who have completed fewer than 24 hours of transferable credit must meet the requirements for entering freshmen. Out of state students must have a minimum 2.0 GPA. 30 of 124 credits required for the bachelor's degree must be completed at UCO.

Visiting: There are regularly scheduled orientations for prospective students, including a brief tour, a question-and-answer period, and access to an information booth. There are guides for informal visits. To schedule a visit, contact Gina Hickey at ghickey@uco.edu.

Financial Aid: In 2013-2014, 82% of all full-time freshmen and 71% of continuing full-time students received some form of financial aid. 55% of all full-time freshmen and 53% of continuing full-time students received need-based aid. The average freshman award was $6,970. Need-based scholarships or need-based grants averaged $2,832; need-based self-help aid (loans and jobs) averaged $2,289; and non-need-based athletic scholarships averaged $197. 13% of undergraduate students work part-time. Average annual earnings from campus work are $3046. The average financial indebtedness of the 2013 graduate was $22,665. The CSS/Profile, FFS, and the college's own financial statement are required. The priority date for freshman financial aid applications for fall entry is May 31. The deadline for filing freshman financial aid applications for fall entry is May 31.

International Students: There are 1421 international students enrolled. The school actively recruits these students. They must take the TOEFL with a minimum score of 500 on the paper-based TOEFL (PBT) or 61 on the Internet-based version (iBT). They must also take the ACT.

Computers: All students may access the system. There are no time limits and no fees.

Graduates: From July 1, 2012 to June 30, 2013, 2329 bachelor's degrees were awarded. The most popular majors were general studies (13%), nursing (5%), and business administration and general studies (5%). 68 companies recruited on campus in 2012-2013. In an average class, 1% graduate in 3 years or less, 11% graduate in 4 years or less, 30% graduate in 5 years or less, and 36% graduate in 6 years or less.

Admissions Contact: Stephanie Kahne, Director of Undergraduate Admissions. E-Mail: *onestop@uco.edu* Web: *http:/www.uco.edu/em/become-a-broncho/apply/Academic-Requirements.asp*

UNIVERSITY OF OKLAHOMA D-3

Norman, OK 73019 **(405) 325-2252**
(800) 234-6868; (405) 325-7124

Full-time: 9034 men, 9070 women
Faculty: 1115; I, --$
Part-time: 1597 men, 1408 women
Ph.D.s: 87%
Graduate: 3260 men, 3138 women
Student/Faculty: 19 to 1
Year: semesters, summer session
Tuition: $7341 ($18,978)
Application Deadline: April 1
Room & Board: $8382
Freshman Class: 11650 applied, 9220 accepted, 4138 enrolled
SAT CR/M: 570/600 **ACT:** 25 **VERY COMPETITIVE+**

The University of Oklahoma, founded in 1890, is a comprehensive research university offering 152 different majors for undergraduate study. There are 14 undergraduate schools and 13 graduate schools. In addition to regional accreditation, OU has baccalaureate program accreditation with AACSB, ABET, ACCE, ACEJMC, CSWE, NAAB, NASM, and NCATE. The 9 libraries contain 5.2 million volumes, 3.6 million microform items, 12,512 audio/video tapes/CDs/DVDs, and subscribe to 147,309 periodicals including electronic. Computerized library services include interlibrary loans, database searching, Internet access, and Wi-Fi capability. Special learning facilities include an art gallery, natural history museum, radio station, TV station, observatory. The 3296-acre campus is in a suburban area 20 miles south of Oklahoma City. Including any residence halls, there are 255 buildings.

Student Life: 68% of undergraduates are from Oklahoma. Others are from 50 states, 115 foreign countries, and Canada. 62% are White. The average age of freshmen is 18; all undergraduates, 22. 16% do not continue beyond their first year; 66% remain to graduate.

Housing: 5836 students can be accommodated in college housing, which includes single-sex and coed dorms, on-campus apartments, and married student housing. In addition, there are honors houses, international floors, honors house, cultural housing, national merit, scholastic and quiet lifestyle floors. On-campus housing is guaranteed for the freshman year only, is available on a first-come, and first-served basis. 67% of students commute. Alcohol is not permitted. All students may keep cars.

Activities: 23% of men belong to 1 local and 29 national fraternities; 30% of women belong to 1 local and 19 national sororities. There are 422 groups on campus, including art, band, cheerleading, chess, choir, chorale, chorus, computers, dance, debate, drama, drill team, environmental, ethnic, film, forensics, gay, honors, international, jazz band, literary magazine, marching band, musical theater, newspaper, opera, orchestra, pep band, photography, political, professional, radio and TV, religious, social, social service, student government, symphony, and yearbook. Popular campus events include CAC Homecoming, Eve of Nations, and CAC Soonerthon.

Sports: There are 10 intercollegiate sports for men and 11 for women, and 26 intramural sports for men and 26 for women. Facilities include a golf course, a field house, an arena, a gymnastics center, tennis courts, a swimming pool complex, a fitness center, a football stadium, track and field facilities, and baseball, soccer, and softball fields. Fitness and Recreation has 25 acres of turf grass maintained for intramural and recreational use.

Disabled Students: 95% of the campus is accessible. Facilities include wheelchair ramps, elevators, special parking, specially equipped restrooms, special class scheduling, lowered drinking fountains, lowered telephones, special housing.

Services: Counseling and information services are available, as is tutoring in some subjects. There is a reader service for the blind, and remedial math, reading, and writing. there are also volunteer note takers, interpreter and real-time reporting services for the deaf or hearing impaired, and alternative testing services.

Campus Safety and Security: Measures include 24-hour foot and vehicle patrol, emergency notification system, self-defense education, and security escort services. There are shuttle buses, emergency telephones, lighted pathways/sidewalks, controlled access to dorms/residences, a bicycle patrol, safe ride program.

Programs of Study: OU confers B.A., B.S., B.Arch., B.B.A., B.F.A., B.Int.Des., B.Mus.Arts, B.Mus.Ed. and B.Mus. degrees. Master's and doctoral degrees are also awarded. Bachelor's degrees are awarded in BIOLOGICAL SCIENCE (biochemistry, botany, microbiology, and zoology), BUSINESS (accounting, banking and finance, business administration and management, business economics, human resources, international business management, management information systems, and marketing/retailing/merchandising), COMMUNICATIONS AND THE ARTS (advertising, Arabic, art, art history and appreciation, broadcasting, Chinese, classics, communications, comparative literature, dance, dramatic arts, English, film arts, French, German, Italian, journalism, language arts, languages, linguistics, music, musical theater, public relations, Russian, Spanish, and video), COMPUTER AND PHYSICAL SCIENCE (astronomy, astrophysics, atmospheric sciences and meteorology, chemistry, computer science, environmental geology, geology, geophysics and seismology, geoscience, information sciences and systems, mathematics, paleontology, and physics), EDUCATION (early childhood education, elementary education, foreign languages education, mathematics education, music education, science education, social studies education, and special education), ENGINEERING AND ENVIRONMENTAL DESIGN (aeronautical engineering, architectural engineering, architecture, aviation administration/management, chemical engineering, civil engineering, computer engineering, construction management, electrical/electronics engineering, engineering, engineering physics, environmental design, environmental engineering, environmental science, industrial engineering, interior design, land use management and reclamation, mechanical engineering, and petroleum/natural gas engineering), HEALTH PROFESSIONS (health science and medical laboratory technology), SOCIAL SCIENCE (African American studies, anthropology, area studies, Asian/Oriental studies, criminal justice, Eastern European studies, economics, European studies, geography, history, human development, interdisciplinary studies, international studies, Judaic studies, Latin American studies, liberal arts/general studies, Native American studies, philosophy, political science/government, psychology, public affairs, religion, Russian and Slavic studies, social work, sociology, and women's studies). Chemistry, finance & accounting, meteorology, petroleum and geological engineering are the strongest academically. Petroleum engineering, psychology, health and exercise science have the largest enrollments.

Required: To graduate, students must have a minimum 2.0 GPA, depending on the major, and complete a minimum of 120 semester hours, the last 30 hours of which must be in residence. The number of hours required in the major varies. A 40-hour general education core includes courses in arts and humanities, oral and symbolic communication, natural science, and social science. All students must take 6 hours each of English composition, American history and government, and general education requirements. Seniors must take a 3-credit-hour capstone experience course integrating their undergraduate studies, and it must include writing.

Special: Co-op programs are available in Arts and Sciences, Business, and Engineering. A variety of voluntary and required internships are available in more than 50 fields of study. OU offers study abroad in over 50 countries, work-study programs, a Washington semester, a general studies degree, dual and student-designed majors, nondegree study, pass/fail options, and credit for life experience. B.A.-B.S. degrees are offered in many subjects and an accelerated degree is offered in 15 majors. The interdisciplinary major in Letters combines the classics, history, philosophy, and languages. There are 17 national honor societies, including Phi Beta Kappa, and a freshman honors program.

Faculty/Classroom: 63% of faculty are male; 37% are female. Graduate students teach 36% of introductory courses. The average class size in an introductory lecture is 42; in a laboratory is 21; and in a regular course is 38.

Admissions: 80% of the 2013-2014 applicants were accepted. The SAT scores for the 2013-2014 freshman class were: Critical Reading--21% below 500, 43% between 500 and 599, 24% between 600 and 699, and 12% between 700 and 800; Math--13% below 500, 41% between 500 and 599, 33% between 600 and 699, and 13% between 700 and 800. The ACT scores were 7% below 21, 23% between 21 and 23, 29% between 24 and 26, 15% between 27 and 28, and 26% above 28. 55% of the current freshmen were in the top fifth of their class; 84% were in the top two fifths. There were 170 National Merit finalists. 252 freshmen graduated first in their class.

Requirements: The SAT or ACT is required. Applicants will be considered for admission using a holistic review and selection process which considers several factors that predict academic success (i.e. high school grade point average, high school course rigor, academic engagement, writing ability, leadership and ACT/SAT scores). Students must have a total of 15 curricular units, including 4 units of English, 3 units of math, 3 units of lab science, I unit of American history, 2 units of citizenship skills, and 2 elective units from areas previously mentioned or computer science or foreign language. Some alternative admission opportunities are available, but limited. AP and CLEP credits are accepted.

Procedure: Freshmen are admitted to all sessions. Entrance exams should be taken during the junior year or the first part of the senior year. There is a rolling admissions plan. Applications should be filed by April 1 for fall entry; November 1 for spring entry; and April 1 for summer entry, along with a $40 fee. Notification is sent on a rolling basis. 1815 applicants were on the 2013 waiting list; 1628 were admitted. Applications are accepted online.

Transfer: 1175 transfer students enrolled in 2012-2013. Applicants with 60 or more semester hours attempted must have a minimum GPA of 2.00. The College of Architecture, College of Atmospheric and Geographic Sciences, College of Business, College of Earth and Energy and College of Fine Arts require a 2.50. The College of Education and College of Journalism and Mass Communication require a 2.75. Nonresident Engineering applicants must have a minimum GPA of 3.00. The Applicants with fewer than 24 semester hours of college-level work must also meet freshman admission requirements. Applicants must be in good standing at the last institution attended. 30 of 120 credits required for the bachelor's degree must be completed at OU.

Visiting: There are regularly scheduled orientations for prospective students, consisting of sessions tailored to individual needs and interests. There are guides for informal visits, visitors may sit in on classes, and stay overnight. To schedule a visit, contact the Prospective Student Services at (405) 325-2151.

Financial Aid: OU is a member of CSS. The FAFSA is required. The priority date for freshman financial aid applications for fall entry is March 1.

International Students: There are 814 international students enrolled. The school actively recruits these students. They must take the TOEFL with a minimum score of 79 on the Internet-based version (iBT).

Computers: All students may access the system 24 hours per day. There are no time limits. The fee is $15.3 crh.

Graduates: From July 1, 2012 to June 30, 2013, 4242 bachelor's degrees were awarded. The most popular majors were multidisciplinary studies (12%), psychology (4%), and accounting (3%). 2590 companies recruited on campus in 2012-2013. In an average class, 1% graduate in 3 years or less, 37% graduate in 4 years or less, 62% graduate in 5 years or less, and 66% graduate in 6 years or less.

Admissions Contact: E-Mail: *admrec@ou.edu* Web: *www.ou.edu*

UNIVERSITY OF SCIENCE AND ARTS OF OKLAHOMA D-3

Chickasha, OK 73018 **(405) 574-1356**
(800) 933-8726; (405) 574-1220

Full-time: 299 men, 564 women	**Faculty:** 55; IIB, --$
Part-time: 45 men, 75 women	**Ph.D.s:** 85%
Graduate: n/av	**Student/Faculty:** 13 to 1
Year: trimesters, summer session	**Tuition:** $5400 ($12,720)
Application Deadline: May 8	**Room & Board:** $5160
Freshman Class: 597 applied, 230 accepted, 187 enrolled	
ACT: 24	

VERY COMPETITIVE

The University of Science and Arts of Oklahoma, founded in 1908, is Oklahoma's only publicly funded liberal arts college, providing interdisciplinary learning opportunities. There is one undergraduate school. In addition to regional accreditation, USAO has baccalaureate program accreditation with NASM and NCATE. The library contains 69,605 volumes, 214 microform items, 3,562 audio/video tapes/CDs/DVDs, and subscribes to 55,000 periodicals including electronic. Computerized library services include interlibrary loans, database searching, and Internet access. Special learning facilities include an art gallery, a commercial art computer lab, TV studio, a child development center, herbarium, art gallery and a speech pathology clinic. The 75-acre campus is in a small town 40 miles southwest of Oklahoma City. Including any residence halls, there are 14 buildings.

Student Life: 86% of undergraduates are from Oklahoma. Others are from 24 states, 19 foreign countries, and Canada. 95% are from public schools. 70% are White; 13% American Indian/Alaska Native. The average age of freshmen is 19; all undergraduates, 24. 39% do not continue beyond their first year; 41% remain to graduate.

Housing: 504 students can be accommodated in college housing, which includes single-sex and coed dorms and on-campus apartments. On-campus housing is guaranteed for the freshman year only, is available on a first-come, and first-served basis. Priority is given to out-of-town students. 54% of students commute. All students may keep cars.

Activities: 1% of men belong to 1 national fraternity; 1% of women belong to 1 national sorority. There are 45 groups on campus, including art, band, cheerleading, choir, chorale, chorus, computers, dance, drama, drill team, ethnic, gay, honors, international, jazz band, literary magazine, musical theater, newspaper, opera, orchestra, pep band, photography, political, professional, radio and TV, religious, social, social service, and student government. Popular campus events include Montmartre Art Festival/Droverstock, Festival of Arts and Ideas and Drover Difference Day.

Sports: There are 5 intercollegiate sports for men and 5 for women, and 5 intramural sports for men and 5 for women. Facilities include a field house, a 2000-seat gym, a 1000-seat auditorium, a ballpark with baseball and softball fields, each seating 200, a soccer field with seating for 250, tennis courts, a weight room, a fitness center, an indoor pool, an outdoor pool, and volleyball courts.

Disabled Students: 95% of the campus is accessible. Facilities include wheelchair ramps, elevators, special parking, specially equipped restrooms, special class scheduling, lowered drinking fountains, and lowered telephones.
Services: Counseling and information services are available, as is tutoring in some subjects, math, writing, and reading. There is remedial math, reading, and writing. Tutors and interpreters are available for hearing-impaired students.
Campus Safety and Security: Measures include 24-hour foot and vehicle patrol and emergency notification system. There are lighted pathways/sidewalks, and security cameras near housing and parking lots.
Programs of Study: USAO confers B.A., B.S. and B.F.A. degrees. Bachelor's degrees are awarded in BIOLOGICAL SCIENCE (biology/biological science), BUSINESS (business administration and management), COMMUNICATIONS AND THE ARTS (art, communications, dramatic arts, English, fine arts, and music), COMPUTER AND PHYSICAL SCIENCE (chemistry, mathematics, natural sciences, and physics), EDUCATION (early childhood education, education of the deaf and hearing impaired, elementary education, and physical education), HEALTH PROFESSIONS (speech pathology/audiology), SOCIAL SCIENCE (American Indian studies, economics, history, political science/government, psychology, and sociology). Humanities and physical science is the strongest academically. Business administration, psychology and art have the largest enrollments.
Required: To graduate, students must complete a total of 124 credit hours with a minimum GPA of 2.0.
Special: USAO offers dual majors, accelerated degree programs in all majors through year-round study, work-study programs, internship placement in community institutions, a Tutorial Scholars Program for student-designed majors, an interdisciplinary studies program, and a limited number of pass/fail options. There are 7 national honor societies, a freshman honors program, and 1 departmental honors programs.
Faculty/Classroom: 49% of faculty are male; 51% are female. All teach undergraduates, 55% do research, and 55% do both. No introductory courses are taught by graduate students. The average class size in an introductory lecture is 20; in a laboratory is 20; and in a regular course is 17.
Admissions: 39% of the 2013-2014 applicants were accepted. The ACT scores were 18% below 21, 29% between 21 and 23, 28% between 24 and 26, 16% between 27 and 28, and 9% above 28. 57% of the current freshmen were in the top fifth of their class; 85% were in the top two fifths.
Requirements: The ACT is required. Applicants must meet one of the following 3 options: (1) have a minimum score of 24 on the ACT or 1090 on the SAT AND (3.0 GPA or top 50% of HS class); (2) have a high school GPA of 3.0 and be in the top 25% of their high school class; or (3) have a minimum GPA of 3.0 in their HS core courses and a minimum score of 22 on the ACT or 1020 on the SAT. USAO requires applicants to be in the upper 50% of their class. A GPA of 3.0 is required. AP and CLEP credits are accepted. Important factors in the admissions decision are evidence of special talent, leadership record, and personality/intangible qualities.
Procedure: Freshmen are admitted to all sessions. Entrance exams should be taken by May of the preceding spring. There is a rolling admissions plan. Applications should be filed by May 8 for fall entry, along with a $40 fee. Notification is sent on a rolling basis. Applications are accepted online.
Transfer: 205 transfer students enrolled in 2012-2013. Applicants must have a minimum GPA of 2.0. Those students with fewer than 30 college-level credit hours must submit a high school transcript or GED and ACT scores. 30 of 124 credits required for the bachelor's degree must be completed at USAO.
Visiting: There are guides for informal visits, visitors may sit in on classes, and stay overnight. To schedule a visit, contact the Admissions Office.
Financial Aid: In 2013-2014, 90% of all full-time freshmen and 83% of continuing full-time students received some form of financial aid. 66% of all full-time freshmen and 64% of continuing full-time students received need-based aid. The average freshman award was $9,174. Need-based scholarships or need-based grants averaged $7,452; need-based self-help aid (loans and jobs) averaged $3,367; non-need-based athletic scholarships averaged $10,594; and other non-need-based awards and non-need-based scholarships averaged $3,376. 20% of undergraduate students work part-time. Average annual earnings from campus work are $2180. The average financial indebtedness of the 2013 graduate was $18,378. The FAFSA and the college's own financial statement, and Institution Information Sheet are required. The priority date for freshman financial aid applications for fall entry is March 15. The deadline for filing freshman financial aid applications for fall entry is rolling.
International Students: There are 63 international students enrolled. The school actively recruits these students. They must take the TOEFL with a minimum score of 500 on the paper-based TOEFL (PBT) or 61 on the Internet-based version (iBT). They must also take the SAT or ACT.
Computers: All students may access the system at any time. There are no time limits and no fees.
Graduates: From July 1, 2012 to June 30, 2013, 188 bachelor's degrees were awarded. The most popular majors were business administration (18%), elementary education (9%), and psychology (9%). 15 companies recruited on campus in 2012-2013. In an average class, 6% graduate in 3 years or less, 28% graduate in 4 years or less, 38% graduate in 5 years or less, and 41% graduate in 6 years or less.
Admissions Contact: Monica Trevino, Director of Admissions. E-Mail: *usao-admissions@usao.edu* Web: *www.usao.edu*

UNIVERSITY OF TULSA E-2

Tulsa, OK 74104 (918) 631-2307
(800) 331-3050; (918) 631-5003

Full-time: 1905 men, 1388 women	**Faculty:** 307; IIA, +$
Part-time: 76 men, 59 women	**Ph.D.s:** 96%
Graduate: 657 men, 512 women	**Student/Faculty:** 11 to 1
Year: semesters, summer session	**Tuition:** $34,835
Application Deadline:	**Room & Board:** $10,476
Freshman Class: 7304 applied, 2965 accepted, 856 enrolled	
SAT CR/M: 620/630	**ACT:** 28 **HIGHLY COMPETITIVE+**

The University of Tulsa, founded in 1894 and affiliated with the Presbyterian Church, is a private comprehensive institution offering over 60 undergraduate major areas of study through its programs in liberal arts and sciences, engineering and natural sciences, and business administration. There are 3 undergraduate schools and 2 graduate schools. In addition to regional accreditation, TU has baccalaureate program accreditation with AACSB, ABET, CSAB, NASM, and TEAC. The 2 libraries contain 1.4 million volumes, 2.6 million microform items, 23,854 audio/video tapes/CDs/DVDs, and subscribe to 53,504 periodicals including electronic. Computerized library services include interlibrary loans, database searching, Internet access, and Wi-Fi capability. Special learning facilities include an art gallery, radio station, and TV station. The 209-acre campus is in an urban area in the city of Tulsa. Including any residence halls, there are 93 buildings.
Student Life: 57% of undergraduates are from out of state, mostly the Southwest. Students are from 44 states, 57 foreign countries, and Canada. 67% are from public schools. 55% are White; 26% Foreign. 44% claim no religious affiliation; 36% Protestant; 13% Catholic. The average age of freshmen is 18; all undergraduates, 21. 10% do not continue beyond their first year; 69% remain to graduate.
Housing: 2684 students can be accommodated in college housing, which includes single-sex and coed dorms, on-campus apartments, off-campus apartments, and married student housing. In addition, there are honors houses, language houses, special-interest houses, fraternity houses, and sorority houses. On-campus housing is guaranteed for the freshman year only, is available on a first-come, first-served basis, and is available on a lottery system for upperclassmen. 74% of students live on campus; of those, 96% remain on campus on weekends. All students may keep cars.
Activities: 21% of men belong to 7 national fraternities; 23% of women belong to 8 national sororities. There are 172 groups on campus, including art, band, cheerleading, chess, choir, chorale, chorus, communications, computers, dance, debate, drama, drill team, environmental, ethnic, film, forensics, gay, honors, international, jazz band, literary magazine, marching band, musical theater, newspaper, opera, orchestra, pep band, photography, political, professional, radio and TV, religious, social, social service, student government, symphony, and yearbook. Popular campus events include Homecoming, Springfest, Black Heritage Month, and International Education Week.
Sports: There are 8 intercollegiate sports for men and 10 for women, and 22 intramural sports for men and 22 for women. Facilities include a 30,000-seat stadium, an 8,355-seat basketball arena, a gym, an athletic field, indoor racquetball courts, basketball and tennis courts, a handball court, a weight room, a dance studio, student fitness center, soccer fields, softball field, track, multi-purpose recreational field, and outdoor track.
Disabled Students: 90% of the campus is accessible. Facilities include wheelchair ramps, elevators, special parking, specially equipped restrooms, special class scheduling, lowered drinking fountains, lowered telephones, special housing.
Services: Counseling and information services are available, as is tutoring in most subjects. There is a reader service for the blind. Special labs are available to students in need of assistance in math and writing.
Campus Safety and Security: Measures include 24-hour foot and vehicle patrol, emergency notification system, self-defense education, and security escort services. There are shuttle buses, emergency telephones, lighted pathways/sidewalks, and controlled access to dorms/residences.
Programs of Study: TU confers B.A., B.S., B.F.A., B.M., B.Mus.Ed., B.S.A.M., B.S.A.T., B.S.B., B.S.B.A., B.S.C., B.S.C.E., B.S.C.S., B.S.D.E., B.S.E.E., B.S.E.P., B.S.E.S.S., B.S.G.S., B.S.I.B.L., B.S.M.E., B.S.N., B.S.P.E., B.S.B.G. and B.S.G.P. degrees. Master's and doctoral degrees are also awarded. Bachelor's degrees are awarded in AGRICULTURE (environmental studies), BIOLOGICAL SCIENCE (biochemistry and biology/biological science), BUSINESS (accounting, banking and finance, business administration and management, business (dual major program),

international business management, management information systems, management science, marketing/retailing/merchandising, organizational behavior, and sports management), COMMUNICATIONS AND THE ARTS (art history, art, arts administration/management, communications, English, film arts, French, German, music, music performance, musical theater, piano/organ, Spanish, theatre arts, and voice), COMPUTER AND PHYSICAL SCIENCE (applied mathematics, chemistry, computer science, geology, geophysics and seismology, geoscience, information sciences and systems, mathematics, and physics), EDUCATION (athletic training, education, education of the deaf and hearing impaired, elementary education, and music education), ENGINEERING AND ENVIRONMENTAL DESIGN (chemical engineering, electrical/electronics engineering, energy management technology, engineering physics, mechanical engineering, and petroleum/natural gas engineering), HEALTH PROFESSIONS (exercise science, nursing, premedicine, and speech pathology/audiology), SOCIAL SCIENCE (anthropology, communication sciences & disorders, economics, history, philosophy, political science/government, prelaw, psychology, religion, Russian and Slavic studies, sociology, and women & gender studies). Petroleum engineering, psychology, and English are the strongest academically. Petroleum engineering, mechanical engineering, and finance have the largest enrollments.

Required: To graduate, students must complete 124 to 136 credit hours, including 24 to 51 in the major, with a minimum GPA determined by the major. Freshmen in liberal arts and business administration must complete the First Seminar. All students must complete the core curriculum, which includes 2 writing courses and at least 1 course in math. All students must also complete the general curriculum, which requires 25 credit hours in 3 categories (aesthetic inquiry and creative expression; historical and social interpretation; and scientific investigation). A foreign language requirement of 2 years for liberal arts and sciences students and 1 year for business majors must be completed.

Special: Internships are available in the Tulsa area during the school year and in cities throughout the United States during the summer. Students may participate in more than 50 study-abroad programs. TU offers a Washington semester, B.A.-B.S. degrees, cross-registration with the 3 undergraduate schools, dual and student-designed majors, accelerated degree programs, non-degree study, work-study programs, and pass/fail options. There are 34 national honor societies, including Phi Beta Kappa, and a freshman honors program.

Faculty/Classroom: 67% of faculty are male; 33% are female. All teach and do research. Graduate students teach 5% of introductory courses. The average class size in an introductory lecture is 21; in a laboratory is 16; and in a regular course is 21.

Admissions: 41% of the 2013-2014 applicants were accepted. The SAT scores for the 2013-2014 freshman class were: Critical Reading--9% below 500, 29% between 500 and 599, 35% between 600 and 699, and 27% between 700 and 800; Math--7% below 500, 27% between 500 and 599, 43% between 600 and 699, and 23% between 700 and 800. The ACT scores were 2% below 21, 10% between 21 and 23, 18% between 24 and 26, 19% between 27 and 28, and 51% above 28. 85% of the current freshmen were in the top fifth of their class; 95% were in the top two fifths. There were 49 National Merit finalists. 23 freshmen graduated first in their class.

Requirements: The SAT or ACT is required. Graduation from an accredited secondary school or satisfactory scores on the GED are also required for admission. The school recommends a minimum of 18 academic credits, including 4 years of English, 4 years of math, 3 years of science and social studies (including history), 2 years of a single foreign language and one year of fine arts and humanities. Computer competency is also expected. An essay and an interview are highly recommended. An audition or a portfolio is required for students applying for music, theater, or art scholarships. AP credits are accepted. Important factors in the admissions decision are advanced placement or honors courses, leadership record, and extracurricular activities record.

Procedure: Freshmen are admitted fall and spring. Entrance exams should be taken during spring of the junior year or fall of the senior year. There are early admissions, deferred admissions, and rolling admissions plans. Application deadlines are open. Application fee is $50. Notification is sent on a rolling basis. Applications are accepted online.

Transfer: 152 transfer students enrolled in 2012-2013. Transfer students must submit official transcripts from all colleges attended and should have a minimum GPA of 2.75 for all college and high school work. Applicants with fewer than 30 credit hours must submit ACT or SAT scores. Those with fewer than 60 credit hours must submit an official high school transcript. Applicants 25 years of age or older are exempt from submitting ACT or SAT scores unless requested to do so by the Admission Office. 45 of 120 credits required for the bachelor's degree must be completed at TU.

Visiting: There are regularly scheduled orientations for prospective students, including overnight programs in the fall and spring. Students stay on campus and attend special information sessions. There are guides for informal visits, visitors may sit in on classes, and stay overnight. To schedule a visit, contact the Office of Admission.

Financial Aid: In 2013-2014, 94% of all full-time freshmen and 88% of continuing full-time students received some form of financial aid. 46% of all full-time freshmen and 42% of continuing full-time students received need-based aid. The average freshman award was $25,426. Need-based scholarships or need-based grants averaged $8,277 ($25,410 maximum); need-based self-help aid (loans and jobs) averaged $6,667 ($11,600 maximum); non-need-based athletic scholarships averaged $24,916 ($46,845 maximum); and other non-need-based awards and non-need-based scholarships averaged $21,162 ($46,845 maximum). 23% of undergraduate students work part-time. Average annual earnings from campus work are $5000. The average financial indebtedness of the 2013 graduate was $26,293. The FAFSA is required. Check with the school for current application deadlines.

International Students: There are 891 international students enrolled. The school actively recruits these students. They must take the TOEFL with a minimum score of 550 on the paper-based TOEFL (PBT) or 80 on the Internet-based version (iBT), a minimum IELTS score of 6.5.

Computers: All students may access the system 24 hours per day. There are no time limits and no fees.

Graduates: From July 1, 2012 to June 30, 2013, 760 bachelor's degrees were awarded. The most popular majors were petroleum engineering (9%), finance (6%), and mechanical engineering (6%). 249 companies recruited on campus in 2012-2013. In an average class, 52% graduate in 4 years or less, 67% graduate in 5 years or less, and 69% graduate in 6 years or less. Of the 2012 graduating class, 27% were enrolled in graduate school within 6 months of graduation, and 87% were employed.

Admissions Contact: Earl Johnson, VP for Enrollment and Student Services. E-Mail: *admission@utulsa.edu* Web: *www.utulsa.edu*

OREGON

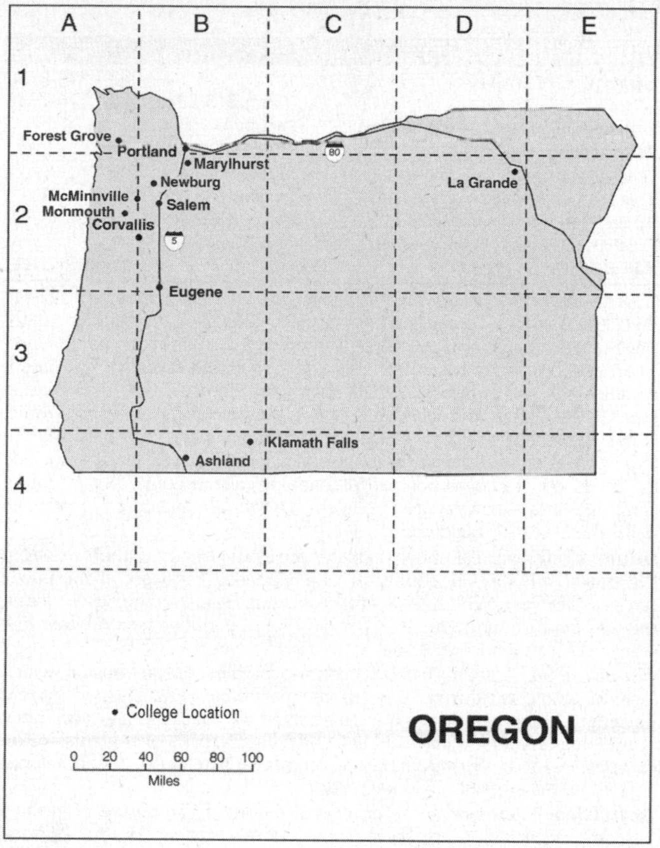

ART INSTITUTE OF PORTLAND

B-1

Portland, OR 97209-2911

(503) 228-6528
(888) 228-6528; (503) 227-1945

Full-time: 470 men, 530 women
Part-time: 150 men, 170 women
Graduate: n/av
Year: trimesters, summer session
Application Deadline: open
Freshman Class: n/av
SAT or ACT: recommended

Faculty: n/av
Ph.D.s: n/av
Student/Faculty: n/av
Tuition: $22,195
Room & Board: n/av

SPECIAL

The Art Institute of Portland is a private institution offering undergraduate programs in interior, graphic, and apparel design; media arts and animation; and multimedia and web design, game art and design, digital media production, and advertising. Some figures in the above capsule and in this profile are approximate. The library contains 22,289 volumes, 1000 audio/video tapes/CDs/DVDs, and subscribes to 200 periodicals including electronic. Computerized library services include interlibrary loans, database searching, and Internet access. Special learning facilities include a learning resource center. The 1-acre campus is in an urban area in downtown Portland. Including any residence halls, there are 2 buildings.

Student Life: 69% of undergraduates are from Oregon. 81% are white. The average age of freshmen is 23; all undergraduates, 25.

Housing: 110 students can be accommodated in college housing, which includes coed off-campus apartments. Housing is available on a first-come, first-served basis. 92% of students commute. Alcohol is not permitted. No one may keep cars.

Activities: There are no fraternities or sororities. There are several groups on campus, including art, communications, computers, film, international, professional, and student government. Popular campus events include portfolio review, animation shows, and Halloween and Valentine's Day activities.

Sports: There is no sports program at AIPD.

Disabled Students: All of the campus is accessible. Facilities include wheelchair ramps, elevators, special parking, specially equipped rest rooms, special class scheduling, lowered drinking fountains, and lowered telephones.

Services: Counseling and information services are available, as is tutoring in most subjects. There is remedial math, reading, and writing.

Campus Safety and Security: There are emergency telephones, lighted pathways/sidewalks, and a night security guard.

Programs of Study: AIPD confers B.S. and B.F.A. degrees. Associate degrees are also awarded. Bachelor's degrees are awarded in COMMUNICATIONS AND THE ARTS (advertising, animation, apparel design, graphic design, media arts, and multimedia), ENGINEERING AND ENVIRONMENTAL DESIGN (interior design). Interior design is the strongest academically. Graphic design has the largest enrollment.

Required: To graduate, students must complete 180 quarter hours, including 111 in the major, with a minimum GPA of 2.0. Distribution requirements include 9 credits each in English composition and history of material culture, 6 credits in basic design, and 3 credits each in drawing, computer fundamentals, physics, math, art history, and critical thinking.

Special: Accelerated degree programs and field trips to San Francisco and annually to Europe are available. Internships are required for most programs.

Faculty/Classroom: 44% of faculty are male; 56% are female. All teach undergraduates. The average class size in an introductory lecture is 25; in a laboratory, 25; and in a regular course, 20.

Requirements: The SAT or ACT is recommended. A high school diploma or GED is required. An interview with an admissions officer and an essay are required. A GPA of 2.5 is required. AP and CLEP credits are accepted. Important factors in the admissions decision are evidence of special talent, personality/intangible qualities, and recommendations by school officials.

Procedure: Freshmen are admitted to all sessions. There are deferred admissions and rolling admissions plans. Application deadlines are open. Application fee is $50. Notification is sent on a rolling basis. Applications are accepted online.

Transfer: Requirements are the same as for new students. 45 of 180 credits required for the bachelor's degree must be completed at AIPD.

Visiting: There are regularly scheduled orientations for prospective students, including college tours, mini-class sessions, financial aid and financial planning meetings, and career assessment. There are guides for informal visits, and visitors may sit in on classes. To schedule a visit, contact the Admissions Office.

Financial Aid: AIPD is a member of CSS. The FAFSA is required. Check with the school for current application deadlines.

International Students: The school actively recruits these students. They must take the TOEFL.

Admissions Contact: Director of Admissions. E-Mail: *aipdadm@aii.edu* Web: *www.artinstitutes.edu*

CONCORDIA UNIVERSITY

B-1

Portland, OR 97211

(503) 280-8501
(800) 321-9371; (503) 280-8531

Full-time: 300 men, 500 women
Part-time: 73 men, 125 women
Graduate: 179 men, 321 women
Year: semesters, summer session
Application Deadline: open
Freshman Class: 804 applied, 532 accepted, 171 enrolled
SAT: required

Faculty: 40
Ph.D.s: 57%
Student/Faculty: 20 to 1
Tuition: $26,900
Room & Board: $8030
ACT: 21

COMPETITIVE

Concordia University, founded in 1905, is a private liberal arts institution affiliated with the Lutheran Church Missouri Synod and is 1 of 10 institutions of the Concordia University System. There are 3 undergraduate schools and 2 graduate schools. The library contains 70,000 volumes, 56,706 microform items, 2,888 audio/video tapes/CDs/DVDs, and subscribes to 424 periodicals including electronic. Computerized library services include interlibrary loans, database searching, and Internet access. Special learning facilities include a The 13-acre campus is in an urban area in Portland. Including any residence halls, there are 20 buildings.

Student Life: 75% of undergraduates are from Oregon. Others are from 14 states, 18 foreign countries, and Canada. 75% are White. 59% are Protestant; 30% claim no religious affiliation. The average age of freshmen is 19; all undergraduates, 25. 25% do not continue beyond their first year; 45% remain to graduate.

Housing: 400 students can be accommodated in college housing, which includes single-sex and coed dorms, on-campus apartments, and married student housing. On-campus housing is guaranteed for the freshman year only, is available on a first-come, first-served basis, and is available on a lottery system for upperclassmen. 59% of students live on campus; of those, 95% remain on campus on weekends. Alcohol is not permitted. All students may keep cars.

Activities: There are no fraternities or sororities. There are 14 groups on campus, including and handbell choir., brass ensemble, choir, chorus, communications, drama, honors, international, literary magazine, newspaper, professional, religious, social, social service, and student government.

Sports: There are 4 intercollegiate sports for men and 5 for women, and 10 intramural sports for men and 10 for women. Facilities include a weight room, a 1200-seat gym, and a baseball/soccer field.

Disabled Students: 80% of the campus is accessible. Facilities include wheelchair ramps, elevators, special parking, specially equipped restrooms, special class scheduling, and lowered telephones.

Services: Counseling and information services are available, as is tutoring in most subjects. There is remedial math, reading, and writing. There is also student-supported individual help and media resources.

Campus Safety and Security: Measures include 24-hour foot and vehicle patrol, self-defense education, and security escort services. There are emergency telephones, lighted pathways/sidewalks, controlled access to dorms/residences, and emergency cell phone available 24 hours.

Programs of Study: Concordia confers B.A., and B.S. degrees. Associate, master's, and doctoral degrees are also awarded. Bachelor's degrees are awarded in BIOLOGICAL SCIENCE (biology/biological science), BUSINESS (business administration and management), COMMUNICATIONS AND THE ARTS (English), COMPUTER AND PHYSICAL SCIENCE (chemistry), EDUCATION (early childhood education, elementary education, and secondary education), ENGINEERING AND ENVIRONMENTAL DESIGN (environmental science), HEALTH PROFESSIONS (health care administration, nursing, and premedicine), SOCIAL SCIENCE (humanities, psychology, social work, theological studies, and youth ministry). Business administration, education, and psychology are the strongest academically. Education and business has the largest enrollments.

Required: To graduate, students must complete a total of 124 semester hours, with a minimum GPA of 2.0. General education requirements total 48 semester hours. All students must take freshman composition and courses in math, phys ed, humanities, religion, science, writing, fine arts, and social sciences. In the major, 45 hours of 300-400 level courses must be taken.

Special: Cross-registration may be arranged through the Concordia University System and with Oregon Independent. There is a dual enrollement program with Portland Community College. There are also internships, study abroad in more than 20 countries, and an accelerated degree program in business, health care administration, and social work. There is 1 national honor society, a freshman honors program, and 1 departmental honors program.

Faculty/Classroom: 67% of faculty are male; 33% are female. All teach undergraduates, and 5% do research. No introductory courses are taught by graduate students. The average class size in an introductory lecture is 19; in a laboratory is 19; and in a regular course is 17.

Admissions: 66% of the 2013-2014 applicants were accepted. The ACT scores were 40% below 21, 35% between 21 and 23, 16% between 24 and 26, 9% between 27 and 28, and 2% above 28. 42% of the current freshmen were in the top fifth of their class; 69% were in the top two fifths.

Requirements: The SAT or ACT is required, with satisfactory SAT verbal scores recommended. Graduation from an accredited secondary school or satisfactory scores on the GED are required. The school recommends that high school courses include 4 units of English, 3 units each of social studies, math, and science, 2 units of a foreign language, and 1 unit of art and music. An interview is recommended. A GPA of 2.5 is required. AP and CLEP credits are accepted. Important factors in the admissions decision are recommendations by school officials, leadership record, and personality/intangible qualities.

Procedure: Freshmen are admitted fall, spring, and summer. Entrance exams should be taken during the junior year or early in the senior year. There is a rolling admissions plan. Early decision applications should be filed by March 1. The fall 2013 application fee was $20. Notification is sent on a rolling basis. Applications are accepted online.

Transfer: 141 transfer students enrolled in 2012-2013. Transfer students must have a minimum GPA of 2.0. 45 of 124 credits required for the bachelor's degree must be completed at Concordia.

Visiting: There are regularly scheduled orientations for prospective students, including class visitations and meetings with program deans and faculty. There are guides for informal visits, visitors may sit in on classes, and stay overnight. To schedule a visit, contact the Admissions Office at admissions@cu-portland.edu.

Financial Aid: The average freshman award was $13,000. The FAFSA is required. Check with the school for current application deadlines.

International Students: There are 15 international students enrolled. The school actively recruits these students. They must take the TOEFL. They must also take the SAT or ACT.

Graduates: From July 1, 2012 to June 30, 2013, 219 bachelor's degrees were awarded. The most popular majors were business administration (36%), education (34%), and nursing . 35 companies recruited on campus in 2012-2013. In an average class, 30% graduate in 4 years or less, 39% graduate in 5 years or less, and 43% graduate in 6 years or less.

Admissions Contact: Office of Admission E-Mail: *admission@cu-portland.edu* Web: *www.cu-portland.edu*

CORBAN UNIVERSITY B-2

Salem, OR 97317 **(503) 375-8180**
(800) 845-3005; (503) 375-7042

Full-time: 335 men, 510 women	**Faculty:** 45
Part-time: 38 men, 66 women	**Ph.D.s:** 68%
Graduate: 94 men, 115 women	**Student/Faculty:** 17 to 1
Year: semesters, summer session	**Tuition:** $26,486 ($27,431)
Application Deadline: August 1	**Room & Board:** $8876
Freshman Class: 2896 applied, 934 accepted, 222 enrolled	
SAT CR/M/W: 517/520/506 **ACT:** 22	**COMPETITIVE**

Corban University is a Christian university offering degrees in biblical-theological studies, business administration, education, humanities, math, phys ed, social sciences, psychology, intercultural studies, and youth work. There are 5 undergraduate schools and 4 graduate schools. The library contains 85,000 volumes, 2,000 microform items, 3,000 audio/video tapes/CDs/DVDs, and subscribes to 552 periodicals including electronic. Computerized library services include interlibrary loans, database searching, Internet access, and Wi-Fi capability. Special learning facilities include an art gallery, radio station, an archaeological museum. The 142-acre campus is in a suburban area in Salem, Oregon. Including any residence halls, there are 28 buildings.

Student Life: 53% of undergraduates are from Oregon. Others are from 29 states, 11 foreign countries, and Canada. 60% are from public schools. 78% are White. 96% are Protestant. The average age of freshmen is 18; all undergraduates, 20. 24% do not continue beyond their first year; 53% remain to graduate.

Housing: 547 students can be accommodated in college housing, which includes single-sex dorms, on-campus apartments, and married student housing. On-campus housing is guaranteed for the freshman year only, is available on a first-come, and first-served basis. 65% of students live on campus; of those, 90% remain on campus on weekends. Alcohol is not permitted. All students may keep cars.

Activities: There are no fraternities or sororities. There are 16 groups on campus, including art, band, choir, chorale, chorus, drama, honors, jazz band, literary magazine, musical theater, newspaper, orchestra, pep band, religious, social, social service, student government, and yearbook. Popular campus events include Sports Weekends, Chapel Services, International Fair, Various Student Led Activities and Contests.

Sports: There are 6 intercollegiate sports for men and 7 for women, and 12 intramural sports for men and 12 for women. Facilities include Corban has a sports center with a gym, soccer fields, baseball fields and the student fitness center.

Disabled Students: 95% of the campus is accessible. Facilities include wheelchair ramps, elevators, special parking, specially equipped restrooms, and lowered telephones.

Services: Counseling and information services are available, as is tutoring in most subjects, US and World History, Math and Sciences, Psychology, Religious Studies, English/Writing, Business, Music and others as needed.

Campus Safety and Security: Measures include 24-hour foot and vehicle patrol, emergency notification system, self-defense education, and security escort services. There are emergency telephones, lighted pathways/sidewalks, controlled access to dorms/residences, 24 hour emergency response not patrol, threat assessment, safety planning, emergency planning, self defense education mentoring, events and mass gatherings, travel security planning, crisis management, executive protection, bomb threats,intellectual property protection, personal protection best practices, loss prevention, security risk assessment, access management, crime prevention through environmental design, Clery compliance and reporting, media relations, money transport, armed and unarmed security, environmental security, business continuity, counter-terrorism, intelligence gathering, security management, and internal investigations.

Programs of Study: Corban confers B.A., and B.S. degrees. Associate, master's, and doctoral degrees are also awarded. Bachelor's degrees are awarded in BUSINESS (accounting, business administration and management, marketing, marketing management, and sports management), COMMUNICATIONS AND THE ARTS (communications, creative writing, English, journalism, music, and music performance), COMPUTER AND PHYSICAL SCIENCE (information sciences and systems and mathematics), EDUCATION (business education, education, elementary education, mathematics education, music education, physical education, social studies education, and sports and wellness studies), HEALTH PROFESSIONS (exercise science, health care administration, health science, predentistry, premedicine, preoptometry, prepharmacy, prephysical therapy, and preveterinary science), SOCIAL SCIENCE (biblical studies, counseling/psychology, criminal justice, crosscultural studies, history, humanities, interdisciplinary studies, ministries, pastoral studies, political science/government, prelaw, psychology, social science, and youth ministry). Education and business is the strongest academically. Psychology, business, and education have the largest enrollments.

Required: To graduate, students must complete 128 credits with 40 to 74 in the major. The minimum required GPA is 2.0 for most programs; the education major requires a 3.0 GPA. The general education core consists of 68 credits. Courses must be taken in Bible, humanities, social sciences, math, science, and phys ed.

Special: Corban offers a pre-seminary co-op program, cross-registration with Oregon Independent Colleges, study abroad in 4 countries, a Washington semester, internships with the approval of a program adviser, accelerated programs in management and communication and in family studies, and student-designed majors with adviser approval. Corban offers at Fast-Track B.S./M.Div. degree, and AMBEX Study Abroad in Germany. There are a freshman honors program.

Faculty/Classroom: 76% of faculty are male; 24% are female. 90% teach undergraduates, 10% do research, and 95% do both. No introductory courses are taught by graduate students. The average class size in a regular course is 15.

Admissions: 32% of the 2013-2014 applicants were accepted. The SAT scores for the 2013-2014 freshman class were: Critical Reading--31% below 500, 41% between 500 and 599, 17% between 600 and 699, and 1% between 700 and 800; Math--24% below 500, 41% between 500 and 599, 18% between 600 and 699, and 1% between 700 and 800; Writing--36% below 500, 36% between 500 and 599, 13% between 600 and 699, and 1% between 700 and 800. The ACT scores were 26% below 21, 30% between 21 and 23, 24% between 24 and 26, 14% between 27 and 28, and 6% above 28. 27% of the current freshmen were in the top fifth of their class; 41% were in the top two fifths. There were 1 National Merit finalists. 15 freshmen graduated first in their class.

Requirements: The SAT or ACT is required. Statement of Faith Essay, and a GPA of 2.7 is required. AP and CLEP credits are accepted. Important factors in the admissions decision are extracurricular activities record, leadership record, and personality/intangible qualities.

Procedure: Freshmen are admitted fall and spring. There is a rolling admissions plan. Applications should be filed by August 1 for fall entry; December 1 for spring entry, along with a $35 fee. Notification is sent on a rolling basis. Applications are accepted online.

Transfer: 78 transfer students enrolled in 2012-2013. Transfer applicants are required to have a minimum 2.0 cumulative college GPA and submit the college transcript and 3 references. 30 of 128 credits required for the bachelor's degree must be completed at Corban.

Visiting: There are regularly scheduled orientations for prospective students, including a campus tour, classroom visit, and activities with the student body. There are guides for informal visits, visitors may sit in on classes, and stay overnight. To schedule a visit, contact The Admissions Office at admissions@corban.edu.

Financial Aid: In 2013-2014, 99% of all full-time freshmen and 99% of continuing full-time students received some form of financial aid. 80% of all full-time freshmen and 83% of continuing full-time students received need-based aid. The average freshman award was $19,976. Need-based scholarships or need-based grants averaged $17,440; need-based self-help aid (loans and jobs) averaged $3,593; non-need-based athletic scholarships averaged $9,418; and other non-need-based awards and non-need-based scholarships averaged $8,428. 37% of undergraduate students work part-time. Average annual earnings from campus work are $1721. The average financial indebtedness of the 2013 graduate was $23,853. The FAFSA is required. The priority date for freshman financial aid applications for fall entry is February 15. The deadline for filing freshman financial aid applications for fall entry is September 1.

International Students: There are 23 international students enrolled. The school actively recruits these students. They must take the TOEFL with a minimum score of 500 on the paper-based TOEFL (PBT) or 61 on the Internet-based version (iBT). They must also take the SAT or ACT.

Graduates: From July 1, 2012 to June 30, 2013, 213 bachelor's degrees were awarded. The most popular majors were psychology (34%), education (16%), and business (14%). 10 companies recruited on campus in 2012-2013. In an average class, 10% graduate in 3 years or less, 49% graduate in 4 years or less, and 53% graduate in 6 years or less.

Admissions Contact: Chris Vetter, Associate Provost of Enrollment Services. E-Mail: *admissions@corban.edu* Web: *www.corban.edu*

EASTERN OREGON UNIVERSITY D-2

La Grande, OR 97850-2807 (541) 962-3393
(800) 452-8639; (541) 962-3418

Full-time: 850 men, 2000 women	**Faculty:** n/av; IIB, --$
Part-time: 420 men, 680 women	**Ph.D.s:** n/av
Graduate: 60 men, 190 women	**Student/Faculty:** n/av
Year: varies, summer session	**Tuition:** $7046
Application Deadline: see profile	**Room & Board:** $8289
Freshman Class: n/av	
SAT or ACT: required	

COMPETITIVE

Eastern Oregon University, founded in 1929, is a public institution that is part of the Oregon University System. It offers programs in liberal and fine arts, agriculture, business, health science, and teacher preparation. There are 3 undergraduate schools and 1 graduate school. The figures in the above capsule and in this profile are approximate. Beginning with the 2012-13 award year, EOU will charge nonresident tuition. In addition to regional accreditation, EOU has baccalaureate program accreditation with NCATE. The library contains 335,455 volumes, 250,834 microform items, 34,176 audio/video tapes/CDs/DVDs, and subscribes to 893 periodicals including electronic. Computerized library services include interlibrary loans, database searching, and Internet access. Special learning facilities include a learning resource center, art gallery, natural history museum, and radio station. The 121-acre campus is in a rural area 260 miles east of Portland. Including any residence halls, there are 13 buildings.

Student Life: 70% of undergraduates are from Oregon. Others are from 42 states, 25 foreign countries, and Canada. 96% are from public schools. 82% are white. The average age of freshmen is 19; all undergraduates, 27. 32% do not continue beyond their first year; 37% remain to graduate.

Housing: 436 students can be accommodated in college housing, which includes single-sex and coed dorms, married student housing, a wellness floor, and an academic focus floor. On-campus housing is available on a first-come, first-served basis. 85% of students commute. All students may keep cars.

Activities: There are no fraternities or sororities. There are 44 groups on campus, including art, band, cheerleading, choir, chorale, chorus, communications, computers, dance, drama, ethnic, international, jazz band, literary magazine, musical theater, newspaper, orchestra, pep band, photography, professional, radio and TV, religious, social, student government, symphony, and yearbook. Popular campus events include Casino Night, Spring Fling, and Spring Symposium.

Sports: There are 6 intercollegiate sports for men and 6 for women, and 6 intramural sports for men and 6 for women. Facilities include racquetball courts, a weight room, 3 gyms, a swimming pool, aerobics facilities, a track, and indoor and outdoor tennis courts.

Disabled Students: 80% of the campus is accessible. Facilities include wheelchair ramps, elevators, special parking, and specially equipped rest rooms.

Services: Counseling and information services are available, as is tutoring in most subjects. There is a reader service for the blind, and remedial math, reading, and writing.

Campus Safety and Security: Measures include 24-hour foot and vehicle patrol, security escort services, emergency telephones, and lighted pathways/sidewalks.

Programs of Study: EOU confers B.A. and B.S degrees. Master's degrees are also awarded. Bachelor's degrees are awarded in AGRICULTURE (agricultural business management, agricultural economics, forestry and related sciences, range/farm management, and soil science), BIOLOGICAL SCIENCE (biology/biological science), BUSINESS (accounting and business administration and management), COMMUNICATIONS AND THE ARTS (art, dramatic arts, English, and music), COMPUTER AND PHYSICAL SCIENCE (chemistry, computer science, mathematics, and physics), EDUCATION (education and physical education), HEALTH PROFESSIONS (health and nursing), SOCIAL SCIENCE (anthropology, history, liberal arts/general studies, psychology, and sociology).

Required: Students must complete 180 credit hours, including 60 hours of general education courses that include 15 hours each of social science, natural science, humanities, art-language, and logic, with a GPA of at least 2.0. They must demonstrate computer competency and pass a writing proficiency exam. A senior capstone experience is required.

Special: There are cooperative and 3-2 engineering degree programs with Oregon State University. The university offers internships, work-study with federal agencies, accelerated degree program, student-designed and dual majors, study abroad in 8 countries, a general studies degree, B.A.-B.S. degrees, a multidisciplinary degree, numerous pre-professional programs, credit by exam and for life/military/work experience, external degrees, and pass/fail options. The university also serves students with course work via telecommunications and video and with a weekend University. There are 6 national honor societies, including Phi Beta Kappa, and 6 departmental honors programs.

Faculty/Classroom: No introductory courses are taught by graduate students. The average class size in an introductory lecture is 60; in a laboratory, 20; and in a regular course, 35.

Requirements: The SAT or ACT is required. A GED is accepted. Applicants must complete 14 academic credits, including 4 years of English, 3 each of math and social studies, and 2 of science. A GPA of 3.0 is required. AP and CLEP credits are accepted. Important factors in the admissions decision are extracurricular activities record and geographical diversity.

Procedure: Freshmen are admitted to all sessions. Entrance exams should be taken in the senior year. There are deferred admissions and rolling admissions plans. Check with the school for current application deadlines. There is no application fee. Notification is sent on a rolling basis.

Transfer: Applicants must have 30 credits of transferable academic work with a GPA of 2.25. 45 of 180 credits required for the bachelor's degree must be completed at EOU.

Visiting: There are regularly scheduled orientations for prospective students, including a campus tour, academic advising, and information sessions on financial aid and residence life. There are guides for informal visits; visitors may sit in on classes and stay overnight. To schedule a visit, contact Admissions/New Student Programs.

Financial Aid: EOU is a member of CSS. The FAFSA is required. Check with the school for application deadlines.

International Students: International students must take the TOEFL with a score of 70 on the Internet-based version (iBT), or the IELTS with a score of 6.

Admissions Contact: Director of Admissions. E-Mail: *admissions@eou.edu* Web: *www.eou.edu*

GEORGE FOX UNIVERSITY B-2

Newberg, OR 97132 **(503) 554-2240**
(800) 765-4369; (503) 554-3110

Full-time: 919 men, 1189 women	**Faculty:** 110; IIA, --$
Part-time: 104 men, 171 women	**Ph.D.s:** 75%
Graduate: 594 men, 708 women	**Student/Faculty:** 14 to 1
Year: semesters, summer session	**Tuition:** $31,120
Application Deadline: February 1	**Room & Board:** $9630

Freshman Class: 2432 applied, 1830 accepted, 619 enrolled
SAT CR/M/W: 540/530/520 **ACT:** 23 **COMPETITIVE+**

George Fox University, founded in 1891, is a Christian university of the humanities, sciences and professional studies. It offers bachelor's degrees in more than 40 majors, adult degree programs, five seminary degrees, and 12 master's and doctoral degrees at its main campus in Newberg, Oregon, and at teaching centers in Portland and Salem, Oregon. There are 6 undergraduate schools and 4 graduate schools. In addition to regional accreditation, George Fox has baccalaureate program accreditation with ABET, ACBSP, CSWE, NASM, and NCATE. The 2 libraries contain 174,988 volumes, 210,708 microform items, and 5,372 audio/video tapes/CDs/DVDs, subscribe to 60,000 periodicals including electronic. Computerized library services include interlibrary loans, database searching, Internet access, and Wi-Fi capability. Special learning facilities include an art gallery, radio station, a television production studio, a pottery kiln, physical therapy, nursing and engineering labs. The 85-acre campus is in a small town 23 miles southwest of Portland. Including any residence halls, there are 80 buildings.

Student Life: 65% of undergraduates are from Oregon. Others are from 27 states, 17 foreign countries, and Canada. 72% are from public schools. 71% are White. 82% are Protestant; 14% claim no religious affiliation. The average age of freshmen is 18; all undergraduates, 21. 18% do not continue beyond their first year; 62% remain to graduate.

Housing: 1211 students can be accommodated in college housing, which includes single-sex dorms and on-campus apartments. In addition, there are special-interest houses. On-campus housing is available on a first-come, first-served basis, and is available on a lottery system for upperclassmen. 56% of students live on campus; of those, 60% remain on campus on weekends. Alcohol is not permitted. All students may keep cars.

Activities: There are no fraternities or sororities. There are 20 groups on campus, including art, band, choir, chorale, chorus, computers, debate, drama, ethnic, film, forensics, honors, international, jazz band, literary magazine, musical theater, newspaper, orchestra, outdoor club, pep band, political, professional, radio and TV, religious, social, social service, student government, symphony, and yearbook. Popular campus events include Serve Day, Juniors Abroad, and Cultural Celebration Week.

Sports: There are 7 intercollegiate sports for men and 8 for women, and 7 intramural sports for men and 7 for women. Facilities include an all-weather track, a fitness center, tennis and handball/racquetball courts, a climbing wall, a 2500-seat gym, and baseball, softball, and soccer fields.

Disabled Students: All of the campus is accessible. Facilities include wheelchair ramps, elevators, special parking, specially equipped restrooms, special class scheduling, lowered drinking fountains, lowered telephones, and special housing.

Services: Counseling and information services are available, as is tutoring in most subjects. There is a reader service for the blind, and remedial math, reading, and writing.

Campus Safety and Security: Measures include 24-hour foot and vehicle patrol, emergency notification system, self-defense education, and security escort services. There are emergency telephones, lighted pathways/sidewalks, controlled access to dorms/residences, parking lot cameras, and video surveillance of key buildings.

Programs of Study: George Fox confers B.A., B.S., B.S.A.T. and B.S.W. degrees. Master's and doctoral degrees are also awarded. Bachelor's degrees are awarded in BIOLOGICAL SCIENCE (biology/biological science), BUSINESS (accounting, business administration and management, business communications, management information systems, management science, and organizational leadership and management), COMMUNICATIONS AND THE ARTS (art, communications, creative writing, dramatic arts, film arts, literature, multimedia, music, and Spanish), COMPUTER AND PHYSICAL SCIENCE (chemistry, computer science, information sciences and systems, and mathematics), EDUCATION (athletic training, elementary education, and music education), ENGINEERING AND ENVIRONMENTAL DESIGN (engineering and applied science), HEALTH PROFESSIONS (allied health, health, health care administration, nursing, predentistry, premedicine, and preveterinary science), SOCIAL SCIENCE (behavioral science, biblical studies, cognitive science, economics, family/consumer studies, history, international studies, ministries, philosophy, political science/government, prelaw, psychology, religion, social science, social work, and sociology). Business, nursing, and elementary education have the largest enrollments.

Required: To graduate, students must have a minimum 2.0 GPA and complete 126 semester hours, including 15 hours of sciences, 11 hours of humanities, 10 hours of Bible and religion, 6 hours each of communication and global and cultural understanding, 3 hours of health and human performance, and a 3 hour senior capstone. Majors require a minimum of 36 hours. A thesis is required in biology, chemistry, and social and behavioral sciences.

Special: Half of George Fox students participate in study abroad programs, which include a three-week faculty-led, subsidized trip in the spring of a student's junior year. The university offers a dual-degree 3/2 program through its applied science major, enabling students to pursue engineering in a discipline such as chemical, environmental or aerospace engineering. Students can complete a semester at the Contemporary Music Center in Martha's Vineyard or the Los Angeles Film Studies Center. George Fox offers internships with area companies, study abroad, and a Washington semester through the Council of Christian Colleges and Universities. Work-study programs, accelerated degrees, dual and student-designed interdisciplinary majors, and pass/fail options in upper-division courses outside of the major also are offered. There are 3 national honor societies, a freshman honors program, and 1 departmental honors program.

Faculty/Classroom: 55% of faculty are male; 45% are female. 64% teach undergraduates. No introductory courses are taught by graduate students. The average class size in an introductory lecture is 36; in a laboratory is 17; and in a regular course is 20.

Admissions: 75% of the 2013-2014 applicants were accepted. The SAT scores for the 2013-2014 freshman class were: Critical Reading--27% below 500, 37% between 500 and 599, 21% between 600 and 699, and 5% between 700 and 800; Math--33% below 500, 40% between 500 and 599, 23% between 600 and 699, and 4% between 700 and 800; Writing--40% below 500, 37% between 500 and 599, 20% between 600 and 699, and 3% between 700 and 800. The ACT scores were 35% below 21, 21% between 21 and 23, 22% between 24 and 26, 8% between 27 and 28, and 13% above 28. 49% of the current freshmen were in the top fifth of their class; 77% were in the top two fifths. 36 freshmen graduated first in their class.

Requirements: The SAT or ACT is required. Applicants need 16 academic credits or 14 Carnegie units, including a suggested 4 units of English, 3 units of social studies, 2 units each of a foreign language, math, and science, and 1 unit of health and physical education. An essay and 2 personal recommendations are required; a portfolio, audition, and interview are recommended in certain majors. A GPA of 2.6 is required. AP and CLEP credits are accepted. Important factors in the admissions decision are advanced placement or honors courses, extracurricular activities record, and leadership record.

Procedure: Freshmen are admitted fall and spring. Entrance exams should be taken in fall or winter. There are early admissions, deferred admissions, and rolling admissions plans. Applications should be filed by February 1 for fall entry; December 1 for spring entry, along with a $40 fee. Notification is sent on a rolling basis. Applications are accepted online.

Transfer: 105 transfer students enrolled in 2012-2013. Transfers must have a minimum 2.6 GPA and 16 semester hours from their previous college. An essay and two personal recommendations are required. 30 of 126 credits required for the bachelor's degree must be completed at George Fox.

Visiting: There are regularly scheduled orientations for prospective students, including observation of classes and talking with professors. There are guides for informal visits, visitors may sit in on classes, and stay overnight. To schedule a visit, contact the Office of Admissions.

Financial Aid: In 2013-2014, 100% of all full-time freshmen and 98% of continuing full-time students received some form of financial aid. 81% of all full-time freshmen and 71% of continuing full-time students received need-based aid. The average freshman award was $28,270. Need-based scholarships or need-based grants averaged $9,606; need-based self-help aid (loans and jobs) averaged $3,704; and other non-need-based awards and non-need-based scholarships averaged $14,960. George Fox is a member of CSS. The FAFSA and the state aid form are required. The priority date for freshman financial aid applications for fall entry is February 1.

International Students: There are 150 international students enrolled. The school actively recruits these students. They must take the TOEFL with a minimum score of 550 on the paper-based TOEFL (PBT) or 80 on the Internet-based version (iBT) and the college's own test.

Graduates: From July 1, 2012 to June 30, 2013, 593 bachelor's degrees were awarded. The most popular majors were business (25%), interdisciplinary studies (12%), and visual and performing arts (7%). 275 companies recruited on campus in 2012-2013. In an average class, 2% graduate in 3 years or less, 50% graduate in 4 years or less, 62% graduate in 5 years or less, and 64% graduate in 6 years or less.

Admissions Contact: Lindsay Knox, Director of Undergraduate Admissions. E-Mail: *admissions@georgefox.edu* Web: *www.georgefox.edu*

LEWIS & CLARK COLLEGE

B-1

Portland, OR 97219

(503) 768-7040
(800) 444-4111; (503) 768-7055

Full-time: 846 men, 1240 women	**Faculty:** 129
Part-time: 22 men, 18 women	**Ph.D.s:** 95%
Graduate: 508 men, 884 women	**Student/Faculty:** 12 to 1
Year: semesters, summer session	**Tuition:** $41,928
Application Deadline: January 15	**Room & Board:** $10,728

Freshman Class: 6459 applied, 4059 accepted, 473 enrolled

VERY COMPETITIVE

Lewis & Clark College, founded in 1867, is a private, independent liberal arts and sciences institution with a global reach. There is 1 undergraduate school and 2 graduate schools. In addition to regional accreditation, L & C has baccalaureate program accreditation with NCATE. The 2 libraries contain 586,144 volumes, 1.5 million microform items, and 23,851 audio/video tapes/CDs/DVDs, and subscribe to 42,560 periodicals including electronic. Computerized library services include interlibrary loans, database searching, Internet access, and Wi-Fi capability. Special learning facilities include an art gallery, radio station, telescope, research astronomical observatory, language lab, greenhouse, and adaptive technology lab. The 137-acre campus is in a suburban area 6 miles south of downtown Portland. Including any residence halls, there are 58 buildings.

Student Life: 88% of undergraduates are from out of state, mostly the West. Students are from 47 states, 78 foreign countries, and Canada. 76% are from public schools. 61% are White; 12% race unknown. 66% claim no religious affiliation. The average age of freshmen is 18; all undergraduates, 20. 13% do not continue beyond their first year; 74% remain to graduate.

Housing: 1394 students can be accommodated in college housing, which includes single-sex and coed dorms and on-campus apartments. In addition, there are language houses, special interest houses, theme communities. On-campus housing is guaranteed for the freshman year only and is available on a lottery system for upperclassmen. 65% of students live on campus. Upperclassmen may keep cars.

Activities: There are no fraternities or sororities. There are 70 groups on campus, including and college outdoors, art, band, choir, chorale, chorus, computers, dance, debate, drama, ethnic, film, forensics, gay, honors, international, jazz band, literary magazine, meridian journal of international and cross-cultural perspectives, newspaper, orchestra, photography, political, professional, radio and TV, religious, social, social service, student government, and symphony. Popular campus events include Gender Studies Symposium, International Affairs Symposium, and Environmental Studies Symposium.

Sports: There are 9 intercollegiate sports for men and 10 for women, and 19 intramural sports for men and 19 for women. Facilities include The main gymnasium in Pamplin Sports Center has three full basketball courts which also serve as volleyball courts and indoor practice facilities for several intercollegiate teams. The gym seats 2,300 in comfortable padded bleachers. The Pamplin Sports Center houses a 3,600-square-foot, fully equipped Weight Room. Eldon Fix Track and Fred Wilson Field at Griswold Stadium is located immediately west of the Sports Center. More than half of Griswold's 3,600 seats are under cover. The field features a state-of-the art Astro-Turf Game Day 3D Synthetic Surface. The Zehntbauer Swimming Pavilion, which houses an eight-lane, 25-yard pool with one and three-meter diving boards. The pavilion, with its fully automatic Colorado timing system, has been the site of an NAIA National Swimming Championship meet.

Disabled Students: 80% of the campus is accessible. Facilities include wheelchair ramps, elevators, special parking, specially equipped restrooms, special class scheduling, lowered drinking fountains, and lowered telephones.

Services: Counseling and information services are available, as is tutoring in every subject. There is a reader service for the blind. There are mentors, note takers, books on tape, and math and writing skills centers.

Campus Safety and Security: Measures include 24-hour foot and vehicle patrol, emergency notification system, self-defense education, and security escort services. There are shuttle buses, emergency telephones, lighted pathways/sidewalks, controlled access to dorms/residences, card key locks in all residence halls.

Programs of Study: L & C confers B.A. degrees. Master's and doctoral degrees are also awarded. Bachelor's degrees are awarded in AGRICULTURE (environmental studies), BIOLOGICAL SCIENCE (biochemistry and biology/biological science), COMMUNICATIONS AND THE ARTS (art history and appreciation, classics, communications, dramatic arts, English, fine arts, languages, music, and studio art), COMPUTER AND PHYSICAL SCIENCE (chemistry, computer mathematics, computer science, mathematics, and physics), SOCIAL SCIENCE (anthropology, East Asian studies, economics, French studies, German area studies, Hispanic American studies, history, interdisciplinary studies, international relations, philosophy, political science/government, psychology, religion, and sociology). Psychology, biology, sociology/anthropology, international affairs, and English, art have the largest enrollments.

Required: To graduate, students must complete a total of 128 semester hours with a 2.0 GPA. A third of this total generally falls in the major program, a third in electives, and a third in general requirements, which includes a required first-year course, 12 hours in scientific and quantitative reasoning, 8 hours in international studies, 3 semesters of a foreign language, 2 semesters of phys ed, and 1 course in creative arts. Certain majors require a thesis or a senior project/recital.

Special: L & C offers cross-registration with the Oregon Independent College Association, which includes Reed College and the University of Portland; internships; study-abroad programs in 60 countries; semesters in Washington and New York City; and dual and student-designed majors. A 3-2 engineering program is available with Columbia and Washington Universities, the University of Southern California. There are 5 national honor societies and including Phi Beta Kappa.

Faculty/Classroom: 50% of faculty are male; 50% are female. No introductory courses are taught by graduate students.

Admissions: 63% of the 2013-2014 applicants were accepted.

Requirements: When admitting new students, our admissions staff look for individuals from diverse backgrounds, with diverse talents and interests – students who will not only meet the rigorous academic challenges of a Lewis & Clark education, but will also take full advantage of the opportunities for individual achievement and growth offered here. Academic Preparation Your high school course load (grades 9-12) should include a minimum of: 4 years of English, 4 years of Mathematics 3-4 years of history and social sciences, 2-3 years of a foreign language, 3 years of lab sciences, 1 year of creative arts Advanced Placement, International Baccalaureate, or honors courses are viewed as further evidence of serious preparation for college-level studies. Successful candidates have taken some of these advanced courses if they are offered at their schools. We look not only at your performance in a challenging curriculum, but at the following criteria as well: SAT or ACT scores (unless applying through the Portfolio Path), Counselor Report (first-year students only) Teacher Recommendation, Personal Essay, Leadership, community service and work experience, and extracurricular involvements, Expressed interest in the College or personal interview (interviews are optional, not required) The committee weighs all of these factors to make a prediction about an applicant's potential for academic success at Lewis & Clark. We want to make sure that any student who has the opportunity to enroll at the College will have the tools they need to flourish in and enjoy our academic program. The committee also looks for students who will contribute to our community – as musicians, leaders, athletes, or community service participants, just to name a few – while they are succeeding academically. A GPA of 2.0 is required. AP credits are accepted.

Procedure: Freshmen are admitted fall and spring. Entrance exams should be taken during spring of the junior year or fall of the senior year. Early decision applications should be filed by November 1; regular applications, by January 15 for fall entry. Notification of early decision is sent December 31; regular decision, April 1. 509 applicants were on the 2013 waiting list; 56 were admitted. Applications are accepted online. Application fees are waived if application is completed online.

Transfer: 46 transfer students enrolled in 2012-2013. Applicants must

submit high school and college transcripts, 2 essays. SAT or ACT scores are required for transfers with fewer than 2 years of transferable credit (60 semester units) 60 of 128 credits required for the bachelor's degree must be completed at L & C.

Visiting: There are regularly scheduled orientations for prospective students, including campus tours, class visits, interviews, special-interest appointments, and 4 open house events. Visitors may sit in on classes and stay overnight. To schedule a visit, contact the Office of Admissions.

Financial Aid: In 2013-2014, 90% of all full-time freshmen and 92% of continuing full-time students received some form of financial aid. 59% of all full-time freshmen and 67% of continuing full-time students received need-based aid. The average freshman award was $28,535. Need-based scholarships or need-based grants averaged $26,945; need-based self-help aid (loans and jobs) averaged $6,233; and other non-need-based awards and non-need-based scholarships averaged $11,869. The average financial indebtedness of the 2013 graduate was $25,134. The CSS/Profile and FAFSA are required. The priority date for freshman financial aid applications for fall entry is February 15.

International Students: There are 207 international students enrolled. The school actively recruits these students. They must take the TOEFL with a minimum score of 575 on the paper-based TOEFL (PBT) or 91 on the Internet-based version (iBT) or take the MELAB, ELPT, or IB English. They must also take the SAT or ACT.

Graduates: From July 1, 2012 to June 30, 2013, 432 bachelor's degrees were awarded. The most popular majors were psychology (14%), sociology/anthropology (8%), and international affairs (8%). 100 companies recruited on campus in 2012-2013. In an average class, 1% graduate in 3 years or less, 68% graduate in 4 years or less, 75% graduate in 5 years or less, and 76% graduate in 6 years or less.

Admissions Contact: Erica Johnson, Director of Admissions. E-Mail: *admissions@lclark.edu* Web: *www.lclark.edu*

LINFIELD COLLEGE-MCMINNVILLE CAMPUS B-2

McMinnville, OR 97128
(503) 883-2213
(800) 640-2287; (503) 883-2472

Full-time: 650 men, 980 women	**Faculty:** 119; IIB, av$
Part-time: 19 men, 22 women	**Ph.D.s:** 93%
Graduate: n/av	**Student/Faculty:** 14 to 1
Year: 4-1-4, summer session	**Tuition:** $36,240
Application Deadline: February 15	**Room & Board:** $9926
Freshman Class: 2139 applied, 1972 accepted, 449 enrolled	
SAT CR/M/W: 530/550/520 **ACT:** 23	**COMPETITIVE**

Linfield College is dedicated exclusively to undergraduate education, and is home to a vibrant community of engaged students. Located in the beautiful Pacific Northwest, the small college offers degrees in the arts, sciences and professional programs. Linfield is a friendly community, where professors know their students' names and help them develop the professional skills and leadership qualities that prepare them for successful careers. The student-faculty ratio of 12:1 allows for a rich education experience that includes collaborative research, creative projects, internships, community service and study abroad; half of all graduates have studied outside the U.S. Linfield welcomes students from diverse backgrounds. The school offers 47 majors and enrolls more than 2,600 students through three programs: a residential liberal arts and sciences program in McMinnville, Ore., the Linfield-Good Samaritan School of Nursing in Portland, Ore., and the Adult Degree Program, which supports students at eight Oregon sites and serves a virtual learning community across the globe. Linfield has been nationally praised for combining affordability and excellence. There are 3 undergraduate schools. In addition to regional accreditation, Linfield has baccalaureate program accreditation with NASM. The library contains 184,441 volumes, 17,491 microform items, 38,152 audio/video tapes/CDs/DVDs, and subscribes to 985 periodicals including electronic. Computerized library services include interlibrary loans, database searching, Internet access, and Wi-Fi capability. Special learning facilities include an art gallery, radio station, Linfield Center for the Northwest, Delkin Recital Hall, Ford Theatre, Linfield Research Institute, Linfield Art Gallery, Linfield Anthropology Museum, Writing Center, Career Development Center, Speaking Center, Academic Advising Office, multimedia studio, science and computer labs. The 189-acre campus is in a small town 40 miles southwest of Portland. Including any residence halls, there are 78 buildings.

Student Life: 51% of undergraduates are from out of state, mostly the Northwest. Students are from 23 states, and 22 foreign countries. 90% are from public schools. 63% are White. The average age of freshmen is 18; all undergraduates, 20. 20% do not continue beyond their first year; 67% remain to graduate.

Housing: 1329 students can be accommodated in college housing, which includes single-sex and coed dorms and on-campus apartments. In addition, there are special-interest houses. On-campus housing is guaranteed for all 4 years. 74% of students live on campus; of those, 80% remain on campus on weekends. All students may keep cars.

Activities: 22% of men belong to 1 local and 3 national fraternities; 25% of women belong to 1 local and 3 national sororities. There are 40 groups on campus, including and others, the Hawaiian Club, Ultimate Frisbee, art, ASL, band, cheerleading, choir, chorale, chorus, computers, dance, debate, drama, environmental, ethnic, forensics, gay, honors, international, jazz band, literary magazine, musical theater, newspaper, opera, orchestra, pep band, photography, political, professional, radio and TV, religious, social, social service, student government, and symphony. Popular campus events include Wildstock (outdoor fair, including music and activities booths), Luau, Hispanic Heritage Day and Homecoming,.

Sports: There are 9 intercollegiate sports for men and 10 for women, and 6 intramural sports for men and 6 for women. Facilities include Football stadium with turf field, all-weather track, soccer field with lights, indoor complex with 2,200-seat gym, 3 basketball courts, 25-yard swimming pool, 2 racquetball courts, 6,000-square-foot weight room, baseball stadium with turf infield and lights, softball stadium with lights, field house with 3 tennis courts and 4 hitting cages, Linfield Wellness Trail, and Linfield Bike Co-op.

Disabled Students: 85% of the campus is accessible. Facilities include wheelchair ramps, elevators, special parking, specially equipped restrooms, special class scheduling, lowered drinking fountains, lowered telephones, and special housing.

Services: Counseling and information services are available, as is tutoring in every subject. There is a reader service for the blind. There is also the Linfield Speaking Center and Linfield Writing Lab.

Campus Safety and Security: Measures include 24-hour foot and vehicle patrol, emergency notification system, self-defense education, and security escort services. There are emergency telephones, lighted pathways/sidewalks, and controlled access to dorms/residences.

Programs of Study: Linfield confers B.A., B.S. and B.S.N. degrees. Bachelor's degrees are awarded in AGRICULTURE (environmental studies), BIOLOGICAL SCIENCE (biochemistry and biology/biological science), BUSINESS (accounting, banking and finance, business administration and management, international business management, and marketing management), COMMUNICATIONS AND THE ARTS (art, communications, creative writing, dramatic arts, English, French, french and francophone studies, German, Japanese, journalism, music, Spanish, studio art, and theatre arts), COMPUTER AND PHYSICAL SCIENCE (applied physics, chemistry, computer science, mathematics, physics, and science), EDUCATION (athletic training, elementary education, health education, music education, and physical education), HEALTH PROFESSIONS (exercise science and nursing), SOCIAL SCIENCE (anthropology, crosscultural studies, economics, German area studies, history, international relations, Japanese studies, philosophy, political science/government, psychology, religion, and sociology). Nursing, accounting, management, exercise science, elementary education, and psychology are the strongest academically. Nursing, accounting, and exercise science have the largest enrollments.

Required: To graduate, students must maintain 2.0 cumulative GPA and complete 125 credit hours, including 35 to 45 in the major. Core requirements include courses from the sciences, literature, fine arts, religion or philosophy, the social sciences, history, and quantitative reasoning. An inquiry seminar in critical thinking and writing is also required. Students must also take courses in American pluralism and global diversity and also 3 credits of activity courses (phys ed, music, or community service).

Special: Linfield is highly ranked among U.S. undergraduate schools for participation in study abroad. Through Linfield's January Term and Semester Abroad programs, students study in 30 locations around the globe, including China, Africa, Europe and Southeast Asia. During the past five years, almost 700 students completed internships off campus, many in the industry of their choice. Some students intern abroad through the IE3 Global Internships program, and others take advantage of off-campus work-study programs that target literacy and disadvantaged youth. Last year more than 50 students collaborated on research projects with their professors, and many presented papers at professional conferences. Education is personalized, and student-designed majors are available. In addition to Linfield's campus-based programs, online degrees and certificates are available, including accelerated degrees. Students are also offered a 3-2 engineering degree as part of a collaboration with the University of Southern California and Oregon and Washington State Universities. Students partner with more than 100 community-based organizations for service learning, sponsored through Linfield's Community Engagement and Service Office. Many outreach projects lead to job opportunities. New students are introduced to college with rich immersion experiences that include First CLAS (Community, Leadership, Action, and Service) and iFocus (for those interested in the sciences) as well as Colloquium and Inquiry Seminars for all. Many also choose to get to know their faculty through the "Take a Professor to Lunch" program. There are 19 national honor societies and 13 departmental honors programs.

Faculty/Classroom: 53% of faculty are male; 47% are female. All teach and do research. No introductory courses are taught by graduate students. The average class size in a regular course is 17.

Admissions: 92% of the 2013-2014 applicants were accepted. The

SAT scores for the 2013-2014 freshman class were: Critical Reading--29% below 500, 43% between 500 and 599, 21% between 600 and 699, and 6% between 700 and 800; Math--24% below 500, 47% between 500 and 599, 26% between 600 and 699, and 3% between 700 and 800; Writing--35% below 500, 48% between 500 and 599, 15% between 600 and 699, and 2% between 700 and 800. The ACT scores were 32% below 21, 20% between 21 and 23, 26% between 24 and 26, 11% between 27 and 28, and 11% above 28.

Requirements: The SAT or ACT is required. Applicants should have 4 years each of English and math, 3 to 4 years each of natural science and social studies, and 2 to 4 years of a foreign language. An essay is required, and an interview is recommended. The GED is accepted. AP and CLEP credits are accepted. Important factors in the admissions decision are advanced placement or honors courses, evidence of special talent, and recommendations by school officials.

Procedure: Freshmen are admitted fall and spring. Entrance exams should be taken during the fall of the senior year of high school. There are early admissions and deferred admissions plans. Applications should be filed by February 15 for fall entry; December 1 for spring entry. Notifications are sent April 1. Applications are accepted online. Application fees are waived if application is completed online.

Transfer: 66 transfer students enrolled in 2012-2013. Applicants must have a minimum 2.0 GPA from an accredited institution to be considered. An interview is also recommended. 30 of 125 credits required for the bachelor's degree must be completed at Linfield.

Visiting: There are regularly scheduled orientations for prospective students, including tours and interviews. There are guides for informal visits, visitors may sit in on classes, and stay overnight. To schedule a visit, contact the Office of Admission.

Financial Aid: In 2013-2014, 98% of all full-time freshmen and 96% of continuing full-time students received some form of financial aid. 78% of all full-time freshmen and 74% of continuing full-time students received need-based aid. The average freshman award was $27,563. Need-based scholarships or need-based grants averaged $24,445; need-based self-help aid (loans and jobs) averaged $6,726; and other non-need-based awards and non-need-based scholarships averaged $17,190. 98% of undergraduate students work part-time. Average annual earnings from campus work are $1500. The average financial indebtedness of the 2013 graduate was $27,955. Linfield is a member of CSS. The FAFSA, and FAFSA Forecaster for Early Action only is required. The priority date for freshman financial aid applications for fall entry is February 1.

International Students: There are 78 international students enrolled. The school actively recruits these students. They must take the TOEFL with a minimum score of 550 on the paper-based TOEFL (PBT) or 80 on the Internet-based version (iBT) or take the MELAB and the college's own test.

Graduates: From July 1, 2012 to June 30, 2013, 288 bachelor's degrees were awarded. The most popular majors were business/marketing (21%), education (12%), and social sciences (10%). In an average class, 1% graduate in 3 years or less, 59% graduate in 4 years or less, 66% graduate in 5 years or less, and 67% graduate in 6 years or less. Of the 2012 graduating class, 10% were enrolled in graduate school within 6 months of graduation, and 75% were employed.

Admissions Contact: Lisa Knodle-Bragiel, Director of Admission. E-Mail: *admission@linfield.edu* Web: *www.linfield.edu*

MARYLHURST UNIVERSITY B-2

Marylhurst, OR 97036 (503) 699-6268
(800) 634-9982; (503) 635-6585

Full-time: n/av	**Faculty:** n/av
Part-time: n/av	**Ph.D.s:** n/av
Graduate: n/av	**Student/Faculty:** 7 to 1
Year: quarters, summer session	**Tuition:** $18,945
Application Deadline: open	**Room & Board:** n/app
Freshman Class: n/av	

NONCOMPETITIVE

Marylhurst University is a liberal arts university rooted in the values of its Catholic heritage that transforms the lives of serious, multigenerational learners through rigorous, relevant learning experiences on a historic campus and online. There are 2 undergraduate schools and 2 graduate schools. In addition to regional accreditation, Marylhurst has baccalaureate program accreditation with NASM. The library contains 95,320 volumes, 179 microform items, 5,250 audio/video tapes/CDs/DVDs, and subscribes to 403 periodicals including electronic. Computerized library services include interlibrary loans, database searching, Internet access, and Wi-Fi capability. Special learning facilities include an art gallery. The 68-acre campus is in a suburban area in the Portland metro area. Including any residence halls, there are 14 buildings.

Student Life: 73% are White. The average age of all undergraduates is 36.

Housing: College-sponsored housing includes coed Priority is given to out-of-town students. Alcohol is not permitted. All students commute. All students may keep cars.

Activities: There are no fraternities or sororities. There are 6 groups on campus, including chorale and symphony.

Sports: There is no sports program at Marylhurst.

Disabled Students: Facilities include wheelchair ramps, elevators, special parking, specially equipped restrooms, special class scheduling, and lowered drinking fountains.

Services: Counseling and information services are available, as is tutoring in some subjects, math and writing There is a reader service for the blind.

Campus Safety and Security: Measures include 24-hour foot and vehicle patrol. There are lighted pathways/sidewalks.

Programs of Study: Marylhurst confers B.A., B.S., B.F.A., B.Music, and B.Music Therapy degrees. Master's degrees are also awarded. Bachelor's degrees are awarded in BUSINESS (business administration and management, management science, real estate, and sustainable management), COMMUNICATIONS AND THE ARTS (art, communications, English literature, English Writing, fine arts, media arts, and music), COMPUTER AND PHYSICAL SCIENCE (science), HEALTH PROFESSIONS (music therapy), SOCIAL SCIENCE (human development, interdisciplinary studies, ministries, psychology, religion, and social science). Business, Interdisciplinary Studies have the largest enrollments.

Required: To earn an undergraduate degree, a student must fulfill the following requirements: Complete a minimum of 180 credits. Complete a minimum of 60 upper-division credits (courses numbered 300 or above). Complete a minimum of 45 residency credits (credits taken at Marylhurst University), including at least 15 credits in each major and at least 9 credits in each minor. Earn a cumulative 2.00 GPA or higher in all coursework taken at Marylhurst. Earn a cumulative 2.00 GPA or higher in all majors and minors (coursework taken at Marylhurst). Complete all requirements of the Marylhurst Core. Complete all requirements of the major and any minors or concentrations.

Special: Classes offered evenings, weekends, and online, accelerated online degree programs in business and real-estate, credit for prior learning, internships, cooperative programs with Montessori Northwest and the Northwest Film Center. There is 1 departmental honors program.

Faculty/Classroom: 42% of faculty are male; 58% are female. No introductory courses are taught by graduate students. The average class size in an introductory lecture is 8 and in a regular course is 8.

Requirements: Minimum high school GPA of 2.50 or average GED score of 500. To best prepare for studies at Marylhurst, it is preferred that a student's high school curriculum include four years of English, three years of math, three years of natural science and three years of social sciences. Minimum GPA of 2.25 and successful academic progress in any college and university coursework. Statement of intent. Letter of recommendation from an academic reference. Participate in an interview with the admissions committee. A GPA of 2.5 is required. AP and CLEP credits are accepted.

Procedure: Freshmen are admitted to all sessions. There is a rolling admissions plan. Application deadlines are open. Application fee is $50. Notification is sent on a rolling basis. Applications are accepted online.

Transfer: 400 transfer students enrolled in 2012-2013. Minimum GPA of 2.25 and successful academic progress in all college and university coursework. Statement of intent. If fewer than 45 quarter credits, minimum high school GPA of 2.50 or average GED score of 500. If fewer than 20 college credits, letter of recommendation from an academic reference (if graduated from high school less than three years ago) and interview. 45 of 180 credits required for the bachelor's degree must be completed at Marylhurst.

Visiting: There are regularly scheduled orientations for prospective students, campus tour, registration and financial aid, academic advising, library, cafeteria, and bookstore. There are guides for informal visits and visitors may sit in on classes. To schedule a visit, contact Admissions Department at admissions@marylhurst.edu.

Financial Aid: The FAFSA, and institutional application is required. Check with the school for current application deadlines.

International Students: There are 18 international students enrolled. They must take the TOEFL with a minimum score of 79 on the Internet-based version (iBT).

Graduates: From July 1, 2012 to June 30, 2013, 202 bachelor's degrees were awarded. The most popular majors were business (35%), interdisciplinary studies (12%), and real estate (10%).

Admissions Contact: Chris Sweet, Director of Admissions. E-Mail: *admissions@marylhurst.edu* Web: *www.marylhurst.edu*

NORTHWEST CHRISTIAN UNIVERSITY B-2

Eugene, OR 97401-3727 (541) 684-7201
(877) 463-6622; (541) 684-7317

Full-time: 150 men, 250 women
Part-time: 10 men, 20 women
Graduate: 50 men, 50 women
Year: trimesters, summer session
Application Deadline: see profile
Freshman Class: n/av
SAT or ACT: required
Faculty: n/av
Ph.D.s: n/av
Student/Faculty: n/av
Tuition: $24,100
Room & Board: $7900

COMPETITIVE

Northwest Christian University was founded in 1895 and is a private institution affiliated with the Christian Church, offering programs in the arts and sciences, business, education, and ministries. Enrollment figures in the above capsule and figures in this profile are approximate. The library contains 60,250 volumes, 766 microform items, 10,367 audio/video tapes/CDs/DVDs, and subscribes to 261 periodicals including electronic. Computerized library services include interlibrary loans, database searching, and Internet access. Special learning facilities include a learning resource center. The 8-acre campus is in an urban area 125 miles south of Portland. Including any residence halls, there are 14 buildings.

Student Life: 92% of undergraduates are from Oregon. Others are from 8 states. 94% are from public schools. 70% are white. 64% claim no religious affiliation; 35% Protestant. The average age of freshmen is 18; all undergraduates, 30.

Housing: 213 students can be accommodated in college housing, which includes single-sex and coed dorms and off-campus apartments. On-campus housing is guaranteed for the freshman year only. 73% of students commute. Alcohol is not permitted. All students may keep cars.

Activities: There are no fraternities or sororities. There are 15 groups on campus, including cheerleading, choir, chorale, debate, drama, forensics, literary magazine, musical theater, newspaper, religious, social service, student government, and yearbook. Popular campus events include Annual Musical, Spirit Week, and Wellness Week.

Sports: There is 1 intercollegiate sport for men and 2 for women, and 4 intramural sports for men and 4 for women. Facilities include an event center with a basketball court, fitness rooms, locker rooms, and a softball practice area.

Disabled Students: 60% of the campus is accessible. Facilities include wheelchair ramps, elevators, special parking, specially equipped rest rooms, special class scheduling, lowered drinking fountains, and lowered telephones.

Services: Counseling and information services are available, as is tutoring in most subjects. There is remedial math, reading, and writing.

Campus Safety and Security: Measures include 24-hour foot and vehicle patrol, security escort services, emergency telephones, and lighted pathways/sidewalks.

Programs of Study: NCU confers B.A. and B.S. degrees. Associate and master's degrees are also awarded. Bachelor's degrees are awarded in BUSINESS (accounting, business administration and management, and management information systems), COMMUNICATIONS AND THE ARTS (communications and music), COMPUTER AND PHYSICAL SCIENCE (computer science), EDUCATION (education and elementary education), HEALTH PROFESSIONS (exercise science and health care administration), SOCIAL SCIENCE (human services, humanities, interdisciplinary studies, international studies, ministries, psychology, and social science).

Required: To graduate, students must complete 124 to 186 quarter credits with at least 40 in the major and a minimum GPA of 2.0. The core curriculum consists of 55 to 86 credit hours in humanities, social sciences, math and science, and Bible; a 1 credit-hour chapel for every term enrolled is also required as are 3 service credits.

Special: NCU offers internships, study abroad in 4 countries, a Washington semester, work-study, accelerated degree programs, and student-designed majors.

Faculty/Classroom: No introductory courses are taught by graduate students. The average class size in an introductory lecture is 40 and in a regular course, 25.

Requirements: The SAT or ACT is required. Students are required to submit a completed admission application, high school transcripts, and 2 references. An interview is recommended. A GPA of 2.5 is required. AP and CLEP credits are accepted. Important factors in the admissions decision are advanced placement or honors courses, recommendations by school officials, and extracurricular activities record.

Procedure: Freshmen are admitted fall and spring. There are early admissions, deferred admissions, and rolling admissions plans. Check with the school for current application deadlines. Notification is sent on a rolling basis. Applications are accepted online.

Transfer: 55 transfer students enrolled in a recent year. Students are required to submit a completed application, official transcripts from each college or university attended, an academic reference, and official high school transcripts if they have fewer than 36 transferable credits. 30 of 124 credits required for the bachelor's degree must be completed at NCU.

Visiting: There are regularly scheduled orientations for prospective students. There are guides for informal visits; visitors may sit in on classes and stay overnight. To schedule a visit, contact Admissions.

Financial Aid: NCU is a member of CSS. The FAFSA and the college's own financial statement are required. Check with the school for current application deadlines.

International Students: International students must take the TOEFL with a score of 500 on the paper-based TOEFL (PBT) or 80 on the Internet-based version (iBT).

Admissions Contact: Director of Admissions. E-Mail: *admissions@nwcu.edu* Web: *www.nwcu.edu*

OREGON INSTITUTE OF TECHNOLOGY B-4

Klamath Falls, OR 97601-8801 (541) 885-1150
(800) 422-2017; (541) 885-1115

Full-time: 1120 men, 850 women
Part-time: 575 men, 560 women
Graduate: 15 men, 5 women
Year: trimesters, summer session
Application Deadline: see profile
Freshman Class: n/av
SAT or ACT: required
Faculty: n/av
Ph.D.s: n/av
Student/Faculty: n/av
Tuition: $7052 ($19,976)
Room & Board: $8900

COMPETITIVE

Oregon Institute of Technology provides degree programs in engineering and health technologies, management, communications, and applied sciences. There are 3 undergraduate schools and 1 graduate school. The figures in the above capsule and in this profile are approximate. In addition to regional accreditation, OIT has baccalaureate program accreditation with ABET and NLN. The library contains 145,988 volumes, 158,278 microform items, 2069 audio/video tapes/CDs/DVDs, and subscribes to 1815 periodicals including electronic. Computerized library services include interlibrary loans and database searching. Special learning facilities include a learning resource center, art gallery, and radio station. The 173-acre campus is in a small town 60 miles east of Medford in south central Oregon. Including any residence halls, there are 12 buildings.

Student Life: 85% of undergraduates are from Oregon. Others are from 35 states and 17 foreign countries. 95% are from public schools. 80% are white. The average age of freshmen is 23; all undergraduates, 26. 26% do not continue beyond their first year; 29% remain to graduate.

Housing: 500 students can be accommodated in college housing, which includes single-sex and coed dorms. On-campus housing is guaranteed for all 4 years. 82% of students commute. All students may keep cars.

Activities: 3% of men belong to 1 local and 1 national fraternity; 3% of women belong to 1 local and 1 national sorority. There are 37 groups on campus, including cheerleading, communications, computers, ethnic, honors, international, newspaper, outdoor, pep band, professional, radio and TV, religious, social, and student government. Popular campus events include Tech Challenge, Family Weekend Tech Fest, and a skills contest for business and math students.

Sports: There are 4 intercollegiate sports for men and 6 for women. Facilities include a 3000-seat stadium, a 2066-seat gym, football, baseball, and softball fields, free weights and aerobics areas, an indoor swimming pool, a track, and tennis, volleyball, basketball, and badminton courts.

Disabled Students: 90% of the campus is accessible. Facilities include wheelchair ramps, elevators, special parking, specially equipped rest rooms, and special class scheduling.

Services: Counseling and information services are available, as is tutoring in math, sciences, and computers. There is a reader service for the blind, and remedial math, reading, and writing.

Campus Safety and Security: Measures include 24-hour foot and vehicle patrol, security escort services, and lighted pathways/sidewalks.

Programs of Study: OIT confers B.S. degrees. Associate and master's degrees are also awarded. Bachelor's degrees are awarded in BUSINESS (management information systems), ENGINEERING AND ENVIRONMENTAL DESIGN (civil engineering, computer technology, electrical/electronics engineering technology, engineering technology, environmental science, industrial administration/management, laser electro-optics technology, manufacturing technology, mechanical engineering technology, and surveying engineering), HEALTH PROFESSIONS (dental hygiene, health science, radiograph medical technology, and ultrasound technology), SOCIAL SCIENCE (industrial and organizational psychology).

Required: General education requirements include 12 hours in social science and 9 hours each in communication, business, and humanities. Students also must take 9 hours in English composition and technical report writing. Completion of 200 quarter hours, with a minimum GPA of 2.0, is required to graduate.

Special: Cross-registration with Klamath Community College, internships in all majors, and co-op programs in all engineering technologies are available. OIT also offers advanced degree programs in software engineering technology and vascular imaging. There are 2 national honor societies.

Faculty/Classroom: No introductory courses are taught by graduate students. The average class size in an introductory lecture is 30; in a laboratory, 18; and in a regular course, 30.

Requirements: The SAT or ACT is required for placement purposes; however, a satisfactory composite score on the SAT or 21 on the ACT is required for applicants who do not meet the minimum GPA requirement. Applicants must have 14 academic units, including 4 years of English, 3 each of math and social sciences, and 2 each of science and a foreign language. The GED is accepted. A GPA of 2.5 is required. AP and CLEP credits are accepted.

Procedure: Freshmen are admitted to all sessions. Entrance exams should be taken during the senior year, and placement tests just prior to registration. There are early admissions and rolling admissions plans. Check with the school for current application deadlines. Application fee is $50. Notification is sent on a rolling basis.

Transfer: Applicants must have a minimum GPA of 2.0 and at least 24 quarter credit hours; students with fewer credit hours must submit high school transcripts or GED scores. An associate degree is recommended. 45 of 190 credits required for the bachelor's degree must be completed at OIT.

Visiting: There are regularly scheduled orientations for prospective students, including tours and meetings with admissions counselors, faculty, and students. There are guides for informal visits; visitors may sit in on classes and stay overnight. To schedule a visit, contact the Admissions Office.

Financial Aid: The FAFSA is required. Check with the school for current application deadlines.

International Students: The school actively recruits these students. They must take the TOEFL with a score of 520 on the paper-based TOEFL (PBT) or 68 on the Internet-based version (iBT), or the IELTS.

Admissions Contact: Director of Admissions. A campus DVD is available. E-Mail: *oit@oit.edu* Web: *www.oit.edu*

OREGON STATE UNIVERSITY — B-2

Corvallis, OR 97331 — **(541) 737-4411; (800) 291-4192**

Full-time: 10137 men, 8349 women	**Faculty:** 982; I, --$
Part-time: 2318 men, 2357 women	**Ph.D.s:** 85%
Graduate: 2442 men, 2322 women	**Student/Faculty:** 19 to 1
Year: quarters, summer session	**Tuition:** $8322 ($23,514)
Application Deadline: September 1	**Room & Board:** $10,695
Freshman Class: 14239 applied, 11303 accepted, 3970 enrolled	
SAT CR/M/W: 540/550/530 **ACT:** 24	**COMPETITIVE+**

Founded in 1868, Oregon State is the state's Land Grant university and is one of only two universities in the U.S. to have Sea Grant, Space Grant and Sun Grant designations. Oregon State is also the only university in Oregon to hold both the Carnegie Foundation's top designation for research institutions and its prestigious Community Engagement classification. There are 10 undergraduate schools and 12 graduate schools. In addition to regional accreditation, Oregon State has baccalaureate program accreditation with AACSB, ABET, ACCE, ACPE, AHEA, CSAB, NASM, NCATE, and SAF. The 4 libraries contain 2.0 million volumes, 2.2 million microform items, 27,256 audio/video tapes/CDs/DVDs, and subscribe to 107,975 periodicals including electronic. Computerized library services include interlibrary loans, database searching, Internet access, and Wi-Fi capability. Special learning facilities include an art gallery, natural history museum, radio station, TV station, an arboretum, a wave research lab, a research farm, research vessel, and the Linus Pauling Collection. The 400-acre campus is in a small town situated 90 miles south of Portland. Including any residence halls, there are 203 buildings.

Student Life: 75% of undergraduates are from Oregon. Others are from 50 states, 64 foreign countries, and Canada. 68% are White. The average age of freshmen is 19; all undergraduates, 23. 16% do not continue beyond their first year; 62% remain to graduate.

Housing: 4641 students can be accommodated in college housing, which includes coed dorms and married student housing. In addition, there are honors houses, special-interest houses, fraternity houses, sorority houses, Housing for international students and housing for entrepreneurship majors. On-campus housing is guaranteed for the freshman year only, is available on a first-come, and first-served basis. 78% of students commute. Alcohol is not permitted. All students may keep cars.

Activities: 13% of men belong to 23 national fraternities; 18% of women belong to 20 national sororities. There are 360 groups on campus, including and adventure club, art, band, cheerleading, chess, choir, chorale, chorus, communications, computers, dance, debate, drama, drill team, drum and bugle corps, environmental, ethnic, film, forensics, gay, honors, international, jazz band, literary magazine, marching band, musical theater, newspaper, orchestra, pep band, photography, political, professional, radio and TV, religious, social, social service, student government, student sustainability initiative, symphony, and yearbook. Popular campus events include Connect Week, Dads Weekend, Civil War, Moms Weekend, Battle of the Bands and Bard in the Quad.

Sports: There are 7 intercollegiate sports for men and 10 for women, and 19 intramural sports for men and 17 for women. Facilities include Dixon Recreation Center is one of the main social hubs of activity on campus. It houses two cardio rooms, two weight rooms, two gyms, six racquetball courts, three squash courts, three multipurpose rooms, a 42ft tall climbing wall, 1/10 mile indoor track, 25-yard pool, a dive well, a hot tub, three sand volleyball courts, and the Adventure Leadership Institute. A Fieldhouse with indoor multipurpose court, turf field, and rock climbing wall. Multiple artificial and natural terf fields around campus, tennis courts, and basketball courts.

Disabled Students: 92% of the campus is accessible. Facilities include wheelchair ramps, elevators, special parking, specially equipped restrooms, special class scheduling, lowered drinking fountains, lowered telephones.

Services: Counseling and information services are available, as is tutoring in most subjects. There is a reader service for the blind, and remedial math, reading, and writing. Facilities include a communication skills center and a math sciences learning center.

Campus Safety and Security: Measures include 24-hour foot and vehicle patrol, emergency notification system, and security escort services. There are shuttle buses, emergency telephones, lighted pathways/sidewalks, and controlled access to dorms/residences.

Programs of Study: Oregon State confers B.A., B.S. and B.F.A. degrees. Master's and doctoral degrees are also awarded. Bachelor's degrees are awarded in AGRICULTURE (agricultural business management, agricultural economics, agriculture, agronomy, animal science, fishing and fisheries, forest engineering, forestry production and processing, forestry and related sciences, horticulture, natural resource management, range/farm management, wildlife management, and wood science), BIOLOGICAL SCIENCE (biochemistry, biology/biological science, biotechnology, botany, ecology, microbiology, nutrition, wildlife biology, and zoology), BUSINESS (accounting, business administration and management, business systems analysis, management information systems, management science, marketing management, marketing/retailing/merchandising, and recreational facilities management), COMMUNICATIONS AND THE ARTS (apparel design, applied art, art, English, French, German, music, Spanish, speech/debate/rhetoric, and visual and performing arts), COMPUTER AND PHYSICAL SCIENCE (chemistry, computer science, earth science, mathematics, medical physics, natural sciences, physics, and science), EDUCATION (education), ENGINEERING AND ENVIRONMENTAL DESIGN (agricultural engineering, bioengineering, chemical engineering, civil engineering, computer engineering, construction management, electrical/electronics engineering, engineering physics, environmental engineering, environmental science, geological engineering, geophysical engineering, industrial engineering, interior design, manufacturing engineering, mechanical engineering, metallurgical engineering, and nuclear engineering), HEALTH PROFESSIONS (exercise science, health, health care administration, medical technology, predentistry, premedicine, preoptometry, prepharmacy, prephysical therapy, prepodiatry, public health, and radiation therapy), SOCIAL SCIENCE (American studies, anthropology, economics, ethnic studies, family/consumer studies, food science, history, human development, international studies, liberal arts/general studies, parks and recreation management, philosophy, political science/government, psychology, sociology, and women's studies). Engineering, agricultural sciences, and forestry are the strongest academically. Business, exercise and sports science, human development and family sciences have the largest enrollments.

Required: To graduate, students must complete at least 180 quarter credits with a GPA of 2.0. The required core curriculum includes writing, mathematics, speech, physical science, biological science, culture, difference and power,technology and society, global issues, fitness. Students must also take a writing-intensive course in their major field and meet additional distribution requirements.

Special: Oregon State University offers a double degree in Education, where a student has a primary degree in any field and then also earns an Education degree. With the Education degree the student also earns an Oregon teaching license. The university began a new program in the Fall of 2012 offering a double degree in Sustainability, students take an additional 36 credits beyond their primary degree. The Sustainability degree is interdisciplinary drawing on courses from many disciplines in the university. OSU has a list of over 200 approved study abroad programs in 77 different countries. There are 14 national honor societies, a freshman honors program, and 40 departmental honors programs.

Faculty/Classroom: 60% of faculty are male; 40% are female. No introductory courses are taught by graduate students. The average class

size in an introductory lecture is 60; in a laboratory is 26; and in a regular course is 38.

Admissions: 79% of the 2013-2014 applicants were accepted. The SAT scores for the 2013-2014 freshman class were: Critical Reading--30% below 500, 43% between 500 and 599, 23% between 600 and 699, and 4% between 700 and 800; Math--25% below 500, 40% between 500 and 599, 28% between 600 and 699, and 7% between 700 and 800; Writing--38% below 500, 41% between 500 and 599, 19% between 600 and 699, and 3% between 700 and 800. The ACT scores were 20% below 21, 25% between 21 and 23, 24% between 24 and 26, 14% between 27 and 28, and 17% above 28. 45% of the current freshmen were in the top fifth of their class; 77% were in the top two fifths. 160 freshmen graduated first in their class.

Requirements: The SAT or ACT is required. Applicants should be high school graduates or hold the GED. Required high school preparation includes 4 years of English; 3 years of math, including algebra II; 3 years of science; 3 years of social science; and 2 years of foreign language. Some subject requirements may be fulfilled by test scores. A GPA of 3.0 is required. AP and CLEP credits are accepted.

Procedure: Freshmen are admitted to all sessions. Entrance exams should be taken during the junior or senior year. There are early admissions, deferred admissions, and rolling admissions plans. Early decision applications should be filed by February 1; regular applications, by September 1 for fall entry; December 8 for winter entry; March 2 for spring entry; and June 22 for summer entry, along with a $60 fee. Notification of early decision is sent March 15; regular decision, Applications are accepted online.

Transfer: 2365 transfer students enrolled in 2012-2013. Applicants must present a GPA of at least 2.25 in previous college work. Students should have completed at least 36 hours of college credit. Must have a C- or better on English Composition and College Algebra. Transfer students must show two years of foreign language in high school or two semesters of foreign language. Either SAT I or ACT scores must be submitted. 72 of 180 credits required for the bachelor's degree must be completed at Oregon State.

Visiting: There are regularly scheduled orientations for prospective students. There are guides for informal visits, visitors may sit in on classes, and stay overnight. To schedule a visit, contact Visitor Center at (541) 737-2626.

Financial Aid: In 2013-2014, 86% of all full-time freshmen and 75% of continuing full-time students received some form of financial aid. 59% of all full-time freshmen and 61% of continuing full-time students received need-based aid. The average freshman award was $12,221. Need-based scholarships or need-based grants averaged $7,526; need-based self-help aid (loans and jobs) averaged $6,201; and non-need-based athletic scholarships averaged $26,895. The average financial indebtedness of the 2013 graduate was $22,831. Oregon State is a member of CSS. The FAFSA is required. The priority date for freshman financial aid applications for fall entry is February 28.

International Students: There are 1222 international students enrolled. The school actively recruits these students. They must take the TOEFL with a minimum score of 80 on the Internet-based version (iBT).

Graduates: From July 1, 2012 to June 30, 2013, 4157 bachelor's degrees were awarded. The most popular majors were engineering (14%), business (13%), and human development and family studies (11%). In an average class, 30% graduate in 4 years or less, 55% graduate in 5 years or less, and 61% graduate in 6 years or less.

Admissions Contact: Noah Buckley, Director of Admissions. E-Mail: *osuadmit@oregonstate.edu* Web: *http:/oregonstate.edu/admissions/*

OREGON UNIVERSITY SYSTEM

The Oregon University System, established in 1929, is a public system in Oregon. It is governed by the Oregon state board of higher education, whose chief administrator is the chancellor. The primary goals of the system are teaching at the undergraduate, graduate, and professional levels, both basic and applied research, and public service to the state and nation. The main priorities are to insure that students are liberally educated, to advance understanding in the areas of arts and sciences, and to be responsive to the particular circumstances of the people of Oregon. The total student enrollment is usually about 69,000 with 4000 faculty members. Altogether there are 182 baccalaureate, 116 master's, and 63 doctoral programs offered in the Oregon University System. Profiles of the 4-year campuses are included in this section.

PACIFIC NORTHWEST COLLEGE OF ART B-1

Portland, OR 97209 **(503) 821-8972; (503) 821-8978**

Full-time: 132 men, 260 women
Part-time: 14 men, 40 women
Graduate: 43 men, 62 women
Year: semesters
Application Deadline: August 15
Freshman Class: 426 applied, 244 accepted, 78 enrolled
Faculty: 24
Ph.D.s: 92%
Student/Faculty: 8 to 1
Tuition: $29,994
Room & Board: $8500
SPECIAL

Pacific Northwest College of Art, founded in 1909, offers professional training in the fine and visual arts. There is one graduate school. In addition to regional accreditation, PNCA has baccalaureate program accreditation with NASAD. The library contains 28,076 volumes, 3,422 audio/video tapes/CDs/DVDs, and subscribes to 112 periodicals including electronic. Computerized library services include interlibrary loans, database searching, Internet access, and Wi-Fi capability. Special learning facilities include an art gallery and radio station. The 1-acre campus is in an urban area in downtown Portland. Including any residence halls, there are 3 buildings.

Student Life: 67% of undergraduates are from out of state, mostly the West. Students are from 34 states, and 3 foreign countries. 76% are White. The average age of freshmen is 19; all undergraduates, 23. 34% do not continue beyond their first year; 43% remain to graduate.

Housing: 75 students can be accommodated in college housing, which includes coed off-campus apartments. On-campus housing is guaranteed for the freshman year only, is available on a first-come, and first-served basis. Alcohol is not permitted.

Activities: There are no fraternities or sororities. Groups on campus include art, gay, photography, professional, and student government. Popular campus events include Time-Based Arts Festival.

Sports: There is no sports program at PNCA.

Disabled Students: 90% of the campus is accessible. Facilities include wheelchair ramps, elevators, specially equipped restrooms, and lowered drinking fountains.

Services: Counseling and information services are available, as is tutoring in most subjects. There is remedial writing.

Campus Safety and Security: Measures include 24-hour foot and vehicle patrol, emergency notification system, self-defense education, and security escort services. There are shuttle buses, emergency telephones, lighted pathways/sidewalks, controlled access to dorms/residences, and guards at building entrances.

Programs of Study: PNCA confers B.F.A. degrees. Master's degrees are also awarded. Bachelor's degrees are awarded in COMMUNICATIONS AND THE ARTS (drawing, fine arts, graphic design, illustration, painting, photography, printmaking, and sculpture). Illustration, General Fine Arts, and Communication Design have the largest enrollments.

Required: To graduate, all students must complete 120 credits, including 45 in liberal arts and science courses and 57 in a studio major. All seniors must earn a 2.0 GPA for both semesters and must complete a thesis, which is critiqued by the faculty and later exhibited.

Special: A joint B.A./B.F.A. degree is offered with Reed College. Students may cross-register with members of the Oregon Independent Colleges Association. There is a Mobility Program for 1 semester or 1 year with member schools of the Association of Schools of Art and Design. Fourth-year communication design majors may undertake a 1-semester professional internship; internships also are strongly encouraged for juniors in all majors. Students may study abroad through PNCA's exchange agreements or in any other country through the programs of other accredited institutions. Nondegree study and student-designed majors are possible.

Faculty/Classroom: 54% of faculty are male; 46% are female. No introductory courses are taught by graduate students. The average class size in a regular course is 18.

Admissions: 57% of the 2013-2014 applicants were accepted.

Requirements: Applicants should be high school graduates or have earned the GED. The application consists of high school transcripts, 2 essays, and a portfolio of at least 12 pieces of artwork. A GPA of 2.0 is required. AP credits are accepted. Important factors in the admissions decision are evidence of special talent.

Procedure: Freshmen are admitted fall and spring. There are deferred admissions and rolling admissions plans. Applications should be filed by August 15 for fall entry; December 15 for spring entry, along with a $35 fee. Notification is sent on a rolling basis. Applications are accepted online.

Transfer: 73 transfer students enrolled in 2012-2013. Applicants must submit official copies of transcripts from high school and all colleges attended. Also required are 2 essays, a resume, a portfolio of 12 to 20 images, and a portfolio index. 48 of 120 credits required for the bachelor's degree must be completed at PNCA.

Visiting: There are guides for informal visits and visitors may sit in on classes. To schedule a visit, contact the Admissions Office.

Financial Aid: The FAFSA is required. The priority date for freshman financial aid applications for fall entry is March 1.

International Students: There are 5 international students enrolled. They must take the TOEFL with a minimum score of 550 on the paper-based TOEFL (PBT).

Graduates: From July 1, 2012 to June 30, 2013, 57 bachelor's degrees were awarded. The most popular majors were illustration (29%), general fine arts (14%), and photography (14%). In an average class, 34% graduate in 4 years or less, 41% graduate in 5 years or less, and 41% graduate in 6 years or less.

Admissions Contact: Jean Hester, Director of Admissions. E-Mail: *admissions@pnca.edu* Web: *www.pnca.edu*

PACIFIC UNIVERSITY A-1

Forest Grove, OR 97116 (503) 359-2218
(800) PAC-UNIV; (503) 359-2975

Full-time: 632 men, 941 women
Part-time: 19 men, 48 women
Graduate: 541 men, 1182 women
Year: 4-1-4, summer session
Application Deadline: February 15
Freshman Class: 2465 applied, 1841 accepted, 475 enrolled
SAT or ACT: required
Faculty: 87
Ph.D.s: 78%
Student/Faculty: 12 to 1
Tuition: $34,512
Room & Board: $10,208

COMPETITIVE

Pacific University, founded in 1849, is an independent institution affiliated with the Congregational Church (United Church of Christ), offering degree programs in liberal arts, science, business, education, and health professions. The figures in above capsule and in this profile are approximate. There are 6 graduate schools. In addition to regional accreditation, Pacific has baccalaureate program accreditation with NASM. The library contains 152,060 volumes, 76,609 microform items, 3,708 audio/video tapes/CDs/DVDs, and subscribes to 945 periodicals including electronic. Computerized library services include interlibrary loans and database searching. Special learning facilities include an art gallery, radio station, TV station, and museum of the history of the university. The 55-acre campus is in a small town 25 miles west of Portland. Including any residence halls, there are 18 buildings.

Student Life: 50% of undergraduates are from out of state, mostly the West. Students are from 31 states, 7 foreign countries, and Canada. 91% are from public schools. 64% are White; 17% Asian American. The average age of freshmen is 18; all undergraduates, 20. 22% do not continue beyond their first year; 54% remain to graduate.

Housing: 680 students can be accommodated in college housing, which includes single-sex and coed dorms and off-campus apartments. In addition, there are special-interest houses. On-campus housing is guaranteed for the freshman year only, is available on a first-come, first-served basis, and is available on a lottery system for upperclassmen. 50% of students commute. All students may keep cars.

Activities: 2% of men belong to 3 local fraternities; 6% of women belong to 3 local sororities. There are 35 groups on campus, including art, band, cheerleading, choir, chorale, chorus, computers, dance, debate, drama, ethnic, forensics, gay, honors, international, jazz band, literary magazine, musical theater, newspaper, opera, orchestra, pep band, photography, political, professional, radio and TV, religious, social, social service, student government, and yearbook. Popular campus events include Hawaiian Club Luau, International Club Banquet, and Japan Day.

Sports: There are 8 intercollegiate sports for men and 8 for women, and 10 intramural sports for men and 10 for women. Facilities include a gym, various courts, a sauna, weight and wrestling rooms, a dance studio, outdoor playing fields, a field house, and racquetball courts.

Disabled Students: 80% of the campus is accessible. Facilities include wheelchair ramps, elevators, special parking, specially equipped restrooms, and lowered drinking fountains.

Services: Counseling and information services are available, as is tutoring in most subjects. There is a reader service for the blind.

Campus Safety and Security: Measures include 24-hour foot and vehicle patrol and security escort services. There are emergency telephones and lighted pathways/sidewalks.

Programs of Study: Pacific confers B.A., B.S. and B.M. degrees. Master's and doctoral degrees are also awarded. Bachelor's degrees are awarded in BIOLOGICAL SCIENCE (biology/biological science), BUSINESS (business administration and management), COMMUNICATIONS AND THE ARTS (creative writing, dramatic arts, Japanese, literature, music, and Spanish), COMPUTER AND PHYSICAL SCIENCE (chemistry, computer science, mathematics, and physics), SOCIAL SCIENCE (economics, history, humanities, philosophy, political science/government, psychology, social work, and sociology). Natural sciences, literature, and creative writing are the strongest academically. Business administration, English and psychology have the largest enrollments.

Required: All students take a core curriculum that includes a first-year seminar and courses in writing, foreign language, social and natural sciences, art, and cross-cultural studies. A cumulative GPA of 2.0 in 124 semester hours is required for graduation. 34 to 64 hours are required in the major, depending on the discipline.

Special: Cross-registration is available with Oregon Independent Colleges and Oregon Graduate Institute of Science and Technology (OGIST). The university also offers cooperative programs with Washington University in St. Louis, OGIST, and Oregon School of Arts and Crafts, as well as study abroad in 13 countries. Full-time, semester-long internships, including one in Washington D.C., are possible. Dual majors, a general studies degree in humanities, nondegree study, 3-2 engineering programs with Washington University in St. Louis and OGIST, and an interdisciplinary program in peace and conflict studies are available. There are 2 national honor societies, a freshman honors program, and 1 departmental honors program.

Faculty/Classroom: 52% of faculty are male; 48% are female. All teach and do research. No introductory courses are taught by graduate students. The average class size in an introductory lecture is 35; in a laboratory is 20; and in a regular course is 19.

Admissions: 75% of a recent year applicants were accepted. The SAT scores for a recent year freshman class were: Critical Reading--29% below 500, 49% between 500 and 599, 17% between 600 and 699, and 5% between 700 and 800; Math--23% below 500, 49% between 500 and 599, 24% between 600 and 699, and 4% between 700 and 800. 18 freshmen graduated first in their class.

Requirements: The SAT or ACT is required. Applicants are expected to be high school graduates or to hold the GED. A personal essay is required, and an interview is recommended. Online applications are available on Pacific's Web pages. Applications are accepted online at the school's web site or through AppliedTechnology (Princeton Review). A GPA of 3.0 is required. AP and CLEP credits are accepted. Important factors in the admissions decision are advanced placement or honors courses, recommendations by school officials, and extracurricular activities record.

Procedure: Freshmen are admitted fall and spring. There are deferred admissions and rolling admissions plans. Applications should be filed by February 15 for fall entry, along with a $40 fee. Applications are accepted online.

Transfer: 67 transfer students enrolled in a recent year. Transfer applicants must present at least a 2.75 GPA in previous college work; those with fewer than 30 semester hours or 45 quarter hours must also submit SAT I or ACT test scores and high school transcripts. A personal interview is strongly recommended. 30 of 124 credits required for the bachelor's degree must be completed at Pacific.

Visiting: There are regularly scheduled orientations for prospective students, including overnight housing with current students, a campus tour, classroom visitations, and meetings with faculty and coaches. There are guides for informal visits, visitors may sit in on classes, and stay overnight. To schedule a visit, contact the Admissions Office.

Financial Aid: In a recent year, 92% of all full-time freshmen and 97% of continuing full-time students received some form of financial aid. 82% of all full-time freshmen and 70% of continuing full-time students received need-based aid. The average freshman award was $12,192. 54% of undergraduate students work part-time. Average annual earnings from campus work are $823. The average financial indebtedness of a recent graduate was $18,500. Pacific is a member of CSS. The FAFSA is required. Check with the school for current application deadlines.

International Students: There are 48 international students enrolled. The school actively recruits these students.

Graduates: In a recent year, 285 bachelor's degrees were awarded. The most popular majors were foreign language and English (11%), business and biology (11%), and physical education (9%). 10 companies recruited on campus in a recent year. In an average class, 44% graduate in 4 years or less, 57% graduate in 5 years or less, and 63% graduate in 6 years or less. Of a recent graduating class, 34% were enrolled in graduate school within 6 months of graduation, and 60% were employed.

Admissions Contact: Beth Woodward, Director of Admissions. E-Mail: *admissions@pacificu.edu* Web: *www.pacificu.edu*

PORTLAND STATE UNIVERSITY B-1

Portland, OR 97207 503-725-5504
(800) 547-8887; 503-725-5525

Full-time: 6935 men, 7582 women
Part-time: 4074 men, 4579 women
Graduate: 2237 men, 3324 women
Year: quarters, summer session
Application Deadline: open
Freshman Class: n/av
SAT CR/M: 520/510
Faculty: n/av; I, --$
Ph.D.s: n/av
Student/Faculty: 18 to 1
Tuition: $7653 ($22,863)
Room & Board: $11,019
ACT: 22

COMPETITIVE

Portland State University (PSU), is a nationally acclaimed leader in sustainability and community-based learning. The University's position in the heart of Oregon's economic and cultural center enables PSU students and faculty to apply scholarly theory to the real-world problems of business and community organizations. Portland State offers more than 220 undergraduate, master's, and doctoral degree options, as well as graduate certificates and continuing education programs. PSU is Oregon's largest and most diverse university, with some 30,000 students who come from all 50 states and from nearly 100 nations around the world. There are 8 undergraduate schools. In addition to regional accreditation, PSU has baccalaureate program accreditation with AACSB, ABET, ASLA, CSWE, NASAD, NASM, and NCATE. Computerized library services include interlibrary loans, database searching, and Internet access. Special learning facilities include an art gallery, radio station, a multicultural center and a Native American center. The 50-acre campus is in an urban area in the center of Portland. Including any residence halls, there are 56 buildings.

Student Life: 89% of undergraduates are from Oregon. Others are from states, and Canada. 65% are White. The average age of all undergraduates is 27. 26% do not continue beyond their first year; 74% remain to graduate.

Housing: 1729 students can be accommodated in college housing, which includes coed dorms, on-campus apartments, and off-campus apartments. On-campus housing is available on a first-come and first-served basis. Priority is given to out-of-town students. 93% of students commute. All students may keep cars.

Activities: There are 246 groups on campus, including and students with disabilities, art, band, cheerleading, chess, choir, chorale, chorus, communications, computers, dance, debate, drama, drill team, environmental, ethnic, film, forensics, gay, honors, international, jazz band, literary magazine, musical theater, newspaper, opera, orchestra, outdoor, pep band, photography, political, professional, radio and TV, religious, social, social service, student government, and symphony. Popular campus events include Portland State of Mind, International Student Cultural Night, Friends of Chamber Music and LunchBox Theater.

Sports: There are 6 intercollegiate sports for men and 9 for women, and 6 intramural sports for men and 6 for women. Facilities include Rec Center, a practice field, an all-weather tennis facility, gyms, circuit training and weight rooms, a golf putting green, running track, and racquetball, handball, and squash courts. Nearby Civic Stadium and Duniway Park provide football, baseball, and track and field facilities.

Disabled Students: 95% of the campus is accessible. Facilities include wheelchair ramps, elevators, special parking, specially equipped restrooms, special class scheduling, lowered drinking fountains, lowered telephones, and special housing.

Services: Counseling and information services are available, as is tutoring in most subjects. There is a reader service for the blind, and remedial math and writing. Student Support Services, provides assistance to students who are low-income, who have a physical disability, or whose parents did not graduate from college.

Campus Safety and Security: Measures include 24-hour foot and vehicle patrol, emergency notification system, self-defense education, and security escort services. There are emergency telephones, lighted pathways/sidewalks, a campus watch newsletter, information lectures, and community liaison.

Programs of Study: PSU confers B.A., B.S. and B.M. degrees. Master's and doctoral degrees are also awarded. Bachelor's degrees are awarded in BIOLOGICAL SCIENCE (biochemistry and biology/biological science), BUSINESS (accounting, business administration and management, management science, marketing/retailing/merchandising, and personnel management), COMMUNICATIONS AND THE ARTS (advertising, art history and appreciation, Chinese, dramatic arts, English, fine arts, French, German, Japanese, languages, music, Russian, Spanish, and speech/debate/rhetoric), COMPUTER AND PHYSICAL SCIENCE (chemistry, computer science, geology, information sciences and systems, mathematics, and physics), EDUCATION (health education), ENGINEERING AND ENVIRONMENTAL DESIGN (architecture, civil engineering, computer engineering, electrical/electronics engineering, and environmental science), SOCIAL SCIENCE (anthropology, child care/child and family studies, community services, economics, geography, history, international studies, law enforcement and corrections, liberal arts/general studies, philosophy, political science/government, psychology, social work, sociology, and women's studies). Electrical engineering, environmental science, and physics are the strongest academically. Psychology, business administration, and art have the largest enrollments.

Required: All students must complete at least 180 quarter credits with a 2.0 GPA in all courses in the major, and in all residence work. Other requirements and the number of hours that must be completed in the major vary by degree program. Freshmen must complete 3 5-credit freshman inquiry courses; sophomores, 3 4-credit courses from different interdisciplinary programs or general education clusters; juniors and seniors, 1 interdisciplinary program or general education cluster (4 3-credit courses); and seniors must complete a Senior Capstone. A thesis is required in the honors program only.

Special: Students may study abroad in 59 countries. Numerous internships, co-op programs, a Washington semester, and work-study programs are available. Most undergraduate programs may be taken on an accelerated basis, and students in all programs may undertake dual majors or design their own majors. A general studies program is available in arts and letters, science, or social science. Nondegree study and pass/fail grading options are possible. Students may enroll for 7 or fewer credits per term without formal admission. There are 8 national honor societies and a freshman honors program.

Faculty/Classroom: 50% of faculty are male; 50% are female. No introductory courses are taught by graduate students.

Admissions: The SAT scores for the 2013-2014 freshman class were: Critical Reading--39% below 500, 39% between 500 and 599, 19% between 600 and 699, and 3% between 700 and 800; Math--42% below 500, 4% between 500 and 599, 16% between 600 and 699, and 1% between 700 and 800; Writing--50% below 500, 36% between 500 and 599, 13% between 600 and 699, and 1% between 700 and 800. The ACT scores were 38% below 21, 26% between 21 and 23, 20% between 24 and 26, 10% between 27 and 28, and 6% above 28.

Requirements: The SAT or ACT is required. A minimum GPA of 3.0 is required. Various combination of test scores and GPA may qualify for admissions under special action by admissions commitee. Applicants should be high school graduates or have earned the GED. Secondary preparation should include 4 years of English, 3 years of math, and 2 years each of science and foreign language and social studies and 1 year of history. In addition, one unit of laboratory science is recommended. A GPA of 3.0 is required. AP and CLEP credits are accepted.

Procedure: Freshmen are admitted to all sessions. Entrance exams should be taken as early as possible. There are deferred admissions and rolling admissions plans. Application deadlines are open. Application fee is $50. Notification is sent on a rolling basis. Applications are accepted online.

Transfer: 2827 transfer students enrolled in 2012-2013. Applicants who are Oregon residents must have earned at least a 2.0 GPA in 30 college credits; those with 12 to 30 credits must meet freshman admission requirements and have a 2.0 GPA in all college work attempted. Nonresident applicants must have at least a 2.25 GPA in 30 hours of college work; those with 12 to 30 hours must meet freshman requirements and have a 2.5 GPA in all college work attempted. 45 of 180 credits required for the bachelor's degree must be completed at PSU.

Visiting: There are regularly scheduled orientations for prospective students, including daily campus tours led by student guides and opportunities for prospective students to meet with faculty, staff, and advisers. There are guides for informal visits, visitors may sit in on classes, and stay overnight. To schedule a visit, contact Campus Tour Coordinator at (503) 725-5555.

Financial Aid: In 2013-2014, 73% of all full-time freshmen and 87% of continuing full-time students received some form of financial aid. 58% of all full-time freshmen and 77% of continuing full-time students received need-based aid. The average freshman award was $11,540. Need-based scholarships or need-based grants averaged $5,350 ($18,500 maximum); need-based self-help aid (loans and jobs) averaged $6,916 ($27,661 maximum); non-need-based athletic scholarships averaged $14,168 ($28,610 maximum); and other non-need-based awards and non-need-based scholarships averaged $3,589 ($33,152 maximum). 80% of undergraduate students work part-time. Average annual earnings from campus work are $1716. The FAFSA and the college's own financial statement are required. Check with the school for current application deadlines.

International Students: There are 880 international students enrolled. The school actively recruits these students. They must take the TOEFL and the college's own test, Only the international TOEFL exam or the PSU institutional TOEFL exam will be accepted.

Graduates: From July 1, 2012 to June 30, 2013, 4320 bachelor's degrees were awarded. The most popular majors were social sciences/general (7%), business administration/management (6%), and psychology/general (6%). In an average class, 11% graduate in 4 years or less, 30% graduate in 5 years or less, and 40% graduate in 6 years or less.

Admissions Contact: Melissa A Trifiletti, Director of New Student Programs. E-Mail: *mtrifi@pdx.edu* Web: *www.pdx.edu/admissions/*

REED COLLEGE — B-1

Portland, OR 97202 — (503) 777-7511; (800) 547-4750; (503) 777-7553

Full-time: 646 men, 711 women
Part-time: 18 men, 21 women
Graduate: 7 men, 9 women
Year: semesters
Application Deadline: January 15
Faculty: 153; IIB, +$
Ph.D.s: 96%
Student/Faculty: 9 to 1
Tuition: $46,010
Room & Board: $11,770
Freshman Class: 2893 applied, 1404 accepted, 356 enrolled
SAT CR/M/W: 710/670/680

MOST COMPETITIVE

Reed College, founded in 1908, is a private, nonsectarian institution offering programs in liberal arts and sciences, and emphasizing instruction through small conference-style classes. There is one undergraduate school and one graduate school. The 2 libraries contain 629,871 volumes,

180,996 microform items, 31,456 audio/video tapes/CDs/DVDs, and subscribe to 17,169 periodicals including electronic. Computerized library services include interlibrary loans, database searching, Internet access, and Wi-Fi capability. Special learning facilities include an art gallery, radio station, a reactor, and centers for bio science, math, quantitative skills, science, and writing. The 116-acre campus is in an urban area in Portland. Including any residence halls, there are 43 buildings.

Student Life: 87% of undergraduates are from out of state, mostly the Southwest. Students are from 47 states, 45 foreign countries, and Canada. 56% are from public schools. 59% are White; 11% Hispanic. The average age of freshmen is 18; all undergraduates, 20. 4% do not continue beyond their first year; 82% remain to graduate.

Housing: 946 students can be accommodated in college housing, which includes coed dorms, on-campus apartments, and off-campus apartments. In addition, there are language houses, special-interest houses, quiet, substance-free, and no-smoking dorms. On-campus housing is guaranteed for the freshman year only, is available on a first-come, first-served basis, and is available on a lottery system for upperclassmen. 67% of students live on campus; of those, 95% remain on campus on weekends. Alcohol is not permitted. All students may keep cars.

Activities: There are no fraternities or sororities. There are 104 groups on campus, including art, chess, choir, chorus, computers, dance, debate, drama, environmental, ethnic, gay, international, jazz band, literary magazine, musical theater, newspaper, orchestra, photography, radio and TV, religious, social service, student government, and symphony. Popular campus events include Performing Arts Festival, Campus Clean Up Day (Canyon Day), and Reed Arts Week (RAW).

Sports: There are 7 intramural sports for men and 6 for women. Facilities include a sports center that houses 2 gyms (1 seating 1,200), an indoor pool, squash and racquetball courts, saunas, a weight room, an exercise room, and a dance studio. Outdoor facilities include tennis courts, a track, and areas for soccer, rugby, volleyball, and baseball.

Disabled Students: Facilities include wheelchair ramps, elevators, special parking, specially equipped restrooms, special class scheduling, lowered drinking fountains, and lowered telephones.

Services: Counseling and information services are available, as is tutoring in every subject. There is a reader service for the blind, and remedial math, reading, and writing.

Campus Safety and Security: Measures include 24-hour foot and vehicle patrol, emergency notification system, self-defense education, and security escort services. There are shuttle buses, emergency telephones, lighted pathways/sidewalks, and controlled access to dorms/residences.

Programs of Study: Reed confers B.A. degrees. Master's degrees are also awarded. Bachelor's degrees are awarded in AGRICULTURE (environmental studies), BIOLOGICAL SCIENCE (biochemistry and biology/biological science), COMMUNICATIONS AND THE ARTS (art, Chinese, classics, dramatic arts, English literature, Germanic languages and literature, linguistics, literature, music, and Russian languages and literature), COMPUTER AND PHYSICAL SCIENCE (chemical physics, chemistry, mathematics, mathematics – economics, and physics), SOCIAL SCIENCE (American studies, anthropology, economics, French studies, history, international political science, philosophy, political science/government, psychology, religion, sociology, and Spanish studies). English, biology, and psychology have the largest enrollments.

Required: All students are required to maintain a C average while fulfilling 120 semester hours of credit. The liberal arts program also requires a year-long humanities course and year-long senior research project, in addition to distribution requirements in literature, philosophy, religion, and the arts; history, social sciences, and psychology; natural sciences; mathematics, logic, or foreign language or linguistics. Students are also required to take 6 quarters of phys ed.

Special: Cross-registration is available through the Oregon Independent Colleges organization and Pacific Northwest College of Art. 3-2 programs are available for computer science with University of Washington and for engineering with CalTech, Columbia University, and Rensselaer Polytechnic Institute. Also available are combined programs with the Pacific Northwest College of Art for Visual Arts. Study abroad in 18 countries, a domestic exchange program with Howard University in Washington, D.C., Sarah Lawrence College, and Sea Education Association (SEA), accelerated degree programs, dual majors, student-designed majors, numerous interdisciplinary majors, nondegree study, and pass/fail options are also offered, including Phi Beta Kappa.

Faculty/Classroom: 56% of faculty are male; 44% are female. All teach and do research. No introductory courses are taught by graduate students.

Admissions: 49% of the 2013-2014 applicants were accepted. The SAT scores for the 2013-2014 freshman class were: Critical Reading--5% between 500 and 599, 36% between 600 and 699, and 59% between 700 and 800; Math--16% between 500 and 599, 49% between 600 and 699, and 35% between 700 and 800; Writing--1% below 500, 8% between 500 and 599, 52% between 600 and 699, and 39% between 700 and 800. The ACT scores were 2% between 21 and 23, 7% between 24 and 26, 18% between 27 and 28, and 73% above 28. 84% of the current freshmen were in the top fifth of their class; 94% were in the top two fifths. 13 freshmen graduated first in their class.

Requirements: The results of either the SAT or ACT are required, and SAT Subject tests are recommended. Reed strongly recommends that applicants have 4 years of English, 3 each of math and science, and 2 each of foreign language, history, and social studies. An essay is required, and an interview is recommended. The GED is accepted. AP credits are accepted. Important factors in the admissions decision are advanced placement or honors courses, personality/intangible qualities, and evidence of special talent.

Procedure: Freshmen are admitted fall. Entrance exams should be taken No later than December of application year. There are early decision and deferred admissions plans. Early decision applications should be filed by November 15; regular applications, by January 15 for fall entry, along with a $50 fee. Notification of early decision is sent December 15; regular decision, April 1. 114 early decision candidates were accepted for the 2013-2014 class. 258 applicants were on the 2013 waiting list; 45 were admitted. Applications are accepted online.

Transfer: 36 transfer students enrolled in 2012-2013. 60 of 120 credits required for the bachelor's degree must be completed at Reed.

Visiting: There are regularly scheduled orientations for prospective students, including an information session, campus tour, and an admission interview. Visitors may sit in on classes and stay overnight. To schedule a visit, contact the Office of Admission.

Financial Aid: In 2013-2014, 50% of all full-time freshmen and 46% of continuing full-time students received some form of financial aid. 49% of all full-time freshmen and 46% of continuing full-time students received need-based aid. The average freshman award was $44,328. Need-based scholarships or need-based grants averaged $41,510; and need-based self-help aid (loans and jobs) averaged $3,895. 39% of undergraduate students work part-time. The average financial indebtedness of the 2013 graduate was $20,079. Reed is a member of CSS. The CSS/Profile, FAFSA, and the college's own financial statement, and parent and student federal tax forms are required. The deadline for filing freshman financial aid applications for fall entry is March 1.

International Students: There are 92 international students enrolled. The school actively recruits these students. They must take the TOEFL with a minimum score of 600 on the paper-based TOEFL (PBT) or 100 on the Internet-based version (iBT). They must also take the SAT or ACT.

Graduates: From July 1, 2012 to June 30, 2013, 341 bachelor's degrees were awarded. The most popular majors were psychology (12%), biology (10%), and English (8%). 110 companies recruited on campus in 2012-2013. In an average class, 70% graduate in 4 years or less, 80% graduate in 5 years or less, and 82% graduate in 6 years or less.

Admissions Contact: Keith Todd, Dean of Admission. E-Mail: *admission@reed.edu* Web: *www.reed.edu*

SOUTHERN OREGON UNIVERSITY B-4

Ashland, OR 97520 **(541) 552-6411; (541) 552-8403**

Full-time: 1655 men, 2071 women	**Faculty:** 199; IIA, --$
Part-time: 656 men, 1032 women	**Ph.D.s:** 93%
Graduate: 216 men, 374 women	**Student/Faculty:** 20 to 1
Year: quarters, summer session	**Tuition:** $7794 ($21,276)
Application Deadline: September 9	**Room & Board:** $10,080
Freshman Class: 1985 applied, 1837 accepted, 637 enrolled	
SAT CR/M/W: 510/500/480 **ACT:** 22	**COMPETITIVE**

Southern Oregon University, founded in 1882, is a public comprehensive university providing undergraduate and graduate programs in humanities, science, business, fine and performing arts, social sciences, and teacher education. There are 3 undergraduate schools and 1 graduate school. In addition to regional accreditation, Southern has baccalaureate program accreditation with ACBSP, NASM, and NCATE. The library contains 336,000 volumes, 807,000 microform items, 90,000 audio/video tapes/CDs/DVDs, and subscribes to 4,300 periodicals including electronic. Computerized library services include interlibrary loans, database searching, Internet access, and Wi-Fi capability. Special learning facilities include an art gallery, radio station, TV station, a center for the visual arts, an art museum, and art galleries, a wildlife forensics lab, a music recital hall, 2 theaters, a greenhouse, and an ecology center. The 175-acre campus is in a small town 10 miles southeast of Medford. Including any residence halls, there are 40 buildings.

Student Life: 69% of undergraduates are from Oregon. Others are from 44 states, 17 foreign countries, and Canada. 85% are from public schools. 54% are White; 28% race unknown. The average age of freshmen is 19; all undergraduates, 25. 30% do not continue beyond their first year; 35% remain to graduate.

Housing: 1300 students can be accommodated in college housing, which includes single-sex and coed dorms, on-campus apartments, off-campus apartments, and married student housing. In addition, there are special-interest houses, 24-hour and 12-hour quiet halls, a wellness hall, a freshman hall, a smoke- and incense-free hall, and an age 21-plus hall. On-campus housing is guaranteed for the freshman year only, is available on a first-come, and first-served basis. 76% of students commute. All students may keep cars.

Activities: There are no fraternities or sororities. There are 125 groups on campus, including art, band, cheerleading, chess, choir, chorale, chorus, communications, computers, dance, drama, environmental, ethnic, film, forensics, gay, honors, international, jazz band, literary magazine, musical theater, newspaper, pep band, photography, political, professional, radio and TV, religious, social, social service, student government, and symphony. Popular campus events include Raider Orientation, Convocation, Southern Oregon Arts and Research Symposium, Commencement Weekend, International Week and One World Series.

Sports: There are 6 intercollegiate sports for men and 7 for women, and 11 intramural sports for men and 7 for women. Facilities include An indoor swimming pool, 6 racquetball courts, 12 tennis courts, 4 gyms, a climbing-wall gym, a dance studio, wrestling and weight rooms, a sauna, a football stadium, an all-weather track, and a soon to be built student fitness and recreations center.

Disabled Students: 95% of the campus is accessible. Facilities include wheelchair ramps, elevators, special parking, specially equipped restrooms, special class scheduling, lowered drinking fountains, lowered telephones, special housing.

Services: Counseling and information services are available, as is tutoring in some subjects, All levels of math and writing. There is a reader service for the blind, and remedial math and writing. Program design is offered for students with learning disabilities.

Campus Safety and Security: Measures include 24-hour foot and vehicle patrol, emergency notification system, self-defense education, and security escort services. There are emergency telephones, lighted pathways/sidewalks, controlled access to dorms/residences, Loud speaker public address system for emergencies.

Programs of Study: Southern confers B.A., B.S. and B.F.A. degrees. Master's degrees are also awarded. Bachelor's degrees are awarded in AGRICULTURE (environmental studies and natural resource management), BIOLOGICAL SCIENCE (biology/biological science), BUSINESS (accounting, business administration and management, business (dual major program), hospitality management services, hotel and restaurant administration, marketing, and marketing/retailing/merchandising), COMMUNICATIONS AND THE ARTS (art history, art, communication, dramatic arts, English, English Writing, film, television and digital media, fine arts, foreign language, graphic design, graphic design & media, languages, music, music business management, music composition, music performance, Spanish, studio art, theatre arts, theatre production, theatre studies, and visual and performing arts), COMPUTER AND PHYSICAL SCIENCE (chemistry, computer mathematics, computer programming, computer information systems, computer science, digital arts/technology, mathematics, mathematics – economics, physics, and science), EDUCATION (early childhood education, education, elementary education, English education, environmental education, physical education, and recreation education), ENGINEERING AND ENVIRONMENTAL DESIGN (environmental science and preengineering), HEALTH PROFESSIONS (biology, biomedical science, health, mental health/human services, nursing, premedicine, prepharmacy, prephysical therapy, and sports medicine), SOCIAL SCIENCE (American Indian studies, anthropology, criminal justice, criminology, economics, gender studies, geography, history, human services, interdisciplinary studies, international studies, liberal arts/general studies, Native American studies, philosophy, political science/government, prelaw, psychology, social science, sociology, and women & gender studies). Fine and performing arts, psychology, criminology/criminal justice, sciences, and social sciences are the strongest academically. Business, psychology, communication, education, and criminology/criminal justice have the largest enrollments.

Required: Students need a minimum GPA of 2.0 earned over 180 quarter hours, with 50 to 100 in the major and at least 60 in upper-division course work. Competency must be demonstrated through course work in writing and research. General education requirements include a yearlong course in speaking, writing, and critical thinking and both lower- and upper-division courses in arts and letters, natural sciences, social sciences, and quantitative reasoning. There is a required senior capstone experience.

Special: Cross-registration through the National Student and Western Student Exchanges, study abroad in 23 countries, internships, and federal work-study are all available. Accelerated degrees in business, communication, computer science, economics, geography, math, political science, foreign languages and literature, and sociology; dual majors in business and chemistry, physics, math, or music, and in math and computer science; and interdisciplinary majors in environmental or international studies are all offered. There are 13 national honor societies, a freshman honors program, and 10 departmental honors programs.

Faculty/Classroom: 55% of faculty are male; 45% are female. All teach undergraduates, and 1% do both. No introductory courses are taught by graduate students. The average class size in a regular course is 25.

Admissions: 93% of the 2013-2014 applicants were accepted. The SAT scores for the 2013-2014 freshman class were: Critical Reading--45% below 500, 36% between 500 and 599, 16% between 600 and 699, and 3% between 700 and 800; Math--49% below 500, 38% between 500 and 599, 11% between 600 and 699, and 2% between 700 and 800; Writing--56% below 500, 32% between 500 and 599, 10% between 600 and 699, and 2% between 700 and 800. The ACT scores were 46% below 21, 26% between 21 and 23, 16% between 24 and 26, 9% between 27 and 28, and 3% above 28.

Requirements: The SAT or ACT is required. A satisfactory score on the SAT is needed if the high school GPA is less than 2.75. Applicants need 14 academic credits, including 4 years of English, 3 each of math and social studies, 2 of science, and 2 years of 1 foreign language. The GED is accepted. A GPA of 2.8 is required. AP and CLEP credits are accepted.

Procedure: Freshmen are admitted to all sessions. Entrance exams should be taken In the students' high school junior or senior year. There are early admissions, deferred admissions, and rolling admissions plans. Application deadlines are open. Application fee is $50. Notification of early decision is sent March 15; regular decision, October 9. Applications are accepted online.

Transfer: 1200 transfer students enrolled in 2012-2013. Transfer students need a minimum GPA of 2.25 and at least 36 quarter credits. 45 of 180 credits required for the bachelor's degree must be completed at Southern.

Visiting: There are regularly scheduled orientations for prospective students, Includes tours of the campus and residence halls and a meeting with an admissions representative. Appointments with faculty and class visits can be arranged. There are guides for informal visits, visitors may sit in on classes, and stay overnight. To schedule a visit, contact The Admissions Office at (800) 482-7672 Ext. 6411.

Financial Aid: In 2013-2014, 75% of all full-time freshmen and 81% of continuing full-time students received some form of financial aid. 56% of all full-time freshmen and 54% of continuing full-time students received need-based aid. The average freshman award was $8,440. Need-based scholarships or need-based grants averaged $6,370; need-based self-help aid (loans and jobs) averaged $3,087; non-need-based athletic scholarships averaged $1,787; and other non-need-based awards and non-need-based scholarships averaged $1,210. 50% of undergraduate students work part-time. Average annual earnings from campus work are $1500. The average financial indebtedness of the 2013 graduate was $29,000. The FAFSA is required. The priority date for freshman financial aid applications for fall entry is March 1.

International Students: There are 166 international students enrolled. The school actively recruits these students. They must take the TOEFL with a minimum score of 520 on the paper-based TOEFL (PBT) or 68 on the Internet-based version (iBT).

Graduates: From July 1, 2012 to June 30, 2013, 795 bachelor's degrees were awarded. The most popular majors were business (16%), psychology (12%), and visual and performing arts (11%). 25 companies recruited on campus in 2012-2013. In an average class, 2% graduate in 3 years or less, 16% graduate in 4 years or less, 28% graduate in 5 years or less, and 32% graduate in 6 years or less.

Admissions Contact: Kelly Moutsatson, Director of Admissions. E-Mail: *admissions@sou.edu* Web: *www.sou.edu*

UNIVERSITY OF OREGON — B-2

Eugene, OR 97403-1226 — **(541) 346-3201**
(800) 232-3825; (541) 346-5815

Full-time: 8400 men, 8570 women	**Faculty:** 844; I, --$
Part-time: 770 men, 770 women	**Ph.D.s:** 96%
Graduate: 1790 men, 2040 women	**Student/Faculty:** n/av
Year: quarters, summer session	**Tuition:** $8883 ($27,738)
Application Deadline: January 15	**Room & Board:** $9501
Freshman Class: n/av	
SAT or ACT: required	

VERY COMPETITIVE

The University of Oregon, founded in 1876, is a public liberal arts institution within the Oregon University System. There are 6 undergraduate schools and 8 graduate schools. Some figures in the above capsule and in this profile are approximate. In addition to regional accreditation, UO has baccalaureate program accreditation with AACSB, ACEJMC, ASLA, FIDER, NAAB, NASM, and NRPA. The 5 libraries contain 3.1 million volumes, 4.2 million microform items, and 112,034 audio/video tapes/CDs/DVDs, and subscribe to 46,879 periodicals including electronic. Computerized library services include interlibrary loans, database searching, Internet access, and laptop Internet portals. Special learning facilities include a learning resource center, art gallery, natural history museum, radio station, an art museum, a natural and cultural history museum, centers for sports marketing, entrepreneurship, instrumentation, and computer music, a chemistry lab, and a longhouse. The 295-acre campus is in a suburban area 110 miles south of Portland. Including any residence halls, there are 107 buildings.

Student Life: 67% of undergraduates are from Oregon. Others are from 49 states, 85 foreign countries, and Canada. 72% are white. The average age of freshmen is 19; all undergraduates, 22. 16% do not continue beyond their first year; 67% remain to graduate.

Housing: 3947 students can be accommodated in college housing, which includes single-sex and coed dorms, on-campus apartments, off-campus apartments, and married student housing. In addition, there are honors houses, language houses, special-interest houses, an international house, and an integrated living-learning center. On-campus housing is available on a first-come, first-served basis. 80% of students commute. All students may keep cars.

Activities: 7% of men belong to 12 national fraternities; 10% of women belong to 1 local sorority and 8 national sororities. There are 250 groups on campus, including art, band, cheerleading, chess, choir, chorale, chorus, computers, dance, debate, drama, drill team, environmental, ethnic, film, forensics, gay, honors, international, jazz band, literary magazine, marching band, musical theater, newspaper, opera, orchestra, pep band, photography, political, professional, radio and TV, religious, social, social service, student government, and symphony. Popular campus events include University Day, Family Weekends, and Convocation.

Sports: There are 7 intercollegiate sports for men and 10 for women, and 13 intramural sports for men and 13 for women. Facilities include a 58,000-seat stadium with 40 private suites, a 9000-seat basketball arena, an 8-lane, 400-meter track-and-field complex with seating for 9500 spectators, a softball complex, 12 tennis courts, a practice putting green, and grass fields for soccer and lacrosse. The student rec center includes several gyms and training facilities with exercise and weight-training equipment, a swimming pool, an indoor track, a climbing wall, and an indoor practice facility for athletic teams.

Disabled Students: 95% of the campus is accessible. Facilities include wheelchair ramps, elevators, special parking, specially equipped rest rooms, special class scheduling, and lowered drinking fountains. An adviser is available for students with disabilities. Other accommodations are made upon request.

Services: Counseling and information services are available, as is tutoring in every subject. There is a reader service for the blind and remedial math and writing. Peer tutors in entry-level undergraduate courses are available through the Academic Learning Services Center. Students can drop in to receive free assistance with math and writing at the center's lab.

Campus Safety and Security: Measures include 24-hour foot and vehicle patrol, emergency notification system, and security escort services. There are shuttle buses, emergency telephones, and lighted pathways/sidewalks. The university has a new campuswide emergency management program, campus emergency operations, and mitigation plans.

Programs of Study: UO confers B.A., B.S., B.Arch., B.Ed., B.F.A., B.I.Arch., B.L.A., and B.Mus. degrees. Master's and doctoral degrees are also awarded. Bachelor's degrees are awarded in AGRICULTURE (environmental studies), BIOLOGICAL SCIENCE (biochemistry, biology/biological science, marine biology, and physiology), BUSINESS (accounting and business administration and management), COMMUNICATIONS AND THE ARTS (advertising, art, art history and appreciation, ceramic art and design, Chinese, classics, communications, comparative literature, dance, design, digital communications, dramatic arts, English, fiber/textiles/weaving, fine arts, French, German, graphic design, Greek, Italian, Japanese, jazz, journalism, Latin, linguistics, metal/jewelry, music, music performance, music theory and composition, painting, photography, printmaking, public relations, romance languages and literature, Russian, sculpture, and Spanish), COMPUTER AND PHYSICAL SCIENCE (chemistry, computer science, digital arts/technology, geology, mathematics, physics, and science), EDUCATION (education and music education), ENGINEERING AND ENVIRONMENTAL DESIGN (architecture, environmental science, interior design, and landscape architecture/design), HEALTH PROFESSIONS (speech pathology/audiology), SOCIAL SCIENCE (anthropology, Asian/Oriental studies, classical/ancient civilization, economics, ethnic studies, family and community services, geography, history, humanities, international studies, Judaic studies, Latin American studies, medieval studies, philosophy, political science/government, psychology, public administration, religion, sociology, and women's studies). Architecture, journalism, and biology are the strongest academically. Business, psychology, and journalism are the largest.

Required: For graduation, at least 180 quarter credits are required of all students, with a minimum GPA of 2.0. A minimum of 36 credits must be in the major, including 24 in upper-division work. Basic courses vary by major, but all students must complete 12 to 16 credits each in the areas of arts and letters, social science, and science, as well as 2 courses in written English and 2 courses in multicultural studies.

Special: UO offers cross-registration with other schools in the Oregon University System, matriculation agreements with more than 25 Oregon and Washington community colleges, dual enrollment with Lane and Southwestern Oregon Community Colleges, study abroad in more than 90 countries, preengineering in conjunction with Lane Community College, and an engineering/physics program with Oregon State University. In addition, numerous internship opportunities, dual majors, a 3-2 engineering degree, and pass/fail options are available. There are 22 national honor societies, including Phi Beta Kappa, a freshman honors program, and 41 departmental honors programs.

Faculty/Classroom: 56% of faculty are male; 44% are female. All teach undergraduates. Graduate students teach 13% of introductory courses. The average class size in an introductory lecture is 43; in a laboratory, 18; and in a regular course, 47.

Admissions: 80% of a recent year's applicants were accepted. 50% of a recent year's freshmen were in the top fifth of their class; 83% were in the top two fifths. There were 13 National Merit finalists. 295 freshmen graduated first in their class.

Requirements: The SAT or ACT is required. The ACT Optional Writing test is also required. In addition, standard freshman admission requirements include a high school GPA of at least 3.0, graduation from a standard or regionally accredited high school, and C- or higher in 14 college preparatory courses. Applications are evaluated based on strength of academic course work, grade trends, class rank, standardized test scores, academic motivation as demonstrated in the application essay, special talents, extracurricular activities, including community service or the need to work to assist your family financially, and ability to enhance the diversity of the university. Applicants can earn automatic admission with a cumulative high school GPA of at least 3.4 and completion of at least 16 college preparatory units with grades of C- or better in each course. AP and CLEP credits are accepted.

Procedure: Freshmen are admitted to all sessions. Entrance exams should be taken after October 15 of the junior year and before March of the senior year. There is a rolling admissions plan. Applications should be filed by January 15 for fall entry, along with a $50 fee. Notification is sent on a rolling basis beginning April 15. Applications are accepted online.

Transfer: 1559 transfer students enrolled in a recent year. If transfer students have completed 35 or fewer transferable quarter credits (23 semester credits), admission will be based on both high school and college work; they must meet admission requirements for both freshmen and transfer students. If transfer students have completed 36 or more quarter credits (24 of which must be graded), admission will be based on college-level course work only. Transfer students must be eligible to return to their most recent institution and have completed 1 college-level composition course and 1 college-level mathematics course with grades of C- or better, P (pass), or S (satisfactory); earned a minimum GPA of 2.25 if they are Oregon residents or 2.5 if they are nonresidents; and demonstrate second-language proficiency. 45 of 180 credits required for the bachelor's degree must be completed at UO.

Visiting: There are regularly scheduled orientations for prospective students, including IntroDUCKtion, a 2-day program scheduled for late July that includes both advising and Web-based registration. There are guides for informal visits, and visitors may sit in on classes. To schedule a visit, contact the Ambassador Program.

Financial Aid: In a recent year, 46% of all full-time freshmen and 43% of continuing full-time students received some form of financial aid. 16% of all full-time freshmen and 21% of continuing full-time students received need-based aid. The average freshman award was $8112. Need-based scholarships or need-based grants averaged $6114; need-based self-help aid (loans and jobs) averaged $4027; non-need-based athletic scholarships averaged $19,746; and other non-need-based awards and non-need-based scholarships averaged $2457. The average financial indebtedness of a recent year's graduate was $18,805. The FAFSA is required. Check with the school for current application deadlines.

International Students: There were 1019 international students enrolled in a recent year. The school actively recruits these students. They must take the TOEFL with a minimum score of 500 on the paper-based TOEFL (PBT) or 61 on the Internet-based version (iBT). They must also take the SAT or ACT.

Graduates: In a recent year, 3568 bachelor's degrees were awarded. The most popular majors were business administration (10%), psychology (8%), and political science (7%). In an average class, 2% graduate in 3 years or less, 45% graduate in 4 years or less, 67% graduate in 5 years or less, and 67% graduate in 6 years or less. 206 companies recruited on campus in a recent year. Of a recent year's graduating class, 28% were enrolled in graduate school within 6 months of graduation.

Admissions Contact: Brian Henley, Director of Admissions. E-Mail: *uoadmit@uoregon.edu* Web: *www.uoregon.edu*

UNIVERSITY OF PORTLAND B-1

Portland, OR 97203 (503) 943-7147
(888) 627-5601; (503) 943-7315

Full-time: 1407 men, 2003 women
Part-time: 31 men, 27 women
Graduate: 181 men, 318 women
Year: semesters, summer session
Application Deadline: February 1
Freshman Class: 9523 applied, 6358 accepted, 835 enrolled
SAT CR/M: 590/600
Faculty: 214; IIA, -$
Ph.D.s: 92%
Student/Faculty: 16 to 1
Tuition: $36,870
Room & Board: $11,004
ACT: required **VERY COMPETITIVE**

The University of Portland, founded in 1901, is an independent institution affiliated with the Roman Catholic Church. It offers degree programs in the arts and sciences, business administration, education, engineering, and nursing. There are 5 undergraduate schools and 1 graduate school. In addition to regional accreditation, UP has baccalaureate program accreditation with AACSB, ABET, CSWE, NASM, and NCATE. The library contains 219,693 volumes, 41,624 microform items, and 15,002 audio/video tapes/CDs/DVDs, and subscribes to 6,830 periodicals including electronic. Computerized library services include interlibrary loans, database searching, Internet access, and Wi-Fi capability. Special learning facilities include an art gallery and radio station. The 155-acre campus is in an urban area 4 miles north of downtown Portland. Including any residence halls, there are 30 buildings.

Student Life: 67% of undergraduates are from out of state, mostly the Northwest. Students are from 44 states, 37 foreign countries, and Canada. 67% are from public schools. 66% are White; 12% Asian American. 47% are Catholic. The average age of freshmen is 19; all undergraduates, 21. 10% do not continue beyond their first year; 79% remain to graduate.

Housing: 1800 students can be accommodated in college housing, which includes single-sex and coed dorms and on-campus apartments. In addition, there are honors houses, language houses, special-interest houses, University-owned rental houses. On-campus housing is guaranteed for the freshman year only and is available on a lottery system for upperclassmen. 55% of students live on campus; of those, 85% remain on campus on weekends. Upperclassmen may keep cars.

Activities: There are no fraternities or sororities. There are 62 groups on campus, including art, band, cheerleading, choir, chorale, chorus, computers, dance, debate, drama, environmental, ethnic, film, gay, honors, international, jazz band, literary magazine, musical theater, newspaper, orchestra, pep band, photography, political, professional, radio and TV, religious, social, social service, student government, symphony, and yearbook. Popular campus events include Dance of the Decade, International Night, Pilotpalooza and Luau.

Sports: There are 6 intercollegiate sports for men and 6 for women, and 20 intramural sports for men and 20 for women. Facilities include weight rooms, an indoor track, a gym, a swimming pool, and a 5000-seat athletic and convocation center. Rental equipment is available for biking and camping activities.

Disabled Students: All of the campus is accessible. Facilities include wheelchair ramps, elevators, special parking, specially equipped restrooms, special class scheduling, lowered drinking fountains, and lowered telephones.

Services: Counseling and information services are available, as is tutoring in most subjects, including English and math. The faculty is available for individual assistance.

Campus Safety and Security: Measures include 24-hour foot and vehicle patrol, emergency notification system, self-defense education, and security escort services. There are shuttle buses, emergency telephones, lighted pathways/sidewalks, and controlled access to dorms/residences.

Programs of Study: UP confers B.A., B.S., B.A.Ed., B.B.A., B.M.Ed., B.S.C.E., B.S.E.E., B.S.E.M., B.S.E.S., B.S.M.E. and B.S.N. degrees. Master's and doctoral degrees are also awarded. Bachelor's degrees are awarded in BIOLOGICAL SCIENCE (biology/biological science), BUSINESS (accounting, banking and finance, entrepreneurial studies, international business management, marketing/retailing/merchandising, and operations management), COMMUNICATIONS AND THE ARTS (communications, dramatic arts, English, music, and Spanish), COMPUTER AND PHYSICAL SCIENCE (chemistry, computer science, mathematics, and physics), EDUCATION (elementary education and secondary education), ENGINEERING AND ENVIRONMENTAL DESIGN (civil engineering, electrical/electronics engineering, engineering, environmental science, and mechanical engineering), HEALTH PROFESSIONS (nursing), SOCIAL SCIENCE (economics, French studies, German area studies, history, interdisciplinary studies, philosophy, political science/government, psychology, social work, sociology, and theological studies). Engineering, nursing, and biology are the strongest academically. Nursing, biology, and mechanical engineering have the largest enrollments.

Required: To graduate, students must complete 120 credit hours, including at least 24 upper-division classes in the major, with a minimum GPA of 2.0. Required courses include 9 hours each of philosophy and theology, 6 each of science, social sciences, and electives, and 3 each of fine arts, history, math, and literature. Some majors may require a comprehensive exam and/or thesis.

Special: UP offers internships through individual departments, cross-registration with members of the Oregon Independent College Association, dual and interdisciplinary majors, including engineering chemistry and organizational communications, work-study programs, and pass/fail options. Study abroad may be arranged in Japan, Mexico, Australia, Chile, and several European countries. There are 9 national honor societies and a freshman honors program.

Faculty/Classroom: 56% of faculty are male; 44% are female. All teach undergraduates. No introductory courses are taught by graduate students. The average class size in an introductory lecture is 25; in a laboratory is 20; and in a regular course is 20.

Admissions: 67% of the 2013-2014 applicants were accepted. The SAT scores for the 2013-2014 freshman class were: Critical Reading--12% below 500, 42% between 500 and 599, 32% between 600 and 699, and 13% between 700 and 800; Math--9% below 500, 39% between 500 and 599, 42% between 600 and 699, and 10% between 700 and 800.

Requirements: The SAT or ACT is required, with a minimum score of 550 on each section of the SAT or a composite of 19 on the ACT. Graduation from an accredited secondary school or satisfactory scores on the GED are required. The high school curriculum should include courses in English composition, math, social studies, science, and a foreign language. 2 essays are required, as is a letter of recommendation from the high school counselor or principal. UP requires applicants to be in the upper 50% of their class. A GPA of 3.0 is required. AP and CLEP credits are accepted.

Procedure: Freshmen are admitted to all sessions. Entrance exams should be taken preferably before February 1 but no later than June 1 of the senior year. There are deferred admissions and rolling admissions plans. Applications should be filed by February 1 for fall entry, along with a $50 fee. Notification is sent on a rolling basis. Applications are accepted online.

Transfer: 100 transfer students enrolled in 2012-2013. Applicants with 26 or more credits must have a minimum GPA of 2.5 and be in good standing at their previous school. Students with fewer credits may need to meet freshman requirements. 30 of 120 credits required for the bachelor's degree must be completed at UP.

Visiting: There are regularly scheduled orientations for prospective students, including a campus tour, class attendance, and a meeting with an admissions counselor. There are guides for informal visits, visitors may sit in on classes, and stay overnight. To schedule a visit, contact the Office of Admissions.

Financial Aid: In 2013-2014, 97% of all full-time freshmen and 94% of continuing full-time students received some form of financial aid. 67% of all full-time freshmen and 64% of continuing full-time students received need-based aid. 36% of undergraduate students work part-time. Average annual earnings from campus work are $2325. The average financial indebtedness of the 2013 graduate was $27,164. The FAFSA is required. The priority date for freshman financial aid applications for fall entry is February 1. The deadline for filing freshman financial aid applications for fall entry is March 1.

International Students: There are 93 international students enrolled. The school actively recruits these students. They must take the TOEFL with a minimum score of 71 on the Internet-based version (iBT).

Graduates: From July 1, 2012 to June 30, 2013, 742 bachelor's degrees were awarded. The most popular majors were nursing (23%), biology (10%), and mechanical engineering (6%). 85 companies recruited on campus in 2012-2013. In an average class, 71% graduate in 4 years or less, 79% graduate in 5 years or less, and 76% graduate in 6 years or less. Of the 2012 graduating class, 15% were enrolled in graduate school within 6 months of graduation.

Admissions Contact: Jason McDonald, Dean of Admissions. E-Mail: *admissio@up.edu* Web: *www.up.edu*

WARNER PACIFIC COLLEGE B-1

Portland, OR 97215 (503) 517-1024
(800) 8041510; (503) 517-1540

Full-time: 532 men, 956 women
Part-time: 19 men, 43 women
Graduate: 49 men, 80 women
Year: semesters, summer session
Application Deadline: open
Freshman Class: n/av
SAT or ACT: required
Faculty: 34
Ph.D.s: 50%
Student/Faculty: 14 to 1
Tuition: $18,290
Room & Board: $7260
COMPETITIVE

Warner Pacific College, founded in 1937, is a private Christian liberal arts college affiliated with the Church of God. There is one undergraduate school and one graduate school. The library contains 67,948 volumes,

2,093 microform items, 2,899 audio/video tapes/CDs/DVDs, and subscribes to 27,038 periodicals including electronic. Computerized library services include interlibrary loans, database searching, and Internet access. Special learning facilities include a The 14-acre campus is in an urban area 5 miles east of downtown Portland. Including any residence halls, there are 30 buildings.

Student Life: 71% of undergraduates are from Oregon. Others are from 18 states, 2 foreign countries, and Canada. 78% are from public schools. 78% are White. 51% claim no religious affiliation; 42% Protestant. The average age of freshmen is 27; all undergraduates, 31. 25% do not continue beyond their first year; 45% remain to graduate.

Housing: 288 students can be accommodated in college housing, which includes single-sex dorms, on-campus apartments, and married student housing. On-campus housing is guaranteed for all 4 years, is available on a first-come, first-served basis, and is available on a lottery system for upperclassmen. Priority is given to out-of-town students. 54% of students live on campus. Alcohol is not permitted. All students may keep cars.

Activities: There are no fraternities or sororities. There are 11 groups on campus, including and spiritual growth groups., art, band, Bible study, choir, chorale, chorus, dance, debate, drama, environmental, ethnic, international, jazz band, literary magazine, newspaper, orchestra, professional, religious, social, social service, student government, and yearbook. Popular campus events include Winter Banquet and Spring Banquet.

Sports: There are 5 intercollegiate sports for men and 6 for women, and 2 intramural sports for men and 2 for women. Facilities include a gym, a weight-training room, and hiking trails.

Disabled Students: 75% of the campus is accessible. Facilities include wheelchair ramps, elevators, special parking, specially equipped restrooms, special class scheduling, lowered drinking fountains.

Services: Counseling and information services are available, as is tutoring in most subjects. There is remedial math, reading, writing, as well as testing and study skills workshops.

Campus Safety and Security: Measures include 24-hour foot and vehicle patrol, emergency notification system, self-defense education, and security escort services. There are emergency telephones, lighted pathways/sidewalks, and controlled access to dorms/residences.

Programs of Study: Warner Pacific confers B.A., and B.S degrees. Associate degrees are also awarded. Bachelor's degrees are awarded in BIOLOGICAL SCIENCE (biology/biological science), BUSINESS (business administration and management), COMMUNICATIONS AND THE ARTS (English and music), EDUCATION (music education and physical education), SOCIAL SCIENCE (American studies, history, human development, liberal arts/general studies, ministries, religious music, social science, and sociology). Biological science and business administration is the strongest academically. Business administration, human development, education, and Christian ministries have the largest enrollments.

Required: To graduate, students must complete 124 credits with a minimum GPA of 2.0. All students must take a core curriculum of 42 credits, consisting of 15 hours in humanities, 9 in communication, 7 to 9 in religion, 6 in social science, 4 in fine arts, and 3 each in science and health and phys ed.

Special: Warner Pacific offers cross-registration through OICA, a Washington semester, a co-op nursing program, 27 majors, accelerated degree programs in human development and business administration, and study abroad in Latin America, the Middle East, and Russia. Internships, work-study programs, double majors, individualized majors, independent study credit for life and military experience, and pass/fail options are available.

Faculty/Classroom: 62% of faculty are male; 38% are female. All teach undergraduates, and 40% do research. No introductory courses are taught by graduate students. The average class size in an introductory lecture is 15; in a laboratory is 10; and in a regular course is 15.

Requirements: The SAT or ACT is required. Applicants must be graduates of an accredited secondary school. The GED is accepted. High school preparation should include 4 years of English, 3 of social studies, and 2 each of math and lab science. A GPA of 2.3 is required. AP and CLEP credits are accepted. Important factors in the admissions decision are evidence of special talent, leadership record, and advanced placement or honors courses.

Procedure: Freshmen are admitted to all sessions. Entrance exams should be taken no later than the early fall of the senior year. There is a rolling admissions plan. Application deadlines are open. Application fee is $50. Applications are accepted online.

Transfer: 170 transfer students enrolled in 2012-2013. Applicants must provide transcripts from their previous college. A minimum GPA of 2.0 is required. 30 of 124 credits required for the bachelor's degree must be completed at Warner Pacific.

Visiting: There are regularly scheduled orientations for prospective students, including 2 campus preview days, 2 Knight Life visit weekends, academic fairs, and scholarship days. There are guides for informal visits, visitors may sit in on classes, and stay overnight. To schedule a visit, contact the Office of Enrollment.

Financial Aid: In 2013-2014, 98% of all full-time freshmen and 98% of continuing full-time students received some form of financial aid. 97% of all full-time freshmen and 97% of continuing full-time students received need-based aid. The average freshman award was $15,003. 5% of undergraduate students work part-time. Average annual earnings from campus work are $2000. The average financial indebtedness of the 2013 graduate was $27,000. Warner Pacific is a member of CSS. The FAFSA is required. Check with the school for current application deadlines.

International Students: There are 12 international students enrolled. The school actively recruits these students. They must take the TOEFL and the college's own test.

Graduates: From July 1, 2012 to June 30, 2013, 149 bachelor's degrees were awarded. The most popular majors were business (35%), human development (30%), and education (10%). In an average class, 2% graduate in 3 years or less, 29% graduate in 4 years or less, 8% graduate in 5 years or less, and 2% graduate in 6 years or less.

Admissions Contact: Shannon Mackey, Exec. Director of Enrollment Management. E-Mail: *admissions@warnerpacific.edu* Web: *www.warnerpacific.edu*

WESTERN OREGON UNIVERSITY — A-2

Monmouth, OR 97361 — (503) 838-8211; (877) 877-1593; (503) 838-8067

Full-time: 1820 men, 2450 women	**Faculty:** 209; IIA, --$
Part-time: 250 men, 350 women	**Ph.D.s:** 72%
Graduate: 240 men, 540 women	**Student/Faculty:** n/av
Year: quarters, summer session	**Tuition:** $7928 ($19,905)
Application Deadline: open	**Room & Board:** $9122
Freshman Class: n/av	
SAT or ACT: required	

COMPETITIVE

Western Oregon University, founded in 1856, is a publicly funded institution and a member of the Oregon University System. WOU offers undergraduate programs through the Colleges of Education and Liberal Arts and Sciences. There are 2 undergraduate schools and 1 graduate school. In addition to regional accreditation, WOU has baccalaureate program accreditation with NASM and NCATE. Computerized library services include interlibrary loans, database searching, Internet access, and laptop Internet portals. Special learning facilities include a learning resource center, art gallery, TV station and the Paul Jensen Arctic Museum. The 157-acre campus is in a rural area 15 miles west of Salem. Including any residence halls, there are 36 buildings.

Student Life: 89% of undergraduates are from Oregon. Others are from 27 states, 22 foreign countries, and Canada. 99% are from public schools. 73% are white. The average age of freshmen is 18; all undergraduates, 22. 30% do not continue beyond their first year; 50% remain to graduate.

Housing: 1350 students can be accommodated in college housing, which includes coed dorms, on-campus apartments, and married student housing. In addition, there are wellness, honors, multicultural, and quiet communities. On-campus housing is guaranteed for the freshman year only. 68% of students commute. Alcohol is not permitted. All students may keep cars.

Activities: There are no fraternities or sororities. There are 50 groups on campus, including art, band, cheerleading, chess, choir, chorale, chorus, computers, dance, debate, drama, drill team, ethnic, gay, honors, international, jazz band, literary magazine, marching band, Model UN, musical theater, newspaper, orchestra, pep band, political, professional, radio and TV, religious, social, social service, and student government. Popular campus events include Annual Christmas Tree Lighting, Alcohol Awareness Week, and Family Day.

Sports: There are 5 intercollegiate sports for men and 6 for women, and 25 intramural sports for men and 25 for women. Facilities include a sports field, a phys ed building, a swimming pool, a weight room, indoor/outdoor tennis courts, handball and racquetball courts, a dance studio, archery facilities, and baseball, softball, and soccer fields.

Disabled Students: 95% of the campus is accessible. Facilities include wheelchair ramps, elevators, special parking, specially equipped restrooms, special class scheduling, lowered drinking fountains, lowered telephones, special housing.

Services: Counseling and information services are available, as is tutoring in most subjects. There is a reader service for the blind, and remedial math, reading, and writing. There is also a student support and services program for first-generation, low-income, and physically disabled students.

Campus Safety and Security: Measures include 24-hour foot and vehicle patrol, self-defense education, and security escort services. There are emergency telephones, lighted pathways/sidewalks. WOU's Safe Ride provides a free and reliable shuttle service to students who would otherwise walk alone at night and risk their safety or possible assault.

Programs of Study: WOU confers B.A., B.S., and B.Mus. degrees. Associate and master's degrees are also awarded. Bachelor's degrees are awarded in BIOLOGICAL SCIENCE (biology/biological science), BUSINESS (business administration and management), COMMUNICATIONS AND THE ARTS (American Sign Language, art, dance, dramatic arts, English, music, Spanish, and speech/debate/rhetoric), COMPUTER AND PHYSICAL SCIENCE (chemistry, computer science, earth science, information sciences and systems, mathematics, and natural sciences), EDUCATION (education and health education), SOCIAL SCIENCE (anthropology, corrections, economics, fire protection, geography, history, humanities, interdisciplinary studies, international studies, interpreter for the deaf, law enforcement and corrections, philosophy, political science/government, psychology, public administration, social science, and sociology). Education, business, and psychology are the strongest academically. Education, criminal justice, and business have the largest enrollments.

Required: To graduate, students must complete a total of 180 quarter hours with a minimum GPA of 2.0. Between 45 and 120 quarter hours are required in the major. All students must fulfill the requirements of the 55-quarter-hour liberal arts core curriculum, which includes 12 credits each of lab science and social sciences, 9 each of literature and fine arts, 4 of phys ed, and 3 each of philosophy, speech, and writing. Students must also satisfy graduation requirements in math, computer science or technology, writing-intensive, and cultural diversity.

Special: Most academic majors in liberal arts and sciences offer a B.A.-B.S degree option. Dual majors, internships, study abroad through international exchange programs and the Oregon University System, and student-designed majors in interdisciplinary studies are available. Nondegree study and pass/fail options are possible. There are 7 national honor societies, a freshman honors program, and 5 departmental honors programs.

Faculty/Classroom: 52% of faculty are male; 48% are female. No introductory courses are taught by graduate students. The average class size in an introductory lecture is 40; in a laboratory is 25; and in a regular course is 30.

Admissions: 89% of a recent year applicants were accepted.

Requirements: The SAT or ACT is required. Graduation from an accredited secondary school or satisfactory scores on the GED are required. Students must have 14 academic credits or Carnegie units. High school courses must include 4 years of English, 3 each of math and social studies, and 2 each of science and a foreign language. A GPA of 2.8 is required. AP and CLEP credits are accepted. Important factors in the admissions decision are evidence of special talent, advanced placement or honors courses, and extracurricular activities record.

Procedure: Freshmen are admitted to all sessions. Entrance exams should be taken during the junior or senior year. There is a rolling admissions plan. Application deadlines are open. Application fee is $50. Applications are accepted online.

Transfer: 503 transfer students enrolled in 2011-2012. Applicants must have a minimum GPA of 2.0. Applicants with fewer than 24 quarter hours must also meet freshman admission requirements. 45 of 180 credits required for the bachelor's degree must be completed at WOU.

Visiting: There are regularly scheduled orientations for prospective students, including seveal spring and summer orientation programs for students and a parent program. All newly admitted students should register during orientation to reserve their enrollment slot; new students can register until the first week of school. There are guides for informal visits and visitors may sit in on classes. To schedule a visit, contact the Admissions Office.

Financial Aid: In a recent year, 83% of all full-time freshmen and 75% of continuing full-time students received some form of financial aid. 61% of all full-time freshmen and 58% of continuing full-time students received need-based aid. The average financial indebtedness of a recent year's graduate was $20,427. The FAFSA, is required. Some campus-based scholarships have separate applications. Check with the school for current application deadlines.

International Students: There are 271 international students enrolled. The school actively recruits these students. They must take the TOEFL with a minimum score of 500 on the paper-based TOEFL (PBT) or 61 on the Internet-based version (iBT).

Graduates: In a recent year, 776 bachelor's degrees were awarded. The most popular majors were education (20%), business (15%), and interdisciplinary studies (9%).

Admissions Contact: Director of Admissions. E-Mail: *wolfgram@wou.edu* Web: *www.wou.edu*

WILLAMETTE UNIVERSITY B-2

Salem, OR 97301 (503) 370-6303
(877) 542-2787; (503) 375-5363

Full-time: 881 men, 1139 women
Part-time: 104 men, 105 women
Graduate: 439 men, 357 women
Year: semesters
Application Deadline: February 1
Freshman Class: 6462 applied, 5370 accepted, 525 enrolled
SAT CR/M/W: 610/600/600 **ACT:** 27 **VERY COMPETITIVE+**
Faculty: 167; IIA, +$
Ph.D.s: 95%
Student/Faculty: 11 to 1
Tuition: $40,874
Room & Board: $10,380

Willamette University, founded in 1842, is an independent liberal arts institution affiliated with the Methodist Church. There are 3 graduate schools. In addition to regional accreditation, Willamette has baccalaureate program accreditation with NASM. The 2 libraries contain 403,135 volumes, 290,140 microform items, and 13,425 audio/video tapes/CDs/DVDs, and subscribe to 26,430 periodicals including electronic. Computerized library services include interlibrary loans, database searching, and Internet access. Special learning facilities include an art gallery, natural history museum, radio station, botanical and Japanese gardens, multimedia center, and "smart" classrooms. The 72-acre campus is in an urban area 50 minutes south of Portland. Including any residence halls, there are 45 buildings.

Student Life: 79% of undergraduates are from out of state, mostly the West. Students are from 42 states, 19 foreign countries, and Canada. 69% are from public schools. 63% are White. 50% claim no religious affiliation; 27% Protestant; 12% Catholic. The average age of freshmen is 18; all undergraduates, 20. 12% do not continue beyond their first year; 78% remain to graduate.

Housing: 1493 students can be accommodated in college housing, which includes coed dorms and on-campus apartments. In addition, there are special-interest houses, fraternity houses, a 24-hour quiet-hour dorm (intensive study), and substance-free options. On-campus housing is guaranteed for the freshman year only and is available on a lottery system for upperclassmen. 68% of students live on campus; of those, 67% remain on campus on weekends. All students may keep cars.

Activities: 18% of men belong to 5 national fraternities; 12% of women belong to 3 national sororities. There are 105 groups on campus, including art, band, cheerleading, choir, chorale, chorus, computers, dance, debate, drama, ethnic, film, forensics, gay, honors, international, jazz band, literary magazine, musical theater, newspaper, orchestra, pep band, photography, political, professional, radio and TV, religious, social, social service, student government, and symphony. Popular campus events include Lu'au, Black Tie Affair, and Wulapalooza.

Sports: There are 10 intercollegiate sports for men and 10 for women, and 10 intramural sports for men and 10 for women. Facilities include a phys ed and recreation center, a 4000-seat football stadium, a 3000-seat indoor gym, a 1200-seat auditorium, a baseball stadium, a soccer field, an all-weather track, a track building, 2 other gyms, a mini-Olympic-size indoor swimming pool, an outdoor swimming pool, 3 indoor and 10 outdoor tennis courts, handball/racquetball courts, weight training facilities, and other practice fields.

Disabled Students: 90% of the campus is accessible. Facilities include wheelchair ramps, elevators, special parking, specially equipped restrooms, special class scheduling, lowered drinking fountains, lowered telephones.

Services: Counseling and information services are available, as is tutoring in most subjects. There is a reader service for the blind. Therapists are available for students on an individual need basis.

Campus Safety and Security: Measures include 24-hour foot and vehicle patrol, emergency notification system, self-defense education, and security escort services. There are emergency telephones, lighted pathways/sidewalks, formal programs and education, and a weekly published campus safety report.

Programs of Study: Willamette confers B.A., and B.M. degrees. Master's and doctoral degrees are also awarded. Bachelor's degrees are awarded in BIOLOGICAL SCIENCE (biology/biological science), COMMUNICATIONS AND THE ARTS (art history and appreciation, comparative literature, dramatic arts, English, French, German, music, music performance, music theory and composition, Spanish, speech/debate/rhetoric, and studio art), COMPUTER AND PHYSICAL SCIENCE (chemistry, computer science, mathematics, physics, and science), EDUCATION (music education), ENGINEERING AND ENVIRONMENTAL DESIGN (environmental science), HEALTH PROFESSIONS (exercise science), SOCIAL SCIENCE (American studies, anthropology, Asian/Oriental studies, classical/ancient civilization, economics, history, humanities, international studies, Japanese studies, Latin American studies, philosophy, political science/government, psychology, religion, sociology, and women's studies). Politics, biology, and economics have the largest enrollments.

Required: To graduate, students must complete a total of 124 semester hours, including a minimum of 32 in the major, with a minimum GPA of

2.0. All students must complete general education requirements in fine arts, humanities, literature, foreign language, interdisciplinary courses, natural sciences, and social sciences, and meet math and English proficiency levels. Freshmen are required to take a World Views seminar. Seniors are required to complete a senior thesis or other project in their major.

Special: Willamette offers internships with the state and city governments, a Chicago semester, a Washington semester, and a 3-2 engineering degree with Washington University, University of Southern California, and Columbia University. Nondegree study, B.A.-B.S. degrees, dual majors, work-study programs with numerous employers in the Salem area and at the university, and credit/no-credit options are also available. Study abroad programs are available in 14 countries. There are 3-2 degrees in management, forestry, and computer science. There are 7 national honor societies and including Phi Beta Kappa.

Faculty/Classroom: 54% of faculty are male; 46% are female. All teach and do research. No introductory courses are taught by graduate students. The average class size in an introductory lecture is 30; in a laboratory is 14; and in a regular course is 16.

Admissions: 83% of the 2013-2014 applicants were accepted. The SAT scores for the 2013-2014 freshman class were: Critical Reading--11% below 500, 38% between 500 and 599, 39% between 600 and 699, and 13% between 700 and 800; Math--9% below 500, 46% between 500 and 599, 34% between 600 and 699, and 12% between 700 and 800; Writing--12% below 500, 42% between 500 and 599, 39% between 600 and 699, and 7% between 700 and 800. The ACT scores were 2% below 21, 9% between 21 and 23, 35% between 24 and 26, 19% between 27 and 28, and 35% above 28. 38 freshmen graduated first in their class.

Requirements: The SAT or ACT is required. The ACT Optional Writing test is also required. Graduation from an accredited secondary school or satisfactory scores on the GED are required. Institutional preferences include 4 years each of English and math, and 3 years each of foreign language, lab science, and social studies or history. 2 essays are required, and an interview is recommended. Portfolios or auditions are recommended for art and music students. A GPA of 2.0 is required. AP credits are accepted. Important factors in the admissions decision are advanced placement or honors courses, recommendations by school officials, parents or siblings attended your school, evidence of special talent, personality/intangible qualities, extracurricular activities record, and geographical diversity.

Procedure: Freshmen are admitted fall and spring. Entrance exams should be taken December 1. There are early admissions and deferred admissions plans. Applications should be filed by February 1 for fall entry; November 1 for spring entry, along with a $50 fee. Notifications are sent April 1. 48 applicants were on the 2013 waiting list; 8 were admitted. Applications are accepted online.

Transfer: 29 transfer students enrolled in 2012-2013. Transfer students must submit transcripts for all college and high school courses. A Transfer Reference (recommendation form)and essay are required. SAT/ACT required for applicants with less than 2 years transferable course work. 60 of 124 credits required for the bachelor's degree must be completed at Willamette.

Visiting: There are regularly scheduled orientations for prospective students, consisting of fall and spring campus preview days, tours, and faculty and student presentations. There are guides for informal visits, visitors may sit in on classes, and stay overnight. To schedule a visit, contact Sue Corner at (877) LIBARTS.

Financial Aid: In 2013-2014, 99% of all full-time freshmen and 95% of continuing full-time students received some form of financial aid. 71% of all full-time freshmen and 61% of continuing full-time students received need-based aid. The average freshman award was $33,644. Need-based scholarships or need-based grants averaged $26,888; and need-based self-help aid (loans and jobs) averaged $6,516. 66% of undergraduate students work part-time. Average annual earnings from campus work are $1500. The average financial indebtedness of the 2013 graduate was $28,849. Willamette is a member of CSS. The FAFSA is required. The priority date for freshman financial aid applications for fall entry is February 1.

International Students: There are 27 international students enrolled. The school actively recruits these students. They must take the TOEFL with a minimum score of 560 on the paper-based TOEFL (PBT) or 83 on the Internet-based version (iBT), and also take the ELPT (English Language Placement Test). They must also take the SAT or ACT.

Graduates: From July 1, 2012 to June 30, 2013, 454 bachelor's degrees were awarded. The most popular majors were biology (10%), political science (9%), and rhetoric & media studies (9%). 109 companies recruited on campus in 2012-2013. In an average class, 69% graduate in 4 years or less, 75% graduate in 5 years or less, and 77% graduate in 6 years or less. Of the 2012 graduating class, 20% were enrolled in graduate school within 6 months of graduation, and 70% were employed.

Admissions Contact: Michael Beseda, Vice President, Enrollment & Communicati. E-Mail: *libarts@willamette.edu* Web: *www.willamette.edu*

PENNSYLVANIA

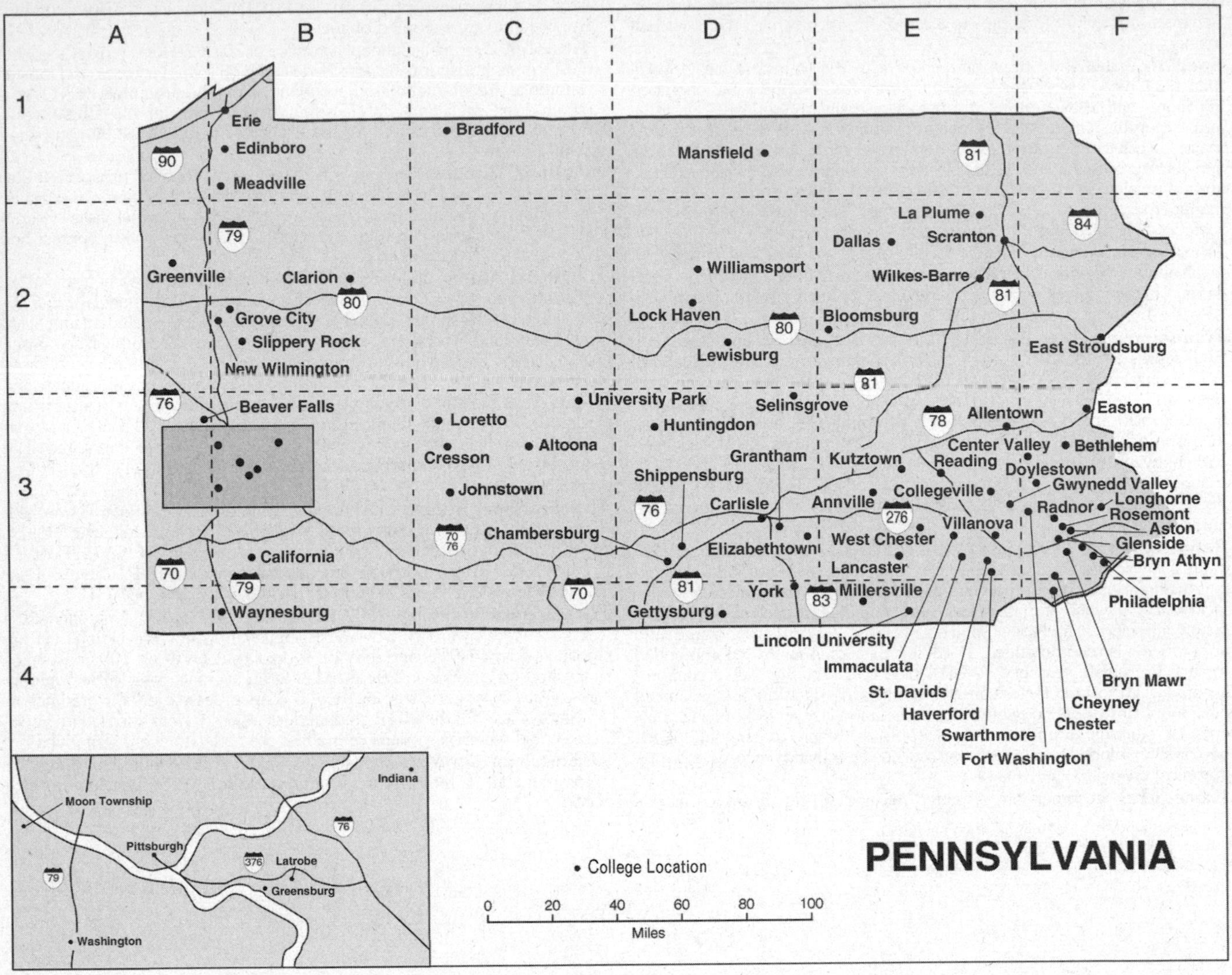

ALBRIGHT COLLEGE E-3

Reading, PA 19612 **(610) 921-7260**
(800) 252-1856; (610) 921-7294

Full-time: 747 men, 970 women
Part-time: 16 men, 18 women
Graduate: none
Year: 4-1-4, summer session
Application Deadline:
Freshman Class: 6060 applied, 3776 accepted, 655 enrolled
SAT CR/M: 510/520
Faculty: 113; IIB, -$
Ph.D.s: 58%
Student/Faculty: 13 to 1
Tuition: $36,660
Room & Board: $10,000

COMPETITIVE

Albright College, founded in 1856, is a private liberal arts institution affiliated with the United Methodist Church. There is one undergraduate school and one graduate school. The library contains 224,174 volumes, and subscribes to 37,520 periodicals including electronic. Computerized library services include interlibrary loans, database searching, Internet access, and Wi-Fi capability. Special learning facilities include an art gallery, radio station, a center for business, Civic and Global Leadership, including a 30,000 square feet of state-of-the-art classrooms, offices and meeting spaces. Our Freedman Gallery has 1,500 items in its permanent collection and hosts 9 - 12 exhibits per year. WXAC 91.3 FM - With studios and offices located in the basement of the Library/Administration Building, Albright College's own radio station offers first-hand opportunities for students to learn about marketing, public relations and communications, as well as the delivery side of the music business industry. Also: satellite dish for foreign language program, transmission and scanning electron microscopes, Holocaust resource center, Center for Excellence in Local Government, center for cultural ecology, center for Latin American studies, Albright community garden. The 118-acre campus is in a suburban area 55 miles west of Philadelphia. Including any residence halls, there are 47 buildings.

Student Life: 60% of undergraduates are from Pennsylvania. Others are from 24 states, and 18 foreign countries. 84% are from public schools. 61% are White; 18% African American. 52% claim no religious affiliation; 23% Unknown Religious affiliation; 22% Catholic. The average age of freshmen is 18; all undergraduates, 20. 25% do not continue beyond their first year; 62% remain to graduate.

Housing: 1192 students can be accommodated in college housing, which includes single-sex and coed dorms. In addition, there are honors houses, special-interest houses, Theme housing. On-campus housing is guaranteed for the freshman year only. 69% of students live on campus; of those, 80% remain on campus on weekends. All students may keep cars.

Activities: 14% of men belong to 4 national fraternities; 19% of women belong to 3 national sororities. There are 72 groups on campus, including band, cheerleading, chess, choir, chorus, computers, dance, debate, drama, environmental, ethnic, film, gay, honors, international, jazz band, literary magazine, musical theater, newspaper, orchestra, pep band, photography, political, professional, radio and TV, religious, social, social service, student government, and yearbook. Popular campus events include Greek Weekend, and Spring Fever Weekend.

Sports: There are 11 intercollegiate sports for men and 12 for women, and 5 intramural sports for men and 3 for women. Facilities include a 5,000-seat stadium, a 2,000-seat gymnasium, baseball, softball, and soccer fields, fitness center, weight room, indoor track, bowling alley, a swimming pool, spin bikes, and racquetball courts.

Disabled Students: 75% of the campus is accessible. Facilities include wheelchair ramps, elevators, special parking, specially equipped restrooms, and special class scheduling.

Services: Counseling and information services are available, as is tutoring in most subjects. There is a reader service for the blind. An academic learning center, a writing center, and an ESL program are available.

Campus Safety and Security: Measures include 24-hour foot and vehicle patrol, emergency notification system, self-defense education, and security escort services. There are shuttle buses, emergency telephones, lighted pathways/sidewalks, controlled access to dorms/residences, a comprehensive crisis action plan, and a bicycle patrol.

Programs of Study: Albright confers B.A., and B.S. degrees. Master's degrees are also awarded. Bachelor's degrees are awarded in BIOLOGICAL SCIENCE (biochemistry and biology/biological science), BUSINESS (accounting, business administration and management, and fashion merchandising), COMMUNICATIONS AND THE ARTS (art, communications, digital communications, dramatic arts, English, French, music business management, and Spanish), COMPUTER AND PHYSICAL SCIENCE (chemistry, computer science, information sciences and systems, mathematics, and physics), EDUCATION (elementary education, secondary education, and special education), ENGINEERING AND ENVIRONMENTAL DESIGN (environmental science), SOCIAL SCIENCE (American studies, child care/child and family studies, criminal justice, economics, history, Latin American studies, philosophy, political science/government, psychobiology, psychology, religion, sociology, textiles and clothing, and women's studies). Visual and performing arts, business, and social sciences have the largest enrollments.

Required: To graduate, students must complete 32 courses, including 13 to 14 in the major, with a minimum GPA of 2.0. All students take one interdisciplinary/synthesis course,one First Year Seminar and they must fulfill the cultural experience requirement. General studies requirements include 11 to 15 courses in English composition, a foreign language, natural science, quantitative reasoning, social science, the arts, and humanities (literature, history, philosophy and religion).

Special: The school offers credit and noncredit internships, a Washington center, an accelerated degree program for working adults, cross-registration, dual majors, student-designed majors, non-degree study, and pass/fail options. Study abroad may be arranged in any country. There are 11 national honor societies and a freshman honors program.

Faculty/Classroom: 46% of faculty are male; 54% are female. All teach undergraduates. No introductory courses are taught by graduate students. The average class size in an introductory lecture is 25; in a laboratory is 15; and in a regular course is 18.

Admissions: 62% of the 2013-2014 applicants were accepted. The SAT scores for the 2013-2014 freshman class were: Critical Reading--42% below 500, 43% between 500 and 599, 14% between 600 and 699, and 1% between 700 and 800; Math--36% below 500, 48% between 500 and 599, 14% between 600 and 699, and 2% between 700 and 800. 49% of the current freshmen were in the top fifth of their class; 69% were in the top two fifths. 4 freshmen graduated first in their class.

Requirements: Graduation from an accredited secondary school or satisfactory scores on the GED are required for admission. Students must have a total of 16 Carnegie units, including 4 years of English, 3 in both math and science, including 1 lab, 2 years each of a foreign language and social studies, and 1 year of both history and visual/performing arts. An essay is required, and an interview recommended. Submission of test scores is optional for admission. Students applying test optional must complete an on-campus admission interview. AP and CLEP credits are accepted. Important factors in the admissions decision are advanced placement or honors courses, leadership record, and recommendations by school officials.

Procedure: Freshmen are admitted fall, spring, and summer. Entrance exams should be taken during the spring of the junior year or the fall of the senior year. There are early admissions, deferred admissions, and rolling admissions plans. Application deadlines are open. Application fee is $25. Applications are accepted online.

Transfer: 20 transfer students enrolled in 2012-2013. Transfer students must have a minimum GPA of 2.5 and be in good standing. 64 of 128 credits required for the bachelor's degree must be completed at Albright.

Visiting: There are regularly scheduled orientations for prospective students, including an interview with a counselor and a tour of the campus with a currently enrolled student. There are guides for informal visits, visitors may sit in on classes, and stay overnight. To schedule a visit, contact the Admissions Office.

Financial Aid: In 2013-2014, 97% of all full-time freshmen and 79% of continuing full-time students received some form of financial aid. 89% of all full-time freshmen and 93% of continuing full-time students received need-based aid. The average freshman award was $35,065. Need-based scholarships or need-based grants averaged $29,190; need-based self-help aid (loans and jobs) averaged $6,281; and other non-need-based awards and non-need-based scholarships averaged $4,708. 40% of undergraduate students work part-time. Average annual earnings from campus work are $1825. The average financial indebtedness of the 2013 graduate was $26,252. Albright is a member of CSS. The FAFSA is required. The priority date for freshman financial aid applications for fall entry is March 1.

International Students: There are 72 international students enrolled. The school actively recruits these students. They must take the TOEFL with a minimum score of 520 on the paper-based TOEFL (PBT) or 68 on the Internet-based version (iBT) or take the MELAB. SAT or ACT considered if submitted.

Graduates: From July 1, 2012 to June 30, 2013, 353 bachelor's degrees were awarded. The most popular majors were visual and performing arts (18%), social sciences (16%), and business/marketing (16%). 25 companies recruited on campus in 2012-2013. In an average class, 54% graduate in 6 years or less. Of the 2012 graduating class, 28% were enrolled in graduate school within 6 months of graduation, and 61% were employed.

Admissions Contact: Gregory E. Eichhorn, Vice President for Enrollment Management and Dean of Admission. E-Mail: *albright@alb.edu* Web: *www.albright.edu*

ALLEGHENY COLLEGE B-1

Meadville, PA 16335 **(814) 332-4351** **(800) 521-5293; (814) 337-0431**

Full-time: 979 men, 1146 women	**Faculty:** 165; IIB, av$
Part-time: 7 men, 29 women	**Ph.D.s:** 93%
Graduate: n/av	**Student/Faculty:** 12 to 1
Year: semesters	**Tuition:** $39,100
Application Deadline: February 15	**Room & Board:** $9920

Freshman Class: 4512 applied, 2927 accepted, 601 enrolled

SAT CR/M/W: 590/600/575 **ACT:** 26 **HIGHLY COMPETITIVE**

Allegheny College has been the premiere college in the country for students with "Unusual Combinations" of interests and talents for nearly 200 years. Because of the academic rigor, experiential focus, and strong reputation behind an Allegheny degree, graduates are well prepared for extraordinary outcomes. The library contains 948,445 volumes, 506,781 microform items, 146,766 audio/video tapes/CDs/DVDs, and subscribes to 21,180 periodicals including electronic. Computerized library services include interlibrary loans, database searching, Internet access, and Wi-Fi capability. Special learning facilities include an art gallery, planetarium, radio station, TV station, observatory, 283-acre experimental research reserve, art studio, 80-acre protected forest, dance studio, Geographic Information Systems Learning Laboratory, language learning center, science complex, seismographic network station, Center for Political Participation, Theater and Communication Arts Center, Living and Learning Residential Communities, environmental roof garden, Richard J. Cook Center for Environmental Science. The 565-acre campus is in a suburban area 90 miles north of Pittsburgh, 35 miles south of Erie. Including any residence halls, there are 41 buildings.

Student Life: 54% of undergraduates are from Pennsylvania. Others are from 45 states, 41 foreign countries, and Canada. 83% are from public schools. 79% are White. 38% claim no religious affiliation; 27% Catholic; 21% Protestant; 11% Buddhist, Hindu, Muslem and other Christian. The average age of freshmen is 19; all undergraduates, 20. 13% do not continue beyond their first year; 79% remain to graduate.

Housing: 1895 students can be accommodated in college housing, which includes single-sex and coed dorms, on-campus apartments, and off-campus apartments. In addition, there are language houses, special-interest houses, fraternity houses, wellness community, quiet study floors, townhouses, civic engagement community, ADA accessible, living and learning residential communities. On-campus housing is guaranteed for all 4 years and is available on a lottery system for upperclassmen. 90% of students live on campus; of those, 80% remain on campus on weekends. All students may keep cars.

Activities: 24% of men belong to 5 national fraternities; 32% of women belong to 5 national sororities. There are 129 groups on campus, including coffee house, music ensembles, outdoor programs, student programming board, academic, art, band, cheerleading, chess, choir, chorale, chorus, computers, dance, drama, environmental, ethnic, gay, honors, international, jazz band, literary magazine, musical theater, newspaper, orchestra, political, professional, radio and TV, religious, social, social service, student government, symphony, and yearbook. Popular campus events include Homecoming, Orchesis Dance Performance, Make A Difference Day, Springfest, Black Heritage Month, Celebrate Asia, International Month, Wingfest, Late Night Events, Relay For Life, and Coming Out Week.

Sports: There are 10 intercollegiate sports for men and 11 for women, and 6 intramural sports for men and 6 for women. Facilities include a comprehensive sports and fitness center that includes a 200 meter training track, weight rooms, cardio machines, 4 multipurpose indoor courts (volleyball, basketball, tennis, badminton, putting green, batting cage), a natatorium, a dance studio, 3 racquetball courts. Outdoor sports complex with a stadium, stadium lights, FieldTurf playing surface, LED graphic display scoreboard, championship style cross-country course, 12 lighted tennis courts, baseball, softball, soccer and rugby grass fields, field for shot put, discuss and hammer throw and a 400 meter double bend 8-lane competition track. In addition, there are 80 wooded acres for mountain biking, hiking, and cross-country skiing.

Disabled Students: 42% of the campus is accessible. Facilities include wheelchair ramps, elevators, special parking, specially equipped restrooms, special class scheduling, lowered drinking fountains, special housing. Reasonable accommodations are made for special needs.

Services: Counseling and information services are available, as is tutoring in some subjects, biology, chemistry, economics, geology, mathematics, modern languages, physics, psychology. other support services available for study skills, technology assistance, time management, a speech consultation, a learning center, writing center, note-taking scribe services, tape recorders, and books on tape.

Campus Safety and Security: Measures include 24-hour foot and vehicle patrol, emergency notification system, self-defense education, and security escort services. There are shuttle buses, emergency telephones, lighted pathways/sidewalks, controlled access to dorms/residences, TTY phones, emergency medical dispatching, motorist assistance, property engraving, on-campus sworn police officers, compliance program.

Programs of Study: Allegheny confers B.A., and B.S. degrees. Bachelor's degrees are awarded in AGRICULTURE (environmental studies), BIOLOGICAL SCIENCE (biochemistry, biology/biological science, and neurosciences), COMMUNICATIONS AND THE ARTS (art, art history and appreciation, communications, dramatic arts, English, French, German, music, Spanish, and studio art), COMPUTER AND PHYSICAL SCIENCE (chemistry, computer science, environmental geology, geology, mathematics, physics, and software engineering), ENGINEERING AND ENVIRONMENTAL DESIGN (environmental science), HEALTH PROFESSIONS (public health), SOCIAL SCIENCE (economics, history, international studies, philosophy, political science/government, psychology, religion, and women's studies). Physical and biological sciences, economics, international studies, psychology and environmental science are the strongest academically. Biology, economics, psychology, political science and English have the largest enrollments.

Required: To graduate, students must complete 128 credit hours with a minimum GPA of 2.0 in both the major and minor. Between 36 and 64 hours are required in the major, including the junior seminar and senior research project. All students must fulfill liberal arts studies requirements of 8 credits in the division least represented in the major and minor and a laboratory course is required for non-natural science majors or minors. Additional required courses include freshman first seminar, freshman second seminar, a sophomore writing and speaking seminar. All graduating seniors complete an independent research project and an oral defense of the project.

Special: Allegheny offers domestic off campus semesters in 7 programs - New York Arts, Oak Ridge Science Center, Philadelphia Center, Washington semester,Duke Marian Lab NC, Ecosystems Center MA, Newberry Seminar Research in the Humanities IL; internships; double majors; independent study; student-designed majors; study abroad in 15 countries; work study. A 3-2 engineering degree is available with Case Western Reserve, Columbia, Duke, University of Pittsburgh, and Washington University. Accelerated masters in public policy & Management, occupational therapy, and physician assistant. Accelerated doctorate in nursing, physical therapy, and osteopathic medicine. Preprofessional programs, graduate school partnerships, and an experiential learning term are also available. There are 15 national honor societies, including Phi Beta Kappa, and 18 departmental honors programs.

Faculty/Classroom: 52% of faculty are male; 48% are female. All teach undergraduates, 84% do research, and 84% do both. No introductory courses are taught by graduate students. The average class size in an introductory lecture is 22; in a laboratory is 19; and in a regular course is 18.

Admissions: 65% of the 2013-2014 applicants were accepted. The SAT scores for the 2013-2014 freshman class were: Critical Reading--11% below 500, 41% between 500 and 599, 39% between 600 and 699, and 9% between 700 and 800; Math--12% below 500, 36% between 500 and 599, 45% between 600 and 699, and 7% between 700 and 800; Writing--6% below 500, 42% between 500 and 599, 36% between 600 and 699, and 6% between 700 and 800. The ACT scores were 7% below 21, 21% between 21 and 23, 25% between 24 and 26, 21% between 27 and 28, and 26% above 28. 62% of the current freshmen were in the top fifth of their class; 88% were in the top two fifths. 17 freshmen graduated first in their class.

Requirements: The SAT or ACT is required. Graduation from an accredited secondary school is required for admission. The GED is accepted. Students must have 16 Carnegie units, including 4 years of English, 3 years each of math, science, and social studies, and 2 years of a foreign language. An essay is required, and an interview is recommended. A college prep program and 2 letters of recommendation (1 from guidance counselor, 1 from teacher) are required. AP and CLEP credits are accepted. Important factors in the admissions decision are advanced placement or honors courses, extracurricular activities record, and leadership record.

Procedure: Freshmen are admitted fall and spring. Entrance exams should be taken by January of the senior year. There are early decision, early admissions, and deferred admissions plans. Early decision applications should be filed by November 15; regular applications, by February 15 for fall entry; and November 1 for spring entry. Notification of early decision is sent December 15; regular decision, April 1. 56 early decision candidates were accepted for the 2013-2014 class. 174 applicants were on the 2013 waiting list; 7 were admitted. Applications are accepted online. Application fees are waived if application is completed online.

Transfer: 22 transfer students enrolled in 2012-2013. Transfer applicants must submit a transcript of all college courses, a high school transcript, standardized test scores, college official's report from prior institutions, essay/personal statement, a letter describing reasons for transfer, and one recommendation from college official. A minimum GPA of 2.5 from college and high school is required, with 3.0 from college recommended. An interview is recommended. 64 of 128 credits required for the bachelor's degree must be completed at Allegheny.

Visiting: There are regularly scheduled orientations for prospective students, consisting of tours, panels, presentations on academic programs, student life, admissions, and financial aid. There are guides for informal visits, visitors may sit in on classes, and stay overnight. To schedule a visit, contact the Office of Admissions.

Financial Aid: In 2013-2014, 100% of all full-time freshmen and 99% of continuing full-time students received some form of financial aid. 74% of all full-time freshmen and 71% of continuing full-time students received need-based aid. The average freshman award was $31,394. Need-based scholarships or need-based grants averaged $26,205 ($46,424 maximum); need-based self-help aid (loans and jobs) averaged $6,324 ($9,500 maximum); other non-need-based awards and non-need-based scholarships averaged $16,665 ($47,020 maximum); and $34,510 from other forms of aid. 70% of undergraduate students work part-time. Average annual earnings from campus work are $1228. The FAFSA is required. The priority date for freshman financial aid applications for fall entry is February 15.

International Students: There are 83 international students enrolled. The school actively recruits these students. They must take the TOEFL with a minimum score of 550 on the paper-based TOEFL (PBT) or 80 on the Internet-based version (iBT). They must also take the SAT or ACT. SAT or ACT can be submitted in place of TOEFL.

Graduates: From July 1, 2012 to June 30, 2013, 463 bachelor's degrees were awarded. The most popular majors were psychology (12%), biology (12%), and economics (12%). 81 companies recruited on campus in 2012-2013. In an average class, 72% graduate in 4 years or less, 77% graduate in 5 years or less, and 79% graduate in 6 years or less. Of the 2012 graduating class, 35% were enrolled in graduate school within 6 months of graduation, and 51% were employed.

Admissions Contact: Brian Dalton, V.P. of Enrollment & Communications. E-Mail: *admissions@allegheny.edu* Web: *www.allegheny.edu/admissions/*

ALVERNIA UNIVERSITY — E-3

Reading, PA 19607 — (610) 796-3005; (888) Alvernia; (610) 796-8336

Full-time: 535 men, 1184 women	**Faculty:** 97
Part-time: 122 men, 530 women	**Ph.D.s:** 66%
Graduate: 184 men, 316 women	**Student/Faculty:** 12 to 1
Year: semesters, summer session	**Tuition:** $29,060
Application Deadline: open	**Room & Board:** $10,190
Freshman Class: 1792 applied, 1391 accepted, 389 enrolled	
SAT CR/M/W: 490/500/480 **ACT:** 20	**COMPETITIVE**

Alvernia College, established in 1958, is a Roman Catholic liberal arts institution. The figures in the above capsule and in this profile are approximate. There are 2 undergraduate schools and one graduate school. In addition to regional accreditation, Alvernia has baccalaureate program accreditation with APTA, CSWE, NCATE, and NLN. The library contains 89,361 volumes, and 2,140 audio/video tapes/CDs/DVDs, and subscribes to 41,005 periodicals including electronic. Computerized library services include interlibrary loans, database searching, Internet access, and Wi-Fi capability. Special learning facilities include an art gallery. The 121-acre campus is in a suburban area 3 miles southwest of Reading. Including any residence halls, there are 20 buildings.

Student Life: 75% of undergraduates are from Pennsylvania. Others are from 18 states, and 4 foreign countries. 71% are White; 14% African American. 56% are Hindu, Muslim, and Buddist; 38% Catholic. The average age of freshmen is 18; all undergraduates, 21. 29% do not continue beyond their first year; 51% remain to graduate.

Housing: 964 students can be accommodated in college housing, which includes single-sex and coed dorms and on-campus apartments. In addition, there are honors houses. On-campus housing is guaranteed for the freshman year only, is available on a first-come, and first-served basis. Priority is given to out-of-town students. 57% of students live on campus; of those, 75% remain on campus on weekends. All students may keep cars.

Activities: There are no fraternities or sororities. There are 35 groups on campus, including band, cheerleading, chorale, chorus, computers, drama, ethnic, honors, international, literary magazine, musical theater, newspaper, political, professional, religious, social, social service, student government, and yearbook. Popular campus events include Christmas on Campus, Spring Fling and Club Fair.

Sports: There are 9 intercollegiate sports for men and 11 for women, and 8 intramural sports for men and 8 for women. Facilities include a gym, a physical fitness and recreation center, playing fields, and outdoor tennis, basketball, and volleyball courts.

Disabled Students: 75% of the campus is accessible. Facilities include wheelchair ramps, elevators, special parking, specially equipped restrooms, special class scheduling, lowered drinking fountains, lowered telephones, and special housing.

Services: Counseling and information services are available, as is tutoring in every subject. There is remedial math, reading, and writing. Facilities include a writing center and a math/science tutorial lab.

Campus Safety and Security: Measures include 24-hour foot and vehicle patrol and security escort services. There are shuttle buses, emergency telephones, lighted pathways/sidewalks, controlled access to dorms/residences, Photo ID cards must be carried by students.

Programs of Study: Alvernia confers B.A., B.S., B.S.N. and B.S.W. degrees. Associate, master's, and doctoral degrees are also awarded. Bachelor's degrees are awarded in BIOLOGICAL SCIENCE (biochemistry, biology/biological science, and forensic science), BUSINESS (accounting, business administration and management, human resources, marketing and distribution, and sports management), COMMUNICATIONS AND THE ARTS (communications, English, and theatre arts), COMPUTER AND PHYSICAL SCIENCE (chemistry, mathematics, and science), EDUCATION (athletic training, elementary education, middle school education, and secondary education), HEALTH PROFESSIONS (health science and nursing), SOCIAL SCIENCE (behavioral science, criminal justice, history, liberal arts/general studies, philosophy, political science/government, psychology, social work, and theological studies). Biology, chemistry, and occupational therapy are the strongest academically. criminal justice, nursing, and business have the largest enrollments.

Required: To graduate, all students must complete at least 123 credit hours with a minimum GPA of 2.0 overall and in the major (2.5 for elementary education and nursing majors). Requirements include 54 to 55 credits in a liberal arts core, consisting of theology and philosophy, social science, communications, literature, fine arts, math, and science. All students also must perform 40 clock hours of service to others before graduation, complete course work in college success skills and in human diversity, and demonstrate computer proficiency.

Special: The college offers co-op programs in business and sports management, internships, cross-registration with Kutztown University, Pennsylvania State University, Albright College, and Reading area community colleges, a Washington semester, dual and student-designed majors, and practicums in psychology, criminal justice, education, addiction studies, social work, athletic training, and occupational therapy. There are 13 national honor societies, a freshman honors program, and 10 departmental honors programs.

Faculty/Classroom: 46% of faculty are male; 54% are female. 93% teach undergraduates. No introductory courses are taught by graduate students. The average class size in an introductory lecture is 19; in a laboratory is 18; and in a regular course is 19.

Admissions: 78% of the 2013-2014 applicants were accepted. The SAT scores for the 2013-2014 freshman class were: Critical Reading--52% below 500, 41% between 500 and 599, 6% between 600 and 699, and 1% between 700 and 800; Math--49% below 500, 43% between 500 and 599, 7% between 600 and 699, and 1% between 700 and 800; Writing--58% below 500, 36% between 500 and 599, 5% between 600 and 699, and 1% between 700 and 800. The ACT scores were 53% below 21, 33% between 21 and 23, 11% between 24 and 26, and 6% between 27 and 28.

Requirements: The SAT or ACT is required. All applicants must be graduates of an accredited secondary school or have a GED certificate. They should have completed at least 16 academic units, including 4 in English and electives and 2 each in math, foreign language, science, and social studies. An interview is required for nursing applicants and strongly recommended for all others. A GPA of 2.0 is required. AP and CLEP credits are accepted. Important factors in the admissions decision are personality/intangible qualities, advanced placement or honors courses, and extracurricular activities record.

Procedure: Freshmen are admitted fall and spring. Entrance exams should be taken in the spring of the junior year or fall of the senior year. There are deferred admissions and rolling admissions plans. Application deadlines are open. Application fee is $25. Notification is sent on a rolling basis. Applications are accepted online.

Transfer: 102 transfer students enrolled in 2012-2013. Applicants must have a college GPA of 2.0 or better. 45 of 123 credits required for the bachelor's degree must be completed at Alvernia.

Visiting: There are regularly scheduled orientations for prospective students, including faculty displays, lunch, tours of the campus, and the opportunity to interact with current students. There are guides for informal visits, visitors may sit in on classes, and stay overnight. To schedule a visit, contact the Admissions Office at admissions@alvernia.edu.

Financial Aid: In 2013-2014, 87% of all full-time freshmen and 85% of continuing full-time students received some form of financial aid. 87% of all full-time freshmen and 83% of continuing full-time students received need-based aid. The average freshman award was $19,880. Need-based scholarships or need-based grants averaged $16,195; need-based self-help aid (loans and jobs) averaged $4,167; and other non-need-based awards and non-need-based scholarships averaged $3,223. Alvernia is a member of CSS. The FAFSA and the state aid form, and the noncustodial parent's statement, if applicable. are required. Check with the school for current application deadlines.

International Students: There are 4 international students enrolled. They must take the TOEFL with a minimum score of 550 on the paper-based TOEFL (PBT) or 75 on the Internet-based version (iBT). They must also take the SAT or ACT.

Graduates: From July 1, 2012 to June 30, 2013, 463 bachelor's degrees were awarded. The most popular majors were health professions (41%), business (21%), and criminal justice (11%). 67 companies recruited on campus in 2012-2013. In an average class, 38% graduate in 4 years or less, 48% graduate in 5 years or less, and 51% graduate in 6 years or less.

Admissions Contact: John McCloskey, Vice President for Enrollment Managment. E-Mail: *john.mccloskey@alvernia.edu* Web: *www.alvernia .edu*

ARCADIA UNIVERSITY F-3

Glenside, PA 19038 (215) 572-2910
(877) ARCADIA; (215) 572-4049

Full-time: 480 men, 1270 women	**Faculty:** 103; IIA, av$
Part-time: 70 men, 140 women	**Ph.D.s:** 89%
Graduate: 350 men, 1100 women	**Student/Faculty:** n/av
Year: semesters, summer session	**Tuition:** $34,650
Application Deadline: open	**Room & Board:** $12,140
Freshman Class: n/av	
SAT or ACT: required	

COMPETITIVE+

Arcadia University, founded in 1853, is a private institution offering undergraduate and graduate programs in the fine arts, the sciences, business, education, and preprofessional fields. There is 1 graduate school. Some figures in the above capsule and in this profile are approximate. In addition to regional accreditation, Arcadia has baccalaureate program accreditation with ACBSP, APTA, CAHEA, and NASAD. The library contains 148,271 volumes, 50,301 microform items, 3236 audio/video tapes/CDs/DVDs, and subscribes to 7832 periodicals including electronic. Computerized library services include interlibrary loans, database searching, Internet access, and laptop Internet portals. Special learning facilities include a learning resource center, art gallery, radio station, observatory, theater, computer graphics and communication labs, and multimedia classrooms. The 76-acre campus is in a suburban area 10 miles north of Philadelphia. Including any residence halls, there are 21 buildings.

Student Life: 68% of undergraduates are from Pennsylvania. Others are from 24 states and 12 foreign countries. 70% are from public schools. 70% are white. 77% claim no religious affiliation; 13% Catholic. The average age of freshmen is 18; all undergraduates, 22. 19% do not continue beyond their first year; 64% remain to graduate.

Housing: 1284 students can be accommodated in college housing, which includes single-sex and coed dorms, on-campus apartments, and off-campus apartments. There is a living and learning community in Grey Towers Castle. On-campus housing is guaranteed for all 4 years. 68% of students live on campus. Upperclassmen may keep cars.

Activities: There are no fraternities or sororities. There are 40 groups on campus, including art, cheerleading, choir, chorale, chorus, communications, computers, dance, drama, ethnic, gay, honors, international, literary magazine, musical theater, newspaper, photography, political, professional, radio and TV, religious, social, social service, student government, and yearbook. Popular campus events include Mr. Beaver contest, Woodstock Weekend, and International Festival.

Sports: There are 6 intercollegiate sports for men and 9 for women, and 5 intramural sports for men and 5 for women. Facilities include a softball field, outdoor tennis and basketball courts, field hockey and soccer/lacrosse fields, and an athletic and recreation center with a 1500-seat gym for basketball and volleyball, an indoor track, an indoor NCAA regulation swimming pool, an aerobics and dance studio, and fitness and training rooms.

Disabled Students: 70% of the campus is accessible. Facilities include wheelchair ramps, elevators, special parking, specially equipped rest rooms, special class scheduling, lowered drinking fountains, and lowered telephones.

Services: Counseling and information services are available, as is tutoring in every subject. There is a reader service for the blind, and remedial math, reading, and writing.

Campus Safety and Security: Measures include 24-hour foot and vehicle patrol, self-defense education, and security escort services. There are shuttle buses, emergency telephones, lighted pathways/sidewalks, alarmed doors, night receptionists, and card access to residence halls.

Programs of Study: Arcadia confers B.A., B.S., and B.F.A. degrees.

Master's and doctoral degrees are also awarded. Bachelor's degrees are awarded in BIOLOGICAL SCIENCE (biology/biological science), BUSINESS (accounting, banking and finance, business administration and management, international business management, marketing/retailing/merchandising, and personnel management), COMMUNICATIONS AND THE ARTS (art history and appreciation, communications, dramatic arts, English, fine arts, graphic design, illustration, photography, and theater design), COMPUTER AND PHYSICAL SCIENCE (chemistry, computer science, mathematics, and science), EDUCATION (art education, early childhood education, elementary education, music education, secondary education, and special education), ENGINEERING AND ENVIRONMENTAL DESIGN (engineering, environmental science, and interior design), HEALTH PROFESSIONS (art therapy, health care administration, predentistry, premedicine, preoptometry, and preveterinary science), SOCIAL SCIENCE (criminal justice, history, international studies, liberal arts/general studies, philosophy, political science/government, prelaw, psychobiology, psychology, and sociology). Biology, psychology, and math are the strongest academically. Fine arts, business, and education have the largest enrollments.

Required: Students must take English composition, math, 2 semesters of a lab science, and a foreign language. They must also fulfill 24 credits of distribution requirements in the arts, humanities, and social sciences; core courses in American pluralism and non-Western cultures; and a final project or thesis. 128 credit hours are required to graduate, including 40 to 52 in the major, with a minimum GPA of 2.0.

Special: Internships are encouraged in all majors. There are study-abroad programs in 13 countries and co-op programs in business, computer science, chemistry, actuarial science, and accounting. There is a 3-2 engineering program with Columbia University and 3-4 optometry programs with Jefferson University and the Pennsylvania College of Optometry. Arcadia also offers a Washington semester, work-study, student-designed majors, a dual major in chemistry and business, interdisciplinary majors in scientific illustration, and credit by exam. There are 13 national honor societies and a freshman honors program.

Faculty/Classroom: 44% of faculty are male; 56% are female. All faculty does research. No introductory courses are taught by graduate students. The average class size in an introductory lecture is 28; in a laboratory, 20; and in a regular course, 16.

Admissions: 85% of a recent year's applicants were accepted. 51% of a recent year's freshmen were in the top fifth of their class; 86% were in the top two fifths. 4 freshmen graduated first in their class.

Requirements: The SAT or ACT is required. Applicants must be graduates of an accredited secondary school or have a GED. A total of 16 academic credits is required, including 4 years of English, 3 each of math and social studies, and 2 each of a foreign language and science. An essay is required. All art and illustration majors (except art education) must submit a portfolio. AP and CLEP credits are accepted. Important factors in the admissions decision are advanced placement or honors courses, recommendations by school officials, and extracurricular activities record.

Procedure: Freshmen are admitted fall and spring. Entrance exams should be taken during orientation. There are early decision, early admissions, deferred admissions, and rolling admissions plans. Application deadlines are open. Application fee is $30 (waived for online applications). Notification is sent on a rolling basis.

Transfer: 167 transfer students enrolled in a recent year. Applicants must have a GPA of 2.5. Art majors must submit a portfolio. The SAT or ACT is required if the student has earned less than 1 year of college credit. An interview is encouraged. 32 of 128 credits required for the bachelor's degree must be completed at Arcadia.

Visiting: There are regularly scheduled orientations for prospective students, including personal interviews Monday through Saturday, open houses, and opportunities to dine on campus and to meet with faculty, financial aid officers, and current students. There are guides for informal visits, and visitors may sit in on classes and stay overnight. To schedule a visit, contact the Office of Enrollment Management.

Financial Aid: In a recent year, 99% of all full-time freshmen and 94% of continuing full-time students received some form of financial aid. 77% of all full-time freshmen received need-based aid. 30% of undergraduate students work part-time. The FAFSA and the college's own financial statement, PHEAA, and parent and student tax returns are required. Check with the school for current application deadlines.

International Students: There were 41 international students enrolled in a recent year. The school actively recruits these students. They must take the TOEFL.

Graduates: In a recent year, 381 bachelor's degrees were awarded. The most popular majors were business (15%), education (15%), and psychology (11%).

Admissions Contact: Director of Admissions. A campus DVD is available. E-Mail: *admiss@arcadia.edu* Web: *www.arcadia.edu*

BLOOMSBURG UNIVERSITY OF PENNSYLVANIA E-2

Bloomsburg, PA 17815 **(570) 389-4316; (570) 389-4741**

Full-time: 3430 men, 4675 women
Part-time: 190 men, 310 women
Graduate: 280 men, 630 women
Year: semesters, summer session
Application Deadline: open
Freshman Class: n/av
SAT or ACT: required

Faculty: 387; IIA, +$
Ph.D.s: 92%
Student/Faculty: n/av
Tuition: $8582 ($17,942)
Room & Board: $7716

COMPETITIVE

Bloomsburg University of Pennsylvania, founded in 1839, is a public institution offering undergraduate programs in the liberal arts, sciences, business, teacher education, technology, and health professions. There are 4 undergraduate schools and 1 graduate school. Some figures in the above capsule and in this profile are approximate. In addition to regional accreditation, BU has baccalaureate program accreditation with AACSB, ABET, CAAHEP, CCNE, CSWE, NASM, NAST, and NCATE. The library contains 489,636 volumes, 2.1 million microform items, 13,502 audio/video tapes/CDs/DVDs, and subscribes to 1710 periodicals including electronic. Computerized library services include interlibrary loans, database searching, Internet access, and laptop Internet portals. Special learning facilities include a learning resource center, art gallery, radio station, and TV station. The 282-acre campus is in a small town 80 miles northeast of Harrisburg. Including any residence halls, there are 72 buildings.

Student Life: 89% of undergraduates are from Pennsylvania. Others are from 22 states, 23 foreign countries, and Canada. 88% are from public schools. 77% are white. The average age of freshmen is 18; all undergraduates, 21. 19% do not continue beyond their first year; 63% remain to graduate.

Housing: 3523 students can be accommodated in college housing, which includes coed dorms, on-campus apartments, and off-campus apartments. In addition, there are honors houses, special-interest houses, and living/learning communities in the residence halls. On-campus housing is guaranteed for the freshman year only. Alcohol is not permitted. All students may keep cars.

Activities: 7% of men belong to 3 local and 12 national fraternities; 9% of women belong to 5 local and 8 national sororities. There are 237 groups on campus, including art, band, cheerleading, chess, choir, chorale, chorus, computers, dance, drama, drill team, ethnic, film, forensics, gay, honors, international, jazz band, literary magazine, marching band, musical theater, newspaper, orchestra, pep band, political, professional, radio and TV, religious, social, social service, student government, and yearbook. Popular campus events include Renaissance Jamboree and Siblings and Children Weekend.

Sports: There are 9 intercollegiate sports for men and 9 for women, and 3 intramural sports for men and 3 for women. Facilities include a 5000-seat stadium, a gym, an athletic field, an indoor track, a 6-lane swimming pool, 9 practice fields, 18 Grasstex tennis courts, racquetball/handball courts, and a 57,000-square-foot recreation facility.

Disabled Students: Facilities include wheelchair ramps, elevators, special parking, specially equipped rest rooms, special class scheduling, lowered drinking fountains, and lowered telephones.

Services: Counseling and information services are available, as is tutoring in some subjects. There is a reader service for the blind, and remedial math, reading, and writing.

Campus Safety and Security: Measures include 24-hour foot and vehicle patrol, emergency notification system, self-defense education, and security escort services. There are shuttle buses, emergency telephones, lighted pathways/sidewalks, controlled access to dorms/residences, monitored surveillance cameras, and strict residence hall security.

Programs of Study: BU confers B.A., B.S., B.S.Ed., B.S.N., and B.S.W. degrees. Associate, master's, and doctoral degrees are also awarded. Bachelor's degrees are awarded in BIOLOGICAL SCIENCE (biology/biological science), BUSINESS (accounting, business administration and management, and business economics), COMMUNICATIONS AND THE ARTS (American Sign Language, art history and appreciation, communications, dramatic arts, English, French, German, music, Spanish, speech/debate/rhetoric, and studio art), COMPUTER AND PHYSICAL SCIENCE (chemistry, computer science, geoscience, mathematics, physics, and radiological technology), EDUCATION (business education, early childhood education, middle school education, secondary education, social studies education, and special education), ENGINEERING AND ENVIRONMENTAL DESIGN (electrical/electronics engineering), HEALTH PROFESSIONS (exercise science, health science, medical laboratory technology, nursing, and speech pathology/audiology), SOCIAL SCIENCE (anthropology, criminal justice, economics, geography, history, philosophy, political science/government, psychology, social work, and sociology). Elementary education, business administration, and special education have the largest enrollments.

Required: To graduate, students must complete 120 credit hours with a minimum GPA of 2.0. BU requires 12 semester hours each in humanities, social sciences, and natural sciences and math. There are specific course requirements in communication, quantitative/analytical reasoning, values, ethics, responsible decision making, and survival, fitness, and recreational skills.

Special: Internships for upperclassmen, study abroad in more than 11 countries, work-study programs, and dual majors are available. BU offers a 3-2 engineering degree with Pennsylvania State and Wilkes Universities. BU has partnered with Luzerne County Community College, Harrisburg Area Community College, and Lehigh Carbon Community College to provide a completion program in early childhood education. There is nondegree study, pass/fail options, and credit for life, military, and work experience. The school uses telecourses and interactive video. There are 9 national honor societies, a freshman honors program, and 15 departmental honors programs.

Faculty/Classroom: 53% of faculty are male; 47% are female. 87% teach undergraduates. No introductory courses are taught by graduate students. The average class size in a laboratory is 16; in a regular course, 31.

Admissions: 64% of a recent year's applicants were accepted. 28% of a recent year's freshmen were in the top fifth of their class; 62% were in the top two fifths. 12 freshmen graduated first in their class.

Requirements: The SAT or ACT is required. Applicants must be graduates of an accredited secondary school. To be competitive, a student should also rank in the top 30% of the high school class with a B average. The GED is accepted. Applicants should complete 4 years each of English and social studies, 3 each of math and science, and 2 of a foreign language. An interview is recommended. AP and CLEP credits are accepted.

Procedure: Freshmen are admitted to all sessions. Entrance exams should be taken during the junior year. There are early decision, early admissions, deferred admissions, and rolling admissions plans. Application deadlines are open. Application fee is $35. Notification is sent on a rolling basis. 215 applicants were on a recent year's waiting list. Applications are accepted online.

Transfer: 568 transfer students enrolled in a recent year. Either the SAT or ACT is required from applicants who have completed fewer than 24 semester hours of college credits. An official secondary school transcript or a GED and official transcripts from any postsecondary schools attended are also required. Applicants must have a minimum GPA of 2.0 (2.5 or 2.8 for some majors) and be in good standing at the college last attended. Those who have completed 30 semester hours must select a major upon entering BU. 30 of 120 credits required for the bachelor's degree must be completed at BU.

Visiting: There are regularly scheduled orientations for prospective students, consisting of a general meeting with admissions staff, a question-and-answer session, a campus tour, lunch, and meetings with academic faculty. There are guides for informal visits, and visitors may sit in on classes. To schedule a visit, contact the Admissions Office.

Financial Aid: In a recent year, 82% of all full-time freshmen and 80% of continuing full-time students received some form of financial aid. 62% of all full-time freshmen and 60% of continuing full-time students received need-based aid. The average freshman award was $11,880. Need-based scholarships or need-based grants averaged $6609; need-based self-help aid (loans and jobs) averaged $4122; non-need-based athletic scholarships averaged $2867; and other non-need-based awards and non-need-based scholarships averaged $2025. The FAFSA and PHEAA Aid Information Request (PAIR) are required. Check with the school for current application deadlines.

International Students: There were 72 international students enrolled in a recent year. They must take the TOEFL with a minimum score of 500 on the paper-based TOEFL (PBT).

Graduates: In a recent year, 1567 bachelor's degrees were awarded. The most popular majors were business administration (17%), elementary education (10%), and special education (6%). In an average class, 40% graduate in 4 years or less, 60% graduate in 5 years or less, and 63% graduate in 6 years or less. 39 companies recruited on campus in a recent year. Of a recent year's graduating class, 19% were enrolled in graduate school within 6 months of graduation, and 72% were employed.

Admissions Contact: Christopher Keller, Director of Admissions. E-mail: *buadmiss@bloomu.edu* Web: *www.bloomu.edu*

BRYN ATHYN COLLEGE OF THE NEW CHURCH F-3

Bryn Athyn, PA 19009	**(267) 502-6044; (267) 502-2593**
Full-time: 93 men, 109 women	**Faculty:** 32
Part-time: 6 men, 5 women	**Ph.D.s:** 56%
Graduate: 12 men, 5 women	**Student/Faculty:** 7 to 1
Year: trimesters	**Tuition:** $17,724
Application Deadline: February 1	**Room & Board:** $10,260
Freshman Class: 396 applied, 207 accepted, 80 enrolled	
SAT CR/M/W: 510/510/470 **ACT:** 22	**COMPETITIVE**

Bryn Athyn College of the New Church, founded in 1877, is a private, independent, liberal arts institution affiliated with the General Church of the New Jerusalem. There is one undergraduate school and one graduate school. The 2 libraries contain 144,475 volumes, 3,593 microform items, 2,017 audio/video tapes/CDs/DVDs, and subscribe to 8,497 periodicals including electronic. Computerized library services include interlibrary loans, database searching, Internet access, and Wi-Fi capability. Special learning facilities include a The 130-acre campus is in a suburban area 15 miles northeast of Philadelphia, PA. Including any residence halls, there are 13 buildings.

Student Life: 71% of undergraduates are from Pennsylvania. Others are from 16 states, 21 foreign countries, and Canada. 39% are from public schools. 67% are White; 19% Foreign. The average age of freshmen is 18; all undergraduates, 21. 9% do not continue beyond their first year; 91% remain to graduate.

Housing: 210 students can be accommodated in college housing, which includes single-sex dorms, on-campus apartments, and off-campus apartments. On-campus housing is guaranteed for all 4 years. 75% of students live on campus; of those, 100% remain on campus on weekends. Alcohol is not permitted. All students may keep cars.

Activities: There are no fraternities or sororities. There are 18 groups on campus, including and college games club, business club, psychology club, chorale, chorus, dance, drama, international, newspaper, Outing club, social, social service, and student government. Popular campus events include Charter Day, Service Day, and Alumni Weekend.

Sports: There are 6 intercollegiate sports for men and 5 for women. Facilities include a 500-seat gym, an open air ice hockey/skating rink, tennis courts, 2 athletic fields, a fitness center, and a dance studio.

Disabled Students: 90% of the campus is accessible. Facilities include wheelchair ramps, elevators, special parking, specially equipped restrooms, lowered drinking fountains, and special housing.

Services: Counseling and information services are available, as is tutoring in most subjects.

Campus Safety and Security: Measures include 24-hour foot and vehicle patrol. There are emergency telephones, lighted pathways/sidewalks, and controlled access to dorms/residences.

Programs of Study: Bryn Athyn College confers B.A., and B.S. degrees. Associate and master's degrees are also awarded. Bachelor's degrees are awarded in BIOLOGICAL SCIENCE (biology/biological science), COMMUNICATIONS AND THE ARTS (English), EDUCATION (education), SOCIAL SCIENCE (history, interdisciplinary studies, psychology, and religion). Interdisciplinary studies, history, and education are the largest.

Required: To graduate, students must complete a total of 130 credit hours with a minimum GPA of 2.0 and must satisfy the Core Program. All students must take required courses in religion, writing, philosophy, and physical education. Some majors require a comprehensive project, exam, or thesis.

Special: Cross-registration is available with Holy Family University, co-op programs, internships, B.A.-B.S. degrees, student-designed majors, nondegree study, and study-abroad opportunities are also available.

Faculty/Classroom: 50% of faculty are male; 50% are female. All teach undergraduates, 24% do research, and 24% do both. No introductory courses are taught by graduate students. The average class size in a regular course is 12.

Admissions: 52% of the 2013-2014 applicants were accepted. The SAT scores for the 2013-2014 freshman class were: Critical Reading--44% below 500, 27% between 500 and 599, 25% between 600 and 699, and 4% between 700 and 800; Math--44% below 500, 35% between 500 and 599, 18% between 600 and 699, and 3% between 700 and 800; Writing--56% below 500, 26% between 500 and 599, 12% between 600 and 699, and 6% between 700 and 800. The ACT scores were 11% below 21, 56% between 21 and 23, 11% between 24 and 26, and 22% above 28.

Requirements: The SAT or ACT is required. Applicants' SAT or ACT scores must reflect promise of success in college work. Applicants must complete and essay. Applicants must be graduates of an accredited secondary school or achieve satisfactory scores on the GED. An interview is recommended. A GPA of 2.2 is required. AP and CLEP credits are accepted. Important factors in the admissions decision are recommendations by school officials, personality/intangible qualities, and advanced placement or honors courses.

Procedure: Freshmen are admitted fall, winter, and spring. Entrance exams should be taken by fall of senior year. There are deferred admissions and rolling admissions plans. Application deadlines are open. Notification is sent on a rolling basis. Applications are accepted online.

Transfer: 20 transfer students enrolled in 2012-2013. Transfer students with less than 30 credits must supply SAT or ACT scores, high school transcript, transcripts from all colleges attended, and a letter of recommendation. An interview is recommended. Transfers with 30+ credits need not supply SAT/ACT and high school transcript. 60 of 130 credits required for the bachelor's degree must be completed at Bryn Athyn College.

Visiting: There are regularly scheduled orientations for prospective students, consisting of touring the campus, attending chapel, and visiting classes. There are guides for informal visits, visitors may sit in on classes, and stay overnight. To schedule a visit, contact Angella Irwin at (267) 502-6044.

Financial Aid: In 2013-2014, 96% of all full-time freshmen and 98% of

continuing full-time students received some form of financial aid. 79% of all full-time freshmen and 63% of continuing full-time students received need-based aid. The average freshman award was $17,130. Need-based scholarships or need-based grants averaged $9,656; need-based self-help aid (loans and jobs) averaged $4,718; and other non-need-based awards and non-need-based scholarships averaged $4,868. 59% of undergraduate students work part-time. Average annual earnings from campus work are $1850. The average financial indebtedness of the 2013 graduate was $17,988. The FAFSA is required. The priority date for freshman financial aid applications for fall entry is February 15. The deadline for filing freshman financial aid applications for fall entry is June 1.

International Students: There are 38 international students enrolled. They must take the TOEFL with a minimum score of 520 on the paper-based TOEFL (PBT) or 70 on the Internet-based version (iBT). They must also take the SAT or ACT.

Graduates: From July 1, 2012 to June 30, 2013, 29 bachelor's degrees were awarded. The most popular majors were interdisciplinary studies (28%), elementary education (24%), and religion and history (14%). Of the 2012 graduating class, 17% were enrolled in graduate school within 6 months of graduation, and 57% were employed.

Admissions Contact: Angella Irwin, Admissions Counselor. E-Mail: *angella.irwin@brynathyn.edu* Web: *www.brynathyn.edu*

BRYN MAWR COLLEGE F-3

Bryn Mawr, PA 19010 (610) 526-5152
(800) 262-1885; (610) 526-7471

Full-time: 1315 women	**Faculty:** 163; IIA, +$
Part-time: 13 women	**Ph.D.s:** 96%
Graduate: 83 men, 327 women	**Student/Faculty:** 8 to 1
Year: semesters, summer session	**Tuition:** $43,900
Application Deadline: January 15	**Room & Board:** $13,800
Freshman Class: 2626 applied, 1086 accepted, 365 enrolled	
SAT CR/M/W: 650/670/670 **ACT:** 28	**MOST COMPETITIVE**

Bryn Mawr College, founded in 1885, is an independent liberal arts institution, primarily for women. The Graduate School of Social Work and Research, the Graduate School of the Arts and Sciences, and the postbaccalaureate premedical programs are coed. There is one undergraduate school and 2 graduate schools. The 4 libraries contain 949,437 volumes, 157,523 microform items, 17,499 audio/video tapes/CDs/DVDs, and subscribe to 68,211 periodicals including electronic. Computerized library services include interlibrary loans, database searching, Internet access, and Wi-Fi capability. Special learning facilities include an art gallery, radio station, an archeological museum, and a language learning center with audio, video, and computer technology. The 136-acre campus is in a suburban area 11 miles west of Philadelphia. Including any residence halls, there are 57 buildings.

Student Life: 85% of undergraduates are from out of state, mostly the Middle Atlantic. Students are from 46 states, 63 foreign countries, and Canada. 64% are from public schools. 37% are White; 23% Foreign; 11% Asian American. The average age of freshmen is 18; all undergraduates, 20. 9% do not continue beyond their first year; 84% remain to graduate.

Housing: 1247 students can be accommodated in college housing, which includes single-sex and coed dorms. In addition, there are language houses, special-interest houses, an African American culture center that houses several students, and an environmental co-op house. On-campus housing is guaranteed for all 4 years. 95% of students live on campus; of those, 90% remain on campus on weekends. Upperclassmen may keep cars.

Activities: There are no fraternities or sororities. There are 100 groups on campus, including and Girl Scouts, investing, media, Model UN, art, business, chess, choir, chorale, chorus, computers, dance, drama, environmental, ethnic, forensics, gay, honors, international, literary magazine, musical theater, orchestra, photography, political, professional, religious, social, social service, and student government. Popular campus events include May Day, Lantern Night and Fall Frolic.

Sports: There are 12 intercollegiate sports for women, and 4 intramural sports for women. Facilities include 3 playing fields with access to an indoor track, a gym with an 8-lane pool and diving well, basketball, badminton, and volleyball courts, a gymnastics room and dance studio, a weight-training and fitness room, a 1,000-seat auditorium, and a student center.

Disabled Students: Facilities include wheelchair ramps, elevators, special parking, specially equipped restrooms, special class scheduling, lowered drinking fountains, lowered telephones, and special housing.

Services: Counseling and information services are available, as is tutoring in every subject. There is a reader service for the blind.

Campus Safety and Security: Measures include 24-hour foot and vehicle patrol, emergency notification system, self-defense education, and security escort services. There are shuttle buses, emergency telephones, lighted pathways/sidewalks, controlled access to dorms/residences, a web page, bicycle registration, and personal safety education (road safety, car maintenance).

Programs of Study: Bryn Mawr confers A.B. degrees. Master's and doctoral degrees are also awarded. Bachelor's degrees are awarded in BIOLOGICAL SCIENCE (biology/biological science), COMMUNICATIONS AND THE ARTS (art history and appreciation, classical languages, classics, comparative literature, English, fine arts, French, German, Greek, Italian, Latin, linguistics, music, romance languages and literature, Russian, and Spanish), COMPUTER AND PHYSICAL SCIENCE (astronomy, chemistry, computer science, geology, mathematics, and physics), SOCIAL SCIENCE (anthropology, archeology, East Asian studies, economics, history, international studies, philosophy, political science/government, psychology, religion, sociology, and urban studies). English, psychology, and math are the largest.

Required: To graduate, students must complete 128 semester hours, with 40 to 60 in the major and a minimum GPA of 2.0. All students must complete 2 courses each in the social sciences, the humanities, and natural sciences or math, including 1 lab science. Additional required courses include 1 college seminar and 1 quantitative skills course. Students must be able to demonstrate proficiency in 1 foreign language.

Special: Students may cross-register with Haverford and Swarthmore Colleges and the University of Pennsylvania. Bryn Mawr sponsors more than 100 grants and internships for summer study in a wide range of disciplines and sponsors/cosponsors study abroad in 27 countries. Student-designed and dual majors are possible. Pass/fail options, work-study programs, a 3-2 degree in engineering with the California Institute of Technology, and a 3-2 degree in city and regional planning with the University of Pennsylvania are offered.

Faculty/Classroom: All teach and do research. No introductory courses are taught by graduate students. The average class size in an introductory lecture is 25; in a laboratory is 15; and in a regular course is 16.

Admissions: 41% of the 2013-2014 applicants were accepted. The SAT scores for the 2013-2014 freshman class were: Critical Reading--3% below 500, 19% between 500 and 599, 45% between 600 and 699, and 33% between 700 and 800; Math--3% below 500, 24% between 500 and 599, 39% between 600 and 699, and 34% between 700 and 800; Writing--1% below 500, 18% between 500 and 599, 45% between 600 and 699, and 37% between 700 and 800. The ACT scores were 7% between 21 and 23, 22% between 24 and 26, 24% between 27 and 28, and 47% above 28. 88% of the current freshmen were in the top fifth of their class; 99% were in the top two fifths.

Requirements: The SAT is required. The ACT may be substituted for the SAT. Requirements for admission are 4 years of English, at least 3 years of math (2 of algebra and 1 of geometry), 3 years of a foreign language or 2 years of 2 languages, and 1 year each of science and history. Most applicants have taken at least 3 lab science courses and trigonometry. An essay is required. An interview is strongly recommended. AP credits are accepted. Important factors in the admissions decision are advanced placement or honors courses, evidence of special talent, and extracurricular activities record.

Procedure: Freshmen are admitted fall. Entrance exams should be taken in the spring of the junior year or the fall of the senior year. There are early decision and deferred admissions plans. Early decision applications should be filed by November 15; regular applications, by January 15 for fall entry, along with a $50 fee. Notification of early decision is sent December 15; regular decision, in April. 194 early decision candidates were accepted for the 2013-2014 class. 846 applicants were on the 2013 waiting list; 5 were admitted. Applications are accepted online.

Transfer: 48 transfer students enrolled in 2012-2013. Applicants for transfer must be in good academic standing at their current institutions. An official SAT score report or ACT score report, 2 professor recommendations, a school official's report, high school transcripts, college transcripts, and the Bryn Mawr Supplement to the College Application for Transfers must be submitted. 96 of 128 credits required for the bachelor's degree must be completed at Bryn Mawr.

Visiting: There are regularly scheduled orientations for prospective students, including student-guided campus tours and interviews can be arranged. There are guides for informal visits, visitors may sit in on classes, and stay overnight. To schedule a visit, contact the Office of Admissions.

Financial Aid: In 2013-2014, 76% of all full-time freshmen and 76% of continuing full-time students received some form of financial aid. 51% of all full-time freshmen and 54% of continuing full-time students received need-based aid. The average freshman award was $40,322. Need-based scholarships or need-based grants averaged $34,201; need-based self-help aid (loans and jobs) averaged $5,485; and other non-need-based awards and non-need-based scholarships averaged $11,970. 63% of undergraduate students work part-time. Average annual earnings from campus work are $2000. The average financial indebtedness of the 2013 graduate was $21,017. Bryn Mawr is a member of CSS. The CSS/Profile and FAFSA, and the prior year's tax returns, the noncustodial parent statement, and the business/farm supplement are required. The deadline for filing freshman financial aid applications for fall entry is February 2.

International Students: There are 255 international students enrolled. The school actively recruits these students. They must take the TOEFL with a minimum score of 600 on the paper-based TOEFL (PBT) or 90 on the

Internet-based version (iBT), or a score of 7 or above on the IELTS. They must also take the SAT or ACT.

Graduates: From July 1, 2012 to June 30, 2013, 331 bachelor's degrees were awarded. The most popular majors were English (11%), anthropology (10%), and biology (9%). 175 companies recruited on campus in 2012-2013. In an average class, 1% graduate in 3 years or less, 78% graduate in 4 years or less, 82% graduate in 5 years or less, and 82% graduate in 6 years or less. Of the 2012 graduating class, 20% were enrolled in graduate school within 6 months of graduation, and 71% were employed.

Admissions Contact: Peaches Valdes, Director of Admissions. E-Mail: *admissions@brynmawr.edu* Web: *www.brynmawr.edu*

BUCKNELL UNIVERSITY D-2

Lewisburg, PA 17837 (570) 577-3000; (570) 577-3538

Full-time: 1677 men, 1827 women	**Faculty:** 370; IIB, +$
Part-time: 10 men, 18 women	**Ph.D.s:** 97%
Graduate: 36 men, 40 women	**Student/Faculty:** 9 to 1
Year: semesters, summer session	**Tuition:** $46,902
Application Deadline: January 15	**Room & Board:** $11,258

Freshman Class: 7947 applied, 2345 accepted, 933 enrolled

SAT CR/M/W: 640/670/650 **ACT:** 30 **MOST COMPETITIVE**

Bucknell University, established in 1846, is a private independent institution offering undergraduate and graduate programs in arts, music, education, humanities, management, engineering, sciences, and social sciences. There are 3 undergraduate schools and one graduate school. In addition to regional accreditation, Bucknell has baccalaureate program accreditation with ABET and NASM. The library contains 946,284 volumes, 36,257 audio/video tapes/CDs/DVDs, and subscribes to 45,521 periodicals including electronic. Computerized library services include interlibrary loans, database searching, Internet access, and Wi-Fi capability. Special learning facilities include an art gallery, radio station, an outdoor natural area, greenhouse, primate facility, observatory, photography lab, race and gender resource center, library resources training lab, electronic classroom, multimedia lab, conference center, performing arts center, and multicultural, writing, craft, environmental, public policy and poetry centers, herbarium, and engineering structural test lab. The 450-acre campus is in a small town 75 miles north of Harrisburg. Including any residence halls, there are 126 buildings.

Student Life: 78% of undergraduates are from out of state, mostly the Middle Atlantic. Students are from 44 states, 50 foreign countries, and Canada. 63% are from public schools. 78% are White. 32% are Catholic; 29% claim no religious affiliation; 25% Protestant. The average age of freshmen is 18; all undergraduates, 21. 6% do not continue beyond their first year; 91% remain to graduate.

Housing: 3032 students can be accommodated in college housing, which includes single-sex and coed dorms and on-campus apartments. In addition, there are special-interest houses, fraternity houses, Sustainable living, substance-free housing. There are also 7 residential colleges for the first year (arts, discovery, environmental, humanities, global, science and technology, languages and cultures and social justice). On-campus housing is guaranteed for all 4 years and is available on a lottery system for upperclassmen. 86% of students live on campus; of those, 85% remain on campus on weekends. Upperclassmen may keep cars.

Activities: 44% of men belong to 11 national fraternities; 41% of women belong to 9 national sororities. There are 150 groups on campus, including art, band, cheerleading, chess, choir, chorale, chorus, communications, computers, dance, debate, drama, environmental, ethnic, film, forensics, gay, honors, international, jazz band, literary magazine, musical theater, newspaper, opera, orchestra, pep band, photography, political, professional, radio station, religious, social, social service, student government, symphony, and yearbook. Popular campus events include Celebration for the Arts, Chrysalis Ball, Family Weekend, Christy's (a capella concert) and Christmas Candlelight Service.

Sports: There are 13 intercollegiate sports for men and 14 for women, and 19 intramural sports for men and 23 for women. Facilities include an athletic and recreation center with an Olympic-size pool; a 16,000-sq.-foot fitness center; a 4,000-seat basketball arena; a 13,000-seat stadium with 8-lane track; hockey and lacrosse fields, baseball fields, and recreational fields for soccer, softball, and other activities; a field house with a 4-lane track, tennis, squash, and racquetball courts, climbing wall, and dance studio; an 18-hole golf course with a training facility; tennis courts and a high-ropes course.

Disabled Students: 75% of the campus is accessible. Facilities include wheelchair ramps, elevators, special parking, specially equipped restrooms, special class scheduling, lowered drinking fountains, lowered telephones, and special housing.

Services: Counseling and information services are available, as is tutoring in some subjects, biology, chemistry, physics, math, and writing across the curriculum.

Campus Safety and Security: Measures include 24-hour foot and vehicle patrol, emergency notification system, self-defense education, and security escort services. There are shuttle buses, emergency telephones, lighted pathways/sidewalks, controlled access to dorms/residences, campus safety alerts, and intrusion alarms in residence halls.

Programs of Study: Bucknell confers B.A., B.S., B.S.B.A., B.S.Env.E., B.S.B.E., B.S.C.E., B.S.C.M., B.S.C.S., B.S.E.D., B.S.E.E., B.S.M.E., B.C.E.N. and B.M.U.S. degrees. Master's degrees are also awarded. Bachelor's degrees are awarded in AGRICULTURE (animal science), BIOLOGICAL SCIENCE (biochemistry, biology/biological science, cell biology, and neurosciences), BUSINESS (accounting and business administration and management), COMMUNICATIONS AND THE ARTS (art, art history and appreciation, classics, dramatic arts, English, fine arts, French, German, music, music history and appreciation, music performance, music theory and composition, Russian, Spanish, and visual and performing arts), COMPUTER AND PHYSICAL SCIENCE (chemistry, computer science, geology, mathematics, physics, and quantitative methods), EDUCATION (early childhood education, education, educational statistics and research, elementary education, music education, and secondary education), ENGINEERING AND ENVIRONMENTAL DESIGN (biomedical engineering, chemical engineering, civil engineering, computer engineering, electrical/electronics engineering, engineering, environmental science, and mechanical engineering), SOCIAL SCIENCE (anthropology, East Asian studies, economics, geography, history, humanities, interdisciplinary studies, international relations, Latin American studies, philosophy, political science/government, psychology, religion, sociology, and women's studies). Humanities, biology, engineering and English are the strongest academically. Management, economics, political science, psychology, biology and civil engineering have the largest enrollments.

Required: The College Core Curriculum is based on an interrelated set of principles that emphasize intellectual and practical skills, transferable tools for integrative learning, and disciplinary perspectives. It recognizes writing, oral communication, and information literacy as central tools for learning and disseminating new knowledge that permeate the entirety of the learning experience. The curriculum is intended to help students understand the synergistic, and complementary relationships among academic disciplines and their varied approaches to describing,analyzing, comprehending, interpreting, and critiquing a range of phenomena in both human cultures, and the physical and natural world. In doing so, it will prepare students to apply the skills, knowledge and sense of responsibility they have gained to new settings and complex problems as engaged citizens in an interconnected world. Although students will satisfy the requirements in different ways each student must devise a program in accordance with the College Core Curriculum, and the University Writing Requirement. AP credit will not count toward any of the requirements that have defined learning goals. AP courses may count for Disciplinary Perspectives courses without defined learning goals.

Special: Bucknell offers internships, study abroad in more than 60 countries, a Washington semester, a 5-year B.A.-B.S. degree in arts and engineering, a 3-2 engineering degree, and dual and student-designed majors. An interdisciplinary major in animal behavior is offered through the biology and psychology departments. Nondegree study is possible, and a pass/fail grading option is offered in some courses. The Residential College program offers opportunities for an academic-residential mix and faculty-student collaborative learning. Undergraduate research opportunities are available in the humanities/social sciences and the sciences and engineering. There are 27 national honor societies, including Phi Beta Kappa, and 55 departmental honors programs.

Faculty/Classroom: 59% of faculty are male; 41% are female. All teach undergraduates, all do research, and all teach and do research. No introductory courses are taught by graduate students. The average class size in an introductory lecture is 24; in a laboratory is 15; and in a regular course is 18.

Admissions: 30% of the 2013-2014 applicants were accepted. The SAT scores for the 2013-2014 freshman class were: Critical Reading--1% below 500, 24% between 500 and 599, 54% between 600 and 699, and 21% between 700 and 800; Math--1% below 500, 14% between 500 and 599, 51% between 600 and 699, and 35% between 700 and 800; Writing--2% below 500, 21% between 500 and 599, 54% between 600 and 699, and 24% between 700 and 800. The ACT scores were 2% between 21 and 23, 13% between 24 and 26, 23% between 27 and 28, and 62% above 28. 83% of the current freshmen were in the top fifth of their class; 96% were in the top two fifths. There were 11 National Merit finalists. 19 freshmen graduated first in their class.

Requirements: The SAT or ACT is required. The ACT Optional Writing test is also required. Applicants must graduate from an accredited secondary school or have a GED. 16 units must be earned, including 4 in English, 3 in math, and 2 each in history, science, social studies, and a foreign language. An essay is required, and campus visit is recommended. Music applicants are required to audition. A portfolio is recommended for art applicants. Both SAT and ACT scores are accepted with no preference for either. AP and CLEP credits are accepted. Important factors in the admissions decision are advanced placement or honors courses, evidence of special talent, and extracurricular activities record.

Procedure: Freshmen are admitted fall. Entrance exams should be taken

before January 1. There are early decision and deferred admissions plans. Early decision applications should be filed by November 15; regular applications, by January 15 for fall entry, along with a $60 fee. Notification of early decision is sent December 15; regular decision, April 1. 427 early decision candidates were accepted for the 2013-2014 class. 816 applicants were on the 2013 waiting list; 38 were admitted. Applications are accepted online.

Transfer: 28 transfer students enrolled in 2012-2013. Transfer students must have a minimum GPA of 2.5 in courses comparable to those offered at Bucknell. The SAT or ACT is required. A minimum of 16 credit hours must have been earned; 32 are recommended. Students are accepted on a space-available basis. 48 of 128 credits required for the bachelor's degree must be completed at Bucknell.

Visiting: There are regularly scheduled orientations for prospective students, including daily visitation schedule. There are guides for informal visits and visitors may sit in on classes. To schedule a visit, contact the Admissions Office.

Financial Aid: In 2013-2014, 62% of all full-time freshmen and 61% of continuing full-time students received some form of financial aid. 45% of all full-time freshmen and 45% of continuing full-time students received need-based aid. The average freshman award was $30,000. Need-based scholarships or need-based grants averaged $25,675; need-based self-help aid (loans and jobs) averaged $4,219; non-need-based athletic scholarships averaged $29,318; and other non-need-based awards and non-need-based scholarships averaged $12,508. 35% of undergraduate students work part-time. Average annual earnings from campus work are $1500. The average financial indebtedness of the 2013 graduate was $22,500. Bucknell is a member of CSS. The CSS/Profile and FAFSA, and noncustodial parent's statement are required. The deadline for filing freshman financial aid applications for fall entry is January 15.

International Students: There are 202 international students enrolled. The school actively recruits these students. They must take the TOEFL with a minimum score of 600 on the paper-based TOEFL (PBT) or 100 on the Internet-based version (iBT). They must also take the SAT or ACT.

Graduates: From July 1, 2012 to June 30, 2013, 850 bachelor's degrees were awarded. The most popular majors were economics (11%), management (11%), and psychology (10%). 750 companies recruited on campus in 2012-2013. In an average class, 87% graduate in 4 years or less, 91% graduate in 5 years or less, and 91% graduate in 6 years or less. Of the 2012 graduating class, 16% were enrolled in graduate school within 6 months of graduation, and 76% were employed.

Admissions Contact: Robert G. Springall, Dean of Admissions. E-Mail: *admissions@bucknell.edu* Web: *www.bucknell.edu*

CABRINI COLLEGE F-3

Radnor, PA 19087 (610) 902-8310
(800) 848-1003; (610) 902-8508

Full-time: 435 men, 793 women	**Faculty:** 68; IIB, -$
Part-time: 47 men, 37 women	**Ph.D.s:** 89%
Graduate: 266 men, 845 women	**Student/Faculty:** 19 to 1
Year: semesters, summer session	**Tuition:** $29,000
Application Deadline:	**Room & Board:** $11,859
Freshman Class: 2127 applied, 1580 accepted, 316 enrolled	
SAT CR/M/W: 450/440/440	**ACT:** 20 **LESS COMPETITIVE**

Students do extraordinary things at Cabrini College, a residential Catholic college welcoming learners of all faiths, cultures and backgrounds. Since its founding in 1957 by the Missionary Sisters of the Sacred Heart of Jesus, Cabrini College has been a national leader among higher education institutions in social justice. Cabrini offers more than 30 majors, pre-professional programs, concentrations and minors to undergraduate students, and graduate programs on campus and at 12 off-site locations. There is one graduate school. In addition to regional accreditation, Cabrini has baccalaureate program accreditation with CSWE. The library contains 140,160 volumes, 2,583 audio/video tapes/CDs/DVDs, and subscribes to 53,883 periodicals including electronic. Computerized library services include interlibrary loans, database searching, Internet access, and Wi-Fi capability. Special learning facilities include a radio station, a communications lab with a TV studio, a graphic design lab, a newsroom for the student newspaper, and a science education and technology building with biology, chemistry, and physics labs. There are also information science labs. The 112-acre campus is in a suburban area 20 miles west of Philadelphia, PA. Including any residence halls, there are 23 buildings.

Student Life: 65% of undergraduates are from Pennsylvania. Others are from 17 states, and 8 foreign countries. 73% are White; 11% African American. 53% are Catholic; 26% claim no religious affiliation. The average age of freshmen is 19; all undergraduates, 21. 29% do not continue beyond their first year; 46% remain to graduate.

Housing: 837 students can be accommodated in college housing, which includes single-sex and coed dorms, on-campus apartments, and off-campus apartments. In addition, there are honors houses and special-interest houses. On-campus housing is available on a first-come, first-served basis, and is available on a lottery system for upperclassmen. Priority is given to out-of-town students. 57% of students live on campus; of those, 50% remain on campus on weekends. Upperclassmen may keep cars.

Activities: There are no fraternities or sororities. There are 50 groups on campus, including cheerleading, choir, chorus, computers, dance, drama, ethnic, gay, honors, international, literary magazine, musical theater, newspaper, photography, political, professional, radio and TV, religious, social, social service, and student government. Popular campus events include Homecoming, Family Weekend, Cabrini Day, Undergraduate Research and Scholarship Symposium, Founders Day, Cabrini Night at the Phillies and Cabrini Spirit Week.

Sports: There are 7 intercollegiate sports for men and 9 for women, and 8 intramural sports for men and 8 for women. Facilities include The Dixon Center is Cabrini's 64,000 square-foot modern sports and recreation complex. The Dixon Center houses a fitness center, two squash courts, a dance/aerobic studio, a state-of-the-art turf field, a competitive pool, classrooms, and a board room. The Nerney Field House is used for varsity sports, intramurals, and clubs with three full-length basketball courts, a basketball court for NCAA Tournament play, and a suspended indoor jogging track.

Disabled Students: 90% of the campus is accessible. Facilities include wheelchair ramps, elevators, special parking, specially equipped restrooms, special class scheduling, lowered drinking fountains, lowered telephones, special housing, special seating in some classrooms. Accommodations are made on an individual basis, with appropriate documentation.

Services: Counseling and information services are available, as is tutoring in every subject. There is a reader service for the blind, and remedial math and writing. Students may enroll in a study skills course or utilize individual tutoring to acquire learning skills.

Campus Safety and Security: Measures include 24-hour foot and vehicle patrol, emergency notification system, and security escort services. There are shuttle buses, emergency telephones, lighted pathways/sidewalks, and controlled access to dorms/residences.

Programs of Study: Cabrini confers B.A., B.S., B.S.Ed. and B.S.W. degrees. Master's degrees are also awarded. Bachelor's degrees are awarded in BUSINESS (accounting, business administration and management, finance, marketing, and sports management), COMMUNICATIONS AND THE ARTS (communication, English, French, graphic design, information technology, music, Spanish, and studio art), COMPUTER AND PHYSICAL SCIENCE (chemistry, computer information systems, information sciences and systems, and mathematics), EDUCATION (education, elementary education, middle school education, secondary education, and special education), ENGINEERING AND ENVIRONMENTAL DESIGN (environmental science), HEALTH PROFESSIONS (biology, exercise science, and premedicine), SOCIAL SCIENCE (African American studies, American studies, criminology, economics, liberal arts/general studies, philosophy, political science/government, psychology, religious studies, social work, and sociology). Business, Education, and Communication have the largest enrollments.

Required: To graduate, students must complete a minimum of 123 credits with a minimum GPA of 2.0. All students must complete a core curriculum, which includes English, math, foreign language, information technology, an interdisciplinary seminar in self-understanding, and a junior seminar exploring the common good, which includes a community service project. Distribution requirements cover science, heritage, cultural diversity, values, the individual and society, contemporary issues, creativity, and religious studies. Most majors require a capstone experience, which can include an internship, student teaching, or a comprehensive project or paper. The average number of hours in the major is 45. A thesis is required in some majors.

Special: Cabrini offers cooperative programs, internships, study abroad, work-study programs, and cross-registration with Eastern University, Rosemont and Valley Forge Colleges, and other SEPCHE colleges and universities. Dual and student-designed majors are available. Credit by exam, credit for life/military/work experience, nondegree study, and pass/fail options are also offered. A Washington semester with the Washington Center for Internships and Academic Seminars are available. There are 18 national honor societies, a freshman honors program, and 11 departmental honors programs.

Faculty/Classroom: 36% of faculty are male; 64% are female. 67% teach undergraduates. No introductory courses are taught by graduate students. The average class size in an introductory lecture is 18; in a laboratory is 15; and in a regular course is 17.

Admissions: 74% of the 2013-2014 applicants were accepted. The SAT scores for the 2013-2014 freshman class were: Critical Reading--70% below 500, 26% between 500 and 599, 4% between 600 and 699, and Math--73% below 500, 23% between 500 and 599, and 4% between 600 and 699; Writing--74% below 500, 24% between 500 and 599, 2% between 600 and 699. The ACT scores were 55% below 21, 23% between 21 and 23, 16% between 24 and 26, 6% between 27 and 28. 16% of the current freshmen were in the top fifth of their class; 37% were in the top two fifths. 1 freshman graduated first in the class.

Requirements: The SAT is required. All students must be graduates of an accredited secondary school or have a GED. Emphasis is placed on the applicant's high school transcript, including course selection, grade-point average in traditional academic subjects, and class rank. The Admissions Office also considers letters of recommendation, standardized test scores, outside interests, and activities. Applicants that meet the following minimum requirements are considered: 1. Graduation from an accredited secondary school (or its equivalent), with the student having accumulated between 17 and 21 units of credit in a college preparatory curriculum distributed as follows - 4 english, 2 language, 3 math, 3 science, 3 social studies, and between 2-6 arts, humanities, and other electives. 2. The Admissions Office also considers applications from students whose high school preparation varies from this pattern, but whose recored gives evidence of ability and promise. 3. Satisfactory academic grade/quality point average and secondary school class rank. 4. Satisfactory Scholastic Achievement Test (SAT) or American College Testing (ACT) scores. AP and CLEP credits are accepted. Important factors in the admissions decision are advanced placement or honors courses, extracurricular activities record, and leadership record.

Procedure: Freshmen are admitted to all sessions. Entrance exams should be taken Before December of the senior year. There are early admissions, deferred admissions, and rolling admissions plans. Application deadlines are open. Application fee is $35. Notification is sent on a Rolling basis. Applications are accepted online.

Transfer: 76 transfer students enrolled in 2012-2013. Admissions accepts students transferring from regionally accredited colleges in the fall and spring semesters. Transfer applicants are considered on the basis of their college performance and final high school transcripts are required if a student has less than 15 college credits depending on the academic major. Generally, Cabrini prefers a grade C or higher. All transfer student candidates for traditional undergraduate degree programs are required to complete a minimum of 45 Cabrini credits and their last 30 credits must be taken at Cabrini. In addition, all students must meet all major and general education requirements. Some programs may have additional requirements. 45 of 123 credits required for the bachelor's degree must be completed at Cabrini.

Visiting: There are regularly scheduled orientations for prospective students, As a component of the First-Year Experience, Cabrini College offers a one-day Summer Orientation Program. Then a New Student Orientation is held in August when the whole class comes together to start their first year at Cabrini. There are guides for informal visits, visitors may sit in on classes, and stay overnight. To schedule a visit, contact Shannon Zottola at (610) 902-8552.

Financial Aid: In 2013-2014, 98% of all full-time freshmen and 98% of continuing full-time students received some form of financial aid. 94% of all full-time freshmen and 84% of continuing full-time students received need-based aid. The average freshman award was $21,594. Need-based scholarships or need-based grants averaged $10,462 ($28,090 maximum); need-based self-help aid (loans and jobs) averaged $4,505 ($3,500 maximum); and other non-need-based awards and non-need-based scholarships averaged $11,588 ($28,090 maximum). 19% of undergraduate students work part-time. Average annual earnings from campus work are $1443. The average financial indebtedness of the 2013 graduate was $27,775. The FAFSA is required. The priority date for freshman financial aid applications for fall entry is February 15. The deadline for filing freshman financial aid applications for fall entry is March 1.

International Students: There are 6 international students enrolled. They must take the TOEFL with a minimum score of 500 on the paper-based TOEFL (PBT) or 173 on the Internet-based version (iBT), Sccessfully complete ESL if not from an English-speaking country. They must also take the SAT or ACT, scoring 800. Sudents from English-speaking countries.

Graduates: From July 1, 2012 to June 30, 2013, 304 bachelor's degrees were awarded. The most popular majors were education (15%), psychology (12%), and communication (8%). In an average class, 49% graduate in 4 years or less, 48% graduate in 5 years or less, and 46% graduate in 6 years or less. Of the 2012 graduating class, 19% were enrolled in graduate school within 6 months of graduation, and 82% were employed.

Admissions Contact: Shannon Zottola, Director of Admissions. E-Mail: *admit@cabrini.edu* Web: *www.cabrini.edu*

CAIRN UNIVERSITY F-3
Philadelphia Biblical University

Langhorne, PA 19047 (215) 752-5800
(800) 366-0049; (215) 702-4248

Full-time: 361 men, 420 women	**Faculty:** 47
Part-time: 32 men, 33 women	**Ph.D.s:** 66%
Graduate: 100 men, 149 women	**Student/Faculty:** 13 to 1
Year: semesters, summer session	**Tuition:** $22,455
Application Deadline: open	**Room & Board:** $8800
Freshman Class: 466 applied, 336 accepted, 184 enrolled	
SAT CR/M: 520/510 **ACT:** 23	**COMPETITIVE**

Cairn University, formerly Philadelphia Biblical University, founded in 1913, is a private institution offering instruction in the Bible, liberal arts and professional theory. There are 5 undergraduate schools and 4 graduate schools. In addition to regional accreditation, Cairn University has baccalaureate program accreditation with CSWE and NASM. The library contains 138,000 volumes, 63,817 microform items, 14,500 audio/video tapes/CDs/DVDs, and subscribes to 30,186 periodicals including electronic. Computerized library services include interlibrary loans, database searching, Internet access, and Wi-Fi capability. The 115-acre campus is in a suburban area 30 miles north of Philadelphia. Including any residence halls, there are 26 buildings.

Student Life: 57% of undergraduates are from Pennsylvania. Others are from 32 states, 29 foreign countries, and Canada. 66% are from public schools. 68% are White; 19% African American. 100% are Protestant. The average age of freshmen is 18; all undergraduates, 23. 26% do not continue beyond their first year; 73% remain to graduate.

Housing: 662 students can be accommodated in college housing, which includes single-sex dorms, on-campus apartments, and married student housing. On-campus housing is guaranteed for all 4 years. 56% of students live on campus. Alcohol is not permitted. All students may keep cars.

Activities: There are no fraternities or sororities. There are 21 groups on campus, including art, band, choir, chorale, chorus, drama, ethnic, honors, international, musical theater, newspaper, opera, orchestra, professional, religious, social, student government, and symphony. Popular campus events include Homecoming, Hoedown and Christmas Celebration.

Sports: There are 6 intercollegiate sports for men and 6 for women, and 7 intramural sports for men and 7 for women. Facilities include gym, baseball diamond, soccer, hockey, softball fields, sand volleyball court, lighted tennis courts, fitness circuit, and a weight room.

Disabled Students: All of the campus is accessible. Facilities include wheelchair ramps, elevators, special parking, specially equipped restrooms, lowered drinking fountains, and special housing.

Services: Counseling and information services are available, as is tutoring in most subjects. The AIMS Program provides academic support for freshmen who need it.

Campus Safety and Security: Measures include 24-hour foot and vehicle patrol, emergency notification system, and security escort services. There are shuttle buses, emergency telephones, lighted pathways/sidewalks, and controlled access to dorms/residences.

Programs of Study: Cairn University confers B.A., B.S., B.Mus., B.S.B.A., B.S.Ed. and B.S.W. degrees. Master's degrees are also awarded. Bachelor's degrees are awarded in BUSINESS (accounting and business administration and management), COMMUNICATIONS AND THE ARTS (English, music, music composition, and music performance), EDUCATION (education, education administration, and music education), SOCIAL SCIENCE (biblical studies, history, liberal arts/general studies, psychology, social work, and youth ministry). Biblical studies is the strongest academically. Teacher education, and social work have the largest enrollments.

Required: Students must complete 30 credits in Biblical Studies. At least 121 credits, with a minimum GPA of 2.0, is required. Approximately 45% of the students are enrolled in dual degree programs and receive the BS in Bible degree plus a baccalaureate or masters in their professional area.

Special: Cairn University offers an accelerated degree program in Biblical Studies, along with multiple internship and study abroad opportunities in the traditional undergraduate programs. There are double degree programs in social work, music, education, and business administration. There are 1 national honor societies and a freshman honors program.

Faculty/Classroom: 64% of faculty are male; 36% are female. 87% teach undergraduates. No introductory courses are taught by graduate students. The average class size in an introductory lecture is 18 and in a regular course is 17.

Admissions: 72% of the 2013-2014 applicants were accepted. The SAT scores for the 2013-2014 freshman class were: Critical Reading--39% below 500, 33% between 500 and 599, 24% between 600 and 699, and 4% between 700 and 800; Math--43% below 500, 40% between 500 and 599, 16% between 600 and 699, and 1% between 700 and 800. The ACT scores were 33% below 21, 19% between 21 and 23, 22% between 24 and 26, 7% between 27 and 28, and 19% above 28. 42% of the current freshmen were in the top fifth of their class; 62% were in the top two fifths.

Requirements: The SAT or ACT is required. A GPA of 2.0 is required. AP and CLEP credits are accepted. Important factors in the admissions decision are advanced placement or honors courses, personality/intangible qualities, and leadership record.

Procedure: Freshmen are admitted fall and spring. Entrance exams should be taken Junior or senior year of high school. There are early admissions, deferred admissions, and rolling admissions plans. Application deadlines are open. Application fee is $25. Notification is sent on a rolling basis. Applications are accepted online.

Transfer: 105 transfer students enrolled in 2012-2013. Transfers must submit an application, a pastor's reference, college transcripts, and a health form. SAT scores and high school transcripts are also required if the student has fewer than 60 college credit hours. 60 of 121 credits required for the bachelor's degree must be completed at Cairn University.

Visiting: There are regularly scheduled orientations for prospective students, including class and chapel visits, a meal in the dining room, and an interview with a counselor. There are guides for informal visits, visitors may sit in on classes, and stay overnight. To schedule a visit, contact the Admissions Office at (215) 702-4235.

Financial Aid: In 2013-2014, 94% of all full-time freshmen and 95% of continuing full-time students received some form of financial aid. 84% of all full-time freshmen and 80% of continuing full-time students received need-based aid. The average freshman award was $17,659. Need-based scholarships or need-based grants averaged $13,969; need-based self-help aid (loans and jobs) averaged $4,173; and other non-need-based awards and non-need-based scholarships averaged $8,933. 55% of undergraduate students work part-time. The average financial indebtedness of the 2013 graduate was $30,633. The FAFSA is required. Check with the school for current application deadlines.

International Students: There are 11 international students enrolled. The school actively recruits these students. They must take the TOEFL with a minimum score of 520 on the paper-based TOEFL (PBT) or 68 on the Internet-based version (iBT).

Graduates: From July 1, 2012 to June 30, 2013, 300 bachelor's degrees were awarded. The most popular majors were philosophy and religious studies (69%), teacher education (13%), and social work (9%). 700 companies recruited on campus in 2012-2013. In an average class, 41% graduate in 4 years or less, 70% graduate in 5 years or less, and 73% graduate in 6 years or less. Of the 2012 graduating class, 27% were enrolled in graduate school within 6 months of graduation, and 85% were employed.

Admissions Contact: Eric Rivera, Dir. of Undergrad Admissions. E-Mail: *admissions@cairn.edu* Web: *www.cairn.edu*

CALIFORNIA UNIVERSITY OF PENNSYLVANIA B-3

California, PA 15419-1394 **(724) 938-4404**
(888) 412-0479; (724) 938-4564

Full-time: 2600 men, 2700 women	**Faculty:** 266; IIA, +$
Part-time: 250 men, 420 women	**Ph.D.s:** 55%
Graduate: 490 men, 760 women	**Student/Faculty:** n/av
Year: semesters, summer session	**Tuition:** $9412 ($13,156)
Application Deadline: open	**Room & Board:** $10,434
Freshman Class: n/av	
SAT or ACT: required	

COMPETITIVE

California University of Pennsylvania, founded in 1852, is a state-supported institution offering degree programs in the arts and sciences, engineering, and education. There are 3 undergraduate schools and 1 graduate school. Some figures in the above capsule and in this profile are approximate. In addition to regional accreditation, the university has baccalaureate program accreditation with CSWE, NCATE, and NLN. The library contains 451,382 volumes, 830,298 microform items, 60,416 audio/video tapes/CDs/DVDs, and subscribes to 822 periodicals including electronic. Computerized library services include interlibrary loans and database searching. Special learning facilities include a learning resource center, art gallery, natural history museum, radio station, and TV station. The 148-acre campus is in a small town 35 miles south of Pittsburgh. Including any residence halls, there are 38 buildings.

Student Life: 95% of undergraduates are from Pennsylvania. Others are from 35 states, 21 foreign countries, and Canada. 95% are from public schools. 93% are white. The average age of freshmen is 19; all undergraduates, 23. 25% do not continue beyond their first year; 50% remain to graduate.

Housing: 1467 students can be accommodated in college housing, which includes single-sex and coed dorms and off-campus apartments. In addition, there are honors houses. On-campus housing is available on a first-come, first-served basis and is available on a lottery system for upperclassmen. 80% of students commute. Alcohol is not permitted. All students may keep cars.

Activities: 10% of men belong to 7 national fraternities; 6% of women belong to 7 national sororities. There are 78 groups on campus, including art, band, cheerleading, chess, choir, chorale, chorus, computers, dance, debate, drama, drill team, ethnic, forensics, honors, international, jazz band, literary magazine, marching band, musical theater, newspaper, pep band, professional, radio and TV, religious, student government, and yearbook.

Sports: There are 12 intercollegiate sports for men and 10 for women, and 13 intramural sports for men and 14 for women. Facilities include tennis and basketball courts, an all-weather track, a swimming pool, and a 4500-seat stadium.

Disabled Students: 95% of the campus is accessible. Facilities include wheelchair ramps, elevators, special parking, specially equipped rest rooms, special class scheduling, lowered drinking fountains, and lowered telephones.

Services: Counseling and information services are available, as is tutoring in most subjects. There is a reader service for the blind, and remedial math, reading, and writing.

Campus Safety and Security: Measures include 24-hour foot and vehicle patrol, self-defense education, and security escort services. There are shuttle buses and lighted pathways/sidewalks.

Programs of Study: The university confers B.A., B.S., B.S.Ed., and B.S.N. degrees. Associate and master's degrees are also awarded. Bachelor's degrees are awarded in BIOLOGICAL SCIENCE (biology/biological science), BUSINESS (accounting, business administration and management, management science, and sports management), COMMUNICATIONS AND THE ARTS (art, dramatic arts, English, French, graphic design, Spanish, and speech/debate/rhetoric), COMPUTER AND PHYSICAL SCIENCE (chemistry, geology, information sciences and systems, mathematics, physical sciences, and physics), EDUCATION (athletic training, early childhood education, education, elementary education, guidance education, reading education, school psychology, secondary education, and special education), ENGINEERING AND ENVIRONMENTAL DESIGN (commercial art, computer technology, electrical/electronics engineering technology, engineering technology, environmental science, and industrial engineering technology), HEALTH PROFESSIONS (medical laboratory technology, mental health/human services, nursing, and physical therapy assistant), SOCIAL SCIENCE (criminal justice, geography, gerontology, history, liberal arts/general studies, parks and recreation management, philosophy, political science/government, psychology, social science, and social work).

Required: Students must complete a minimum of 120 semester credits and must maintain a minimum GPA of 2.5 in teacher education curricula, 2.3 in the student's area of concentration, and 2.0 overall.

Special: Cooperative programs are available in all academic areas when eligibility requirements have been met. Opportunities are provided for internships, and an accelerated degree program in justice studies is also available. There are 25 national honor societies and a freshman honors program.

Faculty/Classroom: 58% of faculty are male; 42% are female. All teach undergraduates. No introductory courses are taught by graduate students. The average class size in an introductory lecture is 30; in a laboratory, 24; and in a regular course, 30.

Admissions: 78% of a recent year's applicants were accepted. 17% of a recent year's freshmen were in the top fifth of their class; 44% were in the top two fifths. 3 freshmen graduated first in their class.

Requirements: The SAT or ACT is required. Graduation from an accredited secondary school is required; a GED will be accepted. Applicants should submit an academic record that includes 4 credits each in English and history, 3 each in math and academic electives, 2 in science, and 1 each in social studies and a foreign language. An essay and an interview are recommended. A GPA of 2.5 is required. AP and CLEP credits are accepted.

Procedure: Freshmen are admitted to all sessions. Entrance exams should be taken during the senior year. There is a rolling admissions plan. Application deadlines are open. Application fee is $25. Applications are accepted online.

Transfer: 619 transfer students enrolled in a recent year. Applicants must submit official transcripts from all previous colleges attended. If fewer than 30 transferable credits are submitted, applicants must also include a high school transcript and standardized test score. Grades of D are not transferable. 30 of 120 credits required for the bachelor's degree must be completed at the university.

Visiting: There are regularly scheduled orientations for prospective students. There are guides for informal visits, and visitors may sit in on classes and stay overnight. To schedule a visit, contact the Admissions Office.

Financial Aid: The FAFSA is required. Check with the school for current application deadlines.

International Students: There were 48 international students enrolled in a recent year. They must take the TOEFL. They must also take the SAT, with a minimum composite score of 800.

Graduates: In a recent year, 983 bachelor's degrees were awarded. The most popular majors were education (21%), business (12%), and justice studies (8%). 62 companies recruited on campus in a recent year. In an average class, 21% graduate in 4 years or less, 43% graduate in 5 years or less, and 49% graduate in 6 years or less. Of a recent year's graduating class, 18% were enrolled in graduate school within 6 months of graduation, and 95% were employed.

Admissions Contact: William Edmonds, Director of Admissions. A campus DVD is available. E-Mail: *inquiry@calu.edu* Web: *www.calu.edu*

CARLOW UNIVERSITY B-3

Pittsburgh, PA 15213 (412) 578-6059
(800) 333-CARLOW; (412) 578-6668

Full-time: 74 men, 1043 women	**Faculty:** 82
Part-time: 124 men, 577 women	**Ph.D.s:** 72%
Graduate: 77 men, 707 women	**Student/Faculty:** 14 to 1
Year: semesters, summer session	**Tuition:** $21,720 ($19,514)
Application Deadline: July 1	**Room & Board:** $8552

Freshman Class: 1205 applied, 743 accepted, 257 enrolled
SAT CR/M/W: 480/470/475 **ACT:** 21 **COMPETITIVE**

Carlow University, founded in 1929, is the first women-centered, liberal arts university in Pennsylvania, prepares students, primarily women, for leadership and service in personal and professional life. There are 6 undergraduate schools and 5 graduate schools. In addition to regional accreditation, Carlow has baccalaureate program accreditation with CSWE. The library contains 133,864 volumes, 11,712 microform items, 5,113 audio/video tapes/CDs/DVDs, and subscribes to 14,784 periodicals including electronic. Computerized library services include interlibrary loans, database searching, Internet access, and Wi-Fi capability. The 15-acre campus is in an urban area in the Oakland section of Pittsburgh. Including any residence halls, there are 14 buildings.

Student Life: 98% of undergraduates are from Pennsylvania. Others are from 11 states, and 7 foreign countries. 90% are from public schools. 56% are White; 14% African American. 43% are Catholic; 17% claim no religious affiliation. The average age of freshmen is 18; all undergraduates, 26. 31% do not continue beyond their first year; 47% remain to graduate.

Housing: 416 students can be accommodated in college housing, which includes single-sex dorms. On-campus housing is available on a first-come, first-served basis, and is available on a lottery system for upperclassmen. 76% of students commute. Alcohol is not permitted. All students may keep cars.

Activities: There are no fraternities or sororities. There are 23 groups on campus, including and campus activities board, students in the natural sciences, band, choir, chorale, chorus, communications, dance, drama, ethnic, honors, literary magazine, musical theater, newspaper, pep band, political, professional, social, social service, student education association, and student government. Popular campus events include Constitution Day, Halloween, and Spring Carnival.

Sports: There are 5 intercollegiate sports for women. Facilities include 2 fitness centers, a pool, and an aerobics room.

Disabled Students: 30% of the campus is accessible. Facilities include wheelchair ramps, elevators, special parking, specially equipped restrooms, special class scheduling, lowered drinking fountains, lowered telephones. 6 power doors, and 1 doorbell.

Services: Counseling and information services are available, as is tutoring in most subjects. There is remedial math, reading, and writing. Professional tutoring is available for reading, writing, study skills, math, and sciences. Peer tutoring is available in other subject areas.

Campus Safety and Security: Measures include 24-hour foot and vehicle patrol, emergency notification system, self-defense education, and security escort services. There are emergency telephones, lighted pathways/sidewalks, an electronically secured dorm entrance and most doors on campus are secured electronically and require an ID badge to enter.

Programs of Study: Carlow confers B.A., B.S., B.S.N. and B.S.W. degrees. Master's and doctoral degrees are also awarded. Bachelor's degrees are awarded in BIOLOGICAL SCIENCE (biology/biological science), BUSINESS (accounting, business administration and management, business communications, and human resources), COMMUNICATIONS AND THE ARTS (art, art history and appreciation, communications, creative writing, English, media arts, Spanish, and technical and business writing), COMPUTER AND PHYSICAL SCIENCE (chemistry, information sciences and systems, and mathematics), EDUCATION (art education, early childhood education, elementary education, journalism education, middle school education, secondary education, and special education), HEALTH PROFESSIONS (art therapy, health care administration, nursing, and scientific/medical marketing), SOCIAL SCIENCE (forensic studies, history, liberal arts/general studies, philosophy, political science/government, psychology, public administration, social work, sociology, and theological studies). Nursing, creative writing, and education are the strongest academically. Nursing, psychology, and business management have the largest enrollments.

Required: A total of 120 credit hours (123 for nursing students), including 27 to 44 in the major, is required for the B.A. Appropriate credits must be earned in the core curriculum. An interdisciplinary course, English, service learning, and communication studies are also required. A minimum GPA of 2.0 is required. All students must demonstrate competence in writing, reading comprehension, and math, and must take basic skills courses in public speaking and research paper writing. All students undergo a comprehensive evaluation in their senior year.

Special: Carlow offers cross-registration to member institutions of the Pittsburgh Council for Higher Education, internships in all areas, and work-study. There are accelerated degree programs, and dual majors are possible in most majors, as are student-designed majors. There are 3-2 engineering programs with Carnegie Mellon University and a 3-2 biology/environmental science and management program with Duquesne University. Students can study abroad in all countries deemed by the government to be safe for travel. There are 4 national honor societies, a freshman honors program, and 31 departmental honors programs.

Faculty/Classroom: 24% of faculty are male; 76% are female. 79% teach undergraduates. No introductory courses are taught by graduate students. The average class size in an introductory lecture is 13; in a laboratory is 10; and in a regular course is 7.

Admissions: 62% of the 2013-2014 applicants were accepted. The SAT scores for the 2013-2014 freshman class were: Critical Reading--58% below 500, 32% between 500 and 599, 8% between 600 and 699, and 2% between 700 and 800; Math--65% below 500, 32% between 500 and 599, and 3% between 600 and 699; Writing--60% below 500, 30% between 500 and 599, 9% between 600 and 699, and 1% between 700 and 800. The ACT scores were 46% below 21, 32% between 21 and 23, 15% between 24 and 26, 3% between 27 and 28, and 4% above 28. 27% of the current freshmen were in the top fifth of their class; 60% were in the top two fifths.

Requirements: The SAT or ACT is required. The minimum scores depend on the major selected. Candidates must be graduates of an accredited secondary school. 18 Carnegie units are required, including 4 each in English and arts/humanities, 3 each in math and science, and 4 in electives. Applicants for nursing must have completed a minimum 4 units in English, 3 in social sciences, and 2 each in math (including algebra) and lab science (including chemistry), as required by the State Board of Nursing. The GED is accepted. An essay and/or interview are recommended. A GPA of 2.0 is required. AP and CLEP credits are accepted.

Procedure: Freshmen are admitted fall, spring, and summer. Entrance exams should be taken late in the junior year or early in the senior year. There are early admissions, deferred admissions, and rolling admissions plans. Early decision applications should be filed by September 30; regular applications, by July 1 for fall entry; and December 1 for spring entry, along with a $20 fee. Notification is sent on a rolling basis. 5 applicants were on the 2013 waiting list; 5 were admitted. Applications are accepted online.

Transfer: 273 transfer students enrolled in 2012-2013. Transfer students must have a minimum GPA of 2.0 and submit college transcripts. Certain programs have higher GPA requireements. An interview is also recommended. 32 of 120 credits required for the bachelor's degree must be completed at Carlow.

Visiting: There are regularly scheduled orientations for prospective students, including a campus tour, information sessions on admission and financial aid, and interaction with faculty and students regarding academic and student life. There are guides for informal visits, visitors may sit in on classes, and stay overnight. To schedule a visit, contact the Admissions Office.

Financial Aid: In 2013-2014, 100% of all full-time freshmen students received some form of financial aid. 86% of all full-time freshmen students received need-based aid. The average freshman award was $25,093. Need-based scholarships or need-based grants averaged $3,381 ($15,352 maximum); need-based self-help aid (loans and jobs) averaged $2,706 ($3,500 maximum); non-need-based athletic scholarships averaged $6,600 ($10,000 maximum); and other non-need-based awards and non-need-based scholarships averaged $4,398 ($20,854 maximum). The average financial indebtedness of the 2013 graduate was $29,536. Carlow is a member of CSS. The FAFSA, and Verification worksheets and tax returns when applicable is required. The priority date for freshman financial aid applications for fall entry is April 1. The deadline for filing freshman financial aid applications for fall entry is rolling.

International Students: There are 2 international students enrolled. They must take the TOEFL with a minimum score of 500 on the paper-based TOEFL (PBT) or 173 on the Internet-based version (iBT). In some cases, the SAT can replace the TOEFL; otherwise the SAT is recommended.

Graduates: From July 1, 2012 to June 30, 2013, 350 bachelor's degrees were awarded. The most popular majors were nursing (30%), biology (10%), and elementary education (9%). 11 companies recruited on campus in 2012-2013. In an average class, 37% graduate in 4 years or less, 46% graduate in 5 years or less, and 47% graduate in 6 years or less. Of the 2012 graduating class, 36% were enrolled in graduate school within 6 months of graduation, and 61% were employed.

Admissions Contact: Susan Winstel, Director of Admissions. E-Mail: *admissions@carlow.edu* Web: *www.carlow.edu*

CARNEGIE MELLON UNIVERSITY B-3

Pittsburgh, PA 15213 **(412) 268-2082; (412) 268-7838**

Full-time: 3430 men, 2430 women	**Faculty:** n/av; I, +$
Part-time: 70 men, 40 women	**Ph.D.s:** 96%
Graduate: 3790 men, 1630 women	**Student/Faculty:** n/av
Year: semesters, summer session	**Tuition:** $44,520
Application Deadline: see profile	**Room & Board:** $11,610
Freshman Class: n/av	
SAT or ACT: required	**MOST COMPETITIVE**

Carnegie Mellon University, established in 1900, is a private nonsectarian institution offering undergraduate programs in liberal arts and science and technology. There are 6 undergraduate schools and 7 graduate schools. The figures in the above capsule and in this profile are approximate. In addition to regional accreditation, Carnegie Mellon has baccalaureate program accreditation with AACSB, ABET, NAAB, NASAD, and NASM. The 4 libraries contain 1.1 million volumes, 1.1 million microform items, 30,729 audio/video tapes/CDs/DVDs, and subscribe to 1955 periodicals including electronic. Computerized library services include interlibrary loans, database searching, Internet access, and laptop Internet portals. Special learning facilities include a learning resource center, art gallery, radio station, and TV station. The 145-acre campus is in a suburban area 4 miles from downtown Pittsburgh. Including any residence halls, there are 80 buildings.

Student Life: 81% of undergraduates are from out of state, mostly the Middle Atlantic. Students are from 49 states, 65 foreign countries, and Canada. 40% are white; 24% Asian American; 15% foreign nationals. The average age of freshmen is 18; all undergraduates, 20. 5% do not continue beyond their first year; 85% remain to graduate.

Housing: 3878 students can be accommodated in college housing, which includes single-sex and coed dorms, on-campus apartments, and off-campus apartments. In addition, there are honors houses, language houses, special-interest houses, fraternity houses, and sorority houses. On-campus housing is guaranteed for all 4 years. 64% of students live on campus. Alcohol is not permitted. Upperclassmen may keep cars.

Activities: 15% of men belong to 16 national fraternities; 10% of women belong to 7 national sororities. There are 225 groups on campus, including art, bagpipe, band, cheerleading, chess, choir, chorale, chorus, computers, debate, drama, ethnic, film, gay, honors, international, jazz band, literary magazine, marching band, musical theater, newspaper, opera, orchestra, pep band, photography, political, professional, radio and TV, religious, social, social service, student government, and symphony. Popular campus events include Spring Carnival, International Festival, and Watson Arts Festival.

Sports: There are 8 intercollegiate sports for men and 8 for women, and 38 intramural sports for men and 38 for women. Facilities include a gym, a football stadium with track, athletic fields, tennis and racquetball courts, and a pool.

Disabled Students: 98% of the campus is accessible. Facilities include wheelchair ramps, elevators, special parking, specially equipped rest rooms, special class scheduling, lowered drinking fountains, and lowered telephones.

Services: Counseling and information services are available, as is tutoring in most subjects. There is a reader service for the blind.

Campus Safety and Security: Measures include 24-hour foot and vehicle patrol, emergency notification system, self-defense education, and security escort services. There are shuttle buses, emergency telephones, lighted pathways/sidewalks, and a SafeWalk Program.

Programs of Study: Carnegie Mellon confers B.A., B.S., B.A.H., B.Arch., B.F.A., and B.S.A. degrees. Master's and doctoral degrees are also awarded. Bachelor's degrees are awarded in BIOLOGICAL SCIENCE (biology/biological science), BUSINESS (business administration and management, business economics, and marketing/retailing/merchandising), COMMUNICATIONS AND THE ARTS (communications, design, dramatic arts, English, fine arts, French, German, journalism, languages, music, and Spanish), COMPUTER AND PHYSICAL SCIENCE (chemistry, computer programming, computer science, information sciences and systems, mathematics, physics, and statistics), EDUCATION (music education), ENGINEERING AND ENVIRONMENTAL DESIGN (chemical engineering, civil engineering, computer engineering, electrical/electronics engineering, engineering, and mechanical engineering), SOCIAL SCIENCE (economics, history, philosophy, political science/government, psychology, public administration, social science, and urban studies). Computer science, engineering, and business administration are the strongest academically. Engineering has the largest enrollments.

Required: To graduate, students must complete requirements in English, history, and computing skills, and they must have a GPA of 2.0. Distribution requirements, the number of credits needed to graduate, and the number of credits required in the major vary by college.

Special: Students may cross-register with other Pittsburgh Council of Higher Education institutions. Also available are internships, work-study programs, study abroad in 49 countries, a Washington semester, accelerated degrees, B.A.-B.S. degrees, co-op programs, dual majors, and limited student-designed majors. There are 10 national honor societies, including Phi Beta Kappa, and a freshman honors program.

Faculty/Classroom: 72% of faculty are male; 28% are female. All teach and do research. No introductory courses are taught by graduate students.

Admissions: 36% of a recent year's applicants were accepted. 88% of a recent year's freshmen were in the top fifth of their class; 97% were in the top two fifths. 69 freshmen graduated first in their class.

Requirements: The SAT or ACT is required. SAT subject tests are not required for drama, design, art, or music applicants. All other applicants must take appropriate tests, preferably by December but no later than January. Applicants must graduate from an accredited secondary school or have a GED. They must earn 16 Carnegie units and must have completed 4 years of English. Applicants to the Carnegie Institute of Technology and the Mellon College of Science must take 4 years of math and 1 year each of biology, chemistry, and physics. Essays are required, and interviews are recommended. Art and design applicants must submit a portfolio. Drama and music applicants must audition. AP credits are accepted.

Procedure: Freshmen are admitted in the fall. There are early decision, early admissions, and deferred admissions plans. Check with the school for current application deadlines. Application fee is $70. Applications are accepted online. A waiting list is maintained.

Transfer: 47 transfer students enrolled in a recent year. Applicants must submit secondary school and college transcripts (including school catalogs with course descriptions so that Carnegie Mellon can evaluate transferable credits).

Visiting: There are regularly scheduled orientations for prospective students, including Saturday group sessions in September, October, November, and April. There are guides for informal visits, and visitors may sit in on classes and stay overnight. To schedule a visit, contact the Admissions Office.

Financial Aid: In a recent year, 76% of all full-time freshmen and 67% of continuing full-time students received some form of financial aid. 53% of all full-time freshmen and 47% of continuing full-time students received need-based aid. The average freshman award was $28,678. 31% of undergraduate students work part-time. The average financial indebtedness of a recent year's graduate was $29,546. Carnegie Mellon is a member of CSS. The FAFSA, the college's own financial statement, and parent and student federal tax returns and W-2 forms are required. Check with the school for current application deadlines.

International Students: There were 933 international students enrolled in a recent year. The school actively recruits these students. They must take the TOEFL with a minimum score of 600 on the paper-based TOEFL (PBT) or 100 on the Internet-based version (iBT) or take the MELAB. They must also take the SAT or ACT.

Graduates: In a recent year, 1349 bachelor's degrees were awarded. The most popular majors were computer science (11%), electrical and computer engineering (10%), and business administration (10%). In an average class, 82% graduate in 5 years or less and 85% graduate in 6 years or less. Of a recent graduating class, 33% were enrolled in graduate school within 6 months of graduation, and 83% were employed.

Admissions Contact: Michael Steidel, Director of Admissions. E-Mail: *undergraduate-admissions@andrew.cmu.edu* Web: *www.cmu.edu*

CEDAR CREST COLLEGE E-3

Allentown, PA 18104 **(610) 740-3780**
(800) 360-1222; (610) 606-4647

Full-time: 33 men, 607 women	**Faculty:** 73; IIB, -$
Part-time: 57 men, 589 women	**Ph.D.s:** 73%
Graduate: 19 men, 181 women	**Student/Faculty:** 9 to 1
Year: semesters, summer session	**Tuition:** $33,550
Application Deadline: open	**Room & Board:** $9690
Freshman Class: 1063 applied, 625 accepted, 141 enrolled	
SAT CR/M/W: 460/470/460 **ACT:** 22	**COMPETITIVE**

Cedar Crest College, founded in 1867, was one of the first women's colleges in the nation. Today it remains an independent, comprehensive liberal arts college for women that combines excellence in scholarship and undergraduate education with an extensive School of Adult and Graduate Education (SAGE) program and growing graduate programs that serve women and men in the surrounding region. There is one undergraduate school and one graduate school. In addition to regional accreditation, Cedar Crest has baccalaureate program accreditation with ACBSP and CSWE. Computerized library services include interlibrary loans, database searching, Internet access, and Wi-Fi capability. Special learning facilities include an art gallery, radio station, an arboretum, theaters, and a sculpture garden. The 84-acre campus is in a suburban area 55 miles north of Philadelphia and 90 miles west of New York City. Including any residence halls, there are 20 buildings.

Student Life: 67% of undergraduates are from Pennsylvania. Others are from 21 states, and 27 foreign countries. 95% are from public schools.

69% are White; 12% Hispanic. The average age of freshmen is 18; all undergraduates, 28. 33% do not continue beyond their first year; 60% remain to graduate.

Housing: 550 students can be accommodated in college housing, which includes single-sex dorms. smoke-free floors, and living learning communities. On-campus housing is guaranteed for all 4 years. 78% of students commute. All students may keep cars.

Activities: There are no fraternities or sororities. There are 51 groups on campus, including art, band, cheerleading, choir, chorus, computers, dance, drama, ethnic, forensics, gay, honors, international, literary magazine, musical theater, newspaper, political, professional, radio and TV, religious, social, social service, student government, and yearbook. Popular campus events include Student Faculty Frolic, Midnight Breakfast and Ring Ceremony.

Sports: There are 8 intercollegiate sports for women, and 4 intramural sports for women. Facilities include 5 tennis courts, softball, field hockey, soccer, and lacrosse fields, a cross-country course, a gym with basketball, volleyball, and badminton courts, dance and aerobics studios, weight training, swim and a fitness center.

Disabled Students: 35% of the campus is accessible. Facilities include wheelchair ramps, elevators, special parking, specially equipped restrooms, special class scheduling, lowered drinking fountains, and lowered telephones.

Services: Counseling and information services are available, as is tutoring in most subjects. There is remedial math and writing. and a computer software skills program for underprepared students.

Campus Safety and Security: Measures include 24-hour foot and vehicle patrol, emergency notification system, self-defense education, and security escort services. There are emergency telephones, lighted pathways/sidewalks, Residence halls are equipped with fire/intrusion alarms, which are monitored 24 hours a day. A keyless access system is in place; exterior doors are locked 24 hours a day.

Programs of Study: Cedar Crest confers B.A., and B.S degrees. Master's degrees are also awarded. Bachelor's degrees are awarded in BIOLOGICAL SCIENCE (biochemistry, biology/biological science, environmental biology, genetics, neurosciences, and nutrition), BUSINESS (accounting, business administration and management, and marketing/retailing/merchandising), COMMUNICATIONS AND THE ARTS (art, communications, dance, dramatic arts, English, fine arts, and music), COMPUTER AND PHYSICAL SCIENCE (chemistry, computer science, information sciences and systems, mathematics, and science), EDUCATION (early childhood education, education, and elementary education), HEALTH PROFESSIONS (nuclear medical technology and nursing), SOCIAL SCIENCE (criminal justice, history, industrial and organizational psychology, political science/government, psychology, social work, and Spanish studies). Sciences, and nursing are the strongest academically. Nursing, social work, and business have the largest enrollments.

Required: To graduate, students must complete 120 credit hours (122 for nursing) with a minimum GPA of 2.0 (some majors have higher requirements). Distribution requirements include 7 credits in natural sciences; 6 each in writing, mathematics and logic, humanities, the arts, and social sciences; and 3 each in global studies and ethics. A major capstone experience is required.

Special: Cross-registration is available through the Lehigh Valley Association of Independent Colleges and Online Consortium. Also available are internships, work-study programs, an accelerated degree program in business, and B.A.-B.S. degrees in math, biology, and psychology. Dual majors, student-designed majors, pass/fail options, and credit for life, military, and work experience are offered. There are 15 national honor societies, a freshman honors program, and 1 departmental honors programs.

Faculty/Classroom: 32% of faculty are male; 68% are female. All teach undergraduates. No introductory courses are taught by graduate students. The average class size in an introductory lecture is 20; in a laboratory is 13; and in a regular course is 14.

Admissions: 59% of the 2013-2014 applicants were accepted. The SAT scores for the 2013-2014 freshman class were: Critical Reading--64% below 500, 30% between 500 and 599, and 6% between 600 and 699; Math--57% below 500, 38% between 500 and 599, and 5% between 600 and 699; Writing--70% below 500, 23% between 500 and 599, and 7% between 600 and 699. 55% of the current freshmen were in the top fifth of their class; 92% were in the top two fifths.

Requirements: The SAT is required. Applicants must be graduates of an accredited secondary school. The GED is accepted. Students should have completed 16 high school academic credits, including 4 years of English, 3 of math, 2 each of science, history, and foreign language, and 1 each of art, music, and social studies. An essay is required. Cedar Crest requires applicants to be in the upper 50% of their class. A GPA of 2.0 is required. AP and CLEP credits are accepted. Important factors in the admissions decision are advanced placement or honors courses, leadership record, and evidence of special talent.

Procedure: Freshmen are admitted fall and spring. Entrance exams should be taken in the junior year or early in the senior year. There are deferred admissions and rolling admissions plans. Application deadlines are open. Applications are accepted online.

Transfer: 49 transfer students enrolled in 2012-2013. Applicants should have a minimum college GPA of 2.0. An interview is recommended. 30 of 120 credits required for the bachelor's degree must be completed at Cedar Crest.

Visiting: There are regularly scheduled orientations for prospective students. There are guides for informal visits, visitors may sit in on classes, and stay overnight. To schedule a visit, contact the Admissions Office at admissions@cedarcrest.edu.

Financial Aid: In 2013-2014, 97% of all full-time freshmen and 99% of continuing full-time students received some form of financial aid. 94% of all full-time freshmen and 95% of continuing full-time students received need-based aid. The average freshman award was $26,840. Need-based scholarships or need-based grants averaged $23,477; need-based self-help aid (loans and jobs) averaged $3,787; and other non-need-based awards and non-need-based scholarships averaged $3,497. 53% of undergraduate students work part-time. Average annual earnings from campus work are $1500. The average financial indebtedness of the 2013 graduate was $27,200. Cedar Crest is a member of CSS. The FAFSA is required. The deadline for filing freshman financial aid applications for fall entry is May 1.

International Students: There are 16 international students enrolled. The school actively recruits these students. They must take the TOEFL with a minimum score of 550 on the paper-based TOEFL (PBT) or 61 on the Internet-based version (iBT).

Graduates: From July 1, 2012 to June 30, 2013, 313 bachelor's degrees were awarded. The most popular majors were nursing (35%), psychology (15%), and business administration (6%). 11 companies recruited on campus in 2012-2013. In an average class, 51% graduate in 4 years or less, 57% graduate in 5 years or less, and 60% graduate in 6 years or less. Of the 2012 graduating class, 7% were enrolled in graduate school within 6 months of graduation, and 70% were employed.

Admissions Contact: Germel Clarke, Director of Admissions. E-Mail: *admissions@cedarcrest.edu* Web: *www.cedarcrest.edu*

CHATHAM UNIVERSITY B-3

Pittsburgh, PA 15232 (412) 365-1290
(800) 837-1290; (412) 365-1609

Full-time: 26 men, 585 women	**Faculty:** 45; IIA, --$
Part-time: 62 men, 304 women	**Ph.D.s:** 88%
Graduate: 243 men, 950 women	**Student/Faculty:** 22 to 1
Year: 4-1-4, summer session	**Tuition:** $32,454
Application Deadline: open	**Room & Board:** $9986
Freshman Class: 594 applied, 361 accepted, 92 enrolled	
SAT CR/M/W: 545/540/545 **ACT:** 22	**VERY COMPETITIVE**

Chatham University, formerly Chatham College and founded in 1869, is a private university offering undergraduate degree programs only to women in more than 30 liberal arts and preprofessional majors. Graduate degree programs in art and architecture, business, counseling psychology, health sciences and nursing, teaching, and writing and other continuing and professional studies programs are open to men as well as women. There is one undergraduate school and 2 graduate schools. The library contains 92,665 volumes, 22,356 microform items, 1,284 audio/video tapes/CDs/DVDs, and subscribes to 31,666 periodicals including electronic. Computerized library services include interlibrary loans, database searching, Internet access, and Wi-Fi capability. Special learning facilities include an art gallery, theaters, a media center, and an arboretum. The 35-acre campus is in an urban area 5 miles east of downtown Pittsburgh. Including any residence halls, there are 33 buildings.

Student Life: 76% of undergraduates are from Pennsylvania. Others are from 47 states, 31 foreign countries, and Canada. 96% are from public schools. 67% are White; 12% race unknown. The average age of freshmen is 19; all undergraduates, 25. 23% do not continue beyond their first year; 61% remain to graduate.

Housing: 509 students can be accommodated in college housing, which includes single-sex dorms, on-campus apartments, and off-campus apartments. In addition, there are special-interest houses, and an intercultural residence hall. On-campus housing is available on a lottery system for upperclassmen. 54% of students live on campus; of those, 75% remain on campus on weekends. Upperclassmen may keep cars.

Activities: There are no fraternities or sororities. There are 67 groups on campus, including choir, dance, drama, environmental, ethnic, feminist, film, gay, honors, international, literary magazine, newspaper, photography, political, professional, religious, social service, and student government. Popular campus events include Fall Festival, Spring Fling and Air Band Contest.

Sports: There are 9 intercollegiate sports for women, and 5 intramural sports for women. Facilities include The Athletic and Fitness Center is an advanced four-level athletic facility designed by the St. Louis, Missouri firm of Hastings and Chivetta. On the lower level is an eight-lane competition swimming pool, whirlpool/sauna/steam room, squash courts, and rock-climbing wall. The athletic training room contains a hydrotherapy room and complete line of rehabilitation equipment. The second level has a smart classroom with an adjoining human performance laboratory. The fitness and cardiovascular rooms contain treadmills, elliptical machines, bikes, free weights, and circuit strength machines. The dance and aerobics studio is a multi-function space that houses Pilates, martial arts, aerobic classes, and dance courses. On the third level, the gymnasium seats 600 spectators for athletic events and up to 1,000 for other events. Finally, the fourth level offers a three-lane walking track and smoothie bar where students may purchase healthy snacks and beverages. There is a out-door field for both soccer and softball.

Disabled Students: 75% of the campus is accessible. Facilities include wheelchair ramps, elevators, special parking, specially equipped restrooms, and special class scheduling.

Services: Counseling and information services are available, as is tutoring in every subject. There is a reader service for the blind, and remedial math, reading, and writing. One-on-one and group tutoring are available by both students and professional specialists, and there is also computer-aided tutoring and an organized study group.

Campus Safety and Security: Measures include 24-hour foot and vehicle patrol, emergency notification system, self-defense education, and security escort services. There are shuttle buses, emergency telephones, and lighted pathways/sidewalks.

Programs of Study: Chatham confers B.A., B.S., B.S.N. and B.S.W. degrees. Master's and doctoral degrees are also awarded. Bachelor's degrees are awarded in AGRICULTURE (environmental studies), BIOLOGICAL SCIENCE (biochemistry and biology/biological science), BUSINESS (accounting, business administration and management, international business management, management information systems, marketing management, and sustainable management), COMMUNICATIONS AND THE ARTS (art history and appreciation, arts administration/management, communications, creative writing, English, English literature, film, television and digital media, media arts, music, Spanish, theatre studies, and visual and performing arts), COMPUTER AND PHYSICAL SCIENCE (chemistry, mathematics, and physics), EDUCATION (early childhood education, education, and elementary education), ENGINEERING AND ENVIRONMENTAL DESIGN (environmental science and interior design), HEALTH PROFESSIONS (exercise science and physical therapy), SOCIAL SCIENCE (crosscultural studies, economics, forensic studies, history, interdisciplinary studies, international relations, political science/government, psychology, public affairs, social work, and women's studies). Nursing, psychology, and biology have the largest enrollments.

Required: To graduate, students must complete 120 credit hours, including a general education curriculum of 7 courses and a senior tutorial, with a minimum GPA of 2.0. Students must also demonstrate proficiencies in writing, math, and computer literacy.

Special: Chatham offers a study-abroad program in 12 countries, cross-registration with other Pittsburgh Council on Higher Education institutions, co-op programs in all majors, internships in the public and private sectors, and a Washington semester in conjunction with American University and the Public Leadership Education Network. Accelerated degree programs, work-study, combined B.A.-B.S. degrees, multidisciplinary majors, and dual and student-designed majors are available. There are 3-2 engineering degrees with Carnegie Mellon and Penn State Universities and the University of Pittsburgh, dual degree programs, and an accelerated Master's program with Carnegie Mellon's Heinz School. There are 11 national honor societies, including Phi Beta Kappa, a freshman honors program, and 30 departmental honors programs.

Faculty/Classroom: 28% of faculty are male; 72% are female. All teach undergraduates. No introductory courses are taught by graduate students. The average class size in an introductory lecture is 13; in a laboratory is 13; and in a regular course is 13.

Admissions: 61% of the 2013-2014 applicants were accepted. The SAT scores for the 2013-2014 freshman class were: Critical Reading--26% below 500, 41% between 500 and 599, 29% between 600 and 699, and 4% between 700 and 800; Math--27% below 500, 53% between 500 and 599, 17% between 600 and 699, and 3% between 700 and 800; Writing--25% below 500, 40% between 500 and 599, 30% between 600 and 699, and 5% between 700 and 800. The ACT scores were 26% below 21, 37% between 21 and 23, 26% between 24 and 26, and 11% above 28. 60% of the current freshmen were in the top fifth of their class; 83% were in the top two fifths.

Requirements: Applicants who choose not to submit the SAT or ACT will be required instead to submit a graded writing sample and resume or list of curricular and cocurricular activities. Applicants will also have the option to submit a portfolio or special project or activity. These materials may also be applied toward Chatham's scholarship review process upon acceptance. AP and CLEP credits are accepted. Important factors in the admissions decision are recommendations by school officials, leadership record, and extracurricular activities record.

Procedure: Freshmen are admitted fall and spring. Entrance exams should be taken by fall of the senior year. There are deferred admissions and rolling admissions plans. Application deadlines are open. Application fee is $35. Notification is sent on a rolling basis. Applications are accepted online. Application fees are waived if application is completed online.

Transfer: 63 transfer students enrolled in 2012-2013. Applicants must present college transcripts 45 of 120 credits required for the bachelor's degree must be completed at Chatham.

Visiting: There are regularly scheduled orientations for prospective students, including campus tours, student and faculty panels, financial aid presentations, and athletic coach meetings. There are guides for informal visits, visitors may sit in on classes, and stay overnight. To schedule a visit, contact the Admissions Office.

Financial Aid: In 2013-2014, 100% of all full-time freshmen and 99% of continuing full-time students received some form of financial aid. 59% of all full-time freshmen and 89% of continuing full-time students received need-based aid. The average freshman award was $29,723. Need-based scholarships or need-based grants averaged $5,327 ($15,936 maximum); need-based self-help aid (loans and jobs) averaged $3,225 ($5,700 maximum); and other non-need-based awards and non-need-based scholarships averaged $12,193 ($35,431 maximum). The average financial indebtedness of the 2013 graduate was $28,416. The FAFSA, and None are required, but students need to complete the FAFSA in order to be considered for need-based grants from the Univ is required. The priority date for freshman financial aid applications for fall entry is March 1. The deadline for filing freshman financial aid applications for fall entry is Rolling.

International Students: There are 94 international students enrolled. The school actively recruits these students. They must take the TOEFL with a minimum score of 550 on the paper-based TOEFL (PBT) or 79 on the Internet-based version (iBT) or take the MELAB, or IELTS. The SAT is required if no TOEFL score is available.

Graduates: From July 1, 2012 to June 30, 2013, 218 bachelor's degrees were awarded. The most popular majors were nursing (22%), psychology (13%), and interior architecture (7%). In an average class, 2% graduate in 3 years or less, 44% graduate in 4 years or less, 49% graduate in 5 years or less, and 50% graduate in 6 years or less.

Admissions Contact: Marylyn Scott, Director of Undergraduate Admissions. E-Mail: *admission@chatham.edu* Web: *www.chatham.edu*

CHESTNUT HILL COLLEGE F-3

Philadelphia, PA 19118 **(215) 248-7001**
(800) 248-0052; (215) 248-7082

Full-time: 410 men, 751 women	**Faculty:** 67
Part-time: 79 men, 267 women	**Ph.D.s:** 84%
Graduate: 144 men, 528 women	**Student/Faculty:** 17 to 1
Year: semesters, summer session	**Tuition:** $30,165 ($31,170)
Application Deadline: open	**Room & Board:** $9808

Freshman Class: 1207 applied, 1058 accepted, 192 enrolled
SAT CR/M/W: 480/470/460 **ACT:** 21 **LESS COMPETITIVE**

Chestnut Hill College, founded in 1924, is a private, liberal arts institution affiliated with the Roman Catholic Church. In addition to the traditional program, CHC also offers an accelerated evening and weekend program for working adults and several graduate programs. Courses in the accelerated program are offered in 6 8-week sessions per year, with 10 career-oriented majors. Graduate programs lead to master's degrees in early level education, middle level education, secondary education, educational leadership, instructional technology, administration of human services, and psychology; and the PsyD in clinical psychology. There are 2 undergraduate schools and one graduate school. In addition to regional accreditation, CHC has baccalaureate program accreditation with NCATE. The library contains 130,355 volumes, 219,532 microform items, 1,776 audio/video tapes/CDs/DVDs, and subscribes to 1,296 periodicals including electronic. Computerized library services include interlibrary loans, database searching, Internet access, and Wi-Fi capability. Special learning facilities include an art gallery, planetarium, radio station, TV station, a planetarium, rotating observatory, and a technology center. The 75-acre campus is in a suburban area 25 miles northwest of downtown Philadelphia, at the very edge of the city. Including any residence halls, there are 17 buildings.

Student Life: 77% of undergraduates are from Pennsylvania. Others are from 22 states, 39 foreign countries, and Canada. 47% are from public schools. 41% are White; 35% African American. 36% claim no religious affiliation; 31% Protestant; 28% Catholic. The average age of freshmen is 18; all undergraduates, 26.5. 26% do not continue beyond their first year; 44% remain to graduate.

Housing: 525 students can be accommodated in college housing, which includes coed dorms and off-campus apartments. In addition, there are honors houses and special-interest houses. On-campus housing is available on a first-come and first-served basis. 65% of students live on campus; of those, 35% remain on campus on weekends. Alcohol is not permitted. Upperclassmen may keep cars.

Activities: There are no fraternities or sororities. There are 31 groups on campus, including chorale, chorus, communications, computers, drama, environmental, ethnic, gay, honors, instrumental ensemble, international, literary magazine, musical theater, newspaper, orchestra, political, professional, radio and TV, religious, social, social service, student government, and yearbook. Popular campus events include Drama Club performances, Musical performances, Empty Bowl Night, Intramural One-Act Play Night, Christmas Decorations and Dance.

Sports: There are 7 intercollegiate sports for men and 7 for women, and 3 intramural sports for men and 3 for women. Facilities include a gym and an auxiliary gym, athletic training room, locker facilities, fitness room, indoor swimming pool, 8 tennis courts, playing fields for hockey, lacrosse, softball, and soccer, as well as neighboring public stables and country club golf course.

Disabled Students: 90% of the campus is accessible. Facilities include wheelchair ramps, elevators, special parking, specially equipped restrooms, a shower area in residence halls.

Services: Counseling and information services are available, as is tutoring in most subjects. There is a reader service for the blind, and remedial math and writing.

Campus Safety and Security: Measures include 24-hour foot and vehicle patrol, emergency notification system, and security escort services. There are emergency telephones, lighted pathways/sidewalks, controlled access to dorms/residences, Doors are locked after 6 p.m. and on weekends and are monitored by cameras. Escorted shuttle cars to parking lots are available.

Programs of Study: CHC confers B.A., B.S. and B.M. degrees. Associate, master's, and doctoral degrees are also awarded. Bachelor's degrees are awarded in BIOLOGICAL SCIENCE (biochemistry, biology/biological science, and molecular biology), BUSINESS (accounting, business administration and management, business communications, human resources, and marketing/retailing/merchandising), COMMUNICATIONS AND THE ARTS (art, communication, communications technology, English literature, French, music, and Spanish), COMPUTER AND PHYSICAL SCIENCE (chemistry, computer management, computer science, information sciences and systems, and mathematics), EDUCATION (early childhood education, elementary education, and music education), ENGINEERING AND ENVIRONMENTAL DESIGN (computer technology and environmental science), HEALTH PROFESSIONS (health care administration), SOCIAL SCIENCE (child care/child and family studies, criminal justice, forensic studies, history, human services, international studies, liberal arts/general studies, political science/government, psychology, and sociology). Biological/computer/physical sciences and humanities is the strongest academically. Business, human services, and education have the largest enrollments.

Required: To graduate, students must complete at least 120 credit hours with a general average of 2.0 overall and in the major. Course work must include 12 to 15 courses in the major, Introduction to the Liberal Arts, Interdisciplinary Global Studies Seminar, a writing course, 2 courses in religious studies, the College Experience; 2 1-credit courses in phys ed, courses in a variety of disciplines including historical, literary, artistic, scientific, and human behavior; a senior seminar and senior thesis. Students may choose from a wide variety of minors.

Special: Cross-registration is available among the seven local members of the Southeasern Pennslvania Consortium of Higher Education. Semesters may be taken at the 10 colleges in the Sisters of St. Joseph College Consortium Student Exchange Program, which are located in various states from Massachusetts to California. The college offers internships; study abroad in England, Spain, Italy, Austria, and France; work-study programs, interdisciplinary majors, and dual and student-designed majors. Up to 6 credits may be given for life experience. Nondegree study and pass/fail options are available. The school offers unique career preparation programs in communications, international studies, environmental science, and international business. There are 16 national honor societies, a freshman honors program, and 14 departmental honors programs.

Faculty/Classroom: 39% of faculty are male; 61% are female. 73% teach undergraduates, 70% do research, and 55% do both. No introductory courses are taught by graduate students. The average class size in an introductory lecture is 25; in a laboratory is 15; and in a regular course is 20.

Admissions: 88% of the 2013-2014 applicants were accepted. The SAT scores for the 2013-2014 freshman class were: Critical Reading--59% below 500, 34% between 500 and 599, 6% between 600 and 699, and 1% between 700 and 800; Math--62% below 500, 30% between 500 and 599, 7% between 600 and 699, and 1% between 700 and 800; Writing--65% below 500, 30% between 500 and 599, and 5% between 600 and 699. The ACT scores were 76% below 21, 12% between 21 and 23, 4% between 24 and 26, 4% between 27 and 28, and 4% above 28. 24% of the current freshmen were in the top fifth of their class; 48% were in the top two fifths.

Requirements: The SAT or ACT is required. Applicants must be graduates of an accredited secondary school. 16 Carnegie units are required, with a recommended 4 units each of English, math, science, and social studies and 3 of foreign language. An interview is recommended for all students. An essay is required. GED is accepted. A GPA of 2.0 is required. AP and CLEP credits are accepted. Important factors in the admissions decision are leadership record, extracurricular activities record, and advanced placement or honors courses.

Procedure: Freshmen are admitted fall, spring, and summer. Entrance exams should be taken early in the senior year. There are deferred admissions and rolling admissions plans. Application deadlines are open. Application fee is $35. Notification is sent on a rolling basis. Applications are accepted online.

Transfer: 73 transfer students enrolled in 2012-2013. Applicants must have a minimum GPA of 2.0; a 2.5 is recommended. 45 of 120 credits required for the bachelor's degree must be completed at CHC.

Visiting: There are regularly scheduled orientations for prospective students, faculty/staff presentations and workshops on specific issues related to admissions (financial aid, curriculum, student life). Opportunities to speak with faculty/staff/students. There are guides for informal visits, visitors may sit in on classes, and stay overnight. To schedule a visit, contact The Admissions Office.

Financial Aid: In 2013-2014, 86% of all full-time freshmen and 80% of continuing full-time students received some form of financial aid. 83% of all full-time freshmen and 75% of continuing full-time students received need-based aid. The average freshman award was $20,730. Need-based scholarships or need-based grants averaged $16,711; and need-based self-help aid (loans and jobs) averaged $4,019. Average annual earnings from campus work are $1000. CHC is a member of CSS. The FAFSA is required. The deadline for filing freshman financial aid applications for fall entry is April 15.

International Students: There are 22 international students enrolled. The school actively recruits these students. They must take the TOEFL with a minimum score of 550 on the paper-based TOEFL (PBT) or 79 on the Internet-based version (iBT). They must also take the SAT or ACT. The college also requires a complete set of academic credentials with English translations.

Graduates: From July 1, 2012 to June 30, 2013, 449 bachelor's degrees were awarded. The most popular majors were education (32%), human services (17%), and criminal justice (10%). 27 companies recruited on campus in 2012-2013. In an average class, 36% graduate in 4 years or less, 44% graduate in 5 years or less, and 47% graduate in 6 years or less. Of the 2012 graduating class, 38% were enrolled in graduate school within 6 months of graduation, and 79% were employed.

Admissions Contact: Jamie Gleason, Director of Admissions. E-Mail: *chcapply@chc.edu* Web: *www.chc.edu*

CHEYNEY UNIVERSITY OF PENNSYLVANIA F-3

Cheyney, PA 19319 (610) 399-2275
(800) 223-3608; (610) 399-2099

Full-time: 571 men, 589 women	**Faculty:** n/av
Part-time: 25 men, 39 women	**Ph.D.s:** 57%
Graduate: 21 men, 39 women	**Student/Faculty:** 14 to 1
Year: semesters, summer session	**Tuition:** $8820 ($13,308)
Application Deadline: May 30	**Room & Board:** $11,552
Freshman Class: 1582 applied, 1379 accepted, 319 enrolled	
SAT or ACT: required	

LESS COMPETITIVE

Cheyney University of Pennsylvania, founded in 1837, is a public, liberal arts institution offering programs in art, business, music, and teacher preparation. Cheyney University of Pennsylvania cherishes its legacy as the oldest historically black institution of higher education. There are 2 undergraduate schools and one graduate school. The library contains 290,000 volumes, 795,000 microform items, 1,451 audio/video tapes/CDs/DVDs, and subscribes to 485 periodicals including electronic. Computerized library services include Internet access. Special learning facilities include an art gallery, planetarium, radio station, TV station, weather station, world cultures center, and theater arts center. The 275-acre campus is in a suburban area 24 miles west of Philadelphia. Including any residence halls, there are 33 buildings.

Student Life: 79% of undergraduates are from Pennsylvania. Others are from 18 states, and 1 foreign countries. 93% are African American. The average age of freshmen is 19; all undergraduates, 22. 35% do not continue beyond their first year; 22% remain to graduate.

Housing: 1048 students can be accommodated in college housing, which includes single-sex and coed dorms. In addition, there are honors houses, special-interest houses, learning communities. On-campus housing is available on a first-come and first-served basis. 58% of students live on campus. Alcohol is not permitted. All students may keep cars.

Activities: There are 30 groups on campus, including art, cheerleading, chess, choir, computers, dance, drama, ethnic, honors, international, jazz band, marching band, modeling club, newspaper, pep band, political, professional, radio and TV, religious, social, social service, and student government. Popular campus events include Founders Day Ball and Wade Wilson Football Classic.

Sports: There are 5 intercollegiate sports for men and 5 for women, and

3 intramural sports for men and 2 for women. Facilities include a track, tennis courts, outdoor and indoor basketball courts, a pool, a gym, and a weight room.

Disabled Students: 90% of the campus is accessible. Facilities include wheelchair ramps, elevators, special parking, specially equipped restrooms, lowered drinking fountains, and lowered telephones.

Services: Counseling and information services are available, as is tutoring in most subjects. There is remedial math, reading, and writing. Both peers and professionals serve as tutors.

Campus Safety and Security: Measures include 24-hour foot and vehicle patrol. There are emergency telephones, lighted pathways/sidewalks, and controlled access to dorms/residences.

Programs of Study: Cheyney confers B.A., B.S., and B.S.Ed. degrees. Associate and master's degrees are also awarded. Bachelor's degrees are awarded in BIOLOGICAL SCIENCE (biology/biological science), BUSINESS (accounting, apparel and accessories marketing, business administration and management, and hotel/motel and restaurant management), COMMUNICATIONS AND THE ARTS (communications, dramatic arts, English, and music), COMPUTER AND PHYSICAL SCIENCE (chemistry, computer science, mathematics, and science), EDUCATION (early childhood education, elementary education, home economics education, and special education), HEALTH PROFESSIONS (medical laboratory technology), SOCIAL SCIENCE (clothing and textiles management/production/services, criminal justice, economics, geography, liberal arts/general studies, parks and recreation management, political science/government, psychology, and social science). Psychology, political science, and social relations are the strongest academically. Business administration and social relations have the largest enrollments.

Required: To graduate, students must complete at least 124 credit hours, with 30 in the major and a minimum GPA of 2.0. Distribution requirements include 6 credits each in communications, humanities, science, and social science, 4 in health and phys ed, and 3 in math.

Special: Internships, study abroad, work-study programs, a chemistry-biology dual degree, nondegree study, pass/fail options, and credit for life, military, and work experience are available. There are 10 national honor societies, a freshman honors program, and 6 departmental honors programs.

Faculty/Classroom: 51% of faculty are male; 49% are female. 76% teach undergraduates. No introductory courses are taught by graduate students.

Admissions: 87% of the 2013-2014 applicants were accepted. The SAT scores for the 2013-2014 freshman class were: Critical Reading--94% below 500, 5% between 500 and 599, 1% between 600 and 699, Math--94% below 500, 6% between 500 and 599, Writing--96% below 500, 3% between 500 and 599, 1% between 600 and 699.

Requirements: The SAT or ACT is required. Applicants must be graduates of an accredited secondary school or hold a GED. An interview is recommended. CLEP credits are accepted. Important factors in the admissions decision are ability to finance college education, extracurricular activities record, and geographical diversity.

Procedure: Freshmen are admitted fall and spring. Entrance exams should be taken during the junior or senior year. There are early admissions and rolling admissions plans. Early decision applications should be filed by November 30; regular applications, by May 30 for fall entry; and November 15 for spring entry. The fall 2013 application fee was $20.

Transfer: 94 transfer students enrolled in 2012-2013. Applicants must have a C average from an accredited postsecondary institution; others may be admitted on probation. Students with fewer than 30 credits must submit a high school transcript. 30 of 124 credits required for the bachelor's degree must be completed at Cheyney.

Visiting: There are regularly scheduled orientations for prospective students. There are guides for informal visits and visitors may sit in on classes. To schedule a visit, contact the Office of Admissions.

Financial Aid: In 2013-2014, 96% of all full-time freshmen and 97% of continuing full-time students received some form of financial aid. 91% of all full-time freshmen and 91% of continuing full-time students received need-based aid. The average freshman award was $11,078. Need-based scholarships or need-based grants averaged $8,169; need-based self-help aid (loans and jobs) averaged $3,438; and other non-need-based awards and non-need-based scholarships averaged $1,298. Cheyney is a member of CSS. The FAFSA is required. The deadline for filing freshman financial aid applications for fall entry is April 15.

International Students: The school actively recruits these students. They must take the TOEFL.

Graduates: From July 1, 2012 to June 30, 2013, 164 bachelor's degrees were awarded. The most popular majors were business administration (24%), social relations (22%), and psychology (12%). In an average class, 10% graduate in 4 years or less, 18% graduate in 5 years or less, and 22% graduate in 6 years or less.

Admissions Contact: Eric Hilton, Executive Director of Enrollment Managem. E-Mail: *admissions@cheyney.edu* Web: *www.cheyney.edu*

CLARION UNIVERSITY OF PENNSYLVANIA B-2

Clarion, PA 16214 **(814) 393-2306; (814) 393-2030**

Full-time: 1715 men, 2658 women
Part-time: 219 men, 607 women
Graduate: 194 men, 687 women
Year: semesters, summer session
Application Deadline: open
Freshman Class: n/av
SAT CR/M/W: 471/477/458
Faculty: 243; IIA, +$
Ph.D.s: 99%
Student/Faculty: 18 to 1
Tuition: $9404 ($12,716)
Room & Board: $7966

COMPETITIVE

Clarion University of Pennsylvania, founded in 1867, is a public institution and part of the Pennsylvania State System of Higher Education. There are 4 undergraduate schools and 4 graduate schools. In addition to regional accreditation, Clarion University has baccalaureate program accreditation with AACSB, NASAD, NASM, and NCATE. The 2 libraries contain 623,893 volumes, 1.5 million microform items, 7,756 audio/video tapes/CDs/DVDs, and subscribe to 23,536 periodicals including electronic. Computerized library services include interlibrary loans, database searching, Internet access, and Wi-Fi capability. Special learning facilities include an art gallery, planetarium, radio station, and TV station. The 201-acre campus is in a small town 85 miles northeast of Pittsburgh. Including any residence halls, there are 54 buildings.

Student Life: 89% of undergraduates are from Pennsylvania. Others are from 47 states, 15 foreign countries, and Canada. 89% are from public schools. 92% are White. The average age of freshmen is 18; all undergraduates, 22. 25% do not continue beyond their first year; 52% remain to graduate.

Housing: 2255 students can be accommodated in college housing, which includes single-sex and coed dorms and off-campus apartments. 77% of students commute. Alcohol is not permitted. All students may keep cars.

Activities: 4% of men belong to 6 national fraternities; 7% of women belong to 8 national sororities. There are 150 groups on campus, including and ski club, dance team, music ensembles, rugby, art, band, cheerleading, choir, chorus, computers, concert band, dance, debate, drama, ethnic, forensics, gay, honors, international, jazz band, literary magazine, marching band, musical theater, newspaper, orchestra, pep band, photography, political, professional, radio and TV, religious, social, social service, student government, and symphony. Popular campus events include Autumn Leaf Festival, Activities Day, and Martin Luther King Cultural Series.

Sports: There are 8 intercollegiate sports for men and 8 for women, and 50 intramural sports for men and 50 for women. Facilities include a 5,000-seat stadium; a gym with a physical fitness center and recreational swimming; a natatorium; baseball, softball, soccer fields; a 48,000-square-foot recreation building with 3 full-size multipurpose courts, a 4-lane elevated track, and a 4,800-square-foot weight room; tennis and basketball courts; sand volleyball pits; and an inline hockey rink.

Disabled Students: 98% of the campus is accessible. Facilities include wheelchair ramps, elevators, special parking, specially equipped restrooms, special class scheduling, lowered drinking fountains, lowered telephones. priority registration.

Services: Counseling and information services are available, as is tutoring in some subjects, math, economics, accounting, biology, chemistry, physics, earth science, history, sociology, political science, psychology, computer information sciences There is a reader service for the blind, and remedial math, reading, and writing. computer-assisted instruction, and a learning skills lab.

Campus Safety and Security: Measures include 24-hour foot and vehicle patrol, emergency notification system, self-defense education, and security escort services. There are emergency telephones, lighted pathways/sidewalks, video surveillance cameras on campus, a bicycle patrol program, and a rape/aggressive defense program.

Programs of Study: Clarion University confers B.A., B.S., B.F.A., B.AS, B.S.B.A., B.S.Ed. and B.S.N. degrees. Associate and master's degrees are also awarded. Bachelor's degrees are awarded in BIOLOGICAL SCIENCE (biology/biological science and molecular biology), BUSINESS (accounting, banking and finance, business administration and management, business economics, international business management, marketing/retailing/merchandising, and real estate), COMMUNICATIONS AND THE ARTS (art, communications, dramatic arts, English, French, Spanish, and speech/debate/rhetoric), COMPUTER AND PHYSICAL SCIENCE (chemistry, computer science, geology, information sciences and systems, mathematics, natural sciences, physics, and radiological technology), EDUCATION (athletic training, early childhood education, elementary education, foreign languages education, library science, music education, secondary education, and special education), ENGINEERING AND ENVIRONMENTAL DESIGN (environmental science and industrial administration/management), HEALTH PROFESSIONS (medical technology, nursing, rehabilitation therapy, and speech pathology/audiology), SOCIAL SCIENCE (anthropology, economics, history, liberal arts/general studies, philosophy, political science/government, psychology, social psychology, social science, and sociology). Education, mass media and journalism, and STEM are the strongest academically. Elementary education, secondary education, and communication have the largest enrollments.

Required: To graduate, students must complete at least 120 credits, with a minimum GPA of 2.0 (2.8 for the College of Education and Human Services). Degree requirements include Writing II, completion of general education courses, including a mandated 12 credits in liberal education skills, 27 credits in liberal knowledge (9 credits each in physical and social sciences, social and behavioral sciences, and arts and humanities), and 3 credits in health and personal performance. Specific degree and class requirements vary by major.

Special: Clarion University has co-op programs in engineering with the University of Pittsburgh and Case Western Reserve University, in speech pathology and audiology with Gallaudet University, and a cooperative M.S.L.S./J.D. with Widener University. Internships, study abroad, work-study programs, and dual and student-designed majors are also available. There are 15 national honor societies and a freshman honors program.

Faculty/Classroom: 46% of faculty are male; 54% are female. All teach undergraduates. No introductory courses are taught by graduate students.

Admissions: The SAT scores for the 2013-2014 freshman class were: Critical Reading--66% below 500, 27% between 500 and 599, and 7% between 600 and 699; Math--68% below 500, 30% between 500 and 599, and 8% between 600 and 699. 19% of the current freshmen were in the top fifth of their class; 48% were in the top two fifths.

Requirements: The SAT is recommended. Applicants must be graduates of an accredited secondary school. The GED is accepted. Clarion University requires 4 years each of English and social studies and 3 years each of math and science and recommends 2 years of a foreign language. An essay and interview are strongly recommended. A GPA of 2.0 is required. AP and CLEP credits are accepted. Important factors in the admissions decision are advanced placement or honors courses, evidence of special talent, and leadership record.

Procedure: Freshmen are admitted fall, spring, and summer. Entrance exams should be taken in the spring of the junior year or early fall of the senior year. There are deferred admissions and rolling admissions plans. Application deadlines are open. Application fee is $30. Applications are accepted online.

Transfer: 331 transfer students enrolled in 2012-2013. Applicants for transfer should have completed at least 6 college credit hours with a GPA of 2.8 for education and communication sciences and disorders majors, 2.5 for business majors, and 2.0 for other programs. An audition is required for music majors, and an interview and national test are required for nursing students. 45 of 120 credits required for the bachelor's degree must be completed at Clarion University.

Visiting: There are regularly scheduled orientations for prospective students, including 12 orientation sessions for new students, 6 in the spring and 6 in the summer. There are guides for informal visits and visitors may sit in on classes. To schedule a visit, contact the Admissions Office.

Financial Aid: In 2013-2014, 78% of all full-time freshmen and 75% of continuing full-time students received some form of financial aid. 77% of all full-time freshmen and 75% of continuing full-time students received need-based aid. The average freshman award was $7,070. Need-based scholarships or need-based grants averaged $4,542. The average financial indebtedness of the 2013 graduate was $29,410. The FAFSA is required. The priority date for freshman financial aid applications for fall entry is April 1. The deadline for filing freshman financial aid applications for fall entry is May 1.

International Students: There are 33 international students enrolled. The school actively recruits these students. They must take the TOEFL.

Graduates: From July 1, 2012 to June 30, 2013, 921 bachelor's degrees were awarded. The most popular majors were business/marketing (18%), education (16%), and health professions (12%). 100 companies recruited on campus in 2012-2013. In an average class, 25% graduate in 4 years or less, 45% graduate in 5 years or less, and 52% graduate in 6 years or less.

Admissions Contact: William Bailey, Dean of Enrollment Management. E-Mail: *admissions@clarion.edu* Web: *www.clarion.edu*

CURTIS INSTITUTE OF MUSIC — F-3

Philadelphia, PA 19103-6187 — **(215) 717-3117; (215) 893-9065**

Full-time: 40 men, 80 women	**Faculty:** n/av
Part-time: none	**Ph.D.s:** n/av
Graduate: 10 men, 10 women	**Student/Faculty:** n/av
Year: varies	**Tuition:** see profile
Application Deadline: open	**Room & Board:** n/app
Freshman Class: n/av	
SAT: required	**SPECIAL**

Curtis Institute of Music, founded in 1924, is a private conservatory offering undergraduate, graduate, and professional programs in music. The institution serves an entirely commuter student body. All applicants are accepted on full-tuition scholarships. However, they must pay about $700 in fees and provide all their living expenses. Figures given in the above capsule and in this profile are approximate. There are 2 graduate schools. In addition to regional accreditation, Curtis has baccalaureate program accreditation with NASM. The library contains 60,000 volumes, 100 microform items, 10,000 audio/video tapes/CDs/DVDs, and subscribes to 40 periodicals including electronic. There are 3 buildings.

Student Life: 92% of undergraduates are from out of state, mostly the Northeast. Students are from 30 states, 21 foreign countries, and Canada. 90% are from public schools. 62% are white. The average age of freshmen is 18. 2% do not continue beyond their first year; 98% remain to graduate.

Housing: There are no residence halls. All students commute.

Activities: There are no fraternities or sororities. Groups on campus include student government.

Sports: There is no sports program at Curtis.

Disabled Students: Facilities include elevators and specially equipped rest rooms.

Services: Counseling and information services are available. Tutoring is provided on an individual basis in every subject.

Programs of Study: Bachelor's degrees are awarded in COMMUNICATIONS AND THE ARTS (music).

Faculty/Classroom: No introductory courses are taught by graduate students.

Requirements: The SAT is required. In addition, applicants must be graduates of an accredited secondary school or have earned a GED. Confidential letters of recommendation from 2 qualified musicians are required. Admission is based primarily on evidence of the applicant's special talent. An audition is required. AP and CLEP credits are accepted.

Procedure: Freshmen are admitted fall. Entrance exams should be taken by March of the senior year. Application deadlines are open. Application fee is $150.

Transfer: 97 of 131 credits required for the bachelor's degree must be completed at Curtis.

Financial Aid: Curtis is a member of CSS. The CSS/Profile and the college's own financial statement are required. Check with the school for current application deadlines.

International Students: They must take the TOEFL. They must also take the SAT.

Admissions Contact: Christopher Hodges, Director of Admissions. E-Mail *www.admissions@curtis.edu* Web: *www.curtis.edu*

DE SALES UNIVERSITY — F-3

Center Valey, PA 18034 — **(610) 282-1100, ext. 1475; (877) 433-7253; (610) 282-0131**

Full-time: n/av	**Faculty:** 110; IIA, --$
Part-time: n/av	**Ph.D.s:** 83%
Graduate: n/av	**Student/Faculty:** 17 to 1
Year: semesters, summer session	**Tuition:** $31,250
Application Deadline:	**Room & Board:** $11,420
Freshman Class: 2624 applied, 1989 accepted, 413 enrolled	
SAT CR/M: 530/550 **ACT:** 25	**COMPETITIVE**

De Sales University, founded in 1964, is a private liberal arts institution affiliated with the Roman Catholic Church. In addition to regional accreditation, DSU has baccalaureate program accreditation with ACBSP and NLN. The library contains 163,935 volumes, 447,834 microform items, 4,233 audio/video tapes/CDs/DVDs, and subscribes to 23,000 periodicals including electronic. Computerized library services include interlibrary loans, database searching, Internet access, and Wi-Fi capability. Special learning facilities include a radio station, TV station, the Gambet Center a brand new state-of-the-art Business and Health Care Building. The state of the art Hurd Science Center, which includes: Senior research activity space. The Labuda Center for the Performing Arts is a state-of-the-art venue is home to: • Main Stage (473 seat proscenium/ thrust theatre) • Schubert Stage (200 seat black box theatre) • Studio Theatre (100 seat lab theatre) • Two dance studios • Shops • Rehearsal and music rooms The Iacocca Studio is a professional, high definition (HD) facility outfitted for multi-camera digital video and music production equipped with: • three cameras • digital switching • a programmable lighting system • an array of studio microphones • multi-track mixing and editing • a digital graphic effects system. Brisson Hall houses: • 10 Avid and Final Cut Pro editing suites that are HD compatible • production office equipped with computers, scriptwriting software, and high-speed Internet access. Classrooms across campus are equipped with video and computer projection systems to enable close study of moving images. The Air Products Theater is a 60-seat projection theater/classroom used for lecture courses as well as a venue for screening student work. The Trexler Library collection includes a diverse range of American and international films as well as a current collection of reference materials related to film, television, and media studies. The 480-acre campus is in a suburban area 50 miles north of Philadelphia. Including any residence halls, there are 32 buildings.

Student Life: 65% of undergraduates are from Pennsylvania. Others are from 18 states, and 5 foreign countries. 93% are White. The average age of freshmen is 18. 15% do not continue beyond their first year; 70% remain to graduate.

Housing: 1156 students can be accommodated in college housing, which includes single-sex dorms. In addition, there are special-interest houses. On-campus housing is guaranteed for all 4 years, is available on a first-come, first-served basis, and is available on a lottery system for upperclassmen. 65% of students live on campus. All students may keep cars.

Activities: There are no fraternities or sororities. Groups on campus include band, cheerleading, choir, chorale, chorus, communications, computers, dance, debate, drama, ethnic, film, honors, international, literary magazine, marching band, musical theater, newspaper, pep band, political, professional, radio and TV, religious, social, social service, student government, and yearbook. Popular campus events include Act 1 Plays, Annual Lecture Series, Fall Fest and Intercollegiate Athletics.

Sports: There are 7 intercollegiate sports for men and 8 for women, and 8 intramural sports for men and 8 for women. Facilities include facilities for soccer, baseball, softball, tennis, basketball, lacrosse, track, cross country, and volleyball; and a sports and recreation facility featuring a fitness center, and multipurpose athletic courts.

Disabled Students: 99% of the campus is accessible. Facilities include wheelchair ramps, elevators, special parking, specially equipped restrooms, special class scheduling, lowered drinking fountains, lowered telephones, and special housing.

Services: Counseling and information services are available, as is tutoring in most subjects. There is a reader service for the blind, and remedial math, reading, and writing. The Academic Resource Center (ARC) provides services (including tutoring) for students.

Campus Safety and Security: Measures include 24-hour foot and vehicle patrol, emergency notification system, self-defense education, and security escort services. There are emergency telephones, lighted pathways/sidewalks, and controlled access to dorms/residences.

Programs of Study: DSU confers B.A., B.S. and B.S.N. degrees. Master's and doctoral degrees are also awarded. Bachelor's degrees are awarded in BIOLOGICAL SCIENCE (biochemistry and biology/biological science), BUSINESS (accounting, banking and finance, business administration and management, human resources, management information systems, marketing/retailing/merchandising, and sports management), COMMUNICATIONS AND THE ARTS (communications, dance, dramatic arts, English, film arts, performing arts, radio/television technology, and Spanish), COMPUTER AND PHYSICAL SCIENCE (chemistry, computer science, and mathematics), EDUCATION (early childhood education and elementary education), HEALTH PROFESSIONS (exercise science, nursing, pharmaceutical science, and physician's assistant), SOCIAL SCIENCE (criminal justice, history, liberal arts/general studies, philosophy, political science/government, psychology, and theological studies). Physician assistant, theatre, nursing, biology and accounting are the strongest academically. Medical studies (Physician Assistant), nursing and theatre have the largest enrollments.

Required: For graduation, students must complete a minimum of 120 credit hours including a maximum of 48 in the major with a minimum GPA of 2.0 overall and in the major. Liberal arts distribution requirements consist of 12 to 16 courses including cultural literacy, modes of thinking, and Christian values and theology, as well as 3 courses in phys ed (one-credit courses). Internships are strongly encouraged for most majors.

Special: Students may cross-register with schools in the Lehigh Valley Association of Independent Colleges (LVAIC). Internships are strongly encouraged in all majors, and study abroad in 10 countries is possible. Dual majors, a Washington semester, pass/fail options, accelerated degree programs, and credit for life, military, and work experience are offered. There are 11 national honor societies and a freshman honors program.

Faculty/Classroom: 49% of faculty are male; 51% are female. All teach undergraduates, all do research, and all teach and do research. No introductory courses are taught by graduate students. The average class size in an introductory lecture is 18; in a laboratory is 24; and in a regular course is 18.

Admissions: 76% of the 2013-2014 applicants were accepted. The SAT scores for the 2013-2014 freshman class were: Critical Reading--31% below 500, 46% between 500 and 599, 18% between 600 and 699, and 5% between 700 and 800; Math--31% below 500, 40% between 500 and 599, 25% between 600 and 699, and 4% between 700 and 800. The ACT scores were 12% below 21, 28% between 21 and 23, 37% between 24 and 26, 13% between 27 and 28, and 10% above 28. 41% of the current freshmen were in the top fifth of their class; 72% were in the top two fifths.

Requirements: The SAT is required. Applicants must be graduates of an accredited secondary school. The GED is accepted. Applicants should have completed 17 college preparatory courses including 4 years each of English, history, and math, 3 years of science, and 2 years of foreign language. The school will accept an essay but strongly recommends an interview. For theater students, a performance appraisal is required. For dance students an audition is required. AP and CLEP credits are accepted. Important factors in the admissions decision are advanced placement or honors courses, leadership record, recommendations by school officials, and evidence of special talent.

Procedure: Freshmen are admitted fall and spring. Entrance exams should be taken during the junior or senior year. There are deferred admissions and rolling admissions plans. Application deadlines are open. Application fee is $30. Notification is sent on a rolling basis. Applications are accepted online.

Transfer: 72 transfer students enrolled in 2012-2013. Applicants for transfer should have completed a minimum of 24 college credit hours with a GPA of 2.5. An interview is recommended. 45 of 120 credits required for the bachelor's degree must be completed at DSU.

Visiting: There are regularly scheduled orientations for prospective students, including meetings with faculty advisers and social activities. There are guides for informal visits, visitors may sit in on classes, and stay overnight. To schedule a visit, contact Mr. Derrick Wetzel at (610) 282-4443.

Financial Aid: In 2013-2014, 84% of all full-time freshmen and 79% of continuing full-time students received some form of financial aid. 83% of all full-time freshmen and 75% of continuing full-time students received need-based aid. The average freshman award was $24,394. Need-based scholarships or need-based grants averaged $19,469 ($31,000 maximum); need-based self-help aid (loans and jobs) averaged $5,047 ($9,500 maximum); and other non-need-based awards and non-need-based scholarships averaged $10,741 ($31,000 maximum). The average financial indebtedness of the 2013 graduate was $25,643. DSU is a member of CSS. The FAFSA, the state aid form, and the college's own financial statement are required. The deadline for filing freshman financial aid applications for fall entry is February 1.

International Students: There are 14 international students enrolled. The school actively recruits these students. They must take the TOEFL with a minimum score of 550 on the paper-based TOEFL (PBT) or 80 on the Internet-based version (iBT). They must also take the SAT or ACT. or the iELTS could be required.

Graduates: From July 1, 2012 to June 30, 2013, 519 bachelor's degrees were awarded. The most popular majors were business, health professions and related sciences, and visual and performing arts. In an average class, 64% graduate in 4 years or less, 66% graduate in 5 years or less, and 70% graduate in 6 years or less.

Admissions Contact: Mary Birkhead, Dean of Enrollment Management. E-Mail: *admiss@desales.edu* Web: *www.desales.edu*

DELAWARE VALLEY COLLEGE F-3

Doylestown, PA 18901-2697 **(215) 489-2211**
(800) 2DELVAL; (215) 230-2968

Full-time: 700 men, 900 women	**Faculty:** 79; IIB, -$
Part-time: 210 men, 190 women	**Ph.D.s:** 62%
Graduate: 30 men, 40 women	**Student/Faculty:** n/av
Year: semesters, summer session	**Tuition:** $29,896
Application Deadline: open	**Room & Board:** $11,242
Freshman Class: n/av	
SAT or ACT: required	

COMPETITIVE

Delaware Valley College, founded in 1896, is a private institution offering undergraduate programs in specialized fields of agriculture, business administration, English, the sciences, math, criminal justice administration, and secondary education. The college also offers graduate programs in educational leadership and in food and agribusiness. Some figures in the above capsule and in this profile are approximate. The library contains 70,000 volumes 162,914 microform items, and subscribes to 728 periodicals including electronic. Computerized library services include interlibrary loans, database searching, Internet access, and laptop Internet portals. Special learning facilities include a learning resource center, radio station, TV station, a dairy science center, a livestock farm, horse facilities, an apiary, a small animal lab, a tissue culture lab, an arboretum, and greenhouses. The 550-acre campus is in a suburban area 20 miles north of Philadelphia. Including any residence halls, there are 36 buildings.

Student Life: 67% of undergraduates are from Pennsylvania. Students are from 22 states, 1 foreign country, and Canada. 85% are from public schools. 80% are white. 35% are Catholic; 32% Protestant; 16% claim no religious affiliation; 14% Buddhist, Seventh-day Adventist, and others. The average age of freshmen is 18; all undergraduates, 21. 26% do not continue beyond their first year; 75% remain to graduate.

Housing: 960 students can be accommodated in college housing, which includes single-sex and coed dorms. In addition, there are honors houses. On-campus housing is available on a first-come, first-served basis, and is available on a lottery system for upperclassmen. 63% of students live on campus; of those, 65% remain on campus on weekends. Upperclassmen may keep cars.

Activities: 4% of men belong to 5 national fraternities; 5% of women belong to 3 national sororities. There are 40 groups on campus, including art, band, cheerleading, chess, choir, chorale, chorus, computers, dance, drama, ethnic, honors, international, literary magazine, newspaper, pep band, photography, professional, radio and TV, religious, social, social service, student government, and yearbook. Popular campus events include A-Day, Parents Day, and Family Weekend.

Sports: There are 8 intercollegiate sports for men and 7 for women, and 9 intramural sports for men and 9 for women. Facilities include 2 gyms, tennis courts, outdoor playing courts and fields, a football stadium, a running track, a small lake, a video game room, picnic areas, nature walks, riding trails, and indoor and outdoor equine facilities.

Disabled Students: 85% of the campus is accessible. Facilities include wheelchair ramps, elevators, special parking, specially equipped rest rooms, special class scheduling, and lowered drinking fountains.

Services: Counseling and information services are available, as is tutoring in most subjects. There is a reader service for the blind, and remedial math, reading, and writing.

Campus Safety and Security: Measures include 24-hour foot and vehicle patrol, self-defense education, and security escort services. There are shuttle buses, emergency telephones, and lighted pathways/sidewalks.

Programs of Study: DVC confers B.A. and B.S. degrees. Associate and master's degrees are also awarded. Bachelor's degrees are awarded in AGRICULTURE (agronomy, animal science, dairy science, equine science, horticulture, and wildlife management), BIOLOGICAL SCIENCE (biology/biological science and zoology), BUSINESS (accounting, business administration and management, marketing/retailing/merchandising, and sports management), COMMUNICATIONS AND THE ARTS (English), COMPUTER AND PHYSICAL SCIENCE (chemistry and computer science), EDUCATION (secondary education), ENGINEERING AND ENVIRONMENTAL DESIGN (environmental science and food services technology), SOCIAL SCIENCE (criminal justice, food production/management/services, and food science). Physical and biological science and animal science are the strongest academically. Business administration and animal science have the largest enrollments.

Required: The bachelor's degree requires completion of at least 128 credits, including 48 in the major, with a minimum GPA of 2.0. The core curriculum consists of 48 credits of liberal arts courses, including cultural enrichment, phys ed, and an introduction to computers. Students must also fulfill employment program requirements.

Special: DVC offers a specialized methods and techniques program that enables students to learn lab techniques and gain experience in the practical aspects of their majors. There is a zoo science major that prepares students for careers in zoo management and animal conservation. There are co-op programs in all majors, dual majors, study abroad in England, internships, and work-study programs in a wide variety of employment and research settings. Cross-registration is available with Rutgers University and Middle Bucks Technical Institute. Nondegree study and pass/fail options are also available. There are 3 national honor societies, a freshman honors program, and 2 departmental honors programs.

Faculty/Classroom: 66% of faculty are male; 34% are female. All teach undergraduates. No introductory courses are taught by graduate students. The average class size in an introductory lecture is 24; in a laboratory, 21; and in a regular course, 20.

Admissions: 79% of a recent year's applicants were accepted. 25% of a recent year's freshmen were in the top fifth of their class; 49% were in the top two fifths. 1 freshman graduated first in the class.

Requirements: The SAT or ACT is required. In addition, applicants must be graduates of accredited secondary schools or have earned a GED. The college requires 15 academic units, including 6 in electives, 3 in English, and 2 each in math, science, and social studies. An interview is recommended. DVC requires applicants to be in the upper 50% of their class. A GPA of 2.8 is required. AP and CLEP credits are accepted. Important factors in the admissions decision are leadership record, personality/intangible qualities, and extracurricular activities record.

Procedure: Freshmen are admitted fall and spring. Entrance exams should be taken in the junior or senior year. There are deferred admissions and rolling admissions plans. Application deadlines are open. Check with the school for the current application fee. Applications are accepted online.

Transfer: 109 transfer students enrolled in a recent year. Applicants must have a minimum GPA of 2.0 and must submit SAT scores. An interview is recommended. 60 of 130 credits required for the bachelor's degree must be completed at DVC.

Visiting: There are regularly scheduled orientations for prospective students, consisting of a student panel, meetings with department chairs, and general information sessions. There are guides for informal visits, and visitors may sit in on classes and stay overnight. To schedule a visit, contact the Admissions Department.

Financial Aid: In a recent year, 98% of all full-time freshmen and 94% of continuing full-time students received some form of financial aid. 78% of all full-time students received need-based aid. The average freshman award was $16,050. 20% of undergraduate students work part-time. Average annual earnings from campus work are $1600. The average financial indebtedness of a recent year's graduate was $17,760. The FAFSA is required. Check with the school for current application deadlines.

International Students: There was 1 international student enrolled in a recent year. International students must take the TOEFL. They must also take the SAT or ACT.

Graduates: In a recent year, 281 bachelor's degrees were awarded. The most popular majors were business administration (30%), animal science (22%), and ornamental horticulture (10%). 310 companies recruited on campus in a recent year. In an average class, 44% graduate in 4 years or less, 54% graduate in 5 years or less, and 57% graduate in 6 years or less. Of a recent year's graduating class, 24% were enrolled in graduate school within 6 months of graduation, and 80% were employed.

Admissions Contact: Director of Admissions. A campus DVD is available. E-Mail: *admitme@deval.edu* Web: *www.deval.edu*

DICKINSON COLLEGE — D-3

Carlisle, PA 17013 — (717) 245-1231; (800) 644-1773; (717) 245-1442

Full-time: 1031 men, 1308 women	**Faculty:** 216; IIB, +$
Part-time: 6 men, 7 women	**Ph.D.s:** 95%
Graduate: n/av	**Student/Faculty:** 11 to 1
Year: semesters, summer session	**Tuition:** $46,094
Application Deadline: February 1	**Room & Board:** $11,568
Freshman Class: 5827 applied, 2590 accepted, 626 enrolled	
SAT CR/M/W: 640/640/635	**ACT:** 29 **HIGHLY COMPETITIVE+**

Dickinson College is a nationally recognized liberal-arts institution chartered in 1783 in Carlisle, Pa. Devoted to its revolutionary roots, the college maintains the mission of founder Benjamin Rush—to provide a useful education in the liberal arts and sciences. Known for its global curriculum, Dickinson offers more than 40 study-abroad programs in 24 countries on six continents. The college is a leader among educational institutions committed to environmental sustainability and green initiatives. The library contains 547,711 volumes, 168,703 microform items, 86,231 audio/video tapes/CDs/DVDs, and subscribes to 5,192 periodicals including electronic. Computerized library services include interlibrary loans, database searching, Internet access, and Wi-Fi capability. Special learning facilities include an art gallery, planetarium, radio station, fiber-optic and satellite telecommunications networks, a telescope observatory, scanning electron microscope, research-quality greenhouse and an archival collection. The 180-acre campus is in a suburban area about 20 miles west of Harrisburg, PA and 2 hours from Washington, D.C. Including any residence halls, there are 146 buildings.

Student Life: 77% of undergraduates are from out of state, mostly the Middle Atlantic. Students are from 42 states, and 44 foreign countries. 60% are from public schools. 76% are White. 26% are Catholic; 25% Protestant; 19% claim no religious affiliation; 12% Jewish. The average age of freshmen is 18; all undergraduates, 20. 10% do not continue beyond their first year; 83% remain to graduate.

Housing: 2038 students can be accommodated in college housing, which includes coed dorms and on-campus apartments. In addition, there are language houses, special-interest houses, fraternity houses, sorority houses, including arts, environmental, learning communities, multicultural and wellness. On-campus housing is guaranteed for all 4 years and is available on a lottery system for upperclassmen. 95% of students live on campus; of those, 85% remain on campus on weekends. Upperclassmen may keep cars.

Activities: 12% of men belong to 4 national fraternities; 20% of women belong to 1 local and 5 national sororities. There are 122 groups on campus, including art, band, cheerleading, chess, choir, chorale, chorus, computers, dance, debate, drama, environmental, ethnic, film, gay, honors, international, jazz band, literary magazine, musical theater, newspaper, orchestra, photography, political, professional, radio and TV, religious, social, social service, student government, symphony, and yearbook. Popular campus events include Public Affairs Symposium, and Clarke Forum Events.

Sports: There are 12 intercollegiate sports for men and 13 for women, and 11 intramural sports for men and 9 for women. Facilities include The fitness center expansion will provide 16,000 square feet and include strength training equipment, cardio respiratory machines and 5 international squash courts. The 38,600 square-foot Kline Center includes a wood floor for Basketball Season and racquetball courts. The gymnasium area features a multi-purpose polyurethane synthetic floor covering that includes an indoor 200-meter, four-lane track with a hidden jump pit. There is a 25-yard competition swimming pool with separate diving well and seating for 350 spectators; tennis courts; a varsity football field; lacrosse and baseball, all comprising nearly 30 acres. A soccer complex that includes a state-of-the-art natural grass field and 500 bleacher seats. There is an outdoor track, jogging trails, bicycle trails, and an indoor rock-climbing wall.

Disabled Students: 68% of the campus is accessible. Facilities include wheelchair ramps, elevators, special parking, specially equipped rest-rooms, special class scheduling, lowered drinking fountains, lowered telephones, and special housing.

Services: Counseling and information services are available, as is tutoring in every subject. Services are provided as necessary on a case-by-case basis. There is a reader service for the blind. There also is a Writing Center

Campus Safety and Security: Measures include 24-hour foot and vehicle patrol, emergency notification system, self-defense education, and security escort services. There are shuttle buses, emergency telephones, lighted pathways/sidewalks, controlled access to dorms/residences, Electronic access to residence halls, and required electronic access for on campus administrative and academic buildings.

Programs of Study: Dickinson confers B.A. and B.S. degrees. Bachelor's degrees are awarded in AGRICULTURE (environmental studies), BIOLOGICAL SCIENCE (biochemistry, biology/biological science, and neurosciences), BUSINESS (international business management), COMMUNICATIONS AND THE ARTS (art history, classical languages, dance, English, French, German, Greek, Latin, music, Russian, Spanish, and theatre arts), COMPUTER AND PHYSICAL SCIENCE (chemistry, computer science, earth science, mathematics, and physics), ENGINEERING AND ENVIRONMENTAL DESIGN (environmental science), SOCIAL SCIENCE (African studies, American studies, anthropology, archeology, classical/ancient civilization, East Asian studies, economics, history, international studies, Italian studies, Judaic studies, Latin American studies, law, medieval studies, Middle Eastern studies, philosophy, political science/government, psychology, public affairs, religion, sociology, and women's studies). International education/foreign languages, sciences, sustainability education and preprofessional programs are the strongest academically. International business and management/international studies, biology, and political science have the largest enrollments.

Required: To graduate, students must complete 32 courses with a minimum GPA of 2.0. The school requires 2 courses each in humanities, social sciences, and lab sciences. Also required are 3 courses of cross-cultural studies (including foreign language, comparative civilizations, and U.S. diversity), a first-year seminar, phys ed, and the completion of a major averaging 9 to 15 courses. Writing-intensive and quantitative reasoning courses are also required.

Special: Students may cross-register with Central Pennsylvania Consortium Colleges. Instruction in 13 languages is available. Internships are available on and off campus. Dickinson now sponsors more than 40 programs on six continents in 24 countries. These options include academic year programs, semester programs, summer programs, globally-integrated courses that include a January international field experience and specialized programs which combine domestic study with international study. A Washington semester, work-study, and accelerated degree programs are available, as are dual majors, student-designed majors, non-degree study, pass/fail options, and a 3-3 law degree with the Dickinson School of Law of Pennsylvania State University. There are 3-2 engineering degrees offered with Case Western Reserve University, Rensselaer Polytechnic Institute, the University of Pennsylvania and with Columbia University. Graduate school agreements are currently in place for: Medicine/Health programs with The Johns Hopkins University School of Nursing; Jefferson School of Population Health at the Jefferson Medical College; Law with The Pennsylvania State University Dickinson School of Law (3-3 Program); Business with The Thunderbird School of Global Management; William E. Simon Graduate School of Business Administration at The University of Rochester; Engineering with Rensselaer Polytechnic Institute (3-2 Program) and Case Western Reserve University (3-2 Program); Columbia University (3-2 Program); International Graduate Education with The Network of Autonomous Schools of the Lombardy Region (Italy); University of Bremen (Bremen, Germany); University of East Anglia (Norwich, England); University of Maine; University of Malaga (Malaga, Spain), and the University of Queensland (Queensland, Australia). There are 16 national honor societies, including Phi Beta Kappa, and 34 departmental honors programs.

Faculty/Classroom: 53% of faculty are male; 47% are female. All teach and do research. No introductory courses are taught by graduate students. The average class size in an introductory lecture is 35 and in a laboratory is 17.

Admissions: 44% of the 2013-2014 applicants were accepted. The SAT scores for the 2013-2014 freshman class were: Critical Reading--3% below 500, 25% between 500 and 599, 53% between 600 and 699, and 18% between 700 and 800; Math--3% below 500, 20% between 500 and 599, 55% between 600 and 699, and 22% between 700 and 800; Writing--4% below 500, 22% between 500 and 599, 57% between 600 and 699, and 17% between 700 and 800. The ACT scores were 2% below 21, 2% between 21 and 23, 11% between 24 and 26, 31% between 27 and 28, and 55% above 28. 70% of the current freshmen were in the top fifth of their class; 92% were in the top two fifths.

Requirements: The SAT or ACT and ACT Writing Test are recommended. The SAT and ACT Subject Tests are optional submissions. The GED is accepted. Applicants should have completed 16 academic credits, including 4 years of English, 3 each of math and science, 2 (preferably 3) of foreign language, 2 of social studies, and 2 additional courses drawn from the above areas. An essay is required, and an interview is recommended. AP credits are accepted. Important factors in the admissions decision are advanced placement or honors courses, extracurricular activities record, and recommendations by school officials.

Procedure: Freshmen are admitted fall. Entrance exams should be taken in the spring of the junior year or the fall of the senior year. There are early decision, early admissions, and deferred admissions plans. Early decision applications should be filed by November 15; regular applications, by February 1 for fall entry, along with a $65 fee. Notification of early decision is sent December 15; regular decision, March 31. 277 early decision candidates were accepted for the 2013-2014 class. 774 applicants were on the 2013 waiting list; 10 were admitted. Applications are accepted online.

Transfer: 20 transfer students enrolled in 2012-2013. Applicants for transfer must have at least a 2.0 cumulative GPA and must submit secondary school and college transcripts and 1 professor recommendation in addition to the standard application for admission. 64 of 128 credits required for the bachelor's degree must be completed at Dickinson.

Visiting: There are regularly scheduled orientations for prospective students, Prospective students can participate in campus tours, individual interviews, group information sessions, class visits, overnight stays in residence halls, and open houses. There are guides for informal visits, visitors may sit in on classes, and stay overnight. To schedule a visit, contact the Admissions Office.

Financial Aid: In 2013-2014, 76% of all full-time freshmen and 74% of continuing full-time students received some form of financial aid. 58% of all full-time freshmen and 56% of continuing full-time students received need-based aid. The average freshman award was $32,929. Need-based scholarships or need-based grants averaged $30,591 ($57,230 maximum); need-based self-help aid (loans and jobs) averaged $6,790 ($10,000 maximum); other non-need-based awards and non-need-based scholarships averaged $10,031 ($53,594 maximum); and $8,815 from other forms of aid. 49% of undergraduate students work part-time. Average annual earnings from campus work are $1133. The average financial indebtedness of the 2013 graduate was $24,739. Dickinson is a member of CSS. The CSS/Profile, FAFSA, and the state aid form, and noncustodial parent statement are required. The priority date for freshman financial aid applications for fall entry is November 15. The deadline for filing freshman financial aid applications for fall entry is February 1.

International Students: There are 170 international students enrolled. The school actively recruits these students. They must take the TOEFL with a minimum score of 89 on the Internet-based version (iBT), IELTS.

Graduates: From July 1, 2012 to June 30, 2013, 526 bachelor's degrees were awarded. The most popular majors were international business and management (8%), biology (7%), and political science (6%). 19 companies recruited on campus in 2012-2013. In an average class, 81% graduate in 4 years or less, 85% graduate in 5 years or less, and 85% graduate in 6 years or less. Of the 2012 graduating class, 38% were enrolled in graduate school within 6 months of graduation, and 64% were employed.

Admissions Contact: Stephanie Balmer, VP for Enrollment and Communication . E-Mail: *admit@dickinson.edu* Web: *www.dickinson.edu*

DREXEL UNIVERSITY F-3

Philadelphia, PA 19104 (215) 895-2400
(800) 2-DREXEL; (215) 895-5939

Full-time: 7920 men, 6057 women	**Faculty:** 989; I, -$
Part-time: 943 men, 1696 women	**Ph.D.s:** 79%
Graduate: 3762 men, 5754 women	**Student/Faculty:** 17 to 1
Year: quarters, summer session	**Tuition:** $37,505
Application Deadline: January 15	**Room & Board:** $14,415
Freshman Class: 43945 applied, 35815 accepted, 3022 enrolled	
SAT CR/M/W: 570/630/570 **ACT:** 27	**HIGHLY COMPETITIVE**

Drexel is a comprehensive national research university ranked among the top 100 in the United States. With 26,132 students, Drexel is one of America's 15 largest private universities. The University has built its global reputation on core achievements that include: leadership in experiential learning through its cooperative education program; a history of academic technology firsts; and recognition as a model of best practices in translational research initiatives. Founded in 1891 in Philadelphia, Drexel now engages with students and communities around the world via three Philadelphia campuses and other regional sites, Drexel University Sacramento, The Academy of Natural Sciences of Drexel University and international research partnerships in several countries around the globe. Drexel Online is one of the oldest and most successful providers of online degree programs. There are 12 undergraduate schools and 14 graduate schools. In addition to regional accreditation, Drexel has baccalaureate program accreditation with AACSB, ABET, ACCE, ADA, CSAB, FIDER, NAAB, and NASAD. The 2 libraries contain 609,339 volumes, 18,133 microform items, 10,923 audio/video tapes/CDs/DVDs, and subscribe to 36,584 periodicals including electronic. Computerized library services include interlibrary loans, database searching, Internet access, and Wi-Fi capability. Special learning facilities include an art gallery, natural history museum, radio station, and TV station. The 109-acre campus is in an urban area in the University City neighborhood of Philadelphia. Including any residence halls, there are 111 buildings.

Student Life: 58% of undergraduates are from out of state, mostly the Middle Atlantic. Students are from 47 states, 132 foreign countries, and Canada. 56% are White; 13% Foreign; 12% Asian American. The average

age of freshmen is 18; all undergraduates, 23. 14% do not continue beyond their first year; 69% remain to graduate.

Housing: 4600 students can be accommodated in college housing, which includes coed dorms, on-campus apartments, and off-campus apartments. In addition, there are fraternity houses, sorority houses, honors floors in residence halls and international student housing. On-campus housing is guaranteed for the freshman year only, is available on a first-come, first-served basis, and is available on a lottery system for upperclassmen. 74% of students commute. All students may keep cars.

Activities: 11% of men belong to 1 local and 16 national fraternities; 10% of women belong to 12 national sororities. There are 340 groups on campus, including art, band, cheerleading, chess, choir, chorus, computers, dance, drama, environmental, ethnic, film, forensics, gay, honors, international, jazz band, literary magazine, musical theater, newspaper, orchestra, pep band, photography, political, professional, radio and TV, religious, social, social service, student government, and yearbook. Popular campus events include Musical, Cultural, and Art Events.

Sports: There are 10 intercollegiate sports for men and 10 for women, and 11 intramural sports for men and 11 for women. Facilities include an athletic center with 3 gyms, 5 squash courts, a 25-yard swimming pool, a diving well, 4 exercise rooms, and 1 wrestling room; a recreation center with 2 gyms, 2 floors of fitness (18,000 square feet), 2 exercise studios, 2 squash courts, a climbing wall, an indoor track, and an armory with 3 multipurpose courts.

Disabled Students: 98% of the campus is accessible. Facilities include wheelchair ramps, elevators, special parking, specially equipped restrooms, special class scheduling, lowered drinking fountains, and special housing.

Services: Counseling and information services are available, as is tutoring in most subjects. There is remedial math, reading, and writing.

Campus Safety and Security: Measures include 24-hour foot and vehicle patrol, emergency notification system, self-defense education, and security escort services. There are shuttle buses, emergency telephones, lighted pathways/sidewalks, controlled access to dorms/residences, residential and commuter safety and security programs.

Programs of Study: Drexel confers B.A., B.S., B.F.A, B.S.N. and B.Arch. degrees. Associate, master's, and doctoral degrees are also awarded. Bachelor's degrees are awarded in BIOLOGICAL SCIENCE (biology/biological science and nutrition), BUSINESS (accounting, business administration and management, business economics, fashion merchandising, hotel/motel and restaurant management, marketing/retailing/merchandising, and sports management), COMMUNICATIONS AND THE ARTS (communications, design, film arts, graphic design, music industry, photography, and video), COMPUTER AND PHYSICAL SCIENCE (chemistry, computer science, digital arts/technology, information sciences and systems, mathematics, physics, science, software engineering, and web technology), EDUCATION (education), ENGINEERING AND ENVIRONMENTAL DESIGN (architectural engineering, architecture, biomedical engineering, chemical engineering, civil engineering, computer engineering, construction management, electrical/electronics engineering, environmental engineering, environmental science, interior design, materials engineering, and mechanical engineering), HEALTH PROFESSIONS (biology, nursing, and premedicine), SOCIAL SCIENCE (economics, fashion design and technology, food production/management/services, history, international studies, philosophy, political science/government, psychology, and sociology). Engineering, business, and design arts are the strongest academically. Business, mechanical engineering, and biological sciences have the largest enrollments.

Required: To graduate, students must complete 180 to 192 term credits with a minimum GPA of 2.0 and must earn the number of Drexel Co-op Units determined by the major. There are requirements in math, computer literacy, English, lab science, humanities, and history.

Special: The Drexel Plan of Cooperative Education enables students to alternate periods of full-time classroom studies and full-time employment with university-approved employers. Participation in cooperative education is mandatory for most students. Cross-registration is available with Indiana University of Pennsylvania and Lincoln University. Drexel also offers study abroad, internships, accelerated degrees, 3-3 engineering degrees, dual majors, nondegree study, and credit/no credit options. There is 1 national honor society and a freshman honors program.

Faculty/Classroom: 53% of faculty are male; 47% are female. No introductory courses are taught by graduate students. The average class size in an introductory lecture is 34; in a laboratory is 21; and in a regular course is 15.

Admissions: 81% of the 2013-2014 applicants were accepted. The SAT scores for the 2013-2014 freshman class were: Critical Reading--18% below 500, 43% between 500 and 599, 31% between 600 and 699, and 8% between 700 and 800; Math--6% below 500, 30% between 500 and 599, 44% between 600 and 699, and 20% between 700 and 800; Writing--19% below 500, 43% between 500 and 599, 31% between 600 and 699, and 7% between 700 and 800. The ACT scores were 3% below 21, 18% between 21 and 23, 23% between 24 and 26, 19% between 27 and 28, and 37% above 28. 52% of the current freshmen were in the top fifth of their class; 81% were in the top two fifths. 17 freshmen graduated first in their class.

Requirements: The SAT is required. Applicants must be graduates of an accredited secondary school. The GED is accepted. A GPA of 2.0 is required. AP and CLEP credits are accepted.

Procedure: Freshmen are admitted fall. There are early admissions and deferred admissions plans. Applications should be filed by January 15 for fall entry, along with a $75 fee. Notifications are sent April 1. Application fees are waived if application is completed online.

Transfer: 1539 transfer students enrolled in 2012-2013. Applicants must have a minimum GPA of 2.5. Other requirements vary among the individual colleges within the university. 45 of 180 credits required for the bachelor's degree must be completed at Drexel.

Visiting: There are regularly scheduled orientations for prospective students, consisting of a 2-day program for new freshmen and their parents in late July. There are guides for informal visits, visitors may sit in on classes, and stay overnight. To schedule a visit, contact the Admissions Office.

Financial Aid: Drexel is a member of CSS. The FAFSA is required. The priority date for freshman financial aid applications for fall entry is February 15.

International Students: There are 2122 international students enrolled. The school actively recruits these students. They must take the TOEFL with a minimum score of 550 on the paper-based TOEFL (PBT) or 79 on the Internet-based version (iBT).

Graduates: From July 1, 2012 to June 30, 2013, 2986 bachelor's degrees were awarded. The most popular majors were business (17%), nursing (8%), and mechanical engineering (6%). 405 companies recruited on campus in 2012-2013. In an average class, 69% graduate in 6 years or less.

Admissions Contact: Director of Admissions E-Mail: *enroll@drexel.edu* Web: *www.drexel.edu*

DUQUESNE UNIVERSITY — B-3

Pittsburgh, PA 15282 — (412) 396-6222; (800) 456-0590; (412) 396-5644

Full-time: 2337 men, 3403 women	**Faculty:** 449; I, --$
Part-time: 129 men, 101 women	**Ph.D.s:** 93%
Graduate: 1592 men, 2342 women	**Student/Faculty:** 15 to 1
Year: semesters, summer session	**Tuition:** $31,385
Application Deadline: July 1	**Room & Board:** $10,632
Freshman Class: 6793 applied, 5033 accepted, 1547 enrolled	
SAT CR/M/W: 561/578/558 **ACT:** 25	**VERY COMPETITIVE**

Duquesne University, founded in 1878 by the Spiritan Congregation, is a private Roman Catholic institution offering programs in liberal arts, natural and environmental sciences, nursing, health sciences, pharmacy, business, music, teacher preparation, preprofessional training, law, and leadership and professional development. There are 9 undergraduate schools and 10 graduate schools. In addition to regional accreditation, Duquesne has baccalaureate program accreditation with AACSB, NASM, and NCATE. The 2 libraries contain 739,768 volumes, 252,149 microform items, 78,797 audio/video tapes/CDs/DVDs, and subscribe to 101,861 periodicals including electronic. Computerized library services include interlibrary loans, database searching, Internet access, and Wi-Fi capability. Special learning facilities include an art gallery, radio station, TV station, 240 multimedia-enhanced teaching facilities: 206 classrooms, 24 labs. The 50-acre campus is in an urban area on a private, self-contained campus in the center of Pittsburgh. Including any residence halls, there are 42 buildings.

Student Life: 75% of undergraduates are from Pennsylvania. Others are from 47 states, 47 foreign countries, and Canada. 84% are White. 54% are Catholic; 25% claim no religious affiliation; 16% Protestant. The average age of freshmen is 18; all undergraduates, 21. 11% do not continue beyond their first year; 75% remain to graduate.

Housing: 4000 students can be accommodated in college housing, which includes coed dorms and on-campus apartments. In addition, there are honors houses, special-interest houses, Fraternity and sorority wings, international wings, and club wings. On-campus housing is available on a first-come, first-served basis, and is available on a lottery system for upperclassmen. 60% of students live on campus; of those, 70% remain on campus on weekends. Some may keep cars.

Activities: 17% of men belong to 1 local and 11 national fraternities; 18% of women belong to 8 national sororities. There are 200 groups on campus, including and social programming, art, band, cheerleading, chess, choir, chorale, chorus, computers, dance, debate, drama, drill team, environmental, ethnic, film, forensics, gay, honors, international, jazz band, literary magazine, marching band, musical theater, newspaper, opera, orchestra, pep band, photography, political, professional, radio and TV, religious, social, social service, student government, symphony, and yearbook. Popular campus events include Carnival, Orientation, Night of Lights, Bluffstock, Greek Week, ISO Week, Christmas Ball, Family Weekend, Multi-cultural Unity Banquet, Commute Day, Spotlight Musical Theater Shows, Program Council Major Concert and Nitespot Late Night Programs.

Sports: There are 6 intercollegiate sports for men and 10 for women, and 6 intramural sports for men and 6 for women. Facilities include The Power Center is a 130,000 square-foot facility; 80,000 square-fee is dedicated to athletic and recreation facilities which feature separate student and staff locker facilities, aerobics space, and 50 cardio fitness viewing machines with personal viewing screens, basketball/volleyball courts, walking/running track, two free weight rooms, and racquetball courts. The A.J. Palumbo Center houses the main arena, two regulation sized basketball courts, a new athletic training room, weight training and cardiovascular areas and locker room facilities for student athletes. McCloskey Field is the center for outdoor Intramural activity. The field is made of artificial turf and is surrounded by a four-lane all-weather track. Aurthur J. Rooney Athletic Field is home to Duquesne University's football, men's and women's soccer, and women's lacrosse teams. Other facilities include a six lane swimming pool, a tennis court and an outdoor basketball/deck hockey court.

Disabled Students: 95% of the campus is accessible. Facilities include wheelchair ramps, elevators, special parking, specially equipped restrooms, special class scheduling, lowered drinking fountains, lowered telephones, and special housing.

Services: Counseling and information services are available, as is tutoring in every subject. There is a reader service for the blind, and remedial math, reading, and writing.

Campus Safety and Security: Measures include 24-hour foot and vehicle patrol, emergency notification system, self-defense education, and security escort services. There are shuttle buses, emergency telephones, lighted pathways/sidewalks, controlled access to dorms/residences, There are security cameras throughout campus that monitor exterior areas 24 hours a day.

Programs of Study: Duquesne confers B.A., B.S., B.M., B.S.A.T., B.S.B.A., B.S.Ed., B.S.H.M.S., B.S.H.S., B.S.N. and B.S.P.S. degrees. Master's and doctoral degrees are also awarded. Bachelor's degrees are awarded in BIOLOGICAL SCIENCE (biochemistry, biology/adolescence education, biology/biological science, and forensic science), BUSINESS (accounting, banking and finance, business administration and management, business communications, business economics, entrepreneurial studies, international business management, management information systems, management science, marketing/retailing/merchandising, nonprofit/public organization management, sports marketing, and supply chain management), COMMUNICATIONS AND THE ARTS (advertising, art history and appreciation, classical languages, communications, dramatic arts, English, Greek (classical), journalism, Latin, literature, modern language, multimedia, music performance, music technology, Spanish, and speech/debate/rhetoric), COMPUTER AND PHYSICAL SCIENCE (chemistry, chemistry/adolescence education, computer science, mathematics, and physics), EDUCATION (athletic training, computer education, early childhood education, education, English education, foreign languages education, health information management, mathematics education, middle school education, music education, physical science secondary school education, secondary education, and social studies education), ENGINEERING AND ENVIRONMENTAL DESIGN (computer technology and environmental science), HEALTH PROFESSIONS (health care administration, music therapy, nursing, occupational therapy, pharmaceutical science, pharmacy, physical therapy, physician's assistant, and speech pathology/audiology), SOCIAL SCIENCE (behavioral science, classical/ancient civilization, economics, history, humanities, international relations, liberal arts/general studies, philosophy, political science/government, psychology, sociology, theological studies, and women and gender studies). Pharmacy, nursing, and accounting have the largest enrollments.

Required: To graduate, students are required to complete at least 120 credit hours, including a specified number in the major (varies by program), with a minimum 2.0 GPA. General requirements vary by department, but there is a 33 credit liberal arts core curriculum.

Special: The university offers cross-registration through the Pittsburgh Council on Higher Education, internships, study abroad in 23 countries, and a Washington semester. Also available are B.A.-B.S. degrees, accelerated degree programs, dual and student-designed majors, a 3-2 engineering program with Case Western Reserve University and University of Pittsburgh, a 3-3 law degree and a 3-2 business degree, pass/fail options, and credit for life, military, and work experience. There are 19 national honor societies and a freshman honors program.

Faculty/Classroom: 55% of faculty are male; 45% are female. 93% teach undergraduates. No introductory courses are taught by graduate students. The average class size in an introductory lecture is 28; in a laboratory is 30; and in a regular course is 28.

Admissions: 74% of the 2013-2014 applicants were accepted. The SAT scores for the 2013-2014 freshman class were: Critical Reading--17% below 500, 59% between 500 and 599, 22% between 600 and 699, and 2% between 700 and 800; Math--13% below 500, 52% between 500 and 599, 32% between 600 and 699, and 3% between 700 and 800; Writing--20% below 500, 53% between 500 and 599, 25% between 600 and 699, and 2% between 700 and 800. The ACT scores were 9% below 21, 30% between 21 and 23, 31% between 24 and 26, 17% between 27 and 28, and 13% above 28. 47% of the current freshmen were in the top fifth of their class; 80% were in the top two fifths. 31 freshmen graduated first in their class.

Requirements: The SAT or ACT is required. The ACT Optional Writing test is also required. Students should have either a high school diploma or the GED. Applicants are required to have 16 academic credits, including 4 each in English and academic electives, and 8 combined in social studies, language, math, and science. An essay is required, and an interview is recommended. An audition is required for music majors. 40 hours shadowing for physical therapy. A GPA of 3.0 is required. AP and CLEP credits are accepted. Important factors in the admissions decision are advanced placement or honors courses, evidence of special talent, ability to finance college education, leadership record, parents or siblings attended your school, personality/intangible qualities, extracurricular activities record, recommendations by alumni, geographical diversity, and recommendations by school officials.

Procedure: Freshmen are admitted to all sessions. Entrance exams should be taken during the spring of the junior year or the fall of the senior year. There are early decision, early admissions, deferred admissions, and rolling admissions plans. Early decision applications should be filed by November 1; regular applications, by July 1 for fall entry; December 1 for spring entry; and April 1 for summer entry, along with a $50 fee. Notification of early decision is sent December 15; regular decision, on a rolling basis. 122 early decision candidates were accepted for the 2013-2014 class. Applications are accepted online.

Transfer: 225 transfer students enrolled in 2012-2013. Applicants must submit complete high school and college transcripts. Students should have a minimum GPA of 2.5 for the university, but some schools require a higher average. A minimum of 12 credits earned is required, and an interview is recommended. 30 of 120 credits required for the bachelor's degree must be completed at Duquesne.

Visiting: There are regularly scheduled orientations for prospective students, consisting of a campus tour and individual interviews with counselors and professors. There are guides for informal visits and visitors may sit in on classes. To schedule a visit, contact Jeannine Cavanaugh at (412) 396-6222.

Financial Aid: In 2013-2014, 100% of all full-time freshmen and 97% of continuing full-time students received some form of financial aid. 72% of all full-time freshmen and 68% of continuing full-time students received need-based aid. The average freshman award was $29,925. Need-based scholarships or need-based grants averaged $15,250 ($25,511 maximum); need-based self-help aid (loans and jobs) averaged $16,660 ($43,830 maximum); non-need-based athletic scholarships averaged $17,307 ($41,887 maximum); and other non-need-based awards and non-need-based scholarships averaged $7,224 ($34,280 maximum). 13% of undergraduate students work part-time. The FAFSA and the college's own financial statement are required. The deadline for filing freshman financial aid applications for fall entry is May 1.

International Students: There are 209 international students enrolled. The school actively recruits these students. They must take the MELAB, Students are required to sit for ENG language placement tests as part of their arrival program.

Graduates: From July 1, 2012 to June 30, 2013, 1303 bachelor's degrees were awarded. The most popular majors were nursing (9%), biology (6%), and psychology (5%). 113 companies recruited on campus in 2012-2013. In an average class, 63% graduate in 4 years or less, 73% graduate in 5 years or less, and 74% graduate in 6 years or less. Of the 2012 graduating class, 29% were enrolled in graduate school within 6 months of graduation, and 60% were employed.

Admissions Contact: Debra Zugates, Director, Admissions. E-Mail: *admissions@duq.edu* Web: *www.duq.edu*

EAST STROUDSBURG UNIVERSITY OF PENNSYLVANIA F-2

East Stroudsburg, PA 18301 **(570) 422-3833**
(877) 230-5547; (570) 422-3933

Full-time: 2423 men, 3072 women	**Faculty:** 301; IIA, +$
Part-time: 339 men, 352 women	**Ph.D.s:** 75%
Graduate: 224 men, 368 women	**Student/Faculty:** 18 to 1
Year: semesters, summer session	**Tuition:** $8990 ($19,114)
Application Deadline: April 1	**Room & Board:** $7646

Freshman Class: 6959 applied, 4814 accepted, 1358 enrolled
SAT CR/M/W: 480/490/480

COMPETITIVE

East Stroudsburg University of Pennsylvania, founded in 1893, is a part of the Pennsylvania State System of Higher Education and offers programs in arts and science, health science and human performance, education, business management, and economics. There are 4 undergraduate schools and one graduate school. In addition to regional accreditation, East Stroudsburg has baccalaureate program accreditation with ABET, NCATE, NLN, and NRPA. The library contains 559,231 volumes, 1.4 million microform items, 12,471 audio/video tapes/CDs/DVDs, and subscribes to 28,670 periodicals including electronic. Computerized library services include interlibrary loans, database searching, and Internet access. Special learning facilities include an art gallery, natural history museum, planetarium, radio station, an observatory, a wildlife museum and greenhouse, and a working restaurant. The 258-acre campus is in a small town 75 miles west of New York City and 85 miles northeast of Philadelphia. Including any residence halls, there are 61 buildings.

Student Life: 75% of undergraduates are from Pennsylvania. Others are from 27 states, 27 foreign countries, and Canada. 64% are White; 12% race unknown. The average age of freshmen is 18; all undergraduates, 21. 29% do not continue beyond their first year; 58% remain to graduate.

Housing: 2250 students can be accommodated in college housing, which includes coed dorms and on-campus apartments. In addition, there are honors houses, special-interest houses, honors floors. On-campus housing is guaranteed for all 4 years. 62% of students commute. Alcohol is not permitted. Upperclassmen may keep cars.

Activities: 4% of men belong to 5 national fraternities; 5% of women belong to 1 local and 4 national sororities. There are 130 groups on campus, including art, band, cheerleading, choir, clubs for most majors, computers, dance, drama, environmental, ethnic, gay, honors, international, jazz band, literary magazine, marching band, musical theater, newspaper, orchestra, pep band, political, professional, radio and TV, religious, social, social service, and student government. Popular campus events include New Student Convocation, Welcome Week, Family Weekend, Homecoming, Diversity Week, African-American History Month, Women's History Month, Greek Week, Community on the Quad, and many Ethnic Festivals.

Sports: There are 8 intercollegiate sports for men and 12 for women, and 11 intramural sports for men and 11 for women. Facilities include Athletic facilities include a field house arena with seating for 2600, a wrestling room, a natatorium and batting cages; two turf fields lined for football, soccer, field hockey and women's lacrosse; five multi-purpose grass fields; a stadium track with bleacher seating for 6000; a softball field and a baseball field with batting cages; and outdoor tennis courts. Recreational facilities include the Mattioli Recreation Center with a 4-court arena for basketball, volleyball, and tennis; an elevated track; a group fitness studio, a boxing zone, a 4800 sq. ft. fitness center, 3 racquetball courts and locker rooms. Also the RecB Fitness Center with a 6000 sq. ft. fitness center, group fitness studio, indoor cycling studio, personal training assessment office, and locker rooms.

Disabled Students: 98% of the campus is accessible. Facilities include wheelchair ramps, elevators, special parking, specially equipped restrooms, special class scheduling, lowered drinking fountains, lowered telephones, special housing.

Services: Counseling and information services are available, as is tutoring in every subject. There is remedial math, reading, and writing.

Campus Safety and Security: Measures include 24-hour foot and vehicle patrol, emergency notification system, self-defense education, and security escort services. There are shuttle buses, emergency telephones, lighted pathways/sidewalks, controlled access to dorms/residences, controlled building access.

Programs of Study: East Stroudsburg confers B.A., and B.S. degrees. Master's degrees are also awarded. Bachelor's degrees are awarded in BIOLOGICAL SCIENCE (biochemistry, biology/biological science, and marine science), BUSINESS (business administration and management and hotel/motel and restaurant management), COMMUNICATIONS AND THE ARTS (art, communications, dramatic arts, English, fine arts, French, media arts, music, and Spanish), COMPUTER AND PHYSICAL SCIENCE (chemistry, computer science, earth science, mathematics, physical sciences, and science), EDUCATION (early childhood education, elementary education, foreign languages education, health education, secondary education, and special education), ENGINEERING AND ENVIRONMENTAL DESIGN (environmental science), HEALTH PROFESSIONS (medical laboratory technology, nursing, premedicine, and speech pathology/audiology), SOCIAL SCIENCE (criminal justice, economics, geography, history, parks and recreation management, philosophy, physical fitness/movement, political science/government, psychology, social studies, and sociology). Biological sciences, business management, and physical education have the largest enrollments.

Required: All students must maintain a GPA of at least 2.0 while taking at least 120 semester hours, including 27 to 83 hours in the major. General education courses total 50 credits, with English composition (3 credits) and phys ed (2 credits) required courses. Distribution requirements include 15 hours each in arts and letters, science, and social science.

Special: Internships are offered in most programs, as are dual majors. Also offered are an accelerated degree program in law, B.A.-B.S. degrees, 3-2 engineering degrees with Pennsylvania State University or the University of Pittsburgh, and a transfer program in podiatry. Nondegree study, study abroad, and cross-registration through the National Student Exchange are possible. There are 23 national honor societies and a freshman honors program.

Faculty/Classroom: 51% of faculty are male; 49% are female. All teach undergraduates. No introductory courses are taught by graduate students. The average class size in an introductory lecture is 40; in a laboratory is 20; and in a regular course is 25.

Admissions: 69% of the 2013-2014 applicants were accepted. The SAT scores for the 2013-2014 freshman class were: Critical Reading--61% below 500, 34% between 500 and 599, and 5% between 600 and 699; Math--52% below 500, 38% between 500 and 599, and 9% between 600 and 699; Writing--62% below 500, 34% between 500 and 599, 4% between 600 and 699, and 1% between 700 and 800. 20% of the current freshmen were in the top fifth of their class; 33% were in the top two fifths. 2 freshmen graduated first in their class.

Requirements: The SAT is required. Applicants must be graduates of an accredited secondary school. The GED is accepted. AP and CLEP credits are accepted. Important factors in the admissions decision are advanced placement or honors courses, evidence of special talent, and leadership record.

Procedure: Freshmen are admitted fall and spring. There is a rolling admissions plan. Applications should be filed by April 1 for fall entry; November 15 for spring entry. The fall 2013 application fee was $35. Notifications are sent December 1. 48 applicants were on the 2013 waiting list; 48 were admitted. Applications are accepted online.

Transfer: 578 transfer students enrolled in 2012-2013. Transfer students must have a 2.0 GPA earned over at least 24 credit hours. 32 of 120 credits required for the bachelor's degree must be completed at East Stroudsburg.

Visiting: There are regularly scheduled orientations for prospective students. There are guides for informal visits and visitors may sit in on classes. To schedule a visit, contact the Admissions Office.

Financial Aid: East Stroudsburg is a member of CSS. The FAFSA is required. The deadline for filing freshman financial aid applications for fall entry is March 1.

International Students: There are 47 international students enrolled. They must take the TOEFL with a minimum score of 79 on the Internet-based version (iBT).

Graduates: From July 1, 2012 to June 30, 2013, 1240 bachelor's degrees were awarded. The most popular majors were business management (10%), elementary education (7%), and sociology (6%). 90 companies recruited on campus in 2012-2013. In an average class, 36% graduate in 4 years or less, 55% graduate in 5 years or less, and 59% graduate in 6 years or less.

Admissions Contact: Jeff Jones, Director, Admissions Office. E-Mail: *undergrads@esu.edu* Web: *www4.esu.edu*

EASTERN UNIVERSITY E-3

St. Davids, PA 19087 800.452.0996
(800) 452-0996; (610) 341-1723

Full-time: 705 men, 1474 women	**Faculty:** n/av
Part-time: 131 men, 391 women	**Ph.D.s:** 69%
Graduate: 534 men, 1028 women	**Student/Faculty:** 11 to 1
Year: semesters, summer session	**Tuition:** $28,090
Application Deadline:	**Room & Board:** $9614
Freshman Class: 1463 applied, 1020 accepted, 366 enrolled	
SAT CR/M/W: 527/520/527 **ACT:** 22	**COMPETITIVE**

Eastern University, founded in 1932, is a private liberal arts institution affiliated with the American Baptist Church. There are 2 graduate schools. In addition to regional accreditation, Eastern has baccalaureate program accreditation with CSWE and NLN. The 4 libraries contain 473,190 volumes, 869,487 microform items, 17,421 audio/video tapes/CDs/DVDs. Computerized library services include interlibrary loans, database searching, and Internet access. Special learning facilities include a planetarium and radio station. The 114-acre campus is in a suburban area 20 miles northwest of Philadelphia. Including any residence halls, there are 23 buildings.

Student Life: 56% of undergraduates are from Pennsylvania. Others are from 38 states, 22 foreign countries, and Canada. 53% are White; 23% African American; 11% Hispanic. 77% are unknown denominations; 15% claim no religious affiliation. The average age of freshmen is 18; all undergraduates, 21. 20% do not continue beyond their first year; 60% remain to graduate.

Housing: 1242 students can be accommodated in college housing, which includes single-sex and coed dorms and on-campus apartments. apartment living by application. On-campus housing is guaranteed for all 4 years. 72% of students live on campus; of those, 75% remain on campus on weekends. Alcohol is not permitted. Upperclassmen may keep cars.

Activities: There are no fraternities or sororities. There are 70 groups on campus, including band, cheerleading, choir, chorale, chorus, communications, computers, dance, drama, drill team, ethnic, honors, international, jazz band, literary magazine, musical theater, newspaper, orchestra, pep band, political, professional, radio and TV, religious, social, social service, student government, and yearbook. Popular campus events include Homecoming, Spring Banquet and World Culture Day.

Sports: There are 5 intercollegiate sports for men and 7 for women, and 3 intramural sports for men and 3 for women. Facilities include a gym, a soccer pitch, a baseball/field hockey/softball field, a weight room, an outdoor track, 4 tennis courts, a health fitness trail, an outdoor pool, and basketball/volleyball courts.

Disabled Students: 75% of the campus is accessible. Facilities include wheelchair ramps, elevators, special parking, specially equipped restrooms, special class scheduling, lowered drinking fountains, lowered telephones, and special housing.

Services: Counseling and information services are available, as is tutoring in every subject. There is a reader service for the blind, and remedial math, reading, and writing.

Campus Safety and Security: Measures include 24-hour foot and vehicle patrol, emergency notification system, self-defense education, and security escort services. There are shuttle buses, emergency telephones, lighted pathways/sidewalks, and controlled access to dorms/residences.

Programs of Study: Eastern confers B.A., B.S., B.S.N. and B.S.W. degrees. Associate, master's, and doctoral degrees are also awarded. Bachelor's degrees are awarded in AGRICULTURE (environmental studies), BIOLOGICAL SCIENCE (biochemistry and biology/biological science), BUSINESS (accounting, business administration and management, entrepreneurial studies, marketing/retailing/merchandising, and organizational leadership and management), COMMUNICATIONS AND THE ARTS (communications, dance, English, music, and Spanish), COMPUTER AND PHYSICAL SCIENCE (chemistry and mathematics), EDUCATION (athletic training, early childhood education, and middle school education), HEALTH PROFESSIONS (exercise science and nursing), SOCIAL SCIENCE (biblical studies, history, missions, philosophy, political science/government, psychology, social work, sociology, theological studies, and youth ministry). Biblical/theological studies is the strongest academically. Education, and business have the largest enrollments.

Required: To graduate, all students must complete at least 127 credit hours with a minimum 2.0 GPA. The required hours in the major vary. Students must take courses in the Old and New Testament, humanities, social sciences, non-Western heritage, natural sciences, college writing, Living and Learning in Community, Heritage of Western Thought and Civilization, Science Technology and Values, and Justice in a Pluralistic Society and complete a capstone.

Special: The college offers cross-registration with Cabrini and Rosemont Colleges, Valley Forge Military Academy, and Villanova University, internships, a Washington semester in the American studies program, and student-designed majors. Also available are accelerated degree programs in organizational management and management of information systems, credit for experience, nondegree study, and pass/fail options. There is a different calendar for the organizational management program. There are 10 national honor societies, a freshman honors program, and 1 departmental honors program.

Faculty/Classroom: 49% of faculty are male; 51% are female. No introductory courses are taught by graduate students.

Requirements: The SAT or ACT is required. A GPA of 2.0 is required. AP and CLEP credits are accepted. Important factors in the admissions decision are advanced placement or honors courses and recommendations by school officials.

Procedure: Freshmen are admitted fall and spring. Entrance exams should be taken as early as possible. There are early admissions, deferred admissions, and rolling admissions plans. Application deadlines are open. Application fee is $25. Notification is sent on a rolling basis. Applications are accepted online.

Transfer: 96 transfer students enrolled in 2012-2013. Applicants should have a 2.0 GPA with more than 24 credits, and a 2.5 GPA with fewer than 24 credits. Candidates must be in good standing at their previous institution. 32 of 127 credits required for the bachelor's degree must be completed at Eastern.

Visiting: There are regularly scheduled orientations for prospective students. There are guides for informal visits, visitors may sit in on classes, and stay overnight. To schedule a visit, contact the Admissions Office.

Financial Aid: Eastern is a member of CSS. The FAFSA and the college's own financial statement are required. Check with the school for current application deadlines.

International Students: There are 54 international students enrolled. The school actively recruits these students. They must take the TOEFL with a minimum score of 79 on the Internet-based version (iBT).

Graduates: From July 1, 2012 to June 30, 2013, 522 bachelor's degrees were awarded. The most popular majors were business/marketing (26%), health professions (26%), and education (17%). 23 companies recruited on campus in 2012-2013. In an average class, 51% graduate in 4 years or less, 7% graduate in 5 years or less, and 1% graduate in 6 years or less. Of the 2012 graduating class, 18% were enrolled in graduate school within 6 months of graduation, and 70% were employed.

Admissions Contact: Michael Dziedziak, Executive Director of Enrollment Management. E-Mail: *ugadm@eastern.edu* Web: *www.eastern.edu/choose_EU*

EDINBORO UNIVERSITY OF PENNSYLVANIA B-1

Edinboro, PA 16444 **(814) 732-2761**
(888) 8GO-BORO; (814) 732-2420

Full-time: 2332 men, 3233 women	**Faculty:** n/av; IIA, av$
Part-time: 213 men, 312 women	**Ph.D.s:** n/av
Graduate: 315 men, 1057 women	**Student/Faculty:** n/av
Year: semesters, summer session	**Tuition:** $8578 ($12,315)
Application Deadline:	**Room & Board:** $7362
Freshman Class: n/av	
SAT CR/M/W: 482/478/462 **ACT:** 20	**LESS COMPETITIVE**

Edinboro University of Pennsylvania, founded in 1857, is a public institution and a member of the Pennsylvania State System of Higher Education. The university offers programs in fine and liberal arts, business, engineering, health science, and teacher preparation. There are 4 undergraduate schools and one graduate school. In addition to regional accreditation, EUP has baccalaureate program accreditation with ABET, ACBSP, ADA, CSWE, NASAD, NASM, NCATE, and NLN. The library contains 485,338 volumes, 691,742 microform items, 10,412 audio/video tapes/CDs/DVDs, and subscribes to 1,024 periodicals including electronic. Computerized library services include interlibrary loans, database searching, Internet access, and Wi-Fi capability. Special learning facilities include an art gallery, planetarium, radio station, TV station, a newspaper. The 585-acre campus is in a small town 18 miles south of Erie. Including any residence halls, there are 46 buildings.

Student Life: 86% of undergraduates are from Pennsylvania. Others are from 42 states, 30 foreign countries, and Canada. 88% are White. The average age of freshmen is 22; all undergraduates, 22. 32% do not continue beyond their first year; 26% remain to graduate.

Housing: 2940 students can be accommodated in college housing, which includes single-sex and coed dorms. In addition, there are honors houses, special-interest houses, floors by academic major and quiet floors. On-campus housing is guaranteed for the freshman year only, is available on a first-come, and first-served basis. 63% of students commute. Alcohol is not permitted. All students may keep cars.

Activities: There are 200 groups on campus, including art, bagpipe, band, cheerleading, chess, chorale, communications, computers, dance, debate, drama, drill team, ethnic, film, forensics, gay, honors, international, jazz band, literary magazine, marching band, musical theater, newspaper, opera, pep band, photography, political, professional, radio and TV, religious, social, social service, student government, and symphony. Popular campus events include Moving in Day/Ice Cream Social, Academic Festival, and Snowfest, Black History and Women's HIstory.

Sports: There are 8 intercollegiate sports for men and 9 for women. Facilities include a field house, a stadium, 6 tennis courts, 4 gyms, a swimming pool, 3 racquetball courts, 2 aerobics rooms, an indoor and outdoor track, a fitness center, men's and women's locker rooms, an athletic training office, a wrestling room, saunas, steamrooms, a weight room, a combative sport room, an outdoor ropes course, a softball field, multiple outdoor sport fields, an outdoor recreation office, and a climbing wall.

Disabled Students: 97% of the campus is accessible. Facilities include wheelchair ramps, elevators, special parking, specially equipped restrooms, special class scheduling, lowered drinking fountains, lowered telephones, special housing.

Services: Counseling and information services are available, as is tutoring in most subjects. There is a reader service for the blind, and remedial math, reading, and writing. Academic aides are available as are services in the academic support library.

Campus Safety and Security: Measures include 24-hour foot and vehicle patrol and self-defense education. There are emergency telephones, lighted pathways/sidewalks, There are 14 commissioned police officers and optional engraving of personal property.

Programs of Study: EUP confers B.A., B.S., B.F.A., B.S.A.E., B.S.Ed. and B.S.N. degrees. Associate and master's degrees are also awarded. Bachelor's degrees are awarded in BIOLOGICAL SCIENCE (biology/biological science), BUSINESS (business administration and management and sports management), COMMUNICATIONS AND THE ARTS (applied art, art, art history and appreciation, communications, dramatic arts, English, English literature, fine arts, graphic design, journalism, media arts, and music), COMPUTER AND PHYSICAL SCIENCE (chemistry, computer science, earth science, geology, information sciences and systems, mathematics, natural sciences, and physics), EDUCATION (art education, early childhood education, elementary education, foreign languages education, health education, mathematics education, middle school education, music education, physical education, science education, secondary education, social studies education, and special education), ENGINEERING AND ENVIRONMENTAL DESIGN (engineering physics, environmental science, and manufacturing technology), HEALTH PROFESSIONS (medical laboratory technology, nuclear medical technology, nursing, premedicine, public health, and speech pathology/audiology), SOCIAL SCIENCE (anthropology, counseling/psychology, criminal justice, economics, forensic studies, geography, history, humanities, liberal arts/general studies, philosophy, political science/government, prelaw, psychology, social science, and social work). Education, visual and performing arts, and health professions have the largest enrollments.

Required: To graduate, students must complete a minimum of 120 semester hours with a minimum GPA of 2.0. General education requirements include 48 hours of courses, consisting of a 21-semester-hour core with 3 hours each in artistic expression, world civilizations, American civilizations, human behavior, cultural diversity and social pluralism, ethics, and science and technology and a 12-hour distribution with 9 hours in English and math skills and 3 hours of health and phys ed.

Special: The university offers cooperative programs in engineering, prelaw, prepharmacy, and osteopathic medicine, and cross-registration through the Pennsylvania State System of Higher Education and the Marine Science Consortium at Wallops Island, Virginia, and with Mercyhurst College and Gannon University. A Harrisburg semester, internships in most majors, a general studies program, student-designed majors, dual majors in education, a 3-2 engineering degree, study abroad in more than 10 countries, and nondegree study are also offered. Students may select pass/fail options and receive credit for life, military, and work experience. There are 10 national honor societies, a freshman honors program, and 9 departmental honors programs.

Faculty/Classroom: 50% of faculty are male; 50% are female. 92% teach undergraduates. No introductory courses are taught by graduate students. The average class size in an introductory lecture is 30.

Admissions: The SAT scores for the 2013-2014 freshman class were: Critical Reading--63% below 500, 29% between 500 and 599, 7% between 600 and 699, and 1% between 700 and 800; Math--62% below 500, 30% between 500 and 599, 7% between 600 and 699, and 1% between 700 and 800. The ACT--1% above 28. 5 freshmen graduated first in their class.

Requirements: The SAT or ACT is required. Candidates for admission should be graduates of an accredited secondary school or the equivalent. The GED is accepted. A GPA of 2.0 is recommended. A portfolio is recommended for art students, and an audition is required for music students. An interview is recommended for all. Admissions decisions are based upon the academic major requested, high school curriculum, grades, GPA, class rank, SAT or ACT scores, and leadership and extracurricular activities record. AP and CLEP credits are accepted. Important factors in the admissions decision are advanced placement or honors courses, extracurricular activities record, and personality/intangible qualities.

Procedure: Freshmen are admitted to all sessions. Entrance exams should be taken in the junior year or early in the senior year. There are early admissions, deferred admissions, and rolling admissions plans. Application deadlines are open. Application fee is $30. Applications are accepted online.

Transfer: 434 transfer students enrolled in 2012-2013. Applicants should have a 2.0 GPA and must submit transcripts from previous institutions. An interview is recommended. 30 of 120 credits required for the bachelor's degree must be completed at Edinboro.

Visiting: There are regularly scheduled orientations for prospective students, including admissions, financial aid, and academic affairs presentations followed by campus tours. There are guides for informal visits, visitors may sit in on classes, and stay overnight. To schedule a visit, contact the Admissions Office.

Financial Aid: In 2013-2014, 83% of all full-time freshmen students received some form of financial aid. 80% of all full-time freshmen students received need-based aid. The FAFSA is required. The priority date for freshman financial aid applications for fall entry is March 15. The deadline for filing freshman financial aid applications for fall entry is May 1.

International Students: There are 80 international students enrolled. The school actively recruits these students. They must take the TOEFL with a minimum score of 500 on the paper-based TOEFL (PBT).

Graduates: From July 1, 2012 to June 30, 2013, 982 bachelor's degrees were awarded. The most popular majors were education (20%), visual and performing arts (12%), and health professions (9%). In an average class, 26% graduate in 4 years or less, 42% graduate in 5 years or less, and 45% graduate in 6 years or less.

Admissions Contact: Admissions Office E-Mail: *eup_admissions@edinboro.edu* Web: *www.edinboro.edu*

ELIZABETHTOWN COLLEGE — D-3

Elizabethtown, PA 17022 — **(717) 361-1400; (717) 361-1365**

Full-time: 653 men, 1155 women	**Faculty:** 132
Part-time: 16 men, 20 women	**Ph.D.s:** 100%
Graduate: 2 men, 46 women	**Student/Faculty:** 14 to 1
Year: semesters, summer session	**Tuition:** $38,200
Application Deadline:	**Room & Board:** $9400
Freshman Class: n/av	
	VERY COMPETITIVE

Elizabethtown College is a community of learners dedicated to educating students intellectually, socially, aesthetically and ethically for lives of service and leadership as citizens of the world. We offer more than four dozen degrees in liberal arts, fine and performing arts, science and engineering, business, communications and education. Through personal attention, creative inspiration and academic challenge, Elizabethtown students are encouraged to expand their intellectual curiosity. Our students become a bigger part of the world through Real-World Learning opportunities which include: collaborative research with faculty mentors, study-abroad experiences in more than 70 locations around the world, civic-engagement outreach, and internships offerings. There are 2 undergraduate schools. In addition to regional accreditation, E-town has baccalaureate program accreditation with ABET, ACBSP, CSWE, and NASM. The library contains 260,258 volumes, 24,078 microform items, 9,750 audio/video tapes/CDs/DVDs, and subscribes to 96,260 periodicals including electronic. Computerized library services include interlibrary loans, database searching, Internet access, and Wi-Fi capability. Special learning facilities include an art gallery, radio station, TV station, the Young Center for Anabaptist and Pietist Studies, a nationally unique academic research facility, and a mineral gallery. The 201-acre campus is in a small town in Lancaster County, PA. It is 10 minutes from Hershey and 25 minutes from Lancaster and Harrisburg. Including any residence halls, there are 52 buildings.

Student Life: 64% of undergraduates are from Pennsylvania. Others are from 26 states, and 24 foreign countries. 85% are from public schools. 88% are White. 33% are Protestant; 28% Catholic. The average age of freshmen is 18; all undergraduates, 20. 18% do not continue beyond their first year; 77% remain to graduate.

Housing: 1494 students can be accommodated in college housing, which includes coed dorms, on-campus apartments, and off-campus apartments. In addition, there are honors houses, special-interest houses, substance free and quiet study. On-campus housing is guaranteed for all 4 years. 80% of students live on campus; of those, 85% remain on campus on weekends. All students may keep cars.

Activities: There are no fraternities or sororities. There are 80 groups on campus, including and residential, learning communities, academic, art, band, cheerleading, choir, chorale, chorus, computers, dance, drama, environmental, ethnic, forensics, gay, honors, international, jazz band, literary magazine, musical theater, newspaper, orchestra, photography, political, professional, radio and TV, religious, social, social service, student government, and yearbook. Popular campus events include Scholarship and Creative Arts Day, Martin Luther king Celebration Week, Hispanic Heritage Month and Into the Streets.

Sports: There are 11 intercollegiate sports for men and 11 for women, and 7 intramural sports for men and 7 for women. Facilities include a 2,200-seat soccer stadium,, a 2,000-seat gymnasium, swimming pool, track and field complex, fitness center, racquetball and tennis courts, sand volleyball courts and baseball, softball, lacrosse, and field hockey fields.

Disabled Students: 75% of the campus is accessible. Facilities include wheelchair ramps, elevators, special parking, specially equipped restrooms, special class scheduling, lowered drinking fountains, lowered telephones, special housing.

Services: Counseling and information services are available, as is tutoring in most subjects. There is a reader service for the blind, and remedial math, reading, and writing. Workshops and individual help with study skills as well as assistive technology is also available.

Campus Safety and Security: Measures include 24-hour foot and vehicle patrol, emergency notification system, self-defense education, and security escort services. There are shuttle buses, emergency telephones, lighted pathways/sidewalks, controlled access to dorms/residences, and a crime prevention program.

Programs of Study: E-town confers B.A., B.S., B.S.W. and B.Mus. degrees. Master's degrees are also awarded. Bachelor's degrees are awarded in AGRICULTURE (forestry and related sciences), BIOLOGICAL SCIENCE (biochemistry, biology/adolescence education, biology/biological science, and biotechnology), BUSINESS (accounting, business administration and management, business economics, business systems analysis, international business management, and marketing management), COMMUNICATIONS AND THE ARTS (art history and appreciation, communications, dramatic arts, English, English literature, English Writing, fine arts, French, German, Japanese, modern language, music, performing arts, Spanish, and studio art), COMPUTER AND PHYSICAL SCIENCE (actuarial science, applied mathematics, chemistry, chemistry/adolescence education, computer science, earth science / adolescence education, information sciences and systems, mathematics, and physics), EDUCATION (art education, early childhood education, education, elementary education, English education, mathematics education, music education, science education, secondary education, social studies education, and social studies secondary school education), ENGINEERING AND ENVIRONMENTAL DESIGN (computer engineering, electrical/electronics engineering, engineering, environmental science, industrial engineering, mechanical engineering, and preengineering), HEALTH PROFESSIONS (music therapy, occupational therapy, predentistry, premedicine, and prephysical therapy), SOCIAL SCIENCE (biblical studies, criminal justice, economics, history, legal studies, philosophy, political science/government, psychology, public administration, religion, social work, and sociology). Business administration, occupational therapy, and biology have the largest enrollments.

Required: The core curriculum includes a first-year seminar and courses in math, language, creative expression, western cultural heritage, nonwestern cultural heritage, the natural and social sciences, and humanities. Distribution requirements include 40 hours in 8 areas of understanding. Students must complete a minimum of 125 credit hours and maintain a GPA of 2.0 overall and in their major. Additional requirements are dependent on the enrolled major.

Special: Students can participate in short-term, semester-long, and year-long study-abroad experiences in 26 different locations worldwide. Also available are work-study programs, internships, a Washington semester, and dual majors, including sociology and anthropology. There is a 5-year cooperative engineering degree where the student will participate in two 7-month co-op rotations; a 3-3 allied health degree and a 3-3 physical therapy degree with Thomas Jefferson University and Widener University; a Premedical Primary Care Program with Penn State University College of Medicine; Biotechnology (B.S.) and Molecular Medicine (M.S.) with Drexel University College of Medicine; a 3-4 B.S. in biology/D.M.D. program with Temple University; a Cardiovascular Invasive Specialty program with Lancaster General College of Nursing and Health Sciences; and a D.O program with Philadelphia College of Osteopathic Medicine. There are 22 national honor societies, a freshman honors program, and 14 departmental honors programs.

Faculty/Classroom: 50% of faculty are male; 50% are female. All teach and do research. No introductory courses are taught by graduate students. The average class size in an introductory lecture is 21; in a laboratory is 19; and in a regular course is 17.

Admissions: 52% of the current freshmen were in the top fifth of their class; 80% were in the top two fifths. 9 freshmen graduated first in their class.

Requirements: The SAT or ACT is required. Recommended composite scores for the SAT range from 1030 to 1230; for the ACT, 21 to 27. Applicants must be graduates of an accredited secondary school or have earned a GED. The college encourages completion of 18 academic credits, based on 4 years of English, 3 of math, 2 each of lab science, social studies, and consecutive foreign language, and 5 additional college preparatory units. An audition is required for music majors and an interview is required for occupational therapy majors. AP credits are accepted. Important factors in the admissions decision are advanced placement or honors courses, recommendations by school officials, and extracurricular activities record.

Procedure: Freshmen are admitted to all sessions. Entrance exams should be taken in spring of the junior year or fall of the senior year. There are deferred admissions and rolling admissions plans. Application deadlines are open. Application fee is $30. 101 applicants were on the 2013 waiting list; 10 were admitted. Applications are accepted online.

Transfer: 27 transfer students enrolled in 2012-2013. Applicants should present a minimum GPA of 3.0 in at least 15 credit hours earned from a community college, or 2.5 from a 4-year institution. 30 of 125 credits required for the bachelor's degree must be completed at E-town.

Visiting: There are regularly scheduled orientations for prospective students, including 5 open houses and weekday appointments throughout the year. Special academic department days are also hosted. There are guides for informal visits, visitors may sit in on classes, and stay overnight. To schedule a visit, contact the Admissions Office.

Financial Aid: In 2013-2014, 99% of all full-time freshmen and 99% of continuing full-time students received some form of financial aid. 77% of all full-time freshmen and 75% of continuing full-time students received need-based aid. The average freshman award was $27,540. Need-based scholarships or need-based grants averaged $23,804 ($38,200 maximum); and need-based self-help aid (loans and jobs) averaged $4,766 ($8,000 maximum). 63% of undergraduate students work part-time. Average annual earnings from campus work are $1192. E-town is a member of CSS. The FAFSA and the college's own financial statement, and family federal tax returns are required. The deadline for filing freshman financial aid applications for fall entry is March 15.

International Students: There are 67 international students enrolled. The school actively recruits these students. They must take the TOEFL with a minimum score of 525 on the paper-based TOEFL (PBT) or 75 on the Internet-based version (iBT). They must also take the SAT or ACT.

Graduates: From July 1, 2012 to June 30, 2013, 440 bachelor's degrees were awarded. The most popular majors were health and occupation (preoccupational therapy) (11%), business administration (9%), and early childhood education (8%). 60 companies recruited on campus in 2012-2013. In an average class, 72% graduate in 4 years or less, 69% graduate in 5 years or less, and 78% graduate in 6 years or less. Of the 2012 graduating class, 24% were enrolled in graduate school within 6 months of graduation, and 68% were employed.

Admissions Contact: Paul Cramer, Vice President for Enrollment. E-Mail: *admissions@etown.edu* Web: *http:/www.etown.edu/admissions/*

ELIZABETHTOWN COLLEGE SCHOOL OF CONTINUING AND PROFESSIONAL STUDIES

Elizabethtown, PA 17022 (717) 361-3750; (717) 361-1466

Full-time: n/av	**Faculty:** n/av
Part-time: 119 men, 253 women	**Ph.D.s:** n/av
Graduate: 30 men, 38 women	**Student/Faculty:** n/av
Year: other, summer session	**Tuition:** n/av
Application Deadline:	**Room & Board:** n/pp
Freshman Class: n/av	

VERY COMPETITIVE

Elizabethtown College is a community of learners dedicated to educating students intellectually, socially, aesthetically and ethically for lives of service and leadership as citizens of the world. We offer more than four dozen degrees in liberal arts, fine and perfoming arts, science and engineering, business,communications and education. Through personal attention, creative inspiration and academic challenge, Elizabethtown students are encouraged to expand their intellectual curiosity. They also are given an opportunity to be a bigger part of the world through experiential learning-collaborative research with caring faculty mentors, study-abroad and civic engagement opportunities, and internships. The library contains 262,101 volumes, 24,078 microform items, and 9,750 audio/video tapes/CDs/DVDs, and subscribes to 96,260 periodicals including electronic. Computerized library services include interlibrary loans, database searching, Internet access, and Wi-Fi capability. Special learning facilities include an art gallery, radio station, TV station, The Young Center for Anabaptist and Pietist Studies, a nationally unique academic research facility, mineral gallery. The 201-acre campus is in a small town 10 minutes from Hershey and 25 minutes from Lancaster and Harrisburg. Including any residence halls, there are 52 buildings.

Student Life: 99% of undergraduates are from Pennsylvania. Others are from 4 states, and 1 foreign countries. 85% are White. The average age of all undergraduates is 31.62.

Housing: All students commute. All students may keep cars.

Activities: There are no fraternities or sororities.

Sports: There is no sports program.

Disabled Students: 75% of the campus is accessible. Facilities include wheelchair ramps, elevators, special parking, specially equipped restrooms, special class scheduling, lowered drinking fountains, and lowered telephones.

Campus Safety and Security: Measures include 24-hour foot and vehicle patrol, emergency notification system, self-defense education, and security escort services. There are shuttle buses, emergency telephones, lighted pathways/sidewalks, controlled access to dorms/residences.

Programs of Study: Elizabethtown College Adult Degrees confers B.A., B.S., and B.P.S. degrees. Associate and master's degrees are also awarded. Bachelor's degrees are awarded in BUSINESS (accounting, business administration and management, human resources, and marketing/retailing/merchandising), COMMUNICATIONS AND THE ARTS (communications and information technology), SOCIAL SCIENCE (addiction studies, behavioral science, criminal justice, human services, public administration, and religion). Business Administration, accounting, human services, have the largest enrollments.

Faculty/Classroom: 52% of faculty are male; 48% are female. All teach undergraduates. No introductory courses are taught by graduate students. The average class size in an introductory lecture is 20.

Procedure: Freshmen are admitted to all sessions. There is a rolling admissions plan. Application deadlines are open. Applications are accepted online.

Transfer: 63 transfer students enrolled in 2012-2013.

Financial Aid: Check with the school for current application deadlines.

Computers: All students may access the system. Any time. There are no time limits and no fees.

Graduates: From July 1, 2012 to June 30, 2013, 110 bachelor's degrees were awarded. The most popular majors were business administration (45%), accounting (21%), and information systems (11%).

Admissions Contact: Barbara Randazzo, Asst. Dean of Enrollment Management. E-Mail: *randazzob@etown.edu* Web: *http:/www.etowndegrees.com*

FRANKLIN AND MARSHALL COLLEGE E-3

Lancaster, PA 17604 (717) 291-3953
(877) 678-9111; (717) 291-4389

Full-time: 1099 men, 1159 women	**Faculty:** 229; IIB, +$
Part-time: 12 men, 27 women	**Ph.D.s:** 93%
Graduate: n/av	**Student/Faculty:** 9 to 1
Year: semesters, summer session	**Tuition:** n/av
Application Deadline: January 15	**Room & Board:** $12,010
Freshman Class: 5174 applied, 2034 accepted, 599 enrolled	
SAT CR/M: 640/662	**ACT:** 29 **MOST COMPETITIVE**

Franklin and Marshall College, founded in 1787, is a private liberal arts institution. The 2 libraries contain 544,913 volumes, 346,078 microform items, 13,410 audio/video tapes/CDs/DVDs, and subscribe to 2,357 periodicals including electronic. Computerized library services include interlibrary loans, database searching, and Internet access. Special learning facilities include an art gallery, natural history museum, planetarium, radio station, TV station, academic technology services, advanced language lab, writing center, and student newspaper. The 209-acre campus is in a suburban area 60 miles west of Philadelphia. Including any residence halls, there are 45 buildings.

Student Life: 70% of undergraduates are from out of state, mostly the Middle Atlantic. Students are from 40 states, 47 foreign countries, and Canada. 57% are from public schools. 67% are White; 11% Foreign. The average age of freshmen is 19; all undergraduates, 20. 8% do not continue beyond their first year; 983% remain to graduate.

Housing: 1570 students can be accommodated in college housing, which includes single-sex and coed dorms, on-campus apartments, and off-campus apartments. In addition, there are language houses, special-interest houses, including a French house, an arts house, an international living center, and a community outreach house. On-campus housing is guaranteed for all 4 years, is guaranteed for the freshman year only, and is available on a lottery system for upperclassmen. 99% of students live on campus. Upperclassmen may keep cars.

Activities: 28% of men belong to 7 national fraternities; 34% of women belong to 3 national sororities. There are 120 groups on campus, including (a student-run club/restaurant), and Ben's Underground, art, band, cheerleading, chess, choir, chorale, chorus, communications, computers, dance, debate, drama, environmental, ethnic, film, forensics, gay, honors, international, jazz band, literary magazine, musical theater, newspaper, opera, orchestra, photography, political, professional, radio and TV, religious, social, social service, student government, symphony, and yearbook. Popular campus events include Spring Arts Weekend, Freshman Feast and Senior Surprise.

Sports: There are 13 intercollegiate sports for men and 13 for women, and 12 intramural sports for men and 12 for women. Facilities include a 3000-seat gym, 4 squash courts, a wrestling room, 54 acres of playing fields, a 400-meter all-weather track, a wellness/aerobic center, a strength training center, and tennis courts. A sports center features a fitness center, 5 multipurpose courts, 2 jogging tracks, and an Olympic-size pool.

Disabled Students: 80% of the campus is accessible. Facilities include wheelchair ramps, elevators, special parking, specially equipped restrooms, special class scheduling, lowered drinking fountains, lowered telephones, and special housing.

Services: Counseling and information services are available, as is tutoring in every subject.

Campus Safety and Security: Measures include 24-hour foot and vehicle patrol, emergency notification system, self-defense education, and security escort services. There are shuttle buses, emergency telephones, lighted pathways/sidewalks, controlled access to dorms/residences, Regular fire safety drills are held in residence halls and academic buildings.

Programs of Study: F & M confers B.A. degrees. Bachelor's degrees are awarded in AGRICULTURE (environmental studies), BIOLOGICAL SCIENCE (biochemistry, biology/biological science, and neurosciences), BUSINESS (business administration and management), COMMUNICATIONS AND THE ARTS (art history and appreciation, classics, dramatic arts, English, fine arts, French, German, Greek, Latin, music, Spanish, and studio art), COMPUTER AND PHYSICAL SCIENCE (astronomy, astrophysics, chemistry, geology, mathematics, and physics), ENGINEERING AND ENVIRONMENTAL DESIGN (environmental science), SOCIAL SCIENCE (African studies, American studies, anthropology, economics, history, interdisciplinary studies, philosophy, political science/government, psychology, religion, and sociology). Chemistry, geosciences, and psychology are the strongest academically. Government, business, organizations and society have the largest enrollments.

Required: General education requirements proceed from 2 foundations courses and a distribution requirement to an upper-level coherent exploration and a major. Students must take at least 1 course in arts, humanities, social science, non-Western cultures, and 1 natural science (including a lab) and a second lab course or natural science in perspective course. 3 semesters of language study are required. Students must also satisfy the writing proficiency requirement. The bachelor's degree requires completion of 32 courses, including a minimum of 8 in the major, with a minimum GPA of 2.0.

Special: There is a 3-2 degree program in forestry and environmental studies with Duke University as well as 3-2 degree programs in engineering with the Pennsylvania State University College of Engineering, Columbia University, Rensselaer Polytechnic Institute, Case Western Reserve, and Washington University at St. Louis. Cross-registration is possible with the Lancaster Theological Seminary, the Central Pennsylvania Consortium, and Millersville University allows students to study at nearby Dickinson College or Gettysburg College. Students may also study architecture and urban planning at Columbia University, studio art at the School of Visual Arts in New York City, theater in Connecticut, oceanography in Massachusetts, and American studies at American University. There are study-abroad programs in England, France, Germany, Greece, Italy, Denmark, India, Japan, and other countries. There are internships for credit, joint majors, many minors, dual majors, student-designed majors, independent study, interdisciplinary studies, optional first-year seminars, collaborative projects, pass/fail options, and nondegree study. There are 12 national honor societies including Phi Beta Kappa.

Faculty/Classroom: 54% of faculty are male; 46% are female. All teach undergraduates, and all teach and do research. No introductory courses are taught by graduate students. The average class size in an introductory lecture is 23; in a laboratory is 19; and in a regular course is 19.

Admissions: 39% of the 2013-2014 applicants were accepted. The SAT scores for the 2013-2014 freshman class were: Critical Reading--2% below 500, 22% between 500 and 599, 53% between 600 and 699, and 23% between 700 and 800; Math--1% below 500, 11% between 500 and 599, 58% between 600 and 699, and 30% between 700 and 800. 83% of the current freshmen were in the top fifth of their class; 96% were in the top two fifths.

Requirements: Standardized tests are optional for students; if this option is selected, 2 recent graded writing samples are required. Applicants must be graduates of accredited secondary schools. Recommended college preparatory study includes 4 years each of English and math, 3 or 4 of foreign language, 3 each of lab science and history/social studies, and 1 or 2 courses in art or music. All students must also submit their high school transcripts, recommendations from a teacher and a counselor, and a personal essay. An interview is recommended. AP and CLEP credits are accepted. Important factors in the admissions decision are advanced placement or honors courses, recommendations by school officials, and extracurricular activities record.

Procedure: Freshmen are admitted fall and spring. Entrance exams should be taken by December of the senior year. There are early decision and deferred admissions plans. Early decision applications should be filed by November 15; regular applications, by January 15 for fall entry, along with a $50 fee. Notification of early decision is sent December 15; regular decision, April 1. 511 applicants were on the 2013 waiting list; 52 were admitted. Applications are accepted online.

Transfer: 27 transfer students enrolled in 2012-2013. Applicants must present a minimum of 4 course credits (16 semester hours) completed at an accredited college. An interview, SAT or ACT scores, college and secondary school transcripts, a dean's form, recommendations from 2 professors, and a letter explaining the reason for transfer are also required. 16 of 32 credits required for the bachelor's degree must be completed at F & M.

Visiting: There are regularly scheduled orientations for prospective students, including a campus tour, an interview, and a class visit. There are guides for informal visits and visitors may sit in on classes. To schedule a visit, contact the Admission Office.

Financial Aid: In 2013-2014, 69% of all full-time freshmen and 70% of continuing full-time students received some form of financial aid. 45% of all full-time freshmen and 41% of continuing full-time students received need-based aid. The average freshman award was $19,861. Need-based scholarships or need-based grants averaged $23,468; need-based self-help aid (loans and jobs) averaged $5,668; and other non-need-based awards and non-need-based scholarships averaged $12,844. 44% of undergraduate students work part-time. The average financial indebtedness of the 2013 graduate was $24,752. F & M is a member of CSS. The CSS/Profile, FAFSA, and the college's own financial statement, and If applicable, the business/farm supplement and noncustodial parents statement are required. are required. The deadline for filing freshman financial aid applications for fall entry is February 1.

International Students: There are 159 international students enrolled. The school actively recruits these students. They must take the TOEFL. They must also take the SAT or ACT.

Graduates: From July 1, 2012 to June 30, 2013, 466 bachelor's degrees were awarded. The most popular majors were government (14%), business, organizations, and society (14%), and English (6%). 26 companies recruited on campus in 2012-2013. In an average class, 79% graduate in 4 years or less, 79% graduate in 5 years or less, and 84% graduate in 6 years or less. Of the 2012 graduating class, 25% were enrolled in graduate school within 6 months of graduation, and 75% were employed.

Admissions Contact: Daniel Lugo, Vice President for Enrollment Management and Dean of Admissions. E-Mail: *admission@fandm.edu* Web: *www.fandm.edu*

GANNON UNIVERSITY B-1

Erie, PA 16541 (814) 871-7240
(800) GANNON U; (814) 871-5803

Full-time: 1082 men, 1474 women	**Faculty:** 175
Part-time: 246 men, 309 women	**Ph.D.s:** 74%
Graduate: 477 men, 623 women	**Student/Faculty:** 15 to 1
Year: semesters, summer session	**Tuition:** $27,546
Application Deadline: open	**Room & Board:** $10,940
Freshman Class: 3983 applied, 3203 accepted, 611 enrolled	
SAT CR/M/W: 520/540/500 **ACT:** 24	**COMPETITIVE**

Gannon University, founded in 1925, is a private liberal arts and teaching-oriented university affiliated with the Roman Catholic Church. There are 3 undergraduate schools and one graduate school. In addition to regional accreditation, Gannon has baccalaureate program accreditation with ABET, ACBSP, and CSWE. The library contains 255,473 volumes, 79 microform items, 4,508 audio/video tapes/CDs/DVDs, and subscribes to 43,323 periodicals including electronic. Computerized library services include interlibrary loans, database searching, Internet access, and Wi-Fi capability. Special learning facilities include an art gallery, radio station, an Environaut - vessel used for research on Lake Erie and a 5800 square foot Patient Simulation Center. The 36-acre campus is in an urban area 128 miles north of Pittsburgh, 99 miles east of Cleveland, and 106 miles southwest of Buffalo. Including any residence halls, there are 45 buildings.

Student Life: 74% of undergraduates are from Pennsylvania. Others are from 32 states, 31 foreign countries, and Canada. 77% are from public schools. 82% are White. 40% are Catholic; 36% claim no religious affiliation; 17% Protestant. The average age of freshmen is 18; all undergraduates, 20. 21% do not continue beyond their first year; 79% remain to graduate.

Housing: 1438 students can be accommodated in college housing, which includes coed dorms, on-campus apartments, and off-campus apartments. In addition, there are language houses, special-interest houses, fraternity houses, and sorority houses. On-campus housing is guaranteed for the freshman year only. Priority is given to out-of-town students. 62% of students commute. Upperclassmen may keep cars.

Activities: 14% of men belong to 6 national fraternities; 18% of women belong to 5 national sororities. There are 71 groups on campus, including activities programming board and a radio station, art, band, cheerleading, choir, chorus, computers, dance, drama, environmental, ethnic, honors, international, literary magazine, newspaper, political, professional, radio and TV, religious, social, social service, student government, and yearbook. Popular campus events include Family Weekend, GIVE Day, Home Coming Weekend, Day of Caring and Springtopia.

Sports: There are 9 intercollegiate sports for men and 9 for women, and 20 intramural sports for men and 20 for women. Facilities include Gannon has a 16000 sq. ft. multi-purpose athletic field that includes five NCAA regulation fields, and seats 2500 people. The Rec Center includes a collegiate-sized swimming pool, six regulation racquetball courts, an indoor running track, weight machines and cardio equipment. There is also a 3000 seat basketball and volleyball, and areas for wrestling and a new acrobatics and tumbling program.

Disabled Students: 70% of the campus is accessible. Facilities include wheelchair ramps, elevators, special parking, specially equipped restrooms, special class scheduling, lowered drinking fountains, and special housing.

Services: Counseling and information services are available, as is tutoring in most subjects. There is a reader service for the blind, and remedial math, reading, and writing. There are math, writing, and advising centers.

Campus Safety and Security: Measures include 24-hour foot and vehicle patrol, emergency notification system, and security escort services. There are shuttle buses, emergency telephones, lighted pathways/sidewalks, controlled access to dorms/residences, security cameras in buildings.

Programs of Study: Gannon confers B.A., B.S., B.S.E., B.S.M., and B.S.N. degrees. Associate, master's, and doctoral degrees are also awarded. Bachelor's degrees are awarded in BIOLOGICAL SCIENCE (bioinformatics, biology/adolescence education, biology/biological science, and nutrition), BUSINESS (accounting, banking and finance, business administration and management, entrepreneurial studies, funeral home services, insurance and risk management, international business management, management information systems, marketing/retailing/merchandising, and sports management), COMMUNICATIONS AND THE ARTS (advertising, communications, dramatic arts, English, and journalism), COMPUTER AND PHYSICAL SCIENCE (chemistry, computer science, information sciences and systems, mathematics, science, and software engineering), EDUCATION (early childhood education, elementary education, English education, foreign languages education, mathematics education, middle school education, secondary education, social studies education, and special education), ENGINEERING AND ENVIRONMENTAL DESIGN (biomedical engineering, electrical/electronics engineering, environmental engineering, environmental science, and mechanical engineering), HEALTH PROFESSIONS (health science, medical technology, nursing, occupational therapy, optometry, physical therapy, physician's assistant, and respiratory therapy), SOCIAL SCIENCE (criminal justice, history, international studies, legal studies, liberal arts/general studies, philosophy, political science/government, psychology, social work, and theological studies). Preprofessional, physicians assistant, and nursing are the strongest academically. Nursing, physician's assistant, sport and exercise science have the largest enrollments.

Required: Students must complete at least 128 hours of academic work. Each academic program has specific course requirements. Students must have a cumulative GPA of at least 2.0.

Special: The university offers study abroad in more than 23 countries, co-op programs, dual majors, summer internships, pass/fail options, work-study programs, a general studies program, accelerated degree programs in law, medicine, optometry, podiatry, veterinary, and pharmacy. Gannon University offers several programs that work in conjunction with other Colleges and Universities such as Charleston School of Pharmacy, LECOM, PCOM, PCO, Ross University School of Medicine, and Duquesne toward degree completion. Gannon also provides students with numerous service and experiential learning opportunities. There are 14 national honor societies, a freshman honors program, and 12 departmental honors programs.

Faculty/Classroom: 53% of faculty are male; 47% are female. 85% teach undergraduates. Graduate students teach 2% of introductory courses. The average class size in an introductory lecture is 20 and in a laboratory is 21.

Admissions: 80% of the 2013-2014 applicants were accepted. The SAT scores for the 2013-2014 freshman class were: Critical Reading--41% below 500, 46% between 500 and 599, 12% between 600 and 699, and 1% between 700 and 800; Math--34% below 500, 42% between 500 and 599, 22% between 600 and 699, and 2% between 700 and 800; Writing--50% below 500, 36% between 500 and 599, 13% between 600 and 699, and 1% between 700 and 800. The ACT scores were 26% below 21, 24% between 21 and 23, 30% between 24 and 26, 10% between 27 and 28, and 10% above 28. 48% of the current freshmen were in the top fifth of their class; 72% were in the top two fifths. 20 freshmen graduated first in their class.

Requirements: The SAT or ACT is required. Candidates should have completed 16 academic units including 4 in English and 12 in social sciences, foreign languages, math, and science, depending on the degree sought. Specific courses in math and science are required for some majors in health sciences and engineering. Essays are required for some programs and encouraged for the general population. The same is true for letters of recommendation. Credits may be earned for those that complete AP exams and IB exams. Gannon accepts the GED in replacement of a high school diploma with appropriate scores earned overall and in each subject matter. AP and CLEP credits are accepted. Important factors in the admissions decision are advanced placement or honors courses, recommendations by school officials, parents or siblings attended your school, personality/intangible qualities, and extracurricular activities record.

Procedure: Freshmen are admitted fall, spring, and summer. Entrance exams should be taken at the end of the junior year or the beginning of the senior year. There are deferred admissions and rolling admissions plans. Application deadlines are open. Application fee is $25. Notification is sent on a rolling basis. 77 applicants were on the 2013 waiting list; 38 were admitted. Applications are accepted online.

Transfer: 114 transfer students enrolled in 2012-2013. Transfer students should be in good standing at their previous institution with at least a 2.0 GPA. They must submit a college clearance from the college most recently attended and transcripts from all institutions attended. A high school transcript is required from transfer students with fewer than 30 credits or for those pursuing a health related field. Some health profession programs offer limited seating. 40 of 128 credits required for the bachelor's degree must be completed at Gannon.

Visiting: There are regularly scheduled orientations for prospective students, Consisting of open houses for prospective students in the fall and spring. Students may meet with faculty, tour the campus, meet with financial aid advisors, and sit in on a variety of presentations. There are guides for informal visits and visitors may stay overnight. To schedule a visit, contact Kris Manczka at (814) 871-7407.

Financial Aid: In 2013-2014, 97% of all full-time freshmen and 95% of continuing full-time students received some form of financial aid. 85% of all full-time freshmen and 80% of continuing full-time students received need-based aid. The average freshman award was $24,500. Need-based scholarships or need-based grants averaged $20,376; need-based self-help aid (loans and jobs) averaged $3,818; non-need-based athletic scholarships averaged $12,381; and other non-need-based awards and non-need-based scholarships averaged $13,332. 20% of undergraduate students work part-time. Average annual earnings from campus work are $1910. The average financial indebtedness of the 2013 graduate was $27,290. Gannon is a member of CSS. The FAFSA and the college's own financial statement are required. The priority date for freshman financial aid applications for fall entry is March 15.

International Students: There are 184 international students enrolled. The school actively recruits these students. They must take the TOEFL with a minimum score of 550 on the paper-based TOEFL (PBT) or 79 on the Internet-based version (iBT).

Graduates: From July 1, 2012 to June 30, 2013, 514 bachelor's degrees were awarded. The most popular majors were health sciences (16%), nursing (14%), and biology (9%). 16 companies recruited on campus in 2012-2013. In an average class, 48% graduate in 4 years or less, 62% graduate in 5 years or less, and 64% graduate in 6 years or less.

Admissions Contact: Patricia Maughn, Coordinator, Admissions Inquiries. E-Mail: *admissions@gannon.edu* Web: *www.gannon.edu*

GENEVA COLLEGE A-3

Beaver Falls, PA 15010 (724) 847-6500
(800) 847-8255; (724) 847-6776

Full-time: 600 men, 730 women
Part-time: 30 men, 30 women
Graduate: 120 men, 180 women
Year: semesters, summer session
Application Deadline: open
Freshman Class: n/av
SAT or ACT: required
Faculty: 75; IIB, -$
Ph.D.s: 76%
Student/Faculty: n/av
Tuition: $23,330
Room & Board: $8560

COMPETITIVE

Geneva College, founded in 1848, is a private institution affiliated with the Reformed Presbyterian Church of North America. The college offers undergraduate programs in the arts and sciences, business, education, health science, biblical and religious studies, engineering, and preprofessional training. Some figures in the above capsule and in this profile are approximate. In addition to the above figures, there are approximately 450 nontraditional undergraduates. In addition to regional accreditation, Geneva has baccalaureate program accreditation with ABET and ACBSP. The library contains 167,206 volumes, 198,624 microform items, 12,901 audio/video tapes/CDs/DVDs, and subscribes to 879 periodicals including electronic. Computerized library services include interlibrary loans, database searching, and Internet access. Special learning facilities include a radio station, TV station, and an observatory. The 50-acre campus is in a small town 35 miles northwest of Pittsburgh. Including any residence halls, there are 30 buildings.

Student Life: 73% of undergraduates are from Pennsylvania. Students are from 37 states, 19 foreign countries, and Canada. 87% are from public schools. 91% are white. 89% are Protestant. The average age of freshmen is 19; all undergraduates, 26. 23% do not continue beyond their first year; 55% remain to graduate.

Housing: 994 students can be accommodated in college housing, which includes single-sex dorms, on-campus apartments, off-campus apartment, and a Discipleship House for those interested in structural growth opportunities. On-campus housing is guaranteed for all 4 years. 73% of students live on campus; of those, 70% remain on campus on weekends. Alcohol is not permitted. Upperclassmen may keep cars.

Activities: There are no fraternities or sororities. There are 50 groups on campus, including band, cheerleading, chess, choir, chorale, chorus, computers, drama, ethnic, forensics, honors, international, literary magazine, marching band, newspaper, photography, political, professional, radio, religious, social, social service, student government, and yearbook. Popular campus events include International Day, Fall Fest, and The Big Event.

Sports: There are 6 intercollegiate sports for men and 5 for women, and 6 intramural sports for men and 5 for women. Facilities include a 5600-seat stadium, a field house, a 3200-seat gym, a practice gym, a track, athletic fields, racquetball and tennis courts, weight training rooms, and the Merriman Athletic Soccer/Track Complex.

Disabled Students: 90% of the campus is accessible. Facilities include wheelchair ramps, elevators, special parking, specially equipped rest rooms, special class scheduling, lowered drinking fountains, and lowered telephones.

Services: Counseling and information services are available, as is tutoring in most subjects. There is remedial math, reading, and writing.

Campus Safety and Security: Measures include security escort services. There are emergency telephones, lighted pathways/sidewalks, an off-duty city policeman on campus from 4:30 p.m. to 7 a.m. daily, and a full-time director of campus security.

Programs of Study: Geneva confers B.A., B.S., B.S.B.A., B.S.E., and B.S.Ed. degrees. Associate and master's degrees are also awarded. Bachelor's degrees are awarded in BIOLOGICAL SCIENCE (biology/biological science), BUSINESS (accounting and business administration and management), COMMUNICATIONS AND THE ARTS (applied music, broadcasting, communications, creative writing, English, music, music business management, Spanish, and speech/debate/rhetoric), COMPUTER AND PHYSICAL SCIENCE (applied mathematics, chemistry, computer science, and physics), EDUCATION (elementary education, mathematics education, and music education), ENGINEERING AND ENVIRONMENTAL DESIGN (aviation administration/management, chemical engineering, and engineering), HEALTH PROFESSIONS (speech pathology/audiology), SOCIAL SCIENCE (biblical studies, counseling/psychology, history, human services, interdisciplinary studies, ministries, philosophy, political science/government, psychology, and sociology). Engineering, business administration, and education are the strongest academically. Elementary education, business administration, and psychology are the largest.

Required: The core curriculum includes 12 hours of humanities, 9 each of biblical studies and social science, 8 to 10 of natural science, 6 of communications, 2 of phys ed, and the 1-hour Freshman Experience course. Students must also fulfill a chapel requirement each semester. To graduate, students must complete 126 to 138 semester hours, including those required for a major, with a minimum GPA of 2.0 in the major.

Special: Cross-registration is offered in conjunction with Pennsylvania State University/Beaver Campus and Community College of Beaver County. There is a 3-1 degree program in cardiovascular technology, and accelerated degree programs in human resources and community ministry. Off-campus study includes programs at the Philadelphia Center for Urban Theological Studies, a Washington semester, a summer program at AuSable, Institute of Environmental Studies in Michigan, art studies in Pittsburgh, CCCU music program in Martha's Vineyard, film studies in Los Angeles, and study abroad in Costa Rica, Egypt, China, England, Russia, and Israel. Geneva also offers internships, independent study, and credit by proficiency exam. Nondegree study is available through adult education programs. There are 2 national honor societies, a freshman honors program, and 1 departmental honors program.

Faculty/Classroom: 76% of faculty are male; 24% are female. 95% teach undergraduates. No introductory courses are taught by graduate students. The average class size in an introductory lecture is 135; in a laboratory, 22; and in a regular course, 20.

Requirements: The SAT or ACT is required. In addition, applicants must be graduates of an accredited secondary school or have earned a GED. Geneva requires 16 academic units, based on 4 each of English and electives, 3 of social studies, 2 each of math and foreign language, and 1 of science. An essay is required and an interview is recommended. A GPA of 2.5 is required. AP and CLEP credits are accepted. Important factors in the admissions decision are recommendations by school officials, advanced placement or honors courses, and leadership record.

Procedure: Freshmen are admitted to all sessions. Entrance exams should be taken during the junior or senior year. There are deferred admissions and rolling admissions plans. Application deadlines are open. Application fee is $40. Notification is sent on a rolling basis. Applications are accepted online.

Transfer: 96 transfer students enrolled in a recent year. Applicants must have a GPA of 2.0, must complete 48 semester hours at Geneva, including 15 in a chosen major, have a high school diploma or GED, and take the SAT or ACT if less than 3 years out of high school. Letters of recommendation are required. 48 of 126 credits required for the bachelor's degree must be completed at Geneva.

Visiting: There are regularly scheduled orientations for prospective students, including class visits, a campus tour, meetings with faculty, admissions, and financial aid counselors, and meetings with coaches. There are guides for informal visits, and visitors may sit in on classes and stay overnight. To schedule a visit, contact the Campus Visit Coordinator.

Financial Aid: In a recent year, 90% of all full-time students received some form of financial aid. 70% of all full-time students received need-based aid. The average freshman award was $13,785. Need-based scholarships or need-based grants averaged $10,241 ($22,000 maximum); need-based self-help aid (loans and jobs) averaged $4212 ($5625 maximum); and non-need-based athletic scholarships averaged $2542 ($14,980 maximum). 75% of undergraduate students work part-time. Average annual earnings from campus work are $1000. The average financial indebtedness of a recent year's graduate was $20,000. Geneva is a member of CSS. The FAFSA is required. Check with the school for current application deadlines.

International Students: There were 18 international students enrolled in a recent year. The school actively recruits these students. They must take the TOEFL and the college's own test.

Graduates: In a recent year, 454 bachelor's degrees were awarded. The most popular majors were business and marketing (40%), philosophy/religion/theology (14%), and education (12%). In an average class, 1% graduate in 3 years or less, 42% graduate in 4 years or less, 55% graduate in 5 years or less, and 56% graduate in 6 years or less.

Admissions Contact: Director of Admissions. A campus DVD is available. E-Mail: *admissions@geneva.edu* Web: *www.geneva.edu*

GETTYSBURG COLLEGE D-4

Gettysburg, PA 17325 (717) 337-6100
(800) 431-0803; (717) 337-6145

Full-time: 1197 men, 1318 women
Part-time: 10 men, 8 women
Graduate: n/av
Year: semesters
Application Deadline: February 1
Freshman Class: 5620 applied, 2264 accepted, 770 enrolled
SAT or ACT: required
Faculty: 221; IIB, +$
Ph.D.s: 95%
Student/Faculty: 10 to 1
Tuition: $45,870
Room & Board: $10,950

HIGHLY COMPETITIVE

Gettysburg College, founded in 1832, is a nationally ranked college offering programs in the liberal arts and sciences. There is one undergraduate school. The library contains 409,241 volumes, 71,368 microform items, 182,931 audio/video tapes/CDs/DVDs, and subscribes to 53,181 periodicals including electronic. Computerized library services include interlibrary loans, database searching, Internet access, and Wi-Fi capability. Special learning facilities include an art gallery, planetarium, radio station, TV station, electron microscopes, spectrometers, an optics lab, plasma physics lab, greenhouse, observatory, child study lab, fine and performing arts facilities, and a state-of-the-art athletic facility. The 200-acre campus is in a suburban area 30 miles south of Harrisburg, 55 miles from Baltimore, MD, and 80 miles from Washington, D.C. Including any residence halls, there are 79 buildings.

Student Life: 73% of undergraduates are from out of state, mostly the Middle Atlantic. Students are from 39 states, and 26 foreign countries. 65% are from public schools. 82% are White. 35% are Protestant; 33% Catholic. The average age of freshmen is 18; all undergraduates, 20. 12% do not continue beyond their first year; 80% remain to graduate.

Housing: 2389 students can be accommodated in college housing, which includes single-sex and coed dorms, on-campus apartments, and off-campus apartments. In addition, there are honors houses, language houses, special-interest houses, fraternity houses, theme housing. On-campus housing is guaranteed for all 4 years and is available on a lottery system for upperclassmen. Upperclassmen may keep cars.

Activities: 41% of men belong to 9 national fraternities; 33% of women belong to 6 national sororities. There are 120 groups on campus, including and dance ensemble, campus activities board, art, band, cheerleading, choir, chorale, chorus, communications, computers, dance, drama, environmental, ethnic, film, gay, honors, international, jazz band, literary magazine, marching band, musical theater, newspaper, opera, orchestra, outdoor recreation program, pep band, photography, political, professional, radio and TV station, religious, social, social service, student government, symphony, and yearbook. Popular campus events include Thanksgiving Dinner, Oceanfest, Snowball and Springfest.

Sports: There are 11 intercollegiate sports for men and 11 for women, and 9 intramural sports for men and 9 for women. Facilities include John F. Jaeger Center for Athletics, recreation and fitness center, natatorium, rock walls, basketball courts, indoor and outdoor tennis courts, several tracks and fields, 2 outdoor turf fields, a field house, and athletic training.

Disabled Students: 90% of the campus is accessible. Facilities include wheelchair ramps, elevators, special parking, specially equipped restrooms, special class scheduling, lowered drinking fountains, and special housing.

Services: Counseling and information services are available, as is tutoring in most subjects.

Campus Safety and Security: Measures include 24-hour foot and vehicle patrol, emergency notification system, self-defense education, and security escort services. There are emergency telephones, lighted pathways/sidewalks, and controlled access to dorms/residences.

Programs of Study: Gettysburg confers B.A.(Music), and B.M.(Performance and Music) degrees. Bachelor's degrees are awarded in BIOLOGICAL SCIENCE (biochemistry and biology/biological science), BUSINESS (business administration and management), COMMUNICATIONS AND THE ARTS (art history and appreciation, classics, dramatic arts, English, French, German, Greek, Latin, music, Spanish, and studio art), COMPUTER AND PHYSICAL SCIENCE (chemistry, computer science, mathematics, mathematics – economics, and physics), EDUCATION (elementary education, foreign languages education, music education, science education, and secondary education), ENGINEERING AND ENVIRONMENTAL DESIGN (environmental science), HEALTH PROFESSIONS (health science, predentistry, and premedicine), SOCIAL SCIENCE (anthropology, economics, history, international relations, Islamic studies, Japanese studies, Judaic studies, Latin American studies, Middle Eastern studies, philosophy, political science/government, prelaw, psychology, religion, sociology, and women's studies). Sciences, psychology, history, management, and political science are the strongest academically. Management, political science, and psychology have the largest enrollments.

Required: All students must complete 32 courses including a concentration in a major field of study culminating with a capstone experience; 1 course each in the arts, humanities, social sciences, quantitative reasoning, diversity: non-western culture, first-year writing; 2 courses in natural sciences and in a foreign language. The minimum GPA is 2.0.

Special: The college offers an extensive study-abroad program and has special centers worldwide. There are summer internships and a Washington semester with American University. Cross-registration is possible with members of the Central Pennsylvania Consortium. There is a United Nations semester at Drew University, and a 3-2 engineering program with Columbia University, Rensselaer Polytechnic, and Washington University in St. Louis. There are also joint programs in optometry with the Pennsylvania College of Optometry, and forestry and environmental studies with Duke University. The college offers double majors, student-designed majors, and B.A.-B.S. degrees in biology, chemistry, physics, biochemistry, and molecular biology, environmental studies and health and exercise sciences. Education certification is also available. There are 29 national honor societies including Phi Beta Kappa.

Faculty/Classroom: 58% of faculty are male; 42% are female. All teach and do research. No introductory courses are taught by graduate students. The average class size in an introductory lecture is 19; in a laboratory is 15; and in a regular course is 18.

Admissions: 40% of the 2013-2014 applicants were accepted. The SAT scores for the 2013-2014 freshman class were: Critical Reading--18% between 500 and 599, 64% between 600 and 699, and 18% between 700 and 800; Math--16% between 500 and 599, 69% between 600 and 699, and 15% between 700 and 800. 92% of the current freshmen were in the top fifth of their class; 99% were in the top two fifths.

Requirements: The SAT or ACT is required. An essay is required. Students planning to major in music must audition and art students can submit a portfolio. An interview and SAT Subject tests are recommended. AP credits are accepted. Important factors in the admissions decision are evidence of special talent, recommendations by school officials, and advanced placement or honors courses.

Procedure: Freshmen are admitted fall and spring. Entrance exams should be taken by the January testing date of the senior year. There are early decision and deferred admissions plans. Early decision applications should be filed by November 15; regular applications, by February 1 for fall entry, along with a $60 fee. Notification of early decision is sent December 15; regular decision, April 1. 343 early decision candidates were accepted for the 2013-2014 class. 659 applicants were on the 2013 waiting list. Applications are accepted online.

Transfer: 17 transfer students enrolled in 2012-2013. Transfer applicants must have a GPA of at least 2.5. An interview is recommended. The high school record, test scores, and a Dean's transfer recommendation form are also required. 16 of 32 credits required for the bachelor's degree must be completed at Gettysburg.

Visiting: There are regularly scheduled orientations for prospective students, visits can include interviews, tours, day and overnight visits, open houses, and group information sessions. There are guides for informal visits and visitors may sit in on classes. To schedule a visit, contact the Admissions Office.

Financial Aid: In 2013-2014, 59% of all full-time freshmen and 55% of continuing full-time students received some form of financial aid. 52% of all full-time freshmen and 54% of continuing full-time students received need-based aid. The average freshman award was $33,317. 46% of undergraduate students work part-time. Average annual earnings from campus work are $1500. The average financial indebtedness of the 2013 graduate was $22,212. Gettysburg is a member of CSS. The CSS/Profile and FAFSA are required. The deadline for filing freshman financial aid applications for fall entry is February 15.

International Students: There are 70 international students enrolled. The school actively recruits these students. They must take the TOEFL. They must also take the SAT or ACT.

Graduates: From July 1, 2012 to June 30, 2013, 739 bachelor's degrees were awarded. The most popular majors were management (10%), history (8%), and English (8%). 160 companies recruited on campus in 2012-2013. In an average class, 80% graduate in 4 years or less, 84% graduate in 5 years or less, and 84% graduate in 6 years or less. Of the 2012 graduating class, 18% were enrolled in graduate school within 6 months of graduation, and 78% were employed.

Admissions Contact: Gail Sweezey, Director of Admissions. E-Mail: *admiss@gettysburg.edu* Web: *www.gettysburg.edu*

GROVE CITY COLLEGE B-2

Grove City, PA 16127 (724) 458-2100; (724) 458-3395

Full-time: 1194 men, 1244 women
Part-time: 32 men, 21 women
Graduate: n/av
Year: semesters, summer session
Application Deadline: February 1
Freshman Class: 1530 applied, 1233 accepted, 648 enrolled
SAT CR/M: 605/601
Faculty: 135
Ph.D.s: 90%
Student/Faculty: 18 to 1
Tuition: n/av
Room & Board: $8108
ACT: 27 **HIGHLY COMPETITIVE**

Grove City College, founded in 1876, is a private, liberal arts and science

Christian college that is committed to providing rigorous academics within a Christian environment at an amazing value. There are 2 undergraduate schools. In addition to regional accreditation, Grove City has baccalaureate program accreditation with ABET. The library contains 162,000 volumes, 4,000 microform items, 3,500 audio/video tapes/CDs/DVDs, and subscribes to 69,679 periodicals including electronic. Computerized library services include interlibrary loans, database searching, Internet access, and Wi-Fi capability. Special learning facilities include an art gallery, radio and TV station, research grade observatory. The 180-acre campus is in a small town 60 miles north of Pittsburgh. Including any residence halls, there are 30 buildings.

Student Life: 52% of undergraduates are from out of state, mostly the Middle Atlantic. Students are from 44 states, 9 foreign countries, and Canada. 60% are from public schools. 93% are White. 52% claim no religious affiliation; 31% Protestant. The average age of freshmen is 18; all undergraduates, 20. 12% do not continue beyond their first year; 82% remain to graduate.

Housing: 2333 students can be accommodated in college housing, which includes single-sex dorms and on-campus apartments. On-campus housing is guaranteed for all 4 years and is available on a lottery system for upperclassmen. 94% of students live on campus; of those, 85% remain on campus on weekends. Alcohol is not permitted. Upperclassmen may keep cars.

Activities: 16% of men belong to 10 local fraternities; 18% of women belong to 9 local sororities. There are 145 groups on campus, including art, band, cheerleading, chess, choir, chorale, chorus, computers, dance, debate, drama, drill team, ethnic, film, forensics, honors, international, jazz band, literary magazine, marching band, musical theater, newspaper, opera, orchestra, pep band, photography, political, professional, radio and TV, religious, social, social service, student government, symphony, and yearbook. Popular campus events include Parents Weekend, Christmas Candlelight Service and President's Gala.

Sports: There are 9 intercollegiate sports for men and 10 for women, and 13 intramural sports for men and 14 for women. Facilities include a field house; a recreation building that includes 2 indoor pools, an indoor running a track, 4 basketball, volleyball, or tennis courts, 3 racquetball courts, bowling lanes, and 2 fitness room, 10 outdoor tennis courts, a turf football stadium with an all-weather track, baseball, soccer, and softball fields, and 3 intramural fields.

Disabled Students: All of the campus is accessible. Facilities include wheelchair ramps, elevators, special parking, specially equipped restrooms, special class scheduling, lowered drinking fountains, lowered telephones, and special housing.

Services: Counseling and information services are available, as is tutoring in most subjects. A student tutoring program is available for a small fee.

Campus Safety and Security: Measures include 24-hour foot and vehicle patrol, emergency notification system, and security escort services. There are emergency telephones, lighted pathways/sidewalks, controlled access to dorms/residences, an emergency response program is in place, which includes a public warning siren and cell phone text message system.

Programs of Study: Grove City confers B.A., B.S., B.Mus., B.S.E.E. and B.S.M.E. degrees. Bachelor's degrees are awarded in BIOLOGICAL SCIENCE (biochemistry and biology/biological science), BUSINESS (accounting, business administration and management, business economics, entrepreneurial studies, finance, international business management, and marketing management), COMMUNICATIONS AND THE ARTS (communications, English, French, music, music business management, music performance, and Spanish), COMPUTER AND PHYSICAL SCIENCE (chemistry, computer information technology, computer science, mathematics, and physics), EDUCATION (early childhood education, elementary education, middle school education, music education, and special education), ENGINEERING AND ENVIRONMENTAL DESIGN (electrical/electronics engineering, industrial administration/management, and mechanical engineering), HEALTH PROFESSIONS (exercise science), SOCIAL SCIENCE (biblical studies, economics, history, philosophy, political science/government, psychology, and religious music). Engineering, computer science, biology, chemistry, and biochemistry are the strongest academically. Biology, mechanical engineering, and communication studies have the largest enrollments.

Required: Students are required to complete a minimum of 128 credit hours. All students must complete the 40-46 semester-hour general education curriculum, which includes 18 hours of humanities; 8 hours of natural science; 3 hours of science, faith, and technology; 3 hours of social science; and 6 hours of quantitative and logical reasoning. Specific courses required include 2 hours of physical/wellness education and 2 years demonstrated proficiency in a foreign language. A minimum GPA of 2.0 is required.

Special: The college offers study abroad; accelerated and double major degrees; semester and summer internships; and a Washington semester. There are 18 national honor societies and 15 departmental honors programs.

Faculty/Classroom: 64% of faculty are male; 36% are female. All teach undergraduates, and 30% do both. No introductory courses are taught by graduate students. The average class size in an introductory lecture is 30; in a laboratory is 20; and in a regular course is 24.

Admissions: 81% of the 2013-2014 applicants were accepted. The SAT scores for the 2013-2014 freshman class were: Critical Reading--8% below 500, 39% between 500 and 599, 40% between 600 and 699, and 13% between 700 and 800; Math--9% below 500, 37% between 500 and 599, 43% between 600 and 699, and 11% between 700 and 800. The ACT scores were 7% below 21, 12% between 21 and 23, 16% between 24 and 26, 23% between 27 and 28, and 42% above 28. 65% of the current freshmen were in the top fifth of their class; 90% were in the top two fifths. There were 7 National Merit finalists. 28 freshmen graduated first in their class.

Requirements: The SAT or ACT is required. An academic or college preparatory curriculum is highly recommended, including 4 units of English; 3 units each of math, science, and a foreign language; and 2 units of history. Two essays are required of all applicants, and an audition is required of music students. An interview is highly recommended. AP and CLEP credits are accepted. Important factors in the admissions decision are extracurricular activities record, personality/intangible qualities, and parents or siblings attended your school.

Procedure: Freshmen are admitted fall and spring. Entrance exams should be taken Spring of the junior year or the fall of the senior year. There are early decision, early admissions, and deferred admissions plans. Early decision applications should be filed by November 15; regular applications, by February 1 for fall entry; and December 15 for spring entry, along with a $50 fee. Notification of early decision is sent December 15; regular decision, March 15. 333 early decision candidates were accepted for the 2013-2014 class. 55 applicants were on the 2013 waiting list; 27 were admitted. Applications are accepted online.

Transfer: 64 transfer students enrolled in 2012-2013. Either the SAT or the ACT is required as well as two letters of recommendation, official high school and college transcripts, and two essays. An interview is highly recommended. 64 of 128 credits required for the bachelor's degree must be completed at Grove City.

Visiting: There are regularly scheduled orientations for prospective students, Daily interviews and tours, 2 high school visitation days in the fall, and 1 visitation day in the spring. There are science, engineering, math, and computer open houses. There are guides for informal visits, visitors may sit in on classes, and stay overnight. To schedule a visit, contact the Admissions Office.

Financial Aid: In 2013-2014, 74% of all full-time freshmen and 69% of continuing full-time students received some form of financial aid. 48% of all full-time freshmen and 37% of continuing full-time students received need-based aid. The average freshman award was $11,905. Need-based scholarships or need-based grants averaged $7,253; need-based self-help aid (loans and jobs) averaged $11,184; and other non-need-based awards and non-need-based scholarships averaged $3,370. 41% of undergraduate students work part-time. Average annual earnings from campus work are $1100. The average financial indebtedness of the 2013 graduate was $29,959. The the college's own financial statement is required. The deadline for filing freshman financial aid applications for fall entry is April 15.

International Students: There are 23 international students enrolled. They must take the TOEFL with a minimum score of 550 on the paper-based TOEFL (PBT) or 79 on the Internet-based version (iBT). They must also take the SAT or ACT, if the TOEFL is not available.

Graduates: From July 1, 2012 to June 30, 2013, 589 bachelor's degrees were awarded. The most popular majors were English (8%), mechanical engineering (7%), and biology (6%). 195 companies recruited on campus in 2012-2013. In an average class, 78% graduate in 4 years or less, 82% graduate in 5 years or less, and 82% graduate in 6 years or less.

Admissions Contact: Sarah E. Gibbs, Director of Admissions. E-Mail: *admissions@gcc.edu* Web: *www.gcc.edu*

GWYNEDD-MERCY COLLEGE F-4

Gwynedd Valley, PA 19437 **(215) 641-5510**
(800) DIAL-GMC; (215) 641-5556

Full-time: 420 men, 1080 women	**Faculty:** 69
Part-time: 170 men, 540 women	**Ph.D.s:** 63%
Graduate: 110 men, 320 women	**Student/Faculty:** n/av
Year: semesters, summer session	**Tuition:** $28,370
Application Deadline: see profile	**Room & Board:** $10,525
Freshman Class: n/av	
SAT or ACT: required	

COMPETITIVE

Gwynedd-Mercy College, founded in 1948, is a private institution affiliated with the Roman Catholic Church and offering degree programs in the arts and sciences, business, education, and health fields. There are 5 undergraduate schools and 2 graduate schools. The figures in the above capsule and in this profile are approximate. In addition to regional accreditation, Gwynedd-Mercy has baccalaureate program accreditation with NLN. The library contains 104,899 volumes and 11,775 audio/video tapes/CDs/DVDs. Computerized library services include interlibrary loans, database searching, Internet access, and laptop Internet portals. Special learning facilities include a learning resource center and a lab school for education majors. The 170-acre campus is in a suburban area 20 miles northwest of Philadelphia. Including any residence halls, there are 21 buildings.

Student Life: 92% of undergraduates are from Pennsylvania. Others are from 14 states and 38 foreign countries. 59% are from public schools. 69% are white; 20% African American. 54% are Catholic; 13% Protestant. The average age of freshmen is 25; all undergraduates, 28. 24% do not continue beyond their first year; 69% remain to graduate.

Housing: 550 students can be accommodated in college housing, which includes coed dorms. On-campus housing is available on a first-come, first-served basis. 72% of students commute. Alcohol is not permitted. All students may keep cars.

Activities: There are no fraternities or sororities. There are 21 groups on campus, including choir, chorus, drama, ethnic, honors, international, literary magazine, newspaper, professional, religious, social, social service, and student government. Popular campus events include Fall Fest, Carol Night, and International Night.

Sports: There are 6 intercollegiate sports for men and 7 for women. Facilities include a recreation center housing men's and women's basketball, women's volleyball, a walking track, indoor racquetball courts, a weight room, team locker rooms, and a sauna. Outdoor facilities include soccer, baseball, softball, and field hockey fields.

Disabled Students: 75% of the campus is accessible. Facilities include wheelchair ramps, elevators, special parking, specially equipped rest rooms, and special class scheduling.

Services: Counseling and information services are available, as is tutoring in most subjects. There is remedial math, reading, and writing. Tutoring is made available in conjunction with student needs.

Campus Safety and Security: Measures include 24-hour foot and vehicle patrol, emergency notification system, and security escort services. There are shuttle buses, emergency telephones, and lighted pathways/sidewalks.

Programs of Study: Gwynedd-Mercy confers B.A., B.S., and B.H.S. degrees. Associate and master's degrees are also awarded. Bachelor's degrees are awarded in BIOLOGICAL SCIENCE (biology/biological science), BUSINESS (accounting, banking and finance, business administration and management, human resources, international business management, management science, marketing and distribution, and sports management), COMMUNICATIONS AND THE ARTS (communications, English, and public relations), COMPUTER AND PHYSICAL SCIENCE (computer science, information sciences and systems, mathematics, natural sciences, and radiological technology), EDUCATION (business education, elementary education, mathematics education, science education, secondary education, social studies education, and special education), HEALTH PROFESSIONS (clinical science, health care administration, medical laboratory technology, medical technology, nursing, radiation therapy, and respiratory therapy), SOCIAL SCIENCE (criminal justice, gerontology, history, human services, psychology, social work, and sociology). Nursing, biology, and medical technology are the strongest academically. Nursing, business, and education have the largest enrollments.

Required: All students must complete at least 125 credit hours, including 60 in the major, with a minimum GPA of 2.0. (Some programs require a higher GPA.) General education courses cover language, literature and fine arts, behavioral and social sciences, humanities, and natural science. Specific courses in English composition, literature, philosophy, and religious studies are required.

Special: The college offers co-op programs in computer science, business administration, and accounting, as well as internships, dual majors, accelerated degree programs, B.A.-B.S. degrees, and pass/fail options. Cross-registration is offered with South Eastern Pennsylvania Consortium for Higher Education. All programs require or have the option for hands-on experience. There is a 3-1 program in medical technology available in which the last year is a hospital rotation. There are 4 national honor societies, a freshman honors program, and 1 departmental honors program.

Faculty/Classroom: 29% of faculty are male; 71% are female. 92% teach undergraduates. No introductory courses are taught by graduate students. The average class size in an introductory lecture, 24; in a laboratory, 15; and in a regular course, 17.

Admissions: 60% of a recent year's applicants were accepted. 18% of a recent year's freshmen were in the top fifth of their class; 42% were in the top two fifths.

Requirements: The SAT or ACT is required. In addition, candidates for admission must be graduates of accredited secondary schools and have completed 16 academic credits/Carnegie units, including 4 credits in English, 3 each in math, science, and college preparatory electives, 2 in a foreign language, and 1 in history. The GED is accepted. An interview is recommended for all candidates and is required for some programs. A GPA of 2.0 is required. AP and CLEP credits are accepted. Important factors in the admissions decision are advanced placement or honors courses, parents or siblings attended your school, and recommendations by alumni.

Procedure: Freshmen are admitted fall and spring. Entrance exams should be taken in the spring of the junior year or the fall of the senior year. There are deferred admissions and rolling admissions plans. Check with the school for current application deadlines. The application fee is $25 (waived for online applications).

Transfer: 198 transfer students enrolled in a recent year. Neither the SAT nor the ACT is required for transfer students out of high school for 2 or more years. A minimum GPA of 2.0 is necessary; some programs require a higher GPA. An interview is recommended. 45 of 125 credits required for the bachelor's degree must be completed at Gwynedd-Mercy.

Visiting: There are regularly scheduled orientations for prospective students, consisting of open houses with formal presentations and campus tours, and class days with class visitations and campus tours. There are guides for informal visits; visitors may sit in on classes and stay overnight. To schedule a visit, contact the Admissions Office.

Financial Aid: In a recent year, 73% of all full-time freshmen and 74% of continuing full-time students received some form of financial aid. 72% of all full-time freshmen and 73% of continuing full-time students received need-based aid. The average freshman award was $14,349. The average financial indebtedness of a recent year's graduate was $20,636. The FAFSA, the college's own financial statement, and federal income tax returns are required. Check with the school for current application deadlines.

International Students: There were 47 international students enrolled in a recent year. They must take the TOEFL with a minimum score of 525 on the paper-based TOEFL (PBT), or score 88 on the MTELP.

Graduates: In a recent year, 358 bachelor's degrees were awarded. The most popular majors were business administration (34%), nursing (21%), and education (15%). In an average class, 1% graduate in 3 years or less, 50% graduate in 4 years or less, 67% graduate in 5 years or less, and 69% graduate in 6 years or less.

Admissions Contact: Michelle Diehl, Director of Undergraduate Admissions. E-Mail: *admissions@gmc.edu* Web: *www.gmc.edu*

HAVERFORD COLLEGE E-4

Haverford, PA 19041 **(610) 896-1350; (610) 896-1338**

Full-time: 568 men, 619 women	**Faculty:** 148; IIB, +$
Part-time: n/av	**Ph.D.s:** 98%
Graduate: n/av	**Student/Faculty:** 9 to 1
Year: semesters	**Tuition:** $45,426
Application Deadline: January 15	**Room & Board:** $13,810
Freshman Class: 3585 applied, 842 accepted, 330 enrolled	
SAT CR/M/W: 710/700/710	**ACT:** 32 **MOST COMPETITIVE**

Haverford College, founded in 1833, is a private liberal arts college. There is one undergraduate school. The 4 libraries contain 592,984 volumes, 8,039 microform items, 16,280 audio/video tapes/CDs/DVDs, and subscribe to 14,775 periodicals including electronic. Computerized library services include interlibrary loans, database searching, Internet access, and Wi-Fi capability. Special learning facilities include an art gallery, planetarium, radio station, an observatory, and an arboretum. The 200-acre campus is in a suburban area 10 miles west of Philadelphia. Including any residence halls, there are 87 buildings.

Student Life: 87% of undergraduates are from out of state, mostly the Middle Atlantic. Students are from 45 states, 39 foreign countries, and Canada. 55% are from public schools. 64% are White. The average age of freshmen is 18; all undergraduates, 20. 2% do not continue beyond their first year; 98% remain to graduate.

Housing: 1187 students can be accommodated in college housing, which includes coed dorms and on-campus apartments. In addition, there are language houses, special-interest houses, and Haverford students may live at Bryn Mawr College through a dorm exchange program. On-campus housing is guaranteed for all 4 years and is available on a lottery system for upperclassmen. 98% of students live on campus; of those, 90% remain on campus on weekends. Upperclassmen may keep cars.

Activities: There are no fraternities or sororities. There are 229 groups on campus, including art, chess, choir, chorale, computers, dance, debate, drama, environmental, ethnic, film, gay, international, jazz band, literary magazine, musical theater, newspaper, orchestra, photography, political, radio and TV, religious, social, social service, student government, and yearbook. Popular campus events include Haverfest, Snowball, and Haverford vs Swarthmore Athletic Events.

Sports: There are 11 intercollegiate sports for men and 13 for women, and 3 intramural sports for men and 3 for women. Facilities include Douglas B. Gardner '83 Integrated Athletic Center: 102,000 square foot facility completed in 2005, contains the Calvin J. Gooding '84 Arena (seating 1,200) for basketball and volleyball; Greg Kannerstein '63 Pavilion for basketball, volleyball and badminton; Arn '76 and Nancy Tellem Fitness Center (7,200 square feet, primarily Cybex exercise equipment, 80 weight and fitness stations); Dana Swan Multipurpose Room for dance, martial arts, fitness, and recreational activities; the Andy Kates Fencing Salle; five International Squash Courts; Tom Glasser '82 Hall of Achievement; extensive sports medicine, locker room, and lobby areas; and a conference/AV room. Built as an ecologically sustainable facility, it was awarded the NCV2 Gold rating in Leadership Energy and Environmental Design (LEED) certification by the United States Green Building Council.

Disabled Students: 60% of the campus is accessible. Facilities include wheelchair ramps, elevators, special parking, specially equipped restrooms, special class scheduling, lowered drinking fountains, lowered telephones, and reasonable accommodations.

Services: Counseling and information services are available, as is tutoring in every subject. There is a reader service for the blind.

Campus Safety and Security: Measures include 24-hour foot and vehicle patrol, emergency notification system, self-defense education, and security escort services. There are shuttle buses, emergency telephones, lighted pathways/sidewalks, controlled access to dorms/residences, and a fire safety program.

Programs of Study: Haverford confers B.A., and B.S. degrees. Bachelor's degrees are awarded in BIOLOGICAL SCIENCE (biology/biological science), COMMUNICATIONS AND THE ARTS (art history and appreciation, classics, comparative literature, English, fine arts, French, German, Greek, Italian, Latin, linguistics, music, romance languages and literature, Russian, Spanish, and visual and performing arts), COMPUTER AND PHYSICAL SCIENCE (astronomy, astrophysics, chemistry, computer science, geology, information sciences and systems, mathematics, and physics), SOCIAL SCIENCE (anthropology, archeology, East Asian studies, economics, history, interdisciplinary studies, liberal arts/general studies, philosophy, political science/government, psychology, religion, sociology, and urban studies). Natural sciences is the strongest academically. English, biology and psychology have the largest enrollments.

Required: All students must take a minimum of 32 course credits, including freshman writing and 3 courses each in social science, natural science, and the humanities. Students must also take 3 semesters of phys ed and demonstrate proficiency in a foreign language. Students must take a minimum of 6 courses in the major and 6 in related fields. Each major includes a capstone experience.

Special: Haverford offers internship programs, cross-registration with Bryn Mawr and Swarthmore Colleges, study abroad in 38 countries, dual majors, and student-designed majors. Pass/fail options are limited to 4 in 4 years. Haverford offers a 3-2 program in engineering with Cal Tech. And a 4-1 program with U of Pennsylvania in engineering.

Faculty/Classroom: All teach undergraduates, and 80% do research. No introductory courses are taught by graduate students. The average class size in an introductory lecture is 20.

Admissions: 23% of the 2013-2014 applicants were accepted. The SAT scores for the 2013-2014 freshman class were: Critical Reading--6% between 500 and 599, 43% between 600 and 699, and 51% between 700 and 800; Math--6% between 500 and 599, 39% between 600 and 699, and 55% between 700 and 800; Writing--6% between 500 and 599, 38% between 600 and 699, and 56% between 700 and 800. The ACT scores were 20% between 27 and 28, and 80% above 28.

Requirements: The SAT or ACT is required. First-year applicants must take the SAT (all 3 tests, including Writing) or the ACT and 2 SAT subject tests before the deadline for the decision plan chosen. Candidates for admission must be graduates of an accredited secondary school and have taken 4 courses in English, 3 each in a foreign language and math, 2 in social studies, and 1 each in science. The GED is accepted. An essay is required, and an interview is recommended. AP credits are accepted. Important factors in the admissions decision are advanced placement or honors courses, leadership record, and recommendations by school officials.

Procedure: Freshmen are admitted fall. Entrance exams should be taken by January 15. There are early decision, early admissions, and deferred admissions plans. Early decision applications should be filed by November 15; regular applications, by January 15 for fall entry, along with a $60 fee. Notification of early decision is sent December 15; regular decision, April 15. 769 applicants were on the 2013 waiting list; 10 were admitted. Applications are accepted online.

Transfer: 2 transfer students enrolled in 2012-2013. Transfer students must be able to enter the sophomore or junior class. Admission depends mainly on the strength of college grades. A minimum GPA of 3.0 is necessary and the SAT is recommended. The equivalent of 1 year of courses must have been earned. A liberal arts curriculum is also recommended. 64 of 128 credits required for the bachelor's degree must be completed at Haverford.

Visiting: There are guides for informal visits, visitors may sit in on classes, and stay overnight. To schedule a visit, contact the Admissions Office.

Financial Aid: In 2013-2014, 55% of all full-time freshmen and 53% of continuing full-time students received some form of financial aid. 51% of all full-time freshmen and 50% of continuing full-time students received need-based aid. The average freshman award was $43,698. Need-based scholarships or need-based grants averaged $40,658; and need-based self-help aid (loans and jobs) averaged $2,456. 64% of undergraduate students work part-time. The average financial indebtedness of the 2013 graduate was $14,110. Haverford is a member of CSS. The CSS/Profile and FAFSA are required. The priority date for freshman financial aid applications for fall entry is February 1. The deadline for filing freshman financial aid applications for fall entry is February 1.

International Students: There are 66 international students enrolled. The school actively recruits these students. They must take the TOEFL with a minimum score of 600 on the paper-based TOEFL (PBT) or 100 on the Internet-based version (iBT). They must also take the SAT or ACT. Haverford requires the SAT (all 3 tests, including Writing) or the ACT plus 2 SAT subject tests.

Graduates: From July 1, 2012 to June 30, 2013, 299 bachelor's degrees were awarded. The most popular majors were Biology (13%), Psychology (12%), and English (10%). 267 companies recruited on campus in 2012-2013. In an average class, 90% graduate in 4 years or less, 92% graduate in 5 years or less, and 93% graduate in 6 years or less. Of the 2012 graduating class, 18% were enrolled in graduate school within 6 months of graduation, and 60% were employed.

Admissions Contact: Jess Lord, Dean of Admission and Financial Aid. E-Mail: *admission@haverford.edu* Web: *www.haverford.edu*

HOLY FAMILY UNIVERSITY F-3

Philadelphia, PA 19114 **(215) 637-7700; (215) 281-1022**

Full-time: 384 men, 1159 women	**Faculty:** 95; IIB, av$
Part-time: 159 men, 436 women	**Ph.D.s:** 77%
Graduate: 232 men, 723 women	**Student/Faculty:** 16 to 1
Year: semesters, summer session	**Tuition:** $27,100
Application Deadline: open	**Room & Board:** $12,930
Freshman Class: n/av	
SAT CR/M/W: 471/476/472	**ACT:** required **LESS COMPETITIVE**

Holy Family University, established in 1954 and affiliated with the Roman Catholic Church, is a private, residential institution with a liberal arts core. There are 4 undergraduate schools and 3 graduate schools. The library contains 145,442 volumes, 3,980 microform items, 5,407 audio/video tapes/CDs/DVDs, and subscribes to 21,932 periodicals including electronic. Computerized library services include interlibrary loans, database searching, and Internet access. Special learning facilities include an art gallery, writing resource center. The 46-acre campus is in a suburban area within city limits. Including any residence halls, there are 8 buildings.

Student Life: 84% of undergraduates are from Pennsylvania. Others are from 16 states, 10 foreign countries, and Canada. 55% are from public schools. 63% are White; 18% race unknown. 57% are Catholic; 12% Protestant. The average age of freshmen is 18; all undergraduates, 21. 24% do not continue beyond their first year; 61% remain to graduate.

Housing: 353 students can be accommodated in college housing, which includes coed dorms, on-campus apartments, and off-campus apartments. On-campus housing is guaranteed for all 4 years and is available on a lottery system for upperclassmen. 83% of students commute. Alcohol is not permitted. All students may keep cars.

Activities: There are no fraternities or sororities. There are 30 groups on campus, including cheerleading, chorale, dance, drama, honors, international, literary magazine, newspaper, professional, radio and TV, religious, social service, student government, and yearbook. Popular campus events include Christmas Rose, Charter Day and Stress Reduction Week.

Sports: There are 5 intercollegiate sports for men and 8 for women, and 5 intramural sports for men and 5 for women. Facilities include fitness center (gym, weight room, etc.), racquetball and lacrosse courts, soccer, tennis, and softball fields.

Disabled Students: 80% of the campus is accessible. Facilities include wheelchair ramps, elevators, special parking, specially equipped restrooms, lowered drinking fountains, and special housing.

Services: There is remedial math, reading, and writing.

Campus Safety and Security: Measures include 24-hour foot and vehicle patrol, emergency notification system, and security escort services. There are shuttle buses, emergency telephones, lighted pathways/sidewalks, and controlled access to dorms/residences.

Programs of Study: Holy Family confers B.A., B.S., B.S.N. and B.S.R.S. degrees. Associate, master's, and doctoral degrees are also awarded. Bachelor's degrees are awarded in BIOLOGICAL SCIENCE (biochemistry and biology/biological science), BUSINESS (accounting, business administration and management, finance, international business information systems, marketing/retailing/merchandising, and sports management), COMMUNICATIONS AND THE ARTS (art, communications, and English), COMPUTER AND PHYSICAL SCIENCE (information sciences and systems, mathematics, and radiological technology), EDUCATION (early childhood education, elementary education, foreign languages education, science education, secondary education, and special education), HEALTH PROFESSIONS (medical laboratory technology and nursing), SOCIAL SCIENCE (criminal justice, fire services administration, history, humanities, industrial and organizational psychology, political science/government, psychology, religion, and sociology). Computer Management Information Systems, Middle Level Education, and Accounting are the strongest academically. Nursing, criminal justice, and psychology have the largest enrollments.

Required: Students must complete 120 to 130 semester hours, including at least 30 in the major, with a minimum GPA of 2.0. Nursing, medical technology, and education majors must maintain a GPA of 2.5. Specific discipline requirements include English, science, math, philosophy, religious studies, social studies, humanities, and foreign language. A core curriculum of communication, quantification, philosophy, humanities, social science, natural sciences, senior ethics, and religious studies must be fulfilled. All majors require satisfactory performance on a comprehensive exam.

Special: Opportunities are provided for study abroad, co-op programs in 23 majors with more than 200 companies, a B.A.-B.S. degree, an accelerated degree program, independent study, credit by exam, nondegree study, and pass/fail options. Students may pursue dual majors in business and French or Spanish, international business and French or Spanish, and elementary and special education. There are 16 national honor societies and a freshman honors program.

Faculty/Classroom: 35% of faculty are male; 65% are female. All teach undergraduates. No introductory courses are taught by graduate students. The average class size in an introductory lecture is 18; in a laboratory is 9; and in a regular course is 19.

Admissions: The SAT scores for the 2013-2014 freshman class were: Critical Reading--71% below 500, 25% between 500 and 599, 4% between 600 and 699, Math--64% below 500, 32% between 500 and 599, 4% between 600 and 699, 32% of the current freshmen were in the top fifth of their class; 68% were in the top two fifths. 2 freshmen graduated first in their class.

Requirements: The SAT or ACT is required. Graduation from an accredited secondary school is required; a GED is accepted. Applicants must submit 16 academic credits, including 4 courses in English, 3 each in history and math, 2 each in foreign language and science, 1 in social studies, and the remainder in academic electives. AP and CLEP credits are accepted. Important factors in the admissions decision are advanced placement or honors courses, extracurricular activities record, and personality/intangible qualities.

Procedure: Freshmen are admitted to all sessions. Entrance exams should be taken by October or November of the senior year. There are early admissions, deferred admissions, and rolling admissions plans. Application deadlines are open. Application fee is $25. Notification is sent on a rolling basis. Applications are accepted online.

Transfer: 198 transfer students enrolled in 2012-2013. Applicants must submit official transcripts from all previous colleges. Grades of D are not transferable. A maximum of 75 credits will be accepted for transfer. 45 of 120 credits required for the bachelor's degree must be completed at Holy Family.

Visiting: There are regularly scheduled orientations for prospective students. There are guides for informal visits, visitors may sit in on classes, and stay overnight. To schedule a visit, contact the Admissions Office.

Financial Aid: In 2013-2014, 88% of all full-time freshmen and 85% of continuing full-time students received some form of financial aid. 88% of all full-time freshmen and 85% of continuing full-time students received need-based aid. The average freshman award was $11,005. Need-based scholarships or need-based grants averaged $17,398; need-based self-help aid (loans and jobs) averaged $5,077; non-need-based athletic scholarships averaged $27,780; other non-need-based awards and non-need-based scholarships averaged $9,774; and $26,323 from other forms of aid. 78% of undergraduate students work part-time. Average annual earnings from campus work are $500. The average financial indebtedness of the 2013 graduate was $35,589. The FAFSA is required. The priority date for freshman financial aid applications for fall entry is March 1. The deadline for filing freshman financial aid applications for fall entry is rolling.

International Students: There are 10 international students enrolled. They must take the TOEFL with a minimum score of 550 on the paper-based TOEFL (PBT) or 79 on the Internet-based version (iBT).

Graduates: From July 1, 2012 to June 30, 2013, 414 bachelor's degrees were awarded. The most popular majors were health professions and related programs (27%), education (23%), and business/marketing (19%). 65 companies recruited on campus in 2012-2013. In an average class, 43% graduate in 4 years or less, 59% graduate in 5 years or less, and 61% graduate in 6 years or less. Of the 2012 graduating class, 24% were enrolled in graduate school within 6 months of graduation, and 68% were employed.

Admissions Contact: Lauren Campbell, Director of Undergraduate Admissions. E-Mail: *admissions@holyfamily.edu* Web: *http:/my.holyfamily.edu/home/index.asp*

IMMACULATA UNIVERSITY E-4

Immaculata, PA 19345 **(610) 647-4400, ext. 3015**
(877) IC-TODAY; (610) 640-0836

Full-time: 327 men, 848 women
Part-time: 284 men, 1424 women
Graduate: 330 men, 904 women
Year: semesters, summer session
Application Deadline: March 1
Freshman Class: 1650 applied, 1314 accepted, 243 enrolled
SAT or ACT: required
Faculty: 100; IIA, --$
Ph.D.s: 74%
Student/Faculty: 10 to 1
Tuition: $30,740
Room & Board: $12,260

COMPETITIVE

Immaculata University, founded in 1920, is a private Catholic, primarily women's liberal arts and career preparation college. There is one graduate school. In addition to regional accreditation, Immaculata has baccalaureate program accreditation with ADA, AHEA, NASM, and NLN. The library contains 130,000 volumes, 1,373 microform items, 1,500 audio/video tapes/CDs/DVDs, and subscribes to 760 periodicals including electronic. Computerized library services include interlibrary loans, database searching, and Internet access. The 400-acre campus is in a suburban area 20 miles west of Philadelphia. Including any residence halls, there are 13 buildings.

Student Life: 69% of undergraduates are from Pennsylvania. Others are from states. 38% are from public schools. 75% are White. 76% are Catholic; 16% Protestant. The average age of freshmen is 18; all undergraduates, 22. 30% do not continue beyond their first year; 55% remain to graduate.

Housing: 380 students can be accommodated in college housing, which includes single-sex and coed dorms and on-campus apartments. On-campus housing is guaranteed for all 4 years. 71% of students live on campus. Alcohol is not permitted. All students may keep cars.

Activities: There are no fraternities or sororities. There are 32 groups on campus, including art, band, choir, chorale, chorus, computers, dance, debate, drama, ethnic, honors, international, jazz band, literary magazine, musical theater, newspaper, orchestra, photography, political, professional, religious, social, social service, and student government. Popular campus events include Rose Arbor Dinner, Class Proms, and Friday's Pub.

Sports: There are 6 intercollegiate sports for women, and 10 intramural sports for women. Facilities include a full gym, tennis courts, a handball gym, an olympic-size swimming pool, hockey and softball fields, and a weight room.

Disabled Students: All of the campus is accessible. Facilities include wheelchair ramps, elevators, special parking, specially equipped restrooms, special class scheduling, lowered drinking fountains, lowered telephones, and special housing.

Services: Counseling and information services are available, as is tutoring in most subjects. There is a reader service for the blind, and remedial math, reading, and writing.

Campus Safety and Security: Measures include 24-hour foot and vehicle patrol, self-defense education, and security escort services. There are emergency telephones and lighted pathways/sidewalks.

Programs of Study: Immaculata confers B.A., B.S., B.Mus. and B.S.N. degrees. Associate, master's, and doctoral degrees are also awarded. Bachelor's degrees are awarded in BIOLOGICAL SCIENCE (biochemistry and biology/biological science), BUSINESS (accounting, banking and finance, business administration and management, and fashion merchandising), COMMUNICATIONS AND THE ARTS (English, French, music, and Spanish), COMPUTER AND PHYSICAL SCIENCE (information sciences and systems and mathematics), EDUCATION (early childhood education, elementary education, foreign languages education, home economics education, middle school education, music education, science education, and secondary education), HEALTH PROFESSIONS (music therapy, nursing, and premedicine), SOCIAL SCIENCE (dietetics, economics, experimental psychology, food science, history, international relations, prelaw, psychology, social science, sociology, and theological studies). Premedicine, education, and dietetics are the strongest academically. Education, business, and music therapy have the largest enrollments.

Required: To graduate, all students must complete 54 credits in liberal arts, including distribution requirements in humanities, social sciences, and sciences. Students must take a minimum of 126 credits, including 36 to 52 in the major. 2 credits of phys ed are also required. The college requires a minimum GPA of 2.0. A thesis, which is the outcome of a required senior seminar, is also required. Internships are required for dietetics, music therapy, and education.

Special: All majors offer opportunities for internships, and most require them. Students may study abroad in 6 countries. The college offers dual-majors, 3 accelerated degree programs in organization dynamics, human resource management, and nursing, and nondegree study and pass/fail options. There are 16 national honor societies, including Phi Beta Kappa, a freshman honors program, and 13 departmental honors programs.

Faculty/Classroom: 40% of faculty are male; 60% are female. 92% teach undergraduates, and 4% do both. No introductory courses are taught by graduate students.

Admissions: 80% of the 2013-2014 applicants were accepted.

Requirements: The SAT or ACT is required. Candidates for admission should be graduates of an accredited secondary school with a minimum of 16 academic credits including 4 in English, 2 each in a foreign language, math, science, and social studies, 1 in history, and 4 more in college preparatory courses. The GED is accepted. An audition is required for music students, and an essay and an interview are recommended for all. A GPA of 2.0 is required. AP and CLEP credits are accepted. Important factors in the admissions decision are advanced placement or honors courses, recommendations by school officials, and extracurricular activities record.

Procedure: Freshmen are admitted fall and spring. Entrance exams should be taken in the spring of the junior year. There are deferred admissions and rolling admissions plans. Applications should be filed by March 1 for fall entry; November 1 for spring entry, along with a $35 fee. Notification of early decision is sent December 1; regular decision, September 15. Applications are accepted online.

Transfer: 44 transfer students enrolled in 2012-2013. In addition, to high school credentials, transfer applicants must present college transcripts. Courses in which the student has achieved a C or better are accepted if they are comparable to Immaculata's courses. A minimum satisfactory score on the SAT is required, as is an interview. Students must have a minimum GPA of 2.0. 64 of 126 credits required for the bachelor's degree must be completed at Immaculata.

Visiting: There are regularly scheduled orientations for prospective students, including an open house and class visit. There are guides for informal visits, visitors may sit in on classes, and stay overnight. To schedule a visit, contact the Office of Admissions.

Financial Aid: In 2013-2014, 81% of all full-time freshmen and 68% of continuing full-time students received some form of financial aid. 74% of all full-time freshmen and 61% of continuing full-time students received need-based aid. The average freshman award was $16,122. Need-based scholarships or need-based grants averaged $5,907; need-based self-help aid (loans and jobs) averaged $4,274; and other non-need-based awards and non-need-based scholarships averaged $6,157. Immaculata is a member of CSS. The FAFSA is required. The priority date for freshman financial aid applications for fall entry is February 15. The deadline for filing freshman financial aid applications for fall entry is April 15.

International Students: The school actively recruits these students. They must take the TOEFL with a minimum score of 550 on the paper-based TOEFL (PBT). They must also take the SAT or ACT.

Graduates: From July 1, 2012 to June 30, 2013, 723 bachelor's degrees were awarded. The most popular majors were health professions (54%), business/marketing (23%), and psychology (3%). In an average class, 52% graduate in 4 years or less, 55% graduate in 5 years or less, and 55% graduate in 6 years or less.

Admissions Contact: Sarah Fox, Assistant Director of Admissions. E-Mail: *admiss@immaculata.edu* Web: *www.immaculata.edu*

INDIANA UNIVERSITY OF PENNSYLVANIA B-3

Indiana, PA 15705 **(724) 357-2230; (800) 442-6830**

Full-time: 5278 men, 6470 women	**Faculty:** 620; I, --$
Part-time: 365 men, 358 women	**Ph.D.s:** 95%
Graduate: 925 men, 1332 women	**Student/Faculty:** 18 to 1
Year: semesters, summer session	**Tuition:** $9080 ($20,216)
Application Deadline: open	**Room & Board:** $11,100

Freshman Class: 9367 applied, 8476 accepted, 2741 enrolled
SAT CR/M/W: 480/490/470

LESS COMPETITIVE

Founded in 1875, IUP is a vibrant, comprehensive, research-based, teaching-focused, student-centered community comprising distinguised faculty members and undergraduate and graduate students from across the nation and around the world. It is one of the largest universities in the 14-member Pennsylvania State System of Higher Education. There are 7 undergraduate schools and 1 graduate school. In addition to regional accreditation, IUP has baccalaureate program accreditation with AACSB, ABET, ADA, CAHEA, NASAD, NASM, and NCATE. The library contains 888,056 volumes, 2.4 million microform items, and 50,101 audio/video tapes/CDs/DVDs, and subscribes to 33,140 periodicals including electronic. Computerized library services include interlibrary loans, database searching, Internet access, and Wi-Fi capability. Special learning facilities include an art gallery, planetarium, radio station, and TV station. The 374-acre campus is in a small town 50 miles northeast of Pittsburgh. Including any residence halls, there are 75 buildings.

Student Life: 93% of undergraduates are from Pennsylvania. Others are from 44 states, 66 foreign countries, and Canada. 76% are White. The average age of freshmen is 18; all undergraduates, 21. 25% do not continue beyond their first year; 50% remain to graduate.

Housing: 4076 students can be accommodated in college housing, which includes single-sex and coed dorms and on-campus apartments. In addition, there are honors houses, 24-hour intensified study floors, substance-free housing, academic specialty housing, and an international house. On-campus housing is guaranteed for the freshman year only and is available on a lottery system for upperclassmen. 68% of students commute. Alcohol is not permitted. All students may keep cars.

Activities: 7% of men belong to 13 national fraternities; 8% of women belong to 11 national sororities. There are 294 groups on campus, including art, band, cheerleading, chess, choir, chorale, chorus, computers, dance, drama, drill team, environmental, ethnic, film, gay, honors, international, jazz band, marching band, musical theater, newspaper, orchestra, pep band, photography, political, professional, radio and TV, religious, social, social service, student government, and symphony. Popular campus events include Panhellenic Recruitment, Homecoming, Family Weekend, IUP Day and International Day.

Sports: There are 8 intercollegiate sports for men and 11 for women, and 10 intramural sports for men and 10 for women. Facilities include 5000-seat athletic complex, a 6500-seat stadium, 2 swimming pools, a fitness/bike trail, 2 softball fields, 2 baseball fields and courts for tennis, badminton, 6 handball/racquetball courts, 6 basketball courts, a rugby field, an outdoor track, 2 soccer fields, 2 grass practice fields, 8 volleyball courts, a sailing base, a frisbee course, 2 fishing ponds, an archery range, a simulated golf range, and 3 fitness centers.

Disabled Students: 98% of the campus is accessible. Facilities include wheelchair ramps, elevators, special parking, specially equipped restrooms, special class scheduling, lowered drinking fountains, and lowered telephones.

Services: Counseling and information services are available, as is tutoring in some subjects. There is a reader service for the blind, and remedial math, reading, and writing.

Campus Safety and Security: Measures include 24-hour foot and vehicle patrol, emergency notification system, self-defense education, and security escort services. There are shuttle buses, emergency telephones, lighted pathways/sidewalks, controlled access to dorms/residences, bicycle registration, operation ID, and crime tip hotline.

Programs of Study: IUP confers B.A., B.S., B.F.A. and B.S.Ed. degrees. Associate, master's, and doctoral degrees are also awarded. Bachelor's degrees are awarded in BIOLOGICAL SCIENCE (biochemistry, biology/adolescence education, biology/biological science, and nutrition), BUSINESS (accounting, business administration and management, fashion merchandising, finance, hotel/motel and restaurant management, human resources, international business management, management information systems, and marketing management), COMMUNICATIONS AND THE ARTS (art, communications, communications technology, English, fine arts, journalism, music, music performance, Spanish, spanish / adolescence education, studio art, and theatre arts), COMPUTER AND PHYSICAL SCIENCE (chemistry, computer science, earth science, geology, mathematics, natural sciences, and physics), EDUCATION (art education, athletic training, early childhood education, health education, music education, physical education, social science education, special education, and vocational education), ENGINEERING AND ENVIRONMENTAL DESIGN (interior design), HEALTH PROFESSIONS (clinical science, nuclear medical technology, nursing, rehabilitation therapy, respiratory therapy, and speech pathology/audiology), SOCIAL SCIENCE (anthropology, architectural studies, Asian/Oriental studies, child care/child and family studies, criminology, economics, family/consumer studies, geography, history, international studies, philosophy, political science/government, psychology, religious studies, safety science, social science, and sociology). Criminology, nursing, and psychology have the largest enrollments.

Required: All candidates for graduation must complete approximately 120 credits, including 48 credits in the liberal studies core. The total number of hours and the minimum GPA vary with the major.

Special: IUP offers co-op programs, cross-registration through the National Student Exchange Consortium, a 3-2 engineering degree with the University of Pittsburgh and Drexel University, and a B.A.-B.S. degree. Internships and dual and student-designed majors are available. Students may study abroad in 56 countries. Also available are work-study programs, a Washington semester, an accelerated degree program, and credit for military experience. There are 23 national honor societies and a freshman honors program.

Faculty/Classroom: 50% of faculty are male; 50% are female. No introductory courses are taught by graduate students.

Admissions: 90% of the 2013-2014 applicants were accepted. The SAT scores for the 2013-2014 freshman class were: Critical Reading--58% below 500, 34% between 500 and 599, 8% between 600 and 699, and 1% between 700 and 800; Math--53% below 500, 38% between 500 and 599, 9% between 600 and 699, and 1% between 700 and 800; Writing--63% below 500, 30% between 500 and 599, and 6% between 600 and 699. 17% of the current freshmen were in the top fifth of their class; 43% were in the top two fifths. 16 freshmen graduated first in their class.

Requirements: The SAT is required. Candidates for admission should be graduates of an accredited secondary school. There are no specific course requirements. Art majors must have a portfolio and music majors must audition. AP and CLEP credits are accepted. Important factors in the admissions decision are advanced placement or honors courses, extracurricular activities record, and evidence of special talent.

Procedure: Freshmen are admitted fall and spring. Entrance exams should be taken by December of the preceding year. There are deferred admissions and rolling admissions plans. Application deadlines are open. Application fee is $50. Notification is sent on a rolling basis. Applications are accepted online.

Transfer: 718 transfer students enrolled in 2012-2013. Transfer students must have a minimum GPA of 2.0 for all subjects. Education students transferring 36 or more credits must have a minimum GPA of 3.0 & those with 35 or less credits must have a minimum gpa of 2.75. Nursing and Speech-Language Pathology students must have a cumulative GPA of 3.0 or higher. 45 of 120 credits required for the bachelor's degree must be completed at Indiana University of Pennsylvania.

Visiting: There are regularly scheduled orientations for prospective students. There are guides for informal visits and visitors may sit in on classes. To schedule a visit, contact the Admissions Office.

Financial Aid: In 2013-2014, 75% of all full-time freshmen and 71% of continuing full-time students received some form of financial aid. 48% of all full-time freshmen and 46% of continuing full-time students received need-based aid. The average freshman award was $9,234. Need-based scholarships or need-based grants averaged $5,997; need-based self-help aid (loans and jobs) averaged $4,667; and non-need-based athletic scholarships averaged $3,682. 14% of undergraduate students work part-time. Average annual earnings from campus work are $2505. The FAFSA is required. The priority date for freshman financial aid applications for fall entry is April 15.

International Students: There are 437 international students enrolled. The school actively recruits these students. They must take the TOEFL with a minimum score of 500 on the paper-based TOEFL (PBT) or 61 on the Internet-based version (iBT).

Graduates: From July 1, 2012 to June 30, 2013, 2470 bachelor's degrees were awarded. The most popular majors were criminology (7%), nursing (6%), and communications media (6%). 141 companies recruited on campus in 2012-2013. In an average class, 47% graduate in 5 years or less and 50% graduate in 6 years or less.

Admissions Contact: Michael Husenits, Director of Undergraduate Admissions. E-Mail: *admissions-inquiry@iup.edu* Web: *www.iup.edu/admissions*

JUNIATA COLLEGE D-3

Huntingdon, PA 16652 **(814) 641-3420**
(877) JUNIATA; (814) 641-3100

Full-time: 695 men, 860 women	**Faculty:** 106; IIB, av$
Part-time: 35 men, 35 women	**Ph.D.s:** 93%
Graduate: 4 men, 6 women	**Student/Faculty:** 13 to 1
Year: semesters, summer session	**Tuition:** $38,630
Application Deadline: March 15	**Room & Board:** $10,710
Freshman Class: 2227 applied, 1650 accepted, 391 enrolled	
SAT CR/M: 570/580	**ACT:** recommended
	VERY COMPETITIVE

Juniata College, founded in 1876, is an independent liberal arts college. In addition to regional accreditation, Juniata has baccalaureate program accreditation with CSWE. The library contains 500,000 volumes, 400 microform items, 2,800 audio/video tapes/CDs/DVDs, and subscribes to 11,000 periodicals including electronic. Computerized library services include interlibrary loans, database searching, Internet access, and Wi-Fi capability. Special learning facilities include an art gallery, radio station, an observatory, an environmental studies field station, a nature preserve, an early childhood education center, and a ceramics studio with an Anagama kiln. The 110-acre campus is in a small town 31 miles south of state college, in the heart of rural Pennsylvania. Including any residence halls, there are 43 buildings.

Student Life: 59% of undergraduates are from Pennsylvania. Others are from 32 states, 44 foreign countries, and Canada. 78% are from public schools. 72% are White. 56% are Protestant; 32% Catholic. The average age of freshmen is 18; all undergraduates, 20. 12% do not continue beyond their first year; 88% remain to graduate.

Housing: 1240 students can be accommodated in college housing, which includes single-sex and coed dorms, on-campus apartments, and off-campus apartments. In addition, there are special-interest houses, and international housing. On-campus housing is guaranteed for all 4 years. 82% of students live on campus; of those, 75% remain on campus on weekends. All students may keep cars.

Activities: There are no fraternities or sororities. There are 87 groups on campus, including art, band, cheerleading, chess, choir, chorale, chorus, computers, dance, debate, drama, environmental, ethnic, forensics, gay, honors, international, jazz band, literary magazine, musical theater, newspaper, orchestra, outing and Model UN club, photography, political, professional, radio and TV, religious, social, social service, student government, and symphony. Popular campus events include Mountain Day, Christmas Madrigal Dinner, and Spring Fest and Relay for Life.

Sports: There are 9 intercollegiate sports for men and 10 for women, and 8 intramural sports for men and 8 for women. Facilities include 2 gyms, a swimming pool, a fitness center, 4 racquetball courts, a multipurpose fitness/dance room, a varsity football field and stadium, baseball, soccer, softball, and hockey fields, an outdoor running track, 7 tennis courts, and 1 outdoor basketball court.

Disabled Students: 75% of the campus is accessible. Facilities include wheelchair ramps, elevators, special parking, specially equipped restrooms, and lowered drinking fountains.

Services: Counseling and information services are available, as is tutoring in most subjects. There is a reader service for the blind. Juniata also offers courses and workshops in study, reading, and writing skills.

Campus Safety and Security: Measures include 24-hour foot and vehicle patrol, emergency notification system, self-defense education, and security escort services. There are emergency telephones, awareness programs, fire safety training, weather alerts, terror alerts, an emergency operation plan, a firearms storage vault, vehicle lockout service, identification processing, and evacuation mapping.

Programs of Study: Juniata confers B.A., and B.S. degrees. Master's degrees are also awarded. Bachelor's degrees are awarded in AGRICULTURE (environmental studies), BIOLOGICAL SCIENCE (biochemistry and biology/biological science), BUSINESS (accounting, banking and finance, business administration and management, human resources, international business management, and marketing/retailing/merchandising), COMMUNICATIONS AND THE ARTS (art history and appreciation, communications, digital communications, dramatic arts, English, French, German, Russian, Spanish, and studio art), COMPUTER AND PHYSICAL SCIENCE (chemistry, computer science, geology, information sciences and systems, mathematics, and physics), EDUCATION (early childhood education, elementary education, English education, foreign languages education, mathematics education, museum studies, science education, secondary education, social studies education, and special education), ENGINEERING AND ENVIRONMENTAL DESIGN (engineering physics and environmental science), SOCIAL SCIENCE (anthropology, economics, history, international studies, peace studies, philosophy, political science/government, psychology, public administration, social work, sociology, and theological studies). Biology, psychology, and business are the strongest academically. Biology, business, and environmental studies/science have the largest enrollments.

Required: Students are required to complete a minimum of 120 credit hours, including courses in fine arts, international studies, social sciences, humanities, and natural sciences, as well as 4 communications-based courses, 2 cultural analysis courses, a math and statistics course, and the college writing seminar. The total number of hours required for the program of emphasis varies from 45 to 60; majors do not exist as such, and students must develop a program of emphasis and complete it to obtain their degree. Students must have a minimum GPA of 2.0.

Special: Juniata offers cooperative programs in marine science, cytogenetics, cytotechnology, marine biology, biotechnology, nursing, medical technology, diagnostic imaging, occupational and physical therapy, dentistry, medicine, optometry, and podiatry. Internships, study abroad in 19 countries, Washington and Philadelphia semesters, and nondegree study are also offered. There are 3-2 engineering degrees with Columbia, Clarkson, Washington, and Pennsylvania State Universities, a 3-3 law program with Duquesne University, and various preprofessional programs, including optometry, chiropractic, medicine, dentistry, pharmacy, physician assistant, and podiatry. With the assistance of faculty advisers, most students design their own majors to meet their individual goals. There are 16 national honor societies, a freshman honors program, and 16 departmental honors programs.

Faculty/Classroom: 58% of faculty are male; 42% are female. All teach undergraduates. No introductory courses are taught by graduate students.

Admissions: 74% of the 2013-2014 applicants were accepted. The SAT scores for the 2013-2014 freshman class were: Critical Reading--17% below 500, 42% between 500 and 599, 31% between 600 and 699, and 10% between 700 and 800; Math--9% below 500, 51% between 500 and 599, 33% between 600 and 699, and 7% between 700 and 800. 59% of the current freshmen were in the top fifth of their class; 89% were in the top two fifths. There were 9 National Merit finalists. 6 freshmen graduated first in their class.

Requirements: The SAT or ACT is recommended. Candidates for admission should be graduates of an accredited secondary school and have completed 16 academic credits, including 4 in English, 2 in a foreign language, and a combination of 10 in math, social studies, and lab science. The GED is accepted, and homeschoolers are encouraged to apply. An essay is required, and an interview is recommended. A GPA of 3.0 is required. AP credits are accepted. Important factors in the admissions decision are advanced placement or honors courses, leadership record, and recommendations by school officials.

Procedure: Freshmen are admitted fall and spring. Entrance exams should be taken by the January test date of the year of admission for fall entry. There are early decision, early admissions, deferred admissions, and rolling admissions plans. Early decision applications should be filed by November 15; regular applications, by March 15 for fall entry; and December 1 for spring entry. Notification of early decision is sent December 31;

regular decision, on a rolling basis. 116 early decision candidates were accepted for the 2013-2014 class. 88 applicants were on the 2013 waiting list. Applications are accepted online. Application fees are waived if application is completed online.

Transfer: 22 transfer students enrolled in 2012-2013. A GPA of 2.5 is required. Applicants must submit a high school transcript, a college transcript, and an essay. SAT scores are required of some students. 30 of 120 credits required for the bachelor's degree must be completed at Juniata.

Visiting: There are regularly scheduled orientations for prospective students, including a campus tour, interviews, attend classes, meet with faculty, coaches, and, members of the financial planning staff. There are guides for informal visits, visitors may sit in on classes, and stay overnight. To schedule a visit, contact Pam Zilch, Campus Visit Coordinator at (814) 641-3428.

Financial Aid: In 2013-2014, 100% of all full-time freshmen and 100% of continuing full-time students received some form of financial aid. 81% of all full-time freshmen and 81% of continuing full-time students received need-based aid. The average freshman award was $31,406. Need-based scholarships or need-based grants averaged $26,089 ($38,030 maximum); and need-based self-help aid (loans and jobs) averaged $4,135 ($6,000 maximum). 48% of undergraduate students work part-time. Average annual earnings from campus work are $992. The average financial indebtedness of the 2013 graduate was $26,573. The FAFSA is required. The priority date for freshman financial aid applications for fall entry is March 1. The deadline for filing freshman financial aid applications for fall entry is May 1.

International Students: There are 166 international students enrolled. The school actively recruits these students. They must take the TOEFL with a minimum score of 550 on the paper-based TOEFL (PBT) or 79 on the Internet-based version (iBT).

Graduates: From July 1, 2012 to June 30, 2013, 326 bachelor's degrees were awarded. The most popular majors were biology/prehealth (15%), business/accounting (12%), and psychology (10%). 70 companies recruited on campus in 2012-2013. In an average class, 70% graduate in 4 years or less, 70% graduate in 5 years or less, and 80% graduate in 6 years or less. Of the 2012 graduating class, 39% were enrolled in graduate school within 6 months of graduation, and 61% were employed.

Admissions Contact: Office of Enrollment E-Mail: *admissions@juniata.edu* Web: *www.juniata.edu*

KEYSTONE COLLEGE E-2

La Plume, PA 18440 (570) 945-8111
(877) 4COLLEGE; (570) 945-7916

Full-time: 558 men, 720 women	**Faculty:** n/av
Part-time: 99 men, 264 women	**Ph.D.s:** 20%
Graduate: 12 men, 38 women	**Student/Faculty:** 10 to 1
Year: semesters, summer session	**Tuition:** $19,920
Application Deadline: July 1	**Room & Board:** $8760
Freshman Class: 778 applied, 739 accepted, 336 enrolled	
SAT CR/M/W: 445/440/445	**ACT:** 17 **LESS COMPETITIVE**

Keystone College, founded in 1868, is a private co-ed, residential, and culturally diverse institution. The library contains 45,967 volumes, 29,352 microform items, 2,243 audio/video tapes/CDs/DVDs, and subscribes to 10,918 periodicals including electronic. Computerized library services include interlibrary loans, database searching, Internet access, and Wi-Fi capability. Special learning facilities include an art gallery, radio station, observatory. The 270-acre campus is in a rural area 15 miles north of Scranton and 40 miles south of Binghamton, New York. Including any residence halls, there are 29 buildings.

Student Life: 89% of undergraduates are from Pennsylvania. Others are from 18 states, and 9 foreign countries. 68% are White. The average age of freshmen is 18; all undergraduates, 24. 39% do not continue beyond their first year; 36% remain to graduate.

Housing: 404 students can be accommodated in college housing, which includes single-sex and coed dorms. single rooms for upperclassmen. On-campus housing is guaranteed for all 4 years. 77% of students commute. Alcohol is not permitted. All students may keep cars.

Activities: There are no fraternities or sororities. There are 19 groups on campus, including and wrestling, professional chefs, rotaract, snow board, art, cheerleading, dance, drama, environmental, ethnic, film, forensics, gay, honors, international, literary magazine, newspaper, photography, professional, radio and TV, religious, social, social service, student government, and yearbook. Popular campus events include Winterfest, Spring Fling, and Independence Day.

Sports: There are 7 intercollegiate sports for men and 8 for women, and 5 intramural sports for men and 5 for women. Facilities include an athletic center (basketball court, weight room, cardio fitness room), tennis courts, playing fields, and a trail system.

Disabled Students: 90% of the campus is accessible. Facilities include wheelchair ramps, elevators, special parking, specially equipped restrooms, special class scheduling, lowered drinking fountains, lowered telephones, and special housing.

Services: Counseling and information services are available, as is tutoring in every subject. There is remedial reading and writing. The writing center is available with some services for those with learning disablities.

Campus Safety and Security: Measures include 24-hour foot and vehicle patrol, emergency notification system, and security escort services. There are shuttle buses, emergency telephones, and lighted pathways/sidewalks.

Programs of Study: Keystone confers B.A., and B.S. degrees. Associate degrees are also awarded. Bachelor's degrees are awarded in AGRICULTURE (natural resource management), BIOLOGICAL SCIENCE (biology/biological science), BUSINESS (accounting, business administration and management, organizational leadership and management, and sports management), COMMUNICATIONS AND THE ARTS (communications and visual and performing arts), COMPUTER AND PHYSICAL SCIENCE (information sciences and systems and natural sciences), EDUCATION (art education, early childhood education, elementary education, mathematics education, and social studies education), ENGINEERING AND ENVIRONMENTAL DESIGN (environmental science), SOCIAL SCIENCE (criminal justice, forensic studies, psychology, and social science). Visual art, environmental resource management, and natural sciences are the strongest academically. Education has the largest enrollment.

Required: To graduate, students must complete 120 to 130 credit hours and maintain a GPA of 2.0. The required core curriculum includes courses in interdisciplinary studies, math, English, speech, computer, and fitness. Distribution requirements and total credit hours vary with the major.

Special: Keystone offers co-op programs in all majors, as well as paid and unpaid internships. Study abroad is available in 14 countries and dependent on major interest or program. The Weekender program accommodates the needs of busy adult students and operates on a trimester basis. There is 1 national honor society and a freshman honors program.

Faculty/Classroom: 45% of faculty are male; 55% are female. All teach undergraduates. No introductory courses are taught by graduate students. The average class size in an introductory lecture is 15; in a laboratory is 11; and in a regular course is 15.

Admissions: 95% of the 2013-2014 applicants were accepted. The SAT scores for the 2013-2014 freshman class were: Critical Reading--80% below 500, 19% between 500 and 599, 1% between 600 and 699, and 1% between 700 and 800; Math--79% below 500, 18% between 500 and 599, 4% between 600 and 699, Writing--82% below 500, 16% between 500 and 599, 1% between 600 and 699, and 1% between 700 and 800. The ACT scores were 86% below 21, 6% between 21 and 23, and 8% above 28. 14% of the current freshmen were in the top fifth of their class; 40% were in the top two fifths.

Requirements: The SAT is required. The ACT Optional Writing test is also required. An interview is recommended for all. An art portfolio is required for all students whose intended major is art or art education. SAT or ACT scores are required (will accept either). A GPA of 2.0 is required. AP and CLEP credits are accepted. Important factors in the admissions decision are extracurricular activities record, leadership record, and advanced placement or honors courses.

Procedure: Freshmen are admitted fall, spring, and summer. Entrance exams should be taken in the spring of the junior year or early fall of the senior year. There are early admissions, deferred admissions, and rolling admissions plans. Applications should be filed by July 1 for fall entry; December 15 for spring entry, along with a $30 fee. Applications are accepted online.

Transfer: 140 transfer students enrolled in 2012-2013. Applicants with more than 12 academic college credits must have a minimum GPA of 2.0. Official transcripts from all colleges attended with a letter of recommendation is required. 45 of 120 credits required for the bachelor's degree must be completed at Keystone.

Visiting: There are regularly scheduled orientations for prospective students, consisting of 7 open houses and 3 visitation days. There are guides for informal visits, visitors may sit in on classes, and stay overnight. To schedule a visit, contact the Admissions Office.

Financial Aid: In 2013-2014, 94% of all full-time freshmen and 93% of continuing full-time students received some form of financial aid. 89% of all full-time freshmen and 89% of continuing full-time students received need-based aid. The average freshman award was $22,348. Need-based scholarships or need-based grants averaged $19,907; need-based self-help aid (loans and jobs) averaged $5,479; and other non-need-based awards and non-need-based scholarships averaged $8,000. 15% of undergraduate students work part-time. Average annual earnings from campus work are $1450. The average financial indebtedness of the 2013 graduate was $21,000. is a member of CSS. The FAFSA and the state aid form are required. The priority date for freshman financial aid applications for fall entry is April. The deadline for filing freshman financial aid applications for fall entry is May.

International Students: There are 13 international students enrolled. They must take the TOEFL with a minimum score of 550 on the paper-based TOEFL (PBT) or 80 on the Internet-based version (iBT) or take the MELAB and the college's own test.

Graduates: From July 1, 2012 to June 30, 2013, 251 bachelor's degrees

were awarded. The most popular majors were business (18%), education (13%), and criminal justice (12%). 20 companies recruited on campus in 2012-2013. In an average class, 24% graduate in 4 years or less, 7% graduate in 5 years or less, and 3% graduate in 6 years or less. Of the 2012 graduating class, 17% were enrolled in graduate school within 6 months of graduation, and 76% were employed.

Admissions Contact: Kathryn Reilly, Director of Admissions. E-Mail: *admissions@keystone.edu* Web: *www.keystone.edu*

KING'S COLLEGE E-2

Wilkes Barre, PA 18711 (570) 208-5858
(888) 546-4772; (570) 208-5971

Full-time: 1009 men, 916 women
Part-time: 93 men, 126 women
Graduate: 63 men, 184 women
Year: semesters, summer session
Application Deadline:
Freshman Class: 2967 applied, 2072 accepted, 514 enrolled
SAT CR/M/W: 519/528/511
Faculty: 132
Ph.D.s: 85%
Student/Faculty: 14 to 1
Tuition: $30,310
Room & Board: $11,368

COMPETITIVE

King's College, founded in 1946, is a private institution affiliated with the Roman Catholic Church. The college offers 35 undergraduate majors plus master's degree programs in health care administration, education with a concentration in reading, and curriculum and instruction. A 5-year physician assistant program is also offered. In addition, King's College offers a 3-2 engineering degree with the University of Notre Dame. There is one graduate school. In addition to regional accreditation, King's has baccalaureate program accreditation with AACSB and NCATE. The library contains 185,081 volumes, 579,953 microform items, 3,381 audio/video tapes/CDs/DVDs, and subscribes to 15,165 periodicals including electronic. Computerized library services include interlibrary loans, database searching, Internet access, and Wi-Fi capability. Special learning facilities include an art gallery, radio station, a TV studio. The 48-acre campus is in an urban area in northeastern Pennsylvania 19 miles south of Scranton. Including any residence halls, there are 29 buildings.

Student Life: 71% of undergraduates are from Pennsylvania. Others are from 18 states, and 4 foreign countries. 74% are from public schools. 80% are White. 56% are Catholic. The average age of freshmen is 18; all undergraduates, 20. 24% do not continue beyond their first year; 70% remain to graduate.

Housing: 1077 students can be accommodated in college housing, which includes single-sex and coed dorms and on-campus apartments. On-campus housing is guaranteed for all 4 years. 38% of students commute. All students may keep cars.

Activities: There are no fraternities or sororities. There are 50 groups on campus, including art, cheerleading, choir, chorale, chorus, computers, dance, drama, environmental, ethnic, film, honors, international, jazz band, literary magazine, musical theater, newspaper, pep band, photography, political, professional, radio and TV, religious, social, social service, student government, and yearbook. Popular campus events include All College Ball, Student Activities Fair and Spring Fling.

Sports: There are 10 intercollegiate sports for men and 9 for women, and 6 intramural sports for men and 6 for women. Facilities include a phys ed center, three multipurpose courts, a fitness center, a wrestling room, racquetball courts, a swimming pool, a multipurpose area, a 2800-seat gym, a free weight area, an outdoor athletic complex with a field house, a multipurpose turf for football, field hockey, soccer, and women's and men's lacrosse; and grass soccer and field hockey fields as well as baseball and softball fields.

Disabled Students: 99% of the campus is accessible. Facilities include wheelchair ramps, elevators, special parking, specially equipped restrooms, special class scheduling, lowered drinking fountains, lowered telephones, and special housing.

Services: Counseling and information services are available, as is tutoring in every subject. The academic skills center provides a writing center, learning skills workshops, a tutoring program, and learning disability services.

Campus Safety and Security: Measures include 24-hour foot and vehicle patrol, emergency notification system, self-defense education, and security escort services. There are shuttle buses, emergency telephones, lighted pathways/sidewalks, and controlled access to dorms/residences.

Programs of Study: King's confers B.A., and B.S. degrees. Associate and master's degrees are also awarded. Bachelor's degrees are awarded in AGRICULTURE (environmental studies), BIOLOGICAL SCIENCE (biology/biological science and neurosciences), BUSINESS (accounting, banking and finance, business administration and management, international business management, marketing/retailing/merchandising, and personnel management), COMMUNICATIONS AND THE ARTS (communications, dramatic arts, English, French, and Spanish), COMPUTER AND PHYSICAL SCIENCE (chemistry, computer science, information sciences and systems, mathematics, physics, and science), EDUCATION (early childhood education, elementary education, foreign languages education, middle school education, science education, secondary education, and special education), HEALTH PROFESSIONS (medical laboratory technology, physician's assistant, predentistry, premedicine, and sports medicine), SOCIAL SCIENCE (criminal justice, economics, history, philosophy, political science/government, prelaw, psychology, sociology, and theological studies). Accounting, English, and biology are the strongest academically. Physician assistant, biology, and accounting have the largest enrollments.

Required: All students must earn a minimum of 120 credits and maintain a GPA of 2.0. The core requirements represent between 52 and 59 credits. The major comprises a maximum of 60 credits, of which up to 40 can be specified in the major department, with the balance designated for related fields.

Special: Cross-registration with Wilkes University and College Misericordia are offered. The Experiential Learning Program provides internship opportunities in all majors with a variety of employers. King's also offers study-abroad through an agreement with Webster University and John Cabot University, a Washington semester, study-abroad programs in 30 countries, an accelerated degree program in health-care administration, B.A.-B.S. degrees in psychology, dual majors, credit for life experience, and pass/fail options on a few courses. Student-designed majors are available through the King's honors program. In addition, King's College offers a 3-2 engineering degree with the University of Notre Dame. There are 11 national honor societies and a freshman honors program.

Faculty/Classroom: 55% of faculty are male; 45% are female. 98% teach undergraduates. No introductory courses are taught by graduate students. The average class size in an introductory lecture is 20; in a laboratory is 14; and in a regular course is 17.

Admissions: 70% of the 2013-2014 applicants were accepted. The SAT scores for the 2013-2014 freshman class were: Critical Reading--38% below 500, 48% between 500 and 599, 13% between 600 and 699, and 1% between 700 and 800; Math--38% below 500, 48% between 500 and 599, 12% between 600 and 699, and 2% between 700 and 800; Writing--45% below 500, 42% between 500 and 599, 11% between 600 and 699, and 2% between 700 and 800. 33% of the current freshmen were in the top fifth of their class; 61% were in the top two fifths. 2 freshmen graduated first in their class.

Requirements: The SAT is recommended. King's requires 16 academic credits, although 24 are recommended, including 4 in English, 3 each in science, math, and social studies, and 2 in foreign language. A GPA of 2.0 is required. AP and CLEP credits are accepted. Important factors in the admissions decision are extracurricular activities record, recommendations by school officials, and leadership record.

Procedure: Freshmen are admitted fall, spring, and summer. Entrance exams should be taken so that scores are received by April 1. There are deferred admissions and rolling admissions plans. Application deadlines are open. Application fee is $30. Notification is sent on a rolling basis. Applications are accepted online.

Transfer: 71 transfer students enrolled in 2012-2013. Applicants must present a minimum GPA of 2.0 to 3.0. Students must have earned at least 12 credit hours at another college. An interview is recommended. 60 of 120 credits required for the bachelor's degree must be completed at King's.

Visiting: There are regularly scheduled orientations for prospective students, consisting of interviews, financial aid presentations, faculty one-on-one meetings, and campus tours. There are guides for informal visits, visitors may sit in on classes, and stay overnight. To schedule a visit, contact the Admissions Office.

Financial Aid: In 2013-2014, 99% of all full-time freshmen and 99% of continuing full-time students received some form of financial aid. 86% of all full-time freshmen and 84% of continuing full-time students received need-based aid. The average freshman award was $23,390. Need-based scholarships or need-based grants averaged $17,373 ($30,310 maximum); need-based self-help aid (loans and jobs) averaged $4,262 ($6,700 maximum); and other non-need-based awards and non-need-based scholarships averaged $10,653 ($30,310 maximum). 34% of undergraduate students work part-time. Average annual earnings from campus work are $1200. The average financial indebtedness of the 2013 graduate was $32,974. King's is a member of CSS. The FAFSA and the college's own financial statement are required. The priority date for freshman financial aid applications for fall entry is February 15.

International Students: There are 4 international students enrolled. The school actively recruits these students. They must take the TOEFL with a minimum score of 530 on the paper-based TOEFL (PBT) or 71 on the Internet-based version (iBT). They must also take the SAT or ACT.

Graduates: From July 1, 2012 to June 30, 2013, 429 bachelor's degrees were awarded. The most popular majors were accounting (10%), business administration (9%), and psychology (9%). 43 companies recruited on campus in 2012-2013. In an average class, 60% graduate in 4 years or less, 64% graduate in 5 years or less, and 66% graduate in 6 years or less. Of the 2012 graduating class, 30% were enrolled in graduate school within 6 months of graduation, and 59% were employed.

Admissions Contact: James Anderson, Director of Admissions. E-Mail: *admissions@kings.edu* Web: *www.kings.edu*

KUTZTOWN UNIVERSITY OF PENNSYLVANIA E-3

Kutztown, PA 19530 (610) 683-4060
(877) 628-1915; (610) 683-1375

Full-time: 3567 men, 4712 women	**Faculty:** 406; IIA, av$
Part-time: 262 men, 274 women	**Ph.D.s:** 82%
Graduate: 180 men, 518 women	**Student/Faculty:** 20 to 1
Year: semesters, summer session	**Tuition:** $8559 ($18,683)
Application Deadline: open	**Room & Board:** $8350

Freshman Class: 8533 applied, 6406 accepted, 1814 enrolled
SAT CR/M/W: 483/486/470 **ACT:** 20 **LESS COMPETITIVE**

Kutztown University of Pennsylvania, founded in 1866, is a public institution within the Pennsylvania State System of Higher Education. The university offers undergraduate programs in the arts and sciences, business, education, and visual and performing arts. There are 4 undergraduate schools and 1 graduate school. In addition to regional accreditation, KU has baccalaureate program accreditation with CSWE, NASAD, NASM, and NCATE. The library contains 401,094 volumes, 1.3 million microform items, 6,341 audio/video tapes/CDs/DVDs, and subscribes to 74,591 periodicals including electronic. Computerized library services include interlibrary loans, database searching, Internet access, and Wi-Fi capability. Special learning facilities include an art gallery, planetarium, radio station, TV station, a women's center, cartography lab, and German Cultural Heritage Center. The 289-acre campus is in a small town 90 miles north of Philadelphia, midway between Reading and Allentown. Including any residence halls, there are 66 buildings.

Student Life: 88% of undergraduates are from Pennsylvania. Others are from 23 states, 25 foreign countries, and Canada. 89% are from public schools. 81% are White. The average age of freshmen is 18; all undergraduates, 21. 27% do not continue beyond their first year; 55% remain to graduate.

Housing: 4500 students can be accommodated in college housing, which includes single-sex and coed dorms and on-campus apartments. In addition, there are honors houses and special-interest houses. On-campus housing is guaranteed for the freshman year only, is available on a first-come, and first-served basis. 56% of students commute. Alcohol is not permitted. All students may keep cars.

Activities: 6% of men belong to 13 national fraternities; 7% of women belong to 8 national sororities. There are 154 groups on campus, including programming board, art, band, cheerleading, chess, choir, chorus, communications, computers, dance, debate, drama, environmental, ethnic, film, gay, honors, international, jazz band, literary magazine, marching band, musical theater, newspaper, orchestra, photography, political, professional, radio and TV, recreational sports, religious, social, social service, student government, symphony, and yearbook. Popular campus events include Bearfest, Home Coming, and Family Day.

Sports: There are 15 intercollegiate sports for men and 17 for women, and 9 intramural sports for men and 9 for women. Facilities include a 5600-seat stadium and outdoor track, a 55,000-sq-ft field house and 200-meter indoor track, a swimming pool, 7 outdoor tennis courts, a 3400-seat arena, athletic fields, a street hockey rink, basketball courts, a rifle range, a fitness center, a free-weight room, and a 64,000-sq-ft student recreation center with fitness center/weight room, 2 fitness studios, 2 racquetball courts, indoor rock climbing wall, a 1 mile suspended jogging track, and locker rooms with Jacuzzis.

Disabled Students: 95% of the campus is accessible. Facilities include wheelchair ramps, elevators, special parking, specially equipped restrooms, special class scheduling, lowered drinking fountains, special housing. All programs are accessible to students with disabilities.

Services: Counseling and information services are available, as is tutoring in most subjects. There is a reader service for the blind, and remedial math, reading, and writing.

Campus Safety and Security: Measures include 24-hour foot and vehicle patrol, emergency notification system, self-defense education, and security escort services. There are shuttle buses, emergency telephones, lighted pathways/sidewalks, controlled access to dorms/residences, a bike patrol, crime prevention programs, automatic fire protection systems, door alarms, safety screens, and student monitors in the dorms.

Programs of Study: KU confers B.A., B.S., B.F.A., B.S.B.A, B.S.Ed., and B.S.W. degrees. Master's degrees are also awarded. Bachelor's degrees are awarded in BIOLOGICAL SCIENCE (biochemistry, biology/biological science, ecology, marine science, microbiology, and molecular biology), BUSINESS (accounting, banking and finance, business administration and management, business economics, international business management, marketing/retailing/merchandising, and recreation and leisure services), COMMUNICATIONS AND THE ARTS (ceramic art and design, crafts, dramatic arts, drawing, English, fiber/textiles/weaving, fine arts, French, German, graphic design, illustration, literature, music, musical theater, painting, photography, printmaking, sculpture, Spanish, speech/debate/rhetoric, studio art, telecommunications, and visual and performing arts), COMPUTER AND PHYSICAL SCIENCE (chemistry, computer science, environmental geology, geology, information sciences and systems, mathematics, physics, and software engineering), EDUCATION (art education, early childhood education, education of the mentally handicapped, education of the physically handicapped, education of the visually handicapped, elementary education, English education, foreign languages education, library science, mathematics education, psychology education, science education, secondary education, social science education, social studies education, special education, and speech correction), ENGINEERING AND ENVIRONMENTAL DESIGN (environmental science and pre-engineering), HEALTH PROFESSIONS (medical laboratory technology, medical technology, nursing, predentistry, premedicine, and speech pathology/audiology), SOCIAL SCIENCE (anthropology, clinical psychology, counseling/psychology, criminal justice, geography, history, industrial and organizational psychology, liberal arts/general studies, paralegal studies, philosophy, philosophy and religion, political science/government, psychology, public administration, social work, and sociology). Physical sciences and education is the strongest academically. Business administration, criminal justice, and leisure and sport studies have the largest enrollments.

Required: General education requirements vary by program, but all students must take phys ed, speech, and English composition. Distribution requirements also include courses in humanities, social sciences, natural sciences, and math. To graduate, students must complete at least 120 semester hours, including 33 to 80 in a major field, with a minimum GPA of 2.0. Students in the College of Liberal Arts and Sciences must take a comprehensive exam.

Special: Students may study abroad in 11 countries. KU offers internships, student-designed majors, dual majors, and a general studies degree. Non degree study is possible. Students may choose from more than 70 study abroad opportunities. Business students can take advantage of our exclusive exchange program with Reutlingen University in Germany. KU offers undergraduate research opportunities, where students conduct original research with members of our esteemed faculty, have the chance to present their findings at professional conferences, and may publish their findings in scholarly journals. KU is the only Pennsylvania state university to offer five-year BS/MS programs in Computer Science and a BSW/MSW program in Social Work. KU boasts one of the few Library Science and Special Education-Visually Impaired programs in the country. KU Electronic Media has earned six Emmy nominations for its productions in the Mid-Atlantic Region, and is the 2013 winner of a Crystal Pillar for Outstanding Achievement in College/University Student Production - Arts and Entertainment/Cultural Affairs. There are 10 national honor societies and a freshman honors program.

Faculty/Classroom: 54% of faculty are male; 46% are female. 98% teach undergraduates. No introductory courses are taught by graduate students. The average class size in an introductory lecture is 37; in a laboratory is 18; and in a regular course is 20.

Admissions: 75% of the 2013-2014 applicants were accepted. The SAT scores for the 2013-2014 freshman class were: Critical Reading--60% below 500, 35% between 500 and 599, and 5% between 600 and 699; Math--58% below 500, 34% between 500 and 599, 7% between 600 and 699, and 1% between 700 and 800; Writing--67% below 500, 29% between 500 and 599, and 4% between 600 and 699. The ACT scores were 58% below 21, 28% between 21 and 23, 10% between 24 and 26, 2% between 27 and 28, and 2% above 28. 14% of the current freshmen were in the top fifth of their class; 39% were in the top two fifths.

Requirements: The SAT or ACT is required. Applicants must be graduates of accredited secondary schools or have earned a GED. Recommended Carnegie units include 4 English, 3 mathematics, 3 social studies, and 3 science, of which at least 2 must be labs. SAT Subject tests in biology/chemistry are required for medical technology. Portfolios or auditions are required for art or music majors. AP and CLEP credits are accepted.

Procedure: Freshmen are admitted fall and spring. Entrance exams should be taken no later than fall of the senior year. There are early admissions, deferred admissions, and rolling admissions plans. Application deadlines are open. Application fee is $35. Notification is sent on a rolling basis. Applications are accepted online.

Transfer: 696 transfer students enrolled in 2012-2013. Applicants must present a GPA of 2.0 (3.0 for education) and official transcripts from all colleges and secondary schools previously attended. Students transferring fewer than 12 credit hours must also submit the SAT or ACT scores. 30 of 120 credits required for the bachelor's degree must be completed at Kutztown.

Visiting: There are regularly scheduled orientations for prospective students, consisting of daily visits, including group tours. There is a comprehensive summer orientation program for enrolling students. There are guides for informal visits and visitors may sit in on classes. To schedule a visit, contact the Admissions Office.

Financial Aid: In 2013-2014, 76% of all full-time freshmen and 72% of continuing full-time students received some form of financial aid. 66% of all full-time freshmen and 61% of continuing full-time students received need-based aid. The average freshman award was $7,426. Need-based scholarships or need-based grants averaged $5,767; need-based self-help aid (loans and jobs) averaged $3,421; non-need-based athletic scholarships averaged $1,989; and other non-need-based awards and non-need-based scholarships averaged $756. 18% of undergraduate students work part-time. Average annual earnings from campus work are $1209. The average financial indebtedness of the 2013 graduate was $32,901. The FAFSA is required. The priority date for freshman financial aid applications for fall entry is March 1.

International Students: There are 90 international students enrolled. They must take the TOEFL with a minimum score of 550 on the paper-based TOEFL (PBT) or 79 on the Internet-based version (iBT).

Graduates: From July 1, 2012 to June 30, 2013, 1795 bachelor's degrees were awarded. The most popular majors were business administration/management (8%), criminal justice (6%), and business administration/marketing (6%). 26 companies recruited on campus in 2012-2013. In an average class, 35% graduate in 4 years or less, 53% graduate in 5 years or less, and 55% graduate in 6 years or less. Of the 2012 graduating class, 19% were enrolled in graduate school within 6 months of graduation, and 57% were employed.

Admissions Contact: Nancy Wunderly, Director of Admissions. E-Mail: *admissions@kutztown.edu* Web: *www.kutztown.edu/admissions*

LA ROCHE COLLEGE — B-3

Pittsburgh, PA 15237 — (412) 536-1275; (800) 838-4LRC; (412) 847-1820

Full-time: 507 men, 623 women	**Faculty:** 60; IIA, --$
Part-time: 78 men, 155 women	**Ph.D.s:** 83%
Graduate: 31 men, 87 women	**Student/Faculty:** 13 to 1
Year: semesters, summer session	**Tuition:** $24,778
Application Deadline: open	**Room & Board:** $10,024
Freshman Class: 1488 applied, 828 accepted, 229 enrolled	
SAT CR/M/W: 460/480/430	**ACT:** 20 — **LESS COMPETITIVE**

La Roche College, founded in 1963, is a private Catholic institution offering undergraduate programs in arts and sciences, business, graphic and interior design, health science, nursing, professional training, and religious studies. There is one undergraduate school and 4 graduate schools. In addition to regional accreditation, La Roche has baccalaureate program accreditation with ACBSP, FIDER, NASAD, and NLN. The library contains 153,338 volumes, 87,229 microform items, 1,210 audio/video tapes/CDs/DVDs, and subscribes to 87,299 periodicals including electronic. Computerized library services include interlibrary loans, database searching, Internet access, and Wi-Fi capability. Special learning facilities include an art gallery, radio station, interior and graphic design studios. The 43-acre campus is in a suburban area 10 miles north of Pittsburgh. Including any residence halls, there are 11 buildings.

Student Life: 95% of undergraduates are from Pennsylvania. Others are from 18 states, 33 foreign countries, and Canada. 91% are from public schools. 65% are White; 13% Foreign; 13% race unknown. 64% claim no religious affiliation; 21% Catholic; 13% Protestant. The average age of freshmen is 19; all undergraduates, 23. 27% do not continue beyond their first year; 52% remain to graduate.

Housing: 569 students can be accommodated in college housing, which includes coed dorms. On-campus housing is guaranteed for all 4 years. 58% of students commute. Alcohol is not permitted. All students may keep cars.

Activities: There are no fraternities or sororities. There are 52 groups on campus, including art, cheerleading, chorus, computers, dance, drama, environmental, ethnic, honors, international, literary magazine, newspaper, photography, political, professional, radio and TV, religious, social, social service, and student government. Popular campus events include Gateway Clipper Cruise, and Globe Fashion Show.

Sports: There are 5 intercollegiate sports for men and 6 for women, and 10 intramural sports for men and 9 for women. Facilities include soccer, softball, and baseball fields, tennis courts, a fitness/sports center that houses a gym, an indoor track, an aerobics room, and a weight room, and a nearby county park with tennis courts and a swimming pool.

Disabled Students: All of the campus is accessible. Facilities include wheelchair ramps, elevators, special parking, specially equipped restrooms, special class scheduling, lowered drinking fountains, lowered telephones, and special housing.

Services: Counseling and information services are available, as is tutoring in every subject. There is a reader service for the blind, and remedial math and writing.

Campus Safety and Security: Measures include 24-hour foot and vehicle patrol, emergency notification system, and security escort services. There are shuttle buses, emergency telephones, lighted pathways/sidewalks, controlled access to dorms/residences, an intercom security system, and residence halls that are locked 24 hours a day.

Programs of Study: La Roche confers B.A., B.S., B.S.I.D. and B.S.N. degrees. Associate and master's degrees are also awarded. Bachelor's degrees are awarded in BIOLOGICAL SCIENCE (biology/biological science), BUSINESS (accounting, banking and finance, business administration and management, institutional management, international business management, marketing management, and real estate), COMMUNICATIONS AND THE ARTS (communications, creative writing, dance, English, graphic design, and Spanish), COMPUTER AND PHYSICAL SCIENCE (chemistry, computer science, information sciences and systems, and mathematics), EDUCATION (elementary education and English education), ENGINEERING AND ENVIRONMENTAL DESIGN (interior design), HEALTH PROFESSIONS (nursing, radiograph medical technology, and respiratory therapy), SOCIAL SCIENCE (criminal justice, history, human services, international relations, liberal arts/general studies, psychology, religion, religious education, safety and security technology, and sociology). Graphic design, interior design, and professional writing are the strongest academically. Psychology, criminal justice, and management have the largest enrollments.

Required: The La Roche Experience is composed of four 1-credit courses taken over four semesters. The course emphasizes the history of La Roche College and introduces students to issues in Diversity and Discrimination, Regions of Conflict, and Economic Justice. Twelve credits in basic skills areas, including English, math and computer applications. Twelve to fifteen credits in liberal arts areas, including history, science, religion or philosophy, aesthetics, literature, and social and cultural systems are required. A 6-credit sequence of 2 interdisciplinary courses. These courses emphasize the integration of knowledge and the interconnections between the local and the global. Students are required to take one Community course and one Global course

Special: There is cross-registration with members of the Pittsburgh Council of Higher Education. Internships, for which students may receive up to 6 credits, are available for juniors and seniors with numerous employers in the Pittsburgh area. La Roche also offers study abroad experiences at no cost after 60 credits, dual majors, credit for life experience, directed research, honors programs, independent study, and pass/fail options. Accelerated degrees may be earned in management, criminal justice, and nursing. A 3-2 engineering degree with the University of Pittsburgh is possible, as are cooperative programs in athletic training, physician's assistant, physical therapy, speech/language pathology, and occupational therapy with Duquesne University. There is a freshman honors program.

Faculty/Classroom: 45% of faculty are male; 55% are female. 93% teach undergraduates. No introductory courses are taught by graduate students. The average class size in an introductory lecture is 24; in a laboratory is 10; and in a regular course is 16.

Admissions: 56% of the 2013-2014 applicants were accepted. The SAT scores for the 2013-2014 freshman class were: Critical Reading--68% below 500, 26% between 500 and 599, 5% between 600 and 699, and 1% between 700 and 800; Math--63% below 500, 31% between 500 and 599, 6% between 600 and 699, Writing--79% below 500, 17% between 500 and 599, 4% between 600 and 699. The ACT scores were 55% below 21, 17% between 21 and 23, 18% between 24 and 26, 5% between 27 and 28, and 5% above 28. 18% of the current freshmen were in the top fifth of their class; 46% were in the top two fifths. 2 freshmen graduated first in their class.

Requirements: The SAT or ACT is required. Applicants must be graduates of accredited secondary schools or have earned a GED. An interview is recommended for all applicants. At least 2 letters of recommendation are required. A GPA of 2.0 is required. AP and CLEP credits are accepted. Important factors in the admissions decision are advanced placement or honors courses, personality/intangible qualities, and recommendations by school officials.

Procedure: Freshmen are admitted fall, spring, and summer. Entrance exams should be taken by the fall of the senior year. There are deferred admissions and rolling admissions plans. Application deadlines are open. Application fee is $50. Applications are accepted online.

Transfer: 167 transfer students enrolled in 2012-2013. Transfer design students must submit all post-secondary trancripts, have a 2.0 GPA, and may be required to submit a portfolio. 30 of 120 credits required for the bachelor's degree must be completed at La Roche.

Visiting: There are regularly scheduled orientations for prospective students, including an overnight stay, information and interactive sessions, class attendance, and meeting with faculty. There are also 1-day visits on Saturday. There are guides for informal visits, visitors may sit in on classes, and stay overnight. To schedule a visit, contact the Admissions Office.

Financial Aid: In 2013-2014, 70% of all full-time freshmen and 73% of continuing full-time students received some form of financial aid. 59% of all full-time freshmen and 55% of continuing full-time students received need-based aid. The average freshman award was $28,128. Need-based scholarships or need-based grants averaged $8,722; and need-based self-help aid (loans and jobs) averaged $7,529. 16% of undergraduate students work part-time. Average annual earnings from campus work are $1416. The average financial indebtedness of the 2013 graduate was $22,985. The FAFSA is required. The deadline for filing freshman financial aid applications for fall entry is May 1.

International Students: There are 174 international students enrolled. The school actively recruits these students. They must take the college's own test, or if their native language is English, they must take the SAT or ACT.

Graduates: From July 1, 2012 to June 30, 2013, 246 bachelor's degrees were awarded. The most popular majors were business (22%), medical imaging (11%), and psychology (9%). In an average class, 5% graduate in 3 years or less, 40% graduate in 4 years or less, 45% graduate in 5 years or less, and 48% graduate in 6 years or less.

Admissions Contact: Terry Kizina, Director of Admissions. E-Mail: *admissions@laroche.edu* Web: *www.laroche.edu*

LA SALLE UNIVERSITY F-3

Philadelphia, PA 19141 (215) 951-1500
(800) 328-1910; (215) 951-1656

Full-time: 1363 men, 2179 women
Part-time: 195 men, 672 women
Graduate: 620 men, 1419 women
Year: semesters, summer session
Application Deadline: April 1
Faculty: n/av; IIA, +$
Ph.D.s: 81%
Student/Faculty: 12 to 1
Tuition: $38,200
Room & Board: $12,070
Freshman Class: 5405 applied, 4370 accepted, 876 enrolled
SAT CR/M: 510/510 **ACT:** 21 **COMPETITIVE**

La Salle University is inspired by St. John Baptist de La Salle, the patron saint of teachers, and shaped by Lasallian and Catholic values. The La Salle University experience prepares students for a lifetime of personal development, service and success. La Salle University provides excellence in teaching and learning, personal attention, a sense of community and a global perspective. La Salle University puts theory into practice by guiding each student's intellectual and spiritual development. Thanks to a creative and practical education, La Salle University graduates go on to make a difference for the greater good. There are 4 undergraduate schools and 24 graduate schools. In addition to regional accreditation, La Salle has baccalaureate program accreditation with AACSB, CSWE, and NLN. The library contains 404,300 volumes, 9,350 microform items, 15,800 audio/video tapes/CDs/DVDs, and subscribes to 7,450 periodicals including electronic. Computerized library services include interlibrary loans, database searching, Internet access, and Wi-Fi capability. Special learning facilities include an art gallery, radio station, TV station, La Salle University Art Museum: a collection of European and American since the Middle Ages. In addition to paintings, the Museum has a collection of Old Master prints and drawings from the 19th and 20th centuries. Collections include: illustrated rare Bibles, Japanese prints, Indian miniatures, African tribal art, pre-Columbian pottery and ancient Greek cotta pottery. La Salle 56 is a cable television station housed in the University's Communication Center. The 133-acre campus is in an urban area 8 miles northwest of Center City, Philadelphia. Including any residence halls, there are 55 buildings.

Student Life: 67% of undergraduates are from Pennsylvania. Others are from 37 states, 29 foreign countries, and Canada. 50% are from public schools. 61% are White; 17% African American. 72% are Catholic; 21% Christian. The average age of freshmen is 18; all undergraduates, 21. 18% do not continue beyond their first year; 65% remain to graduate.

Housing: 2114 students can be accommodated in college housing, which includes single-sex and coed dorms and on-campus apartments. In addition, there are honors houses, special-interest houses, Townhouses - Owned and Operated by La Salle University. On-campus housing is guaranteed for all 4 years, is available on a first-come, first-served basis, and is available on a lottery system for upperclassmen. 55% of students live on campus; of those, 70% remain on campus on weekends. Upperclassmen may keep cars.

Activities: 6% of men belong to 1 local and 4 national fraternities; 18% of women belong to 1 local and 3 national sororities. There are 121 groups on campus, including art, band, cheerleading, choir, chorus, computers, dance, drama, drill team, environmental, ethnic, film, forensics, gay, honors, international, jazz band, literary magazine, musical theater, newspaper, orchestra, pep band, photography, political, professional, radio and TV, religious, social, social service, student government, and yearbook.

Sports: There are 9 intercollegiate sports for men and 13 for women, and 5 intramural sports for men and 4 for women. Facilities include a fitness center, a 4000-seat arena, a 6000-seat lighted stadium and track, swimming pool, wrestling rooms, sauna, and basketball, volleyball and tennis, and squash courts.

Disabled Students: 95% of the campus is accessible. Facilities include wheelchair ramps, elevators, special parking, specially equipped restrooms, special class scheduling, lowered drinking fountains, and special housing.

Services: Counseling and information services are available, as is tutoring in most subjects. There is a reader service for the blind, and remedial writing. A writing center is also available.

Campus Safety and Security: Measures include 24-hour foot and vehicle patrol, emergency notification system, and security escort services. There are shuttle buses, emergency telephones, lighted pathways/sidewalks, controlled access to dorms/residences, and magnetic card access to residence facilities.

Programs of Study: La Salle confers B.A., B.S., B.S.N. and B.S.W. degrees. Associate, master's, and doctoral degrees are also awarded. Bachelor's degrees are awarded in BIOLOGICAL SCIENCE (biochemistry, biology/biological science, and nutrition), BUSINESS (accounting, banking and finance, business administration and management, international economics, management information systems, marketing/retailing/merchandising, and organizational behavior), COMMUNICATIONS AND THE ARTS (classical languages, communications, English, fine arts, French, German, Italian, multimedia, music, Russian, and Spanish), COMPUTER AND PHYSICAL SCIENCE (chemistry, computer science, geology, information sciences and systems, mathematics, and science), EDUCATION (elementary education, foreign languages education, science education, secondary education, social studies education, and special education), ENGINEERING AND ENVIRONMENTAL DESIGN (computer graphics and environmental science), HEALTH PROFESSIONS (nursing, preallied health, predentistry, premedicine, and speech pathology/audiology), SOCIAL SCIENCE (criminal justice, economics, history, philosophy, political science/government, prelaw, psychology, public administration, religion, social work, and sociology). Accounting, education, speech-language and hearing, and biology are the strongest academically. Nursing, communication, and biology have the largest enrollments.

Required: All courses in the core may be counted towards any minor or major barring exclusions by the academic departments sponsoring the minor or major. To complete the core requirements, most School of Arts and Sciences majors must complete a maximum of 19 courses, School of Business Administration majors, a maximum of 16 courses, and School of Nursing majors, a maximum of 15 courses. A major feature of the Core is the Doubles program. All students will be required to enroll in a "Double" during the freshman year. Doubles are thematically linked core courses in different disciplines. In the Doubles program students will explore some or all of the topics in these courses under the guidance of two professors. A sense of academic and social community forms more readily in Doubles courses than in traditional courses because students take both courses with the same small group of students. The First Year Odyssey" refers to the one credit program which introduces students to La Salle University and the city of Philadelphia through activities such as field trips and campus wide programs. Students participate in the First Year Odyssey as part of designated courses or in special First Year Odyssey sections. "Understanding at Home and Abroad" refers to fostering the Christian Brothers' ideals of community, social justice, and compassionate understanding across barriers dividing human beings. Students are required to enroll in one course in the Academic Bulletin designated by the symbol of a "house" (H Understanding at Home) and one course designated by the symbol of a "plane" (Q Understanding Abroad). Some students may fulfill the Understanding at Home or Understanding Abroad requirement through an independent project with the approval of the Department Chair and the Core Director. Faculty and Staff will mentor a limited number of such projects.

Special: Cross-registration is offered in conjunction with Chestnut Hill College, and there is a 2-2 program in allied health with Thomas Jefferson University. La Salle also offers travel study courses, study abroad in Ireland, Austrailia, Rome, Mexico and more, co-op programs, work-study programs, internships in most majors, dual majors, an university-honors program for gifted students, as well as a business scholars co-op program. An integrated science, business, and technology program is offered. La Salle offers a 4-year BS/MBA in Accounting, a 5-year BA/BS/MS in Computer Science, a 5-year BA/MA in History, and a 5-year BS/MA in Speech Language Hearing Science. There are 16 national honor societies, including Phi Beta Kappa, a freshman honors program, and 2 departmental honors programs.

Faculty/Classroom: 47% of faculty are male; 53% are female. No introductory courses are taught by graduate students. The average class size in an introductory lecture is 23; in a laboratory is 14; and in a regular course is 19.

Admissions: 81% of the 2013-2014 applicants were accepted. The SAT scores for the 2013-2014 freshman class were: Critical Reading--41% below 500, 44% between 500 and 599, 13% between 600 and 699, and 2% between 700 and 800; Math--42% below 500, 40% between 500 and 599, 14% between 600 and 699, and 3% between 700 and 800. The ACT scores were 42% below 21, 31% between 21 and 23, 13% between 24 and 26, 7% between 27 and 28, and 7% above 28. 29% of the current freshmen were in the top fifth of their class; 59% were in the top two fifths. 8 freshmen graduated first in their class.

Requirements: The SAT is required. The ACT is recommended. In addition, the SAT: Subject Test in math is recommended. Applicants must be graduates of accredited secondary schools or have earned a GED. La Salle requires 16 academic units, based on 4 years of English, 3 of math, 2 of foreign language, and 1 of history, with the remaining 5 units in academic electives; science and math majors must have an additional one-half unit of math. An essay is required, and an interview is recommended. AP and CLEP credits are accepted. Important factors in the admissions decision are advanced placement or honors courses, leadership record, and recommendations by school officials.

Procedure: Freshmen are admitted fall and spring. Entrance exams should be taken before January of the senior year. There are early admissions, deferred admissions, and rolling admissions plans. Applications should be filed by April 1 for fall entry; December 15 for spring entry, along with a $35 fee. Notifications are sent December 15. Applications are accepted online.

Transfer: 148 transfer students enrolled in 2012-2013. Minimum cumulative GPA of 2.5 (2.75 preferred) required for consideration. Individual programs may have higher GPA requirements. Nursing program applicants must have minimum GPA of 3.0 as well as science GPA of 3.0. Education program applicants should have 3.0 cumulative GPA. Speech, Language and Hearing program applicants should have minimum cumulative GPA of 3.2 (3.4 preferred) for consideration. 50 of 120 credits required for the bachelor's degree must be completed at La Salle.

Visiting: There are regularly scheduled orientations for prospective students, Group Information Sessions and Tours are scheduled 5 days a week. Also, Open Houses in September, October, and February. There are guides for informal visits and visitors may sit in on classes. To schedule a visit, contact the Office of Undergraduate Admissions.

Financial Aid: In 2013-2014, 99% of all full-time freshmen and 96% of continuing full-time students received some form of financial aid. 85% of all full-time freshmen and 79% of continuing full-time students received need based aid. The average freshman award was $28,841. Need-based scholarships or need-based grants averaged $26,749 ($51,670 maximum); need-based self-help aid (loans and jobs) averaged $3,967 ($6,800 maximum); and non-need-based athletic scholarships averaged $16,610 ($50,270 maximum). 7% of undergraduate students work part-time. Average annual earnings from campus work are $4000. The average financial indebtedness of the 2013 graduate was $37,903. The FAFSA is required. The deadline for filing freshman financial aid applications for fall entry is February 15.

International Students: There are 75 international students enrolled. The school actively recruits these students. They must take the TOEFL with a minimum score of 540 on the paper-based TOEFL (PBT) or 80 on the Internet-based version (iBT).

Graduates: From July 1, 2012 to June 30, 2013, 822 bachelor's degrees were awarded. The most popular majors were nursing (27%), communication (8%), and marketing (7%). In an average class, 57% graduate in 4 years or less, 64% graduate in 5 years or less, and 65% graduate in 6 years or less.

Admissions Contact: James Plunkett, Executive Director of Admission. E-Mail: *admiss@lasalle.edu* Web: *www.lasalle.edu*

LAFAYETTE COLLEGE F-3

Easton, PA 18042 **(610) 330-5100; (610) 330-5355**

Full-time: 1297 men, 1138 women	**Faculty:** 221; IIB, +$
Part-time: 29 men, 22 women	**Ph.D.s:** 98%
Graduate: n/av	**Student/Faculty:** 10 to 1
Year: semesters, summer session	**Tuition:** $43,970
Application Deadline: January 15	**Room & Board:** $13,080
Freshman Class: 6766 applied, 2310 accepted, 635 enrolled	
SAT CR/M/W: 617/658/631	**ACT:** 28 **HIGHLY COMPETITIVE+**

Lafayette College, founded in 1826, is a highly selective private, exclusively undergraduate college, emphasizing the liberal arts, sciences, and engineering. In addition to regional accreditation, Lafayette has baccalaureate program accreditation with ABET. The 2 libraries contain 510,000 volumes, 120,000 microform items, and subscribe to 2,600 periodicals including electronic. Computerized library services include interlibrary loans, database searching, and Wi-Fi capability. Special learning facilities include an art gallery, radio station, a geological museum, foreign languages lab, and calculus lab. The 342-acre campus is in a suburban area 70 miles west of New York City. Including any residence halls, there are 81 buildings.

Student Life: 79% of undergraduates are from out of state, mostly the Middle Atlantic. Students are from 43 states, 42 foreign countries, and Canada. 82% are from public schools. 67% are White. 40% claim no religious affiliation; 30% Catholic; 19% Protestant. The average age of freshmen is 18; all undergraduates, 20. 9% do not continue beyond their first year; 88% remain to graduate.

Housing: 2308 students can be accommodated in college housing, which includes single-sex and coed dorms, on-campus apartments, and off-campus apartments. In addition, there are honors houses, special-interest houses, fraternity houses, sorority houses, diversity-oriented houses, arts houses, a black cultural center, and language and special-interest floors. On-campus housing is guaranteed for all 4 years. 92% of students live on campus; of those, 98% remain on campus on weekends. Upperclassmen may keep cars.

Activities: 18% of men belong to 4 national fraternities; 38% of women belong to 6 national sororities. There are 250 groups on campus, including art, band, cheerleading, chess, choir, chorale, chorus, computers, dance, debate, drama, environmental, ethnic, film, forensics, gay, honors, international, jazz band, literary magazine, musical theater, newspaper, orchestra, pep band, photography, political, professional, radio and TV, religious, social, social service, and student government. Popular campus events include 1,000 Nights, Block pARTy, Rivalry Week, All College Day, Earth Day, International Extravaganza, and Presidential Ball.

Sports: There are 11 intercollegiate sports for men and 11 for women, and 18 intramural sports for men and 18 for women. Facilities include an 14,000-seat stadium, sports center containing a 3500-seat gym, a field house, varsity house, a natatorium, fitness center, 2 exercise rooms, weight training room, outdoor track, indoor track, climbing wall, 6 racquet courts, and 3 multipurpose courts. In addition, there is a 230-acre athletic complex for lacrosse, field hockey, soccer, and baseball.

Disabled Students: 95% of the campus is accessible. Facilities include wheelchair ramps, elevators, special parking, specially equipped restrooms, special class scheduling, lowered drinking fountains, and lowered telephones.

Services: Counseling and information services are available, as is tutoring in most subjects, most 100-level and many 200-level classes.

Campus Safety and Security: Measures include 24-hour foot and vehicle patrol, emergency notification system, self-defense education, and security escort services. There are shuttle buses, emergency telephones, lighted pathways/sidewalks, controlled access to dorms/residences, advisers in all residence halls, residence hall lock down from 8 p.m. to 7 a.m.

Programs of Study: Lafayette confers A.B., and B.S. degrees. Bachelor's degrees are awarded in BIOLOGICAL SCIENCE (biochemistry, biology/biological science, and neurosciences), BUSINESS (business economics and international economics), COMMUNICATIONS AND THE ARTS (art, English, French, German, music, and Spanish), COMPUTER AND PHYSICAL SCIENCE (chemistry, computer science, geology, mathematics, and physics), ENGINEERING AND ENVIRONMENTAL DESIGN (chemical engineering, civil engineering, electrical/electronics engineering, engineering, and mechanical engineering), SOCIAL SCIENCE (African studies, American studies, anthropology, Asian/Oriental studies, economics, history, interdisciplinary studies, international relations, philosophy, political science/government, prelaw, psychology, religion, Russian and Slavic studies, and sociology). Engineering, psychology, English and natural sciences are the strongest academically. Economics, political science/government, mechanical engineering have the largest enrollments.

Required: To graduate, students must maintain a GPA of 2.0, and take a minimum of 32 to 36 courses (36 for engineering). The common course of study, designed to build a background in the liberal arts and sciences includes interdisciplinary seminars, a course in humanities, social science, natural science with a lab,and quantitative reasoning. Students must take 2 courses dealing with global and multicultural issues, and must demonstrate elementary proficiency in a foreign language (typically 2 courses). A Science and Technology in a Social Context requirement can be met by taking two classes designated as STSC outside of the student's home division. Finally, student must take one course that explores values in society and four writing intensive courses.

Special: Cross-registration is available through the Lehigh Valley Association of Independent Colleges, internships in all academic departments, study abroad in 3 countries as well as through other individually arranged plans, a Washington semester at American University, and work-study programs with area employers are possible. An accelerated degree plan in all majors, dual and student-designed majors, 5-year dual-degree programs, and pass/fail options in any non major subject also are available. There are 12 national honor societies, including Phi Beta Kappa, and 24 departmental honors programs.

Faculty/Classroom: 63% of faculty are male; 37% are female. All teach and do research. No introductory courses are taught by graduate students. The average class size in a laboratory is 12 and in a regular course is 17.

Admissions: 34% of the 2013-2014 applicants were accepted. The SAT scores for the 2013-2014 freshman class were: Critical Reading--6% below 500, 31% between 500 and 599, 48% between 600 and 699, and 15% between 700 and 800; Math--2% below 500, 18% between 500 and 599, 50% between 600 and 699, and 30% between 700 and 800; Writing--4% below 500, 25% between 500 and 599, 53% between 600 and 699, and 18% between 700 and 800. The ACT scores were 3% below 21, and 37% above 28. 89% of the current freshmen were in the top fifth of their class; 97% were in the top two fifths. There were 2 National Merit finalists. 16 freshmen graduated first in their class.

Requirements: The SAT or ACT is required. The ACT Optional Writing test is also required. Applicants should have taken 4 years of English, 3 of math (4 for science or engineering majors), 2 each of a foreign language and lab science (with physics and chemistry for science or engineering students), and at least an additional 5 units in academic subjects. An essay is required and an interview recommended. Evaluations from the secondary school counselor and a teacher are required. The GED is accepted. AP credits are accepted. Important factors in the admissions decision are advanced placement or honors courses, leadership record, evidence of special talent, extracurricular activities record, ability to finance college education, parents or siblings attended your school, personality/intangible qualities, and geographical diversity.

Procedure: Freshmen are admitted fall. Entrance exams should be taken

by January of the senior year. There are early decision, early admissions, and deferred admissions plans. Early decision applications should be filed by November 15; regular applications, by January 15 for fall entry, along with a $65 fee. Notification of early decision is sent December 15; regular decision, March 25. 304 early decision candidates were accepted for the 2013-2014 class. 459 applicants were on the 2013 waiting list; 23 were admitted. Applications are accepted online.

Transfer: 12 transfer students enrolled in 2012-2013. Acceptance usually depends on college-level performance and achievements. An interview is required if the student lives within 200 miles of the college. No minimum GPA is required, and neither the SAT nor the ACT is needed. The number of credit hours required varies with the program, but usually enough for freshman status with advanced standing is needed. Typically, Lafayette will enroll about 20 transfers in the fall and about 5 in the spring of each year. 16 of 32 credits required for the bachelor's degree must be completed at Lafayette.

Visiting: There are regularly scheduled orientations for prospective students, Student visits include student/faculty panel discussions, tours, and departmental open houses. There are guides for informal visits, visitors may sit in on classes, and stay overnight. To schedule a visit, contact Patricia Lorenz at (610) 330-5100.

Financial Aid: In 2013-2014, 62% of all full-time freshmen and 61% of continuing full-time students received some form of financial aid. 37% of all full-time freshmen and 40% of continuing full-time students received need-based aid. The average freshman award was $39,583. Need-based scholarships or need-based grants averaged $32,358 ($60,200 maximum); need-based self-help aid (loans and jobs) averaged $5,277 ($8,228 maximum); non-need-based athletic scholarships averaged $35,578 ($58,479 maximum); other non-need-based awards and non-need-based scholarships averaged $11,672 ($60,149 maximum); and $12,393 from other forms of aid. 46% of undergraduate students work part-time. Average annual earnings from campus work are $1543. The average financial indebtedness of the 2013 graduate was $25,281. Lafayette is a member of CSS. The CSS/Profile, FAFSA, and the college's own financial statement, and the Business/Farm supplement, and Divorce/Separation parent statement (if applicable) are required. are required. The priority date for freshman financial aid applications for fall entry is January 15. The deadline for filing freshman financial aid applications for fall entry is March 1.

International Students: There are 147 international students enrolled. The school actively recruits these students. They must take the TOEFL with a minimum score of 513 on the paper-based TOEFL (PBT) or 80 on the Internet-based version (iBT) and the Comprehensive English Language Test. They must also take the SAT or ACT.

Graduates: From July 1, 2012 to June 30, 2013, 589 bachelor's degrees were awarded. The most popular majors were social sciences (31%), engineering (21%), and biological life sciences (12%). 83 companies recruited on campus in 2012-2013. In an average class, 85% graduate in 4 years or less, 88% graduate in 5 years or less, and 88% graduate in 6 years or less. Of the 2012 graduating class, 22% were enrolled in graduate school within 6 months of graduation, and 72% were employed.

Admissions Contact: Matthew Hyde, Director of Admissions. E-Mail: *hydem@lafayette.edu* Web: *www.lafayette.edu*

LEBANON VALLEY COLLEGE — E-3

Annville, PA 17003-1400 — (717) 867-6181; (866) LVC-4ADM; (717) 867-6026

Full-time: 700 men, 885 women	**Faculty:** n/av; IIB, av$
Part-time: 65 men, 105 women	**Ph.D.s:** 88%
Graduate: 130 men, 175 women	**Student/Faculty:** n/av
Year: semesters, summer session	**Tuition:** $33,700
Application Deadline: see profile	**Room & Board:** $9300
Freshman Class: n/av	
SAT or ACT: required	

COMPETITIVE

Founded in 1866, Lebanon Valley College is a private institution that offers 34 major fields of study, where students can develop their own individualized major. Check with the school for current application deadlines. LVC offers graduate programs in physical therapy, business, music education, and science education. In addition to regional accreditation, LVC has baccalaureate program accreditation with NASM. The library contains 203,335 volumes, 15,485 microform items, 17,827 audio/video tapes/CDs/DVDs, and subscribes to 792 periodicals including electronic. Computerized library services include interlibrary loans, database searching, Internet access, and laptop Internet portals. Special learning facilities include a learning resource center, art gallery, and a radio station. The 340-acre campus is in a small town 6 miles east of Hershey, PA. Including any residence halls, there are 53 buildings The figures in the above capsule and in this profile are approximate.

Student Life: 80% of undergraduates are from Pennsylvania. Students are from 23 states, 3 foreign countries, and Canada. 94% are from public schools. 92% are white. The average age of freshmen is 18; all undergraduates, 20. 14% do not continue beyond their first year; 71% remain to graduate.

Housing: 1292 students can be accommodated in college housing, which includes single-sex and coed dorms and on-campus apartments. In addition, there are special-interest houses. On-campus housing is guaranteed for all 4 years. 74% of students live on campus; of those, 60% remain on campus on weekends. All students may keep cars.

Activities: 9% of men belong to 2 local and 2 national fraternities; 9% of women belong to 1 local and 3 national sororities. There are 85 groups on campus, including music ensembles, art, band, cheerleading, choir, chorus, concert band, drama, ethnic, gay, honors, international, jazz band, literary magazine, marching band, musical threater, newspaper, orchestra, political, professional, radio and TV, religious, social, social service, student government, and symphony. Popular campus events include Christmas at the Valley, Valley Festival, and Dutchmen Day.

Sports: There are 12 intercollegiate sports for men and 11 for women, and 12 intramural sports for men and 12 for women. Facilities include a 3000-seat stadium, a sports center, more than 60 acres of athletic fields, indoor and outdoor tracks, a 1660 seat gym, playing courts for basketball, handball, squash, and tennis, a 500-seat baseball grandstand, and a football field.

Disabled Students: 80% of the campus is accessible. Facilities include wheelchair ramps, elevators, special parking, specially equipped rest rooms, special class scheduling, lowered drinking fountains, lowered telephones, and special housing.

Services: Counseling and information services are available, as is tutoring in every subject. There is a reader service for the blind.

Campus Safety and Security: Measures include 24-hour foot and vehicle patrol, self-defense education, and security escort services. There are emergency telephones and lighted pathways/sidewalks.

Programs of Study: LVC confers B.A., B.S., B.M., B.S.Ch., and B.S.Med.Tech. degrees. Associates, master's, and doctoral degrees are also awarded. Bachelor's degrees are awarded in BIOLOGICAL SCIENCE (biochemistry and biology/biological science), BUSINESS (accounting and business administration and management), COMMUNICATIONS AND THE ARTS (art, audio technology, communications technology, English, French, German, music, music business management, and Spanish), COMPUTER AND PHYSICAL SCIENCE (actuarial science, chemistry, computer science, mathematics, and physics), EDUCATION (early childhood education, elementary education, music education, and special education), HEALTH PROFESSIONS (health, health care administration, and medical laboratory technology), SOCIAL SCIENCE (American studies, criminal justice, economics, history, philosophy, political science/government, psychobiology, psychology, religion, and sociology). Actuarial science, natural sciences, and education are the strongest academically. Education, business, and natural sciences have the largest enrollments.

Required: The general education program consists of course work in these areas: communications, liberal studies, foreign studies, social diversity studies, and disciplinary perspectives. Students are required to complete 3 writing process courses, and be proficient in computer applications and modes of information access and retrieval. To graduate, students must complete at least 120 credit hours, 2 units of phys ed, and the requirements for the major with a minimum cumulative GPA of 2.0.

Special: Study abroad opportunities are available in Argentina, Australia, England, France, Italy, Germany, Greece, Sweden, Spain, the Netherlands, and New Zealand. There are also 2 off-campus domestic programs in Philadelphia and Washington, D.C. There are 3-2 degree programs in engineering with Penn State University and Case Western Reserve, and in forestry with Duke University. There is also a 2-2 degree program in allied health sciences with Thomas Jefferson University. LVC offers internships in a number of areas. There are 6 national honor societies and 11 departmental honors programs.

Faculty/Classroom: 63% of faculty are male; 37% are female. 90% teach undergraduates. No introductory courses are taught by graduate students. The average class size in an introductory lecture is 23; in a laboratory is 14; and in a regular course is 19.

Requirements: The SAT is required. The ACT Optional Writing test is also required. Applicants must be graduates of an accredited secondary school or have earned a GED. LVC requires 16 academic units or 16 Carnegie units, including 4 in English, 2 each in math and foreign language, and 1 each in science and social studies. An interview is recommended. Students applying as music majors must audition. AP and CLEP credits are accepted. Important factors in the admissions decision are advanced placement or honors courses, leadership record, and personality/intangible qualities.

Procedure: Freshmen are admitted fall and spring. Entrance exams should be taken optional. There is a rolling admissions plan. Application deadlines are open. Application fee is $30. Notifications are sent October 15. Applications are accepted online.

Transfer: 49 transfer students enrolled in a recent year. Requirements for transfer applicants include a minimum GPA of 2.0, SAT scores, and an interview. 30 of 120 credits required for the bachelor's degree must be completed at LVC.

Visiting: There are regularly scheduled orientations for prospective stu-

dents, and visiting students can take tours, and schedule interviews and meetings with professors. There are guides for informal visits and visitors may sit in on classes. To schedule a visit, contact the Director of Admission.

Financial Aid: In a recent year, 99% of all full-time freshmen and 98% of continuing full-time students received some form of financial aid. 85% of all full-time freshmen and 80% of continuing full-time students received need-based aid. The average freshmen award was $24,801, with $20,015 ($22,945 maximum) from need-based scholarships or need-based grants; $5,597 ($9,250 maximum) from need-based self-help aid (loans and jobs); and $12,684 ($29,780 maximum) from other non-need-based awards and non-need-based scholarships. 48% of undergraduate students worked part-time. Average annual earnings from campus work were $1071. LVC is a member of CSS. The FAFSA and the college's own financial statement are required. Check with school for current application deadlines.

International Students: There were 9 international students enrolled in a recent year They must take the TOEFL with a minimum score of 550 on the paper-based TOEFL (PBT) or 80 on the Internet-based version (iBT).

Graduates: In a recent year, 424 bachelor's degrees were awarded. The most popular majors were education (17%), business administration (14%), and social science (11%). 65 companies recruited on campus in a recent year. In an average class, 68% graduate in 4 years or less, 75% graduate in 5 years or less, and 76% graduate in 6 years or less. Of a recent graduating class, 26% were enrolled in graduate school within 6 months of graduation, and 82% were employed.

Admissions Contact: Susan Jones, Director of Admission. E-Mail: *admission@lvc.edu* Web: *www.lvc.edu*

LEHIGH UNIVERSITY F-3

Bethlehem, PA 18015 **(610) 758-3100; (610) 758-4361**

Full-time: 2724 men, 2138 women	**Faculty:** 432
Part-time: 49 men, 20 women	**Ph.D.s:** 97%
Graduate: 1165 men, 1000 women	**Student/Faculty:** 10 to 1
Year: semesters, summer session	**Tuition:** $43,520
Application Deadline: January 1	**Room & Board:** $11,560
Freshman Class: 12589 applied, 3882 accepted, 1198 enrolled	
SAT CR/M: 630/690	**ACT:** 30 **MOST COMPETITIVE**

Lehigh University, founded in 1865, is a private research university offering both undergraduate and graduate programs in liberal arts, sciences, business, education, and engineering. Our students experience interesting, independent research, and work closely with faculty who offer their time and attention on hands-on projects, internships, and innovative studies. There are 3 undergraduate schools and 4 graduate schools. In addition to regional accreditation, Lehigh has baccalaureate program accreditation with AACSB, ABET, and NCATE. The 2 libraries contain 1.2 million volumes, 1.7 million microform items, 15,455 audio/video tapes/CDs/DVDs, and subscribe to 19,752 periodicals including electronic. Computerized library services include interlibrary loans, database searching, Internet access, and Wi-Fi capability. Special learning facilities include an art gallery, radio and TV station, special collections/rare book reading room, digital media studio, financial services lab, and international multimedia resource center. The 1600-acre campus is in a suburban area 50 miles north of Philadelphia and 75 miles southwest of New York City. Including any residence halls, there are 161 buildings.

Student Life: 74% of undergraduates are from out of state, mostly the Middle Atlantic. Students are from 50 states, 58 foreign countries, and Canada. 69% are White. The average age of freshmen is 18; all undergraduates, 20. 6% do not continue beyond their first year; 86% remain to graduate.

Housing: 2541 students can be accommodated in college housing, which includes coed dorms, on-campus apartments, and married student housing. In addition, there are special-interest houses, fraternity houses, sorority houses, substance free housing, UMOJA house, and an ROTC house. On-campus housing is guaranteed for the freshman year only, is available on a first-come, first-served basis, and is available on a lottery system for upperclassmen. 68% of students live on campus; of those, 85% remain on campus on weekends. Upperclassmen may keep cars.

Activities: 40% of men belong to 20 national fraternities; 43% of women belong to 10 national sororities. There are 150 groups on campus, including art, band, cheerleading, chess, choir, chorale, chorus, computers, dance, debate, drama, environmental, ethnic, gay, honors, international, jazz band, literary magazine, marching band, musical theater, newspaper, orchestra, pep band, photography, political, professional, radio and TV, religious, social, social service, student government, symphony, and yearbook. Popular campus events include Greek Week, Spring Fling and International Week.

Sports: There are 12 intercollegiate sports for men and 13 for women, and 14 intramural sports for men and 14 for women. Facilities include a 16,000-seat stadium, a 6500-seat arena, a gym, a champion cross-country course, a field house with basketball and tennis courts, swimming pools, a track, indoor squash and racquetball courts, playing fields including astroturf for field hockey, football, lacrosse, and soccer, weight rooms, a fitness center, climbing wall, indoor tennis center, golf range (driving/chipping/putting).

Disabled Students: Facilities include wheelchair ramps, elevators, special parking, specially equipped restrooms, special class scheduling, lowered drinking fountains, lowered telephones, and special housing.

Services: Counseling and information services are available, as is tutoring in most subjects, calculus, physics, English, accounting, finance, and economics. There is a reader service for the blind. Tutoring is available upon request. Also, there are special programs for students with learning disabilities and English as a Second Language.

Campus Safety and Security: Measures include 24-hour foot and vehicle patrol, emergency notification system, self-defense education, and security escort services. There are shuttle buses, emergency telephones, lighted pathways/sidewalks, controlled access to dorms/residences, LU-alert text messaging system.

Programs of Study: Lehigh confers B.A., and B.S. degrees. Master's and doctoral degrees are also awarded. Bachelor's degrees are awarded in AGRICULTURE (environmental studies), BIOLOGICAL SCIENCE (biochemistry, biology/biological science, and molecular biology), BUSINESS (accounting, business economics, business information systems, finance, marketing management, and supply chain management), COMMUNICATIONS AND THE ARTS (art, art history and appreciation, Chinese, classics, design, English, French, German, journalism, music, music theory and composition, Spanish, and theater design), COMPUTER AND PHYSICAL SCIENCE (applied science, astronomy, astrophysics, chemistry, computer science, earth science, mathematics, physics, science technology, and statistics), ENGINEERING AND ENVIRONMENTAL DESIGN (architecture, bioengineering, chemical engineering, civil engineering, computer engineering, electrical/electronics engineering, engineering mechanics, engineering physics, environmental engineering, environmental science, industrial engineering, materials science and engineering, and mechanical engineering), HEALTH PROFESSIONS (pharmaceutical chemistry, predentistry, premedicine, and preoptometry), SOCIAL SCIENCE (African studies, anthropology, Asian/Oriental studies, behavioral science, classical/ancient civilization, cognitive science, economics, (Social Science) Global Studies, history, international relations, philosophy, political science/government, psychology, religion, social psychology, sociology, and women's studies). Finance, mechanical engineering, accounting have the largest enrollments.

Required: Graduation requirements vary by degree sought, but all students must complete 2 semesters of English, at least 30 credits in the chosen major, and a minimum of 121 credit hours. Students must also maintain a minimum GPA of 2.0.

Special: Lehigh offers many interdisciplinary programs including Integrated Product Development, Computer Science and Business, Integrated Business and Engineering, Integrated Degree in Engineering, Arts and Sciences, Global Citizenship, Lehigh Earth Observatory, and South Mountain College, Lehigh's residential academic program. The university offers co-op programs, cross-registration with the Lehigh Valley Association of Independent Colleges, many combinations of dual majors, study abroad programs in 40 countries, internships, a Washington semester, work-study, a 7-year BA/MD program with Drexel University College of Medicine, a 7-year BA/OD program with SUNY Optometry and a 7-year BA/DMD program with the School of Dental Medicine at the University of Pennsylvania. There are 18 national honor societies, including Phi Beta Kappa, and a freshman honors program.

Faculty/Classroom: 65% of faculty are male; 35% are female. All teach and do research. No introductory courses are taught by graduate students. The average class size in a regular course is 28.

Admissions: 31% of the 2013-2014 applicants were accepted. The SAT scores for the 2013-2014 freshman class were: Critical Reading--5% below 500, 28% between 500 and 599, 50% between 600 and 699, and 17% between 700 and 800; Math--9% between 500 and 599, 46% between 600 and 699, and 45% between 700 and 800. 84% of the current freshmen were in the top fifth of their class; 96% were in the top two fifths. 25 freshmen graduated first in their class.

Requirements: The SAT or ACT is required. The ACT Optional Writing test is also required. Candidates for admission should have completed 4 years of English, 3 years of math and electives, and 2 years each of a foreign language, science, and social science. Most students present 4 years each of science, math, and English. Opportunities for an on-campus interview are made available to prospective students but are not required. Interviews are by appointment only. AP credits are accepted. Important factors in the admissions decision are advanced placement or honors courses, recommendations by school officials, evidence of special talent, and extracurricular activities record.

Procedure: Freshmen are admitted fall and spring. Entrance exams should be taken by the January test date. There are early decision, early admissions, and deferred admissions plans. Early decision applications should be filed by November 15; regular applications, by January 1 for fall entry; and November 1 for spring entry. The fall 2013 application fee was $70. Notification of early decision is sent December 15; regular decision,

April 1. 552 early decision candidates were accepted for the 2013-2014 class. 1250 applicants were on the 2013 waiting list; 39 were admitted. Applications are accepted online.

Transfer: 51 transfer students enrolled in 2012-2013. Transfer candidates should have a minimum GPA of 3.25 and submit high school and college transcripts, an essay, and a statement of good standing from previous institutions. 30 of 121 credits required for the bachelor's degree must be completed at Lehigh.

Visiting: There are regularly scheduled orientations for prospective students, Including group information sessions and tours scheduled Monday through Friday, and some Saturdays, as well as special events and open houses. There are guides for informal visits, visitors may sit in on classes, and stay overnight. To schedule a visit, contact the Office of Admissions.

Financial Aid: In 2013-2014, 41% of all full-time freshmen and 42% of continuing full-time students received some form of financial aid. 41% of all full-time freshmen and 41% of continuing full-time students received need-based aid. The average freshman award was $35,666. Need-based scholarships or need-based grants averaged $30,762; need-based self-help aid (loans and jobs) averaged $5,017 ($7,200 maximum); non-need-based athletic scholarships averaged $35,500 ($54,780 maximum); and other non-need-based awards and non-need-based scholarships averaged $13,876 ($43,220 maximum). 31% of undergraduate students work part-time. Average annual earnings from campus work are $1218. The average financial indebtedness of the 2013 graduate was $33,309. Lehigh is a member of CSS. The CSS/Profile, FAFSA, and the college's own financial statement, and noncustodial profile, and business/farm supplement are required. The deadline for filing freshman financial aid applications for fall entry is February 15.

International Students: There are 334 international students enrolled. The school actively recruits these students. They must take the TOEFL with a minimum score of 570 on the paper-based TOEFL (PBT) or 90 on the Internet-based version (iBT). They must also take the SAT or ACT.

Graduates: From July 1, 2012 to June 30, 2013, 1177 bachelor's degrees were awarded. The most popular majors were finance (12%), mechanical engineering (10%), and accounting (6%). 202 companies recruited on campus in 2012-2013. In an average class, 2% graduate in 3 years or less, 73% graduate in 4 years or less, 84% graduate in 5 years or less, and 86% graduate in 6 years or less. Of the 2012 graduating class, 30% were enrolled in graduate school within 6 months of graduation, and 63% were employed.

Admissions Contact: Bruce Bunnick, Director of Admissions. E-Mail: *admissions@lehigh.edu* Web: *www.lehigh.edu*

LOCK HAVEN UNIVERSITY OF PENNSYLVANIA D-2

Lock Haven, PA 17745 (570) 484-2544
(800) 233-8978; (570) 484-2201

Full-time: 1994 men, 2513 women	**Faculty:** 245; IIB, +$
Part-time: 102 men, 234 women	**Ph.D.s:** 71%
Graduate: 110 men, 295 women	**Student/Faculty:** 21 to 1
Year: semesters, summer session	**Tuition:** $8899 ($16,833)
Application Deadline: open	**Room & Board:** $8688
Freshman Class: 3849 applied, 3311 accepted, 1086 enrolled	
SAT CR/M/W: 472/480/456	**ACT:** 20 **LESS COMPETITIVE**

Lock Haven University, established in 1870, is a public institution offering undergraduate degrees in arts and sciences, education, and human services. The university maintains a branch campus in Clearfield. There are 2 undergraduate schools and one graduate school. In addition to regional accreditation, LHU has baccalaureate program accreditation with ABET, CSWE, NCATE, NLN, and NRPA. Computerized library services include interlibrary loans, database searching, Internet access, and Wi-Fi capability. Special learning facilities include an art gallery, planetarium, radio and TV station. The 135-acre campus is in a rural area 30 miles west of Williamsport.

Student Life: 92% of undergraduates are from Pennsylvania. Others are from 36 states, 23 foreign countries, and Canada. 87% are White. The average age of freshmen is 19; all undergraduates, 21. 30% do not continue beyond their first year; 51% remain to graduate.

Housing: 1898 students can be accommodated in college housing, which includes single-sex and coed dorms and off-campus apartments. On-campus housing is guaranteed for the freshman year only and is available on a lottery system for upperclassmen. 60% of students commute. Alcohol is not permitted. All students may keep cars.

Activities: 3% of men belong to 6 national fraternities; 4% of women belong to 4 national sororities. There are 100 groups on campus, including art, band, cheerleading, chess, choir, chorale, chorus, computers, dance, drama, environmental, ethnic, film, forensics, gay, honors, international, jazz band, literary magazine, marching band, musical theater, newspaper, orchestra, pep band, photography, political, professional, radio and TV, religious, social, social service, student government, symphony, and yearbook. Popular campus events include Family Day, Alcohol Awareness Week, and Spring Carnival.

Sports: There are 8 intercollegiate sports for men and 10 for women. Facilities include a 5,000-seat stadium containing a football field and an all-weather track, a 2,500-seat field house with a wrestling room, a recreation facility, a gym used for intramurals and weight training, and a gym that houses a swimming pool.

Disabled Students: 95% of the campus is accessible. Facilities include wheelchair ramps, elevators, special parking, specially equipped restrooms, special class scheduling, lowered drinking fountains, lowered telephones, and special housing.

Services: Counseling and information services are available, as is tutoring in most subjects. There is a reader service for the blind, and remedial math, reading, and writing. Reader services for the blind can be arranged. There are also writing and math centers.

Campus Safety and Security: Measures include 24-hour foot and vehicle patrol, emergency notification system, and security escort services. There are shuttle buses, emergency telephones, and lighted pathways/sidewalks.

Programs of Study: LHU confers B.A., B.S., B.F.A. and B.S.Ed. degrees. Associate and master's degrees are also awarded. Bachelor's degrees are awarded in BIOLOGICAL SCIENCE (biology/biological science and environmental biology), BUSINESS (business administration and management), COMMUNICATIONS AND THE ARTS (communications, English, fine arts, French, German, journalism, music, Spanish, and speech/debate/rhetoric), COMPUTER AND PHYSICAL SCIENCE (chemistry, computer science, earth science, geology, information sciences and systems, mathematics, and physics), EDUCATION (early childhood education, elementary education, foreign languages education, physical education, science education, secondary education, and special education), HEALTH PROFESSIONS (health science and medical laboratory technology), SOCIAL SCIENCE (criminal justice, economics, geography, history, humanities and social science, international studies, Latin American studies, liberal arts/general studies, paralegal studies, philosophy, political science/government, psychology, social science, social work, and sociology). Health science and biological sciences is the strongest academically. Health science and criminal justice has the largest enrollments.

Required: To graduate, students must complete 60 hours of general education, including 12 in humanities and in social and behavioral sciences, 9 in skills core, 6 in science, 3 in wellness core, and the rest in electives. A total of 120 credit hours is required, including 61 to 68 in the major, with a minimum GPA of 2.0.

Special: There are cooperative programs in music education and engineering, including a 3-2 engineering degree with Pennsylvania State University. Lock Haven also offers study-abroad programs in more than 20 countries, a dual major in education, work-study options, an accelerated degree program for honor students, a student-designed general studies major, and internships, which are required in some majors. Pass/fail grading options are limited to 1 course outside the major per semester, not to exceed 12 credit hours. There are 11 national honor societies and a freshman honors program.

Faculty/Classroom: 52% of faculty are male; 48% are female. All teach undergraduates. No introductory courses are taught by graduate students. The average class size in an introductory lecture is 35 and in a regular course is 25.

Admissions: 86% of the 2013-2014 applicants were accepted. The SAT scores for the 2013-2014 freshman class were: Critical Reading--66% below 500, 29% between 500 and 599, 4% between 600 and 699, and 1% between 700 and 800; Math--60% below 500, 33% between 500 and 599, and 7% between 600 and 699; Writing--74% below 500, 22% between 500 and 599,and 4% between 600 and 699. The ACT scores were 54% below 21, 22% between 21 and 23, 12% between 24 and 26, 4% between 27 and 28, and 8% above 28. 18% of the current freshmen were in the top fifth of their class; 47% were in the top two-fifths.

Requirements: The SAT is required. Applicants must graduate from an accredited secondary school or have a GED. 16 academic credits are required, and a college preparatory course is recommended. AP and CLEP credits are accepted. Important factors in the admissions decision are evidence of special talent and extracurricular activities record.

Procedure: Freshmen are admitted to all sessions. Entrance exams should be taken during the spring of the junior year and the fall of the senior year. There are deferred admissions and rolling admissions plans. Application deadlines are open. Application fee is $25. Applications are accepted online.

Transfer: 192 transfer students enrolled in 2012-2013. Priority is given to applicants who have completed 24 or more transferable credits. A minimum GPA of 2.0 is required. 30 of 120 credits required for the bachelor's degree must be completed at LHU.

Visiting: There are regularly scheduled orientations for prospective students, consisting of an introduction to the administration, sessions with faculty, and an information arena/departmental showcase; small group visits are also scheduled. There are guides for informal visits and visitors may sit in on classes. To schedule a visit, contact the Admissions Office.

Financial Aid: The FAFSA, and PHEAA is required. Check with the school for current application deadlines.

International Students: There are 40 international students enrolled. The school actively recruits these students. They must take the TOEFL.

Graduates: From July 1, 2012 to June 30, 2013, 1026 bachelor's degrees were awarded. The most popular majors were health science (10%), criminal justice (9%), and business administration (7%). In an average class, 28% graduate in 4 years or less, 46% graduate in 5 years or less, and 50% graduate in 6 years or less. Of the 2012 graduating class, 15% were enrolled in graduate school within 6 months of graduation, and 79% were employed.

Admissions Contact: Robin Rocky, Int. Director of Admissions. E-Mail: *rrocky@lhup.edu* Web: *www.lhup.edu*

LYCOMING COLLEGE D-2

Williamsport, PA 17701 (570) 321-4026
(800) 345-3920; (570) 321-4317

Full-time: 566 men, 724 women	**Faculty:** 81
Part-time: 6 men, 11 women	**Ph.D.s:** 94%
Graduate: n/av	**Student/Faculty:** 14 to 1
Year: semesters, summer session	**Tuition:** $33,746
Application Deadline: March 1	**Room & Board:** $9890
Freshman Class: 1737 applied, 1244 accepted, 347 enrolled	
SAT CR/M/W: 520/520/490 **ACT:** 22	**COMPETITIVE**

Lycoming College, established in 1812, is a private, residential, liberal arts institution affiliated with the United Methodist Church. In addition to regional accreditation, Lycoming has baccalaureate program accreditation with AACSB. The library contains 252,483 volumes, 198,862 microform items, 995 audio/video tapes/CDs/DVDs, and subscribes to 50,100 periodicals including electronic. Computerized library services include interlibrary loans, database searching, Internet access, and Wi-Fi capability. Special learning facilities include an art gallery, planetarium, radio station, and TV station. The 35-acre campus is in a small town in north central Pennsylvania. Including any residence halls, there are 25 buildings.

Student Life: 66% of undergraduates are from Pennsylvania. Others are from 29 states, and 11 foreign countries. 81% are from public schools. 78% are White. 24% are Protestant; 20% Catholic. The average age of freshmen is 18; all undergraduates, 20. 21% do not continue beyond their first year; 65% remain to graduate.

Housing: 1213 students can be accommodated in college housing, which includes single-sex and coed dorms, on-campus apartments, and off-campus apartments. In addition, there are language houses, special-interest houses, and nonsmoking, intensive study, and Greek floors. On-campus housing is guaranteed for all 4 years. 87% of students live on campus; of those, 67% remain on campus on weekends. All students may keep cars.

Activities: 16% of men belong to 5 national fraternities; 21% of women belong to 3 local and 2 national sororities. There are 62 groups on campus, including art, band, cheerleading, choir, chorus, computers, dance, drama, environmental, ethnic, film, gay, honors, international, jazz band, literary magazine, musical theater, newspaper, pep band, photography, political, professional, radio and TV, religious, social, social service, student government, and yearbook. Popular campus events include Campus Carnival, Annual Christmas Candlelight Service and Choir Concert.

Sports: There are 9 intercollegiate sports for men and 8 for women, and 7 intramural sports for men and 5 for women. Facilities include an outdoor softball, football, soccer, and lacrosse complex, indoor basketball courts, weight and exercise rooms, indoor pool, and intramural fields.

Disabled Students: 85% of the campus is accessible. Facilities include wheelchair ramps, elevators, special parking, specially equipped restrooms, special class scheduling, lowered drinking fountains, lowered telephones, and special housing.

Services: Counseling and information services are available, as is tutoring in every subject. There is remedial math, reading, and writing.

Campus Safety and Security: Measures include 24-hour foot and vehicle patrol, emergency notification system, self-defense education, and security escort services. There are emergency telephones and lighted pathways/sidewalks.

Programs of Study: Lycoming confers B.A., and B.S. degrees. Bachelor's degrees are awarded in BIOLOGICAL SCIENCE (biology/biological science), BUSINESS (accounting and business administration and management), COMMUNICATIONS AND THE ARTS (art, art history and appreciation, communications, digital communications, dramatic arts, English, French, German, literature, music, Spanish, and studio art), COMPUTER AND PHYSICAL SCIENCE (actuarial mathematics, astronomy, astrophysics, chemistry, mathematics, and physics), SOCIAL SCIENCE (American studies, anthropology, archeology, criminal justice, criminology, economics, history, international studies, philosophy, political science/government, psychology, religion, sociology, and women & gender studies). Archaeology, creative writing, astrophysics, business, biology/environmental studies and chemistry are the strongest academically. Business, psychology, and biology have the largest enrollments.

Required: To graduate, students must complete 128 credits with a minimum overall GPA of 2.0 and a minimum GPA of 2.0 within the major. Distribution requirements include 4 courses in humanities and 2 each in math, fine arts, natural science, and social science, one in English and cultural diversity. Foreign language requirements include a course numbered 101 (unless exempted on the basis of placement) and a course numbered above 101 in the same language. Students must also complete 3 writing intensive courses (1 in major, 1 outside the major, and 1 additional) and 2 semesters of phys ed, wellness, or community service. Several majors offer a capstone course for which a major research paper or project is completed.

Special: Cooperative programs are available with the Ohio and Pennsylvania Colleges of Podiatric Medicine, Pennsylvania College of Optometry, and Penn State and Duke Universities. Cross-registration is available with the Pennsylvania College of Technology. More than 200 internships, including teacher programs, study abroad in 7 countries, and a Washington semester at American University are available. Lycoming offers work-study programs, dual and student-designed majors, and an accelerated degree program in conjunction with the college's Scholar Program in optometry, podiatric medicine, and dentistry. Nondegree study and pass/fail grading options are available. There are 24 national honor societies, a freshman honors program, and 35 departmental honors programs.

Faculty/Classroom: 53% of faculty are male; 47% are female. All teach undergraduates. No introductory courses are taught by graduate students. The average class size in an introductory lecture is 22; in a laboratory is 15; and in a regular course is 18.

Admissions: 72% of the 2013-2014 applicants were accepted. The SAT scores for the 2013-2014 freshman class were: Critical Reading--42% below 500, 41% between 500 and 599, 15% between 600 and 699, and 2% between 700 and 800; Math--38% below 500, 46% between 500 and 599, 15% between 600 and 699, and 2% between 700 and 800; Writing--51% below 500, 38% between 500 and 599, 10% between 600 and 699, and 1% between 700 and 800. The ACT scores were 26% below 21, 36% between 21 and 23, 17% between 24 and 26, 15% between 27 and 28, and 6% above 28. 37% of the current freshmen were in the top fifth of their class; 64% were in the top two fifths. 3 freshmen graduated first in their class.

Requirements: The SAT or ACT is recommended. Applicants must graduate from an accredited secondary school or have a GED. They must have earned 16 academic units including a minimum of 4 years of English, 3 each of math and social studies, and 2 each of lab science, a foreign language, and academic electives. 2 personal letters of recommendation are required. Admissions interview is recommended. Portfolios and auditions may be required for students seeking scholarships in the arts. A GPA of 2.3 is required. AP and CLEP credits are accepted. Important factors in the admissions decision are advanced placement or honors courses, leadership record, and evidence of special talent.

Procedure: Freshmen are admitted fall and spring. Entrance exams should be taken during the junior year or by January of the senior year. There are early admissions, deferred admissions, and rolling admissions plans. Applications should be filed by March 1 for fall entry; December 1 for spring entry, along with a $35 fee. Notification is sent on a rolling basis. Applications are accepted online. Application fees are waived if application is completed online.

Transfer: 34 transfer students enrolled in 2012-2013. Applicants must submit appropriate transcripts and have a minimum GPA of 2.0 in transferable courses. Students who have completed 24 transferable semester hours are not required to submit SAT I or ACT results. 32 of 128 credits required for the bachelor's degree must be completed at Lycoming.

Visiting: There are regularly scheduled orientations for prospective students, consisting of a student-guided tour of campus and an interview with an admissions counselor. Meetings with professors and coaches and attending a class are possible upon request. There are guides for informal visits, visitors may sit in on classes, and stay overnight. To schedule a visit, contact Barb Carlin at admissions@lycoming.edu.

Financial Aid: In 2013-2014, 100% of all full-time freshmen and 99% of continuing full-time students received some form of financial aid. 76% of all full-time freshmen and 80% of continuing full-time students received need-based aid. The average freshman award was $34,012. Need-based scholarships or need-based grants averaged $9,263 ($26,000 maximum); need-based self-help aid (loans and jobs) averaged $3,643 ($5,500 maximum); and other non-need-based awards and non-need-based scholarships averaged $25,748 ($43,025 maximum). 45% of undergraduate students work part-time. Average annual earnings from campus work are $1351. The average financial indebtedness of the 2013 graduate was $35,065. Lycoming is a member of CSS. The FAFSA and the college's own financial statement are required. The priority date for freshman financial aid applications for fall entry is May 1. The deadline for filing freshman financial aid applications for fall entry is May 15.

International Students: There are 53 international students enrolled. The school actively recruits these students. They must take the TOEFL with a minimum score of 525 on the paper-based TOEFL (PBT) or 70 on the Internet-based version (iBT), IELTS.

Graduates: From July 1, 2012 to June 30, 2013, 299 bachelor's degrees were awarded. The most popular majors were business/marketing (25%), social sciences (16%), and psychology (14%). 9 companies recruited on campus in 2012-2013. In an average class, 1% graduate in 3 years or less, 54% graduate in 4 years or less, 62% graduate in 5 years or less, and 64% graduate in 6 years or less. Of the 2012 graduating class, 20% were enrolled in graduate school within 6 months of graduation.

Admissions Contact: James Spencer, VP for Admissions and Financial Aid. E-Mail: *admissions@lycoming.edu* Web: *www.lycoming.edu*

MANSFIELD UNIVERSITY D-1

Mansfield, PA 16933 (570) 662-4243
(800) 577-6826; (570) 662-4121

Full-time: 1036 men, 1417 women	**Faculty:** 136; IIB, +$
Part-time: 73 men, 191 women	**Ph.D.s:** 84%
Graduate: 47 men, 206 women	**Student/Faculty:** 17 to 1
Year: semesters, summer session	**Tuition:** $9192 ($19,316)
Application Deadline:	**Room & Board:** $10,276
Freshman Class: 1870 accepted, 595 enrolled	
SAT CR/M/W: 476/484/451	**ACT:** required **LESS COMPETITIVE**

Mansfield University, founded in 1857, is a public university that is part of the Pennsylvania State System of Higher Education. It offers programs in professional studies and the arts and sciences. There is one graduate school. In addition to regional accreditation, Mansfield has baccalaureate program accreditation with CSWE, NASM, NCATE, and NLN. The library contains 239,560 volumes, 843,728 microform items, 33,404 audio/video tapes/CDs/DVDs, and subscribes to 650 periodicals including electronic. Computerized library services include interlibrary loans, database searching, and Internet access. Special learning facilities include an art gallery, natural history museum, planetarium, radio station, TV station, a high-tech lecture lab. The 175-acre campus is in a rural area 28 miles south of Corning/Elmira, New York, and 58 miles north of Williamsport. Including any residence halls, there are 42 buildings.

Student Life: 80% of undergraduates are from Pennsylvania. Others are from 29 states, 15 foreign countries, and Canada. 81% are White. The average age of freshmen is 18; all undergraduates, 22. 28% do not continue beyond their first year; 50% remain to graduate.

Housing: 1792 students can be accommodated in college housing, which includes coed dorms. In addition, there are special-interest houses, suite-style on-campus residence halls, wellness floors, 24-hour quiet floors, and honors floors in residence halls, plus one freshmen-only residence hall. On-campus housing is guaranteed for all 4 years. 55% of students live on campus. Alcohol is not permitted. All students may keep cars.

Activities: 7% of men belong to 4 national fraternities; 6% of women belong to 4 national sororities. There are 126 groups on campus, including art, band, cheerleading, choir, chorale, chorus, computers, dance, debate, drama, environmental, ethnic, film, forensics, gay, honors, international, jazz band, literary magazine, marching band, musical theater, newspaper, orchestra, pep band, photography, political, professional, radio and TV, religious, social, social service, student government, and symphony. Popular campus events include Fabulous 1890s Weekend.

Sports: There are 6 intercollegiate sports for men and 7 for women, and 16 intramural sports for men and 16 for women. Facilities include a track, a recreation center, a 4000-seat stadium, a 1500-seat indoor gym, a 1200-seat auditorium, and football, baseball, and hockey fields, and a fitness center.

Disabled Students: 80% of the campus is accessible. Facilities include wheelchair ramps, elevators, special parking, specially equipped restrooms, special class scheduling, lowered drinking fountains, lowered telephones, and a wheelchair lift.

Services: Counseling and information services are available, as is tutoring in most subjects. There is a reader service for the blind, and remedial math, reading, and writing.

Campus Safety and Security: Measures include 24-hour foot and vehicle patrol, emergency notification system, self-defense education, and security escort services. There are shuttle buses, emergency telephones, and lighted pathways/sidewalks.

Programs of Study: Mansfield confers B.A., B.S., B.M., B.S.E., B.S.N. and B.S.W. degrees. Associate and master's degrees are also awarded. Bachelor's degrees are awarded in AGRICULTURE (fishing and fisheries), BIOLOGICAL SCIENCE (biochemistry, biology/biological science, and molecular biology), BUSINESS (business administration and management, business economics, international business management, and personnel management), COMMUNICATIONS AND THE ARTS (art history and appreciation, broadcasting, communication, English, French, graphic design, journalism, music, music business management, music performance, public relations, and Spanish), COMPUTER AND PHYSICAL SCIENCE (chemistry, computer science, information sciences and systems, mathematics, and physics), EDUCATION (art education, early childhood education, education of the exceptional child, elementary education, English education, foreign languages education, mathematics education, music education, science education, secondary education, social studies education, and special education), ENGINEERING AND ENVIRONMENTAL DESIGN (city/community/regional planning, environmental science, and preengineering), HEALTH PROFESSIONS (medical technology and nursing), SOCIAL SCIENCE (anthropology, criminal justice, dietetics, economics, geography, history, international studies, liberal arts/general studies, philosophy, political science/government, prelaw, psychology, social work, and sociology). Music, physical sciences, health sciences, and social sciences are the strongest academically. Biology, music, nursing have the largest enrollments.

Required: To graduate, students must complete 120 credit hours with a 2.0 GPA in core courses, distribution requirements, general education electives, and major requirements. Some degrees require a higher GPA.

Special: There are co-op programs in preengineering and medical technology. Students may study abroad in France, Russia, Canada, Australia, Spain, and Germany. There is a 3-2 engineering program with Penn State University. The university also offers work-study, dual majors, a liberal studies degree, credit by exam, credit for military experience, nondegree study, and pass/fail options. There are 6 national honor societies, including Phi Beta Kappa, and a freshman honors program.

Faculty/Classroom: 51% of faculty are male; 49% are female. All teach undergraduates. No introductory courses are taught by graduate students. The average class size in an introductory lecture is 28; in a laboratory is 19; and in a regular course is 30.

Admissions: The SAT scores for the 2013-2014 freshman class were: Critical Reading--60% below 500, 32% between 500 and 599, 7% between 600 and 699, and 1% between 700 and 800; Math--57% below 500, 33% between 500 and 599, 9% between 600 and 699, and 1% between 700 and 800; Writing--77% below 500, 21% between 500 and 599, 5% between 600 and 699, and 1% between 700 and 800. 29% of the current freshmen were in the top fifth of their class; 55% were in the top two fifths. 8 freshmen graduated first in their class.

Requirements: The SAT or ACT is required, with a satisfactory SAT score, or a minimum ACT score of 19. A GED is accepted. Applicants should prepare with 4 credits of English and history, 3 each of math, science, and social studies, 2 of foreign language, and 6 of additional academic electives. Art students must submit a portfolio; music students must audition. A GPA of 2.0 is required. AP and CLEP credits are accepted. Important factors in the admissions decision are advanced placement or honors courses, evidence of special talent, and leadership record.

Procedure: Freshmen are admitted fall and spring. Entrance exams should be taken by the junior or senior year of high school. There are early admissions, deferred admissions, and rolling admissions plans. Check with the school for current application deadlines. The application fee is $25. Notification is sent on a rolling basis. Applications are accepted online.

Transfer: 257 transfer students enrolled in 2012-2013. Applicants must have a GPA of at least 2.0 and must submit all college transcripts. 32 of 120 credits required for the bachelor's degree must be completed at Mansfield.

Visiting: There are regularly scheduled orientations for prospective students. There are guides for informal visits and visitors may sit in on classes. To schedule a visit, contact the Admissions Office.

Financial Aid: In 2013-2014, 91% of all full-time freshmen and 74% of continuing full-time students received some form of financial aid. 55% of all full-time freshmen and 55% of continuing full-time students received need-based aid. The average freshman award was $10,082. Need-based scholarships or need-based grants averaged $4,051; need-based self-help aid (loans and jobs) averaged $2,805; non-need-based athletic scholarships averaged $1,630; and other non-need-based awards and non-need-based scholarships averaged $1,534. 28% of undergraduate students work part-time. Average annual earnings from campus work are $1200. The average financial indebtedness of the 2013 graduate was $22,821. Mansfield is a member of CSS. The FAFSA and the college's own financial statement are required. The priority date for freshman financial aid applications for fall entry is March 15.

International Students: There are 37 international students enrolled. The school actively recruits these students. They must take the TOEFL with a minimum score of 500 on the paper-based TOEFL (PBT) or 61 on the Internet-based version (iBT).

Graduates: From July 1, 2012 to June 30, 2013, 560 bachelor's degrees were awarded. The most popular majors were health majors (13%), visual and performing arts (12%), and criminal justice (11%). 125 companies recruited on campus in 2012-2013. In an average class, 2% graduate in 3 years or less, 33% graduate in 4 years or less, 49% graduate in 5 years or less, and 50% graduate in 6 years or less.

Admissions Contact: Director of Enrollment Services E-Mail: *admissions@mansfield.edu* Web: *www.mansfield.edu*

MARYWOOD UNIVERSITY E-2

Scranton, PA 18509 (570) 348-6234
(866) 279-9663; (570) 961-4763

Full-time: 630 men, 1478 women **Faculty:** n/av; IIA, -$
Part-time: 67 men, 80 women **Ph.D.s:** 91%
Graduate: 248 men, 895 women **Student/Faculty:** 12 to 1
Year: semesters, summer session **Tuition:** $28,175
Application Deadline: open **Room & Board:** $12,520
Freshman Class: 2203 applied, 1543 accepted, 466 enrolled
SAT CR/M/W: 510/520/510 **ACT:** 22 **COMPETITIVE**

Marywood University is a comprehensive, coeducational, Catholic university of 3,300 full-time, part-time and adult students, with over 90 undergraduate, graduate and doctoral degree programs. Established in 1915 by the Sisters, Servants of the Immaculate Heart of Mary, the university houses 1,000 resident students on a national award-winning campus considered one of the most beautiful in the northeast. Marywood University offered the region's first doctoral degree programs in 1996 and is the region's leading provider of graduate education with 34 master's degree programs and 33 certificate offerings. In recent years, the university made $100 million in improvements to campus, including new athletics, residence hall, and dining facilities,and one of the finest studio arts facilities in the northeast. Marywood University consists of four colleges and one school. They are the: Insalaco College of Creative and Performing Arts, Reap College of Education and Human Development, College of Health and Human Services, College of Liberal Arts and Sciences, and the School of Architecture. There are 5 undergraduate schools and 5 graduate schools. In addition to regional accreditation, Marywood has baccalaureate program accreditation with ACBSP, ADA, CSWE, NASAD, NASM, NCATE, and NLN. The library contains 224,294 volumes, 378,244 microform items, 20,970 audio/video tapes/CDs/DVDs, and subscribes to 29,756 periodicals including electronic. Computerized library services include interlibrary loans, database searching, Internet access, and Wi-Fi capability. Special learning facilities include an art gallery, radio station, TV station, Facilities: Five residence halls and 22 townhouse-style apartments on campus with 1,041 full-time students in residence; 450-seat main dining facilities and three campus snack/coffee shops; fully-equipped conference center for groups up to 1,200 (summer conference overnight capacity: 950); academic excellence center; student counseling center; human physiology lab; human development (counseling, psychology) laboratories; biotechnology lab; communication sciences and disorders clinic; nutrition and dietetics lab; assistive technology center; outpatient mental health clinic; multiple "smart" classrooms; multiple computer labs; full-service library; television studio and editing suites; radio station and studio; 60,000-square-foot, studio art center (including ceramic, painting, drawing/foundation, sculpture, glass, metal, clay, wood, photography, fabric, jewelry, and printmaking studios); 15,000-square foot visual arts center (including graphic design and interior architecture computer labs, two art exhibit galleries; Maslow Collection of Contemporary Art; and Maslow Study Gallery); 1,100-seat performance theater; black box theater; 1,500-seat athletics arena (2,500 seats for events); 5,000-square-foot fitness center; NCAA regulation pool and Aquatics Center; additional basketball courts; exterior tennis courts; 1,200-square foot dance/aerobic studio; hydro-therapy room, separate team and student locker facilities; Center for Architectural Studies studios. The 115-acre campus is in a suburban area 120 miles west of New York City and 115 miles north of Philadelphia. Including any residence halls, there are 30 buildings.

Student Life: 71% of undergraduates are from Pennsylvania. Others are from 24 states, and 12 foreign countries. 76% are from public schools. 83% are White. 58% are Catholic; 14% Protestant. The average age of freshmen is 18; all undergraduates, 21. 16% do not continue beyond their first year; 67% remain to graduate.

Housing: 1093 students can be accommodated in college housing, which includes single-sex and coed dorms and on-campus apartments. In addition, there are special-interest houses, Themed Interest communities located within the residence halls. On-campus housing is guaranteed for all 4 years. 50% of students commute. Alcohol is not permitted. All students may keep cars.

Activities: There are no fraternities. There are 60 groups on campus, including film club, art, band, cheerleading, choir, chorus, computers, dance, drama, environmental, ethnic, film, gay, honors, international, jazz band, literary magazine, musical theater, newspaper, orchestra, pep band, photography, political, professional, radio and TV, religious, social, social service, student government, symphony, and volunteer. Popular campus events include Spring Fling, Midnight Madness, and Flapjack Fest.

Sports: There are 8 intercollegiate sports for men and 9 for women, and 28 intramural sports for men and 28 for women. Facilities include The Center for Athletics and Wellness includes a fitness center, a climbing wall, an elevated running track, a dance/aerobic studio, an arena to showcase Pacer sports, and high-tech athletic training areas. Adjacent to this Center is a new eight lane Aquatics Center with 3 and 1 meter boards, team rooms, spectator seating and a safety center. This state of the art facility opened its doors in Spring 2011 and will be home for the Pacer Men's and Women's Swim and Dive teams. Other outdoor facilities include 3 grass fields and 1 multipurpose turf field, tennis courts, a sand volleyball court, and basketball courts.

Disabled Students: 98% of the campus is accessible. Facilities include wheelchair ramps, elevators, special parking, specially equipped restrooms, special class scheduling, lowered drinking fountains, special housing.

Services: Counseling and information services are available, as is tutoring in most subjects, Peer tutoring - tutoring services in most subjects according to the knowledge of current staff There is a reader service for the blind, and remedial math and writing. Individual and small-group tutoring as well as drop-in tutoring centers for math, science and writing.

Campus Safety and Security: Measures include 24-hour foot and vehicle patrol, emergency notification system, self-defense education, and security escort services. There are emergency telephones, lighted pathways/sidewalks, controlled access to dorms/residences, night security in dorms, card access to dorm floors, and transportation on request.

Programs of Study: Marywood confers B.A., B.Arch, B.E.D.A., B.S., B.B.A., B.F.A., B.M., B.S.N. and B.S.W. degrees. Master's and doctoral degrees are also awarded. Bachelor's degrees are awarded in BIOLOGICAL SCIENCE (biology/biological science and biotechnology), BUSINESS (accounting, banking and finance, business administration and management, hospitality management services, international business management, marketing/retailing/merchandising, and retailing), COMMUNICATIONS AND THE ARTS (advertising, arts administration/management, broadcasting, ceramic art and design, communications, digital communications, dramatic arts, English, French, graphic design, illustration, music business management, music performance, musical theater, painting, photography, sculpture, Spanish, studio art, and theater management), COMPUTER AND PHYSICAL SCIENCE (information sciences and systems, mathematics, and science), EDUCATION (art education, athletic training, dance education, early childhood education, education of the deaf and hearing impaired, elementary education, English education, foreign languages education, mathematics education, music education, physical education, science education, secondary education, social science education, and special education), ENGINEERING AND ENVIRONMENTAL DESIGN (architecture, aviation administration/management, environmental design, environmental science, and interior design), HEALTH PROFESSIONS (art therapy, health care administration, health science, medical technology, music therapy, nursing, premedicine, preosteopathy, and speech pathology/audiology), SOCIAL SCIENCE (clinical psychology, criminal justice, dietetics, family/consumer studies, gerontology, history, industrial and organizational psychology, philosophy, physical fitness/movement, political science/government, prelaw, psychology, religion, social science, and social work). Art, business, science, educations, and social science are the strongest academically. Art, and education have the largest enrollments.

Required: To graduate, students must complete a liberal arts core consisting of religious studies, philosophy, math, science, history, social science, literature, writing, foreign language, and fine arts. Additional course requirements include a first year experience course for new undergraduate students who have not transferred from another post-secondary institution and one course with a global studies perspective.

Special: Marywood offers cross-registration with the University of Scranton, internships, study abroad, accelerated degree programs in dietetics and social work, dual majors, and student-designed majors. Students may earn credit for life, military, and work experience. There are 23 national honor societies, a freshman honors program, and 18 departmental honors programs.

Faculty/Classroom: 48% of faculty are male; 52% are female. No introductory courses are taught by graduate students. The average class size in an introductory lecture is 21; in a laboratory is 16; and in a regular course is 19.

Admissions: 70% of the 2013-2014 applicants were accepted. The SAT scores for the 2013-2014 freshman class were: Critical Reading--42% below 500, 46% between 500 and 599, and 11% between 600 and 699; Math--34% below 500, 51% between 500 and 599, and 15% between 600 and 699; Writing--44% below 500, 41% between 500 and 599, and 15% between 600 and 699. The ACT scores were 33% below 21, 32% between 21 and 23, 21% between 24 and 26, 10% between 27 and 28, and 4% above 28. 42% of the current freshmen were in the top fifth of their class; 73% were in the top two fifths. 1 freshman graduated first in the class.

Requirements: The SAT is required. The ACT is recommended. Applicants are expected to be graduates of an accredited secondary school or have the GED. A minimum of 16 academic credits is required, including 4 in English, 3 each in social studies and science (1 as lab), and 2 in math. A letter of support is required in selected majors, as is a portfolio or an audition where appropriate. A personal interview is strongly recommended. A GPA of 2.5 is required. AP and CLEP credits are accepted. Important factors in the admissions decision are advanced placement or honors courses, extracurricular activities record, and leadership record.

Procedure: Freshmen are admitted fall and spring. Entrance exams

should be taken in the junior year or the senior year before February 1. There are deferred admissions and rolling admissions plans. Application deadlines are open. Application fee is $35. Applications are accepted online.

Transfer: 169 transfer students enrolled in 2012-2013. SAT or ACT scores are required of transfer applicants who have earned fewer than 12 college credits; both secondary school and college transcripts are required. Transfer students are required to have earned a minimum GPA of 2.25 at the college most recently attended (3.0 minimum for some majors). A grade of C is the minimum requirement for transfer of academic credit. The SAT is required for nursing transfer students. 60 of 126 credits required for the bachelor's degree must be completed at Marywood.

Visiting: There are regularly scheduled orientations for prospective students, including a campus tour, meetings with an admissions counselor and financial aid counselor, an appointment with an academic advisor, and a full summer orientation program for first-year students. There are guides for informal visits, visitors may sit in on classes, and stay overnight. To schedule a visit, contact the Office of University Admissions.

Financial Aid: In 2013-2014, 99% of all full-time freshmen and 99% of continuing full-time students received some form of financial aid. 88% of all full-time freshmen and 85% of continuing full-time students received need-based aid. The average freshman award was $23,602. Need-based scholarships or need-based grants averaged $16,981 ($38,096 maximum); need-based self-help aid (loans and jobs) averaged $7,790 ($18,439 maximum); other non-need-based awards and non-need-based scholarships averaged $13,690 ($40,968 maximum); and $20,666 from other forms of aid. 31% of undergraduate students work part-time. Average annual earnings from campus work are $2000. The average financial indebtedness of the 2013 graduate was $42,328. The FAFSA and the college's own financial statement are required. The priority date for freshman financial aid applications for fall entry is February 15.

International Students: There are 45 international students enrolled. The school actively recruits these students. They must take the TOEFL with a minimum score of 530 on the paper-based TOEFL (PBT) or 71 on the Internet-based version (iBT), IELTS. Only for certain majors.

Graduates: From July 1, 2012 to June 30, 2013, 478 bachelor's degrees were awarded. The most popular majors were health professions and related sciences (22%), education (18%), and visual and performing arts (17%). In an average class, 51% graduate in 4 years or less, 61% graduate in 5 years or less, and 63% graduate in 6 years or less. Of the 2012 graduating class, 30% were enrolled in graduate school within 6 months of graduation, and 61% were employed.

Admissions Contact: Christian DiGregorio, Director of University Admissions. E-Mail: *yourfuture@marywood.edu* Web: *www.marywood.edu*

MERCYHURST UNIVERSITY B-1

Erie, PA 16546 (814) 824-2980 (800) 825-1926; (814) 824-2071

Full-time: 1390 men, 1988 women	**Faculty:** n/av; IIB, --$
Part-time: 129 men, 333 women	**Ph.D.s:** 60%
Graduate: 140 men, 140 women	**Student/Faculty:** n/av
Year: 4-1-4, summer session	**Tuition:** $30,300
Application Deadline: open	**Room & Board:** $10,400
Freshman Class: 3000 applied, 1900 accepted, 650 enrolled	
SAT CR/M/W: 550/530/510 **ACT:** 23	**COMPETITIVE**

Mercyhurst University, established in 1926, is a private, nonprofit institution affiliated with the Roman Catholic Church. The college offers undergraduate degrees in the arts, business, health science, liberal arts, religious studies, and teacher preparation as well as a degree-directed program for the learning disabled. There is 1 graduate school. In addition to regional accreditation, Mercyhurst has baccalaureate program accreditation with ADA and CSWE. The library contains 165,644 volumes, 50,631 microform items, 9,309 audio/video tapes/CDs/DVDs, and subscribes to 848 periodicals including electronic. Computerized library services include interlibrary loans and database searching. Special learning facilities include an art gallery, planetarium, radio station, TV station, northwestern Pennsylvania historical archives, and archeological institute. The 88-acre campus is in a suburban area within Erie, PA. Including any residence halls, there are 44 buildings.

Student Life: 60% of undergraduates are from Pennsylvania. Others are from 37 states, 14 foreign countries, and Canada. 76% are from public schools. 91% are White. 53% are Catholic; 21% Protestant; 18% claim no religious affiliation. The average age of freshmen is 18; all undergraduates, 26. 20% do not continue beyond their first year; 62% remain to graduate.

Housing: 1718 students can be accommodated in college housing, which includes single-sex and coed dorms, on-campus apartments, and married student housing. On-campus housing is guaranteed for all 4 years. 65% of students live on campus; of those, 91% remain on campus on weekends. Upperclassmen may keep cars.

Activities: There are no fraternities or sororities. There are 49 groups on campus, including art, band, cheerleading, choir, chorus, communications, computers, dance, debate, drama, ethnic, film, gay, honors, international, jazz band, literary magazine, musical theater, newspaper, opera, orchestra, pep band, photography, political, professional, radio and TV, religious, social, social service, and student government. Popular campus events include Activities Day, Parents Weekend, and Winter and Spring Formals.

Sports: There are 13 intercollegiate sports for men and 12 for women, and 9 intramural sports for men and 9 for women. Facilities include indoor crew tanks, football, field hockey, lacrosse, and soccer fields, an ice hockey rink/arena, Nautilus facilities, a free-weight room, a baseball/softball complex, a training room, and a basketball arena.

Disabled Students: 90% of the campus is accessible. Facilities include wheelchair ramps, elevators, special parking, specially equipped restrooms, and lowered drinking fountains.

Services: Counseling and information services are available, as is tutoring in every subject. There is remedial math, reading, and writing.

Campus Safety and Security: Measures include 24-hour foot and vehicle patrol, emergency notification system, and self-defense education. There are shuttle buses, emergency telephones, lighted pathways/sidewalks, controlled access to dorms/residences, and a 24-hour security camera surveillance system.

Programs of Study: Mercyhurst confers B.A., B.S. and B.M. degrees. Associate, master's, and doctoral degrees are also awarded. Bachelor's degrees are awarded in BIOLOGICAL SCIENCE (biochemistry and biology/biological science), BUSINESS (accounting, banking and finance, business administration and management, fashion merchandising, hotel/motel and restaurant management, insurance and risk management, management information systems, and marketing/retailing/merchandising), COMMUNICATIONS AND THE ARTS (advertising, broadcasting, communications, dance, English, graphic design, journalism, languages, music, musical theater, public relations, and studio art), COMPUTER AND PHYSICAL SCIENCE (chemistry, earth science, geology, mathematics, web services, and web technology), EDUCATION (art education, athletic training, business education, early childhood education, elementary education, home economics education, mathematics education, music education, science education, secondary education, social science education, and special education), ENGINEERING AND ENVIRONMENTAL DESIGN (environmental science and interior design), HEALTH PROFESSIONS (art therapy, medical laboratory technology, predentistry, premedicine, preosteopathy, prepharmacy, preveterinary science, and sports medicine), SOCIAL SCIENCE (anthropology, archeology, criminal justice, family/consumer studies, forensic studies, history, philosophy, political science/government, prelaw, psychology, religion, religious education, social work, and sociology). Archeology/anthropology, intelligence studies, and sports medicine are the strongest academically. Business, education, and sports medicine have the largest enrollments.

Required: To graduate, students must complete the core curriculum, which includes English, math, science, religion, philosophy, history, and a computer course. Distribution requirements include American history, cultural appreciation, human behavior, and ethics. A minimum GPA of 2.0 is required, with a 2.5 in the major, and a minimum total of 123 credit hours. The number of credit hours in the major varies, with a minimum of 30. A thesis is necessary for history and English majors.

Special: Mercyhurst offers cross-registration with Gannon University, internships in all majors through the co-op office, and study abroad in London and Dublin. Dual and student-designed majors, credit for life, military, or work experience, nondegree study, work-study, and a pass/fail grading option are also available. There are 7 national honor societies, a freshman honors program, and 4 departmental honors programs.

Faculty/Classroom: 57% of faculty are male; 43% are female. All teach undergraduates, and 30% do research. No introductory courses are taught by graduate students. The average class size in an introductory lecture is 35; in a laboratory is 12; and in a regular course is 25.

Admissions: 63% of the 2013-2014 applicants were accepted. The ACT scores were 21% below 21, 46% between 21 and 23, 33% between 24 and 26, 79% were in the top two fifths. 20 freshmen graduated first in their class.

Requirements: The SAT or ACT is required. Applicants must graduate from an accredited secondary school or have a GED. 16 academic credits are required, including 4 years of English, 3 each of math and social studies, and 2 each of history, science, and a foreign language. Interviews are recommended. Art applicants must submit portfolios; auditions are required of music and dance applicants. Mercyhurst requires applicants to be in the upper 50% of their class. A GPA of 2.8 is required. AP and CLEP credits are accepted. Important factors in the admissions decision are recommendations by alumni, evidence of special talent, and personality/intangible qualities.

Procedure: Freshmen are admitted to all sessions. Entrance exams should be taken during the spring of the junior year. There are deferred admissions and rolling admissions plans. Application deadlines are open. Notification is sent on a rolling basis. Applications are accepted online.

Transfer: 90 transfer students enrolled in 2012-2013. A minimum GPA of 2.0 on previous college work is required 45 of 121 credits required for the bachelor's degree must be completed at Mercyhurst.

Visiting: There are regularly scheduled orientations for prospective students, including tours, class visits, faculty meetings, and interviews with financial aid and admissions counselors. There are guides for informal visits, visitors may sit in on classes, and stay overnight. To schedule a visit, contact the Admissions Office at admug@mercyhurst.edu.

Financial Aid: In 2013-2014, 95% of all full-time freshmen students received some form of financial aid. 76% of all full-time freshmen students received need-based aid. The average freshman award was $15,000. Need-based scholarships or need-based grants averaged $8,000. 60% of undergraduate students work part-time. Average annual earnings from campus work are $1200. The average financial indebtedness of the 2013 graduate was $27,000. Mercyhurst is a member of CSS. The FAFSA is required. The priority date for freshman financial aid applications for fall entry is May 1. The deadline for filing freshman financial aid applications for fall entry is August.

International Students: There are 250 international students enrolled. The school actively recruits these students. They must take the TOEFL. They must also take the SAT or ACT.

Graduates: From July 1, 2012 to June 30, 2013, 800 bachelor's degrees were awarded. 100 companies recruited on campus in 2012-2013.

Admissions Contact: Christopher Coons, Director of Admissions. E-Mail: *admug@mercyhurst.edu* Web: *www.mercyhurst.edu*

MESSIAH COLLEGE D-3

Mechanicsburg, PA 17055 (717) 691-6000
(800) 233-4220; (717) 796-5374

Full-time: 1060 men, 1641 women	**Faculty:** 166; IIB, av$
Part-time: 28 men, 43 women	**Ph.D.s:** 84%
Graduate: 71 men, 241 women	**Student/Faculty:** 13 to 1
Year: semesters, summer session	**Tuition:** $30,470
Application Deadline: open	**Room & Board:** $9070
Freshman Class: 2836 applied, 1869 accepted, 648 enrolled	
SAT CR/M/W: 570/580/560 **ACT:** 25	**VERY COMPETITIVE**

Messiah College, founded in 1909, is a private Christian college of the liberal and applied arts and sciences. The college is committed to the evangelical spirit rooted in the Anabaptist, Pietist, and Wesleyan traditions. There are 4 undergraduate schools and 1 graduate school. In addition to regional accreditation, Messiah has baccalaureate program accreditation with ABET, ACBSP, ADA, CSWE, NASAD, and NASM. The library contains 253,484 volumes, 13 microform items, 22,604 audio/video tapes/CDs/DVDs, and subscribes to 98,644 periodicals including electronic. Computerized library services include interlibrary loans, database searching, Internet access, and Wi-Fi capability. Special learning facilities include an art gallery, natural history museum, and radio station. The 471-acre campus is in a small town 12 miles southwest of Harrisburg. Including any residence halls, there are 53 buildings.

Student Life: 58% of undergraduates are from Pennsylvania. Others are from 37 states, 28 foreign countries, and Canada. 73% are from public schools. 86% are White. 78% are Protestant. The average age of freshmen is 19; all undergraduates, 20. 13% do not continue beyond their first year; 76% remain to graduate.

Housing: 2383 students can be accommodated in college housing, which includes single-sex and coed dorms, on-campus apartments, and off-campus apartments. In addition, there are special-interest houses. On-campus housing is guaranteed for all 4 years. 87% of students live on campus; of those, 70% remain on campus on weekends. Alcohol is not permitted. Upperclassmen may keep cars.

Activities: There are no fraternities or sororities. There are 81 groups on campus, including art, band, choir, chorale, chorus, dance, debate, drama, environmental, ethnic, film, honors, international, jazz band, literary magazine, musical theater, newspaper, orchestra, pep band, political, professional, radio and TV, religious, social, social service, student government, symphony, and yearbook. Popular campus events include Cultural Series, Traveling Music Ensembles, and Theater Productions.

Sports: There are 10 intercollegiate sports for men and 10 for women, and 10 intramural sports for men and 10 for women. Facilities include indoor and outdoor tracks, a pool with separate diving well, wrestling and gymnastics areas, a weight room, numerous playing fields, and courts for racquetball, basketball, and tennis. The campus center provides additional recreational facilities.

Disabled Students: 80% of the campus is accessible. Facilities include wheelchair ramps, elevators, special parking, specially equipped restrooms, special class scheduling, lowered drinking fountains, and special housing.

Services: Counseling and information services are available, as is tutoring in most subjects. There is a reader service for the blind, and remedial math, reading, and writing. supplemental instruction

Campus Safety and Security: Measures include 24-hour foot and vehicle patrol, emergency notification system, self-defense education, and security escort services. There are emergency telephones, lighted pathways/sidewalks, controlled access to dorms/residences, a text messaging alert system.

Programs of Study: Messiah confers B.A., B.S., B.M., B.S.E., B.S.N., B.S.W. and B.F.A. degrees. Master's degrees are also awarded. Bachelor's degrees are awarded in AGRICULTURE (environmental studies), BIOLOGICAL SCIENCE (biochemistry, biology/adolescence education, biology/biological science, molecular biology, and nutrition), BUSINESS (accounting, business administration and management, international business management, management information systems, marketing/retailing/merchandising, sports management, and sustainable management), COMMUNICATIONS AND THE ARTS (art history and appreciation, arts administration/management, broadcasting, communications, dance, dramatic arts, English, film, television and digital media, French, German, journalism, music, music business management, music performance, musical theater, public relations, Spanish, spanish / adolescence education, studio art, and theater management), COMPUTER AND PHYSICAL SCIENCE (chemistry, chemistry/adolescence education, computer science, digital arts/technology, mathematics, and physics), EDUCATION (art education, athletic training, early childhood education, elementary education, English education, environmental education, foreign languages education, mathematics education, music education, physical education, recreation education, science education, social studies education, and sports studies), ENGINEERING AND ENVIRONMENTAL DESIGN (engineering and environmental science), HEALTH PROFESSIONS (exercise science and nursing), SOCIAL SCIENCE (biopsychology, child care/child and family studies, Chinese Studies, criminal justice, dietetics, economics, ethnic studies, family/consumer studies, history, human development, humanities, interdisciplinary studies, ministries, peace studies, philosophy, political science/government, psychology, social work, sociology, Spanish studies, and theological studies). Engineering, nursing, and psychology have the largest enrollments.

Required: All students must complete at least 123 credits with a minimum GPA of 2.0. The last 30 credits must be taken at Messiah College and a minimum of 12 credits must be in the major.

Special: Off-campus study is available, through Brethren Colleges Abroad, at Jerusalem University College at Oxford University, in Thailand, and through Latin American, Central American, Middle East, and Russian studies programs, among others. Off-campus options within the United States include the American and Urban Studies programs, the AuSable Institute of Environmental Studies, Los Angeles Film Studies, Oregon Extension, and others. Students may also spend a semester or year at any of 12 other Christian Consortium colleges in a student exchange program. Numerous internships, practicum's, and ministry opportunities are available. There are 7 national honor societies, a freshman honors program, and 17 departmental honors programs.

Faculty/Classroom: 51% of faculty are male; 49% are female. All teach undergraduates. No introductory courses are taught by graduate students. The average class size in an introductory lecture is 27; in a laboratory is 18; and in a regular course is 24.

Admissions: 66% of the 2013-2014 applicants were accepted. The SAT scores for the 2013-2014 freshman class were: Critical Reading--19% below 500, 44% between 500 and 599, 27% between 600 and 699, and 10% between 700 and 800; Math--19% below 500, 38% between 500 and 599, 35% between 600 and 699, and 8% between 700 and 800; Writing--23% below 500, 43% between 500 and 599, 27% between 600 and 699, and 7% between 700 and 800. The ACT scores were 13% below 21, 19% between 21 and 23, 26% between 24 and 26, 16% between 27 and 28, and 26% above 28. 60% of the current freshmen were in the top fifth of their class; 86% were in the top two fifths. There were 3 National Merit finalists. 7 freshmen graduated first in their class.

Requirements: The SAT or ACT is required. Applicants graduating in the top 20% of their class have a scoreless option that requires an interview. Applicants must have graduated from an accredited high school or the equivalent. Secondary preparation of students who enroll usually includes 4 units in English, 3 or 4 in math, 3 each in natural science, social studies, and foreign languages, and 4 in academic electives. Students who enroll are usually in the top one third of their class and have a B average or better. A campus visit with an information session is recommended. Potential music majors must audition. AP and CLEP credits are accepted. Important factors in the admissions decision are advanced placement or honors courses, recommendations by school officials, and leadership record.

Procedure: Freshmen are admitted fall and spring. Entrance exams should be taken in the spring of the junior year. There is a rolling admissions plan. Application deadlines are open. Application fee is $20. Notification of early decision is sent November 1; regular decision, on a rolling basis. 0 applicants were on the 2013 waiting list; were admitted. Applications are accepted online.

Transfer: 100 transfer students enrolled in 2012-2013. Transfer applicants should have earned a 2.5 GPA in at least 30 college credits. The college prefers that applicants also have composite SAT or ACT scores and that they seek a campus visit. Students with fewer than 30 credits in college should submit a high school transcript as well. 30 of 123 credits required for the bachelor's degree must be completed at Messiah.

Visiting: There are regularly scheduled orientations for prospective students, including a campus tour, academic and career advising, and a financial aid information session. There are guides for informal visits, visitors may sit in on classes, and stay overnight. To schedule a visit, contact the Admissions Office.

Financial Aid: In 2013-2014, 100% of all full-time freshmen and 99% of continuing full-time students received some form of financial aid. 63% of all full-time freshmen and 64% of continuing full-time students received need-based aid. The average freshman award was $13,887. 58% of undergraduate students work part-time. Average annual earnings from campus work are $2175. The average financial indebtedness of the 2013 graduate was $34,122. Messiah is a member of CSS. The FAFSA is required. The priority date for freshman financial aid applications for fall entry is April 1.

International Students: There are 66 international students enrolled. The school actively recruits these students. They must take the TOEFL. They must also take the SAT or ACT.

Graduates: From July 1, 2012 to June 30, 2013, 629 bachelor's degrees were awarded. The most popular majors were nursing (8%), psychology (6%), and engineering (5%). In an average class, 71% graduate in 4 years or less, 75% graduate in 5 years or less, and 76% graduate in 6 years or less. Of the 2012 graduating class, 19% were enrolled in graduate school within 6 months of graduation, and 77% were employed.

Admissions Contact: John Chopka, Vice President for Enrollment Management. E-Mail: *admiss@messiah.edu* Web: *www.messiah.edu*

MILLERSVILLE UNIVERSITY OF PENNSYLVANIA E-4

Millersville, PA 17551 **(717) 872-3371; (717) 871-2147**

Full-time: 2952 men, 3632 women	**Faculty:** 281; IIA, +$
Part-time: 360 men, 444 women	**Ph.D.s:** n/av
Graduate: 239 men, 652 women	**Student/Faculty:** 22 to 1
Year: 4-1-4, summer session	**Tuition:** $8866 ($18,800)
Application Deadline: rolling	**Room & Board:** $9632

Freshman Class: 5455 applied, 3920 accepted, 1299 enrolled

SAT CR/M/W: 500/510/490 **ACT:** 22 **COMPETITIVE**

Millersville University of Pennsylvania is a top-ranked, public university located in the northeast region of the United States. It is committed to offering students a high quality, comprehensive university experience of exceptional value. Dedicated to providing nationally recognized programs that embrace the liberal arts, Millersville offers academic opportunities that are supported by outstanding faculty who are accomplished scholars and practitioners. Founded in 1855 as the first Normal School in Pennsylvania, Millersville University is one of 14 universities within the Pennsylvania State System of Higher Education. The president is Dr. John Anderson. There are 3 undergraduate schools and one graduate school. In addition to regional accreditation, Millersville, MU has baccalaureate program accreditation with ABET, ACBSP, CSWE, NASAD, NASM, NCATE, and NLN. The library contains 364,190 volumes, 8,844 audio/video tapes/CDs/DVDs, and subscribes to 182,653 periodicals including electronic. Computerized library services include interlibrary loans, database searching, Internet access, and Wi-Fi capability. Special learning facilities include an art gallery, radio station, TV station, foreign language lab. weather information center, teleconferencing center, performing art centers, recording studio, Marine Science Consortium (Wallops Island), Atmospheric Research and Aerostat Facility, Center for Disaster Research and Education, and Foucault Pendulum. The 250-acre campus is in a small town 3 miles west of Lancaster. Including any residence halls, there are 93 buildings.

Student Life: 95% of undergraduates are from Pennsylvania. Others are from 23 states, 58 foreign countries, and Canada. 78% are White. The average age of freshmen is 18, all undergraduates, 25. 17% do not continue beyond their first year, 83% remain to graduate.

Housing: 2275 students can be accommodated in college housing, which includes coed dorms, on-campus apartments, and off-campus apartments. In addition, there are honors houses, special-interest houses, For disabled and international students, theme and wellness housing. On-campus housing is available on a first-come, first-served basis, and is available on a lottery system for upperclassmen. 67% of students commute. Alcohol is not permitted. Upperclassmen may keep cars.

Activities: 3% of men belong 7 national fraternities; 4% of women belong to 2 local and 8 national sororities. There are 172 groups on campus, including art, band, cheerleading, chess, choir, chorus, communications, dance, drama, environmental, ethnic, film, gay, honors, international, jazz band, literary magazine, marching band, musical theater, newspaper, orchestra, pep band, political, professional, radio and TV, religious, social, social service, student government, symphony, and yearbook. Popular campus events include Organizational Outbreak, Superfest and Wellness Week, Homecoming, Greek Week, and Spring Concert.

Sports: There are 8 intercollegiate sports for men and 13 for women, and 11 intramural sports for men and 12 for women. Facilities include a football stadium, 2 pools, 2 gyms, 2 fitness centers, a dance studio, a ropes course, wrestling and weight rooms, basketball, volleyball, tennis, and badminton courts, indoor running track, baseball and softball stadium, golf club.

Disabled Students: 85% of the campus is accessible. Facilities include wheelchair ramps, elevators, special parking, specially equipped restrooms, special class scheduling, lowered drinking fountains, lowered telephones, special housing.

Services: Counseling and information services are available, as is tutoring in most subjects. There is a reader service for the blind, and remedial math. Every effort is made to tailor a tutoring program to individual needs. Note takers, interpreters, and some physical aids/ other specialized equipment are provided, as available.

Campus Safety and Security: Measures include 24-hour foot and vehicle patrol, emergency notification system, self-defense education, and security escort services. There are shuttle buses, emergency telephones, lighted pathways/sidewalks, controlled access to dorms/residences, timely warning messages sent via e-mail and text messages and regularly scheduled crime awareness programs.

Programs of Study: Millersville, MU confers B.A., B.S., B.F.A., B.S.Ed., and B.S.N. degrees. Associate and master's degrees are also awarded. Bachelor's degrees are awarded in BIOLOGICAL SCIENCE (biology/biological science), BUSINESS (business administration and management), COMMUNICATIONS AND THE ARTS (art, communications, English, French, German, music, and Spanish), COMPUTER AND PHYSICAL SCIENCE (atmospheric sciences and meteorology, chemistry, computer science, earth science, geology, mathematics, oceanography, and physics), EDUCATION (art education, early childhood education, elementary education, middle school education, music education, social studies education, special education, and technical education), ENGINEERING AND ENVIRONMENTAL DESIGN (industrial engineering technology and occupational safety and health), HEALTH PROFESSIONS (allied health and nursing), SOCIAL SCIENCE (anthropology, economics, geography, history, international studies, philosophy, political science/government, psychology, social work, and sociology). Elementary education, special education, geography, and mathematics are the strongest academically. Business administration, psychology, and biology have the largest enrollments.

Required: All students must complete at least 120 hours, demonstrating proficiency in mathematics and English and maintaining a minimum 2.0 GPA. Students must complete the general education program and complete specific courses in physical education and fundamentals of speech.

Special: Numerous co-op and internship programs, including student teaching opportunities, are available. Millersville has exchange agreements with Franklin and Marshall College, Lancaster Theological Seminary, and Wallops Island Consortium, as well as 3-2 chemical and physical engineering programs with Pennsylvania State University. Study abroad is offered in Australia, Chile, China, England, France, Germany, Japan, Northern Island, Iceland, South Africa, Spain. Dual majors and accelerated degrees are possible in most disciplines. There are 13 national honor societies, a freshman honors program, and 12 departmental honors programs.

Faculty/Classroom: 49% of faculty are male; 51% are female. All teach undergraduates. No introductory courses are taught by graduate students. The average class size in an introductory lecture is 30; in a laboratory is 21; and in a regular course is 30.

Admissions: 72% of the 2013-2014 applicants were accepted. The SAT scores for the 2013-2014 freshman class were: Critical Reading--47% below 500, 41% between 500 and 599, 10% between 600 and 699, and 2% between 700 and 800; Math--42% below 500, 45% between 500 and 599, 12% between 600 and 699, and 1% between 700 and 800; Writing--54% below 500, 37% between 500 and 599, 8% between 600 and 699, and 1% between 700 and 800. The ACT scores were 39% below 21, 26% between 21 and 23, 24% between 24 and 26, 4% between 27 and 28, and 7% above 28. 27% of the current freshmen were in the top fifth of their class; 56% were in the top two fifths.

Requirements: The SAT is required. Applicants must hold a high school diploma or GED. The distribution of high school course units include: 4 units of English, 3 units each in math, science, and social studies, and 2 units of history. Auditions are required for the dance and theater programs. Millersville, MU requires applicants to be in the upper 30% of their class. A GPA of 2.0 is required. AP and CLEP credits are accepted. Important factors in the admissions decision are leadership record, extracurricular activities record, and advanced placement or honors courses.

Procedure: Freshmen are admitted to all sessions. Entrance exams should be taken in the spring of the junior year. There are deferred admissions and rolling admissions plans. Application deadlines are open. Application fee is $50. Notification is sent on a rolling basis. 243 applicants were on the 2013 waiting list; were admitted. Applications are accepted online.

Transfer: 629 transfer students enrolled in 2012-2013. All applicants must submit college transcripts and a statement of good standing from prior institution(s). Preference is given to students with 30 or more transferable credits with a 2.5 GPA or higher.Preference is given to graduates of in-state community colleges or transfers from other Pennsylvania State of

Higher Education schools. Applicants must have at least a 2.0 college GPA. 30 of 120 credits required for the bachelor's degree must be completed at Millersville.

Visiting: There are regularly scheduled orientations for prospective students, including tours of art/humanities facilities, athletic facilities, science and social science facilities, and student service facilities. There are guides for informal visits and visitors may sit in on classes. To schedule a visit, contact the Welcome Center Coordinator (717) 872-3371.

Financial Aid: In 2013-2014, 86% of all full-time freshmen and 82% of continuing full-time students received some form of financial aid. The average financial indebtedness of the 2013 graduate was $31,035. The FAFSA is required. The priority date for freshman financial aid applications for fall entry is March 15.

International Students: There are 55 international students enrolled. The school actively recruits these students. They must take the TOEFL with a minimum score of 550 on the paper-based TOEFL (PBT) or 79 on the Internet-based version (iBT). They must also take the SAT.

Graduates: From July 1, 2012 to June 30, 2013, 1450 bachelor's degrees were awarded. The most popular majors were business/marketing (12%), biology (10%), and psychology (7%). 186 companies recruited on campus in 2012-2013.

Admissions Contact: Brian Hazlett, Vice President for Enrollment Management. E-Mail: *admissions@millersville.edu* Web: *www.millersville.edu/admissions/undergrad/index.php*

MISERICORDIA UNIVERSITY E-2

Dallas, PA 18612 **(570) 674-6400**
(866) 262-6363; (570) 675-2441

Full-time: 620 men, 1170 women	**Faculty:** 95; IIB, av$
Part-time: 144 men, 483 women	**Ph.D.s:** 84%
Graduate: 191 men, 503 women	**Student/Faculty:** 18 to 1
Year: semesters, summer session	**Tuition:** $28,210
Application Deadline:	**Room & Board:** $11,630
Freshman Class: 2125 applied, 1379 accepted, 428 enrolled	
SAT CR/M: 520/540	**ACT:** 23 **COMPETITIVE**

Misericordia University, founded in 1924 by the Sisters of Mercy, is a private liberal arts institution affiliated with the Roman Catholic Church and offers professional programs in health-related fields. There are 3 undergraduate schools. In addition to regional accreditation, has baccalaureate program accreditation with APTA, ASLA, CAHEA, and CSWE. The library contains 81,201 volumes, 4,821 microform items, 11,800 audio/video tapes/CDs/DVDs, and subscribes to 310 periodicals including electronic. Computerized library services include interlibrary loans, database searching, Internet access, and Wi-Fi capability. Special learning facilities include an art gallery, radio station, and TV station. The 120-acre campus is in a suburban area 9 miles north of Wilkes-Barre. Including any residence halls, there are 22 buildings.

Student Life: 77% of undergraduates are from Pennsylvania. Others are from 23 states, and 1 foreign countries. 87% are from public schools. 95% are White. 46% are Catholic; 25% Protestant. The average age of freshmen is 18; all undergraduates, 24. 19% do not continue beyond their first year; 68% remain to graduate.

Housing: 1042 students can be accommodated in college housing, which includes coed dorms. In addition, there are special-interest houses. On-campus housing is guaranteed for the freshman year only, is available on a first-come, first-served basis, and is available on a lottery system for upperclassmen. 58% of students live on campus; of those, 50% remain on campus on weekends. Upperclassmen may keep cars.

Activities: There are no fraternities or sororities. There are 32 groups on campus, including cheerleading, choir, chorale, chorus, drama, ethnic, honors, international, literary magazine, musical theater, newspaper, political, professional, radio and TV, religious, social service, and student government. Popular campus events include Winter Snowball Dance, Homecoming and Spring Fest.

Sports: There are 10 intercollegiate sports for men and 11 for women, and 14 intramural sports for men and 14 for women. Facilities include The athletics facilities at Misericordia University recently underwent major renovations which provide MU's student-athletes with some of the finest competition venues in the region. The facilities - all located on campus - include the Anderson Center, Mangelsdorf Field at the Anderson Outdoor Athletics Complex, Tambur Field, Metz Field House, McGeehan Field, Anderson Softball Field and six tennis courts. The Anderson Center features a six-lane swimming pool, indoor track, racquetball courts, fitness center and an aerobic/dance studio.

Disabled Students: 95% of the campus is accessible. Facilities include wheelchair ramps, elevators, special parking, specially equipped restrooms, special class scheduling, and lowered drinking fountains.

Services: Counseling and information services are available, as is tutoring in every subject. There is a reader service for the blind. Services for students with disabilities are provided through the Alternative Learners Program.

Campus Safety and Security: Measures include 24-hour foot and vehicle patrol, emergency notification system, and security escort services. There are shuttle buses, emergency telephones, lighted pathways/sidewalks, and controlled access to dorms/residences.

Programs of Study: confers B.A., B.S., B.S.N. and B.S.W. degrees. Master's and doctoral degrees are also awarded. Bachelor's degrees are awarded in BIOLOGICAL SCIENCE (biochemistry and biology/biological science), BUSINESS (accounting, business administration and management, marketing/retailing/merchandising, and sports management), COMMUNICATIONS AND THE ARTS (communications and English), COMPUTER AND PHYSICAL SCIENCE (chemistry, computer science, information sciences and systems, and mathematics), EDUCATION (elementary education and special education), HEALTH PROFESSIONS (medical laboratory technology, nursing, occupational therapy, physical therapy, radiograph medical technology, and speech therapy), SOCIAL SCIENCE (history, interdisciplinary studies, liberal arts/general studies, philosophy, psychology, and social work). Occupational therapy, physical therapy, speech language pathology are the strongest academically. Nursing, business, occupational therapy have the largest enrollments.

Required: To graduate, students must earn a minimum of 120 credits. The required core curriculum includes courses in behavioral science, English literature, fine arts, history, math, philosophy, religious studies, and natural science. Within the core curriculum, students must complete one Unviersity Writing Seminar, and two additional courses that are writing intensive. A minimum GPA of 2.0 is required.

Special: Students may cross-register with King's College and Wilkes University. The college offers internships, work-study programs, study abroad, an accelerated degree program in Business, Govt Law and National Security, Applied Behavioral Science, and Nursing for adult students, and a student-designed major. Credit may be granted for life, military, and work experience through prior learning assessment. Nondegree study is also available. The college offers an alternative learner's project, which accepts a limited number of learning disabled students each year. There are 10 national honor societies, a freshman honors program, and 3 departmental honors programs.

Faculty/Classroom: 46% of faculty are male; 54% are female. 86% teach undergraduates, and 10% do both. No introductory courses are taught by graduate students. The average class size in an introductory lecture is 25; in a laboratory is 14; and in a regular course is 20.

Admissions: 65% of the 2013-2014 applicants were accepted. The SAT scores for the 2013-2014 freshman class were: Critical Reading--33% below 500, 52% between 500 and 599, 13% between 600 and 699, and 2% between 700 and 800; Math--23% below 500, 61% between 500 and 599, 15% between 600 and 699, and 1% between 700 and 800. The ACT scores were 26% below 21, 33% between 21 and 23, 23% between 24 and 26, 11% between 27 and 28, and 7% above 28. 45% of the current freshmen were in the top fifth of their class; 77% were in the top two fifths. 3 freshmen graduated first in their class.

Requirements: The SAT is required. In addition, applicants must graduate from an accredited secondary school or have a GED. 16 Carnegie units must be earned, and students must complete 3 years each in English, math, history, and science, and 2 to 3 years in social studies. requires applicants to be in the upper 50% of their class. A GPA of 2.0 is required. AP and CLEP credits are accepted. Important factors in the admissions decision are extracurricular activities record, advanced placement or honors courses, and leadership record.

Procedure: Freshmen are admitted fall and spring. Entrance exams should be taken during the junior year. There are deferred admissions and rolling admissions plans. Application deadlines are open. Application fee is $25. 70 applicants were on the 2013 waiting list; 5 were admitted. Applications are accepted online.

Transfer: 120 transfer students enrolled in 2012-2013. Applicants must have a minimum GPA of 2.0. Requirements may be higher for selected majors.

Visiting: There are regularly scheduled orientations for prospective students, meetings with admissions and financial aid counselors, a tour of the campus, and optional meetings with faculty and coaches. There are guides for informal visits, visitors may sit in on classes, and stay overnight. To schedule a visit, contact the Admissions Office.

Financial Aid: In 2013-2014, 99% of all full-time freshmen and 99% of continuing full-time students received some form of financial aid. 77% of all full-time freshmen and 71% of continuing full-time students received need-based aid. The average freshman award was $27,269. Need-based scholarships or need-based grants averaged $4,139 ($32,850 maximum); need-based self-help aid (loans and jobs) averaged $2,717 ($7,500 maximum); other non-need-based awards and non-need-based scholarships averaged $11,197 ($33,900 maximum); and $8,238 from other forms of aid. is a member of CSS. The FAFSA and the college's own financial statement are required. The priority date for freshman financial aid applications for fall entry is March 1. The deadline for filing freshman financial aid applications for fall entry is May 1.

International Students: There are 1 international students enrolled. The school actively recruits these students. They must take the TOEFL with a minimum score of 500 on the paper-based TOEFL (PBT) or 75 on the Internet-based version (iBT).

Graduates: From July 1, 2012 to June 30, 2013, 513 bachelor's degrees were awarded. The most popular majors were nursing (16%), business (11%), and psychology (10%). In an average class, 64% graduate in 4 years or less, 68% graduate in 5 years or less, and 69% graduate in 6 years or less. Of the 2012 graduating class, 25% were enrolled in graduate school within 6 months of graduation, and 84% were employed.

Admissions Contact: Glenn Bozinski, Director of Admissions. E-Mail: *admiss@misericordia.edu* Web: *www.misericordia.edu*

MOORE COLLEGE OF ART AND DESIGN F-3

Philadelphia, PA 19103 **(215) 568-4515, ext. 1105 (800) 523-2025, ext. 1105; (215) 568-8017**

Full-time: 455 women	**Faculty:** n/av
Part-time: 105 women	**Ph.D.s:** n/av
Graduate: 105 women	**Student/Faculty:** n/av
Year: semesters, summer session	**Tuition:** $31,978
Application Deadline: open	**Room & Board:** $12,323
Freshman Class: n/av	
SAT: recommended	

SPECIAL

Moore College of Art and Design, founded in 1844, is a private professional and fine arts college for women. There is 1 undergraduate school and 1 graduate school. Enrollment figures in the above capsule and figures in this profile are approximate. In addition to regional accreditation, Moore has baccalaureate program accreditation with FIDER and NASAD. The library contains 34,000 volumes and subscribes to 250 periodicals including electronic. Computerized library services include interlibrary loans, database searching, and Internet access. Special learning facilities include 2 art galleries. The 4-acre campus is in an urban area in Philadelphia. Including any residence halls, there are 4 buildings.

Student Life: 61% of undergraduates are from Pennsylvania. Others are from 29 states and 7 foreign countries. 60% are from public schools. 77% are white. The average age of freshmen is 19; all undergraduates, 23. 15% do not continue beyond their first year; 55% remain to graduate.

Housing: 194 students can be accommodated in college housing, which includes dorms and off-campus apartments. On-campus housing is guaranteed for all 4 years. 70% of students commute. Alcohol is not permitted. All students may keep cars.

Activities: There are no fraternities or sororities. There are 10 groups on campus, including computers, environmental action, ethnic, film, gay, international, newspaper, professional, social service, student government, and yearbook. Popular campus events include Spring Fling.

Sports: There is no sports program at Moore. Facilities include a fitness center with a weight room.

Disabled Students: All of the campus is accessible. Facilities include wheelchair ramps, elevators, special parking, specially equipped restrooms, lowered drinking fountains, and lowered telephones.

Services: Counseling and information services are available, as is tutoring in most subjects. English as a second language is offered.

Campus Safety and Security: Measures include 24-hour foot and vehicle patrol, self-defense education, and security escort services. There are shuttle buses, emergency telephones, and lighted pathways/sidewalks.

Programs of Study: Moore confers B.F.A. degrees. Master's degrees are also awarded. Bachelor's degrees are awarded in COMMUNICATIONS AND THE ARTS (fine arts, graphic design, illustration, painting, and sculpture), EDUCATION (art education), ENGINEERING AND ENVIRONMENTAL DESIGN (interior design), SOCIAL SCIENCE (fashion design and technology). Interior design is the strongest academically. Graphic design has the largest enrollment.

Required: All students take 36 credits in basic arts, including design, drawing, color, and art history, and a liberal arts core in history, humanities, and social science. A total of 125.5 to 137 credits, with a 2.0 minimum GPA, is required for graduation. A thesis is required in some programs.

Special: Moore has long-established cooperative relationships with various employers who provide training to supplement academic studies in all majors. Dual majors, nondegree study, study abroad, and continuing education programs are offered.

Faculty/Classroom: 38% of faculty are male; 62% are female. All teach undergraduates. No introductory courses are taught by graduate students. The average class size in an introductory lecture is 20 and in a regular course, 10.

Requirements: The SAT is recommended. Applicants should be graduates of accredited high schools or the equivalent, having taken 4 years of English and 2 years each of social studies, science, and math. At least 2 years of art study are also recommended. The most important part of the application is the portfolio of 8 to 12 original pieces, 6 of which should be drawings from observation. In addition, Moore strongly recommends a personal interview. A GPA of 2.5 is required. AP and CLEP credits are accepted. Important factors in the admissions decision are evidence of special talent, personality/intangible qualities, and extracurricular activities record.

Procedure: Freshmen are admitted fall and spring. There are early admissions, deferred admissions, and rolling admissions plans. Application deadlines are open. Check with the school for current application fee. Notification is sent on a rolling basis.

Transfer: Transfer applicants from non-art programs must meet freshman admission requirements. Others must submit a portfolio for review. Applicants should have at least a 2.0 GPA in previous college work and submit satisfactory SAT scores. A personal interview is required. 50 of 126 credits required for the bachelor's degree must be completed at Moore.

Visiting: There are regularly scheduled orientations for prospective students, including an open house in November. There are guides for informal visits; visitors may sit in on classes and stay overnight. To schedule a visit, contact the Admissions Office.

Financial Aid: Moore is a member of CSS. The CSS/Profile and the college's own financial statement are required. Check with the school for current deadlines.

International Students: The school actively recruits these students. They must take the TOEFL.

Admissions Contact: Heeseung Lee, Director of Admissions and Enrollment Management. E-Mail: *admiss@moore.edu* Web: *www.moore.edu*

MORAVIAN COLLEGE F-3

Bethlehem, PA 18018 **(610) 861-1320 (800) 441-3191; (610) 625-7930**

Full-time: 670 men, 875 women	**Faculty:** n/av; IIB, av$
Part-time: 65 men, 140 women	**Ph.D.s:** n/av
Graduate: 50 men,100 women	**Student/Faculty:** n/av
Year: semesters, summer session	**Tuition:** $34,086
Application Deadline: see profile	**Room & Board:** $9782
Freshman Class: n/av	
SAT or ACT: required	

VERY COMPETITIVE

Moravian College, established in 1742, is a private, liberal arts institution affiliated with the Moravian Church. There are 2 undergraduate schools and 1 graduate school. Figures in the above capsule and figures in this profile are approximate. In addition to regional accreditation, Moravian has baccalaureate program accreditation with CAHEA and NASM. The library contains 263,000 volumes, 11,000 microform items, 5385 audio/video tapes/CDs/DVDs, and subscribes to 15,415 periodicals including electronic. Computerized library services include interlibrary loans, database searching, and Internet access. Special learning facilities include a learning resource center, art gallery, and radio station. The 80-acre campus is in a suburban area 60 miles north of Philadelphia and 90 miles west of New York City. Including any residence halls, there are 127 buildings.

Student Life: 63% of undergraduates are from Pennsylvania. Others are from 20 states and 15 foreign countries. 79% are from public schools. 90% are white. 40% are Catholic; 27% Protestant; 12% claim no religious affiliation. The average age of freshmen is 18; all undergraduates, 20. 14% do not continue beyond their first year; 75% remain to graduate.

Housing: 1093 students can be accommodated in college housing, which includes single-sex and coed dorms and on-campus apartments. In addition, there are special-interest houses, fraternity houses, and sorority houses. On-campus housing is guaranteed for all 4 years. 71% of students live on campus; of those, 65% remain on campus on weekends. Upperclassmen may keep cars.

Activities: 10% of men belong to 1 local and 2 national fraternities; 22% of women belong to 4 national sororities. There are 77 groups on campus, including alumni, art, band, cheerleading, choir, chorale, chorus, communications, computers, dance, debate, drama, environmental, ethnic, gay, honors, international, jazz band, literary magazine, marching band, newspaper, orchestra, outdoor recreation, pep band, photography, political, professional, radio, religious, social, social service, and student government. Popular campus events include Arts and Lecture series, Christmas Vesper services, and Mardi Gras Dance.

Sports: There are 10 intercollegiate sports for men and 10 for women, and 11 intramural sports for men and 11 for women. Facilities include a 1200-seat gym, football, soccer, field hockey, and lacrosse fields, baseball and softball diamonds, indoor and all-weather tracks, indoor and outdoor tennis courts, a field house, a fitness room, an aerobics and dance studio, and 4 multipurpose courts.

Disabled Students: Facilities include wheelchair ramps, elevators, special parking, specially equipped restrooms, special class scheduling, lowered drinking fountains, lowered telephones, and special housing.

Services: Counseling and information services are available, as is tutoring in most subjects. There is a reader service for the blind, peer assistance, and a writing center.

Campus Safety and Security: Measures include 24-hour foot and vehicle patrol, emergency notification system, self-defense education, and

security escort services. There are shuttle buses, emergency telephones, lighted pathways/sidewalks, and an ongoing crime prevention program supervised by a crime prevention officer.

Programs of Study: Moravian confers B.A., B.S., and B.Mus. degrees. Master's degrees are also awarded. Bachelor's degrees are awarded in BIOLOGICAL SCIENCE (biochemistry, biology/biological science, and neurosciences), BUSINESS (accounting, business administration and management, business economics, and international business management), COMMUNICATIONS AND THE ARTS (art history and appreciation, classics, dramatic arts, English, French, German, graphic design, music, Spanish, and studio art), COMPUTER AND PHYSICAL SCIENCE (chemistry, computer science, mathematics, and physics), EDUCATION (art education, elementary education, music education, and secondary education), HEALTH PROFESSIONS (nursing), SOCIAL SCIENCE (criminal justice, economics, German area studies, history, philosophy, political science/government, psychology, religion, social science, and sociology). Physics, chemistry, and computer science are the strongest academically. Psychology, management, and sociology have the largest enrollments.

Required: To graduate, students must complete a Learning in Common curriculum, which includes courses in writing, quantitative reasoning, historical studies, ultimate questions, cultural values and global issues, natural sciences, a foreign language, social sciences, aesthetic expression, literature, moral life, and phys ed. They must maintain a minimum GPA of 2.0 and complete 32 courses equivalent to 128 credits. The number of hours required in the major varies.

Special: The college offers 3-2 engineering degrees in conjunction with Washington University and a 4-1 engineering program with Lehigh University. Moravian also offers cooperative programs in allied health, natural resource management, and geology with Lehigh, Duke, and Thomas Jefferson Universities. Cross-registration is available with Lehigh and DeSales Universities and Lafayette, Muhlenberg, and Cedar Crest Colleges. Internships, study abroad in many countries, a Washington semester, and student-designed majors may be pursued. There are 17 national honor societies and 30 departmental honors programs.

Faculty/Classroom: 51% of faculty are male; 49% are female. All teach and do research. No introductory courses are taught by graduate students. The average class size in an introductory lecture is 19; in a laboratory, 15; and in a regular course, 17.

Requirements: The SAT or ACT is required. Applicants must graduate from an accredited secondary school or have a GED. Moravian requires 16 Carnegie units, based on 4 years each of English and social science, 3 to 4 of math, and 2 each of lab science, a foreign language, and electives. Essays are required and interviews are recommended. For music students, auditions are required; for art students, portfolios are required. AP and CLEP credits are accepted. Important factors in the admissions decision are advanced placement or honors courses, recommendations by school officials, and leadership record.

Procedure: Freshmen are admitted fall and spring. Entrance exams should be taken with enough time to submit scores by the application deadline. There are early decision and deferred admissions plans. Early decision applications should be filed by February 1; check with the school for current application deadlines and fee. Notification of early decision is sent December 15. Applications are accepted online.

Transfer: Applicants must have a minimum GPA of 3.0 and are required to submit recommendations, secondary and postsecondary transcripts, and standardized test scores. 32 of 128 credits required for the bachelor's degree must be completed at Moravian.

Visiting: There are regularly scheduled orientations for prospective students, including information sessions, tours and interviews with admissions staff. There are guides for informal visits; visitors may sit in on classes and stay overnight. To schedule a visit, contact the Office of Admission.

Financial Aid: Moravian is a member of CSS. The CSS/Profile and FAFSA are required. Check with the school for current deadlines.

International Students: The school actively recruits these students. They must take the TOEFL with a minimum score of 550 on the paper-based TOEFL (PBT) or 80 on the Internet-based version (iBT). The SAT or ACT is preferred for all students and required if the student's first language is English.

Admissions Contact: James P. Mackin, Director of Admission. E-Mail: *admissions@moravian.edu* Web: *www.moravian.edu*

MOUNT ALOYSIUS COLLEGE C-3

Cresson, PA 16630 (814) 886-6383
(888) 823-2220; (814) 886-6441

Full-time: 385 men, 881 women	**Faculty:** 68
Part-time: 78 men, 267 women	**Ph.D.s:** 44%
Graduate: 11 men, 27 women	**Student/Faculty:** 19 to 1
Year: semesters, summer session	**Tuition:** $19,520
Application Deadline: rolling	**Room & Board:** $8450
Freshman Class: 1298 applied, 938 accepted, 355 enrolled	
SAT or ACT: required	**COMPETITIVE**

A comprehensive, private, Catholic, co-educational, liberal arts and sciences based college offering undergraduate and graduate education emphasizing career preparation and Mercy values. Our campus overlooks the Allegheny Mountains in the Laurel Highlands of west central Pennsylvania. There are 3 undergraduate schools and 1 graduate school. In addition to regional accreditation, Mount Aloysius College has baccalaureate program accreditation with APTA and NLN. The library contains 77,186 volumes, 4,680 microform items, 2,431 audio/video tapes/CDs/DVDs, and subscribes to 275 periodicals including electronic. Computerized library services include interlibrary loans and database searching. Special learning facilities include an art gallery. The 220-acre campus is in a small town located in the southern Allegheny Mountains between Altoona and Johnstown. Including any residence halls, there are 13 buildings.

Student Life: 90% of undergraduates are from Pennsylvania. Others are from 20 states, 15 foreign countries, and Canada. 80% are from public schools. 94% are White. 40% are Catholic; 35% Protestant. The average age of freshmen is 19; all undergraduates, 25. 30% do not continue beyond their first year; 60% remain to graduate.

Housing: 520 students can be accommodated in college housing, which includes single-sex and coed dorms and on-campus apartments. In addition, there are special-interest houses, Christian Living Community. On-campus housing is guaranteed for all 4 years, is available on a first-come, and first-served basis. Priority is given to out-of-town students. 60% of students commute. Alcohol is not permitted. All students may keep cars.

Activities: There are no fraternities or sororities. There are 100 groups on campus, including and campus ministry (community service organization) and all academic majors have a club, art, cheerleading, choir, chorale, chorus, computers, dance, drama, environmental, ethnic, forensics, honors, international, musical theater, newspaper, photography, political, professional, religious, social, social service, student government, and yearbook. Popular campus events include Madrigal Dinner, Heritage days, and Christmas at MAC.

Sports: There are 6 intercollegiate sports for men and 8 for women, and 13 intramural sports for men and 12 for women. Facilities include an 2000-seat health and physical fitness center with 3 basketball courts, 2 tennis courts, a volleyball court, a weight-and-exercise room equipped with a sauna, and 2 locker rooms.

Disabled Students: All of the campus is accessible. Facilities include wheelchair ramps, elevators, special parking, specially equipped restrooms, special class scheduling, lowered drinking fountains, lowered telephones, and special housing.

Services: Counseling and information services are available, as is tutoring in every subject. There is remedial math, reading, and writing.

Campus Safety and Security: Measures include 24-hour foot and vehicle patrol, emergency notification system, self-defense education, and security escort services. There are shuttle buses, emergency telephones, lighted pathways/sidewalks, and controlled access to dorms/residences.

Programs of Study: Mount Aloysius College confers B.A., and B.S. degrees. Associate and master's degrees are also awarded. Bachelor's degrees are awarded in BIOLOGICAL SCIENCE (biology/biological science, biotechnology, and environmental biology), BUSINESS (accounting, business administration and management, business economics, entrepreneurial studies, human resources, management information systems, management science, marketing management, nonprofit/public organization management, organizational leadership and management, and small business management), COMMUNICATIONS AND THE ARTS (American Sign Language, choral music, English, and voice), COMPUTER AND PHYSICAL SCIENCE (computer security and information assurance, information sciences and systems, radiological technology, science, and web technology), EDUCATION ((Education) Childhood Education, early childhood education, education, elementary education, English education, middle school education, science education, secondary education, and social studies education), ENGINEERING AND ENVIRONMENTAL DESIGN (computational sciences and environmental science), HEALTH PROFESSIONS (allied health, chiropractic, health care administration, medical laboratory technology, medical technology, nuclear medical technology, nursing, nursing home administration, occupational therapy, physical therapy, physical therapy assistant, physician's assistant, preallied health, predentistry, premedicine, preoptometry, preosteopathy, prepharmacy, prephysical therapy, prepodiatry, preventive/wellness health care, preveterinary science, radiation therapy, radiograph medical technology, radiological science, and ultrasound technology), SOCIAL SCIENCE (behavioral science, child care/child and family studies, community psychology, criminal justice, criminology, history, humanities, humanities and social science, interpreter for the deaf, law, law enforcement and corrections, liberal arts/general studies, paralegal studies, political science/government, prelaw, psychology, public administration, religion, social studies, and women's studies). Nursing, medical imaging, allied health sciences, business, accounting, education, pre-law, and criminology are the strongest academically and has the largest enrollments.

Required: Baccalaureate level students are required during their final semester of study to complete 2 3-credit courses designed to integrate and synthesize scientific, behavioral, and moral concepts. Students in allied health programs must complete an approved clinical experience. Courses in research writing and speech are required. A total of 120 credits is required with an overall 2.0 GPA, including a C average in all core courses.

Special: The Professional Studies curriculum provides a student-designed course of study, with an emphasis in behavior and social science, humanities, math/science/computer science, or prelaw. B.A.-B.S. degrees are offered, as are internships in nursing, business, criminology, and student teaching. Our education department offers Early Level Pre K-4/Middle Level 4-8, and secondary education. There are 3 national honor societies, a freshman honors program, and 1 departmental honors program.

Faculty/Classroom: 39% of faculty are male; 61% are female. All teach and do research. No introductory courses are taught by graduate students. The average class size in an introductory lecture is 17; in a laboratory is 12; and in a regular course is 17.

Admissions: 72% of the 2013-2014 applicants were accepted. 5 freshmen graduated first in their class.

Requirements: The SAT or ACT is required. Applicants must graduate from an accredited high school or have the GED. A placement test and any necessary developmental studies classes may need to be taken. Science classes and an interview are required of some allied health programs. AP and CLEP credits are accepted. Important factors in the admissions decision are recommendations by school officials, advanced placement or honors courses, and leadership record.

Procedure: Freshmen are admitted fall and spring. Entrance exams should be taken as early as possible. There is a rolling admissions plan. Check with the school for current application deadlines. The application fee is $30. Notifications are sent in weekly. Applications are accepted online.

Transfer: 250 transfer students enrolled in 2012-2013. Transfer students must have a 2.0 GPA. Only courses with a C or better will be considered for transfer; all other requirements are the same as for freshmen. 30 of 120 credits required for the bachelor's degree must be completed at Mount Aloysius College.

Visiting: There are regularly scheduled orientations for prospective students, on the hour and select Saturdays. There are guides for informal visits, visitors may sit in on classes, and stay overnight. To schedule a visit, contact the Admissions Office at admissions@mtaloy.edu.

Financial Aid: In 2013-2014, 94% of all full-time freshmen and 95% of continuing full-time students received some form of financial aid. 85% of all full-time freshmen and 86% of continuing full-time students received need-based aid. The average freshman award was $11,000. Need-based scholarships or need-based grants averaged $3,000 ($5,000 maximum); need-based self-help aid (loans and jobs) averaged $3,000 ($5,000 maximum); and other non-need-based awards and non-need-based scholarships averaged $3,000 ($7,000 maximum). 65% of undergraduate students work part-time. Average annual earnings from campus work are $750. The average financial indebtedness of the 2013 graduate was $17,125. Mount Aloysius College is a member of CSS. The FAFSA, and Affidavit for International Students is required. The priority date for freshman financial aid applications for fall entry is April 1. The deadline for filing freshman financial aid applications for fall entry is May 1.

International Students: There are 15 international students enrolled. The school actively recruits these students. They must take the TOEFL with a minimum score of 61 on the Internet-based version (iBT) and the Comprehensive English Language Test. They must also take the SAT or ACT. New Jersey Basic Skills Test.

Graduates: From July 1, 2012 to June 30, 2013, 146 bachelor's degrees were awarded. The most popular majors were nursing (12%), RN-BSN (9%), and medical imaging (6%). 50 companies recruited on campus in 2012-2013. In an average class, 33% graduate in 3 years or less, 48% graduate in 4 years or less, 54% graduate in 5 years or less, and 56% graduate in 6 years or less. Of the 2012 graduating class, 22% were enrolled in graduate school within 6 months of graduation, and 97% were employed.

Admissions Contact: Francis Crouse, Vice President for Enrollment Management. E-Mail: *admissions@mtaloy.edu* Web: *www.mtaloy.edu*

MUHLENBERG COLLEGE — E-3

Allentown, PA 18104 — (484) 664-3200; (484) 664-3234

Full-time: 948 men, 1375 women	**Faculty:** 173; IIB, av$
Part-time: 61 men, 64 women	**Ph.D.s:** 88%
Graduate: n/av	**Student/Faculty:** 11 to 1
Year: semesters, summer session	**Tuition:** $42,755
Application Deadline: February 15	**Room & Board:** $10,080
Freshman Class: 5152 applied, 2378 accepted, 579 enrolled	
	HIGHLY COMPETITIVE

Muhlenberg College, established in 1848, is a private liberal arts institution affiliated with the Lutheran Church. The library contains 338,859 volumes, 359,462 microform items, 12,836 audio/video tapes/CDs/DVDs, and subscribes to 39,453 periodicals including electronic. Computerized library services include interlibrary loans, database searching, Internet access, and Wi-Fi capability. Special learning facilities include an art gallery, natural history museum, radio station, TV station, 2 environmental field stations. The 82-acre campus is in a suburban area 50 miles north of Philadelphia and 90 miles west of New York City. Including any residence halls, there are 91 buildings.

Student Life: 79% of undergraduates are from out of state, mostly the Middle Atlantic. Students are from 39 states, and 15 foreign countries. 70% are from public schools. 77% are White; 32% are Jewish; 30% Catholic; 12% Protestant. The average age of freshmen is 18; all undergraduates, 21. 10% do not continue beyond their first year; 86% remain to graduate.

Housing: 2006 students can be accommodated in college housing, which includes single-sex and coed dorms, on-campus apartments, and off-campus apartments. In addition, there are language houses, special-interest houses, fraternity houses, and college-owned houses in the surrounding community. On-campus housing is guaranteed for all 4 years. 92% of students live on campus; of those, 80% remain on campus on weekends. Upperclassmen may keep cars.

Activities: 14% of men belong to 4 national fraternities, 17% of women belong to 1 local and 4 national sororities. There are 126 groups on campus, including and step team, human rights, art, band, cheerleading, chess, choir, chorale, chorus, computers, dance, drama, environmental, ethnic, film, gay, honors, international, jazz band, literary magazine, musical theater, newspaper, opera, orchestra, pep band, photography, political, professional, radio and TV, religious, social, social service, student government, and yearbook. Popular campus events include Spring Fling Weekend, Candlelight Carols and Jefferson Field Day.

Sports: There are 11 intercollegiate sports for men and 11 for women, and 13 intramural sports for men and 13 for women. Facilities include a sports center, which contains a 6-lane swimming pool, racquetball and squash courts, wrestling and weight training rooms; a multipurpose field house with indoor tennis courts, a running track, and basketball and tennis courts, as well as a large aerobic fitness center and weight room; and out door volleyball and a football/lacrosse/field hockey stadium.

Disabled Students: 95% of the campus is accessible. Facilities include wheelchair ramps, elevators, special parking, specially equipped restrooms, special class scheduling, lowered drinking fountains, lowered telephones, special housing.

Services: Counseling and information services are available, as is tutoring in every subject. There is a reader service for the blind. There is also a writing center.

Campus Safety and Security: Measures include 24-hour foot and vehicle patrol, self-defense education, and security escort services. There are shuttle buses, emergency telephones, and lighted pathways/sidewalks.

Programs of Study: Muhlenberg confers B.A., and B.S. degrees. Associate degrees are also awarded. Bachelor's degrees are awarded in BIOLOGICAL SCIENCE (biochemistry, biology/biological science, and neurosciences), BUSINESS (accounting, banking and finance, and business administration and management), COMMUNICATIONS AND THE ARTS (art, communications, dance, dramatic arts, English, film arts, French, German, music, and Spanish), COMPUTER AND PHYSICAL SCIENCE (chemistry, computer science, mathematics, natural sciences, physical sciences, and physics), ENGINEERING AND ENVIRONMENTAL DESIGN (environmental science), SOCIAL SCIENCE (American studies, anthropology, economics, German area studies, history, international studies, philosophy, political science/government, psychology, religion, Russian and Slavic studies, and sociology). Biology, theatre, and psychology are the strongest academically. Biology, business administration, and psychology have the largest enrollments.

Required: The Muhlenberg curriculum is designed to engage students in thoughtful deliberation, critical analysis, and creative thinking. Students will complete a diverse set of general academic requirements and a major in their chosen field of specialization. They will earn no fewer than 34 course units with a cumulative grade point average of not less than 2.00. Skills are acquired through courses emphasizing writing, critical thinking, and language proficiency. Required courses include a First Year Seminar, writing-intensive courses, two semesters of foreign language, and a course in logic or mathematical reasoning. A breadth of knowledge is achieved through study in each of the four academic divisions: Arts (one required), Humanities (three required), Social Sciences (two required), and Natural Sciences (two required). Further, the curriculum encourages students to move between different disciplines in order to learn what sets them apart and how to bring them together. Required courses include a two-course cluster focused on related subject matter approached from different disciplinary angles or points of view, two courses in human difference and global engagement, and a culminating undergraduate experience specified by the major. Students may choose from a wide variety of majors, from accounting to sociology (40 majors in all, plus a self-designed major option). The major provides an in-depth study in the selected field and preparation for work, graduate, or professional school. Majors vary in the number of units required from nine to fifteen, but all students must earn a grade point average of not less than 2.00. A significant percentage of Muhlenberg seniors graduate with double majors, and many majors offer departmental honors programs, senior portfolios, recitals, and mentored research opportunities.

Special: Students may cross-register with Lehigh, Lafayette, Cedar Crest, Moravian, and Allentown Colleges. Internships, work-study programs, B.A-B.S. degrees, study abroad in Asia, Australia, Latin America, Russia, and Europe, and a Washington semester are available. Dual majors and student-designed majors may be pursued. A 3-2 engineering degree is available in cooperation with Columbia and Washington Universities, a 4-4 assured admission medical program is offered with Drexel University College of Medicine, a 3-4 dental program is offered with University of Pennsylvania, and a 3-2 forestry degree is offered in cooperation with Duke University. An army ROTC program is also available. Nondegree study and a pass/fail grading option are also offered. There are 14 national honor societies, including Phi Beta Kappa, a freshman honors program, and 8 departmental honors programs.

Faculty/Classroom: 50% of faculty are male; 50% are female. All teach undergraduates, and 84% do both. No introductory courses are taught by graduate students. The average class size in an introductory lecture is 26; in a laboratory is 16; and in a regular course is 19.

Admissions: 46% of the 2013-2014 applicants were accepted. The SAT scores for the 2013-2014 freshman class were: Critical Reading--3% below 500, 35% between 500 and 599, 45% between 600 and 699, and 17% between 700 and 800; Math--4% below 500, 33% between 500 and 599, 52% between 600 and 699, and 11% between 700 and 800; Writing--3% below 500, 36% between 500 and 599, 45% between 600 and 699, and 16% between 700 and 800. The ACT scores were 23% above 28.

Requirements: Applicants must graduate from an accredited secondary school or have a GED. 16 Carnegie units are required, and students must complete 4 courses in English, 3 in math, and 2 each in history, science, and a foreign language. All students must submit essays. Interviews are recommended and are required for those who do not submit SAT scores. AP and CLEP credits are accepted. Important factors in the admissions decision are geographical diversity, evidence of special talent, personality/intangible qualities, parents or siblings attended your school, extracurricular activities record, recommendations by alumni, recommendations by school officials, ability to finance college education, leadership record, and advanced placement or honors courses.

Procedure: Freshmen are admitted fall and spring. Entrance exams should be taken during the spring of the junior year or the fall of the senior year. There are early decision and deferred admissions plans. Early decision applications should be filed by February 1; regular applications, by February 15 for fall entry, along with a $50 fee. Notifications are sent March 15. 313 early decision candidates were accepted for the 2013-2014 class. 399 applicants were on the 2013 waiting list; 52 were admitted. Applications are accepted online.

Transfer: 12 transfer students enrolled in 2012-2013. A minimum college GPA of 2.5 and an interview are required. 17 of 34 credits required for the bachelor's degree must be completed at Berg.

Visiting: There are regularly scheduled orientations for prospective students, consisting of a tour of the campus and a personal interview. There are 2 open houses in the fall and 1 in the spring. There are guides for informal visits, visitors may sit in on classes, and stay overnight.

Financial Aid: In 2013-2014, 90% of all full-time freshmen and 82% of continuing full-time students received some form of financial aid. 53% of all full-time freshmen and 51% of continuing full-time students received need-based aid. The average freshman award was $24,762. Need-based scholarships or need-based grants averaged $25,175 ($46,700 maximum); need-based self-help aid (loans and jobs) averaged $5,119 ($9,300 maximum); and other non-need-based awards and non-need-based scholarships averaged $12,215 ($26,000 maximum). 20% of undergraduate students work part-time. Average annual earnings from campus work are $1000. The average financial indebtedness of the 2013 graduate was $25,858. Muhlenberg is a member of CSS. The CSS/Profile, FAFSA, and the college's own financial statement, and parent and student tax returns and W-2 forms are required. The priority date for freshman financial aid applications for fall entry is February 15. The deadline for filing freshman financial aid applications for fall entry is February 15.

International Students: There are 15 international students enrolled. The school actively recruits these students. They must take the TOEFL with a minimum score of 550 on the paper-based TOEFL (PBT).

Graduates: From July 1, 2012 to June 30, 2013, 596 bachelor's degrees were awarded. The most popular majors were business (23%), theatre/dance (18%), and psychology (13%). 74 companies recruited on campus in 2012-2013. In an average class, 3% graduate in 3 years or less, 81% graduate in 4 years or less, 85% graduate in 5 years or less, and 86% graduate in 6 years or less. Of the 2012 graduating class, 35% were enrolled in graduate school within 6 months of graduation, and 62% were employed.

Admissions Contact: Christopher Hooker-Haring, Dean of Admissions.
E-Mail: *admissions@muhlenberg.edu* Web: *www.muhlenberg.edu*

NEUMANN UNIVERSITY F-3

Aston, PA 19014 (610) 558-5616
(800) 9NEUMAN; (610) 558-5652

Full-time: 720 men, 1292 women	**Faculty:** 85; IIB, -$
Part-time: 150 men, 339 women	**Ph.D.s:** 63%
Graduate: 191 men, 407 women	**Student/Faculty:** 25 to 1
Year: semesters, summer session	**Tuition:** $21,360
Application Deadline:	**Room & Board:** $9718

Freshman Class: 2358 applied, 2213 accepted, 520 enrolled
SAT: required

LESS COMPETITIVE

Neumann University, founded in 1965 by the Sisters of St. Francis, is a private liberal arts institution affiliated with the Roman Catholic Church. There are 5 graduate schools. In addition to regional accreditation, Neumann has baccalaureate program accreditation with ACBSP, CAHEA, and NLN. The library contains 90,000 volumes, 99,758 microform items, and 36,562 audio/video tapes/CDs/DVDs, and subscribes to 700 periodicals including electronic. Computerized library services include interlibrary loans, database searching, Internet access, and Wi-Fi capability. Special learning facilities include a radio station and TV station. The 50-acre campus is in a suburban area 15 miles southwest of Philadelphia. Including any residence halls, there are 6 buildings.

Student Life: 68% of undergraduates are from Pennsylvania. Others are from 24 states, 8 foreign countries, and Canada. 35% are from public schools. 58% are White; 13% African American. 56% are Catholic; 30% Protestant; 11% claim no religious affiliation. The average age of freshmen is 18; all undergraduates, 20. 26% do not continue beyond their first year; 55% remain to graduate.

Housing: 800 students can be accommodated in college housing, which includes coed dorms and off-campus apartments. On-campus housing is available on a first-come and first-served basis. Priority is given to out-of-town students. 60% of students commute. Alcohol is not permitted. All students may keep cars.

Activities: There are no fraternities or sororities. There are 17 groups on campus, including cheerleading, choir, chorus, dance, drama, ethnic, honors, literary magazine, newspaper, photography, political, professional, radio and TV, religious, social, social service, and student government. Popular campus events include Dinner Dances, Spring Fling, and Charity Fund-raising.

Sports: There are 8 intercollegiate sports for men and 9 for women, and 6 intramural sports for men and 6 for women. Facilities include a 350-seat gym, weight and fitness rooms, tennis courts, baseball and softball fields, an ice hockey rink, video games, and a theater.

Disabled Students: All of the campus is accessible. Facilities include wheelchair ramps, elevators, special parking, specially equipped restrooms, and special class scheduling.

Services: Counseling and information services are available, as is tutoring in every subject. There is a reader service for the blind, and remedial math, reading, and writing.

Campus Safety and Security: Measures include 24-hour foot and vehicle patrol, emergency notification system, self-defense education, and security escort services. There are shuttle buses, emergency telephones, and lighted pathways/sidewalks.

Programs of Study: Neumann confers B.A., and B.S. degrees. Associate, master's, and doctoral degrees are also awarded. Bachelor's degrees are awarded in AGRICULTURE (environmental studies), BIOLOGICAL SCIENCE (biology/biological science), BUSINESS (accounting, business administration and management, international business management, marketing and distribution, and sports management), COMMUNICATIONS AND THE ARTS (communications, digital communications, English, and performing arts), COMPUTER AND PHYSICAL SCIENCE (computer science), EDUCATION (athletic training, early childhood education, and elementary education), HEALTH PROFESSIONS (nursing), SOCIAL SCIENCE (criminal justice, liberal arts/general studies, political science/government, and psychology). Biology, nursing, and elementary education are the strongest academically. Nursing, elementary education, and liberal studies have the largest enrollments.

Required: To graduate, all students must complete 120 to 130 credits, including 44 credits of core requirements, with 30 to 50 in the major. A minimum 2.0 GPA is required.

Special: The college offers co-op programs in all majors, study abroad in England, Italy, Spain, and France, internships, work-study programs, dual majors, and a general studies degree. Credit for life, work, and military experience, nondegree study, an accelerated degree program in liberal studies, and pass/fail options are available. There are 4 national honor societies, a freshman honors program, and 1 departmental honors programs.
Faculty/Classroom: 40% of faculty are male; 60% are female. 96% teach undergraduates, and 15% do both. No introductory courses are taught by graduate students. The average class size in an introductory lecture is 26; in a laboratory is 18; and in a regular course is 19.
Admissions: 94% of the 2013-2014 applicants were accepted. 30% of the current freshmen were in the top fifth of their class; 90% were in the top two fifths.
Requirements: The SAT is required. Applicants must be graduates of an accredited secondary school or have a GED. High school courses must include 4 years of English and 2 years each of a foreign language, history, and science. An interview is recommended. A GPA of 2.0 is required. AP and CLEP credits are accepted. Important factors in the admissions decision are recommendations by school officials.
Procedure: Freshmen are admitted fall and spring. Entrance exams should be taken by December of the senior year. There are deferred admissions and rolling admissions plans. Application deadlines are open. Application fee is $35. Applications are accepted online.
Transfer: 68 transfer students enrolled in 2012-2013. Applicants should submit transcripts from all institutions attended. 30 of 120 credits required for the bachelor's degree must be completed at Neumann.
Visiting: There are regularly scheduled orientations for prospective students, including class visits and informal meetings with faculty. There are guides for informal visits and visitors may sit in on classes. To schedule a visit, contact the Admissions Office.
Financial Aid: In 2013-2014, 95% of all full-time freshmen and 90% of continuing full-time students received some form of financial aid. 90% of all full-time freshmen and 90% of continuing full-time students received need-based aid. The average freshman award was $18,000. Need-based scholarships or need-based grants averaged $15,000 ($18,000 maximum); and need-based self-help aid (loans and jobs) averaged $5,000 ($7,000 maximum). 90% of undergraduate students work part-time. Average annual earnings from campus work are $1600. The average financial indebtedness of the 2013 graduate was $40,000. The FAFSA is required. The deadline for filing freshman financial aid applications for fall entry is March 15.
International Students: There are 55 international students enrolled. They must take the TOEFL with a minimum score of 550 on the paper-based TOEFL (PBT) or 70 on the Internet-based version (iBT). They must also take the SAT.
Graduates: From July 1, 2012 to June 30, 2013, 464 bachelor's degrees were awarded. The most popular majors were liberal studies (30%), nursing (14%), and elementary education (13%). 55 companies recruited on campus in 2012-2013. In an average class, 40% graduate in 4 years or less, 50% graduate in 5 years or less, and 55% graduate in 6 years or less. Of the 2012 graduating class, 20% were enrolled in graduate school within 6 months of graduation, and 95% were employed.
Admissions Contact: Christina Rufo, Director of Admissions. E-Mail: *neumann@neumann.edu* Web: *www.neumann.edu*

PEIRCE COLLEGE F-3

Philadelphia, PA 19102 (215) 670-9214
(888) 467-3472; (888) 467-3472

Full-time: 205 men, 605 women	**Faculty:** n/av
Part-time: 325 men, 850 women	**Ph.D.s:** n/av
Graduate: n/av	**Student/Faculty:** n/av
Year: see profile, summer session	**Tuition:** $16,400
Application Deadline: open	**Room & Board:** n/app
Freshman Class: n/av	

NONCOMPETITIVE

Peirce College, founded in 1865, is a private specialized institution providing practical curricula to primarily working adults. Peirce offers accelerated bachelor's and associate degree programs in business administration, information technology, and paralegal studies, utilizing 3 interchangeable delivery formats: on campus, in Center City Philadelphia; on site at corporate and community locations throughout the region; and online through web-based distance learning. Figures in the above capsule and figures in this profile are approximate. In addition to regional accreditation, Peirce has baccalaureate program accreditation with ACBSP. The library contains 30,000 volumes and subscribes to 25,000 periodicals including electronic. Computerized library services include interlibrary loans, database searching, and Internet access. Special learning facilities include a learning resource center, the Walker Center for Academic Excellence. The 1-acre campus is in an urban area in the Center City Business District. There are 2 buildings.
Student Life: 80% of undergraduates are from Pennsylvania. Others are from 40 states, 30 foreign countries, and Canada. 50% are African American; 31% white. The average age of freshmen is 31; all undergraduates, 33. 7% do not continue beyond their first year; 53% remain to graduate.
Housing: There are no residence halls. All students commute.
Activities: There are no fraternities or sororities. There are 3 groups on campus, including honors and professional. Popular campus events include Student Leadership Retreat, Welcome Back Day, and Annual Awards Induction Ceremony.
Sports: There is no sports program at Peirce.
Disabled Students: All of the campus is accessible. Facilities include wheelchair ramps, elevators, specially equipped restrooms, special class scheduling, lowered drinking fountains, and lowered telephones.
Services: Counseling and information services are available, as is tutoring in most subjects. There is a reader service for the blind, and remedial math, reading, and writing.
Campus Safety and Security: Measures include 24-hour foot and vehicle patrol and security escort services. There are emergency telephones, lighted pathways/sidewalks, and security cameras throughout the campus.
Programs of Study: Peirce confers B.S. degrees. Associates degrees are also awarded. Bachelor's degrees are awarded in BUSINESS (accounting, business administration and management, business law, entrepreneurial studies, human resources, management information systems, marketing management, and real estate), COMPUTER AND PHYSICAL SCIENCE (computer management, computer programming, and information sciences and systems), ENGINEERING AND ENVIRONMENTAL DESIGN (computer technology), SOCIAL SCIENCE (paralegal studies). Paralegal studies is the strongest academically. Business administration has the largest enrollment.
Required: To graduate, all students must complete 121 credit hours, including a core curriculum, and maintain a minimum cumulative GPA of 2.0.
Special: The college offers accelerated degrees and co-op programs in most major programs of study. There are 2 national honor societies.
Faculty/Classroom: 62% of faculty are male; 38% are female. All teach undergraduates. No introductory courses are taught by graduate students. The average class size in an introductory lecture is 19 and in a regular course, 18.
Requirements: Applicants for a degree program must submit an official transcript documenting high school graduation or a copy of the GED or state equivalency diploma and scores. AP and CLEP credits are accepted.
Procedure: Freshmen are admitted to all sessions. Entrance exams are offered continuously. There are deferred admissions and rolling admissions plans. Application deadlines are open. Application fee is $50. Notification is sent on a rolling basis. Applications are accepted online.
Transfer: Transcripts from other colleges attended must be submitted. 31 of 121 credits required for the bachelor's degree must be completed at Peirce.
Visiting: There are regularly scheduled orientations for prospective students, including a campus tour and a meeting with an adviser. There are guides for informal visits, and visitors may sit in on classes. To schedule a visit, contact Enrollment Services.
Financial Aid: The FAFSA and the college's own financial statement are required. Check with the school for current deadlines.
International Students: The school actively recruits these students.
Admissions Contact: Admissions, Enrollment Representative. E-Mail: *info@peirce.edu* Web: *www.peirce.edu*

PENN STATE ERIE/THE BEHREND COLLEGE B-1

Erie, PA 16563 (814) 898-6100
(866) 374-3378; (814) 898-6044

Full-time: 2473 men, 1358 women	**Faculty:** 204; IIB, av$
Part-time: 103 men, 81 women	**Ph.D.s:** 61%
Graduate: 81 men, 26 women	**Student/Faculty:** 16 to 1
Year: semesters, summer session	**Tuition:** $11,500 ($16,500)
Application Deadline: open	**Room & Board:** $6730
Freshman Class: 2590 applied, 2092 accepted, 854 enrolled	
SAT or ACT: required	

COMPETITIVE

Penn State Erie, The Behrend College, founded in 1948, offers 34 baccalaureate programs as well as the first 2 years of most Penn State University Park baccalaureate programs. It offers courses in business, humanities, social sciences, science, engineering technology, and engineering. There are 5 undergraduate schools and 1 graduate school. In addition to regional accreditation, Penn State Erie has baccalaureate program accreditation with AACSB, ABET, and NLN. Computerized library services include interlibrary loans, database searching, Internet access, and laptop Internet portals. Special learning facilities include a learning resource center, radio station, engineering workstation labs, media labs, and an observatory. The 840-acre campus is in a suburban area 5 miles east of Erie. Including any residence halls, there are 45 buildings.

Student Life: 92% of undergraduates are from Pennsylvania. Others are from 28 states, 23 foreign countries, and Canada. 86% are white. The average age of freshmen is 18; all undergraduates, 22. 9% do not continue beyond their first year; 61% remain to graduate.

Housing: 1650 students can be accommodated in college housing, which includes single-sex and coed dorms and on-campus apartments. In addition, there are honors houses, special-interest houses, and a freshman interest groups. On-campus housing is guaranteed for the freshman year only, is available on a first-come, first-served basis, and is available on a lottery system for upperclassmen. 53% of students commute. Alcohol is not permitted. All students may keep cars.

Activities: 5% of men belong to 3 national fraternities; 16% of women belong to 3 national sororities. There are 80 groups on campus, including band, cheerleading, chess, choir, computers, dance, drama, ethnic, gay, honors, international, jazz band, literary magazine, newspaper, pep band, political, professional, radio and TV, religious, social, social service, student government, and yearbook. Popular campus events include a speaker series, parents events, and Black Cultural Awareness Month.

Sports: There are 10 intercollegiate sports for men and 11 for women, and 18 intramural sports for men and 18 for women. Facilities include new athletic center with an indoor track and an 8-lane pool, tennis courts, a weight room, a fitness trail, basketball courts, and baseball, softball, and soccer fields.

Disabled Students: 90% of the campus is accessible. Facilities include wheelchair ramps, elevators, special parking, specially equipped restrooms, special class scheduling, lowered drinking fountains, and lowered telephones.

Services: Counseling and information services are available, as is tutoring in every subject. There is a reader service for the blind, and remedial math, reading, and writing.

Campus Safety and Security: Measures include 24-hour foot and vehicle patrol, self-defense education, and security escort services. There are emergency telephones and lighted pathways/sidewalks.

Programs of Study: Penn State Erie confers B.A., B.S., B.F.A. degrees. Associate and master's degrees are also awarded. Bachelor's degrees are awarded in BIOLOGICAL SCIENCE (biology/biological science), BUSINESS (accounting, banking and finance, business administration and management, business economics, management information systems, and marketing management), COMMUNICATIONS AND THE ARTS (communications and English), COMPUTER AND PHYSICAL SCIENCE (chemistry, computer science, mathematics, physics, and science), ENGINEERING AND ENVIRONMENTAL DESIGN (computer engineering, engineering, engineering technology, mechanical engineering technology, and plastics technology), SOCIAL SCIENCE (economics, history, political science/government, and psychology). Management information systems, psychology, and math are the strongest academically. Engineering, business, and psychology have the largest enrollments.

Required: All baccalaureate degree candidates must take 46 general education credits, including 27 in arts, humanities, natural science, and social and behavioral sciences including a cultural diversity course, 15 in quantification and communication skills including a writing intensive course, and 3 in health, phys ed, and a freshman seminar. All students must complete a minimum of 120 credit hours with a minimum GPA of 2.0. Further requirements vary by degree program.

Special: Internships, study abroad in 14 countries, work-study programs, and accelerated degree programs are available. In addition, a B.A.-B.S. degree in psychology, a 3-2 engineering degree with Edinboro University, dual majors, a general studies degree, and student-designed majors in business and general arts and sciences are offered. Nondegree study and up to 12 credits of pass/fail options are possible. There are 4 national honor societies and a freshman honors program.

Faculty/Classroom: 70% of faculty are male; 30% are female. All teach and do research. No introductory courses are taught by graduate students. The average class size in an introductory lecture is 35; in a laboratory is 18; and in a regular course is 29.

Admissions: 81% of the 2011-2012 applicants were accepted. 25% of the current freshmen were in the top fifth of their class; 40% were in the top two fifths. 12 freshmen graduated first in their class.

Requirements: The SAT or ACT is required. Candidates for admission must have 15 academic credits or 15 Carnegie units, including 5 in social studies, 4 in English, 3 each in math and science, and 2 in foreign language. The GED is accepted. AP and CLEP credits are accepted.

Procedure: Freshmen are admitted to all sessions. Entrance exams should be taken during the junior year. There are deferred admissions and rolling admissions plans. Application deadlines are open. Application fee is $50. Notification is sent on a rolling basis. Applications are accepted online.

Transfer: Transfer candidates need a minimum GPA of 2.4, good academic standing, and 18 or more credits from a regionally accredited institution at the college level. 36 of 120 credits required for the bachelor's degree must be completed at Penn State Erie.

Visiting: There are regularly scheduled orientations for prospective students, including meetings with a counselor and faculty, a campus tour, and a class visit. There are guides for informal visits, visitors may sit in on classes, and stay overnight. To schedule a visit, contact the Admissions Office.

Financial Aid: The FAFSA is required. The priority date for freshman financial aid applications for fall entry is February 15.

International Students: There are 32 international students enrolled. The school actively recruits these students. They must take the TOEFL.

Computers: Wireless access is available. All students may access the system any time by modem or network. There are no time limits and no fees. It is strongly recommended that all students have a personal computer.

Admissions Contact: Mary-Ellen Madigan, Director of Admissions. E-Mail: *behrend.admissions@psu.edu* Web: *www.pserie.psu.edu*

PENN STATE UNIVERSITY/ALTOONA — C-3

Altoona, PA 16601 — **(814) 949-5466; (800) 848-9843**

Full-time: 1955 men, 1815 women	**Faculty:** n/av
Part-time: 115 men, 178 women	**Ph.D.s:** n/av
Graduate: 5 men, 5 women	**Student/Faculty:** n/av
Year: semesters, summer session	**Tuition:** $15,024 ($27,700)
Application Deadline: open	**Room & Board:** $10,500
Freshman Class: n/av	
SAT or ACT: required	

COMPETITIVE

Penn State Altoona, founded in 1939, offers 18 baccalaureate degree programs, 8 associate degrees, and 19 minors. There are 17 undergraduate schools and 1 graduate school. Figures in the above capsule and in this profile are approximate. In addition to regional accreditation, Penn State Altoona has baccalaureate program accreditation with ABET, NASAD, NCATE, and NRPA. The library contains 90,000 audio/video tapes/CDs/DVDs, and subscribes to 500 periodicals including electronic. Computerized library services include interlibrary loans, database searching, Internet access, and laptop Internet portals. Special learning facilities include a learning resource center, art gallery, Pic-Tel teleconferencing, 5 state-of-the-art engineering labs, and CAD/CAM computer lab facilities. The 150-acre campus is in a suburban area. Including any residence halls, there are 33 buildings.

Student Life: 85% of undergraduates are from Pennsylvania. Others are from 28 states, 20 foreign countries, and Canada. 84% are white. The average age of freshmen is 18; all undergraduates, 22. 12% do not continue beyond their first year; 65% remain to graduate.

Housing: 900 students can be accommodated in college housing, which includes single-sex and coed dorms. In addition, there are honors houses, special-interest houses, and alcohol-free and substance-free housing. On-campus housing is available on a first-come, first-served basis and is available on a lottery system for upperclassmen. 78% of students commute. Alcohol is not permitted. All students may keep cars.

Activities: There are 5 local fraternities and 2 local sororities. There are 70 groups on campus, including cheerleading, choir, communications, dance, drama, ethnic, gay, honors, horticulture, international, jazz band, literary magazine, martial arts, newspaper, pep band, political, professional, religious, social, social service, STEP team, student government, and yearbook. Popular campus events include Distinguished Speaker Series, Hoops Hysteria, and Black History and Women's History Month events.

Sports: There are 6 intercollegiate sports for men and 6 for women. Facilities include a large gym, an indoor pool, racquetball courts, a weight room, a fitness loft, tennis courts, an outdoor track, sand volleyball courts, and baseball, softball, and soccer fields.

Disabled Students: 95% of the campus is accessible. Facilities include wheelchair ramps, elevators, special parking, specially equipped restrooms, special class scheduling, lowered drinking fountains, and lowered telephones.

Services: Counseling and information services are available, as is tutoring in most subjects. There is remedial math, reading, and writing.

Campus Safety and Security: Measures include 24-hour foot and vehicle patrol, emergency notification system, self-defense education, and security escort services. There are shuttle buses, emergency telephones, and lighted pathways/sidewalks.

Programs of Study: Penn State Altoona confers B.A. and B.S. degrees. Associates and master's degrees are also awarded. Bachelor's degrees are awarded in AGRICULTURE (environmental studies), BIOLOGICAL SCIENCE (biology/biological science), BUSINESS (business administration and management), COMMUNICATIONS AND THE ARTS (communications, English, and visual and performing arts), COMPUTER AND PHYSICAL SCIENCE (mathematics and science), EDUCATION (elementary education), ENGINEERING AND ENVIRONMENTAL DESIGN (electromechanical technology), HEALTH PROFESSIONS (nursing), SOCIAL SCIENCE (criminal justice, history, human development, and liberal arts/general studies). Engineering and education are the strongest academically.

Business, criminal justice, and elementary education have the largest enrollments.

Required: To graduate, students must complete a minimum of 120 credit hours with a minimum GPA of 2.0. They must complete 46 general education credits, including 27 in arts, humanities, natural science, and social and behavioral sciences and 15 in quantification and communication skills.

Special: Internships, study abroad in 5 countries, work-study programs, B.A.-B.S. degrees, accelerated degree programs, and dual and student-designed majors are available. There is an integrative arts major, which allows students to pursue interest across artistic boundaries. There is a chapter of Phi Beta Kappa and a freshman honors program.

Faculty/Classroom: No introductory courses are taught by graduate students. The average class size in an introductory lecture is 50; in a laboratory, 24; and in a regular course, 28.

Requirements: The SAT or ACT is required. Applicants should have 15 academic or Carnegie units, including 4 in English, 3 each in math, science, and social studies, and 2 in foreign language (required for some majors). The GED is accepted. AP and CLEP credits are accepted.

Procedure: Freshmen are admitted to all sessions. Entrance exams should be taken during the junior year. There are deferred admissions and rolling admissions plans. Application deadlines are open. The application fee is $50. Notification is sent on a rolling basis. Applications are accepted online.

Transfer: High school and college transcripts are required, as is good academic standing. The minimum GPA varies by major. 36 of 120 credits required for the bachelor's degree must be completed at Penn State Altoona.

Visiting: There are regularly scheduled orientations for prospective students, including campus tours and meetings with academic counselors and faculty. There are guides for informal visits; visitors may sit in on classes and stay overnight. To schedule a visit, contact the Admissions Office.

Financial Aid: Some academic scholarships require a specific application, which varies according to the college/major. Check with the school for current deadlines.

International Students: The school actively recruits these students. They must take the TOEFL and also take the SAT or ACT.

Computers: Wireless access is available. All students may access the system. There are no time limits and no fees. It is strongly recommended that all students have a personal computer.

Admissions Contact: Richard Shaffer, Director of Admissions. A campus DVD is available. E-Mail: *rks8@psu.edu* Web: *www.aa.psu.edu*

PENN STATE UNIVERSITY/UNIVERSITY PARK C-3

University Park, PA 16802 **(814) 865-5471; (814) 863-7590**

Full-time: 20070 men, 16884 women	**Faculty:** n/av; I, -$
Part-time: 529 men, 347 women	**Ph.D.s:** 75%
Graduate: 3664 men, 2975 women	**Student/Faculty:** n/av
Year: semesters, summer session	**Tuition:** $16,484 ($28,566)
Application Deadline: November 30	**Room & Board:** $9920
Freshman Class: 41545 applied, 22761 accepted, 7262 enrolled	
SAT CR/M/W: 570/620/590	**ACT:** required **VERY COMPETITIVE**

Penn State University/University Park Campus, founded in 1855, is a public institution that is the oldest and largest of 24 campuses in the Penn State system. The university offers undergraduate and graduate degrees in agricultural sciences, arts and architecture, business, earth and mineral sciences, education, engineering, health and human development, liberal arts, science, communications, and information sciences and technology. Penn State also offers graduate and first professional degrees in medicine and law. There are 15 undergraduate schools and 1 graduate school. In addition to regional accreditation, Penn State has baccalaureate program accreditation with AACSB, ABET, ACEJMC, APTA, ASLA, CSAB, NAAB, NASAD, NASM, NCATE, NLN, and SAF. The 16 libraries contain 5.5 million volumes, 3.6 million microform items, 923,828 audio/video tapes/CDs/DVDs, and subscribe to 309,132 periodicals including electronic. Computerized library services include interlibrary loans, database searching, Internet access, and laptop Internet portals. Special learning facilities include a learning resource center, art gallery, planetarium, radio station, TV station, 5 major museums at University Park house, significant research and educational collections in the fields of agriculture, anthropology, entomology, earth and mineral sciences, and the fine arts. The 8556-acre campus is in a suburban area 90 miles west of Harrisburg, PA. Including any residence halls, there are 933 buildings. The figures in the above capsule and in this profile are approximate.

Student Life: 69% of undergraduates are from Pennsylvania. Others are from 50 states, and Canada. 73% are white. The average age of freshmen is 18; all undergraduates, 20. 7% do not continue beyond their first year; 93% remain to graduate.

Housing: 13642 students can be accommodated in college housing, which includes single-sex and coed dorms, on-campus apartments, and married student housing. In addition, there are honors houses, language houses, special-interest houses, fraternity houses, and sorority houses. On-campus housing is guaranteed for the freshman year only. 63% of students commute. Upperclassmen may keep cars.

Activities: 13% of men belong to 56 national fraternities; 11% of women belong to 30 national sororities. There are 895 groups on campus, including art, band, cheerleading, chess, choir, chorale, chorus, computers, dance, debate, drama, drill team, environmental, ethnic, film, forensics, gay, honors, international, jazz band, literary magazine, marching band, musical theater, newspaper, opera, orchestra, pep band, photography, political, professional, radio and TV, religious, social, social service, student government, symphony, and yearbook. Popular campus events include Late Night Penn State, Dance Marathon, and Penn State football.

Sports: There are 15 intercollegiate sports for men and 14 for women, and 18 intramural sports for men and 18 for women. Facilities include a 107,282-seat football stadium, a baseball field with seating for 6000, a 15,000-seat basketball center, 2 golf courses, an ice skating pavilion, an indoor track/multipurpose field, an outdoor track, a soccer field with seating for 5000, indoor and outdoor swimming pools, bowling lanes, a tennis center, 4 fitness facilities, Shaver's Creek Environmental Center, Stone Valley Recreation Center (fishing, swimming, canoeing, sailing, and kayaking), a rifle range, and facilities for gymnastics, volleyball, field hockey, lacrosse, fencing, and wrestling.

Disabled Students: 95% of the campus is accessible. Facilities include wheelchair ramps, elevators, special parking, specially equipped restrooms, special class scheduling, lowered drinking fountains, lowered telephones, and special housing.

Services: Counseling and information services are available, as is tutoring in most subjects. There is a reader service for the blind, and remedial math, reading, and writing.

Campus Safety and Security: Measures include 24-hour foot and vehicle patrol, emergency notification system, self-defense education, and security escort services. There are shuttle buses, emergency telephones, lighted pathways/sidewalks, and controlled access to dorms/residences.

Programs of Study: Penn State confers B.A., B.S., B.A.E, B.Arch., B.Des., B.Eled. B.F.A., B.Hum., B.L.A., B.M., B.M.A., B.M.E., B.Ph., and B.Sosc. degrees. Associate, master's, and doctoral degrees are also awarded. Bachelor's degrees are awarded in AGRICULTURE (agricultural business management, agricultural mechanics, agriculture, animal science, environmental studies, forestry production and processing, forestry and related sciences, horticulture, natural resource management, and plant protection (pest management)), BIOLOGICAL SCIENCE (biochemistry, biology/biological science, and toxicology), BUSINESS (accounting, hospitality management services, labor studies, management information systems, marketing management, and organizational behavior), COMMUNICATIONS AND THE ARTS (advertising, art, art history and appreciation, Chinese, classics, communications, communications technology, comparative literature, design, English as a second/foreign language, film arts, French, German, graphic design, Italian, Japanese, journalism, music, music performance, Russian, Spanish, and visual and performing arts), COMPUTER AND PHYSICAL SCIENCE (actuarial science, astronomy, atmospheric sciences and meteorology, chemistry, computer science, geology, information sciences and systems, mathematics, physics, and statistics), EDUCATION (educational statistics and research, elementary education, secondary education, and special education), ENGINEERING AND ENVIRONMENTAL DESIGN (aerospace studies, agricultural engineering, architectural engineering, architecture, biomedical engineering, chemical engineering, civil engineering, computer engineering, electrical/electronics engineering, engineering, engineering and applied science, industrial engineering, landscape architecture/design, materials science, mechanical engineering, mining and mineral engineering, nuclear engineering, and petroleum/natural gas engineering), HEALTH PROFESSIONS (health care administration, nursing, premedicine, preveterinary science, rehabilitation therapy, and veterinary science), SOCIAL SCIENCE (African American studies, anthropology, archeology, Asian/Oriental studies, criminal justice, economics, food science, forensic studies, geography, history, human development, international relations, Latin American studies, liberal arts/general studies, medieval studies, parks and recreation management, philosophy, political science/government, psychology, religious education, sociology, and women's studies). Engineering, liberal arts, and business have the largest enrollment.

Required: The typical baccalaureate Penn State academic program requires the completion of between 120 and 130 credits. The General Education requirements are common to all degree programs and compose about one third of the course work (45 credits). All students must also complete a Writing-Across-The-Curriculum course (3 credits), a first-year seminar (1 credit), United States Culture (3 credits), and International Cultures (3 credits) as part of their degree program.

Special: Co-op programs, internships, study-abroad in more than 45 countries, and work-study programs are available. Dual majors and student-designed majors are possible. Accelerated degree programs, a Washington semester, and a 3-2 engineering degree are also offered. There are 38 national honor societies, including Phi Beta Kappa, and a freshman honors program.

Faculty/Classroom: 64% of faculty are male; 36% are female. No introductory courses are taught by graduate students.

Admissions: 55% of the 2011-2012 applicants were accepted. The SAT scores for the 2011-2012 freshman class were: Critical Reading--15% below 500, 47% between 500 and 599, 33% between 600 and 700, and 5% above 700; Math--9% below 500, 30% between 500 and 599, 46% between 600 and 700, and 15% above 700; Writing--13% below 500, 42% between 500 and 599, 38% between 600 and 700, and 7% above 700.

Requirements: The SAT or ACT is required. Applicants may submit an SAT or ACT scores. Admissions decisions for first-year students are made on the basis of several combined factors. Approximately two thirds of the decision for each student is based upon the high school GPA. The remaining one third of the decision is based on the factors, which may include standardized critical reading and math test scores, class rank, personal statement, and activities list. Weighted average or class rank for students who have taken AP/Honors courses are considered. AP and CLEP credits are accepted.

Procedure: Freshmen are admitted fall, spring, and summer. Entrance exams should be taken In the junior year. There are early admissions, deferred admissions, and rolling admissions plans. Applications should be filed by November 30 for fall entry, along with a $50 fee. Notification is sent on a rolling basis. 1315 applicants were on the waiting list; 697 were admitted. Applications are accepted online.

Transfer: 398 transfer students enrolled in a recent year. Transfer applicants need a minimum GPA of 2.0 and good academic standing. 36 of 120 credits required for the bachelor's degree must be completed at Penn State.

Visiting: There are regularly scheduled orientations for prospective students. There are guides for informal visits, visitors may sit in on classes, and stay overnight. To schedule a visit, contact Penn State Undergraduate Admissions.

Financial Aid: The average financial indebtedness of a recent graduate was $31,135. The FAFSA is required. The deadline for filing freshman financial aid applications for fall entry is February 15.

International Students: There are 2136 international students enrolled. The school actively recruits these students. They must take the TOEFL with a minimum score of 550 on the paper-based TOEFL (PBT) or 80 on the Internet-based version (iBT). Students whose native language is English or if U.S. citizen or permanent resident must submit SAT or ACT scores; others submit TOEFL.

Computers: There are more than 50 computer labs and classrooms with about 2952 computers on the University Park campus. There are more than 1000 mobile computing ports that provide users with workstations and peripherals for Windows, Mac, and Unix platforms. The labs are equipped with printers and scanners, as well as more specialized hardware such as digital cameras and CD burners. All students may access the system 24 hours a day, every day. There are no time limits. The fee is $236. It is strongly recommended that all students have a personal computer. Students enrolled in The College of Education, College of Arts & Architecture, College of Engineering must have a personal computer.

Graduates: In a recent year, 11496 bachelor's degrees were awarded. The most popular majors were business (19%), engineering (12%), and communications (9%). 1067 companies recruited on campus in a recent year. In an average class, 65% graduate in 4 years or less, 84% graduate in 5 years or less, and 85% graduate in 6 years or less. Of a recent graduating class, 22% were enrolled in graduate school within 6 months of graduation, and 60% were employed.

Admissions Contact: Anne Rohrbach, Executive Director of Admissions. E-Mail: *admissions@psu.edu* Web: *www.psu.edu*

PENNSYLVANIA COLLEGE OF TECHNOLOGY D-2

Williamsport, PA 17701 **(570) 327-4761**
(800) 367-9222; (570) 321-5551

Full-time: 3201 men, 1573 women	**Faculty:** 295
Part-time: 374 men, 530 women	**Ph.D.s:** 26%
Graduate: n/av	**Student/Faculty:** 17 to 1
Year: semesters, summer session	**Tuition:** $14,940 ($21,180)
Application Deadline: July 1	**Room & Board:** $10,713
Freshman Class: n/av	

NONCOMPETITIVE

Pennsylvania College of Technology, founded in 1989, is a public technical college affiliated with The Pennsylvania State University. There are 6 undergraduate schools. In addition to regional accreditation, Penn College has baccalaureate program accreditation with ABET, ACBSP, ACCE, ADA, NLN, and SAF. The library contains 112,953 volumes, 16,504 microform items, 4,646 audio/video tapes/CDs/DVDs, and subscribes to 31,000 periodicals including electronic. Computerized library services include interlibrary loans, database searching, Internet access, and Wi-Fi capability. Special learning facilities include an art gallery, Le Jeune Chef Restaurant and a dental hygiene clinic are open to the public, as well as the Penn College Children's Learning Center. The 127-acre campus is in a suburban area approximately 65 miles east of State College, and 80 miles west of Wilkes Barre. Including any residence halls, there are 34 buildings.

Student Life: 87% of undergraduates are from Pennsylvania. Others are from 32 states, 14 foreign countries, and Canada. 89% are White. 27% claim no religious affiliation; 18% Catholic; 12% Protestant. The average age of freshmen is 20.5; all undergraduates, 22.5. 31% do not continue beyond their first year; 48% remain to graduate.

Housing: 1725 students can be accommodated in college housing, which includes single-sex and coed dorms and on-campus apartments. On-campus housing is available on a first-come and first-served basis. 70% of students live on campus. Alcohol is not permitted. All students may keep cars.

Activities: There are 61 groups on campus, including art, computers, dance, drama, environmental, ethnic, gay, honors, international, professional, religious, social, social service, and student government. Popular campus events include Cultural Series, Open House Weekend, ComicCom and Career Fair.

Sports: There are 8 intercollegiate sports for men and 8 for women, and 15 intramural sports for men and 15 for women. Facilities include a fitness center, field house, gym, soccer field, tennis courts, sand volleyball court, outdoor basketball court, and an intramural field.

Disabled Students: All of the campus is accessible. Facilities include wheelchair ramps, elevators, special parking, specially equipped restrooms, lowered drinking fountains, lowered telephones, and special housing.

Services: There is a reader service for the blind, and remedial math, reading, and writing. services for hearing-impaired students, adaptive equipment, and note takers are available. Also available is Smarthinking (online tutoring)

Campus Safety and Security: Measures include 24-hour foot and vehicle patrol, emergency notification system, and security escort services. There are shuttle buses, emergency telephones, lighted pathways/sidewalks, controlled access to dorms/residences, Each residence hall complex is surrounded by an 8-foot fence with gates. The gates and all residence hall building doors are secured from 10 p.m. to 5 a.m. each day, and a uniformed police officer works at each complex from 9 p.m. to 5 a.m. each day. Identifications are checked from 10 p.m. to 5 a.m.

Programs of Study: Penn College confers B.S. degrees. Associate degrees are also awarded. Bachelor's degrees are awarded in BUSINESS (accounting, business administration and management, human resources, management information systems, and marketing management), COMMUNICATIONS AND THE ARTS (graphic design), COMPUTER AND PHYSICAL SCIENCE (computer programming, computer security and information assurance, information sciences and systems, and web technology), ENGINEERING AND ENVIRONMENTAL DESIGN (aircraft mechanics, architectural technology, automotive technology, civil engineering technology, computer engineering, computer graphics, construction management, construction technology, drafting and design, electrical/electronics engineering technology, engineering technology, graphic arts technology, manufacturing engineering, mechanical design technology, mechanical engineering, mechanical engineering technology, plastics engineering, printing technology, technological management, and welding engineering), HEALTH PROFESSIONS (dental hygiene, emergency medical technologies, exercise science, health care administration, health science, medical records administration/services, mental health/human services, nursing, occupational therapy, physician's assistant, and radiograph medical technology), SOCIAL SCIENCE (culinary arts and paralegal studies). Health sciences and the school of industrial, computing, and engineering technologies are the strongest academically. Nursing, welding, and physician's assistant have the largest enrollments.

Required: To graduate, students must complete at least 120 credits with a minimum GPA of 2.0 overall and in the major. The core curriculum consists of 18 to 21 credits in humanities, social science, art, and foreign language, 9 in communications, 7 in science, 6 in math, 2 in health and fitness, and a course in computer information.

Special: Penn College offers cooperative and internship programs, opportunities for study abroad experiences, dual- and student-designed majors, and credit by exam and for work and/or life experience.

Faculty/Classroom: 58% of faculty are male; 42% are female. All teach undergraduates. No introductory courses are taught by graduate students. The average class size in a regular course is 19.

Requirements: Applicants must have a high school diploma or GED and must take the college's placement exams. Other admissions criteria vary by program and must be met prior to admittance to these program majors. AP and CLEP credits are accepted. Important factors in the admissions decision are ability to finance college education, leadership record, advanced placement or honors courses, parents or siblings attended your school, evidence of special talent, personality/intangible qualities, extracurricular activities record, recommendations by alumni, geographical diversity, and recommendations by school officials.

Procedure: Freshmen are admitted to all sessions. Entrance exams should be taken prior to scheduling classes. There are early admissions, deferred admissions, and rolling admissions plans. Applications should be filed by July 1 for fall entry. The fall 2013 application fee was $50. Notification is sent on a rolling basis. Applications are accepted online.

Transfer: 441 transfer students enrolled in 2012-2013. Transfer procedures vary with each degree program. Courses are evaluated for transfer equivalency. 60 of 120 credits required for the bachelor's degree must be completed at Penn College.

Visiting: There are regularly scheduled orientations for prospective students, Includes registration, a multimedia presentation, admission and financial aid sessions, a question-and-answer period, a tour of campus facilities, and a reception. There are guides for informal visits. To schedule a visit, contact the Admissions Office.

Financial Aid: The FAFSA and the college's own financial statement are required. The priority date for freshman financial aid applications for fall entry is April 1.

International Students: There are 70 international students enrolled. The school actively recruits these students. They must take the TOEFL with a minimum score of 520 on the paper-based TOEFL (PBT) or 68 on the Internet-based version (iBT). This varies among the program majors.

Computers: All students may access the system. There are no time limits and no fees.

Graduates: From July 1, 2012 to June 30, 2013, 514 bachelor's degrees were awarded. The most popular majors were automotive technology (4%), nursing (4%), and building construction technology (3%). In an average class, 28% graduate in 3 years or less, 38% graduate in 4 years or less, 44% graduate in 5 years or less, and 44% graduate in 6 years or less.

Admissions Contact: Dennis Correll, Assoc Dean for Admissions/ Financial Aid. E-Mail: *admissions@pct.edu* Web: *http:/www.pct.edu/admissions/*

PENNSYLVANIA STATE SYSTEM OF HIGHER EDUCATION

The Pennsylvania State System of Higher Education, established in 1983, is a public system in Pennsylvania. It is governed by a board of governors, whose chief administrator is the chancellor. The primary goal of the system is to provide high-quality liberal arts education at an affordable cost with a central mission of teaching and service. The main priorities are capital facilities matters of maintenance and funding, social equity, and tuition stabilization through appropriate funding. The total student enrollment is usually about 100,000 with 5500 faculty members. Altogether there are 217 baccalaureate, 107 master's, and 6 doctoral programs offered in the Pennsylvania State System of Higer Education. Profiles of the 4-year campuses are included in this section.

PHILADELPHIA UNIVERSITY F-3

Philadelphia, PA 19144 **(215) 951-2700**
(800) 951-7287; (215) 951-2907

Full-time: 940 men, 1739 women	**Faculty:** 110; IIA, av$
Part-time: 60 men, 149 women	**Ph.D.s:** 83%
Graduate: 208 men, 444 women	**Student/Faculty:** 24 to 1
Year: semesters, summer session	**Tuition:** $33,590
Application Deadline:	**Room & Board:** $10,660

Freshman Class: 3602 applied, 2590 accepted, 604 enrolled
SAT or ACT: required

COMPETITIVE

Philadelphia University, founded in 1884, is a private institution offering preprofessional programs in architecture, design, business, sciences, textiles, fashion, and health. There are 6 undergraduate schools and 1 graduate school. In addition to regional accreditation, PhilaU has baccalaureate program accreditation with ABET, FIDER, NAAB, and NASAD. The library contains 109,235 volumes, 125,000 microform items, 50,630 audio/video tapes/CDs/DVDs, and subscribes to 1,011 periodicals including electronic. Computerized library services include interlibrary loans and database searching. Special learning facilities include an art gallery, the Design Center at Philadelphia University. The 100-acre campus is in a suburban area 10 minutes west of metropolitan Philadelphia. Including any residence halls, there are 56 buildings.

Student Life: 52% of undergraduates are from Pennsylvania. Others are from 37 states, 24 foreign countries, and Canada. 65% are from public schools. 72% are White. 18% claim no religious affiliation The average age of freshmen is 23; all undergraduates, 20. 20% do not continue beyond their first year; 56% remain to graduate.

Housing: 1265 students can be accommodated in college housing, which includes single-sex and coed dorms, on-campus apartments, and off-campus apartments. including town houses. On-campus housing is guaranteed for the freshman year only, is available on a first-come, first-served basis, and is available on a lottery system for upperclassmen. Priority is given to out-of-town students. 51% of students commute. Upperclassmen may keep cars.

Activities: 1% of men belong to 1 national fraternity; 1% of women belong to 1 national sorority. There are 30 groups on campus, including cheerleading, choir, dance, drama, ethnic, gay, honors, international, newspaper, professional, religious, social, social service, and student government. Popular campus events include Annual Fashion Show and Design Competition, Welcome Week, and Spring Weekend.

Sports: There are 6 intercollegiate sports for men and 8 for women, and 13 intramural sports for men and 13 for women. Facilities include 2 gyms, a fitness center, 6 tennis courts, 3 athletic fields, and a student center recreation room.

Disabled Students: 85% of the campus is accessible. Facilities include wheelchair ramps, elevators, special parking, specially equipped restrooms, special class scheduling, lowered drinking fountains, and lowered telephones.

Services: Counseling and information services are available, as is tutoring in every subject. There is a reader service for the blind, and remedial math, reading, and writing. Study skills workshops, course-related workshops, math review sessions, writing review sessions, time management and stress reduction workshops.

Campus Safety and Security: Measures include 24-hour foot and vehicle patrol, self-defense education, and security escort services. There are shuttle buses, emergency telephones, and lighted pathways/sidewalks.

Programs of Study: PhilaU confers B.S., and B.Arch. degrees. Associate, master's, and doctoral degrees are also awarded. Bachelor's degrees are awarded in BIOLOGICAL SCIENCE (biochemistry and biology/ biological science), BUSINESS (accounting, banking and finance, fashion merchandising, international business management, management information systems, management science, and marketing/retailing/ merchandising), COMMUNICATIONS AND THE ARTS (graphic design and industrial design), COMPUTER AND PHYSICAL SCIENCE (chemistry, digital arts/technology, and science and management), ENGINEERING AND ENVIRONMENTAL DESIGN (architecture, engineering, environmental science, industrial engineering, interior design, landscape architecture/design, textile engineering, and textile technology), HEALTH PROFESSIONS (physician's assistant and premedicine), SOCIAL SCIENCE (biopsychology, fashion design and technology, and psychology). Physician's assistant, architecture, and engineering are the strongest academically. Architecture, fashion merchandising, and fashion design have the largest enrollments.

Required: All students are required to complete 60-credit residency with courses in math, science, social science, computer literacy, English, history, and the humanities. A total of 121 to 146 credits is required with an overall GPA of 2.0

Special: Internships in all academic majors, study abroad, a dual major in international business, an accelerated business administration degree program, and an integrated major in business and science are available. There is a freshman honors program.

Faculty/Classroom: 58% of faculty are male; 42% are female. All teach undergraduates, and 50% do both. No introductory courses are taught by graduate students. The average class size in an introductory lecture is 25; in a laboratory is 14; and in a regular course is 17.

Admissions: 72% of the 2013-2014 applicants were accepted. 31% of the current freshmen were in the top fifth of their class; 65% were in the top two fifths.

Requirements: The SAT or ACT is required. Applicants should be high school graduates or have earned the GED. Recommended secondary preparation includes 4 years each of English and history, 3 years of math which must include algebra II and geometry, and 3 years of science and 2 years of social studies, and 1 year of history. Potential science majors are strongly urged to take 4 years of math and science. A GPA of 2.5 is required. AP and CLEP credits are accepted. Important factors in the admissions decision are evidence of special talent, extracurricular activities record, and leadership record.

Procedure: Freshmen are admitted fall and spring. There are deferred admissions and rolling admissions plans. Application deadlines are open. Application fee is $40. Notifications are sent November 1. Applications are accepted online.

Transfer: 236 transfer students enrolled in 2012-2013. A 2.5 GPA is usually required, and previously attended college transcripts. An interview is recommended. 60 of 121 credits required for the bachelor's degree must be completed at PhilaU.

Visiting: There are regularly scheduled orientations for prospective students, including an interview and a campus tour. There are guides for informal visits, visitors may sit in on classes, and stay overnight. To schedule a visit, contact the Admissions Office at colemanp@philau.edu.

Financial Aid: In 2013-2014, 78% of all full-time freshmen and 71% of continuing full-time students received some form of financial aid. 78% of all full-time freshmen and 69% of continuing full-time students received need-based aid. The average freshman award was $24,833. Need-based scholarships or need-based grants averaged $20,708; need-based self-help aid (loans and jobs) averaged $5,834; other non-need-based awards and non-need-based scholarships averaged $15,475; and $8,914 from other forms of aid. 28% of undergraduate students work part-time. Average annual earnings from campus work are $1067. The average financial indebtedness of the 2013 graduate was $39,938. The FAFSA is required. The deadline for filing freshman financial aid applications for fall entry is April 15.

International Students: There are 14 international students enrolled.

The school actively recruits these students. They must take the TOEFL with a minimum score of 500 on the paper-based TOEFL (PBT). an English placement test.

Computers: All students may access the system 7 days a week. There are no time limits and no fees.

Graduates: From July 1, 2012 to June 30, 2013, 625 bachelor's degrees were awarded. The most popular majors were business/marketing (35%), visual and performing arts (22%), and architecture (17%). 70 companies recruited on campus in 2012-2013. In an average class, 43% graduate in 4 years or less, 58% graduate in 5 years or less, and 60% graduate in 6 years or less. Of the 2012 graduating class, 19% were enrolled in graduate school within 6 months of graduation, and 71% were employed.

Admissions Contact: Christine Greb, Director of Admissions. E-Mail: *admissions@philau.edu* Web: *www.philau.edu*

POINT PARK UNIVERSITY B-3

Pittsburgh, PA 15222 (412) 392-3430; (412) 392-3902

Full-time: 1070 men, 1481 women
Part-time: 313 men, 362 women
Graduate: 273 men, 342 women
Year: semesters, summer session
Application Deadline: open
Freshman Class: 3237 applied, 2393 accepted, 548 enrolled
SAT or ACT: required
Faculty: n/av; IIA, -$
Ph.D.s: 75%
Student/Faculty: 19 to 1
Tuition: $26,170
Room & Board: $10,220

COMPETITIVE

Point Park is a comprehensive, master's-level university with a strong liberal arts tradition, located in the heart of Downtown Pittsburgh. Point Park currently enrolls 3,841 full- and part-time students in 82 undergraduate programs and 17 graduate programs offered through its School of Arts and Sciences, School of Business, School of Communication, and Conservatory of Performing Arts. The University's students represent 44 states and 56 countries. There are 4 undergraduate schools and 4 graduate schools. In addition to regional accreditation, Point Park has baccalaureate program accreditation with ABET. The library contains 82,565 volumes, 16,275 microform items, 6,831 audio/video tapes/CDs/DVDs, and subscribes to 77,064 periodicals including electronic. Computerized library services include interlibrary loans, database searching, Internet access, and Wi-Fi capability. Special learning facilities include an art gallery, radio station, TV station, Natural sciences labs; engineering technology labs; forensic crime scene house; computer newsrooms; MAC and PC multimedia labs; black/white and color photography darkrooms; digital photography lab; radio station, TV studio/newsroom; cinema production and editing suites; performance and dance studios; performing arts center/theaters; and art galleries. The campus is in an urban area in Downtown Pittsburgh. Including any residence halls, there are 15 buildings.

Student Life: 79% of undergraduates are from Pennsylvania. Others are from 49 states, 25 foreign countries, and Canada. 72% are White; 16% African American. The average age of freshmen is 18; all undergraduates, 24. 26% do not continue beyond their first year; 50% remain to graduate.

Housing: 1022 students can be accommodated in college housing, which includes single-sex and coed dorms and on-campus apartments. living and learning communities. On-campus housing is available on a first-come and first-served basis. 70% of students commute. Some may keep cars.

Activities: There are no fraternities or sororities. There are 34 groups on campus, including choir, chorale, computers, dance, drama, ethnic, film, gay, honors, international, literary magazine, musical theater, newspaper, photography, political, professional, radio and TV, religious, social, social service, and student government.

Sports: There are 5 intercollegiate sports for men and 6 for women, and 8 intramural sports for men and 8 for women. Facilities include an auditorium and a student center which includes a gymnasium, racquetball court and five floors for training, fitness, recreation, sports and meetings.

Disabled Students: 95% of the campus is accessible. Facilities include wheelchair ramps, elevators, specially equipped restrooms, special class scheduling, lowered drinking fountains, lowered telephones, and special housing.

Services: Counseling and information services are available, as is tutoring in some subjects, Learning-disabled services are available on a case-by-case basis. There is a reader service for the blind, and remedial math, reading, and writing.

Campus Safety and Security: Measures include 24-hour foot and vehicle patrol, emergency notification system, self-defense education, and security escort services. There are shuttle buses, emergency telephones, and lighted pathways/sidewalks.

Programs of Study: Point Park confers B.A., B.S. and B.F.A. degrees. Associate and master's degrees are also awarded. Bachelor's degrees are awarded in AGRICULTURE (environmental studies), BIOLOGICAL SCIENCE (biology/biological science, biotechnology, and forensic science), BUSINESS (accounting, business administration and management, finance, funeral home services, human resources, management science, organizational leadership and management, and sports management), COMMUNICATIONS AND THE ARTS (advertising, applied art, arts administration/management, broadcasting, communications, dance, dramatic arts, English, film arts, journalism, media arts, performing arts, photography, public relations, theatre arts, and video), COMPUTER AND PHYSICAL SCIENCE (computer science, digital arts/technology, earth science, and information sciences and systems), EDUCATION ((Education) Childhood Education, dance education, drama education, early childhood education, education, elementary education, secondary education, and special education), ENGINEERING AND ENVIRONMENTAL DESIGN (civil engineering, civil engineering technology, electrical/electronics engineering, electrical/electronics engineering technology, engineering management, engineering technology, environmental science, mechanical engineering, mechanical engineering technology, and systems engineering), HEALTH PROFESSIONS (environmental health science, health care administration, Pre-Health Studies, premedicine, and respiratory therapy), SOCIAL SCIENCE (behavioral science, criminal justice, early childhood studies, history, international studies, law enforcement and corrections, legal studies, liberal arts/general studies, paralegal studies, political science/government, psychology, and public administration). Business, dance, and theater have the largest enrollments.

Required: All majors leading to a baccalaureate degree require a minimum of 120 credits. Most programs require 42 core curriculum credits, with at least 30 completed in residence. A 2.0 GPA is required.

Special: Cross-registration is available through the Pittsburgh Council on Higher Education. The university offers internships, work study, dual and student-designed majors, credit by exam and for life/military/work experience, and nondegree study. Capstone programs are available for students with associate degrees. Accelerated degree programs are available. There are 2 national honor societies and a freshman honors program.

Faculty/Classroom: No introductory courses are taught by graduate students.

Admissions: 74% of the 2013-2014 applicants were accepted. The SAT scores for the 2013-2014 freshman class were: Critical Reading--45% below 500, 39% between 500 and 599, 14% between 600 and 699, and 2% between 700 and 800; Math--57% below 500, 34% between 500 and 599, 8% between 600 and 699, and 1% between 700 and 800; Writing--52% below 500, 35% between 500 and 599, 12% between 600 and 699, and 2% between 700 and 800. The ACT scores were 34% below 21, 22% between 21 and 23, 25% between 24 and 26, 20% between 27 and 28, and 6% above 28.

Requirements: The SAT or ACT is required. Students should have completed 12 academic credits or 16 Carnegie units consisting of 4 in English, 3 in history, science, and math, and 2 years of foreign language. The GED is accepted. Theater and dance students must audition, and an interview is requested for all candidates. A GPA of 2.0 is required. AP and CLEP credits are accepted.

Procedure: Freshmen are admitted to all sessions. Entrance exams should be taken in the junior or senior year. There are deferred admissions and rolling admissions plans. Application deadlines are open. Application fee is $40. Notification is sent on a rolling basis. Applications are accepted online. Application fees are waived if application is completed online.

Transfer: 446 transfer students enrolled in 2012-2013. Applicants must have completed 12 credit hours with at least a 2.0 GPA. The SAT or ACT and an interview are recommended. 30 of 120 credits required for the bachelor's degree must be completed at Point Park.

Visiting: There are regularly scheduled orientations for prospective students. There are guides for informal visits and visitors may sit in on classes. To schedule a visit, contact the Office of Admissions.

Financial Aid: In 2013-2014, 99% of all full-time freshmen and 99% of continuing full-time students received some form of financial aid. 75% of all full-time freshmen and 76% of continuing full-time students received need-based aid. The average freshman award was $29,218. Need-based scholarships or need-based grants averaged $5,664 ($16,000 maximum); need-based self-help aid (loans and jobs) averaged $5,788 ($7,000 maximum); non-need-based athletic scholarships averaged $5,335 ($14,000 maximum); and other non-need-based awards and non-need-based scholarships averaged $11,086 ($31,540 maximum). 16% of undergraduate students work part-time. Average annual earnings from campus work are $2173. The average financial indebtedness of the 2013 graduate was $21,838. The FAFSA is required. The priority date for freshman financial aid applications for fall entry is March 15. The deadline for filing freshman financial aid applications for fall entry is August 15.

International Students: There are 101 international students enrolled. The school actively recruits these students. They must take the TOEFL with a minimum score of 500 on the paper-based TOEFL (PBT) or 61 on the Internet-based version (iBT). Students whose native language is English may submit SAT scores.

Computers: All students may access the system 7 days a week; lab hours vary by facility. There are no time limits and no fees.

Graduates: From July 1, 2012 to June 30, 2013, 719 bachelor's degrees were awarded. The most popular majors were business management (12%), theatre arts (9%), and dance (9%). In an average class, 50% graduate in 6 years or less.

Admissions Contact: Joell Minford E-Mail: *enroll@pointpark.edu* Web: *www.pointpark.edu*

ROBERT MORRIS UNIVERSITY A-3

Moon Township, PA 15108 **(800) 762-0097; (412) 397-2425**

Full-time: 2225 men, 1710 women	**Faculty:** 200; IIA, +$
Part-time: 200 men, 324 women	**Ph.D.s:** 82%
Graduate: 491 men, 494 women	**Student/Faculty:** 15 to 1
Year: semesters, summer session	**Tuition:** $25,114
Application Deadline: May 1	**Room & Board:** $11,585
Freshman Class: 5689 applied, 4580 accepted, 992 enrolled	
SAT CR/M/W: 513/535/500 **ACT:** 23	**COMPETITIVE**

Robert Morris University, founded in 1921, is a private institution offering 34 undergraduate degree programs, and 17 master's and doctoral degree programs. There are 5 undergraduate schools and 5 graduate schools. In addition to regional accreditation, RMU has baccalaureate program accreditation with AACSB, ABET, and TEAC. The library contains 126,886 volumes, 329,226 microform items, 3,664 audio/video tapes/CDs/DVDs, and subscribes to 766 periodicals including electronic. Computerized library services include interlibrary loans, database searching, and Internet access. Special learning facilities include an art gallery, radio station, TV station, a manufacturing lab for engineering and other students. Nursing Students also learn to care for patients in state-of-the-art nursing laboratory, where bedside computers and patient simulators assist in developing clinical decision-making skills. The 230-acre campus is in a suburban area 17 miles southwest of downtown Pittsburgh. Including any residence halls, there are 25 buildings.

Student Life: 85% of undergraduates are from Pennsylvania. Others are from 38 states, 39 foreign countries, and Canada. 90% are from public schools. 76% are White. 41% are Catholic; 35% Protestant. The average age of freshmen is 18; all undergraduates, 22. 19% do not continue beyond their first year; 56% remain to graduate.

Housing: 2015 students can be accommodated in college housing, which includes single-sex and coed dorms and on-campus apartments. On-campus housing is available on a first-come and first-served basis. 56% of students commute. Alcohol is not permitted. All students may keep cars.

Activities: 10% of men belong to 5 national fraternities; 11% of women belong to 4 national sororities. There are 95 groups on campus, including band, cheerleading, choir, computers, drama, environmental, ethnic, film, gay, honors, international, literary magazine, marching band, musical theater, newspaper, pep band, photography, political, professional, radio and TV, religious, social, social service, student government, and yearbook. Popular campus events include Homecoming, Prom and Dances.

Sports: There are 10 intercollegiate sports for men and 13 for women, and 15 intramural sports for men and 15 for women. Facilities include RMU's Moon Campus offers a field house, gym, health club, and 11 athletic fields. The RMU Island Sports Center (4 miles away) has 2 hockey rinks, golf dome, batting cages, health club, and an 8-lane track. Extensive club sport and intramural programs in addition to 23 NCAA sports.

Disabled Students: 75% of the campus is accessible. Facilities include wheelchair ramps, elevators, special parking, specially equipped restrooms, special class scheduling, lowered drinking fountains, lowered telephones, and special housing.

Services: Counseling and information services are available, as is tutoring in most subjects. There is a reader service for the blind, and remedial math, reading, and writing.

Campus Safety and Security: Measures include 24-hour foot and vehicle patrol, emergency notification system, and security escort services. There are shuttle buses, emergency telephones, lighted pathways/sidewalks, and controlled access to dorms/residences.

Programs of Study: RMU confers B.A., B.S., B.F.A., B.S.B.A. and B.S.N. degrees. Master's and doctoral degrees are also awarded. Bachelor's degrees are awarded in BIOLOGICAL SCIENCE (biology/biological science), BUSINESS (accounting, banking and finance, business administration and management, hospitality management services, marketing/retailing/merchandising, organizational behavior, and sports management), COMMUNICATIONS AND THE ARTS (communications, English, and media arts), COMPUTER AND PHYSICAL SCIENCE (actuarial science, applied mathematics, and information sciences and systems), EDUCATION (business education and elementary education), ENGINEERING AND ENVIRONMENTAL DESIGN (engineering, environmental science, and manufacturing engineering), HEALTH PROFESSIONS (health care administration, nuclear medical technology, and nursing), SOCIAL SCIENCE (economics, psychology, and social science). Actuarial science and Engineering is the strongest academically. Accounting, nursing and engineering have the largest enrollments.

Required: All candidates must complete 126 to 135 credit hours, including 24 to 31 in the major, with a 2.0 GPA overall and a 2.5 in the major. A core curriculum varies with each major and consists of humanities, communication skills, social sciences, computing, and math. All students must demonstrate competency in computer software applications.

Special: The university offers internship programs in most majors, cross-registration with the 9 colleges of the Pittsburgh Council of Higher Education, work-study programs, study abroad in 12 countries, and non-degree study. Credit by exam and pass/fail options are available. There are 9 national honor societies, a freshman honors program, and 1 departmental honors program.

Faculty/Classroom: 58% of faculty are male; 42% are female. 99% teach undergraduates, 80% do research, and 80% do both. No introductory courses are taught by graduate students. The average class size in an introductory lecture is 23; in a laboratory is 12; and in a regular course is 23.

Admissions: 81% of the 2013-2014 applicants were accepted. The SAT scores for the 2013-2014 freshman class were: Critical Reading--42% below 500, 44% between 500 and 599, 12% between 600 and 699, and 1% between 700 and 800; Math--32% below 500, 44% between 500 and 599, 20% between 600 and 699, and 3% between 700 and 800; Writing--48% below 500, 40% between 500 and 599, 9% between 600 and 699, and 1% between 700 and 800. 12 freshmen graduated first in their class.

Requirements: The SAT is required. Applicants should be graduates of an accredited secondary school or hold a GED diploma. They must have completed 16 Carnegie units, including 4 in English and Social Studies, 3 in math and 2 in science. An interview is required for some and recommended for all others. A GPA of 2.0 is required. AP and CLEP credits are accepted. Important factors in the admissions decision are advanced placement or honors courses, leadership record, and personality/intangible qualities.

Procedure: Freshmen are admitted fall, spring, and summer. Entrance exams should be taken by fall or late winter of the senior year. There are deferred admissions and rolling admissions plans. Applications should be filed by May 1 for fall entry; December 1 for spring entry, along with a $30 fee. Notification is sent on a rolling basis. 95 applicants were on the 2013 waiting list; 37 were admitted. Applications are accepted online.

Transfer: 330 transfer students enrolled in 2012-2013. Students must have a minimum 2.0 GPA in nondevelopmental academic courses. Those with fewer than 30 earned credits must also submit an official high school transcript and test results of the SAT or ACT. An interview is recommended. 30 of 126 credits required for the bachelor's degree must be completed at RMU.

Visiting: There are regularly scheduled orientations for prospective students, consisting of placement testing, orientation, and academic advising. There are guides for informal visits, visitors may sit in on classes, and stay overnight. To schedule a visit, contact the Enrollment Office.

Financial Aid: In 2013-2014, 90% of all full-time freshmen and 90% of continuing full-time students received some form of financial aid. 99% of all full-time freshmen and 95% of continuing full-time students received need-based aid. The average freshman award was $21,941. Need-based scholarships or need-based grants averaged $16,071; need-based self-help aid (loans and jobs) averaged $6,902; and non need based athletic scholarships averaged $17,587. 100% of undergraduate students work part-time. The average financial indebtedness of the 2013 graduate was $37,857. RMU is a member of CSS. The FAFSA, and PHEAA is required. The deadline for filing freshman financial aid applications for fall entry is May 1.

International Students: There are 170 international students enrolled. The school actively recruits these students. They must take the TOEFL with a minimum score of 500 on the paper-based TOEFL (PBT) or 61 on the Internet-based version (iBT).

Computers: All students may access the system. There are no time limits and no fees.

Graduates: From July 1, 2012 to June 30, 2013, 736 bachelor's degrees were awarded. The most popular majors were management (11%), accounting (11%), and communications (9%). 140 companies recruited on campus in 2012-2013. In an average class, 41% graduate in 4 years or less, 54% graduate in 5 years or less, and 56% graduate in 6 years or less. Of the 2012 graduating class, 7% were enrolled in graduate school within 6 months of graduation, and 86% were employed.

Admissions Contact: Kellie Laurenzi, Dean of Admissions. E-Mail: *enrollmentoffice@rmu.edu* Web: *www.rmu.edu*

ROSEMONT COLLEGE F-4

Rosemont, PA 19010 **(610) 527-0200**
(800) 331-0708; (610) 520-4399

Full-time: 143 men, 283 women	**Faculty:** 28
Part-time: 24 men, 74 women	**Ph.D.s:** 90%
Graduate: 80 men, 304 women	**Student/Faculty:** 8 to 1
Year: semesters	**Tuition:** $30,450
Application Deadline: open	**Room & Board:** $12,380
Freshman Class: 941 applied, 470 accepted, 75 enrolled	
SAT CR/M/W: 504/493/500 **ACT:** 23	**COMPETITIVE**

Rosemont College, founded in 1921, is an independent coeducational liberal arts and sciences college affiliated with the Roman Catholic Church. Accelerated degree and graduate programs are offered in the School of Graduate and Professional Studies. There are 2 undergraduate schools and

1 graduate school. The library contains 165,425 volumes, 22,908 microform items, and 3,425 audio/video tapes/CDs/DVDs, and subscribes to 16,370 periodicals including electronic. Computerized library services include interlibrary loans, database searching, Internet access, and Wi-Fi capability. Special learning facilities include an art gallery. The 56-acre campus is in a suburban area 11 miles west of Philadelphia. Including any residence halls, there are 15 buildings.

Student Life: 75% of undergraduates are from Pennsylvania. Others are from 11 states, and 14 foreign countries. 40% are White; 35% African American. 60% are Catholic; 17% Protestant; 15% Muslim, and Quaker. The average age of freshmen is 18; all undergraduates, 23. 8% do not continue beyond their first year; 72% remain to graduate.

Housing: 391 students can be accommodated in college housing, which includes single-sex and coed dorms. In addition, there are honors houses and special-interest houses. On-campus housing is guaranteed for all 4 years. 73% of students live on campus; of those, 60% remain on campus on weekends. All students may keep cars.

Activities: There are no fraternities or sororities. There are 23 groups on campus, including art, band, choir, chorus, dance, drama, ethnic, gay, honors, international, jazz band, literary magazine, marching band, musical theater, newspaper, orchestra, photography, political, professional, religious, social service, student government, symphony, and yearbook. Popular campus events include Oktoberfest, Founders Day, and International/ Multi-Cultural Festival and Petaltones Concert.

Sports: There are 6 intercollegiate sports for men and 7 for women. Facilities include hockey and softball fields, tennis courts, treadmills, weight equipment, a 500-seat auditorium, and indoor basketball, badminton, and volleyball courts.

Disabled Students: 20% of the campus is accessible. Facilities include wheelchair ramps, elevators, special parking, specially equipped restrooms, special class scheduling, lowered drinking fountains, and lowered telephones.

Services: Counseling and information services are available, as is tutoring in every subject.

Campus Safety and Security: Measures include 24-hour foot and vehicle patrol, emergency notification system, self-defense education, and security escort services. There are shuttle buses, emergency telephones, lighted pathways/sidewalks, electronically operated residence hall entrances activated by security cards.

Programs of Study: Rosemont confers B.A., B.F.A. and B.S. degrees. Master's degrees are also awarded. Bachelor's degrees are awarded in BIOLOGICAL SCIENCE (biochemistry and biology/biological science), BUSINESS (accounting and business administration and management), COMMUNICATIONS AND THE ARTS (communications, English, fine arts, French, German, and Spanish), COMPUTER AND PHYSICAL SCIENCE (chemistry and mathematics), EDUCATION (art education, education, foreign languages education, and secondary education), ENGINEERING AND ENVIRONMENTAL DESIGN (environmental science), HEALTH PROFESSIONS (predentistry and premedicine), SOCIAL SCIENCE (economics, history, humanities, Italian studies, liberal arts/ general studies, philosophy, political science/government, prelaw, psychology, religion, social science, sociology, and women's studies). Biology, chemstry, and liberal arts are the strongest academically. Biology, psychology, business, English literature, and studio art have the largest enrollments.

Required: General education requirements, major requirements, internship, study abroad, service learning. All majors have a comprehensive examination or senior project. 120 minimum credit hours for most majors.

Special: Cross-registration opportunities are available with Villanova, Arcadia, Eastern, Holy Family, Immaculata, and Neumann Universities; Cabrini, Gwynedd-Mercy, and Chestnut Hill Colleges; and the Art Institute International Exchange Program. There is a joint admission program with Temple University School of Dentistry and Drexel University College of Medicine. Internships, study abroad, a Washington semester, dual and student-designed majors, and accelerated degree programs are also available. There are 6 national honor societies and a freshman honors program.

Faculty/Classroom: 40% of faculty are male; 60% are female. All teach undergraduates, and 70% do both. No introductory courses are taught by graduate students. The average class size in an introductory lecture is 20; in a laboratory is 10; and in a regular course is 12.

Admissions: 50% of the 2013-2014 applicants were accepted. The SAT scores for the 2013-2014 freshman class were: Critical Reading--52% below 500, 33% between 500 and 599, 13% between 600 and 699, and 2% between 700 and 800; Math--50% below 500, 41% between 500 and 599, 5% between 600 and 699, and 4% between 700 and 800; Writing--58% below 500, 32% between 500 and 599, 6% between 600 and 699, and 4% between 700 and 800. The ACT scores were 8% below 21, 10% between 21 and 23, 57% between 24 and 26, 18% between 27 and 28, and 7% above 28.

Requirements: The SAT is required. The GED is accepted. Applicants must complete 16 academic units, including 4 in English and 2 each in foreign language, history, math, and science. An interview is recommended. A GPA of 2.0 is required. AP and CLEP credits are accepted. Important factors in the admissions decision are advanced placement or honors courses, leadership record, and recommendations by school officials.

Procedure: Freshmen are admitted fall and spring. Entrance exams should be taken before January of the senior year. There are deferred admissions and rolling admissions plans. Application deadlines are open. Notification is sent on a rolling basis. Applications are accepted online.

Transfer: 27 transfer students enrolled in 2012-2013. Transfer applicants should submit transcripts from each college attended, a letter of good standing from the dean at the last college attended, and catalogs from the colleges from which the student wishes to transfer credits. Students with fewer than 30 credits are required to submit high school transcripts and SAT scores. The minimum GPA is 2.0. An associate degree and interview are recommended. 30 of 120 credits required for the bachelor's degree must be completed at Rosemont.

Visiting: There are regularly scheduled orientations for prospective students, including a campus tour and meetings with financial aid advisers, faculty, and student life representatives. There are guides for informal visits, visitors may sit in on classes, and stay overnight. To schedule a visit, contact the Admissions Office.

Financial Aid: In 2013-2014, 99% of all full-time freshmen and 95% of continuing full-time students received some form of financial aid. 93% of all full-time freshmen and 86% of continuing full-time students received need-based aid. The average freshman award was $25,744. Need-based scholarships or need-based grants averaged $26,427 ($36,530 maximum); and need-based self-help aid (loans and jobs) averaged $3,562 ($11,000 maximum). 27% of undergraduate students work part-time. Average annual earnings from campus work are $805. The average financial indebtedness of the 2013 graduate was $21,622. The FAFSA is required. The priority date for freshman financial aid applications for fall entry is February 15. The deadline for filing freshman financial aid applications for fall entry is March 15.

International Students: There are 4 international students enrolled. The school actively recruits these students. They must take the TOEFL with a minimum score of 550 on the paper-based TOEFL (PBT) or 61 on the Internet-based version (iBT). They must also take the SAT.

Computers: All students may access the system. There are no time limits and no fees.

Graduates: From July 1, 2012 to June 30, 2013, 85 bachelor's degrees were awarded. The most popular majors were business (23%), English/ communication (10%), and biology (8%). 18 companies recruited on campus in 2012-2013. In an average class, 74% graduate in 4 years or less and 77% graduate in 5 years or less. Of the 2012 graduating class, 20% were enrolled in graduate school within 6 months of graduation, and 60% were employed.

Admissions Contact: Kevin McIntyre, Vice President for Enrollment Management. E-Mail: *admissions@rosemont.edu* Web: *www.rosemont.edu*

SAINT FRANCIS UNIVERSITY — C-3

Loretto, PA 15940 — (814) 472-3100; (866) 342-5738; (814) 472-3335

Full-time: 631 men, 967 women	**Faculty:** 90
Part-time: 66 men, 108 women	**Ph.D.s:** 74%
Graduate: 215 men, 464 women	**Student/Faculty:** 13 to 1
Year: semesters, summer session	**Tuition:** $22,444
Application Deadline:	**Room & Board:** $7585
Freshman Class: n/av	
SAT or ACT: required	

LESS COMPETITIVE

Saint Francis University, founded in 1847, is a private Franciscan institution affiliated with the Roman Catholic Church. It offers programs in business, education, humanities, sciences, social science, and preprofessional programs. There are 7 graduate schools. In addition to regional accreditation, Saint Francis has baccalaureate program accreditation with APTA, CAHEA, and CSWE. The library contains 117,870 volumes, 7,648 microform items, 2,701 audio/video tapes/CDs/DVDs, and subscribes to 7,293 periodicals including electronic. Computerized library services include interlibrary loans, database searching, and Internet access. Special learning facilities include an art gallery, radio station, TV station, classroom satellite hookup, art studio, wireless technology lab, and computer assurance lab. The 600-acre campus is in a rural area 85 miles east of Pittsburgh. Including any residence halls, there are 23 buildings. The figures in the above capsule and in this profile are approximate.

Student Life: 79% of undergraduates are from Pennsylvania. Others are from 30 states, 22 foreign countries, and Canada. 66% are from public schools. 85% are White; 11% African American. 55% are Catholic; 40% Protestant. The average age of freshmen is 19; all undergraduates, 21. 21% do not continue beyond their first year; 62% remain to graduate.

Housing: 983 students can be accommodated in college housing, which includes single-sex dorms, on-campus apartments, off-campus apartments, and married student housing. and intensive study floors. On-campus housing is guaranteed for all 4 years. 56% of students live on campus; of those, 20% remain on campus on weekends. Alcohol is not permitted. Upperclassmen may keep cars.

Activities: 1% of men belong to 1 national fraternity; 2% of women belong to 1 local and 2 national sororities. There are 54 groups on campus, including academic department clubs and theater production, art, cheerleading, choir, computers, drama, ethnic, honors, international, literary magazine, newspaper, pep band, photography, political, professional, radio and TV, religious, social, social service, student government, and yearbook. Popular campus events include Days of Reflection, Winter Weekend and Christmas Mass.

Sports: There are 9 intercollegiate sports for men and 12 for women, and 8 intramural sports for men and 8 for women. Facilities include an athletic center with a 6-lane swimming pool, 3 racquetball courts, a suspended running track, a weight room, a 3500-seat basketball arena, and a multipurpose gym. Outdoor facilities include recreational areas and game fields, jogging/walking trails, 9-hole golf course, a lake, and beach volleyball pits.

Disabled Students: Facilities include wheelchair ramps, elevators, special parking, specially equipped restrooms, lowered drinking fountains, lowered telephones, and special housing.

Services: Counseling and information services are available, as is tutoring in most subjects. There is remedial math, reading, and writing.

Campus Safety and Security: Measures include 24-hour foot and vehicle patrol, self-defense education, and security escort services. There are emergency telephones, lighted pathways/sidewalks, and a certified police force.

Programs of Study: Saint Francis confers B.A., B.S., B.S.N. and B.S.W. degrees. Master's degrees are also awarded. Bachelor's degrees are awarded in BIOLOGICAL SCIENCE (biology/biological science), BUSINESS (accounting, management information systems, and management science), COMMUNICATIONS AND THE ARTS (communications, English, French, modern language, and Spanish), COMPUTER AND PHYSICAL SCIENCE (chemistry, computer science, and mathematics), EDUCATION (elementary education and secondary education), HEALTH PROFESSIONS (medical laboratory technology, nursing, occupational therapy, physical therapy, and physician's assistant), SOCIAL SCIENCE (criminal justice, economics, history, international studies, philosophy, political science/government, psychology, public administration, religion, social work, and sociology). Business, and occupational have the largest enrollments.

Required: Students must complete 128 credits, with at least 36 in the major, while maintaining a 2.0 GPA. The core curriculum, totaling 58 credits, includes writing, public speaking, fine arts, foreign language, history, philosophy, religious studies (with required service component), psychology, sociology, political science, and economics. A word processing and research workshop is required in the freshman year. In addition to a comprehensive exam in the major, an English proficiency exam must be taken in the junior year.

Special: The university offers internships, co-op programs, study abroad in 10 countries, a Washington semester, work-study programs, and nondegree study. Student-designed majors and 3-2 engineering degrees with Pennsylvania State and Clarkson Universities and the University of Pittsburgh are available. There is a dual major available in international business/modern languages. Credit by exam and pass/fail options are also offered. There are 11 national honor societies, a freshman honors program, and 10 departmental honors programs.

Faculty/Classroom: 56% of faculty are male; 44% are female. 99% teach undergraduates, 50% do research, and 50% do both. No introductory courses are taught by graduate students. The average class size in an introductory lecture is 23; in a laboratory is 16; and in a regular course is 19.

Admissions: There were 1 National Merit finalists. 5 freshmen graduated first in their class.

Requirements: The SAT or ACT is required. Applicants must be graduates of an accredited secondary school or have earned a GED certificate. All applicants must have completed 16 Carnegie units, consisting of 4 years of English, 2 each of math and social science, 1 lab science, and 7 academic electives. Applicants to biology and allied health majors need an additional unit of science. Chemistry, computer science, engineering, and math applicants need 4 math units and 2 science units. Physical therapy applicants must have 4 units of math and 4 of science. AP and CLEP credits are accepted. Important factors in the admissions decision are advanced placement or honors courses, extracurricular activities record, and recommendations by school officials.

Procedure: Freshmen are admitted to all sessions. Entrance exams should be taken in spring of the junior year and fall of the senior year. There are deferred admissions and rolling admissions plans. Applications should be filed by November 1 for winter entry. The fall 2013 application fee was $30. Notification is sent on a rolling basis. Applications are accepted online.

Transfer: 32 transfer students enrolled in 2012-2013. Applicants must have a minimum GPA of 2.0 for consideration, 2.5 for nursing majors, and 2.75 for physician's assistant majors. 64 of 128 credits required for the bachelor's degree must be completed at Saint Francis.

Visiting: There are regularly scheduled orientations for prospective students, including an interview by financial aid and admission staff, tour, meeting with faculty, and attending class. There are guides for informal visits, visitors may sit in on classes, and stay overnight. To schedule a visit, contact the Admissions Office.

Financial Aid: In 2013-2014, 96% of all full-time freshmen and 91% of continuing full-time students received some form of financial aid. 86% of all full-time freshmen and 83% of continuing full-time students received need-based aid. The average freshman award was $16,962. Need-based scholarships or need-based grants averaged $6,866 ($14,350 maximum); need-based self-help aid (loans and jobs) averaged $2,976 ($4,625 maximum); non-need-based athletic scholarships averaged $1,812 ($26,688 maximum); other non-need-based awards and non-need-based scholarships averaged $3,531 ($18,292 maximum); and $1,777 from other forms of aid. 32% of undergraduate students work part-time. Average annual earnings from campus work are $794. The average financial indebtedness of the 2013 graduate was $17,000. The FAFSA and the college's own financial statement are required. The deadline for filing freshman financial aid applications for fall entry is May 1.

International Students: There are 48 international students enrolled. The school actively recruits these students. They must take the TOEFL. They must also take the SAT or ACT.

Computers: All students may access the system. There are no time limits and no fees.

Graduates: From July 1, 2012 to June 30, 2013, 261 bachelor's degrees were awarded. The most popular majors were elementary education (12%), occupational therapy (11%), and accounting (10%). 60 companies recruited on campus in 2012-2013. In an average class, 1% graduate in 3 years or less, 47% graduate in 4 years or less, 60% graduate in 5 years or less, and 65% graduate in 6 years or less. Of the 2012 graduating class, 23% were enrolled in graduate school within 6 months of graduation, and 75% were employed.

Admissions Contact: Evan Lipp, Dean for Enrollment Management. E-Mail: *admissions@francis.edu* Web: *www.francis.edu*

SAINT JOSEPH'S UNIVERSITY — F-3

Philadelphia, PA 19131 — (610) 660-1300; (888) BE-A-HAWK; (610) 660-1314

Full-time: 2132 men, 2357 women	**Faculty:** 280
Part-time: 366 men, 519 women	**Ph.D.s:** 91%
Graduate: 1391 men, 2189 women	**Student/Faculty:** 16 to 1
Year: semesters, summer session	**Tuition:** $39,040
Application Deadline: February 1	**Room & Board:** $13,232
Freshman Class: 7831 applied, 6165 accepted, 1275 enrolled	
SAT CR/M/W: 550/560/550 **ACT:** 24	**VERY COMPETITIVE**

Founded by the Society of Jesus in 1851, Saint Joseph's University advances the professional and personal ambitions of men and women by providing a demanding, yet supportive, educational experience. One of only 153 schools with a Phi Beta Kappa chapter and AACSB business school accreditation, Saint Joseph's is home to approximately 4,670 traditional undergraduate day students, 610 College of Professional and Liberal Studies and Haub Degree Completion adult undergraduates students, and 3,580 graduate and doctoral students. Saint Joseph's University offers over 50 undergraduate day majors and 50 minors, over 16 College of Professional & Liberal Studies degree and certificate programs as well as over 10 business degree and certificate programs offered through the Haub Degree Completion program, over 30 graduate areas of study including 11 online graduate majors, and an Ed.D. in Educational Leadership. Special programs include Study Abroad, Honors program, Summer Scholars, Service-Learning, and Faith-Justice Studies. Steeped in the 450-year Jesuit tradition of scholarship and service, Saint Joseph's has been named to the President's Higher Education Community Service Honor Roll for General Community Service for seven consecutive years. There are 3 undergraduate schools and 2 graduate schools. In addition to regional accreditation, Saint Joseph's has baccalaureate program accreditation with AACSB. The library contains 353,500 volumes, 860,000 microform items, 4,000 audio/video tapes/CDs/DVDs, and subscribes to 67,400 periodicals including electronic. Computerized library services include interlibrary loans, database searching, Internet access, and Wi-Fi capability. Special learning facilities include an art gallery, radio station, an instructional media center, foreign language labs, Mandeville Hall Wall Street Trading Room, and Claver Honors House, Post Learning Commons. The 114-acre campus is in a suburban area on the western edge of Philadelphia and eastern Montgomery County. Including any residence halls, there are 82 buildings.

Student Life: 53% of undergraduates are from out of state, mostly the Middle Atlantic. Students are from 37 states, and 28 foreign countries. 50% are from public schools. 79% are White. 79% are Catholic; 14% Protestant. The average age of freshmen is 18; all undergraduates, 21. 11% do not continue beyond their first year; 78% remain to graduate.

Housing: 2928 students can be accommodated in college housing, which includes single-sex and coed dorms, on-campus apartments, and off-campus apartments. In addition, there are honors houses, special-interest houses, and special interest floors. On-campus housing is available on a lottery system for upperclassmen. 60% of students live on campus. Upperclassmen may keep cars.

Activities: 9% of men belong to 4 national fraternities; 19% of women belong to 4 national sororities. There are 100 groups on campus, including art, cheerleading, choir, chorale, dance, debate, drama, ethnic, forensics, gay, honors, international, jazz band, literary magazine, musical theater, newspaper, pep band, political, professional, radio, religious, social, social service, and student government. Popular campus events include Community Day, Spring Concert and Hawk-A-Palooza.

Sports: There are 10 intercollegiate sports for men and 10 for women. Facilities include All Saint Joseph's University students are encouraged to participate in intercollegiate, club and intramural activities as well as in the numerous recreational and fitness opportunities that are available. The Athletic Center and the O'Pake Recreation Center, along with Sweeney Field and fields on the Maguire Campus, provide indoor and outdoor locations for athletic and recreational events. These facilities are utilized to enhance the students' physical development under the supervision of Saint Joseph's staff.

Disabled Students: 85% of the campus is accessible. Facilities include wheelchair ramps, elevators, special parking, specially equipped restrooms, special class scheduling, lowered drinking fountains, lowered telephones, special housing. automatic eye doors, curb cuts, a specially equipped van for wheelchairs, a pool lift, and a bell system at major road crossings.

Services: Counseling and information services are available, as is tutoring in most subjects. There is a reader service for the blind. In addition to tutoring, there are study and life skills workshops, supplemental instruction, a writing center, and other educational support services to help students.

Campus Safety and Security: Measures include 24-hour foot and vehicle patrol, emergency notification system, self-defense education, and security escort services. There are shuttle buses, emergency telephones, lighted pathways/sidewalks, controlled access to dorms/residences, and a bicycle patrol.

Programs of Study: Saint Joseph's confers B.A., B.S. and B.B.A. degrees. Associate, master's, and doctoral degrees are also awarded. Bachelor's degrees are awarded in BIOLOGICAL SCIENCE (biochemistry and biology/biological science), BUSINESS (accounting, business administration and management, entrepreneurial studies, finance, human resources, insurance and risk management, international business management, investments and securities, management information systems, marketing management, marketing/retailing/merchandising, organizational leadership and management, and sports marketing), COMMUNICATIONS AND THE ARTS (art, art/art studies, communications, English, French, German, Italian, Latin, music, Spanish, and theatre arts), COMPUTER AND PHYSICAL SCIENCE (actuarial science, chemistry, computer science, information sciences and systems, mathematics, and physics), EDUCATION (art education, early childhood education, elementary education, and special education), ENGINEERING AND ENVIRONMENTAL DESIGN (environmental science), HEALTH PROFESSIONS (health care administration and health science), SOCIAL SCIENCE (asian studies, criminal justice, economics, European studies, French studies, history, international relations, liberal arts/general studies, philosophy, political science/government, psychology, public administration, religious studies, sociology, and theological studies). Biology, and accounting are the strongest academically. Food marketing, marketing, biology, accounting, finance, and interdisciplinary health services have the largest enrollments.

Required: A new General Education Program (GEP) has been implemented beginning with the Fall 2010 freshman. GEP consists of 6 signature core courses; up to 10 variable courses(AP and transfer credits may be accepted); 3 integrative learning courses; and 3 overlay courses focusing on the areas of diversity/globalization, ethics,and writing-intensive.

Special: The University offers internships, a Washington semester, 5-year combined Bachelors/Masters degree programs, dual majors, minor concentrations, and study abroad. There are co-op programs for business majors. There are 23 national honor societies, including Phi Beta Kappa, a freshman honors program, and 16 departmental honors programs.

Faculty/Classroom: 58% of faculty are male; 42% are female. No introductory courses are taught by graduate students. The average class size in a regular course is 25.

Admissions: 79% of the 2013-2014 applicants were accepted. The SAT scores for the 2013-2014 freshman class were: Critical Reading--18% below 500, 58% between 500 and 599, 21% between 600 and 699, and 3% between 700 and 800; Math--16% below 500, 52% between 500 and 599, 28% between 600 and 699, and 3% between 700 and 800; Writing--18% below 500, 53% between 500 and 599, 25% between 600 and 699, and 3% between 700 and 800. The ACT scores were 13% below 21, 30% between 21 and 23, 34% between 24 and 26, 10% between 27 and 28, and 13% above 28.

Requirements: In addition, beginning with the incoming class of 2014, the submission of the SAT and ACT standardized test scores is optional for admission. Academic information, recommendations, and the record of extracurricular involvement and evidence of special talent, leadership and service will be reviewed. Students will continue to have the option to submit an SAT or ACT score if they want additional representation presented to the admissions committee. A variety of factors are considered during the application process including, but not limited to strength of high school, rigor of academic curriculum, service, and overall academic achievement and community involvement. AP and CLEP credits are accepted. Important factors in the admissions decision are advanced placement or honors courses, recommendations by school officials, and leadership record.

Procedure: Freshmen are admitted fall and spring. Entrance exams should be taken in the spring of the junior year and/or the fall of the senior year. There are early admissions and deferred admissions plans. Applications should be filed by February 1 for fall entry; November 15 for spring entry, along with a $60 fee. Notification of early decision is sent December 25; regular decision, March 15. 96 applicants were on the 2013 waiting list; 23 were admitted. Applications are accepted online.

Transfer: 67 transfer students enrolled in 2012-2013. Transfer students requirements include a minimum of 12 transferable credits. Typically, students with a 2.5 cumulative GPA or higher are considered for admission. Transfer applicants must submit high school and college transcripts. 60 of 120 credits required for the bachelor's degree must be completed at Saint Joseph's.

Visiting: There are regularly scheduled orientations for prospective students, consisting of open houses, tours, and information sessions. There are guides for informal visits and visitors may sit in on classes. To schedule a visit, contact the Admissions Office.

Financial Aid: In 2013-2014, 95% of all full-time freshmen and 90% of continuing full-time students received some form of financial aid. The average freshman award was $28,300.. Average annual earnings from campus work are $1500. Saint Joseph's is a member of CSS. The FAFSA is required. The priority date for freshman financial aid applications for fall entry is February 15. The deadline for filing freshman financial aid applications for fall entry is May 1.

International Students: There are 96 international students enrolled. The school actively recruits these students. They must take the TOEFL with a minimum score of 550 on the paper-based TOEFL (PBT) or 79 on the Internet-based version (iBT). They must also take the SAT or ACT, scoring 450. or the TOEFL.

Computers: All students may access the system. There are no time limits and no fees.

Graduates: From July 1, 2012 to June 30, 2013, 1176 bachelor's degrees were awarded. The most popular majors were marketing (12%), finance (9%), and food marketing (9%). 670 companies recruited on campus in 2012-2013. In an average class, 70% graduate in 4 years or less, 78% graduate in 5 years or less, and 78% graduate in 6 years or less. Of the 2012 graduating class, 20% were enrolled in graduate school within 6 months of graduation, and 75% were employed.

Admissions Contact: Maureen Mathis, Assistant Provost. E-Mail: *admit@sju.edu* Web: *www.sju.edu*

SAINT VINCENT COLLEGE B-3

Latrobe, PA 15650 **(724) 805-2500**
(800) SVC-5549; (724) 532-5069

Full-time: 790 men, 742 women	**Faculty:** 99
Part-time: 32 men, 32 women	**Ph.D.s:** 91%
Graduate: 87 men, 130 women	**Student/Faculty:** 16 to 1
Year: semesters, summer session	**Tuition:** $30,350
Application Deadline: April 1	**Room & Board:** $9894
Freshman Class: 2035 applied, 1399 accepted, 472 enrolled	
SAT CR/M/W: 510/520/520 **ACT:** 22	**COMPETITIVE**

Saint Vincent College, founded in 1846, is a private Catholic college of liberal arts and sciences sponsored by Benedictine monks. There are 4 undergraduate schools and 3 graduate schools. In addition to regional accreditation, Saint Vincent has baccalaureate program accreditation with ACBSP. The library contains 287,678 volumes, 99,223 microform items, 7,000 audio/video tapes/CDs/DVDs, and subscribes to 418 periodicals including electronic. Computerized library services include interlibrary loans, database searching, Internet access, and Wi-Fi capability. Special learning facilities include an art gallery, planetarium, radio station, TV station, an observatory, a radio telescope, and a small-business development center. The 200-acre campus is in a suburban area 35 miles east of Pittsburgh. Including any residence halls, there are 22 buildings.

Student Life: 82% of undergraduates are from Pennsylvania. Others are from 27 states, 9 foreign countries, and Canada. 85% are White. 57% are Catholic; 20% Protestant; 11% Unknown denominations. The average age of freshmen is 18; all undergraduates, 20. 15% do not continue beyond their first year; 70% remain to graduate.

Housing: 1283 students can be accommodated in college housing, which includes coed dorms and on-campus apartments. On-campus housing is guaranteed for the freshman year only, is available on a first-come, first-served basis, and is available on a lottery system for upperclassmen. 72% of students live on campus. All students may keep cars.

Activities: There are no fraternities or sororities. There are 63 groups on campus, including art, band, cheerleading, choir, chorus, dance, drama, environmental, ethnic, honors, international, literary magazine, marching band, musical theater, newspaper, pep band, political, professional, radio and TV, religious, social, social service, student government, and yearbook. Popular campus events include Founders' Day, Threshold Lecture Series, and Pittsburgh Steelers Training Camp.

Sports: There are 10 intercollegiate sports for men and 10 for women, and 9 intramural sports for men and 9 for women. Facilities include a 2400-seat gym, a 1050-seat grandstand, basketball and volleyball facilities, a weight and exercise room, an indoor pool, tennis courts, baseball, soccer, and football fields, and a student union and game room area.

Disabled Students: 95% of the campus is accessible. Facilities include wheelchair ramps, elevators, special parking, specially equipped restrooms, lowered drinking fountains, special housing.

Services: Counseling and information services are available, as is tutoring in most subjects. The Opportunity Office provides individual counseling and a study skills class, for first-year students.

Campus Safety and Security: Measures include 24-hour foot and vehicle patrol, emergency notification system, and security escort services. There are emergency telephones, lighted pathways/sidewalks, and controlled access to dorms/residences.

Programs of Study: Saint Vincent confers B.A., and B.S. degrees. Master's and doctoral degrees are also awarded. Bachelor's degrees are awarded in BIOLOGICAL SCIENCE (biochemistry, bioinformatics, and biology/biological science), BUSINESS (accounting, banking and finance, business administration and management, international business management, and marketing/retailing/merchandising), COMMUNICATIONS AND THE ARTS (art, art history and appreciation, arts administration/management, communications, English, fine arts, French, music, music performance, Spanish, studio art, and visual and performing arts), COMPUTER AND PHYSICAL SCIENCE (chemistry, computer science, mathematics, and physics), EDUCATION (art education, business education, early childhood education, middle school education, psychology education, and science education), ENGINEERING AND ENVIRONMENTAL DESIGN (engineering and environmental science), HEALTH PROFESSIONS (occupational therapy, physical therapy, physician's assistant, predentistry, premedicine, prepharmacy, and preveterinary science), SOCIAL SCIENCE (anthropology, economics, history, liberal arts/general studies, philosophy, political science/government, prelaw, psychology, public affairs, sociology, and theological studies). Biology, economics, and psychology are the strongest academically. Biology, psychology, and management have the largest enrollments.

Required: To graduate, students must complete 124 credit hours with a minimum GPA of 2.0. All students are required to take Language and Rhetoric, First Theology, and First Philosophy. The core curriculum includes 9 hours each of social science, theology, and English, 8 of natural sciences, 6 hours each of history, philosophy, and foreign language, and 3/4 of math. Total number of hours in major varies depending on the program. All majors require a culminating activity, such as a thesis, research project, or capstone course/seminar.

Special: There is cross-registration with Seton Hill University, co-op programs, internships, study abroad in Europe and Asia, a work-study program, dual majors, a general studies degree, credit by exam and for life/military/work experience, nondegree study, and pass/fail options. There is a 3-2 engineering option with Boston University, Pennsylvania State University, the University of Pittsburgh, and the Catholic University of America. The college offers teacher certificate courses in early childhood (K-12) and secondary education. There are 16 national honor societies, a freshman honors program, and 13 departmental honors programs.

Faculty/Classroom: 60% of faculty are male; 40% are female. All teach and do research. No introductory courses are taught by graduate students. The average class size in an introductory lecture is 20; in a laboratory is 20; and in a regular course is 25.

Admissions: 69% of the 2013-2014 applicants were accepted. The SAT scores for the 2013-2014 freshman class were: Critical Reading--36% below 500, 45% between 500 and 599, 16% between 600 and 699, and 2% between 700 and 800; Math--28% below 500, 49% between 500 and 599, 21% between 600 and 699, and 2% between 700 and 800; Writing--42% below 500, 42% between 500 and 599, 15% between 600 and 699, and 1% between 700 and 800. The ACT scores were 29% below 21, 30% between 21 and 23, 22% between 24 and 26, 11% between 27 and 28, and 6% above 28. 48% of the current freshmen were in the top fifth of their class; 75% were in the top two fifths. 7 freshmen graduated first in their class.

Requirements: The SAT or ACT is required. Applicants must complete 15 academic credits, including 4 of English, 3 each of social studies and math, 2 of foreign language, and 1 of a lab science. Art students must submit a portfolio, and music and theater students must audition. An essay is required. A GED is accepted. A GPA of 3.2 is required. AP and CLEP credits are accepted. Important factors in the admissions decision are advanced placement or honors courses, evidence of special talent, and recommendations by school officials.

Procedure: Freshmen are admitted fall and spring. Entrance exams should be taken at the end of the junior year or the beginning of the senior year. There are early admissions, deferred admissions, and rolling admissions plans. Applications should be filed by April 1 for fall entry; January 1 for spring entry. The fall 2013 application fee was $25. Applications are accepted online.

Transfer: 47 transfer students enrolled in 2012-2013. Transfer applicants must submit transcripts from postsecondary schools attended and a catalog describing courses taken, plus secondary school transcript(s). 34 of 124 credits required for the bachelor's degree must be completed at Saint Vincent.

Visiting: There are regularly scheduled orientations for prospective students, consisting of a general information session, an informal meeting with faculty, and campus tours. There are guides for informal visits, visitors may sit in on classes, and stay overnight. To schedule a visit, contact the Admission and Financial Aid Office.

Financial Aid: In 2013-2014, 100% of all full-time freshmen and 93% of continuing full-time students received some form of financial aid. 64% of all full-time freshmen and 77% of continuing full-time students received need-based aid. The average freshman award was $19,800. Need-based scholarships or need-based grants averaged $5,690 ($10,807 maximum); need-based self-help aid (loans and jobs) averaged $6,891 ($7,820 maximum); and other non-need-based awards and non-need-based scholarships averaged $19,168 ($39,078 maximum). 44% of undergraduate students work part-time. Average annual earnings from campus work are $1680. The average financial indebtedness of the 2013 graduate was $22,350. The FAFSA is required. The priority date for freshman financial aid applications for fall entry is March 1. The deadline for filing freshman financial aid applications for fall entry is April 1.

International Students: There are 24 international students enrolled. The school actively recruits these students. They must take the TOEFL with a minimum score of 550 on the paper-based TOEFL (PBT). They must also take the SAT or ACT.

Computers: All students may access the system during computer lab hours and 24 hours from dorm rooms. There are no time limits. The fee is $150.

Graduates: From July 1, 2012 to June 30, 2013, 353 bachelor's degrees were awarded. The most popular majors were communication (9%), biology (8%), and psychology (8%). In an average class, 1% graduate in 3 years or less, 63% graduate in 4 years or less, 69% graduate in 5 years or less, and 70% graduate in 6 years or less.

Admissions Contact: Admission and Financial Aid Office E-Mail: *admission@stvincent.edu* Web: *www.stvincent.edu*

SETON HILL UNIVERSITY — B-4

Greensburg, PA 15601-1599 — (724) 838-4255; (800) 826-6234; (724) 830-1294

Full-time: 535 men, 815 women	**Faculty:** n/av; IIB, -$
Part-time: 65 men, 135 women	**Ph.D.s:** 88%
Graduate: 100 men, 310 women	**Student/Faculty:** n/av
Year: semesters, summer session	**Tuition:** $28,154
Application Deadline: open	**Room & Board:** $9626
Freshman Class: n/av	
SAT or ACT: recommended	

COMPETITIVE

Seton Hill University, founded in 1883, is a private university affiliated with the Roman Catholic Church and offers programs in liberal arts and career preparation. The figures in the above capsule and in this profile are approximate. There is 1 graduate school. In addition to regional accreditation, Seton Hill has baccalaureate program accreditation with ADA, CSWE, and NASM. The library contains 123,538 volumes, 5403 microform items, 6684 audio/video tapes/CDs/DVDs, and subscribes to 423 periodicals including electronic. Computerized library services include interlibrary loans, database searching, and Internet access. Special learning facilities include an art gallery, a TV station, a nursery school that functions as laboratory school for education students, a performing arts center, a visual arts center, and a technology wing. The 200-acre campus is in a small town 35 miles east of Pittsburgh. Including any residence halls, there are 19 buildings.

Student Life: 79% of undergraduates are from Pennsylvania. Others are from 32 states, 16 foreign countries, and Canada. 80% are white. The average age of freshmen is 18; all undergraduates, 21. 19% do not continue beyond their first year; 64% remain to graduate.

Housing: 750 students can be accommodated in college housing, which includes single-sex and coed dorms. On-campus housing is guaranteed for all 4 years. 69% of students live on campus. Alcohol is not permitted. All students may keep cars.

Activities: There are no fraternities or sororities. There are 40 groups

on campus, including art, bagpipe, band, cheerleading, choir, chorale, chorus, dance, drama, entrepreneurial, environmental, ethnic, gay, honors, international, jazz band, literary magazine, marching band, musical theater, newspaper, orchestra, pep band, political, professional, religious, social, social service, student government, and symphony. Popular campus events include Christmas on the Hill, Family Weekend, and President's Reception.

Sports: There are 10 intercollegiate sports for men and 12 for women. Facilities include 2 gyms, 1 with a seating capacity of 1200, a fitness center, an aerobics room, a swimming pool, a field house with weight and training rooms, 3 natural grass playing fields, and a football stadium.

Disabled Students: 95% of the campus is accessible. Facilities include wheelchair ramps, elevators, special parking, specially equipped restrooms, special class scheduling, lowered drinking fountains, and lowered telephones.

Services: Counseling and information services are available, as is tutoring in most subjects. There is a reader service for the blind and remedial math and writing.

Campus Safety and Security: Measures include 24-hour foot and vehicle patrol, emergency notification system, self-defense education, and security escort services. There are shuttle buses, emergency telephones, and lighted pathways/sidewalks.

Programs of Study: Seton Hill confers B.A., B.S., B.F.A., B.Mus., B.S.Med.Tech., and B.S.W. degrees. Master's degrees are also awarded. Bachelor's degrees are awarded in BIOLOGICAL SCIENCE (biochemistry and biology/biological science), BUSINESS (accounting, business administration and management, business economics, entrepreneurial studies, human resources, international business management, management information systems, marketing/retailing/merchandising, personnel management, sports management, and tourism), COMMUNICATIONS AND THE ARTS (art history and appreciation, arts administration/management, communications, creative writing, dramatic arts, English, fine arts, graphic design, journalism, music, musical theater, performing arts, Spanish, studio art, theater design, and theater management), COMPUTER AND PHYSICAL SCIENCE (actuarial science, chemistry, computer science, mathematics, and physics), EDUCATION (art education, early childhood education, elementary education, English education, foreign languages education, home economics education, mathematics education, music education, science education, secondary education, social science education, and special education), ENGINEERING AND ENVIRONMENTAL DESIGN (engineering), HEALTH PROFESSIONS (art therapy, medical laboratory technology, music therapy, pharmacy, physician's assistant, predentistry, premedicine, preosteopathy, and preveterinary science), SOCIAL SCIENCE (child care/child and family studies, criminal justice, dietetics, economics, family/consumer resource management, family/consumer studies, food production/management/services, forensic studies, history, human services, international studies, liberal arts/general studies, political science/government, prelaw, psychology, religion, religious music, social work, and sociology). Sciences, education, and fine arts are the strongest academically. Psychology, art, and business have the largest enrollments.

Required: The core curriculum requires 6 credits in Western cultures, 6 credits in writing, and 3 each in theology, philosophy/senior seminar, math, computer science, science, college-level foreign language, U.S. cultures, non-Western cultures, and artistic expression. A total of 120 credit hours with a minimum GPA of 2.0 is required for graduation.

Special: There are cooperative programs in all majors and cross-registration with St. Vincent College, the University of Pittsburgh at Greensburg, and Westmoreland County Community College. Internships are encouraged. Seton Hill offers study abroad, a Washington semester, work-study, dual and student-designed majors, accelerated degree programs, a 3-2 engineering program with Pennsylvania State University and Georgia Institute of Technology, a 2-2 nursing program with Catholic University of America, a 3-2 or 3-1 medical technology program with area hospitals, credit by exam and for life/military/work experience, nondegree study, and pass/fail options. There are 5 national honor societies and a freshman honors program.

Faculty/Classroom: 40% of faculty are male; 60% are female. 87% teach undergraduates, and 60% do research. No introductory courses are taught by graduate students. The average class size in an introductory lecture is 25; in a laboratory, 16; and in a regular course, 17.

Requirements: The SAT or ACT is recommended. 2 graded writing samples are accepted in place of SAT or ACT scores. A total of 15 Carnegie units is required, including 4 each of English and electives, 2 each of math, social studies, and foreign language, and 1 of a lab science. Art students must submit a portfolio; music and theater students must audition. An interview is recommended. The GED is accepted with supporting recommendations. A GPA of 2.5 is required. AP and CLEP credits are accepted. Important factors in the admissions decision are advanced placement or honors courses, evidence of special talent, and leadership record.

Procedure: Freshmen are admitted fall and spring. Entrance exams should be taken in spring of the junior year or fall of the senior year. There are deferred admissions and rolling admissions plans. Application deadlines are open. The application fee is $35. Notification is sent on a rolling basis. Applications are accepted online.

Transfer: Applicants must submit college transcripts and have a GPA of at least 2.0. An interview is recommended, as are supporting letters. 48 of 120 credits required for the bachelor's degree must be completed at Seton Hill.

Visiting: There are regularly scheduled orientations for prospective students, consisting of an introduction, an address by the president or dean, an open reception with faculty, a financial aid session, a student panel, and a campus tour. There are guides for informal visits, and visitors may sit in on classes and stay overnight. To schedule a visit, contact Campus Visit Coordinator.

Financial Aid: The FAFSA and the college's own financial statement are required. Check with school for current application deadlines.

International Students: There were 26 international students enrolled in a recent year. The school actively recruits these students. They must take the TOEFL with a minimum score of 550 on the paper-based TOEFL (PBT) or 79 on the Internet-based version (iBT).

Computers: Wireless access is available. All classrooms, labs, offices, and dorm rooms have Internet access. There are approximately 600 university-owned computers used daily on campus. The Management/Student Information System and the Course Management System as well as all e-mail accounts are accessible from off campus via Internet. All students may access the system 24 hours per day. There are no time limits and no fees.

Graduates: In a recent year, 272 bachelor's degrees were awarded. The most popular majors were business (23%), physician's assistant (7%), and art (4%). 51 companies recruited on campus in a recent year. In an average class, 2% graduate in 3 years or less, 50% graduate in 4 years or less, 54% graduate in 5 years or less, and 59% graduate in 6 years or less. Of a recent graduating class, 31% were enrolled in graduate school within 6 months of graduation and 92% were employed.

Admissions Contact: Director of Admissions. A campus DVD is available. E-mail: *admit@setonhill.edu* Web: *www.setonhill.edu*

SHIPPENSBURG UNIVERSITY OF PENNSYLVANIA D-3

Shippensburg, PA 17257 (717) 477-1231; (717) 477-4016

Full-time: 3187 men, 3176 women	**Faculty:** 310; IIA, +$
Part-time: 149 men, 200 women	**Ph.D.s:** 88%
Graduate: 392 men, 620 women	**Student/Faculty:** 21 to 1
Year: semesters, summer session	**Tuition:** $9154 ($17,374)
Application Deadline:	**Room & Board:** $7910
Freshman Class: 6403 applied, 5158 accepted, 1485 enrolled	
SAT CR/M/W: 490/500/470	**ACT:** 20 **LESS COMPETITIVE**

Shippensburg University, founded in 1871, is a public university that is part of the Pennsylvania State System of Higher Education offering undergraduate and graduate degree programs in the College of Arts and Sciences, College of Business, and College of Education and Human Services. There are 4 undergraduate schools and one graduate school. In addition to regional accreditation, Ship has baccalaureate program accreditation with AACSB, ABET, CSWE, and NCATE. The library contains 369,623 volumes, 1.2 million microform items, 72,601 audio/video tapes/CDs/DVDs, and subscribes to 19,976 periodicals including electronic. Computerized library services include interlibrary loans, database searching, Internet access, and Wi-Fi capability. Special learning facilities include an art gallery, planetarium, radio station, TV station, a closed-circuit television, fashion archives center, vertebrate museum, women's center, on-campus elementary school, electron microscope, greenhouse, and herbarium. The 200-acre campus is in a rural area 40 miles southwest of Harrisburg. Including any residence halls, there are 48 buildings.

Student Life: 94% of undergraduates are from Pennsylvania. Others are from 21 states, and 15 foreign countries. 89% are from public schools. 81% are White. The average age of freshmen is 19; all undergraduates, 21. 32% do not continue beyond their first year; 57% remain to graduate.

Housing: 2641 students can be accommodated in college housing, which includes coed dorms, on-campus apartments, and off-campus apartments. a designated quiet hall and Scholar Hall, a healthy living community, Wellness Center, Honors College, multi-purpose rooms that can be used for academic and/or community programming. On-campus housing is guaranteed for the freshman year only and is available on a lottery system for upperclassmen. 67% of students commute. Alcohol is not permitted. All students may keep cars.

Activities: 6% of men belong to 11 national fraternities; 7% of women belong to 11 national sororities. There are 120 groups on campus, including Vet's Club, BigBrother/Big Sister, ROTC Ranger Challenge Team, Activities Program Board, art, band, cheerleading, choir, chorale, chorus, computers, dance, debate, drama, environmental, ethnic, gay, honors, international, jazz band, literary magazine, marching band, musical theater, newspaper, orchestra, pep band, photography, political, professional, radio and TV, religious, social, social service, student government, and yearbook. Popular campus events include Planetarium Shows, Senior Olympics and Summer Music Festival.

Sports: There are 8 intercollegiate sports for men and 10 for women, and 6 intramural sports for men and 6 for women. Facilities include a 7700-seat stadium for football and track-and-field events and complexes for varsity baseball, softball, and tennis. There is a 450-seat stadium with an artificial turf surface for soccer, field hockey, and lacrosse. Basketball, volleyball, and wrestling competitions are conducted within a 2700-seat facility, with swimming facilities. Outdoor recreational facilities include a 12-acre sports complex. Students also have access to a 64,000-square-foot recreational building.

Disabled Students: 91% of the campus is accessible. Facilities include wheelchair ramps, elevators, special parking, specially equipped restrooms, special class scheduling, lowered drinking fountains, lowered telephones, special housing. enlarged printing, extended time for tests, classroom accessibility, note taking, reader and scribe services for exams, alternative testing sites, priority scheduling. Tech room in Library that has the following software: Kurzweil Reader, Text Help, JAWS, and Zoom Text. At least one resident hall room in each building is handicap accessible, other types of rooms are available as needed.

Services: Counseling and information services are available, as is tutoring in most subjects, most general education courses and writing. JAWS and Zoom Text for the blind and visually impaired. There is remedial math, reading, and writing. Individual meetings with Learning Specialists are available to help students interested in developing individual strategies and group study.

Campus Safety and Security: Measures include 24-hour foot and vehicle patrol, emergency notification system, self-defense education, and security escort services. There are shuttle buses, emergency telephones, lighted pathways/sidewalks, controlled access to dorms/residences, Residence halls are equipped with an automatic heat/smoke detection sprinkler system monitored 24 hours a day by police. A strobe light unit notifies students who are hearing impaired. Residence hall doors are locked 24 hours a day. There are digital cameras at the main entrance to residence halls, computer labs, and other buildings, as well as many exterior cameras covering parking lots and other campus areas. A text emergency message system has also been implemented. Additional cameras and card swipes to gain floor entry into the newly constructed residence halls.

Programs of Study: Ship confers B.A., B.S., B.S.B.A., B.S.Ed. and B.S.W. degrees. Master's degrees are also awarded. Bachelor's degrees are awarded in BIOLOGICAL SCIENCE (biology/biological science and (Biological) Pre-Health Studies), BUSINESS (accounting, banking and finance, business administration and management, management information systems, marketing management, and supply chain management), COMMUNICATIONS AND THE ARTS (art, communications, English, French, journalism, Spanish, and speech/debate/rhetoric), COMPUTER AND PHYSICAL SCIENCE (applied physics, chemistry, computer science, earth science, geoenvironmental studies, mathematics, physics, and software engineering), EDUCATION (art education, business education, early childhood education, elementary education, English education, foreign languages education, mathematics education, middle school education, secondary education, and social studies education), ENGINEERING AND ENVIRONMENTAL DESIGN (computer engineering and environmental science), HEALTH PROFESSIONS (exercise science and health care administration), SOCIAL SCIENCE (criminal justice, early childhood studies, economics, geography, history, interdisciplinary studies, international studies, political science/government, psychology, public administration, social work, and sociology). Psychology, criminal justice, and biology have the largest enrollments.

Required: General education courses include English composition, oral communications, math, and history, as well as courses in logic and numbers for rational thinking; linguistic, literary, artistic, and cultural traditions; lab science; biological and physical science; political, economic, and geographic sciences; and social and behavioral sciences. The core curriculum varies for degree programs. Most degree programs require 120 credit hours, with 22 to 30 hours in the major, and a 2.0 minimum GPA for graduation.

Special: There are 26 national honor societies, a freshman honors program, and 1 departmental honors program.

Faculty/Classroom: 56% of faculty are male; 44% are female. 93% teach undergraduates, and 39% do both. No introductory courses are taught by graduate students.

Admissions: 81% of the 2013-2014 applicants were accepted. The SAT scores for the 2013-2014 freshman class were: Critical Reading--53% below 500, 38% between 500 and 599, 8% between 600 and 699, and 1% between 700 and 800; Math--48% below 500, 40% between 500 and 599, 11% between 600 and 699, and 1% between 700 and 800; Writing--62% below 500, 32% between 500 and 599, and 6% between 600 and 699. The ACT scores were 53% below 21, 30% between 21 and 23, 12% between 24 and 26, 4% between 27 and 28, and 1% above 28. 22% of the current freshmen were in the top fifth of their class; 47% were in the top two fifths. 3 freshmen graduated first in their class.

Requirements: The SAT is required. In addition, applicants are urged to pursue a typical college preparatory program, which should include 4 units of English, 3 social sciences, 3 math, and 3 lab science, and 3 foreign language. A GED is accepted. AP and CLEP credits are accepted. Important factors in the admissions decision are advanced placement or honors courses, recommendations by school officials, and evidence of special talent.

Procedure: Freshmen are admitted fall and spring. Entrance exams should be taken in the junior year and senior year. There are early admissions, deferred admissions, and rolling admissions plans. Application deadlines are open. The fall 2013 application fee was $40. Notification is sent on a rolling basis. Applications are accepted online.

Transfer: 551 transfer students enrolled in 2012-2013. Applicants must provide high school and college transcripts and SAT or ACT scores if they have fewer than 30 college credits. 45 of 120 credits required for the bachelor's degree must be completed at Ship.

Visiting: There are regularly scheduled orientations for prospective students, including daily academic group meetings, campus tours, and 5 weekend open house programs per year. There are guides for informal visits and visitors may sit in on classes. To schedule a visit, contact the Admissions Office.

Financial Aid: In 2013-2014, 91% of all full-time freshmen and 85% of continuing full-time students received some form of financial aid. 70% of all full-time freshmen and 65% of continuing full-time students received need-based aid. The average freshman award was $12,254. Need-based scholarships or need-based grants averaged $5,856 ($20,764 maximum); need-based self help aid (loans and jobs) averaged $7,738 ($24,469 maximum); non-need-based athletic scholarships averaged $2,684 ($10,000 maximum); and other non-need-based awards and non-need-based scholarships averaged $8,415 ($29,812 maximum). 11% of undergraduate students work part-time. Average annual earnings from campus work are $2012. The average financial indebtedness of the 2013 graduate was $27,661. Ship is a member of CSS. The FAFSA, and PHEAA is required. The deadline for filing freshman financial aid applications for fall entry is May 1.

International Students: There are 29 international students enrolled. They must take the TOEFL with a minimum score of 550 on the paper-based TOEFL (PBT) or 66 on the Internet-based version (iBT), Students whose native language is English must submit SAT scores instead of TOEFL.

Computers: All students may access the system 24 hours a day. There are no time limits and no fees.

Graduates: From July 1, 2012 to June 30, 2013, 1386 bachelor's degrees were awarded. The most popular majors were elementary education (15%), criminal justice (9%), and psychology (9%). 44 companies recruited on campus in 2012-2013. In an average class, 40% graduate in 4 years or less, 55% graduate in 5 years or less, and 57% graduate in 6 years or less.

Admissions Contact: William H. Washabaugh, Acting Dean of Enrollment Management. E-Mail: *admiss@ship.edu* Web: *www.ship.edu*

SLIPPERY ROCK UNIVERSITY OF PENNSYLVANIA B-2

Slippery Rock, PA 16057 (724) 738-2015
(800) 929-4778; (724) 738-2913

Full-time: 2865 men, 3570 women	**Faculty:** n/av; IIA, av$
Part-time: 230 men, 420 women	**Ph.D.s:** n/av
Graduate: 240 men, 515 women	**Student/Faculty:** n/av
Year: semesters, summer session	**Tuition:** $9044 ($15,462)
Application Deadline: see profile	**Room & Board:** $9384
Freshman Class: n/av	
SAT: required	**ACT:** recommended

LESS COMPETITIVE

Slippery Rock University of Pennsylvania, founded in 1889, is a public institution that is part of the Pennsylvania State System of Higher Education. It offers programs in business, information, social sciences, education, health, environment, science, humanities, and fine and performing arts. There are 4 undergraduate schools and 1 graduate school. Figures in the above capsule and in this profile are approximate. In addition to regional accreditation, The Rock has baccalaureate program accreditation with ACBSP, APTA, CSWE, NASAD, NASM, NCATE, NLN, and NRPA. The library contains 502,974 volumes, 1.5 million microform items, 22,707 audio/video tapes/CDs/DVDs, and subscribes to 1300 periodicals including electronic. Computerized library services include interlibrary loans, database searching, and Internet access. Special learning facilities include a learning resource center, art gallery, natural history museum, planetarium, radio station, and TV station. The 600-acre campus is in a small town 50 miles north of Pittsburgh. Including any residence halls, there are 60 buildings.

Student Life: 96% of undergraduates are from Pennsylvania. Others are from 35 states, 47 foreign countries, and Canada. 70% are from public schools. 87% are white. The average age of freshmen is 18; all undergraduates, 22. 22% do not continue beyond their first year; 49% remain to graduate.

Housing: 2810 students can be accommodated in college housing, which

includes single-sex and coed dorms, on-campus apartments, off-campus apartments, and married student housing. In addition, there are honors houses, language houses, special-interest houses, fraternity houses, and sorority houses. On-campus housing is guaranteed for the freshman year only and is available on a first-come, first-served basis. 62% of students commute. Alcohol is not permitted. All students may keep cars.

Activities: 7% of men belong to 11 national fraternities; 6% of women belong to 9 national sororities. There are 100 groups on campus, including art, band, cheerleading, chess, choir, chorale, chorus, communications, computers, dance, drama, ethnic, film, gay, honors, international, jazz band, literary magazine, marching band, musical theater, newspaper, orchestra, pep band, photography, political, professional, radio and TV, religious, social, social service, student government, symphony, and yearbook. Popular campus events include Spring Weekend.

Sports: There are 12 intercollegiate sports for men and 12 for women, and 7 intramural sports for men and 7 for women. Facilities include a field house, a gym, and a fitness center. The campus stadium seats 10,000, the indoor gym seats 3000, and the largest auditorium/arena seats 1000.

Disabled Students: 80% of the campus is accessible. Facilities include wheelchair ramps, elevators, special parking, specially equipped restrooms, special class scheduling, lowered drinking fountains, lowered telephones, and special housing.

Services: Counseling and information services are available, as is tutoring in about 60 introductory-level general liberal studies courses. There is a reader service for the blind, and remedial math and writing.

Campus Safety and Security: Measures include 24-hour foot and vehicle patrol, self-defense education, and security escort services. There are shuttle buses, emergency telephones, and lighted pathways/sidewalks. The university maintains its own police department, with officers having the same powers as municipal police.

Programs of Study: The Rock confers B.A., B.S., B.F.A., B.Mus., B.Mus.Ed., B.S.B.A., B.S.Ed., and B.S.N. degrees. Master's and doctoral degrees are also awarded. Bachelor's degrees are awarded in BIOLOGICAL SCIENCE (biology/biological science), BUSINESS (accounting, business administration and management, international business management, and marketing/retailing/merchandising), COMMUNICATIONS AND THE ARTS (communications, dance, English, fine arts, French, German, music, and Spanish), COMPUTER AND PHYSICAL SCIENCE (chemistry, computer science, earth science, geology, information sciences and systems, mathematics, and physics), EDUCATION (early childhood education, elementary education, foreign languages education, health education, music education, science education, secondary education, and special education), HEALTH PROFESSIONS (community health work, medical laboratory technology, and nursing), SOCIAL SCIENCE (anthropology, economics, geography, history, parks and recreation management, philosophy, political science/government, psychology, public administration, social science, social work, and sociology). Business, education, and health science have the largest enrollments.

Required: B.A. students must demonstrate proficiency in a foreign language, and all must complete 42 to 53 credits in a 7-part liberal studies program, including basic competencies, arts, cultural diversity/global perspective, human institutions, science and math, natural experience, and modern age. Specific requirements include public speaking, college writing, algebra, and phys ed. A minimum of 120 credit hours, with at least 30 in the major, is required for graduation.

Special: Study abroad is available in 16 countries. Internships are offered in most majors, and international internships are available in Scotland and England. There is a 3-2 engineering program with Pennsylvania State University. The dual major is an option, and credit is given for military experience. Pass/fail options also are available. There are 26 national honor societies, a freshman honors program, and 33 departmental honors programs.

Faculty/Classroom: 53% of faculty are male; 47% are female. All teach undergraduates. No introductory courses are taught by graduate students. The average class size in an introductory lecture is 33; in a laboratory, 20; and in a regular course, 25.

Requirements: The SAT is required. The ACT is recommended. Students should graduate from an accredited secondary school or have a GED. A total of 16 academic credits is required. The recommended college preparatory program includes 4 years of English and social studies, 3 each of science and math, and 2 of a foreign language. An interview is recommended. AP and CLEP credits are accepted. Important factors in the admissions decision are advanced placement or honors courses, extracurricular activities record, and evidence of special talent.

Procedure: Freshmen are admitted fall, spring, and summer. Entrance exams should be taken in the junior year or fall of the senior year. There are deferred admissions and rolling admissions plans. Check with the school for current application deadlines and fee. Notification is sent on a rolling basis. Applications are accepted online. A waiting list is maintained.

Transfer: Applicants should have completed at least 24 credit hours with a GPA of 2.5. The SAT or ACT, as well as an interview, are recommended. 36 of 120 credits required for the bachelor's degree must be completed at the Rock.

Visiting: There are regularly scheduled orientations for prospective students, including a meeting with faculty, an information fair, and a campus tour. There are guides for informal visits; visitors may sit in on classes and stay overnight. To schedule a visit, contact the Admissions Office.

Financial Aid: The Rock is a member of CSS. The FAFSA is required. Check with the school for current deadlines.

International Students: The school actively recruits these students. They must take the TOEFL.

Computers: All students may access the system. The mainframe system is accessible 24 hours a day. Campus terminal and PC labs are generally open more than 100 hours per week. There are no time limits and no fees.

Admissions Contact: Jim Barrett, Director of Admissions. A campus DVD is available. E-Mail: *asktherock@sru.edu* Web: *www.sru.edu*

SUSQUEHANNA UNIVERSITY — D-3

Selinsgrove, PA 17870 — (570) 372-4260, (800) 326-9672; (570) 372-2722

Full-time: 951 men, 1173 women	**Faculty:** 142; IIB, av$
Part-time: 17 men, 36 women	**Ph.D.s:** 93%
Graduate: 3 men, 5 women	**Student/Faculty:** 12 to 1
Year: semesters, summer session	**Tuition:** $38,780
Application Deadline: March 1	**Room & Board:** $10,390

Freshman Class: 3217 applied, 2327 accepted, 589 enrolled
SAT or ACT: recommended

COMPETITIVE

Susquehanna University, founded in 1858, is an independent, selective, residential institution affiliated with the Lutheran Church. It offers programs through schools of arts and sciences, and business. There are 2 undergraduate schools. In addition to regional accreditation, S.U. has baccalaureate program accreditation with AACSB and NASM. The library contains 644,411 volumes, 32,502 microform items, 10,248 audio/video tapes/CDs/DVDs, and subscribes to 67,437 periodicals including electronic. Computerized library services include interlibrary loans, database searching, Internet access, and Wi-Fi capability. Special learning facilities include an art gallery, radio station, multimedia classrooms, video studios, a campuswide telecommunications network, satellite dishes and distribution system for foreign-language broadcasts, a video conferencing facility, an ecological field station, and observatory, a child development center, and an electronic music lab. The 325-acre campus is in a small town 50 miles north of Harrisburg. Including any residence halls, there are 86 buildings.

Student Life: 51% of undergraduates are from out of state, mostly the Middle Atlantic. Students are from 35 states, 21 foreign countries, and Canada. 79% are from public schools. 82% are White; 33% are Catholic; 32% Protestant; 17% claim no religious affiliation; 16% Buddhist, Muslim, Hindu, Mormon, Eastern and Orthodox. The average age of freshmen is 18; all undergraduates, 20. 16% do not continue beyond their first year; 75% remain to graduate.

Housing: 2042 students can be accommodated in college housing, which includes coed dorms, on-campus apartments, and off-campus apartments. In addition, there are honors houses, special-interest houses, fraternity houses, and sorority houses. On-campus housing is guaranteed for all 4 years. 86% of students live on campus; of those, 85% remain on campus on weekends. All students may keep cars.

Activities: 17% of men belong to 6 national fraternities; 16% of women belong to 5 national sororities. There are 145 groups on campus, including academic clubs (by major/discipline), Asian student coalition, Big brothers/Big sisters, black student union, equestrian, Habitat for Humanity, Hillel, Hispanic organization for student awareness, honor societies, national organization of women, rugby), sports/athletics (Ice hockey, student awareness of the value of the environment, ultimate frisbee, art, band, cheerleading, chess, choir, chorale, chorus, communications, computers, dance, drama, environmental, ethnic, film, gay, honors, international, jazz band, literary magazine, musical theater, newspaper, opera, orchestra, Outdoors club, pep band, photography, political, professional, radio and TV, religious, social, social service, student government, and yearbook. Popular campus events include Thanksgiving Dinner, Spring Weekend, Candlelight Christmas Service, Homecomimg Semi-Formal Ball, Annual Concert and Fall Frenzy.

Sports: There are 11 intercollegiate sports for men and 12 for women, and 7 intramural sports for men and 7 for women. Facilities include a field house with indoor track, tennis, and basketball courts, football stadium and track, soccer, baseball, lacrosse, rugby, and hockey fields, basketball and tennis courts, a swimming pool, racquetball courts, a weight training room, and a fitness center.

Disabled Students: 90% of the campus is accessible. Facilities include wheelchair ramps, elevators, special parking, specially equipped restrooms, special class scheduling, lowered drinking fountains, and lowered telephones.

Services: Counseling and information services are available, as is tutoring in some subjects, writing, math, foreign languages, and study skills. Academic departments also provide tutoring.

Campus Safety and Security: Measures include 24-hour foot and vehicle patrol, emergency notification system, self-defense education, and security escort services. There are emergency telephones, lighted pathways/sidewalks, controlled access to dorms/residences, closed circuit TV cameras in common exterior areas on campus.

Programs of Study: S.U. confers B.A., B.S. and B.M. degrees. Bachelor's degrees are awarded in BIOLOGICAL SCIENCE (biochemistry, biology/biological science, and ecology), BUSINESS (accounting and business administration and management), COMMUNICATIONS AND THE ARTS (art history and appreciation, communications, English, French, German, graphic design, Italian, music, music performance, Spanish, studio art, and visual and performing arts), COMPUTER AND PHYSICAL SCIENCE (chemistry, computer science, earth science, information sciences and systems, mathematics, and physics), EDUCATION (early childhood education and music education), ENGINEERING AND ENVIRONMENTAL DESIGN (environmental science), SOCIAL SCIENCE (anthropology, economics, history, international studies, liberal arts/general studies, philosophy, political science/government, psychology, religion, and sociology). Business, communications, and biology have the largest enrollments.

Required: The Central Curriculum is at the heart of the Susquehanna education experience. The diverse courses in the Central Curriculum comprise 40 percent of the graduation requirement, and are divided into five complementary sections: Richness of Thought, Natural World, Human Interactions, Intellectual Skills, and Connections. As part of the Connections requirement, all students at Susquehanna are required to participate in a unique cross-cultural program that will expose them to different cultures.

Special: Students may register for courses at Bucknell University. Internships are offered in almost all majors and study abroad is available on 6 continents. The School of Business offers a semester in London for junior business majors. Two-week study seminars in Australia, are available, as are a Boston semester, a Washington semester, a United Nations semester, a work and study semester through the Philadelphia Center. The university offers dual and student-designed majors, work-study programs, credit by examination, nondegree study, and pass/fail options. The B.A.-B.S. degree is available in 34 majors. In addition, the university offers a 2-2 program in allied health with Thomas Jefferson University, and a 3-2 program in dentistry with Temple University. Highly motivated students have the option of earning their baccalaureate degree in three years. There are 24 national honor societies and a freshman honors program.

Faculty/Classroom: 53% of faculty are male; 47% are female. All teach and do research. No introductory courses are taught by graduate students. The average class size in an introductory lecture is 22; in a laboratory is 14; and in a regular course is 18.

Admissions: 72% of the 2013-2014 applicants were accepted. The SAT scores for the 2013-2014 freshman class were: Critical Reading--19% below 500, 48% between 500 and 599, 26% between 600 and 699, and 6% between 700 and 800; Math--17% below 500, 49% between 500 and 599, 29% between 600 and 699, and 5% between 700 and 800; Writing--28% below 500, 45% between 500 and 599, 24% between 600 and 699, and 4% between 700 and 800. 45% of the current freshmen were in the top fifth of their class; 28% were in the top two fifths. 12 freshmen graduated first in their class.

Requirements: The SAT or ACT is recommended. All students with a cumulative class rank in the top 20% in a strong college preparatory program. Such students have the option of submitting either the SAT, ACT, or 2 graded writing samples. Students should be graduates of an accredited high school. Preparation should include 4 years of English and math, 3 to 4 years of science, and 2 to 3 years each of social studies and foreign language. In addition, 1 unit of art or music is recommended. An essay is required, as are, for relevant fields, music audition, or writing portfolio. An interview is strongly recommended. AP and CLEP credits are accepted. Important factors in the admissions decision are advanced placement or honors courses, evidence of special talent, and recommendations by school officials.

Procedure: Freshmen are admitted fall and spring. Entrance exams should be taken by January of the senior year. There are early decision, early admissions, deferred admissions, and rolling admissions plans. Early decision applications should be filed by November 1; regular applications, by March 1 for fall entry; and January 1 for spring entry, along with a $35 fee. Notification of early decision is sent November 15; regular decision, January 15. 106 early decision candidates were accepted for the 2013-2014 class. 170 applicants were on the 2013 waiting list; 2 were admitted. Applications are accepted online. Application fees are waived if application is completed online.

Transfer: 37 transfer students enrolled in 2012-2013. Applicants must submit high school and college transcripts, test scores, and a recommendation from a dean. An interview is strongly recommended. A music audition or writing portfolio is required for relevant fields. 65 of 130 credits required for the bachelor's degree must be completed at Susquehanna.

Visiting: There are regularly scheduled orientations for prospective students, special visiting days for prospective students and their parents held in the spring, fall, and summer. These events include sessions with faculty, admissions, financial aid, and placement staff and tours of the campus. There are guides for informal visits, visitors may sit in on classes, and stay overnight. To schedule a visit, contact Chris Markle at (570) 372-4260.

Financial Aid: In 2013-2014, 99% of all full-time freshmen and 94% of continuing full-time students received some form of financial aid. 79% of all full-time freshmen and 70% of continuing full-time students received need-based aid. The average freshman award was $31,277. Need-based scholarships or need-based grants averaged $27,329 ($38,280 maximum); need based self-help aid (loans and jobs) averaged $4,799 ($9,950 maximum); and other non-need-based awards and non-need-based scholarships averaged $16,249 ($38,280 maximum). 49% of undergraduate students work part-time. Average annual earnings from campus work are $1036. The average financial indebtedness of the 2013 graduate was $31,828. S.U. is a member of CSS. The CSS/Profile and FAFSA, and prior year federal tax return for parents and students are required. The priority date for freshman financial aid applications for fall entry is March 15. The deadline for filing freshman financial aid applications for fall entry is May 1.

International Students: There are 30 international students enrolled. The school actively recruits these students. They must take the TOEFL with a minimum score of 550 on the paper-based TOEFL (PBT) or 80 on the Internet-based version (iBT), IELTS.

Computers: All students may access the system 24 hours a day. There are no time limits and no fees.

Graduates: From July 1, 2012 to June 30, 2013, 493 bachelor's degrees were awarded. The most popular majors were business/marketing (19%), communications (15%), and psychology (8%). 50 companies recruited on campus in 2012-2013. In an average class, 68% graduate in 4 years or less, 75% graduate in 5 years or less, and 75% graduate in 6 years or less.

Admissions Contact: Chris Markle, Director of Admissions. E-Mail: *suadmiss@susqu.edu* Web: *www.susqu.edu*

SWARTHMORE COLLEGE — E-3

Swarthmore, PA 19081 — (610) 328-8300; (800) 667-3110; (610) 328-8580

Full-time: 750 men, 787 women	**Faculty:** 171; IIB, ++$
Part-time: 5 men, 10 women	**Ph.D.s:** 100%
Graduate: n/av	**Student/Faculty:** 8 to 1
Year: semesters	**Tuition:** $43,080
Application Deadline: January 1	**Room & Board:** $12,670
Freshman Class: 6589 applied, 935 accepted, 378 enrolled	
SAT CR/M/W: 730/720/730 **ACT:** 32	**MOST COMPETITIVE**

Swarthmore College, a highly selective college of liberal arts and engineering, celebrates the life of the mind. Since its founding in 1864, Swarthmore has given students the knowledge, insight, skills, and experience to become leaders for the common good. The College is private, yet open to all regardless of financial need; and decidedly global in outlook, drawing students from around the world and all 50 states. So much of what Swarthmore stands for, from its commitment to curricular breadth and rigor to its demonstrated interest in facilitating discovery and fostering civic engagement, lies in the quality and passion of its faculty. A student/faculty ratio of 8:1 ensures that students have close, meaningful engagement with their professors, preparing them to translate the skills and understanding gained at Swarthmore into the mark they want to make on the world. The College's Honors program, unique in the U.S., features small groups of accomplished students working closely with engaged faculty, an emphasis on independent learning, a demanding program of study in major and minor fields, and an examination by outside scholars at the end of two years' study. Swarthmore's idyllic, arboretum campus features rolling lawns, a creek, wooded hills, and hiking trails. In addition to regional accreditation, Swarthmore has baccalaureate program accreditation with ABET. The 7 libraries contain 849,268 volumes, 197,650 microform items, and 31,176 audio/video tapes/CDs/DVDs, and subscribe to 17,484 periodicals including electronic. Computerized library services include interlibrary loans, database searching, Internet access, and Wi-Fi capability. Special learning facilities include an art gallery, radio station, The College's LEED-certified integrated science center includes an observatory and robotics and solar energy labs. Arts resources include two galleries, one of which is curated by students, dance studios, cinema, and theater. Research facilities include a music and dance library, a science library, the Friends Historical Library, and the Swarthmore Peace Collection. Students interested in community-based learning are supported by the Lang Center for Civic and Social Responsibility. The 425-acre campus is in a suburban area 11 miles southwest of Philadelphia. Including any residence halls, there are 56 buildings.

Student Life: 88% of undergraduates are from out of state, mostly the Middle Atlantic. Students are from 50 states, 44 foreign countries, and Canada. 57% are from public schools. 44% are White; 14% Asian American; 13% Hispanic. The average age of freshmen is 18; all undergraduates, 20. 3% do not continue beyond their first year; 95% remain to graduate.

Housing: 1429 students can be accommodated in college housing, which

includes single-sex and coed dorms. students of any gender may share rooms and/or bathrooms. On-campus housing is guaranteed for all 4 years. 93% of students live on campus; of those, 100% remain on campus on weekends. Upperclassmen may keep cars.

Activities: 14% of men belong to 1 local and 1 national fraternity. There are 150 groups on campus, including a cappella groups, art, band, chess, choir, chorus, Club sports, computers, dance, debate, drama board, environmental, ethnic, film, gay, honors, international, jazz band, literary magazine, musical theater, newspaper, orchestra, photography, political, radio and TV, religious, social, social service, student government, and yearbook. Popular campus events include Yule Ball, Midnight Breakfast, Worthstock and the Crum Regatta.

Sports: There are 10 intercollegiate sports for men and 12 for women, and 7 intramural sports for men and 7 for women. Athletics facilities include a lighted stadium, a 400-meter durometer track, a synthetic grass playing field, indoor tennis courts, a fitness center with aerobic and Medx equipment, a professionally staffed sports medicine facility with three full-time trainers, and wooded hiking trails.

Disabled Students: 85% of the campus is accessible. Facilities include wheelchair ramps, elevators, special parking, specially equipped restrooms, special class scheduling, lowered drinking fountains, lowered telephones, and special housing.

Services: Counseling and information services are available, as is tutoring in most subjects. There is a reader service for the blind. The campus writing center, student academic mentors, science associates, and math associates provide academic support to students.

Campus Safety and Security: Measures include 24-hour foot and vehicle patrol, emergency notification system, self-defense education, and security escort services. There are shuttle buses, emergency telephones, lighted pathways/sidewalks, and controlled access to dorms/residences.

Programs of Study: Swarthmore confers B.A., and B.S. degrees. Bachelor's degrees are awarded in BIOLOGICAL SCIENCE (biochemistry, biology/biological science, and neurosciences), COMMUNICATIONS AND THE ARTS (art, art history and appreciation, Chinese, classics, comparative literature, dance, dramatic arts, English literature, film arts, French, German, Greek, Latin, linguistics, literature, media arts, music, Russian, Spanish, and theatre arts), COMPUTER AND PHYSICAL SCIENCE (astronomy, astrophysics, chemical physics, chemistry, computer science, mathematics, and physics), EDUCATION (education), ENGINEERING AND ENVIRONMENTAL DESIGN (engineering), SOCIAL SCIENCE (anthropology, Asian/Oriental studies, Chinese Studies, classical/ancient civilization, economics, gender studies, German area studies, history, Japanese studies, medieval studies, peace studies, philosophy, political science/government, psychobiology, psychology, religion, and sociology). Economics, biology, and political science have the largest enrollments.

Required: In order to graduate, students must complete 3 courses in each of 3 divisions consisting of humanities, natural sciences and engineering, and social sciences. Concurrent with distribution and/or major requirements, there is a requirement of 3 writing courses and a science laboratory. Students must demonstrate foreign language competency and fulfill a physical education requirement including a swimming test. Each major has a culminating experience, which may be a thesis, project, or comprehensive exam.

Special: Special educational opportunities at the College include the Honors Program which features small groups of students working closely with faculty and peers; an emphasis on independent learning; and a final examination by outside scholars. Swarthmore offers an engineering major and a program leading toward Teacher Certification. Students may cross-register for courses at Bryn Mawr and Haverford Colleges and the University of Pennsylvania. The Off-Campus Study Office supports students who wish to study abroad, opportunities are widely available and off campus study is encouraged. There are 3 national honor societies, including Phi Beta Kappa, and 31 departmental honors programs.

Faculty/Classroom: 57% of faculty are male; 43% are female. All teach and do research. No introductory courses are taught by graduate students. The average class size in a laboratory is 12 and in a regular course is 16.

Admissions: 14% of the 2013-2014 applicants were accepted. The SAT scores for the 2013-2014 freshman class were: Critical Reading--4% between 500 and 599, 29% between 600 and 699, and 67% between 700 and 800; Math--6% between 500 and 599, 30% between 600 and 699, and 64% between 700 and 800; Writing--4% between 500 and 599, 25% between 600 and 699, and 71% between 700 and 800. The ACT scores were 5% between 24 and 26, 9% between 27 and 28, and 86% above 28. 76% of the current freshmen were in the top fifth of their class; 99% were in the top two fifths. 30 freshmen graduated first in their class.

Requirements: The SAT or ACT is required. The ACT Optional Writing test is also required. Swarthmore does not require a specific high school curriculum. We do, however, recommend the inclusion of four years of English and at least three years each of mathematics, the sciences, and history and social studies; the study of one or two foreign languages; and coursework in art and music. Applicants are required to submit scores for either the SAT and any two SAT Subject tests; or the ACT with writing; or the SAT and the ACT (with or without writing). Two essays are required. Interviews are recommended, though not required for first-year applicants. AP credits are accepted.

Procedure: Freshmen are admitted fall. Entrance exams should be taken in spring of the junior year or fall of the senior year. There are early decision and deferred admissions plans. Early decision applications should be filed by November 15; regular applications, by January 1 for fall entry. The fall 2013 application fee was $60. Notification of early decision is sent December 15; regular decision, April 1. 180 early decision candidates were accepted for the 2013-2014 class. Applications are accepted online.

Transfer: 10 transfer students enrolled in 2012-2013. Applicants for transfer must present both secondary and college transcripts and an official statement of good standing from the tertiary institution. 16 of 32 credits required for the bachelor's degree must be completed at Swarthmore.

Visiting: There are regularly scheduled orientations for prospective students. Tours, information sessions, and interviews are offered throughout the year. There are guides for informal visits, visitors may sit in on classes, and stay overnight. To schedule a visit, contact the Admissions Office.

Financial Aid: In 2013-2014, 49% of all full-time freshmen and 52% of continuing full-time students received some form of financial aid. 49% of all full-time freshmen and 52% of continuing full-time students received need-based aid. The average freshman award was $39,427. Need-based scholarships or need-based grants averaged $37,775 ($58,000 maximum); and need-based self-help aid (loans and jobs) averaged $1,652 ($1,840 maximum). 81% of undergraduate students work part-time. Average annual earnings from campus work are $1890. The average financial indebtedness of the 2013 graduate was $20,020. Swarthmore is a member of CSS. The CSS/Profile, FAFSA, the state aid form, and the college's own financial statement, and tax returns, W-2 statements, and year-end paycheck stubs are required. The priority date for freshman financial aid applications for fall entry is February 15.

International Students: There are 126 international students enrolled. The school actively recruits these students. They must submit scores for either the SAT and any 2 SAT subject tests, the ACT with writing, or the SAT and ACT.

Computers: All students may access the system. There are no time limits and no fees.

Graduates: From July 1, 2012 to June 30, 2013, 375 bachelor's degrees were awarded. The most popular majors were economics (17%), biology (15%), and political science (13%). 50 companies recruited on campus in 2012-2013. In an average class, 1% graduate in 3 years or less, 86% graduate in 4 years or less, 91% graduate in 5 years or less, and 92% graduate in 6 years or less. Of the 2012 graduating class, 21% were enrolled in graduate school within 6 months of graduation, and 39% were employed.

Admissions Contact: James L. Bock, Vice President and Dean of Admissions. E-Mail: *admissions@swarthmore.edu* Web: *www.swarthmore.edu*

TEMPLE UNIVERSITY F-3

Philadelphia, PA 19122 **(215) 204-8556; (888) 340-2222**

Full-time: 12116 men, 12800 women	**Faculty:** 1343; 1, -$
Part-time: 1749 men, 1578 women	**Ph.D.s:** 76%
Graduate: 4204 men, 5174 women	**Student/Faculty:** 18 to 1
Year: semesters, summer session	**Tuition:** $14,096 ($24,122)
Application Deadline: March 1	**Room & Board:** $10,296

Freshman Class: 18813 applied, 12016 accepted, 4390 enrolled

SAT CR/M/W: 558/571/553 **ACT:** 24 **VERY COMPETITIVE**

Temple University, founded in 1888, is part of the Commonwealth System of Higher Education in Pennsylvania. It offers programs in the liberal arts, science and technology, health professions and social work, education, engineering, art, business and management, environmental design, media and communication, music and dance, theater, film and media arts, and tourism and hospitality. Temple has 9 campuses, including 1 in Rome and 1 in Tokyo. There are 17 undergraduate schools. In addition to regional accreditation, Temple has baccalaureate program accreditation with AACSB, ABET, ACEJMC, ACPE, ADA, APTA, ASLA, CSWE, NAAB, NASAD, NASM, NRPA, and TEAC. The 14 libraries contain 4.1 million volumes, 3.4 million microform items, 45,385 audio/video tapes/CDs/DVDs, and subscribe to 67,942 periodicals including electronic. Computerized library services include interlibrary loans, database searching, Internet access, and Wi-Fi capability. Special learning facilities include an art gallery, planetarium, radio station, and TV station. The 330-acre campus is in an urban area approximately 1.5 miles from downtown Philadelphia. Including any residence halls, there are 211 buildings.

Student Life: 79% of undergraduates are from Pennsylvania. Others are from 50 states, 96 foreign countries, and Canada. 56% are White; 12% African American. The average age of freshmen is 18; all undergraduates, 22. 11% do not continue beyond their first year; 66% remain to graduate.

Housing: 5506 students can be accommodated in college housing, which includes coed dorms, on-campus apartments, and off-campus apartments.

In addition, there are honors houses, special-interest houses, and living-learning communities. On-campus housing is guaranteed for the freshman year only. 86% of students commute. Alcohol is not permitted. All students may keep cars.

Activities: 4% of men belong to 19 national fraternities; 4% of women belong to 15 national sororities. There are 329 groups on campus, including art, band, cheerleading, chess, choir, chorale, chorus, communications, computers, dance, debate, drama, drill team, environmental, ethnic, film, forensics, gay, honors, international, jazz band, literary magazine, marching band, musical theater, newspaper, opera, orchestra, pep band, photography, political, professional, radio and TV, religious, social, social service, student government, symphony, and yearbook. Popular campus events include Homecoming, Cherry and White Day.

Sports: There are 12 intercollegiate sports for men and 13 for women, and 14 intramural sports for men and 14 for women. Facilities include Pearson McGonigle Halls is home to several Campus Recreation facilities, including the Climbing Wall, Fitness Mezzanine, and the 3rd Floor Courts. Temple University Fitness (TUF) is a Campus Recreation fitness facility with nearly 16,000-square feet of space that includes: cardio machines, selectorized machines, and areas designated for circuit training, light weights, and stretch/abs/core. Other fitness facilities include: The Liacouras Center (Men's and Women's Basketball); Lincoln Financial Field (Football); Edberg Olson Hall (Football); Pearson-McGonigle Hall (Volleyball, Men's and Women's Gymnastics, Fencing, Men's and Women's Basketball Practice Facility); Geasey Field (Field Hockey and Women's Lacrosse); TU Pavillion (Men's and Women's Tennis); Skip Wilson Field (Baseball); Temple Softball Stadium (Softball); Ambler Soccer Field (Men's and Women's Soccer); Ambler Fieldhouse; Independence Blue Cross Recreaction Center.

Disabled Students: All of the campus is accessible. Facilities include wheelchair ramps, elevators, special parking, specially equipped restrooms, special class scheduling, lowered drinking fountains, lowered telephones, special housing. additional services may be arranged through the Disabled Student Services Office.

Services: Counseling and information services are available, as is tutoring in most subjects. There is a reader service for the blind, and remedial math, reading, and writing.

Campus Safety and Security: Measures include 24-hour foot and vehicle patrol, emergency notification system, self-defense education, and security escort services. There are shuttle buses, emergency telephones, lighted pathways/sidewalks, controlled access to dorms/residences, and 24-hour security in residence halls.

Programs of Study: Temple confers B.A., B.F.A., B.B.A., B.MUS, B.S., B.S. BioE, B.S. Arch, B.S.A.T., B.S.C.E., B.S. Ed., B.S.E.E., B.S.E.T., B.S.M.E., B.S.N. and B.S.W. degrees. Associate, master's, and doctoral degrees are also awarded. Bachelor's degrees are awarded in AGRICULTURE (environmental studies and horticulture), BIOLOGICAL SCIENCE (biochemistry, biology/adolescence education, biology/ biological science, and biophysics), BUSINESS (accounting, banking and finance, business administration and management, entrepreneurial studies, finance, international business management, management information systems, marketing/retailing/merchandising, real estate, sports management, and tourism), COMMUNICATIONS AND THE ARTS (advertising, art, art history and appreciation, broadcasting, ceramic art and design, classics, communications, dance, English, fiber/textiles/weaving, film arts, French, German, glass, graphic design, Italian, jazz, journalism, linguistics, media arts, metal/jewelry, music, music composition, music history and appreciation, music performance, music theory and composition, painting, performing arts, photography, piano/organ, printmaking, public relations, sculpture, Spanish, speech/debate/rhetoric, telecommunications, theater design, theater management, and visual and performing arts), COMPUTER AND PHYSICAL SCIENCE (actuarial science, applied mathematics, chemistry, chemistry/adolescence education, computer science, earth science / adolescence education, geology, information sciences and systems, mathematics, mathematics/computational, mathematics – economics, and physics), EDUCATION (art education, athletic training, career, technical education & training, early childhood education, elementary education, health information management, mathematics education, music education, physical education, secondary education, and technical education), ENGINEERING AND ENVIRONMENTAL DESIGN (architecture, city/community/regional planning, civil engineering, construction management, electrical/electronics engineering, engineering, engineering technology, environmental science, landscape architecture/design, and mechanical engineering), HEALTH PROFESSIONS (music therapy, nursing, predentistry, premedicine, public health, recreation therapy, and speech therapy), SOCIAL SCIENCE (African American studies, American studies, anthropology, Asian/Oriental studies, criminal justice, economics, geography, history, Latin American studies, legal studies, philosophy, physical fitness/movement, political science/government, prelaw, psychology, religion, social science, social work, sociology, and women's studies). Art, journalism, and business are the strongest academically. Biology, psychology, and accounting have the largest enrollments.

Required: The required core curriculum includes nine areas of learning and a total of eleven courses. Areas include: Analytical Reading and Writing, Quantitative Literacy, Mosaic I and Mosaic II, Arts, Human Behavior, Race and Diversity, World Society, Science and Technology, and U.S. Society. All GenEd courses must be completed with a grade of C- or higher to satisfy a GenEd requirement.

Special: Temple offers co-op programs in business/marketing, computer/information sciences, and engineering, internships, study abroad in 15 countries, an extern program in which participating students receive 2 or 3 academic credits, dual majors, distance learning, dual enrollment, ESL, domestic exchange, independent study, and a teacher certification program. There are 3 national honor societies, including Phi Beta Kappa, and a freshman honors program.

Faculty/Classroom: 61% of faculty are male; 39% are female. No introductory courses are taught by graduate students.

Admissions: 64% of the 2013-2014 applicants were accepted. The SAT scores for the 2013-2014 freshman class were: Critical Reading--22% below 500, 48% between 500 and 599, 25% between 600 and 699, and 5% between 700 and 800; Math--17% below 500, 46% between 500 and 599, 30% between 600 and 699, and 7% between 700 and 800; Writing--24% below 500, 46% between 500 and 599, 25% between 600 and 699, and 5% between 700 and 800. The ACT scores were 16% below 21, 27% between 21 and 23, 28% between 24 and 26, 12% between 27 and 28, and 17% above 28. 42% of the current freshmen were in the top fifth of their class; 77% were in the top two fifths. 13 freshmen graduated first in their class.

Requirements: The SAT or ACT is required. Applicants should complete 16 academic credits/Carnegie units, including 4 years of English, 3 of math, 2 each of social studies, foreign language, and science, including 1 of lab science, and 1 each of history and an academic elective. A GED is accepted. A portfolio and audition are required in relevant fields. AP and CLEP credits are accepted. Important factors in the admissions decision are advanced placement or honors courses, parents or siblings attended your school, evidence of special talent, and recommendations by school officials.

Procedure: Freshmen are admitted fall and spring. Entrance exams should be taken by March of the junior year or April of the senior year. There is a rolling admissions plan. Applications should be filed by March 1 for fall entry; November 15 for spring entry. The fall 2013 application fee was $55. Notification is sent on a rolling basis. Applications are accepted online.

Transfer: 3847 transfer students enrolled in 2012-2013. Applicants must have earned at least 15 college credit hours with at least a 2.5 GPA and must submit official high school and college transcripts. 30 of 124 credits required for the bachelor's degree must be completed at Temple.

Visiting: There are regularly scheduled orientations for prospective students. There are guides for informal visits and visitors may sit in on classes. To schedule a visit, contact the Office of Undergraduate Admissions.

Financial Aid: The average freshman award was $15,200. Need-based scholarships or need-based grants averaged $6,193 ; need-based self-help aid (loans and jobs) averaged $3,518; non-need-based athletic scholarships averaged $17,929; and other non-need-based awards and non-need-based scholarships averaged $5,192. The average financial indebtedness of the 2013 graduate was $34,382. The FAFSA and the college's own financial statement, and the PHEAA (Pennsylvania residents) are required. The priority date for freshman financial aid applications for fall entry is March 1.

International Students: There are 1022 international students enrolled. The school actively recruits these students. They must take the TOEFL with a minimum score of 550 on the paper-based TOEFL (PBT) or 79 on the Internet-based version (iBT). They must also take the SAT or ACT.

Computers: All students may access the system 24 hours per day. There are no time limits and no fees.

Graduates: From July 1, 2012 to June 30, 2013, 6080 bachelor's degrees were awarded. The most popular majors were business/marketing (20%), visual and performing arts (11%), and communication/journalism (11%). In an average class, 38% graduate in 4 years or less, 61% graduate in 5 years or less, and 66% graduate in 6 years or less.

Admissions Contact: Karin Mormando, Director of Undergraduate Admissions. E-Mail: *kmormando@temple.edu* Web: *www.temple.edu*

THE LINCOLN UNIVERSITY E-4

Lincoln University, PA 19352	**(484) 365-8000**
	(800) 790-0191; (484) 365-8109
Full-time: 633 men, 936 women	**Faculty:** 97
Part-time: 33 men, 78 women	**Ph.D.s:** 71%
Graduate: 155 men, 266 women	**Student/Faculty:** 17 to 1
Year: semesters, summer session	**Tuition:** $9590 ($14,076)
Application Deadline: open	**Room & Board:** $8404
Freshman Class: 6642 applied, 1689 accepted, 448 enrolled	
SAT CR/M: 410/490	**ACT:** 16 **LESS COMPETITIVE**

The Lincoln University of the Commonwealth of Pennsylvania, founded in

1854 as the nation's first degree-granting historically black college and university, combines the elements of a liberal arts and science-based undergraduate curriculum along with select graduate programs to meet the needs of those living in a highly-technological and global society. Today, the University enrolls a diverse student body of approximately 2,000 men and women. Internationally recognized for preparing and producing world class leaders such as Thurgood Marshall, the first African American U.S. Supreme Court Justice, Lillian Fishburne, the first African American woman promoted to Rear Admiral in the U.S. Navy, Langston Hughes, the noted poet, Kwame Nkrumah, the first President of Ghana and Nnamdi Azikiwe, the first President of Nigeria. There are 3 undergraduate schools and 1 graduate school. The library contains 159,884 volumes, 300,800 microform items, 1,413 audio/video tapes/CDs/DVDs, and subscribes to 133,000 periodicals including electronic. Computerized library services include interlibrary loans, database searching, and Internet access. Special learning facilities include an art gallery, planetarium, radio station, and TV station. The 422-acre campus is in a rural area 45 miles southwest of Philadelphia. Including any residence halls, there are 45 buildings.

Student Life: 57% of undergraduates are from out of state, mostly the Middle Atlantic. Students are from 22 states, 28 foreign countries, and Canada. 79% are African American; 16% race unknown. The average age of freshmen is 21; all undergraduates, 21. 33% do not continue beyond their first year; 38% remain to graduate.

Housing: 1768 students can be accommodated in college housing, which includes single-sex and coed dorms and on-campus apartments. On-campus housing is guaranteed for the freshman year only, is available on a first-come, and first-served basis. 98% of students live on campus; of those, 90% remain on campus on weekends. Alcohol is not permitted. Upperclassmen may keep cars.

Activities: There are 65 groups on campus, including art, band, cheerleading, choir, chorale, computers, dance, drama, drill team, honors, international, jazz band, marching band, newspaper, pep band, political, radio and TV, religious, social, social service, and student government. Popular campus events include Homecoming, Spring Fling, Lectures and Recitals, Black History Month and Convocations.

Sports: There are 7 intercollegiate sports for men and 8 for women, and 2 intramural sports for men and 2 for women. Facilities include a football stadium, a 2000-seat gym, softball and track fields, a fitness trail, a swimming pool, big screen TV, games, table tennis, a pool table, and a bowling alley.

Disabled Students: 80% of the campus is accessible. Facilities include wheelchair ramps, elevators, special parking, specially equipped restrooms, and lowered drinking fountains.

Services: Counseling and information services are available, as is tutoring in every subject. There is a reader service for the blind, and remedial math, reading, and writing.

Campus Safety and Security: Measures include 24-hour foot and vehicle patrol, emergency notification system, self-defense education, and security escort services. There are emergency telephones, lighted pathways/sidewalks, and controlled access to dorms/residences.

Programs of Study: Lincoln University confers B.A. and B.S. degrees. Master's degrees are also awarded. Bachelor's degrees are awarded in BIOLOGICAL SCIENCE (biology/biological science and molecular biology), BUSINESS (accounting, finance, management science, and organizational behavior), COMMUNICATIONS AND THE ARTS (broadcasting, English literature, French, information technology, journalism, music, Spanish, and visual and performing arts), COMPUTER AND PHYSICAL SCIENCE (chemistry, computer science, mathematics, physics, and science), EDUCATION (early childhood education, English education, and health education), ENGINEERING AND ENVIRONMENTAL DESIGN (environmental science), HEALTH PROFESSIONS (health science), SOCIAL SCIENCE (anthropology, biopsychology, clinical psychology, criminal justice, history, human services, philosophy, political science/government, religion, and sociology). Physics, chemistry, and biology are the strongest academically. Business administration, mass communication, social sciences, and health professions have the largest enrollments.

Required: Required credits 3 First Year Experience, 3 African-American Experience, 6 Social Sciences, 2-3 Health Wellness, 9 Humanities, 6 English Composition, 3 Mathematics, 7-8 Natural Sciences, 6-8 Languages or Computer Sciences.

Special: Lincoln offers co-op programs, internships, study abroad in 18 countries, work-study, and pass/fail options. 3-2 engineering degrees are offered with 7 other universities and institutes. Accelerated degree programs, B.A.-B.S. degrees, and dual majors are possible. There are 7 national honor societies, a freshman honors program, and 3 departmental honors programs.

Faculty/Classroom: 63% of faculty are male; 37% are female. 81% teach undergraduates. No introductory courses are taught by graduate students. The average class size in a regular course is 25.

Admissions: 25% of the 2013-2014 applicants were accepted. The SAT scores for the 2013-2014 freshman class were: Critical Reading--88% below 500, 11% between 500 and 599, and 1% between 600 and 699; Math--88% below 500, 11% between 500 and 599, 1% between 600 and 699, Writing--86% below 500, 11% between 500 and 599, 1% between 600 and 699. The ACT scores were 67% below 21, 33% between 21 and 23.

Requirements: The SAT is required. Applicants should complete 21 credit hours, including 4 credits in English, 3 each in math, science, social studies, 2 in art, and 1 in phys ed and 5 academic electives. The GED is accepted. An essay is required and an interview is recommended. Lincoln University requires applicants to be in the upper 50% of their class. A GPA of 2.0 is required. AP and CLEP credits are accepted. Important factors in the admissions decision are advanced placement or honors courses, evidence of special talent, and leadership record.

Procedure: Freshmen are admitted fall and spring. Entrance exams should be taken prior to admission. There are deferred admissions and rolling admissions plans. Application deadlines are open. The fall 2013 application fee was $20. Notification is sent on a rolling basis. Applications are accepted online.

Transfer: 45 transfer students enrolled in 2012-2013. Transfer applicants who are accepted at The Lincoln University must submit a transcript from the school they are currently or have previously attented. The transcript must show satisfactorily completion of 12 hours of transferable credits with a minimum cumulative grade point average of 2.00. 60 of 120 credits required for the bachelor's degree must be completed at Lincoln University.

Visiting: There are regularly scheduled orientations for prospective students. There are guides for informal visits, visitors may sit in on classes, and stay overnight. To schedule a visit, contact the Director of Admissions.

Financial Aid: In 2013-2014, 98% of all full-time freshmen and 99% of continuing full-time students received some form of financial aid. 97% of all full-time freshmen and 89% of continuing full-time students received need-based aid. The average freshman award was $15,894. Need-based scholarships or need-based grants averaged $5,777 ($13,560 maximum); need-based self-help aid (loans and jobs) averaged $6,405 ($12,500 maximum); and other non-need-based awards and non-need-based scholarships averaged $9,239 ($22,500 maximum). 24% of undergraduate students work part-time. Average annual earnings from campus work are $4200. The average financial indebtedness of the 2013 graduate was $28,582. The FAFSA, and PHEAA is required. The deadline for filing freshman financial aid applications for fall entry is April 1.

International Students: There are 39 international students enrolled. The school actively recruits these students. They must take the TOEFL with a minimum score of 550 on the paper-based TOEFL (PBT) or 80 on the Internet-based version (iBT). They must also take the SAT or ACT.

Computers: All students may access the system. There are no time limits and no fees.

Graduates: From July 1, 2012 to June 30, 2013, 229 bachelor's degrees were awarded. The most popular majors were criminal justice (10%), communication (8%), and elementary education (8%). 48 companies recruited on campus in 2012-2013. In an average class, 1% graduate in 3 years or less, 21% graduate in 4 years or less, 36% graduate in 5 years or less, and 38% graduate in 6 years or less.

Admissions Contact: Germel Clark, Director of Admissions. E-Mail: *admiss@lincoln.edu* Web: *www.lincoln.edu*

THIEL COLLEGE A-2

Greenville, PA 16125 **(724) 589-2182**
(800) 24-THIEL; (724) 589-2013

Full-time: 520 men, 435 women	**Faculty:** n/av; IIB, --$
Part-time: 25 men, 40 women	**Ph.D.s:** 79%
Graduate: n/av	**Student/Faculty:** n/av
Year: semesters, summer session	**Tuition:** $23,576
Application Deadline: see profile	**Room & Board:** $10,152
Freshman Class: n/av	

LESS COMPETITIVE

Thiel College, founded in 1866, is a private independent college affiliated with the Lutheran Church. The figures in the above capsule and in this profile are approximate. It offers programs in liberal arts, business, engineering, religion, teacher preparation, and professional programs. The library contains 187,476 volumes, 98,922 microform items, 437 audio/video tapes/CDs/DVDs, and subscribes to 437 periodicals including electronic. Computerized library services include interlibrary loans, database searching, Internet access, and laptop Internet portals. Special learning facilities include a learning resource center, art gallery, radio station, and wildlife sanctuary. The 135-acre campus is in a rural area 75 miles north of Pittsburgh and 75 miles southeast of Cleveland. Including any residence halls, there are 51 buildings.

Student Life: 63% of undergraduates are from Pennsylvania. Others are from 17 states and 9 foreign countries. 90% are from public schools. 59% are white. 44% are Protestant; 22% Catholic; 22% claim no religious affiliation. The average age of freshmen is 18; all undergraduates, 20. 30% do not continue beyond their first year; 41% remain to graduate.

Housing: 1129 students can be accommodated in college housing, which

includes single-sex and coed dorms and on-campus apartments. In addition, there are special-interest houses, fraternity houses, sorority houses, and living-learning centers. On-campus housing is guaranteed for all 4 years. 80% of students live on campus; of those, 60% remain on campus on weekends. Alcohol is not permitted. All students may keep cars.

Activities: 18% of men belong to 4 national fraternities; 26% of women belong to 4 national sororities. There are 40 groups on campus, including art, band, cheerleading, choir, chorus, computers, dance, drama, drill team, ethnic, forensics, gay, honors, international, literary magazine, musical theater, newspaper, pep band, political, professional, radio and TV, religious, social, social service, student government, symphony, and yearbook. Popular campus events include Spring Weekend, Greek Week, and Theatrical Productions.

Sports: There are 10 intercollegiate sports for men and 9 for women, and 4 intramural sports for men and 3 for women. Facilities include a 1200-seat gym, basketball and handball courts, playing fields, a fitness center, tennis courts, and a football stadium.

Disabled Students: 75% of the campus is accessible. Facilities include wheelchair ramps, elevators, special parking, specially equipped rest rooms, and special class scheduling.

Services: Counseling and information services are available, as is tutoring in most subjects. There is remedial math, reading, and writing.

Campus Safety and Security: Measures include 24-hour foot and vehicle patrol, emergency notification system, and security escort services. There are shuttle buses, emergency telephones, and lighted pathways/sidewalks.

Programs of Study: Thiel confers B.A. and B.S. degrees. Associates degrees are also awarded. Bachelor's degrees are awarded in BIOLOGICAL SCIENCE (biology/biological science and neurosciences), BUSINESS (accounting, business administration and management, electronic business, international business management, and management information systems), COMMUNICATIONS AND THE ARTS (art, communications, English, and media arts), COMPUTER AND PHYSICAL SCIENCE (actuarial science, chemistry, computer science, mathematics, physics, and web services), EDUCATION (elementary education and secondary education), ENGINEERING AND ENVIRONMENTAL DESIGN (environmental science and preengineering), HEALTH PROFESSIONS (cytotechnology, medical laboratory technology, physical therapy, predentistry, premedicine, prepharmacy, preveterinary science, and speech pathology/audiology), SOCIAL SCIENCE (criminal justice, history, philosophy, political science/government, prelaw, psychology, religion, religious education, and sociology). Engineering, biology, and chemistry are the strongest academically. Accounting, business administration, and biology have the largest enrollments.

Required: To graduate, students must complete a total of 124 credit hours, with 35 to 55 in the major and a minimum GPA of 2.0. Integrative distribution requirements include 8 hours of Western humanities, 4 hours each of global heritage, health and phys ed, and lab science, and 3 each of religion, humanities, social science, and math/sciences. Math must be college algebra or higher. Some majors require a comprehensive exam or thesis.

Special: Students may spend a semester at Argonne National Laboratories, the Art Institute of Pittsburgh, or Drew University. Special programs include a UN semester, a Washington semester, an Appalachian semester, study at Pittsburgh Institute of Mortuary Science, and a forestry and environmental management semester at Duke University. There is a 3-2 engineering program with Case Western Reserve University, the University of Pittsburgh, and Youngstown State University. Internships, study abroad, work-study, dual majors, nondegree study, cooperative programs in all majors, credit by examination, and credit for life, military, and work experience are also available. There are 11 national honor societies, a freshman honors program, and 10 departmental honors programs.

Faculty/Classroom: 52% of faculty are male; 48% are female. All teach undergraduates. No introductory courses are taught by graduate students. The average class size in an introductory lecture is 25, in a laboratory, 15, and in a regular course, 15.

Requirements: The SAT or ACT is required. The ACT Optional Writing test is also required. Applicants should be high school graduates who have completed 16 academic units, including 4 years of English, 3 of social science, and 2 each of foreign language, math, and science. The GED is accepted. An essay and an interview are recommended. A GPA of 2.0 is required. AP and CLEP credits are accepted. Important factors in the admissions decision are advanced placement or honors courses, evidence of special talent, and leadership record.

Procedure: Freshmen are admitted to all sessions. Entrance exams should be taken by May 1. There are deferred admissions and rolling admissions plans. Check with the school for current application deadlines. Notification is sent on a rolling basis. Applications are accepted online.

Transfer: 52 transfer students enrolled in a recent year. Applicants should meet the same criteria as entering freshmen and should submit official transcripts, statements of good standing, financial aid transcripts, and transfer forms from all colleges previously attended. Students must have a 2.0 GPA to transfer. 30 of 124 credits required for the bachelor's degree must be completed at Thiel.

Visiting: There are regularly scheduled orientations for prospective students, including orientation sessions for students enrolling in the fall and monthly sessions beginning in February. There are guides for informal visits; visitors may sit in on classes and stay overnight. To schedule a visit, contact the Admissions Office.

Financial Aid: In a recent year, 62% of all full-time freshmen and 92% of continuing full-time students received some form of financial aid, including need-based aid. The average freshmen award was $19,698. The CCS/Profile, FAFSA, FFS, or SFS is required; the FAFSA is preferred. Check with school for current application deadlines.

International Students: There were 51 international students enrolled in a recent. The school actively recruits these students. They must take the TOEFL with a minimum score of 503 on the paper-based TOEFL (PBT) or 62 on the Internet-based version (iBT) or take the MELAB.

Computers: Wireless access is available. All students may access the system. There are no time limits and no fees. The college provides an IBM ThinkPad to each of its students.

Graduates: In a recent year, 197 bachelor's degrees were awarded. The most popular majors were business (35%), psychology (12%), and education (6%). 2 companies recruited on campus in a recent year. In an average class, 32% graduate in 4 years or less, 41% graduate in 5 years or less, and 42% graduate in 6 years or less. Of a recent graduating class, 13% were enrolled in graduate school within 6 months of graduation and 87% were employed.

Admissions Contact: Dean of Enrollment Management. Web: *www.thiel.edu*

UNIVERSITY OF PENNSYLVANIA — F-3

Philadelphia, PA 19104 — **215-898-7507; 215-898-9670**

Full-time: 4639 men, 4877 women	**Faculty:** 1397; I, ++$
Part-time: 140 men, 123 women	**Ph.D.s:** 100%
Graduate: 4750 men, 5390 women	**Student/Faculty:** 6 to 1
Year: semesters, summer session	**Tuition:** $42,598
Application Deadline: January 1	**Room & Board:** $12,378

Freshman Class: 31663 applied, 3935 accepted, 2467 enrolled

SAT or ACT: required

MOST COMPETITIVE

The University of Pennsylvania, founded in 1740, is a member of the Ivy League, and has 10,000 undergraduates who make up a dynamic and diverse college community on a beautiful park-like campus in the city of Philadelphia. Current students study in Penn's 4 undergraduate schools--the College, Engineering, Nursing and the Wharton School. The figures in the above capsule and in this profile are approximate. They pursue interdisciplinary study within the schools and across the University's 12 graduate schools, and are engaged in learning in our 165 research centers. There are 4 undergraduate schools and 13 graduate schools. In addition to regional accreditation, Penn has baccalaureate program accreditation with AACSB and ABET. The 15 libraries contain 5.9 million volumes, 4.2 million microform items, 121,233 audio/video tapes/CDs/DVDs, and subscribe to 98,145 periodicals including electronic. Computerized library services include interlibrary loans, database searching, Internet access, and laptop Internet portals. Special learning facilities include a learning resource center, art gallery, natural history museum, planetarium, radio station, TV station, Museum of Archaeology and Anthropology, Institute of Contemporary Art (ICA), Morris Arboretum, Annenberg Center (Theater), Astronomical observatory, Large Animal Research Center, Equine Sports Medicine and Imaging Center, Women's center, Undergraduate Research Center, Wind Tunnel, Cyclotron Facility, Marshak Dairy, Arthur Ross Gallery, Galleries in Van Pelt Library, Galleries in Inn@Penn, Charles Addams Gallery, Kroiz Gallery in Architectural Archives, Kelly Writer's House, ENIAC Museum, Hillel Foundation, Center for Advanced Judaic Studies, LRSM material testing equipment. The 279-acre campus is in an urban area in Philadelphia. Including residence halls, there are 187 buildings.

Student Life: 81% of undergraduates are from out of state, mostly the Middle Atlantic. Students are from 50 states, 92 foreign countries, and Canada. 59% are from public schools. 46% are White; 19% Asian American; 11% foreign nationals. 29% claim no religious affiliation; 26% Protestant; 19% Catholic; 19% Jewish. The average age of freshmen is 18; all undergraduates, 20. 3% do not continue beyond their first year; 96% remain to graduate.

Housing: 6850 students can be accommodated in college housing, which includes coed dorms, on-campus apartments, off-campus apartments, and married student housing. In addition, there are language houses, special-interest houses, fraternity houses, There are over 40 academic residence programs, including the areas of: arts; entrepreneurship; politics, law & society; international studies; media; visual arts; women in science. On-campus housing is guaranteed for the freshman year only, is available on a first-come, first-served basis, and is available on a lottery system for upperclassmen. All students may keep cars.

Activities: 30% of men belong to 36 national fraternities; 17% of women

belong to 13 national sororities. There are 450 groups on campus, including art, band, cheerleading, chess, choir, chorale, chorus, computers, dance, debate, drama, environmental, ethnic, film, forensics, gay, honors, international, jazz band, literary magazine, marching band, musical theater, newspaper, opera, orchestra, pep band, photography, political, professional, radio and TV, religious, social, social service, student government, and symphony.

Sports: There are 17 intercollegiate sports for men and 16 for women, and 11 intramural sports for men and 11 for women. Facilities include 4 gyms, 1 swimming pool, squash courts, indoor and outdoor tennis courts, 7 playing fields, an indoor ice rink, rowing tanks, saunas, weight rooms, exercise facilities, a boathouse, and a stadium.

Disabled Students: 93% of the campus is accessible. Facilities include wheelchair ramps, elevators, special parking, specially equipped restrooms, special class scheduling, lowered drinking fountains, lowered telephones, special housing.

Services: Counseling and information services are available, as is tutoring in most subjects. There is a reader service for the blind. The WHEEL academic support program is available in all residences.

Campus Safety and Security: Measures include 24-hour foot and vehicle patrol, emergency notification system, self-defense education, and security escort services. There are shuttle buses, emergency telephones, lighted pathways/sidewalks, controlled access to dorms/residences, a bicycle patrol, police officers, victim support and special services, Students Together Against Acquaintance Rape, Penn watch, student walking escort, and security guard personnel.

Programs of Study: Penn confers B.A., B.S., B.Applied Sc., B.B.A., B.F.A., B.S.E., and B.S.N. degrees. Associate, master's, and doctoral degrees are also awarded. Bachelor's degrees are awarded in AGRICULTURE (environmental studies), BIOLOGICAL SCIENCE (biochemistry, biology/biological science, and biophysics), BUSINESS (accounting, business administration and management, entrepreneurial studies, human resources, insurance and risk management, logistics, management information systems, marketing/retailing/merchandising, operations management, real estate, retailing, and transportation management), COMMUNICATIONS AND THE ARTS (art history and appreciation, classics, communications, comparative literature, design, dramatic arts, English, fine arts, folklore and mythology, French, German, linguistics, music, Russian, and visual and performing arts), COMPUTER AND PHYSICAL SCIENCE (actuarial science, applied science, chemistry, computer science, digital arts/technology, geology, information sciences and systems, mathematics, physics, science technology, and statistics), EDUCATION (elementary education), ENGINEERING AND ENVIRONMENTAL DESIGN (architecture, bioengineering, chemical engineering, civil engineering, computer engineering, electrical/electronics engineering, and materials engineering), HEALTH PROFESSIONS (health, health care administration, and nursing), SOCIAL SCIENCE (African studies, African American studies, American studies, anthropology, Asian/Oriental studies, cognitive science, economics, gender studies, Hispanic American studies, history, history of science, international relations, international studies, Italian studies, Judaic studies, Latin American studies, law, Middle Eastern studies, Near Eastern studies, philosophy, political science/ government, psychology, public administration, religion, sociology, South Asian studies, urban studies, and women's studies). Finance, economics, nursing, political science, and history have the largest enrollments.

Required: The bachelor's degree requires completion of 32 to 40 course units, depending on the student's major, with 12 to 18 of these units in the major and a GPA of 2.0.

Special: Cross-registration is permitted with Haverford, Swarthmore, and Bryn Mawr Colleges and through the Quaker Consortium. Opportunities are provided for internships, a Washington semester, accelerated degree programs, joint degree programs, preprofessional programs, B.A.-B.S. degrees, dual and student-designed majors, credit by exam, limited pass/ fail options, and study abroad in 39 countries. Through the "one university" concept, students in one undergraduate school may study in any of the other three. There are 11 national honor societies, a freshman honors program, and 27 departmental honors programs.

Faculty/Classroom: 62% of faculty are male; 38% are female. All teach and do research. No introductory courses are taught by graduate students.

Admissions: 12% of a recent year applicants were accepted. The SAT scores for a recent year freshman class were: Critical Reading--6% between 500 and 599, 33% between 600 and 700, and 60% above 700; Math--4% between 500 and 599, 25% between 600 and 700, and 71% above 700; Writing--5% between 500 and 599, 28% between 600 and 700, and 67% above 700. 100% were in the top two fifths of their class.

Requirements: The SAT or ACT is required. Graduation from an accredited secondary school is not required. Recommended preparation includes 4 years of high school English, 3 or 4 each of a foreign language and math, and 3 each of history and social science. An essay is required. A portfolio is recommended for prospective art majors. AP credits are accepted.

Procedure: Freshmen are admitted fall. Entrance exams should be taken by December of the senior year. There are early decision and deferred admissions plans. Early decision applications should be filed by November 1; regular applications, by January 1 for fall entry, along with a $75 fee. Notification of early decision is sent December 15; regular decision, April 1. 1192 early decision candidates were accepted for the 2011-2012 class. 1385 applicants were on the 2011 waiting list; 56 were admitted. Applications are accepted online.

Transfer: 232 transfer students enrolled in a recent year. Applicants must provide college and high school transcripts, essays, and 2 recommendations. SAT or ACT scores are required for transfer students. 16 of 32 credits required for the bachelor's degree must be completed at Penn.

Visiting: There are regularly scheduled orientations for prospective students, including an information session by the Admissions Office and a tour of the campus led by current students. There are guides for informal visits, visitors may sit in on classes, and stay overnight. To schedule a visit, contact the Admissions Office.

Financial Aid: In a recent year, 46% of all full-time freshmen and 46% of continuing full-time students received some form of financial aid. 46% of all full-time freshmen and 46% of continuing full-time students received need-based aid. The average freshman award was $35,264. Need-based scholarships or need-based grants averaged $33,460; and need-based self-help aid (loans and jobs) averaged $2,121. 39% of undergraduate students work part-time. Average annual earnings from campus work are $1740. The average financial indebtedness of a recent year graduate was $18,226. Penn is a member of CSS. The CSS/Profile, FAFSA, the college's own financial statement, and parents' and student's most recently completed income tax returns are required. The priority date for freshman financial aid applications for fall entry is February 15.

International Students: There are 1077 international students enrolled. The school actively recruits these students. They must take the TOEFL. They must also take the SAT subject tests or the ACT with writing.

Computers: Wireless access is available. Wireless Internet access is available in all campus residences and academic buildings, libraries, and public spaces. Many campus buildings are wired for Ethernet, and students residing in campus residences and in Greek houses have an Ethernet connection in their room, in addition to wireless access. They may also use the more than one thousand networked PCs in computer labs, libraries, and other locations on campus. All students may access the system. There are no time limits and no fees. It is strongly recommended that all students have a personal computer.

Graduates: In a recent year, 2475 bachelor's degrees were awarded. The most popular majors were finance (14%), economics (6%), and nursing (6%). In an average class, 88% graduate in 4 years or less and 96% graduate in 6 years or less. Of the recent year graduating class, 20% were enrolled in graduate school within 6 months of graduation, and 60% were employed.

Admissions Contact: A campus DVD is available. E-Mail: *info@admissions.upenn.edu* Web: *http:/www.admissionsug.upenn.edu/request/*

UNIVERSITY OF PITTSBURGH SYSTEM

The University of Pittsburgh System, established in 1787, is a public system in Pennsylvania. It is governed by the board of trustees of the University of Pittsburgh, whose chief administrator is the chancellor. The primary goal of the system is enhancing educational opportunities for the citizens of Pennsylvania and contributing to the state's social, intellectual, and economic development. The main priorities are to engage in research, artistic, and scholarly activities, to provide high-quality undergraduate, graduate, and professional programs, and to offer expertise and educational services to meet the needs of the region and state. The total student enrollment of all 5 campuses is usually 35,581 with 5210 faculty members. Altogether there are 203 baccalaureate, 131 master's, and 94 doctoral programs offered in University of Pittsburgh System. 4-year campuses are located in Pittsburgh, Bradford, Greensburg, and Johnstown. Profiles of the 4-year campuses are included in this section.

UNIVERSITY OF PITTSBURGH AT BRADFORD — C-1

Bradford, PA 16701 — (814) 362-7555; (800) 872-1787; (814) 362-7578

Full-time: 631 men, 730 women	**Faculty:** 75; IIB, -$
Part-time: 40 men, 80 women	**Ph.D.s:** 34%
Graduate: n/av	**Student/Faculty:** 18 to 1
Year: semesters, summer session	**Tuition:** $13,078 ($23,682)
Application Deadline:	**Room & Board:** $8238
Freshman Class: 1599 applied, 464 accepted, 396 enrolled	
SAT CR/M/W: 470/500/450	**ACT:** 20 — **LESS COMPETITIVE**

The University of Pittsburgh at Bradford, established in 1963, is a public, state-related for students who want to earn a world-renowned education in a personalized environment. There is one undergraduate school. In addition to regional accreditation, Pitt-Bradford has baccalaureate program accreditation with NLN. The library contains 101,118 volumes, 1,055 microform items, 4,021 audio/video tapes/CDs/DVDs, and subscribes to 258 periodicals including electronic. Computerized library services include interlibrary loans, database searching, and Internet access. Special learning facilities include an art gallery, radio station, The university also has a crime scene investigation house, a nursing suite with computerized mannequins, a psychology lab, a human performance lab, and athletic training facilities. The 317-acre campus is in a small town 160 miles northeast of Pittsburgh and 80 miles south of Buffalo. Including any residence halls, there are 31 buildings.

Student Life: 85% of undergraduates are from Pennsylvania. Others are from 21 states, and 13 foreign countries. 87% are from public schools. 74% are White. 42% are Protestant; 29% claim no religious affiliation; 22% Catholic. The average age of freshmen is 18; all undergraduates, 22. 30% do not continue beyond their first year; 47% remain to graduate.

Housing: 938 students can be accommodated in college housing, which includes single-sex and coed on-campus apartments. On-campus housing is available on a first-come and first-served basis. 65% of students live on campus; of those, 38% remain on campus on weekends. All students may keep cars.

Activities: 5% of men belong to 5 local fraternities; 4% of women belong to 4 local sororities. There are 63 groups on campus, including art, cheerleading, choir, chorale, computers, dance, drama, environmental, ethnic, gay, honors, international, literary magazine, newspaper, political, professional, radio and TV, religious, social, social service, and student government. Popular campus events include Winter Weekend, Spring Fling, and Alumni Weekend.

Sports: There are 6 intercollegiate sports for men and 7 for women, and 15 intramural sports for men and 15 for women. Facilities include a sport and fitness center that includes a 1200-seat performance arena for basketball, volleyball, and general recreation, a fitness center with physical conditioning equipment; and an exercise arts studio for dance, martial arts, and aerobics. There is also an auxiliary gym for recreated and intramurals, phys ed classes, and other events, and a 6-lane swimming pool. Outdoor facilities include a lighted softball field, a baseball field, tennis courts, 2 handball courts, several basketball courts, football/softball fields, and a sand volleyball court.

Disabled Students: 99% of the campus is accessible. Facilities include elevators, special parking, specially equipped restrooms, lowered drinking fountains, lowered telephones, and special housing.

Services: Counseling and information services are available, as is tutoring in most subjects. There is remedial math, reading, and writing. There is a writing and math center.

Campus Safety and Security: Measures include 24-hour foot and vehicle patrol, emergency notification system, and security escort services. There are shuttle buses, emergency telephones, and lighted pathways/ sidewalks.

Programs of Study: Pitt-Bradford confers B.A., B.S. and B.S.N. degrees. Associate degrees are also awarded. Bachelor's degrees are awarded in AGRICULTURE (environmental studies), BIOLOGICAL SCIENCE (biology/biological science), BUSINESS (accounting, business administration and management, hospitality management services, and sports management), COMMUNICATIONS AND THE ARTS (communications, English, and public relations), COMPUTER AND PHYSICAL SCIENCE (applied mathematics, chemistry, mathematics, and physical sciences), EDUCATION (athletic training, business education, elementary education, English education, environmental education, health education, mathematics education, science education, and social studies education), ENGINEERING AND ENVIRONMENTAL DESIGN (engineering), HEALTH PROFESSIONS (nursing, radiological science, and sports medicine), SOCIAL SCIENCE (criminal justice, economics, history, human development, interdisciplinary studies, liberal arts/general studies, psychology, social science, and sociology). Engineering, nursing, and biology are the strongest academically. Business administration, criminal justice, and biology have the largest enrollments.

Required: To graduate, students must complete a minimum of 120 credits with 30 to 76 in the major, and maintan a minimum GPA of 2.0. At least 30 should be upper-level courses. The core curriculum varies from 12 to 30 credits and distribution requirements from 56 to 59. English, math competency, and phys ed courses are required.

Special: Students may cross-register with colleges in the University of Pittsburgh system. Internships are required or strongly recommended for all majors. The school offers study abroad, dual majors, nondegree study, and a 3-2 engineering degree with the University of Pittsburgh (Oakland campus). Interdisciplinary majors are offered in human relations combining anthropology, psychology, and sociology; social sciences, combining anthropology, economics, history, political science, and sociology; and in interdisciplinary arts, combining art, music, and theater. Professional preparation is available in many areas including premedicine, prelaw, preveterinary science, prepharmacy, and predentistry. Teacher certification is also offered. There are 7 national honor societies.

Faculty/Classroom: 52% of faculty are male; 48% are female. All teach undergraduates. No introductory courses are taught by graduate students. The average class size in an introductory lecture is 23; in a laboratory is 13; and in a regular course is 19.

Admissions: 29% of the 2013-2014 applicants were accepted. The SAT scores for the 2013-2014 freshman class were: Critical Reading--62% below 500, 28% between 500 and 599, and 10% between 600 and 699; Math--49% below 500, 36% between 500 and 599, 13% between 600 and 699, and 2% between 700 and 800; Writing--70% below 500, 25% between 500 and 599, and 5% between 600 and 699. The ACT scores were 58% below 21, 20% between 21 and 23, 15% between 24 and 26, 5% between 27 and 28, and 2% above 28. 18% of the current freshmen were in the top fifth of their class; 50% were in the top two fifths.

Requirements: The SAT or ACT is required. Students must be graduates of an accredited secondary school with 16 Carnegie units, including 4 in English, 3 in history or social studies, and 3 each in science and math. The GED is accepted. Also used in the admissions decision are standardized test scores, rank in class, extracurricular activities, and recommendations. An essay is strongly recommended, as is an interview. A GPA of 2.0 is required. AP and CLEP credits are accepted. Important factors in the admissions decision are advanced placement or honors courses, extracurricular activities record, and leadership record.

Procedure: Freshmen are admitted fall, spring, and summer. Entrance exams should be taken during the junior year or the fall of the senior year. There are deferred admissions and rolling admissions plans. Application deadlines are open. Application fee is $45. Notifications are sent October 16. Applications are accepted online.

Transfer: 112 transfer students enrolled in 2012-2013. A GPA of 2.0 or higher is required. 30 of 120 credits required for the bachelor's degree must be completed at Pitt-Bradford.

Visiting: There are regularly scheduled orientations for prospective students, programs throughout the year, offering a workshop with admissions representatives on academics, admissions, guidance, standardized tests, the application process, and financial aid. Tours led by students, a financial aid presentation , and a special campus event are also offered. There are guides for informal visits and visitors may sit in on classes. To schedule a visit, contact Alexander Nazemetz at (800) 872-1787.

Financial Aid: In 2013-2014, 98% of all full-time freshmen and 94% of continuing full-time students received some form of financial aid. 93% of all full-time freshmen and 85% of continuing full-time students received need-based aid. The average freshman award was $9,318. Need-based scholarships or need-based grants averaged $4,650 ($12,565 maximum); need-based self-help aid (loans and jobs) averaged $4,554 ($14,768 maximum); and other non-need-based awards and non-need-based scholarships averaged $3,948 ($18,969 maximum). 12% of undergraduate students work part-time. Average annual earnings from campus work are $1740. The average financial indebtedness of the 2013 graduate was $35,810. The FAFSA is required. The priority date for freshman financial aid applications for fall entry is March 1.

International Students: There are 48 international students enrolled. They must take the TOEFL with a minimum score of 550 on the paper-based TOEFL (PBT) or 80 on the Internet-based version (iBT). or the IELTS, scoring 6.5.

Computers: All students may access the system. There are no time limits. The fee is $350.

Graduates: From July 1, 2012 to June 30, 2013, 302 bachelor's degrees were awarded. The most popular majors were business management (10%), criminal justice (10%), and sports medicine (7%). 47 companies recruited on campus in 2012-2013. In an average class, 33% graduate in 4 years or less, 51% graduate in 5 years or less, and 54% graduate in 6 years or less. Of the 2012 graduating class, 21% were enrolled in graduate school within 6 months of graduation, and 75% were employed.

Admissions Contact: Alexander P. Nazemetz, Director of Admissions. E-Mail: *admissions@upb.pitt.edu* Web: *www.upb.pitt.edu/Admissions/*

UNIVERSITY OF PITTSBURGH AT GREENSBURG B-3

Greensburg, PA 15601-5898 **(724) 836-9880; (724) 836-7160**

Full-time: 810 men, 855 women
Part-time: 85 men, 85 women
Graduate: n/av
Year: semesters, summer session
Application Deadline: open
Freshman Class: n/av
SAT or ACT: required

Faculty: n/av; IIB, --$
Ph.D.s: n/av
Student/Faculty: n/av
Tuition: $12,626 ($22,818)
Room & Board: $8410

COMPETITIVE

The University of Pittsburgh at Greensburg, established in 1963, is a public state-related institution, offering undergraduate majors that can be completed at Pitt-Greensburg, as well as relocation programs that are begun at Greensburg and completed at another Pitt campus. The figures in the above capsule and in this profile are approximate. The library contains 75,000 volumes, 9458 microform items and 1280 audio/video tapes/ CDs/DVDs. Computerized library services include interlibrary loans, database searching, Internet access, and laptop Internet portals. Special learning facilities include a learning resource center. The 219-acre campus is in a suburban area 33 miles southeast of Pittsburgh. Including any residence halls, there are 25 buildings.

Student Life: 99% of undergraduates are from Pennsylvania. Others are from 5 states, 1 foreign country, and Canada. 94% are white. The average age of freshmen is 18; all undergraduates, 21. 25% do not continue beyond their first year; 55% remain to graduate.

Housing: 585 students can be accommodated in college housing, which includes coed dorms and on-campus apartments. In addition, there are special-interest houses. On-campus housing is available on a first-come, first-served basis. 68% of students commute. Alcohol is not permitted. All students may keep cars.

Activities: There are no fraternities or sororities. There are 44 groups on campus, including academic, band, cheerleading, chess, choir, chorale, chorus, computers, dance, debate, drama, ethnic, honors, literary magazine, newspaper, pep band, political, religious, social, social service, and student government. Popular campus events include a La Cultura study of a different historically significant era each year, the St. Clair history lecture, and Westmoreland Forum on a topic of countywide significance.

Sports: There are 6 intercollegiate sports for men and 6 for women, and 8 intramural sports for men and 8 for women. Facilities include a gym, a weight room, playing fields, and tennis and racquetball courts.

Disabled Students: 95% of the campus is accessible. Facilities include wheelchair ramps, elevators, special parking, specially equipped restrooms, special class scheduling, lowered drinking fountains, lowered telephones, and special housing.

Services: Counseling and information services are available, as is tutoring in math, computer science, and English. There is remedial math, reading, and writing.

Campus Safety and Security: Measures include 24-hour foot and vehicle patrol and security escort services. There are emergency telephones and lighted pathways/sidewalks.

Programs of Study: Pitt-Greensburg confers B.A. and B.S. degrees. Bachelor's degrees are awarded in BIOLOGICAL SCIENCE (biology/biological science), BUSINESS (accounting and management science), COMMUNICATIONS AND THE ARTS (communications, creative writing, and English literature), COMPUTER AND PHYSICAL SCIENCE (applied mathematics and natural sciences), SOCIAL SCIENCE (American studies, anthropology, humanities, political science/government, psychology, and social science). Management and psychology are the strongest academically. Management and administration of justice have the largest enrollments.

Required: To graduate, students must complete 120 to 126 hours, with 24 to 36 in the major, and maintain a minimum GPA of 2.0. General education requirements include 15 credits each in humanities, social sciences, and natural sciences, 6 to 15 in writing courses, 3 each in speech and critical reasoning, and 2 to 3 in math.

Special: Pitt-Greensburg offers cross-registration with the Pittsburgh and Johnstown campuses of the university system and with Seton Hill College and Westmoreland County Community College. Internships are available in all majors and required for English writing and criminology. Double majors, student-designed majors, a Washington semester, nondegree study, and pass/fail options are available. There are 2 national honor societies, including Phi Beta Kappa.

Faculty/Classroom: 52% of faculty are male; 48% are female. All teach undergraduates, and 50% do research. No introductory courses are taught by graduate students. The average class size in an introductory lecture is 30; in a laboratory, 15; and in a regular course, 25.

Requirements: The SAT or ACT is required, including the writing test. Students must be graduates of an accredited secondary school. The GED is also accepted. Students must complete 15 college-preparatory high school units, including 4 each of English and academic electives, 3 of a single foreign language (recommended), 2 of math, and 1 each of history and a lab science; additional units in all but English are recommended. An essay is optional; an interview is recommended. GPA and class rank are also considered heavily. Pitt-Greensburg requires applicants to be in the upper 60% of their class. A GPA of 2.0 is required. AP and CLEP credits are accepted. Important factors in the admissions decision are advanced placement or honors courses, recommendations by school officials, and leadership record.

Procedure: Freshmen are admitted fall and spring. Entrance exams should be taken by November. There are deferred admissions and rolling admissions plans. Application deadlines are open. Check with the school for current application fee. Applications are accepted online.

Transfer: Applicants must have a minimum GPA of 2.0 and at least 12 college credits. 30 of 120 credits required for the bachelor's degree must be completed at Pitt-Greensburg.

Visiting: There are regularly scheduled orientations for prospective students, including Open House, Preview Day, and Junior Jump Start and weekday visits that include campus tours and information sessions. There are guides for informal visits, and visitors may sit in on classes. To schedule a visit, contact the Admissions Office.

Financial Aid: The FAFSA and the college's own financial statement are required. Check with the school for current deadlines.

International Students: They must take the TOEFL.

Computers: Wireless access is available. There are wireless sites at the student union, library, and coffeehouse. All students may access the system. There are no time limits and no fees.

Admissions Contact: Director of Admissions. E-Mail: *upgadmit@pitt.edu* Web: *www.greensburg.pitt.edu*

UNIVERSITY OF PITTSBURGH AT JOHNSTOWN C-3

Johnstown, PA 15904 **(814) 269-7050**
(800) 765-4875; (814) 269-7044

Full-time: 1528 men, 1295 women	**Faculty:** n/av; IIB, -$
Part-time: 60 men, 49 women	**Ph.D.s:** 68%
Graduate: n/av	**Student/Faculty:** n/av
Year: semesters, summer session	**Tuition:** $12,892 ($23,288)
Application Deadline:	**Room & Board:** $7970
Freshman Class: 1570 applied, 1419 accepted, 772 enrolled	
SAT CR/M/W: 505/520/500 **ACT:** 20	**LESS COMPETITIVE**

The University of Pittsburgh at Johnstown is a public institution offering programs in arts and sciences, education, engineering technology, and nursing. In addition to regional accreditation, UPJ has baccalaureate program accreditation with ABET. Computerized library services include interlibrary loans, database searching, and Internet access. Special learning facilities include an art gallery, radio station, and TV station. The 650-acre campus is in a suburban area 70 miles east of Pittsburgh. Including any residence halls, there are 35 buildings.

Student Life: 98% of undergraduates are from Pennsylvania. Others are from 14 states, and 12 foreign countries. 88% are White. The average age of freshmen is 18; all undergraduates, 20. 27% do not continue beyond their first year; 55% remain to graduate.

Housing: 1700 students can be accommodated in college housing, which includes coed dorms, on-campus apartments, and off-campus apartments. In addition, there are special-interest houses, clubs and organizations that provide housing. On-campus housing is guaranteed for all 4 years. 56% of students live on campus; of those, 65% remain on campus on weekends. All students may keep cars.

Activities: 7% of men belong to 5 national fraternities; 7% of women belong to 3 national sororities. There are 85 groups on campus, including band, cheerleading, choir, chorus, computers, dance, drama, environmental, ethnic, gay, honors, literary magazine, musical theater, newspaper, political, professional, radio and TV, religious, social, social service, student government, symphony, and yearbook. Popular campus events include Spring Concert, Pitt Fest and Sephia Fashion Show.

Sports: There are 7 intercollegiate sports for men and 7 for women, and 11 intramural sports for men and 11 for women. Facilities include a 2300-seat gym, a pool, a dance studio, a weight room, a sauna, a cross-country track, basketball courts, and a nature area.

Disabled Students: 80% of the campus is accessible. Facilities include elevators, special parking, specially equipped restrooms, special class scheduling, lowered drinking fountains, lowered telephones, and special housing.

Services: Counseling and information services are available, as is tutoring in most subjects. There is a reader service for the blind, and remedial math.

Campus Safety and Security: Measures include 24-hour foot and vehicle patrol, emergency notification system, self-defense education, and security escort services. There are shuttle buses, emergency telephones, and lighted pathways/sidewalks.

Programs of Study: UPJ confers B.A., and B.S. degrees. Associate degrees are also awarded. Bachelor's degrees are awarded in AGRICULTURE (environmental studies), BIOLOGICAL SCIENCE (biology/biological science), BUSINESS (accounting, banking and finance, business administration and management, and business economics), COMMUNICATIONS AND THE ARTS (communications, creative writing, dramatic arts, English, and journalism), COMPUTER AND PHYSICAL SCIENCE (chemistry, computer science, geology, and mathematics), EDUCATION (elementary education, English education, mathematics education, science education, secondary education, and social science education), ENGINEERING AND ENVIRONMENTAL DESIGN (civil engineering technology, computer engineering, electrical/electronics engineering technology, and mechanical engineering technology), HEALTH PROFESSIONS (medical laboratory technology and nursing), SOCIAL SCIENCE (American studies, criminal justice, economics, geography, history, humanities, political science/government, psychology, social science, and sociology). Business, education, and biology have the largest enrollments.

Required: To graduate, students must complete 120 to 139 credits, with 30 to 36 credits in the major and a minimum GPA of 2.0. The school requires a core set of general education courses to include 12 credits each in humanities, natural sciences, and social sciences.

Special: Students may cross-register with schools in the Pittsburgh Council for Higher Education. Internships are available both on and off campus for credit, pay, or both. The school offers study abroad, work-study programs, accelerated degree programs, dual majors, student-designed majors, nondegree study, and pass/fail options. There are 10 national honor societies.

Faculty/Classroom: 63% of faculty are male; 37% are female. All teach undergraduates. No introductory courses are taught by graduate students. The average class size in an introductory lecture is 25; in a laboratory is 18; and in a regular course is 25.

Admissions: 90% of the 2013-2014 applicants were accepted. The SAT scores for the 2013-2014 freshman class were: Critical Reading--50% below 500, 41% between 500 and 599, 8% between 600 and 699, and 1% between 700 and 800; Math--41% below 500, 43% between 500 and 599, 15% between 600 and 699, and 1% between 700 and 800; Writing--55% below 500, 38% between 500 and 599, 6% between 600 and 699, and 1% between 700 and 800. The ACT scores were 52% below 21, 36% between 21 and 23, 10% between 24 and 26, 1% between 27 and 28, and 1% above 28. 35% of the current freshmen were in the top fifth of their class; 73% were in the top two fifths.

Requirements: The SAT or ACT is required. Applicants must be graduates of an accredited secondary school. The GED is accepted. For admission to freshman standing, 15 academic credits are required, including 4 of English, 3 of math (2 of algebra, 1 of geometry preferred), 2 of foreign language, 1 to 2 of lab science, 1 of social science, and electives. Engineering students must have completed chemistry, physics, and trigonometry. An interview is recommended, and an essay is highly recommended. AP credits are accepted. Important factors in the admissions decision are advanced placement or honors courses, leadership record, and recommendations by school officials.

Procedure: Freshmen are admitted to all sessions. Entrance exams should be taken between April and June of the junior year or by November of the senior year. There are early admissions, deferred admissions, and rolling admissions plans. Application deadlines are open. Application fee is $45. Notification is sent on a rolling basis.

Transfer: 84 transfer students enrolled in 2012-2013. Students wishing to transfer must have a minimum GPA of 2.5 and at least 15 credit hours earned. The SAT or ACT is required. Grades of C or better transfer for credit. 30 of 120 credits required for the bachelor's degree must be completed at UPJ.

Visiting: There are regularly scheduled orientations for prospective students, including 5 programs held on Saturdays in the fall, 2 Saturdays in the spring, 3 Fridays in the spring, and 4 Fridays in the summer. There are guides for informal visits, visitors may sit in on classes, and stay overnight. To schedule a visit, contact the Admissions Office.

Financial Aid: In 2013-2014, 85% of all full-time freshmen and 84% of continuing full-time students received some form of financial aid. 54% of all full-time freshmen and 55% of continuing full-time students received need-based aid. The average freshman award was $12,574. Need-based scholarships or need-based grants averaged $6,362; need-based self-help aid (loans and jobs) averaged $5,429; non-need-based athletic scholarships averaged $4,863; and other non-need-based awards and non-need-based scholarships averaged $4,984. The average financial indebtedness of the 2013 graduate was $26,526. The FAFSA is required. The deadline for filing freshman financial aid applications for fall entry is April 1.

International Students: They must take the TOEFL with a minimum score of 550 on the paper-based TOEFL (PBT) or 80 on the Internet-based version (iBT). The SAT may be required for some students.

Computers: All students may access the system. There are no time limits. The fee is $150 per semester.

Graduates: From July 1, 2012 to June 30, 2013, 494 bachelor's degrees were awarded. The most popular majors were business marketing (27%), education (16%), and engineering technologies (10%). In an average class, 63% graduate in 6 years or less.

Admissions Contact: Therese Grimes, Director of Admissions. E-Mail: *tgrimes@pitt.edu* Web: *www.upj.pitt.edu*

UNIVERSITY OF PITTSBURGH AT PITTSBURGH B-3

Pittsburgh, PA 15260 **(412) 624-PITT; (412) 648-8815**

Full-time: 8691 men, 8792 women	**Faculty:** n/av; I, -$
Part-time: 571 men, 561 women	**Ph.D.s:** 91%
Graduate: 4611 men, 5423 women	**Student/Faculty:** n/av
Year: semesters, summer session	**Tuition:** $17,100 ($27,106)
Application Deadline: open	**Room & Board:** $10,700

Freshman Class: 27634 applied, 15047 accepted, 3925 enrolled

SAT CR/M/W: 625/649/623 **ACT:** 29 **HIGHLY COMPETITIVE+**

The University of Pittsburgh, founded in 1787, is a state-related, public research university with programs in arts and sciences, education, engineering, law, social work, business, health and rehabilitation sciences, nursing, pharmacy, dental medicine, public health, medicine, information sciences, and public and international affairs. There are 9 undergraduate schools and 6 graduate schools. In addition to regional accreditation, Pitt has baccalaureate program accreditation with AACSB, ABET, ADA, and CSWE. The 19 libraries contain 6.8 million volumes, 5.6 million microform items, and 1.2 million audio/video tapes/CDs/DVDs, and subscribe to 186,012 periodicals including electronic. Computerized library services include interlibrary loans, database searching, Internet access, and Wi-Fi capability. Special learning facilities include an art gallery, radio station, international classrooms, located in the 42-story Cathedral of Learning, an observatory, music hall, and a natural history museum very near campus. The 132-acre campus is in a small town 3 miles east of downtown Pittsburgh. Including any residence halls, there are 130 buildings.

Student Life: 72% of undergraduates are from Pennsylvania. Others are from 50 states, 42 foreign countries, and Canada. 77% are White. The average age of all undergraduates is 21. 9% do not continue beyond their first year; 80% remain to graduate.

Housing: 7724 students can be accommodated in college housing, which includes single-sex and coed dorms, on-campus apartments, and off-campus apartments. In addition, there are honors houses, language houses, special-interest houses, fraternity houses, sorority houses, engineering, nursing, business, international living, alcohol free, quiet living, civic engagement and community service, entrepreneurial, leadership development, math, physical sciences, and research communities. On-campus housing is guaranteed for the freshman year only, is available on a first-come, first-served basis, and is available on a lottery system for upperclassmen. 56% of students commute. All students may keep cars.

Activities: 10% of men belong to 20 national fraternities; 9% of women belong to 16 national sororities. There are 485 groups on campus, including art, band, cheerleading, chess, choir, chorale, chorus, communications, computers, dance, debate, drama, ethnic, film, gay, honors, international, jazz band, literary magazine, marching band, musical theater, newspaper, pep band, political, professional, radio and TV, religious, social, social service, student government, and yearbook. Popular campus events include Homecoming Laser and Fireworks Show, Fall Fest and Bigelow Bash.

Sports: There are 8 intercollegiate sports for men and 9 for women, and 10 intramural sports for men and 9 for women. Facilities include Petersen Events Center -a 12,000-seat field house for hosting basketball games and concerts; the complex also has a fitness center for student use as well as a food court and shops; a field house with volleyball, gymnastics, wrestling, and an indoor track and field; a pool, and a gymnastics training center. The new Petersen Sports Complex has a baseball stadium, a soccer stadium, and a softball stadium. There are billiard tables, table tennis, video games, and televisions in the student union.

Disabled Students: 90% of the campus is accessible. Facilities include wheelchair ramps, elevators, special parking, specially equipped restrooms, special class scheduling, lowered drinking fountains, lowered telephones, special housing.

Services: Counseling and information services are available, as is tutoring in some subjects, many lower-level undergraduate science and humanities courses. There is remedial math and writing.

Campus Safety and Security: Measures include 24-hour foot and vehicle patrol, emergency notification system, self-defense education, and security escort services. There are shuttle buses, emergency telephones, lighted pathways/sidewalks, and controlled access to dorms/residences.

Programs of Study: Pitt confers B.A., B.S., B.A.S.W., B.Phil., B.S.B.A., B.S.E., B.S.N. and B.S.P.S. degrees. Master's and doctoral degrees are also awarded. Bachelor's degrees are awarded in AGRICULTURE (environmental studies), BIOLOGICAL SCIENCE (bioinformatics, biology/biological science, ecology, microbiology, molecular biology, and neurosciences), BUSINESS (accounting, banking and finance, business administration and management, business (dual major program), business information systems, economics – statistics, finance, global/general management, human resources, international business management, marketing/retailing/merchandising, and supply chain management), COMMUNICATIONS AND THE ARTS (Chinese, classics, communications, communication rhetoric/communication, communication science, English literature, English Writing, film arts, French, German, Germanic languages and literature, Italian, Japanese, linguistics, media arts, music, physical activity, Polish, Russian, Slavic languages, Spanish, studio art, and theatre arts), COMPUTER AND PHYSICAL SCIENCE (actuarial mathematics, applied mathematics, astronomy, chemistry, computer science, environmental geology, geology, information sciences and systems, mathematics, mathematics – economics, natural sciences, physics, and statistics), EDUCATION (athletic training and health information management), ENGINEERING AND ENVIRONMENTAL DESIGN (bioengineering, chemical engineering, civil engineering, computer engineering, electrical/electronics engineering, engineering physics, industrial engineering, materials engineering, materials science, and mechanical engineering), HEALTH PROFESSIONS (dental hygiene, emergency medical technologies, health services technology, nursing, occupational therapy, pharmaceutical science, and rehabilitation therapy), SOCIAL SCIENCE (administration of justice , africana studies, anthropology, applied psychology, architectural studies, economics, history, history of philosophy, humanities, interdisciplinary studies, international studies, legal studies, liberal arts/general studies, philosophy, political science/government, prelaw, psychology, public administration, public affairs, religion, social science, social work, sociology, and urban studies). engineering, psychology, and nursing have the largest enrollments.

Required: All students in the Kenneth P. Dietrich School of Arts and Sciences must take a minimum of 120 credits. Skills and general education requirements vary but include course work in the humanities, social and natural sciences, and foreign culture. A 2.0 GPA are required. Students must earn their last 30 credits while enrolled in Arts and Sciences and earn at least half of the credits for their majors while enrolled in Arts and Sciences. Requirements for other schools may vary.

Special: Students may cross-register with 9 neighboring colleges and universities. Internships, unlimited study abroad, work-study programs, a dual major in business and any other subject in arts and sciences, and student-designed majors are available. There are freshman seminars and a 5-year joint degree in arts and sciences/engineering. There are co-op programs in engineering, computer science, and chemistry. An accelerated second degree B.S.N. program is available as well as a 3-2 engineering degree. There are 15 national honor societies, including Phi Beta Kappa, and a freshman honors program.

Faculty/Classroom: 60% of faculty are male; 40% are female. No introductory courses are taught by graduate students.

Admissions: 54% of the 2013-2014 applicants were accepted. The SAT scores for the 2013-2014 freshman class were: Critical Reading--3% below 500, 33% between 500 and 599, 48% between 600 and 699, and 16% between 700 and 800; Math--1% below 500, 20% between 500 and 599, 55% between 600 and 699, and 24% between 700 and 800; Writing--3% below 500, 32% between 500 and 599, 49% between 600 and 699, and 16% between 700 and 800. The ACT scores were 1% below 21, 4% between 21 and 23, 24% between 24 and 26, 20% between 27 and 28, and 51% above 28. 79% of the current freshmen were in the top fifth of their class; 98% were in the top two fifths.

Requirements: The SAT or ACT is required. The ACT Optional Writing test is also required. Applicants for admission to the Kenneth P. Dietrich School of Arts and Sciences must be graduates of an accredited secondary school. Students must have 17 high school academic credits, including 4 units of English, 3 to 4 each of math and lab science, 2-3 of social studies, plus 3 to 5 units in academic electives. Pitt recommends that the student have 3 or more years of a single foreign language. An essay is recommended if the student is seeking scholarship consideration. AP and CLEP credits are accepted. Important factors in the admissions decision are advanced placement or honors courses, leadership record, and evidence of special talent.

Procedure: Freshmen are admitted to all sessions. Entrance exams should be taken preferably by January for September admission. There are deferred admissions and rolling admissions plans. Application deadlines are open. Application fee is $45. Notification is sent on a rolling basis. 1738 applicants were on the 2013 waiting list; 289 were admitted. Applications are accepted online.

Transfer: 883 transfer students enrolled in 2012-2013. Applicants for transfer to the Kenneth P. Dietrich School of Arts and Sciences must supply transcripts of all secondary school and college course work and have a minimum GPA of 3.00. An interview is recommended. Grades of C or better transfer for credit. Application deadlines vary by school. 30 of 120 credits required for the bachelor's degree must be completed at Pitt.

Visiting: There are regularly scheduled orientations for prospective students, including information sessions, student-guided tours, and class attendance. There are guides for informal visits and visitors may sit in on classes. To schedule a visit, contact the Office of Admissions and Financial Aid at 1-877-SEE-PITT.

Financial Aid: In 2013-2014, 58% of all full-time freshmen and 57% of continuing full-time students received some form of financial aid. 52% of all full-time freshmen and 53% of continuing full-time students received need-based aid. The average freshman award was $12,039. Need-based scholarships or need-based grants averaged $8,062; need-based self-help aid (loans and jobs) averaged $5,175; and non-need-based athletic scholarships averaged $16,018. The average financial indebtedness of the 2013 graduate was $24,402. The FAFSA is required. The priority date for freshman financial aid applications for fall entry is March 1.

International Students: There are 601 international students enrolled. The school actively recruits these students. They must take the TOEFL with a minimum score of 600 on the paper-based TOEFL (PBT) or 100 on the Internet-based version (iBT). They must also take the SAT or ACT.

Computers: All students may access the system 24 hours a day. There are no time limits and no fees.

Graduates: From July 1, 2012 to June 30, 2013, 4345 bachelor's degrees were awarded. The most popular majors were business (14%), English (9%), and engineering (9%). 465 companies recruited on campus in 2012-2013. In an average class, 80% graduate in 6 years or less.

Admissions Contact: Marc L. Harding, Chief Enrollment Officer. E-Mail: *oafa@pitt.edu* Web: *www.pitt.edu*

UNIVERSITY OF SCRANTON — E-2

Scranton, PA 18510 — (570) 941-7540
(888) SCRANTON; (570) 941-5928

Full-time: 1735 men, 2112 women	**Faculty:** n/av; IIA, +$
Part-time: 88 men, 106 women	**Ph.D.s:** 85%
Graduate: 755 men, 1102 women	**Student/Faculty:** n/av
Year: semesters, summer session	**Tuition:** $38,754
Application Deadline: March 1	**Room & Board:** $13,186

Freshman Class: 9672 applied, 6655 accepted, 971 enrolled
SAT or ACT: required

VERY COMPETITIVE

The University of Scranton, founded in 1888, is a private institution operated by the Jesuit order of the Roman Catholic Church. It offers programs in business, behavioral sciences, education, health science, humanities, math, science, and social science. There are 4 undergraduate schools and 1 graduate school. In addition to regional accreditation, the University has baccalaureate program accreditation with AACSB, ABET, APTA, CSAB, NCATE, and NLN. The library contains 486,650 volumes, 26,241 microform items, 21,285 audio/video tapes/CDs/DVDs, and subscribes to 75,198 periodicals including electronic. Computerized library services include interlibrary loans, database searching, Internet access, and Wi-Fi capability. Special learning facilities include an art gallery, radio station, TV station, The University offers a number of unique facilities including: Hope Horn Gallery in Hyland Hall for paintings and sculpture; the Royal Theater and Studio Theater in the McDade Center for Literary and Performing Arts for University Players productions; television studio and broadcast FM-radio station; 700-seat performance hall in the Houlihan-McLean Center; and the Institute of Molecular Biology and Medicine offering proteomics, genomics and PCR equipment. The 58-acre campus is in an urban area 125 miles north of Philadelphia. Including any residence halls, there are 67 buildings.

Student Life: 60% of undergraduates are from out of state, mostly the Middle Atlantic. Students are from 24 states, and 12 foreign countries. 81% are White. 75% are Catholic. The average age of freshmen is 19; all undergraduates, 21. 12% do not continue beyond their first year; 83% remain to graduate.

Housing: 2647 students can be accommodated in college housing, which includes single-sex and coed dorms, on-campus apartments, and off-campus apartments. In addition, there are special-interest houses. On-campus housing is guaranteed for all 4 years. 64% of students live on campus; of those, 80% remain on campus on weekends. Upperclassmen may keep cars.

Activities: There are no fraternities or sororities. There are 80 groups on campus, including art, band, cheerleading, chess, choir, chorale, chorus, communications, computers, dance, debate, drama, environmental, ethnic, film, forensics, honors, international, jazz band, literary magazine, musical theater, newspaper, orchestra, photography, political, professional, radio and TV, religious, social, social service, student government, symphony, and yearbook. Popular campus events include Spring Fest, Senior Formal, Royal Ball, Shamrockin' Eve, IGNITE Leadershop Conference and Relay for Life.

Sports: There are 9 intercollegiate sports for men and 9 for women, and 20 intramural sports for men and 19 for women. Facilities include a 3000-seat gym, basketball courts, wrestling and weight rooms, handball/racquetball and tennis courts, a sand volleyball court, a soccer/lacrosse field, a softball field, a swimming pool, a physical therapy room, a 3-court multipurpose gym, a fitness center, a sauna and steamroom, a dance aerobics room.

Disabled Students: All of the campus is accessible. Facilities include wheelchair ramps, elevators, special parking, specially equipped restrooms, special class scheduling, lowered drinking fountains, lowered telephones, and special housing.

Services: Counseling and information services are available, as is tutoring in most subjects. There is a reader service for the blind including time management, organizational skills, learning strategies, writing labs, and math labs.

Campus Safety and Security: Measures include 24-hour foot and vehicle patrol, emergency notification system, self-defense education, and security escort services. There are emergency telephones, lighted pathways/sidewalks, and controlled access to dorms/residences.

Programs of Study: the University confers B.A., and B.S. degrees. Associate, master's, and doctoral degrees are also awarded. Bachelor's degrees are awarded in BIOLOGICAL SCIENCE (biochemistry, biology/biological science, biomathematics, biophysics, and neurosciences), BUSINESS (accounting, banking and finance, business administration and management, business economics, electronic business, human resources, information & communication technology, international business management, marketing/retailing/merchandising, and operations management), COMMUNICATIONS AND THE ARTS (communications, English, French, German, Greek, Latin, Spanish, and theatre arts), COMPUTER AND PHYSICAL SCIENCE (chemistry, computer science, information sciences and systems, mathematics, and physics), EDUCATION (early childhood education, elementary education, and secondary education), ENGINEERING AND ENVIRONMENTAL DESIGN (computer engineering, electrical/electronics engineering, and environmental science), HEALTH PROFESSIONS (community health work, exercise science, health care administration, medical laboratory technology, nursing, and occupational therapy), SOCIAL SCIENCE (criminal justice, economics, forensic studies, history, human services, international studies, philosophy, political science/government, psychology, sociology, theological studies, and women's studies). Chemistry, biology, and nursing are the strongest academically. Biology, communication, and nursing have the largest enrollments.

Required: Students take general education requirements according to their area of study. All are required to take philosophy/theology, phys ed, English composition, speech, and computer literacy. The minimum GPA is 2.0, although some majors require a higher GPA.

Special: The university offers dual, student-designed, and interdisciplinary majors, including chemistry-business, chemistry-computers, electronics-business, and international language-business, crdit by exam and for lifr/military/work experience, work-study, nondegree study, and pass/fail options. There are also Honors, Business Leadership Honors & Special Jesuit Liberal Arts Honors Programs; First-year experience courses; Service learning; Faculty/Student Research; Independent Study; Internships Study abroad in over 60 countries; Cross registration IB/AP/College Credit Washington Center; BS/MS Accounting, BS/MS Biochemistry, BS/MS Chemistry, BS/MS Health Administration, BS/MS Nursing, BS/MS Rehabiliation Counseling, BS/MS School Counseling, BS/MS Software Engineering, BS/MS Operations Management, BA/MA Theology, BS/MS Human Resources, and BA/MS or BS/MS Business Administration. There are 32 national honor societies.

Faculty/Classroom: 59% of faculty are male; 41% are female. No introductory courses are taught by graduate students. The average class size in a regular course is 20.

Admissions: 69% of the 2013-2014 applicants were accepted. The SAT scores for the 2013-2014 freshman class were: Critical Reading--15% below 500, 56% between 500 and 599, 25% between 600 and 699, and 4% between 700 and 800; Math--12% below 500, 51% between 500 and 599, 31% between 600 and 699, and 5% between 700 and 800. 11 freshmen graduated first in their class.

Requirements: The SAT or ACT is required. Applicants should be graduates of an accredited secondary school, though in some cases a GED may be accepted. They should complete 18 academic or Carnegie units, including 4 years of high school English, 3 each of math, science, history, and social studies, and 2 of foreign language. 2 letters of reference/recommendation are required. Essays are required. AP and CLEP credits are accepted. Important factors in the admissions decision are advanced placement or honors courses, leadership record, and extracurricular activities record.

Procedure: Freshmen are admitted fall and spring. Entrance exams should be taken by fall of the senior year. There are deferred admissions and rolling admissions plans. Applications should be filed by March 1 for fall entry; December 15 for spring entry; and May 1 for summer entry. Notifications are sent December 15. 1087 applicants were on the 2013 waiting list; 57 were admitted. Applications are accepted online.

Transfer: 89 transfer students enrolled in 2012-2013. Applicants should have earned a GPA of at least 2.5. 60 of 130 credits required for the bachelor's degree must be completed at the University.

Visiting: There are regularly scheduled orientations for prospective students, Group information sessions and tours are available most weekdays and Saturdays throughout the year. There are also personal appointments available with admissions counselors by appointment. There are guides for informal visits and visitors may sit in on classes. To schedule a visit, contact the Office of Admissions.

Financial Aid: In 2013-2014, 90% of all full-time freshmen and 89% of continuing full-time students received some form of financial aid. 69% of all full-time freshmen and 66% of continuing full-time students received need-based aid. The average freshman award was $25,338. The University is a member of CSS. The FAFSA is required. The priority date for freshman financial aid applications for fall entry is February 15.

International Students: There are 40 international students enrolled. The school actively recruits these students. They must take the TOEFL with a minimum score of 500 on the paper-based TOEFL (PBT) or 61 on the Internet-based version (iBT).

Computers: All students may access the system 24 hours a day. There are no time limits and no fees.

Graduates: From July 1, 2012 to June 30, 2013, 902 bachelor's degrees were awarded. The most popular majors were business/marketing (21%), health professions/related sciences (15%), and biological/life sciences (11%). In an average class, 73% graduate in 4 years or less, 79% graduate in 5 years or less, and 80% graduate in 6 years or less. Of the 2012 graduating class, 55% were enrolled in graduate school within 6 months of graduation, and 40% were employed.

Admissions Contact: Joseph M. Roback, Associate Vice President for Admissions and. E-Mail: *admissions@scranton.edu* Web: *www.scranton.edu*

UNIVERSITY OF THE ARTS F-3

Philadelphia, PA 19102 (215) 717-6039
(800) 616-2787; (215) 717-6045

Full-time: 950 men, 1105 women	**Faculty:** n/av
Part-time: 20 men, 40 women	**Ph.D.s:** n/av
Graduate: 65 men, 145 women	**Student/Faculty:** n/av
Year: semesters	**Tuition:** $33,500
Application Deadline: see profile	**Room & Board:** $12,300
Freshman Class: n/av	
SAT or ACT: required	**SPECIAL**

University of the Arts, founded in 1870, is a private institution offering education and professional training in visual, media, and performing arts, with an emphasis on the humanities and interdisciplinary exploration. There are 3 undergraduate schools and 2 graduate schools. Figures in the above capsule and in this profile are approximate. In addition to regional accreditation, UArts has baccalaureate program accreditation with NASAD and NASM. The 3 libraries contain 144,700 volumes, 461 microform items, 21,200 audio/video tapes/CDs/DVDs, and subscribe to 541 periodicals including electronic. Computerized library services include interlibrary loans, database searching, and Internet access. Special learning facilities include an art gallery, several theaters, and music, animation, and recording studios. The 18-acre campus is in an urban area in Philadelphia. Including any residence halls, there are 8 buildings.

Student Life: 61% of undergraduates are from out of state, mostly the Middle Atlantic. Students are from 43 states, 42 foreign countries, and Canada. 73% are from public schools. 67% are white. The average age of freshmen is 18; all undergraduates, 20. 18% do not continue beyond their first year; 55% remain to graduate.

Housing: 690 students can be accommodated in college housing, which includes coed dorms, on-campus apartments, and off-campus apartments. On campus housing is guaranteed for the freshman year only and is available on a first-come, first-served basis. Priority is given to out-of-town students. 65% of students commute. Alcohol is not permitted. No one may keep cars.

Activities: There are no fraternities or sororities. There are 20 groups on campus, including art, band, choir, chorale, chorus, communications, dance, drama, ethnic, film, gay, international, jazz band, musical theater, photography, professional, religious, and student government. Popular campus events include exhibitions and performances.

Sports: There is no sports program at UArts. Athletic facilities are available at area gyms, for which the university provides discount membership.

Disabled Students: 65% of the campus is accessible. Facilities include wheelchair ramps, elevators, specially equipped restrooms, lowered drinking fountains, lowered telephones, and sign language interpreters.

Services: Counseling and information services are available, as is tutoring in every subject. There is remedial math, reading, and writing. There also is assistance with study skills.

Campus Safety and Security: Measures include 24-hour foot and vehicle patrol, self-defense education, security escort services, and lighted pathways/sidewalks.

Programs of Study: UArts confers B.S., B.F.A., and B.M. degrees. Master's degrees are also awarded. Bachelor's degrees are awarded in COMMUNICATIONS AND THE ARTS (communications, dance, film arts, graphic design, illustration, industrial design, multimedia, music performance, music theory and composition, musical theater, painting, photography, printmaking, and sculpture), EDUCATION (dance education). Dance, music, and illustration have the largest enrollments.

Required: All students must complete a core program consisting of liberal arts courses in languages and literature, arts history, philosophy and religion, science and math, and social sciences. A GPA of 2.0 overall for 123 to 143 credits, with 21 to 45 in the major, depending on the curriculum, must be achieved for graduation.

Special: UArts offers cross-registration with the 10-member Consortium East Coast Art Schools. Internships may be arranged, and there are extensive summer programs and opportunities to study abroad.

Faculty/Classroom: 60% of faculty are male; 40% are female. 95% teach undergraduates. No introductory courses are taught by graduate students. The average class size in an introductory lecture is 18 and in a regular course, 14.

Requirements: The SAT or ACT is required. In addition, students must have graduated from an accredited secondary school or hold a GED certificate. A minimum of 16 academic credits consisting of 4 each in English and math and 2 each in music or art and history is recommended. An essay and either a portfolio or an audition are required of all applicants. An interview is recommended. A GPA of 2.0 is required. AP and CLEP credits are accepted. Important factors in the admissions decision are evidence of special talent, advanced placement or honors courses, and personality/intangible qualities.

Procedure: Freshmen are admitted fall and spring. Entrance exams should be taken late in the junior year or early in the senior year. There are deferred admissions and rolling admissions plans. Application deadlines are open. Application fee is $60. Notification is sent on a rolling basis. Applications are accepted online.

Transfer: Candidates must have a minimum 2.0 GPA overall. An interview is recommended, as well as test scores for either the SAT or ACT if English composition has not been completed. 48 of 123 credits required for the bachelor's degree must be completed at UArts.

Visiting: There are regularly scheduled orientations for prospective students, including a spring and fall open house. There are guides for informal visits. To schedule a visit, contact the Office of Admissions.

Financial Aid: The FAFSA is required. Check with the school for current deadlines.

International Students: The school actively recruits these students. They must take the TOEFL.

Computers: Wireless access is available. All students may access the system. There are no time limits and no fees. It is strongly recommended that all students have a personal computer.

Admissions Contact: Director of Admissions. A campus DVD is available. E-Mail: *admissions@uarts.edu* Web: *www.uarts.edu*

UNIVERSITY OF THE SCIENCES F-3

Philadelphia, PA 19104 (215) 596-8815
(888) 996-8747; (215) 596-8821

Full-time: 927 men, 1474 women	**Faculty:** 182
Part-time: 12 men, 25 women	**Ph.D.s:** 84%
Graduate: 146 men, 196 women	**Student/Faculty:** 10 to 1
Year: semesters, summer session	**Tuition:** $34,742
Application Deadline:	**Room & Board:** $13,578
Freshman Class: 4099 applied, 2500 accepted, 440 enrolled	
SAT CR/M/W: 557/603/567	**ACT:** 25 **VERY COMPETITIVE+**

The roots of University of the Sciences reach back to 1821, when the institution was founded as America's first pharmacy college, the Philadelphia College of Pharmacy. Today, USciences continues to build on that esteemed reputation and is now home to 25 undergraduate and 25 graduate programs in five colleges. Our 3,000 students have enrolled in our premier programs in the health sciences, ranging across pharmacy to pre-med to healthcare business and health policy. This is a university that traverses almost the entire range of the health sciences. Students may study traditional sciences such as biology and chemistry or pursue demanding careers in physical and occupational therapy. They may explore fields such as pharmacognosy on the frontiers of learning, or they may be preparing for a life shaping policy for medical and governmental institutions. With careers in healthcare continuing to grow, a USciences' education not only makes for a rewarding choice, but an investment in the future. Key to our distinctive education is a tradition of hands-on research at every level. Our undergraduates participate in highly engaging research in their earliest studies. Our alumni have contributed to progress in every dimension of the health sciences, from pioneering the use of x-rays in the 19th century to unlocking the genetic code in the 20th to discovering countless new medications. Recent graduates have continued this legacy as founders of pharmaceutical companies and companies serving the pharmaceutical and biotech industries. Recent new programs include degrees in physics, cancer biology, cell biology, science and humanities, and exercise science and wellness management, as well as an online master of public health. But what is truly new every day is our students' deepening perspective on how they can make a difference in the critically important arenas of science and healthcare. Discover University of the Sciences: a place where healthcare and science converge. There are 4 undergraduate schools and 4 graduate schools. In addition to regional accreditation, Usciences has baccalaureate program accreditation with ACPE and APTA. The library contains 82,380 volumes, 24,485 microform items, 1,790 audio/video tapes/CDs/DVDs, and subscribes to 22,634 periodicals including electronic. Computerized library services include interlibrary loans, database searching, Internet access, and Wi-Fi capability. Special learning facilities include a The 35-acre campus is in an urban area Philadelphia. Including any residence halls, there are 17 buildings.

Student Life: 58% of undergraduates are from out of state, mostly the Middle Atlantic. Students are from 40 states, 19 foreign countries, and Canada. 46% are White; 36% Asian American. The average age of freshmen is 18; all undergraduates, 21. 12% do not continue beyond their first year; 80% remain to graduate.

Housing: 768 students can be accommodated in college housing, which includes coed dorms and on-campus apartments. In addition, there are honors houses. On-campus housing is available on a first-come, first-served basis, and is available on a lottery system for upperclassmen. Priority is given to out-of-town students. 71% of students commute. Alcohol is not permitted. Upperclassmen may keep cars.

Activities: 7% of men belong to 3 local and 7 national fraternities; 7% of women belong to 3 local and 5 national sororities. There are 83 groups on campus, including band, cheerleading, chess, chorale, chorus, computers, dance, drama, ethnic, gay, honors, international, literary magazine, martial arts, musical theater, newspaper, orchestra, political, professional, religious, social, social service, and student government. Popular campus events include Student Appreciation Weekend, Founder's Day, Usciences Scholarly Day, and Convocation.

Sports: There are 6 intercollegiate sports for men and 7 for women, and 5 intramural sports for men and 5 for women. Facilities include Indoor track, a state of the art gym, a rifle range, tennis courts, a softball field, a jogging path, and recreational areas in the residence halls.

Disabled Students: 90% of the campus is accessible. Facilities include wheelchair ramps, elevators, special parking, specially equipped restrooms, special class scheduling, and individual student accomodation is available.

Services: Counseling and information services are available, as is tutoring in every subject. There is remedial math and writing.

Campus Safety and Security: Measures include 24-hour foot and vehicle patrol, self-defense education, and security escort services. There are shuttle buses, emergency telephones, lighted pathways/sidewalks, controlled access to dorms/residences, required key and student identification for dorm entry; id access only to campus buildings in the evenings.

Programs of Study: Usciences confers B.S., and B.S.H.S. degrees. Master's and doctoral degrees are also awarded. Bachelor's degrees are awarded in BIOLOGICAL SCIENCE (biochemistry, bioinformatics, biology/biological science, microbiology, and toxicology), BUSINESS (marketing management and recreational facilities management), COMPUTER AND PHYSICAL SCIENCE (chemistry, computer science, and physics), ENGINEERING AND ENVIRONMENTAL DESIGN (environmental science), HEALTH PROFESSIONS (health science, medical technology, mental health/human services, occupational therapy, pharmaceutical chemistry, pharmaceutical science, pharmacology, pharmacy, physical therapy, and physician's assistant), SOCIAL SCIENCE (humanities and social science, interdisciplinary studies, and psychology). Pharmacy, physical therapy, physician assistant studies, and occupational therapy are the strongest academically. Pharmacy, physical therapy, and biology have the largest enrollments.

Required: Total credits required for graduation range from 120 to 210 depending on the major, with a 2.0 GPA for BS majors, and higher minimum gpa's for professional programs and other specific programs. (please see our online university catalog). The core curriculum consists of 38 credits including 16 credits of natural science, 6 each of math, social sciences, communication, and an intellectual heritage sequence, 3 of literature, world culture, history, and advanced social sciences, and 1 of phys ed, along with 3 of electives. Students must pass a writing proficiency exam and demonstrate proficiency in computer applications.

Special: USciences offers 5- and 6-year integrated professional programs in occupational therapy, physical therapy, and physician's assistant studies. Internships are required in all health science disciplines. Study abroad is available in Asia, Africa, and Europe through the NYU Study Abroad program. A 1-year undeclared major program is offered, as is a program of curriculum and advisement to prepare students to enter medical school. Students may elect dual majors or a minor in communications, economics, psychology, sociology, math, physics, computer science, biochemistry, biology, chemistry, forensic science, humanities, math, microbiology, social sciences, and writing. There are 5 national honor societies.

Faculty/Classroom: 46% of faculty are male; 54% are female. 99% teach undergraduates. No introductory courses are taught by graduate students. The average class size in an introductory lecture is 100; in a laboratory is 28; and in a regular course is 25.

Admissions: 61% of the 2013-2014 applicants were accepted. The SAT scores for the 2013-2014 freshman class were: Critical Reading--15% below 500, 61% between 500 and 599, 21% between 600 and 699, and 3% between 700 and 800; Math--6% below 500, 43% between 500 and 599, 40% between 600 and 699, and 11% between 700 and 800; Writing--16% below 500, 52% between 500 and 599, 26% between 600 and 699, and 6% between 700 and 800. The ACT scores were 3% below 21, 34% between 21 and 23, 31% between 24 and 26, 16% between 27 and 28, and 16% above 28. 71% of the current freshmen were in the top fifth of their class; 93% were in the top two fifths. 3 freshmen graduated first in their class.

Requirements: The SAT or ACT is required. Applicants must be high school graduates or hold the GED. Minimum academic requirements include 4 credits in English, 1 credit each in American history and social science, and 4 credits in academic electives. Math requirements include 2 years of algebra and 1 year of geometry. The university strongly recommends an additional year of higher-level math, such as pre-calculus or calculus. In addition, 3 science credits are required, and the university strongly recommends that students have 1 credit each in biology, chemistry, and physics. A strong background in English, science, and math is recommended. Usciences requires applicants to be in the upper 50% of their class. AP and CLEP credits are accepted. Important factors in the admissions decision are extracurricular activities record, leadership record, and advanced placement or honors courses.

Procedure: Freshmen are admitted fall. Entrance exams should be taken

by the end of the junior year or the fall of the senior year. There are early admissions, deferred admissions, and rolling admissions plans. Application deadlines are open. Application fee is $45. Notification is sent on a rolling basis. Applications are accepted online. Application fees are waived if application is completed online.

Transfer: 117 transfer students enrolled in 2012-2013. To be considered, pharmacy and physical therapy applicants must present a minimum GPA of 3.0. All other majors must have at least a 2.7 GPA. All applicants must meet high school requirements as well. 51 credits required for the bachelor's degree must be completed at Usciences.

Visiting: There are regularly scheduled orientations for prospective students, Student visits consist of summer open houses for rising seniors, campus day visits, campus tours, and meetings with faculty members. There are guides for informal visits and visitors may sit in on classes. To schedule a visit, contact the Admission Office.

Financial Aid: The FAFSA is required. The priority date for freshman financial aid applications for fall entry is March 15. The deadline for filing freshman financial aid applications for fall entry is open.

International Students: There are 38 international students enrolled. They must take the TOEFL with a minimum score of 550 on the paper-based TOEFL (PBT) or 80 on the Internet-based version (iBT) and the college's own test. They must also take the SAT or ACT.

Computers: All students may access the system. There are no time limits and no fees.

Graduates: From July 1, 2012 to June 30, 2013, 453 bachelor's degrees were awarded. The most popular majors were pharmacy (41%), physical therapy/occup. and health science (32%), and biology (5%). 150 companies recruited on campus in 2012-2013. In an average class, 65% graduate in 4 years or less, 79% graduate in 5 years or less, and 80% graduate in 6 years or less. Of the 2012 graduating class, 14% were enrolled in graduate school within 6 months of graduation, and 74% were employed.

Admissions Contact: Dianna Collins, Executive Director of Admission and Enrollment Services. E-Mail: *admit@usciences.edu* Web: *www.usciences.edu*

URSINUS COLLEGE — E-3

Collegeville, PA 19426 — **(610) 409-3200; (610) 409-3197**

Full-time: 781 men, 801 women	**Faculty:** 125; IIB, +$
Part-time: 2 men, 12 women	**Ph.D.s:** 95%
Graduate: n/av	**Student/Faculty:** 12 to 1
Year: semesters	**Tuition:** $44,530
Application Deadline: February 15	**Room & Board:** $11,100
Freshman Class: 3947 applied, 2618 accepted, 425 enrolled	
SAT CR/M/W: 580/590/590 **ACT:** 26	**VERY COMPETITIVE+**

Ursinus College, founded in 1869, is a private residential college offering programs in the liberal arts. The library contains 420,000 volumes, 201,995 microform items, 32,000 audio/video tapes/CDs/DVDs, and subscribes to 25,883 periodicals including electronic. Computerized library services include interlibrary loans, database searching, Internet access, and Wi-Fi capability. Special learning facilities include an art gallery, planetarium, radio station, TV station, an observatory. The 170-acre campus is in a suburban area 25 miles west of Philadelphia. Including any residence halls, there are 65 buildings.

Student Life: 61% of undergraduates are from Pennsylvania. Others are from 32 states, 13 foreign countries, and Canada. 75% are from public schools. 74% are White. The average age of freshmen is 18; all undergraduates, 20. 8% do not continue beyond their first year; 78% remain to graduate.

Housing: 1650 students can be accommodated in college housing, which includes single-sex and coed dorms, on-campus apartments, and off-campus apartments. In addition, there are special-interest houses, multicultural, wellness, art, physical sciences, community service, literary, international, and quiet houses. On-campus housing is guaranteed for all 4 years. 97% of students live on campus; of those, 90% remain on campus on weekends. Upperclassmen may keep cars.

Activities: 10% of men belong to 5 local and 2 national fraternities; 13% of women belong to 6 local and 1 national sororities. There are 100 groups on campus, including fencing, folk music, gospel choir, men's chorus, art, band, cheerleading, chess, choir, chorale, chorus, computers, dance, debate, drama, environmental, ethnic, film, forensics, gay, honors, international, jazz band, literary magazine, newspaper, pep band, photography, political, professional, radio and TV, religious, social, social service, student government, UCEMS (student EMT group), and yearbook. Popular campus events include Air Band Competition, Relay for Life, and Family Day.

Sports: There are 12 intercollegiate sports for men and 13 for women, and 14 intramural sports for men and 12 for women. Facilities include racquetball and squash courts, a dance studio, tennis courts, a field house, a fitness center, and all types of playing fields.

Disabled Students: 95% of the campus is accessible. Facilities include wheelchair ramps, elevators, special parking, specially equipped restrooms, special class scheduling, lowered drinking fountains, lowered telephones, and special housing.

Services: Counseling and information services are available, as is tutoring in every subject. There is a reader service for the blind. The college provides appropriate services on an as-needed basis.

Campus Safety and Security: Measures include 24-hour foot and vehicle patrol, emergency notification system, self-defense education, and security escort services. There are emergency telephones and lighted pathways/sidewalks.

Programs of Study: Ursinus confers B.A., and B.S. degrees. Bachelor's degrees are awarded in BIOLOGICAL SCIENCE (biochemistry, biology/biological science, and neurosciences), BUSINESS (business economics), COMMUNICATIONS AND THE ARTS (art, classics, communications, dance, dramatic arts, English, French, German, and Spanish), COMPUTER AND PHYSICAL SCIENCE (chemistry, computer science, mathematics, and physics), ENGINEERING AND ENVIRONMENTAL DESIGN (environmental science), HEALTH PROFESSIONS (exercise science), SOCIAL SCIENCE (American studies, anthropology, East Asian studies, history, international relations, philosophy, political science/government, psychology, and sociology). Biology, chemistry, and politics are the strongest academically. Economics, biology, and psychology have the largest enrollments.

Required: All students must fulfill requirements in the common intellectual experience, math or logic, foreign language, humanities, and natural and social science, including an independent learning experience. A total of 128 semester hours, with 32 to 40 in the major, is required, as is a GPA of at least 2.0.

Special: The college offers study abroad, student-designed majors, internships, a Washington semester, dual majors, and a 3-2 engineering degree with Columbia University. Ursinus offers an international studies certificate in addition to a degree in international relations. There are 17 national honor societies, including Phi Beta Kappa, and 27 departmental honors programs.

Faculty/Classroom: 48% of faculty are male; 52% are female. All teach and do research. No introductory courses are taught by graduate students. The average class size in an introductory lecture is 40; in a laboratory is 22; and in a regular course is 18.

Admissions: 66% of the 2013-2014 applicants were accepted. The SAT scores for the 2013-2014 freshman class were: Critical Reading--13% below 500, 45% between 500 and 599, 34% between 600 and 699, and 8% between 700 and 800; Math--7% below 500, 42% between 500 and 599, 40% between 600 and 699, and 11% between 700 and 800; Writing--14% below 500, 43% between 500 and 599, 34% between 600 and 699, and 9% between 700 and 800. The ACT scores were 27% between 24 and 26, 27% between 27 and 28, and 26% above 28. 72% of the current freshmen were in the top fifth of their class; 91% were in the top two fifths. There were 42 National Merit finalists. 6 freshmen graduated first in their class.

Requirements: The SAT or ACT and ACT Writing Test are recommended. In addition, SAT Subject Tests are recommended. Applicants should prepare with 16 academic credits, including 4 years of English, 3 of math, 2 of foreign language, and 1 each of science and social studies. An interview is recommended. A GPA of 2.0 is required. AP credits are accepted. Important factors in the admissions decision are advanced placement or honors courses, recommendations by school officials, and leadership record.

Procedure: Freshmen are admitted fall and spring. Entrance exams should be taken in the junior or senior year. There are early decision, early admissions, deferred admissions, and rolling admissions plans. Early decision applications should be filed by January 15; regular applications, by February 15 for fall entry; and December 1 for spring entry. Notification of early decision is sent January 15; regular decision, April 1. 25 early decision candidates were accepted for the 2013-2014 class. 100 applicants were on the 2013 waiting list. Applications are accepted online.

Transfer: 9 transfer students enrolled in 2012-2013. Transfer applicants must submit transcripts from all institutions attended. 64 of 128 credits required for the bachelor's degree must be completed at Ursinus.

Visiting: There are regularly scheduled orientations for prospective students, including a campus interview and a tour. There are guides for informal visits, visitors may sit in on classes, and stay overnight. To schedule a visit, contact the Admissions Office.

Financial Aid: In 2013-2014, 90% of all full-time freshmen and 90% of continuing full-time students received some form of financial aid. 95% of all full-time freshmen and 69% of continuing full-time students received need-based aid. The average freshman award was $29,150. Need-based scholarships or need-based grants averaged $25,580 ($32,000 maximum); need-based self-help aid (loans and jobs) averaged $4,687 ($7,000 maximum); and other non-need-based awards and non-need-based scholarships averaged $19,000 ($30,000 maximum). 69% of undergraduate students work part-time. Average annual earnings from campus work are $1404. The average financial indebtedness of the 2013 graduate was $35,000. Ursinus is a member of CSS. The CSS/Profile and FAFSA are required. The deadline for filing freshman financial aid applications for fall entry is February 15.

International Students: There are 12 international students enrolled. The school actively recruits these students. They must take the TOEFL with a minimum score of 80 on the Internet-based version (iBT). They must also take the SAT or ACT.

Computers: All students may access the system. There are no time limits and no fees.

Graduates: From July 1, 2012 to June 30, 2013, 339 bachelor's degrees were awarded. The most popular majors were biology (16%), business and economics (13%), and psychology (9%). 60 companies recruited on campus in 2012-2013. In an average class, 76% graduate in 4 years or less, 80% graduate in 5 years or less, and 82% graduate in 6 years or less. Of the 2012 graduating class, 30% were enrolled in graduate school within 6 months of graduation, and 65% were employed.

Admissions Contact: Dana Matassino, Director of Admissions. E-Mail: *admissions@ursinus.edu* Web: *www.ursinus.edu*

VILLANOVA UNIVERSITY — E-3

Villanova, PA 19085 — **(610) 519-4000; (610) 519-6450**

Full-time: 3100 men, 3384 women	**Faculty:** n/av; IIA, +$
Part-time: 252 men, 243 women	**Ph.D.s:** 89%
Graduate: 1820 men, 1835 women	**Student/Faculty:** 12 to 1
Year: semesters, summer session	**Tuition:** $44,580
Application Deadline: January 15	**Room & Board:** $11,856
Freshman Class: n/av	
SAT CR/M/W: 640/670/640	**ACT:** 30 — **MOST COMPETITIVE**

Since 1842, Villanova University's Augustinian Catholic intellectual tradition has been the cornerstone of an academic community in which students learn to think critically, act compassionately and succeed while serving others. There are more than 10,000 undergraduate, graduate and law students in the University's five colleges – the College of Liberal Arts and Sciences, the Villanova School of Business, the College of Engineering, the College of Nursing and the Villanova University School of Law. As students grow intellectually, Villanova prepares them to become ethical leaders who create positive change everywhere life takes them. There are 4 undergraduate schools and 5 graduate schools. In addition to regional accreditation, Villanova has baccalaureate program accreditation with AACSB, ABET, and NLN. The 2 libraries contain 1.2 million volumes, 900,000 microform items, 7,200 audio/video tapes/CDs/DVDs, and subscribe to 16,720 periodicals including electronic. Computerized library services include interlibrary loans, database searching, Internet access, and Wi-Fi capability. Special learning facilities include an art gallery, radio station, TV station, 1 observatory. The 260-acre campus is in a suburban area 12 miles west of Philadelphia. Including any residence halls, there are 69 buildings.

Student Life: 77% of undergraduates are from out of state, mostly the Middle Atlantic. Students are from 46 states, 50 foreign countries, and Canada. 51% are from public schools. 76% are White; 70% are Catholic; 12% Protestant. The average age of freshmen is 18; all undergraduates, 20. 6% do not continue beyond their first year; 94% remain to graduate.

Housing: 4500 students can be accommodated in college housing, which includes single-sex and coed dorms and on-campus apartments. learning communities for freshmen and 1 special sophomore residence hall, a Service Learning Community, and a 24-hour quiet study hall. On-campus housing is available on a lottery system for upperclassmen. 70% of students live on campus; of those, 85% remain on campus on weekends. Upperclassmen may keep cars.

Activities: 18% of men belong to 13 national fraternities; 39% of women belong to 14 national sororities. There are 265 groups on campus, including Day of Service); multicultural; Service and Advocacy, Special Olympics, art, band, cheerleading, choir, chorale, chorus, communications, computers, dance, debate, drama, drill team, environmental, ethnic, film, forensics, gay, honors, international, jazz band, literary magazine, marching band, musical theater, newspaper, pep band, photography, political, professional, radio and TV, religious, social, social service, student government, university service (blue key ambassadors, and yearbook. Popular campus events include Special Olympics, Hoops Mania, Diwahni, Diwali, and Holi.

Sports: There are 11 intercollegiate sports for men and 13 for women, and 10 intramural sports for men and 10 for women. Facilities include a 400-meter outdoor track, 1 swimming pool, weight rooms, a field house, basketball and volleyball courts, softball field, 2 soccer fields and tennis courts. The football stadium seats 12,500; the pavilion, 6,500. The soocer complex seats 1,000; the softball field seats 250.

Disabled Students: 90% of the campus is accessible. Facilities include wheelchair ramps, elevators, special parking, specially equipped restrooms, special class scheduling, lowered drinking fountains, lowered telephones, a specially equipped van for campus transportation, and proximity card readers for several buildings with automatic doors.

Services: Counseling and information services are available, as is tutoring in some subjects. There is a reader service for the blind. Tutoring is open to all students and is not particular to students with disabilities. Some tutoring is offered through individual departments and colleges for first and second year courses. There is a writing center and Math Center for all students. Study skills and academic coaching is available to all students.

Campus Safety and Security: Measures include 24-hour foot and vehicle patrol, emergency notification system, self-defense education, and security escort services. There are shuttle buses, emergency telephones, lighted pathways/sidewalks, and controlled access to dorms/residences.

Programs of Study: Villanova confers B.A., B.S., B.B.A., B.S.N. and B.I.S. degrees. Associate, master's, and doctoral degrees are also awarded. Bachelor's degrees are awarded in AGRICULTURE (environmental studies), BIOLOGICAL SCIENCE (biochemistry and biology/biological science), BUSINESS (accounting, banking and finance, business administration and management, business economics, international business management, management information systems, marketing/retailing/merchandising, and real estate), COMMUNICATIONS AND THE ARTS (art history and appreciation, classics, communications, English, French, Italian, and Spanish), COMPUTER AND PHYSICAL SCIENCE (astronomy, astrophysics, chemistry, computer science, information sciences and systems, mathematics, physics, and science), EDUCATION (secondary education), ENGINEERING AND ENVIRONMENTAL DESIGN (chemical engineering, civil engineering, computer engineering, electrical/electronics engineering, environmental science, and mechanical engineering), HEALTH PROFESSIONS (nursing), SOCIAL SCIENCE (criminal justice, crosscultural studies, economics, gender studies, geography, history, humanities, interdisciplinary studies, Latin American studies, liberal arts/general studies, philosophy, political science/government, psychology, religion, sociology, and theological studies). Nursing, engineering, and business have the largest enrollments.

Required: All students are required to take core courses in humanities, Augustine and Culture, social science, religious studies, natural sciences, philosophy, and math. Students must complete a minimum of 122 credit hours and achieve at least a 2.0 overall G.P.A.

Special: Internships are available for each college in the Philadelphia area as well as in New York City and Washington D.C. Students may study abroad worldwide. Villanova offers a Washington semester, an accelerated degree program in biology for allied health program, dual majors, a general studies degree, and credit by exam. There are 36 national honor societies, including Phi Beta Kappa, and a freshman honors program.

Faculty/Classroom: 55% of faculty are male; 45% are female. 90% teach undergraduates, 74% do research, and 74% do both. Graduate students teach 1% of introductory courses. The average class size in a regular course is 22.

Admissions: The SAT scores for the 2013-2014 freshman class were: Critical Reading--2% below 500, 23% between 500 and 599, 54% between 600 and 699, and 21% between 700 and 800; Math--2% below 500, 13% between 500 and 599, 50% between 600 and 699, and 35% between 700 and 800; Writing--3% below 500, 20% between 500 and 599, 53% between 600 and 699, and 24% between 700 and 800. The ACT scores were 2% between 24 and 26, 36% between 27 and 28, and 62% above 28. 26 freshmen graduated first in their class.

Requirements: The SAT or ACT is required. The ACT Optional Writing test is also required. Applicants must be graduates of an accredited secondary school and should have completed 16 academic units. The specific courses required vary according to college. A GED is accepted. An essay is required. AP and CLEP credits are accepted. Important factors in the admissions decision are leadership record, advanced placement or honors courses, and evidence of special talent.

Procedure: Freshmen are admitted fall. Entrance exams should be taken by December of the senior year. There is a deferred admissions plan. Early decision applications should be filed by November 1; regular applications, by January 15 for fall entry. The fall 2013 application fee was $80. Notification of early decision is sent December 20; regular decision, April 1. 1962 applicants were on the 2013 waiting list; 350 were admitted. Applications are accepted online.

Transfer: 66 transfer students enrolled in 2012-2013. 60 of 122 credits required for the bachelor's degree must be completed at Villanova.

Visiting: There are regularly scheduled orientations for prospective students, Group Admission Presentations and Campus Tours are conducted throughout the year. Please consult our admission web site for a calendar and to register for a visit. There are guides for informal visits and visitors may sit in on classes. To schedule a visit, contact the Office of University Admission.

Financial Aid: In 2013-2014, 66% of all full-time freshmen and 68% of continuing full-time students received some form of financial aid. 51% of all full-time freshmen and 45% of continuing full-time students received need-based aid. The average freshman award was $34,428. Need-based scholarships or need-based grants averaged $22,264 ($43,840 maximum); need-based self-help aid (loans and jobs) averaged $5,064 ($7,500 maximum); non-need-based athletic scholarships averaged $1,690 ($43,840 maximum); and other non-need-based awards and non-need-based scholarships averaged $5,410 ($56,190 maximum). 18% of undergraduate students work part-time. Average annual earnings from campus work are $1378. The average financial indebtedness of the 2013 graduate was $40,354. Villanova is a member of CSS. The CSS/Profile, FAFSA, the state aid form, and the college's own financial statement, and parent and student federal income tax return and W2s are required. The deadline for filing freshman financial aid applications for fall entry is February 7.

International Students: There are 127 international students enrolled. The school actively recruits these students. They must take the TOEFL with a minimum score of 550 on the paper-based TOEFL (PBT) or 81 on the Internet-based version (iBT). They must also take the SAT or ACT.

Computers: All students may access the system. There are no time limits and no fees.

Graduates: From July 1, 2012 to June 30, 2013, 1790 bachelor's degrees were awarded. The most popular majors were business/marketing (29%), nursing (11%), and social sciences (10%). 261 companies recruited on campus in 2012-2013. In an average class, 86% graduate in 4 years or less, 90% graduate in 5 years or less, and 90% graduate in 6 years or less.

Admissions Contact: Michael Gaynor, Director of Admission. E-Mail: *gotovu@villanova.edu* Web: *www.admission.villanova.edu*

WASHINGTON AND JEFFERSON COLLEGE — A-3

Washington, PA 15301 — (724) 223-6025; (888) 926-3529; (724) 223-6534

Full-time: 649 men, 669 women	**Faculty:** 114; IIB, av$
Part-time: 5 men, 5 women	**Ph.D.s:** 92%
Graduate: n/av	**Student/Faculty:** 10 to 1
Year: 4-1-4, summer session	**Tuition:** $39,710
Application Deadline: March 1	**Room & Board:** $10,280
Freshman Class: 7176 applied, 2851 accepted, 326 enrolled	
SAT CR/M: 560/581 — **ACT:** 25	**VERY COMPETITIVE**

Washington & Jefferson College, founded in 1781, is a highly selective, residential, private liberal arts and sciences college located in the rolling hills of Pennsylvania, thirty minutes from Pittsburgh. The College has a ninety-one percent placement rate (employment or graduate school) within six months of graduation. The 4 libraries contain 188,195 volumes, 15,610 microform items, 10,089 audio/video tapes/CDs/DVDs, and subscribe to 43,882 periodicals including electronic. Computerized library services include interlibrary loans, database searching, Internet access, and Wi-Fi capability. Special learning facilities include an art gallery, radio station, biological field station, microplate reader, cell culture labs, isolator lab, X-ray diffraction unit, neuropsychology lab, atomic absorption unit, nuclear magnetic resonance lab, refrigerated centrifuge, global learning unit, language lab, spectrometers, and laser scanning confocal microscope facility. The 60-acre campus is in a small town 27 miles southwest of Pittsburgh, PA. Including any residence halls, there are 53 buildings.

Student Life: 73% of undergraduates are from Pennsylvania. Others are from 37 states, and 18 foreign countries. 83% are from public schools. 83% are White. The average age of freshmen is 18; all undergraduates, 20.

Housing: 1385 students can be accommodated in college housing, which includes single-sex and coed dorms and on-campus apartments. In addition, there are special-interest houses, fraternity houses, sorority houses, on-campus suites, special housing for international students, wellness housing, civics house, pet dorm, quiet house and green house. On-campus housing is guaranteed for all 4 years. 94% of students live on campus; of those, 80% remain on campus on weekends. All students may keep cars.

Activities: 43% of men belong to 6 national fraternities; 46% of women belong to 4 national sororities. There are 79 groups on campus, including and zumba, Asian culture association, dance team, equestrian club, figure skating, film club, Indian student association, Latino culture association, Lion's club, martial arts, pre-vet club, ski club, star wars club, UBELONG, yoga, young entrepreneurs society, art, band, Black student union, cheerleading, chess, choir, chorale, chorus, computers, dance, debate, drama, environmental, ethnic, film, gay, honors, international, jazz band, literary magazine, musical theater, newspaper, pep band, photography, political, professional, radio and TV, religious, social, social service, student government, and yearbook. Popular campus events include International Week, Street Fair (DubJam), Holiday Light-up Night, President's Got Talent Show and Involvement Expo.

Sports: There are 12 intercollegiate sports for men and 12 for women, and 26 intramural sports for men and 26 for women. Facilities include Swimming and diving pools, an all-weather track, a weight room, football, baseball, softball, soccer/lacrosse fields, and basketball, volleyball, squash, and racquetball courts. The stadium seats 3500, the gymnasium 2388.

Disabled Students: 48% of the campus is accessible. Facilities include wheelchair ramps, elevators, special parking, specially equipped restrooms, special class scheduling, lowered drinking fountains, and special housing.

Services: Counseling and information services are available, as is tutoring in most subjects, Accounting, biology, chemistry, computing and information studies, economics, logic, mathematics, modern languages, physics, psychology, and writing.

Campus Safety and Security: Measures include 24-hour foot and vehicle patrol, emergency notification system, self-defense education, and security escort services. There are emergency telephones, lighted pathways/sidewalks, controlled access to dorms/residences, blue light emergency phones; security cameras monitored 24/7.

Programs of Study: W & J confers B.A. degrees. Master's degrees are also awarded. Bachelor's degrees are awarded in AGRICULTURE (environmental studies), BIOLOGICAL SCIENCE (biochemistry, biology/biological science, biophysics, and cell biology), BUSINESS (accounting, business administration and management, and international business management), COMMUNICATIONS AND THE ARTS (art, communication rhetoric/communication, English, French, German, music, Spanish, and theatre arts), COMPUTER AND PHYSICAL SCIENCE (chemistry, computer information technology, mathematics, and physics), EDUCATION (art education and education), SOCIAL SCIENCE (economics, history, interdisciplinary studies, international studies, philosophy, political science/government, psychology, and sociology). Biology, chemistry, and political science are the strongest academically. Business/accounting, psychology, and history have the largest enrollments.

Required: Students must complete the general education requirement of at least 8 courses in 4 divisions. Other requirements include phys ed, first-year seminar, freshman composition, foreign language, cultural diversity, oral communication, quantitative reasoning, academic skills, and 8 to 10 elective courses. A total of 34 courses, with 8 to 10 courses in the major, is required for graduation, as is a 2.0 GPA.

Special: The college offers study abroad in 22 countries (Australia, Austria, Chile, China, Denmark, Ecuador, Egypt, France, the Gambia, Germany, Hong Kong, Ireland, Italy, Japan, Mexico, Netherlands, Norway, Russia, South Africa, South Korea, Spain, United Kingdom), internships in all majors, dual and student-designed majors, credit by exam, and pass/fail options. Concentrations are offered in entrepreneurial studies, film and video studies, graphic design, professional writing and rhetoric. Special programs are offered in education, biological physics, engineering, mind, brain, and behavior, pre-law, ROTC and pre-health professions (pre-physical therapy, pre-occupational therapy, pre-pharmacy, pre-veterinary and pre-dentistry). The college also offers emphasis in financial economics, human resource management, and neuroscience. The BA in financial economics is recognized by the CFA Institute, one of only 77 programs in the U.S. to have been awarded this recognition. Students can take electives in Arabic, Chinese, earth and space science, Japanese, physical education, Russian, and interdisciplinary courses. There is a 3-3 law program with Duquesne University and the University of Pittsburgh, medicine program with Temple University School of Medicine, optometry program with Pennsylvania College of Optometry at Salus University, physician assistant program with Saint Francis University and Chatham University and a physical therapy program with Chatham University. In addition, there is 3-2 engineering program with Case Western Reserve University, Washington University and Columbia University. A Washington semester is available with American University. W&J's proprietary Magellan Project provides financial support for students who wish to pursue summer internships or independent study abroad, making these opportunities available to every W&J student. There are 23 national honor societies, including Phi Beta Kappa, a freshman honors program, and 18 departmental honors programs.

Faculty/Classroom: 55% of faculty are male; 45% are female. All teach and do research. No introductory courses are taught by graduate students. The average class size in an introductory lecture is 16; in a laboratory is 14; and in a regular course is 16.

Admissions: 40% of the 2013-2014 applicants were accepted. The SAT scores for the 2013-2014 freshman class were: Critical Reading--15% below 500, 55% between 500 and 599, 27% between 600 and 699, and 3% between 700 and 800; Math--11% below 500, 50% between 500 and 599, 33% between 600 and 699, and 6% between 700 and 800. The ACT scores were 6% below 21, 16% between 21 and 23, 27% between 24 and 26, 15% between 27 and 28, and 9% above 28. 53% of the current freshmen were in the top fifth of their class; 84% were in the top two fifths. 9 freshmen graduated first in their class.

Requirements: The SAT or ACT is recommended. Applicants must complete 15 academic credits or Carnegie units, including 3 credits of English and math, 2 of foreign language, 1 of history, social science, or nautural science and 6 or more academic courses from the aforementioned areas. An essay is required and interviews are recommended. A GED is accepted. AP credits are accepted. Important factors in the admissions decision are advanced placement or honors courses, evidence of special talent, and personality/intangible qualities.

Procedure: Freshmen are admitted to all sessions. Entrance exams should be taken junior or senior year. There are early decision, early admissions, deferred admissions, and rolling admissions plans. Early decision applications should be filed by December 1; regular applications, by March 1 for fall entry; December 15 for winter entry; and January 15 for spring entry, along with a $25 fee. Notification of early decision is sent December 15; regular decision, April 1. 11 early decision candidates were accepted for the 2013-2014 class. 23 applicants were on the 2013 waiting list; 5

were admitted. Applications are accepted online. Application fees are waived if application is completed online.

Transfer: 28 transfer students enrolled in 2012-2013. Applicants must have a college GPA of at least 2.5. Additionally, transfer students are required to submit an official high school transcript with standardized test results from the SAT or ACT unless they are applying score optional. 64 of 136 credits required for the bachelor's degree must be completed at Washington and Jefferson College.

Visiting: There are regularly scheduled orientations for prospective students, Student visits include a general session, departmental meetings, preprofessional meetings, a financial aid meeting, and class scheduling. There are guides for informal visits, visitors may sit in on classes, and stay overnight. To schedule a visit, contact Lucy Johnson at (724) 223-6025.

Financial Aid: In 2013-2014, 100% of all full-time freshmen and 98% of continuing full-time students received some form of financial aid. 75% of all full-time freshmen and 71% of continuing full-time students received need-based aid. The average freshman award was $30,100. Need-based scholarships or need-based grants averaged $9,030; need-based self-help aid (loans and jobs) averaged $3,311; and other non-need-based awards and non-need-based scholarships averaged $17,759. 41% of undergraduate students work part-time. Average annual earnings from campus work are $1100. The average financial indebtedness of the 2013 graduate was $27,370. The FAFSA is required. The priority date for freshman financial aid applications for fall entry is February 15.

International Students: There are 41 international students enrolled. The school actively recruits these students. They must take the TOEFL with a minimum score of 580 on the paper-based TOEFL (PBT) or 85 on the Internet-based version (iBT).

Computers: All students may access the system any time. There are no time limits and no fees.

Graduates: From July 1, 2012 to June 30, 2013, 330 bachelor's degrees were awarded. The most popular majors were business administration/accounting (19%), psychology (17%), and history (7%). 41 companies recruited on campus in 2012-2013. In an average class, 2% graduate in 3 years or less, 73% graduate in 4 years or less, 75% graduate in 5 years or less, and 77% graduate in 6 years or less. Of the 2012 graduating class, 40% were enrolled in graduate school within 6 months of graduation, and 72% were employed.

Admissions Contact: Alton E. Newell, Vice President for Enrollment . E-Mail: *admission@washjeff.edu* Web: *www.washjeff.edu*

WAYNESBURG UNIVERSITY B-4

Waynesburg, PA 15370 **(724) 852-3248**
(800) 225-7393; (724) 627-8124

Full-time: 595 men, 886 women	**Faculty:** 74; IIB, --$
Part-time: 23 men, 94 women	**Ph.D.s:** 65%
Graduate: 181 men, 411 women	**Student/Faculty:** 21 to 1
Year: semesters, summer session	**Tuition:** $20,540
Application Deadline: open	**Room & Board:** $8560

Freshman Class: 1783 applied, 1573 accepted, 407 enrolled
SAT or ACT: required

COMPETITIVE

Founded in 1849 by the Cumberland Presbyterian Church, Waynesburg University is a private comprehensive Christian university offering doctoral, graduate, and undergraduate programs in more than 70 academic concentrations. There is one graduate school. In addition to regional accreditation, Waynesburg has baccalaureate program accreditation with TEAC. The library contains 93,000 volumes, 5,400 audio/video tapes/CDs/DVDs, and subscribes to 757 periodicals including electronic. Computerized library services include interlibrary loans, database searching, and Internet access. Special learning facilities include an art gallery, natural history museum, radio station, and TV station. The 30-acre campus is in a small town 50 miles south of Pittsburgh. Including any residence halls, there are 29 buildings.

Student Life: 80% of undergraduates are from Pennsylvania. Others are from 33 states, and 4 foreign countries. 90% are from public schools. 79% are White; 15% race unknown. 37% are Protestant; 21% Unknown; 18% Catholic. The average age of freshmen is 18; all undergraduates, 22. 19% do not continue beyond their first year; 53% remain to graduate.

Housing: 1060 students can be accommodated in college housing, which includes single-sex and coed dorms. On-campus housing is guaranteed for all 4 years. 67% of students live on campus; of those, 33% remain on campus on weekends. Alcohol is not permitted. Upperclassmen may keep cars.

Activities: There are no fraternities or sororities. There are 53 groups on campus, including band, cheerleading, choir, chorale, chorus, drama, environmental, ethnic, film, honors, international, jazz band, literary magazine, marching band, musical theater, newspaper, orchestra, pep band, photography, professional, radio and TV, religious, social, social service, student government, and yearbook. Popular campus events include Spring Weekend Formal, VIP Forum and Fine Arts Series.

Sports: There are 9 intercollegiate sports for men and 9 for women, and 7 intramural sports for men and 7 for women. Facilities include a 1500-seat stadium, a 1500-seat gym, a 250-seat arena, a fitness center, basketball and racquetball courts, wrestling and weight rooms, a golf driving net, 3 all-weather tennis courts, and table tennis and billiards tables.

Disabled Students: All of the campus is accessible. Facilities include wheelchair ramps, elevators, special parking, specially equipped restrooms, special class scheduling, and lowered drinking fountains.

Services: Counseling and information services are available, as is tutoring in every subject. There is remedial writing.

Campus Safety and Security: Measures include 24-hour foot and vehicle patrol, emergency notification system, self-defense education, and security escort services. There are emergency telephones, lighted pathways/sidewalks, and 24-hour security access.

Programs of Study: Waynesburg confers B.A., B.S., B.M.L., B.S.B.A., B.S.M.B. and B.S.N. degrees. Master's and doctoral degrees are also awarded. Bachelor's degrees are awarded in BIOLOGICAL SCIENCE (biology/biological science, forensic science, and marine biology), BUSINESS (accounting, entrepreneurial studies, finance, international business management, management science, and marketing/retailing/merchandising), COMMUNICATIONS AND THE ARTS (advertising, art, arts administration/management, broadcasting, communication rhetoric/communication, creative writing, English, graphic design, literature, multimedia, and public relations), COMPUTER AND PHYSICAL SCIENCE (chemistry, computer science, information sciences and systems, and mathematics), EDUCATION (athletic training, early childhood education, elementary education, middle school education, and special education), ENGINEERING AND ENVIRONMENTAL DESIGN (engineering and environmental science), HEALTH PROFESSIONS (exercise science, nursing, predentistry, premedicine, prephysical therapy, and preveterinary science), SOCIAL SCIENCE (biblical studies, criminal justice, history, human services, ministries, prelaw, psychology, social science, and sociology). Nursing, business, and education are the strongest academically. Nursing, business, communication, and criminal justice have the largest enrollments.

Required: To graduate, students must complete a minimum of 124 semester hours, including at least 30 in the major, with a minimum 2.0 GPA. Requirements include 15 credits of humanities and social and behavioral sciences, 8 of natural and physical sciences, 6 each of English and literature/arts, 3 credits each in math and computer science and 1 each of life skills, service learning, and Fiat Lux. Students must also pass an English usage and written competency test as well as a math test.

Special: The college offers internships, an accelerated degree program in marketing and business management, dual majors, a student-designed interdisciplinary major, credit for experience, non-degree study, and pass/fail options. There is a 3-2 engineering degree program with Washington University and Penn State University and a 3-1 in marine biology with Florida Institute of Technology or University of North Carolina Wilmington. A variety of study abroad experiences are available in countries around the world. There are 17 national honor societies and a freshman honors program.

Faculty/Classroom: 54% of faculty are male; 46% are female. No introductory courses are taught by graduate students. The average class size in an introductory lecture is 20; in a laboratory is 15; and in a regular course is 22.

Admissions: 88% of the 2013-2014 applicants were accepted.

Requirements: The SAT or ACT is required. Applicants must be graduates of an accredited secondary school or have a GED certificate and have completed 16 academic credits, including 4 in English, 3 in math, and 2 in sciences, history, or social studies. A GPA of 2.8 is required. AP and CLEP credits are accepted. Important factors in the admissions decision are advanced placement or honors courses, recommendations by school officials, and extracurricular activities record.

Procedure: Freshmen are admitted to all sessions. Entrance exams should be taken in April of the junior year or December of the senior year. There is a rolling admissions plan. Application deadlines are open. Application fee is $20. Applications are accepted online.

Transfer: 45 transfer students enrolled in 2012-2013. Students must submit a high school transcript and complete transcripts from all colleges previously attended. 45 of 124 credits required for the bachelor's degree must be completed at Waynesburg.

Visiting: There are regularly scheduled orientations for prospective students, including visits with faculty, students, administrators, and financial aid officers, and a tour of the campus. There are guides for informal visits, visitors may sit in on classes, and stay overnight. To schedule a visit, contact the Admissions Office.

Financial Aid: In 2013-2014, 97% of all full-time freshmen and 93% of continuing full-time students received some form of financial aid. 90% of all full-time freshmen and 87% of continuing full-time students received need-based aid. The average freshman award was $19,000. Need-based scholarships or need-based grants averaged $6,000 ($29,100 maximum); need-based self-help aid (loans and jobs) averaged $5,500 ($31,500 maximum); and other non-need-based awards and non-need-based scholarships averaged $5,000 ($29,100 maximum). 25% of undergraduate students work part-time. Average annual earnings from campus work are $1500. The average financial indebtedness of the 2013 graduate was $19,000. The FAFSA is required. The priority date for freshman financial aid applications for fall entry is March 15. The deadline for filing freshman financial aid applications for fall entry is rolling.

International Students: There are 4 international students enrolled. The school actively recruits these students. They must take the TOEFL with a minimum score of 557 on the paper-based TOEFL (PBT) or 84 on the Internet-based version (iBT).

Computers: All students may access the system. There are no time limits and no fees.

Graduates: From July 1, 2012 to June 30, 2013, 383 bachelor's degrees were awarded. The most popular majors were health professions & related programs (37%), business/marketing (11%), and criminal justice (8%). In an average class, 45% graduate in 4 years or less, 52% graduate in 5 years or less, and 53% graduate in 6 years or less. Of the 2012 graduating class, 16% were enrolled in graduate school within 6 months of graduation, and 70% were employed.

Admissions Contact: Robin L. King, Sr. V.P. Enrollment and Univ Relation. E-Mail: *admissions@waynesburg.edu* Web: *www.waynesburg.edu*

WEST CHESTER UNIVERSITY OF PENNSYLVANIA E-3

West Chester, PA 19383 (610) 436-3411
(877) 315-2165; (610) 436-2907

Full-time: 4969 men, 7515 women	**Faculty:** n/av; IIA, av$
Part-time: 573 men, 654 women	**Ph.D.s:** n/av
Graduate: 667 men, 1467 women	**Student/Faculty:** n/av
Year: semesters, summer session	**Tuition:** $8850 ($18,784)
Application Deadline: open	**Room & Board:** $7986

Freshman Class: 13438 applied, 6922 accepted, 2298 enrolled
SAT CR/M/W: 530/550/530

COMPETITIVE

West Chester University, founded in 1871, is a public institution that is part of the Pennsylvania State System of Higher Education. It offers programs through the Colleges of Arts and Sciences, Business and Public Affairs, Education, Health Sciences, and Visual and Performing Arts. There are 5 undergraduate schools and 5 graduate schools. In addition to regional accreditation, West Chester University has baccalaureate program accreditation with AACSB, ABET, CSWE, NASAD, NASM, and NCATE. The library contains 1.4 million volumes, 926,544 microform items, 67,347 audio/video tapes/CDs/DVDs, and subscribes to 78,192 periodicals including electronic. Computerized library services include interlibrary loans, database searching, Internet access, and Wi-Fi capability. Special learning facilities include an art gallery, planetarium, radio station, TV station, art gallery, radio station, TV station, planetarium, observatory, an herbarium, a speech and hearing clinic, an autism clinic, a center for government and community affairs, a 151-acre natural area for environmental studies, mineral museum, music library, fully-equipped food preparation laboratory for nutrition and dietetics program, state-of-the-art nursing skills laboratory, athletic training rooms, HEAT (Heat Illness Evaluation Avoidance and Treatment) institute, dance studio, poetry center, outdoor classroom, native plant, ornithology, microsoft demonstration and application center. The 409-acre campus is in a suburban area 25 miles west of Philadelphia. Including any residence halls, there are 115 buildings.

Student Life: 87% of undergraduates are from Pennsylvania. Others are from 28 states, 67 foreign countries, and Canada. 84% are from public schools. 81% are White. The average age of freshmen is 18; all undergraduates, 21. 13% do not continue beyond their first year; 69% remain to graduate.

Housing: 4866 students can be accommodated in college housing, which includes coed dorms and on-campus apartments. In addition, there are special-interest houses, International student sections, and disabled students. On-campus housing is available on a first-come and first-served basis. 61% of students commute. Alcohol is not permitted. Upperclassmen may keep cars.

Activities: 10% of men belong to 11 national fraternities; 13% of women belong to 15 national sororities. There are 252 groups on campus, including art, band, cheerleading, chess, choir, chorale, chorus, communications, computers, dance, debate, drama, drill team, drum and bugle corps, environmental, ethnic, film, forensics, gay, honors, international, jazz band, literary magazine, marching band, musical theater, newspaper, opera, orchestra, pep band, photography, political, professional, radio and TV, religious, social, social service, student government, symphony, and yearbook. Popular campus events include Martin Luther King Day, University Fesitval, Student Involvement Fair, Homecoming, Greek Week and Spring Weekend.

Sports: There are 10 intercollegiate sports for men and 14 for women, and 16 intramural sports for men and 16 for women. Facilities include A 2500-seat field house, a gymnastics room, six gyms, 2 swimming pools and diving well, several practice and game fields, a softball complex, 12 tennis courts, 2,500 seat basketball facility, a 500-seat baseball stadium, 7500-seat stadium, 500 seat field hockey/lacrosse complex two fitness centers, fi mile track, climbing wall, two recreational outdoor pursuits education (ROPE) course.

Disabled Students: Facilities include wheelchair ramps, elevators, special parking, specially equipped restrooms, special class scheduling, lowered drinking fountains, and lowered telephones.

Services: Counseling and information services are available, as is tutoring in some subjects, 100- and 200-level general education courses There is a reader service for the blind, and remedial math, reading, and writing.

Campus Safety and Security: Measures include 24-hour foot and vehicle patrol, emergency notification system, self-defense education, and security escort services. There are shuttle buses, emergency telephones, lighted pathways/sidewalks, controlled access to dorms/residences, bike patrol, card access/security alarms, in all resident halls and resident security officers are posted in residence halls over night and crime prevention programming and alcohol-free alternative events.

Programs of Study: West Chester University confers B.A., B.S., B.F.A., B.Mus., B.S.Ed., B.S.N. and B.S.W. degrees. Master's and doctoral degrees are also awarded. Bachelor's degrees are awarded in AGRICULTURE (environmental studies), BIOLOGICAL SCIENCE (biochemistry, biology/biological science, cell biology, ecology, environmental biology, marine science, microbiology, molecular biology, and nutrition), BUSINESS (accounting, banking and finance, business administration and management, and marketing management), COMMUNICATIONS AND THE ARTS (art, communications, dance, dramatic arts, English, French, German, Latin, literature, music, music history and appreciation, music performance, music theory and composition, musical theater, performing arts, piano performance, Russian, Spanish, studio art, visual and performing arts, and voice), COMPUTER AND PHYSICAL SCIENCE (actuarial science, chemistry, computer science, earth science, geology, geoscience, mathematics, mathematics - actuarial concentration, mathematics/computational, physics, and statistics), EDUCATION (athletic training, early childhood education, elementary education, English education, health education, mathematics education, middle school education, music education, physical education, science education, secondary education, social studies education, and special education), ENGINEERING AND ENVIRONMENTAL DESIGN (engineering physics and urban planning technology), HEALTH PROFESSIONS (exercise science, health, health science, medical technology, nursing, pharmaceutical science, predentistry, premedicine, prephysical therapy, public health, respiratory therapy, and speech pathology/audiology), SOCIAL SCIENCE (American studies, anthropology, criminal justice, dietetics, economics, forensic studies, geography, history, international relations, liberal arts/general studies, philosophy, philosophy and religion, political science/government, prelaw, psychology, social work, sociology, and women's studies). Premedical is the strongest academically. PK-4 early grades prep, psychology, nutrition and dietetics have the largest enrollments.

Required: All students must satisfy requirements in English composition, math, interdisciplinary study, and phys ed. Distribution requirements include 9 hours each of science, behavioral and social science, and humanities, and 3 hours in the arts. A total of 120 (126 or 124 for some degrees) credit hours and a 2.0 GPA are required. Students arrange study abroad programs through a third party. There are also several faculty-led study programs.

Special: There is cross-registration with Cheyney University and a 3-2 engineering program with Pennsylvania State University and Philadelphia University. The university offers some accelerated degree programs, a Washington semester, some student-designed majors, credit by examination for life, military, and work experience, and pass/fail options. There are 29 national honor societies and a freshman honors program.

Faculty/Classroom: No introductory courses are taught by graduate students.

Admissions: 52% of the 2013-2014 applicants were accepted. The SAT scores for the 2013-2014 freshman class were: Critical Reading--28% below 500, 55% between 500 and 599, 16% between 600 and 699, and 1% between 700 and 800; Math--20% below 500, 56% between 500 and 599, 22% between 600 and 699, and 2% between 700 and 800; Writing--32% below 500, 51% between 500 and 599, 17% between 600 and 699, and 1% between 700 and 800. 22% of the current freshmen were in the top fifth of their class; 42% were in the top two fifths. 3 freshmen graduated first in their class.

Requirements: The SAT is required. A college preparatory curriculum in high school, standardized test scores from the SAT, and a personal statement is required. An interview is required for athletic tranning, premedical, and pharmaceutical product development programs, and an audition is required for music. Specific course prerequisites depend on major selection. Additional documentation is required of candidates for the summer academic development program. The GED is acceptable. West Chester University requires applicants to be in the upper 60% of their class. A GPA of 3.0 is required. AP and CLEP credits are accepted.

Procedure: Freshmen are admitted fall and spring. Entrance exams should be taken in spring of the junior year or fall of the senior year. There is a rolling admissions plan. Application deadlines are open. Application fee is $45. Notification is sent on a rolling basis. 561 applicants were on the 2013 waiting list. Applications are accepted online.

Transfer: 1349 transfer students enrolled in 2012-2013. Applicants should have earned at least 30 credits and must have a recommended GPA of at least 2.0 for admissions consideration. Some departments require a higher GPA and specific course requirements. Transfers who have earned fewer than 30 credits must submit a high school transcript and standardized test scores. 30 of 120 credits required for the bachelor's degree must be completed at West Chester University.

Visiting: There are regularly scheduled orientations for prospective students, Campus tours offered four times daily and on selected dates we offer admissions information sessions. During the fall we host two preview days on Saturdays for prospective students and accepted student days on Saturdays in March and April. Our large. There are guides for informal visits and visitors may sit in on class. Contact the Admissions Office.

Financial Aid: In 2013-2014, 79% of all full-time freshmen and 75% of continuing full-time students received some form of financial aid. 67% of all full-time freshmen and 61% of continuing full-time students received need-based aid. The average freshman award was $6,069. Need-based scholarships or need-based grants averaged $5,204 ($12,326 maximum); need-based self-help aid (loans and jobs) averaged $2,980 ($9,900 maximum); non-need-based athletic scholarships averaged $2,400 ($10,000 maximum); and other non-need-based awards and non-need-based scholarships averaged $3,591. 7% of undergraduate students work part-time. Average annual earnings from campus work are $3500. The average financial indebtedness of the 2013 graduate was $30,396. West Chester University is a member of CSS. The FAFSA is required. The priority date for freshman financial aid applications for fall entry is March 1.

International Students: There are 41 international students enrolled. The school actively recruits these students. The SAT is recommended.

Computers: All students may access the system. There are no time limits and no fees.

Graduates: From July 1, 2012 to June 30, 2013, 2972 bachelor's degrees were awarded. The most popular majors were liberal studies (7%), psychology (6%), and communications studies (5%). 161 companies recruited on campus in 2012-2013. In an average class, 42% graduate in 4 years or less, 63% graduate in 5 years or less, and 69% graduate in 6 years or less.

Admissions Contact: Marsha Haug, Director of Admissions. E-Mail: *ugadmiss@wcupa.edu* Web: *www.wcupa.edu*

WESTMINSTER COLLEGE B-2

New Wilmington, PA 16172 (724) 946-7100
(800) 942-8033; (724) 946-6171

Full-time: 510 men, 905 women	**Faculty:** 100; IIB, --$
Part-time: 20 men, 34 women	**Ph.D.s:** 83%
Graduate: 43 men, 86 women	**Student/Faculty:** 14 to 1
Year: semesters, summer session	**Tuition:** $24,220
Application Deadline: open	**Room & Board:** $7070
Freshman Class: 1302 applied, 1006 accepted, 359 enrolled	
SAT: required	**ACT:** 24 **COMPETITIVE+**

Westminster College, founded in 1852, is a private liberal arts institution related to the Presbyterian Church. In addition to regional accreditation, Westminster has baccalaureate program accreditation with NASM. The 2 libraries contain 283,070 volumes, 9,737 microform items, 14,251 audio/video tapes/CDs/DVDs, and subscribe to 848 periodicals including electronic. Computerized library services include interlibrary loans, database searching, Internet access, and Wi-Fi capability. Special learning facilities include an art gallery, planetarium, radio station, TV station, electron microscope labs in the science center, and a graphics computer center. The 350-acre campus is in a rural area 60 miles north of Pittsburgh. Including any residence halls, there are 25 buildings.

Student Life: 79% of undergraduates are from Pennsylvania. Others are from 23 states, and 1 foreign countries. 90% are from public schools. 97% are White. 56% are Protestant; 34% Catholic. The average age of freshmen is 18; all undergraduates, 20. 11% do not continue beyond their first year; 76% remain to graduate.

Housing: 1098 students can be accommodated in college housing, which includes single-sex dorms and on-campus apartments. In addition, there are fraternity houses, Some residence hall floors have 24-hour weekend visitation. On-campus housing is guaranteed for all 4 years. 90% of students live on campus; of those, 70% remain on campus on weekends. Alcohol is not permitted. All students may keep cars.

Activities: 33% of men belong to 5 national fraternities; 34% of women belong to 5 national sororities. There are 60 groups on campus, including band, cheerleading, choir, chorale, chorus, communications, dance, debate, drama, drill team, ethnic, forensics, gay, honors, jazz band, literary magazine, marching band, musical theater, newspaper, orchestra, pep band, political, radio and TV, religious, social, social service, student government, and symphony. Popular campus events include Mock Conventions, Mardi Gras, and Volleyrock.

Sports: There are 9 intercollegiate sports for men and 9 for women, and 7 intramural sports for men and 6 for women. Facilities include a natatorium, racquetball, tennis, and basketball courts, an all-weather track, and weight and aerobics rooms. Canoeing on the lake is available.

Disabled Students: 50% of the campus is accessible. Facilities include wheelchair ramps, elevators, special parking, specially equipped restrooms, and special class scheduling.

Services: Counseling and information services are available, as is tutoring in most subjects, through the learning center There is a reader service for the blind, and remedial math, reading, and writing.

Campus Safety and Security: Measures include 24-hour foot and vehicle patrol, self-defense education, and security escort services. There are shuttle buses, emergency telephones, and lighted pathways/sidewalks.

Programs of Study: Westminster confers B.A., B.S. and B.M. degrees. Master's degrees are also awarded. Bachelor's degrees are awarded in BIOLOGICAL SCIENCE (biology/biological science and molecular biology), BUSINESS (accounting, banking and finance, business administration and management, international business management, and marketing/ retailing/merchandising), COMMUNICATIONS AND THE ARTS (art, broadcasting, communications, dramatic arts, English, fine arts, French, German, Latin, music, music performance, music theory and composition, public relations, and Spanish), COMPUTER AND PHYSICAL SCIENCE (chemistry, computer science, mathematics, and physics), EDUCATION (Christian education, elementary education, guidance education, music education, and secondary education), HEALTH PROFESSIONS (predentistry and premedicine), SOCIAL SCIENCE (criminal justice, economics, history, international relations, philosophy, political science/government, prelaw, psychology, religion, religious music, social science, and sociology). Sciences, business, and education are the strongest academically and have the largest enrollments.

Required: First-year students are required to take Inquiry I and II, as well as writing and a speech course. Students must fulfill a distribution requirement by taking a course in one of each of the Intellectual Perspectives: Visual and Performing Arts, Quantitative Reasoning, Social Thought and Tradition, Humanity and Culture, Scientific Discovery, Foreign Language, and Religious and Philosophical Thought. A capstone experience in their major and community service are also required. Students must complete 132 semester hours with a minimum of 84 outside their majors, and have a minimum of 2.0 GPA in all courses. Majors require between 32 and 60 hours of coursework.

Special: The college offers internships, study abroad in many countries, a Washington semester, various dual and student-designed majors, a 3-2 engineering degree with Case Western Reserve, Pennsylvania State, and Washington Universities, London study at Regent's College, a 3-3 J.D. program with Duquesne, and nondegree study. There are 12 national honor societies and a freshman honors program.

Faculty/Classroom: 53% of faculty are male; 47% are female. All teach undergraduates. No introductory courses are taught by graduate students. The average class size in an introductory lecture is 20; in a laboratory is 20; and in a regular course is 22.

Admissions: 77% of the 2013-2014 applicants were accepted. The ACT scores were 73% below 21, 13% between 21 and 23, 8% between 24 and 26, 2% between 27 and 28, and 3% above 28. 48% of the current freshmen were in the top fifth of their class; 80% were in the top two fifths. 8 freshmen graduated first in their class.

Requirements: The SAT or ACT is required, with a minimum recommended composite score of 900 on the SAT or 20 on the ACT. Applicants must be graduates of an accredited secondary school and have a minimum of 16 academic credits, including 4 units in English, 3 in math, and 2 each in foreign language, science, and social studies. The GED will be considered with a minimum composite score of 270. A portfolio, audition, and interview are recommended. An essay is required. Applications are accepted online. Westminster requires applicants to be in the upper 50% of their class. A GPA of 2.5 is required. AP and CLEP credits are accepted. Important factors in the admissions decision are advanced placement or honors courses, leadership record, and recommendations by school officials.

Procedure: Freshmen are admitted fall, winter, and spring. Entrance exams should be taken during the junior year. There are deferred admissions and rolling admissions plans. Early decision applications should be filed by November 15, along with a $35 fee. Notification of early decision is sent December 1; regular decision, December 1. Applications are accepted online.

Transfer: 11 transfer students enrolled in 2012-2013. Applicants must have a college GPA of 2.0 or better. 60 of 132 credits required for the bachelor's degree must be completed at Westminster.

Visiting: There are regularly scheduled orientations for prospective students, consisting of an introduction, a student panel, a financial aid workshop, a campus tour, a faculty fair, and a lunch. Optional activities include a tour of residence halls and radio and TV stations and a football game. There are 2 visitation days in the fall and 2 in the spring. There are guides for informal visits, visitors may sit in on classes, and stay overnight. To schedule a visit, contact the Office of Admissions.

Financial Aid: In 2013-2014, 98% of all full-time freshmen and 97% of

continuing full-time students received some form of financial aid. 81% of all full-time freshmen and 78% of continuing full-time students received need-based aid. The average freshman award was $16,427. 40% of undergraduate students work part-time. Average annual earnings from campus work are $1650. The average financial indebtedness of the 2013 graduate was $20,386. Westminster is a member of CSS. The FAFSA and the college's own financial statement are required. The deadline for filing freshman financial aid applications for fall entry is May 1.

International Students: There are 2 international students enrolled. They must take the TOEFL or MELAB, or the SAT for students who come from a country where English is the spoken language. They must also take the SAT or ACT.

Computers: All students may access the system. There are no time limits and no fees.

Graduates: From July 1, 2012 to June 30, 2013, 222 bachelor's degrees were awarded. The most popular majors were elementary education (21%), business administration (16%), and social sciences and history (13%). In an average class, 74% graduate in 4 years or less, 75% graduate in 5 years or less, and 76% graduate in 6 years or less. Of the 2012 graduating class, 90% were employed within 6 months of graduation.

Admissions Contact: Louis Levy, Director of Admissions. E-Mail: *llevy@westminstercollege.edu* Web: *www.westminstercollege.edu*

WIDENER UNIVERSITY F-4

Chester, PA 19013 (610) 499-4126
(888)-Widener; (610) 499-4676

Full-time: 1344 men, 1559 women	**Faculty:** 217; IIA, +$
Part-time: 211 men, 420 women	**Ph.D.s:** 84%
Graduate: 981 men, 1796 women	**Student/Faculty:** 12 to 1
Year: semesters, summer session	**Tuition:** $38,028
Application Deadline: February 15	**Room & Board:** $12,340

Freshman Class: 5461 applied, 3673 accepted, 850 enrolled
SAT CR/M: 490/510

COMPETITIVE

Widener University, founded in 1821, is a private liberal arts institution offering undergraduate programs in the arts and sciences, business administration, engineering, nursing, and hospitality management. Other campuses are in Harrisburg and Wilmington, Delaware. There are 7 undergraduate schools and 8 graduate schools. In addition to regional accreditation, Widener has baccalaureate program accreditation with AACSB, ABET, APTA, CSWE, and NCATE. Computerized library services include interlibrary loans, database searching, and Internet access. Special learning facilities include an art gallery, radio station, TV station, a child development center, and a wireless accessible library. The 105-acre campus is in a suburban area 12 miles south of Philadelphia. Including any residence halls, there are 89 buildings.

Student Life: 64% of undergraduates are from Pennsylvania. Others are from 21 states, and 15 foreign countries. 70% are White; 14% African American. The average age of freshmen is 18; all undergraduates, 20. 28% do not continue beyond their first year; 55% remain to graduate.

Housing: 1670 students can be accommodated in college housing, which includes single-sex and coed dorms and on-campus apartments. In addition, there are honors houses, special-interest houses, fraternity houses, sorority houses, substance-free housing, affinity housing, wellness housing, and quiet/study wings. On-campus housing is guaranteed for all 4 years and is available on a lottery system for upperclassmen. 52% of students commute. All students may keep cars.

Activities: 10% of men belong to 6 national fraternities; 9% of women belong to 5 national sororities. There are 106 groups on campus, including men's hockey clubs, ice hockey, model UN, rugby, ski and snowboard, art, cheerleading, chess, choir, chorale, chorus, computers, dance, drama, environmental, ethnic, film, gay, honors, international, jazz band, literary magazine, musical theater, pep band, photography, political, professional, radio and TV, religious, social, social service, student government, and yearbook. Popular campus events include Greek Week, Hundredth Night and Honors Week.

Sports: There are 10 intercollegiate sports for men and 10 for women, and 7 intramural sports for men and 7 for women. Facilities include a 4000-seat stadium, an 1800-seat basketball gym, a field house, a championship pool, a weight training room, an exercise room, tennis courts, outdoor game and practice fields, and an 8-lane, all-weather championship track.

Disabled Students: All of the campus is accessible. Facilities include wheelchair ramps, elevators, special parking, specially equipped restrooms, special class scheduling, lowered drinking fountains, and lowered telephones.

Services: Counseling and information services are available, as is tutoring in every subject. There is a reader service for the blind. Academic support is offered as needed for all students.

Campus Safety and Security: Measures include 24-hour foot and vehicle patrol, emergency notification system, self-defense education, and security escort services. There are shuttle buses, emergency telephones, lighted pathways/sidewalks, controlled access to dorms/residences, residence hall briefings on personal safety, housing security, and enforcement procedures. There are bike patrols.

Programs of Study: Widener confers B.A., B.S., B.S.B., B.S.C.E., B.S.Ch.E., B.S.E.E., B.S. in H.M., B.S.M.E., B.S.N. and B.S.W. degrees. Associate, master's, and doctoral degrees are also awarded. Bachelor's degrees are awarded in BIOLOGICAL SCIENCE (biochemistry and biology/biological science), BUSINESS (accounting, business administration and management, business economics, finance, hospitality management services, international business management, and management information systems), COMMUNICATIONS AND THE ARTS (art, communications, creative writing, English, fine arts, French, media arts, modern language, and Spanish), COMPUTER AND PHYSICAL SCIENCE (chemistry, computer science, information sciences and systems, mathematics, physics, and science), EDUCATION (early childhood education, elementary education, mathematics education, science education, and special education), ENGINEERING AND ENVIRONMENTAL DESIGN (biomedical engineering, chemical engineering, civil engineering, electrical/electronics engineering, engineering, environmental science, mechanical engineering, and preengineering), HEALTH PROFESSIONS (nursing and prephysical therapy), SOCIAL SCIENCE (anthropology, behavioral science, criminal justice, economics, gender studies, history, humanities, international relations, political science/government, psychology, social work, sociology, and women's studies). Computer science, biology, and psychology are the strongest academically. Nursing, psychology, and management have the largest enrollments.

Required: All students must complete 12 credits each in humanities, social sciences, and science/math, and 1 credit in phys ed. For graduation, students must have 121 credit hours and a GPA of 2.0. Hours in the major vary by program. There is a university-wide writing requirement for all students.

Special: Widener offers internships, study abroad in 12 countries, a Washington semester, accelerated degree programs, dual, student-designed, and interdisciplinary majors, including chemistry management, nondegree study, and pass/fail options. Co-op programs are available in business administration, computer science, and engineering and are required in hospitality management. There are 26 national honor societies, a freshman honors program, and 8 departmental honors programs.

Faculty/Classroom: 46% of faculty are male; 54% are female. 82% teach undergraduates, 70% do research, and 70% do both. No introductory courses are taught by graduate students. The average class size in an introductory lecture is 30; in a laboratory is 14; and in a regular course is 24.

Admissions: 67% of the 2013-2014 applicants were accepted. The SAT scores for the 2013-2014 freshman class were: Critical Reading--49% below 500, 43% between 500 and 599, 7% between 600 and 699, and 1% between 700 and 800; Math--36% below 500, 42% between 500 and 599, 17% between 600 and 699, and 2% between 700 and 800. 26% of the current freshmen were in the top fifth of their class; 56% were in the top two fifths. 5 freshmen graduated first in their class.

Requirements: The SAT is required. In addition, applicants must be graduates of an accredited secondary school and have completed 4 units each of English and social studies, 3 units each of math and science, and 1 unit each of art, history, and music. The GED is accepted under limited circumstances. An interview is recommended. A GPA of 3.0 is required. AP credits are accepted. Important factors in the admissions decision are advanced placement or honors courses, recommendations by school officials, and extracurricular activities record.

Procedure: Freshmen are admitted fall and spring. Entrance exams should be taken in the junior year and November or December of the senior year. There are early admissions, deferred admissions, and rolling admissions plans. Applications should be filed by February 15 for fall entry; January 3 for spring entry, along with a $35 fee. Notification of early decision is sent December 15; regular decision, February 15. 17 applicants were on the 2013 waiting list; 4 were admitted. Applications are accepted online.

Transfer: 138 transfer students enrolled in 2012-2013. Applicants must have at least 12 college credits with a minimum GPA of 2.0 (2.5 for nursing students). An associate's degree and an interview are recommended. 45 of 121 credits required for the bachelor's degree must be completed at Widener.

Visiting: There are regularly scheduled orientations for prospective students. There are guides for informal visits, visitors may sit in on classes, and stay overnight. To schedule a visit, contact Office of Admissions at office.admissions@widener.edu.

Financial Aid: In 2013-2014, 99% of all full-time freshmen and 79% of continuing full-time students received some form of financial aid. 75% of all full-time freshmen and 64% of continuing full-time students received need-based aid. The average freshman award was $30,550. Need-based scholarships or need-based grants averaged $7,560; need-based self-help aid (loans and jobs) averaged $4,844, and other non-need-based awards and non-need-based scholarships averaged $19,866. 45% of undergraduate students work part-time. Average annual earnings from campus work are $944. The average financial indebtedness of the 2013 graduate was $40,460. Widener is a member of CSS. The FAFSA is required. The deadline for filing freshman financial aid applications for fall entry is February 15.

International Students: There are 98 international students enrolled. The school actively recruits these students. They must take the TOEFL.

Computers: All students may access the system. Resources are generally available 24 hours a day, 7 days a week. Student computer labs are open from 8 a.m. to 11 p.m. There are no time limits. The fee is $75.

Graduates: The most popular majors were business/marketing (24%), nursing/health professions (20%), and engineering (12%). In an average class, 40% graduate in 4 years or less, 54% graduate in 5 years or less, and 56% graduate in 6 years or less. Of the 2012 graduating class, 20% were enrolled in graduate school within 6 months of graduation, and 70% were employed.

Admissions Contact: Ed Wright, Director of Admissions. E-Mail: *admissions.office@widener.edu* Web: *www.widener.edu*

WILKES UNIVERSITY E-2

Wilkes Barre, PA 18766 (570) 408-4400
(800) WILKESU; (570) 408-4904

Full-time: 1157 men, 1024 women	**Faculty:** n/av; IIA, av$
Part-time: 105 men, 102 women	**Ph.D.s:** 87%
Graduate: 708 men, 1569 women	**Student/Faculty:** 14 to 1
Year: semesters, summer session	**Tuition:** $30,350
Application Deadline: open	**Room & Board:** $12,436
Freshman Class: 3120 applied, 2500 accepted, 586 enrolled	
SAT CR/M/W: 500/530/490	**ACT:** required **COMPETITIVE**

Wilkes University, founded in 1933, is an independent comprehensive university offering undergraduate programs in 40 fields, including the arts and sciences, business, and engineering. There are 5 undergraduate schools and 1 graduate school. In addition to regional accreditation, Wilkes has baccalaureate program accreditation with ABET, ACBSP, and ACPE. The library contains 212,000 volumes, 16,000 microform items, and 2,100 audio/video tapes/CDs/DVDs. Computerized library services include interlibrary loans, database searching, Internet access, and Wi-Fi capability. Special learning facilities include an art gallery, radio station, and TV station. The 27-acre campus is in an urban area 120 miles west of New York City. Including any residence halls, there are 51 buildings.

Student Life: 83% of undergraduates are from Pennsylvania. Others are from 17 states, and 11 foreign countries. 80% are from public schools. 77% are White. The average age of freshmen is 18; all undergraduates, 21. 22% do not continue beyond their first year; 58% remain to graduate.

Housing: 1050 students can be accommodated in college housing, which includes single-sex and coed dorms and on-campus apartments. On-campus housing is guaranteed for all 4 years and is available on a lottery system for upperclassmen. 56% of students commute. Alcohol is not permitted. All students may keep cars.

Activities: There are no fraternities or sororities. There are 80 groups on campus, including art, band, cheerleading, choir, chorus, computers, dance, debate, drama, environmental, ethnic, gay, honors, international, jazz band, literary magazine, musical theater, newspaper, orchestra, pep band, political, professional, radio and TV, religious, social, social service, and student government. Popular campus events include Casino Night, Junior-Senior Dinner Dance and Winter Weekend.

Sports: There are 7 intercollegiate sports for men and 7 for women. Facilities include tennis courts, a 5,000-seat stadium, a 3,500-seat gym, a game room, weight and exercise rooms, and an indoor recreation and athletic center.

Disabled Students: All of the campus is accessible. Facilities include wheelchair ramps, elevators, special parking, specially equipped restrooms, special class scheduling, lowered drinking fountains, and lowered telephones.

Services: Counseling and information services are available, as is tutoring in every subject. There is remedial math, reading, and writing. The Learning Center also provides individual tutoring, group study sessions, and small-group supplemental instruction seminars.

Campus Safety and Security: Measures include 24-hour foot and vehicle patrol, emergency notification system, and security escort services. There are shuttle buses, emergency telephones, lighted pathways/sidewalks, controlled access to dorms/residences, personal alarm devices for students who wish to carry one, and engraving of personal belongings. Students and others may contact security anonymously.

Programs of Study: Wilkes confers B.A., B.S. and B.B.A. degrees. Master's and doctoral degrees are also awarded. Bachelor's degrees are awarded in BIOLOGICAL SCIENCE (biochemistry and biology/biological science), BUSINESS (accounting, business administration and management, entrepreneurial studies, and marketing and distribution), COMMUNICATIONS AND THE ARTS (communications, dramatic arts, English, media arts, musical theater, and Spanish), COMPUTER AND PHYSICAL SCIENCE (chemistry, computer science, earth science, information sciences and systems, and mathematics), EDUCATION (elementary education and middle school education), ENGINEERING AND ENVIRONMENTAL DESIGN (electrical/electronics engineering, engineering and applied science, engineering management, environmental engineering, and mechanical engineering), HEALTH PROFESSIONS (medical technology, nursing, and prepharmacy), SOCIAL SCIENCE (criminology, history, international studies, liberal arts/general studies, philosophy, political science/government, psychology, and sociology). Prepharmacy, biology, and engineering are the strongest academically. Nursing, biology, and mechanical engineering have the largest enrollments.

Required: To graduate, all students must complete at least 120 credit hours, with a minimum of 30 in the major, and a cumulative GPA of at least 2.0 overall and in the major. Students must demonstrate competency in written communication, computer literacy, oral communication, and qualitative reasoning. General education requirements consist of 12 to 15 credits in humanities, 9 to 12 in sciences, 6 to 9 in social sciences, and 3 in fine arts.

Special: Wilkes offers cooperative education, cross-registration with King's College and Misericordia, internships, and study abroad. Dual majors in all disciplines, credit for military experience, and nondegree study are also offered. There are 19 national honor societies and 3 departmental honors programs.

Faculty/Classroom: 54% of faculty are male; 46% are female. No introductory courses are taught by graduate students. The average class size in an introductory lecture is 24; in a laboratory is 19; and in a regular course is 20.

Admissions: 80% of the 2013-2014 applicants were accepted. The SAT scores for the 2013-2014 freshman class were: Critical Reading--45% below 500, 39% between 500 and 599, 15% between 600 and 699, and 1% between 700 and 800; Math--34% below 500, 42% between 500 and 599, 21% between 600 and 699, and 3% between 700 and 800; Writing--51% below 500, 37% between 500 and 599, 11% between 600 and 699, and 1% between 700 and 800. 45% of the current freshmen were in the top fifth of their class; 71% were in the top two fifths.

Requirements: The SAT or ACT is required. Applicants must be graduates of an accredited secondary school or have the GED. Secondary-school preparation should include 4 years of English, 3 years each of math and social studies, and 2 years of science. Theater majors must audition. Wilkes requires applicants to be in the upper 50% of their class. A GPA of 2.5 is required. AP and CLEP credits are accepted. Important factors in the admissions decision are recommendations by school officials, advanced placement or honors courses, and leadership record.

Procedure: Freshmen are admitted fall, spring, and summer. Entrance exams should be taken before the second semester of the senior year in high school. There are early admissions, deferred admissions, and rolling admissions plans. Application deadlines are open. Application fee is $40. Notification is sent on a rolling basis. Applications are accepted online.

Transfer: 165 transfer students enrolled in 2012-2013. Applicants must have a minimum college GPA of 2.0 and at least 30 earned credits. A GPA of 2.5 is required for engineering majors. Students with fewer than 30 credits must submit official high school transcripts and SAT or ACT scores. An interview is recommended. 60 of 120 credits required for the bachelor's degree must be completed at Wilkes.

Visiting: There are regularly scheduled orientations for prospective students, including a general orientation session, a tour of the campus, and a meeting with faculty from the department of the student's intended major. There are guides for informal visits, visitors may sit in on classes, and stay overnight. To schedule a visit, contact the Admissions Office.

Financial Aid: In 2013-2014, 97% of all full-time freshmen and 90% of continuing full-time students received some form of financial aid. 30% of undergraduate students work part-time. Average annual earnings from campus work are $800. The average financial indebtedness of the 2013 graduate was $36,961. The FAFSA is required. The deadline for filing freshman financial aid applications for fall entry is March 1.

International Students: There are 163 international students enrolled. The school actively recruits these students. They must take the TOEFL with a minimum score of 500 on the paper-based TOEFL (PBT) or 60 on the Internet-based version (iBT). They must also take the SAT or ACT.

Computers: All students may access the system 24 hours a day. There are no time limits. There is a fee.

Graduates: From July 1, 2012 to June 30, 2013, 462 bachelor's degrees were awarded. The most popular majors were business (15%), nursing (15%), and engineering (10%). In an average class, 47% graduate in 4 years or less, 56% graduate in 5 years or less, and 58% graduate in 6 years or less. Of the 2012 graduating class, 24% were enrolled in graduate school within 6 months of graduation, and 73% were employed.

Admissions Contact: Melanie Wade, Vice President for Enrollment Services. E-Mail: *melanie.wade@wilkes.edu* Web: *www.wilkes.edu*

WILSON COLLEGE D-4

Chambersburg, PA 17201-1285 (717) 262-2025; (717) 264-1578

Full-time: 15 men, 330 women	**Faculty:** 40
Part-time: 70 men, 315 women	**Ph.D.s:** 78%
Graduate: n/av	**Student/Faculty:** 9 to 1
Year: semesters, summer session	**Tuition:** $28,720
Application Deadline: open	**Room & Board:** $9490
Freshman Class: n/av	
SAT: required	**ACT:** recommended **COMPETITIVE**

Wilson College, founded in 1869, is a private liberal arts institution for women that is affiliated with the Presbyterian Church. There is 1 undergraduate school. The figures in the above capsule and in this profile are approximate. The library contains 175,000 volumes, 10,933 microform items, and 2007 audio/video tapes/CDs/DVDs, and subscribes to 293 periodicals including electronic. Computerized library services include interlibrary loans, database searching, and Internet access. Special learning facilities include a learning resource center, art gallery, natural history museum, radio station, veterinary technology center, transmission electron microscope, classics collection, stables, center for sustainable living, and on-campus equestrian center. The 300-acre campus is in a small town 55 miles south of Harrisburg, 76 miles west of Baltimore, and 90 miles west of Washington, D.C. Including any residence halls, there are 34 buildings.

Student Life: 83% of undergraduates are from Pennsylvania. Others are from 19 states and 10 foreign countries. 91% are from public schools. 85% are white. 51% claim no religious affiliation; 31% Protestant; 11% Catholic. The average age of freshmen is 18; all undergraduates, 30. 33% do not continue beyond their first year; 48% remain to graduate.

Housing: 473 students can be accommodated in college housing, which includes single-sex dorms, on-campus apartments, and single-mother housing for women with children. On-campus housing is guaranteed for all 4 years. 59% of students commute. All students may keep cars.

Activities: There are no fraternities or sororities. There are 23 groups on campus, including art, business, cheerleading, choir, chorale, dance, drama, environmental, equestrian, ethnic, gay, honors, international, literary magazine, newspaper, photography, political, professional, radio and TV, religious, social, social service, and student government. Popular campus events include May Weekend and Thanksgiving, Christmas, and Muhibbah International Dinners.

Sports: There are 8 intercollegiate sports for women, and 8 intramural sports for women. Facilities include a 400-seat gym, field house, pool, gymnastics gym, archery range, hockey field, softball field, tennis courts, 2-lane bowling alley, equestrian center (indoor and outdoor arena), soccer field, and fitness center.

Disabled Students: 55% of the campus is accessible. Facilities include wheelchair ramps, elevators, special parking, specially equipped restrooms, and special class scheduling.

Services: Counseling and information services are available, as is tutoring in every subject. There is remedial math, reading, and writing and study skills workshops.

Campus Safety and Security: Measures include 24-hour foot and vehicle patrol, shuttle buses, emergency telephones, and lighted pathways/sidewalks.

Programs of Study: Wilson confers B.A. and B.S. degrees. Associates degrees are also awarded. Bachelor's degrees are awarded in AGRICULTURE (equine science), BIOLOGICAL SCIENCE (biology/biological science), BUSINESS (accounting and business economics), COMMUNICATIONS AND THE ARTS (communications, English, fine arts, French, languages, and Spanish), COMPUTER AND PHYSICAL SCIENCE (chemistry and mathematics), EDUCATION (elementary education), ENGINEERING AND ENVIRONMENTAL DESIGN (environmental science), HEALTH PROFESSIONS (exercise science and veterinary science), SOCIAL SCIENCE (history, international studies, law, philosophy, political science/government, psychobiology, psychology, religion, and sociology). Business and economics, education, and veterinary medical technology have the largest enrollments.

Required: To graduate, students must complete a minimum of 36 courses with a minimum GPA of 2.0. At least 18 of the 36 courses must be outside any single discipline.

Special: Cross-registration is available with Shippensburg University and Gettysburg College. Wilson offers internships, a Washington semester, student-designed majors, B.A.-B.S. degree in psychology and sociology, credit by exam, pass/fail options, and credit for noncollegiate learning. Students may participate in study-abroad programs sponsored by other colleges. There is a chapter of Phi Beta Kappa and a freshman honors program.

Faculty/Classroom: 47% of faculty are male; 53% are female. All teach undergraduates. No introductory courses are taught by graduate students. The average class size in an introductory lecture is 20; in a laboratory, 14; and in a regular course, 14.

Requirements: The SAT is required. The ACT is recommended. In addition, applicants should prepare with 4 years each of English and social studies/history, 3 of math, and 2 of science with a lab and a foreign language. An essay and at least 1 academic reference are required, and an interview is recommended. Wilson requires applicants to be in the upper 50% of their class. A GPA of 2.5 is required. AP and CLEP credits are accepted. Important factors in the admissions decision are personality/intangible qualities, advanced placement or honors courses, and leadership record.

Procedure: Freshmen are admitted fall and spring. Entrance exams should be taken in the spring of the junior year. There are deferred admissions and rolling admissions plans. Application deadlines are open. Check with the school for current application fee. Notification is sent on a rolling basis. Applications are accepted online.

Transfer: Applicants must have a college GPA of at least 2.0. The SAT or ACT may be waived after discussion with the Admissions Office. 14 of 36 credits required for the bachelor's degree must be completed at Wilson.

Visiting: There are regularly scheduled orientations for prospective students, consisting of a campus tour, meetings with faculty, students, or administration, and an interview with an admissions counselor. There are guides for informal visits; visitors may sit in on classes and stay overnight. To schedule a visit, contact the Office of Admissions.

Financial Aid: The FAFSA and the college's own financial statement are required. Check with the school for current deadlines.

International Students: The school actively recruits these students. They must take the TOEFL and also take the SAT or ACT. The SAT is recommended.

Computers: Wireless access is available. All residence halls and lounges wire to the network. All students may access the system. There are no time limits and no fees.

Admissions Contact: Mary Ann Naso, Vice President for Enrollment. E-Mail: *admissions@wilson.edu* Web: *www.wilson.edu*

YORK COLLEGE OF PENNSYLVANIA D-4

York, PA 17403 (717) 849-1600
(800) 455-8018; (717) 849-1607

Full-time: 2052 men, 2410 women	**Faculty:** 164; IIA, +$
Part-time: 213 men, 342 women	**Ph.D.s:** 87%
Graduate: 91 men, 149 women	**Student/Faculty:** 28 to 1
Year: semesters, summer session	**Tuition:** $14,460
Application Deadline: open	**Room & Board:** $9580
Freshman Class: 9934 applied, 7302 accepted, 1064 enrolled	
SAT CR/M/W: 510/520/500	**ACT:** 22 **COMPETITIVE**

York College of Pennsylvania, founded in 1787, is a private institution offering undergraduate programs in the liberal arts and sciences, as well as professional programs. In addition to regional accreditation, YCP has baccalaureate program accreditation with ABET, ACBSP, NASM, NLN, and NRPA. The library contains 300,000 volumes, 500,000 microform items, 11,000 audio/video tapes/CDs/DVDs, and subscribes to 1,500 periodicals including electronic. Computerized library services include interlibrary loans, database searching, and Internet access. Special learning facilities include an art gallery, radio station, TV station, a telecommunications center, Abraham Lincoln artifacts collection, rare books collection, oral history room, and a nursing education center. The 190-acre campus is in a suburban area 45 miles north of Baltimore. Including any residence halls, there are 46 buildings.

Student Life: 58% of undergraduates are from Pennsylvania. Others are from 32 states, and 7 foreign countries. 85% are from public schools. 83% are White. 36% claim no religious affiliation; 25% Protestant; 24% Catholic; 13% Unknown denominations, and Muslim. The average age of freshmen is 19; all undergraduates, 21. 25% do not continue beyond their first year; 58% remain to graduate.

Housing: 2575 students can be accommodated in college housing, which includes single-sex and coed dorms and on-campus apartments. In addition, there are fraternity houses. On-campus housing is guaranteed for the freshman year only, is available on a first-come, and first-served basis. 52% of students live on campus; of those, 65% remain on campus on weekends. Alcohol is not permitted. All students may keep cars.

Activities: 10% of men belong to 8 national fraternities; 10% of women belong to 6 national sororities. There are 80 groups on campus, including band, cheerleading, chess, choir, chorale, chorus, computers, debate, drama, environmental, ethnic, film, forensics, gay, honors, international, jazz band, literary magazine, musical theater, newspaper, orchestra, photography, political, professional, radio and TV, religious, social, social service, student government, and symphony. Popular campus events include Fall Weekend, Spring Weekend and Spartalooza.

Sports: There are 10 intercollegiate sports for men and 10 for women, and 10 intramural sports for men and 10 for women. Facilities include 2 gyms, a track, a swimming pool, a game room, a fitness center, weight training rooms, tennis courts, and soccer, hockey, baseball, softball, and athletic/intramural fields.

Disabled Students: 90% of the campus is accessible. Facilities include wheelchair ramps, elevators, special parking, specially equipped restrooms, special class scheduling, lowered drinking fountains, and lowered telephones.

Services: Counseling and information services are available, as is tutoring in most subjects. There is remedial math and writing. There is also an education learning resource center.

Campus Safety and Security: Measures include 24-hour foot and vehicle patrol, emergency notification system, and security escort services. There are shuttle buses, emergency telephones, lighted pathways/ sidewalks, safety seminars, crime prevention speakers, a desk monitor in residence halls, and a personal property engraving program.

Programs of Study: YCP confers B.A. and B.S. degrees. Associate, master's, and doctoral degrees are also awarded. Bachelor's degrees are awarded in BIOLOGICAL SCIENCE (biology/biological science), BUSINESS (accounting, banking and finance, business administration and management, entrepreneurial studies, management information systems, marketing/retailing/merchandising, recreation and leisure services, and sports management), COMMUNICATIONS AND THE ARTS (broadcasting, communications, creative writing, dramatic arts, English, English literature, fine arts, graphic design, music, music technology, public relations, and Spanish), COMPUTER AND PHYSICAL SCIENCE (chemistry, computer science, and mathematics), EDUCATION (education, elementary education, English education, mathematics education, music education, science education, secondary education, social studies education, and special education), ENGINEERING AND ENVIRONMENTAL DESIGN (computer engineering, electrical/electronics engineering, engineering, engineering management, and mechanical engineering), HEALTH PROFESSIONS (medical laboratory science, nuclear medical technology, nursing, and respiratory therapy), SOCIAL SCIENCE (behavioral science, criminal justice, economics, history, humanities, parks and recreation management, philosophy, political science/government, psychology, and sociology). Electrical, computer, mechanical engineering, nursing, business, criminal justice and education are the strongest academically. Nursing, education, and criminal justice have the largest enrollments.

Required: To graduate, all students must complete at least 124 credit hours, with 60 to 80 in the major. The required core curriculum consists of English Composition, Writing about Literature, Human Communications, Critical Thinking and Problem Solving in Mathematics, Information Literacy, and physical education. Distribution requirements include 6 credits in fine arts and humanities, 6 in social and behavioral sciences, 6 to 8 in laboratory sciences, 6 in American civilization/government and Western civilization, and 6 in international studies/foreign language. A minimum GPA of 2.0 is required.

Special: YCP offers internships for upper-division students and a co-op program in mechanical engineering. Study abroad is offered in England, Mexico, Japan, Puerto Rico, Korea, and other countries. Dual majors in any combination, nondegree study, and pass/fail options are available. There are 6 national honor societies.

Faculty/Classroom: 57% of faculty are male; 43% are female. All teach undergraduates. No introductory courses are taught by graduate students. The average class size in an introductory lecture is 22; in a laboratory is 17; and in a regular course is 19.

Admissions: 74% of the 2013-2014 applicants were accepted. The SAT scores for the 2013-2014 freshman class were: Critical Reading--41% below 500, 46% between 500 and 599, 12% between 600 and 699, and 1% between 700 and 800; Math--32% below 500, 50% between 500 and 599, 16% between 600 and 699, and 2% between 700 and 800; Writing--47% below 500, 45% between 500 and 599, and 8% between 600 and 699. The ACT scores were 31% below 21, 32% between 21 and 23, 21% between 24 and 26, 12% between 27 and 28, and 4% above 28. 4 freshmen graduated first in their class.

Requirements: The SAT or ACT is required. The ACT Optional Writing test is also required. Applicants must be graduates of an accredited secondary school or have a GED certificate. 15 academic credits are required, including 4 units in English, 3 or 4 in math, 2 or 3 in science, 2 in history, and 1 in social studies. Music students must audition. A GPA of 2.5 is required. AP and CLEP credits are accepted. Important factors in the admissions decision are advanced placement or honors courses, leadership record, and extracurricular activities record.

Procedure: Freshmen are admitted fall and spring. Entrance exams should be taken in the spring of the junior year or the fall of the senior year. There are deferred admissions and rolling admissions plans. Application deadlines are open. Notification is sent on a rolling basis. Applications are accepted online. Application fees are waived if application is completed online.

Transfer: 356 transfer students enrolled in 2012-2013. Applicants must have a minimum GPA of 2.0 from a regionally accredited institution. Students with fewer than 30 credit hours must submit a high school transcript. An interview is recommended. 30 of 124 credits required for the bachelor's degree must be completed at York.

Visiting: There are regularly scheduled orientations for prospective students, including 2 open houses in October/November; 1 junior open house in April; and 2 spring orientation programs in April/May, featuring a general orientation, academic and support services sessions, and campus tours. There are guides for informal visits and visitors may sit in on classes. To schedule a visit, contact the Admissions Office.

Financial Aid: In 2013-2014, 90% of all full-time freshmen and 83% of continuing full-time students received some form of financial aid. 74% of all full-time freshmen and 58% of continuing full-time students received need-based aid. The average freshman award was $13,498. Need-based scholarships or need-based grants averaged $1,961 ($15,100 maximum); need-based self-help aid (loans and jobs) averaged $3,132 ($5,700 maximum); and other non-need-based awards and non-need-based scholarships averaged $5,363 ($27,340 maximum). 20% of undergraduate students work part-time. Average annual earnings from campus work are $1500. The average financial indebtedness of the 2013 graduate was $35,604. YCP is a member of CSS. The FAFSA is required. The priority date for freshman financial aid applications for fall entry is March 1.

International Students: There are 14 international students enrolled. They must take the TOEFL with a minimum score of 530 on the paper-based TOEFL (PBT) or 72 on the Internet-based version (iBT). They must also take the SAT or ACT. IELTS score of 6.

Computers: All students may access the system. There are no time limits and no fees.

Graduates: From July 1, 2012 to June 30, 2013, 975 bachelor's degrees were awarded. The most popular majors were business administration (18%), nursing (14%), and criminal justice (13%). In an average class, 37% graduate in 4 years or less, 55% graduate in 5 years or less, and 58% graduate in 6 years or less.

Admissions Contact: Ines Ramirez, Director of Admissions. E-Mail: *admissions@ycp.edu* Web: *www.ycp.edu*

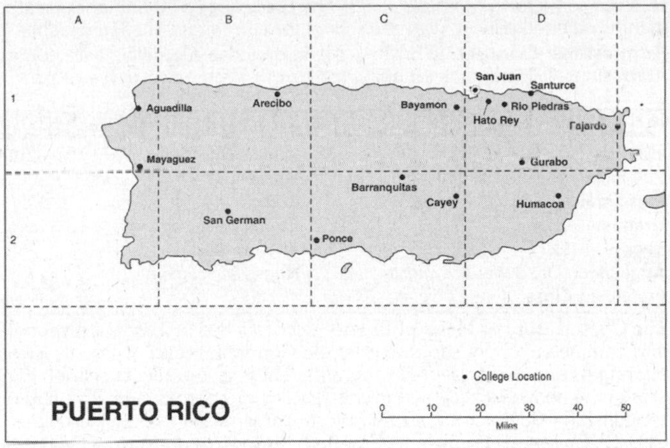

AMERICAN UNIVERSITY OF PUERTO RICO C-1

Bayamon, PR 00960 **(787) 740-6410; (787) 785-7377**

Full-time: n/av
Part-time: n/av
Graduate: n/av
Year: semesters, summer session
Application Deadline: open
Freshman Class: n/av
SAT or ACT: required
Faculty: n/av
Ph.D.s: n/av
Student/Faculty: n/av
Tuition: $5847
Room & Board: n/app

American University of Puerto Rico, founded in 1963, is a private nonsectarian institution offering undergraduate programs in business administration, secretarial training, and computer science. There are 4 undergraduate schools. The 2 libraries contain 10,000 volumes, 1,000 microform items, and 1,000 audio/video tapes/CDs/DVDs, and subscribe to 50 periodicals including electronic. Computerized library services include interlibrary loans and database searching. The 21-acre campus is in an urban area south of San Juan. Including any residence halls, there are 9 buildings.

Student Life: 99% of undergraduates are from Puerto Rico. 80% are from public schools. 100% are Hispanic. The average age of freshmen is 18; all undergraduates, 21. 3% do not continue beyond their first year; 97% remain to graduate.

Housing: Alcohol is not permitted.

Activities: There are no fraternities or sororities. Groups on campus include art and photography.

Sports: There are 3 intercollegiate sports for men and 3 for women, and 3 intramural sports for men and 3 for women. Facilities include an indoor basketball and volleyball court, a soccer field, and a pool.

Disabled Students: All of the campus is accessible. Facilities include wheelchair ramps, elevators, special parking, specially equipped restrooms, lowered drinking fountains, and lowered telephones.

Services: Counseling and information services are available, as is tutoring in every subject.

Campus Safety and Security: Measures include 24-hour foot and vehicle patrol, self-defense education, and security escort services. There are shuttle buses and lighted pathways/sidewalks.

Programs of Study: American confers B.A., and B.B.A. degrees. Associate degrees are also awarded. Business and communications have the largest enrollments.

Required: A GPA of 2.0 is required to graduate.

Special: Work-study programs are available.

Faculty/Classroom: No introductory courses are taught by graduate students.

Requirements: The SAT or ACT is required. A GPA of 2.0 is required.

Procedure: Freshmen are admitted in fall. Application deadlines are open.

Visiting: There are guides for informal visits and visitors may sit in on classes. To schedule a visit, contact the school.

Financial Aid: Check with the school for current application deadlines.

Computers: All students may access the system. There are no time limits and no fees.

Admissions Contact: Admissions Office. Web: *http:/aupr.edu*

CARIBBEAN UNIVERSITY C-1

Bayamon, PR 00960 **(787) 780-0070, ext. 1111**

Full-time: 1250 men, 1903 women
Part-time: 355 men, 423 women
Graduate: 175 men, 729 women
Year: semesters, summer session
Application Deadline:
Freshman Class: n/av
Faculty: n/av
Ph.D.s: n/av
Student/Faculty: n/av
Tuition: $4850
Room & Board: $5525

Caribbean University, founded in 1969, is an independent, commuter institution offering undergraduate programs in business, engineering, health science and liberal arts. There are extension centers in Vega Baja, Carolina and Ponce. There are 6 undergraduate schools and 4 graduate schools. The 4 libraries contain 185,094 volumes, 2,115 audio/video tapes/CDs/DVDs, and subscribe to 78,788 periodicals including electronic. Computerized library services include interlibrary loans, database searching, Internet access, and Wi-Fi capability. Special learning facilities include an art gallery. The 15-acre campus is in an urban area Forest Hill, Bayamon Puerto Rico. Including any residence halls, there are 8 buildings.

Student Life: 100% of undergraduates are from Puerto Rico. 79% are from public schools. 100% are Hispanic. The average age of freshmen is 20.5; all undergraduates, 21.8. 35% do not continue beyond their first year; 65% remain to graduate.

Housing: Alcohol is not permitted. All students commute. All students may keep cars.

Activities: There are no fraternities or sororities. There are 10 groups on campus, including cheerleading, chess, chorale, computers, dance, drama, international, professional, social, social service, and student government.

Sports: There are 10 intercollegiate sports for men and 8 for women, and 2 intramural sports for men and 2 for women. Facilities include a gym, basketball and tennis courts, cheerleading, wresting, soccer, softball, judo, and a track and field arena.

Disabled Students: All of the campus is accessible. Facilities include wheelchair ramps, elevators, special parking, specially equipped restrooms. Special counseling is provided.

Services: Counseling and information services are available, as is tutoring in every subject. There is remedial math, reading, and writing.

Campus Safety and Security: Measures include 24-hour foot and vehicle patrol and emergency notification system. There are emergency telephones, including campus security guards, student ID cards, and regular fire drills.

Programs of Study: Associate and master's degrees are also awarded. Bachelor's degrees are awarded in BIOLOGICAL SCIENCE (biology/biological science), BUSINESS (accounting, banking and finance, business administration and management, marketing/retailing/merchandising, and secretarial studies/office management), COMPUTER AND PHYSICAL SCIENCE (computer programming, computer science, mathematics, and science), EDUCATION (business education, elementary education, middle school education, science education, secondary education, special education, and teaching English as a second/foreign language (TESOL/TEFOL)), ENGINEERING AND ENVIRONMENTAL DESIGN (civil engineering and industrial engineering technology), HEALTH PROFESSIONS (nursing), SOCIAL SCIENCE (criminal justice, social science, and social work). Engineering and nursing is the strongest academically. Nursing, speech theraphy and engineering have the largest enrollments.

Faculty/Classroom: 46% of faculty are male; 54% are female. No introductory courses are taught by graduate students.

Requirements: Applicants must be graduates of an accredited secondary school with a GPA of 2.0 or a CEEB score of 4.0. The GED is accepted. High school preparation should include 3 years each of art, English, Spanish, and social studies, 2 years each of history and math, and 1 year of science. A GPA of 2.0 is required.

Procedure: Freshmen are admitted to all sessions. Entrance exams should be taken in the junior or senior year. There is a rolling admissions plan. Application deadlines are open.

Transfer: 222 transfer students enrolled in 2012-2013. A minimum college GPA of 2.0 is recommended. Applicants should submit two official transcripts and a catalog from each previous college attended, along with a written recommendation from the dean at the last institution. 30 of 135 credits required for the bachelor's degree must be completed at CU.

Visiting: There are regularly scheduled orientations for prospective students. To schedule a visit, contact Rosalie Morales at rmorales@caribbean.edu.

Financial Aid: CU is a member of CSS. The CSS/Profile and FAFSA, and income tax returns are required. Check with the school for current application deadlines.

Computers: All students may access the system. There are no time limits and no fees.

Graduates: From July 1, 2012 to June 30, 2013, 363 bachelor's degrees were awarded. The most popular majors were health professions (37%), engineering (16%), and education (12%). In an average class, 19% graduate in 4 years or less, 24% graduate in 5 years or less, and 27% graduate in 6 years or less.

Admissions Contact: Rosalie Morales, Admission Director. E-Mail: *rmorales@caribbean.edu* Web: *www.caribbean.edu*

CENTRAL UNIVERSITY OF BAYAMON C-1

Bayamon, PR 00960 **(787) 786-3030, ext. 2100**

Full-time: 850 men, 1605 women
Part-time: 160 men, 295 women
Graduate: 100 men, 180 women
Year: semesters, summer session
Application Deadline:
Freshman Class: n/av
Faculty: 61
Ph.D.s: 28%
Student/Faculty: 40 to 1
Tuition: $3850
Room & Board: n/app

Bayamon Central University, founded in 1970, is a private Catholic institution offering degree programs primarily to commuter students in the arts and sciences, business, education, nursing, and religious studies. The figures in the above capsule and in this profile are approximate. There are 4 undergraduate schools and 3 graduate schools. The 2 libraries contain 51,500 volumes, 40 microform items, and subscribe to 370 periodicals including electronic. The 55-acre campus is in an urban area 4 miles west of Bayamon. Including any residence halls, there are 13 buildings.

Student Life: 90% are from public schools. All are Hispanic. The average age of freshmen is 17; all undergraduates, 20.

Housing: There are no residence halls. All students commute.

Activities: There are no fraternities or sororities. There are 13 groups on campus, including computers, film, literary magazine, photography, professional, radio and TV, religious, social service, and student government.

Sports: There are 10 intercollegiate sports for men and 10 for women. Facilities include a 400-seat gym, basketball and volleyball courts, a swimming pool, and a weight-training room.

Disabled Students: All of the campus is accessible. Facilities include wheelchair ramps, elevators, special parking, specially equipped restrooms, special class scheduling, lowered drinking fountains, and lowered telephones.

Services: Counseling and information services are available, as is tutoring in English, Spanish, philosophy, accounting, math, biology, and computer science. There is a reader service for the blind, and remedial math, reading, and writing.

Campus Safety and Security: Measures include 24-hour foot and vehicle patrol.

Programs of Study: UCB confers B.A., B.S., B.B.A., B.S.N. and B.S.S. degrees. Associate and master's degrees are also awarded. Bachelor's degrees are awarded in BIOLOGICAL SCIENCE (biology/biological science), BUSINESS (accounting, business administration and management, and marketing/retailing/merchandising), COMMUNICATIONS AND THE ARTS (journalism and Spanish), COMPUTER AND PHYSICAL SCIENCE (chemistry and computer science), EDUCATION (elementary education, English education, science education, and secondary education), HEALTH PROFESSIONS (nursing and premedicine), SOCIAL SCIENCE (philosophy, psychology, religion, social work, and sociology). Business administration is the strongest academically.

Required: Students must complete 48 credits distributed among specific courses in theology, philosophy, Spanish, English, humanities, social science, math, science, and phys ed. The bachelor's degree requires completion of 124 to 141 credits, including 33 to 43 in the major, with a minimum GPA of 2.0.

Special: The university offers limited pass/fail options, work-study programs, and nondegree study.

Faculty/Classroom: All teach undergraduates. No introductory courses are taught by graduate students. The average class size in an introductory lecture is 35; in a laboratory is 20; and in a regular course is 35.

Requirements: The SAT or the CEEB Spanish equivalent is required. Applicants must be graduates of accredited secondary schools or have earned a GED. They must speak Spanish and have a good knowledge of English. The university requires 15.5 academic credits, including 3 credits each in English, Spanish, math, and science, 1.5 in history, and 1 each in social studies and electives. An interview is recommended. A GPA of 2.0 is required. CLEP credits are accepted. Important factors in the admissions decision are personality/intangible qualities, recommendations by school officials, and ability to finance college education.

Procedure: Freshmen are admitted to all sessions. Entrance exams should be taken by October of the senior year. Check with the school for current application deadlines and fee.

Transfer: A minimum college GPA of 2.0 is required. 30 of 124 credits required for the bachelor's degree must be completed at UCB.

Visiting: There are regularly scheduled orientations for prospective students. There are guides for informal visits, and visitors may sit in on classes. To schedule a visit, contact the Admissions Office.

Financial Aid: In 2013-2014, 94% of all full-time freshmen students received some form of financial aid. The the college's own financial statement is required. Check with the school for current application deadlines.

Admissions Contact: Christine M. Hernandez Cortiella, Director of Admissions. E-Mail: *chernandez@ucb.edu.pr* Web: *www.ucb.edu.pr*

CONSERVATORY OF MUSIC OF PUERTO RICO D-1

San Juan, PR 00918 **(787) 751-0160; (787) 758-8258**

Full-time: 115 men, 35 women
Part-time: 90 men, 35 women
Graduate: n/av
Year: semesters
Application Deadline: see profile
Freshman Class: n/av
Faculty: n/av
Ph.D.s: 2%
Student/Faculty: n/av
Tuition: $2800
Room & Board: n/app

The Conservatory of Music of Puerto Rico, founded in 1959, is a specialized commuter school supported by the Commonwealth of Puerto Rico, offering 4- and 5-year degree programs. There is 1 graduate school. Figures in the above capsule and in this profile are approximate. The library contains 23,608 volumes, 11 microform items, 5000 audio/video tapes/CDs/DVDs, and subscribes to 2 periodicals including electronic. Special learning facilities include a learning resource center and a computer-based ear-training lab. The 3-acre campus is in an urban area in the Hato Rey section of San Juan. Including any residence halls, there are 3 buildings.

Activities: There are no fraternities or sororities.

Sports: There is no sports program at the conservatory.

Programs of Study: The conservatory confers B.F.A., B.M., and B.Perf.Arts degrees. Master's degrees are also awarded.

Required: To graduate, students must complete 142 credit hours (158 for music education) with a minimum GPA of 2.0. Requirements include 4 years of courses in the principal instrument and specific courses in music theory, including solfege, harmony, and counterpoint. All students must present a graduation recital.

Special: A dual major is available in the principal instrument and music education.

Faculty/Classroom: 70% of faculty are male; 30% are female. All teach undergraduates. No introductory courses are taught by graduate students.

Requirements: The SAT is required, or the CEEB's Spanish version. Applicants must be graduates of an accredited secondary school. An interview and audition are required. A GPA of 2.0 is required. AP credits are accepted. Important factors in the admissions decision are leadership record, parents or siblings attended your school, and ability to finance college education.

Procedure: Freshmen are admitted to all sessions. Entrance exams should be taken in May of the junior year or December of the senior year. There is an early admissions plan. Check with the school for current application deadlines and fee. A waiting list is maintained.

Transfer: 100 of 142 credits required for the bachelor's degree must be completed at the conservatory.

Visiting: There are regularly scheduled orientations for prospective students. To schedule a visit, contact the Admissions Office.

Financial Aid: The conservatory is a member of CSS. The CSS/Profile is required. Check with the school for current application deadlines.

Computers: There are no time limits and no fees.

Admissions Contact: Eutimia Santiago, Director of Admissions. Web: *www.cmpr.edu*

ESCUELA DE ARTES PLASTICAS DE PUERTO RICO D-1

San Juan, PR 00902-1112 **(787) 729-0007, ext. 333; (787) 725-8111**

Full-time: 155 men, 210 women
Part-time: 95 men, 100 women
Graduate: n/av
Year: trimesters
Application Deadline: see profile
Freshman Class: n/av
Faculty: n/av
Ph.D.s: 20%
Student/Faculty: n/av
Tuition: $5279 ($8519)
Room & Board: n/app

Escuela de Artes Plasticas de Puerto Rico, founded in 1966, is a public institution considered to be the national art school of Puerto Rico. There is 1 undergraduate school. Figures in the above capsule and in this profile are approximate. The library contains 31,277 volumes, 29,235 microform items, 1477 audio/video tapes/CDs/DVDs, and subscribes to 93 periodicals including electronic. Computerized library services include Internet access. Special learning facilities include a learning resource center, art gallery, Cita laboratory, audiovisual room, and Internet room. The 1-acre campus is in an urban area in Old San Juan. Including any residence halls, there are 3 buildings.

Student Life: 61% are from public schools. All are Hispanic. The average age of freshmen is 18; all undergraduates, 25. 5% do not continue beyond their first year; 35% remain to graduate.

Housing: There are no residence halls. All students commute.
Activities: There are no fraternities or sororities. There are 3 groups on campus, including art, newspaper, and student government. Popular campus events include Student Day, Health Fair, and Halloween Costume Party.
Sports: There is no sports program at EAP.
Disabled Students: All of the campus is accessible. Facilities include wheelchair ramps, elevators, special parking, specially equipped restrooms, and special class scheduling.
Services: Counseling and information services are available, as is tutoring in all the general studies courses. There is remedial writing.
Campus Safety and Security: Measures include 24-hour foot and vehicle patrol and safety training.
Programs of Study: EAP confers B.A. degrees. Bachelor's degrees are awarded in COMMUNICATIONS AND THE ARTS (industrial design, painting, printmaking, and sculpture), EDUCATION (art education), ENGINEERING AND ENVIRONMENTAL DESIGN (computer graphics). Computer graphics has the largest enrollment.
Required: To graduate, students must maintain a minimum GPA of 2.0 in 132 credits, including 36 in art fundamentals and 48 in general education courses.
Special: Accelerated degree programs are offered.
Faculty/Classroom: 57% of faculty are male; 43% are female. All teach undergraduates. No introductory courses are taught by graduate students. The average class size in an introductory lecture is 25 and in a laboratory, 18.
Requirements: The SAT or the CEEB Spanish equivalent of the SAT is required. Applicants must be graduates of an accredited secondary school or have earned a GED. A portfolio and interview are required, with an essay recommended. A GPA of 2.0 is required. Important factors in the admissions decision are evidence of special talent, recommendations by school officials, and personality/intangible qualities.
Procedure: Freshmen are admitted in fall. There is a rolling admissions plan. Check with the school for current application deadlines and fee.
Transfer: Admission requirements are the same as for first-year applicants.
Visiting: There are regularly scheduled orientations for prospective students. There are guides for informal visits. To schedule a visit, contact the Student Affairs Office.
Financial Aid: EAP is a member of CSS. The FAFSA is required. Check with the school for current application deadlines.
International Students: The school actively recruits these students. They must take the SAT or the CEEB Spanish equivalent of the SAT.
Computers: All students may access the system Monday through Saturday from 8 a.m. to 5:30 p.m. There are no fees.
Admissions Contact: Janet Centino, Recruiting Officer. A campus DVD is available. E-Mail: *admissions@eap.edu* Web: *www.eap.edu*

INTER-AMERICAN UNIVERSITY OF PUERTO RICO SYSTEM

The Inter-American University of Puerto Rico System, established in 1912, is a private system in Puerto Rico. It is governed by a board of trustees, whose chief administrator is the president. The primary goal of the system is teaching. The main priorities are to provide quality education and public service, and to devote attention to students' needs. The total student enrollment is usually about 43,000, with 900 faculty members. Altogether there are 35 baccalaureate, 28 master's, and 1 doctoral program offered in Inter-American University of Puerto Rico System. Profiles of the 4-year campuses are included in this section.

INTER-AMERICAN UNIVERSITY OF PUERTO RICO/ AGUADILLA CAMPUS — A-1

Aguadilla, PR 00605 — **(787) 891-0925; (787) 882-3020**

Full-time: 1718 men, 1962 women	**Faculty:** 75
Part-time: 315 men, 362 women	**Ph.D.s:** 32%
Graduate: 89 men, 204 women	**Student/Faculty:** 31 to 1
Year: semesters, summer session	**Tuition:** $6078
Application Deadline: May 1	**Room & Board:** n/app
Freshman Class: 2340 applied, 1641 accepted, 1370 enrolled	

Inter-American University of Puerto Rico/Aguadilla Campus, a private, nonsectarian institution, was founded in 1957 and is a part of the Inter-American University of Puerto Rico. Programs offered include business, fine and liberal arts, health sciences, teacher and professional preparation. There are 5 undergraduate schools and 1 graduate school. In addition to regional accreditation, has baccalaureate program accreditation with NLN. The library contains 70,596 volumes, 460 microform items, 10,271 audio/video tapes/CDs/DVDs, and subscribes to 257 periodicals including electronic. Computerized library services include interlibrary loans, database searching, Internet access, and laptop Internet portals. Special learning facilities include a learning resource center, a multimedia center, an instructional development center, and an electronic classroom. The 54-acre campus is in a suburban area in northwestern Puerto Rico, near the Atlantic Ocean. Including any residence halls, there are 8 buildings.
Student Life: 99% of undergraduates are from Puerto Rico. 90% are from public schools. 100% are Hispanic. The average age of freshmen is 18; all undergraduates, 21. 30% do not continue beyond their first year; 70% remain to graduate.
Housing: There are no residence halls. All students commute.
Activities: There are no fraternities or sororities. There are 26 groups on campus, including cultural, academic, cheerleading, chess, choir, computers, dance, debate, drama, environmental, honors, newspaper, professional, religious, social, social service, and student government. Popular campus events include Flora and Fauna Festival, Achievement Night, and Peace Day.
Sports: There are 13 intercollegiate sports for men and 10 for women, and 10 intramural sports for men and 10 for women. Facilities include a 2000-person-capacity multiuse coliseum with basketball and volleyball courts and a small indoor track. There is also a gym with exercise equipment and an area with 3 platforms for weight-lifting. The recreation facility has table tennis and table and video arcade games.
Disabled Students: 99% of the campus is accessible. Facilities include wheelchair ramps, elevators, special parking, specially equipped restrooms, special class scheduling, lowered drinking fountains, lowered telephones. This Campus does not have a specific LD Program but we provide reasonable accommodation, according to disabled students needs.
Services: Counseling and information services are available, as is tutoring in some subjects. There is a reader service for the blind. There is a computerized center for skills development, and there are language and math labs.
Campus Safety and Security: Measures include 24-hour foot and vehicle patrol and emergency notification system. There are lighted pathways/sidewalks and in-room safes.
Programs of Study: confers B.A., B.S., B.B.A., and B.S.N. degrees. Associate and master's degrees are also awarded. Bachelor's degrees are awarded in BIOLOGICAL SCIENCE (biology/biological science and microbiology), BUSINESS (accounting, business administration and management, hotel/motel and restaurant management, human resources, management information systems, marketing/retailing/merchandising, and secretarial studies/office management), COMPUTER AND PHYSICAL SCIENCE (computer science, information sciences and systems, and radiological technology), EDUCATION (early childhood education, elementary education, physical education, secondary education, and special education), ENGINEERING AND ENVIRONMENTAL DESIGN (electrical/electronics engineering technology), HEALTH PROFESSIONS (mental health/human services and nursing), SOCIAL SCIENCE (criminal justice, forensic studies, psychology, and social work). Criminal justice, biology and nursing have the largest enrollments.
Required: To graduate, students must fulfill 44 to 47 general education credits depending on the major and including 23 credits in basic skills, 9 in historical and social context, 6 in philosophical and esthetic thought, and 3 each in Christian thought and science and technological context. A total of 120 credit hours is required; the number required in the major varies. A 2.0 GPA overall and in the major is required.
Special: The university offers internships in and out of Puerto Rico, work-study, and adult and continuing education programs. There is a freshman honors program.
Faculty/Classroom: 49% of faculty are male; 51% are female. All teach undergraduates. No introductory courses are taught by graduate students.
Admissions: 70% of a recent year applicants were accepted.
Requirements: The SAT is required. Native Spanish speakers may take the Spanish version of the SAT. Applicants must be graduates of an accredited secondary school. An interview may be required. A GPA of 2.0 is required. AP and CLEP credits are accepted.
Procedure: Freshmen are admitted to all sessions. There is a rolling admissions plan. Applications should be filed by May 1 for fall entry; November 15 for winter entry; and April 15 for summer entry. Applications are accepted online.
Transfer: 186 transfer students enrolled in 2010-2011. Transfer applicants must submit all college transcripts and must be in good standing at their previous institution. A minimum of 15 transferable credits with a grade of at least C must have been completed.
Visiting: There are regularly scheduled orientations for prospective students.
Financial Aid: In a recent year, 92% of all full-time freshmen and 94% of continuing full-time students received some form of financial aid. 90% of all full-time freshmen and 94% of continuing full-time students received need-based aid. Need-based scholarships or need-based grants averaged $400 ($600 maximum); need-based self-help aid (loans and jobs) averaged $1,000 ($3,625 maximum); and other non-need-based awards and non-need-based scholarships averaged $780 ($2,000 maximum). 100% of undergraduate students work part-time. Average annual earnings from

campus work are $1000. Inter-American is a member of CSS. The FAFSA and the college's own financial statement are required. The deadline for filing freshman financial aid applications for fall entry is April 28.

International Students: There is 1 international student enrolled.

Computers: Wireless access is available. Open-wireless, network use, and access to the Internet are available to all students. All students may access the system for distance learning, Web browsing, e-mail, and library searches. There are no time limits and no fees.

Graduates: In a recent year, 27 bachelor's degrees were awarded. The most popular majors were criminal justice (16%), teach elemtal K-3 (11%), and nursing (10%). In an average class, 1% graduate in 4 years or less, 3% graduate in 5 years or less, and 4% graduate in 6 years or less.

Admissions Contact: Doris Perez, Director of Admissions. E-Mail: *dperez@aguadilla.inter.edu* Web: *www.aguadilla.inter.edu*

INTER-AMERICAN UNIVERSITY OF PUERTO RICO/ ARECIBO CAMPUS B-1

Arecibo, PR 00614-4050 (787) 878-5195; (787) 880-1624

Full-time: 1110 men, 2210 women	**Faculty:** n/av
Part-time: 280 men, 555 women	**Ph.D.s:** 21%
Graduate: 10 men, 15 women	**Student/Faculty:** n/av
Year: semesters, summer session	**Tuition:** $5096
Application Deadline: see profile	**Room & Board:** n/app
Freshman Class: n/av	

Inter-American University of Puerto Rico/Arecibo campus, founded in 1957, is a private, nonsectarian unit of the Inter-American University of Puerto Rico system. It offers programs in business, health sciences, liberal arts, and teacher preparation. Figures given in above capsule and in this profile are approximate. The library contains 74,991 volumes, 82 microform items, 28,665 audio/video tapes/CDs/DVDs, and subscribes to 739 periodicals including electronic. Computerized library services include interlibrary loans and database searching. Special learning facilities include a learning resource center and a library exhibition area. The 20-acre campus is in a suburban area 50 miles west of San Juan. Including any residence halls, there are 9 buildings.

Student Life: 99% of undergraduates are from Puerto Rico. 93% are from public schools. All are Hispanic. The average age of freshmen is 18; all undergraduates, 24. 11% do not continue beyond their first year.

Housing: There are no residence halls. All students commute.

Activities: There are 2 local fraternities and 1 local sorority. There are 12 groups on campus, including drama, film, honors, newspaper, professional, religious, social, and student government. Popular campus events include Open House, Talent Festival, and sports events.

Sports: There are 7 intercollegiate sports for men and 7 for women, and 10 intramural sports for men and 10 for women. Facilities include a tennis court, a basketball court, and a student center with Ping-Pong tables and weight-lifting equipment.

Disabled Students: Facilities include wheelchair ramps, elevators, special parking, specially equipped restrooms, lowered drinking fountains, and lowered telephones.

Services: Counseling and information services are available, as is tutoring in accounting, secretarial sciences, math, Spanish, English, and computer sciences. There is a reader service for the blind and remedial math.

Campus Safety and Security: Measures include 24-hour foot and vehicle patrol and lighted pathways/sidewalks.

Programs of Study: Inter-American Arecibo confers B.A. and B.S. degrees. Associates and master's degrees are also awarded. Bachelor's degrees are awarded in BIOLOGICAL SCIENCE (biology/biological science and microbiology), BUSINESS (accounting, business administration and management, and marketing and distribution), COMPUTER AND PHYSICAL SCIENCE (chemical technology, chemistry, and computer science), EDUCATION (elementary education, secondary education, special education, and teaching English as a second/foreign language (TESOL/TEFOL)), HEALTH PROFESSIONS (nursing), SOCIAL SCIENCE (criminal justice and social work). Biology, criminal justice, and business administration are the strongest academically. Business administration has the largest enrollment.

Required: To graduate, all students must complete at least 130 credits with a GPA of 2.0. General education requirements include 55 credits in Spanish, English, math, logic, computers, Puerto Rican history, humanities, health, social studies, environment, and religion. Noncredit courses are required in phys ed and orientation.

Special: The university offers 3-2 programs with Pennsylvania State University in engineering and earth and mineral sciences, and with Universidad Catolica Madre y Maestra of the Dominican Republic in medicine. Independent research, work-study, and independent study programs are available. Professional certificate programs are offered in nurse anesthetist and intensive nursing care. There is a freshman honors program.

Faculty/Classroom: 45% of faculty are male; 55% are female. All teach undergraduates. No introductory courses are taught by graduate students. The average class size in an introductory lecture is 27 and in a laboratory, 25.

Requirements: Applicants must present satisfactory scores on the aptitude and English tests of the CEEB. Students whose first language is English may take the SAT. In addition, applicants should be graduates of an accredited high school. The GED is accepted. Secondary school preparation should include 15 to 30 academic credits. Some applicants may be required to schedule an interview. A GPA of 2.0 is required. Important factors in the admissions decision are advanced placement or honors courses, evidence of special talent, and leadership record.

Procedure: Freshmen are admitted to all sessions. Entrance exams should be taken in October or February of the senior year. There are early decision and rolling admissions plans. Check with the school for current application deadlines and fee.

Transfer: Applicants should present a C average in at least 15 college credits. Those with fewer transferable credits must meet freshman entrance requirements.

Visiting: There are regularly scheduled orientations for prospective students. There are guides for informal visits. To schedule a visit, contact the Admissions Office.

Financial Aid: Inter-American Arecibo is a member of CSS. The CSS/Profile and the college's own financial statement are required. Check with the school for current application deadlines.

International Students: They must take the TOEFL and also take the SAT.

Computers: All students may access the system. There are no time limits and no fees. It is strongly recommended that all students have a personal computer.

Admissions Contact: Montalvo Provi, Director of Admissions. Web: *www.arecibo.inter.edu*

INTER-AMERICAN UNIVERSITY OF PUERTO RICO/ BARRANQUITAS C-2

Barranquitas, PR 00794 (787) 857-3600

Full-time: 305 men, 835 women	**Faculty:** n/av
Part-time: 155 men, 430 women	**Ph.D.s:** 1%
Graduate: n/av	**Student/Faculty:** n/av
Year: semesters, summer session	**Tuition:** $5096
Application Deadline: see profile	**Room & Board:** n/app
Freshman Class: n/av	

Inter-American University of Puerto Rico/Barranquitas Regional College, founded in 1957 and part of the Inter-American University system, is a private college whose primary focus is teacher education. There are 6 undergraduate schools. Figures given in the above capsule and in this profile are approximate. The library contains 32,275 volumes, 23,657 microform items, 926 audio/video tapes/CDs/DVDs, and subscribes to 223 periodicals including electronic. Computerized library services include interlibrary loans. Special learning facilities include a learning resource center. The 36-acre campus is in a small town. Including any residence halls, there are 5 buildings.

Student Life: All undergraduates are from Puerto Rico. All are Hispanic. The average age of freshmen is 18; all undergraduates, 22. 4% do not continue beyond their first year; 96% remain to graduate.

Housing: There are no residence halls. All students commute.

Activities: There are no fraternities or sororities. There are 9 groups on campus, including chorus, dance, honors, religious, social, and student government. Popular campus events include Competencias LAI y LIDE, Health Fair, and Open House.

Sports: There are 8 intercollegiate sports for men and 7 for women, and 7 intramural sports for men and 6 for women. Facilities include a student center, a gym, volleyball and basketball courts, and a softball park.

Disabled Students: 1% of the campus is accessible. Facilities include wheelchair ramps and special parking.

Services: Counseling and information services are available, as is tutoring in Spanish, English, and math. There is a reader service for the blind, and remedial math, reading, and writing.

Campus Safety and Security: Measures include 24-hour foot and vehicle patrol, emergency telephones, and lighted pathways/sidewalks.

Programs of Study: Inter-American at Barranquitas confers B.A. and B.B.A. degrees. Associates degrees are also awarded. Bachelor's degrees are awarded in BUSINESS (accounting, business administration and management, and secretarial studies/office management), EDUCATION (early childhood education, elementary education, and secondary education), SOCIAL SCIENCE (criminal justice). Education, business administration, and secretarial studies are the strongest academically.

Required: In order to graduate, students must complete 120 to 132 credit hours with a minimum GPA of 2.0.

Special: Internships are available in education, secretarial studies, and criminal justice. There is 1 national honor society.

Faculty/Classroom: No introductory courses are taught by graduate students.

Requirements: The SAT or ACT is required. SAT subject tests are also required. A GPA of 2.0 is required. AP credits are accepted. Important factors in the admissions decision are evidence of special talent, advanced placement or honors courses, and leadership record.
Procedure: Freshmen are admitted fall, winter, and summer. Entrance exams should be taken in October, February, or June. There are early admissions and rolling admissions plans. Check with the school for current application deadlines and fee.
Transfer: Transfer applicants must submit a university transcript, dean's recommendation, and financial aid transcript. 36 of 120 credits required for the bachelor's degree must be completed at Inter-American at Barranquitas.
Visiting: There are regularly scheduled orientations for prospective students. There are guides for informal visits. To schedule a visit, contact the Admissions Director.
Financial Aid: Inter-American at Barranquitas is a member of CSS. Check with the school for current application deadlines.
International Students: They must take the college's own test and SAT subject tests.
Computers: There are no time limits and no fees.
Admissions Contact: Cintron Edgardo Vega, Director of Admissions. Web: *www.br.uipr.edu*

INTER-AMERICAN UNIVERSITY OF PUERTO RICO/ BAYAMON UNIVERSITY COLLEGE C-1

Bayamon, PR 00957 **(787) 279-1912, ext. 2017; (787) 279-2205**

Full-time: 2366 men, 1846 women	**Faculty:** 100
Part-time: 406 men, 324 women	**Ph.D.s:** 36%
Graduate: 12 men, 30 women	**Student/Faculty:** 22 to 1
Year: semesters, summer session	**Tuition:** $5000
Application Deadline: May 1	**Room & Board:** n/app
Freshman Class: 3107 applied, 1339 accepted, 1090 enrolled	

Inter-American University of Puerto Rico/Bayamon University College, a private, nonsectarian institution founded in 1912, is part of the Inter-American University of Puerto Rico. Students may pursue undergraduate and graduate study in business, health sciences, engineering, and aeronautics There are 3 undergraduate schools. The figures in the above capsule and in this profile are approximatel. In addition to regional accreditation, Inter-American at Bayamon has baccalaureate program accreditation with CSWE. Computerized library services include interlibrary loans, database searching, Internet access, and laptop Internet portals. Special learning facilities include a The 62-acre campus is in an urban area in a medium-size city. Including any residence halls, there are 9 buildings.
Student Life: 67% are from public schools. The average age of freshmen is 19; all undergraduates, 22.
Housing: There are no residence halls. All students commute.
Activities: There are no fraternities or sororities. Groups on campus include band, cheerleading, chess, choir, computers, dance, debate, drama, ethnic, film, honors, international, newspaper, photography, professional, radio and TV, religious, social service, and student government.
Sports: There are 10 intercollegiate sports for men and 10 for women, and 10 intramural sports for men and 10 for women.
Disabled Students: All of the campus is accessible. Facilities include wheelchair ramps, elevators, special parking, lowered drinking fountains, and lowered telephones.
Services: Counseling and information services are available, as is tutoring in some subjects.
Campus Safety and Security: Measures include 24-hour foot and vehicle patrol and security escort services. There are lighted pathways/sidewalks.
Programs of Study: Inter-American at Bayamon confers B.A., B.S., and B.B.A. degrees. Associate and master's degrees are also awarded. Bachelor's degrees are awarded in BIOLOGICAL SCIENCE (bioinformatics, biology/biological science, and biotechnology), BUSINESS (accounting, banking and finance, business administration and management, business economics, human resources, logistics, management information systems, marketing/retailing/merchandising, office supervision and management, and secretarial studies/office management), COMMUNICATIONS AND THE ARTS (communications technology and visual and performing arts), COMPUTER AND PHYSICAL SCIENCE (chemical technology, chemistry, computer science, and mathematics), ENGINEERING AND ENVIRONMENTAL DESIGN (aeronautical science, aeronautical technology, aviation administration/management, aviation computer technology, computer technology, electrical/electronics engineering, electrical/electronics engineering technology, environmental engineering technology, food services technology, industrial administration/management, industrial engineering, and mechanical engineering), SOCIAL SCIENCE (forensic studies). Business administration has the largest enrollment.
Required: To graduate, students must earn a minimum of 110 academic credits, with a minimum GPA of 2.0 overall and in the major.
Faculty/Classroom: 56% of faculty are male; 44% are female. 98% teach undergraduates, and 2% do research. No introductory courses are taught by graduate students.
Admissions: 43% of a recent year applicants were accepted.
Requirements: The Spanish equivalent to the SAT is required. Applicants must be graduates of an accredited secondary school or its equivalent. A GPA of 2.0 is required.
Procedure: Freshmen are admitted to all sessions. Applications should be filed by May 1 for fall entry; November 15 for winter entry; February 15 for spring entry; and April 15 for summer entry. Applications are accepted online.
Transfer: 152 transfer students enrolled in a recent year.
Financial Aid: The FAFSA and the college's own financial statement are required. Check with the school for current application deadlines.
International Students: There are 5 international students enrolled.
Computers: There are no time limits and no fees.
Graduates: In a recent year, 594 bachelor's degrees were awarded. The most popular majors were communications (10%), human resources management (8%), and accounting (7%).
Admissions Contact: Carlos Alicea, Director of Admissions. E-Mail: *calicea@bc.inter.edu* Web: *www.bc.inter.edu*

INTER-AMERICAN UNIVERSITY OF PUERTO RICO/ FAJARDO CAMPUS D-1

Fajardo, PR 00738-7003 **(787) 860-3100, ext. 2210; (787) 860-3470**

Full-time: 1655 men and women	**Faculty:** n/av
Part-time: 525 men and women	**Ph.D.s:** 29%
Graduate: n/av	**Student/Faculty:** n/av
Year: semesters, summer session	**Tuition:** $5500
Application Deadline: see profile	**Room & Board:** n/app
Freshman Class: n/av	

Inter-American University of Puerto Rico/Fajardo Campus, founded in 1912 and a unit of the Inter- American University of Puerto Rico, is a private, nonsectarian college offering undergraduate and graduate degrees in business, fine and liberal arts, health sciences, and teacher preparation. Figures in the above capsule and in this profile are approximate. In addition to regional accreditation, Inter at Fajardo has baccalaureate program accreditation with CSWE. The library contains 39,968 volumes and 1822 audio/video tapes/CDs/DVDs. The 11-acre campus is in an urban area in a small city. Including any residence halls, there are 10 buildings.
Student Life: 90% are from public schools. The average age of freshmen is 18.
Housing: There are no residence halls. All students commute.
Activities: There are no fraternities or sororities. Groups on campus include academic, chorale, cultural, professional, recreational, religious, and social.
Sports: There are 3 intercollegiate sports for men and 2 for women, and 4 intramural sports for men and 3 for women. Facilities include a multipurpose building.
Disabled Students: Facilities include wheelchair ramps, elevators, special parking, and specially equipped restrooms.
Services: There is remedial math and reading.
Programs of Study: Inter at Fajardo confers B.A., B.S., and B.B.A. degrees. Associates, master's, and doctoral degrees are also awarded. Bachelor's degrees are awarded in BIOLOGICAL SCIENCE (biology/biological science), BUSINESS (accounting, banking and finance, business administration and management, insurance, management information systems, marketing/retailing/merchandising, and secretarial studies/office management), COMMUNICATIONS AND THE ARTS (applied music, Spanish, and visual and performing arts), COMPUTER AND PHYSICAL SCIENCE (chemical technology, chemistry, computer science, and mathematics), EDUCATION (early childhood education, elementary education, music education, secondary education, and special education), ENGINEERING AND ENVIRONMENTAL DESIGN (electrical/electronics engineering technology), HEALTH PROFESSIONS (medical technology and nursing), SOCIAL SCIENCE (criminal justice, history, political science/government, psychology, public administration, social work, and sociology). Social work has the largest enrollment.
Required: To graduate, all students must complete 120 credit hours with a minimum GPA of 2.0 overall and in the major. General education requirements total 47 credits including 18 credits in communication skills, 9 in historical-culture heritage, 6 in ability to integrate, apply, and create, 6 in methods of interpreting reality, 5 in reasoning skills, and 3 nonacademic credits each in health, phys ed, or recreation.
Special: Co-op programs in engineering and earth and mineral sciences with Pennsylvania State University, cross-registration, internships, work-study, and adult and continuing education programs are available. There is a freshman honors program and 1 departmental honors program.
Faculty/Classroom: 43% of faculty are male; 57% are female. No introductory courses are taught by graduate students. The average class

size in an introductory lecture is 25; in a laboratory, 20; and in a regular course, 25.

Requirements: The SAT or ACT is required. Native Spanish-speaking students may take the CEEB Spanish version of the SAT. Students must have graduated from an accredited secondary school. An interview may be required. A GPA of 2.0 is required. AP credits are accepted.

Procedure: Freshmen are admitted to all sessions. There is a rolling admissions plan. Check with the school for current application deadlines and fee. Applications are accepted online.

Transfer: Applicants must have completed at least 15 transferable semester credits with a minimum grade of C and must be in good standing at their previous institution. All college transcripts must be submitted.

Financial Aid: The FAFSA and the college's own financial statement are required. Check with the school for current deadlines.

Computers: Wireless access is available. All students may access the system. There are no time limits and no fees.

Admissions Contact: Ada Caraballo, Admissions Director. E-Mail: *adcaraba@inter.edu* Web: *www.fajardo.inter.edu*

INTER-AMERICAN UNIVERSITY OF PUERTO RICO/ METROPOLITAN CAMPUS D-1

San Juan, PR 00919-1293 **(787) 765-1270; (787) 764-6963**

Full-time: 2115 men, 2735 women	**Faculty:** n/av
Part-time: 970 men, 1300 women	**Ph.D.s:** 52%
Graduate: 1125 men, 2320 women	**Student/Faculty:** n/av
Year: varies, summer session	**Tuition:** $7160
Application Deadline: see profile	**Room & Board:** n/app
Freshman Class: n/av	

Inter-American University of Puerto Rico/Metropolitan Campus, a private, nonsectarian institution founded in 1912, is a unit of the Inter-American University of Puerto Rico. Students may pursue undergraduate and graduate study in business, fine and liberal arts, health sciences, and teacher preparation. There are 6 undergraduate schools and 2 graduate schools. Figures in the above capsule and in this profile are approximate. In addition to regional accreditation, Inter American Metro has baccalaureate program accreditation with CSWE. The library contains 112,018 volumes, 638,026 microform items, 1350 audio/video tapes/CDs/DVDs, and subscribes to 2798 periodicals including electronic. Computerized library services include interlibrary loans, database searching, and Internet access. Special learning facilities include a learning resource center, art gallery, audiovisual center, instructional development center, and publication center. The 20-acre campus is in an urban area 9 miles from San Juan. Including any residence halls, there are 13 buildings.

Student Life: 99% of undergraduates are from Puerto Rico. 59% are from public schools. 98% are Hispanic. The average age of freshmen is 18; all undergraduates, 18.

Housing: Alcohol is not permitted. All students commute. All students may keep cars.

Activities: There are no fraternities or sororities. There are 23 groups on campus, including art, cheerleading, chorus, debate, drama, international, jazz band, orchestra, professional, religious, student government, symphony, and yearbook.

Sports: There are 7 intercollegiate sports for men and 7 for women, and 7 intramural sports for men and 7 for women.

Disabled Students: 90% of the campus is accessible. Facilities include wheelchair ramps, elevators, special parking, lowered drinking fountains, and lowered telephones.

Services: Counseling and information services are available, as is tutoring in Spanish, English, and math. There is a reader service for the blind. There also are interpreters for the hearing impaired.

Campus Safety and Security: Measures include 24-hour foot and vehicle patrol.

Programs of Study: Inter-American Metro confers B.A., B.S., and B.B.A. degrees. Associates, master's, and doctoral degrees are also awarded. Bachelor's degrees are awarded in BIOLOGICAL SCIENCE (biology/biological science), BUSINESS (accounting, banking and finance, business administration and management, management information systems, marketing/retailing/merchandising, and secretarial studies/office management), COMMUNICATIONS AND THE ARTS (music performance and Spanish), COMPUTER AND PHYSICAL SCIENCE (chemistry, computer science, and mathematics), EDUCATION (early childhood education, elementary education, secondary education, and special education), HEALTH PROFESSIONS (medical technology and nursing), SOCIAL SCIENCE (criminal justice, history, political science/government, psychology, social work, and sociology). Chemistry is the strongest academically.

Required: To graduate, students must complete 47 general education credits: 23 credits in basic skills, 9 credits in philosophical and esthetic thought, 9 in the historical process of Puerto Rico, 3 in scientific and technological context, and 3 in well-being and quality of life. A total of 120 credit hours must be completed; the number in the major varies. A minimum 2.0 GPA overall and in the major is required.

Special: Cross-registration, internship and work-study programs, and adult education programs are available. There is 1 national honor society and a freshman honors program.

Faculty/Classroom: 49% of faculty are male; 51% are female. 65% teach undergraduates, and 5% also do research. No introductory courses are taught by graduate students. The average class size in an introductory lecture is 20 and in a laboratory, 22.

Requirements: The SAT is recommended. Students whose first language is Spanish may take the CEEB Spanish version of the SAT. A GPA of 2.0 is required.

Procedure: Freshmen are admitted to all sessions. Entrance exams should be taken by October. There is a rolling admissions plan. Check with the school for current application deadlines and fee. Applications are accepted online.

Transfer: Applicants must have completed at least 12 transferable semester credits with a minimum grade of C and be in good standing at the previous institution. 40 of 120 credits required for the bachelor's degree must be completed at Inter-American Metro.

Visiting: There are regularly scheduled orientations for prospective students, including an open house twice a year.

Financial Aid: The FAFSA and the college's own financial statement are required. Check with the school for current deadlines.

Computers: All students may access the system Monday through Saturday. It is recommended that students in economics and administrative sciences have a personal computer.

Admissions Contact: Janice Olivieri, Director of Admissions. A campus DVD is available. E-Mail: *jolivieri@inter.edu* Web: *www.metro.inter.edu*

INTER-AMERICAN UNIVERSITY OF PUERTO RICO/ PONCE C-2

Ponce, PR 00715-2201 **(787) 840-9090; (787) 841-0103**

Full-time: n/av	**Faculty:** n/av
Part-time: n/av	**Ph.D.s:** n/av
Graduate: n/av	**Student/Faculty:** n/av
Year: varies	**Tuition:** $5500
Application Deadline: see profile	**Room & Board:** n/app
Freshman Class: n/av	

Inter-American University of Puerto Rico/Ponce Regional College, founded in 1912 and a unit of the Inter-American University of Puerto Rico, is a private, nonsectarian institution offering undergraduate and graduate programs in business, liberal and fine arts, health sciences, and teacher preparation. There is 1 graduate school. The figures in the above capsule and in this profile are approximate. In addition to regional accreditation, Inter-American at Ponce has baccalaureate program accreditation with CSWE. The campus is in an urban area in a medium-size city.

Activities: There are no fraternities or sororities.

Sports: There is no sports program at Inter-American at Ponce.

Programs of Study: Bachelor's degrees are awarded in BIOLOGICAL SCIENCE (biology/biological science), BUSINESS (accounting, banking and finance, business administration and management, insurance, management information systems, marketing/retailing/merchandising, and secretarial studies/office management), COMMUNICATIONS AND THE ARTS (applied music, Spanish, and visual and performing arts), COMPUTER AND PHYSICAL SCIENCE (chemical technology, chemistry, computer science, and mathematics), EDUCATION (early childhood education, elementary education, music education, secondary education, and special education), ENGINEERING AND ENVIRONMENTAL DESIGN (electrical/electronics engineering technology), HEALTH PROFESSIONS (medical technology and nursing), SOCIAL SCIENCE (criminal justice, history, political science/government, psychology, public administration, social work, and sociology).

Faculty/Classroom: No introductory courses are taught by graduate students.

Procedure: Application deadlines are open.

Financial Aid: The FAFSA and the college's own financial statement are required. Check with the school for current deadlines.

Computers: There are no time limits and no fees.

Admissions Contact: Franco Diaz, Director of Admissions. E-mail: *admisiones@ponce.inter.edu* Web: *www.ponce.inter.edu*

INTER-AMERICAN UNIVERSITY OF PUERTO RICO/ SAN GERMÁN B-2

San Germán, PR 00683-9801 (787) 892-3090; (787) 892-6350

Full-time: 3905 men and women
Part-time: 1205 men and women
Graduate: 955 men and women
Year: semesters, summer session
Application Deadline: see profile
Freshman Class: n/av
Faculty: n/av
Ph.D.s: 43%
Student/Faculty: n/av
Tuition: $5096
Room & Board: $3500

Inter-American University of Puerto Rico/San German, founded in 1912, is a private institution that is part of the Inter-American University of Puerto Rico system. It offers programs in fine and liberal arts, business, health science, and teacher preparation. There are 3 graduate schools. Figures in the above capsule and in this profile are approximate. In addition to regional accreditation, the university has baccalaureate program accreditation with CAHEA. The library contains 153,431 volumes, 571,116 microform items, 30,777 audio/video tapes/CDs/DVDs, and subscribes to 3818 periodicals including electronic. Computerized library services include interlibrary loans. Special learning facilities include a learning resource center, art gallery, and natural history museum. The 260-acre campus is in a rural area 14 miles from Mayaguez. Including any residence halls, there are 64 buildings.

Student Life: 99% of undergraduates are from Puerto Rico. Others are from 9 foreign countries and Canada. 83% are from public schools. 99% are Hispanic. The average age of freshmen is 18; all undergraduates, 22. 28% do not continue beyond their first year; 41% remain to graduate.

Housing: 512 students can be accommodated in college housing, which includes single-sex dorms, on-campus apartments, and married student housing. On-campus housing is guaranteed for all 4 years. 89% of students commute. Alcohol is not permitted. All students may keep cars.

Activities: There are no fraternities or sororities. There are 34 groups on campus, including art, band, choir, chorale, computers, dance, drama, ethnic, honors, international, jazz band, marching band, musical theater, newspaper, orchestra, political, professional, religious, social, social service, and student government. Popular campus events include Feria Tipica and Founders Celebration Dances.

Sports: There are 11 intercollegiate sports for men and 6 for women, and 11 intramural sports for men and 6 for women. Facilities include a gym, dirt and tartan tracks, tennis courts, a jogging course, table tennis, a billiards room, table games, aerobics areas, a small gym in residence halls, and a gym with a basketball court.

Disabled Students: 80% of the campus is accessible. Facilities include wheelchair ramps, special parking, specially equipped restrooms, special class scheduling, lowered drinking fountains, lowered telephones, and elevators in some buildings.

Services: Counseling and information services are available, as is tutoring in Spanish, English, math, and computer science.

Campus Safety and Security: Measures include 24-hour foot and vehicle patrol. There are shuttle buses, emergency telephones, and an electronic security system.

Programs of Study: The university confers B.A., B.S., and B.B.A. degrees. Associates, master's, and doctoral degrees are also awarded. Bachelor's degrees are awarded in BIOLOGICAL SCIENCE (biology/biological science), BUSINESS (accounting, banking and finance, business administration and management, marketing/retailing/merchandising, and secretarial studies/office management), COMMUNICATIONS AND THE ARTS (English, fine arts, music, and Spanish), COMPUTER AND PHYSICAL SCIENCE (chemistry, computer science, and mathematics), EDUCATION (art education, early childhood education, elementary education, health education, music education, science education, secondary education, special education, and teaching English as a second/foreign language (TESOL/TEFOL)), HEALTH PROFESSIONS (medical laboratory technology, nursing, and premedicine), SOCIAL SCIENCE (economics, history, political science/government, psychology, public administration, and sociology). Business administration and medical technology are the strongest academically. Computer science, business administration, and biology have the largest enrollment.

Required: To graduate, students must complete at least 124 credits, with a minimum GPA of 2.5. General education requirements include courses in Spanish, English, mathematical reasoning, logical and critical reasoning, computer programming, and Puerto Rican history. In addition, students must take 6 credits in methods of interpreting reality, 2 in phys ed, computer science, and community service, and 1 each in art, music, ethics, and Puerto Rican culture.

Special: The university offers internships, credit by exam, and nondegree study. A 3-2 engineering degree is available with Penn State University. There are 2 national honor societies and a freshman honors program.

Faculty/Classroom: 48% of faculty are male; 52% are female. 89% teach undergraduates. No introductory courses are taught by graduate students. The average class size in an introductory lecture is 25; in a laboratory, 10; and in a regular course, 25.

Requirements: The SAT is required, or the CEEB Spanish equivalent. Applicants must be high school graduates and have completed 15 credits, including 3 each in Spanish, English, and electives, and 2 each in math and science. A GPA of 2.5 is required. AP and CLEP credits are accepted. Important factors in the admissions decision are advanced placement or honors courses, evidence of special talent, and recommendations by school officials.

Procedure: Freshmen are admitted to all sessions. Entrance exams should be taken in the first or second semester of the senior year. There is an early admissions plan. Check with the school for current deadlines and application fee. Applications are accepted online.

Transfer: Applicants should have at least 15 college credits with a minimum GPA of 2.5. The SAT or the CEEB Spanish version is required, as is a letter of recommendation from the dean of students at the student's previous college. 30 of 124 credits required for the bachelor's degree must be completed at the university.

Visiting: There are regularly scheduled orientations for prospective students during the summer. There are guides for informal visits; visitors may sit in on classes and stay overnight.

Financial Aid: The university is a member of CSS. The FAFSA and the college's own financial statement are required. Check with the school for current deadlines.

Computers: All students may access the system during designated hours. There are no time limits.

Admissions Contact: Mildred Camacho, Director of Admissions. A campus DVD is available. E-Mail: *milcama@sg.inter.edu* Web: *www.sg.inter.edu*

PONTIFICAL CATHOLIC UNIVERSITY OF PUERTO RICO C-2

Ponce, PR 00717-0777 (787) 841-2000, ext. 1000; (787) 651-2044

Full-time: 2285 men, 4475 women
Part-time: 485 men, 795 women
Graduate: 675 men, 1205 women
Year: semesters, summer session
Application Deadline: see profile
Freshman Class: n/av
Faculty: n/av
Ph.D.s: n/av
Student/Faculty: n/av
Tuition: $5206
Room & Board: $4000

Pontifical Catholic University of Puerto Rico, founded in 1948, is a private institution affiliated with the Roman Catholic Church of Puerto Rico. The school offers undergraduate and graduate programs in liberal arts, the sciences, education, and business. There are 4 undergraduate schools and 6 graduate schools. Figures in the above capsule and in this profile are approximate. In addition to regional accreditation, La Catolica has baccalaureate program accreditation with CSWE and NLN. The 2 libraries contain 238,033 volumes, 514,440 microform items, 13,456 audio/video tapes/CDs/DVDs, and subscribe to 58,183 periodicals including electronic. Computerized library services include interlibrary loans and database searching. Special learning facilities include a learning resource center, radio station, TV station, and electronic information center. The 55-acre campus is in an urban area 35 miles south of San Juan. Including any residence halls, there are 40 buildings.

Student Life: All undergraduates are from Puerto Rico. Others are from 4 foreign countries. 80% are from public schools. All are Hispanic. The average age of freshmen is 19; all undergraduates, 22.

Housing: 180 students can be accommodated in college housing, which includes single-sex dorms. Priority is given to out-of-town students. 97% of students commute. Alcohol is not permitted. All students may keep cars.

Activities: 1% of men belong to 11 local fraternities; 1% of women belong to 7 local sororities. There are 50 groups on campus, including art, band, choir, chorale, communications, computers, dance, drama, honors, literary magazine, newspaper, photography, professional, radio and TV, religious, social service, student government, and yearbook. Popular campus events include freshman activities at the beginning of the academic year; religious and social activities celebrated on Thanksgiving, Christmas, and Holy Week, and Puerto Rican Culture Week.

Sports: There are 7 intercollegiate sports for men and 5 for women, and 6 intramural sports for men and 4 for women. Facilities include a gym, a 6000-seat arena, an Olympic-size pool, 5 tennis courts, a baseball field, 3 basketball courts, 3 volleyball courts, and a synthetic track and field.

Disabled Students: 95% of the campus is accessible. Facilities include wheelchair ramps, elevators, special parking, specially equipped restrooms, special class scheduling, lowered drinking fountains, lowered telephones, a braille typewriter, an English and Spanish book reader, and a text enlarger.

Services: Counseling and information services are available, as is tutoring in math, chemistry, physics, English, Spanish, philosophy, statistics, accounting, and political science. There is a reader service for the blind, and remedial math, reading, and writing.

Campus Safety and Security: Measures include 24-hour foot and vehicle patrol, emergency telephones, and lighted pathways/sidewalks.

Programs of Study: La Catolica confers B.A., B.S., B.B.A., and B.S.Ed degrees. Associates, master's, and doctoral degrees are also awarded. Bachelor's degrees are awarded in BIOLOGICAL SCIENCE (biology/biological science), BUSINESS (accounting, banking and finance, business administration and management, business economics, international economics, and marketing/retailing/merchandising), COMMUNICATIONS AND THE ARTS (communications, English, fine arts, public relations, and Spanish), COMPUTER AND PHYSICAL SCIENCE (chemistry, computer programming, mathematics, and physics), EDUCATION (art education, business education, elementary education, home economics education, mathematics education, music education, physical education, science education, secondary education, social studies education, special education, and teaching English as a second/foreign language (TESOL/TEFOL)), HEALTH PROFESSIONS (medical laboratory technology and nursing), SOCIAL SCIENCE (criminology, gerontology, history, liberal arts/general studies, philosophy, political science/government, psychology, public administration, religion, social science, social work, sociology, and theological studies). Physical sciences is the strongest academically. General studies has the largest enrollment.

Required: Bachelor's candidates must complete a 136-credit program in not more than twice the usual number of years and maintain a GPA of 2.0. Required courses include theology, philosophy, humanities, English, Spanish, math, science, phys ed, social or political science, music or art, and basic computer.

Special: The university offers co-op programs in medicine, engineering, veterinary, and pharmacy, as well as cross-registration with the University of Valladolid and a 3-2 engineering degree with Case Western Reserve University. A Washington semester, work-study programs within the university, nondegree study, pass/fail options in elective courses, and a student-designed major in liberal arts are also available. There are 8 national honor societies, a freshman honors program, and 3 departmental honors programs.

Faculty/Classroom: 85% teach undergraduates, and 1% do research. No introductory courses are taught by graduate students. The average class size in an introductory lecture is 35; in a laboratory, 32; and in a regular course, 35.

Requirements: The SAT is required, along with SAT subject tests in math, Spanish, and English as a second language. In addition, applicants must be high school graduates or hold a GED. Students from 3-year senior high schools should have earned 10 units consisting of 3 each of English and Spanish, 2 of math, and 1 each of science and history. Students from 4-year high schools should have earned 15 units consisting of 4 each of English and Spanish, 3 of math, and 2 each of science and history. Students from outside Puerto Rico may substitute 2 years of another foreign language for the Spanish requirement. An interview is required for special programs. A GPA of 2.0 is required. AP and CLEP credits are accepted. Important factors in the admissions decision are advanced placement or honors courses, evidence of special talent, and leadership record.

Procedure: Freshmen are admitted to all sessions. Entrance exams should be taken during the fall of the senior year. There is a rolling admissions plan. Check with the school for current application deadlines. The application fee is $15.

Transfer: Applicants must supply a college transcript. A GPA of 2.0 and 30 credit hours are required. An associate degree is recommended. 30 of 136 credits required for the bachelor's degree must be completed at La Catolica.

Visiting: There are guides for informal visits, and visitors may sit in on classes.

Financial Aid: The FAFSA, the college's own financial statement, and income certification documents are required. Check with the school for current deadlines.

International Students: The school actively recruits these students. They must also take the SAT or ACT.

Computers: All students may access the system 8 a.m. to 10 p.m. Monday through Thursday and 8 a.m. to 5 p.m. Friday and Saturday. There are no time limits. The fee is included in the university fee.

Admissions Contact: Admissions Office. A campus DVD is available.
E-Mail: *admisiones@pucpr.edu* Web: *www.pucpr.edu*

UNIVERSIDAD ADVENTISTA DE LAS ANTILLAS A-1

Mayaguez, PR 00681-0118 **(787) 834-9595, ext. 2261; (787) 834-9597**

Full-time: 295 men, 425 women	**Faculty:** n/av
Part-time: 25 men, 45 women	**Ph.D.s:** n/av
Graduate: 25 men, 60 women	**Student/Faculty:** n/av
Year: semesters, summer session	**Tuition:** $6835
Application Deadline: open	**Room & Board:** $8000
Freshman Class: n/av	

Universidad Adventista de las Antillas, established in 1961 and affiliated with the Seventh-day Adventist Church, offers undergraduate programs in business administration, sciences and computers, education and psychology, nursing and allied health, music and fine arts, religion, and humanities. There are 7 undergraduate schools. Figures in the above capsule and in this profile are approximate. In addition to regional accreditation, UAA has baccalaureate program accreditation with NLN. The library contains 88,432 volumes, 2603 microform items, 1717 audio/video tapes/CDs/DVDs, and subscribes to 392 periodicals including electronic. Computerized library services include interlibrary loans, database searching, and Internet access. Special learning facilities include a learning resource center. The 284-acre campus is in a small town on the west coast of Puerto Rico. Including any residence halls, there are 6 buildings.

Student Life: 72% of undergraduates are from Puerto Rico. Others are from 15 states, 22 foreign countries, and Canada. 50% are from public schools. 96% are Hispanic. 66% are Seventh-day Adventist; 14% claim no religious affiliation; 13% Catholic. The average age of freshmen is 19; all undergraduates, 22. 30% do not continue beyond their first year; 70% remain to graduate.

Housing: 252 students can be accommodated in college housing, which includes single-sex dorms, on-campus apartments, and married student housing. On-campus housing is guaranteed for all 4 years. 70% of students commute. Alcohol is not permitted. All students may keep cars.

Activities: 75% of men belong to 1 local fraternity; 80% of women belong to 1 local sorority. There are 20 groups on campus, including band, choir, chorale, chorus, drama, film, international, literary magazine, newspaper, orchestra, photography, professional, religious, social, social service, and student government. Popular campus events include International Fair, Columbus Day, and Discovering Puerto Rico.

Sports: There are 4 intercollegiate sports for men and 3 for women, and 4 intramural sports for men and 3 for women. Facilities include a gym, a swimming pool, and a tennis court.

Disabled Students: 90% of the campus is accessible. Facilities include wheelchair ramps, special parking, specially equipped restrooms, lowered drinking fountains, and lowered telephones.

Services: Counseling and information services are available, as is tutoring in math, English, and Spanish. There is remedial math, reading, and writing.

Campus Safety and Security: Measures include 24-hour foot and vehicle patrol.

Programs of Study: UAA confers B.A. and B.S. degrees. Associates and master's degrees are also awarded. Bachelor's degrees are awarded in BIOLOGICAL SCIENCE (biology/biological science), BUSINESS (business administration and management and office supervision and management), COMMUNICATIONS AND THE ARTS (music and Spanish), COMPUTER AND PHYSICAL SCIENCE (computer science), EDUCATION (elementary education, music education, and secondary education), HEALTH PROFESSIONS (health science and nursing), SOCIAL SCIENCE (history, pastoral studies, religion, and theological studies). Business administration, nursing, and computer science are the strongest academically. Nursing has the largest enrollment.

Required: Students must complete 128 credits, with 44 to 66 in the major and a minimum GPA of 2.0. General education requirements include courses in religion, music or art, math, phys ed, computer science, Spanish, English, philosophy of education, and biological and physical sciences.

Special: Work-study programs, B.A.-B.S. degrees, credit by exam, and pass/fail options are available. There is a 3-2 engineering degree with Walla Walla University in Washington State.

Faculty/Classroom: 51% of faculty are male; 47% are female. All teach undergraduates. No introductory courses are taught by graduate students. The average class size in an introductory lecture is 30; in a laboratory, 35; and in a regular course, 30.

Requirements: The SAT or ACT is required, with a satisfactory score on the SAT or 18 on the ACT. Graduation from an accredited secondary school is required; the GED is accepted. Applicants must submit 12 to 15 academic credits, including 3 each in English and a foreign language, 2 each in history, math, science, and social studies, and 1 to 2 in other electives. An interview is recommended. A GPA of 2.0 is required. AP and CLEP credits are accepted. Important factors in the admissions decision are advanced placement or honors courses, ability to finance college education, and parents or siblings who attended the school.

Procedure: Freshmen are admitted to all sessions. There is a rolling admissions plan. Application deadlines are open. Check with the school for current application fee.

Transfer: Applicants must be in good standing at the previous institution, with a GPA of at least 2.0, and must submit official transcripts of high school and college credit. An official report of the CEEB Spanish equivalent of the SAT must be provided if the applicant has completed fewer than 24 semester credits. 30 of 128 credits required for the bachelor's degree must be completed at UAA.

Visiting: There are regularly scheduled orientations for prospective students. There are guides for informal visits; visitors may sit in on classes and stay overnight.

Financial Aid: UAA is a member of CSS. The CSS/Profile, FAFSA, and the college's own financial statement are required. Check with the school for current deadlines.

International Students: They must take the college's own test. They must also take the SAT or ACT, or the CEEB Spanish equivalent of the SAT.

Computers: Wireless access is available. All students may access the system 7:30 a.m. to 10 p.m. It is strongly recommended that all students have a personal computer.

Admissions Contact: Evelyn del Valle, Director, Admissions and Continuing Education. A campus DVD is available. E-Mail: *edelvalle@uaa.edu or admissions@uaa.edu* Web: *www.uaa.edu*

UNIVERSIDAD DEL TURABO D-1

Gurabo, PR 00658 **(787) 746-3009**

Full-time: n/av	**Faculty:** n/av
Part-time: n/av	**Ph.D.s:** 33%
Graduate: n/av	**Student/Faculty:** n/av
Year: semesters, summer session	**Tuition:** $5564
Application Deadline: open	**Room & Board:** n/app
Freshman Class: n/av	

Universidad del Turabo, founded in 1972, is a private nonsectarian institution offering undergraduate programs in business administration, education, Spanish, social sciences, natural sciences and technology, and English and communications, and graduate programs in business administration and education. There are 2 graduate schools. Figures given in above capsule and in this profile are approximate. The library contains 126,000 volumes. Computerized library services include database searching. Special learning facilities include a learning resource center, archeological-folkloric museum, and language lab. The 116-acre campus is in a suburban area 15 miles south of San Juan. Including any residence halls, there are 15 buildings.

Activities: There are no fraternities or sororities.

Sports: There is no sports program at the university.

Programs of Study: The university confers B.A., B.S., and B.B.A. degrees. Associates and master's degrees are also awarded. Bachelor's degrees are awarded in BIOLOGICAL SCIENCE (biology/biological science), BUSINESS (accounting, business administration and management, management science, marketing/retailing/merchandising, and secretarial studies/office management), COMMUNICATIONS AND THE ARTS (English and Spanish), COMPUTER AND PHYSICAL SCIENCE (chemistry, computer programming, mathematics, and natural sciences), EDUCATION (elementary education, English education, foreign languages education, mathematics education, physical education, science éducation, secondary education, social science education, and special education), SOCIAL SCIENCE (criminology, economics, history, humanities, psychology, public administration, social science, and sociology).

Required: To graduate, students must complete course requirements with a minimum 2.0 GPA overall and 2.0 to 2.3 in the major.

Special: The university offers a general studies degree, graduate-level night courses in business and education, work-study, and nondegree study. There is 1 departmental honors program.

Faculty/Classroom: 50% of faculty are male; 50% are female. No introductory courses are taught by graduate students.

Procedure: Application deadlines are open.

Financial Aid: The FAFSA is required. Check with the school for current deadlines.

Computers: There are no time limits and no fees.

Admissions Contact: Admissions Office Director.

UNIVERSIDAD METROPOLITANA D-1

Rio Piedras, PR 00928 **(787) 765-6262**

Full-time: n/av	**Faculty:** n/av
Part-time: n/av	**Ph.D.s:** n/av
Graduate: n/av	**Student/Faculty:** n/av
Year: semesters, summer session	**Tuition:** $5564
Application Deadline: open	**Room & Board:** n/app
Freshman Class: n/av	

Universidad Metropolitana, founded in 1980, is a private, commuter institution offering undergraduate programs in the liberal arts and sciences, business, nursing, and education. There are 6 undergraduate schools. Figures given in above capsule and in this profile are approximate. In addition to regional accreditation, UMET has baccalaureate program accreditation with NLN. The library contains 34,445 volumes and 5000 microform items. Special learning facilities include a learning resource center and TV station. The campus is in an urban area. There are 11 buildings.

Activities: There are no fraternities or sororities.

Sports: There is no sports program at UMET.

Programs of Study: UMET confers B.A., B.S., B.B.A., and B.S.N. degrees. Associates and master's degrees are also awarded. Bachelor's degrees are awarded in BUSINESS (accounting, business administration and management, and management science), COMPUTER AND PHYSICAL SCIENCE (natural sciences), EDUCATION (elementary education and secondary education), ENGINEERING AND ENVIRONMENTAL DESIGN (surveying engineering), HEALTH PROFESSIONS (nursing), SOCIAL SCIENCE (humanities, psychology, social science, and sociology). Business is the strongest academically. Education and natural sciences have the largest enrollment.

Required: To graduate, students must complete an average of 135 credits, including at least 30 in the major field. Specific GPA requirements vary by department. All students must take a computer course and complete a general education core.

Special: UMET offers work-study programs, B.A.-B.S. degrees, and an honors program in the natural sciences. The Televised Education Center (CET) offers students an opportunity for independent study. There is 1 departmental honors program.

Faculty/Classroom: 40% of faculty are male; 60% are female. No introductory courses are taught by graduate students.

Requirements: The SAT is required. In addition, applicants must be graduates of an accredited secondary school with a GPA of 2.0. Some programs have higher GPA requirements.

Procedure: Freshmen are admitted to all sessions. There is a rolling admissions plan. Application deadlines are open.

Transfer: All applicants must meet the GPA requirements of the program they wish to enter. Students should submit transcripts from all previous colleges attended as well as a letter of recommendation from the dean of the most recent institution. Grades of C or better transfer for credit.

Financial Aid: The college's own financial statement is required. Check with the school for current deadlines.

Admissions Contact: Office of Admissions. Web: *www.suagm.edu/umet*

UNIVERSIDAD POLITECNICA DE PUERTO RICO D-1

Hato Rey, PR 00918 **(787) 754-8000, ext. 240**

Full-time: 1492 men, 381 women	**Faculty:** 139; IIA, --$
Part-time: 1585 men, 403 women	**Ph.D.s:** 24%
Graduate: 556 men, 229 women	**Student/Faculty:** 13 to 1
Year: trimesters, summer session	**Tuition:** $7548
Application Deadline:	**Room & Board:** $11,704
Freshman Class: 540 applied, 480 accepted, 368 enrolled	
SAT: required	

Polytechnic University of Puerto Rico (PUPR) is a private, co-educational institution specializing in Engineering, Architecture, Land Surveying and Geomatics and Business Administration. Founded in September, 1966, the campus is conveniently located in the island's financial district which is the very core of metropolitan San Juan. Our location affords easy access to many significant cultural and commercial centers of San Juan, our capital city. There are 3 undergraduate schools and 1 graduate school. In addition to regional accreditation, La Poli has baccalaureate program accreditation with ABET and NAAB. The library contains 127,666 volumes, 984 microform items, 3,432 audio/video tapes/CDs/DVDs, and subscribes to 15,377 periodicals including electronic. Computerized library services include interlibrary loans, database searching, Internet access, and Wi-Fi capability. Special learning facilities include a The 8-acre campus is in an urban area in the Hato Rey section of San Juan. Including any residence halls, there are 8 buildings.

Student Life: 99% of undergraduates are from Puerto Rico. 50% are from public schools. 99% are Hispanic. 80% are Catholic. The average age of freshmen is 19.3; all undergraduates, 23.7. 25% do not continue beyond their first year; 22% remain to graduate.

Housing: All students commute. All students may keep cars.

Activities: There are 8 groups on campus, including cheerleading, choir, honors, newspaper, political, professional, religious, and student government. Popular campus events include Student Night, Library Week, and Education Weeks.

Sports: There are 8 intercollegiate sports for men and 5 for women. Facilities include basketball and volleyball courts, and a gym.

Disabled Students: 90% of the campus is accessible. Facilities include wheelchair ramps, elevators, special parking, specially equipped restrooms, and TTY phone.

Services: Counseling and information services are available, as is tutoring in some subjects, Spanish, English, Math, engineering, and science (Physics and Chemistry). There is remedial math.

Campus Safety and Security: Measures include 24-hour foot and vehicle patrol, emergency notification system, and security escort services. There are shuttle buses and lighted pathways/sidewalks.

Programs of Study: La Poli confers B.S., B.B.A. and B.S.E. degrees. Associate and master's degrees are also awarded. Bachelor's degrees are awarded in BUSINESS (business administration and management), COMPUTER AND PHYSICAL SCIENCE (computer science), ENGINEERING AND ENVIRONMENTAL DESIGN (chemical engineering, civil engineering, computer engineering, electrical/electronics engineering, environmental engineering, industrial administration/management, industrial engineering, mechanical engineering, and surveying engineering). Electrical and civil engineering are the strongest programs academically and have the largest enrollments.

Required: All graduating students must complete 128 to 176 quarter credits, with a minimum GPA of 2.0. There are distribution requirements in Spanish, English, humanities, social sciences, and math, and within the chosen field. All students must take 6 credits in computer science. All majors require a practicum course before graduation.

Special: Co-op programs are available in all majors. There are 1 national honor societies, a freshman honors program, and 1 departmental honors programs.

Faculty/Classroom: 65% of faculty are male; 35% are female. 94% teach undergraduates. No introductory courses are taught by graduate students. The average class size in an introductory lecture is 30; in a laboratory is 20; and in a regular course is 22.

Admissions: 89% of the 2013-2014 applicants were accepted.

Requirements: The SAT is required. The CEEB Spanish equivalents of the SAT and subject tests are required. Applicants must be graduates of an accredited secondary school, with 15 high school academic units. An interview is recommended. A GPA of 2.5 is required. AP and CLEP credits are accepted.

Procedure: Freshmen are admitted to all sessions. There are early decision and rolling admissions plans. Application deadlines are open. The fall 2013 application fee was $30. Notification is sent on a rolling basis. Applications are accepted online.

Transfer: 255 transfer students enrolled in 2012-2013. Applicants must present an official transcript and letters of recommendation. They must also have a GPA of 2.0 or higher and approved credits.

Visiting: There are regularly scheduled orientations for prospective students. To schedule a visit, contact Teresa Cardona at (787) 622-8000.

Financial Aid: La Poli is a member of CSS. The FAFSA and the college's own financial statement are required. The deadline for filing freshman financial aid applications for fall entry is April 30.

International Students: the Spanish equivalent of the SAT.

Computers: All students may access the system. There are no time limits. The fee is $35.

Graduates: From July 1, 2012 to June 30, 2013, 510 bachelor's degrees were awarded. The most popular majors were civil engineering (21%), electrical engineering (21%), and business administration (10%). 73 companies recruited on campus in 2012-2013. In an average class, 3% graduate in 4 years or less, 29% graduate in 5 years or less, and 59% graduate in 6 years or less. Of the 2012 graduating class, 19% were enrolled in graduate school within 6 months of graduation.

Admissions Contact: Teresa Cardona, Director of Admissions. E-Mail: *tcardona@pupr.edu* Web: *www.pupr.edu*

UNIVERSITY OF PUERTO RICO SYSTEM

The University of Puerto Rico System, established in 1903, is a public system in Puerto Rico. It is governed by the Puerto Rico council on higher education, whose chief administrator is the president. The primary goal of the system is to serve as a center for scholarly research, to develop academic excellence, and to capitalize on its location as a focal point of the Caribbean region and the international community by developing programs germane to the residents of the region. The main priorities are to improve academic programs in key areas, to strengthen research and research training, and to upgrade physical facilities. The total student enrollment for all eleven campuses is usually 56,000 with 4500 faculty members. Altogether there are 194 baccalaureate, 97 master's, and 15 doctoral programs offered in the University of Puerto Rico System. Profiles of the 4-year campuses are included in this section.

UNIVERSITY OF PUERTO RICO RECINTO DE RIO PIEDRAS — D-1

San Juan, PR 00931-3344 — **(787) 764-0000, ext. 5666; (787) 764-3680, ext. 1375**

Full-time: 4910 men, 9780 women	**Faculty:** n/av
Part-time: 1070 men, 2140 women	**Ph.D.s:** 41%
Graduate: 1290 men, 2770 women	**Student/Faculty:** n/av
Year: semesters, summer session	**Tuition:** $2000
Application Deadline: see profile	**Room & Board:** $6000
Freshman Class: n/av	
SAT: required	

The University of Puerto Rico/Recinto de Rio Piedras, founded in 1903, is a public institution offering undergraduate programs in arts and sciences, business, and education. Nonresident U.S. citizens pay annual tuition and fees equal to what Puerto Rican students would pay at a public university in the home states. Students who do not provide evidence of medical insurance are charged an additional $653 annual fee. There are 8 undergraduate schools and 10 graduate schools. Figures in the above capsule and in this profile are approximate. In addition to regional accreditation, UPR-Rio Piedras has baccalaureate program accreditation with ADA, CSWE, NAAB, and NCATE. The 10 libraries contain 1.8 million volumes, 1.7 million microform items, and subscribe to 5600 periodicals including electronic. Special learning facilities include a learning resource center, art gallery, natural history museum, radio station, audiovisual services, and television production facilities. The 271-acre campus is in an urban area in the Rio Piedras section of San Juan. Including any residence halls, there are 134 buildings.

Student Life: 99% of undergraduates are from Puerto Rico. Others are from 28 foreign countries and Canada. 49% are from public schools. All are Hispanic. The average age of freshmen is 18; all undergraduates, 20. 9% do not continue beyond their first year; 46% remain to graduate.

Housing: 789 students can be accommodated in college housing, which includes coed dorms. On-campus housing is available on a first-come, first-served basis and is available on a lottery system for upperclassmen. Priority is given to out-of-town students. Alcohol is not permitted. All students may keep cars.

Activities: There is 1 local fraternity. There are 63 groups on campus, including art, band, chorus, drama, honors, international, literary magazine, newspaper, pep band, political, professional, radio and TV, religious, social, social service, and student government. Popular campus events include sports events and spring and Christmas concerts.

Sports: There are 12 intercollegiate sports for men and 8 for women, and 15 intramural sports for men and 10 for women. Facilities include a sports complex with a swimming pool, a gym, track and field areas, and tennis, basketball, and volleyball courts.

Disabled Students: 80% of the campus is accessible. Facilities include wheelchair ramps, elevators, special parking, specially equipped restrooms, special class scheduling, lowered drinking fountains, and lowered telephones.

Services: There is a reader service for the blind, and remedial math, reading, and writing.

Campus Safety and Security: Measures include 24-hour foot and vehicle patrol, shuttle buses, emergency telephones, and lighted pathways/sidewalks.

Programs of Study: UPR – Rio Piedras confers B.A., B.S., B.B.A., B.E.D., and B. in Secretarial Science degrees. Master's and doctoral degrees are also awarded. Bachelor's degrees are awarded in AGRICULTURE (natural resource management), BIOLOGICAL SCIENCE (biology/biological science and nutrition), BUSINESS (accounting, banking and finance, business administration and management, business economics, business statistics, labor studies, management science, marketing management, personnel management, and secretarial studies/office management), COMMUNICATIONS AND THE ARTS (comparative literature, dramatic arts, English, fine arts, journalism, languages, music, and romance languages and literature), COMPUTER AND PHYSICAL SCIENCE (applied mathematics, chemistry, computer science, and information sciences and systems), EDUCATION (education, elementary education, secondary education, and special education), ENGINEERING AND ENVIRONMENTAL DESIGN (environmental design), SOCIAL SCIENCE (anthropology, economics, family/consumer studies, geography, history, home economics, interdisciplinary studies, liberal arts/general studies, philosophy, political science/government, psychology, social science, social work, and sociology). Natural sciences is the strongest academically. Secondary education has the largest enrollment.

Required: To graduate, students must complete 117 to 147 credits, with a minimum GPA of 2.0. All students must take basic courses in biological sciences, physical sciences, social sciences, Spanish, humanities, and English. Spanish is the language of instruction in most courses, but students are required to have a working knowledge of English.

Special: The university offers a co-op program in accounting, internships at local government and private agencies, study abroad in 11 countries, a Washington semester, a general studies degree, and nondegree study. There is 1 national honor society.

Faculty/Classroom: 48% of faculty are male; 52% are female. No introductory courses are taught by graduate students. The average class size in an introductory lecture is 23; in a laboratory, 20; and in a regular course, 23.

Requirements: The SAT is required, or the CEEB's Spanish equivalent. Applicants must be graduates of an accredited secondary school. The GED is accepted. Students should have completed 3 courses each of English and Spanish, 2 courses each of math and science, and 3 electives. A GPA of 2.0 is required. AP credits are accepted. Important factors in the admissions decision are advanced placement or honors courses, evidence of special talent, and extracurricular activities record.

Procedure: Freshmen are admitted in fall. Entrance exams should be taken in November or February of the senior year. Check with the school for current application deadlines and fee.

Transfer: Applicants from within Puerto Rico should have a minimum of 48 credits with a 2.5 GPA; out-of-state applicants, 30 credits with a 2.5 GPA.

Visiting: To schedule a visit, contact the Dean of Students.

Financial Aid: The CSS/Profile and the Puerto Rico Income Tax Revenue Report are required. Check with the school for current deadlines.

International Students: The school actively recruits these students. They must take the Spanish or English SAT.

Computers: All students may access the system according to schedules provided during the semester. There are no time limits and no fees.

Admissions Contact: Belinda Cruz Valentin, Admissions Director. Web: *www.uprrp.edu*

UNIVERSITY OF PUERTO RICO/ARECIBO B-1

Arecibo, PR 00613 **(787) 815-0000, ext. 4110; (787) 880-4972**

Full-time: 1155 men, 2345 women	**Faculty:** n/av
Part-time: 200 men, 470 omen	**Ph.D.s:** 22%
Graduate: n/av	**Student/Faculty:** n/av
Year: semesters, summer session	**Tuition:** $2576 ($4598)
Application Deadline: see profile	**Room & Board:** n/app
Freshman Class: n/av	
SAT: required	

University of Puerto Rico/Arecibo, founded in 1967, offers undergraduate programs in business administration, health sciences, natural sciences, education, computer sciences, telecommunications, and others. Figures in the above capsule and in this profile are approximate. In addition to regional accreditation, UPRA has baccalaureate program accreditation with NLN. The library contains 82,316 volumes, 7266 microform items, 2510 audio/video tapes/CDs/DVDs, and subscribes to 1500 periodicals including electronic. Computerized library services include interlibrary loans, database searching, and Internet access. Special learning facilities include a learning resource center and art gallery. The 49-acre campus is in an urban area 40 miles west of San Juan. Including any residence halls, there are 14 buildings.

Student Life: All undergraduates are from Puerto Rico. Others are from 2 foreign countries. 84% are from public schools. All are Hispanic. The average age of freshmen is 18; all undergraduates, 21. 18% do not continue beyond their first year.

Housing: There are no residence halls. All students commute.

Activities: There are no fraternities or sororities. There are 29 groups on campus, including art, band, cheerleading, chorus, computers, dance, drama, film, honors, newspaper, photography, political, professional, radio and TV, religious, social, social service, and student government. Popular campus events include fairs, plays, and concerts.

Sports: There are 8 intercollegiate sports for men and 6 for women, and 4 intramural sports for men and 3 for women. Facilities include basketball and tennis courts, baseball/softball and soccer fields, a gym, track and field facilities, and an activity room.

Disabled Students: 90% of the campus is accessible. Facilities include wheelchair ramps, elevators, special parking, specially equipped restrooms, lowered drinking fountains, and lowered telephones.

Services: Counseling and information services are available, as is tutoring in most subjects. There is a reader service for the blind, and remedial math, reading, and writing.

Campus Safety and Security: Measures include 24-hour foot and vehicle patrol and lighted pathways/sidewalks.

Programs of Study: UPRA confers B.A. B.S. B.B.A. and B.S.N. degrees. Associates degrees are also awarded. Bachelor's degrees are awarded in BIOLOGICAL SCIENCE (microbiology), BUSINESS (accounting, banking and finance, business administration and management, marketing/retailing/merchandising, and secretarial studies/office management), COMMUNICATIONS AND THE ARTS (telecommunications), COMPUTER AND PHYSICAL SCIENCE (computer science), EDUCATION (elementary education and physical education), ENGINEERING AND ENVIRONMENTAL DESIGN (chemical engineering technology), HEALTH PROFESSIONS (nursing), SOCIAL SCIENCE (Iberian studies and industrial and organizational psychology). Microbiology is the strongest academically. Accounting has the largest enrollment.

Required: To graduate, students must have a 2.0 GPA. The total number of credit hours required varies according to major. The core curriculum includes 2 semesters each of English, Spanish, math, and social sciences or humanities.

Special: There are internships, an exchange program with Spain, and a 3-2 engineering degree with the University of Puerto Rico/Mayaguez. There is a freshman honors program.

Faculty/Classroom: 44% of faculty are male; 56% are female. 89% teach undergraduates, and 35% do research. No introductory courses are taught by graduate students. The average class size in an introductory lecture is 25; in a laboratory, 20; and in a regular course, 23.

Requirements: A Spanish version of the SAT or the College Entrance Examination Board test (CEEB) is required. A GPA of 2.0 is required. AP credits are accepted.

Procedure: Freshmen are admitted in fall. Entrance exams should be taken by October of the senior year. There is an early admissions plan. Check with the school for current application deadlines and fee.

Transfer: Applicants should have a minimum of 24 credits with a 2.5 GPA.

Visiting: There are regularly scheduled orientations for prospective students.

Financial Aid: UPRA is a member of CSS. The FAFSA and the college's own financial statement are required. Check with the school for current deadlines.

International Students: They must take the College Entrance Examination Board Test.

Computers: Several computer labs are available to students. Wireless access is available in main buildings. All students may access the system. There are no time limits and no fees.

Admissions Contact: Fernando Gonzalez, Admissions Director. E-Mail: *fernando.gonzalez4@upra.edu* Web: *www.upra.edu*

UNIVERSITY OF PUERTO RICO/BAYAMON A-1

Bayamon, PR 00959-1919 **(787) 786-2885, ext. 2426**

Full-time: 1810 men, 2310 women	**Faculty:** n/av
Part-time: 555 men, 685 women	**Ph.D.s:** 21%
Graduate: n/av	**Student/Faculty:** n/av
Year: semesters, summer session	**Tuition:** $5060
Application Deadline: see profile	**Room & Board:** n/app
Freshman Class: n/av	
SAT or ACT: required	

University of Puerto Rico/Bayamon, formerly Bayamon University College, a commuter institution founded in 1971, is part of the University of Puerto Rico system. The figures in the above capsule and in this profile are approximate. It offers undergraduate business, education, and technical programs. The library contains 67,020 volumes, 247,302 microform items, 5103 audio/video tapes/CDs/DVDs, and subscribes to 273 periodicals including electronic. Computerized library services include database searching. Special learning facilities include a learning resource center. The 78-acre campus is in a suburban area 9 miles west of San Juan. Including any residence halls, there are 20 buildings.

Student Life: All undergraduates are from Puerto Rico. 53% are from public schools. All are Hispanic. The average age of freshmen is 18; all undergraduates, 21. 24% do not continue beyond their first year; 75% remain to graduate.

Housing: There are no residence halls. All students commute.

Activities: There are no fraternities or sororities. There are 15 groups on campus, including art, band, cheerleading, chess, choir, chorus, computers, drama, drill team, honors, professional, religious, social, social service, and student government. Popular campus events include an annual sports tournament, recognition of distinguished athletes, and the college anniversary.

Sports: There are 13 intercollegiate sports for men and 10 for women. Facilities include a basketball/volleyball court, a tennis court, a track and field site, an exercise gym, and a recreation room with table tennis, electronic games, and pool tables.

Disabled Students: 90% of the campus is accessible. Facilities include wheelchair ramps, special parking, specially equipped restrooms, lowered drinking fountains, and lowered telephones.

Services: Counseling and information services are available, as is tutoring in English, math, Spanish, and physics for engineering and electronics students. There is a reader service for the blind and remedial math.

Campus Safety and Security: Measures include 24-hour foot and vehicle patrol.

Programs of Study: UPR-Bayamon confers B.A. degrees. Associates degrees are also awarded. Bachelor's degrees are awarded in BUSINESS (accounting, banking and finance, business administration and management, management engineering, and marketing/retailing/merchandising), COMPUTER AND PHYSICAL SCIENCE (computer science and information sciences and systems), EDUCATION (early childhood education and elementary education), ENGINEERING AND ENVIRONMENTAL DESIGN (electrical/electronics engineering technology). Electronics, computer science, and office systems are the strongest academically. Business administration has the largest enrollment.

Required: General education requirements include courses in Spanish, English, math, social sciences or humanities, and biological or physical sciences. To graduate, students must complete 130 to 135 credits, including 29 to 34 in the major, with a minimum GPA of 2.0.

Special: Students may cross-register with any campus in the University of Puerto Rico system. Work-study programs, dual majors, pass/fail options, and a 3-2 engineering degree with the Mayaguez campus are also available. There is a freshman honors program and 5 departmental honors programs.

Faculty/Classroom: 44% of faculty are male; 56% are female. All teach undergraduates. No introductory courses are taught by graduate students.

The average class size in an introductory lecture is 23 and in a laboratory, 20.

Requirements: The SAT or ACT is required, or the CEEB's Spanish version of the SAT along with SAT subject tests in Spanish, writing, and math. Applicants must be graduates of accredited secondary schools. The GED is accepted. A GPA of 2.0 is required.

Procedure: Freshmen are admitted in fall. Entrance exams should be taken by October of the senior year. There is an early decision admission plan. Check with the school for current application deadlines and fee. Notification of early decision is sent February 15.

Transfer: Applicants must present an associate degree or at least 30 college credits and a minimum GPA of 2.5. 28 of 130 credits required for the bachelor's degree must be completed at UPR-Bayamon.

Visiting: There are regularly scheduled orientations for prospective students. To schedule a visit, contact the Director of Admissions.

Financial Aid: UPR-Bayamon is a member of CSS. The CSS/Profile, the college's own financial statement, and income tax forms, medical receipts, and social security information are required. Check with the school for current deadlines.

International Students: They must take the SAT or the Spanish equivalent version of the SAT.

Computers: All students may access the system daily from 8 a.m. to 10 p.m. and Saturday from 8 a.m. to 4:30 p.m. There are no time limits and no fees.

Admissions Contact: Carmen L. Burgos Montes, Director of Admissions. E-mail: *admisiones@uprb.edu* Web: *www.uprb.edu*

UNIVERSITY OF PUERTO RICO/CAYEY C-2

Cayey, PR 00736 **(787) 738-2161, ext. 2233; 787-738-5633**

Full-time: 905 men, 2310 women	**Faculty:** n/av
Part-time: 155 men, 315 women	**Ph.D.s:** 50%
Graduate: n/av	**Student/Faculty:** n/av
Year: semesters, summer session	**Tuition:** $3376 ($5581)
Application Deadline: see profile	**Room & Board:** n/app
Freshman Class: n/av	
SAT: required	

The University of Puerto Rico at Cayey, is a public, 4-year, liberal arts, coed institution and part of the University of Puerto Rico System. The figures in the above capsule and in this profile are approximate. The library contains 122,907 volumes, 4221 microform items, 8201 audio/video tapes/CDs/DVDs, and subscribes to 517 periodicals including electronic. Computerized library services include interlibrary loans, database searching, Internet access, and laptop Internet portals. Special learning facilities include a learning resource center and art museum. The 167-acre campus is in an urban area 30 miles south of San Juan. There are 54 buildings.

Student Life: All undergraduates are from Puerto Rico. 85% are from public schools. All are Hispanic. The average age of freshmen is 18; all undergraduates, 22. 12% do not continue beyond their first year; 39% remain to graduate.

Housing: There are no residence halls. All students commute.

Activities: There are no fraternities or sororities. There are 35 groups on campus, including art, band, cheerleading, chorus, dance, drama, environmental, honors, marching band, orchestra, political, professional, religious, social, social service, and student government. Popular campus events include Student Day.

Sports: Facilities include a gym, a swimming pool, tennis, basketball, and volleyball courts, and an athletic court.

Disabled Students: All of the campus is accessible. Facilities include wheelchair ramps, elevators, special parking, specially equipped restrooms, lowered drinking fountains, and lowered telephones.

Services: Counseling and information services are available, as is tutoring in most subjects. There is remedial math, reading, and writing.

Campus Safety and Security: Measures include 24-hour foot and vehicle patrol and emergency notification system. There are shuttle buses and lighted pathways/sidewalks.

Programs of Study: UPR Cayey confers B.A., B.S., B.B.A., B.Ed., and B.S.Ed. degrees. Associates degrees are also awarded. Bachelor's degrees are awarded in BIOLOGICAL SCIENCE (biology/biological science), BUSINESS (accounting, business administration and management, management science, and secretarial studies/office management), COMMUNICATIONS AND THE ARTS (English), COMPUTER AND PHYSICAL SCIENCE (chemistry, mathematics, and natural sciences), EDUCATION (elementary education, secondary education, and special education), SOCIAL SCIENCE (economics, Hispanic American studies, history, humanities, and psychology). Natural science is the strongest academically. Biology, accounting, and chemistry have the largest enrollment.

Required: To graduate, students must complete 129 to 135 credits, including 28 in the major, with a minimum GPA of 2.0. There are requirements in humanities, social science, Spanish, English, and natural science. All students must take 2 courses in phys ed.

Special: The university offers cross-registration through the National Student Exchange, study abroad in Toledo, Spain, a Washington semester, and a 3-2 engineering degree with Universidad de Puerto Rico en Mayaguez. There is a chapter of Phi Beta Kappa and a freshman honors program.

Faculty/Classroom: 55% of faculty are male; 45% are female. 98% teach undergraduates, and 2% do research. No introductory courses are taught by graduate students. The average class size in an introductory lecture is 30; in a laboratory, 20; and in a regular course, 30.

Requirements: The SAT or its CEEB Spanish equivalent is required. SAT subject tests in writing, math, and Spanish are required with the SAT. Acceptance is based on a summary of requirements and recommendations, including academic and Carnegie credits, test scores, essay, interview, audition, or portfolio, GED acceptance, and any special circumstances. Applicants must be graduates of an accredited secondary school. The GED is accepted. Students should complete 3 high school courses each in English, Spanish, math, science, and social studies. CLEP credits are accepted. Important factors in the admissions decision are advanced placement or honors courses.

Procedure: Freshmen are admitted in fall. Entrance exams should be taken in October of the senior year. There are early admissions and deferred admissions plans. Check with the school for current application deadlines. Check with the school for application fees. Applications are accepted online.

Transfer: Applicants should have 48 approved credit hours toward the program they are entering.

Visiting: Visitors may sit in on classes.

Financial Aid: The CSS/Profile and FAFSA are required. Check with the school for current deadlines.

International Students: They must take the SAT or the CEEB Spanish equivalent.

Computers: The students have access to the Internet all across the campus via wireless access. All students may access the system 24/7. There are no time limits and no fees.

Admissions Contact: Wilfredo Lopez, Admissions Office Director. E-mail: *admisiones@cayey.upr.edu* Web: *www.cayey.upr.edu*

UNIVERSITY OF PUERTO RICO/HUMACAO D-2

Humacao, PR 00791-4300 **(787) 850-0000, ext. 9301; (787) 850-9428**

Full-time: 1205 men, 2725 women	**Faculty:** n/av
Part-time: 185 men, 455 women	**Ph.D.s:** 34%
Graduate: n/av	**Student/Faculty:** n/av
Year: semesters, summer session	**Tuition:** $3376 (5398)
Application Deadline: see profile	**Room & Board:** n/app
Freshman Class: n/av	
SAT: required	

The University of Puerto Rico at Humacao, founded in 1962, is a public institution offering undergraduate programs in the arts and sciences, business, education, and nursing to an entirely commuter student body. Annual tuition and fees for nonresident U.S. citizens are an amount equal to the nonresident rate at a state university in their home states. The figures in the above capsule and in this profile are approximate. In addition to regional accreditation, UPRH has baccalaureate program accreditation with APTA, CSWE, and NLN. The library contains 119,629 volumes, 66 microform items, 1613 audio/video tapes/CDs/DVDs, and subscribes to 18,697 periodicals including electronic. Computerized library services include interlibrary loans, database searching, and Internet access. Special learning facilities include a learning resource center, museum, observatory, census data center, and web radio. The 62-acre campus is in a suburban area 30 miles southeast of San Juan. There are 29 buildings.

Student Life: 99% of undergraduates are from Puerto Rico. Others are from 9 states and 1 foreign country. 78% are from public schools. All are Hispanic. The average age of freshmen is 18; all undergraduates, 21. 14% do not continue beyond their first year; 86% remain to graduate.

Housing: There are no residence halls. All students commute.

Activities: There are 33 groups on campus, including band, cheerleading, chorus, dance, honors, professional, religious, social, social service, student government, and web radio. Popular campus events include Shakespeare Festival, Women's Week, and Puerto Rican Culture Week.

Sports: There are 8 intercollegiate sports for men and 8 for women, and 3 intramural sports for men and 4 for women. Facilities include a 1000-seat gym, a track, 2 tennis courts, a softball field, a swimming pool, wrestling mats, and a student center.

Disabled Students: 60% of the campus is accessible. Facilities include wheelchair ramps, elevators, special parking, specially equipped restrooms, special class scheduling, lowered drinking fountains, and lowered telephones.

Services: Counseling and information services are available, as is tutoring in English, Spanish, and math. There is a reader service for the blind, and remedial math, reading, and writing.

Campus Safety and Security: Measures include 24-hour foot and vehicle patrol, emergency telephones, and lighted pathways/sidewalks.

Programs of Study: UPRH confers B.A., B.S., and B.B.A. degrees. Associates degrees are also awarded. Bachelor's degrees are awarded in AGRICULTURE (wildlife management), BIOLOGICAL SCIENCE (biology/biological science, marine biology, and microbiology), BUSINESS (accounting, business administration and management, human resources, international business management, and secretarial studies/office management), COMMUNICATIONS AND THE ARTS (English), COMPUTER AND PHYSICAL SCIENCE (chemistry, mathematics, and physics), EDUCATION (elementary education), HEALTH PROFESSIONS (nursing), SOCIAL SCIENCE (social work). Natural sciences is the strongest academically. Business administration has the largest enrollment.

Required: To graduate, students must complete 127 to 136 credit hours, including 18 to 56 in a major field, with a minimum GPA of 2.0. General education requirements include 33 to 73 liberal arts credits, with 6 credits in Spanish and 6 in English, humanities, and social sciences. Other distribution requirements vary by program.

Special: Students may study abroad through the National Student Exchange program. There are also co-op programs, internships in accounting, management, human resources, and physics, work-study programs, credit for work experience, and a pass/fail option in remedial courses. Nondegree study is available through the Division of Continuing Education. The university offers programs in coastal marine biology, industrial microbiology, and industrial chemistry, and sponsors a Puerto Rican plain pigeon conservation project. There is 1 national honor society and a freshman honors program.

Faculty/Classroom: 44% of faculty are male; 56% are female. 87% teach undergraduates, and 1% do research. No introductory courses are taught by graduate students. The average class size in a laboratory is 17 and in a regular course, 21.

Requirements: The SAT is required for U.S. applicants, or the CEEB's Spanish equivalent, as well as SAT subject tests in Spanish and math level I. Applicants must be graduates of an accredited secondary school or have earned the GED. College preparatory study should include 3 credits each in English, Spanish, and math, 2 in history, and 1 in social studies. All courses are conducted in Spanish only. Nonnative speakers of Spanish are required to demonstrate fluency through institutional exam interviews. AP credits are accepted.

Procedure: Freshmen are admitted in fall. Entrance exams should be taken by October or February of the senior year. There is a deferred admissions plan. Notifications are sent in April. Applications are accepted online. Check with the school for current application deadlines.

Transfer: Applicants to the bachelor's programs must have at least 30 college credits with a minimum GPA of 3.0 and must be in good standing at their previous institutions. 30 of 136 credits required for the bachelor's degree must be completed at UPRH.

Visiting: There are regularly scheduled orientations for prospective students.

Financial Aid: The FAFSA is required. Check with the school for current deadlines.

International Students: They must take the CEEB's Spanish version of the SAT. This consists of an aptitude test (verbal and math) and an achievement test battery (Spanish, English, math).

Computers: Wireless access is available. All students may access the system daily until 10 p.m. There are no time limits and no fees.

Admissions Contact: Elizabeth Genera, Director of Admissions. E-Mail: *elizabeth.genera@upr.edu* Web: *www.uprh.edu*

UNIVERSITY OF PUERTO RICO/MAYAGUEZ A-1

Mayaguez, PR 00680 **(787) 265-3811; (787) 834-5265**

Full-time: 5105 men, 4560 women	**Faculty:** n/av
Part-time: 480 men, 580 women	**Ph.D.s:** 64%
Graduate: 550 men, 550 women	**Student/Faculty:** n/av
Year: semesters, summer session	**Tuition:** $2876 ($4030)
Application Deadline: see profile	**Room & Board:** n/app
Freshman Class: n/av	
SAT: required	

The University of Puerto Rico/Mayaguez, founded in 1911, is a bilingual land-grant institution offering undergraduate programs in arts and sciences, business administration, agricultural sciences, and engineering. There are 4 undergraduate schools and 4 graduate schools. Figures in the above capsule and in this profile are approximate. In addition to regional accreditation, the university has baccalaureate program accreditation with ABET and NLN. The library contains 783,905 volumes, 345,052 microform items, and 43,610 audio/video tapes/CDs/DVDs, and subscribes to 2,171 periodicals including electronic. Computerized library services include interlibrary loans, database searching, and Internet access. Special learning facilities include a learning resource center, art gallery, natural history museum, planetarium, sea grant program, and resource center for science and engineering. The 520-acre campus is in an urban area 70 miles west of San Juan. There are 63 buildings.

Student Life: 99% of undergraduates are from Puerto Rico. Others are from 9 foreign countries and Canada. 59% are from public schools. 99% are Hispanic. The average age of freshmen is 18; all undergraduates, 21. 10% do not continue beyond their first year; 52% remain to graduate.

Housing: There are no residence halls. All students commute.

Activities: 5% of men belong to 6 local and 1 national fraternity; 2% of women belong to 3 local sororities. There are 90 groups on campus, including band, cheerleading, chess, choir, chorale, chorus, computers, dance, debate, drama, drill team, drum and bugle corps, ethnic, honors, international, jazz band, literary magazine, marching band, newspaper, orchestra, photography, political, professional, religious, social, social service, student government, and yearbook. Popular campus events include fairs, concerts, and dances.

Sports: There are 12 intercollegiate sports for men and 9 for women, and 15 intramural sports for men and 11 for women. Facilities include a gym, a coliseum, a swimming pool, and 2 playing fields.

Disabled Students: 90% of the campus is accessible. Facilities include wheelchair ramps, elevators, special parking, specially equipped restrooms, special class scheduling, lowered drinking fountains, and lowered telephones.

Services: Counseling and information services are available, as is tutoring in most subjects. There is a reader service for the blind, and remedial math and reading.

Campus Safety and Security: Measures include 24-hour foot and vehicle patrol, shuttle buses, emergency telephones, and lighted pathways/sidewalks.

Programs of Study: The university confers B.A., B.S., B.B.A., and B.S.A. degrees. Associates, master's, and doctoral degrees are also awarded. Bachelor's degrees are awarded in AGRICULTURE (animal science and horticulture), BIOLOGICAL SCIENCE (biochemistry, biology/biological science, biotechnology, and microbiology), BUSINESS (accounting, banking and finance, business administration and management, business economics, and marketing/retailing/merchandising), COMMUNICATIONS AND THE ARTS (English, fine arts, and French), COMPUTER AND PHYSICAL SCIENCE (chemistry, computer science, geology, information sciences and systems, mathematics, and physics), EDUCATION (foreign languages education and teaching English as a second/foreign language (TESOL/TEFOL)), ENGINEERING AND ENVIRONMENTAL DESIGN (chemical engineering, civil engineering, computer engineering, electrical/electronics engineering, engineering, industrial engineering, mechanical engineering, and surveying engineering), HEALTH PROFESSIONS (nursing and premedicine), SOCIAL SCIENCE (economics, history, philosophy, political science/government, psychology, social science, and sociology). Engineering, business administration, and agricultural science are the strongest academically. Electrical, chemical, and civil engineering are the largest.

Required: To graduate, students must complete 172 credit hours with a GPA of 2.0. Required disciplines include humanities, English, Spanish, physical science, biology, social science, math, and phys ed.

Special: The university offers co-op programs in engineering, business, and nursing, as well as some study abroad. There is 1 national honor society and a freshman honors program.

Faculty/Classroom: 65% of faculty are male; 35% are female. 23% do research. No introductory courses are taught by graduate students. The average class size in an introductory lecture is 30; in a laboratory, 20; and in a regular course, 30.

Requirements: The SAT is required, or the CEEB's Spanish equivalent, along with SAT subject tests in writing, Spanish and Spanish reading, and mathematics level I. Applicants must be high school graduates or hold the GED. CLEP credits are accepted.

Procedure: Freshmen are admitted in fall. Entrance exams should be taken during the first semester of the senior year. There is an early admissions plan. Check with the school for current application deadlines. The application fee is $20.

Transfer: Applicants must have 48 college credits with a GPA of 2.0.

Financial Aid: The university is a member of CSS. The college's own financial statement is required. Check with the school for current deadlines.

International Students: The school actively recruits these students. They must take the SAT.

Computers: All students may access the system 24 hours a day. There are no fees.

Admissions Contact: Norma Torres, Director. E-Mail: *norma@rectoria.uprm.edu* Web: *www.uprm.edu*

UNIVERSITY OF THE SACRED HEART D-1

Santurce, PR 00914 (787) 728-1199; (787) 727-7880

Full-time: 1155 men, 2110 women
Part-time: 445 men, 880 women
Graduate: 175 men, 485 women
Year: semesters, summer session
Application Deadline: see profile
Freshman Class: n/av
Faculty: n/av
Ph.D.s: 30%
Student/Faculty: n/av
Tuition: $5500
Room & Board: $3100

University of the Sacred Heart, founded in 1935, is a private, comprehensive Roman Catholic institution. There are 6 undergraduate schools and 4 graduate schools. Figures in the above capsule and in this profile are approximate. In addition to regional accreditation, the university has baccalaureate program accreditation with CAHEA, CSWE, and NLN. The library contains 124,936 volumes, 49,086 microform items, 10,366 audio/video tapes/CDs/DVDs, and subscribes to 1525 periodicals including electronic. Computerized library services include database searching. Special learning facilities include a learning resource center, art gallery, natural history museum, TV station, communication center, and secretarial, human performance, and art labs. The 33-acre campus is in an urban area in San Juan. Including any residence halls, there are 14 buildings.

Student Life: All undergraduates are from Puerto Rico. 44% are from public schools. All are Hispanic. The average age of freshmen is 19; all undergraduates, 22.

Housing: 422 students can be accommodated in college housing, which includes single-sex dorms. On-campus housing is available on a first-come, first-served basis. Alcohol is not permitted. All students may keep cars.

Activities: There are no fraternities or sororities.

Sports: There are 12 intercollegiate sports for men and 10 for women, and 8 intramural sports for men and 8 for women. Facilities include a 1500-seat volleyball and basketball court, Nautilus and free-weight gym, 4 tennis courts, a softball field, 3 beach volley courts, an Olympic swimming pool, a game room, locker area, judo area, and weightlifting area.

Disabled Students: Facilities include wheelchair ramps, elevators, special parking, specially equipped restrooms, lowered drinking fountains, and lowered telephones.

Campus Safety and Security: Measures include 24-hour foot and vehicle patrol.

Programs of Study: The university confers B.A., B.S., B.A.C., B.B.A., B.Ed., B.O.S.A., and B.S.N. degrees. Associates and master's degrees are also awarded. Bachelor's degrees are awarded in BIOLOGICAL SCIENCE (biology/biological science), BUSINESS (accounting, business administration and management, management information systems, marketing/retailing/merchandising, personnel management, secretarial studies/office management, and tourism), COMMUNICATIONS AND THE ARTS (advertising, communications, telecommunications, and visual and performing arts), COMPUTER AND PHYSICAL SCIENCE (chemistry, computer science, and mathematics), EDUCATION (elementary education and physical education), HEALTH PROFESSIONS (medical technology and nursing), SOCIAL SCIENCE (criminal justice, psychology, social work, and urban studies). Business administration and communications have the largest enrollments.

Required: To graduate, students must complete between 133 and 145 credits, including 22 to 45 in the major, with a minimum GPA of 2.1 in the major and 2.0 overall. All students must take 12 credits of English, 9 credits of Spanish, 6 credits each of theology, humanities, social sciences, and biology, and 3 credits each of logic and philosophy, arts, computer science, and physical fitness. Some programs require a fieldwork practicum.

Special: The university offers a Washington semester, work-study, and nondegree programs in continuing education and basic skills. Study in the mainland United States is possible through the National Student Exchange and through independent agreements with various private and public colleges and universities. There are also opportunities for study in Spain and Mexico. A 3-2 engineering degree is offered with Manhattan College in New York. There is 1 national honor society.

Faculty/Classroom: 47% of faculty are male; 53% are female. No introductory courses are taught by graduate students.

Requirements: The SAT is required, or the CEEB's Spanish equivalent, along with SAT subject tests in Spanish, English, and math. Applicants must be graduates of an accredited secondary school. The GED is accepted. The admissions formula is based on GPA (x 600) + CEEB (verbal + math + English). Applicants whose index is 3300 will be admitted to the university. Those who comply with only 1 (GPA or CEEB) will be considered individually by the evaluation committee. A GPA of 2.5 is required. AP credits are accepted.

Procedure: Entrance exams should be taken in October of the senior year. There are early decision, early admissions and rolling admissions plans. Check with the school for current application deadlines and fee. Notification is sent on a rolling basis.

Transfer: Applicants with at least 30 college credits and a high school and college GPA of 2.5 are eligible for transfer. Students must submit CEEB scores and a letter of recommendation. Three quarters of the credits needed in the major must be taken at the university.

Visiting: There are regularly scheduled orientations for prospective students. Visitors may sit in on classes. To schedule a visit, contact the Admission, Promotion, and Recruitment Office.

Financial Aid: The university is a member of CSS. The CSS/Profile, the college's own financial statement, and AFSA are required. Check with the school for current deadlines.

International Students: They must take the SAT or the CEEB's Spanish equivalent.

Computers: All students may access the system. There are no time limits. The fee is $25 to $75. It is strongly recommended that all students have a personal computer.

Admissions Contact: Luis A. Henriquez, Director of Admission and Promotion. A campus DVD is available. E-Mail: *nuevoingreso@sagrado.edu*
Web: *www.sagrado.edu*

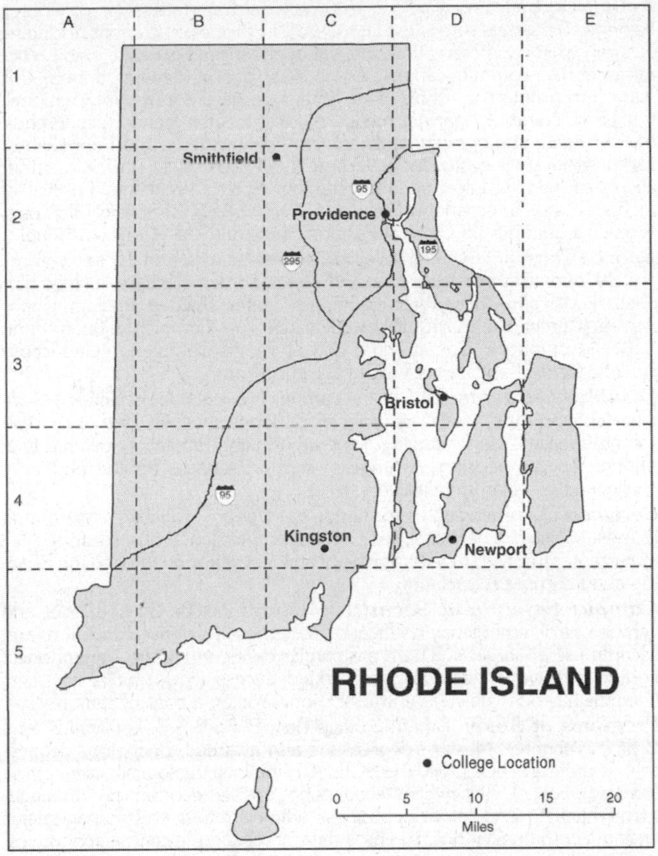

BROWN UNIVERSITY C-2

Providence, RI 02912 **(401) 863-2378; (401) 863-9300**

Full-time: 2977 men, 3137 women **Faculty:** n/av
Part-time: 65 men, 201 women **Ph.D.s:** n/av
Graduate: 1185 men, 1203 women **Student/Faculty:** n/av
Year: semesters, summer session **Tuition:** $42,730
Application Deadline: January 1 **Room & Board:** $11,406
Freshman Class: 30944 applied, 2757 accepted, 1507 enrolled
SAT CR/M/W: 720/730/720 **ACT:** 31 **MOST COMPETITIVE**

Brown University, founded in 1764, is a coeducational liberal arts institution and a member of the Ivy League. The figures given in the above capsule and in this profile are approximate. There are 2 graduate schools. In addition to regional accreditation, Brown has baccalaureate program accreditation with ABET. The 6 libraries contain 3.6 million volumes, 1,000,000 microform items, 28,000 audio/video tapes/CDs/DVDs, and subscribe to 16,000 periodicals including electronic. Computerized library services include interlibrary loans, database searching, and Internet access. Special learning facilities include an art gallery, planetarium, radio station, TV station, an anthropology museum. The 140-acre campus is in a small town 45 miles south of Boston, MA. Including any residence halls, there are 243 buildings.

Student Life: 96% of undergraduates are from out of state, mostly the Middle Atlantic. Students are from 50 states, 81 foreign countries, and Canada. 59% are from public schools. 43% are White; 14% Asian American; 11% Foreign. The average age of freshmen is 18; all undergraduates, 20. 2% do not continue beyond their first year; 96% remain to graduate.

Housing: 4350 students can be accommodated in college housing, which includes single-sex and coed dorms, on-campus apartments, and off-campus apartments. In addition, there are language houses, special-interest houses, fraternity houses, sorority houses, international house, technology house, environmental studies house, and cooperatives. On-campus housing is guaranteed for all 4 years and is available on a lottery system for upperclassmen. Upperclassmen may keep cars.

Activities: 12% of men belong to 10 national fraternities; 2% of women belong to 3 national sororities. There are 350 groups on campus, including ethnic groups, public service, volunteer, art, band, cheerleading, chess, choir, chorale, chorus, computers, dance, debate, drama, environmental, ethnic, film, gay, honors, international, jazz band, literary magazine, marching band, musical theater, newspaper, opera, orchestra, photography, political, professional, radio and TV, religious, social, social service, student government, and yearbook. Popular campus events include Commencement and Spring Weekend.

Sports: There are 17 intercollegiate sports for men and 20 for women, and 15 intramural sports for men and 15 for women. Facilities include a 25,000-seat stadium, an Olympic-size pool, a 200-meter, 6-lane track, a hockey rink, playing fields, weight-training rooms, facilities for wrestling, and courts for squash, racquetball, tennis, basketball, and volleyball.

Disabled Students: Facilities include wheelchair ramps, elevators, special parking, specially equipped restrooms, special class scheduling, lowered drinking fountains, and special housing.

Services: Counseling and information services are available, as is tutoring in most subjects. There is a reader service for the blind. Other services include class note taking, books on tape, diagnostic testing services, oral tests, tutors, and untimed tests.

Campus Safety and Security: Measures include 24-hour foot and vehicle patrol, emergency notification system, self-defense education, and security escort services. There are shuttle buses, emergency telephones, lighted pathways/sidewalks, controlled access to dorms/residences, SafeWALK and SafeRIDE programs.

Programs of Study: Brown confers A.B., and Sc.B. degrees. Master's and doctoral degrees are also awarded. Bachelor's degrees are awarded in BIOLOGICAL SCIENCE (biochemistry, biology/biological science, biophysics, marine biology, molecular biology, and neurosciences), BUSINESS (entrepreneurial studies), COMMUNICATIONS AND THE ARTS (American literature, art, art history and appreciation, classics, comparative literature, English, linguistics, media arts, music, performing arts, Portuguese, and visual and performing arts), COMPUTER AND PHYSICAL SCIENCE (applied mathematics, chemical physics, chemistry, computer science, geology, mathematics, physics, and statistics), EDUCATION (education), ENGINEERING AND ENVIRONMENTAL DESIGN (architectural history, architectural technology, architecture, computational sciences, engineering, and environmental science), HEALTH PROFESSIONS (biomedical science and community health work), SOCIAL SCIENCE (African studies, African American studies, American studies, anthropology, archeology, classical/ancient civilization, cognitive science, developmental psychology, East Asian studies, economics, ethnic studies, French studies, gender studies, German area studies, Hispanic American studies, history, human development, international relations, Italian studies, Judaic studies, Latin American studies, medieval studies, Middle Eastern studies, philosophy, political science/government, psychology, public administration, religion, Russian and Slavic studies, science and society, sociology, South Asian studies, and urban studies). Biological sciences, international relations, and history have the largest enrollments.

Required: To graduate, students must pass 30 of 32 courses taken (4 each semester), including 8 to 21 courses in the major. There are no distribution requirements or specific courses (except for the required courses in a major). Honors thesis are available in each concentration program.

Special: Students may cross-register with Rhode Island School of Design or study abroad in any of 50 programs in 15 countries. A combined A.B.-S.C.B. degree is possible in any major field with 5 years of study. Dual and student-designed majors, community internships, and pass/fail options are available. Students may pursue 5-year programs in the arts or sciences or the 8-year program in the liberal medical education continuum or the Brown/RISD dual degree program. There are including Phi Beta Kappa.

Faculty/Classroom: 67% of faculty are male; 33% are female. All teach undergraduates and do research. Graduate students teach 13% of introductory courses. The average class size in an introductory lecture is 200; in a laboratory is 20; and in a regular course is 40.

Admissions: 9% of the 2013-2014 applicants were accepted. The SAT scores for the 2013-2014 freshman class were: Critical Reading--8% between 500 and 599, 30% between 600 and 699, and 62% between 700 and 800; Math--6% between 500 and 599, 27% between 600 and 699, and 67% between 700 and 800; Writing--6% between 500 and 599, 27% between 600 and 699, and 67% between 700 and 800. The ACT scores were 79% above 28. 99% of the current freshmen were in the top fifth of their class; 99% were in the top two fifths. 158 freshmen graduated first in their class.

Requirements: The SAT or ACT is required. The ACT Optional Writing test is also required. Applicants must be graduates of accredited high schools. Preparation is expected to include courses in English, foreign language, math, lab science, the arts (music or art), and history. A personal essay is required, as are two teacher recommendations. Students must take either the SAT or the ACT. They may submit the SAT along with any 2 SAT Subject tests or they may submit the ACT with Writing. The high school transcript is the central criterion for admission. AP credits are accepted. Important factors in the admissions decision are advanced placement or honors courses, evidence of special talent, and personality/ intangible qualities.

Procedure: Freshmen are admitted fall. Entrance exams should be taken in the junior or senior year. There are early decision and deferred admissions plans. Early decision applications should be filed by November 1; regular applications, by January 1 for fall entry, along with a $75 fee. Notification of early decision is sent December 15; regular decision, April 1. 568 early decision candidates were accepted for the 2013-2014 class. Applications are accepted online.

Transfer: 87 transfer students enrolled in 2012-2013. Transfer applicants must submit high school and college transcripts, 2 recommendations from college professors, scores on the ACT or on the SAT and any 2 SAT Subject tests, a letter of good standing, and a personal essay. 15 of 30 credits required for the bachelor's degree must be completed at Brown.

Visiting: There are regularly scheduled orientations for prospective students, including Group Information Sessions are usually conducted Monday through Friday at 10 a.m. and 2 p.m. from mid-February through November and on Saturday mornings from mid-September to mid-November. There are guides for informal visits and visitors may sit in on classes. To schedule a visit, contact the Admission Office Receptionist.

Financial Aid: In 2013-2014, 49% of all full-time freshmen students received some form of financial aid. 48% of all full-time freshmen received need-based aid. The average freshman award was $37,355. Brown is a member of CSS. The CSS/Profile and FAFSA, and some state forms are required. The deadline for filing freshman financial aid applications for fall entry is January 1.

International Students: There are 593 international students enrolled. The school actively recruits these students. They must take the TOEFL with a minimum score of 100 on the Internet-based version (iBT), If a student receives at least a 600 on their SAT Critical Reading, they need not take the TOEFL. They must also take the SAT or ACT.

Graduates: From July 1, 2012 to June 30, 2013, 1443 bachelor's degrees were awarded. The most popular majors were economics (11%), biological sciences (11%), and international relations (7%). In an average class, 83% graduate in 4 years or less, 94% graduate in 5 years or less, and 95% graduate in 6 years or less. Of the 2012 graduating class, 35% were enrolled in graduate school within 6 months of graduation, and 65% were employed.

Admissions Contact: James S. Miller, Dean of Admission. E-Mail: *admission_undergraduate@brown.edu* Web: *www.brown.edu*

BRYANT UNIVERSITY C-2

Smithfield, RI 02917 **(401) 232-6100**
(800) 622-7001; (401) 232-6741

Full-time: 1324 men, 1876 women	**Faculty:** n/av; IIB, ++$
Part-time: 41 men, 46 women	**Ph.D.s:** 82%
Graduate: 75 men, 92 women	**Student/Faculty:** 18 to 1
Year: semesters, summer session	**Tuition:** $35,939
Application Deadline:	**Room & Board:** $13,240
Freshman Class: 6013 applied, 4603 accepted, 890 enrolled	
SAT CR/M/W: 550/585/545 **ACT:** 25	**VERY COMPETITIVE**

Throughout its 150-year history, Bryant University has earned a distinguished reputation for innovative academic programs and technology that are marketplace driven and highly attuned to the emerging needs of industry and society. There are 2 undergraduate schools and 3 graduate schools. In addition to regional accreditation, Bryant has baccalaureate program accreditation with AACSB. The library contains 256,241 volumes, 14,541 microform items, 2,293 audio/video tapes/CDs/DVDs, and subscribes to 70,129 periodicals including electronic. Computerized library services include interlibrary loans, database searching, Internet access, and Wi-Fi capability. Special learning facilities include a radio station, TV station, George E. Bello Center for Information and Technology, C.V. Star Financial Markets Center, Stepan Grand Hall, Cerce Multi Media Wall; Douglas and Judith Krupp Library, Mahre Periodical Center; Koffler Technology Center and Communications Complex, TV Production Studio; WJMF Radio Station; Janikies Memorial Auditiorium; Koffler Rotunda multimedia student exhibition space; John H. Chafee Center for International Business; Center for Global and Regional Economic Studies; Intercultural Center; Gertrude Meth Hochberg Women's Center; Ronald K. and Kati C. Machtley Interfaith Center; Center for Student Invovlement. The 428-acre campus is in a suburban area 10 miles northwest of Providence, 45 miles southwest of Boston, 190 miles from New York City. Including any residence halls, there are 54 buildings.

Student Life: 85% of undergraduates are from out of state, mostly the Northeast. Students are from 31 states, 65 foreign countries, and Canada. 73% are from public schools. 83% are White. The average age of freshmen is 18; all undergraduates, 20. 13% do not continue beyond their first year; 76% remain to graduate.

Housing: 2882 students can be accommodated in college housing, which includes single-sex and coed dorms and on-campus apartments. In addition, there are honors houses, special-interest houses, quiet, women and international business. On-campus housing is guaranteed for all 4 years. 81% of students live on campus; of those, 87% remain on campus on weekends. All students may keep cars.

Activities: 6% of men belong to 5 national fraternities; 7% of women belong to 5 national sororities. There are 111 groups on campus, including cultural, sports and recreation, art, band, cheerleading, chess, choir, chorale, chorus, communications, computers, dance, debate, drama, drill team, environmental, ethnic, film, forensics, gay, honors, international, jazz band, literary magazine, media, musical theater, newspaper, orchestra, pep band, photography, political, professional, radio and TV, religious, social, social service, student government, and yearbook. Popular campus events include Reunion at Homecoming, Spring Weekend, Festival of Lights, REDay, International Education Week, SASS, RI Special Olympics, Women's Summit, i2i Cultural Fashion Show and Up 'Til Dawn Benefit.

Sports: There are 10 intercollegiate sports for men and 10 for women, and 20 intramural sports for men and 16 for women. Facilities include Elizabeth & Malcolm Chace Wellness Fitness Center; Bulldog Stadium; Chace Athletic Center Main Gym; Bryant Track & Turf Complex; Conaty Park; Softball Complex at Conaty Park; Bryant Tennis Complex; Multipurpose Athletic Center; and Jarvis Varsity Weight Room.

Disabled Students: 90% of the campus is accessible. Facilities include wheelchair ramps, elevators, special parking, specially equipped restrooms, special class scheduling, lowered drinking fountains, lowered telephones, special housing, A range of support services for the physically challenged and learning disabled.

Services: Counseling and information services are available, as is tutoring in most subjects. The Academic Center for Excellence offers tutoring for all currently enrolled students at Bryant and is certified by the College Reading and Learning Association.

Campus Safety and Security: Measures include 24-hour foot and vehicle patrol, emergency notification system, self-defense education, and security escort services. There are shuttle buses, emergency telephones, lighted pathways/sidewalks, controlled access to dorms/residences, Campus has one vehicular entrance monitored by a control station.

Programs of Study: Bryant confers B.A, B.S., B.S.B.A., B.S.I.B. and B.Sc.I.T. degrees. Master's degrees are also awarded. Bachelor's degrees are awarded in BIOLOGICAL SCIENCE (biology/biological science and forensic science), BUSINESS (accounting, applied economics / management, banking and finance, business administration and management, business communications, business data processing, business economics, business information systems, business intelligence and analytics, business law, business statistics, business systems analysis, economics – statistics, entrepreneurial studies, finance, financial services, global/general management, global management, human resources, international accounting, international business, international business information systems, international business management, international economics, investments and securities, international entrepreneurial management, international finance, international marketing, international supply and value chain management, logistics, management information systems, management science. marketing, marketing and distribution, marketing management, marketing/retailing/merchandising, nonprofit/public organization management, and supply chain management), COMMUNICATIONS AND THE ARTS (art and design, art/visual culture, Chinese, communication design , communication, communication studies, communications, communication rhetoric/communication, communication science, comparative literature, English, foreign language, French, information technology, literature, modern language, and Spanish), COMPUTER AND PHYSICAL SCIENCE (actuarial science, actuarial mathematics, applied mathematics, computer management, computer information technology, computer information systems, information sciences and systems, information science, informatics and computer science, mathematics, mathematics - actuarial concentration, mathematics/computational, mathematics – economics, and statistics), EDUCATION (business education, education, education administration, educational statistics and research, English education, foreign languages education, mathematics education, and sports studies), ENGINEERING AND ENVIRONMENTAL DESIGN (computational sciences and environmental science), HEALTH PROFESSIONS (biology), SOCIAL SCIENCE (American studies, applied psychology, applied social science, community services, economics, feminist, gender, sexuality studies, forensic studies, gender studies, (Social Science) Global Studies, history, international studies, law, legal studies, political science/ government, prelaw, psychology, public affairs, and sociology). Accounting, finance, international business, marketing, actuarial math, communications, and entrepreneurship have the largest enrollments.

Required: Students must complete 122-125 credits. First-Year Gateway: 10 credits includes Global Foundations of Character & Leadership, Global Foundations of Organizations and Business, Writing Workshop, and during winter session a 72 hour intensive course, IDEA (Innovation and Design Experience for All) experiential learning generating creative solutions to a real-world situation. Upper Level Gateway: a culminating course across all disciplines. Liberal Arts Core: includes Literary Studies, Micro and Macro-Economics, Mathematics, and Statistics courses. Liberal Arts Distribution: includes two social science, two laboratory science, history, and literature courses. Business Core: includes accounting, finance, information technology, management, and marketing courses. Cross college minors: College of Arts & Sciences majors must minor in a College of Business field, and College of Business majors must minor in a College of Arts & Sciences field. All majors include a senior capstone course, a senior research seminar, and/or a senior practicum combining classroom and work experience related to the major.

Special: First-Year Gateway: 10 credits includes Global Foundations of Character & Leadership, Global Foundations of Organizations and Business, a writing course, and during winter session a 72 hour intensive course, IDEA (Innovation and Design Experience for All) experiential learning generating creative solutions to a real-world situation, plus co-currcular programs with Student Life. Honors Program culminating in a Senior Capstone Project, an interdisciplinary topic of personal interest and aligned to future career or study. Sophomore International Experience (3 credit pre-travel class work plus travel abraod during winter and summer sessions). Study Abroad (semester length via nine providers in over 54 countries). Exchange Programs for semester or year in Japan, Great Britain, and Spain. Service Learning through student organizations and/or coursework in Sociology, Mangement, Literary & Cultural Studies, and/or History; volunteering in community service, learning, reflecting, and devising solutions in classroom and in service. Academic Internships, 3 credits for professional work experience with faculty advisor. Practicum, 6 to 9 credits for professional work experience culminating in a major research project. European Studay Abroad (EUSA) A ten week summer program providing a living, learning and professional working experience in Dublin. The program includes a supervised internship (3 credits); a course taught in Dublin by a Bryant professor (3 credits) and opportunities to explore Dublin, as well as travel in Europe. Internship and housing is provided. The Washington Center, a full-time internship and seminar program offered during the fall, spring and summer semesters in DC. Eligible students can earn 9 to 15 credits for one semester by living, learning and working in DC. The internship placement, seminar program, one evening course and housing is provided. Work Study: Bryant University provides part-time employment opportunities for work-study eligible students to assist them in meeting the cost of education. Army ROTC. There are 10 national honor societies, a freshman honors program, and 12 departmental honors programs.

Faculty/Classroom: 58% of faculty are male; 42% are female. 99% teach undergraduates, 55% do research, and 55% do both. No introductory courses are taught by graduate students. The average class size in an introductory lecture is 26; in a laboratory is 12; and in a regular course is 24.

Admissions: 77% of the 2013-2014 applicants were accepted. The SAT scores for the 2013-2014 freshman class were: Critical Reading--18% below 500, 59% between 500 and 599, 20% between 600 and 699, and 3% between 700 and 800; Math--8% below 500, 48% between 500 and 599, 37% between 600 and 699, and 7% between 700 and 800; Writing--22% below 500, 53% between 500 and 599, 23% between 600 and 699, and 2% between 700 and 800. The ACT scores were 26% between 21 and 23, and 74% above 28. 43% of the current freshmen were in the top fifth of their class; 77% were in the top two fifths. 1 freshman graduated first in the class.

Requirements: In addition, accredited high school diploma or GED. High school general college preparatory program. Academic units: 4 English, 4 Math, 2 Lab Science, 2 Foreign Language, 2 History. Very important: rigor of high school record, GPA. Important: class rank, standardized test scores, application essay, recommendations. AP and CLEP credits are accepted.

Procedure: Freshmen are admitted fall and spring. Entrance exams should be taken by Fall. There are early decision, early admissions, and deferred admissions plans. Early decision applications should be filed by November 15. The fall 2013 application fee was $50. Notification of early decision is sent December 17; regular decision, 116 early decision candidates were accepted for the 2013-2014 class. 383 applicants were on the 2013 waiting list; 95 were admitted. Applications are accepted online.

Transfer: 92 transfer students enrolled in 2012-2013. High school transcript, college transcript, personal essay required. List of course numbers not included on college transcript that the applicant expects to complete before enrollment. 30 credits required for the bachelor's degree must be completed at Bryant.

Visiting: There are regularly scheduled orientations for prospective students, Student-guided tours, admissions staff information sessions, day with class, interviews offered. There are guides for informal visits, visitors may sit in on classes, and stay overnight. To schedule a visit, contact the Office of Admission.

Financial Aid: The average freshman award was $23,109. Need-based scholarships or need-based grants averaged $11,816; need-based self-help aid (loans and jobs) averaged $5,005; non-need-based athletic scholarships averaged $17,835; other non-need-based awards and non-need-based scholarships averaged $3,862; and $12,412 from other forms of aid. The average financial indebtedness of the 2013 graduate was $44,580. Bryant is a member of CSS. The FAFSA is required. Check with the school for current application deadlines.

International Students: There are 247 international students enrolled. The school actively recruits these students. They must take the TOEFL with a minimum score of 550 on the paper-based TOEFL (PBT) or 80 on the Internet-based version (iBT).

Graduates: From July 1, 2012 to June 30, 2013, 783 bachelor's degrees were awarded. The most popular majors were business/marketing (79%), mathematics and statistics (5%), and communications/journalism (5%). 150 companies recruited on campus in 2012-2013. In an average class, 77% graduate in 4 years or less, 80% graduate in 5 years or less, and 80% graduate in 6 years or less. Of the 2012 graduating class, 18% were enrolled in graduate school within 6 months of graduation, and 80% were employed.

Admissions Contact: Michelle Beauregard, Director of Admission. E-Mail: *admission@bryant.edu* Web: *www.bryant.edu*

JOHNSON AND WALES UNIVERSITY/PROVIDENCE CAMPUS C-2

Providence, RI 02903 **(401) 598-1000**

Full-time: 3994 men, 5082 women	**Faculty:** 264
Part-time: 309 men, 454 women	**Ph.D.s:** 25%
Graduate: 427 men, 665 women	**Student/Faculty:** 31 to 1
Year: trimesters, summer session	**Tuition:** $25,407
Application Deadline:	**Room & Board:** $9261

Freshman Class: 13850 applied, 9694 accepted, 2259 enrolled

COMPETITIVE

Johnson & Wales University/Providence Campus, founded in 1914, is the largest of the JWU campuses and offers more than 50 majors in business, hospitality, culinary arts, technology, and graduate programs. The figures in the above capsule and in this profile are approximate. There are 4 undergraduate schools and 2 graduate schools. The 2 libraries contain 108,706 volumes, 439,822 microform items, 3,832 audio/video tapes/CDs/DVDs, and subscribe to 26,160 periodicals including electronic. Computerized library services include interlibrary loans, database searching, Internet access, and Wi-Fi capability. Special learning facilities include a The 166-acre campus is in a small town in Providence, 45 minutes from Boston, Cape Cod, and Newport and 3 hours from New York. Including any residence halls, there are 38 buildings.

Student Life: 81% of undergraduates are from out of state, mostly the Northeast. Students are from 50 states, 91 foreign countries, and Canada. 58% are White. The average age of freshmen is 18; all undergraduates, 19.

Housing: 3534 students can be accommodated in college housing, which includes coed dorms and on-campus apartments. and international housing, technology community, women's community, wellness community, equine community, academic community. All of these are available for first-year students and upperclassmen only. On-campus housing is available on a lottery system for upperclassmen. 70% of students commute. Alcohol is not permitted. All students may keep cars.

Activities: 2% of men belong to 9 national fraternities; 2% of women belong to 7 national sororities. There are 65 groups on campus, including (student newspaper) Multicultural Clubs, Campus Herald, cheerleading, computers, dance, debate, drama, environmental, ethnic, gay, honors, international, musical theater, newspaper, pep band, political, professional, religious, social, social service, student government, and yearbook.

Sports: There is no sports program at JWU. Facilities include state-of-the-art exercise machines and numerous programs, including weight management, personal exercise, wellness programs, body composition analysis, strength training, physical fitness testing, nutritional analysis, physical fitness assessments, life saving, and stress relief days.

Disabled Students: All of the campus is accessible. Facilities include wheelchair ramps, elevators, special parking, specially equipped restrooms, special class scheduling, lowered drinking fountains, and lowered telephones.

Services: Counseling and information services are available, as is tutoring in every subject. Workshops in stress and time management and wellness and learning centers are available.

Campus Safety and Security: Measures include 24-hour foot and vehicle patrol and security escort services. There are shuttle buses, emergency telephones, lighted pathways/sidewalks, 24-hour dorm coverage, a phone hot line for campus emergencies, and crime alerts in the student weekly newspaper.

Programs of Study: JWU confers B.S. degrees. Associate, master's, and doctoral degrees are also awarded. Bachelor's degrees are awarded in AGRICULTURE (equine science), BUSINESS (accounting, business administration and management, entrepreneurial studies, fashion merchandising, hospitality management services, hotel/motel and restaurant management, international business management, management information systems, marketing and distribution, marketing management, marketing/retailing/merchandising, office supervision and management, recreation and leisure services, recreational facilities management, retailing, secretarial studies/office management, small business management, sports management, tourism, and transportation and travel marketing), COMMUNICATIONS AND THE ARTS (advertising), COMPUTER AND

PHYSICAL SCIENCE (computer management, computer science, information sciences and systems, systems analysis, and web services), EDUCATION (marketing and distribution education), ENGINEERING AND ENVIRONMENTAL DESIGN (electrical/electronics engineering, food services technology, and technological management), SOCIAL SCIENCE (clothing and textiles management/production/services, criminal justice, food production/management/services, paralegal studies, parks and recreation management, and systems science). Culinary arts, hotel/restaurant management, and marketing are the strongest academically. Culinary arts, hotel/restaurant management, and sports entertainment event management have the largest enrollments.

Required: To graduate, students must complete 180 quarter credit hours, including at least 36 in the major, with a minimum GPA of 2.0. Required classes include English, math, history, economics, science, psychology, sociology, and professional development.

Special: The university offers 11-week internships in most majors, study abroad in 19 countries, work-study programs, accelerated degree programs, and dual majors. Students have the opportunity to receive hands-on experience through 2 JWU programs: Summer Work Experience (SWEP) and Cooperative Education. There are 1 national honor societies, a freshman honors program, and 5 departmental honors programs.

Faculty/Classroom: 56% of faculty are male; 44% are female. 95% teach undergraduates. No introductory courses are taught by graduate students.

Admissions: 70% of the 2013-2014 applicants were accepted.

Requirements: Although SAT and ACT scores are required only for students applying for honors admissions, students who have taken these tests are encouraged to submit their scores. A GPA of 2.0 is required. AP and CLEP credits are accepted. Important factors in the admissions decision are advanced placement or honors courses, extracurricular activities record, and recommendations by school officials.

Procedure: There are deferred admissions and rolling admissions plans. Application deadlines are open.

Transfer: 358 transfer students enrolled in 2012-2013. Applicants are required to submit official high school and college transcripts and must have earned a minimum college GPA of 2.0. 45 of 180 credits required for the bachelor's degree must be completed at JWU.

Visiting: There are regularly scheduled orientations for prospective students, including tours conducted by JWU students. These tours include an introduction to the academic and social aspects of the campus experience through interactive sessions. There are guides for informal visits, visitors may sit in on classes, and stay overnight. To schedule a visit, contact the Admissions Office.

Financial Aid: Check with the school for current application deadlines.

International Students: There are 949 international students enrolled. The school actively recruits these students.

Graduates: From July 1, 2012 to June 30, 2013, 1583 bachelor's degrees were awarded. The most popular majors were culinary (14%), food service (7%), and hotel management (5%). 462 companies recruited on campus in 2012-2013.

Admissions Contact: William Priante, Dean of Admissions. E-Mail: *admissions.pvd@jwu.edu* Web: *www.jwu.edu*

PROVIDENCE COLLEGE C-2

Providence, RI 02918 (401) 865-2535 (800) 721-6444; (401) 865-2826

Full-time: 1631 men, 2210 women	**Faculty:** 299; IIA, +$
Part-time: 6 men, 5 women	**Ph.D.s:** 80%
Graduate: 248 men, 348 women	**Student/Faculty:** 12 to 1
Year: semesters, summer session	**Tuition:** $41,475
Application Deadline: January 15	**Room & Board:** $12,640
Freshman Class: 9873 applied, 5979 accepted, 982 enrolled	
SAT CR/M/W: 576/583/590	**ACT:** 25 **HIGHLY COMPETITIVE**

Providence College, founded in 1917, is a liberal arts and sciences institution operated by the Dominican Order of the Catholic Church. There are 3 undergraduate schools and 3 graduate schools. The figures in the above capsule and in this profile are approximate. In addition to regional accreditation, Providence has baccalaureate program accreditation with CSWE and NASM. The library contains 795,000 volumes, 245,000 microform items, and subscribes to 39,800 periodicals including electronic. Computerized library services include interlibrary loans, database searching, Internet access, and laptop Internet portals. Special learning facilities include a learning resource center, art gallery, radio station, TV station, Blackfriars Theater, Smith Center for the Arts, Science Center Complex, and computer and language labs. The 105-acre campus is in a suburban area 50 miles south of Boston. Including any residence halls, there are 45 buildings.

Student Life: 89% of undergraduates are from out of state, mostly the Northeast. Students are from 37 states, 26 foreign countries, and Canada. 55% are from public schools. 88% are white. 76% are Catholic. The average age of freshmen is 18; all undergraduates, 20. 3% do not continue beyond their first year; 87% remain to graduate.

Housing: 3072 students can be accommodated in college housing, which includes single-sex and coed dorms and on-campus apartments. On-campus housing is available on a first-come, first-served basis. 78% of students live on campus; of those, 85% remain on campus on weekends. Upperclassmen may keep cars.

Activities: There are no fraternities or sororities. There are 117 groups on campus, including art, band, cheerleading, choir, chorale, chorus, computers, dance, debate, drama, environmental, ethnic, gay, honors, international, jazz band, literary magazine, musical theater, newspaper, pep band, photography, political, professional, radio and TV, religious, social, social service, student government, and yearbook. Popular campus events include Annual Newport Trip, Late Night Madness, and Clam Jam.

Sports: There are 10 intercollegiate sports for men and 12 for women, and 15 intramural sports for men and 15 for women. Facilities include an ice arena, indoor track, courts for tennis, racquetball, handball, squash, basketball, and volleyball, a pool, a nautilus program, facilities for weight lifting, aerobics, a ballet studio, soccer field, softball field, and a turf field.

Disabled Students: 98% of the campus is accessible. Facilities include wheelchair ramps, elevators, special parking, specially equipped restrooms, special class scheduling, lowered drinking fountains, lowered telephones, and special housing.

Services: Counseling and information services are available, as is tutoring in most subjects. There is a reader service for the blind, and remedial math and writing.

Campus Safety and Security: Measures include 24-hour foot and vehicle patrol, emergency notification system, self-defense education, and security escort services. There are shuttle buses, emergency telephones, lighted pathways/sidewalks, controlled access to dorms/residences, and a campuswide computerized card access system for entry into all dorms and apartment buildings.

Programs of Study: Providence confers B.A. and B.S. degrees. Associate and master's degrees are also awarded. Bachelor's degrees are awarded in AGRICULTURE (wildlife management), BIOLOGICAL SCIENCE (biochemistry and biology/biological science), BUSINESS (accounting, banking and finance, business administration and management, business economics, and marketing management), COMMUNICATIONS AND THE ARTS (art history, dramatic arts, English, French, Italian, music, painting, photography, sculpture, Spanish, and studio art), COMPUTER AND PHYSICAL SCIENCE (applied physics, chemistry, computer science, and mathematics), EDUCATION (elementary education, English education, foreign languages education, mathematics education, music education, secondary education, social studies education, and special education), ENGINEERING AND ENVIRONMENTAL DESIGN (preengineering), HEALTH PROFESSIONS (health care administration), SOCIAL SCIENCE (American studies, Asian/American studies, community services, economics, fire science, history, humanities, international studies, liberal arts/general studies, philosophy, political science/government, psychology, social science, social work, sociology, theological studies, and women's studies). Biology, chemistry, and business are the strongest academically. Marketing, business administration, management, and history have the largest enrollments.

Required: To graduate, all students must complete at least 116 credit hours, with 24 upper-division hours in the major, and maintain a GPA of 2.0. Students must also meet an English proficiency requirement, complete 20 credits in Western civilization, and fulfill the 39-credit core curriculum, including 6 credits each in natural science, social science, philosophy (3 must be in ethics), and theology, 3 each in math and fine arts, and 9 in nondepartmental electives.

Special: Providence offers internships in politics, broadcasting, journalism, and business and study abroad in 6 countries. Other opportunities for study abroad are available through AIFS. Also available are dual and student-designed majors, a 3-2 engineering degree with Columbia University or Washington University in St. Louis, nondegree study, a Washington semester, work-study, B.A.-B.S. degrees, and pass/fail options. There are 18 national honor societies and a freshman honors program.

Faculty/Classroom: 59% of faculty are male; 41% are female. All teach undergraduates. No introductory courses are taught by graduate students. The average class size in an introductory lecture is 16; in a laboratory is 15; and in a regular course is 22.

Admissions: 61% of a recent year applicants were accepted. The SAT scores for a recent year freshman class were: Critical Reading--14% below 500, 47% between 500 and 599, 32% between 600 and 700, and 7% above 700; Math--13% below 500, 44% between 500 and 599, 36% between 600 and 700, and 7% above 700; Writing--12% below 500, 40% between 500 and 599, 37% between 600 and 700, and 11% above 700. The ACT scores were 9% below 21, 26% between 21 and 23, 33% between 24 and 26, 15% between 27 and 28, and 17% above 28. 63% of the current freshmen were in the top fifth of their class; 87% were in the top two fifths. 25 freshmen graduated first in their class.

Requirements: Applicants must be graduates of an accredited secondary school. A GPA of 3.25 is recommended. High school preparation should include 4 years of English, 3 years of math, 3 years of 1 foreign language, 2 years of lab science, 2 years of history/social studies, and 2 other academic subjects. An essay and 2 academic letters of recommendation are required. SAT Subject Tests in 2 areas of the applicant's choice are recommended. AP credits are accepted. Important factors in the admissions decision are advanced placement or honors courses, extracurricular activities record, and personality/intangible qualities.

Procedure: Freshmen are admitted fall and spring. Entrance exams should be taken in the junior or senior year. There are early admissions and deferred admissions plans. Early decision applications should be filed by November 1; regular applications, by January 15 for fall entry; and December 1 for spring entry, along with a $55 fee. Notification of early decision is sent January 1; regular decision, April 1. 2204 applicants were on the waiting list; 160 were admitted. Applications are accepted online.

Transfer: 38 transfer students enrolled in a recent year. The application, college transcripts, courses in progress, high school records, a required essay, an intended major, and college disciplinary records are reviewed to ensure that the "match" to PC is a good one. 60 of 116 credits required for the bachelor's degree must be completed at Providence.

Visiting: There are regularly scheduled orientations for prospective students, including campus tours and information sessions. There are guides for informal visits and visitors may sit in on classes. To schedule a visit, contact the Admissions Office.

Financial Aid: In a recent year, 61% of all full-time freshmen and 58% of continuing full-time students received some form of financial aid. 59% of all full-time freshmen and 54% of continuing full-time students received need-based aid. The average freshman award was $26,140. Need-based scholarships or need-based grants averaged $21,557; need-based self-help aid (loans and jobs) averaged $5,969; non-need-based athletic scholarships averaged $21,269; and other non-need-based awards and non-need-based scholarships averaged $19,780. 30% of undergraduate students work part-time. Average annual earnings from campus work are $1400. The average financial indebtedness of a recent graduate was $35,216. Providence is a member of CSS. The CSS/Profile and FAFSA are required. The deadline for filing freshman financial aid applications for fall entry is February 1.

International Students: There are 57 international students enrolled. The school actively recruits these students. They must take the TOEFL with a minimum score of 550 on the paper-based TOEFL (PBT) or 80 on the Internet-based version (iBT).

Graduates: In a recent year, 1138 bachelor's degrees were awarded. The most popular majors were business administration and management (10%), marketing/marketing management (10%), and political science/english/history (7%). In an average class, 85% graduate in 4 years or less, 87% graduate in 5 years or less, and 87% graduate in 6 years or less.

Admissions Contact: Raul A. Fontes, Interim Dean of Admission. E-Mail: *pcadmiss@providence.edu* Web: *www.providence.edu*

RHODE ISLAND COLLEGE C-2

Providence, RI 02908 (401) 456-8234
(800) 669-5760; (401) 456-8817

Full-time: 1864 men, 3594 women	**Faculty:** 302; IIA, -$
Part-time: 565 men, 1238 women	**Ph.D.s:** 89%
Graduate: 159 men, 688 women	**Student/Faculty:** 18 to 1
Year: semesters, summer session	**Tuition:** $7598 ($18,296)
Application Deadline: March 15	**Room & Board:** $9534
Freshman Class: 4492 applied, 3106 accepted, 1071 enrolled	
SAT CR/M/W: 470/460/470 **ACT:** 20	**LESS COMPETITIVE**

Rhode Island College, founded in 1854, is a state-supported liberal arts institution offering undergraduate and graduate programs in the liberal arts and sciences, social work, nursing, business, education, and human development. There are 5 undergraduate schools and 1 graduate school. In addition to regional accreditation, RIC has baccalaureate program accreditation with CSWE, NASAD, NASM, NCATE, and NLN. The library contains 802,729 volumes, 1.3 million microform items, 6,704 audio/video tapes/CDs/DVDs, and subscribes to 1,325,436 periodicals including electronic. Computerized library services include interlibrary loans, database searching, Internet access, and Wi-Fi capability. Special learning facilities include an art gallery and radio station. The 180-acre campus is in a suburban area in Providence. Including any residence halls, there are 43 buildings.

Student Life: 86% of undergraduates are from Rhode Island. Others are from 29 states. 66% are White; 12% race unknown; 11% Hispanic. 39% are Unknown Religious affiliation; 36% Catholic; 25% claim no religious affiliation. The average age of freshmen is 19; all undergraduates, 24. 25% do not continue beyond their first year; 43% remain to graduate.

Housing: 1194 students can be accommodated in college housing, which includes single-sex and coed dorms. In addition, there are honors houses and special-interest houses. On-campus housing is available on a first-come, first-served basis, and is available on a lottery system for upperclassmen. 85% of students commute. Alcohol is not permitted. All students may keep cars.

Activities: 2% of women belong to 1 local and 2 national sororities. There are 75 groups on campus, including art, band, cheerleading, chess, chorale, chorus, dance, debate, drama, environmental, ethnic, film, gay, honors, international, jazz band, literary magazine, musical theater, newspaper, orchestra, political, professional, radio and TV, religious, social, social service, student government, and symphony. Popular campus events include a Fine and Performing Arts Calendar, Banister Gallery, and Diversity Week and Campus Center Activities.

Sports: There are 9 intercollegiate sports for men and 10 for women, and 11 intramural sports for men and 11 for women. Facilities include Rhode Island College is fortunate to have some of the finest athletic and recreation facilities in their conference. The two cornerstone facilities are the Murray Center which houses the intercollegiate athletic program and the newly opened Recreation Center. The Murray Center is home to the college's 28,000 arena which is the home venue for all volleyball, gymnastics and basketball events, and has played host to numerous games leading up to the NCAA championship. The Murray Center also includes a sports' medicine area, varsity weight room, student-athlete lounge, locker rooms, conference space, athletic administration and the Hall of Fame. The Recreation Center is an approximately 80,000 square foot facility which includes a 33,000 square foot fieldhouse with indoor track and three multi-use courts. It also has a swimming pool and a fitness center with the latest in professional fitness equipment. Additionally, there are locker rooms, a student lounge, a sports medicine area, and an intercollegiate athletic wing with a wrestling facility, lockers rooms, coaches offices, and an equipment room. The building also plays host many of the college's major events including concerts. Outdoor facilities an 8.5 acre practice complex, the Anchorman Baseball Complex and the Dana Bazar Softball complex as well as an indoor hitting facility. The varsity competition complex has an NCAA regulation soccer/lacrosse field, is home to the Black Outdoor Track, and seat approximately 5,000 people. There are six all-weather tennis courts also within the campus. A crowning jewel of athletic facilities is the Student-Athlete Success Center which can provide academic support for over 110 student-athletes under state-of-the-art conditions.

Disabled Students: All of the campus is accessible. Facilities include wheelchair ramps, elevators, special parking, specially equipped restrooms, special class scheduling, lowered drinking fountains, lowered telephones, special housing. The Disability Services Office provides accommodations for students with disabilities. Also, an assistive technology computer lab is available at the library.

Services: Counseling and information services are available, as is tutoring in most subjects. There is a reader service for the blind, and remedial math, reading, and writing. There are services for learning-disabled students and any student needing academic assistance.

Campus Safety and Security: Measures include 24-hour foot and vehicle patrol, emergency notification system, and security escort services. There are shuttle buses, emergency telephones, lighted pathways/sidewalks, controlled access to dorms/residences, Bike patrol and Campus wide 911 system.

Programs of Study: RIC confers B.A., B.S., B.F.A., B.M., B.S.N. and B.S.W. degrees. Master's and doctoral degrees are also awarded. Bachelor's degrees are awarded in BIOLOGICAL SCIENCE (biology/biological science), BUSINESS (accounting, banking and finance, business administration and management, and marketing management), COMMUNICATIONS AND THE ARTS (art history and appreciation, communications, dance, dramatic arts, English, film arts, French, music, music performance, Spanish, and studio art), COMPUTER AND PHYSICAL SCIENCE (chemistry, computer science, information sciences and systems, mathematics, physics, and radiological technology), EDUCATION (art education, early childhood education, elementary education, foreign languages education, health education, middle school education, music education, physical education, science education, secondary education, special education, and technical education), HEALTH PROFESSIONS (health care administration, nuclear medical technology, nursing, predentistry, premedicine, and preveterinary science), SOCIAL SCIENCE (addiction studies, African American studies, anthropology, criminal justice, economics, geography, history, Latin American studies, liberal arts/general studies, philosophy, political science/government, prelaw, psychology, public administration, social science, social work, sociology, and women's studies). Nursing, elementary education and psychology have the largest enrollments.

Required: To graduate, students must complete 120 credits and maintain a minimum GPA of 2.0. All students must complete the college's general education program, which consists of 4 core requirements in cultural legacies and critical thinking, and 6 distribution requirements. All students must complete the college writing and mathematics requirements.

Special: Cross-registration is available with Community College of Rhode Island and the University of Rhode Island. The college offers internships, study abroad, work-study programs, a general studies degree, dual and student-designed majors, credit by exam, credit for prior learning, and pass/fail options. There are 4 national honor societies, a freshman honors program, and 36 departmental honors programs.

Faculty/Classroom: 42% of faculty are male; 58% are female. 92% teach undergraduates, 3% do research, and 3% do both. No introductory courses are taught by graduate students. The average class size in an introductory lecture is 30; in a laboratory is 24; and in a regular course is 30.

Admissions: 69% of the 2013-2014 applicants were accepted. The SAT scores for the 2013-2014 freshman class were: Critical Reading--63% below 500, 31% between 500 and 599, 5% between 600 and 699, and 1% between 700 and 800; Math--66% below 500, 28% between 500 and 599, and 6% between 600 and 699; Writing--65% below 500, 30% between 500 and 599, 5% between 600 and 699. The ACT scores were 61% below 21, 23% between 21 and 23, 12% between 24 and 26, 1% between 27 and 28, and 3% above 28. 24% of the current freshmen were in the top fifth of their class; 58% were in the top two fifths.

Requirements: The SAT or ACT is required. The ACT Optional Writing test is also required. Applicants should be graduates of an accredited secondary school with 18 academic credits, including 4 in English, 3 in mathematics, 2 in the same foreign language, 2 in science (biology and chemistry or physics), 2 in social studies, and the remainder in academic electives. The GED is accepted. An essay is required along with a portfolio for art students and an audition for music students. AP and CLEP credits are accepted. Important factors in the admissions decision are recommendations by school officials, advanced placement or honors courses, and evidence of special talent.

Procedure: Freshmen are admitted fall and spring. Entrance exams should be taken by December of the senior year. There is a rolling admissions plan. Applications should be filed by March 15 for fall entry. The fall 2013 application fee was $50. Notifications are sent December 15. Applications are accepted online.

Transfer: 806 transfer students enrolled in 2012-2013. Applicants must submit 24 transferable credits with a minimum GPA of 2.25 with 24 to 29 earned college credits or a minimum GPA of 2.0 with 30 or more earned college credits. 45 of 120 credits required for the bachelor's degree must be completed at RIC.

Visiting: There are regularly scheduled orientations for prospective students, including information sessions and a campus tour. There are guides for informal visits and visitors may sit in on classes. To schedule a visit, contact the Office of Undergraduate Admissions.

Financial Aid: In 2013-2014, 91% of all full-time freshmen and 83% of continuing full-time students received some form of financial aid. 67% of all full-time freshmen and 64% of continuing full-time students received need-based aid. The average freshman award was $10,355. Need-based scholarships or need-based grants averaged $6,149 ($13,420 maximum); need-based self-help aid (loans and jobs) averaged $3,666 ($4,750 maximum); and other non-need-based awards and non-need-based scholarships averaged $4,893 ($30,000 maximum). 10% of undergraduate students work part-time. The average financial indebtedness of the 2013 graduate was $23,089. RIC is a member of CSS. The FAFSA and the college's own financial statement are required. The deadline for filing freshman financial aid applications for fall entry is March 1.

International Students: There are 3 international students enrolled. They must take the TOEFL with a minimum score of 550 on the paper-based TOEFL (PBT) or 79 on the Internet-based version (iBT). They must also take the SAT.

Graduates: From July 1, 2012 to June 30, 2013, 1307 bachelor's degrees were awarded. The most popular majors were nursing (12%), psychology (12%), and management (7%). 212 companies recruited on campus in 2012-2013. In an average class, 14% graduate in 4 years or less, 22% graduate in 5 years or less, and 43% graduate in 6 years or less. Of the 2012 graduating class, 17% were enrolled in graduate school within 6 months of graduation, and 86% were employed.

Admissions Contact: John McLaughlin, Director of Admissions. E-Mail: *jmclaughlin@ric.edu or admissions@ric.edu* Web: *www.ric.edu*

RHODE ISLAND SCHOOL OF DESIGN C-2

Providence, RI 02903 (401) 454-6100
(800) 364-7473; (401) 454-6309

Full-time: 687 men, 1318 women
Part-time: n/av
Graduate: 150 men, 265 women
Year: 4-1-4
Application Deadline: February 1
Freshman Class: 3215 applied, 878 accepted, 460 enrolled
SAT or ACT: required
Faculty: n/av
Ph.D.s: n/av
Student/Faculty: 9 to 1
Tuition: $42,932
Room & Board: $12,272

SPECIAL

Rhode Island School of Design, founded in 1877, is a private institution offering degree programs in fine arts, design, and architecture. In addition to regional accreditation, RISD has baccalaureate program accreditation with NAAB and NASAD. The library contains 150,782 volumes, 4,911 audio/video tapes/CDs/DVDs, and subscribes to 1,631 periodicals including electronic. Computerized library services include interlibrary loans, database searching, Internet access, and Wi-Fi capability. Special learning facilities include an art gallery, the Rhode Island School of Design Museum, Nature Lab, Writing Center. The 13-acre campus is in an urban area 50 miles south of Boston. Including any residence halls, there are 49 buildings.

Student Life: 99% of undergraduates are from out of state, mostly the Middle Atlantic. Students are from 48 states, 64 foreign countries, and Canada. 60% are from public schools. 33% are White; 24% Foreign; 16% Asian American; 12% race unknown. The average age of freshmen is 18; all undergraduates, 20. 8% do not continue beyond their first year; 90% remain to graduate.

Housing: 1503 students can be accommodated in college housing, which includes coed dorms, on-campus apartments, and married student housing. On-campus housing is guaranteed for the freshman year only and is available on a lottery system for upperclassmen. 70% of students live on campus; of those, 90% remain on campus on weekends. Alcohol is not permitted. No one may keep cars.

Activities: There are no fraternities or sororities. There are 47 groups on campus, including art, chorale, computers, drama, environmental, ethnic, film, gay, international, literary magazine, newspaper, photography, political, professional, religious, social, social service, student government, and yearbook. Popular campus events include Student and Alumni Sale, Artists Ball, and RISD By Design.

Sports: There are 7 intramural sports for men and 7 for women. Facilities include a student center with areas and equipment for dance, aerobics, weight and fitness training, a Tillinghast farm. Students may also enroll in activity classes at Brown University and use its athletic complex which includes a swimming pool, an ice skating rink, a track, weight training equipment, and courts for basketball, tennis, and squash.

Disabled Students: Facilities include wheelchair ramps, elevators, special parking, specially equipped restrooms, and special class scheduling.

Services: There is remedial reading and writing. A writing program is available to all students. Taped lectures, note takers, and alternative test-taking procedures are also available, particularly for students with learning disabilities.

Campus Safety and Security: Measures include 24-hour foot and vehicle patrol, emergency notification system, and self-defense education. There are shuttle buses, lighted pathways/sidewalks, controlled access to dorms/residences, building access cards.

Programs of Study: RISD confers B.Arch., B.F.A. degrees. Master's degrees are also awarded. Bachelor's degrees are awarded in COMMUNICATIONS AND THE ARTS (apparel design, ceramic art and design, film arts, glass, graphic design, illustration, industrial design, metal/jewelry, painting, photography, printmaking, and sculpture), ENGINEERING AND ENVIRONMENTAL DESIGN (architecture, furniture design, and interior design), SOCIAL SCIENCE (textiles and clothing). Illustration, industrial design and architecture have the largest enrollments.

Required: To graduate, all students must complete at least 126 credit hours, including 54 in the major, 42 in liberal arts, 18 in the freshman foundation program, and 12 in non-major, art department electives. Liberal arts credits must include 12 each in art/architectural history and electives, and 9 each in Literary Arts and Sciences, and history/philosophy/social science. Core courses include 2 semesters each of foundation drawing, 2-dimensional design, and 3-dimensional design. A minimum GPA of 2.0 and completion of the final-year project are required.

Special: RISD offers cross-registration with Brown University, as well as a RISD/Brown Dual Degree Program, as well as cross-registration through the AICAD mobility program. RISD offers credit or noncredit summer programs, 6-week internships during the midyear winter session, and study abroad in 21 countries and through the European Honors Program in Rome. Students may also elect a liberal arts concentration in art/architectural history, literary studies or social sciences.

Faculty/Classroom: 55% of faculty are male; 45% are female. No introductory courses are taught by graduate students. The average class size in an introductory lecture is 20 and in a laboratory is 17.

Admissions: 27% of the 2013-2014 applicants were accepted.

Requirements: The SAT or ACT is required. In addition, SAT or ACT scores must be substituted. Applicants must be graduates of an accredited secondary school or have a GED. Academic Transcripts, writing samples, assigned drawings, a portfolio, and a statement of purpose are also required. Up to 3 letters of recommendation are recommended. All applicants who speak English as a second language, including US citizens, must submit results from either TOEFL or IELTS. AP credits are accepted.

Procedure: Freshmen are admitted fall and spring. Entrance exams should be taken at least 6 weeks before the application deadline. There are early decision and deferred admissions plans. Early decision applications should be filed by November 1; regular applications, by February 1 for fall entry, along with a $60 fee. Notification of early decision is sent December 1; regular decision, March 15. applicants were on the 2013 waiting list; were admitted. Applications are accepted online.

Transfer: 71 transfer students enrolled in 2012-2013. Applicants must have at least 27 college credits and should submit an essay along with academic transcripts from the previous 3 years. All students must submit a portfolio and complete a drawing assignment. Letters of recommendation are recommended. The SAT or ACT is required for architecture and industrial design applicants. 64 of 126 credits required for the bachelor's degree must be completed at RISD.

Visiting: There are regularly scheduled orientations for prospective students, including a presentation by the admissions staff and a campus tour by a student. Visitors may sit in on classes. To schedule a visit, contact the Admissions Office at admissions@risd.edu.

Financial Aid: 59% of undergraduate students work part-time. Average annual earnings from campus work are $1100. The average financial indebtedness of the 2013 graduate was $32,207. RISD is a member of CSS. The CSS/Profile and FAFSA, and parents' income tax returns are required. The deadline for filing freshman financial aid applications for fall entry is February 15.

International Students: There are 475 international students enrolled. The school actively recruits these students. They must take the TOEFL with a minimum score of 93 on the Internet-based version (iBT), IELTS. They must also take the SAT or ACT.

Graduates: From July 1, 2012 to June 30, 2013, 481 bachelor's degrees were awarded. The most popular majors were visual and performing arts (77%), architecture (15%), and family and consumer sciences (4%). In an average class, 86% graduate in 5 years or less.

Admissions Contact: Edward Newhall, Associate Vice President for Enrollment. E-Mail: *admissions@risd.edu* Web: *www.risd.edu*

ROGER WILLIAMS UNIVERSITY D-3

Bristol, RI 02809 **(401) 254-3500**
(800) 458-7144; (401) 254-3557

Full-time: 1937 men, 1938 women	**Faculty:** n/av; IIB, +$
Part-time: 288 men, 248 women	**Ph.D.s:** 90%
Graduate: 144 men, 177 women	**Student/Faculty:** 19 to 1
Year: semesters, summer session	**Tuition:** $31,668
Application Deadline: February 1	**Room & Board:** $14,120

Freshman Class: 9021 applied, 7305 accepted, 1102 enrolled

COMPETITIVE

Founded in 1956, Roger Williams University, located in Bristol, R.I., is a leading independent, coeducational university with programs in arts and sciences, professional studies, architecture, and law. There are 7 undergraduate schools and 6 graduate schools. In addition to regional accreditation, RWU has baccalaureate program accreditation with AACSB, ABET, ACCE, NAAB, and NASDTEC. The 3 libraries contain 499,355 volumes, 140,689 microform items, 5,347 audio/video tapes/CDs/DVDs, and subscribe to 50,391 periodicals including electronic. Computerized library services include interlibrary loans, database searching, Internet access, and Wi-Fi capability. Special learning facilities include an art gallery, radio station, RWU Marine and Natural Sciences building is home to a marine biology wet-lab and shellfish hatchery. The University also accesses an 80 acre field site on nearby Prudence Island, which includes Jenny's Creek Salt Marsh and the Oyster Nursey Pond. The 140-acre campus is in a small town 18 miles southeast of Providence. Including any residence halls, there are 42 buildings.

Student Life: 83% of undergraduates are from out of state, mostly the Northeast. Students are from 44 states, 62 foreign countries, and Canada. 74% are White. The average age of freshmen is 18; all undergraduates, 22. 17% do not continue beyond their first year; 63% remain to graduate.

Housing: 2995 students can be accommodated in college housing, which includes single-sex and coed dorms, on-campus apartments, off-campus apartments, and married student housing. In addition, there are honors houses, special-interest houses, academic major theme areas. On-campus housing is guaranteed for the freshman year only and is available on a lottery system for upperclassmen. 63% of students live on campus; of those, 70% remain on campus on weekends. Upperclassmen may keep cars.

Activities: There are no fraternities or sororities. There are 70 groups on campus, including art, band, cheerleading, chess, choir, chorale, chorus, communications, computers, dance, drama, environmental, ethnic, film, gay, honors, international, jazz band, literary magazine, musical theater, newspaper, orchestra, photography, political, professional, radio and TV, religious, social service, student government, and yearbook. Popular campus events include Spring Weekend, International Dinner, and Campus Entertainment Network (concerts and comedians).

Sports: There are 11 intercollegiate sports for men and 11 for women, and 17 intramural sports for men and 16 for women. Facilities include The athletic facilities at Roger Williams center around the 124,000 square-foot Campus Recreation Center, completed in 2003. Athletic facilities within the building are highlighted by: An 8,500+ square-foot fitness center on two floors. The Aquatic Center. Two multipurpose dance studios also home to exercise classes. A central gymnasium that seats 1,200 for home events. Two convertible racquetball/squash courts and one regulation squash court. The Field House, utilized for team practices, intramurals, and large tournaments. The campus' athletic facilities extend outdoors, including: The RWU Waterfront, the center for sailing and kayaking. Bayside Field, home to the soccer and lacrosse programs. Paolino Field, home to the softball and baseball teams. Two practice fields located on North Campus. Outdoor tennis, volleyball, and basketball courts.

Disabled Students: Facilities include wheelchair ramps, elevators, special parking, specially equipped restrooms, special class scheduling, lowered drinking fountains, and lowered telephones.

Services: Counseling and information services are available, as is tutoring in every subject. There is a reader service for the blind, and remedial math, reading, and writing.

Campus Safety and Security: Measures include 24-hour foot and vehicle patrol, emergency notification system, and security escort services. There are shuttle buses, emergency telephones, lighted pathways/sidewalks, and controlled access to dorms/residences.

Programs of Study: RWU confers B.A., B.S., B.Arch., B.F.A. and B.G.S degrees. Associate and master's degrees are also awarded. Bachelor's degrees are awarded in BIOLOGICAL SCIENCE (biochemistry, biology/biological science, and marine biology), BUSINESS (accounting, banking and finance, business administration and management, business law, international business management, management science, and marketing/retailing/merchandising), COMMUNICATIONS AND THE ARTS (art history and appreciation, communications, creative writing, dance, dramatic arts, English, graphic design, historic preservation, journalism, languages, media arts, music, theatre arts, and visual and performing arts), COMPUTER AND PHYSICAL SCIENCE (chemistry, computer science, computer security and information assurance, mathematics, web services, and web technology), EDUCATION (education, elementary education, and secondary education), ENGINEERING AND ENVIRONMENTAL DESIGN (architecture, construction management, engineering, environmental science, industrial engineering technology, and technological management), HEALTH PROFESSIONS (health care administration), SOCIAL SCIENCE (American studies, anthropology, community services, criminal justice, economics, history, humanities, international relations, legal studies, paralegal studies, philosophy, political science/government, psychology, public administration, social science, and sociology). Architecture and engineering is the strongest academically. Psychology, criminal justice, and business management have the largest enrollments.

Required: All students must: -Earn a minimum cumulative grade point average (GPA) of 2.0 in order to graduate. Each college or school may also require a minimum GPA in the major. -Successfully complete a minimum of 30 credits of course work in a major, all University Core Curriculum requirements and the Service Learning Requirement -Complete 45 of the last 60 credits at RWU or at an RWU Semester Abroad program. -All financial obligations must be satisfied.

Special: RWU offers co-op programs, internships, accelerated degree programs, study abroad in 30 countries, work-study, individualized majors, and dual majors. There are 16 national honor societies and a freshman honors program.

Faculty/Classroom: 58% of faculty are male; 43% are female. All teach undergraduates. No introductory courses are taught by graduate students.

Admissions: 81% of the 2013-2014 applicants were accepted. 26% of the current freshmen were in the top fifth of their class; 87% were in the top two fifths.

Requirements: Applicants should be graduates of an accredited secondary school with a minimum GPA of 2.0. The GED is accepted. Students should have 4 years of English, 3 years of math, 3 years of social sciences, 3 years of natural sciences (of which 2 must be lab units), 2 years of history and 4 to 6 electives, for a total of 16 Carnegie units. Art and architecture students must submit portfolios. An essay is required, and an interview is recommended. See admission requirements for individual colleges. A GPA of 2.0 is required. AP and CLEP credits are accepted. Important factors in the admissions decision are recommendations by school officials, leadership record, and advanced placement or honors courses.

Procedure: Freshmen are admitted fall and spring. Entrance exams should be taken in September or October of the senior year. There are early admissions, deferred admissions, and rolling admissions plans. Applications should be filed by February 1 for fall entry, along with a $50 fee. Notification of early decision is sent December 15; regular decision, March 15. 130 applicants were on the 2013 waiting list; 5 were admitted. Applications are accepted online.

Transfer: 182 transfer students enrolled in 2012-2013. Applicants need a minimum college GPA of 2.5, college transcripts, an essay or personal statement and a statement of good standing from the prior institution. 45 of 120 credits required for the bachelor's degree must be completed at RWU.

Visiting: There are regularly scheduled orientations for prospective students. There are guides for informal visits and visitors may sit in on classes. To schedule a visit, contact the Office of Admission.

Financial Aid: RWU is a member of CSS. The CSS/Profile and FAFSA are required. The priority date for freshman financial aid applications for fall entry is February 1. The deadline for filing freshman financial aid applications for fall entry is February 1.

International Students: There are 214 international students enrolled. The school actively recruits these students. They must take the TOEFL and the college's own test. SAT scores are required for all education majors.

Graduates: From July 1, 2012 to June 30, 2013, 976 bachelor's degrees were awarded. The most popular majors were business/marketing (24%), architecture (10%), and justice studies (9%). 80 companies recruited on campus in 2012-2013. In an average class, 50% graduate in 4 years or less, 58% graduate in 5 years or less, and 63% graduate in 6 years or less.

Of the 2012 graduating class, 13% were enrolled in graduate school within 6 months of graduation.

Admissions Contact: Amanda Marsili, Director of Admissions Operations. E-Mail: *admit@rwu.edu* Web: *http:/www.rwu.edu/admission-financial-aid/undergraduate-admission*

SALVE REGINA UNIVERSITY D-4

Newport, RI 02840 (401) 341-2908
(888) GO-SALVE; (401) 848-2823

Full-time: 563 men, 1310 women	**Faculty:** 118; IIA, av$
Part-time: 38 men, 115 women	**Ph.D.s:** 81%
Graduate: 227 men, 350 women	**Student/Faculty:** 15 to 1
Year: semesters, summer session	**Tuition:** $34,950
Application Deadline: February 1	**Room & Board:** $12,300

Freshman Class: 5070 applied, 3400 accepted, 465 enrolled
SAT CR/M/W: 550/550/560 **ACT:** 24 **VERY COMPETITIVE**

Salve Regina University, founded in 1934 and sponsored by the Sisters of Mercy, is an independent institution affiliated with the Roman Catholic Church. The university offers programs in liberal arts, business, health science, and professional training. There is one undergraduate school and one graduate school. In addition to regional accreditation, Salve has baccalaureate program accreditation with CSWE and NASAD. The library contains 139,161 volumes, 43,146 microform items, 19,420 audio/video tapes/CDs/DVDs, and subscribes to 1,041 periodicals including electronic. Computerized library services include interlibrary loans, database searching, Internet access, and Wi-Fi capability. Special learning facilities include an art gallery, radio station, biolog and chemistry labs, graphic design and studio art facilities, information systems and computer science labs. The 80-acre campus is in a suburban area on Newport's waterfront, 35 south of Providence and 60 miles south of Boston. Including any residence halls, there are 50 buildings.

Student Life: 75% of undergraduates are from out of state, mostly the Northeast. Students are from 35 states, 21 foreign countries, and Canada. 62% are from public schools. 76% are White; 12% race unknown. The average age of freshmen is 18; all undergraduates, 20. 18% do not continue beyond their first year; 70% remain to graduate.

Housing: 1200 students can be accommodated in college housing, which includes single-sex and coed dorms, on-campus apartments, and off-campus apartments. and living/learning dorms. On-campus housing is available on a first-come, first-served basis, and is available on a lottery system for upperclassmen. 60% of students live on campus; of those, 75% remain on campus on weekends. Upperclassmen may keep cars.

Activities: There are no fraternities or sororities. There are 42 groups on campus, including art, band, cheerleading, choir, chorus, computers, dance, drama, environmental, ethnic, film, gay, honors, international, jazz band, literary magazine, musical theater, newspaper, outdoor, pep band, photography, political, professional, radio and TV, religious, social, social service, student government, and yearbook. Popular campus events include September Welcome-Back Weekend, Octoberfest Weekend, and New Year's Eve Ball.

Sports: There are 8 intercollegiate sports for men and 10 for women, and 8 intramural sports for men and 9 for women. Facilities include a recreation center, tennis courts, outdoor basketball courts, a weight room, a fitness center, and soccer, baseball, and softball fields.

Disabled Students: 75% of the campus is accessible. Facilities include wheelchair ramps, elevators, special parking, specially equipped restrooms, special class scheduling, lowered drinking fountains, and lowered telephones.

Services: Counseling and information services are available, as is tutoring in most subjects. There is remedial math, reading, and writing. There also is a writing center and a computer-based tutorial program.

Campus Safety and Security: Measures include 24-hour foot and vehicle patrol, emergency notification system, self-defense education, and security escort services. There are shuttle buses, emergency telephones, lighted pathways/sidewalks, and controlled access to dorms/residences.

Programs of Study: Salve confers B.A., B.S. and B.A.S. degrees. Associate, master's, and doctoral degrees are also awarded. Bachelor's degrees are awarded in BIOLOGICAL SCIENCE (biology/biological science), BUSINESS (accounting, business administration and management, international business management, management science, and marketing and distribution), COMMUNICATIONS AND THE ARTS (art history and appreciation, communications, communications technology, dramatic arts, English, French, historic preservation, media arts, music, Spanish, and studio art), COMPUTER AND PHYSICAL SCIENCE (chemistry, information sciences and systems, and mathematics), EDUCATION (early childhood education, elementary education, secondary education, and special education), HEALTH PROFESSIONS (nursing), SOCIAL SCIENCE (American studies, criminal justice, economics, history, international studies, philosophy, political science/government, psychology, religion, social work, and sociology). Social work, nursing, and accounting. are the strongest academically. Business, administration of justice, and teacher education have the largest ebnrollments.

Required: To graduate, students must have 120 credit hours, with about 36 in the major, and must maintain a minimum GPA of 2.0. Distribution requirements include 9 credit hours in social science, 6 each in religious studies, science, English, and a foreign language, and 3 each in visual and performing arts, philosophy, and math.

Special: Salve offers internships in most academic disciplines as well as work-study programs on campus. Study abroad in 18 countries, a Washington semester, B.A.-B.S. degrees in biology, business, and economics, dual majors in many programs, and accelerated degree programs in administration of justice, business, international relations, holistic counseling management, and rehabilitation counseling are available. A liberal studies degree, credit for life, military, and work experience, non degree study, and pass/fail options are also offered. There are 15 national honor societies, a freshman honors program, and 10 departmental honors programs.

Faculty/Classroom: 54% of faculty are male; 64% are female. All teach undergraduates, and 50% do both. No introductory courses are taught by graduate students. The average class size in an introductory lecture is 22; in a laboratory is 17; and in a regular course is 18.

Admissions: 67% of the 2013-2014 applicants were accepted. The SAT scores for the 2013-2014 freshman class were: Critical Reading--17% below 500, 59% between 500 and 599, 22% between 600 and 699, and 2% between 700 and 800; Math--16% below 500, 57% between 500 and 599, 24% between 600 and 699, and 2% between 700 and 800; Writing--21% below 500, 52% between 500 and 599, 25% between 600 and 699, and 1% between 700 and 800. The ACT scores were 10% below 21, 37% between 21 and 23, 39% between 24 and 26, 10% between 27 and 28, and 4% above 28. 25% of the current freshmen were in the top fifth of their class; 53% were in the top two fifths. 2 freshmen graduated first in their class.

Requirements: Applicants must be high school graduates or hold a GED. Students should have 16 Carnegie units, consisting of 4 each in English, 3 each in math including algebra and geometry, 2 each in science and foreign language, and 1 in history, and electives. An essay is required. The submission of standardized test scores is optional at Salve Regina unless you are considering a major in education or nursing. Students who decide not to submit scores will not be at any disadvantage during the admission process. A GPA of 2.7 is required. AP and CLEP credits are accepted. Important factors in the admissions decision are advanced placement or honors courses, recommendations by school officials, and leadership record.

Procedure: Freshmen are admitted fall and spring. Entrance exams should be taken as early as possible. There are early admissions and deferred admissions plans. Applications should be filed by February 1 for fall entry; December 1 for spring entry, along with a $50 fee. Notifications are sent March 1. Applications are accepted online.

Transfer: 42 transfer students enrolled in 2012-2013. Applicants must have a college GPA of 2.7 or better. 36 of 120 credits required for the bachelor's degree must be completed at Salve.

Visiting: There are regularly scheduled orientations for prospective students, including information sessions led by an admissions professional with question/answer sessions and a student-led campus tour. There are guides for informal visits, visitors may sit in on classes, and stay overnight. To schedule a visit, contact the Admissions Office.

Financial Aid: In 2013-2014, 97% of all full-time freshmen and 92% of continuing full-time students received some form of financial aid. 80% of all full-time freshmen and 75% of continuing full-time students received need-based aid. The average freshman award was $28,028. 26% of undergraduate students work part-time. Salve is a member of CSS. The FAFSA is required. The priority date for freshman financial aid applications for fall entry is March 1.

International Students: There are 27 international students enrolled. The school actively recruits these students. They must take the TOEFL with a minimum score of 80 on the Internet-based version (iBT). The submission of standardized test scores is optional unless you are considering a major in education or nursing.

Graduates: From July 1, 2012 to June 30, 2013, 431 bachelor's degrees were awarded. The most popular majors were education (23%), nursing (12%), and business (7%). 105 companies recruited on campus in 2012-2013. In an average class, 1% graduate in 3 years or less, 69% graduate in 4 years or less, 72% graduate in 5 years or less, and 72% graduate in 6 years or less. Of the 2012 graduating class, 20% were enrolled in graduate school within 6 months of graduation, and 85% were employed.

Admissions Contact: Colleen Emerson, Dean of Admissions. E-Mail: *sruadmis@salve.edu* Web: *www.salve.edu*

UNIVERSITY OF RHODE ISLAND C-4

Kingston, RI 02881 **(401) 874-1000; (401) 874-5523**

Full-time: 5431 men, 6297 women **Faculty:** n/av; I, --$
Part-time: 769 men, 930 women **Ph.D.s:** 85%
Graduate: 1285 men, 1748 women **Student/Faculty:** n/av
Year: semesters, summer session **Tuition:** $12,450 ($28,016)
Application Deadline: February 1 **Room & Board:** $11,160
Freshman Class: 20637 applied, 15875 accepted, 3258 enrolled
SAT CR/M/W: 530/540/430 **ACT:** 24 **COMPETITIVE+**

The University of Rhode Island, founded in 1892, is a land-grant, sea-grant, and urban-grant institution offering programs in liberal arts, business, engineering, human services, nursing, and pharmacy. Located near the ocean and the bay, the university has strong marine and environmental programs. There are satellite campuses in Providence, West Greenwich, and Narragansett. We are the largest university in the nation's smallest state, but with 13,500 undergraduates and 2,500 graduate students, URI is small enough to be friendly, intimate, safe, and student-centered. Our Students come from most states in the U.S. and dozens of countries all over the world. More than 100 undergraduate and 80 graduate degree programs, plus more than 100 student clubs and activities spark creativity and inspire our students' pioneering spirit. Perfectly located six miles from Rhodes Island's coastal beaches and easy driving distances from Providence, Boston, and New York, our picturesque rural setting is close enough to big-city culture to make anyone feel at home. There are 8 undergraduate schools and 3 graduate schools. In addition to regional accreditation, URI has baccalaureate program accreditation with AACSB, ABET, ACPE, ADA, ASLA, NASM, NCATE, and NLN. The 3 libraries contain 1.4 million volumes, 1.7 million microform items, 14,408 audio/video tapes/CDs/DVDs, and subscribe to 248,194 periodicals including electronic. Computerized library services include interlibrary loans, database searching, Internet access, and Wi-Fi capability. Special learning facilities include an art gallery, planetarium, radio station, TV station, historic textile collection, and early childhood education center. The 1245-acre campus is in a small town. Including any residence halls, there are 145 buildings.

Student Life: 59% of undergraduates are from Rhode Island. Others are from 43 states, 45 foreign countries, and Canada. 68% are White; 11% race unknown. The average age of freshmen is 18; all undergraduates, 21. 19% do not continue beyond their first year; 74% remain to graduate.

Housing: 6759 students can be accommodated in college housing, which includes single-sex and coed dorms, on-campus apartments, off-campus apartments, and married student housing. In addition, there are language houses, special-interest houses, fraternity houses, sorority houses, First year focused residence halls, living learning communities by academic college and program. On-campus housing is guaranteed for the freshman year only and is available on a lottery system for upperclassmen. 56% of students commute. All students may keep cars.

Activities: 15% of men belong to 17 national fraternities; 15% of women belong to 10 national sororities. There are 100 groups on campus, including music ensembles, band, cheerleading, chess, choir, chorale, chorus, computers, concert band, dance, drama, ethnic, gay, honors, international, jazz band, literary magazine, marching band, musical theater, newspaper, pep band, photography, political, professional, radio and TV, religious, social, social service, student government, and yearbook. Popular campus events include First Night, Welcome Week, and Wintefest.

Sports: There are 8 intercollegiate sports for men and 11 for women. Facilities include a 8000-seat area, a 10,000-seat stadium, 3 pools, a multipurpose field house with an indoor 2 betrack, a fitness center, 3 fitness rooms, and courts for basketball, tennis, and volleyball. There are also outdoor tennis courts, an all-weather track, and varsity and practice fields.

Disabled Students: 90% of the campus is accessible. Facilities include wheelchair ramps, elevators, special parking, specially equipped restrooms, special class scheduling, lowered drinking fountains, lowered telephones, special housing.

Services: Counseling and information services are available, as is tutoring in some subjects, ELS and popular freshman courses, including math, physics, chemistry, and biology There is a reader service for the blind, and remedial math, reading, and writing.

Campus Safety and Security: Measures include 24-hour foot and vehicle patrol, emergency notification system, self-defense education, and security escort services. There are shuttle buses, emergency telephones, lighted pathways/sidewalks, and controlled access to dorms/residences.

Programs of Study: URI confers B.A., B.S., B.F.A., B.G.S., B.L.A. and B.M. degrees. Master's and doctoral degrees are also awarded. Bachelor's degrees are awarded in Pharmacy, engineering, and biology are the strongest academically. Nursing, psychology, communication studies, kinesiology, human development and family studies have the largest enrollments.

Required: To graduate, the student must earn 120 to 150 credit hours, at least 30 in the major, with a GPA of 2.0. Distribution requirements include 6 credits each in English communication, fine arts and literature, foreign language or culture, letters, natural science, and social sciences, as well as 3 credits in math and quantitative reasoning.

Special: Cross-registration is available with Rhode Island College and Community College of Rhode Island. URI also offers a Washington semester as well as semester-long internships with businesses and state agencies, study abroad in 40 countries, a B.A.-B.S. degree in German and engineering and in languages and business, a general studies degree, dual majors, pass/fail options, and credit for life, military, and work experience. The College of Engineering offers co-op programs and an international internship. There are 30 national honor societies, including Phi Beta Kappa, and a freshman honors program.

Faculty/Classroom: 54% of faculty are male; 46% are female. No introductory courses are taught by graduate students.

Admissions: 77% of the 2013-2014 applicants were accepted. The SAT scores for the 2013-2014 freshman class were: Critical Reading--26% below 500, 52% between 500 and 599, 19% between 600 and 699, and 3% between 700 and 800; Math--22% below 500, 51% between 500 and 599, 24% between 600 and 699, and 4% between 700 and 800; Writing--26% below 500, 51% between 500 and 599, 20% between 600 and 699, and 2% between 700 and 800. The ACT scores were 7% above 28. 42% of the current freshmen were in the top fifth of their class; 81% were in the top two fifths.

Requirements: The SAT or ACT is required. Applicants should be high school graduates, having completed 18 courses, including 4 of English, 3 to 4 of math, and 2 each of science (chemistry and physics for engineering majors), foreign language, and history or social studies. Remaining units should be college preparatory. Music majors must audition. AP and CLEP credits are accepted. Important factors in the admissions decision are parents or siblings attended your school, extracurricular activities record, geographical diversity, and recommendations by school officials.

Procedure: Freshmen are admitted fall and spring. Entrance exams should be taken during the spring of the junior year or fall of the senior year. There are early admissions, deferred admissions, and rolling admissions plans. Applications should be filed by February 1 for fall entry; December 1 for spring entry. The fall 2013 application fee was $65. Notification is sent on a rolling basis. 1431 applicants were on the 2013 waiting list; 279 were admitted. Applications are accepted online.

Transfer: 600 transfer students enrolled in 2012-2013. Applicants must submit transcripts from high school and all colleges or universities attended. A minimum GPA of 2.5 is required; many programs require higher. An essay or personal statement is required and a statement of good standing from prior institutions. 24 of 120 credits required for the bachelor's degree must be completed at URI.

Visiting: There are regularly scheduled orientations for prospective students, including campus tours and information sessions. Visitors may sit in on classes. To schedule a visit, contact the Admission Office at admission@uri.edu.

Financial Aid: In 2013-2014, 63% of all full-time freshmen and 73% of continuing full-time students received some form of financial aid. 57% of all full-time freshmen and 70% of continuing full-time students received need-based aid. The average freshman award was $16,310. Need-based scholarships or need-based grants averaged $10,113 ($18,245 maximum); need-based self-help aid (loans and jobs) averaged $5,224 ($6,700 maximum); and non-need-based athletic scholarships averaged $990 ($44,256 maximum). 23% of undergraduate students work part-time. Average annual earnings from campus work are $1509. The average financial indebtedness of the 2013 graduate was $25,792. The FAFSA is required. The priority date for freshman financial aid applications for fall entry is March 1.

International Students: There are 45 international students enrolled. The school actively recruits these students. They must take the TOEFL with a minimum score of 550 on the paper-based TOEFL (PBT) or 79 on the Internet-based version (iBT), or the English proficiency test administered by the American Consulate. They must also take the SAT or ACT.

Graduates: From July 1, 2012 to June 30, 2013, 2873 bachelor's degrees were awarded. The most popular majors were communication studies (8%), psychology (6%), and nursing (6%). In an average class, 41% graduate in 4 years or less, 59% graduate in 5 years or less, and 60% graduate in 6 years or less.

Admissions Contact: Cynthia Bonn, Dean of Admissions. E-Mail: *admission@uri.edu* Web: *www.uri.edu/admission*

SOUTH CAROLINA

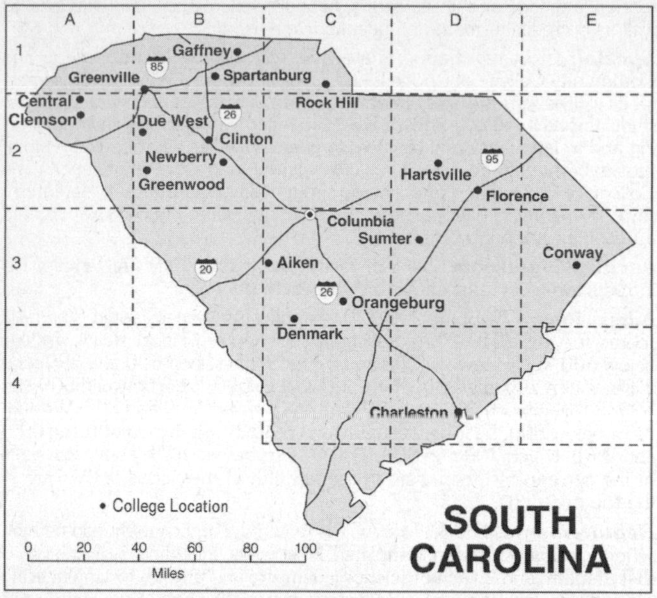

ALLEN UNIVERSITY C-3

Columbia, SC 29204

(803) 376-5735
(888) 425-5360; (803) 376-5715

Full-time: 248 men, 372 women
Part-time: 10 men, 10 women
Graduate: n/av
Year: semesters, summer session
Application Deadline: open
Freshman Class: n/av
Faculty: 14
Ph.D.s: 54%
Student/Faculty: 23 to 1
Tuition: $6500
Room & Board: n/av

NON COMPETITIVE

Allen University, founded in 1870, is a small private institution affiliated with the African Methodist Episcopal Church. It offers undergraduate programs in liberal arts and sciences, business, and social work. The figures in the above capsule are approximate. The library contains 40,558 volumes, 2,883 microform items, 2,527 audio/video tapes/CDs/DVDs, and subscribes to 106 periodicals including electronic. Special learning facilities include a learning resource center. The 4-acre campus is in a small town. Including any residence halls, there are 84 buildings.

Student Life: 70% of undergraduates are from South Carolina. Others are from 20 states, and 9 foreign countries. 95% are from public schools. 99% are African American. 90% are Protestant. The average age of freshmen is 18; all undergraduates, 24. 20% do not continue beyond their first year.

Housing: 405 students can be accommodated in college housing, which includes single-sex dorms and off-campus apartments. On-campus housing is guaranteed for all 4 years. 95% of students live on campus. Alcohol is not permitted. All students may keep cars.

Activities: 8% of men belong to 4 national fraternities; 6% of women belong to 4 national sororities. There are 20 groups on campus, including art, band, cheerleading, choir, chorus, drama, honors, international, newspaper, religious, social service, student government, and yearbook. Popular campus events include Cultural, Academic, and Religious Series (CARS), International Day, and Founders Day.

Sports: There are 2 intercollegiate sports for men.

Disabled Students: All of the campus is accessible.

Services: Counseling and information services are available, as is tutoring in most subjects. There is remedial math, reading, and writing. There are math, science, reading, and writing labs.

Campus Safety and Security: Measures include 24-hour foot and vehicle patrol, self-defense education, and security escort services. There are emergency telephones and lighted pathways/sidewalks.

Programs of Study: Allen confers B.A. and B.S. degrees. Associate degrees are also awarded. Bachelor's degrees are awarded in BIOLOGICAL SCIENCE (biology/biological science), BUSINESS (business administration and management), COMMUNICATIONS AND THE ARTS (English and music), COMPUTER AND PHYSICAL SCIENCE (mathematics), SOCIAL SCIENCE (history, political science/government, and sociology). Sociology/social work and business administration have the largest enrollments.

Required: To graduate, all students must complete 120 credit hours with a minimum 2.0 GPA. Students must demonstrate competence in reading, composition, speech, and fundamental math skills.

Special: Allen offers internships with businesses and federal, state, and local agencies, and work-study with the Columbia Housing Authority. A certificate in gerontology is possible. There is 1 national honor society and 20 departmental honors programs.

Faculty/Classroom: All teach undergraduates. No introductory courses are taught by graduate students.

Requirements: Applicants should be graduates of accredited high schools or have earned the GED. Secondary preparation should total 20 academic credits. A personal interview is recommended. Important factors in the admissions decision are leadership record, advanced placement or honors courses, and evidence of special talent.

Procedure: Freshmen are admitted to all sessions. Entrance exams should be taken in the spring. There is a early decision plan. Application deadlines are open.

Transfer: An official transcript from each school attended is required at least 1 month prior to the beginning of the semester in which admission is desired. 30 of 120 credits required for the bachelor's degree must be completed at Allen.

Visiting: There are regularly scheduled orientations for prospective students. There are guides for informal visits and visitors may sit in on classes. To schedule a visit, contact Dean of Student Development Services.

Financial Aid: Allen is a member of CSS. The CSS/Profile and the college's own financial statement are required. Check with the school for current application deadlines.

International Students: The school actively recruits these students.

Graduates: In an average class, 40% graduate in 4 years or less and 20% graduate in 5 years or less.

Admissions Contact: Admissions Office. E-Mail: *admissions@allenuniversity.edu* Web: *www.allenuniversity.edu*

BENEDICT COLLEGE C-3

Columbia, SC 29204

(803) 705-4491
(800) 868-6598; (803) 253-5167

Full-time: 1275 men, 1310 women
Part-time: 30 men, 25 women
Graduate: n/av
Year: semesters, summer session
Application Deadline: open
Freshman Class: n/av
SAT or ACT: not required
Faculty: n/av
Ph.D.s: 59%
Student/Faculty: n/av
Tuition: $17,688
Room & Board: $7846

NONCOMPETITIVE

Benedict College, founded in 1870, is a private liberal arts institution affiliated with the Baptist Church. There are 4 undergraduate schools. The figures in the above capsule and in this profile are approximate. In addition to regional accreditation, Benedict has baccalaureate program accreditation with CSWE and NCATE. The library contains 119,594 volumes, 164,317 microform items, and 6648 audio/video tapes/CDs/DVDs, and subscribes to 314 periodicals including electronic. Computerized library services include interlibrary loans, database searching, Internet access, and laptop Internet portals. Special learning facilities include a learning resource center and art gallery. The 110-acre campus is in an urban area 90 miles south of Charlotte, North Carolina. Including any residence halls, there are 37 buildings.

Student Life: 60% of undergraduates are from South Carolina. Others are from 34 states and 13 foreign countries. 99% are from public schools. 99% are African American. The average age of freshmen is 19; all undergraduates, 21. 47% do not continue beyond their first year; 28% remain to graduate.

Housing: 2072 students can be accommodated in college housing, which includes single-sex dorms and off-campus apartments. In addition, there are honors houses. On-campus housing is available on a first-come, first-served basis. Priority is given to out-of-town students. 73% of students live on campus. Alcohol is not permitted. Upperclassmen may keep cars.

Activities: 3% of men belong to 4 local and 4 national fraternities; 6% of women belong to 4 local and 4 national sororities. There are 42 groups on campus, including art, cheerleading, choir, chorale, chorus, dance, drama, drill team, honors, international, marching band, newspaper, pep band, photography, religious, social, social service, and student government. Popular campus events include Fall Convocation, Crowning of Miss Benedict, and Religion Emphasis Week.

Sports: There are 7 intercollegiate sports for men and 7 for women, and 2 intramural sports for men. Facilities include a gym and student center.

Disabled Students: 85% of the campus is accessible. Facilities include wheelchair ramps, elevators, and special parking.

Services: Counseling and information services are available, as is tutoring in every subject. There is remedial math, reading, and writing.

Campus Safety and Security: Measures include 24-hour foot and vehicle patrol. There are shuttle buses and lighted pathways/sidewalks.

Programs of Study: Benedict confers B.A., B.S., and B.S.W. degrees. Bachelor's degrees are awarded in BIOLOGICAL SCIENCE (biology/biological science), BUSINESS (accounting and business administration and management), COMMUNICATIONS AND THE ARTS (English, journalism, music, and studio art), COMPUTER AND PHYSICAL SCIENCE (chemistry, computer science, mathematics, and physics), EDUCATION (early childhood education, elementary education, and recreation education), ENGINEERING AND ENVIRONMENTAL DESIGN (computer engineering and electrical/electronics engineering), HEALTH PROFESSIONS (environmental health science and public health), SOCIAL SCIENCE (criminal justice, economics, history, philosophy, political science/government, religion, social science, social work, and sociology). Physics, engineering, and chemistry are the strongest academically. Business administration has the largest enrollment.

Required: Students must complete 125 credit hours, including 24 to 32 in the major, with a minimum GPA of 2.0; some degrees require a higher GPA. The 57-hour general education requirements include 15 hours of English, 9 of social science, 8 of natural science, 6 each of mathematics and a foreign language, 4 of humanities, and 2 each of health education, freshman seminar, physical education, and religion.

Special: Benedict offers work-study programs, a physics/engineering dual major, internships, a B.A./B.S. degree, and preprofessional programs in dentistry, engineering, law, and medicine. There are 6 national honor societies.

Faculty/Classroom: 55% of faculty are male; 45% are female. All teach undergraduates, and 1% do research. The average class size in an introductory lecture is 30; in a laboratory, 27; and in a regular course, 24.

Requirements: Students should have taken 4 secondary school units of English, 3 each of mathematics and social science, 2 of natural science, 7 of electives, and 1 of physical education or ROTC. The GED is accepted. A GPA of 2.0 is required. AP and CLEP credits are accepted.

Procedure: Freshmen are admitted fall and spring. Entrance exams should be taken prior to registration. There are deferred admissions and rolling admissions plans. Application deadlines are open. Application fee is $25.

Transfer: Applicants must submit transcripts from previous institutions attended plus evidence of honorable withdrawal. The SAT is required. Only courses in which a C or better was earned will be considered for credit. 30 of 125 credits required for the bachelor's degree must be completed at Benedict.

Visiting: There are regularly scheduled orientations for prospective students. There are guides for informal visits, and visitors may sit in on classes. To schedule a visit, contact the Admissions Office.

Financial Aid: The CSS/Profile, FAFSA, the college's own financial statement, and South Carolina Tuition Grant applications are required. Check with the school for current deadlines.

International Students: They must take the TOEFL and also take the SAT or ACT. Some students may be required to complete an ESL program.

Admissions Contact: Director of Admissions. A campus DVD is available. E-Mail: *admissions@benedict.edu* Web: *www.benedict.edu*

CHARLESTON SOUTHERN UNIVERSITY — D-4

Charleston, SC 29423-8087 — (843) 863-7050; (800) 947-7474; (843) 863-7070

Full-time: 821 men, 1236 women	**Faculty:** 93; IIB, --$
Part-time: 160 men, 320 women	**Ph.D.s:** 71%
Graduate: 100 men, 140 women	**Student/Faculty:** n/av
Year: semesters, summer session	**Tuition:** $21,100
Application Deadline: open	**Room & Board:** $8500
Freshman Class: n/av	
SAT or ACT: recommended	

COMPETITIVE

Charleston Southern University, founded in 1964, is a private liberal arts institution affiliated with the South Carolina Baptist Convention. There are 4 undergraduate schools and 3 graduate schools. The figures in the above capsule and in this profile are approximate. In addition to regional accreditation, CSU has baccalaureate program accreditation with NASDTEC, NASM, and NLN. The library contains 212,666 volumes, 212,539 microform items, 7527 audio/video tapes/CDs/DVDs, and subscribes to 9788 periodicals including electronic. Computerized library services include database searching. Special learning facilities include a learning resource center, earthquake education center, and field physics laboratory. The 500-acre campus is in a suburban area 20 miles west of Charleston. Including any residence halls, there are 16 buildings.

Student Life: 81% of undergraduates are from South Carolina. Others are from 45 states, 35 foreign countries, and Canada. 85% are from public schools. 47% are white; 27% African American. 50% claim no religious affiliation; 42% Protestant. The average age of freshmen is 18; all undergraduates, 25. 28% do not continue beyond their first year; 31% remain to graduate.

Housing: 1250 students can be accommodated in college housing, which includes single-sex dorms and married student housing. On-campus housing is guaranteed for the freshman year only and is available on a first-come, first-served basis. 56% of students commute. Alcohol is not permitted. All students may keep cars.

Activities: There are no fraternities or sororities. There are 20 groups on campus, including art, band, cheerleading, choir, chorus, drama, honors, jazz band, literary magazine, marching band, newspaper, religious, social service, student government, and yearbook.

Sports: There are 9 intercollegiate sports for men and 9 for women, and 4 intramural sports for men and 4 for women. Facilities include a gym, tennis courts, a track center, football and soccer fields, a baseball diamond, training and weight rooms, a 3-hole golf course with driving range, and a wellness center.

Disabled Students: All of the campus is accessible. Facilities include wheelchair ramps, elevators, special parking, specially equipped rest rooms, and lowered drinking fountains.

Services: Counseling and information services are available, as is tutoring in most subjects. There is remedial math, reading, and writing.

Campus Safety and Security: Measures include 24-hour foot and vehicle patrol and security escort services. There are emergency telephones and lighted pathways/sidewalks.

Programs of Study: CSU confers B.A., B.S., and B.Tech. degrees. Associate and master's degrees are also awarded. Bachelor's degrees are awarded in BIOLOGICAL SCIENCE (biochemistry and biology/biological science), BUSINESS (business administration and management), COMMUNICATIONS AND THE ARTS (dramatic arts, English, fine arts, music, Spanish, and speech/debate/rhetoric), COMPUTER AND PHYSICAL SCIENCE (chemistry, computer science, geology, mathematics, and natural sciences), EDUCATION (early childhood education, elementary education, music education, physical education, and science education), ENGINEERING AND ENVIRONMENTAL DESIGN (environmental science), HEALTH PROFESSIONS (music therapy and nursing), SOCIAL SCIENCE (criminal justice, economics, geography, history, humanities, political science/government, psychology, religion, religious music, social science, sociology, and youth ministry).

Required: To graduate, students must complete 125 credit hours, including all core curriculum, major, and minor requirements, with a GPA of 2.0. At least 45 hours must be in the major. Core courses include 24 hours of communications and fine arts, 11 of natural science/math, and 9 of social studies.

Special: CSU offers internships, cross-registration through the Trident Area Consortium, work-study programs, dual majors, and nondegree study. Nonmajor preprofessional programs are available in dentistry, engineering, law, medicine, and ministry. There are 5 national honor societies, a freshman honors program, and honors programs in all departments.

Faculty/Classroom: 55% of faculty are male; 45% are female. All teach undergraduates. No introductory courses are taught by graduate students. The average class size in an introductory lecture is 40; in a laboratory, 15; and in a regular course, 25.

Requirements: The SAT or ACT is recommended. Applicants must be graduates of an accredited secondary school. The GED is accepted. Character references are preferred. An English proficiency exam is required for all entering students. A GPA of 2.0 is required. AP and CLEP credits are accepted. Important factors in the admissions decision are evidence of special talent, leadership record, and advanced placement or honors courses.

Procedure: Freshmen are admitted to all sessions. Entrance exams should be taken any time before filing for admission. There is a rolling admissions plan. Application deadlines are open. Application fee is $40. Applications are accepted online.

Transfer: Applicants must submit official transcripts from all previous colleges attended. Accepted transfers must take an English proficiency exam. 30 of 125 credits required for the bachelor's degree must be completed at the university.

Visiting: There are regularly scheduled orientations for prospective students, consisting of orientation for students, orientation for parents, placement testing for students, a tour, and lunch. There are guides for informal visits, and visitors may sit in on classes. To schedule a visit, contact the Office of Enrollment Services.

Financial Aid: CSU is a member of CSS. The CSS/Profile and FAFSA are required. Check with the school for current deadlines.

International Students: They must take the TOEFL and also take the SAT or ACT.

Admissions Contact: Director of Enrollment Services. A campus DVD is available. E-Mail: *enroll@csuniv.edu* Web: *www.csuniv.edu*

CITADEL, THE

D-4

Charleston, SC 29409

(843) 953-5230
(800) 868-1842; (843) 953-7036

Full-time: 2353 men, 164 women
Part-time: 129 men, 89 women
Graduate: 370 men, 493 women
Year: semesters, summer session
Application Deadline:
Freshman Class: 2765 applied, 2116 accepted, 645 enrolled
SAT CR/M: 538/549 **ACT:** 23 **COMPETITIVE**

Faculty: n/av; IIA, -$
Ph.D.s: 92%
Student/Faculty: 14 to 1
Tuition: $12,237 ($31,038)
Room & Board: $6265

The Citadel, established in 1842 by the South Carolina legislature, is a liberal arts military college supported by the state and offers degrees in the humanities, business, math, science, engineering, and education. The figures for students in the Corps of Cadets include charges for lab fees, athletic fees, most books, school supplies, uniforms, alterations, and laundry and dry cleaning. There are 5 undergraduate schools and one graduate school. In addition to regional accreditation, The Citadel has baccalaureate program accreditation with AACSB, ABET, and NCATE. The library contains 193,992 volumes, 1.2 million microform items, 5,538 audio/video tapes/CDs/DVDs, and subscribes to 1,260 periodicals including electronic. Computerized library services include interlibrary loans, database searching, Internet access, and Wi-Fi capability. Special learning facilities include a The 300-acre campus is in a suburban area in Charleston, SC. Including any residence halls, there are 69 buildings.

Student Life: 58% of undergraduates are from South Carolina. Others are from 43 states, and 12 foreign countries. 79% are White. The average age of freshmen is 18; all undergraduates, 20. 15% do not continue beyond their first year; 85% remain to graduate.

Housing: 2135 students can be accommodated in college housing, which includes coed dorms. All cadets live in barracks. On-campus housing is guaranteed for all 4 years. Alcohol is not permitted. Upperclassmen may keep cars.

Activities: There are no fraternities or sororities. There are 100 groups on campus, including bagpipe, band, cheerleading, choir, chorale, debate, drill team, ethnic, honors, literary magazine, marching band, newspaper, pep band, political, professional, religious, student government, and yearbook. Popular campus events include Parents Weekend, Corps Day, and Parades most Friday afternoons during Fall and Spring semesters.

Sports: There are 8 intercollegiate sports for men and 6 for women, and 24 intramural sports for men and 24 for women. Facilities include a 22,000-seat stadium, a 6000-seat field house, a golf driving range, a wrestling room, a baseball batting tunnel, weight and wrestling rooms, tennis courts, an all-weather track, and playing fields. The boating center is on campus and The Citadel Beach House is within a half-hour drive of the college.

Disabled Students: 80% of the campus is accessible. Facilities include wheelchair ramps, elevators, special parking, and specially equipped restrooms.

Services: Counseling and information services are available, as is tutoring in every subject.

Campus Safety and Security: Measures include 24-hour foot and vehicle patrol, emergency notification system, and security escort services. There are emergency telephones, lighted pathways/sidewalks, and controlled access to dorms/residences.

Programs of Study: The Citadel confers B.A., B.S., B.S.B.A., B.S.C.E. and B.S.E.E. degrees. Master's degrees are also awarded. Bachelor's degrees are awarded in BIOLOGICAL SCIENCE (biology/biological science), BUSINESS (business administration and management), COMMUNICATIONS AND THE ARTS (English, French, German, and Spanish), COMPUTER AND PHYSICAL SCIENCE (chemistry, computer science, mathematics, and physics), EDUCATION (health education, physical education, and secondary education), ENGINEERING AND ENVIRONMENTAL DESIGN (civil engineering and electrical/electronics engineering), SOCIAL SCIENCE (criminal justice, history, political science/government, and psychology). Engineering is the strongest academically. Business administration has the largest enrollments.

Required: To graduate, students must complete 121 to 139 credit hours, depending on the major, with an overall GPA of 2.0 (2.5 for education and health, exercise, and sport science majors). The required core curriculum for all majors includes study in 5 areas: English, history, math, science, social sciences, computer literacy, and foreign languages. Specific course requirements include 8 semesters of ROTC, 4 of English and science, 2 of math and history, and 1 of social science. In addition, cadets must satisfy disciplinary requirements and observe the honor system.

Special: Work-study programs, internships, dual majors, independent study, and study abroad are available. Qualified students may enroll in a separate honors program. There is a teacher certification program. There are 8 national honor societies, including Phi Beta Kappa, a freshman honors program, and 1 departmental honors program.

Faculty/Classroom: 65% of faculty are male; 35% are female. All teach and do research. No introductory courses are taught by graduate students. The average class size in an introductory lecture is 25 and in a regular course is 20.

Admissions: 77% of the 2013-2014 applicants were accepted. The SAT scores for the 2013-2014 freshman class were: Critical Reading--36% below 500, 46% between 500 and 599, 15% between 600 and 699, and 3% between 700 and 800; Math--23% below 500, 51% between 500 and 599, 23% between 600 and 699, and 3% between 700 and 800. The ACT scores were 22% below 21, 35% between 21 and 23, 27% between 24 and 26, 7% between 27 and 28, and 9% above 28. 30% of the current freshmen were in the top fifth of their class; 59% were in the top two fifths.

Requirements: The SAT or ACT is required. High school diploma is required and GED is accepted. Applicants must be between 17 and 22, unmarried, and must meet certain physical requirements. High school preparation should include 4 units in English; 4 in math, 3 in lab science: biology, chemistry, or physics; 2 each in foreign language and social science; 1 academic elective; 1 in visual/perfoming arts; 1 in phys ed or ROTC; and 1 in American history. AP and CLEP credits are accepted. Important factors in the admissions decision are advanced placement or honors courses, extracurricular activities record, and leadership record.

Procedure: Freshmen are admitted fall. Entrance exams should be taken by February of the senior year. There is a rolling admissions plan. Application deadlines are open. The fall 2013 application fee was $40. Notification is sent on a rolling basis. Applications are accepted online.

Transfer: 117 transfer students enrolled in 2012-2013. Applicants must meet freshmen entrance requirements and submit official transcripts from high school and all previous colleges attended. Transfer students must have completed a minimum of 2 semesters as full-time students (minimum 12 hours each semester) and maintained a GPA of 2.0. A full year of course work, including half the required hours in the major, must be completed at The Citadel. A statement of good standing from prior institutions and an interview are required.

Visiting: There are regularly scheduled orientations for prospective students, Including an interview with an admissions counselor and a campus tour guided by a cadet. There are guides for informal visits, visitors may sit in on classes, and stay overnight. To schedule a visit, contact the Admissions Office.

Financial Aid: In 2013-2014, 84% of all full-time freshmen and 78% of continuing full-time students received some form of financial aid. 61% of all full-time freshmen and 46% of continuing full-time students received need-based aid. 2% of undergraduate students work part-time. Average annual earnings from campus work are $1325. The average financial indebtedness of the 2013 graduate was $33,998. The FAFSA is required. The priority date for freshman financial aid applications for fall entry is March 1.

International Students: There are 26 international students enrolled. They must take the TOEFL with a minimum score of 550 on the paper-based TOEFL (PBT) or 80 on the Internet-based version (iBT).

Graduates: From July 1, 2012 to June 30, 2013, 523 bachelor's degrees were awarded. The most popular majors were business/marketing (25%), engineering (17%), and criminal justice (14%). 145 companies recruited on campus in 2012-2013. In an average class, 60% graduate in 4 years or less, 68% graduate in 5 years or less, and 66% graduate in 6 years or less. Of the 2012 graduating class, 90% were employed within 6 months of graduation.

Admissions Contact: Lt. Col. John Powell, Director of Admissions. E-Mail: *admissions@citadel.edu* Web: *www.citadel.edu*

CLAFLIN UNIVERSITY

C-3

Orangeburg, SC 29115

(803) 535-5382
(800) 922-1246; (803) 535-5385

Full-time: 605 men, 1150 women
Part-time: 27 men, 49 women
Graduate: 30 men, 59 women
Year: semesters, summer session
Application Deadline: open
Freshman Class: 4204 applied, 1453 accepted, 423 enrolled
SAT CR/M: 430/430 **ACT:** 17 **COMPETITIVE+**

Faculty: 116; IIB, --$
Ph.D.s: 78%
Student/Faculty: 14 to 1
Tuition: $13,370
Room & Board: $7520

Claflin University is a comprehensive institution of higher education affiliated with The United Methodist Church. A historically black university founded in 1869, Claflin is committed to providing students with access to exemplary educational opportunities in its undergraduate, graduate and continuing education programs. Claflin seeks to foster a rich community comprised of students, faculty, staff, and administrators who work to nurture and develop the skills and character needed for engaged citizenship and visionary and effective leadership. The figures in the above capsule and in this profile are approximate. In its undergraduate programs, Claflin provides students with the essential foundation of a liberal arts education. Emphasizing critical and analytic thinking, independent research, oral and written communication skills, the University invites students to use disciplined study to explore and confront the substantive challenges facing the global society. Claflin's graduate programs provide opportunities for advanced students to increase their specialization in particular fields of study oriented toward professional enhancement and academic growth. Its continuing education programs provide students with expanded avenues for professional development and personal fulfillment. There are 4 undergraduate schools. In addition to regional accreditation, has baccalaureate program accreditation with ACBSP, NASM, and NCATE. The library contains 163,641 volumes, 65,479 microform items, and 1,169 audio/video tapes/CDs/DVDs, and subscribes to 468 periodicals including electronic. Computerized library services include interlibrary loans, database searching, Internet access, and laptop Internet portals. Special learning facilities include a learning resource center, art gallery, radio station, and TV station. The 46-acre campus is in a suburban area between Columbia and Charleston. Including any residence halls, there are 27 buildings.

Student Life: 79% of undergraduates are from South Carolina. Others are from 28 states, and 10 foreign countries. 98% are from public schools. 93% are African American. 49% are Protestant; 13% claim no religious affiliation. The average age of freshmen is 19; all undergraduates, 23. 30% do not continue beyond their first year; 70% remain to graduate.

Housing: 1141 students can be accommodated in college housing, which includes single-sex dorms and off-campus apartments. In addition, there are honors houses. On-campus housing is available on a first-come and first-served basis. 75% of students live on campus; of those, 70% remain on campus on weekends. Alcohol is not permitted. Upperclassmen may keep cars.

Activities: There are 57 groups on campus, including band, cheerleading, choir, chorale, dance, drama, environmental, ethnic, film, honors, international, jazz band, literary magazine, marching band, newspaper, professional, radio and TV, religious, social, social service, student government, and yearbook. Popular campus events include Founders Day, Pantherfest, and Claflin Pride Day.

Sports: There are 5 intercollegiate sports for men and 7 for women, and 4 intramural sports for men and 4 for women. Facilities include a gym, a game room, and basketball courts.

Disabled Students: 95% of the campus is accessible. Facilities include wheelchair ramps, elevators, special parking, and specially equipped restrooms.

Services: Counseling and information services are available, as is tutoring in most subjects. There is remedial math, reading, and writing.

Campus Safety and Security: Measures include 24-hour foot and vehicle patrol, emergency notification system, and security escort services. There are shuttle buses, emergency telephones, lighted pathways/sidewalks, and controlled access to dorms/residences.

Programs of Study: confers B.A., and B.S. degrees. Master's degrees are also awarded. Bachelor's degrees are awarded in BIOLOGICAL SCIENCE (biochemistry, bioinformatics, biology/biological science, and biotechnology), BUSINESS (business administration and management, management science, marketing/retailing/merchandising, organizational leadership and management, and sports management), COMMUNICATIONS AND THE ARTS (art, communications, English, and music), COMPUTER AND PHYSICAL SCIENCE (chemistry, computer science, digital arts/technology, and mathematics), EDUCATION (art education, early childhood education, elementary education, English education, mathematics education, middle school education, music education, and recreation education), ENGINEERING AND ENVIRONMENTAL DESIGN (computer engineering and environmental science), SOCIAL SCIENCE (African studies, African American studies, American studies, criminal justice, history, philosophy and religion, political science/government, and sociology). Biology, business administration, and sociology are the strongest academically.

Required: To graduate, all students must complete 120 to 130 semester hours with a minimum GPA of 2.0. General education requirements include courses in education, English, humanities, math, phys ed, natural science, computer science, and analytical reasoning. An exit exam is required, and honors college students must complete a capstone project.

Special: Claflin offers co-op and accelerated degree programs in all majors, cross-registration with South Carolina State University, study abroad, B.A.-B.S. degrees in 35 majors, and dual-degree program. There are 6 national honor societies and a freshman honors program.

Faculty/Classroom: 58% of faculty are male; 42% are female. All teach and do research. No introductory courses are taught by graduate students. The average class size in an introductory lecture is 25; in a laboratory is 25; and in a regular course is 25.

Admissions: 35% of a recent year applicants were accepted. The SAT scores for a recent year freshman class were: Critical Reading--78% below 500, 17% between 500 and 599, 4% between 600 and 700; Math--74% below 500, 21% between 500 and 599, 5% between 600 and 700. The ACT scores were 75% below 21, 16% between 21 and 23, 8% between 24 and 26, 1% between 27 and 28. 31% of the current freshmen were in the top fifth of their class; 54% were in the top two fifths. 7 freshmen graduated first in their class.

Requirements: The SAT or ACT is required. Applicants should present evidence of graduating with a diploma from an accredited high school, achieving an overall gpa of at least "C",and successfully completing a curriculum including 24 units in the following: 4 units in English/language arts, 4 units in math, 3 units in science, 2 units in social studies, 1 unit in history, 1 unit in physical education, 1 unit in computer science, 1 unit in foreign language and 7 units in electives. A GPA of 2.0 is required. AP and CLEP credits are accepted. Important factors in the admissions decision are recommendations by school officials, advanced placement or honors courses, parents or siblings who attended the school, evidence of special talent, extracurricular activities record, recommendations by alumni, leadership record, and geographical diversity.

Procedure: Freshmen are admitted fall and spring. There is a rolling admissions plan. Application deadlines are open. The fall application fee was $21. Notification is sent on a rolling basis. Applications are accepted online.

Transfer: 52 transfer students enrolled in a recent year. Applicants with fewer than 60 semester hours of college credit must submit test scores and meet the other criteria for entering freshmen. Official transcripts of all colleges attended are required. 30 of 126 credits required for the bachelor's degree must be completed at Claflin.

Visiting: There are regularly scheduled orientations for prospective students, by appointment. There are guides for informal visits. To schedule a visit, contact the Admissions Office.

Financial Aid: In a recent year, 84% of all full-time freshmen and 82% of continuing full-time students received some form of financial aid. 63% of all full-time freshmen and 60% of continuing full-time students received need-based aid. The average freshman award was $17,310. Need-based scholarships or need-based grants averaged $14,055 ($5,350 maximum); need-based self-help aid (loans and jobs) averaged $7,035 ($9,500 maximum); non-need-based athletic scholarships averaged $3,127 ($8,000 maximum); and other non-need-based awards and non-need-based scholarships averaged $12,990 ($21,566 maximum). Average annual earnings from campus work are $2000. The average financial indebtedness of the 2011 graduate was $33,400. Claflin is a member of CSS. The FAFSA is required. The priority date for freshman financial aid applications for fall entry is April 15. The deadline for filing freshman financial aid applications for fall entry is June 1.

International Students: There are 36 international students enrolled. The school actively recruits these students. They must take the TOEFL with a minimum score of 500 on the paper-based TOEFL (PBT). They must also take the SAT or ACT.

Graduates: In a recent year, 267 bachelor's degrees were awarded. The most popular majors were sociology (21%), criminal justice/law (12%), and organizational management (10%). In an average class, 30% graduate in 4 years or less, 43% graduate in 5 years or less, and 46% graduate in 6 years or less. Of the 2010 graduating class, 20% were enrolled in graduate school within 6 months of graduation.

Admissions Contact: Michael Zeigler, Director of Admissions. E-Mail: *mike.zeigler@claflin.edu* Web: *www.claflin.edu*

CLEMSON UNIVERSITY A-2

Clemson, SC 29634-5124 **(864) 656-2287; (864) 656-0622**

Full-time: 7947 men, 6887 women	**Faculty:** n/av; I, --$
Part-time: 626 men, 376 women	**Ph.D.s:** 88%
Graduate: 2235 men, 1843 women	**Student/Faculty:** 16 to 1
Year: semesters, summer session	**Tuition:** $12,408 ($27,920)
Application Deadline: May 1	**Room & Board:** $7728
Freshman Class: 16282 applied, 10224 accepted, 3386 enrolled	
SAT CR/M/W: 600/630/540 **ACT:** 27	**HIGHLY COMPETITIVE**

Clemson University, founded in 1889, is a public institution with programs in agriculture, architecture, commerce and industry, education, engineering, forest and recreation resources, liberal arts, nursing, and sciences. There are 5 undergraduate schools and 1 graduate school. The figures in the above capsule and in this profile are approximate. In addition to regional accreditation, Clemson has baccalaureate program accreditation with AACSB, ABET, CSAB, NAAB, NCATE, NLN, and NRPA. The 3 libraries contain 1.2 million volumes, 1.2 million microform items, 140,000 audio/video tapes/CDs/DVDs, and subscribe to 11,400 periodicals including electronic. Computerized library services include interlibrary loans, database searching, Internet access, and laptop Internet portals. Special learning facilities include a learning resource center, art gallery, natural history museum, planetarium, radio station, TV station, geology museum, experimental forest, research park, and state botanical gardens. The 1400-acre campus is in a small town 32 miles west of Greenville. Including any residence halls, there are 587 buildings.

Student Life: 69% of undergraduates are from South Carolina. Others are from 50 states, 96 foreign countries, and Canada. 81% are from public schools. 78% are white. The average age of freshmen is 18; all undergraduates, 21. 10% do not continue beyond their first year; 80% remain to graduate.

Housing: 6145 students can be accommodated in college housing, which includes single-sex and coed dorms and on-campus apartments. In addi-

tion, there are honors houses, special-interest houses, fraternity houses, sorority houses, living-learning communities. On-campus housing is guaranteed for the freshman year only and is available on a lottery system for upperclassmen. 63% of students commute. All students may keep cars.

Activities: 18% of men belong to 18 national fraternities; 24% of women belong to 17 national sororities. There are 350 groups on campus, including art, bagpipe, band, cheerleading, choir, chorus, computers, dance, debate, drama, drill team, ethnic, gay, honors, international, jazz band, literary magazine, marching band, musical theater, newspaper, orchestra, pep band, photography, political, professional, radio and TV, religious, social, social service, student government, symphony, and yearbook. Popular campus events include First Friday Parade, Tigerama, Welcome Back Festival, and Annual Shakespeare.

Sports: There are 10 intercollegiate sports for men and 9 for women, and 45 intramural sports for men and 45 for women. Facilities include an indoor tennis facility, a renovated recreation center, an 80,000-seat stadium, and a 10,250-seat coliseum.

Disabled Students: 75% of the campus is accessible. Facilities include wheelchair ramps, elevators, special parking, specially equipped restrooms, special class scheduling, lowered drinking fountains, lowered telephones, and special housing.

Services: Counseling and information services are available, as is tutoring in most subjects. There is a reader service for the blind. Other services include textbooks, testing modifications, library assistance, interpreters, note takers, and letters to faculty members.

Campus Safety and Security: Measures include 24-hour foot and vehicle patrol, emergency notification system, self-defense education, and security escort services. There are shuttle buses, emergency telephones, lighted pathways/sidewalks, electronic card access to residence halls, and limited outdoor surveillance cameras.

Programs of Study: Clemson confers B.A., B.S., B.F.A., and B.L.A. degrees. Master's and doctoral degrees are also awarded. Bachelor's degrees are awarded in AGRICULTURE (agriculture, animal science, forestry production and processing, forestry and related sciences, horticulture, and soil science), BIOLOGICAL SCIENCE (biochemistry, biology/biological science, and microbiology), BUSINESS (accounting, banking and finance, business administration and management, management science, and marketing/retailing/merchandising), COMMUNICATIONS AND THE ARTS (communications, design, English, fine arts, French, German, modern language, and Spanish), COMPUTER AND PHYSICAL SCIENCE (chemistry, computer science, geology, information sciences and systems, mathematics, and physics), EDUCATION (agricultural education, early childhood education, elementary education, industrial arts education, secondary education, and special education), ENGINEERING AND ENVIRONMENTAL DESIGN (agricultural engineering, ceramic engineering, chemical engineering, civil engineering, computer engineering, construction management, electrical/electronics engineering, graphic arts technology, industrial administration/management, industrial engineering, landscape architecture/design, mechanical engineering, and textile technology), HEALTH PROFESSIONS (medical laboratory technology, nursing, predentistry, premedicine, prepharmacy, preveterinary science, and speech pathology/audiology), SOCIAL SCIENCE (economics, food science, history, parks and recreation management, philosophy, political science/government, prelaw, psychology, and sociology). Engineering, architecture, and biological sciences are the strongest academically. Marketing has the largest enrollment.

Required: To graduate, students must complete 120 to 157 credit hours, including 89 to 108 hours in the major, with a GPA of 2.0. Courses are required in English, humanities, math, science, and social science.

Special: Co-op programs are available in all majors except nursing. Work-study programs and study abroad in 39 countries are offered. There are 24 national honor societies, including Phi Beta Kappa, a freshman honors program, and 40 departmental honors programs.

Faculty/Classroom: 66% of faculty are male; 34% are female. 99% teach undergraduates, 73% do research, and 72% do both. Graduate students teach 18% of introductory courses. The average class size in an introductory lecture is 45; in a laboratory is 19; and in a regular course is 29.

Admissions: 63% of the 2011-2012 applicants were accepted. The SAT scores for the 2011-2012 freshman class were: Critical Reading--8% below 500, 41% between 500 and 599, 42% between 600 and 700, and 9% above 700; Math--4% below 500, 25% between 500 and 599, 54% between 600 and 700, and 17% above 700; Writing--24% below 500, 49% between 500 and 599, 23% between 600 and 700, and 2% above 700. The ACT scores were 8% below 21, 15% between 21 and 23, 31% between 24 and 26, 15% between 27 and 28, and 31% above 28. 69% of the current freshmen were in the top fifth of their class; 97% were in the top two fifths. There were 24 National Merit finalists. 179 freshmen graduated first in their class.

Requirements: The SAT or ACT is required. The ACT Optional Writing test is also required. In addition, applicants should be graduates of an accredited secondary school. The GED is accepted. AP and CLEP credits are accepted. Important factors in the admissions decision are advanced placement or honors courses, parents or siblings attended your school, and evidence of special talent.

Procedure: Freshmen are admitted fall, spring, and summer. Entrance exams should be taken during spring of the junior year or fall of the senior year. Applications should be filed by May 1 for fall entry; December 15 for spring entry. The fall application fee was $60. Notifications are sent February 15. Applications are accepted online.

Transfer: 980 transfer students enrolled in a recent year. Transfer applicants must have completed at least 30 semester hours with approximately a 2.5 GPA. 37 of 120 credits required for the bachelor's degree must be completed at Clemson.

Visiting: There are regularly scheduled orientations for prospective students, including a series of 2-day summer programs of advisement, student services presentations, and registration for the fall semester. There are guides for informal visits and visitors may sit in on classes. To schedule a visit, contact the Visitor's Center.

Financial Aid: In a recent year, 87% of all full-time freshmen and 71% of continuing full-time students received some form of financial aid. 28% of all full-time freshmen and 31% of continuing full-time students received need-based aid. The average freshman award was $9,147. Need-based scholarships or need-based grants averaged $1,680 ($7,500 maximum); need-based self-help aid (loans and jobs) averaged $4,113 ($7,125 maximum); non-need-based athletic scholarships averaged $17,653 ($25,390 maximum); and other non-need-based awards and non-need-based scholarships averaged $6,971 ($26,990 maximum). 57% of undergraduate students work part-time. Average annual earnings from campus work are $3353. The average financial indebtedness of a recent graduate was $14,382. The FAFSA is required. The priority date for freshman financial aid applications for fall entry is April 1.

International Students: There are 142 international students enrolled. The school actively recruits these students. They must take the TOEFL with a minimum score of 550 on the paper-based TOEFL (PBT). They must also take the SAT or ACT.

Graduates: In a recent year, 3075 bachelor's degrees were awarded. The most popular majors were management (6%), marketing (6%), and mechanical engineering (5%). 340 companies recruited on campus in a recent year. In an average class, 1% graduate in 3 years or less, 40% graduate in 4 years or less, 68% graduate in 5 years or less, and 72% graduate in 6 years or less.

Admissions Contact: Director of Admissions. A campus DVD is available. E-Mail: *cuadmissions@clemson.edu* Web: *www.clemson.edu*

COASTAL CAROLINA UNIVERSITY E-3

Conway, SC 29528 **(843) 349-2037**
(800) 277-7000; (843) 349-2127

Full-time: 3762 men, 4270 women	**Faculty:** 393; IIB, -$
Part-time: 335 men, 500 women	**Ph.D.s:** 78%
Graduate: 178 men, 433 women	**Student/Faculty:** 19 to 1
Year: semesters, summer session	**Tuition:** $9760 ($22,770)
Application Deadline: June 1	**Room & Board:** $7860
Freshman Class: 14050 applied, 9014 accepted, 2095 enrolled	
SAT CR/M: 490/500	**ACT:** 21 **COMPETITIVE**

Coastal Carolina University, established in 1954, is a public liberal arts institution offering undergraduate programs through the College of Business, College of Science, College of Education,College of Humanities and Fine Arts and University College. Graduate programs are offered through the College of Education, College of Humanities and Fine Arts, College of Science, and the College of Business. There are 5 undergraduate schools and one graduate school. In addition to regional accreditation, Coastal Carolina has baccalaureate program accreditation with AACSB, ABET, NASAD, NASM, and NCATE. The library contains 125,255 volumes, 4,658 microform items, 6,491 audio/video tapes/CDs/DVDs, and subscribes to 36,181 periodicals including electronic. Computerized library services include interlibrary loans, database searching, Internet access, and Wi-Fi capability. Special learning facilities include an art gallery, radio station, a marine science research center. The 630-acre campus is in a suburban area 9 miles west of Myrtle Beach. Including any residence halls, there are 72 buildings.

Student Life: 53% of undergraduates are from South Carolina. Others are from 46 states, 56 foreign countries, and Canada. 92% are from public schools. 70% are White; 20% African American. The average age of freshmen is 18; all undergraduates, 21. 37% do not continue beyond their first year; 46% remain to graduate.

Housing: 3715 students can be accommodated in college housing, which includes coed dorms and off-campus apartments. In addition, there are honors houses and special-interest houses. On-campus housing is available on a first-come, first-served basis, and is available on a lottery system for upperclassmen. 62% of students commute. Alcohol is not permitted. All students may keep cars.

Activities: 3% of men belong to 6 national fraternities; 6% of women belong to 6 national sororities. There are 185 groups on campus, including art, band, cheerleading, chess, choir, chorale, chorus, computers, dance, drama, environmental, ethnic, gay, honors, international, jazz band, literary magazine, marching band, musical theater, newspaper, pep band, political, professional, radio and TV, religious, social, social service, and student government. Popular campus events include CINO Day, Cultural Celebration, Club Recruitment Day, and Homecoming.

Sports: There are 8 intercollegiate sports for men and 9 for women, and 15 intramural sports for men and 15 for women. Facilities include HTC Student Recreation and Convocation Center, a gym, a football stadium, baseball, soccer, and softball fields, tennis, basketball, volleyball, and racquetball courts, an indoor Olympic-size swimming pool, an aerobic dance room, weight rooms, and a track.

Disabled Students: 95% of the campus is accessible. Facilities include wheelchair ramps, elevators, special parking, specially equipped restrooms, special class scheduling, lowered drinking fountains, and special housing.

Services: Counseling and information services are available, as is tutoring in some subjects, English, foreign languages, math and statistics There is a reader service for the blind.

Campus Safety and Security: Measures include 24-hour foot and vehicle patrol, emergency notification system, self-defense education, and security escort services. There are shuttle buses, emergency telephones, and lighted pathways/sidewalks.

Programs of Study: Coastal Carolina confers B.A., B.S., BSN, B.A.Ed., B.A.I.S., B.S.B.A., B.S.Ed., B.S.I.S. and B.S.P.E. degrees. Master's degrees are also awarded. Bachelor's degrees are awarded in BIOLOGICAL SCIENCE (biochemistry, biology/biological science, and marine science), BUSINESS (accounting, banking and finance, business administration and management, marketing/retailing/merchandising, sports management, and tourism), COMMUNICATIONS AND THE ARTS (communications, dramatic arts, English, fine arts, graphic design, music, musical theater, Spanish, and studio art), COMPUTER AND PHYSICAL SCIENCE (chemistry, computer science, information sciences and systems, mathematics, and physics), EDUCATION (early childhood education, elementary education, middle school education, physical education, and special education), HEALTH PROFESSIONS (exercise science, health, health care administration, and nursing), SOCIAL SCIENCE (economics, history, interdisciplinary studies, philosophy, political science/government, psychology, and sociology). Accounting, finance, and management are the strongest academically. Marine science, management, exercise and sport science have the largest enrollments.

Required: Students must successfully complete a minimum of 120 credits, varying with major department requirements, and must maintain a minimum GPA of 2.0. A 4-year core curriculum of 34 to 41 hours is required for proficiency in the broad areas of writing, library research, a foreign language, and computer usage.

Special: Internships are offered in most majors, as well as study abroad in 13 countries. Interdisciplinary studies and a 3-2 engineering degree with Clemson University are available. There are 30 national honor societies and a freshman honors program.

Faculty/Classroom: 52% of faculty are male; 48% are female. 97% teach undergraduates, and 50% do both. No introductory courses are taught by graduate students. The average class size in an introductory lecture is 25; in a laboratory is 20; and in a regular course is 20.

Admissions: 64% of the 2013-2014 applicants were accepted. The SAT scores for the 2013-2014 freshman class were: Critical Reading--54% below 500, 38% between 500 and 599, 7% between 600 and 699, and 1% between 700 and 800; Math--46% below 500, 44% between 500 and 599, 9% between 600 and 699, and 1% between 700 and 800. The ACT scores were 42% below 21, 31% between 21 and 23, 18% between 24 and 26, 6% between 27 and 28, and 3% above 28. 33% of the current freshmen were in the top fifth of their class; 70% were in the top two fifths.

Requirements: The SAT or ACT is required. Graduation from an accredited secondary or homeschool program is required; a GED will be accepted with appropriate scores. Applicants are required to submit complete specific high school credits, including 4 years of college prep English, 4 units of mathematics (algebra II required), 3 units of lab science, 3 units of social sciences (U.S. history required), 2 units of the same foreign language, 1 advanced electives (from computer science, math, additional science, foreign language, social science, humanities, and arts), 1 unit of visual/performing arts, and 1 unit of physical education or ROTC. An interview is recommended. A GPA of 2.7 is required. AP and CLEP credits are accepted. Important factors in the admissions decision are advanced placement or honors courses, recommendations by school officials, and evidence of special talent.

Procedure: Freshmen are admitted to all sessions. Entrance exams should be taken in spring of the junior year or fall of the senior year. There are deferred admissions and rolling admissions plans. Applications should be filed by June 1 for fall entry; December 1 for spring entry, along with a $45 fee. Notification is sent on a rolling basis. Applications are accepted online.

Transfer: 779 transfer students enrolled in 2012-2013. A minimum GPA of 2.0 is required. Transfers with fewer than 30 hours earned must also meet freshman admission requirements. Students must submit college transcripts and be eligible to return to the last institution attended. 30 of 120 credits required for the bachelor's degree must be completed at Coastal Carolina.

Visiting: There are regularly scheduled orientations for prospective students, including sessions for academic requirements, housing, financial aid, and student life, parents' orientation, tours, cookouts, and entertainment. Visitors may sit in on classes. To schedule a visit, contact Holley Aufdemorte at admissions@coastal.edu.

Financial Aid: In 2013-2014, 93% of all full-time freshmen and 86% of continuing full-time students received some form of financial aid. 65% of all full-time freshmen and 62% of continuing full-time students received need-based aid. The average freshman award was $17,516. Need-based scholarships or need-based grants averaged $3,084; need-based self-help aid (loans and jobs) averaged $3,079; non-need-based athletic scholarships averaged $19,015; other non-need-based awards and non-need-based scholarships averaged $5,927; and $10,286 from other forms of aid. 95% of undergraduate students work part-time. Average annual earnings from campus work are $3000. The average financial indebtedness of the 2013 graduate was $30,030. The FAFSA and the college's own financial statement are required. The priority date for freshman financial aid applications for fall entry is March 1.

International Students: There are 137 international students enrolled. They must take the TOEFL with a minimum score of 527 on the paper-based TOEFL (PBT) or 71 on the Internet-based version (iBT). They must also take the SAT or ACT.

Graduates: From July 1, 2012 to June 30, 2013, 1510 bachelor's degrees were awarded. The most popular majors were management (10%), communication (7%), and marketing (6%). 350 companies recruited on campus in 2012-2013. In an average class, 27% graduate in 4 years or less, 42% graduate in 5 years or less, and 46% graduate in 6 years or less.

Admissions Contact: Gregory W. Thornburg, VP, Enrollment Services. E-Mail: *admissions@coastal.edu* Web: *www.coastal.edu/admissions/*

COKER COLLEGE D-2

Hartsville, SC 29550 **(843) 383-8050**
(800) 950-1908; (843) 383-8056

Full-time: 392 men, 617 women	**Faculty:** 62; IIB, --$
Part-time: 43 men, 126 women	**Ph.D.s:** 44%
Graduate: 18 men, 11 women	**Student/Faculty:** 12 to 1
Year: semesters, summer session	**Tuition:** $24,576
Application Deadline: August 1	**Room & Board:** $7680
Freshman Class: 902 applied, 521 accepted, 198 enrolled	
SAT CR/M: 460/480	**ACT:** 19 **LESS COMPETITIVE**

Coker College is a student-centered, comprehensive college. It is dedicated to providing every student enrolled in the Day and Adult Learners Program for Higher Achievement an academic curriculum based upon a uniformly excellent liberal arts core that enhances the structured development of key personal skills. The College's goal is to graduate students with the ability to think analytically and creatively, and to write and speak effectively. Experiences both in and out of the classroom are focused on active student involvement and the practical application of academic knowledge that lead to lifelong learning. Coker measures its success by the personal and professional accomplishments enjoyed by all members of the academic community. There is one undergraduate school and one graduate school. In addition to regional accreditation, Coker has baccalaureate program accreditation with CSWE, NASM, and NCATE. The library contains 79,240 volumes, 15,760 microform items, and 6,075 audio/video tapes/CDs/DVDs, and subscribes to 133 periodicals including electronic. Computerized library services include interlibrary loans, database searching, Internet access, and Wi-Fi capability. Special learning facilities include an art gallery, a botanical garden and a nature preserve. The 37-acre campus is in a small town 25 miles west of Florence, 71 miles northeast of Columbia and 82 miles southeast of Charlotte. Including any residence halls, there are 27 buildings.

Student Life: 78% of undergraduates are from South Carolina. Others are from 28 states, 18 foreign countries, and Canada. 51% are White; 35% African American. The average age of freshmen is 19; all undergraduates, 26. 41% do not continue beyond their first year; 43% remain to graduate.

Housing: 565 students can be accommodated in college housing, which includes single-sex and coed dorms and off-campus apartments. Sophomore Scholars housing, Honors Program housing. On-campus housing is guaranteed for the freshman year only, is available on a first-come, first-served basis, and is available on a lottery system for upperclassmen. 52% of students commute. All students may keep cars.

Activities: There are no fraternities or sororities. There are 34 groups on campus, including art, band, cheerleading, choir, chorus, dance, drama, ethnic, honors, literary magazine, musical theater, photography, political, religious, social service, and student government. Popular campus events include Coker Olympics of Winter (COW Days), Crew Race and Bandfest.

Sports: There are 9 intercollegiate sports for men and 8 for women, and 5 intramural sports for men and 5 for women. Facilities include A gym, a weight room, soccer, baseball and softball fields, tennis courts, a boathouse with canoes and access to a golf course. The gym seats approximately 500.

Disabled Students: 60% of the campus is accessible. Facilities include wheelchair ramps, elevators, special parking, specially equipped restrooms, special class scheduling, lowered drinking fountains, and special housing.

Services: Counseling and information services are available, as is tutoring in most subjects, English, math, and chemistry.

Campus Safety and Security: Measures include 24-hour foot and vehicle patrol, emergency notification system, and security escort services. There are lighted pathways/sidewalks and controlled access to dorms/residences.

Programs of Study: Coker confers B.A., B.S., B.M.E. and B.S.W. degrees. Master's degrees are also awarded. Bachelor's degrees are awarded in BIOLOGICAL SCIENCE (biology/biological science and molecular biology), BUSINESS (business administration and management), COMMUNICATIONS AND THE ARTS (art, communications, dance, dramatic arts, English, graphic design, music, musical theater, photography, and Spanish), COMPUTER AND PHYSICAL SCIENCE (chemistry, computer science, and mathematics), EDUCATION (art education, early childhood education, education, elementary education, English education, mathematics education, music education, physical education, and social science education), HEALTH PROFESSIONS (medical laboratory technology and premedicine), SOCIAL SCIENCE (criminology, history, political science/government, psychology, social work, and sociology). Business administration, social work, sociology and psychology have the largest enrollments.

Required: For undergraduate program: Distribution requirements include 49 hours in Liberal Arts Studies including: 15 hours of core skils, 6 hours of arts, 6 hours of behavioral sciences, 6 hours of cultural diversity, 6 hours of humanities, 7 hours of natural sciences, and 3 hours of US knowledge. A minimum of 120 semester hours including 30 hours in courses number 300 or above is required as well a minimum 2.0 GPA in order to graduate. The final 30 semester hours must be taken in residence at Coker College.

Special: Internships, study abroad in many countries, on-campus and community service work-study programs, cross-registration with Central College and dual and student-designed majors are offered. A 3-1 in medical technology with McLeod Regional Medical Center is possible. Also available are credit for military experience, non-degree study and pass/fail options. The college's round-table approach to teaching allows students and professors to discuss topics and research in small, round-table settings. There are 4 national honor societies, a freshman honors program, and 6 departmental honors programs.

Faculty/Classroom: 48% of faculty are male; 52% are female. 99% teach undergraduates. No introductory courses are taught by graduate students. The average class size in an introductory lecture is 13; in a laboratory is 16; and in a regular course is 20.

Admissions: 58% of the 2013-2014 applicants were accepted. The SAT scores for the 2013-2014 freshman class were: Critical Reading--66% below 500, 24% between 500 and 599, 10% between 600 and 699; Math--58% below 500, 31% between 500 and 599, 10% between 600 and 699, and 1% between 700 and 800. The ACT scores were 60% below 21, 23% between 21 and 23, 16% between 24 and 26. 36% were in the top two fifths.

Requirements: The SAT or ACT is required. Applicants must be graduates of an accredited secondary school or have a GED. SAT or ACT scores are required if the applicant has graduated from high school within the past five years. Additional application information, such as an in-person interview, an essay, letters of recommendation, an audition, portfolio, or additional SAT or ACT scores may also be required. AP and CLEP credits are accepted.

Procedure: Freshmen are admitted fall, spring, and summer. Entrance exams should be taken During the junior year or the first part of the senior year. There are deferred admissions and rolling admissions plans. Application deadlines are open. Application fee is $25. Notifications are sent June 1. Applications are accepted online.

Transfer: 52 transfer students enrolled in 2012-2013. Applicants with fewer than 30 semester hours must submit high school transcripts and SAT scores. A minimum 2.0 GPA is required. 30 of 120 credits required for the bachelor's degree must be completed at Coker.

Visiting: There are regularly scheduled orientations for prospective students, Consisting of orientation, a meal, campus tours and discussions with faculty and a student panel. There are guides for informal visits, visitors may sit in on classes, and stay overnight. To schedule a visit, contact Sarah Peterka at (800) 950-1908.

Financial Aid: In 2013-2014, 99% of all full-time freshmen and 98% of continuing full-time students received some form of financial aid. 87% of all full-time freshmen and 90% of continuing full-time students received need-based aid. The average freshman award was $26,120. Need-based scholarships or need-based grants averaged $6,904 ($23,686 maximum); need-based self-help aid (loans and jobs) averaged $3,676 ($8,500 maximum); non-need-based athletic scholarships averaged $7,693 ($20,241 maximum); and other non-need-based awards and non-need-based scholarships averaged $11,934 ($31,785 maximum). 5% of undergraduate students work part-time. Average annual earnings from campus work are $876. The average financial indebtedness of the 2013 graduate was $35,635. The FAFSA is required. The deadline for filing freshman financial aid applications for fall entry is June 30.

International Students: There are 22 international students enrolled. They must take the TOEFL with a minimum score of 500 on the paper-based TOEFL (PBT) or 61 on the Internet-based version (iBT). They must also take the SAT or ACT.

Graduates: From July 1, 2012 to June 30, 2013, 231 bachelor's degrees were awarded. The most popular majors were business administration (20%), criminology (9%), and sociology (8%). In an average class, 3% graduate in 3 years or less, 33% graduate in 4 years or less, and 8% graduate in 5 years or less. Of the 2012 graduating class, 11% were enrolled in graduate school within 6 months of graduation, and 23% were employed.

Admissions Contact: Adam Connolly, Director of Admissions. E-Mail: *admissions@coker.edu* Web: *www.coker.edu*

COLLEGE OF CHARLESTON — D-4

Charleston, SC 29424 — **(843) 953-5670; (843) 953-6322**

Full-time: 3573 men, 6135 women	**Faculty:** 556; IIA, -$
Part-time: 384 men, 396 women	**Ph.D.s:** 89%
Graduate: 267 men, 864 women	**Student/Faculty:** 16 to 1
Year: semesters, summer session	**Tuition:** $10,230 ($26,694)
Application Deadline: April 1	**Room & Board:** $11,043

Freshman Class: 11532 applied, 8330 accepted, 2116 enrolled

SAT CR/M: 589/579 **ACT:** required **VERY COMPETITIVE**

The College of Charleston is a nationally recognized public liberal arts and sciences university located in the heart of historic Charleston, South Carolina. Founded in 1770, the College is among the nation's top universities for quality education, student life and affordability. The College offers the distinctive combination of a beautiful and historic campus, modern facilities and cutting-edge programs. Students from 50 U.S. states and territories and 63 countries choose the College of Charleston for its small-college feel blended with the advantages and diversity of an urban, mid-sized university. The College provides a creative and intellectually stimulating environment where students are challenged by a committed and caring faculty of distinguished teacher-scholars, all in an incomparable setting. The City of Charleston, world-renowned for its history, culture, architecture and coastal environment, serves our approximately 10,000 undergraduates and 1,500 graduate students as a living and learning laboratory for experiences in business, science, teaching, the humanities, languages and the arts. At the same time, students and faculty are engaged with the community in partnerships to improve education, enhance the business environment and enrich the overall quality of life in the region. There are 6 undergraduate schools and 6 graduate schools. In addition to regional accreditation, C of C has baccalaureate program accreditation with AACSB, ABET, NASM, and NCATE. The library contains 832,011 volumes, 880,146 microform items, and 10,284 audio/video tapes/CDs/DVDs, and subscribes to 72,792 periodicals including electronic. Computerized library services include interlibrary loans, database searching, Internet access, and Wi-Fi capability. Special learning facilities include an art gallery, natural history museum, radio station, an observatory, a communications museum, a marine lab, an African American history and culture research center, and a bronze sculpture foundry. The 52-acre campus is in an urban area in the historic city center of Charleston, SC. Including any residence halls, there are 146 buildings.

Student Life: 63% of undergraduates are from South Carolina. Others are from 50 states, 61 foreign countries, and Canada. 43% are from public schools. 81% are White. The average age of freshmen is 18; all undergraduates, 21. 18% do not continue beyond their first year; 82% remain to graduate.

Housing: 3382 students can be accommodated in college housing, which includes single-sex and coed dorms and on-campus apartments. In addition, there are honors houses, language houses, special-interest houses, fraternity houses, sorority houses, Restored old Charleston houses used as residence halls, some with kitchen facilities in suites. On-campus housing is available on a first-come and first-served basis. 71% of students commute. Upperclassmen may keep cars.

Activities: 16% of men belong to 14 national fraternities; 22% of women belong to 13 national sororities. There are 200 groups on campus, including art, band, chess, choir, chorale, chorus, computers, dance, drama, ethnic, film, forensics, gay, honors, international, jazz band, literary magazine, musical theater, newspaper, opera, orchestra, pep band, political, professional, radio and TV, religious, social, social service, student government, and symphony. Popular campus events include Pep Supper, Homecoming Spirit Cup Competition, Georgestock and Welcome Week.

Sports: There are 8 intercollegiate sports for men and 14 for women, and 11 intramural sports for men and 11 for women. Facilities include Recreation Facilities include A physical education center with racquetball courts, basketball and volleyball courts, a multi-purpose dance room, and a fitness workout deck. The campus student center houses both a swimming pool and a fitness center. Outdoor recreation fields for both sport clubs and intramural play. A newly built fitness center is now available to students as of Fall 2013.

Disabled Students: 70% of the campus is accessible. Facilities include wheelchair ramps, elevators, special parking, specially equipped restrooms, special class scheduling, lowered drinking fountains, and lowered telephones.

Services: Counseling and information services are available, as is tutoring in every subject. There is a reader service for the blind, and remedial math, reading, and writing.

Campus Safety and Security: Measures include 24-hour foot and vehicle patrol, emergency notification system, self-defense education, and security escort services. There are emergency telephones, lighted pathways/sidewalks, and controlled access to dorms/residences.

Programs of Study: C of C confers B.A., B.S. and A.B. degrees. Master's degrees are also awarded. Bachelor's degrees are awarded in BIOLOGICAL SCIENCE (biochemistry, biology/biological science, and marine biology), BUSINESS (accounting, business administration and management, hospitality management services, and international business management), COMMUNICATIONS AND THE ARTS (art history, arts administration/management, classics, communications, dance, English, German, historic preservation, information technology, music, Spanish, studio art, and theatre arts), COMPUTER AND PHYSICAL SCIENCE (astronomy, astrophysics, chemistry, computer science, geology, mathematics, and physics), EDUCATION (athletic training, early childhood education, elementary education, middle school education, physical education, secondary education, and special education), HEALTH PROFESSIONS (exercise science and public health), SOCIAL SCIENCE (anthropology, economics, French studies, history, international studies, Latin American studies, philosophy, political science/government, psychology, sociology, urban studies, and women's studies). Sciences, business and languages are the strongest academically. Biology, communications, and psychology have the largest enrollments.

Required: All students must complete a core curriculum, including English and history courses, 12 hours each of language and humanities, 8 hours of lab science and 6 hours each of English, history, math or logic, and social science. A total of 122 credit hours, including 24 to 43 in the major, with a minimum overall GPA of 2.0 (2.5 in some majors) is required to graduate. The average number of hours required in the major is 40. All entering student with less than one year of college experience are required to complete a First Year Experience (FYE) course with-in their first three consecutive academic terms.

Special: Cross-registration is possible with the Medical University of South Carolina, Trident Technical College, and The Citadel. Co-op programs and internships in all majors, a Washington semester, study abroad in 36 countries, work-study programs, B.A.-B.S. degrees, and dual majors are offered. A 2-2 program in allied health, biometry or nursing is offered with the Medical University of South Carolina. The college's 3-week Maymester session offers unconventional courses and programs using alternative methods of instruction. There is an interdisciplinary honors program available to talented students. There are 6 national honor societies, a freshman honors program, and 10 departmental honors programs.

Faculty/Classroom: 52% of faculty are male; 48% are female. 95% teach undergraduates. No introductory courses are taught by graduate students. The average class size in an introductory lecture is 28; in a laboratory is 14; and in a regular course is 23.

Admissions: 72% of the 2013-2014 applicants were accepted. The SAT scores for the 2013-2014 freshman class were: Critical Reading--12% below 500, 49% between 500 and 599, 31% between 600 and 699, and 7% between 700 and 800; Math--13% below 500, 53% between 500 and 599, 29% between 600 and 699, and 4% between 700 and 800. The ACT scores were 2% below 21, 22% between 21 and 23, 37% between 24 and 26, 19% between 27 and 28, and 19% above 28. 57% of the current freshmen were in the top fifth of their class; 88% were in the top two fifths. There were 4 National Merit finalists. 10 freshmen graduated first in their class.

Requirements: The SAT or ACT is required. Applicants should have completed the following high school units: 4 units of English, 4 units of Math, 3 units of lab science, 3 units of foreign language, 2 units of social studies, 1 unit of history (2 recommended), 3 units of academic electives. 1 unit of computer science (advanced math, computer science or a combination of the two will fulfill this) and 1 unit of fine arts are recommended. The GED is accepted. An essay is required. A GPA of 2.0 is required. AP and CLEP credits are accepted. Important factors in the admissions decision are advanced placement or honors courses, leadership record, and recommendations by school officials.

Procedure: Freshmen are admitted fall and spring. Entrance exams should be taken by March 1. There are early admissions, deferred admissions, and rolling admissions plans. Early decision applications should be filed by November 1; regular applications, by April 1 for fall entry; and November 1 for spring entry, along with a $50 fee. Notification of early decision is sent December 15; regular decision, May 15. 484 applicants were on the 2013 waiting list; 62 were admitted. Applications are accepted online.

Transfer: 747 transfer students enrolled in 2012-2013. Applicants must have 24 hours and must have a 2.6 GPA for in-state residents and 3.0 for out-of-state residents. 30 of 122 credits required for the bachelor's degree must be completed at Charleston.

Visiting: There are regularly scheduled orientations for prospective students, consisting of 1-day open houses throughout the year and 10 2-day orientation sessions throughout the summer, including a family session. Academic requirements and expectations, services offered, placement testing, individual academic advising. There are guides for informal visits and visitors may sit in on classes. To schedule a visit, contact the Admissions Office.

Financial Aid: The FAFSA is required. The priority date for freshman financial aid applications for fall entry is March 1.

International Students: There are 148 international students enrolled. They must take the TOEFL with a minimum score of 600 on the paper-based TOEFL (PBT) or 100 on the Internet-based version (iBT). They must also take the SAT or ACT.

Graduates: From July 1, 2012 to June 30, 2013, 2333 bachelor's degrees were awarded. The most popular majors were business administration (13%), communicaions (10%), and biology (8%). 169 companies recruited on campus in 2012-2013. In an average class, 1% graduate in 3 years or less, 54% graduate in 4 years or less, 64% graduate in 5 years or less, and 66% graduate in 6 years or less. Of the 2012 graduating class, 40% were enrolled in graduate school within 6 months of graduation, and 52% were employed.

Admissions Contact: Suzette Stille, Director of Undergraduate Admissions. E-Mail: *admissions@cofc.edu* Web: *www.cofc.edu*

COLUMBIA COLLEGE C-3

Columbia, SC 29203 **(803) 786-3871**
(800) 277-1301; (803) 786-3674

Full-time: 6 men, 978 women	**Faculty:** n/av; IIB, --$
Part-time: 24 men, 231 women	**Ph.D.s:** 80%
Graduate: 17 men, 255 women	**Student/Faculty:** n/av
Year: semesters, summer session	**Tuition:** $21,650
Application Deadline: August 1	**Room & Board:** $6232
Freshman Class: 1097 applied, 833 accepted, 271 enrolled	
SAT CR/M: 500/500	**ACT:** recommended **COMPETITIVE**

Columbia College, founded in 1854, is a private primarily women's liberal arts college affiliated with the United Methodist Church. The figures in the above capsule and in this profile are approximate. There is one graduate school. In addition to regional accreditation, has baccalaureate program accreditation with CSWE, NASAD, NASDTEC, NASM, and NCATE. The library contains 170,000 volumes, 8,353 microform items, and 29,834 audio/video tapes/CDs/DVDs, and subscribes to 633 periodicals including electronic. Computerized library services include interlibrary loans, database searching, Internet access, and Wi-Fi capability. Special learning facilities include an art gallery, women's leadership center, and a science and technology center. The 53-acre campus is in an urban area in the northern section of Columbia. Including any residence halls, there are 26 buildings.

Student Life: 90% of undergraduates are from South Carolina. Others are from 23 states, and 10 foreign countries. 52% are White; 39% African American. 84% are Protestant; 17% claim no religious affiliation. The average age of freshmen is 18; all undergraduates, 23. 30% do not continue beyond their first year; 70% remain to graduate.

Housing: 650 students can be accommodated in college housing, which includes single-sex dorms. In addition, there are honors houses. On-campus housing is guaranteed for all 4 years. 63% of students live on campus. Alcohol is not permitted. All students may keep cars.

Activities: There are no fraternities or sororities. There are 57 groups on campus, including art, band, choir, chorus, computers, dance, drama, ethnic, honors, international, literary magazine, musical theater, newspaper, opera, photography, political, professional, radio and TV, religious, social, social service, and student government. Popular campus events include Fine Arts Series, Follies, and Ludy Bowl.

Sports: There are 4 intercollegiate sports for women, and 4 intramural sports for women. Facilities include an athletic field, tennis courts, a gym, an Olympic-size pool, a fitness lab, and a dance studio.

Disabled Students: 90% of the campus is accessible. Facilities include wheelchair ramps, elevators, special parking, specially equipped restrooms, and special class scheduling.

Services: Counseling and information services are available. Peer tutoring and remedial instruction are offered in some subjects.

Campus Safety and Security: Measures include 24-hour foot and vehicle patrol, self-defense education, and security escort services. There are emergency telephones and lighted pathways/sidewalks.

Programs of Study: confers B.A., B.F.A. and B.Mus. degrees. Master's degrees are also awarded. Bachelor's degrees are awarded in BIOLOGICAL SCIENCE (biology/biological science), BUSINESS (accounting and business administration and management), COMMUNICATIONS AND THE ARTS (communications, dance, English, French, languages, music, music performance, performing arts, piano/organ, Spanish, and studio art), COMPUTER AND PHYSICAL SCIENCE (chemistry, information sciences and systems, and mathematics), EDUCATION (Christian education, dance education, early childhood education, elementary education, music education, special education, and speech correction), HEALTH PROFESSIONS (medical laboratory technology), SOCIAL SCIENCE (history, political science/government, psychology, public affairs, religion, religious music, social work, and sociology). Education, sciences, and performing arts have the largest enrollments.

Required: To graduate, students must complete 127 semester hours, with a minimum GPA of 2.5 in the major and 2.0 overall. General education requirements for the B.A. degree include 15 hours of communication skills, 12 of social science, 9 of aesthetics, 8 of natural science, 6 of religion, and 3 each of math and phys ed. Students also must satisfy proficiency requirements in English and math.

Special: The Center for Contractual Studies allows qualified students to pursue individualized programs through independent study, practicums, and a senior project. The college also offers internships, study abroad, a Washington semester, dual majors, and credit for life, military, and work experience. Nondegree study and pass/fail options are available. There is a freshman honors program.

Faculty/Classroom: 36% of faculty are male; 64% are female. 95% teach undergraduates. No introductory courses are taught by graduate students. The average class size in an introductory lecture is 20 and in a laboratory is 20.

Admissions: 76% of the 2013-2014 applicants were accepted. The SAT scores for the 2013-2014 freshman class were: Critical Reading--49% below 500, 32% between 500 and 599, 16% between 600 and 699, and 3% between 700 and 800; Math--50% below 500, 36% between 500 and 599, 13% between 600 and 699, and 1% between 700 and 800.

Requirements: The SAT is required. The ACT is recommended. Applicants must be graduates of an accredited secondary school or have earned a GED. They should complete 16 Carnegie units, including 4 years of English, 3 of math, and 2 each of foreign language and lab science, as well as courses in history and social studies. An essay and an interview are recommended, as is a portfolio or an audition for fine or performing arts students. AP and CLEP credits are accepted. Important factors in the admissions decision are recommendations by school officials, advanced placement or honors courses, and leadership record.

Procedure: Freshmen are admitted to all sessions. Entrance exams should be taken near the end of the junior year or by December of the senior year. There is a rolling admissions plan. Applications should be filed by August 1 for fall entry. The fall 2013 application fee was $25. Applications are accepted online.

Transfer: 118 transfer students enrolled in 2012-2013. An interview is recommended for transfer students. Applicants with fewer than 24 semester hours must present ACT or SAT scores and high school transcripts. Grades of C or better transfer for credit. 30 of 127 credits required for the bachelor's degree must be completed at.

Visiting: There are regularly scheduled orientations for prospective students, consisting of meetings with faculty advisers, classroom visits, campus tours, lunch, and student life and financial aid presentations. There are guides for informal visits and visitors may sit in on classes. To schedule a visit, contact the Admissions Office.

Financial Aid: 34% of undergraduate students work part-time. Average annual earnings from campus work are $700. The FAFSA is required. Check with the school for current application deadlines.

International Students: There are 13 international students enrolled. The school actively recruits these students. They must take the TOEFL.

Admissions Contact: Julie A. King, Director of Admissions. E-Mail: *admissions@colacoll.edu* Web: *www.colum.edu*

CONVERSE COLLEGE B-1

Spartanburg, SC 29302 **(864) 596-9040**
(800) 766-1125; (864) 596-9225

Full-time: 608 women	**Faculty:** 76; IIB, --$
Part-time: 82 women	**Ph.D.s:** 89%
Graduate: 120 men, 411 women	**Student/Faculty:** 11 to 1
Year: 4-1-4, summer session	**Tuition:** $28,276
Application Deadline:	**Room & Board:** $8854
Freshman Class: 1383 applied, 710 accepted, 183 enrolled	
SAT CR/M: 530/520 **ACT:** 23	**COMPETITIVE**

Converse College, founded in 1889, is a private women's liberal arts college. Men are admitted to the graduate programs. There are 3 undergraduate schools and 2 graduate schools. In addition to regional accreditation, has baccalaureate program accreditation with NASAD, NASM, and NCATE. The library contains 150,000 volumes, 310 microform items, 12,000 audio/video tapes/CDs/DVDs, and subscribes to 700 periodicals including electronic. Computerized library services include interlibrary loans and database searching. Special learning facilities include an art gallery and natural history museum. The 72-acre campus is in an urban area 80 miles southwest of Charlotte. Including any residence halls, there are 27 buildings.

Student Life: 65% of undergraduates are from South Carolina. Others are from 27 states, 11 foreign countries, and Canada. 70% are from public schools. 45% are White. The average age of freshmen is 18; all undergraduates, 20. 26% do not continue beyond their first year; 54% remain to graduate.

Housing: 700 students can be accommodated in college housing, which includes single-sex dorms and on-campus apartments. a special residence hall for students enrolled in the South Carolina Institute of Leadership for Women, and a wellness dorm. On-campus housing is guaranteed for all 4 years. 85% of students live on campus; of those, 50% remain on campus on weekends. Alcohol is not permitted. All students may keep cars.

Activities: There are no fraternities or sororities. There are 50 groups on campus, including art, cheerleading, choir, chorale, chorus, computers, dance, debate, drama, ethnic, gay, honors, international, literary magazine, musical theater, newspaper, opera, orchestra, photography, political, professional, religious, social service, student government, symphony, and yearbook. Popular campus events include Founders Day, May Day, and Family Weekend.

Sports: There are 9 intercollegiate sports for women, and 6 intramural sports for women. Facilities include Athletic field, field house including training, locker, and weight rooms, a gym, a pool, a dance studio, a weight room, tennis courts, and bowling lanes.

Disabled Students: 75% of the campus is accessible. Facilities include wheelchair ramps, elevators, special parking, and specially equipped restrooms.

Services: Counseling and information services are available, as is tutoring in most subjects. There is a reader service for the blind.

Campus Safety and Security: Measures include 24-hour foot and vehicle patrol, self-defense education, and security escort services. There are emergency telephones and lighted pathways/sidewalks.

Programs of Study: confers B.A., B.S., B.F.A. and B.Mus. degrees. Master's degrees are also awarded. Bachelor's degrees are awarded in BIOLOGICAL SCIENCE (biology/biological science), BUSINESS (accounting and business administration and management), COMMUNICATIONS AND THE ARTS (English, fine arts, French, languages, modern language, music, and Spanish), COMPUTER AND PHYSICAL SCIENCE (chemistry, computer science, and mathematics), EDUCATION (art education, early childhood education, elementary education, foreign languages education, music education, science education, and secondary education), ENGINEERING AND ENVIRONMENTAL DESIGN (interior design), HEALTH PROFESSIONS (art therapy, predentistry, and premedicine), SOCIAL SCIENCE (economics, history, political science/government, prelaw, psychology, and religion). English, politics, and biology are the strongest academically. Music, education, and business have the largest enrollments.

Required: To graduate, students must complete 120 semester hours, including 52 hours across the liberal arts discipline, with a minimum GPA of 2.0. Courses in ideas and culture, computer literacy, public speaking, and phys ed are required.

Special: There are co-op programs and cross-registration with Wofford College. Internships, study abroad, a work-study program, accelerated degree programs, B.A.-B.S. degrees in business, economics, sociology, biology, and chemistry, and dual and student-designed majors are offered. There are 10 national honor societies, a freshman honors program, and 100 departmental honors programs.

Faculty/Classroom: 46% of faculty are male; 54% are female. All teach undergraduates, and 50% do both. No introductory courses are taught by graduate students. The average class size in an introductory lecture is 20; in a laboratory is 15; and in a regular course is 11.

Admissions: 51% of the 2013-2014 applicants were accepted. The SAT scores for the 2013-2014 freshman class were: Critical Reading--29% below 500, 43% between 500 and 599, 25% between 600 and 699, and 3% between 700 and 800; Math--35% below 500, 50% between 500 and 599, 14% between 600 and 699, and 1% between 700 and 800. The ACT scores were 32% below 21, 25% between 21 and 23, 25% between 24 and 26, 13% between 27 and 28, and 6% above 28. 5 freshmen graduated first in their class.

Requirements: The SAT or ACT is recommended. Applicants should be graduates of an accredited secondary school, having completed 20 Carnegie units, including 4 years of English, 3 of math, 2 each of foreign language, science, and social studies, and 1 of history. The GED is accepted. An interview is recommended for all students and an audition is recommended for music students. A GPA of 2.0 is required. AP and CLEP credits are accepted. Important factors in the admissions decision are advanced placement or honors courses, recommendations by school officials, and leadership record.

Procedure: Freshmen are admitted to all sessions. Entrance exams

should be taken by the senior year of high school. There are deferred admissions and rolling admissions plans. Check with the school for current application deadlines.

Transfer: 16 transfer students enrolled in 2012-2013. Transfer applicants should have a minimum GPA of 2.0. 42 of 120 credits required for the bachelor's degree must be completed at Converse.

Visiting: There are regularly scheduled orientations for prospective students, consisting of faculty meetings, panel discussions, campus tours, tours of Spartanburg, and private interview sessions. There are guides for informal visits, visitors may sit in on classes, and stay overnight. To schedule a visit, contact the Admissions Office at admissions@converse.edu.

Financial Aid: In 2013-2014, 100% of all full-time freshmen and 99% of continuing full-time students received some form of financial aid. 86% of all full-time freshmen and 90% of continuing full-time students received need-based aid. The average freshman award was $23,916. Need-based scholarships or need-based grants averaged $20,717; need-based self-help aid (loans and jobs) averaged $4,043; non-need-based athletic scholarships averaged $5,504; and other non-need-based awards and non-need-based scholarships averaged $13,105. The average financial indebtedness of the 2013 graduate was $28,986. The FAFSA is required. The deadline for filing freshman financial aid applications for fall entry is March 15.

International Students: There are 14 international students enrolled. The school actively recruits these students. They must take the TOEFL.

Graduates: From July 1, 2012 to June 30, 2013, 153 bachelor's degrees were awarded. The most popular majors were psychology (10%), biology (8%), and music (5%). 140 companies recruited on campus in 2012-2013. In an average class, 1% graduate in 3 years or less, 48% graduate in 4 years or less, 53% graduate in 5 years or less, and 54% graduate in 6 years or less. Of the 2012 graduating class, 31% were enrolled in graduate school within 6 months of graduation, and 63% were employed.

Admissions Contact: April Lewis, Director of Admissions. Web: *www.converse.edu*

ERSKINE COLLEGE B-2

Due West, SC 29639 (864) 379-8830
(800) 241-8721; (864) 379-2167

Full-time: 250 men, 291 women	**Faculty:** 41; IIB, --$
Part-time: 9 men, 3 women	**Ph.D.s:** 85%
Graduate: n/av	**Student/Faculty:** 11 to 1
Year: semesters, summer session	**Tuition:** $28,160
Application Deadline: open	**Room & Board:** $9200
Freshman Class: 500 applied, 373 accepted, 144 enrolled	
SAT CR/M: 531/543 **ACT:** required	**COMPETITIVE**

Erskine College, founded in 1839, is a private liberal arts college affiliated with the Associate Reformed Presbyterian Church. There is 1 undergraduate school and 1 graduate school. In addition to regional accreditation, Erskine has baccalaureate program accreditation with NCATE. The library contains 217,947 volumes, 63,064 microform items, 2,979 audio/video tapes/CDs/DVDs, and subscribes to 1,125 periodicals including electronic. Computerized library services include interlibrary loans, database searching, Internet access, and laptop Internet portals. The figures in the above capsule and in this profile are approximate. Special learning facilities include an art gallery and radio station. The 85-acre campus is in a rural area 90 miles west of Columbia. Including any residence halls, there are 30 buildings.

Student Life: 76% of undergraduates are from South Carolina. Others are from 19 states, 8 foreign countries, and Canada. 85% are from public schools. 72% are white. The average age of freshmen is 18; all undergraduates, 20. 23% do not continue beyond their first year; 69% remain to graduate.

Housing: 654 students can be accommodated in college housing, which includes single-sex dorms. On-campus housing is guaranteed for all 4 years. 89% of students live on campus; of those, 50% remain on campus on weekends. Alcohol is not permitted. All students may keep cars.

Activities: There are no fraternities or sororities. There are 51 groups on campus, including art, cheerleading, choir, chorale, chorus, computers, dance, drama, ethnic, honors, jazz band, literary magazine, newspaper, pep band, political, professional, radio and TV, religious, social, social service, student government, and yearbook. Popular campus events include Spring Fling, Back to School Bash, and Freshman Follies.

Sports: There are 6 intercollegiate sports for men and 8 for women. Facilities include a physical activities center, 2 gyms, racquetball courts, soccer and baseball fields, tennis and basketball courts, an outdoor pavilion, an outdoor pool, 2 sand volleyball courts, a weight room, a dance/aerobics studio, and a climbing wall.

Disabled Students: 75% of the campus is accessible. Facilities include wheelchair ramps, elevators, special parking, specially equipped restrooms, and special class scheduling.

Services: Counseling and information services are available, as is tutoring in every subject. There is a reader service for the blind.

Campus Safety and Security: Measures include emergency notification system and security escort services. There are lighted pathways/sidewalks.

Programs of Study: Erskine confers A.B. and B.S. degrees. Master's and doctoral degrees are also awarded. Bachelor's degrees are awarded in BIOLOGICAL SCIENCE (biology/biological science), BUSINESS (business administration and management and sports management), COMMUNICATIONS AND THE ARTS (art, English, music, and visual and performing arts), COMPUTER AND PHYSICAL SCIENCE (chemistry, mathematics, natural sciences, and physics), EDUCATION (athletic training, Christian education, early childhood education, elementary education, foreign languages education, physical education, and special education), SOCIAL SCIENCE (American studies, behavioral science, history, philosophy, psychology, religion, and social studies). Mathematics, chemistry, philosophy, and Spanish are the strongest academically. Business administration and biology have the largest enrollments.

Required: Students must complete 124 semester hours with an average of 27 credits in a major and a minimum GPA of 2.0. A basic curriculum of arts and letters, humanities, natural science and math, social sciences, and phys ed is required. Attendance at 17 convocations per semester is also required.

Special: Externships are available during the January term. Study abroad in 5 countries, 3-2 engineering degrees with Clemson University, the University of Tennessee at Knoxville, and Medical University of South Carolina, and pass/fail options are offered. There are 7 national honor societies and 10 departmental honors programs.

Faculty/Classroom: 61% of faculty are male; 39% are female. All teach undergraduates. No introductory courses are taught by graduate students. The average class size in an introductory lecture is 22; in a laboratory is 25; and in a regular course is 14.

Admissions: 75% of a recent applicants were accepted. The SAT scores for a recent freshman class were: Critical Reading--40% below 500, 36% between 500 and 599, 19% between 600 and 700, and 5% above 700; Math--37% below 500, 35% between 500 and 599, 23% between 600 and 700, and 5% above 700. 65% of the current freshmen were in the top fifth of their class; 87% were in the top two fifths.

Requirements: The SAT or ACT is required. In addition, grades from college preparatory courses are weighed twice as heavily as the SAT or ACT scores. Applicants must be graduates of an accredited secondary school. The GED is accepted. Applicants should have a minimum of 14 high school academic credits, including 4 credits of English and 2 credits each of math, science, and history. AP and CLEP credits are accepted. Important factors in the admissions decision are advanced placement or honors courses, recommendations by school officials, and extracurricular activities record.

Procedure: Freshmen are admitted to all sessions. Entrance exams should be taken in the spring of the junior year or the fall of the senior year. There are deferred admissions and rolling admissions plans. Application deadlines are open. The fall application fee was $25. Notification is sent on a rolling basis. Applications are accepted online.

Transfer: 17 transfer students enrolled in a recent year. Transfer applicants should have a minimum GPA of 2.0. An interview is recommended. 60 of 124 credits required for the bachelor's degree must be completed at Erskine.

Visiting: There are guides for informal visits, visitors may sit in on classes, and stay overnight. To schedule a visit, contact Admissions.

Financial Aid: The FAFSA and the college's own financial statement are required. The deadline for filing freshman financial aid applications for fall entry is April 1.

International Students: There are 20 international students enrolled. They must take the TOEFL. They must also take the SAT.

Graduates: In a recent year, 141 bachelor's degrees were awarded. The most popular majors were biology (21%), business (20%), and education (13%). In an average class, 63% graduate in 5 years or less and 69% graduate in 6 years or less.

Admissions Contact: Director of Admissions. E-Mail: *admissions@erskine.edu* Web: *www.erskine.edu*

FRANCIS MARION UNIVERSITY D-2

Florence, SC 29502 (843) 661-1231
(800) 368-7551; (843) 661-4635

Full-time: 1107 men, 2288 women	**Faculty:** 205; IIA, --$
Part-time: 125 men, 260 women	**Ph.D.s:** 82%
Graduate: 52 men, 261 women	**Student/Faculty:** 16 to 1
Year: semesters, summer session	**Tuition:** $9066 ($17,774)
Application Deadline: August 15	**Room & Board:** $6820
Freshman Class: 3908 applied, 2300 accepted, 814 enrolled	
SAT CR/M/W: 475/479/451 **ACT:** 20	**LESS COMPETITIVE**

Francis Marion University, founded in 1970, is a state-supported liberal arts, business, and teachers college. There are 3 undergraduate schools and 3 graduate schools. In addition to regional accreditation, FMU has baccalaureate program accreditation with AACSB, NASAD, NASDTEC,

NCATE, and NLN. The library contains 415,592 volumes, 500,000 microform items, 9,835 audio/video tapes/CDs/DVDs, and subscribes to 860 periodicals including electronic. Computerized library services include interlibrary loans and database searching. Special learning facilities include an art gallery, planetarium, TV station, media center, teaching materials center, and hewn timber cabins. The 400-acre campus is in a rural area 8 miles east of Florence. Including any residence halls, there are 57 buildings.

Student Life: 95% of undergraduates are from South Carolina. Others are from 30 states, 19 foreign countries, and Canada. 92% are from public schools. 49% are African American; 46% White. The average age of freshmen is 18; all undergraduates, 21. 67% do not continue beyond their first year; 40% remain to graduate.

Housing: 1523 students can be accommodated in college housing, which includes single-sex dorms and on-campus apartments. On-campus housing is available on a first-come and first-served basis. 60% of students commute. All students may keep cars.

Activities: 1% of men belong to 7 national fraternities; 2% of women belong to 7 national sororities. There are 46 groups on campus, including art, cheerleading, choir, chorus, dance, drama, ethnic, gay, honors, international, jazz band, literary magazine, newspaper, pep band, photography, political, professional, religious, social, social service, and student government. Popular campus events include Homecoming, University Programming Board, Arts International, and Pee Dee Fiction Festival.

Sports: There are 7 intercollegiate sports for men and 7 for women, and 24 intramural sports for men and 24 for women. Facilities include a 3,200-seat gym; Olympic-size and outdoor leisure pools; new athletic complex for baseball, softball, and soccer; intramural fields; tennis, racquetball, and sand volleyball courts; a track; weight, fitness, and game rooms.

Disabled Students: All of the campus is accessible. Facilities include wheelchair ramps, elevators, special parking, specially equipped restrooms, special class scheduling, and lowered drinking fountains.

Services: . There is a reader service for the blind, and remedial reading and writing.

Campus Safety and Security: Measures include 24-hour foot and vehicle patrol, emergency notification system, and security escort services. There are emergency telephones, lighted pathways/sidewalks, and controlled access to dorms/residences.

Programs of Study: FMU confers B.A., B.S., B.B.A., B.G.S. and B.S.N degrees. Master's degrees are also awarded. Bachelor's degrees are awarded in BIOLOGICAL SCIENCE (biology/biological science), BUSINESS (accounting, banking and finance, business administration and management, business economics, and marketing/retailing/merchandising), COMMUNICATIONS AND THE ARTS (communications, dramatic arts, English, modern language, and music), COMPUTER AND PHYSICAL SCIENCE (chemistry, computer science, information sciences and systems, mathematics, and physics), EDUCATION (art education, early childhood education, elementary education, and middle school education), ENGINEERING AND ENVIRONMENTAL DESIGN (industrial engineering), HEALTH PROFESSIONS (nursing), SOCIAL SCIENCE (economics, history, international studies, liberal arts/general studies, political science/government, psychology, and sociology). Nursing, biology, and physics are the strongest academically. Biology, nursing, and psychology have the largest enrollments.

Required: Students must complete 120 to 132 credit hours, including 30 to 60 in the major, with a GPA of 2.0. Distribution requirements include 15 hours of humanities, 12 each of sciences and basic communications (6 of English composition and 6 of math or logic), up to 12 hours of a foreign language, and 9 of social sciences.

Special: There are co-op programs in civil engineering technology and electronic engineering technology with Florence Darlington Technical College; in engineering, forest management, and aquaculture, fisheries, and wildlife with Clemson University; and in medical technology with the McLeod Regional Medical Center. Internships are required in the communications and health physics programs. Accelerated degree programs, preprofessional programs, and dual majors are possible. Nondegree study is permitted. Self-paced courses are offered in math and French. Study abroad is possible in Australia, Canada, Ecuador, England, France, and Germany, Ireland, Japan, and Mexico. There are 14 national honor societies and a freshman honors program.

Faculty/Classroom: 51% of faculty are male; 49% are female. All teach undergraduates. No introductory courses are taught by graduate students. The average class size in an introductory lecture is 20; in a laboratory is 16; and in a regular course is 20.

Admissions: 57% of the 2013-2014 applicants were accepted. The SAT scores for the 2013-2014 freshman class were: Critical Reading--65% below 500, 26% between 500 and 599, 8% between 600 and 699, and 1% between 700 and 800; Math--64% below 500, 28% between 500 and 599, 7% between 600 and 699, and 1% between 700 and 800; Writing--74% below 500, 24% between 500 and 599, and 2% between 600 and 699. The ACT scores were 69% below 21, 15% between 21 and 23, 12% between 24 and 26, 3% between 27 and 28, and 1% above 28. 33% of the current freshmen were in the top fifth of their class; 68% were in the top two fifths. 8 freshmen graduated first in their class.

Requirements: The SAT or ACT is required. In addition, students should have earned 19 units, consisting of 4 in English, 4 Mathematics, 3 in Science (must include lab), 2 in Foreign Language, 2 in Social Studies, 1 in US History, 1 in Academic Elective, 1 in Visual/Performing Arts, and 1 in either PE or ROTC. A GPA of 2.0 is required. AP and CLEP credits are accepted.

Procedure: Freshmen are admitted to all sessions. Entrance exams should be taken in the fall of the senior year or spring of the junior year. There are deferred admissions and rolling admissions plans. Applications should be filed by August 15 for fall entry, along with a $33 fee. Notifications are sent September 1. Applications are accepted online.

Transfer: 790 transfer students enrolled in 2012-2013. Transfer students should have earned 24 hours of college credit, with a GPA of at least 2.0. 36 of 120 credits required for the bachelor's degree must be completed at the university.

Visiting: There are regularly scheduled orientations for prospective students, including campus tours and registering for classes. There are guides for informal visits and visitors may sit in on classes. To schedule a visit, contact the Admissions Office.

Financial Aid: In 2013-2014, 98% of all full-time freshmen and 93% of continuing full-time students received some form of financial aid. 77% of all full-time freshmen and 50% of continuing full-time students received need-based aid. The average freshman award was $7,320. Need-based scholarships or need-based grants averaged $5,035 ($7,645 maximum); need-based self-help aid (loans and jobs) averaged $3,292 ($9,500 maximum); non-need-based athletic scholarships averaged $8,024 ($19,952 maximum); and other non-need-based awards and non-need-based scholarships averaged $7,510 ($20,919 maximum). 16% of undergraduate students work part-time. Average annual earnings from campus work are $1608. The average financial indebtedness of the 2013 graduate was $30,977. FMU is a member of CSS. The FAFSA and the college's own financial statement are required. The priority date for freshman financial aid applications for fall entry is March 1. The deadline for filing freshman financial aid applications for fall entry is February 15.

International Students: There are 55 international students enrolled. The school actively recruits these students. They must take the TOEFL with a minimum score of 500 on the paper-based TOEFL (PBT) or 61 on the Internet-based version (iBT). TOEFL may be submitted in place of the SAT.

Graduates: From July 1, 2012 to June 30, 2013, 586 bachelor's degrees were awarded. The most popular majors were nursing (17%), biology (15%), and psychology (8%). 173 companies recruited on campus in 2012-2013. In an average class, 18% graduate in 4 years or less, 32% graduate in 5 years or less, and 40% graduate in 6 years or less.

Admissions Contact: Perry Wilson, Director of Admissions. E-Mail: *admission@fmarion.edu* Web: *www.fmarion.edu*

FURMAN UNIVERSITY — B-1

Greenville, SC 29613	**(864) 294-2034; (864) 294-2018**
Full-time: 1122 men, 1500 women	**Faculty:** 240; IIB, +$
Part-time: 64 men, 68 women	**Ph.D.s:** 95%
Graduate: 37 men, 173 women	**Student/Faculty:** 11 to 1
Year: semesters, summer session	**Tuition:** $41,152
Application Deadline: January 15	**Room & Board:** $10,509
Freshman Class: 6035 applied, 4676 accepted, 697 enrolled	
SAT CR/M/W: 600/610/600	**ACT:** 27 **HIGHLY COMPETITIVE**

Founded in 1826, Furman University is an independent liberal arts institution offering undergraduate and graduate programs. The figures in the above capsule and in this profile are approximate. In addition to regional accreditation, Furman has baccalaureate program accreditation with NASM and NCATE. The 3 libraries contain 526,690 volumes, 862,324 microform items, 9,200 audio/video tapes/CDs/DVDs, and subscribe to 13,200 periodicals including electronic. Computerized library services include interlibrary loans, database searching, Internet access, and Wi-Fi capability. Special learning facilities include an art gallery, planetarium, radio station, an observatory, and cable TV with on-campus broadcasting. The 750-acre campus is in a suburban area 5 miles north of Greenville. Including any residence halls, there are 69 buildings.

Student Life: 71% of undergraduates are from out of state, mostly the South. Students are from 46 states, 53 foreign countries, and Canada. 52% are from public schools. 81% are White. 73% are Protestant; 15% Catholic. The average age of freshmen is 18; all undergraduates, 20. 10% do not continue beyond their first year; 84% remain to graduate.

Housing: 2452 students can be accommodated in college housing, which includes single-sex and coed dorms and on-campus apartments. In addition, there are language houses, special-interest houses, small houses, lakeside cabins, an eco-cottage, and a healthy living dorm section. On-campus housing is guaranteed for all 4 years and is available on a lottery system for upperclassmen. 96% of students live on campus; of those, 75% remain on campus on weekends. All students may keep cars.

Activities: 38% of men belong to 7 national fraternities; 51% of women

belong to 7 national sororities. There are 140 groups on campus, including art, band, cheerleading, chess, choir, chorale, chorus, computers, dance, debate, drama, drill team, environmental, ethnic, film, forensics, gay, honors, international, jazz band, literary magazine, marching band, musical theater, newspaper, opera, orchestra, pep band, photography, political, professional, radio and TV, religious, social, social service, student government, symphony, and yearbook. Popular campus events include Beach Weekend and Mountain Weekend.

Sports: There are 9 intercollegiate sports for men and 9 for women, and 20 intramural sports for men and 20 for women. Facilities include a 16500-seat football stadium, a 5800-seat arena, a gym, a pool, an 18-hole golf course, a tennis center with indoor and outdoor courts, a 3000-seat soccer stadium, 12 playing fields, a varsity softball field, and a baseball stadium. The gym includes 6 racquetball courts and a fitness center.

Disabled Students: 99% of the campus is accessible. Facilities include wheelchair ramps, elevators, special parking, specially equipped restrooms, special class scheduling, lowered drinking fountains, lowered telephones, and special housing.

Services: Counseling and information services are available, as is tutoring in every subject. There is a reader service for the blind.

Campus Safety and Security: Measures include 24-hour foot and vehicle patrol, emergency notification system, self-defense education, and security escort services. There are shuttle buses, emergency telephones, lighted pathways/sidewalks, and controlled access to dorms/residences.

Programs of Study: Furman confers B.A., B.S., B.L.A. and B.M. degrees. Master's degrees are also awarded. Bachelor's degrees are awarded in BIOLOGICAL SCIENCE (biology/biological science and neurosciences), BUSINESS (accounting and business administration and management), COMMUNICATIONS AND THE ARTS (art, classics, communications, dramatic arts, English, French, German, Greek, Latin, music, music performance, music theory and composition, and Spanish), COMPUTER AND PHYSICAL SCIENCE (chemistry, computer science, information sciences and systems, mathematics, and physics), EDUCATION (education, elementary education, and music education), ENGINEERING AND ENVIRONMENTAL DESIGN (environmental science and preengineering), HEALTH PROFESSIONS (exercise science and health science), SOCIAL SCIENCE (Asian/Oriental studies, economics, history, philosophy, political science/government, psychology, religion, religious music, sociology, and urban studies). Chemistry, biology, and music are the strongest academically. Political science, health sciences and business administration have the largest enrollments.

Required: Students must complete 1 to 3 courses in foreign languages, 4 empirical studies classes (2 natural world, 2 human and social behavior), 3 courses in human culture, 2 courses in global awareness, 1 course in math and formal reasoning, 1 course in ultimate questions, and 1 course in body and mind. To graduate students must complete 128 credit hours, including 24 to 44 in the major, with a GPA of 2.0.

Special: A 3-2 engineering degree is offered with the Georgia Institute of Technology, Clemson, North Carolina State, and Auburn and Washington Universities. Internships, study abroad in at least 17 countries, a Washington semester with an internship in a government agency or political organization, and work-study programs are offered. B.A.-B.S. degrees, dual majors, interdisciplinary majors such as computer science-math, math-economics, and computing-business, and student-designed majors are available. A bachelor of general studies degree is granted in the evening division. Nondegree study and pass/fail options are possible. Furman features student/faculty research programs. There are 20 national honor societies and including Phi Beta Kappa.

Faculty/Classroom: 63% of faculty are male; 37% are female. All teach undergraduates. No introductory courses are taught by graduate students. The average class size in an introductory lecture is 19; in a laboratory is 10; and in a regular course is 16.

Admissions: 77% of the 2013-2014 applicants were accepted. The SAT scores for the 2013-2014 freshman class were: Critical Reading--12% below 500, 33% between 500 and 599, 43% between 600 and 699, and 12% between 700 and 800; Math--8% below 500, 31% between 500 and 599, 46% between 600 and 699, and 15% between 700 and 800; Writing--14% below 500, 32% between 500 and 599, 42% between 600 and 699, and 12% between 700 and 800. The ACT scores were 7% below 21, 10% between 21 and 23, 24% between 24 and 26, 27% between 27 and 28, and 32% above 28. 64% of the current freshmen were in the top fifth of their class; 86% were in the top two fifths. There were 12 National Merit finalists. 12 freshmen graduated first in their class.

Requirements: The SAT or ACT and ACT Writing Test are recommended. Applicants must be high school graduates or hold a GED. Students should have earned at least 20 units in high school, including 4 of English, 3 each of history, math, and science, and 2 each of social studies and foreign language. A portfolio or an audition, where appropriate, is required. AP credits are accepted. Important factors in the admissions decision are advanced placement or honors courses, evidence of special talent, personality/intangible qualities, extracurricular activities record, leadership record, and parents or siblings attended your school.

Procedure: Freshmen are admitted fall. Entrance exams should be taken by late junior or early senior year. There is a early decision plan. Early decision applications should be filed by November 1; regular applications, by January 15 for fall entry. Notification of early decision is sent December 15; regular decision, April 1. 458 early decision candidates were accepted for the 2013-2014 class. 76 applicants were on the 2013 waiting list; 17 were admitted. Applications are accepted online.

Transfer: 27 transfer students enrolled in 2012-2013. Applicants should complete at least 1 year elsewhere before seeking admission. 64 of 128 credits required for the bachelor's degree must be completed at Furman.

Visiting: There are regularly scheduled orientations for prospective students, consisting of an individual or group session with an admissions officer and a campus tour. There are guides for informal visits, visitors may sit in on classes, and stay overnight. To schedule a visit, contact the Admissions Office at admissions@furman.edu.

Financial Aid: In 2013-2014, 85% of all full-time freshmen and 83% of continuing full-time students received some form of financial aid. 41% of all full-time freshmen and 40% of continuing full-time students received need-based aid. The average freshman award was $26,910. 47% of undergraduate students work part-time. Average annual earnings from campus work are $2400. The average financial indebtedness of the 2013 graduate was $26,661. Furman is a member of CSS. The CSS/Profile, FAFSA, and the state aid form are required. The deadline for filing freshman financial aid applications for fall entry is February 15.

International Students: There are 123 international students enrolled. The school actively recruits these students. They must take the TOEFL.

Graduates: From July 1, 2012 to June 30, 2013, 649 bachelor's degrees were awarded. The most popular majors were political science (12%), business administration (11%), and health sciences (8%). 85 companies recruited on campus in 2012-2013. In an average class, 1% graduate in 3 years or less, 80% graduate in 4 years or less, 84% graduate in 5 years or less, and 85% graduate in 6 years or less. Of the 2012 graduating class, 42% were enrolled in graduate school within 6 months of graduation, and 51% were employed.

Admissions Contact: Brad Pochard, Associate Vice President Admissions. E-Mail: *admission@furman.edu* Web: *www.furman.com*

LANDER UNIVERSITY B-2

Greenwood, SC 29649 **(864) 388-8307**
(888) 4LANDER; (864) 388-8125

Full-time: 740 men, 1360 women	**Faculty:** 137; IIB, --$
Part-time: 80 men, 190 women	**Ph.D.s:** 63%
Graduate: 5 men, 40 women	**Student/Faculty:** n/av
Year: semesters, summer session	**Tuition:** $9504 ($17,976)
Application Deadline: open	**Room & Board:** $7456
Freshman Class: n/av	
SAT or ACT: required	

COMPETITIVE+

Lander University, founded in 1872, is a state-supported institution offering undergraduate programs in liberal arts, science and math, business, education, nursing, and phys ed and exercise studies. The figures in the above capsule and in this profile are approximate. There are 10 undergraduate schools and 1 graduate school. In addition to regional accreditation, Lander has baccalaureate program accreditation with AACSB, NASAD, NASM, and NCATE. The library contains 174,624 volumes, 157,707 microform items, 2592 audio/video tapes/CDs/DVDs, and subscribes to 656 periodicals including electronic. Computerized library services include interlibrary loans, database searching, and Internet access. Special learning facilities include a learning resource center, art gallery, and media center. The 100-acre campus is in a small town 75 miles west of Columbia. Including any residence halls, there are 33 buildings.

Student Life: 92% of undergraduates are from South Carolina. Others are from 23 states, 21 foreign countries, and Canada. 67% are white; 24% African American. The average age of freshmen is 19; all undergraduates, 26. 38% do not continue beyond their first year; 62% remain to graduate.

Housing: 1082 students can be accommodated in college housing, which includes single-sex and coed dorms, on-campus apartments, and off-campus apartments. On-campus housing is available on a first-come, first-served basis. 68% of students commute. Alcohol is not permitted. All students may keep cars.

Activities: 11% of men belong to 5 national fraternities; 12% of women belong to 5 national sororities. There are 65 groups on campus, including art, band, cheerleading, choir, chorale, chorus, computers, dance, drama, ethnic, honors, international, jazz band, literary magazine, musical theater, newspaper, orchestra, pep band, political, professional, religious, social, social service, and student government. Popular campus events include the Greenwood Performing Arts Series.

Sports: There are 5 intercollegiate sports for men and 6 for women, and 11 intramural sports for men and 11 for women. Facilities include a gym, basketball courts, a weight room, a softball field, tennis courts, an indoor pool, and an indoor suspended track.

Disabled Students: All of the campus is accessible. Facilities include

wheelchair ramps, elevators, special parking, specially equipped rest rooms, special class scheduling, lowered drinking fountains, and lowered telephones.

Services: Counseling and information services are available, as is tutoring in most subjects. There is a reader service for the blind, and remedial math, reading, and writing.

Campus Safety and Security: Measures include 24-hour foot and vehicle patrol, emergency notification system, self-defense education, and security escort services. There are emergency telephones, lighted pathways/sidewalks, and controlled access to dorms/residences.

Programs of Study: Lander confers B.A., B.S., and B.M.Ed. degrees. Master's degrees are also awarded. Bachelor's degrees are awarded in BIOLOGICAL SCIENCE (biology/biological science), BUSINESS (business administration and management), COMMUNICATIONS AND THE ARTS (communications, dramatic arts, English, music, Spanish, speech/debate/rhetoric, and visual and performing arts), COMPUTER AND PHYSICAL SCIENCE (chemistry, computer science, and mathematics), EDUCATION (early childhood education, elementary education, music education, physical education, and special education), ENGINEERING AND ENVIRONMENTAL DESIGN (environmental science), HEALTH PROFESSIONS (exercise science, nursing, and sports medicine), SOCIAL SCIENCE (history, interdisciplinary studies, political science/government, psychology, and sociology). Premedical and dual engineering are the strongest academically. Business administration, education, and behavioral science have the largest enrollments.

Required: To graduate, students must complete 125 semester hours, including 36 in the major, with a GPA of 2.0.

Special: Lander offers internships, co-op and work-study programs, accelerated degrees, B.A.-B.S. degrees, dual engineering degrees with Clemson University, student-designed majors in interdisciplinary studies, credit for military experience, and nondegree study. Students in the Honors International Program study abroad in England for 1 semester during their sophomore year. There are 7 national honor societies and a freshman honors program.

Faculty/Classroom: 47% of faculty are male; 53% are female. All teach undergraduates. No introductory courses are taught by graduate students. The average class size in a regular course is 22.

Requirements: The SAT or ACT is required. In addition, applicants must be high school graduates with 20 credits, including 4 each of English and academic electives, 3 each of math and lab science, 2 each of foreign language and social studies, and 1 each of American history and phys ed or ROTC. An interview and a portfolio or an audition, if appropriate, are recommended. A GPA of 2.0 is required. AP and CLEP credits are accepted.

Procedure: Freshmen are admitted to all sessions. Entrance exams should be taken in the junior year. There are early admissions, deferred admissions, and rolling admissions plans. Application deadlines are open. The application fee is $35. Notification is sent on a rolling basis. Applications are accepted online.

Transfer: Applicants must have a minimum college GPA of 2.0; otherwise, they may be considered on the strength of military or work experience. Transcripts from every school attended should be submitted. Students under 21 with fewer than 30 semester credits must submit high school transcripts and SAT or ACT results as well. An interview is recommended. 30 of 125 credits required for the bachelor's degree must be completed at Lander.

Visiting: There are regularly scheduled orientations for prospective students, consisting of open houses. There are guides for informal visits, and visitors may sit in on classes. To schedule a visit, contact the Admissions Office.

Financial Aid: The FAFSA is required. Check with the school for current deadlines.

International Students: The school actively recruits these students. They must take the TOEFL with a minimum score of 550 on the paper-based TOEFL (PBT). They must also take the SAT or ACT.

Admissions Contact: Director of Admissions. E-Mail: *admissions@lander.edu* Web: *www.lander.edu*

LIMESTONE COLLEGE — B-1

Gaffney, SC 29340 — **(864) 489-7151, ext. 4554 (800) 795-7151; (864) 487-8706**

Full-time: 651 men, 390 women	**Faculty:** 75; IIB, --$
Part-time: 9 men, 9 women	**Ph.D.s:** 80%
Graduate: 27 men, 35 women	**Student/Faculty:** 13 to 1
Year: semesters, summer session	**Tuition:** $22,080
Application Deadline: August 27	**Room & Board:** $7800
Freshman Class: 2155 applied, 1175 accepted, 416 enrolled	
SAT CR/M: 480/520	**ACT:** 21 **COMPETITIVE**

Limestone College, founded in 1845, is a private, accredited, coeducational, Christian non-denominational, four-year liberal arts College offering programs in the arts, sciences, business, and teacher preparation. It's programs lead to the Bachelor of Arts, Bachelor of Fine Arts, Bachelor of Science, Bachelor of Social Work, Associate of Arts, and Associate of Science degrees. At the graduate level, a Master of Business Administration is offered. There is one undergraduate school and one graduate school. In addition to regional accreditation, has baccalaureate program accreditation with CSWE, NASM, and NCATE. The library contains 207,115 volumes, 2,924 microform items, 21,408 audio/video tapes/CDs/DVDs, and subscribes to 37,246 periodicals including electronic. Computerized library services include interlibrary loans, database searching, Internet access, and Wi-Fi capability. Special learning facilities include an art gallery, Student Success Center with computer workstations, writing center, math lab, computer graphics art lab, testing center, monitored study halls, and tutorial services. Online math and writing labs. Winnie Davis Hall of Southern History Museum. The 125-acre campus is in a suburban area 50 miles south of Charlotte, NC and 25 miles north of Spartanburg, SC. Including any residence halls, there are 33 buildings.

Student Life: 54% of undergraduates are from South Carolina. Others are from 33 states, 20 foreign countries, and Canada. 55% are White; 29% African American. The average age of freshmen is 19; all undergraduates, 21. 44% do not continue beyond their first year; 61% remain to graduate.

Housing: 539 students can be accommodated in college housing, which includes single-sex dorms, on-campus apartments, and off-campus apartments. On-campus housing is guaranteed for the freshman year only, is available on a first-come, and first-served basis. 58% of students live on campus; of those, 55% remain on campus on weekends. Alcohol is not permitted. All students may keep cars.

Activities: 3% of men belong to 1 national fraternity. There are no sororities. There are 22 groups on campus, including art, band, cheerleading, choir, chorus, computers, dance, drama, honors, international, jazz band, literary magazine, marching band, musical theater, pep band, professional, religious, social, social service, student government, and yearbook. Popular campus events include Christmas on Campus, Homecoming and Saints Festival.

Sports: There are 13 intercollegiate sports for men and 12 for women, and 28 intramural sports for men and 28 for women. Facilities include A 1,500-seat gym, an Olympic-size indoor pool, 8 lighted tennis courts, baseball, softball, soccer, field hockey, and lacrosse fields, 4 practice fields, a student center with game room, a physical education center, a fitness center, and Timken East gym and facilities.

Disabled Students: 75% of the campus is accessible. Facilities include wheelchair ramps, elevators, special parking, specially equipped restrooms, special class scheduling, lowered drinking fountains, special housing. Individual accommodations are made on an as-needed basis.

Services: Counseling and information services are available, as is tutoring in every subject. There is remedial math, reading, and writing. Special assistance is also available to students with documented learning disabilities through the Program for Alternative Learning Styles (PALS) Program.

Campus Safety and Security: Measures include 24-hour foot and vehicle patrol, emergency notification system, and security escort services. There are emergency telephones, lighted pathways/sidewalks, and controlled access to dorms/residences.

Programs of Study: confers B.A., B.S., B.F.A. and B.S.W. degrees. Associate and master's degrees are also awarded. Bachelor's degrees are awarded in BIOLOGICAL SCIENCE (biology/biological science), BUSINESS (accounting, business administration and management, business economics, electronic business, finance, human resources, management science, marketing, marketing and distribution, personnel management, and sports management), COMMUNICATIONS AND THE ARTS (communications, English, English Writing, graphic design, jazz, music, musical theater, studio art, and theatre arts), COMPUTER AND PHYSICAL SCIENCE (chemistry, computer programming, computer information technology, computer science, computer security and information assurance, information sciences and systems, mathematics, web services, and web technology), EDUCATION (athletic training, early childhood education, elementary education, English education, mathematics education, music education, and physical education), ENGINEERING AND ENVIRONMENTAL DESIGN (computer technology), HEALTH PROFESSIONS (health care administration), SOCIAL SCIENCE (criminal justice, economics, history, liberal arts/general studies, physical fitness/movement, prelaw, psychology, and social work). Business administration, sport management, and criminal justice have the largest enrollments.

Required: To graduate a student must complete a minimum of 123 credit hours for a baccalaureate degree or 62 credit hours for an associate degree with a minimum overall GPA of 2.0, including within their major.

Special: The College offers senior internships in public and private organizations for 3 to 6 semester credit hours, as well as a work-study program, on- and off-campus evening courses, and courses on the Internet. The College confers a liberal studies degree and may grant credit for military experience. Double majors are possible; however, granting of 2 baccalaureate degrees requires an additional 31 semester hours. There are 5 national honor societies and a freshman honors program.

Faculty/Classroom: 74% of faculty are male; 26% are female. All teach

undergraduates, and 20% do both. No introductory courses are taught by graduate students. The average class size in an introductory lecture is 22; in a laboratory is 16; and in a regular course is 14.

Admissions: 55% of the 2013-2014 applicants were accepted. The SAT scores for the 2013-2014 freshman class were: Critical Reading--55% below 500, 37% between 500 and 599, 7% between 600 and 699, and 1% between 700 and 800; Math--33% below 500, 57% between 500 and 599, and 10% between 600 and 699. The ACT scores were 41% below 21, 43% between 21 and 23, 11% between 24 and 26, 2% between 27 and 28, and 3% above 28. 13% of the current freshmen were in the top fifth of their class; 38% were in the top two fifths.

Requirements: The SAT or ACT is required. SAT combined score (critical reading and math) of 910 or ACT combined score (English and math) of 19. The College recommends that students present 4 units of English, 3 each of math and social science, and 2 of lab science. The GED is accepted. An interview is recommended. A GPA of 2.0 is required. AP and CLEP credits are accepted. Important factors in the admissions decision are advanced placement or honors courses, leadership record, and evidence of special talent.

Procedure: Freshmen are admitted fall and spring. Entrance exams should be taken During fall of the senior year of high school. There are deferred admissions and rolling admissions plans. Application deadlines are open. Application fee is $25. Notification is sent on a rolling basis. Applications are accepted online. Application fees are waived if application is completed online.

Transfer: 94 transfer students enrolled in 2012-2013. Applicants must have a minimum GPA of 2.0 and be in good standing at their previous school. 31 of 123 credits required for the bachelor's degree must be completed at Limestone.

Visiting: There are regularly scheduled orientations for prospective students, Open House: November 15, 2013; February 21, 2014; and April 11, 2014, or by appointment with Admissions Office. Agenda: President's address, campus tour, science/ business faculty teaching demonstrations, lunch, & tour of athletics & residence halls. There are guides for informal visits, visitors may sit in on classes, and stay overnight. To schedule a visit, contact Cynthia Tubb at (864) 488-4552.

Financial Aid: In 2013-2014, 91% of all full-time freshmen and 94% of continuing full-time students received some form of financial aid. 91% of all full-time freshmen and 92% of continuing full-time students received need-based aid. The average freshman award was $16,350. Need-based scholarships or need-based grants averaged $5,623 ($9,745 maximum); need-based self-help aid (loans and jobs) averaged $6,562 ($12,500 maximum); non-need-based athletic scholarships averaged $6,940 ($24,380 maximum); other non-need-based awards and non-need-based scholarships averaged $4,660 ($28,760 maximum); and $1,445 from other forms of aid. 31% of undergraduate students work part-time. Average annual earnings from campus work are $1565. The average financial indebtedness of the 2013 graduate was $30,580. is a member of CSS. The FAFSA is required. The priority date for freshman financial aid applications for fall entry is February 1. The deadline for filing freshman financial aid applications for fall entry is July 1.

International Students: There are 97 international students enrolled. The school actively recruits these students. They must take the TOEFL with a minimum score of 500 on the paper-based TOEFL (PBT) or 75 on the Internet-based version (iBT). They must also take the SAT or ACT.

Graduates: From July 1, 2012 to June 30, 2013, 155 bachelor's degrees were awarded. The most popular majors were business administration (9%), sport management (9%), and elementary education (8%). In an average class, 20% graduate in 4 years or less, 32% graduate in 5 years or less, and 34% graduate in 6 years or less. Of the 2012 graduating class, 19% were enrolled in graduate school within 6 months of graduation.

Admissions Contact: Chris Phenicie, Vice President for Enrollment Services. E-Mail: *cphenicie@limestone.edu* Web: *www.limestone.edu*

MORRIS COLLEGE D-3

Sumter, SC 29150 (803) 934-3225
(866) 853-1345; (803) 773-8241

Full-time: 363 men, 500 women	**Faculty:** 49
Part-time: 3 men, 8 women	**Ph.D.s:** 73%
Graduate: n/av	**Student/Faculty:** 16 to 1
Year: semesters, summer session	**Tuition:** $11,087
Application Deadline: April 30	**Room & Board:** $4919

Freshman Class: 2177 applied, 1919 accepted, 284 enrolled
SAT or ACT: required

LESS COMPETITIVE

Morris College, founded in 1908, is a private liberal arts institution affiliated with the Baptist Church through the Baptist Educational and Missionary Convention of South Carolina. In addition to regional accreditation, Morris has baccalaureate program accreditation with ACBSP and NCATE. The library contains 123,331 volumes, 228,277 microform items, 3,024 audio/video tapes/CDs/DVDs, and subscribes to 370 periodicals including electronic. Computerized library services include interlibrary loans, database searching, and Internet access. Special learning facilities include a radio station, TV production studio, and photography workroom, forensics center. The 34-acre campus is in a small town 40 miles east of Columbia. Including any residence halls, there are 24 buildings.

Student Life: 79% of undergraduates are from South Carolina. Others are from 19 states. 99% are from public schools. 93% are African American. The average age of freshmen is 19; all undergraduates, 22. 60% do not continue beyond their first year; 31% remain to graduate.

Housing: 820 students can be accommodated in college housing, which includes single-sex dorms. On-campus housing is available on a first-come and first-served basis. 78% of students live on campus; of those, 25% remain on campus on weekends. Alcohol is not permitted. All students may keep cars.

Activities: 4% of men belong to 4 national fraternities; 3% of women belong to 4 national sororities. There are 60 groups on campus, including cheerleading, chess, choir, chorale, dance, drama, honors, literary magazine, newspaper, pep band, photography, political, professional, radio and TV, religious, social, social service, student government, and yearbook. Popular campus events include Coronation of Miss Morris College, Christmas and Gospel Choir Concerts, Martin Luther King Observance and Homecoming.

Sports: There are 4 intercollegiate sports for men and 5 for women, and 3 intramural sports for men and 3 for women. Facilities include a weight room, an athletic field complex, a 1700-seat gym, a 600-seat auditorium and student health and wellness center.

Disabled Students: 73% of the campus is accessible. Facilities include wheelchair ramps, elevators, special parking, specially equipped restrooms, and lowered drinking fountains.

Services: Counseling and information services are available, as is tutoring in every subject. There is remedial math, reading, and writing. Skill-building materials are available on computers.

Campus Safety and Security: Measures include 24-hour foot and vehicle patrol, emergency notification system, and security escort services. There are lighted pathways/sidewalks and controlled access to dorms/residences.

Programs of Study: Morris confers B.A., B.S., B.F.A. and B.S.Ed. degrees. Bachelor's degrees are awarded in BIOLOGICAL SCIENCE (biology/biological science), BUSINESS (business administration and management and recreation and leisure services), COMMUNICATIONS AND THE ARTS (communications and English), COMPUTER AND PHYSICAL SCIENCE (mathematics), EDUCATION (early childhood education, elementary education, English education, mathematics education, science education, and social studies education), HEALTH PROFESSIONS (community health work), SOCIAL SCIENCE (criminal justice, history, liberal arts/general studies, pastoral studies, political science/government, religious education, and sociology). Christian education, English/secondary education, and mathematics are the strongest academically. Business administration, criminal justice, and biology have the largest enrollments.

Required: All students must complete 124 to 146 credit hours, including 36 to 83 in the major, with a 2.0 GPA overall. General education requirements, with a core curriculum of 55 to 61 credits, include 12 credits each in English and social sciences, 8 to 16 in natural sciences, 6 in religion, 4 in fine arts, 3 to 9 in math, 3 in health education, 2 to 3 each in computers and speech, a freshman seminar, a sophomore seminar, and a junior seminar. A comprehensive exam in the major is required prior to graduation.

Special: Internships, co-op programs, and work-study programs on and off campus are offered. A B.S. degree in organizational management is available. A B.S. degree in nursing is offered in conjunction with the University of South Carolina. A cooperative 3-2 engineering degree program with Clemson University and a dual degree in math/engineering with North Carolina A&T University are available. Credit by exam and credit for military experience are possible. There are 1 national honor societies, a freshman honors program, and 1 departmental honors program.

Faculty/Classroom: 54% of faculty are male; 46% are female. All teach undergraduates. No introductory courses are taught by graduate students. The average class size in an introductory lecture is 30; in a laboratory is 20; and in a regular course is 15.

Admissions: 88% of the 2013-2014 applicants were accepted. 3% of the current freshmen were in the top fifth of their class; 16% were in the top two fifths.

Requirements: The SAT or ACT is required. Candidates should be graduates of an accredited secondary school or have the GED. They must have completed 24 Carnegie units, consisting of 4 each in high school English and math, 3 in natural science, 2 in social sciences, and 1 each in U.S. history, phys ed, computer science, and foreign language. Candidate must submit ACT or SAT scores to be used for informational/advising purposes. A GPA of 2.0 is required. AP and CLEP credits are accepted.

Procedure: Freshmen are admitted to all sessions. There are deferred admissions and rolling admissions plans. Applications should be filed by April 30 for fall entry; October 30 for spring entry; and March 30 for summer entry, along with a $20 fee. Applications are accepted online.

Transfer: 50 transfer students enrolled in 2012-2013. Applicants must

submit transcripts and evidence of honorable release. A minimum GPA of 2.0 is required to be admitted in good standing. All other criteria and procedures applicable to freshmen apply to transfers. 30 of 124 credits required for the bachelor's degree must be completed at Morris.

Visiting: There are regularly scheduled orientations for prospective students, consisting of a campus tour, visits with division chairs and faculty members to discuss majors, scheduled activities, and lunch. There are guides for informal visits. To schedule a visit, contact the Admissions Office.

Financial Aid: In 2013-2014, 99% of all full-time freshmen and 99% of continuing full-time students received some form of financial aid. 99% of all full-time freshmen and 98% of continuing full-time students received need-based aid. The average freshman award was $14,500. Need-based scholarships or need-based grants averaged $6,527 ($8,525 maximum); need-based self-help aid (loans and jobs) averaged $3,600 ($5,000 maximum); non-need-based athletic scholarships averaged $1,995 ($5,000 maximum); and other non-need-based awards and non-need-based scholarships averaged $3,792 ($16,806 maximum). 25% of undergraduate students work part-time. Average annual earnings from campus work are $1100. The average financial indebtedness of the 2013 graduate was $19,375. Morris is a member of CSS. The FAFSA and the college's own financial statement are required. The priority date for freshman financial aid applications for fall entry is March 30.

International Students: They must take the TOEFL with a minimum score of 500 on the paper-based TOEFL (PBT).

Graduates: From July 1, 2012 to June 30, 2013, 131 bachelor's degrees were awarded. The most popular majors were criminal justice (18%), business administration (15%), and biology (13%). 52 companies recruited on campus in 2012-2013. In an average class, 16% graduate in 4 years or less, 11% graduate in 5 years or less, and 4% graduate in 6 years or less. Of the 2012 graduating class, 23% were enrolled in graduate school within 6 months of graduation, and 65% were employed.

Admissions Contact: Deborah Calhoun, Director of Admissions and Records. E-Mail: *dcalhoun@morris.edu* Web: *www.morris.edu*

NEWBERRY COLLEGE B-2

Newberry, SC 29108 (803) 321-5127 (800) 845-4955; (803) 321-5138

Full-time: 435 men, 325 women	**Faculty:** 46
Part-time: 10 men, 25 women	**Ph.D.s:** 70%
Graduate: n/av	**Student/Faculty:** 16 to 1
Year: semesters, summer session	**Tuition:** $21,150
Application Deadline: open	**Room & Board:** $5700
Freshman Class: n/av	
SAT or ACT: required	

LESS COMPETITIVE

Newberry College, founded in 1856, is a private liberal arts institution affiliated with the Evangelical Lutheran Church in America. The figures in the above capsule and in this profile are approximate. In addition to regional accreditation, Newberry has baccalaureate program accreditation with NASM and NCATE. The 2 libraries contain 79,464 volumes, 7,153 microform items, and 1,217 audio/video tapes/CDs/DVDs, and subscribe to 258 periodicals including electronic. Computerized library services include interlibrary loans, database searching, and Internet access. Special learning facilities include a radio station, TV station, an herbarium. The 90-acre campus is in a small town 40 miles northwest of Columbia. Including any residence halls, there are 22 buildings.

Student Life: 84% of undergraduates are from South Carolina. Others are from 13 states, 8 foreign countries, and Canada. 90% are from public schools. 71% are White; 26% African American. 80% are Protestant; 12% claim no religious affiliation. The average age of freshmen is 18; all undergraduates, 20. 49% do not continue beyond their first year; 47% remain to graduate.

Housing: 622 students can be accommodated in college housing, which includes single-sex and coed dorms. In addition, there are honors houses. On-campus housing is guaranteed for all 4 years. 77% of students live on campus; of those, 66% remain on campus on weekends. All students may keep cars.

Activities: 11% of men belong to 6 national fraternities; 13% of women belong to 3 national sororities. There are 50 groups on campus, including band, cheerleading, choir, chorale, chorus, computers, dance, drama, ethnic, honors, international, jazz band, literary magazine, marching band, musical theater, newspaper, orchestra, pep band, political, professional, radio and TV, religious, social, social service, student government, and yearbook. Popular campus events include Fall Fling and Spring Fling.

Sports: There are 7 intercollegiate sports for men and 7 for women, and 6 intramural sports for men and 5 for women. Facilities include a 4000-seat stadium, a phys ed complex with a 1600-seat basketball arena and racquetball courts, an outdoor pool, tennis courts, and baseball, softball, and soccer fields.

Disabled Students: 90% of the campus is accessible. Facilities include wheelchair ramps, elevators, special parking, specially equipped restrooms, and special class scheduling.

Services: Counseling and information services are available, as is tutoring in most subjects. There is remedial math, reading, and writing.

Campus Safety and Security: Measures include 24-hour foot and vehicle patrol and security escort services. There are emergency telephones and lighted pathways/sidewalks.

Programs of Study: Newberry confers B.A., B.S., B.M. and B.M.E. degrees. Bachelor's degrees are awarded in BIOLOGICAL SCIENCE (biology/biological science), BUSINESS (business administration and management), COMMUNICATIONS AND THE ARTS (applied music, art, communications, dramatic arts, English, French, German, languages, music, music performance, music theory and composition, and Spanish), COMPUTER AND PHYSICAL SCIENCE (chemistry, computer science, and mathematics), EDUCATION (early childhood education, elementary education, music education, and physical education), HEALTH PROFESSIONS (veterinary science), SOCIAL SCIENCE (history, philosophy, political science/government, psychology, religion, and sociology). Education and natural sciences is the strongest academically. Business administration, education, and physical education have the largest enrollments.

Required: To graduate, students must complete 126 semester hours, with a minimum GPA of 2.0. Core curriculum requirements include 10 to 11 hours of math and natural science, 9 each of communication skills, humanities or fine arts, and history or social sciences, up to 6 of foreign language, 3 of religion, and 2 of phys ed. There is also a 24-event fine arts and lectures requirement. All students must fulfill Communications Across the Curriculum writing projects.

Special: Internships, dual and student-designed majors, study abroad, a Washington semester, work-study programs, independent study, and cooperative education are offered. A 3-2 engineering degree program with Clemson University, a 3-2 forestry program with Duke University, a 3-3 cytotechnology program, and a 3-1 medical technology program are available. Nondegree study is possible. There are 3 national honor societies, a freshman honors program, and 3 departmental honors programs.

Faculty/Classroom: 58% of faculty are male; 41% are female. All teach undergraduates. No introductory courses are taught by graduate students. The average class size in an introductory lecture is 30; in a laboratory is 30; and in a regular course is 25.

Requirements: The SAT or ACT is required. Applicants should have completed 18 high school academic units, including 4 of English, 3 each of math and social science (1 of U.S. history), 2 each of lab science and a foreign language, and 1 elective. The GED is accepted. An essay is recommended. A GPA of 2.0 is required. AP and CLEP credits are accepted. Important factors in the admissions decision are leadership record, evidence of special talent, and recommendations by school officials.

Procedure: Freshmen are admitted to all sessions. Entrance exams should be taken in the spring of the junior year or the fall of the senior year. There are deferred admissions and rolling admissions plans. Application deadlines are open. The fall 2013 application fee was $30.

Transfer: 57 transfer students enrolled in 2012-2013. Applicants must be eligible to return to their previous school. A 2.0 minimum GPA is recommended. 32 of 126 credits required for the bachelor's degree must be completed at Newberry.

Visiting: There are regularly scheduled orientations for prospective students, including a campus tour, informational sessions, and meetings with faculty, staff, and students. There are guides for informal visits, visitors may sit in on classes, and stay overnight. To schedule a visit, contact the Admissions Office.

Financial Aid: In 2013-2014, 91% of all full-time freshmen and 96% of continuing full-time students received some form of financial aid. 63% of all full-time freshmen and 65% of continuing full-time students received need-based aid. The average freshman award was $12,450.. 12% of undergraduate students work part-time. Average annual earnings from campus work are $625. The average financial indebtedness of the 2013 graduate was $3,135. Newberry is a member of CSS. The FAFSA is required. The priority date for freshman financial aid applications for fall entry is March 30. The deadline for filing freshman financial aid applications for fall entry is May 15.

International Students: There are 8 international students enrolled. The school actively recruits these students. They must take the TOEFL and the college's own test. They must also take the SAT or ACT, scoring 900.

Graduates: The most popular majors were business and management (16%), education (13%), and social sciences and history (9%). 124 companies recruited on campus in 2012-2013. Of the 2012 graduating class, 20% were enrolled in graduate school within 6 months of graduation, and 60% were employed.

Admissions Contact: Director of Admissions E-Mail: *admissions@newberry.edu* Web: *www.newberry.edu*

PRESBYTERIAN COLLEGE B-2

Clinton, SC 29325 (864) 833-8258
(800) 960-7583; (864) 833-8195

Full-time: 490 men, 597 women	**Faculty:** 77; IIB, -$
Part-time: 16 men, 20 women	**Ph.D.s:** 96%
Graduate: 92 men, 218 women	**Student/Faculty:** 14 to 1
Year: semesters, summer session	**Tuition:** $33,650
Application Deadline: February 1	**Room & Board:** $9028
Freshman Class: 1650 applied, 1089 accepted, 296 enrolled	
SAT CR/M: 550/550 **ACT:** 24	**VERY COMPETITIVE**

Presbyterian College, founded in 1880, is a private liberal arts institution affiliated with the Presbyterian Church. PC also has a school of pharmacy that offers a doctorate in pharmacy. There is one undergraduate school and one graduate school. In addition to regional accreditation, PC has baccalaureate program accreditation with NASM and NCATE. The library contains 121,499 volumes, 6,866 microform items, 12,866 audio/video tapes/CDs/DVDs, and subscribes to 8,134 periodicals including electronic. Computerized library services include interlibrary loans, database searching, Internet access, and Wi-Fi capability. Special learning facilities include an art gallery. The 240-acre campus is in a small town 40 miles south of Greenville. Including any residence halls, there are 74 buildings.

Student Life: 65% of undergraduates are from South Carolina. Others are from 33 states, and 23 foreign countries. 80% are White; 11% African American. 80% are Protestant. The average age of freshmen is 18; all undergraduates, 20. 14% do not continue beyond their first year; 68% remain to graduate.

Housing: 1151 students can be accommodated in college housing, which includes single-sex and coed dorms, on-campus apartments, and off-campus apartments. In addition, there are special-interest houses, fraternity houses, Carol International House serves as housing for international students and students with an interest in studying abroad or experiencing international cultures. On-campus housing is guaranteed for all 4 years. 100% of students live on campus; of those, 75% remain on campus on weekends. All students may keep cars.

Activities: 38% of men belong to 6 national fraternities; 47% of women belong to 3 national sororities. There are 85 groups on campus, including art, band, cheerleading, choir, chorale, chorus, computers, dance, drama, environmental, ethnic, gay, honors, international, jazz band, literary magazine, newspaper, orchestra, pep band, photography, political, professional, religious, social, social service, student government, and yearbook. Popular campus events include Fall Fling, Spring Swing, and Greek Week.

Sports: There are 7 intercollegiate sports for men and 8 for women, and 9 intramural sports for men and 9 for women. Facilities include A physical education center, tennis courts, a soccer stadium, a baseball complex, a softball complex, and two additional stadiums. Springs Campus Center contains a canteen, table tennis and pool tables, a fitness center, an aerobics room, and a gym.

Disabled Students: 95% of the campus is accessible. Facilities include wheelchair ramps, elevators, special parking, specially equipped restrooms, lowered drinking fountains, and special housing.

Services: Counseling and information services are available, as is tutoring in every subject. There is a reader service for the blind.

Campus Safety and Security: Measures include 24-hour foot and vehicle patrol, emergency notification system, and security escort services. There are shuttle buses, emergency telephones, lighted pathways/sidewalks, controlled access to dorms/residences, 24-hour key card dorm locks.

Programs of Study: PC confers B.A., and B.S. degrees. Doctoral degrees are also awarded. Bachelor's degrees are awarded in BIOLOGICAL SCIENCE (biochemistry and biology/biological science), BUSINESS (business administration and management and business economics), COMMUNICATIONS AND THE ARTS (art, art history and appreciation, dramatic arts, English, French, modern language, music, Spanish, and visual and performing arts), COMPUTER AND PHYSICAL SCIENCE (chemistry, mathematics, medical physics, and physics), EDUCATION (early childhood education, middle school education, and music education), HEALTH PROFESSIONS (pharmacy), SOCIAL SCIENCE (history, international studies, political science/government, psychology, religion, religious education, and sociology). All majors are academically strong. Business administration, biology, and history have the largest enrollments.

Required: To graduate, students must complete a minimum of 122 semester hours, including 30 to 48 in the major, with a minimum GPA of 2.0. Distribution requirements include 8 hours of natural science, 6 each of English, history, social science, and religion, 4 to 6 of intercultural experience, 3 each of math and fine arts, 2 to 3 of phys ed, 1 to 3 each of freshman experience and senior capstone, and up to 7 of foreign language.

Special: Educational internships, study abroad in 25 countries, and a Washington semester are available. Dual majors, work-study programs, accelerated degree programs, B.A.-B.S. degrees, and a 3-2 engineering degree with Auburn, Clemson, and Vanderbilt Universities are offered. There is a forestry environmental studies program with Duke University. Credit for military experience, auditing courses, and pass/fail options are possible. There are 10 national honor societies, a freshman honors program, and 17 departmental honors programs.

Faculty/Classroom: 59% of faculty are male; 41% are female. All teach undergraduates, all do research, and all teach and do research. No introductory courses are taught by graduate students. The average class size in an introductory lecture is 20; in a laboratory is 15; and in a regular course is 15.

Admissions: 66% of the 2013-2014 applicants were accepted. The SAT scores for the 2013-2014 freshman class were: Critical Reading--27% below 500, 46% between 500 and 599, 24% between 600 and 699, and 3% between 700 and 800; Math--18% below 500, 50% between 500 and 599, 28% between 600 and 699, and 4% between 700 and 800. The ACT scores were 16% below 21, 26% between 21 and 23, 24% between 24 and 26, 15% between 27 and 28, and 19% above 28. 52% of the current freshmen were in the top fifth of their class; 84% were in the top two fifths.

Requirements: Applicants must be graduates of an accredited secondary school with 18 academic credits, including 4 years of English, 3 of math, and 2 or more each of foreign language, history, science, and social studies. The GED is accepted. An essay is required. For music scholarships, an audition is required. Depending on high school GPA, some students will be required to submit either SAT or ACT scores. A GPA of 2.0 is required. AP and CLEP credits are accepted. Important factors in the admissions decision are advanced placement or honors courses, recommendations by school officials, and leadership record.

Procedure: Freshmen are admitted to all sessions. Entrance exams should be taken during the spring of the junior year. There are early decision, early admissions, deferred admissions, and rolling admissions plans. Early decision applications should be filed by November 1; regular applications, by February 1 for fall entry; and December 1 for spring entry. Notification of early decision is sent December 1; regular decision, March 15. 35 early decision candidates were accepted for the 2013-2014 class. Applications are accepted online. Application fees are waived if application is completed online.

Transfer: 12 transfer students enrolled in 2012-2013. 48 of 122 credits required for the bachelor's degree must be completed at PC.

Visiting: There are regularly scheduled orientations for prospective students, Academics, student activity, financial aid information, tour, and lunch. There are guides for informal visits, visitors may sit in on classes, and stay overnight. To schedule a visit, contact the Office of Admissions.

Financial Aid: In 2013-2014, 85% of all full-time freshmen and 85% of continuing full-time students received some form of financial aid. 95% of all full-time freshmen and 85% of continuing full-time students received need-based aid. The average freshman award was $31,000. Need-based scholarships or need-based grants averaged $30,263; need-based self-help aid (loans and jobs) averaged $3,438; and non-need-based athletic scholarships averaged $18,000. 41% of undergraduate students work part-time. Average annual earnings from campus work are $1004. The average financial indebtedness of the 2013 graduate was $21,211. PC is a member of CSS. The FAFSA and the college's own financial statement are required. The priority date for freshman financial aid applications for fall entry is March 15. The deadline for filing freshman financial aid applications for fall entry is June 30.

International Students: There are 44 international students enrolled. The school actively recruits these students. They must take the TOEFL with a minimum score of 550 on the paper-based TOEFL (PBT) or 80 on the Internet-based version (iBT). They must also take the SAT or ACT.

Graduates: From July 1, 2012 to June 30, 2013, 266 bachelor's degrees were awarded. The most popular majors were business administration (18%), biology (14%), and English (11%). 60 companies recruited on campus in 2012-2013. In an average class, 60% graduate in 4 years or less, 68% graduate in 5 years or less, and 68% graduate in 6 years or less. Of the 2012 graduating class, 40% were enrolled in graduate school within 6 months of graduation, and 54% were employed.

Admissions Contact: Brian J. Fortman, Dean of Enrollment Management. E-Mail: *admissions@presby.edu* Web: *www.presby.edu*

SOUTH CAROLINA STATE UNIVERSITY C-3

Orangeburg, SC 29117 (803) 536-7186
(800) 260-5956; (803) 536-8990

Full-time: 1600 men, 2000 women	**Faculty:** 211
Part-time: 120 men, 300 women	**Ph.D.s:** 62%
Graduate: 120 men, 530 women	**Student/Faculty:** n/av
Year: semesters, summer session	**Tuition:** $9258 ($18,170)
Application Deadline: May 31	**Room & Board:** $8986
Freshman Class: n/av	
SAT or ACT: required	**LESS COMPETITIVE**

South Carolina State University, a historically black, land-grant institution founded in 1896, offers undergraduate programs in liberal arts and sciences, business, education, engineering technology, and human sciences. There are 5 undergraduate schools and 1 graduate school. The figures in the above capsule and in this profile are approximate. In addition to regional accreditation, SCSU has baccalaureate program accreditation with ABET, ADA, AHEA, CSWE, NASDTEC, and NCATE. The library contains 277,438 volumes, 686,225 microform items, and subscribes to 1394 periodicals including electronic. Computerized library services include interlibrary loans and database searching. Special learning facilities include a learning resource center, art gallery, planetarium, radio station, and instructional media center. The 160-acre campus is in a small town 40 miles east of Columbia. Including any residence halls, there are 60 buildings.

Student Life: 83% of undergraduates are from South Carolina. 95% are African American. The average age of freshmen is 18; all undergraduates, 19. 22% do not continue beyond their first year; 32% remain to graduate.

Housing: 2242 students can be accommodated in college housing, which includes single-sex dorms and married student housing. On-campus housing is available on a first-come, first-served basis and is available on a lottery system for upperclassmen. 80% of students live on campus. Alcohol is not permitted. Upperclassmen may keep cars.

Activities: 25% of men belong to 4 national fraternities; 32% of women belong to 4 national sororities. There are 85 groups on campus, including band, cheerleading, choir, chorus, dance, drama, drill team, honors, international, jazz band, marching band, newspaper, orchestra, pep band, political, religious, social, social service, student government, and yearbook. Popular campus events include Colloquium Series, Game Nights, and Bulldog Fest.

Sports: There are 7 intercollegiate sports for men and 8 for women, and 8 intramural sports for men and 7 for women. Facilities include a student center with a game room and bowling alley, a gym, tennis courts, a 22,000-seat stadium, an 8-lane asphalt track, and swimming pools.

Disabled Students: 60% of the campus is accessible. Facilities include wheelchair ramps, elevators, special parking, specially equipped rest rooms, lowered drinking fountains, and lowered telephones.

Services: Counseling and information services are available, as is tutoring in most subjects. There is a reader service for the blind, and remedial math, reading, and writing. Free counseling is also available.

Campus Safety and Security: Measures include 24-hour foot and vehicle patrol. There are shuttle buses, lighted pathways/sidewalks, and a campus police department with 25 safety and security officers.

Programs of Study: SCSU confers B.A. and B.S. degrees. Master's and doctoral degrees are also awarded. Bachelor's degrees are awarded in AGRICULTURE (agricultural business management), BIOLOGICAL SCIENCE (biology/biological science and nutrition), BUSINESS (accounting, business administration and management, business economics, marketing/retailing/merchandising, and office supervision and management), COMMUNICATIONS AND THE ARTS (dramatic arts, English, fine arts, French, music business management, and Spanish), COMPUTER AND PHYSICAL SCIENCE (chemistry, computer science, mathematics, and physics), EDUCATION (art education, business education, early childhood education, elementary education, guidance education, health education, home economics education, industrial arts education, music education, physical education, reading education, and special education), ENGINEERING AND ENVIRONMENTAL DESIGN (civil engineering technology, electrical/electronics engineering technology, engineering technology, and mechanical engineering technology), HEALTH PROFESSIONS (nursing and speech pathology/audiology), SOCIAL SCIENCE (criminal justice, food science, history, human services, political science/government, psychology, social studies, social work, and sociology). Science, engineering technology, and business education are the strongest academically.

Required: To graduate, all students must complete at least 128 credit hours with a minimum GPA of 2.0. Students must attend the freshman orientation program, take a general education exam in their sophomore year, satisfy the general education program requirements, and pass an English proficiency test.

Special: The university offers co-op education and work-study programs, cross-registration with Claflin College, internships, study abroad in 2 countries, combined B.A.-B.S. degrees, credit for educational and work experience, nondegree study, and pass/fail options for juniors and seniors. Also available are an electrical engineering technology program at Midlands, Greenville, and Trident Technical Colleges, an evening school program, and a program for educationally disadvantaged students who do not meet traditional entrance requirements. There are 12 national honor societies and a freshman honors program.

Faculty/Classroom: No introductory courses are taught by graduate students.

Requirements: The SAT or ACT is required. Applicants must rank in the upper half of their graduating class at an accredited secondary school. The GED is accepted. High school preparation should include 4 units of English, 3 of math, 2 each of foreign language and lab science, and 1 each of history, social studies, and phys ed or ROTC, plus 1/2 unit each in economics and government. A GPA of 2.0 is required. AP and CLEP credits are accepted. Important factors in the admissions decision are advanced placement or honors courses, leadership record, and personality/intangible qualities.

Procedure: Freshmen are admitted fall and spring. Entrance exams should be taken before filing an application. Applications should be filed by May 31 for fall entry and October 31 for spring entry, along with a $25 fee.

Transfer: Transfer applicants should have a college GPA of 2.0. Students with fewer than 30 credit hours must submit high school and college transcripts and SAT or ACT scores. 30 of 128 credits required for the bachelor's degree must be completed at SCSU.

Visiting: There are guides for informal visits, and visitors may sit in on classes. To schedule a visit, contact the Office of Admissions and Recruitment.

Financial Aid: SCSU is a member of CSS. The CSS/Profile is required. Check with the school for current deadlines.

International Students: They must take the TOEFL. They must also take the ACT or SAT, scoring 830 on the SAT.

Admissions Contact: Director of Admissions. E-Mail: *admissions@scsu.edu* Web: *www.scsu.edu*

SOUTHERN WESLEYAN UNIVERSITY A-2

Central, SC 29630-1020 (864) 644-5550
(800) 282-8798; (864) 644-5972

Full-time: 615 men, 1030 women	**Faculty:** 44
Part-time: 10 men, 20 women	**Ph.D.s:** 75%
Graduate: 200 men, 510 women	**Student/Faculty:** n/av
Year: semesters, summer session	**Tuition:** $20,550
Application Deadline: see profile	**Room & Board:** $8050
Freshman Class: n/av	
SAT or ACT: required	
	COMPETITIVE

Southern Wesleyan University, founded in 1906 and affiliated with the Wesleyan Church, is a private liberal arts institution that is a part of the Council for Christian Colleges and Universities. There are 3 undergraduate schools and 3 graduate schools. In addition to regional accreditation, SWU has baccalaureate program accreditation with NASDTEC and NCATE. The library contains 116,200 volumes, 2160 microform items, 5755 audio/video tapes/CDs/DVDs, and subscribes to 510 periodicals including electronic. Computerized library services include interlibrary loans, database searching, and Internet access. Special learning facilities include a learning resource center, electron microscope lab, genealogical research collection, and Freedom's Hill Historic Site. The 325-acre campus is in a small town 30 miles southwest of Greenville and 5 miles from Clemson. Including any residence halls, there are 30 buildings.

Student Life: 83% of undergraduates are from South Carolina. Students are from 23 states, 18 foreign countries, and Canada. 78% are white; 13% African American. 82% are Protestant. The average age of freshmen is 18; all undergraduates, 21. 33% do not continue beyond their first year; 46% remain to graduate.

Housing: 517 students can be accommodated in college housing, which includes single-sex and coed dorms and on-campus apartments. On-campus housing is guaranteed for all 4 years. 62% of students live on campus; of those, 50% remain on campus on weekends. Alcohol is not permitted. All students may keep cars.

Activities: There are no fraternities or sororities. There are 15 groups on campus, including band, cheerleading, choir, chorale, chorus, computers, drama, ethnic, honors, jazz band, literary magazine, musical theater, orchestra, professional, religious, social, social service, student government, and yearbook. Popular campus events include Christmas Banquet, Junior/Senior Banquet, and Coffee House.

Sports: There are 5 intercollegiate sports for men and 5 for women, and 5 intramural sports for men and 4 for women. Facilities include a tennis court, soccer, softball, and baseball fields, a fitness center, and a cross-country trail.

Disabled Students: 80% of the campus is accessible. Facilities include wheelchair ramps, elevators, special parking, specially equipped rest rooms, and special housing.

Services: Counseling and information services are available, as is tutoring in most subjects. There is a reader service for the blind, and remedial math, reading, and writing. Supplemental instruction is available for biology.

Campus Safety and Security: There are emergency telephones, lighted pathways/sidewalks, an overnight security officer, and a patrolled campus.

Programs of Study: SWU confers B.A. and B.S. degrees. Associate and master's degrees are also awarded. Bachelor's degrees are awarded in BIOLOGICAL SCIENCE (biology/biological science), BUSINESS (business administration and management, recreation and leisure services, and sports management), COMMUNICATIONS AND THE ARTS (communications, English, and music), COMPUTER AND PHYSICAL SCIENCE (chemistry, computer science, and mathematics), EDUCATION (early childhood education, elementary education, English education, mathematics education, music education, physical education, and special education), ENGINEERING AND ENVIRONMENTAL DESIGN (computer technology), HEALTH PROFESSIONS (medical laboratory technology), SOCIAL SCIENCE (criminal justice, forensic studies, history, human services, psychology, religion, and social studies). Education, business, and biology have the largest enrollments.

Required: To graduate, students must complete 128 credit hours with 54 hours in general education courses and a minimum GPA of 2.0. All students must take 12 hours each of English and religion, 6 of history, 3 of social sciences, 3 of math or statistics, and 2 science lab courses. Specific required courses include aesthetics, introduction to computer science, phys ed, and interdisciplinary seminars.

Special: Students can participate in the study-abroad program via the CCCU Best Semester Program in Australia, China, Costa Rica, Egypt, England, Russia, and Uganda. Other off-campus study options include the American Studies Program in Washington, D.C., the Los Angeles Film Studies Program, the Contemporary Music Center, and the Summer Institute of Journalism. There are 2 national honor societies, a freshman honors program, and 7 departmental honors programs.

Faculty/Classroom: 62% of faculty are male; 38% are female. All teach and do research. No introductory courses are taught by graduate students. The average class size in an introductory lecture is 22 and in a laboratory is 18.

Admissions: 94% of a recent year's applicants were accepted. 22 freshmen graduated first in their class.

Requirements: The SAT or ACT is required. Applicants should complete 16 Carnegie units, including 4 credits of English and 2 each of math, science, and social studies, as well as 6 electives. The GED is accepted. SWU requires applicants to be in the upper 50% of their class. A GPA of 2.3 is required. AP and CLEP credits are accepted.

Procedure: Freshmen are admitted fall and spring. There are early admissions, deferred admissions, and rolling admissions plans. Application deadlines are open. Application fee is $25. Notification is sent on a rolling basis. Applications are accepted online.

Transfer: 53 transfer students enrolled in a recent year. Transfer students must have a minimum college GPA of 2.0. 30 of 120 credits required for the bachelor's degree must be completed at SWU.

Visiting: There are regularly scheduled orientations for prospective students. There are guides for informal visits, and visitors may sit in on classes, and stay overnight. To schedule a visit, contact the Admissions Office.

Financial Aid: In a recent year, 94% of all full-time freshmen and 93% of continuing full-time students received some form of financial aid, including need-based aid. 76% of undergraduate students work part-time. The average financial indebtedness of a recent year's graduate was $23,055. The FAFSA and the college's own financial statement are required. Check with the school for current application deadlines.

International Students: There were 12 international students enrolled in a recent year. They must take the TOEFL with a minimum score of 500 on the paper-based TOEFL (PBT) or 173 on the Internet-based version (iBT). They must also take the SAT or ACT.

Graduates: In a recent year, 119 bachelor's degrees were awarded. The most popular majors were business (16%), psychology (11%), and religion (9%). In an average class, 34% graduate in 4 years or less, 44% graduate in 5 years or less, and 49% graduate in 6 years or less. Of a recent year's graduating class, 20% were enrolled in graduate school within 6 months of graduation, and 70% were employed.

Admissions Contact: Director of Admissions. E-Mail: *admissions@swu.edu* Web: *www.swu.edu*

UNIVERSITY OF SOUTH CAROLINA SYSTEM

The University of South Carolina System, established in 1801, is a private system in South Carolina. It is governed by a board of trustees, whose chief administrator is the president. The primary goal of the system is to prepare informed and productive citizens in order to adapt to an increasingly complex environment. The main priorities are to foster excellence in undergraduate and graduate education, research, and service programs. The total student enrollment for all 9 campuses is usually 41,148 with 2500 faculty members. Altogether there are 76 baccalaureate, 105 master's, and 56 doctoral programs offered in the University of South Carolina System. Profiles of the 4-year campuses are included in this section.

UNIVERSITY OF SOUTH CAROLINA AT AIKEN — C-3

Aiken, SC 29801 (803) 641-3366
(888) WOW-USCA; (803) 641-3727

Full-time: 875 men, 1540 women	**Faculty:** 142; IIB, --$
Part-time: 276 men, 478 women	**Ph.D.s:** 75%
Graduate: 27 men, 95 women	**Student/Faculty:** 17 to 1
Year: semesters, summer session	**Tuition:** $9308 ($18,340)
Application Deadline: open 1	**Room & Board:** $6970
Freshman Class: n/av	
SAT CR/M/W: 510/500/460	**ACT:** 22 **COMPETITIVE**

The University of South Carolina Aiken, founded in 1961 is a comprehensive liberal arts institution committed to active learning through teaching, faculty and student scholarship, research, creative activities and service. The university offers degrees in the arts and sciences and in the professional disciplines of business, education, and nursing. There are 5 undergraduate schools and 2 graduate schools. In addition to regional accreditation, USCA has baccalaureate program accreditation with AACSB, ABET, NASM, and NCATE. The library contains 211,251 volumes, 79,896 microform items, 4,088 audio/video tapes/CDs/DVDs, and subscribes to 29,776 periodicals including electronic. Computerized library services include interlibrary loans, database searching, Internet access, and Wi-Fi capability. Special learning facilities include an art gallery, planetarium, a science education center, and a language lab. The 453-acre campus is in a suburban area 14 miles east of Augusta, Georgia. Including any residence halls, there are 25 buildings.

Student Life: 87% of undergraduates are from South Carolina. Others are from 35 states, 25 foreign countries, and Canada. 93% are from public schools. 61% are White; 26% African American. The average age of freshmen is 18; all undergraduates, 23. 34% do not continue beyond their first year; 43% remain to graduate.

Housing: 950 students can be accommodated in college housing, which includes coed dorms and on-campus apartments. On-campus housing is available on a first-come, first-served basis, and is available on a lottery system for upperclassmen. 73% of students commute. All students may keep cars.

Activities: 6% of men belong to 6 national fraternities; 11% of women belong to 6 national sororities. There are 100 groups on campus, including and veterans, band, cheerleading, choir, chorus, computers, dance, drama, ethnic, gay, honors, international, jazz band, literary magazine, musical theater, newspaper, nontraditional students, pep band, photography, political, professional, religious, social, social service, and student government. Popular campus events include Waterfest, Homecoming, Greek Life Recruitment Week, Dance Marathon, and Relay for Life.

Sports: There are 5 intercollegiate sports for men and 6 for women, and 9 intramural sports for men and 9 for women. Facilities include an activities center, the Roberto Hernandez baseball stadium, a soccer/intramural/softball field, tennis courts, and a wellness/exercise center.

Disabled Students: All of the campus is accessible. Facilities include wheelchair ramps, elevators, special parking, specially equipped restrooms, lowered drinking fountains, lowered telephones.

Services: Counseling and information services are available, as is tutoring in most subjects, math and writing There is a reader service for the blind.

Campus Safety and Security: Measures include 24-hour foot and vehicle patrol, emergency notification system, self-defense education, and security escort services. There are emergency telephones, lighted pathways/sidewalks, and controlled access to dorms/residences.

Programs of Study: USCA confers B.A., B.S., B.S.(in Business Administration), B.A.Ed, B.S.Ed, B.A.Spec.Ed, B.A.I.S, B.S.N. and B.S.I.S. degrees. Master's degrees are also awarded. Bachelor's degrees are awarded in BIOLOGICAL SCIENCE (biology/biological science), BUSINESS (business administration and management), COMMUNICATIONS AND THE ARTS (communications, English, and fine arts), COMPUTER AND PHYSICAL SCIENCE (applied mathematics, chemistry, and computer mathematics), EDUCATION (early childhood education, elementary education, middle school education, music education, secondary education, and special education), HEALTH PROFESSIONS (exercise science and nursing), SOCIAL SCIENCE (history, interdisciplinary studies, political science/government, psychology, and sociology). English, early childhood education, nursing, and elementary education are the strongest academically. Business, education, and nursing have the largest enrollments.

Required: Students must complete a minimum of 120 credit hours, with at least a 2.0 GPA. USC Aiken has a strong liberal arts emphasis. General education requirements include courses in English, math, applied speech, natural science, social and behavioral sciences, humanities, non-western studies course, and history. In addition, students must complete a critical inquiry course, a prescribed number of writing intensive courses and intercurricular enrichment events.

Special: Cross-registration is permitted with other schools in the University of South Carolina system. Co-op programs,internships, study abroad, student-designed majors, and work-study programs are offered. B.A.-B.S. degrees in Interdisciplinary Studies, nondegree study, and pass/fail options are possible. There are 12 national honor societies, a freshman honors program, and 13 departmental honors programs.

Faculty/Classroom: 49% of faculty are male; 51% are female. All teach undergraduates, 42% do research, and 41% do both. No introductory courses are taught by graduate students. The average class size in an introductory lecture is 17 and in a laboratory is 15.

Admissions: The SAT scores for the 2013-2014 freshman class were: Critical Reading--56% below 500, 35% between 500 and 599, 9% between 600 and 699; Math--60% below 500, 32% between 500 and 599, 8% between 600 and 699; Writing--67% below 500, 28% between 500 and 599, 5% between 600 and 699. The ACT scores were 55% below 21, 23% between 21 and 23, 16% between 24 and 26, 4% between 27 and 28, and 3% above 28. 29% of the current freshmen were in the top fifth of their class; 60% were in the top two fifths. 2 freshmen graduated first in their class.

Requirements: The SAT is required. The ACT and ACT Writing Test are recommended. Admission is based on a combination of an applicant's scores on college entrance exams and high school GPA. Applicants are required to submit 21 academic credits, including 4 years of high school English, 3 units of math, 3 units of social studies, 2 units of foreign language, 3 units of a lab science, 1 of US history, and 1 year of phys ed or ROTC, and 4 electives from 3 different areas such as computer science, English, fine arts, foreign language, humanities, certain lab sciences, a math above algebra II, and social science. It is strongly suggested that 1 be in computer science programming. AP and CLEP credits are accepted. Important factors in the admissions decision are advanced placement or honors courses, recommendations by school officials, and leadership record.

Procedure: Freshmen are admitted to all sessions. Entrance exams should be taken by the fall of the senior year. There are early admissions, deferred admissions, and rolling admissions plans. Application deadlines are open. The fall 2013 application fee was $45. Notification is sent on a rolling basis. Applications are accepted online.

Transfer: 443 transfer students enrolled in 2012-2013. The college GPA is considered. A high school transcript is required of applicants with fewer than 30 semester hours. 30 of 120 credits required for the bachelor's degree must be completed at USCA.

Visiting: There are regularly scheduled orientations for prospective students, including regularly scheduled 3-day orientations for prospective students. There are guides for informal visits and visitors may sit in on classes. To schedule a visit, contact the Admissions Office.

Financial Aid: In 2013-2014, 94% of all full-time freshmen and 89% of continuing full-time students received some form of financial aid. 73% of all full-time freshmen and 66% of continuing full-time students received need-based aid. The average freshman award was $9,839. 2% of undergraduate students work part-time. Average annual earnings from campus work are $664. The average financial indebtedness of the 2013 graduate was $19,848. The FAFSA is required. The priority date for freshman financial aid applications for fall entry is February 15. The deadline for filing freshman financial aid applications for fall entry is March 15.

International Students: There are 50 international students enrolled. They must take the TOEFL with a minimum score of 550 on the paper-based TOEFL (PBT) or 80 on the Internet-based version (iBT). They must also take the SAT or ACT.

Graduates: From July 1, 2012 to June 30, 2013, 536 bachelor's degrees were awarded. The most popular majors were business (24%), nursing (16%), and education (12%). 138 companies recruited on campus in 2012-2013. In an average class, 19% graduate in 4 years or less, 37% graduate in 5 years or less, and 43% graduate in 6 years or less.

Admissions Contact: Andrew Hendrix, Director of Admissions. E-Mail: *AndrewH@usca.edu* Web: *http:/web.usca.edu/*

UNIVERSITY OF SOUTH CAROLINA AT COLUMBIA C-3

Columbia, SC 29208 **(803) 777-7700**
(800) 868-5872; (803) 777-0101

Full-time: 9849 men, 11797 women	**Faculty:** 854; I, --$
Part-time: 898 men, 819 women	**Ph.D.s:** 84%
Graduate: 3268 men, 4657 women	**Student/Faculty:** 25 to 1
Year: semesters, summer session	**Tuition:** $10,816 ($28,528)
Application Deadline: December 1	**Room & Board:** $8909

Freshman Class: 23429 applied, 14199 accepted, 4625 enrolled
SAT CR/M: 590/610 **ACT:** 27 **VERY COMPETITIVE+**

The University of South Carolina at Columbia, founded in 1801, is a publicly assisted institution serving the entire state of South Carolina. In addition to the main campus at Columbia, there are 3 senior campuses at Aiken, Beaufort, and Upstate, and 4 regional campuses at Lancaster, Salkehatchie, Sumter, and Union. There are 11 undergraduate schools and 12 graduate schools. In addition to regional accreditation, USC has baccalaureate program accreditation with AACSB, ABET, ACEJMC, ACPE, CSAB, NASM, NCATE, and NLN. The 7 libraries contain 4.5 million volumes, and 5.5 million microform items. Computerized library services include interlibrary loans, database searching, Internet access, and Wi-Fi capability. Special learning facilities include an art gallery, natural history museum, planetarium, radio station, and TV station. The 444-acre campus is in an urban area in the downtown area of Columbia. Including any residence halls, there are 181 buildings.

Student Life: 65% of undergraduates are from South Carolina. Others are from 50 states, 115 foreign countries, and Canada. 77% are White; 11% African American. The average age of freshmen is 18; all undergraduates, 21. 13% do not continue beyond their first year; 72% remain to graduate.

Housing: 6838 students can be accommodated in college housing, which includes single-sex and coed dorms, on-campus apartments, and married student housing. In addition, there are honors houses, special-interest houses, fraternity houses, sorority houses, Honors, Wellness, Residential College, Pre-Medical, Pre-Law, French, Spanish, Journalism, Engineering, Athletic, Music, Global, Common Courses Programs and Environmentally Friendly. On-campus housing is guaranteed for the freshman year only and is available on a lottery system for upperclassmen. 64% of students commute. All students may keep cars.

Activities: 13% of men belong to 22 national fraternities; 28% of women belong to 16 national sororities. There are 387 groups on campus, including art, band, cheerleading, chess, choir, chorale, chorus, computers, dance, debate, drama, drill team, ethnic, film, forensics, gay, honors, international, jazz band, literary magazine, marching band, musical theater, newspaper, opera, orchestra, pep band, photography, political, professional, radio and TV, religious, social, social service, student government, symphony, and yearbook. Popular campus events include First-Year Reading Experience, Civil Rights Tour, Parents Weekend, Alternative Spring and Fall Break Trips, Homecoming Week and Carolina Cares.

Sports: There are 9 intercollegiate sports for men and 11 for women, and 29 intramural sports for men and 29 for women. Facilities include football and soccer stadiums, a basketball coliseum, a field house, a volleyball and basketball practice facility, baseball, softball, and practice fields, and an all-weather track. There is also a recreation center with badminton, basketball, handball/racquetball, an aquatics center, climbing wall, and weight room.

Disabled Students: 85% of the campus is accessible. Facilities include wheelchair ramps, elevators, special parking, specially equipped restrooms, special class scheduling, lowered drinking fountains, special housing. listening devices, sign language interpreting, and adapted transportation and computers.

Services: Counseling and information services are available, as is tutoring in every subject, reader services for LD students. There is a reader service for the blind.

Campus Safety and Security: Measures include 24-hour foot and vehicle patrol, emergency notification system, self-defense education, and security escort services. There are shuttle buses, emergency telephones, lighted pathways/sidewalks, controlled access to dorms/residences, All police officers have state wide police authority.

Programs of Study: USC confers B.A., B.A.I.S., B.A.I.S., B.A.J.M.C., B.F.A., B.M., B.S., B.S.B.A., B.S.C., B.S.C.S., B.S.E., B.S.I.S., B.S.N., B.S.P.E., B.S.W. and BarSc. degrees. Associate, master's, and doctoral degrees are also awarded. Bachelor's degrees are awarded in BIOLOGICAL SCIENCE (biology/biological science and marine science), BUSINESS (accounting, banking and finance, business administration and management, business economics, hotel/motel and restaurant management, insurance, management science, marketing/retailing/merchandising, office supervision and management, real estate, retailing, and sports management), COMMUNICATIONS AND THE ARTS (advertising, art history and appreciation, broadcasting, classics, communications, comparative literature, dance, dramatic arts, English, fine arts, French, German, journalism, media arts, music, public relations, Russian, Spanish, speech/debate/rhetoric, and studio art), COMPUTER AND PHYSICAL SCIENCE (chemistry, computer science, geology, geophysics and seismology, mathematics, physics, and statistics), EDUCATION (art education, early childhood education, elementary education, middle school education, music education, and physical education), ENGINEERING AND ENVIRONMENTAL DESIGN (biomedical engineering, chemical engineering, civil engineering, computer engineering, electrical/electronics engineering, environmental science, and mechanical engineering), HEALTH PROFESSIONS (exercise science, nursing, and public health), SOCIAL SCIENCE (African American studies, anthropology, criminal justice, economics, European studies, experimental psychology, geography, history, interdisciplinary studies, Latin American studies, philosophy, political science/government, psychology, religion, social work, sociology, and women's studies). Engineering, business, and nursing are the strongest academically. Biology, nursing, experimental psychology, exercise science, and criminology/criminal justice have the largest enrollments.

Required: All students must maintain a GPA of 2.0 in 120 semester hours including 24 in their major. Distribution requirements include 6 hours in English, 6 in Numerical/Analytical Reasoning, 12 in Liberal Arts, 7 in Natural Sciences, and Foreign Language demonstrated proficiency.

Special: USC transmits live interactive televised instruction to more than

20 locations in the state. Cross-registration is offered with the National Technological University in Engineering and through the National Student Exchange. Internships in many fields, study abroad in many countries through the Byrnes International Center, co-op programs, and work-study programs are available. Double majors through the colleges of humanities and social sciences and science and math, student-designed majors, an interdisciplinary studies degree, and a 3-2 engineering degree with the College of Charleston are offered. Credit for military experience, nondegree study, and pass/fail options also are possible. There are 28 national honor societies, including Phi Beta Kappa, and a freshman honors program.

Faculty/Classroom: 59% of faculty are male; 41% are female. All do research, and 61% do both. No introductory courses are taught by graduate students. The average class size in an introductory lecture is 30; in a laboratory is 23; and in a regular course is 29.

Admissions: 61% of the 2013-2014 applicants were accepted. The SAT scores for the 2013-2014 freshman class were: Critical Reading--10% below 500, 45% between 500 and 599, 36% between 600 and 699, and 10% between 700 and 800; Math--5% below 500, 37% between 500 and 599, 48% between 600 and 699, and 11% between 700 and 800. The ACT scores were 3% below 21, 17% between 21 and 23, 29% between 24 and 26, 22% between 27 and 28, and 29% above 28. 57% of the current freshmen were in the top fifth of their class; 88% were in the top two fifths. There were 47 National Merit finalists. 66 freshmen graduated first in their class.

Requirements: The SAT or ACT is required. Admission as a freshman into the University is primarily based upon a combination of grades earned in specific high-school courses and official SAT or ACT scores. Additional factors may be taken into consideration, such as extraordinary personal circumstances, special talents, outstanding extracurricular activities, and evidence of leadership. A GPA of 2.0 is required. AP and CLEP credits are accepted.

Procedure: Freshmen are admitted to all sessions. Entrance exams should be taken during spring of the junior year and fall of the senior year, if necessary. There is a rolling admissions plan. Applications should be filed by December 1 for fall entry; November 1 for spring entry; and May 1 for summer entry, along with a $50 fee. Applications are accepted online.

Transfer: 1961 transfer students enrolled in 2012-2013. Cumulative GPA of 2.25 from all regionally accredited colleges (remedial courses are not included in the GPA computation). Must meet freshman requirements if the student has attempted fewer than 30 semester hours. Transfer requirements are higher for certain majors. 30 of 120 credits required for the bachelor's degree must be completed at USC.

Visiting: There are regularly scheduled orientations for prospective students, Students take placement tests, are advised and register for classes. Day and a half. There are guides for informal visits. To schedule a visit, contact the USC Visitor's Center.

Financial Aid: In 2013-2014, 96% of all full-time freshmen and 87% of continuing full-time students received some form of financial aid. 47% of all full-time freshmen and 46% of continuing full-time students received need-based aid. The average freshman award was $13,526. Need-based scholarships or need-based grants averaged $7,116 ($27,912 maximum); need-based self-help aid (loans and jobs) averaged $2,358 ($15,500 maximum); non-need-based athletic scholarships averaged $11,747; and other non-need-based awards and non-need-based scholarships averaged $5,304. 15% of undergraduate students work part-time. Average annual earnings from campus work are $2396. USC is a member of CSS. The FAFSA is required. The deadline for filing freshman financial aid applications for fall entry is April 15.

International Students: There are 390 international students enrolled. The school actively recruits these students. They must take the TOEFL with a minimum score of 550 on the paper-based TOEFL (PBT) or 77 on the Internet-based version (iBT). The SAT and ACT are recommended.

Graduates: From July 1, 2012 to June 30, 2013, 7162 bachelor's degrees were awarded. The most popular majors were experimental psychology (6%), integrated IT (6%), and biology (5%). 900 companies recruited on campus in 2012-2013. In an average class, 56% graduate in 4 years or less, 70% graduate in 5 years or less, and 72% graduate in 6 years or less. Of the 2012 graduating class, 23% were enrolled in graduate school within 6 months of graduation.

Admissions Contact: R. Scott Verzyl, Associate Vice President for Enrollment . E-Mail: *admissions-ugrad@sc.edu* Web: *http:/www.sc.edu/admissions*

UNIVERSITY OF SOUTH CAROLINA UPSTATE B-1

Spartanburg, SC 29303 **(864) 503-5246**
(800) 277-8727; (864) 503-5727

Full-time: 1430 men, 2759 women | **Faculty:** 202
Part-time: 391 men, 644 women | **Ph.D.s:** 64%
Graduate: 12 men, 122 women | **Student/Faculty:** 17 to 1
Year: semesters, summer session | **Tuition:** $10,198 ($20,226)
Application Deadline: open | **Room & Board:** $7475
Freshman Class: 2971 applied, 1690 accepted, 717 enrolled
SAT CR/M/W: 430/520/410 **ACT:** 20 **LESS COMPETITIVE**

The University of South Carolina Upstate, established in 1967, is a public institution offering undergraduate programs in the liberal arts and sciences, business administration, education, and nursing. There are 4 undergraduate schools and one graduate school. In addition to regional accreditation, USC Upstate has baccalaureate program accreditation with AACSB, NCATE, and NLN. The library contains 235,570 volumes, 51,182 microform items, 6,776 audio/video tapes/CDs/DVDs, and subscribes to 31,063 periodicals including electronic. Computerized library services include interlibrary loans, database searching, Internet access, and Wi-Fi capability. Special learning facilities include an art gallery, including a greenhouse. The 298-acre campus is in an urban area 100 miles north of Columbia. Including any residence halls, there are 20 buildings.

Student Life: 96% of undergraduates are from South Carolina. Others are from 31 states, 26 foreign countries, and Canada. 61% are White; 27% African American. The average age of freshmen is 18; all undergraduates, 23. 34% do not continue beyond their first year; 38% remain to graduate.

Housing: 1016 students can be accommodated in college housing, which includes coed dorms, on-campus apartments, and off-campus apartments. and an honors floor. On-campus housing is guaranteed for the freshman year only, is available on a first-come, and first served basis. 81% of students commute. Alcohol is not permitted. All students may keep cars.

Activities: 6% of men belong to 6 national fraternities; 2% of women belong to 6 national sororities. There are 70 groups on campus, including art, band, cheerleading, choir, chorus, communications, computers, dance, debate, drama, ethnic, film, forensics, gay, honors, international, jazz band, literary magazine, newspaper, pep band, photography, political, professional, religious, social, social service, and student government. Popular campus events include Bowties and Barbecue, Homecoming, Rock the Block, Midnight Madness and Springfest.

Sports: There are 7 intercollegiate sports for men and 8 for women, and 13 intramural sports for men and 12 for women. Facilities include a soccer field, baseball fields, a basketball gym, racquetball courts, and an auxiliary gym.

Disabled Students: 95% of the campus is accessible. Facilities include wheelchair ramps, elevators, special parking, specially equipped restrooms, special class scheduling, lowered drinking fountains, and lowered telephones.

Services: Counseling and information services are available, as is tutoring in most subjects. There is remedial math, reading, and writing.

Campus Safety and Security: Measures include 24-hour foot and vehicle patrol, emergency notification system, self-defense education, and security escort services. There are shuttle buses, emergency telephones, lighted pathways/sidewalks, and controlled access to dorms/residences.

Programs of Study: USC Upstate confers B.A., B.S. and B.S.N. degrees. Master's degrees are also awarded. Bachelor's degrees are awarded in BIOLOGICAL SCIENCE (biology/biological science), BUSINESS (accounting, business administration and management, marketing management, and nonprofit/public organization management), COMMUNICATIONS AND THE ARTS (communications, English, graphic design, music performance, Spanish, and studio art), COMPUTER AND PHYSICAL SCIENCE (chemistry, Computer Engineering Technology, computer science, information sciences and systems, and mathematics), EDUCATION (art education, early childhood education, elementary education, English education, health information management, mathematics education, middle school education, physical education, secondary education, social studies education, and special education), ENGINEERING AND ENVIRONMENTAL DESIGN (commercial art and engineering technology), HEALTH PROFESSIONS (nursing), SOCIAL SCIENCE (criminal justice, economics, history, interdisciplinary studies, liberal arts/general studies, political science/government, psychology, and sociology). Nursing and business administration is the strongest academically. Nursing, education and business administration have the largest enrollments.

Required: Students must complete 120 to 136 credits, including 69 to 82 in the major, with a minimum GPA of 2.0. General education requirements include courses in communications, math, arts and humanities, social and behavioral sciences, natural science, foreign culture, computer studies, and a senior seminar.

Special: Cross-registration is permitted within the University of South Carolina system and with Wofford College and Greenville Technical College. Opportunities are provided for B.A.-B.S. degrees, student-designed majors, a 3-2 engineering degree, nondegree study, credit for military service, and study abroad in Mexico, France, Germany, England, Spain, and Italy. There are 15 national honor societies.

Faculty/Classroom: 43% of faculty are male; 57% are female. 97% teach undergraduates, 3% do research, and all teach and do research. No introductory courses are taught by graduate students. The average class size in an introductory lecture is 22; in a laboratory is 20; and in a regular course is 15.

Admissions: 57% of the 2013-2014 applicants were accepted. The SAT scores for the 2013-2014 freshman class were: Critical Reading--63% below 500, 28% between 500 and 599, 5% between 600 and 699, and 1% between 700 and 800; Math--61% below 500, 33% between 500 and 599, and 6% between 600 and 699; Writing--74% below 500, 23% between 500 and 599, and 3% between 600 and 699. The ACT scores were 64% below 21, 21% between 21 and 23, 10% between 24 and 26, 3% between 27 and 28, and 2% above 28. 29% of the current freshmen were in the top fifth of their class; 61% were in the top two fifths. 5 freshmen graduated first in their class.

Requirements: The SAT is required. Graduation from an accredited secondary school with a GPA of 2.0 is required. The GED is accepted. Applicants must submit 20 academic credits, distributed as follows: 4 years of English, 3 of math, 2 each of lab science, foreign language, and social studies, 1 each of history and phys ed or ROTC, and the remainder in electives. A GPA of 2.0 is required. AP and CLEP credits are accepted.

Procedure: Freshmen are admitted to all sessions. Entrance exams should be taken at the beginning of the senior year. There is a rolling admissions plan. Application deadlines are open. Application fee is $40.

Transfer: 814 transfer students enrolled in 2012-2013. Applicants must have a minimum college GPA of 2.0 and submit final transcripts from all schools attended. Students transferring with fewer than 30 semester credits must submit a minimum SAT score of 700 or ACT score of 18 and meet other freshman requirements. 30 of 120 credits required for the bachelor's degree must be completed at USC Upstate.

Visiting: There are regularly scheduled orientations for prospective students. There are guides for informal visits and visitors may sit in on classes. To schedule a visit, contact the Admissions Office.

Financial Aid: In 2013-2014, 95% of all full-time freshmen and 72% of continuing full-time students received some form of financial aid. 71% of all full-time freshmen and 58% of continuing full-time students received need-based aid. The average freshman award was $6,292. Need-based scholarships or need-based grants averaged $2,424; need-based self-help aid (loans and jobs) averaged $1,744; non-need-based athletic scholarships averaged $3,088; and other non-need-based awards and non-need-based scholarships averaged $2,147. 8% of undergraduate students work part-time. Average annual earnings from campus work are $2000. The average financial indebtedness of the 2013 graduate was $25,780. The FAFSA and CCS/Profile, or FAFSA, or FFS, or SFS are required. The deadline for filing freshman financial aid applications for fall entry is open.

International Students: There are 82 international students enrolled. They must take the TOEFL with a minimum score of 500 on the paper-based TOEFL (PBT) or 61 on the Internet-based version (iBT). They must also take the SAT or ACT.

Graduates: From July 1, 2012 to June 30, 2013, 1132 bachelor's degrees were awarded. The most popular majors were nursing (27%), education (16%), and business administration (14%). 125 companies recruited on campus in 2012-2013. In an average class, 22% graduate in 4 years or less, 35% graduate in 5 years or less, and 38% graduate in 6 years or less. Of the 2012 graduating class, 5% were enrolled in graduate school within 6 months of graduation.

Admissions Contact: Donette Stewart, Assistant Vice Chancellor for Enrollment. E-Mail: *dstewart@uscupstate.edu* Web: *www.uscupstate.edu*

VOORHEES COLLEGE C-3

Denmark, SC 29042 **(803) 780-1023; (803) 780-1430**

Full-time: 231 men, 288 women	**Faculty:** 40
Part-time: 4 men, 10 women	**Ph.D.s:** 40%
Graduate: n/av	**Student/Faculty:** 14 to 1
Year: semesters, summer session	**Tuition:** $10,780
Application Deadline:	**Room & Board:** $7346
Freshman Class: n/av	
SAT or ACT: required	

COMPETITIVE

Voorhees College, founded in 1897, is a historically black liberal arts college affiliated with the Protestant Episcopal Church. Undergraduate programs are offered in Accounting, Biology, Business Administration, Health and Recreation, Mass Communications, Organizational Management, Sociology, Criminal Justice, Computer Science (concentration in Cyber Security), African-American Studies, Sports Management, Education (Child Development, Elementary Education) and Emergency Management and Math. The library contains 309,479 volumes, 26,010 microform items, 298 audio/video tapes/CDs/DVDs, and subscribes to 14,522 periodicals including electronic. Computerized library services include interlibrary loans, database searching, Internet access, and Wi-Fi capability. Special learning facilities include a radio station, an Academic Success Center; Writing Center. The 342-acre campus is in a small town 50 miles south of Columbia. Including any residence halls, there are 25 buildings.

Student Life: 68% of undergraduates are from South Carolina. Others are from 16 states, and 1 foreign countries. 80% are from public schools. 95% are African American. 98% are Protestant. The average age of freshmen is 17; all undergraduates, 23. 40% remain to graduate.

Housing: 537 students can be accommodated in college housing, which includes single-sex dorms. On-campus housing is guaranteed for all 4 years. 75% of students live on campus; of those, 50% remain on campus on weekends. Alcohol is not permitted. All students may keep cars.

Activities: 20% of men belong to 4 national fraternities; 20% of women belong to 4 national sororities. There are 20 groups on campus, including cheerleading, choir, computers, dance, drama, honors, newspaper, political, professional, radio and TV, religious, social, student government, and yearbook. Popular campus events include Career Awareness Week, Black History Month, Religious Emphasis Week, National Women's History Month, Business Week, National Library Week, and Founders Day Week.

Sports: There are 3 intercollegiate sports for men and 4 for women, and 4 intramural sports for men and 4 for women. Facilities include a gym, swimming pool, tennis and basketball courts, baseball and softball fields, track field, a weight room, a dance studio, and a student center.

Disabled Students: 90% of the campus is accessible. Facilities include wheelchair ramps, elevators, special parking, specially equipped restrooms, lowered drinking fountains, and mobile carts.

Services: Counseling and information services are available, as is tutoring in most subjects. There is remedial math, reading, and writing.

Campus Safety and Security: Measures include 24-hour foot and vehicle patrol and emergency notification system. There are lighted pathways/sidewalks.

Programs of Study: Voorhees confers B.A., and B.S. degrees. Bachelor's degrees are awarded in BIOLOGICAL SCIENCE (biology/biological science), BUSINESS (accounting, business administration and management, organizational leadership and management, and recreation and leisure services), COMMUNICATIONS AND THE ARTS (communications and English), COMPUTER AND PHYSICAL SCIENCE (computer science and mathematics), HEALTH PROFESSIONS (health), SOCIAL SCIENCE (criminal justice and sociology). Biology and business administration are the strongest academically. Business and organizational management have the largest enrollments.

Required: To graduate, students must earn at least 122 credit hours, with at least 30 in the major, and have a minimum GPA of 2.0. The 50-hour general education requirement includes 12 hours of English/Speech, 5 hours of Humanities, 3 hours of foreign language, 1 hour of freshmen orientation, 2 hours of physical fitness, 12 hours of economics and history and 15 hours of mathematics, science and technology. A number of free electives and a senior seminar are also required. An English proficiency exam and an exit exam must be passed.

Special: Voorhees offers cooperative education, internships in some programs, work-study, an evening/Saturday program, off-campus summer study, dual majors, credit by exam, and a degree completion program. Cross-registration with Denmark Technical College and interdisciplinary majors, such as health and recreation, are possible. There are 3 national honor societies and 1 departmental honors program.

Faculty/Classroom: All teach undergraduates. No introductory courses are taught by graduate students. The average class size in an introductory lecture is 30; in a laboratory is 20; and in a regular course is 25.

Requirements: The SAT or ACT is required. Applicants must be high school graduates or hold a GED. Students should have earned 24 academic credits in high school, including 4 units of English, 4 units of math, 3 units of science, 1 unit of foreign language (optional), and 1 each of history, social studies, economics/government, 1 unit of physical education, 1 unit of computer science/keyboarding and 7 electives. Letters of recommendation and a campus visit are advised. A GPA of 2.0 is required. AP and CLEP credits are accepted. Important factors in the admissions decision are advanced placement or honors courses, recommendations by school officials, and recommendations by alumni.

Procedure: Freshmen are admitted to all sessions. Entrance exams should be taken in the senior year. There are deferred admissions and rolling admissions plans. Applications should be filed by December 15 for spring entry, along with a $25 fee. Notification of early decision is sent August 15; regular decision, December 15.

Transfer: 35 transfer students enrolled in 2012-2013. Transfer students must submit complete records, including a confidential report from each college attended. The confidential report form is provided by the Office of Admission and Recruitment. Students with fewer than 30 semester hours must submit their high school record with rank in class and GPA. The SAT is recommended; a satisfactory composite score is expected. An interview is advised. 30 of 122 credits required for the bachelor's degree must be completed at Voorhees.

Visiting: There are regularly scheduled orientations for prospective students, consisting of senior visitation days held January through April. There are guides for informal visits, visitors may sit in on classes, and stay overnight. To schedule a visit, contact Adrian West at west@voorhees.edu.

Financial Aid: The average freshman award was $13,967. Need-based self-help aid (loans and jobs) averaged $5,500. Voorhees is a member of CSS. The FAFSA and the college's own financial statement, and or SAR. The FAFSA is preferred. are required. The priority date for freshman financial aid applications for fall entry is April 15.

International Students: They must take the TOEFL. They must also take the SAT or ACT.

Graduates: From July 1, 2012 to June 30, 2013, 131 bachelor's degrees were awarded. The most popular majors were organizational management (28%), criminal justice (11%), and biology (8%). In an average class, 40% graduate in 4 years or less.

Admissions Contact: Paula Payton, Director of Admissions and Recruitment. E-Mail: *ppayton@voorhees.edu* Web: *www.voorhees.edu*

WINTHROP UNIVERSITY C-1

Rock Hill, SC 29733 (803) 323-2191
(800) 946-8476; (803) 323-2137

Full-time: n/av	**Faculty:** 281; IIA, --$
Part-time: n/av	**Ph.D.s:** 87%
Graduate: n/av	**Student/Faculty:** 15 to 1
Year: semesters, summer session	**Tuition:** $13,430 ($26,000)
Application Deadline: May 1	**Room & Board:** $7690
Freshman Class: 4316 applied, 3051 accepted, 1143 enrolled	
SAT CR/M: 525/525	**ACT:** 23 **VERY COMPETITIVE**

Nationally recognized for quality and value, Winthrop University, a public, comprehensive institution in Rock Hill, S.C., blends liberal arts, professional programs, global awareness and civic engagement. No matter what students study at Winthrop, they are prepared for successful careers, engaged in our democratic society, responsive to local and global concerns, and grounded in values that give meaning to their lives. These outcomes reflect the university's commitment to be among the very best institutions of its kind in the nation. Winthrop embodies the characteristics essential to being one of the best – a high-achieving, diverse student body; a national caliber curriculum; an undergraduate residential experience emphasizing community; and institutional values centered around global learning, undergraduate research, and engaged public service. Bolstered by a nationally acclaimed faculty and staff, Winthrop students learn that to be a person of success, they must first be a person of value. As a result, they develop the integrity that makes them stand out as leaders in their communities and in their chosen professions. There are 4 undergraduate schools and 4 graduate schools. In addition to regional accreditation, Winthrop has baccalaureate program accreditation with AACSB, ABET, ACEJMC, CSAB, CSWE, NASAD, NASM, and NCATE. The library contains 476,473 volumes, 1.2 million microform items, 15,277 audio/video tapes/CDs/DVDs, and subscribes to 40,755 periodicals including electronic. Computerized library services include interlibrary loans, database searching, Internet access, and Wi-Fi capability. Special learning facilities include an art gallery, radio station, TV station, an audio recording studio, an early childhood lab school, the MIDI lab, the Instructional Technology Center, Johnson Theatre, Mathematics Tutorial Center, The Writing Center, Academic Success Center and the Conservatory of Music. The 445-acre campus is in a small town 23 miles south of Charlotte, NC. Including any residence halls, there are 75 buildings.

Student Life: Students are from 34 states, 37 foreign countries, and Canada. 62% are White; 28% African American. The average age of freshmen is 18; all undergraduates, 21. 27% do not continue beyond their first year; 58% remain to graduate.

Housing: 2576 students can be accommodated in college housing, which includes single-sex and coed dorms and on-campus apartments. In addition, there are honors houses, special-interest houses, independent, off-campus fraternity and sorority houses. On-campus housing is available on a first-come and first-served basis. 53% of students live on campus; of those, 50% remain on campus on weekends. All students may keep cars.

Activities: 4% of men belong to 7 national fraternities; 9% of women belong to 9 national sororities. There are 160 groups on campus, including art, band, cheerleading, chess, choir, chorale, chorus, computers, dance, drama, environmental, ethnic, gay, honors, international, jazz band, literary magazine, musical theater, newspaper, opera, pep band, political, professional, radio and TV, religious, social, social service, and student government. Popular campus events include Welcome Week, Convocation and Picnic, Basketball Game Tailgaiting, Homecoming Talent Show, Movies at DiGiorgio Campus Center.

Sports: There are 7 intercollegiate sports for men and 9 for women, and 16 intramural sports for men and 16 for women. Facilities include The Lake Area Recreational Complex comprises the Winthrop Coliseum (6k seats), lake, and numerous athletics and recreational fields and Ropes course. Some facilities included there are a challenging 18-hole disc golf course, new 12-court tennis complex, a track and field stadium and a soccer field. On main campus, the Lois Rhame West Health, Physical Ed and Wellness Ctr includes a 2 story climbing wall, raquetball courts, 25 yd pool, basketball courts, 8K sf weight room, cardio room space and aerobic/activity rooms.

Disabled Students: 95% of the campus is accessible. Facilities include wheelchair ramps, elevators, special parking, specially equipped restrooms, special class scheduling, lowered drinking fountains, lowered telephones, and special housing.

Services: Counseling and information services are available, as is tutoring in some subjects, Math and Writing Center available to students, as well as any subjects tutoring program within Residence Halls There is a reader service for the blind. Academic Success Center focuses on helping students achieve academic excellence and earn their college degree. This program provides tutoring opportunities and tools to excel in their classes.

Campus Safety and Security: Measures include 24-hour foot and vehicle patrol, emergency notification system, self-defense education, and security escort services. There are emergency telephones, lighted pathways/sidewalks, and controlled access to dorms/residences.

Programs of Study: Winthrop confers B.A., B.S., B.F.A., B.M., B.M.E. and B.S.W. degrees. Master's degrees are also awarded. Bachelor's degrees are awarded in AGRICULTURE (environmental studies), BIOLOGICAL SCIENCE (biology/biological science and nutrition), BUSINESS (business administration and management, electronic business, and sports management), COMMUNICATIONS AND THE ARTS (art, art history and appreciation, communications, dance, English, English literature, fine arts, French, German, modern language, music, music performance, public relations, Spanish, technical and business writing, and theatre arts), COMPUTER AND PHYSICAL SCIENCE (chemistry, computer science, and mathematics), EDUCATION (athletic training, early childhood education, elementary education, middle school education, music education, physical education, secondary education, special education, and sports and wellness studies), ENGINEERING AND ENVIRONMENTAL DESIGN (environmental science and interior design), HEALTH PROFESSIONS (exercise science and medical laboratory technology), SOCIAL SCIENCE (economics, history, philosophy, philosophy and religion, political science/government, psychology, religion, social work, sociology, and Spanish studies). Business administration, biology, psychology and fine arts have the largest enrollments.

Required: Students must complete a minimum of 124 semester hours, including a 46 to 58-hour general education distribution requirement, and maintain a minimum GPA of 2.0. Specific courses in writing, oral communication, computer information systems, critical issues, and the American Constitution are required.

Special: Cross-registration is permitted with the Charlotte Area Educational Consortium. Internships in Business, Education, Visual and Performing Arts and Arts and Sciences. Study abroad in 20 countries and on-campus work-study programs are offered. Interdisciplinary majors such as science communication, nondegree study, and pass/fail options are possible. There are 15 national honor societies, including Phi Beta Kappa, a freshman honors program, and 24 departmental honors programs.

Faculty/Classroom: 42% of faculty are male; 58% are female. 98% teach undergraduates, and 98% do both. No introductory courses are taught by graduate students. The average class size in an introductory lecture is 32; in a laboratory is 19; and in a regular course is 24.

Admissions: 71% of the 2013-2014 applicants were accepted. The SAT scores for the 2013-2014 freshman class were: Critical Reading--37% below 500, 39% between 500 and 599, 18% between 600 and 699, and 3% between 700 and 800; Math--37% below 500, 43% between 500 and 599, 17% between 600 and 699, and 1% between 700 and 800. The ACT scores were 36% below 21, 28% between 21 and 23, 17% between 24 and 26, 13% between 27 and 28, and 9% above 28. 43% of the current freshmen were in the top fifth of their class; 76% were in the top two fifths.

Requirements: The SAT or ACT is required. Graduation from an accredited secondary school is required; a GED will be accepted. Applicants must have successfully completed 4 credits in high school English, 3 in math, 3 in lab science, 2 each in social studies and foreign language, 1 in United States history, and 4 in Electives that must be taken from at least three different fields selected from among Computer Science, English, Fine Arts, Foreign Languages, Humanities, Laboratory Science (excluding earth science, general physical science,general environmental science, or other introductory science courses for which biology and/or chemistry is not a prerequisite), Mathematics above the level of Algebra II, and Social Sciences. It is suggested that one unit be in Computer Science which includes programming (not just keyboarding) and one unit in Fine Arts (i.e. appreciation of, history, or performance). A GPA of 3.0 is required. AP and CLEP credits are accepted. Important factors in the admissions decision are advanced placement or honors courses, evidence of special talent, and geographical diversity.

Procedure: Freshmen are admitted to all sessions. Entrance exams should be taken December of senior year. There are deferred admissions and rolling admissions plans. Applications should be filed by May 1 for fall entry; January 2 for spring entry. The fall 2013 application fee was $40. Notification is sent on a rolling basis. Applications are accepted online.

Transfer: 359 transfer students enrolled in 2012-2013. Applicants must be eligible to return to the previous institution and submit college transcripts. 30 of 124 credits required for the bachelor's degree must be completed at Winthrop.

Visiting: There are regularly scheduled orientations for prospective students. There are guides for informal visits, visitors may sit in on classes, and stay overnight. To schedule a visit, contact the Admissions Office.

Financial Aid: In 2013-2014, 79% of all full-time freshmen and 70% of continuing full-time students received some form of financial aid. 67% of all full-time freshmen and 60% of continuing full-time students received need-based aid. The average freshman award was $13,298. Need-based scholarships or need-based grants averaged $9,179 ($10,154 maximum); need-based self-help aid (loans and jobs) averaged $3,577 ($4,700 maximum); non-need-based athletic scholarships averaged $9,761 ($28,466 maximum); and other non-need-based awards and non-need-based scholarships averaged $4,262 ($14,006 maximum). 18% of undergraduate students work part-time. Average annual earnings from campus work are $1600. The average financial indebtedness of the 2013 graduate was $22,521. Winthrop is a member of CSS. The FAFSA is required. The priority date for freshman financial aid applications for fall entry is March 1.

International Students: There are 169 international students enrolled. The school actively recruits these students. They must take the TOEFL with a minimum score of 520 on the paper-based TOEFL (PBT) or 68 on the Internet-based version (iBT). They must also take the SAT or ACT.

Graduates: From July 1, 2012 to June 30, 2013, 982 bachelor's degrees were awarded. The most popular majors were business administration (25%), psychology (7%), and biology (5%). 149 companies recruited on campus in 2012-2013. In an average class, 33% graduate in 4 years or less, 18% graduate in 5 years or less, and 53% graduate in 6 years or less. Of the 2012 graduating class, 25% were enrolled in graduate school within 6 months of graduation, and 46% were employed.

Admissions Contact: Deborah Barber, Director of Admissions. E-Mail: *admissions@winthrop.edu* Web: *www.winthrop.edu/admissions*

WOFFORD COLLEGE B-1

Spartanburg, SC 29303 **(864) 597-4130; (864) 597-4147**

Full-time: 800 men, 749 women	**Faculty:** 130; IIB, av$
Part-time: 17 men, 18 women	**Ph.D.s:** 90%
Graduate: n/av	**Student/Faculty:** 11 to 1
Year: 4-1-4, summer session	**Tuition:** $35,515
Application Deadline: February 1	**Room & Board:** $10,280
Freshman Class: 2718 applied, 1870 accepted, 415 enrolled	
SAT CR/M: 585/597 **ACT:** 26	**VERY COMPETITIVE**

Wofford College, founded in 1854, is a private four-year institution affiliated with the United Methodist Church, offering programs in liberal arts and preprofessional studies. It is especially known for leadership in studies abroad, service learning, and its innovative apartment-style housing, known as "The Wofford Village." Wofford has won recent Southern Conference championships in football, baseball, men's basketball and men's soccer. In addition to regional accreditation, Wofford has baccalaureate program accreditation with NASDTEC. The library contains 184,715 volumes, 21,150 microform items, 3,866 audio/video tapes/CDs/DVDs, and subscribes to 47,528 periodicals including electronic. Computerized library services include interlibrary loans, database searching, Internet access, and Wi-Fi capability. Special learning facilities include an art gallery, International studies center with simultaneous translation capabilities, arboretum, greenhouse, the Goodall environmental studies center at Glendale Shoals, Montgomery Music Building, and The Space in The Mungo Center that houses several programs: The Space to: Prepare (houses the Career Services office, the Sophomore Experience and the Institute); The Space to: Impact (a competitive four-year program teaching design thinking, entrepreneurship, project management & the consultative approach to problem solving.; The Space to:Launch (supports students in the concept, development & launch of a business idea.); The Space to: Consult (student consulting group providing business & organizations strategies to improve performance.); The Space to: Explore (helps make the Wofford liberal arts degree global-ready by providing internship & travel opportunities). The 170-acre campus is in an urban area 70 miles southwest of Charlotte. Including any residence halls, there are 72 buildings.

Student Life: 56% of undergraduates are from South Carolina. Others are from 37 states, and 12 foreign countries. 67% are from public schools. 80% are White. 67% are Protestant; 18% Unknown Religious affiliation; 12% Catholic. The average age of freshmen is 18; all undergraduates, 20. 10% do not continue beyond their first year; 82% remain to graduate.

Housing: 1479 students can be accommodated in college housing, which includes coed dorms and on-campus apartments. On-campus housing is guaranteed for all 4 years. 94% of students live on campus; of those, 80% remain on campus on weekends. All students may keep cars.

Activities: 43% of men belong to 8 national fraternities; 55% of women belong to 4 national sororities. There are 98 groups on campus, including and the interfaith youth core, band, cheerleading, choir, chorale, chorus, college bowl team, computers, dance, drama, environmental, ethnic, gay, international, jazz band, literary magazine, newspaper, orchestra, pep band, photography, political, professional, religious, social, social service, student government, and yearbook. Popular campus events include Phi Beta Kappa Day, Honors Day, Novel Experience, and Winter Lighting.

Sports: There are 9 intercollegiate sports for men and 8 for women, and 10 intramural sports for men and 10 for women. Facilities include an 8500-seat campus stadium, a 3500-seat arena, a tennis complex, soccer and baseball fields, and a wellness and athletic center built to the specifications of the Carolina Panthers, sand volleyball court and basketball court.

Disabled Students: 95% of the campus is accessible. Facilities include wheelchair ramps, elevators, special parking, specially equipped restrooms, special class scheduling, lowered drinking fountains, and lowered telephones.

Services: Counseling and information services are available, as is tutoring in every subject. There is a reader service for the blind.

Campus Safety and Security: Measures include 24-hour foot and vehicle patrol, emergency notification system, self-defense education, and security escort services. There are emergency telephones, lighted pathways/sidewalks, and controlled access to dorms/residences.

Programs of Study: Wofford confers B.A., and B.S. degrees. Bachelor's degrees are awarded in AGRICULTURE (environmental studies), BIOLOGICAL SCIENCE (biology/biological science), BUSINESS (accounting, banking and finance, business economics, and finance), COMMUNICATIONS AND THE ARTS (art history, Chinese, creative writing, dramatic arts, English, French, German, Spanish, studio art, and theatre arts), COMPUTER AND PHYSICAL SCIENCE (applied mathematics, chemistry, computer science, mathematics, and physics), SOCIAL SCIENCE (African American studies, crosscultural studies, economics, gender studies, history, humanities, Latin American studies, philosophy, political science/government, psychology, religion, and sociology). Biology, foreign languages, finance/accounting are the strongest academically. Biology, business economics and Spanish have the largest enrollments.

Required: To graduate, students must complete 124 credits, with 24 to 40 credits in the major and a minimum GPA of 2.0. General education requirements include 3 credits each of history/philosophy/religion/mathematics/Cultures & Peoples; 3-4 credits of fine arts; 4-10 credits of foreign languages; 4-16 credits of natural sciences, 6 of English; and 2 of phys ed. Students must complete 4 interim projects, and a freshman humanities seminar.

Special: Special academic programs include study abroad in 70 countries, a Washington semester, and a concentration in Latin American and Caribbean studies. In addition, students can major or minor in multiple fields or complete interdisciplinary, humanities, or intercultural studies majors. The January interim allows students to concentrate on a single study project, internship, or travel experience. (Consistently ranked in top 10, IIE Open Doors Survey) There are 9 national honor societies and including Phi Beta Kappa.

Faculty/Classroom: 60% of faculty are male; 40% are female. All teach undergraduates, and 30% do both. No introductory courses are taught by graduate students. The average class size in an introductory lecture is 21; in a laboratory is 21; and in a regular course is 17.

Admissions: 69% of the 2013-2014 applicants were accepted. The SAT scores for the 2013-2014 freshman class were: Critical Reading--12% below 500, 40% between 500 and 599, 42% between 600 and 699, and 6% between 700 and 800; Math--11% below 500, 35% between 500 and 599, 42% between 600 and 699, and 11% between 700 and 800; Writing--21% below 500, 38% between 500 and 599, 37% between 600 and 699, and 4% between 700 and 800. The ACT scores were 3% below 21, 15% between 21 and 23, 27% between 24 and 26, 23% between 27 and 28, and 32% above 28. 69% of the current freshmen were in the top fifth of their class; 96% were in the top two fifths. 7 freshmen graduated first in their class.

Requirements: The SAT or ACT is required. The ACT Optional Writing test is also required. In addition, Applicants must be graduates of an accredited secondary school. The GED is accepted. Students should have completed 4 years each of high school English and math, 3 of lab science, and 3 each of a foreign language and social studies. An essay is required and an interview is strongly recommended. AP and CLEP credits are accepted. Important factors in the admissions decision are advanced placement or honors courses, leadership record, and personality/intangible qualities.

Procedure: Freshmen are admitted to all sessions. Entrance exams should be taken in the spring of the junior year or fall of the senior year. There are early decision, early admissions, and deferred admissions plans. Early decision applications should be filed by November 1; regular applications, by February 1 for fall entry, along with a $35 fee. Notification of early decision is sent December 1; regular decision, March 15. 1155 early decision candidates were accepted for the 2013-2014 class. 52 applicants were on the 2013 waiting list; 52 were admitted. Applications are accepted online.

Transfer: 19 transfer students enrolled in 2012-2013. Transfers should have a minimum GPA of 2.5 from a 4-year college or 3.0 from a 2-year college, or they may submit ACT or SAT scores. An interview is recommended. 30 of 124 credits required for the bachelor's degree must be completed at Wofford.

Visiting: There are regularly scheduled orientations for prospective students, Information Sessions are offered Mon-Fri at 10:00am and 2:00pm. A visit consists of an information session with an admission counselor and campus tour. There are guides for informal visits, visitors may sit in on classes, and stay overnight. To schedule a visit, contact the Director of Admission at admission@wofford.edu.

Financial Aid: In 2013-2014, 93% of all full-time freshmen and 94% of continuing full-time students received some form of financial aid. 65% of all full-time freshmen and 58% of continuing full-time students received need-based aid. The average freshman award was $27,649. Need-based scholarships or need-based grants averaged $28,257 ; need-based self-help aid (loans and jobs) averaged $3,312; non-need-based athletic scholarships averaged $21,855; and other non-need-based awards and non-need-based scholarships averaged $14,262. 19% of undergraduate students work part-time. Average annual earnings from campus work are $1014. The average financial indebtedness of the 2013 graduate was $24,721. Wofford is a member of CSS. The FAFSA is required. The deadline for filing freshman financial aid applications for fall entry is March 15.

International Students: There are 28 international students enrolled. They must take the TOEFL with a minimum score of 550 on the paper-based TOEFL (PBT) or 80 on the Internet-based version (iBT). They must also take the SAT or ACT.

Graduates: From July 1, 2012 to June 30, 2013, 374 bachelor's degrees were awarded. The most popular majors were business/marketing (26%), biological/life sciences (18%), and foreign languages (12%). 25 companies recruited on campus in 2012-2013. In an average class, 78% graduate in 4 years or less, 81% graduate in 5 years or less, and 82% graduate in 6 years or less.

Admissions Contact: John W. Birney, Director of Admission. E-Mail: *admission@wofford.edu* Web: *www.wofford.edu*

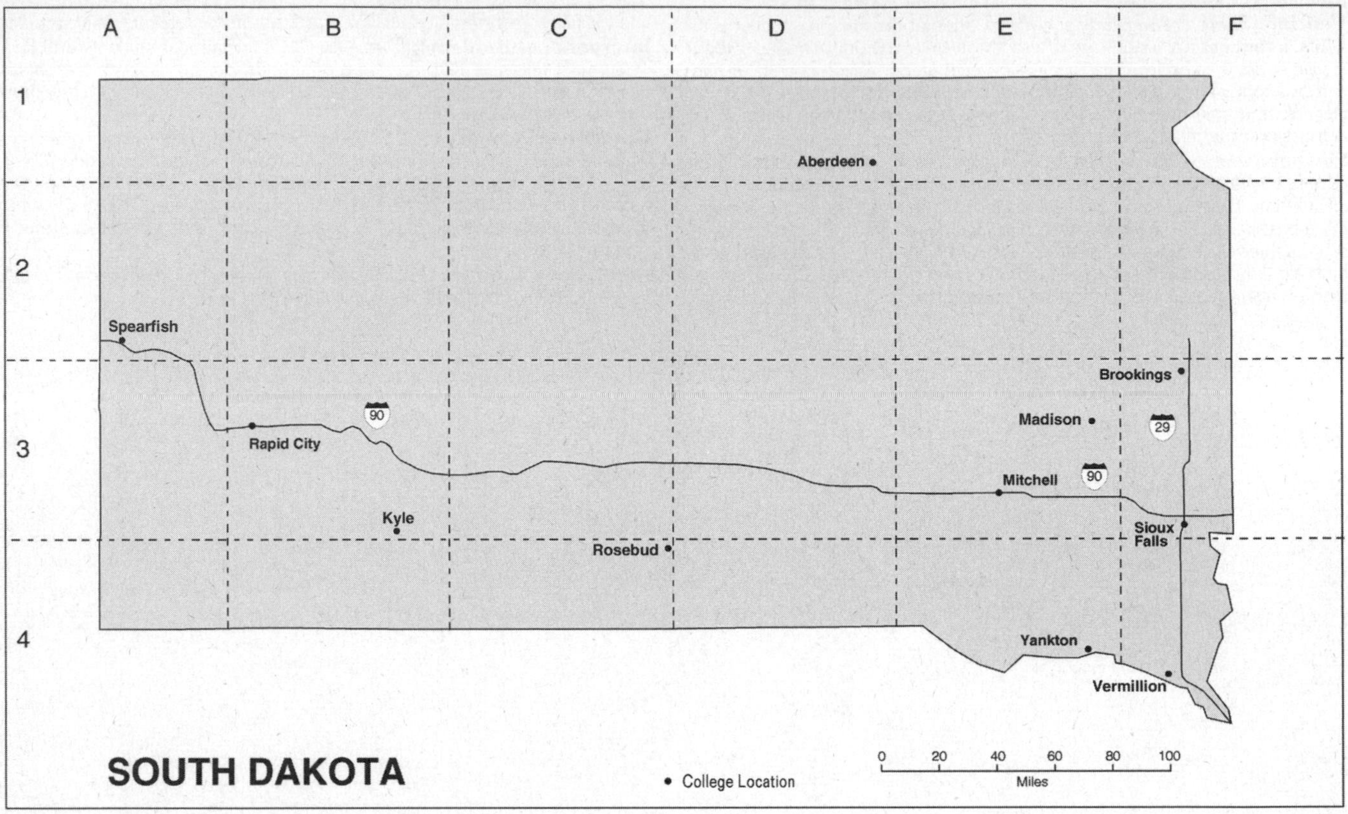

AUGUSTANA COLLEGE F-3

Sioux Falls, SD 57197 (605) 274-5516
(800) 727-2844; (605) 274-5518

Full-time: 635 men, 950 women	**Faculty:** 129; IIB, --$
Part-time: 53 men, 59 women	**Ph.D.s:** 82%
Graduate: 21 men, 47 women	**Student/Faculty:** 12 to 1
Year: 4-1-4, summer session	**Tuition:** $28,630
Application Deadline:	**Room & Board:** $6920
Freshman Class: 1147 applied, 781 accepted, 367 enrolled	
SAT: required **ACT:** 26	**VERY COMPETITIVE**

Augustana College, founded in 1860, is a comprehensive(liberal arts and professional) private college of the Lutheran church. In addition to regional accreditation, has baccalaureate program accreditation with NASM and NCATE. The library contains 233,000 volumes, 8,100 microform items, 7,300 audio/video tapes/CDs/DVDs, and subscribes to 6,150 periodicals including electronic. Computerized library services include interlibrary loans, database searching, Internet access, and Wi-Fi capability. Special learning facilities include an art gallery, and a center for Western studies. The 100-acre campus is in an urban area Sioux Falls, South Dakota. Including any residence halls, there are 47 buildings.

Student Life: 55% of undergraduates are from out of state, mostly the Mid-West. Students are from 30 states, and 43 foreign countries. 85% are from public schools. 87% are White. 47% are Protestant; 20% Catholic. The average age of freshmen is 18; all undergraduates, 20. 19% do not continue beyond their first year; 66% remain to graduate.

Housing: 1225 students can be accommodated in college housing, which includes coed dorms, on-campus apartments, off-campus apartments, and married student housing. In addition, there are special-interest houses, Theme houses. On-campus housing is guaranteed for all 4 years. 73% of students live on campus; of those, 70% remain on campus on weekends. Alcohol is not permitted. All students may keep cars.

Activities: There are no fraternities or sororities. There are 100 groups on campus, including art, band, cheerleading, chess, choir, chorale, chorus, computers, dance, drama, drill team, environmental, ethnic, gay, honors, international, jazz band, literary magazine, musical theater, newspaper, opera, orchestra, pep band, photography, political, professional, religious, social, social service, student government, symphony, and yearbook. Popular campus events include Christmas at Augustana, Viking Days, Boe Forum on Public Affairs and Semester Shutdown.

Sports: There are 9 intercollegiate sports for men and 9 for women, and 18 intramural sports for men and 18 for women. Facilities include a 3600-seat athletic facility, 2 practice gyms, football complex with new stadium, softball and baseball complexes, soccer, baseball,and softball fields, a pool, weight/cardio work-out room, and a health, phys ed, and recreation center.

Disabled Students: 75% of the campus is accessible. Facilities include wheelchair ramps, elevators, special parking, specially equipped restrooms, special class scheduling, lowered drinking fountains, lowered telephones, special housing.

Services: Counseling and information services are available, as is tutoring in most subjects. There is a reader service for the blind, and remedial writing. writing center

Campus Safety and Security: Measures include 24-hour foot and vehicle patrol, emergency notification system, self-defense education, and security escort services. There are emergency telephones, lighted pathways/sidewalks, and controlled access to dorms/residences.

Programs of Study: confers B.A. degrees. Master's degrees are also awarded. Bachelor's degrees are awarded in BIOLOGICAL SCIENCE (biochemistry and biology/biological science), BUSINESS (accounting, business administration and management, business communications, and sports management), COMMUNICATIONS AND THE ARTS (American Sign Language, art, classics, communications, dramatic arts, English, French, German, journalism, modern language, music, Spanish, and theatre arts), COMPUTER AND PHYSICAL SCIENCE (chemical physics, chemistry, computer science, information sciences and systems, mathematics, and physics), EDUCATION (athletic training, drama education, elementary education, middle school education, music education, physical education, social studies education, and special education), ENGINEERING AND ENVIRONMENTAL DESIGN (engineering physics), HEALTH PROFESSIONS (exercise science, medical laboratory science, and nursing), SOCIAL SCIENCE (anthropology, economics, history, interdisciplinary studies, international studies, philosophy, philosophy and religion, physical fitness/movement, political science/government, psychology, religion, and sociology). Nursing, biology, physics, mathematics, business and education are the strongest academically. Nursing, biology, business and education have the largest enrollments.

Required: Students must complete 124 semester hours, with a minimum GPA of 2.0. General education requirements total 59 semester hours, including component courses in writing for graduation. 2 physical education activity courses are required, religion, and a capstone course.

Special: Cross-registration with Upper Midwest Association for Intercultural Education and Higher Education Consortium for Urban Affairs is available. Internships (both national and local), study abroad in unlimited countries, and a 3-2 engineering degree with Washington University in St. Louis, University of Minnesota, and Columbia University are offered. A Washington semester with Lutheran College Washington Consortium or American University is offered. Credit for life experience is possible. There are 12 national honor societies, a freshman honors program, and 21 departmental honors programs.

Faculty/Classroom: 46% of faculty are male; 54% are female. All teach undergraduates, 95% do research, and all teach and do research. No introductory courses are taught by graduate students. The average class size in an introductory lecture is 32; in a laboratory is 18; and in a regular course is 20.

Admissions: 68% of the 2013-2014 applicants were accepted. The ACT scores were 3% below 21, 24% between 21 and 23, 30% between 24 and 26, 28% between 27 and 28, and 15% above 28. 63% of the current freshmen were in the top fifth of their class; 75% were in the top two fifths.

Requirements: The SAT or ACT is required. Applicants may present either ACT or SAT scores. Applicants should have completed 4 years of high school English, 3 each of math and science, and 2 each of a foreign language and history. An essay, a transcript, and a recommendation are required. A GPA of 2.7 is required. AP and CLEP credits are accepted. Important factors in the admissions decision are advanced placement or honors courses, extracurricular activities record, leadership record, and personality/intangible qualities.

Procedure: Freshmen are admitted to all sessions. Entrance exams should be taken in the spring of the junior year or early fall of the senior. There are deferred admissions and rolling admissions plans. Application deadlines are open. Notification is sent on a rolling basis. Applications are accepted online.

Transfer: 55 transfer students enrolled in 2012-2013. Applicants must have a 2.25 GPA in previous college work. 30 of 124 credits required for the bachelor's degree must be completed at Augustana.

Visiting: There are regularly scheduled orientations for prospective students. Explore Augustana offers a campus tour, and visits with professors, current students, and coaches. There are guides for informal visits, visitors may sit in on classes, and stay overnight. To schedule a visit, contact Campus Visit Coordinator at (605) 274-5516.

Financial Aid: In 2013-2014, 99% of all full-time freshmen and 99% of continuing full-time students received some form of financial aid. 77% of all full-time freshmen and 75% of continuing full-time students received need-based aid. The average freshman award was $24,477. Need-based scholarships or need-based grants averaged $20,627; need-based self-help aid (loans and jobs) averaged $5,472; non-need-based athletic scholarships averaged $10,890; and other non-need-based awards and non-need-based scholarships averaged $14,752. 31% of undergraduate students work part-time. Average annual earnings from campus work are $1657. The average financial indebtedness of the 2013 graduate was $27,258. The FAFSA is required. The priority date for freshman financial aid applications for fall entry is March 1.

International Students: There are 139 international students enrolled. The school actively recruits these students. They must take the TOEFL with a minimum score of 550 on the paper-based TOEFL (PBT) or 79 on the Internet-based version (iBT). They must also take the SAT or ACT, scoring 20.

Computers: All students may access the system. There are no time limits and no fees.

Graduates: From July 1, 2012 to June 30, 2013, 359 bachelor's degrees were awarded. The most popular majors were nursing/health professions (18%), business administration (16%), and biology (13%). 25 companies recruited on campus in 2012-2013. In an average class, 1% graduate in 3 years or less, 52% graduate in 4 years or less, 65% graduate in 5 years or less, and 66% graduate in 6 years or less. Of the 2012 graduating class, 28% were enrolled in graduate school within 6 months of graduation, and 98% were employed.

Admissions Contact: Nancy L. Davidson, Vice President of Enrollment. E-Mail: *admission@augie.edu* Web: *www.augie.edu*

BLACK HILLS STATE UNIVERSITY — A-2

Spearfish, SD 57799 — (605) 642-6343; (800) ALL-BHSU; (605) 642-6022

Full-time: 952 men, 1535 women	**Faculty:** 156
Part-time: 533 men, 982 women	**Ph.D.s:** 70%
Graduate: 126 men, 336 women	**Student/Faculty:** 26 to 1
Year: semesters, summer session	**Tuition:** $7617 ($9617)
Application Deadline:	**Room & Board:** $5945
Freshman Class: n/av	
ACT: required	

LESS COMPETITIVE

Black Hills State University is a master's level university that promotes excellence in teaching and learning; supports research, creative and scholarly activities and provides service to the state, region, nation and global community. BHSU provides innovative, high quality undergraduate (associate and baccalaureate) programs in the arts, humanities, education, behavioral sciences, mathematics, social sciences, natural sciences, business and technology as well as selected disciplines of strength at the graduate level. Black Hills State University is the only comprehensive University in western South Dakota. There are 3 undergraduate schools and 1 graduate school. In addition to regional accreditation, BHSU has baccalaureate program accreditation with NCATE. Computerized library services include interlibrary loans, database searching, Internet access, and Wi-Fi capability. Special learning facilities include an art gallery, radio station, TV station, a gymnasium, and theatre. The 123-acre campus is in a small town 45 miles northwest of Rapid City, South Dakota. Including any residence halls, there are 13 buildings.

Student Life: 77% of undergraduates are from South Dakota. Others are from 44 states, and 18 foreign countries. 86% are White. The average age of freshmen is 19; all undergraduates, 24. 48% do not continue beyond their first year; 38% remain to graduate.

Housing: 840 students can be accommodated in college housing, which includes single-sex and coed dorms, on-campus apartments, and married student housing. 79% of students commute. Alcohol is not permitted. All students may keep cars.

Activities: Groups on campus include art, band, cheerleading, choir, chorale, chorus, computers, dance, debate, drama, drill team, environmental, ethnic, forensics, gay, honors, international, jazz band, musical theater, newspaper, pep band, photography, political, professional, radio and TV, religious, social, social service, student government, and yearbook. Popular campus events include Swarm Week and Big 100 Week.

Sports: There are 5 intercollegiate sports for men and 7 for women. Facilities include a stadium, gymnasium (with basketball and volleyball courts), tennis courts, swimming pools, indoor and outdoor tracks, golf course, baseball and softball complex.

Disabled Students: Facilities include wheelchair ramps, elevators, special parking, specially equipped restrooms, lowered drinking fountains, and special housing.

Services: Counseling and information services are available, as is tutoring in most subjects. There is remedial math, reading, and writing.

Campus Safety and Security: Measures include 24-hour foot and vehicle patrol, emergency notification system, and security escort services. There are lighted pathways/sidewalks and controlled access to dorms/residences.

Programs of Study: BHSU confers B.A., B.A.T.S., B.S. and B.S.Ed degrees. Associate and master's degrees are also awarded. Bachelor's degrees are awarded in BIOLOGICAL SCIENCE (biology/biological science), BUSINESS (accounting, business administration and management, hotel/motel and restaurant management, human resources, and marketing/retailing/merchandising), COMMUNICATIONS AND THE ARTS (art, broadcasting, communications, English, fine arts, music, Spanish, and speech/debate/rhetoric), COMPUTER AND PHYSICAL SCIENCE (chemistry, mathematics, and physical sciences), EDUCATION (art education, business education, elementary education, health education, music education, physical education, science education, secondary education, and special education), HEALTH PROFESSIONS (allied health and health care administration), SOCIAL SCIENCE (American Indian studies, history, human services, political science/government, prelaw, psychology, social science, and sociology). Elementary education, biology, and business administration (management) have the largest enrollments.

Required: Contact the school.

Special: There is a Phi Beta Kappa chapter and a freshman honors program.

Faculty/Classroom: No introductory courses are taught by graduate students.

Requirements: The ACT is required. A GPA of 2.0 is required. AP and CLEP credits are accepted.

Procedure: Freshmen are admitted to all sessions. Entrance exams should be taken During the senior year of high school. There are early admissions and rolling admissions plans. Application deadlines are open. Application fee is $20. Applications are accepted online.

Visiting: There are regularly scheduled orientations for prospective students. There are guides for informal visits, visitors may sit in on classes, and stay overnight. To schedule a visit, contact the Admissions Office.

Financial Aid: The FAFSA and state aid form are required. Check with the school for current application deadlines.

International Students: The school actively recruits these students. They must take the TOEFL. They must also take the ACT, scoring 18.

Computers: All students may access the system. There are no time limits and no fees.

Admissions Contact: Admissions Officer, Enrollment Services Center. E-Mail: *admissions@bhsu.edu* Web: *www.bhsu.edu*

DAKOTA STATE UNIVERSITY E-3
Dakota State College

Madison, SD 57042 (605) 256-5139
(888) DSU-9988; (605) 256-5020

Full-time: n/av
Part-time: n/av
Graduate: n/av
Year: semesters, summer session
Application Deadline: open
Freshman Class: 600 accepted, 360 enrolled
SAT or ACT: required
Faculty: n/av
Ph.D.s: n/av
Student/Faculty: n/av
Tuition: $8286 ($10,286)
Room & Board: $5525

COMPETITIVE

Dakota State University, founded in 1881, is a public institution offering undergraduate programs through the Colleges of Business and Information Systems, Education, and Arts and Sciences. There are 3 undergraduate schools and 1 graduate school. In addition to regional accreditation, DSU has baccalaureate program accreditation with ACBSP, AHEA, and NCATE. The library contains 177,454 volumes, 3,669 microform items, 3,426 audio/video tapes/CDs/DVDs, and subscribes to 350 periodicals including electronic. Computerized library services include interlibrary loans, database searching, Internet access, and Wi-Fi capability. Special learning facilities include an art gallery, natural history museum, and radio station. The 56-acre campus is in a rural area 45 miles northwest of Sioux Falls. Including any residence halls, there are 22 buildings.

Housing: 659 students can be accommodated in college housing, which includes single-sex and coed dorms and on-campus apartments. On-campus housing is guaranteed for the freshman year only, is available on a first-come, first-served basis, and is available on a lottery system for upperclassmen. Alcohol is not permitted. All students may keep cars.

Activities: There are no fraternities or sororities. There are 36 groups on campus, including art, band, cheerleading, choir, chorale, chorus, computers, dance, drama, ethnic, honors, international, literary magazine, musical theater, newspaper, pep band, political, professional, radio and TV, religious, social, and student government. Popular campus events include Homecoming, Convocation and Frost Bites Week.

Sports: There are 6 intercollegiate sports for men and 6 for women, and 3 intramural sports for men and 3 for women. Facilities include courts for basketball and racquetball, a football field, a weight room, and a swimming pool.

Disabled Students: 80% of the campus is accessible. Facilities include wheelchair ramps, elevators, special parking, specially equipped restrooms, special class scheduling, and lowered drinking fountains.

Services: Counseling and information services are available, as is tutoring in every subject. There is a reader service for the blind, and remedial math, reading, and writing.

Campus Safety and Security: Measures include self-defense education and security escort services. There are emergency telephones, lighted pathways/sidewalks, controlled access to dorms/residences, a foot patrol.

Programs of Study: DSU confers B.S., B.B.A., B.G.S., and B.S.Ed. degrees. Associate, master's, and doctoral degrees are also awarded. Bachelor's degrees are awarded in BIOLOGICAL SCIENCE (biology/biological science), BUSINESS (business administration and management), COMMUNICATIONS AND THE ARTS (communications technology, English, and information technology), COMPUTER AND PHYSICAL SCIENCE (computer programming, computer game design/development, computer science, computer security and information assurance, digital arts/technology, information sciences and systems, mathematics, and physical sciences), EDUCATION (business education, computer education, elementary education, English education, health education, health information management, marketing and distribution education, mathematics education, and secondary education), ENGINEERING AND ENVIRONMENTAL DESIGN (computer graphics), HEALTH PROFESSIONS (medical records administration/services, premedicine, and respiratory therapy).

Required: All students seeking a bachelor's degree are required to complete 30 credit hours of general education coursework (math, English, science, humanities) as well as 11 credit hours of institutional specific coursework (information technology and personal health). Associate's degree seeking students are required to complete 18 credit hours of general education coursework as well as 6 credit hours of institutional specific coursework. Graduates must have a 2.0 GPA. A general education assessment exam and exit assessment are required of all students.

Special: The university offers co-op programs with South Dakota State University, internships, study abroad in London, and on-campus work-study programs. Also available are the general studies degree, a 3-2 engineering degree with the University of Minnesota/Twin Cities, credit for life, military, and work experience, nondegree study, and pass/fail options. There are 2 national honor societies and a freshman honors program.

Faculty/Classroom: No introductory courses are taught by graduate students.

Admissions: 9 freshmen graduated first in their class.

Requirements: The SAT or ACT is required, with a minimum composite score of 18 on the ACT. In addition, applicants must be graduates of an accredited secondary school or have a GED certificate, and have completed 4 years of English, 3 years each of math, science, and social studies, and 1/2 year of computer science and the fine arts. A GPA of 2.6 is required. AP and CLEP credits are accepted.

Procedure: Freshmen are admitted to all sessions. Entrance exams should be taken before students register for classes. There is a rolling admissions plan. Application deadlines are open. Application fee is $20. Notification is sent on a rolling basis. Applications are accepted online.

Transfer: 67 transfer students enrolled in 2012-2013. Transfer applicants must have a minimum 2.0 GPA. 32 of 128 credits required for the bachelor's degree must be completed at DSU.

Visiting: There are regularly scheduled orientations for prospective students, including general information and academic sessions, a campus tour, and financial aid information. There are guides for informal visits, visitors may sit in on classes, and stay overnight. To schedule a visit, contact the Admissions Office.

Financial Aid: In 2013-2014, 88% of continuing full-time students received some form of financial aid. The average freshman award was $5,836. Need-based scholarships or need-based grants averaged $641. 50% of undergraduate students work part-time. Average annual earnings from campus work are $1405. The average financial indebtedness of the 2013 graduate was $16,588. The FAFSA is required. The deadline for filing freshman financial aid applications for fall entry is March 1.

International Students: There are 120 international students enrolled. The school actively recruits these students. They must take the TOEFL.

Computers: All students may access the system. There are no time limits and no fees.

Graduates: From July 1, 2012 to June 30, 2013, 145 bachelor's degrees were awarded. 25 companies recruited on campus in 2012-2013. In an average class, 24% graduate in 4 years or less, 42% graduate in 5 years or less, and 15% graduate in 6 years or less. Of the 2012 graduating class, 1% were enrolled in graduate school within 6 months of graduation, and 96% were employed.

Admissions Contact: Amy Crissinger, Director of Admission. E-Mail: *admissions@dsu.edu* Web: *www.dsu.edu*

DAKOTA WESLEYAN UNIVERSITY E-3

Mitchell, SD 57301 (605) 995-2650
(800) 333-8506; (605) 995-2699

Full-time: 680 men and women
Part-time: 90 men and women
Graduate: 30 men and women
Year: semesters, summer session
Application Deadline: see profile
Freshman Class: n/av
SAT or ACT: required
Faculty: 51
Ph.D.s: 68%
Student/Faculty: n/av
Tuition: $21,310
Room & Board: $7200

COMPETITIVE

Dakota Wesleyan University, founded in 1885, is a private liberal arts institution affiliated with the United Methodist Church. The figures in the above capsule and in this profile are approximate. There is 1 graduate school. In addition to regional accreditation, DWU has baccalaureate program accreditation with NLN. The library contains 62,500 volumes, 72,500 microform items, 3700 audio/video tapes/CDs/DVDs, and subscribes to 620 periodicals including electronic. Computerized library services include interlibrary loans, database searching, and Internet access. Special learning facilities include a learning resource center and observatory as well as a history museum with art gallery adjacent to the campus. The 50-acre campus is in a small town 70 miles west of Sioux Falls. Including any residence halls, there are 18 buildings.

Student Life: 69% of undergraduates are from South Dakota. Others are from 27 states, 3 foreign countries, and Canada. 99% are from public schools. 86% are white. 50% are Protestant; 24% Catholic. The average age of freshmen is 19; all undergraduates, 23. 32% do not continue beyond their first year.

Housing: 385 students can be accommodated in college housing, which includes single-sex and coed dorms and on-campus apartments. In addition, there are honors houses. On-campus housing is guaranteed for the freshman year only and is available on a first-come, first-served basis. 60% of students commute. Alcohol is not permitted. All students may keep cars.

Activities: There are no fraternities or sororities. There are 30 groups on campus, including academic, art, band, bell choir, brass and woodwind ensembles, cheerleading, choir, chorale, chorus, dance, drama, drill team, ethnic, forensics, honors, international, literary magazine, musical theater, newspaper, political, professional, religious, social, social service, student government, and yearbook. Popular campus events include Spring Week and Family Life Conference.

Sports: There are 7 intercollegiate sports for men and 6 for women, and 3 intramural sports for men and 3 for women. Facilities include a wellness center with a double gym and cardio, weight training, and cybex rooms. City facilities include a 500-seat stadium, a 3200-seat auditorium/arena, a 1500-seat baseball stadium, a 500-seat softball field, and a 1000-seat outdoor track.

Disabled Students: 80% of the campus is accessible. Facilities include wheelchair ramps, elevators, special parking, specially equipped rest rooms, special class scheduling, lowered drinking fountains, lowered telephones, and class relocation.

Services: Counseling and information services are available, as is tutoring in every subject. There is a reader service for the blind, and remedial math, reading, and writing.

Campus Safety and Security: Measures include self-defense education and security escort services. There are emergency telephones, lighted pathways/sidewalks, safety and security personnel trained in first aid and self-defense, 20-hour foot and vehicle patrol, and pamphlets and posters.

Programs of Study: DWU confers B.A. degrees. Associate and master's degrees are also awarded. Bachelor's degrees are awarded in AGRICULTURE (wildlife management), BIOLOGICAL SCIENCE (biology/biological science), BUSINESS (accounting, business administration and management, and sports management), COMMUNICATIONS AND THE ARTS (art, communications, dramatic arts, English, multimedia, and music), COMPUTER AND PHYSICAL SCIENCE (mathematics), EDUCATION (athletic training, elementary education, physical education, special education, and sports and wellness studies), HEALTH PROFESSIONS (nursing), SOCIAL SCIENCE (behavioral science, criminal justice, history, human services, philosophy and religion, psychology, public administration, and sociology). Biochemistry is the strongest academically. Nursing and business have the largest enrollments.

Required: To graduate, students must complete a total of 125 credit hours, including 30 or more in the major, and at least 42 in upper-level courses, with a minimum 2.0 GPA. General education requirements include 6 hours of communication, literature, and the arts, and social, psychological, and political thought, 3 to 5 of physical science, 3 to 4 each of math and cultural awareness, 3 each of history and philosophy/theology, and 2 of physical activities; students must demonstrate basic skills in reading, writing, and math. All new freshmen must take forum and advising courses.

Special: DWU offers internships, study abroad on a limited basis, work-study programs, a general studies degree, dual majors, student-designed minors, credit for experience, and credit/no credit options. There are 4 national honor societies and a freshman honors program.

Faculty/Classroom: 45% of faculty are male; 55% are female. All teach undergraduates. No introductory courses are taught by graduate students. The average class size in an introductory lecture is 20; in a laboratory, 17; and in a regular course, 17.

Requirements: The SAT or ACT is required. In addition, applicants must be graduates of an accredited secondary school or have a GED certificate. An interview is recommended. A GPA of 2.0 is required. AP and CLEP credits are accepted. Important factors in the admissions decision are advanced placement or honors courses, extracurricular activities record, and parents or siblings attended the school.

Procedure: Freshmen are admitted fall, spring, and summer. Entrance exams should be taken during the senior year. There is a rolling admissions plan. Application fee is $25. Check with the school for current application deadlines. Applications are accepted online.

Transfer: Students must submit official transcripts from all previous colleges attended. DWU will accept credits from regionally accredited institutions, but half the credits for the student's major must be completed at DWU. 30 of 125 credits required for the bachelor's degree must be completed at DWU.

Visiting: There are regularly scheduled orientations for prospective students, including a campus tour and meetings with faculty and students. There are guides for informal visits; visitors may sit in on classes and stay overnight. To schedule a visit, contact Enrollment Services.

Financial Aid: DWU is a member of CSS. The FAFSA is required. Check with the school for current application deadlines.

International Students: The school actively recruits these students. They must take the TOEFL with a minimum score of 500 on the paper-based TOEFL (PBT) or 71 on the Internet-based version (iBT), or take the MELAB. They must also take the SAT or ACT.

Computers: Wireless access is available. All students may access the system 24 hours a day. There are no time limits and no fees. It is strongly recommended that all students have a personal computer. Students enrolled in music, education, and computers and technology must have a personal computer.

Admissions Contact: Melissa Herr-Valburg, Director of Admissions. A campus DVD is available. E-Mail: *admissions@dwu.edu* Web: *www.dwu.edu*

MOUNT MARTY COLLEGE — E-4

Yankton, SD 57078 — (605) 668-1545; (800) 658-4552; (605) 668-1607

Full-time: 215 men, 500 women	**Faculty:** 35; IIB, --$
Part-time: 76 men, 301 women	**Ph.D.s:** 64%
Graduate: 50 men, 50 women	**Student/Faculty:** 20 to 1
Year: semesters, summer session	**Tuition:** $22,992
Application Deadline: open	**Room & Board:** $6646
Freshman Class: 397 accepted, 190 enrolled	
ACT: required	

COMPETITIVE

Mount Marty College is a private, Catholic Benedictine liberal arts college, open to students of all faiths and backgrounds. Mount Marty prepares students for a contemporary world of work, service to the human community, and personal growth. There are 2 undergraduate schools and 3 graduate schools. In addition to regional accreditation, Mount Marty has baccalaureate program accreditation with ADA and NLN. The library contains 79,228 volumes, 11,624 microform items, 8,465 audio/video tapes/CDs/DVDs, and subscribes to 439 periodicals including electronic. Computerized library services include interlibrary loans, database searching, Internet access, and Wi-Fi capability. Special learning facilities include an art gallery. The 80-acre campus is in a small town 60 miles northwest of Sioux City, Iowa, and 80 miles southwest of Sioux Falls. Including any residence halls, there are 11 buildings.

Student Life: 60% of undergraduates are from South Dakota. Others are from 25 states, and 5 foreign countries. 79% are from public schools. 94% are White. 42% are Catholic; 36% claim no religious affiliation. The average age of freshmen is 19; all undergraduates, 26. 22% do not continue beyond their first year; 61% remain to graduate.

Housing: 352 students can be accommodated in college housing, which includes single-sex dorms. On-campus housing is guaranteed for all 4 years. 75% of students live on campus; of those, 60% remain on campus on weekends. Alcohol is not permitted. All students may keep cars.

Activities: There are no fraternities or sororities. There are 50 groups on campus, including art, band, choir, chorus, computers, drama, ethnic, forensics, honors, jazz band, literary magazine, musical theater, newspaper, pep band, photography, political, professional, religious, social, social service, and student government. Popular campus events include Blue & Gold Days, Formal Dances, and Benedictine Lecture Series.

Sports: There are 6 intercollegiate sports for men and 6 for women, and 4 intramural sports for men and 4 for women. Facilities include volleyball and basketball courts, a jogging track, 2 racquetball courts, weight and training rooms, a 2220-seat stadium, a 1500-seat indoor gym, and a 700-seat auditorium.

Disabled Students: All of the campus is accessible. Facilities include wheelchair ramps, elevators, special parking, specially equipped restrooms, special class scheduling, lowered drinking fountains, and lowered telephones.

Services: Counseling and information services are available, as is tutoring in most subjects. There is remedial math, reading, and writing.

Campus Safety and Security: Measures include 24-hour foot and vehicle patrol and security escort services. There are emergency telephones and lighted pathways/sidewalks.

Programs of Study: Mount Marty confers B.A., B.S. and B.S.N. degrees. Associate and master's degrees are also awarded. Bachelor's degrees are awarded in BIOLOGICAL SCIENCE (biology/biological science), BUSINESS (accounting and business administration and management), COMMUNICATIONS AND THE ARTS (English, journalism, and music), COMPUTER AND PHYSICAL SCIENCE (chemistry, computer science, mathematics, and radiological technology), EDUCATION (athletic training, elementary education, physical education, secondary education, and special education), ENGINEERING AND ENVIRONMENTAL DESIGN (environmental science), HEALTH PROFESSIONS (health care administration, medical technology, and nursing), SOCIAL SCIENCE (behavioral science, criminal justice, food production/management/services, history, religion, and social science). Nursing, business, and teacher education are the strongest academically.

Required: To graduate, all students must complete at least 128 credit hours, with a minimum GPA of 2.0. General education requirements include 10 credit hours in religious studies/philosophy, 9 in humanities, 6 in English, 4 each in math, natural science, and lab science, and 3 in speech.

Special: Mount Marty offers co-op programs, internships, student-designed majors in selected studies, an accelerated degree program in business administration, credit for work, life, and military experience, and pass/fail options. There are 8 national honor societies, a freshman honors program, and 7 departmental honors programs.

Faculty/Classroom: 54% of faculty are male; 46% are female. All teach undergraduates. No introductory courses are taught by graduate students. The average class size in an introductory lecture is 30; in a laboratory is 15; and in a regular course is 20.

Admissions: The ACT scores were 10% below 21, 50% between 21 and

23, 30% between 24 and 26, 5% between 27 and 28, and 5% above 28. 10% of the current freshmen were in the top fifth of their class; 56% were in the top two fifths. 5 freshmen graduated first in their class.

Requirements: The ACT is required. In addition, Applicants must be graduates of an accredited secondary school or have a GED certificate. An audition and an interview are recommended. A GPA of 2.0 is required. AP and CLEP credits are accepted.

Procedure: Freshmen are admitted fall, spring, and summer. Entrance exams should be taken by October of the senior year. There are deferred admissions and rolling admissions plans. Application deadlines are open. The fall 2013 application fee was $25. Notification is sent on a rolling basis. Applications are accepted online.

Transfer: 60 transfer students enrolled in 2012-2013. Transfer students with fewer than 28 semester hours must submit high school and college transcripts. A minimum GPA of 2.0 and at least 64 credit hours are required. An interview is recommended. 32 of 128 credits required for the bachelor's degree must be completed at Mount Marty.

Visiting: There are regularly scheduled orientations for prospective students, including campus tours, faculty appointments, and admission and financial aid information. There are guides for informal visits, visitors may sit in on classes, and stay overnight. To schedule a visit, contact the Director of Admissions.

Financial Aid: In 2013-2014, 99% of all full-time freshmen and 99% of continuing full-time students received some form of financial aid. 84% of all full-time freshmen and 84% of continuing full-time students received need-based aid. The average freshman award was $12,343. 60% of undergraduate students work part-time. Average annual earnings from campus work are $1500. The average financial indebtedness of the 2013 graduate was $17,407. The FAFSA is required. The deadline for filing freshman financial aid applications for fall entry is March 1.

International Students: There are 5 international students enrolled. The school actively recruits these students. They must take the TOEFL.

Computers: All students may access the system 24 hours, 7 days per week. There are no time limits and no fees.

Graduates: The most popular majors were health professions (28%), business (23%), and education (15%). In an average class, 30% graduate in 4 years or less, 41% graduate in 5 years or less, and 44% graduate in 6 years or less. Of the 2012 graduating class, 5% were enrolled in graduate school within 6 months of graduation, and 94% were employed.

Admissions Contact: Jill Paulson, Director of Admissions. E-Mail: *mmcadmit@mtmc.edu* Web: *www.mtmc.edu*

NATIONAL AMERICAN UNIVERSITY B-3

Rapid City, SD 57701 **(605) 394-4827**
(800) 209-0490; (605) 394-4871

Full-time: 120 men, 230 women
Part-time: 50 men, 80 women
Graduate: 20 men, 20 women
Year: trimesters, summer session
Application Deadline: open
Freshman Class: n/av
Faculty: n/av
Ph.D.s: n/av
Student/Faculty: n/av
Tuition: n/av
Room & Board: n/av

NONCOMPETITIVE

National American University, founded in 1941, is a private institution that offers undergraduate programs in all aspects of business. The figures in the above capsule and in this profile are approximate. There is 1 graduate school. In addition to regional accreditation, NAU has baccalaureate program accreditation with CAHEA. The library contains 31,018 volumes and 71 audio/video tapes/CDs/DVDs, and subscribes to 268 periodicals including electronic. Computerized library services include interlibrary loans, database searching, and Internet access. Special learning facilities include a learning resource center. The Animal Health Care Center and Medical Assisting Room are instructional facilities set up as doctors' offices. The 8-acre campus is in a small town 360 miles from Sioux Falls and 420 miles from Denver, Colorado. Including any residence halls, there are 7 buildings.

Student Life: 85% of undergraduates are from South Dakota. Others are from 18 states, 4 foreign countries, and Canada. 78% are white. The average age of freshmen is 19; all undergraduates, 28. 40% do not continue beyond their first year.

Housing: 260 students can be accommodated in college housing, which includes single-sex and coed dorms. On-campus housing is guaranteed for all 4 years. 82% of students commute. Alcohol is not permitted. All students may keep cars.

Activities: There are no fraternities or sororities. There are 10 groups on campus, including computers, ethnic, international, political, professional, social, social service, and student government. Popular campus events include Maverick Stampede, Spring and Fall Picnics, and Dances.

Sports: There is 1 intercollegiate sport for men and 2 for women, and 2 intramural sports for men and 2 for women. Facilities include a 500-seat gym, a weight room, and rodeo facilities.

Disabled Students: 99% of the campus is accessible. Facilities include wheelchair ramps, elevators, special parking, and lowered drinking fountains.

Services: Counseling and information services are available, as is tutoring in most subjects. There is remedial math, reading, and writing. Some technical classes are tutored by instructors.

Campus Safety and Security: There are emergency telephones, lighted pathways/sidewalks, and security guards on duty all evenings until morning.

Programs of Study: NAU confers B.S. degrees. Associate and master's degrees are also awarded. Bachelor's degrees are awarded in AGRICULTURE (equine science), BUSINESS (accounting and business administration and management), COMPUTER AND PHYSICAL SCIENCE (information sciences and systems), EDUCATION (athletic training), HEALTH PROFESSIONS (health care administration and veterinary science), SOCIAL SCIENCE (paralegal studies). Veterinary technology and business administration are the strongest academically. Business administration, accounting, and equine studies have the largest enrollments.

Required: To graduate, students must complete 192 quarter credit hours with a 2.0 GPA in major courses. Students are required to take 76 hours of general education courses, including 12 hours each of communications, math, social science, and humanities, 8 hours of science, 4 hours of speech, and 16 hours of electives.

Special: NAU offers internships in veterinary technology equine studies and paralegal studies, study abroad, work-study programs on campus and with nonprofit organizations, accelerated degree programs in all majors, and B.A.-B.S. degrees in accounting, computer information systems, management information systems, business administration, paralegal studies, and applied management. A general studies degree, credit for life experience, nondegree study, and pass/fail options are also available. Operation Bootstrap allows qualified U.S. Air Force personnel to complete their college degrees on an accelerated basis. There is 1 national honor society.

Faculty/Classroom: 38% of faculty are male; 62% are female. No introductory courses are taught by graduate students. The average class size in an introductory lecture is 30; in a laboratory, 10; and in a regular course, 25.

Requirements: Applicants must be graduates of an accredited secondary school or have the GED. An interview is recommended. CLEP credits are accepted.

Procedure: Freshmen are admitted to all sessions. Entrance exams should be taken before classes begin. There are deferred admissions and rolling admissions plans. Application deadlines are open. Applications are accepted online.

Transfer: Applicants must submit transcripts of all high school and college work. Grades of C or better transfer for credit. An interview is recommended. 48 of 192 credits required for the bachelor's degree must be completed at NAU.

Visiting: Visits or tours are available anytime with 1 day's notice. Orientations are scheduled at the beginning of each quarter. There are guides for informal visits; visitors may sit in on classes and stay overnight. To schedule a visit, contact the Admissions Office.

Financial Aid: The FAFSA and the college's own financial statement are required. Check with the school for current application deadlines.

International Students: The school actively recruits these students. They must take the TOEFL.

Computers: Wireless access is available. The library has computer labs available for student use. All students may access the system from 7 a.m. to 8 p.m. The time limit is 90 minutes if another student is waiting. There are no fees.

Admissions Contact: Director of Admissions. E-Mail: *rcadmissions@national.edu* Web: *www.national.edu*

NORTHERN STATE UNIVERSITY D-1

Aberdeen, SD 57401 **(605) 626-2544**
(800) 678-5330; (605) 626-2587

Full-time: 704 men, 830 women
Part-time: 487 men, 808 women
Graduate: 112 men, 337 women
Year: semesters, summer session
Application Deadline:
Freshman Class: 1157 applied, 1080 accepted, 398 enrolled
ACT: 22
Faculty: 91
Ph.D.s: 74%
Student/Faculty: 19 to 1
Tuition: $7563 ($9562)
Room & Board: $6458

COMPETITIVE

Northern State University, established in 1901, is a state-supported institution offering undergraduate and graduate programs in the liberal arts and sciences, business, and education. Distance delivery technology is a core mission in all programs, especially all levels of teacher preparation. There are 4 undergraduate schools and 1 graduate school. In addition to regional accreditation, NSU has baccalaureate program accreditation with NASM and NCATE. The library contains 185,340 volumes, 402,685 microform items, 4,500 audio/video tapes/CDs/DVDs, and subscribes to 50,077 periodicals including electronic. Computerized library services include interlibrary loans, database searching, Internet access, and Wi-Fi capability. Special learning facilities include an art gallery, TV station, fine arts center. The 72-acre campus is in an urban area one-half mile south of Aberdeen's city center. Including any residence halls, there are 21 buildings.

Student Life: 75% of undergraduates are from South Dakota. Others are from 35 states, 29 foreign countries, and Canada. 86% are White. The average age of freshmen is 20; all undergraduates, 22. 30% do not continue beyond their first year; 70% remain to graduate.

Housing: 850 students can be accommodated in college housing, which includes coed dorms, on-campus apartments, and married student housing. learning communities. On-campus housing is guaranteed for all 4 years. 58% of students commute. Alcohol is not permitted. All students may keep cars.

Activities: There are no fraternities or sororities. There are 100 groups on campus, including art, band, cheerleading, chess, choir, chorale, chorus, computers, dance, debate, drama, drill team, drum and bugle corps, environmental, ethnic, forensics, gay, honors, international, jazz band, literary magazine, marching band, musical theater, newspaper, orchestra, pep band, photography, political, professional, radio and TV, religious, social, social service, student government, and symphony. Popular campus events include Gypsy Day, Gypsy Week, and I Hate Winter Weekend.

Sports: There are 6 intercollegiate sports for men and 7 for women, and 6 intramural sports for men and 6 for women. Facilities include a sports complex that houses a football stadium and an all-weather track, and a phys ed building that houses a 160-meter track, an Olympic-size pool, a weight room, 3 racquetball courts, a human performance lab, 2 basketball courts, and an 8300-seat arena.

Disabled Students: 90% of the campus is accessible. Facilities include wheelchair ramps, elevators, special parking, specially equipped restrooms, lowered drinking fountains, and curb cuts.

Services: Counseling and information services are available, as is tutoring in most subjects. There is remedial math, reading, and writing. There is an educational media center, a math lab, reading and writing centers, an ASL interpreter for the deaf, and a speech, language, and hearing clinic.

Campus Safety and Security: Measures include emergency notification system, self-defense education, and security escort services. There are emergency telephones, lighted pathways/sidewalks, and controlled access to dorms/residences.

Programs of Study: NSU confers B.A., B.S., B.M.E., B.G.S. and B.S.Ed. degrees. Associate and master's degrees are also awarded. Bachelor's degrees are awarded in BIOLOGICAL SCIENCE (biology/biological science), BUSINESS (accounting, banking and finance, business administration and management, business economics, international business management, marketing/retailing/merchandising, and personnel management), COMMUNICATIONS AND THE ARTS (English, fine arts, French, German, music, and Spanish), COMPUTER AND PHYSICAL SCIENCE (chemistry and mathematics), EDUCATION (art education, business education, early childhood education, elementary education, foreign languages education, health education, middle school education, music education, physical education, science education, secondary education, and special education), ENGINEERING AND ENVIRONMENTAL DESIGN (environmental science), HEALTH PROFESSIONS (medical laboratory technology, predentistry, premedicine, and speech pathology/audiology), SOCIAL SCIENCE (community services, criminal justice, economics, history, human services, physical fitness/movement, political science/government, prelaw, psychology, social science, and sociology). Business and education are the strongest academically.

Required: Students must complete a minimum of 120 semester hours, with 27 to 36 in the major, and must maintain a 2.0 minimum GPA. The core curriculum consists of courses in English, history, fine arts, science, math, and psychology. In addition, there are specific course requirements. All students must pass a comprehensive exam.

Special: Opportunities are provided for internships, a Washington semester, work-study programs, a B.A.-B.S. degree, dual majors, a general studies degree, credit by exam, and nondegree study. Study abroad and a co-op program in international business are available. Technology proficiency certification is available with a diverse selection of certifications. There are 4 national honor societies, including Phi Beta Kappa, a freshman honors program, and 4 departmental honors programs.

Faculty/Classroom: 51% of faculty are male; 49% are female. All teach and do research. No introductory courses are taught by graduate students. The average class size in an introductory lecture is 25 and in a laboratory is 18.

Admissions: 93% of the 2013-2014 applicants were accepted. The SAT scores for the 2013-2014 freshman class were: Critical Reading--58% below 500, 30% between 500 and 599, 11% between 600 and 699, and 1% between 700 and 800; Math--51% below 500, 37% between 500 and 599, 12% between 600 and 699, and 1% between 700 and 800. The ACT scores were 24% below 21, 47% between 21 and 23, 19% between 24 and 26, 5% between 27 and 28, and 5% above 28.

Requirements: The ACT is required. Minimum ACT composite score of 18, or students must earn a high school GPA of at least 2.6 on a 4.0 scale, or rank in the top 60% of their graduating class. Graduation from an accredited secondary school is required; a GED will be accepted. Applicants should submit a minimum academic record distributed as follows: 4 years of English, 3 each of math, science, and social studies, and one year of fine arts. A GPA of 2.0 is required. AP and CLEP credits are accepted. Important factors in the admissions decision are evidence of special talent, advanced placement or honors courses, and extracurricular activities record.

Procedure: Freshmen are admitted fall, spring, and summer. Entrance exams should be taken during the summer before the senior year. There are early admissions, deferred admissions, and rolling admissions plans. Check with the school for current application deadlines. The fall 2013 application fee was $20. Notification is sent on a rolling basis.

Transfer: 110 transfer students enrolled in 2012-2013. Applicants must submit official transcripts from all previous colleges attended. D grades do not transfer. If the applicant has not maintained a C average, an ACT score that places the applicant in the upper 50% of college-bound freshmen may be submitted for consideration. 24 of 120 credits required for the bachelor's degree must be completed at NSU.

Visiting: There are regularly scheduled orientations for prospective students, consisting of a welcome presentation, registration, refreshments, an academic visit, a campus tour, lunch, a financial aid presentation, a student panel, and a cost and scholarship presentation. There are guides for informal visits, visitors may sit in on classes, and stay overnight. To schedule a visit, contact the Admissions Office.

Financial Aid: In 2013-2014, 95% of all full-time freshmen and 90% of continuing full-time students received some form of financial aid. NSU is a member of CSS. The CCS/Profile, or FAFSA, or FFS, or SFS is required. The priority date for freshman financial aid applications for fall entry is March 1.

International Students: There are 107 international students enrolled. The school actively recruits these students. They must take the TOEFL with a minimum score of 525 on the paper-based TOEFL (PBT) or 61 on the Internet-based version (iBT).

Computers: All students may access the system. There are no time limits and no fees.

Graduates: From July 1, 2012 to June 30, 2013, 300 bachelor's degrees were awarded. The most popular majors were business (67%), general studies (64%), and education (22%). 82 companies recruited on campus in 2012-2013. Of the 2012 graduating class, 23% were enrolled in graduate school within 6 months of graduation, and 97% were employed.

Admissions Contact: Allan Vogel, Director of Admissions. E-Mail: *admission2@northern.edu* Web: *www.northern.edu*

PRESENTATION COLLEGE — D-1

Aberdeen, SD 57401 — (605) 225-1634; (800) 437-6060; (605) 229-8518

Full-time: 60 men, 380 women	**Faculty:** 28
Part-time: 20 men, 170 women	**Ph.D.s:** 25%
Graduate: n/av	**Student/Faculty:** 16 to 1
Year: semesters, summer session	**Tuition:** $13,150
Application Deadline: open	**Room & Board:** $4200
Freshman Class: 163 applied, 147 accepted, 73 enrolled	
ACT: 21	

LESS COMPETITIVE

Presentation College, founded in 1922 as Notre Dame Junior College, is an independent Catholic institution offering undergraduate degrees in nursing and allied health service management. The figures in the above capsule and in this profile are apprximate. In addition to regional accreditation, Presentation has baccalaureate program accreditation with AHEA. The library contains 33,725 and subscribes to 221 periodicals including electronic. Computerized library services include interlibrary loans. The 100-acre campus is in a small town. Including any residence halls, there are 8 buildings.

Student Life: 76% of undergraduates are from South Dakota. Others are from 6 states, and Canada. 78% are White. 30% are Catholic; 29% Protestant.

Housing: 137 students can be accommodated in college housing, which includes single-sex dorms. On-campus housing is guaranteed for all 4 years, is available on a first-come, and first-served basis. 81% of students commute. Alcohol is not permitted. All students may keep cars.

Activities: There are no fraternities or sororities. Groups on campus include chorus.

Disabled Students: All of the campus is accessible. Facilities include wheelchair ramps, elevators, special parking, and specially equipped restrooms.

Services: Counseling and information services are available, as is tutoring in every subject. There is remedial math, reading, and writing.

Campus Safety and Security: Measures include 24-hour foot and vehicle patrol. There are emergency telephones and lighted pathways/sidewalks.

Programs of Study: Presentation confers B.S., B.S.N. and B.S.W. degrees. Associate degrees are also awarded. Bachelor's degrees are awarded in BIOLOGICAL SCIENCE (biology/biological science), BUSINESS (business administration and management), COMMUNICATIONS AND THE ARTS (communications), COMPUTER AND PHYSICAL SCIENCE (radiological technology), HEALTH PROFESSIONS (health care administration and nursing), SOCIAL SCIENCE (social work). Nursing has the largest enrollment.

Required: Students must complete 128 semester hours, including 48 in upper-division courses and 36 in the major, with a minimum GPA of 2.0. The core curriculum consists of 18 hours of humanities and fine arts, 12 of social and behavioral sciences, 11 of natural sciences and math, and 10 of religious studies and philosophy.

Special: Certificate programs are available in phlebotomy, surgical technology, administrative assistance, business/accounting, and computer operating. An external degree program offers an accelerated schedule for working adults. Limited credit for experiential learning is possible. There is 1 national honor society and 2 departmental honors programs.

Faculty/Classroom: 32% of faculty are male; 68% are female. All teach undergraduates. No introductory courses are taught by graduate students.

Admissions: 90% of the 2013-2014 applicants were accepted.

Requirements: The ACT is required. In addition, prospective students must graduate from high school or hold a GED, and a GPA of 2.0 is recommended. A GPA of 2.0 is required. AP and CLEP credits are accepted. Important factors in the admissions decision are ability to finance college education, extracurricular activities record, and leadership record.

Procedure: Freshmen are admitted to all sessions. Early decision applications should be filed by April 1. Applications are accepted online.

Transfer: 115 transfer students enrolled in 2012-2013. A 2.0 GPA on previous college work is recommended. 30 of 127 credits required for the bachelor's degree must be completed at Presentation.

Visiting: To schedule a visit, contact the Admissions Office.

Financial Aid: In 2013-2014, 94% of all full-time freshmen and 97% of continuing full-time students received some form of financial aid. 88% of all full-time freshmen and 89% of continuing full-time students received need-based aid. The average freshman award was $11,339. Need-based scholarships or need-based grants averaged $3,933 ($7,050 maximum); need-based self-help aid (loans and jobs) averaged $6,694 ($7,125 maximum); and other non-need-based awards and non-need-based scholarships averaged $9,109 ($11,650 maximum). 100% of undergraduate students work part-time. Average annual earnings from campus work are $1500. The average financial indebtedness of the 2013 graduate was $26,737. Presentation is a member of CSS. The FAFSA is required. The priority date for freshman financial aid applications for fall entry is March 1. The deadline for filing freshman financial aid applications for fall entry is open.

International Students: There are 4 international students enrolled. They must take the TOEFL. They must also take the ACT.

Computers: Computer students may access the system.

Graduates: From July 1, 2012 to June 30, 2013, 116 bachelor's degrees were awarded. The most popular majors were nursing (54%), radiologic technician (7%), and surgical technician (6%).

Admissions Contact: Joddy Meidinger, Director of Admissions and Financial Aid. E-Mail: *meidinger@presentation.edu* Web: *www.presentation.edu*

SINTE GLESKA UNIVERSITY C-4

Rosebud, SD 57570 **(605) 856-8100; (605) 747-2098**

Full-time: 100 men, 240 women	**Faculty:** 23
Part-time: 1 woman	**Ph.D.s:** n/av
Graduate: 120 men, 320 women	**Student/Faculty:** n/av
Year: semesters, summer session	**Tuition:** $4100
Application Deadline: open	**Room & Board:** n/av
Freshman Class: n/av	
	NONCOMPETITIVE

Sinte Gleska University, founded in 1970, is an independent institution offering undergraduate programs in business, fine arts, professional training, and technical studies. The figures in the above capsule and in this profile are approximate. There is 1 graduate school. The library contains 85,000 volumes. The 52-acre campus is in a rural area east of Mission on the Rosebud Reservation. Including any residence halls, there are 7 buildings.

Student Life: 92% of undergraduates are from South Dakota. All are from public schools. 85% are Native American/Eskimo; 15% white. The average age all undergraduates is 31. 10% do not continue beyond their first year; 90% remain to graduate.

Housing: There are no residence halls. All students commute.

Activities: There are no fraternities or sororities. Groups on campus include newspaper and photography. Popular campus events include Founders Day.

Sports: There are 4 intramural sports for men and 3 for women.

Disabled Students: All of the campus is accessible. Facilities include wheelchair ramps, special parking, specially equipped rest rooms, and lowered drinking fountains.

Services: Counseling and information services are available, as is tutoring in every subject.

Campus Safety and Security: There are shuttle buses and an evening security guard.

Programs of Study: Sinte Gleska confers B.A. and B.S. degrees. Associate and master's degrees are also awarded. Bachelor's degrees are awarded in COMMUNICATIONS AND THE ARTS (art), EDUCATION (early childhood education and elementary education), HEALTH PROFESSIONS (mental health/human services), SOCIAL SCIENCE (human services). Education and human services are the strongest academically.

Required: To graduate, students must complete at least 128 credits with a GPA of 2.0; education majors must have a 2.5. All students must fulfill the core curriculum requirements.

Special: The university offers work-study programs, accelerated degree programs, a general studies degree, and pass/fail options.

Faculty/Classroom: No introductory courses are taught by graduate students.

Requirements: Applicants must be graduates of accredited secondary schools or have earned a GED.

Procedure: Freshmen are admitted to all sessions. Entrance exams should be taken before admission. There is a rolling admissions plan. Application deadlines are open.

Transfer: Applicants must submit an official transcript from their previous college. 68 of 128 credits required for the bachelor's degree must be completed at Sinte Gleska.

Visiting: There are regularly scheduled orientations for prospective students. There are guides for informal visits, and visitors may stay overnight. To schedule a visit, contact the Registrar's Office.

Financial Aid: The SFS is required. Check with the school for current application deadlines.

Admissions Contact: Jack Herman, Registrar. Web: *www.sintegleska.edu*

SOUTH DAKOTA BOARD OF REGENTS

The South Dakota Board of Regents, established in 1890, is a public system in South Dakota. It is governed by a Board of Regents, whose chief administrator is the executive director. The primary goal of the system is to provide high quality, diverse educational opportunities and services to the people of South Dakota. The main priorities are excellence in academic programs, diverse campus communities, and resources for economic development efforts. The total student enrollment is usually 32,500, with 1600 faculty members. Altogether there are approximate 437 baccalaureate, 94 master's, and 31 doctoral programs offered in the South Dakota Board of Regents. Profiles of the 4-year campuses are included in this section.

SOUTH DAKOTA SCHOOL OF MINES AND TECHNOLOGY B-3

Rapid City, SD 57701 **(605) 394-2414**
(877) 877-6044; (605) 394-1979

Full-time: 1350 men, 370 women	**Faculty:** 143
Part-time: 223 men, 158 women	**Ph.D.s:** 88%
Graduate: 243 men, 80 women	**Student/Faculty:** 13 to 1
Year: semesters, summer session	**Tuition:** $9370 ($11,310)
Application Deadline: August 15	**Room & Board:** $5890
Freshman Class: 1127 applied, 991 accepted, 454 enrolled	
SAT CR/M/W: 560/600/500 **ACT:** 26	**VERY COMPETITIVE**

South Dakota School of Mines and Technology, founded in 1885, is a public university offering undergraduate and graduate programs in engineering, science, and mathematics. There is one undergraduate school and one graduate school. In addition to regional accreditation, SDSM&T has baccalaureate program accreditation with ABET and CSAB. The library contains 172,180 volumes, 18,958 microform items, and 10,357 audio/video tapes/CDs/DVDs, and subscribes to 7,364 periodicals including electronic. Computerized library services include interlibrary loans, database searching, Internet access, and Wi-Fi capability. Special learning facilities include an art gallery, natural history museum, planetarium, radio station, geology and paleontology museum, and apex gallery. The 120-acre campus is in a suburban area 350 miles northeast of Denver. Including any residence halls, there are 21 buildings.

Student Life: 55% of undergraduates are from South Dakota. Others are from 40 states, 24 foreign countries, and Canada. 82% are White. The average age of freshmen is 19; all undergraduates, 22. 20% do not continue beyond their first year; 55% remain to graduate.

Housing: 671 students can be accommodated in college housing, which includes single-sex and coed dorms and off-campus apartments. In addition, there are fraternity houses and sorority houses. On-campus housing is available on a first-come first-served basis. 67% of students commute. Alcohol is not permitted. All students may keep cars.

Activities: 8% of men belong to 4 national fraternities; 9% of women belong to 2 national sororities. There are 135 groups on campus, including professional, ski club and biking, art, band, cheerleading, choir, chorale, chorus, circle k, computers, dance, drama, drill team, environmental, ethnic, film, gay, honors, international, jazz band, newspaper, orchestra, pep band, political, professional, radio and TV, religious, social, social service, and student government. Popular campus events include M-Week, Christmas Chorale Concert, International Cultural Exposition and Engineers Week.

Sports: There are 7 intercollegiate sports for men and 6 for women, and 10 intramural sports for men and 10 for women. Facilities include a football field, a track, a 2350-seat gym, a sand volleyball court, a swimming pool, squash/racquetball courts, weight room and wellness center.

Disabled Students: 81% of the campus is accessible. Facilities include wheelchair ramps, elevators, special parking, specially equipped restrooms, special class scheduling, lowered drinking fountains, special housing, and an ADA lab with specialized workstations, software, and hardware to aid students with visual, auditory, and mobility impairments and dyslexia.

Services: Counseling and information services are available, as is tutoring in most subjects. There is a reader service for the blind, and remedial math.

Campus Safety and Security: Measures include 24-hour foot and vehicle patrol, emergency notification system, self-defense education, and security escort services. There are emergency telephones, lighted pathways/sidewalks, and controlled access to dorms/residences.

Programs of Study: SDSM&T confers B.S. degrees. Associate, master's, and doctoral degrees are also awarded. Bachelor's degrees are awarded in COMPUTER AND PHYSICAL SCIENCE (chemistry, computer science, geology, mathematics, and physics), ENGINEERING AND ENVIRONMENTAL DESIGN (chemical engineering, civil engineering, computer engineering, electrical/electronics engineering, environmental engineering, geological engineering, industrial engineering, mechanical engineering, metallurgical engineering, and mining and mineral engineering), SOCIAL SCIENCE (interdisciplinary studies). Engineering is the strongest academically. Mechanical engineering, civil engineering, and electrical engineering have the largest enrollments.

Required: Students must complete 120 credits for the science major or 130 credits for the engineering major, and maintain a minimum GPA of 2.0. Included in these requirements are 16 credit hours each of math at a level of calculus and above, basic science, and humanities/social science (for engineering, 3 credits must be at the 300 or above level). State regents mandated distribution requirements include 6 credits each of written communications, social sciences, arts/humanities, science, and cultural diversity; 3 credits each of speech communications and math; and 2 credits of information technology literacy, plus completion of an exam.

Special: Opportunities are provided for study abroad, co-op programs, internships, dual degrees, undergraduate research experiences, interdisciplinary design teams, credit by exam, and nondegree study. There are 5 national honor societies including Phi Beta Kappa.

Faculty/Classroom: 76% of faculty are male; 24% are female. All teach undergraduates, and 31% do research. Graduate students teach 4% of introductory courses. The average class size in an introductory lecture is 38; in a laboratory is 17; and in a regular course is 21.

Admissions: 88% of the 2013-2014 applicants were accepted. The SAT scores for the 2013-2014 freshman class were: Critical Reading--31% below 500, 40% between 500 and 599, 22% between 600 and 699, and 7% between 700 and 800; Math--12% below 500, 40% between 500 and 599, 29% between 600 and 699, and 19% between 700 and 800; Writing--42% below 500, 40% between 500 and 599, 16% between 600 and 699, and 2% between 700 and 800. The ACT scores were 4% below 21, 17% between 21 and 23, 35% between 24 and 26, 20% between 27 and 28, and 24% above 28. 39% of the current freshmen were in the top fifth of their class; 65% were in the top two fifths. There were 6 National Merit finalists. 24 freshmen graduated first in their class.

Requirements: The ACT is required. The SAT is accepted, the ACT is preferred, with a minimum composite score of 920 (420 critical reading/writing and 500 math) on the SAT, or a minimum composite score of 18 on the ACT. Graduation from an accredited secondary school is required. A GED is accepted. Applicants must submit high school credits, distributed as follows: 4 years of English, 3 each of math, lab science, and social studies, and 1/2 year each of fine arts and computer science. A GPA of 2.8 is required. AP and CLEP credits are accepted.

Procedure: Freshmen are admitted fall, spring, and summer. Entrance exams should be taken preferably in October and December. There is a rolling admissions plan. Application deadlines are open. The fall 2013 application fee was $20. Notification is sent on a rolling basis. Applications are accepted online.

Transfer: 103 transfer students enrolled in 2012-2013. Transfer students must submit an official transcript from their High School or GED and their previous college(s)and must have maintained a minimum GPA 2.75 or higher. 30 of 130 credits required for the bachelor's degree must be completed at SDSM&T.

Visiting: There are regularly scheduled orientations for prospective students, including a campus tour, discussions, training, and a meal. There are guides for informal visits, visitors may sit in on classes, and stay overnight. To schedule a visit, contact the Admissions Office.

Financial Aid: In 2013-2014, 60% of all full-time freshmen and 56% of continuing full-time students received some form of financial aid. 44% of all full-time freshmen and 34% of continuing full-time students received need-based aid. The average freshman award was $13,258. Need-based scholarships or need-based grants averaged $4,115; need-based self-help aid (loans and jobs) averaged $3,646; non-need-based athletic scholarships averaged $3,868; and other non-need-based awards and non-need-based scholarships averaged $2,799. 16% of undergraduate students work part-time. Average annual earnings from campus work are $1286. The average financial indebtedness of the 2013 graduate was $18,331. The FAFSA is required. The deadline for filing freshman financial aid applications for fall entry is March 15.

International Students: There are 35 international students enrolled. The school actively recruits these students. They must take the TOEFL with a minimum score of 520 on the paper-based TOEFL (PBT) or 68 on the Internet-based version (iBT). They must also take the ACT. TOEFL's may be submitted in place of SAT or ACT's.

Computers: All students may access the system 24 hours per day. There are no time limits and no fees.

Graduates: From July 1, 2012 to June 30, 2013, 376 bachelor's degrees were awarded. The most popular majors were mechanical engineering (15%), civil engineering (7%), and electrical engineering (6%). 176 companies recruited on campus in 2012-2013. In an average class, 20% graduate in 4 years or less, 46% graduate in 5 years or less, and 55% graduate in 6 years or less. Of the 2012 graduating class, 26% were enrolled in graduate school within 6 months of graduation, and 83% were employed.

Admissions Contact: Office of Admissions E-Mail: *admissions@sdsmt.edu* Web: *www.gotomines.com*

SOUTH DAKOTA STATE UNIVERSITY F-3

Brookings, SD 57007 **(605) 688-4121**
(800) 952-3541; (605) 688-6891

Full-time: n/av	**Faculty:** n/av
Part-time: n/av	**Ph.D.s:** n/av
Graduate: n/av	**Student/Faculty:** n/av
Year: semesters, summer session	**Tuition:** $7713 ($9795)
Application Deadline: open	**Room & Board:** $6583

Freshman Class: 4851 applied, 4458 accepted, 2306 enrolled
ACT: required

COMPETITIVE

South Dakota State University, founded in 1881, is a public land-grant institution, that offers undergraduate programs in agriculture and biological sciences, arts and sciences, engineering, education and human sciences, nursing, pharmacy, and general studies. There are 8 undergraduate schools and 1 graduate school. In addition to regional accreditation, SDSU has baccalaureate program accreditation with ABET, ACCE, ACEJMC, ACPE, NASM, NCATE, and NLN. The library contains 897,150 volumes, 88,489 microform items, 4,682 audio/video tapes/CDs/DVDs, and subscribes to 57,010 periodicals including electronic. Computerized library services include interlibrary loans, database searching, Internet access, and Wi-Fi capability. Special learning facilities include an art gallery, radio station, arboretum, agricultural heritage museum, Northern Plains Biostress Lab, Animal Disease Research and Diagnostic Lab, and South Dakota Art Museum. The 275-acre campus is in a small town 50 miles north of Sioux Falls, 200 miles west of Minneapolis. Including any residence halls, there are 172 buildings.

Student Life: 87% are White.

Housing: 3785 students can be accommodated in college housing, which includes coed dorms, on-campus apartments, and married student housing. In addition, there are honors houses, special-interest houses, fraternity houses, sorority houses, Living Learning Communities. On-campus housing is available on a first-come first-served basis. 68% of students commute. All students may keep cars.

Activities: 4% of men belong to 6 national fraternities; 2% of women belong to 3 national sororities. There are 207 groups on campus, including art, band, cheerleading, chess, choir, chorale, chorus, computers, dance, debate, drama, drill team, environmental, ethnic, film, forensics, gay, honors, international, jazz band, literary magazine, marching band, musical theater, newspaper, opera, orchestra, pep band, photography, political, professional, radio and TV, religious, social, social service, student government, and symphony. Popular campus events include Little International, Engineering Exploration Days, Capers, Cavorts, and Hobo Days.

Sports: There are 9 intercollegiate sports for men and 10 for women, and 16 intramural sports for men and 17 for women. Facilities include a physical education complex, an intramural building, outdoor track, lighted tennis courts, a wellness center, and intramural football, softball, soccer, and Rugby Fields.

Disabled Students: 99% of the campus is accessible. Facilities include

wheelchair ramps, elevators, special parking, specially equipped restrooms, special class scheduling, lowered drinking fountains, lowered telephones, special housing.

Services: Counseling and information services are available, as is tutoring in most subjects, accounting, biology, chemistry, economics, physics, and history There is a reader service for the blind, and remedial math, reading, and writing.

Campus Safety and Security: Measures include 24-hour foot and vehicle patrol, emergency notification system, self-defense education, and security escort services. There are emergency telephones, lighted pathways/sidewalks, and controlled access to dorms/residences.

Programs of Study: SDSU confers B.A., B.G.S., B.S. and B.M.E. degrees. Associate, master's, and doctoral degrees are also awarded. Bachelor's degrees are awarded in AGRICULTURE (agricultural business management, agricultural communications, agricultural economics, agriculture, agronomy, animal science, dairy science, fish and game management, forestry and related sciences, horticulture, natural resource management, plant science, and range/farm management), BIOLOGICAL SCIENCE (biochemistry, biology/biological science, biotechnology, ecology, environmental biology, microbiology, nutrition, and wildlife biology), BUSINESS (apparel and accessories marketing, entrepreneurial studies, and hotel/motel and restaurant management), COMMUNICATIONS AND THE ARTS (art, communications, dramatic arts, English, German, graphic design, journalism, music, and Spanish), COMPUTER AND PHYSICAL SCIENCE (chemistry, computer science, geoscience, mathematics, physics, and software engineering), EDUCATION (agricultural education, art education, athletic training, early childhood education, education, health education, home economics education, music education, physical education, secondary education, technical education, and vocational education), ENGINEERING AND ENVIRONMENTAL DESIGN (agricultural engineering, agricultural engineering technology, architecture, aviation administration/management, aviation maintenance management, civil engineering, construction management, electrical/electronics engineering, electrical/electronics engineering technology, engineering, engineering physics, engineering technology, environmental engineering, industrial administration/management, interior design, landscape architecture/design, manufacturing technology, and mechanical engineering), HEALTH PROFESSIONS (clinical science, exercise science, medical laboratory science, nursing, pharmaceutical science, and pharmacy), SOCIAL SCIENCE (consumer services, early childhood studies, economics, family/consumer resource management, family/consumer studies, food production/management/services, food science, French studies, geography, history, human development, liberal arts/general studies, parks and recreation management, philosophy and religion, political science/government, psychology, rural sociology, safety management, and sociology).

Required: Students must complete at least 120 semester credit hours for the baccalaureate degree (see individual professional college requirements) and 60 semester credit hours for the associate degree. Remedial course credits are not counted as meeting degree requirements. A cumulative grade point average (CGPA) of 2.00 is necessary.

Special: Co-op programs in elementary education and social work, internships, work-study programs, B.A.-B.S. degrees, and interdisciplinary majors including agricultural journalism, environmental management, and wildlife and fisheries science, are available. SDSU offers cross-registration with Dakota State University, Black Hills State University, and the University of South Dakota, Northern State University and South Dakota School of Mines and Technology. Opportunities are provided for dual majors, study abroad in more than 50 countries, credit by examination, student-designed majors, credit for military experience, nondegree study, a general studies degree, and pass/fail options. There are 33 national honor societies and a freshman honors program.

Faculty/Classroom: No introductory courses are taught by graduate students.

Admissions: 92% of the 2013-2014 applicants were accepted.

Requirements: The ACT is required. Students must have an 18 ACT composite score, or be in the top 60% of their class, or have a 2.6 GPA in required classes. Graduation from an accredited secondary school is required. A GED will be accepted. Applicants must submit 4 years of English, 3 years each of social studies, math, and science, and 1 year of fine arts and have a GPA of 2.0 in the required courses. SDSU requires applicants to be in the upper 60% of their class. A GPA of 2.6 is required. AP and CLEP credits are accepted. Important factors in the admissions decision are advanced placement or honors courses, evidence of special talent, and extracurricular activities record.

Procedure: Freshmen are admitted to all sessions. Entrance exams should be taken by spring of the junior year. There is a rolling admissions plan. Application deadlines are open. Application fee is $20. Notification is sent on a rolling basis. Applications are accepted online.

Transfer: To be eligible for transfer, students must have been in good standing at the previous college and must have maintained a minimum GPA of 2.0 to 2.5, depending on the student's major. 30 of 120 credits required for the bachelor's degree must be completed at SDSU.

Visiting: There are regularly scheduled orientations for prospective students, student orientation sessions which are offered each June. Students become acquainted with the university and student resources. They also meet with an academic adviser and register for fall semester classes. Information is sent to all admitted students. There are guides for informal visits, visitors may sit in on classes, and stay overnight. To schedule a visit, contact the Admissions Office at SDSU_Admissions@sdstate.edu.

Financial Aid: SDSU is a member of CSS. The FAFSA is required. The priority date for freshman financial aid applications for fall entry is March 20.

International Students: The school actively recruits these students. They must take the TOEFL with a minimum score of 500 on the paper-based TOEFL (PBT) or 61 on the Internet-based version (iBT).

Computers: All students may access the system. There are no time limits. The fee is $77.33.

Graduates: From July 1, 2012 to June 30, 2013, 1988 bachelor's degrees were awarded.

Admissions Contact: Tracy Welsh, Director. E-Mail: *sdsu.admissions@sdstate.edu* Web: *www.sdstate.edu*

UNIVERSITY OF SIOUX FALLS — F-3

Sioux Falls, SD 57105 — **(605) 331-6600**
(800) 888-1047; (605) 331-6615

Full-time: 490 men, 550 women	**Faculty:** n/av; IIB; $--
Part-time: 110 men, 130 women	**Ph.D.s:** 75%
Graduate: 140 men, 230 women	**Student/Faculty:** n/av
Year: semesters, summer session	**Tuition:** $23,350
Application Deadline: open	**Room & Board:** $7080
Freshman Class: n/av	
SAT or ACT: required	

COMPETITIVE

University of Sioux Falls, founded in 1883, is a private liberal arts institution affiliated with the American Baptist Churches. Some figures in the above capsule and in this profile are approximate. In addition to regional accreditation, USF has baccalaureate program accreditation with CSWE and NCATE. The library contains 78,000 volumes and 4600 audio/video tapes/CDs/DVDs, and subscribes to 450 periodicals including electronic. Computerized library services include interlibrary loans and database searching. Special learning facilities include a learning resource center, radio station, and TV station. The 22-acre campus is in a suburban area 250 miles from Minneapolis/St. Paul, Minnesota, and 180 miles from Omaha, Nebraska. Including any residence halls, there are 15 buildings.

Student Life: 67% of undergraduates are from South Dakota. Others are from 28 states, 5 foreign countries, and Canada. 95% are from public schools. 94% are white. 73% are Protestant; 14% Catholic; 13% claim no religious affiliation. The average age of freshmen is 18; all undergraduates, 21. 32% do not continue beyond their first year; 68% remain to graduate.

Housing: 350 students can be accommodated in college housing, which includes single-sex and coed dorms, on-campus apartments, and married student housing. On-campus housing is guaranteed for the freshman year only, is available on a first-come, first-served basis, and is available on a lottery system for upperclassmen. Priority is given to out-of-town students. 62% of students commute. Alcohol is not permitted. All students may keep cars.

Activities: There are no fraternities or sororities. There are 35 groups on campus, including art, band, cheerleading, choir, chorale, chorus, computers, drama, ethnic, honors, international, jazz band, musical theater, newspaper, opera, orchestra, pep band, photography, political, professional, radio and TV, religious, social, social service, and student government. Popular campus events include Spring Formal and Madrigals.

Sports: There are 9 intercollegiate sports for men and 9 for women. Facilities include a student lounge, a 160-meter running track, volleyball, tennis, badminton, racquetball, and basketball courts, aerobics facilities, exercise machines, a whirlpool, and a 700-seat gym.

Disabled Students: 54% of the campus is accessible. Facilities include wheelchair ramps, elevators, special parking, specially equipped rest rooms, special class scheduling, lowered drinking fountains, and lowered telephones.

Services: Counseling and information services are available, as is tutoring in most subjects. There is remedial math, reading, and writing.

Campus Safety and Security: Measures include self-defense education and security escort services. There are emergency telephones and lighted pathways/sidewalks.

Programs of Study: USF confers B.A. and B.S. degrees. Associate and master's degrees are also awarded. Bachelor's degrees are awarded in BIOLOGICAL SCIENCE (biology/biological science), BUSINESS (accounting, business administration and management, business economics, and marketing/retailing/merchandising), COMMUNICATIONS AND THE ARTS (communications, English, music, and speech/debate/rhetoric), COMPUTER AND PHYSICAL SCIENCE (chemistry, computer science, and mathematics), EDUCATION (art education, early childhood education, elementary education, middle school education, music education, science education, and secondary education), HEALTH PROFESSIONS (medical laboratory technology and premedicine), SOCIAL SCIENCE (history, philosophy, political science/government, prelaw, psychology, religion, social work, and sociology). Business and elementary education are the strongest academically and have the largest enrollments.

Required: To graduate, all students must complete a minimum of 128 credit hours, with 64 hours in the major. Required courses include phys ed, computer science, religion, history, English, science, economics, political science, psychology, math, social science, cross-cultural experience, speech, and fine arts. A writing proficiency test and a minimum 2.0 GPA are also required.

Special: There are co-op programs with Augustana College, the Center for Public Higher Education, Dakota State University, and the North American Baptist Seminary. USF offers internships, study abroad in Japan, Central America, and China, an American Studies Program in Washington, D.C., and a January interim. Also available are on-campus work-study programs, B.A.-B.S. degrees, dual and student-designed interdisciplinary majors, a general studies degree, a 3-2 engineering degree, credit for life and work experience, and pass/fail options. There are 3 national honor societies, a freshman honors program, and 2 departmental honors programs.

Faculty/Classroom: 69% of faculty are male; 31% are female. All teach undergraduates, and 60% do research. No introductory courses are taught by graduate students. The average class size in an introductory lecture is 40; in a laboratory, 15; and in a regular course, 20.

Requirements: The SAT or ACT is required, with a minimum score for the critical reading and math section of the SAT of 1050 or a 22 on the ACT. Applicants must be graduates of an accredited secondary school or have a GED certificate. Students should have completed 4 years each of English and math and 2 years each of foreign language, science, and social studies. USF requires applicants to be in the upper 50% of their class. A GPA of 2.5 is required. AP and CLEP credits are accepted. Important factors in the admissions decision are advanced placement or honors courses, evidence of special talent, and leadership record.

Procedure: Freshmen are admitted to all sessions. Entrance exams should be taken during the junior or senior year of high school. There are early admissions and rolling admissions plans. Application deadlines are open. The application fee is $25; there is no fee for online applications.

Transfer: Transfer students must meet freshman admission requirements and have completed at least 24 hours of college courses with a minimum 2.0 GPA. The SAT or ACT and an interview are recommended. 30 of 128 credits required for the bachelor's degree must be completed at USF.

Visiting: There are regularly scheduled orientations for prospective students, including meetings with faculty and staff, attendance at class, a campus tour, and a financial aid session. There are guides for informal visits, and visitors may sit in on classes and stay overnight. To schedule a visit, contact the Admissions Office.

Financial Aid: USF is a member of CSS. The FAFSA, FFS, CCS/Profile, or SFS is required. Check with the school for current application deadlines.

International Students: The school actively recruits these students. They must take the TOEFL. They must also take the ACT if the examination is available to the student.

Computers: All students may access the system 8 a.m. to 11 p.m. There are no time limits and no fees.

Admissions Contact: Director of New Student Recruitment. E-Mail: *admissions@usiouxfalls.edu* Web: *www.usiouxfalls.edu*

UNIVERSITY OF SOUTH DAKOTA F-4

Vermillion, SD 57069 **(605) 677-5434**
(877) COYOTES; (605) 677-6323

Full-time: 1927 men, 2805 women	**Faculty:** 383; I, --$
Part-time: 895 men, 2006 women	**Ph.D.s:** 85%
Graduate: 1125 men, 1477 women	**Student/Faculty:** 17 to 1
Year: semesters, summer session	**Tuition:** $8022 ($10,104)
Application Deadline: open	**Room & Board:** $7089
Freshman Class: 3606 applied, 3469 accepted, 1342 enrolled	
SAT CR/M: 509/527 **ACT:** 23	**COMPETITIVE**

The University of South Dakota, founded in 1862, is a public institution with undergraduate programs in arts and sciences, education, fine arts, business, health sciences and professional schools of law, medicine, audiology and physcial therapy. There are 6 undergraduate schools and 7 graduate schools. In addition to regional accreditation, USD has baccalaureate program accreditation with AACSB, APTA, CSWE, NASAD, NASM, NCATE, and NLN. The library contains 863,292 volumes, 740,454 microform items, and 15,185 audio/video tapes/CDs/DVDs, and subscribes to 64,575 periodicals including electronic. Computerized library services include interlibrary loans, database searching, Internet access, and Wi-Fi capability. Special learning facilities include an art gallery, natural history museum, radio station, TV station, music museum, historical study center, institutes of American Indian studies, social science research, child welfare training, business and governmental research bureaus, centers for speech and hearing, international studies, fine arts, and telecommunications, natural sciences field station, and archeology and human factors labs. The 284-acre campus is in a small town between Sioux City, Iowa and Sioux Falls, South Dakota. Including any residence halls, there are 69 buildings.

Student Life: 69% of undergraduates are from South Dakota. Others are from 48 states, 27 foreign countries, and Canada. 86% are White. The average age of freshmen is 18; all undergraduates, 22. 25% do not continue beyond their first year; 56% remain to graduate.

Housing: 2218 students can be accommodated in college housing, which includes single-sex and coed dorms, on-campus apartments, and married student housing. In addition, there are fraternity houses and sorority houses. On-campus housing is guaranteed for the freshman year only, is available on a first-come, first-served basis. 72% of students commute. Alcohol is not permitted. All students may keep cars.

Activities: 18% of men belong to 7 national fraternities; 11% of women belong to 8 national sororities. There are 140 groups on campus, including art, band, cheerleading, chess, choir, chorale, chorus, computers, dance, debate, drama, drill team, ethnic, forensics, gay, honors, international, jazz band, literary magazine, marching band, musical theater, newspaper, opera, orchestra, pep band, photography, political, professional, radio and TV, religious, social, social service, student government, and symphony. Popular campus events include Dakota Days, Strollers (a variety production), and Rockfest.

Sports: There are 7 intercollegiate sports for men and 10 for women, and 12 intramural sports for men and 12 for women. Facilities include a completed Wellness Center, an indoor football field, 5 basketball courts, a 25-meter swimming pool, an 8-lane, 200-meter track, a fitness center, a fitness room, batting cages, and racquetball, volleyball, and tennis courts. Outdoor areas include a softball complex, soccer fields, flag football fields, and tennis courts.

Disabled Students: 95% of the campus is accessible. Facilities include wheelchair ramps, elevators, special parking, specially equipped restrooms, special class scheduling, lowered drinking fountains, and lowered telephones.

Services: Counseling and information services are available, as is tutoring in most subjects. There is a reader service for the blind, and remedial math, reading, and writing. There is an academic advising and testing center.

Campus Safety and Security: Measures include 24-hour foot and vehicle patrol, emergency notification system, self-defense education, and security escort services. There are shuttle buses, emergency telephones, and lighted pathways/sidewalks.

Programs of Study: USD confers B.A., B.S., B.B.A., B.F.A., B.G.S., B.M., B.S.Ed, B.S.N. and B.S.R. degrees. Associate, master's, and doctoral degrees are also awarded. Bachelor's degrees are awarded in BIOLOGICAL SCIENCE (biology/biological science), BUSINESS (accounting, banking and finance, management science, and recreation and leisure services), COMMUNICATIONS AND THE ARTS (art, communications technology, dramatic arts, English, German, journalism, music, music performance, and Spanish), COMPUTER AND PHYSICAL SCIENCE (chemistry, computer science, earth science, mathematics, and physics), EDUCATION (art education, elementary education, music education, physical education, secondary education, and special education), HEALTH PROFESSIONS (dental hygiene, health care administration, medical technology, and speech pathology/audiology), SOCIAL SCIENCE (addiction studies, American Indian studies, anthropology, criminal justice, economics, French studies, history, international studies, liberal arts/general studies, philosophy, political science/government, psychology, social work, and sociology). Business, biology, and chemistry are the strongest academically. Business, psychology, and biology have the largest enrollments.

Required: Students must complete 132 hours with a minimum GPA of 2.0. At least 32 hours must be at the 300/400 level. All students should complete 9 hours of interdisciplinary course work, 6 hours each in composition, humanities, social science, natural science, and multicultural diversity, 1 hour in fine arts, and a computer literacy course.

Special: USD offers internships, study abroad in 7 countries, and work-study programs. B.A.-B.S. degrees in 34 majors, a student-designed liberal studies major, dual majors, nondegree study, and pass/fail options are available. The Arts Outreach program provides arts activities and noncredit classes. There are 16 national honor societies, including Phi Beta Kappa, a freshman honors program, and 19 departmental honors programs.

Faculty/Classroom: 50% of faculty are male; 50% are female. 95% teach undergraduates, 5% do research, and all teach and do research. Graduate students teach 8% of introductory courses. The average class size in an introductory lecture is 29; in a laboratory is 19; and in a regular course is 23.

Admissions: 96% of the 2013-2014 applicants were accepted. The SAT scores for the 2013-2014 freshman class were: Critical Reading--46% below 500, 34% between 500 and 599, 18% between 600 and 699, and 2% between 700 and 800; Math--39% below 500, 32% between 500 and

599, 25% between 600 and 699, and 4% between 700 and 800. The ACT scores were 24% below 21, 31% between 21 and 23, 26% between 24 and 26, 11% between 27 and 28, and 8% above 28. 31% of the current freshmen were in the top fifth of their class; 60% were in the top two fifths. 66 freshmen graduated first in their class.

Requirements: The ACT is required. In addition, applicants must have earned a 2.0 GPA in 4 years of English, 3 years each of lab science, math, and social studies, and 2 semesters of fine arts. They must also rank in the top 60% of their graduation class, have an ACT score of 18, or have a high school GPA of 2.6. A GPA of 2.0 is required. AP and CLEP credits are accepted.

Procedure: Freshmen are admitted fall, spring, and summer. There are deferred admissions and rolling admissions plans. Application deadlines are open. Application fee is $20. Applications are accepted online.

Transfer: 635 transfer students enrolled in 2012-2013. Applicants should have a minimum college GPA of 2.0 and be in good standing at their previous school. 32 of 130 credits required for the bachelor's degree must be completed at USD.

Visiting: There are regularly scheduled orientations for prospective students, Student visits include an introductory session with an admission counselor, academic department visits, a campus tour with a student guide, and any other requested units. There are guides for informal visits, visitors may sit in on classes, and stay overnight.

Financial Aid: In 2013-2014, 95% of all full-time freshmen and 88% of continuing full-time students received some form of financial aid. 59% of all full-time freshmen and 62% of continuing full-time students received need-based aid. The average freshman award was $10,479. Need-based scholarships or need-based grants averaged $1,389 ($14,150 maximum); need-based self-help aid (loans and jobs) averaged $2,148 ($10,150 maximum); non-need-based athletic scholarships averaged $609 ($18,818 maximum); and other non-need-based awards and non-need-based scholarships averaged $2,992 ($19,856 maximum). 15% of undergraduate students work part-time. Average annual earnings from campus work are $2007. The average financial indebtedness of the 2013 graduate was $26,629. The FAFSA is required. The priority date for freshman financial aid applications for fall entry is March 15.

International Students: There are 91 international students enrolled. The school actively recruits these students. They must take the TOEFL with a minimum score of 550 on the paper-based TOEFL (PBT).

Computers: All students may access the system 24 hours a day. There are no time limits and no fees.

Graduates: From July 1, 2012 to June 30, 2013, 1055 bachelor's degrees were awarded. The most popular majors were health professions (21%), business/marketing (15%), and education (11%). 72 companies recruited on campus in 2012-2013. In an average class, 2% graduate in 3 years or less, 32% graduate in 4 years or less, 50% graduate in 5 years or less, and 56% graduate in 6 years or less. Of the 2012 graduating class, 30% were enrolled in graduate school within 6 months of graduation, and 60% were employed.

Admissions Contact: Travis Vlasman, Dean of Enrollment. E-Mail: *admission@usd.edu* Web: *www.usd.edu*

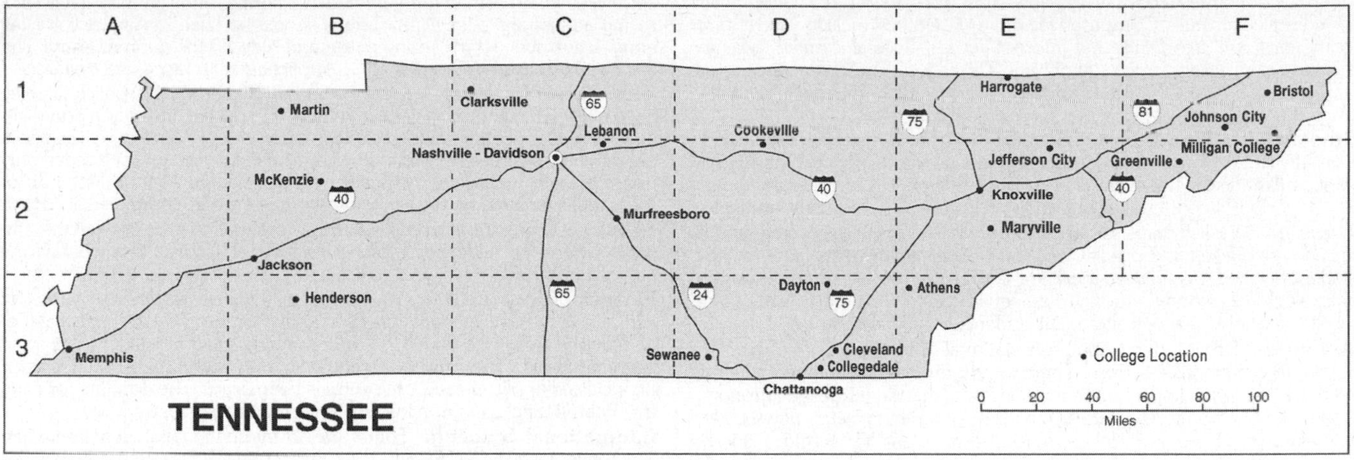

AQUINAS COLLEGE C-2

Nashville, TN 37205
(615) 297-7545 x460
(800) 649-9956; (615) 279-3891

Full-time: 34 men, 153 women
Part-time: 59 men, 262 women
Graduate: 6 men, 62 women
Year: semesters, summer session
Application Deadline:
Faculty: 31
Ph.D.s: 48%
Student/Faculty: 6 to 1
Tuition: $20,550
Room & Board: $8700
Freshman Class: 119 applied, 62 accepted, 36 enrolled
SAT CR/M: 480/415 **ACT:** 24 **COMPETITIVE+**

Aquinas College is committed to the intellectual, moral, and professional development of its students through a rigorous liberal arts curriculum that seeks to develop the whole person. Aquinas College provides students with a foundation for life while preparing them for careers of service in the liberal arts and sciences, business, nursing and, teaching. There are 4 undergraduate schools. In addition to regional accreditation, has baccalaureate program accreditation with NLN. The library contains 70,523 volumes, 140,602 microform items, 2,147 audio/video tapes/CDs/DVDs, and subscribes to 372 periodicals including electronic. Computerized library services include interlibrary loans, database searching, Internet access, and Wi-Fi capability. The 83-acre campus is in an urban area in the western section of metropolitan Nashville. Including any residence halls, there are 6 buildings.

Student Life: 84% of undergraduates are from Tennessee. Others are from 18 states, and 4 foreign countries. 72% are White. 45% are Catholic. The average age of freshmen is 18; all undergraduates, 28. 12% do not continue beyond their first year; 88% remain to graduate.

Housing: 50 students can be accommodated in college housing, which includes single-sex dorms. On-campus housing is available on a first-come and first-served basis. Priority is given to out-of-town students. 92% of students commute. Alcohol is not permitted. All students may keep cars.

Activities: There are no fraternities or sororities. There are 12 groups on campus, including socratic club, student activities board, synaxis of St. John, religious, social, and student ambassadors. Popular campus events include semi-annual Table Tennis and Pool Tournaments, Drive-In-Movie Nights, Fall and Spring Festivals, and St. Thomas Aquinas Feast Day.

Sports: There is no sports program at Aquinas.

Disabled Students: 75% of the campus is accessible. Facilities include wheelchair ramps, special parking, specially equipped restrooms, special class scheduling, and lowered drinking fountains.

Services: Counseling and information services are available, as is tutoring in some subjects, nursing, theology, philosophy, math, writing, and biology. There is remedial math. Write Reason writing center is available to all students for assistance with writing assignments for any course.

Campus Safety and Security: Measures include 24-hour foot and vehicle patrol, emergency notification system, and self-defense education. There are lighted pathways/sidewalks and controlled access to dorms/residences.

Programs of Study: confers B.A., B.B.A., B.S. and B.S.N. degrees. Associate and master's degrees are also awarded. Bachelor's degrees are awarded in BUSINESS (business administration and management), COMMUNICATIONS AND THE ARTS (English), EDUCATION (elementary education and secondary education), HEALTH PROFESSIONS (nursing), SOCIAL SCIENCE (history, interdisciplinary studies, liberal arts/general studies, philosophy, and theological studies). Nursing has the largest enrollment.

Special: The RN-BSN program is offered in an accelerated format. There are 2 national honor societies.

Faculty/Classroom: 23% of faculty are male; 77% are female. All teach undergraduates. No introductory courses are taught by graduate students. The average class size in an introductory lecture is 19; in a laboratory is 10; and in a regular course is 14.

Admissions: 52% of the 2013-2014 applicants were accepted.

Requirements: The SAT or ACT is required. The GED is accepted. A GPA of 2.4 is required. AP and CLEP credits are accepted.

Procedure: Freshmen are admitted to all sessions. There is a rolling admissions plan. Application deadlines are open. Application fee is $25. Applications are accepted online.

Transfer: 157 transfer students enrolled in 2012-2013. Transfer applicants must have a 2.4 GPA in previous college work. Transfer students with less than 30 semester hours of college-level course work must also submit their high school transcripts and SAT/ACT scores. 30 of 120 credits required for the bachelor's degree must be completed at Aquinas.

Visiting: There are regularly scheduled orientations for prospective students, including campus tours and information on admissions, financial aid, student life, and degree programs. There are guides for informal visits and visitors may sit in on classes. To schedule a visit, contact Connie Hansom at admissions@aquinascollege.edu.

Financial Aid: is a member of CSS. The FAFSA and the college's own financial statement are required. The deadline for filing freshman financial aid applications for fall entry is February 15.

International Students: There are 14 international students enrolled. They must take the TOEFL with a minimum score of 525 on the paper-based TOEFL (PBT) or 70 on the Internet-based version (iBT). They must also take the SAT or ACT, scoring 21.

Computers: All students may access the system. all hours of college operation. There are no time limits and no fees.

Graduates: From July 1, 2012 to June 30, 2013, 33 bachelor's degrees were awarded. The most popular majors were nursing (39%), business (33%), and education (15%).

Admissions Contact: Connie Hansom, Director of Admissions. E-Mail: *hansomc@aquinascollege.edu* Web: *http:/www.aquinascollege.edu/admissions/*

AUSTIN PEAY STATE UNIVERSITY C-1

Clarksville, TN 37044
(931) 221-7661
(800) 844-2778; (931) 221-6168

Full-time: 2769 men, 4097 women
Part-time: 1078 men, 1606 women
Graduate: 226 men, 623 women
Year: semesters, summer session
Application Deadline: August 5
Faculty: 360; IIA, --$
Ph.D.s: n/av
Student/Faculty: 18 to 1
Tuition: $6876 ($21,372)
Room & Board: $7774
Freshman Class: 3551 applied, 3054 accepted, 1582 enrolled
ACT: 22
COMPETITIVE

Austin Peay State University, established in 1927, is a public institution offering undergraduate degrees in the liberal arts and sciences and professional preparation. There are 5 undergraduate schools and 1 graduate school. In addition to regional accreditation, APSU has baccalaureate program accreditation with CSWE, NASAD, NASM, NCATE, and NLN. The library contains 225,117 volumes, 672,421 microform items, and 7,143 audio/video tapes/CDs/DVDs, and subscribes to 81,782 periodicals including electronic. Computerized library services include interlibrary loans, database searching, and Internet access. Special learning facilities include an art gallery, radio station, and TV station. The 182-acre campus is in an urban area 47 miles from Nashville. Including any residence halls, there are 80 buildings.

Student Life: 89% of undergraduates are from Tennessee. Others are from 44 states, 23 foreign countries, and Canada. 66% are White; 19% African American. The average age of freshmen is 19; all undergraduates, 25. 34% do not continue beyond their first year; 37% remain to graduate.

Housing: 1818 students can be accommodated in college housing, which includes single-sex and coed dorms, on-campus apartments, and married student housing. In addition, there are honors houses. On-campus housing is available on a first-come and first-served basis. 85% of students commute. Alcohol is not permitted. All students may keep cars.

Activities: 12% of men belong to 9 national fraternities; 11% of women belong to 6 national sororities. There are 86 groups on campus, including art, band, cheerleading, choir, chorus, debate, drama, ethnic, gay, honors, international, jazz band, literary magazine, marching band, newspaper, orchestra, pep band, political, professional, radio and TV, religious, social, social service, student government, and yearbook. Popular campus events include graduation, Parents Day, and Mud Bowl.

Sports: There are 6 intercollegiate sports for men and 9 for women, and 12 intramural sports for men and 12 for women. Facilities include The recreation complex houses 3 multipurpose courts, 4 fully-enclosed racquetball courts, an indoor track, a dynamic climbing area, an expanded fitness area, 2 modern fitness studios, a dedicated indoor cycling studio, and spacious locker rooms. A fitness center and outdoor recreation fields are also available.

Disabled Students: 95% of the campus is accessible. Facilities include wheelchair ramps, elevators, special parking, specially equipped restrooms, special class scheduling, lowered drinking fountains, and lowered telephones.

Services: Counseling and information services are available, as is tutoring in some subjects, including sciences, math, English, and history. There is a reader service for the blind. The university provides help with academic, learning, and test-taking problems.

Campus Safety and Security: Measures include 24-hour foot and vehicle patrol, emergency notification system, self-defense education, and security escort services. There are shuttle buses, emergency telephones, lighted pathways/sidewalks, and controlled access to dorms/residences.

Programs of Study: APSU confers B.A., B.S., B.B.A., B.F.A., B.P.S. and B.S.N. degrees. Associate and master's degrees are also awarded. Bachelor's degrees are awarded in AGRICULTURE (agriculture), BIOLOGICAL SCIENCE (biology/biological science), BUSINESS (business administration and management), COMMUNICATIONS AND THE ARTS (art, communications, English, languages, and music), COMPUTER AND PHYSICAL SCIENCE (chemistry, computer science, geoscience, mathematics, physics, and radiological technology), EDUCATION (health education and special education), ENGINEERING AND ENVIRONMENTAL DESIGN (engineering technology), HEALTH PROFESSIONS (medical technology and nursing), SOCIAL SCIENCE (criminal justice, history, interdisciplinary studies, liberal arts/general studies, philosophy, political science/government, psychology, public administration, social work, and sociology). Biology, nursing, and physics are the strongest academically. General business has the largest enrollment.

Required: To graduate, students must earn a minimum of 120 semester hours, of which 39 hours are in upper division elective courses, earn a cumulative GPA of 2.00, complete a Common General Education Core, and complete the First Year Experience Course.

Special: APSU offers cooperative programs in nuclear medicine with Vanderbilt University and a pre-engineering (2-year transfer) program in which a student will earn a degree in physics and an engineering degree from one of Tennessee's colleges of engineering. Credit may be granted for military experience. Pass/fail grading options and work-study programs are available. There are 11 national honor societies and a freshman honors program.

Faculty/Classroom: 47% of faculty are male; 53% are female. All teach undergraduates. No introductory courses are taught by graduate students. The average class size in an introductory lecture is 24; in a laboratory is 16; and in a regular course is 25.

Admissions: 86% of the 2013-2014 applicants were accepted. The ACT scores were 43% below 21, 30% between 21 and 23, 16% between 24 and 26, 5% between 27 and 28, and 6% above 28. 30% of the current freshmen were in the top fifth of their class; 58% were in the top two fifths.

Requirements: Applicants must be graduates of an accredited secondary school or have a GED. 14 academic units are required, including 4 units of English, 3 units of mathematics, 2 units each of natural/physical science, and a foreign language, and 1 unit each of visual and/or performing arts, social studies, and U.S. history. Applicants who do not meet these requirements may be considered for admission. A GPA of 2.8 is required. AP and CLEP credits are accepted.

Procedure: Freshmen are admitted fall, spring, and summer. There is a rolling admissions plan. Applications should be filed by August 5 for fall entry; December 13 for spring entry; and May 20 for summer entry. The fall 2013 application fee was $15. Applications are accepted online.

Transfer: 900 transfer students enrolled in 2012-2013. Applicants must have a 2.0 GPA and be in good standing with the last institution attended. Grades of D or better will be considered for credit. Application deadlines are the same as those for freshmen. Transfer students having attended only non-regionally accredited institutions are considered new students. 30 of 120 credits required for the bachelor's degree must be completed at APSU.

Visiting: There are regularly scheduled orientations for prospective students. There are guides for informal visits. To schedule a visit, contact the Admissions Office.

Financial Aid: In 2013-2014, 96% of all full-time freshmen and 98% of continuing full-time students received some form of financial aid. 69% of all full-time freshmen and 81% of continuing full-time students received need-based aid. The FAFSA is required. The priority date for freshman financial aid applications for fall entry is February 3. The deadline for filing freshman financial aid applications for fall entry is August 5.

International Students: There are 35 international students enrolled. They must take the TOEFL.

Computers: All students may access the system. There are no time limits and no fees.

Graduates: From July 1, 2012 to June 30, 2013, 1422 bachelor's degrees were awarded. The most popular majors were general business (12%), nursing (7%), and communications (7%). In an average class, 1% graduate in 3 years or less, 16% graduate in 4 years or less, 32% graduate in 5 years or less, and 37% graduate in 6 years or less.

Admissions Contact: Amy Deaton, Director of Admissions. E-Mail: *admission@.apsu.edu* Web: *www.apsu.edu*

BELMONT UNIVERSITY — C-2

Nashville, TN 37212 — (615) 460-6785; (800) 56E-NROL; (615) 460-5434

Full-time: 2066 men, 3051 women	**Faculty:** n/av; IIA, av$
Part-time: 150 men, 239 women	**Ph.D.s:** 82%
Graduate: 502 men, 907 women	**Student/Faculty:** 13 to 1
Year: semesters, summer session	**Tuition:** $27,380
Application Deadline: August 1	**Room & Board:** $10,000
Freshman Class: 5111 applied, 4082 accepted, 1243 enrolled	
SAT CR/M: 590/580	**ACT:** 27 **VERY COMPETITIVE+**

Belmont University, founded in 1890, is a private, Christian liberal arts university. There are 7 undergraduate schools and 6 graduate schools. In addition to regional accreditation, Belmont has baccalaureate program accreditation with AACSB, CSWE, NASM, NCATE, and NLN. The 2 libraries contain 232,140 volumes, 29,999 microform items, 34,506 audio/video tapes/CDs/DVDs, and subscribe to 788 periodicals including electronic. Computerized library services include interlibrary loans, database searching, and Internet access. Special learning facilities include an art gallery, radio station, TV station, and 19th century antebellum mansion. The 69-acre campus is in an urban area in Nashville, TN. Including any residence halls, there are 37 buildings.

Student Life: 65% of undergraduates are from out of state, mostly the South. Students are from 49 states, 29 foreign countries, and Canada. 85% are White. The average age of freshmen is 18; all undergraduates, 21. 17% do not continue beyond their first year; 68% remain to graduate.

Housing: 2851 students can be accommodated in college housing, which includes single-sex dorms and on-campus apartments. On-campus housing is guaranteed for the freshman year only, is available on a first-come, and first-served basis. 50% of students commute. Alcohol is not permitted. All students may keep cars.

Activities: There are 73 groups on campus, including art, band, cheerleading, choir, chorale, chorus, computers, dance, debate, drama, environmental, ethnic, film, forensics, gay, honors, international, jazz band, literary magazine, marching band, musical theater, newspaper, orchestra, pep band, photography, political, professional, radio and TV, religious, social, social service, student government, and symphony.

Sports: There are 7 intercollegiate sports for men and 7 for women, and 8 intramural sports for men and 8 for women. Facilities include The Curb Event Center arena has 5,000 permanent seats in an oval configuration, and a permanent maple hardwood floor. It has three full-size basketball courts and eight suites. Belmont University has partnered with Nashville's Metro Board of Parks and Recreation to provide $8 million worth of enhancements to nearby E.S. Rose Park which would also allow the University to lease space for athletics. Rose Park opened for play in April 2011. The Belmont athletic training department is housed in an 1860 square foot state-of-the-art modern, athletic training facility. Westhaven Golf Club has been added as a practice facility for Belmont men's golf.

Disabled Students: 98% of the campus is accessible. Facilities include

wheelchair ramps, elevators, special parking, specially equipped restrooms, special class scheduling, and lowered drinking fountains.

Services: Counseling and information services are available, as is tutoring in some subjects. Writing and computer labs are available.

Campus Safety and Security: Measures include 24-hour foot and vehicle patrol, self-defense education, and security escort services. There are shuttle buses, emergency telephones, and lighted pathways/sidewalks.

Programs of Study: Belmont confers B.A., B.S., B.B.A., B.F.A., B.M. and B.S.N. degrees. Master's and doctoral degrees are also awarded. Bachelor's degrees are awarded in BIOLOGICAL SCIENCE (biochemistry, biology/biological science, environmental biology, and neurosciences), BUSINESS (accounting, business administration and management, entrepreneurial studies, finance, international business management, international economics, management science, and marketing/retailing/merchandising), COMMUNICATIONS AND THE ARTS (art history, audio technology, classics, communications, design, English, French, German, journalism, multimedia, music, music business management, music performance, music theory and composition, musical theater, public relations, Spanish, studio art, theatre arts, theater design, and visual and performing arts), COMPUTER AND PHYSICAL SCIENCE (applied mathematics, chemistry, computer science, mathematics, medical physics, physics, and web technology), EDUCATION (early childhood education, elementary education, middle school education, and physical education), ENGINEERING AND ENVIRONMENTAL DESIGN (engineering physics), HEALTH PROFESSIONS (exercise science, medical technology, nursing, and pharmaceutical science), SOCIAL SCIENCE (Asian/Oriental studies, biblical languages, biblical studies, Christian studies, economics, European studies, history, liberal arts/general studies, ministries, philosophy, political science/government, psychology, religion, social work, and sociology). Music, business, and humanities are the strongest academically. Business, music, nursing, and music business management have the largest enrollments.

Required: All students must complete at least 128 hours with a C average, including 22 to 24 hours in the major field. B.A. candidates are required to pursue a minor field. All programs except the B.B.A. require a core curriculum, which includes courses in language and literature, humanities (including religion), social sciences, science, math, and phys ed.

Special: Belmont offers study abroad, student-designed majors, and dual majors in math, physics, and chemistry. Dual degree programs are available with Auburn University and the University of Tennessee at Knoxville. Programs require 3 years of study at Belmont followed by 2 years at the other institution. There are 11 national honor societies, a freshman honors program, and 1 departmental honors program.

Faculty/Classroom: 45% of faculty are male; 55% are female. No introductory courses are taught by graduate students.

Admissions: 80% of the 2013-2014 applicants were accepted. The SAT scores for the 2013-2014 freshman class were: Critical Reading--8% below 500, 48% between 500 and 599, 36% between 600 and 699, and 8% between 700 and 800; Math--14% below 500, 45% between 500 and 599, 34% between 600 and 699, and 7% between 700 and 800. The ACT scores were 3% below 21, 24% between 21 and 23, 34% between 24 and 26, 19% between 27 and 28, and 20% above 28. 62% of the current freshmen were in the top fifth of their class; 91% were in the top two fifths.

Requirements: The ACT is required. The SAT is recommended. The university expects a composite score of at least 21 on the ACT and 1000 on the SAT. Applicants should be high school graduates or hold the GED. Secondary preparation should include 4 units of English, 3 of math, and 2 each of a foreign language, history, science, and social studies. Potential music majors must audition. AP and CLEP credits are accepted. Important factors in the admissions decision are advanced placement or honors courses, recommendations by school officials, and evidence of special talent.

Procedure: Freshmen are admitted fall, spring, and summer. Entrance exams should be taken during the junior or senior year. There are early admissions and rolling admissions plans. Applications should be filed by August 1 for fall entry; December 1 for spring entry, along with a $50 fee. Notification is sent on a rolling basis. Applications are accepted online.

Transfer: 466 transfer students enrolled in 2012-2013. Applicants should present an above average GPA in previous college work and be able to meet freshman entrance requirements. Those with fewer than 64 credit hours must also submit SAT or ACT scores. 32 of 128 credits required for the bachelor's degree must be completed at Belmont.

Visiting: There are regularly scheduled orientations for prospective students, consisting of a 2-day program in summer and a 4-day program right before classes begin. There are guides for informal visits, visitors may sit in on classes, and stay overnight. To schedule a visit, contact the Admissions Office.

Financial Aid: The FAFSA is required. The deadline for filing freshman financial aid applications for fall entry is March 1.

International Students: There are 52 international students enrolled. The school actively recruits these students. They must take the TOEFL with a minimum score of 550 on the paper-based TOEFL (PBT) or 80 on the Internet-based version (iBT).

Computers: All students may access the system. There are no time limits and no fees.

Graduates: From July 1, 2012 to June 30, 2013, 1145 bachelor's degrees were awarded. The most popular majors were music business, nursing, and commercial music. 113 companies recruited on campus in 2012-2013. In an average class, 57% graduate in 4 years or less, 67% graduate in 5 years or less, and 68% graduate in 6 years or less.

Admissions Contact: E-Mail: *buadmission@belmont.edu* Web: *www.belmont.edu*

BETHEL UNIVERSITY B-2

McKenzie, TN 38201 **(731) 352-4030; (731) 352-4069**

Full-time: 738 men, 996 women	**Faculty:** 80
Part-time: 147 men, 351 women	**Ph.D.s:** 35%
Graduate: 190 men, 309 women	**Student/Faculty:** 16 to 1
Year: semesters, summer session	**Tuition:** $12,902
Application Deadline: August 30	**Room & Board:** $13,552
Freshman Class: 598 applied, 317 accepted, 198 enrolled	

COMPETITIVE

Bethel University, established in 1842, is a private institution affiliated with the Cumberland Presbyterian Church. The three colleges of Bethel University offer undergraduate degrees through a variety of traditional and nontraditional programs. There is one graduate school. The library contains 79,164 volumes, 185 microform items, and 2,166 audio/video tapes/CDs/DVDs, and subscribes to 1,208 periodicals including electronic. Computerized library services include interlibrary loans, database searching, Internet access, and laptop Internet portals. Special learning facilities include a learning resource center, Jack's Place Pizza Business operated by Students in Free Enterprise (SIFE), and Autism Resource Center. The 100-acre campus is in a small town 120 miles northeast of Memphis. Including any residence halls, there are 18 buildings.

Student Life: 89% of undergraduates are from Tennessee. Others are from 26 states, 25 foreign countries, and Canada. 99% are from public schools. 49% are white; 33% African American. 72% are Protestant. The average age of freshmen is 26; all undergraduates, 31. 38% do not continue beyond their first year; 37% remain to graduate.

Housing: 530 students can be accommodated in college housing, which includes single-sex and coed dorms and on-campus apartments. On-campus housing is available on a first-come and first-served basis. 75% of students commute. Alcohol is not permitted. All students may keep cars.

Activities: 25% of men belong to 5 local fraternities; 25% of women belong to 5 local sororities. There are 25 groups on campus, including art, band, cheerleading, choir, chorale, chorus, drama, honors, marching band, musical theater, pep band, political, professional, religious, social, social service, student government, and yearbook.

Sports: There are 12 intercollegiate sports for men and 12 for women, and 9 intramural sports for men and 8 for women. Facilities include a gym with a heated indoor pool and weight room, a field house, a health and fitness complex, football, soccer, tennis courts, track, and baseball fields.

Disabled Students: 75% of the campus is accessible. Facilities include wheelchair ramps, elevators, special parking, specially equipped restrooms, special class scheduling, and lowered drinking fountains.

Services: Counseling and information services are available, as is tutoring in every subject. There is remedial math, reading, and writing. Tutoring is available free of charge to students.

Campus Safety and Security: Measures include 24-hour foot and vehicle patrol, self-defense education, and security escort services. There are lighted pathways/sidewalks, controlled access to dorms/residences, and security cameras in some buildings.

Programs of Study: Bethel confers B.A., B.S., B.S.N. degrees. Master's degrees are also awarded. Bachelor's degrees are awarded in BIOLOGICAL SCIENCE (biology/biological science), BUSINESS (business administration and management and management science), COMMUNICATIONS AND THE ARTS (English, music, music business management, and theater management), COMPUTER AND PHYSICAL SCIENCE (chemistry and mathematics), EDUCATION (education of the exceptional child, music education, and physical education), HEALTH PROFESSIONS (nursing and premedicine), SOCIAL SCIENCE (child psychology/development, history, human services, psychology, and sociology). Education, physicians assistant studies, and nursing are the strongest academically. Education and organizational management have the largest enrollments.

Required: Requirements for graduation include courses in English, history, lab science, math, phys ed, and religion. Students must complete 128 to 132 hours with a minimum GPA of 2.0. A thesis is required in some majors.

Special: Bethel offers evening classes for adults, in-service training for teachers, off-site classes, an accelerated degree program in organizational management, student-designed majors, internships, work-study, nonde gree study, a pass/fail option, and portfolio credit for prior learning and work experience. There is 1 national honor society, a freshman honors program, and 1 university-wide honors program.

Faculty/Classroom: 54% of faculty are male; 46% are female. All teach undergraduates. No introductory courses are taught by graduate students. The average class size in an introductory lecture, 25, in a laboratory, 15, and in a regular course, 12.

Admissions: In a recent year, 53% applicants were accepted.

Requirements: Applicants must graduate from an accredited secondary school. Those ranking in the upper half of their class or scoring a satisfactory score on the SAT or ACT are granted regular acceptance. Other applicants may be admitted conditionally. Other factors in the admission procedure are standardized test scores, an interview, evidence of special talent, and personality. Open admission is available for the nontraditional bachelor of science in the Management and Organizational Development program. Admission for all other programs is competitive. Bethel requires applicants to be in the upper 50% of their class. A GPA of 2.0 is required. AP and CLEP credits are accepted. Important factors in the admissions decision are advanced placement or honors courses, leadership record, and evidence of special talent.

Procedure: Freshmen are admitted to all sessions. Entrance exams should be taken prior to enrollment, preferably by fall of the senior year. There is a rolling admissions plan. Applications should be filed by August 30 for fall entry, January 10 for spring entry, and June 5 for summer entry, along with a $30 fee. Notification is sent on a rolling basis. Applications are accepted online.

Transfer: 56 transfer students enrolled in a recent year. Applicants must meet the GPA requirements for the number of hours they previously earned. Up to 68 hours may be transferred from community or junior colleges. Students with fewer than 12 semester hours must submit high school transcripts and ACT or SAT scores. 32 of 128 credits required for the bachelor's degree must be completed at Bethel.

Visiting: There are regularly scheduled orientations for prospective students, including about the college, dorms, and the lap-top program; they meet advisers, register for classes, and meet with the financial aid and business office. There are guides for informal visits, visitors may sit in on classes, and stay overnight. To schedule a visit, contact the Admissions Office.

Financial Aid: In a recent year, 95% of all full-time freshmen and 90% of continuing full-time students received some form of financial aid. 67% of all full-time freshmen and 51% of continuing full-time students received need-based aid. 14% of undergraduate students work part-time. Average annual earnings from campus work are $1187. The FAFSA and the college's own financial statement are required. The deadline for filing freshman financial aid applications for fall entry is March 15.

International Students: There are 55 international students enrolled. The school actively recruits these students. They must also take the SAT or ACT.

Computers: Wireless access is available. Each full-time student receives a laptop. Several buildings are wireless and there are hubs across the campus. Additionally, wired access is available in all student dorm rooms. All students may access the system. There are no time limits and no fees. All students are required to have a personal computer.

Graduates: In a recent year, 388 bachelor's degrees were awarded. The most popular majors were management and organizational development (66%), business management (14%), and nursing (9%). In an average class, 16% graduate in 3 years or less, 35% graduate in 4 years or less, 37% graduate in 5 years or less, and 37% graduate in 6 years or less.

Admissions Contact: Tina Hodges, Director of Admissions. A campus DVD is available. E-Mail: *hodgest@bethelu.edu* Web: *www.bethelu.edu*

BRYAN COLLEGE D-3

Dayton, TN 37321-7000 **(423) 775-7204**
(800) 277-9522; (423) 775-7300

Full-time: 453 men, 521 women	**Faculty:** n/av
Part-time: 17 men, 20 women	**Ph.D.s:** 81%
Graduate: 48 men, 24 women	**Student/Faculty:** n/av
Year: semesters, summer session	**Tuition:** $18,740
Application Deadline: open	**Room & Board:** $5454

Freshman Class: 459 applied, 344 accepted, 192 enrolled
SAT or ACT: required

COMPETITIVE

Bryan College, founded in 1930, is a private, Christian institution that is evangelical and interdenominational. Its emphases are on the liberal arts, business, health science, fine arts, Bible and religious studies, music, and teacher preparation. There is 1 undergraduate school. The library contains 150,000 volumes, 13,489 microform items, and 3015 audio/video tapes/CDs/DVDs, and subscribes to 10,000 periodicals including electronic. Computerized library services include interlibrary loans, database searching, Internet access, and laptop Internet portals. The 130-acre campus is in a small town 40 miles north of Chattanooga. Including any residence halls, there are 28 buildings.

Student Life: 55% of undergraduates are from out of state, mostly the South. Students are from 39 states, 6 foreign countries, and Canada. 89% are white. 99% are Protestant. The average age of freshmen is 18; all undergraduates, 20. 24% do not continue beyond their first year; 56% remain to graduate.

Housing: 615 students can be accommodated in college housing, which includes single-sex dorms and married student housing. On-campus housing is guaranteed for all 4 years. 58% of students live on campus; of those, 75% remain on campus on weekends. Alcohol is not permitted. All students may keep cars.

Activities: There are no fraternities or sororities. There are 17 groups on campus, including art, choir, chorale, computers, drama, honors, international, literary magazine, musical theater, newspaper, orchestra, pep band, photography, religious, social, social service, student government, and yearbook. Popular campus events include a fine arts series.

Sports: There are 3 intercollegiate sports for men and 4 for women, and 6 intramural sports for men and 6 for women. Facilities include a 1200-seat gym, soccer fields, baseball field, outdoor swimming pool, and 4 tennis courts.

Disabled Students: All of the campus is accessible. Facilities include wheelchair ramps, elevators, special parking, specially equipped restrooms, and lowered drinking fountains.

Services: Counseling and information services are available, as is tutoring in math and English. There is remedial math, reading, and writing.

Campus Safety and Security: Measures include self-defense education, security escort services, lighted pathways/sidewalks, and a night security patrol.

Programs of Study: Bryan confers B.A. and B.S. degrees. Associate and master's degrees are also awarded. Bachelor's degrees are awarded in BIOLOGICAL SCIENCE (biology/biological science), BUSINESS (business administration and management), COMMUNICATIONS AND THE ARTS (communications, English, music, and Spanish), COMPUTER AND PHYSICAL SCIENCE (computer science and mathematics), EDUCATION (elementary education, physical education, and science education), HEALTH PROFESSIONS (exercise science), SOCIAL SCIENCE (Christian studies, history, liberal arts/general studies, psychology, and religion). Communication studies and business administration have the largest enrollment.

Required: To graduate, students must complete 124 semester hours, with a minimum of 30 in the major, and maintain a GPA of at least 2.0. Distributions requirements include 16 semester hours in Bible, 9 in communications, 7 each in personal development and natural science, and 6 each in the humanities and social science. Specific courses that must be taken include 7 semester hours in science, 6 hours each in freshman English, a foreign language, and history of Western civilization, and 3 each in speech, general psychology, introduction to literature, fine arts, and phys ed. In addition, math and English proficiency must be met; a comprehensive exam in the major is also required.

Special: Special academic programs include psychology internships and practicums in business and psychology. An American Studies Program in Washington and a study-abroad Latin American Studies Program are offered through the Christian College Coalition. There is a freshman honors program.

Faculty/Classroom: 81% of faculty are male; 18% are female. All teach undergraduates. No introductory courses are taught by graduate students. The average class size in an introductory lecture is 27; in a laboratory, 13; and in a regular course, 16.

Requirements: The SAT or ACT is required. The ACT Optional Writing test is also required. Clear admission is granted to applicants who have graduated from an approved high school and who have a minimum GPA of 2.5 with a minimum composite score of 18 on the ACT or 860 on the SAT; clear admission is also granted to applicants with a minimum GPA of 2.0 and a composite score of 20 on the ACT or 920 on the SAT. The high school record should include a minimum of 18 academic credits with a recommended distribution of 4 units of English, 3 each of math, science, and social science/humanities, and 2 of a foreign language. The GED is also accepted. References are required, and an interview is recommended. A GPA of 2.0 is required. AP and CLEP credits are accepted.

Procedure: Freshmen are admitted fall and spring. Entrance exams should be taken before the fall of the senior year in high school. There are deferred admissions and rolling admissions plans. Application deadlines are open. Application fee is $30. Applications are accepted online.

Transfer: 59 transfer students enrolled in a recent year. Applicants need a minimum GPA of 2.0. Transcripts and test scores must be submitted as well as a personal statement or essay. 30 of 124 credits required for the bachelor's degree must be completed at Bryan.

Visiting: There are regularly scheduled orientations for prospective students, consisting of college visitation weekends, which include a tour of the campus, sitting in on classes and chapel, meeting with professors in the area of academic interest, staying with current students in residence halls, and eating meals in the dining room. There are guides for informal visits.

Financial Aid: In a recent year, 78% of all full-time freshmen and 75%

of continuing full-time students received some form of financial aid. At least 74% of all full-time freshmen and at least 66% of continuing full-time students received need-based aid. The average freshman award was $17,870. Need-based scholarships or need-based grants averaged $11,374; need-based self-help aid (loans and jobs) averaged $3734; institutional non-need-based athletic scholarships averaged $6699; and other institutional non-need-based awards and non-need-based scholarships averaged $5307. 45% of undergraduate students work part-time. Average annual earnings from campus work are $1500. The FAFSA and the college's own financial statement are required. The priority date for freshman financial aid applications for fall entry is February 15.

International Students: There are 9 international students enrolled. They must take the TOEFL. They must also take the SAT or ACT.

Computers: Wireless access is available. All students may access the system at all times. There are no time limits and no fees.

Graduates: In a recent year, 213 bachelor's degrees were awarded. The most popular majors were business/marketing (56%), communication/journalism (15%), and education (5%). In an average class, 45% graduate in 4 years or less, 52% graduate in 5 years or less, and 53% graduate in 6 years or less.

Admissions Contact: Director of Admissions. A campus DVD is available. E-mail: *admissions@bryan.edu* Web: *www.bryan.edu*

CARSON-NEWMAN UNIVERSITY E-2

Jefferson City, TN 37760 (865) 471-2000
(800) 678-9061; (865) 471-3502

Full-time: 735 men, 838 women	**Faculty:** n/av; IIB, --$
Part-time: 33 men, 40 women	**Ph.D.s:** 77%
Graduate: 105 men, 216 women	**Student/Faculty:** 12 to 1
Year: semesters, summer session	**Tuition:** $22,652
Application Deadline: August 15	**Room & Board:** $6406

Freshman Class: 2917 applied, 1913 accepted, 453 enrolled
SAT CR/M: 455/520 **ACT:** 23 **COMPETITIVE+**

Carson-Newman, founded in 1851, is a private liberal arts college affiliated with the Tennessee Baptist Convention. There are 2 graduate schools. In addition to regional accreditation, Carson-Newman has baccalaureate program accreditation with ADA, AHEA, NASAD, NASM, NCATE, and NLN. The library contains 300,000 volumes, 221,960 microform items, 15,000 audio/video tapes/CDs/DVDs, and subscribes to 2,000 periodicals including electronic. Computerized library services include interlibrary loans, database searching, and Internet access. Special learning facilities include an art gallery, natural history museum, radio station, and TV station. The 100-acre campus is in a small town 27 miles northeast of Knoxville, TN. Including any residence halls, there are 27 buildings.

Student Life: 86% of undergraduates are from Tennessee. Others are from 29 states, 17 foreign countries, and Canada. 92% are from public schools. 81% are White. 84% are Protestant. The average age of freshmen is 18; all undergraduates, 22. 25% do not continue beyond their first year; 60% remain to graduate.

Housing: 1430 students can be accommodated in college housing, which includes single-sex dorms, on-campus apartments, and married student housing. In addition, there are honors houses. On-campus housing is guaranteed for all 4 years. 50% of students commute. Alcohol is not permitted. All students may keep cars.

Activities: 20% of men belong to 2 local and 1 national fraternities; 20% of women belong to 2 local and 1 national sororities. There are 55 groups on campus, including art, band, cheerleading, chess, choir, chorale, chorus, computers, dance, debate, drama, drill team, ethnic, film, forensics, honors, international, jazz band, literary magazine, marching band, musical theater, newspaper, orchestra, pep band, photography, political, professional, radio and TV, religious, social, social service, student government, and yearbook. Popular campus events include Spring Fest, Fall Formal and Honors Convocation.

Sports: There are 9 intercollegiate sports for men and 8 for women, and 40 intramural sports for men and 40 for women. Facilities include a gym, football stadium, soccer, baseball, softball, and intramural fields, a pool and a student center with 3 racquetball courts, 3 gyms, a weight room, an Olympic-size pool, a Jacuzzi, and an outdoor café.

Disabled Students: 10% of the campus is accessible. Facilities include wheelchair ramps, elevators, special parking, and special class scheduling.

Services: Counseling and information services are available, as is tutoring in most subjects, including English, math, and science. There is remedial math, reading, and writing.

Campus Safety and Security: Measures include 24-hour foot and vehicle patrol, self-defense education, and security escort services. There are lighted pathways/sidewalks.

Programs of Study: Carson-Newman confers B.A., B.S., B.M., B.S.M. and B.S.N. degrees. Associate and master's degrees are also awarded. Bachelor's degrees are awarded in BIOLOGICAL SCIENCE (biology/biological science), BUSINESS (accounting, business administration and management, and business economics), COMMUNICATIONS AND THE ARTS (communications, English, fine arts, French, languages, music, and Spanish), EDUCATION (art education, early childhood education, elementary education, foreign languages education, health education, home economics education, middle school education, music education, science education, and secondary education), HEALTH PROFESSIONS (nursing and physical therapy), SOCIAL SCIENCE (economics, history, philosophy, psychology, religion, social science, and sociology). Nursing, music, and biology are the strongest academically. Nursing, business, and education have the largest enrollments.

Required: All students must complete 128 credit hours, including Composition I and II, Survey of Old Testament, Survey of New Testament, 15 hours in English and communications, 9 in social sciences, 6 each in religion, humanities, and science, and 3 each in history, literature, and math. The major requires 40 to 48 hours. Students must achieve a minimum GPA of 2.0.

Special: The college offers internships, study in England, France, Japan, Hong Kong, and Spain, a Washington semester, on-campus work-study programs, B.A.-B.S. degrees, dual majors, a general studies degree, student-designed majors, and pass/fail options. Students may receive credit for life, military, or work experience. There is 1 national honor society, a freshman honors program, and 16 departmental honors programs.

Faculty/Classroom: 53% of faculty are male; 47% are female. All teach undergraduates, and 40% do research. No introductory courses are taught by graduate students. The average class size in an introductory lecture is 25; in a laboratory is 16; and in a regular course is 17.

Admissions: 66% of the 2013-2014 applicants were accepted. The ACT scores were 35% below 21, 30% between 21 and 23, 20% between 24 and 26, 7% between 27 and 28, and 8% above 28. There were 3 National Merit finalists. 10 freshmen graduated first in their class.

Requirements: The SAT or ACT is required. Students must have a minimum composite score of 19 on the ACT or a satisfactory score on the SAT. Applicants should be graduates of an accredited secondary school. The GED is accepted. 20 academic credits are required, including 4 units of English and 2 units each of history, math, science, and social studies. An essay, a portfolio, an audition, and an interview are recommended. A GPA of 2.3 is required. AP and CLEP credits are accepted. Important factors in the admissions decision are advanced placement or honors courses, leadership record, and parents or siblings attended your school.

Procedure: Freshmen are admitted to all sessions. Entrance exams should be taken in the fall of the senior year or the spring of the junior year. There are deferred admissions and rolling admissions plans. Applications should be filed by August 15 for fall entry; December 15 for spring entry; and April 15 for summer entry, along with a $25 fee. Applications are accepted online.

Transfer: 102 transfer students enrolled in 2012-2013. Transfer students should have a minimum GPA of 2.0. Either the SAT or the ACT is required if the student has fewer than 32 hours of college credit. An interview is recommended. 32 of 128 credits required for the bachelor's degree must be completed at Carson-Newman.

Visiting: There are regularly scheduled orientations for prospective students, including information sessions, meetings with advisers, and preregistration. There are guides for informal visits, visitors may sit in on classes, and stay overnight. To schedule a visit, contact the Admissions Office at admitme@cn.edu.

Financial Aid: Carson-Newman is a member of CSS. The FAFSA and the college's own financial statement are required. The deadline for filing freshman financial aid applications for fall entry is March 1.

International Students: There are 55 international students enrolled. The school actively recruits these students. They must take the TOEFL, or score 4 on the APIEL, and must also take English proficiency and math placement exams.

Computers: All students may access the system until the lab closes at 11 p.m. There are no time limits. The fee is $380.

Graduates: From July 1, 2012 to June 30, 2013, 340 bachelor's degrees were awarded. The most popular majors were education (22%), health professions and related programs (18%), and business/marketing (18%). In an average class, 41% graduate in 4 years or less, 54% graduate in 5 years or less, and 55% graduate in 6 years or less.

Admissions Contact: Melannie Redding, Director of Admissions. E-Mail: *admitme@cn.edu* Web: *www.cn.edu*

CHRISTIAN BROTHERS UNIVERSITY A-3

Memphis, TN 38104-5581 (901) 321-4213
(800) 288-7576; (901) 321-3202

Full-time: 564 men, 631 women
Part-time: 52 men, 104 women
Graduate: 222 men, 255 women
Year: semesters, summer session
Application Deadline: August 1
Freshman Class: 1853 applied, 889 accepted, 290 enrolled
ACT: 25
Faculty: 94; IIB, --$
Ph.D.s: 87%
Student/Faculty: 13 to 1
Tuition: $26,570
Room & Board: $3570
HIGHLY COMPETITIVE

Christian Brothers University, founded in 1871, is a private Catholic university providing undergraduate educational opportunities in the arts, business, engineering, the sciences, and teacher education, and specialized graduate programs. There are 4 undergraduate schools and 3 graduate schools. In addition to regional accreditation, CBU has baccalaureate program accreditation with ABET and NCATE. The figures in the above capsule and in this profile are approximate. The library contains 165,796 volumes, 61,523 microform items, and 2,004 audio/video tapes/CDs/DVDs. Computerized library services include interlibrary loans, database searching, Internet access, and laptop Internet portals. Special learning facilities include a learning resource center and art gallery. The 75-acre campus is in a small town in Memphis, Tennessee. Including any residence halls, there are 27 buildings.

Student Life: 79% of undergraduates are from Tennessee. Others are from 22 states, 22 foreign countries, and Canada. 70% are from public schools. 48% are White; 30% African American. 50% are Protestant; 29% claim no religious affiliation; 20% Catholic. The average age of freshmen is 18; all undergraduates, 23. 26% do not continue beyond their first year; 56% remain to graduate.

Housing: 576 students can be accommodated in college housing, which includes single-sex and coed dorms and on-campus apartments. quiet floors in residence halls and a living/learning community dorm. On-campus housing is available on a first-come, first-served basis, and is available on a lottery system for upperclassmen. Priority is given to out-of-town students. 60% of students commute. All students may keep cars.

Activities: 25% of men belong to 5 national fraternities; 19% of women belong to 6 national sororities. There are 37 groups on campus, including art, chess, chorale, chorus, computers, drama, ethnic, gay, honors, international, literary magazine, musical theater, political, professional, religious, social, social service, student government, and yearbook. Popular campus events include Bacchus, Sofapalooza, and Up Til Dawn.

Sports: There are 5 intercollegiate sports for men and 6 for women, and 10 intramural sports for men and 10 for women. Facilities include a swimming pool, gym, theater, multimedia auditorium, batting cage, jogging track, basketball/volleyball and handball/racquetball courts, baseball and soccer fields, tennis courts, and weight-training facilities.

Disabled Students: 90% of the campus is accessible. Facilities include wheelchair ramps, elevators, special parking, specially equipped restrooms, lowered drinking fountains, and lowered telephones.

Services: Counseling and information services are available, as is tutoring in most subjects. CBU also has centers for math and writing.

Campus Safety and Security: Measures include 24-hour foot and vehicle patrol, emergency notification system, and security escort services. There are emergency telephones, lighted pathways/sidewalks, and controlled access to dorms/residences.

Programs of Study: CBU confers B.A., B.F.A, and B.S. degrees. Master's degrees are also awarded. Bachelor's degrees are awarded in BIOLOGICAL SCIENCE (biochemistry and biology/biological science), BUSINESS (accounting and business administration and management), COMMUNICATIONS AND THE ARTS (English and studio art), COMPUTER AND PHYSICAL SCIENCE (chemistry, computer science, mathematics, natural sciences, and physics), EDUCATION (early childhood education and special education), ENGINEERING AND ENVIRONMENTAL DESIGN (chemical engineering, civil engineering, electrical/electronics engineering, engineering management, engineering physics, and mechanical engineering), HEALTH PROFESSIONS (biomedical science), SOCIAL SCIENCE (applied psychology, history, liberal arts/general studies, philosophy and religion, and psychology). Engineering and biology are the strongest academically. Psychology, business, and electrical have the largest enrollments.

Required: In addition to meeting degree requirements for a particular major, a student at CBU is required to have a broad understanding of self, others, and the contemporary world. The graduate of CBU shall have cultivated, through the arts and sciences, the necessary skills of inquiry, reasoning, and communication, and shall have developed an awareness of the religious dimension of human existence. All students take a broad range of courses; common requirements are 9 hours of English, 3 hours of math, 4 hours of natural and physical sciences, 6 hours of religious studies, 3 hours of moral values, and 6 hours of social science/history for a total of 31 general education hours. Students must take a minimum of 30 hours of general education courses.

Special: Special academic programs include on-campus work-study, study abroad in 4 countries, and internships for all juniors and seniors. There is cross-registration with the Greater Memphis Consortium, Rhodes College, and the University of Memphis. An accelerated degree program is available to all business and psychology majors through the professional studies program, and a general studies degree is offered. Up to 36 hours of nondegree study is possible, as are dual majors, an honors program, and pass/fail options. Numerous teacher licensure programs are also offered. There are 9 national honor societies and a freshman honors program.

Faculty/Classroom: 56% of faculty are male; 44% are female. 83% teach undergraduates. No introductory courses are taught by graduate students. The average class size in an introductory lecture is 17; in a laboratory is 12; and in a regular course is 17.

Admissions: 48% of the 2011-2012 applicants were accepted. The ACT scores were 4% below 21, 42% between 21 and 23, 28% between 24 and 26, 11% between 27 and 28, and 15% above 28. 68% of the current freshmen were in the top fifth of their class; 84% were in the top two fifths. 4 freshmen graduated first in their class.

Requirements: The ACT is required with a score of 21. Also required is a high school GPA of at least 2.5. Other admissions requirements include graduation from an accredited secondary school, with a college-preparatory curriculum recommended. The GED is also accepted. An interview is advised. ACT scores between 18 and 20 with a high school gpa of 3.0 or better are considered. A GPA of 2.5 is required. AP and CLEP credits are accepted. Important factors in the admissions decision are advanced placement or honors courses, leadership record, and recommendations by school officials.

Procedure: Freshmen are admitted to all sessions. Entrance exams should be taken by the end of the junior year. There are deferred admissions and rolling admissions plans. Applications should be filed by August 1 for fall entry; December 1 for spring entry; and May 1 for summer entry, along with a $25 fee. Notifications are sent December 1. Applications are accepted online.

Transfer: 41 transfer students enrolled in a recent year. Transfer students should have a minimum GPA of 2.5 and be in good academic and disciplinary standing. 35 of 122 credits required for the bachelor's degree must be completed at CBU.

Visiting: There are regularly scheduled orientations for prospective students, including attendance at classes, meetings with professors and students, a campus tour, and meetings with admissions and financial aid representatives. There are guides for informal visits, visitors may sit in on classes, and stay overnight. To schedule a visit, contact Dean of Admissions.

Financial Aid: 91% of undergraduate students work part-time. Average annual earnings from campus work are $2400. The average financial indebtedness of a recent graduate was $29,207. The FAFSA is required. Check with the school for current application deadlines.

International Students: There are 35 international students enrolled. The school actively recruits these students. They must take the TOEFL with a minimum score of 500 on the paper-based TOEFL (PBT).

Computers: Wireless is available campus-wide and in the dorms. All students may access the system during the 93.5 hours per week of computer center operation; 24-hour dial-in phone access is available. There are no time limits and no fees.

Graduates: In a recent year, 257 bachelor's degrees were awarded. The most popular majors were business (41%), psychology (15%), and engineering (15%). In an average class, 39% graduate in 4 years or less, 54% graduate in 5 years or less, and 55% graduate in 6 years or less.

Admissions Contact: Dr. Anne Kenworthy, Dean of Admissions. A campus DVD is available. E-Mail: *admissions@cbu.edu* Web: *http:/www.cbu.edu/cbu/Admissions/UndergraduateDay/index.htm*

CUMBERLAND UNIVERSITY C-2

Lebanon, TN 37087 (615) 444-2562, ext. 1225
(800) 467-0562; (615) 444-2569

Full-time: 983 women
Part-time: 372 men, and women
Graduate: 80 men, 185 women
Year: semesters, summer session
Application Deadline: open
Freshman Class: n/av
SAT: recommended
Faculty: n/av
Ph.D.s: 49%
Student/Faculty: 16 to 1
Tuition: $18,700
Room & Board: $6500
ACT: required
COMPETITIVE

Cumberland University, founded in 1842, is a private institution offering undergraduate and graduate degrees in business, education, and social sciences. The figures in the above capsule are approximate. There are 4 graduate schools. In addition to regional accreditation, Cumberland has baccalaureate program accreditation with AACSB and NLN. The library contains 37,056 volumes, 590 microform items, 1260 audio/video tapes/CDs/DVDs, and subscribes to 357 periodicals including electronic. Computerized library services include interlibrary loans, database searching, and Internet access. Special learning facilities include a learning resource center, art gallery, natural history museum, and radio station. The 44-acre campus is in a small town 28 miles east of Nashville. Including any residence halls, there are 17 buildings.

Student Life: 87% of undergraduates are from Tennessee. Others are from 29 states, 29 foreign countries, and Canada. 89% are from public schools. 72% are white; 14% African American. The average age of freshmen is 18; all undergraduates, 22. 44% do not continue beyond their first year; 35% remain to graduate.

Housing: 400 students can be accommodated in college housing, which includes single-sex dorms. On-campus housing is available on a first-come, first-served basis. 62% of students commute. Alcohol is not permitted. All students may keep cars.

Activities: 17% of men belong to 3 national fraternities; 7% of women belong to 2 national sororities. There are 15 groups on campus, including art, band, cheerleading, chorale, chorus, computers, dance, drama, honors, international, jazz band, marching band, musical theater, newspaper, pep band, political, professional, religious, social, social service, and student government. Popular campus events include Fall Frolic, Halloween at CU, and Fall and Spring Preview Days.

Sports: There are 9 intercollegiate sports for men and 8 for women, and 4 intramural sports for men and 5 for women. Facilities include a gym, field house, weight room, baseball and soccer fields, tennis courts, outdoor volleyball courts, football field, and softball field.

Disabled Students: All of the campus is accessible. Facilities include wheelchair ramps, special parking, and lowered telephones.

Services: Counseling and information services are available, as is tutoring in most subjects. There is remedial math, reading, and writing.

Campus Safety and Security: Measures include 24-hour foot and vehicle patrol and emergency notification system. There are emergency telephones and lighted pathways/sidewalks. The outside entrances of the dorms are always secured; only residents have keys.

Programs of Study: Cumberland confers B.A., B.S., B.B.A., and B.S.N. degrees. Associates and master's degrees are also awarded. Bachelor's degrees are awarded in BIOLOGICAL SCIENCE (biology/biological science), BUSINESS (accounting, business administration and management, management science, marketing management, and recreation and leisure services), COMMUNICATIONS AND THE ARTS (English, fine arts, and music), COMPUTER AND PHYSICAL SCIENCE (mathematics), EDUCATION (elementary education, middle school education, music education, physical education, secondary education, and special education), HEALTH PROFESSIONS (nursing), SOCIAL SCIENCE (American studies, criminal justice, history, political science/government, psychology, social science, and sociology). Business, education, and nursing have the largest enrollments.

Required: To graduate, students must complete 120 to 132 (depending on major) semester hours, including a 41-hour core curriculum, and maintain a GPA of 2.0.

Special: Internships with local businesses and with the state legislature are available. Nondegree study, pass/fail options, and an accelerated degree program in general business are offered. There are 13 national honor societies, a freshman honors program, and 5 departmental honors programs.

Faculty/Classroom: 52% of faculty are male; 48% are female. 82% teach undergraduates. No introductory courses are taught by graduate students. The average class size in an introductory lecture is 20; in a laboratory, 20; and in a regular course, 20.

Requirements: The ACT is required. The SAT and ACT Writing Test are recommended. A minimum composite ACT score of 19 and a GPA of 2.5 are expected. Applicants must be high school graduates or have earned the GED with a composite 50 score. A GPA of 2.5 is required. AP and CLEP credits are accepted.

Procedure: Freshmen are admitted fall, spring, and summer. Entrance exams should be taken during spring of the junior year or fall of the senior year. There is a rolling admissions plan. Application deadlines are open. The application fee is $25. Applications are accepted online.

Transfer: 131 transfer students enrolled in a recent year. Transfer applicants should have a GPA of at least 2.0. 33 of 120 credits required for the bachelor's degree must be completed at Cumberland.

Visiting: There are regularly scheduled orientations for prospective students, consisting of campus tours, testing, information sessions pertaining to college life, and academic advising. A parent orientation is provided in conjunction with student orientation programs. There are guides for informal visits and visitors may sit in on classes. To schedule a visit, contact the Admissions Office.

Financial Aid: In a recent year, 95% of all students received some form of financial aid. 33% of students received need-based aid. The average freshmen award was $6133, with $5191 ($9972 maximum) from need-based scholarships or need-based grants; $2800 ($11,500 maximum) from need-based self-help aid (loans and jobs); $7899 ($20,020 maximum) from non-need-based athletic scholarships; and $3212 ($14,710 maximum) from other non-need-based awards and non-need-based scholarships. Average annual earnings from campus work are $1000. The FAFSA and the college's own financial statement are required. Check with the school for current application deadlines.

International Students: There were 40 international students enrolled in a recent year. The school actively recruits these students. They must take the TOEFL with a minimum score of 500 on the paper-based TOEFL (PBT). They must also take the SAT or ACT.

Computers: Wireless access is available. All students may access the system. There are no time limits and no fees.

Graduates: In a recent year, 154 bachelor's degrees were awarded. The most popular majors were nursing (45%), education (27%), and business administration (17%). In an average class, 10% graduate in 4 years or less, 20% graduate in 5 years or less, and 5% graduate in 6 years or less.

Admissions Contact: Eddie Pawlawski, Vice President of Enrollment Management. E-Mail: *epawlawski@cumberland.edu* Web: *cumberland .edu*

EAST TENNESSEE STATE UNIVERSITY — F-1

Johnson City, TN 37614 — **(423) 439-4213**
(800) 462-3878; (423) 439-7156

Full-time: 3400 men, 4550 women	**Faculty:** n/av; IIA, --$
Part-time: 650 men, 980 women	**Ph.D.s:** 75%
Graduate: 620 men, 1225 women	**Student/Faculty:** n/av
Year: semesters, summer session	**Tuition:** $5500 ($14,500)
Application Deadline: open	**Room & Board:** $5500
Freshman Class: n/av	
SAT or ACT: required	

COMPETITIVE

East Tennessee State University, founded in 1911, is a public institution that is part of the State University and Community College System of Tennessee. ETSU's undergraduate and graduate programs stress the liberal arts, business, art, fine arts, professional training, music, teacher preparation, technical studies, and health science. The figures in the above capsule and in this profile are approximate. There are 6 undergraduate schools and 2 graduate schools. In addition to regional accreditation, ETSU has baccalaureate program accreditation with AACSB, ABET, ACEJMC, ADA, CSAB, CSWE, NASAD, NASM, NCATE, and NLN. The library contains 1.1 million volumes, 1.7 million microform items, and 23,658 audio/video tapes/CDs/DVDs, and subscribes to 3714 periodicals including electronic. Computerized library services include interlibrary loans, database searching, and Internet access. Special learning facilities include a learning resource center, art gallery, planetarium, radio station, TV station, and regional art and history museum. The 366-acre campus is in a small town 90 miles northeast of Knoxville. Including any residence halls, there are 68 buildings.

Student Life: 89% of undergraduates are from Tennessee. Others are from 38 states, 46 foreign countries, and Canada. 97% are from public schools. 91% are white. The average age of freshmen is 19; all undergraduates, 23. 33% do not continue beyond their first year; 38% remain to graduate.

Housing: 2478 students can be accommodated in college housing, which includes single-sex and coed dorms, on-campus apartments, and married student housing. On-campus housing is available on a first-come, first-served basis. 79% of students commute. Alcohol is not permitted. All students may keep cars.

Activities: 4% of men belong to 8 national fraternities; 4% of women belong to 1 local and 6 national sororities. There are 200 groups on campus, including art, band, cheerleading, choir, chorale, chorus, computers, dance, drama, drill team, ethnic, forensic, gay, honors, international, jazz band, literary magazine, newspaper, pep band, photography, political, professional, radio and TV, religious, residence hall, social, social service, and student government. Popular campus events include Leadership Retreat, National Clean Up for Hunger, and Winter Cruise.

Sports: There are 6 intercollegiate sports for men and 8 for women, and 8 intramural sports for men and 8 for women. Facilities include a 4000-seat gym and a domed stadium seating 12,000, which includes a basketball arena, tennis and handball/racquetball courts, a track, and weight and training rooms.

Disabled Students: 75% of the campus is accessible. Facilities include wheelchair ramps, elevators, special parking, specially equipped rest rooms, special class scheduling, lowered drinking fountains, lowered telephones, special housing, and adaptive computer equipment.

Services: Counseling and information services are available, as is tutoring in most subjects. There is a reader service for the blind and remedial math, reading, and writing. The office for Students with Disabilities, Student Support Services, and the Undergraduate Academic Advisement administer these services.

Campus Safety and Security: Measures include 24-hour foot and vehicle patrol, self-defense education, and security escort services. There are shuttle buses, emergency telephones, lighted pathways/sidewalks, and engravers available to identify personal property.

Programs of Study: ETSU confers B.A., B.S., B.A.S., B.B.A., B.F.A,

B.G.S., B.M., B.S.D.H., B.S.Ed., B.S.E.H., B.S.M.T., B.S.N., and B.S.W. degrees. Associates, master's, and doctoral degrees are also awarded. Bachelor's degrees are awarded in BIOLOGICAL SCIENCE (biology/biological science), BUSINESS (accounting, management science, and marketing/retailing/merchandising), COMMUNICATIONS AND THE ARTS (art, communications, English, fine arts, music, and speech/debate/rhetoric), COMPUTER AND PHYSICAL SCIENCE (chemistry, computer science, information sciences and systems, mathematics, and physics), EDUCATION (foreign languages education, physical education, and special education), ENGINEERING AND ENVIRONMENTAL DESIGN (engineering technology and survey and mapping technology), HEALTH PROFESSIONS (allied health, dental hygiene, environmental health science, health science, nursing, and public health), SOCIAL SCIENCE (child psychology/development, criminal justice, economics, geography, history, human development, interdisciplinary studies, liberal arts/general studies, philosophy, political science/government, psychology, social work, and sociology). Engineering technology, computer science, and nursing have the largest enrollments.

Required: All students must complete 120 semester hours, with 30 to 60 in the major, and maintain a minimum GPA of 2.0. Distribution requirements, which total 46 semester hours, include English, American history, phys ed, natural science, social and behavioral science, the humanities, analysis, and a 3-hour computer literacy course.

Special: Special academic programs include cooperative education programs, cross-registration with Milligan College, internships in political science, applied human sciences, and management, study abroad in Scotland, England, France, and Spain, B.A.-B.S. degrees, and dual majors in most arts and sciences undergraduate majors. A general studies degree is offered. Credit for military experience may be granted, and nondegree study and pass/fail options are possible. There are 19 national honor societies, a freshman honors program, and 12 departmental honors programs.

Faculty/Classroom: 55% of faculty are male; 45% are female. 85% teach undergraduates. No introductory courses are taught by graduate students. The average class size in an introductory lecture is 30; in a laboratory, 15; and in a regular course, 25.

Requirements: The SAT or ACT is required. Other admissions requirements include graduation from an accredited secondary school, with 20 Carnegie units and 14 academic credits, including 4 of English, 3 of math, 2 each of a foreign language and science, and 1 each of history, social studies, and art. In-state students who pass the Tennessee State Proficiency Test are eligible to apply for admission. Applicants whose ACT/SAT is below a certain score must complete the Academic Assessment Placement Program (AAPP) test battery before registration for classes. The GED is also accepted. A GPA of 2.3 is required. AP and CLEP credits are accepted.

Procedure: Freshmen are admitted to all sessions. Entrance exams should be taken during the junior and/or senior year. There is a rolling admissions plan. Application deadlines are open. The application fee is $15. Notification is sent on a rolling basis. Applications are accepted online.

Transfer: Transfer students must have a minimum GPA of 2.0 in 12 or more semester credit hours of course work from a regionally accredited institution. Transfer students must also satisfy high school unit requirements if deficiencies exist. 34 of 120 credits required for the bachelor's degree must be completed at ETSU.

Visiting: There are regularly scheduled orientations for prospective students, including 5 2-day orientation programs held during spring and summer for new students admitted to fall term. There are guides for informal visits, and visitors may sit in on classes and stay overnight. To schedule a visit, contact the Admissions Office.

Financial Aid: The FAFSA is required. Check with the school for current application deadlines.

International Students: They must take the TOEFL. They must also take the SAT or ACT.

Computers: All students may access the system 24 hours per day. There are no time limits and no fees.

Admissions Contact: Mike Pitts, Director of Admissions. A campus DVD is available. E-Mail: *go2etsu@etsu.edu* Web: *www.etsu.edu*

FISK UNIVERSITY — C-2

Nashville, TN 37208-3051 — (615) 329-8665, (888) 702-0022; (615) 329-8774

Full-time: 245 men, 575 women	**Faculty:** 66
Part-time: 20 men, 30 women	**Ph.D.s:** 76%
Graduate: 20 men, 40 women	**Student/Faculty:** 12 to 1
Year: semesters	**Tuition:** $18,452
Application Deadline: open	**Room & Board:** $12,472
Freshman Class: n/av	
SAT or ACT: required	

COMPETITIVE

Fisk University, founded in 1866, is a private, nonsectarian, liberal arts institution. Established as a college for African Americans, Fisk accepts students regardless of race. The figures in the above capsule and in this profile are approximate. There is 1 graduate school. In addition to regional accreditation, Fisk has baccalaureate program accreditation with NASM. The library contains 210,000 volumes, 114,998 microform items, 3880 audio/video tapes/CDs/DVDs, and subscribes to 844 periodicals including electronic. Computerized library services include database searching, Internet access, and laptop Internet portals. Special learning facilities include an art gallery and a radio station. The 40-acre campus is in an urban area. Including any residence halls, there are 21 buildings.

Student Life: 69% of undergraduates are from out of state, mostly the South. Students are from 39 states and 6 foreign countries. 87% are from public schools. 92% are African American. The average age of freshmen is 18; all undergraduates, 20. 16% do not continue beyond their first year; 68% remain to graduate.

Housing: 852 students can be accommodated in college housing, which includes single-sex dorms and married student housing. On-campus housing is guaranteed for all 4 years. 67% of students live on campus; of those, 80% remain on campus on weekends. Alcohol is not permitted. All students may keep cars.

Activities: 25% of men belong to 4 national fraternities; 20% of women belong to 4 national sororities. There are 102 groups on campus, including cheerleading, choir, dance, drama, honors, international, literary magazine, newspaper, political, professional, radio and TV, religious, social, student government, and yearbook. Popular campus events include Jubilee Day.

Sports: There are 7 intercollegiate sports for men and 8 for women. Facilities include a gym and a student center.

Disabled Students: 80% of the campus is accessible. Facilities include wheelchair ramps and elevators.

Services: Counseling and information services are available, as is tutoring in every subject. There is remedial math, reading, and writing.

Campus Safety and Security: Measures include 24-hour foot and vehicle patrol and security escort services. There are lighted pathways/sidewalks.

Programs of Study: Fisk confers B.A., B.S., and B.M. degrees. Master's degrees are also awarded. Bachelor's degrees are awarded in BIOLOGICAL SCIENCE (biology/biological science), BUSINESS (business administration and management), COMMUNICATIONS AND THE ARTS (dramatic arts, English, fine arts, French, music, Spanish, and speech/debate/rhetoric), COMPUTER AND PHYSICAL SCIENCE (chemistry, computer science, mathematics, and physics), EDUCATION (art education and music education), SOCIAL SCIENCE (economics, history, philosophy, political science/government, psychology, religion, and sociology). Biology, chemistry, and physics are the strongest academically. Biology has the largest enrollment.

Required: To graduate, students must complete 120 credits, including a 32-credit core curriculum in communications, creative arts, humanistic experience and thought, natural sciences or math, social sciences, and world civilization. In addition, students must complete 8 hours of written and computational skills and 24 hours of interdisciplinary courses, plus a foreign language. A minimum 2.0 GPA must be maintained.

Special: Fisk offers cross-registration with Vanderbilt University, study abroad, dual majors in engineering and pharmacy, student-designed majors, and campus work-study. Students may take a 5-year B.S.-B.E. program or a combined B.S.-M.B.A. program with Vanderbilt University. There are 8 national honor societies, including Phi Beta Kappa, and 6 departmental honors programs.

Faculty/Classroom: 61% of faculty are male; 39% are female. All teach undergraduates, 22% do research, and 24% do both. No introductory courses are taught by graduate students. The average class size in an introductory lecture is 30; in a laboratory, 15; and in a regular course, 19.

Requirements: The SAT or ACT is required. Applicants should be high school graduates with 14 academic credits. A GPA of 2.5 is required. AP credits are accepted. Important factors in the admissions decision are advanced placement or honors courses, leadership record, and evidence of special talent.

Procedure: Freshmen are admitted fall and spring. There are early admissions, deferred admissions, and rolling admissions plans. Application deadlines are open. The application fee is $50. Applications are accepted online.

Transfer: Applicants for transfer should have a minimum college GPA of 2.0.

Visiting: There are guides for informal visits, and visitors may sit in on classes and stay overnight. To schedule a visit, contact the Admissions Office.

Financial Aid: The FAFSA and the college's own financial statement are required. Check with the school for current application deadlines.

International Students: They must take the TOEFL.

Computers: All students may access the system. There are no time limits and no fees.

Admissions Contact: Keith Chandler, Director of Admissions. E-Mail: *admit@fisk.edu* Web: *www.fisk.edu*

FREED-HARDEMAN UNIVERSITY B-3

Henderson, TN 38340 (731) 989-6651
(800) 630-3480; (731) 989-6047

Full-time: 653 men, 837 women
Part-time: n/av
Graduate: 482
Year: semesters, summer session
Application Deadline: open
Freshman Class: n/av
ACT: required
Faculty: n/av; IIA, --$
Ph.D.s: 69%
Student/Faculty: 15 to 1
Tuition: $25,000
Room & Board: $7500

VERY COMPETITIVE

Freed-Hardeman University, founded in 1869, is a private, liberal arts institution associated with Churches of Christ. The figures in the above capsule and in this profile are approximate. There are 6 undergraduate schools and 4 graduate schools. In addition to regional accreditation, FHU has baccalaureate program accreditation with ACBSP, CSWE, and NCATE. The library contains 175,748 volumes, 240,000 microform items, 43,000 audio/video tapes/CDs/DVDs, and subscribes to 1650 periodicals including electronic. Computerized library services include interlibrary loans, database searching, and Internet access. Special learning facilities include a learning resource center, art gallery, radio station, TV station, and undergraduate research center. The 120-acre campus is in a small town 85 miles east of Memphis and 13 miles south of Jackson. Including any residence halls, there are 39 buildings.

Student Life: 52% of undergraduates are from out of state, mostly the South. Students are from 38 states, 25 foreign countries, and Canada. 75% are from public schools. 91% are white. 99% are Protestant. The average age of freshmen is 19; all undergraduates, 21. 26% do not continue beyond their first year; 57% remain to graduate.

Housing: 1429 students can be accommodated in college housing, which includes single-sex dorms and on-campus apartments. In addition, there are student-teacher houses. On-campus housing is guaranteed for all 4 years. 75% of students live on campus; of those, 55% remain on campus on weekends. Alcohol is not permitted. All students may keep cars.

Activities: There are no fraternities or sororities. There are 52 groups on campus, including art, band, cheerleading, choir, chorus, communications, computers, drama, drum and bugle corps, ethnic, honors, international, jazz band, musical theater, newspaper, orchestra, pep band, photography, political, professional, radio and TV, religious, social, social service, student government, and yearbook. Popular campus events include Makin' Music and Annual Bible Lectureship.

Sports: There are 3 intercollegiate sports for men and 4 for women, and 7 intramural sports for men and 7 for women. Facilities include 3 gyms, lighted playing fields, lighted tennis courts, a swimming pool, a walking track, a weight room, racquetball courts, and a game room.

Disabled Students: 70% of the campus is accessible. Facilities include wheelchair ramps, elevators, special parking, specially equipped rest rooms, special class scheduling, lowered drinking fountains, and lowered telephones.

Services: Counseling and information services are available, as is tutoring in most subjects. There is remedial math, reading, and writing.

Campus Safety and Security: Measures include 24-hour foot and vehicle patrol, emergency notification system, and security escort services. There are lighted pathways/sidewalks.

Programs of Study: FHU confers B.A., B.S., B.B.A., and B.S.W. degrees. Associates and master's degrees are also awarded. Bachelor's degrees are awarded in BIOLOGICAL SCIENCE (biochemistry and biology/biological science), BUSINESS (accounting, banking and finance, and business administration and management), COMMUNICATIONS AND THE ARTS (art, broadcasting, communications, dramatic arts, English, fine arts, journalism, public relations, and speech/debate/rhetoric), COMPUTER AND PHYSICAL SCIENCE (chemistry, computer programming, computer science, information sciences and systems, mathematics, and physical sciences), EDUCATION (art education, early childhood education, elementary education, health education, middle school education, music education, physical education, science education, secondary education, and special education), ENGINEERING AND ENVIRONMENTAL DESIGN (preengineering), HEALTH PROFESSIONS (predentistry, premedicine, preoptometry, prepharmacy, and preveterinary science), SOCIAL SCIENCE (biblical studies, child care/child and family studies, criminal justice, family/consumer studies, history, ministries, psychology, and social work). Premedicine, preengineering, and business are the strongest academically. Business, Bible, and elementary education have the largest enrollments.

Required: To graduate, students must complete 132 semester hours, including 44 in upper-division courses in Bible, skills, humanities, and science, plus 3 hours of speech communication and 2 hours of phys ed. The major requires a minimum of 30 semester hours, including 15 upper-division hours. Students must maintain a GPA of 2.0. All students must demonstrate, by approved tests or criteria, basic competence in reading, writing, oral communication, math, and computers.

Special: FHU offers study abroad in Belgium and Italy, a B.A.-B.S. degree in Bible, biology, communication, and arts and humanities, co-op programs, a dual major, field practicum opportunities in several majors, student-designed majors, 3-2 engineering degrees with 6 universities, and nondegree study. There are 4 national honor societies, a freshman honors program, and 13 departmental honors programs.

Faculty/Classroom: 68% of faculty are male; 32% are female. 91% teach undergraduates. No introductory courses are taught by graduate students. The average class size in a laboratory is 22 and in a regular course, 20.

Requirements: The ACT is required, with a minimum composite score of 19. Candidates for admission should be graduates of an accredited secondary school. An interview is recommended. A GPA of 2.25 is required. AP and CLEP credits are accepted. Important factors in the admissions decision are personality/intangible qualities, recommendations by school officials, and leadership record.

Procedure: Freshmen are admitted fall, spring, and summer. Entrance exams should be taken in early fall or summer before senior year. There are early admissions and rolling admissions plans. Application deadlines are open. Applications are accepted online.

Transfer: Applicants should have a minimum college GPA of 2.0. Those with fewer than 30 college credits must also submit a high school transcript and ACT or SAT scores. 33 of 132 credits required for the bachelor's degree must be completed at FHU.

Visiting: There are regularly scheduled orientations for prospective students, including an orientation during the 5 days prior to classes beginning in the fall. There are guides for informal visits, and visitors may sit in on classes and stay overnight.

Financial Aid: The FAFSA is required. Check with the school for current application deadlines.

International Students: They must take the TOEFL with a minimum score of 500 on the paper-based TOEFL (PBT) or 61 on the Internet-based version (iBT). They must also take the ACT.

Computers: All students may access the system.

Admissions Contact: Belinda Anderson, Director of Admissions. A campus DVD is available. E-Mail: *banderson@fhu.edu* Web: *www.fhu.edu*

KING UNIVERSITY F-1

Bristol, TN 37620 (423) 652-4861
(800) 362-0014; (423) 652-4727

Full-time: 646 men, 1197 women
Part-time: 52 men, 68 women
Graduate: 141 men, 238 women
Year: semesters, summer session
Application Deadline: open
Freshman Class: 856 applied, 184 accepted, 221 enrolled
SAT CR/M: 485/509
Faculty: 58; IIB, --$
Ph.D.s: 81%
Student/Faculty: 20 to 1
Tuition: $24,960
Room & Board: $8180
ACT: 23

COMPETITIVE

King University is a Presbyterian, master's-level comprehensive university offering more than 80 majors, minors, pre-professional degrees and concentrations in fields such as business, digital media, nursing, forensic science, education, and humanities. Graduate programs are offered in business administration, nursing, and education. A number of off-campus learning opportunities and travel destinations are also available. King University has six academic schools of learning: King College of Arts and Sciences, King School of Business and Economics, King School of Education, King School of Graduatie and Professional Studies & Online Programs, King School of Nursing, and Peeke School of Christian Mission. There are 5 undergraduate schools and 3 graduate schools. The library contains 104,697 volumes, 62,173 microform items, 7,009 audio/video tapes/CDs/DVDs, and subscribes to 349 periodicals including electronic. Computerized library services include interlibrary loans, database searching, Internet access, and Wi-Fi capability. The 135-acre campus is in a small town 2 miles east of Bristol, VA. Including any residence halls, there are 20 buildings.

Student Life: 65% of undergraduates are from Tennessee. Others are from 31 states, 29 foreign countries, and Canada. 89% are from public schools. 77% are White. 68% are Protestant; 18% claim no religious affiliation. The average age of freshmen is 18; all undergraduates, 28.

Housing: 471 students can be accommodated in college housing, which includes single-sex dorms. On-campus housing is guaranteed for all 4 years, is available on a first-come, and first-served basis. 58% of students commute. Alcohol is not permitted. All students may keep cars.

Activities: There are no fraternities or sororities. There are 36 groups on campus, including art, band, cheerleading, choir, chorale, chorus, dance, debate, drama, environmental, honors, international, jazz band, literary magazine, musical theater, newspaper, pep band, photography, political, professional, religious, social service, student government, and yearbook. Popular campus events include International Fair, Fall Ball and Dogwood Ball.

Sports: There are 10 intercollegiate sports for men and 10 for women, and 7 intramural sports for men and 6 for women. Facilities include a gym, soccer and baseball fields, 6 tennis courts, and a fitness trail. A student center complex provides a facility for sporting events, convocations, student activities, and fitness. The 68,000-sq.-ft. building has a basketball court, running track, racquetball courts, offices, board room, weight room, cardio equipment, and a medical suite.

Disabled Students: 80% of the campus is accessible. Facilities include wheelchair ramps, elevators, special parking, and specially equipped restrooms.

Services: Counseling and information services are available, as is tutoring in most subjects. The Academic Center for Excellence (ACE) has a writing center, math center, and speaking center.

Campus Safety and Security: Measures include 24-hour foot and vehicle patrol, emergency notification system, and security escort services. There are emergency telephones, lighted pathways/sidewalks, 24-hour foot and vehicle patrol on weekends, and 12-hour patrol Monday through Friday.

Programs of Study: King confers B.A., B.S., B.B.A., B.Chem., B.S.Med.Tech. and B.S.N. degrees. Master's degrees are also awarded. Bachelor's degrees are awarded in BIOLOGICAL SCIENCE (biochemistry, biology/biological science, and neurosciences), BUSINESS (accounting, business administration and management, business economics, international business management, management information systems, marketing management, and sports management), COMMUNICATIONS AND THE ARTS (digital communications, English, French, modern language, photography, Spanish, technical and business writing, theatre arts, and visual and performing arts), COMPUTER AND PHYSICAL SCIENCE (chemistry, mathematics, and physics), EDUCATION (athletic training, elementary education, music education, physical education, and secondary education), HEALTH PROFESSIONS (health science and nursing), SOCIAL SCIENCE (biblical studies, economics, forensic studies, history, interdisciplinary studies, philosophy, political science/government, psychology, and youth ministry). Business and economics, English, and natural sciences are the strongest academically. Business and economics, nursing, and social sciences have the largest enrollments.

Required: Students must complete a minimum of 124 semester hours with 27 to 53 in the major. The minimum 49 semester hours of core curriculum include courses in English, history, math, Bible, humanities, science, social science, and phys ed. Students must have a minimum GPA of 2.0 in most majors (may vary according to field of study). A comprehensive exam in the student's major area of concentration is required.

Special: King offers co-op programs, cross-registration with Virginia Intermont College, internships, study abroad in approximately 50 countries, a Washington semester, and work-study programs. There are 3-2 engineering degrees available with Vanderbilt University and University of Tennessee. Dual degrees in pharmacy, engineering, and physical therapy are offered. Nondegree study and pass/fail options for special students are available. There is 1 national honor society, a freshman honors program, and 1 departmental honors program.

Faculty/Classroom: 37% of faculty are male; 46% are female. All teach undergraduates, and 45% do both. No introductory courses are taught by graduate students. The average class size in an introductory lecture is 30 and in a laboratory is 30.

Admissions: 21% of the 2013-2014 applicants were accepted. The SAT scores for the 2013-2014 freshman class were: Critical Reading--47% below 500, 47% between 500 and 599, 6% between 600 and 699; Math--36% below 500, 51% between 500 and 599, 12% between 600 and 699, and 1% between 700 and 800. The ACT scores were 6% below 21, 47% between 21 and 23, 43% between 24 and 26, and 4% above 28. 37% of the current freshmen were in the top fifth of their class; 66% were in the top two fifths. 6 freshmen graduated first in their class.

Requirements: The SAT or ACT is required. Graduation from an accredited or recognized secondary institution is required, with a minimum of 16 academic units, distributed as follows: 4 of English; 2 of algebra (Algebra I and II); 1 of geometry; 2 of foreign language; 2 of history and social studies; 1 of natural science; and 4 of other academic electives. A GPA of 2.6 is required. AP and CLEP credits are accepted. Important factors in the admissions decision are advanced placement or honors courses, extracurricular activities record, and leadership record.

Procedure: Freshmen are admitted fall, spring, and summer. Entrance exams should be taken by May 1. There are deferred admissions and rolling admissions plans. Application deadlines are open. Application fee is $20. Applications are accepted online.

Transfer: 97 transfer students enrolled in 2012-2013. Transfer applicants should have a minimum 2.0 GPA and 30 semester hours. If fewer hours have been completed, a 2.4 high school GPA and a minimum ACT composite score of 20 or SAT score of 1000 are required. 50 of 124 credits required for the bachelor's degree must be completed at King.

Visiting: There are regularly scheduled orientations for prospective students, including a campus tour, financial aid seminar, faculty sessions, and admissions counseling. There are guides for informal visits and visitors may sit in on classes. To schedule a visit, contact The Admissions Office.

Financial Aid: In 2013-2014, 83% of all full-time freshmen and 69% of continuing full-time students received some form of financial aid. 80% of all full-time freshmen and 60% of continuing full-time students received need-based aid. The average freshman award was $16,442. Need-based scholarships or need-based grants averaged $14,147; need-based self-help aid (loans and jobs) averaged $4,010; non-need-based athletic scholarships averaged $5,961; and other non-need-based awards and non-need-based scholarships averaged $12,206. 30% of undergraduate students work part-time. Average annual earnings from campus work are $962. The average financial indebtedness of the 2013 graduate was $9,998. King is a member of CSS. The FAFSA and the college's own financial statement are required. The priority date for freshman financial aid applications for fall entry is March 1. The deadline for filing freshman financial aid applications for fall entry is rolling.

International Students: There are 37 international students enrolled. The school actively recruits these students. They must take the TOEFL and the college's own test. Students outside the U.S. where English is the primary language are required to take the SAT in place of the TOEFL.

Computers: All students may access the system. There are no time limits and no fees.

Graduates: From July 1, 2012 to June 30, 2013, 247 bachelor's degrees were awarded. The most popular majors were nursing (51%), business (18%), and psychology (6%). In an average class, 2% graduate in 3 years or less, 47% graduate in 4 years or less, 7% graduate in 5 years or less, and 1% graduate in 6 years or less. Of the 2012 graduating class, 28% were enrolled in graduate school within 6 months of graduation, and 62% were employed.

Admissions Contact: Melinda Clark, Associate Vice President of Enrollment. E-Mail: *admissions@king.edu* Web: *www.king.edu*

LANE COLLEGE — B-3

Jackson, TN 38301-4598 — (731) 426-7533; (800) 960-7533; (731) 426-7559

Full-time: 2,200 men, and women	**Faculty:** n/av
Part-time: n/av	**Ph.D.s:** 60%
Graduate: n/av	**Student/Faculty:** n/av
Year: semesters, summer session	**Tuition:** $8290 ($8500)
Application Deadline: see profile	**Room & Board:** $5700
Freshman Class: n/av	
SAT or ACT: required	

COMPETITIVE

Lane College, founded in 1882, is a private liberal arts institution affiliated with the Christian Methodist Episcopal Church. The figures in the above capsule and in this profile are approximate. The library contains 98,619 volumes, 53,125 microform items, 820 audio/video tapes/CDs/DVDs, and subscribes to 226 periodicals including electronic. Computerized library services include interlibrary loans, database searching, and Internet access. Special learning facilities include a learning resource center, a media center, several computer labs for students majoring in education and other areas, a curriculum lab, a video teleconferencing center, a math lab, a writing center, and a mass communications lab. The 25-acre campus is in a small town 79 miles from Memphis and 122 miles from Nashville. Including any residence halls, there are 23 buildings.

Student Life: 57% of undergraduates are from Tennessee. Others are from 30 states, and 1 foreign country. 85% are from public schools. 99% are African American. 95% are Protestant. The average age of freshmen is 19; all undergraduates, 21. 20% do not continue beyond their first year; 65% remain to graduate.

Housing: 638 students can be accommodated in college housing, which includes single-sex dorms and on-campus apartments. On-campus housing is guaranteed for all 4 years. 63% of students live on campus; of those, 40% remain on campus on weekends. Alcohol is not permitted. All students may keep cars.

Activities: 3% of men belong to 2 local and 2 national fraternities; 9% of women belong to 4 local and 4 national sororities. There are 21 groups on campus, including band, cheerleading, chess, choir, chorus, computers, debate, drama, honors, marching band, newspaper, pep band, religious, social, social service, student government, and yearbook. Popular campus events include Founders Day, Fine Arts Week, and Religious Emphasis Week.

Sports: There are 6 intercollegiate sports for men and 6 for women, and 4 intramural sports for men and 4 for women. Facilities include an Olympic-size swimming pool, a multipurpose/weight room, a gym, off-campus football and baseball fields, and a campus recreation center with a theater area, dance floor, billiards, ping-pong, table games, and a lounge area.

Disabled Students: 70% of the campus is accessible. Facilities include wheelchair ramps, elevators, special parking, specially equipped rest rooms, and wheelchair lifts in some buildings.

Services: Counseling and information services are available, as is tutoring in most subjects. The writing center provides tutoring in writing and the math lab offers tutoring in math. Student Support Services provides tutoring in English, math, reading, computer science, computer literacy, test-taking, and study skills.

Campus Safety and Security: Measures include 24-hour foot and vehicle patrol and security escort services. There are emergency telephones, lighted pathways/sidewalks, a security guard at the entrance to the campus, and camera surveillance in parking lots and dorms.

Programs of Study: Lane confers B.A. and B.S. degrees. Bachelor's degrees are awarded in BIOLOGICAL SCIENCE (biology/biological science), BUSINESS (business administration and management), COMMUNICATIONS AND THE ARTS (communications, English, French, and music), COMPUTER AND PHYSICAL SCIENCE (chemistry, computer science, mathematics, and physics), EDUCATION (physical education), SOCIAL SCIENCE (criminal justice, history, interdisciplinary studies, religion, and sociology). Business, education, and criminal justice are the strongest academically. Education, business, and sociology have the largest enrollments.

Required: Students must complete a minimum of 124 semester hours with a 2.0 GPA. 50 to 69 hours are required in the general studies curriculum, which includes courses in art, music, personal finance, foreign language, speech, composition, literature, history, sociology, math, physical science, biology, computer literacy, foundations of education, religion, and phys ed. The ETS Academic Profile is also required. ETS Major Field Tests are given as exit exams by major.

Special: Cooperative programs are available in engineering with Tennessee State University School of Engineering and Technology. The College also offers work-study programs, dual majors, student-designed majors, and nondegree study. Internships are available in many fields in various corporations, universities, and federal agencies. The college also has a cooperative agreement with Milwaukee Area Technical College. There are 2 national honor societies.

Faculty/Classroom: 72% of faculty are male; 28% are female. All teach undergraduates. The average class size in an introductory lecture is 25; in a laboratory, 16; and in a regular course, 16.

Requirements: The ACT or SAT is required. Graduation from an accredited secondary school is required; a GED will be accepted. Applicants' academic record must include 16 credits, including 4 credits in English and 2 credits each in math, science, and social studies. An additional 2 credits in a foreign language is recommended. An interview is also recommended. A GPA of 2.0 is required. AP and CLEP credits are accepted. Important factors in the admissions decision are evidence of special talent, recommendations by school officials, and ability to finance college education.

Procedure: Freshmen are admitted to all sessions. Entrance exams should be taken by October of the senior year. There are early decision, early admissions and rolling admissions plans. Check with the school for current application deadlines. Notification is sent on a rolling basis. Applications are accepted online.

Transfer: Applicants must submit transcripts from previous colleges attended and be in good standing at the time of application. Students with associate degrees will be given credit for a maximum of 68 semester hours in general education courses with a grade of C or higher. 31 of 124 credits required for the bachelor's degree must be completed at Lane.

Visiting: There are regularly scheduled orientations for prospective students, including meetings on financial aid, residential life, rules and regulations of the college, course requirements, and registration. There are guides for informal visits, and visitors may sit in on classes and stay overnight. To schedule a visit, contact the Office of Recruitment/Admissions.

Financial Aid: The CCS/Profile, or FAFSA, or FFS, or SFS is required. Check with the school for current application deadlines.

International Students: The school actively recruits these students. They must take the TOEFL. They must also take the ACT, scoring 13.

Computers: All students may access the system. There are no time limits and no fees.

Admissions Contact: Evelyn L. Brown, Director of Admissions. A campus DVD is available. E-Mail: *ebrown@lanecollege.edu* Web: *www.lanecollege.edu*

LEE UNIVERSITY — D-3

Cleveland, TN 37311 — (423) 614-8500; (800) 533-9930; (423) 614-8533

Full-time: 1459 men, 2095 women	**Faculty:** 158; IIB, --$
Part-time: 211 men, 251 women	**Ph.D.s:** 73%
Graduate: 143 men, 252 women	**Student/Faculty:** 23 to 1
Year: semesters, summer session	**Tuition:** $12,680
Application Deadline: September 1	**Room & Board:** $6010
Freshman Class: 1777 applied, 1088 accepted, 875 enrolled	
SAT CR/M: 550/530	**ACT:** 24 — **COMPETITIVE+**

Lee University, founded in 1918, is a private liberal arts institution affiliated with the Church of God. There are 4 undergraduate schools and 4 graduate schools. In addition to regional accreditation, Lee has baccalaureate program accreditation with NASM. The 2 libraries contain 271,897 volumes, 51,385 microform items, and 1,671 audio/video tapes/CDs/DVDs, and subscribe to 34,881 periodicals including electronic. Computerized library services include interlibrary loans, database searching, Internet access, and Wi-Fi capability. The 120-acre campus is in a suburban area 20 miles north of Chattanooga. Including any residence halls, there are 50 buildings.

Student Life: 55% of undergraduates are from out of state, mostly the South. Students are from 49 states, 50 foreign countries, and Canada. 83% are White. The average age of freshmen is 18; all undergraduates, 20. 29% do not continue beyond their first year; 48% remain to graduate.

Housing: 1870 students can be accommodated in college housing, which includes single-sex dorms, on-campus apartments, off-campus apartments, and married student housing. On-campus housing is guaranteed for the freshman year only, is available on a first-come, and first-served basis. 56% of students commute. Alcohol is not permitted. All students may keep cars.

Activities: 10% of men belong to 5 local fraternities; 10% of women belong to 5 local sororities. There are 95 groups on campus, including art, band, cheerleading, choir, chorale, chorus, computers, debate, drama, ethnic, film, honors, international, jazz band, literary magazine, musical theater, newspaper, opera, orchestra, pep band, photography, political, professional, radio and TV, religious, social, social service, student government, and symphony. Popular campus events include Lee Day, Parade of Favorites, and Dorm Wars.

Sports: There are 6 intercollegiate sports for men and 6 for women, and 11 intramural sports for men and 11 for women. Facilities include an arena, a recreation complex, a softball field, a tennis center, a soccer field, a baseball field, and a playing field.

Disabled Students: 73% of the campus is accessible. Facilities include wheelchair ramps, elevators, special parking, specially equipped restrooms, special class scheduling, lowered drinking fountains, and lowered telephones.

Services: Counseling and information services are available, as is tutoring in every subject. There is a reader service for the blind, and remedial math, reading, and writing.

Campus Safety and Security: Measures include 24-hour foot and vehicle patrol, emergency notification system, and security escort services. There are shuttle buses, emergency telephones, and lighted pathways/sidewalks.

Programs of Study: Lee confers B.A., B.S., B.C.M., B.M. and B.M.E. degrees. Master's degrees are also awarded. Bachelor's degrees are awarded in BIOLOGICAL SCIENCE (biochemistry and biology/biological science), BUSINESS (accounting and business administration and management), COMMUNICATIONS AND THE ARTS (communications, dramatic arts, English, French, music, music business management, music performance, public relations, Spanish, and telecommunications), COMPUTER AND PHYSICAL SCIENCE (chemistry, information sciences and systems, mathematics, and science), EDUCATION (athletic training, business education, elementary education, health education, mathematics education, middle school education, music education, physical education, and special education), HEALTH PROFESSIONS (health care administration, health science, and medical laboratory technology), SOCIAL SCIENCE (anthropology, biblical studies, crosscultural studies, history, human development, humanities, interdisciplinary studies, ministries, political science/government, psychology, religious music, sociology, and youth ministry). Business administration, communication, human development are the strongest academically. Education, business, and psychology have the largest enrollments.

Required: All students must complete a minimum of 130 credit hours, including a core curriculum and 36 hours in the major, with a 2.0 GPA (2.5 for education majors). A Global Perspectives seminar and cross-cultural experience are required, in addition to a major field test the last semester before graduation in all fields except preprofessional science and teacher licensure.

Special: Lee offers internships, cross-registration with the Coalition for Christian Colleges and Universities, study abroad in 25 countries, a Washington semester, numerous work-study programs, an accelerated degree program in Christian leadership, dual and student-designed majors, nondegree study, and limited pass/fail options. Every student completes a minor in religion. There are 16 national honor societies, a freshman honors program, and 6 departmental honors programs.

Faculty/Classroom: 63% of faculty are male; 37% are female. All teach undergraduates, and 20% do both. No introductory courses are taught by graduate students. The average class size in an introductory lecture is 25; in a laboratory is 15; and in a regular course is 28.

Admissions: 61% of the 2013-2014 applicants were accepted. The SAT scores for the 2013-2014 freshman class were: Critical Reading--34% below 500, 37% between 500 and 599, 23% between 600 and 699, and 6% between 700 and 800; Math--37% below 500, 34% between 500 and 599, 26% between 600 and 699, and 3% between 700 and 800. The ACT scores were 25% below 21, 18% between 21 and 23, 23% between 24 and 26, 18% between 27 and 28, and 16% above 28. 43% of the current freshmen were in the top fifth of their class; 68% were in the top two fifths.

Requirements: The SAT or ACT is recommended. Students must be graduates of accredited secondary schools. The GED is accepted. A portfolio is recommended. A GPA of 2.0 is required. AP and CLEP credits are accepted. Important factors in the admissions decision are advanced placement or honors courses, leadership record, and recommendations by school officials.

Procedure: Freshmen are admitted fall and spring. Entrance exams should be taken prior to registration. There are early admissions, deferred admissions, and rolling admissions plans. Early decision applications should be filed by January 1; regular applications, by September 1 for fall entry, along with a $25 fee. Notifications are sent September 1. Applications are accepted online.

Transfer: 278 transfer students enrolled in 2012-2013. Transfer students must take the SAT or the ACT unless they have 16 credit hours with a GPA of 2.0 or better. Students must have official transcripts from all prior colleges. 30 of 130 credits required for the bachelor's degree must be completed at Lee.

Visiting: There are regularly scheduled orientations for prospective students, The Admissions Office will arrange a complete campus tour upon request. There are guides for informal visits and visitors may sit in on classes. To schedule a visit, contact the Admissions Office.

Financial Aid: In 2013-2014, 96% of all full-time freshmen and 92% of continuing full-time students received some form of financial aid. 68% of all full-time freshmen and 62% of continuing full-time students received need-based aid. Average annual earnings from campus work are $2000. The average financial indebtedness of the 2013 graduate was $27,213. The FAFSA and the college's own financial statement are required. The deadline for filing freshman financial aid applications for fall entry is March 15.

International Students: There are 208 international students enrolled. The school actively recruits these students. They must take the TOEFL. They must also take the SAT or ACT.

Computers: All students may access the system. There are no time limits. The fee is $75.

Graduates: From July 1, 2012 to June 30, 2013, 781 bachelor's degrees were awarded. The most popular majors were education (18%), theology (16%), and business (15%). In an average class, 1% graduate in 3 years or less, 29% graduate in 4 years or less, 44% graduate in 5 years or less, and 49% graduate in 6 years or less.

Admissions Contact: Phil Cook, Vice President for Enrollment. E-Mail: *admissions@leeuniversity.edu* Web: *www.leeuniversity.edu*

LEMOYNE-OWEN COLLEGE A-3

Memphis, TN 38126 (901) 435-1528
(800) 737-7778; (901) 942-6233

Full-time: 640 men and women	**Faculty:** n/av
Part-time: 145 men and women	**Ph.D.s:** 80%
Graduate: n/av	**Student/Faculty:** n/av
Year: semesters, summer session	**Tuition:** $10,598
Application Deadline: see profile	**Room & Board:** $5500
Freshman Class: n/av	
SAT or ACT: required	

COMPETITIVE

LeMoyne-Owen College, established in 1872, is a private, liberal arts college affiliated with the United Church of Christ and the Tennessee Baptist, Missionary and Educational Convention, offering degrees in the liberal arts and sciences and business administration. The figures in the above capsule and in this profile are approximate. In addition to regional accreditation, LOC has baccalaureate program accreditation with NCATE. The library contains 90,000 volumes and 1000 audio/video tapes/CDs/DVDs, and subscribes to 300 periodicals including electronic. Computerized library services include interlibrary loans, database searching, and Internet access. Special learning facilities include a learning resource center and art gallery. The 15-acre campus is in an urban area. Including any residence halls, there are 18 buildings.

Student Life: 86% of undergraduates are from Tennessee. Others are from 20 states and 3 foreign countries. 95% are from public schools. 94% are African American. 90% are Protestant. The average age of all undergraduates is 23. 30% do not continue beyond their first year; 20% remain to graduate.

Housing: 140 students can be accommodated in college housing, which includes single-sex and coed dorms. On-campus housing is available on a first-come, first-served basis. Priority is given to out-of-town students. 80% of students commute. Alcohol is not permitted. All students may keep cars.

Activities: 20% of men belong to 4 local and 4 national fraternities; 20% of women belong to 4 local and 4 national sororities. There are 15 groups on campus, including cheerleading, choir, chorus, community outreach, computers, drama, ethnic, math, newspaper, photography, professional, religious, social service, student government, and yearbook.

Sports: There are 4 intercollegiate sports for men and 5 for women. Facilities include a gym, a pool, and other phys ed installations.

Disabled Students: 80% of the campus is accessible. Facilities include wheelchair ramps and elevators.

Services: Counseling and information services are available, as is tutoring in every subject. There is remedial math, reading, and writing.

Campus Safety and Security: Measures include 24-hour foot and vehicle patrol and security escort services. There are emergency telephones and lighted pathways/sidewalks.

Programs of Study: LOC confers B.A., B.S., and B.B.A. degrees. Bachelor's degrees are awarded in BIOLOGICAL SCIENCE (biology/biological science), BUSINESS (accounting and business administration and management), COMMUNICATIONS AND THE ARTS (art, English, language arts, and music), COMPUTER AND PHYSICAL SCIENCE (chemistry, computer science, mathematics, natural sciences, and science), EDUCATION (early childhood education and special education), SOCIAL SCIENCE (criminal justice, history, humanities, political science/government, social science, social work, and sociology). Business, biology, and education are the strongest academically. Business and biology have the largest enrollments.

Required: To graduate, students must satisfy 42 hours of core requirements in communication, math, natural and computer sciences, literature and the humanities, African and African American history, social and behavioral sciences, and physical fitness. They must have a minimum GPA of 2.0 and grades of C or better in all major courses. The college requires 120 credits for graduation, including at least 45 in upper-division courses. All recent high school graduates must participate in the Freshman-Year Experience Program.

Special: Students may cross-register with other institutions of the Greater Memphis Consortium. The college offers a work-study program, dual and student-designed majors, internships, nondegree study, and a pass/fail grading option. There are dual-degree programs in pharmacy with Xavier School of Pharmacy, in optometry with Southern College of Optometry, and in engineering with Christian Brothers University. There is 1 national honor society, a freshman honors program, and 100 departmental honors programs.

Faculty/Classroom: All teach undergraduates, and 40% do research. The average class size in an introductory lecture is 15; in a laboratory, 15; and in a regular course, 12.

Requirements: The SAT or ACT is required. Applicants must graduate from an accredited secondary school having completed 20 high school units. The college recommends 4 years of English, 2 each of math, science, and social studies, and 1 of a foreign language. Applicants must submit 2 letters of recommendation. Students 23 or older may be admitted to the division of lifelong learning, which accepts the GED. A GPA of 2.0 is required. AP and CLEP credits are accepted. Important factors in the admissions decision are advanced placement or honors courses, evidence of special talent, and parents or siblings attended the school.

Procedure: Freshmen are admitted to all sessions. Entrance exams should be taken in the spring of the junior year. There are early admissions, deferred admissions, and rolling admissions plans. Check with the school for current application deadlines. The application fee is $25.

Transfer: Applicants should have a GPA of 2.0 and must submit 2 copies of official transcripts plus a statement of good standing from the previous college attended. Students with fewer than 28 college credit hours must also submit a high school transcript and, if below age 21, ACT or SAT scores. 30 of 120 credits required for the bachelor's degree must be completed at LOC.

Visiting: There are regularly scheduled orientations for prospective students. There are guides for informal visits and visitors may sit in on classes. To schedule a visit, contact the Admissions Office.

Financial Aid: LOC is a member of CSS. The FAFSA and the college's own financial statement are required. Check with the school for current application deadlines.

International Students: They must take the TOEFL and the ACT.

Computers: All students may access the system. There are no time limits and no fees.

Admissions Contact: Samuel King, Interim Director of Admissions. E-Mail: *admissions@loc.edu* Web: *www.loc.edu*

LINCOLN MEMORIAL UNIVERSITY E-1

Harrogate, TN 37752-0901 (423) 869-3611
(800) 325-0900; (423) 869-6370

Full-time: 350 men, 1000 women	**Faculty:** n/av
Part-time: 85 men, 220 women	**Ph.D.s:** 85
Graduate: 410 men, 1080 women	**Student/Faculty:** n/av
Year: semesters, summer session	**Tuition:** $18,740
Application Deadline: open	**Room & Board:** $6,980
Freshman Class: n/av	
SAT or ACT: required	

COMPETITIVE

Lincoln Memorial University, founded in 1897, is an independent institution offering degree programs in the arts and sciences, business, education, and preprofessional training. The figures in the above capsule are and in this profile are approximate. There are 4 undergraduate schools and 2 graduate schools. In addition to regional accreditation, LMU has baccalaureate program accreditation with CAHEA and NLN. The library contains

200,000 volumes, 160,506 microform items, 254 audio/video tapes/CDs/DVDs, and subscribes to 893 periodicals including electronic. Computerized library services include interlibrary loans, database searching, and Internet access. Special learning facilities include a learning resource center, radio station, TV station, and the Lincoln Museum. The 1000-acre campus is in a rural area 55 miles north of Knoxville. Including any residence halls, there are 32 buildings.

Student Life: 67% of undergraduates are from Tennessee. Others are from 25 states, 22 foreign countries, and Canada. 89% are from public schools. 94% are white. The average age of freshmen is 19; all undergraduates, 23. 20% do not continue beyond their first year; 50% remain to graduate.

Housing: 500 students can be accommodated in college housing, which includes single-sex and coed dorms, on-campus apartments, and married student housing. On-campus housing is guaranteed for the freshman year only and is available on a first-come, first-served basis. Priority is given to out-of-town students. 70% of students commute. Alcohol is not permitted. All students may keep cars.

Activities: There are 3 local fraternities and 3 local sororities. There are 26 groups on campus, including art, cheerleading, choir, chorus, computers, drama, drill team, honors, international, literary magazine, newspaper, photography, radio and TV, religious, social service, student government, and yearbook. Popular campus events include Lincoln Day.

Sports: There are 6 intercollegiate sports for men and 6 for women, and 4 intramural sports for men and 4 for women. Facilities include a 5000-seat arena, a baseball field, a playing field, and a natatorium.

Disabled Students: 60% of the campus is accessible. Facilities include wheelchair ramps, elevators, special parking, and special class scheduling.

Services: Counseling and information services are available, as is tutoring in most subjects. There is remedial math, reading, and writing.

Campus Safety and Security: Measures include 24-hour foot and vehicle patrol. There are lighted pathways/sidewalks.

Programs of Study: LMU confers B.A., B.S., B.B.A., B.S.N., and B.S.W. degrees. Associates and master's degrees are also awarded. Bachelor's degrees are awarded in AGRICULTURE (wildlife management), BIOLOGICAL SCIENCE (biology/biological science), BUSINESS (accounting and business administration and management), COMMUNICATIONS AND THE ARTS (broadcasting, communications, English, and fine arts), COMPUTER AND PHYSICAL SCIENCE (chemistry, information sciences and systems, and mathematics), EDUCATION (athletic training, business education, early childhood education, elementary education, health education, middle school education, science education, and secondary education), ENGINEERING AND ENVIRONMENTAL DESIGN (environmental science), HEALTH PROFESSIONS (medical laboratory technology, nursing, predentistry, premedicine, and veterinary science), SOCIAL SCIENCE (history, prelaw, psychology, social science, and social work). Nursing, business, and education have the largest enrollments.

Required: To graduate, all students must complete at least 128 semester credit hours, including the general studies requirements of the declared major and a minimum of 30 hours of in the major. Students must achieve a minimum GPA of 2.0.

Special: LMU offers pass/fail options and credit for life, military, and work experience. Some internships are available.

Faculty/Classroom: 49% of faculty are male; 51% are female. 80% teach undergraduates. No introductory courses are taught by graduate students. The average class size in an introductory lecture is 20; in a laboratory, 25; and in a regular course, 20.

Requirements: The SAT or ACT is required. Applicants must score 18 on the ACT or 850 on the SAT or graduate with a GPA of at least 3.2. Candidates for admission should be graduates of accredited secondary schools or have the GED. Students should have completed 4 years of English, 2 each of math and science, and 1 each of history and social studies. LMU requires applicants to be in the upper 50% of their class. A GPA of 2.3 is required. AP and CLEP credits are accepted. Important factors in the admissions decision are recommendations by school officials, personality/intangible qualities, and leadership record.

Procedure: Freshmen are admitted fall, spring, and summer. Entrance exams should be taken in the spring of the junior year. There are early admissions, deferred admissions, and rolling admissions plans. Application deadlines are open. The application fee is $25.

Transfer: Trasfer students who have completed 12 or more semester credit hours of potentially transferable course work at a regionally accredited college or uinversity will be considered for transfer admission. Students with fewer than 12 semester credit hours are subject to freshman admission procedures. Official transcripts from all colleges and universities must be sumbmitted. 32 of 128 credits required for the bachelor's degree must be completed at LMU.

Visiting: There are regularly scheduled orientations for prospective students, including introductory sessions for both students and their parents and advising and registration sessions. There are guides for informal visits, and visitors may sit in on classes and stay overnight. To schedule a visit, contact the Office of Admissions and Recruitment.

Financial Aid: LMU is a member of CSS. The CCS/Profile, FAFSA, FFS, or SFS is required. Check with the school for current application deadlines.

International Students: They must take the TOEFL.

Computers: All students may access the system. There are no time limits and no fees. It is strongly recommended that all students have a personal computer.

Admissions Contact: Office of Admissions. E-Mail: *admissions@lmunet.edu* Web: *www.lmunet.edu*

LIPSCOMB UNIVERSITY C-2

Nashville, TN 37204 **(615) 966 1776**
(877) 582-4766; (615) 966-1804

Full-time: 1041 men, 1549 women	**Faculty:** 152; IIA, -$
Part-time: 116 men, 184 women	**Ph.D.s:** 84%
Graduate: 577 men, 1113 women	**Student/Faculty:** 17 to 1
Year: semesters, summer session	**Tuition:** $26,094
Application Deadline: open	**Room & Board:** $9628
Freshman Class: 3467 applied, 1827 accepted, 684 enrolled	
SAT CR/M: 570/590 **ACT:** 25	**VERY COMPETITIVE**

Lipscomb University is a private coeducational institution whose principal focus is undergraduate education in the liberal arts and sciences, combined with a number of undergraduate professional and pre-professional fields, master's and doctoral degree programs. Its primary mission is to integrate Christian faith and practice with academic excellence. This mission is carried out not only in the classroom but also by involvement in numerous services to the church and the larger community. There are 8 undergraduate schools and 15 graduate schools. In addition to regional accreditation, Lipscomb has baccalaureate program accreditation with ABET, ACBSP, ACPE, ADA, CSWE, NASM, NCATE, and NLN. The library contains 267,728 volumes, and 430,988 microform items, and subscribes to 723 periodicals including electronic. Computerized library services include interlibrary loans, database searching, Internet access, and Wi-Fi capability. Special learning facilities include an art gallery, radio station, multimedia production studio. The 75-acre campus is in a suburban area 2 miles south of downtown Nashville. Including any residence halls, there are 25 buildings.

Student Life: 67% of undergraduates are from Tennessee. Others are from 47 states, 39 foreign countries, and Canada. 56% are from public schools. 76% are White. 78% are Protestant; 14% claim no religious affiliation. The average age of freshmen is 18; all undergraduates, 22. 23% do not continue beyond their first year; 64% remain to graduate.

Housing: 1450 students can be accommodated in college housing, which includes single-sex dorms and on-campus apartments. On-campus housing is guaranteed for the freshman year only, is available on a first-come, and first-served basis. 52% of students live on campus; of those, 40% remain on campus on weekends. Alcohol is not permitted. All students may keep cars.

Activities: 16% of men belong to 6 local fraternities; 17% of women belong to 7 local sororities. There are 70 groups on campus, including art, band, cheerleading, choir, chorale, chorus, computers, drama, environmental, ethnic, honors, international, jazz band, musical theater, newspaper, orchestra, pep band, photography, political, professional, radio and TV, religious, social, social service, student government, and yearbook. Popular campus events include Singarama, Annual Service Day, International Square Fair, StompFest, Anteater's Ball, Paint the Herd, and Battle of the Boulevard.

Sports: There are 7 intercollegiate sports for men and 8 for women, and 13 intramural sports for men and 13 for women. Facilities include Allen Arena with a basketball/multi-purpose court and a student activity center with 2 full-size basketball courts, 4 racquetball courts, a jogging course, and weight, aerobics, spinning, and recreation rooms for both men and women.

Disabled Students: All of the campus is accessible. Facilities include wheelchair ramps, elevators, special parking, specially equipped restrooms, special class scheduling, and lowered drinking fountains.

Services: Counseling and information services are available, as is tutoring in some subjects,including math, English, biology, chemistry There is a reader service for the blind, and remedial math, reading, and writing.

Campus Safety and Security: Measures include 24-hour foot and vehicle patrol, emergency notification system, self-defense education, and security escort services. There are shuttle buses, emergency telephones, lighted pathways/sidewalks, controlled access to dorms/residences, residence hall security systems.

Programs of Study: Lipscomb confers B.A., B.S., B.B.A., B.F.A., B.M., B.S.N. and B.S.W. degrees. Associate, master's, and doctoral degrees are also awarded. Bachelor's degrees are awarded in AGRICULTURE (conservation and regulation and environmental studies), BIOLOGICAL SCIENCE (biochemistry, biology/adolescence education, biology/biological science, biophysics, and molecular biology), BUSINESS (accounting, business administration and management, entrepreneurial studies, fashion merchandising, finance, human resources/organizational mgmt, international business management, management information systems, marketing management, marketing/retailing/merchandising, supply chain management, and sustainable management), COMMUNICATIONS AND THE ARTS (art, communications, English, French, German, graphic design, journalism, music, music composition, music performance, musical theater, Spanish, studio art, theatre arts, and visual and performing arts), COMPUTER AND PHYSICAL SCIENCE (applied mathematics, chemistry, chemistry/adolescence education, computer science, mathematics, physics, software engineering, and web services), EDUCATION (art education, early childhood education, education, elementary education, English education, foreign languages education, health education, mathematics education, middle school education, music education, and physical education), ENGINEERING AND ENVIRONMENTAL DESIGN (civil engineering, computer engineering, electrical/electronics engineering, environmental science, mechanical engineering, and preengineering), HEALTH PROFESSIONS (art therapy, exercise science, medical technology, nursing, predentistry, premedicine, preoptometry, and prepharmacy), SOCIAL SCIENCE (American studies, biblical languages, biblical studies, dietetics, economics, European studies, family/consumer studies, food production/management/services, history, interdisciplinary studies, international studies, legal studies, liberal arts/general studies, missions, philosophy, political science/government, prelaw, psychology, social work, textiles and clothing, urban studies, and youth ministry). Biology, education, and engineering are the strongest academically. Business, biology, and nursing have the largest enrollments.

Required: All students must take 18 hours of Bible/theology courses. Other general education requirements include Lipscomb Seminar (freshman seminar class), 6 semester hours each in communications, humanities, science, history, and social science, 3 in math, 2 physical education, and 2 service learning experiences. Students must complete a total of 126 semester hours and have a minimum GPA of 2.0. At least 25% of credit hours must be earned at Lipscomb. Students are required to take and pass a proficiency test of basic computer concepts.

Special: Some majors require an internship. There are study-abroad options on nearly all continents through Lipscomb programs as well as a cooperative with the Council for Christian Colleges & Universities(CCCU). Several programs can be completed in an accelerated three-year format. A B.A.-B.S. option is available in music, and a B.F.A. option is available in art and theatre. There are 5 national honor societies and a freshman honors program.

Faculty/Classroom: 54% of faculty are male; 46% are female. 75% teach undergraduates. No introductory courses are taught by graduate students.

Admissions: 53% of the 2013-2014 applicants were accepted. The SAT scores for the 2013-2014 freshman class were: Critical Reading--17% below 500, 42% between 500 and 599, 28% between 600 and 699, and 13% between 700 and 800; Math--15% below 500, 38% between 500 and 599, 35% between 600 and 699, and 12% between 700 and 800. The ACT scores were 12% below 21, 23% between 21 and 23, 26% between 24 and 26, 15% between 27 and 28, and 24% above 28. 49% of the current freshmen were in the top fifth of their class; 76% were in the top two fifths. There were 11 National Merit finalists. 12 freshmen graduated first in their class.

Requirements: The SAT or ACT is required. Candidates for admission should be graduates of accredited secondary schools. The GED is accepted. 14 academic units are required. Students should have completed 4 units of English and 2 units each of history, math, and science. 2 units of a foreign language are highly recommended. 2 additional units from the areas of English, foreign language, history, math, science, and social studies are also required. A GPA of 2.0 is required. AP and CLEP credits are accepted.

Procedure: Freshmen are admitted to all sessions. There is a rolling admissions plan. Application deadlines are open. Application fee is $50. Applications are accepted online.

Transfer: 145 transfer students enrolled in 2012-2013. College transcripts, an interview, and a statement of good standing from prior institutions are required. 33 of 126 credits required for the bachelor's degree must be completed at Lipscomb.

Visiting: There are regularly scheduled orientations for prospective students. There are guides for informal visits, visitors may sit in on classes, and stay overnight. To schedule a visit, contact Dana Anderson at (615) 966-1776.

Financial Aid: In 2013-2014, 67% of all full-time freshmen and 66% of continuing full-time students received some form of financial aid. 54% of all full-time freshmen and 54% of continuing full-time students received need-based aid. The average freshman award was $19,642. Need-based scholarships or need-based grants averaged $5,104; need-based self-help aid (loans and jobs) averaged $3,993; non-need-based athletic scholarships averaged $18,452; and other non-need-based awards and non-need-based scholarships averaged $12,420. 108% of undergraduate students work part-time. Average annual earnings from campus work are $3500. The average financial indebtedness of the 2013 graduate was $16,647. The FAFSA is required. The priority date for freshman financial aid applications for fall entry is January 31.

International Students: There are 64 international students enrolled. The school actively recruits these students. They must take the TOEFL with a minimum score of 550 on the paper-based TOEFL (PBT) or 80 on the Internet-based version (iBT) or take the MELAB. They must also take the SAT or ACT.

Computers: All students may access the system 24 hours per day, 7 days per week. There are no time limits and no fees.

Graduates: From July 1, 2012 to June 30, 2013, 525 bachelor's degrees were awarded. The most popular majors were business administration and marketing (22%), biological/life sciences (12%), and education (12%). 70 companies recruited on campus in 2012-2013. In an average class, 44% graduate in 4 years or less, 60% graduate in 5 years or less, and 64% graduate in 6 years or less. Of the 2012 graduating class, 90% were enrolled in graduate school within 6 months of graduation, and 90% were employed.

Admissions Contact: Rick Holaway, Senior Director of Admissions. E-Mail: *rick.holaway@lipscomb.edu* Web: *www.lipscomb.edu*

MARYVILLE COLLEGE E-2

Maryville, TN 37804 (865) 981-8206
(800) 597-2687; (865) 981-8005

Full-time: 518 men, 644 women	**Faculty:** 78; IIB, av$
Part-time: 8 men, 6 women	**Ph.D.s:** 01%
Graduate: n/av	**Student/Faculty:** 15 to 1
Year: semesters, summer session	**Tuition:** $ ($25,850)
Application Deadline: March 1	**Room & Board:** $8300

Freshman Class: 1584 applied, 1203 accepted, 317 enrolled
SAT CR/M/W: 537/535/528 **ACT:** 24 **VERY COMPETITIVE**

Maryville College, founded in 1819, is a private liberal arts college affiliated with the Presbyterian Church. The figures in the above capsule and in this profile are approximate. In addition to regional accreditation, Maryville has baccalaureate program accreditation with NASM. The 2 libraries contain 133,686 volumes and 8263 microform items, and subscribe to 16,525 periodicals including electronic. Computerized library services include interlibrary loans, database searching, Internet access, and laptop Internet portals. Special learning facilities include a learning resource center, art gallery, greenhouse, and college woods. The 350-acre campus is in a suburban area 15 miles south of Knoxville. Including any residence halls, there are 22 buildings.

Student Life: 76% of undergraduates are from Tennessee. Others are from 32 states, 20 foreign countries, and Canada. 87% are from public schools. 85% are white. 64% are Protestant. The average age of freshmen is 18; all undergraduates, 21. 28% do not continue beyond their first year; 52% remain to graduate.

Housing: 802 students can be accommodated in college housing, which includes single-sex and coed dorms, on-campus apartments, and off-campus apartments. In addition, there are language houses and special-interest houses. On-campus housing is guaranteed for all 4 years. 69% of students live on campus; of those, 50% remain on campus on weekends. All students may keep cars.

Activities: There are no fraternities or sororities. There are 53 groups on campus, including art, band, cheerleading, choir, chorus, computers, dance, drama, equestrian, ethnic, gay, gospel music, honors, international, jazz band, literary magazine, musical theater, newspaper, orchestra, pep band, photography, political, professional, radio and TV, religious, social service, student government, and symphony. Popular campus events include Dogwood Arts Festival, Blister-in-the-Sun, and Spring Fling.

Sports: There are 7 intercollegiate sports for men and 7 for women, and 12 intramural sports for men and 11 for women. Facilities include a phys ed building with an indoor pool, tennis and racquetball courts, a weight room, football, soccer, baseball, and softball fields, and an off-campus equestrian arena.

Disabled Students: 75% of the campus is accessible. Facilities include wheelchair ramps, elevators, special parking, specially equipped rest rooms, special class scheduling, lowered drinking fountains, lowered telephones, and special housing.

Services: Counseling and information services are available, as is tutoring in every subject. There is a reader service for the blind, remedial math, and sign language interpreters for deaf students.

Campus Safety and Security: Measures include 24-hour foot and vehicle patrol and security escort services. There are lighted pathways/sidewalks.

Programs of Study: Maryville confers B.A. and B.Mus. degrees. Bachelor's degrees are awarded in AGRICULTURE (environmental studies), BIOLOGICAL SCIENCE (biochemistry and biology/biological science), BUSINESS (business administration and management and recreation and leisure services), COMMUNICATIONS AND THE ARTS (American Sign Language, art, art history and appreciation, creative writing, dramatic arts, English, English as a second/foreign language, music, music performance, and Spanish), COMPUTER AND PHYSICAL SCIENCE (chemical physics, chemistry, computer science, and mathematics), EDUCATION (elementary education, music education, physical education, science education, and secondary education), ENGINEERING AND ENVIRONMENTAL

DESIGN (engineering and preengineering), HEALTH PROFESSIONS (nursing, predentistry, and premedicine), SOCIAL SCIENCE (economics, history, international relations, interpreter for the deaf, political science/government, prelaw, psychology, religion, social science, and sociology). Biology, chemistry, and English are the strongest academically. Business, biology, and psychology have the largest enrollments.

Required: Each degree has its own general education requirements, which include humanities and a foreign language. Students must complete at least 128 total credit hours, including 48 in the major, and must maintain a minimum 2.0 GPA. A year-long freshman seminar and orientation are required in addition to a senior thesis in all majors and senior comprehensive exams.

Special: Maryville offers cross-registration with the University of Tennessee and Vanderbilt University, internships, study abroad in 9 countries, a Washington semester, accelerated degree programs, a B.A.-B.S. degree in engineering, and dual and student-designed majors. There are 3-2 engineering degrees offered with regional universities. Nondegree study and pass/fail options are possible. There are 6 national honor societies, a freshman honors program, and 100 departmental honors programs.

Faculty/Classroom: 45% of faculty are male; 55% are female. All teach and do research. The average class size in an introductory lecture is 28; in a laboratory, 15; and in a regular course, 16.

Admissions: 5 freshmen graduated first in their class in a recent year.

Requirements: The SAT or ACT is required. Candidates should be graduates of accredited secondary schools or have the GED. They should also have 15 academic credits with 4 years of English, 3 each of math and science, 2 years of foreign language, and 2 of history or social studies. An essay, portfolio, audition, and interview are all recommended. A GPA of 2.5 is required. AP and CLEP credits are accepted. Important factors in the admissions decision are advanced placement or honors courses, extracurricular activities record, and leadership record.

Procedure: Freshmen are admitted fall, spring, and summer. Entrance exams should be taken by October of the senior year. There are early decisions, early admissions and deferred admissions plans. Early decision applications should be filed by November 15; check with the school for current application deadlines. Notification of early decision is sent December 1. The application fee is $25. Applications are accepted online.

Transfer: 53 transfer students enrolled in a recent year. Transfer applicants must have a minimum GPA of 2.0 and a recommended 15 credit hours earned. An interview is also recommended. 45 of 128 credits required for the bachelor's degree must be completed at Maryville.

Visiting: There are regularly scheduled orientations for prospective students, including an overnight stay in a residence hall, class attendance, meeting with students and faculty, a campus tour, and an interview. There are guides for informal visits and visitors may sit in on classes. To schedule a visit, contact the Admissions Office.

Financial Aid: In a recent year, 100% of all full-time freshmen and 98% of continuing full-time students received some form of financial aid. 82% of all full-time freshmen and 79% of continuing full-time students received need-based aid. The average freshmen award was $26,518, with $17,728 ($36,610 maximum) from need-based scholarships or need-based grants; $2859 ($7500 maximum) from need-based self-help aid (loans and jobs); and $1947 ($23,000 maximum) from other non-need-based awards and non-need-based scholarships. 49% of undergraduate students work part-time. Average annual earnings from campus work are $1559. The average financial indebtedness of a recent graduate was $14,344. Maryville is a member of CSS. The FAFSA is required. Check with the school for current application deadlines.

International Students: There were 44 international students enrolled in a recent year. The school actively recruits these students. They must take the TOEFL, with a minimum score of 525 on the paper-based TOEFL (PBT) or 74 on the Internet-based version (iBT), or the IELTS.

Computers: All students may access the system 7 days a week, 16 hours a day. There are no time limits and no fees. It is strongly recommended that all students have a personal computer.

Graduates: In a recent year, 201 bachelor's degrees were awarded. The most popular majors were business/commerce (16%), child development (11%), and psychology (6%). 80 companies recruited on campus in a recent year. In an average class, 45% graduate in 4 years or less, 50% graduate in 5 years or less, and 52% graduate in 6 years or less. Of a recent graduating class, 28% were enrolled in graduate school within 6 months of graduation and 67% were employed.

Admissions Contact: Bill Silwa, Vice President for Enrollment Management. E-Mail: *bill.silwa@maryvillecollege.edu* Web: *www.maryvillecollege.edu*

MEMPHIS COLLEGE OF ART — A-3

Memphis, TN 38104 — (901) 272-5151; (800) 727-1088; (901) 272-5158

Full-time: 123 men, 220 women	**Faculty:** 26
Part-time: 13 men, 21 women	**Ph.D.s:** 85%
Graduate: 17 men, 39 women	**Student/Faculty:** 11 to 1
Year: semesters, summer session	**Tuition:** $25,050
Application Deadline: open	**Room & Board:** $8500
Freshman Class: 239 applied, 219 accepted, 94 enrolled	
ACT: 22	**SAT:** required — **SPECIAL**

Memphis College of Art, established in 1936, is a private, independent institution offering degree programs in fine arts and design arts, including drawing, painting, photography, printmaking, sculpture, metals, graphic design, illustration, animation, sequential narrative, and digital cinema. There is 1 graduate school. In addition to regional accreditation, MCA has baccalaureate program accreditation with NASAD. The library contains 18,000 volumes, and subscribes to 120 periodicals including electronic. Computerized library services include interlibrary loans and Internet access. Special learning facilities include a learning resource center, art gallery, sound and lighting studios. The 200-acre campus is in an urban area Memphis, Tennessee. Including any residence halls, there are 6 buildings.

Student Life: 60% of undergraduates are from out of state, mostly the South. Students are from 25 states, and 4 foreign countries. 69% are from public schools. 64% are white; 19% African American. The average age of freshmen is 18; all undergraduates, 23. 24% do not continue beyond their first year; 46% remain to graduate.

Housing: 165 students can be accommodated in college housing, which includes single-sex on-campus apartments and off-campus apartments. On-campus housing is available on a first-come first-served basis. Priority is given to out-of-town students. 56% of students commute. Alcohol is not permitted. All students may keep cars.

Activities: There are no fraternities or sororities. There are 5 groups on campus, including art, ethnic, photography, and student government. Popular campus events include Holiday Bazaar, gallery openings, and community dinners.

Sports: There is no sports program at MCA. Facilities include MCA is located in a 340 acre city park, providing space for informal activities. There is an adjacent public golf course, playing fields, and a volleyball court. Regular saturday football, soccer, and bicycling are popular activities.

Disabled Students: All of the campus is accessible. Facilities include wheelchair ramps, elevators, special parking, specially equipped restrooms, lowered drinking fountains, lowered telephones, and special housing.

Services: Counseling and information services are available, as is tutoring in some subjects, liberal studies classes There is remedial writing.

Campus Safety and Security: Measures include 24-hour foot and vehicle patrol, emergency notification system, and security escort services. There are shuttle buses, lighted pathways/sidewalks, card access to campus building and some housing. 24/7 security staff, chaperone, and shuttle service.

Programs of Study: MCA confers B.F.A. degrees. Master's degrees are also awarded. Bachelor's degrees are awarded in COMMUNICATIONS AND THE ARTS (animation, applied art, design, drawing, film arts, fine arts, graphic design, illustration, metal/jewelry, painting, photography, and studio art), COMPUTER AND PHYSICAL SCIENCE (digital arts/technology).

Required: Students must complete 120 credit hours, including 33 in the major, with a minimum GPA of 2.0. Distribution requirements comprise 45 credits in liberal studies, including 12 in art history, 6 in English, and 3 each in literature, social sciences, and natural science or math; 30 credits in elective studio art; and 21 credits in foundation classes, including drawing, 2-D and 3-D design, digital foundations, color foundations, and idea, process, and criticism.

Special: Special academic programs include off-campus internships for juniors and seniors in advertising agencies, design firms, or other educational situations; on- and off-campus work-study; and study abroad in Europe, Canada, Japan, Italy, or Ireland. There are mobility programs with the Association of Independent Colleges of Art and Design (AICAD), and the Memphis Area Consortium.

Faculty/Classroom: 56% of faculty are male; 44% are female. 97% teach undergraduates. No introductory courses are taught by graduate students. The average class size in an introductory lecture is 20 and in a regular course is 17.

Admissions: 92% of the 2011-2012 applicants were accepted. The ACT scores were 23% below 21, 39% between 21 and 23, 23% between 24 and 26, 13% between 27 and 28, and 3% above 28.

Requirements: The SAT or ACT is required. In addition, test scores are used for admissions and placement purposes. Other admissions requirements include a completed application form, high school transcripts (GED is accepted), and a portfolio. An interview is recommended. A GPA of 2.0 is required. AP and CLEP credits are accepted. Important factors in the admissions decision are evidence of special talent, advanced placement or honors courses, and extracurricular activities record.

Procedure: Freshmen are admitted fall and spring. There is a rolling admissions plan. Application deadlines are open. Application fee is $25. Applications are accepted online.

Transfer: 33 transfer students enrolled in 2010-2011. Applicants must submit official college transcripts and a portfolio. 48 of 120 credits required for the bachelor's degree must be completed at MCA.

Visiting: There are regularly scheduled orientations for prospective students. There are guides for informal visits and visitors may sit in on classes. To schedule a visit, contact the Admissions Office.

Financial Aid: In a recent year, 97% of all full-time freshmen and 92% of continuing full-time students received some form of financial aid. 52% of all full-time freshmen and 47% of continuing full-time students received need-based aid. 40% of undergraduate students work part-time. Average annual earnings from campus work are $325. The average financial indebtedness of the 2011 graduate was $34,360. MCA is a member of CSS. The FAFSA is required. The priority date for freshman financial aid applications for fall entry is March 1. The deadline for filing freshman financial aid applications for fall entry is rolling.

International Students: There are 12 international students enrolled. The school actively recruits these students. They must take the TOEFL. They must also take the SAT or ACT.

Computers: All students may access the system. There are no time limits and no fees. It is strongly recommended that all students have a personal computer. A Macintosh is recommended.

Graduates: In a recent year, 53 bachelor's degrees were awarded. The most popular majors were fine arts (38%), design arts (38%), and digital media (13%). 25 companies recruited on campus in a recent year. In an average class, 46% graduate in 6 years or less.

Admissions Contact: Annette Moore, Dean of Admissions. E-Mail: *info@mca.edu* Web: *www.mca.edu*

MIDDLE TENNESSEE STATE UNIVERSITY C-2

Murfreesboro, TN 37132 — **(615) 898-2111; (800) 433-MTSU; (615) 898-5478**

Full-time: 9204 men, 9708 women	**Faculty:** n/av
Part-time: 1577 men, 1810 women	**Ph.D.s:** 68%
Graduate: 963 men, 1926 women	**Student/Faculty:** n/av
Year: semesters, summer session	**Tuition:** $4000 ($11,900)
Application Deadline: July 1	**Room & Board:** $4650
Freshman Class: 9431 applied, 6616 accepted, 1758 enrolled	
SAT: required	**ACT:** 22 — **COMPETITIVE**

Middle Tennessee State University, founded in 1911, is a comprehensive public university that offers undergraduate and graduate programs reflecting an emphasis on research, creative arts, and public and professional service activities. There are 7 undergraduate schools and 1 graduate school. In addition to regional accreditation, MTSU has baccalaureate program accreditation with AACSB, ABET, ACEJMC, ADA, CSAB, CSWE, FIDER, NASAD, NASM, NCATE, NLN, and NRPA. The library contains 702,764 volumes, 1.3 million microform items, and subscribes to 3,798 periodicals including electronic. Computerized library services include interlibrary loans, database searching, and Internet access. Special learning facilities include an art gallery, planetarium, radio station, TV station, numerous research centers. The 500-acre campus is in an urban area 32 miles southeast of Nashville, TN. Including any residence halls, there are 159 buildings.

Student Life: 93% of undergraduates are from Tennessee. Others are from 47 states, 70 foreign countries, and Canada. 80% are White; 14% African American. 45% are Protestant; 43% claim no religious affiliation. The average age of freshmen is 18; all undergraduates, 19.

Housing: 3294 students can be accommodated in college housing, which includes single-sex and coed dorms, on-campus apartments, and married student housing. In addition, there are honors houses, fraternity houses, sorority houses, a First Year Experience program, and various Learning Community programs. On-campus housing is available on a first-come and first-served basis. 85% of students commute. Alcohol is not permitted. All students may keep cars.

Activities: 9% of men belong to 16 national fraternities; 11% of women belong to 1 local and 11 national sororities. There are 153 groups on campus, including art, band, cheerleading, chess, choir, chorale, chorus, computers, dance, debate, drama, drill team, ethnic, film, gay, honors, international, jazz band, literary magazine, marching band, Model UN, musical theater, newspaper, pep band, photography, political, professional, radio and TV, religious, social, social service, student government, and symphony. Popular campus events include Founders Day, Family Day, and African American History Month.

Sports: There are 8 intercollegiate sports for men and 9 for women, and 13 intramural sports for men and 13 for women. Facilities include an athletic center with a 30,000-seat stadium, a 12,000-seat gym, a soccer/track complex, tennis courts, and baseball and softball fields, and a recreation center with 12 courts, an indoor track, indoor and outdoor pools, a rock-climbing wall, and a sand volleyball court.

Disabled Students: All of the campus is accessible. Facilities include wheelchair ramps, elevators, special parking, specially equipped restrooms, special class scheduling, lowered drinking fountains, and lowered telephones.

Services: Counseling and information services are available, as is tutoring in most subjects. There is a reader service for the blind, and remedial math, reading, and writing.

Campus Safety and Security: Measures include 24-hour foot and vehicle patrol, self-defense education, and security escort services. There are shuttle buses, emergency telephones, and lighted pathways/sidewalks.

Programs of Study: MTSU confers B.A., B.S., B.B.A., B.F.A., B.Mus., B.S.N., B.S.W. and B.U.S. degrees. Master's and doctoral degrees are also awarded. Bachelor's degrees are awarded in AGRICULTURE (agricultural business management, animal science, and plant science), BIOLOGICAL SCIENCE (biology/biological science and nutrition), BUSINESS (accounting, banking and finance, business administration and management, entrepreneurial studies, marketing/retailing/merchandising, office supervision and management, and recreation and leisure services), COMMUNICATIONS AND THE ARTS (communications, English, French, German, graphic design, music, music business management, public relations, Spanish, and studio art), COMPUTER AND PHYSICAL SCIENCE (chemistry, computer science, information sciences and systems, mathematics, physics, and science), EDUCATION (art education, athletic training, business education, early childhood education, health education, physical education, and special education), ENGINEERING AND ENVIRONMENTAL DESIGN (engineering technology, environmental science, industrial engineering technology, and interior design), HEALTH PROFESSIONS (health science and nursing), SOCIAL SCIENCE (anthropology, criminal justice, economics, family/consumer studies, geography, history, interdisciplinary studies, international relations, philosophy, political science/government, prelaw, psychology, public administration, social work, sociology, and textiles and clothing). Nursing and science are the strongest academically. Recording industry has the largest enrollment.

Required: To graduate, a total of at least 132 hours, including at least 48 of upper-level courses, is needed with a minimum overall GPA of 2.0. All students must complete the general studies requirements, including 9 hours each of natural science/math and humanities, 6 each of English composition and history, 2 of phys ed., arts/fine arts, social science, demonstrate computer literacy. A major field test and general studies exam are required.

Special: MTSU offers co-op programs in aerospace, computer science, math, engineering technology, and industrial studies, cross-registration with Tennessee State University, internships, study abroad, work-study, double majors, a general studies degree, student-designed majors, nondegree study, and pass/fail options. Credit for life, military, and work experience may be granted. There are 2 national honor societies, a freshman honors program, and 25 departmental honors programs.

Faculty/Classroom: 53% of faculty are male; 47% are female. No introductory courses are taught by graduate students. The average class size in an introductory lecture is 24; in a laboratory is 18; and in a regular course is 23.

Admissions: 70% of the 2013-2014 applicants were accepted. The ACT scores were 32% below 21, 35% between 21 and 23, 20% between 24 and 26, 7% between 27 and 28, and 5% above 28. There were 2 National Merit finalists. 31 freshmen graduated first in their class.

Requirements: The SAT or ACT is required. Applicants must have a minimum composite score of 22 on the ACT if the GPA is less than 3.0. A high school diploma is required, the GED is accepted. The number of academic credits required is 14, including 4 years of English, 3 of math, 2 each of a foreign language and science, and 1 each of social studies, U.S. history, and visual and/or performance arts, with an additional unit of math, language, or art recommended. A GPA of 3.0 is required. AP and CLEP credits are accepted.

Procedure: Freshmen are admitted to all sessions. Entrance exams should be taken in the first half of the senior year. There are deferred admissions and rolling admissions plans. Applications should be filed by July 1 for fall entry, along with a $25 fee. Notification is sent on a rolling basis. Applications are accepted online.

Transfer: Applicants must have a minimum 2.0 GPA and submit official transcripts from all previous colleges attended. If transferring fewer than 9 semester hours, they must also meet freshman admission requirements. 24 of 120 credits required for the bachelor's degree must be completed at MTSU.

Visiting: There are regularly scheduled orientations for prospective students, including campus tours and meeting with a departmental adviser. There are guides for informal visits and visitors may sit in on classes. To schedule a visit, contact the Office of Admissions.

Financial Aid: In 2013-2014, 35% of all full-time freshmen and 52% of continuing full-time students received some form of financial aid. 19% of all full-time freshmen and 29% of continuing full-time students received need-based aid. The average freshman award was $6,265. Need-based scholarships or need-based grants averaged $2,295 ($6,150 maximum); need-based self-help aid (loans and jobs) averaged $1,589 ($10,500 maximum); non-need-based athletic scholarships averaged $11,180 ($9,500 maximum); and other non-need-based awards and non-need-based scholarships averaged $4,057 ($5,000 maximum). 84% of undergraduate students work part-time. Average annual earnings from campus work are $3200. The average financial indebtedness of the 2013 graduate was $19,800. The FAFSA is required. Check with the school for current application deadlines.

International Students: There are 124 international students enrolled. The school actively recruits these students. They must take the TOEFL or MELAB. They must also take the SAT or ACT, scoring 20.

Computers: All students may access the system 24 hours a day. There are no time limits and no fees.

Graduates: From July 1, 2012 to June 30, 2013, 3629 bachelor's degrees were awarded. The most popular majors were business/marketing (20%), visual and performing arts (11%), and interdisciplinary studies (10%).

Admissions Contact: Lynn Palmer, Director of Admissions. E-Mail: *admissions@mtsu.edu* Web: *www.mtsu.edu*

MILLIGAN COLLEGE F-1

Milligan College, TN 37682 (423) 461-8730 (800) 262-8337; (423) 461-8982

Full-time: 338 men, 473 women	**Faculty:** 68; IIB, --$
Part-time: 34 men, 58 women	**Ph.D.s:** 75%
Graduate: 60 men, 137 women	**Student/Faculty:** 12 to 1
Year: semesters, summer session	**Tuition:** $21,860
Application Deadline: August 15	**Room & Board:** $5650
Freshman Class: 643 applied, 438 accepted, 218 enrolled	
SAT CR/M/W: 530/520/510 **ACT:** 23	**COMPETITIVE**

Milligan College, founded in 1866, is a private institution affiliated with the Christian Church and Churches of Christ. Its degree programs stress the liberal arts and biblical studies. There are 3 graduate schools. In addition to regional accreditation, Milligan has baccalaureate program accreditation with NCATE. The library contains 212,861 volumes, 493,520 microform items, and 3,767 audio/video tapes/CDs/DVDs, and subscribes to 79,750 periodicals including electronic. Computerized library services include interlibrary loans, database searching, Internet access, and laptop Internet portals. Special learning facilities include a learning resource center, art gallery, radio station, TV station, editing rooms, and darkroom. The 181-acre campus is in a suburban area 4 miles south of Johnson City. Including any residence halls, there are 23 buildings.

Student Life: 59% of undergraduates are from Tennessee. Others are from 36 states, 15 foreign countries, and Canada. 80% are from public schools. 87% are white. 83% are Protestant. The average age of freshmen is 18; all undergraduates, 22. 23% do not continue beyond their first year; 54% remain to graduate.

Housing: 572 students can be accommodated in college housing, which includes single-sex dorms, on-campus apartments, and married student housing. On-campus housing is guaranteed for all 4 years. 74% of students live on campus. 85% remain on campus on weekends. Alcohol is not permitted. All students may keep cars.

Activities: There are no fraternities or sororities. There are 40 groups on campus, including art, band, cheerleading, choir, chorus, drama, film, honors, jazz band, literary magazine, musical theater, newspaper, orchestra, pep band, photography, political, professional, radio and TV, religious, social, social service, student government, and symphony. Popular campus events include Wonderful Wednesday, campus theater productions, and a faculty auction.

Sports: There are 6 intercollegiate sports for men and 6 for women, and 7 intramural sports for men and 7 for women. Facilities include a 25-meter swimming pool, a basketball court, a 500-seat stadium, a 1500-seat gym, tennis courts, and baseball, softball, and soccer fields.

Disabled Students: 80% of the campus is accessible. Facilities include wheelchair ramps, elevators, special parking, specially equipped rest rooms, and lowered drinking fountains.

Services: Counseling and information services are available, as is tutoring in most subjects. There is remedial math, reading, and writing.

Campus Safety and Security: There are emergency telephones, lighted pathways/sidewalks, and an evening vehicle patrol.

Programs of Study: Milligan confers B.A., B.S., and B.S.N. degrees. Master's degrees are also awarded. Bachelor's degrees are awarded in BIOLOGICAL SCIENCE (biology/biological science), BUSINESS (accounting and business administration and management), COMMUNICATIONS AND THE ARTS (communications, English, fine arts, and music), COMPUTER AND PHYSICAL SCIENCE (chemistry, information sciences and systems, and mathematics), EDUCATION (early childhood education and music education), HEALTH PROFESSIONS (exercise science, nursing, and premedicine), SOCIAL SCIENCE (biblical studies, history, humanities, psychology, religious music, and sociology). Business, nursing, and Bible studies have the largest enrollments.

Required: Students must complete at least 128 semester hours, including 24 to 62 in the major, and 59 to 71 in the general education core, with a minimum GPA of 2.0. Required disciplines include 24 credit hours of humanities, 9 of Bible studies, 8 of lab science, 6 of social science, 3 each of math, speech, and ethnic studies, 2 of phys ed, and 1 of introduction to college; B.A. candidates must also complete 6 to 12 in foreign language. All students must demonstrate computer literacy and attend all required chapel/convocation sessions. Measures of Academic Proficiency and Progress and an exam in the major are also required.

Special: Milligan offers a Washington semester, study abroad in England, Australia, China, Costa Rica, Egypt, Russia, and Uganda, co-op programs and internships in several majors, cross-registration with East Tennessee State University and Emmanuel School of Religion, work-study, nondegree study, and dual majors. 3 credits are offered for students participating in the annual summer tour of Europe. There are 5 national honor societies.

Faculty/Classroom: 49% of faculty are male; 51% are female. 96% teach undergraduates. No introductory courses are taught by graduate students. The average class size in an introductory lecture, 50, in a laboratory, 15, and in a regular course, 15.

Admissions: 68% of a recent year's applicants were accepted. The SAT scores for a recent freshman class were: Critical Reading--34% below 500, 45% between 500 and 599, 18% between 600 and 700, and 3% above 700; Math--38% below 500, 43% between 500 and 599, 15% between 600 and 700, and 3% above 700; Writing--39% below 500, 44% between 500 and 599, 10% between 600 and 700, and 7% above 700. The ACT scores were 26% below 21, 30% between 21 and 23, 26% between 24 and 26, 7% between 27 and 28, and 11% above 28.

Requirements: The SAT or ACT is required. Students must be graduates of an accredited secondary school, with 18 Carnegie units and 18 academic credits, including courses in English, math, science, history and social studies, and speech, music, or art, along with 2 years of a foreign language. Music students must audition. The GED is accepted. Other factors in the admission decision include character, recommendations by school officials, advanced placement or honor courses, ability, preparation, and Christian commitment. AP and CLEP credits are accepted. Important factors in the admissions decision are leadership record, recommendations by school officials, and personality/intangible qualities.

Procedure: Freshmen are admitted to all sessions. Entrance exams should be taken beginning in the spring of the junior year. There are deferred admissions and rolling admissions plans. Applications should be filed by August 15 for fall entry and December 15 for spring entry, along with a $30 fee. Notification is sent on a rolling basis. Applications are accepted online.

Transfer: 70 transfer students enrolled in a recent year. A minimum GPA of 2.5 is preferred. Applicants must submit transcripts of all previous college work. 45 of 128 credits required for the bachelor's degree must be completed at Milligan.

Visiting: There are regularly scheduled orientations for prospective students, consisting of 1-day open houses in November and March that include a campus tour, a financial aid workshop, a meal in the cafeteria, and the opportunity to meet faculty and to learn about student life. There are new student orientation weekends in April, June, and August. There are guides for informal visits; visitors may sit in on classes and stay overnight. To schedule a visit, contact the Campus Visits Coordinator.

Financial Aid: In a recent year, 96% of all full-time freshmen and 99% of continuing full-time students received some form of financial aid. 48% of all full-time freshmen and 56% of continuing full-time students received need-based aid. The average freshman award was $18,709. Need-based scholarships or need-based grants averaged $5,005 ($7,500 maximum); need-based self-help aid (loans and jobs) averaged $4,295 ($7,140 maximum); non-need based athletic scholarships averaged $7,499 ($22,000 maximum); other non-need-based awards and non-need-based scholarships averaged $9,598 ($20,000 maximum); and personnel and tuition and exchange averaged $17,745 (18,900 maximum). 39% of undergraduate students work part-time. Average annual earnings from campus work are $1443. The FAFSA and the college's own financial statement are required. The priority date for freshman financial aid applications for fall entry is March 1.

International Students: There were 18 international students enrolled in a recent year. They must take the TOEFL with a minimum score of 550 on the paper-based TOEFL (PBT) or 79 on the Internet-based version (iBT) or take the MELAB. They must also take the SAT or ACT.

Computers: Wireless access is available. 2 network ports are provided in each residence hall room. Dial-up network service is provided for local commuting students. Wireless access is available in 2 classroom buildings, the student center, the library, and the faculty office building. 102 lab and public access computers are available throughout the campus. All students may access the system. There are no time limits. The fee is $180. It is strongly recommended that all students have a personal computer. An Intel-based Pentium is recommended.

Graduates: In a recent year, 187 bachelor's degrees were awarded. The most popular majors were business administration (20%), communications

(13%), and psychology (8%). 9 companies recruited on campus in a recent year. In an average class, 2% graduate in 3 years or less, 49% graduate in 4 years or less, 59% graduate in 5 years or less, and 59% graduate in 6 years or less.

Admissions Contact: Tracy Brinn, Director of Enrollment Management. E-Mail: *admissions@milligan.edu* Web: *www.milligan.edu*

RHODES COLLEGE — A-3

Memphis, TN 38112 — (901) 843-3700; (800) 844-5969; (901) 843-3631

Full-time: 781 men, 1118 women
Part-time: 5 men, 11 women
Graduate: 10 men, 2 women
Year: semesters, summer session
Application Deadline: January 15
Faculty: 171; IIB, av$
Ph.D.s: 98%
Student/Faculty: 10 to 1
Tuition: $38,092
Room & Board: $9504
Freshman Class: 4138 applied, 2258 accepted, 554 enrolled
SAT CR/M/W: 630/630/620 **ACT:** 28 **HIGHLY COMPETITIVE+**

Rhodes, founded in 1848, is a private, church-affiliated college of arts and sciences. The campus is in a Gothic architectural style, and 13 of its buildings are listed on the National Register of Historic Places. Its 100-acre campus is located in a residential area of Memphis. There is one graduate school. The library contains 302,807 volumes, 106,853 microform items, and 13,346 audio/video tapes/CDs/DVDs, and subscribes to 8,094 periodicals including electronic. Computerized library services include interlibrary loans, database searching, Internet access, and Wi-Fi capability. Special learning facilities include an art gallery, electron microscopes, astronomical observatory, GIS and archeology labs, and Modern Languages Lab. The 100-acre campus is in an urban area Memphis, TN. Including any residence halls, there are 45 buildings.

Student Life: 73% of undergraduates are from out of state, mostly the South. Students are from 47 states, and 19 foreign countries. 53% are from public schools. 75% are White. The average age of freshmen is 18; all undergraduates, 20. 10% do not continue beyond their first year; 81% remain to graduate.

Housing: 1370 students can be accommodated in college housing, which includes single-sex and coed dorms and on-campus apartments. learning communities. On-campus housing is guaranteed for the freshman year only and is available on a lottery system for upperclassmen. 71% of students live on campus; of those, 90% remain on campus on weekends. All students may keep cars.

Activities: 37% of men belong to 8 national fraternities; 54% of women belong to 7 national sororities. There are 103 groups on campus, including Black Student Association, club sports, Contents Under Pressure (comedy improv troupe), Mock Trial Team, Model UN, art, cheerleading, chess, choir, chorale, chorus, computers, dance, debate, drama, environmental, ethnic, gay, Honor Council, honors, international, literary magazine, musical theater, newspaper, orchestra, pep band, photography, political, professional, religious, social, social service, student government, symphony, and yearbook. Popular campus events include Rites of Spring, All-Sing, and Hunger for Homelessness.

Sports: There are 11 intercollegiate sports for men and 12 for women, and 16 intramural sports for men and 16 for women. Facilities include a campus life center, which includes a performance gym, a 3-court multi-use gym, racquetball, and squash courts, a fitness center, and an indoor jogging track. Outdoor facilities include a pool, 10 lighted tennis courts, 2 soccer fields, a football field, a track, and baseball, softball and intramural fields.

Disabled Students: 90% of the campus is accessible. Facilities include wheelchair ramps, elevators, special parking, specially equipped restrooms, special class scheduling, lowered drinking fountains, lowered telephones, and an infrared hearing system in 1 of the auditoriums.

Services: Counseling and information services are available, as is tutoring in some subjects, including math, writing, modern languages, biology, chemistry, economics, business, computer science and physics. There is a reader service for the blind.

Campus Safety and Security: Measures include 24-hour foot and vehicle patrol, emergency notification system, self-defense education, and security escort services. There are emergency telephones, lighted pathways/sidewalks, controlled access to dorms/residences, 24/7 staffed guard house, electronic readers on all gate entrances and residential dorms, security cameras monitored 24 hours a day, a fenced campus, and city cab service billed to student accounts.

Programs of Study: Rhodes confers B.A., and B.S. degrees. Master's degrees are also awarded. Bachelor's degrees are awarded in AGRICULTURE (environmental studies), BIOLOGICAL SCIENCE (biochemistry, biology/biological science, molecular biology, and neurosciences), BUSINESS (business administration and management), COMMUNICATIONS AND THE ARTS (art, English, French, German, music, Spanish, and theatre arts), COMPUTER AND PHYSICAL SCIENCE (chemistry, computer science, mathematics, and physics), ENGINEERING AND ENVIRONMENTAL DESIGN (environmental science), SOCIAL SCIENCE (anthropology, classical/ancient civilization, economics, history, interdisciplinary studies, international studies, Latin American studies, philosophy, political science/government, psychology, religion, Russian and Slavic studies, sociology, and urban studies). Business administration, biology, psychology and English are the strongest academically and have the largest enrollments.

Required: To graduate, students must complete 128 credit hours with a variable number of hours in the major, and maintain a minimum GPA of 2.0. There is a basic degree requirement in 12 foundation areas. Students must complete 3 courses examining questions of meaning and value; 2 courses in writing; 1 course in each of literature, art, math, natural science, human interaction and contemporary institutions, and cultural perspective. Students must further demonstrate intermediate proficiency with a second language, engage in 1 for-credit activity broadening connections between the classroom and the world, participate in three half-semesters of physical education, and complete a senior seminar in the major.

Special: More than half of Rhodes students have an internship experience, in which off-campus work and significant academic work are combined for credit. Study abroad in 11 countries, a Washington semester, cross-registration with Memphis College of Art and Christian Brothers University, and a science semester at Oak Ridge National Laboratory are offered. A 3-2 engineering degree with Washington University is available. The B.A.-B.S. degree and dual majors are offered in any combination, and student-designed majors can be arranged. Nondegree study and pass/fail options are possible. There are 20 national honor societies including Phi Beta Kappa.

Faculty/Classroom: 54% of faculty are male; 46% are female. All teach and do research. No introductory courses are taught by graduate students. The average class size in an introductory lecture is 17; in a laboratory is 17; and in a regular course is 17.

Admissions: 55% of the 2013-2014 applicants were accepted. The SAT scores for the 2013-2014 freshman class were: Critical Reading--3% below 500, 30% between 500 and 599, 44% between 600 and 699, and 23% between 700 and 800; Math--2% below 500, 26% between 500 and 599, 53% between 600 and 699, and 19% between 700 and 800. The ACT scores were 4% between 21 and 23, 22% between 24 and 26, 24% between 27 and 28, and 50% above 28.

Requirements: The SAT or ACT is required. Graduation from an accredited secondary school is required, with 16 or more academic credits, including 4 years of English, 3 of math, and 2 each of a foreign language, science, and social studies/history. The GED is accepted. An essay is required; an interview is recommended. AP credits are accepted. Important factors in the admissions decision are advanced placement or honors courses, recommendations by school officials, and extracurricular activities record.

Procedure: Freshmen are admitted fall and spring. Entrance exams should be taken prior to December of the senior year. There are early decision, early admissions, and deferred admissions plans. Early decision applications should be filed by November 1; regular applications, by January 15 for fall entry; and December 1 for spring entry, along with a $45 fee. Notification of early decision is sent December 1; regular decision, April 1. 30 early decision candidates were accepted for the 2013-2014 class. 435 applicants were on the 2013 waiting list. Applications are accepted online.

Transfer: 15 transfer students enrolled in 2012-2013. Applicants must submit all high school and college transcripts, as well as SAT or ACT scores, and must be in good standing at the last institution they attended. 64 of 128 credits required for the bachelor's degree must be completed at Rhodes.

Visiting: There are regularly scheduled orientations for prospective students, including class visits, meetings with students and faculty, tours, and an overnight stay with students if desired. Interviews also are available. There are guides for informal visits, visitors may sit in on classes, and stay overnight. To schedule a visit, contact the Admissions Office.

Financial Aid: In 2013-2014, 95% of all full-time freshmen and 93% of continuing full-time students received some form of financial aid. 55% of all full-time freshmen and 49% of continuing full-time students received need-based aid. The average freshman award was $34,271. Need-based scholarships or need-based grants averaged $23,691; need-based self-help aid (loans and jobs) averaged $9,770; and other non-need-based awards and non-need-based scholarships averaged $16,832. 33% of undergraduate students work part-time. Average annual earnings from campus work are $2000. The average financial indebtedness of the 2013 graduate was $26,372. Rhodes is a member of CSS. The CSS/Profile and FAFSA are required. The deadline for filing freshman financial aid applications for fall entry is March 1.

International Students: There are 74 international students enrolled. The school actively recruits these students. They must take the TOEFL with a minimum score of 550 on the paper-based TOEFL (PBT) or 80 on the Internet-based version (iBT). They must also take the SAT or ACT.

Computers: All students may access the system 24 hours per day. There are no time limits and no fees.

Graduates: From July 1, 2012 to June 30, 2013, 367 bachelor's degrees were awarded. The most popular majors were business (11%), English and psychology (10%), and biology (8%). 55 companies recruited on campus in 2012-2013. In an average class, 76% graduate in 4 years or less, 81% graduate in 5 years or less, and 81% graduate in 6 years or less.

Admissions Contact: Carey Thompson, VP of Enrollment and Communications. E-Mail: *adminfo@rhodes.edu* Web: *www.rhodes.edu*

SEWANEE: THE UNIVERSITY OF THE SOUTH D-3

Sewanee, TN 37383 (931) 598-1238
(800) 522-2234; (931) 538-3248

Full-time: 791 men, 811 women	**Faculty:** 136; IIB, av$
Part-time: 8 men, 10 women	**Ph.D.s:** 95%
Graduate: 43 men, 38 women	**Student/Faculty:** 11 to 1
Year: semesters, summer session	**Tuition:** $37,100
Application Deadline: February 1	**Room & Board:** $10,600

Freshman Class: 3285 applied, 1980 accepted, 488 enrolled
SAT CR/M/W: 630/610/610 **ACT:** 28 **HIGHLY COMPETITIVE+**

The University of the South, founded in 1857, is an independent liberal arts institution affiliated with the Episcopal Church. There is 1 undergraduate school and 2 graduate schools. The library contains 766,057 volumes, 330,415 microform items, and 26,125 audio/video tapes/CDs/DVDs, and subscribes to 6,033 periodicals including electronic. Computerized library services include interlibrary loans, database searching, Internet access, and Wi-Fi capability. Special learning facilities include an art gallery, radio station, an observatory, a materials analysis lab with an electron scanning microscope, a rare books collection, a music listening room and library. The 13000-acre campus is in a small town 45 miles northwest of Chattanooga. Including any residence halls, there are 102 buildings.

Student Life: 76% of undergraduates are from out of state, mostly the South. Students are from 43 states, 23 foreign countries, and Canada. 55% are from public schools. 82% are White. 59% are Protestant; 24% claim no religious affiliation; 13% Catholic. The average age of freshmen is 18; all undergraduates, 20. 10% do not continue beyond their first year; 78% remain to graduate.

Housing: 1525 students can be accommodated in college housing, which includes single-sex and coed dorms, on-campus apartments, and married student housing. In addition, there are language houses, special-interest houses, fraternity houses, sorority houses, substance-free housing. On-campus housing is guaranteed for all 4 years. 97% of students live on campus; of those, 98% remain on campus on weekends. All students may keep cars.

Activities: 67% of men belong to 2 local and 10 national fraternities; 71% of women belong to 8 local and 1 national sororities. There are 100 groups on campus, including art, cheerleading, choir, chorale, chorus, computers, dance, drama, environmental, ethnic, film, gay, honors, international, jazz band, literary magazine, musical theater, newspaper, orchestra, pep band, photography, political, professional, radio and TV, religious, social, social service, student government, symphony, and yearbook. Popular campus events include Spring Festival Weekend and Performing Arts Series.

Sports: There are 11 intercollegiate sports for men and 12 for women, and 17 intramural sports for men and 16 for women. Facilities include a sport and fitness center with multipurpose volleyball and basketball courts, an indoor pool with diving well, an indoor track, a batting cage, racquetball and squash courts, indoor tennis courts, and dance and fitness studios; a golf course; outdoor tennis courts; a multiweather track; an equestrian center and stables; 15 playing fields, a lake; and areas for rappelling, caving, hiking, and rock climbing.

Disabled Students: 90% of the campus is accessible. Facilities include wheelchair ramps, elevators, special parking, specially equipped restrooms, special class scheduling, lowered drinking fountains, special housing. Special administrative services and a telecommunications device for the deaf are available.

Services: Counseling and information services are available, as is tutoring in most subjects. There is a reader service for the blind. Study skills training is also offered.

Campus Safety and Security: Measures include 24-hour foot and vehicle patrol, emergency notification system, self-defense education, and security escort services. There are shuttle buses, emergency telephones, lighted pathways/sidewalks, and controlled access to dorms/residences.

Programs of Study: Sewanee confers B.A., and B.S. degrees. Master's and doctoral degrees are also awarded. Bachelor's degrees are awarded in AGRICULTURE (environmental studies, forestry and related sciences, and natural resources), BIOLOGICAL SCIENCE (biochemistry, biology/biological science, and environmental biology), COMMUNICATIONS AND THE ARTS (art history, classical languages, English, fine arts, French, German, Greek, Latin, music, Russian, Spanish, and theatre arts), COMPUTER AND PHYSICAL SCIENCE (chemistry, computer science, environmental chemistry, geology, mathematics, and physics), SOCIAL SCIENCE (American studies, anthropology, Asian/Oriental studies, economics, French studies, history, international studies, medieval studies, philosophy, political science/government, psychology, and religion). English, international and global studies, and environmental studies are the strongest academically. English, economics, and biological/life sciences have the largest enrollments.

Required: To graduate, students must complete at least 32 full courses (130 semester hours), 21 of which must be outside the major, with a minimum GPA of 2.0. The core curriculum includes 4 courses in language and literature, 3 in math and natural science, 2 each in social science and phys ed, and 1 each in the arts and in religion or philosophy. Comprehensive exams in the major field of study are required.

Special: Sewanee offers internships in economics and public affairs, study abroad in 13 countries, a Washington semester, and student-designed majors. Teacher certification and Peace Corps, medical, law, and veterinary preparation are available. A 3-2 engineering degree is offered with Columbia, Washington, and Vanderbilt Universities, Georgia Institute of Technology, and Rensselaer Polytechnic Institute. Pass/fail options are possible. There are 10 national honor societies including Phi Beta Kappa.

Faculty/Classroom: 59% of faculty are male; 41% are female. All teach undergraduates. No introductory courses are taught by graduate students. The average class size in an introductory lecture is 20; in a laboratory is 16; and in a regular course is 16.

Admissions: 60% of the 2013-2014 applicants were accepted. The SAT scores for the 2013-2014 freshman class were: Critical Reading--4% below 500, 29% between 500 and 599, 49% between 600 and 699, and 18% between 700 and 800; Math--5% below 500, 38% between 500 and 599, 47% between 600 and 699, and 10% between 700 and 800; Writing--5% below 500, 36% between 500 and 599, 44% between 600 and 699, and 15% between 700 and 800. The ACT scores were 2% below 21, 8% between 21 and 23, 27% between 24 and 26, 26% between 27 and 28, and 37% above 28.

Requirements: The SAT or ACT and ACT Writing Test are recommended. Candidates for admission should have 15 secondary school academic credits, including 4 years of English, 3 of math, and 2 each of lab science, a foreign language, and history or social science. An essay and recommendation are required and an interview is recommended. AP credits are accepted. Important factors in the admissions decision are advanced placement or honors courses, leadership record, and evidence of special talent.

Procedure: Freshmen are admitted fall. Entrance exams should be taken by December of the senior year. There are early decision, early admissions, and deferred admissions plans. Early decision applications should be filed by November 15; regular applications, by February 1 for fall entry. Notification of early decision is sent December 15; regular decision, April 1. 118 early decision candidates were accepted for the 2013-2014 class. 123 applicants were on the 2013 waiting list; 7 were admitted. Applications are accepted online. Application fees are waived if application is completed online.

Transfer: 21 transfer students enrolled in 2012-2013. Applicants should have a minimum GPA of 3.0 and take the SAT or ACT. They must submit official transcripts from all previous colleges attended and 2 letters of recommendation from college instructors, and they must be eligible to continue in their present school. An interview is recommended. 64 of 130 credits required for the bachelor's degree must be completed at Sewanee.

Visiting: There are regularly scheduled orientations for prospective students, including a tour, an interview, class visits, and a meeting with an admission counselor. There are guides for informal visits, visitors may sit in on classes, and stay overnight. To schedule a visit, contact the Office of Admission at (931) 598-1238.

Financial Aid: In 2013-2014, 51% of all full-time freshmen students received some form of financial aid. 51% of all full-time freshmen students received need-based aid. 31% of undergraduate students work part-time. Average annual earnings from campus work are $1500. The FAFSA and the college's own financial statement are required. The deadline for filing freshman financial aid applications for fall entry is March 1.

International Students: There are 50 international students enrolled. The school actively recruits these students. They must take the TOEFL with a minimum score of 550 on the paper-based TOEFL (PBT) or 80 on the Internet-based version (iBT). They must also take the SAT or ACT.

Computers: All students may access the system 24 hours a day. There are no time limits and no fees.

Graduates: From July 1, 2012 to June 30, 2013, 384 bachelor's degrees were awarded. The most popular majors were social sciences (16%), English (13%), and biological/life sciences (12%). 30 companies recruited on campus in 2012-2013. In an average class, 74% graduate in 4 years or less, 78% graduate in 5 years or less, and 78% graduate in 6 years or less. Of the 2012 graduating class, 28% were enrolled in graduate school within 6 months of graduation, and 72% were employed.

Admissions Contact: Lee Ann Backlund, Dean of Admission and Financial Aid. E-Mail: *admiss@sewanee.edu* Web: *www.sewanee.edu*

SOUTHERN ADVENTIST UNIVERSITY D-3

Collegedale, TN 37315 (423) 236-2835
(800) 768-8437; (423) 236-1835

Full-time: 985 men, 1172 women
Part-time: 130 men, 190 women
Graduate: 56 men, 107 women
Year: semesters, summer session
Application Deadline: open
Faculty: 132
Ph.D.s: 64%
Student/Faculty: 16 to 1
Tuition: $21,610
Room & Board: $5,580
Freshman Class: 1513 applied, 1074 accepted, 603 enrolled
SAT: recommended **ACT:** 22 **COMPETITIVE**

Southern Adventist University, founded in 1892, is a private liberal arts institution affiliated with the Seventh-day Adventist Church. The figures in the above capsule and in this profile are approximate. There are 9 undergraduate schools. In addition to regional accreditation, Southern has baccalaureate program accreditation with CSWE, NASM, NCATE, and NLN. The library contains 166,905 volumes, 410,551 microform items, 6,666 audio/video tapes/CDs/DVDs, and subscribes to 2,123 periodicals including electronic. Computerized library services include interlibrary loans, database searching, Internet access, and laptop Internet portals. Special learning facilities include a learning resource center, art gallery, and radio station. The 1000-acre campus is in a small town 18 miles southeast of Chattanooga, TN. Including any residence halls, there are 17 buildings.

Student Life: 78% of undergraduates are from out of state, mostly the South. Students are from 46 states, 42 foreign countries, and Canada. 16% are from public schools. 63% are white; 15% Hispanic; 11% African American. 97% are Protestant. The average age of freshmen is 19; all undergraduates, 21. 31% do not continue beyond their first year; 45% remain to graduate.

Housing: 1837 students can be accommodated in college housing, which includes single-sex dorms, on-campus apartments, and married student housing. On-campus housing is guaranteed for all 4 years. 65% of students live on campus; of those, 70% remain on campus on weekends. Alcohol is not permitted. All students may keep cars.

Activities: There are no fraternities or sororities. There are 30 groups on campus, including band, choir, chorus, drama, ethnic, honors, international, jazz band, newspaper, orchestra, professional, radio and TV, religious, social, student government, symphony, and yearbook. Popular campus events include Alumni Weekend, Strawberry Festival, and Week of Spiritual Emphasis.

Sports: There are 10 intramural sports for men and 10 for women. Facilities include a field house, 8 tennis courts, 3 athletic fields, a pool, 4 racquetball courts, a track, soccer fields, a 23,000-square-foot gym that can seat 3,000 when used as an auditorium, 3 weight rooms, and a 3-hole golf course.

Disabled Students: 70% of the campus is accessible. Facilities include wheelchair ramps, elevators, special parking, specially equipped restrooms, and special class scheduling.

Services: Counseling and information services are available, as is tutoring in most subjects. There is remedial math, reading, and writing.

Campus Safety and Security: Measures include 24-hour foot and vehicle patrol, emergency notification system, and security escort services. There are emergency telephones and lighted pathways/sidewalks.

Programs of Study: Southern confers B.A., B.S., B.B.A., B.F.A., B.Mus., and B.S.W. degrees. Associates and master's degrees are also awarded. Bachelor's degrees are awarded in BIOLOGICAL SCIENCE (biology/biological science), BUSINESS (accounting, banking and finance, business administration and management, entrepreneurial studies, international business management, marketing/retailing/merchandising, and nonprofit/public organization management), COMMUNICATIONS AND THE ARTS (animation, art, broadcasting, communications, English, film arts, fine arts, graphic design, journalism, music, and public relations), COMPUTER AND PHYSICAL SCIENCE (chemistry, computer management, computer science, information sciences and systems, mathematics, physics, and web services), EDUCATION (elementary education, music education, physical education, and recreation education), HEALTH PROFESSIONS (health care administration, health science, medical technology, and nursing), SOCIAL SCIENCE (behavioral science, history, international studies, psychology, public administration, religious education, social work, and theological studies). Business, nursing, and education are the strongest academically. Nursing and business have the largest enrollments.

Required: Students must complete 124 semester hours with at least 30 in the major, and maintain a minimum GPA of 2.0. General education requirements include 12 semester hours of religion; 6 of language, literature, and fine arts; 6 to 9 of English and natural science; 6 of history; 5 of behavioral, family, and health science; 3 each of activity skills, computer competencies, oral communication, and of political and economic systems; and up to 3 of math, depending on the ACT scores.

Special: Internships are available in long-term care, nursing, and journalism. A social work practicum, an accelerated degree program in nursing, and study abroad in Austria, Spain, Argentina, Italy, Germany, Mexico, and France are offered. The B.A.-B.S. degree and dual majors in any combination including business administration and automotive service and business administration and public relations, and interdisciplinary student-designed majors are available. Credit may be granted for 4 years of military experience. Pass/fail options are possible only for phys ed activity classes. There are paraprofessional and pre-professional programs in dentistry and medicine, and various other health-related fields, as well as in law. There are 9 national honors societies.

Faculty/Classroom: 60% of faculty are male; 40% are female. 98% teach undergraduates. No introductory courses are taught by graduate students. The average class size in an introductory lecture is 40; in a laboratory is 25; and in a regular course is 13.

Admissions: In a recent year, 71% of applicants were accepted. The ACT scores were 34% below 21, 27% between 21 and 23, 21% between 24 and 26, 10% between 27 and 28, and 8% above 28. There were 2 National Merit finalists.

Requirements: The ACT is required. The SAT is recommended. Applicants must have a minimum composite score of 22 on the ACT. Students must graduate from an accredited secondary school with 14 academic credits, including 4 units of English and 2 each of a foreign language, math, science, social studies, and history. The GED is accepted. An essay must be submitted if home schooled. A GPA of 2.0 is required. AP and CLEP credits are accepted. Important factors in the admissions decision are advanced placement or honors courses, recommendations by school officials, and leadership record.

Procedure: Freshmen are admitted fall, spring, and summer. Entrance exams should be taken at least prior to admission. There is a rolling admissions plan. Application deadlines are open. Application fee is $25. Notification is sent on a rolling basis. Applications are accepted online.

Transfer: In a recent year, 165 transfer students enrolled. Transfer applicants must have a cumulative GPA of at least 2.0 and a minimum ACT composite score of 18. 2 letters of recommendation are also required. 30 of 124 credits required for the bachelor's degree must be completed at Southern.

Visiting: There are regularly scheduled orientations for prospective students, tour of the campus and dorms, schedule appointments with academic departments, and interview with an admissions officer. There are guides for informal visits, visitors may sit in on classes, and stay overnight. To schedule a visit, contact the Admissions Office.

Financial Aid: In a recent year, 93% of all full-time freshmen and 90% of continuing full-time students received some form of financial aid. 77% of all full-time freshmen and 76% of continuing full-time students received need-based aid. The average freshmen award was $20,130, with $4,697 ($10,000 maximum) from need-based scholarships or need-based grants; $3,740 ($5,800 maximum) from need-based self-help aid (loans and jobs); and $2,290 ($16,205 maximum) from other non-need-based awards and non-need-based scholarships. 43% of undergraduate students work part-time. Average annual earnings from campus work are $3000. The FAFSA is required. The priority date for freshman financial aid applications for fall entry is March 1.

International Students: There are 110 international students enrolled. The school actively recruits these students. They must take the TOEFL with a minimum score of 550 on the paper-based TOEFL (PBT) or 79 on the Internet-based version (iBT) or take the MELAB. They must also take the ACT.

Computers: Wireless access is available. All students may access the system 24 hours per day. There are no time limits and no fees. It is strongly recommended that all students have a personal computer.

Graduates: In a recent year, 371 bachelor's degrees were awarded. The most popular majors were nursing (21%), business (15%), and education (8%). In an average class, 22% graduate in 4 years or less, 36% graduate in 5 years or less, and 48% graduate in 6 years or less. Of a recent graduating class, 15% were enrolled in graduate school within 6 months of graduation, and 41% were employed.

Admissions Contact: Marc Grundy, Director, Enrollment Services. A campus DVD is available. E-Mail: *admissions@southern.edu* Web: *www.southern.edu*

STATE UNIVERSITY AND COMMUNITY COLLEGE SYSTEM OF TENNESSEE

The State University and Community College System of Tennessee, established in 1972, is a private system in Tennessee. It is governed by the Tennessee Board of Regents, whose chief administrator is the chancellor. The primary goal of the system is teaching, research, and public service. The main priorities are to provide quality programs accessible to state residents with equal opportunity in education and employment. In a recent year, the total enrollment was 135,500 with 4200 faculty members. Altogether there are approximately 359 baccalaureate, 195 master's, and 29 doctoral programs offered by the State University and Community College System of Tennessee. Profiles of the 4-year campuses are included in this section.

TENNESSEE STATE UNIVERSITY C-2

Nashville, TN 37209-1561 **(615) 963-5101; (615) 963-5108**

Full-time: 2000 men, 3750 women	**Faculty:** 450; IIA, --$
Part-time: 415 men, 760 women	**Ph.D.s:** 80%
Graduate: 625 men, 1280 women	**Student/Faculty:** 16 to 1
Year: semesters, summer session	**Tuition:** $6100 ($18,50)
Application Deadline: see profile	**Room & Board:** $5900
Freshman Class: n/av	
SAT or ACT: required	

COMPETITIVE

Tennessee State University, founded in 1912, is a state-supported land-grant institution offering undergraduate and graduate programs in arts and sciences, agriculture, health professions, business, education, engineering and technology, and nursing. The figures in the above capsule and in this profile are approximate. There are 7 undergraduate schools and 1 graduate school. In addition to regional accreditation, TSU has baccalaureate program accreditation with AACSB, ABET, AHEA, CSWE, NASAD, NASM, NCATE, and NLN. The 2 libraries contain 463,621 volumes, 754,955 microform items, and 5125 audio/video tapes/CDs/DVDs, and subscribe to 1272 periodicals including electronic. Computerized library services include interlibrary loans and database searching. Special learning facilities include a learning resource center, art gallery, and radio station. The 450-acre campus is in an urban area in Nashville. Including any residence halls, there are 66 buildings.

Student Life: 67% of undergraduates are from Tennessee. Others are from 44 states, 42 foreign countries, and Canada. 90% are from public schools. 74% are African American; 21% white. The average age of freshmen is 18; all undergraduates, 25.

Housing: 3225 students can be accommodated in college housing, which includes single-sex and coed dorms and off campus apartments. In addition, there are honors houses. On-campus housing is guaranteed for all 4 years. 58% of students commute. Alcohol is not permitted. All students may keep cars.

Activities: 1% of men belong to 4 national fraternities; 2% of women belong to 4 national sororities. There are 63 groups on campus, including band, cheerleading, choir, chorale, computers, dance, drama, forensics, honors, jazz band, literary magazine, marching band, newspaper, pep band, professional, radio and TV, religious, social, social service, and student government. Popular campus events include Miss TSU Pageant and Inauguration, Greek Show, and Christmas Tree Lighting Ceremony.

Sports: There are 8 intercollegiate sports for men and 7 for women. Facilities include a major convocation and athletic center that accommodates intramural sports, swimming, handball, and intercollegiate basketball and a campus center that provides extensive recreational facilities.

Disabled Students: 90% of the campus is accessible. Facilities include wheelchair ramps, elevators, special parking, specially equipped rest rooms, and lowered drinking fountains. A campus improvement program makes all new and renovated buildings accessible.

Services: Counseling and information services are available, as is tutoring in some subjects, all general education courses, and many major-field courses. There is a reader service for the blind and remedial math, reading, and writing. A writing clinic, math lab, and reading center provide individualized assistance.

Campus Safety and Security: Measures include 24-hour foot and vehicle patrol. There are shuttle buses, emergency telephones, and lighted pathways/sidewalks.

Programs of Study: TSU confers B.A., B.S., B.B.A., and B.S.N. degrees. Associates, master's, and doctoral degrees are also awarded. Bachelor's degrees are awarded in AGRICULTURE (agriculture), BIOLOGICAL SCIENCE (biology/biological science), BUSINESS (accounting, business administration and management, business economics, and hotel/motel and restaurant management), COMMUNICATIONS AND THE ARTS (art, dramatic arts, English, languages, music, and speech/debate/rhetoric), COMPUTER AND PHYSICAL SCIENCE (chemistry, computer science, mathematics, and physics), EDUCATION (early childhood education, health education, and special education), ENGINEERING AND ENVIRONMENTAL DESIGN (aeronautical technology, architectural engineering, civil engineering, electrical/electronics engineering, and mechanical engineering), HEALTH PROFESSIONS (dental hygiene, health care administration, medical records administration/services, medical technology, nursing, occupational therapy, physical therapy, respiratory therapy, and speech pathology/audiology), SOCIAL SCIENCE (African studies, criminal justice, family/consumer studies, history, interdisciplinary studies, political science/government, psychology, social work, and sociology). Engineering, allied health professions, and nursing are the strongest academically. Allied health, nursing, and engineering have the largest enrollments.

Required: To graduate, students must complete at least 120 semester hours, with 25% in the major, and maintain a minimum GPA of 2.0. Additional requirements include demonstration of proficiency in English composition, completion of a senior project, and courses in English, math, social sciences, American history, humanities, and natural sciences.

Special: Opportunities are provided for co-op programs in business and engineering, cross-registration with Middle Tennessee State University and Meharry Medical College, a B.A.-B.S. degree in interdisciplinary studies, credit by exam, and nondegree study. There are 19 national honor societies, a freshman honors program, and 5 departmental honors programs.

Faculty/Classroom: 55% of faculty are male; 45% are female. 90% teach undergraduates, 20% do research, and 85% do both. No introductory courses are taught by graduate students. The average class size in an introductory lecture is 30; in a laboratory, 35; and in a regular course, 30.

Requirements: The SAT or ACT is required, with a minimum score of 900 on the SAT or 19 on the ACT. Graduation from an accredited secondary school is required; the GED is accepted. Applicants should have 4 credits in English, 3 in math, 2 each in science and a foreign language, and 1 each in history, social studies, and art. A GPA of 2.3 is required. AP and CLEP credits are accepted.

Procedure: Freshmen are admitted to all sessions. Entrance exams should be taken in the junior year. There is an early admissions plan. Check with the school for current application deadlines. The application fee is $25.

Transfer: Applicants must submit official transcripts from all previous colleges attended. Students from other than Tennessee colleges must have maintained a minimum GPA of 2.0. The GPA requirements for students transferring from Tennessee colleges vary according to the number of semester hours being submitted for transfer credit. 30 of 120 credits required for the bachelor's degree must be completed at TSU.

Visiting: There are guides for informal visits, and visitors may sit in on classes and stay overnight. To schedule a visit, contact the recruiting staff.

Financial Aid: The FAFSA is required. Check with the school for current application deadlines.

International Students: There were 63 international students enrolled in a recent year. They must take the TOEFL. They must also take the SAT or ACT.

Computers: All students may access the system. There are no time limits and no fees.

Admissions Contact: Sedric Griffin, Admissions Director. A campus DVD is available. E-Mail: *sgriffin01@tnstate.edu* Web: *www.tnstate.edu*

TENNESSEE TECHNOLOGICAL UNIVERSITY D-2

Cookeville, TN 38505 **(931) 372-3888**
(800) 255-8881; (931) 372-6250

Full-time: 3900 men, 3270 women	**Faculty:** n/av; IIA, -$
Part-time: 415 men, 480 women	**Ph.D.s:** 83%
Graduate: 710 men, 1555 women	**Student/Faculty:** n/av
Year: semesters, summer session	**Tuition:** $6100 ($17,500)
Application Deadline: see profile	**Room & Board:** $7500
Freshman Class: 3254 accepted, 1661 enrolled	
ACT: required	

COMPETITIVE

Tennessee Technological University, founded in 1915 and a member of the state university and community college system of Tennessee, is a public institution offering undergraduate and graduate programs in the liberal arts, business, engineering, agriculture studies, art and fine arts, music, professional training, teacher preparation, nursing, home economics, and crafts. The figures in the above capsule and in this profile are approximate. There are 8 undergraduate schools and 5 graduate schools. In addition to regional accreditation, Tennessee Tech has baccalaureate program accreditation with AACSB, ABET, NASAD, NASM, NCATE, and NLN. The library contains 365,000 volumes, 1 million microform items, and 38,000 audio/video tapes/CDs/DVDs, and subscribes to 3800 periodicals including electronic. Computerized library services include interlibrary loans, database searching, and Internet access. Special learning facilities include a learning resource center, art gallery, radio station, and TV station. The 235-acre campus is in a small town 78 miles east of Nashville. Including any residence halls, there are 97 buildings.

Student Life: 93% of undergraduates are from Tennessee. Others are from 41 states, 55 foreign countries, and Canada. 88% are white. 55% claim no religious affiliation The average age of freshmen is 19; all undergraduates, 22. 27% do not continue beyond their first year; 44% remain to graduate.

Housing: 3100 students can be accommodated in college housing, which includes single-sex and coed dorms, on-campus apartments, and married student housing. In addition, there are honors houses, special-interest houses, and private-room dorms for upper-class students. On-campus housing is guaranteed for all 4 years. 75% of students commute. Alcohol is not permitted. All students may keep cars.

Activities: 10% of men belong to 13 national fraternities; 10% of women belong to 9 national sororities. There are 178 groups on campus, including art, band, cheerleading, chess, choir, chorale, chorus, communications, computers, dance, debate, drama, drill team, ethnic, forensics, gay, honors, international, jazz band, literary magazine, marching band, musical theater, newspaper, opera, orchestra, pep band, photography, political, professional, radio and TV, religious, social, social service, student government, symphony, and yearbook. Popular campus events include intramural events, Greek Week, and Parents Day.

Sports: There are 7 intercollegiate sports for men and 9 for women, and 10 intramural sports for men and 8 for women. Facilities include 2 gyms seating 10,500 and 4000, a 16,500-seat stadium with track facilities, an indoor pool, indoor and outdoor tennis courts, handball and basketball courts, baseball, softball, and football fields, a track, a rifle range, apparatus rooms, and a health and wellness center with an indoor track, 8 racquetball courts, a weight room, an aerobics classroom, a pool, and basketball/volleyball courts.

Disabled Students: 95% of the campus is accessible. Facilities include wheelchair ramps, elevators, special parking, specially equipped rest rooms, special class scheduling, lowered drinking fountains, lowered telephones, and special housing.

Services: Counseling and information services are available, as is tutoring in some subjects, including English and lower levels of math. There is a reader service for the blind and remedial math, reading, and writing.

Campus Safety and Security: Measures include 24-hour foot and vehicle patrol, self-defense education, and security escort services. There are emergency telephones, lighted pathways/sidewalks, and a student safety organization.

Programs of Study: Tennessee Tech confers B.A., B.S., B.F.A., B.M., B.S.Agr., B.S.B.A., B.S.C.E., B.S.Ch.E., B.S.Ed., B.S.E.E., B.S.H.E., B.S.I.E., B.S.Ind.Tech., B.S.M.E., and B.S.N. degrees. Master's and doctoral degrees are also awarded. Bachelor's degrees are awarded in AGRICULTURE (agricultural economics, agriculture, animal science, fish and game management, plant science, soil science, and wildlife management), BIOLOGICAL SCIENCE (biochemistry and biology/biological science), BUSINESS (accounting, banking and finance, business administration and management, management science, and marketing/retailing/merchandising), COMMUNICATIONS AND THE ARTS (English, fine arts, French, German, journalism, Spanish, and technical and business writing), COMPUTER AND PHYSICAL SCIENCE (chemistry, computer science, geology, mathematics, physics, and web technology), EDUCATION (agricultural education, art education, home economics education, music education, physical education, secondary education, and special education), ENGINEERING AND ENVIRONMENTAL DESIGN (chemical engineering, civil engineering, electrical/electronics engineering, engineering, environmental engineering, industrial engineering, industrial engineering technology, manufacturing engineering, and mechanical engineering), HEALTH PROFESSIONS (nursing), SOCIAL SCIENCE (child care/child and family studies, economics, history, human ecology, political science/government, psychology, and sociology). Engineering, business, and education are the strongest academically. Engineering has the largest enrollment.

Required: Students must complete 120 semester hours, with a variable number of hours in the major, and maintain a minimum GPA of 2.0. 9 semester hours of English, 8 of a lab science, 6 of American history, 6 each of social sciences and humanities, and 3 hours each of math and speech are required.

Special: Co-op programs in most academic areas, internships in community-based programs, study abroad, a Washington semester, multidisciplinary majors, and work-study programs are available. Accelerated degree programs are offered in all specified majors with 3 calendar years of continuous studies. A B.A.-B.S. degree is available, as are dual majors in all areas. Credit may be granted for military experience, and nondegree study and pass/fail options are offered. There are 29 national honor societies and a freshman honors program.

Faculty/Classroom: 64% of faculty are male; 36% are female. 99% teach undergraduates, 73% do research, and 70% do both. Graduate students teach 5% of introductory courses. The average class size in an introductory lecture is 27; in a laboratory, 30; and in a regular course, 26.

Admissions: There were 4 National Merit finalists in a recent year.

Requirements: The ACT is required. Applicants must have a minimum composite score of 19 on the ACT (17 if GPA is 2.5 or higher). Other admissions requirements include graduation from an accredited secondary school with 14 academic credits, including 4 of English, 3 of math, 2 each in science and a single foreign language, 1 in American history, 1 in world history, ancient history, modern history, world geography or European history, and 1 in music/art. The GED is also accepted. A GPA of 2.0 is required. AP and CLEP credits are accepted.

Procedure: Freshmen are admitted to all sessions. Entrance exams should be taken during the senior year. There are deferred admissions and rolling admissions plans. Check with the school for current application deadlines. The application fee is $15. Applications are accepted online.

Transfer: 755 transfer students enrolled in a recent year. Transfer students should have a minimum of 12 credit hours earned; the minimum GPA depends on the number of credit hours accumulated. Official transcripts must be submitted, and the ACT is required if the applicant is age 21 or under. If an applicant has fewer than 12 credit hours, admissions requirements are the same as for freshmen. 30 of 120 credits required for the bachelor's degree must be completed at Tennessee Tech.

Visiting: There are regularly scheduled orientations for prospective students, including visits either morning or afternoon each weekday and meetings with an admission officer, faculty member in student's major, and a campus tour. There are guides for informal visits and visitors may sit in on classes. To schedule a visit, contact the Admissions Office.

Financial Aid: In a recent year, 91% of all full-time freshmen and 89% of continuing full-time students received some form of financial aid. 87% of all full-time freshmen and 83% of continuing full-time students received need-based aid. The average freshmen award was $8120. The average financial indebtedness of a recent graduate was $14,478. The FAFSA is required. Check with the school for current application deadlines.

International Students: There were 209 international students enrolled in a recent year. The school actively recruits these students. They must take the TOEFL with a minimum score of 500 on the paper-based TOEFL (PBT) or 61 on the Internet-based version (iBT) and the college's own test. They must also take the SAT or ACT.

Computers: All students may access the system 24 hours a day. There are no time limits and no fees.

Graduates: In a recent year, 1354 bachelor's degrees were awarded. The most popular majors were business (22%), education (20%), and engineering (13%). 475 companies recruited on campus in a recent year. In an average class, 1% graduate in 3 years or less, 17% graduate in 4 years or less, 36% graduate in 5 years or less, and 45% graduate in 6 years or less. Of a recent graduating class, 10% were enrolled in graduate school within 6 months of graduation and 80% were employed.

Admissions Contact: Vanessa Palmer, Director of Admissions. E-Mail: *admissions@tntech.edu* Web: *www.tntech.edu*

TENNESSEE WESLEYAN COLLEGE E-3

Athens, TN 37371-0040 **(423) 746-5286**
(800) PICK-TWC; (423) 744-9968

Full-time: 330 men, 605 women	**Faculty:** 50; IIB, --$
Part-time: 50 men, 85 women	**Ph.D.s:** 70%
Graduate: n/av	**Student/Faculty:** 15 to 1
Year: semesters, summer session	**Tuition:** $16,150
Application Deadline: August	**Room & Board:** $6200
Freshman Class: n/av	

COMPETITIVE

Tennessee Wesleyan College, founded in 1857, is a private institution affiliated with the United Methodist Church. Its undergraduate programs stress the liberal arts, teacher preparation, business, and nursing. The library contains 153,505 volumes, 9,668 microform items, and 3,558 audio/video tapes/CDs/DVDs, and subscribes to 9,663 periodicals including electronic. Computerized library services include interlibrary loans, database searching, and Internet access. Special learning facilities include a learning resource center, art gallery, an education technology lab. The 40-acre campus is in a small town 55 miles south of Knoxville, TN. Including any residence halls, there are 21 buildings.

Student Life: 91% of undergraduates are from Tennessee. Students are from 22 states, and 11 foreign countries. 77% are white. 51% are Protestant. The average age of freshmen is 18; all undergraduates, 33. 38% do not continue beyond their first year; 44% remain to graduate.

Housing: 415 students can be accommodated in college housing, which includes single-sex dorms and on-campus apartments. On-campus housing is guaranteed for all 4 years. 68% of students commute. Alcohol is not permitted. All students may keep cars.

Activities: 7% of men belong to 1 local fraternity; 6% of women belong to 1 local and 1 national sororities. There are 22 groups on campus, including art, band, cheerleading, choir, chorale, computers, dance, drama, ethnic, honors, international, literary magazine, musical theater, newspaper, professional, religious, social, social service, student government, and yearbook. Popular campus events include skiing trips and the annual spring Dodge Ball Tournament.

Sports: There are 7 intercollegiate sports for men and 7 for women. Facilities include a soccer/lacrosse stadium, an air conditioned gym, a fitness center, a baseball field, state-of-the art tennis facility, and a YMCA adjacent to campus, which students may use for a fee.

Disabled Students: 30% of the campus is accessible. Facilities include wheelchair ramps, elevators, special parking, specially equipped restrooms, and special class scheduling.

Campus Safety and Security: Measures include 24-hour foot and vehicle patrol, emergency notification system, self-defense education, and security escort services. There are lighted pathways/sidewalks and controlled access to dorms/residences.

Programs of Study: TWC confers B.A., B.S., B.Applied Sc., B.Mus.Ed., and B.S.N. degrees. Bachelor's degrees are awarded in AGRICULTURE (environmental studies), BIOLOGICAL SCIENCE (biology/biological science), BUSINESS (accounting, banking and finance, business administration and management, human resources, management information systems, and sports management), COMMUNICATIONS AND THE ARTS (English and music), COMPUTER AND PHYSICAL SCIENCE (chemistry and mathematics), EDUCATION (early childhood education, elementary education, physical education, and secondary education), HEALTH PROFESSIONS (exercise science, health, and nursing), SOCIAL SCIENCE (behavioral science, history, human development, human services, interdisciplinary studies, international studies, ministries, pastoral studies, and psychology). Business administration, education, and nursing have the largest enrollments.

Required: Students must complete at least 128 semester hours, fulfilling the requirements of the major and taking 30 semester hours at the upper-division level, and maintain a minimum GPA of 2.0. Distribution requirements include 12 semester hours of the humanities, 9 of social and behavioral sciences, 8 of science, 6 each of math and English composition, and 3 each of speech and fine arts. B.A. candidates must also take 12 hours of a single foreign language. 2 semester hours of phys ed are also needed. Internships are required for human services students, and all students must take an exit exam. The number of hours required for the major varies.

Special: The college offers for credit internships in most majors, study abroad, an accelerated degree program, B.A.-B.S. degrees, and dual and student-designed majors. Students in natural science programs may take summer courses offered by the Gulf Coast Research Laboratory of the University of Southern Mississippi Institute of Marine Sciences. TWC also holds an ambassadorial agreement with the University of St. Augustine for health sciences. There are 5 national honor societies and a freshman honors program.

Faculty/Classroom: 49% of faculty are male; 51% are female. All teach undergraduates. No introductory courses are taught by graduate students. The average class size in an introductory lecture is 14; in a laboratory is 15; and in a regular course is 15.

Admissions: 44% of the current freshmen were in the top fifth of their class; 75% were in the top two fifths. 18 freshmen graduated first in their class.

Requirements: The ACT is required. The SAT is recommended. Other admission requirements include graduation from an accredited secondary school, with 16 academic credits, including 4 units in English, 2 each in math and science, and 1 each in social studies and history. Foreign language is recommended. The GED is also accepted in lieu of a high school diploma and test scores. A GPA of 2.5 is required. AP and CLEP credits are accepted. Important factors in the admissions decision are evidence of special talent and personality/intangible qualities.

Procedure: Freshmen are admitted fall, spring, and summer. Entrance exams should be taken by July of the year they wish to enter the college. There is a rolling admissions plan. Check with the school for current application deadlines. The application fee is $25. Notification is sent on a rolling basis. Applications are accepted online.

Transfer: Transfer students must have a minimum GPA of 2.0; an associate degree is recommended. 15 of 128 credits required for the bachelor's degree must be completed at TWC.

Visiting: There are regularly scheduled orientations for prospective students. There are guides for informal visits, visitors may sit in on classes, and stay overnight. To schedule a visit, contact the Office of Admissions.

Financial Aid: The FAFSA and the college's own financial statement are required. The priority date for freshman financial aid applications for fall entry is March 1.

International Students: There are 18 international students enrolled. They must take the TOEFL with a minimum score of 550 on the paper-based TOEFL (PBT) or 79 on the Internet-based version (iBT). They must also take the SAT or ACT.

Computers: Wireless access is available. There are 4 computer labs on campus that all have Internet access. Additionally, there are computers located in the library with Internet access that may be used for research purposes only. Wireless access is available in all dorms and several campus buildings. Students living in the dorms also get connected to the campus network if they bring their own PCs. All students may access the system. during lab hours; Wireless and dorm access is continuous. Library access is during library hours. There are no time limits and no fees.

Graduates: In a recent year, 194 bachelor's degrees were awarded. The most popular majors were business administration (27%), health professions (21%), and education (20%). 15 companies recruited on campus in a recent year. In an average class, 30% graduate in 4 years or less, 43% graduate in 5 years or less, and 44% graduate in 6 years or less. Of a recent graduating class, 40% were enrolled in graduate school within 6 months of graduation, and 50% were employed.

Admissions Contact: Michelle Boyd, Office Coordinator. E-Mail: *shellyb@twcnet.edu* Web: *www.twcnet.edu*

TREVECCA NAZARENE UNIVERSITY C-2

Nashville, TN 37210 (615) 248-1320
(888) 210-4TNU; (615) 248-7406

Full-time: 471 men, 545 women	**Faculty:** n/av; IIA, --$
Part-time: 196 men, 280 women	**Ph.D.s:** 78%
Graduate: 292 men, 622 women	**Student/Faculty:** 16 to 1
Year: semesters, summer session	**Tuition:** $22,330
Application Deadline: August 1	**Room & Board:** $7788

Freshman Class: 903 applied, 618 accepted, 247 enrolled
SAT CR/M: 540/520 **ACT:** 23 **COMPETITIVE**

Trevecca Nazarene University, founded in 1901, is a private institution affiliated with the Church of the Nazarene. Trevecca offers programs in liberal arts and sciences and a number of professional content areas. The university also provides a variety of nontraditional continuing education professional programs at the undergraduate and graduate levels. There are 4 undergraduate schools and 4 graduate schools. In addition to regional accreditation, TNU has baccalaureate program accreditation with CAHEA, NASM, and NCATE. The library contains 151,985 volumes, and 127 audio/video tapes/CDs/DVDs, and subscribes to 862 periodicals including electronic. Computerized library services include interlibrary loans, database searching, Internet access, and Wi-Fi capability. The 80-acre campus is in an urban area. Including any residence halls, there are 30 buildings.

Student Life: 64% of undergraduates are from Tennessee. Others are from 41 states, 14 foreign countries, and Canada. 70% are White; 14% race unknown. 94% are Protestant. The average age of freshmen is 19; all undergraduates, 25. 26% do not continue beyond their first year; 47% remain to graduate.

Housing: 737 students can be accommodated in college housing, which includes single-sex dorms, on-campus apartments, off-campus apartments, and married student housing. On-campus housing is guaranteed for all 4 years. 53% of students commute. Alcohol is not permitted. All students may keep cars.

Activities: There are no fraternities or sororities. There are 23 groups on campus, including band, cheerleading, choir, chorale, chorus, drama, environmental, forensics, honors, international, jazz band, literary magazine, marching band, musical theater, newspaper, orchestra, pep band, professional, radio and TV, religious, social service, student government, symphony, and yearbook. Popular campus events include drama productions and athletic events.

Sports: There are 5 intercollegiate sports for men and 6 for women, and 9 intramural sports for men and 8 for women. Facilities include a gym, a jogging track, handball, racquetball, and tennis courts, exercise and weight rooms, and playing fields.

Disabled Students: Facilities include wheelchair ramps, elevators, special parking, specially equipped restrooms, and special class scheduling.

Services: Counseling and information services are available, as is tutoring in every subject. There is a reader service for the blind, and remedial math, reading, and writing. An academic enrichment program for students scoring below 19 on the ACT provides tutoring in math, reading, writing, and study skills.

Campus Safety and Security: Measures include 24-hour foot and vehicle patrol and emergency notification system. There are lighted pathways/sidewalks, and weekend and evening foot and vehicle patrols.

Programs of Study: TNU confers B.A., B.S., B.B.A., B.S.N. and B.S.S.W. degrees. Associate, master's, and doctoral degrees are also awarded. Bachelor's degrees are awarded in BIOLOGICAL SCIENCE (biology/biological science), BUSINESS (accounting, business administration and management, electronic business, marketing/retailing/merchandising, and sports management), COMMUNICATIONS AND THE ARTS (communications, digital communications, dramatic arts, English, journalism, music, and music business management), COMPUTER AND PHYSICAL SCIENCE (chemistry, chemistry/adolescence education, information sciences and systems, mathematics, physics, and science), EDUCATION (business education, drama education, early childhood education, education, English education, mathematics education, music education, physical education, science education, secondary education, and special education), HEALTH PROFESSIONS (exercise science and nursing), SOCIAL SCIENCE (behavioral science, criminal justice, history, pastoral studies, political science/government, psychology, religion, social work, and sociology). Teacher education, business, and religion are the strongest academically. Management and human relations, religion, and education have the largest enrollments.

Required: To graduate, students must complete at least 120 semester hours with a minimum 2.0 GPA. The required 54-hour general education curriculum includes courses in English, communications, religion and philosophy, fine arts, history and social science (including foreign language), science, math, and phys ed.

Special: There is cross-registration with other Nazarene colleges and universities in the United States, and work-study programs, internships, a Washington semester, and nondegree study are offered. Study abroad is possible. Three adult degree-completion programs leading to bachelor degrees. A 3-2 nursing program is offered with Belmont University. There are preprofessional studies in physical therapy, medicine, dentistry, pharmacy, veterinary science, law, and engineering. There is 1 national honor society.

Faculty/Classroom: 63% of faculty are male; 37% are female. No introductory courses are taught by graduate students.

Admissions: 68% of the 2013-2014 applicants were accepted. The SAT scores for the 2013-2014 freshman class were: Critical Reading--26% below 500, 49% between 500 and 599, 23% between 600 and 699, and 2% between 700 and 800; Math--37% below 500, 37% between 500 and 599, 21% between 600 and 699, and 5% between 700 and 800. The ACT scores were 23% below 21, 28% between 21 and 23, 25% between 24 and 26, 11% between 27 and 28, and 13% above 28.

Requirements: The SAT or ACT is required. The ACT is preferred, with a composite score of at least 22. Candidates should have completed at least 15 academic secondary credits, including 4 units in English, 2 each in math, foreign language, and social science, and 1 in natural science. A GED of at least 45 is also accepted. The medical technology and teacher education programs have special admission requirements. A GPA of 2.5 is required. AP and CLEP credits are accepted.

Procedure: Freshmen are admitted fall, spring, and summer. Entrance exams should be taken in the junior or senior year. There are deferred admissions and rolling admissions plans. Applications should be filed by August 1 for fall entry; December 1 for spring entry, along with a $25 fee. Applications are accepted online.

Transfer: 73 transfer students enrolled in 2012-2013. Transfer applicants must present official transcripts and recommendations. 30 of 120 credits required for the bachelor's degree must be completed at TNU.

Visiting: There are regularly scheduled orientations for prospective students, including a tour and meetings with admissions and financial aid personnel and faculty. There are guides for informal visits, visitors may sit in on classes, and stay overnight. To schedule a visit, contact the Admissions Office at (888) 210-4TNU.

Financial Aid: In 2013-2014, 94% of all full-time freshmen received some form of financial aid. The FAFSA is required. The priority date for freshman financial aid applications for fall entry is Feb 1.

International Students: There are 17 international students enrolled. They must take the TOEFL with a minimum score of 500 on the paper-based TOEFL (PBT) or 61 on the Internet-based version (iBT). They must also take the SAT or ACT, scoring 18.

Computers: All students may access the system. from 8 a.m. to 11 p.m. every day, with residence hall labs open 24 hours. There are no time limits. The fee is $150.

Graduates: From July 1, 2012 to June 30, 2013, 390 bachelor's degrees were awarded. The most popular majors were business marketing (46%), education (10%), and computer and information sciences (8%). In an average class, 36% graduate in 4 years or less, 45% graduate in 5 years or less, and 47% graduate in 6 years or less.

Admissions Contact: Melinda Miller, Director Undergraduate Admissions. E-Mail: *admissions_und@trevecca.edu* Web: *www.trevecca.edu*

TUSCULUM COLLEGE F-2

Greeneville, TN 37743 (423) 636-7300
(800) 729-0256; (423) 638-7166

Full-time: 915 men, 1460 women	**Faculty:** n/av
Part-time: 35 men, 45 women	**Ph.D.s:** n/av
Graduate: 40 men, 115 women	**Student/Faculty:** 16 to 1
Year: see profile, summer session	**Tuition:** $20,500
Application Deadline: open	**Room & Board:** $8500
Freshman Class: n/av	
SAT or ACT: required	

COMPETITIVE

Tusculum College, a civic arts institution chartered in 1794, is the oldest college in Tennessee and the oldest coeducational college affiliated with the Presbyterian Church. The figures in the above capsule and in this profile are approximate. There is 1 graduate school. The 2 libraries contain 67,202 volumes, 210,798 microform items, and 966 audio/video tapes/CDs/DVDs, and subscribe to 300 periodicals including electronic. Computerized library services include interlibrary loans, database searching, and Internet access. Special learning facilities include an art gallery, radio station, TV station, and the President Andrew Johnson Museum. The 142-acre campus is in a small town 30 miles south of Johnson City, in the foothills of the Great Smoky Mountains. Including any residence halls, there are 21 buildings.

Student Life: 80% of undergraduates are from Tennessee. Others are from 31 states, 22 foreign countries, and Canada. 97% are from public schools. 87% are white. The average age of freshmen is 19; all undergraduates, 28. 40% do not continue beyond their first year; 43% remain to graduate.

Housing: 607 students can be accommodated in college housing, which includes single-sex dorms and on-campus apartments. On-campus housing is guaranteed for all 4 years. 72% of students commute. Alcohol is not permitted. All students may keep cars.

Activities: There are no fraternities or sororities. There are 21 groups on campus, including art, cheerleading, chorale, dance, drama, ethnic, honors, international, newspaper, pep band, photography, professional, radio and TV, religious, social service, student government, and yearbook. Popular campus events include McCormick Day, Opening Convocation, and Honors Convocation.

Sports: There are 7 intercollegiate sports for men and 7 for women, and 12 intramural sports for men and 13 for women. Facilities include a 2000-seat gym, a gym/pool complex, tennis courts, and football, soccer, softball, and baseball fields.

Disabled Students: 50% of the campus is accessible. Facilities include wheelchair ramps, elevators, special parking, specially equipped rest rooms, special class scheduling, lowered drinking fountains, lowered telephones, and special housing. Classes and activities are scheduled in accessible areas.

Services: Counseling and information services are available, as is tutoring in most subjects. There is a reader service for the blind and remedial math, reading, and writing. Math and English tutoring are available on a limited basis through the College Learning Center.

Campus Safety and Security: Measures include 24-hour foot and vehicle patrol and security escort services. There are emergency telephones and lighted pathways/sidewalks.

Programs of Study: Tusculum confers B.A. and B.S. degrees. Master's degrees are also awarded. Bachelor's degrees are awarded in BIOLOGICAL SCIENCE (biology/biological science), BUSINESS (management science, small business management, and sports management), COMMUNICATIONS AND THE ARTS (design, English, and fine arts), COMPUTER AND PHYSICAL SCIENCE (computer science, information sciences and systems, and mathematics), EDUCATION (athletic training, early childhood education, education, elementary education, middle school education, museum studies, physical education, and special education), ENGINEERING AND ENVIRONMENTAL DESIGN (environmental science), HEALTH PROFESSIONS (medical technology, premedicine, and sports medicine), SOCIAL SCIENCE (history, political science/government, and psychology). Management, education, and biology are the strongest academically. Management and education have the largest enrollments.

Required: All students must complete at least 128 hours, with a minimum GPA of 2.0 overall and 2.25 in the major. Specific degree programs have varying requirements. B.S. candidates must take a core curriculum consisting of courses in English, art, music, sociology, economics, and psychology. B.A. candidates must complete a set of interdisciplinary courses, validate 15 competencies, complete a civic arts project, and fulfill the requirements of a major.

Special: Each semester is divided into four 3 1/2-week blocks, with 1 course taken per block. Internships, practicums, and student-teaching opportunities are offered in business administration, professional and special education, social services, psychology, biology, chemistry, and medical technology. The B.S. in applied organizational management is designed for adult students with previous training and work experience. The medical technology program is offered in cooperation with a medical center in Kingsport. Study abroad, independent majors, nondegree study, an accelerated degree program in applied organizational management, work-study programs, student-designed majors, and pass/fail options are available. There is an accelerated evening program for working adults. There is 1 national honor society.

Faculty/Classroom: 67% of faculty are male; 33% are female. 89% teach undergraduates. No introductory courses are taught by graduate students. The average class size in an introductory lecture is 25; in a laboratory, 20; and in a regular course, 15.

Requirements: The SAT or ACT is required. Applicants should be high school graduates or have the GED. Secondary school preparation should include 4 units of English, 2 units each of foreign language, math, and science, and 1 unit of history. A personal essay is also required and an interview may be necessary. Tusculum requires applicants to be in the upper 50% of their class. A GPA of 2.0 is required. AP and CLEP credits are accepted. Important factors in the admissions decision are advanced placement or honors courses, leadership record, and evidence of special talent.

Procedure: Freshmen are admitted to all sessions. Entrance exams should be taken in the spring of the junior year. There are deferred admissions and rolling admissions plans. Application deadlines are open. The application fee is $20. Applications are accepted online.

Transfer: Transfer applicants should present at least a 2.0 GPA in previous college work. Tusculum recommends that applicants also submit SAT or ACT scores. 32 of 128 credits required for the bachelor's degree must be completed at Tusculum.

Visiting: There are regularly scheduled orientations for prospective students, including a fall and spring open house during which students are given campus tours, financial aid information, and application materials.

There are guides for informal visits, and visitors may sit in on classes and stay overnight. To schedule a visit, contact the Admissions Office.

Financial Aid: The FAFSA is required. Check with the school for current application deadlines.

International Students: There were 55 international students enrolled in a recent year. They must take the TOEFL. They must also take the SAT or ACT.

Computers: All students may access the system 24 hours a day, 7 days a week. There are no time limits and no fees.

Admissions Contact: Melissa Ripley, Director of Admissions. E-Mail: *admissions@tusculum.edu* Web: *www.tusculum.edu*

UNION UNIVERSITY B-2

Jackson, TN 38305 (731) 661-5009
(800) 33-UNION; (731) 338-6466

Full-time: 803 men, 1369 women	**Faculty:** 239
Part-time: 303 men, 354 women	**Ph.D.s:** 80%
Graduate: 428 men, 739 women	**Student/Faculty:** 11 to 1
Year: 4-1-4, summer session	**Tuition:** $22,390
Application Deadline: open	**Room & Board:** $5870
Freshman Class: 1930 applied, 1432 accepted, 452 enrolled	
SAT CR/M: 590/590	**ACT:** 25 **VERY COMPETITIVE**

Union University, founded in 1823, is a private, nonprofit institution affiliated with the Southern Baptist Convention. The university offers programs in arts and sciences, education, business, and nursing. There are 5 undergraduate schools and 3 graduate schools. In addition to regional accreditation, Union has baccalaureate program accreditation with AACSB, ABET, CSWE, NASAD, NASM, NCATE, and NLN. The 2 libraries contain 146,055 volumes, 479,357 microform items, 11,088 audio/video tapes/CDs/DVDs, and subscribe to 705 periodicals including electronic. Computerized library services include interlibrary loans, database searching, and Internet access. Special learning facilities include an art gallery, radio and TV lab facilities. The 360-acre campus is in a suburban area 80 miles east of Memphis. Including any residence halls, there are 40 buildings.

Student Life: 69% of undergraduates are from Tennessee. Others are from 44 states, 35 foreign countries, and Canada. 75% are from public schools. 75% are White; 14% African American. 94% are Protestant. The average age of freshmen is 18; all undergraduates, 20. 7% do not continue beyond their first year; 64% remain to graduate.

Housing: 1180 students can be accommodated in college housing, which includes single-sex dorms, on-campus apartments, and married student housing. On-campus housing is guaranteed for all 4 years. 65% of students live on campus; of those, 40% remain on campus on weekends. Alcohol is not permitted. All students may keep cars.

Activities: 27% of men belong to 3 national fraternities; 23% of women belong to 3 national sororities. There are 73 groups on campus, including music ensembles, art, band, cheerleading, choir, chorus, computers, concert band, debate, drama, ethnic, film, honors, international, jazz band, literary magazine, musical theater, newspaper, opera, orchestra, photography, political, professional, radio and TV, religious, social, social service, student government, and symphony. Popular campus events include Campus Day, Parents Weekend, and Variety Show.

Sports: There are 5 intercollegiate sports for men and 5 for women, and 12 intramural sports for men and 12 for women. Facilities include racquetball courts, a student recreation center, an indoor swimming pool, a wellness center, 2 gyms, 2 soccer fields, and baseball and softball complexes.

Disabled Students: 98% of the campus is accessible. Facilities include wheelchair ramps, elevators, special parking, specially equipped restrooms, special class scheduling, lowered drinking fountains, lowered telephones, and special housing.

Services: Counseling and information services are available, as is tutoring in most subjects. There is also assistance with study skills, time management, note taking, reading comprehension, and writing.

Campus Safety and Security: Measures include 24-hour foot and vehicle patrol, emergency notification system, self-defense education, and security escort services. There are emergency telephones and lighted pathways/sidewalks.

Programs of Study: Union confers B.A., B.S., B.M., B.S.B.A., B.S.M.T. and B.S.N. degrees. Associate, master's, and doctoral degrees are also awarded. Bachelor's degrees are awarded in BIOLOGICAL SCIENCE (biology/biological science), BUSINESS (accounting, banking and finance, business administration and management, management science, marketing management, marketing/retailing/merchandising, and sports management), COMMUNICATIONS AND THE ARTS (advertising, art, broadcasting, communications, dramatic arts, English, English as a second/foreign language, English literature, French, graphic design, Greek, journalism, music, music performance, music theory and composition, piano/organ, public relations, Spanish, and voice), COMPUTER AND PHYSICAL SCIENCE (chemistry, computer science, mathematics, physical chemistry, physical sciences, and physics), EDUCATION (education, elementary education, middle school education, music education, physical education, secondary education, special education, and teaching English as a second/foreign language (TESOL/TEFOL)), ENGINEERING AND ENVIRONMENTAL DESIGN (preengineering), HEALTH PROFESSIONS (medical laboratory technology, nursing, predentistry, premedicine, prepharmacy, and sports medicine), SOCIAL SCIENCE (biblical languages, biblical studies, Christian studies, economics, family and community services, history, ministries, missions, pastoral studies, philosophy, political science/government, prelaw, psychology, religion, religious music, social work, sociology, and youth ministry). Business, nursing, and education have the largest enrollments.

Required: All students must complete 128 credit hours, with at least 30 in the major, and maintain a minimum overall GPA of 2.0. The general core requirements are 8 credit hours of lab sciences, 6 each of history, composition, literature, and religion, 3 each of math, oral communication, social sciences/humanities, and fine arts, and 2 of phys ed. Students must pass comprehensive exams in each course and at completion of the major.

Special: Cooperative and accelerated degree programs are available in business department majors. Cross-registration with Freed-Hardeman Universities, internships, study abroad in 7 countries, a Washington semester, work-study programs, composite majors in religion and church ministry, religion and Greek, and religion and philosophy, dual and student-designed majors, 3-2 engineering degrees, and nondegree study are also offered. There are 15 national honor societies, a freshman honors program, and 14 departmental honors programs.

Faculty/Classroom: 53% of faculty are male; 47% are female. All teach undergraduates, and 25% do research. No introductory courses are taught by graduate students. The average class size in an introductory lecture is 25; in a laboratory is 18; and in a regular course is 15.

Admissions: 74% of the 2013-2014 applicants were accepted. The SAT scores for the 2013-2014 freshman class were: Critical Reading--13% below 500, 23% between 500 and 599, 30% between 600 and 699, and 23% between 700 and 800; Math--13% below 500, 35% between 500 and 599, 36% between 600 and 699, and 10% between 700 and 800. The ACT scores were 16% below 21, 21% between 21 and 23, 22% between 24 and 26, 12% between 27 and 28, and 29% above 28. 66% of the current freshmen were in the top fifth of their class; 89% were in the top two fifths. There were 6 National Merit finalists. 44 freshmen graduated first in their class.

Requirements: The SAT or ACT is required. The ACT is preferred. A minimum composite score of 20 on the ACT or 820 on the SAT I is recommended. Candidates must be graduates of an accredited secondary school or have the GED. A minimum of 20 academic credits is required, including at least 14 in English, math, foreign language, and social and natural sciences. An interview is also recommended. Union requires applicants to be in the upper 50% of their class. A GPA of 2.5 is required. AP and CLEP credits are accepted. Important factors in the admissions decision are leadership record, advanced placement or honors courses, and recommendations by school officials.

Procedure: Freshmen are admitted to all sessions. Entrance exams should be taken in the spring of the junior year. There are early decision, early admissions, deferred admissions, and rolling admissions plans. Application deadlines are open. Application fee is $35. 14 early decision candidates were accepted for the 2013-2014 class. Applications are accepted online.

Transfer: 145 transfer students enrolled in 2012-2013. Candidates must have a minimum GPA of 2.0 in more than 12 semester hours and submit a student transfer form from the last institution attended. 32 of 128 credits required for the bachelor's degree must be completed at Union.

Visiting: There are regularly scheduled orientations for prospective students, including campus tours, class visits, and appointments with counselors. There are guides for informal visits, visitors may sit in on classes, and stay overnight. To schedule a visit, contact Robbie Graves at (731) 661-5590.

Financial Aid: 65% of all full-time freshmen and 63% of continuing full-time students received need-based aid. 35% of undergraduate students work part-time. Average annual earnings from campus work are $1000. The FAFSA and the college's own financial statement are required. Check with the school for current application deadlines.

International Students: There are 40 international students enrolled. The school actively recruits these students. They must take the TOEFL.

Computers: All students may access the system 24/7. There are no time limits and no fees.

Graduates: From July 1, 2012 to June 30, 2013, 640 bachelor's degrees were awarded. The most popular majors were business/marketing (26%), health professions and related science (20%), and education (15%). 47 companies recruited on campus in 2012-2013. In an average class, 4% graduate in 3 years or less, 47% graduate in 4 years or less, 59% graduate in 5 years or less, and 60% graduate in 6 years or less. Of the 2012 graduating class, 40% were enrolled in graduate school within 6 months of graduation, and 78% were employed.

Admissions Contact: Rich Grimm, Vice President for Enrollment Service. E-Mail: *info@uu.edu* Web: *www.uu.edu*

UNIVERSITY OF MEMPHIS A-3

Memphis, TN 38152 **(800) 669-2678**

Full-time: 5185 men, 7543 women
Part-time: 1760 men, 3159 women
Graduate: 1826 men, 2666 women
Year: semesters, summer session
Application Deadline: July 1
Freshman Class: 6798 applied, 4243 accepted, 2252 enrolled
ACT: 23

Faculty: n/av; I, av$
Ph.D.s: 80%
Student/Faculty: n/av
Tuition: $8234 ($23,684)
Room & Board: $6860

COMPETITIVE

The University of Memphis, founded in 1912, is a public metropolitan research university and is part of the Tennessee Board of Regents. There are 7 undergraduate schools and 4 graduate schools. In addition to regional accreditation, U of M has baccalaureate program accreditation with AACSB, ABET, ACEJMC, ADA, ASLA, CAHEA, CSWE, FIDER, NASAD, NASM, NCATE, and NLN. Computerized library services include interlibrary loans, database searching, Internet access, and Wi-Fi capability. Special learning facilities include an art gallery, radio station, TV station, an earthquake research center, a center for electron microscopy, Chucalissa Indian Village and Museum, a speech and hearing center, Center for the Humanities, Institute for Intelligent Systems, Institute of Egyptian Art and Archaeology, Ecological Research Center, and Biological Station. The 1607-acre campus is in an urban area in a residential area of Memphis. Including any residence halls, there are 239 buildings.

Student Life: 90% of undergraduates are from Tennessee. Others are from 44 states, 54 foreign countries, and Canada. 50% are White; 39% African American. The average age of freshmen is 18; all undergraduates, 24.

Housing: 2557 students can be accommodated in college housing, which includes single-sex and coed dorms, on-campus apartments, and married student housing. In addition, there are special-interest houses, fraternity houses, family housing. On-campus housing is guaranteed for all 4 years. 87% of students commute. Alcohol is not permitted. All students may keep cars.

Activities: There are 140 groups on campus, including art, band, cheerleading, chess, choir, chorale, chorus, computers, dance, drama, drill team, environmental, ethnic, film, gay, honors, international, jazz band, literary magazine, marching band, musical theater, newspaper, opera, orchestra, pep band, photography, political, professional, radio and TV, religious, social, social service, student government, and symphony. Popular campus events include Black History Month, Step Shows by Greek organizations, and International Night.

Sports: There are 9 intercollegiate sports for men and 9 for women, and 10 intramural sports for men and 10 for women. Facilities include a gym, a football stadium, a baseball field, swimming pools, a track, a weight room, and tennis, handball, and racquetball courts.

Disabled Students: 95% of the campus is accessible. Facilities include wheelchair ramps, elevators, special parking, specially equipped restrooms, special class scheduling, lowered drinking fountains, lowered telephones, special housing, a transportation service.

Services: Counseling and information services are available, as is tutoring in most subjects. There is a reader service for the blind, and remedial math, reading, and writing.

Campus Safety and Security: Measures include 24-hour foot and vehicle patrol, emergency notification system, and security escort services. There are shuttle buses, emergency telephones, lighted pathways/sidewalks, controlled access to dorms/residences, digital video cameras, a computerized entry system, a gated parking lot, parking lot fences, parking lot security towers, campus safety forums, and a personal safety program.

Programs of Study: U of M confers B.A., B.S., B.B.A., B.F.A., B.L.S., B.M., B.P.S., B.S.B.E., B.S.C.E., B.S.Ch., B.S.C.P., B.S.Ed., B.S.E.E., B.S.E.T., B.S.M.E. and B.S.N. degrees. Master's and doctoral degrees are also awarded. Bachelor's degrees are awarded in BIOLOGICAL SCIENCE (biology/biological science and microbiology), BUSINESS (accounting, banking and finance, business economics, hospitality management services, international business management, logistics, management information systems, management science, marketing management, and recreation and leisure services), COMMUNICATIONS AND THE ARTS (art, art history and appreciation, communications, dramatic arts, English, journalism, languages, music, and music business management), COMPUTER AND PHYSICAL SCIENCE (chemistry, computer science, earth science, mathematics, and physics), EDUCATION (physical education and special education), ENGINEERING AND ENVIRONMENTAL DESIGN (architecture, biomedical engineering, civil engineering, computer engineering, computer technology, electrical/electronics engineering, electrical/electronics engineering technology, engineering technology, manufacturing engineering, and mechanical engineering), HEALTH PROFESSIONS (health science and nursing), SOCIAL SCIENCE (African American studies, anthropology, criminal justice, criminology, economics, geography, history, human development, interdisciplinary studies, international studies, liberal arts/general studies, philosophy, political science/government, psychology, social work, and sociology). Nursing, professional studies, psychology, accounting, teaching all learners, criminology and criminal justice have the largest enrollments.

Required: To graduate, students must complete a minimum of 120 credit hours with a GPA of 2.0 and demonstrate proficiency in computer skills. Requirements include 9 hours of humanities and fine arts with at least 1 literature course, 8 hours of natural science, 6 of English composition, 6 of social and behavioral science, 6 of U.S. history, 3 each of math, and 3 of oral communication.

Special: The university offers co-op programs, dual enrollment, internships, study abroad and domestic student exchange, accelerated degree programs, double and student-designed majors, independent study, distance learning, an external degree program, preprofessional and professional studies programs, teacher certification, ESL, nondegree study, and pass/fail options. Students may receive credit for life, military, and work experience. There are 20 national honor societies, a freshman honors program, and 17 departmental honors programs.

Faculty/Classroom: 53% of faculty are male; 47% are female. No introductory courses are taught by graduate students.

Admissions: 62% of the 2013-2014 applicants were accepted.

Requirements: The ACT is required, with a minimum acceptable composite score of 20. Candidates for admission should be graduates of an accredited secondary school and have 15 academic credits or 20 Carnegie units. The GED is accepted. Academic preparation should include 4 units in English, 3 in math, 2 each in science, social studies, and foreign language, 1 in history, and 1 in visual and performing arts. An interview is required for University College applicants, a portfolio is required for art program applicants, and an audition is required for music applicants. A GPA of 2.0 is required. AP and CLEP credits are accepted. Important factors in the admissions decision are advanced placement or honors courses, evidence of special talent, and recommendations by school officials.

Procedure: Freshmen are admitted fall, spring, and summer. Entrance exams should be taken in the spring of the junior year or October of the senior year. There are deferred admissions and rolling admissions plans. Applications should be filed by July 1 for fall entry; December 1 for spring entry; and May 1 for summer entry. The fall 2013 application fee was $25. Notification is sent on a rolling basis. Applications are accepted online.

Transfer: 1682 transfer students enrolled in 2012-2013. Applicants must have honorable dismissal from the last institution attended and have a cumulative GPA that meets the required minimum established by the Tennessee State Board of Regents. 30 of 120 credits required for the bachelor's degree must be completed at U of M.

Visiting: There are regularly scheduled orientations for prospective students, including daily campus tour programs Monday-Friday and the first Saturday of the month. There are guides for informal visits, visitors may sit in on classes, and stay overnight. To schedule a visit, contact Recruitment and Orientation Services at (800) 669-2678.

Financial Aid: In 2013-2014, 72% of all full-time freshmen and 69% of continuing full-time students received some form of financial aid. 51% of all full-time freshmen and 56% of continuing full-time students received need-based aid. The FAFSA is required. The priority date for freshman financial aid applications for fall entry is March 1. The deadline for filing freshman financial aid applications for fall entry is June 1.

International Students: There are 133 international students enrolled. The school actively recruits these students. They must take the TOEFL with a minimum score of 500 on the paper-based TOEFL (PBT) or 61 on the Internet-based version (iBT). They must also take the SAT or ACT. The minimum score is tied to the applicant's GPA.

Computers: All students may access the system. There are no time limits and no fees.

Graduates: From July 1, 2012 to June 30, 2013, 2724 bachelor's degrees were awarded. The most popular majors were professional studies (9%), nursing (8%), and psychology (6%). In an average class, 13% graduate in 4 years or less, 34% graduate in 5 years or less, and 40% graduate in 6 years or less.

Admissions Contact: Steve McKellips, Director of Admissions. E-Mail: *recruitment@memphis.edu* Web: *www.memphis.edu*

UNIVERSITY OF TENNESSEE SYSTEM

The University of Tennessee System, established in 1794, is a land-grand system in Tennessee. It is governed by a board of trustees, whose chief administrator is the president. The primary goal of the system is to provide a full range of teaching, research, and service programs at all levels. The main priorities are to provide quality learning and research opportunities for students from Tennessee and throughout the country. The total student enrollment for all four campuses is usually 38,500 with 3150 faculty members. Altogether there are 182 baccalaureate, 123 master's, and 62 doctoral programs offered in the University of Tennessee System. Profiles of the 4-year campuses are included in this section.

UNIVERSITY OF TENNESSEE AT CHATTANOOGA D-3

Chattanooga, TN 37403 **(423) 425-4662; (423) 425-4157**

Full-time: 4029 men, 5037 women **Faculty:** 453; IIA, --$
Part-time: 586 men, 645 women **Ph.D.s:** 75%
Graduate: 622 men, 755 women **Student/Faculty:** 18 to 1
Year: semesters, summer session **Tuition:** $7554 ($22,760)
Application Deadline: May 1 **Room & Board:** $9329
Freshman Class: n/av
SAT CR/M: 530/530 **ACT:** 23 **COMPETITIVE**

The University of Tennessee at Chattanooga, founded in 1886, is a public institution. Part of the state's university system, it offers programs in liberal and fine arts, business, engineering, health science, and teacher preparation. There are 4 undergraduate schools and 1 graduate school. In addition to regional accreditation, UTC has baccalaureate program accreditation with AACSB, ABET, ACEJMC, AHEA, APTA, CSWE, NASAD, NASM, NCATE, and NLN. The library contains 613,906 volumes, 111 microform items, 22,619 audio/video tapes/CDs/DVDs, and subscribes to 49,911 periodicals including electronic. Computerized library services include interlibrary loans, database searching, Internet access, and Wi-Fi capability. Special learning facilities include an art gallery, radio station, the Jones Observatory, and Challenger Center. The 417-acre campus is in an urban area 120 miles north of Atlanta. Including any residence halls, there are 85 buildings.

Student Life: 94% of undergraduates are from Tennessee. Others are from 43 states, 40 foreign countries, and Canada. 75% are from public schools. 74% are White; 11% African American. The average age of freshmen is 19; all undergraduates, 22. 31% do not continue beyond their first year; 67% remain to graduate.

Housing: 3146 students can be accommodated in college housing, which includes single-sex on-campus apartments. In addition, there are special-interest houses. On-campus housing is guaranteed for the freshman year only, is available on a first-come, and first-served basis. 69% of students commute. Alcohol is not permitted. All students may keep cars.

Activities: 8% of men belong to 14 national fraternities; 18% of women belong to 10 national sororities. There are 130 groups on campus, including band, cheerleading, chess, choir, chorale, chorus, communications, computers, dance, debate, drama, drill team, environmental, ethnic, film, gay, honors, international, jazz band, literary magazine, marching band, musical theater, newspaper, opera, orchestra, pep band, photography, political, professional, radio and TV, religious, social, social service, student government, and symphony. Popular campus events include Homecoming and Welcome Week.

Sports: There are 7 intercollegiate sports for men and 8 for women, and 9 intramural sports for men and 10 for women. Facilities include an aquatic and recreation center, an arena, a tennis and racquet center, a swimming pool, and 2 fields, including a soccer field.

Disabled Students: 95% of the campus is accessible. Facilities include wheelchair ramps, elevators, special parking, specially equipped restrooms, special class scheduling, lowered drinking fountains, and lowered telephones.

Services: Counseling and information services are available, as is tutoring in most subjects. There is a reader service for the blind, and remedial math, reading, and writing.

Campus Safety and Security: Measures include 24-hour foot and vehicle patrol, emergency notification system, self-defense education, and security escort services. There are shuttle buses, emergency telephones, lighted pathways/sidewalks, and controlled access to dorms/residences.

Programs of Study: UTC confers B.A., B.S., B.F.A., B.M., B.S.E., B.S.E.E., B.S.M.E., B.S.N., B.S.W., B.S.ChE. and B.S.C.E. degrees. Master's and doctoral degrees are also awarded. Bachelor's degrees are awarded in BIOLOGICAL SCIENCE (biology/biological science), BUSINESS (business administration and management and recreation and leisure services), COMMUNICATIONS AND THE ARTS (art, communications, dramatic arts, English, fine arts, French, Greek, Latin, music, and Spanish), COMPUTER AND PHYSICAL SCIENCE (applied mathematics, chemistry, computer science, geology, mathematics, and physics), EDUCATION (art education, early childhood education, education, education of the exceptional child, English education, music education, secondary education, and special education), ENGINEERING AND ENVIRONMENTAL DESIGN (chemical engineering, civil engineering, construction management, electrical/electronics engineering, engineering, engineering management, environmental engineering, environmental science, industrial engineering, interior design, mechanical engineering, and nuclear engineering), HEALTH PROFESSIONS (medical laboratory technology, nursing, and rehabilitation therapy), SOCIAL SCIENCE (criminal justice, economics, history, humanities, paralegal studies, philosophy, political science/government, psychology, social work, and sociology). Education, physical therapy and engineering are the strongest academically. Business, health and human performance, and biology have the largest enrollments.

Required: All students must complete at least 120 semester hours and maintain a minimum GPA of 2.0. General education requirements include 9 hours in humanities and fine arts, 6 hours in English and math, 8 hours in natural sciences, 9 hours in cultures and civilizations, and 6 hours in behavioral and social sciences. Students must complete at least 25% of the minimum credit hours under the direction of UTC faculty, complete 60 credit hours at an accredited senior institution, complete the last 24 credit hours at UTC, and complete at least 39 credit hours at the senior (300-400) level. They must also complete a minimum 12 hours at the senior level in the UTC major department or program offering the degree and also complete the senior exit exam. Other requirements vary by major.

Special: Cooperative programs are offered in accounting, business systems, chemistry, communications, engineering, environmental studies, nursing, and psychology. UTC offers internships, study abroad in England, work-study and accelerated degree programs, B.A.-B.S. degrees, dual majors, interdisciplinary majors, including theater and speech, 3-2 engineering degrees, and nondegree study. Credit is given for life, military, or work experience. There are 33 national honor societies, a freshman honors program, and 29 departmental honors programs.

Faculty/Classroom: 52% of faculty are male; 48% are female. 95% teach undergraduates, 2% do research, and 98% do both. Graduate students teach 1% of introductory courses. The average class size in an introductory lecture is 25 and in a laboratory is 10.

Admissions: The SAT scores for the 2013-2014 freshman class were: Critical Reading--36% below 500, 40% between 500 and 599, 17% between 600 and 699, and 7% between 700 and 800; Math--38% below 500, 40% between 500 and 599, 20% between 600 and 699, and 2% between 700 and 800. The ACT scores were 21% below 21, 37% between 21 and 23, 26% between 24 and 26, 10% between 27 and 28, and 6% above 28.

Requirements: The SAT or ACT is required. Secondary school credits should include 4 in English, 4 in math, 3 in Science with labs, 2 in a consecutive foreign language, and 1 each in social studies, history, and fine arts. The GED is accepted. Applications are accepted online at the school's web site. AP and CLEP credits are accepted.

Procedure: Freshmen are admitted fall and spring. Entrance exams should be taken in spring of the junior year. There are deferred admissions and rolling admissions plans. Applications should be filed by May 1 for fall entry; November 1 for spring entry; and April 15 for summer entry, along with a $30 fee. Applications are accepted online.

Transfer: 914 transfer students enrolled in 2012-2013. Transfer students must have pursued courses appropriate to the curriculum at UTC, be eligible to return to their previous institution, and meet UTC's continuation standards. 24 of 120 credits required for the bachelor's degree must be completed at UTC.

Visiting: There are regularly scheduled orientations for prospective students. There are guides for informal visits, visitors may sit in on classes, and stay overnight. To schedule a visit, contact the Admissions Office at utcmocs@utc.edu.

Financial Aid: In 2013-2014, 65% of all full-time freshmen and 62% of continuing full-time students received some form of financial aid. 63% of all full-time freshmen and 53% of continuing full-time students received need-based aid. The average freshman award was $8,765. Need-based scholarships or need-based grants averaged $8,713; need-based self-help aid (loans and jobs) averaged $3,238; non-need-based athletic scholarships averaged $20,128; and other non-need-based awards and non-need-based scholarships averaged $2,857. The average financial indebtedness of the 2013 graduate was $21,585. The FAFSA is required. The priority date for freshman financial aid applications for fall entry is April 1. The deadline for filing freshman financial aid applications for fall entry is April 1.

International Students: There are 136 international students enrolled. The school actively recruits these students. They must take the TOEFL with a minimum score of 500 on the paper-based TOEFL (PBT) or 61 on the Internet-based version (iBT). They must also take the SAT or ACT if it is available in the student's country.

Computers: All students may access the system. There are no time limits and no fees.

Graduates: From July 1, 2012 to June 30, 2013, 1514 bachelor's degrees were awarded. The most popular majors were business administration (22%), education (11%), and psychology (8%). 32 companies recruited on campus in 2012-2013. In an average class, 15% graduate in 4 years or less, 32% graduate in 5 years or less, and 37% graduate in 6 years or less.

Admissions Contact: Lee Pierce, Director of Admissions. E-Mail: *lee-pierce@utc.edu* Web: *www.utc.edu*

UNIVERSITY OF TENNESSEE AT KNOXVILLE E-2

Knoxville, TN 37996 (865) 974-2184

Full-time: 10013 men, 9648 women **Faculty:** 1324; I, --$
Part-time: 712 men, 660 women **Ph.D.s:** 85%
Graduate: 2938 men, 3200 women **Student/Faculty:** 17 to 1
Year: semesters, summer session **Tuition:** $11,194 ($29,684)
Application Deadline: December 1 **Room & Board:** $9170
Freshman Class: 14398 applied, 9693 accepted, 4207 enrolled
SAT CR/M: 580/590 **ACT:** 27 **VERY COMPETITIVE+**

The University of Tennessee is the state's flagship, land grant public research university. Founded as a private college in 1794, it became the first campus of the University of Tennessee in 1879. Programs are offered through the colleges of Agricultural Sciences and Natural Resources; Architecture and Design; Arts and Sciences; Business Administration; Communication and Information; Education, Health, and Human Sciences; Engineering; Law; Nursing; Social Work; and Veterinary Medicine. There are 9 undergraduate schools and 11 graduate schools. In addition to regional accreditation, UT Knoxville has baccalaureate program accreditation with AACSB, ABET, ACEJMC, ACPE, ADA, ASLA, CAHEA, CSWE, FIDER, NAAB, NASAD, NASM, NCATE, NLN, NRPA, and SAF. The 5 libraries contain 3.1 million volumes, 4.7 million microform items, 80,122 audio/video tapes/CDs/DVDs, and subscribe to 58,765 periodicals including electronic. Computerized library services include interlibrary loans, database searching, Internet access, and Wi-Fi capability. Special learning facilities include an art gallery, natural history museum, radio station, and TV station. The 561-acre campus is in an urban area in Knoxville, TN, Including any residence halls, there are 236 buildings.

Student Life: 89% of undergraduates are from Tennessee. Others are from 50 states, 113 foreign countries, and Canada. 81% are White. The average age of freshmen is 18; all undergraduates, 21. 15% do not continue beyond their first year; 85% remain to graduate.

Housing: 7312 students can be accommodated in college housing, which includes single-sex and coed dorms and on-campus apartments. In addition, there are fraternity houses, sorority houses, Honor students have the opportunity to room together. Floors are dedicated in residence houses for honor and special interest students. On-campus housing is guaranteed for the freshman year only, is available on a first-come, and first-served basis. 63% of students commute. Alcohol is not permitted. All students may keep cars.

Activities: 14% of men belong to 24 national fraternities; 21% of women belong to 18 national sororities. There are 296 groups on campus, including art, band, cheerleading, chess, choir, chorale, chorus, computers, dance, debate, drama, environmental, Environmental Law Association, ethnic, film, gay, honors, international, jazz band, literary magazine, marching band, musical theater, newspaper, opera, orchestra, pep band, photography, political, professional, radio and TV, religious, social, social service, student government, symphony, and yearbook. Popular campus events include All-Sing, Torch Night, International Festival, Volapalooza, Vol Night Long, Dance Marathon, Carnius, and Football and Basketball Games.

Sports: There are 9 intercollegiate sports for men and 11 for women, and 50 intramural sports for men and 50 for women. Facilities include a 21,700 seat basketball arena and state-of-the-art basketball practice facility, the third largest collegiate football stadium in the United Sates, an Olympic track, Olympic indoor and outdoor pools, various outdoor facilities, a baseball stadium, and softball and soccer fields.

Disabled Students: 95% of the campus is accessible. Facilities include wheelchair ramps, elevators, special parking, specially equipped restrooms, special class scheduling, lowered drinking fountains, lowered telephones, special housing.

Services: Counseling and information services are available, as is tutoring in some subjects. There is a reader service for the blind. Supplemental instruction in math and chemistry, tutoring in English, math, chemistry and most lower division courses.

Campus Safety and Security: Measures include 24-hour foot and vehicle patrol, emergency notification system, self-defense education, and security escort services. There are shuttle buses, emergency telephones, lighted pathways/sidewalks, campus safety educational programs.

Programs of Study: UT Knoxville confers B.A., B.S., B.Arch., B.F.A., B.M., B.S.ArtEd., B.S.Ag.E., BSAN, BSFS, B.S.F., B.S.P.S., BSID, B.S.C., B.S.B.A., B.A.C., B.S.H.S., B.S.Ed., B.S.Ch.E., B.S.C.E., BSCOME, B.S.C.S., B.S.E.E., B.S.I.E., B.S.A.E., BSBME, B.S.M.E., B.S.N. and B.S.S.W. degrees. Master's and doctoral degrees are also awarded. Bachelor's degrees are awarded in AGRICULTURE (agricultural economics, agriculture, animal science, forestry and related sciences, natural resources, plant science, and soil science), BIOLOGICAL SCIENCE (biology/biological science, nutrition, and wildlife biology), BUSINESS (accounting, business systems analysis, finance, hotel/motel and restaurant management, human resources, logistics, management science, retailing, and sports management), COMMUNICATIONS AND THE ARTS (advertising, art history, art, classics, communications, English, French, German, graphic design, Italian, journalism, music, public relations, Russian, studio art, and theatre arts), COMPUTER AND PHYSICAL SCIENCE (chemistry, computer science, geology, mathematics, physics, and statistics), EDUCATION (education, health information management, marketing and distribution education, recreation education, and special education), ENGINEERING AND ENVIRONMENTAL DESIGN (aerospace studies, architecture, biomedical engineering, chemical engineering, civil engineering, computer engineering, electrical/electronics engineering, environmental science, industrial engineering, interior design, materials engineering, mechanical engineering, and nuclear engineering), HEALTH PROFESSIONS (clinical science, dental hygiene, medical technology, nursing, predentistry, premedicine, prepharmacy, and preveterinary science), SOCIAL SCIENCE (anthropology, child care/child and family studies, economics, food science, geography, Hispanic American studies, history, interdisciplinary studies, philosophy, political science/government, psychology, public administration, religion, social work, and sociology). Engineering, business, nursing, and education are the strongest academically. Logistics, accounting, and psychology have the largest enrollments.

Required: All students must complete at least 120 credits with a minimum 2.0 GPA. Students must take 3 courses in communicating through writing: 1 course in oral communication, 2 courses in quantitative reasoning, 8 courses to develop broadening perspectives: 2 in Natural Sciences, 2 in Arts and Humanities, 2 in Social Sciences, and 2 in Cultures and Civilizations.

Special: Students can design a wide variety of interdisciplinary majors through the College of Arts and Sciences. Honors programs exist within several colleges. University-wide honors programs include the Baker Scholars, Haslam Scholars and Chancellor's Honors Programs. The university offers many dual graduate and professional degrees that include law and business, public administration and law, business and engineering, and recreation and sport management and business. New graduate programs include a master's in landscape architecture, a master's in public health, a master's in business analytics, a doctorate in energy science and engineering, a doctorate of nursing practice, and a doctorate in social work. Study-abroad programs are offered in more than fifty-nine countries. There are 27 national honor societies, including Phi Beta Kappa, and a freshman honors program.

Faculty/Classroom: 58% of faculty are male; 42% are female. 76% teach undergraduates. No introductory courses are taught by graduate students.

Admissions: 67% of the 2013-2014 applicants were accepted. The SAT scores for the 2013-2014 freshman class were: Critical Reading--12% below 500, 46% between 500 and 599, 32% between 600 and 699, and 10% between 700 and 800; Math--12% below 500, 39% between 500 and 599, 38% between 600 and 699, and 10% between 700 and 800. The ACT scores were 12% between 21 and 23, 22% between 24 and 26, 9% between 27 and 28, and 22% above 28. There were 20 National Merit finalists.

Requirements: The SAT or ACT is required. Applicants should be high school graduates or have the GED. Required secondary school courses include 4 credits in English, 4 in math, 3 in science, and 2 foreign language, 1 each in history, social studies, and visual/performing arts. A GPA of 2.0 is required. AP and CLEP credits are accepted. Important factors in the admissions decision are advanced placement or honors courses, evidence of special talent, and extracurricular activities record.

Procedure: Freshmen are admitted to all sessions. Entrance exams should be taken in spring of the junior yearor fall of the senior year. Applications should be filed by December 1 for fall entry; November 1 for spring entry; and December 1 for summer entry, along with a $40 fee. Notifications are sent March 31. 2051 applicants were on the 2013 waiting list; 19 were admitted. Applications are accepted online.

Transfer: 1218 transfer students enrolled in 2012-2013. Transfer applicants should present a minimum 2.0 GPA in previous college work, although many specific programs have higher requirements. Transfer applicants must have completed a minimum of 15 transferable college credits by the date they apply. 30 of 120 credits required for the bachelor's degree must be completed at UT Knoxville.

Visiting: There are regularly scheduled orientations for prospective students, including 2 open houses yearly where prospective students can meet with faculty, administrators, and students to discuss admissions, housing, financial aid, and student activities. There are guides for informal visits and visitors may sit in on classes.

Financial Aid: In 2013-2014, 61% of all full-time freshmen and 58% of continuing full-time students received some form of financial aid. 59% of all full-time freshmen and 52% of continuing full-time students received need-based aid. The average freshman award was $12,866. Need-based scholarships or need-based grants averaged $10,391 ($40,196 maximum); need-based self-help aid (loans and jobs) averaged $4,705 ($40,196 maximum); non-need-based athletic scholarships averaged $12,747 ($42,055 maximum); and other non-need-based awards and non-need-based scholarships averaged $2,783 ($14,850 maximum). 15% of undergraduate students work part-time. Average annual earnings from campus work are $7063. The average financial indebtedness of the 2013 graduate was $22,860. The FAFSA is required. The priority date for freshman financial aid applications for fall entry is March 1.

International Students: There are 385 international students enrolled. The school actively recruits these students. They must take the TOEFL with a minimum score of 523 on the paper-based TOEFL (PBT) or 70 on the Internet-based version (iBT)

Computers: All students may access the system. There are no time limits and no fees.

Graduates: From July 1, 2012 to June 30, 2013, 4771 bachelor's degrees were awarded. The most popular majors were psychology (10%), political science (5%), and logistic/transportation (5%). 527 companies recruited on campus in 2012-2013. In an average class, 36% graduate in 4 years or less, 62% graduate in 5 years or less, and 66% graduate in 6 years or less. Of the 2012 graduating class, 12% were enrolled in graduate school within 6 months of graduation, and 86% were employed.

Admissions Contact: Tom Broadhead, Director of Admissions. E-Mail: *admissions@utk.edu* Web: *www.utk.edu*

UNIVERSITY OF TENNESSEE AT MARTIN B-1

Martin, TN 38238 **(731) 587-7020**
(800) 829-8861; (731) 587-7029

Full-time: 2605 men, 3322 women	**Faculty:** 292
Part-time: 373 men, 725 women	**Ph.D.s:** 74%
Graduate: 128 men, 270 women	**Student/Faculty:** 17 to 1
Year: semesters, summer session	**Tuition:** $7507 ($21,451)
Application Deadline: open	**Room & Board:** $5710

Freshman Class: 3640 applied, 2791 accepted, 1308 enrolled
ACT: 22

COMPETITIVE

UT Martin is a primary campus in the University of Tennessee System and is known for providing high-quality undergraduate and graduate academic programs. From the founding in 1900 of Hall-Moody Institute, through the establishment in 1927 of UT Junior College, to today's status as a comprehensive public university. There are 5 undergraduate schools and 4 graduate schools. In addition to regional accreditation, UT Martin has baccalaureate program accreditation with AACSB, ABET, ACEJMC, ADA, AHEA, CSWE, NASM, NCATE, and NLN. The library contains 379,072 volumes, 709,966 microform items, and 17,122 audio/video tapes/CDs/DVDs. Computerized library services include interlibrary loans, database searching, Internet access, and Wi-Fi capability. Special learning facilities include a natural history museum, radio station, TV station, a teacher resource center, a 680-acre agriculture and natural resources teaching and demonstration complex, a teaching/research facility at Reelfoot Lake State Resort, and a center for global studies and international education. The 250-acre campus is in a rural area 125 miles northeast of Memphis and 150 miles northwest of Nashville. Including any residence halls, there are 49 buildings.

Student Life: 94% of undergraduates are from Tennessee. Others are from 41 states, 17 foreign countries, and Canada. 91% are from public schools. 77% are White; 16% African American. 73% are Protestant. The average age of freshmen is 19; all undergraduates, 23. 30% do not continue beyond their first year; 47% remain to graduate.

Housing: 2382 students can be accommodated in college housing, which includes single-sex and coed dorms, on-campus apartments, and married student housing. In addition, there are honors houses and special-interest houses. On-campus housing is guaranteed for all 4 years, is available on a first-come, and first-served basis. 70% of students commute. Alcohol is not permitted. All students may keep cars.

Activities: 5% of men belong to 13 national fraternities; 10% of women belong to 1 local and 9 national sororities. There are 175 groups on campus, including art, band, cheerleading, choir, chorale, chorus, computers, dance, drama, drill team, environmental, ethnic, film, gay, honors, international, jazz band, literary magazine, marching band, musical theater, newspaper, opera, pep band, photography, political, professional, radio and TV, religious, social, social service, student government, and yearbook. Popular campus events include Greekfest, Homecoming and Pyramid.

Sports: There are 7 intercollegiate sports for men and 10 for women, and 11 intramural sports for men and 11 for women. Facilities include an Olympic-size swimming pool. 7 racquetball courts, a running/walking track, a weight room, 6 basketball, volleyball, badminton and tennis court combinations, and outdoor: a 1.5 mile fitness track, 16 tennis courts, a soccer field, and lighted intramural playing fields.

Disabled Students: All of the campus is accessible. Facilities include wheelchair ramps, elevators, special parking, specially equipped restrooms, special class scheduling, lowered drinking fountains, lowered telephones, and special housing.

Services: Counseling and information services are available, as is tutoring in some subjects including astronomy, biology, chemistry,computer science, English, French, geography, geology, German, history, Japanese, math, psychology, and Spanish.

Campus Safety and Security: Measures include 24-hour foot and vehicle patrol, emergency notification system, and self-defense education. There are emergency telephones, lighted pathways/sidewalks, a bicycle patrol, security cameras in the 4 largest residence halls, Auto-Dialer Alert system, text messaging alert system, and severe weather siren alert system.

Programs of Study: UT Martin confers B.A., B.S., B.A.Mus., B.F.A., B.Mus., B.S.Agri., B.S.Bus.Admn., B.S.Chem., B.S.Crim.Just., B.S.Ed., B.S.Eng., B.S.Fam.C.S., B.S.Health/HP., B.S.N.R.M., B.S.N., B.S.S.W. and B.U.S. degrees. Master's degrees are also awarded. Bachelor's degrees are awarded in AGRICULTURE (agricultural business management, agriculture, animal science, natural resource management, and plant science), BIOLOGICAL SCIENCE (biology/biological science and nutrition), BUSINESS (accounting, business administration and management, business economics, management science, and marketing/retailing/ merchandising), COMMUNICATIONS AND THE ARTS (communications, English, fine arts, French, music, performing arts, and Spanish), COMPUTER AND PHYSICAL SCIENCE (chemistry, computer science, geology, information sciences and systems, and mathematics), EDUCATION (education administration, elementary education, secondary education, and special education), ENGINEERING AND ENVIRONMENTAL DESIGN (engineering), HEALTH PROFESSIONS (health science and nursing), SOCIAL SCIENCE (child care/child and family studies, criminal justice, economics, geography, history, international studies, philosophy, political science/government, psychology, public administration, social work, and sociology). Preprofessional health programs, biology, and engineering are the strongest academically. Agriculture, health and human performance, integrated studies have the largest enrollments.

Required: The number of credit hours required for graduation ranges from 120 to 134 (based on degree). All students must have at least a 2.0 GPA. Specific courses and major requirements vary by the program selected. There is a 1 year or 30 hour UTM residency requirement. The general education core curriculum is 38 hours; English and communications courses are required. Major field and general education tests are required.

Special: UTM offers co-op programs in engineering, agriculture, computer science, business, and chemistry, for-credit internships, cross-registration through the Gulf Coast consortium, study abroad, B.A.-B.S. degrees, dual and student-designed majors, and pass/fail options. There are 11 national honor societies, a freshman honors program, and 6 departmental honors programs.

Faculty/Classroom: 53% of faculty are male; 47% are female. All teach undergraduates, 84% do research, and 84% do both. No introductory courses are taught by graduate students. The average class size in an introductory lecture is 24; in a laboratory is 16; and in a regular course is 18.

Admissions: 77% of the 2013-2014 applicants were accepted. The ACT scores were 34% below 21, 28% between 21 and 23, 19% between 24 and 26, 6% between 27 and 28, and 12% above 28. 49% of the current freshmen were in the top fifth of their class; 80% were in the top two fifths. 19 freshmen graduated first in their class.

Requirements: The ACT is required. Students should have a minimum composite score of 21 on the ACT with a 2.50 minimum GPA, or 18 on the ACT with a minimum 2.85 GPA. Candidates for admission should be graduates of an accredited secondary school with 14 academic credits. The GED is accepted with a score of 500. Secondary school units should include 4 of English, 3 of math, 2 of a foreign language, and 1 each of science, history, social studies, and fine and performing arts. A GPA of 2.5 is required. AP and CLEP credits are accepted.

Procedure: Freshmen are admitted to all sessions. Entrance exams should be taken by the spring of the junior year. There are deferred admissions and rolling admissions plans. Application deadlines are open. Application fee is $30. Notification is sent on a rolling basis. Applications are accepted online.

Transfer: 543 transfer students enrolled in 2012-2013. Transfer students should have a minimum GPA of 2.0. 30 of 120 credits required for the bachelor's degree must be completed at UT Martin.

Visiting: There are regularly scheduled orientations for prospective students, Campus visits include Summer Orientation and Registration (SOAR); 4 sessions conducted for students and parents that include information sessions and class registration. There are guides for informal visits, visitors may sit in on classes, and stay overnight. To schedule a visit, contact the Admissions Office at (800) 829-8861.

Financial Aid: In 2013-2014, 92% of all full-time freshmen and 89% of continuing full-time students received some form of financial aid. 56% of all full time freshmen and 54% of continuing full-time students received need-based aid. The average freshman award was $13,655. Need-based scholarships or need-based grants averaged $6,695 ($9,954 maximum); need-based self-help aid (loans and jobs) averaged $3,376; non-need-based athletic scholarships averaged $10,506; and other non-need-based awards and non-need-based scholarships averaged $2,046 ($2,956 maximum). 39% of undergraduate students work part-time. Average annual earnings from campus work are $2147. The average financial indebtedness of the 2013 graduate was $23,840. The FAFSA is required. The priority date for freshman financial aid applications for fall entry is March 1.

International Students: There are 140 international students enrolled.

The school actively recruits these students. They must take the TOEFL with a minimum score of 500 on the paper-based TOEFL (PBT) or 61 on the Internet-based version (iBT).

Computers: All students may access the system 24 hours. There are no time limits and no fees.

Graduates: From July 1, 2012 to June 30, 2013, 1248 bachelor's degrees were awarded. The most popular majors were business/marketing (17%), interdisciplinary studies (13%), and education (12%). 62 companies recruited on campus in 2012-2013. In an average class, 21% graduate in 4 years or less, 40% graduate in 5 years or less, and 46% graduate in 6 years or less. Of the 2012 graduating class, 25% were enrolled in graduate school within 6 months of graduation, and 68% were employed.

Admissions Contact: Judy Rayburn, Director of Admissions. E-Mail: *jrayburn@utm.edu* Web: *www.utm.edu*

VANDERBILT UNIVERSITY C-2

Nashville, TN 37203 (615) 322-2561
(800) 288-0432; (615) 343-7765

Full-time: 3387 men, 3377 women	**Faculty:** n/av; I, av$
Part-time: 42 men, 29 women	**Ph.D.s:** 96%
Graduate: 2546 men, 3376 women	**Student/Faculty:** 8 to 1
Year: semesters, summer session	**Tuition:** $42,978
Application Deadline: January 3	**Room & Board:** $14,094

Freshman Class: 31099 applied, 3963 accepted, 1613 enrolled
SAT or ACT: required

MOST COMPETITIVE

Vanderbilt University, founded in 1873, is a private university offering programs in liberal and fine arts, business, engineering, health science, religion, law, music, and teacher preparation. There are 4 undergraduate schools and 6 graduate schools. In addition to regional accreditation, Vanderbilt has baccalaureate program accreditation with AACSB, ABET, CAHEA, and NCATE. The 9 libraries contain 2.9 million volumes, 3.0 million microform items, and 63,403 audio/video tapes/CDs/DVDs, and subscribe to 29,173 periodicals including electronic. Computerized library services include interlibrary loans and database searching. Special learning facilities include an art gallery, TV station, two observatories, and a TV news archive. The 330-acre campus is in an urban area in Nashville. Including any residence halls, there are 217 buildings.

Student Life: 88% of undergraduates are from out of state, mostly the South. Students are from 50 states, 53 foreign countries, and Canada. 64% are from public schools. 60% are White. The average age of freshmen is 18; all undergraduates, 20. 3% do not continue beyond their first year; 92% remain to graduate.

Housing: 5500 students can be accommodated in college housing, which includes single-sex and coed dorms, on-campus apartments, and married student housing. In addition, there are language houses and special-interest houses. On-campus housing is guaranteed for the freshman year only, is available on a first-come, first-served basis, and is available on a lottery system for upperclassmen. Priority is given to out-of-town students. 86% of students live on campus. Upperclassmen may keep cars.

Activities: 30% of men belong to 18 national fraternities; 55% of women belong to 16 national sororities. There are 705 groups on campus, including art, band, cheerleading, chess, choir, chorale, chorus, computers, dance, debate, drama, drill team, environmental, ethnic, film, gay, honors, international, jazz band, literary magazine, marching band, musical theater, newspaper, opera, orchestra, pep band, photography, political, professional, radio and TV, religious, social, social service, student government, symphony, video production., and yearbook. Popular campus events include Rites of Spring, Blue Fest and IMPACT Speakers Series.

Sports: There are 6 intercollegiate sports for men and 9 for women, and 45 intramural sports for men and 44 for women. Facilities include a gym, a pool, football and intramural fields, indoor football field, student recreation and tennis centers, basketball and racquetball courts, a suspended indoor track, and a climbing wall.

Disabled Students: 90% of the campus is accessible. Facilities include wheelchair ramps, elevators, special parking, specially equipped restrooms, special class scheduling, lowered drinking fountains, and lowered telephones.

Services: Counseling and information services are available, as is tutoring in most subjects. There is a reader service for the blind.

Campus Safety and Security: Measures include 24-hour foot and vehicle patrol, emergency notification system, self-defense education, and security escort services. There are shuttle buses, emergency telephones, lighted pathways/sidewalks, a bicycle patrol, and student dorm monitors.

Programs of Study: Vanderbilt confers B.A., and B.S. degrees. Master's and doctoral degrees are also awarded. Bachelor's degrees are awarded in BIOLOGICAL SCIENCE (biology/biological science and molecular biology), COMMUNICATIONS AND THE ARTS (classical languages, classics, communications, English, fine arts, French, German, music history and appreciation, music performance, music theory and composition, Russian, Spanish, and theater design), COMPUTER AND PHYSICAL SCIENCE (chemistry, geology, mathematics, and physics), EDUCATION (early childhood education, education, elementary education, secondary education, and special education), ENGINEERING AND ENVIRONMENTAL DESIGN (bioengineering, chemical engineering, civil engineering, computer engineering, electrical/electronics engineering, engineering and applied science, and mechanical engineering), SOCIAL SCIENCE (African American studies, American studies, anthropology, child psychology/development, cognitive science, East Asian studies, economics, European studies, history, human development, interdisciplinary studies, Latin American studies, philosophy, political science/government, psychology, public affairs, religion, sociology, and urban studies). Social science, engineering, and education have the largest enrollments.

Required: All students must take at least 120 total credit hours. General requirements vary, as do specific major requirements, depending on the chosen program. A minimum GPA of 2.0 is usually needed. There is a mandatory writing requirement. Students majoring in human development must complete an internship in the fall semester of the senior year.

Special: Vanderbilt offers cross-registration with Fisk and Howard Universities and Meharry Medical College, study abroad in 18 countries, a Washington semester, a work-study program, B.A.-B.S. degrees, dual and student-designed majors, accelerated degree programs, nondegree study, and pass/fail options. Internships, required for human development majors, are available in human service agencies, city and state government, and businesses. A 3-2 engineering degree is offered with Fisk University. The school belongs to NASA's Tennessee Space Grant Consortium, and the Intercollegiate Center for Classical Studies in Rome. There are 19 national honor societies, including Phi Beta Kappa, a freshman honors program, and 21 departmental honors programs.

Faculty/Classroom: 63% of faculty are male; 37% are female. No introductory courses are taught by graduate students. The average class size in an introductory lecture is 20; in a laboratory is 31; and in a regular course is 19.

Admissions: 13% of the 2013-2014 applicants were accepted. The SAT scores for the 2013-2014 freshman class were: Critical Reading--2% below 500, 3% between 500 and 599, 19% between 600 and 699, and 76% between 700 and 800; Math--1% below 500, 4% between 500 and 599, 15% between 600 and 699, and 80% between 700 and 800; Writing--1% below 500, 5% between 500 and 599, 27% between 600 and 699, and 67% between 700 and 800. The ACT scores were 1% below 21, 1% between 21 and 23, 2% between 24 and 26, 34% between 27 and 28, and 62% above 28. 94% of the current freshmen were in the top fifth of their class; 97% were in the top two fifths. There were 286 National Merit finalists. 99 freshmen graduated first in their class.

Requirements: The SAT or ACT is required. SAT Subject tests are recommended in math level I, II, or IIc, writing, and foreign language. Admission requirements vary by school. Candidates should be graduates of an accredited secondary school with a minimum of 15 academic credits. Most programs require 4 years of English, 3 of math, and 2 of a foreign language and recommend 2 of history and 1 of social studies. An essay is required. An audition is required for Blair School of Music. AP credits are accepted. Important factors in the admissions decision are advanced placement or honors courses, extracurricular activities record, and evidence of special talent.

Procedure: Freshmen are admitted fall. Entrance exams should be taken Spring of the junior year or the fall of the senior year. There are early decision and deferred admissions plans. Early decision applications should be filed by November 1; regular applications, by January 3 for fall entry, along with a $50 fee. Notification of early decision is sent December 15; regular decision, April 1. 687 early decision candidates were accepted for the 2013-2014 class. Applications are accepted online.

Transfer: 206 transfer students enrolled in 2012-2013. Transfers must take the SAT or the ACT. A minimum of 12 hours of college credit must have been earned. Students must meet all freshman requirements and be in good standing at the previous institution attended. Applicants must submit high school and college transcripts and an essay or personal statement. 60 of 120 credits required for the bachelor's degree must be completed at Vanderbilt.

Visiting: There are regularly scheduled orientations for prospective students, including group information sessions and campus tours available Monday through Saturday during the academic year and Monday through Friday during the summer. Schedules vary, so visitors must call in advance. There are guides for informal visits, visitors may sit in on classes, and stay overnight. To schedule a visit, contact the Office of Undergraduate Admissions.

Financial Aid: In 2013-2014, 53% of all full-time freshmen and 49% of continuing full-time students received some form of financial aid. 48% of all full-time freshmen and 45% of continuing full-time students received need-based aid. The average freshman award was $45,413. Need-based scholarships or need-based grants averaged $39,784; need-based self-help aid (loans and jobs) averaged $2,405; non-need-based athletic scholarships averaged $44,311; and other non-need-based awards and non-need-based scholarships averaged $18,797. The average financial indebtedness of the 2013 graduate was $20,303. The CSS/Profile FAFSA, and tax return information are required. The priority date for freshman financial aid applications for fall entry is February 1. The deadline for filing freshman financial aid applications for fall entry is January 3.

International Students: There are 405 international students enrolled. The school actively recruits these students. They must take the TOEFL. They must also take the SAT or ACT.

Computers: All students may access the system any time. There are no time limits and no fees.

Graduates: From July 1, 2012 to June 30, 2013, 1671 bachelor's degrees were awarded. The most popular majors were social sciences (28%), engineering (13%), and interdisciplinary studies (8%). 250 companies recruited on campus in 2012-2013. In an average class, 87% graduate in 4 years or less, 92% graduate in 5 years or less, and 93% graduate in 6 years or less.

Admissions Contact: Admissions Officer E-Mail: *admissions@vanderbilt.edu* Web: *www.vanderbilt.edu*

VICTORY UNIVERSITY A-3

Memphis, TN 38111 (901) 320-9797
(800) 960-9777; (901) 320-9791

Full-time: 200 men, 386 women	**Faculty:** 39
Part-time: 139 men, 282 women	**Ph.D.s:** 56%
Graduate: n/av	**Student/Faculty:** 15 to 1
Year: semesters, summer session	**Tuition:** $11,136
Application Deadline: open	**Room & Board:** $7982
Freshman Class: n/av	
ACT: required	

COMPETITIVE

Victory University, formerly Crichton College, founded in 1941, is an independent Christian liberal arts college offering programs in liberal arts, Bible, business, health science, religion, and teacher preparation. The figures in the above capsule and in this profile are approximate. There are 6 undergraduate schools. In addition to regional accreditation, has baccalaureate program accreditation with NCATE. The library contains 49,855 volumes, 12,519 microform items, and 2,210 audio/video tapes/CDs/DVDs, and subscribes to 174 periodicals including electronic. Computerized library services include interlibrary loans, database searching, and Internet access. The 7-acre campus is in an urban area Memphis, TN. Including any residence halls, there is 1 building.

Student Life: 87% of undergraduates are from Tennessee. Others are from 15 states, 13 foreign countries, and Canada. 68% are African American; 24% White. The average age of freshmen is 21; all undergraduates, 30. 40% do not continue beyond their first year; 33% remain to graduate.

Housing: 153 students can be accommodated in college housing, which includes single-sex off-campus apartments. On-campus housing is guaranteed for all 4 years. 85% of students commute. Alcohol is not permitted. All students may keep cars.

Activities: There are no fraternities or sororities. There are 14 groups on campus, including and Alpha Sigma Lambda, Chi Psi Psychology Club, Crichton Christian Fellowship, Presidential Ambassadors, Psalmos, Science Association, SIFE (Students in Free Enterprise), Sigma Alpha Lambda, Society for HR Management, choir, dance, drama, forensics, honors, international, professional, religious, Sigma Beta Delta (Business Honors Society), social, and student government. Popular campus events include Coffee House, Film Series, and Perkins Lecture Series.

Sports: There are 5 intercollegiate sports for men and 5 for women, and 2 intramural sports for men and 2 for women. Facilities include a campus gym, student center, and membership at local gym.

Disabled Students: All of the campus is accessible. Facilities include wheelchair ramps, elevators, special parking, specially equipped restrooms, lowered drinking fountains, and lowered telephones.

Services: Counseling and information services are available, as is tutoring in most subjects. There is remedial math, reading, and writing.

Campus Safety and Security: Measures include security escort services. There are shuttle buses and lighted pathways/sidewalks.

Programs of Study: confers B.A., and B.S. degrees. Bachelor's degrees are awarded in BIOLOGICAL SCIENCE (biology/biological science), BUSINESS (business administration and management), COMMUNICATIONS AND THE ARTS (English), COMPUTER AND PHYSICAL SCIENCE (chemistry), EDUCATION (education, elementary education, middle school education, science education, and secondary education), HEALTH PROFESSIONS (biomedical science), SOCIAL SCIENCE (biblical studies, history, interdisciplinary studies, liberal arts/general studies, prelaw, psychology, and youth ministry). Business management, elementary education, and psychology have the largest enrollments.

Required: Students must complete a minimum of 120 credit hours, and some disciplines requiring more. The number of hours for the major varies from 48 to 66. The minimum GPA required ito graduate is 2.0, except for teacher education students, who must have a 2.5.

Special: B.A.-B.S. degrees, dual majors, and limited nondegree study are available. The college also offers work study, internships with area businesses and institutions, a study-abroad program through the Best Semester. Accelerated degrees in business administration, psychology, and education are also available. There are 2 national honor societies, a freshman honors program, and 1 departmental honors programs.

Faculty/Classroom: 64% of faculty are male; 36% are female. All teach undergraduates. No introductory courses are taught by graduate students. The average class size in an introductory lecture is 15; in a laboratory is 12; and in a regular course is 17.

Requirements: The ACT is required. Students must have a minimum composite score of 19 on the ACT or 900 combined on the SAT Critical Reading and Math sections. Students must have a high school diploma or hold the GED. A GPA of 2.0 is required. AP and CLEP credits are accepted. Important factors in the admissions decision are advanced placement or honors courses, evidence of special talent, and leadership record.

Procedure: Freshmen are admitted to all sessions. Entrance exams should be taken prior to the beginning of each term. There are deferred admissions and rolling admissions plans. Application deadlines are open. Application fee is $25. Notification is sent on a rolling basis. Applications are accepted online.

Transfer: 225 transfer students enrolled in 2012-2013. Transfer students must have a minimum GPA of 2.0. All transfer students must submit to a COMPASS writing placement test for English placement regardless of previous coursework taken at any other college or university. 32 of 120 credits required for the bachelor's degree must be completed at Victory.

Visiting: There are regularly scheduled orientations for prospective students, a tour and fun activities. There are guides for informal visits, visitors may sit in on classes, and stay overnight. To schedule a visit, contact the Admissions Office.

Financial Aid: In 2013-2014, 93% of all full-time freshmen and 91% of continuing full-time students received some form of financial aid. 93% of all full-time freshmen and 91% of continuing full-time students received need-based aid. The average freshman award was $11,414. Need-based scholarships or need-based grants averaged $3,184 ($4,644 maximum); need-based self-help aid (loans and jobs) averaged $3,422 ($4,500 maximum); non-need-based athletic scholarships averaged $4,490 ($19,734 maximum); and other non-need-based awards and non-need-based scholarships averaged $4,264 ($10,059 maximum). The FAFSA and the college's own financial statement are required. The priority date for freshman financial aid applications for fall entry is April 1. The deadline for filing freshman financial aid applications for fall entry is July 1.

International Students: There are 21 international students enrolled. The school actively recruits these students. They must take the TOEFL with a minimum score of 500 on the paper-based TOEFL (PBT). They must also take the SAT or ACT, scoring 19.

Computers: All students may access the system 24 hours a day, 7 days a week. There are no time limits and no fees.

Graduates: From July 1, 2012 to June 30, 2013, 150 bachelor's degrees were awarded. The most popular majors were business administration (58%), Biblical studies (16%), and education (13%). 12 companies recruited on campus in 2012-2013. In an average class, 12% graduate in 4 years or less, 18% graduate in 5 years or less, and 33% graduate in 6 years or less.

Admissions Contact: Ashley Burns, Director of Admissions. E-Mail: *info@victory.edu* Web: *www.victory.edu*

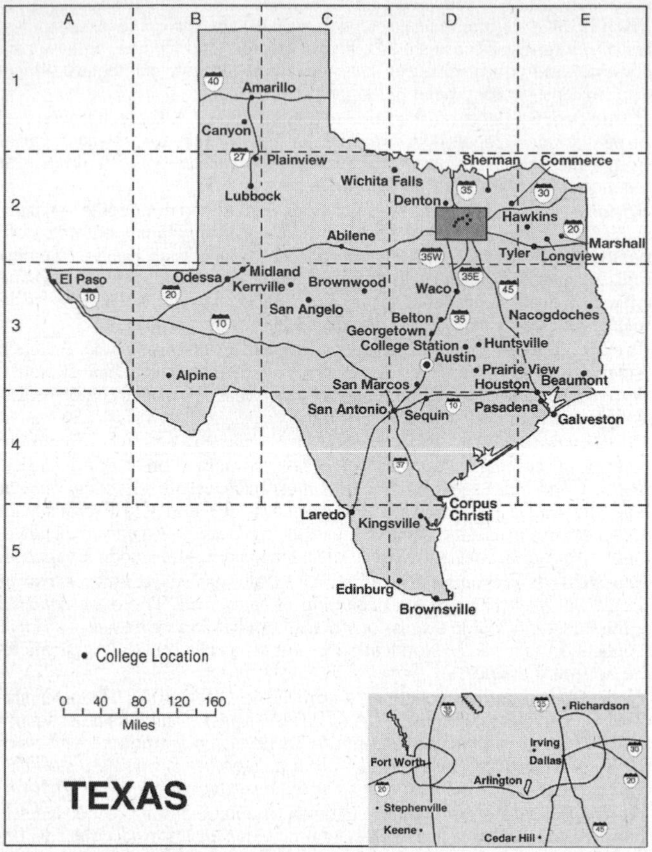

ABILENE CHRISTIAN UNIVERSITY C-2

Abilene, TX 79699 (325) 674-2650
(800) 460-6228; (325) 674-2130

Full-time: 1500 men, 2010 women
Part-time: 99 men, 118 women
Graduate: 294 men, 440 women
Year: semesters, summer session
Application Deadline: February 15
Faculty: 222; IIA, -$
Ph.D.s: 79%
Student/Faculty: 14 to 1
Tuition: $28,350
Room & Board: $8800
Freshman Class: 10188 applied, 4986 accepted, 1030 enrolled
SAT CR/M/W: 532/547/511 **ACT:** 24 **VERY COMPETITIVE**

Abilene Christian University is a selective four-year private Christian university. ACU is the best at providing exceptional academics in a Christ-centered community. It includes the colleges of Arts and Sciences, Biblical Studies, Business Administration, Education and Human Services, and Honors; the Graduate School; the Graduate School of Theology; the School of Information Technology and Computing; the School of Social Work; and the School of Nursing. ACU is affiliated with the Churches of Christ and is one of the largest private universities in the Southwest. There are 8 undergraduate schools and 6 graduate schools. In addition to regional accreditation, ACU has baccalaureate program accreditation with AACSB, ACEJMC, CSWE, FIDER, NASM, and TEAC. The library contains 558,009 volumes, 1.2 million microform items, 66,358 audio/video tapes/CDs/DVDs, and subscribes to 42,083 periodicals including electronic. Computerized library services include interlibrary loans, database searching, Internet access, and Wi-Fi capability. Special learning facilities include an art gallery, planetarium, radio station, TV station, learning commons, writing center, speaking center, AT&T learning studio, maker lab, center for Christian service and leadership, a converged media newsroom, demonstration farm and ranch, and center for restoration studies. The 208-acre campus is in a small town 150 miles west of the Dallas-Fort Worth metroplex. Including any residence halls, there are 46 buildings.

Student Life: 84% of undergraduates are from Texas. Others are from 49 states, 43 foreign countries, and Canada. 64% are from public schools. 69% are White; 11% Hispanic. 48% are Protestant. The average age of freshmen is 18; all undergraduates, 20. 25% do not continue beyond their first year; 60% remain to graduate.

Housing: 1856 students can be accommodated in college housing, which includes single-sex dorms, on-campus apartments, and married student housing. On-campus housing is available on a first-come, first-served basis, and is available on a lottery system for upperclassmen. 52% of students commute. Alcohol is not permitted. All students may keep cars.

Activities: 24% of men belong to 6 local fraternities; 25% of women belong to 5 local sororities. There are 95 groups on campus, including art, band, cheerleading, chess, choir, chorale, chorus, computers, debate, drama, environmental, ethnic, film, forensics, gay, honors, international, jazz band, literary magazine, marching band, musical theater, newspaper, opera, orchestra, photography, political, professional, radio and TV, religious, social, social service, steel drum band., student government, and symphony. Popular campus events include Sing Song Festival, Bible Lectures and Freshman Follies.

Sports: There are 7 intercollegiate sports for men and 7 for women, and 12 intramural sports for men and 12 for women. Facilities include Student Recreation and Wellness Center with fitness center, indoor track, group exercise studios, bouldering wall, indoor swimming pools, gyms, racquetball courts. Also have a coliseum, track, baseball and softball stadiums, soccer field, tennis courts, and a disc golf course.

Disabled Students: 95% of the campus is accessible. Facilities include wheelchair ramps, elevators, special parking, specially equipped restrooms, special class scheduling, lowered drinking fountains, and lowered telephones.

Services: There is a reader service for the blind, remedial math and writing and a sign language interpreter.

Campus Safety and Security: Measures include 24-hour foot and vehicle patrol, emergency notification system, self-defense education, and security escort services. There are shuttle buses, emergency telephones, lighted pathways/sidewalks, and fire safety discussions.

Programs of Study: ACU confers B.A., B.S., B.B.A., B.F.A., B.M., B.S.E. and B.S.N. degrees. Associate, master's, and doctoral degrees are also awarded. Bachelor's degrees are awarded in AGRICULTURE (agricultural business management and animal science), BIOLOGICAL SCIENCE (biochemistry, biology/biological science, and nutrition), BUSINESS (accounting, finance, information & communication technology, management science, and marketing/retailing/merchandising), COMMUNICATIONS AND THE ARTS (advertising, art, communications, communication science, dramatic arts, English, fine arts, game design and development, graphic design, journalism, multimedia, music, public relations, and Spanish), COMPUTER AND PHYSICAL SCIENCE (chemistry, computer game design/development, computer science, information sciences and systems, mathematics, mathematics/computational, and physics), EDUCATION (art education, early childhood education, elementary education, foreign languages education, music education, secondary education, and special education), ENGINEERING AND ENVIRONMENTAL DESIGN (engineering, environmental science, and interior design), HEALTH PROFESSIONS (exercise science and nursing), SOCIAL SCIENCE (biblical studies, criminal justice, family/consumer studies, history, international relations, liberal arts/general studies, ministries, political science/government, psychology, social work, and sociology). Accounting, music, biology, psychology, and English are the strongest academically. Management, biology, and nursing have the largest enrollments.

Required: To graduate, students must complete courses in Bible (15 hours), English, communication, science, mathematics, social science/fine arts/humanities, kinesiology (3 hours), foreign language and cultural awareness. 33 semester hours of advanced work must be taken and a minimum 2.0 GPA maintained. A minimum of 128 credit hours is needed (more in some programs) and 30 to 64 hours of that is in the major, 18 of which must be upper division.

Special: A cooperative engineering degree is offered with the University of Texas at Arlington and an admissions agreement with Texas Tech for applied physics MS program. ACU also offers a Health Professions Cooperative Degree. ACU offers cross-registration with Hardin-Simmons and McMurry Universities and study abroad in 3 countries. Double majors are available; internships are possible in most majors, as are B.A.-B.S. degrees in biology, bio-chemistry, communication, and mathematics. Student designed majors (interdisciplinary studies) are available. There are 14 national honor societies and a freshman honors program.

Faculty/Classroom: 59% of faculty are male; 41% are female. 92% teach undergraduates, and 14% do both. Graduate students teach 1% of introductory courses. The average class size in an introductory lecture is 29; in a laboratory is 17; and in a regular course is 24.

Admissions: 49% of the 2013-2014 applicants were accepted. The SAT scores for the 2013-2014 freshman class were: Critical Reading--36% below 500, 43% between 500 and 599, 15% between 600 and 699, and 6% between 700 and 800; Math--27% below 500, 45% between 500 and 599, 24% between 600 and 699, and 4% between 700 and 800; Writing--46% below 500, 39% between 500 and 599, 13% between 600 and 699, and 2% between 700 and 800. The ACT scores were 18% below 21, 27% between 21 and 23, 26% between 24 and 26, 12% between 27 and 28, and 17% above 28. 49% of the current freshmen were in the top fifth of their class; 78% were in the top two fifths. There were 7 National Merit finalists. 16 freshmen graduated first in their class.

Requirements: The SAT or ACT is required. The ACT Optional Writing test is also required. Satisfactory SAT or ACT score, with at least one writing score. Applicants must be graduates of an accredited secondary school or have the GED and have completed 12 academic credits, including 4 in English, 3 each in math and science, and 2 years of the same foreign language. Art majors need to submit a portfolio, and music and theater majors must audition. ACU requires applicants to be in the upper 50% of their class. AP and CLEP credits are accepted. Important factors in the admissions decision are leadership record, recommendations by alumni, and advanced placement or honors courses.

Procedure: Freshmen are admitted to all sessions. Entrance exams should be taken by February of the senior year. There is an early admissions plan. Applications should be filed by February 15 for fall entry, along with a $50 fee. Notification of early decision is sent November 1; regular decision, February 15. Applications are accepted online.

Transfer: 116 transfer students enrolled in 2012-2013. Transfer students are evaluated for admission on the basis of their college GPA. Entrance exam scores and high school transcripts will be reviewed for students with GPA's below 2.5. 40 of 128 credits required for the bachelor's degree must be completed at Abilene.

Visiting: There are regularly scheduled orientations for prospective students, visits academic department, attend chapel, financial aid and admission information, and special interest sessions. There are guides for informal visits and visitors may sit in on classes. To schedule a visit, contact the Director of Campus Visits.

Financial Aid: In 2013-2014, 99% of all full-time freshmen and 93% of continuing full-time students received some form of financial aid. 70% of all full-time freshmen and 65% of continuing full-time students received need-based aid. The average freshman award was $14,634. Need-based scholarships or need-based grants averaged $16,418; need-based self-help aid (loans and jobs) averaged $5,080; non-need-based athletic scholarships averaged $18,620; and other non-need-based awards and non-need-based scholarships averaged $10,955. 28% of undergraduate students work part-time. Average annual earnings from campus work are $4800. The average financial indebtedness of the 2013 graduate was $39,705. The FAFSA is required. The deadline for filing freshman financial aid applications for fall entry is March 1.

International Students: There are 150 international students enrolled. The school actively recruits these students. They must take the TOEFL with a minimum score of 400 on the paper-based TOEFL (PBT) or 80 on the Internet-based version (iBT). They must also take the SAT or ACT.

Graduates: From July 1, 2012 to June 30, 2013, 805 bachelor's degrees were awarded. The most popular majors were management and business (6%), psychology (6%), and marketing (6%). 163 companies recruited on campus in 2012-2013. In an average class, 2% graduate in 3 years or less, 41% graduate in 4 years or less, 56% graduate in 5 years or less, and 60% graduate in 6 years or less. Of the 2012 graduating class, 29% were enrolled in graduate school within 6 months of graduation, and 53% were employed.

Admissions Contact: Tamera Long, Director of Admissions. E-Mail: *info@admissions.acu.edu* Web: *www.acu.edu*

ANGELO STATE UNIVERSITY — D-4

San Angelo, TX 76909 — (325) 942-2041; (800) 946-8627; (325) 942-2078

Full-time: 2209 men, 2517 women	**Faculty:** 261; IIA, --$
Part-time: 356 men, 464 women	**Ph.D.s:** 75%
Graduate: 319 men, 671 women	**Student/Faculty:** 17 to 1
Year: semesters, summer session	**Tuition:** $7493 ($18,113)
Application Deadline: August 25	**Room & Board:** $7556
Freshman Class: 3267 applied, 3235 accepted, 1475 enrolled	
SAT CR/M/W: 460/480/460 **ACT:** 20	**NONCOMPETITIVE**

Angelo State University, founded in 1928 and part of the Texas Tech University System, offers baccalaureate and master's degrees through the colleges of Arts and Sciences; Business; Education; and Health and Human Services. The university also offers a doctorate in physical therapy. There are 4 undergraduate schools and one graduate school. In addition to regional accreditation, ASU has baccalaureate program accreditation with ACBSP, NCATE, and NLN. The library contains 590,920 volumes, 971,404 microform items, 23,828 audio/video tapes/CDs/DVDs, and subscribes to 45,713 periodicals including electronic. Computerized library services include interlibrary loans, database searching, Internet access, and Wi-Fi capability. Special learning facilities include an art gallery, planetarium, radio station, and TV station. The 268-acre campus is in an urban area in the center of Texas, about 200 miles west of Austin and 250 miles southwest of Dallas-Fort Worth. Including any residence halls, there are 43 buildings.

Student Life: 94% of undergraduates are from Texas. Others are from 44 states, 27 foreign countries, and Canada. 98% are from public schools. 57% are White; 28% Hispanic. The average age of freshmen is 19; all undergraduates, 22. 41% do not continue beyond their first year; 31% remain to graduate.

Housing: 2018 students can be accommodated in college housing, which includes coed dorms and on-campus apartments. There are designated honors rooms in 1 dorm. On-campus housing is available on a first-come and first-served basis. Priority is given to out-of-town students. 80% of students commute. Alcohol is not permitted. All students may keep cars.

Activities: 5% of men belong to 3 national fraternities; 3% of women belong to 2 national sororities. There are 106 groups on campus, including agriculture, art, band, cheerleading, chess, choir, chorale, chorus, computers, dance, debate, drama, drill team, ethnic, film, gay, honors, international, jazz band, literary magazine, marching band, musical theater, newspaper, opera, pep band, photography, political, professional, radio and TV, religious, social, social service, and student government. Popular campus events include Homecoming, Dinner Theatre and Rambunctious Weekend.

Sports: There are 5 intercollegiate sports for men and 8 for women, and 15 intramural sports for men and 15 for women. Facilities include The Center for Human Performance includes a weight room, indoor track and a 40-foot climbing wall plus gymnasium with related basekball, volleyball and racquetball facilities as well as a 25-meter pool. The Intramural Fields support a thriving intramural program. The Junell Center/Stephens Arena is the university's multipurpose arena, seating up to 6300 people for ASU athletic events and concerts. The facility has an auxiliary practice gym, two weight rooms,and a sports medicine area. The LeGrand Sports Complex features a campus track stadium seating 3500.

Disabled Students: 98% of the campus is accessible. Facilities include wheelchair ramps, elevators, special parking, specially equipped restrooms, special class scheduling, lowered drinking fountains, and lowered telephones.

Services: Counseling and information services are available, as is tutoring in most subjects. There is remedial math, reading, and writing.

Campus Safety and Security: Measures include 24-hour foot and vehicle patrol, emergency notification system, self-defense education, and security escort services. There are emergency telephones, lighted pathways/sidewalks, and controlled access to dorms/residences.

Programs of Study: ASU confers B.A., B.S., B.B.A., B.F.A., B.G.S., B.I.S., B.M., B.S.N. and B.S.W. degrees. Master's and doctoral degrees are also awarded. Bachelor's degrees are awarded in AGRICULTURE (agricultural business management, animal science, and natural resource management), BIOLOGICAL SCIENCE (biochemistry, biology/biological science, ecology, and evolutionary biology), BUSINESS (accounting, banking and finance, business administration and management, international business management, management information systems, marketing/ retailing/merchandising, and real estate), COMMUNICATIONS AND THE ARTS (art, communications, English, French, journalism, music, Spanish, studio art, and theatre arts), COMPUTER AND PHYSICAL SCIENCE (applied physics, chemistry, computer science, geoscience, mathematics, and physics), EDUCATION (athletic training), HEALTH PROFESSIONS (exercise science, medical laboratory technology, and nursing), SOCIAL SCIENCE (child psychology/development, criminal justice, history, homeland security, interdisciplinary studies, liberal arts/ general studies, philosophy, political science/government, psychology, social work, and sociology). Math, biology, and physics are the strongest academically. Business-related programs, health sciences and education have the largest enrollments.

Required: To graduate, students must complete a total of 120 to 130 semester hours with a minimum GPA of 2.0 (2.5 for all programs leading to teacher certification). Between 30 and 36 hours are required in the major. General education core courses must be taken in English, government, history and modern language plus electives selected from various fields, including art, communication, drama, mass media, music, philosophy, economics, geography, linguistics, psychology, sociology; and lab science.

Special: ASU provides a variety of cooperative programs with Texas Tech University as well as a broad range of study abroad opportunities in Europe, Asia and South America. There are 19 national honor societies, a freshman honors program, and 10 departmental honors programs.

Faculty/Classroom: 54% of faculty are male; 46% are female. 97% teach undergraduates, and 75% do both. Graduate students teach 3% of introductory courses. The average class size in an introductory lecture is 34; in a laboratory is 23; and in a regular course is 28.

Admissions: 99% of the 2013-2014 applicants were accepted. The SAT scores for the 2013-2014 freshman class were: Critical Reading--66% below 500, 26% between 500 and 599, 6% between 600 and 699, and 1% between 700 and 800; Math--55% below 500, 34% between 500 and 599, 10% between 600 and 699, and 1% between 700 and 800. The ACT scores were 51% below 21, 27% between 21 and 23, 15% between 24 and 26, 5% between 27 and 28, and 3% above 28. 27% of the current freshmen were in the top fifth of their class; 58% were in the top two fifths. 15 freshmen graduated first in their class.

Requirements: The SAT or ACT is required. Applicants must be graduates of an accredited secondary school or have the GED. ASU requires applicants to be in the upper 50% of their class. AP and CLEP credits are accepted.

Procedure: Freshmen are admitted fall, spring, and summer. Entrance exams should be taken during spring of the junior year or fall of the senior year. There are deferred admissions and rolling admissions plans. Applications should be filed by August 25 for fall entry; January 14 for spring entry; and June 3 for summer entry, along with a $35 fee. Notification is sent on a rolling basis. Applications are accepted online.

Transfer: 450 transfer students enrolled in 2012-2013. Transfer students must have a minimum 2.0 GPA; those with fewer than 18 hours must meet high school admission requirements. 30 of 120 credits required for the bachelor's degree must be completed at ASU.

Visiting: There are regularly scheduled orientations for prospective students, orientation, a tour, advising and lunch. There are guides for informal visits, visitors may sit in on classes, and stay overnight. To schedule a visit, contact the Office of Admissions.

Financial Aid: In 2013-2014, 49% of all full-time freshmen and 70% of continuing full-time students received some form of financial aid. 55% of all full-time freshmen and 49% of continuing full-time students received need-based aid. 10% of undergraduate students work part-time. Average annual earnings from campus work are $6214. The average financial indebtedness of the 2013 graduate was $19,149. ASU is a member of CSS. The FAFSA is required. The priority date for freshman financial aid applications for fall entry is April 1. The deadline for filing freshman financial aid applications for fall entry is December 13.

International Students: There are 156 international students enrolled. The school actively recruits these students. They must take the TOEFL with a minimum score of 550 on the paper-based TOEFL (PBT) or 79 on the Internet-based version (iBT), unless English is the native language. They must also take the SAT or ACT, scoring 17.

Graduates: From July 1, 2012 to June 30, 2013, 920 bachelor's degrees were awarded. The most popular majors were interdisciplinary (14%), nursing (10%), and psychology (7%). 141 companies recruited on campus in 2012-2013. In an average class, 16% graduate in 4 years or less, 30% graduate in 5 years or less, and 34% graduate in 6 years or less.

Admissions Contact: Office of Admissions E-Mail: *admissions@angelo.edu* Web: *www.angelo.edu*

AUSTIN COLLEGE D-2

Sherman, TX 75090-4400 (903) 813-3000
(800) 442-5363; (903) 813-3198

Full-time: 614 men, 698 women	**Faculty:** 146; IIB, av$
Part-time: 4 men, 3 women	**Ph.D.s:** 95%
Graduate: 8 men, 16 women	**Student/Faculty:** 12 to 1
Year: semesters, summer session	**Tuition:** $28,700
Application Deadline: March 1	**Room & Board:** $10,000
Freshman Class: 1678 applied, 1190 accepted, 334 enrolled	
SAT CR/M/W: 615/625/595	**ACT:** 26 **HIGHLY COMPETITIVE**

Austin College, founded in 1849, is a private liberal arts institution affiliated with the Presbyterian Church, and offering programs in business, liberal arts, and health fields. There is 1 undergraduate school and 1 graduate school. The figures in the above capsule and in this profile are approximate. The library contains 227,019 volumes, 120,808 microform items, 6,393 audio/video tapes/CDs/DVDs, and subscribes to 5,727 periodicals including electronic. Computerized library services include interlibrary loans, database searching, Internet access, and laptop Internet portals. Special learning facilities include a learning resource center, a social science lab, television studios for media instruction, environmental research areas near Lake Texoma, and a facility for advanced computing and 3-D graphics. The 70-acre campus is in a suburban area 60 miles north of Dallas. Including any residence halls, there are 34 buildings.

Student Life: 93% of undergraduates are from Texas. Others are from 33 states, 21 foreign countries, and Canada. 85% are from public schools. 69% are white; 15% Asian American. 50% are Protestant; 20% claim no religious affiliation; 16% Catholic. The average age of freshmen is 18; all undergraduates, 20. 14% do not continue beyond their first year; 79% remain to graduate.

Housing: 951 students can be accommodated in college housing, which includes single-sex and coed dorms and on-campus apartments. In addition, there are language houses, and a suite-style residence hall. On-campus housing is available on a lottery system for upperclassmen. 70% of students live on campus; of those, 60% remain on campus on weekends. All students may keep cars.

Activities: 26% of men belong to 9 local fraternities; 28% of women belong to 7 local sororities. There are 50 groups on campus, including art, cheerleading, choir, chorale, chorus, drama, ethnic, film, gay, honors, international, jazz band, literary magazine, musical theater, newspaper, orchestra, pep band, photography, political, professional, religious, social, social service, student government, and symphony. Popular campus events include Christmas Pops, Film Series, and Diwali Dinner.

Sports: There are 6 intercollegiate sports for men and 6 for women, and 8 intramural sports for men and 8 for women. Facilities include an athletic/recreation complex that includes 2 gyms, a natatorium, and a fitness pavilion; a tennis stadium; a 2500-seat stadium; and soccer and baseball fields.

Disabled Students: 99% of the campus is accessible. Facilities include wheelchair ramps, elevators, special parking, specially equipped restrooms, special class scheduling, and lowered drinking fountains.

Services: Counseling and information services are available, as is tutoring in some subjects. Individual and group assistance to strengthen reading, writing, and study skills is available.

Campus Safety and Security: Measures include 24-hour foot and vehicle patrol, emergency notification system, self-defense education, and security escort services. There are emergency telephones and lighted pathways/sidewalks.

Programs of Study: AC confers B.A. degrees. Master's degrees are also awarded. Bachelor's degrees are awarded in BIOLOGICAL SCIENCE (biochemistry and biology/biological science), BUSINESS (business administration and management and international economics), COMMUNICATIONS AND THE ARTS (art, classics, communications, English, French, German, Latin, music, and Spanish), COMPUTER AND PHYSICAL SCIENCE (chemistry, computer science, mathematics, and physics), SOCIAL SCIENCE (American studies, economics, history, interdisciplinary studies, international studies, Latin American studies, philosophy, political science/government, psychology, religion, and sociology). Biology, psychology, and political science are the strongest academically. Business administration has the largest enrollments.

Required: Core requirements for graduation include completion of the Foundation Dimension, the Breadth Dimension, and 1 course in Lifetime Sports. To graduate, students must have a minimum 2.0 GPA and a total of 34 course credits (136 semester hours). Students must demonstrate an ability in a modern or classical language other than their own, quantitative competency with an approved course or test, and the required skills in written communication with approved course work. A minor or a 2nd major is required.

Special: AC offers study abroad in 58 countries, internships during the January and summer terms, and fall, spring, and summer internships in Washington, D.C. Work-study, accelerated degree programs in all majors, and dual and student-designed majors are available. There is a 3-2 engineering degree program in conjunction with the University of Texas at Dallas and Washington University in St. Louis, as well as cooperative agreements with Columbia University and Texas A&M University. There are 14 national honor societies, including Phi Beta Kappa.

Faculty/Classroom: 63% of faculty are male; 37% are female. All teach and do research. No introductory courses are taught by graduate students. The average class size in an introductory lecture is 19; in a laboratory is 16; and in a regular course is 20.

Admissions: 71% of a recent year, applicants were accepted. The SAT scores for the 2011-2012 freshman class were: Critical Reading--10% below 500, 31% between 500 and 599, 48% between 600 and 700, and 12% above 700; Math--6% below 500, 27% between 500 and 599, 50% between 600 and 700, and 17% above 700; Writing--16% below 500, 36% between 500 and 599, 36% between 600 and 700, and 12% above 700. The ACT scores were 13% below 21, 20% between 21 and 23, 35% between 24 and 26, 12% between 27 and 28, and 20% above 28. 74% of the current freshmen were in the top fifth of their class; 96% were in the top two fifths. There were 8 National Merit finalists.

Requirements: The SAT or ACT is required. The ACT Optional Writing test is also required. In addition, applicants must be graduates of an accredited secondary school, home school, or have a GED. The minimum recommended academic requirements are 4 credits in English, 3 each in math and science, 2 each in social studies and foreign language, and 1 in art/music/theater. An essay and recommendation are required. AP and CLEP credits are accepted. Important factors in the admissions decision are advanced placement or honors courses, leadership record, and extracurricular activities record.

Procedure: Freshmen are admitted fall and summer. Entrance exams should be taken in the junior year or the fall of the senior year. There are deferred admissions and rolling admissions plans. Applications should be filed by March 1 for fall entry. Notifications are sent April 1. 22 applicants were on the 2011 waiting list; 7 were admitted. Applications are accepted online.

Transfer: 37 transfer students enrolled in a recent year. Applicants must have a minimum 3.0 GPA, submit official college transcripts and 2 recommendations, and be in good standing at most recently attended schools. Students with fewer than 30 credit hours must submit SAT or ACT scores and their high school transcript or GED. 17 of 34 credits required for the bachelor's degree must be completed at Austin.

Visiting: There are regularly scheduled orientations for prospective students, 1-day and 2-day preview programs held for high school juniors, seniors and parents. Individual appointments may be made as well. There are guides for informal visits, visitors may sit in on classes, and stay overnight. To schedule a visit, contact the Admissions Office.

Financial Aid: In a recent year, 98% of all full-time freshmen and 96%

of continuing full-time students received some form of financial aid. 68% of all full-time freshmen and 61% of continuing full-time students received need-based aid. 30% of undergraduate students work part-time. Average annual earnings from campus work are $1700. AC is a member of CSS. The FAFSA is required. The priority date for freshman financial aid applications for fall entry is March 1. The deadline for filing freshman financial aid applications for fall entry is April 1.

International Students: There are 25 international students enrolled. They must take the TOEFL with a minimum score of 550 on the paper-based TOEFL (PBT) or 80 on the Internet-based version (iBT). They must also take the SAT or ACT.

Graduates: In a recent year, 246 bachelor's degrees were awarded. The most popular majors were psychology (17%), business administration (10%), and biology (6%). 43 companies recruited on campus in a recent year. In an average class, 75% graduate in 4 years or less, 77% graduate in 5 years or less, and 79% graduate in 6 years or less. Of the 2010 graduating class, 44% were enrolled in graduate school within 6 months of graduation, and 47% were employed.

Admissions Contact: Nan Davis, VP for Institutional Enrollment. A campus DVD is available. E-Mail: *admission@austincollege.edu* Web: *www.austincollege.edu*

BAYLOR UNIVERSITY D-3

Waco, TX 76798 **(254) 710-3435; (800) BAYLOR-U**

Full-time: 5187 men, 7163 women
Part-time: 106 men, 119 women
Graduate: 1248 men, 1206 women
Year: semesters, summer session
Application Deadline: February 1
Freshman Class: n/av
SAT or ACT: required
Faculty: n/av; I, --$
Ph.D.s: 82%
Student/Faculty: 14 to 1
Tuition: $31,658
Room & Board: $8984

HIGHLY COMPETITIVE

Baylor University in Waco, Texas, is a private Baptist university, and a nationally ranked liberal arts institution. Chartered in 1845 by the Republic of Texas, Baylor is the oldest, continually operating university in the state. Its offerings include undergraduate programs in liberal arts and sciences, business, computer science, education, engineering, music, nursing, social work, and an honors college. There are 8 undergraduate schools and 10 graduate schools. In addition to regional accreditation, Baylor has baccalaureate program accreditation with AACSB, ABET, ADA, CSWE, NASM, and NCATE. The 7 libraries contain 2.5 million volumes, 2.2 million microform items, and 93,815 audio/video tapes/CDs/DVDs. Computerized library services include interlibrary loans, database searching, and Internet access. Special learning facilities include a learning resource center, art gallery, natural history museum, radio station, TV station, a speech/hearing clinic. The 1000-acre campus is in a small town 100 miles south of Dallas/Fort Worth. Including any residence halls, there are 115 buildings.

Student Life: 82% of undergraduates are from Texas. Others are from 50 states, 72 foreign countries, and Canada. 69% are white; 12% Hispanic. 77% are Protestant; 14% Catholic. The average age of freshmen is 19; all undergraduates, 21. 15% do not continue beyond their first year; 72% remain to graduate.

Housing: 4651 students can be accommodated in college housing, which includes single-sex dorms, on-campus apartments, off-campus apartments, and married student housing. In addition, there are honors houses, language houses, special-interest houses, and living-learning centers (partnerships with academic units to create living-learning environments). On-campus housing is guaranteed for the freshman year only, is available on a first-come, and first-served basis. 61% of students commute. Alcohol is not permitted. All students may keep cars.

Activities: 7% of men belong to 3 local and 19 national fraternities; 14% of women belong to 2 local and 17 national sororities. There are 253 groups on campus, including art, band, cheerleading, chess, choir, chorale, chorus, computers, dance, debate, drama, ethnic, film, forensics, honors, international, jazz band, literary magazine, marching band, musical theater, newspaper, opera, orchestra, pep band, photography, political, professional, radio and TV, religious, social, social service, student government, symphony, and yearbook. Popular campus events include Dia del Oso (Day of the Bear), Campus Sing, and Pigskin Review.

Sports: There are 8 intercollegiate sports for men and 10 for women, and 17 intramural sports for men and 17 for women. Facilities include a 50,000-seat football stadium, gyms, intramural fields, tennis courts, a swimming pool, a marina, and a special events center that seats 10,030. A 158,000-square-foot student life center has a 52-foot climbing rock, a fitness center, aerobics room, racquetball/squash courts, basketball courts, a pool, an indoor walking/jogging track, and an outdoor sand volleyball court.

Disabled Students: 95% of the campus is accessible. Facilities include wheelchair ramps, elevators, special parking, specially equipped restrooms, and lowered drinking fountains.

Services: There is a reader service for the blind, and remedial reading and writing. Taped textbooks are available through the Commission for the Blind. The Office of Student Access and Learning provides study skills and time management sessions for students with disabilities.

Campus Safety and Security: Measures include 24-hour foot and vehicle patrol, emergency notification system, and security escort services. There are shuttle buses, emergency telephones, and lighted pathways/sidewalks.

Programs of Study: Baylor confers B.A., B.S., B.B.A., B.F.A., B.M., B.M.E., B.S.Av.Sc., B.S.C., B.S.C.S., B.S.E., B.S.E.C.E., B.S.Ed., B.S.F.C.S., B.S.I., B.S.M.E., B.S.N., and B.S.W. degrees. Master's and doctoral degrees are also awarded. Bachelor's degrees are awarded in AGRICULTURE (forestry and related sciences and soil science), BIOLOGICAL SCIENCE (biochemistry, bioinformatics, biology/biological science, life science, neurosciences, and nutrition), BUSINESS (accounting, banking and finance, business administration and management, business economics, business statistics, business systems analysis, entrepreneurial studies, fashion merchandising, human resources, insurance, international business management, management information systems, marketing/retailing/merchandising, personnel management, real estate, and sports marketing), COMMUNICATIONS AND THE ARTS (applied music, art, art history and appreciation, broadcasting, choral music, classics, communications, creative writing, dramatic arts, English, French, German, Greek (classical), journalism, languages, Latin, literature, music, music history and appreciation, music performance, music theory and composition, performing arts, Russian, Spanish, speech/debate/rhetoric, studio art, telecommunications, and theater design), COMPUTER AND PHYSICAL SCIENCE (applied mathematics, chemistry, computer science, earth science, geology, geophysics and seismology, information sciences and systems, mathematics, and physics), EDUCATION (art education, athletic training, business education, computer education, drama education, elementary education, English education, foreign languages education, health education, home economics education, journalism education, mathematics education, museum studies, music education, physical education, reading education, recreation education, science education, secondary education, social science education, social studies education, and special education), ENGINEERING AND ENVIRONMENTAL DESIGN (airline piloting and navigation, architecture, computer engineering, electrical/electronics engineering, engineering, environmental science, interior design, and mechanical engineering), HEALTH PROFESSIONS (community health work, health science, medical laboratory technology, nursing, optometry, predentistry, premedicine, speech pathology/audiology, and speech therapy), SOCIAL SCIENCE (American studies, anthropology, archeology, Asian/Oriental studies, biblical languages, child care/child and family studies, dietetics, economics, family/consumer studies, fashion design and technology, forensic studies, geography, history, interdisciplinary studies, international public service, Latin American studies, philosophy, physical fitness/movement, political science/government, psychology, public administration, religion, religious education, religious music, Russian and Slavic studies, social work, sociology, and urban studies). Business, biology, and psychology have the largest enrollments.

Required: All degree programs require a minimum of 124 hours and a 2.0 GPA to graduate. Basic requirements for the B.A. degree include 18 semester hours of social science, 12 each of English and science, 6 to 9 of fine arts, 6 of religion, 4 of phys ed, 3 to 16 of foreign language, 3 of math, and 2 semesters of chapel forum. Requirements for other degrees vary.

Special: Baylor offers internships in each school, study abroad and student exchange in more than 30 countries, and pass/fail options. There are also honors and university scholars programs and faculty exchange with 4 schools in China and 1 each in Japan, Thailand, and Russia. There are 36 national honor societies, including Phi Beta Kappa, and a freshman honors program.

Faculty/Classroom: 60% of faculty are male; 40% are female. No introductory courses are taught by graduate students. The average class size in a regular course is 28.

Admissions: 63% of the current freshmen were in the top fifth of their class; 88% were in the top two fifths. There were 62 National Merit Finalists.

Requirements: The SAT or ACT is required. The ACT Optional Writing test is also required. Applicants must be graduates of an accredited secondary school. An interview is recommended. Baylor requires applicants to be in the upper 50% of their class. AP and CLEP credits are accepted.

Procedure: Freshmen are admitted fall, spring, and summer. Entrance exams should be taken in spring of the junior year or fall of the senior year. There is an early admissions plan. Early decision applications should be filed by November 1; regular applications, by February 1 for fall entry, along with a $50 fee. Notification of early decision is sent January 15; regular decision, March 15. Applications are accepted online.

Transfer: 417 transfer students enrolled in 2010-2011. Transfer students should begin studies no later than the end of the sophomore year because of the 60-semester-hour residence requirement for a bachelor's degree. A minimum 2.5 GPA is required. Students with fewer than 30 credit hours earned must meet the entrance requirements for freshmen. 60

of 124 credits required for the bachelor's degree must be completed at Baylor.

Visiting: There are regularly scheduled orientations for prospective students, including day-and-a-half sessions in June and a Welcome Week in August. There are guides for informal visits, visitors may sit in on classes, and stay overnight. To schedule a visit, contact the Campus Visitation Program.

Financial Aid: In 2011-2012, 97% of all full-time freshmen and 89% of continuing full-time students received some form of financial aid. 61% of all full-time freshmen and 55% of continuing full-time students received need-based aid. The average freshman award was $26,362. Need-based scholarships or need-based grants averaged $17,712 ($45,902 maximum); need-based self-help aid (loans and jobs) averaged $5,599 ($15,500 maximum); non-need-based athletic scholarships averaged $20,810 ($44,440 maximum); and other non-need-based awards and non-need-based scholarships averaged $12,918 ($46,902 maximum). 15% of undergraduate students work part-time. Average annual earnings from campus work are $1734. The FAFSA and a residency affirmation are required. The priority date for freshman financial aid applications for fall entry is February 15. The deadline for filing freshman financial aid applications for fall entry is May 1.

International Students: There are 292 international students enrolled. The school actively recruits these students. They must take the TOEFL with a minimum score of 540 on the paper-based TOEFL (PBT) or 76 on the Internet-based version (iBT). They must also take the SAT or ACT.

Graduates: From July 1, 2010 to June 30, 2011, 2709 bachelor's degrees were awarded. The most popular majors were biology (7%), marketing (5%), and psychology (5%). In an average class, 2% graduate in 3 years or less, 51% graduate in 4 years or less, 69% graduate in 5 years or less, and 72% graduate in 6 years or less.

Admissions Contact: Jennifer Carron, Director of Undergraduate Admissions. A campus DVD is available. E-Mail: *admissions@baylor.edu* Web: *www.baylor.edu*

CONCORDIA UNIVERSITY TEXAS — D-3

Austin, TX 78705-2799 — (512) 486-2000; (800) 865-4282; (512) 486-1350

Full-time: 360 men, 420 women	**Faculty:** n/av
Part-time: 100 men, 200 women	**Ph.D.s:** 74%
Graduate: 25 men, 75 women	**Student/Faculty:** n/av
Year: semesters, summer session	**Tuition:** $23,420
Application Deadline: see profile	**Room & Board:** $8960
Freshman Class: n/av	
SAT or ACT: required	
	COMPETITIVE

Concordia University Texas, formerly Concordia University at Austin, was founded in 1926 and is a private college affiliated with the Lutheran Church-Missouri Synod. It offers undergraduate programs in liberal arts, behavioral science, business, communication, education, environmental science, and church music. The figures in the above capsule and in this profile are approximate. There are 4 undergraduate schools. The library contains 56,146 volumes, 8504 microform items, 3213 audio/video tapes/CDs/DVDs, and subscribes to 514 periodicals including electronic. Computerized library services include interlibrary loans and database searching. Special learning facilities include a TV station. The 20-acre campus is in an urban area in the heart of Austin. Including any residence halls, there are 20 buildings.

Student Life: 93% of undergraduates are from Texas. Others are from 21 states and 13 foreign countries. 89% are from public schools. 63% are white; 16% Hispanic. 78% are Protestant; 16% Catholic. The average age of freshmen is 19; all undergraduates, 25. 40% do not continue beyond their first year; 35% remain to graduate.

Housing: 245 students can be accommodated in college housing, which includes single-sex and coed dorms. On-campus housing is guaranteed for the freshman year only and is available on a first-come, first-served basis. 68% of students commute. All students may keep cars.

Activities: There are no fraternities or sororities. There are 9 groups on campus, including band, choir, chorus, dance, drama, ethnic, religious, social, and student government. Popular campus events include Fall Festival Weekend, Parents Day, and Founders Day.

Sports: There are 6 intercollegiate sports for men and 5 for women, and 10 intramural sports for men and 9 for women. Facilities include an activities center, a 1600-seat gym, a 250-seat auditorium, a baseball field, a beach volleyball court, and tennis courts.

Disabled Students: 75% of the campus is accessible. Facilities include wheelchair ramps, elevators, special parking, specially equipped rest rooms, and lowered drinking fountains.

Services: Counseling and information services are available, as is tutoring in most subjects.

Campus Safety and Security: Measures include 24-hour foot and vehicle patrol and security escort services. There are lighted pathways/sidewalks.

Programs of Study: Concordia confers B.A. degrees. Associates and master's degrees are also awarded. Bachelor's degrees are awarded in BUSINESS (accounting and business administration and management), COMMUNICATIONS AND THE ARTS (communications, English, music, and Spanish), COMPUTER AND PHYSICAL SCIENCE (computer science), EDUCATION (elementary education and secondary education), ENGINEERING AND ENVIRONMENTAL DESIGN (environmental science), SOCIAL SCIENCE (behavioral science, history, liberal arts/general studies, Mexican-American/Chicano studies, and religious music). Education is the strongest academically. Business management, education, and communication have the largest enrollments.

Required: To graduate, all students must complete 12 hours each of English, social/behavioral science, and religion, 6 to 8 hours of natural science, and 3 hours each of fine arts, math, phys ed, and speech. Students must earn 128 semester hours, including 39 upper-level hours and 33 to 48 hours in the major. A minimum 2.0 GPA is required, plus a 2.25 GPA in the major.

Special: Concordia offers internships in communications, behavioral science, business, environmental science, and Mexican-American studies, study abroad in Mexico, an accelerated degree program in business management, dual majors, credit for prior experiential learning, nondegree study, pass/fail options, and a preseminary program. There is 1 national honor society.

Faculty/Classroom: 69% of faculty are male; 31% are female. All teach undergraduates. No introductory courses are taught by graduate students. The average class size in a laboratory is 16 and in a regular course is 21.

Requirements: The SAT or ACT is required. The recommended minimum composite score is 860 on the SAT or 17 on the ACT. Applicants must be graduates of an accredited secondary school or have the GED. A GPA of 2.5 is required. AP and CLEP credits are accepted.

Procedure: Freshmen are admitted fall, spring, and summer. There are early admissions, deferred admissions, and rolling admissions plans. Check with the school for current application deadlines. The application fee is $50.

Transfer: Transfer students with fewer than 18 hours earned must meet freshman admissions requirements and submit high school and college transcripts; those with 18 or more hours earned must be in good standing at the previously attended college with a minimum 2.5 GPA. 45 of 128 credits required for the bachelor's degree must be completed at Concordia.

Visiting: There are regularly scheduled orientations for prospective students, consisting of placement exams, scheduling and registration of classes, and information sessions for parents with faculty and administrators. There are guides for informal visits, and visitors may sit in on classes and stay overnight. To schedule a visit, contact the Admissions Office.

Financial Aid: The FAFSA and the college's own financial statement are required. Check with the school for current application deadlines.

International Students: The school actively recruits these students. They must take the TOEFL.

Admissions Contact: Admissions Office. E-Mail: *admissions@concordia.edu* Web: *www.concordia.edu*

DALLAS BAPTIST UNIVERSITY — D-2

Dallas, TX 75211 — (214) 333-5360; (800) 460-1328; (214) 333-5447

Full-time: 1057 men, 1405 women	**Faculty:** 99
Part-time: 376 men, 597 women	**Ph.D.s:** 81%
Graduate: 759 men, 1228 women	**Student/Faculty:** 14 to 1
Year: 4-1-4, summer session	**Tuition:** $22,350
Application Deadline:	**Room & Board:** $6768
Freshman Class: 2631 applied, 1113 accepted, 492 enrolled	
SAT CR/M: 563/560 **ACT:** 22	**COMPETITIVE**

Dallas Baptist University is a Christ-centered comprehensive, liberal arts university offering 68 Bachelor, 23 Accelerated Bachelor/Master, 24 Master, 49 Dual Master, and 2 Doctoral degree programs. DBU integrates faith and academic learning, giving students freedom to explore their faith in the classroom and the encouragement to live out their faith as servant leaders in the world. With online classes as well as weekend and evening classes at locations throughout the Dallas/Fort Worth Metroplex, DBU offers working adults the convenience and flexibility they need to complete their degree. There are 7 undergraduate schools and 24 graduate schools. In addition to regional accreditation, DBU has baccalaureate program accreditation with ACBSP and NASM. The library contains 290,827 volumes, 521,197 microform items, 8,309 audio/video tapes/CDs/DVDs, and subscribes to 25,736 periodicals including electronic. Computerized library services include interlibrary loans, database searching, Internet access, and Wi-Fi capability. Special learning facilities include a The 293-acre campus is in a suburban area 13 miles from downtown Dallas and 29 miles from downtown Fort Worth. Including any residence halls, there are 41 buildings.

Student Life: 90% of undergraduates are from Texas. Others are from 44 states, and 49 foreign countries. 61% are White; 16% African American; 12% Hispanic. 87% are Protestant. The average age of freshmen is 18; all undergraduates, 26. 30% do not continue beyond their first year; 55% remain to graduate.

Housing: 1861 students can be accommodated in college housing, which includes single-sex dorms, on-campus apartments, off-campus apartments, and married student housing. On-campus housing is available on a first-come and first-served basis. 54% of students live on campus; of those, 80% remain on campus on weekends. Alcohol is not permitted. All students may keep cars.

Activities: 7% of men belong to 5 local fraternities, 10% of women belong to 6 local sororities. There are 52 groups on campus, including civil service, community outreach, art, cheerleading, choir, chorale, chorus, communications, dance, drama, drill team, ethnic, honors, international, leadership/mission work, musical theater, opera, pep band, political, professional, religious, social, social service, student government, and yearbook. Popular campus events include Family Weekend, Homecoming, Midnight Madness, Mr. Big Chief, Spring Sing, and SWAT (Student Welcome & Transition).

Sports: There are 8 intercollegiate sports for men and 7 for women, and 13 intramural sports for men and 13 for women. Facilities include a fitness center, tennis courts, baseball field, soccer field, 2 pools, sand volleyball court, basketball court, table tennis, pool table, intramural field, and athletic training center.

Disabled Students: 90% of the campus is accessible. Facilities include wheelchair ramps, elevators, special parking, specially equipped restrooms, special class scheduling, lowered drinking fountains, lowered telephones, and special housing.

Services: Counseling and information services are available, as is tutoring in most subjects, math, science, writing, English, computer, spanish and music There is a reader service for the blind, and remedial math. Other subjects may be available upon request. Student counseling is also available.

Campus Safety and Security: Measures include 24-hour foot and vehicle patrol, emergency notification system, and security escort services. There are shuttle buses, emergency telephones, lighted pathways/sidewalks, and controlled access to dorms/residences.

Programs of Study: DBU confers B.A., B.S., B.A.S., B.B.A., B.B.S., B.M. and B.M.E. degrees. Associate, master's, and doctoral degrees are also awarded. Bachelor's degrees are awarded in BIOLOGICAL SCIENCE (biology/biological science and cell biology), BUSINESS (accounting, banking and finance, business administration and management, finance, hospitality management services, management information systems, marketing/retailing/merchandising, and sports management), COMMUNICATIONS AND THE ARTS (applied music, art, communication design , communications, English, fine arts, music, music business management, music performance, piano performance, and vocal performance), COMPUTER AND PHYSICAL SCIENCE (computer science, mathematics, and natural sciences), EDUCATION (early childhood education, education, elementary education, and physical education), ENGINEERING AND ENVIRONMENTAL DESIGN (environmental science), HEALTH PROFESSIONS (health care administration), SOCIAL SCIENCE (biblical studies, counseling/psychology, criminal justice, history, interdisciplinary studies, liberal arts/general studies, ministries, pastoral studies, philosophy, physical fitness/movement, political science/government, psychology, religious education, religious studies, religious music, and sociology). Education, business, music, music business, psychology, communication, and Biblical studies are the strongest academically. Business administration, interdisciplinary studies, and psychology have the largest enrollments.

Required: To graduate, students must have a minimum GPA of 2.0 and complete a minimum of 126 credit hours, including 24 hours in the major and 42 upper-level hours. Chapel attendance is required. At least 12 credit hours in the major program must be completed at DBU, including 9 upper-level credits. Students must complete a minimum of 25% of credit hours in residence at DBU; complete 30 of the last 36 credit hours with courses offered by DBU; and complete the General Studies requirements including English, history, religion, fine arts, computer science, math, phys ed, natural science, and social science.

Special: Study abroad programs are available in Australia, China, Costa Rica, England, India, Israel, and Uganda. National programs are available through American Studies Program in Washington, D.C., Contemporary Music Center in Nashville, Los Angeles Film Studies Center, and Washington Journalism Center in Washington, D.C. There are 5 national honor societies and a freshman honors program.

Faculty/Classroom: 57% of faculty are male; 43% are female. 77% teach undergraduates. No introductory courses are taught by graduate students. The average class size in a regular course is 13.

Admissions: 42% of the 2013-2014 applicants were accepted. The SAT scores for the 2013-2014 freshman class were: Critical Reading--18% below 500, 48% between 500 and 599, 31% between 600 and 699, and 4% between 700 and 800; Math--14% below 500, 59% between 500 and 599, 25% between 600 and 699, and 2% between 700 and 800. The ACT scores were 36% below 21, 32% between 21 and 23, 22% between 24 and 26, 5% between 27 and 28, and 5% above 28. 6 freshmen graduated first in their class.

Requirements: The SAT or ACT is required. The ACT Optional Writing test is also required. Applicants must be graduates, or expect to graduate, from an accredited secondary school, home school, or have a GED. A composite SAT score of at least 1020 (Critical Reading and Math sections) or a composite ACT score of at least 21 is required, along with a minimum high school GPA of 2.5. An essay is required, and an interview is encouraged. Recommended high school courses should include 4 years each of English and history or social studies, 3 years of math, and 2 to 3 years of a foreign language and science. DBU requires applicants to be in the upper 50% of their class. A GPA of 2.5 is required. AP and CLEP credits are accepted. Important factors in the admissions decision are leadership record, personality/intangible qualities, and extracurricular activities record.

Procedure: Freshmen are admitted to all sessions. Entrance exams should be taken during the spring of the junior year or the fall of the senior year. There are deferred admissions and rolling admissions plans. Application deadlines are open. Application fee is $25. Applications are accepted online. Application fees are waived if application is completed online.

Transfer: 476 transfer students enrolled in 2012-2013. Applicants must submit an essay along with their application and fee, and transcripts of all previous college work, and should have a cumulative GPA of 2.5 or higher. Students with fewer than 30 credit hours must furnish high school transcripts and ACT or SAT scores. 32 of 126 credits required for the bachelor's degree must be completed at DBU.

Visiting: There are regularly scheduled orientations for prospective students, Patriot Preview days each fall, spring, and summer semesters provide parents and students information about life at DBU. Campus tours, visits with faculty and administration, information about admissions, financial aid, and campus life are included. There are guides for informal visits and visitors may sit in on classes. To schedule a visit, contact the Undergraduate Admissions Office.

Financial Aid: In 2013-2014, 96% of all full-time freshmen and 90% of continuing full-time students received some form of financial aid. 60% of all full-time freshmen and 57% of continuing full-time students received need-based aid. The average freshman award was $23,268. Need-based scholarships or need-based grants averaged $5,734 ($12,520 maximum); need-based self-help aid (loans and jobs) averaged $3,566 ($6,500 maximum); non-need-based athletic scholarships averaged $17,579 ($31,260 maximum); other non-need-based awards and non-need-based scholarships averaged $10,436 ($27,990 maximum); and $14,498 from other forms of aid. 25% of undergraduate students work part-time. Average annual earnings from campus work are $3200. The average financial indebtedness of the 2013 graduate was $20,071. The FAFSA and the college's own financial statement are required. The priority date for freshman financial aid applications for fall entry is March 1.

International Students: There are 181 international students enrolled. The school actively recruits these students. They must take the TOEFL with a minimum score of 525 on the paper-based TOEFL (PBT) or 71 on the Internet-based version (iBT), IELTS, or complete the DBU intensive English program.

Graduates: From July 1, 2012 to June 30, 2013, 765 bachelor's degrees were awarded. The most popular majors were multi/interdisciplinary studies (15%), business administration (15%), and religious education (9%). 147 companies recruited on campus in 2012-2013. In an average class, 43% graduate in 4 years or less, 53% graduate in 5 years or less, and 55% graduate in 6 years or less.

Admissions Contact: Bobby Soto, Director of Undergraduate Admissions. E-Mail: *admiss@dbu.edu* Web: *www.dbu.edu*

EAST TEXAS BAPTIST UNIVERSITY — E-2

Marshall, TX 75670 — **(903) 923-2000; (800) 804-ETBU; (903) 923-2001**

Full-time: 505 men, 561 women	**Faculty:** 68; IIB, --$
Part-time: 59 men, 71 women	**Ph.D.s:** 90%
Graduate: 27 men, 24 women	**Student/Faculty:** 13 to 1
Year: semesters, summer session	**Tuition:** $22,590
Application Deadline: August 15	**Room & Board:** $6545
Freshman Class: 709 applied, 522 accepted, 340 enrolled	
SAT CR/M: 470/490	**ACT:** 20 — **COMPETITIVE**

East Texas Baptist University, established in 1912, is a private liberal arts university with a strong Christian emphasis. The educational environment stresses the development of the whole person academically, socially, and spiritually. There are 7 undergraduate schools and 4 graduate schools. In addition to regional accreditation, ETBU has baccalaureate program accreditation with NASM. The library contains 5.2 million volumes, 10,621 microform items, 181,630 audio/video tapes/CDs/DVDs, and subscribes to 28,752 periodicals including electronic. Computerized library services include interlibrary loans, database searching, Internet access, and Wi-Fi capability. Special learning facilities include a radio station, academic center for excellence, math lab, and a writing lab. The 250-acre campus is in a small town 40 miles west of Shreveport, Louisiana, and 150 miles east of Dallas. Including any residence halls, there are 26 buildings.

Student Life: 93% of undergraduates are from Texas. Others are from

18 states, and 6 foreign countries. 89% are from public schools. 63% are White; 19% African American; 11% Hispanic. 68% are Protestant; 25% claim no religious affiliation. The average age of freshmen is 18; all undergraduates, 20. 39% do not continue beyond their first year; 38% remain to graduate.

Housing: 981 students can be accommodated in college housing, which includes single-sex dorms, on-campus apartments, and married student housing. On-campus housing is available on a first-come and first-served basis. 85% of students live on campus; of those, 60% remain on campus on weekends. Alcohol is not permitted. All students may keep cars.

Activities: 2% of men belong to 2 local fraternities; 1% of women belong to 1 local sorority. There are 37 groups on campus, including band, cheerleading, choir, chorale, chorus, debate, drama, ethnic, honors, international, jazz band, literary magazine, marching band, musical theater, newspaper, orchestra, pep band, political, professional, religious, social, social service, student government, symphony, and yearbook. Popular campus events include Connexus, Christmas on the Hill, Welcome Week, Homecoming, Miss ETBU, and Athletic Contests.

Sports: There are 6 intercollegiate sports for men and 6 for women, and 7 intramural sports for men and 7 for women. Facilities include a baseball field, tennis courts, a weight room, a 1500-seat gym, a soccer field, a softball field, an intramural field, a practice gym, football practice fields, a football field, and a stadium.

Disabled Students: 95% of the campus is accessible. Facilities include wheelchair ramps, elevators, special parking, specially equipped restrooms, special class scheduling, and lowered drinking fountains.

Services: Counseling and information services are available, as is tutoring in most subjects.

Campus Safety and Security: Measures include 24-hour foot and vehicle patrol and emergency notification system. There are emergency telephones, lighted pathways/sidewalks, and controlled access to dorms/residences.

Programs of Study: ETBU confers B.A., B.S., B.A.S., B.M., B.S.E. and B.S.N. degrees. Master's degrees are also awarded. Bachelor's degrees are awarded in BIOLOGICAL SCIENCE (biology/biological science and life science), BUSINESS (business administration and management), COMMUNICATIONS AND THE ARTS (communications, dramatic arts, English, music, music performance, piano/organ, Spanish, speech/debate/rhetoric, visual and performing arts, and voice), COMPUTER AND PHYSICAL SCIENCE (chemistry and mathematics), EDUCATION (athletic training, drama education, early childhood education, education, elementary education, English education, foreign languages education, mathematics education, music education, physical education, science education, secondary education, social studies education, and speech correction), HEALTH PROFESSIONS (nursing), SOCIAL SCIENCE (biblical studies, child psychology/development, criminal justice, history, interdisciplinary studies, international studies, ministries, missions, pastoral studies, physical fitness/movement, political science/government, psychology, religion, religious education, religious music, sociology, and youth ministry). Business, teacher education, and nursing have the largest enrollments.

Required: To graduate, students must complete general education requirements and maintain a minimum GPA of 2.0. A total of 120 to 133 semester hours, with at least 30 in the major, is required.

Special: East Texas Baptist University is a member of the Council for Christian Colleges & Universities (CCCU). Through the CCCU, ETBU students have the opportunity to study in many different national and international arenas. Internships are offered in social work, business, religion, education, biology, communication, psychology, and sociology, as is a Washington semester through the American Studies Program. There are 8 national honor societies, a freshman honors program, and 13 departmental honors programs.

Faculty/Classroom: 51% of faculty are male; 49% are female. All teach undergraduates, and 25% do research. No introductory courses are taught by graduate students. The average class size in an introductory lecture is 22; in a laboratory is 13; and in a regular course is 18.

Admissions: 74% of the 2013-2014 applicants were accepted. The SAT scores for the 2013-2014 freshman class were: Critical Reading--64% below 500, 30% between 500 and 599, 6% between 600 and 699; Math--54% below 500, 37% between 500 and 599, 8% between 600 and 699, and 1% between 700 and 800. The ACT scores were 55% below 21, 30% between 21 and 23, 9% between 24 and 26, 4% between 27 and 28, and 2% above 28. 28% of the current freshmen were in the top fifth of their class; 54% were in the top two fifths. 2 freshmen graduated first in their class.

Requirements: The SAT or ACT is required. Applicants must be graduates of an accredited secondary school or have the GED, and must have composite scores of at least 18 on the ACT or 860 on the SAT (critical reading and math), or rank in the top 40% of their graduating class. Students not meeting these requirements may be admitted conditionally for 1 term or semester. ETBU requires applicants to be in the upper 30% of their class. AP and CLEP credits are accepted.

Procedure: Freshmen are admitted fall, spring, and summer. Entrance exams should be taken in the first semester of the senior year. There are deferred admissions and rolling admissions plans. Applications should be filed by August 15 for fall entry; January 3 for spring entry, along with a $25 fee. Applications are accepted online.

Transfer: 134 transfer students enrolled in 2012-2013. Transfer students must have a minimum GPA of 2.0 and be eligible to return to the last college attended. 33 of 120 credits required for the bachelor's degree must be completed at East Texas Baptist University.

Visiting: There are regularly scheduled orientations for prospective students, including campus tours, meals, scholarship interviews/testing, faculty visits, class visits, sports/entertainment, and financial aid seminars. There are guides for informal visits, visitors may sit in on classes, and stay overnight. To schedule a visit, contact the Campus Visit Coordinator at (903) 923-2000.

Financial Aid: In 2013-2014, 99% of all full-time freshmen and 99% of continuing full-time students received some form of financial aid. 76% of all full-time freshmen and 64% of continuing full-time students received need-based aid. The average freshman award was $19,886. Need-based scholarships or need-based grants averaged $6,467 ($14,000 maximum); need-based self-help aid (loans and jobs) averaged $3,996 ($11,320 maximum); and other non-need-based awards and non-need-based scholarships averaged $16,558 ($32,160 maximum). 4% of undergraduate students work part-time. Average annual earnings from campus work are $4800. The average financial indebtedness of the 2013 graduate was $23,937. The FAFSA and the college's own financial statement are required. The priority date for freshman financial aid applications for fall entry is June 1.

International Students: There are 13 international students enrolled. The school actively recruits these students. They must take the TOEFL with a minimum score of 500 on the paper-based TOEFL (PBT) or 61 on the Internet-based version (iBT). They must also take the SAT or ACT, scoring 18.

Graduates: From July 1, 2012 to June 30, 2013, 184 bachelor's degrees were awarded. The most popular majors were education (19%), business (15%), and interdisciplinary studies (14%). 43 companies recruited on campus in 2012-2013. In an average class, 5% graduate in 3 years or less, 23% graduate in 4 years or less, 35% graduate in 5 years or less, and 38% graduate in 6 years or less. Of the 2012 graduating class, 31% were enrolled in graduate school within 6 months of graduation, and 86% were employed.

Admissions Contact: Jason Soles, Director of Admissions. E-Mail: *admissions@etbu.edu* Web: *www.etbu.edu*

HARDIN-SIMMONS UNIVERSITY — C-2

Abilene, TX 79698

(325) 670-1206
(877) 464-7889; (325) 670-1527

Full-time: 800 men, 1000 women
Part-time: 100 men, 175 women
Graduate: 200 men, 230 women
Year: semesters, summer session
Application Deadline: open
Freshman Class: n/av
SAT or ACT: required

Faculty: n/av; IIA, --$
Ph.D.s: 77%
Student/Faculty: n/av
Tuition: $22,500
Room & Board: $7000

COMPETITIVE+

Hardin-Simmons University, founded in 1891, is a private liberal arts institution affiliated with the Baptist General Convention of Texas. The figures in the above capsule and in this profile are approximate. There are 7 undergraduate schools and 1 graduate school. In addition to regional accreditation, HSU has baccalaureate program accreditation with ACBSP, CSWE, and NASM. The 2 libraries contain 262,599 volumes, 23,734 microform items, 12,013 audio/video tapes/CDs/DVDs, and subscribe to 33,942 periodicals including electronic. Computerized library services include interlibrary loans, database searching, Internet access, and laptop Internet portals. Special learning facilities include an art gallery and an observatory. The 209-acre campus is in an urban area 150 miles west of Fort Worth. Including any residence halls, there are 44 buildings.

Student Life: 96% of undergraduates are from Texas. Others are from 23 states, 19 foreign countries, and Canada. 88% are from public schools. 74% are white. 66% are Protestant; 15% unknown; 13% claim no religious affiliation. The average age of freshmen is 18; all undergraduates, 21. 34% do not continue beyond their first year; 49% remain to graduate.

Housing: 1111 students can be accommodated in college housing, which includes single-sex dorms, off-campus apartments, and married student housing. On-campus housing is available on a first-come, first-served basis. 56% of students commute. Alcohol is not permitted. All students may keep cars.

Activities: 5% of men belong to 4 local fraternities; 16% of women belong to 4 local sororities. There are 57 groups on campus, including art, band, cheerleading, choir, chorale, computers, debate, drama, drill team, ethnic, honors, international, literary magazine, marching band, musical theater, newspaper, opera, orchestra, pep band, photography, political, professional, radio and TV, religious, Six White Horse Program, social, social service, student government, and symphony. Popular campus events include Western Heritage Day, All-School SING!, and Founders Day.

Sports: There are 6 intercollegiate sports for men and 6 for women, and 17 intramural sports for men and 17 for women. Facilities include a rodeo arena, 2 running tracks, a practice field, a football stadium, a soccer field, softball and baseball fields, outdoor and indoor swimming pools, 6 bowling alleys, a fitness course, 4 basketball, 4 racquetball, 8 tennis, and 8 badminton/paddleball courts, and a nautilus weight-lifting room.

Disabled Students: All of the campus is accessible. Facilities include wheelchair ramps, elevators, special parking, specially equipped rest rooms, special class scheduling, lowered drinking fountains, lowered telephones, special housing, and an office to coordinate disability services.

Services: Counseling and information services are available, as is tutoring in most subjects. There is remedial math, reading, and writing and free counseling services.

Campus Safety and Security: Measures include 24-hour foot and vehicle patrol. There are emergency telephones and lighted pathways/sidewalks.

Programs of Study: HSU confers B.A., B.S., B.B.A., B.B.S., B.Mus., and B.S.N. degrees. Master's and doctoral degrees are also awarded. Bachelor's degrees are awarded in AGRICULTURE (agricultural business management, agriculture, and animal science), BIOLOGICAL SCIENCE (biochemistry, biology/biological science, and molecular biology), BUSINESS (accounting, banking and finance, business administration and management, management science, and marketing management), COMMUNICATIONS AND THE ARTS (art, broadcasting, communications, dramatic arts, English, graphic design, music, music business management, music history and appreciation, music performance, music theory and composition, piano/organ, public relations, radio/television technology, Spanish, speech/debate/rhetoric, strings, and voice), COMPUTER AND PHYSICAL SCIENCE (chemistry, computer science, geology, mathematics, and physics), EDUCATION (art education, athletic training, business education, computer education, drama education, early childhood education, education, elementary education, English education, foreign languages education, mathematics education, middle school education, music education, physical education, reading education, science education, secondary education, and social studies education), ENGINEERING AND ENVIRONMENTAL DESIGN (environmental science), HEALTH PROFESSIONS (exercise science, health science, nursing, predentistry, premedicine, and speech pathology/audiology), SOCIAL SCIENCE (biblical studies, corrections, criminal justice, economics, history, ministries, missions, philosophy, political science/government, prelaw, psychology, religious music, social work, sociology, theological studies, and youth ministry). English, speech pathology, and music are the strongest academically. Education, biology, and nursing have the largest enrollments.

Required: To graduate, students must complete a minimum of 124 semester hours with a minimum 2.0 GPA. A minimum of 18 to 30 hours are required in the major (18 must be advanced and 12 of the advanced must be from HSU). 42 hours in upper-division courses are required. Core courses that must be taken include 12 to 18 hours of social science, 9 of English, 7 of natural science (from 2 separate fields and 1 requiring a lab), 6 each of Bible and humanities (3 of fine arts and 3 of non-fine arts), 3 to 6 each of math, 3 to 4 of phys ed, 3 of oral communication, and computer science. All students must satisfy chapel attendance requirements and demonstrate proficiency in written English.

Special: Cross-registration may be arranged with Abilene Christian and McMurry Universities. HSU offers cooperative programs, internships, dual majors, credit by exam, nondegree study, and pass/fail options. Students may study abroad in England, Austria, China, Spain, Italy, and Israel, where HSU is involved in an ongoing archeological excavation of early Christian sites. There are 9 national honor societies and a freshman honors program.

Faculty/Classroom: 64% of faculty are male; 36% are female. 87% teach undergraduates. No introductory courses are taught by graduate students. The average class size in an introductory lecture is 23; in a laboratory, 15; and in a regular course, 17.

Requirements: The SAT or ACT is required. The ACT Optional Writing test is also required. Graduation from an accredited secondary school is required; a GED will be accepted. Applicants should submit an academic record of at least 16 units, distributed as follows: 3 units of English, 2 units each of math, science, and social studies, and 7 units of electives, with a GPA of 2.0 or above. 3 letters of recommendation are also required. HSU requires applicants to be in the upper 75% of their class. A GPA of 2.0 is required. AP and CLEP credits are accepted.

Procedure: Freshmen are admitted to all sessions. There are deferred admissions and rolling admissions plans. Application deadlines are open. The application fee is $50. Notification is sent on a rolling basis. Applications are accepted online.

Transfer: Applicants must submit official transcripts from all previous colleges. Students may petition to transfer up to 2 D grades if the overall GPA is 2.0 or higher. Students transferring from a 2-year college may receive credit for up to 66 semester hours of transferable courses. Applicants with fewer than 24 semester hours must submit a high school transcript and official report of ACT or SAT scores. Students ineligible to continue at another institution are not eligible for regular admission to HSU. 31 of 124 credits required for the bachelor's degree must be completed at HSU.

Visiting: There are regularly scheduled orientations for prospective students, including Cowboy Fridays, plus Fall and Winter Preview and Spring Round-Up. There are guides for informal visits and visitors may sit in on classes. To schedule a visit, contact the Visitor Coordinator.

Financial Aid: The FAFSA is required. Check with the school for current application deadlines.

International Students: The school actively recruits these students. They must take the TOEFL with a minimum score of 550 on the paper-based TOEFL (PBT). They must also take the SAT or ACT.

Admissions Contact: Vicki House, Director of Admissions and Recruiting. A campus DVD is available. E-Mail: *vhouse@hsutx.edu* Web: *hsutx.edu*

HOUSTON BAPTIST UNIVERSITY E-3

Houston, TX 77074-3298 (281) 649-3211
(800) 969-3210; (281) 649-3217

Full-time: 684 men, 1,276 women	**Faculty:** 227
Part-time: 69 men, 168 women	**Ph.D.s:** 75%
Graduate: 106 men, 293 women	**Student/Faculty:** 15 to 1
Year: trimesters, summer session	**Tuition:** $24,145
Application Deadline: open	**Room & Board:** $6,975
Freshman Class: n/av	
SAT or ACT: required	

COMPETITIVE+

Houston Baptist University, founded in 1960, is a private institution affiliated with the Baptist General Convention of Texas and offering undergraduate programs in nursing, arts and science, music, and business administration. The figures in the above capsule and in this profile are approximate. There are 7 undergraduate schools and 4 graduate schools. In addition to regional accreditation, HBU has baccalaureate program accreditation with ACBSP and NLN. The library contains 235,026 volumes, 98,065 microform items, 9591 audio/video tapes/CDs/DVDs, and subscribes to 29,992 periodicals including electronic. Computerized library services include interlibrary loans, database searching, Internet access, and laptop Internet portals. Special learning facilities include an art gallery, TV station, Museum of American Architecture and Decorative Arts, Dunham Family Bible in America Museum, Museum of Southern History, and Morris Cultural Arts Center. The 100-acre campus is in an urban area in southwest Houston. Including any residence halls, there are 29 buildings.

Student Life: 97% of undergraduates are from Texas. Others are from 23 states, 38 foreign countries, and Canada. 41% are white; 19% African American; 17% Hispanic; 16% Asian American. 15% are Catholic; 14% Protestant. The average age of freshmen is 19; all undergraduates, 23. 30% do not continue beyond their first year; 70% remain to graduate.

Housing: 568 students can be accommodated in college housing, which includes single-sex dorms and on-campus apartments. On-campus housing is available on a first-come, first-served basis and is available on a lottery system for upperclassmen. Priority is given to out-of-town students. 68% of students commute. Alcohol is not permitted. All students may keep cars.

Activities: 3% of men belong to 1 local and 1 national fraternity; 5% of women belong to 3 national sororities. There are 51 groups on campus, including art, band, cheerleading, choir, chorale, chorus, computers, debate, drama, ethnic, forensics, honors, international, jazz band, newspaper, opera, pep band, photography, political, professional, radio and TV, religious, social service, student government, and symphony. Popular campus events include Welcome Days for new students, Husky Fest Fall Festival, and Winter Formal.

Sports: There are 2 intercollegiate sports for men and 3 for women, and 12 intramural sports for men and 12 for women. Facilities include volleyball, basketball, and tennis courts, an indoor track, softball, baseball, and soccer fields, and areas for track.

Disabled Students: 90% of the campus is accessible. Facilities include wheelchair ramps, elevators, special parking, specially equipped rest rooms, lowered drinking fountains, lowered telephones, and special housing.

Services: There is remedial math and writing.

Campus Safety and Security: Measures include 24-hour foot and vehicle patrol, emergency notification system, and security escort services. There are emergency telephones and lighted pathways/sidewalks.

Programs of Study: HBU confers B.A., B.S., B.B.A., B.M., and B.S.N. degrees. Associates and master's degrees are also awarded. Bachelor's degrees are awarded in BIOLOGICAL SCIENCE (biology/biological science and molecular biology), BUSINESS (accounting, banking and finance, business administration and management, and entrepreneurial studies), COMMUNICATIONS AND THE ARTS (art, communications, English, French, music, music performance, music theory and composition, and Spanish), COMPUTER AND PHYSICAL SCIENCE (chemistry, information sciences and systems, mathematics, and physics), EDUCATION (art education, early childhood education, elementary education, mathematics education, music education, physical education, reading education, secondary education, special education, and teaching English as a second/foreign language (TESOL/TEFOL)), HEALTH PROFESSIONS (nursing), SOCIAL SCIENCE (biblical languages, Christian studies, economics, history, liberal arts/general studies, physical fitness/movement, political science/government, psychology, religious music, and sociology). Premedical studies, health professions, and education are the strongest academically. Biology, nursing, and business administration have the largest enrollments.

Required: To graduate, students must complete a minimum of 130 semester hours, including at least 48 semester hours of upper-level courses and 24 to 36 hours in the major. They must complete courses in Christianity, written and oral communications, math, lab science, computer, kinetics, social and behavioral sciences, humanities, and fine arts. No grade below C within majors and program requirements and a cumulative GPA of 2.0 is required. Proficiency is required in reading, computer, communication, and math. Spiritual Life Program participation is also a graduation requirement.

Special: HBU offers internships through its academic colleges, B.A.-B.S. degrees, and dual majors in most areas, work-study programs, credit for military experience, and pass/fail options. There is a freshman honors program.

Faculty/Classroom: 45% of faculty are male; 55% are female. 94% teach undergraduates. No introductory courses are taught by graduate students. The average class size in a laboratory is 14 and in a regular course is 10.

Requirements: The SAT or ACT is required, with a recommended satisfactory score on the SAT or ACT composite score of 20. The ACT Optional Writing test is also required. 1 counselor or teacher written recommendation and an official high school transcript or GED scores are also required. AP and CLEP credits are accepted. Important factors in the admissions decision are recommendations by school officials, personality/intangible qualities, and advanced placement or honors courses.

Procedure: Freshmen are admitted to all sessions. Entrance exams should be taken in the fall of the senior year. There are early decision and rolling admissions plans. Application deadlines are open. The application fee is $25. Applications are accepted online.

Transfer: Applicants with fewer than 30 semester hours earned must submit high school and college transcripts and SAT or ACT scores. All students must have a minimum 2.0 GPA and submit all previous college transcripts. 32 of 130 credits required for the bachelor's degree must be completed at HBU.

Visiting: There are guides for informal visits; visitors may sit in on classes and stay overnight. To schedule a visit, contact the Office of Admissions.

Financial Aid: The FAFSA and the college's own financial statement are required. Check with the school for current application deadlines.

International Students: The school actively recruits these students. They must take the TOEFL with a minimum score of 550 on the paper-based TOEFL (PBT) or 80 on the Internet-based version (iBT).

Admissions Contact: Eduardo Borges, Director for Admissions. E-Mail: *unadm@hbu.edu* Web: *www.hbu.edu*

HOWARD PAYNE UNIVERSITY — C-3

Brownwood, TX 76801-2794 — **(325) 649-8027**, **(800) 880-4478; (325) 649-8901**

Full-time: 515 men, 545 women	**Faculty:** n/av
Part-time: 165 men, 170 women	**Ph.D.s:** 49%
Graduate: n/av	**Student/Faculty:** n/av
Year: semesters, summer session	**Tuition:** $22,200
Application Deadline: see profile	**Room & Board:** $6622
Freshman Class: n/av	
SAT or ACT: required	

COMPETITIVE

Howard Payne University, founded in 1889 and affiliated with the Baptist General Convention of Texas, offers undergraduate programs in the arts and sciences, business administration, education, Christianity, music, and social sciences. The figures in the above capsule and in this profile are approximate. There are 6 undergraduate schools. In addition to regional accreditation, HPU has baccalaureate program accreditation with CSWE and NASM. The library contains 118,825 volumes and 271,542 microform items, and subscribes to 30,598 periodicals including electronic. Computerized library services include interlibrary loans, database searching, Internet access, and laptop Internet portals. Special learning facilities include a radio station, children's literature center, audio production facility, TV production studio, and video editing facility. The 29-acre campus is in a small town 120 miles southwest of Dallas/Fort Worth. Including any residence halls, there are 31 buildings.

Student Life: 96% of undergraduates are from Texas. Others are from 18 states and 2 foreign countries. 93% are from public schools. 74% are white; 14% Hispanic. 85% are Protestant. The average age of freshmen is 18; all undergraduates, 22. 40% do not continue beyond their first year; 33% remain to graduate.

Housing: 764 students can be accommodated in college housing, which includes single-sex dorms, on-campus apartments, and married student housing. On-campus housing is available on a lottery system for upperclassmen. 54% of students commute. Alcohol is not permitted. All students may keep cars.

Activities: 14% of men belong to 5 local fraternities; 16% of women belong to 6 local sororities. There are 33 groups on campus, including art, band, cheerleading, choir, chorus, drama, drill team, ethnic, honors, jazz band, literary magazine, marching band, musical theater, newspaper, photography, professional, radio and TV, religious, social, social service, student government, and yearbook. Popular campus events include Christian concerts and College Preview Weekends.

Sports: There are 5 intercollegiate sports for men and 5 for women, and 5 intramural sports for men and 5 for women. Facilities include an 8000-seat stadium and an 800-seat auditorium; a remodeled wellness center with basketball and volleyball courts, an indoor walking track, and free weights and exercise equipment; tennis and sand volleyball courts; a practice field; a student union; and nearby baseball and softball parks.

Disabled Students: 90% of the campus is accessible. Facilities include wheelchair ramps, elevators, special parking, specially equipped rest rooms, special class scheduling, and lowered drinking fountains.

Services: Counseling and information services are available, as is tutoring in some subjects, including math and English. There is remedial math, reading, and writing. A writing lab and computer lab are available for English, math, and computer science.

Campus Safety and Security: There are emergency telephones and lighted pathways/sidewalks. In addition, there are 12-hour foot patrols, monthly dorm meetings, 2 security seminars for the entire campus, and 24-hour cell phone availability with on-duty officers.

Programs of Study: HPU confers B.A., B.S., B.A.A.S., B.B.A., and B.M. degrees. Associates degrees are also awarded. Bachelor's degrees are awarded in BIOLOGICAL SCIENCE (biology/biological science), BUSINESS (accounting and business administration and management), COMMUNICATIONS AND THE ARTS (art, communications, dramatic arts, English, multimedia, music, and Spanish), COMPUTER AND PHYSICAL SCIENCE (chemistry, computer science, and mathematics), EDUCATION (athletic training, elementary education, secondary education, and teaching English as a second/foreign language (TESOL/TEFOL)), ENGINEERING AND ENVIRONMENTAL DESIGN (occupational safety and health), HEALTH PROFESSIONS (exercise science), SOCIAL SCIENCE (Christian studies, history, liberal arts/general studies, political science/government, psychology, social work, and sociology). Biology, chemistry, and political science are the strongest academically. Business management, elementary education, and exercise and sports science have the largest enrollments.

Required: To graduate, students must complete a minimum of 128 credit hours, with 49 in general education courses, 30 to 36 in the major, and 18 to 24 in a minor, plus electives. A minimum 2.0 GPA is required. The general education core includes Bible, English, social science, computer science, fine arts, phys ed, lab science, speech, and math courses. Requirements for students not obtaining the B.A. or B.S. vary. All students must complete 6 semester credits of chapel/convocation attendance.

Special: Cross-registration is offered with several hospitals, and internships are available in many fields. HPU offers credit for experience for B.A.A.S. candidates only, study abroad in Israel and England, pass/fail options, and work-study programs. Special programs include the Douglas MacArthur Academy of Freedom, an interdisciplinary honors program in the social sciences, a chemistry honors program, and a provisional program for under prepared students. There are 4 national honor societies, a freshman honors program, and 1 departmental honors program.

Faculty/Classroom: 64% of faculty are male; 36% are female. All teach undergraduates. No introductory courses are taught by graduate students. The average class size in an introductory lecture is 22; in a laboratory, 20; and in a regular course, 18.

Requirements: The SAT or ACT is required. Applicants must be graduates of an accredited secondary school or have a GED. It is recommended that they have completed 4 credits of English, 3 of math including algebra I, 2 1/2 of social studies, 2 of science, 1 1/2 of phys ed, and 1 each of technology applications and a science/social studies elective, along with courses in economics, health, and speech; the remaining credits should be earned in courses approved by the Texas Board of Education. Graduates of high schools or home study programs that are not accredited by a regional or state accrediting agency will have their work reviewed by the admissions committee on an individual basis. A GPA of 3.0 is required. AP and CLEP credits are accepted. Important factors in the admissions decision are recommendations by school officials, leadership record, and personality/intangible qualities.

Procedure: Freshmen are admitted to all sessions. Entrance exams should be taken during the senior year. There are early admissions and rolling admissions plans. Check with the school for current application deadlines and fee. Applications are accepted online.

Transfer: Transfer students must be able to return to the university they

are leaving and submit official transcripts from all previously attended colleges/universities. Students younger than 21 with fewer than 12 semester hours must submit the SAT or ACT scores. The same GPA per number of hours attempted is required of transfers as for continuing HPU students. 32 of 128 credits required for the bachelor's degree must be completed at HPU.
Visiting: There are regularly scheduled orientations for prospective students, including college preview weekends in the fall and spring. There are guides for informal visits, and visitors may sit in on classes and stay overnight. To schedule a visit, contact the Enrollment Services Office.
Financial Aid: The FAFSA is required. Check with the school for current application deadlines.
International Students: The school actively recruits these students. A TOEFL score is not required for international students entering the English as a Second Language (ESL) program. They must take the SAT or ACT. Students must score 19 on the ACT or 830 on the SAT for unconditional admission; otherwise, a provisional program may be available.
Computers: All students may access the system 24 hours a day in 3 labs in the dorms and 8 a.m. to 10 p.m. Monday through Friday in the instructional building labs. There are no time limits and no fees.
Admissions Contact: Cheryl Mangrum, Coordinator of Admissions Services. E-Mail: *enroll@hputx.edu* Web: *www.hputx.edu*

HUSTON-TILLOTSON UNIVERSITY D-3

Austin, TX 78702 (512) 505-3029
(877) 505-3026; (512) 505-3192

Full-time: 400 men, 420 women
Part-time: 15 men, 25 women
Graduate: 20 men, 25 women
Year: semesters, summer session
Application Deadline: see profile
Freshman Class: n/av
SAT or ACT: required
Faculty: 40
Ph.D.s: 75%
Student/Faculty: 16 to 1
Tuition: $24,860
Room & Board: $6946

COMPETITIVE+

Huston-Tillotson University, formed in 1952 by the merger of Tillotson College and Samuel Huston College (both founded in the mid-1870s), is a private liberal arts institution affiliated with the United Church of Christ and the United Methodist Church. The figures in the above capsule and in this profile are approximate. There are 2 undergraduate schools. The library contains 93,034 volumes, 69,945 microform items, and 49,619 audio/video tapes/CDs/DVDs, and subscribes to 2,353 periodicals including electronic. Computerized library services include interlibrary loans, database searching, and Internet access. Special learning facilities include a learning resource center. The 23-acre campus is in an urban area downtown Austin. Including any residence halls, there are 12 buildings.
Student Life: 91% of undergraduates are from Texas. Others are from 24 states, and 10 foreign countries. 85% are from public schools. 76% are African American; 13% Hispanic. 64% are Protestant. The average age of freshmen is 19; all undergraduates, 23. 45% do not continue beyond their first year; 29% remain to graduate.
Housing: 451 students can be accommodated in college housing, which includes single-sex dorms. On-campus housing is guaranteed for all 4 years. 59% of students commute. Alcohol is not permitted. All students may keep cars.
Activities: 3% of men belong to 4 national fraternities; 8% of women belong to 4 local and 4 national sororities. There are 35 groups on campus, including band, cheerleading, choir, chorus, drill team, honors, international, jazz band, newspaper, professional, radio and TV, religious, social, social service, and student government. Popular campus events include Charter Day, Miss UNCF Contest, and the President's Masked Ball.
Sports: There are 5 intercollegiate sports for men and 6 for women, and 2 intramural sports for men and 2 for women. Facilities include an 800-seat gymnasium, a 700-sq.-ft. weight room, and an outdoor practice/activity field.
Disabled Students: 82% of the campus is accessible. Facilities include wheelchair ramps, elevators, special parking, and specially equipped restrooms.
Services: Counseling and information services are available, as is tutoring in every subject. There is remedial math, reading, and writing.
Campus Safety and Security: Measures include 24-hour foot and vehicle patrol and security escort services. There are lighted pathways/sidewalks.
Programs of Study: HT confers B.A. and B.S. degrees. Bachelor's degrees are awarded in BIOLOGICAL SCIENCE (biology/biological science), BUSINESS (business administration and management and marketing/retailing/merchandising), COMMUNICATIONS AND THE ARTS (English and music), COMPUTER AND PHYSICAL SCIENCE (chemistry, computer science, and mathematics), EDUCATION (education, elementary education, and physical education), SOCIAL SCIENCE (criminal justice, history, interdisciplinary studies, political science/government, psychology, and sociology). Biology, computer science, and education are the strongest academically. Business administration and criminal justice have the largest enrollments.
Required: All students must complete 120 credit hours, including 53 in the general education core curriculum, with a minimum GPA of 2.0. Specific core requirements include 18 hours of English and foreign languages, and 3 hours each of fine arts, math, computer science, philosophy and behavioral sciences, 8 of natural science, 4 of phys ed and health, 3 of philosophy, and 1 of psychology.
Special: The university offers co-op programs, internships, study abroad in 3 countries, work-study programs, and dual majors. A 3-2 engineering degree with Prairie View A&M University is also available. There are 4 national honor societies, a freshman honors program, and 2 departmental honors programs.
Faculty/Classroom: 50% of faculty are male; 50% are female. All teach undergraduates, and 4% do research. No introductory courses are taught by graduate students. The average class size in an introductory lecture, 16, in a laboratory, 16, and in a regular course, 20.
Requirements: The SAT or ACT is required. The ACT Optional Writing test is also required. Applicants must be graduates of any accredited high school with a minimum 2.0 GPA, with a satisfactory score on the SAT or 18 on the ACT, with specific academic credits, including 3 credits each in math, English, and science. A GPA of 2.0 is required. AP and CLEP credits are accepted. Important factors in the admissions decision are advanced placement or honors courses, extracurricular activities record, and parents or siblings that attended your school.
Procedure: Freshmen are admitted fall, spring, and summer. There is a rolling admissions plan. Applications are accepted online. Check with the school for current application deadlines and fee.
Transfer: 89 transfer students enrolled in a recent year. Applicants must submit transcripts from all colleges or universities attended and must have an overall GPA of 2.0. Students with fewer than 15 credit hours must meet freshman entrance requirements. 30 of 120 credits required for the bachelor's degree must be completed at HT.
Visiting: There are guides for informal visits; visitors may sit in on classes and stay overnight. To schedule a visit, contact the Director of Admissions.
Financial Aid: The FAFSA and the college's own financial statement are required. Check with the school for current application deadlines.
International Students: There were 26 international students enrolled in a recent year. They must take the TOEFL with a minimum score of 500 on the paper-based TOEFL (PBT) or 61 on the Internet-based version (iBT). They must also take the SAT or ACT.
Graduates: In a recent year, 93 bachelor's degrees were awarded. The most popular majors were business administration (29%), criminal justice (13%), and education (12%). 80 companies recruited on campus in a recent year. In an average class, 15% graduate in 4 years or less, 61% graduate in 5 years or less, and 29% graduate in 6 years or less.
Admissions Contact: Shakitha Stinson, Director of Admission. E-Mail: *slstinson@htu.edu* Web: *www.htu.edu*

JARVIS CHRISTIAN COLLEGE E-2

Hawkins, TX 75765 (903) 730-4890 ext. 2201; (903) 769-1282

Full-time: 317 men, 252 women
Part-time: 45 men, 18 women
Graduate: n/av
Year: semesters, summer session
Application Deadline: August 1
Freshman Class: n/av
Faculty: 29
Ph.D.s: 76%
Student/Faculty: 20 to 1
Tuition: $11,369
Room & Board: $8183

NONCOMPETITIVE

Jarvis Christian College, founded in 1912, is a private liberal arts institution affiliated with the Disciples of Christ. The library contains 74,456 volumes, 135 microform items, 511 audio/video tapes/CDs/DVDs, and subscribes to 3 periodicals including electronic. Computerized library services include interlibrary loans, database searching, Internet access, and Wi-Fi capability. Special learning facilities include an art gallery, natural history museum, archives of the Black Disciples in Texas. The 243-acre campus is in a rural area 100 miles southeast of Dallas. Including any residence halls, there are 43 buildings.
Student Life: 86% of undergraduates are from Texas. Others are from 21 states. 92% are from public schools. 81% are African American. 62% are Baptist, Church of Christ, and Christian Methodist Episcopal; 30% claim no religious affiliation. The average age of freshmen is 19; all undergraduates, 21. 42% do not continue beyond their first year; 58% remain to graduate.
Housing: 700 students can be accommodated in college housing, which includes single-sex dorms, on-campus apartments, and married student housing. On-campus housing is guaranteed for all 4 years. 74% of students live on campus; of those, 71% remain on campus on weekends. Alcohol is not permitted. All students may keep cars.
Activities: 12% of men belong to 4 local fraternities; 2% of women belong to 4 local sororities. There are 26 groups on campus, including band, cheerleading, choir, chorale, computers, dance, drama, honors,

newspaper, political, professional, religious, social, social service, and student government. Popular campus events include Miss/Mr. Jarvis Coronation, Hall of Fame Weekend, Christmas Concert and Founders'/Homecoming Weekend.

Sports: There are 5 intercollegiate sports for men and 4 for women, and 3 intramural sports for men and 2 for women. Facilities include 2 basketball gyms, an indoor pool, tennis courts, volleyball courts, a soccer field, billiards, a flag football field, and a softball/baseball diamond.

Disabled Students: 83% of the campus is accessible. Facilities include wheelchair ramps, special parking, specially equipped restrooms, special class scheduling, lowered drinking fountains, and special housing.

Services: Counseling and information services are available, as is tutoring in every subject. There is remedial math, reading, and writing.

Campus Safety and Security: Measures include 24-hour foot and vehicle patrol, self-defense education, and security escort services. There are lighted pathways/sidewalks.

Programs of Study: Jarvis confers B.A., B.S. and B.B.A. degrees. Bachelor's degrees are awarded in BIOLOGICAL SCIENCE (biology/biological science), BUSINESS (business administration and management), COMMUNICATIONS AND THE ARTS (English), COMPUTER AND PHYSICAL SCIENCE (chemistry and mathematics), EDUCATION (elementary education, secondary education, and special education), SOCIAL SCIENCE (criminal justice, history, religion, social work, and sociology). Biology, criminal justice, social work, kinesiology, and business administration are the strongest academically. Business administration, criminal justice, and kinesiology have the largest enrollments.

Required: A 56-credit general education requirement includes at least 30 hours in the major, plus courses in English, literature, math, religion, science, speech, social science, health, and phys ed. Other graduation requirements include a minimum 2.0 GPA, at least 120 credit hours, math and writing proficiency, and satisfactory scores on the sophomore comprehensive exam. Students planning to enter a graduate or professional school are encouraged to take the GRE, LSAT, MCAT, or GMAT.

Special: Jarvis offers co-op and work-study programs, an accelerated degree in education; internships, dual and student-designed majors. Cross-registration is offered with members of the TADC consortium. Also available are the Brookhaven National Laboratory Semester Program, the UNCF Premedical Summer Program with Fisk University, and the Biomedical Sciences Program with Meharry Medical College. A dual engineering degree is available with University of Texas at Arlington and a dual nursing degree with University of Texas at Tyler. There are 4 national honor societies, a freshman honors program, and 2 departmental honors programs.

Faculty/Classroom: 69% of faculty are male; 31% are female. All teach undergraduates, 28% do research, and 28% do both. No introductory courses are taught by graduate students. The average class size in an introductory lecture is 30; in a laboratory is 18; and in a regular course is 20.

Admissions: 5% of the current freshmen were in the top fifth of their class; 17% were in the top two fifths.

Requirements: The SAT or ACT and ACT Writing Test are recommended. Applicants should graduate from an accredited secondary school with 16 academic credits, including 3 each in English and social science, 2 in math, and 1 in science. The GED is accepted. Graduates of nonaccredited high schools are given conditional admission. Jarvis requires applicants to be in the upper 15% of their class. A GPA of 2.0 is required. AP and CLEP credits are accepted. Important factors in the admissions decision are parents or siblings attended your school and recommendations by alumni.

Procedure: Freshmen are admitted fall, spring, and summer. Entrance exams should be taken Before entrance or during orientation week. There is a rolling admissions plan. Early decision applications should be filed by May 1; regular applications, by August 1 for fall entry; December 1 for spring entry; and May 1 for summer entry, along with a $50 fee. Notifications are sent April 1. Applications are accepted online.

Transfer: 100 transfer students enrolled in 2012-2013. Applicants must submit official transcripts from all schools of higher education attended and provide proof of honorable dismissal from the most recent higher institution, Full credit may be given for courses transferred from unaccredited institutions, but students must validate their work by completing twelve (12) semester hours in residence before transfer credits are accepted at full value. 30 of 120 credits required for the bachelor's degree must be completed at Jarvis.

Visiting: There are regularly scheduled orientations for prospective students, Classroom visits, a tour of the campus, and review of the orientation guidebook. There are guides for informal visits, visitors may sit in on classes, and stay overnight. To schedule a visit, contact Micheline Lambert at (903) 730-4890.

Financial Aid: In 2013-2014, 94% of all full-time freshmen and 99% of continuing full-time students received some form of financial aid. 94% of all full-time freshmen and 99% of continuing full-time students received need-based aid. The average freshman award was $17,596. Need-based scholarships or need-based grants averaged $9,550; need-based self-help aid (loans and jobs) averaged $5,200; and non-need-based athletic scholarships averaged $6,163. 39% of undergraduate students work part-time. Average annual earnings from campus work are $4320. The average financial indebtedness of the 2013 graduate was $4,067. The FAFSA, FFS, and the college's own financial statement are required. The priority date for freshman financial aid applications for fall entry is February 1. The deadline for filing freshman financial aid applications for fall entry is May 1.

International Students: The school actively recruits these students. They must take the TOEFL with a minimum score of 500 on the paper-based TOEFL (PBT). They must also take the SAT or ACT.

Graduates: From July 1, 2012 to June 30, 2013, 42 bachelor's degrees were awarded. The most popular majors were business (33%), biology (14%), and business administration (14%). 52 companies recruited on campus in 2012-2013. In an average class, 7% graduate in 4 years or less, 2% graduate in 5 years or less, and 2% graduate in 6 years or less. Of the 2012 graduating class, 19% were enrolled in graduate school within 6 months of graduation, and 52% were employed.

Admissions Contact: Micheline Lambert, Director. E-Mail: *mlambert@jarvis.edu* Web: *www.jarvis.edu*

LAMAR UNIVERSITY E-3

Beaumont, TX 77710 **(409) 000-0000; (409) 880 8463**

Full-time: 2350 men, 2850 women	**Faculty:** n/av; IIA, -$
Part-time: 1320 men, 1970 women	**Ph.D.s:** 48%
Graduate: 265 men, 310 women	**Student/Faculty:** n/av
Year: semesters, summer session	**Tuition:** $6836 ($16,352)
Application Deadline: see profile	**Room & Board:** $6500
Freshman Class: n/av	
SAT or ACT: required	

LESS COMPETITIVE

Lamar University-Beaumont, founded in 1923, is part of the Lamar University system. The university offers undergraduate degrees in arts and sciences, business, education, engineering, fine arts, communications, health and behavioral science, and technical arts. The figures in the above capsule and in this profile are approximate. There are 7 undergraduate schools and 5 graduate schools. In addition to regional accreditation, LU has baccalaureate program accreditation with AACSB, ABET, CSWE, NASM, and NCATE. The library contains 900,000 volumes and subscribes to 2800 periodicals including electronic. Computerized library services include interlibrary loans and database searching. Special learning facilities include a learning resource center, art gallery, and radio station. The 200-acre campus is in an urban area 90 miles east of Houston. Including any residence halls, there are 90 buildings.

Student Life: 96% of undergraduates are from Texas. Others are from 39 states, 61 foreign countries, and Canada. 95% are from public schools. 79% are white; 16% African American. The average age of freshmen is 19; all undergraduates, 25. 40% do not continue beyond their first year; 19% remain to graduate.

Housing: 1700 students can be accommodated in college housing, which includes dorms and on-campus apartments. In addition, there are special-interest houses, fraternity houses, and sorority houses. On-campus housing is guaranteed for all 4 years. 91% of students commute. Alcohol is not permitted. All students may keep cars.

Activities: 5% of men belong to 11 national fraternities; 5% of women belong to 7 national sororities. There are 120 groups on campus, including art, band, cheerleading, choir, chorale, chorus, communications, computers, dance, drama, ethnic, film, honors, international, jazz band, literary magazine, marching band, musical theater, newspaper, opera, orchestra, pep band, photography, political, professional, radio and TV, religious, social, social service, student government, and symphony. Popular campus events include Springfest, Birdfeed, and Love Lamar Week.

Sports: There are 7 intercollegiate sports for men and 6 for women, and 15 intramural sports for men and 15 for women. Facilities include a 10,000-seat multipurpose facility for basketball and other sports, a student center with games areas and a video lounge, a gym, an indoor/outdoor pool, a track, and a 17,000-seat stadium.

Disabled Students: All of the campus is accessible. Facilities include wheelchair ramps, elevators, special parking, specially equipped rest rooms, special class scheduling, lowered drinking fountains, and lowered telephones.

Services: Counseling and information services are available, as is tutoring in some subjects, including math and English. There is a reader service for the blind and remedial math, reading, and writing.

Campus Safety and Security: Measures include 24-hour foot and vehicle patrol and self-defense education. There are lighted pathways/sidewalks.

Programs of Study: LU confers B.A., B.S., B.A.A.S., B.B.A., B.F.A., B.G.S., B.Mus., and B.S.W. degrees. Associates, master's, and doctoral degrees are also awarded. Bachelor's degrees are awarded in BIOLOGICAL SCIENCE (biology/biological science), BUSINESS (accounting, business administration and management, business economics, business law, marketing/retailing/merchandising, and personnel management), COMMUNICATIONS AND THE ARTS (advertising, communications, design, dramatic arts, English, fine arts, French, music, Spanish, and speech/debate/rhetoric), COMPUTER AND PHYSICAL SCIENCE (chemistry, computer programming, computer science, geology, information sciences and systems, mathematics, and physics), EDUCATION (art education, early childhood education, elementary education, foreign languages education, health education, music education, science education, secondary education, and special education), ENGINEERING AND ENVIRONMENTAL DESIGN (chemical engineering, civil engineering, electrical/electronics engineering, industrial engineering, industrial engineering technology, and mechanical engineering), HEALTH PROFESSIONS (medical laboratory technology, nursing, occupational therapy, pharmacy, physical therapy, predentistry, premedicine, and speech pathology/audiology), SOCIAL SCIENCE (criminal justice, economics, family/consumer studies, history, political science/government, prelaw, psychology, public administration, social science, social work, and sociology). Engineering is the strongest academically. Arts and sciences have the largest enrollments.

Required: To graduate, all students must complete 124 to 132 total credit hours, with 30 hours in the major. Required courses include 12 hours of English, 6 hours each of electives, political science, and American history, and 4 hours each of lab science or math and physical activity and/or marching band and/or ROTC. Students must have a minimum 2.0 GPA.

Special: The university offers internships in social work, work-study programs, B.A.-B.S. degrees, a dual major in biochemistry, the general studies degree, credit for experience, nondegree study, and pass/fail options. There are 2 national honor societies, including Phi Beta Kappa, and a freshman honors program.

Faculty/Classroom: 58% of faculty are male; 42% are female. All teach undergraduates. No introductory courses are taught by graduate students. The average class size in an introductory lecture is 50; in a laboratory, 25; and in a regular course, 24.

Requirements: The SAT or ACT is required. SAT subject tests in math are required for engineering and physical science majors. Applicants must be graduates of an accredited secondary school or have a GED certificate and must have completed 4 credits of English, 3 of math, 2 of science, and 2 1/2 of history. A GPA of 2.0 is required. AP and CLEP credits are accepted. Important factors in the admissions decision are advanced placement or honors courses, evidence of special talent, and leadership record.

Procedure: Freshmen are admitted to all sessions. Entrance exams should be taken in the fall of the senior year. There is a rolling admissions plan. Check with the school for current application deadlines. The application fee is $25.

Transfer: Applicants must have a minimum 2.0 GPA and at least 18 credit hours earned. 30 of 132 credits required for the bachelor's degree must be completed at LU.

Visiting: There are regularly scheduled orientations for prospective students. There are guides for informal visits. To schedule a visit, contact the Admissions Office.

Financial Aid: LU is a member of CSS. The CSS/Profile and the college's own financial statement are required. Check with the school for current application deadlines.

International Students: They must take the TOEFL. They must also take the SAT or ACT, scoring 800 on the SAT.

Admissions Contact: Admissions Office. A campus DVD is available. E-Mail: *admissions@lamar.edu* Web: *www.lamar.edu*

LETOURNEAU UNIVERSITY E-2

Longview, TX 75607 **(903) 233-3000**
(800) 759-8811; (903) 233-3411

Full-time: 938 men, 405 women	**Faculty:** n/av
Part-time: 315 men, 792 women	**Ph.D.s:** n/av
Graduate: 92 men, 301 women	**Student/Faculty:** 15 to 1
Year: semesters, summer session	**Tuition:** $25,740
Application Deadline: August 1	**Room & Board:** $9030
Freshman Class: 1684 applied, 730 accepted, 362 enrolled	
SAT or ACT: required	

COMPETITIVE

Claiming every workplace in every nation as their mission field, LeTourneau University graduates are professionals of ingenuity and Christ-like character who see life's work as a holy calling with eternal impact. From nationally acclaimed academics in fields like engineering and aeronautical science, to excellent programs in business, computer science, education, health care, the humanities, kinesiology, liberal arts, the natural sciences and psychology, LeTourneau emphasizes problem solving, applied knowledge and the integration of faith and learning. LETU's commitment to hands-on learning with personal attention means students don't get lost in the crowd. Instead, they benefit from outstanding faculty, dedicated to an educational experience that is Christ-centered and local but which develops leaders for global impact. International learning opportunities take students around the world. LETU students have participated in ground-breaking research, including biomedical engineering in Africa, visual literacy in Kenya, micro-finance in Ethiopia, or macroeconomics in South America. Students co-author and present research at international conferences. Undergraduate and graduate programs for working adults are offered online and at educational centers in Austin, Bedford, Dallas, Houston, and Tyler. Graduate programs include master's degrees in business administration, counseling, education, engineering, psychology, and strategic leadership. The entering freshman class averages of SAT scores range from approximately 140-160 points above the national average and evidence a strong academic quality. Nearly 20 percent of LETU's traditional enrollment were home schooled. LETU's 55,000 square-foot Paul and Betty Abbott Aviation Center at East Texas Regional Airport features a fleet of 12 airplanes, a 10,000-square foot hangar, classrooms and laboratories equipped with state-of-the-art technology for students majoring in flight science, aircraft systems and an FAA-approved program in air traffic control. Students regularly compete with large public and private schools and take top honors at regional and national competitions in many fields, especially electrical, mechanical and aeronautical design. Life on campus is biblically based, with chapel services, professor-led devotionals, student-led praise and worship and Bible study and prayer times. Students attend weekly chapel services in the state-of-the-art S.E. Belcher Jr. Chapel and Performance center that seats 2,000 and attracts world-class entertainment. There are 6 undergraduate schools and one graduate school. In addition to regional accreditation, LeTourneau has baccalaureate program accreditation with ABET. The library contains 113,322 volumes, 51,621 microform items, 789 audio/video tapes/CDs/DVDs, and subscribes to 77,969 periodicals including electronic. Computerized library services include interlibrary loans, database searching, Internet access, and Wi-Fi capability. Special learning facilities include a The 162-acre campus is in a small town 60 miles west of Shreveport, Louisiana, and 120 miles east of the Dallas/Fort Worth metroplex. Including any residence halls, there are 56 buildings.

Student Life: 47% of undergraduates are from out of state, mostly the West. Students are from states. 61% are White; 31% African American; 15% Hispanic. 26% are non-denominational.

Housing: College-sponsored housing includes single-sex dorms, on-campus apartments, and married student housing. In addition, there are language houses, special-interest houses, Residential societies available, theme housing. On-campus housing is guaranteed for all 4 years. Alcohol is not permitted. All students may keep cars.

Activities: There are no fraternities or sororities. Groups on campus include and music ensembles, drama, film, honors, international, jazz band, literary magazine, newspaper, religious, student government, theater, and yearbook.

Disabled Students: Facilities include wheelchair ramps, elevators, special parking, specially equipped restrooms, special class scheduling, lowered drinking fountains, lowered telephones, special housing, and automated doors.

Services: Counseling and information services are available, as is tutoring in most subjects. There is remedial math and writing.

Campus Safety and Security: Measures include 24-hour foot and vehicle patrol, self-defense education, and security escort services. There are lighted pathways/sidewalks.

Programs of Study: LeTourneau confers B.A., B.S. and B.B.A. degrees. Associate and master's degrees are also awarded. Bachelor's degrees are awarded in BIOLOGICAL SCIENCE (biology/biological science), BUSINESS (accounting, business administration and management, management information systems, marketing management, and marketing/retailing/merchandising), COMMUNICATIONS AND THE ARTS (English), COMPUTER AND PHYSICAL SCIENCE (chemistry, computer mathematics, computer science, and mathematics), EDUCATION (business education, elementary education, physical education, science education, and secondary education), ENGINEERING AND ENVIRONMENTAL DESIGN (aeronautical science, aeronautical technology, computer engineering, computer technology, electrical/electronics engineering, engineering, engineering technology, industrial administration/management, mechanical engineering, and welding engineering), HEALTH PROFESSIONS (health, premedicine, and preveterinary science), SOCIAL SCIENCE (biblical studies, history, interdisciplinary studies, prelaw, psychology, and public administration).

Required: All students must fulfill general curricula requirements, including 12 hours of biblical studies, 9 of English, 3 each of lab science, math, history, and humanities and social science, as well as 2 of phys ed and 1 of introduction to the university. A minimum of 126 semester credit hours, including at least 24 in the major, with a minimum GPA of 2.0 is required to graduate.

Special: Le Tourneau offers co-op programs in engineering, business, accounting, computer science, biology, design technology, and others, internships through business and liberal arts programs, an American studies program with the Council for Christian Colleges and Universities, credit for experience, and study abroad in 7 countries. There is a freshman honors program.

Faculty/Classroom: No introductory courses are taught by graduate students.

Admissions: 43% of the 2013-2014 applicants were accepted. 93 freshmen graduated first in their class.

Requirements: The SAT or ACT is required, with a satisfactory score on the SAT or 20 on the ACT. Applicants must be graduates of an accredited secondary school or have the GED. They should have completed 16 academic credits, including 4 in English, 3 each in math and natural science, 2 in social studies, and 1 in computer science. An essay is required. LeTourneau requires applicants to be in the upper 72% of their class. A GPA of 3.6 is required. AP and CLEP credits are accepted.

Procedure: Freshmen are admitted to all sessions. Entrance exams should be taken by the fall of the senior year. There are deferred admissions and rolling admissions plans. Early decision applications should be filed by December 31; regular applications, by August 1 for fall entry, along with a $35 fee. Notifications are sent August 1. Applications are accepted online.

Transfer: 99 transfer students enrolled in 2012-2013. Applicants with at least 26 semester hours must have a minimum 2.0 GPA. Other students must satisfy freshman entrance requirements. They must provide transcripts from previous colleges attended and a statement of good standing. 36 of 126 credits required for the bachelor's degree must be completed at LeTourneau.

Visiting: There are regularly scheduled orientations for prospective students. Visits are individualized and may include touring the school, attending classes, special events, or chapel, meeting with faculty and financial aid personnel, and staying in a dorm. There are guides for informal visits, visitors may sit in on classes, and stay overnight. To schedule a visit, contact the Visitor Coordinator.

Financial Aid: In 2013-2014, 78% of all full-time freshmen and 31% of continuing full-time students received some form of financial aid. 78% of all full-time freshmen and 31% of continuing full-time students received need-based aid. The average freshman award was $22,004. Need-based scholarships or need-based grants averaged $17,961; need-based self-help aid (loans and jobs) averaged $4,383; and other non-need-based awards and non-need-based scholarships averaged $3,601. The average financial indebtedness of the 2013 graduate was $41,522. LeTourneau is a member of CSS. The FAFSA is required. Check with the school for current application deadlines.

International Students: The school actively recruits these students. They must take the TOEFL. They must also take the SAT or ACT.

Graduates: From July 1, 2012 to June 30, 2013, 635 bachelor's degrees were awarded. The most popular majors were business/marketing (41%), education (21%), and engineering (10%). In an average class, 78% graduate in 4 years or less.

Admissions Contact: James Townsend, Director of Admissions. E-Mail: *admissions@letu.edu* Web: *www.letu.edu*

LUBBOCK CHRISTIAN UNIVERSITY B-2

Lubbock, TX 79407 (806) 720-7151
(800) 933-7601; 806-720-7162

Full-time: 490 men, 768 women	**Faculty:** 92
Part-time: 103 men, 170 women	**Ph.D.s:** 54%
Graduate: 129 men, 342 women	**Student/Faculty:** 12 to 1
Year: semesters, summer session	**Tuition:** $18,740
Application Deadline: open	**Room & Board:** $6778
Freshman Class: 783 applied, 743 accepted, 255 enrolled	
SAT CR/M/W: 500/520/490	**ACT:** 22 **COMPETITIVE**

Lubbock Christian University, founded in 1957 in affiliation with the Churches of Christ, offers undergraduate degrees in liberal arts and professional studies, and graduate degrees in Biblical studies and education, behavioral sciences and nursing. There are 3 undergraduate schools and 2 graduate schools. In addition to regional accreditation, LCU has baccalaureate program accreditation with CSWE and NLN. The library contains 128,890 volumes, 2,250 microform items, 172 audio/video tapes/CDs/DVDs, and subscribes to 404 periodicals including electronic. Computerized library services include interlibrary loans, database searching, Internet access, and Wi-Fi capability. Special learning facilities include an art gallery and radio station. The 65-acre campus is in a suburban area 350 miles from Dallas and 325 miles from Albuquerque. Including any residence halls, there are 22 buildings.

Student Life: 91% of undergraduates are from Texas. Others are from 46 states, 16 foreign countries, and Canada. 86% are from public schools. 71% are White; 19% Hispanic. 89% are Protestant. The average age of freshmen is 18; all undergraduates, 23. 30% do not continue beyond their first year; 70% remain to graduate.

Housing: 589 students can be accommodated in college housing, which includes single-sex dorms, on-campus apartments, and married student housing. On-campus housing is guaranteed for the freshman year only, is available on a first-come, and first-served basis. 67% of students commute. Alcohol is not permitted. All students may keep cars.

Activities: 19% of men belong to 4 local fraternities; 17% of women belong to 3 local sororities. There are 32 groups on campus, including art, band, cheerleading, chorus, drama, ethnic, honors, international, jazz band, musical theater, newspaper, pep band, professional, radio and TV, religious, social, social service, student government, symphony, and yearbook. Popular campus events include Master Follies, Family Weekend and Spiritual Renewal Week.

Sports: There are 5 intercollegiate sports for men and 5 for women, and 7 intramural sports for men and 8 for women. Facilities include the Rip Griffin Center, which serves as the home for the university's intercollegiate teams. The field house is the center for intramural and phys ed activities with an indoor track, badminton, volleyball, and basketball courts, and a fitness center.

Disabled Students: Facilities include wheelchair ramps, elevators, special parking, specially equipped restrooms, special class scheduling, and lowered drinking fountains.

Services: Counseling and information services are available, as is tutoring in every subject. There is a reader service for the blind, and remedial math, reading, and writing.

Campus Safety and Security: Measures include 24-hour foot and vehicle patrol, emergency notification system, and security escort services. There are lighted pathways/sidewalks and controlled access to dorms/residences.

Programs of Study: LCU confers B.A., B.S., B.B.A., B.S.I.S., B.S.N. and B.S.W. degrees. Associate and master's degrees are also awarded. Bachelor's degrees are awarded in AGRICULTURE (agricultural business management, agriculture, and animal science), BIOLOGICAL SCIENCE (biology/biological science), BUSINESS (accounting, banking and finance, business administration and management, finance, organizational leadership and management, and sports management), COMMUNICATIONS AND THE ARTS (American literature, communications, creative writing, and music), COMPUTER AND PHYSICAL SCIENCE (chemistry, information sciences and systems, and mathematics), EDUCATION (art education, business education, early childhood education, elementary education, middle school education, music education, physical education, school psychology, science education, and secondary education), ENGINEERING AND ENVIRONMENTAL DESIGN (engineering), HEALTH PROFESSIONS (exercise science, medical technology, nursing, premedicine, prepharmacy, and prephysical therapy), SOCIAL SCIENCE (biblical studies, criminal justice, family/consumer studies, humanities, ministries, missions, physical fitness/movement, prelaw, psychology, social work, and youth ministry). Education, business administration, and social work are the strongest academically. Organizational management, early childhood/elementary education, and humanities have the largest enrollments.

Required: To graduate, students must complete 120 credit hours, including at least 39 in upper-division courses, 18 in the major, and 15 in residence after achieving senior status, with a minimum GPA of 2.25 overall and 2.5 in the major. All students must fulfill general education and biblical studies course requirements, including courses in English, math, history, science, communication, computer science, and exercise science. The core curriculum totals 33 hours.

Special: LCU offers co-op programs in engineering, medical technology, and criminal justice, internships in several fields, and cross-registration with Texas Tech University and other regional schools. A general studies degree, nondegree study, and pass/fail options are also available. A 3-2 engineering degree with Texas Tech University is offered. There are 3 national honor societies, a freshman honors program, and 1 departmental honors programs.

Faculty/Classroom: 55% of faculty are male; 45% are female. All teach undergraduates. No introductory courses are taught by graduate students. The average class size in an introductory lecture is 19; in a laboratory is 13; and in a regular course is 16.

Admissions: 95% of the 2013-2014 applicants were accepted. The SAT scores for the 2013-2014 freshman class were: Critical Reading--46% below 500, 40% between 500 and 599, 11% between 600 and 699, and 3% between 700 and 800; Math--39% below 500, 44% between 500 and 599, 16% between 600 and 699, and 1% between 700 and 800; Writing--51% below 500, 40% between 500 and 599, and 9% between 600 and 699. The ACT scores were 29% below 21, 29% between 21 and 23, 29% between 24 and 26, 8% between 27 and 28, and 5% above 28. 31% of the current freshmen were in the top fifth of their class; 62% were in the top two fifths. 5 freshmen graduated first in their class.

Requirements: The SAT or ACT is required. Applicants must be graduates of an accredited secondary school or have a GED certificate. Unconditional admission is granted to freshmen who score 18 or higher on the ACT or 860 or higher on the SAT and who meet all other admission requirements. AP and CLEP credits are accepted. Important factors in the admissions decision are personality/intangible qualities, parents or siblings attended your school, and geographical diversity.

Procedure: Freshmen are admitted fall, spring, and summer. Entrance exams should be taken before registration. There are deferred admissions and rolling admissions plans. Application deadlines are open. Application fee is $25. Applications are accepted online.

Transfer: 176 transfer students enrolled in 2012-2013. Transfer stu-

dents with fewer than 16 hours of college credit must meet freshman admission requirements. All transfers must submit an official transcript from previously attended colleges or universities and be in good academic standing. Only courses with a grade of C or above are transferred from another institution. 30 of 126 credits required for the bachelor's degree must be completed at LCU.

Visiting: There are regularly scheduled orientations for prospective students. There are guides for informal visits, visitors may sit in on classes, and stay overnight. To schedule a visit, contact the LCU Admissions.

Financial Aid: In 2013-2014, 48% of all full-time freshmen and 74% of continuing full-time students received some form of financial aid. 47% of all full-time freshmen and 70% of continuing full-time students received need-based aid. The average freshman award was $13,766. Need-based scholarships or need-based grants averaged $9,659; need-based self-help aid (loans and jobs) averaged $4,967; non-need-based athletic scholarships averaged $7,416; and other non-need-based awards and non-need-based scholarships averaged $4,203. 19% of undergraduate students work part-time. Average annual earnings from campus work are $1093. The average financial indebtedness of the 2013 graduate was $29,053. The FAFSA and the college's own financial statement are required. The priority date for freshman financial aid applications for fall entry is June 1.

International Students: There are 27 international students enrolled. They must take the TOEFL with a minimum score of 525 on the paper-based TOEFL (PBT) or 196 on the Internet-based version (iBT) or take the MELAB. They must also take the SAT or ACT, scoring 18.

Graduates: From July 1, 2012 to June 30, 2013, 511 bachelor's degrees were awarded. The most popular majors were health professions and related programs (25%), business/marketing (18%), and education (17%). In an average class, 2% graduate in 3 years or less, 28% graduate in 4 years or less, 9% graduate in 5 years or less, and 2% graduate in 6 years or less.

Admissions Contact: Charles Webb, Director of Admissions. E-Mail: *charles.webb@lcu.edu* Web: *www.lcu.edu*

MCMURRY UNIVERSITY C-2

Abilene, TX 79697 (325) 793-4700
(800) 460-2392; (325) 793-4718

Full-time: 603 men, 613 women	**Faculty:** 78; IIB, --$
Part-time: 141 men, 152 women	**Ph.D.s:** 78%
Graduate: n/av	**Student/Faculty:** 16 to 1
Year: semesters, summer session	**Tuition:** $19,205
Application Deadline: August 13	**Room & Board:** $6757
Freshman Class: 1574 applied, 896 accepted, 320 enrolled	
SAT CR/M: 460/500	**ACT:** 20 **LESS COMPETITIVE**

McMurry University, chartered in 1923, is a private liberal arts institution affiliated with the United Methodist Church. There are 4 undergraduate schools. The library contains 158,395 volumes, 4,519 microform items, 2,171 audio/video tapes/CDs/DVDs, and subscribes to 440 periodicals including electronic. Computerized library services include interlibrary loans, database searching, Internet access, and Wi-Fi capability. Special learning facilities include an art gallery, several special book collections, including the McWhiney collection of Civil War-era books. The 43-acre campus is in an urban area 154 miles west of Fort Worth. Including any residence halls, there are 30 buildings.

Student Life: 96% of undergraduates are from Texas. Others are from 22 states, and 5 foreign countries. 61% are White; 15% African American; 15% Hispanic. 47% are Protestant; 11% Catholic. The average age of freshmen is 18; all undergraduates, 22. 41% do not continue beyond their first year; 42% remain to graduate.

Housing: 672 students can be accommodated in college housing, which includes single-sex dorms and on-campus apartments. On-campus housing is guaranteed for all 4 years, is available on a first-come, and first-served basis. 53% of students commute. Alcohol is not permitted. All students may keep cars.

Activities: 5% of men belong to 5 local fraternities; 9% of women belong to 6 local sororities. There are 45 groups on campus, including art, band, cheerleading, choir, chorale, computers, drama, honors, jazz band, literary magazine, marching band, musical theater, newspaper, political, professional, religious, social, social service, and student government. Popular campus events include Parents Weekend, Sing Song, and Big Event.

Sports: There are 9 intercollegiate sports for men and 8 for women, and 9 intramural sports for men and 9 for women. Facilities include a 4500-seat track and football stadium, a 2200-seat gym, a 1500-seat auditorium, an intramural gym, a swimming pool and diving area, 2 racquetball courts, basketball, volleyball, and badminton courts, a soccer field, and a 875-seat baseball stadium, practice fields. and tennis courts.

Disabled Students: 70% of the campus is accessible. Facilities include wheelchair ramps, elevators, special parking, specially equipped restrooms, special class scheduling, and special housing.

Services: Counseling and information services are available, as is tutoring in most subjects. There is remedial math, reading, and writing.

Campus Safety and Security: Measures include 24-hour foot and vehicle patrol. There are lighted pathways/sidewalks.

Programs of Study: McMurry confers B.A., B.S., B.B.A., B.F.A., B.I.S. and B.S.N. degrees. Bachelor's degrees are awarded in BIOLOGICAL SCIENCE (biochemistry, biology/biological science, and life science), BUSINESS (accounting, banking and finance, business administration and management, management information systems, and marketing/retailing/merchandising), COMMUNICATIONS AND THE ARTS (art, dramatic arts, English, multimedia, music, and Spanish), COMPUTER AND PHYSICAL SCIENCE (chemistry, computer science, mathematics, and physics), EDUCATION (art education, athletic training, business education, elementary education, English education, middle school education, physical education, and secondary education), HEALTH PROFESSIONS (biomedical science, exercise science, and nursing), SOCIAL SCIENCE (history, interdisciplinary studies, political science/government, psychology, religion, social studies, and sociology). Education, biology, and chemistry are the strongest academically.

Required: Students must complete 120 semester hours, including 30 in the major, with a GPA of at least 2.0.Distribution requirements vary with the degree but include courses in English, ethics, fine arts, science, math, social science, religion, political science, sociology, history, foreign language, and health fitness.

Special: McMurry offers internships for seniors with area businesses and cross-registration with Abilene Christian and Hardin-Simmons Universities. There are work-study programs with the university. There are 14 national honor societies, a freshman honors program, and 22 departmental honors programs.

Faculty/Classroom: 58% of faculty are male; 42% are female. All teach undergraduates, and 64% do research. No introductory courses are taught by graduate students.

Admissions: 57% of the 2013-2014 applicants were accepted. The SAT scores for the 2013-2014 freshman class were: Critical Reading--61% below 500, 28% between 500 and 599, 10% between 600 and 699, and 1% between 700 and 800; Math--49% below 500, 38% between 500 and 599, 13% between 600 and 699. The ACT scores were 53% below 21, 19% between 21 and 23, 16% between 24 and 26, 5% between 27 and 28, and 7% above 28. 28% of the current freshmen were in the top fifth of their class; 58% were in the top two fifths.

Requirements: The SAT or ACT is required. Applicants need 16 academic credits, including 4 units of English, 3 each in math and social studies, and 2 each in foreign language and science. An interview is recommended. The GED is accepted with a score of 550 or higher. A GPA of 2.0 is required. AP and CLEP credits are accepted. Important factors in the admissions decision are extracurricular activities record, leadership record, and personality/intangible qualities.

Procedure: Freshmen are admitted fall, spring, and summer. Entrance exams should be taken in the junior year. There are deferred admissions and rolling admissions plans. Applications should be filed by August 13 for fall entry; January 1 for spring entry; and May 13 for summer entry, along with a $20 fee. Notification is sent on a rolling basis. Applications are accepted online.

Transfer: 175 transfer students enrolled in 2012-2013. All transfer students must have a GPA of at least 2.0. Those with fewer than 15 credit hours must submit high school transcripts and SAT I or ACT scores; those with 15 to 23 hours need only school transcripts. 30 of 126 credits required for the bachelor's degree must be completed at McMurry.

Visiting: There are regularly scheduled orientations for prospective students. There are guides for informal visits, visitors may sit in on classes, and stay overnight. To schedule a visit, contact the Admissions Office.

Financial Aid: In 2013-2014, 99% of all full-time freshmen and 98% of continuing full-time students received some form of financial aid. 78% of all full-time freshmen and 78% of continuing full-time students received need-based aid. The average freshman award was $21,613. Need-based scholarships or need-based grants averaged $8,673 ($15,462 maximum); need-based self-help aid (loans and jobs) averaged $4,206 ($8,120 maximum); and other non-need-based awards and non-need-based scholarships averaged $12,007 ($30,229 maximum). 48% of undergraduate students work part-time. Average annual earnings from campus work are $800. The average financial indebtedness of the 2013 graduate was $27,935. The FAFSA is required. The priority date for freshman financial aid applications for fall entry is March 15. The deadline for filing freshman financial aid applications for fall entry is open.

International Students: There are 9 international students enrolled. The school actively recruits these students. They must take the TOEFL with a minimum score of 550 on the paper-based TOEFL (PBT) or 79 on the Internet-based version (iBT).

Graduates: From July 1, 2012 to June 30, 2013, 257 bachelor's degrees were awarded. The most popular majors were business (27%), education (25%), and exercise and sports studies (8%). 10 companies recruited on campus in 2012-2013. In an average class, 2% graduate in 3 years or less, 27% graduate in 4 years or less, 38% graduate in 5 years or less, and 42% graduate in 6 years or less. Of the 2012 graduating class, 27% were enrolled in graduate school within 6 months of graduation, and 73% were employed.

Admissions Contact: Dave Voskuil, VP for Enrollment Management. E-Mail: *admissions@mcm.edu* Web: *www.mcm.edu*

MIDWESTERN STATE UNIVERSITY D-2

Wichita Falls, TX 76308-2099 (940) 397-4334
(800) 842-1922; (940) 397-4672

Full-time: 1,885 men, 2,401 women
Part-time: 565 men, 860 women
Graduate: 234 men, 480 women
Year: semesters, summer session
Application Deadline: see profile
Freshman Class: n/av
SAT or ACT: required
Faculty: 332
Ph.D.s: 68%
Student/Faculty: 19 to 1
Tuition: $11,390
Room & Board: $6300

COMPETITIVE

Midwestern State University, founded in 1922, is a public liberal arts institution offering courses in business administration, education, fine arts, health sciences, humanities, math and science, political science and public administration, and social and behavioral sciences. The figures in the above capsule and in this profile are approximate. There are 6 undergraduate schools and 5 graduate schools. In addition to regional accreditation, MSU has baccalaureate program accreditation with ABET, ACBSP, ADA, NASM, NCATE, and NLN. The library contains 241,000 volumes, 158,000 microform items, 6757 audio/video tapes/CDs/DVDs, and subscribes to 1100 periodicals including electronic. Computerized library services include interlibrary loans and database searching. Special learning facilities include an art gallery, planetarium, TV station, greenhouse, and TTVN studio. The 172-acre campus is in an urban area 135 miles northwest of Dallas. Including any residence halls, there are 31 buildings.

Student Life: 94% of undergraduates are from Texas. Others are from 50 states, 40 foreign countries, and Canada. 67% are white; 13% African American. The average age of freshmen is 18; all undergraduates, 25. 28% do not continue beyond their first year; 30% remain to graduate.

Housing: 733 students can be accommodated in college housing, which includes single-sex and coed dorms, on-campus apartments, off-campus apartments, and married student housing. In addition, there are honors houses and a biology house. On-campus housing is guaranteed for the freshman year only and is available on a first-come, first-served basis. Priority is given to out-of-town students. 80% of students commute. Alcohol is not permitted. All students may keep cars.

Activities: 13% of men belong to 6 national fraternities; 11% of women belong to 6 national sororities. There are 102 groups on campus, including art, band, cheerleading, choir, chorale, chorus, computers, dance, drama, environmental, ethnic, honors, international, jazz band, literary magazine, marching band, newspaper, pep band, political, professional, radio and TV, religious, social, social service, student government, and symphony. Popular campus events include Family Day, Spirit Days, and College Day Preview.

Sports: There are 4 intercollegiate sports for men and 4 for women, and 18 intramural sports for men and 21 for women. Facilities include a 5000-seat gym, a soccer stadium, tennis courts, an indoor swimming pool, a sand volleyball court, and a walking track.

Disabled Students: 99% of the campus is accessible. Facilities include wheelchair ramps, elevators, special parking, specially equipped rest rooms, special class scheduling, lowered drinking fountains, lowered telephones, and special housing.

Services: Counseling and information services are available, as is tutoring in some subjects, including algebra, sciences, and history. There is a reader service for the blind and remedial math, reading, and writing.

Campus Safety and Security: Measures include 24-hour foot and vehicle patrol and self-defense education. There are lighted pathways/sidewalks and seminars on safety and living on campus.

Programs of Study: MSU confers B.A., B.S., B.A.A.S., B.B.A., B.F.A., B.M., B.S.C.J., B.S.D.H., B.S.I.S., B.S.M.T., B.S.N., B.S.R.C., B.S.R.S., and B.S.W. degrees. Associates and master's degrees are also awarded. Bachelor's degrees are awarded in BIOLOGICAL SCIENCE (biology/biological science), BUSINESS (accounting, banking and finance, business administration and management, business economics, international economics, management science, and marketing/retailing/merchandising), COMMUNICATIONS AND THE ARTS (communications, dramatic arts, English, fine arts, music, and Spanish), COMPUTER AND PHYSICAL SCIENCE (chemical technology, chemistry, computer science, geology, information sciences and systems, and mathematics), EDUCATION (music education and physical education), ENGINEERING AND ENVIRONMENTAL DESIGN (engineering technology, environmental science, manufacturing engineering, and preengineering), HEALTH PROFESSIONS (dental hygiene, health care administration, health science, medical laboratory technology, nursing, predentistry, premedicine, prepharmacy, preveterinary science, radiological science, and respiratory therapy), SOCIAL SCIENCE (criminal justice, economics, history, humanities, interdisciplinary studies, political science/government, prelaw, psychology, social work, and sociology). Business and nursing have the largest enrollments.

Required: All students must earn a minimum GPA of 2.0 while taking 120 semester hours, with 24 in the major. Distribution requirements include 7 to 10 hours of natural science, 6 hours of humanities, 6 of social science, and additional phys ed requirements.

Special: An exchange program with the Monterrey Institute of Technology, internships with local firms and agencies, and study abroad in London are available. Dual majors, co-op programs in all majors, a general studies degree, credit for military experience, and nondegree study up to 12 hours are also offered. There are 23 national honor societies and a freshman honors program.

Faculty/Classroom: 50% of faculty are male; 50% are female. All teach undergraduates. Graduate students teach 10% of introductory courses. The average class size in an introductory lecture is 25; in a laboratory, 20; and in a regular course, 25.

Requirements: The SAT or ACT is required. The minimum required composite score on the SAT or ACT is dependent on class rank. For students in the top quarter of the class, there is no minimum requirement. High school credits should include 4 years of English, 3 years of math, 2 years of science, and 6 units of electives. The GED is accepted. AP and CLEP credits are accepted.

Procedure: Freshmen are admitted to all sessions. Entrance exams should be taken before applying for admission. There are early decision and rolling admissions plans. Check with the school for current application deadlines. Applications are accepted online.

Transfer: Transfer students with fewer than 18 semester hours must meet beginning freshman criteria. A minimum GPA of a 2.0, college transcripts, and a statement of good standing from prior institutions are required. 31 of 120 credits required for the bachelor's degree must be completed at MSU.

Visiting: There are regularly scheduled orientations for prospective students, consisting of a college day preview each February, which introduces high school juniors, seniors, and their parents to the campus and faculty. There are also daily tours. There are guides for informal visits, and visitors may sit in on classes and stay overnight. To schedule a visit, contact the Admissions Office.

Financial Aid: MSU is a member of CSS. The FAFSA and the college's own financial statement are required. Check with the school for current application deadlines.

International Students: The school actively recruits these students. They must take the TOEFL with a minimum score of 530 on the paper-based TOEFL (PBT). They must also take the SAT or ACT.

Computers: All students may access the system. There are no time limits and no fees.

Admissions Contact: Director of Admissions. E-Mail: *admissions@mwsu.edu* Web: *www.mwsu.edu*

NORTHWOOD UNIVERSITY D-2

Cedar Hill, TX 75104 (972) 293-5400
(800) 927-9663; (972) 291-3824

Full-time: 275 men, 240 women
Part-time: 5 men, 10 women
Graduate: 25 men, 20 women
Year: semesters, summer session
Application Deadline: see profile
Freshman Class: n/av
SAT or ACT: required
Faculty: n/av
Ph.D.s: 40%
Student/Faculty: n/av
Tuition: $20,540
Room & Board: $9260

LESS COMPETITIVE

Northwood University, founded in 1959 and whose Texas campus opened in 1966, is a private institution offering undergraduate degrees in business administration. The figures in the above capsule and in this profile are approximate. Campuses are located in Florida, Michigan, and Texas. The library contains 9,428 volumes 475 audio/video tapes/CDs/DVDs, and subscribes to 150 periodicals including electronic. Computerized library services include interlibrary loans, database searching, Internet access, and laptop Internet portals. Special learning facilities include a learning resource center and art gallery. The 360-acre campus is in a suburban area 18 miles southwest of Dallas. Including any residence halls, there are 18 buildings.

Student Life: 94% of undergraduates are from Texas. Others are from 17 states, 16 foreign countries, and Canada. 90% are from public schools. 32% are Hispanic; 14% African American. The average age of freshmen is 18; all undergraduates, 21. 36% do not continue beyond their first year; 31% remain to graduate.

Housing: 146 students can be accommodated in college housing, which includes single-sex dorms and on-campus apartments. On-campus housing is guaranteed for the freshman year only, is available on a first-come, and first-served basis. 74% of students commute. All students may keep cars.

Activities: 3% of men belong to 2 local fraternities; 3% of women belong to 2 local sororities. There are 17 groups on campus, including choir, computers, debate, drama, forensics, international, literary magazine, photography, professional, religious, social, social service, and student government. Popular campus events include Sanity Inn (talent show), Spring Formal, Haunted Forest, and International Festival.

Sports: There are 4 intercollegiate sports for men and 4 for women, and 2 intramural sports for men. Facilities include a volleyball court, tennis court, baseball/softball fields, soccer field, jogging trails, along with a state recreational area adjacent to the campus.

Disabled Students: 75% of the campus is accessible. Facilities include wheelchair ramps, special parking, specially equipped restrooms, special class scheduling, lowered drinking fountains, and lowered telephones.

Services: Counseling and information services are available, as is tutoring in most subjects. There is a reader service for the blind, and remedial math, reading, and writing, and tutoring for any subject at student's request.

Campus Safety and Security: Measures include 24 hour foot and vehicle patrol and emergency notification system. There are emergency telephones, lighted pathways/sidewalks, and controlled access to dorms/residences. Traffic is monitored coming onto campus from 9 p.m. to 5 a.m. 7 days a week. In addition, RAs are first-responders and receive CPR/AED certification.

Programs of Study: Northwood confers B.B.A. degrees. Associate and master's degrees are also awarded. Bachelor's degrees are awarded in BUSINESS (accounting and marketing management). Accounting is the strongest academically. Marketing has the largest enrollment.

Required: To graduate, all students must complete at least 123 semester credit hours, including 24 in the major, with a minimum GPA of 2.0. Students must complete the general studies core curriculum and 3 credits of computer science management. Internships are required in some majors.

Special: Study abroad in 15 countries, accelerated degree programs,and internships in some majors are offered. There is a freshman honors program.

Faculty/Classroom: 61% of faculty are male; 38% are female. All teach undergraduates. No introductory courses are taught by graduate students. The average class size in an introductory lecture, 22, in a laboratory, 15, and in a regular course, 19.

Requirements: The SAT or ACT is required. Applicants must have a minimum 2.7 GPA on a 4.0 scale and a score of 17 on the ACT or 830 on the SAT (Critical Reading + Math only). An Admissions Review Committee is available for applicants who do not meet minimum standards and requires a 250-word essay. A GPA of 2.0 is required. AP and CLEP credits are accepted. Important factors in the admissions decision are leadership record, advanced placement or honors courses, and extracurricular activities record.

Procedure: Freshmen are admitted spring and summer. Entrance exams should be taken by December of the senior year. There are deferred admissions and rolling admissions plans. The fee is waived for online applications. Notification is sent on a rolling basis. Applications are accepted online. Check with the school for current application deadlines and fee.

Transfer: 71 transfer students enrolled in a recent year. Applicants must have at least 24 attempted and completed college-level hours and a 2.0 GPA on a 4.0 scale. 31 of 123 credits required for the bachelor's degree must be completed at Northwood.

Visiting: There are regularly scheduled orientations for prospective students, consisting of formal, monthly, customizable recruitment visits that allow students to sit in on a class, tour the campus, meet with students and faculty, and eat lunch in the cafeteria. There are guides for informal visits and visitors may sit in on classes. To schedule a visit, contact the Admissions Office.

Financial Aid: In a recent year, 78% of all full-time freshmen and 70% of continuing full-time students received some form of financial aid. 68% of all full-time freshmen and 60% of continuing full-time students received need-based aid. The average freshmen award was $16,481. Need-based scholarships or need-based grants averaged $5,345 ($11,860 maximum); need-based self-help aid (loans and jobs) averaged $4,709 ($5,600 maximum); non-need based athletic scholarships averaged $5,620 ($17,500 maximum); other non-need based awards and non-need based scholarships averaged $6,980 ($11,500 maximum). 7% of undergraduate students worked part-time. Average annual earnings from campus work were $1539. The FAFSA is required. The deadline for filing freshman financial aid applications for fall entry is rolling.

International Students: There are 48 international students enrolled. The school actively recruits these students. They must take the TOEFL with a minimum score of 500 on the paper-based TOEFL (PBT) or 61 on the Internet-based version (iBT).

Graduates: In a recent year, 93 bachelor's degrees were awarded. The most popular majors were international business (16%), advertising (14%), and promotions management (12%). In an average class, 22% graduate in 4 years or less, 28% graduate in 5 years or less, and 31% graduate in 6 years or less. In a recent year, 93% were employed within 6 months of graduation.

Admissions Contact: Sylvia Correa, Admissions Director. A campus DVD is available. E-Mail: *txadmit@northwood.edu* Web: *www.northwood.edu*

OUR LADY OF THE LAKE UNIVERSITY OF SAN ANTONIO D-4

San Antonio, TX 78207-4689 **(210) 434-6711, ext. 314**
(800) 436-6558; (210) 431-4036

Full- and part-time: 2,751 men and women
Graduate: 1,163 men and women
Year: semesters, summer session
Application Deadline: open
Freshman Class: n/av
SAT or ACT: required
Faculty: n/av
Ph.D.s: n/av
Student/Faculty: 15 to 1
Tuition: $23,256
Room & Board: $7588

LESS COMPETITIVE

Our Lady of the Lake University, founded as a private Catholic institution in 1895 by the Sisters of Divine Providence, offers programs in the arts and sciences, business, education, and social service. The figures in the above capsule and in this profile are approximate. There are 4 undergraduate schools and 4 graduate schools. In addition to regional accreditation, The Lake has baccalaureate program accreditation with ASLA and CSWE. The library contains 163,217 microform items 8891 audio/video tapes/CDs/DVDs, and subscribes to 557 periodicals including electronic. Computerized library services include interlibrary loans, database searching, Internet access, and laptop Internet portals. Special learning facilities include a learning resource center, a demonstration school (early childhood to grade 8), and a communication/learning disorders center. The 52-acre campus is in an urban area about 4 miles west of downtown San Antonio. Including any residence halls, there are 23 buildings.

Student Life: 99% of undergraduates are from Texas. Others are from 17 states and 7 foreign countries. 61% are Hispanic; 19% white. 62% claim no religious affiliation; 24% Catholic; 12% Protestant. The average age of freshmen is 18; all undergraduates, 27. 38% do not continue beyond their first year; 35% remain to graduate.

Housing: 639 students can be accommodated in college housing, which includes coed dorms. In addition, there is honors, quiet, alcohol, drug, and smoke-free housing. On-campus housing is guaranteed for all 4 years. 73% of students commute. All students may keep cars.

Activities: There are no fraternities or sororities. There are 35 groups on campus, including art, cheerleading, choir, chorale, chorus, computers, dance, drama, ethnic, honors, music ensembles, newspaper, orchestra, political, professional, radio and TV, religious, social, social service, student government, and symphony. Popular campus events include Spirit Week.

Sports: There are 9 intramural sports for men and 9 for women. Facilities include playing fields, tennis courts, indoor and outdoor pools, and a gym equipped for weight lifting, and aerobics.

Disabled Students: 90% of the campus is accessible. Facilities include wheelchair ramps, elevators, special parking, specially equipped rest rooms, special class scheduling, lowered drinking fountains, lowered telephones, and special housing.

Services: Counseling and information services are available, as is tutoring in some subjects. There is a reader service for the blind and remedial math, reading, and writing.

Campus Safety and Security: Measures include 24-hour foot and vehicle patrol. There are lighted pathways/sidewalks.

Programs of Study: The Lake confers B.A., B.S., B.A.S., B.B.A., and B.S.W. degrees. Master's and doctoral degrees are also awarded. Bachelor's degrees are awarded in BIOLOGICAL SCIENCE (biology/biological science), BUSINESS (accounting, business administration and management, human resources, management information systems, marketing management, and personnel management), COMMUNICATIONS AND THE ARTS (art, communications, dramatic arts, English, fine arts, music, and Spanish), COMPUTER AND PHYSICAL SCIENCE (chemistry, information sciences and systems, mathematics, and natural sciences), EDUCATION (art education, early childhood education, and special education), HEALTH PROFESSIONS (speech pathology/audiology), SOCIAL SCIENCE (behavioral science, history, liberal arts/general studies, Mexican-American/Chicano studies, philosophy, political science/government, psychology, religion, social studies, social work, and sociology). Biology and chemistry are the strongest academically. Business has the largest enrollment.

Required: A general education requirement includes competencies in English, math, the natural, social, and behavioral sciences, religion, philosophy, literature, art, history, and phys ed. Other graduation requirements are a minimum 2.0 GPA, 128 credit hours, requirements specific to the major, and satisfactory scores on the COMP/ACT.

Special: There is cross-registration through the United Colleges of San Antonio. Dual majors are possible in the B.A.-B.B.A. programs. A 3-2 engineering degree is offered with Washington University. Credit by exam and for life/work/military experience is available, as is a special degree program for working adults/nontraditional students through the Weekend College.

Faculty/Classroom: No introductory courses are taught by graduate students.

Requirements: The SAT or ACT is required. Applicants should graduate from an accredited secondary school with 16 academic credits, including 4 in English, 3 in social studies, and 2 each in math and lab science. A combination of SAT or ACT scores and high school GPA or class rank determines admission. A GED with a satisfactory SAT or ACT score is also acceptable. Mature students returning to school may waive the SAT/ACT requirement for the college's own testing. AP and CLEP credits are accepted.

Procedure: Freshmen are admitted to all sessions. Entrance exams should be taken prior to December of the senior year. There are deferred admissions and rolling admissions plans. Application deadlines are open. The application fee is $25 (waived for online applications). Applications are accepted online.

Transfer: Transfer applicants with 30 or more credit hours and a minimum 2.0 GPA are accepted. Others are evaluated by the same criteria as freshmen applicants. 30 of 128 credits required for the bachelor's degree must be completed at the Lake.

Visiting: There are regularly scheduled orientations for prospective students. There are guides for informal visits; visitors may sit in on classes and stay overnight. To schedule a visit, contact the Admissions Office.

Financial Aid: The FAFSA and FFS are required. Check with the school for current application deadlines.

International Students: The school actively recruits these students. They must take the TOEFL.

Admissions Contact: Dean of Enrollment Management. E-Mail: *admission@lake.ollusa.edu* Web: *www.ollusa.edu*

PAUL QUINN COLLEGE — D-2

Dallas, TX 75241 (214) 302-3575 or 302-3520 (214) 302-3559

Full-time: 92 men, 98 women	**Faculty:** n/av
Part-time: 1 men, 2 women	**Ph.D.s:** n/av
Graduate: n/av	**Student/Faculty:** n/av
Year: semesters	**Tuition:** $12,400
Application Deadline:	**Room & Board:** $7350
Freshman Class: n/av	
SAT or ACT: required	
	LESS COMPETITIVE

Paul Quinn College, founded in 1872, is a coeducational liberal arts college affiliated with the African Methodist Episcopal Church. There are 5 undergraduate schools. In addition to regional accreditation, PQC has baccalaureate program accreditation with CSWE. The library contains 88,187 volumes, 30,550 microform items, and subscribes to 167 periodicals including electronic. Computerized library services include interlibrary loans, database searching, Internet access, and Wi-Fi capability. Special learning facilities include a The 130-acre campus is in an urban area 12 miles from downtown Dallas. Including any residence halls, there are 8 buildings.

Student Life: 74% of undergraduates are from Texas. Others are from 9 states. 92% are from public schools. 88% are African American; 11% Hispanic. 97% are Protestant. The average age of freshmen is 18; all undergraduates, 20. 20% do not continue beyond their first year.

Housing: 236 students can be accommodated in college housing, which includes coed dorms. In addition, there are honors houses. On-campus housing is guaranteed for all 4 years. 51% of students commute. Alcohol is not permitted. All students may keep cars.

Activities: 40% of men belong to 4 national fraternities; 30% of women belong to 3 national sororities. There are 20 groups on campus, including cheerleading, choir, chorale, computers, dance, drama, ethnic, musical theater, newspaper, religious, social, social service, student government, and yearbook. Popular campus events include Honors Day, and Founders Day.

Sports: There are 3 intercollegiate sports for men and 3 for women, and 5 intramural sports for men and 5 for women.

Disabled Students: All of the campus is accessible. Facilities include wheelchair ramps, elevators, special parking, specially equipped restrooms, special class scheduling, and lowered drinking fountains.

Services: Counseling and information services are available, as is tutoring in every subject. There is remedial math, reading, and writing. Tutoring is available.

Campus Safety and Security: Measures include 24-hour foot and vehicle patrol and security escort services. There are controlled access to dorms/residences.

Programs of Study: PQC confers B.S. degrees. Bachelor's degrees are awarded in BUSINESS (accounting, business administration and management, and entrepreneurial studies), COMMUNICATIONS AND THE ARTS (communications and English), SOCIAL SCIENCE (humanities, legal studies, liberal arts/general studies, political science/government, and psychology). Legal studies is the strongest academically. Business administration -management has the largest enrollments.

Special: There is a freshman honors program.

Faculty/Classroom: No introductory courses are taught by graduate students.

Requirements: The SAT or ACT is required, and high school transcripts must be submitted. A GPA of 2.0 is required. CLEP credits are accepted. Important factors in the admissions decision are leadership record, advanced placement or honors courses, and recommendations by school officials.

Procedure: Check with the school for current application deadlines.

Transfer: Applicants must meet the basic admissions requirements. 30 of 128 credits required for the bachelor's degree must be completed at PQC.

Visiting: There are regularly scheduled orientations for prospective students. There are guides for informal visits, visitors may sit in on classes, and stay overnight. To schedule a visit, contact the Director of Admissions.

Financial Aid: PQC is a member of CSS. The FAFSA, and and the previous year's student's/parents' tax forms is required. Check with the school for current application deadlines.

International Students: They must take the TOEFL. They must also take the SAT or ACT, scoring 700.

Admissions Contact: Ralph Spencer, Admissions Officer. Web: *www.pqc.edu*

PRAIRIE VIEW A&M UNIVERSITY — D-3

Prairie View, TX 77446 (936) 261-1000; (936) 857-2699

Full-time: 2549 men, 3732 women	**Faculty:** n/av
Part-time: 192 men, 284 women	**Ph.D.s:** 111%
Graduate: 441 men, 1138 women	**Student/Faculty:** 17 to 1
Year: semesters, summer session	**Tuition:** $7738 ($18,268)
Application Deadline: June 1	**Room & Board:** $7467
Freshman Class: 9602 applied, 3975 accepted, 1588 enrolled	
SAT CR/M/W: 410/420/417 **ACT:** 17	**LESS COMPETITIVE**

Prairie View A&M University, established in 1876, is a comprehensive unit of the Texas A&M University System, offering undergraduate and graduate degree programs in applied sciences and engineering technology, business, engineering, nursing, arts and sciences, education, agriculture and human sciences, architecture, juvenile justice, and psychology. There are 8 undergraduate schools and 7 graduate schools. In addition to regional accreditation, PVAMU has baccalaureate program accreditation with AACSB, ABET, CSWE, NAAB, NCATE, and NLN. The library contains 388,559 volumes, 712,773 microform items, 3,307 audio/video tapes/CDs/DVDs, and subscribes to 33,733 periodicals including electronic. Computerized library services include interlibrary loans, database searching, Internet access, and Wi-Fi capability. Special learning facilities include an art gallery, radio station, a solar observatory. The 1440-acre campus is in a small town 40 miles northwest of Houston. Including any residence halls, there are 153 buildings.

Student Life: 93% of undergraduates are from Texas. Others are from 38 states, and 34 foreign countries. 90% are from public schools. 89% are African American. The average age of freshmen is 19; all undergraduates, 22. 24% do not continue beyond their first year; 39% remain to graduate.

Housing: 3084 students can be accommodated in college housing, which includes coed on-campus apartments. In addition, there are special-interest houses, and intensive learning community housing for 600 upperclass students. On-campus housing is guaranteed for the freshman year only, is available on a first-come, and first-served basis. 53% of students live on campus; of those, 50% remain on campus on weekends. Alcohol is not permitted. All students may keep cars.

Activities: 5% of men belong to 5 national fraternities; 5% of women belong to 4 national sororities. There are 30 groups on campus, including band, cheerleading, choir, chorus, dance, drama, drill team, ethnic, honors, international, jazz band, marching band, newspaper, orchestra, photography, political, professional, radio and TV, religious, social, social service, and student government. Popular campus events include Honors Week, Family Day and Trail Rides.

Sports: There are 8 intercollegiate sports for men and 10 for women, and 6 intramural sports for men and 6 for women. Facilities include a 5000-seat stadium and a large athletic and recreation complex.

Disabled Students: 5% of the campus is accessible. Facilities include wheelchair ramps, elevators, special parking, and specially equipped restrooms.

Services: Counseling and information services are available, as is tutoring in some subjects. There is a reader service for the blind, and remedial math, reading, and writing.

Campus Safety and Security: Measures include 24-hour foot and vehicle patrol. There are emergency telephones, lighted pathways/sidewalks, and a 24-hour department of traffic and security.

Programs of Study: PVAMU confers B.A., B.S., B.Arch., B.A.S.W., B.B.A., B.S.Ag., B.S.C.E., B.S.C.E.T., B.S.C.H.E., B.S.C.J., B.S.Diet., B.S.E.E., B.S.E.E.T., B.S.H.S., B.S.I.S., B.S.I.T., B.S.M.E., B.S.N. and B.S.T.C.H. degrees. Master's and doctoral degrees are also awarded. Bachelor's degrees are awarded in AGRICULTURE (agricultural business management, agricultural economics, agronomy, and animal science), BIOLOGICAL SCIENCE (biology/biological science), BUSINESS (accounting, banking and finance, business administration and management, and marketing/retailing/merchandising), COMMUNICATIONS AND THE ARTS (art, broadcasting, communications, dramatic arts, English, journalism, music, Spanish, and speech/debate/rhetoric), COMPUTER AND PHYSICAL SCIENCE (chemistry, computer science, mathematics, and physics), EDUCATION (physical education), ENGINEERING AND ENVIRONMENTAL DESIGN (architecture, chemical engineering, civil engineering, computer engineering, electrical/electronics engineering, engineering technology, industrial engineering technology, and mechanical engineering), HEALTH PROFESSIONS (health, medical technology, and nursing), SOCIAL SCIENCE (criminal justice, dietetics, family and community services, geography, history, interdisciplinary studies, political science/government, psychology, social work, and sociology). Engineering and nursing is the strongest academically. Nursing, educational administration, and counseling have the largest enrollments.

Required: All students must complete at least 120 semester hours, with a minimum GPA of 2.5 or higher, depending on the major. Completion of a 42-hour core curriculum is required. Some majors require a comprehensive exam or thesis.

Special: Cooperative programs and internships in various majors, study abroad, work-study programs, and combined B.A.-B.S. degrees in chemistry, biology, math, and computer science are offered. There are 12 national honor societies, including Phi Beta Kappa, and a freshman honors program.

Faculty/Classroom: 60% of faculty are male; 40% are female. Graduate students teach 1% of introductory courses. The average class size in an introductory lecture is 23 and in a laboratory is 30.

Admissions: 41% of the 2013-2014 applicants were accepted. The SAT scores for the 2013-2014 freshman class were: Critical Reading--85% below 500, 13% between 500 and 599, 1% between 600 and 699; Math--82% below 500, 16% between 500 and 599, 2% between 600 and 699. The ACT scores were 57% below 21, 36% between 21 and 23, 4% between 24 and 26, and 4% between 27 and 28. 19% of the current freshmen were in the top fifth of their class; 46% were in the top two fifths. 3 freshmen graduated first in their class.

Requirements: The SAT or ACT is required. In addition, a GPA of at least 2.0 is necessary for financial aid eligibility. Applicants should be graduates of accredited high schools or have earned the GED. Secondary school preparation should include 4 years each of English and academic electives, 3 years each of math and social studies, and 2 years of science. A GPA of 2.5 is required. AP and CLEP credits are accepted. Important factors in the admissions decision are leadership record, advanced placement or honors courses, and recommendations by school officials.

Procedure: Freshmen are admitted to all sessions. Entrance exams should be taken during the junior or senior year of high school. There is a deferred admissions plan. Applications should be filed by June 1 for fall entry; November 1 for spring entry; and April 1 for summer entry, along with a $25 fee. Notification is sent on a rolling basis. Applications are accepted online.

Transfer: 401 transfer students enrolled in 2012-2013. Transfer applicants must present at least a 2.0 GPA from the last college attended. 30 of 120 credits required for the bachelor's degree must be completed at PVAMU.

Visiting: There are regularly scheduled orientations for prospective students, consisting of an orientation held 2 days prior to registration. There are guides for informal visits, visitors may sit in on classes, and stay overnight. To schedule a visit, contact the Student Recruitment.

Financial Aid: In 2013-2014, 76% of all full-time freshmen and 71% of continuing full-time students received some form of financial aid. 76% of all full-time freshmen and 71% of continuing full-time students received need-based aid. The average freshman award was $14,745. Need-based scholarships or need-based grants averaged $4,120; need-based self-help aid (loans and jobs) averaged $2,500; non-need-based athletic scholarships averaged $10,051; other non-need-based awards and non-need-based scholarships averaged $3,875; and $6,385 from other forms of aid. The average financial indebtedness of the 2013 graduate was $27,500. The CSS/Profile, FAFSA, and the college's own financial statement are required. The priority date for freshman financial aid applications for fall entry is March 17. The deadline for filing freshman financial aid applications for fall entry is August 1.

International Students: There are 93 international students enrolled. They must take the TOEFL with a minimum score of 500 on the paper-based TOEFL (PBT). They must also take the SAT or ACT. a satisfactory score on the SAT or ACT.

Graduates: From July 1, 2012 to June 30, 2013, 1026 bachelor's degrees were awarded. The most popular majors were health professions and related programs (20%), business/marketing (14%), and homeland security (11%). In an average class, 14% graduate in 4 years or less, 18% graduate in 5 years or less, and 39% graduate in 6 years or less.

Admissions Contact: Mary Gooch, Director of Undergraduate Admissions. E-Mail: *admissions@pvamu.edu* Web: *www.pvamu.edu*

RICE UNIVERSITY E-3

Houston, TX 77251-1892 (713) 348-7423
(800) 527-OWLS; (713) 348-5952

Full-time: 1600 men, 1475 women	**Faculty:** 670; I, +$
Part-time: 25 men, 15 women	**Ph.D.s:** 96%
Graduate: 1430 men, 810 women	**Student/Faculty:** 6 to 1
Year: semesters, summer session	**Tuition:** $33,620
Application Deadline: see profile	**Room & Board:** $12,250
Freshman Class: n/av	
SAT or ACT: required	

MOST COMPETITIVE

Rice University, founded in 1912, is a comprehensive research university offering undergraduate and graduate programs through its schools of Engineering, Natural Sciences, Humanities, Social Sciences, Music, and Architecture; Rice's School of Business offers graduate degrees and an undergraduate minor. The figures in the above capsule and in this profile are approximate. There are 6 undergraduate schools and 7 graduate schools. In addition to regional accreditation, Rice has baccalaureate program accreditation with ABET and NAAB. The library contains 2.6 million volumes, 3.3 million microform items, 62,279 audio/video tapes/CDs/DVDs, and subscribes to 72,352 periodicals including electronic. Computerized library services include interlibrary loans, database searching, Internet access, and laptop Internet portals. Special learning facilities include an art gallery, radio station, TV station, a media center, and an observatory. The 300-acre campus is in an urban area 3 miles southwest of downtown Houston. Including any residence halls, there are 75 buildings.

Student Life: 55% of undergraduates are from Texas. Others are from 50 states, 44 foreign countries, and Canada. 48% are white; 21% Asian American; 12% Hispanic. 33% are Protestant; 32% claim no religious affiliation; 18% Catholic. The average age of freshmen is 18; all undergraduates, 20. 3% do not continue beyond their first year; 93% remain to graduate.

Housing: 2080 students can be accommodated in college housing, which includes coed dorms. On-campus housing is guaranteed for the freshman year plus 2 of the 3 upperclass years and is available on a lottery system for upperclassmen. 67% of students live on campus; of those, 95% remain on campus on weekends. All students may keep cars.

Activities: There are no fraternities or sororities. There are 225 groups on campus, including academic, art, band, cheerleading, chess, choir, chorale, chorus, computers, dance, debate, drama, environmental, ethnic, film, forensics, gay, honors, international, jazz band, literary magazine, marching band, musical theater, newspaper, opera, orchestra, pep band, photography, political, professional, radio and TV, religious, social, social service, student government, symphony, and yearbook. Popular campus events include Baker Shakespeare Festival, Biking Relay Race, Archi Arts, and Costume Ball.

Sports: There are 19 intercollegiate sports for men and 18 for women, and 14 intramural sports for men and 13 for women. Facilities include a 103,000-square-foot recreation center with a 2400-square-foot recreation pool, a 50-meter competition pool, 2 indoor and 2 outdoor basketball courts, an indoor soccer and hockey arena, 4 racquetball courts, 2 squash courts, a 9000-square-foot weight and cardio workout room, and 4 multipurpose rooms for group fitness and dance classes; a 5000-seat gym; a pool; a track stadium; fields for soccer, lacrosse, and rugby; courts for tennis, squash, racquetball, volleyball, and basketball; and a 70,000-seat stadium.

Disabled Students: 90% of the campus is accessible. Facilities include wheelchair ramps, elevators, special parking, specially equipped rest rooms, special class scheduling, lowered drinking fountains, lowered telephones, special housing, and a stair lift.

Services: Counseling and information services are available, as is tutoring in every subject.

Campus Safety and Security: Measures include 24-hour foot and vehicle patrol, emergency notification system, self-defense education, and security escort services. There are shuttle buses, emergency telephones, lighted pathways/sidewalks, controlled access to dorms/residences, and a campus police department with a variety of outreach programs.

Programs of Study: Rice confers B.A., B.S., B.Arch., B.F.A., B.Mus., and B.S.E degrees. Master's and doctoral degrees are also awarded. Bachelor's degrees are awarded in BIOLOGICAL SCIENCE (biology/biological science), BUSINESS (management science), COMMUNICATIONS AND THE ARTS (art history and appreciation, classics, English, linguistics, music, music history and appreciation, music performance, music theory and composition, and visual and performing arts), COMPUTER AND PHYSICAL SCIENCE (applied mathematics, chemistry, computer science, earth science, geology, geophysics and seismology, mathematics, physics, and statistics), ENGINEERING AND ENVIRONMENTAL DESIGN (architectural engineering, architecture, bioengineering, chemical engineering, civil engineering, electrical/electronics engineering, environmental engineering, and mechanical engineering), HEALTH PROFESSIONS (exercise science), SOCIAL SCIENCE (anthropology, Asian/Oriental studies, classical/ancient civilization, cognitive science, economics, French studies, German area studies, Hispanic American studies, history, medieval studies, philosophy, political science/government, psychology, public affairs, religion, sociology, and women's studies). Biochemistry and cell biology, mechanical engineering, and political science have the largest enrollments.

Required: All students must complete at least 120 credits, with a 1.67 overall GPA and a 2.0 GPA in the major field. Distribution requirements include 12 credit/semester hours in natural sciences, social sciences, or humanities, depending on the major, and additional courses in these fields to meet distribution requirements. All students take 2 semesters of phys ed. At least 48 semester hours in upper-level courses are required.

Special: An 8-year guaranteed medical school program with the Baylor College of Medicine; a 5-year joint degree program for the B.S.E./M.S.E. in engineering; a 5-year joint degree for the B.S.E./M.B.A. in engineering and business; and a 3-2 engineering degree are possible, as are cross-registration, internships, study abroad, work-study, dual majors, and student-designed majors. There are 10 national honor societies, including Phi Beta Kappa, and 9 departmental honors programs.

Faculty/Classroom: 69% of faculty are male; 31% are female. All teach undergraduates and do research. No introductory courses are taught by graduate students. The average class size in a regular course is 14.

Requirements: The SAT or ACT is required. The ACT Optional Writing test is also required. In addition, official high school transcripts, 1 counselor recommendation, and 1 teacher recommendation are required. To satisfy the testing requirement, students must submit either (a) the SAT plus 2 SAT subject tests or (b) the ACT with the Writing Test. Music students must arrange an audition. Architecture students must submit a portfolio. An interview is recommended but not required. Candidates should have completed 16 college preparatory units, including 4 years of English, 3 of math, and 2 each of social studies, foreign language, and lab science. AP credits are accepted.

Procedure: Freshmen are admitted in the fall. Entrance exams should be taken no later than December of the senior year for regular decision and no later than November for early decision. Early decision applications should be filed by November 1; check with the school for current application deadlines for regular decision applications. The application fee is $65. Notification of early decision is sent December 15; regular decision, April 1. Applications are accepted online. A waiting list is maintained.

Transfer: 84 transfer students enrolled in a recent year. Transfer applicants should present at least a 3.2 GPA in previous college work, SAT scores, 2 college teacher recommendations, high school and college transcripts, and a letter from the dean of their current college. 60 of 120 credits required for the bachelor's degree must be completed at Rice.

Visiting: There are regularly scheduled orientations for prospective students, consisting of information sessions and tours available year-round. There are guides for informal visits, and visitors may sit in on classes and stay overnight. To schedule a visit, contact the Office of Admissions.

Financial Aid: In a recent year, all full-time students received some form of financial aid. 35% of all full-time freshmen and 37% of continuing full-time students received need-based aid. Need-based scholarships or need-based grants averaged $28,392; need-based self-help aid (loans and jobs) averaged $1624; non-need-based athletic scholarships averaged $16,276; and other non-need-based awards and non-need-based scholarships averaged $9589. Rice is a member of CSS. The CSS/Profile, the FAFSA, and parent and student tax returns are required. Check with the school for current application deadlines.

International Students: There were 220 international students enrolled in a recent year. The school actively recruits these students. They must take the TOEFL. They must also take the SAT or ACT.

Graduates: In a recent year, 978 bachelor's degrees were awarded. The most popular majors were economics (7%), biochemistry and cell biology (7%), and psychology (6%). In an average class, 82% graduate in 4 years or less, 92% graduate in 5 years or less, and 93% graduate in 6 years or less. Of a recent year graduating class, 43% were enrolled in graduate school within 6 months of graduation, and 49% were employed.

Admissions Contact: Julie M. Browning, Dean for Undergraduate Enrollment. Web: *www.rice.edu*

SAINT MARY'S UNIVERSITY D-4

San Antonio, TX 78228 210.436.3126
(800) FOR-STMU; 210.431.6742

Full-time: 1000 men, 1284 women	**Faculty:** 162; IIA, +$
Part-time: 50 men, 57 women	**Ph.D.s:** 93%
Graduate: 777 men, 698 women	**Student/Faculty:** 12 to 1
Year: semesters, summer session	**Tuition:** $25,188
Application Deadline: open	**Room & Board:** $8666
Freshman Class: 5147 applied, 2997 accepted, 596 enrolled	
SAT CR/M/W: 510/530/490 **ACT:** 22	**COMPETITIVE**

Saint Mary's University, established in 1852, is a private Roman Catholic institution in the Marianist tradition, offering undergraduate programs in humanities and social sciences, business and administration, and science, engineering, and technology. There are 3 undergraduate schools and 2 graduate schools. In addition to regional accreditation, St. Mary's has baccalaureate program accreditation with AACSB and ABET. The 2 libraries contain 222,220 volumes, 367,294 microform items, 5,741 audio/video tapes/CDs/DVDs, and subscribe to 36,954 periodicals including electronic. Computerized library services include interlibrary loans, database searching, Internet access, and Wi-Fi capability. Special learning facilities include an art gallery, natural history museum, The Learning Assistance Center is a learner-oriented service that provides academic support and instructional resources to the students, staff and faculty of St. Mary's University. The 135-acre campus is in a suburban area 5 miles northwest of downtown San Antonio. Including any residence halls, there are 45 buildings.

Student Life: 7% of undergraduates are from out of state, mostly the Southwest. Students are from 32 states, 36 foreign countries, and Canada. 68% are from public schools. 72% are Hispanic; 14% White. 41% are Catholic; 15% Baptist, Buddhist, Eastern Orthodox, Episcopal and Hindu. The average age of freshmen is 18; all undergraduates, 21. 27% do not continue beyond their first year; 64% remain to graduate.

Housing: 1454 students can be accommodated in college housing, which includes coed dorms. theme housing. On-campus housing is guaranteed for the freshman year only, is available on a first-come, and first-served basis. Priority is given to out-of-town students. 58% of students live on campus; of those, 80% remain on campus on weekends. All students may keep cars.

Activities: 15% of men belong to 1 local and 4 national fraternities; 13% of women belong to 1 local and 3 national sororities. There are 55 groups on campus, including art, band, cheerleading, choir, chorale, dance, drama, ethnic, honors, international, jazz band, newspaper, pep band, photography, political, professional, religious, social, social service, and student government. Popular campus events include Campus Ministry Retreat, Hunger Awareness Week, Fiesta Oyster Bake, President's Peace Commision, and Lin Great Speaker.

Sports: There are 5 intercollegiate sports for men and 5 for women, and 28 intramural sports for men and 28 for women. Facilities include a gym, weight room, tennis, handball, basketball courts, pools, tracks, dance movement studio, baseball and softball stadium, batting cages, soccer field and sports arena.

Disabled Students: 80% of the campus is accessible. Facilities include wheelchair ramps, elevators, special parking, specially equipped restrooms, special class scheduling, lowered drinking fountains, and special housing.

Services: Counseling and information services are available, as is tutoring in most subjects, Biology, chemistry, physics, psychology, languages, math, writing, accounting, statistics, English, and engineering There is remedial math, reading, and writing. Biochemistry, organic chemistry, programming, macro/micro economics, philosphy, electronics

Campus Safety and Security: Measures include 24-hour foot and vehicle patrol, emergency notification system, self-defense education, and security escort services. There are emergency telephones, lighted pathways/sidewalks, controlled access to dorms/residences, a crime prevention awareness program each semester.

Programs of Study: St. Mary's confers B.A., B.S. and B.B.A. degrees. Master's and doctoral degrees are also awarded. Bachelor's degrees are awarded in BIOLOGICAL SCIENCE (biochemistry and biology/biological science), BUSINESS (accounting, banking and finance, business administration and management, human resources, international business management, and marketing/retailing/merchandising), COMMUNICATIONS AND THE ARTS (communications, English, French, German, music, Spanish, and speech/debate/rhetoric), COMPUTER AND PHYSICAL SCIENCE (chemistry, computer science, earth science, mathematics, and physics), EDUCATION (business education, elementary education, science education, and secondary education), ENGINEERING AND ENVIRONMENTAL DESIGN (computer engineering, electrical/electronics engineering, engineering, environmental science, industrial engineering, and mechanical engineering), HEALTH PROFESSIONS (predentistry and premedicine), SOCIAL SCIENCE (criminal justice, economics, history, international relations, international studies, Latin American studies, philosophy, political science/government, prelaw, psychology, sociology, and theological studies). Biology, accounting, and political science are the strongest academically. Biology, business, and political science have the largest enrollments.

Required: All students must complete at least 128 semester hours, 24 to 30 in the major, with a minimum 2.0 GPA. Core curriculum requirements include courses in fine arts, English, foreign language, speech, natural science, math, social science, philosophy, and theology. Students must also take computer science, demonstrate computer literacy, and take interdisciplinary electives. 128 hours includes CORE, Major and Minor (if applicable), and elective requirements. 6 advanced writing, intensive courses in major.

Special: St. Mary's offers cooperative programs and internships in all majors, depending on the student's needs. Students may cross-register at any of the United Colleges of San Antonio, spend a semester in Washington, D.C., or study in England, Austria, or Mexico. Dual majors are possible in computer science and engineering and public justice and sociology, political science, or psychology. Accelerated degree programs are offered in law, (J.D./M.B.A.) and dentistry (B.A. in combined science and dentistry). Required theology courses may be taken on a pass/fail basis. There are 10 national honor societies, a freshman honors program, and 3 departmental honors programs.

Faculty/Classroom: 63% of faculty are male; 37% are female. 75% teach undergraduates. No introductory courses are taught by graduate students. The average class size in an introductory lecture is 30; in a laboratory is 60; and in a regular course is 25.

Admissions: 58% of the 2013-2014 applicants were accepted. The SAT scores for the 2013-2014 freshman class were: Critical Reading--43% below 500, 42% between 500 and 599, 12% between 600 and 699, and 2% between 700 and 800; Math--31% below 500, 51% between 500 and 599, 17% between 600 and 699, and 1% between 700 and 800; Writing--52% below 500, 38% between 500 and 599, 9% between 600 and 699, and 1% between 700 and 800. The ACT scores were 25% below 21, 42% between 21 and 23, 21% between 24 and 26, 6% between 27 and 28, and 6% above 28. 3 freshmen graduated first in their class.

Requirements: The SAT or ACT is required. All applicants must be high school graduates or have the GED, rank in the upper half of their graduating classes, and score in the 50th percentile on SAT I or ACT. Secondary school preparation should include 4 units of English, 3 each of math and academic electives, and 3 each of social science, natural science, and foreign language. Potential science and engineering majors should have 4 units of math and 3 of lab science, including chemistry or physics. AP and CLEP credits are accepted. Important factors in the admissions decision are leadership record, advanced placement or honors courses, and personality/intangible qualities.

Procedure: Freshmen are admitted fall and spring. Entrance exams should be taken by the fall of the senior year. There are early admissions, deferred admissions, and rolling admissions plans. Application deadlines are open. The fall 2013 application fee was $30. Notification is sent on a rolling basis. Applications are accepted online.

Transfer: 124 transfer students enrolled in 2012-2013. Prospective transfer students possessing the aptitude and motivation to succeed at St. Mary's are encouraged to apply for admission. To be considered for admission, a minimum cumulative grade point average of 2.5 (on a 4.0 scale) in all academic work attempted and good standing at the college or university last attended are required. Applicants in good standing with the last institution attended and who present a grade point average between 2.0 and 2.49 (on a 4.0 scale) may be considered for probationary admission. (Developmental or technical course work is not considered in the evaluation of the academic GPA.) Possession of the minimum grade point average for consideration does not imply admissibility to St. Mary's University. The merits of each application are considered on a case-by-case basis. Academic credits ordinarily will be accepted in transfer from another college if the grade(s) earned is/are at least C (2.0 on a 4.0 scale). The school(s) must be accredited by one of the six regional accrediting associations. 45 of 126 credits required for the bachelor's degree must be completed at St. Mary's.

Visiting: There are regularly scheduled orientations for prospective students, Campus tour, admissions/financial aid session, overnight stay, student only activities, parent only activities, and placement testing. There are guides for informal visits, visitors may sit in on classes, and stay overnight. To schedule a visit, contact Undergraduate Admissions Office.

Financial Aid: St. Mary's is a member of CSS. The CSS/Profile is required. The deadline for filing freshman financial aid applications for fall entry is April 1.

International Students: There are 117 international students enrolled. The school actively recruits these students. They must take the TOEFL with a minimum score of 550 on the paper-based TOEFL (PBT) or 80 on the Internet-based version (iBT), International English LanguageTesting System (IELTS). They must also take the SAT or ACT.

Graduates: From July 1, 2012 to June 30, 2013, 513 bachelor's degrees were awarded. The most popular majors were psychology (7%), criminal justice (6%), and political science (6%). 30 companies recruited on campus in 2012-2013. In an average class, 33% graduate in 4 years or less, 53% graduate in 5 years or less, and 55% graduate in 6 years or less.

Admissions Contact: Nelson Delgado, Acting Director of Undergrad Admissions. E-Mail: *uadm@stmarytx.edu* Web: *www.stmarytx.edu/admission*

SAM HOUSTON STATE UNIVERSITY D-3

Huntsville, TX 77341 (936) 294-1845
(866) 232-7528; (936) 294-3758

Full-time: 5429 men, 7010 women
Part-time: 1041 men, 1515 women
Graduate: 911 men, 1711 women
Year: semesters, summer session
Application Deadline: open
Faculty: 582; IIA, -$
Ph.D.s: 95%
Student/Faculty: 20 to 1
Tuition: $9938 ($19,083)
Room & Board: $8144
Freshman Class: 7070 applied, 5473 accepted, 2069 enrolled
SAT or ACT: required

COMPETITIVE

Sam Houston University, founded in 1879, is a public institution offering programs in fine arts and mass communication, applied sciences, business administration, criminal justice, education, and humanities and social sciences. There are 6 undergraduate schools and 6 graduate schools. In addition to regional accreditation, Sam Houston State has baccalaureate program accreditation with AACSB, ABET, ADA, NASM, and NCATE. The library contains 1.3 million volumes, 3,744 audio/video tapes/CDs/DVDs, and subscribes to 7,175 periodicals including electronic. Computerized library services include interlibrary loans, database searching, Internet access, and laptop Internet portals. Special learning facilities include a learning resource center, planetarium, radio station, TV station, the Sam Houston Museum. The 1256-acre campus is in a small town 70 miles north of Houston. Including any residence halls, there are 228 buildings.

Student Life: 98% of undergraduates are from Texas. Others are from 48 states, 59 foreign countries, and Canada. 71% are white; 14% African American; 12% Hispanic. The average age of freshmen is 18; all undergraduates, 22. 31% do not continue beyond their first year; 40% remain to graduate.

Housing: 3293 students can be accommodated in college housing, which includes single-sex and coed dorms, on-campus apartments, and off-campus apartments. In addition, there are honors houses, special-interest houses, fraternity houses, and sorority houses. On-campus housing is guaranteed for all 4 years. 73% of students commute. All students may keep cars.

Activities: 9% of men belong to 15 local fraternities; 5% of women belong to 13 local sororities. There are 235 groups on campus, including art, band, cheerleading, choir, chorale, chorus, computers, dance, drama, drill team, environmental, ethnic, film, forensics, gay, honors, international, jazz band, marching band, musical theater, newspaper, orchestra, pep band, photography, political, professional, radio and TV, religious, social, social service, student government, and symphony. Popular campus events include Organization Fair, Greek Week, and Welcome Week.

Sports: There are 7 intercollegiate sports for men and 7 for women, and 13 intramural sports for men and 13 for women. Facilities include a 14,000-seat stadium, a 5,200-seat gym, 4 basketball courts, 10 racquetball courts, 3 swimming pools, and 2 weight rooms.

Disabled Students: 90% of the campus is accessible. Facilities include wheelchair ramps, elevators, special parking, specially equipped restrooms, lowered drinking fountains. closed-circuit television (CCTV), computer workstations with large print and speech output capabilities, and telecommunication devices for the disabled.

Services: Counseling and information services are available, as is tutoring in every subject. There is a reader service for the blind, and remedial math, reading, and writing.

Campus Safety and Security: Measures include 24-hour foot and vehicle patrol, emergency notification system, and security escort services. There are emergency telephones and lighted pathways/sidewalks.

Programs of Study: Sam Houston State confers B.A., B.S., B.A.A.S., B.B.A., B.F.A., and B.M. degrees. Master's and doctoral degrees are also awarded. Bachelor's degrees are awarded in AGRICULTURE (agriculture, animal science, and horticulture), BIOLOGICAL SCIENCE (biology/biological science), BUSINESS (accounting, banking and finance, business administration and management, and marketing/retailing/merchandising), COMMUNICATIONS AND THE ARTS (art, dance, dramatic arts, English, French, German, graphic design, journalism, music, music performance, music theory and composition, musical theater, photography, Spanish, and speech/debate/rhetoric), COMPUTER AND PHYSICAL SCIENCE (chemistry, computer science, geology, mathematics, and physics), EDUCATION (physical education), ENGINEERING AND ENVIRONMENTAL DESIGN (environmental science), HEALTH PROFESSIONS (health, medical technology, and music therapy), SOCIAL SCIENCE (criminal justice, economics, geography, history, law enforcement and corrections, philosophy, physical fitness/movement, political science/government, psychology, and sociology). Criminal justice, general business, and psychology have the largest enrollments.

Required: All students must maintain a GPA of 2.0 while taking 128 semester hours, including 30 in the major. The core curriculum includes 15 hours of social and behavioral sciences, 9 hours of humanities and visual and performing arts, 8 hours of natural sciences, 6 hours of communication, 4 hours of an institutionally designated option, and 3 hours of math.

Special: Work-study programs with the university, study abroad in 6 countries, second degrees, and B.A.-B.S. degrees are available. There are 10 national honor societies and a freshman honors program.

Faculty/Classroom: 53% of faculty are male; 47% are female. All teach and do research. Graduate students teach 5% of introductory courses.

Admissions: 77% of a recent year, applicants were accepted. 32% of the current freshmen were in the top fifth of their class; 67% were in the top two fifths. 10 freshmen graduated first in their class.

Requirements: The SAT or ACT is required. Applicants must have secondary school credits as follows: 4 of English, 2 each of math, history, and science, 1 1/2 of phys ed, and a half credit each of social studies and health education. The GED is accepted. A GPA of 2.0 is required. AP and CLEP credits are accepted.

Procedure: Freshmen are admitted fall, spring, and summer. There are early admissions and rolling admissions plans. Application deadlines are open. The fall application fee was $40. Notification is sent on a rolling basis.

Transfer: 2153 transfer students enrolled in a recent year. Transfer applicants must present a 2.0 GPA on all previous college work. 42 of 128 credits required for the bachelor's degree must be completed at Sam Houston.

Visiting: There are regularly scheduled orientations for prospective students, including a tour of the campus, dorms, and departments. There are guides for informal visits. To schedule a visit, contact the Visitor Center.

Financial Aid: In a recent year, 61% of continuing full-time students received some form of financial aid. 45% of continuing full-time students received need-based aid. 5% of undergraduate students work part-time. The average financial indebtedness of a recent graduate was $19,188. The FAFSA is required. The priority date for freshman financial aid applications for fall entry is March 31. The deadline for filing freshman financial aid applications for fall entry is May 31.

International Students: There are 105 international students enrolled. The school actively recruits these students. They must take the TOEFL with a minimum score of 550 on the paper-based TOEFL (PBT). They must also take the SAT or ACT.

Graduates: In a recent year, 3188 bachelor's degrees were awarded. The most popular majors were business/marketing (25%), homeland security (16%), and interdisciplinary studies (13%). 34 companies recruited on campus in a recent year. In an average class, 17% graduate in 4 years or less and 41% graduate in 6 years or less.

Admissions Contact: Trevor Thorn, Director of Undergraduate Admissions. A campus DVD is available. E-Mail: *admissions@shsu.edu* Web: *www.shsu.edu*

SCHREINER UNIVERSITY C-3

Kerrville, TX 78028 **800.343.4919**

Full-time: 440 men, 589 women	**Faculty:** n/av
Part-time: 16 men, 20 women	**Ph.D.s:** 80%
Graduate: 26 men, 45 women	**Student/Faculty:** 14 to 1
Year: semesters, summer session	**Tuition:** $22,484
Application Deadline: August 1	**Room & Board:** $10,250

Freshman Class: 894 applied, 828 accepted, 299 enrolled

SAT or ACT: required

LESS COMPETITIVE

Schreiner University, founded in 1923, is an independent liberal arts institution affiliated with the Presbyterian Church. There are 3 undergraduate schools and 2 graduate schools. The library contains 100,000 volumes, 593 microform items, 1,068 audio/video tapes/CDs/DVDs, and subscribes to 203 periodicals including electronic. Computerized library services include interlibrary loans, database searching, and Internet access. The 205-acre campus is in a rural area 60 miles northwest of San Antonio. Including any residence halls, there are 59 buildings.

Student Life: 96% of undergraduates are from Texas. Others are from 20 states, and 2 foreign countries. 63% are White; 29% Hispanic. 19% are Catholic. The average age of freshmen is 18; all undergraduates, 21. 67% do not continue beyond their first year; 41% remain to graduate.

Housing: 768 students can be accommodated in college housing, which includes coed dorms and on-campus apartments. In addition, there are special-interest houses, Learning Communities. On-campus housing is guaranteed for all 4 years. 69% of students live on campus. All students may keep cars.

Activities: 3% of men belong to 2 national fraternities; 3% of women belong to 2 national sororities. There are 38 groups on campus, including art, cheerleading, choir, chorale, drama, honors, international, literary magazine, newspaper, pep band, photography, political, professional, religious, social, and student government. Popular campus events include Bingo Night, Fall Ball, and Outdoor Movie Nights.

Sports: Facilities include basketball and volleyball courts, baseball and softball diamonds, 3 handball/racquetball courts, a track, 8 tennis courts, a swimming pool, soccer and intramural fields, a golf driving range, and a recreation room.

Disabled Students: 95% of the campus is accessible. Facilities include wheelchair ramps, elevators, special parking, specially equipped restrooms, special class scheduling, lowered drinking fountains, and lowered telephones.

Services: Counseling and information services are available, as is tutoring in every subject, introductory-level courses There is remedial math, reading, and writing. There also are workshops, a certified peer-tutoring program, a math lab, a self-management orientation course, and computer-assisted instruction for learning skills.

Campus Safety and Security: Measures include emergency notification system and security escort services. There are emergency telephones, a night vehicle patrol.

Programs of Study: Schreiner confers B.A., B.B.A., B.G.S., B.S. and B.S.N. degrees. Associate and master's degrees are also awarded. Bachelor's degrees are awarded in BIOLOGICAL SCIENCE (biochemistry and biology/biological science), BUSINESS (accounting, business administration and management, and management information systems), COMMUNICATIONS AND THE ARTS (art, dramatic arts, English, graphic design, music, theatre arts, and visual and performing arts), COMPUTER AND PHYSICAL SCIENCE (chemistry and mathematics), EDUCATION (early childhood education, education, elementary education, English education, mathematics education, middle school education, music education, physical education, science education, secondary education, and social science education), HEALTH PROFESSIONS (exercise science and nursing), SOCIAL SCIENCE (history, humanities, liberal arts/general studies, philosophy, political science/government, prelaw, psychology, and religion). Nursing, Graphic Design, and Sciences are the strongest academically. Sciences, English, and business have the largest enrollments.

Required: To graduate, all students must have a minimum GPA of 2.0 for 120 semester hours, including 24 hours in the major. The core curriculum includes courses from English composition, oral communication, foreign language, history, natural science, math, philosophy or religion, computer studies, government, business administration, literature and fine arts, social science, and fitness. B.A. candidates must complete a senior capstone project, thesis, or course; B.B.A. candidates may substitute an internship.

Special: Schreiner offers study abroad, work-study with the university, second majors, a general studies degree, nondegree study, and a 3-2 engineering degree with the University of Texas, Texas Tech University, and Texas A&M University. There are 6 national honor societies and a freshman honors program.

Faculty/Classroom: 49% of faculty are male; 51% are female. All teach undergraduates. No introductory courses are taught by graduate students.

Admissions: 93% of the 2013-2014 applicants were accepted. The SAT scores for the 2013-2014 freshman class were: Critical Reading--55% below 500, 34% between 500 and 599, 8% between 600 and 699, and 3% between 700 and 800; Math--41% below 500, 48% between 500 and 599, 10% between 600 and 699, and 1% between 700 and 800; Writing--68% below 500, 26% between 500 and 599, 5% between 600 and 699, and 1% between 700 and 800.

Requirements: The SAT or ACT is required. AP and CLEP credits are accepted.

Procedure: Freshmen are admitted to all sessions. Entrance exams should be taken in the spring of the junior year. There are early admissions, deferred admissions, and rolling admissions plans. Applications should be filed by August 1 for fall entry; December 1 for spring entry; and May 1 for summer entry. The fall 2013 application fee was $25. Notification is sent on a rolling basis. Applications are accepted online.

Transfer: 64 transfer students enrolled in 2012-2013. Applicants with fewer than 15 transferable credit hours must meet freshman admissions requirements. For those with more, the SAT or ACT is not required. A 2.0 minimum GPA is necessary. 30 of 120 credits required for the bachelor's degree must be completed at Schreiner.

Visiting: There are regularly scheduled orientations for prospective students, including guided tours, financial aid information, and faculty and student discussions. There are guides for informal visits, visitors may sit in on classes, and stay overnight. To schedule a visit, contact the Admission Office at admissions@schreiner.edu.

Financial Aid: The average financial indebtedness of the 2013 graduate was $24,539. The FAFSA is required. The priority date for freshman financial aid applications for fall entry is April 1. The deadline for filing freshman financial aid applications for fall entry is August 1.

International Students: There are 5 international students enrolled. They must take the TOEFL with a minimum score of 550 on the paper-based TOEFL (PBT) or 79 on the Internet-based version (iBT). They must also take the SAT or ACT.

Graduates: From July 1, 2012 to June 30, 2013, 191 bachelor's degrees were awarded. The most popular majors were exercise science/sport management (18%), nursing (12%), and education (10%). In an average class, 35% graduate in 4 years or less, 40% graduate in 5 years or less, and 41% graduate in 6 years or less.

Admissions Contact: E-Mail: *admissions@schreiner.edu* Web: *www.schreiner.edu*

SOUTHERN METHODIST UNIVERSITY D-2

Dallas, TX 75275 (214) 768-2058
(800) 323-0672; (214) 768-0103

Full-time: 3019 men, 3100 women
Part-time: 118 men, 120 women
Graduate: 2674 men, 1898 women
Year: semesters, summer session
Application Deadline: January 15
Faculty: 727; I, +$
Ph.D.s: 84%
Student/Faculty: 11 to 1
Tuition: $43,800
Room & Board: $13,955
Freshman Class: 12080 applied, 6125 accepted, 1431 enrolled
MOST COMPETITIVE

Southern Methodist University, founded in 1911, is a private nonsectarian institution affiliated with the United Methodist Church. SMU offers undergraduate and graduate programs in humanities and sciences, business, arts, education, engineering and applied sciences. There are 5 undergraduate schools and 7 graduate schools. In addition to regional accreditation, SMU has baccalaureate program accreditation with AACSB, ABET, NASAD, and NASM. The 8 libraries contain 3.1 million volumes, 2.0 million microform items, 58,145 audio/video tapes/CDs/DVDs, and subscribe to 29,852 periodicals including electronic. Computerized library services include interlibrary loans, database searching, Internet access, and Wi-Fi capability. Special learning facilities include an art gallery, natural history museum, radio station, TV station, Meadows Museum houses one of the finest Spanish art collections outside Spain; SMU's engineering school is the nation's first to host a Lockheed Martin Skunk Works Lab modeled after the California research facility; performance facilities include theatres with classical thrust stage, proscenium stage and black box area; journalism complex includes digital newsroom and TV studio. The 235-acre campus is in a suburban area 5 miles north of downtown Dallas. Including any residence halls, there are 76 buildings.

Student Life: 50% of undergraduates are from out of state, mostly the South. Students are from 49 states, 101 foreign countries, and Canada. 59% are from public schools. 62% are White; 11% Foreign. 18% are Protestant; 15% Catholic. The average age of freshmen is 18; all undergraduates, 20. 7% do not continue beyond their first year; 79% remain to graduate.

Housing: 2000 students can be accommodated in college housing, which includes coed dorms, on-campus apartments, and married student housing. In addition, there are honors houses, special-interest houses, fraternity houses, sorority houses, Living-learning communities with some classes taught in residence hall classrooms. On-campus housing is guaranteed for the freshman year only, is available on a first-come, and first-served basis. 62% of students commute. Alcohol is not permitted. All students may keep cars.

Activities: 34% of men belong to 15 national fraternities; 47% of women belong to 14 national sororities. There are 180 groups on campus, including art, band, cheerleading, choir, chorale, chorus, computers, dance, drama, drill team, ethnic, forensics, gay, honors, international, jazz band, literary magazine, marching band, musical theater, opera, orchestra, pep band, photography, political, professional, religious, social, social service, student government, and symphony. Popular campus events include Celebration of Lights and Community Service Day.

Sports: There are 6 intercollegiate sports for men and 11 for women, and 20 intramural sports for men and 20 for women. Facilities include gymnastic and weight rooms, a dance studio, indoor and outdoor jogging tracks, indoor and outdoor pools, a 2400-seat outdoor stadium, a 6500-seat indoor stadium, and courts for basketball, volleyball, tennis, badminton, and racquetball.

Disabled Students: 95% of the campus is accessible. Facilities include wheelchair ramps, elevators, special parking, specially equipped restrooms, special class scheduling, lowered drinking fountains, lowered telephones, and automatic doors.

Services: Counseling and information services are available, as is tutoring in most subjects. There is a reader service for the blind, and remedial reading and writing. The Learning Enhancement Center provides study skills workshops, note-taking techniques, and time management skills seminars.

Campus Safety and Security: Measures include 24-hour foot and vehicle patrol, emergency notification system, self-defense education, and security escort services. There are shuttle buses, emergency telephones, lighted pathways/sidewalks, controlled access to dorms/residences, card-key devices, issued to all students living in residence halls, must be used to enter these buildings.

Programs of Study: SMU confers B.A., B.S., B.B.A., B.F.A., B.M., B.S.C.P.E., B.S.C.E., B.S.E.E., B.S.Env.E. and B.S.M.E. degrees. Master's and doctoral degrees are also awarded. Bachelor's degrees are awarded in BIOLOGICAL SCIENCE (biochemistry and biology/biological science), BUSINESS (accounting, banking and finance, business administration and management, management information systems, management science, marketing/retailing/merchandising, organizational behavior, and real estate), COMMUNICATIONS AND THE ARTS (advertising, art history and appreciation, broadcasting, communications, communications technology, creative writing, dance, dramatic arts, English, film arts, French, German, journalism, languages, media arts, music performance, music theory and composition, performing arts, piano/organ, public relations, Russian, Spanish, studio art, telecommunications, and video), COMPUTER AND PHYSICAL SCIENCE (chemistry, computer science, environmental geology, geology, geophysics and seismology, mathematics, physics, and statistics), EDUCATION (art education, dance education, elementary education, health education, music education, and physical education), ENGINEERING AND ENVIRONMENTAL DESIGN (civil engineering, computer engineering, electrical/electronics engineering, engineering management, environmental engineering, environmental science, and mechanical engineering), HEALTH PROFESSIONS (music therapy and speech pathology/audiology), SOCIAL SCIENCE (African American studies, anthropology, criminal justice, economics, German area studies, history, humanities, international studies, Italian studies, Latin American studies, liberal arts/general studies, medieval studies, Mexican-American/Chicano studies, philosophy, physical fitness/movement, political science/government, psychology, public affairs, religion, Russian and Slavic studies, social science, sociology, and Southwest American studies). Economics, finance, accounting, psychology and advertising have the largest enrollments.

Required: Basic requirements consist of 122 semester hours, including the major requirements for one of SMU's over 100 majors, as well as the University Curriculum (UC), which consists of three, main course-based components: Foundations, Pillars and Capstone. The Foundations emphasize reading and writing, quantitative reasoning, applied critical thinking, and wellness. The five UC Pillars cover the natural sciences, the arts and humanities, and the social and behavioral sciences. The Capstone completes each student's general education. In addition to the three core components, there are eight proficiencies and experiences that can be satisfied through coursework or out-of-class activities.

Special: SMU offers a co-op program in engineering, work-study programs, B.A.-B.S. degrees, study abroad in 50 countries with 150 programs, dual majors in any combination, student-designed majors, numerous internships, and interdisciplinary majors, including economics with finance applications and economics with systems analysis. A 3-2 advanced degree in business is available, as are evening degree programs in humanities and social sciences, and teacher certification programs. There are 30 national honor societies, including Phi Beta Kappa, and a freshman honors program.

Faculty/Classroom: 62% of faculty are male; 38% are female. 89% teach undergraduates, and 89% do both. No introductory courses are taught by graduate students.

Admissions: 51% of the 2013-2014 applicants were accepted.

Requirements: The SAT or ACT is recommended. Applicants should graduate from an accredited high school with a minimum of 15 academic credits: 4 in English, 3 in higher math, including algebra I, II, and plane geometry, 3 each in natural science and social science, and 2 in a foreign language. Home School Certificate applicants may qualify with the SAT or ACT and 3 SAT Subject Tests in math, literature, and science. Performing arts majors must audition. AP and CLEP credits are accepted. Important factors in the admissions decision are advanced placement or honors courses, leadership record, and recommendations by school officials.

Procedure: Freshmen are admitted to all sessions. Entrance exams should be taken by December of the senior year. There are early decision, deferred admissions, and rolling admissions plans. Early decision applications should be filed by November 1; regular applications, by January 15 for fall entry, along with a $60 fee. Notification of early decision is sent April 1; regular decision, on a rolling basis. 1496 applicants were on the 2013 waiting list; 179 were admitted. Applications are accepted online.

Transfer: 325 transfer students enrolled in 2012-2013. A minimum 2.5 GPA is generally required for transfer, but specific requirements vary according to the program of study. Candidates must demonstrate math proficiency. A foreign language requirement may be met through high school or college work. 60 of 122 credits required for the bachelor's degree must be completed at SMU.

Visiting: There are regularly scheduled orientations for prospective students, including information about academic studies, financial aid sessions, discussions with current students, lunch with faculty and students, and a tour of the campus. There is also a Spring Fest visitation in March for high school sophomores & juniors. There are guides for informal visits, visitors may sit in on classes, and stay overnight. To schedule a visit, contact the Undergraduate Admissions Office.

Financial Aid: In 2013-2014, 72% of all full-time freshmen and % of continuing full-time students received some form of financial aid. The average freshman award was $36,804. Need-based scholarships or need-based grants averaged $18,892; need-based self-help aid (loans and jobs) averaged $6,504; non-need-based athletic scholarships averaged $45,015; and other non-need-based awards and non-need-based scholarships averaged $18,627. The average financial indebtedness of the 2013 graduate was $29,829. SMU is a member of CSS. The CSS/Profile and FAFSA are required. The priority date for freshman financial aid applications for fall entry is February 15.

International Students: There are 420 international students enrolled.

The school actively recruits these students. They must take the TOEFL with a minimum score of 550 on the paper-based TOEFL (PBT) or 80 on the Internet-based version (iBT), or the IELTS, with a minimum score of 6.5. SAT or ACT are not required for non-US citizens attending high school outside of the US.

Graduates: From July 1, 2012 to June 30, 2013, 1617 bachelor's degrees were awarded. The most popular majors were economics (9%), finance (8%), and accounting (7%). In an average class, 67% graduate in 4 years or less, 76% graduate in 5 years or less, and 79% graduate in 6 years or less.

Admissions Contact: Wes Waggoner, Dean, Undergraduate Admission . E-Mail: *enrol_serv@mail.smu.edu* Web: *www.smu.edu/admissions*

SOUTHWESTERN ADVENTIST UNIVERSITY D-2

Keene, TX 76059 (817) 202- 6733
(800) 433-2240; (817) 202-6753

Full-time: 340 men, 400 women
Part-time: 54 men, 91 women
Graduate: 16 men, 7 women
Year: semesters, summer session
Application Deadline: August 27 5
Freshman Class: n/av
SAT: required
Faculty: 50
Ph.D.s: 63%
Student/Faculty: 15 to 1
Tuition: $17,800
Room & Board: $5226

LESS COMPETITIVE

Southwestern Adventist College, founded in 1893, is a Seventh-day Adventist institution offering liberal arts and professional degree programs. There is one graduate school. In addition to regional accreditation, SWAU has baccalaureate program accreditation with NLN. The library contains 110,261 volumes, 7,031 microform items, 1,741 audio/video tapes/CDs/DVDs, and subscribes to 439 periodicals including electronic. Computerized library services include interlibrary loans, database searching, Internet access, and Wi-Fi capability. Special learning facilities include a natural history museum, radio station, TV station, and observatory. The 150-acre campus is in a rural area 35 miles south of Fort Worth. Including any residence halls, there are 24 buildings.

Student Life: 21% of undergraduates are from out of state, mostly the Southwest. Students are from 28 states, 67 foreign countries, and Canada. 44% are from public schools. 38% are White; 22% Hispanic; 15% Foreign; 13% African American. 77% claim no religious affiliation; 23% Protestant. The average age of all undergraduates is 26. 23% do not continue beyond their first year; 33% remain to graduate.

Housing: 420 students can be accommodated in college housing, which includes single-sex dorms and married student housing. On-campus housing is guaranteed for all 4 years. 56% of students commute. Alcohol is not permitted. All students may keep cars.

Activities: There are no fraternities or sororities. There are 22 groups on campus, including art, band, choir, chorale, chorus, computers, drama, ethnic, film, honors, international, newspaper, orchestra, pep band, photography, professional, radio and TV, religious, SIFE/ENACTUS, social, social service, student government, symphony, and yearbook. Popular campus events include University Days, Basketball Tournament, Music Festival and Memosa Memories.

Sports: There are 6 intramural sports for men and 6 for women. Facilities include jogging and fitness tracks, weight and aerobics rooms, courts for tennis, racquetball, and basketball, and fields for soccer, football and baseball.

Disabled Students: 78% of the campus is accessible. Facilities include wheelchair ramps, elevators, special parking, specially equipped restrooms, and lowered drinking fountains.

Services: Counseling and information services are available, as is tutoring in most subjects. There is remedial math and writing.

Campus Safety and Security: Measures include 24-hour foot and vehicle patrol and emergency notification system. There are lighted pathways/sidewalks, controlled access to dorms/residences, and a 12-hour night foot patrol.

Programs of Study: SWAU confers B.A., B.S., and B.B.A. degrees. Associate and master's degrees are also awarded. Bachelor's degrees are awarded in BIOLOGICAL SCIENCE (biology/biological science), BUSINESS (business administration and management, international economics, management science, and office supervision and management), COMMUNICATIONS AND THE ARTS (broadcasting, communications, English, journalism, music, and speech/debate/rhetoric), COMPUTER AND PHYSICAL SCIENCE (chemistry, computer science, information sciences and systems, mathematics, and physics), EDUCATION (business education, elementary education, physical education, and secondary education), HEALTH PROFESSIONS (exercise science, health, medical technology, and nursing), SOCIAL SCIENCE (history, international relations, psychology, religion, social science, social studies, social work, and theological studies). Nursing, business, biology, and religion are the strongest academically. Education, nursing, and business have the largest enrollments.

Required: To graduate, students will complete at least 128 hours, including 40 credit hours in upper-division courses, and earn a minimum cumulative grade point average of 2.00 and 2.25 in the major field of specialization. Classes listed as cognates are included in the major with 12 hours in the major field taken in residence. Graduates must complete 32 of the last 38 credit hours in residence and take the College Base General Education examination prior to graduation.

Special: Cooperative programs in medical technology are available with several area hospitals. Internships are arranged on an individual basis. Students may study abroad in Argentina, Italy, Germany, France, or Spain. Student-designed majors, interdisciplinary majors, including mathematical physics, and an adult degree program are offered. There are a freshman honors program and 1 departmental honors programs.

Faculty/Classroom: 63% of faculty are male; 37% are female. All teach undergraduates, and 8% do both. No introductory courses are taught by graduate students. The average class size in an introductory lecture is 30; in a laboratory is 15; and in a regular course is 20.

Requirements: The SAT is required. Applicants should be high school graduates or hold the GED. Secondary preparation is expected to include 12 academic credits in English, foreign language, math, natural or physical science, and social science. Potential nursing or education majors and Seventh-day Adventist ministers must meet additional requirements. AP and CLEP credits are accepted. Important factors in the admissions decision are recommendations by alumni, ability to finance college education, and leadership record.

Procedure: Freshmen are admitted fall and spring. Entrance exams should be taken before registration. There are early admissions, deferred admissions, and rolling admissions plans. Applications should be filed by August 27 5 for fall entry; January 11 for spring entry; and May 5 for summer entry. Applications are accepted online.

Transfer: An official transcript from each college or university the student has attended must be mailed directly to SWAU's Admissions Office. Transfer students with less than a C average may be accepted on a probationary basis. Nursing, education, and theology majors have additional requirements. 32 of 128 credits required for the bachelor's degree must be completed at SWAU.

Visiting: There are regularly scheduled orientations for prospective students, Scheduled visitation programs in fall and spring that consist of meeting the administration, touring the campus, and receiving financial and academic counseling. There are guides for informal visits, visitors may sit in on classes, and stay overnight. To schedule a visit, contact the Enrollment Office at (800) 433-2240.

Financial Aid: The FAFSA and the college's own financial statement are required. Check with the school for current application deadlines.

International Students: There are 139 international students enrolled. The school actively recruits these students. They must take the TOEFL or MELAB. They must also take the SAT or ACT, scoring 760. SAT/ACT scores are required of students from English-speaking countries.

Graduates: From July 1, 2012 to June 30, 2013, 200 bachelor's degrees were awarded. The most popular majors were education (21%), business (15%), and nursing (15%). In an average class, 3% graduate in 3 years or less, 20% graduate in 4 years or less, 30% graduate in 5 years or less, and 33% graduate in 6 years or less.

Admissions Contact: Rahneeka Hazelton, Director for Admissions. E-Mail: *admissions@swau.edu* Web: *www.swau.edu*

SOUTHWESTERN UNIVERSITY D-3

Georgetown, TX 78626 (512) 863-1200
(800) 252-3166; (512) 863-9601

Full-time: 652 men, 867 women
Part-time: 3 men, 13 women
Graduate: n/av
Year: semesters, summer session
Application Deadline: February 1
Freshman Class: 3546 applied, 1850 accepted, 491 enrolled
SAT CR/M: 590/580
Faculty: 116; IIB, av$
Ph.D.s: 100%
Student/Faculty: 13 to 1
Tuition: n/av
Room & Board: $10,420
ACT: 26

VERY COMPETITIVE

Southwestern University, founded in 1840, is a private, national liberal arts institution affiliated with the United Methodist Church. There are 2 undergraduate schools. In addition to regional accreditation, Southwestern has baccalaureate program accreditation with NASM. The library contains 391,040 volumes, 65,316 microform items, 21,371 audio/video tapes/CDs/DVDs, and subscribes to 1,578 periodicals including electronic. Computerized library services include interlibrary loans, database searching, Internet access, and Wi-Fi capability. Special learning facilities include an art gallery, radio station, observatory. The 700-acre campus is in a suburban area 28 miles north of Austin. Including any residence halls, there are 36 buildings.

Student Life: 88% of undergraduates are from Texas. Others are from 36 states, and 9 foreign countries. 81% are from public schools. 67% are White; 19% Hispanic. 68% are Protestant; 25% Catholic. The average age of freshmen is 18; all undergraduates, 20. 13% do not continue beyond their first year; 75% remain to graduate.

Housing: 1108 students can be accommodated in college housing, which

includes single-sex and coed dorms and on-campus apartments. In addition, there are fraternity houses. On-campus housing is available on a first-come, first-served basis, and is available on a lottery system for upperclassmen. 77% of students live on campus; of those, 80% remain on campus on weekends. All students may keep cars.

Activities: 29% of men belong to 4 national fraternities; 20% of women belong to 4 national sororities. There are 99 groups on campus, including art, band, cheerleading, choir, chorale, chorus, computers, dance, debate, drama, environmental, ethnic, film, gay, honors, international, jazz band, literary magazine, musical theater, newspaper, opera, orchestra, pep band, political, professional, radio and TV, religious, social, social service, and student government. Popular campus events include Homecoming, Sing, ClusterFest Musical Festival and Brown Symposium.

Sports: There are 10 intercollegiate sports for men and 10 for women, and 20 intramural sports for men and 20 for women. Facilities include a recreation center that includes: a 2000-seat performance gym, recreation gym, locker rooms, indoor jogging track, racquetball & handball courts, indoor swimming pool, weight room and fitness area. Outdoor facilities: baseball, softball, soccer and lacrosse fields, tennis courts, recreational fields. Including an athletic field house with locker room, weight room, athletic training center, offices and meeting rooms, football practice fields, outdoor track and field complex. Also sand volleyball and cove with food, billiards, and friday night live.

Disabled Students: 90% of the campus is accessible. Facilities include wheelchair ramps, elevators, special parking, specially equipped restrooms, special class scheduling, lowered drinking fountains, lowered telephones, and special housing.

Services: Counseling and information services are available, as is tutoring in some subjects, English, math, computer science, and sciences There is a reader service for the blind, and remedial writing.

Campus Safety and Security: Measures include 24-hour foot and vehicle patrol, emergency notification system, self-defense education, and security escort services. There are emergency telephones, lighted pathways/sidewalks, and controlled access to dorms/residences.

Programs of Study: Southwestern confers B.A., B.S., B.F.A., B.Ed., and B.Mus. degrees. Bachelor's degrees are awarded in AGRICULTURE (animal science and environmental studies), BIOLOGICAL SCIENCE (biochemistry and biology/biological science), BUSINESS (accounting and business administration and management), COMMUNICATIONS AND THE ARTS (art history, art, classics, communications, dramatic arts, English, French, German, Greek, Latin, music, and Spanish), COMPUTER AND PHYSICAL SCIENCE (applied science, chemistry, mathematics, mathematics/computational, and physics), EDUCATION (education), HEALTH PROFESSIONS (exercise science), SOCIAL SCIENCE (anthropology, economics, history, international studies, Latin American studies, philosophy, political science/government, psychology, religion, sociology, and women's studies). biology, business, and communication have the largest enrollments.

Required: All degrees require a 2.0 or higher GPA in 127 or more credits. Each requires a First Year Seminar, 2 Fitness and Recreational Activity Credits, at least 1 course (3-4 credits) tagged for each of Social Justice, Intercultural Perspectives, Math or Computer Science, Fine Arts Performance, Fine Arts Lecture, and Natural Science with lab. Two tagged courses in both Humanities and Social Science are required, as is 4th semester proficiency in a foreign language. Major requirements vary, but require a minimum of 30 credits, including a capstone.

Special: Students may study abroad in a multitude of countries. The university offers a Fall London semester, Washington semester, dual, student-designed, and independent majors, and internships in government, fine arts, psychology, sociology, science, and other fields, including those in the New York Arts Program. A Physical Science major allows students to spend several years at Southwestern, then finish their SU degree with a year's qualifying engineering coursework at another university. There are 7 national honor societies, including Phi Beta Kappa, and 37 departmental honors programs.

Faculty/Classroom: 50% of faculty are male; 50% are female. All teach undergraduates, and 68% do both. No introductory courses are taught by graduate students. The average class size in an introductory lecture is 19; in a laboratory is 18; and in a regular course is 13.

Admissions: 52% of the 2013-2014 applicants were accepted. The SAT scores for the 2013-2014 freshman class were: Critical Reading--16% below 500, 39% between 500 and 599, 35% between 600 and 699, and 10% between 700 and 800; Math--7% below 500, 44% between 500 and 599, 37% between 600 and 699, and 9% between 700 and 800. The ACT scores were 9% below 21, 20% between 21 and 23, 28% between 24 and 26, 16% between 27 and 28, and 26% above 28. 65% of the current freshmen were in the top fifth of their class; 90% were in the top two fifths. There were 2 National Merit finalists. 11 freshmen graduated first in their class.

Requirements: The SAT or ACT is required. Applicants should be graduates of an accredited high school or have the GED. Secondary preparation should include, at a minimum, 4 years each of English and math, 3 each of science and social science or history, 2 of a foreign language, and 1 of an academic elective. An essay, an SAT or ACT score and a counselor recommendation are required, and an interview is recommended. AP and CLEP credits are accepted. Important factors in the admissions decision are advanced placement or honors courses, recommendations by school officials, and leadership record.

Procedure: Freshmen are admitted fall. Entrance exams should be taken in the fall or early spring of the senior year. There are early admissions and deferred admissions plans. Applications should be filed by February 1 for fall entry. Notifications are sent April 15. 7 applicants were on the 2013 waiting list; 0 were admitted. Applications are accepted online.

Transfer: 65 transfer students enrolled in 2012-2013. Preference is given to students having a 3.0 in all college work. 64 of 127 credits required for the bachelor's degree must be completed at Southwestern.

Visiting: There are regularly scheduled orientations for prospective students, including 3 or 4 group overnight options and individually arranged visits throughout the year. All visits typically include tours, faculty appointments and interview, and may also include an overnight on campus and class visit. There are guides for informal visits, visitors may sit in on classes, and stay overnight. To schedule a visit, contact the Admission Office.

Financial Aid: In 2013-2014, 99% of all full-time freshmen and 95% of continuing full-time students received some form of financial aid. 68% of all full-time freshmen and 63% of continuing full-time students received need-based aid. The average freshman award was $30,216. Need-based scholarships or need-based grants averaged $25,793; need-based self-help aid (loans and jobs) averaged $4,863; and other non-need-based awards and non-need-based scholarships averaged $18,874. 53% of undergraduate students work part-time. Average annual earnings from campus work are $1301. The average financial indebtedness of the 2013 graduate was $34,997. Southwestern is a member of CSS. The FAFSA is required. The priority date for freshman financial aid applications for fall entry is March 1. The deadline for filing freshman financial aid applications for fall entry is March 1.

International Students: There are 22 international students enrolled. The school actively recruits these students. They must take the TOEFL with a minimum score of 570 on the paper-based TOEFL (PBT) or 88 on the Internet-based version (iBT). They must also take the SAT or ACT.

Graduates: From July 1, 2012 to June 30, 2013, 338 bachelor's degrees were awarded. The most popular majors were biology (10%), psychology (9%), and business (9%). 5 companies recruited on campus in 2012-2013. In an average class, 2% graduate in 3 years or less, 67% graduate in 4 years or less, 73% graduate in 5 years or less, and 75% graduate in 6 years or less.

Admissions Contact: Christine Bowman, Director of Admissions. E-Mail: *admission@southwestern.edu* Web: *www.southwestern.edu/admission/*

ST. EDWARD'S UNIVERSITY D-3

Austin, TX 78704 **(512) 448-8500**
(800) 555-0164; (512) 464-8877

Full-time: 1400 men, 2070 women	**Faculty:** n/av; IIA, -$
Part-time: 390 men, 525 women	**Ph.D.s:** 90%
Graduate: 350 men, 600 women	**Student/Faculty:** n/av
Year: semesters, summer session	**Tuition:** $30,710
Application Deadline: see profile	**Room & Board:** $8850
Freshman Class: n/av	
SAT or ACT: required	
	VERY COMPETITIVE

Saint Edward's University, founded in 1885, is an independent Catholic liberal arts institution offering undergraduate courses in business, behavioral and social sciences, humanities, education, and natural sciences, and graduate courses in human service, business administration, counseling, liberal arts, computer information systems, teaching, college student development, organizational leadership and ethics. There are 6 undergraduate schools and 11 graduate schools. In addition to regional accreditation, SEU has baccalaureate program accreditation with CSWE. The library contains 201,930 volumes, 6,73 microform items, 3934 audio/video tapes/CDs/DVDs, and subscribes to 1909 periodicals including electronic. Computerized library services include interlibrary loans, database searching, Internet access, and laptop Internet portals. Special learning facilities include a learning resource center, art gallery, and digital photography lab. The 160-acre campus is in an urban area in Austin. Including any residence halls, there are 58 buildings.

Student Life: 90% of undergraduates are from Texas. Others are from 46 states and 28 foreign countries. 76% are from public schools. 55% are white; 30% Hispanic. 53% are Catholic; 29% Protestant. The average age of freshmen is 18; all undergraduates, 20. 18% do not continue beyond their first year; 66% remain to graduate.

Housing: 1372 students can be accommodated in college housing, which includes single-sex and coed dorms and on-campus apartments. In addition, there are 2 living learning communities: global understanding and social justice. On-campus housing is guaranteed for the freshman year only, is available on a first-come, first-served basis, and is available on a lottery system for upperclassmen. 62% of students commute. All students may keep cars.

Activities: There are no fraternities or sororities. There are 95 groups on campus, including art, cheerleading, choir, chorale, chorus, computers, dance, drama, drill team, environmental, ethnic, film, forensics, gay, honors, international, literary magazine, musical theater, newspaper, orchestra, photography, political, professional, radio and TV, religious, social, social service, sports club, and student government. Popular campus events include Festival of Lights and The Big Event Service Project.

Sports: There are 5 intercollegiate sports for men and 6 for women, and 10 intramural sports for men and 10 for women. Facilities include 2 gyms, baseball and softball fields, 2 soccer fields, tennis, basketball, racquetball/handball, and volleyball courts, an indoor/outdoor pool, and a fitness center, plus 1 outdoor basketball and 2 outdoor sand volleyball courts and a multipurpose field.

Disabled Students: 95% of the campus is accessible. Facilities include wheelchair ramps, elevators, special parking, specially equipped restrooms, special class scheduling, lowered drinking fountains, lowered telephones, and special housing.

Services: Counseling and information services are available, as is tutoring in most subjects. There is a reader service for the blind, and remedial math, reading, and writing. There is also a learning strategies course.

Campus Safety and Security: Measures include 24-hour foot and vehicle patrol, emergency notification system, self-defense education, and security escort services. There are emergency telephones, lighted pathways/sidewalks, and controlled access to dorms/residences.

Programs of Study: SEU confers B.A., B.S., B.A.A.S., B.B.A., and B.L.S. degrees. Master's degrees are also awarded. Bachelor's degrees are awarded in BIOLOGICAL SCIENCE (biochemistry, bioinformatics, and biology/biological science), BUSINESS (accounting, banking and finance, business administration and management, entrepreneurial studies, international business management, and marketing management), COMMUNICATIONS AND THE ARTS (art, communications, creative writing, digital communications, dramatic arts, English literature, graphic design, photography, and Spanish), COMPUTER AND PHYSICAL SCIENCE (chemistry, computer science, information sciences and systems, and mathematics), EDUCATION (art education, drama education, English education, foreign languages education, mathematics education, physical education, science education, and social studies education), ENGINEERING AND ENVIRONMENTAL DESIGN (preengineering), HEALTH PROFESSIONS (predentistry and premedicine), SOCIAL SCIENCE (criminal justice, criminology, economics, forensic studies, history, interdisciplinary studies, international relations, Latin American studies, liberal arts/general studies, philosophy, physical fitness/movement, political science/government, prelaw, psychology, religion, religious education, social work, and sociology). Psychology, communication, and biology have the largest enrollments.

Required: All students must maintain a minimum GPA of 2.0 while taking 120 semester hours, including 36 to 81 in the major. The core curriculum includes courses from Foundational Skills, Cultural Foundations, and Foundations for Values and Decisions. In the required capstone class, seniors identify a problem in society, research it, present their solutions orally and in writing, and perform a civic engagement activity that supports their position. All students must pass a computer competency test.

Special: Internships and study abroad in a variety of countries through the ISEP, SEU, and other university programs are available. Student-designed majors, credit for life experience, nondegree study, and pass/fail options also are possible. A flexible program for working adults is offered through New College. There are 10 national honor societies and a freshman honors program.

Faculty/Classroom: 53% of faculty are male; 47% are female. 87% teach undergraduates. No introductory courses are taught by graduate students. The average class size in a laboratory is 13 and in a regular course, 19.

Requirements: The SAT or ACT is required. The ACT Optional Writing test is also required. If SAT Writing is taken also, ACT Writing is not required. Successful applicants should be in the top half of their graduating class with testing at or above a combined critical reading and math score of 1000 on the SAT, or a composite score, not including writing, of 21 on the ACT. The GED is accepted. An interview is recommended. An essay is required. AP and CLEP credits are accepted. Important factors in the admissions decision are advanced placement or honors courses, extracurricular activities record, and leadership record.

Procedure: Freshmen are admitted fall and spring. Entrance exams should be taken in spring of the junior year or in summer or fall of the senior year. There are deferred admissions and rolling admissions plans. Notification is sent on a rolling basis. Applications are accepted online. Check with the school for current application deadlines.

Transfer: 277 transfer students enrolled in a recent year. Transfer applicants must have a minimum GPA of 2.25. Transfers with less than 30 hours must submit high school transcripts. 30 of 120 credits required for the bachelor's degree must be completed at St. Edward's University.

Visiting: There are regularly scheduled orientations for prospective students, including a tour, financial aid and academic sessions, class visits, and entertainment. There are guides for informal visits, and visitors may stay overnight. To schedule a visit, contact the Admissions Office.

Financial Aid: In a recent year, 92% of all full-time freshmen and 88% of continuing full-time students received some form of financial aid. 71% of all full-time freshmen and 63% of continuing full-time students received need-based aid. The average freshman award was $24,020. Need-based scholarships or need-based grants averaged $13,063 ($27,450 maximum); need-based self-help aid (loans and jobs) averaged $3683 ($7500 maximum); non-need-based athletic scholarships averaged $15,598 ($32,984 maximum); and other non-need-based awards and non-need-based scholarships averaged $7568 ($36,600 maximum). 21% of undergraduate students worked part-time. Average annual earnings from campus work were $1836. SEU is a member of CSS. The FAFSA is required. Check with the school for current application deadlines.

International Students: There were 102 international students enrolled in a recent year. The school actively recruits these students. They must take the TOEFL with a minimum score of 500 on the paper-based TOEFL (PBT) or 61 on the Internet-based version (iBT). The SAT or ACT, IELTS, PTE Academic, GCE & GCSE, IB (English Higher Level), and AP (English Language or English Literature) are also accepted to demonstrate English proficiency.

Graduates: In a recent year, 978 bachelor's degrees were awarded. The most popular majors were psychology (11%), business and management (10%), and communication (10%). 158 companies recruited on campus in a recent year. In an average class, 2% graduate in 3 years or less, 51% graduate in 4 years or less, 65% graduate in 5 years or less, and 66% graduate in 6 years or less.

Admissions Contact: Tracy Manier, Associate Vice President and Dean of Undergraduate Admission. E-mail: *seu.admit@stedwards.edu* Web: *www.gotostedwards.com*

STEPHEN F. AUSTIN STATE UNIVERSITY — E-3

Nacogdoches, TX 75962 — **(936) 468-2504; (936) 468-3849**

Full-time: 3647 men, 5908 women	**Faculty:** n/av
Part-time: 658 men, 1056 women	**Ph.D.s:** 73%
Graduate: 617 men, 1068 women	**Student/Faculty:** n/av
Year: semesters, summer session	**Tuition:** $7498 ($16,798)
Application Deadline: open	**Room & Board:** $8170
Freshman Class: 9190 applied, 5993 accepted, 2177 enrolled	
SAT CR/M/W: 470/490/460 **ACT:** 20	**COMPETITIVE**

Stephen F. Austin State University, founded in 1923, is a public regional university offering undergraduate and graduate degree programs through 6 colleges. There are 6 undergraduate schools and 1 graduate school. In addition to regional accreditation, SFA has baccalaureate program accreditation with AACSB, ABET, ADA, CSWE, FIDER, NASAD, NASM, NCATE, NLN, and SAF. The library contains 741,055 volumes, 854,752 microform items, 24,256 audio/video tapes/CDs/DVDs, and subscribes to 1,195 periodicals including electronic. Computerized library services include interlibrary loans, database searching, Internet access, and laptop Internet portals. The figures in the above capsule and in this profile are approximate. Special learning facilities include a learning resource center, art gallery, planetarium, radio station, TV station, arboretum, beef and poultry research centers, experimental forest, and biotechnology and environmental science research centers. The 430-acre campus is in a small town 140 miles northeast of Houston. Including any residence halls, there are 120 buildings.

Student Life: 98% of undergraduates are from Texas. Others are from 43 states, 34 foreign countries, and Canada. 97% are from public schools. 62% are white; 23% African American. The average age of freshmen is 18; all undergraduates, 22. 36% do not continue beyond their first year; 45% remain to graduate.

Housing: 4509 students can be accommodated in college housing, which includes single-sex and coed dorms. In addition, there are honors houses, special-interest houses, and an enrichment hall with required study hall hours. On-campus housing is guaranteed for all 4 years. 58% of students commute. Alcohol is not permitted. All students may keep cars.

Activities: 10% of men belong to 24 national fraternities; 9% of women belong to 12 local sororities. There are 211 groups on campus, including art, band, cheerleading, choir, chorale, chorus, computers, dance, debate, drama, drill team, ethnic, film, flag corps, gay, honors, international, jazz band, literary magazine, marching band, musical theater, newspaper, opera, orchestra, pep band, photography, political, professional, radio and TV, religious, social, social service, student government, and symphony. Popular campus events include Showcase Saturday and Big Dip Mentor Ring Ceremony.

Sports: There are 6 intercollegiate sports for men and 9 for women. Facilities include There are gyms for basketball, volleyball and badminton; outdoor basketball courts; sand volleyball courts; courts for handball, tennis and raquetball; weight and gymnastics rooms; indoor pool; outdoor pool with lap lanes and a lazy river; a rock-climbing wall; and intramural fields.

Disabled Students: All of the campus is accessible. Facilities include wheelchair ramps, elevators, special parking, specially equipped restrooms, special class scheduling, lowered drinking fountains, and lowered telephones.

Services: Counseling and information services are available, as is tutoring in most subjects. There is a reader service for the blind, and remedial math, reading, and writing.

Campus Safety and Security: Measures include 24-hour foot and vehicle patrol, emergency notification system, self-defense education, and security escort services. There are shuttle buses, emergency telephones, and lighted pathways/sidewalks.

Programs of Study: SFA confers B.A., B.A.A.S., B.B.A., B.F.A., B.M., B.S., B.S.A.G., B.S.F., B.S.I.S., B.S.N., B.S.R.H.B., and B.S.W. degrees. Master's and doctoral degrees are also awarded. Bachelor's degrees are awarded in AGRICULTURE (agricultural business management, agricultural mechanics, agriculture, animal science, fish and game management, forestry production and processing, forestry and related sciences, horticulture, poultry science, and wildlife management), BIOLOGICAL SCIENCE (biology/biological science and nutrition), BUSINESS (accounting, banking and finance, business administration and management, fashion merchandising, hospitality management services, international business management, management information systems, management science, marketing management, and marketing/retailing/merchandising), COMMUNICATIONS AND THE ARTS (art, broadcasting, communications, dance, dramatic arts, English, French, journalism, music, radio/television technology, Spanish, and speech/debate/rhetoric), COMPUTER AND PHYSICAL SCIENCE (chemistry, computer programming, computer science, geology, information sciences and systems, mathematics, and physics), EDUCATION (agricultural education, education of the deaf and hearing impaired, and education of the visually handicapped), ENGINEERING AND ENVIRONMENTAL DESIGN (environmental science and interior design), HEALTH PROFESSIONS (health science, nursing, rehabilitation therapy, and speech therapy), SOCIAL SCIENCE (child psychology/development, corrections, criminal justice, dietetics, economics, family/consumer studies, geography, history, interdisciplinary studies, law enforcement and corrections, paralegal studies, parks and recreation management, philosophy, physical fitness/movement, political science/government, psychology, public administration, social work, and sociology). Interdisciplinary studies, nursing, and kinesiology have the largest enrollements.

Required: Most programs require that students must complete at least 120 hours with a minimum 2.0 GPA. The B.A. program requires courses in communication skills, math and natural science, humanities, social science, and physical activity.

Special: Internships, dual majors, and dual degrees are possible in some programs. Study abroad is available in more than 40 countries. Preengineering and 3-2 engineering programs with Texas A&M are offered, as are preprofessional programs and a general studies degree. There is a freshman honors program.

Faculty/Classroom: 49% of faculty are male; 51% are female. No introductory courses are taught by graduate students. The average class size in an introductory lecture is 36; in a laboratory is 24; and in a regular course is 26.

Admissions: 65% of the 2011-2012 applicants were accepted. The SAT scores for the 2011-2012 freshman class were: Critical Reading--62% below 500, 29% between 500 and 599, 8% between 600 and 700, and 1% above 700; Math--55% below 500, 35% between 500 and 599, 10% between 600 and 700, and 1% above 700; Writing--67% below 500, 28% between 500 and 599, 5% between 600 and 700, and 1% above 700. The ACT scores were 52% below 21, 26% between 21 and 23, 16% between 24 and 26, 4% between 27 and 28, and 2% above 28. 31% of the current freshmen were in the top fifth of their class; 68% were in the top two fifths. 19 freshmen graduated first in their class.

Requirements: The SAT or ACT is required. AP and CLEP credits are accepted.

Procedure: Freshmen are admitted fall, spring, and summer. Entrance exams should be taken during the junior year. There is a rolling admissions plan. Application deadlines are open. Application fee is $35. Notification is sent on a rolling basis. Applications are accepted online.

Transfer: Applicants with fewer than 15 hours of college work must meet freshman admission requirements. Those with more than 15 hours must have at least a 2.0 GPA. Those with GPAs lower than 2.0 may be admitted to the summer school on probation. 42 of 120 credits required for the bachelor's degree must be completed at SFA.

Visiting: There are regularly scheduled orientations for prospective students, including 5 3-day summer orientations for incoming freshmen and their families and 3 1-day sessions for incoming transfer students. Showcase Saturdays are 1-day open house programs held in the fall and spring for prospective students. There are guides for informal visits and visitors may sit in on classes. To schedule a visit, contact the Office of Admissions.

Financial Aid: In a recent year, 66% of all full-time freshmen and 62% of continuing full-time students received some form of financial aid. 52% of all full-time freshmen and 51% of continuing full-time students received need-based aid. The average freshman award was $9,746. Need-based scholarships or need-based grants averaged $6,407; need-based self-help aid (loans and jobs) averaged $3,625; non-need-based athletic scholarships averaged $6,511; and other non-need-based awards and non-need-based scholarships averaged $3,404. The average financial indebtedness of a recent graduate was $19,309. The FAFSA and the college's own financial statement are required. The priority date for freshman financial aid applications for fall entry is April 1. The deadline for filing freshman financial aid applications for fall entry is rolling.

International Students: There are 107 international students enrolled. The school actively recruits these students. They must take the TOEFL with a minimum score of 550 on the paper-based TOEFL (PBT) or 79 on the Internet-based version (iBT). They must also take the SAT or ACT.

Graduates: From July 1, 2010 to June 30, 2011, 1838 bachelor's degrees were awarded. The most popular majors were interdisciplinary studies (13%), kinesiology (7%), and nursing (6%). In an average class, 22% graduate in 4 years or less, 40% graduate in 5 years or less, and 45% graduate in 6 years or less.

Admissions Contact: Monique Cossich, Executive Director of Enrollment Management. A campus DVD is available. E-Mail: *admissions@sfasu.edu* Web: *www.sfasu.edu*

SUL ROSS STATE UNIVERSITY B-3

Alpine, TX 79832 **432-837-8343; 432-837-8343**

Full-time: 580 men, 456 women	**Faculty:** 80; IIA, --$
Part-time: 123 men, 151 women	**Ph.D.s:** 69%
Graduate: 247 men, 344 women	**Student/Faculty:** 16 to 1
Year: semesters, summer session	**Tuition:** $6600 ($17,220)
Application Deadline: open	**Room & Board:** $6810
Freshman Class: n/av	
SAT or ACT: required	

LESS COMPETITIVE

Sul Ross State University, founded in 1917, is a public institution offering programs in the liberal arts and sciences, fine arts and music, range animal science, business, and education. In addition, an upper-level and graduate center offers courses in Uralde, Del Rio, and Eagle Pass, Texas. There are 3 undergraduate schools and one graduate school. The library contains 248,598 volumes, 444,950 microform items, 13,011 audio/video tapes/CDs/DVDs, and subscribes to 1,951 periodicals including electronic. Computerized library services include interlibrary loans and database searching. Special learning facilities include an art gallery, natural history museum, planetarium, radio station, and extensive geology/chemistry lab equipment, including a scanning electron microscope. The 600-acre campus is in a rural area 165 miles from Odessa. Including any residence halls, there are 22 buildings.

Student Life: 98% of undergraduates are from Texas. Others are from 18 states, and 7 foreign countries. 98% are from public schools. 55% are Hispanic; 32% White. The average age of freshmen is 20; all undergraduates, 24. 55% do not continue beyond their first year; 24% remain to graduate.

Housing: 769 students can be accommodated in college housing, which includes single-sex and coed dorms, on-campus apartments, and married student housing. On-campus housing is guaranteed for the freshman year only, is available on a first-come, and first-served basis. 67% of students commute. Alcohol is not permitted. All students may keep cars.

Activities: There are no fraternities or sororities. There are 41 groups on campus, including art, cheerleading, choir, drama, ethnic, honors, international, literary magazine, musical theater, newspaper, pep band, political, professional, religious, student government, and yearbook. Popular campus events include Cultural Events, Fall on the Mall, and Honors Day.

Sports: There are 5 intercollegiate sports for men and 4 for women, and 4 intramural sports for men and 3 for women. Facilities include a gym and an undergraduate center.

Disabled Students: 90% of the campus is accessible. Facilities include wheelchair ramps, elevators, special parking, specially equipped restrooms, special class scheduling, and lowered drinking fountains.

Services: Counseling and information services are available, as is tutoring in some subjects, math, reading, and English There is remedial math, reading, and writing.

Campus Safety and Security: Measures include 24-hour foot and vehicle patrol. There are lighted pathways/sidewalks.

Programs of Study: Sully confers B.A., B.S., B.B.A. and B.F.A. degrees. Associate and master's degrees are also awarded. Bachelor's degrees are awarded in AGRICULTURE (agricultural business management, animal science, natural resource management, and wildlife management), BIOLOGICAL SCIENCE (biology/biological science), BUSINESS (accounting, business administration and management, and office supervision and management), COMMUNICATIONS AND THE ARTS (communications, dramatic arts, English, fine arts, and Spanish), COMPUTER AND PHYSICAL SCIENCE (computer science, geology, and mathematics), EDUCATION (art education and elementary education), SOCIAL SCIENCE (criminal justice, history, physical fitness/movement, political science/government, psychology, and social science). Behavioral and social sciences, education, and fine arts are the strongest academically. Phys ed, criminal justice, and education have the largest enrollments.

Required: All students must complete a general education requirement of 53 to 57 hours, including courses in English, history, foreign language, political science, math, the arts, social science, and natural science. A minimum 2.0 GPA and 130 credit hours are required to graduate. There are additional requirements for some degree programs. All students must take 2 courses in phys ed and 1 in computer science. The total number of hours required in the major varies.

Special: Sully offers unpaid internships in several departments, including psychology and criminal justice, as well as work-study programs and nondegree study. There is also a freshman honors program.

Faculty/Classroom: 69% of faculty are male; 31% are female. 95% teach undergraduates, and 85% do both. No introductory courses are taught by graduate students. The average class size in an introductory lecture is 42; in a laboratory is 15; and in a regular course is 21.

Requirements: The SAT or ACT is required. In addition, applicants should be graduates of an accredited secondary school and have a minimum of 14 credits, including 4 in English, 3 in math, 2 each in science, history, and phys ed/health, and 1 in government/economics. Applicants must meet 1 of the following criteria for full admission: present a minimum composite score of 20 on the ACT or 920 on the SAT; or graduate in the upper half of their class. Probationary admission is possible for students who do not meet the admissions standards. AP and CLEP credits are accepted.

Procedure: Freshmen are admitted to all sessions. Entrance exams should be taken preferably early in the senior year. There are early decision, early admissions, and rolling admissions plans. Application deadlines are open. Application fee is $25. Applications are accepted online.

Transfer: The GPA required for transfer students varies according to the number of college credits completed. 30 of 130 credits required for the bachelor's degree must be completed at Sully.

Visiting: There are regularly scheduled orientations for prospective students, consisting of 1 1/2-day programs in January, late August, June, and July. There are guides for informal visits, visitors may sit in on classes, and stay overnight. To schedule a visit, contact the Office of Admissions.

Financial Aid: In 2013-2014, 80% of all full-time freshmen and % of continuing full-time students received some form of financial aid. 52% of all full-time freshmen and 21% of continuing full-time students received need-based aid. The average freshman award was $5,489. 7% of undergraduate students work part-time. Average annual earnings from campus work are $2000. Sully is a member of CSS. The CSS/Profile and FAFSA are required. Check with the school for current application deadlines.

International Students: They must take the TOEFL with a minimum score of 550 on the paper-based TOEFL (PBT) or 213 on the Internet-based version (iBT). They must also take the SAT or ACT.

Graduates: From July 1, 2012 to June 30, 2013, 342 bachelor's degrees were awarded. The most popular majors were interdisciplinary studies (22%), criminal justice (14%), and business administration (9%). In an average class, 16% graduate in 4 years or less, 24% graduate in 5 years or less, and 30% graduate in 6 years or less.

Admissions Contact: MaryBeth Marks, Director of Admissions. E-Mail: *mmarks2@sulross.edu* Web: *www.sulross.edu*

TARLETON STATE UNIVERSITY — D-2

Stephenville, TX 76402 — (254) 968-9125; (800) 687-8236; (254) 968-9951

Full-time: 2978 men, 4435 women	**Faculty:** 292
Part-time: 846 men, 1326 women	**Ph.D.s:** 65%
Graduate: 491 men, 861 women	**Student/Faculty:** 19 to 1
Year: semesters, summer session	**Tuition:** $5856 ($14,352)
Application Deadline: August 1	**Room & Board:** $7633
Freshman Class: 5262 applied, 4338 accepted, 1919 enrolled	
SAT CR/M/W: 470/500/460	**ACT:** 20 **LESS COMPETITIVE**

Tarleton State University, founded in 1899 and a part of the Texas A&M University System, is a public institution offering undergraduate and graduate programs in agriculture and technology, arts and sciences, business, and education and fine arts. There are 5 undergraduate schools and 1 graduate school. In addition to regional accreditation, Tarleton has baccalaureate program accreditation with ABET, ACBSP, CSWE, NASM, and NCATE. The library contains 400,000 volumes, 920,000 microform items, 9,500 audio/video tapes/CDs/DVDs, and subscribes to 25,800 periodicals including electronic. Computerized library services include interlibrary loans, database searching, Internet access, and Wi-Fi capability. Special learning facilities include an art gallery, planetarium, radio station, a 600-acre farm, a 1,200-acre ranch, an equine center, and a center for industrial history of Texas. The 125-acre campus is in a small town 67 miles southwest of Fort Worth. Including any residence halls, there are 84 buildings.

Student Life: 98% of undergraduates are from Texas. Others are from 42 states, 25 foreign countries, and Canada. 91% are from public schools. 73% are White; 15% Hispanic. The average age of freshmen is 18; all undergraduates, 24. 32% do not continue beyond their first year; 43% remain to graduate.

Housing: 3151 students can be accommodated in college housing, which includes single-sex and coed dorms, on-campus apartments, off-campus apartments, and married student housing. On-campus housing is guaranteed for the freshman year only, is available on a first-come, and first-served basis. 70% of students commute. Alcohol is not permitted. All students may keep cars.

Activities: 9% of men belong to 9 national fraternities; 7% of women belong to 9 national sororities. There are 117 groups on campus, including art, band, cheerleading, choir, communications, computers, dance, debate, drama, drill team, environmental, ethnic, film, gay, honors, international, jazz band, literary magazine, marching band, musical theater, newspaper, pep band, photography, political, professional, radio and TV, religious, social, social service, student government, and yearbook. Popular campus events include Howdy Week, Spring Fest, and Tarleton Christmas.

Sports: There are 5 intercollegiate sports for men and 7 for women, and 12 intramural sports for men and 12 for women. Facilities include a fully equipped complex with a heated pool, track, courts for basketball, volleyball, tennis, and racquetball and various playing fields. There is also a 7,000-seat stadium, a 3,300-seat gym, a fully lighted 550-seat baseball stadium, and a softball stadium.

Disabled Students: 90% of the campus is accessible. Facilities include wheelchair ramps, elevators, special parking, special class scheduling, lowered drinking fountains, lowered telephones, and easy-access doors.

Services: Counseling and information services are available, as is tutoring in most subjects, math, science, English, and social studies. The Teaching and Learning center provides tutoring assistance in all academic areas.

Campus Safety and Security: Measures include 24-hour foot and vehicle patrol, emergency notification system, self-defense education, and security escort services. There are shuttle buses, emergency telephones, and lighted pathways/sidewalks.

Programs of Study: Tarleton confers B.A., B.S., B.A.A.S., B.A.T, B.B.A., B.F.A., B.M., B.S.N. and B.S.W. degrees. Associate, master's, and doctoral degrees are also awarded. Bachelor's degrees are awarded in AGRICULTURE (agricultural business management, agricultural economics, agricultural mechanics, agriculture, agronomy, animal science, horticulture, international agriculture, plant science, and range/farm management), BIOLOGICAL SCIENCE (biology/biological science and wildlife biology), BUSINESS (accounting, banking and finance, business administration and management, fashion merchandising, human resources, management science, marketing and distribution, marketing/retailing/merchandising, office supervision and management, and personnel management), COMMUNICATIONS AND THE ARTS (art, dramatic arts, English, fine arts, music, Spanish, and speech/debate/rhetoric), COMPUTER AND PHYSICAL SCIENCE (chemistry, computer programming, computer science, earth science, geology, information sciences and systems, mathematics, and physics), EDUCATION (agricultural education, art education, business education, home economics education, industrial arts education, and physical education), ENGINEERING AND ENVIRONMENTAL DESIGN (industrial engineering technology), HEALTH PROFESSIONS (medical laboratory technology, nursing, physical therapy, predentistry, premedicine, prepharmacy, and preveterinary science), SOCIAL SCIENCE (criminal justice, dietetics, economics, history, home economics, human development, interdisciplinary studies, law enforcement and corrections, physical fitness/movement, political science/government, prelaw, social work, sociology, and water resources). Science and business are the strongest academically. Business and education has the largest enrollments.

Required: All students must complete at least 120 hours, including 24 hours in the major, with a 2.0 GPA. The 42-hour required core curriculum includes courses in English, U.S. and Texas government, U.S. history, lab science, communications, computer information systems, and wellness. There are also distributional requirements that must be met in humanities and social sciences, and a writing proficiency exam.

Special: Tarleton offers work-study programs, internships, limited nondegree study, study abroad in 10 countries. There is a 3-2 engineering degree available with Texas A&M University. Special degree programs may be designed to meet unusual requirements. There are 11 national honor societies, a freshman honors program, and 9 departmental honors programs.

Faculty/Classroom: 51% of faculty are male; 49% are female. 91% teach undergraduates. Graduate students teach 2% of introductory courses. The average class size in an introductory lecture is 26; in a laboratory is 21; and in a regular course is 25.

Admissions: 82% of the 2013-2014 applicants were accepted. The SAT scores for the 2013-2014 freshman class were: Critical Reading--60% below 500, 31% between 500 and 599, 8% between 600 and 699, and 1% between 700 and 800; Math--48% below 500, 41% between 500 and 599, 10% between 600 and 699, and 1% between 700 and 800; Writing-

-68% below 500, 27% between 500 and 599, 4% between 600 and 699. The ACT scores were 47% below 21, 32% between 21 and 23, 16% between 24 and 26, 3% between 27 and 28, and 1% above 28. 26% of the current freshmen were in the top fifth of their class; 66% were in the top two fifths. 5 freshmen graduated first in their class.

Requirements: The SAT or ACT is required. Requirements vary with rank in class. Students in the top 10 percent of their graduating class should provide SAT/ACT scores and also complete a Recommended or Distinguished program. All applicants must provide SAT/ACT scores (a minimum total of 950 on the critical reading and math components of the SAT) and must also include the essay writing component from the SAT or ACT. Students in the lower half of their class must score higher. Secondary preparation should include 9 hours of English (including 3 of speech), 3 of college preparatory math, 3 of visual or performing arts, 3 of humanities (literature or philosophy, 15 of history and government, and 3 of electives. AP and CLEP credits are accepted. Important factors in the admissions decision are advanced placement or honors courses, evidence of special talent, and extracurricular activities record.

Procedure: Freshmen are admitted to all sessions. Entrance exams should be taken in the junior year. There is a rolling admissions plan. Applications should be filed by August 1 for fall entry; December 1 for spring entry; and May 1 for summer entry, along with a $30 fee. Notification is sent on a rolling basis. Applications are accepted online.

Transfer: 1251 transfer students enrolled in 2012-2013. Applicants with 30 or more transferable credits must present a 2.0 GPA; those with fewer than 30 credits must present a 2.8 GPA. A GPA of 2.0 to 2.79 may be admitted provided transfers also meet regular admission standards of first-time freshman applicants. 30 of 120 credits required for the bachelor's degree must be completed at Tarleton.

Visiting: There are regularly scheduled orientations for prospective students, including a tour of the campus. There are guides for informal visits and visitors may sit in on classes. To schedule a visit, contact the Office of School Relations, Tarleton Center at (254) 968-9845.

Financial Aid: In 2013-2014, 68% of all full-time freshmen and 75% of continuing full-time students received some form of financial aid. 65% of all full-time freshmen and 95% of continuing full-time students received need-based aid. The average freshman award was $7,653. Need-based scholarships or need-based grants averaged $3,439; need-based self-help aid (loans and jobs) averaged $3,240; and other non-need-based awards and non-need-based scholarships averaged $3,237. 18% of undergraduate students work part-time. Average annual earnings from campus work are $2200. The average financial indebtedness of the 2013 graduate was $15,548. Tarleton is a member of CSS. The FAFSA and FFS are required. The priority date for freshman financial aid applications for fall entry is April 1. The deadline for filing freshman financial aid applications for fall entry is November 1.

International Students: There are 44 international students enrolled. The school actively recruits these students. They must take the TOEFL with a minimum score of 520 on the paper-based TOEFL (PBT) or 69 on the Internet-based version (iBT). They must also take the SAT or ACT.

Graduates: From July 1, 2012 to June 30, 2013, 1811 bachelor's degrees were awarded. The most popular majors were business/marketing (17%), interdisciplinary studies (16%), and agriculture (11%). 367 companies recruited on campus in 2012-2013. In an average class, 2% graduate in 3 years or less, 18% graduate in 4 years or less, 31% graduate in 5 years or less, and 39% graduate in 6 years or less. Of the 2012 graduating class, 5% were enrolled in graduate school within 6 months of graduation, and 80% were employed.

Admissions Contact: Cindy Hess, Director of Undergraduate Admissions. E-Mail: *uadm@tarleton.edu* Web: *www.tarleton.edu/admissions*

TEXAS A&M UNIVERSITY SYSTEM

The Texas A&M University System, established in 1876, is a public system in Texas. It is governed by a 9-member board of regents, whose chief administrator is the chancellor. The primary goal of the system is teaching, research, and service. The main priorities are to provide undergraduate and graduate students with a quality education, and to be a world leader in the development and dissemination of new knowledge. The total student enrollment for all 8 campuses is usually about 71,500 with 4000 faculty members. Altogether there are 496 baccalaureate, 352 master's, 105 doctoral programs offered in Texas A&M University System. Profiles of the 4-year campuses are included in this section.

TEXAS A&M UNIVERSITY — D-3

College Station, TX 77843 — **(979) 845-3741; (979) 847-8737**

Full-time: 20604 men, 19009 women — **Faculty:** n/av; I, -$
Part-time: 2401 men, 2058 women — **Ph.D.s:** 88%
Graduate: 6411 men, 4895 women — **Student/Faculty:** 22 to 1
Year: semesters, summer session — **Tuition:** $8506 ($25,126)
Application Deadline: February 15 — **Room & Board:** $8450
Freshman Class: 31388 applied, 21725 accepted, 10241 enrolled
SAT CR/M/W: 570/610/550 — **ACT:** 26 — **VERY COMPETITIVE+**

Texas A&M University, founded in 1876, is part of the Texas A&M University system. Undergraduate degrees are offered in agriculture and life sciences, architecture, business administration, education, engineering, geosciences, liberal arts, science, and biomedical science. There are 9 undergraduate schools and 11 graduate schools. In addition to regional accreditation, Texas A&M has baccalaureate program accreditation with AACSB, ABET, ACCE, ACEJMC, ADA, ASLA, CSAB, NAAB, NCATE, and SAF. The 7 libraries contain 4.9 million volumes, 5.6 million microform items, 93,362 audio/video tapes/CDs/DVDs, and subscribe to 114,154 periodicals including electronic. Computerized library services include interlibrary loans, database searching, Internet access, and Wi-Fi capability. Special learning facilities include an art gallery, radio station, TV station, weather station, observatory, cyclotron, wind tunnel, visualization lab, nuclear reactor, ocean wave pool, and the Bush Museum and Library. The 8300-acre campus is in an urban area 90 miles northwest of Houston. Including any residence halls, there are 796 buildings.

Student Life: 96% of undergraduates are from Texas. Others are from 50 states, 87 foreign countries, and Canada. 68% are White; 20% Hispanic. The average age of freshmen is 18; all undergraduates, 20. 9% do not continue beyond their first year; 81% remain to graduate.

Housing: 9661 students can be accommodated in college housing, which includes single-sex and coed dorms, on-campus apartments, off-campus apartments, married student housing. In addition, there are honors houses, fraternity houses, sorority houses, and honors dorm. On-campus housing is available on a first-come and first-served basis. 75% of students commute. All students may keep cars.

Activities: 6% of men belong to 5 local and 15 national fraternities; 11% of women belong to 3 local and 33 national sororities. There are 800 groups on campus, including art, band, cheerleading, chess, choir, chorale, chorus, computers, dance, drama, drill team, drum and bugle corps, ethnic, film, gay, honors, international, jazz band, literary magazine, marching band, musical theater, newspaper, opera, orchestra, photography, political, professional, radio and TV, religious, social, social service, student government, symphony, and yearbook. Popular campus events include Midnight Yell Practice, Silver Taps and Muster.

Sports: There are 9 intercollegiate sports for men and 12 for women, and 23 intramural sports for men and 23 for women. Facilities include a coliseum, a natatorium, 11 basketball/volleyball courts, 27 handball/racquetball courts, badminton, weight and activity rooms, jogging trails, 14 tennis courts, a squash court, an 18-hole golf course, a 2500-seat auditorium/arena, a driving range, flag football fields, 4 soccer fields, 4 outdoor basketball courts, and 5 walking trails. Intercollegiate athletic facilities include a 70,210-seat football stadium, a 7200-seat indoor basketball and volleyball coliseum, a 7053-seat baseball stadium, a 1750-seat softball complex, a 1000-seat soccer complex, a 2000-seat natatorium, a 3000-seat track-and-field complex, a 1500-seat tennis center, and an 18,000-square-foot physical strength and conditioning lab.

Disabled Students: 85% of the campus is accessible. Facilities include wheelchair ramps, elevators, special parking, specially equipped restrooms, special class scheduling, lowered drinking fountains, lowered telephones, and an office of support services for students with disabilities.

Services: Counseling and information services are available, as is tutoring in most subjects. There is a reader service for the blind, and remedial math, reading, and writing. Workshops in time management, basic study techniques, and test-taking skills are available.

Campus Safety and Security: Measures include 24-hour foot and vehicle patrol, emergency notification system, self-defense education, and security escort services. There are shuttle buses, emergency telephones, lighted pathways/sidewalks, a security awareness committee, and crime-watch and safety tip lines. Crime bulletins are available on the university police web site.

Programs of Study: Texas A&M confers B.A., B.S., B.B.A., B.Ed. and B.L.A. degrees. Master's and doctoral degrees are also awarded. Bachelor's degrees are awarded in AGRICULTURE (agricultural business management, agricultural communications, agricultural economics, agronomy, animal science, dairy science, fish and game management, fishing and fisheries, forestry and related sciences, horticulture, poultry science, and range/farm management), BIOLOGICAL SCIENCE (biochemistry, biology/biological science, botany, entomology, genetics, microbiology, and zoology), BUSINESS (accounting, banking and finance, business systems analysis, management science, marketing/retailing/merchandising, and personnel management), COMMUNICATIONS AND THE ARTS

(English, French, German, journalism, performing arts, Russian, Spanish, and speech/debate/rhetoric), COMPUTER AND PHYSICAL SCIENCE (atmospheric sciences and meteorology, chemistry, computer science, geology, geophysics and seismology, mathematics, and physics), EDUCATION (agricultural education, elementary education, health education, physical education, and secondary education), ENGINEERING AND ENVIRONMENTAL DESIGN (aeronautical engineering, agricultural engineering, bioengineering, biomedical engineering, chemical engineering, civil engineering, computer engineering, construction engineering, electrical/electronics engineering, engineering technology, environmental design, environmental science, industrial engineering technology, landscape architecture/design, mechanical engineering, nuclear engineering, and petroleum/natural gas engineering), HEALTH PROFESSIONS (biomedical science), SOCIAL SCIENCE (anthropology, economics, history, international studies, parks and recreation management, philosophy, political science/government, psychology, and sociology). Biomedical science, business administration, biology, engineering, and agriculture are the strongest academically.

Required: To graduate, students must complete at least 128 credit hours, including 30 to 33 in the major. A minimum 2.0 GPA is required. Students must complete a core curriculum of 48 hours in 8 subject areas, including courses in American history and government, phys ed, computers, foreign language, speech and writing skills, math/logical reasoning, science, humanities, and social science. Requirements in the major vary.

Special: The university offers extensive opportunities through the Career Center and Study Abroad Office. B.A.- B.S. degrees, study abroad in 12 countries, internships, a Washington semester, credit for military experience, nondegree study, co-op programs, dual majors, and pass/fail options are available. A 5-year graduate business/liberal arts program is offered, as well as a 3-2 engineering degree with Sam Houston State University. There are 41 national honor societies, including Phi Beta Kappa, and a freshman honors program.

Faculty/Classroom: 71% of faculty are male; 29% are female. 70% teach undergraduates, 72% do research, and 47% do both. Graduate students teach 11% of introductory courses. The average class size in an introductory lecture is 78; in a laboratory is 28; and in a regular course is 58.

Admissions: 69% of the 2013-2014 applicants were accepted. The SAT scores for the 2013-2014 freshman class were: Critical Reading--18% below 500, 41% between 500 and 599, 33% between 600 and 699, and 8% between 700 and 800; Math--8% below 500, 33% between 500 and 599, 45% between 600 and 699, and 14% between 700 and 800; Writing--25% below 500, 44% between 500 and 599, 26% between 600 and 699, and 5% between 700 and 800. The ACT scores were 5% below 21, 15% between 21 and 23, 26% between 24 and 26, 18% between 27 and 28, and 36% above 28. 84% of the current freshmen were in the top fifth of their class; 97% were in the top two fifths. There were 170 National Merit finalists. 341 freshmen graduated first in their class.

Requirements: The SAT or ACT is required. The ACT Optional Writing test is also required. In addition, secondary school graduation is a condition of freshman admission. Required high school courses include 4 credits in English, 3 1/2 credits in math, 3 credits in science (2 from biology, chemistry, or physics), 2 credits of social studies and the same foreign language, and 1 of history. AP and CLEP credits are accepted. Important factors in the admissions decision are leadership record, evidence of special talent, and extracurricular activities record.

Procedure: Freshmen are admitted fall, spring, and summer. Entrance exams should be taken during the spring of the junior year or by December of the senior year. There is a rolling admissions plan. Applications should be filed by February 15 for fall entry; October 15 for spring entry; and February 15 for summer entry, along with a $60 fee. Applications are accepted online.

Transfer: 2309 transfer students enrolled in 2012-2013. Applicants must submit transcripts from previously attended colleges. Requirements vary, depending on how many semester hours were attempted and the grades for those hours. 30 of 128 credits required for the bachelor's degree must be completed at Texas A&M.

Visiting: There are regularly scheduled orientations for prospective students, Some 20 new-student conferences are held for students to meet with academic advisers to select courses, become acquainted with student life activities, and tour the campus. There are guides for informal visits and visitors may sit in on classes. To schedule a visit, contact the Aggieland Visitor Center at (979) 845-5851.

Financial Aid: In 2013-2014, 73% of all full-time freshmen and 64% of continuing full-time students received some form of financial aid. 52% of all full-time freshmen and 53% of continuing full-time students received need-based aid. The average freshman award was $12,576. Need-based scholarships or need-based grants averaged $10,556 ($39,606 maximum); need-based self-help aid (loans and jobs) averaged $5,221 ($32,994 maximum); non-need-based athletic scholarships averaged $5,265 ($17,925 maximum); other non-need-based awards and non-need-based scholarships averaged $5,685 ($51,397 maximum); and $4,447 from other forms of aid. 20% of undergraduate students work part-time. Average annual earnings from campus work are $3100. The average financial indebtedness of the 2013 graduate was $24,291. The FAFSA is required. The priority date for freshman financial aid applications for fall entry is March 15.

International Students: There are 669 international students enrolled. They must take the TOEFL with a minimum score of 550 on the paper-based TOEFL (PBT) or 80 on the Internet-based version (iBT). The SAT or ACT is required for graduates of U.S. high schools only.

Graduates: From July 1, 2012 to June 30, 2013, 9570 bachelor's degrees were awarded. The most popular majors were business/marketing (17%), engineering (14%), and agriculture (11%). 150 companies recruited on campus in 2012-2013. In an average class, 1% graduate in 3 years or less, 51% graduate in 4 years or less, 77% graduate in 5 years or less, and 81% graduate in 6 years or less.

Admissions Contact: Admissions Counseling E-Mail: *admissions@tamu.edu* Web: *www.tamu.edu*

TEXAS A&M UNIVERSITY AT COMMERCE — D-2

Commerce, TX 75429-3011 — **(903) 886-5072; (903) 468-8685**

Full-time: 1575 men, 2475 women	**Faculty:** n/av; I, -$
Part-time: 445 men, 735 women	**Ph.D.s:** 65%
Graduate: 1420 men, 2430 women	**Student/Faculty:** n/av
Year: semesters, summer session	**Tuition:** $6628 ($16,647)
Application Deadline: see profile	**Room & Board:** $6750
Freshman Class: n/av	
SAT or ACT: required	
	COMPETITIVE

Texas A&M University at Commerce, founded in 1889, offers undergraduate and graduate programs in business and technology, arts and sciences, and education. The figures in the above capsule and this profile are approximate. There are 3 undergraduate schools and 1 graduate school. In addition to regional accreditation, TAMU-C has baccalaureate program accreditation with AACSB, CSWE, NASM, and NCATE. The library contains 1.2 million volumes, 1.2 million microform items, and subscribes to 16,222 periodicals including electronic. Computerized library services include interlibrary loans, database searching, Internet access, and laptop Internet portals. Special learning facilities include a planetarium, radio station, TV station, performing arts center, and farm. The 1883-acre campus is in a small town 65 miles northeast of Dallas. Including any residence halls, there are 121 buildings.

Student Life: 97% of undergraduates are from Texas. Others are from 30 states, 21 foreign countries, and Canada. 98% are from public schools. 65% are white; 17% African American. The average age of freshmen is 19; all undergraduates, 25. 42% do not continue beyond their first year; 57% remain to graduate.

Housing: 1910 students can be accommodated in college housing, which includes single-sex and coed dorms, on-campus apartments, off-campus apartments, and married student housing. In addition, there are honors houses, special-interest houses, fraternity houses, and sorority houses. On-campus housing is guaranteed for the freshman year only and is available on a first-come, first-served basis. 71% of students commute. Alcohol is not permitted. All students may keep cars.

Activities: 15% of men belong to 9 national fraternities; 12% of women belong to 7 national sororities. There are 96 groups on campus, including art, band, cheerleading, chess, choir, chorale, chorus, dance, drama, ethnic, film, gay, honors, international, jazz band, literary magazine, marching band, musical theater, newspaper, orchestra, pep band, photography, political, professional, radio and TV, religious, social, social service, and student government. Popular campus events include Sam Rayburn Symposium, Christmas Feast of Carols, and Springfest.

Sports: There are 5 intercollegiate sports for men and 5 for women, and 7 intramural sports for men. Facilities include a 1700-seat auditorium, a 10,000-seat stadium, a gym, handball and racquetball courts, a bowling alley, a swimming pool, a weight room, tennis courts, a field house, and intramural fields.

Disabled Students: All of the campus is accessible. Facilities include wheelchair ramps, elevators, special parking, and specially equipped rest rooms.

Services: Counseling and information services are available, as is tutoring in some subjects, including math and writing. There is remedial math, reading, and writing.

Campus Safety and Security: Measures include 24-hour foot and vehicle patrol, self-defense education, and security escort services. There are emergency telephones, lighted pathways/sidewalks, a victim assistance officer, a police service for special and social events, crime and date-rape prevention presentations, and motorist assistance.

Programs of Study: TAMU-C confers B.A., B.S., B.A.C.J., B.B.A., B.F.A., B.G.S., B.M., B.M.Ed., B.S.C.J., B.S.Lib.Sci., and B.S.W. degrees. Master's and doctoral degrees are also awarded. Bachelor's degrees are awarded in AGRICULTURE (agricultural economics, agriculture, animal science, and wildlife management), BIOLOGICAL SCIENCE (biology/biological science and botany), BUSINESS (accounting, banking and finance, business administration and management, and marketing/retailing/merchandising), COMMUNICATIONS AND THE ARTS (advertising, broadcasting, dramatic arts, English, fine arts, French, German, journalism, languages, music, photography, printmaking, and Spanish), COMPUTER AND PHYSICAL SCIENCE (chemistry, computer science, earth science, geology, mathematics, and physics), EDUCATION (agricultural education, business education, early childhood education, elementary education, guidance education, health education, industrial arts education, music education, science education, and secondary education), ENGINEERING AND ENVIRONMENTAL DESIGN (engineering technology and preengineering), HEALTH PROFESSIONS (predentistry, premedicine, and prepharmacy), SOCIAL SCIENCE (anthropology, criminal justice, economics, geography, history, political science/government, prelaw, psychology, religion, social work, and sociology). Education, computer science, and business administration are the strongest programs academically and has the largest enrollments.

Required: To graduate, all students must earn a GPA of 2.0 while taking at least 126 semester hours, including 24 hours in the major. Distribution requirements include 24 in culture courses such as American history and foreign languages, 12 each in English composition, math, and speech skills, 8 in sciences, 6 in upper-division courses, and 4 in phys ed.

Special: TAMU-C offers co-op programs with E-Systems Inc. and numerous other firms, cross-registration by independent arrangement, study abroad in England, and work-study programs. B.A.-B.S. degrees, second degrees, dual majors, a general studies degree, credit for life experience, internships, nondegree study, and pass/fail options are also available. There are 18 national honor societies, a freshman honors program, and 26 departmental honor programs.

Faculty/Classroom: 53% of faculty are male; 47% are female. 77% teach undergraduates, 46% do research, and 37% do both. Graduate students teach 21% of introductory courses. The average class size in an introductory lecture is 30; in a laboratory, 20; and in a regular course, 25.

Requirements: The SAT or ACT is required, with a minimum recommended composite score of 800 or 20, respectively. Applicants need not be graduates of an accredited secondary school, although high school graduation is required. The GED is also accepted. A GPA of 2.0 is required. AP and CLEP credits are accepted.

Procedure: Freshmen are admitted to all sessions. Entrance exams should be taken prior to enrollment. There are deferred admissions and rolling admissions plans. Check with the school for current application guidelines and fee. Notification is sent on a rolling basis.

Transfer: Applicants must have a college GPA of 2.0 with a minimum of 21 credit hours. The SAT or ACT is not required. College transcripts and a statement of good standing from the prior institution are required. 30 of 126 credits required for the bachelor's degree must be completed at TAMU-C.

Visiting: There are regularly scheduled orientations for prospective students. There are guides for informal visits and visitors may sit in on classes. To schedule a visit, contact the Admissions Office.

Financial Aid: The FAFSA and the college's own financial statement are required. Check with the school for current application deadlines.

International Students: They must take the TOEFL. They must also take the SAT or ACT.

Admissions Contact: Director of Admissions. A campus DVD is available. E-Mail: *admissions@tamu-commerce.edu* Web: *www.tamu-commerce.edu*

TEXAS A&M UNIVERSITY AT CORPUS CHRISTI — D-4

Corpus Christi, TX 78412 — (361) 825-2624; (800) 482-6822; (361) 825-5887

Full-time: 2040 men, 3215 women
Part-time: 545 men, 785 women
Graduate: 540 men, 1110 women
Year: semesters, summer session
Application Deadline: see profile
Freshman Class: n/av
SAT or ACT: required
Faculty: 1,400
Ph.D.s: 74%
Student/Faculty: 20 to 1
Tuition: $6900 ($16,300)
Room & Board: $9100

LESS COMPETITIVE

Texas A&M University at Corpus Christi, part of the Texas A&M University System since 1989, is a public institution offering 34 undergraduate degree programs and 27 graduate degree programs. The figures in the above capsule and this profile are approximate. The library contains 433,785 volumes, 654,518 microform items, 6245 audio/video tapes/CDs/DVDs, and subscribes to 1706 periodicals including electronic. The university is located on its own 240-acre island approximately 10 miles from downtown Corpus Christi.

Student Life: 98% of undergraduates are from Texas. 57% are white; 37% Hispanic. The average age of freshmen is 19; all undergraduates, 23.

Housing: College-sponsored housing includes single-sex and coed dorms. In addition, there are apartments for single students.

Activities: There are no fraternities or sororities. Groups on campus include band, choir, dance, drama, film, jazz band, literary magazine, marching band, musical theater, newspaper, opera, pep band, student government, symphony, and yearbook.

Sports: Facilities include a field house with a full-size gym, a weight room, and 4 racquetball/handball courts. Adjacent to the gym are 6 lighted tennis courts, a practice court, a 25-meter swimming pool, and lighted playing fields. A wellness center offers a free-weight area, weight machines, cardiovascular equipment, a wellness resource area, 2 aerobic studios, and a game room.

Programs of Study: Texas A&M Corpus Christi confers B.A., B.S., B.B.A., B.F.A., B.M., B.S.H.S., B.S.I.S., and B.S.N. degrees. Master's and doctoral degrees are also awarded. Bachelor's degrees are awarded in BIOLOGICAL SCIENCE (biology/biological science), BUSINESS (accounting, banking and finance, business administration and management, management information systems, and marketing/retailing/merchandising), COMMUNICATIONS AND THE ARTS (art, communications, dramatic arts, English, music, Spanish, and speech/debate/rhetoric), COMPUTER AND PHYSICAL SCIENCE (chemistry, computer science, geology, and mathematics), EDUCATION (education), ENGINEERING AND ENVIRONMENTAL DESIGN (engineering technology, environmental science, and mechanical engineering technology), HEALTH PROFESSIONS (clinical science, health science, and nursing), SOCIAL SCIENCE (criminal justice, geography, history, political science/government, psychology, and sociology).

Required: To graduate, a minimum of 124 semester hours must be completed. A minimum of 45 semester hours of upper-division credit is required, as is a minimum GPA of 2.0 overall and in the major. In addition, all students must complete the core curriculum requirement, including 6 credit hours each of communication (English rhetoric/composition), natural science, U.S. history, and political science and 3 each of math, visual and performing arts, humanities, and social/behavioral science. Students must also meet foreign language and computer literacy requirements and take a first-year seminar.

Special: Cooperative programs, internships, dual majors, and distance learning are available.

Faculty/Classroom: 57% of faculty are male; 43% are female. No introductory courses are taught by graduate students.

Requirements: The SAT or ACT is required. Graduation from secondary school is required, with 4 units of English, 3 each of math, science, and social studies, and 2 of a foreign language. The GED is accepted. AP and CLEP credits are accepted. Important factors in the admissions decision are advanced placement or honors courses.

Procedure: Freshmen are admitted fall, spring, and summer. Check with the school for current application deadlines. The application fee is $25. Applications are accepted online.

Transfer: College transcripts, a statement of good standing from prior institutions, and a GPA of 2.0 are required. 79 of 124 credits required for the bachelor's degree must be completed at Texas A&M Corpus Christi.

Visiting: There are regularly scheduled orientations for prospective students, including a tour of the campus and or introduction to various services on campus. To schedule a visit, contact the Office of Admissions.

Financial Aid: The FAFSA is required. Check with the school for current application deadlines.

International Students: They must take the TOEFL.

Admissions Contact: Director of Admissions. E-mail: *admiss@tamucc.edu* Web: *www.tamucc.edu*

TEXAS A&M UNIVERSITY AT GALVESTON — E-4

Galveston, TX 77553-1675 — (409) 740-4414; (877) 322-4443; (409) 740-4731

Full-time: 875 men, 600 women
Part-time: 65 men, 60 women
Graduate: 20 men, 50 women
Year: semesters, summer session
Application Deadline: open
Freshman Class: n/av
SAT or ACT: required
Faculty: n/av
Ph.D.s: 40%
Student/Faculty: n/av
Tuition: $9500 ($18,500)
Room & Board: $7500

COMPETITIVE

Texas A&M University at Galveston, founded in 1962, is a public institution that offers marine and maritime-related programs. It is part of the Texas A&M University system. The figures in the above capsule and this profile are approximate. There are 9 undergraduate schools and 1 graduate school. In addition to regional accreditation, TAMUG has baccalaureate program accreditation with ABET. The library contains 43,000 volumes 52,984 microform items, and subscribes to 970 periodicals including electronic. Computerized library services include interlibrary loans and database searching. Special learning facilities include a learning resource center and a training ship, the T/S Texas Clipper, used for an annual summer training cruise. The 120-acre campus is in a suburban area 50 miles south of Houston on the Gulf of Mexico. Including any residence halls, there are 14 buildings.

Student Life: 81% of undergraduates are from Texas. Others are from

43 states and 8 foreign countries. 94% are from public schools. 85% are white. The average age of freshmen is 18; all undergraduates, 20. 28% do not continue beyond their first year; 52% remain to graduate.

Housing: 650 students can be accommodated in college housing, which includes coed dorms. On-campus housing is guaranteed for the freshman year only, is available on a first-come, and first-served basis. 58% of students commute. Alcohol is not permitted. All students may keep cars.

Activities: There are no fraternities or sororities. There are 39 groups on campus, including chorale, drama, ethnic, international, literary magazine, newspaper, political, professional, religious, social, social service, student government, and yearbook. Popular campus events include Springfest, Mardi Grass, and Maritime Ball.

Sports: There are 2 intercollegiate sports for men and 1 for women, and 6 intramural sports for men and 5 for women. Facilities include tennis courts, a volleyball court, a swimming pool, and a basketball court.

Disabled Students: 85% of the campus is accessible. Facilities include wheelchair ramps, elevators, special parking, specially equipped rest rooms, special class scheduling, and lowered drinking fountains.

Services: Counseling and information services are available, as is tutoring in most subjects. There is a reader service for the blind and remedial math, reading, and writing.

Campus Safety and Security: Measures include 24-hour foot and vehicle patrol, emergency notification system, and security escort services. There are shuttle buses and lighted pathways/sidewalks.

Programs of Study: TAMUG confers B.A., B.S. degrees. Master's degrees are also awarded. Bachelor's degrees are awarded in AGRICULTURE (environmental studies, fishing and fisheries, and natural resource management), BIOLOGICAL SCIENCE (biology/biological science, environmental biology, marine biology, and marine science), BUSINESS (international business management, recreation and leisure services, and transportation management), COMPUTER AND PHYSICAL SCIENCE (earth science, geoscience, hydrology, natural sciences, oceanography, and science and management), ENGINEERING AND ENVIRONMENTAL DESIGN (civil engineering, electrical/electronics engineering technology, electromechanical technology, environmental science, land use management and reclamation, marine engineering, maritime science, mechanical engineering technology, naval architecture and marine engineering, ocean engineering, systems engineering, and transportation engineering), SOCIAL SCIENCE (archeology, geography, humanities and social science, liberal arts/general studies, and water resources). Marine systems engineering is the strongest academically. Marine biology has the largest enrollment.

Required: Depending on the major, students must complete 130 to 160 credit hours with a GPA of 2.0 overall as well as in the major. The required core curriculum includes courses in math, political science, American history, and macroeconomics. Distribution requirements include 6 credits each in English, calculus, humanities, and social sciences; 8 credits in science; and 12 credits in citizenship. Students must also complete a 2-semester sequence of a foreign language and 1 computer language course. Total number of hours in the major is 36.

Special: TAMUG offers dual majors in all majors, dual degrees, internships in marine biology and oceanography, a summer semester at sea, and credit for military service. Students may challenge any course for credit by exam. A pass/fail option is available for electives taken by juniors or seniors who have a minimum 2.5 GPA. Selected majors may earn a ship's officer license with a degree program.

Faculty/Classroom: 65% of faculty are male; 35% are female. All teach undergraduates. No introductory courses are taught by graduate students. The average class size in an introductory lecture is 48; in a laboratory, 14; and in a regular course, 24.

Requirements: The SAT or ACT is required. Acceptable test scores depend on high school rank, with minimum composite scores of 1000 for the SAT and 24 for the ACT. Applicants must be graduates of an accredited high school or hold a GED. A minimum of 16 academic credits is required, including 4 units of English, 3 1/2 units of math, 2 1/2 units of either history or social studies, 2 units each of a foreign language and science, and the rest in electives. AP and CLEP credits are accepted. Important factors in the admissions decision are leadership record, extracurricular activities record, and recommendations by school officials.

Procedure: Freshmen are admitted to all sessions. Entrance exams should be taken late in the junior year or early in the senior year. There are early decision, early admissions, deferred admissions, and rolling admissions plans. Application deadlines are open. Notification is sent on a rolling basis. Applications are accepted on-line.

Transfer: Applicants must have a cumulative 2.0 GPA in a minimum of 24 completed credit hours as well as a 2.0 GPA in each of the last 2 terms attended. 30 of 130 credits required for the bachelor's degree must be completed at TAMUG.

Visiting: There are regularly scheduled orientations for prospective students, including campus tours conducted Monday and Friday at 10 a.m. There are guides for informal visits and visitors may sit in on classes. To schedule a visit, contact the Student Relations Department.

Financial Aid: The FAFSA is required. Check with the school for current application deadlines.

International Students: They must take the TOEFL and the college's own test. They must also take the SAT or ACT.

Admissions Contact: Director of Admissions. A campus DVD is available. E-Mail: *seaaggie@tamug.edu* Web: *www.tamug.edu*

TEXAS A&M UNIVERSITY AT KINGSVILLE D-5

Kingsville, TX 78363 **(361) 593-2315**
(800) 687-6000; (361) 595-2195

Full-time: 2140 men, 2000 women	**Faculty:** n/av; IIA, --$
Part-time: 610 men, 910 women	**Ph.D.s:** 71 %
Graduate: 620 men, 720 women	**Student/Faculty:** 16 to 1
Year: semesters, summer session	**Tuition:** $9,500 ($19,338)
Application Deadline: open	**Room & Board:** $7500
Freshman Class: n/av	
SAT or ACT: required	

LESS COMPETITIVE

Texas A&M University at Kingsville, founded in 1925 as South Texas Teachers College, is a comprehensive university and part of the Texas A&M University system. Graduate and undergraduate programs are offered in agriculture and home economics, arts and sciences, business administration, education, and engineering. The figures in the above capsule and this profile are approximate. There are 5 undergraduate schools and 5 graduate schools. In addition to regional accreditation, TAMUK has baccalaureate program accreditation with ABET, ADA, NASM, and NCATE. The library contains 358,466 volumes, 183,416 microform items, 3224 audio/video tapes/CDs/DVDs, and subscribes to 2304 periodicals including electronic. Computerized library services include interlibrary loans and database searching. Special learning facilities include a learning resource center, art gallery, natural history museum, planetarium, radio station, TV station, and wildlife and citrus research facilities. The 246-acre campus is in a small town 40 miles southwest of Corpus Christi. Including any residence halls, there are 82 buildings.

Student Life: 95% of undergraduates are from Texas. Others are from 35 states, 44 foreign countries, and Canada. 98% are from public schools. 62% are Hispanic; 29% white. The average age of freshmen is 19; all undergraduates, 23. 45% do not continue beyond their first year; 22% remain to graduate.

Housing: 1200 students can be accommodated in college housing, which includes single-sex and coed dorms and married student housing. On-campus housing is guaranteed for all 4 years. 70% of students commute. All students may keep cars.

Activities: 3% of men belong to 6 national fraternities; 3% of women belong to 3 national sororities. There are 106 groups on campus, including art, band, cheerleading, choir, chorale, chorus, communications, computers, dance, debate, drama, drill team, ethnic, honors, international, jazz band, marching band, mariachi, musical theater, newspaper, pep band, political, professional, radio and TV, religious, social, and student government. Popular campus events include Campus Capers, Fall Carnival, and Spring Block Party.

Sports: There are 3 intercollegiate sports for men and 3 for women, and 2 intramural sports for men and 2 for women. Facilities include 2 gyms, an Olympic-size swimming pool, courts for tennis and racquetball, an all-weather track, and various playing fields. There are facilities for archery, bowling, golf, fencing, weight training, and jogging.

Disabled Students: 90% of the campus is accessible. Facilities include wheelchair ramps, elevators, special parking, specially equipped rest rooms, lowered drinking fountains, and lowered telephones.

Services: Counseling and information services are available, as is tutoring in every subject. There is a reader service for the blind and remedial math, reading, and writing.

Campus Safety and Security: Measures include 24-hour foot and vehicle patrol, self-defense education, and security escort services. There are emergency telephones and lighted pathways/sidewalks.

Programs of Study: TAMUK confers B.A., B.S., B.A.A.S., B.B.A., B.F.A., B.M., B.S.A., B.S.C.E., B.S.Ch.E., B.S.C.S., B.S.E.E., B.S.I.E., B.S. in Hum.Sci., B.S. in Nat. Gas Eng., B.S.I.T., and B.S.M.E. degrees. Master's and doctoral degrees are also awarded. Bachelor's degrees are awarded in AGRICULTURE (agricultural business management, animal science, plant science, range/farm management, and soil science), BIOLOGICAL SCIENCE (biology/biological science), BUSINESS (accounting, banking and finance, business administration and management, business economics, fashion merchandising, management science, marketing/retailing/merchandising, and real estate), COMMUNICATIONS AND THE ARTS (communications, dramatic arts, English, fine arts, music, and Spanish), COMPUTER AND PHYSICAL SCIENCE (chemistry, computer science, geology, mathematics, and physics), EDUCATION (agricultural education, elementary education, health education, music education, physical education, and secondary education), ENGINEERING AND ENVIRONMENTAL DESIGN (chemical engineering, civil engineering, electrical/electronics engineering, engineering management, industrial engineering technology, interior design, mechanical engineering, and petroleum/natural gas engineering), HEALTH PROFESSIONS (medical laboratory technology, nursing, predentistry, premedicine, prepharmacy, preveterinary science, and speech pathology/audiology), SOCIAL SCIENCE (anthropology, child care/child and family studies, food production/management/services, food science, geography, history, home economics, political science/government, prelaw, psychology, public administration, and sociology). Engineering is the strongest academically. Education has the largest enrollment.

Required: All students must complete 124 to 135 semester hours, including a minimum of 24 in the major and 45 in advanced work, with at least a 2.0 GPA. General education requirements include courses in oral and written communication, math and reasoning, U.S. and Texas government, social sciences, American and world history, lab sciences, fine arts, and phys ed.

Special: There are co-op programs in engineering, business, and agriculture, and internships, B.A.-B.S. degrees, and dual majors in most programs. A nontraditional Bachelor of Applied Arts and Sciences program is offered to students with vocational or technical training or experience. The Center for Continuing Education offers noncredit enrichment courses in a variety of subjects, a professional development program in organizational management, and a number of seminars and short courses that are held abroad. The university also offers a work-study program and the College I Freshman program. There are 10 national honor societies, a freshman honors program, and 20 departmental honors programs.

Faculty/Classroom: 66% of faculty are male; 34% are female. All teach undergraduates. No introductory courses are taught by graduate students. The average class size in an introductory lecture is 30; in a laboratory, 20; and in a regular course, 25.

Requirements: The SAT or ACT is required. Applicants should be high school graduates or have a GED. Secondary preparation must include 7 units of electives, no more than 4 of which may be in vocational subjects, 3 units of English, 2 units each of math (including algebra), foreign language, and natural science, and 1 unit each of history and another social science. The university sets minimum admissible scores each year. An interview is encouraged. AP and CLEP credits are accepted.

Procedure: Freshmen are admitted to all sessions. Entrance exams should be taken before graduation from high school. There are early admissions and rolling admissions plans. Application deadlines are open. The application fee is $15. Notification is sent on a rolling basis.

Transfer: All applicants must present a GPA of at least 2.0. 24 of 124 credits required for the bachelor's degree must be completed at TAMUK.

Visiting: There are regularly scheduled orientations for prospective students, including advisement, tours, stays in dorms, entertainment, registration, and financial information. There are guides for informal visits, and visitors may sit in on classes and stay overnight. To schedule a visit, contact the Office of School Relations.

Financial Aid: TAMUK is a member of CSS. The FAFSA is required. Check with the school for current application deadlines.

International Students: They must take the TOEFL and the college's own test. They must also take the SAT or ACT.

Admissions Contact: Director of Admissions. E-Mail: *admissions@tamuk.edu* Web: *www.tamuk.edu*

TEXAS CHRISTIAN UNIVERSITY — D-2

Fort Worth, TX 76129 — **(817) 257-7490**
(800) TCU-FROG; (817) 257-7268

Full-time: 3338 men, 4988 women	**Faculty:** n/av; I, -$
Part-time: 157 men, 157 women	**Ph.D.s:** n/av
Graduate: 582 men, 703 women	**Student/Faculty:** n/av
Year: semesters, summer session	**Tuition:** $36,590
Application Deadline: February 15	**Room & Board:** $10,980

Freshman Class: 18551 applied, 8791 accepted, 1936 enrolled
SAT or ACT: required

HIGHLY COMPETITIVE

Texas Christian University, founded in 1873, is a private university affiliated with the Christian Church (Disciples of Christ). TCU is a teaching and research institution offering undergraduate programs in arts, sciences, business, education, fine arts, communications, nursing, and engineering. There are 8 undergraduate schools and 8 graduate schools. In addition to regional accreditation, TCU has baccalaureate program accreditation with AACSB, ABET, ACEJMC, ADA, CSWE, NASAD, and NASM. The library contains 1.4 million volumes, 511,879 microform items, 67,874 audio/video tapes/CDs/DVDs, and subscribes to 87,509 periodicals including electronic. Computerized library services include interlibrary loans, database searching, Internet access, and Wi-Fi capability. Special learning facilities include an art gallery, natural history museum, radio station, TV station, observatory, speech and hearing clinic. The 277-acre campus is in a suburban area 5 miles southwest of downtown Fort Worth. Including any residence halls, there are 112 buildings.

Student Life: 58% of undergraduates are from Texas. Others are from 50 states, 66 foreign countries, and Canada. 59% are from public schools. 73% are White. 45% are Protestant; 29% claim no religious affiliation; 20% Catholic. The average age of freshmen is 18; all undergraduates, 20. 10% do not continue beyond their first year; 76% remain to graduate.

Housing: 4100 students can be accommodated in college housing, which includes single-sex and coed dorms and on-campus apartments. In addition, there are honors houses, fraternity houses, and sorority houses. On-campus housing is available on a lottery system for upperclassmen. 52% of students commute. All students may keep cars.

Activities: 42% of men belong to 20 national fraternities; 53% of women belong to 1 local and 19 national sororities. There are 234 groups on campus, including art, band, cheerleading, choir, chorale, chorus, communications, computers, dance, debate, drama, drill team, environmental, ethnic, film, forensics, gay, honors, international, jazz band, literary magazine, marching band, musical theater, newspaper, opera, orchestra, pep band, photography, political, professional, radio and TV, religious, social, social service, student government, symphony, and yearbook. Popular campus events include Frog Camp, Frogs First Weekend, Family Weekend, Homecoming, Christmas Tree Lighting, Carols by Candlelight, Senior Fiesta.

Sports: There are 8 intercollegiate sports for men and 10 for women. Facilities include a recreation center, a climbing wall and challenge course, fitness and wellness programs, and a pool.

Disabled Students: All of the campus is accessible. Facilities include wheelchair ramps, elevators, special parking, specially equipped restrooms, lowered drinking fountains, lowered telephones.

Campus Safety and Security: Measures include 24-hour foot and vehicle patrol, emergency notification system, self-defense education, and security escort services. There are shuttle buses, emergency telephones, lighted pathways/sidewalks, controlled access to dorms/residences, bike patrol, and video monitoring of some parking lots.

Programs of Study: TCU confers B.A., B.B.A., B.F.A., B.G.S., B.Mus., B.S., B.S.Ed., B.S.N., B.S.S.W., B.C.J., B.Mus.Ed. and B.Ath.Trng. degrees. Master's and doctoral degrees are also awarded. Bachelor's degrees are awarded in AGRICULTURE (ranch management), BIOLOGICAL SCIENCE (biochemistry, biology/biological science, environmental earth resources, life science secondary school education, neurosciences, and nutrition), BUSINESS (accounting, business information systems, entrepreneurial studies, fashion merchandising, finance, international accounting, international business information systems, international economics, international entrepreneurial management, international finance, international real estate finance, international marketing, international supply and value chain management, marketing management, real estate finance, supply chain management, and professional program in accounting), COMMUNICATIONS AND THE ARTS (art history, ballet, ballet modern dance, ceramic art and design, church music, communications, English, film, television and digital media, French, German, graphic design, instrumental performance, instrumental music education, journalism, keyboard - piano concentration, modern dance, music, music theory and composition, musical theater, organ performance, painting, photography, piano pedagogy, printmaking, sculpture, Spanish, sports media, strategic communication, strings, studio art, theatre acting, theatre arts, theater design, theatre production, theatre studies, vocal performance, vocal music education, and writing), COMPUTER AND PHYSICAL SCIENCE (astronomy and physics, chemistry, computer information technology, computer science, geology, geoscience, mathematics, mathematics - actuarial concentration, and physics), EDUCATION (art education, athletic training, bilingual early childhood education, early childhood education, English education, general studies, mathematics education, middle school education, music education, physical education, physical science secondary school education, science education, secondary education, social studies education, and social studies secondary school education), ENGINEERING AND ENVIRONMENTAL DESIGN (electrical/electronics engineering, engineering, environmental science, interior design, and mechanical engineering), HEALTH PROFESSIONS (habilitation of the deaf, health, movement science, nursing, Pre-Health Studies, speech pathology/audiology, and sports psychology), SOCIAL SCIENCE (anthropology, child psychology/development, criminal justice, dietetics, economics, food production/management/services, geography, history, international political science, philosophy, political science/government, psychology, religion, social work, and sociology). General business, nursing, and liberal arts pre-major have the largest enrollments.

Required: TCU requires completion of university curriculum requirements, which are divided into foundations (composition, mathematics, oral communication, and advanced writing) and explorations (humanities, fine arts, social sciences and natural sciences). These are normally satisfied with 15 to 18 courses. At least 124 credit hours (58 of which must be in residence) with a 2.000 GPA; 42 hours of upper division work; at least the last 30 hours in residence; a major or concentration.

Special: A general studies degree and a combined B.A.-B.S. degree in numerous majors are offered. TCU also accepts credit by exam and credit for life, military, and work experience. 4-1 programs are available in education. Internships are available in almost all major areas. The university also offers a Washington semester, student exchange programs, and study abroad in 26 countries. TCU also offers study at its London Center and study through the American Airlines Leadership for the Americas program. An accelerated degree program in nursing is also offered. TCU also offers a B.S.W. and B.S.C.J. There are 33 national honor societies, including Phi Beta Kappa, and a freshman honors program.

Faculty/Classroom: No introductory courses are taught by graduate students. The average class size in an introductory lecture is 33 and in a laboratory is 21.

Admissions: 47% of the 2013-2014 applicants were accepted. 66% of the current freshmen were in the top fifth of their class; 91% were in the top two fifths.

Requirements: Either the SAT or the ACT is required, but not both. Candidates should be graduates of an accredited secondary school and have completed 15 Carnegie units, including 4 years of English, 3 years each of math, science, and social studies, and 2 each of the same foreign language and of academic electives. TCU also requires an essay and counselor's recommendation. A personal interview is optional. AP and CLEP credits are accepted. Important factors in the admissions decision are advanced placement or honors courses, leadership record, and extracurricular activities record.

Procedure: Freshmen are admitted fall, spring, and summer. Entrance exams should be taken during or before the fall semester of the senior year. There are early decision, early admissions, and deferred admissions plans. Early decision applications should be filed by November 1; regular applications, by February 15 for fall entry; and December 1 for spring entry, along with a $40 fee. Notification of early decision is sent January 1; regular decision, April 1. 1680 applicants were on the 2013 waiting list; 67 were admitted. Applications are accepted online.

Transfer: 401 transfer students enrolled in 2012-2013. The recommended GPA is 2.7 and a minimum GPA of 2.0 is required. Applicants must complete an application form and submit official transcripts from each college attended. If fewer than 24 semester hours of transferable work have been completed at the time of application, SAT or ACT scores and secondary school transcripts are required. 58 credits required for the bachelor's degree must be completed at TCU.

Visiting: There are regularly scheduled orientations for prospective students, including student-led campus tours, group information sessions, optional personal interviews, and departmental visits. There are guides for informal visits, visitors may sit in on classes, and stay overnight. To schedule a visit, contact TCU Admissions Office.

Financial Aid: In 2013-2014, 75% of all full-time freshmen and 69% of continuing full-time students received some form of financial aid. 41% of all full-time freshmen and 41% of continuing full-time students received need-based aid. The average freshman award was $23,648. Need-based scholarships or need-based grants averaged $13,813 ($50,265 maximum); need-based self-help aid (loans and jobs) averaged $2,638 ($9,000 maximum); non-need-based athletic scholarships averaged $35,063 ($60,248 maximum); and other non-need-based awards and non-need-based scholarships averaged $12,589 ($50,790 maximum). 15% of undergraduate students work part-time. Average annual earnings from campus work are $1500. The average financial indebtedness of the 2013 graduate was $38,317. TCU is a member of CSS. The CSS/Profile and FAFSA are required. The priority date for freshman financial aid applications for fall entry is March 15. The deadline for filing freshman financial aid applications for fall entry is March 15.

International Students: There are 410 international students enrolled. The school actively recruits these students. They must take the TOEFL with a minimum score of 550 on the paper-based TOEFL (PBT) or 80 on the Internet-based version (iBT), SAT, ACT, TOEFL or IELTS. They must also take the SAT or ACT. SAT or ACT required for freshmen whose high school was taught in English or who want to be considered for scholarship.

Graduates: From July 1, 2012 to June 30, 2013, 1732 bachelor's degrees were awarded. The most popular majors were nursing (10%), strategic communication (7%), and communication studies (5%). In an average class, 1% graduate in 3 years or less, 59% graduate in 4 years or less, 74% graduate in 5 years or less, and 76% graduate in 6 years or less. Of the 2012 graduating class, 30% were enrolled in graduate school within 6 months of graduation, and 66% were employed.

Admissions Contact: Ray Brown, Dean of Admissions. E-Mail: *frogmail@tcu.edu* Web: *www.tcu.edu*

TEXAS LUTHERAN UNIVERSITY D-4

Seguin, TX 78155 (830) 372-8050
(800) 771-8521; (830) 372-8096

Full-time: 609 men, 649 women	**Faculty:** 76; IIB, --$
Part-time: 34 men, 37 women	**Ph.D.s:** 80%
Graduate: 8 men, 4 women	**Student/Faculty:** 16 to 1
Year: semesters, summer session	**Tuition:** $25,890
Application Deadline: June 1	**Room & Board:** $8180
Freshman Class: 1734 applied, 882 accepted, 346 enrolled	
SAT CR/M/W: 500/530/490 **ACT:** 22	**COMPETITIVE**

Texas Lutheran University, founded in 1891, is an exclusively undergraduate university of the liberal arts, sciences, and professional studies. The university's mission is to prepare students academically, spiritually, and socially for lives of leadership and service. There is one undergraduate school and one graduate school. In addition to regional accreditation, TLU has baccalaureate program accreditation with ACBSP, NASM, and TEAC. The library contains 155,280 volumes, 119,086 microform items, 5,776 audio/video tapes/CDs/DVDs, and subscribes to 149,122 periodicals including electronic. Computerized library services include interlibrary loans, database searching, Internet access, and Wi-Fi capability. Special learning facilities include an art gallery and natural history museum. The 184-acre campus is in a small town 37 miles east of San Antonio and 50 miles south of Austin. Including any residence halls, there are 37 buildings.

Student Life: 97% of undergraduates are from Texas. Others are from 19 states, 7 foreign countries, and Canada. 94% are from public schools. 57% are White; 30% Hispanic. 69% are Protestant; 18% Catholic. The average age of freshmen is 18; all undergraduates, 21. 30% do not continue beyond their first year; 52% remain to graduate.

Housing: 848 students can be accommodated in college housing, which includes single-sex and coed dorms, on-campus apartments, and married student housing. On-campus housing is guaranteed for all 4 years, is guaranteed for the freshman year only, is available on a first-come, and first-served basis. 56% of students live on campus; of those, 50% remain on campus on weekends. All students may keep cars.

Activities: 7% of men belong to 3 local and 1 national fraternities; 10% of women belong to 3 local sororities. There are 52 groups on campus, including art, band, cheerleading, choir, chorus, computers, dance, drama, environmental, ethnic, forensics, gay, honors, international, jazz band, literary magazine, musical theater, newspaper, orchestra, pep band, political, professional, religious, science, social, social service, student government, and symphony. Popular campus events include Christmas Vespers, Spring Fling and Student Academic Symposium.

Sports: There are 6 intercollegiate sports for men and 8 for women, and 14 intramural sports for men and 14 for women. Facilities include a 2,200-seat gym, a fitness center, an 8-lane swimming pool, softball, baseball, and soccer fields, intramural/recreation fields, golf practice greens, a lighted walking track, practice gym, lighted sand volleyball courts, tennis courts, and racquetball courts.

Disabled Students: 90% of the campus is accessible. Facilities include wheelchair ramps, elevators, special parking, specially equipped restrooms, special class scheduling, lowered drinking fountains, and special housing.

Services: Counseling and information services are available, as is tutoring in most subjects. There is a reader service for the blind. Assistance with writing assignments is also available.

Campus Safety and Security: Measures include 24-hour foot and vehicle patrol, self-defense education, and security escort services. There are lighted pathways/sidewalks, and coded locks in residence halls.

Programs of Study: TLU confers B.A., B.S., B.B.A. and B.M. degrees. Master's degrees are also awarded. Bachelor's degrees are awarded in BIOLOGICAL SCIENCE (biology/biological science), BUSINESS (accounting and business administration and management), COMMUNICATIONS AND THE ARTS (art, communications, dramatic arts, English, music, and Spanish), COMPUTER AND PHYSICAL SCIENCE (applied science, chemistry, computer science, information sciences and systems, mathematics, and physics), EDUCATION (athletic training, education, and physical education), SOCIAL SCIENCE (economics, history, international studies, philosophy, political science/government, psychology, sociology, and theological studies). Business, biology, and psychology are the strongest academically. Business, kinesiology, and psychology have the largest enrollments.

Required: All students must complete 124 semester hours, including 24 to 54 in their major, with a 2.0 GPA. Between 45 and 49 hours of distribution courses are required. A senior seminar, project, or concert is required in all majors.

Special: Internships are available in most majors. Study abroad in all countries affiliated with ISEP, Augsburg College, Central College, Equador Exchange, and Kansai Gaidai, a Washington semester with American University, and work-study programs are available. The college offers student-designed majors and dual majors. There is a 3-2 engineering program with Texas A&M, Baylor University and Southern Methodist University. There are 11 national honor societies, a freshman honors program, and 20 departmental honors programs.

Faculty/Classroom: 53% of faculty are male; 47% are female. All teach undergraduates. No introductory courses are taught by graduate students. The average class size in an introductory lecture is 20; in a laboratory is 20; and in a regular course is 18.

Admissions: 51% of the 2013-2014 applicants were accepted. The SAT scores for the 2013-2014 freshman class were: Critical Reading--48% below 500, 38% between 500 and 599, 13% between 600 and 699, and 1% between 700 and 800; Math--33% below 500, 50% between 500 and 599, 16% between 600 and 699, and 1% between 700 and 800; Writing--54% below 500, 37% between 500 and 599, 8% between 600 and 699, and 1% between 700 and 800. The ACT scores were 35% below 21, 31% between 21 and 23, 23% between 24 and 26, 7% between 27 and 28, and 4% above 28. 45% of the current freshmen were in the top fifth of their class; 75% were in the top two fifths. 3 freshmen graduated first in their class.

Requirements: The SAT or ACT is required. Applicants must have 16 Carnegie units, including a recommended 4 years in English, 3 each of social studies, math, and science, and 2 in foreign language. The GED is accepted. A GPA of 2.5 is required. AP and CLEP credits are accepted. Important factors in the admissions decision are advanced placement or honors courses, recommendations by school officials, and extracurricular activities record.

Procedure: Freshmen are admitted fall and spring. Entrance exams should be taken in the spring of the junior year or the summer before the senior year. There is a rolling admissions plan. Applications should be filed by June 1 for fall entry; December 1 for spring entry, along with a $40 fee. Notification is sent on a rolling basis. Applications are accepted online.

Transfer: 72 transfer students enrolled in 2012-2013. Applicants for transfer must have a GPA of at least 2.25 and be in good academic standing. 33 of 124 credits required for the bachelor's degree must be completed at TLU.

Visiting: There are regularly scheduled orientations for prospective students, including a campus tour, classroom visits, a financial aid presentation, a study abroad session, an athlete session, and a student panel. There are guides for informal visits, visitors may sit in on classes, and stay overnight. To schedule a visit, contact the Admissions Office.

Financial Aid: In 2013-2014, 97% of all full-time freshmen and 98% of continuing full-time students received some form of financial aid. 85% of all full-time freshmen and 84% of continuing full-time students received need-based aid. The average freshman award was $24,051. Need-based scholarships or need-based grants averaged $19,502 ($24,000 maximum); need-based self-help aid (loans and jobs) averaged $9,624 ($16,080 maximum); and other non-need-based awards and non-need-based scholarships averaged $14,647 ($25,760 maximum). 31% of undergraduate students work part-time. Average annual earnings from campus work are $3403. The average financial indebtedness of the 2013 graduate was $29,787. The FAFSA is required. The priority date for freshman financial aid applications for fall entry is March 1.

International Students: There are 2 international students enrolled. The school actively recruits these students. They must take the TOEFL with a minimum score of 550 on the paper-based TOEFL (PBT) or 79 on the Internet-based version (iBT). They must also take the SAT or ACT, scoring 960.

Graduates: From July 1, 2012 to June 30, 2013, 235 bachelor's degrees were awarded. The most popular majors were business administration (21%), kinesiology (17%), and Education (11%). 29 companies recruited on campus in 2012-2013. In an average class, 31% graduate in 4 years or less, 48% graduate in 5 years or less, and 52% graduate in 6 years or less.

Admissions Contact: Adam Navarro-Jusino, Director of Admissions. E-Mail: *admissions@tlu.edu* Web: *www.tlu.edu*

TEXAS SOUTHERN UNIVERSITY E-3

Houston, TX 77004 **(713) 313-6861; (713) 313-1878**

Full-time: 2541 men, 3364 women	**Faculty:** 159
Part-time: 462 men, 654 women	**Ph.D.s:** 70%
Graduate: 1012 men, 1613 women	**Student/Faculty:** 19 to 1
Year: semesters, summer session	**Tuition:** $7646 ($16,946)
Application Deadline: August 15	**Room & Board:** $10,566
Freshman Class: 9393 applied, 4991 accepted, 1349 enrolled	
SAT CR/M/W: 400/420/400	**ACT:** 17 **LESS COMPETITIVE**

Texas Southern University, founded in 1947, is a state-supported institution offering undergraduate programs in the arts and sciences, education and behavioral sciences, pharmacy and health science, business, and technology. There are 7 undergraduate schools and 7 graduate schools. In addition to regional accreditation, TSU has baccalaureate program accreditation with AACSB, ABET, ACPE, and NCATE. The 3 libraries contain 263,210 volumes, 504,754 microform items, 1,953 audio/video tapes/CDs/DVDs, and subscribe to 109,317 periodicals including electronic. Computerized library services include interlibrary loans, database searching, and Internet access. Special learning facilities include an art gallery and radio station. The 150-acre campus is in an urban area 3 miles southeast of downtown Houston. Including any residence halls, there are 45 buildings.

Student Life: 89% of undergraduates are from Texas. Others are from 42 states, 23 foreign countries, and Canada. 82% are African American. The average age of freshmen is 18; all undergraduates, 23. 39% do not continue beyond their first year.

Housing: 1600 students can be accommodated in college housing, which includes single-sex dorms and off-campus apartments. On-campus housing is available on a first-come and first-served basis. Priority is given to out-of-town students. 76% of students commute. Alcohol is not permitted. All students may keep cars.

Activities: There are 146 groups on campus, including accounting, and pharmaceutical, business, consumer services, health, art, band, cheerleading, choir, chorus, computers, dance, debate, drama, ethnic, film, honors, international, jazz band, marching band, newspaper, orchestra, photography, political, professional, radio and TV, religious, science, social, social service, student government, symphony, and yearbook. Popular campus events include Senior Day, Christmas Tree Lighting, TSU Relays, Convocation, Honors day and Homecoming.

Sports: There are 7 intercollegiate sports for men and 9 for women, and 4 intramural sports for men and 7 for women. Facilities include a health and phys ed complex that seats 8100, a 7000-seat football stadium, 2 gyms, the larger seating 1000, and a recreational facility with a food court.

Disabled Students: 95% of the campus is accessible. Facilities include wheelchair ramps, elevators, special parking, specially equipped restrooms, lowered drinking fountains, and lowered telephones.

Services: Counseling and information services are available, as is tutoring in most subjects. There is remedial math, reading, and writing.

Campus Safety and Security: Measures include 24-hour foot and vehicle patrol, emergency notification system, self-defense education, and security escort services. There are shuttle buses, emergency telephones, and lighted pathways/sidewalks.

Programs of Study: TSU confers B.A., B.S., B.B.A.,B.S.I.T., B.S.P.A., B.F.A., B.S.C.S., B.S.Ed, B.A.Ed, B.S.H.E., B.S.M.T, B.S.Pharm, and B.S.Phys.Ther. degrees. Master's and doctoral degrees are also awarded. Bachelor's degrees are awarded in BIOLOGICAL SCIENCE (biology/biological science and nutrition), BUSINESS (accounting, banking and finance, business administration and management, and marketing/retailing/merchandising), COMMUNICATIONS AND THE ARTS (art, communications, dramatic arts, English, music, and Spanish), COMPUTER AND PHYSICAL SCIENCE (chemistry, computer science, and mathematics), EDUCATION (English education, foreign languages education, mathematics education, and physical education), ENGINEERING AND ENVIRONMENTAL DESIGN (aviation administration/management, civil engineering technology, drafting and design technology, electrical/electronics engineering technology, engineering technology, environmental engineering technology, and industrial engineering technology), HEALTH PROFESSIONS (environmental health science, health, health care administration, medical technology, and respiratory therapy), SOCIAL SCIENCE (administration of justice , criminal justice, dietetics, economics, history, human services, interdisciplinary studies, liberal arts/general studies, physical fitness/movement, political science/government, psychology, public affairs, social work, and sociology). Prepharmacy is the strongest academically. Biology and business have the largest enrollments.

Required: Students must complete between 136 and 148 semester hours, depending on the field of study, and amintain a minimum GPA of 2.0. The core curriculum is 44 hours. A minimum of 30 hours is required in the major. A course in phys ed is also required.

Special: Cross-registration is available with North Harris and Houston Community Colleges, as well as in military science with the University of Houston. Study abroad in Africa, internships, B.A.-B.S. degrees, and work-study programs are also available There are 7 national honor societies, a freshman honors program, and 1 departmental honors programs.

Faculty/Classroom: 49% of faculty are male; 51% are female. 69% teach undergraduates. No introductory courses are taught by graduate students. The average class size in an introductory lecture is 21 and in a laboratory is 7.

Admissions: 53% of the 2013-2014 applicants were accepted. The SAT scores for the 2013-2014 freshman class were: Critical Reading--90% below 500, 9% between 500 and 599, and 1% between 600 and 699; Math--86% below 500, 13% between 500 and 599, 1% between 600 and 699; Writing--92% below 500, 8% between 500 and 599. The ACT scores were 93% below 21, 5% between 21 and 23, 2% between 24 and 26. 18% of the current freshmen were in the top fifth of their class; 46% were in the top two fifths. 1 freshman graduated first in the class.

Requirements: The SAT or ACT is recommended. Candidates should be graduates of an accredited secondary school or have the GED. Official high school transcript showing date of graduation, or GED Test Report. Official SAT or ACT test scores; ACT 17 (composite) or 820 SAT Critical Reading and Mathematics combined. A GPA of 2.5 is required. AP and CLEP credits are accepted.

Procedure: Freshmen are admitted fall, spring, and summer. Entrance exams should be taken by the semester prior to enrollment. There are early admissions and rolling admissions plans. Applications should be filed by August 15 for fall entry; December 15 for spring entry; and May 15 for summer entry, along with a $42 fee. Notification is sent on a rolling basis. Applications are accepted online.

Transfer: 618 transfer students enrolled in 2012-2013. The applicant must be a student in good standing and must submit an official transcripts. The SAT or ACT is required. 30 of 120 credits required for the bachelor's degree must be completed at TSU.

Visiting: There are regularly scheduled orientations for prospective stu-

dents, including a required orientation for freshmen and transfer students. Orientation dates, including early registration, are posted in the orientation application. There are guides for informal visits and visitors may stay overnight. To schedule a visit, contact the Office of Recruitment at (713) 313-7849.

Financial Aid: In 2013-2014, 93% of all full-time freshmen and 87% of continuing full-time students received some form of financial aid. The average freshman award was $7,110. Need-based scholarships or need-based grants averaged $7,741; need-based self-help aid (loans and jobs) averaged $7,151; non-need-based athletic scholarships averaged $8,872; and other non-need-based awards and non-need-based scholarships averaged $6,663. Average annual earnings from campus work are $1649. The average financial indebtedness of the 2013 graduate was $36,798. The FAFSA is required. The deadline for filing freshman financial aid applications for fall entry is April 15.

International Students: There are 304 international students enrolled. They must take the TOEFL with a minimum score of 500 on the paper-based TOEFL (PBT) or 61 on the Internet-based version (iBT). They must also take the SAT or ACT, scoring 820.

Graduates: From July 1, 2012 to June 30, 2013, 774 bachelor's degrees were awarded. The most popular majors were business (23%), health professional (14%), and security/homeland security/law enforcement/firefighting/protective services (10%). In an average class, 3% graduate in 4 years or less, 8% graduate in 5 years or less, and 12% graduate in 6 years or less. Of the 2012 graduating class, 32% were enrolled in graduate school within 6 months of graduation.

Admissions Contact: Brian Armstrong, Director of Admissions. E-Mail: *armstrong_bj@tsu.edu* Web: *http:/www.tsu.edu/admissions/admissions_main.php*

TEXAS STATE UNIVERSITY SYSTEM

The Texas State University System, established in 1911, is a public system in Texas. It is governed by a 9-member board of regents, whose chief administrator is the chancellor. The primary mission of the system is teaching. The main priorities are the teacher education, business and liberal arts. The total student enrollment for all five campuses is usually about 43,500 with 1400 faculty members. Altogether there are 325 baccalaureate programs, 200 master's, 1 doctoral programs offered in Texas State University System. Profiles of the 4-year campuses are included in this section.

TEXAS STATE UNIVERSITY — D-3

San Marcos, TX 78666 — **(512) 245-2364; (512) 245-8044**

Full-time: 11201 men, 14464 women	**Faculty:** 1195; IIA, -$
Part-time: 2566 men, 2801 women	**Ph.D.s:** 77%
Graduate: 1713 men, 2823 women	**Student/Faculty:** 21 to 1
Year: semesters, summer session	**Tuition:** $9151 ($19,771)
Application Deadline: May 1	**Room & Board:** $7344
Freshman Class: 18937 applied, 13976 accepted, 5181 enrolled	
SAT CR/M/W: 540/551/509 **ACT:** 24	**VERY COMPETITIVE**

Texas State University was founded in 1899 and is part of the Texas State University System. Texas State offers programs in general studies, applied arts and technology, business, education, fine arts, health professions, liberal arts, and science and engineering. Texas State offers 96 Bachelor degrees, 86 Master degrees, 11 Doctoral degrees and 1 Special Professional degree. There are 8 undergraduate schools and 1 graduate school. In addition to regional accreditation, Texas State has baccalaureate program accreditation with AACSB, ABET, ACCE, ACEJMC, ADA, AHEA, CSAB, CSWE, FIDER, NASM, and NRPA. The library contains 1.5 million volumes, 2.0 million microform items, and 116,439 audio/video tapes/CDs/DVDs, and subscribes to 14,762 periodicals including electronic. Computerized library services include interlibrary loans, database searching, Internet access, and Wi-Fi capability. Special learning facilities include an art gallery, planetarium, radio station, recording studio, 17 inch telescope, clean room for manufacturing micro chips, anthropology forensics laboratory, and special collections library in southwest writing and photography. The 456-acre campus is in a suburban area 30 miles south of Austin and 45 miles northeast of San Antonio. Including any residence halls, there are 265 buildings.

Student Life: 98% of undergraduates are from Texas. Others are from 49 states, 37 foreign countries, and Canada. 98% are from public schools. 54% are White; 31% Hispanic. The average age of freshmen is 18; all undergraduates, 22. 23% do not continue beyond their first year; 57% remain to graduate.

Housing: 5749 students can be accommodated in college housing, which includes single-sex and coed dorms, on-campus apartments, and married student housing. In addition, there are honors houses, special-interest houses, special residences for international students, single parents, upper-division students, and freshmen experience. On-campus housing is guaranteed for the freshman year only, is available on a first-come, and first-served basis. 81% of students commute. All students may keep cars.

Activities: 5% of men belong to 6 local and 15 national fraternities; 5% of women belong to 12 national sororities. There are 365 groups on campus, including art, band, cheerleading, chess, choir, chorale, chorus, computers, dance, debate, drama, drill team, ethnic, gay, honors, international, jazz band, literary magazine, marching band, musical theater, newspaper, nontraditional students, opera, orchestra, pep band, photography, political, professional, radio and TV, religious, social, social service, student government, symphony, and yearbook. Popular campus events include Welcome Week, Cricket Fest, RecJam and Moonlight Breakfast.

Sports: There are 5 intercollegiate sports for men and 7 for women, and 10 intramural sports for men and 10 for women. Facilities include Sport facilities include a 30,000-seat stadium, a 7200-seat gym, 2000-seat baseball stadium, and 1000-seat softball stadium. There are tennis courts, a spring-fed pool, an aquatic sports center. A student recreation center with basketball and volleyball courts, racquetball courts, an indoor jogging/walking track, weight-lifting equipment, exercise machines, and rooms for fitness, dance, and aerobics.

Disabled Students: 88% of the campus is accessible. Facilities include wheelchair ramps, elevators, special parking, specially equipped restrooms, special class scheduling, lowered drinking fountains, lowered telephones, special housing. curb cuts, pay TTY text telephones, adaptive computer technology, sign language interpreter, and reading recorder services for the visually impaired.

Services: Counseling and information services are available, as is tutoring in most subjects. There is a reader service for the blind, and remedial math, reading, and writing. Tutoring is available for all core curriculum classes.

Campus Safety and Security: Measures include 24-hour foot and vehicle patrol, emergency notification system, self-defense education, and security escort services. There are shuttle buses, emergency telephones, and lighted pathways/sidewalks.

Programs of Study: Texas State confers B.A., B.A.A.S., B.A.I.S., B.B.A., B.E.S.S., B.F.A., B.G.S., B.H.A., B.H.W.P., B.M., B.P.A., B.S., B.S.A.G., B.S.A.S., B.S.C.L.S., B.S.C.D., B.S.C.J., B.S.F.C.S., B.S.H.I.M., B.S.H.P., B.S.N, B.S.R.A., B.S.R.C., B.S.R.T., B.S.T. and B.S.W. degrees. Master's and doctoral degrees are also awarded. Bachelor's degrees are awarded in AGRICULTURE (agricultural business management, agriculture, and animal science), BIOLOGICAL SCIENCE (biochemistry, biology/biological science, marine biology, microbiology, nutrition, physiology, wildlife biology, and zoology), BUSINESS (accounting, banking and finance, business administration and management, business economics, fashion merchandising, marketing/retailing/merchandising, recreational facilities management, and tourism), COMMUNICATIONS AND THE ARTS (advertising, applied art, art, audio technology, broadcasting, communication design, communications, dance, dramatic arts, English, French, German, jazz, journalism, music, music performance, musical theater, photography, public relations, Spanish, studio art, and theatre arts), COMPUTER AND PHYSICAL SCIENCE (chemistry, computer information systems, computer science, mathematics, and physics), EDUCATION (athletic training, early childhood education, elementary education, health education, physical education, special education, and technical education), ENGINEERING AND ENVIRONMENTAL DESIGN (cartography, city/community/regional planning, construction management, construction technology, electrical/electronics engineering, engineering technology, environmental science, industrial engineering, industrial engineering technology, interior design, land use management and reclamation, manufacturing engineering, manufacturing technology, urban planning technology, and water and wastewater technology), HEALTH PROFESSIONS (clinical science, exercise science, health care administration, medical records administration/services, nursing, radiation therapy, respiratory therapy, and speech pathology/audiology), SOCIAL SCIENCE (American studies, anthropology, Asian/Oriental studies, child care/child and family studies, corrections, criminal justice, economics, European studies, family/consumer studies, gender studies, geography, history, interdisciplinary studies, international relations, international studies, law enforcement and corrections, liberal arts/general studies, Middle Eastern studies, philosophy, political science/government, psychology, public administration, social work, and sociology). Geography, education, nursing, anthropology, and engineering are the strongest academically. Education, business, psychology, and exercise and sports science have the largest enrollments.

Required: All students must earn a minimum GPA of 2.0 while taking at least 120 semester hours, including 30 SCH in their major. The core curriculum includes basic skills, history and political science, natural science, social science, philosophy, international perspectives, literature, fine arts, and physical fitness.

Special: Co-op programs in medicine, dentistry, engineering, architecture, law, pharmacy, nursing, occupational therapy, and veterinary medicine, internships in many departments, study abroad in 26 countries, and Washington semesters are available. Dual majors, credit for life experience, and non-degree study also are possible. Two summer sessions are offered in most programs. A 3-2 engineering degree is possible with the University of Texas, Texas A&M, Texas Tech University, and University of Texas at San Antonio. There are 24 national honor societies, a freshman honors program, and 1 departmental honors programs.

Faculty/Classroom: 51% of faculty are male; 49% are female. 91%

teach undergraduates, and 10% do research. Graduate students teach 5% of introductory courses. The average class size in an introductory lecture is 43; in a laboratory is 22; and in a regular course is 31.

Admissions: 74% of the 2013-2014 applicants were accepted. The SAT scores for the 2013-2014 freshman class were: Critical Reading--27% below 500, 53% between 500 and 599, 17% between 600 and 699, and 3% between 700 and 800; Math--17% below 500, 59% between 500 and 599, 22% between 600 and 699, and 2% between 700 and 800; Writing--44% below 500, 45% between 500 and 599, 10% between 600 and 699, and 1% between 700 and 800. The ACT scores were 8% below 21, 41% between 21 and 23, 31% between 24 and 26, 11% between 27 and 28, and 9% above 28. 35% of the current freshmen were in the top fifth of their class; 76% were in the top two fifths. 17 freshmen graduated first in their class.

Requirements: The SAT or ACT is required. The ACT Optional Writing test is also required. Minimum test scores are determined by high school class rank. Applicants need 24 academic credits, including 4 units in English, 3.5 in social science and electives, 3 in math and science, 2 in foreign language, 1.5 in physical education, 1 in technology applications and fine arts and .5 in speech, economics, health education, 1 in fine arts, and 3.5 in electives The GED is accepted; applicants with a GED are treated as though they were in the 4th quarter of their graduating class. AP and CLEP credits are accepted. Important factors in the admissions decision are advanced placement or honors courses, leadership record, and extracurricular activities record.

Procedure: Freshmen are admitted to all sessions. Entrance exams should be taken at the end of the junior year. There is a rolling admissions plan. Applications should be filed by May 1 for fall entry; December 1 for spring entry; and May 1 for summer entry, along with a $60 fee. Applications are accepted online.

Transfer: 3740 transfer students enrolled in 2012-2013. Transfer students with 29 or fewer credits must meet freshman requirements; those with 30 or more credits must submit official transcripts to verify a minimum 2.25 GPA. 30 of 120 credits required for the bachelor's degree must be completed at Texas State.

Visiting: There are regularly scheduled orientations for prospective students, consisting of a 2-day event, with registration required. First-time freshmen parents may attend. Students receive registration instructions, academic advising, and information concerning Texas State's academic policies, procedures, and student services. Time is allotted to register for classes. There are guides for informal visits and visitors may sit in on classes. To schedule a visit, contact the Admissions Office.

Financial Aid: In 2013-2014, 82% of all full-time freshmen and 76% of continuing full-time students received some form of financial aid. 60% of all full-time freshmen and 54% of continuing full-time students received need-based aid. The average freshman award was $15,548. Need-based scholarships or need-based grants averaged $7,244 ($16,300 maximum); need-based self-help aid (loans and jobs) averaged $3,444 ($8,100 maximum); non-need-based athletic scholarships averaged $8,710 ($22,011 maximum); and other non-need-based awards and non-need-based scholarships averaged $11,868 ($31,660 maximum). 56% of undergraduate students work part-time. Average annual earnings from campus work are $5376. The average financial indebtedness of the 2013 graduate was $23,575. The FAFSA is required. The priority date for freshman financial aid applications for fall entry is April 1.

International Students: There are 156 international students enrolled. They must take the TOEFL with a minimum score of 550 on the paper-based TOEFL (PBT) or 78 on the Internet-based version (iBT). They must also take the SAT or ACT.

Graduates: From July 1, 2012 to June 30, 2013, 5436 bachelor's degrees were awarded. The most popular majors were interdisciplinary studies (education) (9%), management (6%), and psychology (6%). 889 companies recruited on campus in 2012-2013. In an average class, 1% graduate in 3 years or less, 29% graduate in 4 years or less, 49% graduate in 5 years or less, and 57% graduate in 6 years or less. Of the 2012 graduating class, 22% were enrolled in graduate school within 6 months of graduation, and 83% were employed.

Admissions Contact: Stephanie Anderson, Assistant VP for Enrollment Management. E-Mail: *admissions@txstate.edu* Web: *www.txstate.edu*

TEXAS TECH UNIVERSITY — B-2

Lubbock, TX 79409-5005 — **(806) 742-1480; (806) 742-0062**

Full-time: 11,700 men, 9450 women	**Faculty:** n/av; I, --$
Part-time: 1200 men, 800 women	**Ph.D.s:** 92%
Graduate: 2760 men, 2500 women	**Student/Faculty:** n/av
Year: semesters, summer session	**Tuition:** $10,500 ($18,155)
Application Deadline: see profile	**Room & Board:** $8095
Freshman Class: n/av	
SAT or ACT: required	

COMPETITIVE

Texas Tech University, founded in 1923, is a large, comprehensive public university offering undergraduate and graduate programs in a variety of professional fields. The figures in the above capsule and this profile are approximate. There are 10 undergraduate schools and 1 graduate school. In addition to regional accreditation, Texas Tech has baccalaureate program accreditation with AACSB, ABET, ACEJMC, ASLA, CSWE, NAAB, NASAD, NASM, and NCATE. The 5 libraries contain 4.9 million volumes, 2.3 million microform items, 85,909 audio/video tapes/CDs/DVDs, and subscribe to 22,717 periodicals including electronic. Computerized library services include interlibrary loans, database searching, Internet access, and laptop Internet portals. Special learning facilities include a learning resource center, art gallery, natural history museum, planetarium, radio station, TV station, ranching heritage center, international cultural center, international textile center, and Southwest collection. The 1839-acre campus is in an urban area in Lubbock. Including any residence halls, there are 138 buildings.

Student Life: 93% of undergraduates are from Texas. Others are from 47 states, 121 foreign countries, and Canada. 75% are white; 12% Hispanic. The average age of freshmen is 19; all undergraduates, 21. 17% do not continue beyond their first year; 56% remain to graduate.

Housing: 6763 students can be accommodated in college housing, which includes single-sex and coed dorms and on-campus apartments. In addition, there are honors houses, special-interest houses, living/learning communities, intensive study floors, substance-free floors, nonsmoking floors, and summer housing. On-campus housing is guaranteed for the freshman year only and is available on a first-come, first-served basis. 73% of students commute. Alcohol is not permitted. All students may keep cars.

Activities: 14% of men belong to 25 national fraternities; 18% of women belong to 1 local and 17 national sororities. There are 400 groups on campus, including art, band, cheerleading, chess, choir, chorale, chorus, communications, computers, dance, debate, drama, drill team, drum and bugle corps, environmental, ethnic, film, forensics, gay, honors, international, jazz band, literary magazine, marching band, musical theater, newspaper, opera, orchestra, pep band, photography, political, professional, radio and TV, religious, social, social service, student government, symphony, and yearbook. Popular campus events include Parents Day, Carol of the Lights, and Madrigal Dinner.

Sports: There are 7 intercollegiate sports for men and 8 for women, and 27 intramural sports for men and 27 for women. Facilities include an athletic training center, a student recreation center, an aquatic center, and an athletic study/learning center.

Disabled Students: All of the campus is accessible. Facilities include wheelchair ramps, elevators, special parking, specially equipped rest rooms, special class scheduling, lowered drinking fountains, lowered telephones, and special housing.

Services: Counseling and information services are available, as is tutoring in every subject. There is a reader service for the blind and remedial math, reading, and writing. There are books on tape, note-taking services, tape recorders, a learning center that provides peer tutoring, a computer video lab, academic skills assessments, and testing accommodations for students with disabilities.

Campus Safety and Security: Measures include 24-hour foot and vehicle patrol and emergency notification system. There are shuttle buses, emergency telephones, lighted pathways/sidewalks, and presentations on crime prevention.

Programs of Study: Texas Tech confers B.A., B.S., B.F.A., B.G.S., B.I.D., B.Land.Arch., B.M., B.S.ARCH., B.S.C.E., B.S.Ch.E., B.S.E.E., B.S. Eng. Physics, B.S. Eng. Tech., B.S.Envir. Eng., B.S. in Family and Consumer Sciences, B.S. Home Eco., B.S. Indust. Eng., B.S. Int'l Eco., B.S in Community, Family, and Addiction Services, B.S.M.E., B.S.P.E., and B.S.R.H.I.M degrees. Master's and doctoral degrees are also awarded. Bachelor's degrees are awarded in AGRICULTURE (agricultural business management, agricultural communications, agricultural economics, agronomy, animal science, conservation and regulation, fish and game management, horticulture, plant protection (pest management), range/farm management, and wildlife management), BIOLOGICAL SCIENCE (biochemistry, biology/biological science, cell biology, microbiology, molecular biology, nutrition, and zoology), BUSINESS (banking and finance, business administration and management, business economics, hotel/motel and restaurant management, international business management, international economics, management information systems, marketing and distribution, and retailing), COMMUNICATIONS AND THE ARTS (advertising, apparel design, art history and appreciation, broadcasting, classics, communications, dance, design, dramatic arts, English, French, German, journalism, music, music performance, music theory and composition, performing arts, photography, public relations, Spanish, studio art, telecommunications, theater design, and visual and performing arts), COMPUTER AND PHYSICAL SCIENCE (chemistry, computer science, geology, geophysics and seismology, geoscience, mathematics, and physics), EDUCATION (early childhood education, middle school education, and science education), ENGINEERING AND ENVIRONMENTAL DESIGN (architecture, chemical engineering, civil engineering, construction technology, electrical/electronics engineering, electrical/electronics engineering technology, energy management technology, engineering,

engineering physics, engineering technology, environmental engineering, industrial engineering, interior design, landscape architecture/design, mechanical engineering, and mechanical engineering technology), HEALTH PROFESSIONS (exercise science and health), SOCIAL SCIENCE (addiction studies, anthropology, child psychology/development, clothing and textiles management/production/services, dietetics, economics, family/consumer resource management, family/consumer studies, food production/management/services, food science, geography, history, home economics, human development, Latin American studies, liberal arts/general studies, philosophy, political science/government, psychology, Russian and Slavic studies, social work, and sociology). Business, exercise and sports sciences, and mechanical engineering have the largest enrollments.

Required: All students seeking a bachelor's degree must meet the requirements of the core curriculum. A minimum of 120 credits hours is required, depending on the degree program. A minimum GPA of 2.0 is required. The last 30 hours and 25% of all credit hours must be from Texas Tech.

Special: Texas Tech offers many bachelor-to-masters accelerated degree programs, internships, study abroad, dual degrees, dual majors, extended studies, and pass/fail options. There are 20 national honor societies, including Phi Beta Kappa, and a freshman honors program.

Faculty/Classroom: 62% of faculty are male; 38% are female. All teach undergraduates, 46% do research, and 46% do both. No introductory courses are taught by graduate students. The average class size in an introductory lecture is 45; in a laboratory, 21; and in a regular course, 35.

Requirements: The SAT or ACT is required. Applicants should be graduates of an accredited high school or have the GED. The university requires 11 credits of academic work in high school, including 4 credits in English, 3 in math, 2 in lab sciences, and 2 in foreign language. AP and CLEP credits are accepted.

Procedure: Freshmen are admitted fall, spring, and summer. Entrance exams should be taken before registering for classes. There are early admissions and rolling admissions plans. Check with the school for current application deadlines. The application fee is $60. Notification is sent on a rolling basis. Applications are accepted online.

Transfer: To transfer 24 or more hours, the GPA must be a minimum of 2.25. To transfer 12 to 23 hours, applicants must have a 2.5 GPA. To transfer fewer than 12 hours, applicants must have a 2.0 GPA and meet freshman requirements for admission. 30 of 120 credits required for the bachelor's degree must be completed at Texas Tech.

Visiting: There are regularly scheduled orientations for prospective students, including summer orientation conferences offering new students an opportunity to meet with advisers, register early for the fall semester, and get acquainted with the campus. There are guides for informal visits. To schedule a visit, contact Visitor Center.

Financial Aid: The FAFSA is required. Check with the school for current application deadlines.

International Students: They must take the TOEFL, scoring 550 on the paper-based TOEFL (PBT) or 80 on the Internet-based version (iBT), or take the IELTS. They must also take the SAT or ACT.

Admissions Contact: Admissions Office. A campus DVD is available. E-Mail: *admissions@tamu.edu* Web: *www.tamu.edu*

TEXAS WESLEYAN UNIVERSITY D-2

Fort Worth, TX 76105 **(817) 531-4422**
(800) 580-8980; (817) 531-7515

Full-time: 748 men, 681 women	**Faculty:** n/av; IIA, av$
Part-time: 217 men, 295 women	**Ph.D.s:** 91%
Graduate: 249 men, 424 women	**Student/Faculty:** 15 to 1
Year: semesters, summer session	**Tuition:** $22,040
Application Deadline: open	**Room & Board:** $7846
Freshman Class: 2394 applied, 998 accepted, 273 enrolled	
SAT CR/M/W: 512/521/471	**ACT:** 21 **COMPETITIVE**

Texas Wesleyan University, founded in 1890, is a liberal arts institution affiliated with the United Methodist Church. There are 4 undergraduate schools and 3 graduate schools. In addition to regional accreditation, Texas Wesleyan has baccalaureate program accreditation with AACSB, ACBSP, and NASM. The library contains 186,701 volumes, 20,069 microform items, 6,113 audio/video tapes/CDs/DVDs, and subscribes to 1,545 periodicals including electronic. Computerized library services include interlibrary loans, database searching, Internet access, and Wi-Fi capability. Special learning facilities include an art gallery, a theater. The 79-acre campus is in an urban area 2 miles east of downtown Fort Worth. Including any residence halls, there are 37 buildings.

Student Life: 75% of undergraduates are from Texas. Others are from 28 states, 33 foreign countries, and Canada. 93% are from public schools. 36% are White; 21% Foreign; 20% race unknown; 19% Hispanic; 15% African American. 80% are Baptist, Christian, Methodist, and Church of Christ; 36% claim no religious affiliation. The average age of freshmen is 19; all undergraduates, 23. 29% do not continue beyond their first year; 71% remain to graduate.

Housing: 432 students can be accommodated in college housing, which includes single-sex and coed dorms and on-campus apartments. On-campus housing is available on a first-come and first-served basis. 81% of students commute. Alcohol is not permitted. All students may keep cars.

Activities: 3% of men belong to 3 local and 2 national fraternities; 5% of women belong to 3 local and 2 national sororities. There are 35 groups on campus, including art, band, cheerleading, choir, chorale, computers, drama, ethnic, forensics, gay, honors, international, jazz band, literary magazine, musical theater, newspaper, opera, political, professional, radio and TV, religious, social, social service, and student government. Popular campus events include We Are Wesleyan Concert, RAM JAM and University College Day.

Sports: There are 5 intercollegiate sports for men and 5 for women, and 11 intramural sports for men and 11 for women. Facilities include a 1,500-seat athletic center, 2 tennis courts, an off-campus baseball park, and softball and soccer fields.

Disabled Students: Facilities include wheelchair ramps, elevators, special parking, specially equipped restrooms, special class scheduling, and lowered telephones.

Services: Counseling and information services are available, as is tutoring in most subjects. There is remedial math, reading, and writing.

Campus Safety and Security: Measures include 24-hour foot and vehicle patrol, self-defense education, and security escort services. There are emergency telephones, lighted pathways/sidewalks, and residence hall programs.

Programs of Study: Texas Wesleyan confers B.A., B.B.A., B.F.A., B.M. and B.S. degrees. Master's and doctoral degrees are also awarded. Bachelor's degrees are awarded in BIOLOGICAL SCIENCE (biochemistry and biology/biological science), BUSINESS (accounting, business administration and management, business economics, management information systems, marketing management, marketing/retailing/merchandising, and sports management), COMMUNICATIONS AND THE ARTS (advertising, art, broadcasting, dramatic arts, English, journalism, music, Spanish, and theater design), COMPUTER AND PHYSICAL SCIENCE (chemistry, computer science, and mathematics), EDUCATION (athletic training, education, elementary education, foreign languages education, mathematics education, physical education, social science education, social studies education, and teaching English as a second/foreign language (TESOL/TEFOL)), HEALTH PROFESSIONS (exercise science), SOCIAL SCIENCE (criminal justice, economics, history, industrial and organizational psychology, interdisciplinary studies, international relations, paralegal studies, political science/government, prelaw, psychology, religion, religious education, and sociology). Education, liberal studies and general business have the largest enrollments.

Required: A minimum GPA of 2.0 and a minimum of 124 credit hours are required to graduate. All students must complete a general education requirement of 51 credits, including courses in writing, literature, religion, lab science, history, math, political or economic systems, fine arts, humanities, phys ed, and social science, philosophy, or psychology. The total number of hours in the major varies.

Special: Study abroad is offered in more than 25 countries. A 3-2 engineering degree is offered in conjunction with a number of universities. Pass/fail options are available, as are B.A.-B.S. degrees and internships in sports management, business, psychology, mass communication, and sociology. A predentistry program is available. There are 15 national honor societies and 8 departmental honors programs.

Faculty/Classroom: 47% of faculty are male; 53% are female. 56% teach undergraduates. No introductory courses are taught by graduate students. The average class size in an introductory lecture is 15.

Admissions: 42% of the 2013-2014 applicants were accepted. The SAT scores for the 2013-2014 freshman class were: Critical Reading--52% below 500, 37% between 500 and 599, 10% between 600 and 699, and 1% between 700 and 800; Math--40% below 500, 57% between 500 and 599, 7% between 600 and 699, and 1% between 700 and 800; Writing--64% below 500, 29% between 500 and 599, 8% between 600 and 699. The ACT scores were 67% below 21, 20% between 21 and 23, 10% between 24 and 26, 1% between 27 and 28. 3 freshmen graduated first in their class.

Requirements: The SAT or ACT is required. Applicants must be graduates of an accredited secondary school or have a GED equivalent, with satisfactory scores of 19 ACT composite score or 920 SAT combined score in critical reading and math only. Texas Wesleyan requires applicants to be in the upper 50% of their class. A GPA of 2.5 is required. AP and CLEP credits are accepted. Important factors in the admissions decision are leadership record, extracurricular activities record, and recommendations by alumni.

Procedure: Freshmen are admitted to all sessions. Entrance exams should be taken as early as possible. There is a rolling admissions plan. Application deadlines are open. The fall 2013 application fee was $25. Applications are accepted online.

Transfer: 267 transfer students enrolled in 2012-2013. Applicants with fewer than 30 credit hours must submit a high school transcript and the results of either the SAT or the ACT. A minimum GPA of 2.0 is required.

45 of 124 credits required for the bachelor's degree must be completed at Texas Wesleyan.

Visiting: There are regularly scheduled orientations for prospective students. There are guides for informal visits, visitors may sit in on classes, and stay overnight. To schedule a visit, contact the Office of Admissions.

Financial Aid: In 2013-2014, 90% of all full-time freshmen and 90% of continuing full-time students received some form of financial aid. 90% of all full-time freshmen students received need-based aid. The FAFSA and the college's own financial statement are required. Check with the school for current application deadlines.

International Students: There are 393 international students enrolled. The school actively recruits these students. They must take the TOEFL with a minimum score of 520 on the paper-based TOEFL (PBT) or 68 on the Internet-based version (iBT). an IELTS score of at least 6.0. The score must be less than 2 years old.

Graduates: From July 1, 2012 to June 30, 2013, 296 bachelor's degrees were awarded. The most popular majors were elementary education (17%), liberal studies (9%), and psychology and criminal justice (8%). 56 companies recruited on campus in 2012-2013. In an average class, 15% graduate in 4 years or less, 36% graduate in 5 years or less, and 41% graduate in 6 years or less.

Admissions Contact: Denelle Rodriguez, Interim Director Admissions. E-Mail: *admission@txwes.edu* Web: *www.txwes.edu*

TEXAS WOMAN'S UNIVERSITY D-2

Denton, TX 76204 (940) 898-3188
(866) 809-6130, ext. 3188; (940) 898-3081

Full-time: 587 men, 5988 women	**Faculty:** 381; I, --$
Part-time: 340 men, 2528 women	**Ph.D.s:** 70%
Graduate: 743 men, 4982 women	**Student/Faculty:** 21 to 1
Year: semesters, summer session	**Tuition:** $6703 ($17,232)
Application Deadline: July 15	**Room & Board:** $6930

Freshman Class: 4268 applied, 3679 accepted, 1159 enrolled
SAT or ACT: required

LESS COMPETITIVE

Texas Woman's University, founded in 1901, is a comprehensive public university primarily for women, offering degree programs in the liberal arts, education, music and fine arts, and the business and health professions. There are 7 undergraduate schools and 8 graduate schools. In addition to regional accreditation, TWU has baccalaureate program accreditation with ACBSP, ADA, APTA, CSWE, NASM, and NLN. The 2 libraries contain 688,461 volumes, 1.6 million microform items, 11,675 audio/video tapes/CDs/DVDs, and subscribe to 2,445 periodicals including electronic. Computerized library services include interlibrary loans, database searching, and Internet access. Special learning facilities include an art gallery, medical centers and clinics. The 270-acre campus is in an urban area 38 miles north of Dallas. Including any residence halls, there are 62 buildings.

Student Life: 93% of undergraduates are from Texas. Others are from 44 states, 72 foreign countries, and Canada. 62% are White; 18% African American; 11% Hispanic. The average age of freshmen is 19; all undergraduates, 25. 25% do not continue beyond their first year; 35% remain to graduate.

Housing: 1346 students can be accommodated in college housing, which includes single-sex and coed dorms, on-campus apartments, off-campus apartments, and married student housing. In addition, there are honors houses, special-interest houses, fraternity houses, sorority houses, housing for honors, living learning communities. On-campus housing is guaranteed for the freshman year only, is available on a first-come, and first-served basis. 81% of students commute. All students may keep cars.

Activities: 6% of women belong to 2 local and 8 national sororities. There are 100 groups on campus, including art, band, choir, chorale, chorus, communications, computers, dance, drama, ethnic, gay, honors, international, jazz band, musical theater, newspaper, opera, orchestra, political, professional, radio and TV, religious, social, social service, spirit organization, and student government. Popular campus events include Black Awareness Week, Fall and Mexican Festivals.

Sports: There are 5 intercollegiate sports for women, and 11 intramural sports for men and 11 for women. Facilities include a gym, rock-climbing wall, indoor and outdoor swimming pools, weight-training and fitness rooms, tennis and racquetball courts, a golf course, an indoor track, and aerobic exercise classrooms.

Disabled Students: 95% of the campus is accessible. Facilities include wheelchair ramps, elevators, special parking, specially equipped restrooms, lowered drinking fountains, lowered telephones.

Services: Counseling and information services are available, as is tutoring in some subjects, math, science, English (writing), and computer science. There is remedial math, reading, and writing.

Campus Safety and Security: Measures include 24-hour foot and vehicle patrol, emergency notification system, self-defense education, and security escort services. There are emergency telephones and lighted pathways/sidewalks.

Programs of Study: TWU confers B.A., B.S., B.B.A., B.F.A. B.G.S., and B.S.W. degrees. Master's and doctoral degrees are also awarded. Bachelor's degrees are awarded in BIOLOGICAL SCIENCE (biology/biological science), BUSINESS (accounting, business administration and management, fashion merchandising, and marketing/retailing/merchandising), COMMUNICATIONS AND THE ARTS (art, communications, dance, dramatic arts, English, fine arts, and music), COMPUTER AND PHYSICAL SCIENCE (chemistry, computer science, and mathematics), HEALTH PROFESSIONS (dental hygiene, health science, medical technology, music therapy, and nursing), SOCIAL SCIENCE (child psychology/development, consumer services, criminal justice, dietetics, family/consumer studies, fashion design and technology, history, interdisciplinary studies, physical fitness/movement, political science/government, psychology, social work, and sociology). Nursing, interdisciplinary studies, and psychology have the largest enrollments.

Required: Core curriculum includes 6 units each of history, political science, composition, and science, 3 each of math, fine arts, multicultural studies, literature, and women's studies, plus 15 additional hours. General education requirements vary according to the degree. A 2.0 GPA, successful completion of the Texas-mandated examination in reading, writing, and math, and a minimum of 124 hours are needed to graduate.

Special: Co-op programs in most majors, study abroad, and internships are available. Cross-registration is possible with the University of North Texas and East Texas State University. A 3-2 engineering program exists with the University of Texas at Dallas and Texas A&M University. There are 14 national honor societies, a freshman honors program, and 15 departmental honors programs.

Faculty/Classroom: 20% of faculty are male; 80% are female. No introductory courses are taught by graduate students.

Admissions: 86% of the 2013-2014 applicants were accepted.

Requirements: The SAT or ACT is required. In addition, a minimum combined score of 950 is required on SAT I, or a score of 20 on the ACT. Applicants should be graduates of an accredited secondary school or have a GED certificate and have completed 4 secondary school units in English, 3 each in math and social studies, and 2 in science, plus 3 in academic electives. A GPA of 2.0 is required. AP and CLEP credits are accepted.

Procedure: Freshmen are admitted to all sessions. Entrance exams should be taken during the junior or the senior year of high school. There are early admissions, deferred admissions, and rolling admissions plans. Applications should be filed by July 15 for fall entry; November 1 for spring entry, along with a $50 fee.

Transfer: 1485 transfer students enrolled in 2012-2013. Transfer students must possess at least a 2.0 GPA and be in good standing at all previously attended institutions. Coursework must be from an accredited college or university. 30 of 124 credits required for the bachelor's degree must be completed at TWU.

Visiting: There are regularly scheduled orientations for prospective students, including admissions and financial aid sessions, and a campus tour. There are guides for informal visits, visitors may sit in on classes, and stay overnight. To schedule a visit, contact the Office of Admissions.

Financial Aid: In 2013-2014, 72% of all full-time freshmen and 54% of continuing full-time students received some form of financial aid. 47% of all full-time freshmen and 62% of continuing full-time students received need-based aid. The average freshman award was $9,331. Need-based scholarships or need-based grants averaged $7,931; need-based self-help aid (loans and jobs) averaged $3,919; non-need-based athletic scholarships averaged $4,833; other non-need-based awards and non-need-based scholarships averaged $4,573; and $1,591 from other forms of aid. 73% of undergraduate students work part-time. Average annual earnings from campus work are $3090. The average financial indebtedness of the 2013 graduate was $25,155. TWU is a member of CSS. The FAFSA and the college's own financial statement are required. The priority date for freshman financial aid applications for fall entry is March 1. The deadline for filing freshman financial aid applications for fall entry is April 1.

International Students: There are 143 international students enrolled. The school actively recruits these students. They must take the TOEFL.

Graduates: From July 1, 2012 to June 30, 2013, 824 bachelor's degrees were awarded. The most popular majors were health professions and related programs (34%), business/marketing (17%), and interdisciplinary studies (8%). 190 companies recruited on campus in 2012-2013. In an average class, 18% graduate in 4 years or less, 31% graduate in 5 years or less, and 35% graduate in 6 years or less.

Admissions Contact: Erma Nieto-Brecht, Director of Admissions. E-Mail: *admissions@twu.edu* Web: *www.twu.edu*

TRINITY UNIVERSITY D-4

San Antonio, TX 78212 (210) 999-7207
(800) TRINITY; (210) 999-8164

Full-time: 1069 men, 1248 women
Part-time: 18 men, 18 women
Graduate: 60 men, 112 women
Year: semesters, summer session
Application Deadline: February 1
Faculty: 240; IIA, +$
Ph.D.s: 98%
Student/Faculty: 9 to 1
Tuition: n/av
Room & Board: $10,496
Freshman Class: 4402 applied, 2831 accepted, 596 enrolled
SAT CR/M/W: 620/620/600 **ACT:** 29 **HIGHLY COMPETITIVE+**

Trinity University, founded in 1869, is a private liberal arts university. There is one undergraduate school and one graduate school. In addition to regional accreditation, Trinity has baccalaureate program accreditation with AACSB, ABET, NASM, and NCATE. The library contains 879,879 volumes, 307,774 microform items, 36,208 audio/video tapes/CDs/DVDs, and subscribes to 2,500 periodicals including electronic. Computerized library services include interlibrary loans and database searching. Special learning facilities include an art gallery, radio station, and TV station. The 117-acre campus is in an urban area 3 miles north of downtown San Antonio. Including any residence halls, there are 45 buildings.

Student Life: 66% of undergraduates are from Texas. Others are from 44 states, 70 foreign countries, and Canada. 62% are from public schools. 60% are White; 15% Hispanic. 27% are Protestant; 25% claim no religious affiliation; 23% Catholic; 18% unknown. The average age of freshmen is 18; all undergraduates, 20. 11% do not continue beyond their first year; 80% remain to graduate.

Housing: 1900 students can be accommodated in college housing, which includes coed dorms. In addition, there are language houses and special-interest houses. On-campus housing is guaranteed for all 4 years. 75% of students live on campus. All students may keep cars.

Activities: 13% of men belong to 5 local fraternities; 12% of women belong to 5 local sororities. There are 130 groups on campus, including gaming, art, band, cheerleading, chess, choir, chorale, chorus, computers, dance, debate, drama, drill team, ethnic, film, forensics, gay, honors, international, jazz band, literary magazine, musical theater, newspaper, opera, orchestra, pep band, photography, political, professional, radio and TV, religious, social, social service, student government, symphony, wind ensemble, and yearbook. Popular campus events include Tower Party, and Trinity Night at the San Antonio Spurs Game.

Sports: There are 9 intercollegiate sports for men and 9 for women, and 20 intramural sports for men and 17 for women. Facilities include an indoor Olympic pool and diving center, a 5000-seat stadium, and a 3000-seat auditorium/arena.

Disabled Students: 99% of the campus is accessible. Facilities include wheelchair ramps, elevators, special parking, specially equipped restrooms, lowered drinking fountains, lowered telephones. Learning disabled services are determined through Counseling and Career Services (one on one).

Services: Counseling and information services are available, as is tutoring in most subjects.

Campus Safety and Security: Measures include 24-hour foot and vehicle patrol, emergency notification system, self-defense education, and security escort services. There are emergency telephones, lighted pathways/sidewalks, and shuttle carts.

Programs of Study: Trinity confers B.A., B.S. and B.M. degrees. Master's degrees are also awarded. Bachelor's degrees are awarded in BIOLOGICAL SCIENCE (biochemistry and biology/biological science), BUSINESS (business administration and management), COMMUNICATIONS AND THE ARTS (art, art history and appreciation, Chinese, classics, communications, dramatic arts, English, French, German, Greek, Latin, music, Russian, Spanish, and speech/debate/rhetoric), COMPUTER AND PHYSICAL SCIENCE (chemistry, computer science, geoscience, mathematics, and physics), ENGINEERING AND ENVIRONMENTAL DESIGN (engineering and applied science), SOCIAL SCIENCE (anthropology, economics, history, international relations, philosophy, political science/government, psychology, religion, sociology, and urban studies). Business, communication, and modern languages and literatures have the largest enrollments.

Required: To graduate, students must satisfy the common curriculum and residency requirements and complete a minimum of 124 credit hours (129 for a B.S. in engineering science and 141 for a B.M. in performance and composition). Students must take at least 60 hours outside the major and 30 hours in upper-division courses. A minimum 2.0 GPA is required.

Special: The university offers study abroad in 35 countries. A Washington semester, accelerated programs, dual majors, student-designed majors, and pass/fail options are also available, as well as teacher certification and a liberal arts/career combination. There are 5 national honor societies, including Phi Beta Kappa, and 14 departmental honors programs.

Faculty/Classroom: 58% of faculty are male; 42% are female. All teach undergraduates. No introductory courses are taught by graduate students. The average class size in a regular course is 21.

Admissions: 64% of the 2013-2014 applicants were accepted. The SAT scores for the 2013-2014 freshman class were: Critical Reading--3% below 500, 34% between 500 and 599, 44% between 600 and 699, and 18% between 700 and 800; Math--2% below 500, 27% between 500 and 599, 54% between 600 and 699, and 17% between 700 and 800; Writing--9% below 500, 35% between 500 and 599, 41% between 600 and 699, and 14% between 700 and 800. The ACT scores were 7% between 21 and 23, 21% between 24 and 26, 23% between 27 and 28, and 49% above 28. 73% of the current freshmen were in the top fifth of their class; 94% were in the top two fifths. There were 11 National Merit finalists. 8 freshmen graduated first in their class.

Requirements: The SAT or ACT is required. In addition, applicants should have completed 4 years of English, 3 1/2 of math, 3 each of lab science and social studies, and 2 of foreign language. A personal essay, an official high school transcript, a recommendation from a high school counselor, and a teacher's evaluation are also required. A campus visit and a visit with the university's counselor are also recommended. AP credits are accepted. Important factors in the admissions decision are advanced placement or honors courses, recommendations by school officials, and extracurricular activities record.

Procedure: Freshmen are admitted fall, spring, and summer. Entrance exams should be taken late in the junior year or early in the senior year. There are early decision, early admissions, and deferred admissions plans. Early decision applications should be filed by November 1; regular applications, by February 1 for fall entry; and November 15 for spring entry, along with a $50 fee. Notification of early decision is sent December 15; regular decision, April 1. 37 early decision candidates were accepted for the 2013-2014 class. 269 applicants were on the 2013 waiting list; 118 were admitted. Applications are accepted online.

Transfer: A 3.0 college GPA, high school and college transcripts, an essay, standardized test scores, and a statement of good standing from the prior institution are required. An interview is recommended. 60 of 124 credits required for the bachelor's degree must be completed at Trinity.

Visiting: There are regularly scheduled orientations for prospective students, including a campus tour, an admissions and financial aid session, student panels, specialty tours and breakout sessions, a faculty fair, and lunch in the dining hall. There are guides for informal visits, visitors may sit in on classes, and stay overnight. To schedule a visit, contact the Admissions Office.

Financial Aid: In 2013-2014, 94% of all full-time freshmen and 86% of continuing full-time students received some form of financial aid. 57% of all full-time freshmen and 46% of continuing full-time students received need-based aid. The average freshman award was $27,189. Need-based scholarships or need-based grants averaged $23,658; need-based self-help aid (loans and jobs) averaged $5,777; and other non-need-based awards and non-need-based scholarships averaged $13,185. The average financial indebtedness of the 2013 graduate was $42,987. The FAFSA is required. The priority date for freshman financial aid applications for fall entry is February 15. The deadline for filing freshman financial aid applications for fall entry is April 1.

International Students: There are 168 international students enrolled. The school actively recruits these students. They must take the TOEFL with a minimum score of 600 on the paper-based TOEFL (PBT) or 100 on the Internet-based version (iBT). They must also take the SAT or ACT.

Graduates: From July 1, 2012 to June 30, 2013, 561 bachelor's degrees were awarded. The most popular majors were business/marketing (20%), communication (9%), and modern language and literature (7%). In an average class, 1% graduate in 3 years or less, 70% graduate in 4 years or less, 79% graduate in 5 years or less, and 80% graduate in 6 years or less.

Admissions Contact: Christopher Ellertson, Dean of Admissions and Financial Aid. E-Mail: *admissions@trinity.edu* Web: *www.trinity.edu*

UNIVERSITY OF DALLAS D-2

Irving, TX 75062 (972) 721-5266
(800) 628-6999; (972) 721-5017

Full-time: 638 men, 691 women
Part-time: 15 men, 9 women
Graduate: 731 men, 489 women
Year: semesters, summer session
Application Deadline: March 1
Faculty: 81; IIA, --$
Ph.D.s: 88%
Student/Faculty: 12 to 1
Tuition: $33,010
Room & Board: $10,500
Freshman Class: 1178 applied, 1032 accepted, 354 enrolled
SAT CR/M/W: 610/580/580 **ACT:** 26 **VERY COMPETITIVE+**

The University of Dallas, founded in 1955, is a private liberal arts institution affiliated with the Roman Catholic Church. Undergraduate programs are offered through the Constantin College of Liberal Arts, and the Braniff Graduate School has liberal arts and management divisions. There are 3 undergraduate schools and 4 graduate schools. In addition to regional accreditation, UD has baccalaureate program accreditation with AACSB. The library contains 364,691 volumes, 4,526 microform items, 432 audio/video tapes/CDs/DVDs, and subscribes to 64,000 periodicals including electronic. Computerized library services include interlibrary loans, database searching, Internet access, and Wi-Fi capability. Special learning facilities include an art gallery, an 80-seat theater, and an observatory. The 750-acre campus is in an urban area 12 miles west of Dallas. Including any residence halls, there are 31 buildings.

Student Life: 52% of undergraduates are from out of state, mostly the Mid-West. Students are from 50 states, 15 foreign countries, and Canada. 45% are from public schools. 69% are White; 17% Hispanic. 84% are Catholic. The average age of freshmen is 18; all undergraduates, 20. 20% do not continue beyond their first year; 69% remain to graduate.

Housing: 838 students can be accommodated in college housing, which includes single-sex and coed dorms and on-campus apartments. On-campus housing is guaranteed for the freshman year only, is available on a first-come, and first-served basis. 65% of students live on campus; of those, 90% remain on campus on weekends. All students may keep cars.

Activities: There are no fraternities or sororities. There are 40 groups on campus, including art, chamber ensemble, chess, choir, chorale, chorus, computers, dance, debate, drama, film, honors, international, literary magazine, musical theater, newspaper, opera, photography, political, professional, religious, social, social service, student government, symphony, and yearbook. Popular campus events include Charity Week, Groundhog Celebration and Spring Formal.

Sports: There are 7 intercollegiate sports for men and 7 for women, and 6 intramural sports for men and 3 for women. Facilities include Athletic center with a gym, weight room, and aerobics equipment and locker facilities. An outdoor pool, and outdoor tennis courts. A collegiate soccer field, a baseball field, a multipurpose field, and 5 miles of jogging trails are also available.

Disabled Students: 70% of the campus is accessible. Facilities include wheelchair ramps, elevators, special parking, specially equipped restrooms, special class scheduling, and lowered drinking fountains.

Services: Counseling and information services are available, as is tutoring in most subjects. There is remedial math and writing. There are writing and math labs, an academic success office, and department sponsored tutoring.

Campus Safety and Security: Measures include 24-hour foot and vehicle patrol, emergency notification system, self-defense education, and security escort services. There are emergency telephones, lighted pathways/sidewalks, and controlled access to dorms/residences.

Programs of Study: UD confers B.A., and B.S. degrees. Master's and doctoral degrees are also awarded. Bachelor's degrees are awarded in BIOLOGICAL SCIENCE (biochemistry and biology/biological science), BUSINESS (business administration and management), COMMUNICATIONS AND THE ARTS (art history and appreciation, ceramic art and design, classics, dramatic arts, English, French, German, painting, printmaking, sculpture, and Spanish), COMPUTER AND PHYSICAL SCIENCE (chemistry, computer science, mathematics, and physics), EDUCATION (art education and elementary education), SOCIAL SCIENCE (economics, history, philosophy, political science/government, psychology, and theological studies). Classics, English, and politics are the strongest academically. English, biology, and business have the largest enrollments.

Required: To graduate with a B.A., students must complete at least 120 credits, including 38 in advanced credits, which included 12 in the major, with a 2.0 GPA. Completion of core curriculum requirements as well as major requirements is required. To graduate with a B.S degree, students must complete the above requirements for a B.A. plus 12 additional hours in the major. Seniors must pass a comprehensive exam in their major.

Special: UD offers internships in field experience or an off-campus research semester, summer study abroad, on-campus work-study programs, B.A.-B.S. degrees, and double majors. There are 5 national honor societies, including Phi Beta Kappa, and 4 departmental honors programs.

Faculty/Classroom: 64% of faculty are male; 36% are female. 90% teach undergraduates. No introductory courses are taught by graduate students. The average class size in an introductory lecture is 22; in a laboratory is 16; and in a regular course is 19.

Admissions: 88% of the 2013-2014 applicants were accepted. The SAT scores for the 2013-2014 freshman class were: Critical Reading--7% below 500, 36% between 500 and 599, 39% between 600 and 699, and 18% between 700 and 800; Math--12% below 500, 44% between 500 and 599, 29% between 600 and 699, and 15% between 700 and 800; Writing--13% below 500, 40% between 500 and 599, 30% between 600 and 699, and 17% between 700 and 800. The ACT scores were 4% below 21, 22% between 21 and 23, 29% between 24 and 26, 14% between 27 and 28, and 31% above 28. 68% of the current freshmen were in the top fifth of their class; 80% were in the top two fifths. There were 14 National Merit finalists.

Requirements: The SAT or ACT is required. The university seeks high school students who have pursued a curriculum of college preparatory courses including English, social science, math, science, and a foreign language. Applicants pursuing a discipline in the sciences should have 4 years of math. Depth in a foreign language is advised. Although the university is flexible in its admission requests, applicants should be in the upper third of their graduating class and should present satisfactory SAT or ACT scores. AP and CLEP credits are accepted. Important factors in the admissions decision are leadership record, extracurricular activities record, and advanced placement or honors courses.

Procedure: Freshmen are admitted fall and spring. Entrance exams should be taken During the junior year or by the fall of the senior year. There are early admissions, deferred admissions, and rolling admissions plans. Applications should be filed by March 1 for fall entry; December 1 for spring entry, along with a $40 fee. Notification is sent on a rolling basis. Applications are accepted online.

Transfer: 42 transfer students enrolled in 2012-2013. Applicants must have a minimum 2.5 GPA from an accredited college or university. An associate degree and an interview are recommended. Official transcripts from all previous colleges attended, a writing sample, a personal statement, and an academic letter of recommendation are required. Students with fewer than 30 transferable credits must also submit SAT or ACT scores and an official high school transcript. 60 of 120 credits required for the bachelor's degree must be completed at UD.

Visiting: There are regularly scheduled orientations for prospective students, including a campus tour, scholarship competition, visits to residence halls and classes, meetings with students, mass, parents' meetings, and departmental advising. There are guides for informal visits, visitors may sit in on classes, and stay overnight. To schedule a visit, contact the Admission Office.

Financial Aid: In 2013-2014, 99% of all full-time freshmen and 94% of continuing full-time students received some form of financial aid. 68% of all full-time freshmen and 58% of continuing full-time students received need-based aid. The average freshman award was $26,613. Need-based scholarships or need-based grants averaged $22,328; need-based self-help aid (loans and jobs) averaged $5,208; and other non-need-based awards and non-need-based scholarships averaged $14,168. 15% of undergraduate students work part-time. Average annual earnings from campus work are $1650. The average financial indebtedness of the 2013 graduate was $31,446. The FAFSA is required. The priority date for freshman financial aid applications for fall entry is March 1.

International Students: There are 34 international students enrolled. The school actively recruits these students. They must take the TOEFL with a minimum score of 79 on the Internet-based version (iBT). They must also take the SAT or ACT. SAT or ACT scores may be submitted in place of the TOEFL.

Computers: All students may access the system. There are no time limits and no fees.

Graduates: From July 1, 2012 to June 30, 2013, 310 bachelor's degrees were awarded. The most popular majors were social science (16%), business (14%), and English (12%). 26 companies recruited on campus in 2012-2013. In an average class, 60% graduate in 4 years or less, 66% graduate in 5 years or less, and 69% graduate in 6 years or less. Of the 2012 graduating class, 23% were enrolled in graduate school within 6 months of graduation, and 61% were employed.

Admissions Contact: Jill Corbin, Assistant Vice President of Enrollment. E-Mail: *ugadmis@udallas.edu* Web: *www.udallas.edu*

UNIVERSITY OF HOUSTON SYSTEM

The University of Houston System, established in 1977, is a private system in Texas. It is governed by a 9-member board of regents, whose chief administrator is the chancellor. The primary goal of the system is the overall coordination of teaching, research, and service. The main priorities are long-range planning, governmental and private representation, and overall executive management. The total student enrollment for all four campuses is usually 48,907 with 3,218 faculty members. Altogether there are 180 baccalaureate, 163 master's, and 51 doctural programs offered in the University of Houston System. Profiles of the 4-year campuses are included in this section.

UNIVERSITY OF HOUSTON

E-3

Houston, TX 77004 **(713) 743-1010; (800) 741-4449**

Full-time: 11297 men, 11532 women	**Faculty:** 898; I, -$
Part-time: 4577 men, 4181 women	**Ph.D.s:** 86%
Graduate: 3980 men, 3973 women	**Student/Faculty:** 25 to 1
Year: semesters, summer session	**Tuition:** $10,272 ($20,298)
Application Deadline: April 1	**Room & Board:** $8912

Freshman Class: 17407 applied, 10167 accepted, 3434 enrolled

SAT CR/M: 551/588 **ACT:** 24 **VERY COMPETITIVE**

The University of Houston is a Carnegie-designated Tier-One public research university that is recognized throughout the world as a leader in energy research, which is centered in a visionary Energy Research Park, law, business, and environmental education. Located in America's fourth-largest city, the University of Houston is the most ethnically diverse metropolitan research university in the United States. It's 39,500 students hail from 119 countries. In addition to preparing its students to succeed in today's global economy, the University of Houston also is a catalyst within its own community - changing lives through health, education and outreach projects that help build a future for children in Houston, in Texas and in the world. Other distinctive merits of the University of Houston include a strong student experience, a historic Division I athletic programs, top-level arts programs and an internationally recognized faculty including a Nobel Laureate; winners of the National Medal of Science, Pulitzer and Tony awards; and members of prestigious National Academies. Discover the greatness of the University of Houston's dynamic tree-lined campus of more than 650 acres - nestled just minutes from Houston's bustling theater and museum districts - where world-class teaching, revolutionary research and nationally recognized students work together to create a globally competitive educational environment. There are 8 undergraduate schools and 4 graduate schools. In addition to regional accreditation, UH has baccalaureate program accreditation with AACSB, ABET, ACCE, ACPE, NAAB, NASM, and NCATE. The 5 libraries contain 2.4 million volumes, 6.0 million microform items, 31,106 audio/video tapes/CDs/DVDs, and subscribe to 77,827 periodicals including electronic. Computerized library services include interlibrary loans, database searching, Internet access, and Wi-Fi capability. Special learning facilities include an art gallery, radio station, TV station, observatory. The 594-acre campus is in an urban area 3 miles from downtown Houston, Texas. Including any residence halls, there are 152 buildings.

Student Life: 94% of undergraduates are from Texas. Others are from 49 states, 101 foreign countries, and Canada. 93% are from public schools. 31% are White; 26% Hispanic; 19% Asian American; 11% African American. The average age of freshmen is 18; all undergraduates, 22. 15% do not continue beyond their first year; 48% remain to graduate.

Housing: 8008 students can be accommodated in college housing, which includes coed dorms, on-campus apartments, off-campus apartments, and married student housing. In addition, there are honors houses, special-interest houses, fraternity houses, and sorority houses. On-campus housing is available on a first-come and first-served basis. 83% of students commute. All students may keep cars.

Activities: 4% of men belong to 23 national fraternities; 3% of women belong to 19 national sororities. There are 357 groups on campus, including art, band, cheerleading, chess, choir, chorale, chorus, computers, dance, debate, drama, drill team, environmental, ethnic, film, forensics, gay, honors, international, jazz band, literary magazine, marching band, musical theater, newspaper, opera, orchestra, pep band, photography, political, professional, radio and TV, religious, social, social service, student government, symphony, and yearbook. Popular campus events include Frontier Fiesta, Homecoming and Cat's Back.

Sports: There are 7 intercollegiate sports for men and 10 for women, and 23 intramural sports for men and 23 for women. Facilities include The Department of Intercollegiate Athletics operates seven athletics facilities Cougar Field (baseball), Cougar Softball Stadium (softball), Hofheinz Pavilion (men's and women's basketball), Yeoman Fieldhouse inside the Athletics/Alumni Center (Athletics administrative offices, volleyball, indoor men's and women's track), Tom Tellez Track at Carl Lewis International Complex (women's soccer, men's and women's outdoor track), John E. Hoff Tennis Courts (women's tennis) and football practice fields. The eighth and newest facility will be opened in August 2014 – the new Houston Football Stadium – 40,000 seat, state-of-the-art, on-campus venue. The Athletics facilities are located on the northeast corner of the UH campus, and Hofheinz Pavilion, Softball Stadium and Cougar Field (baseball) are equipped for NCAA postseason events.

Disabled Students: 98% of the campus is accessible. Facilities include wheelchair ramps, elevators, special parking, specially equipped restrooms, special class scheduling, lowered drinking fountains, lowered telephones, special housing.

Services: Counseling and information services are available, as is tutoring in most subjects, core requirements There is a reader service for the blind, and remedial math, reading, and writing. Accommodation assistance for students taking exams, tutors assisting with course work, and other accommodations are available.

Campus Safety and Security: Measures include 24-hour foot and vehicle patrol, emergency notification system, self-defense education, and security escort services. There are shuttle buses, emergency telephones, lighted pathways/sidewalks, controlled access to dorms/residences, community dialogues, and assistance with disabled vehicles.

Programs of Study: UH confers B.A., B.S, B.A.C.Y., B.Arch., B.B.A., B.F.A, B.M., B.S.C.E., B.S.Ch.E, B.S.C.P.E., B.S.E.E., B.S.I.E., B.S.M.E, B.S.B.E. and B.S.P.E.T.E. degrees. Master's and doctoral degrees are also awarded. Bachelor's degrees are awarded in BIOLOGICAL SCIENCE (biology/biological science), BUSINESS (accounting, hotel/motel and restaurant management, management information systems, marketing and distribution, and supply chain management), COMMUNICATIONS AND THE ARTS (American Sign Language, applied music, art, Chinese, communications, dance, English, French, industrial design, Spanish, and studio art), COMPUTER AND PHYSICAL SCIENCE (chemistry, geology, mathematics, and physics), ENGINEERING AND ENVIRONMENTAL DESIGN (architecture, biomedical engineering, chemical engineering, civil engineering, computer engineering, construction management, electrical/electronics engineering, environmental design, environmental science, industrial engineering, mechanical engineering, mechanical engineering technology, and petroleum/natural gas engineering), HEALTH PROFESSIONS (health and pharmaceutical science), SOCIAL SCIENCE (anthropology, interdisciplinary studies, Italian studies, liberal arts/general studies, and philosophy). Business, and engineering are the strongest academically. Psychology, accounting, and biology have the largest enrollments.

Required: To graduate, student must complete 120 semester credit hours, including at least 36 in advance-level courses, with a minimum GPA of 2.0. Core Curriculum requirements include 6 hours each in communication, history, government, natural sciences; also 3 hours each in math, math/reasoning, humanities, visual & performing arts, social/behavioral sciences, and writing in the disciplines courses.

Special: Many colleges at the University of Houston offer internships and cooperative education opportunities in areas such as business, engineering, government/policy, education, hospitality, research, healthcare/health education, communications/media, sports, and science, math and technology. UH also offers a 3-2 program with the School of Nursing at the University of Texas Health Science Center. Partnering with The University of Texas Health Science Center at Houston (UTHealth) and The University of Texas Medical Branch at Galveston (UTMB), UH will allow entering students to earn credit hours toward both a Bachelor of Science (B.S.) degree from UH and a Doctor of Medicine (M.D.) from either UTHealth or UTMB in seven years. Study abroad programs include Faculty-Led programs, such as those offered through the Department of Modern and Classical Languages to China and France, and through the African American Studies Program to Africa; Special Programs under the direction of the Department of Hispanic Studies to Latin America and Spain; Affiliated Programs through organizations such as the Council on International Education and Exchange (CIEE), and the University Study Abroad Consortium (USAC), which have established programs all over the world; and Reciprocal Exchange Studies. There are 18 national honor societies, a freshman honors program, and 40 departmental honors programs.

Faculty/Classroom: 61% of faculty are male; 39% are female. 57% teach undergraduates. Graduate students teach 19% of introductory courses. The average class size in an introductory lecture is 70; in a laboratory is 24; and in a regular course is 10.

Admissions: 58% of the 2013-2014 applicants were accepted. The SAT scores for the 2013-2014 freshman class were: Critical Reading--25% below 500, 45% between 500 and 599, 24% between 600 and 699, and 6% between 700 and 800; Math--11% below 500, 43% between 500 and 599, 38% between 600 and 699, and 8% between 700 and 800. The ACT scores were 17% below 21, 28% between 21 and 23, 27% between 24 and 26, 12% between 27 and 28, and 16% above 28. 61% of the current freshmen were in the top fifth of their class. There were 25 National Merit finalists. 26 freshmen graduated first in their class.

Requirements: The SAT or ACT is required. Automatic enrollment granted to applicants who rank in top-tenth of secondary school class and submit a completed application by April 1. All other students are reviewed using a holistic administration process. A GPA of 2.0 is required. AP and CLEP credits are accepted. Important factors in the admissions decision are evidence of special talent, advanced placement or honors courses, and recommendations by school officials.

Procedure: Freshmen are admitted to all sessions. Entrance exams should be taken Priority deadline of December 1st. There is a rolling admissions plan. Early decision applications should be filed by December 1; regular applications, by April 1 for fall entry; December 1 for spring entry; and April 1 for summer entry, along with a $50 fee. Notifications are sent 04 15. Applications are accepted online.

Transfer: 3423 transfer students enrolled in 2012-2013. Applicants must be eligible to return to their last college. A 2.0 GPA is required for students with 30 or more semester hours of college credit, a 2.5 GPA for those with 15 to 29. 30 of 120 credits required for the bachelor's degree must be completed at UH.

Visiting: There are regularly scheduled orientations for prospective students, Students receive a tour, information sessions that help with the transition from high school to college and have scheduled time with an academic advisor. There are guides for informal visits and visitors may stay overnight. To schedule a visit, contact Admissions Staff at the Welcome Center at vc@uh.edu.

Financial Aid: In 2013-2014, 85% of all full-time freshmen and 75% of continuing full-time students received some form of financial aid. 55% of all full-time freshmen and 58% of continuing full-time students received need-based aid. The average freshman award was $13,250. Need-based scholarships or need-based grants averaged $7,935 ($20,708 maximum); need-based self-help aid (loans and jobs) averaged $3,341 ($5,500 maximum); non-need-based athletic scholarships averaged $12,976 ($18,822 maximum); and other non-need-based awards and non-need-based scholarships averaged $6,956 ($38,604 maximum). The average financial indebtedness of the 2013 graduate was $18,244. UH is a member of CSS. The FAFSA is required. The priority date for freshman financial aid applications for fall entry is April 1. The deadline for filing freshman financial aid applications for fall entry is May 1.

International Students: There are 1219 international students enrolled. The school actively recruits these students. They must take the TOEFL with

a minimum score of 550 on the paper-based TOEFL (PBT) or 79 on the Internet-based version (iBT). They must also take the SAT or ACT.

Computers: All students may access the system. There are no time limits and no fees.

Graduates: From July 1, 2012 to June 30, 2013, 5757 bachelor's degrees were awarded. The most popular majors were psychology (8%), accounting (5%), and interdisciplinary studies (5%). In an average class, 16% graduate in 4 years or less, 38% graduate in 5 years or less, and 48% graduate in 6 years or less.

Admissions Contact: Djuana Young, Admissions Director. E-Mail: *admissions@uh.edu* Web: *http:/www.uh.edu/admissions/*

UNIVERSITY OF HOUSTON-DOWNTOWN E-3

Houston, TX 77002 **(713) 221-8522; (713) 223-7468**

Full-time: 2827 men, 4069 women **Faculty:** 337; IIB, -$
Part-time: 2618 men, 3972 women **Ph.D.s:** 84%
Graduate: 123 men, 148 women **Student/Faculty:** 21 to 1
Year: semesters, summer session **Tuition:** $6267 ($16,887)
Application Deadline: rolling **Room & Board:** n/app
Freshman Class: 3096 applied, 2944 accepted, 1130 enrolled
LESS COMPETITIVE

University of Houston-Downtown, founded in 1974 and part of the University of Houston System, is a commuter university and a designated Hispanic Serving Institution and Minority Serving Institution. It offers 50 bachelor's and master's degrees and provides access to hundreds of internships and service opportunities in Houston. There are 5 undergraduate schools and 3 graduate schools. In addition to regional accreditation, UHD has baccalaureate program accreditation with AACSB, ABET, and CSWE. The library contains 206,585 volumes, 5,688 microform items, 3,536 audio/video tapes/CDs/DVDs, and subscribes to 9,731 periodicals including electronic. Computerized library services include interlibrary loans, database searching, Internet access, and Wi-Fi capability. Special learning facilities include an art gallery. The 24-acre campus is in an urban area on the northern edge of the city's business district, on the city's light rail line. Including any residence halls, there are 7 buildings.

Student Life: 97% of undergraduates are from Texas. Others are from 27 states, 65 foreign countries, and Canada. 44% are Hispanic; 26% African American; 19% White; 11% Asian American. The average age of freshmen is 19; all undergraduates, 27. 33% do not continue beyond their first year; 12% remain to graduate.

Housing: Alcohol is not permitted. All students commute. All students may keep cars.

Activities: 1% of men belong to 4 national fraternities; 1% of women belong to 6 national sororities. There are 63 groups on campus, including, model UN, campus ministries, cheerleading, computers, drama, environmental, ethnic, gay, honors, international, jazz band, literary magazine, newspaper, photography, political, professional, religious, social, social service, and student government. Popular campus events include Activities Day, Fall Family Festival and Culture on the Bayou.

Sports: There are 10 intramural sports for men and 10 for women. Facilities include a three-level, 30,000-square-foot Student Life Center with 2 ball courts equipped for basketball, volleyball, and badminton, a multipurpose studio for aerobics and martial arts, and a fitness center with weight equipment and cardiovascular units.

Disabled Students: 95% of the campus is accessible. Facilities include wheelchair ramps, elevators, special parking, specially equipped restrooms, lowered drinking fountains, and lowered telephones.

Services: Counseling and information services are available, as is tutoring in some subjects, and science. There is a reader service for the blind, and remedial math, reading, and writing. Special labs for math, reading, writing and statistics are available. The university also offers supplemental instruction, in which targeted courses have free study sessions and exam reviews led by UHD students who have taken and excelled in the course for which they are study leaders. Writing Associates are upper-division students who serve as sympathetic readers, offering written, constructive feedback regarding students' argument, analysis, organization, development and writing style.

Campus Safety and Security: Measures include 24-hour foot and vehicle patrol, emergency notification system, self-defense education, and security escort services. There are shuttle buses, emergency telephones, lighted pathways/sidewalks, and controlled access to dorms/residences.

Programs of Study: UHD confers B.A., B.A.A.S., B.B.A., B.S., B.S.W. and B.S.E.T. degrees. Master's degrees are also awarded. Bachelor's degrees are awarded in BIOLOGICAL SCIENCE (biology/biological science, biotechnology, and microbiology), BUSINESS (accounting, banking and finance, business administration and management, insurance and risk management, international business management, marketing/retailing/merchandising, and supply chain management), COMMUNICATIONS AND THE ARTS (communications, English, fine arts, Spanish, and technical and business writing), COMPUTER AND PHYSICAL SCIENCE (applied mathematics, chemistry, computer science, information sciences and systems, mathematics, and statistics), ENGINEERING AND ENVIRONMENTAL DESIGN (engineering technology and fire protection engineering), SOCIAL SCIENCE (criminal justice, history, humanities, interdisciplinary studies, philosophy, political science/government, psychology, safety management, social science, social work, and sociology). Accounting, psychology, criminal justice and interdisciplinary studies have the largest enrollments.

Required: For degree completion, at least 25% of the semester credit hours must be earned through instruction offered by UHD. The final 30 semester credit hours of course work toward the degree must be taken at the University of Houston-Downtown. At least 18 of these hours must be at the upper level and be approved by the student's major department. Only the appropriate academic dean may waive any portion of these requirements and only upon petition by a student who has extraordinary reasons. A minimum grade point average of 2.0 calculated on all grades earned at UHD is required for graduation. In addition, a grade point average of 2.0 is required for all courses taken at UHD that apply toward the degree.

Special: The university offers internships, study abroad in 6 countries, general studies degrees, nondegree study, and pass/fail options. There are 12 national honor societies.

Faculty/Classroom: 51% of faculty are male; 49% are female. All teach undergraduates. No introductory courses are taught by graduate students. The average class size in an introductory lecture is 30; in a laboratory is 23; and in a regular course is 27.

Admissions: 95% of the 2013-2014 applicants were accepted. The SAT scores for the 2013-2014 freshman class were: Critical Reading--81% below 500, 17% between 500 and 599, 2% between 600 and 699; Math--67% below 500, 29% between 500 and 599, 4% between 600 and 699. The ACT scores were 38% below 21, 62% between 21 and 26. 20% of the current freshmen were in the top fifth of their class; 50% were in the top two fifths.

Requirements: The SAT or ACT is recommended. Applicants must be graduates of an accredited secondary school or have a GED certificate. High school courses must include English, math, science, and social studies. AP and CLEP credits are accepted.

Procedure: Freshmen are admitted to all sessions. Entrance exams should be taken before attending orientation. There are early admissions and rolling admissions plans. Check with the school for current application deadlines. The application fee is $35. Applications are accepted online.

Transfer: 2236 transfer students enrolled in 2012-2013. Transfer students must have completed a minimum of 15 credit hours. 30 of 120 credits required for the bachelor's degree must be completed at Houston-Downtown.

Visiting: There are regularly scheduled orientations for prospective students, Individual tours include a 30 minute walking tour. Group tours include a 30 minute presentation and a 45 minute tour. Other opportunities such as class visits, financial aid workshop, placement testing are available with advance notice. There are guides for informal visits and visitors may sit in on classes. To schedule a visit, contact Jordan Green at (713) 221-8021.

Financial Aid: In 2013-2014, 81% of all full-time freshmen and 73% of continuing full-time students received some form of financial aid. 77% of all full-time freshmen and 69% of continuing full-time students received need-based aid. The average freshman award was $8,573. Need-based scholarships or need-based grants averaged $5,955; need-based self-help aid (loans and jobs) averaged $3,441; other non-need-based awards and non-need-based scholarships averaged $8,294; and $3,529 from other forms of aid. 4% of undergraduate students work part-time. Average annual earnings from campus work are $3057. The average financial indebtedness of the 2013 graduate was $19,440. The FAFSA is required. The priority date for freshman financial aid applications for fall entry is April 15.

International Students: There are 259 international students enrolled. They must take the TOEFL with a minimum score of 550 on the paper-based TOEFL (PBT) or 80 on the Internet-based version (iBT). They must also take the SAT or ACT.

Computers: All students may access the system 7 days a week. There are no time limits and no fees.

Graduates: From July 1, 2012 to June 30, 2013, 2388 bachelor's degrees were awarded. The most popular majors were business/marketing (36%), interdisciplinary studies (26%), and homeland security (10%). 120 companies recruited on campus in 2012-2013. In an average class, 1% graduate in 4 years or less, 7% graduate in 5 years or less, and 12% graduate in 6 years or less.

Admissions Contact: Spencer Lightsy, Director of Admissions. E-Mail: *uhdadmit@uhd.edu* Web: *www.uhd.edu/admissions/*

UNIVERSITY OF MARY HARDIN-BAYLOR D-3

Belton, TX 76513 (254) 295-4513
(800) 727-8642; (254) 295-5049

Full-time: 1058 men, 1731 women	**Faculty:** n/av
Part-time: 104 men, 163 women	**Ph.D.s:** 72%
Graduate: 184 men, 252 women	**Student/Faculty:** 16 to 1
Year: semesters, summer session	**Tuition:** $25,200
Application Deadline:	**Room & Board:** $6750

Freshman Class: 5540 applied, 4691 accepted, 675 enrolled
SAT CR/M/W: 516/530/485 **ACT:** 24 **COMPETITIVE+**

The University of Mary Hardin-Baylor, founded in 1845, is a private facility affiliated with the Baptist General Convention of Texas. It offers undergraduate degrees in liberal arts, fine arts, music, business, education, nursing, and social work, as well as graduate degrees in business, information systems, education, psychology/counseling, and nursing,and a doctorate in educational administration. The figures in the above capsule and in this profile are approximate. There are 7 undergraduate schools and 7 graduate schools. In addition to regional accreditation, UMHB has baccalaureate program accreditation with CSWE. The library contains 204,979 volumes, 9,696 microform items, and 8,781 audio/video tapes/CDs/DVDs, and subscribes to 80,771 periodicals including electronic. Computerized library services include interlibrary loans, database searching, Internet access, and Wi-Fi capability. Special learning facilities include an art gallery, and nature walk. The 170-acre campus is in a small town in central Texas halfway between San Antonio and Dallas/Fort Worth. Including any residence halls, there are 71 buildings.

Student Life: 98% of undergraduates are from Texas. Others are from 29 states, 14 foreign countries, and Canada. 60% are White; 17% Hispanic; 14% African American. 20% claim no religious affiliation; 13% Catholic. The average age of freshmen is 18; all undergraduates, 22. 34% do not continue beyond their first year; 47% remain to graduate.

Housing: 1567 students can be accommodated in college housing, which includes single-sex dorms and on-campus apartments. On-campus housing is guaranteed for all 4 years. 50% of students commute. Alcohol is not permitted. All students may keep cars.

Activities: There are no fraternities or sororities. There are 59 groups on campus, including art, band, cheerleading, chess, choir, chorale, chorus, computers, debate, drama, drill team, ethnic, forensics, honors, international, jazz band, literary magazine, marching band, musical theater, newspaper, opera, orchestra, pep band, photography, political, professional, religious, social service, student government, symphony, and yearbook. Popular campus events include Miss UMHB Pageants, Mr. Crusader Knights, Play Day, and Easter Pageant.

Sports: There are 6 intercollegiate sports for men and 6 for women, and 21 intramural sports for men and 21 for women. Facilities include a football stadium, a football training facility, 2 football practice fields, a tennis center, and soccer fields, and a campus recreation center housing a pool, 2 basketball courts, and cardio and weight equipment.

Disabled Students: 85% of the campus is accessible. Facilities include wheelchair ramps, elevators, special parking, specially equipped restrooms, special class scheduling, lowered drinking fountains, lowered telephones, special housing.

Services: Counseling and information services are available, as is tutoring in most subjects. There is a reader service for the blind, and remedial math, reading, and writing. Academic counselors and software for the blind are also available.

Campus Safety and Security: Measures include 24-hour foot and vehicle patrol, emergency notification system, self-defense education, and security escort services. There are emergency telephones, lighted pathways/sidewalks, a campus police force.

Programs of Study: UMHB confers B.A., B.S., B.B.A., B.C.M., B.F.A., B.G.S., B.M., B.S.N. and B.S.W. degrees. Master's and doctoral degrees are also awarded. Bachelor's degrees are awarded in BIOLOGICAL SCIENCE (biology/adolescence education and biology/biological science), BUSINESS (accounting, business administration and management, finance, international business, marketing/retailing/merchandising, and sports management), COMMUNICATIONS AND THE ARTS (art, church music, communications, English, journalism, multimedia, music, music performance, performing arts, Spanish, speech/debate/rhetoric, and visual design), COMPUTER AND PHYSICAL SCIENCE (chemistry, chemistry/adolescence education, clinical laboratory science, computer science, information sciences and systems, and mathematics), EDUCATION (art education, early childhood education, elementary education, English education, foreign languages education, mathematics education, middle school education, music education, physical education, reading education, science education, secondary education, social studies education, and special education), ENGINEERING AND ENVIRONMENTAL DESIGN (computer graphics and engineering science), HEALTH PROFESSIONS (exercise science and nursing), SOCIAL SCIENCE (biblical studies, Christian studies, criminal justice, economics, history, ministries, political science/government, psychology, religion, social work, and sociology). Education, business, and nursing are the strongest academically. Nursing has the largest enrollment.

Required: To graduate all students must complete at least 124 credits, including at least 24 in the major field and at least 36 upper-level credits, with a 2.0 GPA. Requirements include 6 credits each in English, social sciences, religion, and electives, 3 each in math and communication, an additional 3 to 4 in math, lab science, or foreign language, and a 1-credit Success in Academics course. There is a chapel attendance requirement for full-time students and a residency requirement of 31 hours.

Special: Study abroad in 5 countries, internships, a work-study program, dual majors, a professional studies degree, an applied science bachelor's degree, post-baccalaureate certification in education, and a 5-year B.B.A./M.B.A. accounting specialization are offered. There are 7 national honor societies and a freshman honors program.

Faculty/Classroom: 43% of faculty are male; 57% are female. No introductory courses are taught by graduate students. The average class size in an introductory lecture is 25; in a laboratory is 20; and in a regular course is 17.

Admissions: 85% of the 2013-2014 applicants were accepted. The SAT scores for the 2013-2014 freshman class were: Critical Reading--42% below 500, 44% between 500 and 599, 12% between 600 and 699, and 2% between 700 and 800; Math--34% below 500, 49% between 500 and 599, 16% between 600 and 699, and 1% between 700 and 800; Writing--60% below 500, 32% between 500 and 599, 7% between 600 and 699, and 1% between 700 and 800. The ACT scores were 28% below 21, 30% between 21 and 23, 22% between 24 and 26, 11% between 27 and 28, and 9% above 28.

Requirements: The SAT or ACT is required. Students who rank in the top half of their high school graduating class must score a minimum of 950 on the SAT or 20 on the ACT. Those who graduate in the lower half of their class must score a minimum of 990 on the SAT or 21 on the ACT. There is no minimum test score for students who rank in the top 10% of their high school graduating class. All students should be graduates of an accredited high school and have 22 units of credit, including 4 in English, 3 in math, and 2.5 in social science. AP and CLEP credits are accepted. Important factors in the admissions decision are advanced placement or honors courses, recommendations by school officials, and extracurricular activities record.

Procedure: Freshmen are admitted fall, spring, and summer. Entrance exams should be taken by the fall of the senior year. There is a rolling admissions plan. Application deadlines are open. Application fee is $35. Notification is sent on a rolling basis. Applications are accepted online.

Transfer: 301 transfer students enrolled in 2012-2013. Applicants must present at least a 2.0 GPA, be in good standing at their previous institutions, and submit all college transcripts. Those with fewer than 12 transferable credits must also meet freshman requirements. 31 of 124 credits required for the bachelor's degree must be completed at UMHB.

Visiting: There are regularly scheduled orientations for prospective students, consisting of campus tours and visits with counselors to discuss admissions, financial aid, housing, and degree plans. There are guides for informal visits, visitors may sit in on classes, and stay overnight. To schedule a visit, contact the Admissions Office.

Financial Aid: In 2013-2014, 78% of all full-time freshmen and 81% of continuing full-time students received some form of financial aid. 78% of all full-time freshmen and 80% of continuing full-time students received need-based aid. The average freshman award was $16,940. Need-based scholarships or need-based grants averaged $13,883 ($19,537 maximum); need-based self-help aid (loans and jobs) averaged $3,971 ($6,300 maximum); and other non-need-based awards and non-need-based scholarships averaged $7,926 ($20,000 maximum). 15% of undergraduate students work part-time. Average annual earnings from campus work are $2300. The average financial indebtedness of the 2013 graduate was $28,458. The FAFSA and the college's own financial statement are required. The priority date for freshman financial aid applications for fall entry is March 1. The deadline for filing freshman financial aid applications for fall entry is September 1.

International Students: There are 83 international students enrolled. The school actively recruits these students.

Computers: All students may access the system any time. There are no time limits and no fees.

Graduates: From July 1, 2012 to June 30, 2013, 609 bachelor's degrees were awarded. The most popular majors were nursing (23%), education (16%), and business (10%). In an average class, 28% graduate in 4 years or less, 42% graduate in 5 years or less, and 47% graduate in 6 years or less.

Admissions Contact: Brent Burks, Director of Admissions & Recruiting.
E-Mail: *admissions@umhb.edu* Web: *www.umhb.edu*

UNIVERSITY OF NORTH TEXAS D-2

Denton, TX 76203 (940) 565-2681
(800) UNT-8211; (940) 565-2408

Full-time: 10503 men, 11964 women	**Faculty:** 613; I, --$
Part-time: 2925 men, 2829 women	**Ph.D.s:** 80%
Graduate: 3065 men, 4719 women	**Student/Faculty:** 28 to 1
Year: semesters, summer session	**Tuition:** $8842 ($18,232)
Application Deadline: August 1	**Room & Board:** $7392

Freshman Class: 13737 applied, 8969 accepted, 3746 enrolled

SAT CR/M/W: 540/550/520 **ACT:** 23 **COMPETITIVE**

The University of North Texas, founded in 1890, is a public institution offering students 12 undergraduate schools and 1 graduate school. In addition to regional accreditation, UNT has baccalaureate program accreditation with AACSB, ABET, ACCE, ACEJMC, CSAB, CSWE, FIDER, NASM, NCATE, and NRPA. The 5 libraries contain 2.3 million volumes, 3.9 million microform items, 232,620 audio/video tapes/CDs/DVDs, and subscribes to 95,958 periodicals including electronic. The figures in the above capsule and in this profile are approximate. Computerized library services include interlibrary loans, database searching, Internet access, and laptop Internet portals. Special learning facilities include a learning resource center, art gallery, planetarium, radio station, TV station, an observatory, and a TV and film production unit. The 875-acre campus is in a suburban area 35 miles north of Dallas/Fort Worth. Including any residence halls, there are 165 buildings.

Student Life: 97% of undergraduates are from Texas. Others are from 50 states, 139 foreign countries, and Canada. 60% are white; 14% Hispanic; 12% African American. The average age of freshmen is 18; all undergraduates, 22. 22% do not continue beyond their first year; 48% remain to graduate.

Housing: 5895 students can be accommodated in college housing, which includes single-sex and coed dorms, on-campus apartments, off-campus apartments, and married student housing. In addition, there are honors houses, special-interest houses, fraternity houses, and sorority houses. On-campus housing is available on a first-come and first-served basis. 81% of students commute. All students may keep cars.

Activities: 4% of men belong to 25 national fraternities; 5% of women belong to 16 national sororities. There are 440 groups on campus, including band, cheerleading, chess, choir, chorale, chorus, computers, dance, debate, drama, ethnic, film, gay, honors, international, jazz band, literary magazine, marching band, musical theater, newspaper, opera, orchestra, pep band, photography, political, professional, radio and TV, religious, social, social service, student government, and symphony. Popular campus events include Howdy Week, Taste of North Texas, Union Day, and Earth Day.

Sports: There are 6 intercollegiate sports for men and 10 for women, and 22 intramural sports for men and 19 for women. Facilities include a brand new football stadium, a weight-training building, tennis courts, 3 indoor swimming pools, 3 gyms, 8 handball and racquetball courts, gymnastics equipment, intramural fields, and a recreational sports complex.

Disabled Students: 90% of the campus is accessible. Facilities include wheelchair ramps, elevators, special parking, specially equipped restrooms, special class scheduling, lowered drinking fountains, lowered telephones, and dorm rooms adapted for disabled students.

Services: Counseling and information services are available, as is tutoring in most subjects. There is a reader service for the blind, and remedial math, reading, and writing.

Campus Safety and Security: Measures include 24-hour foot and vehicle patrol, emergency notification system, self-defense education, and security escort services. There are shuttle buses, emergency telephones, lighted pathways/sidewalks, controlled access to dorms/residences. In addition, there is a crime prevention program, sexual assault information services, and a full-time crime prevention officer on duty.

Programs of Study: UNT confers B.A., B.A.A.S., B.B.A., B.F.A., B.M., B.S., B.S.B.C., B.S.Bio, B.S.Chem., B.S.Eco., B.S.E.P., B.S.E.T., B.S.Math., B.S.M.T., B.S.Phy., and B.S.W. degrees. Master's and doctoral degrees are also awarded. Bachelor's degrees are awarded in BIOLOGICAL SCIENCE (biochemistry and biology/biological science), BUSINESS (accounting, banking and finance, business administration and management, electronic business, entrepreneurial studies, hospitality management services, human resources, insurance, investments and securities, logistics, management information systems, management science, marketing/retailing/merchandising, operations management, organizational behavior, organizational leadership and management, purchasing/inventory management, real estate, and recreation and leisure services), COMMUNICATIONS AND THE ARTS (applied art, art, art history and appreciation, broadcasting, choral music, communications, dance, design, dramatic arts, English, French, German, jazz, journalism, music, music history and appreciation, music performance, music theory and composition, musical theater, performing arts, radio/television technology, Spanish, studio art, telecommunications, theater design, theater management, and visual and performing arts), COMPUTER AND PHYSICAL SCIENCE (chemistry, computer science, information sciences and systems, mathematics, and physics), ENGINEERING AND ENVIRONMENTAL DESIGN (aviation administration/management, commercial art, computer engineering, construction engineering, electrical/electronics engineering, electrical/electronics engineering technology, emergency/disaster science, engineering physics, engineering technology, interior design, manufacturing engineering, mechanical engineering, mechanical engineering technology, and nuclear engineering technology), HEALTH PROFESSIONS (cytotechnology, health, medical laboratory technology, rehabilitation therapy, and speech pathology/audiology), SOCIAL SCIENCE (anthropology, applied psychology, child care/child and family studies, criminal justice, economics, fashion design and technology, geography, history, home furnishings and equipment management/production/services, human services, interdisciplinary studies, international studies, liberal arts/general studies, philosophy, physical fitness/movement, political science/government, psychology, social science, social work, and sociology). Jazz studies, public administration, and accounting are the strongest academically. Biology, psychology, and interdisciplinary studies have the largest enrollments.

Required: All students must complete at least 120 semester hours, including a minimum of 42 hours in the major, with a 2.0 GPA. The core requirements include English, natural science, U.S. history, political science, visual/performing arts, and humanities. Proficiency in English composition must be demonstrated.

Special: UNT offers co-op programs, internships, and work-study programs with the university. Students may study abroad in several locations. An accelerated degree program in math and science allows Texas high school students to obtain 2 years of college credit during their last 2 years in high school. Dual degrees, a general studies degree, and pass/fail options are also offered. There are 42 national honor societies and a freshman honors program.

Faculty/Classroom: 55% of faculty are male; 45% are female. 80% teach undergraduates. Graduate students teach 34% of introductory courses. The average class size in an introductory lecture is 52 and in a laboratory is 51.

Admissions: 65% of a recent year, applicants were accepted. The SAT scores for a recent freshman class were: Critical Reading--29% below 500, 44% between 500 and 599, 23% between 600 and 700, and 4% above 700; Math--23% below 500, 45% between 500 and 599, 25% between 600 and 700, and 6% above 700; Writing--39% below 500, 42% between 500 and 599, 17% between 600 and 700, and 2% above 700. The ACT scores were 21% below 21, 31% between 21 and 23, 25% between 24 and 26, 13% between 27 and 28, and 11% above 28. 40% of the current freshmen were in the top fifth of their class; 75% were in the top two fifths. There were 9 National Merit finalists.

Requirements: The SAT or ACT is required. Applicants must be graduates of an accredited high school and submit a high school transcript. The required minimum score for entrance exams is determined by high school class rank. AP and CLEP credits are accepted.

Procedure: Freshmen are admitted fall, spring, and summer. Entrance exams should be taken at least 2 months before admissions deadlines. There are early admissions, deferred admissions, and rolling admissions plans. Applications should be filed by August 1 for fall entry; December 3 for spring entry; and May 12 for summer entry, along with a $60 fee. Notification is sent on a rolling basis. Applications are accepted online.

Transfer: 5835 transfer students enrolled in a recent year. Applicants with fewer than 30 hours from an accredited college must have a 2.5 GPA and meet freshman entrance requirements. Applicants with at least 30 but no more than 44 transferable hours must have a 2.3 GPA; those with more than 44 hours must have a 2.0 GPA. 30 of 120 credits required for the bachelor's degree must be completed at UNT.

Visiting: There are regularly scheduled orientations for prospective students, including 3-day, 2-night sessions throughout the summer. There are guides for informal visits, visitors may sit in on classes, and stay overnight.

Financial Aid: 7% of undergraduate students work part-time. The FAFSA is required. The priority date for freshman financial aid applications for fall entry is March 31. The deadline for filing freshman financial aid applications for fall entry is June 1.

International Students: There are 578 international students enrolled. The school actively recruits these students. They must take the TOEFL with a minimum score of 550 on the paper-based TOEFL (PBT) or 79 on the Internet-based version (iBT) or take the MELAB, ECPE, FCE, CAE, CPE, IELTS, or ELPT. U.S. high school graduates who are not U.S. citizens may take either the SAT or ACT instead of the TOEFL.

Computers: Wireless access is available. Wireless Internet is available across campus. All dorm rooms are wired for Internet. All students may access the system 24 hours a day. There are no time limits.

Graduates: In a recent year, 6062 bachelor's degrees were awarded. The most popular majors were elementary education (7%), applied arts and sciences (6%), and sociology (6%). 628 companies recruited on campus in a recent year. In an average class, 1% graduate in 3 years or less, 19% graduate in 4 years or less, 41% graduate in 5 years or less, and 48% graduate in 6 years or less.

Admissions Contact: Rebecca Lothringer, Director of Undergraduate Admissions. E-Mail: *undergrad@abn.unt.edu* Web: *www.unt.edu*

UNIVERSITY OF ST. THOMAS - HOUSTON E-3

Houston, TX 77006 (713) 525-3500; (713) 525-3558

Full-time: 443 men, 826 women	**Faculty:** 113; IIA, -$
Part-time: 152 men, 189 women	**Ph.D.s:** 94%
Graduate: 553 men, 1426 women	**Student/Faculty:** 11 to 1
Year: semesters, summer session	**Tuition:** $28,240
Application Deadline: May 1	**Room & Board:** $8250
Freshman Class: 780 applied, 602 accepted, 237 enrolled	
SAT CR/M/W: 540/560/530 **ACT:** 25	**VERY COMPETITIVE**

Committed to educating leaders of faith and character, the University of St. Thomas in Houston offers a Catholic liberal arts education for a lifetime of opportunities. Liberal arts degrees provide invaluable training to a range of careers including business, teaching and health. UST offers 31 undergraduate and 10 graduate degree programs. There are 4 undergraduate schools and 4 graduate schools. In addition to regional accreditation, UST has baccalaureate program accreditation with AACSB and ACBSP. The 4 libraries contain 323,847 volumes, 611,505 microform items, 13,282 audio/video tapes/CDs/DVDs, and subscribe to 80,504 periodicals including electronic. Computerized library services include interlibrary loans, database searching, and Internet access. Special learning facilities include an art gallery, meditation graden. The 21-acre campus is in an urban area 3 miles from Downtown Houston. Including any residence halls, there are 67 buildings.

Student Life: 96% of undergraduates are from Texas. Others are from 28 states, 39 foreign countries, and Canada. 37% are Hispanic; 32% White; 12% Asian American. 61% are Catholic; 13% claim no religious affiliation; 13% Buddhist, Muslim, Ortodox and Unitarian; 12% Protestant. The average age of freshmen is 18; all undergraduates, 25. 23% do not continue beyond their first year; 51% remain to graduate.

Housing: 348 students can be accommodated in college housing, which includes coed dorms and on-campus apartments. In addition, there are special-interest houses, Residents are grouped by classification. On-campus housing is available on a first-come and first-served basis. Priority is given to out-of-town students. 82% of students commute. All students may keep cars.

Activities: There are no fraternities or sororities. There are 80 groups on campus, including art, cheerleading, choir, communications, dance, drama, environmental, ethnic, film, forensics, honors, international, jazz band, literary magazine, musical theater, newspaper, orchestra, political, professional, religious, social, social service, and student government. Popular campus events include Research Symposium, Mass of Holy Spirit, Mass of St. Thomas Aquinas and Deck the Mall.

Sports: There are 3 intercollegiate sports for men and 3 for women, and 7 intramural sports for men and 7 for women. Facilities include a large gym, 3 racquetball courts, weight room, fitness room, dance room, swimming pool, 2 tennis courts, sand in front of volleyball court, men's and women's locker rooms. Outdoor facilities include 2 lighted playing fields, 2 batting cages, pitching machine, half basketball court and soccer goals.

Disabled Students: 95% of the campus is accessible. Facilities include wheelchair ramps, elevators, special parking, specially equipped restrooms, special class scheduling, lowered drinking fountains, lowered telephones.

Services: Counseling and information services are available, as is tutoring in most subjects. There is remedial math, reading, and writing. Kurzweil Educational software for the visually impaired. There are remedial classes, but if a student has special needs, tutoring services will provide remedial tutoring.

Campus Safety and Security: Measures include 24-hour foot and vehicle patrol, emergency notification system, self-defense education, and security escort services. There are shuttle buses, emergency telephones, lighted pathways/sidewalks, controlled access to dorms/residences, fire suppression system, fire extinguishers and smoke detectors. Annual fire drills; IP security cameras.

Programs of Study: UST confers B.A., B.F.A., B.S., B.S.N., B.B.A. and B.B.A., degrees. Master's and doctoral degrees are also awarded. Bachelor's degrees are awarded in AGRICULTURE (environmental studies), BIOLOGICAL SCIENCE (biochemistry, bioinformatics, and biology/biological science), BUSINESS (accounting, banking and finance, business administration and management, finance, marketing, and marketing/retailing/merchandising), COMMUNICATIONS AND THE ARTS (communications, dramatic arts, English, French, music, Spanish, and studio art), COMPUTER AND PHYSICAL SCIENCE (applied mathematics, chemistry, computer science, mathematics, and physics), EDUCATION (business education, education, music education, and nursing education), ENGINEERING AND ENVIRONMENTAL DESIGN (environmental science), HEALTH PROFESSIONS (nursing), SOCIAL SCIENCE (economics, history, international studies, liberal arts/general studies, philosophy, political science/government, psychology, religion, and theological studies). Biology is the strongest academically. Biology, finance, and psychology have the largest enrollments.

Required: To graduate, students must complete the core curriculum and 30 to 48 hours in their selected majors. In some cases, students need to complete special projects according to the requirements of specific majors. Students must have a minimum 2.0 GPA in a total of 126 credit hours, including 36 hours of upper-division credits and the final 36 hours competed in residence at the University.

Special: UST has a cooperative 3-2 engineering program with the University of Houston, Texas A&M University, University of Notre Dame and Catholic University of America. Internships in the major field of study and study abroad in 11 countries are also available. Dual and joint majors and 5 year joint bachelor's and master's degree programs, combining BBA/MBA are available. There are 22 national honor societies, a freshman honors program, and 1 departmental honors programs.

Faculty/Classroom: 53% of faculty are male; 47% are female. 64% teach undergraduates. No introductory courses are taught by graduate students. The average class size in an introductory lecture is 14 and in a laboratory is 13.

Admissions: 77% of the 2013-2014 applicants were accepted. The SAT scores for the 2013-2014 freshman class were: Critical Reading--28% below 500, 48% between 500 and 599, 19% between 600 and 699, and 5% between 700 and 800; Math--21% below 500, 45% between 500 and 599, 32% between 600 and 699, and 2% between 700 and 800; Writing--32% below 500, 46% between 500 and 599, 20% between 600 and 699, and 1% between 700 and 800. The ACT scores were 8% below 21, 21% between 21 and 23, 40% between 24 and 26, 8% between 27 and 28, and 23% above 28. 44% of the current freshmen were in the top fifth of their class; 72% were in the top two fifths. 1 freshman graduated first in the class.

Requirements: The SAT or ACT is required. The ACT Optional Writing test is also required. Applicants must graduate from an accredited secondary school, home school program or successfully complete the GED. Additionally, applicants should have competitive grades (mimimum high school GPA of 2.80 on a 4.0 scale) in a minimum of 18 college preparatory high school units: including 4 units of English, 3 units of social science, 3 units of mathematics, 3 units of science, 2 units of the same classical or modern language other than English, and 3 units of electives in college preparatory classes. Applicants should also have competitive official SAT or ACT scores and competitive class rank if high school ranks graduates. If appropriate, applicants should submit official transcripts of home school coursework. Home schooled students may also need to submit course descriptions, reading lists, or other information if requested. UST requires applicants to be in the upper 50% of their class. A GPA of 2.5 is required. AP and CLEP credits are accepted. Important factors in the admissions decision are advanced placement or honors courses, recommendations by school officials, and extracurricular activities record.

Procedure: Freshmen are admitted fall, spring, and summer. Entrance exams should be taken as early as possible. There are early admissions and deferred admissions plans. Early decision applications should be filed by December 1; regular applications, by May 1 for fall entry; December 1 for spring entry; and May 1 for summer entry. Notification of early decision is sent 12 15; regular decision, on a rolling basis. Applications are accepted online. Application fees are waived if application is completed online.

Transfer: 186 transfer students enrolled in 2012-2013. Transfer students must have a minimum 2.50 GPA college GPA a minimum high school GPA of 2.80 and have a high school diploma or GED. 36 of 126 credits required for the bachelor's degree must be completed at UST.

Visiting: There are regularly scheduled orientations for prospective students, tours, class visitations, introductions to faculty, administrative members, and currently enrolled students, financial aid sessions and social activities. There are guides for informal visits, visitors may sit in on classes, and stay overnight. To schedule a visit, contact the Admissions Counselor.

Financial Aid: In 2013-2014, 93% of all full-time freshmen and 85% of continuing full-time students received some form of financial aid. 70% of all full-time freshmen and 63% of continuing full-time students received need-based aid. The average freshman award was $22,631. Need-based scholarships or need-based grants averaged $18,536; need-based self-help aid (loans and jobs) averaged $4,042; non-need-based athletic scholarships averaged $5,685; and other non-need-based awards and non-need-based scholarships averaged $11,153. The average financial indebtedness of the 2013 graduate was $35,358. The FAFSA is required. The priority date for freshman financial aid applications for fall entry is April 15.

International Students: There are 139 international students enrolled. The school actively recruits these students. They must take the TOEFL with a minimum score of 550 on the paper-based TOEFL (PBT) or 79 on the Internet-based version (iBT). They must also take the SAT or ACT, scoring 23.

Computers: All students may access the system 24 hours a day, 7 days a week. There are no time limits and no fees.

Graduates: From July 1, 2012 to June 30, 2013, 330 bachelor's degrees were awarded. The most popular majors were psychology (11%), finance

(9%), and education (8%). In an average class, 27% graduate in 4 years or less, 46% graduate in 5 years or less, and 51% graduate in 6 years or less.

Admissions Contact: Arthur Ortiz, Assistant Vice President for Enrollment. E-Mail: *admissions@stthom.edu* Web: *www.stthom.edu*

UNIVERSITY OF TEXAS AT ARLINGTON D-2

Arlington, TX 76019 (817) 272-6287; (817) 272-3435

Full-time: 6600 men, 7350 women
Part-time: 2600 men, 3060 women
Graduate: 2735 men, 2700 women
Year: semesters, summer session
Application Deadline: see profile
Freshman Class: n/av
SAT or ACT: required
Faculty: n/av; I, --$
Ph.D.s: 81%
Student/Faculty: 22 to 1
Tuition: $9378 ($17,516)
Room & Board: $7500

LESS COMPETITIVE

The University of Texas at Arlington, founded in 1895, is part of the University of Texas System and is organized into colleges and schools, including business administration, engineering, liberal arts, science, architecture, nursing, social work, graduate studies, urban and public affairs, and education. There are 9 undergraduate schools and 10 graduate schools. The figures in the above capsule and this profile are approximate. In addition to regional accreditation, UTA has baccalaureate program accreditation with AACSB, ABET, ASLA, CSWE, FIDER, NAAB, NASM, and NLN. The 3 libraries contain 1.1 million volumes, 1.5 million microform items, 3468 audio/video tapes/CDs/DVDs, and subscribe to 5073 periodicals including electronic. Computerized library services include interlibrary loans and database searching. Special learning facilities include a learning resource center, art gallery, planetarium, cartographic history library, and nano lab. The 395-acre campus is in an urban area in the center of the Dallas/Fort Worth metroplex. Including any residence halls, there are 100 buildings.

Student Life: 92% of undergraduates are from Texas. Others are from 45 states, 88 foreign countries, and Canada. 56% are white; 12% African American; 11% foreign nationals. The average age of freshmen is 18; all undergraduates, 24. 31% do not continue beyond their first year; 31% remain to graduate.

Housing: 3303 students can be accommodated in college housing, which includes single-sex and coed dorms, on-campus apartments, off-campus apartments, and married student housing. In addition, there are honors houses, fraternity houses, and sorority houses. On-campus housing is available on a first-come, first-served basis. 86% of students commute. Alcohol is not permitted. All students may keep cars.

Activities: 6% of men belong to 12 national fraternities; 4% of women belong to 10 national sororities. There are 225 groups on campus, including art, band, cheerleading, chess, choir, chorale, chorus, communications, computers, dance, drama, drill team, drum and bugle corps, ethnic, forensics, gay, honors, international, jazz band, marching band, opera, orchestra, photography, political, professional, religious, social, social service, student government, symphony, and yearbook. Popular campus events include Charity Week, The Big Event, and Last Day Blast.

Sports: There are 6 intercollegiate sports for men and 6 for women, and 10 intramural sports for men and 10 for women. Facilities include 12 racquetball, 4 basketball and volleyball courts, 12 lighted tennis courts, an inside track, 1 Olympic-size pool, 3 weight rooms, a 12,000-seat stadium, and a 3000-seat gym.

Disabled Students: All of the campus is accessible. Facilities include wheelchair ramps, elevators, special parking, specially equipped rest rooms, special class scheduling, lowered drinking fountains, and lowered telephones.

Services: Counseling and information services are available, as is tutoring in most subjects, including English, math, computer science, and foreign languages. There is a reader service for the blind, remedial math, reading, and writing, a math tutorial clinic, a nursing learning resource center, a reading lab, a science learning center, and a writing lab.

Campus Safety and Security: Measures include 24-hour foot and vehicle patrol, self-defense education, and security escort services. There are shuttle buses, emergency telephones, lighted pathways/sidewalks, crime prevention programs, and an emergency on-campus phone number.

Programs of Study: UTA confers B.A., B.S., B.A.I.S., B.B.A., B.F.A., B.M., B.S.A.S.E., B.S.C.E., B.S.C.S., B.S.C.S.E., B.S.E.E., B.S.I.E., B.S.I.S., B.S.M.E., B.S.N., and B.S.W. degrees. Master's and doctoral degrees are also awarded. Bachelor's degrees are awarded in BIOLOGICAL SCIENCE (biochemistry, biology/biological science, and microbiology), BUSINESS (accounting, banking and finance, business administration and management, business economics, management science, marketing/retailing/merchandising, and real estate), COMMUNICATIONS AND THE ARTS (art history and appreciation, broadcasting, communications, dramatic arts, English, French, German, journalism, music, Russian, Spanish, speech/debate/rhetoric, and studio art), COMPUTER AND PHYSICAL SCIENCE (chemistry, computer science, geology, information sciences and systems, mathematics, and physics), EDUCATION (physical education), ENGINEERING AND ENVIRONMENTAL DESIGN (architecture, civil engineering, computer engineering, electrical/electronics engineering, industrial engineering technology, interior design, landscape architecture/design, and mechanical engineering), HEALTH PROFESSIONS (medical technology and nursing), SOCIAL SCIENCE (anthropology, classical/ancient civilization, criminal justice, economics, history, interdisciplinary studies, philosophy, political science/government, psychology, social work, and sociology). Liberal arts, business, and engineering have the largest enrollments.

Required: All students must earn a GPA of 2.0 while taking at least 124 semester hours, including 30 in their major. The core curriculum requires 8 hours of science, 6 each of English composition, math, U.S. history, and U.S. political science, and 3 each of literature, liberal arts, social/cultural studies, and fine arts/philosophy. Students must demonstrate proficiency in oral presentations and computer use. Proficiency exams, or completion of a department-designated course, may be required by the major department. Theses are required of members of the Honors College.

Special: Cooperative education programs provide opportunities to gain experience in local business through the colleges of engineering and business. Cross-registration with the Summer Institute of Linguistics and the University of Texas Health Science Center, as well as with other members of the University of Texas System, is available. Study abroad in 10 countries, work-study at the university, B.A.-B.S. degrees, dual majors, student-designed interdisciplinary majors, credit for military experience, and pass/fail options are also offered. There are 2 national honor societies, a freshman honors program, and 10 departmental honor programs.

Faculty/Classroom: 60% of faculty are male; 40% are female. Graduate students teach 17% of introductory courses. The average class size in an introductory lecture is 47 and in a laboratory is 25.

Requirements: The SAT or ACT is required. Students ranked in the top 10% of their high school class are admitted regardless of SAT/ACT. The GED is accepted under certain circumstances. Applicants must have 20 academic credits, including 4 units of English, 3 each of math, social studies, and science, and 2 units of foreign language. AP and CLEP credits are accepted. Important factors in the admissions decision are advanced placement or honors courses, leadership record, and evidence of special talent.

Procedure: Freshmen are admitted to all sessions. Entrance exams should be taken during the fall of the senior year. There are early admissions, deferred admissions, and rolling admissions plans. Check with the school for current application deadlines and fee. Notification is sent on a rolling basis. Applications are accepted online.

Transfer: Transfer students with 30 or more transferable semester hours need a 2.0 GPA or evidence of high school or GED completion and SAT or ACT scores comparable to the high school associated rank (varies by student). Transfer students with fewer than 30 transferable semester hours must have a 2.0 GPA and also meet admission requirements for entering freshmen. 25 credits required for the bachelor's degree must be completed at UTA.

Visiting: There are regularly scheduled orientations for prospective students, including overnight summer orientations for freshmen and 1-day orientations for transfers and returning adult students. There are guides for informal visits and visitors may sit in on classes. To schedule a visit, contact the Admissions Office.

Financial Aid: The FAFSA and income tax returns are required. Check with the school for current application deadlines.

International Students: They must take the TOEFL. They must also take the SAT, scoring 900.

Computers: All students may access the system at all times. There are no time limits and no fees.

Admissions Contact: Director of Admissions. A campus DVD is available. E-mail: *beamaverick@uta.edu* Web: *www.uta.edu*

UNIVERSITY OF TEXAS AT AUSTIN D-3

Austin, TX 78712 (512) 475-7440; (512) 475-7475

Full-time: 16,500 men, 18,110 women
Part-time: 1480 men, 1375 women
Graduate: 5685 men, 5230 women
Year: semesters, summer session
Application Deadline: see profile
Freshman Class: n/av
SAT or ACT: required
Faculty: 1100; I, avg$
Ph.D.s: 84%
Student/Faculty: 13 to 1
Tuition: $9500 ($35,000)
Room & Board: $9500

HIGHLY COMPETITIVE

University of Texas at Austin, founded in 1883, is a major research institution within the University of Texas System and provides a broad range of degree programs. There are 12 undergraduate schools and 15 graduate schools. The figures in the above capsule and this profile are approximate. In addition to regional accreditation, UT has baccalaureate program accreditation with AACSB, ABET, ACEJMC, ACPE, ADA, CSWE, FIDER, NAAB, NASAD, and NASM. The 17 libraries contain 8.2 million volumes, 6.1 million microform items, 991,469 audio/video tapes/CDs/DVDs, and subscribe to 50,014 periodicals including electronic. Computerized library services include interlibrary loans, database searching, Internet access, and laptop Internet portals. Special learning facilities include a learning resource center, art gallery, natural history museum, radio station, TV station, observatory, marine science institute, fusion reactor, and Lyndon Baines Johnson Library and Museum. The 350-acre campus is in an urban area near downtown Austin, just off the interstate. Including any residence halls, there are 120 buildings.

Student Life: 92% of undergraduates are from Texas. Others are from 50 states, 125 foreign countries, and Canada. 56% are white; 18% Hispanic; 17% Asian American. The average age of freshmen is 18; all undergraduates, 21. 8% do not continue beyond their first year; 78% remain to graduate.

Housing: 6815 students can be accommodated in college housing, which includes single-sex and coed dorms, off-campus apartments, and married student housing. In addition, there are honors houses and living-learning centers (for freshmen). On-campus housing is available on a first-come, first-served basis. 80% of students commute. All students may keep cars.

Activities: 9% of men belong to 27 national fraternities; 14% of women belong to 23 national sororities. There are 100 groups on campus, including art, band, cheerleading, chess, choir, chorale, chorus, computers, dance, drama, ethnic, film, forensics, gay, honors, international, jazz band, literary magazine, marching band, musical theater, newspaper, opera, orchestra, pep band, photography, political, professional, radio and TV, religious, social, social service, student government, and symphony. Popular campus events include Gone to Texas (welcome for new students), Cinco de Mayo, and Texas Revue (talent show).

Sports: There are 8 intercollegiate sports for men and 10 for women, and 45 intramural sports for men and 45 for women. Facilities include an 80,106-seat football stadium, a 16,175-seat basketball center, a 4400-seat volleyball arena, a 6649-seat baseball stadium, a 2600-seat Olympic swimming facility, 6 multipurpose indoor recreational/athletic facilities of various sizes available for basketball, volleyball, racquetball, swimming, weight training, and related activities, and 3 outdoor facilities covering nearly 40 acres available for swimming, tennis, basketball, racquetball, and various field sports. There is also a 1252-seat softball stadium and a 20,000-seat track and soccer stadium.

Disabled Students: 98% of the campus is accessible. Facilities include wheelchair ramps, elevators, special parking, specially equipped rest rooms, lowered drinking fountains, lowered telephones. specially equipped reading rooms, a speech and hearing center, academic accommodations specific to the student's disability, and interpreters for the hearing impaired.

Services: Counseling and information services are available, as is tutoring in most subjects. There is a reader service for the blind and remedial math, reading, and writing.

Campus Safety and Security: Measures include 24-hour foot and vehicle patrol, self-defense education, and security escort services. There are shuttle buses, emergency telephones, and lighted pathways/sidewalks. There is also a crime prevention unit and closed-circuit TV covering some parking areas and offices.

Programs of Study: UT confers B.A., B.S., B.Arch., B.B.A., B.F.A., B.M., B.J., and B.S.W. degrees. Master's and doctoral degrees are also awarded. Bachelor's degrees are awarded in BIOLOGICAL SCIENCE (biochemistry, biology/biological science, microbiology, molecular biology, and nutrition), BUSINESS (accounting, banking and finance, business administration and management, management information systems, management science, and marketing management), COMMUNICATIONS AND THE ARTS (advertising, applied music, Arabic, art history and appreciation, classics, dance, design, dramatic arts, English, film arts, French, German, Greek, Hebrew, Italian, journalism, Latin, linguistics, music, music theory and composition, Portuguese, public relations, Russian, Scandinavian languages, Slavic languages, Spanish, speech/debate/rhetoric, studio art, and visual and performing arts), COMPUTER AND PHYSICAL SCIENCE (astronomy, chemistry, computer science, geology, geophysics and seismology, mathematics, and physics), ENGINEERING AND ENVIRONMENTAL DESIGN (aerospace studies, architectural engineering, architecture, biomedical engineering, chemical engineering, civil engineering, electrical/electronics engineering, geophysical engineering, interior design, landscape architecture/design, mechanical engineering, and petroleum/natural gas engineering), HEALTH PROFESSIONS (medical technology, nursing, pharmacy, and speech pathology/audiology), SOCIAL SCIENCE (American studies, anthropology, archeology, Asian/Oriental studies, child care/child and family studies, classical/ancient civilization, dietetics, Eastern European studies, economics, ethnic studies, geography, history, human ecology, humanities, Islamic studies, Judaic studies, Latin American studies, liberal arts/general studies, Middle Eastern studies, philosophy, physical fitness/movement, political science/government, psychology, religion, Russian and Slavic studies, social work, sociology, textiles and clothing, and urban studies). Biological sciences, electrical, computer engineering, and government have the largest enrollments.

Required: All students must maintain a GPA of 2.0 while satisfactorily completing 120 to 167 semester hours. Distribution requirements include 6 hours each in American government, American history, natural science, and courses containing a substantial writing component (with at least 3 hours being upper-division); 3 hours each in math, social science, English composition, literature, and humanities/fine arts; plus 3 additional hours in either math, natural science, computer science, or social science; and a fourth semester proficiency in a single foreign language.

Special: Cooperative programs are available in most engineering courses, microbiology, chemistry, computer science, geology, and actuarial studies. Cross-registration is provided in pharmacy with the University of Texas at San Antonio. Internships, study abroad, B.A.-B.S. degrees, dual majors, student-designed majors for humanities students, and pass/fail options are offered. There are 45 national honor societies, including Phi Beta Kappa, a freshman honors program, and 50 departmental honor programs.

Faculty/Classroom: 64% of faculty are male; 36% are female. All teach and do research. No introductory courses are taught by graduate students.

Requirements: The SAT or ACT is required. The ACT Optional Writing test is also required. All students graduating in the top 10% of their class from an accredited Texas high school are eligible for admission. Applicants not meeting that requirement are reviewed based on SAT or ACT scores, class rank, writing samples, and related factors; consideration may be given to socioeconomic and geographic information. In addition, applicants need 15.5 academic credits, including 4 in English, 3 each in math and social studies, 2 each in science and foreign language, and 1.5 in electives. An audition is required for applied music majors. The GED is accepted, with supportive information. Home-schooled students are required to submit the results of either the SAT: Subject tests or AP exams in English, math, and a third subject of the student's choosing. AP and CLEP credits are accepted. Important factors in the admissions decision are leadership record, evidence of special talent, and extracurricular activities record.

Procedure: Freshmen are admitted fall, spring, and summer. Entrance exams should be taken in the junior year or early in the senior year. There are deferred admissions and rolling admissions plans. Check with the school for current application deadlines and fee. Applications are accepted online.

Transfer: Applicants must have at least 24 transferable hours (30 for business). 60 of 120 credits required for the bachelor's degree must be completed at UT.

Visiting: There are regularly scheduled orientations for prospective students. There are guides for informal visits and visitors may sit in on classes. To schedule a visit, contact the Office of Admissions, Freshman Admissions Center.

Financial Aid: UT is a member of CSS. The FAFSA is required. Check with the school for current application deadlines.

International Students: They must take the TOEFL with a minimum score of 550 on the paper-based TOEFL (PBT) or 79 on the Internet-based version (iBT). They must also take the SAT or ACT.

Computers: Wireless access is available. Complete Internet access is available in every dorm room, all libraries, and a multitude of departmental computer labs and classrooms. Several public wireless sites exist. All students may access the system 24 hours a day. There are no time limits and no fees. Students enrolled in College of Education teacher preparation program must have a personal computer.

Admissions Contact: Freshman Admissions Center. E-mail: *www.utexas.edu/student/admissions/about/email.html* Web: *www.utexas.edu*

UNIVERSITY OF TEXAS AT DALLAS D-2

Richardson, TX 75080 **(972) 883-2270; (972) 883-2599**

Full-time: 6069 men, 4566 women	**Faculty:** 445; I, +$
Part-time: 1357 men, 1057 women	**Ph.D.s:** 93%
Graduate: 4529 men, 3615 women	**Student/Faculty:** 22 to 1
Year: semesters, summer session	**Tuition:** $11,806 ($30,378)
Application Deadline: July 1	**Room & Board:** $9240

Freshman Class: 8750 applied, 5125 accepted, 2233 enrolled

SAT CR/M/W: 600/640/590 **ACT:** 27 **HIGHLY COMPETITIVE**

The University of Texas at Dallas, founded in 1969 as part of the University of Texas system, offers undergraduate and graduate programs in the liberal arts and sciences, business, engineering, computer science, cognitive science, and neuroscience. There are 7 undergraduate schools and 7 graduate schools. In addition to regional accreditation, UTD has baccalaureate program accreditation with AACSB and ABET. The library contains 2.7 million volumes, 2.4 million microform items, 14,950 audio/video tapes/CDs/DVDs, and subscribes to 67,950 periodicals including electronic. Computerized library services include interlibrary loans, database searching, and Internet access. Special learning facilities include an art gallery, radio station, TV station, a center for communications disorders, a rare books library, and special library collections on aviation history, geophysics, philatelic research, and botanicals. The 550-acre campus is in a suburban area 18 miles north of downtown Dallas. Including any residence halls, there are 140 buildings.

Student Life: 93% of undergraduates are from Texas. Others are from

50 states, 80 foreign countries, and Canada. 92% are from public schools. 36% are White; 23% Foreign; 19% Asian American; 12% Hispanic. The average age of freshmen is 18; all undergraduates, 23. 11% do not continue beyond their first year; 63% remain to graduate.

Housing: 5154 students can be accommodated in college housing, which includes coed dorms, on-campus apartments, and married student housing. privately owned campus apartments, students can request to be assigned to a living learning group. On-campus housing is available on a first-come and first-served basis. 75% of students commute. All students may keep cars.

Activities: 3% of men belong to 10 national fraternities; 2% of women belong to 6 national sororities. There are 276 groups on campus, including art, band, cheerleading, chess, choir, chorale, chorus, computers, dance, debate, drama, ethnic, film, forensics, gay, honors, international, jazz band, literary magazine, musical theater, newspaper, opera, orchestra, pep band, political, professional, radio and TV, religious, social, social service, and student government. Popular campus events include Homecoming, Holiday Sing, Oozeball and Green Lecture Series.

Sports: There are 6 intercollegiate sports for men and 7 for women, and 27 intramural sports for men and 27 for women. Facilities include 4 racquetball courts, 3 squash courts, 10 lighted tennis courts, indoor and outdoor basketball courts, a sand volleyball court, a 1-mile gravel track, 4 soccer fields, 4 softball fields, a junior Olympic pool/natatorium, and a 4000-seat gym.

Disabled Students: All of the campus is accessible. Facilities include wheelchair ramps, elevators, special parking, specially equipped restrooms, lowered drinking fountains, lowered telephones.

Services: Counseling and information services are available, as is tutoring in most subjects. There is a reader service for the blind, and remedial math, reading, and writing.

Campus Safety and Security: Measures include 24-hour foot and vehicle patrol, emergency notification system, self-defense education, and security escort services. There are emergency telephones, lighted pathways/sidewalks, controlled access to dorms/residences, campus crime watch bulletins, bicycle patrols, crime prevention programs, ID engraving, police liaison who works with students on security issues.

Programs of Study: UTD confers B.A., B.S., B.S.E.E. and B.S.T.E. degrees. Master's and doctoral degrees are also awarded. Bachelor's degrees are awarded in BIOLOGICAL SCIENCE (biochemistry, biology/biological science, molecular biology, and neurosciences), BUSINESS (accounting, banking and finance, business administration and management, international business management, and marketing management), COMMUNICATIONS AND THE ARTS (fine arts, literature, media arts, telecommunications, Telecommunications Engineering Technology, and visual and performing arts), COMPUTER AND PHYSICAL SCIENCE (actuarial science, chemistry, computer science, geoscience, information sciences and systems, mathematics, physics, and software engineering), ENGINEERING AND ENVIRONMENTAL DESIGN (biomedical engineering, computer engineering, electrical/electronics engineering, and mechanical engineering), HEALTH PROFESSIONS (speech pathology/audiology), SOCIAL SCIENCE (American studies, child psychology/development, cognitive science, criminology, economics, geography, history, humanities, interdisciplinary studies, international public service, political science/government, psychology, public administration, and sociology). Electrical engineering, biology, and biochemistry are the strongest academically. Business administration, biology, and accounting have the largest enrollments.

Required: To graduate, students must complete at least 120 credit hours, including 30 in the major and 51 in upper-division courses, with a minimum GPA of 2.0. Core courses include 15 credits in social science (with 6 each in U.S./Texas government and U.S./Texas history), 9 in natural science, and 6 each in communications, math, and humanities/fine arts. Magna and summa cum laude graduates must complete a thesis.

Special: Cross-registration is available with other University of Texas campuses. Accelerated degree programs and B.A.-B.S. degrees are offered in several majors, as is a 3-2 engineering degree. Co-op programs, internships, work-study programs with several major corporations, dual majors, student-designed majors and Washington semester are also possible. In addition, students may study abroad in Europe, Asia, Mexico and New Zealand. There are 5 national honor societies, a freshman honors program, and 16 departmental honors programs.

Faculty/Classroom: 66% of faculty are male; 34% are female. 59% teach undergraduates, 3% do research, and 38% do both. Graduate students teach 9% of introductory courses. The average class size in an introductory lecture is 52; in a laboratory is 28; and in a regular course is 43.

Admissions: 59% of the 2013-2014 applicants were accepted. The SAT scores for the 2013-2014 freshman class were: Critical Reading--9% below 500, 35% between 500 and 599, 38% between 600 and 699, and 18% between 700 and 800; Math--3% below 500, 21% between 500 and 599, 48% between 600 and 699, and 28% between 700 and 800; Writing--13% below 500, 40% between 500 and 599, 34% between 600 and 699, and 13% between 700 and 800. The ACT scores were 3% below 21, 10% between 21 and 23, 20% between 24 and 26, 20% between 27 and 28, and 47% above 28. 63% of the current freshmen were in the top fifth of their class; 85% were in the top two fifths. There were 88 National Merit finalists. 48 freshmen graduated first in their class.

Requirements: The SAT or ACT is required. The ACT Optional Writing test is also required. Applicants should be graduates of an accredited secondary school. In-state students who rank in the top 10% of their class gain automatic admission to UTD. Credentials for other students must include completion of 4 units of English, 3.5 of math, 3 each of social science and lab science, 2 of a foreign language, and course work in fine arts and electives, with health and phys ed courses recommended. AP and CLEP credits are accepted. Important factors in the admissions decision are advanced placement or honors courses, leadership record, and evidence of special talent.

Procedure: Freshmen are admitted to all sessions. Entrance exams should be taken at the end of the junior year or beginning of the senior year. There are deferred admissions and rolling admissions plans. Applications should be filed by July 1 for fall entry; November 1 for spring entry; and April 1 for summer entry, along with a $50 fee. Applications are accepted online.

Transfer: 1704 transfer students enrolled in 2012-2013. Sophomore applicants must present a GPA of 3.0 and 12 credits in the general education core. Upper-division applicants should have a GPA of 2.5 and be in good standing at the last school attended. 30 of 120 credits required for the bachelor's degree must be completed at UTD.

Visiting: There are regularly scheduled orientations for prospective students, including meetings with faculty and an admissions counselor, and a campus tour. There are guides for informal visits and visitors may sit in on classes. To schedule a visit, contact the Office of Enrollment Services at (972) 883-2270.

Financial Aid: In 2013-2014, 51% of all full-time freshmen and 53% of continuing full-time students received some form of financial aid. 47% of all full-time freshmen and 47% of continuing full-time students received need-based aid. The average freshman award was $15,466. Need-based scholarships or need-based grants averaged $11,195; need-based self-help aid (loans and jobs) averaged $4,603; and other non-need-based awards and non-need-based scholarships averaged $13,766. 9% of undergraduate students work part-time. Average annual earnings from campus work are $7112. The average financial indebtedness of the 2013 graduate was $19,565. The FAFSA is required. The priority date for freshman financial aid applications for fall entry is March 31. The deadline for filing freshman financial aid applications for fall entry is April 15.

International Students: There are 502 international students enrolled. They must take the TOEFL with a minimum score of 550 on the paper-based TOEFL (PBT) or 80 on the Internet-based version (iBT). They must also take the SAT or ACT.

Computers: All students may access the system 8 a.m. to midnight in most labs. There are no time limits and no fees.

Graduates: From July 1, 2012 to June 30, 2013, 2761 bachelor's degrees were awarded. The most popular majors were accounting (10%), business administration (9%), and biology (8%). 1250 companies recruited on campus in 2012-2013. In an average class, 6% graduate in 3 years or less, 46% graduate in 4 years or less, 59% graduate in 5 years or less, and 63% graduate in 6 years or less. Of the 2012 graduating class, 35% were enrolled in graduate school within 6 months of graduation, and 47% were employed.

Admissions Contact: Matthew Sanchez, Director, Enrollment Services. E-Mail: *interest@utdallas.edu* Web: *www.utdallas.edu*

UNIVERSITY OF TEXAS AT EL PASO — A-3

El Paso, TX 79968 — **(915) 747-5890; (915) 747-8893**

Full-time: 4970 men, 5880 women	**Faculty:** 1,241; IIA, av$
Part-time: 2165 men, 2800 women	**Ph.D.s:** n/av
Graduate: 1135 men, 1465 women	**Student/Faculty:** n/av
Year: semesters, summer session	**Tuition:** $7300 ($16,800)
Application Deadline: see profile	**Room & Board:** $9500
Freshman Class: n/av	
SAT or ACT: required	

NONCOMPETITIVE

The University of Texas at El Paso, founded in 1913 and the second oldest academic member of the University of Texas System, was originally called the Texas School of Mines and Metallurgy. The figures in the above capsule and in this profile are approximate. It now offers classes through the schools and colleges of business, education, engineering, liberal arts, nursing and allied health, and science. There are 6 undergraduate schools and 1 graduate school. The figures in the above capsule and this profile are approximate. In addition to regional accreditation, UTEP has baccalaureate program accreditation with AACSB, ABET, and NLN. The library contains 1.1 million volumes, 1.8 million microform items, 9995 audio/video tapes/CDs/DVDs, and subscribes to 3005 periodicals including electronic. Computerized library services include interlibrary loans, database searching, and Internet access. Special learning facilities include a learning resource center, art gallery, natural history museum, radio station, TV station, seismic observatory, and the El Paso Centennial Museum. The 366-acre campus is in an urban area. Including any residence halls, there are 87 buildings.

Student Life: 97% of undergraduates are from Texas. Others are from 49 states, 84 foreign countries, and Canada. 95% are from public schools. 75% are Hispanic. The average age of freshmen is 19; all undergraduates, 22. 31% do not continue beyond their first year; 27% remain to graduate.

Housing: 443 students can be accommodated in college housing, which includes coed on-campus apartments. In addition, there are fraternity houses, sorority houses, suites, private rooms, and 24-hour quiet floors. On-campus housing is available on a first-come, first-served basis. Alcohol is not permitted. All students may keep cars.

Activities: There are 100 groups on campus, including art, band, cheerleading, chess, choir, chorale, computers, dance, drama, drill team, drum and bugle corps, ethnic, film, honors, international, jazz band, literary magazine, marching band, musical theater, newspaper, opera, orchestra, pep band, photography, political, professional, radio and TV, religious, social, social service, student government, symphony, and yearbook. Popular campus events include Women's History and Hispanic Cultural weeks and St. Patrick's Engineering Initiation.

Sports: There are 6 intercollegiate sports for men and 5 for women, and 1 intramural sport for men and 1 for women. Facilities include basketball, volleyball, badminton, racquetball, and tennis courts, grass fields for multiple use, an Outdoor Adventure Program with backpacking, bicycling, rafting, and ski trips, a 52,000-seat football stadium, a 12,222-seat basketball gym, a swimming pool, a bowling alley, and a weight room.

Disabled Students: Facilities include wheelchair ramps, elevators, special parking, specially equipped rest rooms, special class scheduling, lowered drinking fountains, and special housing.

Services: Counseling and information services are available, as is tutoring in every subject. There is a reader service for the blind and remedial math, reading, and writing.

Campus Safety and Security: There are shuttle buses and lighted pathways/sidewalks.

Programs of Study: UTEP confers B.A., B.S., B.B.A., B.F.A., B.I.S., B.M., B.S.C.E., B.S.C.S., B.S.Ed., B.S.E.E., B.S.I.E., B.S.MeT.E., B.S.N., and B.S.W. degrees. Master's and doctoral degrees are also awarded. Bachelor's degrees are awarded in BIOLOGICAL SCIENCE (biology/biological science and microbiology), BUSINESS (accounting, banking and finance, business economics, management information systems, management science, and marketing/retailing/merchandising), COMMUNICATIONS AND THE ARTS (art, communications, dramatic arts, English, French, German, journalism, languages, linguistics, music, Spanish, speech/debate/rhetoric, and theater management), COMPUTER AND PHYSICAL SCIENCE (applied mathematics, chemistry, computer science, earth science, geology, geophysics and seismology, mathematics, physics, science, and statistics), ENGINEERING AND ENVIRONMENTAL DESIGN (civil engineering, electrical/electronics engineering, industrial engineering technology, mechanical engineering, and metallurgical engineering), HEALTH PROFESSIONS (allied health, clinical science, health science, medical laboratory technology, and nursing), SOCIAL SCIENCE (anthropology, criminal justice, economics, history, interdisciplinary studies, Latin American studies, Mexican-American/Chicano studies, philosophy, physical fitness/movement, political science/government, psychology, social work, and sociology). Business, nursing, and engineering are the strongest academically. Criminal justice, interdisciplinary studies, and kinesiology have the largest enrollments.

Required: All students must have a minimum GPA of 2.0 while taking 125 to 130 semester hours. Students also must complete a distribution of courses through the general foundation program. Course work is required in the areas of arts/fine arts, computer literacy, English, including composition, foreign languages, history, humanities, math, sciences, and social sciences.

Special: Cross-registration with the University of Texas and the University of Texas Health Science Center is available. Internships, mainly at the graduate level, study abroad in London and Hildesheim, Germany, work-study programs, nondegree study, and pass/fail options are available. There also is the Inter-American Sciences and Humanities Program for students from Spanish-speaking countries whose English is less than adequate for normal study in the United States. The Center for Inter-American and Border Studies also promotes teaching, research, and outreach programs to further the understanding of Latin America. Similar studies are offered through the Cross-Cultural Southwest Ethnic Study Center. An accelerated degree, co-op programs in information science, public health, nursing, pharmacy, and border studies, double majors, dual enrollment, distance learning, ESL, independent study, teacher certification, and weekend college programs are also offered. There is a freshman honors program.

Faculty/Classroom: 59% of faculty are male; 41% are female. No introductory courses are taught by graduate students. The average class size in an introductory lecture is 25; in a laboratory, 15; and in a regular course, 22.

Requirements: The SAT or ACT is required. Satisfactory scores on the ACT or SAT are required for citizens or permanent residents of the United States who have graduated within the past 5 years. UTEP recommends high school preperation that includes of 4 years of English, 3 to 4 of math, (more for science and engineering students), 3 of natural science, and 2 each of social studies, history, and foreign language. The GED is accepted. A GPA of 2.0 is required. AP and CLEP credits are accepted. Important factors in the admissions decision are extracurricular activities record, evidence of special talent, and recommendations by alumni.

Procedure: Freshmen are admitted to all sessions. There are early admissions, deferred admissions, and rolling admissions plans. Check with the school for current application deadlines. Applications are accepted online.

Transfer: Transfer applicants must have at least a C average and must be eligible to return to all previous institutions attended. Transcripts must be provided. 30 of 125 credits required for the bachelor's degree must be completed at UTEP.

Visiting: There are regularly scheduled orientations for prospective students, including preenrollment counseling and campus tours. There are guides for informal visits, and visitors may sit in on classes and stay overnight. To schedule a visit, contact the Recruiting Office.

Financial Aid: The FAFSA and the college's own financial statement are required. Check with the school for current application deadlines.

International Students: The school actively recruits these students. They must take the TOEFL or the PAA. They must also take the SAT or ACT.

Admissions Contact: Director of Admissions. A campus DVD is available. E-Mail: *futureminer@utep.edu* Web: *www.utep.edu*

UNIVERSITY OF TEXAS AT SAN ANTONIO D-4

San Antonio, TX 78249 **(210) 458-4536**
(800) 669-0919; (210) 458-7857

Full-time: 10455 men, 9578 women	**Faculty:** 784; IIA, av$
Part-time: 2359 men, 1950 women	**Ph.D.s:** 74%
Graduate: 1909 men, 2372 women	**Student/Faculty:** 23 to 1
Year: semesters, summer session	**Tuition:** $8737 ($19,455)
Application Deadline: July 1	**Room & Board:** $9635
Freshman Class: n/av	

COMPETITIVE

The University of Texas at San Antonio is dedicated to the advancement of knowledge through research and discovery, teaching and learning, community engagement and public service. As an institution of access and excellence, UTSA embraces multicultural traditions, and serves as a center for intellectual and creative resources as well as a catalyst for socioeconomic development and the commercialization of intellectual property – for Texas, the nation and the world. There are 9 undergraduate schools and 7 graduate schools. In addition to regional accreditation, UTSA has baccalaureate program accreditation with AACSB, ABET, NASAD, and NASM. The 3 libraries contain 1.9 million volumes, 2.9 million microform items, 3.6 million audio/video tapes/CDs/DVDs, and subscribe to 70,467 periodicals including electronic. Computerized library services include interlibrary loans, database searching, Internet access, and Wi-Fi capability. Special learning facilities include an art gallery, the Institute of Texan Cultures. The 725-acre campus is in a suburban area approximately 18 miles northwest of downtown San Antonio. Including any residence halls, there are 121 buildings.

Student Life: 98% of undergraduates are from Texas. Others are from 50 states, 96 foreign countries, and Canada. 47% are Hispanic; 29% White. The average age of freshmen is 18; all undergraduates, 23. 37% do not continue beyond their first year; 34% remain to graduate.

Housing: 4298 students can be accommodated in college housing, which includes single-sex and coed dorms and on-campus apartments. On-campus housing is available on a first-come and first-served basis. 95% of students commute. All students may keep cars.

Activities: 3% of men belong to 12 national fraternities; 3% of women belong to 10 national sororities. There are 217 groups on campus, including art, band, cheerleading, chess, choir, chorale, chorus, computers, dance, debate, drama, environmental, ethnic, film, forensics, gay, honors, international, jazz band, marching band, newspaper, orchestra, pep band, political, professional, religious, social, social service, student government, and symphony. Popular campus events include Fiesta UTSA, Best Fest and Rowdy Rampage Fireworks Spectacular.

Sports: There are 7 intercollegiate sports for men and 8 for women, and 26 intramural sports for men and 26 for women. Facilities include numerous gyms, including those for basketball, volleyball, badminton, indoor soccer, and inline hockey, weight rooms, a 400-meter track, a tennis center, a cardio room, 4 dance studios, racquetball courts, wallyball courts, a rock wall, an indoor 1/6-mile track, a climbing wall, a swimming pool, sand volleyball courts, an outdoor basketball court, 4 outdoor multipurpose fields, a Frisbee golf course, and locker rooms.

Disabled Students: All of the campus is accessible. Facilities include wheelchair ramps, elevators, special parking, specially equipped restrooms, special class scheduling, lowered drinking fountains, lowered telephones, and special housing.

Services: Counseling and information services are available, as is tutoring in some subjects. There is a reader service for the blind, and remedial math, reading, and writing.

Campus Safety and Security: Measures include 24-hour foot and vehicle patrol, emergency notification system, self-defense education, and security escort services. There are shuttle buses, emergency telephones, lighted pathways/sidewalks, and controlled access to dorms/residences.

Programs of Study: UTSA confers B.A., B.S., B.A.A.S., B.B.A., B.F.A., B.M., B.S.C.E., B.S.E.E., B.P.A. and B.S.M.E. degrees. Master's and doctoral degrees are also awarded. Bachelor's degrees are awarded in BIOLOGICAL SCIENCE (biochemistry and biology/biological science), BUSINESS (accounting, business administration and management, business statistics, finance, human resources, management science, and marketing management), COMMUNICATIONS AND THE ARTS (art, art history and appreciation, classics, communications, English, modern language, music, and Spanish), COMPUTER AND PHYSICAL SCIENCE (actuarial science, actuarial mathematics, chemistry, computer science, computer security and information assurance, geology, information sciences and systems, mathematics, physics, and statistics), EDUCATION ((Education) Childhood Education, early childhood education, and education), ENGINEERING AND ENVIRONMENTAL DESIGN (architecture, biomedical engineering, civil engineering, computer engineering, construction management, electrical/electronics engineering, engineering, environmental science, interior design, and mechanical engineering), HEALTH PROFESSIONS (health), SOCIAL SCIENCE (American studies, anthropology, child care/child and family studies, criminal justice, economics, geography, history, humanities, interdisciplinary studies, Mexican-American/Chicano studies, philosophy, philosophy and religion, political science/government, public administration, sociology, and women's studies). Honors college, business, engineering and sciences are the strongest academically. Business, biology, psychology and kinesiology have the largest enrollments.

Required: In order to receive a bachelor's degree from UTSA, a student must meet these minimum requirements: Complete a minimum of 120 semester credit hours, at least 39 of which must be upper-division level. Complete the University Core Curriculum requirements outlined in this chapter. Complete at least one course in the University Core Curriculum designated as a Q-course to satisfy the Quantitative Scholarship requirement. Complete the major and support work requirements and the free elective requirements for the desired degree. Free electives refer to any semester credit hours accepted by UTSA in transfer or awarded by UTSA that, for degree purposes, are not applied to Core Curriculum, major, minor, or support work requirements. Meet all requirements for a degree as put forth by the Texas State Education Code, including the following: Meet the minimum UTSA residence requirements. Achieve an overall 2.0 grade point average in all work attempted at UTSA and a 2.0 grade point average in all work included in the major. Be in good academic standing at UTSA. Apply formally for the degree before the deadline in the Office of the Registrar.

Special: UTSA offers a wide variety of programs to enrich educational opportunities for students. Programs such as University College, ROTC and the Honors College are designed to provide opportunities for research, service and leadership. There are also programs for Pre-Professional Studies (Pre-Med and Pre-Law), internships and a newly offered degree in Multidisciplinary Studies where students have an opportunity to choose three focus areas. There are 40 national honor societies, a freshman honors program, and 17 departmental honors programs.

Faculty/Classroom: 58% of faculty are male; 42% are female. 81% teach undergraduates. Graduate students teach 13% of introductory courses. The average class size in an introductory lecture is 55 and in a laboratory is 21.

Admissions: 62% of the 2013-2014 applicants were accepted. The SAT scores for the 2013-2014 freshman class were: Critical Reading--49% below 500, 36% between 500 and 599, 13% between 600 and 699, and 2% between 700 and 800; Math--35% below 500, 45% between 500 and 599, 18% between 600 and 699, and 2% between 700 and 800. The ACT scores were 38% below 21, 29% between 21 and 23, 21% between 24 and 26, 7% between 27 and 28, and 5% above 28. 23 freshmen graduated first in their class.

Requirements: The SAT or ACT is required. Admission is based on a formula derived from high school class rank and SAT or ACT scores. Applicants must be graduates of accredited high schools or have earned the GED. AP and CLEP credits are accepted.

Procedure: Freshmen are admitted to all sessions. Entrance exams should be taken in the spring of the junior year. There is a rolling admissions plan. Applications should be filed by July 1 for fall entry; November 15 for spring entry; and May 2 for summer entry, along with a $60 fee. Notification is sent on a rolling basis. Applications are accepted online.

Transfer: 2463 transfer students enrolled in 2012-2013. Admissions requirements for transfer students with 30+ hours completed at time of application (work in progress is not considered) must: have at least a cumulative 2.25 GPA on a 4.0 scale in all transferable college coursework from a regionally accredited institutions. Submit your official transcripts from EACH college or university attended, including Dual Credit work Be eligible to return to most recent institution (includes academic and disciplinary actions)* Note: When calculating the cumulative grade point average for admission, ALL attempted work is considered. Repeated courses are NOT excluded. A student currently on suspension at a previous institution will not be considered for admission. 30 of 120 credits required for the bachelor's degree must be completed at UTSA.

Visiting: There are regularly scheduled orientations for prospective students. There are guides for informal visits. To schedule a visit, contact the Visitor Center.

Financial Aid: In 2013-2014, 46% of all full-time freshmen and 53% of continuing full-time students received some form of financial aid. 45% of all full-time freshmen and 52% of continuing full-time students received need-based aid. The average freshman award was $10,434. Need-based scholarships or need-based grants averaged $7,557; need-based self-help aid (loans and jobs) averaged $3,301; non-need-based athletic scholarships averaged $8,557; and other non-need-based awards and non-need-based scholarships averaged $1,518. 7% of undergraduate students work part-time. Average annual earnings from campus work are $5855. The average financial indebtedness of the 2013 graduate was $25,140. The FAFSA and the college's own financial statement are required. The priority date for freshman financial aid applications for fall entry is March 15. The deadline for filing freshman financial aid applications for fall entry is June 30.

International Students: There are 1104 international students enrolled. The school actively recruits these students. They must take the TOEFL with a minimum score of 500 on the paper-based TOEFL (PBT) or 61 on the Internet-based version (iBT), or take the IELTS, with a minimum score of 5. They must also take the SAT or ACT.

Computers: All students may access the system 24 hours a day wireless access. There are no time limits and no fees.

Graduates: From July 1, 2012 to June 30, 2013, 4371 bachelor's degrees were awarded. The most popular majors were business/marketing (25%), interdisciplinary studies (9%), and biological/life sciences (7%). 111 companies recruited on campus in 2012-2013. In an average class, 11% graduate in 4 years or less, 20% graduate in 5 years or less, and 31% graduate in 6 years or less.

Admissions Contact: Beverly Woodson Day, Director of Admissions. E-Mail: *prospects@utsa.edu* Web: *http:/www.utsa.edu/admissions*

UNIVERSITY OF TEXAS-PAN AMERICAN D-5

Edinburg, TX 78539 **(956) 665-2999; (956) 665-2687**

Full-time: 5795 men, 7420 women	**Faculty:** n/av
Part-time: 2045 men, 2342 women	**Ph.D.s:** n/av
Graduate: 985 men, 1466 women	**Student/Faculty:** n/av
Year: semesters, summer session	**Tuition:** $5173 ($13,787)
Application Deadline: August 8	**Room & Board:** $7259
Freshman Class: 9313 applied, 5790 accepted, 3102 enrolled	
SAT CR/M/W: 460/490/450 **ACT:** 19	**LESS COMPETITIVE**

The University of Texas-Pan American, founded in 1927, is a state-supported institution offering programs in the arts and sciences, education, business, and health-related professions. It is part of the University of Texas system. There are 7 undergraduate schools and 7 graduate schools. In addition to regional accreditation, UT Pan American has baccalaureate program accreditation with AACSB, ABET, ADA, CSWE, and NASM. The library contains 869,617 volumes, 32,963 microform items, 8,137 audio/video tapes/CDs/DVDs, and subscribes to 57,310 periodicals including electronic. Computerized library services include interlibrary loans, database searching, Internet access, and Wi-Fi capability. Special learning facilities include an art gallery, planetarium, a coastal studies lab. laptop Internet portals, chat services, text services, online request for books, journal articles, online delivery of journal articles, embedded librarian services to distance ed students. The 331-acre campus is in a small town close to the Mexican border and the Gulf of Mexico. Including any residence halls, there are 70 buildings.

Student Life: 98% of undergraduates are from Texas. Others are from 39 states, 43 foreign countries, and Canada. 88% are Hispanic. The average age of freshmen is 19; all undergraduates, 22. 24% do not continue beyond their first year; 76% remain to graduate.

Housing: 892 students can be accommodated in college housing, which includes single-sex and coed dorms and on-campus apartments. On-campus housing is available on a first-come and first-served basis. All students may keep cars.

Activities: 2% of men belong to 9 national fraternities; 1% of women belong to 5 national sororities. There are 194 groups on campus, including academic, art, band, cheerleading, choir, chorale, chorus, computers, dance, drama, ethnic, film, gay, honors, international, jazz band, literary magazine, musical theater, newspaper, opera, orchestra, pep band, photography, political, professional, radio and TV, religious, social, social service, student government, and symphony. Popular campus events include Cinco de Mayo, Spirit Week and Bronco Day.

Sports: There are 7 intercollegiate sports for men and 7 for women, and 14 intramural sports for men and 14 for women. Facilities include a 4000-seat field house, baseball and tennis stadiums, a track, a soccer field, and the Wellness and Recreation Sports Complex.The WRSC is approximately 100,000 square feet in size and consists of the following indoor spaces: Main Gym (2-courts), Multi-purpose Gym, Racquetball Courts (3), Weight Room, Cardio Theatre, Dance Studios (2), Climbing Wall, Indoor Track (1/10th mile), Classroom/Audiovisual Theatre, Relaxation Lounges, Wellness Energy Zone, and Fitness Assessment Room. Outdoor spaces include: Swimming Pool, Hot Tub, Basketball Courts (2), Beach Volleyball Courts (2), Tennis Courts (2), Palapa/Barbecue area, Softball Field, Intramural Sports Fields (2).

Disabled Students: 95% of the campus is accessible. Facilities include wheelchair ramps, elevators, special parking, specially equipped restrooms, special class scheduling, lowered drinking fountains, lowered telephones, special housing.

Services: Counseling and information services are available, as is tutoring in some subjects, American Sign Language, biology, chemistry,French, history, math, philosophy, physics, political scienceand Spanish. There is a reader service for the blind, and remedial math, reading, and writing. The Learning Assistance Center provides small-group and individual tutoring and computer-aided instruction.

Campus Safety and Security: Measures include 24-hour foot and vehicle patrol, emergency notification system, self-defense education, and security escort services. There are shuttle buses, emergency telephones, lighted pathways/sidewalks, and a university police department.

Programs of Study: UT Pan American confers B.A., B.S., B.A.S.C., B.B.A., B.F.A., B.G.S., B.I.S.,BM, B.S.C.E., B.S.C.J., B.S.C.S., B.S.E.E., B.S.M.E., B.S.M., B.S.N., B.S.P.A.S. and B.S.W. degrees. Master's and doctoral degrees are also awarded. Bachelor's degrees are awarded in BIOLOGICAL SCIENCE (biology/biological science), BUSINESS (accounting, banking and finance, finance, international business management, management science, and marketing/retailing/merchandising), COMMUNICATIONS AND THE ARTS (art, communications, dance, dramatic arts, English, journalism, music, performing arts, and Spanish), COMPUTER AND PHYSICAL SCIENCE (chemistry, computer information systems, computer science, information sciences and systems, mathematics, physical sciences, and physics), ENGINEERING AND ENVIRONMENTAL DESIGN (civil engineering, computer engineering, electrical/electronics engineering, environmental science, manufacturing engineering, and mechanical engineering), HEALTH PROFESSIONS (clinical science, health, nursing, physician's assistant, rehabilitation therapy, and speech pathology/audiology), SOCIAL SCIENCE (anthropology, criminal justice, dietetics, early childhood studies, economics, French studies, history, interdisciplinary studies, Latin American studies, liberal arts/general studies, Mexican-American/Chicano studies, philosophy, physical fitness/movement, political science/government, psychology, social studies, social work, and sociology). Engineering and business is the strongest academically. Biology, nursing, and criminal justice have the largest enrollments.

Required: To graduate, students must complete 124 to 137 semester hours with a 2.0 GPA. At least 30 hours are required in the major. Students must also fulfill a general education requirement of 48 hours by taking 18 hours in humanities (including English and a foreign language), 15 hours of social science (including U.S. history and Texas government), 11 hours of lab science and math, and 2 hours each of phys ed and computer science. Other requirements vary according to degree.

Special: Internships, co-op programs, study abroad, work-study programs, dual majors, and nondegree study are available. There are 9 national honor societies, a freshman honors program, and 6 departmental honors programs.

Faculty/Classroom: No introductory courses are taught by graduate students.

Admissions: 62% of the 2013-2014 applicants were accepted. The SAT scores for the 2013-2014 freshman class were: Critical Reading--67% below 500, 26% between 500 and 599, 6% between 600 and 699, and 1% between 700 and 800; Math--52% below 500, 39% between 500 and 599, 8% between 600 and 699, and 2% between 700 and 800; Writing--72% below 500, 23% between 500 and 599, and 4% between 600 and 699. The ACT scores were 66% below 21, 23% between 21 and 23, 8% between 24 and 26, 2% between 27 and 28, and 1% above 28.

Requirements: The SAT or ACT is required. The ACT is preferred. Applicants must be graduates of an accredited high school or have the GED. 21 academic units are required, including 4 units of English; 3 units of math, at least 1 of which must be algebra; 2 units of science; 1 unit each of world history and U.S. history; and 1/2 unit each of U.S. government, economics, phys ed, and health education. An additional 7 units may be taken in electives. AP and CLEP credits are accepted.

Procedure: Freshmen are admitted to all sessions. Entrance exams should be taken preferably in the junior year of high school. There is a rolling admissions plan. Applications should be filed by August 8 for fall entry; December 18 for spring entry; and April 25 for summer entry. Notification is sent on a rolling basis. Applications are accepted online.

Transfer: 1252 transfer students enrolled in 2012-2013. Transfer applicants must meet the same criteria as entering freshmen. 31 of 120 credits required for the bachelor's degree must be completed at UT Pan American.

Visiting: There are regularly scheduled orientations for prospective students. There are guides for informal visits and visitors may sit in on classes. To schedule a visit, contact the Admissions Office.

Financial Aid: The FAFSA is required. The priority date for freshman financial aid applications for fall entry is March 15.

International Students: There are 350 international students enrolled. The school actively recruits these students. They must take the TOEFL with a minimum score of 500 on the paper-based TOEFL (PBT) or 61 on the Internet-based version (iBT). They must also take the SAT or ACT, scoring ACT Composite 18; SAT 860 (Critical Reading + Math.

Computers: All students may access the system. There are no time limits. The fee is $10.3/SCH.

Graduates: From July 1, 2012 to June 30, 2013, 2734 bachelor's degrees were awarded. The most popular majors were multi/interdisciplinary studies (9%), biology, and general (8%), and criminal justice and corrections (8%). In an average class, 17% graduate in 4 years or less, 34% graduate in 5 years or less, and 39% graduate in 6 years or less.

Admissions Contact: Dr. Magdalena Hinojosa, Sr. Assoc VP for Enrollment Services. E-Mail: *admissions@utpa.edu* Web: *www.utpa.edu/admissions*

UNIVERSITY OF THE INCARNATE WORD — D-4

San Antonio, TX 78209 — (210) 829-6005; (800) 749-WORD; (210) 829-3921

Full-time: 1609 men, 2592 women	**Faculty:** n/av; IIA, -$
Part-time: 909 men, 1381 women	**Ph.D.s:** 61%
Graduate: 868 men, 1296 women	**Student/Faculty:** 14 to 1
Year: semesters, summer session	**Tuition:** n/av
Application Deadline: open	**Room & Board:** $10,410
Freshman Class: 4062 applied, 3781 accepted, 1045 enrolled	
SAT CR/M/W: 470/490/460	**ACT:** 20 — **LESS COMPETITIVE**

University of the Incarnate Word, founded in 1881, is a liberal arts institution affiliated with the Catholic Church that offers undergraduate programs in art, business, health science, education, music, religious studies, nursing, and fine arts. There are 7 undergraduate schools and 4 graduate schools. In addition to regional accreditation, UIW has baccalaureate program accreditation with ACBSP, ADA, AHEA, CAHEA, NCATE, and NLN. The library contains 274,159 volumes, 301,272 microform items, 15,414 audio/video tapes/CDs/DVDs, and subscribes to 96,890 periodicals including electronic. Computerized library services include interlibrary loans, database searching, Internet access, and Wi-Fi capability. Special learning facilities include an art gallery, radio station, and TV station. The 200-acre campus is in an urban area about 3 miles north of downtown San Antonio. Including any residence halls, there are 45 buildings.

Student Life: 94% of undergraduates are from Texas. Others are from 43 states, 33 foreign countries, and Canada. 59% are Hispanic; 21% White. 40% are Catholic; 20% claim no religious affiliation. The average age of freshmen is 18; all undergraduates, 27. 30% do not continue beyond their first year; 40% remain to graduate.

Housing: 1251 students can be accommodated in college housing, which includes single-sex and coed dorms and on-campus apartments. On-campus housing is available on a first-come and first-served basis. 88% of students commute. All students may keep cars.

Activities: 1% of men belong to 3 national fraternities; 1% of women belong to 1 local and 3 national sororities. There are 70 groups on campus, including art, cheerleading, choir, chorale, chorus, dance, drama, drill team, ethnic, honors, international, jazz band, literary magazine, marching band, musical theater, newspaper, orchestra, pep band, political, professional, radio and TV, religious, social, social service, and student government. Popular campus events include Welcome Week, Light the Way and Golden Harvest.

Sports: There are 9 intercollegiate sports for men and 10 for women, and 10 intramural sports for men and 11 for women. Facilities include football and soccer fields, a pool, tennis courts, baseball and softball fields, a basketball and vollyball complex and a fully-equipped weight traning room.

Disabled Students: 88% of the campus is accessible. Facilities include wheelchair ramps, elevators, special parking, specially equipped restrooms, special class scheduling, lowered drinking fountains, lowered telephones, and special housing.

Services: Counseling and information services are available, as is tutoring in most subjects. There is remedial math, reading, and writing.

Campus Safety and Security: Measures include 24-hour foot and vehicle patrol, emergency notification system, self-defense education, and security escort services. There are shuttle buses, emergency telephones, lighted pathways/sidewalks, and controlled access to dorms/residences.

Programs of Study: UIW confers B.A., B.S., B.B.A. and B.M. degrees.

Associate, master's, and doctoral degrees are also awarded. Bachelor's degrees are awarded in BIOLOGICAL SCIENCE (biology/biological science and nutrition), BUSINESS (business administration and management, fashion merchandising, human resources, and sports management), COMMUNICATIONS AND THE ARTS (art, communications, dramatic arts, English, music, music business management, and Spanish), COMPUTER AND PHYSICAL SCIENCE (chemistry, information sciences and systems, and mathematics), EDUCATION (art education, athletic training, elementary education, music education, physical education, and secondary education), ENGINEERING AND ENVIRONMENTAL DESIGN (engineering management, environmental science, and interior design), HEALTH PROFESSIONS (music therapy, nuclear medical technology, and nursing), SOCIAL SCIENCE (child care/child and family studies, fashion design and technology, history, philosophy, political science/government, prelaw, psychology, religion, and sociology). Nursing, and business are the strongest academically. Nursing, pharmacy, and business have the largest enrollments.

Required: To graduate, students must complete at least 128 credit hours, with a minimum GPA of 2.0. An extensive required core curriculum of 53 credit hours includes world literature, dimensions of wellness, computer literacy, and a capstone. A total of 45 hours of community service also is required.

Special: UIW offers cross-registration with Our Lady of the Lake and Saint Mary's Universities, internships, work-study programs, and study abroad. There are 7 national honor societies, a freshman honors program, and 1 departmental honors program.

Faculty/Classroom: 47% of faculty are male; 53% are female. All teach undergraduates. No introductory courses are taught by graduate students.

Admissions: 93% of the 2013-2014 applicants were accepted. The SAT scores for the 2013-2014 freshman class were: Critical Reading--61% below 500, 30% between 500 and 599, 8% between 600 and 699, and 1% between 700 and 800; Math--53% below 500, 36% between 500 and 599, 10% between 600 and 699, and 1% between 700 and 800; Writing--69% below 500, 25% between 500 and 599, 5% between 600 and 699, and 1% between 700 and 800. The ACT scores were 53% below 21, 27% between 21 and 23, 14% between 24 and 26, 4% between 27 and 28, and 2% above 28. 33% of the current freshmen were in the top fifth of their class; 62% were in the top two fifths.

Requirements: The SAT or ACT is required. Students must have a minimum GPA of 2.0 with mimium composite scores of 920 on the SAT I or 18 on the ACT. Applicants must be graduates of an accredited secondary school or have the GED, and have completed 16 Carnegie units, including at least 4 units of English, 3 of math, science and social studies, 2 of foreign language, and 1 of fine arts. In some cases, applicants may be asked to take an assessment test and/or arrange for a personal interview to provide further information upon which a decision will be based. A GPA of 2.0 is required. AP and CLEP credits are accepted.

Procedure: Freshmen are admitted to all sessions. Entrance exams should be taken in the junior or senior year of high school. There are deferred admissions and rolling admissions plans. Application deadlines are open. Application fee is $20. Notification is sent on a rolling basis. Applications are accepted online.

Transfer: 744 transfer students enrolled in 2012-2013. Applicants are advised to have at least a cumulative GPA of 2.5 or better for unconditional admission. Students may be admitted with less than a 2.5 GPA on the recommendation of the Admissions Committee. The Committee reserves the right to place conditions or requirements on the admittance of such a student. Applicants with fewer than 24 transferrable hours must submit an official high school transcript with the scores of any SAT or ACT exam (s) previously taken. Transfer applicants out of high school for more than 2 years, or who are GED recipients, are not required to submit SAT or ACT exam scores. 36 of 128 credits required for the bachelor's degree must be completed at UIW.

Visiting: There are regularly scheduled orientations for prospective students, consisting of an introduction to services, a campus tour, assessment testing, advisement, and registration. There are guides for informal visits, visitors may sit in on classes, and stay overnight. To schedule a visit, contact the Office of Admissions.

Financial Aid: In 2013-2014, 90% of all full-time freshmen students received some form of financial aid. 83% of all full-time freshmen students received need-based aid. The average freshman award was $18,453. Need-based scholarships or need-based grants averaged $13,981; need-based self-help aid (loans and jobs) averaged $3,843; non-need-based athletic scholarships averaged $9,375; and other non-need-based awards and non-need-based scholarships averaged $8,410. 57% of undergraduate students work part-time. Average annual earnings from campus work are $2000. The FAFSA is required. The priority date for freshman financial aid applications for fall entry is April 1.

International Students: There are 252 international students enrolled. The school actively recruits these students. They must take the TOEFL with a minimum score of 550 on the paper-based TOEFL (PBT) or 83 on the Internet-based version (iBT).

Computers: All students may access the system 24 hours a day, 7 days a week. There are no time limits and no fees.

Graduates: From July 1, 2012 to June 30, 2013, 1201 bachelor's degrees were awarded. The most popular majors were business/marketing (37%), health professions and related programs (9%), and biological/life sciences (8%). In an average class, 19% graduate in 4 years or less, 36% graduate in 5 years or less, and 40% graduate in 6 years or less.

Admissions Contact: Andrea Cyterski-Acosta, Director of Admissions. E-Mail: *cyterski@uiwtx.edu* Web: *www.uiw.edu*

WAYLAND BAPTIST UNIVERSITY — B-2

Plainview, TX 79072 — **(806) 291-3500**

Full-time: 579 men, 432 women	**Faculty:** 101
Part-time: 182 men, 192 women	**Ph.D.s:** 67%
Graduate: 178 men, 261 women	**Student/Faculty:** 11 to 1
Year: semesters, summer session	**Tuition:** $11,900
Application Deadline: open	**Room & Board:** $4158
Freshman Class: n/av	

LESS COMPETITIVE

Wayland Baptist University, founded in 1908, is a private liberal arts school affiliated with the Baptist General Convention of Texas (Southern Baptist). There are 9 undergraduate schools and one graduate school. In addition to regional accreditation, Wayland has baccalaureate program accreditation with NASM. The library contains 131,163 volumes, 283,041 microform items, 11,893 audio/video tapes/CDs/DVDs, and subscribes to 2,661 periodicals including electronic. Computerized library services include interlibrary loans, database searching, and Internet access. Special learning facilities include an art gallery, natural history museum, radio station, and TV station. The 80-acre campus is in a small town 45 miles north of Lubbock. Including any residence halls, there are 41 buildings.

Student Life: 82% of undergraduates are from Texas. Others are from 42 states, 20 foreign countries, and Canada. 88% are from public schools. 45% are White; 29% Hispanic; 12% African American. 52% are Protestant; 35% unknown non-denominational; 13% Catholic. The average age of freshmen is 19; all undergraduates, 22. 34% do not continue beyond their first year; 37% remain to graduate.

Housing: 730 students can be accommodated in college housing, which includes single-sex dorms and married student housing. On-campus housing is guaranteed for all 4 years, is available on a first-come, and first-served basis. 81% of students live on campus. Alcohol is not permitted. All students may keep cars.

Activities: 2% of men belong to 2 local and 1 national fraternities; 5% of women belong to 1 local and 1 national sororities. There are 32 groups on campus, including art, band, cheerleading, choir, chorale, chorus, computers, dance, drama, environmental, honors, international, marching band, musical theater, newspaper, photography, political, professional, radio and TV, religious, social, social service, student government, and yearbook. Popular campus events include Pride Week, Big Weekend, and Miss Wayland.

Sports: There are 8 intercollegiate sports for men and 7 for women, and 7 intramural sports for men and 7 for women. Facilities include a 3,000-seat gym, basketball/volleyball,tennis courts, baseball field, track, soccer field and weight training facility. Laney Center: 50,000 square foot recreational student facility featuring an elevated indoor jogging track, cardiac strength center, 25 foot climbing wall, aerobic room, classrooms/offices, pool and ping-pong tables, snack bar and double gymnasium with electronic scoreboards.

Disabled Students: All of the campus is accessible. Facilities include wheelchair ramps, elevators, special parking, specially equipped restrooms, special class scheduling, and lowered drinking fountains.

Services: Counseling and information services are available, as is tutoring in every subject. There is a reader service for the blind, and remedial math, reading, and writing.

Campus Safety and Security: Measures include emergency notification system and self-defense education. There are lighted pathways/sidewalks, controlled access to dorms/residences, and a security service on campus.

Programs of Study: Wayland confers B.A., B.A.S., B.B.A., B.C.M., B.M., B.S., B.S.I.S. and B.S.N. degrees. Associate and master's degrees are also awarded. Bachelor's degrees are awarded in AGRICULTURE (environmental studies), BIOLOGICAL SCIENCE (biology/biological science and life science), BUSINESS (accounting, business administration and management, and management information systems), COMMUNICATIONS AND THE ARTS (art, communications, dramatic arts, English, graphic design, music, and Spanish), COMPUTER AND PHYSICAL SCIENCE (chemistry, geology, mathematics, physical sciences, and science), EDUCATION (business education, early childhood education, music education, physical education, and vocational education), ENGINEERING AND ENVIRONMENTAL DESIGN (environmental science and preengineering), HEALTH PROFESSIONS (health care administration, nursing, and premedicine), SOCIAL SCIENCE (Christian studies, criminal justice, economics, history, human services, interdisciplinary studies, philosophy, political science/government, prelaw, psychology, religion, religious education, religious music, social science, social studies, and sociology). Religion, education, business and social science are the strongest academically. Education, business, math and science have the largest enrollments.

Required: To graduate, all students must earn a GPA of at least 2.0 while taking 124 to 145 semester hours, with 30 to 42 in their majors and 36 to 42 in upper-division hours. Distribution requirements include 12 hours of English; 8 to 16 in science; 6 each in Bible, history, and humanities; up to 6 in foreign language; 4 in phys ed; 3 to 6 in math; 3 in computer science; and 3 in philosophy, sociology, or psychology. Chapel attendance is also required. Honors students must complete a thesis.

Special: A cooperative education program with Texas Tech University, internships in social science, business administration, religion, education, and social work, study abroad, and work-study plans through the Social Security Administration are available. In addition, credit for life and military experience is given in the individualized occupational education program. Nondegree study in the Community Classroom program is also offered. There are composite science, composite social science, all-level phys ed, and music programs available. There are 7 national honor societies and a freshman honors program.

Faculty/Classroom: 68% of faculty are male; 32% are female. All teach undergraduates. No introductory courses are taught by graduate students. The average class size in an introductory lecture is 16; in a laboratory is 13; and in a regular course is 13.

Admissions: 19% of the current freshmen were in the top fifth of their class; 41% were in the top two fifths. 2 freshmen graduated first in their class.

Requirements: The SAT or ACT is required. Wayland requires graduation from an accredited secondary school with 3 years of English and 2 years each of science, math, and social science. The GED is accepted. AP and CLEP credits are accepted.

Procedure: Freshmen are admitted to all sessions. There is a rolling admissions plan. Application deadlines are open. Application fee is $35. Applications are accepted online.

Transfer: 102 transfer students enrolled in 2012-2013. Applicants need a minimum GPA of 2.0 and must be able to reenter all colleges previously attended. 30 of 124 credits required for the bachelor's degree must be completed at Wayland.

Visiting: There are regularly scheduled orientations for prospective students. There are guides for informal visits, visitors may sit in on classes, and stay overnight. To schedule a visit, contact the Admissions Office at admityou@wbu.edu.

Financial Aid: In 2013-2014, 61% of all full-time freshmen and 86% of continuing full-time students received some form of financial aid. 60% of all full-time freshmen and 83% of continuing full-time students received need-based aid. The average freshman award was $10,100. Need-based scholarships or need-based grants averaged $7,946 ($9,994 maximum); need-based self-help aid (loans and jobs) averaged $2,856 ($9,921 maximum); non-need-based athletic scholarships averaged $6,538 ($22,178 maximum); and other non-need-based awards and non-need-based scholarships averaged $6,447 ($16,400 maximum). 13% of undergraduate students work part-time. Average annual earnings from campus work are $2472. The average financial indebtedness of the 2013 graduate was $30,461. Wayland is a member of CSS. The FAFSA and the college's own financial statement are required. Check with the school for current application deadlines.

International Students: There are 33 international students enrolled. The school actively recruits these students. They must take the TOEFL with a minimum score of 500 on the paper-based TOEFL (PBT) or 61 on the Internet-based version (iBT). They must also take the SAT or ACT.

Computers: All students may access the system during posted lab hours. There are no time limits and no fees.

Graduates: From July 1, 2012 to June 30, 2013, 184 bachelor's degrees were awarded. The most popular majors were business administration (26%), education (25%), and justics administration (6%). In an average class, 7% graduate in 3 years or less, 34% graduate in 4 years or less, 44% graduate in 5 years or less, and 10% graduate in 6 years or less.

Admissions Contact: Debbie Stennett, Director of Admissions. E-Mail: *admityou@wbu.edu* Web: *www.wbu.edu*

WEST TEXAS A&M UNIVERSITY B-1

Canyon, TX 79016 **(806) 651-2020**
(800) 99-WTAMU; (806) 651-5285

Full-time: 1900 men, 2450 women
Part-time: 550 men, 700 women
Graduate: 550 men, 900 women
Year: semesters, summer session
Application Deadline: open
Freshman Class: n/av
SAT or ACT: required

Faculty: 252, IIA, --$
Ph.D.s: 70%
Student/Faculty: 252
Tuition: $6430 ($15,820)
Room & Board: $6000

COMPETITIVE

West Texas A&M University, a member of the Texas A&M University System and founded in 1910, is a public institution offering programs in the liberal arts and sciences, fine arts, agriculture, nursing, and education. There are 4 undergraduate schools and 1 graduate school. Figures in the above capsule and this profile are approximate. In addition to regional accreditation, WTAMU has baccalaureate program accreditation with ACBSP, CSWE, and NASM. The 2 libraries contain 1.1 million volumes, 1.3 million microform items, and 1555 audio/video tapes/CDs/DVDs, and subscribe to 16,973 periodicals including electronic. Computerized library services include interlibrary loans, database searching, Internet access, and laptop Internet portals. Special learning facilities include a learning resource center, art gallery, natural history museum, radio station, alternative energy institute, electronic learning center, communications disorders center, and nursing learning center. The 135-acre campus is in a small town 17 miles south of Amarillo. Including any residence halls, there are 82 buildings.

Student Life: 90% of undergraduates are from Texas. Others are from 39 states, 26 foreign countries, and Canada. 93% are from public schools. 76% are white; 14% Hispanic. The average age of freshmen is 18; all undergraduates, 24. 36% do not continue beyond their first year; 66% remain to graduate.

Housing: 1520 students can be accommodated in college housing, which includes single-sex and coed dorms. In addition, there are special-interest houses, sorority units within the residence halls, 24-hour quiet areas, and an honors hall. On-campus housing is guaranteed for all 4 years. 82% of students commute. Alcohol is not permitted. All students may keep cars.

Activities: 4% of men belong to 1 local and 4 national fraternities; 4% of women belong to 2 local and 3 national sororities. There are 97 groups on campus, including academic, art, band, cheerleading, choir, chorale, chorus, computers, dance, debate, drama, ethnic, film, forensics, honors, international, jazz band, literary magazine, marching band, musical theater, newspaper, opera, orchestra, photography, political, professional, radio and TV, religious, social, social service, student government, and symphony. Popular campus events include Workathon, RHA Mud Pull, and Buffalo Branding.

Sports: There are 6 intercollegiate sports for men and 6 for women, and 39 intramural sports for men and 39 for women. Facilities include a swimming pool, an 8-lane bowling alley, weight-training rooms, a 20,000-seat stadium, an event center, handball, racquetball, tennis, badminton, basketball, and volleyball courts, a flag football field, and softball fields.

Disabled Students: All of the campus is accessible. Facilities include wheelchair ramps, elevators, special parking, specially equipped rest rooms, special class scheduling, lowered drinking fountains, lowered telephones, and special housing.

Services: Counseling and information services are available, as is tutoring in most subjects, including core curriculum courses. There is a reader service for the blind and remedial math, reading, and writing.

Campus Safety and Security: Measures include 24-hour foot and vehicle patrol, self-defense education, and security escort services. There are shuttle buses, emergency telephones, lighted pathways/sidewalks, and shuttle buses provided by city transport.

Programs of Study: WTAMU confers B.A., B.S., B.A.A.S., B.B.A., B.F.A., B.G.S., B.M., B.S.M.T., and B.S.N. degrees. Master's and doctoral degrees are also awarded. Bachelor's degrees are awarded in AGRICULTURE (agricultural business management, agricultural economics, agriculture, animal science, plant protection (pest management), plant science, and soil science), BIOLOGICAL SCIENCE (biology/biological science, biotechnology, and wildlife biology), BUSINESS (accounting, banking and finance, business administration and management, business economics, management science, and marketing/retailing/merchandising), COMMUNICATIONS AND THE ARTS (applied art, art, broadcasting, dance, dramatic arts, English, graphic design, music, music theory and composition, musical theater, performing arts, public relations, publishing, Spanish, speech/debate/rhetoric, and studio art), COMPUTER AND PHYSICAL SCIENCE (chemistry, computer science, geology, information sciences and systems, mathematics, and physics), EDUCATION (art education, athletic training, business education, drama education, English education, foreign languages education, mathematics education, music education, physical education, reading education, science education, social studies education, and special education), ENGINEERING AND ENVIRONMENTAL DESIGN (emergency/disaster science, engineering technology, environmental science, mechanical engineering, and preengineering), HEALTH PROFESSIONS (allied health, exercise science, medical technology, music therapy, nursing, predentistry, premedicine, prepharmacy, preveterinary science, and speech pathology/audiology), SOCIAL SCIENCE (criminal justice, economics, geography, history, interdisciplinary studies, liberal arts/general studies, political science/government, prelaw, psychology, public administration, social science, social work, and sociology). Education and music are the strongest academically. Education is the largest.

Required: A general education requirement of 46 hours includes courses in analytic reasoning and communication skills, cultural heritage, English, computer literacy, math, science, history, political science, humanities, and sports and exercise sciences. Additional core requirements vary according to major. A minimum 2.0 GPA and 127 credit hours, including at least 36 of advanced work, up to a maximum of 60, 30 of which must be at WTAMU, are required to graduate. At least 33 hours must be earned in residence at WTAMU, including at least 24 of the last 30 hours counted toward a degree.

Special: WTAMU offers work-study programs, a Washington semester, internships, co-op programs, credit by exam, B.A.-B.S. degrees, a general studies degree, interdisciplinary studies in elementary/secondary education fields, nondegree study, and pass/fail options. There are 12 national honor societies, a freshman honors program, and 14 departmental honor programs.

Faculty/Classroom: 56% of faculty are male; 44% are female. 95% teach undergraduates, 47% do research, and 44% do both. Graduate students teach 16% of introductory courses. The average class size in an introductory lecture is 28; in a laboratory, 23; and in a regular course, 26.

Requirements: The SAT or ACT is required. In addition, applicants should have graduated from an accredited secondary school or have a GED. Admission requires graduation in the top 50% of the student's high school class or a minimum composite score of 20 on the ACT or 950 on the SAT. AP and CLEP credits are accepted.

Procedure: Freshmen are admitted to all sessions. Entrance exams should be taken in the fall of the senior year. There are deferred admissions and rolling admissions plans. Application deadlines are open. The application fee is $25. Applications are accepted online.

Transfer: A 2.0 GPA is generally required for transfer students. 30 of 127 credits required for the bachelor's degree must be completed at WTAMU.

Visiting: There are regularly scheduled orientations for prospective students, including a tour of campus, admissions and financial services sessions, selection of a major, and a visit with faculty. There are guides for informal visits, and visitors may sit in on classes and stay overnight. To schedule a visit, contact the Admissions Office.

Financial Aid: The FAFSA is required. Check with the school for current application deadlines.

International Students: The school actively recruits these students. They must take the TOEFL. They must also take the SAT or ACT.

Computers: All students may access the system. There are no time limits.

Admissions Contact: Director of Admissions. A campus DVD is available. E-mail: *admissions@wtamu.edu* Web: *www.wtamu.edu*

WILEY COLLEGE E-2

Marshall, TX 75670 (903) 927-3311
(800) 658-6889; (903) 938-8100

Full-time: 1237 men and women	**Faculty:** n/av
Part-time: n/av	**Ph.D.s:** 63%
Graduate: n/av	**Student/Faculty:** 16 to 1
Year: semesters, summer session	**Tuition:** $9470
Application Deadline: open	**Room & Board:** $6636
Freshman Class: n/av	
SAT or ACT: required	

LESS COMPETITIVE

Wiley College, founded in 1873 as an institution for black students, is affiliated with the United Methodist Church. The college offers programs in the liberal arts, sciences, and teacher training. The figures in the above capsule and in this profile are approximate. The library contains 80,000 volumes and subscribes to 298 periodicals including electronic. The 58-acre campus is in a small town 35 miles west of Shreveport.

Housing: 45% of students commute.

Activities: There are no fraternities or sororities.

Sports: There are 3 intercollegiate sports for men and 3 for women.

Programs of Study: Wiley confers B.A., B.S., and B.B.A. degrees. Bachelor's degrees are awarded in BIOLOGICAL SCIENCE (biology/biological science), BUSINESS (business administration and management, hotel/motel and restaurant management, and office supervision and management), COMMUNICATIONS AND THE ARTS (communications, English, music, and music performance), COMPUTER AND PHYSICAL SCIENCE (chemistry, computer science, mathematics, and physics), EDUCATION (business education, elementary education, English education, mathematics education, music education, physical education, secondary education, social science education, and special education), SOCIAL SCIENCE (history, liberal arts/general studies, philosophy, religion, social science, and sociology).

Required: Core requirements include courses in education, English, humanities, history, religion, science, and math. 2 credits in phys ed and 3 in computer science are required. A 2.0 GPA and 124 semester hours are needed to graduate.

Faculty/Classroom: All teach undergraduates.

Requirements: The SAT or ACT is required. Applicants must be graduates of an accredited secondary school or have scored at least 40 on the GED. A letter of recommendation from a high school counselor or teacher is required. A GPA of 2.0 is required.

Procedure: There are early decision and early admissions plans. Application deadlines are open.

Transfer: Transfer applicants must be in good standing at their last college. 30 of 124 credits required for the bachelor's degree must be completed at Wiley.

Visiting: There are regularly scheduled orientations for prospective students, including campus tours Monday through Friday at 10:30 a.m. and 2:30 p.m. and Saturdays by appointment. To schedule a visit, contact the Office of Admissions.

Financial Aid: Check with the school for current application deadlines.

International Students: They must take the TOEFL.

Computers: All students may access the system. There are no time limits and no fees.

Admissions Contact: Director of Admissions. E-mail: *admissions@wileyc.edu* Web: *www.wileyc.edu*

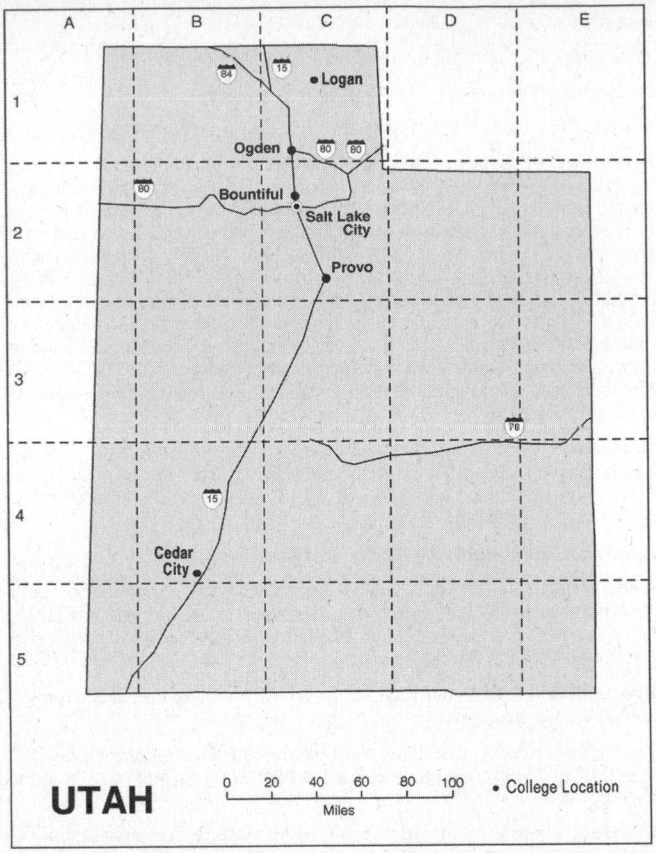

BRIGHAM YOUNG UNIVERSITY C-2

Provo, UT 84602 (801) 422-2500; (801) 422-0005

Full-time: 13,536 men, 11,550 women
Part-time: 1422 men, 1259 women
Graduate: 2021 men, 1335 women
Year: quarters, summer session
Application Deadline: February 15
Freshman Class: 12557 applied, 6895 accepted, 5526 enrolled
ACT: required
Faculty: n/av
Ph.D.s: 98%
Student/Faculty: 23 to 1
Tuition: $5350
Room & Board: $7750

HIGHLY COMPETITIVE

Brigham Young University, founded in 1875, is a private university affiliated with the Church of Jesus Christ of Latter-day Saints. The university follows a semester calendar with spring and summer terms. Tuition figures in this profile are for members of the church. Students who are not members of the Church of Jesus Christ of Latter-day Saints pay twice the tuition amount listed. Living costs are identical for members and non-members. There are 10 undergraduate schools and 1 graduate school. In addition to regional accreditation, BYU has baccalaureate program accreditation with AACSB, ABET, ACCE, ACEJMC, ADA, ASLA, CSAB, CSWE, NASAD, NASDTEC, NASM, NCATE, NLN, and NRPA. The 2 libraries contain 4.0 million volumes, 3.5 million microform items, 304,688 audio/video tapes/CDs/DVDs, and subscribe to 198,871 periodicals including electronic. Computerized library services include interlibrary loans, database searching, Internet access, and Wi-Fi capability. Special learning facilities include an art gallery, natural history museum, planetarium, radio station, TV station, an archeological museum, an earth science museum, reading and writing labs, and math, language, and computer labs. The 557-acre campus is in a suburban area 45 miles south of Salt Lake City. Including any residence halls, there are 330 buildings.

Student Life: 71% of undergraduates are from out of state, mostly the West. Students are from 50 states, 121 foreign countries, and Canada. 86% are White. The average age of freshmen is 19; all undergraduates, 22. 11% do not continue beyond their first year; 77% remain to graduate.

Housing: 8040 students can be accommodated in college housing, which includes single-sex dorms, on-campus apartments, and married student housing. In addition, there are honors houses, language houses, special-interest houses, family housing contracts for 1324 student family residences. On-campus housing is available on a first-come and first-served basis. 80% of students commute. Alcohol is not permitted. All students may keep cars.

Activities: There are no fraternities or sororities. There are 390 groups on campus, including art, band, cheerleading, chess, choir, chorale, chorus, computers, dance, debate, drama, drill team, environmental, ethnic, film, honors, international, jazz band, literary magazine, marching band, musical theater, newspaper, opera, orchestra, pep band, photography, political, professional, radio and TV, religious, social, social service, student government, and symphony. Popular campus events include Fall and Spring Fling and Preference Dances.

Sports: There are 10 intercollegiate sports for men and 11 for women, and 34 intramural sports for men and 32 for women. Facilities include pools, tennis and racquetball courts, gyms, tracks, fields, and a strength and conditioning complex.

Disabled Students: 97% of the campus is accessible. Facilities include wheelchair ramps, elevators, special parking, specially equipped restrooms, special class scheduling, lowered drinking fountains, lowered telephones, special housing.

Services. Counseling and information services are available, as is tutoring in most subjects. There is a reader service for the blind, and remedial math, reading, and writing.

Campus Safety and Security: Measures include, emergency notification system, self-defense education, and security escort services. There are emergency telephones, lighted pathways/sidewalks, a bicycle patrol, academic building security officers from 7 p.m. to 2 a.m., and limited access to dorms.

Programs of Study: BYU confers B.A., B.S., B.F.A., B.G.S., B.M. and B.Mus. degrees. Master's and doctoral degrees are also awarded. Bachelor's degrees are awarded in AGRICULTURE (agricultural business management, environmental studies, plant science, and wildlife management), BIOLOGICAL SCIENCE (biochemistry, bioinformatics, biology/biological science, biophysics, biotechnology, botany, microbiology, molecular biology, neurosciences, nutrition, physiology, plant genetics, and plant physiology), BUSINESS (accounting, business administration and management, management information systems, management science, marketing management, recreation and leisure services, and tourism), COMMUNICATIONS AND THE ARTS (advertising, animation, art, art history and appreciation, audio technology, Chinese, classical languages, classics, communications, comparative literature, dance, dramatic arts, English, fine arts, French, German, graphic design, Greek, illustration, industrial design, Italian, Japanese, jazz, Korean, Latin, linguistics, literature, media arts, music, music performance, music technology, music theory and composition, musical theater, performing arts, photography, Portuguese, public relations, Russian, Spanish, studio art, and visual and performing arts), COMPUTER AND PHYSICAL SCIENCE (actuarial science, astronomy, chemistry, computer science, geology, information sciences and systems, mathematics, physics, and statistics), EDUCATION (art education, dance education, drama education, early childhood education, elementary education, English education, home economics education, mathematics education, music education, science education, social science education, special education, and technical education), ENGINEERING AND ENVIRONMENTAL DESIGN (chemical engineering, city/community/regional planning, civil engineering, computer engineering, construction management, electrical/electronics engineering, electrical/electronics engineering technology, environmental design, food services technology, landscape architecture/design, manufacturing engineering, manufacturing technology, and mechanical engineering), HEALTH PROFESSIONS (clinical science, exercise science, health science, nursing, and speech pathology/audiology), SOCIAL SCIENCE (American studies, anthropology, archeology, Asian/American studies, Asian/Oriental studies, classical/ancient civilization, dietetics, economics, family/consumer studies, food science, geography, history, human development, humanities, international relations, Latin American studies, Middle Eastern studies, Near Eastern studies, philosophy, political science/government, psychology, social work, and sociology). Engineering, accounting and business are the strongest academically. Business, communications and exercise science have the largest enrollments.

Required: To graduate, students must complete 120 semester hours with a minimum GPA of 2.0. All students must take a total of 14 semester hours of religion and 2 hours of phys ed. There are general education requirements in English, advanced writing, foreign language or math, arts and letters, natural sciences, social sciences, and American heritage.

Special: Brigham Young offers cooperative programs, national and international internships, study abroad in 55 countries, a Washington semester, dual majors, nondegree study, and credit for life and work experience. There are 22 national honor societies, including Phi Beta Kappa, a freshman honors program, and 100 departmental honors programs.

Faculty/Classroom: 72% of faculty are male; 28% are female. No introductory courses are taught by graduate students.

Admissions: 55% of the 2013-2014 applicants were accepted. The SAT

scores for the 2013-2014 freshman class were: Critical Reading--6% below 500, 28% between 500 and 599, 43% between 600 and 699, and 23% between 700 and 800; Math--4% below 500, 24% between 500 and 599, 50% between 600 and 699, and 22% between 700 and 800; Writing--10% below 500, 37% between 500 and 599, 41% between 600 and 699, and 12% between 700 and 800. The ACT scores were 2% below 21, 6% between 21 and 23, 20% between 24 and 26, 25% between 27 and 28, and 47% above 28. 80% of the current freshmen were in the top fifth of their class.

Requirements: The ACT is required. Applicants must be graduates of an accredited secondary school. Either the ACT or SAT is required. The GED is accepted. The school recommends that applicants complete 4 years of English, 3 years of math, and 2 courses in foreign language, lab science, history, and literature or writing. Essays and letters of recommendation are required with the application. AP and CLEP credits are accepted. Important factors in the admissions decision are advanced placement or honors courses, recommendations by school officials, and evidence of special talent.

Procedure: Freshmen are admitted to all sessions. Entrance exams should be taken by December of the senior year. There are early admissions, deferred admissions, and rolling admissions plans. Applications should be filed by February 15 for fall entry; October 1 for winter entry; February 15 for spring entry; and February 15 for summer entry, along with a $35 fee. Applications are accepted online.

Transfer: 783 transfer students enrolled in 2012-2013. For applicants, primary consideration will be given to basic general education subjects (English, math, history, and foreign languages) and major subjects. The GPA from those subjects must be near 3.5 to be competitive for admission. 30 credits required for the bachelor's degree must be completed at BYU.

Visiting: There are regularly scheduled orientations for prospective students, including a campus tour, visits with the prospective major's department and advisement center, and an interview with a school relations counselor. There are guides for informal visits and visitors may sit in on classes. To schedule a visit, contact the Admissions Office.

Financial Aid: In 2013-2014, 63% of all full-time freshmen and 69% of continuing full-time students received some form of financial aid. 19% of all full-time freshmen and 42% of continuing full-time students received need-based aid. The average freshman award was $4,990. Need-based scholarships or need-based grants averaged $4,515; need-based self-help aid (loans and jobs) averaged $3,249; non-need-based athletic scholarships averaged $5,168; and other non-need-based awards and non-need-based scholarships averaged $3,641. 44% of undergraduate students work part-time. The FAFSA is required. The deadline for filing freshman financial aid applications for fall entry is June 30.

International Students: There are 1400 international students enrolled. They must take the TOEFL with a minimum score of 550 on the paper-based TOEFL (PBT) or 80 on the Internet-based version (iBT). They must also take the SAT or ACT.

Computers: All students may access the system any time. There are no time limits and no fees.

Graduates: From July 1, 2012 to June 30, 2013, 7177 bachelor's degrees were awarded. The most popular majors were business marketing (13%), biological/life sciences (12%), and education (9%). 430 companies recruited on campus in 2012-2013. In an average class, 22% graduate in 4 years or less, 38% graduate in 5 years or less, and 77% graduate in 6 years or less.

Admissions Contact: Tom Gourley, Director of Admissions Office. E-Mail: *admissions@byu.edu* Web: *www.byu.edu*

SOUTHERN UTAH UNIVERSITY B-4

Cedar City, UT 84720 **(435) 586-7740; (435) 865-8223**

Full-time: 1900 men, 2400 women	**Faculty:** n/av; IIA, --$
Part-time: 300 men, 400 women	**Ph.D.s:** 99%
Graduate: 175 men, 200 women	**Student/Faculty:** n/av
Year: semesters, summer session	**Tuition:** $6,500 ($17,000)
Application Deadline: see profile	**Room & Board:** $8500
Freshman Class: n/av	
SAT or ACT: required	

COMPETITIVE

Southern Utah University, founded in 1897, is part of the Utah System of Higher Education and offers undergraduate degrees in arts and letters, science, education, and business. There are 6 undergraduate schools and 3 graduate schools. Figures in the above capsule and this profile are approximate. In addition to regional accreditation, SUU has baccalaureate program accreditation with AACSB, ACBSP, NASDTEC, NASM, and NLN. The library contains 202,784 volumes, 673,985 microform items, 17,969 audio/video tapes/CDs/DVDs, and subscribes to 1100 periodicals including electronic. Computerized library services include interlibrary loans and database searching. Special learning facilities include a learning resource center, art gallery, natural history museum, planetarium, radio station, and TV station. The 133-acre campus is in a small town 170 miles north of Las Vegas. Including any residence halls, there are 76 buildings.

Student Life: 86% of undergraduates are from Utah. Others are from 45 states, 32 foreign countries, and Canada. 98% are from public schools. 31% claim no religious affiliation. The average age of freshmen is 18; all undergraduates, 23. 41% do not continue beyond their first year; 34% remain to graduate.

Housing: 395 students can be accommodated in college housing, which includes single-sex and coed dorms and on-campus apartments. In addition, there are fraternity houses and sorority houses. On-campus housing is available on a first-come, first-served basis. Priority is given to out-of-town students. 87% of students commute. Alcohol is not permitted. All students may keep cars.

Activities: 4% of men belong to 2 national fraternities; 3% of women belong to 1 local and 2 national sororities. There are 48 groups on campus, including art, bagpipe, band, cheerleading, choir, chorale, chorus, communications, computers, dance, drama, drill team, ethnic, forensics, gay, honors, international, jazz band, literary magazine, marching band, musical theater, newspaper, opera, orchestra, pep band, political, professional, radio and TV, religious, social, social service, student government, symphony, and yearbook. Popular campus events include Founders Day, dances, and service programs.

Sports: There are 7 intercollegiate sports for men and 8 for women, and 13 intramural sports for men and 13 for women. Facilities include a 10,000-seat stadium for football and for track and field, a baseball field, recreation grounds, a 5300-seat special events facility for basketball, volleyball, and gymnastics, tennis and racquetball courts, and large, all-weather practice areas. SUU owns and operates a 1000-acre farm and a 3700-acre ranch.

Disabled Students: 95% of the campus is accessible. Facilities include wheelchair ramps, elevators, special parking, specially equipped rest rooms, special class scheduling, lowered drinking fountains, lowered telephones, and special housing.

Services: Counseling and information services are available, as is tutoring in most subjects. There is a reader service for the blind and remedial math, reading, and writing.

Campus Safety and Security: Measures include self-defense education and security escort services. There are emergency telephones and lighted pathways/sidewalks.

Programs of Study: SUU confers B.A., B.S., and B.I.S. degrees. Associate and master's degrees are also awarded. Bachelor's degrees are awarded in AGRICULTURE (agriculture), BIOLOGICAL SCIENCE (biology/biological science), BUSINESS (accounting, banking and finance, business administration and management, marketing management, and marketing/retailing/merchandising), COMMUNICATIONS AND THE ARTS (art, communications, dance, dramatic arts, English, French, German, music, and Spanish), COMPUTER AND PHYSICAL SCIENCE (chemistry, computer science, geology, information sciences and systems, and mathematics), EDUCATION (art education, athletic training, business education, dance education, drama education, elementary education, English education, foreign languages education, mathematics education, music education, physical education, science education, social science education, social studies education, and special education), ENGINEERING AND ENVIRONMENTAL DESIGN (construction management and engineering technology), SOCIAL SCIENCE (criminal justice, economics, family/consumer studies, history, interdisciplinary studies, political science/government, psychology, and sociology). Business, science, and education are the strongest academically. Business and education have the largest enrollments.

Required: To graduate, all students must complete at least 122 credit hours with a minimum 2.0 GPA. Students must satisfy general education, major, minor, and basic skills requirements, including 4 courses each in social and physical sciences, 2 each in English, fine arts, and humanities, 1 each in math, phys ed, and communications, and a course in either history, political science, or economics to fulfill the U.S. government requirement. Other courses required for graduation include computer literacy and philosophy.

Special: SUU offers co-op programs with Weber State University, work-study programs, study abroad, dual majors, student-designed majors leading to a B.I.S. degree, and internships with government officials in Washington, D.C. Other programs offered include distance learning, ESL, independent study, liberal arts/career combinations, a teacher certification program, and weekend college. There are 3 national honor societies and 3 departmental honors programs.

Faculty/Classroom: 66% of faculty are male; 34% are female. All teach undergraduates, and 65% both teach and do research. No introductory courses are taught by graduate students. The average class size in an introductory lecture is 29 and in a laboratory is 14.

Requirements: The SAT or ACT is required; the ACT is recommended. In addition, applicants should be graduates of an accredited secondary school or have a GED and should have completed 4 years of English, (composition and literature emphasis), 3 of math, at least 2 of which are elementary algebra or beyond, 3 each of biological/physical sciences (1 with a lab) and social studies including U.S. history/government, and 2 years of a foreign language. A GPA of 2.0 is required. AP and CLEP credits are accepted.

Procedure: Freshmen are admitted to all sessions. There are early admissions, deferred admissions, and rolling admissions plans. Check with the school for current application deadlines. The application fee is $45. Applications are accepted online.

Transfer: Applicants must submit transcripts from previously attended colleges and have a minimum 2.25 GPA in college courses and a 2.0 high school GPA. ACT scores as well as high school transcripts are required from students who have not completed English or math courses at another institution or who have not completed a minimum of 30 credit hours at an institution of higher education. 30 of 122 credits required for the bachelor's degree must be completed at SUU.

Visiting: There are regularly scheduled orientations for prospective students, including campus tours, which can be arranged by appointment. There are guides for informal visits, and visitors may sit in on classes and stay overnight. To schedule a visit, contact the Director of School Relations.

Financial Aid: The FAFSA and the college's own financial statement are required. Check with the school for current application deadlines.

International Students: The school actively recruits these students. They must take the TOEFL. They must also take the SAT or ACT.

Computers: All students may access the system.

Admissions Contact: Director of Admissions. E-mail: *adminfo@suu.edu* Web: *www.suu.edu*

UNIVERSITY OF UTAH C-2

Salt Lake City, UT 84112 — 801-581-8761; 800-685-8856; 801-585-3257

Full-time: 9709 men, 7809 women	**Faculty:** 1359; I, -$
Part-time: 4097 men, 3225 women	**Ph.D.s:** 80%
Graduate: 4215 men, 3333 women	**Student/Faculty:** 13 to 1
Year: semesters, summer session	**Tuition:** $6763 ($21,389)
Application Deadline: April 1	**Room & Board:** $6699

Freshman Class: 11118 applied, 9187 accepted, 3494 enrolled

SAT CR/M/W: 580/580/550 **ACT:** 24 **VERY COMPETITIVE**

The flagship of the Utah System of Higher Education, the University of Utah was founded in 1850 and offers graduate and undergraduate programs in various disciplines. There are 14 undergraduate schools and 15 graduate schools. In addition to regional accreditation, U of U has baccalaureate program accreditation with AACSB, ABET, ACEJMC, ACPE, APTA, CSWE, NAAB, NASM, and NLN. The 3 libraries contain 4.2 million volumes, 3.0 million microform items, and 96,897 audio/video tapes/CDs/DVDs, and subscribe to 86,266 periodicals including electronic. Computerized library services include interlibrary loans, database searching, Internet access, and Wi-Fi capability. Special learning facilities include an art gallery, natural history museum, radio station, TV station, an arboretum. The 1535-acre campus is in an urban area Salt Lake City. Including any residence halls, there are 354 buildings.

Student Life: 82% of undergraduates are from Utah. Others are from 50 states, 118 foreign countries, and Canada. 95% are from public schools. 72% are White. The average age of freshmen is 19; all undergraduates, 24. 12% do not continue beyond their first year; 59% remain to graduate.

Housing: 4827 students can be accommodated in college housing, which includes single-sex and coed dorms, on-campus apartments, off-campus apartments, and married student housing. In addition, there are honors houses, special-interest houses, fraternity houses, sorority houses, theme houses, limited visitation and 24-hour quiet housing. On-campus housing is available on a first-come, first-served basis. 86% of students commute. Alcohol is not permitted. All students may keep cars.

Activities: 3% of men belong to 8 national fraternities; 4% of women belong to 6 national sororities. There are 487 groups on campus, including art, band, cheerleading, chess, choir, chorale, chorus, computers, dance, debate, drama, drill team, drum and bugle corps, environmental, ethnic, film, forensics, gay, honors, international, jazz band, marching band, musical theater, newspaper, opera, orchestra, pep band, photography, political, professional, radio and TV, religious, social, social service, student government, and symphony. Popular campus events include Redfest, Plazafest, and Welcome Week.

Sports: There are 7 intercollegiate sports for men and 10 for women, and 11 intramural sports for men and 10 for women. Facilities include a 45,635-seat stadium, a 15,500-seat basketball arena, 6 indoor gyms, indoor tennis courts, a sand volleyball court, 3 indoor swimming pools, a gymnastics room, 5 weight rooms, 19 handball/racquetball/squash courts, a 200-meter indoor track, 400-meter outdoor track, a disc golf course, 3 outdoor playing fields, and a 10-lane bowling alley.

Disabled Students: All of the campus is accessible. Facilities include wheelchair ramps, elevators, special parking, specially equipped restrooms, special class scheduling, lowered drinking fountains, lowered telephones, and special housing.

Services: Counseling and information services are available, as is tutoring in most subjects. There is a reader service for the blind, and remedial math and writing. There are also support services for the deaf, including readers, scribes, tutors, and interpreters. The on-campus Center for Disability Services directs students to on-campus services for people with disabilities and provides a supportive environment so they can achieve their academic goals.

Campus Safety and Security: Measures include an emergency notification system, self-defense education, and security escort services. There are shuttle buses, emergency telephones, lighted pathways/sidewalks, and controlled access to dorms/residences.

Programs of Study: U of U confers B.A., B.F.A., B.Mus., B.S., B.S.W. and B.U.S. degrees. Master's and doctoral degrees are also awarded. Bachelor's degrees are awarded in AGRICULTURE (environmental studies), BIOLOGICAL SCIENCE (biology/biological science), BUSINESS (accounting, business administration and management, entrepreneurial studies, finance, management information systems, management science, marketing management, marketing/retailing/merchandising, operations management, and recreation and leisure services), COMMUNICATIONS AND THE ARTS (Arabic, art history, art, art history and appreciation, ballet, Chinese, classics, communications, comparative literature, dance, dramatic arts, English, film arts, fine arts, French, German, Hebrew, Japanese, linguistics, media arts, music, Russian, Spanish, theatre arts, and visual and performing arts), COMPUTER AND PHYSICAL SCIENCE (applied mathematics, atmospheric sciences and meteorology, chemistry, computer science, earth science, environmental geology, geology, geophysics and seismology, geoscience, information sciences and systems, mathematics, and physics), EDUCATION (art education, elementary education, English education, health education, social science education, special education, and teaching English as a second/foreign language (TESOL/TEFOL)), ENGINEERING AND ENVIRONMENTAL DESIGN (architecture, bioengineering, biomedical engineering, chemical engineering, civil engineering, computer engineering, electrical/electronics engineering, engineering, geological engineering, materials engineering, materials science, mechanical engineering, metallurgical engineering, mining and mineral engineering, and urban planning technology), HEALTH PROFESSIONS (exercise science, medical laboratory science, medical laboratory technology, medical science, nursing, occupational therapy, pharmacy, physical therapy, public health, and speech pathology/audiology), SOCIAL SCIENCE (anthropology, architectural studies, Asian/Oriental studies, behavioral science, consumer services, economics, ethnic studies, family/consumer studies, gender studies, geography, history, human development, humanities, international studies, Latin American studies, Middle Eastern studies, parks and recreation management, peace studies, philosophy, political science/government, psychology, social science, social work, sociology, urban studies, and women's studies). Biology, business administration, exercise and sport science, communication, and economics have the largest enrollments.

Required: To graduate, all students must satisfy requirements in the general education and intellectual exploration programs. General education requirements include 1 course each in American institutions and lower-division writing; 2 in quantitative reasoning; and 2 each in fine arts, humanities, physical science, and social science, excluding the major area. Students must complete at least 122 credit hours, with 45 to 60 in the major. A minimum 2.0 GPA is required.

Special: The university offers numerous opportunities for cooperative programs, cross-registration through the Western Undergraduate Exchange (WUC) as part of the Western Interstate Commission for Higher Education (WICHE), study abroad in more than 30 countries, internships, work-study and accelerated degree programs, and B.A.-B.S. degrees. Also available are the general studies degree, a Washington semester, student-designed and dual majors, credit for telecourses and military experience, nondegree study, and pass/fail options. There are 40 national honor societies, including Phi Beta Kappa, a freshman honors program, and 27 departmental honors programs.

Faculty/Classroom: 58% of faculty are male; 42% are female. Graduate students teach 23% of introductory courses. The average class size in an introductory lecture is 54; in a laboratory is 21; and in a regular course is 44.

Admissions: 83% of the 2013-2014 applicants were accepted. The SAT scores for the 2013-2014 freshman class were: Critical Reading--18% below 500, 42% between 500 and 599, 30% between 600 and 699, and 10% between 700 and 800; Math--19% below 500, 36% between 500 and 599, 34% between 600 and 699, and 11% between 700 and 800; Writing--25% below 500, 42% between 500 and 599, 28% between 600 and 699, and 5% between 700 and 800. The ACT scores were 20% below 21, 23% between 21 and 23, 26% between 24 and 26, 12% between 27 and 28, and 19% above 28. 41% of the current freshmen were in the top fifth of their class; 70% were in the top two fifths.

Requirements: The ACT is required. The SAT is accepted. Applicants must be graduates of an accredited secondary school or have the GED. Academic credits required include 4 years each of English and electives, 2 years each of foreign language and math, 3 years of biological and/or physical science, and 1 year of history. A GPA of 2.6 is required. AP and CLEP credits are accepted. Important factors in the admissions decision are advanced placement or honors courses, leadership record, and personality/intangible qualities.

Procedure: Freshmen are admitted fall, spring, and summer. Entrance exams should be taken in the junior year of high school. There are deferred admissions and rolling admissions plans. Applications should be filed by April 1 for fall entry; November 1 for spring entry; and March 15 for summer entry, along with a $45 fee. Notification is sent on a rolling basis. Applications are accepted online.

Transfer: 2183 transfer students enrolled in 2012-2013. Transfer students must have completed at least 45 quarter (30 semester) hours with a minimum 2.6 GPA. 30 of 122 credits required for the bachelor's degree must be completed at U of U.

Visiting: There are regularly scheduled orientations for prospective students, including an information session with an admissions counselor to discuss academic and student involvement opportunities, scholarships, financial aid, admissions requirements, and deadlines, along with a campus tour and tour of residence halls. If time permits, prospective students are encouraged to meet with academic advisers on various majors, visit classrooms, and stay overnight in a residence hall. There are guides for informal visits, visitors may sit in on classes, and stay overnight. To schedule a visit, contact The Office of Admissions, Welcome Center at (801) 581-6295.

Financial Aid: In 2013-2014, 42% of all full-time freshmen and 43% of continuing full-time students received some form of financial aid. 34% of all full-time freshmen and 38% of continuing full-time students received need-based aid. The average freshman award was $14,194. Need-based scholarships or need-based grants averaged $7,065 ($32,378 maximum); need-based self-help aid (loans and jobs) averaged $6,685 ($25,192 maximum); non-need-based athletic scholarships averaged $18,708 ($38,466 maximum); and other non-need-based awards and non-need-based scholarships averaged $6,945 ($26,654 maximum). 6% of undergraduate students work part-time. Average annual earnings from campus work are $3500. The average financial indebtedness of the 2013 graduate was $20,796. The FAFSA and the college's own financial statement are required. The priority date for freshman financial aid applications for fall entry is March 15.

International Students: There are 1505 international students enrolled. They must take the TOEFL with a minimum score of 550 on the paper-based TOEFL (PBT) or 80 on the Internet-based version (iBT). They must also take the SAT or ACT.

Computers: All students may access the system 24 hours per day. There are no time limits and no fees.

Graduates: From July 1, 2012 to June 30, 2013, 4919 bachelor's degrees were awarded. The most popular majors were mass communications (6%), psychology (6%), and economics (5%). 230 companies recruited on campus in 2012-2013. In an average class, 22% graduate in 4 years or less, 46% graduate in 5 years or less, and 59% graduate in 6 years or less.

Admissions Contact: Matthew Lopez, Director of Admissions. E-Mail: *admissions@utah.edu* Web: *www.admissions.utah.edu*

UTAH STATE UNIVERSITY — C-1

Logan, UT 84322 (435) 797-1079
(800) 488-8108; (435) 797-3708

Full-time: 7436 men, 7824 women	**Faculty:** 750; I, --$
Part-time: 3780 men, 5345 women	**Ph.D.s:** 80%
Graduate: 1508 men, 1919 women	**Student/Faculty:** 22 to 1
Year: semesters, summer session	**Tuition:** $6183 ($17,886)
Application Deadline: April 1	**Room & Board:** $5620
Freshman Class: 10935 applied, 10768 accepted, 3970 enrolled	
SAT: recommended **ACT:** 23	**COMPETITIVE**

Utah State University, founded in 1888, is a public institution that offers degree programs in the liberal arts and sciences, agriculture and natural resources, engineering, business, education, fine arts, music, family life, and the sciences. The figures in the above capsule and in this profile are approximate. There are 8 undergraduate schools and one graduate school. In addition to regional accreditation, USU has baccalaureate program accreditation with AACSB, ABET, ADA, AHEA, ASLA, CSWE, FIDER, NASM, NCATE, NRPA, and SAF. The 3 libraries contain 1.5 million volumes, 2.7 million microform items, 18,027 audio/video tapes/CDs/DVDs, and subscribe to 10,281 periodicals including electronic. Computerized library services include interlibrary loans, database searching, Internet access, and Wi-Fi capability. Special learning facilities include an art gallery, natural history museum, radio station, a laboratory school, a historical farm, a fine arts center, and a developmental center for people who are disabled. The 332-acre campus is in a small town 86 miles north of Salt Lake City. Including any residence halls, there are 104 buildings.

Student Life: 76% of undergraduates are from Utah. Others are from 50 states, 88 foreign countries, and Canada. 75% are White; 12% race unknown. The average age of freshmen is 19.2; all undergraduates, 23.8. 28% do not continue beyond their first year; 52% remain to graduate.

Housing: 3301 students can be accommodated in college housing, which includes single-sex dorms, on-campus apartments, and married student housing. In addition, there are honors houses, special-interest houses, fraternity houses, and sorority houses. On-campus housing is available on a first-come, first-served basis. Alcohol is not permitted. All students may keep cars.

Activities: 2% of men belong to 1 local and 5 national fraternities; 2% of women belong to 1 local and 3 national sororities. There are 225 groups on campus, including art, bagpipe, band, cheerleading, choir, chorale, chorus, computers, dance, drama, drill team, environmental, ethnic, film, gay, honors, international, jazz band, literary magazine, marching band, musical theater, newspaper, opera, orchestra, pep band, photography, political, professional, radio and TV, religious, social, social service, student government, and symphony. Popular campus events include Festival of the American West, Halloween Howl, Homecoming, and A-Day.

Sports: There are 7 intercollegiate sports for men and 9 for women, and 23 intramural sports for men and 23 for women. Facilities include 5 gyms, indoor and outdoor tennis courts, 2 swimming pools, 40 acres of grass for outdoor sports, a field house, and golf and skiing areas. The campus stadium seats 30,257, and the largest auditorium seats 10,000.

Disabled Students: 97% of the campus is accessible. Facilities include wheelchair ramps, elevators, special parking, specially equipped restrooms, special class scheduling, lowered drinking fountains, lowered telephones. special phones to receive calls from the deaf, and a disability resource center.

Services: Counseling and information services are available, as is tutoring in most subjects. There is a reader service for the blind, and remedial math, reading, and writing. There is also a writing lab and a tutor room.

Campus Safety and Security: Measures include self-defense education, and security escort services. There are shuttle buses, emergency telephones, lighted pathways/sidewalks, and campus police.

Programs of Study: USU confers B.A., B.S., B.F.A., B.I.D., B.L.A. and B.M. degrees. Associate, master's, and doctoral degrees are also awarded. Bachelor's degrees are awarded in AGRICULTURE (agricultural business management, agricultural economics, animal science, dairy science, forestry and related sciences, international agriculture, natural resource management, plant science, range/farm management, soil science, and wildlife management), BIOLOGICAL SCIENCE (biochemistry, biology/biological science, and microbiology), BUSINESS (accounting, banking and finance, business administration and management, business economics, fashion merchandising, international business management, management information systems, marketing/retailing/merchandising, and personnel management), COMMUNICATIONS AND THE ARTS (dance, dramatic arts, English, fine arts, French, German, journalism, music, and Spanish), COMPUTER AND PHYSICAL SCIENCE (chemistry, computer science, earth science, geology, information sciences and systems, mathematics, physics, and statistics), EDUCATION (agricultural education, art education, business education, early childhood education, elementary education, foreign languages education, health education, home economics education, industrial arts education, mathematics education, music education, physical education, science education, secondary education, and special education), ENGINEERING AND ENVIRONMENTAL DESIGN (agricultural engineering, civil engineering, electrical/electronics engineering, engineering, environmental science, industrial engineering, industrial engineering technology, interior design, landscape architecture/design, and mechanical engineering), HEALTH PROFESSIONS (medical laboratory technology, music therapy, predentistry, premedicine, public health, speech pathology/audiology, and veterinary science), SOCIAL SCIENCE (American studies, child care/child and family studies, economics, food science, geography, history, home economics, human development, international relations, liberal arts/general studies, parks and recreation management, philosophy, political science/government, prelaw, psychology, social work, and sociology). Natural resources, engineering, and special education are the strongest academically. Humanities, business, education have the largest enrollments.

Required: The core curriculum of 30 semester credits includes at least 6 of writing; the total number of credits required for graduation is 120. Students must maintain a minimum GPA of 2.5. The number of credits required in the major varies, but there is a minimum of 40 in major classes.

Special: Internships are available in most departments through the Cooperative Education Program. The National Student Exchange Program allows students to cross-register in designated institutions and programs, and the International Student Exchange Program enables students to study abroad. There is also cross-registration with the University of the Americas of Mexico. A general studies degree and student-designed majors are available. Nondegree study, work-study programs, co-op programs, B.A.-B.S. degrees, pass/fail options, and credit for military experience are offered. There are 11 national honor societies, a freshman honors program, and 35 departmental honors programs.

Faculty/Classroom: 62% of faculty are male; 38% are female. Graduate students teach 5% of introductory courses. The average class size in an introductory lecture is 35; in a laboratory is 20; and in a regular course is 25.

Admissions: 98% of the 2013-2014 applicants were accepted. The ACT scores were 23% below 21, 27% between 21 and 23, 23% between 24 and 26, 11% between 27 and 28, and 16% above 28. 37% of the current freshmen were in the top fifth of their class; 74% were in the top two fifths. 168 freshmen graduated first in their class.

Requirements: The ACT is required. The SAT is recommended. The ACT is preferred. Students should graduate from an accredited secondary school with 15 academic units, including 4 in English, 3 each in math and science, and 1 in social sciences. GED equivalency is accepted, provided ACT scores are 19 or higher. Students not meeting entrance requirements may be considered for admission on a provisional basis. A GPA of 2.7 is required. AP and CLEP credits are accepted. Important factors in the admissions decision are evidence of special talent, parents or siblings attended your school, and recommendations by school officials.

Procedure: Freshmen are admitted to all sessions. Entrance exams should be taken in the spring of the junior year. There are deferred admissions and rolling admissions plans. Applications should be filed by April 1 for fall entry; October 1 for spring entry; and April 1 for summer entry, along with a $40 fee. Applications are accepted online.

Transfer: 1076 transfer students enrolled in 2012-2013. A minimum 2.2 GPA, higher for some majors, is required for transfer students. Those applicants with fewer than 45 credits must also submit ACT scores. 30 of 120 credits required for the bachelor's degree must be completed at USU.

Visiting: There are regularly scheduled orientations for prospective students, consisting of a campus tour, including a meeting with an academic adviser, lunch, and a housing tour, available at 10:30 a.m. and 1:30 p.m., September to May, and 1:30 p.m., June to August. There are guides for informal visits, visitors may sit in on classes, and stay overnight. To schedule a visit, contact Admissions Office.

Financial Aid: In 2013-2014, 51% of all full-time freshmen and 57% of continuing full-time students received some form of financial aid. 44% of all full-time freshmen and 50% of continuing full-time students received need-based aid. The average freshman award was $8,137. Need-based scholarships or need-based grants averaged $6,389; need-based self-help aid (loans and jobs) averaged $5,654; non-need-based athletic scholarships averaged $5,837; and other non-need-based awards and non-need-based scholarships averaged $1,876. 21% of undergraduate students work part-time. Average annual earnings from campus work are $3200. The average financial indebtedness of the 2013 graduate was $15,200. The FAFSA and Federal Tax Forms are required. The priority date for freshman financial aid applications for fall entry is December 1. The deadline for filing freshman financial aid applications for fall entry is February 1.

International Students: There are 492 international students enrolled. They must take the TOEFL with a minimum score of 525 on the paper-based TOEFL (PBT) or 71 on the Internet-based version (iBT) or take the MELAB. The TOEFL is preferred.

Computers: All students may access the system 24 hours a day, 7 days a week. There are no time limits. The fee is $10 to 27.

Graduates: From July 1, 2012 to June 30, 2013, 3557 bachelor's degrees were awarded. The most popular majors were communicative disorders and deaf education (11%), economics (7%), and interdisciplinary studies (5%). 225 companies recruited on campus in 2012-2013. In an average class, 52% graduate in 6 years or less.

Admissions Contact: Katie Nielsen, Director of Admissions Office. E-Mail: *admit@usu.edu* Web: *www.usu.edu*

UTAH SYSTEM OF HIGHER EDUCATION

WEBER STATE UNIVERSITY C-1

Ogden, UT 84408 **(801) 626-7670; (801) 626-6747**

Full-time: 5774 men, 6010 women	**Faculty:** 439; IIA, --$
Part-time: 6407 men, 7677 women	**Ph.D.s:** 82%
Graduate: 365 men, 299 women	**Student/Faculty:** 22 to 1
Year: semesters, summer session	**Tuition:** $4761 ($12,858)
Application Deadline: August 21	**Room & Board:** $6600

Freshman Class: 5561 applied, 5561 accepted, 2954 enrolled

ACT: 21

Weber State University provides associate, baccalaureate and master degree programs in liberal arts, sciences, technical and professional fields. Encouraging freedom of expression and valuing diversity, the university provides excellent educational experiences for students through extensive personal contact among faculty, staff and students in and out of the classroom. Through academic programs, research, artistic expression, public service and community-based learning, the university serves as an educational, cultural and economic leader for the region. There are 7 undergraduate schools and 11 graduate schools. In addition to regional accreditation, WSU has baccalaureate program accreditation with AACSB, ABET, ACCE, ADA, CSWE, NASAD, NASM, NCATE, and NLN. The library contains 708,606 volumes, 623,973 microform items, and 22,957 audio/video tapes/CDs/DVDs, and subscribes to 793 periodicals including electronic. Computerized library services include interlibrary loans, database searching, and Internet access. Special learning facilities include an art gallery, natural history museum, planetarium, radio station, TV station, and a working crime lab. The 526-acre campus is in an urban area located in the foothills of the Wasatch Mountains, 33 miles north of Salt Lake City. Including any residence halls, there are 61 buildings.

Student Life: 92% of undergraduates are from Utah. Others are from 50 states, 45 foreign countries, and Canada. 99% are from public schools. 54% are White; 32% race unknown.. The average age of freshmen is 23; all undergraduates, 26. 26% do not continue beyond their first year.

Housing: 864 students can be accommodated in college housing, which includes single-sex and coed dorms, on-campus apartments, and married student housing. On-campus housing is guaranteed for all 4 years, is available on a first-come, first-served basis. 97% of students commute. Alcohol is not permitted. All students may keep cars.

Activities: There are 229 groups on campus, including art, band, cheerleading, chess, choir, chorale, chorus, communications, computers, dance, debate, drama, drill team, drum and bugle corps, environmental, ethnic, forensics, gay, honors, international, jazz band, literary magazine, marching band, musical theater, newspaper, opera, orchestra, pep band, photography, political, professional, radio and TV, religious, social, social service, student government, symphony, and The Latter-day Saint Student Association (LDSSA) is established by the Ogden Institute of Religion to help students attending a Weber State University have a balanced secular and spiritual educational experience during their years of formal education.. Popular campus events include homecoming, graduation, and student elections.

Sports: There are 5 intercollegiate sports for men and 7 for women, and 8 intramural sports for men and 8 for women. Facilities include Weber State University is home to many athletic and recreation facilities including: an indoor track, a strength-training center, indoor basketball and volleyball courts, group fitness areas, the Swenson Pool, racquetball and tennis courts, the 17,000-seat Wildcat Stadium, the 11,592-seat Dee Events Center, the 7,800-seat Val A. Browning Center for the Performing Arts, outdoor playing fields, fitness centers located at University Village and Davis Campus, a 1-mile jogging trail, and the Weber Rocks Climbing Wall.

Disabled Students: 99% of the campus is accessible. Facilities include wheelchair ramps, elevators, special parking, specially equipped restrooms, special class scheduling, lowered drinking fountains, lowered telephones, and special housing.

Services: Counseling and information services are available, as is tutoring in every subject. There is a reader service for the blind, and remedial math, reading, and writing. Translators are offered for the hearing impaired.

Campus Safety and Security: Measures include self-defense education, and security escort services. There are shuttle buses, emergency telephones, and lighted pathways/sidewalks.

Programs of Study: WSU confers B.A., B.S., B.F.A., B.I.S., B.M. and B.M.E. degrees. Associate and master's degrees are also awarded. Bachelor's degrees are awarded in BIOLOGICAL SCIENCE (biology/biological science, botany, microbiology, and zoology), BUSINESS (accounting, banking and finance, business administration and management, business economics, human resources, international economics, management information systems, marketing management, personnel management, purchasing/inventory management, and supply chain management), COMMUNICATIONS AND THE ARTS (art, communications, dance, dramatic arts, English, fine arts, French, German, graphic design, journalism, media arts, music, music performance, musical theater, photography, piano/organ, public relations, Spanish, theatre arts, visual and performing arts, and voice), COMPUTER AND PHYSICAL SCIENCE (chemistry, computer programming, computer science, earth science, geology, information sciences and systems, mathematics, physical sciences, and physics), EDUCATION (art education, athletic training, business education, early childhood education, education, elementary education, English education, foreign languages education, health education, mathematics education, music education, physical education, science education, secondary education, social science education, special education, and teaching English as a second/foreign language (TESOL/TEFOL)), ENGINEERING AND ENVIRONMENTAL DESIGN (automotive technology, computer engineering, construction management, electrical/electronics engineering, electrical/electronics engineering technology, environmental science, interior design, manufacturing engineering, manufacturing technology, mechanical engineering technology, plastics engineering, and plastics technology), HEALTH PROFESSIONS (clinical science, dental hygiene, health care administration, nursing, radiation therapy, radiograph medical technology, radiological science, and respiratory therapy), SOCIAL SCIENCE (anthropology, child care/child and family studies, criminal justice, early childhood studies, economics, family/consumer studies, geography, gerontology, history, interdisciplinary studies, liberal arts/general studies, philosophy, political science/government, psychology, social work, and sociology). Keyboard performance/pedagogy, master of taxation, and vocal performance/pedagogy are the strongest academically. Nursing, business administration, and accounting have the largest enrollments.

Required: To graduate, students must demonstrate math competency and complete courses in government/history, English, humanities, math, biological/physical sciences, and social sciences. At least 120 semester credit hours, with 45 at the upper-division level, and a minimum GPA of 2.0 are required. Hours in the major and distribution requirements vary with the degree.

Special: Weber State University offers co-op programs and internships in many majors, a Washington semester, study abroad in Mexico and England, work-study programs with community businesses, B.A.-B.S. degrees, dual majors in many combinations, student-designed majors resulting in a B.I.S. degree, a general studies degree, credit for military experience, non-degree study, and pass/fail options. There are 20 national honor societies, a freshman honors program, and 17 departmental honors programs.

Faculty/Classroom: 53% of faculty are male; 47% are female. All teach undergraduates. No introductory courses are taught by graduate students. The average class size in an introductory lecture is 34 and in a laboratory is 26.

Admissions: 100% of the 2013-2014 applicants were accepted. The ACT scores were 46% below 21, 25% between 21 and 23, 18% between 24 and 26, 7% between 27 and 28, and 5% above 28.

Requirements: The ACT is recommended. Applicants must be graduates of an accredited secondary school or have a GED. Other requirements vary by department. Out-of-state residents must have a minimum high school GPA of 2.0. AP and CLEP credits are accepted.

Procedure: Freshmen are admitted to all sessions. Entrance exams should be taken Junior or senior year of high school. There are early admissions, deferred admissions, and rolling admissions plans. Applications should be filed by August 21 for fall entry, along with a $30 fee. Applications are accepted online.

Transfer: 1249 transfer students enrolled in 2012-2013. Transfer students must submit official transcripts from previously attended colleges or universities and have a minimum GPA of 2.0. 30 of 120 credits required for the bachelor's degree must be completed at WSU.

Visiting: There are regularly scheduled orientations for prospective students. There are guides for informal visits, visitors may sit in on classes, and stay overnight. To schedule a visit, contact Laura Albright at (801) 626-6050.

Financial Aid: In 2013-2014, 77% of all full-time freshmen and 72% of continuing full-time students received some form of financial aid. 47% of all full-time freshmen and 55% of continuing full-time students received need-based aid. The average freshman award was $6,154. Need-based scholarships or need-based grants averaged $3,999 ($9,273 maximum); need-based self-help aid (loans and jobs) averaged $3,492 ($18,647 maximum); non-need-based athletic scholarships averaged $8,403 ($20,024 maximum); and other non-need-based awards and non-need-based scholarships averaged $3,601 ($26,483 maximum). 1% of undergraduate students work part-time. Average annual earnings from campus work are $8514. The FAFSA and the college's own financial statement are required. The deadline for filing freshman financial aid applications for fall entry is March 1.

International Students: There are 441 international students enrolled. The school actively recruits these students.

Computers: All students may access the system. There are no time limits and no fees.

Graduates: From July 1, 2012 to June 30, 2013, 2157 bachelor's degrees were awarded. The most popular majors were teacher education (8%), sales and service technology (7%), and nursing (5%). In an average class, 8% graduate in 4 years or less, 23% graduate in 5 years or less, and 43% graduate in 6 years or less.

Admissions Contact: Scott Teichert, Director of Admissions. E-Mail: *ScottTeichert@weber.edu* Web: *www.weber.edu*

WESTMINSTER COLLEGE C-2

Salt Lake City, UT 84105 (801) 832-2200
(800) 748-4753; (801) 832-3101

Full-time: 1020 men, 1276 women	**Faculty:** 147; IIB, av$
Part-time: 138 men, 115 women	**Ph.D.s:** 71%
Graduate: 413 men, 396 women	**Student/Faculty:** 10 to 1
Year: semesters, summer session	**Tuition:** $27,682
Application Deadline: rolling	**Room & Board:** $8184
Freshman Class: 3414 applied, 2321 accepted, 513 enrolled	
SAT CR/M: 550/560	**ACT:** 25 **VERY COMPETITIVE**

Westminster College, founded in 1875, is a private, comprehensive, liberal arts institution offering undergraduate programs through the Bill and Vieve Gore school of business, the St. Mark's Westminster school of nursing and health sciences, the School of arts and sciences and education. There are 4 undergraduate schools and 4 graduate schools. In addition to regional accreditation, has baccalaureate program accreditation with ACBSP and NLN. The library contains 123,552 volumes, 256,182 microform items, 5,733 audio/video tapes/CDs/DVDs, and subscribes to 20,117 periodicals including electronic. Computerized library services include interlibrary loans, database searching, Internet access, and laptop Internet portals. Special learning facilities include a learning resource center, a multipurpose theater, networked classrooms, a flight simulation center, a center for financial analysis, and a health and wellness recreation center. The 27-acre campus is in an urban area 6 miles southeast of downtown Salt Lake City. Including any residence halls, there are 31 buildings.

Student Life: 51% of undergraduates are from Utah. Others are from 47 states, 37 foreign countries, and Canada. 81% are from public schools. 71% are white. 77% claim no religious affiliation; 18% Buddhist, Greek Orthodox, Christian, LDS, Presbyterian, and Episcopal. The average age of freshmen is 18.21; all undergraduates, 21.93. 20% do not continue beyond their first year; 66% remain to graduate.

Housing: 647 students can be accommodated in college housing, which includes single-sex and coed dorms, on-campus apartments, and off-campus apartments. On-campus housing is guaranteed for the freshman year only, is available on a first-come, first-served basis, and is available on a lottery system for upperclassmen. Priority is given to out-of-town students. 74% of students commute. All students may keep cars.

Activities: There are no fraternities or sororities. There are 60 groups on campus, including art, choir, chorale, chorus, computers, dance, debate, drama, environmental, ethnic, film, gay, honors, international, jazz band, literary magazine, musical theater, newspaper, orchestra, photography, political, professional, religious, social service, student government, and symphony. Popular campus events include Westminster welcome week, pizza tasting, and halloween dance.

Sports: There are 8 intercollegiate sports for men and 9 for women, and 10 intramural sports for men and 10 for women. Facilities include a health and wellness recreation center, including basketball courts, a weight room, a lap pool, racquetball courts, a dance studio, 2 floors of cardio equipment, and a climbing wall.

Disabled Students: 99% of the campus is accessible. Facilities include wheelchair ramps, elevators, special parking, specially equipped restrooms, special class scheduling, lowered drinking fountains, lowered telephones, and special housing.

Services: Counseling and information services are available, as is tutoring in most subjects. There is a reader service for the blind, and remedial math, reading, and writing.

Campus Safety and Security: Measures include 24-hour foot and vehicle patrol, emergency notification system, self-defense education, and security escort services. There are emergency telephones, lighted pathways/sidewalks, controlled access to dorms/residences, and separate dorm security.

Programs of Study: confers B.A., B.S., and B.F.A. degrees. Master's degrees are also awarded. Bachelor's degrees are awarded in AGRICULTURE (environmental studies), BIOLOGICAL SCIENCE (biology/biological science and neurosciences), BUSINESS (accounting, banking and finance, business administration and management, international business management, investments and securities, and marketing/retailing/merchandising), COMMUNICATIONS AND THE ARTS (art, arts administration/management, communications, dramatic arts, English, fine arts, and music), COMPUTER AND PHYSICAL SCIENCE (chemistry, computer science, information sciences and systems, mathematics, and physics), EDUCATION (early childhood education, elementary education, and special education), ENGINEERING AND ENVIRONMENTAL DESIGN (aviation administration/management and aviation computer technology), HEALTH PROFESSIONS (nursing), SOCIAL SCIENCE (criminal justice, economics, history, philosophy, political science/government, prelaw, psychology, social science, sociology, and Spanish studies). Nursing, biology, and English are the strongest academically. Business, nursing, and psychology have the largest enrollments.

Required: To graduate, all students must complete at least 124 credit hours, with a minimum 2.0 GPA and 40 to 80 hours in the major. Students are also required to complete a Learning Community, which is 2 courses linked together by a common theme, and courses in humanities (10 to 12 credits), science/mathematics (9 to 12 credits), social sciences (8 credits), arts (5 to 8 credits), writing and other communication skills (7 credits), living arts (2 to 4 credits), and a diversity course.

Special: The college offers internships in every major, study abroad, dual and student-designed majors, an accelerated degree, co-op, work-study, independent study, weekend college, and freshman seminar courses. A 3-2 engineering degree with USC in Los Angeles or Washington University in St. Louis, Missouri, is also possible. There are 2 national honor societies, including Phi Beta Kappa, a freshman honors program, and 1 departmental honors program.

Faculty/Classroom: 46% of faculty are male; 54% are female. All teach undergraduates. No introductory courses are taught by graduate students.

Admissions: 68% of a recent year applicants were accepted. The SAT scores for a recent year freshman class were: Critical Reading--24% below 500, 38% between 500 and 599, 22% between 600 and 700, and 12% above 700; Math--18% below 500, 48% between 500 and 599, 24% between 600 and 700, and 8% above 700. The ACT scores were 13% below 21, 23% between 21 and 23, 32% between 24 and 26, 14% between 27 and 28, and 16% above 28. 49% of the current freshmen were in the top fifth of their class; 77% were in the top two fifths. There were 16 National Merit finalists. 14 freshmen graduated first in their class.

Requirements: The SAT or ACT is required. In addition, applicants must be graduates of an accredited secondary school or have a GED certificate. College preparatory work should include 4 units of English, 3 of science, 2 each of math, foreign language, social studies, and electives, and 1 of history. An interview is recommended. AP and CLEP credits are accepted. Important factors in the admissions decision are evidence of special talent, extracurricular activities record, and advanced placement or honors courses.

Procedure: Freshmen are admitted to all sessions. Entrance exams should be taken in the junior or senior year of high school. There are deferred admissions and rolling admissions plans. Application deadlines are open. The fall of a recent year application fee was $50. Applications are accepted online.

Transfer: 215 transfer students enrolled in a recent year. Transfer students must have a minimum 2.5 GPA and be in good standing at all previously attended institutions. They must provide college transcripts and submit an essay. An interview is recommended. Some students may need to present standardized test scores and high school transcripts. 36 of 124 credits required for the bachelor's degree must be completed at Westminster.

Visiting: There are regularly scheduled orientations for prospective students, including a welcome program, lunch, various workshops, a campus tour, and meetings with faculty. There are guides for informal visits, visitors may sit in on classes, and stay overnight. To schedule a visit, contact Director of Admissions.

Financial Aid: In a recent year, 97% of all full-time freshmen and 91% of continuing full-time students received some form of financial aid. 67% of all full-time freshmen and 63% of continuing full-time students received need-based aid. The average freshman award was $23,700. Need-based scholarships or need-based grants averaged $17,628 ($26,712 maximum); need-based self-help aid (loans and jobs) averaged $5,457 ($9,000 maximum); non-need-based athletic scholarships averaged $2,350 ($20,212 maximum); and other non-need-based awards and non-need-based scholarships averaged $12,958 ($14,000 maximum). 73% of undergraduate students work part-time. Average annual earnings from campus work are $2250. The average financial indebtedness of a recent graduate was $22,557. Westminster is a member of CSS. The FAFSA is required. The priority date for freshman financial aid applications for fall entry is April 15. The deadline for filing freshman financial aid applications for fall entry is rolling.

International Students: There are 141 international students enrolled. The school actively recruits these students. They must take the TOEFL with a minimum score of 550 on the paper-based TOEFL (PBT).

Computers: Wireless access is available. Westminster College provides wireless service in all academic areas including the residential halls. Every student has access to the Westminster network, including an e-mail account, 1 GB of storage space, and free on-campus Internet access. Computer labs are also available for student use around campus; the lab in Giovale Library has over 50 workstations. All students may access the system. There are no time limits. The fee is $125. All students are required to have a personal computer. Students enrolled in all programs must have a personal computer.

Graduates: In a recent year, 461 bachelor's degrees were awarded. The most popular majors were business (26%), health professions (19%), and social science (9%). 30 companies recruited on campus in a recent year. In an average class, 46% graduate in 4 years or less, 61% graduate in 5 years or less, and 66% graduate in 6 years or less. Of a recent graduating class, 13% were enrolled in graduate school within 6 months of graduation, and 74% were employed.

Admissions Contact: Elizabeth Key, Director of Admissions. E-Mail: *admission@westminstercollege.edu* Web: *www.westminstercollege.edu*

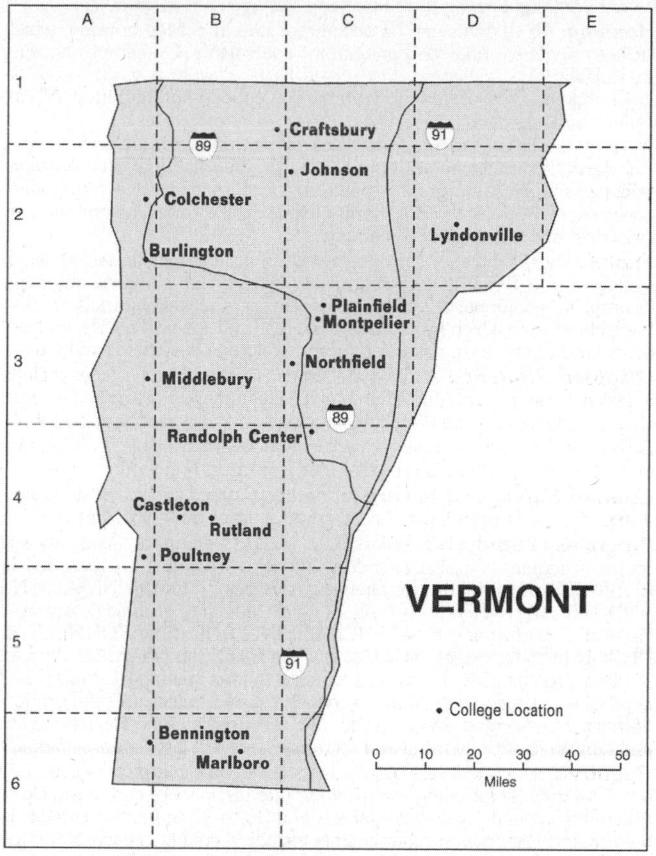

BENNINGTON COLLEGE

A-6

Bennington, VT 05201

(802) 440-4312
(800) 833-6845; (802) 440-4320

Full-time: 244 men, 440 women
Part-time: 1 men, 3 women
Graduate: 27 men, 111 women
Year: other
Application Deadline: January 3
Freshman Class: 1236 applied, 779 accepted, 197 enrolled
SAT CR/M/W: 690/610/660
Faculty: 64
Ph.D.s: 70%
Student/Faculty: 11 to 1
Tuition: $44,220
Room & Board: $12,770
ACT: 29
HIGHLY COMPETITIVE+

Bennington College, founded in 1932, is a private liberal arts institution characterized by cross-disciplinary learning, a close working relationship between student and teacher, a self-directed academic planning process, and a connection to the world through it's winter internship term. There are 4 graduate schools. The 2 libraries contain 125,000 volumes, 6,000 audio/video tapes/CDs/DVDs, and subscribe to 14,500 periodicals including electronic. Computerized library services include interlibrary loans, database searching, Internet access, and Wi-Fi capability. Special learning facilities include an art gallery, radio station, Center for the Advancement of Public Action with unique tiered symposium space for U.N.-style dialogue and web-casting; observatory; greenhouse; digital arts lab; art gallery; architecture, drawing, painting, printmaking, and sculpture studios; ceramics studio and kilns; photography darkrooms; film and video editing studio; several fully equipped theaters; dance studios; scripts library; costume shop; electronic music and sound recording studios; music practice rooms and music library; student-run cafe and bar; and 440 acres of forest, ponds, wetlands and fields for recreation and scientific study. The 440-acre campus is in a small town in the southwestern corner of Vermont, 160 miles north of New York City and 150 miles west of Boston. Including any residence halls, there are 70 buildings.

Student Life: 96% of undergraduates are from out of state, mostly the Middle Atlantic. Students are from 46 states, 35 foreign countries, and Canada. 57% are from public schools. 77% are White. The average age of freshmen is 18; all undergraduates, 20. 17% do not continue beyond their first year; 64% remain to graduate.

Housing: 661 students can be accommodated in college housing, which includes coed dorms, on-campus apartments, and off-campus apartments. In addition, there are special-interest houses. On-campus housing is guaranteed for all 4 years. 95% of students live on campus; of those, 75% remain on campus on weekends. All students may keep cars.

Activities: There are no fraternities or sororities. There are 37 groups on campus, including campus activities board, student educational policies committee, student endowment for the arts, sustainability committee, art, chess, choir, chorale, chorus, computers, dance, debate, drama, environmental, ethnic, film, gay, international, jazz band, literary magazine, musical theater, newspaper, opera, outing club, photography, political, radio and TV, religious, social, social service, student government, and symphony. Popular campus events include Sunfest, Faculty Concerts, and Student-Work Performances.

Sports: There are 2 intercollegiate sports for men and 2 for women, and 15 intramural sports for men and 15 for women. Facilities include Recreation barn (includes aerobic room, free weights, weight training equipment, yoga and martial arts equipment, cardiovascular machines), rock climbing wall, dance studio, tennis courts, soccer field, and basketball court. Swimming, horseback riding, rock climbing, canoeing, caving, snowshoeing, whitewater rafting, and skiing facilities are available in the surrounding area.

Disabled Students: 80% of the campus is accessible. Facilities include wheelchair ramps, elevators, special parking, specially equipped restrooms, lowered drinking fountains, special housing.

Services: Counseling and information services are available, as is tutoring in some subjects. There is remedial writing. Tutoring for learning disabilities is available in the town of Bennington at a cost to the student.

Campus Safety and Security: Measures include 24-hour foot and vehicle patrol, emergency notification system, and security escort services. There are shuttle buses, emergency telephones, and lighted pathways/sidewalks.

Programs of Study: Bennington confers B.A. degrees. Master's degrees are also awarded. Bachelor's degrees are awarded in AGRICULTURE (environmental studies), BIOLOGICAL SCIENCE (biology/biological science, botany, ecology, environmental biology, evolutionary biology, and zoology), COMMUNICATIONS AND THE ARTS (American literature, animation, art, ceramic art and design, Chinese, comparative literature, creative writing, dance, design, digital communications, dramatic arts, drawing, English, English literature, film arts, fine arts, French, Germanic languages and literature, illustration, Italian, Japanese, jazz, journalism, languages, literature, multimedia, music, music performance, music theory and composition, painting, performing arts, photography, piano/organ, playwriting/screenwriting, printmaking, sculpture, Spanish, strings, studio art, theater design, video, visual and performing arts, and voice), COMPUTER AND PHYSICAL SCIENCE (astronomy, chemistry, computer science, digital arts/technology, mathematics, physical sciences, physics, and science), EDUCATION (drama education, early childhood education, education, elementary education, foreign languages education, mathematics education, middle school education, and secondary education), ENGINEERING AND ENVIRONMENTAL DESIGN (architecture and environmental science), HEALTH PROFESSIONS (premedicine), SOCIAL SCIENCE (American studies, anthropology, child psychology/development, European studies, fashion design and technology, history, humanities, humanities and social science, interdisciplinary studies, international relations, international studies, Judaic studies, Latin American studies, liberal arts/general studies, philosophy, political science/government, prelaw, psychology, social psychology, social science, sociology, and women's studies). Literature, languages, and visual and performing arts are the strongest academically. Literature, and interdisciplinary studies have the largest enrollments.

Required: A minimum of 128 credit hours is required to graduate. Students must also complete a Field Work Term (job/internship) for each year in residence. Student's programs must reflect breadth and depth in curricular choices, and their academic plan process must be approved by a faculty committee.

Special: 7-week work/internships (during January and February) are required each year in residence. Cross-registration with Williams College, Southern Vermont College, and Massachusetts College of Liberal Arts is possible. In addition, study abroad, dual, and student-designed majors are offered. Students receive narrative evaluations with the option of letter grades.

Faculty/Classroom: 51% of faculty are male; 49% are female. All teach undergraduates, all do research, and all teach and do research. No introductory courses are taught by graduate students. The average class size in an introductory lecture is 16; in a laboratory is 15; and in a regular course is 10.

Admissions: 63% of the 2013-2014 applicants were accepted. The SAT scores for the 2013-2014 freshman class were: Critical Reading--13% between 500 and 599, 46% between 600 and 699, and 41% between 700 and 800; Math--2% below 500, 38% between 500 and 599, 48%

between 600 and 699, and 13% between 700 and 800; Writing--2% below 500, 21% between 500 and 599, 51% between 600 and 699, and 27% between 700 and 800. The ACT scores were 5% below 21, 23% between 24 and 26, 23% between 27 and 28, and 50% above 28. 56% of the current freshmen were in the top fifth of their class; 84% were in the top two fifths.

Requirements: In addition, Bennington admits students who have demonstrated a passion for learning and academic excellence. The Common Application as well as the Bennington Supplement are required. Submission of standardized test scores is optional. A majority of applicants are interviewed in person or by phone.

Procedure: Freshmen are admitted fall and spring. Entrance exams should be taken during the spring of the junior year or the fall of the senior year. There are early decision, early admissions, and deferred admissions plans. Early decision applications should be filed by November 15; regular applications, by January 3 for fall entry; and November 15 for spring entry, along with a $60 fee. Notification of early decision is sent December 20; regular decision, April 1. 21 early decision candidates were accepted for the 2013-2014 class. 152 applicants were on the 2013 waiting list; 27 were admitted. Applications are accepted online.

Transfer: 15 transfer students enrolled in 2012-2013. Applicants must submit the common application for transfer students, including essays, secondary school reports, college transcripts, and recommendations from 2 faculty members at the college from which they are transferring. They must also interview with a member of the admissions staff. Submission of SAT or ACT scores is optional. 64 of 128 credits required for the bachelor's degree must be completed at Bennington.

Visiting: There are regularly scheduled orientations for prospective students, including a tour of campus, classes, lunch in the dining hall, and meeting with an admissions counselor. Overnight visits are also possible during the term. There are guides for informal visits, visitors may sit in on classes, and stay overnight. To schedule a visit, contact the Admissions Office at (800) 833-6845.

Financial Aid: In 2013-2014, 95% of all full-time freshmen and 90% of continuing full-time students received some form of financial aid. 58% of all full-time freshmen and 63% of continuing full-time students received need-based aid. The average freshman award was $33,336. Need-based scholarships or need-based grants averaged $23,448; need-based self-help aid (loans and jobs) averaged $4,696; and other non-need-based awards and non-need-based scholarships averaged $13,019. 20% of undergraduate students work part-time. Average annual earnings from campus work are $2214. The average financial indebtedness of the 2013 graduate was $25,716. Bennington is a member of CSS. The CSS/Profile, FAFSA, the college's own financial statement, and student and parent tax returns and W-2s are required. The priority date for freshman financial aid applications for fall entry is February 1. The deadline for filing freshman financial aid applications for fall entry is February 15.

International Students: There are 48 international students enrolled. The school actively recruits these students. They must take the TOEFL with a minimum score of 577 on the paper-based TOEFL (PBT) or 90 on the Internet-based version (iBT).

Computers: All students may access the system. There are no time limits and no fees.

Graduates: From July 1, 2012 to June 30, 2013, 151 bachelor's degrees were awarded. The most popular majors were visual and performing arts (46%), social sciences (10%), and English language and literature (10%). In an average class, 59% graduate in 4 years or less, 63% graduate in 5 years or less, and 64% graduate in 6 years or less.

Admissions Contact: Janet Marsden, Vice President for Admissions. E-Mail: *admissions@bennington.edu* Web: *www.bennington.edu*

BURLINGTON COLLEGE A-2

Burlington, VT 05401 (802) 862-9616
(800) 862-9616; (802) 660-4331

Full-time: 88 men, 72 women	**Faculty:** 7
Part-time: 25 men, 34 women	**Ph.D.s:** 34%
Graduate: 8 men, 16 women	**Student/Faculty:** 8 to 1
Year: semesters, summer session	**Tuition:** $22,885
Application Deadline: August	**Room & Board:** $9625
Freshman Class: 199 applied, 165 accepted, 45 enrolled	
SAT or ACT: recommended	**SPECIAL**

Burlington College, founded in 1972, is an independent liberal arts college that offers a nontraditional, individualized approach in which classes are small and discussion based, narrative evaluations replace traditional grades, and students direct their own education. The library contains 12,000 volumes, and 1,000 audio/video tapes/CDs/DVDs, and subscribes to 60 periodicals including electronic. Computerized library services include interlibrary loans, database searching, Internet access, and Wi-Fi capability. Special learning facilities include an art gallery, digital video and audio editing suites, and a film-production studio. The 32-acre campus is in an urban area overlooking Lake Champlain. Including any residence halls, there are 6 buildings.

Student Life: 56% of undergraduates are from Vermont. Others are from 26 states, 3 foreign countries, and Canada. 74% are White; 16% race unknown. The average age of freshmen is 21; all undergraduates, 29. 43% do not continue beyond their first year; 20% remain to graduate.

Housing: 46 students can be accommodated in college housing, which includes single-sex and coed on-campus apartments. On-campus housing is available on a first-come, first-served basis. Priority is given to out-of-town students. 79% of students commute. Alcohol is not permitted. All students may keep cars.

Activities: There are no fraternities or sororities. Groups on campus include art, communications, ethnic, film, gay, international, literary magazine, newspaper, photography, political, social, social service, and student government. Popular campus events include coffeehouses, community service trips, and film society screenings.

Sports: There is no sports program at BC. Facilities include sailing, windsurfing, and a 9-mile bike path are available on or along nearby Lake Champlain, additional bicycling, roller-blading, and walking trails are also available nearby, which has a pool, basketball and sqauash courts, and students have access to the exercise rooms, weight and aerobic condtioning.

Disabled Students: All of the campus is accessible. Facilities include wheelchair ramps, special parking, specially equipped restrooms, special class scheduling, lowered drinking fountains, and lowered telephones.

Services: Counseling and information services are available, as is tutoring in most subjects. There is remedial math, reading, and writing.

Campus Safety and Security: There are lighted pathways/sidewalks, distribution of campus safety and security policies and procedures.

Programs of Study: BC confers B.A., and B.F.A degrees. Associate and master's degrees are also awarded. Bachelor's degrees are awarded in BUSINESS (hospitality management services), COMMUNICATIONS AND THE ARTS (creative writing, film arts, fine arts, graphic design, and visual and performing arts), ENGINEERING AND ENVIRONMENTAL DESIGN (woodworking), SOCIAL SCIENCE (Caribbean studies, human services, legal studies, liberal arts/general studies, paralegal studies, and psychology). Psychology, human services, cinema studies and film production are the strongest academically. Individualized majors, cinema studies and film production, writing and literature have the largest enrollments.

Required: All students are required to satisfactorily complete at least 120 semester credits, including an 18-credit interdisciplinary core curriculum, 40 credits in general education areas, and 36 to 45 upper-level credits in their major. Distribution requirements include 3 credits in each of the following areas: responsible action, creative expression, quantitative reasoning, media literacy, historical consciousness, cultural awareness, social awareness, written and oral communication, critical thinking, research methods, scientific thought. Students are also required to take college-level math and 2 writing courses, to demonstrate competency in the use of computers, and to complete both a 6-credit capstone project and a 3-credit practicum.

Special: Cross-registration is available with the University of Vermont, St. Michael's College, Champlain College, and the Community College of Vermont internships through various organizations, study abroad, and work-study programs with nonprofit organizations are also available. The college offers dual majors, interdisciplinary majors, individualized majors, independent study, a non-residential degree program, and credit for life experience. Professional certificates are offered in film studies, paralegal studies and woodworking.

Faculty/Classroom: 47% of faculty are male; 53% are female. All teach undergraduates. No introductory courses are taught by graduate students. The average class size in a regular course is 7.

Admissions: 83% of the 2013-2014 applicants were accepted.

Requirements: The SAT or ACT is recommended. Photography, Graphic Design, Film, Fine Art and Woodworking portfolios are required for B.F.A degrees. AP and CLEP credits are accepted. Important factors in the admissions decision are personality/intangible qualities, extracurricular activities record, and recommendations by school officials.

Procedure: Freshmen are admitted fall, spring, and summer. There are deferred admissions and rolling admissions plans. Check with the school for current application deadlines. The application fee is $50. Notification is sent on a rolling basis. Applications are accepted online.

Transfer: Transfer students must meet the same requirements as new students. High school transcripts precede acceptance. The Independent Degree Program requires 30 college credits prior to entrance. Transcripts precede acceptance. 30 of 120 credits required for the bachelor's degree must be completed at BC.

Visiting: There are guides for informal visits and visitors may sit in on classes. To schedule a visit, contact the Admissions Office at admissions@burlington.edu.

Financial Aid: In 2013-2014, 81% of all full-time freshmen and 79% of continuing full-time students received some form of financial aid. 74% of all full-time freshmen and 74% of continuing full-time students received need-based aid. The average freshman award was $14,856. Need-based scholarships or need-based grants averaged $10,670 ($11,590 maximum); and need-based self-help aid (loans and jobs) averaged $5,101

($19,285 maximum). 22% of undergraduate students work part-time. Average annual earnings from campus work are $1000. The average financial indebtedness of the 2013 graduate was $27,665. The FAFSA and the state aid form are required. Check with the school for current application deadlines.

International Students: There are 2 international students enrolled. They must take the TOEFL with a minimum score of 550 on the paper-based TOEFL (PBT).

Computers: All students may access the system 80 hours per week. There are no time limits and no fees.

Graduates: From July 1, 2012 to June 30, 2013, 29 bachelor's degrees were awarded. The most popular majors were cinema studies and film production (27%), individualized majors (17%), and integral pyschology (17%). In an average class, 23% graduate in 5 years or less.

Admissions Contact: Meghan Daly, Administrative Assistant of Admissions. E-Mail: *admissions@burlington.edu* Web: *burlington.edu*

CASTLETON STATE COLLEGE B-4

Castleton, VT 05735 (802) 468-1213
(800) 639-8521; (802) 468-1476

Full-time: 945 men, 961 women	**Faculty:** 94; IIB, -$
Part-time: 49 men, 104 women	**Ph.D.s:** 96%
Graduate: 25 men, 72 women	**Student/Faculty:** 14 to 1
Year: semesters, summer session	**Tuition:** $10,286 ($24,014)
Application Deadline: open	**Room & Board:** $9138

Freshman Class: 2737 applied, 2084 accepted, 487 enrolled
SAT CR/M/W: 490/500/470 **ACT:** 20 **COMPETITIVE**

Castleton State College, founded in 1787, is the oldest institution of higher learning in Vermont. As part of the Vermont State Colleges system, it offers a state-supported undergraduate and graduate program in liberal arts, teacher preparation, and professional studies. There is one graduate school. In addition to regional accreditation, Castleton has baccalaureate program accreditation with CSWE and NLN. The library contains 206,845 volumes, 613,114 microform items, and 15,520 audio/video tapes/CDs/DVDs, and subscribes to 49,645 periodicals including electronic. Computerized library services include interlibrary loans, database searching, Internet access, and Wi-Fi capability. Special learning facilities include an art gallery, radio station, TV studio, observatory, and theater. The 165-acre campus is in a rural area 12 miles west of Rutland. Including any residence halls, there are 24 buildings.

Student Life: 71% of undergraduates are from Vermont. Others are from 25 states, 6 foreign countries, and Canada. 88% are White. The average age of freshmen is 18; all undergraduates, 21. 30% do not continue beyond their first year; 41% remain to graduate.

Housing: 1100 students can be accommodated in college housing, which includes single-sex and coed dorms and off-campus apartments. substance-free housing. On-campus housing is guaranteed for the freshman year only and is available on a lottery system for upperclassmen. 54% of students live on campus; of those, 70% remain on campus on weekends. All students may keep cars.

Activities: There are no fraternities or sororities. There are 40 groups on campus, including art, band, cheerleading, choir, chorale, chorus, computers, dance, drama, ethnic, film, gay, honors, international, jazz band, literary magazine, marching band, musical theater, newspaper, pep band, photography, political, professional, radio and TV, religious, social, social service, student government, and sustainability club. Popular campus events include spring, winter and alumni weekends.

Sports: There are 10 intercollegiate sports for men and 10 for women, and 11 intramural sports for men and 11 for women. Facilities include a 6-lane swimming pool, 2 racquetball courts, 2 fitness centers, a recreation gym, an ice hockey rink, and an extensive trail system for hiking, running, and x-c skiing.

Disabled Students: 95% of the campus is accessible. Facilities include wheelchair ramps, elevators, special parking, specially equipped restrooms, special class scheduling, lowered drinking fountains, and lowered telephones.

Services: Counseling and information services are available, as is tutoring in every subject. There is a reader service for the blind, and remedial math, reading, and writing.

Campus Safety and Security: Measures include 24-hour foot and vehicle patrol, emergency notification system, self-defense education, and security escort services. There are emergency telephones, lighted pathways/sidewalks, and controlled access to dorms/residences.

Programs of Study: Castleton confers B.A., B.S., B.M. and B.S.W. degrees. Associate and master's degrees are also awarded. Bachelor's degrees are awarded in BIOLOGICAL SCIENCE (biology/biological science), BUSINESS (business administration and management and sports management), COMMUNICATIONS AND THE ARTS (art, communications, dramatic arts, literature, music, and Spanish), COMPUTER AND PHYSICAL SCIENCE (computer science, geology, mathematics, and natural sciences), EDUCATION (athletic training, health education, music education, and physical education), ENGINEERING AND ENVIRONMENTAL DESIGN (environmental science), HEALTH PROFESSIONS (exercise science, health science, and nursing), SOCIAL SCIENCE (area studies, criminal justice, history, liberal arts/general studies, philosophy, psychology, social science, social work, and sociology). Business, and teacher preparation have the largest enrollments.

Required: All students must maintain a GPA of 2.0 while taking 122 semester hours, including 30 or more in their major. Distribution requirements include 3 courses each in literature and the arts, 2 each in math and natural sciences, and 1 each in foreign cultures, history, philosophy and psychology, and social analysis. Specific courses include computers, communication, and an introduction to liberal arts.

Special: Cross-registration with other Vermont State Colleges, co-op programs, internships, study abroad, and work-study programs are available. In addition, B.A.-B.S. degrees, dual majors, student-designed majors in history, math, and social sciences, credit for life experience, nondegree study, and pass/fail options are offered. There are 8 national honor societies, a freshman honors program, and 4 departmental honors programs.

Faculty/Classroom: 52% of faculty are male; 48% are female. All teach undergraduates, and 50% do both. No introductory courses are taught by graduate students. The average class size in an introductory lecture is 25; in a laboratory is 14; and in a regular course is 18.

Admissions: 76% of the 2013-2014 applicants were accepted. The SAT scores for the 2013-2014 freshman class were: Critical Reading--54% below 500, 38% between 500 and 599, 6% between 600 and 699, and 2% between 700 and 800; Math--56% below 500, 35% between 500 and 599, and 9% between 600 and 699; Writing--69% below 500, 27% between 500 and 599, and 4% between 600 and 699.

Requirements: The SAT or ACT is required. The college requires that candidates have 4 years of English, 3 year of math, 3 years of social studies or history, 3 years of sciences (two of which must be a lab). The college recommends 2 years of a foreign language. The GED is accepted. An interview is recommended. A GPA of 2.9 is required. AP and CLEP credits are accepted. Important factors in the admissions decision are advanced placement or honors courses, leadership record, and recommendations by school officials.

Procedure: Freshmen are admitted fall and spring. Entrance exams should be taken during the spring of the junior year or fall of the senior year. There are early admissions, deferred admissions, and rolling admissions plans. Application deadlines are open. Application fee is $40. Applications are accepted online.

Transfer: 182 transfer students enrolled in 2012-2013. All transfer applicants must have a 2.0 GPA and submit both previous college transcipts and an dessay/personal statement. Some transfer applicants will be asked to submit high school transripts, standardized test scores, and a statement of good standing from the prior institution. An interview may also be required of some transfer students. 30 of 122 credits required for the bachelor's degree must be completed at Castleton.

Visiting: There are regularly scheduled orientations for prospective students, including meetings with admissions counselors, faculty, and coaches as well as a campus tour. There are guides for informal visits and visitors may sit in on classes. To schedule a visit, contact the Admissions Office at (800) 639-8521.

Financial Aid: Castleton is a member of CSS. The FAFSA is required. The deadline for filing freshman financial aid applications for fall entry is April 1.

International Students: There are 27 international students enrolled. The school actively recruits these students. They must take the TOEFL with a minimum score of 550 on the paper-based TOEFL (PBT) or 80 on the Internet-based version (iBT).

Computers: All students may access the system. There are no time limits and no fees.

Graduates: From July 1, 2012 to June 30, 2013, 271 bachelor's degrees were awarded. The most popular majors were business (30%), communication (10%), and psychology (10%). 63 companies recruited on campus in 2012-2013. In an average class, 25% graduate in 4 years or less, 39% graduate in 5 years or less, and 41% graduate in 6 years or less.

Admissions Contact: Maurice Ouimet, Admissions Director. E-Mail: *info@castleton.edu* Web: *www.castleton.edu*

CHAMPLAIN COLLEGE A-2

Burlington, VT 05402 (802) 860-2727
(800) 570-5858; (802) 860-2767

Full-time: 1368 men, 841 women	**Faculty:** 100
Part-time: 26 men, 16 women	**Ph.D.s:** 69%
Graduate: 158 men, 249 women	**Student/Faculty:** 21 to 1
Year: semesters, summer session	**Tuition:** $31,350
Application Deadline: February 1	**Room & Board:** $13,500

Freshman Class: 5097 applied, 3574 accepted, 594 enrolled
SAT CR/M/W: 568/556/544 **ACT:** 25 **VERY COMPETITIVE**

Champlain College, founded in 1878, has been carrying out its mission to prepare students for successful careers for 125 years. There is 1 undergraduate school and 5 graduate schools. In addition to regional accreditation, Champlain has baccalaureate program accreditation with CSWE. The library contains 167,149 volumes, 661 audio/video tapes/CDs/DVDs, and subscribes to 55,155 periodicals including electronic. Computerized library services include interlibrary loans, database searching, Internet access, and Wi-Fi capability. Special learning facilities include a The 22-acre campus is in an urban area of Burlington, Vermont. Including any residence halls, there are 46 buildings.

Student Life: 76% of undergraduates are from out of state, mostly the Northeast. Students are from 41 states, 22 foreign countries, and Canada. 86% are White; 28% race unknown. The average age of freshmen is 18; all undergraduates, 20. 21% do not continue beyond their first year; 62% remain to graduate.

Housing: 1361 students can be accommodated in college housing, which includes single-sex and coed dorms, on-campus apartments, and off-campus apartments. In addition, there are special-interest houses, performing arts, international, and wellness dorms. On-campus housing is guaranteed for all 4 years, is available on a first-come, first-served basis, and is available on a lottery system for upperclassmen. 34% of students commute. Alcohol is not permitted. No one may keep cars.

Activities: There are no fraternities or sororities. There are 22 groups on campus, including flash animation, skiing and sailing, art, chorale, chorus, computers, drama, environmental, ethnic, gay, honors, international, literary magazine, musical theater, newspaper, outing, photography, professional, radio and TV, religious, social, social service, and student government. Popular campus events include skiing, snowboarding trips and spring meltdown.

Sports: There are 16 intramural sports for men and 16 for women. Facilities include a fitness center, games center, and a gym.

Disabled Students: 79% of the campus is accessible. Facilities include wheelchair ramps, elevators, special parking, specially equipped restrooms, special class scheduling, lowered drinking fountains, and lowered telephones.

Services: Counseling and information services are available, as is tutoring in some subjects, math, accounting, and writing. Peer tutoring is available.

Campus Safety and Security: Measures include 24-hour foot and vehicle patrol, emergency notification system, self-defense education, and security escort services. There are shuttle buses, emergency telephones, lighted pathways/sidewalks, and controlled access to dorms/residences.

Programs of Study: Champlain confers B.S., B.F.A., B.S.W. and B.B.A. degrees. Associate and master's degrees are also awarded. Bachelor's degrees are awarded in BUSINESS (accounting, business administration and management, electronic business, international business management, management science, and marketing management), COMMUNICATIONS AND THE ARTS (advertising, broadcasting, communications, communications technology, film arts, fine arts, graphic design, information technology, journalism, media arts, multimedia, public relations, and technical and business writing), COMPUTER AND PHYSICAL SCIENCE (computer game design/development, computer information technology, computer science, computer security and information assurance, information sciences and systems, radiological technology, software engineering, and web services), EDUCATION (early childhood education, elementary education, health information management, middle school education, and secondary education), ENGINEERING AND ENVIRONMENTAL DESIGN (computational sciences), SOCIAL SCIENCE (criminal justice, forensic studies, legal studies, liberal arts/general studies, psychology, and social work). Information systems, electronic game art, design, and development are the strongest academically. Digital forensics, electronic gaming, and psychology have the largest enrollments.

Required: A GPA of 2.0 and 120 credits are required for Baccalaureate degrees. Students must take between 40 and 60 hours in the major. Every undergraduate takes Champlain's Core Curriculum, a four-year course of interdisciplinary study that cultivates the intellectual leadership prized by a complex economy and a rapidly changing world. All undergraduate students also participate in LEAD (Life Experience and Action Dimension), a four-year program designed to help you develop life skills that are practical, meaningful and useful and that will serve you throughout your entire lifetime.

Special: Cross-registration with St. Michael's College, co-op programs (with Federal Law Enforcement Training Center, the Vermont police academy, and student teaching), internships, and study abroad opportunities through school-sponsored programs in Montreal, Ireland, England, France, Sweden, and Switzerland are available. Study abroad in other countries is also available. Champlain College has a special agreement with NYU's School of Continuing and Professional Studies. Students with a G.P.A. of 3.25 or greater can be granted "auto-admission" to one of 14 masters programs offered through NYU including an M.S. in Management and Systems and an M.S. in Global Affairs. Through a special agreement with the prestigious Thunderbird School, Champlain students may be able to pursue a Certificate of Advanced Global Studies during the fall of the fourth year, and upon successful completion, have those credits apply towards one of Thunderbird's masters programs. Students are also eligible for a 15% reduction in price per credit hour for certain master's programs. Dual majors are possible through the professional studies and computer information systems programs. Accelerated degree programs, such as the 5-year B.S./M.B.A. with Clarkson and Southern New Hampshire Universities, and student-designed majors are also available.

Faculty/Classroom: 63% of faculty are male; 37% are female. All teach undergraduates. No introductory courses are taught by graduate students. The average class size in a regular course is 14.

Admissions: 70% of the 2013-2014 applicants were accepted. The SAT scores for the 2013-2014 freshman class were: Critical Reading--22% below 500, 42% between 500 and 599, 27% between 600 and 699, and 9% between 700 and 800; Math--25% below 500, 41% between 500 and 599, 29% between 600 and 699, and 5% between 700 and 800; Writing--28% below 500, 47% between 500 and 599, 22% between 600 and 699, and 3% between 700 and 800. The ACT scores were 17% below 21, 19% between 21 and 23, 29% between 24 and 26, 15% between 27 and 28, and 20% above 28.

Requirements: The SAT or ACT is required. Applicants must be graduates of an accredited high school or the equivalent. AP and CLEP credits are accepted. Important factors in the admissions decision are extracurricular activities record, recommendations by school officials, and advanced placement or honors courses.

Procedure: Freshmen are admitted fall and spring. Entrance exams should be taken prior to applying. There are early decision and deferred admissions plans. Early decision applications should be filed by November 15; regular applications, by February 1 for fall entry; and December 1 for spring entry. Notification of early decision is sent December 15; regular decision, March 15. 318 early decision candidates were accepted for the 2013-2014 class. 75 applicants were on the 2013 waiting list; 31 were admitted. Applications are accepted online.

Transfer: 105 transfer students enrolled in 2012-2013. High school and college transcripts are required. 45 of 120 credits required for the bachelor's degree must be completed at Champlain.

Visiting: There are regularly scheduled orientations for prospective students, including a group information session followed by a tour. Personal interviews are also available with an admissions counselor. There are guides for informal visits and visitors may sit in on classes. To schedule a visit, contact the Admissions Office at admission@champlain.edu.

Financial Aid: The FAFSA is required. The deadline for filing freshman financial aid applications for fall entry is February 15.

International Students: There are 24 international students enrolled. The school actively recruits these students. They must take the TOEFL with a minimum score of 550 on the paper-based TOEFL (PBT) or 79 on the Internet-based version (iBT). They must also take the SAT or ACT.

Computers: All students may access the system. There are no time limits and no fees.

Graduates: From July 1, 2012 to June 30, 2013, 506 bachelor's degrees were awarded. The most popular majors were business (21%), graphic design (17%), and computer and information sciences and support services (11%). 985 companies recruited on campus in 2012-2013. In an average class, 52% graduate in 4 years or less, 59% graduate in 5 years or less, and 62% graduate in 6 years or less. Of the 2012 graduating class, 5% were enrolled in graduate school within 6 months of graduation, and 84% were employed.

Admissions Contact: Sarah Adriano, Director of Admissions. E-Mail: *admission@champlain.edu* Web: *www.champlain.edu*

COLLEGE OF ST JOSEPH — B-4

Rutland, VT 05701 — **802-776-5206**
(877) 270-9998; (802) 776-5258

Full-time: 62 men, 58 women	**Faculty:** 10
Part-time: 22 men, 34 women	**Ph.D.s:** 75%
Graduate: 26 men, 69 women	**Student/Faculty:** 10 to 1
Year: semesters, summer session	**Tuition:** $21,200
Application Deadline: open	**Room & Board:** $9400
Freshman Class: 183 applied, 125 accepted, 33 enrolled	
SAT CR/M/W: 417/427/435	**ACT:** 17 **LESS COMPETITIVE**

The College of St. Joseph, founded in 1956, is a private Catholic institution offering undergraduate programs in the arts and sciences, business, criminal justice, education, psychology, and human services, and graduate programs in business, education, psychology, and human services. The college serves a range of students from traditional age to adult learners. There are 3 graduate schools. The library contains 148,090 volumes, 19,739 microform items, and 1,406 audio/video tapes/CDs/DVDs, and subscribes to 49,053 periodicals including electronic. Computerized library services include interlibrary loans, database searching, Internet access, and Wi-Fi capability. The 117-acre campus is in a small town 1 mile west of Rutland. Including any residence halls, there are 11 buildings.

Student Life: 69% of undergraduates are from Vermont. Others are from 16 states, 1 foreign countries, and Canada. 84% are White; 14% African

American. The average age of freshmen is 19; all undergraduates, 24. 25% do not continue beyond their first year; 75% remain to graduate.

Housing: 150 students can be accommodated in college housing, which includes single-sex dorms and on-campus apartments. On-campus housing is guaranteed for all 4 years. 54% of students commute. All students may keep cars.

Activities: There are no fraternities or sororities. There are 13 groups on campus, including environmental, honors, professional, religious, social, social service, and student government. Popular campus events include spring fling, cultural event series (year round), and student leadership-academic awards dinner.

Sports: There are 2 intercollegiate sports for men and 2 for women, and 2 intramural sports for men and 2 for women. Facilities include a 1000-seat gym, a fitness center, racquetball courts, an aerobics studio, a cross-country skiing/running trail, a softball diamond, a soccer field, and indoor batting cage.

Disabled Students: All of the campus is accessible. Facilities include wheelchair ramps, elevators, special parking, specially equipped restrooms, special class scheduling, lowered drinking fountains, lowered telephones, and special housing.

Services: Counseling and information services are available, as is tutoring in every subject. There is remedial math, reading, and writing. There are also counseling services and spiritual counseling offered on campus.

Campus Safety and Security: Measures include emergency notification system. There are emergency telephones, lighted pathways/sidewalks, and a night-time security patrol from 8 p.m. to 6 a.m.

Programs of Study: CSJ confers B.A., and B.S. degrees. Associate and master's degrees are also awarded. Bachelor's degrees are awarded in BUSINESS (accounting, business administration and management, organizational leadership and management, and sports management), COMMUNICATIONS AND THE ARTS (English), COMPUTER AND PHYSICAL SCIENCE (radiological technology), EDUCATION (elementary education and secondary education), HEALTH PROFESSIONS (health science), SOCIAL SCIENCE (criminal justice, history, human services, liberal arts/general studies, and psychology). Business is the strongest academically. Business administration, criminal justice and psychology have the largest enrollments.

Required: To graduate, students must complete 127 credit hours with a minimum GPA of 2.0, (2.5 is required for acceptance to teacher certification program), including 12 credits in English/speech, 9 in social/behavioral sciences, 6 in math, philosophy/religious studies, and natural sciences, and 3 in fine arts. Human services majors must complete 2 internships. The number of hours in the major varies, from 36 to 39 for arts and sciences, to 51 to 60 for business and education, and 40 to 58 for psychology and human services.

Special: The college offers internships in history, political science, business, human services, psychology, and criminal justice, and in Rutland County businesses, human service agencies, and elementary and secondary schools. In addition, dual majors, study abroad, and independent and directed study options are available. An accelerated degree program is available in organizational leadership and behavioral sciences. There are 6 national honor societies and 5 departmental honors programs.

Faculty/Classroom: 66% of faculty are male; 34% are female. All teach undergraduates. No introductory courses are taught by graduate students. The average class size in an introductory lecture is 14; in a laboratory is 5; and in a regular course is 7.

Admissions: 68% of the 2013-2014 applicants were accepted. The SAT scores for the 2013-2014 freshman class were: Critical Reading--25% below 500, 75% between 500 and 599; Math--100% below 500; Writing--25% below 500, 75% between 500 and 599. The ACT scores were 100% below 21. 10% of the current freshmen were in the top fifth of their class; 60% were in the top two fifths.

Requirements: The SAT is required. The ACT is recommended. Applicants should be graduates of accredited secondary schools. College preparatory study must include 4 years of English, 3 of math, 2 each of science and social studies, and 5 other academic electives. The college prefers that students rank in the upper 50% of their graduating class. An essay is required and an interview is recommended. AP and CLEP credits are accepted.

Procedure: Freshmen are admitted fall and spring. Entrance exams should be taken by December of the senior year. There are deferred admissions and rolling admissions plans. Application deadlines are open. Application fee is $25. Applications are accepted online.

Transfer: 8 transfer students enrolled in 2012-2013. Transfers must present a minimum GPA of 2.0. 33 of 127 credits required for the bachelor's degree must be completed at CSJ.

Visiting: There are regularly scheduled orientations for prospective students, including a campus tour, admissions interview, and visits to classes during fall and spring. There are guides for informal visits, visitors may sit in on classes, and stay overnight. To schedule a visit, contact the Admissions Office.

Financial Aid: In 2013-2014, 100% of all full-time freshmen and 99% of continuing full-time students received some form of financial aid. 97% of all full-time freshmen and 93% of continuing full-time students received need-based aid. The average freshman award was $27,444. Need-based scholarships or need-based grants averaged $20,591 ($35,445 maximum); need-based self-help aid (loans and jobs) averaged $5,653 ($11,000 maximum); and other non-need-based awards and non-need-based scholarships averaged $14,500 ($14,500 maximum). 33% of undergraduate students work part-time. Average annual earnings from campus work are $844. The average financial indebtedness of the 2013 graduate was $20,623. The FAFSA, the state aid form, and the college's own financial statement are required. The priority date for freshman financial aid applications for fall entry is March 1.

International Students: There is 1 international student enrolled. They must take the TOEFL with a minimum score of 550 on the paper-based TOEFL (PBT) or 79 on the Internet-based version (iBT). They must also take the SAT or ACT.

Computers: All students may access the system. There are no time limits and no fees.

Graduates: From July 1, 2012 to June 30, 2013, 38 bachelor's degrees were awarded. The most popular majors were human services (16%), liberal studies (16%), and organizational leadership (16%). In an average class, 3% graduate in 3 years or less, 16% graduate in 4 years or less, 23% graduate in 5 years or less, and 23% graduate in 6 years or less. Of the 2012 graduating class, 16% were enrolled in graduate school within 6 months of graduation, and 52% were employed.

Admissions Contact: Judy Morgan, Director of Admissions. E-Mail: *judy.morgan@csj.edu* Web: *www.csj.edu*

GODDARD COLLEGE — C-3

Plainfield, VT 05667 — (800) 906-8312; (800) 468-4888; (802) 454-1029

Full-time: 73 men, 171 women	**Faculty:** n/av
Part-time: n/av	**Ph.D.s:** n/av
Graduate: 137 men, 322 women	**Student/Faculty:** n/av
Year: semesters	**Tuition:** $14,930
Application Deadline: open	**Room & Board:** $1488
Freshman Class: 10 applied, 7 accepted, 6 enrolled	
	VERY COMPETITIVE

Goddard College, founded in 1863, is a private college that stresses progressive, individualized education for personal and community transformation, based on John Dewey's learning-by-engagement philosophy. There is one graduate school. The library contains 115,100 volumes, and 400 audio/video tapes/CDs/DVDs, and subscribes to 10,000 periodicals including electronic. Computerized library services include interlibrary loans, database searching, Internet access, and Wi-Fi capability. Special learning facilities include a radio station. The 200-acre campus is in a rural area 10 miles from Montpelier, the state capital. Including any residence halls, there are 28 buildings.

Student Life: 85% of undergraduates are from out of state, mostly the Northeast. Students are from states, and Canada. 65% are White; 13% race unknown. The average age of freshmen is 32; all undergraduates, 34.

Housing: 175 students can be accommodated in college housing, which includes single-sex and coed dorms. In addition, there are special-interest houses. 100% of students commute. All students commute. All students may keep cars.

Activities: There are no fraternities or sororities. There are 9 groups on campus, including art, drama, literary magazine, radio and TV, and student government.

Sports: There is no sports program at Goddard. Facilities include Workout room, hiking and cross-country ski trails.

Disabled Students: 60% of the campus is accessible. Facilities include wheelchair ramps, elevators, special parking, and specially equipped restrooms.

Services: There is remedial writing.

Campus Safety and Security: Measures include 24-hour foot and vehicle patrol. There are lighted pathways/sidewalks and controlled access to dorms/residences.

Programs of Study: Goddard confers B.A., B.F.A. degrees. Master's degrees are also awarded. Bachelor's degrees are awarded in AGRICULTURE (environmental studies), BIOLOGICAL SCIENCE (nutrition), BUSINESS (sustainable management), COMMUNICATIONS AND THE ARTS (applied art, art, comparative literature, creative writing, dramatic arts, English, English Writing, fine arts, folklore and mythology, intermedia/multimedia, literature, media arts, photography, playwriting/screenwriting, and visual and performing arts), EDUCATION (art education, collaborative education, early childhood education, education, elementary education, English education, health education, learner designed area of study, middle school education, and secondary education), HEALTH PROFESSIONS (health, health promotion, and health science), SOCIAL SCIENCE (addiction studies, clinical psychology, counseling/psychology, crosscultural studies, cultural studies/critical theory & analysis, ethics, politics, and social policy, history, human development, human ecology, humanities and social science, industrial and organizational psychology, interdisciplinary studies, justice and society, liberal arts/general studies, psychology, social psychology, social science, and women and gender studies). Creative writing, interdisciplinary arts, cultural studies, gender studies, and psychology are the strongest academically.

Required: Students come to campus for eight days at the beginning of each semester, then study independently the rest of the term, at home or elsewhere. Collaborating with a faculty advisor, students design and carry out programs of study specifically tailored to their own personal and professional interests and goals. Assessment takes the form of narrative evaluations rather than letter grades. There are no declared majors, but in the last semester of enrollment, all students must complete a culminating senior study or project that may be multidisciplinary and requires foundation work comparable to a major. A total of 120 credits is required to graduate. Students must conduct, or transfer in, substantive studies in the arts, humanities, social sciences, natural sciences, and quantitative reasoning.

Special: The BA/MA Fast Track in Psychology saves students a semester toward earning an MA while completing their bachelor's degree. All programs entail students designing their own studies. The B.A. in Sustainability, B.A. in Education, B.A. in Health Arts & Sciences, and B.F.A. in Creative Writing are upper-division programs, requiring 60 prior credits. The main undergraduate program encompasses both lower and upper divisions.

Faculty/Classroom: No introductory courses are taught by graduate students.

Admissions: 70% of the 2013-2014 applicants were accepted.

Requirements: Goddard admits students who can contribute to its learning community and who will thrive in a self-directed degree program. The admissions decision is based on the application, including essays, letters of recommendation, transcripts, samples of the student's creative or academic work, and an interview. Standardized test scores are unhelpful and not required. Homeschooled students are welcome to apply. AP and CLEP credits are accepted. Important factors in the admissions decision are personality/intangible qualities, recommendations by alumni, and evidence of special talent.

Procedure: Freshmen are admitted to all sessions. There are deferred admissions and rolling admissions plans. Check with the school for current application deadlines. The application fee is $40. Notification is sent on a rolling basis. Applications are accepted online.

Transfer: Official transcripts from previous institutions, writing samples, personal statements, letters of recommendation, and interviews are required. 45 of 120 credits required for the bachelor's degree must be completed at Goddard.

Visiting: There are regularly scheduled orientations for prospective students, consisting of Discover Goddard Days held in fall and spring, one visiting day during each residency, and individual meetings by appointment. There are guides for informal visits and visitors may sit in on classes. To schedule a visit, contact Respective admissions counselor for the program.

Financial Aid: The FAFSA is required. Check with the school for current application deadlines.

International Students: There are 2 international students enrolled.

Computers: All students may access the system 24 hours a day, 7 days a week. There are no time limits and no fees.

Admissions Contact: Jen Morin, Admissions Counselor. E-Mail: *admissions@.goddard.edu* Web: *www.goddard.edu*

GREEN MOUNTAIN COLLEGE — A-4

Poultney, VT 05764 — (802) 287-8000; (800) 776-6675; (802) 287-8099

Full-time: 400 men, 375 women	**Faculty:** n/av
Part-time: 10 men, 10 women	**Ph.D.s:** 93%
Graduate: 25 men, 35 women	**Student/Faculty:** n/av
Year: semesters	**Tuition:** $26,400
Application Deadline: open	**Room & Board:** $10,000
Freshman Class: n/av	
SAT: required	**ACT:** recommended

LESS COMPETITIVE

Green Mountain College, established in 1834, is a private, environmental liberal arts institution. There are 2 graduate schools. Figures in the above capsule and this profile are approximate. In addition to regional accreditation, GMC has baccalaureate program accreditation with NRPA. The library contains 60,000 volumes, 10,000 microform items, 2000 audio/video tapes/CDs/DVDs, and subscribes to 300 periodicals including electronic. Computerized library services include interlibrary loans, database searching, Internet access, and laptop Internet portals. Special learning facilities include a learning resource center, an art gallery, a radio station, an organic farm, a rope course, an ice-climbing wall, the Dean Nature Preserve, the Poultney River watershed, and Welsh Heritage Center. The 155-acre campus is in a small town 20 miles southwest of Rutland. Including any residence halls, there are 26 buildings.

Student Life: 84% of undergraduates are from out of state, mostly the Northeast. Students are from 32 states, 12 foreign countries, and Canada. 83% are from public schools. 70% are white. The average age of freshmen is 18; all undergraduates, 21. 28% do not continue beyond their first year; 40% remain to graduate.

Housing: 595 students can be accommodated in college housing, which includes coed dorms. In addition, there are honors houses, special-interest houses, and adventure-recreation, creative arts, quiet, substance-free, and sustainable living floors. On-campus housing is guaranteed for all 4 years. 95% of students live on campus; of those, 80% remain on campus on weekends. All students may keep cars.

Activities: There are no fraternities or sororities. There are 30 groups on campus, including art, bagpipe, band, Big Brother/Big Sister, cheerleading, choir, chorale, chorus, communications, dance, drama, environmental club, ethnic, gay, honors, international, jazz band, literary magazine, newspaper, orchestra, photography, professional, radio and TV, religious, rugby, social, social service, student government, ultimate Frisbee, and women's. Popular campus events include family weekend, Honors Banquet, and Welsh Heritage Harvest Festival.

Sports: There are 7 intercollegiate sports for men and 7 for women, and 8 intramural sports for men and 7 for women. Facilities include a gym with an indoor pool, weight room, playing fields, tennis courts, a par course, a fitness trail, and a ropes course.

Disabled Students: 70% of the campus is accessible. Facilities include wheelchair ramps, elevators, special parking, specially equipped rest rooms, special class scheduling, and lowered drinking fountains.

Services: Counseling and information services are available, as is tutoring in every subject. There is remedial math, reading, and writing.

Campus Safety and Security: Measures include 24-hour foot and vehicle patrol and security escort services. There are shuttle buses and lighted pathways/sidewalks.

Programs of Study: GMC confers B.A., B.S., and B.F.A. degrees. Master's degrees are also awarded. Bachelor's degrees are awarded in AGRICULTURE (environmental studies and natural resource management), BIOLOGICAL SCIENCE (biology/biological science), BUSINESS (business administration and management, hospitality management services, hotel/motel and restaurant management, recreation and leisure services, and recreational facilities management), COMMUNICATIONS AND THE ARTS (art, arts administration/management, communications, creative writing, English, fine arts, and visual and performing arts), EDUCATION (art education, elementary education, English education, secondary education, social studies education, and special education), HEALTH PROFESSIONS (recreation therapy), SOCIAL SCIENCE (behavioral science, history, liberal arts/general studies, philosophy, psychology, and sociology). Recreation, environmental studies, and education have the largest enrollment and are the strongest academically.

Required: To graduate, students must complete 37 hours in environmental liberal arts, including 4 core courses, a 1-credit orientation course, and 8 additional courses chosen from 4 distribution categories. A minimum GPA of 2.0 is required. Students must complete 120 to 125 credit hours, with 42 to 65 hours in the major. 33 credits must be completed in upper division courses.

Special: Semester-long internships are required in all majors. Students may study abroad in Wales, Korea, England, Spain, Japan, France, and Italy. Work-study programs and a self-designed major are available. Co-op and accelerated degree programs are available in resort management and hospitality management. There is 1 national honor society, a freshman honors program, and 4 departmental honors programs.

Faculty/Classroom: 64% of faculty are male; 36% are female. 66% teach undergraduates, and 34% both teach and do research. No introductory courses are taught by graduate students. The average class size in an introductory lecture is 25; in a laboratory, 9; and in a regular course, 14.

Requirements: The SAT is required. The ACT is recommended. In addition, applicants must graduate from an accredited secondary school or have a GED. 16 academic credits are required. Students must complete 4 years in English, 3 years in math, 2 to 3 years in science, and 2 years each in history and social studies. An essay is required. Test scores are optional. A GPA of 2.4 is required. AP and CLEP credits are accepted. Important factors in the admissions decision are personality/intangible qualities, advanced placement or honors courses, and evidence of special talent.

Procedure: Freshmen are admitted fall and spring. Entrance exams should be taken in the fall of the senior year of high school. There are deferred admissions and rolling admissions plans. Application deadlines are open. Check with the school for current application fee. Applications are accepted online.

Transfer: 49 transfer students enrolled in a recent year. Transfer students need a GPA of 2.0. They must have earned a minimum of 12 credits and are required to submit an essay. The SAT or ACT is required, along with 2 letters of recommendation and a dean's statement from last school attended. 30 of 120 credits required for the bachelor's degree must be completed at GMC.

Visiting: There are regularly scheduled orientations for prospective students, including a campus tour, presentations by administrators, student panel, lunch in dining hall, and academic offerings. There are guides for informal visits, visitors may sit in on classes, and stay overnight. To schedule a visit, contact the Campus Visit Coordinator.

Financial Aid: In a recent year, 90% of all full-time freshmen and 78% of continuing full-time students received some form of financial aid. 90% of all full-time freshmen and 72% of continuing full-time students received need-based aid. The average freshmen award was $12,500. 45% of undergraduate students work part-time. Average annual earnings from campus work are $1500. The average financial indebtedness of a recent graduate was $20,000. The FAFSA is required. Check with the school for current application deadlines.

International Students: There were 10 international students enrolled in a recent year. The school actively recruits these students. They must take the TOEFL. They must also take the SAT or ACT.

Computers: Wireless access is available. There are 80 PCs and Macs available for student use and two network jacks in each dorm room. Wireless access is available in the library. All students may access the system 24 hours/7 days a week. There are no time limits and no fees.

Graduates: In a recent year, 107 bachelor's degrees were awarded. The most popular majors were recreation (18%), environmental studies (14%), and education (12%). 21 companies recruited on campus in a recent year. In an average class, 24% graduate in 4 years or less, 37% graduate in 5 years or less, and 40% graduate in 6 years or less. Of a recent graduating class, 4% were enrolled in graduate school within 6 months of graduation, and 75% were employed.

Admissions Contact: Dean of Enrollment. A campus DVD is available. E-mail: *admiss@greenmtn.edu* Web: *www.greenmtn.edu*

JOHNSON STATE COLLEGE — B-2

Johnson, VT 05656 — (802) 635-1219; (800) 635-2356; (802) 635-1230

Full-time: 550 men, 660 women	**Faculty:** n/av; IIB, -$
Part-time: 100 men, 375 women	**Ph.D.s:** 90%
Graduate: 75 men, 225 women	**Student/Faculty:** n/av
Year: semesters, summer session	**Tuition:** $9400 ($19,500)
Application Deadline: open	**Room & Board:** $8700
Freshman Class: n/av	
SAT or ACT: required	

COMPETITIVE

Johnson State College, founded in 1828, is a public liberal arts and science college, offering more than 30 academic and professional degree programs. There is 1 graduate school. Figures in the above capsule and this profile are approximate. The library contains 96,584 volumes, 180,158 microform items, 7200 audio/video tapes/CDs/DVDs, and subscribes to 631 periodicals including electronic. Computerized library services include interlibrary loans, database searching, Internet access, and laptop Internet portals. Special learning facilities include a learning resource center, art gallery, radio station, and a 24-hour study room. The 350-acre campus is in a small town 45 miles northeast of Burlington. Including any residence halls, there are 12 buildings.

Student Life: 63% of undergraduates are from Vermont. Others are from 23 states, 6 foreign countries, and Canada. 90% are white. The average age of freshmen is 19; all undergraduates, 21. 30% do not continue beyond their first year; 45% remain to graduate.

Housing: 549 students can be accommodated in college housing, which includes coed dorms, on-campus apartments, and married student housing. In addition, there are special-interest houses and an alcohol-free residence hall. On-campus housing is guaranteed for all 4 years. 57% of students live on campus. Alcohol is not permitted. All students may keep cars.

Activities: There are no fraternities or sororities. There are 35 groups on campus, including art, band, choir, chorus, dance, debate, drama, environmental, gay, hospitality, jazz band, leadership, literary magazine, musical theater, newspaper, outdoor, photography, political, professional, radio and TV, religious, social, social service, and student government. Popular campus events include Winter Carnival and Coffee House (weekly live entertainment).

Sports: There are 6 intercollegiate sports for men and 6 for women, and 20 intramural sports for men and 20 for women. Facilities include a 7000-square-foot multiuse facility with health monitoring and exercise equipment, 2 gyms, a state-of-the-art weight room, a 25-yard indoor pool, a 700-seat varsity basketball court, 2 racquetball courts, a 26-foot indoor climbing and bouldering wall, and 1 squash court.

Disabled Students: 60% of the campus is accessible. Facilities include wheelchair ramps, elevators, special parking, specially equipped rest rooms, special class scheduling, and lowered drinking fountains.

Services: Counseling and information services are available, as is tutoring in most subjects. There is a reader service for the blind, and remedial math, reading, and writing. The Academic Support Services Department provides accommodations for students with a documented learning disability.

Campus Safety and Security: Measures include 24-hour foot and vehicle patrol, self-defense education, and security escort services. There are shuttle buses, emergency telephones, and lighted pathways/sidewalks.

Programs of Study: Johnson State confers B.A., B.S., and B.F.A. degrees. Associate and master's degrees are also awarded. Bachelor's degrees are awarded in AGRICULTURE (natural resource management), BIOLOGICAL SCIENCE (biology/biological science and cell biology), BUSINESS (business administration and management, business systems analysis, hospitality management services, recreational facilities management, small business management, and tourism), COMMUNICATIONS AND THE ARTS (art, creative writing, English, fine arts, jazz, journalism, music, music business management, music history and appreciation, music performance, performing arts, studio art, theater design, theater management, and visual and performing arts), COMPUTER AND PHYSICAL SCIENCE (mathematics), EDUCATION (art education, athletic training, education, elementary education, English education, environmental education, mathematics education, middle school education, music education, physical education, recreation education, science education, and secondary education), ENGINEERING AND ENVIRONMENTAL DESIGN (environmental science), HEALTH PROFESSIONS (allied health, health science, and premedicine), SOCIAL SCIENCE (anthropology, behavioral science, history, humanities, liberal arts/general studies, physical fitness/movement, political science/government, prelaw, psychology, and sociology). Environmental science, elementary/secondary/middle school education, and wellness and alternative medicine have the largest enrollments.

Required: The bachelor's degree requires completion of at least 120 credit hours of course work (not including basic skills credits), with a minimum cumulative GPA of 2.0. In addition, students must complete the general education core curriculum and an approved major as well as take a writing proficiency exam.

Special: All students are encouraged to complete an internship. Through the National Student Exchange program, students may study at another institution or abroad for a semester or a year. Co-op programs are offered in business, tourism, hospitality management, and education, and cross-registration is available with other Vermont state colleges. There is 1 national honor society.

Faculty/Classroom: 58% of faculty are male; 42% are female. All teach undergraduates. No introductory courses are taught by graduate students.

Requirements: The SAT or ACT is required. In addition, successful candidates for admission have generally completed a college preparatory curriculum consisting of 4 years of English, 3 of math (2 of algebra, 1 of geometry), 3 of social sciences, and 2 of science (including 1 lab science). An official high school transcript or GED test score must be submitted with the application. In addition, 1 letter of recommendation, preferably from a guidance counselor, and SAT or ACT scores should be sent with the application or under separate cover. A GPA of 2.3 is required. AP and CLEP credits are accepted. Important factors in the admissions decision are advanced placement or honors courses, recommendations by school officials, and extracurricular activities record.

Procedure: Freshmen are admitted fall and spring. There are deferred admissions and rolling admissions plans. Application deadlines are open. Check with the school for current application fee. Applications are accepted online.

Transfer: A GPA of at least 2.0 is required. 30 of 120 credits required for the bachelor's degree must be completed at Johnson State.

Visiting: There are regularly scheduled orientations for prospective students, including a campus tour and an admission interview. Students may request to meet with a faculty member. There are guides for informal visits, and visitors may sit in on classes. To schedule a visit, contact Admissions Receptionist.

Financial Aid: Johnson State is a member of CSS. The FAFSA is required. Check with the school for current application deadlines.

International Students: International students must take the TOEFL with a minimum score of 500 on the paper-based TOEFL (PBT) or 61 on the Internet-based version (iBT). Students with scores between 500 and 549 on the paper-based TOEFL or between 61 and 80 on the Internet-based version will be required to expand their proficiency in English. Students must also take the SAT or ACT, scoring 1400 on the SAT.

Computers: Wireless access is available. All students may access the system. There are no time limits and no fees.

Admissions Contact: Associate Dean of Enrollment Services. E-mail: *jscadmissions@jsc.edu* Web: *www.jsc.edu*

LYNDON STATE COLLEGE D-2

Lyndonville, VT 05851 (802) 626-6413
(800) 225-1998; (802) 626-6335

Full-time: 560 men, 570 women
Part-time: 70 men, 230 women
Graduate: 1 men, 5 women
Year: semesters, summer session
Application Deadline: see profile
Freshman Class: n/av
SAT or ACT: required
Faculty: n/av; IIB, --$
Ph.D.s: 60%
Student/Faculty: n/av
Tuition: $19,856
Room & Board: $8946

COMPETITIVE

Lyndon State College, founded in 1911 as a teachers' college, became a liberal arts school in 1962, offering undergraduate and graduate courses. There is 1 graduate school. Figures in the above capsule and this profile are approximate. In addition to regional accreditation, LSC has baccalaureate program accreditation with NRPA. The library contains 100,000 volumes, 10,000 microform items, 3600 audio/video tapes/CDs/DVDs, and subscribes to 545 periodicals including electronic. Computerized library services include interlibrary loans, database searching, and Internet access. Special learning facilities include a learning resource center, art gallery, radio station, TV station, founder's museum, and meteorology lab. The 175-acre campus is in a small town in northeastern Vermont, 184 miles north of Boston. Including any residence halls, there are 17 buildings.

Student Life: 60% of undergraduates are from Vermont. Others are from 24 states, 12 foreign countries, and Canada. 99% are white. The average age of freshmen is 18; all undergraduates, 24. 33% do not continue beyond their first year; 41% remain to graduate.

Housing: 600 students can be accommodated in college housing, which includes single-sex and coed dorms. In addition, there are special-interest houses. On-campus housing is available on a first-come, first-served basis. Priority is given to out-of-town students. 56% of students commute. All students may keep cars.

Activities: There are no fraternities or sororities. There are 22 groups on campus, including cheerleading, choir, chorale, chorus, communications, dance, drama, film, gay, honors, international, jazz band, literary magazine, newspaper, photography, political, professional, radio and TV, religious, social, social service, student government, and yearbook. Popular campus events include Family Weekend, Alumni Weekend, and a concert series.

Sports: There are 5 intercollegiate sports for men and 5 for women, and 12 intramural sports for men and 12 for women. Facilities include a fitness center, which includes a wide variety of cardiovascular, selectorized and free weight equipment; racquetball courts, an auxiliary gym, and an Olympic-size pool; outdoor tennis courts; cross-country ski trails and running trails; access to an ice rink, nearby mountains, and a ski resort; and softball, soccer, basketball and rugby fields.

Disabled Students: 70% of the campus is accessible. Facilities include wheelchair ramps, elevators, special parking, specially equipped rest rooms, and lowered drinking fountains.

Services: Counseling and information services are available, as is tutoring in every subject. There is remedial math, reading, and writing. A math lab and a writing center are available for student use.

Campus Safety and Security: Measures include 24-hour foot and vehicle patrol, self-defense education, and security escort services. There are emergency telephones, lighted pathways/sidewalks, and a security and safety service on campus as well as a 24-hour emergency rescue squad.

Programs of Study: LSC confers B.A. and B.S. degrees. Associate and master's degrees are also awarded. Bachelor's degrees are awarded in BUSINESS (accounting, business administration and management, recreation and leisure services, and sports management), COMMUNICATIONS AND THE ARTS (communications, English, graphic design, journalism, multimedia, and radio/television technology), COMPUTER AND PHYSICAL SCIENCE (atmospheric sciences and meteorology, mathematics, natural sciences, and science), EDUCATION (early childhood education, elementary education, English education, physical education, recreation education, and science education), SOCIAL SCIENCE (human services, interdisciplinary studies, psychology, and social science). Meteorology, natural science, and math are the strongest academically. Education, communications, and business have the largest enrollments.

Required: All students must maintain a minimum GPA of 2.0 while taking 122 semester hours, including 42 hours in liberal arts. Distribution requirements include 28 credits in arts, humanities, math and science, and social and behavioral sciences. Required courses include freshman English and college algebra.

Special: Cooperative programs in a variety of businesses, including local ski areas, social agencies, and radio and TV stations, internships in recreation programs and communications, and study abroad in Nova Scotia and England are available. B.A.-B.S. degrees, work-study, a general studies degree, dual and student-designed majors, a 3-2 engineering degree with Norwich University in Vermont, credit for life experience, nondegree study, cross-registration, work study, accelerated degree programs, and pass/fail options also are offered. There is 1 national honor society, a freshman honors program, and 1 departmental honors program.

Faculty/Classroom: 66% of faculty are male; 34% are female. All teach undergraduates. No introductory courses are taught by graduate students. The average class size in an introductory lecture is 20; in a laboratory, 16; and in a regular course, 16.

Requirements: The SAT or ACT is required. In addition, LSC recommends that applicants have 4 years of English and 2 each of math, foreign language, history, and science. An essay is required, as is a recommendation from the high school principal or guidance counselor. An interview is recommended. The GED is accepted. A GPA of 2.0 is required. AP and CLEP credits are accepted. Important factors in the admissions decision are advanced placement or honors courses, recommendations by school officials, and leadership record.

Procedure: Freshmen are admitted fall and spring. There are early decision, early admissions, deferred admissions, and rolling admissions plans. Check with the school for current application deadlines and fee. Applications are accepted online.

Transfer: Interviews are recommended for transfer students. An official transcript from each college attended is required. 30 of 122 credits required for the bachelor's degree must be completed at LSC.

Visiting: There are regularly scheduled orientations for prospective students, including a tour, an information session, and faculty presentations. There are guides for informal visits, and visitors may sit in on classes and stay overnight. To schedule a visit, contact the Admissions Office.

Financial Aid: LSC is a member of CSS. The FAFSA and parent and student income tax forms, if requested, are required. Check with the school for current application deadlines.

International Students: They must take the TOEFL.

Computers: All students may access the system 24 hours a day, 7 days a week. There are no time limits and no fees. It is strongly recommended that all students have a personal computer. A Dell or Apple computer is recommended.

Admissions Contact: Admissions. E-mail: *admissions@lyndonstate.edu* Web: *www.lsv.vsc.edu*

MARLBORO COLLEGE B-6

Marlboro, VT 05344 (802) 258-9261
(800) 343-0049; (802) 258-9300

Full-time: 126 men, 201 women
Part-time: 4 men, 5 women
Graduate: n/av
Year: semesters
Application Deadline: February 15
Freshman Class: n/av
SAT or ACT: required
Faculty: 35
Ph.D.s: 77%
Student/Faculty: 9 to 1
Tuition: $37,060
Room & Board: $10,140

VERY COMPETITIVE

Marlboro College, established in 1946, is a small private institution offering degrees in the liberal and fine arts and humanities, and employing self-designed programs of study. The figures in the above capsule and in this profile are approximate. There is one graduate school. The library contains 65,216 volumes, 5,799 microform items, and 2,990 audio/video tapes/CDs/DVDs, and subscribes to 188 periodicals including electronic. Computerized library services include interlibrary loans, database searching, Internet access, and Wi-Fi capability. Special learning facilities include an art gallery, planetarium, observatory. The 366-acre campus is in a rural area 9 miles west of Brattleboro, 2 1/2 hours from Boston. Including any residence halls, there are 36 buildings.

Student Life: 89% of undergraduates are from out of state, mostly the Northeast. Students are from 36 states, 5 foreign countries, and Canada. 70% are from public schools. 83% are White. The average age of freshmen is 19; all undergraduates, 21. 28% do not continue beyond their first year; 48% remain to graduate.

Housing: 266 students can be accommodated in college housing, which includes single-sex and coed dorms, on-campus apartments, and married student housing. alcohol-free and smoke-free dorms. On-campus housing is guaranteed for the freshman year only, is available on a first-come, and first-served basis. 84% of students live on campus; of those, 90% remain on campus on weekends. All students may keep cars.

Activities: There are no fraternities or sororities. There are 25 groups on campus, including art, chess, chorus, communications, computers, dance, drama, film, gay, international, jazz band, literary magazine, musical theater, newspaper, photography, political, social, social service, and student government. Popular campus events include Green-up Day, Creativity Lecture Series, and Visiting Writers Series.

Sports: There are 1 intercollegiate sports for men and 1 for women, and 1 intramural sports for men and 1 for women. Facilities include a soccer field, a volleyball court, cross-country trails, a basketball court, a weight room, a climbing wall, and field trips for canoeing, white-water rafting, and skiing.

Disabled Students: 90% of the campus is accessible. Facilities include

wheelchair ramps, special parking, specially equipped restrooms, and special class scheduling.

Services: Counseling and information services are available, as is tutoring in some subjects, including writing, languages, math, and organic chemistry.

Campus Safety and Security: Measures include self-defense education. alcohol-free and smoke-free dorms.

Programs of Study: Marlboro confers B.A., and B.S. degrees. Master's degrees are also awarded. Bachelor's degrees are awarded in BIOLOGICAL SCIENCE (biochemistry, biology/biological science, botany, and microbiology), COMMUNICATIONS AND THE ARTS (creative writing, dance, dramatic arts, English, fine arts, French, German, Greek, Italian, Latin, linguistics, music, photography, Russian, and Spanish), COMPUTER AND PHYSICAL SCIENCE (chemistry, computer science, mathematics, and physics), HEALTH PROFESSIONS (premedicine), SOCIAL SCIENCE (anthropology, economics, history, interdisciplinary studies, international studies, philosophy, political science/government, prelaw, psychology, social science, and sociology). Sciences, humanities, and world studies are the strongest academically. Literature, biology, and sociology have the largest enrollments.

Required: To graduate, students must complete a plan of concentration, a writing requirement, and a freshman seminar. A minimum GPA of 2.0 is required. Students must earn 120 credits, with 50 credits in the major, and complete a thesis and an oral exam.

Special: Marlboro offers a variety of internships, cross registration with Huron University in London, and study abroad in many countries. The World Studies Program combines liberal arts with international studies, including 5 to 8 months of internship work in another culture. Accelerated and B.A.-B.S. degree programs are available. Students may pursue dual majors. Majors reflect an integrated course of study designed by students and their faculty advisers during the junior year.

Faculty/Classroom: 62% of faculty are male; 38% are female. All teach undergraduates. No introductory courses are taught by graduate students. The average class size in an introductory lecture is 10; in a laboratory is 8; and in a regular course is 8.

Admissions: 78% of the 2013-2014 applicants were accepted. The ACT scores were 35% between 21 and 23, 29% between 24 and 26, 29% between 27 and 28, and 7% above 28. 46% of the current freshmen were in the top fifth of their class; 82% were in the top two fifths. 2 freshmen graduated first in their class.

Requirements: The SAT or ACT is required. In addition, applicants typically graduate from an accredited secondary school or have a GED. They are encouraged to earn 16 Carnegie units and complete 4 years of English and 3 years each of math, science, history, and a foreign language. Essays and interviews are required. AP and CLEP credits are accepted. Important factors in the admissions decision are advanced placement or honors courses, evidence of special talent, and extracurricular activities record.

Procedure: Freshmen are admitted fall and spring. Entrance exams should be taken by October before entry. There are early decision, early admissions, and deferred admissions plans. Early decision applications should be filed by November 15; regular applications, by February 15 for fall entry; and December 1 for spring entry. The fall 2013 application fee was $50. Notification of early decision is sent December 15; regular decision, April 1. Applications are accepted online.

Transfer: Transfers must have a minimum GPA of 2.0. 42 of 120 credits required for the bachelor's degree must be completed at Marlboro.

Visiting: There are regularly scheduled orientations for prospective students, including a tour, faculty interview, and discussions with admissions and financial aid. There are guides for informal visits, visitors may sit in on classes, and stay overnight. To schedule a visit, contact the Office of Admissions.

Financial Aid: In 2013-2014, 85% of all full-time freshmen and 85% of continuing full-time students received some form of financial aid. 68% of all full-time freshmen and 80% of continuing full-time students received need-based aid. The average freshman award was $20,907. Need-based scholarships or need-based grants averaged $15,969 ($24,250 maximum); need-based self-help aid (loans and jobs) averaged $4,289 ($4,555 maximum); and other non-need-based awards and non-need-based scholarships averaged $11,723 ($20,950 maximum). 68% of undergraduate students work part-time. Average annual earnings from campus work are $1118. Marlboro is a member of CSS. The CSS/Profile and FAFSA are required. The priority date for freshman financial aid applications for fall entry is February 15. The deadline for filing freshman financial aid applications for fall entry is March 1.

International Students: There are 6 international students enrolled. The school actively recruits these students. They must take the TOEFL.

Computers: All students may access the system 24 hours a day. There are no time limits and no fees.

Graduates: In an average class, 48% graduate in 5 years or less.

Admissions Contact: Brigid Lawler, Dean of Admissions. E-Mail: *blawler@marlboro.edu* Web: *www.marlboro.edu*

MIDDLEBURY COLLEGE — A-3

Middlebury, VT 05753 — **(802) 443-3000; (802) 443-2065**

Full-time: 1207 men, 1270 women	**Faculty:** 267; IIB, +$
Part-time: 12 men, 6 women	**Ph.D.s:** 95%
Graduate: n/av	**Student/Faculty:** 9 to 1
Year: 4-1-4	**Tuition:** $45,314
Application Deadline: January 1	**Room & Board:** $12,156

Freshman Class: 9109 applied, 1595 accepted, 625 enrolled

SAT CR/M/W: 688/692/697 **ACT:** 31 **MOST COMPETITIVE**

Founded in 1800, Middlebury College is a small, private liberal arts institution offering degree programs in languages, humanities, and social and natural sciences. There is one undergraduate school and 3 graduate schools. The 2 libraries contain 3.0 million volumes, 702 microform items, 43,589 audio/video tapes/CDs/DVDs, and subscribe to 78,711 periodicals including electronic. Computerized library services include interlibrary loans, database searching, Internet access, and Wi-Fi capability. Special learning facilities include an art gallery, planetarium, and radio station. The 355-acre campus is in a small town 35 miles south of Burlington. Including any residence halls, there are 115 buildings.

Student Life: 94% of undergraduates are from out of state, mostly the Northeast. Students are from 52 states, 74 foreign countries, and Canada. 66% are White; 11% Foreign. The average age of freshmen is 18; all undergraduates, 20. 5% do not continue beyond their first year; 94% remain to graduate.

Housing: 2433 students can be accommodated in college housing, which includes single-sex and coed dorms, on-campus apartments, and married student housing. In addition, there are language houses, special-interest houses, coed social, multicultural and environmental houses. On-campus housing is guaranteed for all 4 years and is available on a lottery system for upperclassmen. 95% of students live on campus. All students may keep cars.

Activities: There are no fraternities or sororities. There are 150 groups on campus, including art, band, cheerleading, chess, choir, chorus, communications, computers, dance, debate, drama, environmental, ethnic, film, gay, honors, international, jazz band, literary magazine, Middlebury Mountain Club, musical theater, newspaper, orchestra, pep band, photography, political, professional, radio and TV, religious, social, social service, student government, and yearbook. Popular campus events include Winter Carnival, Student Concert Series, and Clifford Symposium.

Sports: There are 12 intercollegiate sports for men and 11 for women, and 16 intramural sports for men and 16 for women. Facilities include Middlebury's well-maintained playing fields and outstanding athletic facilities rank among the best in the country. Facilities include a 3,500-seat football and lacrosse complex, baseball and softball fields, 18-hole golf course, 3.5-km cross country trail, 2,200-seat hockey arena, Olympic-size natatorium, new squash courts, tennis courts, climbing wall, gymnasium, 6,500-square-foot fitness center, astro-turf fields, all-weather outdoor track.

Disabled Students: 65% of the campus is accessible. Facilities include wheelchair ramps, elevators, special parking, specially equipped restrooms, special class scheduling, lowered drinking fountains, lowered telephones, and special housing.

Services: Counseling and information services are available, as is tutoring in every subject. There is a reader service for the blind.

Campus Safety and Security: Measures include 24-hour foot and vehicle patrol, emergency notification system, self-defense education, and security escort services. There are shuttle buses, emergency telephones, lighted pathways/sidewalks, controlled access to dorms/residences, a paid student patrol, a ski patrol at the Snow Bowl, and a special events staff.

Programs of Study: Midd confers A.B. degrees. Master's and doctoral degrees are also awarded. Bachelor's degrees are awarded in AGRICULTURE (environmental studies), BIOLOGICAL SCIENCE (biochemistry, biology/biological science, molecular biology, and neurosciences), BUSINESS (international economics), COMMUNICATIONS AND THE ARTS (Arabic, Chinese, classics, comparative literature, dance, dramatic arts, English, film arts, French, German, Italian, Japanese, music, Russian, Spanish, and studio art), COMPUTER AND PHYSICAL SCIENCE (chemistry, computer science, geology, mathematics, and physics), ENGINEERING AND ENVIRONMENTAL DESIGN (architectural history), SOCIAL SCIENCE (African American studies, American studies, anthropology, East Asian studies, economics, European studies, geography, history, Latin American studies, liberal arts/general studies, Middle Eastern studies, philosophy, political science/government, psychology, religion, Russian and Slavic studies, sociology, South Asian studies, and women's studies). Foreign languages, international studies, and sciences are the strongest academically. Economics, environmental studies, and political science have the largest enrollments.

Required: Candidates for the Bachelor of Arts degree must complete 36 courses. At least 18 of these courses must be Middlebury courses. Courses taken at Middlebury summer Language Schools or at the Middlebury Schools Abroad will count in the 18-course total and the grades will count in the undergraduate grade point average.

Special: In addition to extensive study abroad opportunities, Middlebury

College offers Pre-Professional Combined Programs as well as Washington Semester, Maritime Studies, and Exchange Programs with Spelman and Swarthmore Colleges and the Association of Vermont Independent Colleges. Other opportunities include a semester at Woods Hole Marine Biological Laboratory and Dual-Degree Engineering Programs with Dartmouth and Columbia. There is Phi Beta Kappa chapter and 36 departmental honors programs.

Faculty/Classroom: 54% of faculty are male; 46% are female. All teach undergraduates. No introductory courses are taught by graduate students. The average class size in an introductory lecture is 20 and in a regular course is 20.

Admissions: 18% of the 2013-2014 applicants were accepted. The SAT scores for the 2013-2014 freshman class were: Critical Reading--1% below 500, 13% between 500 and 599, 34% between 600 and 699, and 52% between 700 and 800; Math--1% below 500, 9% between 500 and 599, 38% between 600 and 699, and 52% between 700 and 800; Writing--1% below 500, 10% between 500 and 599, 34% between 600 and 699, and 56% between 700 and 800. The ACT scores were 2% between 21 and 23, 25% between 24 and 26, and 73% above 28.

Requirements: The SAT or ACT is required. AP credits are accepted. Important factors in the admissions decision are leadership record, advanced placement or honors courses, evidence of special talent, personality/intangible qualities, extracurricular activities record, geographical diversity, recommendations by school officials, and parents or siblings attended the school.

Procedure: Freshmen are admitted fall and spring. Entrance exams should be taken by December of the senior year. There are early decision, early admissions, and deferred admissions plans. Early decision applications should be filed by November 1; regular applications, by January 1 for fall entry, along with a $65 fee. Notification of early decision is sent January 1; regular decision, March 30. 352 early decision candidates were accepted for the 2013-2014 class. Applications are accepted online.

Transfer: 1 transfer students enrolled in 2012-2013. Transfer students must have the strongest academic record possible through high school and a minimum 3.0 average in college. 18 of 36 credits required for the bachelor's degree must be completed at Midd.

Visiting: There are regularly scheduled orientations for prospective students, including campus tours and a group or individual interview. There are guides for informal visits and visitors may sit in on classes. To schedule a visit, contact the Admissions Office.

Financial Aid: In 2013-2014, 46% of all full-time freshmen and 40% of continuing full-time students received some form of financial aid. 45% of all full-time freshmen and 40% of continuing full-time students received need-based aid. The average freshman award was $41,606. Need-based scholarships or need-based grants averaged $38,981; and need-based self-help aid (loans and jobs) averaged $3,320. The average financial indebtedness of the 2013 graduate was $17,715. Midd is a member of CSS. The CSS/Profile and FAFSA, and federal tax forms, non-custodial profile are required. The priority date for freshman financial aid applications for fall entry is November 15. The deadline for filing freshman financial aid applications for fall entry is February 1.

International Students: There are 252 international students enrolled. The school actively recruits these students. They must take the TOEFL. They must also take the SAT or ACT and fulfill the same requirements as first-year applicants.

Computers: All students may access the system 24 hours a day. There are no time limits and no fees.

Graduates: From July 1, 2012 to June 30, 2013, 656 bachelor's degrees were awarded. The most popular majors were economics (13%), political science (7%), and environmental studies (7%). In an average class, 87% graduate in 4 years or less, 93% graduate in 5 years or less, and 94% graduate in 6 years or less. Of the 2012 graduating class, 12% were enrolled in graduate school within 6 months of graduation, and 49% were employed.

Admissions Contact: Greg Buckles, Dean of Admissions. E-Mail: *admissions@middlebury.edu* Web: *www.middlebury.edu*

NORWICH UNIVERSITY C-3

Northfield, VT 05663
(802) 485-2001
(800) 468-6679; (802) 485-2032

Full-time: 1360 men, 500 women	**Faculty:** n/av; IIA, -$
Part-time: 35 men, 10 women	**Ph.D.s:** 85%
Graduate: 540 men, 215 women	**Student/Faculty:** n/av
Year: semesters, summer session	**Tuition:** $30,500
Application Deadline: open	**Room & Board:** $11,500
Freshman Class: n/av	
SAT or ACT: required	

COMPETITIVE

Norwich University, founded in 1819, offers programs in the arts and sciences, architecture, engineering, health and physical science, criminal justice, history, international studies, studies in war and peace, management, and accounting. There are 6 undergraduate schools and 2 graduate schools. Figures in the above capsule and this profile are approximate. In addition to regional accreditation, Norwich has baccalaureate program accreditation with ABET, ACBSP, and NLN. The library contains 245,931 volumes, 90,435 microform items, and 2872 audio/video tapes/CDs/DVDs, and subscribes to 815 periodicals including electronic. Computerized library services include interlibrary loans, database searching, Internet access, and laptop Internet portals. Special learning facilities include a learning resource center, art gallery, natural history museum, radio station, greenhouse, and 3 computer labs. The 1125-acre campus is in a rural area 11 miles south of Montpelier. Including any residence halls, there are 36 buildings.

Student Life: 80% of undergraduates are from out of state, mostly the Northeast. Students are from 39 states, 13 foreign countries, and Canada. 82% are white. The average age of freshmen is 18; all undergraduates, 21. 25% do not continue beyond their first year; 52% remain to graduate.

Housing: 1598 students can be accommodated in college housing, which includes single-sex and coed dorms. On-campus housing is guaranteed for the freshman year only and is available on a lottery system for upperclassmen. Priority is given to out-of-town students. 83% of students live on campus; of those, 85% remain on campus on weekends. Alcohol is not permitted. Upperclassmen may keep cars.

Activities: There are no fraternities or sororities. There are 75 groups on campus, including band, cheerleading, chess, choir, chorus, communications, computers, drama, drill team, ethnic, honors, international, jazz band, literary magazine, marching band, musical theater, newspaper, orchestra, pep band, photography, political, professional, radio and TV, religious, social service, and student government. Popular campus events include Regimental Ball, Winter Carnival, and Junior Weekend.

Sports: There are 12 intercollegiate sports for men and 7 for women, and 8 intramural sports for men and 8 for women. Facilities include an ice hockey arena, a field house with an indoor track, an indoor swimming pool, an aerobics room, weight and wrestling rooms, playing fields, an outdoor track, a 1200-seat basketball arena, and a 1000-seat hockey arena.

Disabled Students: Facilities include wheelchair ramps, elevators, special parking, specially equipped rest rooms, and lowered drinking fountains.

Services: Counseling and information services are available, as is tutoring in most subjects. There is remedial math, reading, and writing.

Campus Safety and Security: Measures include 24-hour foot and vehicle patrol. There are lighted pathways/sidewalks.

Programs of Study: Norwich confers B.A., B.S., and B.Arch. degrees. Associate degrees are also awarded. Bachelor's degrees are awarded in BIOLOGICAL SCIENCE (biochemistry and biology/biological science), BUSINESS (accounting, business administration and management, and business economics), COMMUNICATIONS AND THE ARTS (communications and English), COMPUTER AND PHYSICAL SCIENCE (chemistry, computer science, computer security and information assurance, geology, information sciences and systems, mathematics, and physics), EDUCATION (physical education), ENGINEERING AND ENVIRONMENTAL DESIGN (architecture, civil engineering, computer engineering, electrical/electronics engineering, environmental science, mechanical engineering, and military science), HEALTH PROFESSIONS (medical laboratory technology, nursing, and sports medicine), SOCIAL SCIENCE (criminal justice, history, international studies, liberal arts/general studies, peace studies, political science/government, and psychology). Engineering and architecture are the strongest academically. Criminal justice and nursing have the largest enrollments.

Required: The total number of required credits and courses vary by program. All students are required to complete 3 credit hours in history and English 101-102 and 2 semesters in phys ed. A 2.0 GPA is required to graduate.

Special: Norwich offers internships, a Washington semester, work-study on and off campus for service organizations and criminal justice programs, a B.A.-B.S. degree in communications, and study abroad in 15 countries through other schools and organizations and through the Vermont Overseas Studies Program. International studies majors must study abroad in a country whose language they are studying. There are 5 national honor societies, including Phi Beta Kappa, and 5 departmental honors programs.

Faculty/Classroom: 74% of faculty are male; 26% are female. 82% teach undergraduates, and 82% do both. No introductory courses are taught by graduate students. The average class size in an introductory lecture is 20; in a laboratory, 13; and in a regular course, 18.

Requirements: The SAT or ACT is required. In addition, applicants should graduate from an accredited secondary school with 18 academic credits or achieve the GED equivalent. AP and CLEP credits are accepted. Important factors in the admissions decision are leadership record, extracurricular activities record, and evidence of special talent.

Procedure: Freshmen are admitted fall and spring. Entrance exams should be taken starting with spring of the junior year. There is a rolling admissions plan. Application deadlines are open. Check with the school for current application fee. Applications are accepted online.

Transfer: Transfer students should present a 2.0 GPA and meet all standards for entering freshmen. 60 of 116 credits required for the bachelor's degree must be completed at Norwich.

Visiting: There are regularly scheduled orientations for prospective students, including meetings with representatives from admissions, financial aid, academic offices, including Dean of Students or Commandant's Office, athletics (if desired), and a campus tour. There are guides for informal visits, and visitors may sit in on classes and stay overnight. To schedule a visit, contact Admissions, Main Office.

Financial Aid: Norwich is a member of CSS. The CSS/Profile and FAFSA are required. Check with the school for current application deadlines.

International Students: They must take the TOEFL.

Computers: Wireless access is available. There is open access. Dorms are wired and there is no limitation to Internet access or other use of the network. All students may access the system 24 hours per day. There are no time limits. It is strongly recommended that all students have a personal computer. Students enrolled in architecture must have a personal computer.

Admissions Contact: Dean of Enrollment Management. E-mail: *nuadm@norwich.edu* Web: *www.norwich.edu*

SAINT MICHAEL'S COLLEGE A-2

Colchester, VT 05439 (802) 654-3000
(800) 762-8000; (802) 654-2906

Full-time: 904 men, 1044 women	**Faculty:** 155; IIB, --$
Part-time: 12 men, 11 women	**Ph.D.s:** 86%
Graduate: 103 men, 336 women	**Student/Faculty:** 13 to 1
Year: semesters, summer session	**Tuition:** $39,015
Application Deadline: February 1	**Room & Board:** $9725
Freshman Class: 4578 applied, 3570 accepted, 547 enrolled	
SAT CR/M/W: 580/570/570 **ACT:** 25	**VERY COMPETITIVE**

Saint Michael's College, was founded in 1904 by the Society of Saint Edmund. We are a selective Catholic liberal arts college, with a community of 2,000 students in residence and over 150 full-time faculty members. We are located on a 440 acre campus overlooking the Green Mountains and Burlington, Vermont. There is one graduate school. The library contains 277,282 volumes, 137,000 microform items, and 12,812 audio/video tapes/CDs/DVDs, and subscribes to 82,500 periodicals including electronic. Computerized library services include interlibrary loans, database searching, Internet access, and Wi-Fi capability. Special learning facilities include an art gallery, radio station, an observatory. The 440-acre campus is in a suburban area 2 miles east of Burlington, Vermont. Including any residence halls, there are 51 buildings.

Student Life: 79% of undergraduates are from out of state, mostly the Northeast. Students are from 35 states, 16 foreign countries, and Canada. 68% are from public schools. 87% are White. 54% are Catholic; 20% Protestant; 20% claim no religious affiliation. The average age of freshmen is 18; all undergraduates, 20. 10% do not continue beyond their first year; 79% remain to graduate.

Housing: 1900 students can be accommodated in college housing, which includes single-sex and coed dorms and on-campus apartments. In addition, there are honors houses, special-interest houses, theme housing, and substance-free housing. On-campus housing is guaranteed for all 4 years. 96% of students live on campus; of those, 85% remain on campus on weekends. All students may keep cars.

Activities: There are no fraternities or sororities. There are 50 groups on campus, including cand cycling, skiing, wilderness program, art, band, cheerleading, choir, chorale, chorus, communications, dance, drama, environmental, ethnic, fire and rescue, gay, honors, international, jazz band, literary magazine, musical theater, newspaper, pep band, photography, political, professional, radio and TV, religious, social, social service, student government, and yearbook. Popular campus events include Family Weekend, Christmas and Spring Semi-Formals and Spring Weekend.

Sports: There are 10 intercollegiate sports for men and 11 for women, and 22 intramural sports for men and 22 for women. Facilities include a 2,500-seat gym and field house with basketball, volleyball, tennis, and badminton courts, 4 multipurpose courts, a 6-lane swimming pool, fitness center, training room, weight room, climbing wall, pool, table tennis, suspended track, soccer, racquetball and squash courts, field hockey, lacrosse, baseball, and softball fields.

Disabled Students: 75% of the campus is accessible. Facilities include wheelchair ramps, elevators, special parking, specially equipped restrooms, special class scheduling, lowered drinking fountains, lowered telephones, special housing. Other accommodations are provided on an individual basis.

Services: Counseling and information services are available, as is tutoring in every subject. Tutoring can be arranged on an individual basis. The following are available: peer tutoring, writing center, quantitative skills, study skills.

Campus Safety and Security: Measures include 24-hour foot and vehicle patrol, emergency notification system, self-defense education, and security escort services. There are shuttle buses, emergency telephones, lighted pathways/sidewalks, controlled access to dorms/residences, a campus fire and rescue squad.

Programs of Study: Saint Michael's confers B.A., and B.S. degrees. Master's degrees are also awarded. Bachelor's degrees are awarded in AGRICULTURE (environmental studies), BIOLOGICAL SCIENCE (biochemistry and biology/biological science), BUSINESS (accounting and business administration and management), COMMUNICATIONS AND THE ARTS (dramatic arts, English, fine arts, French, journalism, music, and Spanish), COMPUTER AND PHYSICAL SCIENCE (chemistry, computer science, information sciences and systems, mathematics, physical sciences, and physics), EDUCATION (art education, elementary education, foreign languages education, science education, and secondary education), ENGINEERING AND ENVIRONMENTAL DESIGN (preengineering), HEALTH PROFESSIONS (preallied health and prepharmacy), SOCIAL SCIENCE (American studies, anthropology, economics, gender studies, history, philosophy, political science/government, prelaw, psychology, religion, and sociology). Business administration, psychology, and biology have the largest enrollments.

Required: To earn the degree of Bachelor of Arts or the degree of Bachelor of Science a student must: Complete a minimum of 128 credit hours (equivalent to 32 full-courses). Complete the degree requirements of one of the established majors or a special major approved by the Curriculum and Education Policy Committee. Complete the Liberal Studies Curriculum requirements (see below). Achieve a minimum cumulative quality point average of 2.0 and a minimum of a 2.0 average in courses taken in the major. Complete a minimum of twenty-four of the last thirty-two credits at Saint Michael's. Transfer students, must earn a minimum of sixty four credits at Saint Michael's College. The Liberal Studies Curriculum (LSC) is fulfilled through specific course requirement options and courses within the student's major field. Areas of study within the LSC include: Fundamental Philosophical Questions, Study of Christian Traditions and Thought, Ethical Decision Making, Global Issues that Impact the Common Good, Historical Studies, Literary Studies, Processes of Scientific Reasoning, Quantitative Reasoning, Second Language (depending on placement), Social and Institutional Dimensions of Human Behavior, Artistic Experience, Experiential Learning, Oral and Written Communication.

Special: A variety of special academic programs and enriching academic experiences are available at Saint Michael's College. During the most recent academic year over 40% of our graduates participated in a "for credit" internship, most of which were associated with the student's major. On-campus work-study opportunities are available in departments and offices throughout the College. Students can choose from more than 100 study abroad programs in countries spanning the globe (see our website for specific destinations). There are also opportunities for semester long domestic "study away" programs including a Washington semester with American University. Student-designed majors may be pursued and nearly 20% of our most recent graduating class completed a double major. 43% of the most recent graduating class participated in "for credit" study abroad experiences including summer and winter sessions as well as short term faculty led programs. The college offers a 3-2 engineering degree program in cooperation with Clarkson University and the University of Vermont and a 4+1 graduate business program is available with Clarkson University. A B.S./Pharm.D. degree is also available with the Albany College of Pharmacy and Health Services. Non-degree study and pass/fail grading options are offered on a limited basis. Independent research and undergraduate research opportunities with faculty are available through many departments. There are 11 national honor societies, including Phi Beta Kappa, a freshman honors program, and 1 departmental honors program.

Faculty/Classroom: 54% of faculty are male; 46% are female. All teach and do research. No introductory courses are taught by graduate students. The average class size in an introductory lecture is 24; in a laboratory is 16; and in a regular course is 18.

Admissions: 78% of the 2013-2014 applicants were accepted. The SAT scores for the 2013-2014 freshman class were: Critical Reading--13% below 500, 43% between 500 and 599, 39% between 600 and 699, and 5% between 700 and 800; Math--15% below 500, 46% between 500 and 599, 34% between 600 and 699, and 5% between 700 and 800; Writing--15% below 500, 47% between 500 and 599, 33% between 600 and 699, and 5% between 700 and 800. The ACT scores were 14% below 21, 14% between 21 and 23, 32% between 24 and 26, 17% between 27 and 28, and 23% above 28. 49% of the current freshmen were in the top fifth of their class; 73% were in the top two fifths. 11 freshmen graduated first in their class.

Requirements: The SAT or ACT and ACT Writing Test are recommended. Applicants must graduate from an accredited secondary school or have a GED. They must complete 16 Carnegie units. The college requires 4 credits in English, 3 to 4 credits in math and science, and 3 each in history (social studies) and a foreign language. An essay is required and an interview is recommended. Stanardized tests are optional. There are three application deadlines: Early Action 1-(November 1st), Early Action 2-(December 1st), Regular Decision-(February 1st). AP and CLEP credits are accepted. Important factors in the admissions decision are advanced placement or honors courses, evidence of special talent, and recommendations by school officials.

Procedure: Freshmen are admitted fall and spring. Entrance exams should be taken in the fall of the senior year. There is a deferred admissions plan. Applications should be filed by February 1 for fall entry; November 1 for spring entry, along with a $50 fee. Notifications are sent April 1. 100 applicants were on the 2013 waiting list; 21 were admitted. Applications are accepted online.

Transfer: 34 transfer students enrolled in 2012-2013. Transfer applicants must have a minimum GPA of 2.5; generally, those admitted have a GPA of at least 3.0. The SAT is optional. An interview is recommended. 64 of 128 credits required for the bachelor's degree must be completed at Saint Michael's.

Visiting: There are regularly scheduled orientations for prospective students, typically a campus visit includes a group information session, a video about the school, a campus tour, and a meeting with a staff member to review admissions criteria. There are guides for informal visits and visitors may sit in on classes. To schedule a visit, contact the Admissions Office.

Financial Aid: In 2013-2014, 96% of all full-time freshmen and 94% of continuing full-time students received some form of financial aid. 78% of all full-time freshmen and 69% of continuing full-time students received need-based aid. The average freshman award was $26,539. Need-based scholarships or need-based grants averaged $21,468 ($46,860 maximum); need-based self-help aid (loans and jobs) averaged $5,952 ($13,300 maximum); non-need-based athletic scholarships averaged $46,860 ($46,860 maximum); and other non-need-based awards and non-need-based scholarships averaged $12,993 ($46,860 maximum). 44% of undergraduate students work part-time. Average annual earnings from campus work are $1574. The average financial indebtedness of the 2013 graduate was $33,054. Saint Michael's is a member of CSS. The FAFSA, federal tax forms from both student and parents, and W-2 forms are required. The deadline for filing freshman financial aid applications for fall entry is February 15.

International Students: There are 47 international students enrolled. The school actively recruits these students. They must take the TOEFL with a minimum score of 550 on the paper-based TOEFL (PBT) or 79 on the Internet-based version (iBT). The SAT or ACT is optional for international students but recommended. The TOEFL may be used in place of the SAT.

Computers: All students may access the system. There are no time limits and no fees.

Graduates: From July 1, 2012 to June 30, 2013, 470 bachelor's degrees were awarded. The most popular majors were business administration and accounting (22%), psychology (12%), and biological/life sciences (9%). 100 companies recruited on campus in 2012-2013. In an average class, 74% graduate in 4 years or less, 78% graduate in 5 years or less, and 79% graduate in 6 years or less. Of the 2012 graduating class, 17% were enrolled in graduate school within 6 months of graduation, and 83% were employed.

Admissions Contact: Jacqueline Murphy, Director of Office of Admission. E-Mail: *admission@smcvt.edu* Web: *www.smcvt.edu*

SOUTHERN VERMONT COLLEGE — A-6

Bennington, VT 05201 (802) 447-6300 (800) 378-2782; (802) 447-4695

Full-time: 188 men, 349 women	**Faculty:** 25
Part-time: 18 men, 46 women	**Ph.D.s:** 50%
Graduate: n/av	**Student/Faculty:** 17 to 1
Year: semesters, summer session	**Tuition:** $21,180
Application Deadline: August 15	**Room & Board:** $9560
Freshman Class: 498 applied, 466 accepted, 242 enrolled	
SAT CR/M/W: 450/450/0 **ACT:** 19	**LESS COMPETITIVE**

Southern Vermont College, established in 1926, is a private institution offering a career-oriented, liberal arts education to a student body from diverse academic backgrounds. In addition to regional accreditation, SVC has baccalaureate program accreditation with NLN. The library contains 17,000 volumes and subscribes to 1,050 periodicals including electronic. Computerized library services include interlibrary loans, database searching, Internet access, and laptop Internet portals. Special learning facilities include a learning resource center and art gallery. The 371-acre campus is in a small town 40 miles east of Albany, New York. Including any residence halls, there are 12 buildings.

Student Life: 66% of undergraduates are from out of state, mostly the Northeast. Students are from 14 states, and 3 foreign countries. 75% are white; 11% African American. The average age of freshmen is 18; all undergraduates, 20. 44% do not continue beyond their first year; 42% remain to graduate.

Housing: 330 students can be accommodated in college housing, which includes coed dorms. Quiet, nonsmoking, and first-year student residence halls are available. On-campus housing is guaranteed for the freshman year only and is available on a lottery system for upperclassmen. 60% of students live on campus. All students may keep cars.

Activities: There are no fraternities or sororities. There are 20 groups on campus, including nursing club, radiology club, art, band, criminal justice, dance, drama, ethnic, gay, honors, newspaper, photography, professional, radio and TV, social, social service, student government, and yearbook. Popular campus events include homecoming, Winterfest, Moosapalooza, family weekend, and welcome week.

Sports: There are 5 intercollegiate sports for men and 5 for women, and 3 intramural sports for men and 3 for women. Facilities include a multipurpose field for softball, baseball, soccer, and rugby, a volleyball court, and a field house, including gym and fitness center.

Disabled Students: 50% of the campus is accessible. Facilities include wheelchair ramps, special parking, and specially equipped restrooms.

Services: Counseling and information services are available, as is tutoring in every subject. There is also a learning differences support program.

Campus Safety and Security: Measures include 24-hour foot and vehicle patrol and security escort services. There are shuttle buses and lighted pathways/sidewalks.

Programs of Study: SVC confers B.A., B.S., and B.S.N. degrees. Associate degrees are also awarded. Bachelor's degrees are awarded in BUSINESS (business administration and management, entrepreneurial studies, and sports management), COMMUNICATIONS AND THE ARTS (communications, creative writing, and English), HEALTH PROFESSIONS (health care administration, nursing, and radiological science), SOCIAL SCIENCE (criminal justice, history, liberal arts/general studies, and psychology). Nursing, criminal justice, psychology, and business are the largest.

Required: To graduate, students must complete a 42-credit core requirement consisting of course work in economics, English, environmental studies, government, history, cultural arts, math (including computer science), natural sciences, philosophy, psychology, and sociology. Minors are required in some programs. A minimum GPA of 2.0 is required. Students must earn a minimum of 120 credits, with 30 in the major.

Special: The individualized degree program allows students to formulate their own degree. Independent study, individualized study, and internships, dual majors, student-designed majors, and cross-registration with Bennington College are available. There is 1 national honor society.

Faculty/Classroom: 36% of faculty are male; 64% are female. All teach undergraduates. No introductory courses are taught by graduate students. The average class size in an introductory lecture is 18; in a laboratory is 13; and in a regular course is 12.

Admissions: 94% of the 2011-2012 applicants were accepted. The SAT scores for the 2011-2012 freshman class were: Critical Reading--78% below 500, 19% between 500 and 599, 2% between 600 and 700, and 1% above 700; Math--75% below 500, 24% between 500 and 599, 1% between 600 and 700; Writing--78% below 500, 19% between 500 and 599, 1% between 600 and 700.

Requirements: The SAT is required. The ACT is recommended. Applicants must graduate from an accredited secondary school or have a GED. The college requires 4 years of English and 3 of math. SVC requires applicants to be in the upper 67% of their class. A GPA of 2.0 is required. AP and CLEP credits are accepted. Important factors in the admissions decision are ability to finance college education, leadership record, advanced placement or honors courses, personality/intangible qualities, extracurricular activities record, recommendations by alumni, and recommendations by school officials.

Procedure: Freshmen are admitted fall and spring. There are early admissions, deferred admissions, and rolling admissions plans. Application deadlines are open. Application fee is $30. Applications are accepted online.

Transfer: 70 transfer students enrolled in 2010-2011. Applicants must have a GPA of 2.0 and be in good standing. Interviews are recommended, and a dean's report is required. 30 of 120 credits required for the bachelor's degree must be completed at SVC.

Visiting: There are regularly scheduled orientations for prospective students. There are guides for informal visits and visitors may sit in on classes. To schedule a visit, contact Admissions.

Financial Aid: In 2011-2012, 95% of all full-time freshmen and 92% of continuing full-time students received some form of financial aid. 90% of all full-time freshmen and 90% of continuing full-time students received need-based aid. The average freshman award was $8,000. Need-based scholarships or need-based grants averaged $8,000 ($14,000 maximum); need-based self-help aid (loans and jobs) averaged $3,500 ($33,424 maximum); and other non-need-based awards and non-need-based scholarships averaged $8,000 ($14,000 maximum). 100% of undergraduate students work part-time. Average annual earnings from campus work are $750. The average financial indebtedness of the 2011 graduate was $26,000. SVC is a member of CSS. The FAFSA and the college's own financial statement are required. The priority date for freshman financial aid applications for fall entry is February 15.

International Students: There are 2 international students enrolled. They must take the TOEFL.

Computers: Wireless access is available. Students use the college's network and wireless system inside and outside the residential areas, in the library, and in the main academic building. All students may access the system. There are no time limits and no fees.

Graduates: From July 1, 2010 to June 30, 2011, 67 bachelor's degrees were awarded. The most popular majors were psychology (25%), nursing (13%), and criminal justice (12%). 25 companies recruited on campus in 2010-2011. In an average class, 8% graduate in 3 years or less, 28% graduate in 4 years or less, 33% graduate in 5 years or less, and 42% graduate in 6 years or less. Of the 2010 graduating class, 50% were enrolled in graduate school within 6 months of graduation, and 35% were employed.

Admissions Contact: Jeremy Gibbons, Director of Admissions. E-Mail: *admissions@svc.edu* Web: *www.svc.edu*

STERLING COLLEGE B-1

Craftsbury Common, VT 05827 (802) 586-7711, ext. 135; (800) 648-3591; (802) 586-2596

Full-time: 57 men, 46 women
Part-time: 1 men, 1 women
Graduate: n/av
Year: semesters
Application Deadline: February 15
Freshman Class: 97 applied, 74 accepted, 30 enrolled
SAT or ACT: recommended
Faculty: 14
Ph.D.s: 29%
Student/Faculty: 7 to 1
Tuition: $25,500
Room & Board: $8500

COMPETITIVE

Sterling College offers a liberal arts curriculum with an environmental focus. It combines traditional and experiential academics and offers internships and global field studies. The 2 libraries contain 13,630 volumes, and 600 audio/video tapes/CDs/DVDs, and subscribe to 127 periodicals including electronic. Computerized library services include interlibrary loans, database searching, Internet access, and laptop Internet portals.The figures in the above capsule and in this profile are approximate. Special learning facilities include a learning resource center, art gallery, woodshop, darkroom, managed woodlot, organic garden, working livestock farm, 30-foot-tall climbing wall, bouldering wall, greenhouse, blacksmithshop, sugar house, and a 300-acre boreal forest/wetland research area. The 430 acre campus is in a rural area 40 miles north of Montpelier and 60 miles from Burlington. Including any residence halls, there are 16 buildings.

Student Life: 82% of undergraduates are from out of state, mostly the Northeast. Students are from 22 states. 70% are white. The average age of freshmen is 19; all undergraduates, 21. 33% do not continue beyond their first year; 60% remain to graduate.

Housing: 90 students can be accommodated in college housing, which includes coed dorms. On-campus housing is guaranteed for all 4 years. 77% of students live on campus. All students may keep cars.

Activities: There are no fraternities or sororities. Groups on campus include activism theater, diversity, folk music, art, dance, environmental, film, literary magazine, outing, photography, student government, and yearbook. Popular campus events include All-College Work Days, Earth Day, and Annual Wood-Projects show.

Sports: There is no sports program at Sterling. Facilities include a climbing tower, nature trails on campus, and nationally recognized cross-country ski trails managed by a nearby sports center. There is a soccer field and access to a gym at a local high school.

Disabled Students: All of the campus is accessible. Facilities include wheelchair ramps and specially equipped restrooms.

Services: Counseling and information services are available, as is tutoring in every subject. There is remedial math. Students seek assistance directly from faculty or teacher assistants. In addition, there is a learning support liaison and counselor as well as a writing center.

Campus Safety and Security: Measures include emergency notification system. There are lighted pathways/sidewalks, weekly community meetings address personal safety and security when necessary.

Programs of Study: Sterling confers B.A. degrees. Bachelor's degrees are awarded in AGRICULTURE (agriculture, conservation and regulation, natural resource management, and wildlife management), EDUCATION (recreation education), SOCIAL SCIENCE (area studies). Conservation ecology, northern studies, and sustainable agriculture are the strongest academically.

Required: Candidates for the B.A. degree must earn a minimum of 120 credits with a minimum cumulative GPA of 2.0 and pass the mathematics competency test. Candidates must also complete all required core courses, complete 6 credits each of natural science, social science, and humanities electives, including a minimum of 2 credits emphasizing textual analysis and written critical response, and complete an approved major. All resident students must receive a satisfactory grade in Sterling's Work program during their final semester of academic enrollment. Nonresident students must receive a satisfactory grade in their final semester of record in the Work Program.

Special: Internships are required in the second year of study. Study abroad, work study, and student-designed majors are available.

Faculty/Classroom: 50% of faculty are male; 50% are female. All teach undergraduates. No introductory courses are taught by graduate students. The average class size in an introductory lecture is 12; in a laboratory is 12; and in a regular course is 12.

Admissions: 76% of a recent year applicants were accepted. 20% of the current freshmen were in the top fifth of their class; 40% were in the top two fifths.

Requirements: The SAT or ACT is recommended. In addition, essays, quality of the interview, and the comments provided by references are equal to the value of high school and college transcripts. Home-schooled students are strongly encouraged to contact the admissions office to discuss their particular needs and interests. A GPA of 2.0 is required. AP credits are accepted. Important factors in the admissions decision are advanced placement or honors courses, recommendations by school officials, and leadership record.

Procedure: Freshmen are admitted fall and spring. There are early decision, early admissions, and deferred admissions plans. Early decision applications should be filed by December 15; regular applications, by February 15. Notification of early decision is sent January 15; regular decision, April 1. Applications are accepted online. Check with the school for current application fee.

Transfer: 15 transfer students enrolled in a recent year. In addition to the standard application, transfer students must provide copies of college transcripts. They may begin in the spring semester. 30 of 120 credits required for the bachelor's degree must be completed at Sterling.

Visiting: There are regularly scheduled orientations for prospective students, including a student-led campus tour, an interview with admissions, and a meal in the dining hall. Weekend Open Houses offer a more comprehensive view of the college. There are 2 open houses per year. Monday Visit Days are similar to open houses, but students may sit in on classes. There are guides for informal visits and visitors may sit in on classes. To schedule a visit, contact the Admissions Office.

Financial Aid: 90% of undergraduate students work part-time. Average annual earnings from campus work are $1500. The FAFSA and the college's own financial statement are required. The priority date for freshman financial aid applications for fall entry is March 1.

International Students: They must take the TOEFL with a minimum score of 500 on the paper-based TOEFL (PBT).

Computers: Wireless access is available. Students have access to PCs on campus in the library, the Career Resource Center, and Environmental Science Computer Lab. These PCs are available for Internet access, student e-mailing, course work, searching library databases, access to the shared network, and laboratory-related uses. Wireless connection throughout campus makes network/Internet available from most locations and laptops. All students may access the system. There are no time limits and no fees. It is strongly recommended that all students have a personal computer.

Graduates: In a recent year, 16 bachelor's degrees were awarded. The most popular majors were self-designed (25%), circumpolar studies (25%), and conservation ecology (19%). 30 companies recruited on campus in a recent year. In an average class, 40% graduate in 4 years or less, 52% graduate in 5 years or less, and 56% graduate in 6 years or less. Of a recent graduating class, 30% were employed within 6 months of graduation.

Admissions Contact: Director of Admissions. E-Mail: *admissions@sterlingcollege.edu* Web: *www.sterlingcollege.edu*

UNIVERSITY OF VERMONT A-2

Burlington, VT 05405 (802) 656-3370; (802) 656-8611

Full-time: 4310 men, 5454 women
Part-time: 461 men, 687 women
Graduate: 779 men, 1032 women
Year: semesters, summer session
Application Deadline: January 15
Freshman Class: 22381 applied, 17357 accepted, 2495 enrolled
SAT CR/M/W: 590/595/595 **ACT:** 26
Faculty: n/av; I, --$
Ph.D.s: 77%
Student/Faculty: 17 to 1
Tuition: $15,718 ($36,646)
Room & Board: $10,402

VERY COMPETITIVE+

The University of Vermont, established in 1791, is a public, land-grant, comprehensive institution with a dual focus on teaching and research. Its undergraduate and graduate offerings include the liberal arts, business administration, engineering, math, natural resources, agricultural studies, fine arts, teacher preparation, social services, environmental studies, and health science, including nursing. There are 7 undergraduate schools and 2 graduate schools. In addition to regional accreditation, UVM has baccalaureate program accreditation with AACSB, ABET, APTA, ASLA, CAHEA, CSWE, and NCATE. The 2 libraries contain 2.5 million volumes. Computerized library services include interlibrary loans, database searching, and Internet access. Special learning facilities include an art gallery, radio station, TV station, a health care center, 4 research farms, the Fleming Museum, geology museum, 9 natural areas, lakeshore science center, and aquatic research vessel. The 460-acre campus is in a suburban area 90 miles south of Montreal, 200 miles north of Boston, on the shore of Lake Champlain. Including any residence halls, there are 119 buildings.

Student Life: 66% of undergraduates are from out of state, mostly the Northeast. Students are from 48 states, 32 foreign countries, and Canada.

84% are White. 40% claim no religious affiliation; 26% Catholic; 20% Protestant. The average age of freshmen is 18; all undergraduates, 20. 14% do not continue beyond their first year; 86% remain to graduate.

Housing: 5500 students can be accommodated in college housing, which includes coed dorms, on-campus apartments, off-campus apartments, and married student housing. In addition, there are honors houses, language houses, special-interest houses, fraternity houses, sorority houses, In addition, the living/learning center provides an integrated, theme-based academic and residential option. On-campus housing is guaranteed for all 4 years and is available on a lottery system for upperclassmen. 51% of students live on campus; of those, 90% remain on campus on weekends. Upperclassmen may keep cars.

Activities: 8% of men belong to 2 local and 9 national fraternities; 5% of women belong to 7 national sororities. There are 170 groups on campus, including and environmental, outing, art, band, cheerleading, chess, choir, chorale, chorus, community service, computers, dance, drama, environmental, ethnic, gay, honors, international, jazz band, literary magazine, musical theater, orchestra, pep band, photography, political, professional, religious, social, social service, and student government. Popular campus events include Winterfest, Community Serve-a-thon, and Sugar on Snow day.

Sports: There are 8 intercollegiate sports for men and 10 for women, and 24 intramural sports for men and 24 for women. Facilities include a 3228-seat gym, a 4000-seat ice hockey stadium, turffield, a field house, soccer and baseball fields, a fitness center, indoor and outdoor tracks, a natatorium, indoor tennis courts, a racquetball court, a climbing facility, a dance studio, and a gymnastics facility.

Disabled Students: 90% of the campus is accessible. Facilities include wheelchair ramps, elevators, special parking, specially equipped restrooms, special class scheduling, lowered drinking fountains, lowered telephones. first-priority routes in poor weather, a TTY phone system for hearing-impaired students, and closed-caption video decoders.

Services: Counseling and information services are available, as is tutoring in most subjects. There is a reader service for the blind. There is also supplemental instruction, note-taking and test-taking seminars, time management instruction, outreach programs, exam proctoring, and writing tutors, as well as support for ESL students.

Campus Safety and Security: Measures include 24-hour foot and vehicle patrol, emergency notification system, self-defense education, and security escort services. There are shuttle buses, emergency telephones, lighted pathways/sidewalks, controlled access to dorms/residences, bike registration, identification of property, and 18 fully certified police officers.

Programs of Study: UVM confers B.A., B.S., B.Mus., B.S.A.E., B.S.B.A., B.S.Ed., B.S.C.E., B.S.C.S., B.S.E.E., B.S.E.M., B.S.M., B.S.M.E. and B.S.M.S. degrees. Master's and doctoral degrees are also awarded. Bachelor's degrees are awarded in AGRICULTURE (agriculture, animal science, environmental studies, fishing and fisheries, forestry and related sciences, horticulture, natural resource management, and plant science), BIOLOGICAL SCIENCE (biochemistry, biology/biological science, botany, genetics, microbiology, molecular biology, neurosciences, nutrition, wildlife biology, and zoology), BUSINESS (business administration and management, entrepreneurial studies, and international economics), COMMUNICATIONS AND THE ARTS (art, art history and appreciation, Chinese, classics, communications, dramatic arts, English, film arts, French, German, Greek, Japanese, Latin, linguistics, music, Russian, and Spanish), COMPUTER AND PHYSICAL SCIENCE (chemistry, computer science, geology, information sciences and systems, mathematics, physics, and statistics), EDUCATION (art education, athletic training, early childhood education, education, elementary education, English education, foreign languages education, mathematics education, middle school education, music education, physical education, science education, secondary education, social studies education, and special education), ENGINEERING AND ENVIRONMENTAL DESIGN (civil engineering, electrical/electronics engineering, engineering, engineering management, environmental engineering, environmental science, landscape architecture/design, and mechanical engineering), HEALTH PROFESSIONS (biomedical science, exercise science, medical laboratory science, nuclear medical technology, nursing, radiation therapy, and speech pathology/audiology), SOCIAL SCIENCE (anthropology, area studies, Asian/Oriental studies, child care/child and family studies, dietetics, economics, ethnic studies, European studies, food science, gender studies, geography, history, human development, Italian studies, Latin American studies, parks and recreation management, philosophy, political science/government, psychology, religion, Russian and Slavic studies, social work, and sociology). Business administration, psychology, and biology/biological science have the largest enrollments.

Required: Degree requirements vary among the individual colleges, but all require at least a 2.0 GPA and 122 credit hours to graduate. Most students must enroll in at least 30 distribution credits (approximately 10 courses) in the arts, humanities, social sciences, languages, literature, math, and the sciences. All academic units require a 2 courses in Race and Culture.

Special: Special academic programs include co-op programs, internships in every discipline, study abroad in 110 countries, a Washington semester, work-study, an accelerated degree program in computer science,secondary education, and public administration, RN-BS-MS, dual majors, and student-designed majors. In addition, a 3-4 veterinary medicine degree is offered with Tufts University. There are 25 national honor societies, including Phi Beta Kappa, a freshman honors program, and 14 departmental honors programs.

Faculty/Classroom: 51% of faculty are male; 49% are female. Graduate students teach 3% of introductory courses. The average class size in a regular course is 30.

Admissions: 78% of the 2013-2014 applicants were accepted. The SAT scores for the 2013-2014 freshman class were: Critical Reading--10% below 500, 41% between 500 and 599, 39% between 600 and 699, and 10% between 700 and 800; Math--10% below 500, 41% between 500 and 599, 41% between 600 and 699, and 8% between 700 and 800; Writing--10% below 500, 42% between 500 and 599, 39% between 600 and 699, and 9% between 700 and 800. The ACT scores were 3% below 21, 15% between 21 and 23, 32% between 24 and 26, 23% between 27 and 28, and 27% above 28. 50% of the current freshmen were in the top fifth of their class; 88% were in the top two fifths.

Requirements: The SAT or ACT is required. The ACT Optional Writing test is also required. Other admissions requirements include graduation from an accredited secondary school with 16 Carnegie units. Required high school course work includes 4 years of English, 3 years each of social science and math, including algebra I and II and geometry, and 2 years each of the same foreign language and science (one of which must be a lab science). Some academic units require additional course work. An essay must be submitted. The GED is also accepted. AP and CLEP credits are accepted. Important factors in the admissions decision are advanced placement or honors courses, extracurricular activities record, and recommendations by school officials.

Procedure: Freshmen are admitted fall and spring. Entrance exams should be taken by November of the senior year. There are early admissions and deferred admissions plans. Early decision applications should be filed by November 1; regular applications, by January 15 for fall entry; and November 1 for spring entry, along with a $55 fee. Notification of early decision is sent December 15; regular decision, March 15. 2288 applicants were on the 2013 waiting list; 159 were admitted. Applications are accepted online.

Transfer: 444 transfer students enrolled in 2012-2013. Successful transfer students have a cumulative grade point average of at least 2.8 in credited courses and meet the same entrance requirements as freshmen. Considerations include the college and high school records, the major indicated, and availability of space at UVM. 30 of 122 credits required for the bachelor's degree must be completed at University of Vermont.

Visiting: There are regularly scheduled orientations for prospective students, consisting of information sessions and tours most weekdays and many Saturdays year round. Visitors may sit in on classes. To schedule a visit, contact the Admissions Office.

Financial Aid: In 2013-2014, 94% of all full-time freshmen and 84% of continuing full-time students received some form of financial aid. 59% of all full-time freshmen and 59% of continuing full-time students received need-based aid. The average financial indebtedness of the 2013 graduate was $27,772. The FAFSA is required. The priority date for freshman financial aid applications for fall entry is February 10.

International Students: There are 242 international students enrolled. The school actively recruits these students. They must take the TOEFL with a minimum score of 79 on the Internet-based version (iBT), or ELPT. They must also take the SAT or ACT.

Computers: All students may access the system at any time. There are no time limits and no fees.

Graduates: From July 1, 2012 to June 30, 2013, 2562 bachelor's degrees were awarded. The most popular majors were business (10%), psychology (8%), and political science (7%). 170 companies recruited on campus in 2012-2013. In an average class, 65% graduate in 4 years or less, 74% graduate in 5 years or less, and 75% graduate in 6 years or less. Of the 2012 graduating class, 19% were enrolled in graduate school within 6 months of graduation, and 85% were employed.

Admissions Contact: Dr. Beth A. Wiser, Director of Admission. E-Mail: *admissions@uvm.edu* Web: *www.uvm.edu*

VERMONT STATE COLLEGES

The Vermont State Colleges, established in 1962, is a public system in Vermont. It is governed by a board of trustees, whose chief administrator is the chancellor. The primary goal of the system is teaching. The main priorities are to insure all citizens have access to higher education and continuous learning opportunities, and to provide educational programs that are affordable, high quality, student centered and accessible to maintain the quality of cultural, social, and economic life in Vermont. The total student enrollment of all 5 campuses was 9,050 with 285 faculty members. Altogether there are 60 baccalaureate, and 5 master's programs offered in the

Vermont State Colleges. Profiles of the 4-year campuses are included in this section.

VERMONT TECHNICAL COLLEGE C-4

Randolph Center, VT 05061 **(802) 728-1000**

Full-time: 655 men, 380 women	**Faculty:** n/av; III, --$
Part-time: 165 men, 160 women	**Ph.D.s:** 54%
Graduate: n/av	**Student/Faculty:** n/av
Year: semesters	**Tuition:** $12,500 ($21,500)
Application Deadline: open	**Room & Board:** $8500
Freshman Class: n/av	
SAT or ACT: required	

COMPETITIVE

Vermont Technical College, founded in 1910, is one of the 5 institutions in the Vermont State Colleges System and is the state's only public technical college. The figures in the above capsule and this profile are approximate. In addition to regional accreditation, VTC has baccalaureate program accreditation with ABET. The library contains 59,480 volumes, 5920 microform items, and 4122 audio/video tapes/CDs/DVDs, and subscribes to 348 periodicals including electronic. Computerized library services include interlibrary loans, database searching, and Internet access. Special learning facilities include a learning resource center, radio station, and Vermont Interactive Television. The 544-acre campus is in a rural area. Including any residence halls, there are 19 buildings.

Student Life: 60% of undergraduates are from Vermont. Others are from 12 states and 2 foreign countries. 90% are from public schools. 94% are white. The average age of freshmen is 25; all undergraduates, 26. 25% do not continue beyond their first year; 55% remain to graduate.

Housing: 550 students can be accommodated in college housing, which includes single-sex and coed dorms. On-campus housing is guaranteed for all 4 years. 60% of students commute. All students may keep cars.

Activities: There are no fraternities or sororities. Groups on campus include chess, computers, drama, ethnic, gay, international, photography, professional, radio and TV, religious, social, social service, and student government. Popular campus events include Harvest Days, Winter Carnival, and Spring Fling.

Sports: There are 6 intercollegiate sports for men and 5 for women, and 21 intramural sports for men and 21 for women. Facilities include a double-court gym, 2 racquetball courts, a 6-lane 25-yard pool, a fitness center, outdoor soccer, baseball, and softball fields, trails for cross-country skiing, and a downhill ski run.

Disabled Students: All of the campus is accessible. Facilities include wheelchair ramps, elevators, special parking, specially equipped rest rooms, special class scheduling, lowered drinking fountains, and lowered telephones.

Services: Counseling and information services are available, as is tutoring in every subject.

Campus Safety and Security: Measures include 24-hour foot and vehicle patrol, self-defense education, and security escort services. There are emergency telephones and lighted pathways/sidewalks.

Programs of Study: VTC confers B.S. degrees. Associates degrees are also awarded. Bachelor's degrees are awarded in COMPUTER AND PHYSICAL SCIENCE (information sciences and systems and software engineering), EDUCATION (business education), ENGINEERING AND ENVIRONMENTAL DESIGN (architectural engineering, computer engineering, and electromechanical technology). Electromechanical engineering technology is the strongest academically. Architectural engineering technology and business have the largest enrollments.

Required: To graduate, students must complete 120 to 130 credit hours with a minimum GPA of 2.0. Required courses include those in English, technical communications, math, and computer.

Special: Cross-registration, internships, work-study programs, and dual majors are offered. There are 2 national honor societies, a freshman honors program, and 2 departmental honors programs.

Faculty/Classroom: 58% of faculty are male; 42% are female. All teach undergraduates. The average class size in an introductory lecture is 28; in a laboratory, 16; and in a regular course, 32.

Requirements: The SAT or ACT is required. AP and CLEP credits are accepted.

Procedure: Freshmen are admitted fall and spring. There is a rolling admissions plan. Application deadlines are open. The application fee is $42. Applications are accepted online. A waiting list is maintained.

Transfer: Transcripts are required from all colleges attended. 50 of 120 credits required for the bachelor's degree must be completed at VTC.

Visiting: There are regularly scheduled orientations for prospective students. There are guides for informal visits, and visitors may sit in on classes and stay overnight. To schedule a visit, contact Admissions.

Financial Aid: The FAFSA is required. Check with the school for current application deadlines.

International Students: They must take the TOEFL. They must also take the SAT or ACT and the college's own entrance exam.

Computers: All students may access the system. There are no time limits and no fees. It is strongly recommended that all students have a personal computer.

Admissions Contact: Office of Admissions. E-mail: *admissions@vtc.edu* Web: *www.vtc.edu*

WOODBURY INSTITUTE OF CHAMPLAIN COLLEGE IN BURLINGTON C-3

Montpelier, VT 05602 **(802) 229-0516** **(800) 639-6039; (802) 229-2141**

Full-time: 15 men, 80 women	**Faculty:** n/av
Part-time: 10 men, 30 women	**Ph.D.s:** 75%
Graduate: 5 men, 10 women	**Student/Faculty:** n/av
Year: semesters	**Tuition:** $28,350
Application Deadline: see profile	**Room & Board:** $12,500
Freshman Class: n/av	

LESS COMPETITIVE

Woodbury Institute of Champlain College, formerly Woodbury College, was established in 1975 and offers adult-focused, career-oriented programs in legal and paralegal studies, mediation/conflict management, and prevention and community development. Figures in the above capsule and this profile are approximate. The library contains 17,000 volumes and subscribes to 20,000 periodicals including electronic. Computerized library services include interlibrary loans and database searching. The 8-acre campus is in a small town 1 1/2 miles north of the center of Montpelier and the Vermont state government district. There is 1 building.

Student Life: 97% of undergraduates are from Vermont. Others are from 3 states and 1 foreign country. 96% are white. The average age of freshmen is 35; all undergraduates, 35. 15% do not continue beyond their first year; 85% remain to graduate.

Housing: College-sponsored housing consists of dorms and on-campus apartments.

Activities: There are no fraternities or sororities. Popular campus events include town meetings and community luncheons.

Sports: There is no sports program at Woodbury.

Disabled Students: Facilities include wheelchair ramps, elevators, special parking, and specially equipped rest rooms.

Services: Counseling and information services are available, as is tutoring in most subjects.

Programs of Study: Woodbury confers B.S. degrees. Associate degrees are also awarded. Bachelor's degrees are awarded in SOCIAL SCIENCE (community services, human services, interdisciplinary studies, law, and paralegal studies). Paralegal and mediation and applied conflict studies are the largest.

Required: Each student must demonstrate satisfactory competency in core courses and program requirements. A total of 120 credit hours must be completed, with 48 in the major.

Special: Internships are required for all undergraduate students. A student-designed major in interdisciplinary studies is possible. Certificate programs are offered.

Faculty/Classroom: 39% of faculty are male; 61% are female. All teach undergraduates. No introductory courses are taught by graduate students. The average class size in an introductory lecture is 12; in a laboratory, 12; and in a regular course, 12.

Requirements: Students must submit a completed application, a high school diploma or GED, and an essay. An interview is optional. AP and CLEP credits are accepted. Important factors in the admissions decision are personality/intangible qualities, recommendations by alumni, and recommendations by school officials.

Procedure: Freshmen are admitted to all sessions. There are deferred admissions and rolling admissions plans. Check with the school for current application deadlines and fee. Notification is sent on a rolling basis. Applications are accepted online.

Transfer: Requirements are the same as for incoming freshmen, including high school transcripts, and an essay. 45 of 120 credits required for the bachelor's degree must be completed at Woodbury.

Visiting: There are regularly scheduled orientations for prospective students, including an introductory meeting, a school philosophy presentation, a financial aid discussion, a free class, a meal, and a Q&A session. There are guides for informal visits and visitors may stay overnight. To schedule a visit, contact Admissions.

Financial Aid: The FAFSA and the college's own financial statement are required. Check with the school for current application deadlines.

Computers: All students may access the system.

Admissions Contact: Admissions Director. E-Mail: *admission@champlain.edu* Web: *www.champlain.edu*

VIRGINIA

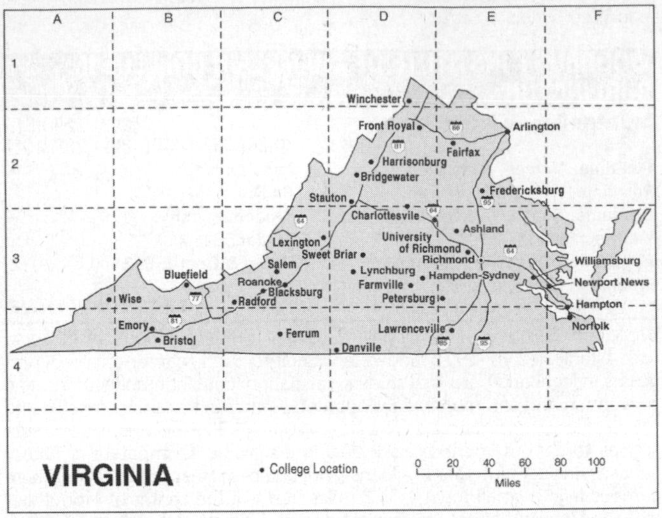

AVERETT UNIVERSITY D-4

Danville, VA 24541 (434) 791-0000
(800) 283-7388; (434) 791-2784

Full-time: 435 men, 423 women
Part-time: 9 men, 19 women
Graduate: 12 men, 17 women
Year: semesters, summer session
Application Deadline: July 15
Faculty: 61; IIA, --$
Ph.D.s: 75%
Student/Faculty: 12 to 1
Tuition: $27,500
Room & Board: $8500
Freshman Class: 1697 applied, 1491 accepted, 241 enrolled
SAT CR/M: 470/480 **ACT:** 19 **LESS COMPETITIVE**

Founded in 1859 as a school for young women, Averett grew to a fully accredited, co-educational, four-year college in 1971. Today, the university attracts students from across the nation as well as around the world and offers degree programs at numerous Virginia locations. Averett is an innovative, small, private university that gives students the individual attention traditionally associated with small liberal arts colleges along with the advantages found at comprehensive universities. There is one graduate school. The library contains 162,878 volumes, 101,773 microform items, and 688 audio/video tapes/CDs/DVDs, and subscribes to 36,957 periodicals including electronic. Computerized library services include interlibrary loans, database searching, Internet access, and Wi-Fi capability. The 252-acre campus is in a small town 45 miles from Greensboro, NC. Including any residence halls, there are 15 buildings.

Student Life: 70% of undergraduates are from Virginia. Others are from 22 states, 22 foreign countries, and Canada. 62% are White; 25% African American.. The average age of freshmen is 18; all undergraduates, 21. 58% do not continue beyond their first year; 38% remain to graduate.

Housing: 501 students can be accommodated in college housing, which includes single-sex and coed dorms and on-campus apartments. On-campus housing is guaranteed for all 4 years. 57% of students live on campus; of those, 75% remain on campus on weekends. Alcohol is not permitted. All students may keep cars.

Activities: There are no fraternities; 1% of women belong to 1 local sororities. There are 30 groups on campus, including American chemical society, anime association, Averett players, campus activities board, flying cougers, gay-straight alliance; equestrian and environmental clubs, habitat for humanity, IMPACT, science association, sisters implementing sisterhood, writer's folio club, art, cheerleading, choir, dance, drama, environmental, ethnic, gay, Gospel choir, honors, international, literary magazine, musical theater, newspaper, photography, political, professional, religious, social, social service, and student government. Popular campus events include Spring Formal, Senior Pinning, and late breakfast.

Sports: There are 8 intercollegiate sports for men and 7 for women, and 5 intramural sports for men and 5 for women. Facilities include tennis courts, a 100-acre equestrian center, and a 70-acre athletic center.

Disabled Students: 58% of the campus is accessible. Facilities include wheelchair ramps, elevators, special parking, and specially equipped restrooms.

Services: Counseling and information services are available, as is tutoring in most subjects. There is remedial math, reading, and writing.

Programs of Study: Averett confers B.A., B.S., B.A.S., B.B.A., M.B.A. and M.E.D. degrees. Associate and master's degrees are also awarded. Bachelor's degrees are awarded in AGRICULTURE (equine science), BIOLOGICAL SCIENCE (biology/biological science and environmental biology), BUSINESS (business administration and management and marketing management), COMMUNICATIONS AND THE ARTS (art, dramatic arts, English, journalism, modern language, music, music performance, and performing arts), COMPUTER AND PHYSICAL SCIENCE (computer science, information sciences and systems, and mathematics), EDUCATION (art education, athletic training, drama education, early childhood education, education, elementary education, English education, health education, mathematics education, middle school education, physical education, science education, secondary education, social studies education, and sports and wellness studies), ENGINEERING AND ENVIRONMENTAL DESIGN (airline piloting and navigation, aviation administration/management, and environmental science), HEALTH PROFESSIONS (biomedical science and health), SOCIAL SCIENCE (criminal justice, history, interdisciplinary studies, liberal arts/general studies, political science/government, prelaw, psychology, religion, social science, and sociology). Mathematics and biology are the strongest academically. Business administration, education, sociology/criminal justice, and physical education have the largest enrollments.

Required: Students may earn a Bachelor of Arts or Bachelor of Science degree by completing the core general education requirements along with a major area of study. A minimum of 120 semester hours is required for graduation. Requirements for specific majors may be found in departmental descriptions.

Special: Averett offers co-op programs and internships in several majors. Students may design their own majors with approval, or select dual majors or double majors. An interdisciplinary degree and nondegree study are offered. Senior equestrian studies majors may spend a semester or summer in England preparing for the British Horse Society A.I. certificate. Study abroad is available. There are 4 national honor societies, a freshman honors program, and 3 departmental honors programs.

Faculty/Classroom: 50% of faculty are male; 50% are female. All teach undergraduates. No introductory courses are taught by graduate students. The average class size in an introductory lecture is 15; in a laboratory is 14; and in a regular course is 14.

Admissions: 88% of the 2013-2014 applicants were accepted. The SAT scores for the 2013-2014 freshman class were: Critical Reading--66% below 500, 29% between 500 and 599, 4% between 600 and 699, and 1% between 700 and 800; Math--60% below 500, 35% between 500 and 599, and 4% between 600 and 699. The ACT scores were 71% below 21, 14% between 21 and 23, 13% between 24 and 26, 1% between 27 and 28, and 1% above 28. 16% of the current freshmen were in the top fifth of their class; 40% were in the top two fifths.

Requirements: The SAT or ACT is required. Applicants should have a high school diploma or its equivalent. 16 Carnegie units in college prep coursework should include a minimum of 3 in college prep math and 3 in lab sciences, 4 in English, 3 in social sciences, and 3 electives (foreign language recommended). Interviews are recommended with a campus visit. Auditions are required for music majors. Portfolios are recommended for art majors. GEDS are accepted. Recommendation letters are recommended but not required. A GPA of 2.2 is required. AP and CLEP credits are accepted. Important factors in the admissions decision are extracurricular activities record, leadership record, and advanced placement or honors courses.

Procedure: Freshmen are admitted to all sessions. Entrance exams should be taken in the junior year or the fall of the senior year. There are deferred admissions and rolling admissions plans. Applications should be filed by July 15 for fall entry; November 15 for spring entry. Notification is sent on a rolling basis. Applications are accepted online.

Transfer: 78 transfer students enrolled in 2012-2013. Applicants must present at least a 2.0 GPA on a 4.0 scale and be eligible to return to their previous college. 30 of 120 credits required for the bachelor's degree must be completed at Averett.

Visiting: There are regularly scheduled orientations for prospective students, including sessions with admissions, student life, financial aid, academics, athletics, campus tours, and lunch. There are guides for informal visits, visitors may sit in on classes, and stay overnight.

Financial Aid: In 2013-2014, 87% of all full-time freshmen and 86% of continuing full-time students received some form of financial aid. 87% of all full-time freshmen and 86% of continuing full-time students received need-based aid. 16% of undergraduate students work part-time. Average annual earnings from campus work are $902. The FAFSA and the college's own financial statement are required. The priority date for freshman financial aid applications for fall entry is April 1.

International Students: There are 79 international students enrolled. The school actively recruits these students. They must take the TOEFL with a minimum score of 500 on the paper-based TOEFL (PBT) or 61 on the Internet-based version (iBT). They must also take the SAT or ACT, scoring 850.

Graduates: From July 1, 2012 to June 30, 2013, 152 bachelor's degrees were awarded. The most popular majors were education (28%), business/marketing (17%), and pre-medicine (13%). In an average class, 1% graduate in 3 years or less, 23% graduate in 4 years or less, 28% graduate in 5 years or less, and 40% graduate in 6 years or less.

Admissions Contact: Joel Nester, Director of Admissions. Web: *www.averett.edu*

BLUEFIELD COLLEGE B-3

Bluefield, VA 24605 (276) 326-4339
(800) 872 0175; (276) 326-4288

Full-time: 287 men, 405 women	**Faculty:** 33; IIB, --$
Part-time: 27 men, 57 women	**Ph.D.s:** 61%
Graduate: none	**Student/Faculty:** 21 to 1
Year: semesters, summer session	**Tuition:** $12,000
Application Deadline: open	**Room & Board:** $5800
Freshman Class: 731 applied, 358 accepted, 110 enrolled	
SAT: required **ACT:** 21	**COMPETITIVE+**

Bluefield College is a Christ-centered liberal arts college in covenant with the Baptist General Association of Virginia. We offer a challenging academic experience within a diverse Christian environment. Our academic and co-curricular programs transform students' lives by integrating liberal arts with career-oriented studies and service to God and the global community. We are committed to graduating students who think critically, communicate effectively, and adapt readily to a changing world. There is one undergraduate school. In addition to regional accreditation, BC has baccalaureate program accreditation with TEAC. The library contains 47,000 volumes, and 3,477 audio/video tapes/CDs/DVDs, and subscribes to 70,000 periodicals including electronic. Computerized library services include interlibrary loans, database searching, and Internet access. The 82-acre campus is in a small town 100 miles west of Roanoke on the Virginia-West Virginia state line. Including any residence halls, there are 26 buildings.

Student Life: 80% of undergraduates are from Virginia. Others are from 19 states, and 2 foreign countries. 79% are White; 18% African American.

Housing: 330 students can be accommodated in college housing, which includes single-sex dorms, on-campus apartments, and married student housing. On-campus housing is available on a lottery system for upperclassmen. 65% of students live on campus; of those, 60% remain on campus on weekends. Alcohol is not permitted. All students may keep cars.

Activities: 5% of men belong to 2 local fraternities; 10% of women belong to 2 local sororities. There are 15 groups on campus, including art, cheerleading, choir, chorale, chorus, communications, dance, drama, honors, literary magazine, musical theater, newspaper, orchestra, professional, religious, social, and student government. Popular campus events include Homecoming and Mud Pig Day.

Sports: There are 6 intramural sports for men and 6 for women. Facilities include a gym with game courts, excercise facility, a student activities center, a game room, tennis courts, and a sand volleyball court.

Disabled Students: 95% of the campus is accessible. Facilities include wheelchair ramps, elevators, special parking, specially equipped restrooms, and lowered drinking fountains.

Services: Counseling and information services are available, as is tutoring in most subjects. There is remedial math and writing.

Campus Safety and Security: Measures include 24-hour foot and vehicle patrol, emergency notification system, and security escort services. There are lighted pathways/sidewalks and controlled access to dorms/residences.

Programs of Study: BC confers B.A., and B.S. degrees. Bachelor's degrees are awarded in BIOLOGICAL SCIENCE (biology/biological science), BUSINESS (business administration and management), COMMUNICATIONS AND THE ARTS (communications, English, fine arts, and music), COMPUTER AND PHYSICAL SCIENCE (chemistry and mathematics), EDUCATION (middle school education and secondary education), HEALTH PROFESSIONS (exercise science), SOCIAL SCIENCE (Christian studies, criminal justice, history, interdisciplinary studies, psychology, religion, and social studies). Business, teacher education, and biology are the strongest academically. Business, organizational management and development, and criminal justice have the largest enrollments.

Required: To graduate, students must have completed a minimum of 126 semester hours, including a liberal arts requirement of 51 to 53 hours, with 30 to 45 hours in the major, and a minimum 2.0 GPA. Other requirements vary per program. All graduates must demonstrate computer proficiency by testing, passing computer courses, or having components in required courses.

Special: The college offers credit for life/military/work experience, nondegree study through the Fine Arts Community School, study abroad in England, an accelerated degree program in organizational management and development and in criminal justice, and internships in criminal justice, psychology, and recreation. There are 4 national honor societies, a freshman honors program, and 7 departmental honors programs.

Faculty/Classroom: 70% of faculty are male; 30% are female. All teach undergraduates, 30% do research, and 30% do both. No introductory courses are taught by graduate students. The average class size in an introductory lecture is 17; in a laboratory is 12; and in a regular course is 10.

Admissions: 49% of the 2013-2014 applicants were accepted. The ACT scores were 57% below 21, 20% between 21 and 23, 13% between 24 and 26, 3% between 27 and 28, and 7% above 28. 38% of the current freshmen were in the top fifth of their class; 64% were in the top two fifths.

Requirements: The SAT or ACT is required. Applicants must be graduates of an accredited secondary school or have a GED certificate, and have completed 4 years of English, 2 of social sciences, 1 of science, and 5 of electives. A GPA of 2.0 is required. AP and CLEP credits are accepted. Important factors in the admissions decision are leadership record, advanced placement or honors courses, and recommendations by school officials.

Procedure: Freshmen are admitted to all sessions. Entrance exams should be taken early in the senior year. There are deferred admissions and rolling admissions plans. Application deadlines are open. Application fee is $30. Notification is sent on a rolling basis. Applications are accepted online.

Transfer: 337 transfer students enrolled in 2012-2013. Prospective students must submit transcripts of all academic work, a financial aid transcript, and SAT or ACT scores if they have fewer than 30 hours of college level work. 32 of 126 credits required for the bachelor's degree must be completed at BC.

Visiting: There are regularly scheduled orientations for prospective students, including campus tours, opportunities to develop class schedules, and financial aid workshops. Visitors may sit in on classes and stay overnight. To schedule a visit, contact the Admissions Office.

Financial Aid: The FAFSA and the college's own financial statement are required. The deadline for filing freshman financial aid applications for fall entry is March 10.

International Students: There are 2 international students enrolled. The school actively recruits these students. They must take the TOEFL.

Graduates: From July 1, 2012 to June 30, 2013, 246 bachelor's degrees were awarded. 4 companies recruited on campus in 2012-2013. In an average class, 1% graduate in 3 years or less, 47% graduate in 4 years or less, 50% graduate in 5 years or less, and 55% graduate in 6 years or less. Of the 2012 graduating class, 16% were enrolled in graduate school within 6 months of graduation.

Admissions Contact: Admissions Office Web: *www.bluefield.edu*

BRIDGEWATER COLLEGE D-2

Bridgewater, VA 22812-1599 (540) 828-5469
(800) 759-8328; (540) 828-5481

Full-time: 830 men, 1010 women	**Faculty:** 106; IIB, --$
Part-time: 4 men, 4 women	**Ph.D.s:** 82%
Graduate: n/av	**Student/Faculty:** 17 to 1
Year: 4-1-4, summer session	**Tuition:** $29,090
Application Deadline: open	**Room & Board:** $10,790
Freshman Class: 5401 applied, 2967 accepted, 536 enrolled	
SAT CR/M/W: 520/510/490 **ACT:** 23	**COMPETITIVE**

Bridgewater College, founded in 1880, is a private liberal arts institution affiliated with the Church of the Brethren. The library contains 152,808 volumes, 2,163 microform items, and 5,992 audio/video tapes/CDs/DVDs, and subscribes to 47,649 periodicals including electronic. Computerized library services include interlibrary loans, database searching, Internet access, and Wi-Fi capability. Special learning facilities include an art gallery, radio station, museum of the Shenandoah Valley and Church of the Brethren. The 300-acre campus is in a small town 8 miles south of Harrisonburg. Including any residence halls, there are 44 buildings.

Student Life: 78% of undergraduates are from Virginia. Others are from 28 states, 16 foreign countries, and Canada. 93% are from public schools. 79% are White. 64% are Protestant; 21% claim no religious affiliation; 12% Catholic. The average age of freshmen is 18; all undergraduates, 20. 24% do not continue beyond their first year; 60% remain to graduate.

Housing: 1491 students can be accommodated in college housing, which includes single-sex and coed dorms and on-campus apartments. In addition, there are honors houses. On-campus housing is guaranteed for all 4 years. 83% of students live on campus; of those, 60% remain on campus on weekends. Alcohol is not permitted. All students may keep cars.

Activities: There are no fraternities or sororities. There are 68 groups on campus, including art, band, cheerleading, choir, chorale, chorus, communications, dance, drama, ethnic, gay, honors, international, jazz band, literary magazine, musical theater, newspaper, pep band, professional, radio and TV, religious, social, social service, student government, and yearbook. Popular campus events include Homecoming, Welcome Week Activities and Spring Fest Concert.

Sports: There are 9 intercollegiate sports for men and 11 for women, and 22 intramural sports for men and 22 for women. Facilities include a gym, a 2500-seat football stadium, a swimming pool, tennis courts, an all-weather track, playing fields for baseball, lacrosse, softball, football, field hockey, and soccer, and a 34,000-square-foot fitness center with basketball, volleyball, and racquetball courts, an indoor track, a cardiac and weight-training center, aerobics/dance rooms, and a 75-acre equestrian center that includes 2 barns with 50 stalls in total, fully equipped classrooms and offices, and 1 indoor and 2 outdoor arenas.

Disabled Students: 95% of the campus is accessible. Facilities include wheelchair ramps, elevators, special parking, specially equipped restrooms, lowered drinking fountains, lowered telephones, special housing.

Services: Counseling and information services are available, as is tutoring in every subject. There is a reader service for the blind. The academic support center provides students with academic assistance through an academic coach program, departmental help sessions, learning strategy workshops, transition program, tutoring services, learning skill websites, and support for students with learning disabilities.

Campus Safety and Security: Measures include 24-hour foot and vehicle patrol, emergency notification system, and self-defense education. There are emergency telephones, lighted pathways/sidewalks, and controlled access to dorms/residences.

Programs of Study: Bridgewater confers B.A., B.S. and B.G.S. degrees. Bachelor's degrees are awarded in BIOLOGICAL SCIENCE (biology/biological science and nutrition), BUSINESS (business administration and management and management information systems), COMMUNICATIONS AND THE ARTS (art, communications, English, French, music, and Spanish), COMPUTER AND PHYSICAL SCIENCE (applied physics, chemistry, computer science, mathematics, and physics), EDUCATION (athletic training and physical education), ENGINEERING AND ENVIRONMENTAL DESIGN (environmental science), HEALTH PROFESSIONS (exercise science), SOCIAL SCIENCE (economics, family/consumer studies, history, international relations, liberal arts/general studies, philosophy, political science/government, psychology, religion, and sociology). Biology, chemistry, and English are the strongest academically. Biology, business administration, and health/exercise science have the largest enrollments.

Required: To graduate, all students must complete a minimum of 123 credit hours, with a minimum of 48 credit hours chosen from junior/senior level courses. A major consists of 32 to 54 credit hours. A minimum 2.0 GPA is required, overall and in the major. The BA degree requires completion of a foreign language through the intermediate level, and the BS degree requires completion of a foreign language through the elementary level or additional courses in the global/Europe area along with additional science/math courses. Students must complete a course in Critical Inquiry in the Liberal Arts and a senior portfolio requirement. Other general education requirements include core courses in writing, oral communication, math, wellness, and exercise science; and courses from global perspectives, humanities, social sciences, and natural science. A minimum of 33 credit hours with 30 of the last 33 credits hours earned in residence at the college. A thesis is required for graduation with honors at the magna or summa level.

Special: Bridgewater offers internships to junior and seniors; study abroad in over 40 countries; and a teacher certification program in elementary and secondary education. Interdisciplinary majors include environmental science, history and political science, global studies, liberal studies, nutrition and wellness, philosophy and religion, and physics and math. Dual-degree programs are offered in engineering with George Washington University (3-2) and Virginia Tech (3-2), in physical therapy with Shenandoah University (3-4), and in nursing with Vanderbilt University (3-2). There are 8 national honor societies, a freshman honors program, and 16 departmental honors programs.

Faculty/Classroom: 53% of faculty are male; 47% are female. All teach undergraduates, 50% do research, and 50% do both. No introductory courses are taught by graduate students. The average class size in an introductory lecture is 24; in a laboratory is 16; and in a regular course is 19.

Admissions: 55% of the 2013-2014 applicants were accepted. The SAT scores for the 2013-2014 freshman class were: Critical Reading--41% below 500, 44% between 500 and 599, 13% between 600 and 699, and 2% between 700 and 800; Math--42% below 500, 42% between 500 and 599, 15% between 600 and 699, and 1% between 700 and 800; Writing--54% below 500, 35% between 500 and 599, and 11% between 600 and 699. The ACT scores were 27% below 21, 24% between 21 and 23, 36% between 24 and 26, 5% between 27 and 28, and 8% above 28. 38% of the current freshmen were in the top fifth of their class; 68% were in the top two fifths. 8 freshmen graduated first in their class.

Requirements: The SAT or ACT is required. The SAT is preferred. An interview is recommended. Applicants must be graduates of an accredited secondary school or have a GED certificate, and have completed 15 units, including 4 in English, 3 in math, 2 in science, 2 in history and social studies, and 4 in electives. Bridgewater requires applicants to be in the upper 50% of their class. A GPA of 2.0 is required. AP credits are accepted. Important factors in the admissions decision are advanced placement or honors courses, recommendations by school officials, and leadership record.

Procedure: Freshmen are admitted to all sessions. Entrance exams should be taken in spring of the junior year or fall of the senior year. There are deferred admissions and rolling admissions plans. Application deadlines are open. The fall 2013 application fee was $30. 61 applicants were on the 2013 waiting list. Applications are accepted online. Application fees are waived if application is completed online.

Transfer: 59 transfer students enrolled in 2012-2013. A degree from an accredited high school and a 2.2 GPA in all undergraduate work are required. 33 of 123 credits required for the bachelor's degree must be completed at Bridgewater.

Visiting: There are regularly scheduled orientations for prospective students, including a meeting with a faculty adviser, course scheduling and registration, and social activities. There are guides for informal visits and visitors may sit in on classes. To schedule a visit, contact the Admissions Office at (800) 759-8328.

Financial Aid: In 2013-2014, 100% of all full-time freshmen and 99% of continuing full-time students received some form of financial aid. 87% of all full-time freshmen and 82% of continuing full-time students received need-based aid. The average freshman award was $26,981. Need-based scholarships or need-based grants averaged $23,811 ($36,765 maximum); need-based self-help aid (loans and jobs) averaged $4,699 ($7,000 maximum); and other non-need-based awards and non-need-based scholarships averaged $17,135 ($32,970 maximum). 27% of undergraduate students work part-time. Average annual earnings from campus work are $743. The average financial indebtedness of the 2013 graduate was $33,493. Bridgewater is a member of CSS. The FAFSA and the state aid form are required. The priority date for freshman financial aid applications for fall entry is March 1.

International Students: There are 21 international students enrolled. The school actively recruits these students. They must take the TOEFL with a minimum score of 500 on the paper-based TOEFL (PBT) or 65 on the Internet-based version (iBT). The SAT may replace the TOEFL.

Graduates: From July 1, 2012 to June 30, 2013, 291 bachelor's degrees were awarded. The most popular majors were biology (11%), business administration (11%), and health and exercise science (10%). 59 companies recruited on campus in 2012-2013. In an average class, 52% graduate in 4 years or less, 59% graduate in 5 years or less, and 60% graduate in 6 years or less. Of the 2012 graduating class, 23% were enrolled in graduate school within 6 months of graduation, and 57% were employed.

Admissions Contact: Jarret L. Smith, Director of Admissions. E-Mail: *admissions@bridgewater.edu* Web: *www.bridgewater.edu*

CHRISTENDOM COLLEGE — D-2

Front Royal, VA 22630 — (540) 636-2900; (800) 877-5456; (540) 636-1655

Full-time: 192 men, 215 women	**Faculty:** 20
Part-time: 1 men, 1 women	**Ph.D.s:** 65%
Graduate: 32 men, 28 women	**Student/Faculty:** 15 to 1
Year: semesters	**Tuition:** $20,434
Application Deadline: March 1	**Room & Board:** $7656
Freshman Class: 228 applied, 211 accepted, 104 enrolled	
SAT CR/M/W: 632/570/616 **ACT:** 25	**VERY COMPETITIVE**

Christendom College, founded in 1977, is a private liberal arts institution affiliated with the Roman Catholic Church. There is one graduate school. The library contains 90,000 volumes, 860 microform items, 1,345 audio/video tapes/CDs/DVDs, and subscribes to 279 periodicals including electronic. Computerized library services include interlibrary loans and database searching. The 120-acre campus is in a rural area 65 miles west of Washington, D.C. Including any residence halls, there are 21 buildings.

Student Life: 74% of undergraduates are from out of state, mostly the Middle Atlantic. Students are from 43 states, 2 foreign countries, and Canada. 91% are White. 99% are Catholic. The average age of freshmen is 18; all undergraduates, 20. 7% do not continue beyond their first year; 70% remain to graduate.

Housing: College-sponsored housing includes single-sex dorms and on-campus apartments. On-campus housing is guaranteed for all 4 years. 95% of students live on campus; of those, 100% remain on campus on weekends. Alcohol is not permitted. All students may keep cars.

Activities: There are no fraternities or sororities. There are 15 groups on campus, including chess, choir, chorale, computers, debate, drama, film, literary magazine, musical theater, newspaper, photography, political, professional, religious, social, social service, student government, and yearbook. Popular campus events include Christmas Dinner Dance, Coffee House, and St. Patrick's Day.

Sports: There are 4 intercollegiate sports for men and 3 for women, and 7 intramural sports for men and 7 for women. Facilities include indoor basketball and volleyball courts, racquetball courts, playing fields, table games, a recreation center, and an outdoor swimming pool.

Disabled Students: 60% of the campus is accessible. Facilities include wheelchair ramps, elevators, special parking, and specially equipped restrooms.

Campus Safety and Security: Measures include 24-hour foot and

vehicle patrol and security escort services. There are emergency telephones and lighted pathways/sidewalks.

Programs of Study: Christendom confers B.A. degrees. Associate and master's degrees are also awarded. Bachelor's degrees are awarded in COMMUNICATIONS AND THE ARTS (English), SOCIAL SCIENCE (classical/ancient civilization, history, philosophy, political science/government, and theological studies). Philosophy is the strongest academically and has the largest enrollment.

Required: To graduate, all students must complete a total of 126 credit hours, including a 30-hour major and an 86-credit core curriculum, which includes 18 hours each in theology and philosophy. A minimum 2.0 GPA is required. All students must demonstrate proficiency in a foreign language and complete a thesis.

Special: Christendom offers summer internships in Washington, D.C. for political science students and also sponsors a semester in Rome during the junior year. Students may pursue dual majors. There is a work-study program with the college. There are 5 departmental honors programs.

Faculty/Classroom: 76% of faculty are male; 24% are female. All teach undergraduates. No introductory courses are taught by graduate students. The average class size in an introductory lecture is 22 and in a regular course is 20.

Admissions: 93% of the 2013-2014 applicants were accepted. The SAT scores for the 2013-2014 freshman class were: Critical Reading--5% below 500, 33% between 500 and 599, 33% between 600 and 699, and 29% between 700 and 800; Math--20% below 500, 46% between 500 and 599, 24% between 600 and 699, and 10% between 700 and 800; Writing--11% below 500, 24% between 500 and 599, 43% between 600 and 699, and 22% between 700 and 800. The ACT scores were 3% below 21, 28% between 21 and 23, 50% between 24 and 26, 12% between 27 and 28, and 7% above 28. 40% of the current freshmen were in the top fifth of their class; 85% were in the top two fifths.

Requirements: The SAT or ACT is required, the SAT is preferred. A minimum composite score of 1650 on the newest SAT or 24 on the ACT is required. Applicants need not be graduates of an accredited secondary school. GED certificates are accepted. Essays and letters of recommendation are required. A campus visit and a meeting with the Admissions Director are highly recommended. Christendom requires applicants to be in the upper 50% of their class. A GPA of 3.0 is required. AP credits are accepted.

Procedure: Freshmen are admitted fall and spring. Entrance exams should be taken in the spring of the junior year or fall of the senior year. There is an early admissions plan. Early decision applications should be filed by December 1; regular applications, by March 1 for fall entry; and January 2 for spring entry, along with a $25 fee. Notification of early decision is sent December 15; regular decision, April 1. Applications are accepted online.

Transfer: 13 transfer students enrolled in 2012-2013. Students must have a minimum 2.0 GPA and meet all other applicable standard admissions requirements. The SAT or ACT is recommended. 36 of 126 credits required for the bachelor's degree must be completed at Christendom.

Visiting: There are guides for informal visits, visitors may sit in on classes, and stay overnight. To schedule a visit, contact the Admissions Counselor.

Financial Aid: In 2013-2014, 69% of all full-time freshmen and 56% of continuing full-time students received some form of financial aid. 56% of all full-time freshmen and 54% of continuing full-time students received need-based aid. The average freshman award was $14,725. Need-based scholarships or need-based grants averaged $6,270; need-based self-help aid (loans and jobs) averaged $7,530; and other non-need-based awards and non-need-based scholarships averaged $7,290. 40% of undergraduate students work part-time. Average annual earnings from campus work are $2000. The average financial indebtedness of the 2013 graduate was $25,875. The the college's own financial statement is required. Check with the school for current application deadlines.

International Students: There are 4 international students enrolled. They must take the TOEFL.

Graduates: From July 1, 2012 to June 30, 2013, 98 bachelor's degrees were awarded. 8 companies recruited on campus in 2012-2013. In an average class, 70% graduate in 4 years or less and 70% graduate in 6 years or less. Of the 2012 graduating class, 12% were enrolled in graduate school within 6 months of graduation, and 75% were employed.

Admissions Contact: Thomas L. McFadden, Jr., Director of Admissions and Marketing. E-Mail: *admissions@christendom.edu* Web: *www.christendom.edu*

CHRISTOPHER NEWPORT UNIVERSITY — F-3

Newport News, VA 23606 — **(757) 594-7015**
(800) 333-4268; (757) 594-7333

Full-time: 2139 men, 2823 women	**Faculty:** 268; IIB, av$
Part-time: 64 men, 68 women	**Ph.D.s:** 85%
Graduate: 45 men, 93 women	**Student/Faculty:** 19 to 1
Year: semesters, summer session	**Tuition:** $11,092 ($20,992)
Application Deadline: February 1	**Room & Board:** $9958

Freshman Class: 7016 applied, 4141 accepted, 1276 enrolled
SAT CR/M: 580/580 **ACT:** 25 **VERY COMPETITIVE**

Christopher Newport University (CNU) is a public school offering a private school experience. There are 3 undergraduate schools and 1 graduate school. In addition to regional accreditation, CNU has baccalaureate program accreditation with AACSB, ABET, CSWE, and NASM. The library contains 244,893 volumes, 199,332 microform items, and 8,262 audio/video tapes/CDs/DVDs, and subscribes to 55,865 periodicals including electronic. Computerized library services include interlibrary loans, database searching, Internet access, and Wi-Fi capability. Special learning facilities include an art gallery, radio station, TV station, Ferguson Center for the Arts, and the Mariner's Museum Library at Christopher Newport University. The 260-acre campus is in a suburban area three hours south of Washington, D.C., 45 minutes from the Virginia Beach oceanfront, and 20 minutes east of historic Williamsburg. Including any residence halls, there are 44 buildings.

Student Life: 93% of undergraduates are from Virginia. Others are from 29 states, 34 foreign countries, and Canada. 76% are White. The average age of freshmen is 18; all undergraduates, 20. 16% do not continue beyond their first year; 66% remain to graduate.

Housing: 3708 students can be accommodated in college housing, which includes coed dorms and on-campus apartments. In addition, there are fraternity houses, sorority houses, Learning Communities. On-campus housing is available on a lottery system for upperclassmen. 73% of students live on campus; of those, 75% remain on campus on weekends. Alcohol is not permitted. All students may keep cars.

Activities: 16% of men belong to 10 national fraternities; 18% of women belong to 8 national sororities. There are 225 groups on campus, including art, band, cheerleading, chess, choir, chorale, chorus, computers, dance, drama, ethnic, film, gay, honors, international, jazz band, literary magazine, marching band, musical theater, newspaper, orchestra, pep band, political, professional, radio and TV, religious, social, social service, student government, and symphony. Popular campus events include Campus Tie Dye, Candelight Ceremony, Captain's Ball, Club Fair, Day of Service, FallFest, Family Weekend, Ferguson Center for the Arts concerts/performances (over 50 events each year), Food 4 Thought, Friday at Four Concerts on the Lawn, GSSU Drag B.

Sports: There are 11 intercollegiate sports for men and 12 for women, and 6 intramural sports for men and 6 for women. Facilities include The Freeman Center is home to Christopher Newport University's volleyball, men's and women's basketball and indoor track and field programs. Opened in 2000, The Freeman Center can seat up to 2.500 fans for basketball and volleyball contests and plays host to thousands of collegiate and high school track and field athletes annually. There is a 200-meter indoor track, 5 basketball courts (2 housed in a separate Auxiliary gymnasium) and a 13,500 square foot fitness pavilion with state of the are fitness equipment. CNU has a football stadium which includes a 400-meter track, 6 outdoor tennis courts, individual state of the art fields for soccer, field hockey, baseball and softball.

Disabled Students: 96% of the campus is accessible. Facilities include wheelchair ramps, elevators, special parking, specially equipped restrooms, special class scheduling, lowered drinking fountains, special housing.

Services: Counseling and information services are available, as is tutoring in most subjects.

Campus Safety and Security: Measures include 24-hour foot and vehicle patrol, emergency notification system, self-defense education, and security escort services. There are emergency telephones, lighted pathways/sidewalks, controlled access to dorms/residences, a campus police department, and a full time communication center for emergency radio and telephone communications.

Programs of Study: CNU confers B.A., B.S., B.M., B.S.B.A. and B.S.I.S. degrees. Master's degrees are also awarded. Bachelor's degrees are awarded in BIOLOGICAL SCIENCE (biochemistry, biology/biological science, environmental biology, and neurosciences), BUSINESS (accounting, business administration and management, finance, and marketing), COMMUNICATIONS AND THE ARTS (classical languages, communications, English, fine arts, French, German, music, romance languages and literature, Spanish, and theatre arts), COMPUTER AND PHYSICAL SCIENCE (applied mathematics, applied physics, chemistry, computer science, information sciences and systems, and mathematics), ENGINEERING AND ENVIRONMENTAL DESIGN (computer engineering and environmental science), HEALTH PROFESSIONS (predentistry, premedicine, preoptometry, prepharmacy, prephysical therapy, and preveterinary science), SOCIAL SCIENCE (American studies, economics, history, interdisciplinary studies, philosophy, political science/government, prelaw, psychology, social work, and sociology). Biology, business, and psychology have the largest enrollments.

Required: To graduate, all students must fulfill the liberal learning core, including mathematics, language, written communication, global and multicultural perspectives, identity institutions and societies, creative expressions, laboratory science, western traditions, and formal and informal reasoning, with a minimum of 120 semester hours and with 45 credits in residence. In addition, students must complete all requirements specific to the major and present an overall and an 'in-major' GPA of at least 2.0.

Special: CNU offers cross-registration with Thomas Nelson Community College, Tidewater Community College, Hampton University and Old Dominion University, dual majors, a student-designed interdisciplinary studies major, internships, and study abroad. Special course offerings: Honors Program, the President's Leadership Program and Freshman Learning Communities. There are 15 national honor societies and a freshman honors program.

Faculty/Classroom: 53% of faculty are male; 47% are female. All teach undergraduates. No introductory courses are taught by graduate students.

Admissions: 59% of the 2013-2014 applicants were accepted. The SAT scores for the 2013-2014 freshman class were: Critical Reading--7% below 500, 53% between 500 and 599, 34% between 600 and 699, and 6% between 700 and 800; Math--7% below 500, 57% between 500 and 599, 33% between 600 and 699, and 3% between 700 and 800. The ACT scores were 7% below 21, 24% between 21 and 23, 31% between 24 and 26, 19% between 27 and 28, and 19% above 28. 42% of the current freshmen were in the top fifth of their class; 81% were in the top two fifths. 10 freshmen graduated first in their class.

Requirements: CNU requires Virginia's Advanced Studies Diploma (ASD) or similar college preparatory diploma from an accredited high school with a satisfactory score on the SAT verbal and math or ACT composite. The GED is not accepted in lieu of a final high school transcript for freshman admission, as GED recipients do not meet ASD requirements. A total of 24 academic credits are recommended, including 4 units of English, 4 each of social science, math, and science and either 3 units of 1 foreign language (preferred) or 2 years of 2 foreign languages. An essay and a personal statement are required. SAT or ACT scores are not required for students with a 3.5 or higher high school GPA in a rigorous curriculum that includes college level work. Letters of recommendation and interviews are strongly recommended but not required. A GPA of 3.0 is required. AP and CLEP credits are accepted. Important factors in the admissions decision are recommendations by school officials, extracurricular activities record, and evidence of special talent.

Procedure: Freshmen are admitted fall and spring. Entrance exams should be taken before the senior year. There are early decision, early admissions, and deferred admissions plans. Early decision applications should be filed by November 15; regular applications, by February 1 for fall entry; and October 1 for spring entry. The fall 2013 application fee was $50. Notification of early decision is sent December 15; regular decision, March 15. 345 early decision candidates were accepted for the 2013-2014 class. 524 applicants were on the 2013 waiting list; 137 were admitted. Applications are accepted online.

Transfer: 240 transfer students enrolled in 2012-2013. Applicants must present a minimum 3.0 GPA, and be eligible to return to the most recently attended college or university. All transfer applicants must submit official college and high school transcripts. SAT or ACT scores are required if high school graduation is within the last five years. In addition applicants must submit letters of recommendation and an essay. 45 of 120 credits required for the bachelor's degree must be completed at CNU.

Visiting: There are regularly scheduled orientations for prospective students, Information sessions and walking campus tours are available Monday through Friday at 10 a.m. and 2 p.m.; Saturday information session and tour at 11 a.m. Special on and off campus events and receptions as scheduled annually. Visitors may sit in on classes and stay overnight. To schedule a visit, contact the Admission Office.

Financial Aid: In 2013-2014, 74% of all full-time freshmen and 67% of continuing full-time students received some form of financial aid. 42% of all full-time freshmen and 43% of continuing full-time students received need-based aid. The average freshman award was $9,725. Need-based scholarships or need-based grants averaged $6,066 ($7,000 maximum); need-based self-help aid (loans and jobs) averaged $3,356 ($5,500 maximum); and other non-need-based awards and non-need-based scholarships averaged $5,947 ($30,751 maximum). 1% of undergraduate students work part-time. Average annual earnings from campus work are $1447. The average financial indebtedness of the 2013 graduate was $22,967. The FAFSA is required. The priority date for freshman financial aid applications for fall entry is March 1. The deadline for filing freshman financial aid applications for fall entry is June 30.

International Students: There are 12 international students enrolled. The school actively recruits these students. They must take the TOEFL with a minimum score of 530 on the paper-based TOEFL (PBT) or 71 on the Internet-based version (iBT). They must also take the SAT or ACT.

Graduates: From July 1, 2012 to June 30, 2013, 1057 bachelor's degrees were awarded. The most popular majors were psychology (14%), biology (10%), and communications (10%). 383 companies recruited on campus in 2012-2013. In an average class, 1% graduate in 3 years or less, 57% graduate in 4 years or less, 66% graduate in 5 years or less, and 66% graduate in 6 years or less.

Admissions Contact: Rob Lange, Dean of Admissions. E-Mail: *admit@cnu.edu* Web: *www.cnu.edu*

COLLEGE OF WILLIAM & MARY — E-3

Williamsburg, VA 23187 — (757) 221-4223; (757) 221-1242

Full-time: 2777 men, 3418 women	**Faculty:** n/av; 1, -$
Part-time: 37 men, 39 women	**Ph.D.s:** n/av
Graduate: 975 men, 1130 women	**Student/Faculty:** n/av
Year: semesters, summer session	**Tuition:** $15,463 ($38,440)
Application Deadline: January 1	**Room & Board:** $9622
Freshman Class: n/av	

MOST COMPETITIVE

Founded by Royal Charter in 1693, the College of William & Mary is the second-oldest college in the country. It has a long history of liberal arts education and a growing research and science curriculum that demonstrates a strong commitment to undergraduate research. There are 3 undergraduate schools and 5 graduate schools. In addition to regional accreditation, William & Mary has baccalaureate program accreditation with AACSB and NCATE. The 5 libraries contain 2.2 million volumes, 2.5 million microform items, and 39,752 audio/video tapes/CDs/DVDs, and subscribe to 105,829 periodicals including electronic. Computerized library services include interlibrary loans, database searching, Internet access, and Wi-Fi capability. Special learning facilities include an art gallery, radio station, an anthropology museum, an art studio, a greenhouse, the Center for Archaeological Research, and the Omohundro Institute of Early American History and Culture. The 1200-acre campus is in a small town 50 miles southeast of Richmond. Including any residence halls, there are 183 buildings.

Student Life: 67% of undergraduates are from Virginia. Others are from 49 states, 51 foreign countries, and Canada. 60% are White. The average age of freshmen is 18; all undergraduates, 20. 4% do not continue beyond their first year; 90% remain to graduate.

Housing: College-sponsored housing includes single-sex and coed dorms, on-campus apartments, and off-campus apartments. In addition, there are honors houses, language houses, special-interest houses, fraternity houses, sorority houses, an international studies hall; smoke-free and multicultural housing; and Africana, Community Scholars, and Eco-House. On-campus housing is guaranteed for the freshman year only and is available on a lottery system for upperclassmen. 73% of students live on campus. Upperclassmen may keep cars.

Activities: There are 380 groups on campus, including art, band, cheerleading, chess, choir, chorale, chorus, computers, dance, debate, drama, drill team, environmental, ethnic, film, gay, honors, international, jazz band, literary magazine, musical theater, newspaper, opera, orchestra, pep band, photography, political, professional, radio and TV, religious, social, social service, student government, symphony, and yearbook. Popular campus events include Yule Log Ceremony, King and Queen Ball, and Opening Convocation.

Sports: There are 10 intercollegiate sports for men and 11 for women, and 28 intramural sports for men and 26 for women. Facilities include Zable football stadium with a seating capacity of 12,259; Jimmye Laycock Football Center with 30,000-square feet; Kaplan basketball arena with 8,600 seats; Plumeri Park lighted baseball facility with 1,000 seats; Albert-Daly natural grass field for lacrosse and soccer; McCormack-Nagelsen Tennis Center with six indoor tennis courts; Busch Courts with eight individual hard tennis court surfaces; Busch Field Hockey field with a seating capacity of 2,271; Adair Gymnasium with a 25 yard, 6-lane pool, a basketball court, and two volleyball courts; Joseph W. Montgomery Strength Training Center with 5,000 square feet; Recreation Center with a 25 yard, 8-lane pool, the Alan B. Miller Gymnasium, a fitness room, two weight rooms, five racquetball courts, two squash courts, and a host of other amenities.

Disabled Students: 95% of the campus is accessible. Facilities include wheelchair ramps, elevators, special parking, specially equipped restrooms, special class scheduling, lowered drinking fountains. modified recreational facilities, braille signage, Kurzweil reader, and a special learning lab for the visually impaired. Individual accommodations are made on a case-by-case basis.

Services: Counseling and information services are available, as is tutoring in most subjects. There is a reader service for the blind.

Campus Safety and Security: Measures include 24-hour foot and vehicle patrol, emergency notification system, self-defense education, and security escort services. There are shuttle buses, emergency telephones, lighted pathways/sidewalks, controlled access to dorms/residences, crime prevention programs.

Programs of Study: William & Mary confers B.A., B.S. and B.B.A. degrees. Master's and doctoral degrees are also awarded. Bachelor's degrees are awarded in BIOLOGICAL SCIENCE (biology/biological science and neurosciences), BUSINESS (accounting, banking and finance, business administration and management, entrepreneurial studies, and marketing management), COMMUNICATIONS AND THE ARTS (art, art history and appreciation, Chinese, dramatic arts, English, French, German, linguistics, modern language, and music), COMPUTER AND PHYSICAL SCIENCE (chemistry, computer science, geology, mathematics, and physics), EDUCATION (athletic training), HEALTH PROFESSIONS (health science), SOCIAL SCIENCE (African studies, American studies, anthropology, classical/ancient civilization, economics, history, interdisciplinary studies, international relations, Latin American studies, medieval studies, philosophy, political science/government, psychology, public affairs, religion, sociology, and women's studies). Biology, government, and psychology have the largest enrollments.

Required: To graduate, students must demonstrate proficiencies in foreign language, writing, and computing. Freshman seminars are required. Students must complete 120 credit hours, with 33 to 48 in the major, a minimum 2.0 GPA, and a minimum of 60 credit hours in residence at the College. Distribution requirements include courses in math and quantitative reasoning, natural sciences, social sciences, world cultures and history, literature and history of the arts, and philosophical, religious, and social thought.

Special: William and Mary has various special academic programs available to students: Study abroad in 23 countries over the world; Work-study programs with various employer including campus departments and off-campus community agencies; Washington Program which is open to students in all majors and disciplines; Accelerated degree program in Computer Science and Public Policy with an option whereby a small number of current W&M undergraduates will be able to earn both a Bachelor's degree and a Master degree in a total of five years of coursework; Student Self-designed majors in Interdisciplinary Studies; Combined Degree Programs with engineering schools of Columbia University; Joint degree program with University of St Andrews in Scotland; The Department Honors programs administered by the Roy R. Charles Center; Internships for credit; and Dual major in all majors. There are 29 national honor societies, including Phi Beta Kappa, a freshman honors program, and 35 departmental honors programs.

Faculty/Classroom: No introductory courses are taught by graduate students.

Admissions: 95% of the current freshmen were in the top fifth of their class; 99% were in the top two fifths.

Requirements: The SAT or ACT is required. The Common Application, William & Mary Supplement to the Common Application, Secondary School Report form complete with a high school transcript and counselor letter of recommendation, Midyear School Report form, and official report of standardized test scores, application fee, or a fee waiver request. AP credits are accepted. Important factors in the admissions decision are advanced placement or honors courses, extracurricular activities record, and recommendations by school officials.

Procedure: Freshmen are admitted fall. Entrance exams should be taken in spring of the junior year or fall of the senior year. There are early decision and deferred admissions plans. Early decision applications should be filed by November 1; regular applications, by January 1 for fall entry; and November 1 for spring entry. The fall 2013 application fee was $70. Notification of early decision is sent December 1; regular decision, April 1. 552 early decision candidates were accepted for the 2013-2014 class. 3196 applicants were on the 2013 waiting list; 1474 were admitted. Applications are accepted online.

Transfer: 185 transfer students enrolled in 2012-2013. William & Mary recommends that students interested in transferring to the College take challenging courses in the liberal arts and sciences. Typically, competitive transfer applicants have a GPA of 3.5 or higher at their current institution. 60 of 120 credits required for the bachelor's degree must be completed at William & Mary.

Visiting: There are regularly scheduled orientations for prospective students, group information session followed by a student-led tour. There are guides for informal visits and visitors may sit in on classes. To schedule a visit, contact the Office of Admissions.

Financial Aid: The FAFSA and the college's own financial statement, and the CSS Profile is required for early decision enrollees. are required. The priority date for freshman financial aid applications for fall entry is March 1. The deadline for filing freshman financial aid applications for fall entry is March 1.

International Students: The school actively recruits these students. They must take the TOEFL with a minimum score of 600 on the paper-based TOEFL (PBT) or 100 on the Internet-based version (iBT). They must also take the SAT or ACT. SAT II: subject tests are considered if they are submitted.

Graduates: From July 1, 2012 to June 30, 2013, 1517 bachelor's degrees were awarded. In an average class, 90% graduate in 6 years or less.

Admissions Contact: E-Mail: *admission@wm.edu* Web: *www.wm.edu/admission*

EASTERN MENNONITE UNIVERSITY D-2

Harrisonburg, VA 22802 (540) 432-4118
(800) 368-2665; (540) 432-4444

Full-time: 345 men, 522 women	**Faculty:** 89; IIA, --$
Part-time: 15 men, 15 women	**Ph.D.s:** 71%
Graduate: 107 men, 307 women	**Student/Faculty:** 10 to 1
Year: semesters, summer session	**Tuition:** $29,350
Application Deadline: open	**Room & Board:** $9500
Freshman Class: 636 applied, 490 accepted, 206 enrolled	
SAT: required **ACT:** 25	**VERY COMPETITIVE**

Eastern Mennonite University, founded in 1917, is a private Christian liberal arts university affiliated with the Mennonite Church. The university offers programs in the arts and sciences, education, biology, and nursing. EMU also offers master's degrees in several areas. EMU's Lancaster site provides some programs in Lancaster, Pennsylvania. There are 7 graduate schools. In addition to regional accreditation, EMU has baccalaureate program accreditation with ACPE, CSWE, NCATE, and NLN. The library contains 167,242 volumes, 92,096 microform items, and 3,723 audio/video tapes/CDs/DVDs, and subscribes to 1,056 periodicals including electronic. Computerized library services include interlibrary loans, database searching, Internet access, and Wi-Fi capability. Special learning facilities include an art gallery, natural history museum, planetarium, radio station, an arboretum and greenhouse, nursing laboratory, and cadaver laboratory. The 97-acre campus is in a small town. 110 miles southwest of Washington, D.C. Including any residence halls, there are 44 buildings.

Student Life: 57% of undergraduates are from out of state, mostly the Middle Atlantic. Students are from 32 states, 19 foreign countries, and Canada. 58% are from public schools. 81% are White. 91% are Protestant. The average age of freshmen is 18; all undergraduates, 21. 23% do not continue beyond their first year; 62% remain to graduate.

Housing: 683 students can be accommodated in college housing, which includes single-sex and coed dorms, on-campus apartments, off-campus apartments, and married student housing. an intentional community. On-campus housing is guaranteed for all 4 years. 57% of students live on campus; of those, 75% remain on campus on weekends. Alcohol is not permitted. All students may keep cars.

Activities: There are no fraternities or sororities. There are 51 groups on campus, including art, chess, choir, chorale, chorus, computers, dance, drama, environmental, ethnic, film, honors, international, jazz band, literary magazine, musical theater, newspaper, orchestra, pep band, photography, political, professional, radio and TV, religious, social, social service, student government, student women's association and peace fellowship, and yearbook. Popular campus events include Spring Fling, Fall Festival, and Multicultural Week.

Sports: There are 7 intercollegiate sports for men and 8 for women, and 15 intramural sports for men and 15 for women. Facilities include a fitness center, aerobics room, indoor track, and climbing wall. The gym includes 1 regular varsity court and 2 courts for team practice. Outside facilities include a lighted artificial turf playing field, lighted tennis courts, baseball, softball, and soccer fields, a rubberized outdoor track, as well as basketball and sand volleyball courts.

Disabled Students: 75% of the campus is accessible. Facilities include wheelchair ramps, elevators, special parking, specially equipped restrooms, special class scheduling, lowered drinking fountains, special housing. Newer buildings on campus have accessible telephones.

Services: Counseling and information services are available, as is tutoring in most subjects, core curriculum courses There is a reader service for the blind, and remedial reading and writing. EMU owns technology, such as the ability to burn textbooks onto CD's, for visually impaired students and those with other special learning needs. Technology for the hearing impaired will be provided as needed.

Campus Safety and Security: Measures include self-defense education and security escort services. There are emergency telephones, lighted pathways/sidewalks, There is a 12-hour foot or vehicle watchman.

Programs of Study: EMU confers B.A., and B.S. degrees. Associate and master's degrees are also awarded. Bachelor's degrees are awarded in AGRICULTURE (international agriculture), BIOLOGICAL SCIENCE (biochemistry and biology/biological science), BUSINESS (accounting, business administration and management, international business management, and recreational facilities management), COMMUNICATIONS AND THE ARTS (art, communications, dramatic arts, English, French, German, music, and Spanish), COMPUTER AND PHYSICAL SCIENCE (chemistry, computer management, computer science, and mathematics), EDUCATION (early childhood education, elementary education, physical education, secondary education, and special education), ENGINEERING AND ENVIRONMENTAL DESIGN (environmental science), HEALTH PROFESSIONS (medical laboratory technology and nursing), SOCIAL SCIENCE (biblical studies, development economics, economics, history, liberal arts/general studies, ministries, peace studies, philosophy, psychology, religion, social science, social work, sociology, and theological studies). Biology/pre-med, education, and nursing are the strongest academically. Business, education, and nursing have the largest enrollments.

Required: To graduate, students must complete interdisciplinary core courses, courses in Bible and religion, cross-cultural study, writing, speech, and math, a major (minors are optional), and a variety of electives for a minimum of 128 semester hours. A minimum cumulative GPA of 2.0 is required while some majors require a higher GPA in the major or overall.

Special: EMU offers study-abroad programs each semester and during the summer at a variety of locations around the world. Students may also choose to study 1 or 2 semesters in Washington, D.C. There are internships in a variety of majors, dual majors, a student-designed major, and a 2 year general studies degree. There is 1 national honor society and a freshman honors program.

Faculty/Classroom: 58% of faculty are male; 42% are female. 75% teach undergraduates, 38% do research, and 35% do both. No introductory courses are taught by graduate students. The average class size in an introductory lecture is 40; in a laboratory is 17; and in a regular course is 18.

Admissions: 77% of the 2013-2014 applicants were accepted. The ACT scores were 17% below 21, 21% between 21 and 23, 30% between 24 and 26, 9% between 27 and 28, and 23% above 28. 36% of the current freshmen were in the top fifth of their class; 65% were in the top two fifths. 7 freshmen graduated first in their class.

Requirements: The SAT or ACT is required. In addition, with a minimum composite score of 920 or 20, respectively. Applicants must be graduates of an accredited secondary school or have a GED certificate. The university recommends that students have completed 4 credits of English, 3 each of math, science, and social studies, 2 or more of foreign language and chemistry for nursing majors. A personal reference is required and an interview is recommended. A GPA of 2.2 is required. AP and CLEP credits are accepted. Important factors in the admissions decision are leadership record, extracurricular activities record, and recommendations by school officials.

Procedure: Freshmen are admitted fall and spring. Entrance exams should be taken in the spring of the junior year or the fall of the senior year. There are deferred admissions and rolling admissions plans. Application deadlines are open. The fall 2013 application fee was $25. Applications are accepted online.

Transfer: 77 transfer students enrolled in 2012-2013. Transfer students must have a minimum college GPA of 2.0. 32 of 128 credits required for the bachelor's degree must be completed at EMU.

Visiting: There are regularly scheduled orientations for prospective students, including an address by the president, a financial aid seminar, a review of general education, and attendance at a chapel; the opportunity to sit in on classes, meet with professors and admissions representatives, sleep in residence halls, eat in the cafeteria, and attend special campus events. There are guides for informal visits. To schedule a visit, contact the Admissions Office.

Financial Aid: In 2013-2014, 97% of all full-time freshmen and 96% of continuing full-time students received some form of financial aid. 89% of all full-time freshmen and 87% of continuing full-time students received need-based aid. The average freshman award was $16,515. Need-based scholarships or need-based grants averaged $2,700; need-based self-help aid (loans and jobs) averaged $6,015; and other non-need-based awards and non-need-based scholarships averaged $7,800. 35% of undergraduate students work part-time. Average annual earnings from campus work are $1300. The average financial indebtedness of the 2013 graduate was $18,208. EMU is a member of CSS. The FAFSA and the state aid form are required. The deadline for filing freshman financial aid applications for fall entry is April 15.

International Students: There are 40 international students enrolled. They must take the TOEFL. They must also take the SAT or ACT, scoring 920.

Graduates: From July 1, 2012 to June 30, 2013, 315 bachelor's degrees were awarded. The most popular majors were business (30%), nursing (16%), and education (9%). 15 companies recruited on campus in 2012-2013. In an average class, 45% graduate in 4 years or less, 59% graduate in 5 years or less, and 62% graduate in 6 years or less. Of the 2012 graduating class, 8% were enrolled in graduate school within 6 months of graduation, and 86% were employed.

Admissions Contact: Bonnie Lofton E-Mail: *admiss@emu.edu* Web: *www.emu.edu*

EMORY AND HENRY COLLEGE B-4

Emory, VA 24327 (276) 944-6133
(800) 848-5493; (276) 944-6935

Full-time: 464 men, 410 women
Part-time: 12 men, 11 women
Graduate: 14 men, 34 women
Year: semesters, summer session
Application Deadline: April 15
Freshman Class: n/av
SAT or ACT: required

Faculty: 72; IIB, --$
Ph.D.s: n/av
Student/Faculty: 10 to 1
Tuition: $28,966
Room & Board: $9780

COMPETITIVE

Emory and Henry College, founded in 1836, is a private liberal arts institution affiliated with the United Methodist Church. The library contains 271,209 volumes, 207,000 microform items, and 7,950 audio/video tapes/CDs/DVDs, and subscribes to 352 periodicals including electronic. Computerized library services include interlibrary loans, database searching, and Internet access. Special learning facilities include an art gallery, radio station, and TV station. The 331-acre campus is in a rural area in Emory, southwest Virginia.

Student Life: 64% of undergraduates are from Virginia. Others are from 26 states, 5 foreign countries, and Canada. 99% are from public schools. 80% are White. The average age of freshmen is 18; all undergraduates, 20.

Housing: College-sponsored housing includes single-sex and coed dorms, on-campus apartments, and off-campus apartments. In addition, there are honors houses and special-interest houses. On-campus housing is guaranteed for all 4 years. 77% of students live on campus; of those, 50% remain on campus on weekends. Alcohol is not permitted. All students may keep cars.

Activities: 15% of men belong to 9 local fraternities; 30% of women belong to 6 local sororities. There are 50 groups on campus, including art, band, cheerleading, choir, chorus, dance, debate, drama, ethnic, gay, international, literary magazine, musical theater, newspaper, opera, pep band, photography, political, professional, radio and TV, religious, social, social service, student government, and yearbook. Popular campus events include Homecoming, Founder's Day, Martin Luther King Junior Day, Fall Formals, Parents Day, Greek Air Band, and the Literary Festival.

Sports: Facilities include a gym, pool, racquetball court, outdoor volleyball courts, tennis courts, a weight room, dance room, golf course, baseball and football fields, and a horseshoe area.

Disabled Students: 50% of the campus is accessible. Facilities include wheelchair ramps, elevators, special parking, specially equipped restrooms, special class scheduling, lowered drinking fountains, and special housing.

Services: Counseling and information services are available, as is tutoring in most subjects. There is a reader service for the blind, and remedial math and writing.

Campus Safety and Security: Measures include 24-hour foot and vehicle patrol, self-defense education, and security escort services. There are lighted pathways/sidewalks.

Programs of Study: E and H confers B.A., and B.S. degrees. Master's degrees are also awarded. Bachelor's degrees are awarded in BIOLOGICAL SCIENCE (biology/biological science), BUSINESS (business administration and management), COMMUNICATIONS AND THE ARTS (art, communications, creative writing, dramatic arts, English literature, journalism, literature, modern language, music performance, and music theory and composition), COMPUTER AND PHYSICAL SCIENCE (chemistry, computer management, computer science, mathematics, and physics), EDUCATION (English education, mathematics education, and physical education), ENGINEERING AND ENVIRONMENTAL DESIGN (environmental science), SOCIAL SCIENCE (community services, East Asian studies, economics, European studies, geography, history, interdisciplinary studies, international studies, Middle Eastern studies, philosophy, political science/government, psychology, public affairs, religion, and sociology).

Required: All students must complete a general studies curriculum covering Western traditions, great books, religion, ethical values inquiry, and global studies and must demonstrate proficiency in oral skills. Specific courses include a first-year writing course, 1 each from 3 disciplines, including social sciences, humanities and arts, and natural sciences, and according to major, either a foreign language or quantitative methods. A total of 120 semester hours for a B.A. or 124 for a B.S., with a GPA of 2.0, is required for graduation. The total number of hours in the major varies.

Special: A cooperative program in medical technology and 2-2, 4-1, and 3-2 engineering degrees are available. Dual and student-designed majors, an interdisciplinary English major, combined B.A.-B.S. degrees, internships, a Washington Semester, work-study, nondegree study, and pass/fail options are also available. There are 10 national honor societies and 8 departmental honors programs.

Faculty/Classroom: 59% of faculty are male; 41% are female. All teach undergraduates. No introductory courses are taught by graduate students. The average class size in an introductory lecture is 25; in a laboratory is 13; and in a regular course is 22.

Requirements: The SAT or ACT is required. Applicants should be high school graduates. High school courses required include 4 years of English, 3 or more units of math including algebra I, algebra II, and geometry, 2 or more units of lab science, 2 units of a single foreign language, and 2 or more units of social studies and history. One additional unit in fine arts is strongly recommended. A personal essay is required. AP credits are accepted. Important factors in the admissions decision are advanced placement or honors courses, recommendations by school officials, and evidence of special talent.

Procedure: Freshmen are admitted fall, spring, and summer. Entrance exams should be taken in November of the senior year. There are early decision, deferred admissions, and rolling admissions plans. Early decision applications should be filed by November 1; regular applications, by April 15 for fall entry, along with a $30 fee. Applications are accepted online.

Transfer: 64 transfer students enrolled in 2012-2013. Transfers must have at least a 2.5 GPA in previous college work. Those with at least 24 credits may be admitted without high school data; those with fewer than 24 credits must meet freshman admission standards. 33 of 120 credits required for the bachelor's degree must be completed at E and H.

Visiting: There are regularly scheduled orientations for prospective students, including a program for students to meet faculty and staff and to attend education sessions on college life. There are guides for informal visits, visitors may sit in on classes, and stay overnight. To schedule a visit, contact the Admissions Office.

Financial Aid: 13% of undergraduate students work part-time. Average annual earnings from campus work are $1200. The FAFSA, the state aid form, and the college's own financial statement are required. The priority date for freshman financial aid applications for fall entry is April 1. The deadline for filing freshman financial aid applications for fall entry is August 1.

International Students: There are 5 international students enrolled. The school actively recruits these students. They must take the TOEFL.

Admissions Contact: David Hawsey, Vice President of Enrollment Management. E-Mail: *ehadmiss@ehc.edu* Web: *www.ehc.edu*

FERRUM COLLEGE — C-4

Ferrum, VA 24088 (540) 365-4290; (800) 868-9797; (540) 365-4266

Full-time: 685 men, 535 women	**Faculty:** 69; II B, --$
Part-time: 15 men, 15 women	**Ph.D.s:** 68%
Graduate: n/av	**Student/Faculty:** n/av
Year: semesters	**Tuition:** $26,250
Application Deadline: open	**Room & Board:** $9000
Freshman Class: n/av	
SAT or ACT: required	

LESS COMPETITIVE

Ferrum College, founded in 1913, is a private, primarily residential institution offering both professional and liberal arts majors. Figures in the above capsule and this profile are approximate. In addition to regional accreditation, Ferrum has baccalaureate program accreditation with CSWE. The library contains 219,774 volumes, 7578 microform items, and 2285 audio/video tapes/CDs/DVDs, and subscribes to 21,014 periodicals including electronic. Computerized library services include interlibrary loans, database searching, Internet access, and laptop Internet portals. Special learning facilities include a learning resource center, art gallery, radio station, folk life museum, and living history museum. The 740-acre campus is in a rural area 35 miles south of Roanoke. Including any residence halls, there are 54 buildings.

Student Life: 86% of undergraduates are from Virginia. Others are from 24 states and 5 foreign countries. 59% are white; 25% African American. 29% claim no religious affiliation. The average age of freshmen is 18; all undergraduates, 21. 40% do not continue beyond their first year; 35% remain to graduate.

Housing: 1300 students can be accommodated in college housing, which includes single-sex and coed dorms, on-campus apartments, off-campus apartments, and married student housing. In addition, there is theme housing by floors in dorms. On-campus housing is guaranteed for all 4 years. 86% of students live on campus; of those, 50% remain on campus on weekends. All students may keep cars.

Activities: 6% of men belong to 2 local fraternities; 9% of women belong to 3 local sororities. There are 63 groups on campus, including art, cheerleading, choir, chorale, chorus, communications, computers, dance, drama, environmental, ethnic, film, gay, honors, international, jazz band, literary magazine, musical theater, newspaper, photography, political, professional, radio and TV, religious, social, social service, and student government. Popular campus events include Spring Fling, Blue Ridge Folklife Festival, and Snow Ball.

Sports: There are 7 intercollegiate sports for men and 7 for women, and 13 intramural sports for men and 13 for women. Facilities include a gym, a field house, tennis courts, a weight room, an indoor pool, an outdoor volleyball court, a football stadium, a soccer field, a baseball field, a women's softball field, a recreation center (with indoor basketball courts, racquetball courts, and universal weights), and hiking/mountain biking trails.

Disabled Students: 75% of the campus is accessible. Facilities include wheelchair ramps, elevators, special parking, specially equipped restrooms, special class scheduling, and lowered drinking fountains.

Services: Counseling and information services are available, as is tutoring in most subjects. There is remedial math, reading, and writing. College skills classes, individual assistance for study strategies, and subject-specific tutoring by professors and students are available.

Campus Safety and Security: Measures include 24-hour foot and vehicle patrol, self defense education, and security escort services. There are emergency telephones, lighted pathways/sidewalks, and controlled access to dorms/residences.

Programs of Study: Ferrum confers B.A., B.S., B.F.A., and B.S.W. degrees. Bachelor's degrees are awarded in AGRICULTURE (agriculture and horticulture), BIOLOGICAL SCIENCE (biology/biological science), BUSINESS (accounting, business administration and management, recreation and leisure services, and sports management), COMMUNICATIONS AND THE ARTS (art, dramatic arts, English, performing arts, Russian, and Spanish), COMPUTER AND PHYSICAL SCIENCE (chemistry, information sciences and systems, and mathematics), EDUCATION (physical education), ENGINEERING AND ENVIRONMENTAL DESIGN (environmental science), HEALTH PROFESSIONS (health science), SOCIAL SCIENCE (criminal justice, history, international studies, liberal arts/general studies, philosophy, political science/government, psychology, religion, social studies, and social work). Chemistry, biology, and environmental science are the strongest academically. Business administration, criminal justice, and liberal arts/teacher education have the largest enrollments.

Required: To graduate, students must complete at least 121 semester hours with a minimum GPA of 2.0. There are 37 hours of distribution requirements, including social sciences, natural sciences, English, religion/philosophy, math, literature, fine arts, and phys ed. A major may require up to 57 semester hours, and 30 hours of the total must be in upper-level courses.

Special: The college encourages internships, and some majors require them. Study abroad, work-study programs, dual majors, an accelerated degree program in social work, and B.A.-B.S. degrees are offered. A liberal studies degree and nondegree study are available. There are 6 national honor societies, a freshman honors program, and 33 departmental honors programs.

Faculty/Classroom: 57% of faculty are male; 43% are female. All teach and do research. The average class size in an introductory lecture is 20; in a laboratory, 15; and in a regular course, 13.

Requirements: The SAT or ACT is required. Applicants must be graduates of an accredited secondary school or receive a GED certificate. Applicants should complete 18 high school academic credits. The Admissions Committee considers courses taken, grades, extracurricular activities, SAT or ACT scores, and recommendations. Personal interviews may be required for students lacking appropriate GPA or standardized test scores. AP and CLEP credits are accepted. Important factors in the admissions decision are advanced placement or honors courses, leadership record, and evidence of special talent.

Procedure: Freshmen are admitted to all sessions. There are deferred admissions and rolling admissions plans. Application deadlines are open. The application fee is $25. Notification is sent on a rolling basis. Applications are accepted online.

Transfer: Applicants for transfer must be in good academic standing at their current schools. 32 of 127 credits required for the bachelor's degree must be completed at Ferrum.

Visiting: There are regularly scheduled orientations for prospective students, including faculty information sessions, parent-to-parent and student-to-student sessions, and tours of the campus and residence halls. There are guides for informal visits; visitors may sit in on classes and stay overnight. To schedule a visit, contact the Director of Admissions.

Financial Aid: The FAFSA and the state aid form are required. Check with the school for current application deadlines.

International Students: The school actively recruits these students. They must take the TOEFL. They must also take the SAT or ACT.

Admissions Contact: Gilda Woods, Director of Admissions. E-mail: *admissions@ferrum.edu* Web: *www.ferrum.edu*

GEORGE MASON UNIVERSITY — E-2

Fairfax, VA 22030-4444 (703) 993-2400; (703) 993-4622

Full-time: 7150 men, 8050 women	**Faculty:** n/av; I, -$
Part-time: 2200 men, 2300 women	**Ph.D.s:** 90%
Graduate: 5120 men, 7250 women	**Student/Faculty:** 15 to 1
Year: semesters, summer session	**Tuition:** $9566 ($26,044)
Application Deadline: see profile	**Room & Board:** $9000
Freshman Class: n/av	
ACT: recommended	

VERY COMPETITIVE

George Mason University, founded in 1972, is an entrepreneurial public institution with national distinction in a range of academic fields. The university has undergraduate and graduate degree programs in engineering, information technology, biotechnology, and health care. There are 8 undergraduate schools and 11 graduate schools. The figures in the above capsule and this profile are approximate. In addition to regional accreditation, Mason has baccalaureate program accreditation with AACSB, ABET, CSAB, CSWE, NASM, and NCATE. The 5 libraries contain 1.9 million volumes, 3.2 million microform items, and 43,289 audio/video tapes/CDs/DVDs, and subscribe to 56,433 periodicals including electronic. Computerized library services include interlibrary loans, database searching, Internet access, and laptop Internet portals. Special learning facilities include a learning resource center, art gallery, radio station, TV station, astronomy observatory, and the Smithsonian Conservation and Research Center. The 806-acre campus is in a suburban area in the Greater Washington Metropolitan area, 21 miles southwest of Washington, D.C. Including any residence halls, there are 115 buildings.

Student Life: 88% of undergraduates are from Virginia. Others are from 50 states, 131 foreign countries, and Canada. 86% are from public schools. 59% are white; 16% Asian American. The average age of freshmen is 18; all undergraduates, 23. 15% do not continue beyond their first year; 69% remain to graduate.

Housing: 5057 students can be accommodated in college housing, which includes single-sex and coed dorms, on-campus apartments, and off-campus apartments. In addition, there are honors houses and special-interest houses. On-campus housing is guaranteed for new freshmen for all 4 years and is available to other students on a first-come, first-served basis. 74% of students commute. All students may keep cars. Alcohol is permitted on campus with certain restrictions.

Activities: 7% of men belong to 23 national fraternities; 6% of women belong to 15 national sororities. There are 255 groups on campus, including art, band, cheerleading, chess, choir, chorale, chorus, computers, dance, drama, environmental, ethnic, film, forensics, gay, honors, international, jazz band, literary magazine, musical theater, newspaper, opera, orchestra, pep band, photography, political, professional, radio and TV, religious, social, social service, student government, symphony, and yearbook. Popular campus events include Welcome Week, Mason Day, and Patriot Day.

Sports: There are 11 intercollegiate sports for men and 11 for women, and 11 intramural sports for men and 11 for women. Facilities include a 10,000-seat arena for basketball, indoor soccer, and concerts; a sports and recreation complex that includes a 200-meter track, basketball, handball/racquetball, tennis, and volleyball courts, baseball and softball diamonds, batting cages, a weight room, saunas, and a golf and archery net; a 400-meter outdoor track; and playing fields. The aquatic and fitness center offers a 2-story fitness area with 3000 sq. ft. of cardio and 5000 sq. ft. of weight training equipment, a recreational pool, an Olympic-size competition pool and diving well, a hot tub, and a dry sauna.

Disabled Students: 95% of the campus is accessible. Facilities include wheelchair ramps, elevators, special parking, specially equipped restrooms, special class scheduling, lowered drinking fountains, lowered telephones, and special housing. Special arrangements can be made for testing, readers, note takers, and interpreters.

Services: Counseling and information services are available, as is tutoring in most subjects. There is a reader service for the blind. Additional tutoring is offered for a fee.

Campus Safety and Security: Measures include 24-hour foot and vehicle patrol, emergency notification system, self-defense education, and security escort services. There are shuttle buses, lighted pathways/sidewalks, controlled access to dorms/residences, and security call boxes located throughout the campus.

Programs of Study: Mason confers B.A., B.S., B.F.A., B.I.S., B.S.E.D., and B.S.N. degrees. Master's and doctoral degrees are also awarded. Bachelor's degrees are awarded in AGRICULTURE (environmental studies), BIOLOGICAL SCIENCE (biology/biological science and neurosciences), BUSINESS (accounting, banking and finance, business administration and management, marketing/retailing/merchandising, operations management, and tourism), COMMUNICATIONS AND THE ARTS (art history and appreciation, communications, communications technology, dance, dramatic arts, English, film arts, French, music, Spanish, video, and visual and performing arts), COMPUTER AND PHYSICAL SCIENCE (astronomy, chemistry, computer science, earth science, geology, information sciences and systems, mathematics, physics, science and management, and software engineering), EDUCATION (athletic training and physical education), ENGINEERING AND ENVIRONMENTAL DESIGN (civil engineering, computational sciences, computer engineering, electrical/electronics engineering, industrial engineering, and systems engineering), HEALTH PROFESSIONS (community health work, health science, medical technology, and nursing), SOCIAL SCIENCE (anthropology, criminal justice, economics, geography, history, interdisciplinary studies, international relations, Latin American studies, parks and recreation management, philosophy, political science/government, psychology, public administration, religion, Russian and Slavic studies, social work, and sociology). Accounting, biology, and psychology have the largest enrollments.

Required: To graduate, all students must complete a core of study that includes 6 credits written communication, 3 to 4 credits information technology, 4 credits lab science, 3 credits each oral communication, quantitative reasoning, literature, arts, Western civilization/world history, social and behavioral science, natural science, and global understanding, and 1 to 6 credits synthesis as well as at least 45 hours of upper-division work. Hours in the major vary. A minimum 2.0 GPA is required, and a total of 120 to 133 credit hours must be completed.

Special: Mason offers internships through academic departments and on-campus work-study programs. Also available are dual and student-designed majors, accelerated degrees, non-degree study, and pass/fail options. New Century College is an integrated program of study that emphasizes collaboration, experimental learning, and self-reflection. Mason also offers the Smithsonian Semester, a 16-credit resident program in conservation studies at the Smithsonian Conservation and Research Center in Front Royal, Virginia. There are 4 national honor societies, a freshman honors program, several departmental honors programs, and a universitywide honors program.

Faculty/Classroom: 55% of faculty are male; 45% are female. 84% teach undergraduates. Graduate students teach 12% of introductory courses. The average class size in an introductory lecture is 43; in a laboratory, 23; and in a regular course, 25.

Requirements: The ACT is recommended. A score-optional review of applications allows applicants to be considered for admission without submitting test scores. Applicants must be graduates of an accredited secondary school or have a GED certificate. A minimum high school GPA of 3.5 is recommended. A minimum of 18 academic credits is required, including 4 years of English, 3 each of math, science, lab science, social studies, and academic electives, and 2 of foreign language. A written personal statement is required. A GPA of 2.0 is required. AP and CLEP credits are accepted. Important factors in the admissions decision are advanced placement or honors courses, evidence of special talent, and recommendations by school officials.

Procedure: Freshmen are admitted fall, spring, and summer. Entrance exams should be taken during the spring of the junior year. There are early action and deferred admissions plan. Check with the school for current application deadlines and fee. Applications are accepted online. A waiting list is maintained.

Transfer: 2600 transfer students enrolled in a recent year. Applicants must have a minimum 2.0 GPA and generally have completed 30 or more transferable credits from an accredited college or university. Official transcripts (including high school if 30 credits or less have been completed) are required. SAT or ACT scores must be submitted if 30 credits or less have been completed unless applicant graduated from high school more than 5 years before application. 30 of 120 credits required for the bachelor's degree must be completed at Mason.

Visiting: There are regularly scheduled orientations for prospective students, including campus tours and an information session. There are guides for informal visits, and visitors may sit in on classes. To schedule a visit, contact the Admissions Office.

Financial Aid: In a recent year, 67% of all full-time freshmen and 61% of continuing full-time students received some form of financial aid. 43% of all full-time freshmen and 44% of continuing full-time students received need-based aid. The average freshman award was $12,012. Need-based scholarships or need-based grants averaged $7182 ($24,800 maximum); need-based self-help aid (loans and jobs) averaged $3660 ($8500 maximum); non-need-based athletic scholarships averaged $16,156 ($36,533 maximum); and other non-need-based awards and non-need-based scholarships averaged $5940 ($33,540 maximum). The average financial indebtedness of a recent graduate was $19,582. The FAFSA is required. Check with the school for current deadlines.

International Students: There were 488 international students enrolled in a recent year. The school actively recruits these students. They must take the TOEFL with a minimum score of 570 on the paper-based TOEFL (PBT) or 88 on the Internet-based version (iBT). They must also take the SAT or ACT.

Computers: Wireless access is available. Information regarding computer lab locations and hours of operation, quantity of PCs, and the university's wireless system is available at GMU's Classroom Technologies web site. All students may access the system 24 hours per day. There are no time limits and no fees. Students in some programs are encouraged to have a personal computer.

Graduates: In a recent year, 4009 bachelor's degrees were awarded. The most popular majors were business/marketing (22%), social sciences (14%), and English (9%). 546 companies recruited on campus in a recent year. In an average class, 2% graduate in 3 years or less, 39% graduate in 4 years or less, 58% graduate in 5 years or less, and 63% graduate in 6 years or less.

Admissions Contact: Andrew Flagel, Dean of Undergraduate Admissions. E-mail: *admissions@gmu.edu* Web: *www.gmu.edu*

HAMPDEN-SYDNEY COLLEGE D-3

Hampden-Sydney, VA 23943 (434) 223-6120
(800) 755-0733; (434) 223-6346

Full-time: 1069 men, 1 women | **Faculty:** 92; IIB, av$
Part-time: n/av | **Ph.D.s:** 86%
Graduate: n/av | **Student/Faculty:** 11 to 1
Year: semesters, summer session | **Tuition:** $37,352
Application Deadline: March 1 | **Room & Board:** $11,726
Freshman Class: 2623 applied, 1439 accepted, 292 enrolled
SAT CR/M/W: 555/562/524 **ACT:** 23 **COMPETITIVE**

Hampden-Sydney College, founded in 1775, is a private men's liberal arts institution affiliated with the Presbyterian Church. There is one undergraduate school. The library contains 269,245 volumes, 4,545 microform items, 7,064 audio/video tapes/CDs/DVDs, and subscribes to 140 periodicals including electronic. Computerized library services include interlibrary loans, database searching, Internet access, and Wi-Fi capability. Special learning facilities include an art gallery, planetarium, radio station, an international communications center, college history museum, and observatory. The 1340-acre campus is in a rural area 60 miles southwest of Richmond. Including any residence halls, there are 118 buildings.

Student Life: 71% of undergraduates are from Virginia. Others are from 32 states, 15 foreign countries, and Canada. 66% are from public schools. 81% are White. 33% are Protestant; 18% claim no religious affiliation; 16% Catholic. The average age of freshmen is 18; all undergraduates, 20. 20% do not continue beyond their first year; 68% remain to graduate.

Housing: 1122 students can be accommodated in college housing, which includes single-sex dorms, on-campus apartments, off-campus apartments, and married student housing. In addition, there are honors houses, language houses, special-interest houses, fraternity houses, Minority Student House, and International Student House. On-campus housing is guaranteed for all 4 years. 95% of students live on campus; of those, 60% remain on campus on weekends. All students may keep cars.

Activities: 30% of men belong to 8 national fraternities. There are no sororities. There are 83 groups on campus, including art, band, chess, choir, chorale, chorus, computers, debate, drama, environmental, ethnic, gay, honors, international, literary magazine, newspaper, pep band, photography, political, professional, radio and TV, religious, social, social service, student government, and yearbook. Popular campus events include Greek Week, Macon Week, and Midwinters CAC events.

Sports: There are 9 intercollegiate sports for men, and 8 intramural sports for men. Facilities include a field house with 3 basketball courts, 5 racquetball/handball courts, an outdoor track, a pool, squash courts, a weight room, a gym, tennis courts, and many playing fields. Gammon gym has been renovated and is now Snyder Hall, and now also includes an Athletic Hall of Fame.

Disabled Students: 80% of the campus is accessible. Facilities include wheelchair ramps, elevators, special parking, specially equipped rest rooms, special class scheduling, and lowered telephones.

Services: Counseling and information services are available, as is tutoring in every subject.

Campus Safety and Security: Measures include 24-hour foot and vehicle patrol, emergency notification system, and self-defense education. There are emergency telephones, lighted pathways/sidewalks, controlled access to dorms/residences, There also is a fire department on campus and a first responder unit for emergency medical assistance. The dorm phone lines are hooked into 911.

Programs of Study: Hampden-Sydney confers B.A., and B.S. degrees. Bachelor's degrees are awarded in BIOLOGICAL SCIENCE (biology/biological science), BUSINESS (business economics), COMMUNICATIONS AND THE ARTS (classics, English, fine arts, French, German, Greek, Latin, and Spanish), COMPUTER AND PHYSICAL SCIENCE (applied mathematics, chemistry, computer science, mathematics, and physics), SOCIAL SCIENCE (economics, history, humanities, philosophy, political science/government, psychology, and religion). Sciences, economics, and rhetoric are the strongest academically. Economics, history, and biology have the largest enrollments.

Required: To graduate, students must complete 120 credit hours with a minimum GPA of 2.0. Distribution requirements include 7 courses in humanities, 4 in math and natural sciences, and 3 in social sciences. All students must also take rhetoric and foreign language and pass a rhetoric exam.

Special: The college offers co-op programs with Longwood, Randolph-Macon, Randolph College, Sweet Briar, Hollins, and Mary Baldwin Colleges and Washington and Lee University. Cross-registration with Longwood College, internships, study abroad, a 3-2 engineering program with the University of Virginia, dual-degree program in Physics and Engineering from Hampden-Sydney College and Old Dominion University, Eastern Virginaia Medical School Joint program, The George Washington University School of Medicine Ealry Selection program, the VCU-MCV early slection program, Duke University Fuqua School of Business Early Admission program - Master of Management Studies, The UVA Darden School of Business preferred consideration program - Master of Business Administration, Washington semester, work-study programs, B.A.-B.S. degree, and dual majors are available. There is a public service concentration in all majors. There are 15 national honor societies, including Phi Beta Kappa, a freshman honors program, and 10 departmental honors programs.

Faculty/Classroom: 70% of faculty are male; 30% are female. All teach and do research. No introductory courses are taught by graduate students. The average class size in an introductory lecture is 13; in a laboratory is 13; and in a regular course is 14.

Admissions: 55% of the 2013-2014 applicants were accepted. The SAT scores for the 2013-2014 freshman class were: Critical Reading--25% below 500, 48% between 500 and 599, 22% between 600 and 699, and 5% between 700 and 800; Math--21% below 500, 46% between 500 and 599, 28% between 600 and 699, and 5% between 700 and 800. 28% of the current freshmen were in the top fifth of their class; 85% were in the top two fifths. 4 freshmen graduated first in their class.

Requirements: The SAT or ACT is required. The school recommends the SAT. Applicants must be graduates of an accredited secondary school and have completed 16 high school academic credits, including 4 of English, 3 of math, 2 each of foreign language and science, and 1 of social studies. An essay is required and an interview is recommended. The GED is accepted. A GPA of 2.5 is required. AP credits are accepted. Important factors in the admissions decision are advanced placement or honors courses, recommendations by school officials, and leadership record.

Procedure: Freshmen are admitted fall and spring. Entrance exams should be taken during the junior or senior year of high school. There are early decision and early admissions plans. Early decision applications should be filed by November 15; regular applications, by March 1 for fall entry; and December 1 for spring entry, along with a $30 fee. Notification of early decision is sent December 15; regular decision, April 15. 55 early decision candidates were accepted for the 2013-2014 class. Applications are accepted online.

Transfer: 21 transfer students enrolled in 2012-2013. Applicants must have a minimum GPA of 2.5 and must take either the SAT or the ACT. An interview is recommended. 60 of 120 credits required for the bachelor's degree must be completed at Hampden-Sydney.

Visiting: There are regularly scheduled orientations for prospective students, consisting of lectures, information sessions, tours, lunch, and an athletic event. There are guides for informal visits, visitors may sit in on classes, and stay overnight. To schedule a visit, contact Mary Brooks at (434) 223-6123.

Financial Aid: In 2013-2014, 98% of all full-time freshmen and 99% of continuing full-time students received some form of financial aid. 70% of all full-time freshmen and 64% of continuing full-time students received need-based aid. The average freshman award was $36,940. Need-based scholarships or need-based grants averaged $24,799 ($31,000 maximum); need-based self-help aid (loans and jobs) averaged $4,547 ($11,000 maximum); and other non-need-based awards and non-need-based scholarships averaged $14,967 ($30,000 maximum). 22% of undergraduate students work part-time. Average annual earnings from campus work are $1385. The average financial indebtedness of the 2013 graduate was $28,651. The FAFSA is required. The deadline for filing freshman financial aid applications for fall entry is March 1.

International Students: There are 19 international students enrolled. They must take the TOEFL with a minimum score of 114 on the Internet-based version (iBT). They must also take the SAT or ACT.

Computers: All students may access the system. There are no time limits and no fees.

Graduates: From July 1, 2012 to June 30, 2013, 206 bachelor's degrees were awarded. The most popular majors were economics (30%), history (19%), and psychology (10%). 40 companies recruited on campus in 2012-2013. In an average class, 66% graduate in 4 years or less, 67% graduate in 5 years or less, and 68% graduate in 6 years or less. Of the 2012 graduating class, 20% were enrolled in graduate school within 6 months of graduation, and 60% were employed.

Admissions Contact: Anita H. Garland, Dean of Admissions. E-Mail: *hsapp@hsc.edu* Web: *www.hsc.edu*

HAMPTON UNIVERSITY F-3

Hampton, VA 23668 (757) 727-5328
(800) 624-3328; (757) 727-5095

Full-time: 1242 men, 2222 women | **Faculty:** 323
Part-time: 151 men, 236 women | **Ph.D.s:** 74%
Graduate: 314 men, 589 women | **Student/Faculty:** 10 to 1
Year: semesters, summer session | **Tuition:** $19,738
Application Deadline: March 1 | **Room & Board:** $8790
Freshman Class: n/av
SAT CR/M: 514/517 **ACT:** 20 **COMPETITIVE**

Hampton, founded in 1868, is a multicultural, historically-black, private university. Programs are offered through the following schools: Business, Engineering and Technology; Liberal Arts; Nursing; Pharmacy; Science;

College of Education and Continuing Studies; and the Graduate College. There are 8 undergraduate schools and 1 graduate school. In addition to regional accreditation, HU has baccalaureate program accreditation with ABET, ACEJMC, ASLA, CSAB, NAAB, NASM, NCATE, and NLN. The 4 libraries contain 526,154 volumes, 1.1 million microform items, and 5,835 audio/video tapes/CDs/DVDs, and subscribe to 32,187 periodicals including electronic. Computerized library services include interlibrary loans, database searching, and Internet access. Special learning facilities include an art gallery, natural history museum, radio station, and TV station. The 314-acre campus is in an urban area 15 miles west of Norfolk. Including any residence halls, there are 125 buildings.

Student Life: 67% of undergraduates are from out of state, mostly the Middle Atlantic. Students are from 44 states, 27 foreign countries, and Canada. 92% are from public schools. 89% are African American. The average age of freshmen is 18; all undergraduates, 20. 22% do not continue beyond their first year; 78% remain to graduate.

Housing: 3066 students can be accommodated in college housing, which includes single-sex and coed dorms and off-campus apartments. In addition, there are honors houses, student cottages. On-campus housing is available on a first-come, first-served basis, and is available on a lottery system for upperclassmen. 53% of students live on campus; of those, 65% remain on campus on weekends. Alcohol is not permitted. Upperclassmen may keep cars.

Activities: 5% of men belong to 6 national fraternities; 4% of women belong to 3 national sororities. There are 110 groups on campus, including art, band, cheerleading, choir, chorale, chorus, communications, dance, debate, drama, drill team, ethnic, honors, international, jazz band, marching band, newspaper, orchestra, pep band, photography, political, radio and TV, religious, social service, student government, symphony, and yearbook. Popular campus events include Career Day, High School Day, Parents' Weekend, Homecoming, Founder's Day and Convocation.

Sports: There are 5 intercollegiate sports for men and 6 for women, and 2 intramural sports for men and 1 for women. Facilities include Football stadium, Convocation Center, 12 outdoor tennis courts, open fields for intramural sports, 2 basketball courts, 2 swimming pools, volleyball court, exercise nd training room, a new student center with a health center, bowling alley, movie theater, indoor track, and restaurants.

Disabled Students: 90% of the campus is accessible. Facilities include wheelchair ramps, elevators, special parking, specially equipped restrooms, lowered drinking fountains, and lowered telephones.

Services: Counseling and information services are available, as is tutoring in most subjects. There is remedial math, reading, and writing.

Campus Safety and Security: Measures include 24-hour foot and vehicle patrol and self-defense education. There are emergency telephones, lighted pathways/sidewalks, Bike patrols, on-campus police officers, video cameras, gated campus, identification of valuables, limited access to campus, smoke detectors in residence halls, motorist assistance, and civilian support team.

Programs of Study: HU confers B.A., B.S. and B.S.Nurs. degrees. Associate, master's, and doctoral degrees are also awarded. Bachelor's degrees are awarded in BIOLOGICAL SCIENCE (biology/biological science), BUSINESS (accounting, banking and finance, business administration and management, marketing/retailing/merchandising, and sports management), COMMUNICATIONS AND THE ARTS (art, communications, dramatic arts, English, and music), COMPUTER AND PHYSICAL SCIENCE (chemistry, computer science, information sciences and systems, mathematics, and physics), EDUCATION (physical education), ENGINEERING AND ENVIRONMENTAL DESIGN (architecture, chemical engineering, and electrical/electronics engineering), HEALTH PROFESSIONS (nursing, recreation therapy, and speech pathology/audiology), SOCIAL SCIENCE (economics, history, political science/government, psychology, and sociology). Architecture, biology, and physics are the strongest academically. Biology, psychology, business management, nursing, and journalism have the largest enrollments.

Required: To graduate, students must complete 120 credit hours, with 74 hours in the major, related subjects, and free electives, and a GPA of 2.0.(The average GPA of the graduating class is 3.1.) There is a 44 to 48 hour distribution requirement in freshman studies, history, language, arts and humanities, English, social sciences, math, pure and applied sciences, speech, and health and phys ed.

Special: The college offers co-op programs in most majors, cross-registration with 6 schools, internships, and student-designed majors. Work study, study abroad, and dual majors are also available. Students may receive credit for life, military, and work experience. There are pass/fail options. There are 15 national honor societies and a freshman honors program.

Faculty/Classroom: 49% of faculty are male; 51% are female. 90% teach undergraduates, and 10% do research. No introductory courses are taught by graduate students. The average class size in an introductory lecture is 50; in a laboratory is 20; and in a regular course is 25.

Admissions: The SAT scores for the 2013-2014 freshman class were: Critical Reading--45% below 500, 43% between 500 and 599, 10% between 600 and 699, and 2% between 700 and 800; Math--44% below 500, 44% between 500 and 599, 12% between 600 and 699, and 1% between 700 and 800. The ACT scores were 40% below 21, 34% between 21 and 23, 15% between 24 and 26, 1% between 27 and 28, and 1% above 28. 45% of the current freshmen were in the top fifth of their class; 45% were in the top two fifths. There were 224 National Merit finalists. 49 freshmen graduated first in their class.

Requirements: Applicants must be graduates of an accredited secondary school, or the GED is accepted. Students should complete 17 Carnegie units, including 4 units of English, 3 units of math, (algebra I and II and geometry), 2 years of science (chemistry and biology), 2 years of social studies, and 6 academic electives. An interview is recommended. Additional important factors that may be considered into the admissions decision are demonstrated leadership qualities, essays, and extracurricular activities. A GPA of 2.5 is required. AP and CLEP credits are accepted. Important factors in the admissions decision are advanced placement or honors courses, personality/intangible qualities, leadership record, extracurricular activities record, recommendations by school officials, and recommendations by alumni.

Procedure: Freshmen are admitted fall and spring. Entrance exams should be taken During the junior year or fall of the senior year. There are early admissions, deferred admissions, and rolling admissions plans. Early decision applications should be filed by November 1; regular applications, by March 1 for fall entry; and November 1 for spring entry, along with a $35 fee. Notification of early decision is sent December 31; regular decision, on a Rolling basis. Applications are accepted online.

Transfer: 183 transfer students enrolled in 2012-2013. Applicants for transfer must have a minimum GPA of 2.5 and 15 transferable hours. Students must have at least 60 semester or 90 quarter hours. 30 of 120 credits required for the bachelor's degree must be completed at HU.

Visiting: There are regularly scheduled orientations for prospective students, Years of academic tradition and success are here to greet you. We invite you to visit the campus and experience our diverse culture, beautiful scenery, and meet future classmates through group, personal, online, or virtual tour options. There are guides for informal visits and visitors may sit in on classes. To schedule a visit, contact the Office of Admission at (757) 727-5328.

Financial Aid: In 2013-2014, 58% of all full-time freshmen and 54% of continuing full-time students received some form of financial aid. 56% of all full-time freshmen and 51% of continuing full-time students received need-based aid. The average freshman award was $5,045. Need-based scholarships or need-based grants averaged $5,424; need-based self-help aid (loans and jobs) averaged $5,291; non-need-based athletic scholarships averaged $24,257; and other non-need-based awards and non-need-based scholarships averaged $12,047. Average annual earnings from campus work are $1400. The average financial indebtedness of the 2013 graduate was $15,374. The FAFSA is required. The deadline for filing freshman financial aid applications for fall entry is February 15.

International Students: There are 58 international students enrolled. The school actively recruits these students. They must take the TOEFL with a minimum score of 550 on the paper-based TOEFL (PBT).

Computers: All students may access the system 24 hours per day. There are no time limits and no fees.

Graduates: From July 1, 2012 to June 30, 2013, 830 bachelor's degrees were awarded. The most popular majors were psychology (13%), nursing (8%), and biology (7%). 376 companies recruited on campus in 2012-2013. In an average class, 43% graduate in 4 years or less, 50% graduate in 5 years or less, and 65% graduate in 6 years or less. Of the 2012 graduating class, 26% were enrolled in graduate school within 6 months of graduation, and 93% were employed.

Admissions Contact: Angela Boyd, Director of Admission. E-Mail: *angela.boyd@hamptonu.edu* Web: *www.hamptonu.edu*

HOLLINS UNIVERSITY C-3

Roanoke, VA 24020 (540) 362-6214
(800) 456-9595; (540) 362-6218

Full-time: 591 women	**Faculty:** 71; IIB, -$
Part-time: 19 women	**Ph.D.s:** 100%
Graduate: 39 men, 129 women	**Student/Faculty:** 9 to 1
Year: 4-1-4	**Tuition:** $32,075
Application Deadline: May 1	**Room & Board:** $11,220
Freshman Class: 814 applied, 537 accepted, 128 enrolled	
SAT CR/M/W: 586/526/559 **ACT:** 24	**VERY COMPETITIVE**

Founded in 1842 and Virginia's first chartered women's college, Hollins offers a broad liberal arts curriculum. There is one undergraduate school and one graduate school. In addition to regional accreditation, Hollins has baccalaureate program accreditation with TEAC. The library contains 626,085 volumes, 12,985 microform items, and 13,796 audio/video tapes/CDs/DVDs, and subscribes to 38,349 periodicals including electronic. Computerized library services include interlibrary loans, database searching, Internet access, and Wi-Fi capability. Special learning facilities include an art gallery, radio station, and TV station. The 475-acre campus is in a suburban area in Roanoke County. Including any residence halls, there are 73 buildings.

Student Life: 57% of undergraduates are from Virginia. Others are from 42 states, and 13 foreign countries. 80% are from public schools. 72% are White; 11% African American. 43% are Agnostic, Buddhist, Hindu, Muslim, Wicca and Unitarian; 28% Protestant; 16% Catholic; 12% claim no religious affiliation. The average age of freshmen is 19; all undergraduates, 22. 30% do not continue beyond their first year; 70% remain to graduate.

Housing: 725 students can be accommodated in college housing, which includes single-sex dorms and on-campus apartments. In addition, there are language houses and special-interest houses. On-campus housing is guaranteed for all 4 years. 77% of students live on campus; of those, 50% remain on campus on weekends. All students may keep cars.

Activities: There are no fraternities or sororities. There are 36 groups on campus, including art, choir, chorale, dance, drama, environmental, ethnic, film, gay, honors, international, literary magazine, musical theater, newspaper, political, radio and TV, religious, social, social service, student government, and yearbook. Popular campus events include Literary Festival, Classics Symposium, Tinker Day, Ring Night, Holiday Tea, Dance and Theatre Productions.

Sports: There are 8 intercollegiate sports for women, and 1 intramural sports for women. Facilities include a swimming center, a fitness center and weight rooms, a gym, an auxilary gym, an equestrian center, a 1.5-mile jogging loop, 9 outdoor tennis courts, 2 playing fields, a putting green, an exercise studio, 2 training rooms, 2 saunas, and a climbing wall.

Disabled Students: 42% of the campus is accessible. Facilities include wheelchair ramps, elevators, special parking, specially equipped restrooms, special class scheduling, lowered drinking fountains, special housing.

Services: Counseling and information services are available, as is tutoring in most subjects. There is a reader service for the blind, and remedial writing.

Campus Safety and Security: Measures include 24-hour foot and vehicle patrol, emergency notification system, self-defense education, and security escort services. There are emergency telephones, lighted pathways/sidewalks, emergency buttons located along walkways and in labs.

Programs of Study: Hollins confers B.A., B.S., and B.A./B.F.A. degrees. Master's degrees are also awarded. Bachelor's degrees are awarded in AGRICULTURE (environmental studies), BIOLOGICAL SCIENCE (biology/biological science), BUSINESS (business administration and management), COMMUNICATIONS AND THE ARTS (art history and appreciation, communications, dance, dramatic arts, English, film arts, French, music, Spanish, and studio art), COMPUTER AND PHYSICAL SCIENCE (chemistry, mathematics, and physics), SOCIAL SCIENCE (classical/ancient civilization, economics, gender studies, history, interdisciplinary studies, international studies, philosophy, political science/government, psychology, religion, and sociology). Art history, classical studies, French, and theatre are the strongest academically. English/creative writing, psychology, studio art, and biology have the largest enrollments.

Required: To graduate, students must complete 128 credits for the B.A., 140 credits for the B.S., and 150 credits for the B.A./B.F.A., plus 4 short terms. At least 32 hours in the major and a 2.0 GPA are required. All students must fulfill Hollins' general education program (Education Through Skills and Perspectives). Students are also required to take 2 semesters of phys ed or participate in a varsity sport. A thesis is required for some majors.

Special: Hollins offers internships during the January term, dual majors, student-designed majors, accelerated degrees, and study abroad in 16 countries. There is cross-registration with the Virginia Seven College Exchange and Roanoke College. A Washington Semester is availalbe through The American University. There are 16 national honor societies, including Phi Beta Kappa, and 22 departmental honors programs.

Faculty/Classroom: 41% of faculty are male; 64% are female. All teach undergraduates. Graduate students teach 1% of introductory courses. The average class size in an introductory lecture is 11; in a laboratory is 11; and in a regular course is 14.

Admissions: 66% of the 2013-2014 applicants were accepted. The SAT scores for the 2013-2014 freshman class were: Critical Reading--19% below 500, 33% between 500 and 599, 34% between 600 and 699, and 14% between 700 and 800; Math--33% below 500, 45% between 500 and 599, 20% between 600 and 699, and 2% between 700 and 800; Writing--32% below 500, 33% between 500 and 599, 25% between 600 and 699, and 10% between 700 and 800. The ACT scores were 20% below 21, 26% between 21 and 23, 16% between 24 and 26, 23% between 27 and 28, and 15% above 28. 48% of the current freshmen were in the top fifth of their class; 83% were in the top two fifths. 1 freshman graduated first in the class.

Requirements: The SAT or ACT is required. Applicants must be graduates of an accredited secondary school. With proper documentation, the GED and home-schooled students are accepted. Applicants should complete 16 high school academic credits, including 4 credits of English and 3 credits each of foreign language, math, science, and social studies. Official high school transcripts and letters of recommendation are required. An essay is also required, and an interview is recommended. AP credits are accepted. Important factors in the admissions decision are advanced placement or honors courses, recommendations by school officials, and parents or siblings attended the school.

Procedure: Freshmen are admitted fall and spring. Entrance exams should be taken by January of the senior year. There are early decision, deferred admissions, and rolling admissions plans. Early decision applications should be filed by November 1; regular applications, by May 1 for fall entry; and December 1 for spring entry, along with a $40 fee. Notification of early decision is sent November 15; regular decision, on a rolling basis. 11 early decision candidates were accepted for the 2013-2014 class. 7 applicants were on the 2013 waiting list; 2 were admitted. Applications are accepted online.

Transfer: 32 transfer students enrolled in 2012-2013. Applicants for transfer should have a minimum college GPA of 2.5. Other criteria are the same as for entering freshmen. 64 of 128 credits required for the bachelor's degree must be completed at Hollins.

Visiting: There are regularly scheduled orientations for prospective students, Includes 2 open houses for Seniors, 1 in October and 1 in November. Sophomores and Juniors are invited to Spring Visit Days in March and May. Admitted students are invited to campus in April. There are guides for informal visits, visitors may sit in on classes, and stay overnight. To schedule a visit, contact the Campus Visit Coordinator at (540) 362-6401.

Financial Aid: In 2013-2014, 100% of all full-time freshmen and 98% of continuing full-time students received some form of financial aid. 75% of all full-time freshmen and 76% of continuing full-time students received need-based aid. The average freshman award was $29,987. Need-based scholarships or need-based grants averaged $9,806 ($31,490 maximum); need-based self-help aid (loans and jobs) averaged $4,315 ($8,000 maximum); other non-need-based awards and non-need-based scholarships averaged $21,450 ($36,990 maximum); and $4,516 from other forms of aid. 49% of undergraduate students work part-time. Average annual earnings from campus work are $1935. The average financial indebtedness of the 2013 graduate was $29,576. The FAFSA and the state aid form are required. The priority date for freshman financial aid applications for fall entry is February 15.

International Students: There are 30 international students enrolled. The school actively recruits these students. They must take the TOEFL with a minimum score of 550 on the paper-based TOEFL (PBT) or 79 on the Internet-based version (iBT). SAT scores may be submitted in lieu of the TOEFL; however, if SAT scores are low the TOEFL may also be required.

Computers: All students may access the system 24 hours a day, 7 days a week. There are no time limits. The fee is $150.

Graduates: From July 1, 2012 to June 30, 2013, 185 bachelor's degrees were awarded. The most popular majors were English/creative writing (25%), psychology (13%), and business (10%). 4 companies recruited on campus in 2012-2013. In an average class, 51% graduate in 4 years or less, 56% graduate in 5 years or less, and 56% graduate in 6 years or less. Of the 2012 graduating class, 29% were enrolled in graduate school within 6 months of graduation, and 68% were employed.

Admissions Contact: Stefanie Niles, VP, Enrollment. E-Mail: *huadm@hollins.edu* Web: *www.hollins.edu*

JAMES MADISON UNIVERSITY D-2

Harrisonburg, VA 22807 **(540) 568-5681; (540) 568-3332**

Full-time: 6999 men, 10330 women	**Faculty:** 840; IIA, -$
Part-time: 400 men, 378 women	**Ph.D.s:** 78%
Graduate: 559 men, 1261 women	**Student/Faculty:** 20 to 1
Year: semesters, summer session	**Tuition:** $9176 ($23,654)
Application Deadline: January 15	**Room & Board:** $8873

Freshman Class: 22648 applied, 14392 accepted, 4325 enrolled

SAT CR/M/W: 570/580/565 **ACT:** required **VERY COMPETITIVE**

James Madison University, founded in 1908, is a public institution with programs in science and math, business, education, arts and letters, visual and performing arts, and integrated science and technology. There are 7 undergraduate schools and 1 graduate school. In addition to regional accreditation, JMU has baccalaureate program accreditation with AACSB, ABET, ADA, AHEA, CSWE, FIDER, NASAD, NASM, and NCATE. The 3 libraries contain 645,740 volumes, 1.1 million microform items, and 42,676 audio/video tapes/CDs/DVDs, and subscribe to 12,662 periodicals including electronic. Computerized library services include interlibrary loans, database searching, and Internet access. Special learning facilities include an art gallery, planetarium, radio station, an arboretum, a music library, CISAT Library Services, a mineral museum, and Science on a Sphere. The 712-acre campus is in a small town 123 miles southwest of Washington, D.C. Including any residence halls, there are 111 buildings.

Student Life: 71% of undergraduates are from Virginia. Others are from

45 states, 55 foreign countries, and Canada. 81% are White. 32% are Catholic; 26% Protestant; 23% claim no religious affiliation. The average age of freshmen is 18; all undergraduates, 21. 8% do not continue beyond their first year; 81% remain to graduate.

Housing: 6100 students can be accommodated in college housing, which includes coed dorms and off-campus apartments. In addition, there are honors houses, special-interest houses, fraternity houses, sorority houses, Substance-free and international communities, and learning communities for education, health, psychology, community service, biology, ecology, wellness housing and special housing for disabled students, theme housing. On-campus housing is guaranteed for the freshman year only. 64% of students commute. Upperclassmen may keep cars.

Activities: 12% of men belong to 15 national fraternities; 12% of women belong to 9 national sororities. There are 298 groups on campus, including art, band, cheerleading, chess, choir, chorale, chorus, computers, dance, drama, environmental, ethnic, gay, honors, international, jazz band, literary magazine, marching band, musical theater, newspaper, opera, orchestra, pep band, photography, political, professional, radio and TV, religious, social, social service, student government, symphony, and yearbook. Popular campus events include Madison Symposium, James Madison Week, and International Week.

Sports: There are 6 intercollegiate sports for men and 12 for women, and 10 intramural sports for men and 10 for women. Facilities include a 12800-seat stadium, a convocation center, an all-weather track, a gym, a natatorium, tennis courts, a lighted Astroturf field, and baseball, soccer, and softball fields. A recreation center houses a fitness center, racquetball courts, basketball gyms, an indoor track, a pool, and a climbing wall.

Disabled Students: 90% of the campus is accessible. Facilities include wheelchair ramps, elevators, special parking, specially equipped restrooms, special class scheduling, lowered drinking fountains, lowered telephones, special housing.

Services: Counseling and information services are available, as is tutoring in every subject, through various learning centers There is a reader service for the blind. Support is also available in time management, organization, test preparation, and test taking.

Campus Safety and Security: Measures include 24-hour foot and vehicle patrol, emergency notification system, self-defense education, and security escort services. There are emergency telephones, lighted pathways/sidewalks, controlled access to dorms/residences, and public bus transportation routes through the campus.

Programs of Study: JMU confers B.A., B.S., B.B.A., B.F.A., B.I.S., B.M., B.S.N. and B.S.W. degrees. Master's and doctoral degrees are also awarded. Bachelor's degrees are awarded in BIOLOGICAL SCIENCE (biology/biological science and biotechnology), BUSINESS (accounting, banking and finance, business administration and management, business economics, hospitality management services, international business management, marketing/retailing/merchandising, recreation and leisure services, and tourism), COMMUNICATIONS AND THE ARTS (art, art history and appreciation, communications, communications technology, dance, dramatic arts, English, fine arts, media arts, modern language, music, and speech/debate/rhetoric), COMPUTER AND PHYSICAL SCIENCE (chemistry, computer science, geology, information sciences and systems, mathematics, physics, quantitative methods, science technology, and statistics), EDUCATION (athletic training), ENGINEERING AND ENVIRONMENTAL DESIGN (engineering), HEALTH PROFESSIONS (health care administration, health science, nursing, and speech pathology/audiology), SOCIAL SCIENCE (anthropology, criminal justice, dietetics, economics, geography, history, international studies, liberal arts/general studies, philosophy, physical fitness/movement, political science/government, psychology, public administration, religion, social science, social work, and sociology). Interdisciplinary liberal studies, health science, and kinesiology have the largest enrollments.

Required: To graduate, students must complete a minimum of 120 credit hours, with a GPA of at least 2.0., meet the general education requirements and the requirements of their major, have been enrolled at JMU a minimum of two regular semesters, and have earned a minimum of 30 credit hours at JMU during that period of enrollment.

Special: JMU offers internships, work-study programs, a Washington semester, and study abroad in London, Antwerp, Florence, and Salamanca. There is a combined program in forestry with Virginia Tech. An individualized study degree, nondegree study, pass/fail options, and credit for life, military, and work experience are available. There are 28 national honor societies, including Phi Beta Kappa, a freshman honors program, and 82 departmental honors programs.

Faculty/Classroom: 52% of faculty are male; 48% are female. 92% teach undergraduates. Graduate students teach 1% of introductory courses. The average class size in an introductory lecture is 39; in a laboratory is 22; and in a regular course is 31.

Admissions: 64% of the 2013-2014 applicants were accepted. The SAT scores for the 2013-2014 freshman class were: Critical Reading--13% below 500, 52% between 500 and 599, 31% between 600 and 699, and 4% between 700 and 800; Math--10% below 500, 47% between 500 and 599, 39% between 600 and 699, and 4% between 700 and 800; Writing--14% below 500, 51% between 500 and 599, 31% between 600 and 699, and 4% between 700 and 800. 21 freshmen graduated first in their class.

Requirements: The SAT or ACT is required. Applicants must be graduates of an accredited secondary school. They must show solid achievement in 4 or more academic courses each year of high school including some honors or advanced course work. A personal statement is optional. Art students must present a portfolio. Theater, dance, and music students must audition. Nursing students must apply to the nursing department in addition to applying for undergraduate admission. AP credits are accepted. Important factors in the admissions decision are advanced placement or honors courses, recommendations by school officials, and extracurricular activities record.

Procedure: Freshmen are admitted fall. Entrance exams should be taken in the spring of the junior year or the fall of the senior year. There are early admissions and deferred admissions plans. Early decision applications should be filed by November 1; regular applications, by January 15 for fall entry, along with a $50 fee. Notification of early decision is sent January 15; regular decision, April 1. 1431 applicants were on the 2013 waiting list; 7 were admitted. Applications are accepted online.

Transfer: 628 transfer students enrolled in 2012-2013. Applicants must have a minimum GPA of 2.0 and must submit a complete application, official college transcripts, and secondary school records or a copy of their GED. A one-page personal statement is optional. If applicants have fewer than 30 credit hours completed at the time of application, they must submit SAT scores unless they are 25 years old or older. 30 of 120 credits required for the bachelor's degree must be completed at JMU.

Visiting: There are regularly scheduled orientations for prospective students, including daily campus tours during the week and on Saturdays, and tours following group conferences with admissions counselors. There are guides for informal visits. To schedule a visit, contact the Admissions Office.

Financial Aid: In 2013-2014, 32% of all full-time freshmen and 33% of continuing full-time students received some form of financial aid. 35% of all full-time freshmen and 31% of continuing full-time students received need-based aid. The average freshman award was $9,509. Need-based scholarships or need-based grants averaged $7,560; need-based self-help aid (loans and jobs) averaged $4,736; non-need-based athletic scholarships averaged $18,500; other non-need-based awards and non-need-based scholarships averaged $4,695; and $3,384 from other forms of aid. 20% of undergraduate students work part-time. Average annual earnings from campus work are $1885. The average financial indebtedness of the 2013 graduate was $23,562. The FAFSA is required. The deadline for filing freshman financial aid applications for fall entry is March 1.

International Students: There are 272 international students enrolled. The school actively recruits these students. They must take the TOEFL with a minimum score of 550 on the paper-based TOEFL (PBT) or 81 on the Internet-based version (iBT).

Computers: All students may access the system 24 hours a day. There are no time limits and no fees.

Graduates: From July 1, 2012 to June 30, 2013, 4096 bachelor's degrees were awarded. The most popular majors were health professions and related programs (15%), business/marketing (14%), and communication/journalism (9%). 194 companies recruited on campus in 2012-2013. In an average class, 64% graduate in 4 years or less, 80% graduate in 5 years or less, and 81% graduate in 6 years or less. Of the 2012 graduating class, 27% were enrolled in graduate school within 6 months of graduation, and 46% were employed.

Admissions Contact: Michael D. Walsh, Director of Admissions. E-Mail: *admissions@jmu.edu* Web: *www.jmu.edu*

LIBERTY UNIVERSITY D-3

Lynchburg, VA 24502 (434) 582-7307
(800) 543-5317; (434) 582-2421

Full-time: 2800 men, 3300 women	**Faculty:** 200
Part-time: 110 men, 120 women	**Ph.D.s:** 67%
Graduate: n/av	**Student/Faculty:** 31 to 1
Year: semesters, summer session	**Tuition:** $14,000
Application Deadline:	**Room & Board:** $5401
Freshman Class: n/av	
SAT or ACT: required	
	COMPETITIVE

Liberty University, founded in 1971, is a private liberal arts institution affiliated with the Baptist Church. The figures in the above capsule and in this profile are approximate. There are 6 undergraduate schools and 5 graduate schools. In addition to regional accreditation, Liberty has baccalaureate program accreditation with NASM and NLN. The library contains 211,092 volumes, 95,329 microform items, and 7,149 audio/video tapes/CDs/DVDs, and subscribes to 10,806 periodicals including electronic. Computerized library services include interlibrary loans, database searching, and Internet access. Special learning facilities include a radio station and TV station. The 160-acre campus is in a suburban area 45 miles east of Roanoke. Including any residence halls, there are 73 buildings.

Student Life: 60% of undergraduates are from out of state, mostly the Middle Atlantic. Students are from 48 states, 76 foreign countries, and Canada. 78% are White; 11% African American. 89% are Protestant. The average age of freshmen is 19; all undergraduates, 21.

Housing: 4303 students can be accommodated in college housing, which includes single-sex dorms and on-campus apartments. On-campus housing is guaranteed for all 4 years. 64% of students live on campus; of those, 90% remain on campus on weekends. Alcohol is not permitted. All students may keep cars.

Activities: There are no fraternities or sororities. There are 40 groups on campus, including band, cheerleading, choir, chorale, chorus, communications, computers, debate, drama, drill team, ethnic, honors, international, marching band, musical theater, newspaper, opera, orchestra, pep band, political, professional, radio and TV, religious, social service, student government, and yearbook. Popular campus events include Super Conference and Missions Emphasis Week.

Sports: There are 9 intercollegiate sports for men and 8 for women, and 16 intramural sports for men and 16 for women. Facilities include an 11000-seat football stadium, an 8000-seat basketball arena/convention center, baseball and soccer fields, a track complex and a tennis center.

Disabled Students: 90% of the campus is accessible. Facilities include wheelchair ramps, elevators, special parking, specially equipped restrooms, special class scheduling, lowered drinking fountains, lowered telephones, and special housing.

Services: Counseling and information services are available, as is tutoring in every subject. There is remedial math, reading, and writing.

Campus Safety and Security: Measures include 24-hour foot and vehicle patrol, self-defense education, and security escort services. There are shuttle buses and lighted pathways/sidewalks.

Programs of Study: Liberty confers B.A., B.S., B.M. and B.S.N. degrees. Associate, master's, and doctoral degrees are also awarded. Bachelor's degrees are awarded in BIOLOGICAL SCIENCE (biology/biological science), BUSINESS (accounting, business administration and management, management information systems, and sports management), COMMUNICATIONS AND THE ARTS (communications, English, English as a second/foreign language, music, and Spanish), COMPUTER AND PHYSICAL SCIENCE (computer science and mathematics), EDUCATION (athletic training, elementary education, and physical education), HEALTH PROFESSIONS (community health work, exercise science, and nursing), SOCIAL SCIENCE (family/consumer studies, history, interdisciplinary studies, international studies, liberal arts/general studies, political science/government, psychology, religion, and social science). Education, psychology, and business are the strongest academically. Business, psychology, and education have the largest enrollments.

Required: Students must complete 120 to 123 credit hours to graduate, with a minimum GPA of 2.0. With few exceptions, by major, all must complete 18 hours of foundational studies in English, math, speech communications, and general education. An additional 42 credits of investigative studies are required; these vary according to the degree sought, either B.A. or B.S., but include English, natural sciences, history, arts, music, languages, government, social sciences, philosophy, theology, Bible studies, and integrated studies.

Special: Liberty offers internships, B.A.-B.S. degrees, and student-designed majors in interdisciplinary and general studies. There are 8 national honor societies, including Phi Beta Kappa, and a freshman honors program.

Faculty/Classroom: 67% of faculty are male; 33% are female. 90% teach undergraduates. No introductory courses are taught by graduate students. The average class size in an introductory lecture is 43; in a laboratory is 22; and in a regular course is 23.

Admissions: There were 5 National Merit finalists.

Requirements: The SAT or ACT is required. Applicants must have completed 16 high school academic credits. The GED is accepted. An essay is required. A GPA of 2.0 is required. AP and CLEP credits are accepted. Important factors in the admissions decision are ability to finance college education, recommendations by school officials, and advanced placement or honors courses.

Procedure: Freshmen are admitted to all sessions. Entrance exams should be taken during the junior year. There are early decision, early admissions, deferred admissions, and rolling admissions plans. Application deadlines are open. Application fee is $35. Notification is sent on a rolling basis. Applications are accepted online.

Transfer: 743 transfer students enrolled in 2012-2013. Applicants for transfer must have a GPA of 2.0. If transferring fewer than 60 hours, a high school transcript and test scores are required. 30 of 120 credits required for the bachelor's degree must be completed at Liberty.

Visiting: There are regularly scheduled orientations for prospective students, including College for a Weekend, a 2-day program offering a chance to attend classes and special meetings. There are guides for informal visits, visitors may sit in on classes, and stay overnight. To schedule a visit, contact the Visitor's Center at visitorscenter@liberty.edu.

Financial Aid: In 2013-2014, 98% of all full-time freshmen and 88% of continuing full-time students received some form of financial aid. 64% of all full-time freshmen and 64% of continuing full-time students received need-based aid. The average freshman award was $8,506. Need-based scholarships or need-based grants averaged $1,800 ($4,000 maximum); need-based self-help aid (loans and jobs) averaged $3,725 ($3,940 maximum); non-need-based athletic scholarships averaged $8,172 ($18,850 maximum); and other non-need-based awards and non-need-based scholarships averaged $4,667 ($15,220 maximum). 15% of undergraduate students work part-time. Average annual earnings from campus work are $2500. The average financial indebtedness of the 2013 graduate was $15,619. The FAFSA and Singlefile Form (preferred) are required. The deadline for filing freshman financial aid applications for fall entry is March 1.

International Students: There are 238 international students enrolled. The school actively recruits these students. They must take the TOEFL or MELAB. They must also take the SAT or ACT.

Computers: All students may access the system. 24 hours a day Sunday through Thursday and 7:30 a.m. to 9 p.m. Friday and Saturday. There are no time limits. The fee is $200 per semester.

Graduates: From July 1, 2012 to June 30, 2013, 945 bachelor's degrees were awarded. The most popular majors were psychology (17%), business (16%), and religion (14%).

Admissions Contact: David Hart, Associate Director of Admissions. E-Mail: *admissions@liberty.edu* Web: *www.liberty.edu*

LONGWOOD UNIVERSITY D-3

Farmville, VA 23909 **(434) 395-2060**
(800) 281-4677; (434) 395-2332

Full-time: 540 men, 2733 women	**Faculty:** 238; IIA, --$
Part-time: 144 men, 1080 women	**Ph.D.s:** 77%
Graduate: 154 men, 309 women	**Student/Faculty:** 18 to 1
Year: semesters, summer session	**Tuition:** $11,340 ($24,210)
Application Deadline: March 1	**Room & Board:** $9584
Freshman Class: 4055 applied, 3299 accepted, 1111 enrolled	
SAT CR/M: 500/500 **ACT:** 21	**COMPETITIVE**

Longwood University, founded in 1839, is a state-supported institution with programs in liberal arts, business, and teacher preparation. There are 3 undergraduate schools and 1 graduate school. In addition to regional accreditation, Longwood has baccalaureate program accreditation with AACSB, CSWE, NASM, NCATE, and NRPA. The library contains 362,151 volumes, 667,409 microform items, and 23,331 audio/video tapes/CDs/DVDs. Computerized library services include interlibrary loans, database searching, Internet access, and Wi-Fi capability. Special learning facilities include an art gallery, radio station, a greenhouse, a language lab, 6 computer labs, and a psychology lab. The 160-acre campus is in a small town 60 miles west of Richmond and 60 miles south of Charlottesville. Including any residence halls, there are 44 buildings.

Student Life: 96% of undergraduates are from Virginia. Others are from 22 states, 19 foreign countries, and Canada. 93% are from public schools. 82% are White. The average age of freshmen is 18; all undergraduates, 19. 20% do not continue beyond their first year; 60% remain to graduate.

Housing: College-sponsored housing includes single-sex and coed dorms and off-campus apartments. In addition, there are honors houses, a substance-free dorm, and international studies, fraternity/sorority, and ecology floors. On-campus housing is guaranteed for the freshman year only, is available on a first-come, first-served basis, and is available on a lottery system for upperclassmen. 74% of students live on campus; of those, 60% remain on campus on weekends. Upperclassmen may keep cars.

Activities: 22% of men belong to 12 national fraternities; 22% of women belong to 10 national sororities. There are 176 groups on campus, including art, band, cheerleading, chess, choir, chorus, computers, dance, drama, ethnic, gay, honors, international, jazz band, musical theater, newspaper, pep band, photography, political, professional, radio and TV, religious, social, social service, and student government. Popular campus events include Spring Weekend, and Oktoberfest.

Sports: There are 6 intercollegiate sports for men and 8 for women, and 14 intramural sports for men and 16 for women. Facilities include a 9-hole golf course, a weight training facility, 1 gym, racquetball courts, 11 lighted tennis courts, 2 pools, a bowling alley, 2 outdoor sand volleyball courts, a 10-station fitness trail, a frisbee golf course, outdoor basketball courts, and soccer, baseball, and softball fields.

Disabled Students: Facilities include wheelchair ramps, elevators, special parking, special class scheduling, lowered drinking fountains, lowered telephones, special housing. The campus is mostly accessible with continuous monitoring for accessibility.

Services: Counseling and information services are available, as is tutoring in some subjects, Learning strategies, study skills, organizational skills and time management There is a reader service for the blind, and remedial writing. There is also assistance in study skills, learning strategies, advocacy training, and compensatory strategy instruction.

Campus Safety and Security: Measures include 24-hour foot and

vehicle patrol, emergency notification system, self-defense education, and security escort services. There are shuttle buses, emergency telephones, lighted pathways/sidewalks, controlled access to dorms/residences, electronic card key entry into dorms, and video cameras.

Programs of Study: Longwood confers B.A., B.S., B.F.A., B.M. and B.S.B.A. degrees. Master's degrees are also awarded. Bachelor's degrees are awarded in BIOLOGICAL SCIENCE (biology/biological science), BUSINESS (business administration and management), COMMUNICATIONS AND THE ARTS (art, communications, English, modern language, music, and visual and performing arts), COMPUTER AND PHYSICAL SCIENCE (chemistry, computer science, mathematics, and physics), EDUCATION (art education, athletic training, elementary education, music education, physical education, and special education), HEALTH PROFESSIONS (community health work, nursing, and recreation therapy), SOCIAL SCIENCE (anthropology, criminal justice, criminology, economics, history, liberal arts/general studies, political science/government, psychology, social work, and sociology). Natural sciences and secondary education are the strongest academically. Business, biology and elementary education have the largest enrollments.

Required: To graduate, students must complete 120 to 145 credits, including 36 to 77 in the major, with a minimum GPA of 2.0 overall. A 41-hour general education core curriculum, 4 intensive writing courses, a phys ed course, and 30 upper-level credit hours are also required.

Special: Longwood offers internships or directed research projects in all majors, study abroad in 15 countries, and B.A.-B.S. degrees in many majors. Cross-registration is possible with Hampden-Sydney College, as are 3-2 engineering degrees with several regional universities. Also, there is a 3-3 preprofessional program in physical therapy with University of Virginia, Old Dominion, and Virginia Commonwealth Universities. There are 10 national honor societies and a freshman honors program.

Faculty/Classroom: 45% of faculty are male; 55% are female. All teach undergraduates, and 50% do both. No introductory courses are taught by graduate students. The average class size in an introductory lecture is 21 and in a regular course is 21.

Admissions: 81% of the 2013-2014 applicants were accepted. The SAT scores for the 2013-2014 freshman class were: Critical Reading--43% below 500, 44% between 500 and 599, 10% between 600 and 699, and 1% between 700 and 800; Math--44% below 500, 45% between 500 and 599, and 9% between 600 and 699.

Requirements: The SAT or ACT is required. Applicants must be graduates of an accredited secondary school; the GED is accepted. Students should complete 4 years of high school English, 2 years each of foreign language and 3 years science (including 2 lab courses), 2 years of history, and algebra I, II, and geometry. A personal statement is required. An audition is required for music students. AP and CLEP credits are accepted. Important factors in the admissions decision are advanced placement or honors courses, leadership record, and evidence of special talent.

Procedure: Freshmen are admitted to all sessions. Entrance exams should be taken in the fall of the senior year. There are early admissions and rolling admissions plans. Early decision applications should be filed by December 1; regular applications, by March 1 for fall entry; October 15 for winter entry; October 15 for spring entry; and March 1 for summer entry, along with a $50 fee. Notification is sent on a rolling basis. Applications are accepted online.

Transfer: 214 transfer students enrolled in 2012-2013. Applicants for transfer must have a GPA of at least 2.5 in all college course work attempted. Other criteria are the same as for entering freshmen. 30 of 120 credits required for the bachelor's degree must be completed at Longwood.

Visiting: There are regularly scheduled orientations for prospective students, including informational and tour programs, and open houses September - December and March - May. Visitors may sit in on classes and stay overnight. To schedule a visit, contact the Admissions Office at admissions@longwood.edu.

Financial Aid: The FAFSA is required. The priority date for freshman financial aid applications for fall entry is March 1.

International Students: The school actively recruits these students. They must take the TOEFL with a minimum score of 550 on the paper-based TOEFL (PBT) or 79 on the Internet-based version (iBT). They must also take the SAT or ACT.

Computers: All students may access the system. There are no time limits and no fees.

Graduates: In an average class, 1% graduate in 3 years or less, 40% graduate in 4 years or less, 56% graduate in 5 years or less, and 59% graduate in 6 years or less.

Admissions Contact: Sallie McMullin, Dean of Admissions. E-Mail: *admissions@longwood.edu* Web: *www.longwood.edu/admissions*

LYNCHBURG COLLEGE D-3

Lynchburg, VA 24501 **(800) 426-8101; (800) 426-8101**

Full-time: 842 men, 1247 women	**Faculty:** n/av; IIA, --$
Part-time: 31 men, 58 women	**Ph.D.s:** 82%
Graduate: 192 men, 343 women	**Student/Faculty:** 12 to 1
Year: semesters, summer session	**Tuition:** $33,565
Application Deadline: open	**Room & Board:** $9080

Freshman Class: 5695 applied, 3627 accepted, 512 enrolled

SAT CR/M/W: 500/500/490 **ACT:** 21 **COMPETITIVE**

Lynchburg College, established in 1903, is a private institution affiliated with the Christian Church (Disciples of Christ). LC offers bachelor's degrees in 39 majors, master's degrees in 12 programs, and 2 doctoral degrees (Physical Therapy & Leadership Studies). There are 6 undergraduate schools and 1 graduate school. In addition to regional accreditation, L.C. has baccalaureate program accreditation with ACBSP. The library contains 379,947 volumes, 466,605 microform items, 7,994 audio/video tapes/CDs/DVDs, and subscribes to 38,522 periodicals including electronic. Computerized library services include interlibrary loans, database searching, and Internet access. Special learning facilities include an art gallery, astronomical observatory, Claytor Nature Center (470 acre farm used for science classes), theatre and cadaver lab. The 250-acre campus is in a suburban area 180 miles southwest of Washington, D.C., and 120 west of Richmond. Including any residence halls, there are 40 buildings.

Student Life: 68% of undergraduates are from Virginia. Others are from 39 states, and 9 foreign countries. 77% are White; 11% African American. The average age of freshmen is 18; all undergraduates, 21. 22% do not continue beyond their first year; 57% remain to graduate.

Housing: 1750 students can be accommodated in college housing, which includes single-sex and coed dorms and on-campus apartments. In addition, there are honors houses, language houses, special-interest houses, fraternity houses, and sorority houses. On-campus housing is guaranteed for all 4 years. 73% of students live on campus. Upperclassmen may keep cars.

Activities: 11% of men belong to 5 national fraternities; 14% of women belong to 5 national sororities. There are 80 groups on campus, including art, cheerleading, choir, chorus, communications, computers, dance, drama, environmental, ethnic, gay, honors, international, jazz band, literary magazine, musical theater, newspaper, orchestra, political, professional, religious, social, social service, and student government. Popular campus events include Homecoming, Turkey Bowl and Campus Days.

Sports: There are 10 intercollegiate sports for men and 11 for women, and 12 intramural sports for men and 12 for women. Facilities include a weight room, exercise physiology lab, field house, athletic fields, and ropes course.

Disabled Students: 95% of the campus is accessible. Facilities include wheelchair ramps, elevators, special parking, specially equipped restrooms, special class scheduling, lowered drinking fountains, lowered telephones, and special housing.

Services: Counseling and information services are available, as is tutoring in most subjects.

Campus Safety and Security: Measures include 24-hour foot and vehicle patrol, emergency notification system, and security escort services. There are emergency telephones, lighted pathways/sidewalks, controlled access to dorms/residences, All residence halls are locked 24 hours a day. Admission is only by scanning an ID card.

Programs of Study: L.C. confers B.A., and B.S. degrees. Master's and doctoral degrees are also awarded. Bachelor's degrees are awarded in AGRICULTURE (environmental studies), BIOLOGICAL SCIENCE (biology/biological science), BUSINESS (accounting, business administration and management, human resources, management science, marketing/retailing/merchandising, and sports management), COMMUNICATIONS AND THE ARTS (art, communications, English, French, music, Spanish, and theatre arts), COMPUTER AND PHYSICAL SCIENCE (chemistry, computer science, mathematics, and physics), EDUCATION (athletic training, education, and elementary education), ENGINEERING AND ENVIRONMENTAL DESIGN (environmental science), HEALTH PROFESSIONS (biomedical science, exercise science, health promotion, and nursing), SOCIAL SCIENCE (criminology, economics, history, international relations, philosophy, physical fitness/movement, political science/government, psychology, religion, and sociology). Communication studies, nursing, elementary education, business administration have the largest enrollments.

Required: The 51 hour core includes foreign language, fine arts, written composition, history, lab science, literature, math, oral communications, philosophy, religious studies, social science, and wellness. A senior symposium is also required, as is a thesis in some programs. Students must complete 124 credit hours to graduate, with a 2.0 GPA, and 30 to 69 hours in their major.

Special: Students may cross-register with Sweet Briar and Randolph Colleges, and they may study abroad in 20 countries. There is a Washington semester available, B.A.-B.S. degrees in chemistry, internships, and a work-study program. A 3-2 engineering degree is available in cooperation with Old Dominion University and the University of Virginia. There are 14 national honor societies and a freshman honors program.

Faculty/Classroom: 44% of faculty are male; 56% are female. 95% teach undergraduates. No introductory courses are taught by graduate students.

Admissions: 64% of the 2013-2014 applicants were accepted. The SAT scores for the 2013-2014 freshman class were: Critical Reading--50% below 500, 38% between 500 and 599, 10% between 600 and 699, and 2% between 700 and 800; Math--49% below 500, 36% between 500 and 599, 14% between 600 and 699, and 1% between 700 and 800; Writing--54% below 500, 36% between 500 and 599, and 10% between 600 and 699. The ACT scores were 41% below 21, 28% between 21 and 23, 17% between 24 and 26, 8% between 27 and 28, and 6% above 28.

Requirements: The SAT or ACT is required. In addition, SAT: Subject Tests are recommended. GED's are reviewed on a case-by-case basis. Applicants should have earned between 16 to 20 academic high school credits in English, math and social science, lab science, and foreign language. AP and CLEP credits are accepted. Important factors in the admissions decision are advanced placement or honors courses, leadership record, and recommendations by school officials.

Procedure: Freshmen are admitted fall, spring, and summer. Entrance exams should be taken in the junior year and in the first semester of the senior year. There are early decision and rolling admissions plans. Early decision applications should be filed by November 15, along with a $30 fee. Notification of early decision is sent December 15; regular decision, 117 early decision candidates were accepted for the 2013-2014 class. Applications are accepted online. Application fees are waived if application is completed online.

Transfer: 125 transfer students enrolled in 2012-2013. Transfer students must have a minimum GPA of 2.0 to be considered, and must be in good academic and social standing. The SAT or ACT is not required for transfer students. An interview is recommended. 48 of 124 credits required for the bachelor's degree must be completed at L.C.

Visiting: There are regularly scheduled orientations for prospective students, including individual appointments. There are guides for informal visits, visitors may sit in on classes, and stay overnight. To schedule a visit, contact the Admissions Office at admissions@lynchburg.edu.

Financial Aid: In 2013-2014, 82% of all full-time freshmen and 76% of continuing full-time students received some form of financial aid. 82% of all full-time freshmen and 76% of continuing full-time students received need-based aid. The average freshman award was $26,707. Need-based scholarships or need-based grants averaged $23,105; and need-based self-help aid (loans and jobs) averaged $4,570. 37% of undergraduate students work part-time. Average annual earnings from campus work are $2000. The average financial indebtedness of the 2013 graduate was $35,000. L.C. is a member of CSS. The FAFSA and the state aid form are required. The deadline for filing freshman financial aid applications for fall entry is March 1.

International Students: There are 26 international students enrolled. The school actively recruits these students. They must take the TOEFL with a minimum score of 550 on the paper-based TOEFL (PBT) or 78 on the Internet-based version (iBT). They must also take the SAT or ACT.

Computers: All students may access the system 24 hours a day, 7 days a week. There are no time limits and no fees.

Graduates: From July 1, 2012 to June 30, 2013, 465 bachelor's degrees were awarded. The most popular majors were elementary education (10%), communication studies (9%), and nursing (7%). In an average class, 1% graduate in 3 years or less, 46% graduate in 4 years or less, 54% graduate in 5 years or less, and 56% graduate in 6 years or less.

Admissions Contact: Sharon Walters-Bower, Director of Admissions. E-Mail: *admissions@lynchburg.edu* Web: *http:/www.lynchburg.edu/undergraduate-admission*

MARY BALDWIN COLLEGE D-2

Staunton, VA 24401 (540) 887-7279
(800) 468-2262; (540) 887-7292

Full-time: 46 men, 986 women	**Faculty:** 75; IIB, --$
Part-time: 46 men, 353 women	**Ph.D.s:** 96%
Graduate: 37 men, 230 women	**Student/Faculty:** 10 to 1
Year: 4-1-4, summer session	**Tuition:** $28,710
Application Deadline: April 15	**Room & Board:** $8400

Freshman Class: 3129 applied, 1638 accepted, 272 enrolled
SAT CR/M/W: 500/480/480 **ACT:** 21 **COMPETITIVE**

Mary Baldwin College, founded in 1842, is one of the nation's oldest women's colleges and, at the same time, a forward-looking master's level university offering a variety of coeducational, nonresidential adult and graduate programs. There are 4 undergraduate schools and 3 graduate schools. In addition to regional accreditation, MBC has baccalaureate program accreditation with CSWE and TEAC. The library contains 147,624 volumes, 65,502 microform items, and 7,907 audio/video tapes/CDs/DVDs, and subscribes to 36,606 periodicals including electronic. Computerized library services include interlibrary loans, database searching, Internet access, and Wi-Fi capability. Special learning facilities include an art gallery, radio station, TV station, a military/leadership museum, and Spencer Center for Civic and Global Engagement. The 54-acre campus is in a small town. Including any residence halls, there are 40 buildings.

Student Life: 65% of undergraduates are from Virginia. Others are from 36 states, and 7 foreign countries. 80% are from public schools. 42% are White; 34% African American.. The average age of freshmen is 18; all undergraduates, 19. 31% do not continue beyond their first year; 49% remain to graduate.

Housing: 775 students can be accommodated in college housing, which includes single-sex dorms and on-campus apartments. In addition, there are honors houses, special-interest houses, lofts and suites. On-campus housing is guaranteed for all 4 years. 82% of students live on campus; of those, 70% remain on campus on weekends. All students may keep cars.

Activities: There are no fraternities or sororities. There are 60 groups on campus, including and Wellness, Student Government, art, cheerleading, choir, chorale, chorus, dance, drama, drill team, drum and bugle corps, environmental, ethnic, film, gay, Hiking, honors, international, literary magazine, marching band, musical theater, newspaper, orchestra, photography, political, professional, radio and TV, religious, social, social service, student government, and yearbook. Popular campus events include Apple Day, Junior Dads, Family Weekend, Signature Ball, Halloween Pumpkin Carving, Las Posadas, Kwanzaa, International Festival, and Capstone Festival.

Sports: There are 6 intercollegiate sports for women, and 6 intramural sports for women. Facilities include main gym (basketball and volleyball courts), dance hall and fencing studio, racquetball courts, cardio and strength equipment, tennis courts, soccer field, softball field, track, parade ground.

Disabled Students: 30% of the campus is accessible. Facilities include wheelchair ramps, elevators, special parking, and specially equipped restrooms.

Services: Counseling and information services are available, as is tutoring in most subjects. There is a reader service for the blind, and remedial math and writing.

Campus Safety and Security: Measures include 24-hour foot and vehicle patrol, emergency notification system, self-defense education, and security escort services. There are emergency telephones, lighted pathways/sidewalks, controlled access to dorms/residences, 24-hour locked residence halls; video surveillance in all-night computer labs and access areas; video surveillance for early college residence hall.

Programs of Study: MBC confers B.A., B.S. and B.S.W. degrees. Master's and doctoral degrees are also awarded. Bachelor's degrees are awarded in BIOLOGICAL SCIENCE (biology/biological science), BUSINESS (business administration and management, international economics, and marketing management), COMMUNICATIONS AND THE ARTS (art, art history and appreciation, arts administration/management, communications, dramatic arts, English, music, Spanish, and studio art), COMPUTER AND PHYSICAL SCIENCE (applied mathematics, chemistry, mathematics, and physics), EDUCATION (education), HEALTH PROFESSIONS (clinical science and health care administration), SOCIAL SCIENCE (American studies, anthropology, Asian/Oriental studies, criminal justice, East Asian studies, economics, history, international relations, philosophy, political science/government, psychology, religion, social psychology, social work, and sociology). Psychology, business, biology, chemistry, English, history, political science, and education are the strongest academically. Education, psychology, and art have the largest enrollments.

Required: To graduate, students must complete a minimum of 126 semester hours including at least 18 in the major and 6 hours or more each in natural sciences, social sciences, arts, and humanities and history; 6 hours each in courses focused on writing, quantitative reasoning, and diverse cultures in a global context (foreign language, cross-cultural studies, and/or study abroad); 3 hours each in courses emphasizing oral communication, role of race and ethnicity, role of gender, and experiential education; 2 hours of health and phys ed; and 1 hour of community involvement credit. A minimum GPA of 2.0 is required. Most disciplines require upper-level seminars and significant projects consisting of some type of original research.

Special: MBC and 6 other colleges in Virginia (Hampden-Sydney College, Hollins University, Randolph-Macon College, Randolph College, Sweet Briar College, and Washington and Lee University) form a consortium through which students may attend another of the participating colleges for a semester or a year. Students in the Women's Institute for Leadership program may participate in an exchange program with Norwich University. Students may earn a bachelor's degree in physics by taking courses at Washington and Lee as well as MBC. MBC has a guaranteed admission agreement with the entire Virginia Community College System. MBC offers a minor in public history through a partnership with the Woodrow Wilson Presidential Library. Internships, study abroad, B.A.-B.S. degrees in biology, biochemistry, chemistry, and psychology, and work-study programs are available. The college offers an accelerated degree program as well as dual and student-designed majors. There are two combined bachelor's-master's degree programs solely at MBC, as well as 3-2 programs available in engineering with the University of Virginia and in nursing with Vanderbilt University. There is an advanced degree program in teaching with the University of Virginia and a Virginia State Teacher Licensure program. Credit for life, military, and work experience may be granted. Nondegree study and a pass/fail grading option are also available. There are 17 national honor societies, including Phi Beta Kappa, a freshman honors program, and 29 departmental honors programs.

Faculty/Classroom: 36% of faculty are male; 64% are female. 88% teach undergraduates. No introductory courses are taught by graduate students. The average class size in an introductory lecture is 15; in a laboratory is 22; and in a regular course is 19.

Admissions: 52% of the 2013-2014 applicants were accepted. The SAT scores for the 2013-2014 freshman class were: Critical Reading--58% below 500, 28% between 500 and 599, 12% between 600 and 699, and 2% between 700 and 800; Math--70% below 500, 22% between 500 and 599, and 8% between 600 and 699; Writing--63% below 500, 26% between 500 and 599, 9% between 600 and 699, and 2% between 700 and 800. The ACT scores were 31% below 21, 31% between 21 and 23, 27% between 24 and 26, and 4% between 27 and 28. 20% of the current freshmen were in the top fifth of their class; 81% were in the top two fifths.

Requirements: The SAT or ACT is required. In addition, Applicants must graduate from an accredited secondary school, have a GED, or meet state equivalency requirements for homeschooling. A minimum of 16 academic units are required, including 4 in English, 3 in math, 2 to 3 in social studies, and 2 each in a foreign language and science. Either the SAT or the ACT (not both) is required. Essays and interviews are recommended. A GPA of 2.0 is required. AP and CLEP credits are accepted. Important factors in the admissions decision are extracurricular activities record, leadership record, and advanced placement or honors courses.

Procedure: Freshmen are admitted fall and spring. Entrance exams should be taken in the junior or senior year. There are early admissions, deferred admissions, and rolling admissions plans. Applications should be filed by April 15 for fall entry; December 15 for spring entry. Applications are accepted online. Application fees are waived if application is completed online.

Transfer: 30 transfer students enrolled in 2012-2013. Transfer applicants must have at least a 2.0 GPA from the institution where they are currently enrolled. 66 of 126 credits required for the bachelor's degree must be completed at MBC.

Visiting: There are regularly scheduled orientations for prospective students, consisting of a tour, an interview, meet faculty, attend class, eat in dining hall, student events, athletic tours, and other activities as requested or available. There are guides for informal visits, visitors may sit in on classes, and stay overnight. To schedule a visit, contact Allison Burch or anyone in the Admissions Office at admit@mbc.edu.

Financial Aid: In 2013-2014, 96% of all full-time freshmen and 90% of continuing full-time students received some form of financial aid. 88% of all full-time freshmen and 83% of continuing full-time students received need-based aid. The average freshman award was $29,826. Need-based scholarships or need-based grants averaged $6,350 ($15,416 maximum); need-based self-help aid (loans and jobs) averaged $7,265 ($18,500 maximum); and other non-need-based awards and non-need-based scholarships averaged $20,516 ($37,600 maximum). 28% of undergraduate students work part-time. Average annual earnings from campus work are $1400. The average financial indebtedness of the 2013 graduate was $21,763. The FAFSA and the state aid form are required. The priority date for freshman financial aid applications for fall entry is February 15. The deadline for filing freshman financial aid applications for fall entry is May 1.

International Students: There are 24 international students enrolled. The school actively recruits these students. They must take the TOEFL with a minimum score of 500 on the paper-based TOEFL (PBT) or 61 on the Internet-based version (iBT).

Computers: All students may access the system. There are no time limits and no fees.

Graduates: From July 1, 2012 to June 30, 2013, 235 bachelor's degrees were awarded. The most popular majors were psychology (14%), history (10%), and business administration (7%). 17 companies recruited on campus in 2012-2013. In an average class, 3% graduate in 3 years or less, 45% graduate in 4 years or less, 47% graduate in 5 years or less, and 50% graduate in 6 years or less. Of the 2012 graduating class, 20% were enrolled in graduate school within 6 months of graduation, and 84% were employed.

Admissions Contact: Roberta Palmer, Director of Admissions. E-Mail: *admit@mbc.edu* Web: *www.mbc.edu*

MARYMOUNT UNIVERSITY E-2

Arlington, VA 22207 (703) 284-1500
(800) 548-7638; (703) 522-0349

Full-time: 658 men, 1517 women	**Faculty:** 122; IIA, -$
Part-time: 84 men, 211 women	**Ph.D.s:** 89%
Graduate: 278 men, 954 women	**Student/Faculty:** 18 to 1
Year: semesters, summer session	**Tuition:** n/av
Application Deadline: rolling	**Room & Board:** $11,000

Freshman Class: 1945 applied, 1561 accepted, 375 enrolled
SAT CR/M/W: 500/490/490 **ACT:** 21 **COMPETITIVE**

Marymount, founded in 1950, is a Catholic-affiliated, comprehensive university. Programs are offered through the Schools of Arts and Sciences, Business Administration, Education and Human Services, and Health Professions. There are 4 undergraduate schools and 4 graduate schools. In addition to regional accreditation, Marymount has baccalaureate program accreditation with ACBSP and NCATE. The library contains 237,587 volumes, 198,465 microform items, and 14,084 audio/video tapes/CDs/DVDs, and subscribes to 57,490 periodicals including electronic. Computerized library services include interlibrary loans, database searching, Internet access, and Wi-Fi capability. Special learning facilities include an art gallery, and instructional media center. The 21-acre campus is in a suburban area 6 miles southwest of Washington, D.C. Including any residence halls, there are 15 buildings.

Student Life: 56% of undergraduates are from Virginia. Others are from 37 states, and 57 foreign countries. 82% are from public schools. 42% are White; 16% African American; 15% Hispanic. 36% are Catholic; 31% claim no religious affiliation; 21% Protestant; 11% Muslim (7%), Orthodox (2%), Hindu (1%), and Buddhist (1%). The average age of freshmen is 18; all undergraduates, 23. 26% do not continue beyond their first year; 50% remain to graduate.

Housing: 858 students can be accommodated in college housing, which includes single-sex and coed dorms and off-campus apartments, and theme housing. On-campus housing is available on a lottery system for upperclassmen. 66% of students commute. Upperclassmen may keep cars.

Activities: There are no fraternities or sororities. There are 37 groups on campus, including art, cheerleading, choir, chorus, communications, dance, drama, ethnic, honors, international, literary magazine, newspaper, political, professional, religious, social, social service, student government, and yearbook. Popular campus events include Portfolio in Motion (Fashion Show), Snowball (Winter Formal Dance), and International Week.

Sports: There are 6 intercollegiate sports for men and 6 for women, and 6 intramural sports for men and 7 for women. Facilities include Basketball arena, practice field, recreational gymnasium, swimming pool, aerobics and weight rooms, and off-campus baseball field.

Disabled Students: Facilities include wheelchair ramps, elevators, special parking, specially equipped restrooms, special class scheduling, lowered drinking fountains, lowered telephones, and special housing.

Services: Counseling and information services are available, as is tutoring in most subjects. There is a reader service for the blind, and remedial math, reading, and writing.

Campus Safety and Security: Measures include 24-hour foot and vehicle patrol, emergency notification system, and security escort services. There are shuttle buses, emergency telephones, lighted pathways/sidewalks, and controlled access to dorms/residences.

Programs of Study: Marymount confers B.A., B.S., B.B.A. and B.S.N. degrees. Master's and doctoral degrees are also awarded. Bachelor's degrees are awarded in BIOLOGICAL SCIENCE (biology/biological science), BUSINESS (business administration and management and fashion merchandising), COMMUNICATIONS AND THE ARTS (art, communications, English, graphic design, and information technology), COMPUTER AND PHYSICAL SCIENCE (mathematics), EDUCATION (art education, English education, health information management, mathematics education, and special education), ENGINEERING AND ENVIRONMENTAL DESIGN (interior design), HEALTH PROFESSIONS (health science and nursing), SOCIAL SCIENCE (criminal justice, economics, fashion design and technology, forensic studies, history, liberal arts/general studies, paralegal studies, philosophy, political science/government, psychology, sociology, and theological studies). Business administration, nursing, and biology have the largest enrollments.

Required: To graduate, students must complete all course requirements with a minimum cumulative grade point average of 2.0. Core curriculum includes courses in writing, humanities, math, sciences, social science, health and wellness, and freshman seminar. Students must earn 120 credits by completing all liberal arts requirements, all general education requirements, and all major requirements.

Special: Students can cross-register with the Consortium of Universities of the Washington Metropolitan Area or study abroad in various countries. Marymount offers dual and student-designed majors and accelerated degrees in nursing and interior design. An internship, clinical, or student teaching experience is required in all majors except nursing. There are 12 national honor societies and a freshman honors program.

Faculty/Classroom: 35% of faculty are male; 65% are female. 77%

teach undergraduates. No introductory courses are taught by graduate students. The average class size in an introductory lecture is 23; in a laboratory is 13; and in a regular course is 17.

Admissions: 80% of the 2013-2014 applicants were accepted. The SAT scores for the 2013-2014 freshman class were: Critical Reading--46% below 500, 43% between 500 and 599, 9% between 600 and 699, and 2% between 700 and 800; Math--52% below 500, 38% between 500 and 599, and 10% between 600 and 699; Writing--51% below 500, 40% between 500 and 599, 8% between 600 and 699, and 1% between 700 and 800. The ACT scores were 43% below 21, 32% between 21 and 23, 19% between 24 and 26, 3% between 27 and 28, and 3% above 28. 24% of the current freshmen were in the top fifth of their class; 52% were in the top two fifths. 2 freshmen graduated first in their class.

Requirements: The SAT or ACT is required. Applicants must graduate from an accredited secondary school or have a GED. Marymount requires 15 academic credits in preparatory courses and strongly recommends biology and chemistry for Nursing candidates. Average incoming freshman SAT score is 1000. If both SAT and ACT scores are submitted, the highest equivalent test score will be used. A letter of recommendation and writing sample also are required. A GPA of 2.6 is required. AP and CLEP credits are accepted. Important factors in the admissions decision are advanced placement or honors courses, extracurricular activities record, and evidence of special talent.

Procedure: Freshmen are admitted fall, spring, and summer. Entrance exams should be taken Scores must be received by August 15 for fall-term admission. There are deferred admissions and rolling admissions plans. Application deadlines are open. Application fee is $40. Notification is sent on a rolling basis. Applications are accepted online.

Transfer: 336 transfer students enrolled in 2012-2013. One letter of recommendation required. Transfer applicants with fewer than 30 credits must meet freshman admission requirements. Additional requirements for Nursing and International applicants. 36 of 120 credits required for the bachelor's degree must be completed at Marymount.

Visiting: There are regularly scheduled orientations for prospective students, including Campus Visit Days, Information Nights, and new student summer orientation. There are guides for informal visits, visitors may sit in on classes, and stay overnight. To schedule a visit, contact the Admissions Office.

Financial Aid: In 2013-2014, 74% of all full-time freshmen and 64% of continuing full-time students received some form of financial aid. 53% of all full-time freshmen and 48% of continuing full-time students received need-based aid. The average freshman award was $19,058. Need-based scholarships or need-based grants averaged $4,051; need-based self-help aid (loans and jobs) averaged $4,892; and other non-need-based awards and non-need-based scholarships averaged $12,575. 10% of undergraduate students work part-time. Average annual earnings from campus work are $2400. The average financial indebtedness of the 2013 graduate was $25,598. The FAFSA is required. The priority date for freshman financial aid applications for fall entry is March 1.

International Students: There are 237 international students enrolled. The school actively recruits these students. They must take the TOEFL with a minimum score of 550 on the paper-based TOEFL (PBT) or 79 on the Internet-based version (iBT). They must also take the SAT or ACT, scoring 950.

Computers: All students may access the system. There are no time limits. The fee is $8.25/credit.

Graduates: From July 1, 2012 to June 30, 2013, 579 bachelor's degrees were awarded. The most popular majors were nursing (31%), business administration (16%), and psychology (6%). In an average class, 37% graduate in 4 years or less, 47% graduate in 5 years or less, and 50% graduate in 6 years or less. Of the 2012 graduating class, 75% were employed within 6 months of graduation.

Admissions Contact: Dr. Chris E. Domes, Vice President for Enrollment Management. E-Mail: *admissions@marymount.edu* Web: *http:/www.marymount.edu*

NORFOLK STATE UNIVERSITY F-4

Norfolk, VA 23504 (757) 823-8396 (800) 274-1821; (757) 823-2078

Full-time: 1735 men, 2690 women	**Faculty:** n/av
Part-time: 315 men, 600 women	**Ph.D.s:** 63%
Graduate: 180 men, 585 women	**Student/Faculty:** n/av
Year: semesters, summer session	**Tuition:** $7200 ($20,800)
Application Deadline: see profile	**Room & Board:** $9000
Freshman Class: n/av	
SAT or ACT: required	

LESS COMPETITIVE

Norfolk State University, founded in 1935, is an independent institution offering undergraduate and graduate programs in the liberal arts and sciences, business education, health-related professions, and vocational, technical, and professional training. There are 5 undergraduate schools and 1 graduate school. The figures in the above capsule and this profile are approximate. In addition to regional accreditation, NSU has baccalaureate program accreditation with AACSB, ACEJMC, ADA, CSAB, CSWE, NASM, NCATE, and NLN. The library contains 341,068 volumes, 60,882 microform items, 27 audio/video tapes/CDs/DVDs, and subscribes to 1186 periodicals including electronic. Computerized library services include interlibrary loans, database searching, and Internet access. Special learning facilities include a learning resource center, art gallery, planetarium, radio station, TV station, and musical theater. The 134-acre campus is in an urban area in the port city of Norfolk. Including any residence halls, there are 31 buildings.

Student Life: 87% of undergraduates are from Virginia. Others are from 40 states and 34 foreign countries. 87% are African American. The average age of freshmen is 18; all undergraduates, 23. 30% do not continue beyond their first year; 27% remain to graduate.

Housing: 2070 students can be accommodated in college housing, which includes single-sex dorms. On-campus housing is available on a first-come, first-served basis. 62% of students commute. Alcohol is not permitted. Upperclassmen may keep cars.

Activities: 10% of men belong to 12 national fraternities; 10% of women belong to 8 national sororities. There are 112 groups on campus, including art, band, cheerleading, choir, chorus, computers, dance, debate, drama, drill team, ethnic, honors, international, jazz band, literary magazine, marching band, newspaper, pep band, political, professional, radio and TV, religious, social, social service, student government, and yearbook. Popular campus events include Martin Luther King commemorative activities and Black History Month activities.

Sports: There are 6 intercollegiate sports for men and 7 for women, and 8 intramural sports for men and 7 for women. Facilities include a stadium and track seating 28,088, an arena seating 7500, a baseball field, a softball field, a gym, a swimming pool, tennis courts, and a bowling alley.

Disabled Students: 80% of the campus is accessible. Facilities include wheelchair ramps, elevators, special parking, specially equipped rest rooms, special class scheduling, lowered telephones, and special housing.

Services: Counseling and information services are available, as is tutoring in most subjects. There is a reader service for the blind.

Campus Safety and Security: Measures include 24-hour foot and vehicle patrol and security escort services. There are shuttle buses, emergency telephones, lighted pathways/sidewalks, and town meetings.

Programs of Study: NSU confers B.A., B.S., B.Mus., and B.S.W. degrees. Associate, master's, and doctoral degrees are also awarded. Bachelor's degrees are awarded in BIOLOGICAL SCIENCE (biology/biological science and environmental biology), BUSINESS (accounting, banking and finance, and hospitality management services), COMMUNICATIONS AND THE ARTS (communications, English, fine arts, graphic design, and journalism), COMPUTER AND PHYSICAL SCIENCE (chemistry, computer science, mathematics, and physics), EDUCATION (business education, early childhood education, music education, and technical education), ENGINEERING AND ENVIRONMENTAL DESIGN (computer technology, construction technology, drafting and design technology, electrical/electronics engineering technology, and military science), HEALTH PROFESSIONS (exercise science, health care administration, health science, medical records administration/services, medical technology, and nursing), SOCIAL SCIENCE (history, interdisciplinary studies, political science/government, psychology, public administration, and sociology). Social work and computer science are the strongest academically. Business, computer science, and nursing have the largest enrollments.

Required: Students must complete at least 120 semester hours with a minimum 2.0 GPA, including general education courses such as communication, humanities, social science, natural science, health ed, phys ed, and computer literacy. They must also demonstrate writing competence.

Special: NSU offers cross-registration with other institutions in the Tidewater Consortium, a student-exchange program with Old Dominion University, co-op education, a second baccalaureate degree with a minimum of 30 additional semester hours earned, a B.A.-B.S. degree, and a general studies degree. Credit for military experience is possible. There are 14 national honor societies and a freshman honors program.

Faculty/Classroom: 55% of faculty are male; 45% are female. No introductory courses are taught by graduate students. The average class size in an introductory lecture is 20; in a laboratory, 16; and in a regular course, 17.

Requirements: The SAT or ACT is required. Applicants should be graduates of an accredited secondary school or have the GED equivalent and have completed 22 academic units: 4 in English, 3 in history/social studies, 3 each in math and science, and 9 in electives. Nursing applicants must meet additional requirements. A GPA of 2.0 is required. AP and CLEP credits are accepted.

Procedure: Freshmen are admitted fall, spring, and summer. Entrance exams should be taken by March of the senior year. There are deferred admissions and rolling admissions plans. Check with the school for current application deadlines. The application fee is $45. Applications are accepted online.

Transfer: Transfers must meet freshman admissions criteria. 30 of 120 credits required for the bachelor's degree must be completed at NSU.

Visiting: There are regularly scheduled orientations for prospective students, including registration, a general information session, visits to academic departments, admissions, and a tour. There are guides for informal visits, and visitors may sit in on classes and stay overnight. To schedule a visit, contact the Admissions Office.

Financial Aid: NSU is a member of CSS. The FAFSA and the SAR are required. Check with the school for current application deadline.

International Students: The school actively recruits these students. They must take the TOEFL. They must also take the SAT or ACT, scoring 800 on the SAT.

Computers: All students may access the system any time. There are no time limits and no fees. It is strongly recommended that all students have a personal computer. A Gateway is recommended.

Admissions Contact: Director of Admissions. A campus DVD is available. E-mail: *admissions@nsu.edu* Web: *www.nsu.edu*

OLD DOMINION UNIVERSITY — F-4

Norfolk, VA 23529 — (757) 683-3648; (800) 348-7926; (757) 683-3255

Full-time: 7106 men, 7996 women	**Faculty:** 560; I, --$
Part-time: 2011 men, 2706 women	**Ph.D.s:** 83%
Graduate: 2082 men, 2927 women	**Student/Faculty:** 27 to 1
Year: semesters, summer session	**Tuition:** $8820 ($24,480)
Application Deadline: February 1	**Room & Board:** $9842
Freshman Class: 10202 applied, 7834 accepted, 2942 enrolled	
SAT CR/M: 510/510	**ACT:** 21 — **COMPETITIVE**

Old Dominion University, founded in 1930, is a public institution with programs in arts and letters, business and public administration, engineering, education, sciences, and health sciences. There are 6 undergraduate schools and 6 graduate schools. In addition to regional accreditation, ODU has baccalaureate program accreditation with AACSB, ABET, ADA, APTA, NASAD, NASM, NCATE, and NRPA. The 3 libraries contain 1.2 million volumes, 1.9 million microform items, and 54,133 audio/video tapes/CDs/DVDs, and subscribe to 24,257 periodicals including electronic. Computerized library services include interlibrary loans, database searching, Internet access, and Wi-Fi capability. Special learning facilities include an art gallery, planetarium, radio station, a music library and composers collections, university special collections and archives, an art library, and a digital library. The 251-acre campus is in an urban area in the Norfolk Hampton Roads Metropolitan region. Including any residence halls, there are 126 buildings.

Student Life: 92% of undergraduates are from Virginia. Others are from 44 states, 63 foreign countries, and Canada. 90% are from public schools. 50% are White; 27% African American. The average age of freshmen is 19; all undergraduates, 22. 20% do not continue beyond their first year; 51% remain to graduate.

Housing: 4678 students can be accommodated in college housing, which includes single-sex and coed dorms and on-campus apartments. In addition, there are honors houses, special-interest houses, Living Learning Communities (Honors; Health Professionals; Women in Math; Science and Engineering; and Engineering. On-campus housing is guaranteed for the freshman year only, is available on a first-come, first-served basis, and is available on a lottery system for upperclassmen. 76% of students commute. Upperclassmen may keep cars.

Activities: 6% of men belong to 19 national fraternities; 5% of women belong to 10 national sororities. There are 285 groups on campus, including art, band, cheerleading, chess, choir, chorale, chorus, communications, computers, dance, debate, drama, drill team, environmental, ethnic, film, forensics, gay, honors, international, jazz band, marching band, musical theater, newspaper, pep band, political, professional, radio and TV, religious, social, and student government. Popular campus events include International Festival, Exam Jam, Campus Chaos, Homecoming, Greek Week and Relay for Life.

Sports: There are 9 intercollegiate sports for men and 9 for women, and 22 intramural sports for men and 22 for women. Facilities include an indoor tennis center (8 indoor courts, 12 outdoor courts), baseball stadium, basketball arena, varsity soccer game field and soccer practice field, practice gym, wrestling practice room, turf field stadium for field hockey and lacrosse, practice football fields, football game stadium, 9-hole golf course with a 2-tier heated driving range, sailing centers, and a water area for varsity rowing, erg room, 8 lane swimming pool.

Disabled Students: 95% of the campus is accessible. Facilities include wheelchair ramps, elevators, special parking, specially equipped restrooms, special class scheduling, lowered drinking fountains, special housing.

Services: Counseling and information services are available, as is tutoring in some subjects. There is a reader service for the blind, and remedial writing.

Campus Safety and Security: Measures include 24-hour foot and vehicle patrol, emergency notification system, self-defense education, and security escort services. There are shuttle buses, emergency telephones, lighted pathways/sidewalks, controlled access to dorms/residences, a bicycle patrol.

Programs of Study: ODU confers B.A., B.S., B.F.A., B.M., B.S.B.A., B.S.C.E., B.S.C.O.M.E., B.S.C.S., B.S.D.H., B.S.E.E., B.S.E.H., B.S.E.T., B.S.H.S., B.S.M.&S.E., B.S.M.E., B.S.M.T., B.S.N. and B.S.N.M.T. degrees. Master's and doctoral degrees are also awarded. Bachelor's degrees are awarded in BIOLOGICAL SCIENCE (biochemistry, biology/biological science, and marine biology), BUSINESS (accounting, banking and finance, business administration and management, business intelligence and analytics, electronic business, fashion merchandising, insurance, international business management, management information systems, marketing management, real estate, recreation and leisure services, and sports management), COMMUNICATIONS AND THE ARTS (art history and appreciation, communications, dance, dramatic arts, English, film arts, fine arts, French, German, graphic design, journalism, linguistics, literature, music, music business management, music performance, music theory and composition, performing arts, Spanish, studio art, and theater design), COMPUTER AND PHYSICAL SCIENCE (applied mathematics, chemistry, computer science, earth science, geology, information sciences and systems, mathematics, oceanography, physics, and statistics), EDUCATION (art education, dance education, drama education, early childhood education, elementary education, English education, foreign languages education, health education, mathematics education, music education, physical education, science education, secondary education, social studies education, and special education), ENGINEERING AND ENVIRONMENTAL DESIGN (civil engineering, civil engineering technology, computer engineering, electrical/electronics engineering, electrical/electronics engineering technology, engineering technology, mechanical engineering, mechanical engineering technology, and nuclear engineering technology), HEALTH PROFESSIONS (cytotechnology, dental hygiene, environmental health science, exercise science, health science, medical technology, nuclear medical technology, nursing, ophthalmic technology, public health, and speech pathology/audiology), SOCIAL SCIENCE (African studies, African American studies, Asian/Oriental studies, criminal justice, economics, geography, history, human services, interdisciplinary studies, international studies, philosophy, political science/government, psychology, sociology, and women's studies). Criminal justice, accounting, speech pathology, nursing, biology, English, business, exercise science, civil engineering are the strongest academically. Biology, psychology, and criminal justice have the largest enrollments.

Required: At least 120 credits, with a minimum GPA of 2.0, are required to graduate. Students must complete the university's general education program, consisting of specific skills and perspectives courses outside the student's major. English composition is a required course, and students must earn a C or better in ENGL 110, ENGL 211/221/231 and a W (writing extensive) course.

Special: Old Dominion offers cross-registration with schools in the Tidewater Consortium program. There are co-op programs, guaranteed internships, study abroad in 56 countries, and a work-study program. Students may take a B.A.-B.S. degree in engineering and liberal arts. An interdisciplinary program, dual majors, 3-2 engineering degrees in business and engineering, nondegree study, pass/fail options, and credit for military and life experience are available. There are 23 national honor societies and a freshman honors program.

Faculty/Classroom: 59% of faculty are male; 41% are female. 78% teach undergraduates, and 2% do research. No introductory courses are taught by graduate students. The average class size in an introductory lecture is 34; in a laboratory is 23; and in a regular course is 32.

Admissions: 77% of the 2013-2014 applicants were accepted. The SAT scores for the 2013-2014 freshman class were: Critical Reading--42% below 500, 44% between 500 and 599, 13% between 600 and 699, and 1% between 700 and 800; Math--41% below 500, 43% between 500 and 599, 15% between 600 and 699, and 1% between 700 and 800. The ACT scores were 49% below 21, 26% between 21 and 23, 16% between 24 and 26, 5% between 27 and 28, and 4% above 28. 25% of the current freshmen were in the top fifth of their class; 59% were in the top two fifths. 7 freshmen graduated first in their class.

Requirements: The SAT or ACT is required. Applicants must be graduates of an accredited secondary school. The GED is accepted. Applicants should have completed 4 years of math and 3 years each of English, foreign languages, science, and social science. An essay and recommendation are required. A list of extracurricular activities is required. Applications are accepted online via CollegeNET. A GPA of 2.7 is required. AP and CLEP credits are accepted. Important factors in the admissions decision are advanced placement or honors courses, recommendations by school officials, and leadership record.

Procedure: Freshmen are admitted fall, spring, and summer. Entrance exams should be taken in May of the junior year or November/December of the senior. There are early admissions, deferred admissions, and rolling admissions plans. Applications should be filed by February 1 for fall entry; October 1 for spring entry; and March 15 for summer entry, along with a $50 fee. Notification is sent on a rolling basis. Applications are accepted online.

Transfer: 2284 transfer students enrolled in 2012-2013. Applicants

must have a minimum GPA of 2.5 and at least 24 semester hour credits. Applicants with fewer semester hours must meet the same requirements as freshmen. 30 of 120 credits required for the bachelor's degree must be completed at ODU.

Visiting: There are regularly scheduled orientations for prospective students, Academic Advising, tours, college presentations, registration. There are guides for informal visits and visitors may sit in on classes. To schedule a visit, contact the Admissions Office at (757) 683-3685.

Financial Aid: In 2013-2014, 70% of all full-time freshmen and 68% of continuing full-time students received some form of financial aid. 64% of all full-time freshmen and 61% of continuing full-time students received need-based aid. The average freshman award was $11,235. Need-based scholarships or need-based grants averaged $7,761 ($21,660 maximum); need-based self-help aid (loans and jobs) averaged $3,550 ($21,660 maximum); non-need-based athletic scholarships averaged $17,885 ($21,660 maximum); and other non-need-based awards and non-need-based scholarships averaged $2,944 ($21,660 maximum). 5% of undergraduate students work part-time. Average annual earnings from campus work are $4800. The average financial indebtedness of the 2013 graduate was $25,585. The FAFSA is required. The priority date for freshman financial aid applications for fall entry is February 15.

International Students: There are 201 international students enrolled. The school actively recruits these students. They must take the TOEFL with a minimum score of 550 on the paper-based TOEFL (PBT) or 79 on the Internet-based version (iBT) and the college's own test.

Computers: All students may access the system 24 hours a day. There are no time limits and no fees.

Graduates: From July 1, 2012 to June 30, 2013, 3938 bachelor's degrees were awarded. The most popular majors were interdisciplinary studies (7%), psychology (7%), and criminology (7%). 400 companies recruited on campus in 2012-2013. In an average class, 1% graduate in 3 years or less, 23% graduate in 4 years or less, 45% graduate in 5 years or less, and 51% graduate in 6 years or less.

Admissions Contact: Shereen Williams, Customer Service Manager, Admissions. E-Mail: *admissions@odu.edu* Web: *www.odu.edu/admissions*

RADFORD UNIVERSITY C-3

Radford, VA 24142 **(540) 831-5371; (540) 831-5038**

Full-time: 3771 men, 4774 women	**Faculty:** 377; IIA, -$
Part-time: 170 men, 198 women	**Ph.D.s:** 82%
Graduate: 266 men, 749 women	**Student/Faculty:** 18 to 1
Year: semesters, summer session	**Tuition:** $8976 ($20,695)
Application Deadline: February 1	**Room & Board:** $8156
Freshman Class: 7774 applied, 6088 accepted, 1986 enrolled	
SAT CR/M/W: 490/490/480	**ACT:** 20 **LESS COMPETITIVE**

Radford University, founded in 1910, is a comprehensive, coeducational student-focused public institution with diverse curricula in science and technology; business and economics; nursing, allied health and human services; education and human development; visual and performing arts; and graduate and professional studies. There are 6 undergraduate schools and 1 graduate school. In addition to regional accreditation, RU has baccalaureate program accreditation with AACSB, ABET, CSAB, CSWE, FIDER, NASM, NCATE, and NRPA. The library contains 306,885 volumes, 1.4 million microform items, and 27,110 audio/video tapes/CDs/DVDs. Computerized library services include interlibrary loans, database searching, Internet access, and Wi-Fi capability. Special learning facilities include an art gallery, natural history museum, planetarium, radio station, TV station. The 191-acre campus is in a small town 36 miles southwest of Roanoke. Including any residence halls, there are 55 buildings.

Student Life: 94% of undergraduates are from Virginia. Others are from 39 states, 50 foreign countries, and Canada. 92% are from public schools. 79% are White. The average age of freshmen is 18; all undergraduates, 21. 22% do not continue beyond their first year; 59% remain to graduate.

Housing: 3291 students can be accommodated in college housing, which includes coed dorms, on-campus apartments, and off-campus apartments. In addition, there are honors houses and special-interest houses. On-campus housing is guaranteed for the freshman year only. 64% of students commute. Alcohol is not permitted. All students may keep cars.

Activities: 9% of men belong to 12 national fraternities; 12% of women belong to 12 national sororities. There are 235 groups on campus, including art, band, cheerleading, choir, chorale, computers, dance, drama, environmental, ethnic, gay, honors, international, jazz band, literary magazine, musical theater, newspaper, orchestra, pep band, political, professional, radio and TV, religious, social, social service, and student government.

Sports: There are 8 intercollegiate sports for men and 11 for women, and 35 intramural sports for men and 35 for women. Facilities include Slated for completion in fall 2014 is a new Student Fitness and Wellness Center that will be a state-of-the-art facility that will incorporate a two-story indoor sloped running track, gymnasium, multi-purpose activity courts, basketball courts, weight and cardio rooms,and fitness and nutritional instruction classrooms. Construction is also projected to begin on a new intramural complex that will provide additional fields for intramural soccer, lacrosse, flag football and rugby. A 3200-seat multipurpose facility including a natatorium with an 8-lane swimming pool, a 1/6-mile jogging track, steam rooms, basketball and volleyball courts, a pole vault practice runway, an indoor golf room, and student-athlete support facilities such as a weight room, a rehabilitaion and training room, and an academic center. Outdoor facilities include a jogging trail, 12 tennis courts, and facilities for baseball,track, soccer, field hockey, and softball.

Disabled Students: 94% of the campus is accessible. Facilities include wheelchair ramps, elevators, special parking, specially equipped restrooms, special class scheduling, lowered drinking fountains, lowered telephones, and special housing.

Services: Counseling and information services are available, as is tutoring in most subjects.

Campus Safety and Security: Measures include 24-hour foot and vehicle patrol, emergency notification system, self-defense education, and security escort services. There are shuttle buses, emergency telephones, lighted pathways/sidewalks, and controlled access to dorms/residences.

Programs of Study: RU confers B.A., B.S., B.B.A., B.F.A., B.M., B.S.N. and B.S.W. degrees. Master's and doctoral degrees are also awarded. Bachelor's degrees are awarded in BIOLOGICAL SCIENCE (biology/biological science), BUSINESS (accounting, banking and finance, business administration and management, marketing/retailing/merchandising, and recreation and leisure services), COMMUNICATIONS AND THE ARTS (art, communications, dance, design, English, fine arts, media arts, music, speech/debate/rhetoric, and theatre arts), COMPUTER AND PHYSICAL SCIENCE (chemistry, computer science, geology, information sciences and systems, mathematics, and physics), EDUCATION (athletic training, foreign languages education, and physical education), HEALTH PROFESSIONS (nursing and speech pathology/audiology), SOCIAL SCIENCE (anthropology, criminal justice, dietetics, economics, geography, history, interdisciplinary studies, philosophy and religion, political science/government, psychology, social science, social work, and sociology). Nursing and education are the strongest academically. Interdisciplinary studies, criminal justice, exercise, sport and health education have the largest enrollments.

Required: To graduate, students must complete at least 120 credit hours, including 30 to 90 in the major, with a 2.0 GPA. There are core curriculum requirements in English, communication, math, natural sciences, humanities, visual and performing arts, social and behavioral sciences, U.S. and global perspectives, and health and wellness.

Special: RU offers internships, study abroad in 16 countries, and on-campus work-study. There are accelerated degree programs in criminal justice, nursing, and communication, and dual and student-designed majors are possible. There are 3-2 engineering, chemistry, physics, and math degree programs with Virginia Tech. There are 24 national honor societies and a freshman honors program.

Faculty/Classroom: 51% of faculty are male; 49% are female. 87% teach undergraduates. Graduate students teach 8% of introductory courses. The average class size in an introductory lecture is 37; in a laboratory is 21; and in a regular course is 34.

Admissions: 78% of the 2013-2014 applicants were accepted. The SAT scores for the 2013-2014 freshman class were: Critical Reading--54% below 500, 37% between 500 and 599, 9% between 600 and 699, and 1% between 700 and 800; Math--54% below 500, 38% between 500 and 599, and 8% between 600 and 699; Writing--62% below 500, 34% between 500 and 599, and 4% between 600 and 699. The ACT scores were 57% below 21, 25% between 21 and 23, 14% between 24 and 26, 2% between 27 and 28, and 2% above 28. 22% of the current freshmen were in the top fifth of their class; 44% were in the top two fifths. There were 8 National Merit finalists. 7 freshmen graduated first in their class.

Requirements: The SAT or ACT is required. In addition, most successful applicants have taken 4 units each of English, math, and social sciences, including American history, and 3 or 4 units each of laboratory sciences and foreign language. The GED is accepted. AP and CLEP credits are accepted.

Procedure: Freshmen are admitted fall, spring, and summer. There are early admissions and deferred admissions plans. Applications should be filed by February 1 for fall entry, along with a $50 fee. Notifications are sent April 1. 1102 applicants were on the 2013 waiting list; 442 were admitted. Applications are accepted online.

Transfer: 770 transfer students enrolled in 2012-2013. Applicants must have a minimum GPA of 2.0 for consideration. Those with fewer than 24 semester hours of college work must submit their high school record. 45 of 120 credits required for the bachelor's degree must be completed at RU.

Visiting: There are regularly scheduled orientations for prospective students, consisting of open houses in the fall, information sessions and tours Monday through Friday, and Admitted Student Days in the spring. There are guides for informal visits and visitors may sit in on classes. To schedule a visit, contact the Office of Admissions at admissions@radford.edu.

Financial Aid: In 2013-2014, 75% of all full-time freshmen and 74% of

continuing full-time students received some form of financial aid. 56% of all full-time freshmen and 53% of continuing full-time students received need-based aid. The average freshman award was $13,203. Need-based scholarships or need-based grants averaged $6,836 ($24,505 maximum); need-based self-help aid (loans and jobs) averaged $7,564 ($32,851 maximum); non-need-based athletic scholarships averaged $11,044 ($30,477 maximum); and other non-need-based awards and non-need-based scholarships averaged $9,622 ($33,140 maximum). 13% of undergraduate students work part-time. Average annual earnings from campus work are $7247. The average financial indebtedness of the 2013 graduate was $25,895. The FAFSA is required. The deadline for filing freshman financial aid applications for fall entry is February 1.

International Students: There are 56 international students enrolled. The school actively recruits these students. They must take the TOEFL with a minimum score of 520 on the paper-based TOEFL (PBT) or 68 on the Internet-based version (iBT). They must also take the SAT.

Computers: All students may access the system. There are no time limits and no fees.

Graduates: From July 1, 2012 to June 30, 2013, 1761 bachelor's degrees were awarded. The most popular majors were interdisciplinary studies (10%), criminal justice (8%), and psychology (7%). 291 companies recruited on campus in 2012-2013. In an average class, 41% graduate in 4 years or less, 56% graduate in 5 years or less, and 59% graduate in 6 years or less. Of the 2012 graduating class, 13% were enrolled in graduate school within 6 months of graduation.

Admissions Contact: James Pennix, Dean of Admissions. E-Mail: *admissions@radford.edu* Web: *www.radford.edu*

RANDOLPH COLLEGE D-3

Lynchburg, VA 24503 (434) 947-8100
(800) 745-7692; (434) 947-8996

Full-time: 229 men, 420 women	**Faculty:** 69; IIB, -$
Part-time: 9 men, 7 women	**Ph.D.s:** 96%
Graduate: 5 men, 12 women	**Student/Faculty:** 9 to 1
Year: semesters	**Tuition:** $32,750
Application Deadline: March 15	**Room & Board:** $11,210

Freshman Class: 1051 applied, 881 accepted, 216 enrolled
SAT CR/M/W: 550/535/535 **ACT:** 25 **VERY COMPETITIVE**

Randolph College, founded in 1891, is an independent, coeducational, liberal arts institution. The college's curriculum offers the best feature of an honors education with a global outlook. Students are encouraged to travel, to take on real problems, to pursue and achieve a goal with personal meaning. Embedded within a student's education are opportunities to study abroad, both national and international internships, career guidance, leadership development, and one-on-one faculty advising. There is one undergraduate school and one graduate school. In addition to regional accreditation, Randolph has baccalaureate program accreditation with NASDTEC and TEAC. The library contains 197,332 volumes, 187,000 microform items, and 3,600 audio/video tapes/CDs/DVDs, and subscribes to 618 periodicals including electronic. Computerized library services include interlibrary loans, database searching, and Internet access. Special learning facilities include an art gallery, radio station, an observatory, acclaimed collection of American art housed in the Maier Museum, 2 theaters, recital hall, organic garden, a 100-acre equestrian center, and 3 nature preserves. The 100-acre campus is in a suburban area within minutes of the Blue Ridge Mountains, 1 hour southwest of Charlottesville. Including any residence halls, there are 18 buildings.

Student Life: 59% of undergraduates are from Virginia. Others are from 36 states, 32 foreign countries, and Canada. 72% are from public schools. 67% are White; 13% Foreign. 55% are Protestant; 15% Catholic; 15% claim no religious affiliation; 12% Muslim, Hindu, Buddhist, and Orthodox. The average age of freshmen is 18; all undergraduates, 20. 20% do not continue beyond their first year; 64% remain to graduate.

Housing: 675 students can be accommodated in college housing, which includes single-sex and coed dorms. In addition, there are special-interest houses, shared housing for prime time students, and women's dorms, theme housing, and coed dorms. On-campus housing is guaranteed for all 4 years. 90% of students live on campus; of those, 80% remain on campus on weekends. All students may keep cars.

Activities: There are no fraternities or sororities. There are 35 groups on campus, including and outdoor adventures, environmental, equestrian, art, chorale, chorus, dance, debate, drama, environmental, ethnic, film, foreign language, gay, honors, international, literary magazine, newspaper, pep band, photography, political, professional, radio and TV, religious, social, social service, student government, and yearbook. Popular campus events include Tacky Party, Never-ending Weekend, Senior Dinner Dance and Dell Parties.

Sports: There are 6 intercollegiate sports for men and 8 for women, and 6 intramural sports for men and 6 for women. Facilities include a multipurpose playing field and track, gym, an indoor heated swimming pool, dance studios, aerobic and weight rooms, 8 tennis courts, 2 athletic fields, frisbee golf course, 100-acre riding center with teaching and amphitheater show rings and indoor and outdoor arenas, and a 900-seat auditorium.

Disabled Students: 50% of the campus is accessible. Facilities include wheelchair ramps, elevators, special parking, specially equipped restrooms, special class scheduling, special housing, a wheelchair lift, and TDY telephone for hearing impaired.

Services: Counseling and information services are available, as is tutoring in every subject.

Campus Safety and Security: Measures include 24-hour foot and vehicle patrol, emergency notification system, self-defense education, and security escort services. There are emergency telephones, lighted pathways/sidewalks, and controlled access to dorms/residences.

Programs of Study: Randolph confers B.A., B.S. and B.F.A. degrees. Master's degrees are also awarded. Bachelor's degrees are awarded in AGRICULTURE (environmental studies), BIOLOGICAL SCIENCE (biology/biological science), BUSINESS (business administration and management), COMMUNICATIONS AND THE ARTS (art, classics, communications, dance, dramatic arts, English, French, music, and Spanish), COMPUTER AND PHYSICAL SCIENCE (chemistry, mathematics, and physics), EDUCATION (education and physical education), ENGINEERING AND ENVIRONMENTAL DESIGN (engineering physics and environmental science), HEALTH PROFESSIONS (health science), SOCIAL SCIENCE (economics, history, international studies, philosophy, political science/government, psychology, religion, and sociology). Biology, psychology, political science, and English have the largest enrollments.

Required: To graduate, all students must complete at least 124 credit hours with a minimum GPA of 2.0. Students must satisfy the requirements for the general education and major programs and must have a minimum GPA of 2.0 in the major.

Special: Randolph offers a spring semester American Culture Program, as well as study abroad in 11 countries, including its own program in England, and both domestic and international internships. A Washington semester at American University is available, as is the Tri-College Consortium with Sweet Briar and Lynchburg Colleges, and the Seven-College Exchange Program with Hampden-Sydney, Hollins, Mary Baldwin, Randolph-Macon, and Sweet Briar Colleges, and Washington and Lee University. There is a 3-2 nursing program with Johns Hopkins University and Vanderbilt University and a 3-2 engineering degree with several institutions. There are 17 national honor societies, including Phi Beta Kappa, and 16 departmental honors programs.

Faculty/Classroom: 46% of faculty are male; 54% are female. All teach undergraduates, 58% do research, and 58% do both. No introductory courses are taught by graduate students. The average class size in an introductory lecture is 16; in a laboratory is 11; and in a regular course is 12.

Admissions: 84% of the 2013-2014 applicants were accepted. The SAT scores for the 2013-2014 freshman class were: Critical Reading--26% below 500, 44% between 500 and 599, 23% between 600 and 699, and 3% between 700 and 800; Math--34% below 500, 41% between 500 and 599, 22% between 600 and 699, and 3% between 700 and 800; Writing--34% below 500, 41% between 500 and 599, 20% between 600 and 699, and 5% between 700 and 800. 71% of the current freshmen were in the top fifth of their class; 91% were in the top two fifths.

Requirements: The SAT or ACT is required. In addition, applicants must be graduates of an accredited secondary school with at least 16 academic credits, including 4 units in English, 3 to 4 in a foreign language, 3 in math, 2 in biology, chemistry, or physics with lab work, and 1 to 2 in electives from other academic study. An interview is strongly encouraged. AP and CLEP credits are accepted. Important factors in the admissions decision are advanced placement or honors courses, recommendations by school officials, and leadership record.

Procedure: Freshmen are admitted fall and spring. Entrance exams should be taken in the junior or senior year. There are early admissions and deferred admissions plans. Early decision applications should be filed by December 1; regular applications, by March 15 for fall entry; and December 1 for spring entry, along with a $35 fee. Notification of early decision is sent December 15; regular decision, on a rolling basis. Applications are accepted online.

Transfer: 24 transfer students enrolled in 2012-2013. Transfer students must submit college and high school transcripts, a letters of recommendation from a college official. An interview is recommended. 62 of 124 credits required for the bachelor's degree must be completed at Randolph.

Visiting: There are regularly scheduled orientations for prospective students, including a campus tour, student panels, faculty panels, class visits, and individual sessions with admissions and financial planning counselor. There are guides for informal visits, visitors may sit in on classes, and stay overnight. To schedule a visit, contact the Admissions Office.

Financial Aid: In 2013-2014, 99% of all full-time freshmen and 99% of continuing full-time students received some form of financial aid. 76% of all full-time freshmen and 74% of continuing full-time students received need-based aid. The average freshman award was $23,278. Need-based scholarships or need-based grants averaged $5,907; need-based self-help aid (loans and jobs) averaged $4,614; other non-need-based awards and non-need-based scholarships averaged $6,350; and $14,208 from other forms of aid. 66% of undergraduate students work part-time. Average annual earnings from campus work are $1100. The average financial indebtedness of the 2013 graduate was $12,454. The FAFSA and the state aid form are required. The priority date for freshman financial aid applications for fall entry is March 1.

International Students: There are 66 international students enrolled. The school actively recruits these students. They must take the TOEFL with a minimum score of 550 on the paper-based TOEFL (PBT) or 79 on the Internet-based version (iBT).

Computers: All students may access the system. There are no time limits and no fees.

Graduates: From July 1, 2012 to June 30, 2013, 118 bachelor's degrees were awarded. The most popular majors were social sciences (16%), psychology (11%), and history (10%). In an average class, 2% graduate in 3 years or less, 63% graduate in 4 years or less, 64% graduate in 5 years or less, and 64% graduate in 6 years or less. Of the 2012 graduating class, 35% were enrolled in graduate school within 6 months of graduation, and 60% were employed.

Admissions Contact: Margaret Blount, Director of Recruitment. E-Mail: *admissions@randolphcollege.edu* Web: *www.randolphcollege.edu*

RANDOLPH-MACON COLLEGE — E-3

Ashland, VA 23005 (804) 752-7305
(800) 888-1762; (804) 752-4707

Full-time: 615 men, 680 women	**Faculty:** 94; IIB, -$
Part-time: 8 men, 12 women	**Ph.D.s:** 99%
Graduate: n/av	**Student/Faculty:** 14 to 1
Year: 4-1-4, summer session	**Tuition:** $34,850
Application Deadline: March 1	**Room & Board:** $10,236

Freshman Class: 2997 applied, 1909 accepted, 382 enrolled
SAT CR/M/W: 547/545/530 **ACT:** 24 **COMPETITIVE**

Randolph-Macon College, established in 1830, is a private liberal arts college historically affiliated with the United Methodist Church. There is one undergraduate school. In addition to regional accreditation, Randolph-Macon has baccalaureate program accreditation with NCATE. The library contains 173,817 volumes, 337,743 microform items, and 6,644 audio/video tapes/CDs/DVDs, and subscribes to 4,892 periodicals including electronic. Computerized library services include interlibrary loans, database searching, Internet access, and Wi-Fi capability. Special learning facilities include an art gallery, radio station, TV station, an observatory, a radio telescope, a darkroom, and a greenhouse. The 116-acre campus is in a suburban area 15 miles north of Richmond and 90 miles south of Washington, D.C. Including any residence halls, there are 70 buildings.

Student Life: 74% of undergraduates are from Virginia. Others are from 29 states, 23 foreign countries, and Canada. 80% are from public schools. 76% are White. 46% are Protestant; 14% Catholic. The average age of freshmen is 18; all undergraduates, 20. 23% do not continue beyond their first year; 61% remain to graduate.

Housing: 1074 students can be accommodated in college housing, which includes single-sex and coed dorms and on-campus apartments. In addition, there are honors houses, language houses, special-interest houses, fraternity houses, sorority houses, senior apartments, Greek housing, and several college-owned houses. On-campus housing is guaranteed for all 4 years and is available on a lottery system for upperclassmen. 80% of students live on campus; of those, 77% remain on campus on weekends. All students may keep cars.

Activities: 31% of men belong to 8 national fraternities; 40% of women belong to 4 national sororities. There are 80 groups on campus, including and Residence Hall Association, art, Campus Events Committee, cheerleading, choir, chorale, chorus, communications, computers, dance, debate, drama, environmental, ethnic, film, forensics, gay, honors, international, jazz band, literary magazine, musical theater, newspaper, opera, pep band, photography, political, professional, radio and TV, religious, social, social service, and student government. Popular campus events include Cultural Arts Series, Dance Marathon, Monster Bash and Beat Hampden-Sydney Week.

Sports: There are 8 intercollegiate sports for men and 9 for women, and 15 intramural sports for men and 15 for women. Facilities include 6 tennis courts, several playing fields for men's and women's sports, 2 gyms, an indoor track, an indoor pool, a football field, a weight room, and an exercise room. A sports and recreation center includes racquetball and squash courts, a 25-yard pool, a weight room, an aerobics room, a 3-lane track, a multipurpose gym, and a climbing wall.

Disabled Students: 85% of the campus is accessible. Facilities include wheelchair ramps, elevators, special parking, specially equipped restrooms, special class scheduling, special housing, and advisers for learning-disabled students.

Services: Counseling and information services are available, as is tutoring in every subject. There is a reader service for the blind.

Campus Safety and Security: Measures include 24-hour foot and vehicle patrol, emergency notification system, self-defense education, and security escort services. There are emergency telephones, lighted pathways/sidewalks, and controlled access to dorms/residences.

Programs of Study: Randolph-Macon confers B.A., and B.S. degrees. Bachelor's degrees are awarded in AGRICULTURE (environmental studies), BIOLOGICAL SCIENCE (biology/biological science), BUSINESS (accounting and business economics), COMMUNICATIONS AND THE ARTS (art history and appreciation, arts administration/management, classics, communications, dramatic arts, English, French, German, Greek, Latin, music, Spanish, and studio art), COMPUTER AND PHYSICAL SCIENCE (chemistry, computer science, mathematics, and physics), ENGINEERING AND ENVIRONMENTAL DESIGN (engineering physics), SOCIAL SCIENCE (archeology, Asian/Oriental studies, economics, history, international studies, philosophy, political science/government, psychology, religion, sociology, and women's studies). Biology, psychology, economics/business have the largest enrollments.

Required: To graduate, students must complete 110 credit hours, with 30 to 42 hours in the major and a minimum GPA of 2.0. All students must complete a Capstone course culminating the academic experience. All students must satisfy requirements in math, social science, lab science, literature, philosophy/theology, phys ed, fine arts, foreign language, history, and writing. There are also requirements for Western, non-Western, computing, multidisciplinary, and experiential courses. All first-year students must complete the First-Year Experience, a yearlong course team-taught by 2 professors in different disciplines.

Special: The college offers special programs in engineering with Columbia University and the University of Virginia, in forestry with Duke University, and in accounting with Virginia Commonwealth University and Union University. The college has a Guaranteed Admission Agreement with the George Washington University School of Nursing. A new Early Assurance Program (EAP) exists with the Eastern Virginia Medical School (EVMS) Physician Assistant program. There is cross-registration with Hollins, Sweet Briar, Randolph College, Hampden-Sydney, Washington and Lee, and Mary Baldwin. Study-abroad programs are offered in 45 countries. Internships, dual majors, and a Washington semester are available. B.A.-B.S. degrees are possible in all majors. There are 19 national honor societies, including Phi Beta Kappa, and a freshman honors program.

Faculty/Classroom: 56% of faculty are male; 44% are female. All teach and do research. No introductory courses are taught by graduate students. The average class size in an introductory lecture is 15; in a laboratory is 12; and in a regular course is 16.

Admissions: 64% of the 2013-2014 applicants were accepted. The SAT scores for the 2013-2014 freshman class were: Critical Reading--26% below 500, 51% between 500 and 599, 19% between 600 and 699, and 4% between 700 and 800; Math--28% below 500, 48% between 500 and 599, 22% between 600 and 699, and 3% between 700 and 800; Writing--36% below 500, 44% between 500 and 599, 19% between 600 and 699, and 1% between 700 and 800. 34% of the current freshmen were in the top fifth of their class; 73% were in the top two fifths. 2 freshmen graduated first in their class.

Requirements: The SAT is required. Applicants must be graduates of an accredited secondary school or have completed their GED. Applicants should complete a minimum of 16 high school academic credits, including 4 years of English, 3 to 4 years each of math and science, and 2 to 3 years of foreign language, history, and social studies. An essay is required, and an interview is recommended. A GPA of 2.0 is required. AP and CLEP credits are accepted. Important factors in the admissions decision are advanced placement or honors courses, recommendations by school officials, and extracurricular activities record.

Procedure: Freshmen are admitted fall and spring. Entrance exams should be taken by January of the senior year. There are early admissions and deferred admissions plans. Early decision applications should be filed by November 15; regular applications, by March 1 for fall entry; and December 1 for spring entry, along with a $30 fee. Notification of early decision is sent January 1; regular decision, April 1. 224 applicants were on the 2013 waiting list; 60 were admitted. Applications are accepted online.

Transfer: 28 transfer students enrolled in 2012-2013. Applicants must have a minimum GPA of 2.0 and must be eligible to return to their previous institution. They must submit high school and college transcripts and SAT scores (the SAT requirement is waived for students who have earned an associate degree).

Visiting: There are regularly scheduled orientations for prospective students, including interviews, information sessions, tours, open houses, and visitation days. There are guides for informal visits, visitors may sit in on classes, and stay overnight. To schedule a visit, contact the Office of Admissions at (800) 888-1762.

Financial Aid: In 2013-2014, 100% of all full-time freshmen and 99% of continuing full-time students received some form of financial aid. 79% of all full-time freshmen and 99% of continuing full-time students received need-based aid. The average freshman award was $25,716. Need-based scholarships or need-based grants averaged $22,331; need-based self-help aid (loans and jobs) averaged $4,267; and other non-need-based awards and non-need-based scholarships averaged $16,073. 46% of undergraduate students work part-time. Average annual earnings from campus work are $1500. The average financial indebtedness of the 2013 graduate was

$32,020. The FAFSA, the state aid form, and the college's own financial statement are required. The priority date for freshman financial aid applications for fall entry is February 15. The deadline for filing freshman financial aid applications for fall entry is March 1.

International Students: There are 44 international students enrolled. The school actively recruits these students. They must take the TOEFL with a minimum score of 550 on the paper-based TOEFL (PBT) or 80 on the Internet-based version (iBT).

Computers: All students may access the system. Computer labs are open from 8 a.m. to 1 a.m. There are no time limits and no fees.

Graduates: From July 1, 2012 to June 30, 2013, 255 bachelor's degrees were awarded. The most popular majors were biology (11%), sociology (10%), and economics/business (9%). 54 companies recruited on campus in 2012-2013. In an average class, 2% graduate in 3 years or less, 58% graduate in 4 years or less, 60% graduate in 5 years or less, and 61% graduate in 6 years or less. Of the 2012 graduating class, 12% were enrolled in graduate school within 6 months of graduation, and 40% were employed.

Admissions Contact: David Lesesne, VP Enrollment, Dean of Admissions. E-Mail: *admissions@rmc.edu* Web: *http:/www.rmc.edu/admissions.aspx*

ROANOKE COLLEGE C-3

Salem, VA 24153 **(540) 375-2270**
(800) 388-2276; (540) 375-2267

Full-time: 806 men, 1158 women	**Faculty:** 167; IIB, av$
Part-time: 35 men, 30 women	**Ph.D.s:** 83%
Graduate: n/av	**Student/Faculty:** 12 to 1
Year: semesters, summer session	**Tuition:** $36,472
Application Deadline: March 15	**Room & Board:** $11,524
Freshman Class: 4167 applied, 3034 accepted, 542 enrolled	
SAT CR/M/W: 540/540/530 **ACT:** 24	**COMPETITIVE+**

Roanoke College provides its 2,100 students with a true classic college experience with a focus on personal connections. Students receive a strong liberal arts foundation through a unique Intellectual Inquiry core curriculum emphasizing learning firsthand through topic based courses where fundamental concepts and skills are taught and then applied to real problems and issues. The college offers undergraduate programs in the arts and sciences and in business administration. There is one undergraduate school. In addition to regional accreditation, Roanoke has baccalaureate program accreditation with ACBSP and TEAC. The library contains 224,958 volumes, 157,966 microform items, and 7,962 audio/video tapes/CDs/DVDs, and subscribes to 82,673 periodicals including electronic. Computerized library services include interlibrary loans, database searching, Internet access, and Wi-Fi capability. Special learning facilities include an art gallery, radio station, media classrooms, a video production facility, and multimedia computer labs. The 80-acre campus is in a suburban area 7 miles west of Roanoke, VA, in the Blue Ridge Mountains. Including any residence halls, there are 69 buildings.

Student Life: 53% of undergraduates are from Virginia. Others are from 38 states, 27 foreign countries, and Canada. 79% are from public schools. 86% are White. 34% are Protestant; 22% claim no religious affiliation; 18% Catholic. The average age of freshmen is 18; all undergraduates, 20. 19% do not continue beyond their first year; 65% remain to graduate.

Housing: 1572 students can be accommodated in college housing, which includes single-sex and coed dorms and on-campus apartments. In addition, there are honors houses, special-interest houses, fraternity houses, sorority houses, Five different Living Learning Communities within Residence Life. On-campus housing is guaranteed for the freshman year only, is available on a first-come, first-served basis, and is available on a lottery system for upperclassmen. Priority is given to out-of-town students. 79% of students live on campus. All students may keep cars.

Activities: 22% of men belong to 5 national fraternities; 26% of women belong to 5 national sororities. There are 100 groups on campus, including art, band, cheerleading, choir, chorale, chorus, computers, dance, debate, drama, environmental, ethnic, gay, honors, international, jazz band, literary magazine, newspaper, orchestra, pep band, photography, political, professional, radio and TV, religious, social, social service, and student government. Popular campus events include Family weekend, President's Ball, Fridays on the Quad (FOTQ), Winterfest and Alumni Weekend.

Sports: There are 9 intercollegiate sports for men and 10 for women, and 11 intramural sports for men and 9 for women. Facilities include A 1400 seat FieldTurf stadium, a 2400-seat gym, lighted turf athletic fields, an all-weather track, practice and playing fields, tennis and racquetball courts, a swimming pool, and a fitness center with weight training and physical conditioning equipment.

Disabled Students: 85% of the campus is accessible. Facilities include wheelchair ramps, elevators, special parking, specially equipped restrooms, special class scheduling, and special housing.

Services: Counseling and information services are available, as is tutoring in every subject. A supervised peer tutoring program is available at no charge to students, as well as a writing center and the Center for Learning and Teaching.

Campus Safety and Security: Measures include 24-hour foot and vehicle patrol, emergency notification system, self-defense education, and security escort services. There are shuttle buses, emergency telephones, lighted pathways/sidewalks, and controlled access to dorms/residences.

Programs of Study: Roanoke confers B.A., B.S. and B.B.A. degrees. Bachelor's degrees are awarded in AGRICULTURE (environmental studies), BIOLOGICAL SCIENCE (biochemistry and biology/biological science), BUSINESS (business administration and management and sports management), COMMUNICATIONS AND THE ARTS (art, art history and appreciation, communications, creative writing, French, literature, music, Spanish, and theatre arts), COMPUTER AND PHYSICAL SCIENCE (chemistry, computer science, mathematics, and physics), EDUCATION (athletic training and physical education), HEALTH PROFESSIONS (exercise science), SOCIAL SCIENCE (Christian studies, criminal justice, economics, history, international relations, philosophy, political science/government, psychology, religion, and sociology). Biology, chemistry, philosophy, and religious studies are the strongest academically. Business, biology, psychology have the largest enrollments.

Required: Requirements for graduation include completion of 33.5 courses, including about 9 to 12 in the major and about 11 to 14 in the Intellectual Inquiry core curriculum. The core consists of 2 first-year seminars; 5 to 7 topical courses drawn from the mathematical and natural sciences, the social sciences, and the humanities; a capstone that addresses a contemporary issue; and an intensive learning course. Students must also demonstrate competency in a foreign language at an intermediate level and complete 2 physical education courses. A 2.0 GPA is required.

Special: We offer cross-registration with Hollins University and study abroad in many countries. Roanoke also offers internships, research with faculty, a Washington semester, the Virginia at Oxford Program, a dual degree engineering degree with Virginia Polytechnic Institute and State University, credit by exam, and pass/fail options. A special May Term offers unique intensive travel and local experiences. Nondegree study is available to those students admitted with special status. There are 31 national honor societies, including Phi Beta Kappa, a freshman honors program, and 15 departmental honors programs.

Faculty/Classroom: 51% of faculty are male; 49% are female. All teach undergraduates, 78% do research, and 78% do both. No introductory courses are taught by graduate students. The average class size in an introductory lecture is 18; in a laboratory is 18; and in a regular course is 18.

Admissions: 73% of the 2013-2014 applicants were accepted. The SAT scores for the 2013-2014 freshman class were: Critical Reading--26% below 500, 46% between 500 and 599, 24% between 600 and 699, and 4% between 700 and 800; Math--28% below 500, 50% between 500 and 599, 21% between 600 and 699, and 2% between 700 and 800; Writing--30% below 500, 49% between 500 and 599, 18% between 600 and 699, and 3% between 700 and 800. The ACT scores were 22% below 21, 27% between 21 and 23, 28% between 24 and 26, 13% between 27 and 28, and 10% above 28. 35% of the current freshmen were in the top fifth of their class; 66% were in the top two fifths. There were 2 National Merit finalists. 5 freshmen graduated first in their class.

Requirements: The SAT or ACT is required. Recommendations, an essay, and an interview are recommended. Applicants must be graduates of accredited secondary schools or have earned a GED. The college requires 16 (20 recommended) academic units, based on 4 years of English, 3 courses in math, 4 courses in foreign language (recommended), and 2 courses each in lab science and social studies. An audition is also recommended for performing arts majors. AP and CLEP credits are accepted. Important factors in the admissions decision are advanced placement or honors courses, personality/intangible qualities, and leadership record.

Procedure: Freshmen are admitted fall and spring. Entrance exams should be taken by January of the senior year. There are early decision, deferred admissions, and rolling admissions plans. Early decision applications should be filed by November 1; regular applications, by March 15 for fall entry, along with a $30 fee. Notification of early decision is sent December 1; regular decision, on a Rolling basis. 164 early decision candidates were accepted for the 2013-2014 class. 112 applicants were on the 2013 waiting list; 12 were admitted. Applications are accepted online. Application fees are waived if application is completed online.

Transfer: 74 transfer students enrolled in 2012-2013. Transfers must have a minimum GPA of 2.2. SAT scores and an interview are recommended. Transfers must be in good academic standing with their previous institution. 17 of 34 credits required for the bachelor's degree must be completed at Roanoke.

Visiting: There are regularly scheduled orientations for prospective students, Open houses that provide a sampling of college life at Roanoke as well as discussing financial aid and admissions. Student/Faculty panels answer questions, and campus tours are given. There are guides for informal visits, visitors may sit in on classes, and stay overnight. To schedule a visit, contact the Admissions Office at (540) 375-2270.

Financial Aid: In 2013-2014, 97% of all full-time freshmen and 97% of continuing full-time students received some form of financial aid. 76% of all full-time freshmen and 74% of continuing full-time students received

need-based aid. The average freshman award was $29,320. Need-based scholarships or need-based grants averaged $25,205; and need-based self-help aid (loans and jobs) averaged $4,929. 33% of undergraduate students work part-time. Average annual earnings from campus work are $1681. The average financial indebtedness of the 2013 graduate was $32,311. The FAFSA and the state aid form are required. The priority date for freshman financial aid applications for fall entry is March 1.

International Students: There are 49 international students enrolled. The school actively recruits these students. They must take the TOEFL with a minimum score of 520 on the paper-based TOEFL (PBT) or 68 on the Internet-based version (iBT). They must also take the SAT or ACT.

Computers: All students may access the system any time. There are no time limits. The fee is $984.

Graduates: From July 1, 2012 to June 30, 2013, 452 bachelor's degrees were awarded. The most popular majors were business administration (18%), psychology (13%), and history (9%). 119 companies recruited on campus in 2012-2013. In an average class, 1% graduate in 3 years or less, 58% graduate in 4 years or less, 63% graduate in 5 years or less, and 64% graduate in 6 years or less. Of the 2012 graduating class, 39% were enrolled in graduate school within 6 months of graduation, and 87% were employed.

Admissions Contact: Dr. Brenda Poggendorf, Vice President of Enrollment. E-Mail: *admissions@roanoke.edu* Web: *www.roanoke.edu*

SAINT PAUL'S COLLEGE E-4

Lawrenceville, VA 23868 (434) 848-6492
(800) 678-7071; (434) 848-1862

Full-time: 330 men, 310 women	**Faculty:** n/av
Part-time: 10 men, 40 women	**Ph.D.s:** 59%
Graduate: n/av	**Student/Faculty:** n/av
Year: semesters, summer session	**Tuition:** $13,100
Application Deadline: open	**Room & Board:** $7700
Freshman Class: n/av	
SAT: required	NONCOMPETITIVE

Saint Paul's College, founded in 1888, is a small, private liberal arts college affiliated with the Protestant Episcopal Church offering undergraduate programs in arts and sciences, business, and teacher education. The figures in the above capsule and this profile are approximate. The library contains 41,500 volumes, 29,000 microform items, and 914 audio/video tapes/CDs/DVDs, and subscribes to 167 periodicals including electronic. Computerized library services include interlibrary loans, database searching, and Internet access. Special learning facilities include a learning resource center. The 180-acre campus is in a small town 55 miles south of Petersburg and 80 miles South of Richmond. Including any residence halls, there are 34 buildings.

Student Life: 67% of undergraduates are from Virginia. Others are from 19 states and 6 foreign countries. 99% are from public schools. 96% are African American. 90% are Protestant. The average age of freshmen is 19; all undergraduates, 21. 45% do not continue beyond their first year; 55% remain to graduate.

Housing: 431 students can be accommodated in college housing, which includes single-sex dorms. In addition, there are special-interest houses and single-parent housing. On-campus housing is guaranteed for the freshman year only and is available on a lottery system for upperclassmen. 62% of students live on campus; of those, 52% remain on campus on weekends. Alcohol is not permitted. All students may keep cars.

Activities: 7% of men belong to 5 national fraternities; 5% of women belong to 3 national sororities. There are 22 groups on campus, including art, cheerleading, chess, choir, communications, dance, drama, ethnic, honors, pep band, political, religious, social service, student government, Students in Free Enterprise, and Virginia Highway Safety Project. Popular campus events include a lecture and concert series, College for a Day, and Founders Day.

Sports: There are 7 intercollegiate sports for men and 7 for women, and 2 intramural sports for men and 2 for women. Facilities include a gym, baseball and football fields, practice fields, and tennis courts.

Disabled Students: 30% of the campus is accessible. Facilities include wheelchair ramps, elevators, special parking, specially equipped restrooms, and lowered drinking fountains.

Services: Counseling and information services are available, as is tutoring in most subjects. There is remedial math, reading, and writing.

Campus Safety and Security: Measures include 24-hour foot and vehicle patrol, self-defense education, and security escort services. There are shuttle buses, emergency telephones, and lighted pathways/sidewalks.

Programs of Study: SPC confers B.A., B.S., and B.S.Ed. degrees. Bachelor's degrees are awarded in BIOLOGICAL SCIENCE (biology/biological science, marine biology, and marine science), BUSINESS (business administration and management), COMMUNICATIONS AND THE ARTS (English), COMPUTER AND PHYSICAL SCIENCE (mathematics), EDUCATION (business education, elementary education, and secondary education), ENGINEERING AND ENVIRONMENTAL DESIGN (environmental science), SOCIAL SCIENCE (law enforcement and corrections, political science/government, social science, and sociology). Organizational management is the strongest academically. Business administration has the largest enrollment.

Required: All students must complete 42 semester hours of general education requirements, including courses in humanities, natural science and math, social sciences, health and phys ed, and computer information systems. A minimum of 120 hours, including at least 30 in the major, with at least a 2.0 GPA is required to graduate. Students in the Organizational Management Program (OMP) are required to write a thesis. All students must take PRAXIS for teacher certification.

Special: Cross-registration is possible with members of the Southside Higher Education Consortium and with Richard Bland College and Parkland College. Minors and the B.A.-B.S. degree are offered in most disciplines. Nonmajor preprofessional programs are available in the health professions. Endorsements in early childhood, middle, and secondary education are available in appropriate majors. Co-op programs in aquatic science and environmentive science, a general studies degree, and work-study programs are available. Nondegree study is possible. There are 2 national honor societies, a freshman honors program, and 3 departmental honors programs.

Faculty/Classroom: 62% of faculty are male; 38% are female. All teach undergraduates, and 6% both teach and do research. The average class size in an introductory lecture is 15; in a laboratory, 8; and in a regular course, 10.

Requirements: The SAT is required. In addition, applicants should be graduates of an accredited secondary school and have completed 16 academic units, including English, math, science, and social sciences. A GPA of 2.0 is required. AP and CLEP credits are accepted. Important factors in the admissions decision are recommendations by school officials, leadership record, and evidence of special talent.

Procedure: Freshmen are admitted fall and spring. Entrance exams should be taken during the senior year of high school. There are early decision, early admissions and rolling admissions plans. Application deadlines are open. The application fee is $20. Notification is sent on a rolling basis.

Transfer: Transfer applicants must supply all former official high school and college transcripts as well as a background form completed by the former college. 30 of 120 credits required for the bachelor's degree must be completed at SPC.

Visiting: There are regularly scheduled orientations for prospective students, including an open house, College for a Day, and Honors Convocation. There are guides for informal visits; visitors may sit in on classes and stay overnight. To schedule a visit, contact Vice President for Student Affairs.

Financial Aid: SPC is a member of CSS. The FAFSA and the state aid form are required. Check with the school for current application deadlines.

International Students: They must take the TOEFL. They must also take the SAT or ACT.

Computers: All students may access the system Monday through Friday from 3 a.m. to 6 p.m. There are no time limits. It is strongly recommended that all students have a personal computer.

Admissions Contact: Admissions Office. E-Mail: *admissions@saintpauls.edu* Web: *www.saintpauls.edu*

SHENANDOAH UNIVERSITY D-1

Winchester, VA 22601 (540) 665-4581
(800) 432-2266; (540) 665-4627

Full-time: 771 men, 1020 women	**Faculty:** 166	
Part-time: 77 men, 282 women	**Ph.D.s:** 79%	
Graduate: 533 men, 1320 women	**Student/Faculty:** 11 to 1	
Year: semesters, summer session	**Tuition:** $29,704	
Application Deadline: open	**Room & Board:** $9564	
Freshman Class: 1619 applied, 1362 accepted, 418 enrolled		
SAT CR/M/W: 480/490/470	**ACT:** 21	COMPETITIVE

Shenandoah University, founded in 1875, is a private university, affiliated with the United Methodist Church and offering undergraduate programs in arts and sciences, nursing, respiratory care, business, music, theater, and dance. Graduate programs include: business, music, performance, pedagogy, music education, education, nursing and pharmacy; health professions include: athletic training, occupational therapy, physical therapy, and physician assistant studies. There are 4 undergraduate schools and 7 graduate schools. In addition to regional accreditation, Shenandoah, SU has baccalaureate program accreditation with AACSB, ACPE, NASM, NLN, and TEAC. The 2 libraries contain 130,954 volumes, 56,680 microform items, and 24,193 audio/video tapes/CDs/DVDs, and subscribe to 86,490 periodicals including electronic. Computerized library services include interlibrary loans, database searching, Internet access, and Wi-Fi capability. Special learning facilities include an art gallery, Children's Literature Center in the library, Claude Moore Center for Literacy in the School of Education, Pharmacy Apothecary Museum, arts and media centers, conservatory, recording studio, Feltner Museum, Environmental Studies green rooftop garden, launched All Steinway School initiative, Cool Spring Campus, a model computer classroom in the School of Education, as well as the Academic Enrichment Center. The 315-acre campus is in a small town 72 miles west of Washington, D.C. Including any residence halls, there are 47 buildings.

Student Life: 65% of undergraduates are from Virginia. Others are from 47 states, 55 foreign countries, and Canada. 66% are White; 13% African American. 49% are Protestant; 21% claim no religious affiliation; 11% Catholic. The average age of freshmen is 18; all undergraduates, 21. 34% do not continue beyond their first year; 37% remain to graduate.

Housing: 914 students can be accommodated in college housing, which includes coed dorms and off-campus apartments. In addition, there are honors houses and special-interest houses. On-campus housing is guaranteed for the freshman year only, is available on a first-come, first-served basis, and is available on a lottery system for upperclassmen. 60% of students commute. All students may keep cars.

Activities: There are no fraternities or sororities. There are 75 groups on campus, including art, band, Campus Activity Network- a group of students that work with the department of student activities to provide activities on campus, cheerleading, choir, chorale, chorus, dance, drama, environmental, ethnic, film, honors, international, jazz band, literary magazine, musical theater, newspaper, orchestra, pep band, political, professional, religious, social, social service, student government, and symphony. Popular campus events include Movie Nights, Wine Tasting, Jazz Trio Social, Relay for Life, Welcome Back, Sun Block Party, International Days, Homecoming and Family Weekend.

Sports: There are 10 intercollegiate sports for men and 10 for women, and 7 intramural sports for men and 7 for women. Facilities include Shentel Stadium for football, men's and women's soccer, field hockey, and men's and women's lacrosse; 1 practice soccer field, 1 practice football field, Shingleton Gym for men's and women's basketball and volleyball, 4-lane 400-meter track, 1 multi-use grass field for practice and intramurals; indoor athletics facility with batting cages, armory, 1 weight room, 1 fitness room. The fitness room in the Brandt Center has cardio equipment, dumbbells, and selectorized weights. The weight room in Aikens has racks, weights, benches, and free weights. Armory has indoor athletics facility with batting cages.

Disabled Students: 91% of the campus is accessible. Facilities include wheelchair ramps, elevators, special parking, specially equipped restrooms, special class scheduling, lowered drinking fountains, special housing.

Services: Counseling and information services are available, as is tutoring in every subject.

Campus Safety and Security: Measures include 24-hour foot and vehicle patrol, emergency notification system, self-defense education, and security escort services. There are shuttle buses, emergency telephones, lighted pathways/sidewalks, controlled access to dorms/residences, Lockout car and dead-car battery jump assistance; online ICE program - In Case of Emergency, online program: Safer in 60 Seconds; orientation attendees get an emergency preparedness list; Emergency Operation Plan Program, each campus building has an emergency coordinator and outfitted with emergency preparedness items.

Programs of Study: Shenandoah, SU confers B.A., B.S., B.B.A., B.F.A, B.M. and B.M.T. degrees. Master's and doctoral degrees are also awarded. Bachelor's degrees are awarded in BIOLOGICAL SCIENCE (biology/biological science), BUSINESS (business administration and management, entrepreneurial studies, and sports management), COMMUNICATIONS AND THE ARTS (acting, church music, collaborative piano, communications, composition, costume design, dance, dramatic arts, English, jazz, music, music production/recording technology, music performance, music technology, music theatre accompanying , music theory and composition, musical theater, performing arts, piano/organ, scenic and lighting design, Spanish, theatre arts, theater design, and theater management), COMPUTER AND PHYSICAL SCIENCE (chemistry and mathematics), EDUCATION (core studies, dance education, music education, outdoor leadership/education, and university studies), ENGINEERING AND ENVIRONMENTAL DESIGN (environmental science), HEALTH PROFESSIONS (exercise science, health care administration, kinesiology, music therapy, nursing, public health, and respiratory therapy), SOCIAL SCIENCE (criminal justice, history, law enforcement and corrections, liberal arts/general studies, physical fitness/movement, political science/ government, psychology, public administration, religion, religious music, social science, and sociology). Political science, math, and dance are the strongest academically. Nursing, business administration, and kinesiology have the largest enrollments.

Required: To graduate, all students must have taken the required core curriculum with a cumulative grade-point average of 2.0. Some programs require higher grade-point average in the major. The minimum number of credit hours required for a baccalaureate degree is 120. Other requirements vary depending on the program of study. Twenty-four of the last 30 credit hours required in a baccalaureate degree program must be earned at Shenandoah University.

Special: Internships; dual majors (Pharm-MBA, MSN-MBA, DPT/MSAT); Accelerated degree programs: ASD NUR.BS, 3+2 model with AT, 3+4 model with PharmD); cross-registration consortiums (Collaborative Agreements) with James Madison University (Nursing), Johns Hopkins School of Nursing, Marshall University School of Nursing, Old Dominion University School of Nursing, Radford University School of Nursing, West Virginia Wesleyan Department of Nursing, George Washington University (Pharmacy); B.A. interdisciplinary studies; study abroad: Choice of 166 Global Partner institutions among 55 nations; no work-study programs; non-degree study is possible. There are 5 national honor societies.

Faculty/Classroom: 44% of faculty are male; 56% are female. 70% teach undergraduates. No introductory courses are taught by graduate students. The average class size in an introductory lecture is 17; in a laboratory is 12; and in a regular course is 13.

Admissions: 84% of the 2013-2014 applicants were accepted. The SAT scores for the 2013-2014 freshman class were: Critical Reading--57% below 500, 34% between 500 and 599, 7% between 600 and 699, and 2% between 700 and 800; Math--55% below 500, 33% between 500 and 599, 11% between 600 and 699, and 1% between 700 and 800; Writing--63% below 500, 27% between 500 and 599, 8% between 600 and 699, and 2% between 700 and 800. The ACT scores were 46% below 21, 28% between 21 and 23, 13% between 24 and 26, 6% between 27 and 28, and 7% above 28. 18% of the current freshmen were in the top fifth of their class; 51% were in the top two fifths. 3 freshmen graduated first in their class.

Requirements: The SAT is required. The high school transcript should indicate courses pursued, grades earned, grade point average and credits earned. It is required that the coursework include: four units of English, three units of Mathematics (Algebra I, Algebra II and Geometry), and two units of science (including one laboratory science). Two units of a foreign language are strongly recommended. Other classes may be appropriate for some curricula and will be evaluated on an individual basis by the Office of Admissions. Applicants are strongly recommended to indicate community and extra-curricular involvement. Shenandoah Conservatory applicants are also required to successfully complete an audition or portfolio review. The most heavily weighted factor in the applicant's total profile is actual academic performance, as indicated by the high school transcript. A GPA of 2.5 is required. AP and CLEP credits are accepted. Important factors in the admissions decision are advanced placement or honors courses, extracurricular activities record, and evidence of special talent.

Procedure: Freshmen are admitted fall and spring. Entrance exams should be taken By junior year or early in the senior year. There are deferred admissions and rolling admissions plans. Application deadlines are open. Application fee is $30. Notification is sent on a rolling basis. Applications are accepted online.

Transfer: 130 transfer students enrolled in 2012-2013. Transfer applicants must submit evidence of good standing at the college last attended and an official transcript(s) of credits earned at all institutions previously attended, showing entrance credits accepted and results of standardized tests administered. Transfer applicants who have completed fewer than 24 credits must also submit official high school transcripts. 30 of 120 credits required for the bachelor's degree must be completed at Shenandoah, SU.

Visiting: There are regularly scheduled orientations for prospective students, including information sessions with faculty and staff, student-guided campus tours, and lunch in the dining hall. There are guides for informal visits, visitors may sit in on classes, and stay overnight. To schedule a visit, contact Andrew Woodall at (800) 432-2266.

Financial Aid: In 2013-2014, 96% of all full-time freshmen and 98% of continuing full-time students received some form of financial aid. 76% of all full-time freshmen and 75% of continuing full-time students received need-based aid. The average freshman award was $25,688. Need-based scholarships or need-based grants averaged $6,992 ($10,000 maximum); need-based self-help aid (loans and jobs) averaged $4,268 ($5,500 maximum); and other non-need-based awards and non-need-based scholarships averaged $9,641 ($28,000 maximum). 49% of undergraduate students work part-time. Average annual earnings from campus work are $2000. The average financial indebtedness of the 2013 graduate was $28,738. The FAFSA the state aid form, and Virginia United Methodist Scholarship Application are required. Check with the school for current application deadlines.

International Students: There are 90 international students enrolled. The school actively recruits these students. They must take the TOEFL with a minimum score of 500 on the paper-based TOEFL (PBT) or 71 on the Internet-based version (iBT).

Computers: All students may access the system 24/7. There are no time limits. The fee is $160.

Graduates: From July 1, 2012 to June 30, 2013, 471 bachelor's degrees were awarded. The most popular majors were nursing (24%), kinesiology (10%), and psychology (7%). 59 companies recruited on campus in 2012-2013. In an average class, 25% graduate in 4 years or less, 35% graduate in 5 years or less, and 37% graduate in 6 years or less. Of the 2012 graduating class, 18% were enrolled in graduate school within 6 months of graduation, and 54% were employed.

Admissions Contact: Andrew Woodall, Exe Director of Recruitment & Admissions. E-Mail: *admit@su.edu* Web: *www.su.edu*

SWEET BRIAR COLLEGE D-3

Sweet Briar, VA 24595 (434) 381-6142
(800) 381-6142; (434) 381-6152

Full-time: 25 men, 670 women	**Faculty:** 78; IIB, -$
Part-time: 3 men, 25 women	**Ph.D.s:** 85%
Graduate: 16 women	**Student/Faculty:** 8 to 1
Year: semesters	**Tuition:** $32,325
Application Deadline: February 1	**Room & Board:** $11,440

Freshman Class: 763 applied, 605 accepted, 176 enrolled
SAT CR/M/W: 560/510/530 **ACT:** 25 **COMPETITIVE+**

Sweet Briar College, founded in 1901, is a private women's liberal arts institution. In addition to regional accreditation, Sweet Briar has baccalaureate program accreditation with ABET. The library contains 290,290 volumes, 400,024 microform items, and 10,280 audio/video tapes/CDs/DVDs. Computerized library services include interlibrary loans, database searching, Internet access, and Wi-Fi capability. Special learning facilities include an art gallery, radio station, college museum, observatory, and environmental education/nature center. The 3250-acre campus is in a rural area 165 miles southwest of Washington, D.C., 120 miles west of Richmond, 12 miles north of Lynchburg. Including any residence halls, there are 34 buildings.

Student Life: 50% of undergraduates are from out of state, mostly the South. Students are from 41 states, and 3 foreign countries. 85% are from public schools. 77% are White. The average age of freshmen is 18; all undergraduates, 20. 26% do not continue beyond their first year; 62% remain to graduate.

Housing: 625 students can be accommodated in college housing, which includes single-sex dorms and on-campus apartments. substance-free, first-year, and international housing for those interested in international affairs and languages. On-campus housing is guaranteed for all 4 years and is available on a lottery system for upperclassmen. 93% of students live on campus. All students may keep cars.

Activities: There are no fraternities or sororities. There are 52 groups on campus, including riding clubs, chemistry, outdoor, art, choir, chorus, communications, computers, dance, drama, environmental, ethnic, gay, health-related, honors, international, literary magazine, musical theater, newspaper, orchestra, photography, political, professional, radio and TV, religious, social, social service, student government, symphony, and yearbook. Popular campus events include Spring Fling, Step Singing and Dell Parties.

Sports: There are 6 intercollegiate sports for women, and 3 intramural sports for women. Facilities include a natatorium, a gym, a weight room, a pathway and trail system for walking, biking, and a riding, 14 tennis courts, a riding center, soccer/lacrosse/field hockey fields, a fitness circuit, primitive campgrounds, and 2 lakes.

Disabled Students: Facilities include wheelchair ramps, elevators, special parking, specially equipped restrooms, lowered drinking fountains, lowered telephones, and special housing.

Services: Counseling and information services are available, as is tutoring in most subjects.

Campus Safety and Security: Measures include 24-hour foot and vehicle patrol, emergency notification system, self-defense education, and security escort services. There are shuttle buses, emergency telephones, lighted pathways/sidewalks, controlled access to dorms/residences, gates manned by security personnel from 6 p.m. to 6 a.m., and locked dorms with student key access.

Programs of Study: Sweet Briar confers B.A., B.S. and B.F.A. degrees. Master's degrees are also awarded. Bachelor's degrees are awarded in AGRICULTURE (environmental studies), BIOLOGICAL SCIENCE (biochemistry and biology/biological science), BUSINESS (business administration and management), COMMUNICATIONS AND THE ARTS (art history and appreciation, creative writing, dance, dramatic arts, English, French, German, modern language, music, musical theater, Spanish, and studio art), COMPUTER AND PHYSICAL SCIENCE (chemistry, mathematics, and physics), ENGINEERING AND ENVIRONMENTAL DESIGN (engineering and applied science, engineering management, and environmental science), SOCIAL SCIENCE (anthropology, archeology, classical/ancient civilization, economics, German area studies, history, interdisciplinary studies, international relations, liberal arts/general studies, philosophy, political science/government, psychology, religion, sociology, and Spanish studies). Business, biology, and psychology have the largest enrollments.

Required: To graduate, students must complete 120 credits, of which 60 must be earned at Sweet Briar, with a minimum GPA of 2.0. 30 to 36 must be in the major. In addition to major requirements, specific degree requirements include English: Thought and Expression. Students must take 7 hours in scientific theory and experiment; 6 in global cultures; 4 in study or practice of the arts; 3 each in Western culture, social science, literature, and economic, political, or legal systems; and 2 in physical activity. Students must demonstrate proficiency in oral and written communication, quantitative reasoning, and a foreign language. A senior capstone course/experience is also required.

Special: The college offers a coordinate program in general business management and arts management, as well as internships to explore career opportunities and gain work experience. Study abroad, a Washington semester with American University, student-designed and interdisciplinary majors, accelerated degree programs, and 3-2 engineering degrees with Columbia University, Washington University in St. Louis, Virginia Polytechnic Institute, and University of Virginia are available. Cross-registration with Lynchburg and Randolph-Macon Woman's Colleges (the Tri-College Consortium) and the Seven College Exchange is also possible. There are 10 national honor societies, including Phi Beta Kappa, and a freshman honors program.

Faculty/Classroom: 50% of faculty are male; 50% are female. All teach undergraduates, and all teach and do research. No introductory courses are taught by graduate students. The average class size in a regular course is 11.

Admissions: 79% of the 2013-2014 applicants were accepted. The SAT scores for the 2013-2014 freshman class were: Critical Reading--28% below 500, 42% between 500 and 599, 24% between 600 and 699, and 6% between 700 and 800; Math--42% below 500, 42% between 500 and 599, 13% between 600 and 699, and 3% between 700 and 800; Writing--39% below 500, 37% between 500 and 599, 23% between 600 and 699, and 1% between 700 and 800. The ACT scores were 15% below 21, 23% between 21 and 23, 32% between 24 and 26, 17% between 27 and 28, and 12% above 28.

Requirements: The SAT or ACT is required. The Admissions Committee looks for qualities such as independent thinking, ethical principles, assertiveness, initiative, and appreciation of diversity. Requirements normally include a minimum of 4 units in English, 3 in math, 3 in social studies, 2 sequential years in a foreign language, and 3 units in science, as well as additional units in these subjects to total 16. Most candidates have 20 such academic units. An interview is strongly encouraged but not required. AP credits are accepted. Important factors in the admissions decision are recommendations by school officials, leadership record, and advanced placement or honors courses.

Procedure: Freshmen are admitted fall and spring. Entrance exams should be taken by Spring of the junior year and/or fall of the senior year. There are early admissions and deferred admissions plans. Applications should be filed by February 1 for fall entry; November 1 for spring entry, along with a $40 fee. Notifications are sent March 1. Applications are accepted online.

Transfer: 21 transfer students enrolled in 2012-2013. Transfer applicants must submit official transcripts from high school and college, test scores, a college catalog, and recommendations from a previous dean and professor, and a statement explaining why the applicant wishes to transfer, and why the applicant is interested in Sweet Briar. 60 of 120 credits required for the bachelor's degree must be completed at Sweet Briar.

Visiting: There are regularly scheduled orientations for prospective students, consisting of attendance at classes and campus events, meetings with faculty and coaches, an overnight stay in a dorm, a campus tour, and more. There are guides for informal visits, visitors may sit in on classes, and stay overnight. To schedule a visit, contact Campus Visit Coordinator at (800) 381-6142.

Financial Aid: In 2013-2014, 100% of all full-time freshmen and 97% of continuing full-time students received some form of financial aid. 66% of all full-time freshmen and 53% of continuing full-time students received need-based aid. The average freshman award was $29,040. Need-based scholarships or need-based grants averaged $21,729 ($44,276 maximum); need-based self-help aid (loans and jobs) averaged $9,747 ($29,031 maximum); and other non-need-based awards and non-need-based scholarships averaged $12,567 ($31,850 maximum). 70% of undergraduate students work part-time. Average annual earnings from campus work are $1000. The average financial indebtedness of the 2013 graduate was $23,596. The FAFSA and the college's own financial statement, and non-custodial parents statement are required. The priority date for freshman financial aid applications for fall entry is February 15. The deadline for filing freshman financial aid applications for fall entry is April 15.

International Students: There are 15 international students enrolled. The school actively recruits these students. They must take the TOEFL with a minimum score of 550 on the paper-based TOEFL (PBT). They must also take the SAT or ACT.

Computers: All students may access the system 24 hours a day. There are no time limits and no fees.

Graduates: From July 1, 2012 to June 30, 2013, 154 bachelor's degrees were awarded. The most popular majors were business management (17%), biology (14%), and English and creative writing (10%). 49 companies recruited on campus in 2012-2013. In an average class, 2% graduate in 3 years or less, 61% graduate in 4 years or less, 62% graduate in 5 years or less, and 62% graduate in 6 years or less. Of the 2012 graduating class, 34% were enrolled in graduate school within 6 months of graduation, and 64% were employed.

Admissions Contact: Steven Nape, Dean of Enrollment Management. E-Mail: *admissions@sbc.edu* Web: *www.sbc.edu*

UNIVERSITY OF MARY WASHINGTON E-2

Fredericksburg, VA 22401 (540) 654-2000
(800) 468-5614; (540) 654-1857

Full-time: 1357 men, 2524 women **Faculty:** 244; IIB, av$
Part-time: 244 men, 390 women **Ph.D.s:** 89%
Graduate: 176 men, 402 women **Student/Faculty:** 14 to 1
Year: semesters, summer session **Tuition:** $9546 ($21,560)
Application Deadline: February 1 **Room & Board:** $10,238
Freshman Class: 4847 applied, 3724 accepted, 955 enrolled
SAT CR/M/W: 570/560/560 **ACT:** 25 **VERY COMPETITIVE**

The University of Mary Washington is a premier, selective public liberal arts and sciences university in Virginia, highly respected for its commitment to academic excellence, strong undergraduate liberal arts and sciences program, and dedication to life-long learning. The university, with a total enrollment of more than 5,000, features colleges of business, education and arts and sciences, and three campuses, including a residential campus in Fredericksburg, Va., a second one in nearby Stafford and a third in Dahlgren, Va., which serves as a center of development of educational and research partnerships between the Navy, higher education institutions and the region's employers. There are 3 undergraduate schools and 2 graduate schools. In addition to regional accreditation, has baccalaureate program accreditation with NASM. The 2 libraries contain 424,417 volumes, 610,498 microform items, and 2,206 audio/video tapes/CDs/DVDs, and subscribe to 62,985 periodicals including electronic. Computerized library services include interlibrary loans, database searching, Internet access, and Wi-Fi capability. Special learning facilities include an art gallery, radio station, the Center for Historic Preservation, Leidecker Center for Asian Studies, and James Farmer Multicultural Center. The 176-acre campus is in a suburban area 50 miles south of Washington, D.C., and 50 miles north of Richmond. Including any residence halls, there are 48 buildings.

Student Life: 87% of undergraduates are from Virginia. Others are from 38 states, 23 foreign countries, and Canada. 87% are from public schools. 64% are White; 14% race unknown. The average age of freshmen is 18; all undergraduates, 22. 17% do not continue beyond their first year; 76% remain to graduate.

Housing: 2820 students can be accommodated in college housing, which includes single-sex and coed dorms and on-campus apartments. In addition, there are language houses, special-interest houses, Living and learning communities, including gender neutral and international housing. On-campus housing is available on a lottery system for upperclassmen. 61% of students live on campus; of those, 80% remain on campus on weekends. Upperclassmen may keep cars.

Activities: There are no fraternities or sororities. There are 140 groups on campus, including Students Helping Honduras, art, bagpipe, cheerleading, choir, chorale, chorus, Class council, computers, dance, debate, drama, environmental, ethnic, film, gay, honors, international, jazz band, literary magazine, musical theater, newspaper, opera, orchestra, pep band, photography, political, professional, radio and TV, religious, social, social service, student government, symphony, and yearbook. Popular campus events include Rocktoberfest, Junior Ring Dance and Multicultural Fair.

Sports: There are 10 intercollegiate sports for men and 12 for women, and 16 intramural sports for men and 20 for women. Facilities include a lighted, all-weather-turf recreational sports field, 6-lane, 25-yard indoor pool, regulation basketball and volleyball courts, a weight room, batting cages, training rooms, playing fields for all outdoor sports, a running course, handball/racquetball courts, an 8-lane, 400-meter track, a 20,000-square-foot fitness and recreation facility, and an indoor tennis center.

Disabled Students: 75% of the campus is accessible. Facilities include wheelchair ramps, elevators, special parking, specially equipped restrooms, lowered drinking fountains, lowered telephones, and special housing.

Services: Counseling and information services are available, as is tutoring in most subjects. There is a reader service for the blind.

Campus Safety and Security: Measures include 24-hour foot and vehicle patrol, emergency notification system, self-defense education, and security escort services. There are emergency telephones, lighted pathways/sidewalks, and controlled access to dorms/residences.

Programs of Study: confers B.A., B.S. and B.L.S. degrees. Master's degrees are also awarded. Bachelor's degrees are awarded in BIOLOGICAL SCIENCE (biology/biological science), BUSINESS (business administration and management), COMMUNICATIONS AND THE ARTS (art history and appreciation, classics, dramatic arts, English, French, German, historic preservation, music, Spanish, and studio art), COMPUTER AND PHYSICAL SCIENCE (chemistry, computer science, mathematics, and physics), ENGINEERING AND ENVIRONMENTAL DESIGN (environmental science), SOCIAL SCIENCE (American studies, anthropology, economics, geography, history, international relations, liberal arts/general studies, philosophy, political science/government, psychology, religion, and sociology). Historic preservation, history, political science, international affairs, English, biology, psychology, earth and environmental sciences are the strongest academically. Business administration, psychology, biology, English, and history have the largest enrollments.

Required: To graduate, students must complete 120 credit hours and a minimum GPA of 2.0. Hours required in the major vary. The B.A. and B.S. general education curriculum includes a first-year seminar, courses in quantitative reasoning, natural science, human experience and society, global inquiry, language, arts, literature and performance, and experiential learning. The experiential learning requirement may be fulfilled through study abroad, service learning, undergraduate research, or career internships. Students complete 4 writing-intensive courses and 2 speaking-intensive courses from across the curriculum. A thesis is required in some majors and programs of study. The B.L.S. degreee program is a flexible, adult-oriented alternative that features slightly different requirements.

Special: Study abroad anywhere in the world, a Washington semester, and credit for off-campus work experience are available. The university offers dual majors, work-study programs, student-designed majors, and pass/fail options. More than 500 internships for credit are also available. Teacher licensure preparation is offered for elementary and secondary education. Elementary education is a 5-year bachelor's-master's degree program. There are 23 national honor societies, including Phi Beta Kappa, and a freshman honors program.

Faculty/Classroom: 51% of faculty are male; 49% are female. All teach undergraduates. No introductory courses are taught by graduate students. The average class size in an introductory lecture is 27; in a laboratory is 22; and in a regular course is 20.

Admissions: 77% of the 2013-2014 applicants were accepted. The SAT scores for the 2013-2014 freshman class were: Critical Reading--10% below 500, 42% between 500 and 599, 37% between 600 and 699, and 10% between 700 and 800; Math--14% below 500, 47% between 500 and 599, 34% between 600 and 699, and 4% between 700 and 800; Writing--12% below 500, 45% between 500 and 599, 37% between 600 and 699, and 6% between 700 and 800. The ACT scores were 7% below 21, 24% between 21 and 23, 34% between 24 and 26, 18% between 27 and 28, and 17% above 28. There were 3 National Merit finalists. 5 freshmen graduated first in their class.

Requirements: The SAT or ACT and ACT Writing Test are recommended. Applicants must be graduates of an accredited secondary school or hold the GED. The Admissions Committee recommends that applicants complete 4 years of each of math, English, foreign language, science, and social studies. A SAT subject test is strongly recommended. Application essays are required. A counselor or teacher recommendation is also required. AP and CLEP credits are accepted. Important factors in the admissions decision are advanced placement or honors courses, evidence of special talent, and recommendations by school officials.

Procedure: Freshmen are admitted fall and spring. Entrance exams should be taken by January of the senior year. There are early admissions and deferred admissions plans. Applications should be filed by February 1 for fall entry; November 1 for spring entry, along with a $50 fee. Notifications are sent April 1. 352 applicants were on the 2013 waiting list; 73 were admitted. Applications are accepted online.

Transfer: 309 transfer students enrolled in 2012-2013. The university recommends that applicants for transfer have a minimum GPA of 3.0 and 30 college credits. The SAT and high school transcripts are required. Graduates from Virginia community colleges are given preference for admission. 30 of 120 credits required for the bachelor's degree must be completed at UMW.

Visiting: There are regularly scheduled orientations for prospective students, including information sessions, available Monday through Friday at 10:30 a.m. and 2 p.m., followed by a student-guided tour, and 2 Saturday open houses each semester. Visitors may sit in on classes and stay overnight. To schedule a visit, contact the Office of Admissions.

Financial Aid: In 2013-2014, 66% of all full-time freshmen and 63% of continuing full-time students received some form of financial aid. 34% of all full-time freshmen and 32% of continuing full-time students received need-based aid. The average freshman award was $4,800. Need-based scholarships or need-based grants averaged $6,493 ($2,455 maximum); need-based self-help aid (loans and jobs) averaged $3,324 ($7,500 maximum); and other non-need-based awards and non-need-based scholarships averaged $15,423 ($30,371 maximum). 28% of undergraduate students work part-time. Average annual earnings from campus work are $2175. The average financial indebtedness of the 2013 graduate was $23,300. The FAFSA and the college's own financial statement are required. The deadline for filing freshman financial aid applications for fall entry is March 1.

International Students: There are 38 international students enrolled. The school actively recruits these students. They must take the TOEFL with a minimum score of 88 on the Internet-based version (iBT). They must also take the SAT or ACT.

Computers: All students may access the system. There are no time limits and no fees.

Graduates: From July 1, 2012 to June 30, 2013, 868 bachelor's degrees were awarded. The most popular majors were English (11%), business administration (11%), and psychology (9%). 100 companies recruited on campus in 2012-2013. In an average class, 69% graduate in 4 years or less, 75% graduate in 5 years or less, and 76% graduate in 6 years or less. Of the 2012 graduating class, 24% were enrolled in graduate school within 6 months of graduation, and 95% were employed.

Admissions Contact: Carol Descak, Assoc Provost, Admissions & Finan Aid. E-Mail: *admit@umw.edu* Web: *www.umw.edu*

UNIVERSITY OF RICHMOND E-3

University of Richmond, VA 23173 (804) 289-8640 (800) 700-1662; (804) 287-6003

Full-time: 1393 men, 1549 women	**Faculty:** 318; IIB, +$
Part-time: 28 men, 13 women	**Ph.D.s:** 93%
Graduate: 303 men, 245 women	**Student/Faculty:** 9 to 1
Year: semesters, summer session	**Tuition:** $45,320
Application Deadline: January 15	**Room & Board:** $10,270
Freshman Class: 9825 applied, 3061 accepted, 805 enrolled	
SAT CR/M/W: 640/660/650	**ACT:** 30

The University of Richmond provides a collaborative learning and research environment unlike any other in higher education, offering students an extraordinary combination of the liberal arts with law, business and leadership studies. There are 3 undergraduate schools and 2 graduate schools. In addition to regional accreditation, UR has baccalaureate program accreditation with AACSB. The 3 libraries contain 526,568 volumes, 13,558 microform items, and 30,034 audio/video tapes/CDs/DVDs, and subscribe to 333,950 periodicals including electronic. Computerized library services include interlibrary loans, database searching, Internet access, and Wi-Fi capability. Special learning facilities include an art gallery, radio station, Joel and Lila Harnett Print Study Center, the Museum of Art and The Lora Robins Gallery of Design from Nature. The 350-acre campus is in a suburban area 6 miles west of Richmond. Including any residence halls, there are 95 buildings.

Student Life: 80% of undergraduates are from out of state, mostly the Northeast. Students are from 46 states, 74 foreign countries, and Canada. 57% are from public schools. 57% are White; 12% Foreign. The average age of freshmen is 18; all undergraduates, 20. 6% do not continue beyond their first year; 94% remain to graduate.

Housing: 2786 students can be accommodated in college housing, which includes single-sex and coed dorms and on-campus apartments. In addition, there are special-interest houses. On-campus housing is available on a first-come, first-served basis, and is available on a lottery system for upperclassmen. 87% of students live on campus; of those, 90% remain on campus on weekends. All students may keep cars.

Activities: 13% of men belong to 7 national fraternities; 22% of women belong to 7 national sororities. There are 177 groups on campus, including art, band, cheerleading, choir, chorale, chorus, communications, computers, dance, debate, drama, drill team, environmental, ethnic, gay, honors, international, jazz band, literary magazine, musical theater, newspaper, orchestra, pep band, political, professional, radio and TV, religious, social, social service, and student government. Popular campus events include Proclamation Night, Investiture Ceremony and Midnight Mayhem.

Sports: There are 7 intercollegiate sports for men and 9 for women. Facilities include a 10,000-seat gym, a football stadium, a soccer/track complex, lighted intramural fields, an intramural gym, aerobics and weight rooms, a swimming pool, and tennis, racquetball, and squash courts.

Disabled Students: 90% of the campus is accessible. Facilities include wheelchair ramps, elevators, special parking, specially equipped restrooms, and lowered drinking fountains.

Services: Counseling and information services are available, as is tutoring in most subjects. There are support centers for help with academic skills, writing, and speech.

Campus Safety and Security: Measures include 24-hour foot and vehicle patrol, emergency notification system, self-defense education, and security escort services. There are shuttle buses, emergency telephones, lighted pathways/sidewalks, a card-access system in all residence halls, vehicle assistance, emergency first aid service, fingerprinting, firearms storage, and personal property engraving and identification.

Programs of Study: UR confers B.A., B.S. and B.S.B.A. degrees. Master's and doctoral degrees are also awarded. Bachelor's degrees are awarded in AGRICULTURE (environmental studies), BIOLOGICAL SCIENCE (biochemistry, biology/biological science, and molecular biology), BUSINESS (accounting and business administration and management), COMMUNICATIONS AND THE ARTS (art history, communication rhetoric/communication, dance, English, French, german studies, Greek, journalism, Latin, music, Spanish, studio art, and theatre arts), COMPUTER AND PHYSICAL SCIENCE (chemistry, computer science, mathematics, and physics), SOCIAL SCIENCE (American studies, anthropology, Chinese Studies, classical/ancient civilization, cognitive science, criminal justice, economics, history, interdisciplinary studies, international studies, philosophy, political science/government, psychology, religion, Russian and Slavic studies, sociology, and women's studies). Business adminstration, international studies, and accounting are the largest.

Required: A candidate for the Bachelor of Arts, Bachelor of Science, or Bachelor of Science in Business Administration degree must satisfactorily complete all degree requirements and 35 units. Undergraduate degree candidates must earn a grade point average of not less than 2.00 on all coursework attempted and must receive credit for attendance at assemblies and convocations, as required. All undergraduate degrees at the University of Richmond require satisfactory completion of one major (9 -18.5 total units). Multiple majors and/or minors may also be pursued and upon completion will be recorded on the permanent academic record. In the Robins School of Business and Jepson School of Leadership Studies a student must complete the requirements for the degree, as stated in the catalog at the time of entrance, within five years from the date of original entry.

Special: Study abroad in Argentina, Australia, Austria, Barbados, Belgium, Bolivia, Bonaire, Botswana, Brazil, Cameroon, Chile, China, Costa Rica, the Czech Republic, Denmark, the Dominican Republic, Ecuador, France, Germany, Ghana, India, Indonesia, Ireland, Israel, Italy, Jamaica, Japan, Jordan, Kenya Coast Republic, Madagascar, Mali, Mexico, Mongolia, Morocco, Nepal, the Netherlands, New Zealand, Nicaragua, Panama, Peru, Poland, Portugal, the Russian Federation, Rwanda, Senegal, South Africa, South Korea, Spain, Sweden, Switzerland, Taiwan, Tanzania, Thailand, Trinidad and Tobago, Tunisia, Turkey, Turks and Caicos, Uganda, the United Kingdom, and Vietnam. -A 3-2 engineering degree program with Columbia University School of Engineering and Applied Science. There are 8 national honor societies, including Phi Beta Kappa, and 10 departmental honors programs.

Faculty/Classroom: 56% of faculty are male; 44% are female. All teach undergraduates. No introductory courses are taught by graduate students. The average class size in an introductory lecture is 15 and in a regular course is 16.

Admissions: 31% of the 2013-2014 applicants were accepted. The SAT scores for the 2013-2014 freshman class were: Critical Reading--4% below 500, 22% between 500 and 599, 52% between 600 and 699, and 21% between 700 and 800; Math--2% below 500, 16% between 500 and 599, 48% between 600 and 699, and 34% between 700 and 800; Writing--4% below 500, 19% between 500 and 599, 52% between 600 and 699, and 25% between 700 and 800. The ACT scores were 2% below 21, 2% between 21 and 23, 8% between 24 and 26, 19% between 27 and 28, and 69% above 28. 87% of the current freshmen were in the top fifth of their class; 99% were in the top two fifths. There were 6 National Merit finalists.

Requirements: The SAT or ACT is required. Candidates for admission must have a high school diploma (or recognized equivalent), and must have completed a minimum of 16 units of secondary school coursework. Minimum requirements include four units in English, three in college preparatory mathematics (including Algebra I, II, and Geometry), and at least two each in history, laboratory science, and foreign language (two units of the same language, not including American Sign Language, which will not satisfy the requirement for foreign language). Competitive candidates for admission typically exceed the minimum requirements and have taken four units in all five core areas at the highest levels available in their school setting. Applicants should submit the Common Application, and may submit SAT or ACT test scores. The University of Richmond's application review is need-blind, and the university guarantees to meet 100% of each family's demonstrated need. AP and CLEP credits are accepted.

Procedure: Freshmen are admitted fall. Entrance exams should be taken by February 1 of the senior year. There are early decision and deferred admissions plans. Early decision applications should be filed by November 15; regular applications, by January 15 for fall entry, along with a $50 fee. Notification of early decision is sent December 15; regular decision, April 1. 340 early decision candidates were accepted for the 2013-2014 class. 1641 applicants were on the 2013 waiting list; 95 were admitted. Applications are accepted online.

Transfer: 49 transfer students enrolled in 2012-2013. Applicants must have earned a minimum of 24 credit hours in transferable courses. A minimum GPA of 2.0 is required. 60 credits required for the bachelor's degree must be completed at UR.

Visiting: There are regularly scheduled orientations for prospective students, All first-time visitors are encouraged to schedule a regular campus visit, which typically includes an information session (a 45-minute presentation by an admission representative) and a campus tour (90-minute walking tour of campus led by a student). There are guides for informal visits and visitors may sit in on classes. To schedule a visit, contact the Admissions Office at (800) 289-8640.

Financial Aid: In 2013-2014, 57% of all full-time freshmen and 66% of continuing full-time students received some form of financial aid. 41% of all full-time freshmen and 40% of continuing full-time students received need-based aid. The average freshman award was $40,700. Need-based scholarships or need-based grants averaged $35,240; need-based self-help aid (loans and jobs) averaged $3,830; non-need-based athletic scholarships averaged $29,380; and other non-need-based awards and non-need-based scholarships averaged $39,785. 48% of undergraduate students work part-time. Average annual earnings from campus work are $1515. The average financial indebtedness of the 2013 graduate was $22,225. UR is a member of CSS. The CSS/Profile, FAFSA, the college's own financial statement, copies of parent and student federal tax return, and noncustodial parent profile are required. The deadline for filing freshman financial aid applications for fall entry is February 15.

International Students: There are 346 international students enrolled. The school actively recruits these students. They must take the TOEFL with a minimum score of 550 on the paper-based TOEFL (PBT) or 80 on the Internet-based version (iBT), . They must also take the SAT or ACT.

Computers: All students may access the system. There are no time limits and no fees.

Graduates: From July 1, 2012 to June 30, 2013, 858 bachelor's degrees were awarded. The most popular majors were business/marketing (39%), social sciences (16%), and biological/life sciences (9%). 139 companies recruited on campus in 2012-2013. In an average class, 81% graduate in 4 years or less, 85% graduate in 5 years or less, and 85% graduate in 6 years or less. Of the 2012 graduating class, 17% were enrolled in graduate school within 6 months of graduation, and 94% were employed.

Admissions Contact: Gil Villanueva, Dean of Admissions. E-Mail: *admissions@richmond.edu* Web: *http:/admissions.richmond.edu/*

UNIVERSITY OF VIRGINIA D-3

Charlottesville, VA 22904 **(434) 982-3200; (434) 924-3587**

Full-time: 6763 men, 8327 women	**Faculty:** n/av; I, +$
Part-time: 379 men, 618 women	**Ph.D.s:** 90%
Graduate: 3612 men, 3765 women	**Student/Faculty:** 16 to 1
Year: semesters, summer session	**Tuition:** $12,458 ($39,844)
Application Deadline: January 1	**Room & Board:** $9717
Freshman Class: 29021 applied, 8728 accepted, 3516 enrolled	
SAT CR/M/W: 670/680/670	**ACT:** 30 **MOST COMPETITIVE**

The University of Virginia, founded in 1819, is a public institution with undergraduate programs in architecture, arts and sciences, commerce, education, engineering and applied science, and nursing. There are 6 undergraduate schools and 10 graduate schools. In addition to regional accreditation, UVA has baccalaureate program accreditation with AACSB, ABET, ASLA, NAAB, and TEAC. The 15 libraries contain 5.1 million volumes, 4.2 million microform items, and 191,044 audio/video tapes/CDs/DVDs, and subscribe to 187,148 periodicals including electronic. Computerized library services include interlibrary loans, database searching, Internet access, and Wi-Fi capability. Special learning facilities include an art gallery, radio station, TV station, an art museum, and observatory. The 1167-acre campus is in a suburban area 70 miles northwest of Richmond, VA. Including any residence halls, there are 537 buildings.

Student Life: 73% of undergraduates are from Virginia. Others are from 49 states, 119 foreign countries, and Canada. 73% are from public schools. 61% are White; 12% Asian American. The average age of freshmen is 18; all undergraduates, 20. 3% do not continue beyond their first year; 93% remain to graduate.

Housing: 6213 students can be accommodated in college housing, which includes coed dorms, on-campus apartments, and married student housing. In addition, there are honors houses, language houses, and special-interest houses. On-campus housing is guaranteed for the freshman year only, is available on a first-come, first-served basis, and is available on a lottery system for upperclassmen. 59% of students commute. Upperclassmen may keep cars.

Activities: 25% of men belong to 27 national fraternities; 28% of women belong to 16 national sororities. Groups on campus include and tour guides, art, band, cheerleading, chess, choir, chorale, chorus, computers, dance, debate, drama, environmental, ethnic, film, forensics, gay, honors, international, jazz band, judiciary, literary magazine, marching band, musical theater, newspaper, opera, orchestra, pep band, photography, political, professional, radio and TV, religious, social, social service, student government, and symphony. Popular campus events include Culturefest and Family Weekend.

Sports: There are 11 intercollegiate sports for men and 12 for women, and 18 intramural sports for men and 18 for women. Facilities include a 61,500-seat stadium, a 16,000 seat arena, and 4 recreation centers including an aquatics and fitness center.

Disabled Students: All of the campus is accessible. Facilities include wheelchair ramps, elevators, special parking, specially equipped restrooms, special class scheduling, lowered drinking fountains, lowered telephones. curb cuts, voice synthesizers, braille printers, and large-screen monitors.

Services: Counseling and information services are available, as is tutoring in every subject. There is a reader service for the blind. There are transcribers, note takers, and taped readings for disabled students.

Campus Safety and Security: Measures include 24-hour foot and vehicle patrol, emergency notification system, self-defense education, and security escort services. There are shuttle buses, emergency telephones, lighted pathways/sidewalks, controlled access to dorms/residences, bicycle registration.

Programs of Study: UVA confers B.A., B.S., B.Ar.H., B.I.S., B.S.C., B.S.Ed., B.S.N. and B.U.E.P. degrees. Master's and doctoral degrees are also awarded. Bachelor's degrees are awarded in BIOLOGICAL SCIENCE (biology/biological science), BUSINESS (business administration and management), COMMUNICATIONS AND THE ARTS (art, classics, comparative literature, dramatic arts, English, French, German, Italian, music, Slavic languages, and Spanish), COMPUTER AND PHYSICAL SCIENCE (astronomy, chemistry, computer science, mathematics, and physics), ENGINEERING AND ENVIRONMENTAL DESIGN (aerospace studies, architectural history, architecture, biomedical engineering, chemical engineering, city/community/regional planning, civil engineering, computer engineering, electrical/electronics engineering, engineering and applied science, environmental science, mechanical engineering, systems engineering, and urban design), HEALTH PROFESSIONS (nursing and speech pathology/audiology), SOCIAL SCIENCE (African American studies, anthropology, area studies, economics, history, interdisciplinary studies, international relations, philosophy, political science/government, psychology, public administration, religion, and sociology). English, history, and biology are the strongest academically. Commerce, psychology, and biology have the largest enrollments.

Required: To graduate, students must complete 120 credit hours, with 18 to 42 hours in the major and a minimum GPA of 2.0. Distribution requirements include 12 hours of math and science, 6 hours each of humanities, composition, and social sciences, 4 semesters of foreign languages, 3 hours of historical studies, and 3 hours of non-Western perspectives.

Special: The college offers internships, study abroad, accelerated degree programs, B.A.-B.S. degrees in biology, environmental sciences, chemistry and physics, co-op programs in engineering, and nondegree study. Dual majors in most arts and sciences programs, student-designed majors, an interdisciplinary major and Echols, and Rodman Scholars program (invited students design own curricula with many requirements waived), and pass/fail options are available. There is a including Phi Beta Kappa chapter, a freshman honors program, and 35 departmental honors programs.

Faculty/Classroom: 65% of faculty are male; 35% are female. 50% teach undergraduates. Graduate students teach 36% of introductory courses. The average class size in an introductory lecture is 44 and in a regular course is 33.

Admissions: 30% of the 2013-2014 applicants were accepted. The SAT scores for the 2013-2014 freshman class were: Critical Reading--2% below 500, 14% between 500 and 599, 47% between 600 and 699, and 37% between 700 and 800; Math--2% below 500, 12% between 500 and 599, 40% between 600 and 699, and 46% between 700 and 800; Writing--2% below 500, 12% between 500 and 599, 47% between 600 and 699, and 39% between 700 and 800. The ACT scores were 1% below 21, 3% between 21 and 23, 7% between 24 and 26, 12% between 27 and 28, and 77% above 28. 97% of the current freshmen were in the top fifth of their class; 99% were in the top two fifths.

Requirements: The SAT is required. Applicants can substitute the ACT for the SAT if the optional ACT Writing Test is also taken. Two SAT subject tests of the student's choosing are strongly recommended. With few exceptions, candidates graduate from accredited secondary schools. While the GED is accepted, it is rare for candidates for first-year admission who have this credential to be competitive in the admissions process. Applicants should complete 16 high school academic courses, including 4 courses of English, 4 courses of math, 2 courses of physics, biology, or chemistry (3 if applying to engineering), 2 years of foreign language, and 1 course of social science. A letter of recommendation (preferably from the secondary school) is required; also, a teacher's recommendation is recommended. AP credits are accepted.

Procedure: Freshmen are admitted fall. Entrance exams should be taken by December of the senior year. There are early admissions and deferred admissions plans. Applications should be filed by January 1 for fall entry, along with a $60 fee. Notifications are sent April 1. 2606 applicants were on the 2013 waiting list; 185 were admitted. Applications are accepted online.

Transfer: 594 transfer students enrolled in 2012-2013. For the largest school (Arts and Sciences) "an applicant for transfer admission must be in good academic and social standing at any college that he or she is currently attending or has previously attended and must be eligible to return there. To be competitive for admission, we recommend that a transfer student have a cumulative grade point average of B+ or better in all college work attempted 60 of 120 credits required for the bachelor's degree must be completed at UVA.

Visiting: There are regularly scheduled orientations for prospective students, Visits consist of comprehensive information sessions and campus tours. There are guides for informal visits, visitors may sit in on classes, and stay overnight. To schedule a visit, contact the Monroe Society at (434) 924-3321.

Financial Aid: In 2013-2014, 33% of all full-time freshmen and 31% of continuing full-time students received some form of financial aid. 30% of all full-time freshmen and 27% of continuing full-time students received need-based aid. The average financial indebtedness of the 2013 graduate was $21,815. The FAFSA and the college's own financial statement are required. The deadline for filing freshman financial aid applications for fall entry is March 1.

International Students: There are 941 international students enrolled. The school actively recruits these students. They must take the TOEFL or International English Language Testing System (IELTS). They must also take the SAT or ACT, as well as the same tests as all other entering students.

Computers: All students may access the system 24 hours a day, 7 days a week. There are no time limits. The fee is $210.

Graduates: From July 1, 2012 to June 30, 2013, 3738 bachelor's degrees were awarded. The most popular majors were commerce (9%), foreign affairs (9%), and economics (8%). 500 companies recruited on campus in 2012-2013. In an average class, 2% graduate in 3 years or less, 86% graduate in 4 years or less, 92% graduate in 5 years or less, and 93% graduate in 6 years or less.

Admissions Contact: Gregory W. Roberts, Dean of Admissions. E-Mail: *undergradadmission@virginia.edu* Web: *www.virginia.edu*

UNIVERSITY OF VIRGINIA'S COLLEGE AT WISE — A-3

Wise, VA 24293 — (276) 328-0322; (888) 282-9324; (276) 328-0251

Full-time: 710 men, 735 women	**Faculty:** n/av; IIB, -$
Part-time: 125 men, 335 women	**Ph.D.s:** 70%
Graduate: n/av	**Student/Faculty:** n/av
Year: semesters, summer session	**Tuition:** $7721 ($21,336)
Application Deadline: see profile	**Room & Board:** $8000
Freshman Class: n/av	
SAT or ACT: required	**COMPETITIVE**

The University of Virginia's College at Wise, founded in 1954, offers undergraduate programs through the departments of business studies, education, languages and literature, behavioral and social sciences, natural sciences, math and computer science, history and philosophy, visual and performing arts, and nursing. The figures in the above capsule and this profile are approximate. In addition to regional accreditation, UVA's College at Wise has baccalaureate program accreditation with NLN. The library contains 143,265 volumes, 66,230 microform items, and 4786 audio/video tapes/CDs/DVDs, and subscribes to 2265 periodicals including electronic. Computerized library services include interlibrary loans, database searching, and Internet access. The 396-acre campus is in a small town 60 miles northwest of Bristol. Including any residence halls, there are 42 buildings.

Student Life: 95% of undergraduates are from Virginia. Others are from 11 states and 7 foreign countries. 99% are from public schools. 89% are white. The average age of freshmen is 18; all undergraduates, 24. 35% do not continue beyond their first year; 29% remain to graduate.

Housing: 575 students can be accommodated in college housing, which includes single-sex and coed dorms, on-campus apartments, and off-campus apartments. In addition, there are special-interest houses. On-campus housing is available on a first-come, first-served basis and is available on a lottery system for upperclassmen. 75% of students commute. All students may keep cars.

Activities: 7% of men belong to 1 local and 3 national fraternities; 7% of women belong to 3 local and 1 national sorority. There are 53 groups on campus, including art, band, cheerleading, chess, choir, chorale, chorus, communications, dance, drama, ethnic, film, gay, honor court, honors, inter-Greek council, international, jazz band, literary magazine, musical theater, multicultural alliance, newspaper, pep band, political, professional, radio and TV, religious, resident hall association, social, social service, student activities board, and student government. Popular campus events include the Holly Ball, Jam for Man, and Extramural Flag Football Scramble.

Sports: There are 6 intercollegiate sports for men and 5 for women, and 56 intramural sports for men and 56 for women. Facilities include baseball and softball fields, a gym, tennis courts, a swimming pool, 3 practice football fields, a football stadium, a racquetball court, a fitness center, and a dance practice room.

Disabled Students: All of the campus is accessible. Facilities include wheelchair ramps, elevators, special parking, specially equipped restrooms, special class scheduling, lowered drinking fountains, and special housing.

Services: Counseling and information services are available, as is tutoring in every subject. There is a reader service for the blind and remedial math and writing. Tutoring is free to all registered students.

Campus Safety and Security: Measures include 24-hour foot and vehicle patrol, self-defense education, and security escort services. There are emergency telephones, lighted pathways/sidewalks, and a crime prevention office.

Programs of Study: UVA's College at Wise confers B.A., B.S., and B.S.N. degrees. Bachelor's degrees are awarded in BIOLOGICAL SCIENCE (biology/biological science), BUSINESS (accounting and business administration and management), COMMUNICATIONS AND THE ARTS (art, communications, dramatic arts, English, French, and Spanish), COMPUTER AND PHYSICAL SCIENCE (chemistry, information sciences and systems, and mathematics), ENGINEERING AND ENVIRONMENTAL DESIGN (environmental science), HEALTH PROFESSIONS (medical laboratory technology and nursing), SOCIAL SCIENCE (criminal justice, economics, history, international studies, law enforcement and corrections, liberal arts/general studies, political science/government, psychology, and social science). Natural science, accounting, and math are the strongest academically. Business administration, history, and education have the largest enrollments.

Required: To graduate, all students must complete 52 hours of general education requirements including courses in liberal arts, art, humanities, social sciences, natural sciences, English composition, literature, math, foreign lanquage, phys ed, and Western heritage. At least 120 credit hours are required, with a minimum 2.0 GPA overall and in the major area.

Special: The college offers co-op programs in all majors, internships in education, social sciences, and communication, on-campus work-study programs, B.A.-B.S. degrees in most majors, dual and student-designed majors, and pass/fail options for classes not required for the major. There are 4 national honor societies, a freshman honors program, and 9 departmental honors programs.

Faculty/Classroom: 60% of faculty are male; 40% are female. All teach undergraduates, 50% do research, and 50% do both. The average class size in an introductory lecture is 20; in a laboratory, 17; and in a regular course, 18.

Requirements: The SAT or ACT is required. All applicants must be graduates of approved secondary schools or hold a GED. Preference is given to students who earn an Advanced Studies Diploma or its equivalent, rank in the top half of their graduating class, have a satisfactory score on the SAT (18 on the ACT), and complete 4 years of English, 3 or more courses in math, including algebra I and II and a course selected from among geometry, trigonometry, advanced math, or calculus, 2 or more years of natural science beyond general science, 2 or more years of a foreign language, and 1 year each of American history and world history. A GPA of 2.4 is required. AP credits are accepted. Important factors in the admissions decision are advanced placement or honors courses, recommendations by school officials, and leadership record.

Procedure: Freshmen are admitted to all sessions. Entrance exams should be taken by January 1 of the application year. There are early admissions, deferred admissions, and rolling admissions plans. Check with the school for current application deadlines and fee. Notification is sent on a rolling basis. Applications are accepted online.

Transfer: Transfer students must meet all general admissions requirements and submit secondary school transcripts or GED results and transcripts of all previous college work. A minimum 2.2 GPA is required. Students who have a minimum of 30 semester hours of college work, have an associate degree, or who are at least 25 years old need not submit the SAT or ACT scores. For others, a satisfactory score on the SAT or 18 on the ACT is recommended. 58 of 120 credits required for the bachelor's degree must be completed at UVA's College at Wise.

Visiting: There are regularly scheduled orientations for prospective students, including an interview, a campus tour, a meal, and class visitation. There are guides for informal visits and visitors may sit in on classes. To schedule a visit, contact the Admissions Office.

Financial Aid: The FAFSA and the college's own financial statement are required. Check with the school for current application deadlines.

International Students: The school actively recruits these students. They must take the TOEFL. They must also take the SAT or ACT.

Computers: All students may access the system 24 hours per day. There are no time limits and no fees.

Admissions Contact: Russell Necessary, Vice Chancellor for Enrollment Management. A campus DVD is available. E-mail: *admissions@uvawise.edu* Web: *www.uvawise.edu*

VIRGINIA COMMONWEALTH UNIVERSITY — E-3

Richmond, VA 23284 — (804) 828-8476; (800) 841-3638; (804) 828-1899

Full-time: 8727 men, 11283 women	**Faculty:** n/av; I, --$	
Part-time: 1737 men, 2204 women	**Ph.D.s:** n/av	
Graduate: 2927 men, 4874 women	**Student/Faculty:** 18 to 1	
Year: semesters, summer session	**Tuition:** $9885 ($23,912)	
Application Deadline: January 15	**Room & Board:** $8748	
Freshman Class: 14659 applied, 9488 accepted, 3617 enrolled		
SAT CR/M/W: 550/550/540	**ACT:** 23	**COMPETITIVE**

Virginia Commonwealth University is a major public research university located in Richmond, the state capital of Virginia. There are 13 undergraduate schools and 14 graduate schools. In addition to regional accreditation, VCU has baccalaureate program accreditation with AACSB, ABET, ACEJMC, ACPE, ADA, APTA, CSAB, CSWE, FIDER, NASAD, NAS-

DTEC, NASM, NCATE, NLN, and NRPA. The 2 libraries contain 2.5 million volumes, 3.3 million microform items, and 75,270 audio/video tapes/CDs/DVDs, and subscribe to 61,000 periodicals including electronic. Computerized library services include interlibrary loans, database searching, Internet access, and Wi-Fi capability. Special learning facilities include an art gallery, radio station, and TV station. The 144-acre campus is in an urban area 2 miles west of downtown Richmond and 90 miles from Washington, D.C. Including any residence halls, there are 211 buildings.

Student Life: 90% of undergraduates are from Virginia. Others are from 48 states, 109 foreign countries, and Canada. 54% are White; 16% African American; 11% Asian American. The average age of freshmen is 18; all undergraduates, 21. 85% remain to graduate.

Housing: 5321 students can be accommodated in college housing, which includes coed dorms and on-campus apartments. In addition, there are honors houses, ASPIRE- is an innovative and comprehensive community engagement-focused living-learning program for sophmores at VCU. On-campus housing is guaranteed for the freshman year only, is available on a first-come, and first-served basis. 78% of students commute. All students may keep cars.

Activities: There are 477 groups on campus, including art, band, cheerleading, chess, choir, chorale, chorus, computers, dance, debate, drama, ethnic, film, forensics, gay, honors, international, jazz band, literary magazine, musical theater, newspaper, opera, pep band, photography, political, professional, radio and TV, religious, social, social service, student government, symphony, and yearbook. Popular campus events include Annual Fall Step Show, Fest, Greek Week, Homecoming International Festival, Spring Fest, and Welcome Week.

Sports: There are 8 intercollegiate sports for men and 8 for women, and 21 intramural sports for men and 21 for women. Facilities include Facilities include a multipurpose indoor facility for intercollegiate athletics and recreational sports; a 24,495-square-foot recreation space with a fitness center, an activity center, and a wellness resource center; a 3,250-seat stadium for soccer and track and field events; a 250-seat tennis center open year-round, and a 25,990-square-foot recreation complex containing gym, handball/racquetball courts, weight room, and cardiovascular fitness space. Facilities also include a 1,200-seat field and jogging track with artificial turf; a baseball field; and a 42,989-square-foot aquatic and recreational facility with a 6-lane pool and spa, handball/racquetball and squash courts, and gyms.

Disabled Students: 90% of the campus is accessible. Facilities include wheelchair ramps, elevators, special parking, specially equipped restrooms, special class scheduling, and lowered drinking fountains.

Services: Counseling and information services are available, as is tutoring in most subjects. There is a reader service for the blind, and remedial math, reading, and writing.

Campus Safety and Security: Measures include 24-hour foot and vehicle patrol, emergency notification system, self-defense education, and security escort services. There are shuttle buses, emergency telephones, lighted pathways/sidewalks, controlled access to dorms/residences, formal presentations, online crime prevention program, annual security report, crime prevention through environmental design, community police officers/certified prevention specialists, security inspections of facilities, operation ID bike and computer registration, and victim/witness assistance program.

Programs of Study: VCU confers B.A., B.S., B.I.S., B.M., B.S.W. and B.F.A. degrees. Master's and doctoral degrees are also awarded. Bachelor's degrees are awarded in AGRICULTURE (environmental studies), BIOLOGICAL SCIENCE (bioinformatics and biology/biological science), BUSINESS (accounting, business administration and management, marketing/retailing/merchandising, and sports management), COMMUNICATIONS AND THE ARTS (art history and appreciation, communications, crafts, dance, dramatic arts, English, film arts, graphic design, languages, media arts, music, painting, photography, and sculpture), COMPUTER AND PHYSICAL SCIENCE (chemistry, computer science, information sciences and systems, mathematics, physics, and science), EDUCATION (art education, foreign languages education, and health education), ENGINEERING AND ENVIRONMENTAL DESIGN (bioengineering, biomedical engineering, chemical engineering, computer engineering, electrical/electronics engineering, electrical/electronics engineering technology, interior design, and mechanical engineering), HEALTH PROFESSIONS (clinical science, dental hygiene, and nursing), SOCIAL SCIENCE (African American studies, anthropology, criminal justice, economics, fashion design and technology, forensic studies, history, homeland security, interdisciplinary studies, international studies, philosophy, philosophy and religion, political science/government, psychology, religion, safety science, social work, sociology, and urban studies). Business, visual and performing arts, and psychology have the largest enrollments.

Required: All degree requirements must be completed prior to the graduation date. A minmum of 45 credits in 300 to 500 level courses or the equivalent is required for a bachelor's degree. A minimum of 120 credits total and cumulative grade point average of 2.0 or better are required to receive a baccalaureate degree. Some programs may require higher sum for earned hours or cumulative GPA.

Special: The university has these special study options: Accelerated programs, cooperative education program, distance learning, double major, dual enrollment, English as a second language (ESL), Honors program, independent study, internships, student-designed major, study abroad and teacher certification program. There are 18 national honor societies and a freshman honors program.

Faculty/Classroom: 57% of faculty are male; 43% are female. No introductory courses are taught by graduate students. The average class size in an introductory lecture is 41; in a laboratory is 31; and in a regular course is 33.

Admissions: 65% of the 2013-2014 applicants were accepted. The SAT scores for the 2013-2014 freshman class were: Critical Reading--22% below 500, 49% between 500 and 599, 24% between 600 and 699, and 5% between 700 and 800; Math--21% below 500, 49% between 500 and 599, 24% between 600 and 699, and 4% between 700 and 800; Writing--29% below 500, 47% between 500 and 599, 20% between 600 and 699, and 4% between 700 and 800. The ACT scores were 18% below 21, 34% between 21 and 23, 26% between 24 and 26, 11% between 27 and 28, and 12% above 28. 26 freshmen graduated first in their class.

Requirements: The SAT is required. The ACT Optional Writing test is also required. The ACT is recommended. In addition, candidates for admission to VCU are reviewed base on their academic performance in an accredited high school or on GED scores and either SAT Test or ACT scores. The college preparatory curriculum is highly preferred, and a minimum of 20 units is required for admission to all programs on the Monroe Park Campus. Extracurricular activities and employement experience may strengthen an application. Essays are required for scholarship consideration and for School fot he Arts applicants. Freshman also are required to take SATs and have a personal computer. Freshman applicants udner 22yrs must submit official SAT or ACT scores. Applicants whos native language is one other than English must submit scores for the test of English as a Foreign Language (TOEFL) in addition to any other required test scores. A GPA of 2.0 is required. AP and CLEP credits are accepted.

Procedure: Freshmen are admitted fall and spring. Entrance exams should be taken. SAT or ACT scores must be received for fall term admission by March. There are early admissions, deferred admissions, and rolling admissions plans. Applications should be filed by January 15 for fall entry; November 1 for spring entry. The fall 2013 application fee was $40. Notifications are sent April 1. 494 applicants were on the 2013 waiting list. Applications are accepted online.

Transfer: 2021 transfer students enrolled in 2012-2013. To be considered for admission students applying to lower division programs offered on the Monroe Park Campus must present a cumulative GPA of C or better in all nondevelopmental hours attempted at all accredited colleges attended. Transfer applicants with fewer than 30 semester/45 quarter hours also are evaluated on their high school acdemic performance and if under 22 years of age at the time of enrollment, SAT or ACT scores.

Visiting: There are regularly scheduled orientations for prospective students, daily tours every Monday-Saturday except holidays and holiday weekends. The information session is followed by an hour-long guided walk tour of the Monroe Park. Reservations are not required for attendance at these daily sessions. To schedule a visit, contact the Office of Admissions.

Financial Aid: In 2013-2014, 78% of all full-time freshmen and 71% of continuing full-time students received some form of financial aid. 57% of all full-time freshmen and 55% of continuing full-time students received need-based aid. The average freshman award was $14,518. Need-based scholarships or need-based grants averaged $6,428 ($22,446 maximum); need-based self-help aid (loans and jobs) averaged $3,722 ($9,000 maximum); non-need-based athletic scholarships averaged $12,903 ($24,520 maximum); and other non-need-based awards and non-need-based scholarships averaged $6,713 ($42,967 maximum). 4% of undergraduate students work part-time. Average annual earnings from campus work are $1738. The average financial indebtedness of the 2013 graduate was $28,889. The FAFSA is required. The priority date for freshman financial aid applications for fall entry is March 1.

International Students: There are 962 international students enrolled. The school actively recruits these students. They must take the TOEFL with a minimum score of 550 on the paper-based TOEFL (PBT) or 80 on the Internet-based version (iBT) and the college's own test.

Computers: All students may access the system. There are no time limits and no fees.

Graduates: From July 1, 2012 to June 30, 2013, 4666 bachelor's degrees were awarded. The most popular majors were business, management, marketing and related support service (14%), visual and performing arts (13%), and psychology (8%). In an average class, 1% graduate in 3 years or less, 34% graduate in 4 years or less, 51% graduate in 5 years or less, and 57% graduate in 6 years or less.

Admissions Contact: Sybil C. Halloran, Director of Admissions. E-Mail: *ugrad@vcu.edu* Web: *www.vcu.edu*

VIRGINIA INTERMONT COLLEGE B-4

Bristol, VA 24201 (276) 466-7851
(800) 451-1842; (276) 466-7855

Full-time: 143 men, 304 women
Part-time: 12 men, 37 women
Graduate: n/av
Year: semesters, summer session
Application Deadline: open
Freshman Class: n/av
SAT: required
Faculty: 45
Ph.D.s: 52%
Student/Faculty: 22 to 1
Tuition: $24,642
Room & Board: $7769
ACT: 20 **LESS COMPETITIVE**

Virginia Intermont College, founded in 1884, is a private institution affiliated with the Baptist General Association of Virginia. In addition to regional accreditation, V.I. College has baccalaureate program accreditation with CSWE. The library contains 54,735 volumes, 9,205 microform items, and 2,275 audio/video tapes/CDs/DVDs, and subscribes to 15,004 periodicals including electronic. Computerized library services include interlibrary loans, database searching, and Internet access. Special learning facilities include an art gallery, an equestrian center, a ballet center, and a film lab. The 13-acre campus is in an urban area 144 miles southwest of Roanoke and 120 miles northeast of Knoxville, TN. Including any residence halls, there are 18 buildings.

Student Life: 55% of undergraduates are from Virginia. Others are from 38 states, 30 foreign countries, and Canada. 85% are from public schools. 89% are White. 44% are Protestant; 40% claim no religious affiliation; 11% Catholic. The average age of freshmen is 19; all undergraduates, 24. 39% do not continue beyond their first year; 35% remain to graduate.

Housing: 470 students can be accommodated in college housing, which includes single-sex and coed dorms, off-campus apartments, and married student housing. In addition, there are honors houses. On-campus housing is guaranteed for all 4 years. 80% of students commute. Alcohol is not permitted. All students may keep cars.

Activities: There are no fraternities or sororities. There are 15 groups on campus, including art, choir, communications, computers, dance, drama, environmental, ethnic, gay, honors, literary magazine, musical theater, newspaper, photography, political, professional, religious, social service, and student government. Popular campus events include May Court, Family Weekend and Spring Fling.

Sports: There are 8 intercollegiate sports for men and 8 for women, and 12 intramural sports for men and 12 for women. Facilities include a gym, a 1,200-seat amphitheater, a 900-seat auditorium, lighted tennis courts, a swimming pool, a fitness center, and an equine center.

Disabled Students: 35% of the campus is accessible. Facilities include wheelchair ramps, elevators, special parking, specially equipped restrooms, special class scheduling, and special housing.

Services: Counseling and information services are available, as is tutoring in every subject. There is a reader service for the blind, and remedial math and reading.

Campus Safety and Security: Measures include 24-hour foot and vehicle patrol, self-defense education, and security escort services. There are lighted pathways/sidewalks.

Programs of Study: V.I. College confers B.A., B.S., B.F.A. and B.S.W. degrees. Associate degrees are also awarded. Bachelor's degrees are awarded in AGRICULTURE (equine science), BIOLOGICAL SCIENCE (biology/biological science), BUSINESS (business administration and management and sports management), COMMUNICATIONS AND THE ARTS (art, dance, dramatic arts, English, fine arts, performing arts, and photography), COMPUTER AND PHYSICAL SCIENCE (information sciences and systems), EDUCATION (education and secondary education), HEALTH PROFESSIONS (premedicine and preveterinary science), SOCIAL SCIENCE (criminal justice, culinary arts, history, interdisciplinary studies, liberal arts/general studies, paralegal studies, political science/government, psychology, public administration, religion, and social work). Equine studies, business, and photography have the largest enrollments.

Required: To graduate, students must complete 124 credits with a minimum GPA of 2.0. Required courses are English compostition, English literature, world history, computer fundamentals, college math, natural science, performing arts, visual arts, psychology or sociology, economics or political science, philosophy or religion, speech, and phys ed.

Special: V.I. College offers cross-registration with King College and internships in paralegal studies, social work, business, art, dance, photography, sports management, political science, psychology, and theater. Dual majors, study abroad, a general studies degree, and nondegree study are available. Evening degree programs in management and leadership, interdisciplinary studies, computer information management, graphic design, and social work are designed for working adults. There are 4 national honor societies and a freshman honors program.

Faculty/Classroom: 57% of faculty are male; 43% are female. All teach undergraduates. No introductory courses are taught by graduate students. The average class size in an introductory lecture is 19; in a laboratory is 10; and in a regular course is 12.

Admissions: The ACT scores were 60% below 21, 21% between 21 and 23, 16% between 24 and 26, 2% between 27 and 28, and 1% above 28. 24% of the current freshmen were in the top fifth of their class; 35% were in the top two fifths. 7 freshmen graduated first in their class.

Requirements: The SAT or ACT is required, with a minimum composite score of 780 on the SAT I or 18 on the ACT. Applicants must be graduates of an accredited secondary school or home school. The GED is accepted. Applicants should complete 15 academic credits, including 4 credits of English, 2 each of social science and math, 1 of a lab science, and 6 electives. An essay is required of students not meeting the normal admissions requirements. A GPA of 2.0 is required. AP and CLEP credits are accepted. Important factors in the admissions decision are advanced placement or honors courses, evidence of special talent, and ability to finance college education.

Procedure: Freshmen are admitted to all sessions. Entrance exams should be taken late in the junior year or early in the senior year. There are early admissions, deferred admissions, and rolling admissions plans. Application deadlines are open. The fall 2013 application fee was $15. Applications are accepted online.

Transfer: 106 transfer students enrolled in 2012-2013. Applicants for transfer should have a minimum GPA of 2.0. An interview is recommended. 30 of 124 credits required for the bachelor's degree must be completed at V.I. College.

Visiting: There are regularly scheduled orientations for prospective students, consisting of a campus tour, an admissions interview, meetings with faculty, auditions for performance scholarships, and planning sessions with financial aid staff. There are guides for informal visits, visitors may sit in on classes, and stay overnight. To schedule a visit, contact the Admissions Office.

Financial Aid: In 2013-2014, 67% of all full-time freshmen and 78% of continuing full-time students received some form of financial aid. 65% of all full-time freshmen and 73% of continuing full-time students received need-based aid. The average freshman award was $12,445. Need-based scholarships or need-based grants averaged $1,000 ($2,000 maximum); need-based self-help aid (loans and jobs) averaged $4,125 ($4,125 maximum); and other non-need-based awards and non-need-based scholarships averaged $5,000 ($13,900 maximum). 60% of undergraduate students work part-time. Average annual earnings from campus work are $1500. The average financial indebtedness of the 2013 graduate was $17,125. V.I. College is a member of CSS. The FAFSA is required. The deadline for filing freshman financial aid applications for fall entry is April 15.

International Students: There are 63 international students enrolled. The school actively recruits these students. They must take the TOEFL. They must also take the SAT or ACT.

Computers: All students may access the system. There are no time limits and no fees.

Graduates: From July 1, 2012 to June 30, 2013, 224 bachelor's degrees were awarded. The most popular majors were interdisciplinary studies (32%), business administration (23%), and visual and performing arts (13%). 22 companies recruited on campus in 2012-2013. In an average class, 20% graduate in 4 years or less, 29% graduate in 5 years or less, and 29% graduate in 6 years or less. Of the 2012 graduating class, 15% were enrolled in graduate school within 6 months of graduation, and 92% were employed.

Admissions Contact: Roger Lowe, Director of Admissions. E-Mail: *viadmit@vic.edu* Web: *www.vic.edu*

VIRGINIA MILITARY INSTITUTE C-3

Lexington, VA 24450 (540) 464-7211
(800) 767-4207; (540) 464-7746

Full-time: 1270 men, 115 women
Part-time: n/av
Graduate: n/av
Year: semesters, summer session
Application Deadline: see profile
Freshman Class: n/av
SAT or ACT: required
Faculty: n/av; IIB, av$
Ph.D.s: 94%
Student/Faculty: n/av
Tuition: $13,000 ($32,000)
Room & Board: $7500
COMPETITIVE

Virginia Military Institute, established in 1839, is the nation's first state-supported military college. It offers academic programs in engineering, sciences, and liberal arts. All students are members of the Corps of Cadets, live in barracks, eat together in the mess hall, wear uniforms, and adhere to the honor system. The figures in the above capsule and in this profile are approximate. In addition to regional accreditation, VMI has baccalaureate program accreditation with ABET. The 2 libraries contain 240,000 volumes, 12,963 microform items, and 5747 audio/video tapes/CDs/DVDs, and subscribe to 26,789 periodicals including electronic. Computerized library services include interlibrary loans, database searching, Internet access, and laptop Internet portals. Special learning facilities include a learning resource center, an observatory, a research library, and 2 history museums. The 134-acre campus is in a small town 50 miles north of Roanoke. Including any residence halls, there are 68 buildings.

Student Life: 59% of undergraduates are from Virginia. Others are from

45 states, 9 foreign countries, and Canada. 78% are from public schools. 85% are white. 64% are Protestant; 28% Catholic. The average age of freshmen is 18; all undergraduates, 20. 20% do not continue beyond their first year; 74% remain to graduate.

Housing: 1389 students can be accommodated in college housing, which includes coed dorms. On-campus housing is guaranteed for all 4 years. Alcohol is not permitted. Upperclassmen may keep cars.

Activities: There are no fraternities or sororities. There are 50 groups on campus, including bagpipe, band, cheerleading, choir, chorus, communications, dance, drama, drill team, ethnic, historical, honors, international, investment, jazz band, literary magazine, marching band, musical theater, newspaper, orchestra, pep band, photography, political, professional, religious, social, social service, and student government. Popular campus events include Ring Figure, Virginia Transportation Conference, and dance and concert weekends.

Sports: There are 11 intercollegiate sports for men and 6 for women, and 4 intramural sports for men and 4 for women. Facilities include basketball, racquetball, and tennis courts, fields for lacrosse, football, baseball, and soccer, a swimming pool, a rifle range, indoor and outdoor running tracks, a wrestling facility, access to a golf course, weight training and aerobic facility, and auxiliary indoor and outdoor basketball courts.

Disabled Students: 75% of the campus is accessible. Facilities include wheelchair ramps, elevators, special parking, and specially equipped rest rooms.

Services: Counseling and information services are available, as is tutoring in some subjects, including French, Spanish, German, Arabic, chemistry, math, physics, economics, business, writing, and most required freshman classes. Tutoring for intercollegiate athletes, paid for by the NCAA, also is available.

Campus Safety and Security: Measures include 24-hour foot and vehicle patrol and self-defense education. There are emergency telephones, lighted pathways/sidewalks, and a 24-hour student guard team.

Programs of Study: VMI confers B.A. and B.S. degrees. Bachelor's degrees are awarded in BIOLOGICAL SCIENCE (biology/biological science), BUSINESS (business economics), COMMUNICATIONS AND THE ARTS (English), COMPUTER AND PHYSICAL SCIENCE (chemistry, computer science, mathematics, and physics), ENGINEERING AND ENVIRONMENTAL DESIGN (civil engineering, electrical/electronics engineering, and mechanical engineering), SOCIAL SCIENCE (history, international studies, and psychology). Engineering (civil, electrical, and mechanical) and sciences are the strongest academically. History, business/economics, and civil and mechanical engineering have the largest enrollments.

Required: To graduate, students must complete 136 to 144 semester hours, with a GPA of 2.0. All students must pass chemistry, English, history, math, phys ed, ROTC, and public speaking. In addition, all cadets must pass swimming, boxing, and wrestling.

Special: Study abroad in 14 countries and work-study programs are available, as are for-credit internships in English and international studies and summer internships in foreign countries. VMI offers dual majors in any combination and B.A.-B.S. degrees in liberal arts, physical sciences, and engineering. Minors are offered in each field of study. There are 11 national honor societies, a freshman honors program, and 3 departmental honors programs.

Faculty/Classroom: 80% of faculty are male; 20% are female. All teach undergraduates and do research. No introductory courses are taught by graduate students. The average class size in an introductory lecture is 17; in a laboratory is 13; and in a regular course is 12.

Requirements: The SAT or ACT is required. In addition, applicants must be graduates of an accredited secondary school. Applicants should complete 19 to 20 high school academic units, including 4 years of English and math, 3 of science, history, and foreign language, and 2 of social studies. An essay is encouraged and an interview is recommended. A GPA of 2.0 is required. AP credits are accepted. Important factors in the admissions decision are advanced placement or honors courses, extracurricular activities record, and leadership record.

Procedure: Freshmen are admitted fall. Entrance exams should be taken spring of the junior year or fall of the senior year. There are early decision, early admissions and rolling admissions plans. Early decision applications should be filed by November 15; regular applications, by February 1 for fall entry. Notification of early decision is sent December 15. The application fee is $40. Applications are accepted online.

Transfer: Applicants for transfer must have a minimum GPA of 2.0, 24 transferable credit hours, and a satisfactory high school record. Either the SAT or the ACT is required. 135 of 135 credits required for the bachelor's degree must be completed at VMI.

Visiting: There are regularly scheduled orientations for prospective students, consisting of tours, conferences with academic and ROTC instructors, and interaction with current freshmen. There are guides for informal visits; visitors may sit in on classes and stay overnight. To schedule a visit, contact Admissions.

Financial Aid: VMI is a member of CSS. The FAFSA and the college's own financial statement are required. Check with the school for current application deadlines.

International Students: The school actively recruits these students. They must take the TOEFL. International students who will play intercollegiate athletics must take the SAT or ACT.

Computers: Wireless access is available. There are 200 common PCs available in locations across campus. All students may access the system. There are no time limits and no fees. It is strongly recommended that all students have a personal computer.

Admissions Contact: Col. Vernon L. Beitzel, Director, Admissions. A campus DVD is available. E-Mail: *admissions@vmi.edu* Web: *www.vmi.edu*

VIRGINIA POLYTECHNIC INSTITUTE AND STATE UNIVERSITY C-3

Blacksburg, VA 24061 **(540) 231-6267; (540) 231-3242**

Full-time: 15886 men, 11992 women **Faculty:** n/av; I, av$
Part-time: 1689 men, 1288 women **Ph.D.s:** 90%
Graduate: 4086 men, 2853 women **Student/Faculty:** n/av
Year: semesters, summer session **Tuition:** $9500 ($22,800)
Application Deadline: January 15 **Room & Board:** $7000
Freshman Class: 21201 applied, 12947 accepted, 5177 enrolled
SAT CR/M/W: 590/621/586 **ACT:** required
HIGHLY COMPETITIVE

Virginia Polytechnic Institute and State University, founded in 1872, is a public land-grant institution. It offers a cadet program within the larger, nonmilitary student body. There are 7 undergraduate schools and 2 graduate schools. In addition to regional accreditation, Virginia Tech has baccalaureate program accreditation with AACSB, ABET, ACCE, ADA, AHEA, ASLA, FIDER, NAAB, NCATE, and SAF. The 4 libraries contain 2.3 million volumes, 6.3 million microform items, and 27,574 audio/video tapes/CDs/DVDs, and subscribe to 35,596 periodicals including electronic. Computerized library services include interlibrary loans, database searching, and Internet access. Special learning facilities include a learning resource center, art gallery, natural history museum, radio station, TV station, airport, wind tunnels, agricultural stations, radio/visual observatories, satellite up-link station, multimedia, digital music, writing, CAD/CAM labs, math emporium, and CAVE (cave automatic virtual environment). The 2600-acre campus is in a rural area 40 miles southwest of Roanoke. Including any residence halls, there are 110 buildings.

Student Life: 74% of undergraduates are from Virginia. Others are from 49 states, 77 foreign countries, and Canada. 77% are white. The average age of freshmen is 18; all undergraduates, 20. 11% do not continue beyond their first year; 78% remain to graduate.

Housing: 9125 students can be accommodated in college housing, which includes single-sex and coed dorms. In addition, there are honors houses, special-interest houses, fraternity houses, and sorority houses. On-campus housing is guaranteed for the freshman year only and is available on a lottery system for upperclassmen. 60% of students commute. Upperclassmen may keep cars.

Activities: 13% of men belong to 43 national fraternities; 19% of women belong to 21 national sororities. There are 600 groups on campus, including art, band, cheerleading, chess, choir, chorale, chorus, computers, dance, drama, drill team, drum and bugle corps, ethnic, film, gay, honors, international, jazz band, literary magazine, marching band, musical theater, newspaper, orchestra, pep band, photography, political, professional, radio and TV, religious, social, social service, student government, and symphony. Popular campus events include Quad Jams, Ring Dance, and German's Mid-Winter Dance.

Sports: There are 11 intercollegiate sports for men and 10 for women, and 24 intramural sports for men and 24 for women. Facilities include a football stadium, a basketball coliseum, a field house, an indoor tennis pavilion, a 9-hole golf course, soccer and baseball fields, a swimming pool, a diving well, basketball, volleyball, racquetball, handball, squash, and tennis courts, a gymnastics room, a weight-lifting room, lighted multipurpose recreation fields, and a pond for ice skating. Residential quads are also equipped with weight-room and exercise facilities; there are also 2 gyms.

Disabled Students: 60% of the campus is accessible. Facilities include wheelchair ramps, elevators, special parking, specially equipped restrooms, special class scheduling, lowered drinking fountains, lowered telephones, special housing, and a special services library room for the visually impaired.

Services: Counseling and information services are available, as is tutoring in most subjects. There is a reader service for the blind, and remedial reading.

Campus Safety and Security: Measures include 24-hour foot and vehicle patrol, emergency notification system, self-defense education, and security escort services. There are shuttle buses, emergency telephones, and lighted pathways/sidewalks.

Programs of Study: Virginia Tech confers B.A., B.S., B.Arch., B.F.A., B.Land.Arch., B.S.Bus., B.S.E., and B.S.Ed. degrees. Master's and doctoral degrees are also awarded. Bachelor's degrees are awarded in AGRICULTURE (agricultural economics, animal science, dairy science, forestry and related sciences, horticulture, poultry science, and soil science), BIOLOGICAL SCIENCE (biochemistry, biology/biological science, and nutrition), BUSINESS (accounting, apparel and accessories marketing, banking and finance, business economics, entrepreneurial studies, hotel/motel and restaurant management, management science, marketing management, and tourism), COMMUNICATIONS AND THE ARTS (art, communications, dramatic arts, English, French, German, industrial design, music, and Spanish), COMPUTER AND PHYSICAL SCIENCE (chemistry, computer science, geology, mathematics, physics, planetary and space science, and statistics), EDUCATION (agricultural education, business education, environmental education, foreign languages education, science education, and secondary education), ENGINEERING AND ENVIRONMENTAL DESIGN (aerospace studies, agricultural engineering, architecture, chemical engineering, civil engineering, computer engineering, construction engineering, construction management, electrical/electronics engineering, engineering mechanics, environmental science, industrial engineering, interior design, landscape architecture/design, materials engineering, mechanical engineering, mining and mineral engineering, and ocean engineering), HEALTH PROFESSIONS (physical therapy, predentistry, and premedicine), SOCIAL SCIENCE (dietetics, economics, food science, geography, history, human development, interdisciplinary studies, international studies, interpreter for the deaf, parks and recreation management, philosophy, physical fitness/movement, political science/government, prelaw, psychology, public affairs, sociology, and urban studies). Engineering, architecture, and business are the strongest academically. Engineering, computer science, and biology have the largest enrollments.

Required: To graduate, students must complete between 120 and 156 credit hours (depending on the major), with a minimum GPA of 2.0. There is a required core curriculum that includes 8 hours of science and 6 hours each of humanities, social science, math, and writing and discourse. Students must also meet a foreign language requirement.

Special: Students may cross-register with Miami University in Ohio, Oxford Polytechnic Institute, California Polytechnic Institute, and Florida A & M. Study abroad in 36 countries, internships in nearly every major, a Washington semester, and a wide range of work-study programs are available, as well as co-ops in 48 majors. There are honors options for most majors, B.A.-B.S. degrees, dual and student-designed majors, credit for independent study or research, nondegree study, and pass/fail options. The Corps of Cadets, a militarily structured organization, is open to men and women. Undergraduate advising programs are available to students wishing to prepare for professional school in law, dentistry, medicine, pharmacy, physical therapy, or veterinary medicine. There are 13 national honor societies, including Phi Beta Kappa, and a freshman honors program.

Faculty/Classroom: 69% of faculty are male; 31% are female. 74% teach undergraduates, and all do research. Graduate students teach 12% of introductory courses. The average class size in an introductory lecture, 46, and in a laboratory, 30.

Admissions: 61% of the 2009-2010 applicants were accepted. 82% of the current freshmen were in the top fifth of their class; 97% were in the top two fifths.

Requirements: The SAT or ACT is required. Applicants must be graduates of an accredited secondary school, or the GED is accepted. Applicants should complete 18 high school academic credits, including 4 years of English, 3 of math, including algebra II and geometry, 2 of lab science, to be chosen from biology, chemistry, or physics, and 1 each of history and social studies. An additional 3 years from college preparatory courses and 4 from any credit course offerings are required. AP and CLEP credits are accepted. Important factors in the admissions decision are advanced placement or honors courses, evidence of special talent, and extracurricular activities record.

Procedure: Freshmen are admitted to all sessions. Entrance exams should be taken by January 1 of the senior year. There is a early decision and a deferred admissions plan. Applications should be filed for early decision by November 1, and for regular decision by January 15 for fall entry, October 1 for spring entry, and April 22 for summer entry, along with a $50 fee. Notification of early decision is sent December 15; regular decision, April 1. Applications are accepted online. 2919 applicants were on a recent waiting list, 308 were accepted.

Transfer: 925 transfer students enrolled in a recent year. Applicants must have a minimum GPA of 2.0 and must specify a major. Competitive GPA is 3.0. 30 of 120 credits required for the bachelor's degree must be completed at Virginia Tech.

Visiting: There are regularly scheduled orientations for prospective students, consisting of a Fall Open House Series: half-day on-campus programs that include presentations, tours, and question-and-answer sessions. There are guides for informal visits and visitors may sit in on classes. To schedule a visit, contact Office of Undergraduate Admissions.

Financial Aid: In a recent year, 36% of all full-time freshmen and 35% of continuing full-time students received some form of financial aid. 29% of all full-time freshmen and 28% of continuing full-time students received need-based aid. The average freshman award was $11,609. Need-based scholarships or need-based grants averaged $6,924; need-based self-help aid (loans and jobs) averaged $4,002 and other non-need based awards and non-need based scholarships averaged $2,562. The FAFSA is required. Check with the school for current application deadlines.

International Students: The school actively recruits these students. They must take the TOEFL. They must also take the SAT or ACT.

Computers: Wireless access is available. Each student brings a personal computer and has access to high-speed Ethernet connections in all residence halls, laboratories, and lecture rooms, as well as wireless access in all academic buildings. There are 912 university owned workstations available for general student use. All students may access the system any time. All students are required to have a personal computer. Requirements vary by major.

Graduates: In a recent year, 5538 bachelor's degrees were awarded. 250 companies recruited on campus in a recent year. In an average class, 51% graduate in 4 years or less, 74% graduate in 5 years or less, and 78% graduate in 6 years or less. Of a recent graduating class, 19% were enrolled in graduate school within 6 months of graduation, and 57% were employed.

Admissions Contact: Office of Undergraduate Admissions A campus DVD is available. E-Mail: *vtadmiss@vt.edu* Web: *www.vt.edu*

VIRGINIA STATE UNIVERSITY — E-3

Petersburg, VA 23806 — (804) 524-5902; (800) 871-7611; (804) 524-5055

Full-time: 1405 men, 1805 women	**Faculty:** n/av
Part-time: 205 men, 205 women	**Ph.D.s:** 74%
Graduate: 225 men, 585 women	**Student/Faculty:** n/av
Year: semesters, summer session	**Tuition:** $7000 ($15,000)
Application Deadline: see profile	**Room & Board:** $8000
Freshman Class: n/av	
SAT or ACT: required	

COMPETITIVE+

Virginia State University is a historically black public land-grant institution of higher education providing academic programs that integrate instruction, research, and extension/public service. The figures in this capsule and profile are approximate. There are 4 undergraduate schools and 1 graduate school. In addition to regional accreditation, VSU has baccalaureate program accreditation with ABET, ADA, CSWE, NASM, and NCATE. The library contains 280,599 volumes, 662,075 microform items, and 3,939 audio/video tapes/CDs/DVDs, and subscribes to 1,198 periodicals including electronic. Computerized library services include interlibrary loans and database searching. Special learning facilities include a learning resource center, art gallery, radio station, and TV station. The 652-acre campus is in a suburban area 25 miles south of Richmond. Including any residence halls, there are 52 buildings.

Student Life: 65% of undergraduates are from Virginia. Others are from 35 states, and 1 foreign country. 96% are from public schools. 90% are African American. The average age of freshmen is 18; all undergraduates, 21. 40% do not continue beyond their first year; 18% remain to graduate.

Housing: 2050 students can be accommodated in college housing, which includes single-sex dorms. In addition, there are honors houses. On-campus housing is guaranteed for the freshman year only, is available on a first-come, and first-served basis. 52% of students live on campus; of those, 20% remain on campus on weekends. Alcohol is not permitted. Upperclassmen may keep cars.

Activities: 10% of men belong to 4 national fraternities; 10% of women belong to 4 national sororities. There are 44 groups on campus, including band, cheerleading, chess, choir, chorus, computers, dance, drama, drill team, ethnic, honors, international, jazz band, marching band, musical theater, newspaper, orchestra, pep band, photography, political, professional, radio and TV, religious, social, student government, symphony, and yearbook. Popular campus events include High School Day, VSU Day, and Commencement.

Sports: There are 7 intercollegiate sports for men and 6 for women, and 5 intramural sports for men and 6 for women. Facilities include a gym, an Olympic-size pool, a dance studio, tennis courts, a track field, a football field, a baseball field, and indoor and outdoor basketball courts.

Disabled Students: 75% of the campus is accessible. Facilities include wheelchair ramps, elevators, special parking, and specially equipped rest rooms.

Services: Counseling and information services are available, as is tutoring in most subjects. There is a reader service for the blind.

Campus Safety and Security: Measures include 24-hour foot and vehicle patrol. There are emergency telephones and lighted pathways/sidewalks.

Programs of Study: VSU confers B.A., B.S., B.F.A., B.I.S., and B.Mus. degrees. Master's degrees are also awarded. Bachelor's degrees are awarded in AGRICULTURE (agriculture), BIOLOGICAL SCIENCE (biology/biological science), BUSINESS (accounting, business administration and management, hotel/motel and restaurant management, management information systems, and marketing management), COMMUNICATIONS AND THE ARTS (English literature, music performance, and visual and performing arts), COMPUTER AND PHYSICAL SCIENCE (chemistry, mathematics, and physics), EDUCATION (athletic training, business education, physical education, and trade and industrial education), ENGINEERING AND ENVIRONMENTAL DESIGN (engineering technology), SOCIAL SCIENCE (economics, history, home economics, interdisciplinary studies, political science/government, psychology, public administration, social work, and sociology). Business administration, accounting, and business information systems have the largest enrollments.

Required: To graduate, students must have a minimum GPA of 2.0. They must earn at least 120 credits, with the last 27 semester hours in residence. Requirements include those in phys ed, freshman writing, math, biology, social or physical science, history, and psychology. Freshman orientation must also be completed.

Special: VSU offers dual majors, a general studies degree, a 3-2 engineering degree program, nondegree study, and a pass/fail grading option. There are 10 national honor societies, including Phi Beta Kappa, a freshman honors program, and 7 departmental honors programs.

Faculty/Classroom: 67% of faculty are male; 33% are female. Graduate students teach 2% of introductory courses.

Requirements: The SAT or ACT is required. Applicants must graduate from an accredited secondary school with 16 academic credits and 12 Carnegie units, or have a GED. Students must take 4 years of English, 2 each of a foreign language, math, and science, and 1 each of history and social studies. Essays, 2 letters of recommendation, evidence of physical condition, interviews, and, if appropriate, auditions are required. A GPA of 2.2 is required. AP and CLEP credits are accepted. Important factors in the admissions decision are advanced placement or honors courses, recommendations by school officials, and leadership record.

Procedure: Freshmen are admitted fall and spring. There are deferred admissions and rolling admissions plans. Check with the school for current application fees. Applications are accepted online.

Transfer: Applicants must have a minimum GPA of 2.0. Those transferring fewer than 25 semester hours must meet freshman standards. 30 of 120 credits required for the bachelor's degree must be completed at VSU.

Visiting: There are regularly scheduled orientations for prospective students. There are guides for informal visits and visitors may sit in on classes. To schedule a visit, contact Admissions.

Financial Aid: VSU is a member of CSS. The CSS/Profile and the college's own financial statement are required. Check with the school for current application deadlines.

International Students: They must take the TOEFL. They must also take the SAT or ACT.

Computers: All students may access the system 8 a.m. to 10 p.m. Monday through Friday and 8 a.m. to 4 p.m. Saturdays. There are no time limits and no fees. It is strongly recommended that all students have a personal computer.

Admissions Contact: Irene Logan, Director of Admissions. A campus DVD is available. E-Mail: *ilogan@vsu.edu* Web: *www.vsu.edu*

VIRGINIA UNION UNIVERSITY — E-3

Richmond, VA 23220 — (804) 342-3570; (800) 368-3227; (804) 342-3511

Full-time: 1210 men and women	**Faculty:** n/av
Part-time: n/av	**Ph.D.s:** 55%
Graduate: 310 men and women	**Student/Faculty:** n/av
Year: semesters, summer session	**Tuition:** $14,000
Application Deadline: see profile	**Room & Board:** $7000
Freshman Class: n/av	
SAT: required	

COMPETITIVE

Virginia Union University, established in 1865 and affiliated with the Baptist Church, is a private institution offering undergraduate programs in education and psychology, business, humanities, natural science and math, and social sciences. The figures in the above capsule and in this profile are approximate. There are 2 undergraduate schools and 1 graduate school. In addition to regional accreditation, VUU has baccalaureate program accreditation with ACBSP and CSWE. The library contains 145,305 volumes, 62,079 microform items, and 1,523 audio/video tapes/CDs/DVDs, and subscribes to 308 periodicals including electronic. Computerized library services include database searching. Special learning facilities include a learning resource center and art gallery. The 72-acre campus is in an urban area in the city of Richmond. Including any residence halls, there are 18 buildings.

Student Life: 52% of undergraduates are from Virginia. Others are from 27 states, and 4 foreign countries. 85% are from public schools. 98% are African American. The average age of freshmen is 18. 31% do not continue beyond their first year; 55% remain to graduate.

Housing: 700 students can be accommodated in college housing, which includes single-sex dorms. In addition, there are honors houses. On-campus housing is available on a first-come and first-served basis. Priority is given to out-of-town students. Alcohol is not permitted. All students may keep cars.

Activities: There are 32 groups on campus, including cheerleading, drama, international, newspaper, religious, student government, and yearbook. Popular campus events include films, lectures, and concerts.

Sports: There are 6 intercollegiate sports for men and 6 for women, and 3 intramural sports for men and 2 for women. Facilities include a gym-auditorium and a 10,000-seat stadium.

Disabled Students: 90% of the campus is accessible. Facilities include wheelchair ramps, elevators, and special parking.

Services: Counseling and information services are available, as is tutoring in every subject. There is remedial math, reading, and writing.

Campus Safety and Security: Measures include 24-hour foot and vehicle patrol and security escort services. There are emergency telephones and lighted pathways/sidewalks.

Programs of Study: VUU confers B.A., B.S., and B.S.W. degrees. Master's and doctoral degrees are also awarded. Bachelor's degrees are awarded in BIOLOGICAL SCIENCE (biology/biological science), BUSINESS (accounting, banking and finance, and business administration and management), COMMUNICATIONS AND THE ARTS (English, journalism, and music), COMPUTER AND PHYSICAL SCIENCE (chemistry and mathematics), EDUCATION (art education, business education, early childhood education, elementary education, music education, secondary education, and special education), SOCIAL SCIENCE (criminology, history, political science/government, psychology, religion, social work, and sociology). Teacher education, accounting, and history/political science are the strongest academically. Teacher education, criminology, and business administration have the largest enrollments.

Required: To graduate, all students must complete at least 124 credit hours with a GPA of at least 2.0. Courses in religion, English, math, science, social science, a foreign language, and phys ed are required. There are also chapel and VUU events with attendance requirements. All students must successfully complete a computer science course and must take an English essay exam, usually by the end of the junior year, as well as a comprehensive exam in their major.

Special: The university offers cross-registration with Virginia Commonwealth and Virginia State Universities, and the University of Richmond. Internships, co-op programs, federal work-study programs, a general studies degree, a joint law degree with St. John's University School of Law in New York, a 3-2 degree in engineering with the Universities of Michigan and Iowa and Howard University, and exchange programs are also offered. There are 2 national honor societies and a freshman honors program.

Faculty/Classroom: 55% of faculty are male; 45% are female. 86% teach undergraduates. No introductory courses are taught by graduate students. The average class size in an introductory lecture is 28; in a laboratory is 20; and in a regular course is 22.

Requirements: The SAT is required. Graduation from an accredited secondary school is required; the GED is accepted. Sixteen academic units are required, including 4 of English, 3 each of math and academic electives, and 2 each of foreign language, social science, and natural science. Special consideration is given to disadvantaged students. Children of alumni are given some preference. A GPA of 2.0 is required. AP and CLEP credits are accepted. Important factors in the admissions decision are extracurricular activities record, advanced placement or honors courses, and leadership record.

Procedure: Freshmen are admitted fall and spring. Entrance exams should be taken between March of the junior year and March of the senior year. There are early admissions, deferred admissions, and rolling admissions plans. Check with the school for current application deadlines and fees. Notification is sent on a rolling basis.

Transfer: Transfer students must be in good standing at their previous institutions and must submit all college transcripts. 30 of 124 credits required for the bachelor's degree must be completed at VUU.

Visiting: There are guides for informal visits and visitors may sit in on classes. To schedule a visit, contact the Admissions Office.

Financial Aid: VUU is a member of CSS. The CSS/Profile is required. Check with the school for current application deadlines.

International Students: They must take the TOEFL. They must also take the SAT or ACT.

Computers: All students may access the system. There are no time limits and no fees. It is strongly recommended that all students have a personal computer.

Admissions Contact: Gil Powell, Director of Admissions. E-Mail: *admissions@vuu.edu* Web: *www.vuu.edu*

VIRGINIA WESLEYAN COLLEGE F-4

Norfolk, VA 23502-5599 (757) 455-3208
(800) 737-8684; (757) 461-5238

Full-time: 1405 men and women	**Faculty:** n/av; IIB, -$
Part-time: n/av	**Ph.D.s:** 85%
Graduate: n/av	**Student/Faculty:** n/av
Year: semesters, summer session	**Tuition:** $25,000
Application Deadline: open	**Room & Board:** $8000
Freshman Class: n/av	
SAT: required	**ACT:** 20 LESS COMPETITIVE

Virginia Wesleyan College, established in 1961, is a private institution affiliated with the United Methodist Church, offering undergraduate degrees in the humanities, the social sciences, the natural sciences, and math. The figures in the above capsule and in this profile are approximate. In addition to regional accreditation, Virginia Wesleyan has baccalaureate program accreditation with NRPA. The library contains 121,373 volumes, 15,869 microform items, and 3,813 audio/video tapes/CDs/DVDs, and subscribes to 800 periodicals including electronic. Computerized library services include interlibrary loans, database searching, and Internet access. Special learning facilities include a learning resource center, art gallery, radio station, a greenhouse, the Center for the Study of Religious Freedom, 142 acres of woodland used as a lab for biological and environmental sciences, a social sciences lab, the Center for Sacred Music, and an apiary. The 300-acre campus is in a suburban area 8 miles east of downtown Norfolk and 10 miles west of the Virginia Beach oceanfront. Including any residence halls, there are 31 buildings.

Student Life: 79% of undergraduates are from Virginia. Others are from 33 states, 7 foreign countries, and Canada. 82% are from public schools. 77% are white; 15% African American. 46% are Protestant; 22% Catholic; 22% claim no religious affiliation. The average age of freshmen is 18; all undergraduates, 24. 34% do not continue beyond their first year; 42% remain to graduate.

Housing: 696 students can be accommodated in college housing, which includes single-sex and coed dorms and on-campus apartments. In addition, there are honors houses, special-interest houses, fraternity, sorority, and international residence halls. On-campus housing is guaranteed for all 4 years. 58% of students commute. All students may keep cars.

Activities: 10% of men belong to 2 national fraternities; 15% of women belong to 4 national sororities. There are 62 groups on campus, including, cheerleading, chorus, commuter, dance, departmental drama, ethnic, gay, honors, international, literary magazine, model UN, musical theater, newspaper, political, professional, radio and TV, religious, social, social service, student government, women's, and yearbook. Popular campus events include TGIF Series and seafood party in the Dell.

Sports: There are 8 intercollegiate sports for men and 9 for women, and 5 intramural sports for men and 5 for women. Facilities include the student center, which includes a multiactivity athletic center, a 36-foot-high climbing wall, NCAA regulation swimming pool, indoor running track, and racquetball and basketball courts. Also baseball, softball, lacrosse, field hockey, and soccer fields, and tennis courts are available.

Disabled Students: 90% of the campus is accessible. Facilities include wheelchair ramps, elevators, special parking, specially equipped rest rooms, special class scheduling, lowered drinking fountains, and lowered telephones.

Services: Counseling and information services are available, as is tutoring in most subjects. There is a reader service for the blind, and remedial math, reading, and writing. Note takers, special co-advising, test proctoring, and Learning Plus for Praxis are available.

Campus Safety and Security: Measures include 24-hour foot and vehicle patrol, self-defense education, and security escort services. There are shuttle buses, emergency telephones, lighted pathways/sidewalks, and a bicycle patrol.

Programs of Study: Virginia Wesleyan confers B.A. and B.S. degrees. Bachelor's degrees are awarded in AGRICULTURE (environmental studies), BIOLOGICAL SCIENCE (biology/biological science), BUSINESS (business administration and management), COMMUNICATIONS AND THE ARTS (art, classics, communications, dramatic arts, English, French, German, journalism, languages, music, and Spanish), COMPUTER AND PHYSICAL SCIENCE (chemistry, computer science, earth science, mathematics, and natural sciences), EDUCATION (art education, elementary education, secondary education, and social studies education), SOCIAL SCIENCE (American studies, criminal justice, history, human ecology, humanities, interdisciplinary studies, international relations, liberal arts/general studies, parks and recreation management, philosophy, political science/government, psychology, religion, social science, social studies, social work, sociology, and women's studies). Art, history, and math are the strongest academically. Biology, education, and liberal arts management program have the largest enrollments.

Required: To graduate, students must complete general studies requirements, which include English, math, a foreign language, and Frames of Reference courses. These include: Empirical Knowledge; Aesthetic Understanding and Activity; Ethical Values, World Views, Faith Perspectives; Historical Perspective; Communications; and Institutional and Cultural Systems. Students must earn 120 credits, including 40 in the major, with a minimum 2.0 GPA. Students must complete 3 credits designated to fulfill a Senior Integrative Experience requirement. Students must complete at least one-fifth of their Virginia Wesleyan work courses designated as writing courses for transfer students, the required number of writing courses depends upon hours of credit upon admission. A First Year Seminar Introduction to Inquiry is also required for first-time college students. All graduates must demonstrate computer literacy in a manner related to their field and designated by their major program. Oral communications proficiency also must be demonstrated in a manner prescribed by the major program. The number of hours required for the major varies; the maximum is 50.

Special: Students may cross-register with Old Dominion University, the College of William and Mary, or Norfolk State University through the Virginia Tidewater Consortium. Internships are available and are usually completed during the senior year. The college offers study-abroad programs and international internships through partnerships and exchange programs in several countries, additional arrangements for study abroad can be made in almost any country. Dual majors, individualized and interdivisional majors, and interdisciplinary majors are available. Work-study programs with Virginia Wesleyan are offered. Credit may be granted for life, military, and work experience. Nondegree study and pass/fail options are also available. There are 16 national honor societies and a freshman honors program.

Faculty/Classroom: 55% of faculty are male; 45% are female. All teach undergraduates. No introductory courses are taught by graduate students. The average class size in a regular course is 12.

Requirements: The SAT or ACT is required. Applicants must graduate from an accredited secondary school or have a GED. The college recommends 15 academic credits. Students should complete 4 years of English, 3 of social studies/history, math, and science, and 2 of foreign language. Essays are required and interviews are recommended. Home-schooled graduates are reviewed individually. A GPA of 2.0 is required. AP and CLEP credits are accepted. Important factors in the admissions decision are advanced placement or honors courses, extracurricular activities record, and leadership record.

Procedure: Freshmen are admitted fall and spring. Entrance exams should be taken in the spring of the junior year and the fall of the senior year. There are early admissions, deferred admissions, and rolling admissions plans. Application deadlines are open. Notification is sent on a rolling basis. Applications are accepted online.

Transfer: Applicants must have a minimum GPA of 2.0 in courses to be transferred. For applicants who have not completed 12 semester hours of college work, official transcripts of college and high school records (including SAT or ACT scores) are required. All others must submit a high school diploma or GED in addition to official college transcripts. 30 of 120 credits required for the bachelor's degree must be completed at Virginia Wesleyan.

Visiting: There are regularly scheduled orientations for prospective students, consisting of 3 Open House Days on Saturdays for prospective students to meet faculty and current students, and to tour the campus. There are guides for informal visits; visitors may sit in on classes and stay overnight. To schedule a visit, contact the Admissions Office.

Financial Aid: The FAFSA is required. Check with school for current application deadlines.

International Students: The school actively recruits these students. They must take the TOEFL. They must also take the SAT or ACT.

Computers: Wireless access is available. Approximately 100 classrooms and labs are linked to the college's network. Wireless access is available at the student center and the library. Residential rooms are equipped with Internet access. All students may access the system 5:30 a.m. to 1 a.m. There are no time limits and no fees. It is strongly recommended that all students have a personal computer. A Dell OptiPlex or Latitude is recommended.

Admissions Contact: Richard T. Hinshaw, Vice President for Enrollment Management. E-Mail: *admissions@vwc.edu* Web: *www.vwc.edu*

WASHINGTON AND LEE UNIVERSITY C-3

Lexington, VA 24450 (540) 458-8710; (540) 458-8062

Full-time: 929 men, 906 women	**Faculty:** 209; IIB, +$
Part-time: 1 men, 2 women	**Ph.D.s:** 96%
Graduate: 259 men, 205 women	**Student/Faculty:** 8 to 1
Year: n/app	**Tuition:** $43,362
Application Deadline: January 1	**Room & Board:** $9450
Freshman Class: 5972 applied, 1163 accepted, 479 enrolled	
SAT CR/M/W: 691/693/683	**ACT:** 30 MOST COMPETITIVE

Washington and Lee is a private, highly selective liberal arts university. Founded in 1749, its 430-acre campus is located in Lexington, Virginia, approximately 50 miles northeast of Roanoke and 190 miles southwest of Washington, DC. There are 2 undergraduate schools and 1 graduate school. In addition to regional accreditation, Washington and Lee has baccalaureate program accreditation with AACSB and ACEJMC. The 3 libraries contain 973,445 volumes, 1.4 million microform items, and 18,522 audio/video tapes/CDs/DVDs, and subscribe to 11,794 periodicals including electronic. Computerized library services include interlibrary loans, database searching, Internet access, and Wi-Fi capability. Special learning facilities include an art gallery, radio station, TV station. The 430-acre campus is in a small town 50 miles northeast of Roanoke, Virginia and 190 miles southwest of Washington, DC. Including any residence halls, there are 112 buildings.

Student Life: 86% of undergraduates are from out of state, mostly the South. Students are from 53 states, 31 foreign countries, and Canada. 55% are from public schools. 83% are White. 50% are Protestant; 22% Catholic; 19% claim no religious affiliation. The average age of freshmen is 18; all undergraduates, 20. 5% do not continue beyond their first year; 90% remain to graduate.

Housing: 1267 students can be accommodated in college housing, which includes coed dorms and on-campus apartments. In addition, there are language houses, special-interest houses, fraternity houses, and sorority houses. On-campus housing is available on a lottery system for upperclassmen. 59% of students live on campus; of those, 95% remain on campus on weekends. All students may keep cars.

Activities: 81% of men belong to 17 national fraternities; 82% of women belong to 7 national sororities. There are 128 groups on campus, including and leadership, Spanish, sports, volunteer, cheerleading, choir, chorale, chorus, communications, dance, debate, drama, environmental, ethnic, film, forensics, gay, honors, international, jazz band, literary magazine, musical theater, newspaper, orchestra, Outing, pep band, photography, political, professional, radio and TV, religious, social, social service, student government, symphony, and yearbook. Popular campus events include Presidential Mock Convention, Fancy Dress Ball and NABORS Service Day.

Sports: There are 12 intercollegiate sports for men and 12 for women, and 19 intramural sports for men and 17 for women. Facilities include Gymnasium, 2400-seat arena, 7000-seat stadium, pool with a 500-seat gallery, fitness center, weight training and exercise rooms, handball, racquetball, squash, and tennis courts, outdoor track, baseball and practice fields, indoor tennis facility, 1000-seat soccer/lacrosse stadium, and a 1000-seat turf field for field hockey and lacrosse.

Disabled Students: 55% of the campus is accessible. Facilities include wheelchair ramps, elevators, special parking, specially equipped restrooms, special class scheduling, lowered drinking fountains, and special housing.

Services: Counseling and information services are available, as is tutoring in every subject. There is a reader service for the blind.

Campus Safety and Security: Measures include 24-hour foot and vehicle patrol, emergency notification system, self-defense education, and security escort services. There are shuttle buses, emergency telephones, lighted pathways/sidewalks, controlled access to dorms/residences, Required safety programs for first-year students.

Programs of Study: Washington and Lee confers B.A., and B.S. degrees. Master's and doctoral degrees are also awarded. Bachelor's degrees are awarded in BIOLOGICAL SCIENCE (biochemistry, biology/biological science, and neurosciences), BUSINESS (accounting and business administration and management), COMMUNICATIONS AND THE ARTS (art history and appreciation, classics, dramatic arts, English, French, German, Germanic languages and literature, journalism, music, romance languages and literature, Russian languages and literature, Spanish, and studio art), COMPUTER AND PHYSICAL SCIENCE (chemistry, computer science, geology, mathematics, natural sciences, and physics), ENGINEERING AND ENVIRONMENTAL DESIGN (chemical engineering, engineering physics, and environmental science), SOCIAL SCIENCE (anthropology, archeology, East Asian studies, economics, history, interdisciplinary studies, medieval studies, philosophy, political science/government, psychology, public affairs, religion, and sociology). Mass communications, neuroscience, business administration, accounting, and chemistry are the strongest academically. Business administration, economics, politics, accounting, and biology have the largest enrollments.

Required: To graduate, students must achieve proficiency in a foreign language and English composition and complete at least 1 course in fine arts and humanities, lab science and math, and literature and 2 courses in social sciences. A total of 113 credits, with a minimum GPA of 2.0, is required. All students must take 4 skills courses in physical education and pass a swimming test.

Special: Special academic programs are available throughout The College and The Williams School of Commerce. Internship opportunities include the Washington Term, First-Year Internship Program, and study abroad opportunities in over 50 countries. Students may earn dual degrees and double majors; over 30 departments offer honors programs. Teacher certification is offered in consortium with Virginia Military Institute and Southern Virginia University. There are 17 national honor societies, including Phi Beta Kappa, and 31 departmental honors programs.

Faculty/Classroom: 66% of faculty are male; 34% are female. 86% teach undergraduates, all do research, and 86% do both. No introductory courses are taught by graduate students. The average class size in an introductory lecture is 19; in a laboratory is 17; and in a regular course is 15.

Admissions: 19% of the 2013-2014 applicants were accepted. The SAT scores for the 2013-2014 freshman class were: Critical Reading--4% between 500 and 599, 47% between 600 and 699, and 49% between 700 and 800; Math--3% between 500 and 599, 50% between 600 and 699, and 47% between 700 and 800; Writing--10% between 500 and 599, 44% between 600 and 699, and 46% between 700 and 800. The ACT scores were 27% between 27 and 28, and 73% above 28. 96% of the current freshmen were in the top fifth of their class; 100% were in the top two fifths. There were 14 National Merit finalists. 36 freshmen graduated first in their class.

Requirements: The SAT or ACT is required. The ACT Optional Writing test is also required. A high school diploma is not required. Applicants must earn 17 units (24 recommended), including 4 units in English, 3 in math (4 recommended), 3 in a foreign language (4 recommended), and 1 each in history (2 recommended) and natural science (4 recommended with 1 lab science). Course work in social sciences(1) is also required (2 recommended). Essays, test scores, a transcript, and recommendation letters are needed to apply. An interview is recommended. AP credits are accepted. Important factors in the admissions decision are advanced placement or honors courses, leadership record, extracurricular activities record, and recommendations by school officials.

Procedure: Freshmen are admitted fall. Entrance exams should be taken Prior to January of the senior year. There are early decision and deferred admissions plans. Early decision applications should be filed by November 1; regular applications, by January 1 for fall entry. The fall 2013 application fee was $50. Notification of early decision is sent December 21; regular decision, April 1. 261 early decision candidates were accepted for the 2013-2014 class. 2002 applicants were on the 2013 waiting list; 89 were admitted. Applications are accepted online.

Transfer: 1 transfer students enrolled in 2012-2013. Transfer applicants must have a GPA of at least 2.0 (at least 3.5 to be competitive); no more than 56 credits will transfer. There is a 2-year residency requirement. 57 of 113 credits required for the bachelor's degree must be completed at Washington and Lee.

Visiting: There are regularly scheduled orientations for prospective students, including hourly interviews and campus tours, 2 group information sessions daily, seasonal Saturday tours and interviews. There are guides for informal visits and visitors may sit in on classes. To schedule a visit, contact the Admissions Office.

Financial Aid: In 2013-2014, 49% of all full-time freshmen and 49% of continuing full-time students received some form of financial aid. 44% of all full-time freshmen and 41% of continuing full-time students received need-based aid. The average freshman award was $44,349. Need-based scholarships or need-based grants averaged $39,120; need-based self-help aid (loans and jobs) averaged $2,043; and other non-need-based awards and non-need-based scholarships averaged $44,427. 17% of undergraduate students work part-time. Average annual earnings from campus work are $780. The average financial indebtedness of the 2013 graduate was $23,409. Washington and Lee is a member of CSS. The CSS/Profile and FAFSA, and Federal tax returns for parents and students and business tax returns are required. The priority date for freshman financial aid applications for fall entry is February 1. The deadline for filing freshman financial aid applications for fall entry is February 1.

International Students: There are 79 international students enrolled. The school actively recruits these students. They must take the TOEFL with a minimum score of 600 on the paper-based TOEFL (PBT) or 100 on the Internet-based version (iBT), APIEL or ELPT. They must also take the SAT or ACT.

Computers: All students may access the system 24 hours a day, 7 days a week while classes are in session. There are no time limits. The fee is $300.

Graduates: From July 1, 2012 to June 30, 2013, 421 bachelor's degrees were awarded. The most popular majors were business administration (14%), economics (10%), and politics (10%). 65 companies recruited on campus in 2012-2013. In an average class, 88% graduate in 4 years or less, 90% graduate in 5 years or less, and 90% graduate in 6 years or less. Of the 2012 graduating class, 32% were enrolled in graduate school within 6 months of graduation, and 83% were employed.

Admissions Contact: William M. Hartog, Dean of Admissions and Financial Aid. E-Mail: *admissions@wlu.edu* Web: *www.wlu.edu*

WASHINGTON

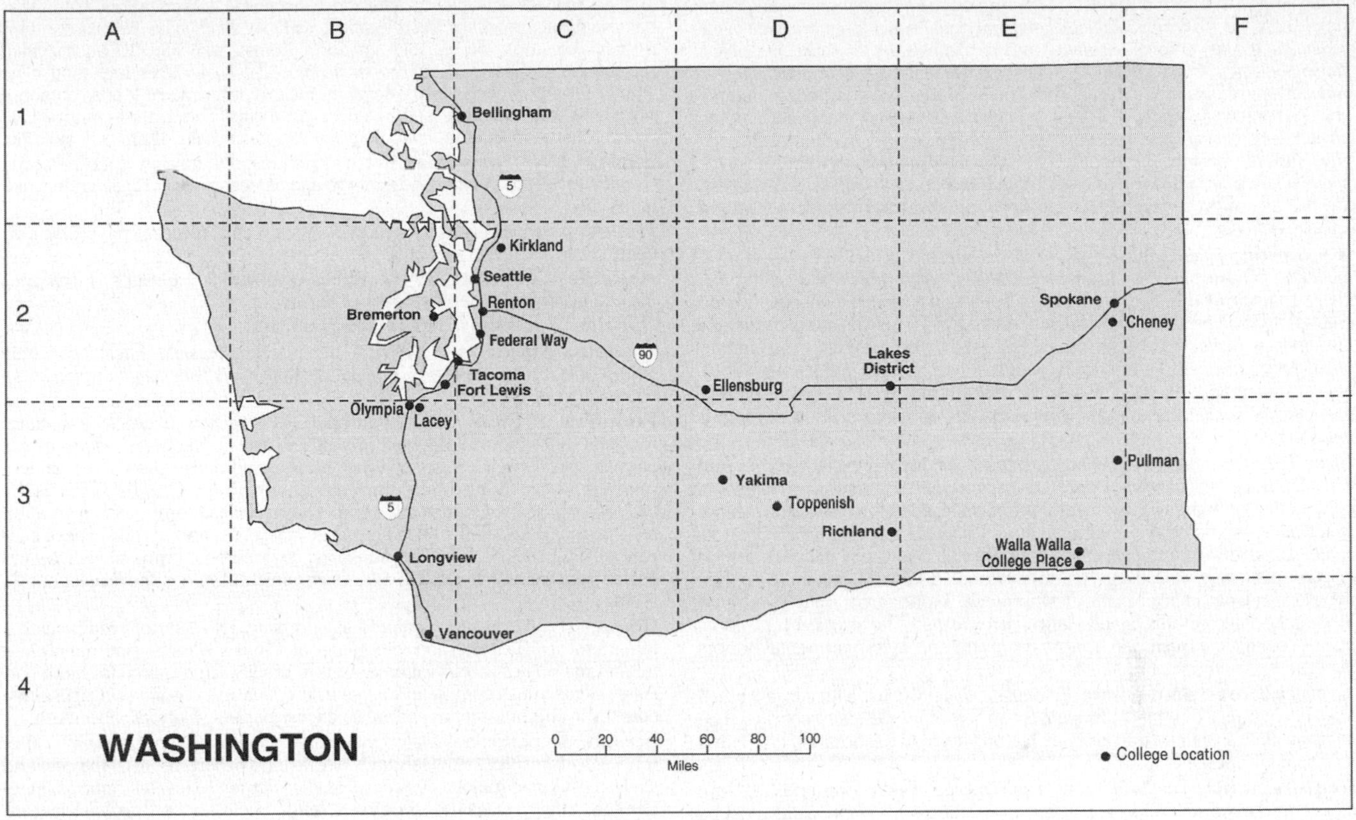

CENTRAL WASHINGTON UNIVERSITY D-2

Ellensburg, WA 98926
(509) 963-1211
(866) 298-4968; (509) 963-3022

Full-time: 7500 men and women
Part-time: n/av
Graduate: 500 men and women
Year: trimesters, summer session
Application Deadline: see profile
Freshman Class: n/av
SAT or ACT: required
Faculty: n/av; IIA, --$
Ph.D.s: 90%
Student/Faculty: n/av
Tuition: $6500 ($15,500)
Room & Board: $7500

COMPETITIVE

Central Washington University is a public institution offering undergraduate programs in the arts and sciences, business administration, and education. There are 4 undergraduate schools and 1 graduate school. Figures in the above capsule and in this profile are approximate. In addition to regional accreditation, CWU has baccalaureate program accreditation with ABET, ACCE, ADA, NASM, NCATE, and NRPA. The library contains 546,025 volumes, 1.2 million microform items, and 9500 audio/video tapes/CDs/DVDs. Computerized library services include interlibrary loans and database searching. Special learning facilities include a learning resource center, art gallery, natural history museum, planetarium, radio station, anthropology museum, botanical greenhouse, and primate research lab. The 380-acre campus is in a rural area 100 miles east of Seattle. Including any residence halls, there are 74 buildings.

Student Life: 97% of undergraduates are from Washington. Others are from 35 states, 32 foreign countries, and Canada. 95% are from public schools. 78% are white. The average age of freshmen is 19; all undergraduates, 23. 24% do not continue beyond their first year; 52% remain to graduate.

Housing: 2525 students can be accommodated in college housing, which includes coed dorms, on-campus apartments, off-campus apartments, and married student housing. In addition, there are special-interest houses, a freshman-only enrichment hall, and a residence hall for transfers and upperclassmen only. On-campus housing is guaranteed for the freshman year only and is available on a first-come, first-served basis. All students may keep cars.

Activities: There are no fraternities or sororities. There are 80 groups on campus, including art, band, cheerleading, chess, choir, chorale, chorus, computers, dance, drama, ethnic, film, gay, honors, international, jazz band, literary magazine, marching band, musical theater, newspaper, opera, orchestra, pep band, photography, political, professional, radio and TV, religious, social, social service, student government, and symphony. Popular campus events include Tower Theater productions and Jazz Night.

Sports: There are 8 intercollegiate sports for men and 8 for women, and 9 intramural sports for men and 9 for women. Facilities include a 3500-seat stadium, swimming pool, arena, weight training room, athletic field, and 3 gyms.

Disabled Students: All of the campus is accessible. Facilities include wheelchair ramps, elevators, special parking, specially equipped rest rooms, special class scheduling, lowered drinking fountains, and lowered telephones.

Services: Counseling and information services are available, as is tutoring in most subjects. There is a reader service for the blind, and remedial math, reading, and writing.

Campus Safety and Security: Measures include 24-hour foot and vehicle patrol, self-defense education, and security escort services. There are shuttle buses, emergency telephones, lighted pathways/sidewalks, and controlled-entry residence halls.

Programs of Study: CWU confers B.A., B.S., B.A.Ed., B.F.A., and B.M. degrees. Master's degrees are also awarded. Bachelor's degrees are awarded in BIOLOGICAL SCIENCE (biology/biological science), BUSINESS (accounting, banking and finance, business administration and management, business economics, fashion merchandising, international business management, marketing/retailing/merchandising, recreation and leisure services, and tourism), COMMUNICATIONS AND THE ARTS (art, broadcasting, Chinese, communications, dramatic arts, English, fine arts, French, German, guitar, Japanese, journalism, language arts, music, music business management, music theory and composition, percussion, piano/organ, public relations, Russian, Spanish, speech/debate/rhetoric, strings, studio art, visual and performing arts, and voice), COMPUTER AND PHYSICAL SCIENCE (actuarial science, chemistry, computer programming, computer science, earth science, geology, information sciences and systems, mathematics, physics, and software engineering), EDUCATION (art education, business education, early childhood education, elementary education, English education, foreign languages education, health education, home economics education, industrial arts education, marketing and distribution education, mathematics education, middle school education, music education, physical education, science education, secondary education, social studies education, and special education), ENGINEERING AND

ENVIRONMENTAL DESIGN (aeronautical technology, aviation administration/management, aviation maintenance management, construction management, electrical/electronics engineering, engineering technology, industrial engineering technology, and mechanical engineering), HEALTH PROFESSIONS (community health work, emergency medical technologies, exercise science, and public health), SOCIAL SCIENCE (anthropology, Asian/Oriental studies, criminal justice, economics, family and community services, family/consumer studies, food science, geography, gerontology, history, liberal arts/general studies, paralegal studies, parks and recreation management, philosophy, political science/government, prelaw, psychology, public administration, safety science, social science, social work, and sociology). Accounting, music, and geology are the strongest academically. Business and education have the largest enrollments.

Required: Students must complete a minimum of 180 quarter credits, including 60 in upper-division courses and a minimum of 45 in the major plus a minor or 60 in the major. Core curriculum requirements include 61 credits of Basic and Breadth courses, including 15 credits each in arts and humanities, social and behavioral sciences, and natural science, 6 credits of English composition, and a philosophy logic or finite math course. Students must maintain a 2.3 GPA in the major and 2.0 GPA overall. A comprehensive exam in reading comprehension, sentence skills, and math is required.

Special: Students may study abroad; there is a formal exchange program with Japanese universities. There are 3-2 engineering degree programs in conjunction with the University of Puget Sound, the University of Washington, and Washington State University. CWU also offers co-op programs, cross-registration, internships, work-study programs, an accelerated degree program, credit/no credit options, dual and student-designed majors, and credit for military experience. Nondegree study is offered through adult/continuing education programs. There are 11 national honor societies, a freshman honors program, and 12 departmental honors programs.

Faculty/Classroom: 58% of faculty are male; 42% are female. All teach and do research. Graduate students teach 7% of introductory courses. The average class size in an introductory lecture is 45; in a laboratory is 20; and in a regular course is 40.

Requirements: The SAT or ACT is required. Test scores and GPA are considered in combination according to a sliding scale. Applicants must be graduates of accredited secondary schools or have earned a GED. The university requires 15 academic credits or Carnegie units: 4 years of English, 3 each of math and social studies, 2 of the same foreign language, 2 of science, and 1 of performing arts or an academic elective. A GPA of 2.0 is required. AP and CLEP credits are accepted. Important factors in the admissions decision are leadership record, personality/intangible qualities, and recommendations by school officials.

Procedure: Freshmen are admitted to all sessions. Entrance exams should be taken before the fall of the senior year. There is a rolling admissions plan. Check with the school for current application deadlines. The application fee is $50. Notification is sent on a rolling basis. Applications are accepted online.

Transfer: Students presenting an associate degree need a minimum GPA of 2.5 for automatic offer of admission; those with a GPA of 2.5 to 2.0 will be asked to provide additional information for review. 45 of 180 credits required for the bachelor's degree must be completed at CWU.

Visiting: There are regularly scheduled orientations for prospective students, consisting of an information session, a tour of residence halls, a tour of the campus, prearranged appointments with faculty, and a financial aid presentation. There are guides for informal visits; visitors may sit in on classes and stay overnight. To schedule a visit, contact the Admissions Office.

Financial Aid: The FAFSA is required. Check with the school for current application deadlines.

International Students: The school actively recruits these students. They must take the TOEFL. They must also take the SAT or ACT.

Computers: All students may access the system 24 hours a day. There are no time limits.

Admissions Contact: Director of Admissions. E-Mail: *cwuadmis@cwu.edu* Web: *www.cwu.edu*

CITY UNIVERSITY OF SEATTLE C-2

Seattle, WA 98121 (206) 239-4500; (800) 426-5596

Full-time: 287 men, 351 women
Part-time: 248 men, 304 women
Graduate: 379 men, 606 women
Year: quarters, summer session
Application Deadline: open
Freshman Class: n/av
Faculty: 14
Ph.D.s: n/av
Student/Faculty: 15 to 1
Tuition: $14,880
Room & Board: n/app

NONCOMPETITIVE

City University, established in 1973, is a private (non-profit) institution offering undergraduate, graduate, and doctoral programs in many different delivery modes including online, face to face, or a combination of both, and at a variety of instructional sites including locations in Washington State, Canada, Mexico, Europe, and Asia. There are 2 undergraduate schools and 4 graduate schools. In addition to regional accreditation, CityU has baccalaureate program accreditation with ACBSP. The library contains 46,663 volumes, 551,736 microform items, and 13,000 audio/video tapes/CDs/DVDs, and subscribes to 75,430 periodicals including electronic. Computerized library services include interlibrary loans, database searching, Internet access, and Wi-Fi capability. The 1-acre campus is in an urban area in Seattle. Including any residence halls, there is 1 building.

Student Life: Students are from 45 states, 24 foreign countries, and Canada. 68% are White. The average age of freshmen is 32; all undergraduates, 34.

Housing: Alcohol is not permitted. All students commute. No one may keep cars.

Activities: There are no fraternities or sororities. Groups on campus include international and student government.

Sports: There is no sports program at CityU.

Disabled Students: 90% of the campus is accessible. Facilities include wheelchair ramps, elevators, special parking, and specially equipped restrooms.

Programs of Study: CityU confers B.A., and B.S. degrees. Associate, master's, and doctoral degrees are also awarded. Bachelor's degrees are awarded in BUSINESS (accounting, business administration and management, and marketing/retailing/merchandising), COMPUTER AND PHYSICAL SCIENCE (computer programming and computer information technology), EDUCATION (elementary education and middle school education), SOCIAL SCIENCE (counseling/psychology, criminal justice, and liberal arts/general studies). Business administration has the largest enrollment.

Required: Students are required to complete 180 quarter credits, with a minimum of 45 of these credits taken at City University, and maintain a minimum GPA of 2.0. A minimum of 30 credits are required in the major. All students must complete 55 general education credits, which include courses in the humanities, social sciences, natural sciences, and math.

Special: Opportunities are provided for cooperative programs with other schools, internships, study abroad, work-study programs, dual majors, and student-designed majors. A general studies degree, pass/fail options, independent study, weekend programs, and credit for military service are offered.

Faculty/Classroom: No introductory courses are taught by graduate students. The average class size in an introductory lecture is 25.

Requirements: Graduation from an accredited secondary school is not required; a GED will be accepted. An interview is recommended. AP and CLEP credits are accepted.

Procedure: Freshmen are admitted to all sessions. There are deferred admissions and rolling admissions plans. Application deadlines are open. Application fee is $50.

Transfer: 134 transfer students enrolled in 2012-2013. Students applying for transfer must submit official transcripts from all colleges previously attended. Applicants may transfer up to 135 quarter credits from accredited 4-year colleges, with at least 45 of these credits in upper-level courses. Up to 90 quarter credits may be transferred from 2-year colleges. 45 of 180 credits required for the bachelor's degree must be completed at CityU.

Visiting: To schedule a visit, contact the Student Affairs Office.

Financial Aid: The FAFSA and the college's own financial statement are required. The deadline for filing freshman financial aid applications for fall entry is July 9.

International Students: There are 350 international students enrolled. The school actively recruits these students. They must take the TOEFL and the college's own English placement exam to determine placement in ESL classes if necessary.

Computers: All students may access the system. There are no time limits and no fees.

Graduates: From July 1, 2012 to June 30, 2013, 289 bachelor's degrees were awarded. The most popular majors were business/marketing (72%), education (18%), and computer and information sciences (6%).

Admissions Contact: Student Affairs/Admissions E-Mail: *info@cityu.edu* Web: *www.cityu.edu*

CORNISH COLLEGE OF THE ARTS C-2

Seattle, WA 98121 (206) 726-5016
(800) 726-ARTS; (206) 720-1011

Full-time and part-time: 800
Graduate: n/av
Year: semesters, summer session
Application Deadline: see profile
Faculty: 145
Ph.D.s: 59%
Student/Faculty: 8 to 1
Tuition: $28,750
Room & Board: n/av
Freshman Class: n/av
SAT or ACT: recommended

SPECIAL

Cornish College of the Arts, founded in 1914, is an independent commuter institution offering undergraduate programs in the fine arts, dance, design, music, theater, and performance production. There are 6 undergraduate schools. The figures in the above capsule and in this profile are approximate. In addition to regional accreditation, Cornish has baccalaureate program accreditation with NASAD. The library contains 17,914 volumes, 4570 audio/video tapes/CDs/DVDs, and subscribes to 104 periodicals including electronic. Computerized library services include database searching and Internet access. Special learning facilities include a learning resource center, art gallery, dance studios, large black box theater, studio theater, concert hall, rehearsal facilities, photography, printmaking, painting, sculpture studios, and digital labs. The 4-acre campus is in an urban area in the Capitol Hill and downtown neighborhoods of Seattle. Including any residence halls, there are 5 buildings.

Student Life: 55% of undergraduates are from Washington. Others are from 28 states, 10 foreign countries, and Canada. 67% are white. The average age of freshmen is 23; all undergraduates, 23. 20% do not continue beyond their first year; 50% remain to graduate.

Housing: There are no residence halls. All students commute.

Activities: There are no fraternities or sororities. There are 12 groups on campus, including art, band, chess, choir, chorus, communications, computers, dance, drama, ethnic, film, gay, international, jazz band, literary magazine, musical theater, newspaper, opera, orchestra, photography, political, professional, religious, social, and student government. Popular campus events include Theater Seniors Productions, Costume Design Tea and Fashion Show, and Dance Theater Performances.

Sports: There is no sports program at Cornish.

Disabled Students: 50% of the campus is accessible. Facilities include wheelchair ramps, elevators, special parking, specially equipped rest rooms, lowered drinking fountains, and lowered telephones.

Services: Counseling and information services are available, as is tutoring in every subject. There is a reader service for the blind, and remedial writing. There is a staffed writing center with computers.

Campus Safety and Security: Measures include 24-hour foot and vehicle patrol, self-defense education, and security escort services. There are shuttle buses, emergency telephones, lighted pathways/sidewalks, and card-key access during nonbusiness hours.

Programs of Study: Cornish confers B.F.A. and B.M. degrees. Bachelor's degrees are awarded in COMMUNICATIONS AND THE ARTS (dance, design, dramatic arts, fine arts, music, and theater design). Design and dance are the strongest academically. Fine arts and theater are the largest.

Required: General education requirements include 30 semester hours in the humanities and sciences, as well as 6 to 8 in arts electives. To graduate, students must complete at least 127 semester hours, including 94 in their specific discipline, and maintain a minimum GPA of 2.0 during their senior year.

Special: Cornish offers a premajor first year of study to those music students who initially need more fundamental training. Internships are available to upperclassmen in all majors. Students may earn credit by examination in humanities and science courses, as well as credit for life experience in all majors where appropriate. Work-study programs and nondegree study are also offered.

Faculty/Classroom: 49% of faculty are male; 51% are female. All teach undergraduates. No introductory courses are taught by graduate students. The average class size in an introductory lecture is 18; in a laboratory is 15; and in a regular course is 15.

Requirements: The SAT or ACT is recommended. The required audition or portfolio review is the single most important criterion in the admissions decision. Applicants should be graduates of accredited secondary schools or have earned a GED. In addition to providing evidence of their artistic talent, students must submit 2 essays and arrange for an interview. AP and CLEP credits are accepted. Important factors in the admissions decision are evidence of special talent, personality/intangible qualities, and recommendations by school officials.

Procedure: Freshmen are admitted in the fall. There are deferred admissions and rolling admissions plans. Check with the school for current application deadlines. The application fee is $40. Applications are accepted online.

Transfer: Applicants must meet the same requirements as freshmen. 60 of 127 credits required for the bachelor's degree must be completed at Cornish.

Visiting: There are regularly scheduled orientations for prospective students, consisting of Preview Days during which applicants can attend classes, interact with students and faculty, and experience campus life. There are guides for informal visits and visitors may sit in on classes. To schedule a visit, contact the Admissions Office.

Financial Aid: Cornish is a member of CSS. The FAFSA and the college's own financial statement are required. Check with the school for current application deadlines.

International Students: They must take the TOEFL.

Computers: All students may access the system. There are no time limits. Students enrolled in design must have a personal computer.

Admissions Contact: Jane Buckman, Associate Dean of Enrollment Services. E-Mail: *admissions@cornish.edu* Web: *www.cornish.edu*

EASTERN WASHINGTON UNIVERSITY E-2

Cheney, WA 99004 **509.359.2397; (509) 359-6692**

Full-time: 4490 men, 5225 women	**Faculty:** 408; IIA, --$
Part-time: 882 men, 1081 women	**Ph.D.s:** 98%
Graduate: 364 men, 749 women	**Student/Faculty:** 23 to 1
Year: quarters, summer session	**Tuition:** $7976 ($18,719)
Application Deadline: May 15	**Room & Board:** $8412
Freshman Class: n/av	

COMPETITIVE

Eastern Washington University, founded in 1882, is a comprehensive public university that provides programs in the arts and sciences, business, health sciences and nursing, and technology. There are 4 undergraduate schools and 1 graduate school. In addition to regional accreditation, EWU has baccalaureate program accreditation with AACSB, ABET, ADA, APTA, ASLA, CSAB, CSWE, NASM, NCATE, NLN, and NRPA. The library contains 846,241 volumes, 820,642 microform items, and 56,880 audio/video tapes/CDs/DVDs, and subscribes to 75,183 periodicals including electronic. Computerized library services include interlibrary loans, database searching, Internet access, and Wi-Fi capability. Special learning facilities include an art gallery, planetarium, radio station, Riverpoint Health Sciences complex, Weissenborn Map Library, Indian Education Center, State Digital Archives building, State Crime Lab, and Turnbull Nature Preserve. The 35-acre campus is in a small town 18 miles southwest of Spokane. Including any residence halls, there are 32 buildings.

Student Life: 94% of undergraduates are from Washington. Others are from 43 states, 21 foreign countries, and Canada. 98% are from public schools. 73% are White. The average age of freshmen is 18; all undergraduates, 22. 24% do not continue beyond their first year; 46% remain to graduate.

Housing: 2066 students can be accommodated in college housing, which includes coed dorms, on-campus apartments, and married student housing. In addition, there are special-interest houses, fraternity houses, sorority houses, living and learning communities, all-male, all-female, academic, music, and drama floors, and floors for older students, theme housing, wellness housing, and special housing for disabled students. On-campus housing is available on a first-come, first-served basis. 80% of students commute. Alcohol is not permitted. All students may keep cars.

Activities: 5% of men belong to 9 national fraternities; 5% of women belong to 1 local and 9 national sororities. There are 98 groups on campus, including and sports clubs, art, band, cheerleading, chess, choir, chorale, chorus, computers, dance, debate, drama, environmental, ethnic, film, gay, honors, international, jazz band, literary magazine, marching band, musical theater, newspaper, orchestra, outdoor recreation, pep band, photography, political, professional, radio and TV, religious, social, social service, student government, symphony, and yearbook. Popular campus events include Cinco de Mayo, Hawaii Luau, Homecoming, Pass Through the Pillars, World Party, Mardi Gras, Greek Week Neighbor Festival, Day of Silence.

Sports: There are 12 intercollegiate sports for men and 14 for women, and 13 intramural sports for men and 13 for women. Facilities include a recreation center, a 200-meter indoor track, 12 racquetball courts, an indoor swimming pool, wrestling rooms, a dance studio, a 7000-seat stadium & red turf, a 5800-seat indoor gym, a fitness studio, and volleyball, baseball, and basketball courts.

Disabled Students: 93% of the campus is accessible. Facilities include wheelchair ramps, elevators, special parking, specially equipped restrooms, special class scheduling, lowered drinking fountains, lowered telephones, special housing.

Services: Counseling and information services are available, as is tutoring in every subject. There is a reader service for the blind, and remedial math, reading, and writing.

Campus Safety and Security: Measures include 24-hour foot and vehicle patrol, emergency notification system, self-defense education, and security escort services. There are emergency telephones, lighted pathways/sidewalks, controlled access to dorms/residences, crisis lines, and emergency contact light standards.

Programs of Study: EWU confers B.A., B.S., B.A.B., B.A.E., B.D.H., B.F.A., B.Mus. and B.S.N. degrees. Master's degrees are also awarded. Bachelor's degrees are awarded in BIOLOGICAL SCIENCE (biochemistry, biology/biological science, botany, and microbiology), BUSINESS (accounting, banking and finance, business administration and management, management science, marketing/retailing/merchandising, personnel management, and recreation and leisure services), COMMUNICATIONS AND THE ARTS (art, art history and appreciation, broadcasting, communications, creative writing, dance, dramatic arts, English, French, German, graphic design, journalism, literature, music, music performance, Spanish, speech/debate/rhetoric, and studio art), COMPUTER AND PHYSICAL SCIENCE (chemistry, computer science, geology, information sciences and systems, mathematics, and physics),

EDUCATION (art education, computer education, elementary education, foreign languages education, guidance education, health education, marketing and distribution education, mathematics education, middle school education, music education, physical education, recreation education, science education, secondary education, and social science education), ENGINEERING AND ENVIRONMENTAL DESIGN (computer technology, engineering, engineering technology, mechanical engineering technology, and military science), HEALTH PROFESSIONS (dental hygiene, health care administration, medical laboratory technology, nursing, predentistry, premedicine, preveterinary science, recreation therapy, and speech pathology/audiology), SOCIAL SCIENCE (anthropology, criminal justice, economics, geography, history, humanities, international relations, parks and recreation management, philosophy, political science/government, prelaw, psychology, social science, social work, sociology, and urban studies). Health sciences, biology, and computer science are the strongest academically. Business, education, and social science have the largest enrollments.

Required: All students must complete 180 quarter credits, including 60 to 110 in their major, while earning a minimum GPA of 2.0. Specific requirements include English composition and math courses to demonstrate competency. Distribution requirements include 11 total courses from 3 breadth areas: humanities, natural sciences and math, and social sciences. Seniors must complete a capstone course.

Special: Cooperative programs in nursing, cross-registration with the Intercollegiate School of Nursing, internships with area businesses, and work-study based on federal financial aid are available. B.A.-B.S. degrees, dual majors in any subject, study abroad in 12 countries, 3 types of general studies degrees, student-designed majors, and a 3-2 engineering degree with Washington State University are offered. Credit for military experience, nondegree study, and pass/fail options for nonmajor or nonminor courses also are possible. There are 9 national honor societies, including Phi Beta Kappa, and a freshman honors program.

Faculty/Classroom: 52% of faculty are male; 48% are female. 99% teach undergraduates. No introductory courses are taught by graduate students. The average class size in an introductory lecture is 30; in a laboratory is 20; and in a regular course is 30.

Admissions: 78% of the 2013-2014 applicants were accepted. The SAT scores for the 2013-2014 freshman class were: Critical Reading--57% below 500, 33% between 500 and 599, 9% between 600 and 699, and 1% between 700 and 800; Math--51% below 500, 38% between 500 and 599, 11% between 600 and 699; Writing--64% below 500, 30% between 500 and 599, and 6% between 600 and 699. The ACT scores were 20% below 21, 55% between 21 and 23, and 25% above 28.

Requirements: The SAT or ACT is required. Admission is determined by an index coordinating the GPA with entrance exam scores. The GED is accepted. EWU requires 4 years of English, 3 each of math and social science, 2 each of science (including a lab science) and a single foreign language (ASL accepted), and 1 of fine arts or academic electives. A GPA of 2.0 is required. AP and CLEP credits are accepted.

Procedure: Freshmen are admitted to all sessions. Entrance exams should be taken during the spring of the junior year or fall of the senior year. There are deferred admissions and rolling admissions plans. Applications should be filed by May 15 for fall entry, along with a $50 fee. Notifications are sent November 1. Applications are accepted online.

Transfer: 1423 transfer students enrolled in 2012-2013. Applicants with fewer than 40 credits must submit high school and college transcripts and test scores; those with more than 40 credits acceptable by Eastern or who have earned an associate degree from a Washington community college must submit a college transcript. 45 of 180 credits required for the bachelor's degree must be completed at EWU.

Visiting: There are regularly scheduled orientations for prospective students, consisting of overnight programs for students and parents that present informational sessions on campus life and academic survival skills, academic advising, course registration, and social functions. There are guides for informal visits, visitors may sit in on classes, and stay overnight. To schedule a visit, contact the Visitors Center at (509) 359-6555.

Financial Aid: In 2013-2014, 66% of all full-time freshmen and 65% of continuing full-time students received some form of financial aid. 51% of all full-time freshmen and 50% of continuing full-time students received need-based aid. The average freshman award was $12,975. Need-based scholarships or need-based grants averaged $7,455; need-based self-help aid (loans and jobs) averaged $2,591; and non-need-based athletic scholarships averaged $8,895. 89% of undergraduate students work part-time. Average annual earnings from campus work are $3000. The average financial indebtedness of the 2013 graduate was $22,925. The FAFSA is required. The priority date for freshman financial aid applications for fall entry is February 15.

International Students: There are 399 international students enrolled. The school actively recruits these students. They must take the TOEFL with a minimum score of 525 on the paper-based TOEFL (PBT) or 71 on the Internet-based version (iBT). They must also take the SAT or ACT.

Computers: All students may access the system throughout the school day plus evenings and weekends. There are no time limits. The fee is $35 per term.

Graduates: From July 1, 2012 to June 30, 2013, 2252 bachelor's degrees were awarded. The most popular majors were business/marketing (18%), health professions and related programs (10%), and social sciences (9%). 60 companies recruited on campus in 2012-2013. In an average class, 20% graduate in 4 years or less, 39% graduate in 5 years or less, and 47% graduate in 6 years or less.

Admissions Contact: Shannon Carr, Director of Admissions. E-Mail: *Admissions@ewu.edu* Web: *http:/www.ewu.edu/Admissions.xml*

EVERGREEN STATE COLLEGE — B-3

Olympia, WA 98505 — **(360) 867-6170; (360) 867-6576**

Full-time: 2176 men, 2618 women	**Faculty:** 247
Part-time: 510	**Ph.D.s:** 87%
Graduate: 100 men, 210 women	**Student/Faculty:** 23 to 1
Year: trimesters, summer session	**Tuition:** $20,500
Application Deadline: see profile	**Room & Board:** $8500
Freshman Class: n/av	
SAT or ACT: required	

COMPETITIVE+

Evergreen State College, founded in 1967, is a public liberal arts and sciences college offering interdisciplinary, collaborative, and team-taught academic programs. There are 3 graduate schools. Figures in the above capsule and in this profile are approximate. The library contains 471,406 volumes, 494,714 microform items, 89,195 audio/video tapes/CDs/DVDs, and subscribes to 12,579 periodicals including electronic. Computerized library services include interlibrary loans, database searching, Internet access, and laptop Internet portals. Special learning facilities include a learning resource center, art gallery, radio station, TV station, organic farm and community gardens, Longhouse Education and Cultural Center, Evergreen Art Galleries, animation and design studio, ceramics studio, metal shop, wood shop, photography studios and darkrooms, science laboratories, and access to media equipment, computer labs, and scientific equipment. The 1000-acre campus is in a small town 7 miles west of Olympia. Including any residence halls, there are 73 buildings.

Student Life: 77% of undergraduates are from Washington. Others are from 48 states, 9 foreign countries, and Canada. 69% are white. The average age of freshmen is 19; all undergraduates, 25. 32% do not continue beyond their first year; 57% remain to graduate.

Housing: 925 students can be accommodated in college housing, which includes coed dorms, on-campus apartments, and married student housing. In addition, there are special-interest houses, drug-and alcohol-free housing, first-year experience, quiet housing, Community Action House, and Sustainability House. On-campus housing is guaranteed for the freshman year only and is available on a first-come, first-served basis. 78% of students commute. Alcohol is not permitted. All students may keep cars.

Activities: There are no fraternities or sororities. There are 78 groups on campus, including art, choir, chorale, communications, dance, drama, environmental, ethnic, film, gay, international, literary magazine, newspaper, photography, political, professional, radio and TV, religious, social, social service, and student government. Popular campus events include Super Saturday, Evergreen Expressions Series (performance/media art), and Olympia Film Society.

Sports: There are 3 intercollegiate sports for men and 4 for women, and 10 intramural sports for men and 10 for women. Facilities include a recreation center, which houses an 11-lane swimming pool, a diving well, exercise and weight training rooms, 5 racquetball courts, and indoor climbing walls. There is a 3100-seat gym, a covered pavilion, 4 tennis courts, and 5 playing fields.

Disabled Students: All of the campus is accessible. Facilities include wheelchair ramps, elevators, special parking, specially equipped rest rooms, lowered drinking fountains, and lowered telephones.

Services: Counseling and information services are available, as is tutoring in some subjects. The Writing Center offers assistance in writing; the Quantitive and Symbolic Reasoning Center offers assistance with all levels of math, economics, statistics, chemistry, biology, physics, and computer science. There is a reader service for the blind.

Campus Safety and Security: Measures include 24-hour foot and vehicle patrol, self-defense education, and security escort services. There are emergency telephones and lighted pathways/sidewalks.

Programs of Study: Evergreen confers B.A., B.S., and B.A.S degrees. Master's degrees are also awarded. Bachelor's degrees are awarded in COMPUTER AND PHYSICAL SCIENCE (natural sciences), SOCIAL SCIENCE (liberal arts/general studies).

Required: Students must earn a minimum of 180 quarter hours of credit to receive a B.A. or B.S. degree. For a B.A. 45 of the last 90 credits must be earned at Evergreen (for transfer students). For a B.S. students must have completed 72 credits of science, math, or computer science, 48 of which must be upper division. For a B.A.S. dual degree 225 credits are required and students must meet the requirements of a B.A. and B.S.

Special: All work at the college is interdisciplinary, and the programs of study change annually. The college's credit-generating options include the comprehensive Coordinated Study Program, which allows students and faculty to work together intensively. Credits may be earned through cooperative programs, work-study programs, internships, independent contracts, or from prior learning and military experience.

Faculty/Classroom: 51% of faculty are male; 49% are female. 91% teach undergraduates. No introductory courses are taught by graduate students. The average class size in an introductory lecture is 50; in a laboratory is 23; and in a regular course is 25.

Requirements: The SAT or ACT is required. Candidates should be graduates of an accredited secondary school and have completed 15 academic credits, consisting of 4 in English, 3 each in math and social studies, 2 each in foreign language and science (one of which must be a lab science in biology, chemistry, or physics), and 1 in fine, visual, or performing arts or other college preparatory elective from another area mentioned in list. A GED is acceptable. A GPA of 2.0 is required. AP and CLEP credits are accepted. Important factors in the admissions decision are advanced placement or honors courses, evidence of special talent, and ability to finance college education.

Procedure: Freshmen are admitted fall, winter, and spring. Entrance exams should be taken during the spring of the junior year or fall of the senior year. Check with the school for current application deadlines and fee. Applications are accepted online.

Transfer: Applicants with fewer than 40 credits must submit SAT or ACT scores and a high school transcript. A 2.0 minimum GPA is required. An associate degree is recommended. All applicants must submit all college transcripts. 45 of 180 credits required for the bachelor's degree must be completed at Evergreen.

Visiting: There are regularly scheduled orientations for prospective students, including an admissions session, a class visit, and a campus tour. There are guides for informal visits; visitors may sit in on classes and stay overnight. To schedule a visit, contact the Student Visitor Program.

Financial Aid: Evergreen is a member of CSS. The FAFSA and the college's own financial statement are required. Check with the school for current application deadlines.

International Students: They must take the TOEFL with a minimum score of 550 on the paper-based TOEFL (PBT) or 79 on the Internet-based version (iBT). They must also take the SAT or ACT.

Computers: Open wireless is available on much of the core campus and residential areas. Ethernet is available in campus housing. All dorms are wired for access to the network, online course registration, and student access to academic records and student account information, off-campus access to campus network, wireless network, student web hosting, and online library. There is extensive multimedia equipment available for student use. Multiple computer labs exist on campus that provide both general use and discipline specific access to technology resources. All students may access the system 24 hours. There are no time limits and no fees.

Admissions Contact: Admissions Office. E-Mail: *admissions@evergreen.edu* Web: *www.evergreen.edu*

GONZAGA UNIVERSITY — E-2

Spokane, WA 99258 — (509) 313-6591; (800) 322-2584; (509) 313-5780

Full-time: 2206 men, 2620 women	**Faculty:** 350
Part-time: 34 men, 36 women	**Ph.D.s:** 83%
Graduate: 1061 men, 1648 women	**Student/Faculty:** 11 to 1
Year: semesters, summer session	**Tuition:** $35,127
Application Deadline: February 1	**Room & Board:** $9120
Freshman Class: 7031 applied, 4790 accepted, 1238 enrolled	
SAT CR/M: 596/605	**ACT:** 27 **HIGHLY COMPETITIVE**

Gonzaga University, founded in 1887, is a private, liberal arts institution affiliated with the Roman Catholic Church and the Society of Jesus (Jesuits). The university offers undergraduate and graduate degrees in arts and sciences, business, education, engineering, nursing, and human physiology. The figures in the above capsule and in this profile are approximate. There are 5 undergraduate schools and 7 graduate schools. In addition to regional accreditation, Gonzaga has baccalaureate program accreditation with AACSB, ABET, and NCATE. The 2 libraries contain 527,693 volumes, 6,808 audio/video tapes/CDs/DVDs, and subscribe to 48,895 periodicals including electronic. Computerized library services include interlibrary loans, database searching, Internet access, and Wi-Fi capability. Special learning facilities include an art gallery, radio station, and TV station. The 131-acre campus is in an urban area near downtown Spokane. Including any residence halls, there are 105 buildings.

Student Life: 54% of undergraduates are from out of state, mostly the West. Students are from 43 states, 26 foreign countries, and Canada. 63% are from public schools. 73% are White. 50% are Catholic; 22% claim no religious affiliation; 15% Protestant. The average age of freshmen is 18; all undergraduates, 20. 6% do not continue beyond their first year; 82% remain to graduate.

Housing: 3028 students can be accommodated in college housing, which includes single-sex and coed dorms, on-campus apartments, off-campus apartments, and married student housing. In addition, there are special-interest houses, Living and Learning Communities within residence halls. On-campus housing is guaranteed for the freshman year only, is available on a first-come, first-served basis, and is available on a lottery system for upperclassmen. 59% of students live on campus; of those, 75% remain on campus on weekends. All students may keep cars.

Activities: There are no fraternities or sororities. There are 102 groups on campus, including art, band, cheerleading, chess, choir, chorale, chorus, communications, computers, dance, debate, drama, drill team, environmental, ethnic, gay, honors, international, jazz band, literary magazine, mock trial, musical theater, newspaper, orchestra, pep band, photography, political, professional, radio and TV, religious, social, social service, student government, symphony, and yearbook. Popular campus events include Search and other spiritual retreats, GEL Weekend, Charity Ball and Fall Family Weekend.

Sports: There are 7 intercollegiate sports for men and 7 for women, and 26 intramural sports for men and 26 for women. Facilities include Basketball arena, 2 basketball/volleyball courts, indoor golf and tennis building (six courts), outdoor grass soccer practice facility adjoined to an outdoor grass game field, outdoor baseball stadium and field, indoor rowing room, athletic weight room, student fitness center with cardiovascular and weight areas, multipurpose synthetic turf field, 3 multipurpose courts, 4 racquetball courts, 2 aerobics rooms, indoor running track, and a 6-lane 25-yard swimming pool.

Disabled Students: 90% of the campus is accessible. Facilities include wheelchair ramps, elevators, special parking, specially equipped restrooms, special class scheduling, lowered drinking fountains, lowered telephones. Academic adjustments are provided for students with disabilities who provide appropriate documentation and request services from Disabilities, Resources, Education, and Access Management (DREAM). Accessible rooms exist in some residence halls and apartments.

Services: Counseling and information services are available, as is tutoring in most subjects. There is a reader service for the blind. Informal peer tutoring in English and math is available.

Campus Safety and Security: Measures include 24-hour foot and vehicle patrol, emergency notification system, self-defense education, and security escort services. There are shuttle buses, emergency telephones, lighted pathways/sidewalks, and controlled access to dorms/residences.

Programs of Study: Gonzaga confers B.A., B.S., B.B.A., B.Ed., and B.S.N. degrees. Master's and doctoral degrees are also awarded. Bachelor's degrees are awarded in AGRICULTURE (environmental studies), BIOLOGICAL SCIENCE (biochemistry and biology/biological science), BUSINESS (accounting, business administration and management, and business economics), COMMUNICATIONS AND THE ARTS (art, broadcasting, classics, communications, dramatic arts, English, French, journalism, literature, music, public relations, Spanish, and speech/debate/rhetoric), COMPUTER AND PHYSICAL SCIENCE (chemistry, computer science, mathematics, and physics), EDUCATION (music education, physical education, and special education), ENGINEERING AND ENVIRONMENTAL DESIGN (civil engineering, computer engineering, electrical/electronics engineering, and mechanical engineering), HEALTH PROFESSIONS (exercise science and nursing), SOCIAL SCIENCE (classical/ancient civilization, criminal justice, economics, history, interdisciplinary studies, international studies, Italian studies, liberal arts/general studies, philosophy, political science/government, psychology, religion, and sociology). Engineering and business administration are the strongest academically. Business, engineering, and liberal arts have the largest enrollments.

Required: All students must complete at least 128 credit hours with a minimum 2.0 GPA. The major requirements are 18 hours in upper-division courses and supporting courses required by the major department. Students must complete 9 credits each of philosophy and religious studies, 7 credits in English, speech, and critical thinking, and 3 credits each in math and English literature.

Special: Cross-registration with Whitworth University, internships, study abroad in 40 countries, a Washington semester, an summer faculty-led program in Alaska and on- and off-campus work-study programs are offered. High school juniors and seniors may take 6 credits per semester in certain areas. There is a limited pass/fail option, and dual majors are possible. There are 12 national honor societies and a freshman honors program.

Faculty/Classroom: 56% of faculty are male; 44% are female. 80% teach undergraduates. No introductory courses are taught by graduate students. The average class size in an introductory lecture is 23; in a laboratory is 18; and in a regular course is 23.

Admissions: 68% of the 2013-2014 applicants were accepted. The SAT scores for the 2013-2014 freshman class were: Critical Reading--6% below 500, 44% between 500 and 599, 40% between 600 and 699, and 10% between 700 and 800; Math--3% below 500, 40% between 500 and 599, 46% between 600 and 699, and 11% between 700 and 800. The ACT scores were 12% between 21 and 23, 33% between 24 and 26, 20% between 27 and 28, and 35% above 28. There was 1 National Merit finalist.

Requirements: The SAT or ACT is required. Applicants should be graduates of an accredited secondary school. They must have completed 17 academic credits consisting of 4 years of English, 3 to 4 years of math, 2 to 3 years of the same foreign language; world language preferred, ASL accepted, 3 years of history and/or social science, and 3 to 4 years of natural or physical laboratory science. An essay and letters of recommendation are required. An interview is optional but recommended for students with a GPA lower than 3.1 or SAT score less than 1070 for Verbal/Critical plus Math, or 23 ACT Composite. AP credits are accepted. Important factors in the admissions decision are advanced placement or honors courses, leadership record, and extracurricular activities record.

Procedure: Freshmen are admitted fall and spring. Entrance exams should be taken by time of application. There are early admissions and deferred admissions plans. Early decision applications should be filed by November 15; regular applications, by February 1 for fall entry; and November 15 for spring entry, along with a $50 fee. Notification of early decision is sent January 15; regular decision, April 1. 160 applicants were on the 2013 waiting list; 55 were admitted. Applications are accepted online.

Transfer: 121 transfer students enrolled in 2012-2013. A minimum GPA of 2.7 is required. An interview is recommended. 30 of 128 credits required for the bachelor's degree must be completed at Gonzaga.

Visiting: There are regularly scheduled orientations for prospective students, Day visits are permitted Monday through Friday; overnight visits, Sunday through Thursday (except for holiday periods). There are guides for informal visits, visitors may sit in on classes, and stay overnight. To schedule a visit, contact the Gonzaga Visit Office at (509) 13-6531.

Financial Aid: In 2013-2014, 98% of all full-time freshmen and 96% of continuing full-time students received some form of financial aid. 74% of all full-time freshmen and 72% of continuing full-time students received need-based aid. The average freshman award was $23,496. Need-based scholarships or need-based grants averaged $7,342 ($32,859 maximum); need-based self-help aid (loans and jobs) averaged $5,654 ($13,300 maximum); non-need-based athletic scholarships averaged $22,966 ($45,340 maximum); and other non-need-based awards and non-need-based scholarships averaged $13,227 ($48,654 maximum). 25% of undergraduate students work part-time. Average annual earnings from campus work are $2291. The average financial indebtedness of the 2013 graduate was $26,740. Gonzaga is a member of CSS. The FAFSA is required. The deadline for filing freshman financial aid applications for fall entry is February 1.

International Students: There are 62 international students enrolled. The school actively recruits these students. They must take the TOEFL with a minimum score of 550 on the paper-based TOEFL (PBT) or 80 on the Internet-based version (iBT) or take the MELAB or the ESL Exit Exam, which includes a writing test.

Computers: All students may access the system 24 hours per day. There are no time limits and no fees.

Graduates: From July 1, 2012 to June 30, 2013, 1444 bachelor's degrees were awarded. The most popular majors were business and management (24%), social sciences (13%), and engineering (9%). 100 companies recruited on campus in 2012-2013. In an average class, 1% graduate in 3 years or less, 71% graduate in 4 years or less, 81% graduate in 5 years or less, and 82% graduate in 6 years or less. Of the 2012 graduating class, 21% were enrolled in graduate school within 6 months of graduation, and 91% were employed.

Admissions Contact: Julie McCulloh, Dean of Admissions. E-Mail: *mcculloh@gu.gonzaga.edu* Web: *www.gonzaga.edu*

HERITAGE UNIVERSITY D-3

Toppenish, WA 98948 **(509) 865-8697; (509) 865-4469**

Full-time: 150 men, 502 women	**Faculty:** 55
Part-time: 51 men, 173 women	**Ph.D.s:** 40%
Graduate: 80 men, 172 women	**Student/Faculty:** 12 to 1
Year: semesters, summer session	**Tuition:** $17,664
Application Deadline: open	**Room & Board:** n/app
Freshman Class: n/av	
SAT or ACT: recommended	

NONCOMPETITIVE

Heritage College, founded in 1982, is a private, nonprofit commuter college offering undergraduate and graduate programs in liberal arts and teacher education, half of which are given on evenings and weekends. There are 2 undergraduate schools and 2 graduate schools. In addition to regional accreditation, Heritage has baccalaureate program accreditation with CSWE. The library contains 93,254 volumes, 152,244 microform items, and 1,190 audio/video tapes/CDs/DVDs, and subscribes to 18,320 periodicals including electronic. Computerized library services include interlibrary loans, database searching, Internet access, and Wi-Fi capability. The 48-acre campus is in a rural area 20 miles south of Yakima. Including any residence halls, there are 34 buildings.

Student Life: 99% of undergraduates are from Washington. Others are from 5 states. 57% are Hispanic; 25% White. The average age of freshmen is 24; all undergraduates, 30. 43% do not continue beyond their first year; 57% remain to graduate.

Housing: College-sponsored housing includes Alcohol is not permitted. All students commute. All students may keep cars.

Activities: There are no fraternities or sororities. There are 5 groups on campus, including HUNAC (Native American), Social Work, art, choir, computers, dance, ENACTUS (business), ethnic, honors, professional, religious, social, social service, and student government. Popular campus events include Spring Faire, and Academic Convocation.

Sports: There are 2 intramural sports for men and 2 for women. Facilities include a track and field used for soccer, flag football, and volleyball, and a basketball court.

Disabled Students: 95% of the campus is accessible. Facilities include wheelchair ramps, special parking, specially equipped restrooms, special class scheduling, and lowered drinking fountains.

Services: Counseling and information services are available, as is tutoring in some subjects. There is remedial math, reading, and writing.

Campus Safety and Security: Measures include emergency notification system and security escort services. There are emergency telephones and lighted pathways/sidewalks.

Programs of Study: Heritage confers B.A., B.S., and B.A.Ed. and B.S.W. degrees. Associate and master's degrees are also awarded. Bachelor's degrees are awarded in BUSINESS (accounting and business administration and management), COMMUNICATIONS AND THE ARTS (art and English), COMPUTER AND PHYSICAL SCIENCE (computer science, mathematics, and science), EDUCATION (art education, early childhood education, elementary education, science education, and secondary education), ENGINEERING AND ENVIRONMENTAL DESIGN (environmental science), HEALTH PROFESSIONS (biomedical science), SOCIAL SCIENCE (interdisciplinary studies, Native American studies, psychology, and social work). Education has the largest enrollment.

Required: All students must complete 44 to 45 credits of general college requirements, which include 12 credits each in arts and letters, 10 credits in science and math, 9 credits in social sciences, 1 year of English, a computer course, a math course above the 100-level, and a world civilization course. At least 126 semester credit hours must be completed, with at least 48 upper-division credits. Education majors must have a minimum GPA of 2.5; others must have a 2.0.

Special: Heritage provides individualized assistance. Credit by examination is available in many courses, and credit may be given for work experience. The college also has cooperative programs with 3 school districts, internships in local businesses, social service agencies, and cross-registration with Northwest Indian College. Pass/fail options are possible for some courses. An accelerated degree program is available in business adminstration. There is a freshman honors program.

Faculty/Classroom: 41% of faculty are male; 59% are female. 82% teach undergraduates. No introductory courses are taught by graduate students. The average class size in an introductory lecture is 14; in a laboratory is 12; and in a regular course is 9.

Requirements: The SAT or ACT and ACT Writing Test are recommended. AP and CLEP credits are accepted.

Procedure: Freshmen are admitted to all sessions. Entrance exams should be taken before registering. There is a rolling admissions plan. Application deadlines are open.

Transfer: 104 transfer students enrolled in 2012-2013. Students must have complete 30 credits. 32 of 126 credits required for the bachelor's degree must be completed at Heritage.

Visiting: There are regularly scheduled orientations for prospective students, consisting of a day and an evening fall orientation. There are guides for informal visits and visitors may sit in on classes. To schedule a visit, contact the Director of Admissions.

Financial Aid: In 2013-2014, 98% of all full-time freshmen and 93% of continuing full-time students received some form of financial aid. 98% of all full-time freshmen and 93% of continuing full-time students received need-based aid. The average freshman award was $18,033. Need-based scholarships or need-based grants averaged $13,241 ($18,465 maximum); need-based self-help aid (loans and jobs) averaged $5,886 ($12,500 maximum); and other non-need-based awards and non-need-based scholarships averaged $339 ($8,233 maximum). 6% of undergraduate students work part-time. Average annual earnings from campus work are $5200. The average financial indebtedness of the 2013 graduate was $24,356. Heritage is a member of CSS. The CSS/Profile, FAFSA, and the college's own financial statement are required. The priority date for freshman financial aid applications for fall entry is February 10.

International Students: They must take the TOEFL.

Computers: All students may access the system during open hours. There are no time limits and no fees.

Graduates: From July 1, 2012 to June 30, 2013, 141 bachelor's degrees were awarded. The most popular majors were education (51%), social work (11%), and business (11%).

Admissions Contact: Olivia Gutierrez, Director of Admissions. E-Mail: *Gutierrez_O@heritage.edu* Web: *www.heritage.edu*

NORTHWEST UNIVERSITY C-2

Kirkland, WA 98033 (425) 889-5231
(800) 669-3781; (425) 889-5224

Full-time: 365 men, 610 women
Part-time: 40 men, 50 women
Graduate: 30 men, 55 women
Year: semesters, summer session
Application Deadline: see profile
Freshman Class: n/av
SAT or ACT: required
Faculty: n/av; IIB, --$
Ph.D.s: 41%
Student/Faculty: n/av
Tuition: $12,000
Room & Board: $8000

COMPETITIVE

Northwest University, founded in 1934, is a private institution offering programs in ministry, business, nursing, and education. There are 2 graduate schools. The figures in the above capsule and this profile are approximate. The library contains 174,100 volumes, 40,800 microform items, and 5000 audio/video tapes/CDs/DVDs, and subscribes to 900 periodicals including electronic. Computerized library services include interlibrary loans, database searching, and Internet access. Special learning facilities include a radio station. The 56-acre campus is in a suburban area in Kirkland, 10 miles east of Seattle and overlooking Lake Washington. Including any residence halls, there are 27 buildings.

Student Life: 79% of undergraduates are from Washington. Others are from 23 states, 15 foreign countries, and Canada. 60% are white. 99% are Protestant. The average age of freshmen is 19; all undergraduates, 25. 34% do not continue beyond their first year; 34% remain to graduate.

Housing: 544 students can be accommodated in college housing, which includes single-sex dorms, on-campus apartments, and married student housing. On-campus housing is guaranteed for all 4 years. 63% of students live on campus; of those, 80% remain on campus on weekends. Alcohol is not permitted. All students may keep cars.

Activities: There are no fraternities or sororities. There are 20 groups on campus, including and radio, band, choir, chorale, chorus, communications, debate, drama, forensics, international, jazz band, literary magazine, musical theater, newspaper, orchestra, photography, professional, religious, social, social service, student government, and yearbook. Popular campus events include Christmas Holiday Social, All-School Banquet, and Roomies Night-out.

Sports: There are 4 intercollegiate sports for men and 4 for women, and 2 intramural sports for men and 2 for women. Facilities include a gym pavilion, outdoor tennis courts, a practice field for soccer and intramural football, access to the Seattle Seahawks' fields, outdoor basketball, and sand volleyball.

Disabled Students: 75% of the campus is accessible. Facilities include wheelchair ramps, elevators, special parking, specially equipped rest rooms, and residence hall restrooms and shower facilities.

Services: There is a reader service for the blind and remedial writing. The Student Success Office provides assistance in most areas, including study skills.

Campus Safety and Security: Measures include 24-hour foot and vehicle patrol and security escort services. There are shuttle buses, emergency telephones, and lighted pathways/sidewalks.

Programs of Study: NC confers B.A. degrees. Associates and master's degrees are also awarded. Bachelor's degrees are awarded in BIOLOGICAL SCIENCE (life science), BUSINESS (business administration and management), COMMUNICATIONS AND THE ARTS (communications, English, journalism, music, and music business management), COMPUTER AND PHYSICAL SCIENCE (computer management), EDUCATION (education, elementary education, middle school education, physical education, secondary education, and special education), ENGINEERING AND ENVIRONMENTAL DESIGN (environmental science), HEALTH PROFESSIONS (nursing), SOCIAL SCIENCE (behavioral science, biblical studies, counseling/psychology, history, interdisciplinary studies, liberal arts/general studies, ministries, missions, pastoral studies, philosophy, psychology, religion, religious education, religious music, theological studies, and youth ministry). Teacher education, business, and psychology are the strongest academically. Teacher education, church ministries, and business have the largest enrollments.

Required: Students must complete 18 credits in humanities, 16 in religion, 12 in social science, and 10 each in science and math. At least 125 semester credits (up to 139 for teacher education), with a minimum GPA of 2.0, are required. The number of semester credits needed in the major varies from 36 to 50.

Special: Northwest offers study in several locations in the U.S. and foreign countries through the Council for Christian Colleges and Universities. Dual majors are available. There are 2 national honor societies and 1 departmental honors program.

Faculty/Classroom: 65% of faculty are male; 35% are female. All teach undergraduates. No introductory courses are taught by graduate students. The average class size in an introductory lecture is 30, in a laboratory, 20, and in a regular course, 24.

Requirements: The SAT or ACT is required. A GPA of 2.3 is required. AP and CLEP credits are accepted. Important factors in the admissions decision are personality/intangible qualities, recommendations by alumni, and leadership record.

Procedure: Freshmen are admitted to all sessions. Entrance exams should be taken in the spring of the junior year. There are early decision, deferred admissions, and rolling admissions plans. Check with the school for current application deadlines and fee.

Transfer: Transfers must have a minimum 2.3 GPA from high school and college and must submit SAT or ACT scores, an essay, and 2 letters of reference. 30 of 125 credits required for the bachelor's degree must be completed at NC.

Visiting: There are regularly scheduled orientations for prospective students, including Northwest Fridays. There are guides for informal visits; visitors may sit in on classes and stay overnight.

Financial Aid: The FAFSA and the college's own financial statement are required. Check with the school for application deadlines.

International Students: They must take the TOEFL.

Computers: All students may access the system. There are set hours for labs; residence halls are always connected. There are no time limits. It is strongly recommended that all students have a personal computer. An IBM or Microsoft Windows Office-compatible computer is recommended.

Admissions Contact: Undergraduate Admissions. A campus DVD is available. E-Mail: *admissions@northwestu.edu* Web: *www.northwestu .edu*

PACIFIC LUTHERAN UNIVERSITY C-2

Tacoma, WA 98447-0003 (253) 535-7151
(800) 274-6758; (253) 536-5136

Full-time: 1158 men, 1870 women
Part-time: 60 men, 78 women
Graduate: 100 men, 207 women
Year: 4-1-4, summer session
Application Deadline:
Freshman Class: 2818 applied, 2643 accepted, 648 enrolled
SAT CR/M: 548/550
Faculty: 254; IIA, --$
Ph.D.s: 88%
Student/Faculty: 15 to 1
Tuition: $24,740
Room & Board: $10,100
ACT: 25

VERY COMPETITIVE

Pacific Lutheran University, founded in 1890, is a coeducational, independent institution affiliated with the Evangelical Lutheran Church in America. The figures in the above capsule and in this profile are approximate. There are 7 undergraduate schools and 5 graduate schools. In addition to regional accreditation, PLU has baccalaureate program accreditation with AACSB, ABET, CSWE, NASM, and NCATE. The library contains 610,134 volumes, 236,411 microform items, 13,521 audio/video tapes/CDs/DVDs, and subscribes to 4,474 periodicals including electronic. Computerized library services include interlibrary loans, database searching, Internet access, and Wi-Fi capability. Special learning facilities include an art gallery, radio station, TV station, an herbarium, invertebrate and vertebrate museums, a biology field station, Northwest history collections, a Scandinavian history collection, and a language resource center. The 126-acre campus is in a suburban area 7 miles south of Tacoma. Including any residence halls, there are 41 buildings.

Student Life: 76% of undergraduates are from Washington. Others are from 40 states, 21 foreign countries, and Canada. 97% are from public schools. 71% are White. 61% are Protestant. The average age of freshmen is 18; all undergraduates, 21. 17% do not continue beyond their first year; 69% remain to graduate.

Housing: 1700 students can be accommodated in college housing, which includes single-sex and coed dorms, on-campus apartments, and married student housing. In addition, there are honors houses, language houses, and special-interest houses. On-campus housing is guaranteed for the freshman year only. 51% of students live on campus; of those, 75% remain on campus on weekends. All students may keep cars.

Activities: There are no fraternities or sororities. There are 67 groups on campus, including advertising, and commuter, comedy, adult student, art, band, cheerleading, choir, chorale, chorus, computers, dance, debate, drama, environmental, ethnic, film, forensics, gay, honors, international, jazz band, literary magazine, musical theater, newspaper, opera, orchestra, pep band, photography, political, professional, radio and TV, religious, social, social service, student government, and symphony. Popular campus events include Songfest, Family Weekend, Homecoming, PLUtonic Concerts, Clay Crows, and Dance Ensemble.

Sports: There are 11 intercollegiate sports for men and 10 for women, and 8 intramural sports for men and 8 for women. Facilities include a 3500-seat gym/auditorium, 800-seat center for the performing arts, a 150-seat black box theatre, Lagerquist Concert Hall fitness center, a swimming pool, racquetball, and tennis courts. There is additional recreational space in Memorial Gym for volleyball and basketball. All weather soccer field, softball and baseball fields and other fields for practice.

Disabled Students: 90% of the campus is accessible. Facilities include wheelchair ramps, elevators, special parking, specially equipped restrooms, special class scheduling, lowered drinking fountains, and lowered telephones.

Services: Counseling and information services are available, as is tutoring

in most subjects. There is a reader service for the blind. Study groups and pretest and posttest reviews are also available.

Campus Safety and Security: Measures include 24-hour foot and vehicle patrol, emergency notification system, self-defense education, and security escort services. There are emergency telephones, lighted pathways/sidewalks, and controlled access to dorms/residences.

Programs of Study: PLU confers B.A., B.S., B.A.E., B.A.P.E., B.A.Rec., B.B.A., B.F.A., B.M., B.M.A., B.M.Ed., B.S.N. and B.S.P.E. degrees. Master's degrees are also awarded. Bachelor's degrees are awarded in BIOLOGICAL SCIENCE (biology/biological science), BUSINESS (business administration and management and recreation and leisure services), COMMUNICATIONS AND THE ARTS (art, classics, communications, English, fine arts, French, German, music, music performance, music theory and composition, piano/organ, Scandinavian languages, Spanish, and voice), COMPUTER AND PHYSICAL SCIENCE (applied physics, chemistry, computer programming, computer science, geoscience, mathematics, and physics), EDUCATION (education, music education, and physical education), ENGINEERING AND ENVIRONMENTAL DESIGN (computer engineering, engineering and applied science, and environmental science), HEALTH PROFESSIONS (nursing), SOCIAL SCIENCE (anthropology, Asian/Oriental studies, economics, history, international studies, philosophy, political science/government, psychology, religion, Scandinavian studies, social work, sociology, and women's studies). Business administration, education, and nursing have the largest enrollments.

Required: All students must complete 128 credit hours, with a maximum of 40 in the major. Candidates for degrees in nursing, business administration, and education need a cumulative 2.5 GPA; all others must have a 2.0 GPA. The required curriculum is 36 credit hours of distributive core courses in arts/literature, natural sciences/math, philosophy, religious studies, and social sciences; writing and critical conversation courses; and diversity classes. There is a senior capstone project required.

Special: PLU offers 2 different bachelor's degrees simultaneously, 3-2 engineering degrees with Washington University in St. Louis and Columbia University, and accelerated degree programs in most majors. Dual majors and student-designed majors can be arranged. Extensive internships with local businesses and nonprofit organizations, work-study programs, nondegree study, and pass/fail options are also available. The Wang Center for International Programs supports the university's internationally focused academic programs. There are study-abroad programs in 28 countries. There are 6 national honor societies and a freshman honors program.

Faculty/Classroom: 44% of faculty are male; 56% are female. 99% teach undergraduates, 90% do research, and 90% do both. No introductory courses are taught by graduate students. The average class size in an introductory lecture is 23; in a laboratory is 16; and in a regular course is 17.

Admissions: 94% of the 2013-2014 applicants were accepted. The SAT scores for the 2013-2014 freshman class were: Critical Reading--28% below 500, 41% between 500 and 599, 26% between 600 and 699, and 5% between 700 and 800; Math--29% below 500, 41% between 500 and 599, 24% between 600 and 699, and 6% between 700 and 800; Writing--33% below 500, 43% between 500 and 599, 21% between 600 and 699, and 3% between 700 and 800. The ACT scores were 4% below 21, 24% between 21 and 23, 27% between 24 and 26, 15% between 27 and 28, and 18% above 28. 64% of the current freshmen were in the top fifth of their class; 87% were in the top two fifths.

Requirements: The SAT or ACT is required. In addition, applicants should be graduates of accredited secondary schools, although GED certificates are accepted. PLU requires 2 years each of college preparatory math and a foreign language and recommends 4 years of English, 2 each of social studies and lab science, 1 of fine or performing arts, and 3 of electives. An essay is required. A GPA of 2.0 is required. AP and CLEP credits are accepted. Important factors in the admissions decision are advanced placement or honors courses, leadership record, and evidence of special talent.

Procedure: Freshmen are admitted fall and spring. Entrance exams should be taken by January of the senior year. There are deferred admissions and rolling admissions plans. Application deadlines are open. Application fee is $40. Notification is sent on a rolling basis. Applications are accepted online. Application fees are waived if application is completed online.

Transfer: 240 transfer students enrolled in 2012-2013. Candidates must be in good academic and personal standing at the institutions last attended full time. Although it does not guarantee admission, a 2.5 GPA in all college work is usually required. For applicants with fewer than 30 semester hours or 45 quarter hours, secondary school records and standardized test scores must be submitted. All students must meet the foreign language and math entrance requirements. 32 of 128 credits required for the bachelor's degree must be completed at PLU.

Visiting: There are regularly scheduled orientations for prospective students, consisting of activities based on the students' individual interests - tour, class visits, meeting with coaches and/or faculty, overnight stays. There are guides for informal visits, visitors may sit in on classes, and stay overnight. To schedule a visit, contact the Office of Admissions.

Financial Aid: In 2013-2014, 99% of all full-time freshmen and 95% of continuing full-time students received some form of financial aid. 81% of all full-time freshmen and 73% of continuing full-time students received need-based aid. The average freshman award was $32,992. Need-based scholarships or need-based grants averaged $22,233 ($42,308 maximum); need-based self-help aid (loans and jobs) averaged $10,608; and other non-need-based awards and non-need-based scholarships averaged $17,076 ($48,308 maximum). 48% of undergraduate students work part-time. Average annual earnings from campus work are $3336. The average financial indebtedness of the 2013 graduate was $26,866. The FAFSA is required. The priority date for freshman financial aid applications for fall entry is January 31.

International Students: There are 186 international students enrolled. The school actively recruits these students. They must take the TOEFL with a minimum score of 550 on the paper-based TOEFL (PBT) or 79 on the Internet-based version (iBT).

Computers: All students may access the system 24 hours. There are no time limits and no fees.

Graduates: From July 1, 2012 to June 30, 2013, 727 bachelor's degrees were awarded. The most popular majors were social sciences (11%), health professions (11%), and business (9%). 53 companies recruited on campus in 2012-2013. In an average class, 59% graduate in 4 years or less, 67% graduate in 5 years or less, and 69% graduate in 6 years or less.

Admissions Contact: Admissions Office. E-Mail: *admission@plu.edu* Web: *www.plu.edu*

SAINT MARTIN'S UNIVERSITY — B-3

Lacey, WA 98503 (360) 438-4596
(800) 368-8803; (360) 412-6189

Full-time: 544 men, 599 women	**Faculty:** 72; IIB, --$
Part-time: 189 men, 147 women	**Ph.D.s:** 56%
Graduate: 126 men, 218 women	**Student/Faculty:** 12 to 1
Year: semesters, summer session	**Tuition:** $28,722
Application Deadline: March 1	**Room & Board:** $9360
Freshman Class: 808 applied, 665 accepted, 228 enrolled	
SAT CR/M/W: 519/630/503	**ACT:** 22 **COMPETITIVE**

Saint Martin's University, founded in 1895, is a private, non-profit Roman Catholic institution conducted by the Benedictine order, offering undergraduate and graduate programs in liberal arts and sciences, business, education, and engineering. There are 4 undergraduate schools and 6 graduate schools. In addition to regional accreditation, has baccalaureate program accreditation with ABET and TEAC. The library contains 213,275 volumes, 163,992 microform items, 2,315 audio/video tapes/CDs/DVDs, and subscribes to 4,369 periodicals including electronic. Computerized library services include interlibrary loans, database searching, and Internet access. Special learning facilities include an art gallery. The 380-acre campus is in a suburban area 3 miles from Olympia and 60 miles south of Seattle. Including any residence halls, there are 17 buildings.

Student Life: 75% of undergraduates are from Washington. Others are from 25 states, 13 foreign countries, and Canada. 85% are from public schools. 51% are White; 16% Hispanic. 43% claim no religious affiliation; 23% Catholic. The average age of freshmen is 18; all undergraduates, 24. 26% do not continue beyond their first year; 54% remain to graduate.

Housing: 630 students can be accommodated in college housing, which includes coed dorms. On-campus housing is guaranteed for the freshman year only, is available on a first-come, and first-served basis. 67% of students commute. Alcohol is not permitted. All students may keep cars.

Activities: There are no fraternities or sororities. There are 30 groups on campus, including band, choir, drama, ethnic, honors, international, jazz band, musical theater, newspaper, pep band, political, religious, social, social service, and student government. Popular campus events include Career Fair, International Day, and Capital Food and Wine Festival.

Sports: There are 6 intercollegiate sports for men and 7 for women, and 9 intramural sports for men and 9 for women. Facilities include a 5300-seat multipurpose pavilion, new recreation center, athletic fields, and nearby golf courses, lakes, and mountains.

Disabled Students: 90% of the campus is accessible. Facilities include wheelchair ramps, elevators, special parking, specially equipped restrooms, lowered drinking fountains, lowered telephones.

Services: Counseling and information services are available, as is tutoring in some subjects, writing There is a reader service for the blind.

Campus Safety and Security: Measures include 24-hour foot and vehicle patrol, emergency notification system, and security escort services. There are emergency telephones, lighted pathways/sidewalks, controlled access to dorms/residences, There is a security patrol from dark to dawn.

Programs of Study: confers B.A., B.S., B.S.W., B.S.N., B.S.C.E. and B.S.M.E. degrees. Master's degrees are also awarded. Bachelor's degrees are awarded in BIOLOGICAL SCIENCE (biology/biological science), BUSINESS (accounting and business administration and management),

COMMUNICATIONS AND THE ARTS (English, music, and theatre arts), COMPUTER AND PHYSICAL SCIENCE (chemistry, computer science, and mathematics), EDUCATION (elementary education and special education), ENGINEERING AND ENVIRONMENTAL DESIGN (civil engineering and mechanical engineering), HEALTH PROFESSIONS (nursing), SOCIAL SCIENCE (community services, criminal justice, history, interdisciplinary studies, political science/government, psychology, religion, social work, and sociology). Engineering and math/sciences are the strongest academically. Psychology, business, and education have the largest enrollments.

Required: All students must complete freshman composition and general education requirements, including 2 courses in social sciences, 1 course each in literature, philosophy, the arts, religious studies, natural science with lab, math (precalculus), U.S. history, and non-U.S. history, as well as 2 credits of phys ed. A total of 128 semester credits with a 2.0 GPA is required. 1 year of a world language is required if the student did not take 2 years of a single foreign language in high school.

Special: Double majors, work-study with the state of Washington, nonprofit organizations, and Saint Martin's, internships in all disciplines, a Washington semester with American University, and pass/fail options are offered. The FOCUS program offers credit for job experience. Nondegree study and study abroad is possible. There are 2 national honor societies and 2 departmental honors programs.

Faculty/Classroom: 55% of faculty are male; 45% are female. 96% teach undergraduates. No introductory courses are taught by graduate students. The average class size in an introductory lecture is 20; in a laboratory is 12; and in a regular course is 12.

Admissions: 82% of the 2013-2014 applicants were accepted. The SAT scores for the 2013-2014 freshman class were: Critical Reading--39% below 500, 41% between 500 and 599, 16% between 600 and 699, and 4% between 700 and 800; Math--35% below 500, 42% between 500 and 599, 21% between 600 and 699, and 2% between 700 and 800; Writing--45% below 500, 44% between 500 and 599, and 11% between 600 and 699. The ACT scores were 63% below 21, 17% between 21 and 23, 12% between 24 and 26, 2% between 27 and 28, and 6% above 28.

Requirements: The SAT or ACT is required. Applicants must be graduates of an accredited secondary school or have a GED, with a minimum of 16 academic units, including 4 in English, 2 or 3 in math, 2 in history/social science, 1 or 2 each in foreign language and lab science, and 7 in electives. Class standing also is considered. An essay and recommendation from a teacher or counselor are required. Students should have a score of 800 on the SAT I and a 2.5 GPA. AP and CLEP credits are accepted. Important factors in the admissions decision are advanced placement or honors courses, recommendations by school officials, and personality/intangible qualities.

Procedure: Freshmen are admitted fall, spring, and summer. There is a rolling admissions plan. Applications should be filed by March 1 for fall entry; December 15 for spring entry. Notification is sent on a rolling basis. Applications are accepted online.

Transfer: 177 transfer students enrolled in 2012-2013. Transfer applicants must submit transcripts from all colleges previously attended and have a 2.0 GPA. 30 of 128 credits required for the bachelor's degree must be completed at.

Visiting: There are regularly scheduled orientations for prospective students, including a campus tour and faculty, student service, and financial aid presentations. There are guides for informal visits, visitors may sit in on classes, and stay overnight. To schedule a visit, contact the Admissions Office at (800) 368-8803.

Financial Aid: 63% of continuing full-time students received need-based aid. The FAFSA, and International Student's Certification of Finances are required. The deadline for filing freshman financial aid applications for fall entry is March 1.

International Students: There are 68 international students enrolled. The school actively recruits these students. They must take the TOEFL with a minimum score of 525 on the paper-based TOEFL (PBT) or 71 on the Internet-based version (iBT).

Computers: All students may access the system. There are no time limits and no fees.

Graduates: From July 1, 2012 to June 30, 2013, 300 bachelor's degrees were awarded. The most popular majors were business (29%), psychology (17%), and education (14%). In an average class, 40% graduate in 4 years or less, 52% graduate in 5 years or less, and 54% graduate in 6 years or less.

Admissions Contact: Sarah Weiss, Director of Admissions. E-Mail: *admissions@stmartin.edu* Web: *www.stmartin.edu*

SEATTLE PACIFIC UNIVERSITY C-2

Seattle, WA 98119 (206) 281-2021
(800) 366-3344; (206) 281-2669

Full-time: 1102 men, 2146 women | **Faculty:** n/av; IIA, av$
Part-time: 45 men, 102 women | **Ph.D.s:** 87%
Graduate: 269 men, 606 women | **Student/Faculty:** 15 to 1
Year: quarters, summer session | **Tuition:** $32,067
Application Deadline: March 1 | **Room & Board:** $9492
Freshman Class: 5165 applied, 3726 accepted, 767 enrolled
SAT CR/M/W: 570/570/550 **ACT:** 25 **VERY COMPETITIVE+**

Seattle Pacific University, founded in 1891, is a private, institution affiliated with the Free Methodist Church. It offers programs in business and economics, education, fine and performing arts, health science, humanities, natural and mathematical sciences, phys ed and athletics, religion, and social and behavioral sciences. There are 6 undergraduate schools and 6 graduate schools. In addition to regional accreditation, SPU has baccalaureate program accreditation with AACSB, ABET, NASM, NCATE, and NLN. The library contains 217,369 volumes, 497,248 microform items, 7,414 audio/video tapes/CDs/DVDs, and subscribes to 2,729 periodicals including electronic. Computerized library services include interlibrary loans, database searching, Internet access, and Wi-Fi capability. Special learning facilities include an art gallery, a science center, performing arts theater, writing lab, and a media center. The 35-acre campus is in an urban area seven minutes from downtown Seattle. Including any residence halls, there are 94 buildings.

Student Life: 62% of undergraduates are from Washington. Others are from 44 states, 20 foreign countries, and Canada. 65% are White; 11% Asian American.. The average age of freshmen is 18; all undergraduates, 21. 15% do not continue beyond their first year; 70% remain to graduate.

Housing: 1761 students can be accommodated in college housing, which includes single-sex and coed dorms, on-campus apartments, off-campus apartments, and married student housing. theme houses. 51% of students live on campus. Alcohol is not permitted. All students may keep cars.

Activities: There are no fraternities or sororities. There are 51 groups on campus, including art, chess, choir, chorale, drama, ethnic, honors, international, jazz band, literary magazine, newspaper, orchestra, pep band, political, professional, radio, religious, social, social service, student government, and symphony. Popular campus events include Family Weekend, Talent Show, and Ivy Cutting at Graduation.

Sports: There are 5 intercollegiate sports for men and 7 for women, and 9 intramural sports for men and 9 for women. Facilities include a soccer field, an oval track, tennis and basketball courts, a gym and crew house, a crew dock, a 2600-seat indoor gym, an 800-seat campus auditorium, and a community swimming pool available to students with free passes.

Disabled Students: 70% of the campus is accessible. Facilities include wheelchair ramps, elevators, special parking, specially equipped restrooms, and special class scheduling.

Services: Counseling and information services are available, as is tutoring in most subjects. There is a reader service for the blind, and remedial math and writing. In addition, there is priority registration for disabled students.

Campus Safety and Security: Measures include 24-hour foot and vehicle patrol, emergency notification system, and security escort services. There are emergency telephones, lighted pathways/sidewalks, controlled access to dorms/residences, closed-circuit TV monitors.

Programs of Study: SPU confers B.A., and B.S. degrees. Master's and doctoral degrees are also awarded. Bachelor's degrees are awarded in BIOLOGICAL SCIENCE (biochemistry and biology/biological science), BUSINESS (accounting and business administration and management), COMMUNICATIONS AND THE ARTS (art, classics, communications, creative writing, English, fine arts, French, German, language arts, Latin, linguistics, literature, music, Russian, and Spanish), COMPUTER AND PHYSICAL SCIENCE (chemistry, computer science, information sciences and systems, mathematics, and physics), EDUCATION (education, elementary education, home economics education, mathematics education, music education, nursing education, physical education, science education, secondary education, social science education, special education, and teaching English as a second/foreign language (TESOL/TEFOL)), ENGINEERING AND ENVIRONMENTAL DESIGN (electrical/electronics engineering, engineering, engineering and applied science, and interior design), HEALTH PROFESSIONS (exercise science and nursing), SOCIAL SCIENCE (Christian studies, clinical psychology, economics, European studies, family/consumer resource management, family/consumer studies, food science, history, Latin American studies, liberal arts/general studies, philosophy, physical fitness/movement, political science/government, prelaw, psychology, social science, sociology, and theological studies). Education, nursing, and business administration have the largest enrollments.

Required: All students must demonstrate competency in math and English. Students must complete 15 quarter credits in Christian heritage and values, 56 in general education, plus up to 15 credits of foreign language competency, and at least 45 to 60 in the major, depending on the program. A minimum of 180 credits is needed for the bachelor's degree, with a 2.0 GPA overall. At least 60 credits must be earned in 3000-level courses or higher.

Special: There is a cooperative program with Fashion Institute of Technology in New York City, Fashion Institute of Design and Merchandising in Los Angeles, and Han Nam University in Korea, cross-registration with the Christian College Consortium and Christian College Coalition, and a Washington semester in American studies through the Christian College Coalition. SPU offers internships, study abroad in more than 5 countries, work-study programs, dual and student-designed majors, interdisciplinary majors such as language arts, and a liberal studies major for associate degree graduates. A general studies degree, pass/no credit options, and nondegree study are available. There are 5 national honor societies, a freshman honors program, and 10 departmental honors programs.

Faculty/Classroom: 29% of faculty are male; 41% are female. No introductory courses are taught by graduate students. The average class size in a regular course is 18.

Admissions: 72% of the 2013-2014 applicants were accepted. The SAT scores for the 2013-2014 freshman class were: Critical Reading--16% below 500, 47% between 500 and 599, 28% between 600 and 699, and 9% between 700 and 800; Math--19% below 500, 46% between 500 and 599, 32% between 600 and 699, and 3% between 700 and 800; Writing--23% below 500, 45% between 500 and 599, 27% between 600 and 699, and 5% between 700 and 800. The ACT scores were 9% below 21, 22% between 21 and 23, 30% between 24 and 26, 18% between 27 and 28, and 21% above 28.

Requirements: The SAT or ACT is required. The SAT I is preferred, with a minimum required composite score of 950. Candidates should be graduates of an accredited secondary school with a minimum high school GPA of 2.5 or hold a GED certificate. A strong college preparatory program in high school is recommended, including 4 years of English, 3 each of math, science, and foreign language, 2 of history, and 1 of social studies. An essay and 2 letters of recommendation are required, and an interview is recommended. AP and CLEP credits are accepted. Important factors in the admissions decision are advanced placement or honors courses, leadership record, and extracurricular activities record.

Procedure: Freshmen are admitted to all sessions. Entrance exams should be taken by January of the senior year. There are early decision and rolling admissions plans. Early decision applications should be filed by November 15; regular applications, by March 1 for fall entry, along with a $45 fee. Notification of early decision is sent February 15; regular decision, on a rolling basis. Applications are accepted online.

Transfer: 237 transfer students enrolled in 2012-2013. A minimum 2.5 GPA is required, and an interview is recommended. Transcripts from all previous colleges attended and from high school are required, along with 2 letters of recommendation and an essay or personal statement. Evidence of honorable dismissal from the previous school is also required. Students with at least 30 credits earned are not required to take the SAT or ACT. 45 of 180 credits required for the bachelor's degree must be completed at SPU.

Visiting: There are regularly scheduled orientations for prospective students. There are guides for informal visits, visitors may sit in on classes, and stay overnight. To schedule a visit, contact the Admissions Office.

Financial Aid: The FAFSA is required. The deadline for filing freshman financial aid applications for fall entry is June 30.

International Students: The school actively recruits these students. They must take the TOEFL.

Computers: All students may access the system during lab hours, Monday through Saturday, during the academic year. There are no time limits and no fees.

Graduates: From July 1, 2012 to June 30, 2013, 728 bachelor's degrees were awarded. The most popular majors were psychology (10%), nursing (9%), and business administration (9%).

Admissions Contact: Jobe Korb-Nice, Director of Undergraduate Admissions. E-Mail: *admissions@spu.edu* Web: *www.spu.edu*

SEATTLE UNIVERSITY C-2

Seattle, WA 98122 (206) 296-2000
(800) 426-7123; (206) 296-5656

Full-time: 1814 men, 2615 women	**Faculty:** 302
Part-time: 124 men, 113 women	**Ph.D.s:** n/av
Graduate: 1122 men, 1634 women	**Student/Faculty:** 14 to 1
Year: quarters, summer session	**Tuition:** $36,464
Application Deadline: February 1	**Room & Board:** $10,545
Freshman Class: 7161 applied, 5244 accepted, 971 enrolled	
SAT CR/M/W: 580/580/580 **ACT:** 27	**VERY COMPETITIVE+**

Seattle University is Seattle's university. That means a centralized urban location in one of the world's most innovative, vibrant and culturally rich metropolitan cities. There are 5 undergraduate schools and 7 graduate schools. In addition to regional accreditation, Seattle U has baccalaureate program accreditation with AACSB, ABET, CAHEA, NCATE, and NLN. The 2 libraries contain 597,754 volumes, 1.8 million microform items, and 7,521 audio/video tapes/CDs/DVDs, and subscribe to 61,700 periodicals including electronic. Computerized library services include interlibrary loans, database searching, Internet access, and Wi-Fi capability. Special learning facilities include an art gallery, planetarium, radio station, an electron microscope, a recording studio, and MRI. The 46-acre campus is in an urban area east of downtown Seattle in the Capitol Hill neighborhood. Including any residence halls, there are 34 buildings.

Student Life: 56% of undergraduates are from out of state, mostly the West. Students are from 44 states, 88 foreign countries, and Canada. 59% are White; 18% Asian American. 26% are Catholic; 25% Protestant; 14% claim no religious affiliation. The average age of freshmen is 18; all undergraduates, 20. 14% do not continue beyond their first year; 77% remain to graduate.

Housing: 2085 students can be accommodated in college housing, which includes coed dorms and on-campus apartments. In addition, there are language houses, 24-hour quiet floors, and single-sex floors. On-campus housing is available on a lottery system for upperclassmen. Priority is given to out-of-town students. 55% of students commute. Some may keep cars.

Activities: There are no fraternities or sororities. There are 61 groups on campus, including art, cheerleading, choir, chorale, communications, dance, debate, drama, environmental, ethnic, forensics, gay, honors, international, jazz band, literary magazine, musical theater, newspaper, photography, political, professional, radio and TV, religious, social, social service, and student government. Popular campus events include Hawaiian Luau, Quad Stock and International Student Dinner.

Sports: There are 8 intercollegiate sports for men and 10 for women, and 14 intramural sports for men and 14 for women. Facilities include a 180,000 sq. ft of recreational, fitness and athletic space center with 2 swimming pools, cardio and weight rooms, group exercise, a yoga and martial arts classrooms, racquetball and squash courts, 3 basketball courts, outdoor track, soccer and softball fields and tennis courts, and an astroturf gym for indoor soccer/tennis with 2 batting cages.

Disabled Students: 95% of the campus is accessible. Facilities include wheelchair ramps, elevators, special parking, specially equipped restrooms, special class scheduling, lowered drinking fountains, and lowered telephones.

Services: Counseling and information services are available, as is tutoring in most subjects, inclusing math, English, accounting, language, and science. There is a reader service for the blind and a writing center.

Campus Safety and Security: Measures include 24-hour foot and vehicle patrol, emergency notification system, self-defense education, and security escort services. There are shuttle buses, emergency telephones, lighted pathways/sidewalks, and controlled access to dorms/residences.

Programs of Study: Seattle U confers B.A., B.S., B.A.B.A., B.A.E., B.A.H., B.C.J., B.M., B.F.A., B.S.B., B.S.B.C., B.S.P., B.S.C.E., B.S.C.S., B.S.D.U., B.S.E.E., B.S.E.S., B.S.G.S., B.S.M., B.S.M.E., B.S.N. and B.S.W. degrees. Master's and doctoral degrees are also awarded. Bachelor's degrees are awarded in AGRICULTURE (environmental studies), BIOLOGICAL SCIENCE (biochemistry, biology/adolescence education, biology/biological science, cell biology, and marine biology), BUSINESS (accounting, business administration and management, business economics, finance, international business management, international economics, and marketing management), COMMUNICATIONS AND THE ARTS (art history, communications, creative writing, English, film arts, fine arts, French, journalism, music, photography, Spanish, strings, theatre arts, and visual and performing arts), COMPUTER AND PHYSICAL SCIENCE (applied mathematics, chemistry, chemistry/adolescence education, computer science, digital arts/technology, mathematics, mathematics - actuarial concentration, mathematics/theoretical, physics, science, and Urban Ecology), EDUCATION (environmental education and mathematics education), ENGINEERING AND ENVIRONMENTAL DESIGN (civil engineering, computer engineering, electrical/electronics engineering, environmental engineering, environmental science, and mechanical engineering), HEALTH PROFESSIONS (exercise science, medical technology, nursing, and ultrasound technology), SOCIAL SCIENCE (anthropology, asian studies, criminal justice, economics, forensic studies, history, humanities, international studies, liberal arts/general studies, philosophy, political science/government, psychology, public administration, religion, social work, sociology, theological studies, and women & gender studies). Nursing, criminal justice, business, creative writing, environmental science, computer science, humanities for leadership, and engineering are the strongest academically. Nursing, psychology, and business have the largest enrollments.

Required: Students must complete 180 to 192 quarter hours, depending on the degree, with 70 to 90 in the major, and maintain a minimum GPA of 2.25 to 2.5. Core curriculum requirements include 12 courses (60 credits) and a major-specific capstone course divided into four modules: Engaging Academic Inquiry, Exploring the Self and Others, Engaging the World, and Reflection.

Special: Seattle University provides many opportunities for dual majors, local, national and international internships, and on and off-campus work study positions. In addition, distinctive programs include: International Development Intership Program (IDIP). There are a freshman honors program and 8 departmental honors programs.

Faculty/Classroom: 48% of faculty are male; 52% are female. No introductory courses are taught by graduate students. The average class size in a regular course is 18.

Admissions: 73% of the 2013-2014 applicants were accepted. The SAT scores for the 2013-2014 freshman class were: Critical Reading--11% below 500, 46% between 500 and 599, 34% between 600 and 699, and 9% between 700 and 800; Math--11% below 500, 50% between 500 and 599, 32% between 600 and 699, and 7% between 700 and 800, Writing--12% below 500, 45% between 500 and 599, 36% between 600 and 699, and 7% between 700 and 800.

Requirements: The SAT or ACT is required. Admissions requirements include graduation from an accredited secondary school, with 16 academic credits, including 4 years of English, 3 each of math and social studies, 2 of foreign language, 2 of lab science, and 2 academic electives; 4 years of math and lab physics and chemistry are required of science and engineering students; lab biology and chemistry are needed by nursing students. The GED is also accepted. A GPA of 2.7 is required. AP and CLEP credits are accepted.

Procedure: Freshmen are admitted to all sessions. Entrance exams should be taken during the fall of the senior year. There are early admissions, deferred admissions, and rolling admissions plans. Applications should be filed by February 1 for fall entry; November 1 for winter entry; February 1 for spring entry; and May 1 for summer entry, along with a $50 fee. Notifications are sent March 1. 1386 applicants were on the 2013 waiting list; 180 were admitted. Applications are accepted online.

Transfer: 424 transfer students enrolled in 2012-2013. Generally, transfer students should have a college GPA of at least 2.25. An associate degree is recommended; a 2.75 GPA is required for nursing and business administration students. 45 of 180 credits required for the bachelor's degree must be completed at Seattle U.

Visiting: There are regularly scheduled orientations for prospective students, Inclused an info session with a brief overview of the university and our admissions and scholarship process and a campus tour including classroom space, a residence hall room, dining and fitness facilities, and the Student Center. There are guides for informal visits, visitors may sit in on classes, and stay overnight. To schedule a visit, contact Admissions Office at (800) 426-7123.

Financial Aid: In 2013-2014, 67% of all full-time freshmen students received some form of financial aid. 61% of all full-time freshmen students received need-based aid. The average freshman award was $28,080. Need-based scholarships or need-based grants averaged $15,592; need-based self-help aid (loans and jobs) averaged $9,339; non-need-based athletic scholarships averaged $18,582; and other non-need-based awards and non-need-based scholarships averaged $9,927. The average financial indebtedness of the 2013 graduate was $29,498. The FAFSA and the college's own financial statement are required. The priority date for freshman financial aid applications for fall entry is February 1.

International Students: There are 476 international students enrolled. The school actively recruits these students. They must take the TOEFL with a minimum score of 520 on the paper-based TOEFL (PBT) or 68 on the Internet-based version (iBT).

Computers: All students may access the system. There are no time limits and no fees.

Graduates: From July 1, 2012 to June 30, 2013, 1250 bachelor's degrees were awarded. The most popular majors were business/marketing (26%), health professions and related sciences (14%), and engineering (6%). In an average class, 59% graduate in 4 years or less, 74% graduate in 5 years or less, and 77% graduate in 6 years or less.

Admissions Contact: Melore Nielsen, Dean of Admissions. E-Mail: *admissions@seattleu.edu* Web: *www.seattleu.edu*

UNIVERSITY OF PUGET SOUND — C-2

Tacoma, WA 98416 — **(253) 879-3211; (253) 879-3993**

Full-time: 1081 men, 1439 women	**Faculty:** 207
Part-time: 17 men, 4 women	**Ph.D.s:** 90%
Graduate: 66 men, 207 women	**Student/Faculty:** 12 to 1
Year: semesters, summer session	**Tuition:** $41,868
Application Deadline: January 15	**Room & Board:** $10,780
Freshman Class: 4588 applied, 3910 accepted, 670 enrolled	
SAT CR/M/W: 620/590/610	**ACT:** 27 **HIGHLY COMPETITIVE+**

We're a classic, forward-thinking and entrepreneurial liberal arts college with a renowned School of Music and an innovative business and leadership program. There is one undergraduate school and 3 graduate schools. In addition to regional accreditation, Puget Sound has baccalaureate program accreditation with NASM. The library contains 530,281 volumes, 172,308 microform items, and 16,122 audio/video tapes/CDs/DVDs, and subscribes to 47,432 periodicals including electronic. Computerized library services include interlibrary loans, database searching, Internet access, and Wi-Fi capability. Special learning facilities include an art gallery, natural history museum, radio station, sculpture building, theatres, greenhouse, transmission and scanning electron microscopes, confocal microscope, DNA sequencer, NMR, X-ray diffractometer, microcomputer labs, sedimentology lab, stereoscopic and petrographic microscopes, computerized plotting/digitizing board and image analysis system, portable seismograph, gravimeter, proton precession magnetometer, ICP, GPS GIS lab, electronic music composition lab, electronic music keyboard lab with MIDI workstations, three electronic music classrooms, and one music v-room. The 97-acre campus is in a small town in the North End neighborhood of Tacoma, Washington, 45 minutes south of Seattle and 30 minutes north of Olympia. Including any residence halls, there are 135 buildings.

Student Life: Students are from 42 states, 8 foreign countries, and Canada. 74% are from public schools. 57% claim no religious affiliation; 24% Protestant.

Housing: 1751 students can be accommodated in college housing, which includes single-sex and coed dorms and on-campus apartments. In addition, there are honors houses, language houses, special-interest houses, fraternity houses, and sorority houses. On-campus housing is guaranteed for the freshman year only, is available on a first-come, first-served basis, and is available on a lottery system for upperclassmen. All students may keep cars.

Activities: There are 125 groups on campus, including and diversity awareness, health and wellness, sports, art, band, cheerleading, choir, chorale, chorus, computers, dance, debate, drama, environmental, ethnic, forensics, gay, gender, honors, international, jazz band, literary magazine, musical theater, newspaper, opera, orchestra, pep band, photography, political, professional, radio and TV, religious, social, social service, student government, symphony, and yearbook. Popular campus events include Foolish Pleasures (student film festival), Mistletoast Holiday, Hawaiian Luau, and Drag Show.

Sports: There are 11 intercollegiate sports for men and 12 for women, and 8 intramural sports for men and 8 for women. Facilities include 3,000-seat basketball and volleyball gym; 6-lane pool; 2,488-seat football, soccer, lacrosse, and track stadium; 6 indoor tennis courts; fitness center with free weights and aerobics equipment, dance studio, track, baseball, softball, and intramural fields (one of which is synthetic), indoor climbing wall; auxiliary gym for intramurals and recreation.

Disabled Students: 80% of the campus is accessible. Facilities include wheelchair ramps, elevators, special parking, specially equipped restrooms, special class scheduling, lowered drinking fountains, lowered telephones, and special housing.

Services: Counseling and information services are available, as is tutoring in most subjects. There is a reader service for the blind.

Campus Safety and Security: Measures include 24-hour foot and vehicle patrol, emergency notification system, and security escort services. There are emergency telephones, lighted pathways/sidewalks, controlled access to dorms/residences, 24-hour live dispatch.

Programs of Study: Puget Sound confers B.A., B.M. and B.S. degrees. Master's and doctoral degrees are also awarded. Bachelor's degrees are awarded in BIOLOGICAL SCIENCE (biochemistry, biology/biological science, cell biology, and molecular biology), BUSINESS (business administration and management and international economics), COMMUNICATIONS AND THE ARTS (art, Chinese, classics, communications, dramatic arts, East Asian languages and literature, English, French, German, Japanese, music, music performance, and Spanish), COMPUTER AND PHYSICAL SCIENCE (chemistry, computer science, geology, mathematics, natural sciences, and physics), EDUCATION (music education), HEALTH PROFESSIONS (exercise science), SOCIAL SCIENCE (Asian/Oriental studies, economics, history, philosophy, political science/government, psychology, religion, science and society, and sociology). Music, biology, and business have the largest enrollments.

Required: In order to receive the baccalaureate degree from the University of Puget Sound, a student must earn a minimum of 32 units.

Special: Special academic programs include study abroad in over 50 countries as well as local, national, and international internships in conjunction with an internship seminar. There is a 3-2 engineering degree offered with Washington University in St. Louis, Columbia University, Duke University, and the University of Southern California. Cross-disciplinary majors include foreign language and international affairs, music and business, computer science and business. Double-majoring is encouraraged. Unique programs include a 9-month 8-country Pacific Rim/Asia study-travel program, an intensive 4-year study of the classics of Western civilization, and the Business Leadership Program which combines traditional business and liberal arts study. There are 15 national honor societies, including Phi Beta Kappa, a freshman honors program, and 13 departmental honors programs.

Faculty/Classroom: 53% of faculty are male; 47% are female. 89% teach undergraduates. No introductory courses are taught by graduate students. The average class size in an introductory lecture is 18; in a laboratory is 12; and in a regular course is 15.

Admissions: 85% of the 2013-2014 applicants were accepted. The SAT

scores for the 2013-2014 freshman class were: Critical Reading--5% below 500, 32% between 500 and 599, 44% between 600 and 699, and 18% between 700 and 800; Math--7% below 500, 37% between 500 and 599, 45% between 600 and 699, and 11% between 700 and 800; Writing--5% below 500, 38% between 500 and 599, 43% between 600 and 699, and 14% between 700 and 800. The ACT scores were 11% between 21 and 23,59% between 27 and 28, and 29% above 28.

Requirements: The SAT or ACT is required. Puget Sound only accepts the Common Application for undergraduate admission. Admission requirements include graduation from an accredited secondary school with a recommended 4 years of English, 3 to 4 of mathematics, 3 to 4 years of natural, and/or physical, laboratory science, 3 of social studies or history, 2 to 3 of foreign language, and 1 year of fine, visual, or performing arts. Also required are letters of personal recommendation from a teacher and counselor. An essay must be submitted, and an interview is recommended. The GED is also accepted. AP credits are accepted. Important factors in the admissions decision are advanced placement or honors courses, evidence of special talent, and personality/intangible qualities.

Procedure: Freshmen are admitted fall and spring. Entrance exams should be taken during the fall of the senior year. There are early decision and deferred admissions plans. Early decision applications should be filed by November 15; regular applications, by January 15 for fall entry; and November 1 for spring entry, along with a $50 fee. Notification of early decision is sent December 15; regular decision, April 1. 104 early decision candidates were accepted for the 2013-2014 class. Applications are accepted online.

Transfer: 59 transfer students enrolled in 2012-2013. Applicants must have had an honorable dismissal from the institution(s) previously attended and be in good academic standing with a minimum GPA of 2.0. All college transcripts and the rigor of prior course work and resulting grades are evaluated. High school transcripts and SAT or ACT scores are required if less than 1 year of college has been completed. An interview is recommended. An essay is required. Puget Sound only accepts the Common Application for undergraduate transfer admission. 64 of 128 credits required for the bachelor's degree must be completed at Puget Sound.

Visiting: There are regularly scheduled orientations for prospective students, tour of campus, meetings with counselors, faculty, and coaches, classroom visits, overnight stays (if desired). There are guides for informal visits, visitors may sit in on classes, and stay overnight. To schedule a visit, contact Carolyn Johnson.

Financial Aid: The average freshman award was $29,075. Need-based scholarships or need-based grants averaged $23,395 ; need-based self-help aid (loans and jobs) averaged $7,353; other non-need-based awards and non-need-based scholarships averaged $5,778; and $14,321 from other forms of aid. Puget Sound is a member of CSS. The CSS/Profile and FAFSA are required February 1.

International Students: There are 16 international students enrolled. They must take the TOEFL with a minimum score of 550 on the paper-based TOEFL (PBT) or 80 on the Internet-based version (iBT). They must also take the SAT or ACT. all freshman applicants and transfers with less than 1 full year of college work must take the SAT or ACT.

Computers: All students may access the system. There are no time limits and no fees.

Graduates: From July 1, 2012 to June 30, 2013, 641 bachelor's degrees were awarded. The most popular majors were business (13%), psychology (11%), and politics and government (8%). 68 companies recruited on campus in 2012-2013. In an average class, 68% graduate in 4 years or less, 76% graduate in 5 years or less, and 78% graduate in 6 years or less. Of the 2012 graduating class, 16% were enrolled in graduate school within 6 months of graduation, and 62% were employed.

Admissions Contact: Carolyn Johnson, Senior Associate Director of Admission. E-Mail: *admission@pugetsound.edu* Web: *http:/www.pugetsound.edu/admission*

UNIVERSITY OF WASHINGTON C-2

Seattle, WA 98195 **(206) 543-9686**

Full-time: 11612 men, 12597 women	**Faculty:** n/av
Part-time: 2141 men, 2220 women	**Ph.D.s:** 89%
Graduate: 5354 men, 6294 women	**Student/Faculty:** n/av
Year: trimesters, summer session	**Tuition:** $12,397 ($31,971)
Application Deadline:	**Room & Board:** $10,752

Freshman Class: 17877 applied, 11586 accepted, 5338 enrolled

SAT or ACT: required

VERY COMPETITIVE

The University of Washington, founded in 1861, is a public institution offering a broad range of degree programs. There are 12 undergraduate schools and 1 graduate school. In addition to regional accreditation, UW has baccalaureate program accreditation with AACSB, ABET, NCATE, and NLN. The 16 libraries contain 7.0 million volumes. Computerized library services include interlibrary loans, database searching, Internet access, and Wi-Fi capability. Special learning facilities include an art gallery, natural history museum, planetarium, radio station, TV station, state museum, full teaching hospital, marine science lab, 200-acre arboretum, and field research forest. The 643-acre campus is in an urban area 5 miles from downtown Seattle. Including any residence halls, there are 279 buildings.

Student Life: 80% of undergraduates are from Washington. Others are from 44 states, 107 foreign countries, and Canada. 51% are White; 26% Asian American. The average age of freshmen is 18; all undergraduates, 21. 8% do not continue beyond their first year; 75% remain to graduate.

Housing: 5200 students can be accommodated in college housing, which includes coed dorms, on-campus apartments, and married student housing. In addition, there are honors houses, special-interest houses, fraternity houses, sorority houses, and a freshman house, business, engineering, international, pre-health science, substance and alcohol free environment. On-campus housing is guaranteed for all 4 years. 80% of students commute. Alcohol is not permitted. All students may keep cars.

Activities: 6% of men belong to 27 national fraternities; 5% of women belong to 16 national sororities. There are 550 groups on campus, including band, cheerleading, chess, choir, chorale, chorus, communications, computers, dance, debate, drama, ethnic, film, gay, honors, international, jazz band, literary magazine, marching band, musical theater, newspaper, opera, orchestra, pep band, political, professional, radio and TV, religious, social, social service, student government, and symphony. Popular campus events include Convocation, Dawg Daze, and Washington Weekend.

Sports: There are 11 intercollegiate sports for men and 12 for women, and 13 intramural sports for men and 12 for women. Facilities include a 72,500-seat football stadium, a baseball field, a track and field complex, lakeside facilities, tennis courts, the intramurals building, a golf driving range, and a swimming pool.

Disabled Students: 95% of the campus is accessible. Facilities include wheelchair ramps, elevators, special parking, specially equipped restrooms, special class scheduling, lowered drinking fountains, lowered telephones, and special housing.

Services: Counseling and information services are available, as is tutoring in every subject. There is a reader service for the blind, and remedial math, reading, and writing.

Campus Safety and Security: Measures include 24-hour foot and vehicle patrol, emergency notification system, self-defense education, and security escort services. There are shuttle buses, emergency telephones, lighted pathways/sidewalks, and emergency telephone numbers.

Programs of Study: UW confers B.A., B.S., B.A.B.A., B.C.H.S., B.L.Arch., B.Mus., B.S.A.&A., B.S.B.C., B.S.Cer.E., B.S.Comp.E., B.S.F., B.S.Fish., B.S.I.E., B.S.M.E., B.S.Med.Tech., B.S.Met.E. and B.S.Nur. degrees. Master's and doctoral degrees are also awarded. Bachelor's degrees are awarded in AGRICULTURE (fishing and fisheries, forest engineering, and forestry production and processing), BIOLOGICAL SCIENCE (biochemistry, biology/biological science, botany, microbiology, neurosciences, and zoology), BUSINESS (accounting, banking and finance, business administration and management, business economics, international business management, marketing/retailing/merchandising, and personnel management), COMMUNICATIONS AND THE ARTS (art history and appreciation, classics, communications, comparative literature, dance, dramatic arts, English, French, Germanic languages and literature, graphic design, Italian, Japanese, jazz, music history and appreciation, music performance, painting, photography, Scandinavian languages, sculpture, Slavic languages, Spanish, speech/debate/rhetoric, studio art, and technical and business writing), COMPUTER AND PHYSICAL SCIENCE (astronomy, atmospheric sciences and meteorology, computer science, geology, information sciences and systems, mathematics, oceanography, physics, quantitative methods, and statistics), EDUCATION (music education), ENGINEERING AND ENVIRONMENTAL DESIGN (aeronautical engineering, ceramic engineering, chemical engineering, civil engineering, computer engineering, construction engineering, electrical/electronics engineering, engineering, landscape architecture/design, materials science, ocean engineering, and paper and pulp science), HEALTH PROFESSIONS (dental hygiene, environmental health science, health care administration, medical laboratory technology, nursing, and speech pathology/audiology), SOCIAL SCIENCE (African American studies, anthropology, Asian/American studies, Asian/Oriental studies, Canadian studies, economics, ethnic studies, food science, geography, history, international relations, Judaic studies, liberal arts/general studies, Near Eastern studies, philosophy, political science/government, psychology, religion, Russian and Slavic studies, social work, sociology, South Asian studies, and women's studies). Business, political science, and art have the largest enrollments.

Required: All students must maintain a GPA of 2.0 while taking 180 quarter credits, with 50 in the major. Distribution requirements include 40 credits from the humanities, social sciences, and math/natural sciences, with 12 credits in English composition/writing and a course in quantitative/symbolic reasoning.

Special: A wide variety of internships, including those for minority students in engineering, concurrent dual majors, study abroad in 60 countries, a Washington semester, a general studies degree, and co-op programs are available. Work-study programs, cross-registration with the National Student Exchange, credit/no credit options, student-designed majors, accelerated degree programs, nondegree study, and a 5-year B.A.-B.S. degree also are offered. There are 20 national honor societies, including Phi Beta Kappa, a freshman honors program, and 36 departmental honors programs.

Faculty/Classroom: 62% of faculty are male; 38% are female. 85% do both. No introductory courses are taught by graduate students.

Admissions: 65% of the 2013-2014 applicants were accepted. The SAT scores for the 2013-2014 freshman class were: Critical Reading--16% below 500, 36% between 500 and 599, 36% between 600 and 699, and 12% between 700 and 800; Math--9% below 500, 32% between 500 and 599, 44% between 600 and 699, and 16% between 700 and 800; Writing--17% below 500, 42% between 500 and 599, 34% between 600 and 699, and 8% between 700 and 800. The ACT scores were 9% below 21, 16% between 21 and 23, 27% between 24 and 26, 20% between 27 and 28, and 28% above 28. 97% of the current freshmen were in the top fifth of their class; 99% were in the top two fifths. There were 39 National Merit finalists.

Requirements: The SAT or ACT is required. The ACT Optional Writing test is also required. Applicants must have completed 15 academic units, including 4 years of English, 3 each of math and social sciences, 2 each of foreign language and science, and 1/2 year each in fine/visual performing arts and electives. Admission is based on a comprehensive review. A GPA of 2.0 is required. AP credits are accepted.

Procedure: Freshmen are admitted to all sessions. Entrance exams should be taken by December of the senior year. Applications should be filed by September 15 for winter entry; December 15 for spring entry; and January 15 for summer entry, along with a $50 fee. Notifications are sent March 15. 773 applicants were on the 2013 waiting list; 332 were admitted. Applications are accepted online.

Transfer: 2709 transfer students enrolled in 2012-2013. The school gives priority to Washington community colleges students. Admission is based on a comprehensive review. 45 of 180 credits required for the bachelor's degree must be completed at UW.

Visiting: There are regularly scheduled orientations for prospective students, including attending a class, a meeting with an admissions counselor and/or academic advisor, going on a campus tour, and attending information sessions. There are guides for informal visits and visitors may sit in on classes. To schedule a visit, contact the Student Visitation Program at (206) 543-5429.

Financial Aid: In 2013-2014, 50% of all full-time freshmen and 45% of continuing full-time students received some form of financial aid. 32% of all full-time freshmen and 37% of continuing full-time students received need-based aid. The average financial indebtedness of the 2013 graduate was $16,116. The FAFSA is required. The priority date for freshman financial aid applications for fall entry is February 28.

International Students: There are 1095 international students enrolled. They must take the TOEFL with a minimum score of 540 on the paper-based TOEFL (PBT) or 57 on the Internet-based version (iBT).

Computers: All students may access the system 24 hours daily. There are no time limits and no fees.

Graduates: From July 1, 2012 to June 30, 2013, 7024 bachelor's degrees were awarded. The most popular majors were social sciences (19%), biological/life sciences (10%), and business/marketing (10%). 212 companies recruited on campus in 2012-2013. In an average class, 48% graduate in 4 years or less, 71% graduate in 5 years or less, and 75% graduate in 6 years or less.

Admissions Contact: Office of Admissions Web: *www.washington.edu*

WALLA WALLA UNIVERSITY E-3

College Place, WA 99324-1198 (509) 527-2608
(800) 541-8900; (509) 527-2397

Full-time: 768 men, 700 women
Part-time: 47 men, 48 women
Graduate: 64 men, 173 women
Year: quarters, summer session
Application Deadline: open
Freshman Class: n/av
ACT: required
Faculty: n/av; IIA, --$
Ph.D.s: 48%
Student/Faculty: n/av
Tuition: $23,954
Room & Board: $6100

NONCOMPETITIVE

Walla Walla University, founded in 1892, is a private comprehensive institution affiliated with the Seventh-day Adventist Church, and offers liberal arts, professional, and technical programs. The figures in the above capsule and in this profile are approximate. There are 6 undergraduate schools and 4 graduate schools. In addition to regional accreditation, WWU has baccalaureate program accreditation with ABET, ACBSP, CSWE, NASM, and NLN. The 3 libraries contain 184,493 volumes, 151,946 microform items, and 3,451 audio/video tapes/CDs/DVDs, and subscribe to 3,727 periodicals including electronic. Computerized library services include interlibrary loans and database searching. Special learning facilities include a learning resource center, art gallery, radio station, TV station, audio listening/music library, and observatory. The 55-acre campus is in a small town 120 miles southwest of Spokane. Including any residence halls, there are 34 buildings.

Student Life: 60% of undergraduates are from out of state. The average age of freshmen is 19; all undergraduates, 21.

Housing: 1500 students can be accommodated in college housing, which includes single-sex dorms, on-campus apartments, off-campus apartments, and married student housing. In addition, there are off-campus houses. On-campus housing is guaranteed for all 4 years. 63% of students live on campus. Alcohol is not permitted. All students may keep cars.

Activities: There are no fraternities or sororities. Groups on campus include art, band, choir, chorale, chorus, drama, ethnic, honors, international, jazz band, literary magazine, newspaper, orchestra, photography, professional, radio and TV, religious, social service, student government, and symphony. Popular campus events include the Mud Bowl football game and the Sonneberg Series basketball tournament.

Sports: There are 6 intercollegiate sports for men and 3 for women, and 9 intramural sports for men and 8 for women. Facilities include a track, tennis and racquetball courts, a gymnastics gym, a pool, a climbing wall, a gym, several weight rooms, and residence hall health spas.

Disabled Students: 90% of the campus is accessible. Facilities include wheelchair ramps, elevators, special parking, specially equipped restrooms, special class scheduling, and special housing.

Services: Counseling and information services are available, as is tutoring in most subjects, including math, languages, sciences, business, and engineering. There is remedial math, reading, and writing.

Campus Safety and Security: Measures include 24-hour foot and vehicle patrol, emergency notification system, self-defense education, and security escort services. There are emergency telephones and lighted pathways/sidewalks.

Programs of Study: WWU confers B.A., B.S., B.B.A., B.Mus., B.S.E., and B.S.W. degrees. Associate and master's degrees are also awarded. Bachelor's degrees are awarded in BIOLOGICAL SCIENCE (biochemistry, biology/biological science, and biophysics), BUSINESS (business administration and management), COMMUNICATIONS AND THE ARTS (art, communications, English, French, German, graphic design, music, music performance, Spanish, and speech/debate/rhetoric), COMPUTER AND PHYSICAL SCIENCE (chemistry, computer science, digital arts/technology, information sciences and systems, mathematics, and physics), EDUCATION (business education, elementary education, music education, physical education, and special education), ENGINEERING AND ENVIRONMENTAL DESIGN (automotive technology, aviation computer technology, bioengineering, engineering, and environmental science), HEALTH PROFESSIONS (health and nursing), SOCIAL SCIENCE (biblical languages, history, humanities, psychology, religion, social work, sociology, and theological studies). Social work, business, and engineering are the strongest academically.

Required: To graduate, students must successfully complete 192 quarter hours, including at least 45 in the major and at least 60 in upper-level work, with a minimum GPA of 2.0. Grades below C- will not apply toward the major. Students must also meet a general studies requirement that includes 16 to 20 quarter hours in religion and theology, 13 to 21 in language arts, 12 to 20 in history and social science, 12 to 16 in humanities and math/natural science, and 2 to 6 in health and phys ed. A comprehensive exam is required, as is attendance at chapel and assemblies.

Special: Opportunities are provided for internships, co-op programs, cross-registration with Whitman College, study abroad in 6 countries, work-study programs, a B.A.-B.S. degree, dual majors, credit by exam, and nondegree study. There is a freshman honors program and 6 departmental honors programs.

Faculty/Classroom: 54% of faculty are male; 46% are female. All teach undergraduates. No introductory courses are taught by graduate students. The average class size in an introductory lecture, 24, and in a regular course, 13.

Requirements: The ACT is required. Scores are used for placement and academic advisement. Graduation from an accredited secondary school is required; a GED will be accepted. Applicants should submit an academic record containing at a minimum 4 years of English, and 2 each of history, science, and math, including algebra and geometry, along with a letter of recommendation from a teacher or school official. A GPA of 2.0 is required. AP and CLEP credits are accepted. Important factors in the admissions decision are advanced placement or honors courses, recommendations by school officials, and leadership record.

Procedure: Freshmen are admitted to all sessions. Entrance exams should be taken during the junior or senior year. There are early decision, early admissions, deferred admissions, and rolling admissions plans. Application deadlines are open. Application fee is $40. Applications are accepted online.

Transfer: 143 transfer students enrolled in a recent year. Applicants should have a 2.0 minimum GPA and must submit all college transcripts and a letter of recommendation (3 for nursing majors) from a former teacher or school official. 36 of 192 credits required for the bachelor's degree must be completed at WWU.

Visiting: There are guides for informal visits; visitors may sit in on classes and stay overnight.

Financial Aid: The FAFSA and the college's own financial statement are required. Check with the school for current application deadlines.

International Students: The school actively recruits these students. They must take the TOEFL with a minimum score of 550 on the paper-based TOEFL (PBT) or 79 on the Internet-based version (iBT). They must also take the SAT or ACT.

Computers: Wireless access is available. Several computer labs are available for student use. All students may access the system. The labs are open 6:30 a.m. to 11 p.m. Sunday through Thursday and 6:30 a.m. to 3:30 p.m. Fridays. There are no time limits and no fees.

Admissions Contact: Dallas Weis, Director of Admissions. A campus DVD is available. E-Mail: *dallas.weis@wallawalla.edu* Web: *www.wallawalla.edu*

WASHINGTON STATE UNIVERSITY E-3

Pullman, WA 99164 (509) 335-5586
(000) 400-0970; (509) 005-4902

Full-time: 9982 men, 9818 women	**Faculty:** n/av; I, --$
Part-time: 1139 men, 1824 women	**Ph.D.s:** 90%
Graduate: 2094 men, 2470 women	**Student/Faculty:** 16 to 1
Year: semesters, summer session	**Tuition:** $11,299 ($22,577)
Application Deadline: January 31	**Room & Board:** $10,162
Freshman Class: n/av	
SAT or ACT: required	

COMPETITIVE

Founded as a land-grant institution in 1890, Washington State University in Pullman is today a major research university. Its undergraduate and graduate offerings span the liberal arts and sciences, business, education, engineering and architecture, agricultural, human and natural resource sciences, and the health sciences, including nursing, pharmacy, and veterinary medicine. There are 12 undergraduate schools and 1 graduate school. In addition to regional accreditation, Washington State has baccalaureate program accreditation with AACSB, ABET, ACCE, ACPE, ADA, ASLA, FIDER, NAAB, NASM, NCATE, NRPA, and SAF. The 6 libraries contain 2.2 million volumes, 4.0 million microform items, 424,265 audio/video tapes/CDs/DVDs, and subscribe to 42,987 periodicals including electronic. Computerized library services include interlibrary loans, database searching, Internet access, and Wi-Fi capability. Special learning facilities include an art gallery, natural history museum, planetarium, radio station, TV station, Specialized teaching and research labs for science and engineering, a planetarium and observatory, virtual reality computer-integrated manufacturing lab, fine arts studio facilities with specialized equipment, museums, displays and collections, and art galleries, digital recording studio; music listening library; radio and television studios; livestock centers, labs, and barns, a wildlife center, a bear center (live grizzly bears in captivity for research, education, and conservation), human anatomy lab, greenhouses, vivaria, and an herbarium, financial markets lab (trading room), food sensory evaluation facility, a veterinary teaching hospital, a social and economic sciences research center, a water research center, a laboratory for atmospheric research, nuclear radiation center. The 620-acre campus is in a small town 80 miles south of Spokane, and 285 miles east of Seattle. Including any residence halls, there are 549 buildings.

Student Life: 88% of undergraduates are from Washington. Others are from 50 states, 57 foreign countries, and Canada. 69% are White. The average age of freshmen is 17; all undergraduates, 23. 16% do not continue beyond their first year; 72% remain to graduate.

Housing: 8507 students can be accommodated in college housing, which includes single-sex and coed dorms, on-campus apartments, and married student housing. In addition, there are honors houses, language houses, special-interest houses, fraternity houses, sorority houses, living-learning communities. On-campus housing is guaranteed for the freshman year only. 64% of students commute. All students may keep cars.

Activities: 21% of men belong to 25 national fraternities; 20% of women belong to 14 national sororities. There are 380 groups on campus, including art, band, cheerleading, chess, choir, chorale, chorus, computers, dance, debate, drama, environmental, ethnic, film, forensics, gay, honors, international, jazz band, literary magazine, marching band, musical theater, newspaper, opera, orchestra, pep band, photography, political, professional, radio and TV, religious, social, social service, student government, symphony, and yearbook. Popular campus events include Convocation, All-Campus Picnic, and Civic Engagement Week.

Sports: There are 7 intercollegiate sports for men and 10 for women, and 12 intramural sports for men and 12 for women. Facilities include a 40,000-seat stadium, a 12,000-seat coliseum, full 200-meter NCAA indoor and outdoor tracks, tennis courts, a 165,500-square-foot student recreation center, an 18-hole championship golf course, an indoor practice facility with roll-out turf system, baseball and soccer fields, indoor swimming pools, racquetball and squash courts, a climbing wall, ballrooms, gyms, an indoor rowing facility, an outdoor recreation center, basketball courts, sand volleyball courts, and intramural playing fields.

Disabled Students: Facilities include wheelchair ramps, elevators, special parking, specially equipped restrooms, special class scheduling, lowered drinking fountains, lowered telephones, special housing, and a van to provide transportation to and from classes.

Services: Counseling and information services are available, as is tutoring in most subjects. There is a reader service for the blind. Learning assistance is available in workshops that address study skills, note taking, test preparation, time management, career/major choice, stress management, and life skills

Campus Safety and Security: Measures include 24-hour foot and vehicle patrol, emergency notification system, self-defense education, and security escort services. There are shuttle buses, emergency telephones, lighted pathways/sidewalks, controlled access to dorms/residences, crime prevention and personal safety education, monitored lighting levels on campus, a women's transit service, residence hall security hours, a police intern program, and housing patrols.

Programs of Study: Washington State confers B.A., B.S., B.F.A., B.L.A. and B.M. degrees. Master's and doctoral degrees are also awarded. Bachelor's degrees are awarded in AGRICULTURE (agricultural business management, agricultural communications, agricultural economics, agricultural mechanics, agriculture, agronomy, animal science, horticulture, natural resource management, plant protection (pest management), plant science, range/farm management, soil science, and wildlife management), BIOLOGICAL SCIENCE (biochemistry, biology/biological science, cell biology, entomology, genetics, microbiology, neurosciences, plant genetics, plant pathology, wildlife biology, and zoology), BUSINESS (accounting, business administration and management, business economics, business law, business statistics, entrepreneurial studies, hotel/motel and restaurant management, international business management, management information systems, marketing management, operations management, and sports management), COMMUNICATIONS AND THE ARTS (advertising, broadcasting, Chinese, communications, digital communications, English, fine arts, French, journalism, linguistics, multimedia, music, music performance, music theory and composition, public relations, and Spanish), COMPUTER AND PHYSICAL SCIENCE (applied mathematics, chemistry, computer science, digital arts/technology, geology, mathematics, physical sciences, physics, and science), EDUCATION (agricultural education, athletic training, bilingual/bicultural education, early childhood education, education, English education, foreign languages education, physical education, science education, secondary education, social studies education, and special education), ENGINEERING AND ENVIRONMENTAL DESIGN (agricultural engineering, architecture, bioengineering, biomedical engineering, chemical engineering, civil engineering, computer engineering, construction management, electrical/electronics engineering, environmental science, interior design, landscape architecture/design, manufacturing engineering, materials engineering, and mechanical engineering), HEALTH PROFESSIONS (biomedical science, exercise science, nursing, predentistry, premedicine, preoptometry, prepharmacy, prephysical therapy, preveterinary science, and speech pathology/audiology), SOCIAL SCIENCE (anthropology, Asian/Oriental studies, clothing and textiles management/production/services, criminal justice, crosscultural studies, economics, ethnic studies, family/consumer studies, food science, history, human development, humanities, interdisciplinary studies, liberal arts/general studies, philosophy, political science/government, prelaw, psychology, religion, social science, social studies, sociology, and women's studies). Organic agriculture, interior design, and international business are the strongest academically. Business administration, general social sciences, and nursing have the largest enrollments.

Required: Students must complete 120 semester hours, with fulfillment of a major and 40 hours of upper-division work, and maintain a minimum GPA of 2.0. Specific disciplines to be taken vary within majors. General university requirements include 10 hours of science, 9 of arts and humanities and social sciences, 6 of world civilization, 6 of communication, and 3 each of math, intercultural studies, and American diversity. Students must complete a writing portfolio, undergo a mid-career assessment, and pass a writing qualifying exam prior to graduation.

Special: Undergraduates can become involved in faculty research, internships, study-abroad programs in 95 countries, an Honors College, academic club projects and competitions, civic engagement projects, work-study programs, and co-op programs in numerous majors. Dual majors are available, as are B.A.-B.S. degrees in computer science and psychology and student-designed majors in general studies. Interior design and veterinary medicine programs offer accelerated paths to advanced degrees. Credit may be granted for military service, and nondegree and pass/fail options are offered. Cross-registration is available with the Universities of Idaho and Washington, Eastern Washington University, and Wenatchee Valley College. The WSU College of Nursing is a consortium of Washington State, Eastern Washington, and Whitworth Universities. There are 34 national honor societies, including Phi Beta Kappa, a freshman honors program, and 100 departmental honors programs.

Faculty/Classroom: 58% of faculty are male; 42% are female. Graduate students teach 18% of introductory courses. The average class size in a regular course is 36.

Requirements: The SAT or ACT is required. Students should be graduates of an accredited secondary school with 4 years of English, 3 each of math (1 year each of algebra, geometry, and advanced math) and social science, and 2 each of a world language (includes Native American languages and American Sign Language), science, and 1 year of fine, visual or performing arts, or elective from any of the other required subjects. A combination of the high school GPA and test scores is considered. The GED is also accepted. A GPA of 2.0 is required. AP and CLEP credits are accepted. Important factors in the admissions decision are advanced placement or honors courses, evidence of special talent, and personality/intangible qualities.

Procedure: Freshmen are admitted fall, spring, and summer. Entrance exams should be taken during spring of the junior year or fall of the senior year. Applications should be filed by January 31 for fall entry; November 15 for spring entry, along with a $50 fee. Notifications are sent November 1. applicants were on the 2013 waiting list; were admitted. Applications are accepted online.

Transfer: 1233 transfer students enrolled in 2012-2013. Transfer applicants who have less than a full year of college-level academic work may be required to submit a high school transcript, test scores, and/or a personal statement. 30 of 120 credits required for the bachelor's degree must be completed at Washington State.

Visiting: There are regularly scheduled orientations for prospective students, consisting of a campus tour and a presentation about admissions, financial aid, and scholarship opportunities. There are guides for informal visits and visitors may sit in on classes.

Financial Aid: In 2013-2014, 86% of all full-time freshmen and 76% of continuing full-time students received some form of financial aid. 49% of all full-time freshmen and 53% of continuing full-time students received need-based aid. The average freshman award was $18,745. Need-based scholarships or need-based grants averaged $8,523 ($16,326 maximum); need-based self-help aid (loans and jobs) averaged $3,988 ($10,000 maximum); non-need-based athletic scholarships averaged $19,085 ($34,834 maximum); and other non-need-based awards and non-need-based scholarships averaged $4,077 ($28,750 maximum). 26% of undergraduate students work part-time. Average annual earnings from campus work are $3367. The average financial indebtedness of the 2013 graduate was $20,544. The FAFSA is required. The priority date for freshman financial aid applications for fall entry is February 15.

International Students: There are 779 international students enrolled. The school actively recruits these students. They must take the TOEFL with a minimum score of 550 on the paper-based TOEFL (PBT) or 79 on the Internet-based version (iBT) or take the MELAB, IELTS, IB with a passing score in English, or SAT with a reading/writing score of 500.

Computers: All students may access the system 24 hours a day. There are no time limits and no fees.

Graduates: From July 1, 2012 to June 30, 2013, 4907 bachelor's degrees were awarded. The most popular majors were business administration (18%), social sciences (13%), and communication (11%). 275 companies recruited on campus in 2012-2013. In an average class, 38% graduate in 4 years or less, 62% graduate in 5 years or less, and 69% graduate in 6 years or less.

Admissions Contact: Wendy Peterson, Director of Admissions. E-Mail: *admissions@wsu.edu* Web: *www.wsu.edu*

WESTERN WASHINGTON UNIVERSITY C-1

Bellingham, WA 98225	**(360) 650-2422; (360) 650-7369**
Full-time: 5689 men, 7226 women	**Faculty:** n/av; IIA, -$
Part-time: 552 men, 458 women	**Ph.D.s:** 88%
Graduate: 342 men, 582 women	**Student/Faculty:** 20 to 1
Year: quarters, summer session	**Tuition:** $8863 ($19,752)
Application Deadline: March 1	**Room & Board:** $9656
Freshman Class: 9791 applied, 7799 accepted, 2688 enrolled	
SAT CR/M/W: 550/550/530 **ACT:** 25	**VERY COMPETITIVE**

Western Washington University, founded in 1893, is a nonprofit, public institution whose emphasis is on the liberal arts and sciences, business and business administration, and economics, art, fine arts, and performing arts, music, teacher preparation, interdisciplinary learning, and environmental studies. There are 7 undergraduate schools and 1 graduate school. In addition to regional accreditation, WWU has baccalaureate program accreditation with AACSB, ABET, ASLA, NASM, NCATE, and NRPA. The 2 libraries contain 1.3 million volumes, 1.4 million microform items, and 93,199 audio/video tapes/CDs/DVDs, and subscribe to 129,895 periodicals including electronic. Computerized library services include interlibrary loans, database searching, Internet access, and Wi-Fi capability. Special learning facilities include an art gallery, planetarium, radio station, a marine lab, neutron generator lab, motor vehicle research lab, a wind tunnel, air pollution lab, an electronic music studio, and performing arts center. The 195-acre campus is in a small town 60 miles south of Vancouver, British Columbia and 90 miles north of Seattle. Including any residence halls, there are 80 buildings.

Student Life: 91% of undergraduates are from Washington. Others are from states, and Canada. 75% are White. The average age of freshmen is 18; all undergraduates, 21. 15% do not continue beyond their first year; 85% remain to graduate.

Housing: 4040 students can be accommodated in college housing, which includes coed dorms, on-campus apartments, off-campus apartments, and married student housing. a fitness/wellness hall, freshman interest groups, substance-free living, quiet and smoke-free areas. On-campus housing is available on a first-come and first-served basis. 71% of students commute. All students may keep cars.

Activities: There are no fraternities or sororities. There are 225 groups on campus, including and environmental., art, band, cheerleading, chess, choir, chorale, chorus, computers, dance, debate, drama, environmental, ethnic, film, forensics, gay, honors, international, jazz band, literary magazine, musical theater, newspaper, opera, orchestra, pep band, photography, political, professional, recreational, religious, social, social service, student government, and symphony. Popular campus events include The Western Jam Talent Show, Casino Night and Cinco de Mayo.

Sports: There are 6 intercollegiate sports for men and 9 for women, and 13 intramural sports for men and 13 for women. Facilities include Facilities include a 96,000 square feet center with a pool, rock wall, 10,000 square feet of weight and fitness equipment, 3 basketball courts, and 1 multi-activity court. In addition, there is an artificial-surfaced soccer practice field, a six lane track, and a softball complex.

Disabled Students: All of the campus is accessible. Facilities include wheelchair ramps, elevators, special parking, specially equipped restrooms, special class scheduling, lowered drinking fountains, lowered telephones.

Services: Counseling and information services are available, as is tutoring in most subjects, including English, humanities, social sciences, math and natural sciences. There is a reader service for the blind.

Campus Safety and Security: Measures include 24-hour foot and vehicle patrol, emergency notification system, self-defense education, and security escort services. There are shuttle buses, emergency telephones, and lighted pathways/sidewalks.

Programs of Study: WWU confers B.A., B.S., B.A.E., B.F.A. and B.Mus. degrees. Master's degrees are also awarded. Bachelor's degrees are awarded in AGRICULTURE (environmental studies), BIOLOGICAL SCIENCE (biochemistry, biology/biological science, cell biology, ecology, life science, marine biology, marine science, and molecular biology), BUSINESS (accounting, business administration and management, fashion merchandising, human resources, international business management, international economics, management information systems, management science, marketing/retailing/merchandising, and operations management), COMMUNICATIONS AND THE ARTS (apparel design, art, ceramic art and design, classics, communications, creative writing, dance, design, dramatic arts, English, fine arts, French, German, Japanese, journalism, linguistics, multimedia, music, music history and appreciation, painting, photography, Russian, sculpture, Spanish, theater design, and visual and performing arts), COMPUTER AND PHYSICAL SCIENCE (applied mathematics, applied physics, chemistry, computer science, earth science, geology, mathematics, physics, and polymer science), EDUCATION (art education, early childhood education, education administration, elementary education, foreign languages education, health education, music education, physical education, reading education, recreation education, science education, secondary education, special education, and technical education), ENGINEERING AND ENVIRONMENTAL DESIGN (electrical/electronics engineering, electrical/electronics engineering technology, engineering technology, environmental science, industrial engineering technology, manufacturing technology, mechanical design technology, mechanical engineering technology, plastics engineering, and technology and public affairs), HEALTH PROFESSIONS (nursing, rehabilitation therapy, and speech pathology/audiology), SOCIAL SCIENCE (American studies, anthropology, behavioral science, Canadian studies, child psychology/development, East Asian studies, economics, geography, history, human services, interdisciplinary studies, parks and recreation management, philosophy, political science/government, psychology, public affairs, social studies, and sociology). Industrial technology, materials science, business, and computer science are the strongest academically. Business and marketing, social sciences, visual and performing arts have the largest enrollments.

Required: Students must complete at least 180 quarter hours, with fulfillment of a major and at least 60 credits in upper-division study, and maintain at least a 2.0 GPA or that prescribed by departments/divisions. General university requirements include 70 to 75 credits, and students must satisfy writing proficiency requirements as well. Fairhaven College has a separate interdisciplinary core program.

Special: Special academic programs include internships through various academic departments and study abroad in 75 countries. Dual majors are available through various departments. There is a general studies degree, and a B.A. in humanities. A 3-2 engineering degree is possible with the University of Washington. WWU is in the process of starting an Engineering Program that will replace the 3-2. Student-designed majors are offered through the liberal studies department in the College of Arts and Sciences and through Fairhaven College, which affords an unusual degree of student involvement in the structure and content of their own programs and which uses faculty narrative for students' academic evaluations. In addition, Huxley College of Environmental Studies provides specialized education and research. Up to 30 credits of electives may be granted for military service, and nondegree study and pass/fail options are possible. There are 12 national honor societies, a freshman honors program, and 12 departmental honors programs.

Faculty/Classroom: 50% of faculty are male; 50% are female. No introductory courses are taught by graduate students.

Admissions: 80% of the 2013-2014 applicants were accepted. The SAT scores for the 2013-2014 freshman class were: Critical Reading--25% below 500, 43% between 500 and 599, 27% between 600 and 699, and 5% between 700 and 800; Math--25% below 500, 47% between 500 and 599, 26% between 600 and 699, and 3% between 700 and 800; Writing--32% below 500, 45% between 500 and 599, 21% between 600 and 699, and 2% between 700 and 800. The ACT scores were 13% below 21, 26% between 21 and 23, 28% between 24 and 26, 15% between 27 and 28, and 18% above 28.

Requirements: The SAT or ACT is required. Other admissions requirements include completion of 16 academic units, comprised of 4 years of college preparatory English composition and literature courses; 3 units of college preparatory math, including 2 years of algebra; 3 units of social studies/history; 2 units of science, including 1 unit of a chemistry or physics with an algebra prerequisite; 2 units of the same foreign language; 1 unit of fine and performing arts; and 1 semester in another academic field. Freshman applicants meeting minimum GPA and subject requirements are ranked by an index combining the GPA and a standardized test score. The GED is also accepted. Other factors taken into consideration include curricular rigor (level of difficulty of courses), grade trends, leadership, community involvement, special talent, multicultural experience, and personal hardship or circumstances. A GPA of 2.5 is required. AP credits are accepted. Important factors in the admissions decision are advanced placement or honors courses, leadership record, and personality/intangible qualities.

Procedure: Freshmen are admitted to all sessions. Entrance exams should be taken by fall of the senior year. Applications should be filed by March 1 for fall entry; October 15 for winter entry; January 15 for spring entry; and March 1 for summer entry. The fall 2013 application fee was $55. Notifications are sent March 15. 905 applicants were on the 2013 waiting list; 454 were admitted. Applications are accepted online.

Transfer: Applicants with fewer than 40 quarter credits are eligible for consideration if they have completed the last term before transferring with a GPA of at least 2.0, and if they satisfy the requirements for freshman admission. Those with 40 or more transferable quarter credits are eligible if they have achieved a cumulative GPA of at least 2.0. Admission is selective. 90 of 180 credits required for the bachelor's degree must be completed at WWU.

Visiting: There are regularly scheduled orientations for prospective students, Student visits include tours, class visits and advisement. There are guides for informal visits, visitors may sit in on classes, and stay overnight. To schedule a visit, contact the STARS Program at (360) 650-3861.

Financial Aid: In 2013-2014, 51% of all full-time freshmen and 48% of continuing full-time students received some form of financial aid. 41% of all full-time freshmen and 42% of continuing full-time students received need-based aid. The average freshman award was $13,143. Need-based scholarships or need-based grants averaged $8,828; and need-based self-help aid (loans and jobs) averaged $4,098. 10% of undergraduate students work part-time. Average annual earnings from campus work are $2156. The FAFSA is required. The deadline for filing freshman financial aid applications for fall entry is February 15.

International Students: There are 126 international students enrolled. They must take the TOEFL with a minimum score of 550 on the paper-based TOEFL (PBT) or 80 on the Internet-based version (iBT). They must also take the SAT or ACT.

Computers: All students may access the system. There are no time limits and no fees.

Graduates: From July 1, 2012 to June 30, 2013, 2996 bachelor's degrees were awarded. The most popular majors were business and marketing (14%), social sciences (14%), and English (6%). 72 companies recruited on campus in 2012-2013. In an average class, 35% graduate in 4 years or less, 26% graduate in 5 years or less, and 67% graduate in 6 years or less. Of the 2012 graduating class, 13% were enrolled in graduate school within 6 months of graduation, and 94% were employed.

Admissions Contact: Clara Capron, Director. E-Mail: *admit@cc.wwu.edu* Web: *www.wwu.edu*

WHITMAN COLLEGE E-3

Walla Walla, WA 99362 (509) 527-5176
(877) 462-9448; (509) 527-4967

Full-time: 645 men, 859 women
Part-time: 21 men, 16 women
Graduate: n/av
Year: semesters
Application Deadline: January 15
Freshman Class: 2600 applied, 1473 accepted, 392 enrolled
SAT CR/M/W: 670/660/660
Faculty: 151; IIB, +$
Ph.D.s: 94%
Student/Faculty: 10 to 1
Tuition: $43,500
Room & Board: $10,900
ACT: 30 **MOST COMPETITIVE**

Whitman College, founded in 1883, is a nonprofit, private, independent residential liberal arts and sciences college. There is one undergraduate school. The library contains 566,989 volumes, and 8,407 audio/video tapes/CDs/DVDs, and subscribes to 66,049 periodicals including electronic. Computerized library services include interlibrary loans, database searching, Internet access, and Wi-Fi capability. Special learning facilities include an art gallery, natural history museum, planetarium, radio station, an electron microscope lab, an indoor planetarium, an off-campus an observatory and on-campus astronomical telescopes, an Asian art collection, a video-conferencing center, an outdoor sculpture walk, an organic garden, and indoor and outdoor rock climbing walls. The 117-acre campus is in a small town 150 miles south of Spokane, 260 miles southeast of Seattle, and 235 miles east of Portland. Including any residence halls, there are 41 buildings.

Student Life: 65% of undergraduates are from out of state, mostly the Northwest. Students are from 42 states, 25 foreign countries, and Canada. 68% are from public schools. 72% are White. The average age of freshmen is 18; all undergraduates, 20. 6% do not continue beyond their first year; 94% remain to graduate.

Housing: 882 students can be accommodated in college housing, which includes single-sex and coed dorms and off-campus apartments. In addition, there are language houses, special-interest houses, and fraternity houses. On-campus housing is guaranteed for the freshman year only and is available on a lottery system for upperclassmen. All students may keep cars.

Activities: 46% of men belong to 4 national fraternities; 40% of women belong to 4 national sororities. There are 117 groups on campus, including art, choir, chorale, chorus, dance, debate, drama, environmental, ethnic, film, forensics, gay, honors, international, jazz band, literary magazine, musical theater, newspaper, opera, orchestra, photography, political, professional, radio and TV, religious, social, social service, student government, symphony, and yearbook. Popular campus events include Renaissance Fair, Choral Contest, and Interest House Block Party.

Sports: There are 7 intercollegiate sports for men and 7 for women, and 10 intramural sports for men and 9 for women. Facilities include a stadium, two gyms, squash and handball courts, saunas, climbing walls, and an aerobic/dance room. There is an athletics center with a 10,000-square-foot weights/cardiovascular area, 8-lane swimming pool, 6 outdoor tennis courts, 4 indoor tennis courts, a soccer field, a dance studio, and an off-campus sports complex, including soccer, baseball, and track facilities.

Disabled Students: 96% of the campus is accessible. Facilities include wheelchair ramps, elevators, special parking, specially equipped restrooms, lowered drinking fountains, lowered telephones. Any modifications necessary for specific cases will be made.

Services: Counseling and information services are available, as is tutoring in most subjects. There is a reader service for the blind. There are also centers for study skills and writing.

Campus Safety and Security: Measures include emergency notification system, self-defense education, and security escort services. There are emergency telephones, lighted pathways/sidewalks, controlled access to dorms/residences, 24-hour foot patrol.

Programs of Study: confers B.A. degrees. Bachelor's degrees are awarded in AGRICULTURE (environmental studies), BIOLOGICAL SCIENCE (biochemistry), COMMUNICATIONS AND THE ARTS (art history, classics, dance, English, film arts, fine arts, French, German, music, Spanish, speech/debate/rhetoric, studio art, and theatre arts), COMPUTER AND PHYSICAL SCIENCE (astronomy, chemistry, geology, mathematics, and physics), ENGINEERING AND ENVIRONMENTAL DESIGN (environmental science), HEALTH PROFESSIONS (biology), SOCIAL SCIENCE (anthropology, Asian/Oriental studies, economics, ethnic studies, history, philosophy, political science/government, psychology, religion, and sociology). Biology, psychology, and politics have the largest enrollments.

Required: Students must complete 124 credits, with 32 to 36 in the major, and maintain a minimum GPA of 2.0. Distribution requirements include a minimum of 6 credits in social sciences, humanities, fine arts, and science (including 1 course with a lab); 1 course of 3 or more credits in quantitative analysis; and 2 courses that fulfill the alternative voices requirement. Freshman must take the year-long Encounters (great works) course. All majors require an oral exam as well as a thesis project or comprehensive written exam.

Special: Special academic programs include more than 500 internships, over 80 semester or year-long study abroad programs in 40 countries, a Washington semester, and study programs in Chicago and Philadelphia. Dual majors are available in any area, and student-designed majors are offered. There is a 3-2 environmental management and forestry program with Duke University and a 3-2 engineering program with Washington University in St. Louis, California Institute of Technology and Applied Science, Columbia and Duke Universities, and University of Washington. A 3-3 law program is offered through Columbia University. A 4-1 education program is available through Bank Street College of Education and University of Puget Sound Cooperative. Certification is offered for elementary and secondary education. A pass-D-fail option is available. A 3-2 program in international studies is available with the Monterey Institute of International Studies. A 3-2 program in oceanography is available with University of Washington. There are 3 national honor societies, including Phi Beta Kappa, and a freshman honors program.

Faculty/Classroom: 55% of faculty are male; 45% are female. All teach undergraduates, all do research, and all teach and do research. No introductory courses are taught by graduate students. The average class size in an introductory lecture is 24; in a laboratory is 23; and in a regular course is 18.

Admissions: 57% of the 2013-2014 applicants were accepted. The SAT scores for the 2013-2014 freshman class were: Critical Reading--4% below 500, 15% between 500 and 599, 42% between 600 and 699, and 39% between 700 and 800; Math--2% below 500, 20% between 500 and 599, 53% between 600 and 699, and 25% between 700 and 800; Writing--5% below 500, 16% between 500 and 599, 53% between 600 and 699, and 26% between 700 and 800. The ACT scores were 6% between 21 and 23, 12% between 24 and 26, 15% between 27 and 28, and 67% above 28. 80% of the current freshmen were in the top fifth of their class; 95% were in the top two fifths.

Requirements: The SAT or ACT is required. Applicants must submit either ACT or SAT scores. The GED is accepted. 3 essays must be submitted, and an interview is recommended. Credit by challenge examination is accepted. AP credits are accepted. Important factors in the admissions decision are advanced placement or honors courses, personality/intangible qualities, evidence of special talent, recommendations by alumni, recommendations by school officials, and extracurricular activities record.

Procedure: Freshmen are admitted fall and spring. Entrance exams should be taken by fall of the senior year. There are early decision and deferred admissions plans. Early decision applications should be filed by November 15; regular applications, by January 15 for fall entry. The fall 2013 application fee was $50. Notification of early decision is sent December 21; regular decision, March 29. 125 early decision candidates were accepted for the 2013-2014 class. Applications are accepted online.

Transfer: 20 transfer students enrolled in 2012-2013. Transfer applicants must submit the common application, a transfer supplement, a teacher/counselor recommendation, a statement of good standing from prior institutions, their high school and college transcripts, SAT or ACT scores (required for some), and the application fee. 54 of 124 credits required for the bachelor's degree must be completed at Whitman.

Visiting: There are regularly scheduled orientations for prospective students. There are guides for informal visits, visitors may sit in on classes, and stay overnight. To schedule a visit, contact Mary Beth Ehrhardt at (509) 527-5176.

Financial Aid: In 2013-2014, 77% of all full-time freshmen and 73% of continuing full-time students received some form of financial aid. 51% of all full-time freshmen and 43% of continuing full-time students received need-based aid. The average freshman award was $33,588. Need-based scholarships or need-based grants averaged $28,689; need-based self-help aid (loans and jobs) averaged $6,256; and other non-need-based awards and non-need-based scholarships averaged $8,427. The average financial indebtedness of the 2013 graduate was $15,027. The CSS/Profile and FAFSA are required. The priority date for freshman financial aid applications for fall entry is November 15. The deadline for filing freshman financial aid applications for fall entry is February 1.

International Students: There are 53 international students enrolled. The school actively recruits these students. They must take the TOEFL with a minimum score of 560 on the paper-based TOEFL (PBT) or 85 on the Internet-based version (iBT). They must also take the SAT or ACT.

Computers: All students may access the system 24 hours a day. There are no time limits and no fees.

Graduates: From July 1, 2012 to June 30, 2013, 365 bachelor's degrees were awarded. The most popular majors were biology (12%), psychology (8%), and English (7%). In an average class, 80% graduate in 4 years or less, 87% graduate in 5 years or less, and 88% graduate in 6 years or less.

Admissions Contact: Tony Cabasco, Dean of Admission and Financial Aid. E-Mail: *admission@whitman.edu* Web: *www.whitman.edu*

WHITWORTH UNIVERSITY E-2

Spokane, WA 99251 (509) 777-4348
(800) 533-4668; (509) 777-3758

Full-time: 916 men, 1400 women
Part-time: 17 men, 25 women
Graduate: 77 men, 133 women
Year: 4-1-4, summer session
Application Deadline: March 1
Faculty: 148; IIB, --$
Ph.D.s: 82%
Student/Faculty: 11 to 1
Tuition: $36,012
Room & Board: $9814
Freshman Class: 4043 applied, 2610 accepted, 593 enrolled
SAT CR/M/W: 600/600/590 **ACT:** 26 **VERY COMPETITIVE+**

Whitworth University, founded in 1890, is an independent, comprehensive institution affiliated with the Presbyterian Church. The emphasis of its undergraduate and graduate programs is on the liberal arts, business, art and fine arts, music, religious studies, and teacher preparation. There are 4 undergraduate schools and 3 graduate schools. In addition to regional accreditation, Whitworth has baccalaureate program accreditation with NASM, NCATE, and NLN. The 2 libraries contain 286,000 volumes, 10,000 microform items, and 9,000 audio/video tapes/CDs/DVDs, and subscribe to 3,000 periodicals including electronic. Computerized library services include interlibrary loans, database searching, Internet access, and Wi-Fi capability. Special learning facilities include an art gallery, radio station, a writing center. The 200-acre campus is in a suburban area 7 miles north of Spokane. Including any residence halls, there are 40 buildings.

Student Life: 61% of undergraduates are from Washington. Others are from 32 states, 27 foreign countries, and Canada. 88% are from public schools. 79% are White. 81% are Protestant. The average age of freshmen is 18; all undergraduates, 21. 11% do not continue beyond their first year; 77% remain to graduate.

Housing: 1352 students can be accommodated in college housing, which includes single-sex and coed dorms, on-campus apartments, and off-campus apartments. In addition, there are language houses, special-interest houses, and theme houses. On-campus housing is guaranteed for all 4 years. 62% of students live on campus; of those, 90% remain on campus on weekends. Alcohol is not permitted. All students may keep cars.

Activities: There are no fraternities or sororities. There are 45 groups on campus, including art, band, cheerleading, choir, chorale, chorus, computers, dance, drama, environmental, ethnic, forensics, honors, international, jazz band, literary magazine, musical theater, newspaper, orchestra, photography, political, radio and TV, religious, social, social service, and student government. Popular campus events include Guest Speakers, Student Research Conference, and Community Building Day.

Sports: There are 9 intercollegiate sports for men and 9 for women, and 10 intramural sports for men and 8 for women. Facilities include a new university recreation center complete with climbing walls, a 2000-seat stadium, a 1200-seat gym, a field house, an aquatic center, and playing fields.

Disabled Students: 70% of the campus is accessible. Facilities include wheelchair ramps, elevators, special parking, specially equipped rest rooms, special class scheduling, lowered drinking fountains, and lowered telephones.

Services: Counseling and information services are available, as is tutoring in most subjects, including biology, chemistry, computer science, French, German, Spanish, math, physics, and writing.

Campus Safety and Security: Measures include 24-hour foot and vehicle patrol, emergency notification system, and security escort services. There are emergency telephones, lighted pathways/sidewalks, and controlled access to dorms/residences.

Programs of Study: Whitworth confers B.A. and B.S. degrees. Master's degrees are also awarded. Bachelor's degrees are awarded in BIOLOGICAL SCIENCE (biology/biological science and biophysics), BUSINESS (accounting, business administration and management, international business management, and marketing management), COMMUNICATIONS AND THE ARTS (art, communications, dramatic arts, English, French, journalism, music, Spanish, and speech/debate/rhetoric), COMPUTER AND PHYSICAL SCIENCE (applied physics, chemistry, computer science, mathematics, physics, and quantitative methods), EDUCATION (athletic training, elementary education, English education, foreign languages education, mathematics education, music education, science education, secondary education, and social studies education), ENGINEERING AND ENVIRONMENTAL DESIGN (engineering physics), HEALTH PROFESSIONS (health science, nursing, predentistry, and premedicine), SOCIAL SCIENCE (American studies, crosscultural studies, economics, history, international studies, peace studies, philosophy, political science/government, prelaw, psychology, sociology, theological studies, and women's studies). Music, sciences, and education are the strongest academically. Biology, health sciences, and psychology have the largest enrollments.

Required: Students must complete 126 credit hours, with about 45 in the major, and maintain a GPA of at least 2.0. The curriculum includes 3 core courses on religious, rationalist, and scientific traditions; distribution requirements are comprised of 3 phys ed activity courses, 2 each in a foreign language and science/math, and 1 course each in biblical literature, oral communication, fine arts, social science, and humanities. Additionally, global perspectives and an American diversity course must be fulfilled.

Special: Special academic programs include many work-study opportunities, 1 to 3 internship course credits that may be earned by juniors and seniors, and a January Washington term. Study abroad is available in 15 countries. There is cross-registration with the Intercollegiate Language Study Consortium. Accelerated degree programs are possible, as is a 3-2 engineering degree, and students may choose to specialize in an area of concentration in lieu of a major. Credit may be granted for life, military, or work experience. Nondegree study is possible for those auditing or in seminars, and there is 1 pass/fail option allowed per year. A special feature of the school is the modified semester calendar, which affords unusual opportunities for internships, study tours, and other activities. There is a freshman honors program.

Faculty/Classroom: 58% of faculty are male; 42% are female. All teach undergraduates. No introductory courses are taught by graduate students. The average class size in an introductory lecture is 30; in a laboratory is 15; and in a regular course is 19.

Admissions: 65% of the 2013-2014 applicants were accepted. The SAT scores for the 2013-2014 freshman class were: Critical Reading--11% below 500, 36% between 500 and 599, 44% between 600 and 699, and 9% between 700 and 800; Math--11% below 500, 38% between 500 and 599, 43% between 600 and 699, and 8% between 700 and 800; Writing--11% below 500, 42% between 500 and 599, 39% between 600 and 699, and 8% between 700 and 800. 42 freshmen graduated first in their class.

Requirements: The ACT is recommended. Other admissions criteria include 4 high school credits in English, 3 each in math, science, and history/social studies, and 2 of a foreign language. An essay must be submitted, and an interview is recommended. Music students are advised to audition. AP and CLEP credits are accepted. Important factors in the admissions decision are advanced placement or honors courses, extracurricular activities record, and leadership record.

Procedure: Freshmen are admitted fall, winter, and spring. Entrance exams should be taken by fall of the senior year, though spring of the junior year is preferred. There are deferred admissions and rolling admissions plans. Early decision applications should be filed by November 30; regular applications, by March 1 for fall entry. Notification of early decision is sent December 20; regular decision, March 15. 150 applicants were on the 2013 waiting list; 60 were admitted. Applications are accepted online.

Transfer: 90 transfer students enrolled in 2012-2013. Transfer students must have a GPA of at least 2.75 and a recommended 45 quarter credits earned. The SAT or ACT is recommended. 32 of 126 credits required for the bachelor's degree must be completed at Whitworth.

Visiting: There are regularly scheduled orientations for prospective students, including a class visit, a tour, and an overnight stay, if desired. There are guides for informal visits, visitors may sit in on classes, and stay overnight. To schedule a visit, contact Megan Thompson at admissions@whitworth.edu.

Financial Aid: 100% of undergraduate students work part-time. Average annual earnings from campus work are $1402. The average financial indebtedness of the 2013 graduate was $24,465. The CCS/Profile, or FAFSA, or FFS, or SFS is required. The deadline for filing freshman financial aid applications for fall entry is March 1.

International Students: There are 48 international students enrolled. The school actively recruits these students. They must take the TOEFL.

Computers: All students may access the system. There are no time limits and no fees.

Graduates: From July 1, 2012 to June 30, 2013, 513 bachelor's degrees were awarded. The most popular majors were business management (14%), sciences (13%), and social sciences (10%). 60 companies recruited on campus in 2012-2013. In an average class, 5% graduate in 3 years or less, 66% graduate in 4 years or less, 73% graduate in 5 years or less, and 74% graduate in 6 years or less. Of the 2012 graduating class, 20% were enrolled in graduate school within 6 months of graduation, and 72% were employed.

Admissions Contact: Greg Orwig, Vice President, Admissions and Fin Aid. E-Mail: *admission@whitworth.edu* Web: *www.whitworth.edu*

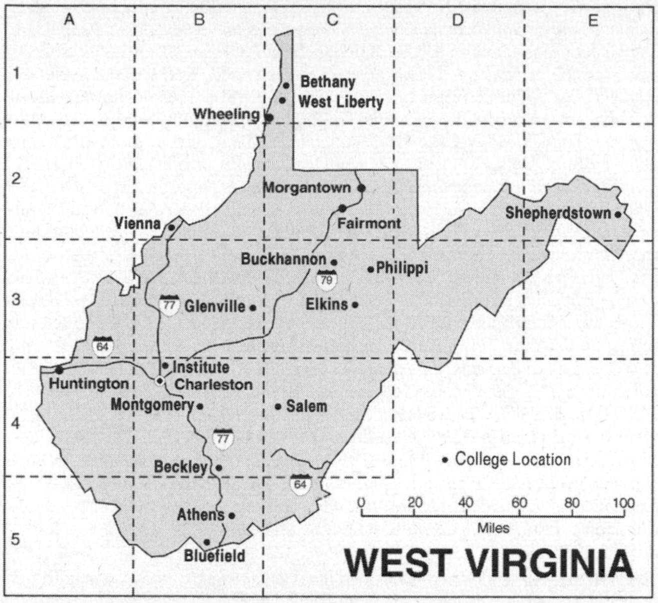

ALDERSON BROADDUS UNIVERSITY C-3

Philippi, WV 26416 (304) 457-6256
(800) 263-1549; (304) 457-6239

Full-time: 531 men, 464 women
Part-time: 12 men, 45 women
Graduate: 22 men, 43 women
Year: semesters, summer session
Application Deadline: August 1
Freshman Class: 597 applied, 441 accepted, 162 enrolled
SAT CR/M/W: 470/470/470
Faculty: 60
Ph.D.s: 47%
Student/Faculty: 11 to 1
Tuition: $21,654
Room & Board: $7002
ACT: 21
COMPETITIVE

Alderson-Broaddus University is a private institution, founded in 1871 and affiliated with American Baptist Churches. It offers a strong liberal arts foundation, with selected programs in the health sciences, humanities, natural sciences, and education. The figures in the above capsule and in this profile are approximate. There is one undergraduate school and one graduate school. In addition to regional accreditation, AB has baccalaureate program accreditation with NLN and TEAC. The library contains 60,000 volumes, 40,000 microform items, and 1,500 audio/video tapes/CDs/DVDs, and subscribes to 59,000 periodicals including electronic. Computerized library services include interlibrary loans, database searching, and Internet access. Special learning facilities include an art gallery, radio station, TV station, a gross anatomy lab, a hydrotherapy pool, and a simulation lab. The 170-acre campus is in a small town 100 miles south of Pittsburgh and 100 miles north of Charleston. Including any residence halls, there are 15 buildings.

Student Life: 56% of undergraduates are from out of state, mostly the Middle Atlantic. Students are from 40 states, 13 foreign countries, and Canada. 90% are from public schools. 74% are White; 16% African American. 14% claim no religious affiliation; 11% Catholic. The average age of freshmen is 19; all undergraduates, 21. 29% do not continue beyond their first year; 39% remain to graduate.

Housing: 580 students can be accommodated in college housing, which includes single-sex and coed dorms, on-campus apartments, off-campus apartments, and married student housing. On-campus housing is guaranteed for all 4 years. 64% of students live on campus; of those, 25% remain on campus on weekends. Alcohol is not permitted. All students may keep cars.

Activities: 9% of men belong to 2 local fraternities; 6% of women belong to 3 local sororities. There are 49 groups on campus, including art, band, choir, chorale, chorus, computers, debate, drama, ethnic, forensics, honors, jazz band, musical theater, newspaper, opera, photography, political, professional, radio and TV, religious, social, social service, student government, and yearbook. Popular campus events include Final Fling, Monte Carlo Night, and Spring Festival Weekend.

Sports: There are 5 intercollegiate sports for men and 6 for women, and 10 intramural sports for men and 11 for women. Facilities include baseball, soccer, softball, and intramural fields, a swimming pool, a basketball court, a fitness center, racquetball/handball courts, auxiliary gyms, a batting cage, a reconditioned tennis court, an outdoor basketball court, and a sand volleyball court.

Disabled Students: 75% of the campus is accessible. Facilities include wheelchair ramps, elevators, special parking, specially equipped restrooms, special class scheduling, and special housing.

Services: Counseling and information services are available, as is tutoring in every subject. There is remedial math, reading, and writing. There is also an academic support network.

Campus Safety and Security: Measures include emergency notification system and self-defense education. There are lighted pathways/sidewalks, and a foot and vehicle patrol evenings and weekends.

Programs of Study: AB confers B.A., and B.S. degrees. Associate and master's degrees are also awarded. Bachelor's degrees are awarded in BIOLOGICAL SCIENCE (biology/biological science), BUSINESS (accounting, business administration and management, human resources, marketing/retailing/merchandising, organizational leadership and management, and recreational facilities management), COMMUNICATIONS AND THE ARTS (communications, creative writing, music, and visual and performing arts), COMPUTER AND PHYSICAL SCIENCE (chemistry, computer science, mathematics, and natural sciences), EDUCATION (athletic training, elementary education, music education, physical education, recreation education, and secondary education), ENGINEERING AND ENVIRONMENTAL DESIGN (environmental science), HEALTH PROFESSIONS (health science, nursing, radiograph medical technology, and recreation therapy), SOCIAL SCIENCE (Christian studies, criminology, family/consumer studies, history, interdisciplinary studies, political science/government, and psychology). Nursing, health sciences, and biology are the strongest academically.

Required: Each graduate is required to complete at least 1 major and Liberal Studies Program requirements amounting to 45 semester hours plus electives for a minimum of 128 semester hours. The Liberal Studies requirements include courses in English, literature, math, computer literacy, physical and biological science, philosophy/religion, social science, history, aesthetic expression, and health. All graduates must have attained a GPA of 2.0 overall and in the major. Certain disciplines may require a GPA higher than the minimum to continue in the major and to graduate.

Special: Internships in numerous majors, study abroad through the college's programs in Austria, and work scholarships at the college are available. In addition, the college offers dual majors, a general studies degree, the B.A.-B.S. degree, nondegree study, and an accelerated B.A. degree in natural science. There are 2 national honor societies, a freshman honors program, and 1 departmental honors program.

Faculty/Classroom: 44% of faculty are male; 56% are female. All teach undergraduates. No introductory courses are taught by graduate students. The average class size in an introductory lecture is 40; in a laboratory is 30; and in a regular course is 20.

Admissions: 74% of the 2013-2014 applicants were accepted. The SAT scores for the 2013-2014 freshman class were: Critical Reading--57% below 500, 38% between 500 and 599, and 5% between 600 and 699; Math--61% below 500, 32% between 500 and 599, and 7% between 600 and 699; Writing--69% below 500, 29% between 500 and 599, and 2% between 600 and 699. The ACT scores were 47% below 21, 29% between 21 and 23, 19% between 24 and 26, 3% between 27 and 28, and 2% above 28. 35% of the current freshmen were in the top fifth of their class; 68% were in the top two fifths. 9 freshmen graduated first in their class.

Requirements: The SAT or ACT is required. The recommended composite score for the SAT is 950 (critical reading and math); for the ACT, 21. Applicants who are graduates of secondary schools or have passed the GED are considered for admission. An audition for certain majors and an interview are recommended. A GPA of 2.5 is required. AP and CLEP credits are accepted. Important factors in the admissions decision are advanced placement or honors courses, leadership record, and recommendations by school officials.

Procedure: Freshmen are admitted to all sessions. Entrance exams should be taken in spring of the junior year. There are deferred admissions and rolling admissions plans. Applications should be filed by August 1 for fall entry; January 1 for spring entry, along with a $25 fee. Notification is sent on a rolling basis. Applications are accepted online.

Transfer: 30 transfer students enrolled in 2012-2013. Transfer applicants must have a minimum 2.0 GPA. If they have fewer than 29 transfer credit hours, ACT or SAT results and a high school diploma are required. 32 of 128 credits required for the bachelor's degree must be completed at AB.

Visiting: There are regularly scheduled orientations for prospective students, including placement tests and social programs. There are guides for informal visits, visitors may sit in on classes, and stay overnight. To schedule a visit, contact the Admissions Office.

Financial Aid: In 2013-2014, 99% of all full-time freshmen students received some form of financial aid. 94% of all full-time freshmen and 92% of continuing full-time students received need-based aid. The average freshman award was $24,997. Need-based scholarships or need-based grants averaged $15,885 ($31,776 maximum); need-based self-help aid (loans and jobs) averaged $5,620 ($6,900 maximum); non-need-based athletic scholarships averaged $1,195 ($19,465 maximum); and other non-need-based awards and non-need-based scholarships averaged $3,690 ($30,900 maximum). 50% of undergraduate students work part-time. Average annual earnings from campus work are $1400. The average financial indebtedness of the 2013 graduate was $31,369. The FAFSA and the college's own financial statement are required. The priority date for freshman financial aid applications for fall entry is March 1. The deadline for filing freshman financial aid applications for fall entry is September 1.

International Students: The school actively recruits these students. They must take the TOEFL with a minimum score of 500 on the paper-based TOEFL (PBT). They must also take the SAT or ACT.

Computers: All students may access the system. There are no time limits and no fees.

Graduates: From July 1, 2012 to June 30, 2013, 124 bachelor's degrees were awarded. The most popular majors were nursing (27%), health science (15%), and biology (8%). In an average class, 28% graduate in 4 years or less, 37% graduate in 5 years or less, and 39% graduate in 6 years or less. Of the 2012 graduating class, 15% were enrolled in graduate school within 6 months of graduation.

Admissions Contact: Zachary Ward, Director of Admissions. E-Mail: *wardza@ab.edu* Web: *www.ab.edu*

BETHANY COLLEGE C-1

Bethany, WV 26032 (304) 829-7611
(800) 922-7611; (304) 829-7142

Full-time: 388 men, 302 women	**Faculty:** 48
Part-time: 2 men, 2 women	**Ph.D.s:** 77%
Graduate: 16 men, 17 women	**Student/Faculty:** 14 to 1
Year: 4-1-4	**Tuition:** $25,736
Application Deadline:	**Room & Board:** $9546
Freshman Class: 1736 applied, 859 accepted, 183 enrolled	
SAT CR/M/W: 450/430/460	**ACT:** 21 **COMPETITIVE**

Bethany College, founded in 1840, is a liberal arts institution affiliated with the Christian Church (Disciples of Christ). In addition to regional accreditation, Bethany has baccalaureate program accreditation with CSWE and NCATE. The library contains 256,917 volumes, 546 microform items, and 3,633 audio/video tapes/CDs/DVDs, and subscribes to 96 periodicals including electronic. Computerized library services include interlibrary loans, database searching, Internet access, and Wi-Fi capability. Special learning facilities include an art gallery, radio station, and TV station. The 1300-acre campus is in a rural area 14 miles north of Wheeling and 40 miles southwest of Pittsburgh. Including any residence halls, there are 34 buildings.

Student Life: 80% of undergraduates are from out of state, mostly the Middle Atlantic. Students are from 26 states, 5 foreign countries, and Canada. 90% are from public schools. 58% are White; 21% African American; 15% race unknown. 59% are Protestant; 30% Catholic. The average age of freshmen is 19; all undergraduates, 20. 36% do not continue beyond their first year; 60% remain to graduate.

Housing: 912 students can be accommodated in college housing, which includes single-sex and coed dorms, on-campus apartments, and off-campus apartments. In addition, there are fraternity houses and sorority houses. On-campus housing is guaranteed for all 4 years. 96% of students live on campus. All students may keep cars.

Activities: 20% of men belong to 5 national fraternities; 35% of women belong to 1 local and 3 national sororities. There are 82 groups on campus, including art, band, chess, choir, chorale, chorus, computers, dance, drama, environmental, ethnic, gay, honors, international, jazz band, literary magazine, marching band, musical theater, newspaper, orchestra, outdoor club and athletic clubs, pep band, political, professional, radio and TV, religious, social, social service, and student government. Popular campus events include Spring Weekend, Starlight Breakfasts and Homecoming.

Sports: There are 11 intercollegiate sports for men and 11 for women, and 12 intramural sports for men and 12 for women. Facilities include 24-hour fitness center, weight room, 2000-seat stadium, 1000-seat gym, natatorium/swimming pool, racquetball courts, indoor track, and separate football, soccer, baseball, and softball fields.

Disabled Students: 65% of the campus is accessible. Facilities include wheelchair ramps, elevators, special parking, specially equipped restrooms, special class scheduling, lowered drinking fountains, special housing.

Services: Counseling and information services are available, as is tutoring in every subject. There is a reader service for the blind, and remedial math, reading, and writing.

Campus Safety and Security: Measures include 24-hour foot and vehicle patrol, emergency notification system, self-defense education, and security escort services. There are lighted pathways/sidewalks and controlled access to dorms/residences.

Programs of Study: Bethany confers B.A., and B.S. degrees. Master's degrees are also awarded. Bachelor's degrees are awarded in AGRICULTURE (equine science), BIOLOGICAL SCIENCE (biochemistry, biology/adolescence education, biology/biological science, and forensic science), BUSINESS (accounting, business administration and management, finance, international economics, management science, and sports management), COMMUNICATIONS AND THE ARTS (communications, creative writing, digital communications, English, English literature, fine arts, graphic communications management, languages, Spanish, spanish / adolescence education, sports media, theatre acting, theatre arts, and theatre production), COMPUTER AND PHYSICAL SCIENCE (applied mathematics, chemistry, chemistry/adolescence education, computer mathematics, computer science, mathematics, mathematics - actuarial concentration, mathematics – economics, and physical sciences), EDUCATION (art education, education, elementary education, English education, mathematics education, middle school education, physical education, psychology education, science education, secondary education, social science education, and social studies education), ENGINEERING AND ENVIRONMENTAL DESIGN (environmental science), HEALTH PROFESSIONS (prephysical therapy and preveterinary science), SOCIAL SCIENCE (economics, history, interdisciplinary studies, international relations, political science/government, psychology, religion, social studies, and social work). Education, social work, economics, and mathematics are the strongest academically. Education, communications, and psychology have the largest enrollments.

Required: All students must complete 128 semester hours, including 24 to 48 in the major, while maintaining a 2.0 GPA. A freshman seminar is required. Distribution credits must be earned in contemporary society and institutions, creative arts, cultural awareness, human behavior, international understanding, life science, literature, mathematical understanding, physical science, and the Western tradition. Students must complete a writing proficiency requirement, a senior project thesis, and a senior comprehensive exam (oral and written) to graduate.

Special: Bethany offers a 3-2 engineering degree with Columbia and Case Western Reserve Universities, a 3-3 law degree with Duquesne University, several dual master's degree programs with Carnegie Mellon University, a joint Digital Design program with The Art Institute of Pittsburgh, internships (required in many majors), study abroad in France, Spain, England, Germany, Canada, Japan, Puerto Rico, Argentina, Ireland, and Sweden, a Washington semester, and work-study programs. B.A.-B.S. degrees and dual majors in all majors, student-designed majors in interdisciplinary studies, and pass/fail options in non-major courses also are offered. There is also a voluntary January term (required for first-year students). There are 21 national honor societies.

Faculty/Classroom: 60% of faculty are male; 40% are female. All teach undergraduates. No introductory courses are taught by graduate students. The average class size in an introductory lecture is 30; in a laboratory is 14; and in a regular course is 14.

Admissions: 49% of the 2013-2014 applicants were accepted. The SAT scores for the 2013-2014 freshman class were: Critical Reading--64% below 500, 26% between 500 and 599, 9% between 600 and 699, and 1% between 700 and 800; Math--65% below 500, 30% between 500 and 599, and 5% between 600 and 699; Writing--74% below 500, 19% between 500 and 599, 6% between 600 and 699, and 1% between 700 and 800. The ACT scores were 45% below 21, 27% between 21 and 23, 22% between 24 and 26, 4% between 27 and 28, and 1% above 28. 26% of the current freshmen were in the top fifth of their class; 43% were in the top two fifths. 1 freshman graduated first in the class.

Requirements: Applicants must have 15 Carnegie units, which should include 4 years of English, 3 each in math and science, and 2 each in foreign language, history, and social studies. An essay, an interview, a portfolio, and an audition are recommended, depending on the major. The GED is accepted. AP and CLEP credits are accepted. Important factors in the admissions decision are leadership record, recommendations by school officials, and advanced placement or honors courses.

Procedure: Freshmen are admitted to all sessions. Entrance exams should be taken during the junior year. There are deferred admissions and rolling admissions plans. Application deadlines are open. Notification is sent on a rolling basis. Applications are accepted online. Application fees are waived if application is completed online.

Transfer: 52 transfer students enrolled in 2012-2013. Transfer students must have a minimum GPA of 2.0. 48 of 128 credits required for the bachelor's degree must be completed at Bethany.

Visiting: There are regularly scheduled orientations for prospective students, tour and meetings with faculty, coaches, financial aid, & admissions. There are guides for informal visits, visitors may sit in on classes, and stay overnight. To schedule a visit, contact the Office of Enrollment at admission@bethanywv.edu.

Financial Aid: In 2013-2014, 99% of all full-time freshmen and 100%

of continuing full-time students received some form of financial aid. 89% of all full-time freshmen and 84% of continuing full-time students received need-based aid. The average freshman award was $32,249. Need-based scholarships or need-based grants averaged $15,429 ($26,226 maximum); need-based self-help aid (loans and jobs) averaged $4,347 ($7,500 maximum); and other non-need-based awards and non-need-based scholarships averaged $15,207 ($42,944 maximum). 70% of undergraduate students work part-time. Average annual earnings from campus work are $1100. The average financial indebtedness of the 2013 graduate was $25,326. The FAFSA is required. The priority date for freshman financial aid applications for fall entry is March 1.

International Students: There are 9 international students enrolled. The school actively recruits these students. They must take the TOEFL with a minimum score of 500 on the paper-based TOEFL (PBT) or 90 on the Internet-based version (iBT).

Computers: All students may access the system 24 hours daily. There are no time limits and no fees.

Graduates: From July 1, 2012 to June 30, 2013, 146 bachelor's degrees were awarded. The most popular majors were psychology (21%), communications (14%), and physical education (13%). 80 companies recruited on campus in 2012-2013. In an average class, 1% graduate in 3 years or less, 39% graduate in 4 years or less, 44% graduate in 5 years or less, and 48% graduate in 6 years or less.

Admissions Contact: Mollie Cecere, Director of Enrollment. E-Mail: *admission@bethanywv.edu* Web: *http://www.bethanywv.edu/prospective-students/*

BLUEFIELD STATE COLLEGE B-5

Bluefield, WV 24701 (304) 327-4068
(800) 654-7798; (304) 325-7747

Full-time: 627 men, 959 women — **Faculty:** 79; IIB, --$
Part-time: 135 men, 342 women — **Ph.D.s:** 52%
Graduate: n/av — **Student/Faculty:** 30 to 1
Year: semesters, summer session — **Tuition:** $3640 ($7514)
Application Deadline: open — **Room & Board:** n/av
Freshman Class: 558 applied, 383 accepted, 292 enrolled
SAT: recommended — **ACT:** 18 — **LESS COMPETITIVE**

Bluefield State College, founded in 1895, is a state-supported commuter college offering programs in engineering technologies, business, teacher education, arts and sciences, health science professions, and a variety of career fields. The college also offers a wide variety of off-campus courses. Figures in the above capsule and in this profile are approximate. In addition to regional accreditation, Bluefield State has baccalaureate program accreditation with ABET and NCATE. The library contains 75,803 volumes, 5,195 microform items, and 7,500 audio/video tapes/CDs/DVDs, and subscribes to 6,258 periodicals including electronic. Computerized library services include interlibrary loans, database searching, and Internet access. Special learning facilities include a learning resource center and art gallery. The 40-acre campus is in a small town 90 miles south of Charleston. Including any residence halls, there are 9 buildings.

Student Life: 95% of undergraduates are from West Virginia. Others are from 12 states, 10 foreign countries, and Canada. 99% are from public schools. 90% are white. The average age of freshmen is 21; all undergraduates, 27. 34% do not continue beyond their first year; 52% remain to graduate.

Housing: There are no residence halls. All students commute.

Activities: 3% of men belong to 3 local and 3 national fraternities; 1% of women belong to 3 local and 1 national sororities. There are 42 groups on campus, including cheerleading, choir, ethnic, honors, international, jazz band, newspaper, student government, and yearbook. Popular campus events include dances and sports events.

Sports: There are 5 intercollegiate sports for men and 5 for women, and 20 intramural sports for men and 15 for women. Facilities include a gym, a pool, tennis courts, an athletic field, and physical fitness and aerobics rooms.

Disabled Students: All of the campus is accessible. Facilities include wheelchair ramps, elevators, special parking, specially equipped restrooms, and lowered drinking fountains.

Services: Counseling and information services are available, as is tutoring in most subjects. There is a reader service for the blind.

Campus Safety and Security: Measures include 24-hour foot and vehicle patrol and self-defense education. There are emergency telephones and lighted pathways/sidewalks.

Programs of Study: Bluefield State confers B.A., B.S., B.S.E.T., and B.S.N. degrees. Associate degrees are also awarded. Bachelor's degrees are awarded in BIOLOGICAL SCIENCE (biology/biological science), BUSINESS (accounting and business administration and management), COMPUTER AND PHYSICAL SCIENCE (computer science), EDUCATION (elementary education and middle school education), ENGINEERING AND ENVIRONMENTAL DESIGN (engineering technology), HEALTH PROFESSIONS (nursing), SOCIAL SCIENCE (criminal justice, humanities, and social science). Engineering, technology, and health science are the strongest academically. Business is the largest.

Required: The minimum requirement for graduation is a 2.0 GPA overall and in the student's major and minor, and 128 semester hours. All graduating students must have completed the general program specific to their degree and a core curriculum of 40 hours among humanities, social science, lab science, basic skills, and computer science.

Special: A general studies degree and life experience credentials are offered through the Regents Bachelor of Arts Degree Program, designed for adults. Nondegree study is offered. There are 2 national honor societies, a freshman honors program, and 1 departmental honors program.

Faculty/Classroom: 62% of faculty are male; 38% are female. All teach undergraduates, and 10% do research. No introductory courses are taught by graduate students. The average class size in an introductory lecture is 40; in a laboratory is 25; and in a regular course is 25.

Admissions: 69% of the 2011-2012 applicants were accepted. The SAT scores for a recent freshman class were: Critical Reading--55% below 500, 43% between 500 and 599, 2% between 600 and 700; Math--57% below 500, 33% between 500 and 599, and 10% between 600 and 700. The ACT scores were 73% below 21, 17% between 21 and 23, 8% between 24 and 26, 1% between 27 and 28, and 1% above 28. 27% of the current freshmen were in the top fifth of their class; 46% were in the top two fifths.

Requirements: The ACT is required. The SAT is recommended. Regular admission is granted to students meeting GED requirements or having a high school diploma, with an overall 2.0 GPA or a composite score of at least 17 on the ACT or 680 on the SAT. They also must have successfully completed minimum high school curricular unit requirements consisting of 4 units in English, 3 in social studies, 2 in math (algebra I and higher), and 2 in lab science. Other students not meeting these requirements may be admitted on a conditional basis. AP and CLEP credits are accepted.

Procedure: Freshmen are admitted to all sessions. Entrance exams should be taken before enrolling. There are early admissions, deferred admissions, and rolling admissions plans. Application deadlines are open. Applications are accepted online.

Transfer: 146 transfer students enrolled in 2010-2011. Applicants must be in good standing at the institution from which they are transferring. 32 of 128 credits required for the bachelor's degree must be completed at Bluefield State.

Visiting: There are regularly scheduled orientations for prospective students. There are guides for informal visits and visitors may sit in on classes. To schedule a visit, contact the Admissions Office.

Financial Aid: In a recent year, 70% of all full-time freshmen and 70% of continuing full-time students received some form of financial aid. 60% of all full-time freshmen and 60% of continuing full-time students received need-based aid. The average freshman award was $4,200. Need-based scholarships or need-based grants averaged $500 ($2,000 maximum); need-based self-help aid (loans and jobs) averaged $4,000 ($10,500 maximum); and non-need-based athletic scholarships averaged $2,000 ($3,200 maximum). 75% of undergraduate students work part-time. Average annual earnings from campus work are $1600. The average financial indebtedness of the 2011 graduate was $7,500. The FAFSA and the college's own financial statement are required. The deadline for filing freshman financial aid applications for fall entry is March 15.

International Students: There are 27 international students enrolled. They must take the TOEFL. They must also take the ACT.

Computers: All students may access the system during class and lab hours. There are no time limits and no fees.

Graduates: In a recent year, 196 bachelor's degrees were awarded. The most popular majors were education (18%), nursing (14%), and business administration (13%). In an average class, 15% graduate in 4 years or less, 23% graduate in 5 years or less, and 35% graduate in 6 years or less. Of the 2010 graduating class, 7% were enrolled in graduate school within 6 months of graduation, and 95% were employed.

Admissions Contact: John C. Cardwell, Vice President for Enrollment Management. E-Mail: *bscadmit@bluefieldstate.edu* Web: *www.bluefieldstate.edu*

CONCORD UNIVERSITY B-5

Athens, WV 24712 (304) 384-5248
(888) 384-5249; (304) 384-9044

Full-time: 1033 men, 1344 women — **Faculty:** 119
Part-time: 93 men, 182 women — **Ph.D.s:** 49%
Graduate: 54 men, 182 women — **Student/Faculty:** 16 to 1
Year: semesters, summer session — **Tuition:** $5716 ($12,698)
Application Deadline: open — **Room & Board:** $7386
Freshman Class: 2495 applied, 1224 accepted, 573 enrolled
SAT CR/M: 486/482 — **ACT:** 21 — **COMPETITIVE**

Concord University, founded in 1872, is a public institution with undergraduate programs in liberal arts and professional training. There is one undergraduate school and one graduate school. In addition to regional accreditation, Concord has baccalaureate program accreditation with

CSWE and NCATE. The library contains 168,164 volumes, 240,089 microform items, and 3,800 audio/video tapes/CDs/DVDs, and subscribes to 140 periodicals including electronic. Computerized library services include interlibrary loans, database searching, Internet access, and Wi-Fi capability. Special learning facilities include an art gallery, radio station, and TV station. The 123-acre campus is in a small town 85 miles south of Charleston. Including any residence halls, there are 21 buildings.

Student Life: 83% of undergraduates are from West Virginia. Others are from 29 states, 22 foreign countries, and Canada. 97% are from public schools. 89% are White. 40% are Protestant; 40% claim no religious affiliation; 15% Catholic. The average age of freshmen is 19; all undergraduates, 23. 38% do not continue beyond their first year; 39% remain to graduate.

Housing: 1125 students can be accommodated in college housing, which includes single-sex dorms and married student housing. honor floors in residence halls and housing for international students. On-campus housing is guaranteed for all 4 years and is guaranteed for the freshman year only. 68% of students commute. All students may keep cars.

Activities: 20% of men belong to 1 local and 4 national fraternities; 20% of women belong to 4 national sororities. There are 70 groups on campus, including art, bagpipe, band, cheerleading, choir, chorale, computers, dance, drama, environmental, film, gay, honors, international, jazz band, literary magazine, marching band, newspaper, pep band, political, professional, radio and TV, religious, social, social service, student government, and yearbook. Popular campus events include Big-name Concerts, Alumni Day, Faculty and Student Plays, Homecoming and Spring Fling.

Sports: There are 8 intercollegiate sports for men and 8 for women, and 15 intramural sports for men and 15 for women. Facilities include 5 tennis courts, 4 racquetball courts, 2 gyms, a Nautilus fitness room, a pool, a dance studio, and various outdoor fields. The campus stadium seats 4000, the larger gym 2700, and the largest auditorium 900.

Disabled Students: 90% of the campus is accessible. Facilities include wheelchair ramps, elevators, special parking, specially equipped restrooms, special class scheduling, lowered drinking fountains, lowered telephones, and special housing.

Services: Counseling and information services are available, as is tutoring in every subject. There is a reader service for the blind, and remedial math, reading, and writing.

Campus Safety and Security: Measures include 24-hour foot and vehicle patrol, emergency notification system, and security escort services. There are emergency telephones, lighted pathways/sidewalks, controlled access to dorms/residences, foot and vehicle patrol is available 24 hours Monday through Friday and is on call Saturday and Sunday.

Programs of Study: Concord confers B.A., B.S., B.B.A., B.S.C.I.S., B.S.Ed., B.S.Med.Tech. and B.S.W. degrees. Associate and master's degrees are also awarded. Bachelor's degrees are awarded in BIOLOGICAL SCIENCE (biology/biological science), BUSINESS (accounting, banking and finance, business administration and management, hotel/motel and restaurant management, marketing/retailing/merchandising, office supervision and management, and small business management), COMMUNICATIONS AND THE ARTS (broadcasting, communications, and English), COMPUTER AND PHYSICAL SCIENCE (chemistry, computer programming, computer science, information sciences and systems, and mathematics), EDUCATION (art education, business education, early childhood education, elementary education, middle school education, music education, science education, secondary education, and special education), HEALTH PROFESSIONS (medical laboratory technology, predentistry, premedicine, and prepharmacy), SOCIAL SCIENCE (geography, history, parks and recreation management, political science/government, prelaw, psychology, social science, social work, and sociology). Teacher education, business, and preprofessional biology are the strongest academically. Teacher education, business, biology, psychology have the largest enrollments.

Required: To graduate, students must earn 120 credit hours, including 36 to 50 in the major, with a minimum GPA of 2.0 (2.5 in many departments). All students must complete the college's general studies curriculum. Required courses include 14 to 15 semester hours of math and science, 12 of English and literature, 12 of social studies, 6 of fine arts, 3 of speech, and 2 of phys ed, 1 of univ 100.

Special: Students may serve internships in medical technology, social work, travel industry management, commercial art/advertising, and communications arts. Concord offers a Washington semester, cross-registration with Bluefield State College, dual majors, interdisciplinary student-designed majors, and nondegree study. Credit for life, military, and work experience is granted to adult students through the Regents Bachelor of Arts Degree Program. There are 5 national honor societies and a freshman honors program.

Faculty/Classroom: 48% of faculty are male; 52% are female. All teach undergraduates, all do research, and all teach and do research. No introductory courses are taught by graduate students. The average class size in an introductory lecture is 23; in a laboratory is 17; and in a regular course is 22.

Admissions: 49% of the 2013-2014 applicants were accepted. The SAT scores for the 2013-2014 freshman class were: Critical Reading--58% below 500, 32% between 500 and 599, and 10% between 600 and 699; Math--58% below 500, 34% between 500 and 599, 7% between 600 and 699, and 1% between 700 and 800; Writing--68% below 500, 23% between 500 and 599, 8% between 600 and 699, and 1% between 700 and 800.

Requirements: The SAT or ACT is required. The ACT is preferred. Applicants must be high school graduates or hold a GED. Students should present 17 academic credits, including 4 in English, 3 each in social studies and science, 4 in math and 1 each in history and health/phys ed. An interview is recommended and, where appropriate, a portfolio or an audition. A GPA of 2.0 is required. AP and CLEP credits are accepted.

Procedure: Freshmen are admitted to all sessions. Entrance exams should be taken in the junior year or preferably early in the senior year. There are deferred admissions and rolling admissions plans. Application deadlines are open. Notification is sent on a rolling basis. Applications are accepted online.

Transfer: Applicants must have a GPA of at least 2.0. Concord recommends a minimum of 15 credit hours of college work completed and an interview. 36 of 120 credits required for the bachelor's degree must be completed at Concord.

Visiting: There are regularly scheduled orientations for prospective students. There are guides for informal visits, visitors may sit in on classes, and stay overnight. To schedule a visit, contact the Admissions Office.

Financial Aid: In 2013-2014, 93% of all full-time freshmen and 80% of continuing full-time students received some form of financial aid. 41% of all full-time freshmen and 40% of continuing full-time students received need-based aid. The average freshman award was $12,103. 26% of undergraduate students work part-time. Average annual earnings from campus work are $2100. The average financial indebtedness of the 2013 graduate was $17,000. The FAFSA is required. The priority date for freshman financial aid applications for fall entry is March 1. The deadline for filing freshman financial aid applications for fall entry is April 15.

International Students: There are 85 international students enrolled. The school actively recruits these students. They must take the TOEFL with a minimum score of 500 on the paper-based TOEFL (PBT) or 60 on the Internet-based version (iBT). They must also take the SAT or ACT.

Computers: All students may access the system. There are no time limits and no fees.

Graduates: From July 1, 2012 to June 30, 2013, 432 bachelor's degrees were awarded. The most popular majors were education (23%), business/marketing (16%), and liberal arts/general studies (14%). In an average class, 19% graduate in 4 years or less, 32% graduate in 5 years or less, and 38% graduate in 6 years or less.

Admissions Contact: Kent Gamble, Director of Enrollment. E-Mail: *admissions@concord.edu* Web: *www.concord.edu*

DAVIS AND ELKINS COLLEGE C-3

Elkins, WV 26241 (304) 637-1326
(800) 624-3157; (304) 637-1800

Full-time: 347 men, 450 women	**Faculty:** 66; IIB, --$
Part-time: 4 men, 23 women	**Ph.D.s:** 73%
Graduate: none	**Student/Faculty:** 9 to 1
Year: semesters, summer session	**Tuition:** $24,992
Application Deadline: open	**Room & Board:** $8750
Freshman Class: n/av	
SAT or ACT: required	

COMPETITIVE

Davis and Elkins College, founded in 1904 and affiliated with the Presbyterian Church, offers programs in the liberal arts, business, professional training, teacher preparation, nursing, and recreation management. In addition to regional accreditation, D&E has baccalaureate program accreditation with TEAC. Computerized library services include interlibrary loans, database searching, Internet access, and Wi-Fi capability. The 170-acre campus is in a small town 200 miles west of Washington, D.C. Including any residence halls, there are 22 buildings.

Housing: 572 students can be accommodated in college housing, which includes single-sex and coed dorms. On-campus housing is guaranteed for all 4 years. All students may keep cars.

Activities: There are no fraternities or sororities. Groups on campus include art, choir, computers, drama, honors, international, jazz band, musical theater, newspaper, pep band, religious, student government, and yearbook. Popular campus events include Parents Weekend, Deja Vu, and International Week.

Sports: There are 6 intercollegiate sports for men and 6 for women, and 10 intramural sports for men and 10 for women. Facilities include a 2000-seat gym, 1300-seat arena, fields, fitness center and fitness trails, tennis court, and pool.

Disabled Students: 80% of the campus is accessible. Facilities include wheelchair ramps, elevators, special parking, specially equipped restrooms, special class scheduling, lowered drinking fountains, and lowered telephones.

Services: Counseling and information services are available, as is tutoring in every subject. There is remedial math, reading, and writing. Learning disabilities services also are available.

Campus Safety and Security: Measures include self-defense education and security escort services. There are lighted pathways/sidewalks. The campus security service is on duty from 6 p.m. to 5 a.m.

Programs of Study: D&E confers B.A., and B.S. degrees. Associate degrees are also awarded. Bachelor's degrees are awarded in BIOLOGICAL SCIENCE (biology/biological science), BUSINESS (accounting, business administration and management, hospitality management services, management science, and marketing/retailing/merchandising), COMMUNICATIONS AND THE ARTS (art, communications, dramatic arts, English, languages, and music), COMPUTER AND PHYSICAL SCIENCE (chemistry, computer science, and mathematics), EDUCATION (elementary education, physical education, and secondary education), ENGINEERING AND ENVIRONMENTAL DESIGN (environmental science), HEALTH PROFESSIONS (predentistry and premedicine), SOCIAL SCIENCE (economics, history, political science/government, prelaw, psychology, religion, and sociology). Business, psychology, and biology are the strongest academically. Business, nursing, and hospitality management have the largest enrollments.

Required: To graduate, students must complete 124 credit hours, including 30 to 40 in the major, with a GPA of 2.0. General education requirements include 7 hours of natural science, 6 each of history, social science, English composition, philosophy, religion, literature, and math, 5 of fine arts, and 2 of phys ed, as well as a course in computer literacy. A freshman experience class and a public speaking course are also required.

Special: Students may study abroad or take a Washington semester. The college offers co-op programs with Syracuse University and SUNY, as well as internships. Students may take dual majors in psychology/human services, biology/environmental sciences, and history/political science, and student-designed majors are permitted through a contract degree program. The college awards credit for life, military, and work experience. Nondegree study is allowed, and pass/fail options are open. The college's mentor-assisted degree-completion program allows adults to earn degrees through credit for life experience and off-campus study. There are 6 national honor societies, a freshman honors program, and 100 departmental honors programs.

Faculty/Classroom: 61% of faculty are male; 39% are female. All teach undergraduates. No introductory courses are taught by graduate students. The average class size in an introductory lecture is 15; in a laboratory is 11; and in a regular course is 11.

Requirements: The SAT or ACT is required, with a minimum composite score of 900 on the the SAT I or 19 on the ACT. Applicants should be high school graduates or hold a GED. Students should have earned 16 academic credits, including 4 in English, 3 in social studies, 3 in math, including a minimum of algebra I and geometry, and 3 in natural science, including a lab course. Two years of foreign language is recommended. A GPA of 2.0 is required. AP and CLEP credits are accepted. Important factors in the admissions decision are advanced placement or honors courses, recommendations by school officials, and leadership record.

Procedure: Freshmen are admitted to all sessions. Entrance exams should be taken during the fall of the senior year. There are early decision, deferred admissions, and rolling admissions plans. Application deadlines are open. Notification is sent on a rolling basis. Applications are accepted online.

Transfer: Transfer applicants should have earned 62 credit hours, with a GPA of 2.0. An associate degree is recommended. 15 of 124 credits required for the bachelor's degree must be completed at D&E.

Visiting: There are regularly scheduled orientations for prospective students, including meals, a tour of campus, and panel discussions. There are guides for informal visits, visitors may sit in on classes, and stay overnight. To schedule a visit, contact the Admissions Office.

Financial Aid: In 2013-2014, 89% of all full-time freshmen and 89% of continuing full-time students received some form of financial aid. 69% of all full-time freshmen and 70% of continuing full-time students received need-based aid. The average freshman award was $16,512. Need-based scholarships or need-based grants averaged $2,807 ($5,550 maximum); need-based self-help aid (loans and jobs) averaged $2,587 ($6,125 maximum); non-need-based athletic scholarships averaged $3,402 ($8,000 maximum); and other non-need-based awards and non-need-based scholarships averaged $7,716 ($10,000 maximum). 40% of undergraduate students work part-time. Average annual earnings from campus work are $1200. The average financial indebtedness of the 2013 graduate was $15,000. The FAFSA, is required. Check with the school for current application deadlines.

International Students: The school actively recruits these students. They must take the TOEFL or MELAB. They must also take the SAT or ACT.

Computers: All students may access the system. There are no time limits and no fees.

Admissions Contact: Renee Heckel, Director of Admissions. E-Mail: *admiss@davisandelkins.edu* Web: *www.davisandelkins.edu*

FAIRMONT STATE UNIVERSITY C-2

Fairmont, WV 26554 (304) 367-4892
(800) 641-5678; (304) 367-4789

Full-time: 1744 men, 2042 women	**Faculty:** n/av
Part-time: 178 men, 398 women	**Ph.D.s:** 65%
Graduate: 113 men, 234 women	**Student/Faculty:** 23 to 1
Year: semesters, summer session	**Tuition:** $5672 ($11,404)
Application Deadline: open	**Room & Board:** $7426
Freshman Class: 3400 applied, 2692 accepted, 1220 enrolled	
SAT CR/M: 468/484	**ACT:** 21 **LESS COMPETITIVE**

Fairmont State University, formerly Fairmont State College, and founded in 1865, is a public institution offering programs in business, education, engineering technology, and health careers. In addition to regional accreditation, Fairmont State has baccalaureate program accreditation with ABET, ACBSP, NCATE, and NLN. The library contains 275,000 volumes, 54,241 microform items, and 12,000 audio/video tapes/CDs/DVDs, and subscribes to 1,175 periodicals including electronic. Computerized library services include interlibrary loans and database searching. Special learning facilities include a learning resource center. The 120-acre campus is in a small town 75 miles south of Pittsburgh. Including any residence halls, there are 12 buildings.

Student Life: 95% of undergraduates are from West Virginia. Others are from 24 states, and 19 foreign countries. 98% are from public schools. 90% are white. The average age of freshmen is 19; all undergraduates, 23. 34% do not continue beyond their first year; 67% remain to graduate.

Housing: 1150 students can be accommodated in college housing, which includes single-sex and coed dorms, on-campus apartments, and married student housing. On-campus housing is guaranteed for the freshman year only, is available on a first-come, first-served basis. 82% of students commute. Alcohol is not permitted. All students may keep cars.

Activities: 4% of men belong to 1 local and 2 national fraternities; 4% of women belong to 1 local and 3 national sororities. There are 85 groups on campus, including art, band, cheerleading, choir, chorus, computers, debate, drama, gay, honors, jazz band, literary magazine, marching band, musical theater, newspaper, pep band, photography, political, professional, religious, service, social, student government, and symphony. Popular campus events include multicultural events.

Sports: There are 7 intercollegiate sports for men and 6 for women, and 24 intramural sports for men and 24 for women. Facilities include a phys ed center, a 5000-seat stadium, a 4000-seat basketball arena, and playing fields.

Disabled Students: All of the campus is accessible. Facilities include wheelchair ramps, elevators, special parking, specially equipped restrooms, special class scheduling, lowered drinking fountains, and lowered telephones.

Services: Counseling and information services are available, as is tutoring in most subjects. There is a reader service for the blind, and remedial math, reading, and writing.

Campus Safety and Security: Measures include 24-hour foot and vehicle patrol and emergency notification system. There are emergency telephones and lighted pathways/sidewalks.

Programs of Study: Fairmont State confers B.A., B.S., B.S.E.T., and B.S.N. degrees. Associate and master's degrees are also awarded. Bachelor's degrees are awarded in BIOLOGICAL SCIENCE (biology/biological science), BUSINESS (accounting, banking and finance, business administration and management, business economics, and marketing/retailing/merchandising), COMMUNICATIONS AND THE ARTS (communications, English, French, and speech/debate/rhetoric), COMPUTER AND PHYSICAL SCIENCE (chemistry, computer science, and mathematics), EDUCATION (art education, business education, early childhood education, elementary education, foreign languages education, health education, middle school education, music education, science education, and secondary education), ENGINEERING AND ENVIRONMENTAL DESIGN (architectural technology, civil engineering technology, electrical/electronics engineering technology, engineering technology, manufacturing technology, and mechanical engineering technology), SOCIAL SCIENCE (criminal justice, family/consumer studies, history, political science/government, psychology, and sociology). Engineering technology, and education are the strongest academically. Business, health careers, and criminal justice have the largest enrollments.

Required: To graduate, students must complete 128 hours with a GPA of 2.0. (2.5 in education specializations). Students must complete 50 core curriculum hours for the B.S. or B.A. degree. All students must take 2 hours of phys ed. Course and distribution requirements vary according to the program.

Special: The college offers internships in teacher education, retailing, and psychology, and awards a B.S. degree in chemistry/math. There are 4 national honor societies, a freshman honors program, and 4 departmental honors programs.

Faculty/Classroom: 49% of faculty are male; 51% are female. All teach undergraduates. No introductory courses are taught by graduate students.

The average class size in an introductory lecture is 35; in a laboratory is 20; and in a regular course is 30.

Admissions: 79% of a recent year, applicants were accepted. The SAT scores for a recent freshman class were: Critical Reading--69% below 500, 29% between 500 and 599, 2% between 600 and 700; Math--65% below 500, 33% between 500 and 599, 2% between 600 and 700.

Requirements: The SAT or ACT is required. For students who have graduated from high school or completed GED requirements fewer than 5 years prior to seeking admission. A satisfactory score is required on the SAT or 17 on the ACT. Applicants must be high school graduates or hold a GED. The college requires 4 credits in English, and 3 each in social studies (1 in U.S. history), math (algebra I and at least 1 higher), and lab science. A foreign language is recommended. A GPA of 2.5 is required. AP and CLEP credits are accepted.

Procedure: Freshmen are admitted fall, spring, and summer. Entrance exams should be taken during the fall of the senior year. There is a rolling admissions plan. Check with the school for current application deadlines. Applications are accepted online.

Transfer: 463 transfer students enrolled in a recent year. Applicants must have a GPA of 2.0. The ACT is required for applicants with fewer than 30 college credits. 60 of 128 credits required for the bachelor's degree must be completed at Fairmont State.

Visiting: There are regularly scheduled orientations for prospective students. There are guides for informal visits and visitors may sit in on classes. To schedule a visit, contact the Office of Admissions.

Financial Aid: Fairmont State is a member of CSS. The FAFSA is required. The deadline for filing freshman financial aid applications for fall entry is March 1.

International Students: There are 69 international students enrolled. The school actively recruits these students. They must take the TOEFL. They must also take the SAT or ACT. If ACT or SAT scores are not supplied, the ACT must be taken upon arrival on campus.

Computers: There are over 1000 public stations available at the various campuses, classrooms, library, and student center. All students may access the system 24 hours a day, 7 days a week. There are no time limits and no fees. It is strongly recommended that all students have a personal computer.

Graduates: In a recent year, 663 bachelor's degrees were awarded. The most popular majors were business (21%), health professions (10%), and homeland security (10%). 75 companies recruited on campus in 2010-2011. In an average class, 15% graduate in 4 years or less, 30% graduate in 5 years or less, and 35% graduate in 6 years or less. Of a recent graduating class, 18% were enrolled in graduate school within 6 months of graduation, and 80% were employed.

Admissions Contact: Office of Admissions A campus DVD is available. E-Mail: *admit@fairmontstate.edu* Web: *http:/www.fairmontstate.edu/admit/*

GLENVILLE STATE COLLEGE — B-3

Glenville, WV 26351 — (304) 462-4128; (800) 924-2010; (304) 462-8619

Full-time: 600 men, 550 women	**Faculty:** n/av; IIB, --$
Part-time: 375 men, 200 women	**Ph.D.s:** 53%
Graduate: n/av	**Student/Faculty:** 19 to 1
Year: semesters, summer session	**Tuition:** $5852 ($13,220)
Application Deadline: open	**Room & Board:** $8400
Freshman Class: n/av	
SAT or ACT: required	

NONCOMPETITIVE

Glenville State College, founded in 1872, is a public college offering programs in education, the arts and sciences, and business. The figures in the above capsule and this profile are approximate. In addition to regional accreditation, GSC has baccalaureate program accreditation with NCATE and SAF. The library contains 116,220 volumes, 604,256 microform items, and 2968 audio/video tapes/CDs/DVDs, and subscribes to 22,835 periodicals including electronic. Computerized library services include interlibrary loans, database searching, Internet access, and laptop Internet portals. Special learning facilities include a learning resource center and art gallery. The 360-acre campus is in a rural area 100 miles northeast of Charleston. Including any residence halls, there are 27 buildings.

Student Life: 89% of undergraduates are from West Virginia. Others are from 27 states, 3 foreign countries, and Canada. 98% are from public schools. 83% are white; 14% African American. The average age of freshmen is 19; all undergraduates, 25. 39% do not continue beyond their first year; 31% remain to graduate.

Housing: 599 students can be accommodated in college housing, which includes single-sex dorms, on-campus apartments, and married student housing. On-campus housing is guaranteed for all 4 years. 67% of students commute. Alcohol is not permitted. All students may keep cars.

Activities: 4% of men belong to 1 local fraternity and 1 national fraternity; 4% of women belong to 4 local sororities. There are 41 groups on campus, including art, band, cheerleading, chess, choir, chorus, computers, drama, drill team, environmental, ethnic, gay, honors, international, jazz band, literary magazine, marching band, musical theater, newspaper, pep band, political, professional, religious, social, social service, and student government. Popular campus events include Friends and Family Weekend and Social Science Colloquium Services.

Sports: There are 5 intercollegiate sports for men and 6 for women, and 4 intramural sports for men and 3 for women. Facilities include a field house, 5000-seat football stadium, running track, tennis courts, softball field, 700-seat gym, swimming pool, fitness center, and weight room.

Disabled Students: 98% of the campus is accessible. Facilities include wheelchair ramps, elevators, special parking, specially equipped restrooms, lowered drinking fountains, lowered telephones, and special housing. Adaptations are made to class delivery locations to accommodate student needs.

Services: Counseling and information services are available, as is tutoring in most subjects. There is a reader service for the blind, and remedial math, reading, and writing. Arrangements can be made for one-on-one tutoring should the Academic Support Center not offer tutoring in a particular subject.

Campus Safety and Security: Measures include security escort services. There are shuttle buses, emergency telephones, lighted pathways/sidewalks, and electronically operated dorm entrances.

Programs of Study: GSC confers B.A. and B.S. degrees. Associate degrees are also awarded. Bachelor's degrees are awarded in AGRICULTURE (forestry and related sciences and natural resource management), BIOLOGICAL SCIENCE (biology/biological science), BUSINESS (accounting, business administration and management, marketing/retailing/merchandising, recreational facilities management, and sports management), COMMUNICATIONS AND THE ARTS (English), COMPUTER AND PHYSICAL SCIENCE (chemistry and information sciences and systems), EDUCATION (business education, early childhood education, elementary education, English education, health education, mathematics education, middle school education, music education, physical education, science education, secondary education, social studies education, and special education), ENGINEERING AND ENVIRONMENTAL DESIGN (environmental science and survey and mapping technology), HEALTH PROFESSIONS (nursing), SOCIAL SCIENCE (criminal justice, history, liberal arts/general studies, and psychology). Teacher education is the strongest academically. Business has the largest enrollment.

Required: All students must take the general studies programs, consisting of 43 hours in English, math, science, the social sciences, humanities, and phys ed. Information science is also required. To graduate, students must complete 128 credit hours, with 42 in the major. Non-education majors must maintain a 2.0 GPA; education majors, a 2.5.

Special: The college offers B.A.-B.S. degrees in numerous majors, credit by exam, student-designed majors in interdisciplinary studies, and pass/fail options. Some programs of study require internships. There are 7 national honor societies.

Faculty/Classroom: 56% of faculty are male; 44% are female. 99% teach undergraduates, and 1% do research. No introductory courses are taught by graduate students.

Requirements: The SAT or ACT is required. In addition, at least a 2.0 high school GPA and an ACT composite score of 18 or a 3.0 high school GPA regardless of ACT are required. Applicants should be graduates of an accredited secondary school and have taken 4 courses in English, 3 in social studies, 4 units in higher math, 3 units in science, 1 unit in art, and 2 units of foreign language. GED admission is also possible. A GPA of 2.0 is required. AP and CLEP credits are accepted. Important factors in the admissions decision are ability to finance college education, extracurricular activities record, and evidence of special talent.

Procedure: Freshmen are admitted to all sessions. Entrance exams should be taken at the end of the junior year of high school. There is a rolling admissions plan. Application deadlines are open. Application fee is $20. Notification is sent on a rolling basis. Applications are accepted online.

Transfer: 83 transfer students enrolled in a recent year. Applicants must be in good standing at their previous institution. 32 of 128 credits required for the bachelor's degree must be completed at GSC.

Visiting: There are regularly scheduled orientations for prospective students in which prospective students can meet with an admissions officer and/or a division officer and they can also schedule a campus tour. There are guides for informal visits, visitors may sit in on classes, and stay overnight. To schedule a visit, contact Office of Enrollment Services.

Financial Aid: In a recent year, 83% of all full-time freshmen and 81% of continuing full-time students received some form of financial aid. 75% of all full-time freshmen and 82% of continuing full-time students received need-based aid. 13% of undergraduate students work part-time. The average financial indebtedness of a recent graduate was $19,666. The FAFSA and the state aid form (first-time students) are required. Check with the school for current deadlines.

International Students: There were 3 international students enrolled in a recent year. The school actively recruits these students. They must take the TOEFL with a minimum score of 550 on the paper-based TOEFL (PBT). They must also take the SAT or ACT, scoring 810 on the SAT Math and Verbal Subject tests or 18 on the ACT.

Computers: PCs are available for students in the library, residence halls, and labs. Most of campus has wireless capabilities. Dorm rooms that do not have wireless have LAN access. All students may access the system. There are no time limits and no fees. A Dell is recommended.

Graduates: In a recent year, 191 bachelor's degrees were awarded. The most popular majors were business (31%), teacher education (22%), and behavioral science (18%). 53 companies recruited on campus in a recent year. In an average class, 7% graduate in 3 years or less, 21% graduate in 4 years or less, 30% graduate in 5 years or less, and 31% graduate in 6 years or less.

Admissions Contact: Enrollment Services. Web: *www.glenville.edu*

MARSHALL UNIVERSITY A-4

Huntington, WV 25755 (304) 696-3160
(800) 642-3499; (304) 696-3135

Full-time: 3643 men, 4629 women
Part-time: 605 men, 885 women
Graduate: 1247 men, 2047 women
Year: semesters, summer session
Application Deadline:
Freshman Class: n/av
SAT or ACT: required
Faculty: n/av; IIA, --$
Ph.D.s: 77%
Student/Faculty: 18 to 1
Tuition: $6216 ($14,446)
Room & Board: $8604

COMPETITIVE

Marshall University, founded in 1837 and part of the University of West Virginia system, is a comprehensive public institution offering programs in Liberal Arts, Science, Business, Education, Journalism and Mass Communications, Arts & Media, Information Technology and Engineering, and Health Professions. There are 10 undergraduate schools and 3 graduate schools. In addition to regional accreditation, Marshall has baccalaureate program accreditation with AACSB, ABET, ACEJMC, CSWE, NASM, NCATE, and NRPA. The 2 libraries contain 2.2 million volumes, 1.0 million microform items, and 43,449 audio/video tapes/CDs/DVDs, and subscribe to 45,508 periodicals including electronic. Computerized library services include interlibrary loans, database searching, and Internet access. Special learning facilities include an art gallery, natural history museum, radio station, TV station, a greenhouse. The 100-acre campus is in an urban area 126 miles east of Lexington, Kentucky, and 50 miles west of Charleston, West Virginia. Including any residence halls, there are 55 buildings.

Student Life: 79% of undergraduates are from West Virginia. Others are from 47 states, 51 foreign countries, and Canada. 82% are White. The average age of freshmen is 19; all undergraduates, 23.

Housing: 2499 students can be accommodated in college housing, which includes single-sex and coed dorms. Honors floors, Living Learning Communities, and Freshman Interest Groups. On-campus housing is available on a first-come and first-served basis. Alcohol is not permitted. All students may keep cars.

Activities: There are 194 groups on campus, including art, band, cheerleading, choir, chorale, chorus, communications, computers, dance, debate, drama, environmental, ethnic, forensics, gay, honors, international, jazz band, literary magazine, marching band, musical theater, newspaper, opera, orchestra, pep band, photography, political, professional, radio and TV, religious, social, social service, student government, symphony, and yearbook. Popular campus events include Week of Welcome, Parents Weekend, Homecoming, Springfest and International Festival.

Sports: There are 8 intercollegiate sports for men and 10 for women, and 9 intramural sports for men and 9 for women. Facilities include a 10,500-seat basketball arena, a 30,000-seat football stadium, tennis courts, a baseball field, an Olympic-size pool, an auxiliary gym, a health and fitness center, racquetball courts, a human performance enhancement lab, the Marshall Recreation Center which is a 123,000 square-foot, state-of-the art facility.

Disabled Students: All of the campus is accessible. Facilities include wheelchair ramps, elevators, special parking, specially equipped restrooms, special class scheduling, lowered drinking fountains, lowered telephones, special housing.

Services: Counseling and information services are available, as is tutoring in most subjects. There is a reader service for the blind, and remedial math, reading, and writing.

Campus Safety and Security: Measures include 24-hour foot and vehicle patrol, emergency notification system, self-defense education, and security escort services. There are emergency telephones, lighted pathways/sidewalks, and controlled access to dorms/residences.

Programs of Study: Marshall confers B.A., B.S., B.B.A., B.F.A., B.S.Cyotech, B.S.Chem, B.S.N., B.S.W. and B.S.E. degrees. Associate, master's, and doctoral degrees are also awarded. Bachelor's degrees are awarded in AGRICULTURE (natural resource management), BIOLOGICAL SCIENCE (anatomy, biochemistry, biology/biological science, biotechnology, cell biology, ecology, evolutionary biology, molecular biology, and nutrition), BUSINESS (accounting, banking and finance, business economics, finance, international business management, management information systems, marketing/retailing/merchandising, and sports management), COMMUNICATIONS AND THE ARTS (advertising, applied art, art, broadcasting, ceramic art and design, classics, communications, communication rhetoric/communication, creative writing, English, English literature, French, German, graphic design, information technology, Japanese, jazz, journalism, literature, music, music performance, music theory and composition, painting, percussion, photography, piano/organ, public relations, radio/television technology, sculpture, Spanish, sports media, strings, theatre arts, theater design, and voice), COMPUTER AND PHYSICAL SCIENCE (applied mathematics, chemistry, computer game design/development, computer science, computer security and information assurance, environmental chemistry, geology, information sciences and systems, mathematics, physics, and science technology), EDUCATION (athletic training, (Education) Childhood Education, early childhood education, education, elementary education, English education, foreign languages education, middle school education, music education, physical education, secondary education, social studies education, and special education), ENGINEERING AND ENVIRONMENTAL DESIGN (civil engineering, engineering, environmental science, occupational safety and health, and preengineering), HEALTH PROFESSIONS (allied health, cytotechnology, exercise science, health science, medical laboratory technology, nursing, Pre-Health Studies, predentistry, premedicine, preoptometry, preosteopathy, prepharmacy, prephysical therapy, prepodiatry, public health, respiratory therapy, and speech pathology/audiology), SOCIAL SCIENCE (criminal justice, dietetics, economics, forensic studies, geography, history, humanities, international relations, parks and recreation management, philosophy, physical fitness/movement, political science/government, prelaw, psychology, safety and security technology, safety management, social work, sociology, and women's studies). Biological science, elementary education, and secondary education have the largest enrollments.

Required: Marshall utilizes a Core Curriculum that applies through all colleges and majors which incorporates critical thinking, multicultural, writing intensive, and international components. Most degrees require 120 for graduation. Overall and major-specific GPAs vary with degrees.

Special: Many programs require or offer internships. Work-study opportunities are available on campus. Students participate in student exchange and study abroad programs. B.A.-B.S. degrees, dual majors and minors, nondegree study, credit for life experience, and credit/no-credit options are available. There are 20 national honor societies and a freshman honors program.

Faculty/Classroom: 54% of faculty are male; 46% are female. No introductory courses are taught by graduate students. The average class size in a regular course is 22.

Requirements: The SAT or ACT is required. General freshman admission is open to all applicants with a high school diploma with an overall GPA of 2.00 on a 4.00 scale and an ACT composite score of 19 or a SAT combined score 900 (critical reading + math) or an overall GPA of 3.00 on a 4.00 scale and an ACT composite score of 16 or a SAT combined score 770 (critical reading + math). The GED is also accepted. The following high school units are recommended for admission: 4 years of English (including courses in grammar, composition, literature), 3 years of social studies (including U.S. history), 4 years of math (including Algebra I and at least two higher units), 3 years of laboratory science, 2 years of the same foreign language, 1 year of fine arts. A GPA of 2.0 is required. AP and CLEP credits are accepted.

Procedure: Freshmen are admitted to all sessions. Entrance exams should be taken during the junior year or early in the senior year. There is a rolling admissions plan. Check with the school for current application deadlines. The application fee is $30. Notification is sent on a rolling basis. Applications are accepted online.

Transfer: 978 transfer students enrolled in 2012-2013. All transfer students must be eligible to return to the institution they most recently attended. In addition, transfer students who have fewer than 26 earned semester hours must meet one of the following criteria: must meet the current freshman admission standards, or have earned 12 graded college-level semester hours and completed all prerequisite courses for English and math while maintaining a 2.00 cumulative college GPA.

Visiting: There are regularly scheduled orientations for prospective students. There are guides for informal visits, visitors may sit in on classes, and stay overnight. To schedule a visit, contact the Office of Recruitment at (304) 696-3646.

Financial Aid: In 2013-2014, 87% of all full-time freshmen and 89% of continuing full-time students received some form of financial aid. 75% of all full-time freshmen and 74% of continuing full-time students received need-based aid. The average freshman award was $10,915. Need-based scholarships or need-based grants averaged $5,260 ($23,172 maximum); need-based self-help aid (loans and jobs) averaged $5,622 ($15,000 maximum); non-need-based athletic scholarships averaged $11,892 ($24,560 maximum); and other non-need-based awards and non-need-based scholarships averaged $5,164 ($25,769 maximum). 3% of undergraduate students work part-time. Average annual earnings from campus work are $1598. The average financial indebtedness of the 2013 graduate was $26,727. Marshall is a member of CSS. The FAFSA is required. The priority date for freshman financial aid applications for fall entry is March 1. The deadline for filing freshman financial aid applications for fall entry is March 1.

International Students: There are 132 international students enrolled. The school actively recruits these students. They must take the TOEFL with a minimum score of 80 on the Internet-based version (iBT).

Computers: All students may access the system during scheduled hours, 7 days a week. There are no time limits and no fees.

Graduates: From July 1, 2012 to June 30, 2013, 1562 bachelor's degrees were awarded. The most popular majors were arts (16%), elementary education (7%), and management (7%). In an average class, 45% graduate in 6 years or less.

Admissions Contact: Admissions Office, Staff. E-Mail: *admissions@marshall.edu* Web: *www.marshall.edu*

MOUNTAIN STATE UNIVERSITY B-4

Beckley, WV 25801 (304) 929-1334
(800) 766-6067; (304) 929-1710

Full-time: 1104 men, 2163 women	**Faculty:** 96
Part-time: 511 men, 1112 women	**Ph.D.s:** 31%
Graduate: 238 men, 422 women	**Student/Faculty:** 34 to 1
Year: semesters, summer session	**Tuition:** $8180
Application Deadline: open	**Room & Board:** $7150

Freshman Class: 1633 applied, 1633 accepted, 763 enrolled
SAT or ACT: recommended

NONCOMPETITIVE

Mountain State University, founded in 1933, is a private institution offering more than 50 professionally oriented degree programs in leadership, health and human services, business and technology, and arts and sciences, along with such specialized fields as culinary arts and legal studies. Graduate programs in executive leadership and psychology are also offered. There are 4 undergraduate schools and 1 graduate school. In addition to regional accreditation, MSU has baccalaureate program accreditation with APTA and CSWE. The library contains 133,365 volumes, 1,427 microform items, and 4,913 audio/video tapes/CDs/DVDs, and subscribes to 157 periodicals including electronic. Computerized library services include interlibrary loans, database searching, and Internet access. Special learning facilities include a learning resource center, a greenhouse, medicinal-botanical gardens, and a gross anatomy (cadaver) lab. The 35-acre campus is in a small town approximately 50 miles south of Charleston, WV, and approximately 180 miles north of Charlotte, NC. Including any residence halls, there are 39 buildings.

Student Life: 69% of undergraduates are from West Virginia. Others are from 48 states, 40 foreign countries, and Canada. 63% are white. The average age of freshmen is 30; all undergraduates, 31. 48% do not continue beyond their first year; 28% remain to graduate.

Housing: 396 students can be accommodated in college housing, which includes coed dorms and off-campus apartments. housing for athletes. On-campus housing is guaranteed for the freshman year only, is available on a first-come, and first-served basis. 63% of students commute. Alcohol is not permitted. All students may keep cars.

Activities: There are 16 groups on campus, including cheerleading, chorale, drama, ethnic, forensics, gay, honors, international, literary magazine, pep band, professional, religious, SGA newsletter, social, social service, and student government. Popular campus events include Appalachian Vision series, Business and Technology show, and Performing Arts series.

Sports: There are 4 intercollegiate sports for men and 4 for women, and 5 intramural sports for men and 4 for women. Facilities include a pool, a track, racquetball courts, exercise equipment, and an aerobics area. MSU students receive a membership in the local YMCA.

Disabled Students: 85% of the campus is accessible. Facilities include wheelchair ramps, elevators, special parking, specially equipped restrooms, special class scheduling, lowered drinking fountains, lowered telephones.

Services: Counseling and information services are available, as is tutoring in most subjects. There is a reader service for the blind, and remedial math and writing.

Campus Safety and Security: Measures include 24-hour foot and vehicle patrol, emergency notification system, and security escort services. There are emergency telephones, lighted pathways/sidewalks, and controlled access to dorms/residences.

Programs of Study: MSU confers B.A., B.S., B.S.N., and B.S.W. degrees. Associate, master's, and doctoral degrees are also awarded. Bachelor's degrees are awarded in AGRICULTURE (environmental studies and wildlife management), BIOLOGICAL SCIENCE (biology/biological science), BUSINESS (accounting, business administration and management, business law, electronic business, marketing and distribution, marketing/retailing/merchandising, organizational behavior, and organizational leadership and management), COMMUNICATIONS AND THE ARTS (graphic design), COMPUTER AND PHYSICAL SCIENCE (computer science, information sciences and systems, and radiological technology), EDUCATION (early childhood education and health education), ENGINEERING AND ENVIRONMENTAL DESIGN (aviation administration/management, computer technology, engineering, mining and mineral engineering, and occupational safety and health), HEALTH PROFESSIONS (emergency medical technologies, health care administration, nursing, occupational therapy, physician's assistant, and ultrasound technology), SOCIAL SCIENCE (criminal justice, culinary arts, forensic studies, humanities, interdisciplinary studies, law, liberal arts/general studies, paralegal studies, psychology, religion, and social work). Physician assistant, radiologist technician, are the strongest academically. Organizational leadership, psychology, and strategic leadership have the largest enrollments.

Required: Requirements for graduation are a 2.0 GPA overall and completion of all required course credit hours. All students must complete 36 hours of general studies and the required hours of the program's core curriculum.

Special: Internships and a degree completion program are available. B.A.-B.S. degrees and student-designed majors are offered in interdisciplinary studies. There is an acclererated B.S. degree in organizational leadership. There are 5 national honor societies.

Faculty/Classroom: 31% of faculty are male; 68% are female. All teach undergraduates, 15% do research, and 15% do both. No introductory courses are taught by graduate students. The average class size in an introductory lecture is 13; in a laboratory is 20; and in a regular course is 14.

Admissions: 100% of a recent year applicants were accepted. The SAT scores for a recent freshman class were: Math--50% below 500, 50% between 500 and 599. The ACT scores were 73% below 21, 15% between 21 and 23, 9% between 24 and 26, 3% between 27 and 28. 10% of the current freshmen were in the top fifth of their class; 29% were in the top two fifths.

Requirements: The SAT or ACT and ACT Writing Test are recommended. The GED is accepted. AP and CLEP credits are accepted. Important factors in the admissions decision are recommendations by school officials, parents or siblings who attended the school, and ability to finance college education.

Procedure: Freshmen are admitted to all sessions. Entrance exams should be taken any time prior to application. There are early admissions, deferred admissions, and rolling admissions plans. Application deadlines are open. Application fee is $25. Notification is sent on a rolling basis. Applications are accepted online.

Transfer: 763 transfer students enrolled in a recent year. Applicants must submit official transcripts from all colleges attended. 30 of 120 credits required for the bachelor's degree must be completed at MSU.

Visiting: There are regularly scheduled orientations for prospective students, including a campus tour, registration, financial aid information, and sign-up for housing and meal plans. There are guides for informal visits, visitors may sit in on classes, and stay overnight. To schedule a visit, contact Admissions Department.

Financial Aid: In a recent year, 81% of continuing full-time students received some form of financial aid. 68% of continuing full-time students received need-based aid. The average freshman award was $5,778. Need-based scholarships or need-based grants averaged $2,644 ($4,075 maximum); need-based self-help aid (loans and jobs) averaged $3,823 ($9,456 maximum); non-need-based athletic scholarships averaged $3,459 ($14,491 maximum); and other non-need-based awards and non-need-based scholarships averaged $6,354 ($6,354 maximum). 8% of undergraduate students work part-time. Average annual earnings from campus work are $552. The FAFSA and the college's own financial statement are required. The deadline for filing freshman financial aid applications for fall entry is March 1.

International Students: There are 276 international students enrolled. The school actively recruits these students. They must take the TOEFL with a minimum score of 500 on the paper-based TOEFL (PBT) or 61 on the Internet-based version (iBT). The ACT is recommended for placement.

Computers: Wireless access is available. MSU has 5 computer labs on the main campus in addition to PC availability in the library and a computer lab on each of the branch campuses. In total, there are 230 student-accessible computers. There are Internet connections in all student housing rooms and wireless access at the main campus and the branch campuses. All students may access the system. Wireless and in-room network connectivity are available at all times. There are no time limits and no fees.

Graduates: In a recent year, 814 bachelor's degrees were awarded. The most popular majors were nursing (28%), organizational leadership (22%), and administration of criminal justice (9%). 69 companies recruited on campus in 2010-2011. In an average class, 4% graduate in 4 years or less, 6% graduate in 5 years or less, and 10% graduate in 6 years or less. Of the

2010 graduating class, 16% were enrolled in graduate school within 6 months of graduation, and 84% were employed.

Admissions Contact: Director of Admissions Process. A campus DVD is available. Web: *www.mountainstate.edu*

OHIO VALLEY UNIVERSITY B-2

Vienna, WV 26105 **(304) 865-6202; (304) 865-6175**

Full-time: 250 men, 275 women	**Faculty:** 21; IIB, --$
Part-time: 12 men, 22 women	**Ph.D.s:** 75%
Graduate: n/av	**Student/Faculty:** 18 to 1
Year: semesters, summer session	**Tuition:** $14,364
Application Deadline: open	**Room & Board:** $5660
Freshman Class: 304 applied, 170 accepted, 85 enrolled	
ACT: 23	**COMPETITIVE**

Ohio Valley University, founded in 1960, is a liberal arts institution affiliated with the Church of Christ. There are 4 undergraduate schools and 1 graduate school. The library contains 31,750 volumes, 51,530 microform items, and 2,946 audio/video tapes/CDs/DVDs, and subscribes to 165 periodicals including electronic. Computerized library services include interlibrary loans, database searching, Internet access, and Wi-Fi capability. The 270-acre campus is in a suburban area OVU is located in beautiful Vienna, West Virginia, on the Ohio River in the historic Mid-Ohio Valley. Including any residence halls, there are 9 buildings.

Student Life: 65% of undergraduates are from out of state, mostly the Mid-West. Students are from 28 states, 13 foreign countries, and Canada. 97% are from public schools. 88% are White. 97% are Protestant. The average age of freshmen is 18; all undergraduates, 22. 26% do not continue beyond their first year; 35% remain to graduate.

Housing: 500 students can be accommodated in college housing, which includes single-sex dorms, on campus apartments, and married student housing. On-campus housing is guaranteed for all 4 years. 55% of students live on campus; of those, 30% remain on campus on weekends. Alcohol is not permitted. All students may keep cars.

Activities: There are no fraternities or sororities. There are 16 groups on campus, including band, cheerleading, choir, chorale, chorus, communications, drama, jazz band, newspaper, pep band, religious, social, and student government. Popular campus events include Expressions, a school-wide musical review.

Sports: There are 5 intercollegiate sports for men and 4 for women, and 11 intramural sports for men and 10 for women. Facilities include a weight room, a student union with recreation facilities, an activity center, and 2 gyms.

Disabled Students: 30% of the campus is accessible. Facilities include wheelchair ramps, elevators, special parking, specially equipped restrooms, special class scheduling, and lowered telephones.

Services: Counseling and information services are available, as is tutoring in most subjects. There is remedial math, reading, and writing.

Campus Safety and Security: Measures include 24-hour foot and vehicle patrol.

Programs of Study: Ohio Valley confers B.A., and B.S. degrees. Associate degrees are also awarded. Bachelor's degrees are awarded in BIOLOGICAL SCIENCE (biochemistry), BUSINESS (accounting, business administration and management, organizational leadership and management, and sports management), COMMUNICATIONS AND THE ARTS (English), COMPUTER AND PHYSICAL SCIENCE (computer information technology and mathematics), EDUCATION (elementary education, English education, health education, mathematics education, and science education), HEALTH PROFESSIONS (biology and health), SOCIAL SCIENCE (biblical studies, criminal justice, history, humanities, interdisciplinary studies, psychology, and sociology). Business is the strongest academically. Elementary education, psychology, business administration have the largest enrollments.

Required: To graduate, students must complete 128 credit hours, including 53 to 60 in the major, with a minimum GPA of 2.0. General requirements include 4 courses of Bible studies, 2 of English composition, 1 to 2 of history, and 1 each of speech, computer literacy, math, and social science. There is also a phys ed requirement. Students must attend chapel daily and take 1 Bible class each semester.

Special: Ohio Valley offers internships with churches for student ministers. Study abroad programs are frequently offered in England, France and Italy. OVU is also affiliated with the Washington Center for Internships and Academic Seminars. There is 1 national honor societty and 1 departmental honors program.

Faculty/Classroom: 68% of faculty are male; 32% are female. All teach undergraduates. No introductory courses are taught by graduate students. The average class size in an introductory lecture is 30; in a laboratory is 20; and in a regular course is 15.

Admissions: 56% of the 2013-2014 applicants were accepted. The ACT scores were 75% below 21, 25% between 21 and 23, 9% between 24 and 26, 3% between 27 and 28, and 2% above 28. 10% of the current freshmen were in the top fifth of their class; 32% were in the top two fifths. 10 freshmen graduated first in their class.

Requirements: The ACT is required. Applicants should be graduates of an accredited secondary school or have earned a GED. Ohio Valley requires applicants to be in the upper 50% of their class. A GPA of 2.0 is required. AP and CLEP credits are accepted. Important factors in the admissions decision are recommendations by school officials, personality/intangible qualities, and leadership record.

Procedure: Freshmen are admitted fall and spring. Entrance exams should be taken during the senior year. There are early admissions and rolling admissions plans. Application deadlines are open. Notification is sent on a rolling basis.

Transfer: Transfer applicants must provide high school, college, and financial aid transcripts, and test scores. 32 of 128 credits required for the bachelor's degree must be completed at Ohio Valley.

Visiting: There are guides for informal visits, visitors may sit in on classes, and stay overnight. To schedule a visit, contact the Office of Admissions.

Financial Aid: In 2013-2014, 95% of all full-time freshmen and 98% of continuing full-time students received some form of financial aid. 70% of all full-time freshmen and 65% of continuing full-time students received need-based aid. The average freshman award was $9,768. Need-based scholarships or need-based grants averaged $7,219; need-based self-help aid (loans and jobs) averaged $3,248 ($5,500 maximum); non-need-based athletic scholarships averaged $5,442 ($16,796 maximum); and other non-need-based awards and non-need-based scholarships averaged $7,732 ($15,000 maximum). 44% of undergraduate students work part-time. Average annual earnings from campus work are $800. The average financial indebtedness of the 2013 graduate was $9,035. Ohio Valley is a member of CSS. The FAFSA is required. The priority date for freshman financial aid applications for fall entry is February 14.

International Students: There are 33 international students enrolled. The school actively recruits these students. They must take the TOEFL with a minimum score of 500 on the paper-based TOEFL (PBT) or 61 on the Internet-based version (iBT). They must also take the SAT or ACT, scoring 18.

Computers: All students may access the system. There are no time limits and no fees.

Graduates: From July 1, 2012 to June 30, 2013, 101 bachelor's degrees were awarded. The most popular majors were business (46%), education (25%), and psychology (16%). In an average class, 18% graduate in 4 years or less, 35% graduate in 5 years or less, and 27% graduate in 6 years or less.

Admissions Contact: Rob E. Dudley, Director of Admissions. E-Mail: *admissions@ovc.edu* Web: *www.ovc.edu*

SALEM INTERNATIONAL UNIVERSITY C-4

Salem, WV 26426 **(304) 782-5336**
(800) 283-4562; (304) 782-5592

Full-time: 165 men, 175 women	**Faculty:** n/av
Part-time: 10 men, 10 women	**Ph.D.s:** 88%
Graduate: 55 men, 95 women	**Student/Faculty:** n/av
Year: see profile, summer session	**Tuition:** $14,000
Application Deadline: open	**Room & Board:** $6500
Freshman Class: n/av	
SAT: required	**ACT:** 21 **COMPETITIVE**

Salem International University, founded in 1888, is a private institution offering both liberal arts and career-oriented degree programs, including international business, biotechnology, Japanese studies, and equine careers and industry management. The figures in the above capsule and in this profile are approximate. There are 3 graduate schools. In addition to regional accreditation, SIU has baccalaureate program accreditation with ACBSP. The library contains 105,437 volumes, 284,302 microform items, 974 audio/video tapes/CDs/DVDs, and subscribes to 94 periodicals including electronic. Computerized library services include interlibrary loans and database searching. Special learning facilities include a learning resource center, art gallery, radio station, TV station, Fort New Salem (an 1800s settlement), an equestrian center, and a greenhouse. The 300-acre campus is in a rural area 120 miles south of Pittsburgh, Pennsylvania. Including any residence halls, there are 19 buildings.

Student Life: 69% of undergraduates are from out of state, mostly the Middle Atlantic. Others are from 34 states, 26 foreign countries, and Canada. 53% are white; 22% foreign nationals. The average age of freshmen is 19; all undergraduates, 21. 37% do not continue beyond their first year; 51% remain to graduate.

Housing: 550 students can be accommodated in college housing, which includes single-sex and coed dorms. In addition, there are honors houses and special-interest houses. On-campus housing is guaranteed for all 4 years. 90% of students live on campus; of those, 75% remain on campus on weekends. All students may keep cars.

Activities: 10% of men belong to 2 local fraternities; 12% of women belong to 3 local sororities. There are 25 groups on campus, including cheerleading, ethnic, gay, honors, international, newspaper, professional, radio and TV, religious, social, social service, student government, and yearbook. Popular campus events include Winterfest, Spring Arts Series, and Spring Fling.

Sports: There are 6 intercollegiate sports for men and 6 for women, and 12 intramural sports for men and 12 for women. Facilities include a gym, a pool, a weight room, tennis courts, a soccer stadium, a fitness trail, racquetball courts, and horseback-riding trails.

Disabled Students: 90% of the campus is accessible. Facilities include wheelchair ramps, elevators, special parking, specially equipped rest rooms, special class scheduling, and special wheelchair lifting equipment.

Services: Counseling and information services are available, as is tutoring in most subjects, most classes have a tutoring option. There is a reader service for the blind, and remedial math, reading, and writing.

Campus Safety and Security: Measures include 24-hour foot and vehicle patrol and security escort services. There are emergency telephones, lighted pathways/sidewalks, and Dial-a-Ride on weekends.

Programs of Study: SIU confers B.A. and B.S. degrees. Associates and master's degrees are also awarded. Bachelor's degrees are awarded in AGRICULTURE (equine science), BIOLOGICAL SCIENCE (biology/biological science and molecular biology), BUSINESS (business administration and management and sports management), COMMUNICATIONS AND THE ARTS (communications and English as a second/foreign language), COMPUTER AND PHYSICAL SCIENCE (computer mathematics and information sciences and systems), EDUCATION (athletic training, elementary education, and secondary education), ENGINEERING AND ENVIRONMENTAL DESIGN (aviation administration/management and environmental science), SOCIAL SCIENCE (criminal justice, human services, Japanese studies, and liberal arts/general studies). Molecular biology and Japanese studies are the strongest academically. Management studies, equine, and criminal justice have the largest enrollments.

Required: All students must take 57 hours in the core curriculum, including courses in communication skills, humanities, science/math, social studies, psychology, and health and phys ed. A minimum 2.0 GPA overall, with a minimum 2.25 GPA in the major, and 128 credit hours are required to graduate.

Special: A student may cross-register with another college within the Mountain State Association of Colleges. Many internships are available. Study abroad is offered. Dual majors, credit by exam, and credit for life experience may be arranged. There are 2 national honor societies.

Faculty/Classroom: 54% of faculty are male; 46% are female. All teach and do research. No introductory courses are taught by graduate students. The average class size in an introductory lecture is 25; in a laboratory is 10; and in a regular course is 14.

Requirements: The SAT or ACT is required. Applicants should be graduates of an accredited secondary school with 15 academic courses, including 4 in English, 3 each in math, science, and social studies, and 2 in a foreign language. A GPA of 2.0 is required. AP and CLEP credits are accepted. Important factors in the admissions decision are advanced placement or honors courses, evidence of special talent, and extracurricular activities record.

Procedure: Freshmen are admitted to all sessions. Entrance exams should be taken in the junior year or fall of the senior year. There are deferred admissions and rolling admissions plans. Application deadlines are open. Application fee is $25. Notification is sent on a rolling basis. Applications are accepted online.

Transfer: A minimum GPA of 2.0 is required for acceptance as a transfer student. 32 of 128 credits required for the bachelor's degree must be completed at SIU.

Visiting: There are regularly scheduled orientations for prospective students, consisting of meetings with academic and administrative department heads, tours, question-and-answer sessions, and a reception. There are guides for informal visits; visitors may sit in on classes and stay overnight. To schedule a visit, contact the Admissions Office.

Financial Aid: SIU is a member of CSS. The FAFSA is required. Check with the school for current application deadlines.

International Students: The school actively recruits these students. They must take the TOEFL.

Computers: All students may access the system. There are no time limits. The fee is $40. It is strongly recommended that all students have a personal computer.

Admissions Contact: Director of Admissions. E-Mail: *admissions@salemiu.edu* Web: *www.salemiu.edu*

SHEPHERD UNIVERSITY — E-2

Shepherdstown, WV 25443 — (304) 876-5212; (800) 344-5231; (304) 876-5165

Full-time: 1351 men, 1938 women	**Faculty:** 140; IIB, -$
Part-time: 352 men, 349 women	**Ph.D.s:** 85%
Graduate: 77 men, 154 women	**Student/Faculty:** 23 to 1
Year: semesters, summer session	**Tuition:** $6256 ($15,840)
Application Deadline:	**Room & Board:** $8740

Freshman Class: 1746 applied, 1647 accepted, 684 enrolled

SAT CR/M: 490/480 **ACT:** 21 **COMPETITIVE**

Shepherd University, founded in 1871, is a state-supported institution offering programs in the liberal and creative arts, business administration, teacher education, social and natural sciences, health fields, and other career-oriented areas. There are 4 undergraduate schools and 1 graduate school. In addition to regional accreditation, Shepherd has baccalaureate program accreditation with CSWE, NASM, and NCATE. The library contains 192,979 volumes, 26,733 microform items, and 4,964 audio/video tapes/CDs/DVDs, and subscribes to 51,466 periodicals including electronic. Computerized library services include interlibrary loans, database searching, Internet access, and Wi-Fi capability. Special learning facilities include an art gallery, radio station, a nursery school, 3 theaters, the Center for the Study of the Civil War, and the Robert C. Byrd Center for Legislative Studies. The 323-acre campus is in a small town 70 miles northwest of Washington, D.C., and Baltimore. Including any residence halls, there are 52 buildings.

Student Life: 63% of undergraduates are from West Virginia. Others are from 46 states, and 13 foreign countries. 83% are from public schools. 83% are White. The average age of freshmen is 19; all undergraduates, 23. 32% do not continue beyond their first year; 38% remain to graduate.

Housing: 1300 students can be accommodated in college housing, which includes coed dorms and on-campus apartments. In addition, there are honors houses and special-interest houses. On-campus housing is guaranteed for all 4 years. 67% of students commute. All students may keep cars.

Activities: 3% of men belong to 4 national fraternities; 4% of women belong to 3 national sororities. There are 85 groups on campus, including art, band, cheerleading, choir, chorale, chorus, computers, dance, drama, drill team, environmental, ethnic, gay, honors, international, jazz band, literary magazine, marching band, musical theater, newspaper, opera, orchestra, pep band, political, professional, radio and TV, religious, social, social service, student government, and symphony. Popular campus events include Family Day, Shepfest, Midnight Breakfast and Relay for Life.

Sports: There are 6 intercollegiate sports for men and 6 for women, and 12 intramural sports for men and 12 for women. Facilities include a 5000-seat football and women's lacrosse field, 2 soccer fields, baseball and softball fields, a 3000-seat gym, 9 outdoor and 2 indoor tennis courts, 2 outdoor sand volleyball courts, a fitness/wellness center, and a swimming pool.

Disabled Students: 90% of the campus is accessible. Facilities include wheelchair ramps, elevators, special parking, specially equipped restrooms, special class scheduling, lowered drinking fountains, lowered telephones.

Services: Counseling and information services are available, as is tutoring in most subjects. There is remedial math, reading, and writing and tutorial assistance for students with learning disabilities.

Campus Safety and Security: Measures include 24-hour foot and vehicle patrol, emergency notification system, and security escort services. There are shuttle buses, emergency telephones, lighted pathways/sidewalks, and controlled access to dorms/residences.

Programs of Study: Shepherd confers B.A., B.S., B.F.A., B.M.E., B.S.N., B.S.W. and R.B.A. degrees. Master's degrees are also awarded. Bachelor's degrees are awarded in AGRICULTURE (environmental studies), BIOLOGICAL SCIENCE (biology/biological science), BUSINESS (accounting, business administration and management, and recreation and leisure services), COMMUNICATIONS AND THE ARTS (art, communications, English, music, and Spanish), COMPUTER AND PHYSICAL SCIENCE (chemistry, computer science, information sciences and systems, and mathematics), EDUCATION (art education, elementary education, English education, health education, home economics education, mathematics education, music education, physical education, science education, secondary education, and social studies education), ENGINEERING AND ENVIRONMENTAL DESIGN (computer engineering and computer technology), HEALTH PROFESSIONS (nursing), SOCIAL SCIENCE (economics, family/consumer studies, history, political science/government, psychology, social work, and sociology). Biology, education, art, nursing, music, and social work are the strongest academically. Nursing, education, and business have the largest enrollments.

Required: To graduate, students must complete a minimum of 120 semester hours with a 2.0 GPA overall and in the major and minor fields. The general studies core totals 42: written Engilsh, 6; mathematics, 3; history, 3; sciences, 8; first-year experience, 1; arts, 3; humanities, 6; social sciences, 9; and wellness, 3. Students pursuing the Bachelor of Arts degree (not including education) are required to complete 12 semester hours in the same foreign language, except music students whose requirements must be approved by the chairs of the Music and English and Modern Languages departments. Two years of German or French or both are recommended for students who anticipate going to graduate or professional school. The foreign language requirement for the B.A. degree can be satisfied through advanced placement or CLEP tests.

Special: Shepherd offers study abroad, a B.A.-B.S. degree in communication and new media, and internships and co-op programs that are available in most majors. There is a Washington semester, and dual majors are possible in any 2 majors. Credit by exam, life experience credentialing through the Regents degree, nondegree study, and pass/fail options for electives are offered. There are 9 national honor societies, a freshman honors program, and 19 departmental honors programs.

Faculty/Classroom: 51% of faculty are male; 49% are female. 99% teach undergraduates, 81% do research, and 81% do both. No introductory courses are taught by graduate students. The average class size in an introductory lecture is 23; in a laboratory is 21; and in a regular course is 15.

Admissions: 94% of the 2013-2014 applicants were accepted. The SAT scores for the 2013-2014 freshman class were: Critical Reading--49% below 500, 37% between 500 and 599, 11% between 600 and 699, and 3% between 700 and 800; Math--55% below 500, 35% between 500 and 599, and 10% between 600 and 699. The ACT scores were 43% below 21, 27% between 21 and 23, 19% between 24 and 26, 7% between 27 and 28, and 4% above 28.

Requirements: The SAT or ACT is required. In addition, with a minimum composite score of 910 on the SAT (critical reading and math) or 19 on the ACT. Applicants should be graduates of an accredited secondary school and have earned academic credits including 4 each in English and math, 3 each in social science (1 in American history) and lab science, 1 in art, and the rest in computer, foreign language, and other academic electives. Applicants must have a minimum 2.0 academic core GPA. The GED is accepted. A GPA of 2.0 is required. AP and CLEP credits are accepted. Important factors in the admissions decision are advanced placement or honors courses, leadership record, and extracurricular activities record.

Procedure: Freshmen are admitted fall, spring, and summer. Entrance exams should be taken during the junior year. There are early decision, early admissions, deferred admissions, and rolling admissions plans. Application deadlines are open. Application fee is $45. Notification is sent on a rolling basis. 107 early decision candidates were accepted for the 2013-2014 class. Applications are accepted online.

Transfer: 353 transfer students enrolled in 2012-2013. Applicants must have a 2.0 cumulative GPA in a minimum of 26 semester hours of college-level work completed and must submit a transcript from each college attended. 32 of 120 credits required for the bachelor's degree must be completed at Shepherd.

Visiting: There are regularly scheduled orientations for prospective students, consisting of 3 fall open houses and 2 spring open houses, and weekday campus tours. There are guides for informal visits, visitors may sit in on classes, and stay overnight. To schedule a visit, contact the Admissions Office at admissions@shepherd.edu.

Financial Aid: In 2013-2014, 91% of all full-time freshmen and 82% of continuing full-time students received some form of financial aid. 64% of all full-time freshmen and 63% of continuing full-time students received need-based aid. The average freshman award was $10,667. Need-based scholarships or need-based grants averaged $4,728 ($5,550 maximum); need-based self-help aid (loans and jobs) averaged $3,056 ($5,500 maximum); and non-need-based athletic scholarships averaged $4,990 ($14,000 maximum). 11% of undergraduate students work part-time. Average annual earnings from campus work are $2284. The average financial indebtedness of the 2013 graduate was $23,397. The FAFSA and the state aid form are required. The priority date for freshman financial aid applications for fall entry is March 1.

International Students: There are 13 international students enrolled. The school actively recruits these students. They must take the TOEFL with a minimum score of 550 on the paper-based TOEFL (PBT) or 79 on the Internet-based version (iBT). They must also take the SAT or ACT, scoring 910.

Computers: All students may access the system 24 hours daily. There are no time limits and no fees.

Graduates: The most popular majors were regents bachelor of arts (18%), education (12%), and business administration (10%). 89 companies recruited on campus in 2012-2013. In an average class, 18% graduate in 4 years or less, 34% graduate in 5 years or less, and 38% graduate in 6 years or less. Of the 2012 graduating class, 24% were enrolled in graduate school within 6 months of graduation, and 69% were employed.

Admissions Contact: Michael Konopski, Interim VP, Enrollment Management. E-Mail: *admissions@shepherd.edu* Web: *www.shepherd.edu*

UNIVERSITY OF CHARLESTON — B-4

Charleston, WV 25304	**(304) 357-4750; (800) 995-4682**
Full-time: 513 men, 737 women	**Faculty:** 74
Part-time: 64 men, 72 women	**Ph.D.s:** 56%
Graduate: 281 men, 268 women	**Student/Faculty:** 17 to 1
Year: varies, summer session	**Tuition:** $19,650
Application Deadline:	**Room & Board:** $9000
Freshman Class: n/av	
SAT CR/M: 470/480 **ACT:** 22	**COMPETITIVE**

The University of Charleston prepares students for a life of productive work, enlightened living and community involvement. UC is a private, non-profit institution with locations in Charleston, Beckley and Martinsburg, West Virginia as well as online. There are 3 undergraduate schools and 3 graduate schools. In addition to regional accreditation, UC has baccalaureate program accreditation with ACPE, NLN, and TEAC. The library contains 94,267 volumes, 229,551 microform items, and 5,000 audio/video tapes/CDs/DVDs, and subscribes to 150 periodicals including electronic. Computerized library services include interlibrary loans, database searching, Internet access, and Wi-Fi capability. Special learning facilities include an art gallery, academic success center, and career center. The 40-acre campus is in a small town.

Student Life: 65% of undergraduates are from West Virginia. Others are from 33 states, 36 foreign countries, and Canada. 64% are White; 12% African American; 11% race unknown. The average age of freshmen is 18; all undergraduates, 23. 34% do not continue beyond their first year; 46% remain to graduate.

Housing: 944 students can be accommodated in college housing, which includes coed dorms and married student housing. Housing available on Charleston and Beckley campuses. On-campus housing is guaranteed for the freshman year only, is available on a first-come, and first-served basis. Priority is given to out-of-town students. 54% of students commute. All students may keep cars.

Activities: Groups on campus include art, cheerleading, chess, choir, chorale, communications, computers, debate, ethnic, film, honors, international, newspaper, pep band, photography, political, professional, religious, social, social service, and student government. Popular campus events include Governor's Cup Regatta and World-fest.

Sports: There are 8 intercollegiate sports for men and 9 for women. Facilities include a gym, a game room, a Nautilus center, an indoor pool, soccer, softball, and baseball fields, racquetball, volleyball, and tennis courts, and a new fitness center.

Disabled Students: 85% of the campus is accessible. Facilities include wheelchair ramps, elevators, special parking, specially equipped restrooms, lowered drinking fountains, lowered telephones, and special housing.

Services: Counseling and information services are available, as is tutoring in most subjects. There is a reader service for the blind, and remedial math, reading, and writing.

Campus Safety and Security: Measures include 24-hour foot and vehicle patrol, emergency notification system, self-defense education, and security escort services. There are shuttle buses, emergency telephones, lighted pathways/sidewalks, controlled access to dorms/residences, There are burglar alarms in dorms, safety and date-rape seminars, drug awareness programs, surveillance cameras at dorms (used in conjunction with card access), and emergency radio communications.

Programs of Study: UC confers B.A., B.S. and B.S.N. degrees. Associate, master's, and doctoral degrees are also awarded. Bachelor's degrees are awarded in BIOLOGICAL SCIENCE (biology/biological science), BUSINESS (accounting, business administration and management, finance, and sports management), COMMUNICATIONS AND THE ARTS (art and communications), COMPUTER AND PHYSICAL SCIENCE (chemistry), EDUCATION (athletic training, elementary education, English education, physical education, science education, social studies education, and special education), ENGINEERING AND ENVIRONMENTAL DESIGN (interior design), HEALTH PROFESSIONS (diagnostic medical sonography, nursing, and radiological science), SOCIAL SCIENCE (criminal justice, culinary arts, history, liberal arts/general studies, political science/government, psychology, and social work). Health sciences is the strongest academically. Business, nursing, and biology have the largest enrollments.

Required: Students must obtain degree objective within 150% of the normal time frame for degree completion. For example, in a baccalaureate program requiring 120 credit hours, students must obtain degrees within 180 attempted credit hours (120 X 1.50 = 180). For associate programs of 60 credit hours, students must complete within 90 attempted hours. Graduate students in master degree programs requiring 68 hours must complete within 102 attempted credit hours. Doctoral students have a maximum of 219 attempted credit hours. This maximum time frame is based upon student classification in the University's academic records. Students who are pursuing a course of study with greater credit hour requirements need to notify the Financial Aid Office in order to have a review done on a case-by-case basis. This request for review will not be considered an appeal. The student is responsible for completing all requirements of his or her major program, including mastery of exit-level outcomes at designated standards, and for meeting all University requirements, including meeting all Liberal Learning Outcomes, before they will be allowed to graduate. Students should confer with major advisors and mentors, and refer to the Academic Catalog, to assure satisfactory progress toward graduation.

Special: The university offers credit by exam and credit for prior learning, self-acquired competency (SAC) credits, and credits for educational experiences in the armed services. Internships, on-campus work-study, and hospital clinical experience in qualified programs are available. There are 6 national honor societies.

Faculty/Classroom: 68% teach undergraduates. No introductory courses are taught by graduate students. The average class size in an introductory lecture is 24 and in a laboratory is 20.

Admissions: 69% of the 2013-2014 applicants were accepted. The SAT scores for the 2013-2014 freshman class were: Critical Reading--69% below 500, 24% between 500 and 599, 4% between 600 and 699, and 4% between 700 and 800; Math--58% below 500, 29% between 500 and 599, 11% between 600 and 699, and 1% between 700 and 800. The ACT scores were 38% below 21, 29% between 21 and 23, 21% between 24 and 26, 6% between 27 and 28, and 7% above 28.

Requirements: The SAT or ACT is required. In addition, six semesters of high school, with a minimum 2.25 academic grade point average (on a 4-point scale), or GED score of 500. AP and CLEP credits are accepted.

Procedure: Freshmen are admitted to all sessions. Entrance exams should be taken by December of the senior year. There are deferred admissions and rolling admissions plans. Application deadlines are open. Application fee is $25. Notification is sent on a rolling basis. Applications are accepted online.

Transfer: 93 transfer students enrolled in 2012-2013. Applicants who have earned 12 or more college-level credits (generally, courses numbered 100 and above) at another institution, have a minimum 2.25 grade point average (on a 4.0 point scale) and are in good standing at the institution last attended.

Visiting: There are regularly scheduled orientations for prospective students, including meetings with faculty, financial aid and student life information sessions, a campus tour, and meetings with coaches for athletes. There are guides for informal visits, visitors may sit in on classes, and stay overnight. To schedule a visit, contact the Admissions Office at (800) 995-4682 (GO UC).

Financial Aid: In 2013-2014, 100% of all full-time freshmen students received some form of financial aid. UC is a member of CSS. The FAFSA and the college's own financial statement are required. The priority date for freshman financial aid applications for fall entry is March 1. The deadline for filing freshman financial aid applications for fall entry is September 15.

International Students: There are 101 international students enrolled. The school actively recruits these students. They must take the TOEFL with a minimum score of 500 on the paper-based TOEFL (PBT) or 61 on the Internet-based version (iBT) or take the MELAB and the college's own test. They must also take the SAT or ACT.

Computers: All students may access the system. There are no time limits and no fees.

Graduates: From July 1, 2012 to June 30, 2013, 331 bachelor's degrees were awarded. The most popular majors were business/marketing (40%), biological/life studies (9%), and social sciences (7%). In an average class, 5% graduate in 3 years or less, 35% graduate in 4 years or less, 41% graduate in 5 years or less, and 46% graduate in 6 years or less.

Admissions Contact: Joan Clark, Vice President for Admissions. E-Mail: *admissions@ucwv.edu* Web: *http:/www.ucwv.edu/Admissions/*

WEST LIBERTY UNIVERSITY — C-1

West Liberty, WV 26074 — (304) 336-8076; (800) 732-6204; (304) 336-8403

Full-time: 1008 men, 1323 women	**Faculty:** n/av
Part-time: 134 men, 222 women	**Ph.D.s:** 60%
Graduate: 10 men, 31 women	**Student/Faculty:** 18 to 1
Year: semesters, summer session	**Tuition:** $4,880 ($12,750)
Application Deadline: see profile	**Room & Board:** $7,310
Freshman Class: n/av	
SAT or ACT: required	

LESS COMPETITIVE

West Liberty University, formerly West Liberty State College, founded in 1837, is a state-assisted university offering programs in teacher education, liberal and fine arts, sciences, business, and preprofessional and technical fields. There are 4 undergraduate schools. The figures in the above capsule and this profile are approximate. In addition to regional accreditation, West Liberty has baccalaureate program accreditation with ADA, CAHEA, NASM, NCATE, and NLN. The library contains 196,338 volumes, 131,000 microform items, and subscribes to 485 periodicals including electronic. Computerized library services include interlibrary loans and database searching. Special learning facilities include a learning resource center, art gallery, radio station, TV station, and a publication area. The 263-acre campus is in a rural area 10 miles north of Wheeling and 56 miles southwest of Pittsburgh. Including any residence halls, there are 22 buildings.

Student Life: 72% of undergraduates are from West Virginia. Others are from 21 states, 9 foreign countries, and Canada. 90% are from public schools. 95% are white. The average age of freshmen is 18; all undergraduates, 22. 30% do not continue beyond their first year; 43% remain to graduate.

Housing: College-sponsored housing includes single-sex and coed dorms, on-campus apartments, and married student housing. In addition, there are honors houses and an honors dorm. On-campus housing is available on a first-come, first-served basis. 55% of students commute. Alcohol is not permitted. All students may keep cars.

Activities: 6% of men belong to 4 local fraternities; 10% of women belong to 1 local and 3 national sororities. There are 48 groups on campus, including art, cheerleading, choir, chorus, communications, drama, ethnic, honors, hospitality, jazz band, literary magazine, marching band, musical theater, newspaper, pep band, photography, professional, radio and TV, religious, social, social service, steel drum band, student government, and tourism. Popular campus events include Multi-Cultural Day, Greek Week, and Spring Fling.

Sports: There are 8 intercollegiate sports for men and 7 for women, and 8 intramural sports for men and 7 for women. Facilities include handball and racquetball courts, training rooms, 3 gyms, indoor track, wellness center, and indoor swimming pool. There is also a game area with pool tables and table tennis, 8 all-weather-surface tennis courts, and football and softball/baseball fields.

Disabled Students: 90% of the campus is accessible. Facilities include wheelchair ramps, elevators, special parking, specially equipped rest rooms, lowered drinking fountains, and lowered telephones.

Services: Counseling and information services are available, as is tutoring in every subject. There is a reader service for the blind, and remedial math and writing.

Campus Safety and Security: Measures include 24-hour foot and vehicle patrol, self-defense education, and security escort services. There are emergency telephones, lighted pathways/sidewalks, and late night transport.

Programs of Study: West Liberty confers B.A., B.S., and B.S.N. degrees. Associates degrees are also awarded. Bachelor's degrees are awarded in BIOLOGICAL SCIENCE (biology/biological science), BUSINESS (accounting, banking and finance, business administration and management, business economics, management science, marketing/retailing/merchandising, and tourism), COMMUNICATIONS AND THE ARTS (communications, English, fine arts, graphic design, and music), COMPUTER AND PHYSICAL SCIENCE (chemistry, information sciences and systems, and mathematics), EDUCATION (art education, early childhood education, elementary education, health education, middle school education, music education, physical education, science education, secondary education, and special education), ENGINEERING AND ENVIRONMENTAL DESIGN (preengineering), HEALTH PROFESSIONS (clinical science, dental hygiene, nursing, predentistry, premedicine, prepharmacy, and speech pathology/audiology), SOCIAL SCIENCE (criminal justice, economics, history, interdisciplinary studies, physical fitness/movement, political science/government, prelaw, psychology, social science, and sociology). Business, natural sciences, and health sciences are the strongest academically. Business, elementary education, and criminal justice have the largest enrollments.

Required: The required core curriculum varies for B.A. and B.S. candidates, but both include courses in communications, fine arts and humanities, natural science and math, social science and history, and phys ed and health. A minimum GPA of 2.0 and 128 credit hours are required to graduate.

Special: Communications, exercise physiology, criminal justice, hospitality, tourism management, sports management, and golf management require an on-campus internship. The Washington Center Program, an internship, is also offered. However, students may also choose to complete an internship in the areas of business, clinical lab science, phys ed, or nursing. Interdisciplinary studies is a student-designed degree taken as either a B.A. or B.S. Biology, chemistry, and math are offered as a B.S. degree but may also be taken as a B.A. degree in education. Work and life experience credit is accepted in the Regents B.A. degree program. There are 10 national honor societies, a freshman honors program, and 6 departmental honors programs.

Faculty/Classroom: 59% of faculty are male; 41% are female. All teach undergraduates. No introductory courses are taught by graduate students. The average class size in an introductory lecture is 25; in a laboratory is 20; and in a regular course is 20.

Requirements: The SAT or ACT is required. Applicants must graduate from an accredited secondary school with a minimum GPA of 2.0, or have a composite minimum score of 17 on the ACT or a satisfactory score on the SAT. Students must have completed 4 years of English, 3 of social sciences, including U.S. history, 2 of math (algebra I and higher), and 2 of lab science. The GED is accepted. AP and CLEP credits are accepted.

Procedure: Freshmen are admitted to all sessions. Entrance exams should be taken in time so that all admissions credentials, including test scores, are received 2 weeks prior to the beginning of the term. There are deferred admissions and rolling admissions plans. Check with the school for current application deadlines and fees. Applications are accepted online.

Transfer: Students must be eligible to return to the institution from which they wish to transfer. An official college transcript and a minimum GPA of 2.0 overall are required. Admissions criteria are the same as for freshmen if the student has completed fewer than 28 hours of college-level course work. 36 of 128 credits required for the bachelor's degree must be completed at West Liberty.

Visiting: There are guides for informal visits; visitors may sit in on classes and stay overnight. To schedule a visit, contact the Office of Admissions.

Financial Aid: The FAFSA is required. Check with the school for current application deadlines.

International Students: They must take the TOEFL. They must also take the SAT or ACT, scoring 17.

Computers: All students may access the system. There are no time limits and no fees. It is strongly recommended that all students have a personal computer.

Admissions Contact: Director of Admissions and Recruitment. Web: *www.westliberty.edu*

WEST VIRGINIA STATE UNIVERSITY B-4

Institute, WV 25112-1000 (304) 766-3221
(800) 987-2112; (304) 766-5182

Full-time: 1050 men, 1350 women	**Faculty:** n/av
Part-time: 380 men, 680 women	**Ph.D.s:** 48%
Graduate: 20 men, 20 women	**Student/Faculty:** n/av
Year: varies, summer session	**Tuition:** $5038 ($11,778)
Application Deadline: see profile	**Room & Board:** $6154
Freshman Class: n/av	
SAT: recommended	**ACT:** required **NONCOMPETITIVE**

West Virginia State University, founded in 1891, is a state-supported institution offering broad programs in the arts and sciences and in preprofessional studies, including business and education. It also offers a comprehensive evening class schedule. The figures in the above capsule and this profile are approximate. In addition to regional accreditation, State University has baccalaureate program accreditation with ABET, CSWE, NCATE, and NRPA. The library contains 30,000 volumes, 500,000 microform items, and 6000 audio/video tapes/CDs/DVDs, and subscribes to 700 periodicals including electronic. Computerized library services include interlibrary loans and database searching. Special learning facilities include a learning resource center, art gallery, and TV station. The 91-acre campus is in a suburban area 8 miles west of Charleston. Including any residence halls, there are 40 buildings.

Student Life: 94% of undergraduates are from West Virginia. Others are from 34 states and 8 foreign countries. 99% are from public schools. 84% are white; 14% African American. The average age of freshmen is 26; all undergraduates, 27. 30% do not continue beyond their first year; 64% remain to graduate.

Housing: 794 students can be accommodated in college housing, which includes single-sex dorms, on-campus apartments, and married student housing. 93% of students commute. Alcohol is not permitted. All students may keep cars.

Activities: 1% of men belong to 1 local and 4 national fraternities; 1% of women belong to 3 national sororities. There are 42 groups on campus, including art, band, cheerleading, choir, chorale, chorus, drama, drill team, ethnic, film, honors, international, jazz band, literary magazine, newspaper, orchestra, pep band, photography, political, radio and TV, religious, social, social service, student government, and yearbook. Popular campus events include movies, comedy shows, and plays.

Sports: There are 5 intercollegiate sports for men and 4 for women, and 8 intramural sports for men and 7 for women. Facilities include a 6000-seat stadium, swimming pool, sports center, 1500-seat gym, student union, and student mall/plaza.

Disabled Students: Facilities include wheelchair ramps, elevators, special parking, specially equipped rest rooms, special class scheduling, and lowered drinking fountains.

Services: Counseling and information services are available, as is tutoring in most subjects, economics, political science, upper-division math, and accounting. There is remedial math, reading, and writing.

Campus Safety and Security: Measures include 24-hour foot and vehicle patrol and lighted pathways/sidewalks. There are formal educational sessions held in the dormitories each semester.

Programs of Study: State University confers B.A., B.S., and B.S.Ed. degrees. Associates degrees are also awarded. Bachelor's degrees are awarded in BIOLOGICAL SCIENCE (biology/biological science), BUSINESS (accounting, banking and finance, business administration and management, and marketing/retailing/merchandising), COMMUNICATIONS AND THE ARTS (communications, English, and fine arts), COMPUTER AND PHYSICAL SCIENCE (applied mathematics, chemistry, and mathematics), EDUCATION (art education, early childhood education, elementary education, and secondary education), HEALTH PROFESSIONS (recreation therapy), SOCIAL SCIENCE (criminal justice, economics, history, political science/government, psychology, social work, and sociology). Biology is the strongest academically. Education and business have the largest enrollments.

Required: Bachelor's degree candidates must take 52 to 53 semester credits of general studies courses, including freshman seminar, English, math, natural science, literature, fine arts, history, and cultural studies. To graduate, students must complete 121 to 128 credits with a minimum 2.0 GPA overall and in the major.

Special: State University offers internships, a Washington semester, work-study programs, and B.A.-B.S. degrees in communications, psychology, and biology. Credit by exam and for life/military/work experience is available. Nondegree study and pass/fail options are possible. There are 7 national honor societies, a freshman honors program, and 7 departmental honors programs.

Faculty/Classroom: 49% of faculty are male; 51% are female. All teach undergraduates. No introductory courses are taught by graduate students. The average class size in a regular course is 25.

Requirements: The ACT is required. The SAT is recommended. A minimum ACT composite score of 14 or a 2.0 GPA is required for regular admission. Applicants should be graduates of an accredited secondary school and have completed a minimum of 4 years each in English and academic electives, 3 in social studies, and 2 each in math and science. The GED is accepted. AP and CLEP credits are accepted. Important factors in the admissions decision are evidence of special talent, leadership record, and advanced placement or honors courses.

Procedure: Freshmen are admitted to all sessions. Entrance exams should be taken 6 months prior to entry. There are early decision and rolling admissions plans. Check with the school for current application deadlines and fees. Notification is sent on a rolling basis. Applications are accepted online.

Transfer: Applicants must submit ACT scores and high school and college transcripts, and must have a 2.0 GPA. 30 of 121 credits required for the bachelor's degree must be completed at State University.

Visiting: There are regularly scheduled orientations for prospective students, including both academic and social activities. There are guides for informal visits; visitors may sit in on classes and stay overnight. To schedule a visit, contact Office of Admissions.

Financial Aid: The CSS/Profile is required. Check with the school for current application deadlines.

International Students: They must take the TOEFL. They must also take the ACT.

Computers: All students may access the system Monday through Thursday, 9 a.m. to 10 p.m., Friday, 9 a.m. to 7 p.m., and Saturday, 9 a.m. to 2 p.m. Each student is allocated $200 of use per semester.

Admissions Contact: Interim Director of Admissions. Web: *wvstateu .edu*

WEST VIRGINIA UNIVERSITY C-2

Morgantown, WV 26506 (304) 293-2121
(800) 344-9881; (304) 293-3080

Full-time: 11587 men, 9440 women	**Faculty:** n/av; I, --$
Part-time: 739 men, 991 women	**Ph.D.s:** 81%
Graduate: 2995 men, 3714 women	**Student/Faculty:** 21 to 1
Year: semesters, summer session	**Tuition:** $6456 ($19,632)
Application Deadline: August 1	**Room & Board:** $9338
Freshman Class: 16079 applied, 13713 accepted, 4913 enrolled	
SAT CR/M: 516/536	**ACT:** 24 **COMPETITIVE+**

West Virginia University, founded in 1867, is a comprehensive, public land-grant research university offering more than 100 undergraduate degrees in liberal arts and sciences, health science, and professional training. The figures in the above capsule and in this profile are approximate. There are 15 undergraduate schools and 13 graduate schools. In addition to regional accreditation, WVU has baccalaureate program accreditation with AACSB, ABET, ACEJMC, ACPE, ADA, APTA, ASLA, CAHEA, CSWE, FIDER, NASAD, NASM, NCATE, NLN, NRPA, and SAF. The 5 libraries contain 2.5 million volumes, 263,203 microform items, 15,663 audio/video tapes/CDs/DVDs, and subscribe to 83,495 periodicals including electronic. Computerized library services include interlibrary loans, database searching, Internet access, and Wi-Fi capability. Special learning facilities include an art gallery, planetarium, radio station, a discovery lab for inventors, a coal, mining, and minerals history museum, a pharmacy museum, art museum, and an arboretum. The 2800-acre campus is in a small town 75 miles south of Pittsburgh, and 200 miles west of Baltimore. Including any residence halls, there are 255 buildings.

Student Life: 51% of undergraduates are from out of state, mostly the Middle Atlantic. Students are from 50 states, 109 foreign countries, and Canada. 83% are White. The average age of freshmen is 19; all undergraduates, 21. 56% remain to graduate.

Housing: 5781 students can be accommodated in college housing, which includes single-sex and coed dorms, on-campus apartments, off-campus apartments, and married student housing. In addition, there are honors houses, language houses, special-interest houses, fraternity houses, sorority houses, and sections within residence halls designated for special programming. On-campus housing is available on a first-come, first-served basis, and is available on a lottery system for upperclassmen. 76% of students commute. Alcohol is not permitted. All students may keep cars.

Activities: 7% of men belong to 16 national fraternities; 7% of women belong to 1 local and 8 national sororities. There are 390 groups on campus, including art, band, cheerleading, chess, choir, chorale, chorus, computers, dance, debate, drama, environmental, ethnic, film, forensics, gay, honors, international, jazz band, literary magazine, marching band, newspaper, opera, orchestra, pep band, photography, political, professional, radio and TV, religious, social, social service, student government, symphony, and yearbook. Popular campus events include Mountaineer Week, Greek Week and Fall Fest.

Sports: There are 7 intercollegiate sports for men and 9 for women, and 17 intramural sports for men and 17 for women. Facilities include The rec center utilizes 5 lighted tennis courts which are located near the building; the rec center has 17,000 fee of dedicated weight and exercise space. There is a one nineth mile jogging track located in the rec center and approximately one half mile outside of the rec center. There is a grass and turf field located next to the rec center. Soccer, football, lacrosse, Frisbee can all be played in that area. There are three swimming pools, 7 basketball courts, a 50 foot high climbing wall,in the center; There is a natatorium with swimming and diving pools; rifle facilities; tennis courts; a weight room; indoor/outdoor tracks; a bowling alley; lacrosse, baseball, football, and soccer fields; a 63,500-seat stadium; a 14,000-seat gym; a coliseum offering basketball, wrestling, volleyball, and gymnastics; and a soccer stadium.

Disabled Students: 90% of the campus is accessible. Facilities include wheelchair ramps, elevators, special parking, specially equipped restrooms, special class scheduling, lowered drinking fountains, lowered telephones, special housing. Academic programs are made accessible by transferring class to an architecturally accessible facility. Other facilities include tactile signage, specially designed lab facilities, portable lab stations, a Kurzweil reading machine, and a specially equipped van for inner-city transportation.

Services: Counseling and information services are available, as is tutoring in most subjects. There is a reader service for the blind, and remedial math, reading, and writing.

Campus Safety and Security: Measures include 24-hour foot and vehicle patrol, emergency notification system, self-defense education, and security escort services. There are shuttle buses, emergency telephones, lighted pathways/sidewalks, neighborhood watch programs, and sexual assault prevention booths staffed by city and university police.

Programs of Study: WVU confers B.A., B.S., B.F.A., B.M., B.Md.S., B.S.A.E., B.S.Agr., B.S.B.Ad., B.S.B.S., B.S.C.E., B.S.Ch.E., B.S.Cp.E., B.S.E.E., B.S.F., B.S.C.S., B.S.I.E., B.S.J., B.S.L.A., B.S.M.E., B.S.Min.E., B.S.N., B.S.Pnge., B.S.R., R.B.A. and B.S.W. degrees. Master's and doctoral degrees are also awarded. Bachelor's degrees are awarded in AGRICULTURE (agriculture, agronomy, animal science, fish and game management, fishing and fisheries, forestry and related sciences, horticulture, natural resource management, and plant science), BIOLOGICAL SCIENCE (biology/biological science and nutrition), BUSINESS (accounting, banking and finance, business administration and management, fashion merchandising, marketing and distribution, recreation and leisure services, sports management, and tourism), COMMUNICATIONS AND THE ARTS (advertising, art, broadcasting, communications, dramatic arts, English, journalism, music, public relations, speech/debate/rhetoric, and visual and performing arts), COMPUTER AND PHYSICAL SCIENCE (chemistry, computer science, geology, geoscience, mathematics, physics, and science), EDUCATION (athletic training, English education, environmental education, foreign languages education, mathematics education, and physical education), ENGINEERING AND ENVIRONMENTAL DESIGN (aeronautical engineering, aerospace studies, chemical engineering, civil engineering, computer engineering, electrical/electronics engineering, engineering, environmental science, interior design, landscape architecture/design, mechanical engineering, mining and mineral engineering, petroleum/natural gas engineering, and systems engineering), HEALTH PROFESSIONS (dental hygiene, medical technology, nursing, occupational therapy, pharmacy, physical therapy, speech pathology/audiology, and veterinary science), SOCIAL SCIENCE (anthropology, child care/child and family studies, economics, family/consumer resource management, geography, history, interdisciplinary studies, international studies, liberal arts/general studies, parks and recreation management, philosophy, political science/government, psychology, social work, and sociology). Engineering and mineral resources, psychology, and political science are the strongest academically. Business and economics, engineering and mineral resources, and health sciences have the largest enrollments.

Required: All students are required to take 12 credit hours in each of 3 areas: humanities and fine arts, social and behavioral sciences, and natural sciences and math. The 36 credit hours must include international/minority/gender studies, math, composition, and an advanced course emphasizing writing skills. A minimum 2.0 GPA and at least 128 credit hours are required to graduate.

Special: A co-op program in engineering and cross-registration with schools in the Southern Regional Education Board through the Academic Common Market are possible. Internships, study abroad in 25 countries, a Washington semester, student-designed majors, dual majors in business and foreign languages, and B.A.-B.S. degrees in economics, chemistry, physics, biology, math, psychology, and geology are available. A liberal studies degree, credit by exam, credit for life experience, nondegree study, and pass/fail options are also offered. There are 30 national honor societies, including Phi Beta Kappa, and a freshman honors program.

Faculty/Classroom: 55% of faculty are male; 45% are female. No introductory courses are taught by graduate students.

Admissions: 85% of the 2013-2014 applicants were accepted. The SAT scores for the 2013-2014 freshman class were: Critical Reading--41% below 500, 44% between 500 and 599, 13% between 600 and 699, and 2% between 700 and 800; Math--33% below 500, 45% between 500 and 599, 19% between 600 and 699, and 3% between 700 and 800. The ACT scores were 54% below 21, 20% between 21 and 23, 18% between 24 and 26, 7% between 27 and 28, and 2% above 28.

Requirements: The SAT or ACT is required. West Virginia residents must have a minimim GPA of 2.0 and either a composite ACT score of 19 or a combined SAT score of 910 (critical reading and math). Nonresidents must have a minimum GPA of 2.5 and either 21 on the ACT or 990 on the SAT. A GPA of 2.0 is required. AP and CLEP credits are accepted. Important factors in the admissions decision are leadership record, evidence of special talent, and advanced placement or honors courses.

Procedure: Freshmen are admitted fall, spring, and summer. Entrance exams should be taken by spring of the junior year. There are deferred admissions and rolling admissions plans. Applications should be filed by August 1 for fall entry, along with a $35 fee. Applications are accepted online.

Transfer: 1101 transfer students enrolled in 2012-2013. Students must have a minimum 2.0 GPA in all college work attempted. Those with fewer than 12 transferable credit hours must also meet freshman admission standards. Some programs have different course and higher GPA requirements. 30 of 128 credits required for the bachelor's degree must be completed at WVU.

Visiting: There are regularly scheduled orientations for prospective students, including 2-day sessions with campus tours, placement testing, academic and advisement meetings, parent/student orientation discussions, and transitional meetings. There are guides for informal visits and visitors may sit in on classes. To schedule a visit, contact the Visitors Resource Center at (304) 293-3489.

Financial Aid: In 2013-2014, 72% of all full-time freshmen and 60% of continuing full-time students received some form of financial aid. 42% of all full-time freshmen and 35% of continuing full-time students received need-based aid. The average freshman award was $6,616. Need-based scholarships or need-based grants averaged $5,159; need-based self-help aid (loans and jobs) averaged $4,492; non-need-based athletic scholarships averaged $18,266; and other non-need-based awards and non-need-based scholarships averaged $2,604. The average financial indebtedness of the 2013 graduate was $23,641. The FAFSA and the state aid form are required. The deadline for filing freshman financial aid applications for fall entry is March 1.

International Students: There are 906 international students enrolled. The school actively recruits these students. They must take the TOEFL with a minimum score of 500 on the paper-based TOEFL (PBT) or 61 on the Internet-based version (iBT). They must also take the SAT or ACT, scoring 950.

Computers: All students may access the system 24 hours a day, 7 days a week. There are no time limits and no fees.

Graduates: From July 1, 2012 to June 30, 2013, 4078 bachelor's degrees were awarded. The most popular majors were business (12%), engineering (12%), and health field (9%). 1200 companies recruited on campus in 2012-2013. In an average class, 34% graduate in 4 years or less, 52% graduate in 5 years or less, and 56% graduate in 6 years or less.

Admissions Contact: Stephen Lee, Ex Director of Admissions and Records. E-Mail: *wvuadmissions@arc.wvu.edu* Web: *www.wvu.edu*

WEST VIRGINIA UNIVERSITY INSTITUTE OF TECHNOLOGY B-4

Montgomery, WV 25136 **(304) 442-3164; (888) 554-TECH**

Full-time: 1100 men, 590 women
Part-time: 400 men, 310 women
Graduate: n/av
Year: semesters, summer session
Application Deadline:
Freshman Class: n/av
SAT or ACT: required
Faculty: 120
Ph.D.s: 52%
Student/Faculty: 14 to 1
Tuition: $5808 ($14,616)
Room & Board: $8286

NONCOMPETITIVE

West Virginia University Institute of Technology, part of the Western Virginia University system and founded in 1895, is a public institution offering programs in business and accounting, psychology and sciences, nursing,and engineering and engineering technology. There are 3 undergraduate schools. In addition to regional accreditation, WVU Tech has baccalaureate program accreditation with ABET, ADA, and NLN. The library contains 166,967 volumes, 438,232 microform items, and subscribes to 510 periodicals including electronic. Computerized library services include interlibrary loans and database searching. Special learning facilities include an art gallery. The 112-acre campus is in a small town 28 miles southeast of Charleston. Including any residence halls, there are 15 buildings.

Student Life: 91% of undergraduates are from West Virginia. Others are from 25 states, 24 foreign countries, and Canada. 95% are from public schools. 87% are White. The average age of freshmen is 19; all undergraduates, 24. 35% do not continue beyond their first year; 40% remain to graduate.

Housing: 500 students can be accommodated in college housing, which includes single-sex and coed dorms. quiet floors. On-campus housing is guaranteed for all 4 years, is available on a first-come, and first-served basis. 69% of students commute. Alcohol is not permitted. All students may keep cars.

Activities: 10% of men belong to 5 national fraternities; 8% of women belong to 2 national sororities. There are 42 groups on campus, including art, cheerleading, computers, drama, ethnic, international, newspaper, photography, political, professional, religious, social, social service, and student government. Popular campus events include Comedy and Film Series, Black History Month and Greek Week.

Sports: There are 5 intercollegiate sports for men and 4 for women, and 8 intramural sports for men and 8 for women. Facilities include a gym, weight room, tennis courts, a student union, a football field and 3000-seat stadium, an Olympic-size swimming pool, game rooms, and a fitness center.

Disabled Students: 60% of the campus is accessible. Facilities include wheelchair ramps, elevators, special parking, specially equipped restrooms, special class scheduling, and lowered drinking fountains.

Services: Counseling and information services are available, as is tutoring in most subjects. There is remedial math, reading, and writing.

Campus Safety and Security: Measures include 24-hour foot and vehicle patrol, self-defense education, and security escort services. There are lighted pathways/sidewalks.

Programs of Study: WVU Tech confers B.A., B.S., B.E.T., B.M.E.T., B.S.C.E., B.S.E. and B.S.E.E. degrees. Bachelor's degrees are awarded in BIOLOGICAL SCIENCE (biology/biological science), BUSINESS (accounting and business administration and management), COMPUTER AND PHYSICAL SCIENCE (chemistry, computer programming, computer science, and physics), ENGINEERING AND ENVIRONMENTAL DESIGN (chemical engineering, civil engineering, electrical/electronics engineering, electrical/electronics engineering technology, engineering technology, industrial administration/management, industrial engineering technology, and mechanical engineering), HEALTH PROFESSIONS (health care administration and nursing), SOCIAL SCIENCE (history and public administration). Engineering is the strongest academically. Nursing has the largest enrollment.

Required: Core curriculum requirements include 8 hours of lab science, 6 to 12 each of humanities and social science, 6 each of English and math/computer science, and 2 of phys ed and health. Other requirements vary according to the degree sought. To graduate, students must complete 128 semester hours with a minimum 2.0 GPA overall and in the major.

Special: An extensive co-op program is offered in all areas as well as a number of internships in public service and industrial relations. Credit for armed service experience and credit by departmental exam are available.

Faculty/Classroom: 70% of faculty are male; 30% are female. All teach undergraduates, and 10% do research. No introductory courses are taught by graduate students. The average class size in an introductory lecture is 30; in a laboratory is 15; and in a regular course is 20.

Admissions: 11 freshmen graduated first in their class.

Requirements: The SAT or ACT is required with a minimum composite score of 870 on the SAT or 18 on the ACT (higher for engineering and health majors). Applicants should be graduates from an accredited secondary school or have qualifying scores on the GED. A GPA of 2.0 is required. AP and CLEP credits are accepted.

Procedure: Freshmen are admitted to all sessions. Entrance exams should be taken in sufficient time for the scores to reach the Institute by the application deadline. There are early admissions and rolling admissions plans. Applications should be filed by December 15 for spring entry; May 1 for summer entry.

Transfer: 192 transfer students enrolled in 2012-2013. Minimum of 30 credit hours with a gpa of 2.0 30 of 128 credits required for the bachelor's degree must be completed at WVU Tech.

Visiting: There are regularly scheduled orientations for prospective students. There are guides for informal visits, visitors may sit in on classes, and stay overnight. To schedule a visit, contact the Admissions Office at tech-admissions@mail.wvu.edu.

Financial Aid: In 2013-2014, 86% of all full-time freshmen and 54% of continuing full-time students received some form of financial aid. 49% of all full-time freshmen and 45% of continuing full-time students received need-based aid. The average freshman award was $2,480.. 15% of undergraduate students work part-time. Average annual earnings from campus work are $1000. The average financial indebtedness of the 2013 graduate was $13,000. WVU Tech is a member of CSS. The FAFSA is required. The priority date for freshman financial aid applications for fall entry is March 1.

International Students: There are 74 international students enrolled. The school actively recruits these students. They must take the TOEFL with a minimum score of 62 on the Internet-based version (iBT). They must also take the SAT or ACT.

Computers: All students may access the system 24 hours a day. There are no time limits and no fees.

Graduates: From July 1, 2012 to June 30, 2013, 261 bachelor's degrees were awarded. The most popular majors were engineering (42%), business (21%), and health (10%). 68 companies recruited on campus in 2012-2013. In an average class, 2% graduate in 3 years or less, 30% graduate in 4 years or less, 10% graduate in 5 years or less, and 2% graduate in 6 years or less.

Admissions Contact: Reeta Piirala-Skoglund, Director of Enrollment. E-Mail: *tech-admissions@mail.wvu.edu* Web: *www.wvutech.edu*

WEST VIRGINIA WESLEYAN COLLEGE C-3

Buckhannon, WV 26201 **(304) 473-8510**
(800) 722-9933; (304) 473-8108

Full-time: 600 men, 700 women
Part-time: 15 men, 10 women
Graduate: 20 men, 30 women
Year: semesters, summer session
Application Deadline: see profile
Freshman Class: n/av
SAT or ACT: required
Faculty: 171; IIB, --$
Ph.D.s: 77%
Student/Faculty: 13 to 1
Tuition: $23,870
Room & Board: $7,390

COMPETITIVE

West Virginia Wesleyan College, founded in 1890, is an independent liberal and applied arts college affiliated with the United Methodist Church. The figures in the above capsule and this profile are approximate. In addition to regional accreditation, WVWC has baccalaureate program accreditation with NCATE and NLN. The library contains 116,240 volumes, 39,119 microform items, and 6322 audio/video tapes/CDs/DVDs, and subscribes to 14,126 periodicals including electronic. Computerized library services include interlibrary loans, database searching, Internet access, and laptop Internet portals. Special learning facilities include a learning resource center, art gallery, planetarium, and radio station. The 80-acre campus is in a small town in the Appalachian foothills, 135 miles south of Pittsburgh, Pennsylvania. Including any residence halls, there are 23 buildings.

Student Life: 53% of undergraduates are from West Virginia. Others are from 37 states, 12 foreign countries, and Canada. 85% are from public schools. 88% are white. 53% are Protestant; 20% Catholic. The average age of freshmen is 18; all undergraduates, 21.

Housing: 1275 students can be accommodated in college housing, which includes single-sex and coed dorms and on-campus apartments. In addition, there are honors houses, quiet study living areas and substance-free small group living units. On-campus housing is guaranteed for all 4 years. 83% of students live on campus; of those, 65% remain on campus on weekends. Alcohol is not permitted. All students may keep cars.

Activities: 25% of men belong to 5 national fraternities; 25% of women belong to 5 national sororities. There are 75 groups on campus, including art, band, cheerleading, choir, chorale, chorus, communications, computers, dance, drama, ethnic, forensics, honors, international, jazz band, literary magazine, musical theater, newspaper, political, professional, radio and TV, religious, social, social service, student government, and yearbook. Popular campus events include Founders Day, Festivals of Lessons and Carols, and Spring Sing.

Sports: There are 9 intercollegiate sports for men and 8 for women, and

9 intramural sports for men and 8 for women. Facilities include baseball and football fields with seating for 3500, as well as a phys ed center with a 3800-seat intercollegiate basketball court, 2 intramural practice courts, 4 handball courts, an auxiliary gym, indoor tennis courts, volleyball courts, golf and wrestling practice areas, sauna baths, a dance studio, and gymnastics and weight rooms. A state park is near the campus.

Disabled Students: 75% of the campus is accessible. Facilities include wheelchair ramps, elevators, special parking, specially equipped rest rooms, special class scheduling, and lowered drinking fountains.

Services: Counseling and information services are available, as is tutoring in every subject. There is a reader service for the blind, and remedial math, reading, and writing.

Campus Safety and Security: Measures include 24-hour foot and vehicle patrol, self-defense education, and security escort services. There are emergency telephones, lighted pathways/sidewalks, rape awareness educational programs, and appropriate training for residence hall staff.

Programs of Study: WVWC confers B.A., B.S., B.M.E., and B.S.N. degrees. Master's degrees are also awarded. Bachelor's degrees are awarded in BIOLOGICAL SCIENCE (biology/biological science and nutrition), BUSINESS (accounting, business administration and management, and marketing/retailing/merchandising), COMMUNICATIONS AND THE ARTS (dramatic arts, English, music, public relations, and speech/debate/rhetoric), COMPUTER AND PHYSICAL SCIENCE (chemistry, computer science, mathematics, and physics), EDUCATION (art education, elementary education, music education, physical education, and secondary education), ENGINEERING AND ENVIRONMENTAL DESIGN (engineering physics), HEALTH PROFESSIONS (nursing), SOCIAL SCIENCE (economics, history, international studies, philosophy, political science/government, psychology, religion, religious education, social science, and sociology). Physical and natural sciences and accounting are the strongest academically. Business, biology, and education have the largest enrollments.

Required: To graduate, students must earn 120 semester hours with a minimum GPA of 2.0; 24 to 51 hours must be in the major, 48 to 53 in general studies. Required disciplines are cultural studies, natural science and math, social sciences, health and phys ed, religion, philosophy, humanities and fine arts, and communications.

Special: WVWC offers cross-registration with the Mountain State Association of Colleges. Students may participate in a wide variety of internships, including a Washington center internship and work-study and study-abroad programs; there are exchange agreements in Korea, the People's Republic of China, Norway, and Bulgaria. Nondegree and pass/fail study, dual, student-designed, and contract majors, and credit for life, military, and work experience are available. A 3-2 engineering degree offered with West Virginia University and the University of Virginia. There is 1 national honor society and a freshman honors program.

Faculty/Classroom: 79% of faculty are male; 21% are female. All teach undergraduates. No introductory courses are taught by graduate students. The average class size in an introductory lecture is 24; in a laboratory is 12; and in a regular course is 21.

Requirements: The SAT or ACT is required. A satisfactory score is needed on the SAT or 18 on the ACT. Applicants must be high school graduates, or hold a GED. Students should have earned 26 academic credits, consisting of 4 in English, 3 each in math, science, and academic electives, and 2 each in foreign language, lab science, and social studies, as well as a total of 7 academic credits in fine arts, technology education, health, and phys ed. An essay and an interview are recommended. A GPA of 2.2 is required. AP and CLEP credits are accepted. Important factors in the admissions decision are extracurricular activities record, recommendations by school officials, and leadership record.

Procedure: Freshmen are admitted fall and spring. Entrance exams should be taken in fall of the senior year or spring/summer of the junior year. There are early decision, deferred admissions, and rolling admissions plans. Check with the school for current application deadlines and fees. Applications are accepted online.

Transfer: Transfer applicants must supply a high school transcript if their GPA for college work is less than 2.5. An associate degree and an interview are recommended. 30 of 120 credits required for the bachelor's degree must be completed at WVWC.

Visiting: There are regularly scheduled orientations for prospective students. There are guides for informal visits; visitors may sit in on classes and stay overnight. To schedule a visit, contact the Director of Admission.

Financial Aid: The FAFSA is required. Check with the school for current application deadlines.

International Students: The school actively recruits these students. They must take the TOEFL. They must also take the SAT or ACT if they are seeking scholarships.

Computers: Wireless access is available. All students may access the system. There are no time limits and no fees. All students are required to have a personal computer.

Admissions Contact: Director of Admission. A campus DVD is available. E-Mail: *admissions@wvwc.edu* Web: *www.wvwc.edu*

WHEELING JESUIT UNIVERSITY — C-1

Wheeling, WV 26003 — (304) 243-2359; (800) 624-6992; (304) 243-2397

Full-time: 424 men, 505 women — **Faculty:** 82; IIA, --$
Part-time: 64 men, 180 women — **Ph.D.s:** 69%
Graduate: 109 men, 281 women — **Student/Faculty:** 11 to 1
Year: semesters, summer session — **Tuition:** $25,640
Application Deadline: open — **Room & Board:** $9028
Freshman Class: 1401 applied, 880 accepted, 279 enrolled
SAT CR/M/W: 500/510/480 — **ACT:** 22 — **COMPETITIVE**

Wheeling Jesuit University, founded in 1954, is an independent college affiliated with the Society of Jesus, offering undergraduate programs in the liberal arts and sciences, nursing, allied health, business, and education, and graduate programs in business administration and organizational leadership, nursing, education, and physical therapy. There is 1 undergraduate school and 3 graduate schools. In addition to regional accreditation, Wheeling Jesuit has baccalaureate program accreditation with ACBSP and TEAC. The library contains 159,511 volumes, 135,030 microform items, and 45,450 audio/video tapes/CDs/DVDs, and subscribes to 232 periodicals including electronic. Computerized library services include interlibrary loans, database searching, Internet access, and Wi-Fi capability. Special learning facilities include a radio station, NASA Challenger Learning Center, Center for Educational Technologies. The 65-acre campus is in a suburban area 60 miles southwest of Pittsburgh. Including any residence halls, there are 16 buildings.

Student Life: 68% of undergraduates are from out of state, mostly the Middle Atlantic. Students are from 28 states, 16 foreign countries, and Canada. 68% are from public schools. 67% are White; 22% race unknown. 52% claim no religious affiliation; 32% Catholic; 12% Protestant. The average age of freshmen is 18; all undergraduates, 22. 28% do not continue beyond their first year; 60% remain to graduate.

Housing: 979 students can be accommodated in college housing, which includes single-sex and coed dorms, off-campus apartments, and married student housing. In addition, there are honors houses and special-interest houses. On-campus housing is guaranteed for all 4 years. 84% of students live on campus; of those, 80% remain on campus on weekends. All students may keep cars.

Activities: There are no fraternities or sororities. There are 26 groups on campus, including band, cheerleading, choir, chorale, chorus, communications, computers, dance, drama, environmental, ethnic, film, honors, international, literary magazine, musical theater, newspaper, pep band, political, professional, radio and TV, religious, social, social service, student government, and yearbook. Popular campus events include Culture Fest, Last Blast Carnival and Family Weekend.

Sports: There are 10 intercollegiate sports for men and 9 for women, and 8 intramural sports for men and 8 for women. Facilities include The Alma Grace McDonough Health and Recreation Center is an 107,000 square foot facility that houses a performance gymnasium with seating for 2200, a practice gymnasium, two raquetball courts, an indoor natatorium with a regulation pool, an indoor running/walking track, weight room, and a fully equipped fitness center. The Outdoor Athletic Complex includes soccer fields, two lighted tennis courts, a softball field, an 8-lane, 400m track, and a throwing area for field events. The complex features a 1400 seat grandstand, pressbox, heated locker rooms, and lighting system.

Disabled Students: 85% of the campus is accessible. Facilities include wheelchair ramps, elevators, special parking, specially equipped restrooms, lowered drinking fountains, lowered telephones, and special housing.

Services: Counseling and information services are available, as is tutoring in most subjects. There is a reader service for the blind, and remedial math, reading, and writing.

Campus Safety and Security: Measures include 24-hour foot and vehicle patrol, emergency notification system, self-defense education, and security escort services. There are lighted pathways/sidewalks and controlled access to dorms/residences.

Programs of Study: Wheeling Jesuit confers B.A., B.S. and B.S.N. degrees. Master's and doctoral degrees are also awarded. Bachelor's degrees are awarded in AGRICULTURE (environmental studies), BIOLOGICAL SCIENCE (biology/biological science), BUSINESS (accounting, business administration and management, management science, marketing management, organizational leadership and management, and sports management), COMMUNICATIONS AND THE ARTS (American literature, communications, communication rhetoric/communication, creative writing, digital communications, English, English literature, French, literature, English and Professional Communication, romance languages and literature, and Spanish), COMPUTER AND PHYSICAL SCIENCE (applied physics, chemistry, computer science, information sciences and systems, mathematics, and physics), EDUCATION (athletic training, early childhood education, education, elementary education, English education, foreign languages education, mathematics education, middle school education, science education, secondary education, social studies education, and special education), ENGINEERING AND ENVIRONMENTAL DESIGN (engineering, environmental science, and preengineering), HEALTH PROFESSIONS (health science, nuclear medical technology, nursing, predentistry, premedicine, preoptometry, preosteopathy, prepharmacy, prephysical therapy, preveterinary science, and respiratory therapy), SOCIAL SCIENCE (criminal justice, criminology, ethics, politics, and social policy, (Social Science) Global Studies, history, international studies, liberal arts/ general studies, philosophy, philosophy and religion, political science/ government, prelaw, psychology, religion, and theological studies). Biology, chemistry and English literature are the strongest academically. Business administration, nursing and psychology have the largest enrollments.

Required: To graduate, students must complete 120 credit hours with a GPA of no less than 2.0. The core curriculum consists of 52 credits in English composition, fine arts, mathematics, modern languages, literature, history, social science, global perspectives, natural science, philosophy, theology, and 1 course in ethics or Christian morality, as well as particpation in the first year program.

Special: The university offers internships with many businesses and institutions as well as a Washington semester and study abroad. Students may obtain a 3-2 engineering degree with Case Western Reserve University or West Virginia University. Accelerated programs are available in nursing and education. The school permits dual and student-designed majors. There are 20 national honor societies, a freshman honors program, and 15 departmental honors programs.

Faculty/Classroom: 53% of faculty are male; 47% are female. 88% teach undergraduates, 80% do research, and 70% do both. No introductory courses are taught by graduate students. The average class size in an introductory lecture is 15; in a laboratory is 10; and in a regular course is 15.

Admissions: 63% of the 2013-2014 applicants were accepted. The SAT scores for the 2013-2014 freshman class were: Critical Reading 41% below 500, 46% between 500 and 599, and 13% between 600 and 699; Math--35% below 500, 52% between 500 and 599, 10% between 600 and 699, and 2% between 700 and 800; Writing--57% below 500, 38% between 500 and 599, and 5% between 600 and 699. The ACT scores were 31% below 21, 31% between 21 and 23, 23% between 24 and 26, 9% between 27 and 28, and 6% above 28. 38% of the current freshmen were in the top fifth of their class; 65% were in the top two fifths.

Requirements: The SAT or ACT is required. Students must submit official results of either the SAT or ACT. In addition, applicants must be high school graduates or hold a GED. Letters of recommendation and a list of extracurricular activities are also encouraged. Students should have earned 15 academic credits consisting of 4 in English, 2 each in math and history or social science, 1 in lab science (2 are recommended for science majors), and 6 in academic electives, with a foreign language recommended. Exceptions are made, especially if the high school GPA is 3.0 or better. Students entering programs in the natural sciences should have taken 1 course each of chemistry and biology. Applicants interested in preparing for future study in the physical therapy doctorate program should have a minimum of 3 years of lab science (including physics). A GPA of 3.0 is required. AP and CLEP credits are accepted. Important factors in the admissions decision are leadership record, recommendations by school officials, and extracurricular activities record.

Procedure: Freshmen are admitted to all sessions. There are deferred admissions and rolling admissions plans. Application deadlines are open. Application fee is $25. Notification is sent on a rolling basis. Applications are accepted online.

Transfer: 42 transfer students enrolled in 2012-2013. Applicants must have a cummulative college GPA of 2.3 or higher and submit official transcripts of all previous college work. Candidates may be asked to submit an official high school transcript. Transfer credit is only awarded for course work completed at accredited institutions in which a student earned a grade of C or higher. Grades of C- are not accepted. For those students who have earned an associate's degree from a regionally accredited institution, the University will accept that associate's degree (and all related credits) in total for transfer. 30 of 120 credits required for the bachelor's degree must be completed at Wheeling Jesuit.

Visiting: There are regularly scheduled orientations for prospective students, including meetings with faculty, discussions by students and parents, meals, and campus tours. There are guides for informal visits, visitors may sit in on classes, and stay overnight. To schedule a visit, contact the Campus Visit Coordinator at (304) 243-2318.

Financial Aid: In 2013-2014, 97% of all full-time freshmen and 98% of continuing full-time students received some form of financial aid. 54% of all full-time freshmen and 53% of continuing full-time students received need-based aid. The average freshman award was $16,595. Need-based scholarships or need-based grants averaged $6,143 ($11,000 maximum); need-based self-help aid (loans and jobs) averaged $5,470 ($9,700 maximum); non-need-based athletic scholarships averaged $7,006 ($23,530 maximum); and other non-need-based awards and non-need-based scholarships averaged $10,040 ($23,530 maximum). 43% of undergraduate students work part-time. Average annual earnings from campus work are $1856. The average financial indebtedness of the 2013 graduate was $30,516. The FAFSA is required. The priority date for freshman financial aid applications for fall entry is February 15.

International Students: There are 36 international students enrolled. The school actively recruits these students. They must take the TOEFL with a minimum score of 550 on the paper-based TOEFL (PBT) or 80 on the Internet-based version (iBT).

Computers: All students may access the system continuously. There are no time limits and no fees.

Graduates: From July 1, 2012 to June 30, 2013, 192 bachelor's degrees were awarded. The most popular majors were nursing (39%), business administration (20%), and psychology (5%). 60 companies recruited on campus in 2012-2013. In an average class, 49% graduate in 4 years or less, 58% graduate in 5 years or less, and 60% graduate in 6 years or less. Of the 2012 graduating class, 15% were enrolled in graduate school within 6 months of graduation, and 60% were employed.

Admissions Contact: Larry Vallar, Vice President for Enrollment Management. E-Mail: *admiss@wju.edu* Web: *www.wju.edu*

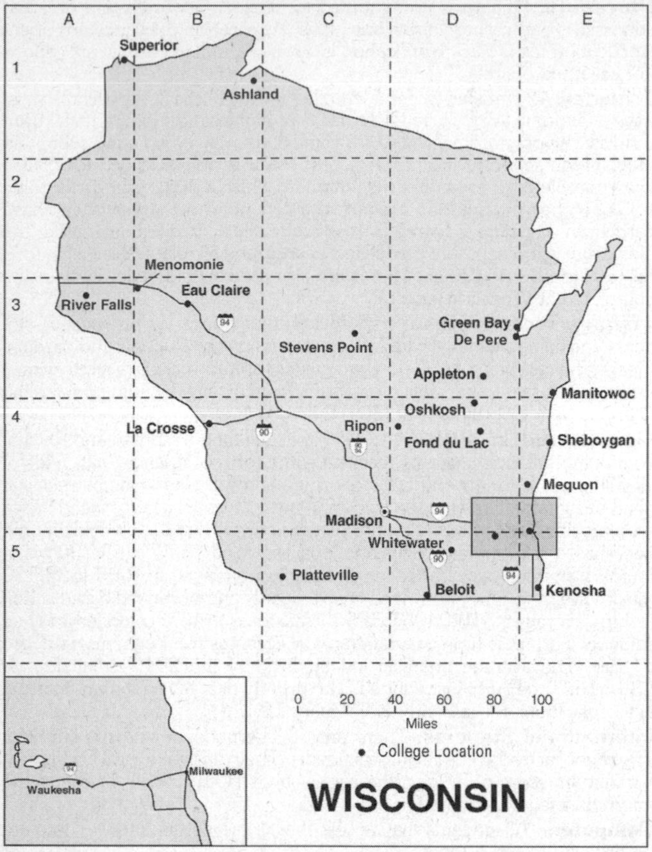

ALVERNO COLLEGE E-4

Milwaukee, WI 53234 (414) 382-6108
(800) 933-3401; (414) 382-6055

Full-time: 1360 women
Part-time: 3 men, 499 women
Graduate: 70 men, 604 women
Year: semesters, summer session
Application Deadline: August 1
Freshman Class: 582 applied, 459 accepted, 208 enrolled
ACT: 19

Faculty: 112; IIB, --$
Ph.D.s: 93%
Student/Faculty: 12 to 1
Tuition: $23,231
Room & Board: $7252

LESS COMPETITIVE

Alverno College is a four-year, liberal arts, independent, Catholic college for women located in Milwaukee, Wisconsin. The school was founded in 1887 by the School Sisters of St. Francis and has been developed in the Franciscan traditions of service, citizenship, and respect for the individual, her background and goals, Alverno has created a model of teaching that builds on the diversity of the students and their experiences. There are 4 undergraduate schools and 5 graduate schools. In addition to regional accreditation, Alverno has baccalaureate program accreditation with NASM and NCATE. The library contains 191,248 volumes, 246,730 microform items, 4,747 audio/video tapes/CDs/DVDs, and subscribes to 49,710 periodicals including electronic. Computerized library services include interlibrary loans, database searching, Internet access, and Wi-Fi capability. Special learning facilities include an art gallery, radio station, art and culture gallery, nursing skills lab, student-centered multimedia production facility, computer center, science labs, theater venue, and conferencing center. The 46-acre campus is in a small town on the southwest edge of Milwaukee. Including any residence halls, there are 11 buildings.

Student Life: 96% of undergraduates are from Wisconsin. Others are from 8 states, 12 foreign countries, and Canada. 58% are White; 17% African American; 15% Hispanic. 30% are Catholic; 28% claim no religious affiliation; 16% Protestant. The average age of freshmen is 19; all undergraduates, 25. 28% do not continue beyond their first year; 39% remain to graduate.

Housing: 220 students can be accommodated in college housing, which includes single-sex dorms. On-campus housing is guaranteed for all 4 years. 89% of students commute. All students may keep cars.

Activities: There are no fraternities; 1% of women belong to 4 national sororities. There are 37 groups on campus, including CIRCLE K, Dance Team, PSE, art, choir, chorus, dance, drama, environmental, ethnic, honors, international, literary magazine, newspaper, political, professional, radio and TV, religious, SIFE, social, social service, and student government. Popular campus events include Career Day, Fine Arts Performances and Community Day.

Sports: There are 7 intercollegiate sports for women, and 4 intramural sports for women. Facilities include NCAA regulation soccer field with World Cup-style goals and scoreboard, NCAA regulation softball field with 190' fence, a gym with regulation intercollegiate volleyball and basketball courts, a fitness center with state-of-the-art free motion fitness and cardio equipment, an outdoor volleyball court, a multipurpose room for dancing, aerobics, and cardio kickboxing.

Disabled Students: 95% of the campus is accessible. Facilities include wheelchair ramps, elevators, special parking, specially equipped restrooms, lowered drinking fountains, lowered telephones.

Services: Counseling and information services are available, as is tutoring in most subjects, academic assistance: course-based study groups, communication (writing, reading, speaking) center, math resource center, ESL instruction and support, objective test taking prep seminars, and support services and accommodations for students with disabilities. There is remedial math, reading, and writing.

Campus Safety and Security: Measures include 24-hour foot and vehicle patrol, emergency notification system, and security escort services. There are emergency telephones, lighted pathways/sidewalks, controlled access to dorms/residences, electronically operated and video-surveillanced dorm entrances, walkways, buildings; a security staff equipped with 2-way radios, pagers, and cell phones; and motion detector and audible alarms in buildings.

Programs of Study: Alverno confers B.A., B.M., B.S., B.S.Ed. and B.S.N. degrees. Associate and master's degrees are also awarded. Bachelor's degrees are awarded in BIOLOGICAL SCIENCE (biology/biological science and molecular biology), BUSINESS (accounting, business administration and management, international business management, management information systems, and marketing management), COMMUNICATIONS AND THE ARTS (art, communications, communications technology, English, media arts, and music), COMPUTER AND PHYSICAL SCIENCE (chemistry, mathematics, and science), EDUCATION (art education, elementary education, middle school education, science education, and secondary education), ENGINEERING AND ENVIRONMENTAL DESIGN (computer technology and environmental science), HEALTH PROFESSIONS (art therapy, music therapy, and nursing), SOCIAL SCIENCE (community services, history, international relations, philosophy, political science/government, psychology, religion, sociology, and women's studies). Nursing, elementary education, and psychology have the largest enrollments.

Required: Students must complete a learning program that integrates accomplishment in required areas of knowledge, with the achievement of required competence levels in the following eight core abilities: communication, analysis, problem solving, valuing in decision-making, social interaction, developing a global perspective, effective citizenship, and aesthetic engagement. This is accomplished through general education courses in history, English, philosophy, religious studies, arts, sciences, math, psychology, and social science; through completion of a major and minor area of study; and completion of at least one required internship or practice.

Special: Alverno offers internships, dual majors, nondegree study, and pre-professional programs in dentistry, law, medicine, pharmacy, physician's assistant, and veterinary medicine. Alverno offers study abroad in more than 15 countries and also offers courses that include an international travel component. Alverno can arrange other programs through a worldwide consortium of facilities. The school's interactive curriculum is outcome-oriented and performance-based; letter grades are not assigned. There is 1 national honor society.

Faculty/Classroom: 19% of faculty are male; 81% are female. All teach and do research. No introductory courses are taught by graduate students. The average class size in a regular course is 20.

Admissions: The ACT scores were 66% below 21, 23% between 21 and 23, 7% between 24 and 26, 3% between 27 and 28, and 1% above 28.

Requirements: The ACT is required. Applicants must be graduates of an accredited secondary school, having completed 17 academic credits with college preparatory courses. The GED is accepted. A GPA of 2.4 is required. AP and CLEP credits are accepted.

Procedure: Freshmen are admitted fall and spring. Entrance exams should be taken as early as possible. There are deferred admissions and rolling admissions plans. Application deadlines are open. Notification is sent on a rolling basis. Applications are accepted online. Application fees are waived if application is completed online.

Transfer: 298 transfer students enrolled in 2012-2013. Applicants

should have a minimum college GPA of 2.0 and must submit transcripts from all schools previously attended.

Visiting: There are regularly scheduled orientations for prospective students, consisting of open houses and overnight events that include tours of the campus, classroom visits, and meetings with faculty and current students. There are guides for informal visits, visitors may sit in on classes, and stay overnight. To schedule a visit, contact the Admissions Office at admissions@alverno.edu.

Financial Aid: In 2013-2014, 100% of all full-time freshmen and 99% of continuing full time students received some form of financial aid. 92% of all full-time freshmen and 92% of continuing full-time students received need-based aid. The average freshman award was $20,255. Need-based scholarships or need-based grants averaged $14,377; need-based self-help aid (loans and jobs) averaged $2,598; other non-need-based awards and non-need-based scholarships averaged $3,086; and $1,852 from other forms of aid. 24% of undergraduate students work part-time. Average annual earnings from campus work are $3600. The average financial indebtedness of the 2013 graduate was $36,021. The FAFSA and the college's own financial statement are required. The priority date for freshman financial aid applications for fall entry is March 15.

International Students: There are 12 international students enrolled. The school actively recruits these students. They must take the TOEFL with a minimum score of 520 on the paper-based TOEFL (PBT) or 68 on the Internet-based version (iBT).

Computers: All students may access the system. There are no time limits and no fees.

Graduates: From July 1, 2012 to June 30, 2013, 341 bachelor's degrees were awarded. The most popular majors were nursing (44%), business management (13%), and elementary education (6%). 78 companies recruited on campus in 2012-2013. In an average class, 30% graduate in 5 years or less and 39% graduate in 6 years or less. Of the 2012 graduating class, 13% were enrolled in graduate school within 6 months of graduation, and 94% were employed.

Admissions Contact: Christy Stone, Director of Admissions. E Mail: *admissions@alverno.edu* Web: *www.alverno.edu*

BELOIT COLLEGE D-5

Beloit, WI 53511 (608) 363-2500
(800) 9-BELOIT; (608) 363-2075

Full-time: 515 men, 739 women	**Faculty:** 115; IIB, -$
Part-time: 18 men, 34 women	**Ph.D.s:** 98%
Graduate: n/av	**Student/Faculty:** 11 to 1
Year: semesters, summer session	**Tuition:** $42,500
Application Deadline: January 15	**Room & Board:** $7470
Freshman Class: 2253 applied, 1524 accepted, 299 enrolled	
SAT CR/M: 630/600 **ACT:** 27	**HIGHLY COMPETITIVE**

Beloit College, founded in 1846, is a private liberal arts institution. The library contains 505,586 volumes, 7,314 microform items, 9,301 audio/video tapes/CDs/DVDs, and subscribes to 1,052 periodicals including electronic. Computerized library services include interlibrary loans, database searching, and Internet access. Special learning facilities include an art gallery, natural history museum, planetarium, radio station, TV station, a comprehensive language lab, an observatory, and a theater complex. The 44-acre campus is in a small town 50 miles south of Madison, Wisconsin, 90 miles northwest of Chicago. Including any residence halls, there are 70 buildings.

Student Life: 80% of undergraduates are from out of state, mostly the Mid-West. Students are from 49 states, 34 foreign countries, and Canada. 76% are from public schools. 71% are White. The average age of freshmen is 18; all undergraduates, 20. 9% do not continue beyond their first year; 76% remain to graduate.

Housing: 1180 students can be accommodated in college housing, which includes single-sex and coed dorms and on-campus apartments. In addition, there are language houses, special-interest houses, fraternity houses, and sorority houses. On-campus housing is guaranteed for all 4 years. 93% of students live on campus; of those, 95% remain on campus on weekends. All students may keep cars.

Activities: 8% of men belong to 3 national fraternities; 6% of women belong to 2 local and 1 national sororities. There are 95 groups on campus, including science fiction and fantasy, student radio, art, band, chess, choir, chorus, computers, dance, drama, entrepreneurial, environmental, ethnic, film, gay, honors, international, jazz band, literary magazine, musical theater, newspaper, orchestra, pep band, photography, political, professional, radio and TV, religious, social, social service, student government, and symphony. Popular campus events include Great Lecture Series, Advising Day, Folk and Blues Weekend and Spring Day.

Sports: There are 10 intercollegiate sports for men and 9 for women, and 7 intramural sports for men and 5 for women. Facilities include a sports center that houses a 2,250-seat arena for basketball and volleyball, racquetball/handball courts, a fitness center, and a natatorium; a field house that contains a running track, an indoor soccer area, a batting/pitching cage, and space for indoor tennis; a 3,500-seat stadium hosting football, soccer, lacrosse, and track and field; outdoor playing fields; a dance studio; and a new tennis court complex. There are facilities nearby for sailing, ice skating, and other recreation.

Disabled Students: 35% of the campus is accessible. Facilities include wheelchair ramps, elevators, special parking, specially equipped restrooms, special class scheduling, lowered drinking fountains, and lowered telephones.

Services: Counseling and information services are available, as is tutoring in most subjects, most introductory and many advanced courses (as available and requested).

Campus Safety and Security: Measures include 24-hour foot and vehicle patrol, emergency notification system, and security escort services. There are emergency telephones, lighted pathways/sidewalks, and controlled access to dorms/residences.

Programs of Study: Beloit confers B.A., and B.S. degrees. Bachelor's degrees are awarded in AGRICULTURE (agriculture), BIOLOGICAL SCIENCE (biochemistry, biology/biological science, cell biology, ecology, and environmental biology), BUSINESS (business administration and management), COMMUNICATIONS AND THE ARTS (art history and appreciation, classical languages, comparative literature, creative writing, dramatic arts, East Asian languages and literature, English, French, German, literature, modern language, music, Russian, Spanish, speech/debate/rhetoric, and studio art), COMPUTER AND PHYSICAL SCIENCE (applied physics, chemistry, computer science, environmental geology, geology, mathematics, and physics), EDUCATION (art education and education), ENGINEERING AND ENVIRONMENTAL DESIGN (environmental science), HEALTH PROFESSIONS (predentistry, premedicine, and preveterinary science), SOCIAL SCIENCE (anthropology, area studies, classical/ancient civilization, economics, history, interdisciplinary studies, international relations, philosophy, political science/government, prelaw, psychology, religion, sociology, and women's studies). Anthropology, creative writing, and sociology are the strongest academically. Anthropology, psychology, and international relations have the largest enrollments.

Required: To graduate, students must complete 31 units, including 8 to 15 in the major, with a minimum GPA of 2.0. Students must complete 3 writing designated courses, 1 quantitative reasoning designated course, and 1 intercultural literacy designated course. Breadth requirements include 1 courses in each of the following domains: Conceptual and Foundational Systems, Artistic and Creative Practices, Social Analysis of Human Behavior, Scientific Inquiry into the Physical and Biological Universe, and Textual Cultures and Analysis. Students are also expected to complete a liberal arts in practice experience that integrates learning from inside and outside the classroom, typically in the junior year, and a capstone experience, typically in the senior year.

Special: Beloit offers cross-registration with the University of Wisconsin/Madison, internships, study abroad in more than 38 countries, and a Washington semester. Dual majors, student-designed and interdisciplinary majors, and nondegree study are available. A 3-2 engineering degree is offered with 9 institutions, and co-op programs are available in social services, forestry and environmental management, engineering, and business administration. An intensive summer language program is offered in Russian, Arabic, Japanese, and Chinese. There are 6 national honor societies, including Phi Beta Kappa.

Faculty/Classroom: 49% of faculty are male; 51% are female. All teach and do research. No introductory courses are taught by graduate students. The average class size in an introductory lecture is 15; in a laboratory is 15; and in a regular course is 15.

Admissions: 68% of the 2013-2014 applicants were accepted. The SAT scores for the 2013-2014 freshman class were: Critical Reading--14% below 500, 30% between 500 and 599, 28% between 600 and 699, and 29% between 700 and 800; Math--14% below 500, 36% between 500 and 599, 36% between 600 and 699, and 15% between 700 and 800. The ACT scores were 2% below 21, 22% between 21 and 23, 47% between 27 and 28, and 30% above 28. 49% of the current freshmen were in the top fifth of their class; 69% were in the top two fifths. There were 2 National Merit finalists.

Requirements: The SAT or ACT is required. In addition, Beloit does not use the SAT writing test for either admissions or placement decisions. Applicants must be graduates of an accredited secondary school or homeschool program, with 4 years of English, 3 each of math, science, and history/social sciences, and 2 of foreign language. The GED is accepted. An essay and a letter of recommendation are required, and an interview is strongly recommended. AP and CLEP credits are accepted. Important factors in the admissions decision are advanced placement or honors courses, recommendations by school officials, and leadership record.

Procedure: Freshmen are admitted fall and spring. Entrance exams should be taken before the end of the first semester of the senior year. There are early decision, early admissions, deferred admissions, and rolling admissions plans. Early decision applications should be filed by November 30; regular applications, by January 15 for fall entry. Notification of early decision is sent November 30; regular decision, March 15. 30 applicants were on the 2013 waiting list; 2 were admitted. Applications are accepted online.

Transfer: 23 transfer students enrolled in 2012-2013. Applicants must have a minimum GPA of 2.5 and submit official transcripts of all college work completed. The SAT or the ACT is required, and an interview is recommended. A letter of recommendation from a professor at a current/previous institution is also required. 16 of 31 credits required for the bachelor's degree must be completed at Beloit.

Visiting: There are regularly scheduled orientations for prospective students, including an interview, a tour, class visits, and meetings with professors. Enrolled students serve as tour guides and hosts for overnight stays. There are guides for informal visits, visitors may sit in on classes, and stay overnight. To schedule a visit, contact the Office of Admissions.

Financial Aid: In 2013-2014, 96% of all full-time freshmen and 93% of continuing full-time students received some form of financial aid. 71% of all full-time freshmen and 67% of continuing full-time students received need-based aid. The average freshman award was $31,215. Need-based scholarships or need-based grants averaged $26,401; need-based self-help aid (loans and jobs) averaged $5,801; other non-need-based awards and non-need-based scholarships averaged $16,146; and $4,590 from other forms of aid. 79% of undergraduate students work part-time. Average annual earnings from campus work are $1636. The average financial indebtedness of the 2013 graduate was $16,438. Beloit is a member of CSS. The FAFSA and the college's own financial statement are required. The deadline for filing freshman financial aid applications for fall entry is March 1.

International Students: There are 138 international students enrolled. The school actively recruits these students. They must also take the SAT or ACT. Applicants from selected countries must also supply a school-leaving exam/certificate.

Computers: All students may access the system at any time. There are no time limits and no fees.

Graduates: From July 1, 2012 to June 30, 2013, 298 bachelor's degrees were awarded. The most popular majors were social sciences (26%), visual and performing arts (11%), foreign languages, literatures, and and linguistics (10%). In an average class, 68% graduate in 4 years or less, 78% graduate in 5 years or less, and 78% graduate in 6 years or less. Of the 2012 graduating class, 14% were enrolled in graduate school within 6 months of graduation, and 76% were employed.

Admissions Contact: James Zielinski, Director of Admissions. E-Mail: *admiss@beloit.edu* Web: *www.beloit.edu*

CARDINAL STRITCH UNIVERSITY — E-4

Milwaukee, WI 53217-7516 — **(414) 410-4040**
(800) 347-8822; (414) 410-4049

Full-time: 920 men, 2010 women	**Faculty:** n/av
Part-time: 60 men, 180 women	**Ph.D.s:** 54%
Graduate: 830 men, 1910 women	**Student/Faculty:** n/av
Year: semesters, summer session	**Tuition:** $23,220
Application Deadline: see profile	**Room & Board:** $7500
Freshman Class: n/av	
SAT or ACT: required	

COMPETITIVE

Cardinal Stritch University, founded in 1937 as a college, is a private, Catholic institution sponsored by the Sisters of St. Francis. The figures in the above capsule and in this profile are approximate. There are 4 undergraduate schools and 1 graduate school. In addition to regional accreditation, Stritch has baccalaureate program accreditation with NCATE and NLN. The library contains 132,293 volumes, 173,216 microform items, and 6,310 audio/video tapes/CDs/DVDs, and subscribes to 1,309 periodicals including electronic. Computerized library services include interlibrary loans and database searching. Special learning facilities include a learning resource center, art gallery,and radio station. The 40-acre campus is in a suburban area 10 miles north of Milwaukee. Including any residence halls, there are 9 buildings.

Student Life: 89% of undergraduates are from Wisconsin. Others are from 16 states, 27 foreign countries, and Canada. 60% are from public schools. 72% are white; 16% African American. 27% are Catholic. The average age of freshmen is 19; all undergraduates, 32. 27% do not continue beyond their first year; 43% remain to graduate.

Housing: 278 students can be accommodated in college housing, which includes coed dorms. On-campus housing is available on a first-come and first-served basis. 95% of students commute. All students may keep cars.

Activities: There are no fraternities or sororities. There are 50 groups on campus, including art, band, cheerleading, choir, chorus, computers, dance, drama, ethnic, film, honors, international, jazz band, musical theater, newspaper, orchestra, photography, political, professional, radio and TV, religious, social, social service, student government, and yearbook. Popular campus events include Thursday Night events and weekly activities, such as sporting events and plays.

Sports: There are 5 intercollegiate sports for men and 5 for women, and 2 intramural sports for men and 2 for women. Facilities include basketball and volleyball courts, an indoor track, a weight and exercise room, an area for table tennis and billiards, and a soccer field.

Disabled Students: 80% of the campus is accessible. Facilities include wheelchair ramps, special parking, specially equipped rest rooms, special class scheduling, and lowered telephones.

Services: Counseling and information services are available, as is tutoring in every subject. There is remedial math, reading, and writing.

Campus Safety and Security: Measures include 24-hour foot and vehicle patrol. There are lighted pathways/sidewalks.

Programs of Study: Stritch confers B.A., B.S. and B.F.A. degrees. Associates, master's, and doctoral degrees are also awarded. Bachelor's degrees are awarded in BIOLOGICAL SCIENCE (biology/biological science), BUSINESS (accounting, business administration and management, and international business management), COMMUNICATIONS AND THE ARTS (art, communications, creative writing, dramatic arts, English, fine arts, French, music, public relations, and Spanish), COMPUTER AND PHYSICAL SCIENCE (chemistry, computer science, and mathematics), EDUCATION (early childhood education, elementary education, middle school education, secondary education, and special education), HEALTH PROFESSIONS (nursing, predentistry, premedicine, preoptometry, and preveterinary science), SOCIAL SCIENCE (history, prelaw, psychology, religion, social science, and sociology). Education in general and special education in particular are the strongest academically. Business, education, and nursing have the largest enrollments.

Required: To graduate, students must complete 128 credits, 34 to 72 in the major, with a GPA of at least 2.0. Required disciplines include history, foreign language, literature, written communication, and communication arts. 5 courses are required in humanities, 3 in social/behavioral sciences, 2 each in communication arts and written communication, and 1 each in math and natural science. An English proficiency exam must be taken.

Special: Students may participate in a variety of internships with Milwaukee businesses and organizations. Stritch offers an accelerated degree program and a B.A.-B.S. degree in business, dual majors, a general studies degree, and nondegree study. There is study abroad, work-study programs, pass/fail options, and credit for life, military, and work experience. An accelerated evening program and a management program are offered for working adults. There are 9 national honor societies and a freshman honors program.

Faculty/Classroom: 49% of faculty are male; 51% are female. All teach undergraduates. No introductory courses are taught by graduate students. The average class size in a laboratory is 12 and in a regular course is 11.

Requirements: The SAT or ACT is required, with a recommended minimum composite score of 20 on the ACT or a satisfactory score on the SAT. Applicants must be graduates of an accredited secondary school, with 16 academic credits, including 4 years of English and 2 years each of math (algebra required), science, and social studies. The GED is accepted. Stritch requires an essay and recommends an interview. A GPA of 2.0 is required. AP and CLEP credits are accepted. Important factors in the admissions decision are leadership record, evidence of special talent, and advanced placement or honors courses.

Procedure: Freshmen are admitted to all sessions. Entrance exams should be taken as early as possible. There are deferred admissions and rolling admissions plans. Check with the school for current application deadlines. Notification is sent on a rolling basis. Applications are accepted online.

Transfer: Applicants for transfer should have a minimum GPA of 2.0, and be eligible for return to the previous institution. 32 of 128 credits required for the bachelor's degree must be completed at Stritch.

Visiting: There are regularly scheduled orientations for prospective students, including a campus tour, meetings with admissions and financial aid counselors, and possible meetings with department chairs. There are guides for informal visits; visitors may sit in on classes and stay overnight. To schedule a visit, contact the Admissions Office.

Financial Aid: The FAFSA and the college's own financial statement are required. Check with the school for current application deadlines.

International Students: They must take the TOEFL. They must also take the SAT or ACT, and the college's own entrance exam.

Computers: All students may access the system. There are no time limits and no fees.

Admissions Contact: David Wegener, Director of Admissions. E-Mail: *admityou@stritch.edu* Web: *www.stritch.edu*

CARROLL UNIVERSITY D-5

Waukesha, WI 53186 (262) 524-7220
(800) CARROLL; (262) 524-7139

Full-time: n/av
Part-time: 193 men, 375 women
Graduate: 62 men, 177 women
Year: semesters, summer session
Application Deadline: open
Freshman Class: 2429 applied, 1912 accepted, 598 enrolled
SAT: required
Faculty: 101; IIB, --$
Ph.D.s: 71%
Student/Faculty: 23 to 1
Tuition: $20,900
Room & Board: $5810
ACT: 23
COMPETITIVE

Carroll University, founded in 1846, is an independent, co-educational comprehensive college grounded in the liberal arts tradition. There are 2 undergraduate schools and 3 graduate schools. In addition to regional accreditation, Carroll has baccalaureate program accreditation with APTA and NLN. The library contains 150,000 volumes, 21,637 microform items, 1,400 audio/video tapes/CDs/DVDs, and subscribes to 14,000 periodicals including electronic. Computerized library services include interlibrary loans, database searching, Internet access, and Wi-Fi capability. Special learning facilities include an art gallery, radio station, a studio theater, and recital hall. The 52-acre campus is in a suburban area 15 miles west of Milwaukee. Including any residence halls, there are 31 buildings.

Student Life: 77% of undergraduates are from Wisconsin. Others are from 25 states, 31 foreign countries, and Canada. 85% are from public schools. 91% are White. The average age of freshmen is 19; all undergraduates, 22. 23% do not continue beyond their first year; 58% remain to graduate.

Housing: 1289 students can be accommodated in college housing, which includes single-sex and coed dorms and on-campus apartments. 50% of students commute. All students may keep cars.

Activities: 3% of men belong to 2 local fraternities; 8% of women belong to 4 national sororities. There are 40 groups on campus, including activities board, Greek life, art, band, cheerleading, choir, chorale, chorus, computers, dance, diversity, drama, ethnic, film, gay, honors, international, jazz band, literary magazine, musical theater, newspaper, orchestra, photography, political, professional, radio and TV, religious, social, social service, student government, symphony, and yearbook. Popular campus events include International Folk Fair, Madrigal Dinner and Spring Fling.

Sports: There are 10 intercollegiate sports for men and 10 for women, and 5 intramural sports for men and 5 for women. Facilities include an all-purpose field house, gym including volleyball court, 2 basketball courts, and an indoor track, 6 tennis courts, 6-lane pool, 2 sand volleyball courts, football/soccer field, practice field, softball diamond, batting cages, athletic training rooms, exercise/physiology laboratory, weight room, fitness weight room, dance studio, and a campus center which houses ping pong tables, pool tables, dart machine and video games.

Disabled Students: 20% of the campus is accessible. Facilities include wheelchair ramps, elevators, special parking, specially equipped restrooms, and special class scheduling.

Services: Counseling and information services are available, as is tutoring in most subjects. There is a reader service for the blind. Academic coaching is available.

Campus Safety and Security: Measures include 24-hour foot and vehicle patrol, self-defense education, and security escort services. There are shuttle buses, emergency telephones, and lighted pathways/sidewalks.

Programs of Study: Carroll confers B.A., B.S. and B.S.N. degrees. Master's degrees are also awarded. Bachelor's degrees are awarded in BIOLOGICAL SCIENCE (biochemistry, biology/biological science, and marine biology), BUSINESS (accounting, business administration and management, organizational behavior, recreational facilities management, and small business management), COMMUNICATIONS AND THE ARTS (art, communications, dramatic arts, English, music, and Spanish), COMPUTER AND PHYSICAL SCIENCE (actuarial science, chemistry, computer science, information sciences and systems, and mathematics), EDUCATION (art education, athletic training, early childhood education, elementary education, foreign languages education, music education, physical education, and science education), ENGINEERING AND ENVIRONMENTAL DESIGN (environmental science and graphic arts technology), HEALTH PROFESSIONS (clinical science, exercise science, and nursing), SOCIAL SCIENCE (criminal justice, history, international relations, political science/government, psychology, religion, and sociology). Computer science, education, and business are the strongest academically. Nursing, communication, and criminal justice have the largest enrollments.

Required: To graduate, students must complete 128 credit hours, 32 to 88 in the major, with a minimum GPA of 2.0. Students must take 7 courses from the Liberal Studies Progarm and a first-year seminar and writing seminar, 1 computer science course and a math course are needed for the B.S.; 12 credits of modern language or the humanities and math competency is needed for the B.A.

Special: A Washington semester at American University and a United Nations semester are offered, as are internships and individually designed majors. Under the International and Off-Campus Program, short-and long-term study abroad programs are offered to sophomores,juniors and seniors so that they may travel to places that are culturally different from their own. IOP offers programs in such areas as Western and Eastern Europe, Latin America, Africa, or Asia. A capstone experience bridges the student's college work to employment or graduate school. There are 5 national honor societies and a freshman honors program.

Faculty/Classroom: 45% of faculty are male; 55% are female. All teach undergraduates, 41% do research, and 41% do both. No introductory courses are taught by graduate students. The average class size in a laboratory is 18 and in a regular course is 23.

Admissions: 79% of the 2013-2014 applicants were accepted. The ACT scores were 31% below 21, 34% between 21 and 23, 22% between 24 and 26, 9% between 27 and 28, and 4% above 28. 34% of the current freshmen were in the top fifth of their class; 65% were in the top two fifths. There were 1 National Merit finalists. 18 freshmen graduated first in their class.

Requirements: The SAT or ACT is required. Applicants must be graduates of an accredited secondary school. The GED is accepted. An essay and interview are recommended for all students, and a portfolio or audition is advised for art and music students, respectively. Carroll requires applicants to be in the upper 50% of their class. A GPA of 2.0 is required. AP and CLEP credits are accepted. Important factors in the admissions decision are advanced placement or honors courses, recommendations by school officials, and evidence of special talent.

Procedure: Freshmen are admitted fall and spring. Entrance exams should be taken during the junior year. There are deferred admissions and rolling admissions plans. Application deadlines are open. Applications are accepted online.

Transfer: 197 transfer students enrolled in 2012-2013. Applicants for transfer must have a minimum GPA of 2.0. An interview is required. 32 of 128 credits required for the bachelor's degree must be completed at Carroll.

Visiting: There are regularly scheduled orientations for prospective students, consisting of a campus tour, financial aid/admissions counseling, academic department meetings, and extracurricular activities meetings. There are guides for informal visits, visitors may sit in on classes, and stay overnight. To schedule a visit, contact the Office of Admissions.

Financial Aid: In 2013-2014, 98% of all full-time freshmen and 98% of continuing full-time students received some form of financial aid. 63% of all full-time freshmen and 70% of continuing full-time students received need-based aid. The average freshman award was $15,039. Need-based scholarships or need-based grants averaged $11,100; need-based self-help aid (loans and jobs) averaged $3,607; and $360 from other forms of aid. 59% of undergraduate students work part-time. Average annual earnings from campus work are $850. The average financial indebtedness of the 2013 graduate was $15,195. Carroll is a member of CSS. The FAFSA is required. The deadline for filing freshman financial aid applications for fall entry is September 1.

International Students: There are 40 international students enrolled. The school actively recruits these students. They must take the TOEFL.

Computers: All students may access the system 24 hours every day. There are no time limits and no fees.

Graduates: From July 1, 2012 to June 30, 2013, 487 bachelor's degrees were awarded. The most popular majors were education (19%), business (13%), and nursing (11%). 5 companies recruited on campus in 2012-2013. In an average class, 39% graduate in 4 years or less, 54% graduate in 5 years or less, and 58% graduate in 6 years or less. Of the 2012 graduating class, 33% were enrolled in graduate school within 6 months of graduation, and 97% were employed.

Admissions Contact: James V. Wiseman, Vice President of Enrollment.
E-Mail: *cc.info@ccadmin.cc.edu* Web: *www.carrollu.edu*

CARTHAGE COLLEGE E-5

Kenosha, WI 53140 (262) 551-6000
(800) 351-4058; (262) 551-5762

Full-time: 2525 men and women
Part-time: 950 men and women
Graduate: n/av
Year: semesters, summer session
Application Deadline: open
Freshman Class: n/av
SAT or ACT: required
Faculty: n/av; IIB, av$
Ph.D.s: 90%
Student/Faculty: n/av
Tuition: $31,800
Room & Board: $9100
COMPETITIVE

Carthage College, founded in 1847, is an independent liberal arts institution affiliated with the Evangelical Lutheran Church in America. There is 1 graduate school. The figures in the above capsule and in this profile are approximate. In addition to regional accreditation, Carthage has baccalaureate program accreditation with CSWE and NASM. The library contains 130,000 volumes, 9,000 microform items, 1,300 audio/video tapes/CDs/DVDs, and subscribes to 450 periodicals including electronic. Computerized library services include interlibrary loans and database searching.

Special learning facilities include a learning resource center, art gallery, and radio station. The 75-acre campus is in a suburban area 30 miles south of Milwaukee and 60 miles north of Chicago, on the shore of Lake Michigan. Including any residence halls, there are 16 buildings.

Student Life: 52% of undergraduates are from out of state, mostly the Mid-West. Students are from 23 states, 14 foreign countries, and Canada. 88% are from public schools. 89% are white. 31% are Catholic; 26% claim no religious affiliation; 13% are Protestant. The average age of freshmen is 18; all undergraduates, 20. 24% do not continue beyond their first year; 50% remain to graduate.

Housing: 1250 students can be accommodated in college housing, which includes single-sex and coed dorms. In addition, there are study-intensive floors and a health and wellness floor. On-campus housing is guaranteed for all 4 years. 68% of students live on campus; of those, 75% remain on campus on weekends. Alcohol is not permitted. All students may keep cars.

Activities: 20% of men and women belong to 15 fraternities and sororities. There are 90 groups on campus, including art, band, cheerleading, choir, chorus, computers, debate, drama, ethnic, film, forensics, gay, Habitat for Humanity, honors, international, jazz band, literary magazine, musical theater, newspaper, orchestra, pep band, photography, political, professional, radio and TV, religious, social, social service, student government, and yearbook. Popular campus events include May Madness, Little Sibling Weekend, and Casino Night.

Sports: There are 10 intercollegiate sports for men and 10 for women, and 10 intramural sports for men and 5 for women. Facilities include a phys ed center, a 3000-seat stadium, a 3500-seat gym, tennis courts, baseball, soccer, and softball fields, and a natatorium.

Disabled Students: 90% of the campus is accessible. Facilities include wheelchair ramps, elevators, special parking, specially equipped rest rooms, special class scheduling, lowered drinking fountains, and lowered telephones.

Services: Counseling and information services are available, as is tutoring in most subjects.

Campus Safety and Security: Measures include 24-hour foot and vehicle patrol, self-defense education, and security escort services. There are emergency telephones, lighted pathways/sidewalks, and electronic exit locks on residence halls.

Programs of Study: Carthage confers B.A. degrees. Master's degrees are also awarded. Bachelor's degrees are awarded in BIOLOGICAL SCIENCE (biology/biological science), BUSINESS (accounting, business administration and management, international economics, and marketing management), COMMUNICATIONS AND THE ARTS (art, English, fine arts, French, German, graphic design, languages, music, performing arts, Spanish, and studio art), COMPUTER AND PHYSICAL SCIENCE (chemistry, mathematics, natural sciences, and physics), EDUCATION (elementary education, English education, foreign languages education, mathematics education, middle school education, music education, physical education, and secondary education), SOCIAL SCIENCE (criminal justice, economics, geography, history, philosophy, political science/government, psychology, religion, social science, social work, and sociology). Education, business, and sciences are the strongest academically. Business and education have the largest enrollments.

Required: To graduate, students must complete 138 credits, with up to 56 in the major and a minimum GPA of 2.0 (education requires 2.75). Students must complete 50 credits in liberal arts studies, including the Heritage Seminar Series, which includes 3 courses that help develop competencies in cultural studies, writing, thinking, reading, speaking, and listening. 2 courses each are required in religion and foreign language, and 1 in math. There is also a phys ed requirement. Each student must complete one of the junior symposia, a series of 3 interdependent courses, and a senior project in the major.

Special: Internships are available during the January term or, in some cases, for a semester. Carthage offers study abroad in 5 countries, cross-registration with the University of Wisconsin, a Washington semester, a general studies degree, an accelerated degree program in business administration, work-study programs, and dual and student-designed majors. Students may take a 3-2 engineering degree with Case Western Reserve and Washington Universities or the Universities of Minnesota-Twin Cities and Wisconsin/Madison, or a 3-2 occupational therapy degree with Washington University. There are pass/fail options and credit for military and work experience. There are 3 national honor societies and a freshman honors program.

Faculty/Classroom: 68% of faculty are male; 32% are female. All teach undergraduates. No introductory courses are taught by graduate students. The average class size in an introductory lecture is 19; in a laboratory is 19; and in a regular course is 19.

Requirements: The SAT or ACT is required. Applicants should be graduates of an accredited secondary school, having earned 16 academic credits, including English, foreign language, math, science, and social studies. The GED is accepted. An interview is recommended. A GPA of 2.0 is required. AP and CLEP credits are accepted. Important factors in the admissions decision are advanced placement or honors courses, leadership record, and extracurricular activities record.

Procedure: Freshmen are admitted to all sessions. Entrance exams should be taken in spring of the junior year or fall of the senior year. There are deferred admissions and rolling admissions plans. Application deadlines are open. Check with the school for the current application fee. Notification is sent on a rolling basis. Applications are accepted online.

Transfer: Transfer students are accepted based on academic performance at their previous school; they should have a GPA greater than 2.0. If they have fewer than 12 credits, the high school record is considered. Either the SAT or ACT and an interview are recommended. 32 of 138 credits required for the bachelor's degree must be completed at Carthage.

Visiting: There are regularly scheduled orientations for prospective students, including small group meetings with a first-year adviser and faculty members, class selection, and curriculum overview. Informational sessions for parents are offered. There are guides for informal visits, visitors may sit in on classes, and stay overnight. To schedule a visit, contact the visit coordinator in the Office of Admissions.

Financial Aid: The FAFSA is required. Check with the school for current financial aid deadlines.

International Students: The school actively recruits these students. They must take the TOEFL.

Computers: All students may access the system 24 hours on weekdays, and 8 a.m. to 8 p.m. on weekends. There are no time limits and no fees.

Admissions Contact: Director of Admissions and Financial Aid. E-mail: *admissions@carthage.edu* Web: *www.carthage.edu*

CONCORDIA UNIVERSITY WISCONSIN E-4

Mequon, WI 53097	**(414) 243-4500; (414) 243-4545**
Full-time: n/av	**Faculty:** 99; IIB, av$
Part-time: n/av	**Ph.D.s:** 75%
Graduate: n/av	**Student/Faculty:** 11 to 1
Year: 4-1-4, summer session	**Tuition:** $20,990
Application Deadline: August 1	**Room & Board:** $7990
Freshman Class: 1130 accepted, 402 enrolled	
SAT: required	**ACT:** 22 **COMPETITIVE**

Concordia University Wisconsin, established in 1881, is a private institution affiliated with the Lutheran Church-Missouri Synod. There are 4 undergraduate schools and one graduate school. In addition to regional accreditation, CUW has baccalaureate program accreditation with NLN. The library contains 120,000 volumes, 270,602 microform items, 4,152 audio/video tapes/CDs/DVDs, and subscribes to 37,000 periodicals including electronic. Computerized library services include interlibrary loans, database searching, and Internet access. Special learning facilities include an art gallery, radio station, a curriculum library for education students, health and fitness facility, sustainable environmental center, state of the art residence hall. The 155-acre campus is in a suburban area 15 miles north of Milwaukee. Including any residence halls, there are 20 buildings.

Student Life: 60% of undergraduates are from Wisconsin. Others are from 47 states, and 25 foreign countries. 75% are White; 17% African American. 79% are Protestant; 21% Catholic. The average age of freshmen is 18; all undergraduates, 20. 20% do not continue beyond their first year; 60% remain to graduate.

Housing: 1500 students can be accommodated in college housing, which includes single-sex dorms. On-campus housing is guaranteed for all 4 years, is available on a first-come, and first-served basis. 69% of students live on campus; of those, 50% remain on campus on weekends. Alcohol is not permitted. All students may keep cars.

Activities: There are no fraternities or sororities. There are 20 groups on campus, including art, band, cheerleading, choir, chorale, drama, drill team, ethnic, honors, international, jazz band, literary magazine, musical theater, newspaper, orchestra, pep band, political, professional, radio and TV, religious, and student government. Popular campus events include Winterfest and Springfest.

Sports: There are 11 intercollegiate sports for men and 10 for women, and 10 intramural sports for men and 9 for women. Facilities include a field house, stadium, and fitness center, new athletic fields including state of the art baseball stadium.

Disabled Students: All of the campus is accessible. Facilities include wheelchair ramps, elevators, special parking, and specially equipped restrooms.

Services: Counseling and information services are available, as is tutoring in every subject. There is a reader service for the blind, and remedial math, reading, and writing.

Campus Safety and Security: Measures include 24-hour foot and vehicle patrol and emergency notification system. There are lighted pathways/sidewalks, controlled access to dorms/residences, Security guards are on duty from 4 p.m. to 8 a.m. on weekdays and 24 hours a day on weekends.

Programs of Study: CUW confers B.A., B.S. and B.S.N. degrees. Associate, master's, and doctoral degrees are also awarded. Bachelor's degrees are awarded in BIOLOGICAL SCIENCE (biology/biological science), BUSINESS (accounting, banking and finance, business administration and management, management science, and marketing/retailing/ merchandising), COMMUNICATIONS AND THE ARTS (art, communications, English, graphic design, music, Spanish, speech/debate/rhetoric, and telecommunications), COMPUTER AND PHYSICAL SCIENCE (mathematics and radiological technology), EDUCATION (athletic training, early childhood education, elementary education, physical education, and secondary education), ENGINEERING AND ENVIRONMENTAL DESIGN (interior design), HEALTH PROFESSIONS (nursing, occupational therapy, and sports medicine), SOCIAL SCIENCE (biblical languages, criminal justice, history, humanities, ministries, paralegal studies, pastoral studies, psychology, religion, religious music, social science, social work, and theological studies). Education, business, and health sciences are the strongest academically.

Required: To graduate, students must complete 126 credits, including at least 30 in the major, with a minimum GPA of 2.0. The 47 1/2 credit core curriculum includes theology/philosophy, humanities, cross culture, social science, natural science, communication, math, and phys ed.

Special: Internships, study abroad, pass/fail options, and credit for life, military, and work experience are available. Concordia offers a general studies degree, dual, student-designed, and interdisciplinary majors, including justice and public policy, and nondegree study. Accelerated degree programs are available in several fields. There is 1 national honor society.

Faculty/Classroom: 43% of faculty are male; 57% are female. All teach undergraduates. No introductory courses are taught by graduate students. The average class size in a regular course is 17.

Requirements: The SAT or ACT is required. A satisfactory score on the SAT or on the ACT is required. Applicants must be graduates of an accredited secondary school, having completed 16 academic credits, including 3 of English and 2 each of math, science, and social studies. The GED is accepted. A GPA of 2.5 is required. AP and CLEP credits are accepted. Important factors in the admissions decision are leadership record, recommendations by school officials, and personality/intangible qualities.

Procedure: Freshmen are admitted to all sessions. Entrance exams should be taken in the junior year. There is a rolling admissions plan. Applications should be filed by August 1 for fall entry. The fall 2013 application fee was $35.

Transfer: 104 transfer students enrolled in 2012-2013. Applicants for transfer must have a minimum GPA of 2.0 and meet the same entrance exam criteria as entering freshmen. 36 of 126 credits required for the bachelor's degree must be completed at CUW.

Visiting: There are regularly scheduled orientations for prospective students, including a tour and financial aid and academic information sessions. There are guides for informal visits, visitors may sit in on classes, and stay overnight. To schedule a visit, contact the Admission Office.

Financial Aid: The CSS/Profile, FAFSA, and the college's own financial statement, and income tax forms are required. The deadline for filing freshman financial aid applications for fall entry is April 30.

International Students: There are 49 international students enrolled. The school actively recruits these students. They must take the TOEFL and the college's own test, If the student's TOEFL score is below 500, the student must take an English proficiency exam for placement.

Computers: All students may access the system. There are no time limits and no fees.

Graduates: Of the 2012 graduating class, 52% were employed within 6 months of graduation.

Admissions Contact: Robert Nowak, Director of Admissions. E-Mail: *admission@cuw.edu* Web: *www.cuw.edu*

EDGEWOOD COLLEGE C-4

Madison, WI 53711 **(608) 663-2294**
(800) 444-4861 ext. 2294; (608) 663-2214

Full-time: 600 men, 1100 women	**Faculty:** 86
Part-time: 145 men, 361 women	**Ph.D.s:** 80%
Graduate: 219 men, 404 women	**Student/Faculty:** 18 to 1
Year: 4-1-4, summer session	**Tuition:** $24,666
Application Deadline: August 25	**Room & Board:** $8628

Freshman Class: 1035 applied, 835 accepted, 309 enrolled
ACT: 22

COMPETITIVE

Edgewood College, established in 1927, is a private Catholic institution sponsored by the Sinsinawa Dominican Sisters. There is one graduate school. In addition to regional accreditation, Edgewood has baccalaureate program accreditation with NCATE. The library contains 88,329 volumes, 94,050 microform items, 3,946 audio/video tapes/CDs/DVDs, and subscribes to 494 periodicals including electronic. Computerized library services include interlibrary loans and database searching. Special learning facilities include an art gallery. The 55-acre campus is in a suburban area 5 miles southwest of Madison. Including any residence halls, there are 15 buildings.

Student Life: 90% of undergraduates are from Wisconsin. Others are from 11 states, and 10 foreign countries. 75% are from public schools. 84% are White. 27% are Catholic. The average age of freshmen is 18; all undergraduates, 21. 20% do not continue beyond their first year; 58% remain to graduate.

Housing: 560 students can be accommodated in college housing, which includes single-sex and coed dorms and on-campus apartments. On-campus housing is guaranteed for all 4 years and is available on a lottery system for upperclassmen. 65% of students commute. Upperclassmen may keep cars.

Activities: There are no fraternities or sororities. There are 30 groups on campus, including art, band, choir, chorale, chorus, communications, drama, environmental, ethnic, gay, honors, international, literary magazine, musical theater, newspaper, orchestra, pep band, political, religious, social, social service, student government, and symphony. Popular campus events include Homecoming, Springfest and Winter Frost.

Sports: There are 5 intercollegiate sports for men and 7 for women, and 9 intramural sports for men and 9 for women. Facilities include a 1000-seat gym, soccer, baseball, and softball fields, a fitness center, and access to tennis courts.

Disabled Students: 85% of the campus is accessible. Facilities include wheelchair ramps, elevators, special parking, specially equipped restrooms, special class scheduling, lowered drinking fountains, lowered telephones, special housing. automated doors in the library, science center, activities center, and residence halls and a chairlift.

Services: Counseling and information services are available, as is tutoring in every subject, most sciences, introductory math courses, and Spanish. There is a reader service for the blind, and remedial math, reading, and writing.

Campus Safety and Security: Measures include self-defense education and security escort services. There are emergency telephones, lighted pathways/sidewalks, Residence halls have alarms, a security card system, and campus security guards. RAs are on duty 24 hours a day, weekends 7a.m. to 3 p.m. and 8 p.m. to 4 a.m. weekdays.

Programs of Study: Edgewood confers B.A., and B.S. degrees. Master's degrees are also awarded. Bachelor's degrees are awarded in BIOLOGICAL SCIENCE (biology/biological science), BUSINESS (accounting and business administration and management), COMMUNICATIONS AND THE ARTS (art, English, French, graphic design, music, performing arts, and Spanish), COMPUTER AND PHYSICAL SCIENCE (chemistry, information sciences and systems, mathematics, and natural sciences), EDUCATION (early childhood education, education of the exceptional child, elementary education, science education, and social studies education), ENGINEERING AND ENVIRONMENTAL DESIGN (preengineering), HEALTH PROFESSIONS (art therapy, cytotechnology, medical technology, and nursing), SOCIAL SCIENCE (child care/child and family studies, criminal justice, economics, history, international relations, political science/government, prelaw, psychology, public administration, religion, and sociology). Liberal arts is the strongest academically. Business, education, and nursing have the largest enrollments.

Required: To graduate, students must complete a minimum of 120 credit hours with a minimum cumulative GPA of 2.0. There are general education requirements, and each student must complete a major field of study and a Human Issues study.

Special: Students may cross-register with the University of Wisconsin/ Madison. Internships, study abroad, dual and student-designed majors, nondegree study, pass/fail options, and credit for prior learning. experience are available. There is a weekend degree program. There is an accelerated undergraduate degree program for working adults. There are 5 national honor societies and a freshman honors program.

Faculty/Classroom: All teach undergraduates. No introductory courses are taught by graduate students. The average class size in a regular course is 18.

Admissions: 81% of the 2013-2014 applicants were accepted. The ACT scores were 38% below 21, 31% between 21 and 23, 22% between 24 and 26, 7% between 27 and 28, and 3% above 28. 25% of the current freshmen were in the top fifth of their class; 59% were in the top two fifths. 1 freshman graduated first in the class.

Requirements: The ACT is recommended. Candidates for admission to Edgewood are expected to present a 2.5 cumulative high school GPA, rank in the upper half of their class, and have a composite score of 18 on the ACT or a satisfactory score on the SAT. The GED is accepted. Applicants should complete 16 Carnegie units, 12 of which should be chosen from the following fields: natural science, speech, social science, English, foreign language, history, religious studies, and mathematics. 2 years of the same foreign language in grades 9-12 with grades of C or better are also recommended. Edgewood requires applicants to be in the upper 50% of their class. A GPA of 2.5 is required. AP and CLEP credits are accepted.

Procedure: Freshmen are admitted fall and spring. Entrance exams should be taken by the senior year. There is a rolling admissions plan. Applications should be filed by August 25 for fall entry; January 12 for spring entry, along with a $25 fee. Applications are accepted online.

Transfer: Transfer students must complete an Application for Undergraduate Admission and have official transcripts from each high school, college and univeristy attended sent directly to the Office of Admissions. High school transcripts should include class rank and cumulative GPA. GEDs are accepted. Students are expected to present a minimum of 12 academic-level credits and a cumulative college grade point average of 2.0 (on a 4.0 scale) from an accredited institution. Students dismissed from a previous college must wait one full year prior to applying to Edgewood and supply additional information. 32 of 120 credits required for the bachelor's degree must be completed at Edgewood.

Visiting: There are regularly scheduled orientations for prospective students, including Experience Edgewood Days, a program where admitted freshmen spend a day on campus as if they were Edgewood College Students. They choose their own schedule for the day, which may include sitting in on classes, attending athletics presentations, and learning about study abroad opportunities, residence life and student activities. Students also have the opportunity to take campus tours and exclusive tours of the residence halls. Complimentary lunch is included. There are guides for informal visits, visitors may sit in on classes, and stay overnight. To schedule a visit, contact the Admissions Office.

Financial Aid: 85% of undergraduate students work part-time. Average annual earnings from campus work are $2000. Edgewood is a member of CSS. The FAFSA and the college's own financial statement, and and a tax return are required. Check with the school for current application deadlines.

International Students: The school actively recruits these students. They must take the TOEFL or MELAB.

Computers: All students may access the system. There are no time limits and no fees.

Graduates: From July 1, 2012 to June 30, 2013, 334 bachelor's degrees were awarded. The most popular majors were nursing (31%), education (17%), and business (13%). 35 companies recruited on campus in 2012-2013. In an average class, 40% graduate in 4 years or less, 57% graduate in 5 years or less, and 58% graduate in 6 years or less.

Admissions Contact: Christine Benedict, Director of Undergraduate Admissions. E-Mail: *admissions@edgewood.edu* Web: *www.edgewood .edu*

LAKELAND COLLEGE E-4

Sheboygan, WI 53082 **(920) 565-1217**
(800) 242-3347; (920) 565-1206

Full-time: 390 men, 400 women	**Faculty:** 41; IIB, --$
Part-time: 20 men, 30 women	**Ph.D.s:** 59%
Graduate: 50 men, 130 women	**Student/Faculty:** 19 to 1
Year: semesters, summer session	**Tuition:** $17,595
Application Deadline:	**Room & Board:** $6195
Freshman Class: n/av	
SAT or ACT: required	

COMPETITIVE

Lakeland College, established in 1862, is a private institution affiliated with the United Church of Christ. The 4-4-1 academic calendar consists of 4-month fall and spring terms, and an optional 3-week May term. There is one graduate school. The library contains 57,447 volumes, 33,169 microform items, 2,099 audio/video tapes/CDs/DVDs, and subscribes to 322 periodicals including electronic. Computerized library services include interlibrary loans and database searching. Special learning facilities include an art gallery, and a college history museum. The 240-acre campus is in a rural area 10 miles northwest of Sheboygan. Including any residence halls, there are 24 buildings.

Student Life: 79% of undergraduates are from Wisconsin. Others are from 16 states, 31 foreign countries, and Canada. 90% are from public schools. 76% are White. 32% are Protestant; 29% Catholic; 25% claim no religious affiliation. The average age of all undergraduates is 22. 32% do not continue beyond their first year; 43% remain to graduate.

Housing: 488 students can be accommodated in college housing, which includes single-sex and coed dorms and on-campus apartments. In addition, there are honors houses, male-only, female-only, and housing for students with senior standing. On-campus housing is guaranteed for all 4 years. 57% of students live on campus; of those, 60% remain on campus on weekends. All students may keep cars.

Activities: 17% of men belong to 3 local fraternities; 11% of women belong to 3 local sororities. There are 27 groups on campus, including band, choir, chorus, dance team, drama, ethnic, honors, international, literary magazine, newspaper, pep band, professional, radio and TV, religious, social, student government, and yearbook. Popular campus events include Winter Carnival, and Spring Celebration.

Sports: There are 8 intercollegiate sports for men and 7 for women, and 2 intramural sports for men and 2 for women. Facilities include a sports complex, a fitness lab, 3 full-size basketball courts, a weight room, indoor and outdoor tennis courts, indoor pitching and batting facilities, and softball, baseball, football, soccer, and practice fields.

Disabled Students: 83% of the campus is accessible. Facilities include wheelchair ramps, elevators, special parking, specially equipped restrooms, lowered drinking fountains. though not at every building.

Services: Counseling and information services are available, as is tutoring in every subject. There is a reader service for the blind, and remedial math, reading, and writing.

Campus Safety and Security: Measures include security escort services. There are emergency telephones, lighted pathways/sidewalks, and foot patrol on weekends and evenings.

Programs of Study: Lakeland confers B.A. degrees. Master's degrees are also awarded. Bachelor's degrees are awarded in BIOLOGICAL SCIENCE (biology/biological science), BUSINESS (accounting, business administration and management, business economics, hospitality management services, international business management, and marketing management), COMMUNICATIONS AND THE ARTS (art, creative writing, dramatic arts, English, German, music, and Spanish), COMPUTER AND PHYSICAL SCIENCE (chemistry, computer science, and mathematics), EDUCATION (business education, early childhood education, elementary education, music education, and secondary education), SOCIAL SCIENCE (behavioral science, criminal justice, economics, history, philosophy, physical fitness/movement, psychology, public administration, religion, and sociology). Business, education, and accounting are the strongest academically. Education, business, and computer science have the largest enrollments.

Required: To graduate, students must complete 128 semester hours, with at least 32 in the major and a minimum 2.0 GPA. There are requirements in history, humanities, natural sciences, social sciences, and religion.

Special: Internships in all majors, study abroad in Germany and Japan, a Washington semester, and work-study programs are available. There are some dual majors, a general studies degree, a 3-2 engineering degree with the University of Wisconsin/Madison, a 2-2 1/2 nursing program with Bellin College of Nursing, and nondegree study. There is a freshman honors program and 10 departmental honors programs.

Faculty/Classroom: 51% of faculty are male; 49% are female. All teach and do research. No introductory courses are taught by graduate students. The average class size in an introductory lecture is 20; in a laboratory is 15; and in a regular course is 16.

Requirements: The SAT or ACT is required, with a minimum composite score of 950 on the SAT I or 19 on the ACT. Applicants must be graduates of an accredited secondary school or have the GED. An interview is recommended. Applications are accepted online via the college's web site. A GPA of 2.0 is required. AP and CLEP credits are accepted. Important factors in the admissions decision are advanced placement or honors courses, leadership record, and evidence of special talent.

Procedure: Freshmen are admitted fall, spring, and summer. Entrance exams should be taken after the enrollment commitment is made. There is a rolling admissions plan. Applications should be filed by December 15 for spring entry, along with a $20 fee. Notification is sent on a rolling basis. Applications are accepted online.

Transfer: 115 transfer students enrolled in 2012-2013. Applicants should have a GPA of at least 2.0. Lakeland recommends an interview. 36 of 128 credits required for the bachelor's degree must be completed at Lakeland.

Visiting: There are regularly scheduled orientations for prospective students, consisting of meetings with faculty and financial aid personnel, activities meetings, and a campus tour. There are guides for informal visits, visitors may sit in on classes, and stay overnight. To schedule a visit, contact the Admissions Office.

Financial Aid: In 2013-2014, 100% of all full-time freshmen and 97% of continuing full-time students received some form of financial aid. 86% of all full-time freshmen and 90% of continuing full-time students received need-based aid. The average freshman award was $11,895. 30% of undergraduate students work part-time. Average annual earnings from campus work are $1000. The average financial indebtedness of the 2013 graduate was $20,558. Lakeland is a member of CSS. The FAFSA and the college's own financial statement are required. The deadline for filing freshman financial aid applications for fall entry is July 1.

International Students: There are 100 international students enrolled. The school actively recruits these students. They must take the TOEFL.

Computers: All students may access the system. 7 a.m. to 2 a.m.

Graduates: From July 1, 2012 to June 30, 2013, 145 bachelor's degrees were awarded. The most popular majors were education (28%), business administration (17%), and computer science (10%). In an average class, 13% graduate in 3 years or less, 30% graduate in 4 years or less, 43% graduate in 5 years or less, and 46% graduate in 6 years or less. Of the 2012 graduating class, 10% were enrolled in graduate school within 6 months of graduation, and 95% were employed.

Admissions Contact: Leo Gavrilos, Director of Admissions. E-Mail: *admissions@lakeland.edu* Web: *www.lakeland.edu*

LAWRENCE UNIVERSITY D-3

Appleton, WI 54911 (920) 832-6500
(800) 227-0982; (920) 832-6782

Full-time: 656 men, 787 women
Part-time: 29 men, 24 women
Graduate: n/av
Year: trimesters
Application Deadline: January 15
Freshman Class: 2422 applied, 1405 accepted, 326 enrolled
Faculty: 163; IIB, av$
Ph.D.s: 96%
Student/Faculty: 8 to 1
Tuition: $38,481
Room & Board: $7890

HIGHLY COMPETITIVE

Lawrence University, founded in 1847, is a private liberal arts institution with a conservatory of music. There is one undergraduate school. In addition to regional accreditation, Lawrence has baccalaureate program accreditation with NASM. The library contains 420,502 volumes, 102,629 microform items, 25,897 audio/video tapes/CDs/DVDs, and subscribes to 2,505 periodicals including electronic. Computerized library services include interlibrary loans, database searching, Internet access, and Wi-Fi capability. Special learning facilities include an art gallery, natural history museum, and radio station. The 84-acre campus is in an urban area 100 miles north of Milwaukee, 30 miles south of Green Bay. Including any residence halls, there are 58 buildings.

Student Life: 69% of undergraduates are from out of state, mostly the Mid-West. Students are from 45 states, 35 foreign countries, and Canada. 75% are from public schools. 77% are White. 69% claim no religious affiliation. The average age of freshmen is 18; all undergraduates, 20. 12% do not continue beyond their first year; 76% remain to graduate.

Housing: 1364 students can be accommodated in college housing, which includes single-sex and coed dorms, on-campus apartments, and married student housing. In addition, there are language houses, special-interest houses, theme houses- students with like interests. On-campus housing is guaranteed for all 4 years. 98% of students live on campus; of those, 90% remain on campus on weekends. All students may keep cars.

Activities: 22% of men belong to 5 national fraternities; 18% of women belong to 3 national sororities. There are 100 groups on campus, including art, band, chess, choir, chorale, chorus, computers, dance, drama, environmental, ethnic, film, gay, honors, international, jazz band, literary magazine, musical theater, newspaper, opera, orchestra, pep band, photography, political, professional, radio and TV, religious, social, social service, student government, symphony, and yearbook. Popular campus events include Midwest Trivia Contest, International Cabaret, Mardis Gras, and Shack-a-thon.

Sports: There are 12 intercollegiate sports for men and 10 for women, and 23 intramural sports for men and 23 for women. Facilities include a 5255-seat lighted football stadium, 8-lane state-of-the-art outdoor track, 4-lane indoor track, baseball, soccer, practice fields, 6 tennis, 1 squash, and 4 racquetball/handball courts, 2 gyms for basketball, volleyball, and badminton, 3 batting cages, an 8-lane swimming pool with diving well, 3 weight rooms, 2 cardio exercise rooms, and sauna rooms, and a dance studio.

Disabled Students: 95% of the campus is accessible. Facilities include wheelchair ramps, elevators, special parking, specially equipped restrooms, special class scheduling, lowered drinking fountains, and special housing.

Services: Counseling and information services are available, as is tutoring in every subject. There is a reader service for the blind. The writing lab focuses on enhancing writing skills, as well as remedial writing.

Campus Safety and Security: Measures include 24-hour foot and vehicle patrol, emergency notification system, self-defense education, and security escort services. There are emergency telephones, lighted pathways/sidewalks, controlled access to dorms/residences, the Whistle Stop Program.

Programs of Study: Lawrence confers B.A., B.Mus., and B.A.-B.Mus degrees. Bachelor's degrees are awarded in AGRICULTURE (environmental studies), BIOLOGICAL SCIENCE (biochemistry and biology/biological science), COMMUNICATIONS AND THE ARTS (art history and appreciation, Chinese, classics, dramatic arts, English, French, German, Japanese, linguistics, music performance, music theory and composition, Russian, Spanish, and studio art), COMPUTER AND PHYSICAL SCIENCE (chemistry, computer science, geology, mathematics, and physics), EDUCATION (music education), SOCIAL SCIENCE (anthropology, cognitive science, East Asian studies, economics, gender studies, history, international studies, philosophy, political science/government, and psychology). Biology, music, physics, theatre, psychology and government are the strongest academically. Psychology, biology and English have the largest enrollments.

Required: Students must complete 216 units (270 units for a double-degree program), including 48 to 72 in the major, with a minimum GPA of 2.0. All students must take Freshmen Studies. Distribution requirements include 12 units each in humanities, social sciences, and natural sciences, including a lab course, and 6 units in fine arts. Competency requirements must also be met in writing, speaking, foreign language, and quantitative analysis. Some majors require a comprehensive exam or a thesis.

Special: Lawrence offers Chicago-based programs in urban studies, urban education, and the arts, a humanities program at the Newberry Library, and a science internship at Oak Ridge National Laboratory. There are study-abroad programs in 28 countries, a Washington semester, limited pass/fail options, student-designed majors, and nondegree study. Students may take a 3-2 engineering degree with Columbia or Washington Universities, or Rensselaer Polytechnic Institute. Also available are 3-2 programs in forestry and environmental studies with Duke University, in occupational therapy with Washington University in St. Louis. A 5-year B.A.-B.Mus. degree is offered. There are 5 national honor societies including Phi Beta Kappa.

Faculty/Classroom: 62% of faculty are male; 38% are female. All teach and do research. No introductory courses are taught by graduate students. The average class size in an introductory lecture is 24; in a laboratory is 15; and in a regular course is 15.

Admissions: 58% of the 2013-2014 applicants were accepted. 74% of the current freshmen were in the top fifth of their class; 95% were in the top two fifths. There were 13 National Merit finalists. 13 freshmen graduated first in their class.

Requirements: Applicants should complete 16 high school academic credits. Lawrence requires an essay, reports from a teacher and counselor, and an audition for music majors. The school recommends an interview, and a portfolio for art majors. AP credits are accepted. Important factors in the admissions decision are advanced placement or honors courses, evidence of special talent, and extracurricular activities record.

Procedure: Freshmen are admitted fall. Entrance exams should be taken in the spring of the junior year or fall of the senior year. There are early decision, early admissions, and deferred admissions plans. Early decision applications should be filed by November 15; regular applications, by January 15 for fall entry, along with a $40 fee. Notification of early decision is sent December 1; regular decision, April 1. 43 early decision candidates were accepted for the 2013-2014 class. 483 applicants were on the 2013 waiting list; 93 were admitted. Applications are accepted online.

Transfer: 16 transfer students enrolled in 2012-2013. Applicants must present official transcripts of their college and secondary school work, and the recommendation of a college professor. Typically, candidates with a college GPA of 2.75 or higher will receive serious consideration. 108 of 216 credits required for the bachelor's degree must be completed at Lawrence.

Visiting: There are regularly scheduled orientations for prospective students, Visiting students can participate in an extensive day-long program with many choices of classes and presentations. There are guides for informal visits, visitors may sit in on classes, and stay overnight. To schedule a visit, contact Visit Coordinator in the Office of Admissions.

Financial Aid: In 2013-2014, 95% of all full-time freshmen and 94% of continuing full-time students received some form of financial aid. 64% of all full-time freshmen and 58% of continuing full-time students received need-based aid. The average freshman award was $29,500. Need-based scholarships or need-based grants averaged $22,700 ($38,205 maximum); need-based self-help aid (loans and jobs) averaged $6,800 ($8,000 maximum); and other non-need-based awards and non-need-based scholarships averaged $11,817 ($38,205 maximum). 72% of undergraduate students work part-time. Average annual earnings from campus work are $1400. The average financial indebtedness of the 2013 graduate was $25,673. Lawrence is a member of CSS. The FAFSA and the college's own financial statement are required. The priority date for freshman financial aid applications for fall entry is March 1.

International Students: There are 104 international students enrolled. The school actively recruits these students. They must take the TOEFL with a minimum score of 577 on the paper-based TOEFL (PBT) or 90 on the Internet-based version (iBT).

Computers: All students may access the system 24 hours a day. There are no time limits and no fees.

Graduates: From July 1, 2012 to June 30, 2013, 310 bachelor's degrees were awarded. The most popular majors were music performance (11%), biology (10%), and psychology (8%). 10 companies recruited on campus in 2012-2013. In an average class, 1% graduate in 3 years or less, 68% graduate in 4 years or less, 70% graduate in 5 years or less, and 76% graduate in 6 years or less. Of the 2012 graduating class, 30% were enrolled in graduate school within 6 months of graduation, and 50% were employed.

Admissions Contact: Ken Anselment, Dean of Admissions and Financial Aid. E-Mail: *excel@lawrence.edu* Web: *www.lawrence.edu*

MARIAN UNIVERSITY D-4

Fond du Lac, WI 54935 (920) 923-7650
(800) 2-MARIAN; (920) 923-8755

Full-time: 376 men, 963 women
Part-time: 106 men, 243 women
Graduate: 131 men, 369 women
Year: semesters, summer session
Application Deadline: open
Freshman Class: 1021 applied, 772 accepted, 248 enrolled
ACT: 20
Faculty: 84; IIA, --$
Ph.D.s: 59%
Student/Faculty: 16 to 1
Tuition: $24,650
Room & Board: $6330

LESS COMPETITIVE

Marian University, founded in 1936, is a private, Catholic, liberal arts based institution offering degree programs in the arts and sciences, business, education, and health fields. There are 4 undergraduate schools and 3 graduate schools. In addition to regional accreditation, Marian has baccalaureate program accreditation with CSWE, NCATE, and NLN. The library contains 118,008 volumes, 11,000 microform items, 61,034 audio/video tapes/CDs/DVDs, and subscribes to 1,503 periodicals including electronic. Computerized library services include interlibrary loans, database searching, Internet access, and Wi-Fi capability. The 78-acre campus is in a small town 60 miles north of Milwaukee. Including any residence halls, there are 30 buildings.

Student Life: 90% of undergraduates are from Wisconsin. Others are from 19 states, 10 foreign countries, and Canada. 70% are from public schools. 86% are White. 41% are Catholic; 28% Protestant; 26% claim no religious affiliation. The average age of freshmen is 18; all undergraduates, 25. 31% do not continue beyond their first year; 48% remain to graduate.

Housing: 498 students can be accommodated in college housing, which includes single-sex and coed dorms and on-campus apartments. In addition, there are fraternity houses, sorority houses, and a chemical-free wellness residence hall. On-campus housing is guaranteed for all 4 years. 67% of students commute. All students may keep cars.

Activities: 5% of men belong to 1 national fraternity; 5% of women belong to 1 local and 2 national sororities. There are 38 groups on campus, including band, cheerleading, chess, choir, chorus, dance, drama, environmental, ethnic, gay, honors, international, jazz band, multicultural and campus ministry, newspaper, orchestra, photography, political, professional, religious, social, social service, student government, and symphony. Popular campus events include Technology Symposium, Academic Symposium, and Big Band.

Sports: There are 8 intercollegiate sports for men and 9 for women, and 8 intramural sports for men and 6 for women. Facilities include a new baseball field, a soccer field, a softball field, a gym, a game room, outdoor volleyball, and a weight room.

Disabled Students: All of the campus is accessible. Facilities include wheelchair ramps, elevators, special parking, specially equipped restrooms, and lowered telephones.

Services: Counseling and information services are available, as is tutoring in most subjects. There is a reader service for the blind, and remedial math, reading, and writing.

Campus Safety and Security: Measures include 24-hour foot and vehicle patrol, emergency notification system, self-defense education, and security escort services. There are emergency telephones, lighted pathways/sidewalks, and controlled access to dorms/residences.

Programs of Study: Marian confers B.A., B.S., B.A.J., B.B.A., B.I.S, B.O.C., B.S.B.A., B.S.Ed., B.S.I.S., B.S.M.T., B.S.N., B.S.R.T. and B.S.W. degrees. Master's and doctoral degrees are also awarded. Bachelor's degrees are awarded in BIOLOGICAL SCIENCE (biology/biological science), BUSINESS (accounting, business administration and management, management science, marketing/retailing/merchandising, and sports management), COMMUNICATIONS AND THE ARTS (art, communications, English, music, music business management, and Spanish), COMPUTER AND PHYSICAL SCIENCE (chemistry, information sciences and systems, mathematics, and radiological technology), EDUCATION (art education, early childhood education, elementary education, English education, mathematics education, middle school education, music education, science education, secondary education, and social science education), HEALTH PROFESSIONS (cytotechnology and nursing), SOCIAL SCIENCE (criminal justice, economics, history, homeland security, interdisciplinary studies, psychology, and social work). Nursing, education, and business have the largest enrollments.

Required: To graduate, students must complete 128 credits with a minimum GPA of 2.0 (social work, 2.75; nursing and education, 3.0). Core requirements include 25 credits in arts and humanities, 12 to 13 in social and behavioral science, and 12 in math and natural science, as well as a freshman seminar.

Special: Internships are offered in most areas of study, cooperative education programs in all majors, and accelerated-degree programs in nursing, business administration, and operation management. Student-designed and dual majors, credit for prior learning, work-study, nondegree study, and cooperative education (paid work experience) are available. Study abroad at Harlaxton College, England, and in Spain is possible. There are evening degree completion programs for working adults. There are 7 national honor societies and a freshman honors program.

Faculty/Classroom: 48% of faculty are male; 52% are female. 83% teach undergraduates. No introductory courses are taught by graduate students. The average class size in an introductory lecture is 22; in a laboratory is 16; and in a regular course is 13.

Admissions: 76% of the 2013-2014 applicants were accepted. The ACT scores were 58% below 21, 24% between 21 and 23, 13% between 24 and 26, 4% between 27 and 28, and 1% above 28. 23% of the current freshmen were in the top fifth of their class; 51% were in the top two fifths. 4 freshmen graduated first in their class.

Requirements: The ACT is required. The required minimum ACT composite score is 18. Applicants must be graduates of an accredited secondary school or have earned a GED. An interview is recommended. A GPA of 2.0 is required. AP and CLEP credits are accepted. Important factors in the admissions decision are advanced placement or honors courses, ability to finance college education, and personality/intangible qualities.

Procedure: Freshmen are admitted to all sessions. Entrance exams should be taken in the junior year. There are early admissions, deferred admissions, and rolling admissions plans. Application deadlines are open. Application fee is $20. Notification is sent on a rolling basis. Applications are accepted online.

Transfer: 168 transfer students enrolled in 2012-2013. The school recommends a minimum GPA of 2.0, the SAT or ACT (if <30 credits), and an interview. 32 of 128 credits required for the bachelor's degree must be completed at Marian.

Visiting: There are regularly scheduled orientations for prospective students, consisting of sessions in April, May, June, and July for course selection and meeting with advisors. There are guides for informal visits, visitors may sit in on classes, and stay overnight. To schedule a visit, contact the Admissions Office.

Financial Aid: In 2013-2014, 94% of all full-time freshmen and 86% of continuing full-time students received some form of financial aid. 94% of all full-time freshmen and 86% of continuing full-time students received need-based aid. The average freshman award was $22,515. Need-based scholarships or need-based grants averaged $14,412 ($28,640 maximum); need-based self-help aid (loans and jobs) averaged $6,021 ($18,354 maximum); and other non-need-based awards and non-need-based scholarships averaged $9,250 ($17,000 maximum). 30% of undergraduate students work part-time. Average annual earnings from campus work are $1340. The average financial indebtedness of the 2013 graduate was $27,850. The FAFSA and the college's own financial statement are required. The deadline for filing freshman financial aid applications for fall entry is March 15.

International Students: There are 41 international students enrolled. The school actively recruits these students. They must take the TOEFL with a minimum score of 525 on the paper-based TOEFL (PBT) or 70 on the Internet-based version (iBT).

Computers: All students may access the system. There are no time limits and no fees.

Graduates: From July 1, 2012 to June 30, 2013, 407 bachelor's degrees were awarded. The most popular majors were nursing (38%), business administration (20%), and criminal justice (13%). 27 companies recruited on campus in 2012-2013. In an average class, 28% graduate in 4 years or less, 44% graduate in 5 years or less, and 47% graduate in 6 years or less. Of the 2012 graduating class, 7% were enrolled in graduate school within 6 months of graduation, and 80% were employed.

Admissions Contact: Shannon Laluzerne, Director of Admissions. E-Mail: *SLaLuzerne@marianuniversity.edu* Web: *www.marianuniversity.edu*

MARQUETTE UNIVERSITY E-4

Milwaukee, WI 53201 (414) 288-7302
(800) 222-6544; (414) 288-3764

Full-time: 3814 men, 4155 women
Part-time: 177 men, 147 women
Graduate: 1690 men, 1766 women
Year: semesters, summer session
Application Deadline: December 1
Freshman Class: 22900 applied, 12644 accepted, 1928 enrolled
SAT CR/M/W: 580/600/580
Faculty: 588; I, -$
Ph.D.s: 90%
Student/Faculty: 14 to 1
Tuition: $33,244
Room & Board: $10,420
ACT: 27

VERY COMPETITIVE+

Marquette University, established in 1881, is a private Roman Catholic Jesuit institution. There are 8 undergraduate schools and 4 graduate schools. In addition to regional accreditation, Marquette has baccalaureate program accreditation with AACSB, ABET, ACEJMC, ADA, APTA, and NCATE. The 2 libraries contain 1.7 million volumes, 820,669 microform items, 19,560 audio/video tapes/CDs/DVDs, and subscribe to 39,040 periodicals including electronic. Computerized library services include interlibrary loans, database searching, Internet access, and Wi-Fi capability. Special learning facilities include an art gallery, radio station, and TV station. The 98-acre campus is in an urban area in the heart of Milwaukee. Including any residence halls, there are 69 buildings.

Student Life: 64% of undergraduates are from out of state, mostly the Mid-West. Students are from 48 states, 37 foreign countries, and Canada. 57% are from public schools. 75% are White. 55% are Catholic; 13% Protestant. The average age of freshmen is 18; all undergraduates, 20. 12% do not continue beyond their first year; 80% remain to graduate.

Housing: 4800 students can be accommodated in college housing, which includes single-sex and coed dorms and on-campus apartments. In addition, there are honors houses, specified majors, social justice, and multicultural floors. On-campus housing is guaranteed for the freshman year only and is available on a lottery system for upperclassmen. 54% of students live on campus; of those, 90% remain on campus on weekends. All students may keep cars.

Activities: 11% of men belong to 11 national fraternities; 14% of women belong to 13 national sororities. There are 270 groups on campus, including and recreational, art, band, cheerleading, chess, choir, chorale, chorus, community awareness, computers, dance, debate, drama, drill team, ethnic, film, gay, honors, international, jazz band, literary magazine, musical theater, newspaper, orchestra, pep band, photography, political, professional, radio and TV, religious, social, social service, student government, and symphony. Popular campus events include Student Organizational Fest, Winter Flurry and Hunger Clean Up.

Sports: There are 7 intercollegiate sports for men and 7 for women, and 40 intramural sports for men and 40 for women. Facilities include 2 recreation centers and Valley Fields, an outdoor soccer, track, and football facility.

Disabled Students: 90% of the campus is accessible. Facilities include wheelchair ramps, elevators, special parking, specially equipped restrooms, special class scheduling, lowered drinking fountains, lowered telephones, and special housing.

Services: Counseling and information services are available, as is tutoring in some subjects, many lower-division classes taken by freshmen and sophomores There is a reader service for the blind. Book taping and note taking are available for the physically disabled.

Campus Safety and Security: Measures include 24-hour foot and vehicle patrol, emergency notification system, self-defense education, and security escort services. There are shuttle buses, emergency telephones, lighted pathways/sidewalks, controlled access to dorms/residences, Closed-circuit cameras in selected parking lots and buildings throughout the campus. Public Safety has bicycle patrols and the Milwaukee police conduct patrols on horseback. Secure storage for bicycles in parking ramps, monitored by Public Safety using closed-circuit cameras.

Programs of Study: Marquette confers B.A., B.S., B.S.N., B.S.B.E., B.S.C.E., B.S.C.M., B.S.C.O., B.S.E.E. and B.S.M.E. and B.S.N. degrees. Master's and doctoral degrees are also awarded. Bachelor's degrees are awarded in BIOLOGICAL SCIENCE (biochemistry, biology/biological science, molecular biology, and physiology), BUSINESS (accounting, business administration and management, business economics, entrepreneurial studies, finance, human resources, international business management, management information systems, marketing/retailing/merchandising, operations management, organizational leadership and management, real estate, and supply chain management), COMMUNICATIONS AND THE ARTS (advertising, broadcasting, classical languages, classics, communications, dramatic arts, English, French, German, information technology, journalism, media arts, public relations, Spanish, and theatre arts), COMPUTER AND PHYSICAL SCIENCE (chemistry, computer science, mathematics, physics, and statistics), EDUCATION (athletic training, education, and secondary education), ENGINEERING AND ENVIRONMENTAL DESIGN (bioengineering, biomedical engineering, civil engineering, computational sciences, computer engineering, construction engineering, electrical/electronics engineering, engineering, environmental engineering, and mechanical engineering), HEALTH PROFESSIONS (biomedical science, clinical science, exercise science, medical laboratory science, nursing, premedicine, and speech pathology/audiology), SOCIAL SCIENCE (anthropology, criminology, economics, history, interdisciplinary studies, international relations, peace studies, philosophy, political science/government, psychology, sociology, and theological studies). Biomedical engineering, nursing, and premedicine are the strongest academically. Biomedical sciences, nursing and accounting have the largest enrollments.

Required: To graduate, students must complete a total of 126 to 135 credit hours and maintain a minimum GPA of 2.0, or 2.5 in accounting. The 36-credit-hour core of common studies includes 6 credit hours each of rhetoric, human nature and ethics, and theology, and 3 each of mathematical reasoning, individual and social behavior, science and nature, histories of cultures and societies, literature and performing arts, and diverse cultures. The total number of hours in the major varies.

Special: Marquette offers co-op programs in engineering, internships, study abroad in 16 countries, a Washington summer term, and work-study programs. Dual and student-designed majors, nondegree study, an accelerated degree program for pre-dental and pre-law students, and pass/fail options are available. Cross-registration is possible with Milwaukee Institute of Art and Design, and there is a 2-2 engineering program with Waukesha County Technical College. The Freshman Frontier Program offers academic support for selected freshmen who do not meet regular admission requirements but show potential for success. The Educational Opportunity Program affords students from minority groups and low-income families the opportunity to attend the school. There are 22 national honor societies, including Phi Beta Kappa, a freshman honors program, and 42 departmental honors programs.

Faculty/Classroom: 58% of faculty are male; 42% are female. 78% teach undergraduates. No introductory courses are taught by graduate students.

Admissions: 55% of the 2013-2014 applicants were accepted. The SAT scores for the 2013-2014 freshman class were: Critical Reading--13% below 500, 44% between 500 and 599, 36% between 600 and 699, and 7% between 700 and 800; Math--10% below 500, 36% between 500 and 599, 45% between 600 and 699, and 10% between 700 and 800; Writing--14% below 500, 44% between 500 and 599, 37% between 600 and 699, and 5% between 700 and 800. The ACT scores were 3% below 21, 13% between 21 and 23, 27% between 24 and 26, 23% between 27 and 28, and 35% above 28. 38% of the current freshmen were in the top fifth of their class; 60% were in the top two fifths. There were 5 National Merit finalists. 43 freshmen graduated first in their class.

Requirements: The SAT or ACT is required. In addition, Marquette requires either the ACT or the SAT test. Applicants must be graduates of an accredited secondary school with a recommended 18 credits, including 4 years of English, 3 each of social studies and math, 2 each of sciences and foreign language, and 4 of additional academic subjects. Most students rank in the upper quarter of their high school class. The GED is accepted, with a minimum score of 225. Applicants must demonstrate ability, preparation, and motivation. An interview is recommended. AP and CLEP credits are accepted. Important factors in the admissions decision are advanced placement or honors courses, recommendations by school officials, and leadership record.

Procedure: Freshmen are admitted to all sessions. Entrance exams should be taken in the junior year and repeated early in the senior year if necessary. There is a deferred admissions plan. Applications should be filed by December 1 for fall entry. The fall 2013 application fee was $30. Notifications are sent January 31. 1459 applicants were on the 2013 waiting list; 505 were admitted. Applications are accepted online.

Transfer: 149 transfer students enrolled in 2012-2013. Applicants for transfer must have a minimum GPA of 2.0; some programs require a higher average. The SAT or ACT is required if the applicant has completed fewer than 12 hours of college-level work. 30 of 126 credits required for the bachelor's degree must be completed at Marquette.

Visiting: There are regularly scheduled orientations for prospective students, including an agenda for visits that varies according to the specific program; open houses are available on scheduled weekends throughout the academic year. There are guides for informal visits, visitors may sit in on classes, and stay overnight. To schedule a visit, contact the Office of Undergraduate Admissions at (800) 222-6544.

Financial Aid: In 2013-2014, 99% of all full-time freshmen and 98% of continuing full-time students received some form of financial aid. 55% of all full-time freshmen and 51% of continuing full-time students received need-based aid. The average freshman award was $22,040. Need-based scholarships or need-based grants averaged $7,717 ($30,950 maximum); need-based self-help aid (loans and jobs) averaged $4,800 ($13,000 maximum); non-need-based athletic scholarships averaged $21,977 ($44,624 maximum); and other non-need-based awards and non-need-based scholarships averaged $12,118. 50% of undergraduate students work part-time. Average annual earnings from campus work are $2000. The average financial indebtedness of the 2013 graduate was $34,602. Marquette is a member of CSS. The FAFSA is required. The priority date for freshman financial aid applications for fall entry is February 1.

International Students: There are 258 international students enrolled. The school actively recruits these students. Marquette requires success in final external secondary exams according to the student's country of education.

Computers: All students may access the system 24 hours a day. There are no time limits and no fees.

Graduates: From July 1, 2012 to June 30, 2013, 1722 bachelor's degrees were awarded. The most popular majors were biomedical sciences (8%), accounting (6%), and psychology (5%). 183 companies recruited on campus in 2012-2013. In an average class, 60% graduate in 4 years or less, 78% graduate in 5 years or less, and 80% graduate in 6 years or less.

Admissions Contact: Robert Blust, Dean of Admissions. E-Mail: *admissions@marquette.edu* Web: *www.marquette.edu*

MILWAUKEE INSTITUTE OF ART AND DESIGN E-4

Milwaukee, WI 53202-6003 (414) 291-8070
(888) 749-MIAD; (414) 291-8077

Full- and part-time: 675 men and women
Graduate: n/av
Year: semesters, summer session
Application Deadline: see profile
Freshman Class: n/av
SAT or ACT: recommended

Faculty: 32
Ph.D.s: 85%
Student/Faculty: 19 to 1
Tuition: $26,800
Room & Board: $9100

SPECIAL

Milwaukee Institute of Art and Design, founded in 1974, is a private, 4-year professional college of art and design. The figures in the above capsule and in this profile are approximate. In addition to regional accreditation, MIAD has baccalaureate program accreditation with NASAD. The library contains 31,600 volumes 900 audio/video tapes/CDs/DVDs, and subscribes to 120 periodicals including electronic. Computerized library services include interlibrary loans, database searching, Internet access, and laptop Internet portals. Special learning facilities include a learning resource center, art gallery, and museum. The campus is in an urban area in downtown Milwaukee. Including any residence halls, there are 4 buildings.

Student Life: 72% of undergraduates are from Wisconsin. Others are from 20 states. 80% are from public schools. 82% are white. The average age of freshmen is 19; all undergraduates, 23. 21% do not continue beyond their first year; 73% remain to graduate.

Housing: 165 students can be accommodated in college housing, which includes coed dorms. On-campus housing is available on a first-come, first-served basis. 77% of students commute. Alcohol is not permitted. All students may keep cars.

Activities: There are no fraternities or sororities. There are 25 groups on campus, including art, ethnic, gay, literary magazine, photography, political, professional, religious, social, and student government. Popular campus events include visiting artist lectures and workshops, student and faculty exhibitions, and a scholarship show.

Sports: There is no sports program at MIAD.

Disabled Students: All of the campus is accessible. Facilities include wheelchair ramps, elevators, specially equipped rest rooms, lowered drinking fountains, and lowered telephones.

Services: Counseling and information services are available, as is tutoring in some subjects, including liberal studies. There is remedial writing. There is a program in developmental freshman English as well as student tutoring, and a writing center.

Campus Safety and Security: Measures include security escort services. There are emergency telephones and lighted pathways/sidewalks.

Programs of Study: MIAD confers B.F.A. degrees. Bachelor's degrees are awarded in COMMUNICATIONS AND THE ARTS (drawing, fine arts, graphic design, illustration, industrial design, painting, photography, printmaking, and sculpture), ENGINEERING AND ENVIRONMENTAL DESIGN (interior design). Graphic design, illustration, and industrial design have the largest enrollments.

Required: About 66% of the graduation credits are in studio courses. Students must complete 124 credits, with 81 studio credits, 43 in liberal studies, and a minimum GPA of 2.0. MIAD requires 12 credits in art history and at least 12 credits in English/writing and 19 credits in the humanities and sciences.

Special: Students may cross-register with Marquette University and 29 other nationally accredited art colleges. Study abroad in Japan, Germany, Poland, and France, a semester at New York Artists Studio, and internships in all design fields and photography are available. Nondegree study and credit for life, military, and work experience are possible. There are 23 departmental honors programs.

Faculty/Classroom: 60% of faculty are male; 40% are female. All teach undergraduates. The average class size in a regular course is 16.

Admissions: 74% of a recent year's applicants were accepted.

Requirements: The SAT or ACT is recommended. Applicants must be graduates of an accredited secondary school. 4 years of art are recommended. A portfolio review and an interview are required. A GPA of 2.0 is required. AP and CLEP credits are accepted. Important factors in the admissions decision are evidence of special talent, advanced placement or honors courses, and personality/intangible qualities.

Procedure: Freshmen are admitted fall and spring. There are deferred admissions and rolling admissions plans. Check with the school for current application deadlines. Notification is sent on a rolling basis.

Transfer: 60 transfer students were enrolled in a recent year. A transfer portfolio evaluation is done. Transcripts are reviewed for courses comparable to MIAD's programs. A grade of C or better is required for transfer. 30 of 124 credits required for the bachelor's degree must be completed at MIAD.

Visiting: There are guides for informal visits and visitors may sit in on classes. To schedule a visit, contact the Admissions Office.

Financial Aid: In a recent year, 84% of all full-time freshmen and 89% of continuing full-time students received some form of financial aid. 82% of all full-time freshmen and 87% of continuing full-time students received need-based aid. The average freshman award was $18,085. The average financial indebtedness of a recent graduate was $36,217. The FAFSA is required. Check with the school for current financial aid deadlines.

International Students: In a recent year, there were 23 international students enrolled. The school actively recruits these students. They must take the TOEFL.

Computers: All facilities are both wireless and optically wired. Access to the wireless system is through IT service account request. The Institute has both PC and Mac labs. 172 student-access workstations (18 workstations per studio for digital majors and an open lab) are available. There is also additional access in the library and open access in hallway hubs. All students may access the system more than 80 hours a week. It is strongly recommended that all students have a personal computer. An Apple or Dell, based upon industry standards for digital majors, is recommended.

Graduates: In a recent year, 121 bachelor's degrees were awarded. The most popular majors were communication design (22%), illustration (17%), and industrial design (15%). In an average class, 33% graduate in 4 years or less, 41% graduate in 5 years or less, and 42% graduate in 6 years or less. 15 companies recruited on campus in a recent year. Of a recent graduating class, 1% were enrolled in graduate school within 6 months of graduation, and 90% were employed.

Admissions Contact: Director of Admissions. A campus DVD is available. E-mail: *admissions@miad.edu* Web: *www.miad.edu*

MILWAUKEE SCHOOL OF ENGINEERING E-4

Milwaukee, WI 53202 (414) 277-6762
(800) 332-6763; (414) 277-7475

Full-time: 1705 men, 488 women
Part-time: 160 men, 25 women
Graduate: 143 men, 43 women
Year: quarters, summer session
Application Deadline:
Freshman Class: 2014 applied, 1147 accepted, 490 enrolled
SAT CR/M: 570/630

Faculty: 22; IIB, av$
Ph.D.s: 80%
Student/Faculty: 16 to 1
Tuition: $31,920
Room & Board: $8028
ACT: 27

VERY COMPETITIVE+

Milwaukee School of Engineering, established in 1903, is a private university offering bachelor's and master's degrees in the areas of engineering, business, mathematics and nursing. There are 5 undergraduate schools and 2 graduate schools. In addition to regional accreditation, MSOE has baccalaureate program accreditation with ABET and ACCE. The library contains 52,805 volumes, 80,654 microform items, and 2,451 audio/video tapes/CDs/DVDs, and subscribes to 101,951 periodicals including electronic. Computerized library services include interlibrary loans, database searching, Internet access, and Wi-Fi capability. Special learning facilities include an art gallery and radio station. The 20-acre campus is in an urban area in Milwaukee, Wisconsin. Including any residence halls, there are 14 buildings.

Student Life: 69% of undergraduates are from Wisconsin. Others are from 33 states, 27 foreign countries, and Canada. 80% are from public schools. 78% are White. The average age of freshmen is 19.47; all undergraduates, 22. 25% do not continue beyond their first year; 57% remain to graduate.

Housing: 930 students can be accommodated in college housing, which includes coed dorms. In addition, there are special-interest houses, There are suites for upperclassmen with kitchens, bathrooms, and living rooms. On-campus housing is guaranteed for all 4 years. 56% of students commute. Alcohol is not permitted. All students may keep cars.

Activities: 10% of men belong to 1 local and 3 national fraternities; 12% of women belong to 2 local and 1 national sororities. There are 72 groups on campus, including and ultimate frisbee, bowling, paintball, tae kwon do, cheerleading, chess, choir, computers, dance, drama, environmental, ethnic, gay, honors, international, jazz band, literary magazine, pep band, political, professional, radio and TV, religious, rugby, social, social service, student government, and symphony. Popular campus events include St. Patrick's Week, Greek Week and Sub-Zero Days.

Sports: There are 12 intercollegiate sports for men and 7 for women, and 9 intramural sports for men and 9 for women. Facilities include The Kern Center is a 210,000-square-foot recreation, athletic, health and wellness center. It contains an ice arena, fitness center, wrestling room, field house, counseling center, health services, campus ministry, basketball arena, and an indoor track facility.

Disabled Students: 95% of the campus is accessible. Facilities include wheelchair ramps, elevators, special parking, specially equipped restrooms, special class scheduling, lowered drinking fountains, lowered telephones, and special housing.

Services: Counseling and information services are available, as is tutoring in every subject. There is a reader service for the blind, and remedial math, reading, and writing.

Campus Safety and Security: Measures include 24-hour foot and vehicle patrol and security escort services. There are shuttle buses, emergency telephones, lighted pathways/sidewalks, and 24-hour security in residence halls.

Programs of Study: MSOE confers B.A., and B.S. degrees. Master's degrees are also awarded. Bachelor's degrees are awarded in BIOLOGICAL SCIENCE (molecular biology), BUSINESS (business administration and management, international business management, management information systems, management science, and operations research), COMMUNICATIONS AND THE ARTS (technical and business writing), COMPUTER AND PHYSICAL SCIENCE (actuarial science and software engineering), ENGINEERING AND ENVIRONMENTAL DESIGN (architectural engineering, biomedical engineering, computer engineering, construction management, electrical/electronics engineering, engineering, engineering technology, industrial engineering, and mechanical engineering), HEALTH PROFESSIONS (nursing). Biomedical engineering and computer engineering is the strongest academically. Architectural, mechanical, and electrical engineering have the largest enrollments.

Required: To graduate, students must complete approximately 197 quarter credits with a minimum GPA of 2.0 overall and in the major. There are requirements in speech, composition, computer programming, ethics, and business.

Special: MSOE offers internships in the student's discipline, study-abroad in France, Germany, India, and Czech Republic, on-campus work-study programs, and nondegree study. A number of dual degrees along with a 5-year freshman-to-master's degree in civil engineering, are available. There are 6 national honor societies and 5 departmental honors programs.

Faculty/Classroom: 71% of faculty are male; 29% are female. 92% teach undergraduates, 2% do research, and 18% do both. No introductory courses are taught by graduate students. The average class size in an introductory lecture is 22; in a laboratory is 16; and in a regular course is 22.

Admissions: 57% of the 2013-2014 applicants were accepted. The SAT scores for the 2013-2014 freshman class were: Critical Reading--17% below 500, 53% between 500 and 599, 19% between 600 and 699, and 11% between 700 and 800; Math--8% below 500, 19% between 500 and 599, 58% between 600 and 699, and 15% between 700 and 800. The ACT scores were 3% below 21, 13% between 21 and 23, 29% between 24 and 26, 35% between 27 and 28, and 20% above 28.

Requirements: The ACT is required. The SAT is recommended. In addition, applicants must be graduates of an accredited secondary school, having completed 15 academic credits, including 4 units of English, 2 units each of science and math, and 1 unit each of social studies and history. More units in math, science, and English are strongly advised; 1 unit in computer science is recommended. The GED is accepted. An essay is required, and an interview is recommended. A GPA of 2.5 is required. AP and CLEP credits are accepted. Important factors in the admissions decision are advanced placement or honors courses, leadership record, and personality/intangible qualities.

Procedure: Freshmen are admitted to all sessions. Entrance exams should be taken during the junior year. There are deferred admissions and rolling admissions plans. Application deadlines are open. Applications are accepted online.

Transfer: 144 transfer students enrolled in 2012-2013. Applicants for transfer should have a minimum GPA of 2.75 and must have completed 24 semester or 36 quarter credits. 100 of 197 credits required for the bachelor's degree must be completed at MSOE.

Visiting: There are regularly scheduled orientations for prospective students, consisting of personal visits, Spring and Fall Open Houses, Accepted Student Days and Senior Visit Days. There are guides for informal visits, visitors may sit in on classes, and stay overnight. To schedule a visit, contact the Admission Office.

Financial Aid: In 2013-2014, 100% of all full-time freshmen and 98% of continuing full-time students received some form of financial aid. 81% of all full-time freshmen and 83% of continuing full-time students received need-based aid. The average freshman award was $23,772. Need-based scholarships or need-based grants averaged $21,207 ($42,738 maximum); need-based self-help aid (loans and jobs) averaged $2,886 ($9,000 maximum); other non-need-based awards and non-need-based scholarships averaged $12,170 ($31,920 maximum); and $7,930 from other forms of aid. 68% of undergraduate students work part-time. Average annual earnings from campus work are $1988. The average financial indebtedness of the 2013 graduate was $38,038. The FAFSA is required. The priority date for freshman financial aid applications for fall entry is March 15.

International Students: There are 65 international students enrolled. The school actively recruits these students. They must take the TOEFL with a minimum score of 79 on the Internet-based version (iBT).

Computers: All students may access the system. There are no time limits and no fees.

Graduates: From July 1, 2012 to June 30, 2013, 470 bachelor's degrees were awarded. The most popular majors were mechanical engineering (24%), business (17%), and architectural engineering (15%). 248 companies recruited on campus in 2012-2013. In an average class, 39% graduate in 4 years or less, 53% graduate in 5 years or less, and 56% graduate in 6 years or less. Of the 2012 graduating class, 6% were enrolled in graduate school within 6 months of graduation, and 88% were employed.

Admissions Contact: Seandra Mitchell, Director of Admission. E-Mail: *mitchell@msoe.edu* Web: *www.msoe.edu*

MOUNT MARY UNIVERSITY E-4

Milwaukee, WI 53222 **(414) 256-1219 ex. 399; (414) 256-0180**

Full-time: 3 men, 682 women	**Faculty:** n/av
Part-time: 18 men, 223 women	**Ph.D.s:** 74%
Graduate: 51 men, 504 women	**Student/Faculty:** 10 to 1
Year: semesters, summer session	**Tuition:** $25,098
Application Deadline:	**Room & Board:** $7738

Freshman Class: 477 applied, 258 accepted, 114 enrolled
ACT: 20

LESS COMPETITIVE

Mount Mary University, founded in 1913, is a private women's liberal arts institution sponsored by the School Sisters of Notre Dame, and affiliated with the Roman Catholic Church. There are 4 undergraduate schools and one graduate school. In addition to regional accreditation, Mount Mary has baccalaureate program accreditation with CAHEA, CSWE, FIDER, and NLN. The library contains 317,954 volumes, 4,828 audio/video tapes/CDs/DVDs, and subscribes to 61,920 periodicals including electronic. Computerized library services include interlibrary loans, database searching, Internet access, and Wi-Fi capability. Special learning facilities include an art gallery, computer centers, CAD labs, S.M.A.R.T. classrooms, and a historic costume collection. The 80-acre campus is in an urban area 7 miles west of downtown Milwaukee. Including any residence halls, there are 8 buildings.

Student Life: 96% of undergraduates are from Wisconsin. Others are from 10 states, and 15 foreign countries. 52% are White; 22% African American; 14% Hispanic. The average age of freshmen is 20; all undergraduates, 24. 29% do not continue beyond their first year; 42% remain to graduate.

Housing: 184 students can be accommodated in college housing, which includes single-sex dorms. On-campus housing is available on a first-come and first-served basis. 82% of students commute. All students may keep cars.

Activities: There are no fraternities or sororities. There are 37 groups on campus, including and department-affiliated clubs, art, choir, chorale, chorus, dance, drama, ethnic, honors, international, literary magazine, newspaper, political, professional, religious, social, social service, and student government. Popular campus events include Freshman Investiture, Spring Formal, and Christmas on the Mound.

Sports: There are 6 intercollegiate sports for women. Facilities include gym, exercise room, weight room, soccer field.

Disabled Students: 98% of the campus is accessible. Facilities include wheelchair ramps, elevators, special parking, specially equipped restrooms, and lowered drinking fountains.

Services: Counseling and information services are available, as is tutoring in most subjects. There is a reader service for the blind, and remedial math, reading, and writing. A tutoring language lab is also available.

Campus Safety and Security: Measures include 24-hour foot and vehicle patrol, emergency notification system, self-defense education, and security escort services. There are lighted pathways/sidewalks and controlled access to dorms/residences.

Programs of Study: Mount Mary confers B.A., and B.S. degrees. Master's and doctoral degrees are also awarded. Bachelor's degrees are awarded in BIOLOGICAL SCIENCE (biology/biological science), BUSINESS (accounting, business administration and management, fashion merchandising, and marketing/retailing/merchandising), COMMUNICATIONS AND THE ARTS (communications, English, fine arts, graphic design, public relations, Spanish, and technical and business writing), COMPUTER AND PHYSICAL SCIENCE (chemistry, mathematics, and radiological technology), EDUCATION (art education, bilingual/bicultural education, business education, early childhood education, elementary education, English education, foreign languages education, music education, science education, and secondary education), ENGINEERING AND ENVIRONMENTAL DESIGN (interior design), HEALTH PROFESSIONS (art therapy, occupational therapy, predentistry, and premedicine), SOCIAL SCIENCE (behavioral science, criminal justice, dietetics, fashion design and technology, history, international studies, liberal arts/general studies, philosophy, prelaw, psychology, social work, and theological studies). Occupational therapy, apparel fashion design, amd merchandise managment are the strongest academically. Psychology, occupational therapy, and business administration have the largest enrollments.

Required: To graduate, students must complete 128 credit hours, including at least 24 (but as many as 74) in the major, while maintaining a GPA of at least 2.0, with many majors requiring a higher GPA. A 48-credit liberal arts core curriculum and demonstrated math competency are required.

Special: Mount Mary College offers internships, accelerated degree programs in business administration, business/professional communication, and marketing, and study abroad in many countries. Student-designed majors, a pre-nursing program with Columbia College of Nursing, pass/fail options, and credit for life, military, and work experience are available. There are 14 national honor societies and a freshman honors program.

Faculty/Classroom: 22% of faculty are male; 78% are female. No introductory courses are taught by graduate students. The average class size in a laboratory is 12 and in a regular course is 12.

Admissions: 54% of the 2013-2014 applicants were accepted. The ACT scores were 61% below 21, 12% between 21 and 23, 19% between 24 and 26, 3% between 27 and 28, and 5% above 28. 48% of the current freshmen were in the top fifth of their class; 70% were in the top two fifths. 2 freshmen graduated first in their class.

Requirements: The ACT is required. Applicants must be graduates of an accredited secondary school. The GED is accepted. Students should have completed 16 credits, including 4 in English, and 2 each in history, social sciences, math, science and academic elective. Mount Mary requires applicants to be in the upper 40% of their class. A GPA of 2.5 is required. AP and CLEP credits are accepted. Important factors in the admissions decision are advanced placement or honors courses, recommendations by school officials, and leadership record.

Procedure: Freshmen are admitted fall and spring. Entrance exams should be taken in the junior year or fall of the senior year. There are deferred admissions and rolling admissions plans. Application deadlines are open. Applications are accepted online. Application fees are waived if application is completed online.

Transfer: 61 transfer students enrolled in 2012-2013. Applicants should have a minimum GPA of 2.0, though each department has its own admission requirements. The school recommends either the SAT or ACT. 32 of 128 credits required for the bachelor's degree must be completed at Mount Mary.

Visiting: There are regularly scheduled orientations for prospective students, including tours, meetings with faculty and staff, and information sessions. There are guides for informal visits, visitors may sit in on classes, and stay overnight. To schedule a visit, contact Admissions Office at mmu-admiss@mtmary.edu.

Financial Aid: The FAFSA is required. The priority date for freshman financial aid applications for fall entry is March 1.

International Students: There are 20 international students enrolled. The school actively recruits these students. They must take the TOEFL with a minimum score of 76 on the Internet-based version (iBT).

Computers: All students may access the system. 7 days a week, 24 hours a day. There are no time limits and no fees.

Graduates: From July 1, 2012 to June 30, 2013, 165 bachelor's degrees were awarded. The most popular majors were business/marketing (23%), visual and performing arts (17%), and public administration and social services (9%). In an average class, 21% graduate in 4 years or less, 36% graduate in 5 years or less, and 42% graduate in 6 years or less.

Admissions Contact: Rachel Sonnentag, Director of Undergraduate Admissions. E-Mail: *mmu-admiss@mtmary.edu* Web: *www.mtmary.edu*

NORTHLAND COLLEGE B-1

Ashland, WI 54806 (715) 682-1224
(800) 753-1840; (715) 682-1258

Full- and part-time: 750 men and women	**Faculty:** n/av
Graduate: n/av	**Ph.D.s:** 84%
Year: varies, summer session	**Student/Faculty:** n/av
Application Deadline: see profile	**Tuition:** $26,225
	Room & Board: $7710
Freshman Class: n/av	
SAT or ACT: required	

COMPETITIVE

Northland College, founded in 1892, is a private liberal arts institution affiliated with the United Church of Christ and offers undergraduate programs in the arts and sciences, business, education, health professions, and social sciences. There are 3 undergraduate schools. The figures in the above capsule and in this profile are approximate. The library contains 77,700 volumes and 9,300 microform items, and subscribes to 350 periodicals including electronic. Computerized library services include interlibrary loans and database searching. Special learning facilities include a learning resource center, art gallery, natural history museum, environmental research acreage, community garden, and wind tower. The 100-acre campus is in a small town 70 miles east of Duluth, Minnesota. Including any residence halls, there are 20 buildings.

Student Life: 65% of undergraduates are from out of state, mostly the Mid-West. Students are from 42 states, 7 foreign countries, and Canada. 90% are from public schools. 89% are white. The average age of freshmen is 20; all undergraduates, 21. 20% do not continue beyond their first year; 44% remain to graduate.

Housing: 530 students can be accommodated in college housing, which includes single-sex and coed dorms and on-campus apartments. In addition, there are special-interest houses and a farmhouse. On-campus housing is guaranteed for all 4 years. 60% of students live on campus; of those, 80% remain on campus on weekends. Alcohol is not permitted. All students may keep cars.

Activities: 2% of men belong to 1 local and 1 national fraternity; 2% of women belong to 2 local sororities. There are 25 groups on campus, including art, band, cheerleading, choir, chorale, chorus, computers, drama, ethnic, gay, honors, international, jazz band, literary magazine, newspaper, orchestra, photography, political, professional, religious, social, social service, student government, symphony, and yearbook. Popular campus events include Snow Festival and Spring Fling.

Sports: There are 4 intercollegiate sports for men and 4 for women, and 11 intramural sports for men and 11 for women. Facilities include an Olympic-size pool, a weight-lifting room, tennis and racquetball courts, a ropes course, and an outdoor recreation program.

Disabled Students: 90% of the campus is accessible. Facilities include wheelchair ramps, elevators, special parking, specially equipped rest rooms, and special class scheduling.

Services: Counseling and information services are available, as is tutoring in every subject. There is a reader service for the blind, and remedial math, reading, and writing.

Campus Safety and Security: Measures include security escort services. There are emergency telephones and lighted pathways/sidewalks.

Programs of Study: Northland confers B.A. and B.S. degrees. Bachelor's degrees are awarded in AGRICULTURE (natural resource management), BIOLOGICAL SCIENCE (biology/biological science), BUSINESS (business administration and management and business economics), COMMUNICATIONS AND THE ARTS (creative writing, English, and fine arts), COMPUTER AND PHYSICAL SCIENCE (atmospheric sciences and meteorology, chemistry, earth science, information sciences and systems, and mathematics), EDUCATION (elementary education, middle school education, music education, and secondary education), ENGINEERING AND ENVIRONMENTAL DESIGN (environmental science), SOCIAL SCIENCE (history, parks and recreation management, peace studies, psychology, public administration, religion, and sociology). Biology, natural resources, and meteoroloy are the strongest academically. Biology, natural resources, and outdoor education have the largest enrollments.

Required: Students must complete 124 credits, including 35 to 60 in the major, with a minimum GPA of 2.0. All students must meet requirements that include courses in English composition, literature, history, philosophy, social and natural sciences, physical science, fine arts, phys ed, and studies of other cultures.

Special: Opportunities are provided for cooperative programs in many majors and with other schools, internships, work-study programs with state and federal agencies, student-designed majors, credit for life experience, pass/fail options, and study abroad in 7 countries. Cross-registration is offered with Spring Term Consortium Schools, Allegheny and Beloit Colleges, and Kansai Gaidai University in Japan. 3-2 engineering degrees are available in conjunction with Michigan Technological University and Washington University in St. Louis. A 3-2 degree program in forestry is also available. There are 2 national honor societies.

Faculty/Classroom: 81% of faculty are male; 19% are female. All teach undergraduates. The average class size in an introductory lecture is 30; in a laboratory, 30; and in a regular course, 22.

Requirements: The SAT or ACT is required. In addition, graduation from an accredited secondary school is required; the GED is accepted. An essay and interview are recommended. A GPA of 2.0 is required. AP and CLEP credits are accepted. Important factors in the admissions decision are advanced placement or honors courses, extracurricular activities record, and recommendations by school officials.

Procedure: Freshmen are admitted fall and winter. Entrance exams should be taken in the fall. There are early decision, early admissions, deferred admissions, and rolling admissions plans. Early decision applications should be filed by November 22; check with the school for current application deadlines. Notification of early decision is sent December 22. Applications are accepted online.

Transfer: Applicants must have maintained a minimum GPA of 2.0 in previously attended colleges. 30 of 124 credits required for the bachelor's degree must be completed at Northland.

Visiting: There are regularly scheduled orientations for prospective students, including an interview, a tour, class visits, and an overnight stay in a dorm. There are guides for informal visits, visitors may sit in on classes, and stay overnight. To schedule a visit, contact the Admissions Office.

Financial Aid: Northland is a member of CSS. The FAFSA and the college's own financial statement are required. Check with the school for current financial aid deadlines.

International Students: The school actively recruits these students. They must take the TOEFL or MELAB.

Computers: All students may access the system. There are no time limits and no fees.

Admissions Contact: Director of Admissions. A campus DVD is available. E-mail: *admit@northland.edu* Web: *www.northland.edu*

RIPON COLLEGE D-4

Ripon, WI 54971 (920) 748-8185
(800) 94-RIPON; (920) 748-8335

Full-time: 508 men, 546 women
Part-time: 4 men, 7 women
Graduate: n/av
Year: semesters
Application Deadline: August 1
Freshman Class: 1160 applied, 899 accepted, 289 enrolled
SAT CR/M: 500/528
Faculty: 64; IIB, --$
Ph.D.s: 75%
Student/Faculty: 15 to 1
Tuition: $28,689
Room & Board: $8270
ACT: 24 **COMPETITIVE+**

Ripon College, established in 1851, is a private, residential, liberal arts institution. The library contains 183,000 volumes, 10,000 microform items, 600 audio/video tapes/CDs/DVDs, and subscribes to 300 periodicals including electronic. Computerized library services include interlibrary loans, database searching, Internet access, and Wi-Fi capability. Special learning facilities include an art gallery, radio station, a music library, an art slide library, and college archives. The 250-acre campus is in a small town 80 miles north of Milwaukee. Including any residence halls, there are 26 buildings.

Student Life: 74% of undergraduates are from Wisconsin. Others are from 31 states, 18 foreign countries, and Canada. 60% are from public schools. 86% are White. The average age of freshmen is 18; all undergraduates, 20. 15% do not continue beyond their first year; 76% remain to graduate.

Housing: 1056 students can be accommodated in college housing, which includes single-sex and coed dorms and on-campus apartments. theme and interest groups may form living areas in the residence halls. On-campus housing is guaranteed for all 4 years and is available on a lottery system for upperclassmen. 90% of students live on campus; of those, 80% remain on campus on weekends. All students may keep cars.

Activities: 34% of men belong to 2 local and 3 national fraternities; 28% of women belong to 1 local and 3 national sororities. There are 80 groups on campus, including art, band, cheerleading, choir, chorale, chorus, dance, drama, environmental, ethnic, film, forensics, gay, honors, international, jazz band, literary magazine, musical theater, newspaper, orchestra, pep band, photography, political, professional, radio and TV, religious, social, social service, student government, symphony, and yearbook. Popular campus events include Spring and Winter Festivals, Milwaukee Symphony Concerts, and Theater Events.

Sports: There are 10 intercollegiate sports for men and 11 for women, and 12 intramural sports for men and 12 for women. Facilities include a phys ed center, 2 fields, tennis courts, a recreation center, and an exercise room and a fitness center in the residence halls. The campus is within 5 miles of lakes and cross-country skiing opportunities.

Disabled Students: 50% of the campus is accessible. Facilities include wheelchair ramps, elevators, special parking, specially equipped restrooms, special class scheduling, and lowered drinking fountains.

Services: Counseling and information services are available, as is tutoring in most subjects. Tutoring and services are also available for learning-disabled students.

Campus Safety and Security: Measures include 24-hour foot and vehicle patrol and security escort services. There are emergency telephones, lighted pathways/sidewalks, and a paging system.

Programs of Study: confers A.B. degrees. Bachelor's degrees are awarded in BIOLOGICAL SCIENCE (biochemistry and biology/biological science), BUSINESS (business administration and management), COMMUNICATIONS AND THE ARTS (art, art history and appreciation, communications, dramatic arts, English, French, German, music, and Spanish), COMPUTER AND PHYSICAL SCIENCE (chemistry, computer science, mathematics, physical sciences, and physics), EDUCATION (early childhood education, elementary education, middle school education, and secondary education), ENGINEERING AND ENVIRONMENTAL DESIGN (environmental science), HEALTH PROFESSIONS (exercise science), SOCIAL SCIENCE (anthropology, economics, history, international studies, Latin American studies, philosophy, political science/government, psychobiology, psychology, religion, and sociology). Sciences and education is the strongest academically. Business, biology, and history have the largest enrollments.

Required: To graduate, students must complete 124 credit hours, including usually 24 in the major, with a minimum GPA of 2.0. Required courses include 1 course each in fine arts, humanities, natural sciences, and social and behavioral sciences, a first-year seminar, a first-year writing course, 1 phys ed course, and a capstone experience.

Special: Students may cross-register with the Associated Colleges of the Midwest. Internships, study abroad in 13 countries, through 7 domestic programs, and a Washington semester are available. The college offers 3-year degrees in all areas, dual and student-designed majors, and pass/fail options. A 3-2 engineering degree is available with Rensselaer Polytechnic Institute, Washington University, and the University of Madison; other 3-2 programs are in environmental studies and in forestry with Duke University. There are 12 national honor societies, including Phi Beta Kappa, and a freshman honors program.

Faculty/Classroom: 58% of faculty are male; 42% are female. All teach and do research. No introductory courses are taught by graduate students. The average class size in an introductory lecture is 25; in a laboratory is 15; and in a regular course is 19.

Admissions: 78% of the 2013-2014 applicants were accepted. The SAT scores for the 2013-2014 freshman class were: Critical Reading--53% below 500, 35% between 500 and 599, 9% between 600 and 699, and 3% between 700 and 800; Math--36% below 500, 38% between 500 and 599, 23% between 600 and 699, and 3% between 700 and 800. The ACT scores were 19% below 21, 29% between 21 and 23, 28% between 24 and 26, 14% between 27 and 28, and 10% above 28. 48% of the current freshmen were in the top fifth of their class; 80% were in the top two fifths. 14 freshmen graduated first in their class.

Requirements: The SAT or ACT is required. Applicants must be graduates of an accredited secondary school. The GED is accepted. Applicants should complete at least 17 Carnegie units, including 4 of English, 2 to 4 each of math, social studies, and natural sciences, and up to 7 of other college-preparatory electives. An essay may be required, and an interview is recommended. requires applicants to be in the upper 50% of their class. A GPA of 2.0 is required. AP and CLEP credits are accepted. Important factors in the admissions decision are leadership record, recommendations by school officials, and advanced placement or honors courses.

Procedure: Freshmen are admitted fall and spring. Entrance exams should be taken in the junior year or the fall of the senior year. There are deferred admissions and rolling admissions plans. Applications should be filed by August 1 for fall entry; December 15 for spring entry, along with a $30 fee. Notification is sent on a rolling basis. Applications are accepted online.

Transfer: 16 transfer students enrolled in 2012-2013. Applicants must have a minimum 2.0 GPA and be in good standing at their previous college. The SAT or ACT, a personal statement, and an interview are recommended. 32 of 124 credits required for the bachelor's degree must be completed at Ripon.

Visiting: There are regularly scheduled orientations for prospective students, including a tour, an interview, and meetings with professors and coaches. There are guides for informal visits and visitors may sit in on classes. To schedule a visit, contact the Admission Office.

Financial Aid: In 2013-2014, 96% of all full-time freshmen and 90% of continuing full-time students received some form of financial aid. 86% of all full-time freshmen and 83% of continuing full-time students received need-based aid. The average freshman award was $28,771. Need-based scholarships or need-based grants averaged $20,300 ($33,736 maximum); need-based self-help aid (loans and jobs) averaged $5,364 ($8,800 maximum); and other non-need-based awards and non-need-based scholarships averaged $14,703 ($33,500 maximum). 45% of undergraduate students work part-time. Average annual earnings from campus work are $1877. The average financial indebtedness of the 2013 graduate was $24,795. The FAFSA is required. The priority date for freshman financial aid applications for fall entry is March 1.

International Students: There are 31 international students enrolled. The school actively recruits these students. They must take the TOEFL with a minimum score of 550 on the paper-based TOEFL (PBT) or 79 on the Internet-based version (iBT).

Computers: All students may access the system. There are no time limits and no fees.

Graduates: From July 1, 2012 to June 30, 2013, 213 bachelor's degrees were awarded. The most popular majors were business (16%), psychology (12%), and English (11%). 14 companies recruited on campus in 2012-2013. In an average class, 1% graduate in 3 years or less, 60% graduate in 4 years or less, 76% graduate in 5 years or less, and 76% graduate in 6 years or less. Of the 2012 graduating class, 34% were enrolled in graduate school within 6 months of graduation, and 64% were employed.

Admissions Contact: Steven M. Schuetz, Vice President for Admissions and Financial Aid. E-Mail: *schuetz@ripon.edu* Web: *www.ripon.edu*

SILVER LAKE COLLEGE E-3

Manitowoc, WI 54220 (920) 686-6187
(800) 236-4752, ext. 175; (920) 684-7082

Full- and part-time: 310 men, 710 women
Graduate: n/av
Year: semesters, summer session
Application Deadline: open
Freshman Class: n/av
SAT or ACT: required
Faculty: n/av
Ph.D.s: 49%
Student/Faculty: n/av
Tuition: $21,580
Room & Board: $8500
LESS COMPETITIVE

Silver Lake College, founded in 1935, is a private Catholic liberal arts institution offering undergraduate and graduate programs. There are 3 graduate schools. The figures in the above capsule and in this profile are approximate. In addition to regional accreditation, Silver Lake College has baccalaureate program accreditation with NASM. The library contains

60,400 volumes, 2,100 microform items, 12,500 audio/video tapes/CDs/DVDs, and subscribes to 300 periodicals including electronic. Computerized library services include interlibrary loans and database searching. Special learning facilities include a learning resource center and a special education clinic used for the training of special education teachers. The 30-acre campus is in a rural area 4 miles west of Manitowoc. Including any residence halls, there are 2 buildings.

Student Life: 99% of undergraduates are from Wisconsin. Others are from 4 states and 4 foreign countries. 89% are from public schools. 94% are white. The average age of freshmen is 19; all undergraduates, 27. 18% do not continue beyond their first year; 50% remain to graduate.

Housing: 30 students can be accommodated in college housing, which includes coed off-campus apartments. On-campus housing is guaranteed for the freshman year only. 73% of students commute. Alcohol is not permitted. All students may keep cars.

Activities: There are no fraternities or sororities. There are 18 groups on campus, including art, band, choir, chorus, communications, computers, dance, honors, jazz band, literary magazine, newspaper, orchestra, professional, religious, and student government. Popular campus events include Fine Arts Series, Campus Ministry programs, and Parents Day.

Sports: There is 1 intercollegiate sport for women, and 2 intramural sports for men and 2 for women. Facilities include a YMCA and the Two Rivers and Manitowoc Recreation Department.

Disabled Students: 95% of the campus is accessible. Facilities include wheelchair ramps, elevators, special parking, specially equipped rest rooms, and special class scheduling.

Services: Counseling and information services are available, as is tutoring in most subjects and study groups as needed. There is a reader service for the blind, and remedial math, reading, and writing.

Campus Safety and Security: There are emergency telephones and lighted pathways/sidewalks.

Programs of Study: Silver Lake College confers B.A., B.S., B.B.A., and B.M. degrees. Associate and master's degrees are also awarded. Bachelor's degrees are awarded in BIOLOGICAL SCIENCE (biology/biological science), BUSINESS (accounting, business administration and management, human resources, and personnel management), COMMUNICATIONS AND THE ARTS (English, fine arts, music, and studio art), COMPUTER AND PHYSICAL SCIENCE (computer science, information sciences and systems, and mathematics), EDUCATION (art education, early childhood education, elementary education, music education, secondary education, and special education), SOCIAL SCIENCE (history, psychology, public administration, religion, and social science). Elementary education and special education are the strongest academically. Business administration and management have the largest enrollments.

Required: To graduate, students must complete at least 120 credit hours with a minimum GPA of 2.0. 45 to 50 credits of liberal arts studies must be taken.

Special: Silver Lake offers cross-registration with several Wisconsin technical colleges, internships, B.A.-B.S. degrees, dual majors, work-study programs, and student-designed majors. Nondegree study, pass/fail options, and credit for life, military, and work experience are available. An accelerated degree program in business management, accounting, human resources, and public administration is offered. There are 4 national honor societies and 4 departmental honors programs.

Faculty/Classroom: 37% of faculty are male; 63% are female. 85% teach undergraduates, and 1% do research. No introductory courses are taught by graduate students. The average class size in an introductory lecture is 19; in a laboratory, 7; and in a regular course, 10.

Requirements: The SAT or ACT is required. Applicants must be graduates of an accredited secondary school. The GED is accepted. Applicants should complete 3 units of high school English, 2 each of math and history or social studies, and 1 of lab science. A GPA of 2.0 is required. AP and CLEP credits are accepted. Important factors in the admissions decision are recommendations by school officials, evidence of special talent, and advanced placement or honors courses.

Procedure: Freshmen are admitted fall and spring. Entrance exams should be taken in the spring of the junior year. There is a rolling admissions plan. Application deadlines are open. Check with the school for the current fee. Applications are accepted online.

Transfer: Applicants who have 30 acceptable credits must have a minimum GPA of 2.0; those with fewer credits must meet the requirements for entering freshmen, except that the SAT or ACT is not required. 30 of 120 credits required for the bachelor's degree must be completed at Silver Lake College.

Visiting: There are regularly scheduled orientations for prospective students, including a tour and meetings with an admissions counselor, an adviser, the financial aid department, and the housing director. There are guides for informal visits and visitors may sit in on classes. To schedule a visit, contact the Admissions Office.

Financial Aid: The FAFSA, the college's own financial statement, and tax returns are required. Check with the school for current financial aid deadlines.

International Students: They must take the TOEFL.

Computers: All students may access the system. There are no time limits and no fees.

Admissions Contact: Admissions Office. E-mail: *admslc@silver.sl.edu*
Web: *www.sl.edu*

ST. NORBERT COLLEGE — D-3

De Pere, WI 54115
(920) 403-3005
(800) 236-4878; (920) 403-4072

Full-time: 876 men, 1239 women	**Faculty:** 137; IIB, -$
Part-time: 17 men, 28 women	**Ph.D.s:** 88%
Graduate: 20 men, 34 women	**Student/Faculty:** 14 to 1
Year: semesters, summer session	**Tuition:** $31,866
Application Deadline: open	**Room & Board:** $8126

Freshman Class: 2088 applied, 1711 accepted, 539 enrolled
ACT: 25

VERY COMPETITIVE

With a liberal arts foundation that teaches critical thinking, problem-solving and leadership skills, St. Norbert College offers academic excellence and faculty members who make student success their top priority. Students have a multitude of programs and internship opportunities, and can study abroad in nearly 30 countries on six continents. Undergraduates here regularly experience graduate-level collaborative research with faculty. Academic advisors guide students throughout their college career, and an active alumni community provides valuable career networking. There are 3 graduate schools. The library contains 239,049 volumes, 16,055 microform items, 2,885 audio/video tapes/CDs/DVDs, and subscribes to 79,664 periodicals including electronic. Computerized library services include interlibrary loans, database searching, Internet access, and Wi-Fi capability. Special learning facilities include an art gallery, radio station, TV station, innovation studio; center for women's and gender studies; center for peace, justice and public understanding; marina; fine and performing arts centers; center for international education; center for leadership and service; children's center; center for Norbertine studies; language labs; media center with satellite hookup; and environmental sciences research craft. The 108-acre campus is in a suburban area 5 miles south of Green Bay. Including any residence halls, there are 41 buildings.

Student Life: 76% of undergraduates are from Wisconsin. Others are from 29 states, 18 foreign countries, and Canada. 72% are from public schools. 91% are White. 47% are Catholic; 35% Protestant; 16% claim no religious affiliation. The average age of freshmen is 18; all undergraduates, 20. 19% do not continue beyond their first year; 75% remain to graduate.

Housing: 1681 students can be accommodated in college housing, which includes single-sex and coed dorms and on-campus apartments. In addition, there are special-interest houses, a townhouse complex, a living center, and off-campus houses. On-campus housing is guaranteed for all 4 years. 75% of students live on campus; of those, 80% remain on campus on weekends. All students may keep cars.

Activities: 13% of men belong to 4 national fraternities; 10% of women belong to 4 national sororities. There are 69 groups on campus, including art, band, cheerleading, chess, choir, chorale, chorus, computers, dance, drama, E2K Entertainment Tonight, environmental, ethnic, film, gay, honors, international, jazz band, literary magazine, musical theater, newspaper, opera, pep band, photography, political, professional, radio and TV, religious, social, social service, student government, and yearbook. Popular campus events include Opening Campus Picnic/convocation, E2K Homecoming and SNC Day.

Sports: There are 10 intercollegiate sports for men and 10 for women, and 7 intramural sports for men and 7 for women. Facilities include a 3,100-seat stadium, a sports complex, an 1,800-seat sports center, and an activity center.

Disabled Students: 78% of the campus is accessible. Facilities include wheelchair ramps, elevators, special parking, specially equipped restrooms, special class scheduling, lowered drinking fountains, lowered telephones, and special housing.

Services: Counseling and information services are available, as is tutoring in most subjects. There is a reader service for the blind, and remedial math, reading, and writing.

Campus Safety and Security: Measures include 24-hour foot and vehicle patrol, emergency notification system, self-defense education, and security escort services. There are emergency telephones, lighted pathways/sidewalks, controlled access to dorms/residences, motorist assistance, and a crime prevention program.

Programs of Study: St. Norbert confers B.A., B.B.A., B.Mus. and B.S. degrees. Master's degrees are also awarded. Bachelor's degrees are awarded in BIOLOGICAL SCIENCE (biology/biological science), BUSINESS (accounting, business administration and management, and international business management), COMMUNICATIONS AND THE ARTS (art, communications, English, French, German, graphic design, music, Spanish, and theatre arts), COMPUTER AND PHYSICAL SCIENCE (chemistry, computer science, geology, mathematics, natural sciences, and physics), EDUCATION (elementary education and music education), ENGINEERING AND ENVIRONMENTAL DESIGN (commercial art and environmental science), SOCIAL SCIENCE (economics, history, humanities, international relations, philosophy, political science/government, psychology, religion, and sociology). Business administration, communications and elementary education have the largest enrollments.

Required: To graduate, students must complete 128 credits with at least a 2.0 GPA and a minimum of 40 semester credits in a particular major and a major GPA of at least a 2.0. There are general education requirements in the areas of religious studies, human nature, human relationships, natural science, creative expression, U.S. heritage, foreign heritages, foreign language, quantitative skills, Western tradition, global society, a writing-intensive course, and Senior Colloquium.

Special: A partnership program with Bellin College Nursing, cross-registration in Arabic courses with the University of Wisconsin-Green Bay, internships, study abroad in more than 31 countries, a Washington semester, and work-study programs are available. The college offers dual and student-designed majors, B.A.-B.S. degrees, nondegree study, and limited credit for military experience and work training. The Leadership and Service Program and leadership minor help students improve their leadership abilities through courses and activities. A 3-2 engineering degree is available with Michigan Tech University. A Masters of Science in Applied Economics (MSAE) degree preparation agreement with Marquette University. There are 8 national honor societies and a freshman honors program.

Faculty/Classroom: 58% of faculty are male; 42% are female. All teach undergraduates. No introductory courses are taught by graduate students. The average class size in an introductory lecture is 21 and in a regular course is 21.

Admissions: 82% of the 2013-2014 applicants were accepted. The ACT scores were 9% below 21, 29% between 21 and 23, 32% between 24 and 26, 17% between 27 and 28, and 13% above 28. 48% of the current freshmen were in the top fifth of their class; 77% were in the top two fifths. 24 freshmen graduated first in their class.

Requirements: The ACT is required. Admissions requirements are either graduation from an accredited secondary school with 16 units recommended, including 4 English, 3 math, 3 lab sciences, 2 foreign language 2 social studies, 2 history; or a GED recommended score in the 55% range; and either an SAT or ACT entrance exam. AP and CLEP credits are accepted. Important factors in the admissions decision are advanced placement or honors courses, extracurricular activities record, and recommendations by school officials.

Procedure: Freshmen are admitted to all sessions. Entrance exams should be taken by the end of the junior year. There are deferred admissions and rolling admissions plans. Application deadlines are open. Application fee is $25. Notification of early decision is sent December 15; regular decision, on a rolling basis. Applications are accepted online.

Transfer: 44 transfer students enrolled in 2012-2013. Applicants should have a minimum GPA of 2.5. At least their senior year and 25% of their major credits must be taken at St. Norbert. 32 of 128 credits required for the bachelor's degree must be completed at St. Norbert.

Visiting: There are regularly scheduled orientations for prospective students, Including preregistrations, meetings with advisers, and meetings regarding programming and activities, housing, and student life. There are guides for informal visits, visitors may sit in on classes, and stay overnight. To schedule a visit, contact the Office of Admissions.

Financial Aid: In 2013-2014, 99% of all full-time freshmen received some form of financial aid. 77% of all full-time freshmen and 72% of continuing full-time students received need-based aid. The average freshman award was $25,106. The average financial indebtedness of the 2013 graduate was $21,656. The FAFSA is required. The priority date for freshman financial aid applications for fall entry is March 1.

International Students: There are 67 international students enrolled. The school actively recruits these students. They must take the TOEFL with a minimum score of 555 on the paper-based TOEFL (PBT) or 80 on the Internet-based version (iBT). They must also take the SAT or ACT.

Computers: All students may access the system. There are no time limits and no fees.

Graduates: From July 1, 2012 to June 30, 2013, 447 bachelor's degrees were awarded. The most popular majors were business administration (16%), elementary education (15%), and communications (10%). 64 companies recruited on campus in 2012-2013. In an average class, 69% graduate in 4 years or less, 74% graduate in 5 years or less, and 75% graduate in 6 years or less. Of the 2012 graduating class, 13% were enrolled in graduate school within 6 months of graduation.

Admissions Contact: Edward Lamm, V.P. of Enrollment Mgmt. & Communication. E-Mail: *admit@snc.edu* Web: *www.snc.edu/futurestudents*

UNIVERSITY OF WISCONSIN SYSTEM

The University of Wisconsin System, established in 1971, is a public system in Wisconsin. It is governed by an 18-member appointed board of regents, whose chief administrator is president. The primary goal of the system is teaching, research, and public service. The main priorities are to develop human resources; to discover and disseminate knowledge; and to extend knowledge and its application. The total student enrollment of all 26 campuses is usually 181,000 with 11,500 faculty members. Altogether there are 700 baccalaureate, 329 master's, and 149 doctoral programs offered in the University of Wisconsin System. Profiles of the 4-year campuses are included in this section.

UNIVERSITY OF WISCONSIN/EAU CLAIRE B-3

Eau Claire, WI 54701 **(715) 836-5415**
(888) INFO-UWE; (715) 836-2409

Full-time: 3908 men, 5539 women	**Faculty:** 439; IIA, --$
Part-time: 344 men, 592 women	**Ph.D.s:** 78%
Graduate: 206 men, 313 women	**Student/Faculty:** 21 to 1
Year: semesters, summer session	**Tuition:** $8710 ($16,283)
Application Deadline:	**Room & Board:** $6720
Freshman Class: 5885 applied, 4724 accepted, 2017 enrolled	
SAT: recommended	**ACT:** 24 **VERY COMPETITIVE**

The University of Wisconsin-Eau Claire fosters in one another creativity, critical insight, empathy, and intellectual courage, the hallmarks of a transformative liberal education and the foundation for active citizenship and lifelong inquiry. There are 4 undergraduate schools. In addition to regional accreditation, UW-Eau Claire has baccalaureate program accreditation with AACSB, ABET, ACEJMC, CSWE, and NASM. The library contains 1.2 million volumes, 530,353 microform items, 24,662 audio/video tapes/CDs/DVDs, and subscribes to 63,825 periodicals including electronic. Computerized library services include interlibrary loans, database searching, Internet access, and Wi-Fi capability. Special learning facilities include an art gallery, planetarium, radio station, TV station, a human development center, natural preserve, ropes course, materials science center, college of nursing and health sciences clinical simulation/skills lab. The 337-acre campus is in an urban area 95 miles east of Minneapolis, Minnesota. Including any residence halls, there are 28 buildings.

Student Life: 74% of undergraduates are from Wisconsin. Others are from 45 states, 41 foreign countries, and Canada. 90% are White. The average age of freshmen is 18; all undergraduates, 21. 18% do not continue beyond their first year; 82% remain to graduate.

Housing: 3924 students can be accommodated in college housing, which includes single-sex and coed dorms and on-campus apartments. In addition, there are special-interest houses, theme housing, and wellness housing. On-campus housing is available on a first-come and first-served basis. 74% of students commute. All students may keep cars.

Activities: 1% of men belong to 3 local fraternities; 1% of women belong to 3 local sororities. There are 270 groups on campus, including art, band, cheerleading, chess, choir, chorale, chorus, communications, computers, dance, debate, drama, environmental, ethnic, film, forensics, gay, honors, international, jazz band, literary magazine, marching band, musical theater, newspaper, opera, orchestra, pep band, photography, political, professional, radio and TV, religious, social, social service, student government, and symphony. Popular campus events include Winter Carnival, Homecoming and Blugold Organizations Bash.

Sports: There are 9 intercollegiate sports for men and 11 for women. Facilities include a gym, a pool, 30 acres of intramural and recreation fields, a game room, bowling and billiards, a Nautilus fitness center, racquetball courts, a weight room, a ropes course, a 3212-seat stadium, tennis courts, and a climbing wall.

Disabled Students: 80% of the campus is accessible. Facilities include wheelchair ramps, elevators, special parking, specially equipped restrooms, special class scheduling, lowered drinking fountains, and lowered telephones.

Services: Counseling and information services are available, as is tutoring in some subjects, writing, math/problem solving, and reading/study skills There is a reader service for the blind, and remedial math, reading, and writing. Entry-level courses in foreign languages, humanities, and social and physical sciences are available.

Campus Safety and Security: Measures include 24-hour foot and vehicle patrol, emergency notification system, and self-defense education. There are shuttle buses, emergency telephones, lighted pathways/sidewalks, and controlled access to dorms/residences.

Programs of Study: UW-Eau Claire confers B.A., B.S., B.B.A., B.F.A., B.L.S., B.P.S., B.M., B.M.E., B.S.E.Ph., B.S.N. and B.S.W. degrees. Associate, master's, and doctoral degrees are also awarded. Bachelor's degrees are awarded in BIOLOGICAL SCIENCE (biochemistry and biology/biological science), BUSINESS (accounting, banking and finance, business administration and management, international business, marketing, and organizational leadership and management), COMMUNICATIONS AND THE ARTS (art, communications, English, French, German, journalism, music, Spanish, and theatre arts), COMPUTER AND PHYSICAL SCIENCE (chemistry, computer science, geology, information sciences and systems, mathematics, physical sciences, and physics), EDUCATION (athletic training, elementary education, physical education, science education, and special education), ENGINEERING AND ENVIRONMENTAL DESIGN (materials science), HEALTH PROFESSIONS (health care administration, nursing, predentistry, premedicine, preoptometry, prepharmacy, prephysical therapy, preveterinary science, and public health), SOCIAL SCIENCE (American Indian studies, communication sciences & disorders, criminal justice, economics, geography, history, Latin American studies, liberal arts/general studies, philosophy, political science/government, prelaw, psychology, religious studies, social studies, social work, sociology, and women's studies). Nursing, Biology, and Kinesiology have the largest enrollments.

Required: All students must complete 39 hours in general education, including 9-15 each in social sciences, humanities, and natural sciences, and 6 in communications/math. All students must also meet the writing requirement, take 2 credits in wellness, complete a minimum of 3 credits that contain significant content dealing with race and ethnicity, and must complete 30 or more hours of service-learning. A minimum 2.0 GPA and 120 credit hours are required to graduate.

Special: Numerous internships, work-study programs, and study abroad in 26 countries are offered. Dual majors and interdisciplinary majors are possible. Credit by examination, non-degree study, and pass/fail options are offered. There are 26 national honor societies, a freshman honors program, and 17 departmental honors programs.

Faculty/Classroom: 48% of faculty are male; 52% are female. All teach undergraduates. No introductory courses are taught by graduate students. The average class size in an introductory lecture is 31 and in a laboratory is 21.

Admissions: 80% of the 2013-2014 applicants were accepted. The SAT scores for the 2013-2014 freshman class were: Critical Reading--29% below 500, 31% between 500 and 599, 34% between 600 and 699, and 6% between 700 and 800; Math--9% below 500, 40% between 500 and 599, 31% between 600 and 699, and 20% between 700 and 800. The ACT scores were 11% below 21, 9% between 21 and 23, 36% between 24 and 26, 34% between 27 and 28, and 10% above 28. There were 3 National Merit finalists. 52 freshmen graduated first in their class.

Requirements: The ACT is required. The SAT is recommended. Applicants should graduate from an accredited secondary school or present its equivalent, with 17 academic credits including 4 in English, 3 each in social studies, college prep math, and science and 2 years of a single foreign language. Each application is given a comprehensive review. In addition to a rigorous curriculum, academic factors include: class rank, GPA, trends in grades, and test scores. Secondary non-academic factors include: leadership, service, achievement in arts, athletics, etc, and diversity in personal background and experience. AP and CLEP credits are accepted. Important factors in the admissions decision are advanced placement or honors courses, evidence of special talent, and leadership record.

Procedure: Freshmen are admitted fall, winter, spring, and summer. Entrance exams should be taken by December of the senior year. There are early admissions and rolling admissions plans. Application deadlines are open. The fall 2013 application fee was $44. Applications are accepted online.

Transfer: 568 transfer students enrolled in 2012-2013. Transfer applicants mustcarry a minimum 2.0 GPA. Preference is given to transfers who have completed the equivalent of freshman composition and college algebra. Students with less than 30 semester credits must meet the freshman admissions requirements. 30 of 120 credits required for the bachelor's degree must be completed at UW-Eau Claire.

Visiting: There are regularly scheduled orientations for prospective students, during which students meet with academic advisers, develop a class schedule, register for classes, and tour the campus. There are guides for informal visits and visitors may sit in on classes. To schedule a visit, contact the Admissions Office at admissions@uwec.edu.

Financial Aid: In 2013-2014, 81% of all full-time freshmen and 71% of continuing full-time students received some form of financial aid. 56% of all full-time freshmen and 52% of continuing full-time students received need-based aid. The average freshman award was $8,055. Need-based scholarships or need-based grants averaged $5,433; need-based self-help aid (loans and jobs) averaged $5,251; and other non-need-based awards and non-need-based scholarships averaged $5,847. 32% of undergraduate students work part-time. Average annual earnings from campus work are $2244. The average financial indebtedness of the 2013 graduate was $22,658. The FAFSA is required. The deadline for filing freshman financial aid applications for fall entry is April 15.

International Students: There are 254 international students enrolled. The school actively recruits these students. They must take the TOEFL with a minimum score of 550 on the paper-based TOEFL (PBT) or 79 on the Internet-based version (iBT). They must also take the SAT or ACT.

Computers: All students may access the system 24 hours a day, 7 days per week. There are no time limits and no fees.

Graduates: From July 1, 2012 to June 30, 2013, 2129 bachelor's degrees were awarded. The most popular majors were marketing (21%), health professionals (16%), and education (8%). In an average class, 30% graduate in 4 years or less, 63% graduate in 5 years or less, and 68% graduate in 6 years or less.

Admissions Contact: Heather Kretz, Interim Director of Admissions. E-Mail: *admissions@uwec.edu* Web: *www.uwec.edu*

UNIVERSITY OF WISCONSIN/GREEN BAY D-3

Green Bay, WI 54311 **(920) 465-2111; (920) 465-2765**

Full-time: 1602 men, 2712 women
Part-time: 627 men, 1503 women
Graduate: 81 men, 142 women
Year: semesters, summer session
Application Deadline: January 1
Freshman Class: 2343 applied, 1928 accepted, 809 enrolled
ACT: 23

Faculty: 191; IIA, --$
Ph.D.s: 84%
Student/Faculty: 23 to 1
Tuition: $7676 ($15,249)
Room & Board: $7224

COMPETITIVE

The University of Wisconsin/Green Bay, founded in 1968, is a public institution offering programs in humanities and fine arts, natural sciences, social sciences, business, education, health, and pre-professional areas. There are 2 undergraduate schools and 1 graduate school. In addition to regional accreditation, UW-Green Bay has baccalaureate program accreditation with ADA, CSWE, NASM, and NLN. The library contains 366,860 volumes, 1.4 million microform items, 47,943 audio/video tapes/CDs/DVDs, and subscribes to 3,234 periodicals including electronic. Computerized library services include interlibrary loans, database searching, Internet access, and Wi-Fi capability. Special learning facilities include an art gallery, natural history museum, radio station, TV station, a 270-acre arboretum, and a regional performing arts center. The 700-acre campus is in a suburban area 111 miles north of Milwaukee. Including any residence halls, there are 49 buildings.

Student Life: 95% of undergraduates are from Wisconsin. Others are from 37 states, 30 foreign countries, and Canada. 95% are from public schools. 88% are White. 40% are Catholic; 40% Protestant; 15% claim no religious affiliation. The average age of freshmen is 19; all undergraduates, 25. 28% do not continue beyond their first year; 50% remain to graduate.

Housing: 2000 students can be accommodated in college housing, which includes coed dorms and on-campus apartments. In addition, there are special-interest houses, and dorm suites with private bedrooms. On-campus housing is available on a first-come, first-served basis, and is available on a lottery system for upperclassmen. 67% of students commute. All students may keep cars.

Activities: 1% of men belong to 1 national fraternity; 1% of women belong to 2 national sororities. There are 116 groups on campus, including art, band, cheerleading, choir, chorale, chorus, computers, dance, drama, drill team, environmental, ethnic, film, gay, honors, international, jazz band, literary magazine, musical theater, newspaper, orchestra, pep band, photography, political, professional, radio and TV, religious, social, social service, and student government. Popular campus events include Frost Fest, GB Week, and Pow Wow.

Sports: There are 7 intercollegiate sports for men and 9 for women, and 7 intramural sports for men and 7 for women. Facilities include Full service sports center with a 5000-seat arena for campus-wide ceremonies, concerts and events, auxiliary courts (basketball practice, student recreation), elevated running track, 28-foot climbing tower, two weight areas with Magnum machines and free weights, group aerobics/fitness studio (cardio deck with stationary bikes, stair-climbers, elliptical machines, treadmills, video monitors), indoor turf gym, pool, and offices and team rooms for Green Bay Phoenix athletics.

Disabled Students: All of the campus is accessible. Facilities include wheelchair ramps, elevators, special parking, specially equipped restrooms, lowered drinking fountains, lowered telephones. automatic door openers. All academic buildings on campus are connected by an underground concourse system which is widely accessed by the entire campus community and which makes the campus particularly accessible to wheelchair transportation.

Services: Counseling and information services are available, as is tutoring in most subjects. There is a reader service for the blind, and remedial math, reading, and writing. There is an academic support office, language and writing centers, student health services, and individual counseling. Available equipment includes a visual enlarger, automatic page turner, accessible computer station with attached voice syntheizer, slow speed cassette recorders, and a TDD device. Note takers, typists, readers, and aids are available for students.

Campus Safety and Security: Measures include 24-hour foot and vehicle patrol and security escort services. There are emergency telephones, lighted pathways/sidewalks, and controlled access to dorms/residences.

Programs of Study: UW-Green Bay confers B.A., B.S., B.A.S., B.B.A., B.M., B.S.N. and B.S.W. degrees. Associate and master's degrees are also awarded. Bachelor's degrees are awarded in AGRICULTURE (environmental studies), BIOLOGICAL SCIENCE (biology/biological science), BUSINESS (accounting, business administration and management, finance, human resources, and sustainable management), COMMUNICATIONS AND THE ARTS (art, arts administration/management, communications, creative writing, design, dramatic arts, English, English as a second/foreign language, fine arts, French, German, Germanic languages and literature, music, Spanish, and theatre arts), COMPUTER AND

PHYSICAL SCIENCE (chemistry, computer science, earth science, geoscience, information sciences and systems, and mathematics), EDUCATION (art education, education, elementary education, English education, foreign languages education, health information management, mathematics education, middle school education, music education, and secondary education), ENGINEERING AND ENVIRONMENTAL DESIGN (city/community/regional planning, engineering technology, and environmental science), HEALTH PROFESSIONS (exercise science and nursing), SOCIAL SCIENCE (American Indian studies, dietetics, economics, French studies, gender studies, history, human development, humanities, interdisciplinary studies, liberal arts/general studies, philosophy, political science/government, psychology, public administration, social work, urban studies, and women's studies). Education, environmental science, human biology, psychology and accounting are the strongest academically. Business, human biology, and human development have the largest enrollments.

Required: All students must complete at least 120 semester hours, including an average of 36 in the major, with a minimum GPA of 2.0, depending on the major. A 31-credit requirement in general education consists of 9 credits in humanities, 3 in fine arts, 9 in social sciences, and 10 in natural sciences. Students must declare an interdisciplinary minor or major and must complete at least 30 credits in the discipline. Courses in Other Culture Studies and Ethnic Studies are required; other course requirements vary by major.

Special: UW-Green Bay offers cross-registration with Bellin College of Nursing and the University of Wisconsin at Milwaukee or Oshkosh. There are study-abroad programs and travel courses in numerous countries. Students can receive credit by examination or for life, military, or work experience. There are internships in almost all fields; interdisciplinary majors, including communication and the arts, human biology, and regional planning; and dual and student-designed majors, work-study, B.A.-B.S. degrees in most areas, nondegree study, a general studies degree, and pass/fail options. A 3-2 engineering degree with the University of Wisconsin/Milwaukee is offered. There are 6 national honor societies and 34 departmental honors programs.

Faculty/Classroom: 47% of faculty are male; 53% are female. All teach undergraduates, 85% do research, and 85% do both. No introductory courses are taught by graduate students. The average class size in an introductory lecture is 45; in a laboratory is 20; and in a regular course is 25.

Admissions: 82% of the 2013-2014 applicants were accepted. The ACT scores were 24% below 21, 35% between 21 and 23, 28% between 24 and 26, 9% between 27 and 28, and 4% above 28.

Requirements: The ACT is required. Candidates must be graduates of an accredited secondary school or hold a GED certificate. They must have completed 17 academic credits consisting of 4 in English, 3 in social sciences, 3 each in science and math, 2 in any of the above areas or a foreign language, and 2 other electives. Home schooled applicants are encouraged to apply and should contact the admissions office for additional information. AP and CLEP credits are accepted. Important factors in the admissions decision are advanced placement or honors courses, extracurricular activities record, and leadership record.

Procedure: Freshmen are admitted to all sessions. Entrance exams should be taken between the junior and senior years. There are deferred admissions and rolling admissions plans. Applications should be filed by January 1 for fall entry; November 1 for spring entry, along with a $44 fee. Notification is sent on a rolling basis. 43 applicants were on the 2013 waiting list; 27 were admitted. Applications are accepted online.

Transfer: 1200 transfer students enrolled in 2012-2013. Transfer students must have a minimum GPA of 2.0 based on at least 15 transferable credits; priority for admission is given to students with 24 credits and a minimum GPA of 2.5. 31 of 120 credits required for the bachelor's degree must be completed at UW-Green Bay.

Visiting: There are regularly scheduled orientations for prospective students, including Campus Preview Days, which consist of information sessions, academic area workshops, and campus tours. There are guides for informal visits and visitors may sit in on classes. To schedule a visit, contact the Office of Admissions.

Financial Aid: In 2013-2014, 74% of all full-time freshmen and 72% of continuing full-time students received some form of financial aid. 53% of all full-time freshmen and 47% of continuing full-time students received need-based aid. The average freshman award was $9,584. Need-based scholarships or need-based grants averaged $5,443 ($20,000 maximum); need-based self-help aid (loans and jobs) averaged $5,746 ($12,000 maximum); non-need-based athletic scholarships averaged $7,367 ($23,000 maximum); and other non-need-based awards and non-need-based scholarships averaged $1,490 ($5,000 maximum). 80% of undergraduate students work part-time. Average annual earnings from campus work are $3000. The average financial indebtedness of the 2013 graduate was $26,510. The FAFSA and FFS are required. The deadline for filing freshman financial aid applications for fall entry is April 15.

International Students: There are 115 international students enrolled. The school actively recruits these students. They must take the TOEFL with a minimum score of 500 on the paper-based TOEFL (PBT) or 61 on the Internet-based version (iBT).

Computers: All students may access the system, 7 a.m. to 12 p.m.; 24 hours a day through network or modem. There are no time limits and no fees.

Graduates: From July 1, 2012 to June 30, 2013, 1303 bachelor's degrees were awarded. The most popular majors were business administration (14%), psychology (11%), and human biology (10%). 60 companies recruited on campus in 2012-2013. In an average class, 1% graduate in 3 years or less, 20% graduate in 4 years or less, 45% graduate in 5 years or less, and 50% graduate in 6 years or less. Of the 2012 graduating class, 25% were enrolled in graduate school within 6 months of graduation, and 83% were employed.

Admissions Contact: Pam Harvey-Jacobs, Director of Admissions. E-Mail: *admissions@uwgb.edu* Web: *www.uwgb.edu*

UNIVERSITY OF WISCONSIN/LA CROSSE — B-4

La Crosse, WI 54601 — **(608) 785-8000; (608) 785-8940**

Full-time: 3778 men, 5180 women	**Faculty:** n/av; IIA, --$
Part-time: 223 men, 260 women	**Ph.D.s:** 67%
Graduate: 256 men, 530 women	**Student/Faculty:** 20 to 1
Year: semesters, summer session	**Tuition:** $8755 ($16,328)
Application Deadline:	**Room & Board:** $6000
Freshman Class: 6908 applied, 4904 accepted, 1888 enrolled	
SAT: required **ACT:** 25	**VERY COMPETITIVE**

The University of Wisconsin/La Crosse, founded in 1909, is a public institution offering undergraduate and graduate studies in arts and sciences, health and human services, business administration, education, phys ed and recreation, professional development, and educational administration. The figures in the above capsule and in this profile are approximate. There are 6 undergraduate schools and 1 graduate school. In addition to regional accreditation, UW-L has baccalaureate program accreditation with AACSB, APTA, NASM, and NCATE. The library contains 500,370 volumes, 581,624 microform items, 14,372 audio/video tapes/CDs/DVDs, and subscribes to 10,697 periodicals including electronic. Computerized library services include interlibrary loans and database searching. Special learning facilities include an art gallery, planetarium, radio station, TV station, the River Studies Center and the Allied Health Center. The 121-acre campus is in a small town 140 miles west of Madison and 150 miles southeast of Minneapolis/St. Paul, WI. Including any residence halls, there are 32 buildings.

Student Life: 16% of undergraduates are from out of state, mostly the Mid-West. 90% are from public schools. 94% are White. The average age of freshmen is 18; all undergraduates, 20. 13% do not continue beyond their first year; 61% remain to graduate.

Housing: 3180 students can be accommodated in college housing, which includes single-sex and coed dorms. In addition, there are special-interest houses, fraternity houses, sorority houses, a residence hall for international students and students 21 years or older, substance free, and first year experience housing. On-campus housing is available on a first-come, first-served basis, and is available on a lottery system for upperclassmen. 65% of students commute. All students may keep cars.

Activities: 1% of men belong to 3 national fraternities; 1% of women belong to 2 national sororities. There are 140 groups on campus, including art, band, cheerleading, chess, choir, chorale, chorus, computers, dance, drama, ethnic, gay, honors, international, jazz band, literary magazine, marching band, musical theater, newspaper, orchestra, pep band, photography, political, professional, radio and TV, religious, social, social service, student government, and symphony. Popular campus events include Parents Weekend, Community-Sponsored Oktoberfest and Various Cultural Events.

Sports: There are 9 intercollegiate sports for men and 10 for women, and 11 intramural sports for men and 11 for women. Facilities include a wrestling room, an indoor track, 6 indoor tennis courts, 16 outdoor tennis courts, an Olympic-size swimming pool, 2 strength-training centers, a dance studio, racquetball courts, a 4363-seat stadium, a 2880-seat gym, and an 880-seat auditorium.

Disabled Students: 98% of the campus is accessible. Facilities include wheelchair ramps, elevators, special parking, specially equipped restrooms, special class scheduling, lowered drinking fountains, lowered telephones, special housing.

Services: Counseling and information services are available, as is tutoring in most subjects. There is a reader service for the blind, and remedial math and writing. There is also a counseling and testing center and a writing lab.

Campus Safety and Security: Measures include 24-hour foot and vehicle patrol, self-defense education, and security escort services. There are emergency telephones and lighted pathways/sidewalks.

Programs of Study: UW-L confers B.A., and B.S. degrees. Associate and master's degrees are also awarded. Bachelor's degrees are awarded in BIOLOGICAL SCIENCE (biology/biological science and microbiology), BUSINESS (accounting, banking and finance, business administration and management, international business management, and marketing/retailing/merchandising), COMMUNICATIONS AND THE ARTS (art, communications, dramatic arts, English, fine arts, French, music, Spanish, and speech/debate/rhetoric), COMPUTER AND PHYSICAL SCIENCE (chemistry, computer science, information sciences and systems, mathematics, and physics), EDUCATION (athletic training, elementary education, health education, physical education, science education, secondary education, and social studies education), HEALTH PROFESSIONS (community health work, exercise science, medical laboratory technology, nuclear medical technology, occupational therapy, physician's assistant, radiation therapy, and recreation therapy), SOCIAL SCIENCE (archeology, economics, geography, German area studies, history, parks and recreation management, philosophy, political science/government, psychology, public administration, and sociology). Microbiology, nuclear medicine technology, and physics are the strongest academically. Business administration, elementary education, and biology have the largest enrollments.

Required: To graduate, students must earn 120 semester credits, including 68 in subjects outside the major and at least 40 in 300- or 400-level courses. The minimum GPA is 2.0, though it is considerably higher for some programs. Distribution requirements include 30 to 40 credits in liberal studies and 13 to 19 credits in skill courses.

Special: Cooperative programs and cross-registration are available with Viterbo College. There are study-abroad programs in 14 countries and an international student exchange program. UW-L also offers a 3-2 engineering degree with the University of Wisconsin/Madison, the University of Wisconsin/Milwaukee, Platteville, and the University of Minnesota, work-study programs, internships, nondegree study, credit by exam, and pass/fail options. There are 10 national honor societies, a freshman honors program, and 11 departmental honors programs.

Faculty/Classroom: 50% of faculty are male; 50% are female. 95% teach undergraduates, 5% do research, and 80% do both. No introductory courses are taught by graduate students. The average class size in an introductory lecture is 37; in a laboratory is 20; and in a regular course is 30.

Admissions: 71% of the 2013-2014 applicants were accepted. The ACT scores were 5% below 21, 28% between 21 and 23, 41% between 24 and 26, 17% between 27 and 28, and 9% above 28. 77% of the current freshmen were in the top fifth of their class; 98% were in the top two fifths. 49 freshmen graduated first in their class.

Requirements: The SAT or ACT is required. Applicants must be graduates of an accredited secondary school or hold a GED certificate. They must have completed 17 academic credits, including 4 courses in English, 3 each in social studies, math, and science, 2 in algebra and 1 in geometry, and 4 other academic courses. Students completing rigorous courses, including in the senior year, will be stronger candidates for admission. Students must rank in the top 35% of their high school graduating class and score at least 22 on the ACT or the top 40% and score 25 on the ACT. UW-L requires applicants to be in the upper 40% of their class. A GPA of 2.0 is required. AP and CLEP credits are accepted. Important factors in the admissions decision are advanced placement or honors courses, leadership record, and recommendations by school officials.

Procedure: Freshmen are admitted to all sessions. Entrance exams should be taken by the junior year or at the beginning of the senior year. There are early admissions and rolling admissions plans. Application deadlines are open. Application fee is $44. Notification is sent on a rolling basis. Applications are accepted online.

Transfer: 490 transfer students enrolled in 2012-2013. Transfer admission is likely with a GPA of 3.2; however, with a GPA of 2.0 to 2.74, admission is on a space-available basis. High School and college transcripts are required and a statement of good standing from prior institutions. 18 of 120 credits required for the bachelor's degree must be completed at UW-L.

Visiting: There are regularly scheduled orientations for prospective students, including 2 academic sessions, a parent panel, a UW-L student panel, and a tour of the campus. There are guides for informal visits and visitors may sit in on classes. To schedule a visit, contact the Admissions Office.

Financial Aid: The FAFSA and the college's own financial statement are required. The priority date for freshman financial aid applications for fall entry is March 15.

International Students: There are 256 international students enrolled. The school actively recruits these students. They must take the TOEFL and the college's own test, and also take the La Crosse Battery (based on MELAB), and write a 30-minute composition.

Computers: All students may access the system, 7 a.m. to midnight. There are no time limits and no fees.

Graduates: From July 1, 2012 to June 30, 2013, 1586 bachelor's degrees were awarded. In an average class, 37% graduate in 4 years or less, 42% graduate in 5 years or less, and 71% graduate in 6 years or less.

Admissions Contact: Corey Sjoquist, Director of Admissions. E-Mail: *admissions@uwlax.edu* Web: *www.uwlax.edu*

UNIVERSITY OF WISCONSIN/MADISON C-4

Madison, WI 53706 **(608) 262-3961; (608) 262-7706**

Full-time: 13887 men, 14706 women
Part-time: 1376 men, 1350 women
Graduate: 5996 men, 5960 women
Year: semesters, summer session
Application Deadline: February 1
Faculty: n/av; I, --$
Ph.D.s: 90%
Student/Faculty: 17 to 1
Tuition: $10,403 ($26,653)
Room & Board: $8354
Freshman Class: 29675 applied, 15161 accepted, 6339 enrolled
SAT or ACT: required

HIGHLY COMPETITIVE

The University of Wisconsin - Madison, founded in 1849, is a public, land-grant institution offering undergraduate and graduate study in almost every major field. There are 9 undergraduate schools and 13 graduate schools. In addition to regional accreditation, Wisconsin has baccalaureate program accreditation with AACSB, ABET, ADA, ASLA, CSWE, FIDER, NASAD, NASM, and SAF. The 43 libraries contain 8.6 million volumes. Computerized library services include interlibrary loans, database searching, Internet access, and Wi-Fi capability. Special learning facilities include an art gallery, natural history museum, planetarium, radio station, and TV station. The 936-acre campus is in an urban area 75 miles west of Milwaukee and 150 miles northwest of Chicago.

Student Life: 67% of undergraduates are from Wisconsin. Others are from 50 states, 130 foreign countries, and Canada. 77% are White. The average age of freshmen is 18; all undergraduates, 20. 5% do not continue beyond their first year; 84% remain to graduate.

Housing: 7414 students can be accommodated in college housing, which includes single-sex and coed dorms, on-campus apartments, and married student housing. In addition, there are honors houses, language houses, special-interest houses, co-op housing, residential learning communities, housing for student families. No one may keep cars.

Activities: There are 907 groups on campus, including art, band, cheerleading, chess, choir, chorale, chorus, communications, computers, dance, debate, drama, environmental, ethnic, film, forensics, gay, honors, international, jazz band, literary magazine, marching band, musical theater, newspaper, opera, orchestra, pep band, photography, political, professional, radio and TV, religious, social, social service, student government, symphony, and yearbook.

Sports: There are 12 intercollegiate sports for men and 12 for women, and 14 intramural sports for men and 14 for women.

Disabled Students: 90% of the campus is accessible. Facilities include wheelchair ramps, elevators, special parking, specially equipped restrooms, special class scheduling, lowered drinking fountains, and lowered telephones.

Services: Counseling and information services are available, as is tutoring in most subjects. There is a reader service for the blind.

Campus Safety and Security: Measures include 24-hour foot and vehicle patrol, emergency notification system, self-defense education, and security escort services. There are shuttle buses, emergency telephones, lighted pathways/sidewalks, and controlled access to dorms/residences.

Programs of Study: Wisconsin confers B.A., B.S., B.B.A., B.F.A., B.M., B.S.Ed. and B.N.S. degrees. Master's and doctoral degrees are also awarded. Bachelor's degrees are awarded in AGRICULTURE (agricultural business management, agricultural communications, agricultural economics, agronomy, animal science, dairy science, environmental studies, forestry and related sciences, horticulture, poultry science, and soil science), BIOLOGICAL SCIENCE (biochemistry, biology/biological science, botany, entomology, genetics, microbiology, molecular biology, nutrition, plant pathology, wildlife biology, and zoology), BUSINESS (accounting, banking and finance, human resources, insurance and risk management, international business management, marketing/retailing/merchandising, nonprofit/public organization management, operations management, personal financial planning, real estate, and retailing), COMMUNICATIONS AND THE ARTS (African languages, art, art history and appreciation, Chinese, classics, communications, communication science, comparative literature, dance, dramatic arts, English, French, German, Hebrew, Italian, Japanese, journalism, Latin, linguistics, music, music performance, Polish, Portuguese, Russian, Spanish, and theatre arts), COMPUTER AND PHYSICAL SCIENCE (actuarial science, applied mathematics, astronomy, atmospheric sciences and meteorology, chemistry, computer science, geology, geophysics and seismology, information sciences and systems, mathematics, physics, and statistics), EDUCATION (art education, athletic training, elementary education, music education, physical education, secondary education, and special education), ENGINEERING AND ENVIRONMENTAL DESIGN (bioengineering, biomedical engineering, cartography, chemical engineering, civil engineering, computer engineering, electrical/electronics engineering, engineering mechanics, engineering physics, environmental science, geological engineering, industrial engineering, interior design, landscape architecture/design, materials science, mechanical engineering, naval architecture and marine engineering, nuclear engineering, and textile technology), HEALTH PROFESSIONS (kinesiology, medical science, nursing, pharmacology, physician's assistant, and speech pathology/audiology), SOCIAL SCIENCE (African American studies, anthropology, Asian/Oriental studies, child care/child and family studies, economics, family/consumer studies, food science, gender studies, geography, history, history of science, human development, international relations, international studies, Judaic studies, Latin American studies, law, philosophy, political science/government, psychology, religion, rural sociology, Scandinavian studies, social studies, social work, sociology, textiles and clothing, and women's studies). Biology, economics, and political science have the largest enrollments.

Required: Required courses vary with individual programs. A total of 120 to 136 credit hours, with at least 30 in the major, and a cumulative GPA of 2.0 are minimum requirements for graduation. In addition to courses required for each major, all students must complete general education in communication, quantitative reasoning, breadth (science, math, humanities, and social science), and ethnic studies.

Special: Co-op programs, internships, study abroad, work-study programs, and accelerated degrees in any major are available. B.A.-B.S. degrees and dual and student-designed majors also are available. There is a Phi Beta Kappa chapter and a freshman honors program.

Faculty/Classroom: 61% of faculty are male; 39% are female. No introductory courses are taught by graduate students.

Admissions: 51% of the 2013-2014 applicants were accepted. The SAT scores for the 2013-2014 freshman class were: Critical Reading--7% below 500, 39% between 500 and 599, 40% between 600 and 699, and 14% between 700 and 800; Math--1% below 500, 14% between 500 and 599, 40% between 600 and 699, and 45% between 700 and 800; Writing--5% below 500, 24% between 500 and 599, 52% between 600 and 699, and 19% between 700 and 800.

Requirements: The SAT or ACT is required. The ACT Optional Writing test is also required. Applicants must have completed the following number of units in high school (these are minimums; the number of units recommended is higher): 17 total units including 4 English, 4 math, 3 each of science, social studies, and foreign language, and 2 academics/fine arts electives. AP and CLEP credits are accepted.

Procedure: Freshmen are admitted fall, spring, and summer. Entrance exams should be taken in the junior year. There are deferred admissions and rolling admissions plans. Applications should be filed by February 1 for fall entry; October 1 for spring entry; and February 1 for summer entry, along with a $44 fee. Notification is sent on a rolling basis. Applications are accepted online.

Transfer: 1087 transfer students enrolled in 2012-2013. Admission is competitive and varies by program. Generally, applicants must have at least sophomore standing. 30 of 120 credits required for the bachelor's degree must be completed at Wisconsin.

Visiting: There are regularly scheduled orientations for prospective students, including an admission information session, a tour, and class visits. There are guides for informal visits, visitors may sit in on classes, and stay overnight. To schedule a visit, contact the Visitor and Information Program at (608) 263-2400.

Financial Aid: The average financial indebtedness of the 2013 graduate was $25,664. Wisconsin is a member of CSS. The FAFSA is required. Check with the school for current application deadlines.

International Students: There are 2138 international students enrolled. The school actively recruits these students. They must take the TOEFL with a minimum score of 550 on the paper-based TOEFL (PBT) or 80 on the Internet-based version (iBT). They must also take the SAT or ACT.

Computers: All students may access the system. There are no time limits and no fees.

Graduates: From July 1, 2012 to June 30, 2013, 6422 bachelor's degrees were awarded. The most popular majors were biology (8%), economics (8%), and political science (7%). In an average class, 57% graduate in 4 years or less, 82% graduate in 5 years or less, and 84% graduate in 6 years or less.

Admissions Contact: Office of Admissions and Recruitment E-Mail: *onwisconsin@admissions.wisc.edu* Web: *www.wisc.edu*

UNIVERSITY OF WISCONSIN/MILWAUKEE E-4

Milwaukee, WI 53211 **(414) 229-2222; 414-229-3788**

Full-time: 9385 men, 9544 women	**Faculty:** n/av; I, --$
Part-time: 1918 men, 2157 women	**Ph.D.s:** 76%
Graduate: 1943 men, 2837 women	**Student/Faculty:** 18 to 1
Year: semesters, summer session	**Tuition:** $9300 ($19,029)
Application Deadline: July 1	**Room & Board:** $9136

Freshman Class: 8311 applied, 7347 accepted, 3256 enrolled

ACT: 22

COMPETITIVE

UW-Milwaukee is Wisconsin's premier public urban research university. With a student body of more than 27,000, UWM is the first choice university for individuals seeking access to success. Peck School of the Arts, Wisconsin's only school of the arts, the School of Architecture and Urban Planning, Wisconsin's largest colleges of nursing and health sciences and far-ranging programs are designed for educating the next generation of engineers, scientists and teachers. UWM also offers one of the nation's few combinations of social welfare and criminal justice tracks in a single academic school and features a rapidly expanding school of business with Wisconsin's longest-running executive MBA program. With over 150 baccalaureate, masters, and doctoral degree programs, research and learning are intertwined. UW-Milwaukee also provides enhanced educational opportunities to over 7,000 area residents through its School of Continuing Education. By focusing on the two primary strategic goals of successful students and research excellence, UWM is focused on refining the quality and increasing the capacity of its programs, all with an eye towards the subsequent economic impact for the State of Wisconsin. There are 10 undergraduate schools and 3 graduate schools. In addition to regional accreditation, UWM has baccalaureate program accreditation with AACSB, ABET, APTA, CAHEA, CSWE, NAAB, NASM, and NLN. The library contains 2.6 million volumes, 1.8 million microform items, 977,767 audio/video tapes/CDs/DVDs, and subscribes to 85,593 periodicals including electronic. Computerized library services include interlibrary loans, database searching, Internet access, and Wi-Fi capability. Special learning facilities include an art gallery, planetarium, radio station, The American Geographical Society Library, Institute of Visual Arts. The 104-acre campus is in an urban area in Milwaukee, Wisconsin. Including any residence halls, there are 58 buildings.

Student Life: 91% of undergraduates are from Wisconsin. Others are from 46 states, 51 foreign countries, and Canada. 92% are from public schools. 72% are White. The average age of freshmen is 19; all undergraduates, 23. 30% do not continue beyond their first year.

Housing: 4288 students can be accommodated in college housing, which includes coed dorms, off-campus apartments, and married student housing. In addition, there are honors houses, language houses, and special-interest houses. On-campus housing is available on a first-come and first-served basis. 84% of students commute. Some may keep cars.

Activities: There are 296 groups on campus, including art, band, cheerleading, chess, choir, chorale, chorus, communications, computers, dance, debate, drama, environmental, ethnic, film, gay, honors, international, jazz band, literary magazine, musical theater, newspaper, orchestra, pep band, photography, political, professional, religious, social, social service, student government, and symphony. Popular campus events include Fall Welcome, PantherFest, Concerts, Art Exhibitions and Dance Performances.

Sports: There are 6 intercollegiate sports for men and 7 for women, and 12 intramural sports for men and 12 for women. Facilities include a basketball court, volleyball court, baseball field, soccer field, natatorium, indoor track, exercise facilities, and racquetball courts.

Disabled Students: 95% of the campus is accessible. Facilities include wheelchair ramps, elevators, special parking, specially equipped restrooms, special class scheduling, lowered drinking fountains, lowered telephones, special housing. UWM will make the necessary accommodations students need for housing, but no dorms are exclusively for those with disabilities.

Services: Counseling and information services are available, as is tutoring in some subjects. There is a reader service for the blind, and remedial math, reading, and writing.

Campus Safety and Security: Measures include 24-hour foot and vehicle patrol, emergency notification system, self-defense education, and security escort services. There are shuttle buses, emergency telephones, lighted pathways/sidewalks, and controlled access to dorms/residences.

Programs of Study: UWM confers B.A., B.B.A., B.F.A., B.S., B.S.E. and B.S.N. degrees. Master's and doctoral degrees are also awarded. Bachelor's degrees are awarded in BIOLOGICAL SCIENCE (biochemistry, biology/biological science, microbiology, molecular biology, and nutrition), BUSINESS (accounting, business administration and management, entrepreneurial studies, finance, human resources, international business, management information systems, marketing management, operations management, and real estate), COMMUNICATIONS AND THE ARTS (art, art history and appreciation, classics, communications, comparative literature, dance, dramatic arts, English, film arts, French, Germanic languages and literature, information technology, linguistics, music, and Russian languages and literature), COMPUTER AND PHYSICAL SCIENCE (actuarial science, applied mathematics, atmospheric sciences and meteorology, chemistry, computer science, geology, information sciences and systems, mathematics, physics, and web services), EDUCATION (art education, athletic training, education, music education, and special education), ENGINEERING AND ENVIRONMENTAL DESIGN (architecture, civil engineering, computer engineering, electrical/electronics engineering, engineering, environmental science, industrial engineering, materials engineering, mechanical engineering, and urban planning technology), HEALTH PROFESSIONS (exercise science, hospital administration, nursing, occupational therapy, premedicine, recreation therapy, and speech pathology/audiology), SOCIAL SCIENCE (African American studies, anthropology, Asian/American studies, behavioral science, criminal justice, economics, ethnic studies, forensic studies, geography, history, interdisciplinary studies, international studies, Italian studies, Judaic studies, Latin American studies, liberal arts/general studies, Near Eastern studies, peace studies, philosophy, political science/government, psychology, religion, Scandinavian studies, social work, sociology, Spanish studies, urban studies, and women's studies). Education, business, and psychology have the largest enrollments.

Required: Generally, to be a candidate for the Bachelor's Degree, students must satisfactorily complete the following: English composition and math proficiency exams must be passed with satisfactory scores. A minimum of 120 undergraduate credits in courses numbered 100 through 500. The General Education requirements, university requirements and all major and/or minor requirements. Distribution requirements include 6 credits each in humanities, natural sciences, and socials sciences, and 3 credits each in the arts and cultural diversity. A minimum GPA of 2.000 or better both overall and in the major and minor fields; Business Administration and Accounting majors must have a cumulative GPA of 2.500 overall. A minimum of 30 credits overall and half of upper-level credits in majors and minors must be earned in residence at UW-Milwaukee. Other specific graduation criteria are set by individual colleges and schools.

Special: UWM offers cooperative education programs in computer science and engineering, accelerated degree programs, dual majors, student-designed majors, and study abroad opportunities in Africa, Asia, Europe, and South America. UWM also has a consortial nursing program with UW-Parkside, a graduate exchange program for graduate students with Marquette University, and a collaborative doctoral program in biomedical and health informatics with the Medical College of Wisconsin. There are 4 national honor societies, including Phi Beta Kappa, and a freshman honors program.

Faculty/Classroom: 50% of faculty are male; 50% are female. No introductory courses are taught by graduate students.

Admissions: 88% of the 2013-2014 applicants were accepted. The ACT scores were 38% below 21, 30% between 21 and 23, 21% between 24 and 26, 7% between 27 and 28, and 5% above 28. 19% of the current freshmen were in the top fifth of their class; 25% were in the top two fifths. 25 freshmen graduated first in their class.

Requirements: The ACT is required. All freshmen applicants under the age of 21 must submit ACT or SAT scores; scores submitted via high school transcripts are acceptable. A GED certificate is accepted. Music, dance, and theatre majors must audition and art majors must submit a portfolio. For the School of Architecture and Urban Planning, higher rank and ACT requirements apply. Each application receives a comprehensive review, taking all factors into consideration. In addition to academic preparation, other factors considered include demonstrated leadership skills, motivation, and maturity, as addressed in a student's personal statement and/or recommendations. UWM provides broad access to individuals from many walks of life and encourages all interested students to apply. Certain programs, including Architecture, Engineering, and Nursing are more selective and higher standardized test scores may be required. AP and CLEP credits are accepted. Important factors in the admissions decision are advanced placement or honors courses, leadership record, and evidence of special talent.

Procedure: Freshmen are admitted to all sessions. Entrance exams should be taken in the spring of the junior year. There are deferred admissions and rolling admissions plans. Applications should be filed by July 1 for fall entry; December 1 for spring entry, along with a $44 fee. Notification is sent on a rolling basis. Applications are accepted online.

Transfer: 2585 transfer students enrolled in 2012-2013. Students applying with less than 12 transferable credits must meet freshman admission requirements 30 of 120 credits required for the bachelor's degree must be completed at UWM.

Visiting: There are regularly scheduled orientations for prospective students, New Student Orientation is a one and a half day (overnight) program packed with information about UWM. At orientation new students will meet other students, learn about campus resources and student life, meet with advisors and register for classes. There are guides for informal visits, visitors may sit in on classes, and stay overnight. To schedule a visit, contact the Department of Admissions and Recruitment.

Financial Aid: In 2013-2014, 70% of all full-time freshmen and 67% of continuing full-time students received some form of financial aid. 70% of all full-time freshmen and 56% of continuing full-time students received need-based aid. The average freshman award was $7,224. Need-based scholarships or need-based grants averaged $6,054; need-based self-help aid (loans and jobs) averaged $3,801; non-need-based athletic scholarships averaged $7,705; and other non-need-based awards and non-need-based scholarships averaged $2,644. The average financial indebtedness of the 2013 graduate was $32,371. The FAFSA is required. The priority date for freshman financial aid applications for fall entry is March 1. The deadline for filing freshman financial aid applications for fall entry is December 1.

International Students: There are 606 international students enrolled. The school actively recruits these students. They must take the TOEFL with a minimum score of 520 on the paper-based TOEFL (PBT) or 68 on the Internet-based version (iBT), International English Language Testing System (IELTS). All applicants to the College of Engineering and Applied Science must also submit official ACT or SAT scores.

Computers: All students may access the system any time. There are no time limits and no fees.

Graduates: From July 1, 2012 to June 30, 2013, 3984 bachelor's degrees were awarded. The most popular majors were finance (8%), marketing (8%), and nursing (7%).

Admissions Contact: Department of Admissions and Recruitment E-Mail: *uwmlook@uwm.edu* Web: *www.uwm.edu*

UNIVERSITY OF WISCONSIN/OSHKOSH — D-4

Oshkosh, WI 54901 — **(920) 424-3164; (920) 424-1207**

Full- and part-time: 11,650 men and women
Graduate: 1450 men and women
Year: semesters, summer session
Application Deadline: see profile
Freshman Class: n/av
SAT or ACT: required

Faculty: n/av; IIA, --$
Ph.D.s: 81%
Student/Faculty: n/av
Tuition: $7501 ($15,200)
Room & Board: $7542

LESS COMPETITIVE

The University of Wisconsin/Oshkosh, founded in 1871, is a public institution offering undergraduate and graduate programs in education, business, the arts and sciences, and health fields. The figures in the above capsule and in this profile are approximate. There are 4 undergraduate schools and one graduate school. In addition to regional accreditation, UW/Oshkosh has baccalaureate program accreditation with AACSB, ACEJMC, CSWE, NASM, NCATE, and NLN. The library contains 487,000 volumes, 1.3 million microform items, 7,000 audio/video tapes/CDs/DVDs, and subscribes to 1,850 periodicals including electronic. Computerized library services include interlibrary loans and database searching. Special learning facilities include a learning resource center, art gallery, planetarium, radio station, TV station, and speech and hearing clinic. The 170-acre campus is in an urban area 90 miles north of Milwaukee. Including any residence halls, there are 52 buildings.

Student Life: 96% of undergraduates are from Wisconsin. Others are from 30 states, 32 foreign countries, and Canada. 94% are white. The average age of freshmen is 18; all undergraduates, 22. 29% do not continue beyond their first year; 55% remain to graduate.

Housing: 3667 students can be accommodated in college housing, which includes single-sex and coed dorms. In addition, there are designated quiet floors, designated smoke-free floors, and a university learning community floor. On-campus housing is guaranteed for all 4 years. 66% of students commute. All students may keep cars.

Activities: 5% of men belong to 8 national fraternities; 5% of women belong to 5 national sororities. There are 175 groups on campus, including art, band, cheerleading, chess, choir, communications, computers, dance, debate, ethnic, film, forensics, gay, honors, international, jazz band, literary magazine, musical theater, newspaper, opera, pep band, political, professional, radio and TV, religious, social, social service, student government, and symphony. Popular campus events include Winter Carnival, Taste of UW Oshkosh, and Celebration of Racial Inclusiveness.

Sports: There are 10 intercollegiate sports for men and 11 for women, and 15 intramural sports for men and 15 for women. Facilities include a hall for basketball, swimming, and volleyball, a sports center for basketball, tennis, and indoor track, a pool, a 10,400-seat stadium for football and outdoor track, a 2500-seat indoor gym, and a 5808-seat arena.

Disabled Students: Some of the campus is accessible. Facilities include wheelchair ramps, elevators, special parking, specially equipped rest rooms, special class scheduling, lowered drinking fountains, and lowered telephones.

Services: Counseling and information services are available, as is tutoring in most subjects. There is a reader service for the blind, and remedial math, reading, and writing.

Campus Safety and Security: Measures include 24-hour foot and vehicle patrol, self-defense education, and security escort services. There are emergency telephones and lighted pathways/sidewalks.

Programs of Study: UW/Oshkosh confers B.A., B.S., B.Art Ed., B.B.A., B.F.A., B.L.S., B.M., B.M.E., B.S.N., and B.S.W. degrees. Associate and master's degrees are also awarded. Bachelor's degrees are awarded in BIOLOGICAL SCIENCE (biology/biological science and microbiology), BUSINESS (accounting, banking and finance, business administration and management, human resources, management information systems, and marketing/retailing/merchandising), COMMUNICATIONS AND THE ARTS (art, English, fine arts, French, German, journalism, music, Spanish, and speech/debate/rhetoric), COMPUTER AND PHYSICAL SCIENCE (chemistry, computer science, geology, mathematics, and physics), EDUCATION (art education, elementary education, music education, physical education, science education, secondary education, social science education, and special education), HEALTH PROFESSIONS (medical laboratory technology, music therapy, nursing, and speech pathology/audiology), SOCIAL SCIENCE (anthropology, criminal justice, economics, geography, history, human services, international studies, liberal arts/general studies, philosophy, political science/government, psychology, religion, social work, sociology, and urban studies). Business, education, and nursing have the largest enrollments.

Required: All students must complete a minimum of 120 credit hours with at least a 2.0 GPA. A minimum of 42 credits in general education requirements includes 9 credits each in humanities and social science, 8 in natural science, 6 in English composition, 3 each in math or logic, non-Western culture, and speech, and 2 in phys ed.

Special: UW/Oshkosh offers internships and study abroad. There are 15 national honor societies and a freshman honors program.

Faculty/Classroom: 56% of faculty are male; 44% are female. No introductory courses are taught by graduate students. The average class size in an introductory lecture is 31 and in a laboratory, 21.

Requirements: The ACT or SAT is required. Students must graduate from an accredited secondary school or have a GED diploma. They should have completed 17 academic credits, including 4 in English, 3 each in math, social sciences, and natural sciences, and 4 in electives. AP and CLEP credits are accepted.

Procedure: Freshmen are admitted to all sessions. Entrance exams should be taken in spring of the junior year or early fall of the senior year. There are deferred admissions and rolling admissions plans. Check with the school for current application deadlines and fee. Notification is sent on a rolling basis. Applications are accepted online.

Transfer: Candidates should have completed 30 or more semester credits; if not, high school transcripts are reviewed. Students must have at least a 2.0 cumulative GPA. 30 of 120 credits required for the bachelor's degree must be completed at UW/Oshkosh.

Visiting: There are regularly scheduled orientations for prospective students, including preview days, campus tours, and an individual appointment with an admissions counselor. There are guides for informal visits, visitors may sit in on classes, and stay overnight. To schedule a visit, contact the Admissions Office.

Financial Aid: UW/Oshkosh is a member of CSS. The FAFSA is required. Check with the school for current financial aid deadlines.

International Students: They must take the TOEFL.

Computers: All students may access the system 24 hours, 7 days a week. There are no time limits and no fees.

Admissions Contact: Jill Endries, Director of Admissions. A campus DVD is available. E-mail: *oshadmuw@uwosh.edu* Web: *www.uwosh.edu*

UNIVERSITY OF WISCONSIN/PARKSIDE E-5

Kenosha, WI 53141-2000 **(262) 595-2355; (262) 595-2008**

Full-time: 3750 men and women	**Faculty:** n/av; IIA, --$
Part-time: 1550 men and women	**Ph.D.s:** 97%
Graduate: 150 men and women	**Student/Faculty:** n/av
Year: semesters, summer session	**Tuition:** $7430 ($14,974)
Application Deadline: see profile	**Room & Board:** $7542
Freshman Class: n/av	
SAT or ACT: required	

LESS COMPETITIVE

The University of Wisconsin/Parkside, founded in 1968, offers undergraduate programs in liberal arts, business, education, and science and technology. There are 4 undergraduate schools and 3 graduate schools. Figures in the above capsule and in this profile are approximate. The library contains 350,000 volumes, 150,000 microform items, 10,200 audio/video tapes/CDs/DVDs, and subscribes to 1,500 periodicals including electronic. Special learning facilities include a learning resource center, art gallery, and radio station. The 700-acre campus is in a suburban area 30 miles south of Milwaukee. Including any residence halls, there are 11 buildings.

Student Life: 92% of undergraduates are from Wisconsin. 73% are white. The average age of freshmen is 18; all undergraduates, 21. 34% do not continue beyond their first year; 60% remain to graduate.

Housing: 400 students can be accommodated in college housing, which includes coed on-campus apartments and off-campus apartments. In addition, there are special-interest houses. On-campus housing is guaranteed for all 4 years. 63% of students commute. All students may keep cars.

Activities: There are no fraternities or sororities. There are 60 groups on campus, including art, band, cheerleading, choir, chorale, chorus, computers, drama, ethnic, gay, honors, international, jazz band, literary magazine, musical theater, newspaper, orchestra, political, professional, religious, social, social service, student government, and yearbook. Popular campus events include Cinco de Mayo, Winter Carnival, and Black History Month.

Sports: There are 8 intercollegiate sports for men and 6 for women. Facilities include a cross-country course, tennis courts, playing fields, and an all-purpose phys ed building with a 3000-seat auditorium for athletic events and concerts.

Disabled Students: All of the campus is accessible. Facilities include wheelchair ramps, elevators, special parking, specially equipped rest rooms, lowered drinking fountains, and lowered telephones.

Services: Counseling and information services are available, as is tutoring in every subject. There is a reader service for the blind, and remedial math, reading, and writing.

Campus Safety and Security: There are shuttle buses, emergency telephones, and lighted pathways/sidewalks.

Programs of Study: UW/Parkside confers B.A. and B.S. degrees. Master's degrees are also awarded. Bachelor's degrees are awarded in BIOLOGICAL SCIENCE (biology/biological science), BUSINESS (business administration and management), COMMUNICATIONS AND THE ARTS (communications, dramatic arts, English, fine arts, French, German, music, and Spanish), COMPUTER AND PHYSICAL SCIENCE (chemistry, computer science, geology, mathematics, physics, and science), EDUCATION (education), ENGINEERING AND ENVIRONMENTAL DESIGN (industrial administration/management), SOCIAL SCIENCE (economics, geography, history, humanities, international studies, philosophy, political science/government, psychology, and sociology). Social sciences and physical sciences are the strongest academically. Business has the largest enrollment.

Required: A total of 120 credits with at least 30 in the major and a GPA of 2.0 are required for graduation. Students must complete a minimum of 12 credits in humanities and the arts, 12 in social and behavioral sciences, and 9 in natural sciences. Nonengineering majors with fewer than 2 units of foreign language in high school must also fulfill a foreign language requirement.

Special: UW/Parkside offers on-campus work-study programs, internships, study abroad, student-designed majors, and an accelerated premedicine program. Nondegree study and credit by exam are possible. There is a freshman honors program.

Faculty/Classroom: No introductory courses are taught by graduate students. The average class size in an introductory lecture is 150; in a laboratory, 50; and in a regular course, 30.

Requirements: The ACT or SAT is required. Candidates must be graduates of an accredited secondary school or hold a GED diploma. At least 17 academic credits are required, including 4 in English, 3 each in social sciences, natural sciences, and math, and 4 electives. AP and CLEP credits are accepted. Important factors in the admissions decision are geographical diversity, extracurricular activities record, and ability to finance college education.

Procedure: Freshmen are admitted fall and spring. Entrance exams should be taken by the fall of the senior year. There are early admissions, deferred admissions, and rolling admissions plans. Check with the school for current application deadlines and fee.

Transfer: Students must have a GPA of 2.0 and be in good standing with the previous institution attended. 30 of 120 credits required for the bachelor's degree must be completed at UW/Parkside.

Visiting: There are regularly scheduled orientations for prospective students, including open houses and campus tours. There are guides for informal visits and visitors may sit in on classes. To schedule a visit, contact the Admissions Office.

Financial Aid: The CSS/Profile, FFS, and the college's own financial statement are required. Check with the school for current application deadlines.

International Students: They must take the TOEFL.

Computers: Two general-purpose labs are available to all students. All students may access the system. There are no time limits and no fees.

Admissions Contact: Admissions Director. E-mail: *admissions@uwp.edu* Web: *www.uwp.edu*

UNIVERSITY OF WISCONSIN/PLATTEVILLE C-5

Platteville, WI 53818 **(608) 342-1125 (800) 362-5515; (608) 342-1122**

Full-time: 4587 men, 2413 women	**Faculty:** n/av
Part-time: 459 men, 223 women	**Ph.D.s:** n/av
Graduate: 441 men, 382 women	**Student/Faculty:** 25 to 1
Year: semesters, summer session	**Tuition:** $7484 ($15,057)
Application Deadline: open	**Room & Board:** $6790
Freshman Class: 4030 applied, 3194 accepted, 1612 enrolled	
ACT: 23	

COMPETITIVE

The University of Wisconsin-Platteville takes its roots from the Platteville Normal School State Teachers College (1866) and the Wisconsin Mining Trade School (1908). Since then, the university's teaching mission has remained the same, develop strong graduates who can take their experience as a student directly to the workforce in an impactful way. Rich in its academic programs, the University of Wisconsin-Platteville consists of three colleges – the College of Business, Industry, Life Science and Agriculture; the College of Engineering, Mathematics and Science; and the College of Liberal Arts and Education. We have particular strengths in agriculture, biology, business, criminal justice, education, engineering, and industrial technology. There are 3 undergraduate schools and 1 graduate school. In addition to regional accreditation, UW-Platteville has baccalaureate program accreditation with ABET, NASM, and NCATE. The 2 libraries contain 208,065 volumes, 17,300 microform items, and 5,673 audio/video tapes/CDs/DVDs. Computerized library services include interlibrary loans, database searching, Internet access, and Wi-Fi capability. Special learning facilities include an art gallery, radio station, and TV station. The 821-acre campus is in a small town 20 miles northeast of Dubuque, Iowa, and 75 miles southwest of Madison, Wisconsin. Including any residence halls, there are 33 buildings.

Student Life: 77% of undergraduates are from Wisconsin. 90% are from public schools. 92% are White. The average age of freshmen is 18; all undergraduates, 21. 23% do not continue beyond their first year; 52% remain to graduate.

Housing: College-sponsored housing includes single-sex and coed dorms. 57% of students commute. All students may keep cars.

Activities: 6% of men belong to 2 local and 7 national fraternities; 8% of women belong to 2 local and 5 national sororities. There are 220 groups on campus, including art, band, cheerleading, choir, chorale, chorus, computers, debate, drama, ethnic, film, forensics, gay, honors, international, jazz band, literary magazine, marching band, musical theater, newspaper, opera, orchestra, pep band, photography, political, professional, radio and TV, religious, social, social service, student government, and symphony. Popular campus events include Homecoming, Pioneer Distinguished Lecturer Presentation, Mudfest Rugby Tournament, Lighting and Whitewashing of the M.

Sports: There are 7 intercollegiate sports for men and 7 for women, and 13 intramural sports for men and 12 for women. Facilities include We have a 2000 seat gym, a 10,000 seat stadium, a 200 meter indoor track, a 400 meter outdoor track, 7 basketball and 7 volleyball courts, 6 tennis and 3 racquetball courts, a weight room, a swimming pool, 2 baseball diamonds, and soccer fields.

Disabled Students: 95% of the campus is accessible. Facilities include wheelchair ramps, elevators, special parking, specially equipped restrooms, special class scheduling, lowered drinking fountains, lowered telephones, and special housing.

Services: Counseling and information services are available, as is tutoring in most subjects. There is remedial math, reading, and writing.

Campus Safety and Security: Measures include 24-hour foot and vehicle patrol, emergency notification system, and security escort services. There are shuttle buses, emergency telephones, lighted pathways/sidewalks, and controlled access to dorms/residences.

Programs of Study: UW-Platteville confers B.A., and B.S. degrees. Associate and master's degrees are also awarded. Bachelor's degrees are awarded in AGRICULTURE (agricultural business management, animal science, horticulture, and soil science), BIOLOGICAL SCIENCE (biology/biological science), BUSINESS (accounting and business administration and management), COMMUNICATIONS AND THE ARTS (art, English, German, music, Spanish, and visual and performing arts), COMPUTER AND PHYSICAL SCIENCE (chemistry, computer science, mathematics, physical sciences, physics, and software engineering), EDUCATION (agricultural education, art education, education, elementary education, middle school education, music education, physical education, secondary education, and technical education), ENGINEERING AND ENVIRONMENTAL DESIGN (civil engineering, electrical/electronics engineering, engineering, environmental engineering, industrial engineering, industrial engineering technology, land use management and reclamation, and mechanical engineering), SOCIAL SCIENCE (criminal justice, forensic studies, geography, history, international studies, liberal arts/general studies, philosophy, political science/government, psychology, and social science). Mechanical engineering, business administration and criminal justice have the largest enrollments.

Required: To graduate, students must complete a minimum of 120 credit hours, with a minimum GPA of 2.0 overall and within the major. Course requirements include 12 credits in humanities and fine arts, 9 each in social sciences and natural sciences, 4 in ethnic and gender studies, and 3 in international education. Other competency requirements include 6 credits in English composition, 3 in math, and 2 each in speech and phys ed.

Special: UWP offers internships in business, industry, and communication, a co-op program in engineering, and study abroad in 16 countries. Credit by exam, credit for life, military, and work experience, work-study programs, dual majors, student-designed majors, non-degree study, and pass/fail options are also available. There are 12 national honor societies, a freshman honors program, and 4 departmental honors programs.

Faculty/Classroom: No introductory courses are taught by graduate students.

Admissions: 79% of the 2013-2014 applicants were accepted. The ACT scores were 21% below 21, 32% between 21 and 23, 26% between 24 and 26, 11% between 27 and 28, and 10% above 28.

Requirements: The ACT is required. Applicants must have successfully completed 17 college preparatory units, including 4 units of English, 3 of math (algebra and higher), 3 of social science, 3 of natural science (2 must inlcude lab experiences), 4 from the above academic areas, foreign language, fine arts, computer science, or courses in vocational areas. Standard admission will be given to those students who are in the top 50% of their graduating class or have an ACT composite of 22 (SAT equivalency). UW-Platteville requires applicants to be in the upper 50% of their class. AP and CLEP credits are accepted.

Procedure: Freshmen are admitted to all sessions. Entrance exams should be taken in April or June of the junior year. There are deferred admissions and rolling admissions plans. Application deadlines are open. Application fee is $44. Applications are accepted online.

Transfer: 403 transfer students enrolled in 2012-2013. Applicants must have a cumulative GPA of at least 2.0 and be in good standing at the institution they are currently attending or have attended. 32 of 120 credits required for the bachelor's degree must be completed at UW-Platteville.

Visiting: There are regularly scheduled orientations for prospective students, The Pioneer Previews, held on 6 dates each year, include group tours, an admissions briefing, and visits to specific colleges and departments. Daily visits (Monday through Friday) are also available. There are guides for informal visits, visitors may sit in on classes, and stay overnight. To schedule a visit, contact the Prospective Student Services Office at (877) UWPLATT.

Financial Aid: The FAFSA is required. The priority date for freshman financial aid applications for fall entry is March 15.

International Students: There are 67 international students enrolled. The school actively recruits these students. They must take the TOEFL with a minimum score of 500 on the paper-based TOEFL (PBT) or 61 on the Internet-based version (iBT). Wisconsin English and math placement exam.

Computers: All students may access the system. There are no time limits and no fees.

Graduates: From July 1, 2012 to June 30, 2013, 1222 bachelor's degrees were awarded. The most popular majors were engineering (23%), criminal justice (12%), and business/marketing (10%). In an average class, 52% graduate in 6 years or less.

Admissions Contact: Angela Udelhofen, Enrollment Services/Assistant Chancellor. E-Mail: *admit@uwplatt.edu* Web: *www.uwplatt.edu/admission.html*

UNIVERSITY OF WISCONSIN/RIVER FALLS — A-3

River Falls, WI 54022 — **(715) 425-3500; (715) 425-0676**

Full- and part-time: 5750 men and women
Graduate: 350 men and women
Year: semesters, summer session
Application Deadline: open
Freshman Class: n/av
SAT or ACT: required

Faculty: n/av; IIA, --$
Ph.D.s: 85%
Student/Faculty: n/av
Tuition: $7770 ($15,850)
Room & Board: $7074

LESS COMPETITIVE

The University of Wisconsin/River Falls, founded in 1874, is a public institution offering undergraduate programs in arts and sciences, education, agriculture, and food and environmental sciences. There are 4 undergraduate schools and 1 graduate school. The figures in the above capsule and in this profile are approximate. In addition to regional accreditation, UW/River Falls has baccalaureate program accreditation with ACEJMC, ASLA, CSWE, NASM, and NCATE. The library contains 221,400 volumes, 726,000 microform items, 8,400 audio/video tapes/CDs/DVDs, and subscribes to 1,300 periodicals including electronic. Computerized library services include interlibrary loans, database searching, and Internet access. Special learning facilities include a learning resource center, art gallery, planetarium, radio station, TV station, greenhouse, climbing wall, communicative disorders lab, educational technology center, food science and meat facilities, 2 campus lab farms, and sundial. The 226-acre campus is in a suburban area 29 miles east of Minneapolis-St. Paul, Minnesota. Including any residence halls, there are 26 buildings.

Student Life: 52% of undergraduates are from Wisconsin. Others are from 25 states, 13 foreign countries, and Canada. 95% are from public schools. 95% are white. The average age of freshmen is 18; all undergraduates, 21. 25% do not continue beyond their first year; 54% remain to graduate.

Housing: 2172 students can be accommodated in college housing, which includes single-sex and coed dorms. On-campus housing is guaranteed for all 4 years. 59% of students commute. All students may keep cars.

Activities: 5% of men belong to 5 national fraternities; 5% of women belong to 4 national sororities. There are 120 groups on campus, including academic, agriculture, art, band, cheerleading, choir, chorus, communications, computers, dance, debate, drama, drug awareness, ethnic, forensics, gay, honors, international, jazz band, literary magazine, musical theater, newspaper, orchestra, pep band, political, professional, radio and TV, religious, rodeo, social, student government, and symphony. Popular campus events include Winter Carnival, Annual Rodeo, and Unity in the Community.

Sports: There are 7 intercollegiate sports for men and 11 for women, and 11 intramural sports for men and 12 for women. Facilities include an ice arena, a 4550-seat stadium, 2 multipurpose phys ed centers, a swimming pool, a 2600-seat gym and a smaller gym, handball courts, a field house, an indoor track, an indoor rock-climbing wall, and basketball, tennis, and volleyball courts.

Disabled Students: 95% of the campus is accessible. Facilities include wheelchair ramps, elevators, special parking, specially equipped rest rooms, special class scheduling, lowered drinking fountains, and lowered telephones.

Services: Counseling and information services are available, as is tutoring in every subject. There is a reader service for the blind, and remedial math, reading, and writing.

Campus Safety and Security: Measures include 24-hour foot and vehicle patrol, self-defense education, and security escort services. There are emergency telephones and lighted pathways/sidewalks.

Programs of Study: UW/River Falls confers B.A., B.S., B.F.A, B.M.E., and B.S.W. degrees. Master's degrees are also awarded. Bachelor's degrees are awarded in AGRICULTURE (agricultural business management, agronomy, animal science, conservation and regulation, horticulture, and soil science), BIOLOGICAL SCIENCE (biology/biological science and biotechnology), BUSINESS (accounting and business administration and management), COMMUNICATIONS AND THE ARTS (art, communications, English, fine arts, journalism, modern language, music, and speech/debate/rhetoric), COMPUTER AND PHYSICAL SCIENCE (chemistry, computer programming, geology, mathematics, physics, and science), EDUCATION (agricultural education, art education, elementary education, foreign languages education, music education, physical education, and secondary education), ENGINEERING AND ENVIRONMENTAL DESIGN (agricultural engineering and land use management and reclamation), HEALTH PROFESSIONS (premedicine, prepharmacy, and speech pathology/audiology), SOCIAL SCIENCE (economics, food science, geography, history, political science/government, prelaw, psychology, social studies, social work, and sociology). Physics, chemistry, and elementary education are the strongest academically. Business, elementary education, and animal science have the largest enrollments.

Required: To graduate, students must complete at least 120 semester hours, with a GPA of 2.0 overall and 2.25 in the major field. General education requirements include 39 semester hours in English composition, speech and humanities, natural and social sciences, math, and phys ed.

Special: Co-op programs in food science and environmental science, on-campus work-study, and accelerated degree programs in several preprofessional areas are available. UW/River Falls also offers internships, student-designed majors, credit by examination, nondegree study, and pass/fail options. Study abroad is available through the National Student Exchange and the International Student Exchange Program in some 15 countries. There are 11 national honor societies and a freshman honors program.

Faculty/Classroom: 70% of faculty are male; 30% are female. All teach undergraduates. No introductory courses are taught by graduate students. The average class size in an introductory lecture is 30; in a laboratory, 24; and in a regular course, 20.

Requirements: The ACT or SAT is required. Candidates must be graduates of an accredited secondary school and have completed at least 17 academic credits, including 4 in English, 3 each in social sciences, math, and science, and 4 electives. A GED certificate is accepted. AP and CLEP credits are accepted.

Procedure: Freshmen are admitted to all sessions. Entrance exams should be taken in the spring of the junior year. There are early admissions, deferred admissions, and rolling admissions plans. Application deadlines are open. Check with the school for the current application fee. Applications are accepted online. A waiting list is maintained.

Transfer: Priority admission is given to students with a college GPA of 2.6 or higher. Students with a GPA of 2.0 to 2.6 are placed on a waiting list. Transfers in elementary education must have a GPA of 3.0. 30 of 120 credits required for the bachelor's degree must be completed at UW/River Falls.

Visiting: There are regularly scheduled orientations for prospective students, including College Visit Days and tours. There are guides for informal visits and visitors may sit in on classes. To schedule a visit, contact the Admissions Office.

Financial Aid: UW/River Falls is a member of CSS. The FAFSA is required. Check with the school for current financial aid deadlines.

International Students: They must take the TOEFL and the ACT or SAT.

Computers: All students may access the system more than 80 hours per week, and by telephone request when labs are closed. There are no time limits and no fees.

Admissions Contact: Admissions Director. E-mail: *admit@uwrf.edu* Web: *http:/www.uwrf.edu*

UNIVERSITY OF WISCONSIN/STEVENS POINT C-3

Stevens Point, WI 54481	**(715) 346-2441; (715) 346-2441**
Full-time: 4159 men, 4476 women	**Faculty:** 413; IIA, --$
Part-time: 219 men, 264 women	**Ph.D.s:** 67%
Graduate: 93 men, 288 women	**Student/Faculty:** 20 to 1
Year: semesters, summer session	**Tuition:** $7505 ($15,078)
Application Deadline: open	**Room & Board:** $6538
Freshman Class: 4915 applied, 3672 accepted, 1637 enrolled	
SAT CR/M/W: 546/536/528	**ACT:** 23 **COMPETITIVE**

The University of Wisconsin/Stevens Point, founded in 1894, offers undergraduate programs in natural resources, education, business, arts and sciences, and professional studies. There are 4 undergraduate schools and one graduate school. In addition to regional accreditation, UWSP has baccalaureate program accreditation with ABET, ASLA, and NASAD. The library contains 813,123 volumes, 50,349 microform items, 25,357 audio/video tapes/CDs/DVDs, and subscribes to 44,876 periodicals including electronic. Computerized library services include interlibrary loans, database searching, Internet access, and Wi-Fi capability. Special learning facilities include an art gallery, natural history museum, planetarium, radio station, TV station, There is also an observatory, map center, 275-acre nature preserve, groundwater center, and wellness Institute. The 400-acre campus is in a small town 110 miles north of Madison. Including any residence halls, there are 35 buildings.

Student Life: 89% of undergraduates are from Wisconsin. Others are from 30 states, 29 foreign countries, and Canada. 98% are from public schools. 89% are White. The average age of freshmen is 19; all undergraduates, 22. 20% do not continue beyond their first year; 61% remain to graduate.

Housing: 3414 students can be accommodated in college housing, which includes single-sex and coed dorms. In addition, there are special-interest houses. 62% of students commute. All students may keep cars.

Activities: 1% of men belong to 1 local and 4 national fraternities; 1% of women belong to 2 local and 1 national sororities. There are 201 groups on campus, including art, band, cheerleading, choir, chorale, chorus, computers, dance, drama, environmental, ethnic, film, gay, honors, international, jazz band, literary magazine, musical theater, newspaper, orchestra, pep band, photography, political, professional, radio and TV, religious, social, social service, student government, and symphony. Popular campus events include Trivia Contest, International Club Dinner, and Spud Bowl.

Sports: There are 8 intercollegiate sports for men and 10 for women, and 16 intramural sports for men and 16 for women. Facilities include 2 gyms, a health enhancement center, a cardio center, aquatic center, and the University Center. The campus stadium seats 5500, the indoor gym, 3500. There is also a 391-seat auditorium and numerous outdoor fields.

Disabled Students: All of the campus is accessible. Facilities include wheelchair ramps, elevators, special parking, specially equipped restrooms, special class scheduling, lowered drinking fountains, lowered telephones.

Services: Counseling and information services are available, as is tutoring in most subjects. There is a reader service for the blind, and remedial math, reading, and writing.

Campus Safety and Security: Measures include 24-hour foot and vehicle patrol, emergency notification system, and security escort services. There are emergency telephones, lighted pathways/sidewalks, and controlled access to dorms/residences.

Programs of Study: UWSP confers B.A., B.S., B.F.A. and B.M. degrees. Associate, master's, and doctoral degrees are also awarded. Bachelor's degrees are awarded in AGRICULTURE (fishing and fisheries, forestry and related sciences, natural resource management, and soil science), BIOLOGICAL SCIENCE (biochemistry, biology/biological science, nutrition, and wildlife biology), BUSINESS (accounting and business administration and management), COMMUNICATIONS AND THE ARTS (art, arts administration/management, communications, dance, dramatic arts, English, fine arts, French, German, music, and Spanish), COMPUTER AND PHYSICAL SCIENCE (chemistry, geoscience, information sciences and systems, mathematics, natural sciences, physics, and web services), EDUCATION (athletic training, early childhood education, education, education of the exceptional child, elementary education, health education, music education, and physical education), ENGINEERING AND ENVIRONMENTAL DESIGN (computer technology, interior design, and paper and pulp science), HEALTH PROFESSIONS (clinical science, health science, and speech pathology/audiology), SOCIAL SCIENCE (American studies, dietetics, economics, family/consumer studies, geography, history, international studies, liberal arts/general studies, philosophy, political science/government, psychology, public administration, social science, social work, and sociology). Natural resources, education and social sciences have the largest enrollments.

Required: To graduate, students must complete 120 credit hours (30 from UWSP and 40 at 300/400 level), with a minimum GPA of 2.0. Core curriculum requirements must also be fulfilled, along with courses in writing, natural science, non-Western culture, minorities studies, social science, humanities, and wellness, and 3 credits in phys ed. Some majors require additional credits and higher minimum GPAs.

Special: A co-op program in nursing is offered with UW/Eau Claire and St. Joseph's Hospital. Internships, study abroad in 9 countries, work-study programs, dual and student-designed majors, independent study, and pass/fail options are also available. Credit is given for military, life, and work experience. There are 13 national honor societies and 3 departmental honors programs.

Faculty/Classroom: 64% of faculty are male; 46% are female. All teach undergraduates, and 98% do both. No introductory courses are taught by graduate students.

Admissions: 75% of the 2013 2014 applicants were accepted. The SAT scores for the 2013-2014 freshman class were: Critical Reading--23% below 500, 55% between 500 and 599, 14% between 600 and 699, and 9% between 700 and 800; Math--32% below 500, 41% between 500 and 599, 23% between 600 and 699, and 5% between 700 and 800; Writing--46% below 500, 32% between 500 and 599, 23% between 600 and 699. The ACT scores were 27% below 21, 37% between 21 and 23, 23% between 24 and 26, 8% between 27 and 28, and 5% above 28. 27% of the current freshmen were in the top fifth of their class; 61% were in the top two fifths. 28 freshmen graduated first in their class.

Requirements: The SAT or ACT is required. Applicants should have a high school rank of top 35% or above, or a cumulative high school GPA of 3.20 or higher, with an ACT composite score of 21 (SAT equivalent) or above; or rank in the top 50% of high school class with an ACT composite score of 21 or above. The ACT is preferred. The GED is accepted. Required academic preparation includes 4 years of English, 3 of social studies, and 3 each of math and lab science, along with 4 electives; 2 years of foreign language are recommended. The following non-academic factors are considered: involvement through work experience, extracurricular activities, and volunteerism; personal characteristics and accomplishments including special talents and abilities, honors, awards and personal qualities; diversity in background and experience; and life circumstances. While non-academic factors are considered, they will not necessarily make an applicant with a weak academic background a strong candidate for admission. AP and CLEP credits are accepted.

Procedure: Freshmen are admitted fall and spring. Entrance exams should be taken previous fall or spring. There are deferred admissions and rolling admissions plans. Application deadlines are open. Application fee is $44. 119 applicants were on the 2013 waiting list; 98 were admitted. Applications are accepted online.

Transfer: 786 transfer students enrolled in 2012-2013. Applicants must submit high school and college transcripts, as well as a statement of good standing from prior institutions. A high school minimum GPA of 2.25 is required. If fewer than 12 credits have been completed, the student must enroll as a freshman. 30 of 120 credits required for the bachelor's degree must be completed at UWSP.

Visiting: There are regularly scheduled orientations for prospective students, Students and parents can visit campus on a scheduled daily visit or participate in a one-day specialized program called ViewPoint, which is offered several times each fall and spring. UWSP also offers Info Nights in communities throughout WI and in IL to introduce students and parents to the university and answer detailed questions. There are guides for informal visits. To schedule a visit, contact the Office of Admissions.

Financial Aid: In 2013-2014, 58% of all full-time freshmen and 60% of continuing full-time students received some form of financial aid. 31% of all full-time freshmen and 34% of continuing full-time students received need-based aid. The average freshman award was $6,571. Need-based scholarships or need-based grants averaged $5,406; need-based self-help aid (loans and jobs) averaged $4,107; other non-need-based awards and non-need-based scholarships averaged $2,237; and $3,960 from other forms of aid. 38% of undergraduate students work part-time. Average annual earnings from campus work are $1887. The average financial indebtedness of the 2013 graduate was $22,788. The FAFSA is required. The priority date for freshman financial aid applications for fall entry is March 15. The deadline for filing freshman financial aid applications for fall entry is May 1.

International Students: There are 206 international students enrolled. The school actively recruits these students. They must take the TOEFL with a minimum score of 70 on the Internet-based version (iBT).

Computers: All students may access the system. There are no time limits and no fees.

Graduates: From July 1, 2012 to June 30, 2013, 1717 bachelor's degrees were awarded. The most popular majors were natural resources and conservation (13%), education (10%), and social sciences (10%). 124 companies recruited on campus in 2012-2013. In an average class, 22% graduate in 4 years or less and 59% graduate in 6 years or less. Of the 2012 graduating class, 17% were enrolled in graduate school within 6 months of graduation, and 55% were employed.

Admissions Contact: Terri Crumley, Director of Admissions. E-Mail: *admiss@uwsp.edu* Web: *www.uwsp.edu/admissions*

UNIVERSITY OF WISCONSIN/STOUT B-3

Menomonie, WI 54751 **(715) 232-1411**
(800) 447-8688; (715) 232-1667

Full- and part-time: 7980 men and women
Graduate: 1045 men and women
Year: semesters, summer session
Application Deadline: open
Freshman Class: n/av
SAT or ACT: required

Faculty: n/av; IIA, --$
Ph.D.s: 78%
Student/Faculty: n/av
Tuition: $9150 ($16,790
Room & Board: $6384

COMPETITIVE

The University of Wisconsin/Stout, founded in 1891, offers undergraduate programs in liberal studies, human environmental sciences, industry and technology, education, and human services. There are 4 undergraduate schools and 1 graduate school. The figures in the above capsule and in this profile are approximate. In addition to regional accreditation, UW-Stout has baccalaureate program accreditation with ABET, ACCE, ADA, FIDER, and NASAD. The library contains 231,600 volumes, 1.2 million microform items, 14,200 audio/video tapes/CDs/DVDs, and subscribes to 73,500 periodicals including electronic. Computerized library services include interlibrary loans, database searching, Internet access, and laptop Internet portals. Special learning facilities include a learning resource center, art gallery, radio station, and TV station. The 131-acre campus is in a rural area 60 miles east of Minneapolis/St. Paul. Including any residence halls, there are 43 buildings.

Student Life: 69% of undergraduates are from Wisconsin. Others are from 26 states, 39 foreign countries, and Canada. 93% are white. The average age of freshmen is 18; all undergraduates, 22. 27% do not continue beyond their first year.

Housing: 2936 students can be accommodated in college housing, which includes coed dorms. In addition, there is smoke-free, alcohol-free, upperclassmen-only, and freshman student housing. On-campus housing is guaranteed for all 4 years. 60% of students commute. All students may keep cars.

Activities: 2% of men belong to 3 local and 2 national fraternities; 3% of women belong to 3 national sororities. There are 117 groups on campus, including art, band, cheerleading, choir, chorale, chorus, computers, dance, debate, drama, ethnic, film, forensics, gay, honors, international, jazz band, literary magazine, marching band, musical theater, newspaper, pep band, photography, political, professional, radio, religious, social, social service, and student government. Popular campus events include Family Weekend, Cheese Week, and Biggest House Party.

Sports: There are 6 intercollegiate sports for men and 8 for women, and 20 intramural sports for men and 19 for women. Facilities include baseball, soccer, and football fields, indoor and outdoor tracks, and a field house with basketball, racquetball, and volleyball courts, a pool, weight and gymnastics rooms, and indoor and outdoor tennis courts.

Disabled Students: All of the campus is accessible. Facilities include wheelchair ramps, elevators, special parking, specially equipped rest rooms, special class scheduling, lowered drinking fountains, lowered telephones, and special housing.

Services: Counseling and information services are available, as is tutoring in most subjects. There is a reader service for the blind, and remedial math, reading, and writing.

Campus Safety and Security: Measures include 24-hour foot and vehicle patrol. There are lighted pathways/sidewalks and training sessions.

Programs of Study: UW-Stout confers B.A., B.S., and B.F.A. degrees. Master's degrees are also awarded. Bachelor's degrees are awarded in BUSINESS (business administration and management, hospitality management services, management science, marketing/retailing/merchandising, and retailing), COMMUNICATIONS AND THE ARTS (apparel design, art, communications, fine arts, and telecommunications), COMPUTER AND PHYSICAL SCIENCE (applied mathematics, applied science, and science), EDUCATION (art education, early childhood education, home economics education, marketing and distribution education, technical education, and vocational education), ENGINEERING AND ENVIRONMENTAL DESIGN (construction technology, engineering technology, graphic arts technology, graphic and printing production, industrial administration/management, industrial engineering technology, and manufacturing engineering), HEALTH PROFESSIONS (rehabilitation therapy), SOCIAL SCIENCE (child care/child and family studies, dietetics, family/consumer studies, food production/management/services, and psychology). General business administration, art, and hotel, restaurant, and tourism management have the largest enrollments.

Required: Students must complete a minimum of 124 credits, including a general education component. Some degree programs have specific general education courses that must be taken in order to satisfy certification, accreditation, or prerequisite standards. Students must also fulfill an ethnic studies requirement.

Special: UW-Stout offers business and industry internships, cooperative programs, work-study programs, and study abroad in London. Dual majors, credit by examination, credit for life, military, and work experience, nondegree study, and pass/fail options are also available. There is 1 national honor society, a freshman honors program, and 3 departmental honors programs.

Faculty/Classroom: 58% of faculty are male; 42% are female. All teach and do research. No introductory courses are taught by graduate students. The average class size in an introductory lecture is 28 and in a laboratory, 20.

Requirements: The SAT or ACT is required, with the ACT preferred. Minimum test scores are waived if students rank in the upper 50% of their class. Some programs require higher class rank. Applicants should graduate from an accredited secondary school. The GED is accepted if applicants are over 21, or if their graduating class has been out for at least 2 years.

Secondary school preparation should include 4 academic credits in English, 3 each in social studies, math, and science, and 4 in electives. AP and CLEP credits are accepted.

Procedure: Freshmen are admitted fall, spring, and summer. Entrance exams should be taken in June of the junior year. There is a rolling admissions plan. Application deadlines are open. Check with the school for the current application fee. Notification is sent on a rolling basis. Applications are accepted online. A waiting list is maintained.

Transfer: A minimum college GPA of 2.0 is required for student transfers from UW system institutions. A 2.2 GPA is required for those transferring from outside the UW system. A high school transcript and a statement of good standing from prior institutions are required. 32 of 124 credits required for the bachelor's degree must be completed at UW-Stout.

Visiting: There are regularly scheduled orientations for prospective students, including an interview with an admissions counselor and a campus tour. There are also campus preview days throughout the academic year. There are guides for informal visits, visitors may sit in on classes, and stay overnight. To schedule a visit, contact the Admissions Office.

Financial Aid: UW-Stout is a member of CSS. The FAFSA is required. Check with the school for current financial aid deadlines.

International Students: The school actively recruits these students. They must take the TOEFL.

Computers: All students may access the system 24 hours a day, 7 days a week. There are no time limits and no fees. All students are required to have a personal computer. A Compaq is recommended.

Admissions Contact: Director of Admissions. A campus DVD is available. E-mail: *admissions@uwstout.edu* Web: *www.uwstout.edu*

UNIVERSITY OF WISCONSIN/SUPERIOR — A-1

Superior, WI 54880 — **(715) 394-8264; (715) 394-8407**

Full-time: 868 men, 1150 women — **Faculty:** 130; IIA, --$
Part-time: 146 men, 358 women — **Ph.D.s:** 63%
Graduate: 35 men, 99 women — **Student/Faculty:** 13 to 1
Year: semesters, summer session — **Tuition:** $7946 ($15,519)
Application Deadline: August 1 — **Room & Board:** $6160
Freshman Class: 910 applied, 605 accepted, 325 enrolled
ACT: 22

COMPETITIVE

The University of Wisconsin/Superior, founded in 1893, offers undergraduate programs in the liberal arts and sciences, business, education, fine arts, applied arts, and social sciences. In addition to regional accreditation, UW/Superior has baccalaureate program accreditation with CSWE and NASM. Computerized library services include interlibrary loans, database searching, Internet access, and Wi-Fi capability. Special learning facilities include an art gallery, planetarium, radio station, TV station, an aquatic lab. The 230-acre campus is in an urban area Superior, Wisconsin, a city of 27,000 at the western tip of Lake Superior. Superior is accessible by Interstate 35 in Minnesota and U.S. Highway 53 in Wisconsin. Including any residence halls, there are 17 buildings.

Student Life: 51% of undergraduates are from Wisconsin. Others are from 34 states, 38 foreign countries, and Canada. 90% are from public schools. 84% are White. The average age of freshmen is 18; all undergraduates, 22. 34% do not continue beyond their first year; 41% remain to graduate.

Housing: 820 students can be accommodated in college housing, which includes coed dorms. On-campus housing is guaranteed for the freshman year only. 72% of students commute. All students may keep cars.

Activities: There are no fraternities or sororities. There are 61 groups on campus, including art, band, cheerleading, choir, chorale, chorus, computers, dance, drama, ethnic, gay, honors, international, jazz band, newspaper, orchestra, pep band, photography, political, professional, radio and TV, religious, social, social service, student government, and symphony. Popular campus events include World Culture Night and Winterfest.

Sports: There are 6 intercollegiate sports for men and 8 for women, and 19 intramural sports for men and 19 for women. Facilities include a 3000-seat gym, an ice arena, a swimming pool, a weight training room, a dance studio, racquetball courts, an all-weather track, a climbing wall, and softball and baseball fields.

Disabled Students: 95% of the campus is accessible. Facilities include wheelchair ramps, elevators, special parking, specially equipped restrooms, special class scheduling, lowered drinking fountains, and lowered telephones.

Services: Counseling and information services are available, as is tutoring in every subject. There is remedial math and writing.

Campus Safety and Security: Measures include 24-hour foot and vehicle patrol, emergency notification system, self-defense education, and security escort services. There are emergency telephones, lighted pathways/sidewalks, and controlled access to dorms/residences.

Programs of Study: UW/Superior confers B.A., B.S., B.F.A., B.M. and B.M.E. degrees. Associate and master's degrees are also awarded. Bachelor's degrees are awarded in BIOLOGICAL SCIENCE (biology/biological science), BUSINESS (accounting, business administration and management, finance, international business management, sustainable management, and transportation management), COMMUNICATIONS AND THE ARTS (art history, art, communications, dramatic arts, English, fine arts, music, music performance, speech/debate/rhetoric, studio art, theatre arts, visual and performing arts, and writing), COMPUTER AND PHYSICAL SCIENCE (chemistry, computer science, and mathematics), EDUCATION (art education, elementary education, English education, health education, mathematics education, music education, physical education, science education, secondary education, social science education, and social studies secondary school education), HEALTH PROFESSIONS (art therapy, biology, community health work, exercise science, health, health and physical activity, and health promotion), SOCIAL SCIENCE (criminal justice, economics, history, interdisciplinary studies, international studies, law, political science/government, psychology, public administration, social studies, social work, and sociology). Business administration, elementary education, and biology are the strongest academically. Business administration, elementary education, and communicating arts have the largest enrollments.

Required: To graduate, students must complete 120 credit hours, with a GPA of 2.0. A minimum of 54 hours must be credited toward completion of 1 comprehensive major, 2 majors, or 1 major and 1 minor. The required core curriculum includes 55 credits in Communications, English, Math, Phys Ed, World Culture, Contemporary Society, Aesthetic Experience, Natural Science, and Human Behavior. A comprehensive exam and a senior project are required.

Special: UW/Superior offers work-study and co-op programs in business and internships in social work, business, mass communication, and criminal justice. There is a comprehensive program of student-designed majors, along with a cooperative program in marine studies with Texas A&M University, and 3-2 engineering and forestry programs with Michigan Technological University. Students may cross-register for 2 classes per semester at the University of Minnesota/Duluth or the College of St. Scholastica. An extended degree is offered. Credit for life experience and pass/fail options are available. There are 4 national honor societies and 4 departmental honors programs.

Faculty/Classroom: 52% of faculty are male; 48% are female. 95% teach undergraduates. No introductory courses are taught by graduate students. The average class size in an introductory lecture is 22; in a laboratory is 20; and in a regular course is 17.

Admissions: 66% of the 2013-2014 applicants were accepted. The ACT scores were 38% below 21, 31% between 21 and 23, 22% between 24 and 26, 5% between 27 and 28, and 5% above 28. 20% of the current freshmen were in the top fifth of their class; 54% were in the top two fifths. 7 freshmen graduated first in their class.

Requirements: The ACT is required. Out-of-state residents may submit SAT scores instead. Applicants must graduate from an accredited secondary school or the equivalent. Applicant must rank in at least the upper 50% of their graduating class or achieve a minimum composite score of 21 on the ACT. AP and CLEP credits are accepted.

Procedure: Freshmen are admitted fall, spring, and summer. Entrance exams should be taken spring of junior year or early fall of senior year. There are deferred admissions and rolling admissions plans. Applications should be filed by August 1 for fall entry; January 5 for spring entry, along with a $44 fee. Notification is sent on a rolling basis. Applications are accepted online.

Transfer: 317 transfer students enrolled in 2012-2013. A college GPA of 2.0 is required. 30 of 120 credits required for the bachelor's degree must be completed at UW/Superior.

Visiting: There are regularly scheduled orientations for prospective students, consisting of 2 days of social and educational programs. There are guides for informal visits, visitors may sit in on classes, and stay overnight. To schedule a visit, contact the Admissions Office.

Financial Aid: In 2013-2014, 65% of all full-time freshmen and 69% of continuing full-time students received some form of financial aid. 38% of all full-time freshmen and 49% of continuing full-time students received need-based aid. The average freshman award was $10,523. Need based scholarships or need-based grants averaged $5,386; and need-based self-help aid (loans and jobs) averaged $4,600. The average financial indebtedness of the 2013 graduate was $27,871. The FAFSA is required. The priority date for freshman financial aid applications for fall entry is April 1.

International Students: There are 141 international students enrolled. The school actively recruits these students. They must take the TOEFL with a minimum score of 500 on the paper-based TOEFL (PBT) or 61 on the Internet-based version (iBT) or take the MELAB, completion of ELS language center program (if necessary). ACT or SAT score is required if International student is native English speaking.

Computers: All students may access the system 24 hours a day. There are no time limits and no fees.

Graduates: From July 1, 2012 to June 30, 2013, 478 bachelor's degrees were awarded. The most popular majors were business/marketing (21%), education (15%), and communication/journalism (12%). In an average

class, 1% graduate in 3 years or less, 16% graduate in 4 years or less, 38% graduate in 5 years or less, and 41% graduate in 6 years or less.
Admissions Contact: Tonya Roth, Director of Admissions. E-Mail: *admissions@uwsuper.edu* Web: *www.uwsuper.edu*

UNIVERSITY OF WISCONSIN/WHITEWATER D-5

Whitewater, WI 53190 **(262) 472-1440; (262) 472-1515**

Full-time: 4722 men, 5325 women	**Faculty:** 384; IIA, --$
Part-time: 269 men, 371 women	**Ph.D.s:** 73%
Graduate: 479 men, 780 women	**Student/Faculty:** 22 to 1
Year: semesters, summer session	**Tuition:** $7528 ($15,101)
Application Deadline: open	**Room & Board:** $5786
Freshman Class: 7000 applied, 5600 accepted, 2150 enrolled	
SAT CR/M/W: 530/520/525	**ACT:** recommended **COMPETITIVE**

The University of Wisconsin/Whitewater, founded in 1868, offers programs in teacher education, business, liberal arts, preprofessional studies, fine arts and music. There are 4 undergraduate schools and 1 graduate school. In addition to regional accreditation, UW-Whitewater has baccalaureate program accreditation with AACSB, ASLA, CSWE, NASM, and NCATE. The library contains 356,000 volumes, 993,000 microform items, and 7,300 audio/video tapes/CDs/DVDs, and subscribes to 5,000 periodicals including electronic. Computerized library services include interlibrary loans and database searching. Special learning facilities include an art gallery, radio station, TV station, observatory and weather station. The 385-acre campus is in a small town 50 miles southwest of Milwaukee. Including any residence halls, there are 45 buildings.
Student Life: 85% of undergraduates are from Wisconsin. Others are from 26 states, 38 foreign countries, and Canada. 70% are from public schools. 87% are White. The average age of freshmen is 19; all undergraduates, 22. 20% do not continue beyond their first year; 63% remain to graduate.
Housing: 4300 students can be accommodated in college housing, which includes single-sex and coed dorms and off-campus apartments. On-campus housing is available on a first-come and first-served basis. 8% of students commute. All students may keep cars.
Activities: 5% of men belong to 1 local and 6 national fraternities; 5% of women belong to 1 local and 4 national sororities. There are 130 groups on campus, including art, band, cheerleading, choir, chorus, communications, computers, dance, drama, drill team, ethnic, film, gay, honors, international, marching band, musical theater, newspaper, orchestra, pep band, photography, political, professional, radio and TV, religious, social, social service, student government, symphony, and yearbook. Popular campus events include Job Fair, Performing Arts Series, and Athletic Contests.
Sports: There are 9 intercollegiate sports for men and 8 for women, and 12 intramural sports for men and 12 for women. Facilities include tennis courts, pools, playing fields, a 13,000-seat stadium, and a 3500-seat gym.
Disabled Students: 85% of the campus is accessible. Facilities include wheelchair ramps, elevators, special parking, specially equipped restrooms, special class scheduling, lowered drinking fountains, lowered telephones.
Services: Counseling and information services are available, as is tutoring in most subjects. There is a reader service for the blind, and remedial math, reading, and writing.
Campus Safety and Security: Measures include 24-hour foot and vehicle patrol, self-defense education, and security escort services. There are shuttle buses, emergency telephones, and lighted pathways/sidewalks.
Programs of Study: UW-Whitewater confers B.A., B.S., B.B.A., B.F.A., B.M. and B.S.Ed. degrees. Associate and master's degrees are also awarded. Bachelor's degrees are awarded in BIOLOGICAL SCIENCE (biology/biological science), BUSINESS (accounting, banking and finance, business administration and management, business economics, marketing/retailing/merchandising, office supervision and management, and personnel management), COMMUNICATIONS AND THE ARTS (art history and appreciation, communications, dramatic arts, English, French, German, journalism, music, public relations, Spanish, and speech/debate/rhetoric), COMPUTER AND PHYSICAL SCIENCE (chemistry, computer programming, mathematics, and physics), EDUCATION (art education, business education, early childhood education, elementary education, foreign languages education, middle school education, music education, physical education, science education, secondary education, social studies education, and special education), SOCIAL SCIENCE (economics, geography, history, international studies, political science/government, prelaw, psychology, public administration, safety and security technology, social work, sociology, and women's studies). Accounting, education and marketing are the strongest academically. Business/accounting, education, letters and sciences has the largest enrollments.
Required: Students must complete 50 credits of general studies, a writing competency requirement, and 3 credits in minority issues. A GPA of 2.0 and 120 hours are required to graduate.
Special: Internships, study abroad in 9 nations, accelerated degree programs in safety studies and speech communication, student-designed majors, and a general studies degree are available. Credit by examination, nondegree study, and pass/fail options are also offered. There are 14 national honor societies, a freshman honors program, and 7 departmental honors programs.
Faculty/Classroom: 57% of faculty are male; 43% are female. All teach undergraduates, and 78% do research. No introductory courses are taught by graduate students. The average class size in a regular course is 26.
Admissions: 80% of the 2013-2014 applicants were accepted.
Requirements: The SAT or ACT is recommended. Applicants should graduate from an accredited secondary school or with 17 academic units, including 4 in English and 3 each in social studies, math, and science. The GED may be accepted. Applicants should rank in the upper 40% of their graduating class or achieve a combined high school and ACT/SAT percentile rank of 100% or above. A GPA of 2.8 is required. AP and CLEP credits are accepted. Important factors in the admissions decision are evidence of special talent, advanced placement or honors courses, and recommendations by school officials.
Procedure: Freshmen are admitted to all sessions. There are early admissions and rolling admissions plans. Application deadlines are open. Notification is sent on a rolling basis.
Transfer: Applicants should have a minimum college GPA of 2.0. 30 of 120 credits required for the bachelor's degree must be completed at UW-Whitewater.
Visiting: There are regularly scheduled orientations for prospective students. There are guides for informal visits and visitors may sit in on classes. To schedule a visit, contact the Admissions Office.
Financial Aid: In 2013-2014, 73% of all full-time freshmen and 73% of continuing full-time students received some form of financial aid. 45% of all full-time freshmen and 45% of continuing full-time students received need-based aid. The average freshman award was $6,000. UW-Whitewater is a member of CSS. The FAFSA is required. Check with the school for current application deadlines.
International Students: The school actively recruits these students. They must take the TOEFL or MELAB.
Computers: All students may access the system. 24 hours if they have their own terminal or 8 a.m. to 11 p.m. Monday through Thursday and varied weekend hours in the general lab. There are no time limits and no fees.
Graduates: In an average class, 50% graduate in 6 years or less.
Admissions Contact: Jeff Blahnik, Director of Admissions. E-Mail: *uwwadmit@mail.uww.edu* Web: *www.uww.edu*

VITERBO UNIVERSITY B-4

La Crosse, WI 54601 **(608) 796-3010**
(800) 848-3726; (608) 796-3020

Full-time: 437 men, 1132 women	**Faculty:** 107; IIA, --$
Part-time: 125 men, 411 women	**Ph.D.s:** 60%
Graduate: 211 men, 514 women	**Student/Faculty:** 12 to 1
Year: semesters, summer session	**Tuition:** $22,670
Application Deadline: open	**Room & Board:** $7400
Freshman Class: 1655 applied, 1145 accepted, 304 enrolled	
ACT: 23	**COMPETITIVE**

Viterbo University, Catholic, Franciscan ecumenical university, prepares students for leadership and service by providing a student-centered, values-based, learning-focused liberal arts education rooted in the values of human dignity and respect for the world. Viterbo offers a wide variety of programs that encourage and challenge students to be thoughtful, creative, competent, and independent thinkers. We offer a seamless education that blends undergraduate and graduate courses with liberal arts courses so as to develop a whole, value-based person. By encouraging leadership and service students become capable and socially responsible in using their talents, energy, resources, and time to conceive and implement worthy vocations and projects for the good of people and the world. Viterbo University's Center for Ethics in Leadership assists the entire school community in its commitment to inoculate ethics across all aspects of university life. There are 5 undergraduate schools and 5 graduate schools. In addition to regional accreditation, Viterbo has baccalaureate program accreditation with CSWE, NASM, NCATE, and NLN. The library contains 92,300 volumes, 307 microform items, and 5,110 audio/video tapes/CDs/DVDs, and subscribes to 229 periodicals including electronic. Computerized library services include interlibrary loans, database searching, Internet access, and Wi-Fi capability. Special learning facilities include an art gallery, music resource center. The 72-acre campus is in a suburban area 150 miles from Minneapolis - St. Paul, 105 miles from Madison, and 230 miles from Chicago. Including any residence halls, there are 18 buildings.
Student Life: 76% of undergraduates are from Wisconsin. Others are from 34 states, and 11 foreign countries. 93% are from public schools. 92% are White. 43% are Catholic; 34% Protestant; 14% unidentified religions. The average age of freshmen is 18; all undergraduates, 25. 26% do not continue beyond their first year; 52% remain to graduate.

Housing: 686 students can be accommodated in college housing, which includes single-sex and coed dorms and on-campus apartments. In addition, there are special-interest houses, On-campus houses and special-interest floors. On-campus housing is guaranteed for the freshman year only, is available on a first-come, and first-served basis. 10% of students commute. Alcohol is not permitted. Upperclassmen may keep cars.

Activities: There are no fraternities or sororities. There are 32 groups on campus, including art, choir, chorale, chorus, dance, drama, drill team, environmental, ethnic, gay, honors, international, literary magazine, musical theater, newspaper, opera, pep band, political, professional, religious, social, social service, and student government. Popular campus events include Orientation Weekend, Welcome Back Bash, Viterbo Days (Family Day), St. Francis Day Celebration, and Courtyard Carni.

Sports: There are 7 intercollegiate sports for men and 8 for women, and 14 intramural sports for men and 14 for women. Facilities include a student activity center with weight training and fitness rooms and courts for basketball, volleyball, and racquetball. The nearby Mississippi River and Mt. LaCrosse provide additional recreational opportunities. A 12.5-acre outdoor athletic complex has facilities for soccer, baseball, and softball, located 2 1/2 miles from campus. There also are on-campus sand volleyball and paved basketball outdoor courts. The nearby Mississippi River and Mt. La Crosse provide opportunities for canoeing and skiing.

Disabled Students: 90% of the campus is accessible. Facilities include wheelchair ramps, elevators, special parking, specially equipped restrooms, special class scheduling, lowered drinking fountains, and lowered telephones.

Services: Counseling and information services are available, as is tutoring in every subject. There is a reader service for the blind, and remedial math, reading, and writing.

Campus Safety and Security: Measures include emergency notification system, self-defense education, and security escort services. There are shuttle buses, emergency telephones, lighted pathways/sidewalks, controlled access to dorms/residences, an emergency evacuation plan, 24 hours a day, 7 days a week, phone access to security personnel, security patrol from 5 p.m. to 7 a.m., ID check-in in dorms after 10 p.m., and card access to all campus buildings after regular hours, and 6 emergency blue lights.

Programs of Study: Viterbo confers B.A., B.S., B.Art.Ed., B.B.A., B.F.A., B.I.L., B.L.S., B.M., B.S.T., B.S.VC., B.S.Community-Medical Dietetics, B.S.Ed., and B.S.N. degrees. Associate and master's degrees are also awarded. Bachelor's degrees are awarded in AGRICULTURE (environmental studies), BIOLOGICAL SCIENCE (biochemistry and biology/biological science), BUSINESS (accounting, management information systems, management science, marketing/retailing/merchandising, organizational leadership and management, sports management, and sustainable management), COMMUNICATIONS AND THE ARTS (art, arts administration/management, communication, dramatic arts, English, graphic design, music performance, Spanish, studio art, and theatre studies), COMPUTER AND PHYSICAL SCIENCE (chemistry, digital arts/technology, mathematics, and natural sciences), EDUCATION (art education, business education, elementary education, English education, mathematics education, music education, science education, social studies education, and technology & science education), HEALTH PROFESSIONS (health care administration and nursing), SOCIAL SCIENCE (addiction studies, biopsychology, criminal justice, dietetics, history, liberal arts/general studies, philosophy, psychology, religious education, religious studies, social studies, social work, and sociology). Life Sciences, nutrition/dietetics, and natural sciences are the strongest academically. Health professions, business, and education have the largest enrollments.

Required: Students must complete a minimum of 128 semester hours of credit. A minimum of 43 of these must be upper division level. All students must complete the General Education requirements (45 credit hours from various disciplines) and competencies, as well as all of the specified requirements for their major. Also, students must complete a service component designed by their major program. All students must have a GPA of at least 2.0; and must take as a minimum the last 30 consecutive semester hours at Viterbo University or complete 45 of the last 60 semester hours from Viterbo. Students seeking a B.S. must complete 7 credits of natural science and/or math in addition to the 4 credits of natural science in the General Education requirements. Students seeking a B.A. must complete the equivalent of 14 semester hours of the same modern foreign language.

Special: Students may cross-register at the University of Wisconsin/LaCrosse, enroll for independent study, or earn a dual degree. Co-op programs, study abroad in 7 countries, double majors, student-designed majors, accelerated degree programs, work-study, internships in many areas, credit by exam, and credit/no credit options are available. There are 2 national honor societies, including Phi Beta Kappa, and a freshman honors program.

Faculty/Classroom: 48% of faculty are male; 63% are female. 90% teach undergraduates, 53% do research, and 53% do both. No introductory courses are taught by graduate students. The average class size in an introductory lecture is 17; in a laboratory is 16; and in a regular course is 15.

Admissions: 69% of the 2013-2014 applicants were accepted. The ACT scores were 24% below 21, 34% between 21 and 23, 29% between 24 and 26, 8% between 27 and 28, and 5% above 28. 37% of the current freshmen were in the top fifth of their class; 72% were in the top two fifths. 6 freshmen graduated first in their class.

Requirements: The ACT is required. Graduation from an accredited secondary school is required; the GED is accepted. Secondary preparation should include 16 credits, with 3 or 4 in English and 2 each in math, natural science, and social science or history. Fine arts students may be required to audition or submit a portfolio. Nursing, dietetics, and pre-medical students must have high school chemistry. A GPA of 2.0 is required. AP and CLEP credits are accepted.

Procedure: Freshmen are admitted to all sessions. Entrance exams should be taken at orientation, prior to registration. There is a rolling admissions plan. Application deadlines are open. Application fee is $25. Notification is sent on a rolling basis. Applications are accepted online.

Transfer: 274 transfer students enrolled in 2012-2013. Transfer students must have a cumulative GPA of at least 2.0, are free to return to their previous school, and are considered to be in good academic standing both at their previous school and at Viterbo. They must submit an application, the official transcripts of coursework in high school, official transcripts from all post-secondary institutions, and ACT/SAT results, if already taken. 30 of 128 credits required for the bachelor's degree must be completed at Viterbo.

Visiting: There are regularly scheduled orientations for prospective students, including a meeting with an admissions staff member, a tour of the campus, and optional meetings with a financial aid officer and faculty members. There are guides for informal visits and visitors may sit in on classes. To schedule a visit, contact the Admission Office.

Financial Aid: In 2013-2014, 98% of all full-time freshmen students received some form of financial aid. 100% of undergraduate students work part-time. Average annual earnings from campus work are $1167. The FAFSA and the college's own financial statement are required. The priority date for freshman financial aid applications for fall entry is March 15.

International Students: There are 24 international students enrolled. The school actively recruits these students. They must take the TOEFL with a minimum score of 525 on the paper-based TOEFL (PBT) or 93 on the Internet-based version (iBT).

Computers: All students may access the system, 6 a.m. to 1 a.m. daily. There are no time limits and no fees.

Graduates: From July 1, 2012 to June 30, 2013, 453 bachelor's degrees were awarded. The most popular majors were health (44%), letters and science (26%), and business (15%). 80 companies recruited on campus in 2012-2013. In an average class, 33% graduate in 4 years or less and 52% graduate in 6 years or less. Of the 2012 graduating class, 7% were enrolled in graduate school within 6 months of graduation, and 97% were employed.

Admissions Contact: Robert Forget, Dean, Admission. E-Mail: *admission@viterbo.edu* Web: *www.viterbo.edu*

WISCONSIN LUTHERAN COLLEGE — E-4

Milwaukee, WI 53226 — (414) 443-8811; (888) 947-5884; (414) 443-8547

Full- and part-time: 800 men and women	**Faculty:** n/av
Graduate: n/av	**Ph.D.s:** 70%
Year: semesters, summer session	**Student/Faculty:** n/av
Application Deadline: see profile	**Tuition:** $23,330
	Room & Board: $8740
Freshman Class: n/av	
SAT or ACT: required	
	VERY COMPETITIVE

Wisconsin Lutheran College, founded in 1973 in affiliation with the Wisconsin Evangelical Lutheran Synod, offers higher education in the arts and sciences within a conservative Christian environment. The figures in the above capsule and in this profile are approximate. The library contains 72,600 volumes, 9,200 microform items, 4,600 audio/video tapes/CDs/DVDs, and subscribes to 990 periodicals including electronic. Computerized library services include interlibrary loans, database searching, and Internet access. Special learning facilities include a learning resource center, art gallery, sound studio, electronic music lab, and language lab. The 21-acre campus is in a suburban area on the western edge of Milwaukee. Including any residence halls, there are 27 buildings.

Student Life: 80% of undergraduates are from Wisconsin. Others are from 26 states and 10 foreign countries. 41% are from public schools. 95% are white. 88% are Protestant. The average age of freshmen is 18; all undergraduates, 20. 20% do not continue beyond their first year; 74% remain to graduate.

Housing: 600 students can be accommodated in college housing, which includes single-sex dorms and on-campus apartments. On-campus housing is guaranteed for all 4 years. 74% of students live on campus. Alcohol is not permitted. All students may keep cars.

Activities: There are no fraternities or sororities. There are 30 groups

on campus, including Ambassador Club (admissions), art, band, cheerleading, choir, dance, drama, ethnic, international, jazz band, musical theater, newspaper, pep band, photography, political, professional, religious, social, social service, student government, and yearbook. Popular campus events include musical and theater events, Winterfest, and Commencement Weekend.

Sports: There are 7 intercollegiate sports for men and 8 for women, and 5 intramural sports for men and 5 for women. Facilities include 3 full basketball courts, a 2500-seat gym, weight room, a fitness center, a dance/aerobics room, training and therapy rooms, and a walking/running track.

Disabled Students: 90% of the campus is accessible. Facilities include wheelchair ramps, elevators, special parking, specially equipped restrooms, lowered drinking fountains, and lowered telephones.

Services: Counseling and information services are available, as is tutoring in some subjects, including math, writing, and foreign language.

Campus Safety and Security: Measures include 24-hour foot and vehicle patrol, self-defense education, and security escort services. There are shuttle buses, lighted pathways/sidewalks, a security service, and electronically operated dorm entrances.

Programs of Study: Wisconsin Lutheran confers B.A. and B.S. degrees. Bachelor's degrees are awarded in BIOLOGICAL SCIENCE (biology/biological science), BUSINESS (business economics), COMMUNICATIONS AND THE ARTS (art, communications, dramatic arts, English, music, and Spanish), COMPUTER AND PHYSICAL SCIENCE (chemistry and mathematics), EDUCATION (elementary education), SOCIAL SCIENCE (history, interdisciplinary studies, political science/government, psychology, social science, and theological studies). Chemistry, education, and biology are the strongest academically. Music, theology, and education have the largest enrollments.

Required: Composition, speech, math, and foreign language competencies are required. All students must complete a core curriculum that includes courses in theology, aesthetics, literature, natural science, history, social science, and intellectual diversity, plus 1 credit in phys ed/lifetime sport and 2 freshman seminars. A minimum overall GPA of 2.0 and 2.5 in the major (some require a higher GPA) plus 128 credit hours are required to graduate.

Special: Student-designed majors and study abroad are offered. Internships are available in most departments.

Faculty/Classroom: 70% of faculty are male; 30% are female. All teach and do research. The average class size in an introductory lecture is 20; in a laboratory, 10; and in a regular course, 16.

Requirements: The ACT or SAT is required, with a minimum composite or combined score of 21 or 1000, respectively. Students should be graduates of an accredited high school or its equivalent with a minimum of 16 high school units, including 4 in English, 3 each in academic electives and math, and 2 each in science, foreign language, and social studies/history. Students must rank in the upper half of their graduating class or have a minimum GPA of 2.7. The Academic Recommendation Form must be submitted. A portfolio for art grants and an audition for music and drama grants are required. AP and CLEP credits are accepted. Important factors in the admissions decision are leadership record and personality/intangible qualities.

Procedure: Freshmen are admitted fall and spring. Entrance exams should be taken in the spring of the junior year. There is a rolling admissions plan. Check with the school for current application deadlines and fee. Notification is sent on a rolling basis. Applications are accepted online.

Transfer: Students should have a GPA of at least 2.5 for transfer credit. The Transfer Recommendation Form is required. 30 of 128 credits required for the bachelor's degree must be completed at Wisconsin Lutheran.

Visiting: There are regularly scheduled orientations for prospective students, including a tour of the campus, a meal, meetings with admissions, financial aid, cocurriculars, and faculty in academic areas of interest. There are guides for informal visits, visitors may sit in on classes, and stay overnight. To schedule a visit, contact the Admissions Office.

Financial Aid: The FAFSA and the college's own financial statement are required. Check with the school for current application deadlines.

International Students: They must take the TOEFL. They must also take the SAT or ACT.

Computers: All students may access the system. There are no time limits and no fees. It is strongly recommended that all students have a personal computer.

Admissions Contact: Craig Swiontek, Director of Admissions. E-mail: *admissions@wlc.edu* Web: *www.wlc.edu*

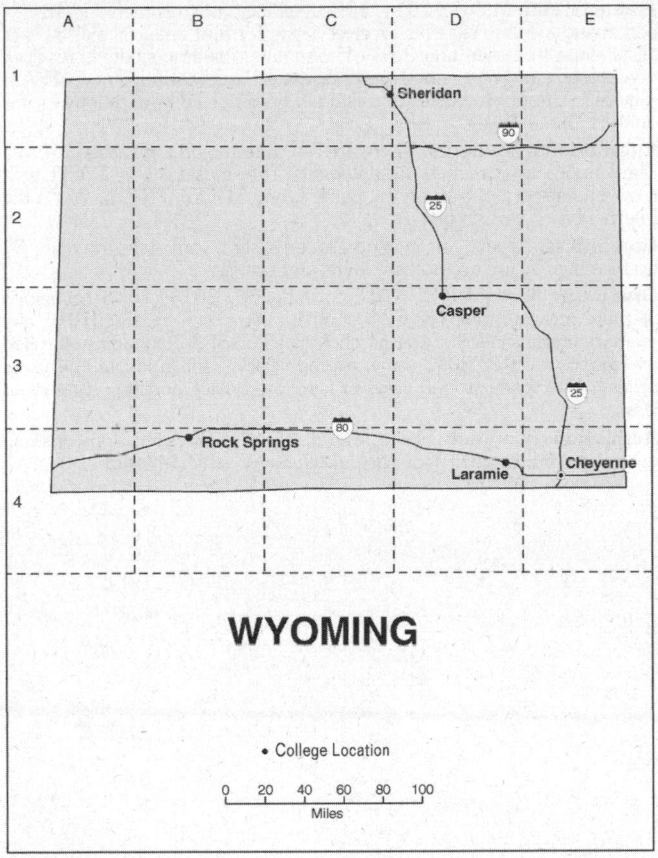

UNIVERSITY OF WYOMING D-4

Laramie, WY 82071 **(307) 766-5160**
(800) 342-5996; (307) 766-4042

Full-time: 4224 men, 4087 women
Part-time: 638 men, 1245 women
Graduate: 1303 men, 1406 women
Year: semesters, summer session
Application Deadline: August 10
Freshman Class: 4181 applied, 4001 accepted, 1584 enrolled
SAT CR/M: 543/557
Faculty: 744; I, --$
Ph.D.s: 83%
Student/Faculty: 11 to 1
Tuition: $4404 ($14,124)
Room & Board: $9451
ACT: 24 **COMPETITIVE+**

The University of Wyoming, founded in 1886, is a public institution offering programs in agriculture and natural resources, arts and sciences, business, education, engineering and applied science, health sciences, and law. There are 7 undergraduate schools and 8 graduate schools. In addition to regional accreditation, UW has baccalaureate program accreditation with AACSB, ABET, ACPE, ADA, CSAB, CSWE, NASM, and NCATE. The 5 libraries contain 1.6 million volumes, 2.9 million microform items, 15,925 audio/video tapes/CDs/DVDs, and subscribe to 103,083 periodicals including electronic. Computerized library services include interlibrary loans, database searching, Internet access, and Wi-Fi capability. Special learning facilities include an art gallery, natural history museum, planetarium, TV station, The American Heritage Center, specialized science and agriculture labs, Williams Botany Conservatory, Wyoming Infrared Observatory, Geology-Brinkerhoff Geology Library, Law Library, Library Annex, NPS UW Research Library, Rocky Mountain Herbarium. The 785-acre campus is in a small town 128 miles north of Denver and 50 miles west of Cheyenne. Including any residence halls, there are 161 buildings.

Student Life: 67% of undergraduates are from Wyoming. Others are from 52 states, 91 foreign countries, and Canada. 77% are White. The average age of freshmen is 19; all undergraduates, 24. 26% do not continue beyond their first year; 53% remain to graduate.

Housing: 2620 students can be accommodated in college housing, which includes single-sex and coed dorms, on-campus apartments, off-campus apartments, and married student housing. In addition, there are honors houses, special-interest houses, fraternity houses, sorority houses, academic, single-gender, coed, upperclassmen, quiet-living, substance-free and freshman interest-group floors. On-campus housing is guaranteed for all 4 years. 77% of students commute. All students may keep cars.

Activities: 5% of men belong to 7 national fraternities; 4% of women belong to 5 national sororities. There are 244 groups on campus, including art, band, cheerleading, choir, chorale, chorus, communications, computers, dance, debate, drama, drill team, environmental, ethnic, film, forensics, gay, honors, international, jazz band, literary magazine, marching band, musical theater, newspaper, opera, orchestra, pep band, photography, political, professional, radio and TV, religious, social, social service, student government, and symphony. Popular campus events include President's Welcome, Family Weekend, and Homecoming.

Sports: There are 8 intercollegiate sports for men and 9 for women, and 47 intramural sports for men and 43 for women. Facilities include a 30,514-seat stadium, a 15,000-seat indoor gym and arena, basketball, volleyball, and racquetball courts, running tracks, 2 pools, weight rooms, an indoor tennis complex, a baseball and track stadium, a football training center, a 6,855-yard golf course, a sports complex, a climbing wall, and a wrestling room.

Disabled Students: 95% of the campus is accessible. Facilities include wheelchair ramps, elevators, special parking, specially equipped restrooms, special class scheduling, lowered drinking fountains, lowered telephones, special housing.

Services: Counseling and information services are available, as is tutoring in most subjects. There is a reader service for the blind. note-taking services, tape recorders, and interpreters for the hearing impaired.

Campus Safety and Security: Measures include 24-hour foot and vehicle patrol, emergency notification system, self-defense education, and security escort services. There are shuttle buses, emergency telephones, lighted pathways/sidewalks, and controlled access to dorms/residences.

Programs of Study: UW confers B.A., B.S., B.A.S., B.F.A., B.M., B.S.A.R., B.S.C.E., B.S.Ch., B.S.C.P., B.S.C.S., B.S.D.H., B.S.E.E., B.S.E.S.E., B.S.F.C., B.S.M.E., B.S.N., B.S.P.E. and B.S.W. degrees. Master's and doctoral degrees are also awarded. Bachelor's degrees are awarded in AGRICULTURE (agricultural business management, agricultural communications, agricultural economics, agriculture, animal science, environmental studies, fish and game management, and range/farm management), BIOLOGICAL SCIENCE (botany, ecology, microbiology, molecular biology, physiology, wildlife biology, and zoology), BUSINESS (accounting, business administration and management, business economics, finance, management information systems, management science, marketing, organizational leadership and management, and recreation and leisure services), COMMUNICATIONS AND THE ARTS (art, communication, English, French, German, journalism, music, music performance, music theory and composition, Russian, Spanish, and theatre acting), COMPUTER AND PHYSICAL SCIENCE (astronomy and physics, chemistry, computer science, earth science, environmental geology, geology, mathematics, physics, and statistics), EDUCATION (agricultural education, elementary education, health education, home economics education, music education, physical education, secondary education, special education, technical education, and trade and industrial education), ENGINEERING AND ENVIRONMENTAL DESIGN (architectural engineering, chemical engineering, civil engineering, computer engineering, electrical/electronics engineering, energy management technology, energy systems technology, mechanical engineering, and petroleum/natural gas engineering), HEALTH PROFESSIONS (biology, dental hygiene, health science, kinesiology, nursing, and speech pathology/audiology), SOCIAL SCIENCE (American Indian studies, American studies, anthropology, counseling/psychology, criminal justice, economics, family/consumer studies, geography, history, humanities, interdisciplinary studies, international studies, philosophy, political science/government, psychology, religious studies, social science, social work, sociology, and women & gender studies). Nursing, elementary education, and psychology have the largest enrollments.

Required: To graduate, students must complete 120 to 157 credit hours, depending on the major, with a minimum GPA of 2.0. The core curriculum includes a required 30 to 36 hours of general education courses in the University Studies Program.

Special: UW offers internships, study abroad in many countries, national student exchange, Washington and U.N. semesters, work-study programs, dual and interdisciplinary majors, pass/fail options, student-designed majors, credit by exam, accelerated degree programs, and credit for life, military, and work experience. There are 46 national honor societies, including Phi Beta Kappa, and a freshman honors program.

Faculty/Classroom: 61% of faculty are male; 39% are female. 97% teach undergraduates. No introductory courses are taught by graduate students. The average class size in an introductory lecture is 39 and in a regular course is 39.

Admissions: 96% of the 2013-2014 applicants were accepted. The SAT scores for the 2013-2014 freshman class were: Critical Reading--33% below 500, 38% between 500 and 599, 25% between 600 and 699, and 4% between 700 and 800, Math 25% below 500, 39% between 500 and

599, 30% between 600 and 699, and 6% between 700 and 800. The ACT scores were 16% below 21, 28% between 21 and 23, 28% between 24 and 26, 12% between 27 and 28, and 15% above 28. 42% of the current freshmen were in the top fifth of their class; 73% were in the top two fifths. 78 freshmen graduated first in their class.

Requirements: The SAT or ACT is required for students under 21; the ACT is preferred. Applicants must be graduates of an accredited secondary school or hold a GED certificate. Secondary preparation should include at least 19 academic credits consisting of 4 years each of English, Math, and Science, 3 years of Social Science, 2 years of foreign language, and 2 years chosen from fine & performing arts, social & behavioral studies, humanities, additional foreign language, or career-technical courses. A visit is suggested. A GPA of 3.0 is required. AP and CLEP credits are accepted.

Procedure: Freshmen are admitted fall, spring, and summer. Entrance exams should be taken in the spring of the junior year or fall of the senior year. There are deferred admissions and rolling admissions plans. Applications should be filed by August 10 for fall entry; December 10 for spring entry, along with a $40 fee. Applications are accepted online.

Transfer: 1119 transfer students enrolled in 2012-2013. Applicants with 30 or more transferable college-level credits must have a minimum GPA of 2.0. All applicants with fewer credits must apply as a new freshman. Those students under age 21 must also present SAT or ACT scores. 30 credits required for the bachelor's degree must be completed at University of Wyoming.

Visiting: There are regularly scheduled orientations for prospective students, including campus tours and meetings with academic advisers. There are guides for informal visits. To schedule a visit, contact Pre-College and Student Visit Program at (307) 766-4075.

Financial Aid: In 2013-2014, 50% of all full-time freshmen and 48% of continuing full-time students received some form of financial aid. 31% of all full-time freshmen and 33% of continuing full-time students received need-based aid. The average freshman award was $9,259. The FAFSA is required. The priority date for freshman financial aid applications for fall entry is March 1.

International Students: There are 340 international students enrolled. The school actively recruits these students. They must take the TOEFL with a minimum score of 540 on the paper-based TOEFL (PBT) or 76 on the Internet-based version (iBT).

Computers: All students may access the system some labs are open 24 hours a day. There are no time limits and no fees.

Graduates: From July 1, 2012 to June 30, 2013, 2053 bachelor's degrees were awarded. The most popular majors were nursing (10%), elementary education (8%), and psychology (5%). 323 companies recruited on campus in 2012-2013. In an average class, 24% graduate in 4 years or less, 47% graduate in 5 years or less, and 54% graduate in 6 years or less.

Admissions Contact: Shelley Dodd, Director of Admissions. E-Mail: *admissions@uwyo.edu* Web: *http:/www.uwyo.edu/admissions/*

ARIZONA

ARIZONA CHRISTIAN UNIVERSITY — C-4

Phoenix, AZ 85032 (602) 386-4133; (602) 404-2159

Full-time: 233 men, 215 women
Part-time: none
Graduate: none
Application Deadline: see profile
SAT CR/M: 516/495
Faculty: 55
Tuition: $19,468
Room & Board: $8074
ACT: 22

Arizona Christian University, founded in 1960, is affiliated with Non-denominational. Its mission is Transforming culture with the truth. The figures in the above capsule are approximate. In addition to regional accreditation, the college is accredited by AABC and NCA. Arizona Christian University awards the B.A. and B.S. in elementary education, biblical studies, Christian ministries, secondary education, business administration, behavioral health, family studies, and music education. The school also awards associate and bachelor's degrees. Web: *http:/www.arizonachristian.edu*

ARKANSAS

CENTRAL BAPTIST COLLEGE — C-3

Conway, AR 72032 (501) 329-6872; (501) 329-2941

Full-time: 280 men, 250 women
Part-time: 60 men, 50 women
Graduate: n/av
Application Deadline: August 15
ACT: required
Faculty: n/av
Tuition: $10,500
Room & Board: $6,500

Central Baptist College, founded in 1952, is affiliated with the Baptist Missionary Association of Arkansas. The figures in the above capsule are approximate. It's mission is to develop a community of learners dedicated to the integration of Christian faith and academic excellence and exists to instill in our students a commitment to lifelong learning, spiritual development and service to God, through a program characterized by academic rigor, practical experience, and spiritual direction of a Christ focused environment. In addition to regional accreditation, the college is accredited by NCA. Central Baptist College awards the B.A., B.S., and B.B.A. in Bible studies, church music, organizational management, management information systems, social service, music, general studies, leadership and ministry, psychology, biology, and missions. The school also awards associate and bachelor's degrees. Web: *www.centralbaptist.edu*

CALIFORNIA

PATTEN UNIVERSITY — B-3

Oakland, CA 94601 (510) 261-8500; (510) 534-8564

Full-time: 75 men, 140 women
Part-time: 300 men, 150 women
Graduate: 3 men, 23 women
Application Deadline: March 31
Faculty: 125
Tuition: $15,500
Room & Board: $7880

Patten University, founded in 1944, is affiliated with Christian Evangelical Churches of America/Church of God, Cleveland, Tennessee. Its mission is to provide an excellent education on the undergraduate and graduate levels that integrates growing faith and quality learning to inspire and equip men and women for Christian ministry and service. The figures in the above capsule are approximate. In addition to regional accreditation, the college is accredited by WASC. Patten University awards the B.A. and B.S. in biblical studies, Christian leadership, communication, intercultural-urban ministry, liberal studies, pastoral studies, music and worship leadership, organizational management, psychology, and youth ministry. The school also awards associate, bachelor's, and master's degrees. Web: *www.patten.edu*

WILLIAM JESSUP UNIVERSITY — B-3

Rocklin, CA 95678 (916) 577-2226; (916) 577-2220

Full-time: 260 men, 399 women
Part-time: 7 men, 6 women
Graduate: n/av
Application Deadline: June 1
ACT: 20
Faculty: 74
Tuition: $22,300
Room & Board: $9140

William Jessup University, founded in 1939, is affiliated with nondenominational. Its mission is to prepare Christians for leadership and service in church and society through Christian higher education, spiritual formation, and directed experiences. The figures in the above capsule are approximate. In addition to regional accreditation, the college is accredited by AABC. William Jessup University awards the B.A. and B.S. in Bible and theology, pastoral ministry, yourth ministry, Christian education, Intercultural studies, counseling, music and worship, business management, liberal arts education. and Christian leadership. The school also awards associate and bachelor's degrees. Web: *www.jessup.edu*

CONNECTICUT

HOLY APOSTLES COLLEGE AND SEMINARY — C-2

Cromwell, CT 06416 (860) 632-3022; (860) 632-3075

Full-time: 25 men, 7 women
Part-time: 7 men, 17 women
Graduate: 178 men, 82 women
Application Deadline: open
SAT: required
Faculty: 25
Tuition: $9950
Room & Board: n/av

Holy Apostles College and Seminary, founded in 1956, is affiliated with the Roman Catholic Church. Its mission is to cultivate lay, consecrated, and ordained Catholic leaders for the purpose of evangelization and to maintain excellence in teaching/learning, research/discovery, and service/engagement through the liberal arts, philosophy, and theology. The figures in the above capsule are approximate. In addition to regional accreditation, the college is accredited by NEASC. Holy Apostles College and Seminary awards the B.A. in English in the humanities, history in the social sciences, philosophy, and theology. The school also awards associate, bachelor's, and master's degrees. Web: *www.holyapostles.edu*

FLORIDA

BAPTIST COLLEGE OF FLORIDA — B-1

Graceville, FL 32440 (800) 328-2660, ext. 460; (850) 263-9026

Full-time: 237 men, 177 women
Part-time: 103 men, 29 women
Graduate: n/av
Application Deadline: August 1
Faculty: 57
Tuition: $8800
Room & Board: $4200

Baptist College of Florida, founded in 1943, is affiliated with Florida Baptist Convention. Its mission is to promote, provide for, operate, and control a program of education and training for ministers and other religious workers. In addition to regional accreditation, the college is accredited by SACS. Baptist College of Florida awards the B.A. in biblical studies, Christian counseling, Christian education, Christian studies, elementary education, English, English secondary education, history and social studies, history and social studies secondary education, leadership, ministry, missions, and music ministry. The figures in the above capsule are approximate. The school also awards associate and bachelor's degrees. Web: *www.baptistcollege.edu*

JOHNSON UNIVERSITY Florida Christian College — D-3

Kissimmee, FL 34744 (407) 569-1172; (407) 847-3925

Full-time: 105 men, 110 women
Part-time: 30 men, 30 women
Graduate: n/av
Application Deadline: July 15
ACT: 24
Faculty: 24
Tuition: $11,670
Room & Board: $3200 (room only)

Johnson University, formerly Florida Christian College, founded in 1976, is affiliated with Christian Churches/Churches of Christ/Independent. Its mission is to conduct a course of study educating men and women for Christian service, to provide a program of instruction on the college level, to grant appropriate degrees, and to serve as a resource to churches, especially in Florida. In addition to regional accreditation, the college is accredited by AABC and SACS. Johnson University awards the B.A., B.S., and B.Th. in Bible, Christian education ministries, and Christian ministries. The figures in the above capsule are approximate. The school also awards associate and bachelor's degrees. Web: *www.fcc.edu*

ST. JOHN VIANNEY COLLEGE SEMINARY — E-5

Miami, FL 33165 (305) 223-4561; (305) 223-0650

Full-time: 74 men, no women
Faculty: 23
Part-time: 1 men, 1 women
Tuition: $21,347
Graduate: n/av
Room & Board: $8643
Application Deadline: open

St. John Vianney College Seminary, founded in 1959, is affiliated with the Roman Catholic Church. The figures in the above capsule are approximate. Its mission is to provide an undergraduate education preparatory for students whose stated objective is to serve the Catholic Church in the priesthood, and to provide spiritual and intellectual formation within an Anglo-Hispanic bilingual, bicultural setting. In addition to regional accreditation, the college is accredited by SACS. St. John Vianney College Seminary awards the B.A. and B.Phil. in philosophy. The school also awards bachelor's degrees. Web: *www.sjvcs.edu*

GEORGIA

POINT UNIVERSITY — B-2
Atlanta Christian College

West Point, GA 31833 (706) 385-1201; (706) 645-9473

Full-time: 586 men, 697 women
Faculty: 140
Part-time: 53 men, 103 women
Tuition: $17,400
Graduate: none
Room & Board: $6200
Application Deadline: August 1

Point University, founded in 1937, is affiliated with Christian Churches and Churches of Christ. Its mission is The mission of Point University is to educate students for Christ-centered service and leadership throughout the world. In addition to regional accreditation, the college is accredited by SACSCOC. Point University awards the B.A., B.S., and B.B.A. in accounting, biblical studies, biblical studies and preaching ministry (dual major), biology, business administration, child and youth development, Christian ministry, counseling and human services, criminal justice, early childhood education, English, English and biblical studies (dual major), exercise science, history, human relations, humanities, humanities and biblical studies (dual major), management, marketing, middle grades education, music, organizational leadership, psychology, sociology with specialization in social work. The school also awards associate and bachelor's degrees. Web: *www.point.edu*

ILLINOIS

LINCOLN CHRISTIAN UNIVERSITY — D3

Lincoln, IL 62656-2111 (217) 732-3168, ext. 2351; (217) 732-4199

Full-time: 273 men, 265 women
Faculty: 99
Part-time: 52 men, 53 women
Tuition: $14,840
Graduate: 233 men, 117 women
Room & Board: $7179
Application Deadline: open
ACT: 23

Lincoln Christian University, founded in 1944, is affiliated with the Christian Church/Church of Christ. Its mission is a Christian higher education community whose mission it is to nurture and equip Christians with a Biblical worldview to serve and lead in the church and the world. The figures in the above capsule are approximate. In addition to regional accreditation, the college is accredited by AABC and NCACS. Lincoln Christian University awards the B.A. and B.S. in Bible, business administration, Christian leadership and management, general ministry, intercultural studies, preaching ministry, youth ministry, Biblical exposition, children and family ministry, Christian spiritual formation, general studies, philosophy, psychology, worship ministry,and youth and preaching ministry. The school also awards associate, bachelor's, master's, and doctorate degrees. Web: *www.lincolnchristian.edu*

MOODY BIBLE INSTITUTE — E-2

Chicago, IL 60610 (312) 329-2050; (312) 329-8955

Full-time: 848 men, 730 women
Faculty: 95
Part-time: 436 men, 389 women
Tuition: $2286
Graduate: 261 men, 152 women
Room & Board: $8160
Application Deadline: December 1 or March 1
ACT: 26

Moody Bible Institute, founded in 1886, is affiliated with Evangelical Protestant. Its mission is to educate and train individuals to proclaim the gospel of the Lord Jesus Christ, to promote evangelism, and to serve the Evangelical Christian Church vocationally and/or avocationally in its worldwide ministry. In addition to regional accreditation, the college is accredited by AABC and NCA. Moody Bible Institute awards the B.A., B.S., and B.Mus. in missionary aviation technology, biblical studies, evangelism/discipleship, communication, educational ministries, world missions, pastoral studies, religious education, church music, sacred music, Bible-theology, applied linguistics, youth ministry, urban ministry, Jewish and modern Israel studies, family ministries, women's ministries, and teaching English to speakers of other languages. The figures in the above capsule are approximate. The school also awards associate, bachelor's, and master's degrees. Web: *http:/www.moody.edu*

IOWA

DIVINE WORD COLLEGE — E-2

Epworth, IA 52045-0380 (800) 553-3321; (563) 876-5515

Full-time: 80 men, 34 women
Faculty: 29
Part-time: n/av
Tuition: $12,725
Graduate: n/av
Room & Board: $4150
Application Deadline: July 15

Divine Word College, founded in 1912, is affiliated with Roman Catholic. Its mission is DWC combines a liberal arts education with a cross-cultural program of missionary formation for Divine Word Missionaries and other leaders in the Roman Catholic Church. The figures in the above capsule are approximate. In addition to regional accreditation, the college is accredited by NCA. Divine Word College awards the BA in Philosophy, Cross-Cultural Studies, and Religious Studies. The school also awards associate and bachelor's degrees. Web: *www.dwci.edu*

FAITH BAPTIST BIBLE COLLEGE AND THEOLOGICAL SEMINARY — C-3

Ankeny, IA 50023 (888) FAITH 4 U; (515) 964-1638

Full-time: 120 men, 186 women
Faculty: 36
Part-time: 22 men, 23 women
Tuition: 14,314
Graduate: 52 men, 14 women
Room & Board: $6010
Application Deadline: August 1
SAT CR/M/W: 590/555/605
ACT: 22

Faith Baptist Bible College and Theological Seminary, founded in 1921, is affiliated with The Baptist Church. Its mission is to provide an intensive biblical and vocational education on the college level with the goal of preparing students to minister effectively in Christian service through leadership positions in fundamental Baptist churches and other organizations of like convictions. In addition to regional accreditation, the college is accredited by AABC and NCA. The figures in the above capsule are approximate. Faith Baptist Bible College and Theological Seminary awards the B.A. and B.S. in Bible and theology, assistant pastor, Christian education, Christian school, missions, music ministries, and pastoral training. The school also awards associate, bachelor's, and master's degrees. Web: *www.faith.edu*

KENTUCKY

CLEAR CREEK BAPTIST BIBLE COLLEGE — F-3

Pineville, KY 40977-9752 (606) 337-3196; (606) 337-2372

Full-time: 110 men, 25 women
Faculty: n/av
Part-time: 60 men, 15 women
Tuition: $5580
Graduate: n/av
Room & Board: $3728
Application Deadline: July 15

Clear Creek Baptist Bible College, founded in 1926, is affiliated with the Southern Baptist Church. The figures in the above capsule are approximate. Its mission is providing theological education for adults called to Christian service. In addition to regional accreditation, the college is accredited by AABC and SACS. Clear Creek Baptist Bible College awards the B.A. in Bible, as well as associate and bachelor's degrees. Web:*www.ccbbc.edu*

MID-CONTINENT UNIVERSITY — A-4

Mayfield, KY 42066-0357 (270) 247-8521, ext. 228; (270) 247-3115

Full-time: 734 men, 1173 women
Faculty: 155
Part-time: 96 men, 176 women
Tuition: $13,850
Graduate: 31 men, 60 women
Room & Board: $7300
Application Deadline: August 15

Mid-Continent University, founded in 1949, is affiliated with The Baptist Church. Its mission is to educate students for Christian leadership and service throughout the world. The figures in the above capsule are approximate. In addition to regional accreditation, the college is accredited by

SACS. Mid-Continent University awards the B.A., B.S., and B.Min. in biblical languages, biblical studies, business management, Christian education and leadership, Christian ministry, evangelism, missions, psychology and counseling, behavioral studies, English, general studies, social studies, elementary teacher education, mathematics, organizational leadership, and business administration (management emphasis). The school also awards associate, bachelor's, and master's degrees. Web: *www.midcontinent.edu*

LOUISIANA

SAINT JOSEPH AND ABBEY SEMINARY COLLEGE D-3

St. Benedict, LA 70457 (985) 867-2248; (985) 867-2270

Full-time: 80 men
Part-time: 70 men
Graduate: n/av
Application Deadline: open
Faculty: n/av
Tuition: $12,860
Room & Board: $12,440

Saint Joseph and Abbey Seminary College, founded in 1891, is affiliated with the Roman Catholic Church. Figures in the above capsule are approximate. Its mission is to educate and train men for the priesthood in the Roman Catholic Church and to support preparation for lay ministry. In addition to regional accreditation, the college is accredited by SACS. Saint Joseph Seminary College awards the B.A. in philosophy and the liberal arts, and philosophy and theological studies. The school also awards bachelor's degrees. Web:*www.sjasc.edu*

MICHIGAN

SACRED HEART MAJOR SEMINARY E-5

Detroit, MI 48206 (313) 883-8512; (313) 883-8682

Full-time: 46 men, 6 women
Part-time: 108 men, 102 women
Graduate: 124 men, 44 women
Application Deadline: August 15
Faculty: 78
Tuition: $15,770
Room & Board: $8768

Sacred Heart Major Seminary, founded in 1919, is affiliated with The Roman Catholic Church. It is an institution of higher education that primarily prepares candidates for the Roman Catholic Priesthood and, further, prepares individuals for the diaconate, lay ministry and other leadership roles. Sacred Heart Major Seminary seeks to provide an excellent undergraduate formation based on an emphasis in Philosophy and ministry that will serve as a sound foundation to pursue theological studies. The graduate Theology programs seek to ensure a clearly Catholic professional and academic formation for ministerial service. In addition to regional accreditation, the college is accredited by NCA and ATS. Sacred Heart Major Seminary awards the A.B. and B.Phil. in Philosophy, Pastoral Theology. The school also awards associate, bachelor's, and master's degrees. Web: *www.shms.edu*

MINNESOTA

CROWN COLLEGE C-4

Saint Bonifacius, MN 55375 (952) 446-4142; (952) 446-4149

Full-time: 348 men, 465 women
Part-time: 96 men, 122 women
Graduate: 100 men, 67 women
Application Deadline: see profile
ACT: 23
Faculty: n/av
Tuition: $21,970
Room & Board: $7880

Crown College, founded in 1916, is affiliated with the Christian and Missionary Alliance. Its mission is to provide a Biblically based education for Christian leadership in the Christian and Missionary Alliance, the church at large, and the world. In addition to regional accreditation, the college is accredited by NCA. Crown College awards the B.A., B.S., B.Mus.Ed., and B.S.N. in Biblical and Theological Studies, Biology, Business Administration, Child and Family Ministries, Communication, Criminal/Social Justice, Discipleship Ministries, Elementary Education, English, English Education, ESL Education, General Studies, History, Intercultural Studies, Liberal Arts, Linguistics, Management, Music, Music Education, New Testament, Nursing, Pastoral Leadership, Physical Education, Psychology, Science Education, Social Entrepreneurship, Social Studies Education, Sport Management, TESOL, Urban Studies, Worship Arts, Youth and Family, and Youth/Social Ministry. The school also awards associate, bachelor's, and master's degrees. Web: *www.crown.edu*

MARTIN LUTHER COLLEGE C-4

New Ulm, MN 56073-3300 (507) 354-8221 ext.377; (507) 354-8225

Full-time: 515 men, 525 women
Part-time: 8 men, 9 women
Graduate: n/av
Application Deadline: April 15
ACT: 24
Faculty: 98
Tuition: $11,820
Room & Board: $4890

Martin Luther College, founded in 1995, is affiliated with the Wisconsin Evangelical Lutheran Synod. Its mission is to provide training for elementary and secondary teaching, preseminary training for pastoral students, and training for other church vocations through the Staff Ministry Program. The figures in the above capsule are approximate. In addition to regional accreditation, the college is accredited by NCACS. Martin Luther College awards the B.A. and B.S.Ed. in education and preseminary studies. The school also awards bachelor's degrees. Web: *www.mlc-wels.edu*

OAK HILLS CHRISTIAN COLLEGE B-2

Bemidji, MN 56601 (218) 751-1249; (218) 444-1311

Full-time: 75 men, 75 women
Part-time: 15 men, 20 women
Graduate: n/av
Application Deadline: see profile
ACT: required
Faculty: 18
Tuition: $14,230
Room & Board: $5580

Oak Hills Christian College, founded in 1946, is interdenominational. The figures in the above capsule are approximate. Its mission is Integrating faith and learning through biblical training. The college awards the B.A., B.S. in biblical studies, applied psychology, applied studies, campus ministry, contemporary worship, contemporary Christian ministry, intercultural studies, pastoral ministry, and youth ministry. The school also awards associate and bachelor's degrees. Web: *www.oakhills.edu*

MISSOURI

CONCEPTION SEMINARY COLLEGE A-1

Conception, MO 64433 (660) 944-2886; (660) 944-2829

Full-time: 85 men, no women
Part-time: 2 men, 50 women
Graduate: n/av
Application Deadline: July 31
ACT: 22
Faculty: 30
Tuition: $16,910
Room & Board: $10,236

Conception Seminary College, founded in 1886, is affiliated with The Roman Catholic Church. Its mission is to prepare men who are discerning for the Roman Catholic priesthood. Conception Seminary College places emphasis on spiritual, personal, and academic formation. The figures in the above capsule are approximate. In addition to regional accreditation, the college is accredited by NCA. Conception Seminary College awards the B.A. in liberal arts. The school also awards bachelor's degrees. Web: *www.conceptionabbey.org*

NORTH CAROLINA

MID-ATLANTIC CHRISTIAN UNIVERSITY F-2

Elizabeth City, NC 27909-4054 (866) 996-MACU(6228); (252) 334-2064

Full-time: 87 men, 48 women
Part-time: 12 men, 22 women
Graduate: none
Application Deadline: see profile
SAT CR/M: 480/480
Faculty: 23
Tuition: $11,700
Room & Board: $7900
ACT: 20

Mid-Atlantic Christian University, founded in 1948, is affiliated with The Christian Church/Church of Christ. Its mission is Mid-Atlantic Christian University is an undergraduate institution of Christian higher education whose mission is to impact the world by transforming ordinary people into extraordinary Christian leaders. In addition to regional accreditation, the college is accredited by AABC and SACS. Mid-Atlantic Christian University awards the B.A., B.S., B.Th. in Biblical Exposition and Cross-Cultural Ministry, Biblical Exposition and General Ministry, Biblical Exposition and Missions Aviation, Biblical Exposition and Preaching, Biblical Exposition with Youth & Family Ministry, Biblical Exposition & Applied Linguistics, Biblical Studies with Counseling & Psychology, Biblical Studies with Leadership & Administration, Biblical Studies, and Biblical Exposition. The school also awards associate and bachelor's degrees. Web: *www.macuniversity.edu*

NORTH DAKOTA

TRINITY BIBLE COLLEGE E-4

Ellendale, ND 58436 **(888) TBC-2DAY; (701) 349-5443**

Full-time: 131 men, 143 women **Faculty:** 30
Part-time: 8 men, 25 women **Tuition:** $13,590
Graduate: n/av **Room & Board:** $5550
Application Deadline: August 15

Trinity Bible College, founded in 1948, is affiliated with The Assemblies of God. Its mission is to prepare pastors, church leaders, and Christian professionals in various fields in a Bible-based Pentecostal environment of academic excellence. The figures in the above capsule are approximate. In addition to regional accreditation, the college is accredited by AABC and NCACS. Trinity Bible College awards the B.A. in biblical studies, business administration, elementary education, ministerial studies, and missions. The school also awards associate and bachelor's degrees. Web: *www.trinitybiblecollege.edu*

OHIO

CINCINNATI CHRISTIAN UNIVERSITY A-5

Cincinnati, OH 45204-3200 **(800) 949-4CCU ext. 8485; (513) 244-8111**

Full-time: 270 men, 236 women **Faculty:** 85
Part-time: 85 men, 44 women **Tuition:** $14,604
Graduate: 169 men, 86 women **Room & Board:** $6730
Application Deadline: August 10

Cincinnati Christian University, founded in 1924, is affiliated with Christian Churches/Churches of Christ. Its mission is to teach men and women to live by biblical principles and to equip and empower them with skills, insight, and vision both to lead the church and to impact society for Christ. In addition to regional accreditation, the college is accredited by AABC and NCA. Cincinnati Christian University awards the B.A., B.S., and B.Mus. in biblical studies (primary major), education, ministries, (second major), and signing interpreter's training program, psychology, preaching, youth ministry, worship, music, children's ministry, urban/intercultural ministry, music education and history. The school also awards associate, bachelor's, and master's degrees. Web: *www.CCUniversity.edu*

OHIO CHRISTIAN UNIVERSITY

Circleville, OH 43113 **(740) 477-7701 or (877) 762-8669 (740) 420-5921**

Full-time: 372 men, 429 women **Faculty:** 135
Part-time: 55 men, 75 women **Tuition:** $16,600
Graduate: n/av **Room & Board:** $7386
Application Deadline: Priority deadline is May
SAT CR/M/W: 478/418/514 **ACT:** 19

Ohio Christian University, founded in 1948, is affiliated with Churches of Christ in Christian Union (CCCU). Its mission is to provide a holistic Bible college education in the Wesleyan tradition that equips students to grow spiritually and intellectually and to serve effectively in society and the church. The figures in the above capsule are approximate. In addition to regional accreditation, the college is accredited by AABC and NCA. Ohio Christian University awards the B.A. in religion, business management, psychology, nursing, teacher education, international studies, ministries, music education, youth ministries, and christian ministries. The school also awards associate and bachelor's degrees. Web: *www.ohiochristian.edu*

PONTIFICAL COLLEGE JOSEPHINUM C-3

Columbus, OH 43235 **(888) 252-5812; (614) 885-2307**

Full-time: 78 men **Faculty:** 41
Part-time: n/av **Tuition:** $18,439
Graduate: 51 men, 2 women **Room & Board:** $8646
Application Deadline: July 31
SAT CR/M/W: 550/570/520 **ACT:** 24

Pontifical College Josephinum, founded in 1888, is affiliated with The Roman Catholic Church. Its mission is to prepare young men for the priesthood. The figures in the above capsule are approximate. In addition to regional accreditation, the college is accredited by NCACS and ATS. Pontifical College Josephinum awards the B.A. in philosophy and the humanities (English literature, Hispanic studies, history, and classical studies). The school also awards bachelor's and master's degrees. Web: *pcj.edu*

OKLAHOMA

MID-AMERICA CHRISTIAN UNIVERSITY D-3

Oklahoma City, OK 73170 **(405) 692-3188; (405) 692-3165**

Full-time: 338 men, 387 women **Faculty:** 45
Part-time: 87 men, 94 women **Tuition:** $14,500
Graduate: 116 men, 158 women **Room & Board:** $5500
Application Deadline: open

Mid-America Christian University, founded in 1953, is affiliated with Church of God in Anderson, Indiana. The university equips students to impact their world for Christ through achieving Bible-based academic excellence in a Christian environment so that students professionally serve in their chosen vocation/ministry. The figures in the above capsule are approximate. In addition to regional accreditation, the college is accredited by NCA. Mid-America Christian University awards the B.A. and B.S. in behavioral science, elementary education, English, music, performance, pastoral ministry, worship and music ministries, secondary education, specialized ministries, management and ethics, English/business, and business administration. The school also awards associate, bachelor's, and master's degrees. Web: *www.macu.edu*

SOUTHWESTEN CHRISTIAN UNIVERSITY

Bethany, OK 73008 **(405) 789-7661, ext. 3436; (405) 495-0078**

Full-time: 91 men, 92 women **Faculty:** 35
Part-time: 11 men, 15 women **Tuition:** $8750
Graduate: 58 men, 20 women **Room & Board:** $2600
Application Deadline: open
ACT: 18

Southwesten Christian University, founded in 1946, is affiliated with Pentecostal Holiness. Its mission is the education and training for Christian service leading toward professional competence in the practice of various ministry forms. In addition to regional accreditation, the college is accredited by NCA. Southwesten Christian University awards the B.A. and B.S. and B.B.A. in Bibical studies, church growth, church music, music perfomace, missions, Christian education, Christian elementary education, pastoral ministry, youth ministry religion, Biblicial leadership, human and family services, business leadership, nonprofit organizational leadership, and business administration. The school also awards associate, bachelor's, and master's degrees. Web:http:/www.swcu.edu

OREGON

MOUNT ANGEL SEMINARY B-2

St. Benedict, OR 97373 **(503) 845-3543; (503) 845-3126**

Full-time: 85 men **Faculty:** 40
Part-time: n/av **Tuition:** $14,184
Graduate: 87 men, 12 women **Room & Board:** $9434
Application Deadline: July 15

Mount Angel Seminary, founded in 1889, is affiliated with The Roman Catholic Church. Its mission is to prepare students of the Roman Catholic priesthood for religious orders and dioceses. In addition to regional accreditation, the college is accredited by NASC. Mount Angel Abby and Seminary awards the B.A. in philosophy and literature. The figures in the above capsule are approximate. The school also awards bachelor's and master's degrees. Web: *www.seminary.mtangel.edu*

PENNSYLVANIA

BAPTIST BIBLE COLLEGE OF PENNSYLVANIA E-2

Clarks Summit, PA 18411 **(570) 586-2400 or (800) 451-7664 (570) 585-9400**

Full-time: 226 men, 346 women **Faculty:** 32
Part-time: 10 men, 30 women **Tuition:** $17,500
Graduate: 177 men and women **Room & Board:** $6,800
Application Deadline: August 15
SAT CR/M: 520/510 **ACT:** 22

Baptist Bible College of Pennsylvania, founded in 1932, is affiliated with the Baptist Church. Its mission is to prepare men and women for service in selected Christian ministries as pastors, missionaries, Christian education workers, and teachers for Christian schools, counselors, church musicians, and secretaries for Christian organizations. In addition to regional accreditation, the college is accredited by AABC and MSACS. Baptist Bible College of Pennsylvania awards the B.S. in Bible and B.S.M. in church music, communications, elementary education, general missions, local church ministries, music education, outreach and evangelism pastor, pastoral ministry, pastor of Christian education, preseminary, secondary education, secretarial ministries, sports ministries, youth pastor, precounseling, general ministries, women's ministries, early childhood education, and office professionals. The figures in the above capsule are approximate. The school also awards associate, master's, and doctorate degrees. Web: *http:/www.bbc.edu*

LANCASTER BIBLE COLLEGE & GRADUATE EDUCATION AND SEMINARY E-3
Lancaster Bible & Graduate School

Lancaster, PA 17601 (717) 560-8271 ext.5395; (717) 560-8213

Full-time: 302 men, 286 women — **Faculty:** 86
Part-time: 110 men, 105 women — **Tuition:** $16,340
Graduate: 90 men, 85 women — **Room & Board:** $7280
Application Deadline: open
SAT CR/M: 520/500 — **ACT:** 23

Lancaster Bible College & Graduate Education and Seminary, founded in 1933, is nondenominational. Its mission is to educate Christian men and women to live according to a biblical worldview and to serve through professional Christian ministries. In addition to regional accreditation, the college is accredited by AABC and MSA. The college awards the B.S. in Bible and B.S.Ed. in Bible education, Bible ministry, children and family ministry, counseling (professional), cross-cultural ministry, elementary education/early level, elementary education/middle level, music education, music performance, pastoral ministry, pre-seminary, social work, spiritual formation and discipleship, student ministry, TESOL, women in Christian ministry, and worship arts. The college also awards associate, bachelor's, and master's degrees. Web: *www.lbc.edu*

SAINT CHARLES BORROMEO SEMINARY F-3

Wynnewood, PA 19096 (610) 785-6252; (610) 617-9267

Full-time: 90 men, no women — **Faculty:** 65
Part-time: 25 men, 35 women — **Tuition:** $18,928
Graduate: 90 men, 30 women — **Room & Board:** $11,972
Application Deadline: July 1

Saint Charles Borromeo Seminary, founded in 1832, is affiliated with The Roman Catholic Church. Its mission is to prepare and educate men for the Roman Catholic priesthood and to provide undergraduate and graduate programs for men and women pursuing theological studies. The figures in the above capsule are approximate. In addition to regional accreditation, the college is accredited by MSACS. The school awards the B.A. in philosophy, as well as bachelor's and master's degrees. Web: *www.scs.edu*

SOUTH CAROLINA

COLUMBIA INTERNATIONAL UNIVERSITY C-3

Columbia, SC 29230 (803) 807-5019; (803) 786-4041

Full-time: 215 men, 259 women — **Faculty:** 49
Part-time: 33 men, 43 women — **Tuition:** $21,275
Graduate: 214 men, 186 women — **Room & Board:** $6710
Application Deadline: open
ACT: 24

Columbia International University, founded in 1923, is a multidenominational Christian school. Its mission is to prepare students to grow in spiritual maturity, Bible knowledge, and ministry skills in preparation for vocational or lay Christian ministry. In addition to regional accreditation, the college is accredited by AABC and SACS. Columbia International University awards the B.A. and B.S. in Bible, general studies, intercultural studies, psychology, biblical languages, music, Bible teaching, youth ministry, middle eastern studies, family and church education, teacher education, humanities, pastoral ministries, and communications. The figures in the above capsule are approximate. The school also awards associate, bachelor's, master's, and doctorate degrees. Web: *www.ciu.edu*

TENNESSEE

JOHNSON UNIVERSITY E-3

Knoxville, TN 37998 (865) 251-3403; (865) 251-2337

Full-time: 343 men, 306 women — **Faculty:** 62
Part-time: 15 men, 16 women — **Tuition:** $9930
Graduate: 69 men, 67 women — **Room & Board:** $5750
Application Deadline: June 1

Johnson University, founded in 1893, is Christian centered. Its mission is to educate students for specialized Christian ministries. In addition to regional accreditation, the college is accredited by AABC and SACS. All students who graduate from Johnson University with a Bachelor of Arts or a Bachelor of Science degree major in Bible. In addition, five professional programs require a second major. They are: counseling, preaching, interdisciplinary major with focus on teacher education, music, and youth ministry/preaching. The school also awards associate, bachelor's, and master's degrees. Web: *jscjultz@johnsonu.edu*

WELCH COLLEGE C-2
Free Will Baptist Bible College

Nashville, TN 37205 (615) 844-5078; (615) 269-6028

Full-time: 100 men, 92 women — **Faculty:** 55
Part-time: 54 men, 36 women — **Tuition:** $14,806
Graduate: n/av — **Room & Board:** $6542
Application Deadline: open
ACT: 22

Welch College, formerly Free Will Baptist Bible College, founded in 1942, is affiliated with National Association of Free Will Baptists. Its mission is to educate leaders to serve Christ, His Church and His world through Biblical thought and life. The figures in the above capsule are approximate. In addition to regional accreditation, the college is accredited by AABC, SACS, and ABHE. Welch College awards the B.A. and B.S. in biblical studies, biblical and ministry studies, business administration, church music, church music and youth ministry, English, elementary education, music education, music performance, sports medicine, physical education, secondary English education, and psychology and learning. The school also awards associate and bachelor's degrees. Web: *www.fwbbc.edu*

TEXAS

AUSTIN GRADUATE SCHOOL OF THEOLOGY D-3

Austin, TX 78752 (512) 476-2772; (512) 476-3919

Full-time: 4 men, no women — **Faculty:** 10
Part-time: 15 men, 7 women — **Tuition:** $825
Graduate: 25 men, 5 women — **Room & Board:** n/av
Application Deadline: July 1 (recommended)

Austin Graduate School of Theology, founded in 1917, is affiliated with The Church of Christ. Its mission is to equip ministers and other Christians for service in the kingdom of God. The figures in the above capsule are approximate. In addition to regional accreditation, the college is accredited by SACS. Austin Graduate School of Theology awards the B.A. in Christian studies as well as bachelor's and master's degrees. Web: *http:/www.austingrad.edu*

BAPTIST MISSIONARY ASSOCIATION THEOLOGICAL SEMINARY E-2

Jacksonville, TX 75766 (903) 586-2501; (903) 586-0378

Full-time: 23 men, 1 women — **Faculty:** 13
Part-time: 26 men, 22 women — **Tuition:** $4500
Graduate: 49 men, 8 women — **Room & Board:** $4500
Application Deadline: open

Baptist Missionary Association Theological Seminary, founded in 1955, is affiliated with The Baptist Missionary Association. Its mission is to train individuals for Christian ministry. In addition to regional accreditation, the college is accredited by SACS. Baptist Missionary Association Theological Seminary awards the B.A.R. in religion, as well as associate, bachelor's, and master's degrees. The figures in the above capsule are approximate. Web: *http:/www.bmats.edu*

CRISWELL COLLEGE D-2

Dallas, TX 75246 (214) 818-1326; (214) 818-1310

Full-time: 140 men, 30 women — **Faculty:** 27
Part-time: 160 men, 50 women — **Tuition:** $7032
Graduate: 100 men, 20 women — **Room & Board:** n/app
Application Deadline: July 15

Criswell College, founded in 1970, is affiliated with The Southern Baptist Church. Its mission is to educate and train laymen and full-time Christian workers in biblical, theological, and professional studies so they can serve effectively in evangelistic, educational, pastoral, and missionary vocations of the Christian church. Enrollment and faculty figures in the above capsule are approximate. In addition to regional accreditation, the college is accredited by SACS. Criswell College awards the B.A. in biblical studies, counseling, missions, evangelism, pastoral, and urban ministries. The school also awards associate, bachelor's, and master's degrees. Web: *http:/www.criswell.edu*

SOUTHWESTERN ASSEMBLIES OF GOD UNIVERSITY D-2

Waxahachie, TX 75165 (972) 825-4634; (972) 923-0006

Full-time: 587 men, 604 women **Faculty:** 129
Part-time: 145 men, 122 women **Tuition:** $16,230
Graduate: 168 men, 148 women **Room & Board:** $6321
Application Deadline: open

Southwestern Assemblies of God University, founded in 1927, is affiliated with Assemblies of God. Its mission is to prepare undergraduate and graduate students spiritually, academically, professionally, and cross culturally so as to successfully fill evangelistic, missionary and church ministry roles and to provide quality educational and professional Christian service wherever needed throughout the world. In addition to regional accreditation, the college is accredited by AABC and SACS. Southwestern Assemblies of God University awards the B.A. and B.S. in Accounting, Ancient Studies, Biblical Studies, Business Administration, Children & Family Ministries, Church Ministries, Church Planting & Revitalization, Communication Counseling, Counseling Ministries, Criminal Justice, Digital Media, Arts Drama, Education, Bilingual Education, Elementary Education, Middle & Secondary English, Language Arts/Reading, Social Studies/History, Music Education, Instrumental Piano Vocal, Physical Education, English, History, Human Services, Management, Management Information Systems, Marketing Media, Ministries, Music Ministries, Music Performance, Pastoral Ministries, Professional Development, Psychology, Social Work, Sports Management, Theological Studies, World Ministries, and Youth & Student Ministries. The school also awards associate, bachelor's, and master's degrees. Web: *www.sagu.edu*

WASHINGTON

TRINITY LUTHERAN COLLEGE C-2

Everett, WA 98201 (425) 249-4741

Full-time: 47 men, 65 women **Faculty:** 26
Part-time: 2 men, 3 women **Tuition:** $22,260
Graduate: n/av **Room & Board:** $8500
Application Deadline: see profile
SAT CR/M: 475/450 **ACT:** 20

Trinity Lutheran College, founded in 1944, is affiliated with The Lutheran Church. Its mission is to prepare students, through a living-learning environment, for rewarding careers by learning to integrate faith, ethics, and service along with key learning objectives. The figures in the above capsule are approximate. A Trinity education requires students to have the courage to take responsibility for their own faith, thought, and actions. In addition to regional accreditation, the college is accredited by NASC. Trinity Lutheran College awards the B.A. in biblical studies; music and worship; early childhood education; children, youth and family studies; intercultural studies; communications; business, leadership and management; psychology; and social work. The school also awards associate and bachelor's degrees. Web: *www.tlc.edu*

WISCONSIN

MARANATHA BAPTIST BIBLE COLLEGE D-4

Watertown, WI 53094 (920) 261-9300; (920) 261-9109

Full-time: 350 men, 404 women **Faculty:** 57
Part-time: 31 men, 45 women **Tuition:** $5780
Graduate: 27 men, 3 women **Room & Board:** $3400
Application Deadline: see profile
ACT: 21

Maranatha Baptist Bible College, founded in 1968, is affiliated with The Baptist Church. Its mission is to produce students who are spiritually and academically prepared to serve the Lord. The figures in the above capsule are approximate. We want to develop servants of Christ who are disciplined, creative, and passionate about the field to which they have been called. In addition to regional accreditation, the college is accredited by NCA. Maranatha Baptist Bible College awards the B.A. and B.S. in Bible, church ministries, education, general studies, fine arts, business, nursing, office administration, biology, and premed. The school also awards associate, bachelor's, and master's degrees. Web: *www.mbbc.edu*

AIR FORCE

In the Air Force ROTC program, young men and women may earn commissions while attending college. The amount of academic credit given for Air Force ROTC varies from school to school.

Most new Air Force officers come through the Air Force ROTC program. It offers students the opportunity to attend a civilian college while studying officership as part of their undergraduate curriculum.

The AFROTC program begins with the General Military Course. Freshmen or sophomores attend one hour of ROTC classes and one to two hours of leadership laboratory weekly. During these first two years, study is focused on the history of the Air Force and the part it plays in the world today. During the summer between sophomore and junior years, students attend a four-week basic training course located at an Air Force base.

The Professional Officer Course is completed during the junior and senior years. Study includes management principles and defense policy and offers the opportunity for managing, organizing, directing, and evaluating the cadet corps activities. Cadets who are medically qualified will have the opportunity to compete for pilot or navigator positions. Upon graduation, students are commissioned as Second Lieutenants.

For academically qualified students in selected majors, the AFROTC offers scholarships, including tuition, fees and books, and a monthly nontaxable allowance during the school year.

The majority of scholarships are awarded in the technical degree areas of engineering and computer science, but there are opportunities in nontechnical areas as well. Scholarships are based on individual merit, not financial need. Those who receive a scholarship must still apply and be accepted by the school they wish to attend and notify the AFROTC headquarters of their selection.

The scholarship program is broken down into different types and durations. All scholarships include full or partial tuition, fees, textbook allowance, and $250–$400 per month tax-free allowance during the academic year. Type 1 pays full tuition at any school offering AFROTC. Type 2 pays tuition and fees up to a maximum of $18,000 per year. There are two variations of the Type 7 scholarship. A Type 7 scholarship winner can attend any post-secondary institution (public or private) where tuition does not exceed $9,000 per year, or he/she can attend any public post-secondary institution where the student qualifies for in-state tuition rates.

The application deadline is December 1 of the senior year, but priority consideration is given to those who get the application in early. AFROTC only accepts on-line applications and they are available during the spring prior to the senior year of high school.

Further information can be obtained from the professor of aerospace studies at any of the host campuses where Air Force ROTC is offered. The listing that follows represents the host schools that offer these programs. Hundreds more schools have crosstown agreements with these institutions to make AFROTC more accessible to students. Please be sure to contact the school directly for more details. You may also find useful and current information at the Air Force Reserve Officer Training Corps web site, *www.afrotc.com*.

ALABAMA
- Alabama State University
- Auburn University at Montgomery
- Samford University
- Troy University
- Tuskegee University
- University of Alabama
- University of South Alabama

ALASKA
- University of Alaska - Anchorage

ARIZONA
- Arizona State University
- Embry-Riddle Aeronautical University
- Loyola Marymount University
- Northern Arizona University
- University of Arizona

ARKANSAS
- University of Arkansas

CALIFORNIA
- California State University, Fresno
- California State University, Sacramento
- California State University, San Bernadino
- Loyola Marymount University
- San Diego State University
- San Jose State University
- University of California at Berkeley
- University of California at Los Angeles
- University of Southern California

COLORADO
- Colorado State University
- University of Colorado at Boulder

CONNECTICUT
- University of Connecticut
- Yale University

DELAWARE
- University of Delaware

DISTRICT OF COLUMBIA
- Howard University

FLORIDA
- Embry-Riddle Aeronautical University
- Florida State University
- University of Central Florida
- University of Florida
- University of Miami
- University of South Florida

GEORGIA
- Georgia Institute of Technology
- University of Georgia
- Valdosta State University

HAWAII
- University of Hawaii at Manoa

ILLINOIS
- Illinois Institute of Technology
- Saint Louis University
- Southern Illinois University
- University of Illinois at Champaign/Urbana

INDIANA
- Indiana State University
- Indiana University
- Purdue University
- University of Notre Dame

IOWA
- Iowa State University
- University of Iowa

KANSAS
- Kansas State University
- University of Kansas

KENTUCKY
- University of Kentucky
- University of Louisville

LOUISIANA
- Louisiana State University and Agricultural and Mechanical College
- Louisiana Tech University
- Tulane University

MARYLAND
- University of Maryland

MASSACHUSETTS

- Boston University
- Massachusetts Institute of Technology
- Rensselaer Polytechnic Institute
- University of Massachusetts
- University of Massachusetts, Lowell
- Worcester Polytechnic Institute

MICHIGAN

- Michigan State University
- Michigan Technological University
- University of Michigan

MINNESOTA

- University of Minnesota/Duluth
- University of Minnesota
- University of Saint Thomas

MISSISSIPPI

- Jackson State University
- Mississippi State University
- University of Mississippi
- University of Southern Mississippi

MISSOURI

- Missouri University of Science and Technology
- St. Louis University
- University of Missouri/Columbia

MONTANA

- Montana State University

NEBRASKA

- University of Nebraska at Lincoln
- University of Nebraska at Omaha

NEVADA

- University of Nevada—Las Vegas

NEW HAMPSHIRE

- University of New Hampshire

NEW JERSEY

- New Jersey Institute of Technology
- Rutgers University

NEW MEXICO

- New Mexico State University
- University of New Mexico

NEW YORK

- Clarkson University
- Cornell University
- Manhattan College
- Rensselaer Polytechnic Institute
- Rochester Institute of Technology
- Syracuse University

NORTH CAROLINA

- Duke University
- East Carolina University
- Fayetteville State University
- North Carolina A & T State University
- North Carolina State University
- University of North Carolina at Chapel Hill
- University of North Carolina at Charlotte

NORTH DAKOTA

- North Dakota State University

OHIO

- Bowling Green University
- Kent State University
- Miami University
- Ohio State University, The
- Ohio University
- University of Cincinnati
- Wright State University

OKLAHOMA

- Oklahoma State University
- University of Oklahoma

OREGON

- Oregon State University
- University of Portland

PENNSYLVANIA

- Pennsylvania State University/ Main Campus
- Saint Joseph's University
- University of Pittsburgh
- Wilkes University

PUERTO RICO

- University of Puerto Rico/Mayaguez
- University of Puerto Rico/Río Piedras

SOUTH CAROLINA

- Charleston Southern University
- The Citadel
- Clemson University
- University of South Carolina/ Columbia

SOUTH DAKOTA

- South Dakota State University

TENNESSEE

- Tennessee State University
- University of Memphis
- University of Tennessee

TEXAS

- Angelo State University
- Baylor University
- Texas A & M University
- Texas Christian University
- Texas State University/San Marcos
- Texas Tech University
- University of Houston
- University of North Texas
- University of Texas at Austin
- University of Texas at San Antonio

UTAH

- Brigham Young University
- University of Utah
- Utah State University

VERMONT

- Norwich University

VIRGINIA

- University of Virginia
- Virginia Military Institute
- Virginia Polytechnic Institute

WASHINGTON

- Central Washington University
- University of Washington
- Washington State University

WEST VIRGINIA

- West Virginia University

WISCONSIN

- Marquette University
- University of Wisconsin/Madison

WYOMING

- University of Wyoming

ARMY

The Army Reserve Officers' Training Corps (ROTC) provides college students with the opportunity to combine leadership and management training with their other academic studies. The curriculum, which consists of a series of classroom and hands-on leadership training experiences, provides students with the necessary foundation to serve successfully in positions of responsibility in either the U.S. Army or the corporate world.

Those with a strong academic background, an active mindset, and the ability to rapidly assimilate information thrive in the program. These scholar-athlete-leaders note that the leadership skills developed through their participation in the program are further honed during their period of service as Army officers. After service as an Army lieutenant, many graduates elect to continue their service in uniform. Others elect to enter the corporate world where their leadership skills and experience as ROTC-trained Army officers allow them to advance rapidly.

Although the program is designed to be completed in four years, students may complete all requirements within a two-year period through participation in a summer training session called the Leaders' Training Course, normally held during the summer between the sophomore and junior years. A generous series of merit-based scholarships that cover tuition, fees, textbooks, and supplies exist to help students and their families defray the cost of college. For more information on the program, call (800) USA-ROTC, or contact the professor of military science at a college that offers Army ROTC. Detailed information about the program is also available at *www.armyrotc.com*.

ALABAMA

- Alabama A&M University
- Auburn University
- Auburn University at Montgomery
- Jacksonville State University
- Marion Military Institute
- The University of Alabama
- Tuskegee University
- University of Alabama at Birmingham
- University of North Alabama
- University of South Alabama

ALASKA

- University of Alaska/Fairbanks

ARIZONA

- Arizona State University
- Northern Arizona University
- University of Arizona

ARKANSAS

- Arkansas State University
- University of Arkansas
- University of Arkansas at Pine Bluff
- University of Central Arkansas

CALIFORNIA

- California Polytechnic State University at San Luis Obispo
- California State University at Fresno
- California State University at Fullerton
- Claremont McKenna College
- San Diego State University
- Santa Clara University
- University of California at Berkeley
- University of California at Davis
- University of California at Los Angeles
- University of California at Santa Barbara
- University of San Francisco
- University of Southern California

COLORADO

- Colorado State University
- University of Colorado at Boulder
- University of Colorado at Colorado Springs

CONNECTICUT

- University of Connecticut

DELAWARE

- University of Delaware

DISTRICT OF COLUMBIA

- Georgetown University
- Howard University

FLORIDA

- Embry-Riddle Aeronautical University
- Florida A & M University
- Florida Institute of Technology
- Florida International University
- Florida Southern College
- Florida State University
- University of Central Florida
- University of Florida
- University of South Florida
- University of Tampa
- University of West Florida

GEORGIA

- Columbus State University
- Fort Valley State University
- Georgia Institute of Technology
- Georgia Military College
- Georgia Regents University
- Georgia Southern University
- Georgia State University
- University of North Georgia
- University of Georgia

HAWAII

- University of Hawaii at Manoa

IDAHO

- Boise State University
- University of Idaho

ILLINOIS

- Eastern Illinois University
- Illinois State University
- Loyola University
- Northern Illinois University
- Southern Illinois University at Carbondale
- Southern Illinois University at Edwardsville
- University of Illinois at Chicago
- University of Illinois at Urbana-Champaign
- Western Illinois University
- Wheaton College

INDIANA

- Ball State University
- Indiana University-Purdue University at Indianapolis
- Indiana University at Bloomington
- Purdue University
- Rose-Hulman Institute of Technology
- University of Notre Dame

IOWA

- Iowa State University
- University of Iowa
- University of Northern Iowa

KANSAS

- Kansas State University
- Pittsburg State University
- University of Kansas

KENTUCKY

- Eastern Kentucky University
- Morehead State University
- University of Kentucky
- University of Louisville
- Western Kentucky University

LOUISIANA

- Grambling State University
- Louisiana State University
- Northwestern State University
- Southern University and A & M College
- Tulane University

MAINE

- University of Maine

MARYLAND

- Bowie State University
- Loyola University Maryland
- McDaniel College
- Morgan State University
- The Johns Hopkins University
- University of Maryland at College Park

MASSACHUSETTS

- Boston University
- Massachusetts Institute of Technology
- Northeastern University
- University of Massachusetts
- Worcester Polytechnic Institute

MICHIGAN

- Central Michigan University
- Eastern Michigan University
- Michigan State University
- Michigan Technological University
- Northern Michigan University
- University of Michigan
- Western Michigan University

MINNESOTA

- Minnesota State University, Mankato
- Saint John's University
- University of Minnesota/Twin Cities

MISSISSIPPI

- Alcorn State University
- Jackson State University
- Mississippi State University
- University of Mississippi
- University of Southern Mississippi

MISSOURI

- Lincoln University
- Missouri State University
- Missouri University of Science and Technology
- Missouri Western State University
- Truman State University
- University of Central Missouri
- University of Missouri/Columbia
- Washington University
- Wentworth Military Academy

MONTANA

- Montana State University
- University of Montana

NEBRASKA

- Chadron State College
- Creighton University
- University of Nebraska at Lincoln

NEVADA

- University of Nevada/Reno

NEW HAMPSHIRE

- University of New Hampshire

NEW JERSEY

- Princeton University
- Rutgers University
- Seton Hall University

NEW MEXICO

- New Mexico Military Institute
- New Mexico State University
- University of New Mexico

NEW YORK

- Canisius College
- City University of New York (CUNY)
- Clarkson University
- Cornell University
- Fordham University
- Hofstra University
- Niagara University
- Rochester Institute of Technology
- Saint Bonaventure University
- Saint John's University New York
- Siena College
- State University of New York (SUNY)/Brockport
- Syracuse University

NORTH CAROLINA

- Appalachian State University
- Campbell University
- Duke University
- East Carolina University
- Elizabeth City State University
- North Carolina Agricultural and Technical State University
- North Carolina State University
- Saint Augustine's College
- University of North Carolina at Chapel Hill
- University of North Carolina at Charlotte
- Wake Forest University

NORTH DAKOTA

- North Dakota State University
- University of North Dakota

OHIO

- Bowling Green State University
- Capital University
- Central State University
- John Carroll University
- Kent State University
- The Ohio State University
- Ohio University
- The University of Akron
- University of Cincinnati
- University of Dayton
- University of Toledo
- Wright State University
- Xavier University

OKLAHOMA

- Cameron University
- Oklahoma State University
- University of Central Oklahoma
- University of Oklahoma

OREGON

- Oregon State University
- University of Oregon
- University of Portland

PENNSYLVANIA

- Bucknell University
- Dickinson College
- Drexel University
- Edinboro University of Pennsylvania
- Gannon University
- Indiana University of Pennsylvania
- Lehigh University
- Lock Haven University of Pennsylvania
- Pennsylvania State University
- Shippensburg University
- Slippery Rock University
- Temple University
- University of Pittsburgh
- University of Scranton
- Valley Forge Military College
- Widener University

PUERTO RICO

- University of Puerto Rico/Mayaguez
- University of Puerto Rico/Río Piedras

RHODE ISLAND

- Providence College
- University of Rhode Island

SOUTH CAROLINA

- The Citadel
- Clemson University
- Furman University
- Presbyterian College
- South Carolina State University
- University of South Carolina
- Wofford College

SOUTH DAKOTA

- South Dakota School of Mines
- South Dakota State University
- University of South Dakota

TENNESSEE

- Austin Peay State University
- Carson-Newman College
- East Tennessee State University
- Middle Tennessee State University
- Tennessee Tech University
- University of Memphis
- University of Tennessee at Knoxville
- University of Tennessee at Martin
- Vanderbilt University

TEXAS

- Prairie View A & M University
- Saint Mary's University
- Sam Houston State University
- Stephen F. Austin State University
- Tarleton State University
- Texas A & M University-College Station
- Texas A & M-Corpus Christi
- Texas A & M University at Kingsville
- Texas Christian University
- Texas State University
- Texas Tech University
- University of Houston
- University of Texas at Arlington
- University of Texas at Austin
- University of Texas at El Paso
- University of Texas at San Antonio
- University of Texas-Pan American

UTAH

- Brigham Young University
- University of Utah
- Weber State University

VERMONT

- Norwich University
- University of Vermont

VIRGINIA

- College of William and Mary
- George Mason University
- Hampton University
- James Madison University
- Norfolk State University
- Old Dominion University
- University of Richmond
- University of Virginia
- Virginia Military Institute
- Virginia State University
- Virginia Tech

WASHINGTON

- Central Washington University
- Eastern Washington University
- Gonzaga University
- Pacific Lutheran University
- Seattle University
- University of Washington
- Washington State University

WEST VIRGINIA

- Marshall University
- West Virginia State College
- West Virginia University

WISCONSIN

- Marquette University
- University of Wisconsin/La Crosse
- University of Wisconsin/Madison
- University of Wisconsin/Oshkosh
- University of Wisconsin/Stevens Point

WYOMING

- University of Wyoming

NAVY

The NROTC Program educates and trains qualified young men and women for service as commissioned officers in the unrestricted line Navy or Marine Corps. Two programs are available: the NROTC Scholarship Program and the NROTC College Program.

The NROTC Scholarship Program plays an important role in preparing young men and women for leadership and management positions in an increasingly technical Navy and Marine Corps. The four-year NROTC Scholarship Program is available to qualified students who graduate from high school before August 1 of the year they intend to start college. The two-year NROTC Scholarship Program is available to qualified college sophmores who have completed one year of differential and integral calculus with a grade of C or better and maintain a minimum GPA of 2.5.

Selected applicants for NROTC Scholarship Programs (four-year and two-year) are awarded scholarships through a highly competitive national selection process, and receive full tuition, fees, book stipend, and other financial benefits at many of the country's leading colleges and universities. Upon graduation, midshipmen are commissioned as officers in the unrestricted line Navy or Marine Corps.

Students selected for the NROTC Scholarship Program make their own arrangements for college enrollment and room and board, and take the normal course load required by the college or university for degree completion. Additionally, scholarship midshipmen are required to follow specific academic guidelines. Full information concerning the NROTC Scholarship Program is available from any of the colleges and universities with NROTC units or from Navy and Marine Corps recruiters.

For information on the NROTC scholarship programs, call 1-800-USA-NAVY or 1-800-NAV-ROTC, e-mail *PNSC_NROTC.scholarship@navy.mil*; or visit *https://www.nrotc.navy.mil*. Electronic application for the four-year scholarship program must be submitted by January 31.

The NROTC College Program may be either two or four years. Additional points include:

- Applicants are selected from students already attending or accepted by colleges with the NROTC program.
- Students selected for "advance standing" receive a stipend for a maximum of 20 months. Advance standing is only available starting in the junior year of college. Stipend per academic month is $350 junior year and $400 senior year.
- Students will complete naval science and other university courses, a few specific university courses, and attend one summer training session, normally at sea for Navy-option midshipmen and in Quantico, VA for Marine Corps-option midshipmen.

The following list shows the colleges and universities that have an NROTC unit on campus. Many more institutions offer the program through cross-town arrangements. We recommend that you visit *https://www.nrotc.navy.mil* for a listing of participating colleges and universities. Contact the schools directly for the most current and accurate information.

ALABAMA

- Auburn University
- Tuskegee University

ARIZONA

- Arizona State University
- University of Arizona

CALIFORNIA

- University of California/Berkeley
- University of California/Los Angeles
- University of San Diego
- University of Southern California

COLORADO

- University of Colorado at Boulder

CONNECTICUT

- Yale University

DISTRICT OF COLUMBIA

- George Washington University

FLORIDA

- Embry Riddle Aeronautical University
- Florida A & M University
- Jacksonville University
- University of Florida
- University of South Florida

GEORGIA

- Georgia Institute of Technology
- Morehouse College
- Savannah State College

IDAHO

- University of Idaho

ILLINOIS

- Illinois Institute of Technology
- Northwestern University
- University of Illinois at Urbana-Champaign

INDIANA

- Purdue University/West Lafayette
- University of Notre Dame

IOWA

- Iowa State University

KANSAS

- University of Kansas

LOUISIANA

- Southern University and A & M College
- Tulane University

MAINE

- Maine Maritime Academy

MASSACHUSETTS

- Boston University
- College of the Holy Cross
- Massachusetts Institute of Technology

MICHIGAN

- University of Michigan

MINNESOTA

- University of Minnesota

MISSISSIPPI

- University of Mississippi

MISSOURI

- University of Missouri

NEBRASKA

- University of Nebraska at Lincoln

NEW JERSEY

- Rutgers University

NEW MEXICO

- University of New Mexico

NEW YORK

- Cornell University
- Rensselaer Polytechnic Institute
- State University of New York/Maritime College
- University of Rochester

NORTH CAROLINA

- Duke University
- North Carolina State University
- University of North Carolina at Chapel Hill

OHIO

- Miami University
- Ohio State University

OKLAHOMA

- University of Oklahoma

OREGON

- Oregon State University

PENNSYLVANIA

- Carnegie Mellon University
- Pennsylvania State University Park Campus
- University of Pennsylvania
- Villanova University

SOUTH CAROLINA

- The Citadel
- University of South Carolina

TENNESSEE

- University of Memphis
- Vanderbilt University

TEXAS

- Prairie View A & M University
- Rice University
- Texas A & M University
- University of Texas at Austin

UTAH

- University of Utah

VERMONT

- Norwich University

VIRGINIA

- Hampton University
- Norfolk State University
- Old Dominion University
- University of Virginia
- Virginia Military Institute
- Virginia Polytechnic Institute and State University

WASHINGTON

- University of Washington

WISCONSIN

- Marquette University
- University of Wisconsin/Madison

ENROLLMENT IN CANADIAN SCHOOLS

Recently, Canadian universities hosted a record 70,000 full-time international students. International students account for 6 percent of full-time undergraduate students and 18 percent at the graduate level. Most Canadian universities admit international students—although some have a quota on the number they will accept—and will give interested students information on how their academic qualifications are equated with Canadian requirements.

The Association of Universities and Colleges of Canada (AUCC) represents 92 universities and university-level colleges. These institutions account for almost 99 percent of the total university enrollment in Canada. Almost all Canadian colleges are coeducational. This section contains individual profiles for those English-language universities that enroll more than 10,000 students.

Affiliated with each of these universities are a number of general, theological, or residential colleges, which also have been listed here. The names and addresses of the three French-speaking colleges with enrollments of more than 10,000 may be found at the end of this introduction.

Admissions Requirements

Each university has its own entrance requirements and will assess you on an individual basis. The university will determine the equivalency of your academic credentials. There is no nationwide set of entrance exams. For more details about this or any other part of the application process, contact the registrar at the university you wish to attend.

Admissions Procedure

Once you have determined which universities meet your needs, contact the registrar's office at each institution to obtain an application for a bachelor's program or a professional degree. If you anticipate pursuing postgraduate studies in Canada, you may obtain more information by contacting the dean of graduate studies at the universities that interest you. It is important to apply early. Remember that the Canadian academic year usually starts in September. Some programs, however, do admit students to courses that start in January and May.

The AUCC's web site *www.aucc.ca* has links to the web pages of all Canadian universities, the majority of which accept applications via e-mail.

To study at a Canadian university, you will need a study permit. You may also need a visitor's visa, which will be issued to you at the same time as your study permit. To apply for a study permit, please contact your nearest Canadian diplomatic post.

You will have to arrange for medical coverage before you arrive in Canada. Medical coverage varies from province to province and sometimes from university to university within each province. Please ask an official at the nearest Canadian diplomatic post for detailed information. Also, check whether the universities you are applying to have any medical insurance plans for international students.

Degrees Offered

Canadian universities, like those in the United States, grant three levels of degrees: bachelor's and first professional, master's, and doctoral as well as undergraduate certificates and diplomas and graduate diploma programs.

Earning the first degree can take three to five years. A general, or unspecialized, program leading to a Bachelor of Arts or Bachelor of Science usually can be completed in three years. An honors degree, earned in a specialized program, usually requires four years. Students must meet more rigorous requirements to enter an honors-degree program and must maintain high grades to remain in it. First professional degrees in some fields may take more than four years to earn, and students may be required to undertake two or three years of university study before enrolling in the professional program. Students who enter graduate programs with a general degree usually must study a year longer than those with honors degrees. Undergraduate diplomas and certificates may be from one to three years' duration and may (although not necessarily) be used as a basis for entry to a degree program. A graduate diploma may be considered as conferring a qualification that is intermediate between the bachelor's (or first professional degree) and master's degree. It may be completed in as little as two or as long as three academic years.

Organizations

Virtually all universities have organizations for international students, and sponsor international student centers and advisers. There also are national organizations that aid international students, including the World University Service of Canada and the Canadian Bureau for International Education, which arranges for representatives to meet international students arriving at Canadian airports.

Tuition, Fees, and Aid

Universities and colleges are heavily subsidized by provincial and federal governments, and tuition fees actually cover one third of university operating costs. Canadian institutions charge different fees for different programs, unlike American institutions, which charge the same tuition regardless of the program of study. Each profile in this book lists the range of tuitions, which may or may not include student fees. Some universities have higher fees for international students, and where that is the case, the profile includes just the international fees. All costs are given in Canadian (CDN) dollars. In all cases, you should check with the university in which you are interested to obtain the most up-to-date information about tuition and room-and-board charges.

Most awards available to international students through Canadian universities or from the Canadian government are restricted to graduate and post graduate studies. Some of the scholarship programs for international students to study in Canada include the Commonwealth Scholarship and Fellowship Plan, the Canadian International Development Agency awards, the Government of Canada awards program of cultural exchanges and the Programme canadien de bourses de la Francophonie. Students interested in applying for aid should contact a Canadian diplomatic mission in their home countries and, for information on cultural exchange programs, their own nation's education department or ministry.

Additional Information

Association of Universities and Colleges of Canada
600-350 Albert Street
Ottawa, ON, K1R 1B1 Canada
(613) 563-1236
Fax: (613) 563-9745
E-mail: info@aucc.ca
www.aucc.ca
(publications include *Notes for International Students, and The Directory of Canadian Universities*)

The Canadian Bureau for International Education
220 Laurier Avenue West, Suite 1550
Ottawa, ON K1P 5Z9 Canada
(613) 237-4820
Fax: (613) 237-1073
E-mail: info@cbie.ca
www.cbie.ca

Canada Immigration & Citizenship
www.cic.gc.ca
(publications include *Study in Canada: Visas, Work and Immigration for International Students, downloadable pdf Publication*)

Consulate General of Canada in New York
1251 Avenue of the Americas
Concourse Level (between 49th & 50th Streets, Midtown Manhattan)
New York, NY 10020-1175
(212) 596-1628
Fax: (212) 596-1790
Monday–Friday, 9am–5pm
E-mail: cngnyg@international.gc.ca
www.can-am.gc.ca/new-york

The Department of Foreign Affairs, Trade and Development
125 Sussex Drive
Ottawa, ON K1A 0G2 Canada
(613) 996-9709
1 (800) 267-8376
Fax: (613) 996-9709
E-mail: has online form on website
www.international.gc.ca/international/index.aspx

Social Sciences and Humanities Research Council of Canada
350 Albert Street, P.O. Box 1610
Ottawa, ON K1P 6G4, Canada
(613) 992-3027
E-mail: strategic@sshrc-crsh.gc.ca
www.sshrc-crsh.gc.ca

Statistics Canada
150 Tunney's Pasture Driveway
Ottawa, Ontario K1A 0T6 Canada
Monday–Friday, 8:30am–4:30pm
1 (800) 263-1136
or (514) 283-8300 (international)
Fax: (877) 287-4369
E-mail: infostats@statcan.gc.ca
www.statcan.ca

World University Service of Canada
1404 Scott Street
Ottawa, ON K1Y 4M8 Canada
(613) 798-7477
(800) 267-8699
Fax: (613) 798-0990
E-mail: wusc@wusc.ca
www.wusc.ca

CANADA

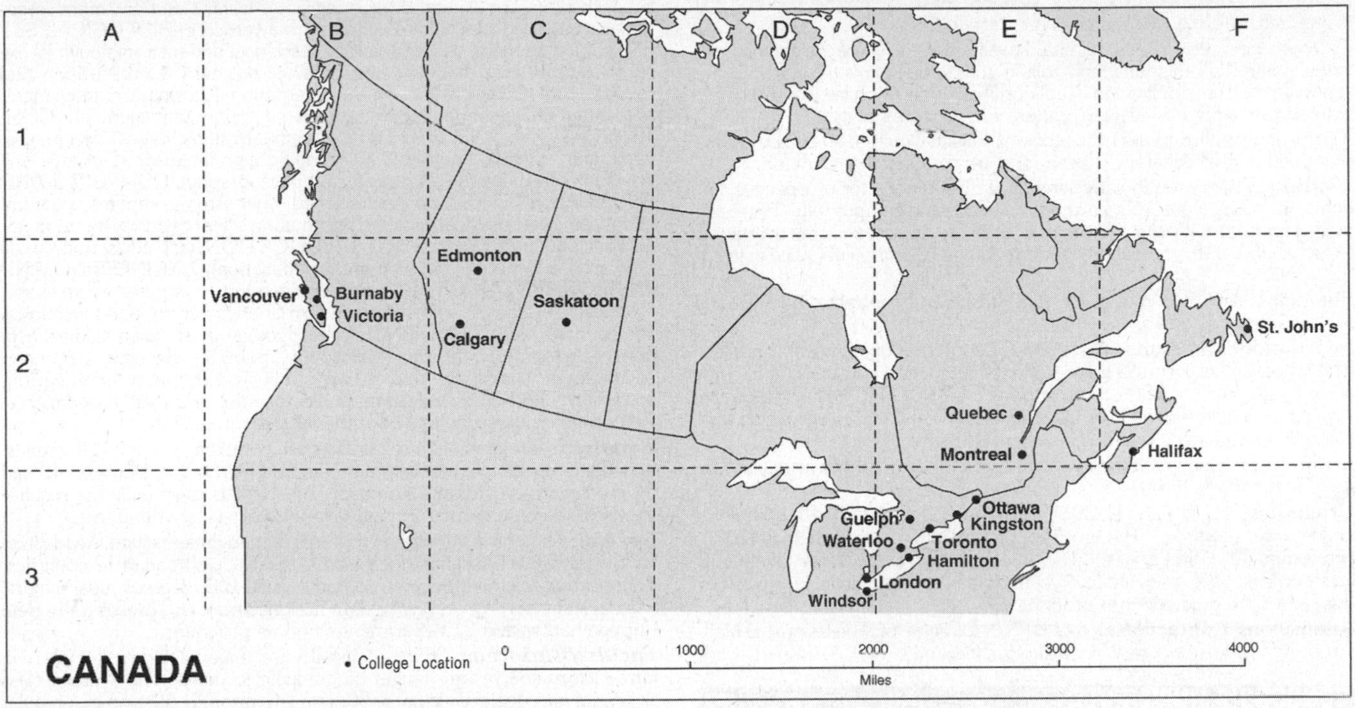

CARLETON UNIVERSITY E-3

Ottawa, ON K1S 5B6 **(613) 520-3609; (613) 520-3517**

Full-time: 9000 men, 9406 women	**Faculty:** n/av
Part-time: 1502 men, 1216 women	**Ph.D.s:** 93%
Graduate: 1937 men, 1699 women	**Student/Faculty:** n/av
Year: semesters, summer session	**Tuition:** $8101 ($2573)
Application Deadline: May	**Room & Board:** $10,200
Freshman Class: n/av	

Carleton University, founded in 1942, is a public institution operated by the province of Ontario. There are 14 undergraduate and 14 graduate degree programs offered. The figures in the above capsule and in this profile are approximate. There are 5 undergraduate schools and 1 graduate school. The library contains 1.8 million volumes, 1.4 million microform items, and 22,370 audio/video tapes/CDs/DVDs, and subscribes to 40,607 periodicals including electronic. Computerized library services include interlibrary loans, database searching, Internet access, and Wi-Fi capability. Special learning facilities include an art gallery, radio station, and an environmental biology laboratories annex. The 152-acre campus is in a small town in Ottawa. Including any residence halls, there are 29 buildings.

Student Life: 80% of undergraduates are from Ontario. The average age of freshmen is 19; all undergraduates, 21. 13% do not continue beyond their first year; 72% remain to graduate.

Housing: 2873 students can be accommodated in college housing, which includes single-sex and coed dorms. On-campus housing is available on a lottery system for upperclassmen. Priority is given to out-of-town students. All students may keep cars.

Activities: There are no fraternities or sororities. There are 80 groups on campus, including cheerleading, chess, choir, computers, drama, environmental, ethnic, film, gay, international, jazz band, newspaper, pep band, photography, political, radio and TV, religious, social, social service, and student government. Popular campus events include orientation.

Sports: There are 16 intercollegiate sports for men and 18 for women, and 4 intramural sports for men and 3 for women. Facilities include a physical recreation center with an Olympic-size pool, squash courts, Nautilus and fitness centers, and a double gym. Outdoor tennis courts and playing fields are also available.

Disabled Students: All of the campus is accessible. Facilities include wheelchair ramps, elevators, special parking, specially equipped restrooms, lowered drinking fountains, lowered telephones. including automatic doors in some buildings, tactile control panels in elevators, tunnels connecting buildings, specially equipped residence rooms, and attendant services.

Services: Counseling and information services are available, as is tutoring in most subjects. There is a reader service for the blind. Study skills workshops are available in essay writing and preparation and writing of exams. There is special exam scheduling and a study center for disabled students and a PASS program (peer tutoring).

Campus Safety and Security: Measures include 24-hour foot and vehicle patrol, emergency notification system, and security escort services. There are emergency telephones, lighted pathways/sidewalks, controlled access to dorms/residences, and bike patrol, rape defence classes and student safety patrol.

Programs of Study: Carleton confers B.A., B.Sc., B.Arch., B.Comm., B.C.S., B.Eng., B.Hum., B.I.B., B.I.D., B.I.T., B.J., B.Math., B.Mus., B.P.A.P.M. and B.S.W. degrees. Master's and doctoral degrees are also awarded. Bachelor's degrees are awarded in BIOLOGICAL SCIENCE (biochemistry, biology/biological science, biometrics and biostatistics, biotechnology, and neurosciences), BUSINESS (accounting, business systems analysis, human resources, international business management, marketing and distribution, marketing/retailing/merchandising, and operations research), COMMUNICATIONS AND THE ARTS (art history and appreciation, classics, communications, communications technology, English, English literature, film arts, French, German, industrial design, Italian, journalism, linguistics, music, Russian, and Spanish), COMPUTER AND PHYSICAL SCIENCE (chemistry, computer mathematics, computer programming, computer science, geology, information sciences and systems, mathematics, physical sciences, physics, and statistics), EDUCATION (teaching English as a second/foreign language (TESOL/TEFOL)), ENGINEERING AND ENVIRONMENTAL DESIGN (aeronautical engineering, architecture, civil engineering, computer engineering, electrical/electronics engineering, engineering, engineering physics, environmental engineering, environmental science, mechanical engineering, and systems engineering), SOCIAL SCIENCE (anthropology, Canadian studies, child care/child and family studies, classical/ancient civilization, cognitive science, criminology, Eastern European studies, economics, European studies, geography, German area studies, history, human ecology, interdisciplinary studies, law, liberal arts/general studies, philosophy, political science/government, psychology, public administration, religion, social work, sociology, and women's studies). Arts, engineering, and commerce have the largest enrollments.

Required: Requirements for graduation vary according to programs.

Special: Carleton offers co-op programs in many majors and an exchange program with the University of Ottawa. Study abroad, internships in industrial design, dual and student-designed majors, accelerated degree programs, and interdisciplinary programs are available. The university also utilizes instructional television.

Faculty/Classroom: 65% of faculty are male; 35% are female. No introductory courses are taught by graduate students. The average class size in an introductory lecture is 166 and in a regular course is 107.

Requirements: In addition, Applicants must be graduates of an accredited secondary school. Architecture, humanities, and industrial design students must present a portfolio; social work students should submit a personal information form; music students must audition. A GPA of 3.0 is required. AP and CLEP credits are accepted.

Procedure: Freshmen are admitted to all sessions. There are early admissions, deferred admissions, and rolling admissions plans. Check with the school for current application deadlines. The application fee is $100. Notifications are sent in May. Applications are accepted on-line.

Transfer: Applicants are evaluated on individual merits. 30 of 120 credits required for the bachelor's degree must be completed at Carleton.

Visiting: There are regularly scheduled orientations for prospective students, including a general information session and campus tour. There are guides for informal visits, visitors may sit in on classes, and stay overnight. To schedule a visit, contact the Undergraduate Recruitment Office at (613) 520-3663.

Financial Aid: The deadline for filing freshman financial aid applications for fall entry is February 1.

International Students: There are 1565 international students enrolled. The school actively recruits these students. They must take the TOEFL with a minimum score of 580 on the paper-based TOEFL (PBT) or 86 on the Internet-based version (iBT) or take the MELAB and the college's own test, Canadian Academic English Language Assessment.

Computers: Students who have an account for the mainframe may access the system at any time.

Graduates: From July 1, 2012 to June 30, 2013, 3640 bachelor's degrees were awarded. The most popular majors were psychology (10%), economics (4%), and English (4%). In an average class, 3% graduate in 3 years or less, 38% graduate in 4 years or less, 62% graduate in 5 years or less, and 67% graduate in 6 years or less.

Admissions Contact: Janice O'Farrell, Director of Admissions. E-Mail: *admissions@carleton.ca* Web: *www.carleton.ca*

CONCORDIA UNIVERSITY E-2

Montreal, PQ H3G IM8 **(514) 848-4971; (514) 848-2837**

Full-time: n/av	**Faculty:** 714
Part-time: n/av	**Ph.D.s:** 84%
Graduate: n/av	**Student/Faculty:** 17 to 1
Year: semesters, summer session	**Tuition:** $2659 ($17,391)
Application Deadline: March 1	**Room & Board:** $5000
Freshman Class: n/av	
SAT or ACT: recommended	

Concordia University, established in 1974, is a public institution operated by the province of Quebec. There are 5 undergraduate schools and 1 graduate school. In addition to regional accreditation, has baccalaureate program accreditation with AACSB. The 2 libraries contain 3.0 million volumes, 75,000 microform items, and 2,000 audio/video tapes/CDs/DVDs, and subscribe to 5,500 periodicals including electronic. Computerized library services include interlibrary loans and database searching. Special learning facilities include an art gallery, radio station, TV station, a greenhouse, audiovisual instruction service, and specialized research center. The 1555-acre campus is in an urban area in downtown Montreal and in suburban Loyola. Including any residence halls, there are 80 buildings.

Student Life: 90% of undergraduates are from Quebec. Others are from 29 states, 128 foreign countries. The average age of freshmen is 21; all undergraduates, 25. 11% do not continue beyond their first year; 52% remain to graduate.

Housing: 144 students can be accommodated in college housing, which includes single-sex and coed dorms and off-campus apartments. In addition, there are fraternity houses and sorority houses. On-campus housing is available on a first-come and first-served basis. Priority is given to out-of-town students. 98% of students commute. All students may keep cars.

Activities: 1% of men belong to 3 national fraternities; 1% of women belong to 3 national sororities. There are 125 groups on campus, including art, choir, chorale, chorus, computers, dance, drama, ethnic, film, gay, honors, international, jazz band, literary magazine, musical theater, newspaper, orchestra, photography, political, professional, radio and TV, religious, social, social service, student government, symphony, and yearbook.

Sports: There are 9 intercollegiate sports for men and 7 for women, and 16 intramural sports for men and 12 for women. Facilities include an arena, a gym, and a football stadium.

Disabled Students: 75% of the campus is accessible. Facilities include wheelchair ramps, elevators, special parking, specially equipped restrooms, special class scheduling, lowered drinking fountains, lowered telephones.

Services: Counseling and information services are available, as is tutoring in most subjects. There is a reader service for the blind, and remedial math, reading, and writing.

Campus Safety and Security: Measures include 24-hour foot and vehicle patrol, self-defense education, and security escort services. There are shuttle buses, emergency telephones, and lighted pathways/sidewalks.

Programs of Study: confers B.A., B.Admin., B.Comm., B.Comp.Sci., B.Ed., B.Eng., B.F.A. and B.S.C. degrees. Master's and doctoral degrees are also awarded. Bachelor's degrees are awarded in BIOLOGICAL SCIENCE (biochemistry, biology/biological science, and microbiology), BUSINESS (accounting, banking and finance, business administration and management, business economics, international business management, marketing/retailing/merchandising, and personnel management), COMMUNICATIONS AND THE ARTS (communications, dance, design, dramatic arts, English, English as a second/foreign language, film arts, fine arts, journalism, languages, music, and photography), COMPUTER AND PHYSICAL SCIENCE (actuarial science, chemistry, computer programming, computer science, geology, information sciences and systems, mathematics, physics, and statistics), EDUCATION (art education, early childhood education, and elementary education), ENGINEERING AND ENVIRONMENTAL DESIGN (civil engineering, computer engineering, electrical/electronics engineering, industrial engineering, and mechanical engineering), SOCIAL SCIENCE (anthropology, East Asian studies, economics, geography, history, philosophy, political science/government, psychology, sociology, and urban studies). Computer engineering, accounting, and communication studies are the strongest academically. Accounting and psychology have the largest enrollments.

Required: To graduate, students must complete 90 to 120 credits, depending on the degree, with a minimum GPA of 2.0. Between 42 and 54 credits are required in the major. All students must fulfill the requirements of the core curriculum and take the university writing test.

Special: The university offers programs in many majors with the Institute for Co-operative Education, internships, and study abroad in 12 countries. There are accelerated degree programs, B.A.-B.S. degrees, dual majors, a general studies degree, and student-designed majors. There is a Phi Beta Kappa chapter and 21 departmental honors programs.

Faculty/Classroom: 65% of faculty are male; 35% are female. No introductory courses are taught by graduate students. The average class size in an introductory lecture is 50; in a laboratory is 50; and in a regular course is 50.

Requirements: The SAT or ACT is recommended. Applicants must be graduates of an accredited secondary school. The GED is accepted. An essay, an interview, a portfolio, or an audition may be required for some programs. A GPA of 2.5 is required. AP and CLEP credits are accepted. Important factors in the admissions decision are advanced placement or honors courses and recommendations by school officials.

Procedure: Freshmen are admitted to all sessions. There are early decision, early admissions, and rolling admissions plans. Early decision applications should be filed by February 1; regular applications, by March 1 for fall entry; November 1 for winter entry; and April 15 for summer entry, along with a $50 fee.

Transfer: Applicants must have a minimum GPA of 2.2. 45 of 90 credits required for the bachelor's degree must be completed at Concordia.

Visiting: There are regularly scheduled orientations for prospective students. There are guides for informal visits and visitors may sit in on classes. To schedule a visit, contact the Office of Student Recruitment at (514) 848-4779.

Financial Aid: Check with the school for current application deadlines.

International Students: There are 1235 international students enrolled. The school actively recruits these students. They must take the TOEFL or MELAB and the college's own test.

Computers: All students may access the system from 8:30 a.m. to 11:30 p.m. There are no time limits and no fees.

Graduates: From July 1, 2012 to June 30, 2013, 4291 bachelor's degrees were awarded. The most popular majors were arts and science (55%), commerce and administration (25%), and fine arts (10%). 500 companies recruited on campus in 2012-2013.

Admissions Contact: Pete Regimbald, Assistant Registrar. E-Mail: *admreg@alcor.concordia.ca* Web: *www.concordia.ca*

DALHOUSIE UNIVERSITY F-2

Halifax, NS B3H 4R2 **(902) 494-2450; (902) 494-1630**

Full-time: n/av	**Faculty:** n/av
Part-time: n/av	**Ph.D.s:** n/av
Graduate: n/av	**Student/Faculty:** n/av
Year: semesters, summer session	**Tuition:** $7531
Application Deadline:	**Room & Board:** $9220
Freshman Class: n/av	

Dalhousie University, founded in 1818, is located in Nova Scotia, Canada. 18,500 students study at the undergraduate, graduate and professional levels in more than 180 programs in 12 faculties. Computerized library services include interlibrary loans, database searching, and Internet access. Special learning facilities include an art gallery, natural history museum, planetarium, and radio station. The campus is in an urban area in Halifax and Truro, Nova Scotia.

Housing: 2200 students can be accommodated in college housing, which

includes single-sex and coed dorms, on-campus apartments, off-campus apartments, and married student housing. In addition, there are special-interest houses. On-campus housing is available on a first-come, first-served basis, and is available on a lottery system for upperclassmen. Some may keep cars.

Activities: There are no fraternities or sororities. There are 280 groups on campus, including cheerleading, chess, chorale, communications, computers, dance, debate, drama, environmental, ethnic, gay, honors, international, musical theater, newspaper, photography, political, professional, radio and TV, religious, social, social service, and student government.

Sports: Facilities include recreation facilities available in both Halifax and Truro. Cardio and weight training equipment, soccer fields, outdoor tennis courts, a track, an Olympic-size swimming pool, squash and volleyball courts, a climbing wall, and dance studio are amongst the university's athletic facilities.

Disabled Students: The Advising and Access Services Centre is available to assist students who require support.

Services: Counseling and information services are available, as is tutoring in most subjects. There is a reader service for the blind, and remedial math and writing.

Campus Safety and Security: Measures include 24-hour foot and vehicle patrol, emergency notification system, self-defense education, and security escort services. There are shuttle buses, emergency telephones, lighted pathways/sidewalks, and controlled access to dorms/residences.

Programs of Study: Master's and doctoral degrees are also awarded. Bachelor's degrees are awarded in AGRICULTURE (agricultural economics, agricultural sciences, and animal science), BIOLOGICAL SCIENCE (biochemistry, biology/biological science, marine biology, microbiology, and neurosciences), BUSINESS (accounting, banking and finance, business administration and management, business economics, and recreation and leisure services), COMMUNICATIONS AND THE ARTS (classics, dramatic arts, English, French, German, music, Russian, and Spanish), COMPUTER AND PHYSICAL SCIENCE (chemistry, computer science, earth science, mathematics, physics, and statistics), EDUCATION (health education), ENGINEERING AND ENVIRONMENTAL DESIGN (chemical engineering, city/community/regional planning, and engineering), HEALTH PROFESSIONS (dental hygiene, nursing, occupational therapy, pharmacy, physical therapy, predentistry, and premedicine), SOCIAL SCIENCE (Canadian studies, economics, history, international studies, law, philosophy, physical fitness/movement, political science/government, psychology, religion, social work, sociology, and women's studies).

Special: There is a freshman honors program.

Faculty/Classroom: No introductory courses are taught by graduate students.

Requirements: For 2014-15 applicants from the US must have an SAT result of at least 1650 or an ACT composite score of 23 and no individual score less than 20. Grade 12 credit in English is required. An audition is necessary for music students. AP credits are accepted.

Procedure: Freshmen are admitted to all sessions. There are early decision, early admissions, deferred admissions, and rolling admissions plans. Check with the school for current application deadlines. The application fee is $65. Applications are accepted on-line.

Transfer: Applicants are assessed on an individual basis.

Visiting: There are regularly scheduled orientations for prospective students. There are guides for informal visits and visitors may sit in on classes. To schedule a visit, contact Campus Tours at (902) 494-2587.

Financial Aid: Check with the school for current application deadlines.

International Students: The school actively recruits these students. They must take the SAT or ACT.

Computers: All students may access the system. There are no time limits and no fees.

Admissions Contact: E-Mail: *admissions@dal.ca* Web: *www.dal.ca*

LAVAL UNIVERSITY E-2

Quebec, PQ G1K 7P4 (418) 656-2764
(877) 785-2825; (418) 656-5216

Full-time: 9000 men, 13000 women	**Faculty:** n/av
Part-time: 3345 men, 5487 women	**Ph.D.s:** 90%
Graduate: 4914 men, 5458 women	**Student/Faculty:** n/av
Year: semesters, summer session	**Tuition:** $2092 ($10,749)
Application Deadline:	**Room & Board:** $9100

Freshman Class: 28717 applied, 20234 accepted, 10726 enrolled

Laval University, founded in 1852, is the oldest French-language university in North America. It offers undergraduate and graduate programs through 17 faculties and 9 institutes. There are 16 undergraduate schools and 17 graduate schools. In addition to regional accreditation, has baccalaureate program accreditation with AACSB. The 2 libraries contain 3.4 million volumes, 1.3 million microform items, and 37,832 audio/video tapes/CDs/DVDs, and subscribe to 17,625 periodicals including electronic. Computerized library services include interlibrary loans, database searching, and Internet access. Special learning facilities include an art gallery, natural history museum, radio station, a language lab, and business simulations. The 465-acre campus is in an urban area 2 miles west of old Quebec City. Including any residence halls, there are 35 buildings.

Student Life: 94% of undergraduates are from Quebec. The average age of all undergraduates is 26.

Housing: 2400 students can be accommodated in college housing, which includes single-sex and coed on-campus apartments. On-campus housing is available on a first-come, first-served basis. All students may keep cars.

Activities: There are no fraternities or sororities. There are 150 groups on campus, including art, band, chess, choir, chorale, computers, dance, drama, ethnic, film, forensics, gay, international, jazz band, literary magazine, musical theater, newspaper, opera, orchestra, photography, political, radio and TV, religious, social, social service, student government, and symphony. Popular campus events include Thematic Weeks, Rendez-vous Laval, and Student Festivals.

Sports: There are 13 intercollegiate sports for men and 10 for women, and 7 intramural sports for men and 7 for women. Facilities include a covered stadium with a 200-meter running track and 4 tennis courts; a 50-meter swimming pool with a 10-meter diving tower; a double ice arena; 1 triple and 2 single gyms; 4 squash courts; 4 handball and racquetball courts; judo, karate, and self-defense rooms; a dance studio; an open-air stadium with a 400-meter running track; softball, football, and soccer fields; 6 outdoor tennis courts; 3 physical training rooms; a golf driving range; an indoor golf practice room; 2 outdoor basketball courts; a 1-kilometer hiking trail; and a jogging track.

Disabled Students: 95% of the campus is accessible. Facilities include wheelchair ramps, elevators, special parking, specially equipped restrooms, special class scheduling, lowered drinking fountains, lowered telephones. teletype machines for the deaf, computerized classrooms for the visually disabled, electric doors, sidewalks adjusted for physically disabled students, elevators equipped with speaking devices, and a campus plan in braille.

Services: There is a reader service for the blind, and remedial math and writing. Tutoring in French grammar is available

Campus Safety and Security: Measures include 24-hour foot and vehicle patrol and security escort services. There are emergency telephones, lighted pathways/sidewalks, services include 24-hour camera surveillance in pedestrian tunnels and trained evacuating teams in all buildings. Security training for social events is offered to all student associations.

Programs of Study: confers B.A., B.Sc., B.A.A., B.A.V., B.Ed., B.Ens., B.Ing., B.Mus., B.Pharm., B.Sc.A., B.Sc.Arch., B.Serv.Soc., B.Th. and LL.B. degrees. Master's and doctoral degrees are also awarded. Bachelor's degrees are awarded in AGRICULTURE (agricultural business management, agricultural economics, agronomy, forest engineering, forestry and related sciences, and wood science), BIOLOGICAL SCIENCE (biochemistry, biology/biological science, microbiology, and nutrition), BUSINESS (business administration and management), COMMUNICATIONS AND THE ARTS (art, art history and appreciation, communications, dramatic arts, English, English as a second/foreign language, French, languages, linguistics, literature, music, and visual and performing arts), COMPUTER AND PHYSICAL SCIENCE (actuarial science, chemistry, computer science, geology, geoscience, mathematics, physics, software engineering, and statistics), EDUCATION (art education, athletic training, early childhood education, education, elementary education, music education, physical education, secondary education, and technical education), ENGINEERING AND ENVIRONMENTAL DESIGN (agricultural engineering, architecture, chemical engineering, civil engineering, computer engineering, electrical/electronics engineering, engineering and applied science, engineering physics, geological engineering, graphic arts technology, industrial administration/management, mechanical engineering, metallurgical engineering, and mining and mineral engineering), HEALTH PROFESSIONS (nursing, occupational therapy, pharmacy, physical therapy, predentistry, and premedicine), SOCIAL SCIENCE (anthropology, classical/ancient civilization, consumer services, counseling/psychology, economics, food science, French studies, geography, history, interdisciplinary studies, international studies, Judaic studies, law, philosophy, physical fitness/movement, political science/government, psychology, social work, sociology, Spanish studies, and theological studies). Business administration, sciences, and education have the largest enrollments.

Required: Requirements for graduation vary according to the program. A minimum GPA of 2.0 out of 4.33 is required per 30 credits.

Special: Laval offers co-op programs in forest operation, mining, metallurgical engineering, mineral engineering, and wood processing engineering, and study abroad in 65 countries. Dual majors are possible in anthropology and ethnology, economics and politics, international studies and modern languages, historical sciences and patrimonial studies, French language and professional writing, math and computer science. Intensive French courses are offered during the summer.

Faculty/Classroom: All teach undergraduates. No introductory courses are taught by graduate students.

Admissions: 70% of the 2013-2014 applicants were accepted.

Requirements: The only general requirement is the D.E.C. (Diploma of

Collegial Studies 13 years of scholarity) or the equivalent. Some programs have specific requirements. All undergraduate students (except those who are nonfrancophones) must show a sufficient knowledge of the French language to obtain their bachelor's degree.

Procedure: Freshmen are admitted to all sessions. Check with the school for current application deadlines. Applications are accepted on-line.

Transfer: 1662 transfer students enrolled in 2012-2013. Applicants must have the D.E.C. or the equivalent.

Visiting: There are regularly scheduled orientations for prospective students. There are guides for informal visits and visitors may stay overnight. To schedule a visit, contact the Public Affairs Office at (877) 785-2825.

Financial Aid: The deadline for filing freshman financial aid applications for fall entry is June 30.

International Students: There are 1013 international students enrolled. The school actively recruits these students.

Computers: All students may access the system 24 hours a day. There are no time limits and no fees.

Graduates: From July 1, 2012 to June 30, 2013, 6734 bachelor's degrees were awarded. The most popular majors were administration (18%), science and engineering (14%), and letters (13%). 14000 companies recruited on campus in 2012-2013. Of the 2012 graduating class, 83% were employed within 6 months of graduation.

Admissions Contact: Public Affairs Office E-Mail: *accveil@*dap.ulaval.ca Web: *www.ulaval.ca/bip*

MCGILL UNIVERSITY — E-2

Montreal, PQ H3A oG4 — **(514) 398-3910; (514) 398-5544**

Full-time: 6899 men, 10952 women	**Faculty:** n/av
Part-time: 1200 men, 2056 women	**Ph.D.s:** 95%
Graduate: 3464 men, 3900 women	**Student/Faculty:** n/av
Year: semesters, summer session	**Tuition:** $2826 ($6018)
Application Deadline: March 1	**Room & Board:** $7964
Freshman Class: 18963 applied, 10689 accepted, 4834 enrolled	
SAT: required	**ACT:** 29

McGill University, founded in 1821, is a publicly funded private institution that grants undergraduate, graduate, and professional degrees. Tuition fees may vary depending on program. Higher rates are charged to international students. There are 11 undergraduate schools and 79 graduate schools. In addition to regional accreditation, McGill has baccalaureate program accreditation with APTA. The 14 libraries contain 3.3 million volumes, 1.6 million microform items, and 71,765 audio/video tapes/CDs/DVDs, and subscribe to 22,513 periodicals including electronic. Computerized library services include interlibrary loans and database searching. Special learning facilities include a natural history museum, radio station, McCord Museum of Canadian History, Mont St. Hilaire Nature Conservation Center, an herbarium, an arboretum, a subarctic research station, the Institute of Air and Space Law, the Institute of Islamic Studies, the Redpath Museum of Natural History, the Lyman Entomological Museum, the Ecomuseum, the Osler Library of the History of Medicine, and the Lande Canadiana Collection. The 80-acre campus is in an urban area in downtown Montreal, with the MacDonald campus located on the far west end of the island. Including any residence halls, there are 150 buildings.

Student Life: 53% of undergraduates are from Quebec. Others are from 140 foreign countries. 17% are Foreign. The average age of freshmen is 19; all undergraduates, 21.

Housing: 2080 students can be accommodated in college housing, which includes single-sex and coed dorms, off-campus apartments, and married student housing. On-campus housing is available on a lottery system for upperclassmen. Priority is given to out-of-town students. 83% of students commute.

Activities: 4% of men belong to 1 local and 12 national fraternities; 2% of women belong to 4 national sororities. There are 180 groups on campus, including and drive-safe program, walk-safe, band, cheerleading, chess, choir, chorale, chorus, computers, dance, debate, drama, ethnic, film, gay, honors, international, jazz band, literary magazine, Model UN, musical theater, newspaper, opera, orchestra, photography, political, professional, radio and TV, religious, social, social service, student government, symphony, and yearbook. Popular campus events include Multicultural Festivals, 4-Floor Parties, Music, Film and Theatrical Productions.

Sports: There are 23 intercollegiate sports for men and 24 for women, and 23 intramural sports for men and 15 for women. Facilities include a 20,000-seat stadium; a 1,000-seat competition hall; 2 double gyms for basketball, volleyball, and badminton; 8 outdoor tennis courts; 4 indoor tennis courts; a 400-meter outdoor track and a banked 6-lane 200-meter indoor track; 2 weight-training rooms; dance, aerobics, and martial arts rooms; 1 pool; a gymnastics facility; 3 sports fields; a fitness center; a sport medicine center; and hyperbaric chamber.

Disabled Students: 80% of the campus is accessible. Facilities include wheelchair ramps, elevators, special parking, specially equipped restrooms, special class scheduling, lowered telephones. Braille, variable-speed tape recorders, talking calculators, books on tape, exam accommodations, adapted computers (voice synthesis and voice recognition), sign language interpreters, computerized note taking, note takers, print enlargement, readers, and adapted transport.

Services: Counseling and information services are available, as is tutoring in every subject. There is a reader service for the blind, and remedial math, reading, and writing.

Campus Safety and Security: Measures include 24-hour foot and vehicle patrol and security escort services. There are emergency telephones and lighted pathways/sidewalks.

Programs of Study: McGill confers B.A., B.C.L., B.Com., B.Ed., B.Eng., B.Mus., B.Sc., B.Sc.Agr., B.Sc.Agr.Eng., B.Sc.Arch., B.Sc.F.Sc., B.Sc.N., B.Sc.Nutr.Sc., B.Sc.Occ.Ther., B.Sc.Phys.Ther., B.S.W., B.Th. and LL.B. degrees. Master's and doctoral degrees are also awarded. Bachelor's degrees are awarded in AGRICULTURE (agricultural economics, agriculture, animal science, conservation and regulation, plant science, and soil science), BIOLOGICAL SCIENCE (anatomy, biochemistry, biology/biological science, botany, cell biology, environmental biology, microbiology, molecular biology, nutrition, physiology, wildlife biology, and zoology), BUSINESS (accounting, banking and finance, entrepreneurial studies, human resources, institutional management, insurance and risk management, international business management, labor studies, management information systems, management science, marketing management, and organizational behavior), COMMUNICATIONS AND THE ARTS (art history and appreciation, classics, English, French, jazz, linguistics, modern language, music history and appreciation, music performance, music technology, music theory and composition, Russian, and Spanish), COMPUTER AND PHYSICAL SCIENCE (applied mathematics, atmospheric sciences and meteorology, chemistry, computer science, earth science, geology, geophysics and seismology, information sciences and systems, mathematics, physics, planetary and space science, and software engineering), EDUCATION (elementary education, foreign languages education, music education, physical education, secondary education, special education, teaching English as a second/foreign language (TESOL/TEFOL), and vocational education), ENGINEERING AND ENVIRONMENTAL DESIGN (agricultural engineering, architecture, chemical engineering, civil engineering, computer engineering, electrical/electronics engineering, environmental science, mechanical engineering, metallurgical engineering, and mining and mineral engineering), HEALTH PROFESSIONS (clinical science, exercise science, nursing, occupational therapy, and physical therapy), SOCIAL SCIENCE (African studies, American studies, anthropology, Canadian studies, Caribbean studies, dietetics, East Asian studies, economics, food science, French studies, geography, German area studies, Hispanic American studies, history, humanities, international studies, Italian studies, Judaic studies, Latin American studies, law, Middle Eastern studies, philosophy, political science/government, psychology, religion, social work, sociology, Western civilization/culture, and women's studies).

Required: To graduate, students must successfully complete a required number of approved credits, usually between 90 and 120. Students must also be in satisfactory standing, with a minimum cumulative GPA of 2.0.

Special: There is cross-registration with area universities. Study abroad, work-study within the university, co-op programs in mining and metallurgical engineering, dual majors, internships, and student-designed majors are available. There are 6 departmental honors programs.

Faculty/Classroom: 67% of faculty are male; 33% are female. No introductory courses are taught by graduate students. The average class size in an introductory lecture is 30; in a laboratory is 25; and in a regular course is 45.

Admissions: 56% of the 2013-2014 applicants were accepted.

Requirements: The SAT is required. The ACT may be submitted instead of the SAT. McGill requires applicants to be in the upper 25% of their class. A GPA of 3.3 is required. AP credits are accepted. Important factors in the admissions decision are advanced placement or honors courses, recommendations by school officials, and evidence of special talent.

Procedure: Freshmen are admitted fall. Entrance exams should be taken during the spring of the junior year and/or fall of the senior year. There are deferred admissions and rolling admissions plans. Applications should be filed by March 1 for fall entry, along with a $60 fee. Applications are accepted on-line.

Transfer: 528 transfer students enrolled in 2012-2013. Requirements vary with the program. Standard admission requirements must also be met. Students must submit high school and college transcripts and have a 3.0 GPA in college coursework. 60 of 90 credits required for the bachelor's degree must be completed at McGill.

Visiting: There are regularly scheduled orientations for prospective students, with a varying agenda (including campus tours and student for a day programs). There are guides for informal visits, visitors may sit in on classes, and stay overnight. To schedule a visit, contact the Welcome Center at (514) 398-6555 (tours).

Financial Aid: In 2013-2014, 30% of all full-time freshmen and 17% of continuing full-time students received some form of financial aid. The average freshman award was $5,855. Need-based scholarships or need-based grants averaged $3,022; and need-based self-help aid (loans and jobs) averaged $6,146. McGill is a member of CSS. The FAFSA and the college's own financial statement are required. The deadline for filing freshman financial aid applications for fall entry is June 1.

International Students: There are 3732 international students enrolled. The school actively recruits these students. They must take the TOEFL or MELAB. A McGill Certificate of Proficiency in English must be earned. SAT and/or ACT tests are required for U.S.

Computers: All students may access the system any time. There are no fees.

Graduates: From July 1, 2012 to June 30, 2013, 4277 bachelor's degrees were awarded. The most popular majors were social sciences (18%), health professions (11%), and biological/life sciences (10%). In an average class, 65% graduate in 4 years or less, 81% graduate in 5 years or less, and 83% graduate in 6 years or less.

Admissions Contact: Admissions, Recruitment, and Registrar's Office E-Mail: *admissions@mcgill.ca* Web: *www.mcgill.ca*

MCMASTER UNIVERSITY E-3

Hamilton, ON L8S 4K1 **(905) 525-4600; (905) 527-1105**

Full-time: 5400 men, 7000 women	**Faculty:** 927
Part-time: 900 men, 1900 women	**Ph.D.s:** n/av
Graduate: 1190 men, 1030 women	**Student/Faculty:** 13 to 1
Year: n/app	**Tuition:** $6000 ($18,000)
Application Deadline:	**Room & Board:** $6700
Freshman Class: n/av	

McMaster University is a public nonsectarian institution, offering programs in the arts and sciences, business, engineering, health sciences, kinesiology, and social work. There are 2 graduate schools. The 4 libraries contain 1.7 million volumes, 1.4 million microform items, 19,500 audio/video tapes/CDs/DVDs, and subscribe to 11,976 periodicals including electronic. Computerized library services include interlibrary loans and database searching. Special learning facilities include an art gallery, planetarium, radio station, a nuclear reactor, tandem accelerator, a greenhouses, Chedoke-McMaster Hospital, a communication research lab, Bertrand Russell archives, Humanities Communication Centre, and computing labs. The 300-acre campus is in an urban area 60 miles southwest of Toronto. Including any residence halls, there are 44 buildings.

Student Life: 95% of undergraduates are from Ontario. Others are from 12 states, and 79 foreign countries. The average age of freshmen is 20; all undergraduates, 22. 1% do not continue beyond their first year.

Housing: 2765 students can be accommodated in college housing, which includes single-sex and coed dorms and on-campus apartments. In addition, there are language houses, La Maison Francaise, an international house, and a quiet house. On-campus housing is guaranteed for the freshman year only and is available on a lottery system for upperclassmen. Priority is given to out-of-town students. 77% of students commute. All students may keep cars.

Activities: There are no fraternities or sororities. There are 100 groups on campus, including academic, art, band, cheerleading, chess, choir, chorale, chorus, computers, debate, drama, ethnic, gay, international, jazz band, musical theater, newspaper, orchestra, photography, political, radio and TV, religious, social, student government, and yearbook. Popular campus events include Marauder Weekend.

Sports: There are 16 intercollegiate sports for men and 14 for women, and 16 intramural sports for men and 14 for women. Facilities include an outdoor track and field, a mini-weight room, a swimming pool, cross-country trails, rugby, soccer, and football fields, tennis, squash, and handball courts, and a state-of-the-art fitness facility.

Disabled Students: 60% of the campus is accessible. Facilities include wheelchair ramps, elevators, special parking, specially equipped restrooms, special class scheduling, lowered telephones, and basement-level and above-ground tunnels with connecting walkways.

Services: Counseling and information services are available, as is tutoring in some subjects. There is a reader service for the blind. and may be arranged through individual departments.

Campus Safety and Security: Measures include 24-hour foot and vehicle patrol and security escort services. There are shuttle buses, emergency telephones, lighted pathways/sidewalks, additional services include the Emergency First-Response Team, Mac Alert bulletins, a campus watch program, a prevention programs officer, and video monitoring in some parking areas.

Programs of Study: Mac confers B.A., B.S., B.A.S., B.A./B.S.W., B.C., B.Eng., B.Eng./Management, B.Eng./Society, B.H.S., B.Kinesiology, B.Mus. and B.S.N. degrees. Master's and doctoral degrees are also awarded. Bachelor's degrees are awarded in BIOLOGICAL SCIENCE (biochemistry, biology/biological science, and life science), BUSINESS (business administration and management and labor studies), COMMUNICATIONS AND THE ARTS (art, art history and appreciation, classics, comparative literature, dramatic arts, English, French, linguistics, modern language, music, and Russian), COMPUTER AND PHYSICAL SCIENCE (chemistry, computer science, earth science, geology, mathematics, physical sciences, physics, science, and statistics), ENGINEERING AND ENVIRONMENTAL DESIGN (chemical engineering, civil engineering, computer engineering, electrical/electronics engineering, engineering physics, environmental science, manufacturing engineering, materials engineering, materials science, and mechanical engineering), HEALTH PROFESSIONS (medical science, nursing, occupational therapy, and physical therapy), SOCIAL SCIENCE (anthropology, economics, geography, German area studies, gerontology, history, interdisciplinary studies, Japanese studies, Latin American studies, liberal arts/general studies, philosophy, physical fitness/movement, political science/government, psychology, religion, social work, sociology, and women's studies).

Required: Requirements for graduation vary according to the program of study. A minimum 3.5 GPA in 90 to 150 units is required for most programs.

Special: Many opportunities exist to combine 2 subjects of study within 1 faculty, or between 2 faculties. All honors students have the option of taking a minor in a second subject area. Nondegree study is possible through the Center for Continuing Education. Internships and study abroad are offered. Students may repeat failed courses provided they are eligible to continue in the program. There are 37 departmental honors programs.

Faculty/Classroom: 71% of faculty are male; 29% are female. All teach and do research. No introductory courses are taught by graduate students.

Requirements: U.S. applicants must have a high school grade average of 80. Applicants must be graduates of an accredited secondary school. The required high school courses should include 5 years each of English and math. A portfolio is required for art students and an audition for music students. A supplementary application form is required for some programs. Offers of admission are made based on academic standing and audition/portfolio/supplementary application requirements where necessary. A GPA of 80.0 is required. Important factors in the admissions decision are evidence of special talent, extracurricular activities record, and leadership record.

Procedure: Freshmen are admitted to all sessions. There is a early decision plan. Check with the school for current application deadlines.

Transfer: Applicants are considered on an individual basis. Review of high school, college, and/or university work determines admission status.

Visiting: There are regularly scheduled orientations for prospective students, including campus tours, information sessions, and panel discussions. There are guides for informal visits and visitors may sit in on classes. To schedule a visit, contact Tour Coordinator, Division of Student Liaison.

Financial Aid: 50% of all full-time freshmen students received need-based aid. 12% of undergraduate students work part-time. Average annual earnings from campus work are $1411. The deadline for filing freshman financial aid applications for fall entry is July 15.

International Students: The school actively recruits these students. They must take the TOEFL or MELAB.

Computers: All students may access the system any time. There are no time limits and no fees.

Graduates: From July 1, 2012 to June 30, 2013, 3000 bachelor's degrees were awarded.

Admissions Contact: Sam Digiandomenico, Associate Registrar Admissions. E-Mail: *macadmit@mcmail.mcmaster.ca* Web: *www.mcmaster.ca*

MEMORIAL UNIVERSITY OF NEWFOUNDLAND F-2

St. John's, NF A1C 5S7 **(709) 737-3705**
(866) 354-8896; (709) 737-2337

Full-time: 5000 men, 7000 women	**Faculty:** 932
Part-time: 690 men, 1350 women	**Ph.D.s:** 50%
Graduate: 840 men, 760 women	**Student/Faculty:** 12 to 1
Year: varies, summer session	**Tuition:** $4202 ($7510)
Application Deadline: March 1	**Room & Board:** $4686
Freshman Class: n/av	

Memorial University of Newfoundland, founded in 1925, is a public liberal arts institution. The figures in the above capsule and in this profile are approximate. There are 13 undergraduate schools and 12 graduate schools. The 3 libraries contain 2.5 million volumes, and subscribe to 700 periodicals including electronic. Computerized library services include interlibrary loans and database searching. Special learning facilities include an art gallery, natural history museum, planetarium, radio station, TV station, a language labs. The 220-acre campus is in an urban area within St. John's. Including any residence halls, there are 40 buildings.

Student Life: 98% of undergraduates are from Newfoundland.

Housing: 1750 students can be accommodated in college housing, which includes single-sex and coed dorms, on-campus apartments, off-campus apartments, and married student housing. On-campus housing is available on a first-come and first-served basis. Priority is given to out-of-town students. 89% of students commute. All students may keep cars.

Activities: There are no fraternities or sororities. There are 100 groups on campus, including and academic., band, cheerleading, chess, choir, chorale, computers, dance, debate, drama, ethnic, gay, international, jazz band, literary magazine, musical theater, newspaper, orchestra, photography, political, professional, radio and TV, religious, single parent, social, social service, student government, symphony, and yearbook. Popular campus events include Winter Carnival and Orientation.

Sports: There are 6 intercollegiate sports for men and 6 for women, and 6 intramural sports for men and 6 for women. Facilities include a gym, squash courts, a rifle range, a weight room, a soccer field, and swimming facilities.

Disabled Students: 85% of the campus is accessible. Facilities include wheelchair ramps, elevators, special parking, specially equipped restrooms, special class scheduling, lowered drinking fountains, lowered telephones. classroom aids, note-taking volunteers, and other facilities based on individual needs.

Services: There is a reader service for the blind, and remedial math, reading, and writing. Students staying in residence have access to tutoring in every subject. In addition, lectures are offered on topics such as public speaking, speed reading, and time management.

Campus Safety and Security: Measures include 24-hour foot and vehicle patrol, self-defense education, and security escort services. There are emergency telephones and lighted pathways/sidewalks.

Programs of Study: MUN confers B.A., B.Sc., B.Comm.(Co-op.), B.Comm.(Gen.), B.Ed., B.Eng., B.F.A., B.Kin., B.M.S., B.Mus., B.Mus.Ed., B.Med.Sc., B.N., B.P.E., B.Rec., B.Sc.(Pharm.), B.Spec.Ed., B.S.W., B.Tech. and B.Voc.Ed. degrees. Master's and doctoral degrees are also awarded. Bachelor's degrees are awarded in AGRICULTURE (forestry and related sciences), BIOLOGICAL SCIENCE (biochemistry, biology/biological science, cell biology, ecology, entomology, environmental biology, evolutionary biology, marine biology, marine science, microbiology, and neurosciences), BUSINESS (entrepreneurial studies, human resources, labor studies, management science, marketing/retailing/merchandising, organizational behavior, and small business management), COMMUNICATIONS AND THE ARTS (dramatic arts, English, English literature, fine arts, folklore and mythology, French, German, linguistics, literature, music, music history and appreciation, music performance, music theory and composition, Russian, Spanish, and visual and performing arts), COMPUTER AND PHYSICAL SCIENCE (applied mathematics, applied physics, chemistry, computer science, earth science, information sciences and systems, mathematics, oceanography, and statistics), EDUCATION (athletic training, education, elementary education, guidance education, middle school education, music education, physical education, recreation education, secondary education, and special education), ENGINEERING AND ENVIRONMENTAL DESIGN (civil engineering, electrical/electronics engineering, engineering technology, maritime science, mechanical engineering, naval architecture and marine engineering, and ocean engineering), HEALTH PROFESSIONS (medical science, nursing, and pharmacy), SOCIAL SCIENCE (anthropology, archeology, Canadian studies, criminology, dietetics, economics, French studies, geography, German area studies, history, humanities, medieval studies, philosophy, physical fitness/movement, political science/government, psychology, religion, social studies, social work, sociology, Spanish studies, and women's studies). Marine biology, naval architecture, and business are the strongest academically. Arts, science, business, and engineering have the largest enrollments.

Required: Students must complete 40 to 50 credits to graduate. Each discipline has different requirements for graduation.

Special: The university offers co-op programs in commerce, phys ed, recreation, kinesiology, and engineering. Internships are available in education and nursing. Study abroad may be arranged in at least 20 countries. Work-study programs, dual majors, and B.A.-B.S. degrees are available. There are 3 departmental honors programs.

Faculty/Classroom: 80% of faculty are male; 20% are female. All teach and do research. Graduate students teach 71% of introductory courses. The average class size in an introductory lecture is 40.

Requirements: Admission is based on a 70% high school average as computed from university preparatory courses required for admission. Applications are accepted on-line. A GPA of 70.0 is required. AP credits are accepted.

Procedure: Freshmen are admitted to all sessions. There is a rolling admissions plan. Applications should be filed by March 1 for fall entry; October 1 for winter entry; February 1 for spring entry; and February 1 for summer entry. The fall 2013 application fee was $80.

Transfer: 499 transfer students enrolled in 2012-2013. Applicants must be in good academic standing at the previous institution. 10 of 40 credits required for the bachelor's degree must be completed at MUN.

Visiting: There are regularly scheduled orientations for prospective students, including various student activities, mock lectures, campus tours, and educational sessions. There are guides for informal visits and visitors may sit in on classes. To schedule a visit, contact the Student Development at (709) 737-2192.

Financial Aid: Average annual earnings from campus work are $1000. Check with the school for current application deadlines.

International Students: There are 135 international students enrolled. The school actively recruits these students. They must take the TOEFL or MELAB.

Computers: All students may access the system. There are no time limits and no fees.

Graduates: From July 1, 2012 to June 30, 2013, 2317 bachelor's degrees were awarded. The most popular majors were business (13%), biology (7%), and sociology (6%). In an average class, 75% graduate in 4 years or less, 20% graduate in 5 years or less, and 5% graduate in 6 years or less. Of the 2012 graduating class, 24% were enrolled in graduate school within 6 months of graduation, and 63% were employed.

Admissions Contact: Phyllis McCann, Manager of Admissions. E-Mail: *pmccann@morgan.ucs.mun.ca*

QUEEN'S UNIVERSITY E-3

Kingston, ON K7L 3N6 **(613) 533-2218; (613) 533-6810**

Full-time: n/av	**Faculty:** 973
Part-time: n/av	**Ph.D.s:** n/av
Graduate: n/av	**Student/Faculty:** 13 to 1
Year: semesters, summer session	**Tuition:** $5800 ($13,000)
Application Deadline:	**Room & Board:** $0000
Freshman Class: n/av	
SAT: required	

Queen's University, founded in 1841, is a public institution offering undergraduate and graduate programs in the arts and sciences, business, engineering, health sciences, and teacher education. The figures in the above capsule and in this profile are approximate. There are 10 undergraduate schools and 5 graduate schools. The 8 libraries contain 1.8 million volumes, 2.0 million microform items, and 7,000 audio/video tapes/CDs/DVDs, and subscribe to 15,000 periodicals including electronic. Computerized library services include interlibrary loans and database searching. Special learning facilities include an art gallery, radio station, TV station, a geology museum, and observatory. The 160-acre campus is in an urban area 150 miles east of Toronto. Including any residence halls, there are 100 buildings.

Student Life: 85% of undergraduates are from Ontario. Others are from 80 foreign countries. 89% are from public schools. 5% do not continue beyond their first year; 90% remain to graduate.

Housing: 3071 students can be accommodated in college housing, which includes single-sex and coed dorms, on-campus apartments, off-campus apartments, and married student housing. In addition, there are language houses, special-interest houses, study floors, and nonsmoking floors. On-campus housing is guaranteed for the freshman year only. 80% of students commute. All students may keep cars.

Activities: There are no fraternities or sororities. There are 220 groups on campus, including art, bagpipe, band, cheerleading, chess, choir, chorale, chorus, computers, dance, debate, drama, ethnic, film, gay, international, jazz band, literary magazine, marching band, musical theater, newspaper, orchestra, photography, political, professional, radio and TV, religious, social, social service, student government, symphony, and yearbook. Popular campus events include Orientation Week, Alumni Weekend, and Applied Science Formal.

Sports: There are 19 intercollegiate sports for men and 21 for women, and 39 intramural sports for men and 39 for women. Facilities include a pool, an indoor track, a hockey arena, tennis, squash, racquetball courts, a weight room, a dance studio, and a projectile range. There is also a 5000-seat indoor gym and a 12000-seat football stadium.

Disabled Students: 80% of the campus is accessible. Facilities include wheelchair ramps, elevators, special parking, specially equipped restrooms, special class scheduling, lowered drinking fountains, and lowered telephones.

Services: Counseling and information services are available, as is tutoring in most subjects. There is a reader service for the blind, and remedial math, reading, and writing.

Campus Safety and Security: Measures include 24-hour foot and vehicle patrol, self-defense education, and security escort services. There are shuttle buses, emergency telephones, and lighted pathways/sidewalks.

Programs of Study: Queen's confers B.A., B.Sc., B.A./B.Ed., B.A./B.Phe., B.Comm., B.F.A., B.Mus., B.N.Sc., B.Sc./B.Ed., B.Sc./B.Phe., B.S.C.E., B.Sc.O.T. and B.Sc.P.T. degrees. Master's and doctoral degrees are also awarded. Bachelor's degrees are awarded in BIOLOGICAL SCIENCE (biochemistry, biology/biological science, and life science), COMMUNICATIONS AND THE ARTS (art history and appreciation, classics, dramatic arts, English, film arts, fine arts, French, German, Greek, Italian, Latin, music, and Spanish), COMPUTER AND PHYSICAL SCIENCE (chemistry, computer science, geology, mathematics, physics, and statistics), EDUCATION (elementary education, middle school education, and secondary education), ENGINEERING AND ENVIRONMENTAL DESIGN (chemical engineering, civil engineering, electrical/electronics engineering, engineering physics, geological engineering, and mechanical engineering), HEALTH PROFESSIONS (health, nursing, occupational therapy, and physical therapy), SOCIAL SCIENCE (economics, geography, history, Judaic studies, philosophy, political science/government, psychology, religion, sociology, and women's studies). Arts, science, and engineering have the largest enrollments.

Required: Each faculty and school establishes the academic requirements for the graduation of its students.

Special: Internships are available in life science, commerce, and engineering. Students may study abroad in 25 countries. Dual majors are available. Cross-registration with St. Lawrence College for the B.S.N. is possible. There are a freshman honors program and 20 departmental honors programs.

Faculty/Classroom: 72% of faculty are male; 27% are female. All teach undergraduates. No introductory courses are taught by graduate students. The average class size in a laboratory is 40.

Requirements: The SAT is required. Candidates for admission are required to submit a school profile. Applications are accepted on-line. A GPA of 70.0 is required. Important factors in the admissions decision are evidence of special talent, leadership record, and extracurricular activities record.

Procedure: Freshmen are admitted fall. There are deferred admissions and rolling admissions plans. Check with the school for current application deadlines. The application fee is $125. Notifications are sent May 27. Applications are accepted on-line.

Transfer: 151 transfer students enrolled in 2012-2013. Admission requirements for transfer applicants vary by program. 10 of 19 credits required for the bachelor's degree must be completed at Queen's.

Visiting: There are regularly scheduled orientations for prospective students, consisting of a short briefing session and a walking tour. There are guides for informal visits, visitors may sit in on classes, and stay overnight. To schedule a visit, contact Student Recruitment at (613) 533-2217.

Financial Aid: 9% of all full-time freshmen students received need-based aid. The deadline for filing freshman financial aid applications for fall entry is May 13.

International Students: There are 396 international students enrolled. The school actively recruits these students. They must take the TOEFL or MELAB. They must also take the SAT, scoring 1200.

Computers: All students may access the system 24 hours.

Graduates: From July 1, 2012 to June 30, 2013, 3506 bachelor's degrees were awarded.

Admissions Contact: Dr. David Walker, Dean. E-Mail: *deanfhs@.queensu.ca* Web: *www.queensu.ca*

RYERSON UNIVERSITY — E-3

Toronto, ON M5B 2K3 — **(416) 979-5036; (416) 979-5067**

Full-time: n/av	**Faculty:** n/av
Part-time: n/av	**Ph.D.s:** 63%
Graduate: n/av	**Student/Faculty:** 23 to 1
Year: semesters, summer session	**Tuition:** $6500 ($17,500)
Application Deadline: February 1	**Room & Board:** $10,500
Freshman Class: n/av	
SAT or ACT: recommended	

Ryerson Polytechnic University, founded in 1948, is a public institution offering undergraduate programs in arts, applied arts, business, community services, and engineering and applied science. There are 50 undergraduate schools and 37 graduate schools. In addition to regional accreditation, Ryerson has baccalaureate program accreditation with FIDER. The figures in the above capsule and in this profile are approximate. The library contains 477,739 volumes, 842,963 microform items, and 20,235 audio/video tapes/CDs/DVDs, and subscribes to 60,809 periodicals including electronic. Computerized library services include interlibrary loans, database searching, Internet access, and laptop Internet portals. Special learning facilities include a learning resource center, radio station, the BlackStar Historical Black and White Photography Collection, Heidelberg Centre, George Vari Engineering and Computing Centre. The 20-acre campus is in an urban area in downtown Toronto. Including any residence halls, there are 35 buildings.

Student Life: 90% of undergraduates are from Ontario.

Housing: 852 students can be accommodated in college housing, which includes coed dorms. On-campus housing is available on a first-come and first-served basis. Priority is given to out-of-town students. 96% of students commute. All students may keep cars.

Activities: There are no fraternities or sororities. There are 150 groups on campus, including choir, chorale, computers, drama, environmental, ethnic, film, gay, international, literary magazine, musical theater, newspaper, political, professional, radio and TV, religious, social, social service, student government, and yearbook. Popular campus events include orientation, parade, and picnic.

Sports: There are 7 intercollegiate sports for men and 8 for women, and 20 intramural sports for men and 20 for women. Facilities include a recreation and athletic center, 7 squash courts, a fitness training center that includes an indoor running track and weight-training equipment, a rehabilitation center, a 25-yard pool, saunas, 3 studios, and 6 gyms.

Disabled Students: The campus is accessible. Facilities include wheelchair ramps, elevators, special parking, specially equipped restrooms, special class scheduling, lowered drinking fountains, lowered telephones, special housing. test and exam adaptations, computer-equipped exam and study rooms, assistive listening devices for personal use and for use in auditorium settings, advocacy services, individual needs assessment, and access to a wide range of technical devices.

Services: Counseling and information services are available, as is tutoring in most subjects. There is a reader service for the blind, and remedial math, reading, and writing. Services are available in study skills development, critical reading seminars, time management skills, and exam workshops.

Campus Safety and Security: Measures include 24-hour foot and vehicle patrol, emergency notification system, self-defense education, and security escort services. There are emergency telephones, lighted pathways/sidewalks, controlled access to dorms/residences, sexual assault training, harassment prevention and crime prevention programs, and community policing programs.

Programs of Study: Ryerson confers B.A., B.Arch.Sc., B.A.Sc., B.Comm., B.Des., B.Eng., B.H.Sc., B.Sc., B.S.W., B.Tech., and B.U.R.P.I. degrees. Master's and doctoral degrees are also awarded. Bachelor's degrees are awarded in BUSINESS (business administration and management, hospitality management services, and management information systems), COMMUNICATIONS AND THE ARTS (broadcasting, journalism, and photography), COMPUTER AND PHYSICAL SCIENCE (computer programming), EDUCATION (early childhood education), ENGINEERING AND ENVIRONMENTAL DESIGN (aeronautical engineering, architecture, chemical engineering, civil engineering, electrical/electronics engineering, graphic and printing production, industrial engineering, interior design, mechanical engineering, and urban planning technology), HEALTH PROFESSIONS (environmental health science and nursing), SOCIAL SCIENCE (child care/child and family studies, family/consumer studies, fashion design and technology, geography, public administration, and social work). Business management, nursing, and information technology management have the largest enrollments.

Required: To graduate, students must have a 2.0 GPA and complete the requirements of their program of study.

Special: The university offers co-op programs in applied chemistry and biology, chemical engineering, and midwifery. Accelerated degree programs are available in journalism, radio and television arts, nurse practitioner, and nursing, and many programs have a work-study component. There is 1 national honor society and a freshman honors program.

Faculty/Classroom: 32% are female. No introductory courses are taught by graduate students. The average class size in a regular course is 30.

Admissions: 36% of a recent year's applicants were accepted.

Requirements: The SAT or ACT and ACT Writing Test are recommended. In addition, students should be high school graduates with a minimum B overall average. A GPA of 3.0 is required. AP credits are accepted.

Procedure: Freshmen are admitted fall. Applications should be filed by February 1 for fall entry, along with a $130 fee. Notifications are sent in March. Applications are accepted on-line. 7000 applicants were on a recent waiting list.

Transfer: 700 transfer students enrolled in a recent year. Transfer applicants must have completed 1 year at the college level. Acceptance of transfer credits is at the discretion of the Office of Admissions/Liaison/Curriculum Advising. Half of the required credits for a particular degree program must be completed at Ryerson.

Visiting: There are regularly scheduled orientations for prospective students, Student visits include a half-day tour and discussion session featuring campus tours and visits to specific schools and departments. There are guides for informal visits and visitors may sit in on classes. To schedule a visit, contact Undergraduate Admissions and Recruitment.

Financial Aid: Ryerson is a member of CSS. Check with the school for current application deadlines.

International Students: There are 1000 international students enrolled. The school actively recruits these students. They must take the TOEFL with a minimum score of 560 on the paper-based TOEFL (PBT) or 83 on the Internet-based version (iBT) or take the MELAB and the college's own test.

Computers: Wireless access is available. All students may access the system. There are no time limits and no fees.

Admissions Contact: Michelle Beaton, Manager, International Recruitment. E-Mail: *international@ryerson.ca* Web: *www.ryerson.ca*

SIMON FRASER UNIVERSITY B-2

Burnaby, BC V5A 1S6 (778) 782-3995; (778) 782-4969

Full-time: n/av
Part-time: n/av
Graduate: n/av
Year: varies, summer session
Application Deadline: May 1
Freshman Class: n/av
SAT: required
Faculty: n/av
Ph.D.s: 88%
Student/Faculty: n/av
Tuition: $6724 ($17,984)
Room & Board: $7484

Simon Fraser University, established in 1965, is a public institution offering undergraduate and graduate programs in the arts, sciences, business, education, and applied sciences. In addition to its main campus, the university maintains the Harbour Centre campus in downtown Vancouver to provide mid-career education to the urban population and the new SFU Surrey campus offering programs in information technology and interactive arts. There are 8 undergraduate schools and 35 graduate schools. The 3 libraries contain 2.6 million volumes, 936,808 microform items, and 22,649 audio/video tapes/CDs/DVDs, and subscribe to 67,000 periodicals including electronic. Computerized library services include interlibrary loans, database searching, Internet access, and Wi-Fi capability. Special learning facilities include an art gallery, radio station, archeology museum, special literature and map collections, fine and performing arts theater, hypo/hyperbaric chamber, back test unit, rock climbing wall, apiary, underwater lab, television and photography studios, and dance floors. The 400-acre campus is in a suburban area 9 miles east of Vancouver, Canada. Including any residence halls, there are 51 buildings.

Student Life: 89% of undergraduates are from British Columbia. Others are from states, 107 foreign countries, and Canada. 92% are from public schools. The average age of freshmen is 19; all undergraduates, 23.

Housing: 1750 students can be accommodated in college housing, which includes single-sex and coed dorms, on-campus apartments, and married student housing. In addition, there are special-interest houses. On-campus housing is guaranteed for the freshman year only. Priority is given to out-of-town students. 92% of students commute. All students may keep cars.

Activities: There are no fraternities or sororities. There are 35 groups on campus, including gaming, hobbies and preprofessional, special interest, athletic, bagpipe, chess, choir, computers, ethnic, gay, international, newspaper, political, professional, religious, social, social service, and student government. Popular campus events include Terry Fox Day, Gung Hagis Fat Choi, and Robbie Burns Day.

Sports: There are 8 intercollegiate sports for men and 9 for women, and 8 intramural sports for men and 7 for women. Facilities include 3 gyms, swimming and diving pools, a running track, weight rooms, saunas, playing fields, a combative room, tennis, squash, and racquetball courts, and a fitness center.

Disabled Students: 95% of the campus is accessible. Facilities include wheelchair ramps, elevators, special parking, specially equipped restrooms, lowered drinking fountains, lowered telephones, special housing, a braille printer, a visualtek machine, closed-circuit TV for text or graphic enlargement, note taking tutor support, adaptive technology, exam modifications, sign language interpreters, closed captioning in lectures, and alternate format texts.

Services: There is a reader service for the blind. There are taped library books. Some lectures are taped.

Campus Safety and Security: Measures include 24-hour foot and vehicle patrol and security escort services. There are emergency telephones, lighted pathways/sidewalks, controlled access to dorms/residences, safe-walk stations, and student patrols.

Programs of Study: SFU confers B.A., B.A.Sc., B.B.A., B.E.D., B.F.A., B.G.S. and B.Sc. degrees. Master's and doctoral degrees are also awarded. Bachelor's degrees are awarded in BIOLOGICAL SCIENCE (biology/biological science, molecular biology, and physiology), BUSINESS (business administration and management and management science), COMMUNICATIONS AND THE ARTS (art, communications, dance, dramatic arts, English, film arts, French, linguistics, music, and visual and performing arts), COMPUTER AND PHYSICAL SCIENCE (actuarial science, applied mathematics, applied physics, chemistry, computer science, earth science, mathematics, physics, science, and statistics), EDUCATION (education), ENGINEERING AND ENVIRONMENTAL DESIGN (engineering and applied science and environmental science), SOCIAL SCIENCE (anthropology, archeology, Canadian studies, cognitive science, criminology, economics, geography, history, humanities, liberal arts/general studies, philosophy, physical fitness/movement, political science/government, psychology, sociology, and women's studies). Engineering science is the strongest academically. Business administration, psychology, and computing science have the largest enrollments.

Required: General bachelor's degrees require completion of 120 semester hours with a 2.0 cumulative GPA. For a honors degrees, students must complete 132 hours. Some programs require a thesis.

Special: Simon Fraser offers cooperative education in most areas of study, study abroad in 47 countries, many opportunities for joint majors, a general studies degree, work-study programs, dual-majors, student-designed majors, and a variety of certificate and diploma programs, as well as non-degree and evening study. Interdisciplinary majors are offered in such areas as chemical physics, management and systems science, mathematical physics, and physics and physiology. There is a freshman honors program and 48 departmental honors programs.

Faculty/Classroom: 71% of faculty are male; 29% are female. No introductory courses are taught by graduate students.

Requirements: The SAT is required. The ACT is recommended. The SAT is required for U.S. applicants. Applicants must be graduates of an accredited secondary school and have a minimum grade average of 70%. A GPA of 3.2 is required. AP credits are accepted.

Procedure: Freshmen are admitted to all sessions. There are early decision and early admissions plans. Early decision applications should be filed by April 1; regular applications, by May 1 for fall entry; September 30 for spring entry; and February 2 for summer entry. The fall 2013 application fee was $45. Notification of early decision is sent April 15; regular decision, June 30. Applications are accepted on-line.

Transfer: 2603 transfer students enrolled in 2012-2013. Applicants must have a minimum GPA of 2.0 and be in good standing at their previous school. 60 of 120 credits required for the bachelor's degree must be completed at SFU.

Visiting: There are regularly scheduled orientations for prospective students, consisting of regularly scheduled 1-day campus orientations for prospective students. There are guides for informal visits and visitors may stay overnight. To schedule a visit, contact the Residence and Housing Office at (778) 782-4201.

Financial Aid: The average financial indebtedness of the 2013 graduate was $20,000. The FAFSA is required. The deadline for filing freshman financial aid applications for fall entry is July 1.

International Students: There are 2889 international students enrolled. The school actively recruits these students. They must take the TOEFL, or IELTS (minimum score 6.5 on academic modules).

Computers: All students may access the system any time. There are no time limits and no fees.

Graduates: From July 1, 2012 to June 30, 2013, 4160 bachelor's degrees were awarded. The most popular majors were business (14%), education (11%), and economics (8%). In an average class, 65% graduate in 5 years or less and 68% graduate in 6 years or less.

Admissions Contact: Mehran Kiai, Enrollment Services. E-Mail: *undergraduate-admissions@sfu.ca* Web: *www.students@sfu.ca*

UNIVERSITÉ DE MONTRÉAL E-2

Montreal, PQ H3C 3J7 (514) 343-7076; (514) 343-5788

Full-time: 13,028 men, 17,940 women
Part-time: 5422 men, 9055 women
Graduate: 6789 men, 8363 women
Year: trimesters, summer session
Application Deadline: March 1
Freshman Class: 31,100 applied, 13,923 accepted, 13,174 enrolled
Faculty: n/av
Ph.D.s: 96%
Student/Faculty: n/av
Tuition: $3300
Room & Board: $4700

Université de Montréal, founded in 1878, is the largest French-language university in North America, with 13 faculties, 2 affiliated schools, 62 teaching departments, and more than 170 research units. Cost figures above are for 8 months. There are 16 undergraduate schools and 15 graduate schools. The 19 libraries contain 3.0 million volumes, 1.6 million microform items, 2.0 million audio/video tapes/CDs/DVDs, and subscribe to 50,000 periodicals including electronic. Computerized library services include interlibrary loans, database searching, Internet access, and laptop Internet portals. Special learning facilities include a learning resource center, art gallery, natural history museum, radio station, concert hall. The 145-acre campus is in an urban area in Montreal, Canada. Including any residence halls, there are 38 buildings.

Student Life: Students are from 11 states. 88% are from public schools. The average age of freshmen is 22; all undergraduates, 24. 20% do not continue beyond their first year; 80% remain to graduate.

Housing: 1164 students can be accommodated in college housing, which includes coed off-campus apartments. On-campus housing is available on a first-come and first-served basis. 98% of students commute. All students may keep cars.

Activities: There are no fraternities or sororities. There are 100 groups on campus, including art, cheerleading, choir, chorale, computers, dance, debate, drama, environmental, ethnic, film, international, jazz band, literary magazine, newspaper, orchestra, photography, political, radio and TV, religious, social, social service, student government, and yearbook. Popular campus events include Multicultural Week and Welcoming Week.

Sports: There are 8 intercollegiate sports for men and 6 for women, and 12 intramural sports for men and 12 for women. Facilities include a skating rink, a football field, a gym, squash and racquetball courts, an Olympic-size pool, a diving pool, a running field with tennis courts, and aerobic and muscular exercise equipment.

Disabled Students: 95% of the campus is accessible. Facilities include

wheelchair ramps, elevators, special parking, specially equipped restrooms, lowered drinking fountains, lowered telephones, special housing, and specialized equipment center for students with disabilities.

Services: Counseling and information services are available, as is tutoring in some subjects. There is a reader service for the blind, and remedial math, reading, and writing.

Campus Safety and Security: Measures include 24-hour foot and vehicle patrol, emergency notification system, and security escort services. There are emergency telephones, lighted pathways/sidewalks, controlled access to dorms/residences, and in-room safes.

Programs of Study: UdeM confers B.A., B.Sc., B.A.A., B.A.P., B.D.I., B.Gest, B.Ed., B.Ing., B.Int., B.Mus., and B.Th. degrees. Associates, master's, and doctoral degrees are also awarded. Bachelor's degrees are awarded in BIOLOGICAL SCIENCE (biochemistry, biology/biological science, biometrics and biostatistics, and nutrition), BUSINESS (business administration and management), COMMUNICATIONS AND THE ARTS (art history and appreciation, classics, English, film arts, French, German, industrial design, linguistics, and music), COMPUTER AND PHYSICAL SCIENCE (chemistry, computer science, mathematics, and physics), EDUCATION (education, physical education, and psychology education), ENGINEERING AND ENVIRONMENTAL DESIGN (architectural engineering, architecture, engineering, industrial administration/management, and landscape architecture/design), HEALTH PROFESSIONS (health science, nursing, occupational therapy, pharmacy, physical therapy, predentistry, premedicine, preveterinary science, speech pathology/audiology, and veterinary science), SOCIAL SCIENCE (anthropology, Asian/Oriental studies, criminology, economics, geography, history, law, philosophy, political science/government, psychology, social work, sociology, Spanish studies, theological studies, and urban studies). Law, medicine, and nursing have the largest enrollments.

Required: To graduate, students must have a GPA of 2.0 on a 4.3 scale. The total number of credits required in most programs is 90, although it can range up to 187. Professional programs, particularly those in health-related fields, require more hours.

Special: The university offers co-op programs in math, translation, mining, and civil, chemical, and software material engineering; and work-study programs in hospitals and businesses in Quebec. Dual majors in math and economics, math and physics, math and computer science, communication and politics, economics and politics, and 3-2 engineering degrees may also be arranged. Study abroad is available in 31 countries. There is a freshman honors program and 45 departmental honors programs.

Faculty/Classroom: 71% of faculty are male; 29% are female. All teach undergraduates. No introductory courses are taught by graduate students. The average class size in an introductory lecture is 48; in a laboratory is 19; and in a regular course is 40.

Admissions: 45% of a recent year's applicants were accepted.

Requirements: In a recent year's, applicants in certain programs must take the university's admissions tests. An interview is also required in some programs.

Procedure: Freshmen are admitted fall and winter. Applications should be filed by March 1 for fall entry, November 1 for winter entry, March 1 for spring entry, and March 1 for summer entry, along with a $100 fee. Notifications are sent March 15. Applications are accepted on-line. A waiting list is maintained.

Transfer: Transfers are considered if there are openings in the second or third year of the university's programs. 90 credits required for the bachelor's degree must be completed at UdeM.

Visiting: There are regularly scheduled orientations for prospective students, visits include Orientation and Employment Week in November, guided tours February through May, and open house in January and August. There are guides for informal visits. To schedule a visit, contact Direction des communications et du recrutement.

Financial Aid: In a recent year, 42% of all full-time freshmen and 50% of continuing full-time students received some form of financial aid. 42% of all full-time freshmen and 50% of continuing full-time students received need-based aid. The average freshmen award was $6,000. 57% of undergraduate students work part-time. Average annual earnings from campus work are $4500. The deadline for filing freshman financial aid applications for fall entry is March 31.

International Students: The school actively recruits these students.

Computers: Wireless access is available. There are many computers in the libraries and in public rooms. In addition, there is access to the Internet from the rooms of housing services. All students may access the system 24 hours per day. There are no time limits and no fees. It is strongly recommended that all students have a personal computer. Students enrolled in management programs, pharmacy, and architecture must have a personal computer. A ThinkPad is recommended.

Graduates: In a recent year, 4221 bachelor's degrees were awarded. The most popular majors were law (8%), medicine (5%), and nursing (5%). In an average class, 66% graduate in 4 years or less.

Admissions Contact: Jacinthe Gauthier, Responsible admissions. E-Mail: *admissions@regis.umontreal.ca* Web: *http:/www.etudes.umontreal.ca*

UNIVERSITY OF ALBERTA C-2

Edmonton, AB T6G 2M7 **(780) 492-3113; (780) 492-7172**

Full-time: 12346 men, 15665 women **Faculty:** 1659
Part-time: 691 men, 1147 women **Ph.D.s:** 92%
Graduate: 3550 men, 3594 women **Student/Faculty:** n/av
Year: semesters, summer session **Tuition:** $5829 ($18,459)
Application Deadline: May 1 **Room & Board:** $6502
Freshman Class: 10587 applied, 6131 accepted, 4812 enrolled
SAT: recommended

The University of Alberta, founded in 1908, is a publicly supported institution offering undergraduate and graduate programs in arts and science, agricultural sciences, business, education, engineering, nursing, phys ed, native studies, and professional studies. The figures in the above capsule and in this profile are approximate. There are 18 undergraduate schools and 1 graduate school. The 13 libraries contain 5.4 million volumes, and 3.7 million microform items. Computerized library services include interlibrary loans, database searching, Internet access, and Wi-Fi capability. Special learning facilities include an art gallery, radio station, an agricultural meteorological research station, ecological sanctuary, botanical garden, the Kurimoto Japanese Garden farm, and Timms Centre for the Arts. The 155-acre campus is in an urban area 2 miles southwest of downtown Edmonton, Canada. Including any residence halls, there are 90 buildings.

Student Life: Students are from 130 foreign countries, and Canada. The average age of freshmen is 19; all undergraduates, 22.

Housing: 4900 students can be accommodated in college housing, which includes single-sex and coed dorms, on-campus apartments, off-campus apartments, and married student housing. In addition, there are honors houses, language houses, special-interest houses, fraternity houses, and sorority houses. 88% of students commute. All students may keep cars.

Activities: There are 400 groups on campus, including art, band, cheerleading, chess, choir, chorale, chorus, computers, dance, debate, drama, environmental, ethnic, film, forensics, gay, honors, international, jazz band, musical theater, newspaper, opera, orchestra, pep band, photography, political, radio and TV, religious, social, social service, student government, and symphony. Popular campus events include WOW (Week of Welcome) and AntiFreeze (winter activity).

Sports: There are 12 intercollegiate sports for men and 13 for women, and 60 intramural sports for men and 45 for women. Facilities include a stadium, swimming pools, gyms, combatives and weight rooms, ballet/fencing and aerobics studios, a 400-meter outdoor track, an ice arena, racquetball and squash courts, a wrestling gym, an indoor field house, a sports medicine clinic, a training center for disabled athletes, curling rinks, and tennis courts.

Disabled Students: 98% of the campus is accessible. Facilities include wheelchair ramps, elevators, special parking, specially equipped restrooms, special class scheduling, lowered drinking fountains, lowered telephones.

Services: Counseling and information services are available, as is tutoring in most subjects. There is a reader service for the blind, and remedial math, reading, and writing.

Campus Safety and Security: Measures include 24-hour foot and vehicle patrol, emergency notification system, self-defense education, and security escort services. There are emergency telephones, lighted pathways/sidewalks, and controlled access to dorms/residences.

Programs of Study: U of A confers B.A., B.Comm., B.Ed., B.F.A., B.Mus., B.P.E., B.S.C., B.S.Cn. and B.des. degrees. Master's and doctoral degrees are also awarded. Bachelor's degrees are awarded in AGRICULTURE (agricultural economics, agriculture, animal science, and soil science), BIOLOGICAL SCIENCE (biochemistry, biology/biological science, botany, cell biology, entomology, genetics, microbiology, physiology, and zoology), BUSINESS (accounting, management science, and marketing/retailing/merchandising), COMMUNICATIONS AND THE ARTS (classics, comparative literature, dance, dramatic arts, English, film arts, French, Germanic languages and literature, linguistics, music, romance languages and literature, and Slavic languages), COMPUTER AND PHYSICAL SCIENCE (applied mathematics, chemistry, computer science, earth science, geology, geophysics and seismology, mathematics, physical sciences, physics, and statistics), EDUCATION (education of the deaf and hearing impaired, education of the multiply handicapped, elementary education, physical education, secondary education, special education, and vocational education), ENGINEERING AND ENVIRONMENTAL DESIGN (chemical engineering technology, civil engineering, computer engineering, electrical/electronics engineering, engineering physics, mechanical engineering, metallurgical engineering, mining and mineral engineering, and petroleum/natural gas engineering), HEALTH PROFESSIONS (medical laboratory science, nursing, occupational therapy, pharmacy, and physical therapy), SOCIAL SCIENCE (anthropology, Canadian studies, clothing and textiles management/production/services, criminology, East Asian studies, Eastern European studies, economics, geography, history, law, philosophy, political science/government, psychology, sociology, and women's studies). Arts, science, and engineering have the largest enrollments.

Required: The requirements for graduation vary according to the program. A minimum GPA of 2.0 and at least 120 credit hours are required for graduation.

Special: The university offers co-op programs in business and engineering. Opportunities for study abroad, internships, dual majors, bilingual classes in French and English, credit by exam (special assessment), and pass/fail options are also available. There is 1 national honor society and a freshman honors program.

Faculty/Classroom: All teach and do research. No introductory courses are taught by graduate students. The average class size in an introductory lecture is 90; in a laboratory is 20; and in a regular course is 35.

Admissions: 58% of the 2013-2014 applicants were accepted.

Requirements: The SAT is recommended. Graduation from an accredited secondary school is required. A minimum grade average of 70 is required in all courses submitted for academic credit. Depending on the program selected by the student, an essay, portfolio, audition, or interview may be required. A GPA of 70.0 is required. AP credits are accepted.

Procedure: Freshmen are admitted to all sessions. There is an early admissions plan. Applications should be filed by May 1 for fall entry; November 15 for winter entry; and March 1 for spring entry, along with a $115 fee. Notification of early decision is sent January 2; regular decision, August 1. Applications are accepted on-line.

Transfer: 4609 transfer students enrolled in 2012-2013. Applicants must meet minimum matriculation requirements or complete 24 credits of transferable work with satisfactory standing. 60 of 120 credits required for the bachelor's degree must be completed at U of A.

Visiting: There are regularly scheduled orientations for prospective students, including University Open House on the first weekend in October and Orientation for new students held on campus 2 days before classes begin in the fall term. There are guides for informal visits, visitors may sit in on classes, and stay overnight. To schedule a visit, contact the Office of the Registrar and Student Awards.

Financial Aid: Check with the school for current application deadlines.

International Students: There are 1885 international students enrolled. The school actively recruits these students. They must take the TOEFL with a minimum score of 580 on the paper-based TOEFL (PBT) or 86 on the Internet-based version (iBT) or take the MELAB and the college's own test.

Computers: All students may access the system 24 hours a day. There are no time limits and no fees.

Graduates: From July 1, 2012 to June 30, 2013, 7073 bachelor's degrees were awarded.

Admissions Contact: Office of the Registrar and Student Awards E-Mail: *www.registrar.ualberta.ca/contact* Web: *www.ualberta.ca*

UNIVERSITY OF BRITISH COLUMBIA B-2

Vancouver, BC V6T 1Z1 (604) 822-3014
(877) 272-1422; (604) 822-3599

Full-time: 10,044 men, 11,331 women	**Faculty:** n/av
Part-time: 3357 men, 4085 women	**Ph.D.s:** 99%
Graduate: 6861 men, 8293 women	**Student/Faculty:** 15 to 1
Year: see profile, summer session	**Tuition:** $5554
Application Deadline: February 28	**Room & Board:** $7150

Freshman Class: 23102 applied, 12285 accepted, 6225 enrolled
SAT or ACT: required

The University of British Columbia, established in 1908, is a publicly supported institution offering a wide range of undergraduate, graduate, and professional programs in the arts, sciences, and other fields of study. The winter session lasts from early September through April; some courses extend into May. Summer session begins in May and goes to mid-August, consisting of 2 terms. There are 16 undergraduate schools and one graduate school. The 22 libraries contain 5.6 million volumes, 5.2 million microform items, and 840,000 audio/video tapes/CDs/DVDs, and subscribe to 63,000 periodicals including electronic. Computerized library services include interlibrary loans, database searching, Internet access, and laptop Internet portals. Special learning facilities include a learning resource center, art gallery, natural history museum, radio station, a learning center, an anthropology museum, Canada's largest accelerator for subatomic physics, a space observatory, a center for integrated computer systems research, a center for the study of global issues, and a center for the performing arts. The 1000-acre campus is in an urban area 6 miles from the center of Vancouver, Canada. Including any residence halls, there are 500 buildings.

Student Life: 87% of undergraduates are from British Columbia. Others are from 43 states, 140 foreign countries, and Canada. 98% are from public schools. 14% are Foreign. The average age of freshmen is 20; all undergraduates, 21. 8% do not continue beyond their first year; 92% remain to graduate.

Housing: 9500 students can be accommodated in college housing, which includes single-sex and coed dorms, on-campus apartments, and married student housing. In addition, there are special-interest houses, International houses: Japanese, Korean, Mexican and Hong Kong. On-campus housing is guaranteed for the freshman year only, is available on a first-come, first-served basis, and is available on a lottery system for upperclassmen. Priority is given to out-of-town students. 80% of students commute. All students may keep cars.

Activities: 6% of men belong to 7 national fraternities; 2% of women belong to 7 national sororities. There are 250 groups on campus, including varsity outdoors., art, band, cheerleading, chess, choir, chorale, chorus, computers, dance, debate, drama, environmental, ethnic, film, gay, honors, international, jazz band, literary magazine, musical theater, newspaper, opera, orchestra, photography, political, professional, radio and TV, religious, ski and snowboard, social, social service, student government, symphony, and yearbook. Popular campus events include Storm the Wall, Day of the Longboat, and Great Trek Run.

Sports: There are 13 intercollegiate sports for men and 11 for women, and 18 intramural sports for men and 18 for women. Facilities include a winter sports center, a 3500-seat stadium, a gym, an aquatic center, playing fields, a recreation center, a tennis center, and a rowing centre.

Disabled Students: 95% of the campus is accessible. Facilities include wheelchair ramps, elevators, special parking, specially equipped restrooms, special class scheduling, lowered drinking fountains, lowered telephones, special housing, accessible shower stalls in fitness facilities, tactile maps, TTY pay phones, an accessible security bus, and audible street crossing signals.

Services: Counseling and information services are available, as is tutoring in most subjects. There is a reader service for the blind, and remedial math, reading, and writing.

Campus Safety and Security: Measures include 24-hour foot and vehicle patrol and security escort services. There are shuttle buses, emergency telephones, lighted pathways/sidewalks, controlled access to dorms/residences, Royal Canadian mounted police detachment on campus, awareness programs on theft, and personal safety lectures.

Programs of Study: UBC confers B.A., B.A.H.S., B.A.Sc., B.B.R.E., B.Com.B.C.S., B.D.Sc., B.Ed., B.End., B.F.A., B.H.E., B.H.K., B.Mgt., B.M.LSc., B.Mus., B.Mw., B.Sc., B.Sc.Die., B.Sc.F., B.Sc.Pharm., B.S.F., B.S.N., B.S.W., and L.L.B. degrees. Master's and doctoral degrees are also awarded. Bachelor's degrees are awarded in AGRICULTURE (agricultural economics, animal science, forestry production and processing, forestry and related sciences, horticulture, natural resource management, and soil science), BIOLOGICAL SCIENCE (biochemistry, biology/biological science, biophysics, biotechnology, microbiology, nutrition, physiology, and zoology), BUSINESS (accounting, banking and finance, business administration and management, business economics, human resources, international business management, management information systems, marketing/retailing/merchandising, real estate, recreational facilities management, and transportation management), COMMUNICATIONS AND THE ARTS (art history and appreciation, Chinese, classics, creative writing, dramatic arts, English, film arts, fine arts, French, German, Italian, Japanese, linguistics, music, music history and appreciation, music performance, music theory and composition, romance languages and literature, and Spanish), COMPUTER AND PHYSICAL SCIENCE (astronomy, atmospheric sciences and meteorology, chemistry, computer science, earth science, geophysics and seismology, mathematics, oceanography, physics, science, and statistics), EDUCATION (elementary education, museum studies, and physical education), ENGINEERING AND ENVIRONMENTAL DESIGN (chemical engineering, civil engineering, computer engineering, electrical/electronics engineering, engineering, engineering physics, environmental design, environmental engineering, environmental science, geological engineering, mechanical engineering, metallurgical engineering, and mining and mineral engineering), HEALTH PROFESSIONS (exercise science, health, nursing, pharmacology, preveterinary science, and speech pathology/audiology), SOCIAL SCIENCE (anthropology, archeology, Asian/Oriental studies, Canadian studies, classical/ancient civilization, cognitive science, dietetics, economics, European studies, family/consumer studies, food production/management/services, food science, geography, Hispanic American studies, history, home economics, human ecology, international relations, Latin American studies, medieval studies, Native American studies, philosophy, political science/government, psychology, religion, sociology, South Asian studies, and women's studies). Applied sciences and commerce are the strongest academically. Education and arts are the largest.

Required: To graduate, students must complete 120 credits in arts or science, more for applied science. Total number of hours required in a major varies by faculty. English is required for all majors.

Special: UBC offers co-op programs in science, applied science, commerce, arts, and forestry, and study abroad through 190 student exchange opportunities in 41 countries. Non-degree study is possible. A B.A.-B.A.Sc. degree, student-designed majors, dual majors in most faculties, and work-study programs are available. There is 1 national honor society and 10 departmental honors programs.

Faculty/Classroom: 62% of faculty are male; 38% are female. No introductory courses are taught by graduate students.

Admissions: 53% of the 2013-2014 applicants were accepted. 96% of the current freshmen were in the top fifth of their class.

Requirements: The SAT or ACT is required. The ACT Optional Writing test is also required. In addition, graduation from an accredited secondary school is required. General admission for students following a U.S. system is based on 4 years of English and 3 of math. There are also specific program requirements in math, chemistry, physics, and biology for students applying to science-based programs U.S. curriculum students are required to submit SAT or ACT and writing scores. Exemptions may begin where these tests are not available. A GPA of 2.6 is required. AP credits are accepted. Important factors in the admissions decision are extracurricular activities record, leadership record, and recommendations by school officials.
Procedure: Freshmen are admitted fall and spring. There are early admissions, deferred admissions, and rolling admissions plans. Applications should be filed by February 28 for fall entry; February 28 for spring entry; and February 28 for summer entry, along with a $100 fee. Applications are accepted on-line.
Transfer: 1829 transfer students enrolled in 2012-2013. Official transcripts, completion of the equivalent of 24 course credits, and no failures are required. A competitive GPA is required to get into the program at the second or third year. Applicants must have attended an accredited post-secondary institution. 60 of 120 credits required for the bachelor's degree must be completed at UBC.
Visiting: There are regularly scheduled orientations for prospective students, Monday through Saturday. There are guides for informal visits, visitors may sit in on classes, and stay overnight.
Financial Aid: The FAFSA and the college's own financial statement are required. Check with the school for current application deadlines.
International Students: There are 4442 international students enrolled. The school actively recruits these students. They must also take the SAT or ACT.
Computers: Wireless access is available. PCs and wireless access are available across the campus. All students may access the system 24 hours per day. There are no time limits and no fees. It is strongly recommended that all students have a personal computer.
Graduates: In a recent year, 5740 bachelor's degrees were awarded. The most popular majors were psychology (9%), biology (7%), and English (6%). In an average class, 34% graduate in 4 years or less, 70% graduate in 5 years or less, and 77% graduate in 6 years or less.
Admissions Contact: Office of the Registrar Web: *www.askme.ubc.ca*

UNIVERSITY OF CALGARY C-2

Calgary, AB T2N 1N4 **(403) 210-7625; (403) 220-0762**

Full-time: 10,000 men, 12,000 women	**Faculty:** n/av
Part-time: 1293 men, 1901 women	**Ph.D.s:** n/av
Graduate: 2578 men, 2556 women	**Student/Faculty:** 13 to 1
Year: semesters, summer session	**Tuition:** $7100 ($16,000)
Application Deadline: May 1	**Room & Board:** $6700
Freshman Class: n/av	
SAT or ACT: required	

The University of Calgary, founded in 1945, is a public institution offering undergraduate programs in numerous liberal arts and professional fields. There are 15 undergraduate schools and 2 graduate schools. The 6 libraries contain 2.5 million volumes, 3.6 million microform items, and 36,920 audio/video tapes/CDs/DVDs, and subscribe to 20,237 periodicals including electronic. Computerized library services include interlibrary loans, database searching, Internet access, and laptop Internet portals. Special learning facilities include a learning resource center, art gallery, radio station, TV station, environmental research center, observatory, human performance and theater labs, arts museum, children's hospital, and Foothills medical centre. The 526-acre campus is in an urban area in northwest Calgary, Alberta, Canada. Including any residence halls, there are 36 buildings.
Student Life: 80% of undergraduates are from Alberta. Students are from 32 states, 90 foreign countries, and Canada. 50% are from public schools. The average age of freshmen is 19; all undergraduates, 23. 6% do not continue beyond their first year; 92% remain to graduate.
Housing: 1500 students can be accommodated in college housing, which includes coed dorms, on-campus apartments, and married student housing. In addition, there are honors houses, language houses, Global Village, and living and learning academic community. On-campus housing is guaranteed for all 4 years and is guaranteed for the freshman year only. Priority is given to out-of-town students. 30% of students commute. All students may keep cars.
Activities: There are no fraternities or sororities. There are 221 groups on campus, including art, band, chess, choir, chorus, computers, dance, debate, drama, environmental, ethnic, film, gay, international, jazz band, musical theater, newspaper, orchestra, political, professional, radio and TV, religious, social, social service, and student government. Popular campus events include Bermuda Shorts Day (last day of classes in April), Orientation Week, and KickOff.
Sports: There are 9 intercollegiate sports for men and 9 for women, and 20 intramural sports for men and 18 for women. Facilities include 3 gyms, a 50-meter swimming pool, a 200-meter indoor track, a 3-story climbing wall, an indoor speed-skating arena, an outdoor stadium, rooms for weight training, aerobics, and combatives, and squash, tennis, and racquetball courts. There is also a 200-seat lecture theater, a games area, and an outdoor recreation center.
Disabled Students: All of the campus is accessible. Facilities include wheelchair ramps, elevators, special parking, specially equipped restrooms, special class scheduling, lowered drinking fountains, lowered telephones, and special housing.
Services: Counseling and information services are available, as is tutoring in most subjects. There is a reader service for the blind, and remedial math and writing.
Campus Safety and Security: Measures include 24-hour foot and vehicle patrol, emergency notification system, and security escort services. There are emergency telephones, lighted pathways/sidewalks, and controlled access to dorms/residences.
Programs of Study: U of C confers B.A., B.Sc., B.Comm., B.C.R., B.C.S., B.Ed., B.F.A., B.G.S., B.H.R.M., B.H.Sc., B.Kin., B.Mus., B.N., B.Sc.Eng., B.S.W., and LL.B. degrees. Master's and doctoral degrees are also awarded. Bachelor's degrees are awarded in BIOLOGICAL SCIENCE (biochemistry, bioinformatics, biology/biological science, botany, cell biology, ecology, and zoology), BUSINESS (accounting, business administration and management, hotel/motel and restaurant management, and marketing/retailing/merchandising), COMMUNICATIONS AND THE ARTS (communications, dance, dramatic arts, English, fine arts, French, German, linguistics, music, music history and appreciation, music performance, music theory and composition, Russian, and Spanish), COMPUTER AND PHYSICAL SCIENCE (actuarial science, applied mathematics, astrophysics, chemical physics, chemistry, computer science, earth science, geology, geophysics and seismology, mathematics, natural sciences, physics, and statistics), EDUCATION (education, elementary education, and secondary education), ENGINEERING AND ENVIRONMENTAL DESIGN (chemical engineering, civil engineering, computer engineering, electrical/electronics engineering, environmental science, mechanical engineering, petroleum/natural gas engineering, and surveying engineering), HEALTH PROFESSIONS (biomedical science, exercise science, nursing, public health, and sports medicine), SOCIAL SCIENCE (anthropology, archeology, Asian/Oriental studies, Canadian studies, classical/ancient civilization, economics, geography, history, international relations, Latin American studies, law, liberal arts/general studies, philosophy, physical fitness/movement, political science/government, psychology, religion, social work, sociology, urban studies, and women's studies). Engineering and medicine are the strongest academically. Management, and engineering, have the largest enrollments.
Required: To graduate, all students must satisfy the required courses, course sequences, and credit distribution in their particular program. Students must maintain a minimum 2.0 GPA and complete 7 to 10 full-course equivalents in the major field.
Special: The university offers co-op programs in applied chemistry, management, and many other fields. Dual majors, work-study programs, internships in engineering and computer science, combined degrees in many disciplines, and study abroad in 61 countries are also available. Students may cross-register with any of 8 member colleges in the Big Country Education Consortium. U of C sponsors or is affiliated with 20 research institutes and groups. There is 1 national honor society, a freshman honors program, and 2 departmental honors programs.
Faculty/Classroom: No introductory courses are taught by graduate students. The average class size in an introductory lecture is 89; in a laboratory is 24; and in a regular course is 60.
Requirements: The SAT or ACT is required. U.S. applicants must be graduates of a secondary school. AP credits are accepted.
Procedure: Freshmen are admitted fall. There is an early admissions plan. Applications should be filed by May 1 for fall entry, along with a $145 fee. Applications are accepted on-line.
Transfer: Applicants must have a cumulative GPA of 2.0 or above on all transfer courses. 20 of 40 credits required for the bachelor's degree must be completed at U of C.
Visiting: There are regularly scheduled orientations for prospective students, campus tours and admissions advising. There are guides for informal visits and visitors may stay overnight. To schedule a visit, contact Student Enrollment Services.
Financial Aid: In a recent year, 40% of all full-time freshmen received some form of financial aid. 20% of all full-time freshmen and 20% of continuing full-time students received need-based aid. The priority date for freshman financial aid applications for fall entry is April 1. The deadline for filing freshman financial aid applications for fall entry is April 1.
International Students: There are 1300 international students enrolled. The school actively recruits these students. They must take the TOEFL with a minimum score of 83 on the Internet-based version (iBT), or take the IELTS, the CAEL, or the university's English program. They must also take the SAT or ACT, scoring 1100.
Computers: Wireless access is available. The campus is wireless, and has

15 computer labs with over 1,000 computers available for public use. All students may access the system. 800 terminals are available 24 hours per day. There are no time limits and no fees. It is strongly recommended that all students have a personal computer.

Graduates: In a recent year, 5102 bachelor's degrees were awarded. The most popular majors were science (30%), arts (25%), and engineering (10%). 60 companies recruited on campus in a recent year.

Admissions Contact: David Johnson, Assistant Vice-President . E-Mail: *future.students@ucalgary.ca* Web: *www.ucalgary.ca*

UNIVERSITY OF GUELPH E-3

Guelph, ON N1G 2W1 **(519) 821-2130; (519) 766-9481**

Full-time: n/av
Part-time: n/av
Graduate: n/av
Year: varies, summer session
Application Deadline: March 1
Freshman Class: 18852 applied, 13765 accepted, 3479 enrolled
SAT or ACT: required
Faculty: 800
Ph.D.s: 98%
Student/Faculty: 19 to 1
Tuition: $5982 ($16,982)
Room & Board: $8100

The University of Guelph, founded in 1964, is a public institution offering programs in arts and sciences, agriculture, engineering, commerce, landscape architecture, veterinary medicine, applied science, and technology. There are 7 undergraduate schools and 56 graduate schools. The library contains 2.0 million volumes, 1.5 million microform items, and 17,000 audio/video tapes/CDs/DVDs, and subscribes to 7,600 periodicals including electronic. Computerized library services include interlibrary loans, database searching, Internet access, and Wi-Fi capability. Special learning facilities include an art gallery, radio station, an observatory, a learning commons, a research park, and arboretum. The 1017-acre campus is in a suburban area 2 miles south of the center of Guelph, Canada. Including any residence halls, there are 80 buildings.

Student Life: 93% of undergraduates are from Ontario. Others are from 100 foreign countries. The average age of freshmen is 18; all undergraduates, 21. 9% do not continue beyond their first year; 89% remain to graduate.

Housing: 5500 students can be accommodated in college housing, which includes single-sex and coed dorms, on-campus apartments, off-campus apartments, and married student housing. In addition, there are language houses, special-interest houses, an international house, La Maison Francaise, Eco house, an arts house, and study intensive and academic clusters. On-campus housing is guaranteed for the freshman year only, is available on a first-come, first-served basis, and is available on a lottery system for upperclassmen. 67% of students commute. All students may keep cars.

Activities: There are no fraternities or sororities. There are 100 groups on campus, including art, cheerleading, chess, choir, chorale, computers, dance, debate, drama, environmental, ethnic, gay, international, jazz band, literary magazine, newspaper, photography, political, professional, radio and TV, religious, social, social service, student government, and yearbook. Popular campus events include College Royal open house weekend in March.

Sports: There are 15 intercollegiate sports for men and 15 for women, and 17 intramural sports for men and 17 for women. Facilities include a twin-pad arena, with an Olympic size ice surface, 5 squash courts, a fitness gym, weight-training rooms, a 6-lane swimming pool and an Olympic-size pool, a fitness circuit, and 3 gyms. Outdoor facilities include 4 tennis courts, a running track, lighted football, field hockey, soccer, rugby and fastball fields, jogging trails, and multipurpose fields. There are also 2 dance studios, a climbing wall, a wrestling/combatives room, a covered field with artificial turf, and a 200-meter track.

Disabled Students: 90% of the campus is accessible. Facilities include wheelchair ramps, elevators, special parking, specially equipped restrooms, special class scheduling, lowered drinking fountains, lowered telephones, special housing. special library services, equipment, and software.

Services: Counseling and information services are available, as is tutoring in most subjects. There is a reader service for the blind. ESL, learning, studying, and writing resources are available.

Campus Safety and Security: Measures include 24-hour foot and vehicle patrol, emergency notification system, self-defense education, and security escort services. There are shuttle buses, emergency telephones, lighted pathways/sidewalks, controlled access to dorms/residences, there is a campus safe walk and a campus police patrol.

Programs of Study: U of G confers B.A., B.A.S., B.A.Sc., B.B.R.M., B.Comm., B.Comp., B.L.A., B.Sc., B.Sc.Agr., B.Sc.Eng., B.Sc.Env. and B.Sc.(Tech). degrees. Master's and doctoral degrees are also awarded. Bachelor's degrees are awarded in AGRICULTURE (agricultural economics, agriculture, agronomy, animal science, horticulture, and natural resource management), BIOLOGICAL SCIENCE (biochemistry, biology/biological science, biophysics, ecology, environmental biology, marine science, microbiology, molecular biology, nutrition, wildlife biology, and zoology), BUSINESS (hospitality management services, human resources, marketing management, and real estate), COMMUNICATIONS AND THE ARTS (art history and appreciation, classical languages, English, music, Spanish, and studio art), COMPUTER AND PHYSICAL SCIENCE (chemical physics, chemistry, computer science, earth science, information sciences and systems, physical sciences, physics, and statistics), ENGINEERING AND ENVIRONMENTAL DESIGN (biomedical engineering, engineering, environmental engineering, and landscape architecture/design), SOCIAL SCIENCE (anthropology, child care/child and family studies, classical/ancient civilization, criminal justice, economics, food science, French studies, geography, gerontology, history, interdisciplinary studies, philosophy, political science/government, psychology, public administration, rural sociology, sociology, water resources, and women's studies). Biological and physical sciences and veterinary medicine are the strongest academically. Biological and physical sciences, arts, and social sciences have the largest enrollments.

Required: To graduate, students must complete 30 credits (half courses) for a general degree and 40 credits (half courses) for an honors degree. U of G requires a minimum of 10 credits in the major.

Special: U of G offers co-op programs in 30 majors, study abroad in 29 countries, and work-study programs. Accelerated degree programs, dual majors, a general studies degree, and non-degree study are available. There are a freshman honors program and 33 departmental honors programs.

Faculty/Classroom: No introductory courses are taught by graduate students. The average class size in an introductory lecture is 300 and in a laboratory is 25.

Admissions: 73% of the 2013-2014 applicants were accepted.

Requirements: The SAT or ACT is required. The ACT Optional Writing test is also required. In addition, U.S. applicants must have a grade point average of 3.0 from a regionally accredited high school, and a combined math and critical reading SAT score of 1100 or ACT score of 24. Where class rankings are reported on the transcript, a ranking in the top quarter is preferred. Students should include among their senior level courses, specific courses that are required for admission to the degree program of their choice. Particular attention is paid to performance in program prerequisites. Students should ensure that senior year final grades from first and second semester interim grades are submitted before the document deadline date. AP credits are accepted. Important factors in the admissions decision are advanced placement or honors courses, extracurricular activities record, and leadership record.

Procedure: Freshmen are admitted fall. There are early decision and deferred admissions plans. Early decision applications should be filed by January 1; regular applications, by March 1 for fall entry. The fall 2013 application fee was $200. Notifications are sent in March. 5000 early decision candidates were accepted for the 2013-2014 class. Applications are accepted on-line.

Transfer: Applicants must meet general admissions requirements and have a B average in all college-level courses.

Visiting: There are regularly scheduled orientations for prospective students, Student visits include daily tours of the campus, Fall Preview Day, and Campus Days and Connection Conference in the Spring. . There are guides for informal visits and visitors may sit in on classes. To schedule a visit, contact the Tour Coordinator at (519) 824-4120, ext. 58712.

Financial Aid: 30% of undergraduate students work part-time. The FAFSA, the college's own financial statement, and the Federal and Provincial Government Canadian Form are required. Check with the school for current application deadlines.

International Students: There are 700 international students enrolled. The school actively recruits these students. They must take the TOEFL with a minimum score of 600 on the paper-based TOEFL (PBT) or 89 on the Internet-based version (iBT), and also take the TWE and TSE. The IELTS or MELAB may be substituted for these tests. U.S. students are required to submit SAT or ACT scores, with minimum acceptable scores.

Computers: All students may access the system at any time. There are no time limits and no fees.

Admissions Contact: Admission Services, Reception. E-Mail: *admisssion@registrar.uoguelph.ca* Web: *www.uoguelph.ca/admissions*

UNIVERSITY OF OTTAWA E-3

Ottawa, ON K1N 6N5 **(613) 562-5700 (877) 868-8292; (613) 562-5323**

Full-time: 11,124 men, 17,521 women
Part-time: 2177 men, 3095 women
Graduate: 2430 men, 3252 women
Year: semesters, summer session
Application Deadline: open
Freshman Class: n/av
SAT: required
Faculty: n/av
Ph.D.s: 96%
Student/Faculty: 22 to 1
Tuition: $6606 ($16,944)
Room & Board: $6860

The University of Ottawa, founded in 1848, is a bilingual (French/English) institution offering undergraduate and graduate degrees through the faculties of Arts, Law, Health Sciences, Medicine, Science, Engineering, Management, Social Sciences and Education. There are 9 undergraduate schools and 9 graduate schools. The figures in the above capsule and in this profile are approximate. In addition to regional accreditation, Ottawa has baccalaureate program accreditation with AACSB. The 8 libraries contain 2.2 million volumes, 1.9 million microform items, and 777,349 audio/video tapes/CDs/DVDs, and subscribe to 60,522 periodicals including electronic. Computerized library services include interlibrary loans, database searching, Internet access, and laptop Internet portals. Special learning facilities include a learning resource center, art gallery, radio station, TV station, Museum of Classical Antiquities. The 43-acre campus is in an urban area in Ottawa, Ontario, Canada. Including any residence halls, there are 40 buildings.

Student Life: 80% of undergraduates are from Ontario.

Housing: 2870 students can be accommodated in college housing, which includes single-sex and coed dorms, on-campus apartments, and married student housing. On-campus housing is available on a first-come, first-served basis, and is available on a lottery system for upperclassmen. All students may keep cars.

Activities: There are no fraternities or sororities. There are 100 groups on campus, including art, band, cheerleading, chess, choir, chorale, computers, dance, debate, drama, environmental, ethnic, film, gay, honors, international, jazz band, newspaper, orchestra, photography, political, professional, radio and TV, religious, social, social service, student government, and symphony. Popular campus events include University of Ottawa Day, Gee-gees football games, and International Week.

Sports: There are 5 intercollegiate sports for men and 7 for women, and 13 intramural sports for men and 11 for women. Facilities include 2 sports complexes that include: weight-training and combat rooms, a 50-meter swimming pool, gyms, racquetball and squash courts, billiards and ping pong tables, indoor arena, and a multipurpose sports field.

Disabled Students: 75% of the campus is accessible. Facilities include wheelchair ramps, elevators, special parking, specially equipped restrooms, special class scheduling, lowered drinking fountains, lowered telephones, special housing, automatic doors, and specialized equipment.

Services: Counseling and information services are available, as is tutoring in most subjects. There is a reader service for the blind, and remedial math, reading, and writing.

Campus Safety and Security: Measures include 24-hour foot and vehicle patrol, emergency notification system, self-defense education, and security escort services. There are shuttle buses, emergency telephones, lighted pathways/sidewalks, controlled access to dorms/residences, and a community crime-stoppers program.

Programs of Study: Ottawa confers B.A., B.Ad., B.A.Sc., B.Com., B.Ed., B.F.A., B.Mus., B.Sc., B.Sc.N., B.Soc.Sc., B.Jour., and B.H.Sc. degrees. Master's and doctoral degrees are also awarded. Bachelor's degrees are awarded in AGRICULTURE (environmental studies), BIOLOGICAL SCIENCE (biochemistry, biology/biological science, biotechnology, and life science), BUSINESS (accounting, banking and finance, electronic business, human resources, management information systems, management science, and marketing/retailing/merchandising), COMMUNICATIONS AND THE ARTS (Arabic, art history and appreciation, arts administration/management, classics, communications, English, English as a second/foreign language, French, German, Italian, journalism, Latin, linguistics, modern language, music, Spanish, and visual and performing arts), COMPUTER AND PHYSICAL SCIENCE (chemistry, computer science, earth science, geology, mathematics, physics, and software engineering), EDUCATION (education, elementary education, foreign languages education, and middle school education), ENGINEERING AND ENVIRONMENTAL DESIGN (biomedical engineering, chemical engineering, civil engineering, computer engineering, electrical/electronics engineering, environmental engineering, environmental science, and mechanical engineering), HEALTH PROFESSIONS (biomedical science, health science, nursing, and ophthalmic technology), SOCIAL SCIENCE (anthropology, Canadian studies, criminology, economics, ethics, politics, and social policy, ethnic studies, geography, gerontology, history, international studies, law, medieval studies, philosophy, political science/government, psychology, public administration, religion, Russian and Slavic studies, sociology, and women's studies). Law, medicine, and education are the strongest academically. Arts, social sciences, and science have the largest enrollments.

Required: Students must maintain a GPA of 3.5 out of 10 for all courses, including those in the major. Students must also complete a second language requirement: French for English students, and English for French students.

Special: Opportunities are provided for cooperative programs, study abroad in over 56 countries, a general studies degree in arts and in sciences, and combined programs in all fields in arts and in social sciences. There are 40 departmental honors programs.

Faculty/Classroom: 63% of faculty are male; 37% are female. All teach and do research. No introductory courses are taught by graduate students. The average class size in an introductory lecture is 60; in a laboratory is 30; and in a regular course is 30.

Requirements: The SAT is required. Graduation from an accredited secondary school is required. Those students planning to major in occupational or physical therapy must speak French. A portfolio is required for fine arts students, and an audition for music students. AP credits are accepted.

Procedure: Freshmen are admitted fall and winter. There are early decision, early admissions, and rolling admissions plans. Check with the school for current application deadlines. The fall application fee was $105.

Transfer: Admissions requirements vary according to program. 60 of 90 credits required for the bachelor's degree must be completed at Ottawa.

Visiting: There are regularly scheduled orientations for prospective students. There are guides for informal visits and visitors may sit in on classes. To schedule a visit, contact Liaison Office.

Financial Aid: In a recent year, an average annual earnings from campus work were $3000. Check with the school for current application deadlines.

International Students: There were 2234 international students enrolled in a recent year. The school actively recruits these students. They must take the TOEFL with a minimum score of 580 on the paper-based TOEFL (PBT) or 92 on the Internet-based version (iBT) or take the MELAB and the college's own test.

Computers: Wireless access is available. PCs are available in campus labs, in wireless zones throughout the campus, and in all residence rooms. All students may access the system 24 hours/day. There are no time limits and no fees.

Graduates: In a recent year, 6836 bachelor's degrees were awarded.

Admissions Contact: Andre-Pierre Lepage E-Mail: *eureka@uottawa.ca* Web: *www.admission.uottowa.ca*

UNIVERSITY OF SASKATCHEWAN C-2

Saskatoon, SK S7N 5A2 **(306) 966-5788; (306) 966-2115**

Full-time: n/av	**Faculty:** n/av
Part-time: n/av	**Ph.D.s:** 87%
Graduate: n/av	**Student/Faculty:** n/av
Year: semesters, summer session	**Tuition:** $6500
Application Deadline: April 1	**Room & Board:** $8100
Freshman Class: n/av	

The University of Saskatchewan, founded in 1907, is a public institution offering programs in business, agriculture, arts and sciences, education, engineering, and health professions. The figures in the above capsule and in this profile are approximate. There are 14 undergraduate schools and one graduate school. The 8 libraries contain 2.5 million volumes, 3.1 million microform items, and subscribe to 47,055 periodicals including electronic. Computerized library services include interlibrary loans, database searching, Internet access, and laptop Internet portals. Special learning facilities include a learning resource center, art gallery, natural history museum, and planetarium. The 1865-acre campus is in an urban area in Saskatoon.

Student Life: 77% remain to graduate.

Housing: 1600 students can be accommodated in college housing, which includes single-sex dorms, off-campus apartments, and married student housing. On-campus housing is available on a first-come and first-served basis. All students may keep cars.

Activities: There are no fraternities or sororities. Groups on campus include band, cheerleading, chess, choir, chorale, chorus, computers, drama, ethnic, gay, international, jazz band, literary magazine, newspaper, orchestra, photography, political, professional, religious, social, social service, and student government. Popular campus events include Powwow in the Bowl, Experience US!, and Greystone Scholar Spend-a-Day.

Sports: There are 8 intercollegiate sports for men and 7 for women, and 17 intramural sports for men and 17 for women. Facilities include The PAC, Physical Activity Complex, houses a 40-foot climbing wall, gym, state-of-the art fitness centre and weight room, walk/job track, squash and racquetball courts, dance studio, gymnastics areas and swimming pool. There also are a football stadium, hockey rink, curling rink, track and field area, and outdoor soccer field.

Disabled Students: All of the campus is accessible. Facilities include wheelchair ramps, elevators, special parking, specially equipped restrooms, special class scheduling, lowered drinking fountains, lowered telephones. There is also a coordinator of services for students with disabilities, special funding application assistance, and special exam scheduling and accommodations. Adaptive computerized equipment is located in the main library building.

Services: Counseling and information services are available, as is tutoring in most subjects. There is remedial math and writing.

Campus Safety and Security: Measures include 24-hour foot and vehicle patrol, emergency notification system, self-defense education, and security escort services. There are emergency telephones, lighted pathways/sidewalks, and controlled access to dorms/residences.

Programs of Study: U of S confers B.A., B.Sc., B.A.Sc., B.Comm., B.E., B.Ed., B.F.A., B.Mus., B.Mus/Mus.Ed., B.S.A., B.S.N., B.S.P., and B.Sc.Kin./Kin.Ed. degrees. Master's and doctoral degrees are also awarded. Bachelor's degrees are awarded in AGRICULTURE (agricultural business management, agricultural economics, agronomy, animal science, environmental studies, horticulture, plant science, range/farm management, and soil science), BIOLOGICAL SCIENCE (anatomy, biochemistry, bioinformatics, biology/biological science, biotechnology, cell biology, environmental biology, microbiology, nutrition, and physiology), BUSINESS (accounting, banking and finance, business administration and management, business economics, human resources, marketing/retailing/merchandising, and operations management), COMMUNICATIONS AND THE ARTS (art, art history and appreciation, dramatic arts, English, fine arts, French, German, Hebrew, Latin, linguistics, modern language, music, music performance, music theory and composition, musicology/ethnomusicology, Russian, Spanish, and studio art), COMPUTER AND PHYSICAL SCIENCE (applied mathematics, chemistry, computer science, environmental geology, geology, geophysics and seismology, mathematics, and physics), EDUCATION (education, elementary education, home economics education, physical education, secondary education, and teaching English as a second/foreign language (TESOL/TEFOL)), ENGINEERING AND ENVIRONMENTAL DESIGN (agricultural engineering, bioengineering, bioresource engineering, chemical engineering, civil engineering, computer engineering, electrical/electronics engineering, electrical/electronics engineering technology, engineering physics, environmental engineering, environmental engineering technology, environmental science, geological engineering, land use management and reclamation, mechanical engineering, and urban planning technology), HEALTH PROFESSIONS (biomedical science, exercise science, health science, nursing, pharmacology, pharmacy, physical therapy, and veterinary science), SOCIAL SCIENCE (anthropology, archeology, dietetics, economics, food science, gender studies, geography, history, international studies, law, Native American studies, Near Eastern studies, philosophy, political science/government, psychology, public administration, religion, social work, sociology, and women's studies).

Required: Requirements for graduation vary according to the program of study.

Special: The University of Saskatchewan offers interdisciplinary majors, including agricultural biology, agricultural chemistry, agricultural and bioresource engineering, agricultural extension, and anthropology and archaeology. Co-op programs are offered through the Program for Agricultural Cooperative Education. There are computer science internships, as well as internships offered through the Engineering Professional Internship program. The university has exchange agreements with 41 countries.

Faculty/Classroom: 65% of faculty are male; 35% are female. No introductory courses are taught by graduate students.

Requirements: Applicants must be graduates of an accredited secondary school. The decision is based solely on academic achievement in secondary school. In direct-entry programs, priority is given to Saskatchewan residents, with the exception being the College of Arts and Science. A GPA of 70.0 is required. AP credits are accepted.

Procedure: Freshmen are admitted to all sessions. There is a early decision plan. Applications should be filed by April 1 for fall entry; September 1 for winter entry; February 1 for spring entry; and March 1 for summer entry, along with a $90 fee. Applications are accepted on-line.

Transfer: Applicants must meet promotion levels for the college to which transfer is sought.

Visiting: There are regularly scheduled orientations for prospective students. To schedule a visit, contact Recruitment & Admissions.

Financial Aid: Check with the school for current application deadlines.

International Students: There are 1863 international students enrolled. The school actively recruits these students. They must take the TOEFL with a minimum score of 550 on the paper-based TOEFL (PBT) or 80 on the Internet-based version (iBT) or take the MELAB or IELTS.

Computers: Wireless access is available. Computer labs are open 7 days a week, 365 days a year. Each computer is equipped with Internet access and access to the university network. All students may access the system 24/7. There are no time limits and no fees.

Admissions Contact: Recruitment and Admission E-Mail: *admissions@usask.ca* Web: *explore.usask.ca*

UNIVERSITY OF TORONTO E-3

Toronto, ON M5S 1A1 **(416) 978-2190; (416) 978-6089**

Full-time: 24,724 men, 31,037 women
Part-time: 3179 men, 3547 women
Graduate: 6843 men, 8339 women
Year: see profile, summer session
Application Deadline: see profile
Freshman Class: n/av
SAT: required
Faculty: n/av
Ph.D.s: 91%
Student/Faculty: n/av
Tuition: $7100 ($23,500)
Room & Board: $11,000

The University of Toronto, founded in 1827, is a public institution offering undergraduate programs in applied science and engineering, arts and science, education, dentistry, law, medicine, music, nursing, pharmacy, physical and health education, and radiation sciences. Degrees are also offered at the graduate level in a wide range of programs. The figures in the above capsule and in this profile are approximate. There are 20 undergraduate schools and 1 graduate school. The 32 libraries contain 11.4 million volumes, 5.5 million microform items, 374,046 audio/video tapes/CDs/DVDs, and subscribe to 74,545 periodicals including electronic. Computerized library services include interlibrary loans, database searching, Internet access, and laptop Internet portals. Special learning facilities include a learning resource center, art gallery, radio station, and an observatory. The 1767-acre campus is in an urban area with 3 campuses in downtown and suburban Toronto. Including any residence halls, there are 242 buildings.

Student Life: 88% of undergraduates are from Ontario. The average age of freshmen is 18; all undergraduates, 21. 5% do not continue beyond their first year; 83% remain to graduate.

Housing: 7903 students can be accommodated in college housing, which includes single-sex and coed dorms, on-campus apartments, off-campus apartments, and married student housing. On-campus housing is guaranteed for the freshman year only and is available on a first-come, first-served basis. Priority is given to out-of-town students. 80% of students commute. All students may keep cars.

Activities: There are no fraternities or sororities. There are 200 groups on campus, including art, band, cheerleading, chess, choir, chorus, computers, dance, debate, drama, ethnic, film, gay, international, jazz band, literary magazine, musical theater, newspaper, opera, orchestra, photography, political, radio and TV, religious, social, student government, symphony, and yearbook. Popular campus events include U of T Day, concerts, and theater productions.

Sports: There are 27 intercollegiate sports for men and 26 for women, and 29 intramural sports for men and 29 for women. Facilities include swimming pools, an outdoor hockey rink, weight and exercise rooms, gyms, squash and multipurpose courts, a rifle range, dance studios, playing fields, a stadium, an arena, and a 200-meter indoor running track.

Disabled Students: Facilities include wheelchair ramps, elevators, special parking, specially equipped restrooms, lowered drinking fountains, and lowered telephones.

Services: Counseling and information services are available, as is tutoring in every subject. There is a reader service for the blind.

Campus Safety and Security: Measures include 24-hour foot and vehicle patrol, self-defense education, and security escort services. There are shuttle buses, emergency telephones, and lighted pathways/sidewalks.

Programs of Study: U of T confers B.A., B.Sc., B.A.Sc., B.B.A., B.Com., B.Ed., B.Sc.Med.Rad.Sc., B.Sc.N., B.Sc.O.T., B.Sc.Phm., B.Sc.P.T., B.S.P.H.E., and Mus.Bac. degrees. Master's and doctoral degrees are also awarded. Bachelor's degrees are awarded in AGRICULTURE (environmental studies, forestry and related sciences, and natural resource management), BIOLOGICAL SCIENCE (biochemistry, biology/biological science, biophysics, biotechnology, botany, cell biology, ecology, evolutionary biology, life science, microbiology, molecular biology, neurosciences, nutrition, physiology, toxicology, and zoology), BUSINESS (banking and finance, business administration and management, business economics, electronic business, and human resources), COMMUNICATIONS AND THE ARTS (art history and appreciation, arts administration/management, classics, communications, communications technology, comparative literature, dramatic arts, English, film arts, French, German, Greek, Italian, journalism, Latin, linguistics, media arts, modern language, music, music history and appreciation, music theory and composition, musicology/ethnomusicology, Polish, Portuguese, Russian languages and literature, Slavic languages, Spanish, technical and business writing, and visual and performing arts), COMPUTER AND PHYSICAL SCIENCE (actuarial science, applied mathematics, applied physics, astronomy, astrophysics, chemical physics, chemistry, computer science, digital arts/technology, earth science, geology, mathematics, paleontology, physical sciences, physics, planetary and space science, statistics, and systems analysis), EDUCATION (education, education of the exceptional child, foreign languages education, music education, and physical education), ENGINEERING AND ENVIRONMENTAL DESIGN (architecture, chemical engineering, civil engineering, computer engineering, electrical/electronics engineering, engineering and applied science, environmental science, industrial engineering, materials engineering, materials science, mechanical engineering, mining and mineral engineering, and water and wastewater technology), HEALTH PROFESSIONS (environmental health science, health, nursing, occupational therapy, pharmacology, pharmacy, physical therapy, physician's assistant, and radiological science), SOCIAL SCIENCE (African studies, American studies, anthropology, applied psychology, archeology, behavioral science, Canadian studies, Caribbean studies, Celtic studies, Christian studies, classical/ancient civilization, cognitive science, criminology, East Asian studies, economics, ethics, politics, and social policy, European studies, forensic studies, geography, German area studies, Hispanic American studies, history, history of science, human ecology, humanities, international relations, international studies, Judaic studies, medieval studies, Middle Eastern studies, Native American studies, Pacific area studies, peace studies, philosophy, political science/government, psychology, public affairs, religion, Russian and Slavic studies, Scandinavian studies, sociology, South Asian studies, urban studies, and women's studies). Arts and science, applied science, and engineering have the largest enrollments.

Required: Arts and science students must satisfy a breadth requirement, which includes 3 courses from outside the major. Students must complete 20 credits for a 4-year degree, plus prerequisite subjects.

Special: The university offers co-op programs in management, arts management, management and information technology, cell and molecular biology, computer science, mathematical and physical sciences, sociology, applied psychology, public policy, humanities, international development studies, psychology (including mental health studies), sciences, social sciences, and neuroscience. Study abroad, interdisciplinary programs, and various work-study programs are also available.

Faculty/Classroom: 55% of faculty are male; 45% are female. No introductory courses are taught by graduate students.

Requirements: The SAT is required. The faculties of Arts and Science, Music, and Physical Education and Health will consider grade 12 applicants from an accredited U.S. high school with a high GPA and good scores on the SAT. The ACT will also be considered. Engineering will consider excellent grade 12 students with high SAT scores who also are completing at least 2 advanced placement courses. The SAT subject tests and AP courses and exams must include math, physics, and chemistry. Other requirements may apply. Architecture students must submit a questionnaire and a portfolio. Music students must audition. A GPA of 3.0 is required. AP credits are accepted.

Procedure: Freshmen are admitted fall. There are early decision, early admissions, deferred admissions, and rolling admissions plans. Check with the school for current application deadlines and fee. Notification is sent on a rolling basis.

Transfer: 786 transfer students enrolled in a recent year. For the Arts and Science divisions, normally a B average is required. 5 of 20 credits required for the bachelor's degree must be completed at U of T.

Visiting: There are regularly scheduled orientations for prospective students. There are guides for informal visits. To schedule a visit, contact the Student Recruitment Office.

International Students: There were 6884 international students enrolled in a recent year. The school actively recruits these students. They must take the TOEFL with a minimum score of 600 on the paper-based TOEFL (PBT) or 100 on the Internet-based version (iBT) or take the MELAB, the ELDA/COPE, the IELTS Academic Module, or the University of Toronto's School of Continuing Studies Academic English Course. They must also take the SAT or ACT, scoring at least 1800 on the SAT or 26 on the ACT. Students must score at least 500 on SAT subject tests.

Computers: Wireless access is available. All students may access the system. There are no time limits and no fees.

Graduates: In a recent year, 9724 bachelor's degrees were awarded. In an average class, 83% graduate in 4 years or less.

Admissions Contact: Admissions Counselor. A video is available on-line. E-mail: *admissions.help@utoronto.ca* Web: *www.utoronto.ca*

UNIVERSITY OF VICTORIA B-2

Victoria, BC V8W 3P2 **(250) 721-8121; (250) 721-6225**

Full-time: 11,000 men and women	**Faculty:** n/av
Part-time: 5900 men and women	**Ph.D.s:** n/av
Graduate: 2500 men and women	**Student/Faculty:** n/av
Year: semesters, summer session	**Tuition:** $6700 ($17,100)
Application Deadline: see profile	**Room & Board:** $7700
Freshman Class: n/av	

The University of Victoria, founded in 1903 as Victoria College, is a public institution operated by the province of British Columbia. It offers undergraduate and graduate programs in the arts and sciences, business, education, engineering, fine arts, human and social development, and law. There are 8 undergraduate schools and 1 graduate school. Some figures in the above capsule and in this profile are approximate. The 4 libraries contain 1.9 million volumes, 2.3 million microform items, and 110,600 audio/video tapes/CDs/DVDs, and subscribe to 40,000 periodicals including electronic. Computerized library services include interlibrary loans, database searching, Internet access, and laptop Internet portals. Special learning facilities include a learning resource center, art gallery, radio station, and language labs. The 400-acre campus is in an urban area in Victoria. Including any residence halls, there are 107 buildings.

Student Life: 86% of undergraduates are from British Columbia. 92% are from public schools. The average age of freshmen is 21.

Housing: 2200 students can be accommodated in college housing, which includes single-sex and coed dorms, on-campus apartments, and married student housing. There is an off-campus housing registry service. On-campus housing is guaranteed for the freshman year only, is available on a first-come, first-served basis, and is available on a lottery system for upperclassmen. Priority is given to out-of-town students. 89% of students commute. All students may keep cars.

Activities: There are no fraternities or sororities. Groups on campus include art, chess, choir, chorus, computers, dance, debate, drama, environmental, ethnic, gay, honors, international, jazz band, musical theater, newspaper, orchestra, photography, political, radio and TV, religious, social, social service, student government, symphony, and yearbook. Popular campus events include Week of Welcome, the President's BBQ, and Experience UVic (spring open house).

Sports: There are 7 intercollegiate sports for men and 7 for women, and 12 intramural sports for men and 12 for women. Facilities include 3 gyms, a dance studio, 2 weight and fitness training rooms, racquetball and squash courts, playing fields, an outdoor stadium, tennis courts, 2 swimming pools, a sailing compound, and jogging trails.

Disabled Students: 95% of the campus is accessible. Facilities include wheelchair ramps, elevators, special parking, specially equipped restrooms, lowered drinking fountains, lowered telephones, and special housing.

Services: Counseling and information services are available, as is tutoring in most subjects. There is remedial reading and writing.

Campus Safety and Security: Measures include 24-hour foot and vehicle patrol, self-defense education, and security escort services. There are emergency telephones and lighted pathways/sidewalks.

Programs of Study: UVic confers B.A., B.S., B.Com., B.Ed., B.Eng., B.F.A., B.Mus., B.Sc., B.S.N., B.S.W., and L.L.B. degrees. Master's and doctoral degrees are also awarded. Bachelor's degrees are awarded in AGRICULTURE (environmental studies), BIOLOGICAL SCIENCE (biochemistry, biology/biological science, and microbiology), BUSINESS (business administration and management, hospitality management services, international business management, and recreation and leisure services), COMMUNICATIONS AND THE ARTS (art history and appreciation, classics, creative writing, dramatic arts, English, French, Germanic languages and literature, linguistics, music, and visual and performing arts), COMPUTER AND PHYSICAL SCIENCE (astronomy, chemistry, computer science, earth science, mathematics, physics, software engineering, and statistics), EDUCATION (elementary education, physical education, and secondary education), ENGINEERING AND ENVIRONMENTAL DESIGN (computer engineering, electrical/electronics engineering, and mechanical engineering), HEALTH PROFESSIONS (health science and nursing), SOCIAL SCIENCE (anthropology, child care/child and family studies, economics, geography, Hispanic American studies, history, Italian studies, Latin American studies, medieval studies, Pacific area studies, philosophy, political science/government, psychology, Russian and Slavic studies, social work, sociology, and women's studies). Writing is the strongest academically.

Required: To graduate, students must complete the university English requirement, a minimum of 60 units above the 100 level, at least 21 of which must be upper level, and have a 2.0 GPA.

Special: A number of co-op and internship programs are available in specific disciplines as are many dual majors, including biochemistry/microbiology and Hispanic/Italian studies. Work-study is possible on a limited basis for Canadian students only. Study abroad is offered in 19 countries. There are 37 departmental honors programs.

Faculty/Classroom: 61% of faculty are male; 39% are female. All teach undergraduates and do research. No introductory courses are taught by graduate students. The average class size in an introductory lecture is 53; in a regular course, 30.

Admissions: 73% of a recent year's applicants were accepted.

Requirements: Application requires high school graduation with a 2.5 GPA or higher, 4 semesters of English, 2 each of social science, math, science, and language, and 6 semesters of 2.5 work at grade 12 level. Applications are accepted on-line at the school's web site. AP credits are accepted.

Procedure: Freshmen are admitted to all sessions. There are early admissions and deferred admissions plans. Check with the school for current application deadlines. Application fee is $60 ($100 for international students). Applications are accepted on-line.

Transfer: 2000 transfer students enrolled in a recent year. Requirements vary with the program and the individual. 30 of 60 credits required for the bachelor's degree must be completed at UVic.

Visiting: There are regularly scheduled orientations for prospective students. There are guides for informal visits, and visitors may sit in on classes and stay overnight. To schedule a visit, contact Campus Tours.

International Students: There were 2000 international students enrolled in a recent year. The school actively recruits these students. They must take the TOEFL with a minimum score of 530 on the paper-based TOEFL (PBT) or 71 on the Internet-based version (iBT) or take the MELAB or IELTS.

Computers: Wireless is available across campus. All students may access the system at any time. There are no time limits and no fees.

Graduates: In a recent year, 3285 bachelor's degrees were awarded.

Admissions Contact: Admissions Officer. Web: *http:/web.uvic.ca/adms*

UNIVERSITY OF WATERLOO E-3

Waterloo, ON N2L 3G1 (519) 888-4567, ext. 33777; (519) 746-8088

Full-time: 12,879 men, 9451 women	**Faculty:** n/av
Part-time: 391 men, 555 women	**Ph.D.s:** 93%
Graduate: 2421 men, 1509 women	**Student/Faculty:** 25 to 1
Year: varies, summer session	**Tuition:** $6500 ($18,500)
Application Deadline: March 31	**Room & Board:** $9000

Freshman Class: 29,859 applied, 20,942 accepted, 6970 enrolled

The University of Waterloo, founded in 1957, is a public institution that offers undergraduate and graduate programs in applied health sciences, arts, engineering, environment, math, and science. Students have a home base in 1 of 6 faculties or 4 affiliated institutions. Most programs are offered in either the traditional or the cooperative system of study. There are 10 undergraduate schools and 6 graduate schools. The figures in the above capsule and in this profile are approximate. The 8 libraries contain 2.0 million volumes, 1.7 million microform items, and 1,179 audio/video tapes/CDs/DVDs, and subscribe to 24,074 periodicals including electronic. Computerized library services include interlibrary loans, database searching, Internet access, and laptop Internet portals. Special learning facilities include a learning resource center, art gallery, radio station, 4 museums, 2 theaters, and an observatory. The 1000-acre campus is in a suburban area 60 miles southwest of Toronto. Including any residence halls, there are 65 buildings.

Student Life: 95% of undergraduates are from Ontario. Others are from 13 states.

Housing: 6100 students can be accommodated in college housing, which includes single-sex and coed dorms, on-campus apartments, and off-campus apartments. In addition, there are special-interest houses, language floors, and an off-campus housing service. On-campus housing is guaranteed for the freshman year only. Priority is given to out-of-town students. All students may keep cars.

Activities: 1% of men belong to 1 national fraternity; 1% of women belong to 1 national sorority. There are 150 groups on campus, including and social dance, juggling, martial arts, band, bridge, cheerleading, chess, choir, computers, dance, debate, drama, environmental, ethnic, film, gay, honors, international, literary magazine, marching band, musical theater, newspaper, photography, political, professional, radio and TV, religious, social, social service, student government, and yearbook. Popular campus events include Oktoberfest and Canada Day.

Sports: There are 18 intercollegiate sports for men and 18 for women, and 16 intramural sports for men and 16 for women. Facilities include outdoor playing fields, an ice arena, a swimming pool, a diving tank, squash courts, weight rooms, 2 gyms, a dance studio, tennis courts, and activity areas.

Disabled Students: All of the campus is accessible. Facilities include wheelchair ramps, elevators, special parking, specially equipped restrooms, special class scheduling, lowered drinking fountains, lowered telephones, and up-to-date technical equipment for the visually disabled and the hearing impaired.

Services: Counseling and information services are available, as is tutoring in most subjects. There is a reader service for the blind, and remedial math, reading, and writing.

Campus Safety and Security: Measures include 24-hour foot and vehicle patrol, emergency notification system, self-defense education, and security escort services. There are shuttle buses, emergency telephones, and lighted pathways/sidewalks.

Programs of Study: Waterloo confers B.A., B.Sc., B.A.S., B.A.Sc., B.A.F.M., B. Arch., B.C.F.M., B.C.S., B.E.S., B.I.S., B.Math, BSc. Phm., B.S.E., B.S.W., and B.K.I. degrees. Master's and doctoral degrees are also awarded. Bachelor's degrees are awarded in AGRICULTURE (environmental studies), BIOLOGICAL SCIENCE (biochemistry, bioinformatics, biology/biological science, and biotechnology), BUSINESS (accounting, business administration and management, human resources, management engineering, management science, operations research, and recreation and leisure services), COMMUNICATIONS AND THE ARTS (art history and appreciation, arts administration/management, classics, dramatic arts, English, English literature, film arts, fine arts, French, German, music, Russian, Spanish, speech/debate/rhetoric, and studio art), COMPUTER AND PHYSICAL SCIENCE (actuarial science, applied mathematics, chemistry, computer mathematics, computer science, digital arts/technology, earth science, information sciences and systems, mathematics, physics, science, science and management, software engineering, and statistics), EDUCATION (foreign languages education, mathematics education, and science education), ENGINEERING AND ENVIRONMENTAL DESIGN (architecture, chemical engineering, city/community/regional planning, civil engineering, computational sciences, computer engineering, electrical/electronics engineering, engineering, environmental engineering, environmental science, geological engineering, mechanical engineering, and systems engineering), HEALTH PROFESSIONS (health, health science, optometry, preallied health, preoptometry, and respiratory therapy), SOCIAL SCIENCE (anthropology, economics, French studies, geography, history, international studies, medieval studies, philosophy, physical fitness/movement, political science/government, psychology, religion, Russian and Slavic studies, social work, sociology, and women's studies). Engineering, accounting, and math are the strongest academically. The arts program has the largest enrollment.

Required: To graduate, all students must satisfy specific program requirements. These include a writing skills requirement. The total number of credits and minimum grade average vary.

Special: Cross-registration with Wilfrid Laurier University, study abroad in 30 countries, dual, student-designed, and interdisciplinary majors, a combined bachelor's-master's degree in accounting and engineering, and noncredit courses are available. Students may study under the regular or cooperative system, which allows off-campus work terms in education, professional organizations and agencies, business, industry, or government. There are concurrent education programs in conjunction with the faculties of education at Brock and Queen's Universities. There are 55 departmental honors programs.

Faculty/Classroom: 75% of faculty are male; 25% are female. All teach and do research. No introductory courses are taught by graduate students.

Admissions: 70% of a recent year's applicants were accepted.

Requirements: Candidates from the United States must have a high school diploma with exceptionally high standing and AP exams in prerequisite subjects or first-year university standing in acceptable subjects from an accredited university. An audition, portfolio, and/or interview may be required for certain programs. A GPA of 3.0 is required. AP credits are accepted. Important factors in the admissions decision are advanced placement or honors courses, extracurricular activities record, and leadership record.

Procedure: Freshmen are admitted fall, winter, and spring. Entrance exams should be taken by the junior year. There are early admissions and deferred admissions plans. Applications should be filed by March 31 for fall entry, October 31 for winter entry, and March 1 for spring entry, along with a $130 fee. Notifications are sent May 25. Applications are accepted on-line.

Transfer: Applicants are considered on an individual basis. 10 of 20 credits required for the bachelor's degree must be completed at Waterloo.

Visiting: There are regularly scheduled orientations for prospective students. Student visits include tours and individual and group information sessions. There are guides for informal visits and visitors may sit in on classes. To schedule a visit, contact the Visitors Reception Center.

Financial Aid: The FAFSA is required. Check with the school for current application deadlines.

International Students: There are 2398 international students enrolled. The school actively recruits these students. They must take the TOEFL and also take the TWE and the TSE. The MELAB or the IELTS may also be submitted.

Computers: Wireless access is available. All students may access the system. Some restrictions may apply in some faculties. There are no time limits and no fees.

Graduates: In a recent year, 4466 bachelor's degrees were awarded. The most popular majors were arts (32%), mathematics (21%), and engineering (18%).

Admissions Contact: Undergraduate Recruitment Web: *www.findoutmore.uwaterloo.ca*

UNIVERSITY OF WESTERN ONTARIO D-3

London, ON N6A 3K7 (519) 661-2100; (519) 661-3710

Full-time: 11,675 men, 14,288 women	**Faculty:** 1381
Part-time: 699 men, 973 women	**Ph.D.s:** n/av
Graduate: 2622 men, 2723 women	**Student/Faculty:** 20 to 1
Year: varies, summer session	**Tuition:** $6986 ($19,350)
Application Deadline: May 15	**Room & Board:** $9270

Freshman Class: 32163 applied, 17817 accepted, 9644 enrolled
SAT: required

The University of Western Ontario is one of Canada's oldest and largest universities--founded in 1878. There are 12 undergraduate schools and 1 graduate school. In addition to regional accreditation, UWO, Western has baccalaureate program accreditation with ASLA. The 7 libraries contain 3.7 million volumes, 4.1 million microform items, 2.1 million audio/video tapes/CDs/DVDs, and subscribe to 86,179 periodicals including electronic. Computerized library services include interlibrary loans, database searching, Internet access, and laptop Internet portals. Special learning facilities include a learning resource center, art gallery, radio station, TV station, International Centre for Olympic Studies, Fowler-Kennedy Sports Medicine Clinic, Cronyn Observatory, and Boundary Layer Wind Tunnel. The 1125-acre campus is in an urban area 120 miles from both Detroit, Michigan and Toronto, Ontario. Including any residence halls, there are 116 buildings.

Student Life: 94% of undergraduates are from Ontario. Others are from 116 foreign countries. The average age of freshmen is 19; all undergraduates, 21. 7% do not continue beyond their first year.

Housing: 5077 students can be accommodated in college housing, which includes single-sex and coed dorms, on-campus apartments, and married student housing. In addition, there are honors houses and special-interest houses. On-campus housing is guaranteed for the freshman year only and is available on a lottery system for upperclassmen. Priority is given to out-of-town students. 75% of students commute. All students may keep cars.

Activities: There are no fraternities or sororities. There are 184 groups on campus, including art, band, cheerleading, chess, choir, chorale, chorus, computers, dance, debate, drama, environmental, ethnic, film, gay, international, jazz band, marching band, musical theater, newspaper, opera, orchestra, photography, political, professional, radio and TV, religious, social, social service, and student government. Popular campus events include Western homecoming, fall preview day, and summer academic orientation.

Sports: There are 20 intercollegiate sports for men and 21 for women, and 20 intramural sports for men and 19 for women. Facilities include Thompson Recreation and Athletic Centre, and TD Waterhouse Stadium.

Disabled Students: 92% of the campus is accessible. Facilities include wheelchair ramps, elevators, special parking, specially equipped restrooms, special class scheduling, lowered drinking fountains, lowered telephones, and special housing.

Services: Counseling and information services are available, as is tutoring in most subjects. There is a reader service for the blind, and remedial math, reading, and writing. Details available through Learning Skills Services at the Student Development Centre.

Campus Safety and Security: Measures include 24-hour foot and vehicle patrol, emergency notification system, and security escort services. There are emergency telephones, lighted pathways/sidewalks, controlled access to dorms/residences, campus community police, SERT: Student Emergency Response Team, and Western foot patrol.

Programs of Study: Western confers B.A., B.Sc., B.Ed., B.E.Sc., B.F.A., B.H.Sc, B.M.O.S., B.M.Sc., B.Mus., B.Mus.A., B.A.H.Ec., B.Sc.H.Ec., B.Sc.FN, B.Sc.N., B.S.W.Hons., J.D., and B.Th degrees. Master's and doctoral degrees are also awarded. Bachelor's degrees are awarded in AGRICULTURE (environmental studies, natural resource management, and plant science), BIOLOGICAL SCIENCE (anatomy, biochemistry, bioinformatics, biology/biological science, biophysics, cell biology, ecology, genetics, microbiology, nutrition, physiology, and toxicology), BUSINESS (accounting, business administration and management, business communications, and human resources), COMMUNICATIONS AND THE ARTS (applied music, art, art history and appreciation, arts administration/management, Chinese, classical languages, classics, communications, communications technology, comparative literature, creative writing, digital communications, English, English literature, film arts, fine arts, French, German, Germanic languages and literature, Greek, Italian, Japanese, Latin, linguistics, media arts, modern language, music, music business management, music history and appreciation, music performance, music theory and composition, musicology/ethnomusicology, opera, piano/organ, public relations, radio/television technology, Russian, Spanish, strings, studio art, and visual and performing arts), COMPUTER AND PHYSICAL SCIENCE (actuarial science, applied mathematics, astronomy, astrophysics, chemistry, computer mathematics, computer programming, computer science, cybernetics, earth science, geology, geophysics and seismology, information sciences and systems, mathematics, medical physics, physics, planetary and space science, science, software engineering, and statistics), EDUCATION (education, elementary education, middle school education, museum studies, music education, physical education, and secondary education), ENGINEERING AND ENVIRONMENTAL DESIGN (aviation administration/management, biomedical engineering, chemical engineering, civil engineering, computer engineering, computer technology, electrical/electronics engineering, engineering, engineering management, environmental engineering, environmental science, materials engineering, materials science, and mechanical engineering), HEALTH PROFESSIONS (health science, medical science, nursing, and pharmacology), SOCIAL SCIENCE (American studies, anthropology, Asian/American studies, Asian/Oriental studies, biblical studies, Canadian studies, child psychology/development, classical/ancient civilization, clinical psychology, criminology, East Asian studies, economics, family/consumer studies, food science, French studies, gender studies, geography, gerontology, history, home economics, human ecology, humanities, humanities and social science, interdisciplinary studies, international relations, Italian studies, Japanese studies, Latin American studies, law, liberal arts/general studies, Native American studies, peace studies, philosophy, philosophy and religion, physical fitness/movement, political science/government, psychology, public administration, religion, social science, social work, sociology, Spanish studies, theological studies, urban studies, Western civilization/culture, and women's studies).

Faculty/Classroom: 69% of faculty are male; 31% are female. No introductory courses are taught by graduate students.

Admissions: 55% of a recent year applicants were accepted.

Requirements: The SAT is required. A GPA of 3.5 is required. AP credits are accepted. Important factors in the admissions decision are advanced placement or honors courses, recommendations by school officials, and leadership record.

Procedure: Freshmen are admitted fall. There are deferred admissions and rolling admissions plans. Early decision applications should be filed by May 15; regular applications, by May 15 for fall entry. The fall application fee was $125. Notifications are sent February 1. Applications are accepted on-line.

Transfer: 381 transfer students enrolled in a recent year. A minimum 3.0 GPA is required of transfer applicant; a maximum of 10.0 credits may be transferred. At least 5 credits in a 15-credit degree program or 10 credits in an honors program must be completed at The University of Western Ontario to earn a bachelor's degree. 5 of 15 credits required for the bachelor's degree must be completed at Western.

Visiting: There are regularly scheduled orientations for prospective students, academic counseling appointments and campus tours. There are guides for informal visits and visitors may sit in on classes. To schedule a visit, contact the Liaison Officer and Events Planner.

Financial Aid: Western is a member of CSS. The FAFSA and the college's own financial statement are required. Check with the school for current application deadlines.

International Students: The school actively recruits these students. They must take the TOEFL with a minimum score of 550 on the paper-based TOEFL (PBT) or 83 on the Internet-based version (iBT) or take the MELAB.

Computers: Wireless access is available. All students may access the system. There are no time limits and no fees.

Graduates: In a recent year, 6791 bachelor's degrees were awarded. 393 companies recruited on campus in 2010-2011. Of the 2010 graduating class, 94% were employed within 6 months of graduation.

Admissions Contact: Lori Gribbon, Director, Recruitment and Admissions. E-Mail: *reg-admissions@uwo.ca* Web: *http:/welcome.uwo.ca/*

UNIVERSITY OF WINDSOR — D-3

Windsor, ON N9B 3P4 (519) 253-3000, ext. 3315; (519) 971-3653

Full-time: 5176 men, 6196 women	**Faculty:** 592
Part-time: 1190 men, 1273 women	**Ph.D.s:** 92%
Graduate: 859 men, 850 women	**Student/Faculty:** 18 to 1
Year: trimesters, summer session	**Tuition:** $8400 ($21,300)
Application Deadline: open	**Room & Board:** $9900
Freshman Class: n/av	
SAT or ACT: required	

The University of Windsor, founded in 1857, is a public liberal arts institution offering undergraduate and graduate programs through 10 faculties and 6 schools. There are 11 undergraduate schools and one graduate school. The 2 libraries contain 1.7 million volumes, 1.5 million microform items, and 10,792 audio/video tapes/CDs/DVDs, and subscribe to 76,378 periodicals including electronic. Computerized library services include interlibrary loans, database searching, Internet access, and laptop Internet portals. Special learning facilities include a learning resource center, art gallery, natural history museum, radio station, a video-conferencing center, a computing services theater, the Chrysler Canada/University of Windsor Research Center, and the Great Lakes Institute. The 125-acre campus is in an urban area 2 kilometers from downtown Windsor, and 3 kilometers from downtown Detroit, Michigan. Including any residence halls, there are 58 buildings.

Student Life: 90% of undergraduates are from Ontario. Others are from states, 90 foreign countries, and Canada. 95% are from public schools. The average age of freshmen is 18; all undergraduates, 22. 10% do not continue beyond their first year.

Housing: 1500 students can be accommodated in college housing, which includes coed dorms, on-campus apartments, and married student housing. On-campus housing is guaranteed for the freshman year only and is available on a lottery system for upperclassmen. 90% of students commute. All students may keep cars.

Activities: 1% of men belong to 3 national fraternities; 1% of women belong to 3 national sororities. There are 135 groups on campus, including cheerleading, chess, choir, chorale, computers, dance, debate, drama, environmental, ethnic, film, forensics, gay, honors, international, jazz band, literary magazine, musical theater, newspaper, orchestra, political, professional, radio and TV, religious, social, and student government. Popular campus events include Head Start Orientation, Windsor Welcome Week and Homecoming.

Sports: There are 7 intercollegiate sports for men and 6 for women, and 11 intramural sports for men and 9 for women. Facilities include a 6-lane 200-meter track, a multiuse gym, a field house, a stadium, an indoor pool, weight rooms, and a sports therapy clinic.

Disabled Students: 90% of the campus is accessible. Facilities include wheelchair ramps, elevators, special parking, specially equipped restrooms, special class scheduling, lowered drinking fountains, lowered telephones. , and specially equipped residence rooms.

Services: Counseling and information services are available, as is tutoring in most subjects. There is a reader service for the blind, and remedial math, reading, and writing.

Campus Safety and Security: Measures include 24-hour foot and

vehicle patrol, emergency notification system, self-defense education, and security escort services. There are emergency telephones, lighted pathways/sidewalks, and controlled access to dorms/residences.

Programs of Study: U of W confers B.A., B.Sc., B.A.S., B.A.Sc., B.Comm., B.C.S., B.Ed., B.E.S., B.F.A., B.F.S., B.H.K., B. Math, B.Mus., B.Mus.Th., B.Sc.N., B.S.W. and L.L.B. degrees. Master's and doctoral degrees are also awarded. Bachelor's degrees are awarded in AGRICULTURE (environmental studies), BIOLOGICAL SCIENCE (biochemistry, biology/biological science, and biotechnology), BUSINESS (business administration and management and international business management), COMMUNICATIONS AND THE ARTS (art history and appreciation, classics, communications, comparative literature, creative writing, dramatic arts, English, French, languages, modern language, music, Spanish, and visual and performing arts), COMPUTER AND PHYSICAL SCIENCE (chemistry, computer science, geology, mathematics, physics, science, software engineering, and statistics), EDUCATION (drama education, education, and science education), ENGINEERING AND ENVIRONMENTAL DESIGN (automotive technology, civil engineering, electrical/electronics engineering, engineering, environmental engineering, environmental science, industrial engineering, and mechanical engineering), HEALTH PROFESSIONS (music therapy and nursing), SOCIAL SCIENCE (anthropology, Canadian studies, criminology, crosscultural studies, developmental psychology, economics, family/consumer studies, forensic studies, geography, history, international relations, law, philosophy, physical fitness/movement, political science/government, psychology, social work, sociology, urban studies, and women's studies). Science, engineering, and human kinetics are the strongest academically. Business, science, and education have the largest enrollments.

Required: To graduate, students must complete a total of 90 credit hours, including 30 in the major, with a C average. Honors students must complete 120 hours, including 60 in the major, with a B average. All students must fulfill the requirements of the core curriculum.

Special: The university offers a variety of co-op programs and internships. Cross-registration may be arranged with the University of Detroit Mercy, Wayne State University, the University of Central Florida, and the University of Darby (England). There are 30 departmental honors programs.

Faculty/Classroom: 54% of faculty are male; 46% are female. All teach and do research. No introductory courses are taught by graduate students. The average class size in an introductory lecture is 100; in a laboratory is 25; and in a regular course is 50.

Requirements: The SAT or ACT is required. Advanced Placement Examinations in certain prerequisite subjects may also be required. AP credits are accepted.

Procedure: Freshmen are admitted to all sessions. Entrance exams should be taken as early as possible. There are early decision, early admissions and rolling admissions plans. Check with the school for current application deadlines. Applications are accepted on-line. A waiting list is maintained.

Transfer: Applicants must present an official transcript and be in good academic standing.

Visiting: There are regularly scheduled orientations for prospective students, visits include a tour, counseling, and classes if requested. There are guides for informal visits and visitors may sit in on classes. To schedule a visit, contact Office of Liason & Student Recruitment.

Financial Aid: Check with the school for current application deadlines.

International Students: There are 1209 international students enrolled. The school actively recruits these students. They must take the TOEFL or MELAB.

Computers: Wireless access is available. On average, there are approximately 35 computers per computer lab on our campus. Network access is available in the dorms, and dorm lounges. Students can also remotely access the web and get their email through our connection. Our campus is completly wireless. All students may access the system. There are no time limits and no fees.

Admissions Contact: Charlene Yates, Manager, Undergraduate Admissions. E-Mail: *liaison@uwindsor.ca* Web: *www.windsor.ca/futurestudents*

YORK UNIVERSITY E-3

Toronto (North York), ON M3J 1P3 **(416) 736-5000; (416) 736-5536**

Full-and part-time: 47,000 men and women
Graduate: 6100 men and women
Year: semesters, summer session
Application Deadline: see profile
Freshman Class: n/av
SAT or ACT: required

Faculty: 1300
Ph.D.s: 98%
Student/Faculty: n/av
Tuition: $7100 ($17,000)
Room & Board: $8300

York University, founded in 1959, is a public institution offering programs in computer science, design, education, environmental studies, fine arts, business, social science, law, engineering, health, humanities, human resources, pure and applied sciences, and social work. There are 10 undergraduate schools and 43 graduate schools. The 5 libraries contain 2.5 million volumes, 4.0 million microform items, and 54,184 audio/video tapes/CDs/DVDs, and subscribe to 24,576 periodicals including electronic. Computerized library services include interlibrary loans, database searching, Internet access, and Wi-Fi capability. Special learning facilities include an art gallery, radio station, TV station, observatory, language labs, writing center, geographical information systems lab, computer science labs, science-related labs, and fine arts studios and labs (editing studios). The 635-acre campus is in an urban area of Toronto. Including any residence halls, there are 96 buildings.

Student Life: 90% of undergraduates are from Ontario. Others are from states, and 159 foreign countries. The average age of freshmen is 18; all undergraduates, 22. 97% remain to graduate.

Housing: 4000 students can be accommodated in college housing, which includes single-sex and coed dorms, on-campus apartments, and married student housing. In addition, there are language houses, special-interest houses, co-op housing. On-campus housing is available on a first-come, first-served basis, and is available on a lottery system for upperclassmen. Priority is given to out-of-town students. 93% of students commute. All students may keep cars.

Activities: There are no fraternities or sororities. There are 249 groups on campus, including art, band, cheerleading, chess, choir, communications, computers, dance, debate, drama, ethnic, film, gay, international, jazz band, literary magazine, musical theater, newspaper, orchestra, photography, political, professional, radio and TV, religious, social, social service, student government, and yearbook. Popular campus events include The Blue Bowl (football), Orientation Week, and Multicultural Week.

Sports: There are 11 intercollegiate sports for men and 12 for women, and 17 intramural sports for men and 17 for women. Facilities include a stadium, a 6-rink ice arena, 5-sport playing fields, 4 softball diamonds, a cricket pitch, an indoor and outdoor track and field center, and 26 indoor and outdoor tennis courts. There is a fitness center with 29 cardio machines and free weights, a 25-meter swimming pool, 4 gyms, 7 squash courts, 3 dance/aerobic studios, a spinning studio, and a sports therapy clinic. There is a combative room, 3 teaching labs, and an outdoor events facility.

Disabled Students: 65% of the campus is accessible. Facilities include wheelchair ramps, elevators, special parking, specially equipped restrooms, special class scheduling, lowered drinking fountains, lowered telephones. The office for persons with disabilities offers a variety of additional services.

Services: Counseling and information services are available, as is tutoring in most subjects. There is a reader service for the blind. a writing support center, and a multimedia language center. The Counseling and Development Center offers a variety of services and workshops.

Campus Safety and Security: Measures include 24-hour foot and vehicle patrol, self-defense education, and security escort services. There are shuttle buses, emergency telephones, lighted pathways/sidewalks, There is also a bicycle patrol team monitoring the campuses.

Programs of Study: York confers B.A., B.Sc., B.A.S., B.B.A., B.Des., B.Ed., B.E.S., B.F.A., B.H.R.M., B.H.S., B.Sc.N., B.S.W., I.B.B.A. and L.L.B. degrees. Master's and doctoral degrees are also awarded. Bachelor's degrees are awarded in AGRICULTURE (conservation and regulation and environmental studies), BIOLOGICAL SCIENCE (biochemistry, biology/biological science, biotechnology, and ecology), BUSINESS (accounting, banking and finance, business administration and management, business economics, business statistics, entrepreneurial studies, human resources, international business management, international economics, labor studies, management science, marketing and distribution, and organizational behavior), COMMUNICATIONS AND THE ARTS (art history and appreciation, classics, communications, creative writing, dance, design, dramatic arts, English, film arts, fine arts, French, German, Greek, Italian, linguistics, music, photography, Russian, Spanish, video, and visual and performing arts), COMPUTER AND PHYSICAL SCIENCE (applied mathematics, astronomy, atmospheric sciences and meteorology, chemistry, computer science, earth science, information sciences and systems, mathematics, physics, science, science technology, and statistics), EDUCATION (education, education of the deaf and hearing impaired, elementary education, middle school education, and secondary education), ENGINEERING AND ENVIRONMENTAL DESIGN (computer engineering, engineering, environmental science, and industrial administration/management), HEALTH PROFESSIONS (community health work, environmental health science, exercise science, health, health care administration, health science, nursing, and rehabilitation therapy), SOCIAL SCIENCE (African studies, anthropology, Canadian studies, Caribbean studies, cognitive science, criminal justice, criminology, East Asian studies, economics, European studies, French studies, geography, German area studies, gerontology, Hispanic American studies, history, humanities, international studies, Judaic studies, Latin American studies, law, liberal arts/general studies, peace studies, philosophy, physical fitness/movement, political science/government, psychology, public administration, religion, Russian and Slavic studies, science and society, social science, social work, sociology, South Asian studies, Third World studies, urban studies, and women's studies). Business, science, and some fine arts and liberal arts programs are the strongest academically. Psychology, administrative studies, and sociology are the largest.

Required: Students must maintain at least a C average in 90 credits to receive an ordinary degree and a C+ in 120 credits to receive an honors degree. Requirements for graduation vary according to the program.

Special: Co-op programs and cross-registration with Seneca, Centennial, Sheridan, and Humber Colleges, internships, study abroad in more than 100 countries, and work-study are available. York offers dual, student-designed, multi-, and interdisciplinary majors, including atmospheric chemistry, physics and astronomy, science, technology, culture, and society, social and political thought, space and communication sciences, and translation. Independent study and nondegree study are also possible. There are a freshman honors program.

Faculty/Classroom: 59% of faculty are male; 41% are female. All teach and do research. No introductory courses are taught by graduate students. The average class size in an introductory lecture is 72 and in a laboratory is 25.

Requirements: For U.S. students, a satisfactory score on the SAT or ACT is required. In addition, U.S. applicants must have an overall average of B in academic courses in grades 11 and 12. Secondary school record, SAT or ACT scores, and teacher or counselor recommendation are taken into consideration. Applicants to a fine arts program are required to successfully pass an audition or evaluation, and business administration applicants are required to submit a supplementary application. Admission averages and course prerequisites vary by faculty. AP credits are accepted.

Procedure: Freshmen are admitted to all sessions. Entrance exams should be taken in the fall of the senior year. There are early admissions and rolling admissions plans. Check with the school for current application deadlines and fee. Notification is sent on a rolling basis. Applications are accepted on-line.

Transfer: Requirements vary depending on the program. Postsecondary transcripts are required.

Visiting: There are regularly scheduled orientations for prospective students, consisting of a general information session and a campus tour and 1 week of orientation prior to the start of classes. There are guides for informal visits, and visitors may sit in on classes and stay overnight. To schedule a visit, contact the Office of Admissions.

Financial Aid: The FAFSA is required. Check with the school for current application deadlines.

International Students: The school actively recruits these students. They may have to take the TOEFL, YELT, or IELTS.

Computers: Wireless access is available. All students may access the system 24 hours per day. There are no time limits and no fees.

Admissions Contact: Office of Admissions. Web: *http:/futurestudents.yorku.ca*

STUDY ABROAD

Study abroad programs are now available in more than 60 countries in fields that range from Costa Rican tropical biology to Finnish architecture. Program directors have responded to the vocational interests of the student of the 21st century by organizing programs in international management, health care administration, and other career-oriented fields.

In fact, study in both traditional and nontraditional fields is enriched by overseas experience. An international perspective can benefit study of environmental sciences, anthropology, political science, urban planning, oceanography, hotel administration, psychology, social work, journalism, marketing and law, as well as film, art history, theater, music and dance.

The vast majority of U.S. students enter European schools through organized, ongoing programs sponsored and managed by the colleges and universities in which they are already enrolled. In this way, they automatically earn U.S. academic credit from their home institution for their overseas course work. Academic credit *directly* earned at a foreign institution is often not acceptable toward a U.S. degree. Applying directly to a foreign school is not difficult but unusual.

There are colleges and universities located in foreign nations that are organized on the U.S. system and accredited by U.S. accrediting agencies, e.g., American University of Paris. A list of accredited U.S. institutions overseas is provided in the annual *Accredited Institutions of Postsecondary Education,* published for the Commission on Recognition of Postsecondary Accreditation by the American Council on Education, and is available from the American Council on Education, One Dupont Circle NW, Washington, DC 20036-1193, (202) 939-9300, *www.acenet.edu*

According to the Institute of International Education, in their *Open Doors 2013 Report on International Educational Exchange,* based on a recent academic year, 283,323 U.S. students studied abroad. This reflected an increase of 3.4% since the previous year. The number of U.S. students studying abroad has increased over 80% in the last decade. Europe still hosts the largest number of students. However, there is growing interest in non-traditional destinations—including Costa Rica (9%), Brazil (17%), Ecuador (15%), Peru (10%), and Japan (28%). The five leading destinations measured in 2012/2013 were the United Kingdom, Italy, Spain, France, and China. The top five fields of study for international students included: business & management (22%), engineering (19%), math/computer (10%), physical & life sciences (8%), and social sciences (9%).

The report also indicated that during a recent academic year, 819,644 international students were studying in the United States. This represented an increase of 7.2% from the previous year. The largest fields of study were business and management (22%) and engineering (19%).

A Productive Experience

If you are interested in study abroad, plan ahead by taking the following steps to ensure that the experience is productive:

- **Assess the ways in which study abroad will benefit your educational and career plans.** Study abroad can be a casual choice or a pleasant way to spend a semester but you will derive the greatest benefit if you bring more thought to it: How will the overseas experience complement your other courses or your educational major? Can you maximize its value by seeking language as well as academic study or by combining independent study or an internship with traditional course work?
- **Consult your campus study-abroad adviser.** Most colleges and universities have a person or an office charged with the responsibility of counseling students on overseas study. The study-abroad adviser is best qualified to help you make the right choices.
- **Make sure your college will accept credit earned at the study-abroad program you have chosen.** Speak with both your academic adviser and your study-abroad adviser and resolve any issues before you leave. Many students have assumed incorrectly that credit is granted automatically for another institution's program. You cannot take this for granted.
- **Be realistic about your foreign language proficiency.** It is one thing to be able to order a meal or buy a train ticket in a foreign language. It is quite another to follow a professor lecturing on a complex subject. If you discover that your linguistic ability is inadequate, it is quite possible that you can find abroad the subject matter you want taught in English. You will get more out of the overseas experience however, if you make the effort to function in the language of the chosen country.
- **Look carefully at costs.** If you are dealing with a program sponsor that is not your home institution, it is wise to read program literature carefully. Ask questions before you go if you have any qualms! Are charges clearly specified? Does the literature specify what services *are* covered and more important, what services are *not* covered? What is the refund policy, if any? Is there a clearly identified organization with an official base in the United States which would be legally responsible in the event of disaster?

  While drawing up your budget, think about the extras. You will want to make the small side trips to new places that help to make overseas living rewarding. Try to give yourself some financial flexibility in working out your budget.
- **Think about what it means to live abroad.** Be sure to arrange for substitutes for the support systems you take for granted at home. Will your medical insurance cover you? Do you need vaccinations or a doctor who can manage your specific health problems while you are living abroad? What about visas?

  It is critically important to find out about housing before you leave. Student housing is difficult to find almost everywhere. Be sure to find out whether securing housing abroad is your responsibility and what the alternatives are in the country in which you plan to live.
- **Don't assume that you can work abroad.** Because of foreign labor laws, students should not plan to seek paid employment. The practice of working one's way through college is not common abroad, nor are the relatively high-paying part-time jobs that make it possible in the United States. However, increasing numbers of students are looking to combine practical work experience with study abroad. There are many work exchanges, volunteer opportunities, and internships available. Contact the Council on International Exchange, 300 Fore Street, Portland, ME 04101, (207) 553-4000, Fax: (207) 553-4299 for further information.
- **Find out what you can about the sponsoring agency, especially if it is not an accredited U.S. college or university.** Talk to your study-abroad adviser if you have any doubts. Most private agencies engaged in study abroad are legitimate organizations but their basic purposes may not match yours. Does the organization have experience in placing students in an academic environment, not just in arranging travel? Are descriptions of its study program specific or vague? Does it make unverifiable claims about the academic reputation of its programs, or their recognition by U.S. higher educational institutions?

For further information, consult:

Institute of International Education
809 United Nations Plaza
New York, NY 10017
(212) 984-5367 Fax: (212) 984-5496

For further information, consult the following publications:
IIE Passport: Study Abroad Directories, which are available at *www.iiebooks.org*

Council on International Educational Exchange (CIEE)
300 Fore Street
Portland, ME 04101
9am–5pm
(207) 553-4000 Fax: (207) 553-4299
E-mail: contact@ciee.org
Website: *www.ciee.org*

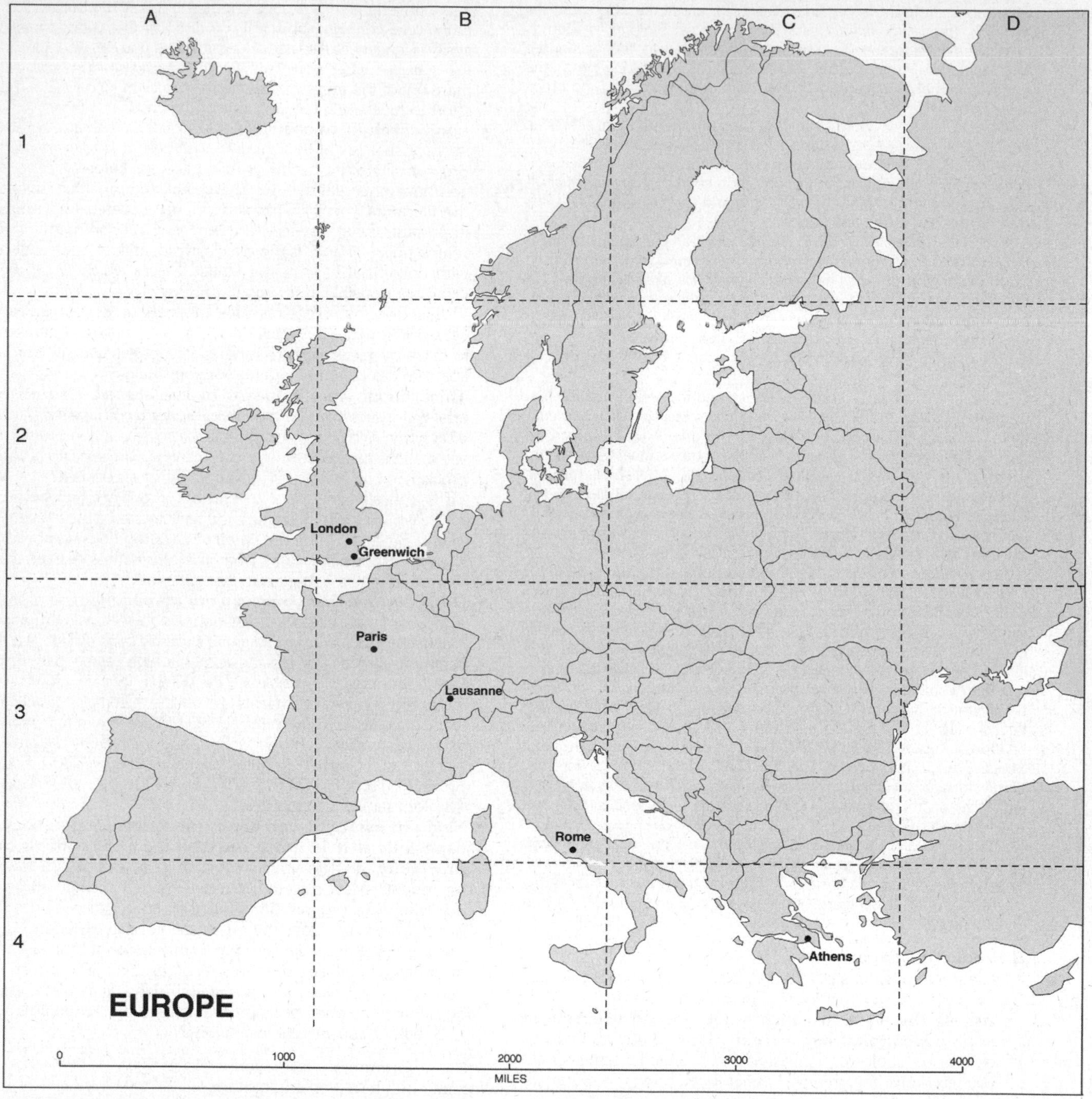

AMERICAN UNIVERSITY OF CAIRO

New Cairo, (212) 730-8800 (Egypt 20-2 615-2233); (212) 730-1600

Full-time: n/av
Part-time: n/av
Graduate: n/av
Year: semesters, summer session
Application Deadline: June 1
Faculty: 362
Ph.D.s: 66%
Student/Faculty: 14 to 1
Tuition: $20,676
Room & Board: $5500
Freshman Class: 1543 applied, 1520 accepted, 1252 enrolled
SAT or ACT: required

The American University in Cairo, founded in 1919, is a private liberal arts institution offering accredited American undergraduate and graduate programs in Egypt. There are 4 undergraduate schools. In addition to regional accreditation, AUC has baccalaureate program accreditation with AACSB, ABET, and CSAB. The 2 libraries contain 538,680 volumes, 190,536 microform items, 2,790 audio/video tapes/CDs/DVDs, and subscribe to 82,000 periodicals including electronic. Computerized library services include interlibrary loans, database searching, Internet access, and Wi-Fi capability. Special learning facilities include an art gallery, radio station, a theater. The 260-acre campus is in an urban area in New Cairo, Egypt. The figures in the above capsule and in this profile are approximate. Including any residence halls, there are 16 buildings.

Student Life: The average age of freshmen is 18; all undergraduates, 20. 6% do not continue beyond their first year; 82% remain to graduate.

Housing: 830 students can be accommodated in college housing, which includes single-sex dorms and off-campus apartments. On-campus housing is guaranteed for all 4 years, is available on a first-come, and first-served basis. 91% of students commute. Alcohol is not permitted. All students may keep cars.

Activities: There are no fraternities or sororities. There are 62 groups on campus, including anit-cancer team. , art, chess, choir, chorus, dance, debate, drama, ethnic, international, literary magazine, musical theater, newspaper, photography, political, professional, radio and TV, social, social service, student government, and yearbook. Popular campus events include International Day, National University Cultural Activities Competition and Model United Nations.

Sports: There are 23 intercollegiate sports for men and 17 for women, and 10 intramural sports for men and 8 for women. Facilities include an tennis courts, multipurpose courts, an exercise gym, a weight room, and a 400-seat stadium. There are also private clubs in the area and other provisions for horseback riding, rowing, swimming and scuba diving, track and field, water polo, squash, and soccer.

Disabled Students: All of the campus is accessible. Facilities include wheelchair ramps, elevators, and specially equipped restrooms.

Services: There is remedial reading and writing.

Campus Safety and Security: Measures include 24-hour foot and vehicle patrol, emergency notification system, and security escort services. There are shuttle buses, lighted pathways/sidewalks, controlled access to dorms/residences, security personnel at all open entrances 24 hours a day.

Programs of Study: AUC confers B.A., and B.S. degrees. Master's degrees are also awarded. Bachelor's degrees are awarded in BUSINESS (accounting and business administration and management), COMMUNICATIONS AND THE ARTS (Arabic, art, communications, English, journalism, and theater design), COMPUTER AND PHYSICAL SCIENCE (actuarial science, chemistry, computer science, mathematics, and physics), EDUCATION (journalism education), ENGINEERING AND ENVIRONMENTAL DESIGN (architectural engineering, computer engineering, construction engineering, engineering, and mechanical engineering), SOCIAL SCIENCE (anthropology, economics, history, Middle Eastern studies, philosophy, political science/government, psychology, and sociology). Journalism, business administration and political science have the largest enrollments.

Required: All students must maintain a C average and must complete from 120 to 162 semester credits, depending on the major. Core courses include a writing program, an interdisciplinary seminar in humanities, natural science, and social science, a scientific-thinking course, and Arab literature, history, and society.

Special: Study abroad through a consortium of U.S. schools, work-study programs with the university, and non-degree study are available.

Faculty/Classroom: 51% of faculty are male; 49% are female. No introductory courses are taught by graduate students. The average class size in an introductory lecture is 20; in a laboratory is 13; and in a regular course is 17.

Admissions: 99% of the 2013-2014 applicants were accepted.

Requirements: The SAT or ACT is required. The ACT Optional Writing test is also required. U.S. applicants must also be graduates of an accredited secondary school and submit complete transcripts and a copy of their diploma. Others must submit the Egyptian Thanawiya Amma certificate or other national high school certificate recognized by the university as equivalent to it, or the GCE, GCSE, or IGCSE. A minimum high school GPA of 2.0 is required. Students should have taken courses in 3 of the following subjects: languages and humanities, math, social studies, and biological and physical sciences. AP credits are accepted. Important factors in the admissions decision are ability to finance college education, evidence of special talent, and extracurricular activities record.

Procedure: Freshmen are admitted fall and spring. Entrance exams should be taken by July for fall admission. There is a rolling admissions plan. Early decision applications should be filed by April 1; regular applications, by June 1 for fall entry; and November 1 for spring entry. The fall 2013 application fee was $45. Applications are accepted on-line.

Transfer: 20 transfer students enrolled in a recent year. Transfer students must have a C average on secondary school and college transcripts. 45 of 120 credits required for the bachelor's degree must be completed at AUC.

Visiting: There are regularly scheduled orientations for prospective students. There are guides for informal visits, visitors may sit in on classes, and stay overnight. To schedule a visit, contact the General Director of Admission in Egypt at 20-2 797-5551.

Financial Aid: In a recent year, 55% of all full-time freshmen students received some form of financial aid. 43% of all full-time freshmen students received need-based aid. 5% of undergraduate students work part-time. The the college's own financial statement is required. The deadline for filing freshman financial aid applications for fall entry is September 15.

International Students: There are 351 international students enrolled. The school actively recruits these students. Graduates of U.S. high schools must take the SAT or ACT.

Computers: All students may access the system. There are no time limits and no fees.

Graduates: In a recent year, 778 bachelor's degrees were awarded. The most popular majors were business administration (24%), journalism and mass communication (18%), and political science (10%). 424 companies recruited on campus in a recent year. In an average class, 3% graduate in 3 years or less, 35% graduate in 4 years or less, 70% graduate in 5 years or less, and 82% graduate in 6 years or less.

Admissions Contact: American University in Cairo's, New York Office. E-Mail: *aucegypt@aucnyo.edu* Web: *www.aucegypt.edu*

AMERICAN UNIVERSITY OF PARIS — B-3

Paris, 75007 — (33) (1) 40 62 07 20

Full-time: 194 men, 432 women	**Faculty:** 62
Part-time: 26 men, 45 women	**Ph.D.s:** 84%
Graduate: 37 men, 155 women	**Student/Faculty:** 11 to 1
Year: semesters, summer session	**Tuition:** $36,887
Application Deadline:	**Room & Board:** n/app
Freshman Class: n/av	
SAT or ACT: recommended	

The American University of Paris, founded in 1962, is a private institution that provides a liberal arts program in an international context. It has regional U.S. accreditation and is recognized by the French government as an institute of higher learning. Classes are in English except for foreign language and literature courses. There is one undergraduate school and one graduate school. The library contains 76,000 volumes, 1,000 microform items, 1,200 audio/video tapes/CDs/DVDs, and subscribes to 40,000 periodicals including electronic. Computerized library services include interlibrary loans, database searching, Internet access, and Wi-Fi capability. Special learning facilities include an art gallery and radio station. The campus is in an urban area in Paris, France. Including any residence halls, there are 8 buildings.

Student Life: The average age of freshmen is 19; all undergraduates, 21.

Housing: 475 students can be accommodated in college housing, which includes coed off-campus apartments. On-campus housing is available on a first-come and first-served basis. All students commute. No one may keep cars.

Activities: There are no fraternities or sororities. Groups on campus include and Wine Society, Fashion Club, art, cheerleading, chess, computers, dance, debate, drama, environmental, ethnic, film, forensics, gay, honors, international, literary magazine, Music, newspaper, photography, political, professional, radio and TV, religious, social, social service, and student government.

Sports: There are 3 intercollegiate sports for men and 3 for women, and 6 intramural sports for men and 6 for women. Facilities include AUP has approval to rent gyms in and around Paris to provide regular practice and work out time.

Disabled Students: 50% of the campus is accessible. Facilities include wheelchair ramps, elevators, specially equipped restrooms, and special class scheduling.

Services: Counseling and information services are available, as is tutoring in most subjects. There is remedial writing. Tutoring Programs in ARC, ARC, Writing Lab, Tech/Media, Faculty Instruction, Disability Support 1) ARC-Link program (disciplinary): Response: Some subjects; Elementary Arabic I, Financial Accounting, Managerial Accounting, Computer Science, Corporate Finance, Entrepreneurial Finance, Environmental Science, International Financial Markets, Information Systems, Principles of Microeconomics, Principles of Macroeconomics, International Economic Relations, Intermediate Macroeconomics, Introduction to Econometrics, Elementary French and Culture I, Elementary French and Culture II, Intermediate French and Culture I, Intermediate French and Culture II, Elementary Latin I, Elementary Latin II, Intermediate Latin I, Greek , Math for Life, Applied Finite Mathematics, Applied Statistics I, Calculus I, Web Authoring 2) Writing Lab, Academic Writing (both remedial and advanced, but we never refer to it as "remedial"), Citation and Plagiarism Workshops, Resume building, Graduate Writing Lab: advanced tutoring/thesis support 3) Tech/Media, computer programs, software training, digital media (Adobe Creative Suite, FinalCutPro), presentation training, faculty training for course sites 4) Other , faculty project support and pedagogical workshops, plagiarism-detection training and consultation, survey-building training, and disability support.

Programs of Study: AUP confers B.A., and B.S. degrees. Master's degrees are also awarded. Bachelor's degrees are awarded in BUSINESS (business administration and management, entrepreneurial studies, international business management, international economics, international finance, management information systems, and marketing), COMMUNICATIONS AND THE ARTS (art history, communication, comparative literature, and film arts), COMPUTER AND PHYSICAL SCIENCE (computer science), ENGINEERING AND ENVIRONMENTAL DESIGN (environmental science), SOCIAL SCIENCE (economics, European studies, history, international political science, Middle Eastern studies, philosophy, psychology, and urban studies). Art history, international economics, and comparative literature are the strongest academically. International business administration, global communications, and international comparative politics are the largest.

Required: Undergraduate students must maintain a minimum GPA of 2.0 and earn at least 128 semester credits. The 128 credits required to graduate, include core major requirements, general education requirements and general electives. The general education requirement includes; Mathematics, English, French, Social Sciences, Science, and Humanities courses.

Special: There are co-operative partnership programs with, Eugene Lang

College of the New School, The Fashion Institute of Technology, The George Washington University, The Goizueta Business School of Emory University, Loyola University in Maryland, Northeastern University, Salve Regina University, The University of Miami, The University of San Francisco, l' Université de Paris-Sorbonne, The American University of Cairo in Egypt, The University of Cape Town in South Africa, and The University of Oslo in Norway. Cross-registration is available in foreign language programs at 3 other French colleges. Juniors and seniors with good academic standing are encouraged to undertake internships. Study abroad, second degrees, non-degree study, and pass/fail options also are offered. There are 1 national honor societies and 10 departmental honors programs.

Faculty/Classroom: 67% of faculty are male; 33% are female. No introductory courses are taught by graduate students. The average class size in an introductory lecture is 13; in a laboratory is 8; and in a regular course is 13.

Requirements: The SAT or ACT is recommended. Candidates must be graduates of an accredited secondary school. An essay and 2 letters of recommendation are also needed. Knowledge of French is not required. Students may apply either through the AUP website, www.aup.edu, or through the Common Application. A GPA of 2.8 is required. AP credits are accepted. Important factors in the admissions decision are advanced placement or honors courses, recommendations by school officials, personality/intangible qualities, and extracurricular activities record.

Procedure: Freshmen are admitted fall and spring. There are deferred admissions and rolling admissions plans. Application deadlines are open. Application fee is $70. Applications are accepted on-line.

Transfer: 80 transfer students enrolled in 2012-2013. Transfer applicants must submit college and high school transcripts, and SAT I or ACT scores if they have fewer than 45 credits. Two letters of recommendation, and an essay are required. 64 of 128 credits required for the bachelor's degree must be completed at AUP.

Visiting: There are regularly scheduled orientations for prospective students, by appointment. There are guides for informal visits and visitors may sit in on classes. To schedule a visit, contact the Admissions Office at +331 40 62 0720.

Financial Aid: In 2013-2014, 43% of all full-time freshmen and 36% of continuing full-time students received some form of financial aid. 26% of all full-time freshmen and 28% of continuing full-time students received need-based aid. The average freshman award was $8,943. AUP is a member of CSS. The FAFSA and the college's own financial statement are required. The priority date for freshman financial aid applications for fall entry is March 15.

International Students: There are 697 international students enrolled. The school actively recruits these students. They must take the TOEFL and the college's own test, TOEIC, or IELTS.

Computers: All students may access the system. There are no time limits and no fees.

Graduates: From July 1, 2012 to June 30, 2013, 131 bachelor's degrees were awarded. The most popular majors were global communications (17%), international and comparative politics (14%), and international business administration (14%). In an average class, 18% graduate in 3 years or less, 40% graduate in 4 years or less, 45% graduate in 5 years or less, and 46% graduate in 6 years or less.

Admissions Contact: Brad Walp, Director of Admissions. E-Mail: *admissions@aup.edu* Web: *www.aup.edu*

AMERICAN UNIVERSITY OF ROME B-3

Rome, 00153 — **011 39 6 58330919 (888)791-8327; 011 396 58330992**

Full-time: 525 men	**Faculty:** 16
Part-time: n/av	**Ph.D.s:** 73%
Graduate: n/av	**Student/Faculty:** 31 to 1
Year: semesters, summer session	**Tuition:** $18,500
Application Deadline: March 1	**Room & Board:** $9735
Freshman Class: n/av	
SAT or ACT: required	

The American University of Rome, founded in 1969, is a private institution offering programs in archeology, art history, business, communications, film and digital media, international relations, Italian studies, international relations, Italian studies, and liberal arts. The library contains 15,000 volumes, 10,000 microform items, and 1,200 audio/video tapes/CDs/DVDs. Computerized library services include interlibrary loans, database searching, and Internet access. Special learning facilities include a learning resource center, a multimedia lab and digital film making. The figures in the above capsule and in this profile are approximate. The campus is in a suburban area on the Janiculum Hill, 15 minutes walking distance from downtown Rome. Including any residence halls, there are 3 buildings.

Student Life: Students are from 40 foreign countries and Canada. 20% are from public schools. 83% are white. The average age of freshmen is 18; all undergraduates, 20. 30% remain to graduate.

Housing: 350 students can be accommodated in college housing, which includes single-sex off-campus apartments. On-campus housing is available on a first-come and first-served basis. 85% of students live on campus; of those, 85% remain on campus on weekends. Alcohol is not permitted. No one may keep cars.

Activities: There are no fraternities or sororities. Groups on campus include art, choir, dance, debate, drama, film, gay, honors, international, literary magazine, newspaper, photography, political, professional, religious, social, social service, and student government. Popular campus events include the Guest Lecture Series, liberal arts and business excursions, and international relations debates.

Sports: There are 1 intercollegiate sports for men and 1 for women, and 3 intramural sports for men and 3 for women. Facilities include off-campus access to soccer, tennis, swimming facilities, and performing arts.

Disabled Students: 30% of the campus is accessible.

Services: Counseling and information services are available, as is tutoring in some subjects, Italian language There is remedial math and writing.

Programs of Study: AUR confers B.A. and B.S. degrees. Associate degrees are also awarded. Bachelor's degrees are awarded in BUSINESS (business administration and management), COMMUNICATIONS AND THE ARTS (art history and appreciation, communications, and film arts), SOCIAL SCIENCE (archeology, international relations, international studies, and Italian studies). Business administration, international relations, and communications have the largest enrollment.

Required: To graduate, students must complete 120 credits, including 60 in the major, with a minimum GPA of 2.0. Distribution requirements include general education requirements, including Italian language, requirements in the major and free electives. A comprehensive exam in business and a thesis in other disciples is required.

Special: Internships in business, international relations, communications, Italian studies, art history, film and digital media, and archeology are available. Study abroad programs are available. There are 99 departmental honors programs.

Faculty/Classroom: 40% of faculty are male; 60% are female. All teach undergraduates, and 70% do research. No introductory courses are taught by graduate students. The average class size in an introductory lecture is 18; in a laboratory is 12; and in a regular course is 18.

Requirements: The SAT or ACT is required. A high school diploma and transcript or the non-American equivalent is required, as are a letter of recommendation and an essay. The GED is accepted. A GPA of 2.5 is required. AP and CLEP credits are accepted. Important factors in the admissions decision are recommendations by school officials, advanced placement or honors courses, and personality/intangible qualities.

Procedure: Freshmen are admitted to all sessions. There are early decision, early admissions, deferred admissions, and rolling admissions plans. Applications should be filed by March 1 for fall entry; October 1 for spring entry; and March 30 for summer entry, along with a $60 fee. Applications are accepted on-line.

Transfer: Applicants must submit an application, a high school transcript, a diploma, all transcripts of universities attended, a letter of recommendation, and an essay. 45 of 120 credits required for the bachelor's degree must be completed at AUR.

Visiting: There are regularly scheduled orientations for prospective students, which AUR organizes directly and through its agents in many U.S. states and in other countries. Orientation is assisted by use of audiovisual materials. There are guides for informal visits and visitors may sit in on classes. To schedule a visit, contact Enrollment Services.

Financial Aid: In a recent year, 38% of all full-time freshmen and 43% of continuing full-time students received some form of financial aid. 20% of all full-time freshmen and 17% of continuing full-time students received need-based aid. The FAFSA is required. Check with the school for current application deadlines.

International Students: There are 240 international students enrolled. The school actively recruits these students. They must take the TOEFL or MELAB and the college's own test.

Computers: Wireless access is available. All students may access the system 8:30 a.m. to 8:30 p.m. Monday through Friday and 10 a.m. to 6 p.m. on weekends. There are no time limits and no fees. It is strongly recommended that all students have a personal computer.

Graduates: Of the 2010 graduating class, 32% were enrolled in graduate school within 6 months of graduation, and 48% were employed.

Admissions Contact: Stefania Lorio, Associate Dean of Enrollment Services. A campus DVD is available. E-Mail: *admissions@aur.edu* Web: *www.aur.edu*

AMERICAN COLLEGE OF GREECE, DEREE C-4

Athens, **+30210 600-9800, ext. 1472; +30210 608-2344**

Full-time: 662 men, 700 women	**Faculty:** 141
Part-time: 850 men, 832 women	**Ph.D.s:** 70%
Graduate: n/av	**Student/Faculty:** 12 to 1
Year: semesters, summer session	**Tuition:** $12,000
Application Deadline: July 25	**Room & Board:** n/app
Freshman Class: 852 applied, 727 accepted, 651 enrolled	
SAT or ACT: recommended	

Deree is the undergraduate and graduate division of The American College (ACG) of Greece, which was founded in 1875 as the American School for Girls. ACG has 5 divisions and 2 campuses in Athens. Deree offers bachelor's degrees in 15 areas of the liberal arts and business. The graduate school offers masters in psychology, communications, finance, and business. There is one undergraduate school and one graduate school. The 3 libraries contain 180,000 volumes, 4,000 microform items, 1,700 audio/video tapes/CDs/DVDs, and subscribe to 6,370 periodicals including electronic. The figures in the above capsule and in this profile are approximate. Computerized library services include interlibrary loans, database searching, Internet access, and laptop Internet portals. Special learning facilities include a learning resource center, art gallery, a museum of the history of the college, and writing centers. The 64-acre campus is in an urban area 6 miles northeast of Athens, Greece. Including any residence halls, there are 12 buildings.

Student Life: 52% are from public schools. The average age of freshmen is 19; all undergraduates, 23. 5% do not continue beyond their first year; 88% remain to graduate.

Housing: Alcohol is not permitted. All students commute. No one may keep cars.

Activities: There are no fraternities or sororities. There are 38 groups on campus, including environmental, film, health, radio, art, chess, choir, coin/stamp, computers, dance, debate, drama, drill team, ethnic, film, international, literary magazine, newspaper, orchestra, photography, radio and TV, social service, student government, and yearbook. Popular campus events include Career Forum, Film Previews, and May Fest.

Sports: There are 5 intercollegiate sports for men and 5 for women, and 8 intramural sports for men and 2 for women. Facilities include a gym, a fitness center, 2 dance studios, aerobic rooms, 4 outdoor tennis courts, a 50-meter swimming pool, a 400-meter track, and a soccer field. Designated as an official training site for the U.S. Olympic Committee.

Disabled Students: 90% of the campus is accessible. Facilities include wheelchair ramps, elevators, special parking, specially equipped restrooms, special class scheduling, and lowered drinking fountains.

Services: Counseling and information services are available, as is tutoring in some subjects, math, accounting and finance, and economics. There is remedial writing.

Campus Safety and Security: Measures include 24-hour foot and vehicle patrol and security escort services. There are shuttle buses and lighted pathways/sidewalks.

Programs of Study: Deree confers B.A. and B.S. degrees. Associate and master's degrees are also awarded. Bachelor's degrees are awarded in BUSINESS (accounting, business administration and management, international business management, management information systems, marketing/retailing/merchandising, and tourism), COMMUNICATIONS AND THE ARTS (art history and appreciation, communications, English, music, and visual and performing arts), SOCIAL SCIENCE (economics, history, philosophy, psychology, and sociology). English, psychology, and marketing are the strongest academically. Marketing, management, accounting, and communications have the largest enrollments.

Required: All students must maintain a minimum CI (cumulative index) of 2.0 and complete 128 semester hours, including 47 hours in general education, at least 30 in the concentration, and must meet the College's residency requirements by completing at least 30 credits (beyond the introductory level courses). Distribution requirements vary with the major but include composition, public speaking, humanities, ethics, computer, and social science.

Special: Study abroad, work-study programs, and dual majors in all disciplines are offered. Non-degree study and pass/fail options are available.

Faculty/Classroom: 44% of faculty are male; 56% are female. All teach undergraduates. No introductory courses are taught by graduate students. The average class size in an introductory lecture is 25; in a laboratory is 20; and in a regular course is 19.

Admissions: 85% of the 2013-2014 applicants were accepted.

Requirements: The SAT or ACT and ACT Writing Test are recommended. Applicants must be graduates of an accredited secondary school. The GED is accepted. English speakers are required to pass an English language proficiency test. A GPA of 2.0 is required. AP and CLEP credits are accepted. Important factors in the admissions decision are recommendations by school officials, extracurricular activities record, and personality/intangible qualities.

Procedure: Freshmen are admitted to all sessions. There are deferred admissions and rolling admissions plans. Applications should be filed by July 25 for fall entry; December 15 for winter entry; January 25 for spring entry; and June 1 for summer entry. Notification is sent on a rolling basis.

Transfer: 42 transfer students enrolled in 2012-2013. Applicants must have a minimum GPA of 2.0 and submit high school transcripts, an official catalog, and a diploma. English proficiency also must be demonstrated, if students are not native speakers of English. 30 of 128 credits required for the bachelor's degree must be completed at Deree.

Visiting: There are regularly scheduled orientations for prospective students, consisting of information sessions and campus tours. There are guides for informal visits and visitors may sit in on classes. To schedule a visit, contact the Office of Admissions at 0030-210 6009800 ext.1254.

Financial Aid: In a recent year, 4% of all full-time freshmen students received some form of financial aid. 1% of all full-time freshmen students received need-based aid. The average freshman award was $3,626. Need-based scholarships or need-based grants averaged $7,542 ($12,980 maximum). Deree is a member of CSS. The the college's own financial statement, and Internal Revenue statement is required. The deadline for filing freshman financial aid applications for fall entry is September 1.

International Students: There are 400 international students enrolled. The school actively recruits these students.

Computers: Wireless access is available. There are 226 PC's in 16 different locations around campus for student use. All students may access the system 8 a.m. to 10 p.m. daily. There are no time limits. The fee is $50. It is strongly recommended that all students have a personal computer.

Graduates: In a recent year, 584 bachelor's degrees were awarded. The most popular majors were management (15%), communications (12%), and marketing (10%). 123 companies recruited on campus in a recent year. In an average class, 1% graduate in 3 years or less, 17% graduate in 4 years or less, 48% graduate in 5 years or less, and 17% graduate in 6 years or less. Of the 2010 graduating class, 12% were enrolled in graduate school within 6 months of graduation, and 36% were employed.

Admissions Contact: Nancy Parkes, Dean of Admissions. E-Mail: *admission@acg.edu* Web: *www.acg.edu*

FRANKLIN UNIVERSITY SWITZERLAND B-3

Sorengo, 6924 **(718) 335-6800, (011-41-91-986-3613); (718) 335-6733, (011-41-91-993-3906)**

Full-time: 140 men, 276 women	**Faculty:** 25
Part-time: 3 women	**Ph.D.s:** 76%
Graduate: 4 men, 1 women	**Student/Faculty:** 16 to 1
Year: semesters, summer session	**Tuition:** $39,600
Application Deadline: March 15	**Room & Board:** $8050
Freshman Class: n/av	
SAT: required	

Franklin University Switzerland, founded in 1969, is a private institution providing a liberal education through courses that are international in perspective and cross-cultural in content. The baccalaureate degree offers concentrations in international management, art history, modern languages (French, Italian, German), international relations, history/literature, and visual and communication arts. There is one undergraduate school and one graduate school. The library contains 33,500 volumes, 15 microform items, 1,620 audio/video tapes/CDs/DVDs, and subscribes to 174 periodicals including electronic. Computerized library services include interlibrary loans and database searching. Special learning facilities include a radio station. The 4-acre campus is in a suburban area on a hillside above Lugano in the southern region of Switzerland called the Ticino. Including any residence halls, there are 8 buildings.

Student Life: Students are from 23 states, 55 foreign countries, and Canada. The average age of freshmen is 18; all undergraduates, 20. 48% do not continue beyond their first year.

Housing: College-sponsored housing includes single-sex dorms, on-campus apartments, and off-campus apartments. 85% of students live on campus; of those, 60% remain on campus on weekends. All students may keep cars.

Activities: There are no fraternities or sororities. Groups on campus include art, drama, international, literary magazine, newspaper, photography, social, student government, and yearbook.

Sports: There are 3 intramural sports for men and 2 for women.

Services: Counseling and information services are available, as is tutoring in most subjects.

Campus Safety and Security: There are emergency telephones and lighted pathways/sidewalks.

Programs of Study: confers B.A. degrees. Associate and master's degrees are also awarded. Bachelor's degrees are awarded in BUSINESS (international business management and international economics), COMMUNICATIONS AND THE ARTS (art history and appreciation, literature, media arts, and modern language), SOCIAL SCIENCE (European studies, history, and international relations). International management/international relations are the strongest academically.

Required: All students must complete 125 credit hours. A general core requirement of 48 credit hours includes 12 credit hours in foreign languages, 9 in humanities, 6 in math/science and history, and 3 in English. Academic travel is required each year (each travel program is 1 academic credit). A minimum GPA of 2.0 overall and 42 credits or more in the major, with a C or better, are also required. Some majors require a thesis.

Special: Cross-registration with most U.S. colleges having an international management major, internships, study abroad as part of the academic travel requirement, accelerated degree programs in any major, and dual majors are offered. There are 4 departmental honors programs.

Faculty/Classroom: 50% of faculty are male; 50% are female. All teach undergraduates. No introductory courses are taught by graduate students. The average class size in an introductory lecture is 15; in a laboratory is 10; and in a regular course is 15.

Requirements: The SAT is required. The college recommends that applicants have completed 4 years of English, 3 years each of history and a foreign language, and 2 years each of science and math. Electives in art, music, and computers are recommended. An essay, a personal statement, and academic references are required. An interview is strongly encouraged. A GPA of 2.0 is required. AP credits are accepted. Important factors in the admissions decision are leadership record, personality/intangible qualities, and extracurricular activities record.

Procedure: Freshmen are admitted to all sessions. Entrance exams should be taken in the fall prior to the desired entrance. There are early decision, early admissions, deferred admissions, and rolling admissions plans. Early decision applications should be filed by December 15; regular applications, by March 15 for fall entry; November 15 for spring entry; and May 1 for summer entry, along with a $50 fee. Notification of early decision is sent January 15; regular decision, on a rolling basis.

Transfer: Applicants must have a C average and provide 1 recommendation. 60 of 120 credits required for the bachelor's degree must be completed at FUS.

Visiting: There are guides for informal visits and visitors may sit in on classes. To schedule a visit, contact the New York Admissions Office.

Financial Aid: In 2013-2014, 47% of all full-time freshmen and 28% of continuing full-time students received some form of financial aid. 36% of all full-time freshmen and 12% of continuing full-time students received need-based aid. The average freshman award was $6,667. 30% of undergraduate students work part-time. Average annual earnings from campus work are $1000. The FAFSA and the college's own financial statement are required. The deadline for filing freshman financial aid applications for fall entry is May 1.

International Students: The school actively recruits these students. They must take the TOEFL. They must also take the SAT or ACT.

Computers: All students may access the system. There are no time limits and no fees.

Graduates: From July 1, 2012 to June 30, 2013, 72 bachelor's degrees were awarded. The most popular majors were international management (35%), international relations (15%), and international economics (11%). In an average class, 20% graduate in 3 years or less and 80% graduate in 4 years or less.

Admissions Contact: Karen Ballard, U.S. Associate Director of Admissions. E-Mail: *kballard@fc.edu* Web: *www.fc.edu*

JOHN CABOT UNIVERSITY B-3

Rome, 00165 **(39) 066 819 1328; 1-855-528-7662**

Full-time: n/av	**Faculty:** 20
Part-time: n/av	**Ph.D.s:** 80%
Graduate: n/av	**Student/Faculty:** 32 to 1
Year: semesters, summer session	**Tuition:** $22,000
Application Deadline: July 15	**Room & Board:** n/app
Freshman Class: n/av	
SAT CR/M/W: 541/507/521	**ACT:** recommended

John Cabot University, founded in 1972, is an independent, four year liberal arts college offering an American university education in the heart of Rome, Italy. In addition to our 700 degree seeking students from over 60 countries, the University is home to visiting students from 130 U.S. colleges and universities each semester. John Cabot students enrich their international academic experience by pursuing international internships, taking part in student athletics and organizations, and traveling on educational exchange programs with John Cabot's partner universities abroad. There is one undergraduate school. The library contains 28,000 volumes, 1,300 audio/video tapes/CDs/DVDs, and subscribes to 72 periodicals including electronic. Computerized library services include interlibrary loans, database searching, Internet access, and Wi-Fi capability. The campus is in an urban area of Trastevere, a historic neighborhood in Rome, Italy. Including any residence halls, there are 4 buildings.

Student Life: Students are from 30 states, 70 foreign countries, and Canada. The average age of freshmen is 18; all undergraduates, 22. 13% do not continue beyond their first year; 87% remain to graduate.

Housing: 500 students can be accommodated in college housing, which includes single-sex dorms, on-campus apartments, and off-campus apartments. In addition, there are special-interest houses. On-campus housing is guaranteed for all 4 years. Some may keep cars.

Activities: There are no fraternities or sororities. There are 15 groups on campus, including art, chess, dance, debate, drama, environmental, ethnic, film, gay, international, jazz band, musical theater, newspaper, opera, photography, political, professional, social, social service, student government, and yearbook. Popular campus events include Trips to Florence, Capri, and Venice, the annual Presidential Gala, 2 Musical Theater Productions per year, and Presidental Lecture Series.

Sports: There are 4 intercollegiate sports for men and 4 for women, and 8 intramural sports for men and 10 for women. Facilities include an on-campus gym, off-campus pool, courts, fields, and training facilities leased by the university.

Disabled Students: Facilities include wheelchair ramps, elevators, and specially equipped restrooms.

Services: Counseling and information services are available, as is tutoring in some subjects, Italian, French, and Spanish. There is remedial math, reading, and writing.

Campus Safety and Security: Measures include 24-hour foot and vehicle patrol, emergency notification system, self-defense education, and security escort services. There are emergency telephones, controlled access to dorms/residences, guards on duty 24/7 in dormitories; 8am-10pm M-Friday, 12pm-10pm Saturday, Sunday in academic buildings.

Programs of Study: JCU confers B.A., and B.B.A. degrees. Associate degrees are also awarded. Bachelor's degrees are awarded in BUSINESS (business administration and management and marketing management), COMMUNICATIONS AND THE ARTS (art history and appreciation, classics, communication, and English literature), SOCIAL SCIENCE (economics, history, humanities, international studies, Italian studies, and political science/government). Business administration and International Affairs has the largest enrollments.

Required: To graduate, students must complete 120 semester hours with a GPA of 2.0, including required courses in writing, math, and foreign language.

Special: Qualifying students may intern through John Cabot Career Services with multinational and Italian businesses, governmental organizations, and embassies. Workstudy opportunities are also avaailable. Students may also study abroad at one of John Cabot's partner institutions in the United States, Europe, and Australia. There are a freshman honors program.

Faculty/Classroom: 60% of faculty are male; 40% are female. All teach undergraduates, and 40% do research. No introductory courses are taught by graduate students. The average class size in an introductory lecture is 15 and in a regular course is 25.

Requirements: The SAT or ACT and ACT Writing Test are recommended. SAT or ACT tests are required of U.S. high school graduates and are recommended for students graduating from other educational systems. Also required are a personal essay and 2 letters of academic recommendation. An interview is recommended; the GED diploma may be recognized for admission. A GPA of 2.8 is required. AP and CLEP credits are accepted. Important factors in the admissions decision are advanced placement or honors courses, leadership record, recommendations by school officials, and extracurricular activities record.

Procedure: Freshmen are admitted to all sessions. Entrance exams should be taken at the orientation session. There are early decision, early admissions, deferred admissions, and rolling admissions plans. Applications should be filed by July 15 for fall entry; November 15 for spring entry, along with a $50 fee. 20 early decision candidates were accepted for the 2013-2014 class. Applications are accepted on-line.

Transfer: 80 transfer students enrolled in 2012-2013. Transfer applicants must be in good academic standing at the previous institution. 60 of 120 credits required for the bachelor's degree must be completed at JCU.

Visiting: There are regularly scheduled orientations for prospective students, Visits are conducted Monday-Friday at 10am and 2pm. Open Houses are scheduled monthly on Saturdays. There are guides for informal visits and visitors may sit in on classes. To schedule a visit, contact the Admissions Office at +39-06-6819121.

Financial Aid: In 2013-2014, 70% of all full-time freshmen students received some form of financial aid. The average freshman award was $5,000. 10% of undergraduate students work part-time. The FAFSA and the college's own financial statement are required. Check with the school for current application deadlines.

International Students: There are 467 international students enrolled. The school actively recruits these students. They must take the TOEFL with a minimum score of 85 on the Internet-based version (iBT) and the college's own test, IELTS also accepted. They must also take the SAT or ACT.

Computers: All students may access the system. There are no time limits and no fees.

Graduates: From July 1, 2012 to June 30, 2013, 102 bachelor's degrees were awarded. The most popular majors were business administration (35%), international affairs (25%), and communications (10%). 32 companies recruited on campus in 2012-2013.

Admissions Contact: Danette Anderson, Enrollment Manager. E-Mail: *admissions@johncabot.edu* Web: *www.johncabot.edu*

RICHMOND, THE AMERICAN INTERNATIONAL UNIVERSITY IN LONDON B-2

Richmond, Surrey, TW10 6JP **+44 (0) 20 8332 9000; +44 (0) 20 8832 1596**

Full-time: 565 men, 570 women	**Faculty:** 50
Part-time: 6 men, 57 women	**Ph.D.s:** 72%
Graduate: 50 men, 50 women	**Student/Faculty:** 22 to 1
Year: semesters, summer session	**Tuition:** $21,000
Application Deadline: March 1	**Room & Board:** $10,970
Freshman Class: n/av	
SAT or ACT: required	

Richmond College, The American University in London, established in 1972, is an independent, international, liberal arts and professional studies university. It occupies the campus of the original Richmond College, founded in 1843 and part of the University of London, and is incorporated as a not-for-profit educational institution in the state of Delaware. There are 2 graduate schools. The 2 libraries contain 60,000 volumes and they subscribe to 300 periodicals including electronic. Computerized library services include database searching. The 5-acre campus is in a suburban area 8 miles southwest of London. Including any residence halls, there are 3 buildings.

Activities: There are no fraternities or sororities.

Sports: There is no sports program at Richmond.

Programs of Study: Richmond confers B.A., and B.S. degrees. Associate and master's degrees are also awarded. Bachelor's degrees are awarded in BUSINESS (business administration and management and international business management), COMMUNICATIONS AND THE ARTS (art history and appreciation, communications, literature, performing arts, and studio art), COMPUTER AND PHYSICAL SCIENCE (computer programming and mathematics), ENGINEERING AND ENVIRONMENTAL DESIGN (environmental science and systems engineering), SOCIAL SCIENCE (anthropology, economics, history, international relations, political science/government, psychology, and sociology). Business and economics has the largest enrollments.

Required: Students must complete 12 courses in 7 fields: English, humanities, social science, intercultural studies, math, science, and the creative arts. Proficiency in English composition, math, and computer skills is required. A 2.0 GPA and 120 credit hours are needed to graduate.

Special: The International Internship Program utilizes London-based businesses and institutions. Study abroad is offered at the university's study centers in Florence, Italy and Shizuoka, Japan. A field study project in a developing country may be arranged during the summer. A limited number of students can be placed in family helper/au pair positions with British families. Joint degrees are offered in engineering with George Washington University. There is a freshman honors program.

Faculty/Classroom: 65% of faculty are male; 35% are female. 97% teach undergraduates. No introductory courses are taught by graduate students. The average class size in an introductory lecture is 22; in a laboratory is 12; and in a regular course is 17.

Requirements: The SAT or ACT is required. U.S. applicants should have completed secondary school with a 2.5 GPA. A GED equivalent is acceptable. An autobiographical essay is an important part of the application. A GPA of 2.5 is required. AP and CLEP credits are accepted. Important factors in the admissions decision are advanced placement or honors courses, geographical diversity, and recommendations by school officials.

Procedure: Freshmen are admitted to all sessions. There are deferred admissions and rolling admissions plans. Application deadlines are open. The fall 2013 application fee was $35.

Transfer: 48 transfer students enrolled in 2012-2013. A 2.0 GPA, official transcripts from all previous institutions, and 2 references are required for admission. 45 of 120 credits required for the bachelor's degree must be completed at Richmond.

Visiting: There are regularly scheduled orientations for prospective students. There are guides for informal visits, visitors may sit in on classes, and stay overnight. To schedule a visit, contact the Admissions Counselor in the U.K.

Financial Aid: In 2013-2014, 27% of all full-time freshmen received some form of financial aid. The average freshman award was $8,735. The FAFSA and the college's own financial statement are required. The deadline for filing freshman financial aid applications for fall entry is April 15.

International Students: The school actively recruits these students. The school also requires placement exams in math and English.

Computers: All students may access the system daily from 8:30 a.m. to 10 p.m. There are no time limits and no fees.

Graduates: From July 1, 2012 to June 30, 2013, 184 bachelor's degrees were awarded.

Admissions Contact: Julie Williams, Director of Undergraduate Admissions. E-Mail: *enroll@richmond.ac.uk* Web: *www.richmond.ac.uk*

STUDY IN THE UNITED STATES

More and more American colleges and universities are welcoming students from foreign countries. Did you know that there are nearly 750,000 international students enrolled in U.S. institutions of higher learning, and that number continues to increase?

Why Colleges and Universities Seek International Students

There are several reasons why American colleges and universities seek international students. First, they recognize that international students help educate the American students on campus by introducing them to different ideas and cultures. Second, the number of college-age American students is declining, and international students can fill places that otherwise would go unfilled. Third, the money that international students spend on tuition and other expenses helps the U.S. economy; education is a valuable export for the United States. And fourth, education has long been an important part of America's foreign aid program, providing foreign nationals with skills that they can use to improve life in their homelands.

Why International Students Seek to Study in the United States

There are also a number of reasons why international students seek to study in the United States. For some students, colleges and universities in the United States offer opportunities to study major fields that are not available in their own countries. For other students, American colleges and universities offer an alternative to colleges and universities in their own countries where places may not be available for all of the qualified students who wish to attend. For still other students, study in the United States provides them not only with an education but also with experiences in living in another culture and in exchanging ideas with students from many nations.

Whatever *your* reason may be for studying in the United States, this book will help you make decisions and plans.

Investigating a College or University

Although most of the colleges and universities in the United States are very honest about their programs and services, a few have been known to misrepresent themselves. When choosing a college or university, as when making any other major purchase, you should investigate carefully. In addition to checking whether your exact major field is offered, you should compare the special services for international students offered by the schools that you are considering. You will want to know whether a representative of the school will pick you up at the airport when you arrive, whether dormitories or other housing is available, and whether there is a foreign student adviser to help you with decisions that you will have to make and problems that you may have to solve after you arrive.

The Difference Between a College and a University

Most international students want to know the difference between a college and a university. This is a difficult question because there is more than one correct answer. In fact, there are three definitions for the word *college* (as it refers to a college in the United States) listed in the *American Heritage Dictionary of the English Language*.

According to the dictionary, a *college* is (1) a school of higher learning that grants a bachelor's degree (undergraduate degree) in arts or sciences or both; (2) an undergraduate division of a university that offers courses and grants undergraduate degrees in a particular field of study; or (3) a technical or professional school, often affiliated with a university, that grants a bachelor's or master's degree in that field.

A *university* is a school of higher learning that grants a bachelor's degree (undergraduate degree), master's degree, and doctorate (Ph.D.) through various colleges within the university.

The Comparison of a College and a University

Many international students ask whether a university is better than a college. The answer is that a university has advantages and disadvantages for an international student, and a college has advantages and disadvantages.

The advantages of a university are that there are usually more research and recreational facilities, and more different kinds of courses offered. The disadvantages of a university are that courses taught to first-year students are often taught by teaching assistants who are graduate students themselves, and that the classes can be very large. The advantages of a college are that the courses are almost always taught by professors, and that the classes are usually small. The disadvantages of a college are that there are usually fewer research and recreational facilities.

Remember, as you decide what is best for you, that there are excellent colleges and there are excellent universities.

Accreditation

Unlike most countries, the United States does not have a national ministry of education that approves the programs at colleges and universities throughout the country. Instead, programs are approved by professional organizations and regional associations. This approval is called accreditation.

All of the schools listed in this book are accredited or are in the process of being accredited.

Requirements for Admission

Academic Preparation

To study in the United States, an international student should begin preparing in secondary school. A good secondary school report is one of the most important requirements for admission to a college or university. When applying to a college or university, you must submit an English translation of your grades with a seal and signature on it. This grade report is called a transcript. In addition, most colleges and universities require undergraduate students to submit standardized test scores. Some of the most common tests are the ACT (American College Test), the SAT (Scholastic Aptitude Test), and the SAT Subject Tests. Each test is described below.

ACT Achievement Test	A test of general academic preparation
SAT Reasoning Test	An aptitude test for college
SAT Subject Tests	Skill tests in academic subjects

The ACT is a national college admission examination that measures your general educational development in English, mathematics, reading, and science, as well as your writing ability in a thirty-minute essay. The SAT is a test that measures your general skills in critical reading, mathematics, and writing. In addition, the SAT Subject Tests measure your knowledge in key academic areas such as languages, social sciences, natural sciences, and mathematics. Some highly selective schools require applicants to take several SAT Subject Tests in addition to the SAT Reasoning Test. Both the SAT and the ACT are administered by Educational Testing Service for the College Board. For more information, visit *www.ets.org* or *www.collegeboard.com*.

The following books are available from Barron's Educational Series, Inc., 250 Wireless Boulevard, Hauppauge, New York 11788, USA, to help you prepare for the ACT and the SAT:

Barron's ACT
Pass Key to the ACT
Barron's SAT 2400 (available with CD-ROM)
Barron's SAT (available with CD Rom)
Pass Key to the SAT
Barron's 6 SAT Practice Tests
Picture These SAT Words
SAT Flash Cards
SAT Word Master

SAT Vocabulary Flashcards
Barron's SAT Math Workbook
Barron's SAT Critical Reading Workbook
Barron's SAT Writing Workbook
Hot Words for the SAT

Barron's also has a series of study guides for the SAT Subject Tests in the following areas: Biology, Physics, Chemistry, Math, U.S. History, World History, Literature, French, and Spanish.

Barron's books are available worldwide at major bookstores or directly from the publisher at *www.barronseduc.com*. Click on Test Preparation for further information.

English Language Proficiency

In addition, if your native language is not English, you will probably have to take a test of your ability to use English. The most widely used of these tests is the TOEFL (Test of English as a Foreign Language), given at official test centers throughout the world. Two TOEFL® formats are being used in different parts of the world while the TOEFL® iBT is being phased in: The Internet-Based TOEFL (iBT), and the Supplemental Paper-Based TOEFL (PBT). The Michigan English Language Assessment Battery (MELAB) and the IELTS (International English Language Testing System) are sometimes accepted as proof of English language proficiency also. These tests are described as follows:

TOEFL® iBT	An Internet-based test. The newest TOEFL format, being phased in throughout the world. A test of listening, speaking, reading, and writing.
Supplemental PBT	A pencil and paper alternative to the iBT available in remote locations or by special arrangement with the test administrator. A test of listening, structure, and reading, with a separate essay. A speaking part is being developed for the PBT.
MELAB	The Michigan English Language Assessment Battery, which is sometimes accepted as evidence of English language proficiency instead of the TOEFL. A test of listening, writing, and multiple-choice items in grammar, vocabulary, and reading.
IELTS	The International English Language Testing System is available in academic or general formats. Listening, speaking, reading, and writing modules are included.

You can take the TOEFL at an official test center. To register, visit *www.ets.org* or register by mail or fax, using the form in the *TOEFL Bulletin of Information,* which can be downloaded from the web site or obtained in print at one of the regional registration sites or counseling centers around the world. For more information about the test, visit *www.ets.org/toefl*. For information about preparing for the test, visit *www.teflprep.com*. To download a bulletin or to register for the MELAB, visit the official web site at *www.lsa.umich.edu/eli* or write to the MELAB Office at the following address: English Language Institute, 555 South Forest Avenue, Ann Arbor, MI 48104-2584. Phone: (734) 764-2413. E-mail: eli-information@umich.edu

To register for IELTS, visit the official web site at *www.ielts.org* or go to a local IELTS center.

Barron's TOEFL books are available worldwide at major bookstores or directly from the publisher at *www.barronseduc.com*. Click on Test Preparation, and then click on TOEFL/TOEIC/IELTS.

Barron's TOEFL iBT (available as book only, book with audio CDs, and book with CD-ROM)
Barron's TOEFL Superpack (includes TOEFL book, 10 CD audio pack, and Essential Words for the TOEFL)
Barron's Practice Exercises for the TOEFL
Barron's PASS KEY to the TOEFL iBT
Barron's Writing for the TOEFL iBT
Barron's Essential Words for the TOEFL
Barron's Michigan Test Battery
Barron's IELTS
Essential Words for the IELTS
IELTS Practice Exams
IELTS Superpack (includes IELTS, IELTS Practice Exams, and Essential Words for the TOEFL)

Financial Guarantees

All schools require that international students show proof of their ability to pay tuition, fees, and living expenses. Most schools require a statement from a bank that shows adequate finances for one year's study. If the name on the account is not the same as the name of the student, a signed letter from the person who has the account must accompany the bank statement. In the letter this person promises to support the international student while the student is in the United States. This person is called the student's sponsor.

Application Procedures

Select a few schools and write for information

When you are ready to apply—usually about a year before the date on which you hope to enter college—write to the schools that interest you for application materials. You should include the field you wish to study, a brief outline of your previous education, the number of years you have studied English, the amount of money you can spend, and the proposed date of enrollment. The college admissions officers will review this information and should let you know if the college cannot meet your needs. You should also ask the schools for information about special programs and organizations for international students.

Remember, this book provides general information about the requirements for admission to colleges and universities, but each school has the authority to set its own standards for admission. For the specific requirements for admission, you must write directly to the schools that most interest you. Some schools will be glad to send you a catalog free of charge; most schools will charge you a fee for the catalog.

Libraries of college catalogs also can be found at the offices of the Institute of International Education, a private, nonprofit, international educational exchange agency administered in 13 international locations. To find an office near you, visit *www.iie.org*. Counseling centers, generally located at U.S. embassies and the offices of binational and Fulbright commissions, also have collections of college catalogs. The Department of State supports a network of advising centers around the world. To find a center near you, visit *www.educationusa.info*. Another web site that offers limited free access to college catalogs is *www.collegesource.org*. After a search for three catalogs and a time limit of ten days, a subscription is required to continue looking through their database. Online catalogs are available for many schools on their websites.

Apply to more than one school

Remember, most American students apply to more than one college or university, and you should, too, especially if you are interested in competitive schools with very high admissions standards. By using this book and by reviewing catalogs from the schools that interest you, you can select several colleges and universities to which you can apply. Because the application fees are almost always nonrefundable, you should truly be serious about the schools where you make application.

Be sure that you have selected some schools where you are likely to be accepted. If you were an average student in high school and your standardized test scores are average, you have little chance of being accepted by a highly competitive school. Evaluate yourself realistically.

Remember, too, that the rating of colleges and universities in this book is based upon information about American students only. Although it is usually accurate for international students as well, some large state universities that are listed as noncompetitive have open admission for state residents. This means that anyone with a high school diploma who is a resident of that state may attend the state school. These schools, listed as noncompetitive, may actually be very competitive for students from other states and for international students. Nevertheless, the rating scale will be useful to you, especially for schools that are not large state universities.

Be sure that you submit all of the documents that the schools require along with application fees. The most common reason for delays in admission to American colleges and universities is because international students do not send everything that is required along with their application forms.

When you are ready to apply to the schools of your choice, consider the following points:

1. Be sure that the schools offer your major field of study.
2. Be sure that the schools are accredited.
3. Be sure that you apply to more than one school.
4. Be sure that you apply to schools where you meet the requirements for admission.
5. Be sure that you submit all of the documents and fees with your application to avoid delays.

Make a Decision

Some international students choose a school in the United States because their friends are going there. It is nice to have friends on campus, but the right school for your friend may not be the right school for you. There is no list of the best schools in the United States. A school may be the best in one major field and only average in another major field. It may have famous professors who only do research and do not teach. It may be well known but not academically excellent.

Consider the following points in making a decision where you will go to school.

1. Be sure that the school offers your major field of study or a premajor for your major field of study.
2. Be sure that the school is accredited.
3. Be sure that the school offers an English program if you need one.
4. Be sure that you understand how much credit you will receive if you are transferring from another school.
5. Be sure that the school has a foreign-student adviser or someone assigned to help international students.
6. Be sure that the expenses for the school are within your budget.

Going to the United States

You should start investigating requirements for visas from the United States and from your home country (if applicable) as soon as you decide to study overseas. You cannot apply for an American visa, however, until you have been accepted by a school in the United States. You must apply for the visa at a U.S. embassy or consulate. You probably will need the following items.

1. A passport (except for Canadians) from your own country.
2. A passport-sized photograph.
3. A Form I-20 (Certificate of Eligibility for Non-Immigrant Student Status) from the school that has accepted you.
4. A notarized bank statement or other proof that you have enough money available and/or financial aid promised to cover your expenses for the entire term of your program. (If you have been accepted to a bachelor's degree program, for instance, the term is four years.)
5. Evidence that you are in good health, including a recent chest X-ray and, in some countries, proof that you have been vaccinated against smallpox within the past three years.
6. A supplemental visa application, and a fee for the Student and Exchange Visitor Information Service, or other security information.

Most students are admitted to the United States under an F-1 (foreign student) visa. Those who come under certain grant or scholarship programs may qualify for a J-1 (exchange visitor) visa. After you have qualified for your visa, any spouse and children of yours may be admitted under F-2 or J-2 visas. You must provide evidence that there is enough money to support them while you are studying. For more information, visit *www.immigrationsupport.org*.

You may want to consider participating in predeparture orientation programs offered by education services abroad and by the U.S. Information Service. Information about these programs is available from the agency or from any U.S. embassy or consulate.

Many schools send representatives to meet students at local airports and bus and train stations, if they have correct arrival information. If your school offers this service, take advantage of it. Send your travel plans to the foreign-student adviser on your campus.

Arriving on Campus

As soon as you arrive on campus, you should visit the foreign-student adviser, an official who is responsible for the welfare of students from other countries. If your college has no such official, you should see the dean of students. Bring your passport and immigration documents.

Your university will also assign a faculty member to advise you on your academic program. Other services available through the school may include psychological counseling and health-care services. Although some schools provide limited health care to students at no charge, you should keep in mind that, in the United States, medical care is the responsibility of the individual, not the government. You would be wise to obtain health insurance. Many colleges offer such plans (some *require* foreign students to have health insurance) and your foreign-student adviser can provide information on them.

Most colleges and universities offer campus orientation programs for all new students; some also hold special orientations for foreign students. The latter are generally held during the summer and may continue on after the academic year has begun. On- and off-campus tours and placement exams may be included.

English Language and Cultural Orientation Programs

Many American colleges and universities provide English language instruction often in conjunction with courses and activities that orient foreign students to the various phases of life in the United States. Full-time English language programs generally involve at least 15 hours of intensive instruction per week and usually include orientation activities. Single courses involve fewer hours and are generally taken to help students engaged in academic courses.

You should know that your ability to speak and write English will affect your admission to most American colleges and universities. If your ability falls below that required for admission, you may be accepted conditionally, with the understanding that you will participate in an intensive English course or program. Some schools require that all foreign students enroll in such a course or program.

For more information, you should refer to the booklet *Intensive English Programs in the USA,* published by the Institute of International Education, 809 United Nations Plaza, New York, New York 10017 and available in their overseas offices and many U.S. embassy libraries as well as their web site, *www.iiebooks.org*. This publication gives detailed information on the intensive English-language courses and programs at many of the institutions in this book.

Expenses

Most colleges will expect you to pay all fixed costs—tuition, room-and-board, if you live and eat in college facilities and student fees—in U.S dollars at the beginning of each academic term. Some colleges provide installment plans, under which these costs may be paid monthly over the course of the term.

Keep in mind when determining your probable expenses that personal expenses, including travel, entertainment, and textbooks may be considerable and generally are not listed as part of a college's tuition schedule. While some colleges will provide an estimate of a typical student's personal expenses, you should generally expect to spend considerably more.

International students generally are not permitted to hold jobs in the United States. Work permits are issued only when there is unexpected economic need. Part-time jobs on campus, however, are permitted and do not require government approval.

Financial aid may be available from your government, the U.S. government cultural exchange programs, corporations, the college you attend, or religious, fraternal, or special-interest groups. For information, contact a U.S. embassy or consulate and your government's ministry or department of education. If you are already in the United States, see your foreign-student adviser.

Pamela J. Sharpe, Ph.D.
Author, *Barron's TOEFL® iBT, 14th Edition*

INDEX